The STRONGEST NASB EXHAUSTIVE CONCORDANCE

UPDATED NASB

The STRONGEST

NASB EXHAUSTIVE CONCORDANCE

ZONDERVAN®

ZONDERVAN.com/
AUTHORTRACKER
follow your favorite authors

Strongest NASB Exhaustive Concordance

This editon published by special arrangement with The Lockman Foundation in 2000 by
Zondervan, *Grand Rapids, Michigan 49530*

Original edition published in English under the title
New American Standard Updated Edition Exhaustive Concordance of the Bible

Requests for information should be addressed to:

Zondervan, *Grand Rapids, Michigan 49530*

Library of Congress Cataloging-in-Publication Data

NASB exhaustive concordance.
The strongest NASB exhaustive concordance.
p. cm.
Originally published: Grand Rapids, Mich. : Zondervan, 2004, in series: Premier reference series.
ISBN-10: 0-310-26284-4
ISBN-13: 978-0-310-26284-8
1. Bible—Concordances, English—New American Standard. 2. Hebrew language—Dictionaries—English.
3. Aramaic language—Dictionaries—English. 4. Greek language, Biblical—Dictionaries—English.
I. Zondervan Bible Publishers (Grand Rapids, Mich.) II. Title.
BS425.N27 2004
220.5'208 – dc22

2004010497

Printed in the United States of America

14 15 16 17 18 19 20 21 22 23 • 23 22 21 20 19 18 17 16 15 14

CONTENTS

ACKNOWLEDGMENTS

A symphony not a solo

New American Standard Exhaustive Concordance
Project Staff

Based on the original 1981 edition
Robert L. Thomas, Th.D., General Editor
Reuben A. Olson, D.D., Project Chairman 1970-1976
Peter P. Ahn, Ph.D., Director of Research 1971-1976
Robert G. Lambeth, President, B.S., CPA, LL.D.
of
The Lockman Foundation

NASB Update Edition
revised and edited 1998
W. Don Wilkins, M.A., Th.M., Ph.D.

Robert G. Lambeth, President, B.S., CPA, LL.D.

Daniel L. Fox
Brian J. Harris
Eduardo Hernández
Dennis R. Hukel

R. S. Pike Lambeth
Sam P. Molina
Emilio A. Núñez, Jr.
Duane L. Wetzler, Ph.D.

of
The Lockman Foundation

The Lockman Foundation expresses gratitude to all the people who have had a part in the completion of the project. A special 'thank you' is also given to Phoebe N. Lambeth, Audrey Bartsch, Myrtle L. Larson, Margaret McKinstry McKay, Gladys Read, Marilyn J. Saliby, Elizabeth H. Storey, and Pamela J. Williams for their contribution to this work.

The grass withers, the flower fades, but the word of our God stands forever.
Isaiah 40:8

PREFACE

The most important tool for Bible study is a good concordance. It shows the reader where a particular verse is found in the Bible, just as a good map shows the location of a particular place. All Bible concordances list the words of the Bible in alphabetical order along with references to the verses in which they are found.

Like maps, however, concordances vary in completeness; often many words and verses are omitted. The NEW AMERICAN STANDARD EXHAUSTIVE CONCORDANCE lists every word which may be used to locate a verse* as well as complete references to all the verses in which that word occurs. The NEW AMERICAN STANDARD EXHAUSTIVE CONCORDANCE also notes the original Hebrew, Aramaic or Greek word from which the English word was translated. Abridged dictionaries of the original languages are provided which are based upon standard up-to-date reference works and give not only definitions but also English spellings of the words, translations and other useful information.

Because of its many features, the NEW AMERICAN STANDARD EXHAUSTIVE CONCORDANCE lends great flexibility to Bible study. Any verse in the NEW AMERICAN STANDARD BIBLE UPDATE may be found even when the reference is unknown to the reader. It is also possible to determine which verses in the Bible contain a certain word (e.g. 'love' or 'God'). The Hebrew, Aramaic or Greek for any listed word may be traced to find its general meaning and the ways in which it is translated in the NEW AMERICAN STANDARD BIBLE UPDATE. All of this may be done through a convenient reference system which requires no knowledge of the original languages. This reference system is based on the same numbering system for Hebrew, Aramaic and Greek words as that of Strong's *Exhaustive Concordance of the Bible* (King James Version).

Although other concordances listing the various words and their occurrences can be created for any Bible version, such an extensive reference system as that found in the NEW AMERICAN STANDARD EXHAUSTIVE CONCORDANCE is most effective for a translation that is both accurate and literal. The NEW AMERICAN STANDARD BIBLE UPDATE meets these requirements. The NEW AMERICAN STANDARD BIBLE UPDATE, in addition to its smoothly-flowing style, dignity, and readability, offers a word-for-word literalness which makes direct comparisons with the original languages possible.

The NEW AMERICAN STANDARD EXHAUSTIVE CONCORDANCE, like the NEW AMERICAN STANDARD BIBLE, is the result of monumental effort. The original NEW AMERICAN STANDARD EXHAUSTIVE CONCORDANCE was the product of more than ten years of work, much of which involved matching the English words to the corresponding words in the original languages. The nature of this work required that it be done by hand, though computers were used in most other tasks. A great deal of time has more recently been spent in revising the NEW AMERICAN STANDARD EXHAUSTIVE CONCORDANCE, in order to make it more consistent both with the NEW AMERICAN STANDARD BIBLE Updated Edition and with modern research on Biblical manuscripts and Greek etymology.

More than seventy dedicated people have faithfully worked on the project. Each staff member played a vital role whether as proofreader, assistant editor, language specialist, computer specialist, production coordinator, administrative assistant or in any of numerous other capacities.

All those who participated in this work share the hope that the NEW AMERICAN STANDARD EXHAUSTIVE CONCORDANCE will enrich personal Bible study and help to open the door to the marvelous treasures in God's Word.

The Lockman Foundation

*Frequently occurring words which would not be of practical use in locating a reference are not included in the NEW AMERICAN STANDARD EXHAUSTIVE CONCORDANCE. These words are:

a	be	her	is	of	that	unto	were
an	but	him	it	on	the	up	with
and	by	his	its	our	their	upon	you
are	for	I	me	out	them	us	your
as	from	in	my	shall	they	was	
at	he	into	not	she	to	we	

NEW AMERICAN STANDARD

EXHAUSTIVE CONCORDANCE OF THE BIBLE

HEBREW — ARAMAIC AND GREEK DICTIONARIES

Updated Edition

HOW TO USE THE CONCORDANCE

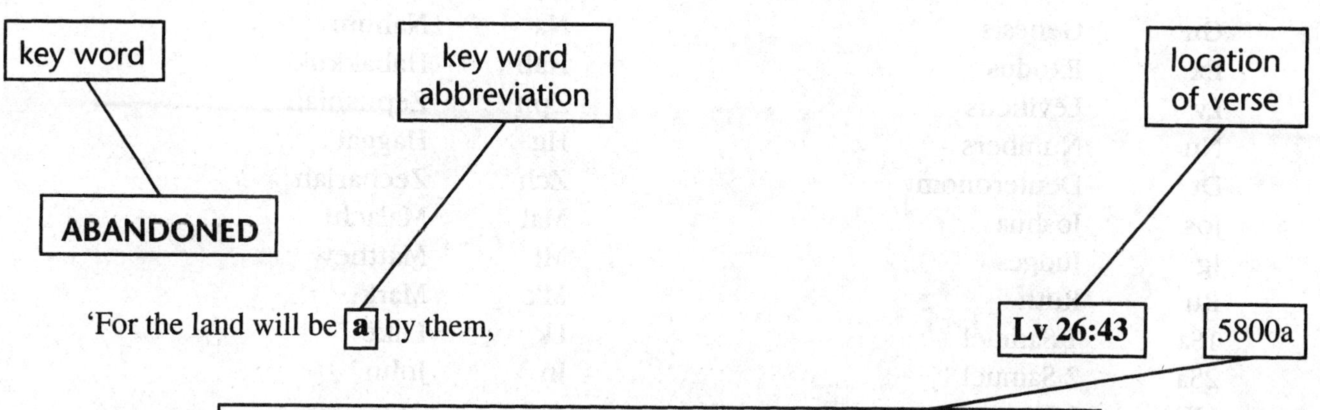

Reference number of the Hebrew-Aramaic (roman type) or Greek *(italic type)* word from which the English key word was translated. The numbers correspond to those found in Strong's *Exhaustive Concordance of the Bible* (KJV).

The lower case letter following some numbers indicates a word not listed as a separate entry in Strong's volume.

If a reference number is not found next to the verse reference, it indicates that the key word has been supplied to complete the English sentence or that the key word is part of an idiomatic expression.

HINTS TO HELP

Different forms of the same word, such as *abandon, abandoned,* or *abandons* are listed as separate key words.

Book titles, topical headings, Psalm titles, and explanatory statements found at the end of some books are not included because they are not part of the text of the Bible.

Words printed in italic type in the Bible are not included since they indicate words which are not found in the original Hebrew, Aramaic or Greek, but are implied by it.

A verse may be located which contains an Arabic numeral such as *10*. The list of key numbers follows the key words.

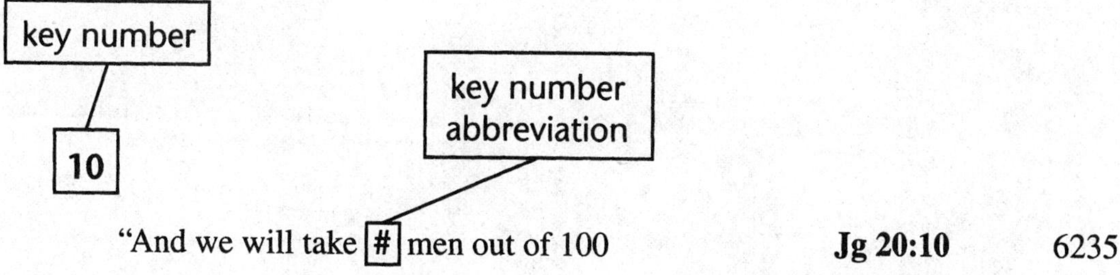

BIBLE BOOK ABBREVIATIONS

The following are the abbreviations of the books of the Bible used in this volume:

Gn	Genesis	Na	Nahum
Ex	Exodus	Hab	Habakkuk
Lv	Leviticus	Zph	Zephaniah
Nu	Numbers	Hg	Haggai
Dt	Deuteronomy	Zch	Zechariah
Jos	Joshua	Mal	Malachi
Jg	Judges	Mt	Matthew
Ru	Ruth	Mk	Mark
1Sa	1 Samuel	Lk	Luke
2Sa	2 Samuel	Jn	John
1Ki	1 Kings	Ac	Acts
2Ki	2 Kings	Ro	Romans
1Ch	1 Chronicles	1Co	1 Corinthians
2Ch	2 Chronicles	2Co	2 Corinthians
Ezr	Ezra	Ga	Galatians
Ne	Nehemiah	Eph	Ephesians
Es	Esther	Php	Philippians
Jb	Job	Col	Colossians
Ps	Psalms	1Th	1 Thessalonians
Pr	Proverbs	2Th	2 Thessalonians
Ec	Ecclesiastes	1Tm	1 Timothy
SS	Song of Solomon	2Tm	2 Timothy
Is	Isaiah	Ti	Titus
Jer	Jeremiah	Phm	Philemon
La	Lamentations	Heb	Hebrews
Ezk	Ezekiel	Jas	James
Da	Daniel	1Pe	1 Peter
Hos	Hosea	2Pe	2 Peter
Jl	Joel	1Jn	1 John
Am	Amos	2Jn	2 John
Ob	Obadiah	3Jn	3 John
Jon	Jonah	Jude	Jude
Mi	Micah	Rv	Revelation

A

AARON

not your brother **A** the Levite? Ex 4:14 175
Now the LORD said to **A**, Ex 4:27 175
Moses told **A** all the words of Ex 4:28 175
Then Moses and **A** went and Ex 4:29 175
and **A** spoke all the words which Ex 4:30 175
and **A** came and said to Pharaoh, Ex 5:1 175
"Moses and **A**, why do you draw the Ex 5:4 175
A as they were waiting for them. Ex 5:20 175
the LORD spoke to Moses and to **A**, Ex 6:13 175
and she bore him **A** and Moses; Ex 6:20 175
A married Elisheba, the Ex 6:23 175
It was *the same* **A** and Moses to Ex 6:26 175
it was *the same* Moses and **A**. Ex 6:27 175
brother **A** shall be your prophet. Ex 7:1 175
and your brother **A** shall speak to Ex 7:2 175
So Moses and **A** did *it;* Ex 7:6 175
years old and **A** eighty-three, Ex 7:7 175
Now the LORD spoke to Moses and **A**, Ex 7:8 175
miracle,' then you shall say to **A**, Ex 7:9 175
So Moses and **A** came to Pharaoh, Ex 7:10 175
and **A** threw his staff down before Ex 7:10 175
Moses, "Say to **A**, 'Take your staff Ex 7:19 175
So Moses and **A** did even as the Ex 7:20 175
"Say to **A**, 'Stretch out your hand Ex 8:5 175
So **A** stretched out his hand over Ex 8:6 175
called for Moses and **A** and said, Ex 8:8 175
Moses and **A** went out from Pharaoh, Ex 8:12 175
Moses, "Say to **A**, 'Stretch out your Ex 8:16 175
and **A** stretched out his hand with Ex 8:17 175
called for Moses and **A** and said, Ex 8:25 175
Then the LORD said to Moses and **A**, Ex 9:8 175
Then Pharaoh sent for Moses and **A**, Ex 9:27 175
Moses and **A** went to Pharaoh Ex 10:3 175
A were brought back to Pharaoh, Ex 10:8 175
hurriedly called for Moses and **A**, Ex 10:16 175
Moses and **A** performed all Ex 11:10 175
Moses and **A** in the land of Egypt, Ex 12:1 175
LORD had commanded Moses and **A**, Ex 12:28 175
for Moses and **A** at night and said, Ex 12:31 175
The LORD said to Moses and **A**, Ex 12:43 175
LORD had commanded Moses and **A**. Ex 12:50 175
Moses and **A** in the wilderness. Ex 16:2 175
So Moses and **A** said to all the Ex 16:6 175
Then Moses said to **A**, Ex 16:9 175
It came about as **A** spoke to Ex 16:10 175
Moses said to **A**, Ex 16:33 175
so **A** placed it before the Ex 16:34 175
and Moses, **A**, and Hur went up to Ex 17:10 175
A and Hur supported his hands, Ex 17:12 175
and **A** came with all the elders of Ex 18:12 175
come up *again,* you and **A** with you; Ex 19:24 175
"Come up to the LORD, you and **A**, Ex 24:1 175
Then Moses went up with **A**, Ex 24:9 175
behold, **A** and Hur are with you; Ex 24:14 175
A and his sons shall keep it in Ex 27:21 175
near to yourself **A** your brother, Ex 28:1 175
to minister as priest to Me—**A**, Ex 28:1 175
holy garments for **A** your brother, Ex 28:2 175
for **A** your brother and his sons, Ex 28:4 175
and **A** shall bear their names Ex 28:12 175
"**A** shall carry the names of Ex 28:29 175
and **A** shall carry the judgment of Ex 28:30 175
shall be on **A** when he ministers; Ex 28:35 175
and **A** shall take away the iniquity Ex 28:38 175
"You shall put them on **A** your Ex 28:41 175
"They shall be on **A** and on Ex 28:43 175
"Then you shall bring **A** and his Ex 29:4 175
and put on **A** the tunic and the Ex 29:5 175
them with sashes, **A** and his sons, Ex 29:9 175
you shall ordain **A** and his sons. Ex 29:9 175
and **A** and his sons shall lay their Ex 29:10 175
and **A** and his sons shall lay their Ex 29:15 175
and **A** and his sons shall lay their Ex 29:19 175
it on **A** and on his garments and Ex 29:21 175
of **A** and in the hands of his sons, Ex 29:24 175
from the one which was for **A** and Ex 29:27 175
"It shall be for **A** and his Ex 29:28 175
"The holy garments of **A** shall Ex 29:29 175
"**A** and his sons shall eat the Ex 29:32 175
you shall do to **A** and to his sons, Ex 29:35 175
I will also consecrate **A** and his Ex 29:44 175
"**A** shall burn fragrant Ex 30:7 175
A trims the lamps at twilight, Ex 30:8 175
"**A** shall make atonement on Ex 30:10 175
"**A** and his sons shall wash Ex 30:19 175
for **A** and his descendants Ex 30:21 175
You shall anoint **A** and his sons, Ex 30:30 175
holy garments for **A** the priest, Ex 31:10 175
the people assembled about **A** and Ex 32:1 175
A said to them, Ex 32:2 175
their ears and brought *them* to **A**. Ex 32:3 175
Now when **A** saw *this,* he built an Ex 32:5 175
A made a proclamation and said, Ex 32:5 175
Then Moses said to **A**, Ex 32:21 175
A said, "Do not let the anger Ex 32:22 175
for **A** had let them get out of control Ex 32:25 175
with the calf which **A** had made. Ex 32:35 175
So when **A** and all the sons of Ex 34:30 175
and **A** and all the rulers in the Ex 34:31 175
holy garments for **A** the priest and Ex 35:19 175
Ithamar the son of **A** the priest. Ex 38:21 175
holy garments which were for **A**, Ex 39:1 175
woven linen for **A** and his sons, Ex 39:27 175
the holy garments for **A** the priest Ex 39:41 175
"Then you shall bring **A** and his Ex 40:12 175
the holy garments on **A** and anoint Ex 40:13 175
From it Moses and **A** and his Ex 40:31 175
'The sons of **A** the priest Lv 1:7 175
belongs to **A** and his sons: Lv 2:3 175
belongs to **A** and his sons: Lv 2:10 175
and the sons of **A** shall sprinkle Lv 3:13 175
"Command **A** and his sons, saying, Lv 6:9 175
the sons of **A** shall present it Lv 6:14 175
of it **A** and his sons are to eat. Lv 6:16 175
among the sons of **A** may eat it; Lv 6:18 175
"This is the offering which **A** and Lv 6:20 175
"Speak to **A** and to his sons, Lv 6:25 175
shall belong to all the sons of **A**, Lv 7:10 175
shall belong to **A** and his sons. Lv 7:31 175
'The one among the sons of **A** who Lv 7:33 175
and have given them to **A** the Lv 7:34 175
that which is consecrated to **A** and Lv 7:35 175
"Take **A** and his sons with him, Lv 8:2 175
had **A** and his sons come near and Lv 8:6 175
and **A** and his sons laid their Lv 8:14 175
and **A** and his sons laid their Lv 8:18 175
and **A** and his sons laid their Lv 8:22 175
of **A** and on the hands of his sons and Lv 8:27 175
the altar and sprinkled it on **A**, Lv 8:30 175
and he consecrated **A**, Lv 8:30 175
Moses said to **A** and to his sons, Lv 8:31 175
'**A** and his sons shall eat it.' Lv 8:31 175
Thus **A** and his sons did all the Lv 8:36 175
eighth day that Moses called **A** and Lv 9:1 175
and he said to **A**, Lv 9:2 175
Moses then said to **A**, Lv 9:7 175
So **A** came near to the altar and Lv 9:8 175
thigh **A** presented as a wave offering Lv 9:21 175
Then **A** lifted up his hands toward Lv 9:22 175
A went into the tent of meeting. Lv 9:23 175
Nadab and Abihu, the sons of **A**, Lv 10:1 175
Then Moses said to **A**, Lv 10:3 175
So **A**, therefore, kept silent. Lv 10:3 175
Then Moses said to **A** and to his Lv 10:6 175
The LORD then spoke to **A**, Lv 10:8 175
Then Moses spoke to **A**, Lv 10:12 175
But **A** spoke to Moses, Lv 10:19 175
spoke again to Moses and to **A**, Lv 11:1 175
the LORD spoke to Moses and to **A**, Lv 13:1 175
shall be brought to **A** the priest or Lv 13:2 175
further spoke to Moses and to **A**, Lv 14:33 175
LORD also spoke to Moses and to **A**, Lv 15:1 175
the death of the two sons of **A**, Lv 16:1 175
"Tell your brother **A** that he Lv 16:2 175
"**A** shall enter the holy place Lv 16:3 175
"Then **A** shall offer the bull for Lv 16:6 175
"**A** shall cast lots for the Lv 16:8 175
"Then **A** shall offer the goat on Lv 16:9 175
"Then **A** shall offer the bull of Lv 16:11 175
"Then **A** shall lay both of his Lv 16:21 175
"Then **A** shall come into the tent Lv 16:23 175
"Speak to **A** and to his sons and Lv 17:2 175
to the priests, the sons of **A**, Lv 21:1 175
"Speak to **A**, saying, Lv 21:17 175
the descendants of **A** the priest who Lv 21:21 175
So Moses spoke to **A** and to his Lv 21:24 175
"Tell **A** and his sons to be Lv 22:2 175
'No man of the descendants of **A**, Lv 22:4 175
"Speak to **A** and to his sons and Lv 22:18 175
A shall keep it in order from Lv 24:3 175
It shall be for **A** and his sons, Lv 24:9 175
you and **A** shall number them by Nu 1:3 175
So Moses and **A** took these men who Nu 1:17 175
whom Moses and **A** numbered, Nu 1:44 175
the LORD spoke to Moses and to **A**, Nu 2:1 175
generations of **A** and Moses at the Nu 3:1 175
are the names of the sons of **A**: Nu 3:2 175
are the names of the sons of **A**, Nu 3:3 175
in the lifetime of their father **A**. Nu 3:4 175
and set them before **A** the priest, Nu 3:6 175
the Levites to **A** and to his sons; Nu 3:9 175
"So you shall appoint **A** and his Nu 3:10 175
and Eleazar the son of **A** the Nu 3:32 175
are Moses and **A** and his sons, Nu 3:38 175
whom Moses and **A** numbered at the Nu 3:39 175
them, to **A** and to his sons." Nu 3:48 175
ransom money to **A** and to his sons, Nu 3:51 175
the LORD spoke to Moses and to **A**, Nu 4:1 175
A and his sons shall go in and Nu 4:5 175
"When **A** and his sons have Nu 4:15 175
Eleazar the son of **A** the priest Nu 4:16 175
the LORD spoke to Moses and to **A**, Nu 4:17 175
A and his sons shall go in and Nu 4:19 175
at the command of **A** and his sons; Nu 4:27 175
Ithamar the son of **A** the priest. Nu 4:28 175
Ithamar the son of **A** the priest." Nu 4:33 175
So Moses and **A** and the leaders of Nu 4:34 175
whom Moses and **A** numbered Nu 4:37 175
whom Moses and **A** numbered Nu 4:41 175
whom Moses and **A** numbered Nu 4:45 175
whom Moses and **A** and the leaders Nu 4:46 175
"Speak to **A** and to his sons, Nu 6:23 175
Ithamar the son of **A** the priest. Nu 7:8 175
"Speak to **A** and say to him, Nu 8:2 175
A therefore did so; Nu 8:3 175
"**A** then shall present the Levites Nu 8:11 175
Levites stand before **A** and before Nu 8:13 175
Levites as a gift to **A** and to his sons Nu 8:19 175
Thus did Moses and **A** and all the Nu 8:20 175
and **A** presented them as a wave Nu 8:21 175
A also made atonement for them to Nu 8:21 175
before **A** and before his sons; Nu 8:22 175
before Moses and **A** on that day. Nu 9:6 175
"The priestly sons of **A**, Nu 10:8 175
Then Miriam and **A** spoke against Nu 12:1 175
said to Moses and **A** and to Miriam, Nu 12:4 175
tent, and He called **A** and Miriam. Nu 12:5 175
As **A** turned toward Miriam, behold, Nu 12:10 175
Then **A** said to Moses, Nu 12:11 175
proceeded to come to Moses and **A** Nu 13:26 175
grumbled against Moses and **A**; Nu 14:2 175
Then Moses and **A** fell on their Nu 14:5 175
The LORD spoke to Moses and **A**, Nu 14:26 175
wood brought him to Moses and **A** and Nu 15:33 175
together against Moses and **A**, Nu 16:3 175
but as for **A**, who is he that you Nu 16:11 175
both you and they along with **A**. Nu 16:16 175
A *shall* each *bring* his firepan." Nu 16:17 175
tent of meeting, with Moses and **A**. Nu 16:18 175
the LORD spoke to Moses and **A**, Nu 16:20 175
Eleazar, the son of **A** the priest, Nu 16:37 175
descendants of **A** should come near Nu 16:40 175
grumbled against Moses and **A**, Nu 16:41 175
had assembled against Moses and **A**, Nu 16:42 175
Then Moses and **A** came to the front Nu 16:43 175
Moses said to **A**, Nu 16:46 175
A took *it* as Moses had spoken, Nu 16:47 175
Then **A** returned to Moses at the Nu 16:50 175
the rod of **A** among their rods. Nu 17:6 175
the rod of **A** for the house of Levi Nu 17:8 175
"Put back the rod of **A** before the Nu 17:10 175
So the LORD said to **A**, Nu 18:1 175
Then the LORD spoke to **A**, Nu 18:8 175
Then the LORD said to **A**, Nu 18:20 175
LORD's offering to **A** the priest. Nu 18:28 175
the LORD spoke to Moses and **A**, Nu 19:1 175
themselves against Moses and **A**. Nu 20:2 175
Then Moses and **A** came in from the Nu 20:6 175
and you and your brother **A** Nu 20:8 175
and Moses and **A** gathered the Nu 20:10 175
But the LORD said to Moses and **A**, Nu 20:12 175
spoke to Moses and **A** at Mount Hor Nu 20:23 175
"**A** will be gathered to his Nu 20:24 175
"Take **A** and his son Eleazar and Nu 20:25 175
and strip **A** of his garments and Nu 20:26 175
So **A** will be gathered *to his* Nu 20:26 175
After Moses had stripped **A** of Nu 20:28 175
A died there on the mountain top. Nu 20:28 175
congregation saw that **A** had died, Nu 20:29 175
of Israel wept for **A** thirty days. Nu 20:29 175
Eleazar, the son of **A** the priest, Nu 25:7 175
Eleazar, the son of **A** the priest, Nu 25:11 175
Eleazar the son of **A** the priest, Nu 26:1 175
against **A** in the company of Korah, Nu 26:9 175
A and Moses and their sister Nu 26:59 175
To **A** were born Nadab and Abihu, Nu 26:60 175
by Moses and **A** the priest, Nu 26:64 175
people, as **A** your brother was; Nu 27:13 175
the leadership of Moses and **A**. Nu 33:1 175
Then **A** the priest went up to Mount Nu 33:38 175
A was one hundred twenty-three Nu 33:39 175
enough with **A** to destroy him; Dt 9:20 175
prayed for **A** at the same time. Dt 9:20 175
There **A** died and there he was Dt 10:6 175
as **A** your brother died on Mount Dt 32:50 175
And the sons of **A** the priest, who Jos 21:4 175
and they were for the sons of **A**, Jos 21:10 175
of **A** the priest they gave Hebron, Jos 21:13 175
All the cities of the sons of **A**, Jos 21:19 175
'Then I sent Moses and **A**, Jos 24:5 175
And Eleazar the son of **A** died; Jos 24:33 175
LORD who appointed Moses and **A** 1Sa 12:6 175
then the LORD sent Moses and **A** who 1Sa 12:8 175
The children of Amram *were* **A**, 1Ch 6:3 175
And the sons of **A** *were* Nadab, 1Ch 6:3 175
But **A** and his sons offered on the 1Ch 6:49 175
These are the sons of **A**: 1Ch 6:50 175
To the sons of **A** of the families 1Ch 6:54 175
To the sons of **A** they gave the 1Ch 6:57 175
was the leader of *the house of* **A**, 1Ch 12:27 175
gathered together the sons of **A** and 1Ch 15:4 175
sons of Amram were **A** and Moses. 1Ch 23:13 175
And **A** was set apart to sanctify 1Ch 23:13 175
assist the sons of **A** with the service 1Ch 23:28 175
of the sons of **A** their relatives, 1Ch 23:32 175
the descendants of **A** *were these:* 1Ch 24:1 175
the sons of **A** *were* Nadab, Abihu, 1Ch 24:1 175
to them through **A** their father, 1Ch 24:19 175
sons of **A** in the presence of David 1Ch 24:31 175
the son of Kemuel; for **A**, Zadok; 1Ch 27:17 175
the sons of **A** and the Levites, 2Ch 13:9 175
and the sons of **A** are ministering 2Ch 13:10 175
the sons of **A** who are consecrated 2Ch 26:18 175
the priests, the sons of **A**, 2Ch 29:21 175
Also for the sons of **A** the priests 2Ch 31:19 175
the priests, the sons of **A**, 2Ch 35:14 175
for the priests, the sons of **A**. 2Ch 35:14 175
son of **A** the chief priest. Ezr 7:5 175
The priest, the son of **A**, Ne 10:38 175
portion for the sons of **A**. Ne 12:47 175
flock By the hand of Moses and **A**. Ps 77:20 175
and **A** were among His priests, Ps 99:6 175
servant, *And* **A**, whom He had chosen. Ps 105:26 175
of Moses in the camp, And of **A**, Ps 106:16 175
O house of **A**, trust in the LORD; Ps 115:10 175
He will bless the house of **A**; Ps 115:12 175
Oh let the house of **A** say, Ps 118:3 175
O house of **A**, bless the LORD; Ps 135:19 175
And I sent before you Moses, **A**, and Mi 6:4 175
a wife from the daughters of **A**, Lk 1:5 2
SAYING TO **A**, 'MAKE FOR US GODS Ac 7:40 2
is called by God, even as **A** was. Heb 5:4 2

according to the order of A? **Heb 7:11** *2*
AARON'S
A son Eleazar married one of **Ex 6:25** 175
But A staff swallowed up their **Ex 7:12** 175
Miriam the prophetess, A sister, **Ex 15:20** 175
Eleazar and Ithamar, A sons. **Ex 28:1** 175
make A garments to consecrate him, **Ex 28:3** 175
and they shall be over A heart **Ex 28:30** 175
"It shall be on A forehead, **Ex 28:38** 175
For A sons you shall make tunics; **Ex 28:40** 175
lobe of A right ear and on the lobes **Ex 29:20** 175
the breast of A ram of ordination, **Ex 29:26** 175
and A sons the priests shall **Lv 1:5** 175
'Then A sons the priests shall **Lv 1:8** 175
before the LORD, and A sons the **Lv 1:11** 175
'He shall then bring it to A sons the **Lv 2:2** 175
the tent of meeting, and A sons the **Lv 3:2** 175
'Then A sons shall offer *it* up in **Lv 3:5** 175
and A sons shall sprinkle its **Lv 3:8** 175
oil on A head and anointed him, **Lv 8:12** 175
Next Moses had A sons come near **Lv 8:13** 175
put it on the lobe of A right ear, **Lv 8:23** 175
He also had A sons come near; **Lv 8:24** 175
A sons presented the blood to **Lv 9:9** 175
and A sons handed the blood to him **Lv 9:12** 175
and A sons handed the blood to him **Lv 9:18** 175
the sons of A uncle Uzziel, **Lv 10:4** 175
So he was angry with A surviving **Lv 10:16** 175
write A name on the rod of Levi; **Nu 17:3** 175
the son of Eleazar, A son, **Jg 20:28** 175
down upon the beard, *Even* A beard, **Ps 133:2** 175
the manna, and A rod which budded, **Heb 9:4** *2*
ABADDON
before Him, And A has no covering. **Jb 26:6** 11
"A and Death say, **Jb 28:22** 11
would be fire that consumes to A, **Jb 31:12** 11
the grave, Your faithfulness in A? **Ps 88:11** 11
and A *lie open* before the LORD, **Pr 15:11** 11
Sheol and A are never satisfied, **Pr 27:20** 11
his name in Hebrew is A, **Rv 9:11** *3*
ABAGTHA
Biztha, Harbona, Bigtha, A, **Es 1:10** 5
ABANAH
"Are not A and Pharpar, the **2Ki 5:12** 71
ABANDON
more a them in the wilderness, **Nu 32:15** 5117
"Do not a your servants; **Jos 10:6**
7503, 3027, 4480
they did not a their practices or **Jg 2:19** 5307
"For the LORD will not a His **1Sa 12:22** 5203
'I will a the remnant of My **2Ki 21:14** 5203
You will not a my soul to Sheol; **Ps 16:10** 5800a
Do not a me nor forsake me, O God **Ps 27:9** 5203
the LORD will not a His people, **Ps 94:14** 5203
Do not a my instruction. **Pr 4:2** 5800a
So a the quarrel before it breaks **Pr 17:14** 5203
How much more do his friends a him! **Pr 19:7** 7368
you, do not a your position, **Ec 10:4** 5117
given birth only to a *her young,* **Jer 14:5** 5800a
The LORD declares, 'I will a you.' **Jer 23:33** 5203
thus says the LORD—so I will a **Jer 24:8** 5414
I will a you to the wilderness, **Ezk 29:5** 5203
YOU WILL NOT A MY SOUL TO HADES, **Ac 2:27** *1459*
ABANDONED
'For the land will be a by them, **Lv 26:43** 5800a
But now the LORD has a us and **Jg 6:13** 5203
dead, they a the cities and fled; **1Sa 31:7** 5800a
They a their idols there, so **2Sa 5:21** 5800a
They a their gods there; **1Ch 14:12** 5800a
They a the house of the LORD, **2Ch 24:18** 5800a
Therefore You a them to the hand of **Ne 9:28** 5800a
your sake is the earth to be a, **Jb 18:4** 5800a
He a the dwelling place at Shiloh, **Ps 78:60** 5203
They have a the LORD, They have **Is 1:4** 5800a
For You have a Your people, the **Is 2:6** 5203
a nest, And as one gathers a eggs, **Is 10:14** 5800a
they a before the sons of Israel; **Is 17:9** 5800a
Because the palace has been a, **Is 32:14** 5203
My house, I have a My inheritance; **Jer 12:7** 5203
His altar, He has a His sanctuary; **La 2:7** 5010
For Gaza will be a And **Zph 2:4** 5800a
that HE WAS NEITHER A TO HADES, **Ac 2:31** *1459*
our being saved was gradually a. **Ac 27:20** *4014*
also the men a the natural function **Ro 1:27** *863*
domain, but a their proper abode, **Jude 1:6** *620*
ABANDONS
For she a her eggs to the earth And **Jb 39:14** 5800a
ABARIM
"Go up to this mountain of A, **Nu 27:12** 5682
and camped in the mountains of A, **Nu 33:47** 5682
journeyed from the mountains of A and **Nu 33:48** 5682
"Go up to this mountain of the A, **Dt 32:49** 5682
Cry out also from A, **Jer 22:20** 5682
ABASE
on the haughty *whom* You a. **2Sa 22:28** 8213
But haughty eyes You a. **Ps 18:27** 8213
And a the haughtiness of the **Is 13:11** 8213
is low and a that which is high. **Ezk 21:26** 8213
ABASED
the man *of importance* has been a, **Is 2:9** 8213
The proud look of man will be a And **Is 2:11** 8213
is lifted up, That he may be a. **Is 2:12** 8213
the loftiness of men will be a; **Is 2:17** 8213
and the man of *importance* a, **Is 5:15** 8213
eyes of the proud also will be a. **Is 5:15** 8213
And those who are lofty will be a. **Is 10:33** 8213
and a before all the people, **Mal 2:9** 8217
ABASHED
will be a and the sun ashamed, **Is 24:23** 2659
ABATED
was a from the face of the land; **Gn 8:8** 7043
the water was a from the earth. **Gn 8:11** 7043
eye was not dim, nor his vigor a. **Dt 34:7** 5127
ABBA
And He was saying, "A! Father! **Mk 14:36** *5*
by which we cry out, "A! Father!" **Ro 8:15** *5*
into our hearts, crying, "A! Father!" **Ga 4:6** *5*
ABDA
and Adoniram the son of A *was* over **1Ki 4:6** 5653
and A the son of Shammua, the son **Ne 11:17** 5653
ABDEEL
and Shelemiah the son of A to **Jer 36:26** 5655
ABDI
the son of Kishi, the son of A, **1Ch 6:44** 5660
Kish the son of A and Azariah the **2Ch 29:12** 5660
Mattaniah, Zechariah, Jehiel, A, **Ezr 10:26** 5660
ABDIEL
Ahi the son of A, the son of Guni, **1Ch 5:15** 5661
ABDOMEN
thigh waste away and your a swell; **Nu 5:21** 990
and make your a swell and your **Nu 5:22** 990
and her a will swell and her thigh **Nu 5:27** 990
His a is carved ivory Inlaid with **SS 5:14** 4578
ABDON
lands, A with its pasture lands, **Jos 21:30** 5658
Now A the son of Hillel the **Jg 12:13** 5658
Then A the son of Hillel the **Jg 12:15** 5658
lands, A with its pasture lands, **1Ch 6:74** 5658
A, Zichri, Hanan, **1Ch 8:23** 5658
and his firstborn son *was* A, **1Ch 8:30** 5658
and his firstborn son *was* A, **1Ch 9:36** 5658
of Shaphan, A the son of Micah, **2Ch 34:20** 5658
ABED-NEGO
Mishael Meshach and to Azariah A. **Da 1:7** 5664
Meshach and A over the **Da 2:49** 5665
namely Shadrach, Meshach and A. **Da 3:12** 5665
to bring Shadrach, Meshach and A; **Da 3:13** 5665
it true, Shadrach, Meshach and A, **Da 3:14** 5665
A replied to the king, **Da 3:16** 5665
toward Shadrach, Meshach and A. **Da 3:19** 5665
to tie up Shadrach, Meshach and A in **Da 3:20** 5665
up Shadrach, Meshach and A. **Da 3:22** 5665
men, Shadrach, Meshach and A, **Da 3:23** 5665
"Shadrach, Meshach and A, **Da 3:26** 5665
Meshach and A came out of the **Da 3:26** 5665
God of Shadrach, Meshach and A, **Da 3:28** 5665
Meshach and A shall be torn limb **Da 3:29** 5665
Meshach and A to prosper in the **Da 3:30** 5665
ABEL
she gave birth to his brother A. **Gn 4:2** 1893
And A was a keeper of flocks, but **Gn 4:2** 1893
A, on his part also brought of **Gn 4:4** 1893
regard for A and for his offering; **Gn 4:4** 1893
Cain told A his brother. **Gn 4:8** 1893
A his brother and killed him. **Gn 4:8** 1893
"Where is A your brother?" **Gn 4:9** 1893
another offspring in place of A, **Gn 4:25** 1893
of Israel to A, even Beth-maacah, **2Sa 20:14** 59
and besieged him in A Beth-maacah, **2Sa 20:15** 62
'They will surely ask *advice* at A,' **2Sa 20:18** 59
A to the blood of Zechariah, **Mt 23:35** *6*
of A to the blood of Zechariah, **Lk 11:51** *6*
By faith A offered to God a better **Heb 11:4** *6*
speaks better than *the blood* of A. **Heb 12:24** *6*
ABEL-BETH-MAACAH
Ijon, Dan, A and all Chinneroth, **1Ki 15:20** 62
Ijon and A and Janoah and Kedesh **2Ki 15:29** 62
ABEL-KERAMIM
twenty cities, and as far as A. **Jg 11:33** 64
ABEL-MAIM
and they conquered Ijon, Dan, A and **2Ch 16:4** 66
ABEL-MEHOLAH
Zererah, as far as the edge of A, **Jg 7:22** 65
from Beth-shean to A as far as the **1Ki 4:12** 65
Elisha the son of Shaphat of A you **1Ki 19:16** 65
ABEL-MIZRAIM
Therefore it was named A, **Gn 50:11** 67
ABEL-SHITTIM
as far as A in the plains of Moab. **Nu 33:49** 63
ABHOR
for My soul shall a you. **Lv 26:30** 1602
I so a them as to destroy them, **Lv 26:44** 1602
it and you shall utterly a it, **Dt 7:26** 8581
And my own clothes would a me. **Jb 9:31** 8581
"All my associates a me, **Jb 19:19** 8581
"They a me *and* stand aloof from **Jb 30:10** 8581
curse him, nations will a him; **Pr 24:24** 2194
a him who speaks *with* integrity. **Am 5:10** 8581
Who a justice And twist everything **Mi 3:9** 8581
You who a idols, do you rob **Ro 2:22** *948*
A what is evil; cling to what is good. **Ro 12:9** *655*
ABHORRED
and therefore I have a them. **Lv 20:23** 6973
and their soul a My statutes. **Lv 26:43** 1602
he a Israel and reigned over Aram. **1Ki 11:25** 6973
For He has not despised nor a the **Ps 22:24** 8262
with wrath And greatly a Israel; **Ps 78:59** 3988a
people And He a His inheritance. **Ps 106:40** 8581
Their soul a all kinds of food, **Ps 107:18** 8581
One, To the One a by the nation, **Is 49:7** 8581
were a on the day you were born. **Ezk 16:5** 1604
ABHORRENCE
will be an a to all mankind." **Is 66:24** 1860
ABHORRENT
and they shall be a to you; **Lv 11:11** 8263
have fins and scales is a to you. **Lv 11:12** 8263
they are a, not to be eaten: **Lv 11:13** 8263
takes his brother's wife, it is a; **Lv 20:21** 5079
the king's command was a to Joab. **1Ch 21:6** 8581
gold will become an a thing; **Ezk 7:19** 5079
I will make it an a thing to them. **Ezk 7:20** 5079
ABHORS
and if your soul a My ordinances **Lv 26:15** 1602
The LORD a the man of bloodshed **Ps 5:6** 8581
ABI
was A the daughter of Zechariah. **2Ki 18:2** 21
ABI-ALBON
A the Arbathite, Azmaveth the **2Sa 23:31** 45
ABIASAPH
Assir and Elkanah and A; **Ex 6:24** 23
ABIATHAR
the son of Ahitub, named A, **1Sa 22:20** 54
A told David that Saul had **1Sa 22:21** 54
Then David said to A, **1Sa 22:22** 54
when A the son of Ahimelech fled **1Sa 23:6** 54
so he said to A the priest, **1Sa 23:9** 54
Then David said to A the priest, **1Sa 30:7** 54
So A brought the ephod to David. **1Sa 30:7** 54
the son of A *were* priests, **2Sa 8:17** 54
and A came up until all the people **2Sa 15:24** 54
Ahimaaz and Jonathan the son of A. **2Sa 15:27** 54
Therefore Zadok and A returned the **2Sa 15:29** 54
and A the priests with you there? **2Sa 15:35** 54
report to Zadok and A the priests. **2Sa 15:35** 54
to Zadok and to A the priests, **2Sa 17:15** 54
sent to Zadok and A the priests, **2Sa 19:11** 54
and Zadok and A were priests; **2Sa 20:25** 54
of Zeruiah and with A the priest; **1Ki 1:7** 54
the sons of the king and A the priest **1Ki 1:19** 54
of the army and A the priest, **1Ki 1:25** 54
the son of A the priest came. **1Ki 1:42** 54
for him, for A the priest, **1Ki 2:22** 54
to A the priest the king said, **1Ki 2:26** 54
A from being priest to the LORD, **1Ki 2:27** 54
the priest in the place of A. **1Ki 2:35** 54
and Zadok and A *were* priests; **1Ki 4:4** 54
for Zadok and A the priests, **1Ch 15:11** 54
the son of A *were* priests, **1Ch 18:16** 54
priest, Ahimelech the son of A, **1Ch 24:6** 54
and A succeeded Ahithophel; **1Ch 27:34** 54
in the time of A *the* high priest, **Mk 2:26** *8*
ABIATHAR'S
Zadok's son and Jonathan, A son; **2Sa 15:36** 54
ABIB
"On this day in the month of A, **Ex 13:4** 24
the appointed time in the month A, **Ex 23:15** 24
appointed time in the month of A, **Ex 34:18** 24
month of A you came out of Egypt. **Ex 34:18** 24
"Observe the month of A and **Dt 16:1** 24
for in the month of A the LORD **Dt 16:1** 24
ABIDA
Epher and Hanoch and A and Eldaah. **Gn 25:4** 28
were Ephah, Epher, Hanoch, A **1Ch 1:33** 28
ABIDAN
of Benjamin, A the son of Gideoni; **Nu 1:11** 27
A the son of Gideoni, **Nu 2:22** 27
day *it was* A the son of Gideoni, **Nu 7:60** 27
offering of A the son of Gideoni. **Nu 7:65** 27
and A the son of Gideoni over the **Nu 10:24** 27
ABIDE
know its ways Nor a in its paths. **Jb 24:13** 3427
O Lord, who may a in Your tent? **Ps 15:1**
1481a, 7931
His soul will a in prosperity, And **Ps 25:13** 3885a
do good, So you will a forever. **Ps 37:27** 7931
He will a before God forever; **Ps 61:7** 3427
a in the shadow of the Almighty. **Ps 91:1** 3885a
But You, O LORD, a forever **Ps 102:12** 3427
He makes the barren woman a in the **Ps 113:9** 3427
will a in the fertile field. **Is 32:16** 3427
"A in Me, and I in you. **Jn 15:4** *3306*
can you unless you a in Me. **Jn 15:4** *3306*
"If anyone does not a in Me, **Jn 15:6** *3306*
"If you a in Me, and My words **Jn 15:7** *3306*
in Me, and My words a in you, **Jn 15:7** *3306*
have also loved you; a in My love. **Jn 15:9** *3306*
you will a in My love; **Jn 15:10** *3306*
commandments and a in His love. **Jn 15:10** *3306*
But now faith, hope, love, a these **1Co 13:13** *3306*
CURSED IS EVERYONE WHO DOES NOT A **Ga 3:10** *1696*
let that a in you which you heard **1Jn 2:24** *3306*
a in the Son and in the Father. **1Jn 2:24** *3306*
it has taught you, you a in Him. **1Jn 2:27** *3306*
Now, little children, a in Him, **1Jn 2:28** *3306*
how does the love of God a in him? **1Jn 3:17** *3306*
that we a in Him and He in us, **1Jn 4:13** *3306*
not a in the teaching of Christ, **2Jn 1:9** *3306*
ABIDES
tent of meeting which a with them **Lv 16:16** 7931
But the LORD a forever; **Ps 9:7** 3427
cannot be moved but a forever. **Ps 125:1** 3427
but the wrath of God a on him." **Jn 3:36** *3306*
flesh and drinks My blood a in Me, **Jn 6:56** *3306*
know Him because He a with you and **Jn 14:17** *3306*
itself unless it a in the vine, **Jn 15:4** *3306*
he who a in Me and I in him, he **Jn 15:5** *3306*
the *law* of liberty, and a by it, **Jas 1:25** *3887*
the one who says he a in Him ought **1Jn 2:6** *3306*

The one who loves his brother **a** in 1Jn 2:10 *3306*
and the word of God **a** in you, 1Jn 2:14 *3306*
heard from the beginning **a** in you, 1Jn 2:24 *3306*
you received from Him **a** in you, 1Jn 2:27 *3306*
No one who **a** in Him sins; 1Jn 3:6 *3306*
sin, because His seed **a** in him; 1Jn 3:9 *3306*
He who does not love **a** in death. 1Jn 3:14 *3306*
keeps His commandments **a** in Him, 1Jn 3:24 *3306*
We know by this that He **a** in us, 1Jn 3:24 *3306*
we love one another, God **a** in us, 1Jn 4:12 *3306*
is the Son of God, God **a** in him, 1Jn 4:15 *3306*
one who **a** in love abides in God, 1Jn 4:16 *3306*
one who abides in love **a** in God, 1Jn 4:16 *3306*
abides in God, and God **a** in him. 1Jn 4:16 *3306*
for the sake of the truth which **a** 2Jn 1:2 *3306*
the one who **a** in the teaching, he 2Jn 1:9 *3306*

ABIDING
My Spirit is **a** in your midst; Hg 2:5 5975
You do not have His word **a** in you, Jn 5:38 *3306*
the Father **a** in Me does His works. Jn 14:10 *3306*
spoken to you while **a** with you. Jn 14:25 *3306*
has eternal life **a** in him. 1Jn 3:15 *3306*

ABIEL
whose name was Kish the son of **A**, 1Sa 9:1 22
father of Abner *was* the son of **A**. 1Sa 14:51 22
brooks of Gaash, **A** the Arbathite, 1Ch 11:32 22

ABIEZER
for the sons of **A** and for the sons Jos 17:2 44
better than the vintage of **A**? Jg 8:2 44
A the Anathothite, Mebunnai the 2Sa 23:27 44
bore Ishhod and **A** and Mahlah. 1Ch 7:18 44
the Tekoite, **A** the Anathothite, 1Ch 11:28 44
ninth month *was* **A** the Anathothite 1Ch 27:12 44

ABIEZRITE
which belonged to Joash the **A** as Jg 6:11 33

ABIEZRITES
it is still in Ophrah of the **A**. Jg 6:24 33
and the **A** were called together to Jg 6:34 44
father Joash, in Ophrah of the **A**. Jg 8:32 33

ABIGAIL
Nabal, and his wife's name was **A**. 1Sa 25:3 26
But one of the young men told **A**, 1Sa 25:14 26
Then **A** hurried and took two 1Sa 25:18 26
When **A** saw David, she hurried and 1Sa 25:23 26
Then David said to **A**, 1Sa 25:32 26
Then **A** came to Nabal, and behold, 1Sa 25:36 26
Then David sent a proposal to **A**, 1Sa 25:39 26
of David came to **A** at Carmel, 1Sa 25:40 26
Then **A** quickly arose, and rode on 1Sa 25:42 26
and **A** the Carmelitess, 1Sa 27:3 26
Ahinoam the Jezreelitess and **A** the 1Sa 30:5 26
Ahinoam the Jezreelitess and **A** the 2Sa 2:2 26
by **A** the widow of Nabal the 2Sa 3:3 26
in to **A** the daughter of Nahash, 2Sa 17:25 26
their sisters *were* Zeruiah and **A**. 1Ch 2:16 26
A bore Amasa, and the father 1Ch 2:17 26
was Daniel, by **A** the Carmelitess; 1Ch 3:1 26

ABIHAIL
of Merari *was* Zuriel the son of **A**. Nu 3:35 32
The name of Abishur's wife *was* **A**, 1Ch 2:29 32
These *were* the sons of **A**, 1Ch 5:14 32
son of David *and of* **A** the daughter 2Ch 11:18 32
the daughter of **A** the uncle of Es 2:15 32
Then Queen Esther, daughter of **A**, Es 9:29 32

ABIHU
and she bore him Nadab and **A**, Ex 6:23 30
Nadab and **A** and seventy of the Ex 24:1 30
went up with Aaron, Nadab and **A**, Ex 24:9 30
as priest to Me—Aaron, Nadab and **A**, Ex 28:1 30
Now Nadab and **A**, the sons of Lv 10:1 30
Nadab the firstborn, and **A**, Nu 3:2 30
But Nadab and **A** died before the Nu 3:4 30
To Aaron were born Nadab and **A**, Nu 26:60 30
But Nadab and **A** died when they Nu 26:61 30
the sons of Aaron *were* Nadab, **A**, 1Ch 6:3 30
the sons of Aaron *were* Nadab, **A**, 1Ch 24:1 30
But Nadab and **A** died before their 1Ch 24:2 30

ABIHUD
Bela had sons: Addar, Gera, **A**, 1Ch 8:3 31
Zerubbabel was the father of **A**, Mt 1:13 *10*
A the father of Eliakim, and Eliakim Mt 1:13 *10*

ABIJAH
and the name of his second, **A**; 1Sa 8:2 29
At that time **A** the son of Jeroboam 1Ki 14:1 29
of Hezron in Caleb-ephrathah, **A**, 1Ch 2:24 29
son *was* Rehoboam, **A** *was* his son, 1Ch 3:10 29
were Joel the firstborn, and **A** 1Ch 6:28 29
Elioenai, Omri, Jeremoth, **A**, 1Ch 7:8 29
for Hakkoz, the eighth for **A**, 1Ch 24:10 29
of Absalom, and she bore him **A**, 2Ch 11:20 29
Rehoboam appointed **A** the son 2Ch 11:22 29
son **A** became king in his place. 2Ch 12:16 29
A became king over Judah. 2Ch 13:1 29
was war between **A** and Jeroboam. 2Ch 13:2 29
A began the battle with an 2Ch 13:3 29
Then **A** stood on Mount Zemaraim, 2Ch 13:4 29
and all Israel before **A** and Judah. 2Ch 13:15 29
A and his people defeated them 2Ch 13:17 29
A pursued Jeroboam and 2Ch 13:19 29
recover strength in the days of **A**; 2Ch 13:20 29
But **A** became powerful; and took 2Ch 13:21 29
Now the rest of the acts of **A**, 2Ch 13:22 29
So **A** slept with his fathers, and 2Ch 14:1 29
And his mother's name *was* **A**, 2Ch 29:1 29
Meshullam, **A**, Mijamin, Ne 10:7 29
Iddo, Ginnethoi, **A**, Ne 12:4 29
of **A**, Zichri; of Miniamin, Ne 12:17 29
Rehoboam the father of **A**, Mt 1:7 *7*
A the father of Asa. Mt 1:7 *7*
Zacharias, of the division of **A**; Lk 1:5 *7*

ABIJAM
And **A** his son became king in his 1Ki 14:31 38
Nebat, **A** became king over Judah. 1Ki 15:1 38
the acts of **A** and all that he did, 1Ki 15:7 38
was war between **A** and Jeroboam. 1Ki 15:7 38
And **A** slept with his fathers and 1Ki 15:8 38

ABILENE
and Lysanias was tetrarch of **A**, Lk 3:1 *9*

ABILITY
"Now with all my **a** I have 1Ch 29:2 3581b
According to their **a** they gave to Ezr 2:69 3581b
"We according to our **a** have Ne 5:8 1767
discerning nor favor to men of **a**; Ec 9:11 3045
and who had **a** for serving in the Da 1:4 3581b
one, each according to his own **a**; Mt 25:15 *1411*
testify that according to their **a**, 2Co 8:3 *1411*
and beyond their **a**, *they gave* of 2Co 8:3 *1411*
the completion of it by your **a**. 2Co 8:11 *2192*
herself received **a** to conceive, Heb 11:11 *1411*

ABIMAEL
and Obal and **A** and Sheba Gn 10:28 39
Ebal, **A**, Sheba, 1Ch 1:22 39

ABIMELECH
So **A** king of Gerar sent and took Gn 20:2 40
came to **A** in a dream of the night, Gn 20:3 40
Now **A** had not come near her; Gn 20:4 40
So **A** arose early in the morning Gn 20:8 40
Then **A** called Abraham and said to Gn 20:9 40
And **A** said to Abraham, Gn 20:10 40
A then took sheep and oxen and Gn 20:14 40
A said, "Behold, my land Gn 20:15 40
A and his wife and his maids, Gn 20:17 40
household of **A** because of Sarah, Gn 20:18 40
at that time that **A** and Phicol, Gn 21:22 40
But Abraham complained to **A** Gn 21:25 40
the servants of **A** had seized. Gn 21:25 40
And **A** said, "I do not know who Gn 21:26 40
and oxen and gave them to **A** Gn 21:27 40
A said to Abraham, Gn 21:29 40
and **A** and Phicol, the commander of Gn 21:32 40
to **A** king of the Philistines. Gn 26:1 40
that **A** king of the Philistines Gn 26:8 40
Then **A** called Isaac and said, Gn 26:9 40
A said, "What is this you have Gn 26:10 40
So **A** charged all the people, Gn 26:11 40
Then **A** said to Isaac, Gn 26:16 40
Then **A** came to him from Gerar with Gn 26:26 40
him a son, and he named him **A**. Jg 8:31 40
And **A** the son of Jerubbaal went to Jg 9:1 40
they were inclined to follow **A**, Jg 9:3 40
A hired worthless and reckless fellows, Jg 9:4 40
and they went and made **A** king, Jg 9:6 40
and integrity in making **A** king, Jg 9:16 40
on one stone, and have made **A**, Jg 9:18 40
his house this day, rejoice in **A**, Jg 9:19 40
let fire come out from **A** and Jg 9:20 40
from Beth-millo, and consume **A**." Jg 9:20 40
there because of **A** his brother. Jg 9:21 40
A ruled over Israel three years. Jg 9:22 40
between **A** and the men of Shechem; Jg 9:23 40
dealt treacherously with **A**, Jg 9:23 40
might be laid on **A** their brother, Jg 9:24 40
and it was told to **A**. Jg 9:25 40
and ate and drank and cursed **A**. Jg 9:27 40
"Who is **A**, and who is Shechem, Jg 9:28 40
Then I would remove **A**." Jg 9:29 40
And he said to **A**, Jg 9:29 40
sent messengers to **A** deceitfully, Jg 9:31 40
So **A** and all the people who *were* Jg 9:34 40
and **A** and the people who *were* with Jg 9:35 40
is **A** that we should serve him?' Jg 9:38 40
of Shechem and fought with **A**. Jg 9:39 40
A chased him, and he fled Jg 9:40 40
Then **A** remained at Arumah, but Jg 9:41 40
the field, and it was told to **A**. Jg 9:42 40
Then **A** and the company who was Jg 9:44 40
A fought against the city all Jg 9:45 40
It was told **A** that all the Jg 9:47 40
So **A** went up to Mount Zalmon, he Jg 9:48 40
and **A** took an axe in his hand and Jg 9:48 40
one his branch and followed **A**, Jg 9:49 40
Then **A** went to Thebez, and he Jg 9:50 40
So **A** came to the tower and fought Jg 9:52 40
men of Israel saw that **A** was dead, Jg 9:55 40
God repaid the wickedness of **A**, Jg 9:56 40
Now after **A** died, Tola the son of Jg 10:1 40
down **A** the son of Jerubbesheth? 2Sa 11:21 40
and Zadok the son of Ahitub and **A** 1Ch 18:16 40

ABIMELECH'S
an upper millstone on **A** head, Jg 9:53 40

ABINADAB
into the house of **A** on the hill, 1Sa 7:1 41
Then Jesse called **A** and 1Sa 16:8 41
and the second to him **A**, 1Sa 17:13 41
A and Malchi-shua the sons of Saul. 1Sa 31:2 41
house of **A** which was on the hill; 2Sa 6:3 41
and Uzzah and Ahio, the sons of **A**, 2Sa 6:3 41
ark of God from the house of **A**, 2Sa 6:4 41
his firstborn, then **A** the second, 1Ch 2:13 41
father of Jonathan, Malchi-shua, **A** and 1Ch 8:33 41
father of Jonathan, Malchi-shua, **A** and 1Ch 9:39 41
down Jonathan, **A** and Malchi-shua, 1Ch 10:2 41
on a new cart from the house of **A**, 1Ch 13:7 41

ABINOAM
the son of **A** from Kedesh-naphtali, Jg 4:6 42
of **A** had gone up to Mount Tabor. Jg 4:12 42
the son of **A** sang on that day, Jg 5:1 42
away your captives, O son of **A**. Jg 5:12 42

ABIRAM
son of Levi, with Dathan and **A**, Nu 16:1 48
sent a summons to Dathan and **A**, Nu 16:12 48
of Korah, Dathan and **A**.' " Nu 16:24 48
arose and went to Dathan and **A**, Nu 16:25 48
dwellings of Korah, Dathan and **A**; Nu 16:27 48
and Dathan and **A** came out *and* Nu 16:27 48
Nemuel and Dathan and **A**. Nu 26:9 48
These are the Dathan and **A** who Nu 26:9 48
and what He did to Dathan and **A**, Dt 11:6 48
with the *loss of* **A** his firstborn, 1Ki 16:34 48
And engulfed the company of **A**. Ps 106:17 48

ABISHAG
and found **A** the Shunammite, 1Ki 1:3 49
and **A** the Shunammite was 1Ki 1:15 49
me **A** the Shunammite as a wife." 1Ki 2:17 49
"Let **A** the Shunammite be given to 1Ki 2:21 49
A the Shunammite for Adonijah? 1Ki 2:22 49

ABISHAI
and to **A** the son of Zeruiah, 1Sa 26:6 52
A said, "I will go down with you." 1Sa 26:6 52
and **A** came to the people by night, 1Sa 26:7 52
Then **A** said to David, 1Sa 26:8 52
But David said to **A**, 1Sa 26:9 52
were there, Joab and **A** and Asahel; 2Sa 2:18 52
But Joab and **A** pursued Abner, and 2Sa 2:24 52
So Joab and **A** his brother killed 2Sa 3:30 52
in the hand of **A** his brother, 2Sa 10:10 52
before **A** and entered the city. 2Sa 10:14 52
Then **A** the son of Zeruiah said to 2Sa 16:9 52
said to **A** and to all his servants, 2Sa 16:11 52
command of **A** the son of Zeruiah, 2Sa 18:2 52
king charged Joab and **A** and Ittai, 2Sa 18:5 52
king charged you and **A** and Ittai, 2Sa 18:12 52
But **A** the son of Zeruiah said 2Sa 19:21 52
And David said to **A**, 2Sa 20:6 52
Then Joab and **A** his brother 2Sa 20:10 52
A the son of Zeruiah helped him, 2Sa 21:17 52
A, the brother of Joab, the 2Sa 23:18 52
Moreover **A** the son of Zeruiah 1Ch 18:12 52

ABISHALOM
name was Maacah the daughter of **A**. 1Ki 15:2 53
name was Maacah the daughter of **A**. 1Ki 15:10 53

ABISHUA
Phinehas became the father of **A**, 1Ch 6:4 50
and **A** became the father of Bukki, 1Ch 6:5 50
son, Phinehas his son, **A** his son, 1Ch 6:50 50
A, Naaman, Ahoah, 1Ch 8:4 50
son of **A**, son of Phinehas, son of Ezr 7:5 50

ABISHUR
sons of Shammai *were* Nadab and **A**. 1Ch 2:28 51

ABISHUR'S
The name of **A** wife *was* Abihail, 1Ch 2:29 51

ABITAL
fifth, Shephatiah the son of **A**; 2Sa 3:4 37
the fifth *was* Shephatiah, by **A**; 1Ch 3:3 37

ABITUB
became the father of **A** and Elpaal. 1Ch 8:11 36

ABLAZE
among the brands you have set **a**. Is 50:11 1197a
His throne *was* **a** with flames, Its Da 7:9 7631
that is coming will set them **a**," Mal 4:1 3857

ABLE
were not **a** to remain together. Gn 13:6 3201
if you are **a** to count them." Gn 15:5 3201
no one will be **a** to see the land. Ex 10:5 3201
all the people **a** men who fear God, Ex 18:21 2428
you, then you will be **a** to endure, Ex 18:23 3201
chose **a** men out of all Israel and Ex 18:25 2428
Moses was not **a** to enter the Ex 40:35 3201
whoever *is* **a** *to* go out to war in Nu 1:3
whoever *was* **a** *to* go out to war, Nu 1:20
whoever *was* **a** *to* go out to war, Nu 1:22
whoever *was* **a** *to* go out to war, Nu 1:24
whoever *was* **a** *to* go out to war, Nu 1:26
whoever *was* **a** *to* go out to war, Nu 1:28
whoever *was* **a** *to* go out to war, Nu 1:30
whoever *was* **a** *to* go out to war, Nu 1:32
whoever *was* **a** *to* go out to war, Nu 1:34
whoever *was* **a** *to* go out to war, Nu 1:36
whoever *was* **a** *to* go out to war, Nu 1:38
whoever *was* **a** *to* go out to war, Nu 1:40
whoever *was* **a** *to* go out to war, Nu 1:42
whoever *was* **a** *to* go out to war in Nu 1:45
am not **a** to carry all this people, Nu 11:14 3201
not **a** to go up against the people, Nu 13:31 3201
perhaps I may be **a** to defeat them Nu 22:6 3201
I may be **a** to fight against them and Nu 22:11 3201
Am I **a** to speak anything at all? Nu 22:38 3201
is **a** to go out to war in Israel." Nu 26:2
'I am not **a** to bear *the burden* of Dt 1:9 3201
a to put an end to them quickly, Dt 7:22 3201
no man will be **a** to stand before Dt 7:24
"Because the LORD was not **a** to Dt 9:28 3201
"No man will be **a** to stand before you; Dt 11:25
you are not **a** to bring *the tithe*, Dt 14:24 3201
"Every man shall give as he is **a**, Dt 16:17 3027
I am no longer **a** to come and go, Dt 31:2 3201
"No man will *be* **a** *to* stand Jos 1:5
will not be **a** to serve the LORD, Jos 24:19 3201
a to do in comparison with you?" Jg 8:3 3201
"Who is **a** to stand before the 1Sa 6:20 3201

is a to fight with me and kill me, 1Sa 17:9 3201
"You are not a to go against this 1Sa 17:33 3201
For who is a to judge this great 1Ki 3:9 3201
And all who were a to put on armor 2Ki 3:21 3201
if you are a on your part to set 2Ki 18:23 3201
be a to deliver you from my hand; 2Ki 18:29 3201
1,760 very a men for the work of 1Ch 9:13 2428
relatives *were* a men with strength for 1Ch 26:8 2428
we should be a to offer as generously 1Ch 29:14 6113, 3581b
who is a to build a house for Him, 2Ch 2:6 6113, 3581b
a to contain the burnt offering, 2Ch 7:7 3201
a to go to war *and* handle 2Ch 25:5 3201
nations of the lands a at all to deliver 2Ch 32:13 3201
be a to deliver you from my hand? 2Ch 32:14 3201
kingdom was a to deliver his people 2Ch 32:15 3201
but they were not a to give Ezr 2:59 3201
we are not a to stand in the open. Ezr 10:13 3581b
lived in Jerusalem were 468 a men. Ne 11:6 2428
and none of them was a to speak Ne 13:24 5234
widows will not be a to weep. Jb 27:15
so that they were not a to rise; Ps 18:38 3201
me, so that I am not a to see; Ps 40:12 3201
Man is not a to tell *it*. Ec 1:8 3201
For who is a to straighten what He Ec 7:13 3201
if you are a on your part to set Is 36:8 3201
he will not be a to deliver you; Is 36:14 3201
Perhaps you will be a to profit, Is 47:12 3201
they will not be a to escape; Jer 11:11 3201
LORD was no longer a to endure *it*, Jer 44:22 3201
will not be a to conceal himself; Jer 49:10 3201
against whom I am not a to stand. La 1:14 3201
gold will not be a to deliver them Ezk 7:19 3201
not be a to live by his righteousness Ezk 33:12 3201
lambs as much as he is a to give, Ezk 46:5 3027
with the lambs as much as he is a, Ezk 46:7 5381, 3027
lambs as much as one is a to give, Ezk 46:11 3027
"Are you a to make known to me Da 2:26 3546
are a to declare *it* to the king. Da 2:27 3202
been a to reveal this mystery." Da 2:47 3202
our God whom we serve is a to Da 3:17 3202
who is a to deliver in this way." Da 3:29 3202
wise men of my kingdom is a to make Da 4:18 3202
but you are a, for a spirit of the Da 4:18 3546
and He is a to humble those who Da 4:37 3202
you are a to give interpretations Da 5:16 3202
Now if you are a to read the Da 5:16 3202
a to deliver you from the lions?" Da 6:20 3202
and no one will *be* a *to* withstand Da 11:16
their gold Will be a to deliver them Zph 1:18 3201
that from these stones God is a to Mt 3:9 *1410*
believe that I am a to do this?" Mt 9:28 *1410*
but rather fear Him who is a to Mt 10:28 *1410*
He who is a to accept *this*, let Mt 19:12 *1410*
Are you a to drink the cup that I Mt 20:22 *1410*
They said to Him, "We are a." Mt 20:22 *1410*
No one was a to answer Him a word, Mt 22:46 *1410*
'I am a to destroy the temple of Mt 26:61 *1410*
that house will not be a to stand. Mk 3:25 *1410*
to them, so far as they were a to hear it; Mk 4:33 *1410*
no one was a to bind him anymore, Mk 5:3 *1410*
"Where will anyone be a *to find* Mk 8:4 *1410*
and be a soon afterward to speak Mk 9:39 *1410*
a to drink the cup that I drink, Mk 10:38 *1410*
They said to Him, "We are a." Mk 10:39 *1410*
from these stones God is a Lk 3:8 *1410*
seek to enter and will not be a. Lk 13:24 *2480*
and is not a to finish, Lk 14:29 *2480*
to build and was not a to finish.' Lk 14:30 *2480*
from here to you will not be a, Lk 16:26 *1410*
will be a to resist or refute. Lk 21:15 *1410*
and no one is a to snatch *them* out Jn 10:29 *1410*
and then they were not a to haul Jn 21:6 *2480*
will not be a to overthrow them; Ac 5:39 *1410*
nor we have been a to bear? Ac 15:10 *2480*
which is a to build *you* up and to Ac 20:32 *1410*
you will be a to ascertain the Ac 24:8 *1410*
we were scarcely a to get the Ac 27:16 *2480*
He was a also to perform. Ro 4:21 *1415*
for it is not even a *to do so*, Ro 8:7 *1410*
will be a to separate us from the Ro 8:39 *1410*
God is a to graft them in again. Ro 11:23 *1415*
the Lord is a to make him stand. Ro 14:4 *1414*
a also to admonish one another. Ro 15:14 *1410*
Now to Him who is a to establish Ro 16:25 *1410*
you were not yet a *to receive it*. 1Co 3:2 *1410*
even now you are not yet a, 1Co 3:2 *1410*
one wise man who will be a to decide 1Co 6:5 *1410*
if you are a also to become free, 1Co 7:21 *1410*
be tempted beyond what you are a, 1Co 10:13 *1410*
that you will be a to endure it. 1Co 10:13 *1410*
so that we will be a to comfort those 2Co 1:4 *1410*
And God is a to make all grace 2Co 9:8 *1414*
given which was a to impart life, Ga 3:21 *1410*
may be a to comprehend with all Eph 3:18 *1840*
Now to Him who is a to do Eph 3:20 *1410*
that you will be a to stand firm Eph 6:11 *1410*
be a to resist in the evil day, Eph 6:13 *1410*
with which you will be a to extinguish Eph 6:16 *1410*
hospitable, a to teach, 1Tm 3:2 *1317*
am convinced that He is a to guard 2Tm 1:12 *1415*
will be a to teach others also. 2Tm 2:2 *2425*
but be kind to all, a to teach, 2Tm 2:24 *1317*
always learning and never a to 2Tm 3:7 *1410*
sacred writings which are a to give 2Tm 3:15 *1410*
that he will be a both to exhort in Ti 1:9 *1415*
He is a to come to the aid of Heb 2:18 *1410*
not a to enter because of unbelief. Heb 3:19 *1410*
and a to judge the thoughts and Heb 4:12 *2924*
the One a to save Him from death, Heb 5:7 *1410*
He is a also to save forever those who Heb 7:25 *1410*
He considered that God is a to Heb 11:19 *1415*
which is a to save your souls. Jas 1:21 *1410*
a to bridle the whole body as well. Jas 3:2 *1415*
who is a to save and to destroy; Jas 4:12 *1410*
be a to call these things to mind. 2Pe 1:15 *2192*
is a to keep you from stumbling, Jude 1:24 *1410*
the earth was a to open the book Rv 5:3 *1410*
and who is a to stand?" Rv 6:17 *1410*
who is a to wage war with him?" Rv 13:4 *1410*
one will be a to buy or to sell, Rv 13:17 *1410*
and no one was a to enter the Rv 15:8 *1410*

ABNER

of his army was A the son of Ner, 1Sa 14:50 74
father of A *was* the son of Abiel. 1Sa 14:51 74
to A the commander of the army, 1Sa 17:55 74
"A, whose son is this young man?" 1Sa 17:55 74
And A said, "By your life, O king, 1Sa 17:55 74
A took him and brought him before 1Sa 17:57 74
up and A sat down by Saul's side, 1Sa 20:25 74
Saul lay, and A the son of Ner, 1Sa 26:5 74
and A and the people were lying 1Sa 26:7 74
people and to A the son of Ner, 1Sa 26:14 74
"Will you not answer, A?" 1Sa 26:14 74
Then A replied, 1Sa 26:14 74
So David said to A, 1Sa 26:15 74
But A the son of Ner, commander of 2Sa 2:8 74
Now A the son of Ner, went out 2Sa 2:12 74
Then A said to Joab, 2Sa 2:14 74
and A and the men of Israel were 2Sa 2:17 74
Asahel pursued A and did not 2Sa 2:19 74
or to the left from following A. 2Sa 2:19 74
Then A looked behind him and said, 2Sa 2:20 74
So A said to him, 2Sa 2:21 74
A repeated again to Asahel, 2Sa 2:22 74
therefore A struck him in the 2Sa 2:23 74
But Joab and Abishai pursued A, 2Sa 2:24 74
behind A and became one band, 2Sa 2:25 74
Then A called to Joab and said, 2Sa 2:26 74
A and his men then went through 2Sa 2:29 74
Joab returned from following A; 2Sa 2:30 74
that A was making himself strong 2Sa 3:6 74
and Ish-bosheth said to A, 2Sa 3:7 74
Then A was very angry over the 2Sa 3:8 74
"May God do so to A, 2Sa 3:9 74
could no longer answer A a word, 2Sa 3:11 74
Then A sent messengers to David in 2Sa 3:12 74
Then A said to him, 2Sa 3:16 74
Now A had consultation with the 2Sa 3:17 74
A also spoke in the hearing of 2Sa 3:19 74
and in addition A went to speak in 2Sa 3:19 74
Then A and twenty men with him 2Sa 3:20 74
A and the men who were with him. 2Sa 3:20 74
A said to David, 2Sa 3:21 74
So David sent A away, and he went 2Sa 3:21 74
A was not with David in Hebron, 2Sa 3:22 74
"A the son of Ner came to the 2Sa 3:23 74
Behold, A came to you; 2Sa 3:24 74
"You know A the son of Ner, that 2Sa 3:25 74
David, he sent messengers after A, 2Sa 3:26 74
So when A returned to Hebron, Joab 2Sa 3:27 74
of the blood of A the son of Ner. 2Sa 3:28 74
Abishai his brother killed A because 2Sa 3:30 74
sackcloth and lament before A." 2Sa 3:31 74
Thus they buried A in Hebron; 2Sa 3:32 74
voice and wept at the grave of A, 2Sa 3:32 74
chanted a *lament* for A and said, 2Sa 3:33 74
"Should A die as a fool dies? 2Sa 3:33 74
to put A the son of Ner to death. 2Sa 3:37 74
heard that A had died in Hebron, 2Sa 4:1 74
it in the grave of A in Hebron. 2Sa 4:12 74
of Israel, to A the son of Ner, 1Ki 2:5 74
A the son of Ner, commander of the 1Ki 2:32 74
A the son of Ner and Joab the son 1Ch 26:28 74
Benjamin, Jaasiel the son of A; 1Ch 27:21 74

ABNER'S

down many of Benjamin and A men, 2Sa 2:31 74

ABOARD

Your wise men, O Tyre, were a; Ezk 27:8
Phoenicia, we went a and set sail. Ac 21:2 *1910*
for Italy, and he put us a it. Ac 27:6 *1688*

ABODE

And I cursed his a immediately. Jb 5:3 5116a
visit your a and fear no loss. Jb 5:24 5116a
which God has desired for His a? Ps 68:16 3427
soul would soon have dwelt in *the* a Ps 94:17
of jackals *And* an a of ostriches. Is 34:13 2681
bless you, O a of righteousness, Jer 31:23 5116a
to him and make Our a with him. Jn 14:23 *3438*
but abandoned their proper a, Jude 1:6 *3613*

ABOLISH

And I will a the bow, the sword and Hos 2:18 7665
came to a the Law or the Prophets; Mt 5:17 *2647*
I did not come to a but Mt 5:17 *2647*

ABOLISHED

that the regular sacrifice is a and Da 12:11 5493
when He has a all rule and all 1Co 15:24 *2673*
enemy that will be a is death. 1Co 15:26 *2673*
block of the cross has been a. Ga 5:11 *2673*
Savior Christ Jesus, who a death and 2Tm 1:10 *2673*

ABOLISHING

by a in His flesh the enmity, Eph 2:15 *2673*

ABOMINABLE

do not practice any of the a customs Lv 18:30 8441
for every a act which the LORD Dt 12:31 8441
removed the a idols from all the land 2Ch 15:8 8251
they have committed a deeds; Ps 14:1 8581
and have committed a injustice; Ps 53:1 8581
Both of them are a to the LORD. Pr 20:10 8441
unjust man is a to the righteous, Pr 29:27 8441
in the way is a to the wicked. Pr 29:27 8441
do this a thing which I hate." Jer 44:4 8441
street and made your beauty a Ezk 16:25 8581
drinking parties and a idolatries. 1Pe 4:3 *111*
and unbelieving and a and murderers Rv 21:8 *948*

ABOMINABLY

acted very a in following idols, 1Ki 21:26 8581
which you acted more a than they, Ezk 16:52 8581

ABOMINATION

God what is an a to the Egyptians. Ex 8:26 8441
If we sacrifice what is an a to Ex 8:26 8441
as one lies with a female; it is an a. Lv 18:22 8441
it is an a to the LORD your God. Dt 7:25 8441
not bring an a into your house, Dt 7:26 8441
this a has been done among you, Dt 13:14 8441
is an a to the LORD your God. Dt 22:5 8441
are an a to the LORD your God. Dt 23:18 8441
for that is an a before the LORD, Dt 24:4 8441
is an a to the LORD your God. Dt 25:16 8441
a molten image, an a to the LORD, Dt 27:15 8441
Ashtoreth the a of the Sidonians, 2Ki 23:13 8251
and for Chemosh the a of Moab, 2Ki 23:13 8251
Milcom the a of the sons of Ammon, 2Ki 23:13 8251
devious are an a to the LORD; Pr 3:32 8441
Yes, seven which are an a to Him: Pr 6:16 8441
And wickedness is an a to my lips. Pr 8:7 8441
false balance is an a to the LORD, Pr 11:1 8441
in heart are an a to the LORD, Pr 11:20 8441
Lying lips are an a to the LORD, Pr 12:22 8441
an a to fools to turn away from evil. Pr 13:19 8441
of the wicked is an a to the LORD, Pr 15:8 8441
of the wicked is an a to the LORD, Pr 15:9 8441
Evil plans are an a to the LORD, Pr 15:26 8441
in heart is an a to the LORD; Pr 16:5 8441
It is an a for kings to commit Pr 16:12 8441
them alike are an a to the LORD. Pr 17:15 8441
weights are an a to the LORD, Pr 20:23 8441
sacrifice of the wicked is an a, Pr 21:27 8441
And the scoffer is an a to men. Pr 24:9 8441
the law, Even his prayer is an a. Pr 28:9 8441
no longer, Incense is an a to Me. Is 1:13 8441
He who chooses you is an a. Is 41:24 8441
I make the rest of it into an a, Is 44:19 8441
And My inheritance you made an a. Jer 2:7 8441
because of the a they have done? Jer 6:15 8441
because of the a they had done? Jer 8:12 8441
mind that they should do this a, Jer 32:35 8441
eyes to the idols *and* commits a, Ezk 18:12 8441
a with his neighbor's wife and Ezk 22:11 8441
will set up the a of desolation. Da 11:31 8251
and the a of desolation is set up, Da 12:11 8251
and an a has been committed in Mal 2:11 8441
"Therefore when you see the A OF Mt 24:15 *946*
"But when you see the A OF Mk 13:14 *946*
no one who practices a and lying, Rv 21:27 *946*

ABOMINATIONS

and shall not do any of these a, Lv 18:26 8441
before you have done all these a, Lv 18:27 8441
'For whoever does any of these a, Lv 18:29 8441
their a and their idols *of* wood, Dt 29:17 8251
With a they provoked Him to anger. Dt 32:16 8441
They did according to all the a of 1Ki 14:24 8441
according to the a of the nations 2Ki 16:3 8441
according to the a of the nations 2Ki 21:2 8441
king of Judah has done these a, 2Ki 21:11 8441
idols and all the a that were seen 2Ki 23:24 8251
according to the a of the nations 2Ch 28:3 8441
the a of the nations whom the LORD 2Ch 33:2 8441
Josiah removed all the a from 2Ch 34:33 8441
Jehoiakim and the a which he did, 2Ch 36:8 8441
all the a of the nations; 2Ch 36:14 8441
the lands, according to their a, Ezr 9:1 8441
with their a which have filled it Ezr 9:11 8441
the peoples who commit these a? Ezr 9:14 8441
there are seven a in his heart. Pr 26:25 8441
their soul delights in their a, Is 66:3 8251
you may do all these a? Jer 7:10 8441
in the field, I have seen your a. Jer 13:27 8251
idols and with their a." Jer 16:18 8441
of the a which you have committed; Jer 44:22 8441
'And because of all your a, Ezk 5:9 8441
idols and with all your a, Ezk 5:11 8441
have committed, for all their a. Ezk 6:9 8441
the evil a of the house of Israel, Ezk 6:11 8441
bring all your a upon you. Ezk 7:3 8441
you, and your a will be among you; Ezk 7:4 8441
ways and bring on you all your a. Ezk 7:8 8441
while your a are in your midst; Ezk 7:9 8441
images of their a *and* their detestable Ezk 7:20 8441
the great a which the house of Ezk 8:6 8441
you will see still greater a." Ezk 8:6 8441
a that they are committing here." Ezk 8:9 8441
a which they are committing." Ezk 8:13 8441
see still greater a than these." Ezk 8:15 8441
to commit the a which they have Ezk 8:17 8441
groan over all the a which are being Ezk 9:4 8441
things and all its a from it. Ezk 11:18 8441
their detestable things and a, Ezk 11:21 8441
may tell all their a among the nations Ezk 12:16 8441
your faces away from all your a. Ezk 14:6 8441
make known to Jerusalem her a Ezk 16:2 8441
"Besides all your a and Ezk 16:22 8441

on top of all your *other* **a**. Ezk 16:43 8441
ways or done according to their **a**; Ezk 16:47 8441
haughty and committed **a** before Me. Ezk 16:50 8441
multiplied your **a** more than they. Ezk 16:51 8441
your **a** which you have committed. Ezk 16:51 8441
penalty of your lewdness and **a**," Ezk 16:58 8441
He has committed all these **a**, Ezk 18:13 8441
all the **a** that a wicked man does, Ezk 18:24 8441
them know the **a** of their fathers; Ezk 20:4 8441
Then cause her to know all her **a**. Ezk 22:2 8441
Then declare to them their **a**. Ezk 23:36 8441
rely on your sword, you commit **a** and Ezk 33:26 8441
a which they have committed." Ezk 33:29 8441
for your iniquities and your **a**. Ezk 36:31 8441
their **a** which they have committed. Ezk 43:8 8441
"Enough of all your **a**, Ezk 44:6 8441
in addition to all your **a**. Ezk 44:7 8441
their **a** which they have committed. Ezk 44:13 8441
and on the wing of **a** *will come* one Da 9:27 8251
gold cup full of **a** and of the unclean Rv 17:4 946
HARLOTS AND OF THE **A** OF Rv 17:5 946

ABORT

His cow calves and does not **a**. Jb 21:10 7921

ABOUND

will make you **a** in prosperity, Dt 28:11 3498
when their grain and new wine **a**. Ps 4:7 7231
man will **a** with blessings, Pr 28:20 7227a
"May your peace **a**! Da 4:1 7680
"May your peace **a**! Da 6:25 7680
Man, Jesus Christ, **a** to the many. Ro 5:15 4052
that you will **a** in hope by the Ro 15:13 4052
seek to **a** for the edification of 1Co 14:12 4052
of righteousness **a** in glory. 2Co 3:9 4052
thanks to **a** to the glory of God. 2Co 4:15 4052
But just as you **a** in everything, 2Co 8:7 4052
you **a** in this gracious work also, 2Co 8:7 4052
able to make all grace **a** to you, 2Co 9:8 4052
that your love may **a** still more Php 1:9 4052
in me may **a** in Christ Jesus through Php 1:26 4052
and **a** in love for one another, 1Th 3:12 4052

ABOUNDED

the truth of God **a** to His glory, Ro 3:7 4052
increased, grace **a** all the more, Ro 5:20 5248

ABOUNDING

and **a** in lovingkindness and truth; Ex 34:6 7227a
to anger and **a** in lovingkindness; Ne 9:17 7227a
to anger and **a** in lovingkindness. Ps 103:8 7227a
were no springs **a** with water. Pr 8:24 3513
to anger, **a** in lovingkindness And Jl 2:13 7227a
this woman was **a** with deeds of Ac 9:36 4134
a in riches for all who call on Ro 10:12 4147
always **a** in the work of the Lord, 1Co 15:58 4052

ABOUNDS

man **a** in transgression. Pr 29:22 7227a
a all the more toward you, 2Co 7:15 4053

ABOUT

the tree **a** which I commanded you, Gn 3:17
So it came **a** in the course of time Gn 4:3
a when they were in the field, Gn 4:8
Now it came **a**, when men began to Gn 6:1
I am **a** to destroy them with the Gn 6:13
It came **a** after the seven days, Gn 7:10
came **a** at the end of forty days, Gn 8:6
Now it came **a** in the six hundred Gn 8:13
"It shall come **a**, Gn 9:14
It came **a** as they journeyed east, Gn 11:2
came **a** when he came near to Egypt, Gn 12:11
came **a** when Abram came into Egypt, Gn 12:14
walk **a** the land through its length Gn 13:17
And it came **a** in the days of Gn 14:1
It came **a** when the sun had set, Gn 15:17
from Abraham what I am **a** to do, Gn 18:17
what He has spoken **a** him." Gn 18:19 5921
we are **a** to destroy this place, Gn 19:13
Thus it came **a**, when God destroyed Gn 19:29
and it came **a**, when God caused me Gn 20:13
and wandered **a** in the wilderness Gn 21:14
opposite him, **a** a bowshot away, Gn 21:16
Now it came **a** at that time that Gn 21:22
Now it came **a** after these things, Gn 22:1
Now it came **a** after these things, Gn 22:20
mother's household **a** these things. Gn 24:28
came **a** after the death of Abraham, Gn 25:11
"Behold, I am **a** to die; Gn 25:32 1980
men of the place asked **a** his wife, Gn 26:7
It came **a**, when he had been Gn 26:8
Now it came **a** on the same day, Gn 26:32
him **a** the well which they had dug, Gn 26:32 5921, 182
Now it came **a**, when Isaac was old and Gn 27:1
Now it came **a**, as soon as Isaac Gn 27:30
come **a** when you become restless, Gn 27:40
So it came **a** in the morning that, Gn 29:25
a when Rachel had borne Joseph, Gn 30:25
"And it came **a** at the time when Gn 31:10
Now it came **a** on the third day, Gn 34:25
came **a** as her soul was departing Gn 35:18
It came **a** while Israel was Gn 35:22
bad report **a** them to their father. Gn 37:2
"Go now and see **a** the welfare of Gn 37:14
So it came **a**, when Joseph reached Gn 37:23
And it came **a** at that time, that Gn 38:1
Now it was **a** three months later Gn 38:24
It came **a** at the time she was Gn 38:27
came **a** as he drew back his hand, Gn 38:29
It came **a** that from the time Gn 39:5
It came **a** after these events Gn 39:7
Then it came **a** after these things Gn 40:1
Thus it came **a** on the third day, Gn 40:20
and I have heard it said **a** you, Gn 41:15 5921
to Pharaoh what He is **a** to do. Gn 41:25
to Pharaoh what He is **a** to do. Gn 41:28
and God will quickly bring it **a**. Gn 41:32 6213a
the dreams which he had **a** them, Gn 42:9
Now it came **a** as they were Gn 42:35
So it came **a** when they had Gn 43:2
a us and our relatives, Gn 43:7
and it came **a** when we came to the Gn 43:21
he asked them **a** their welfare, Gn 43:27
"Thus it came **a** when we went up Gn 44:24
Now it came **a** after these things Gn 48:1
"Behold, I am **a** to die, but God Gn 48:21
am **a** to be gathered to my people; Gn 49:29
"Behold, I am **a** to die; Gn 50:5
to bring **a** this present result, Gn 50:20 6213a
"I am **a** to die, but God will Gn 50:24
Now it came **a** in those days, when Ex 2:11
Now it came **a** in *the course of* Ex 2:23
"I am indeed concerned **a** you and Ex 3:16
Now it came **a** at the lodging place Ex 4:24
the LORD was concerned **a** the sons Ex 4:31
to Pharaoh king of Egypt **a** bringing Ex 6:27
Now it came **a** on the day when the Ex 6:28
"Behold, **a** this time tomorrow, I Ex 9:18
'**A** midnight I am going out into Ex 11:4
Now it came **a** at midnight that the Ex 12:29
a six hundred thousand men on Ex 12:37
of Abib, you are **a** to go forth. Ex 13:4
'It came **a**, when Pharaoh was Ex 13:15
was stubborn **a** letting us go, Ex 13:15
It came **a** as Aaron spoke to Ex 16:10
So it came **a** at evening that the Ex 16:13
It came **a** on the seventh day Ex 16:27
a when Moses held his hand up, Ex 17:11
It came **a** the next day that Ex 18:13
and the people stood **a** Moses from Ex 18:13 5921
the people stand **a** you from morning Ex 18:14 5921
So it came **a** on the third day, Ex 19:16
'Set bounds **a** the mountain and Ex 19:23
any lost thing **a** which one says, Ex 22:9
a that when he cries out to Me, Ex 22:27
I will speak to you **a** all that I Ex 25:22
the people assembled **a** Aaron and Ex 32:1 5921
mind **a** *doing* harm to Your people. Ex 32:12 5921
So the LORD changed His mind **a** the Ex 32:14 5921
It came **a**, as soon as Moses Ex 32:19
and **a** three thousand men of the Ex 32:28
And it came **a**, whenever Moses went Ex 33:8
and it will come **a**, Ex 33:22
It came **a** when Moses was Ex 34:29
and lied **a** it and sworn falsely, Lv 6:3
anything **a** which he swore falsely; Lv 6:5
Now it came **a** on the eighth day Lv 9:1
which the LORD has brought **a**. Lv 10:6
'You shall not go **a** as a slanderer Lv 19:16
the water, then it shall come **a**, Nu 5:27
Then it came **a** when the ark set Nu 10:35
The people would go **a** and gather Nu 11:8 7751a
a a day's journey on this side and Nu 11:31
and **a** two cubits *deep* on the Nu 11:31
"But if the LORD brings **a** an Nu 16:30 1254a
It came **a**, however, when the Nu 16:42
"It will come **a** that the rod Nu 17:5
and it shall come **a**, Nu 21:8
and it came **a**, that if a serpent Nu 21:9
Then it came **a** in the morning that Nu 22:41
Then it came **a** after the plague, Nu 26:1
then it shall come **a** that those Nu 33:55
the LORD our God is **a** to give us. Dt 1:20
the LORD our God is **a** to give us.' Dt 1:25
"So it came **a** when all the men of Dt 2:16
into which you are **a** to cross. Dt 3:21
"Then it shall come **a** when the Dt 6:10
"Then it shall come **a**, Dt 7:12
"It shall come **a** if you ever Dt 8:19
"It came **a** at the end of Dt 9:11
you are **a** to cross to possess it; Dt 11:8
you are **a** to cross to possess it, Dt 11:11
"It shall come **a**, Dt 11:13
"It shall come **a**, Dt 11:29
"For you are **a** to cross the Dt 11:31
then it shall come **a** that the Dt 12:11
It shall come **a** if he says to you, Dt 15:16
"Now it shall come **a** when he sits Dt 17:18
'It shall come **a** that whoever Dt 18:19
does not come **a** or come true, Dt 18:22
you are **a** to enter to possess. Dt 23:20
"Therefore it shall come **a** when Dt 25:19
"But it shall come **a**, Dt 28:15
"It shall come **a** that as the Dt 28:63
by the way **a** which I spoke to you, Dt 28:68
are **a** to cross the Jordan to possess." Dt 31:13
a to lie down with your fathers; Dt 31:16
"Then it shall come **a**, Dt 31:21
It came **a**, when Moses finished Dt 31:24
which you are **a** to cross the Dt 32:47
Now it came **a** after the death of Jos 1:1
"It came **a** when *it was time* Jos 2:5
and it shall come **a** when the LORD Jos 2:14
"It shall come **a** that anyone Jos 2:19
of **a** 2,000 cubits by measure. Jos 3:4
"It shall come **a** when the Jos 3:13
a 40,000 equipped for war, Jos 4:13
It came **a** when the priests who Jos 4:18
Now it came **a** when all the kings Jos 5:1
came **a** when Joshua was by Jericho, Jos 5:13
only **a** two or three thousand men Jos 7:3
So **a** three thousand men from the Jos 7:4
down **a** thirty-six of their men, Jos 7:5
And he took **a** 5,000 men and set Jos 8:12
came **a** when the king of Ai saw *it*, Jos 8:14
Now it came **a** when all the kings Jos 9:1
It came **a** at the end of three Jos 9:16
Now it came **a** when Adoni-zedek Jos 10:1
to go *down* for **a** a whole day. Jos 10:13
It came **a** when Joshua and the Jos 10:20
It came **a** at sunset that Jos 10:27
Then it came **a**, when Jabin king of Jos 11:1
give me this hill country **a** which Jos 14:12
up to Addar and turned **a** to Karka. Jos 15:3 5437
The border turned **a** from Jos 15:10 5437
came **a** that when she came *to him*, Jos 15:18
a eastward to Taanath-shiloh and Jos 16:6 5437
It came **a** when the sons of Jos 17:13
'It shall also come **a** if they say Jos 22:28
Now it came **a** after many days, Jos 23:1
"It shall come **a** that just as Jos 23:15
It came **a** after these things Jos 24:29
Now it came **a** after the death of Jg 1:1
it came **a** when she came *to him*, Jg 1:14
came **a** when Israel became strong, Jg 1:28
But it came **a** when the judge died, Jg 2:19
It came **a** when he had finished Jg 3:18
It came **a** when he had arrived, Jg 3:27
that time **a** ten thousand Moabites, Jg 3:29
journey that you are **a** to take, Jg 4:9
Now it came **a** when the sons of Jg 6:7
which our fathers told us **a**, Jg 6:13
when they searched **a** and inquired, Jg 6:29
came **a** that the LORD said to him, Jg 7:9
armies with them, **a** 15,000 men, Jg 8:10
Then it came **a**, as soon as Gideon Jg 8:33
Now it came **a** the next day, that Jg 9:42
died, **a** a thousand men and women. Jg 9:49
gathered themselves **a** Jephthah, Jg 11:3 413
It came **a** after a while that Jg 11:4
For it came **a** when the flame went Jg 13:20
Then it came **a** on the fourth day Jg 14:15
After this it came **a** that he loved Jg 16:4
It came **a** when she pressed him Jg 16:16
And **a** 3,000 men and women were on Jg 16:27
a which you uttered a curse in my Jg 17:2
Now it came **a** in those days, when Jg 19:1
the field, **a** thirty men of Israel. Jg 20:31
and kill **a** thirty men of Israel, Jg 20:39
Israel, has this come **a** in Israel, Jg 21:3
It came **a** the next day that Jg 21:4
"It shall come **a**, Jg 21:22
Now it came **a** in the days when the Ru 1:1
And they lived there **a** ten years. Ru 1:4
and it was **a** an ephah of barley. Ru 2:17
Now it came **a**, as she continued 1Sa 1:12
It came **a** in due time, after 1Sa 1:20
I am **a** to do a thing in Israel at 1Sa 3:11
"For I have told him that I am **a** 1Sa 3:13
Philistines who killed **a** four thousand 1Sa 4:2
was pregnant and **a** to give birth; 1Sa 4:19
And **a** the time of her death the 1Sa 4:20
And it came **a** when Samuel was old 1Sa 8:1
cease *to be concerned* **a** the donkeys 1Sa 9:5 4480
perhaps he can tell us **a** our 1Sa 9:6
"**A** this time tomorrow I will send 1Sa 9:16
invited, who were **a** thirty men. 1Sa 9:22
ceased to be concerned **a** the donkeys 1Sa 10:2
"What shall I do **a** my son?"' 1Sa 10:2
those signs came **a** on that day. 1Sa 10:9
It came **a**, when all who knew 1Sa 10:11
But he did not tell him **a** the 1Sa 10:16
with him, **a** six hundred men. 1Sa 13:15
So it came **a** on the day of battle 1Sa 13:22
with him *were* **a** six hundred men, 1Sa 14:2
his armor bearer made was **a** twenty 1Sa 14:14
within **a** half a furrow in an acre of 1Sa 14:14
who has brought **a** this great 1Sa 14:45 6213a
and it shall come **a** when the evil 1Sa 16:16
So it came **a** whenever the *evil* 1Sa 16:23
Now it came **a** when he had finished 1Sa 18:1
Now it came **a** on the next day that 1Sa 18:10
it came **a** at the time when Merab, 1Sa 18:19
I will speak with my father **a** you; 1Sa 19:3
and the LORD brought **a** a great 1Sa 19:5 6213a
then would I not tell you **a** it?" 1Sa 20:9
my father **a** this time tomorrow, 1Sa 20:12
It came **a** the next day, the 1Sa 20:27
Now it came **a** in the morning that 1Sa 20:35
arrows which I am **a** to shoot." 1Sa 20:36
and David knew **a** the matter. 1Sa 20:39
'Let no one know anything **a** the 1Sa 21:2
were **a** four hundred men with him. 1Sa 22:2
I have brought **a** *the death of* 1Sa 22:22 5437
Now it came **a**, when Abiathar the 1Sa 23:6
David and his men, **a** six hundred, 1Sa 23:13
and learn **a** all the hiding places 1Sa 23:23 4480
I am **a** to give your enemy into 1Sa 24:4
It came **a** afterward that 1Sa 24:5
And it came **a** while he was 1Sa 25:2
and **a** four hundred men went up 1Sa 25:13
as long as we went **a** with them, 1Sa 25:15
It came **a** as she was riding on 1Sa 25:20
A ten days later, the LORD 1Sa 25:38
"Otherwise they will tell **a** us, 1Sa 27:11 5921
Now it came **a** in those days that 1Sa 28:1
for my life to bring **a** my death?" 1Sa 28:9
It came **a** on the next day when 1Sa 31:8
it came **a** after the death of Saul, 2Sa 1:1
And it came **a** when he came to 2Sa 1:2

Then it came **a** afterwards that	2Sa 2:1	
And it came **a** that all who came to	2Sa 2:23	
It came **a** while there was war	2Sa 3:6	
Now it came **a** when the king lived	2Sa 7:1	
I have been moving **a** in a tent,	2Sa 7:6	
Now after this it came **a** that	2Sa 8:1	
sent and inquired **a** the woman.	2Sa 11:3	
Now it came **a** after two full years	2Sa 13:23	
from me that I am **a** to ask you."	2Sa 14:18	
Now it came **a** after this that	2Sa 15:1	
Now it came **a** at the end of forty	2Sa 15:7	
it came **a** when Hushai the Archite,	2Sa 16:16	
It came **a** after they had	2Sa 17:21	
flee, they will not care **a** us;	2Sa 18:3	413
us die, they will not care **a** us.	2Sa 18:3	413
silent **a** bringing the king back?"	2Sa 19:10	
as he was **a** to cross the Jordan.	2Sa 19:18	
then are you angry **a** this matter?	2Sa 19:42	5921
Now it came **a** after this that	2Sa 21:18	
a a great victory that day;	2Sa 23:10	6213a
LORD brought **a** a great victory.	2Sa 23:12	6213a
"Go **a** now through all the tribes	2Sa 24:2	7751a
had gone **a** through the whole land,	2Sa 24:8	7751a
"Otherwise it will come **a**,	1Ki 1:21	
of war on his belt **a** his waist,	1Ki 2:5	
turned **a** and become my brother's,	1Ki 2:15	5437
came **a** at the end of three years,	1Ki 2:39	
peace on all sides around **a** him.	1Ki 4:24	5439
Now it came **a** in the four hundred	1Ki 6:1	
round **a** with carved engravings	1Ki 6:29	4524
Then the king faced **a** and blessed	1Ki 8:14	5437
Now it came **a** when Solomon had	1Ki 9:1	
It came **a** at the end of twenty	1Ki 9:10	
the queen of Sheba heard **a** the fame	1Ki 10:1	
him **a** all that was in her heart.	1Ki 10:2	
land **a** your words and your wisdom.	1Ki 10:6	5921
For it came **a**, when David was in	1Ki 11:15	
It came **a** at that time, when	1Ki 11:29	
It came **a** when all Israel	1Ki 12:20	
Now it came **a**, as they were	1Ki 13:20	
It came **a** after he had eaten	1Ki 13:23	
It came **a** as soon as he was	1Ki 15:29	
It came **a** when he became	1Ki 16:11	
It came **a**, as though it had	1Ki 16:31	
Now it came **a** after these things that	1Ki 17:17	
"It will come **a** when I leave	1Ki 18:12	
a the altar which they made.	1Ki 18:26	5921
It came **a** at noon, that Elijah	1Ki 18:27	
It came **a** at the seventh *time*,	1Ki 18:44	
of them by tomorrow **a** this time."	1Ki 19:2	
"It shall come **a**,	1Ki 19:17	
but **a** this time tomorrow I will	1Ki 20:6	
Now it came **a** after these things that	1Ki 21:1	
a when Ahab heard these words,	1Ki 21:27	
sackcloth and went **a** despondently.	1Ki 21:27	
together, **a** four hundred men,	1Ki 22:6	
girdle bound **a** his loins."	2Ki 1:8	
And it came **a** when the LORD was	2Ki 2:1	
the LORD was **a** to take up Elijah by	2Ki 2:1	
And it came **a**, when the minstrel	2Ki 3:15	
It happened in the morning **a**	2Ki 3:20	
slingers went **a** *it* and struck it.	2Ki 3:25	5437
to the place **a** which the man of God	2Ki 6:10	
Now it came **a** after this, that	2Ki 6:24	
'Tomorrow **a** this time a measure of	2Ki 7:1	
will be *sold* tomorrow **a** this time	2Ki 7:18	
a and fled and said to Ahaziah,	2Ki 9:23	2015, 3027
at Jezreel tomorrow **a** this time."	2Ki 10:6	
Then it came **a**, as soon as he had	2Ki 10:25	
But it came **a** that in the	2Ki 12:6	
Now it came **a**, as soon as the	2Ki 14:5	
Now *this* came **a** because the sons	2Ki 17:7	
a in the third year of Hoshea,	2Ki 18:1	
Me **a** Sennacherib king of Assyria,	2Ki 19:20	413
It came **a** as he was worshiping	2Ki 19:37	
of the LORD *this* came **a** in Jerusalem	2Ki 24:20	
it came **a** in the seventh month,	2Ki 25:25	
Now it came **a** in the	2Ki 25:27	
It came **a** the next day, when	1Ch 10:8	
when he was **a** to go to battle with	1Ch 12:19	
wandered **a** from nation to nation,	1Ch 16:20	
And it came **a**, when David dwelt in	1Ch 17:1	
It came **a** the same night that	1Ch 17:3	
Now after this it came **a** that	1Ch 18:1	
Now it came **a** after this, that	1Ch 19:1	
went and told David **a** the men.	1Ch 19:5	5921
Now it came **a** after this, that war	1Ch 20:4	
but as he was **a** to destroy *it*, the	1Ch 21:15	
I am **a** to build a house for the	2Ch 2:4	
I am **a** to build *will be* great,	2Ch 2:5	
for the house which I am **a** to	2Ch 2:9	
Then the king faced **a** and blessed	2Ch 6:3	5437
Now it came **a** at the end of the	2Ch 8:1	
him **a** all that was on her heart.	2Ch 9:1	
land **a** your words and your wisdom.	2Ch 9:5	5921
a in King Rehoboam's fifth year,	2Ch 12:2	
and worthless men gathered **a** him,	2Ch 13:7	5921
Now it came **a** after this that the	2Ch 20:1	
it came **a** in the course of time,	2Ch 21:19	
It came **a** when Jehu was	2Ch 22:8	
Now it came **a** after this that	2Ch 24:4	
It came **a** whenever the chest	2Ch 24:11	
Now it came **a** as soon as the	2Ch 25:3	
for he had brought **a** a lack of	2Ch 28:19	
because the thing came **a** suddenly.	2Ch 29:36	
a this and cried out to heaven.	2Ch 32:20	5921
speak **a** Josiah in their lamentations	2Ch 35:25	5921
All those **a** them encouraged	Ezr 1:6	5439
When I heard **a** this matter,	Ezr 9:3	
the captivity, and **a** Jerusalem.	Ne 1:2	5921
And it came **a** in the month Nisan,	Ne 2:1	
the Ammonite official heard **a** *it*,	Ne 2:10	
and also **a** the king's words which	Ne 2:18	
Now it came **a** that when Sanballat	Ne 4:1	
they were speaking **a** his good	Ne 6:19	
learned **a** the evil that Eliashib had	Ne 13:7	
It came **a** that just as it grew	Ne 13:19	
"Do we then hear **a** you that you	Ne 13:27	
So it came **a** when the command and	Es 2:8	
Now it came **a** on the third day	Es 5:1	
speak to the king **a** hanging Mordecai	Es 6:4	
and edict were **a** to be executed,	Es 9:1	
this second letter **a** Purim.	Es 9:29	
"From roaming **a** on the earth and	Jb 1:7	7751a
"Have You not made a hedge **a** him	Jb 1:10	1157
"From roaming **a** on the earth and	Jb 2:2	7751a
And that You are concerned **a** him,	Jb 7:17	413
"He wanders **a** for food, saying,	Jb 15:23	
flock, And their children skip **a**.	Jb 21:11	7540
to go **a** naked without clothing,	Jb 24:10	
me **a** as the collar of my coat.	Jb 30:18	
"I go **a** mourning without comfort;	Jb 30:28	
new wineskins it is **a** to burst.	Jb 32:19	
He spreads His lightning **a** Him,	Jb 36:30	5921
"Do you know **a** the layers of the	Jb 37:16	5921
to God And wander **a** without food?	Jb 38:41	
It came **a** after the LORD had	Jb 42:7	
You, O LORD, are a shield **a** me,	Ps 3:3	1157
set themselves against me round **a**.	Ps 3:6	5439
The wicked strut **a** on every side When	Ps 12:8	
And I will go **a** Your altar,	Ps 26:6	5437
When I kept silent **a** *my sin*, my	Ps 32:3	
I went **a** as though it were my	Ps 35:14	
every man walks **a** as a phantom;	Ps 39:6	
Walk **a** Zion and go around her;	Ps 48:12	5437
They wander **a** for food And growl	Ps 59:15	
who sit in the gate talk **a** me,	Ps 69:12	
camp, Round **a** their dwellings.	Ps 78:28	5439
like water round **a** Jerusalem;	Ps 79:3	5439
They walk **a** in darkness;	Ps 82:5	
and **a** to die from my youth on;	Ps 88:15	
burns up His adversaries round **a**.	Ps 97:3	5439
the beasts of the forest prowl **a**.	Ps 104:20	7430
wandered **a** from nation to nation,	Ps 105:13	
Let his children wander **a** and beg;	Ps 109:10	
head And ornaments **a** your neck.	Pr 1:9	
When you walk **a**, they will guide	Pr 6:22	
He who goes **a** as a talebearer	Pr 11:13	
he who pursues evil *will bring* **a**	Pr 11:19	
He who goes **a** as a slanderer	Pr 20:19	
evil report **a** you will not pass away.	Pr 25:10	
Do not boast **a** tomorrow, For you	Pr 27:1	
from wisdom that you ask **a** this.	Ec 7:10	5921
while mourners go **a** in the street.	Ec 12:5	5437
must arise now and go **a** the city;	SS 3:2	5437
of wheat Fenced **a** with lilies.	SS 7:2	5473
will come **a** that In the last days The	Is 2:2	
Now it will come **a** that instead of	Is 3:24	
It will come **a** that he who is	Is 4:3	
Now it came **a** in the days of Ahaz,	Is 7:1	
And it will come **a** in that day,	Is 7:23	
the Lord is **a** to bring on them the	Is 8:7	
will be the belt **a** His loins,	Is 11:5	
faithfulness the belt **a** His waist.	Is 11:5	
come **a** when Moab presents himself,	Is 16:12	
Damascus is **a** to be removed from	Is 17:1	
cloud and is **a** to come to Egypt;	Is 19:1	
The oracle **a** Arabia.	Is 21:13	
LORD is **a** to hurl you headlong,	Is 22:17	
And He is **a** to grasp you firmly	Is 22:17	
"Then it will come **a** in that day,	Is 22:20	
And tie your sash securely **a** him.	Is 22:21	
Take *your* harp, walk **a** the city,	Is 23:16	5437
It will come **a** at the end of	Is 23:17	
the LORD is **a** to come out from His	Is 26:21	
It will come **a** also in that day	Is 27:13	
more **a** the Holy One of Israel."	Is 30:11	
be to you Like a breach **a** to fall,	Is 30:13	
As locusts rushing **a** men	Is 33:4	4944
rushing about men rush **a** on it.	Is 33:4	8264
his ears from hearing **a** bloodshed And	Is 33:15	
Me **a** Sennacherib king of Assyria,	Is 37:21	413
It came **a** as he was worshiping	Is 37:38	
I will wander **a** all my years	Is 38:15	
tells his sons **a** Your faithfulness.	Is 38:19	413
Do not anxiously look **a** you,	Is 41:10	
look **a** us and fear together.	Is 41:23	
"Ask Me **a** the things to come	Is 45:11	5921
Who carry **a** their wooden idol And	Is 45:20	
And destruction **a** which you do not	Is 47:11	
For My salvation is **a** to come And	Is 56:1	7138
"Lift up your eyes round **a** and	Is 60:4	5439
and against all its walls round **a** and	Jer 1:15	5439
"It shall come **a** in that day,"	Jer 4:9	
they are against her round **a**,	Jer 4:17	5439
have lied **a** the LORD And said,	Jer 5:12	
"It shall come **a** when they say,	Jer 5:19	
Going **a** as a talebearer.	Jer 6:28	
neighbor goes **a** as a slanderer.	Jer 9:4	
"Behold, I am **a** to punish them!	Jer 11:22	
"Behold I am **a** to uproot them	Jer 12:14	
"And it will come **a** that after I	Jer 12:15	
"Behold I am **a** to fill all the	Jer 13:13	
Have gone roving **a** in the land that	Jer 14:18	5503
turn aside to ask **a** your welfare?	Jer 15:5	
"But it will come **a**,	Jer 17:24	
"Behold I am **a** to bring a	Jer 19:3	
I am **a** to bring on this city and	Jer 19:15	
I am **a** to turn back the weapons of	Jer 21:4	
I am **a** to attend to you for the	Jer 23:2	
against all these nations round **a**;	Jer 25:9	5439
And all the people gathered **a**	Jer 26:9	413
change His mind **a** the misfortune	Jer 26:13	413
and the LORD changed His mind **a**	Jer 26:19	413
now this word which I am **a** to speak	Jer 28:7	
I am **a** to remove you from the face	Jer 28:16	
I am **a** to punish Shemaiah the	Jer 29:32	
that I am **a** to do to My people,"	Jer 29:32	
'It shall come **a** on that day,'	Jer 30:8	
and they who go **a** with flocks.	Jer 31:24	5265
I am **a** to give this city into the	Jer 32:3	
I am **a** to give this city into the	Jer 32:28	
Jerusalem heard the report **a** them,	Jer 37:5	
"Let no man know **a** these words	Jer 38:24	
of Babylon gave orders **a** Jeremiah	Jer 39:11	5921
I am **a** to bring My words on this	Jer 39:16	
you are telling a lie **a** Ishmael."	Jer 40:16	413
Gedaliah, when no one knew **a** *it*,	Jer 41:4	
famine, **a** which you are anxious,	Jer 42:16	
I have built I am **a** to tear down,	Jer 45:4	
I have planted I am **a** to uproot,	Jer 45:4	
the rivers whose waters surge **a**?	Jer 46:7	
the rivers whose waters surge **a**;	Jer 46:8	
a the coming of Nebuchadnezzar king	Jer 46:13	
For each time you speak **a** him you	Jer 48:27	
boastful you are **a** the valleys!	Jer 49:4	
'But it will come **a** in the last	Jer 49:39	
Because you skip **a** like a	Jer 50:11	6335a
has heard the report **a** them,	Jer 50:43	
has brought **a** our vindication;	Jer 51:10	3318
the anger of the LORD *this* came **a** in	Jer 52:3	
Now it came **a** in the ninth year of	Jer 52:4	
Now it came **a** in the	Jer 52:31	
a him should be his adversaries;	La 1:17	5439
a flaming fire Consuming round **a**.	La 2:3	5439
it came **a** in the thirtieth year,	Ezk 1:1	
wherever the spirit was **a** to go,	Ezk 1:12	
of them were full of eyes round **a**.	Ezk 1:18	5439
Wherever the spirit was **a** to go,	Ezk 1:20	
It came **a** in the sixth year,	Ezk 8:1	
were **a** twenty-five men with their	Ezk 8:16	
It came **a** when He commanded	Ezk 10:6	
Now it came **a** as I prophesied,	Ezk 11:13	
should never come **a** nor happen.	Ezk 16:16	
came **a** after all your wickedness	Ezk 16:23	
'Then nations heard **a** him;	Ezk 19:4	413
'And he walked **a** among the lions;	Ezk 19:6	
into your mind will not come **a**,	Ezk 20:32	
I am **a** to kindle a fire in you,	Ezk 20:47	
I am **a** to take from you the desire	Ezk 24:16	
I am **a** to profane My sanctuary,	Ezk 24:21	
any round **a** them who scorned them;	Ezk 28:24	5439
all who scorn them round **a** them.	Ezk 28:26	5439
her graves are round **a** her.	Ezk 32:22	5439
her company is round **a** her grave.	Ezk 32:23	5439
your fellow citizens who talk **a**	Ezk 33:30	
of the nations which are round **a**,	Ezk 36:4	5439
of Israel, that I am **a** to act,	Ezk 36:22	
left round **a** you will know that I,	Ezk 36:36	5439
me to pass among them round **a**,	Ezk 37:2	5439
"I will turn you **a** and	Ezk 38:4	7725
that are assembled **a** you,	Ezk 38:7	5921
"It will come **a** on that day, that	Ezk 38:10	
It shall come **a** in the last days	Ezk 38:16	
"It will come **a** on that day,	Ezk 38:18	
the gate *extended* round **a** to the	Ezk 40:14	5439
around **a** the house on every side.	Ezk 41:5	5439
round **a** their three stories,	Ezk 41:16	5439
on its edge round **a** one span;	Ezk 43:13	5439
its base *shall be* a cubit round **a**;	Ezk 43:17	5439
ledge and on the border round **a**;	Ezk 43:20	5439
within all its boundary round **a**.	Ezk 45:1	5439
the holy place a square round **a** five	Ezk 45:2	5439
cubits for its open space round **a**.	Ezk 45:2	5439
a row *of masonry* round **a** in them,	Ezk 46:23	5439
were made under the rows round **a**.	Ezk 46:23	5439
"It will come **a** that every	Ezk 47:9	
"And it will come **a** that	Ezk 47:10	
shall be 18,000 *cubits* round **a**;	Ezk 48:35	5439
a which the king consulted them,	Da 1:20	
informed Daniel **a** the matter.	Da 2:15	
Mishael and Azariah, **a** the matter,	Da 2:17	
a which the king has inquired,	Da 2:27	
four men loosed *and* walking **a**	Da 3:25	
"Now I have heard **a** you that a	Da 5:14	5922
"But I personally have heard **a** you,	Da 5:16	5922
kingdom at the age of sixty-two.	Da 5:31	
the king **a** the king's injunction,	Da 6:12	5922
"How long will the vision **a**	Da 8:13	
weariness **a** the time of the evening	Da 9:21	
a to tell you and stand upright,	Da 10:11	
the prince of Greece is **a** to come.	Da 10:20	
"It will come **a** in that day,"	Hos 2:16	
"It will come **a** in that day	Hos 2:21	
Tell your sons **a** it, And *let* your	Jl 1:3	
"It will come **a** after this	Jl 2:28	
"And it will come **a** that whoever	Jl 2:32	
And it came **a**, when it had	Am 7:2	
The LORD changed His mind **a** this.	Am 7:3	5921
The LORD changed His mind **a** this.	Am 7:6	5921
"Behold I am **a** to put a plumb	Am 7:8	
the Nile, And it will be tossed **a** And	Am 8:8	1644
"It will come **a** in that day,"	Am 8:9	
that the ship was **a** to break up.	Jon 1:4	
a us so that we will not perish."	Jon 1:6	
was extremely happy **a** the plant.	Jon 4:6	5921

reason to be angry **a** the plant?" Jon 4:9 5921
And it will come **a** in the last Mi 4:1
That He may teach us **a** His ways Mi 4:2 4480
"And it will come **a** that He who Na 3:7
All who hear **a** you Will clap *their* Na 3:19 8088
the report **a** You *and* I fear. Hab 3:2
"Then it will come **a** on the day Zph 1:8
"It will come **a** at that time Zph 1:12
"I will gather those who grieve **a** Zph 3:18 4480
'It will come **a** that just as Zch 8:13
"It will come **a** in that day Zch 12:3
I will set **a** to destroy all the nations Zch 12:9 1245
"It will come **a** in that day," Zch 13:2
"Also it will come **a** in that day Zch 13:4
It will come **a** in all the land," Zch 13:8
but it will come **a** that at evening Zch 14:7
It will come **a** in that day Zch 14:13
Then it will come **a** that any who Zch 14:16
skip **a** like calves from the stall. Mal 4:2 6335a
a Him spread throughout all Syria; Mt 4:24
do not be worried **a** your life, *as* Mt 6:25 *3588*
why are you worried **a** clothing? Mt 6:28 *4012*
"So do not worry **a** tomorrow; for Mt 6:34 *1519*
"See that no one knows **a** *this!*" Mt 9:30
the news **a** Him throughout all that land. Mt 9:31
a how or what you are to say; Mt 10:19
to speak to the crowds **a** John, Mt 11:7 *4012*
is the one **a** whom it is written, Mt 11:10 *4012*
tetrarch heard the news **a** Jesus, Mt 14:1
Now when Jesus heard **a** *John,* He Mt 14:13
were **a** five thousand men who ate, Mt 14:21 *5616*
spoken to them **a** John the Baptist. Mt 17:13 *4012*
a anything that they may ask, Mt 18:19 *4012*
are you asking Me **a** what is good? Mt 19:17 *4012*
"And he went out **a** the third hour Mt 20:3 *4012*
a the sixth and the ninth hour, Mt 20:5 *4012*
a the eleventh *hour* he went out and Mt 20:6 *4012*
hired **a** the eleventh hour came, Mt 20:9 *4012*
Jesus was **a** to go up to Jerusalem, Mt 20:17 *3195*
the cup that I am **a** to drink?" Mt 20:22 *3195*
THIS CAME **A** FROM THE LORD, AND IT Mt 21:42
that He was speaking **a** them. Mt 21:45 *4012*
"What do you think **a** the Christ, Mt 22:42 *4012*
"For *it is* just like a man **a** Mt 25:14
not know what you are talking **a**." Mt 26:70
A the ninth hour Jesus cried out with Mt 27:46 *4012*
Immediately the news **a** Him Mk 1:28
they spoke to Jesus **a** her. Mk 1:30 *4012*
a these things in your hearts? Mk 2:8
Looking **a** at those who were Mk 3:34 *4017*
began asking Him **a** Mk 4:10
the sea, **a** two thousand *of them* Mk 5:13 *5613*
man, and *all* **a** the swine. Mk 5:16 *4012*
after hearing **a** Jesus, she came up in Mk 5:27 *4012*
that no one should know **a** this, Mk 5:43
When his disciples heard **a** *this,* Mk 6:29
a the fourth watch of the night He Mk 6:48 *4012*
and ran **a** that whole country and Mk 6:55 *4063*
questioned Him **a** the parable. Mk 7:17
A four thousand were *there;* Mk 8:9 *5613*
warned them to tell no one **a** Him. Mk 8:30 *4012*
He did not want anyone to know **a** *it.* Mk 9:30
questioning Him **a** this again. Mk 10:10 *4012*
THIS CAME **A** FROM THE LORD, AND IT Mk 12:11
in the *passage* **a** *the burning* Mk 12:26 *1909*
beforehand **a** what you are to say, Mk 13:11
what you are talking **a**." Mk 14:68
know this man you are talking **a**!" Mk 14:71
know the exact truth **a** the things you Lk 1:4 *4012*
stayed with her **a** three months, Lk 1:56 *5613*
being talked **a** in all the hill country Lk 1:65 *1255*
had been told them **a** this Child. Lk 2:17 *4012*
which were being said **a** Him. Lk 2:33 *4012*
"And *what* **a** us, what shall we Lk 3:14
wondering in their hearts **a** John, Lk 3:15 *4012*
Himself was **a** thirty years of age, Lk 3:23 *5616*
and news **a** Him spread through all Lk 4:14 *4012*
And the report **a** Him was spreading Lk 4:37 *4012*
But the news **a** Him was spreading Lk 5:15 *4012*
by him, was sick and **a** to die. Lk 7:2 *3195*
When he heard **a** Jesus, Lk 7:3 *4012*
to him **a** all these things. Lk 7:18 *4012*
to speak to the crowds **a** John, Lk 7:24 *4012*
is the one **a** whom it is written, Lk 7:27 *4012*
only daughter, **a** twelve years old, Lk 8:42 *5613*
man **a** whom I hear such things?" Lk 9:9 *4012*
He *began* speaking to them **a** the Lk 9:11 *4012*
there were **a** five thousand men.) Lk 9:14 *5616*
eat in groups of **a** fifty each." Lk 9:14 *5616*
was **a** to accomplish at Jerusalem. Lk 9:31 *3195*
to ask Him **a** this statement. Lk 9:45 *4012*
and bothered **a** so many things; Lk 10:41 *4012*
do not worry **a** how or Lk 12:11
do not worry **a** *your* life, *as* Lk 12:22 *3588*
do you worry **a** other matters? Lk 12:26 *4012*
reported to Him **a** the Galileans whose Lk 13:1 *4012*
'What is this I hear **a** you? Lk 16:2 *4012*
God bring **a** justice for His elect who Lk 18:7 *4160*
bring **a** justice for them quickly. Lk 18:8 *4160*
written through the prophets **a** the Son Lk 18:31
He was **a** to pass through that way. Lk 19:4 *3195*
in the *passage* **a** *the burning* bush, Lk 20:37
Him any longer **a** anything. Lk 20:40
some were talking **a** the temple, Lk 21:5 *4012*
things are **a** to take place?" Lk 21:7 *3195*
things that are **a** to take place, Lk 21:36 *3195*
from them **a** a stone's throw, Lk 22:41 *5616*
After **a** an hour had passed, Lk 22:59 *5616*
not know what you are talking **a**." Lk 22:60
because he had been hearing **a** Him Lk 23:8 *4012*
It was now **a** the sixth hour, Lk 23:44 *5616*
and the Sabbath was **a** to begin. Lk 23:54 *2020*
While they were perplexed **a** this, Lk 24:4 *4012*
was **a** seven miles from Jerusalem. Lk 24:13
were talking with each other **a** all Lk 24:14 *4012*
"The things **a** Jesus the Nazarene, Lk 24:19 *4012*
written **a** Me in the Law of Moses Lk 24:44 *4012*
He came as a witness, to testify **a** Jn 1:7 *4012*
but *he came* to testify **a** Jn 1:8 *4012*
John testified **a** Him and cried out, Jn 1:15 *4012*
What do you say **a** yourself?" Jn 1:22 *4012*
day, for it was **a** the tenth hour. Jn 1:39 *5613*
with a Jew **a** purification. Jn 3:25 *4012*
It was **a** the sixth hour. Jn 4:6 *5613*
to eat that you do not know **a**." Jn 4:32 *3609a*
"If I *alone* testify **a** Myself, Jn 5:31 *4012*
that the testimony which He gives **a** Jn 5:32 *4012*
very works that I do—testify **a** Jn 5:36 *4012*
it is these that testify **a** Me; Jn 5:39 *4012*
for he wrote **a** Me. Jn 5:46 *4012*
down, in number **a** five thousand. Jn 6:10 *5613*
had rowed **a** three or four miles, Jn 6:19 *5613*
Jews were grumbling **a** Him, Jn 6:41 *4012*
muttering these things **a** Him, Jn 7:32 *4012*
"You are testifying **a** Yourself; Jn 8:13 *4012*
"Even if I testify **a** Myself, My Jn 8:14 *4012*
"I am He who testifies **a** Myself, Jn 8:18 *4012*
the Father who sent Me testifies **a** Me." Jn 8:18 *4012*
speaking to them **a** the Father. Jn 8:27
"What do you say **a** Him, since He Jn 9:17 *4012*
and is not concerned **a** the sheep. Jn 10:13 *4012*
John said **a** this man was true." Jn 10:41 *4012*
near Jerusalem, **a** two miles off; Jn 11:18 *5613*
he was concerned **a** the poor, Jn 12:6 *4012*
continued to testify **a** *Him.* Jn 12:17
He will testify **a** Me, Jn 15:26 *4012*
not know what He is talking **a**." Jn 16:18
you deliberating together **a** this, Jn 16:19 *4012*
that day you will not question Me **a** Jn 16:23
questioned Jesus **a** His disciples, Jn 18:19 *4012*
His disciples, and **a** His teaching. Jn 18:19 *4012*
kind of death He was **a** to die. Jn 18:32 *3195*
or did others tell you **a** Me?" Jn 18:34 *4012*
it was **a** the sixth hour. Jn 19:14 *5613*
aloes, **a** a hundred pounds *weight* Jn 19:39 *5613*
but **a** one hundred yards away, Jn 21:8 *5613*
"Lord, and what **a** this man?" Jn 21:21
a all that Jesus began to do and Ac 1:1 *4012*
of **a** one hundred and twenty persons Ac 1:15 *5616*
there were added **a** three thousand souls. Ac 2:41 *5616*
and John **a** to go into the temple, Ac 3:3 *3195*
restoration of all things **a** which God Ac 3:21 *4012*
men came to be **a** five thousand. Ac 4:4 *5613*
for we cannot stop speaking **a** what we Ac 4:20
an interval of **a** three hours, Ac 5:7 *5613*
into the temple **a** daybreak and Ac 5:21 *5259*
they were greatly perplexed **a** them Ac 5:24 *4012*
and a group of **a** four hundred men Ac 5:36 *5613*
EGYPT WHO KNEW NOTHING **A** JOSEPH. Ac 7:18 *3609a*
went **a** preaching the word. Ac 8:4 *1330*
the good news **a** the kingdom of God Ac 8:12 *4012*
I have heard from many **a** this man, Ac 9:13 *4012*
them, moving **a** freely in Jerusalem, Ac 9:28 *1531, 2532, 1607*
A the ninth hour of the day he Ac 10:3 *5616, 4012*
housetop **a** the sixth hour to pray. Ac 10:9 *4012*
and *how* He went **a** doing good and Ac 10:38 *1330*
The news **a** them reached the Ac 11:22 *4012*
Now **a** that time Herod the king Ac 12:1 *2596*
Herod was **a** to bring him forward, Ac 12:6 *3195*
and he went **a** seeking those who Ac 13:11 *4013*
"For a period of **a** forty Ac 13:18 *5613*
a four hundred and fifty years. Ac 13:19 *5613*
God first concerned Himself **a** taking Ac 15:14 *1980a*
But **a** midnight Paul and Silas were Ac 16:25 *2596*
sword and was **a** to kill himself, Ac 16:27 *3195*
when Paul was **a** to open his mouth, Ac 18:14 *3195*
but if there are questions **a** words Ac 18:15 *4012*
concerned **a** any of these things. Ac 18:17
There were in all **a** twelve men. Ac 19:7 *5616*
them **a** the kingdom of God. Ac 19:8 *4012*
Jesus, and I know **a** Paul, Ac 19:15 *1987*
A that time there occurred no small Ac 19:23 *2596*
as they shouted for **a** two hours, Ac 19:34 *5613*
as he was **a** to set sail for Syria, Ac 20:3 *3195*
I went **a** preaching the kingdom, Ac 20:25 *1330*
and they have been told **a** you, Ac 21:21 *4012*
which they have been told **a** you, Ac 21:24 *4012*
As Paul was **a** to be brought Ac 21:37 *3195*
approaching Damascus **a** noontime, Ac 22:6 *4012*
not accept your testimony **a** Me.' Ac 22:18 *4012*
'What are you **a** to do? Ac 22:26 *3195*
Therefore those who were **a** to Ac 22:29 *3195*
somewhat more thoroughly **a** him. Ac 23:20 *4012*
and was **a** to be slain by them, Ac 23:27 *3195*
over questions **a** their Law, Ac 23:29 *4012*
a more exact knowledge **a** the Way, Ac 24:22 *4012*
him *speak* **a** faith in Christ Jesus. Ac 24:24 *4012*
he himself was **a** to leave shortly. Ac 25:4 *3195*
there is anything wrong **a** the man, Ac 25:5 *1722*
of disagreement with him **a** their own Ac 25:19 *4012*
religion and **a** a dead man, Ac 25:19 *4012*
you see this man **a** whom all the Ac 25:24 *4012*
a him to write to my lord. Ac 25:26 *4012*
that I am **a** to make my defense Ac 26:2 *3195*
a me for a long time, Ac 26:5
the king knows **a** these matters, Ac 26:26 *4012*
which was **a** to sail to the regions Ac 27:2 *3195*
driven **a** in the Adriatic Sea, Ac 27:27 *1308*
a midnight the sailors *began* to Ac 27:27 *2596*
Until the day was **a** to dawn, Ac 27:33 *3195*
expecting that he was **a** to swell up Ac 28:6 *3195*
brethren, when they heard **a** us, Ac 28:15 *4012*
or spoken anything bad **a** you. Ac 28:21 *4012*
testifying **a** the kingdom of God and Ac 28:23
apostleship to bring **a** *the* obedience Ro 1:5 *1519*
a God is evident within them; Ro 1:19
he has something to boast **a**, Ro 4:2 *2745*
for the Law brings **a** wrath, Ro 4:15 *2716*
he was **a** a hundred years old, Ro 4:19 *4225*
tribulation brings **a** perseverance; Ro 5:3 *2716*
for I would not have known **a** Ro 7:7 *3609a*
For I testify **a** them that they have a Ro 10:2
not knowing **a** God's righteousness and Ro 10:3
the Scripture says in *the passage* **a** Ro 11:2
from Jerusalem and round **a** as far Ro 15:19 *2945*
the things **a** which you wrote, 1Co 7:1
Do not worry **a** it; 1Co 7:21
a the things of the Lord, 1Co 7:32
a the things of the world, 1Co 7:33
a the things of the Lord, 1Co 7:34
a the things of the world, 1Co 7:34
God is not concerned **a** oxen, 1Co 9:9
come **a** the saying that is written, 1Co 15:54
always carrying **a** in the body the 2Co 4:10 *4064*
I have boasted to him **a** you, 2Co 7:14 *5228*
of our reason for boasting **a** you. 2Co 8:24 *5228*
you **a** this ministry to the saints; 2Co 9:1 *4012*
I boast **a** you to the Macedonians, 2Co 9:2 *5228*
that our boasting **a** you may not be 2Co 9:3 *5228*
somewhat further **a** our authority, 2Co 10:8 *4012*
matter **a** which they are boasting. 2Co 11:12
will rather boast **a** my weaknesses, 2Co 12:9 *1722*
not recognize this **a** yourselves, 2Co 13:5
a the truth of the gospel, Ga 2:14 *4314*
my tone, for I am perplexed **a** you. Ga 4:20 *1722*
which He brought **a** in Christ, Eph 1:20 *1754*
a by every wind of doctrine, Eph 4:14 *4064*
also may know **a** my circumstances, Eph 6:21 *2596*
so that you may know **a** us, Eph 6:22 *4012*
for me to feel this way **a** you all, Php 1:7 *5228*
and I may be less concerned **a** *you.* Php 2:28
that you may know **a** our circumstances Col 4:8 *4012*
you **a** the whole situation here. Col 4:9
(**a** whom you received instructions; Col 4:10 *4012*
For they themselves report **a** us 1Th 1:9 *4012*
sent to find out **a** your faith, 1Th 3:5
a you through your faith; 1Th 3:7 *1909*
brethren, **a** those who are asleep, 1Th 4:13 *4012*
matters **a** which they make confident 1Tm 1:7 *4012*
a things not proper *to mention.* 1Tm 5:13
questions and disputes **a** words, 1Tm 6:4 *3055*
which He will bring **a** at the 1Tm 6:15
of God not to wrangle **a** words, 2Tm 2:14 *3054*
having nothing bad to say **a** us. Ti 2:8 *4012*
and strife and disputes **a** the Law, Ti 3:9
THAT YOU ARE CONCERNED **A** HIM? Heb 2:6 *1980a*
elementary teaching **a** the Christ, Heb 6:1
of instruction **a** washings and Heb 6:2
he was **a** to erect the tabernacle; Heb 8:5 *3195*
God testifying **a** his gifts, Heb 11:4 *1909*
by God **a** things not yet seen, Heb 11:7 *4012*
they went **a** in sheepskins, in Heb 11:37 *4022*
of the soil, being patient **a** it, Jas 5:7 *1909*
a His calling and choosing you; 2Pe 1:10
Lord is not slow **a** His promise, 2Pe 3:9
teaches you **a** all things, 1Jn 2:27 *4012*
write you **a** our common salvation, Jude 1:3 *4012*
and argued **a** the body of Moses, Jude 1:9 *4012*
It was also **a** these men *that* Enoch, Jude 1:14
not fear what you are **a** to suffer. Rv 2:10 *3195*
the devil is **a** to cast some of you Rv 2:10 *3195*
that remain, which were **a** to die; Rv 3:2 *3195*
is **a** to come upon the whole world, Rv 3:10 *3195*
in heaven for **a** half an hour. Rv 8:1 *5613*
three angels who are **a** to sound!" Rv 8:13 *3195*
had spoken, I was **a** to write; Rv 10:4 *3195*
angel, when he is **a** to sound, Rv 10:7 *3195*
the woman who was **a** to give birth, Rv 12:4 *3195*
a naked and men will not see his Rv 16:15 *4043*
a one hundred pounds each, Rv 16:21 *5613*
and is **a** to come up out of the Rv 17:8 *3195*

ABOVE

waters which were **a** the expanse; Gn 1:7 4480, 5921
and let birds fly **a** the earth in Gn 1:20 5921
ark, so that it rose **a** the earth. Gn 7:17 4480, 5921
from the dew of heaven from **a**. Gn 27:39 5921
the LORD stood **a** it and said, Gn 28:13 5921
you With blessings of heaven **a**, Gn 49:25 4480, 5921
in heaven **a** or on the earth beneath Ex 20:4 4480, 4605
and from **a** the mercy seat, from Ex 25:22 5921
a covering of porpoise skins **a**. Ex 26:14 4480, 4605
a the skillfully woven band of the Ex 28:27 4480, 4605
a covering of porpoise skins **a**. Ex 36:19 4480, 4605
a the woven band of the ephod. Ex 39:20 4480, 4605
it, to fasten it on the turban **a**, Ex 39:31 4480, 4605

those which have **a** their feet Lv 11:21 4480, 4605
speaking to him from **a** the mercy seat Nu 7:89 5921
over the tabernacle, staying **a** it, Nu 9:22 5921
a the assembly of the LORD?" Nu 16:3 5921
heaven **a** and on the earth below; Dt 4:39 4480, 4605
in heaven **a** or on the earth beneath Dt 5:8 4480, 4605
shall be blessed **a** all peoples; Dt 7:14 4480
them, *even* you **a** all peoples, Dt 10:15 4480
as the heavens *remain* **a** the earth. Dt 11:21 5921
not be lifted up **a** his countrymen Dt 17:20 4480
a all nations which He has made, Dt 26:19 5921
a all the nations of the earth. Dt 28:1 5921
the tail, and you only will be **a**, Dt 28:13 4605
rise **a** you higher and higher, Dt 28:43 5921
in heaven **a** and on earth beneath. Jos 2:11 4480, 4605
from **a** will stand in one heap." Jos 3:13 4480, 4605
a stood *and* rose up in one heap, Jos 3:16 4480, 4605
and honor your sons **a** Me, 1Sa 2:29 4480
of the LORD of hosts who sits **a** 1Sa 4:4
LORD of hosts who is enthroned **a** 2Sa 6:2
who chose me **a** your father and 2Sa 6:21 4480
your father and **a** all his house, 2Sa 6:21 4480
me **a** those who rise up against me; 2Sa 22:49 4480
It was paneled with cedar **a** 1Ki 7:3 4605, 5921
And **a** were costly stones, stone 1Ki 7:11 4480, 4605
even **a** *and* close to the rounded 1Ki 7:20 4480, 4605
the frames there *was* a pedestal **a**, 1Ki 7:29 4480, 4605
over the ark and its poles from **a**. 1Ki 8:7 4480, 4605
in heaven **a** or on earth beneath, 1Ki 8:23 4480, 4605
who are enthroned **a** the cherubim, 2Ki 19:15
his throne **a** the throne of the kings 2Ki 25:28 4480, 5921
the LORD who is enthroned **a** 1Ch 13:6
also is to be feared **a** all gods. 1Ch 16:25 5921
over and **a** all that I have already 1Ch 29:3 4480, 4605
a the people and said to them, 2Ch 24:20 4480, 5921
were high **a** them he chopped down; 2Ch 34:4 4605
iniquities have risen **a** our heads and Ezr 9:6 4605
A the Horse Gate the priests Ne 3:28 4480, 5921
he was standing **a** all the people; Ne 8:5 4480, 5921
exalted **a** all blessing and praise! Ne 9:5 5921
the wall **a** the house of David Ne 12:37 4480, 5921
the wall, **a** the Tower of Furnaces, Ne 12:38 4480, 5921
and **a** the Gate of Ephraim, by the Ne 12:39 4480, 5921
and how he had promoted him **a** the Es 5:11 5921
Let not God **a** care for it, Nor Jb 3:4 4605
And his lamp goes out **a** him. Jb 18:6 5921
And his branch is cut off **a**. Jb 18:16 4480, 4605
of wisdom is **a** *that of* pearls. Jb 28:18 4480
what is the portion of God from **a** Jb 31:2 4605
For I would have denied God **a**. Jb 31:28 4480, 4605
Nor regards the rich **a** the poor, Jb 34:19 6440
Your splendor **a** the heavens! Ps 8:1 5921
me **a** those who rise up against me; Ps 18:48 4480
lifted up **a** my enemies around me, Ps 27:6 5921
With the oil of joy **a** Your fellows. Ps 45:7 4480
He summons the heavens **a**, Ps 50:4 4480, 5921
Be exalted **a** the heavens, O God; Ps 57:5 5921
Let Your glory *be* **a** all the earth. Ps 57:5 5921
Be exalted **a** the heavens, O God; Ps 57:11 5921
Let Your glory *be* **a** all the earth. Ps 57:11 5921
Yet He commanded the clouds **a** And Ps 78:23 4480, 4605
You who are enthroned **a** Ps 80:1
a all those who are around Him? Ps 89:7 5921
God And a great King **a** all gods, Ps 95:3 5921
He is to be feared **a** all gods. Ps 96:4 5921
You are exalted far **a** all gods. Ps 97:9 5921
He is enthroned **a** the cherubim, Ps 99:1
He is exalted **a** all the peoples. Ps 99:2 5921
as the heavens are **a** the earth, Ps 103:11 5921
were standing **a** the mountains. Ps 104:6 5921
is great **a** the heavens, Ps 108:4 4480, 5921
Be exalted, O God, **a** the heavens, Ps 108:5 5921
And Your glory **a** all the earth. Ps 108:5 5921
The LORD is high **a** all nations; Ps 113:4 5921
His glory is **a** the heavens. Ps 113:4 5921
I love Your commandments **A** gold, Ps 119:127 4480
Above gold, yes, **a** fine gold. Ps 119:127 4480
And that our Lord is **a** all gods. Ps 135:5 4480
spread out the earth **a** the waters, Ps 136:6 5921
exalt Jerusalem **A** my chief joy. Ps 137:6 5921
the waters that are **a** the heavens! Ps 148:4 4480, 5921
His glory is **a** earth and heaven. Ps 148:13 5921
When He made firm the skies **a**, Pr 8:28 4480, 4605
is to be chosen **a** silver. Pr 16:16 4480
For her worth is far **a** jewels. Pr 31:10 4480
And will be raised **a** the hills; Is 2:2 4480
Seraphim stood **a** Him, each having Is 6:2 4605
my throne **a** the stars of God, Is 14:13 4605
a the heights of the clouds; Is 14:14 5921
For the windows **a** are opened, and Is 24:18 4480, 4791
who is enthroned **a** the cherubim, Is 37:16
who sits **a** the circle of the earth, Is 40:22 5921
"Drip down, O heavens, from **a**, Is 45:8 4605
mourn And the heavens **a** be dark, Jer 4:28 4480, 4605
"If the heavens **a** can be Jer 31:37 4480, 4605
which was **a** the chamber of Jer 35:4 4480, 4605
his throne **a** the thrones of the kings Jer 52:32 4480, 4605
Their wings were spread out **a**; Ezk 1:11 4480, 4605
And there came a voice from **a** the Ezk 1:25 5921
Now **a** the expanse that was over Ezk 1:26 4480, 4605
a throne, appeared **a** them. Ezk 10:1 5921
And its height was raised **a** the Ezk 19:11 5921, 996
lift itself up **a** the nations. Ezk 29:15 5921
in three stories, one **a** another, Ezk 41:6 413
From the ground to **a** the entrance Ezk 41:20 4480, 5921
and magnify himself **a** every god and Da 11:36 5921
will magnify himself **a** *them* all. Da 11:37 5921
who was **a** the waters of the river, Da 12:6 4480, 4605
who was **a** the waters of the river, Da 12:7 4480, 4605
his fruit **a** and his root below. Am 2:9 4480, 4605
It will be raised **a** the hills, Mi 4:1 4480
will not be magnified **a** Judah. Zch 12:7 5921
"A disciple is not **a** his teacher, Mt 10:24 *5228*
teacher, nor a slave **a** his master. Mt 10:24 *5228*
And **a** His head they put up Mt 27:37 *1883*
they removed the roof **a** Him; Mk 2:4 *3699*
"A pupil is not **a** his teacher; Lk 6:40 *5228*
was also an inscription **a** Him, Lk 23:38 *1909*
"He who comes from **a** is above all, Jn 3:31 *509*
"He who comes from above is **a** all, Jn 3:31 *1883*
He who comes from heaven is **a** all. Jn 3:31 *1883*
"You are from below, I am from **a**; Jn 8:23 *507*
it had been given you from **a**; Jn 19:11 *509*
I WILL GRANT WONDERS IN THE SKY **A** Ac 2:19 *507*
One person regards one day **a** another, Ro 14:5 *3844*
But the Jerusalem **a** is free; Ga 4:26 *507*
far **a** all rule and authority and Eph 1:21 *5231*
ascended far **a** all the heavens, Eph 4:10 *5231*
the name which is **a** every name, Php 2:9 *5228*
children of God **a** reproach in the Php 2:15 *299b*
Christ, keep seeking the things **a**, Col 3:1 *507*
Set your mind on the things **a**, Col 3:2 *507*
who opposes and exalts himself **a** 2Th 2:4 *1909*
then, must be **a** reproach, 1Tm 3:2 *423*
so that they may be **a** reproach. 1Tm 5:7 *423*
namely, if any man is **a** reproach, Ti 1:6 *410*
be **a** reproach as God's steward, Ti 1:7 *410*
OF GLADNESS **A** YOUR COMPANIONS." Heb 1:9 *3844*
sinners and exalted **a** the heavens; Heb 7:26
and **a** it *were* the cherubim of Heb 9:5 *5231*
saying **a**, "SACRIFICES AND OFFERINGS Heb 10:8 *511*
and every perfect gift is from **a**, Jas 1:17 *509*
not that which comes down from **a**, Jas 3:15 *509*
the wisdom from **a** is first pure, Jas 3:17 *509*
But **a** all, my brethren, do not Jas 5:12 *4253*
A all, keep fervent in your love 1Pe 4:8 *4253*

ABRAHAM

Abram, But your name shall be **A**; Gn 17:5 85
God said further to **A**, Gn 17:9 85
Then God said to **A**, Gn 17:15 85
A fell on his face and laughed, Gn 17:17 85
And **A** said to God, Gn 17:18 85
with him, God went up from **A**. Gn 17:22 85
Then **A** took Ishmael his son, and Gn 17:23 85
Now **A** was ninety-nine years old Gn 17:24 85
very same day **A** was circumcised, Gn 17:26 85
So **A** hurried into the tent to Gn 18:6 85
A also ran to the herd, and took a Gn 18:7 85
Now **A** and Sarah were old, advanced Gn 18:11 85
And the LORD said to **A**, Gn 18:13 85
and **A** was walking with them to Gn 18:16 85
hide from **A** what I am about to do, Gn 18:17 85
since **A** will surely become a great Gn 18:18 85
A what He has spoken about him." Gn 18:19 85
while **A** was still standing before Gn 18:22 85
A came near and said, Gn 18:23 85
And **A** replied, Gn 18:27 85
speaking to **A** the LORD departed, Gn 18:33 85
and **A** returned to his place. Gn 18:33 85
Now **A** arose early in the morning Gn 19:27 85
the valley, that God remembered **A**, Gn 19:29 85
Now **A** journeyed from there toward Gn 20:1 85
A said of Sarah his wife, Gn 20:2 85
called **A** and said to him, Gn 20:9 85
And Abimelech said to **A**, Gn 20:10 85
A said, "Because I thought, Gn 20:11 85
servants, and gave them to **A**, Gn 20:14 85
A prayed to God, Gn 20:17 85
bore a son to **A** in his old age, Gn 21:2 85
A called the name of his son Gn 21:3 85
Then **A** circumcised his son Isaac Gn 21:4 85
Now **A** was one hundred years old Gn 21:5 85
"Who would have said to **A** that Gn 21:7 85
and **A** made a great feast on the Gn 21:8 85
Egyptian, whom she had borne to **A**, Gn 21:9 85
Therefore she said to **A**, Gn 21:10 85
A greatly because of his son. Gn 21:11 85
But God said to **A**, Gn 21:12 85
So **A** rose early in the morning and Gn 21:14 85
commander of his army, spoke to **A**, Gn 21:22 85
A said, "I swear it." Gn 21:24 85
But **A** complained to Abimelech Gn 21:25 85
A took sheep and oxen and Gn 21:27 85
Then **A** set seven ewe lambs of the Gn 21:28 85
Abimelech said to **A**, Gn 21:29 85
A planted a tamarisk tree at Gn 21:33
And **A** sojourned in the land of the Gn 21:34 85
these things, that God tested **A**, Gn 22:1 85
Abraham, and said to him, "**A**!" Gn 22:1 85
So **A** rose early in the morning and Gn 22:3 85
On the third day **A** raised his eyes Gn 22:4 85
A said to his young men, Gn 22:5 85
A took the wood of the burnt Gn 22:6 85
spoke to **A** his father and said, Gn 22:7 85
A said, "God will provide for Gn 22:8 85
and **A** built the altar there and Gn 22:9 85
A stretched out his hand and Gn 22:10 85
"**A**, Abraham!" And he said, "Here Gn 22:11 85
"Abraham, **A**!" And he said, "Here Gn 22:11 85
Then **A** raised his eyes and looked, Gn 22:13 85
and **A** went and took the ram and Gn 22:13 85
A called the name of that Gn 22:14 85
to **A** a second time from heaven, Gn 22:15 85
So **A** returned to his young men, Gn 22:19 85
and **A** lived at Beersheba. Gn 22:19 85
these things, that it was told **A**, Gn 22:20 85
and **A** went in to mourn for Sarah Gn 23:2 85
Then **A** rose from before his dead, Gn 23:3 85
The sons of Heth answered **A**, Gn 23:5 85
So **A** rose and bowed to the people Gn 23:7 85
Ephron the Hittite answered **A** in the Gn 23:10 85
And **A** bowed before the people of Gn 23:12 85
Then Ephron answered **A**, Gn 23:14 85
A listened to Ephron; Gn 23:16 85
and **A** weighed out for Ephron the Gn 23:16 85
to **A** for a possession in the Gn 23:18 85
A buried Sarah his wife in the Gn 23:19 85
were deeded over to **A** for a burial Gn 23:20 85
Now **A** was old, advanced in age; Gn 24:1 85
LORD had blessed **A** in every way. Gn 24:1 85
A said to his servant, the Gn 24:2 85
Then **A** said to him, Gn 24:6 85
under the thigh of **A** his master, Gn 24:9 85
"O LORD, the God of my master **A**, Gn 24:12 85
lovingkindness to my master **A**. Gn 24:12 85
the LORD, the God of my master **A**, Gn 24:27 85
'O LORD, the God of my master **A**, Gn 24:42 85
the LORD, the God of my master **A**, Gn 24:48 85
Now **A** took another wife, whose Gn 25:1 85
A gave all that he had to Isaac; Gn 25:5 85
A gave gifts while he was still Gn 25:6 85
A breathed his last and died Gn 25:8 85
the field which **A** purchased from Gn 25:10 85
there **A** was buried with Sarah his Gn 25:10 85
came about after the death of **A**, Gn 25:11 85
Egyptian, Sarah's maid, bore to **A**; Gn 25:12 85
A became the father of Isaac; Gn 25:19 85
had occurred in the days of **A**. Gn 26:1 85
which I swore to your father **A**. Gn 26:3 85
A obeyed Me and kept My charge, Gn 26:5 85
dug in the days of **A** his father, Gn 26:15 85
dug in the days of his father **A**, Gn 26:18 85
them up after the death of **A**; Gn 26:18 85
"I am the God of your father **A**; Gn 26:24 85
For the sake of My servant **A**." Gn 26:24 85
also give you the blessing of **A**, Gn 28:4 85
which God gave to **A**." Gn 28:4 85
father **A** and the God of Isaac; Gn 28:13 85
God of my father, the God of **A**, Gn 31:42 85
"The God of **A** and the God of Gn 31:53 85
A and God of my father Isaac, Gn 32:9 85
land which I gave to **A** and Isaac, Gn 35:12 85
where **A** and Isaac had sojourned. Gn 35:27 85
my fathers **A** and Isaac walked, Gn 48:15 85
names of my fathers **A** and Isaac; Gn 48:16 85
which **A** bought along with the Gn 49:30 85
they buried **A** and his wife Sarah, Gn 49:31 85
which **A** had bought along with the Gn 50:13 85
which He promised on oath to **A**, Gn 50:24 85
remembered His covenant with **A**, Ex 2:24 85
God of your father, the God of **A**, Ex 3:6 85
God of your fathers, the God of **A**, Ex 3:15 85
God of your fathers, the God of **A**, Ex 3:16 85
of their fathers, the God of **A**, Ex 4:5 85
and I appeared to **A**, Ex 6:3 85
land which I swore to give to **A**, Ex 6:8 85
"Remember **A**, Isaac, and Israel, Ex 32:13 85
to the land of which I swore to **A**, Ex 33:1 85
and My covenant with **A** as well, Lv 26:42 85
see the land which I swore to **A**, Nu 32:11 85
to give to your fathers, to **A**, Dt 1:8 85
which He swore to your fathers, **A**, Dt 6:10 85
LORD swore to your fathers, to **A**, Dt 9:5 85
'Remember Your servants, **A**, Dt 9:27 85
as He swore to your fathers, to **A**, Dt 29:13 85
LORD swore to your fathers, to **A**, Dt 30:20 85
is the land which I swore to **A**, Dt 34:4 85

of A and the father of Nahor, Jos 24:2 85
father A from beyond the River, Jos 24:3 85
"O LORD, the God of A, 1Ki 18:36 85
because of His covenant with A, 2Ki 13:23 85
Abram, that is A. 1Ch 1:27 85
sons of A *were* Isaac and Ishmael. 1Ch 1:28 85
A became the father of Isaac. 1Ch 1:34 85
The covenant which He made with A, 1Ch 16:16 85
"O LORD, the God of A, 1Ch 29:18 85
of A Your friend forever? 2Ch 20:7 85
return to the LORD GOD of A, 2Ch 30:6 85
Chaldees, And gave him the name A. Ne 9:7 85
as the people of the God of A, Ps 47:9 85
O seed of A, His servant, O sons Ps 105:6 85
The covenant which He made with A, Ps 105:9 85
His holy word *With* A His servant; Ps 105:42 85
says the LORD, who redeemed A, Is 29:22 85
chosen, Descendant of A My friend, Is 41:8 85
"Look to A your father And to Is 51:2 85
Father, though A does not know us And Is 63:16 85
rulers over the descendants of A, Jer 33:26 85
'A was *only* one, yet he possessed Ezk 33:24 85
to Jacob *And* unchanging love to A, Mi 7:20 85
the son of David, the son of A: Mt 1:1 11
A was the father of Isaac, Mt 1:2 11
the generations from A to David are Mt 1:17 11
'We have A for our father'; Mt 3:9 11
able to raise up children to A. Mt 3:9 11
and recline *at the table* with A, Mt 8:11 11
'I AM THE GOD OF A, AND THE GOD OF Mt 22:32 11
'I AM THE GOD OF A, AND THE GOD OF Mk 12:26 11
To A and his descendants forever." Lk 1:55 11
which He swore to A our father, Lk 1:73 11
'We have A for our father,' for I Lk 3:8 11
able to raise up children to A. Lk 3:8 11
the son of Isaac, the son of A, Lk 3:34 11
woman, a daughter of A as she is, Lk 13:16 11
when you see A and Isaac and Jacob Lk 13:28 11
in torment, and saw A far away and Lk 16:23 11
'Father A, have mercy on me, and Lk 16:24 11
"But A said, 'Child, remember that Lk 16:25 11
"But A said, 'They have Moses and Lk 16:29 11
'No, father A, but if someone goes Lk 16:30 11
because he, too, is a son of A. Lk 19:9 11
he calls the Lord THE GOD OF A, Lk 20:37 11
"A is our father." Jn 8:39 11
children, do the deeds of A. Jn 8:39 11
this A did not do. Jn 8:40 11
A died, and the prophets *also* Jn 8:52 11
are not greater than our father A, Jn 8:53 11
father A rejoiced to see My day, Jn 8:56 11
years old, and have You seen A?" Jn 8:57 11
I say to you, before A was born, Jn 8:58 11
"The God of A, Isaac and Jacob, Ac 3:13 11
with your fathers, saying to A, Ac 3:25 11
A when he was in Mesopotamia, Ac 7:2 11
and so A became the father of Ac 7:8 11
and laid in the tomb which A had Ac 7:16 11
which God had assured to A, Ac 7:17 11
THE GOD OF A AND ISAAC AND JACOB.' Ac 7:32 11
What then shall we say that A, Ro 4:1 11
For if A was justified by works, Ro 4:2 11
"A BELIEVED GOD, AND IT WAS Ro 4:3 11
CREDITED TO A AS RIGHTEOUSNESS." Ro 4:9 11
faith of our father A which he had Ro 4:12 11
For the promise to A or to his Ro 4:13 11
those who are of the faith of A, Ro 4:16 11
an Israelite, a descendant of A, Ro 11:1 11
Are they descendants of A? 2Co 11:22 11
Even so A BELIEVED GOD, AND IT WAS Ga 3:6 11
are of faith who are sons of A. Ga 3:7 11
the gospel beforehand to A, Ga 3:8 11
are of faith are blessed with A, Ga 3:9 11
of A might come to the Gentiles, Ga 3:14 11
were spoken to A and to his seed. Ga 3:16 11
it to A by means of a promise. Ga 3:18 11
it is written that A had two sons, Ga 4:22 11
gives help to the descendant of A. Heb 2:16 11
when God made the promise to A, Heb 6:13 11
who met A as he was returning from Heb 7:1 11
to whom also A apportioned a tenth Heb 7:2 11
how great this man was to whom A, Heb 7:4 11
these are descended from A. Heb 7:5 11
them collected a tenth from A and Heb 7:6 11
so to speak, through A even Levi, Heb 7:9 11
By faith A, when he was called, Heb 11:8 11
By faith A, when he was tested, Heb 11:17 11
A our father justified by works when Jas 2:21 11
"AND A BELIEVED GOD, AND IT WAS Jas 2:23 11
as Sarah obeyed A, 1Pe 3:6 11

ABRAHAM'S

male among the men of A household, Gn 17:23 85
because of Sarah, A wife. Gn 20:18 85
Milcah bore to Nahor, A brother. Gn 22:23 85
the wife of A brother Nahor, Gn 24:15 85
So he said, "I am A servant. Gn 24:34 85
When A servant heard their words, Gn 24:52 85
nurse with A servant and his men. Gn 24:59 85
the years of A life that he lived, Gn 25:7 85
the generations of Ishmael, A son, Gn 25:12 85
the generations of Isaac, A son: Gn 25:19 85
the daughter of Ishmael, A son, Gn 28:9 85
The sons of Keturah, A concubine, 1Ch 1:32 85
away by the angels to A bosom; Lk 16:22 11
"We are A descendants and have Jn 8:33 11
"I know that you are A descendants; Jn 8:37 11
"If you are A children, do the Jn 8:39 11
"Brethren, sons of A family, Ac 13:26 11
because they are A descendants, Ro 9:7 11
Christ, then you are A descendants, Ga 3:29 11

ABRAM

years, and became the father of A. Gn 11:26 87
Terah became the father of A, Gn 11:27 87
A and Nahor took wives for Gn 11:29 87
Terah took A his son, and Lot Gn 11:31 87
Now the LORD said to A, Gn 12:1 87
So A went forth as the LORD had Gn 12:4 87
Now A was seventy-five years old Gn 12:4 87
A took Sarai his wife and Lot Gn 12:5 87
A passed through the land as Gn 12:6 87
The LORD appeared to A and said, Gn 12:7 87
A journeyed on, continuing Gn 12:9 87
so A went down to Egypt to sojourn Gn 12:10 87
came about when A came into Egypt, Gn 12:14 87
he treated A well for her sake; Gn 12:16 87
Then Pharaoh called A and said, Gn 12:18 87
So A went up from Egypt to the Gn 13:1 87
Now A was very rich in livestock, Gn 13:2 87
and there A called on the name of Gn 13:4 87
Now Lot, who went with A, Gn 13:5 87
So A said to Lot, Gn 13:8 87
A settled in the land of Canaan, Gn 13:12 87
The LORD said to A, Gn 13:14 87
Then A moved his tent and came and Gn 13:18 87
came and told A the Hebrew. Gn 14:13 87
and these were allies with A. Gn 14:13 87
When A heard that his relative Gn 14:14 87
"Blessed be A of God Most High, Gn 14:19 87
The king of Sodom said to A, Gn 14:21 87
A said to the king of Sodom, Gn 14:22 87
'I have made A rich.' Gn 14:23 87
of the LORD came to A in a vision, Gn 15:1 87
"Do not fear, A, I am a shield to Gn 15:1 87
A said, "O Lord GOD, what Gn 15:2 87
And A said, "Since You have given Gn 15:3 87
carcasses, and A drove them away. Gn 15:11 87
down, a deep sleep fell upon A; Gn 15:12 87
God said to A, Gn 15:13 87
the LORD made a covenant with A, Gn 15:18 87
So Sarai said to A, Gn 16:2 87
And A listened to the voice of Gn 16:2 87
After A had lived ten years in Gn 16:3 87
her to her husband A as his wife. Gn 16:3 87
And Sarai said to A, Gn 16:5 87
But A said to Sarai, Gn 16:6 87
So Hagar bore A a son; Gn 16:15 87
and A called the name of his son, Gn 16:15 87
A was eighty-six years old Gn 16:16 87
when A was ninety-nine years old, Gn 17:1 87
appeared to A and said to him, Gn 17:1 87
A fell on his face, and God Gn 17:3 87
shall your name be called A, Gn 17:5 87
A, that is Abraham. 1Ch 1:27 87
Who chose A And brought him out Ne 9:7 87

ABRAM'S

The name of A wife was Sarai; Gn 11:29 87
his daughter-in-law, his son A wife; Gn 11:31 87
plagues because of Sarai, A wife. Gn 12:17 87
was strife between the herdsmen of A Gn 13:7 87
They also took Lot, A nephew, Gn 14:12 87
A wife had borne him no *children*, Gn 16:1 87
A wife Sarai took Hagar the Gn 16:3 87

ABROAD

of the Canaanite were spread a. Gn 10:18
otherwise we will be scattered a over the Gn 11:4
So the LORD scattered them a from Gn 11:8
LORD scattered them a over the face Gn 11:9
sound a ram's horn a on the tenth day Lv 25:9
you scatter the burning coals a. Nu 16:37 1973
the earth, And he has no name a. Jb 18:17
6440, 2351
Then You spread them a. Ps 44:2
O peoples, And sound His praise a, Ps 66:8
You shed a a plentiful rain, Ps 68:9 5130
your springs be dispersed a, Pr 5:16 2351
Let its spices be wafted a. SS 4:16
a to the right and to the left. Is 54:3 6555
until you have scattered them a, Ezk 34:21 2351
of God who are scattered a. Jn 11:52 1287
"HE SCATTERED A, HE GAVE TO THE 2Co 9:9
twelve tribes who are dispersed a: Jas 1:1

ABRONAH

from Jotbathah and camped at A. Nu 33:34 5684
They journeyed from A and Nu 33:35 5684

ABSALOM

the third, A the son of Maacah, 2Sa 3:3 53
Now it was after this that A the 2Sa 13:1 53
the sister of my brother A." 2Sa 13:4 53
Then A her brother said to her, 2Sa 13:20 53
But A did not speak to Amnon 2Sa 13:22 53
for A hated Amnon because he had 2Sa 13:22 53
A had sheepshearers in Baal-hazor, 2Sa 13:23 53
and A invited all the king's sons. 2Sa 13:23 53
A came to the king and said, 2Sa 13:24 53
But the king said to A, 2Sa 13:25 53
A said, "If not, please let my brother 2Sa 13:26 53
But when A urged him, he let Amnon 2Sa 13:27 53
A commanded his servants, 2Sa 13:28 53
The servants of A did to Amnon 2Sa 13:29 53
to Amnon just as A had commanded. 2Sa 13:29 53
"A has struck down all the king's 2Sa 13:30 53
because by the intent of A this 2Sa 13:32 53
Now A had fled. And the young man 2Sa 13:34 53
Now A fled and went to Talmai the 2Sa 13:37 53
So A had fled and gone to Geshur, 2Sa 13:38 53
King David longed to go out to A; 2Sa 13:39 53
king's heart *was inclined* toward A. 2Sa 14:1 53
bring back the young man A." 2Sa 14:21 53
and brought A to Jerusalem. 2Sa 14:23 53
So A turned to his own house and 2Sa 14:24 53
was no one as handsome as A, 2Sa 14:25 53
To A there were born three sons, 2Sa 14:27 53
Now A lived two full years in 2Sa 14:28 53
Then A sent for Joab, to send him 2Sa 14:29 53
to A at his house and said to him, 2Sa 14:31 53
A answered Joab, 2Sa 14:32 53
and told him, he called for A. 2Sa 14:33 53
the king, and the king kissed A. 2Sa 14:33 53
that A provided for himself a chariot 2Sa 15:1 53
A used to rise early and stand 2Sa 15:2 53
A would call to him and say, 2Sa 15:2 53
Then A would say to him, 2Sa 15:3 53
Moreover, A would say, 2Sa 15:4 53
In this manner A dealt with 2Sa 15:6 53
so A stole away the hearts of the 2Sa 15:6 53
years that A said to the king, 2Sa 15:7 53
But A sent spies throughout all 2Sa 15:10 53
'A is king in Hebron.'" 2Sa 15:10 53
men went with A from Jerusalem, 2Sa 15:11 53
And A sent for Ahithophel the 2Sa 15:12 53
increased continually with A. 2Sa 15:12 53
of the men of Israel are with A." 2Sa 15:13 53
none of us will escape from A. 2Sa 15:14 53
among the conspirators with A." 2Sa 15:31 53
return to the city, and say to A, 2Sa 15:34 53
city, and A came into Jerusalem. 2Sa 15:37 53
into the hand of your son A. 2Sa 16:8 53
Then A and all the people, the men 2Sa 16:15 53
Archite, David's friend, came to A, 2Sa 16:16 53
to Absalom, that Hushai said to A, 2Sa 16:16 53
A said to Hushai, 2Sa 16:17 53
Then Hushai said to A, 2Sa 16:18 53
Then A said to Ahithophel, 2Sa 16:20 53
Ahithophel said to A, 2Sa 16:21 53
pitched a tent for A on the roof, 2Sa 16:22 53
and A went in to his father's 2Sa 16:22 53
regarded by both David and A. 2Sa 16:23 53
Furthermore, Ahithophel said to A, 2Sa 17:1 53
A and all the elders of Israel. 2Sa 17:4 53
Then A said, "Now call Hushai 2Sa 17:5 53
When Hushai had come to A, 2Sa 17:6 53
come to Absalom, A said to him, 2Sa 17:6 53
So Hushai said to A, 2Sa 17:7 53
among the people who follow A.' 2Sa 17:9 53
Then A and all the men of Israel 2Sa 17:14 53
LORD might bring calamity on A. 2Sa 17:14 53
A and the elders of Israel, 2Sa 17:15 53
a lad did see them and told A; 2Sa 17:18 53
And A crossed the Jordan, he and 2Sa 17:24 53
A set Amasa over the army in 2Sa 17:25 53
A camped in the land of Gilead. 2Sa 17:26 53
my sake with the young man A." 2Sa 18:5 53
all the commanders concerning A. 2Sa 18:5 53
Now A happened to meet the 2Sa 18:9 53
For A was riding on *his* mule, and 2Sa 18:9 53
I saw A hanging in an oak." 2Sa 18:10 53
'Protect for me the young man A!' 2Sa 18:12 53
thrust them through the heart of A 2Sa 18:14 53
and struck A and killed him. 2Sa 18:15 53
They took A and cast him into 2Sa 18:17 53
Now A in his lifetime had taken 2Sa 18:18 53
"Is it well with the young man A?" 2Sa 18:29 53
"Is it well with the young man A?" 2Sa 18:32 53
"O my son A, my son, my son 2Sa 18:33 53
my son Absalom, my son, my son A! 2Sa 18:33 53
I had died instead of you, O A, 2Sa 18:33 53
is weeping and mourns for A." 2Sa 19:1 53
"O my son A, O Absalom, my son, 2Sa 19:4 53
"O my son Absalom, O A, 2Sa 19:4 53
for I know this day that if A were 2Sa 19:6 53
has fled out of the land from A. 2Sa 19:9 53
"However, A, whom we anointed 2Sa 19:10 53
will do us more harm than A; 2Sa 20:6 53
and he was born after A. 1Ki 1:6 53
when I fled from A your brother. 1Ki 2:7 53
although he had not followed A. 1Ki 2:28 53
the third *was* A the son of Maacah, 1Ch 3:2 53
he took Maacah the daughter of A, 2Ch 11:20 53
loved Maacah the daughter of A more 2Ch 11:21 53

ABSALOM'S

desolate in her brother A house. 2Sa 13:20 53
So A servants set the field on 2Sa 14:30 53
Then A servants came to the woman 2Sa 17:20 53
is called A Monument to this day. 2Sa 18:18 53

ABSENCE

only, but now much more in my a, Php 2:12 666

ABSENT

when we are a one from the other. Gn 31:49 5641
a in body but present in spirit, 1Co 5:3 548
the body we are a from the Lord 2Co 5:6 1553
and prefer rather to be a from the 2Co 5:8 1553
ambition, whether at home or a, 2Co 5:9 1553
you, but bold toward you when a! 2Co 10:1 548
we are in word by letters when a, 2Co 10:11 548
and though now a I say in advance 2Co 13:2 548
I am writing these things while a, 2Co 13:10 548
I come and see you or remain a, Php 1:27 548
For even though I am a in body, Col 2:5 548

ABSHAI

the three sons of Zeruiah *were* A, 1Ch 2:16 52
As for A the brother of Joab, he 1Ch 11:20 52
in the hand of A his brother; 1Ch 19:11 52
also fled before A his brother and 1Ch 19:15 52

ABSOLUTELY

a refuses to give her to him, Ex 22:17 3985

ABSORBED
Take pains with these things; be a 1Tm 4:15
ABSTAIN
a from wine and strong drink; Nu 6:3 5144b
I weep in the fifth month and a, Zch 7:3 5144a
that they a from things contaminated Ac 15:20 568
that you a from things sacrificed Ac 15:29 568
should a from meat sacrificed to idols Ac 21:25 5442
that you a from sexual immorality; 1Th 4:3 568
a from every form of evil. 1Th 5:22 568
of the Lord is to a from wickedness." 2Tm 2:19 868
strangers to a from fleshly lusts which 1Pe 2:11 568
ABSTAINING
and advocate a from foods which 1Tm 4:3 568
ABSURD
a to me in sending a prisoner, Ac 25:27 249
ABUNDANCE
And an a of grain and new wine; Gn 27:28 7230
seven years of great a are coming Gn 41:29 7647
and all the a will be forgotten in Gn 41:30 7647
"So the a will be unknown in the Gn 41:31 7647
of Egypt in the seven years of a. Gn 41:34 7647
great a like the sand of the sea, Gn 41:49 3966
heart, for the a of all things; Dt 28:47 7230
will draw out the a of the seas, Dt 33:19 8228
which is on the seashore in a; 1Sa 13:5 7230
the sand that is by the sea in a, 2Sa 17:11 7230
oxen and fatlings and sheep in a, 1Ki 1:19 7230
oxen and fatlings and sheep in a, 1Ki 1:25 7230
sand that is on the seashore in a; 1Ki 4:20 7230
Never again did such a of spices 1Ki 10:10 7230
stones and alabaster in a. 1Ch 29:2 7230
all this a that we have provided 1Ch 29:16 1995
sacrifices in a for all Israel. 1Ch 29:21 7230
to prepare timber in a for me, 2Ch 2:9 7230
and he gave them food in a. 2Ch 11:23 7230
in a the first fruits of grain, 2Ch 31:5 7235a
acquired flocks and herds in a, 2Ch 32:29 7230
sorts of wine were furnished in a. Ne 5:18 7235a
olive groves, Fruit trees in a. Ne 9:25 7230
see, And an a of water covers you. Jb 22:11 8229
their a the fire has consumed.' Jb 22:20 3499a
He gives food in a. Jb 36:31 3527
that an a of water will cover you? Jb 38:34 8229
And leave their a to their babes. Ps 17:14 3499a
them, And lightning flashes in a, Ps 18:14 7227a
their fill of the a of Your house; Ps 36:8 1880
Than the a of many wicked. Ps 37:16 1995
days of famine they will have a. Ps 37:19 7646
boast in the a of their riches? Ps 49:6 7230
trusted in the a of his riches Ps 52:7 7230
brought us out into a place of a. Ps 66:12 7310
And a of peace till the moon is no Ps 72:7 7230
May there be a of grain in the Ps 72:16 6451
And waters of a are drunk by them. Ps 73:10 4392
He sent them food in a. Ps 78:25 7648
But in a of counselors there is Pr 11:14 7230
There is gold, and an a of jewels; Pr 20:15 7230
And in a of counselors there is Pr 24:6 7230
he who loves a with its income. Ec 5:10 1995
because of the a of the milk produced Is 7:22 7230
Therefore the a which they have Is 15:7 3502
good, And delight yourself in a. Is 55:2 1880
Because the a of the sea will be Is 60:5 1995
His compassion And according to the a Is 63:7 7230
the soul of the priests with a, Jer 31:14 1880
to them an a of peace and truth. Jer 33:6 6283
wine and summer fruit in great a. Jer 40:12 7235a
they have lost the a it produced. Jer 48:36 3502
of the a of all kinds of wealth; Ezk 27:12 7230
because of the a of your goods; Ezk 27:16 7230
because of the a of your goods, Ezk 27:18 7230
of the a of all kinds of wealth, Ezk 27:18 7230
With the a of your wealth and your Ezk 27:33 7230
"By the a of your trade You were Ezk 28:16 7230
silver and garments in great a. Zch 14:14 7230
be given, and he will have an a; Mt 13:12 4052
be given, and he will have an a; Mt 25:29 4052
for not even when one has an a Lk 12:15 4052
those who receive the a of grace Ro 5:17 4050
sufferings of Christ are ours in a, 2Co 1:5 4052
their a of joy and their deep poverty 2Co 8:2 4050
a being a supply for their need, 2Co 8:14 4051
that their a also may become a 2Co 8:14 4051
may have an a for every good deed; 2Co 9:8 4052
of having a and suffering need. Php 4:12 4052
everything in full and have an a; Php 4:18 4052
ABUNDANT
to anger and a in lovingkindness, Nu 14:18 7227a
Assyria come and find a water?" 2Ch 32:4 7227a
"Its a produce is for the Ne 9:37 7235a
"The a in years may not be wise, Jb 32:9 7227a
to justice and a righteousness. Jb 37:23 7230
by Your a lovingkindness I will Ps 5:7 7230
themselves in a prosperity. Ps 37:11 7230
a drink like the ocean depths. Ps 78:15 7227a
And a in lovingkindness to all who Ps 86:5 7227a
and a in lovingkindness and truth. Ps 86:15 7227a
not remember Your a kindnesses, Ps 106:7 7227a
And with Him is a redemption. Ps 130:7 7235a
the memory of Your a goodness Ps 145:7 7227a
is our Lord and a in strength; Ps 147:5 7227a
A food is in the fallow ground of Pr 13:23 7230
and a waters of the Euphrates, Is 8:7 7227a
of an a spoil will be divided; Is 33:23 4766
by many waters, A in treasures, Jer 51:13 7227a
According to His a lovingkindness. La 3:32 7230
sound of a waters as they went, Ezk 1:24 7227a
daughters had arrogance, a food and Ezk 16:49 7654
He placed it beside a waters; Ezk 17:5 7227a
in good soil beside a waters, Ezk 17:8 7227a
of branches Because of a waters. Ezk 19:10 7227a
was beautiful and its fruit a, Da 4:12 7690
was beautiful and its fruit a, Da 4:21 7690
to anger and a in lovingkindness, Jon 4:2 7227a
and a grace was upon them all. Ac 4:33 3173
on these we bestow more a honor, 1Co 12:23 4053
giving more a honor to that member 1Co 12:24 4053
our comfort is a through Christ. 2Co 1:5 4052
grace of our Lord was more than a, 1Tm 1:14 5250
ABUNDANTLY
they may breed a on the earth, Gn 8:17 8317
the earth a and multiply in it." Gn 9:7 8317
plenty the land brought forth a. Gn 41:47 7062
and water came forth a, Nu 20:11 7227a
a in all the work of your hand, Dt 30:9 3498
brought in a the tithe of all. 2Ch 31:5 7230
insight you have a provided! Jb 26:3 7230
pour down, They drip upon man a. Jb 36:28 7227a
You water its furrows a Ps 65:10 7301
I will give thanks a to the LORD; Ps 109:30 3966
"I will a bless her provision; Ps 132:15 1288
to our God, For He will a pardon. Is 55:7 7235a
have life, and have it a. Jn 10:10 4053
Him who is able to do far more a Eph 3:20 5238b
Christ will be a supplied to you. 2Pe 1:11 4146
ABUSE
uncircumcised will come and a me." 1Ch 10:4 5953a
into their hand and they will a me." Jer 38:19 5953a
passing by were hurling a at Him, Mt 27:39 987
passing by were hurling a at Him, Mk 15:29 987
hanged there was hurling a at Him, Lk 23:39 987
ABUSED
and a her all night until morning, Jg 19:25 5953a
ABUSIVE
and a speech from your mouth. Col 3:8 148
arise envy, strife, a language, 1Tm 6:4 988
ABYSS
command them to go away into the a. Lk 8:31 12
'WHO WILL DESCEND INTO THE A?' Ro 10:7 12
over them, the angel of the a; Rv 9:11 12
of the a will make war with them, Rv 11:7 12
of the a and go to destruction. Rv 17:8 12
a and a great chain in his hand. Rv 20:1 12
and he threw him into the a, Rv 20:3 12
ACACIA
dyed red, porpoise skins, a wood, Ex 25:5 7848
They shall construct an ark of a wood Ex 25:10 7848
"You shall make poles of a Ex 25:13 7848
You shall make a table of a wood, Ex 25:23 7848
You shall make the poles of a wood Ex 25:28 7848
for the tabernacle of a wood, Ex 26:15 7848
you shall make bars of a wood, Ex 26:26 7848
pillars of a overlaid with gold, Ex 26:32 7848
five pillars of a for the screen and Ex 26:37 7848
shall make the altar of a wood, Ex 27:1 7848
for the altar, poles of a wood, Ex 27:6 7848
you shall make it of a wood. Ex 30:1 7848
You shall make the poles of a wood Ex 30:5 7848
and porpoise skins, and a wood, Ex 35:7 7848
who had in his possession a wood Ex 35:24 7848
for the tabernacle of a wood, Ex 36:20 7848
Then he made bars of a wood, Ex 36:31 7848
He made four pillars of a for it, Ex 36:36 7848
Bezalel made the ark of a wood; Ex 37:1 7848
He made poles of a wood and Ex 37:4 7848
Then he made the table of a wood, Ex 37:10 7848
He made the poles of a wood Ex 37:15 7848
the altar of incense of a wood: Ex 37:25 7848
He made the poles of a wood Ex 37:28 7848
altar of burnt offering of a wood, Ex 38:1 7848
He made the poles of a wood Ex 38:6 7848
"So I made an ark of a wood and Dt 10:3 7848
cedar in the wilderness, The a and Is 41:19 7848
ACCAD
Babel and Erech and A and Calneh, Gn 10:10 390
ACCEPT
price of the field, a it from me that Gn 23:13 3947
perhaps he will a me." Gn 32:20
5375, 6440
and its owner shall a it, Ex 22:11 3947
nor shall you a any such from the Lv 22:25 7126
"A these things from them, that Nu 7:5 3947
And a the work of his hands; Dt 33:11 7521
which you will a from their hand. 1Sa 10:4 3947
against me, let Him a an offering; 1Sa 26:19 7381a
"May the LORD your God a you." 2Sa 24:23 7521
from him, but he did not a them. Es 4:4 6901
Shall we indeed a good from God Jb 2:10 6901
from God and not a adversity?" Jb 2:10 6901
pray to God, and He will a him, Jb 33:26 7521
For I will a him so that I may not Jb 42:8
6440, 5375
O a the freewill offerings of my Ps 119:108 7521
"They would not a my counsel, Pr 1:30 14
Hear, my son, and a my sayings And Pr 4:10 3947
He will not a any ransom, Nor will Pr 6:35
5375, 6440
to counsel and a discipline, Pr 19:20 6901
who criticize will a instruction. Is 29:24 3925
LORD their God or a correction; Jer 7:28 3947
the LORD does not a them; Jer 14:10 7521
I am not going to a them. Jer 14:12 7521
there I will a them and there I Ezk 20:40 7521
"As a soothing aroma I will a you Ezk 20:41 7521
and I will a you,' declares the Ezk 43:27 7521
the righteous and a bribes And Am 5:12 3947
offerings, I will not a them; Am 5:22 7521
will revere Me, A instruction.' Zph 3:7 3947
"nor will I a an offering from you. Mal 1:10 7521
"And if you are willing to a it, Mt 11:14 1209
"Not all men can a this Mt 19:11 5562
He who is able to a this, Mt 19:12 5562
to accept this, let him a it." Mt 19:12 5562
and they hear the word and a it and Mk 4:20 3858
and you do not a our testimony. Jn 3:11 2983
lawful for us to a or to observe, Ac 16:21 3858
not a your testimony about Me.' Ac 22:18 3858
a the one who is weak in faith, Ro 14:1 4355
Therefore, a one another, just as Ro 15:7 4355
But a natural man does not a the 1Co 2:14 1209
a partner, a him as you would me. Phm 1:17 4355
them, does not a what we say. 3Jn 1:9 1926
ACCEPTABLE
man make himself a to his lord? 1Sa 29:4 7521
that they may offer a sacrifices Ezr 6:10 5208
of my heart Be a in Your sight, Ps 19:14 7522
And find your burnt offering a! Ps 20:3 1878
is to You, O LORD, at an a time; Ps 69:13 7522
righteous bring forth what is a, Pr 10:32 7522
of the wise makes knowledge a, Pr 15:2 3190
sacrifices will be a on My altar; Is 56:7 7522
a fast, even an a day to the LORD? Is 58:5 7522
Your burnt offerings are not a And Jer 6:20 7522
and holy sacrifice, a to God, Ro 12:1 2101
which is good and a and perfect. Ro 12:2 2101
is a to God and approved by men. Ro 14:18 2101
of the Gentiles may become a, Ro 15:16 2144
may prove a to the saints; Ro 15:31 2144
"AT THE A TIME I LISTENED TO YOU, 2Co 6:2 1184
Behold, now is "THE A TIME," 2Co 6:2 2144
is a according to what a person has, 2Co 8:12 2144
a fragrant aroma, an a sacrifice, Php 4:18 1184
This is good and a in the sight of 1Tm 2:3 587
for this is a in the sight of God. 1Tm 5:4 587
we may offer to God an a service Heb 12:28 2102
a to God through Jesus Christ. 1Pe 2:5 2144
ACCEPTANCE
will go up with a on My altar, Is 60:7 7522
their a be but life from the dead? Ro 11:15 4356
statement, deserving full a, 1Tm 1:15 594
statement deserving full a. 1Tm 4:9 594
ACCEPTED
they may be a before the LORD. Ex 28:38 7522
that he may be a before the LORD. Lv 1:3 7522
that it may be a for him to make Lv 1:4 7521
he who offers it will not be a, Lv 7:18 7521
offer it so that you may be a. Lv 19:5 7522
it will not be a. Lv 19:7 7521
for you to be a—it must be a male Lv 22:19 7522
for it will not be a for you. Lv 22:20 7522
flock, it must be perfect to be a; Lv 22:21 7522
but for a vow it will not be a. Lv 22:23 7521
they shall not be a for you.' Lv 22:25 7521
day on it shall be a as a sacrifice Lv 22:27 7521
sacrifice it so that you may be a. Lv 22:29 7522
before the LORD for you to be a; Lv 23:11 7522
He would not have a a burnt Jg 13:23 3947
So the priests and the Levites a Ezr 8:30 6901
and the LORD a Job. Jb 42:9
5375, 6440
They a no chastening. Jer 2:30 3947
She a no instruction. Zph 3:2 3947
one who eats, for God has a him. Ro 14:3 4355
also a us to the glory of God. Ro 15:7 4355
For he not only a our appeal, but 2Co 8:17 1209
gospel which you have not a, 2Co 11:4 1209
you a it not as the word of men, 1Th 2:13 1209
and a joyfully the seizure of your Heb 10:34 4327
ACCEPTING
tortured, not a their release, Heb 11:35 4327
Name, a nothing from the Gentiles. 3Jn 1:7 2983
ACCEPTS
'Cursed is he who a a bribe to Dt 27:25 3947
a his father's discipline, Pr 13:1
or a it with favor from your hand. Mal 2:13 3947
ACCESS
who had a to the king's presence Es 1:14 7200
and I will grant you free a among Zch 3:7 1980
our a in one Spirit to the Father. Eph 2:18 4318
confident a through faith in Him. Eph 3:12 4318
ACCIDENT
"It is an a, he is not clean, 1Sa 20:26 4745
ACCLAIM
and they began to a Him, Mk 15:18 782
ACCO
drive out the inhabitants of A, Jg 1:31 5910
ACCOMPANIED
the people of Israel a the king. 2Sa 19:40 5674a
lifted up their voice a by trumpets 2Ch 5:13
a by the instruments of David, 2Ch 29:27
Their banquets are a by lyre Is 5:12
a by a large crowd with swords Mt 26:47
3326, 846
a by a crowd with swords and Mk 14:43
3326, 846
with Him, a by a large crowd. Lk 7:11 2532
women who a Him from Galilee were Lk 23:49 4870
the men who have a us all the time Ac 1:21 4905
of the brethren from Joppa a him. Ac 10:23 4905
And he was a by Sopater of Berea, Ac 20:4 4902b
and entered the auditorium a Ac 25:23 4862

Context	Reference	Number
put out to sea **a** by Aristarchus,	Ac 27:2	1510, 4862
great gain when **a** by contentment.	1Tm 6:6	3326

ACCOMPANIMENT

Context	Reference	Number
and with songs *to the* **a** of	Ne 12:27	

ACCOMPANY

Context	Reference	Number
to the young men who **a** my lord.	1Sa 25:27	1980, 7272
in the sight of the men who **a** you	Jer 19:10	1980, 854
Him that he might **a** Him.	Mk 5:18	3326, 1510
And He allowed no one to **a** Him,	Mk 5:37	4870
will **a** those who have believed:	Mk 16:17	3877
begging Him that he might **a** Him;	Lk 8:38	1510, 4862
and **a** them without misgivings,	Ac 10:20	4198, 4862
you, and things that **a** salvation,	Heb 6:9	2192

ACCOMPANYING

Context	Reference	Number
And they were **a** him to the ship.	Ac 20:38	4311

ACCOMPLISH

Context	Reference	Number
which He will **a** for you today;	Ex 14:13	6213a
both **a** much and surely prevail."	1Sa 26:25	6213a
to David, I do not **a** this for him,	2Sa 3:9	6213a
Then you shall **a** my desire by	1Ki 5:9	6213a
sinned, what do you **a** against Him?	Jb 35:6	6466
The LORD will **a** what concerns me;	Ps 138:8	1584
"What does it **a**?"	Ec 2:2	6213a
of the LORD of hosts will **a** this.	Is 9:7	6213a
We could not **a** deliverance for the	Is 26:18	6213a
I will **a** all My good pleasure';	Is 46:10	6213a
to **a** My anger against them in the	Ezk 20:8	3615
to **a** My anger against them in the	Ezk 20:21	3615
will **a** what his fathers never did,	Da 11:24	6213a
He was about to **a** at Jerusalem.	Lk 9:31	4137
who sent Me and to **a** His work.	Jn 4:34	5048
the Father has given Me to **a**	Jn 5:36	5048
of a righteous man can **a** much.	Jas 5:16	1754
whatever you **a** for the brethren,	3Jn 1:5	2038b

ACCOMPLISHED

Context	Reference	Number
has **a** deliverance in Israel."	1Sa 11:13	6213a
been **a** with the help of our God.	Ne 6:16	6213a
"It will be **a** before his time,	Jb 15:32	4390
"Who has performed and **a** *it,*	Is 41:4	6213a
He has **a** The intent of His heart;	Jer 30:24	6965
His idle boasts have **a** nothing.	Jer 48:30	6213a
He has **a** His word Which He	La 2:17	1214
The LORD has **a** His wrath, He has	La 4:11	3615
from the Law until all is **a**.	Mt 5:18	1096
account of the things **a** among us,	Lk 1:1	4135
and **a** redemption for His people,	Lk 1:68	4160
how distressed I am until it is **a**!	Lk 12:50	5055
about the Son of Man will be **a**.	Lk 18:31	5055
having **a** the work which You have	Jn 17:4	5048
all things had already been **a**,	Jn 19:28	5055
God for the work that they had **a**.	Ac 14:26	4137
what Christ has **a** through me,	Ro 15:18	2716
been **a** in the sphere of another.	2Co 10:16	2092
the proclamation might be fully **a**,	2Tm 4:17	4135
and when sin is **a**, it brings forth	Jas 1:15	658
experiences of suffering are being **a**	1Pe 5:9	2005
you do not lose what we have **a**,	2Jn 1:8	2038b

ACCOMPLISHES

Context	Reference	Number
To God who **a** *all things* for me.	Ps 57:2	1584

ACCOMPLISHING

Context	Reference	Number
Me empty, Without **a** what I desire,	Is 55:11	6213a
Pilate saw that he was **a** nothing,	Mt 27:24	5623
FOR I AM **A** A WORK IN YOUR DAYS, A	Ac 13:41	2038b

ACCOMPLISHMENTS

Context	Reference	Number
a of his authority and strength,	Es 10:2	4639

ACCORD

Context	Reference	Number
statutes, to live in **a** with them;	Lv 18:4	
either good or bad, of my own **a**.	Nu 24:13	3820
with one **a** to fight with Joshua	Jos 9:2	6310
in **a** with all the good that he had	Jg 8:35	
answered him in **a** with this word,	1Sa 17:27	
Men who are not in **a** with Your law.	Ps 119:85	
But they too, with one **a**,	Jer 5:5	3162
ready or act in **a** with his will,	Lk 12:47	4314
voices to God with one **a** and said,	Ac 4:24	3661
with one **a** in Solomon's portico.	Ac 5:12	3661
The crowds with one **a** were	Ac 8:6	3661
and with one **a** they came to him,	Ac 12:20	3661
the Jews with one **a** rose up	Ac 18:12	3661
with one **a** into the theater,	Ac 19:29	3661
that with one **a** you may with one	Ro 15:6	3661
ability, *they gave* of their own **a**,	2Co 8:3	830
he has gone to you of his own **a**.	2Co 8:17	830
in **a** with the activity of Satan,	2Th 2:9	2596

ACCORDANCE

Context	Reference	Number
you in **a** with all these words."	Ex 24:8	5921
for in **a** with these words I have	Ex 34:27	5921, 6310
shall perform in **a** with all that	Ex 36:1	
Moses spoke to the sons of Israel in **a**	Nu 29:40	
In **a** with the command of the LORD	Jos 19:50	5921
In **a** with all these words and all	2Sa 7:17	
gatekeepers in **a** with the command	Ne 12:45	
So I bought the waistband in **a**	Jer 13:2	
So he reported to them in **a** with	Jer 38:27	
your God in **a** with your words;	Jer 42:4	
if we do not act in **a** with the	Jer 42:5	
in **a** with all Your righteous acts,	Da 9:16	
I will chastise them in **a** with the	Hos 7:12	
Reap in **a** with kindness;	Hos 10:12	6310
in **a** with our ways and our deeds,	Zch 1:6	
soldiers, in **a** with their orders,	Ac 23:31	2596
that is in **a** with the Law and	Ac 24:14	2596
that *it may be* in **a** with grace,	Ro 4:16	2596
God, but not in **a** with knowledge.	Ro 10:2	2596
in **a** with the authority which the	2Co 13:10	2596
These are in **a** with the working of	Eph 1:19	2596
This was in **a** with the eternal	Eph 3:11	2596
in **a** with the lusts of deceit,	Eph 4:22	2596
a with the commandments and	Col 2:22	2596
in **a** with the prophecies	1Tm 1:18	2596
in **a** to their own desires,	2Tm 4:3	2596
which is in **a** with the teaching,	Ti 1:9	2596

ACCORDED

Context	Reference	Number
each *is tested* by the praise **a** him.	Pr 27:21	6310

ACCORDING

Context	Reference	Number
in Our image, **a** to Our likeness;	Gn 1:26	
his own likeness, **a** to his image,	Gn 5:3	
a to all that God had commanded	Gn 6:22	
Noah did **a** to all that the	Gn 7:5	
every one **a** to his language,	Gn 10:5	
his language, **a** to their families,	Gn 10:5	
sons of Ham, **a** to their families,	Gn 10:20	
families, **a** to their languages,	Gn 10:20	
sons of Shem, **a** to their families,	Gn 10:31	
families, **a** to their languages,	Gn 10:31	
their lands, **a** to their nations.	Gn 10:31	
of Noah, **a** to their genealogies,	Gn 10:32	
done entirely **a** to its outcry,	Gn 18:21	
but **a** to the kindness that I have	Gn 21:23	
twelve princes **a** to their tribes.	Gn 25:16	
"Good, let it be **a** to your word."	Gn 30:34	
a to the pace of the cattle that	Gn 33:14	
and **a** to the pace of the children,	Gn 33:14	
I will give **a** as you say to me;	Gn 34:12	
a to their *various* chiefs in the	Gn 36:30	
a to their families *and* their	Gn 36:40	
a to their habitations in the land	Gn 36:43	
will put Pharaoh's cup into his hand **a**	Gn 40:13	
each of us dreamed **a** to the	Gn 41:11	
he interpreted **a** to his *own* dream.	Gn 41:12	
and **a** to your command all my	Gn 41:40	5921
the firstborn **a** to his birthright	Gn 43:33	
and the youngest **a** to his youth,	Gn 43:33	
let it also be **a** to your words;	Gn 44:10	
a to the command of Pharaoh,	Gn 45:21	5921
with food, **a** to their little ones.	Gn 47:12	6310
of Levi **a** to their generations:	Ex 6:16	
and Shimei, **a** to their families.	Ex 6:17	
Levites **a** to their generations.	Ex 6:19	
the Levites **a** to their families.	Ex 6:25	
land of Egypt **a** to their hosts."	Ex 6:26	5921
"*May it be* **a** to your word, that	Ex 8:10	
LORD did **a** to the word of Moses,	Ex 8:13	
a to their fathers' households,	Ex 12:3	
take one **a** to the number of persons	Ex 12:4	
a to what each man should eat, you	Ex 12:4	6310
lambs **a** to your families,	Ex 12:21	
had done **a** to the word of Moses,	Ex 12:35	
you shall take an omer apiece **a** to	Ex 16:16	
Sin, **a** to the command of the LORD,	Ex 17:1	5921
her **a** to the custom of daughters.	Ex 21:9	
be done to him **a** to the same rule.	Ex 21:31	
them, nor do **a** to their deeds;	Ex 23:24	
"**A** to all that I am going to show	Ex 25:9	
shall erect the tabernacle **a** to its plan	Ex 26:30	
the other stone, **a** to their birth.	Ex 28:10	
engrave the two stones **a** to the names	Ex 28:11	5921
"The stones shall be **a** to the	Ex 28:21	5921
twelve, **a** to their names;	Ex 28:21	5921
each **a** to his name for the twelve	Ex 28:21	5921
a to all that I have commanded you;	Ex 29:35	
half a shekel **a** to the shekel of	Ex 30:13	
a to the shekel of the sanctuary,	Ex 30:24	
they are to make *them* **a** to all	Ex 31:11	
a to the command of Moses,	Ex 38:21	5921
a to the shekel of the sanctuary.	Ex 38:24	
a to the shekel of the sanctuary;	Ex 38:25	
half a shekel **a** to the shekel of	Ex 38:26	
a to the names of the sons of	Ex 39:6	5921
and the sons of Israel did **a** to	Ex 39:32	
did all the work **a** to all that the LORD	Ex 39:42	
a to all that the LORD had	Ex 40:16	
burnt offering **a** to the ordinance.	Lv 5:10	
a to your valuation in silver by	Lv 5:15	
the flock, **a** to your valuation,	Lv 5:18	
the flock, **a** to your valuation,	Lv 6:6	
and offered it **a** to the ordinance.	Lv 9:16	
they did **a** to the word of Moses.	Lv 10:7	
he is to sell to you **a** to the	Lv 25:15	
on you seven times **a** to your sins.	Lv 26:21	
he *shall be valued* **a** to your	Lv 27:2	
a to the means of the one who	Lv 27:8	5921, 6310
a to your valuation it shall stand.	Lv 27:17	
redeem it **a** to your valuation and	Lv 27:27	
shall be sold **a** to your valuation.	Lv 27:27	
a to the number of names,	Nu 1:2	
a to the number of names,	Nu 1:18	
a to the number of names,	Nu 1:20	
men, **a** to the number of names,	Nu 1:22	
a to the number of names,	Nu 1:24	
a to the number of names,	Nu 1:26	
a to the number of names,	Nu 1:28	
a to the number of names,	Nu 1:30	
a to the number of names,	Nu 1:32	
a to the number of names,	Nu 1:34	
a to the number of names,	Nu 1:36	
a to the number of names,	Nu 1:38	
a to the number of names,	Nu 1:40	
a to the number of names,	Nu 1:42	
own standard, **a** to their armies.	Nu 1:52	
a to all which the LORD had	Nu 1:54	
a to all that the LORD commanded	Nu 2:34	
a to his father's household.	Nu 2:34	5921
them **a** to the word of the LORD,	Nu 3:16	5921
a to their fathers' households.	Nu 3:20	
a to all the service concerning	Nu 3:26	
a to all their service in the tent	Nu 4:33	
whom Moses and Aaron numbered **a** to	Nu 4:37	5921
whom Moses and Aaron numbered **a** to	Nu 4:41	5921
whom Moses and Aaron numbered **a** to	Nu 4:45	5921
A to the commandment of the LORD	Nu 4:49	5921
to the LORD **a** to his separation,	Nu 6:21	5921
a to his vow which he takes, so he	Nu 6:21	
a to the law of his separation."	Nu 6:21	5921
to each man **a** to his service."	Nu 7:5	6310
of Gershon, **a** to their service,	Nu 7:7	6310
of Merari, **a** to their service,	Nu 7:8	6310
a to the shekel of the sanctuary,	Nu 7:13	
a to the shekel of the sanctuary,	Nu 7:19	
a to the shekel of the sanctuary,	Nu 7:25	
a to the shekel of the sanctuary,	Nu 7:31	
a to the shekel of the sanctuary,	Nu 7:37	
a to the shekel of the sanctuary,	Nu 7:43	
a to the shekel of the sanctuary,	Nu 7:49	
a to the shekel of the sanctuary,	Nu 7:55	
a to the shekel of the sanctuary,	Nu 7:61	
a to the shekel of the sanctuary,	Nu 7:67	
a to the shekel of the sanctuary,	Nu 7:73	
a to the shekel of the sanctuary,	Nu 7:79	
a to the shekel of the sanctuary;	Nu 7:85	
a to the shekel of the sanctuary,	Nu 7:86	
a to the pattern which the LORD	Nu 8:4	
a to all that the LORD had	Nu 8:20	
you shall observe it **a** to all its	Nu 9:3	
and **a** to all its ordinances."	Nu 9:3	
a to all that the LORD had	Nu 9:5	
a to all the statute of the	Nu 9:12	
a to the statute of the Passover	Nu 9:14	
Passover and **a** to its ordinance,	Nu 9:14	
a to the command of the LORD they	Nu 9:20	5921
Then **a** to the command of the LORD	Nu 9:20	5921
a to the command of the LORD	Nu 9:23	5921
a to the commandment of the LORD	Nu 10:13	5921
sons of Judah, **a** to their armies,	Nu 10:14	
camp of Reuben, **a** to their armies,	Nu 10:18	5921
of Ephraim, **a** to their armies,	Nu 10:22	
sons of Dan, **a** to their armies,	Nu 10:25	
the iniquity of this people **a** to	Nu 14:19	
have pardoned *them* **a** to your word;	Nu 14:20	
a to your complete number from	Nu 14:29	
'**A** to the number of days which you	Nu 14:34	
'**A** to the number that you prepare,	Nu 15:12	
do for everyone **a** to their number.	Nu 15:12	
its drink offering, **a** to the ordinance,	Nu 15:24	
a to their fathers' households.	Nu 17:2	
a to their fathers' households,	Nu 17:6	
a to the shekel of the sanctuary,	Nu 18:16	
of Simeon **a** to their families:	Nu 26:12	
sons of Gad **a** to their families:	Nu 26:15	
families of the sons of Gad **a** to those	Nu 26:18	
of Judah **a** to their families were:	Nu 26:20	
These are the families of Judah **a**	Nu 26:22	
of Issachar **a** to their families:	Nu 26:23	
families of Issachar **a** to those who	Nu 26:25	
of Zebulun **a** to their families:	Nu 26:26	
families of the Zebulunites **a** to those	Nu 26:27	
of Joseph **a** to their families:	Nu 26:28	
of Ephraim **a** to their families:	Nu 26:35	
the sons of Ephraim **a** to those who	Nu 26:37	
of Joseph **a** to their families.	Nu 26:37	
of Benjamin **a** to their families:	Nu 26:38	
of Benjamin **a** to their families;	Nu 26:41	
sons of Dan **a** to their families:	Nu 26:42	
of Dan **a** to their families.	Nu 26:42	
a to those who were numbered of	Nu 26:43	
sons of Asher **a** to their families:	Nu 26:44	
sons of Asher **a** to those who were	Nu 26:47	
of Naphtali **a** to their families:	Nu 26:48	
of Naphtali **a** to their families;	Nu 26:50	
a to the number of names.	Nu 26:53	
their inheritance **a** to those who were	Nu 26:54	6310
their inheritance **a** to the names	Nu 26:55	
"**A** to the selection by lot, their	Nu 26:56	5921, 6310
the Levites **a** to their families:	Nu 26:57	
offerings, **a** to their ordinance,	Nu 29:6	
their number **a** to the ordinance;	Nu 29:18	
their number **a** to the ordinance;	Nu 29:21	
their number **a** to the ordinance;	Nu 29:24	
their number **a** to the ordinance;	Nu 29:27	
their number **a** to the ordinance;	Nu 29:30	
their number **a** to the ordinance;	Nu 29:33	
their number **a** to the ordinance;	Nu 29:37	
he shall do **a** to all that proceeds	Nu 30:2	
starting places **a** to their journeys	Nu 33:2	
a to their starting places.	Nu 33:2	
land by lot **a** to your families;	Nu 33:54	
a to the tribes of your fathers.	Nu 33:54	
land of Canaan **a** to its borders.	Nu 34:2	
a to its borders all around.' "	Nu 34:12	
a to their fathers' households,	Nu 34:14	
Gad **a** to their fathers' households,	Nu 34:14	
avenger **a** to these ordinances.	Nu 35:24	5921
Israel **a** to the word of the LORD,	Nu 36:5	5921
a to all that the LORD had	Dt 1:3	
a to the blessing of the LORD your	Dt 12:15	

a to the blessing of the LORD your Dt 16:17
is giving you, **a** to your tribes, Dt 16:18
"You shall do **a** to the terms Dt 17:10 5921
a to all that they teach you. Dt 17:10
"**A** to the terms of the law which Dt 17:11 5921
and **a** to the verdict which they Dt 17:11 5921
"This is **a** to all that you asked Dt 18:16
they may not teach you to do **a** to all Dt 20:18
diligently observe and do **a** to all that Dt 24:8
number of stripes **a** to his guilt. Dt 25:2 1767
a to all Your commandments which Dt 26:13
I have done **a** to all that You Dt 26:14
a to all the curses of the Dt 29:21
with all your heart and soul **a** to all Dt 30:2
and you shall do to them **a** to all Dt 31:5
A to the number of the sons of Israel. Dt 32:8
and bronze, And **a** to your days, Dt 33:25
Moab, **a** to the word of the LORD. Dt 34:5 5921
be careful to do **a** to all the law Jos 1:7
do **a** to all that is written in it; Jos 1:8
"**A** to your words, so be it." Jos 2:21
a to the number of the tribes of Jos 4:5
a to the number of the tribes of Jos 4:8
a to all that Moses had commanded Jos 4:10
do *it* **a** to the word of the LORD. Jos 8:8
a to the word of the LORD which He Jos 8:27
a to all that is written in the Jos 8:34
a to all that he had done to Jos 10:32
a to all that he had done to Jos 10:35
a to all that he had done to Eglon. Jos 10:37
a to all that the LORD had spoken Jos 11:23
for an inheritance to Israel **a** to their Jos 11:23
a possession **a** to their divisions, Jos 12:7
of Reuben **a** to their families. Jos 13:15
of Reuben **a** to their families, Jos 13:23
sons of Gad, **a** to their families. Jos 13:24
sons of Gad **a** to their families, Jos 13:28
of Manasseh **a** to their families. Jos 13:29
of Machir **a** to their families. Jos 13:31
the sons of Judah **a** to their families Jos 15:1
sons of Judah **a** to their families. Jos 15:12
a to the command of the LORD to Jos 15:13 413
sons of Judah **a** to their families. Jos 15:20
of Ephraim **a** to their families: Jos 16:5
of Ephraim **a** to their families, Jos 16:8
of Manasseh **a** to their families: Jos 17:2
son of Joseph **a** to their families. Jos 17:2
So **a** to the command of the LORD he Jos 17:4 413
of it **a** to their inheritance; Jos 18:4 6310
of Israel **a** to their divisions. Jos 18:10
came up **a** to their families, Jos 18:11
a to their families *and* according Jos 18:20
and **a** to its borders all around. Jos 18:20
sons of Benjamin **a** to their families Jos 18:21
of Benjamin **a** to their families. Jos 18:28
of Simeon **a** to their families, Jos 19:1
of Simeon **a** to their families. Jos 19:8
of Zebulun **a** to their families. Jos 19:10
of Zebulun **a** to their families, Jos 19:16
of Issachar **a** to their families. Jos 19:17
of Issachar **a** to their families, Jos 19:23
sons of Asher **a** to their families. Jos 19:24
sons of Asher **a** to their families, Jos 19:31
of Naphtali **a** to their families. Jos 19:32
of Naphtali **a** to their families, Jos 19:39
sons of Dan **a** to their families. Jos 19:40
sons of Dan **a** to their families, Jos 19:48
a to the command of the LORD. Jos 21:3 413
The sons of Merari **a** to their Jos 21:7
the Gershonites **a** to their families Jos 21:33
of Merari **a** to their families, Jos 21:40
a to all that He had sworn to Jos 21:44
a to the command of the LORD Jos 22:9 5921
a to the vow which he had made; Jg 11:39
and took wives **a** to their number Jg 21:23
and did **a** to all that her mother-in-law Ru 3:6
faithful priest who will do **a** to what 1Sa 2:35
tumors and five golden mice **a** *to* 1Sa 6:4
and the golden mice, **a** to 1Sa 6:18
a to the appointed time set by 1Sa 13:8
I am with you **a** to your desire." 1Sa 14:7
servants of Saul reported to him **a** to 1Sa 18:24
come down **a** to all the desire of 1Sa 23:20
they spoke to Nabal **a** to all these 1Sa 25:9
and told him **a** to all these words. 1Sa 25:12
LORD does for my lord **a** to all 1Sa 25:30
the evildoer **a** to his evil." 2Sa 3:39
word, and **a** to Your own heart, 2Sa 7:21
a to all that we have heard with 2Sa 7:22
"**A** to all that my lord the king 2Sa 9:11
a to your servant's word, so it 2Sa 13:35
rewarded me **a** to my righteousness; 2Sa 22:21
A to the cleanness of my hands He 2Sa 22:21
me **a** to my righteousness, 2Sa 22:25
A to my cleanness before His eyes. 2Sa 22:25
went up **a** to the word of Gad, 2Sa 24:19
a to what is written in the Law of 1Ki 2:3
"So act **a** to your wisdom, and do 1Ki 2:6
a as he walked before You in 1Ki 3:6 3512c
I have done **a** to your words. 1Ki 3:12
should be, each **a** to his charge. 1Ki 4:28
servants **a** to all that you say, 1Ki 5:6
its parts and **a** to all its plans. 1Ki 6:38
stones, of stone cut **a** to measure, 1Ki 7:9
stones, stone cut **a** to measure, 1Ki 7:11
a to the clear space on each, 1Ki 7:36
giving him **a** to his righteousness. 1Ki 8:32
render to each **a** to all his ways, 1Ki 8:39
and do **a** to all for which the 1Ki 8:43

Israel, **a** to all that He promised; 1Ki 8:56
doing **a** to all that I have 1Ki 9:4
and gold **a** to all his desire), 1Ki 9:11
he gave her **a** to his royal bounty. 1Ki 10:13
and he spoke to them **a** to the 1Ki 12:14
way **a** to the word of the LORD. 1Ki 12:24
a to the sign which the man of God 1Ki 13:5
a to the word of the LORD which He 1Ki 13:26
a to the word of the LORD which He 1Ki 14:18
They did **a** to all the abominations 1Ki 14:24
them, **a** to the word of the LORD, 1Ki 15:29
Baasha, **a** to the word of the LORD, 1Ki 16:12
Segub, **a** to the word of the LORD, 1Ki 16:34
and did **a** to the word of the LORD, 1Ki 17:5
and did **a** to the word of Elijah, 1Ki 17:15
a to the word of the LORD which He 1Ki 17:16
cut themselves **a** to their custom 1Ki 18:28
Elijah took twelve stones **a** to 1Ki 18:31
"It is **a** to your word, my lord, O 1Ki 20:4
a to all that the Amorites had 1Ki 21:26
a to the word of the LORD which He 1Ki 22:38
God of Israel to anger, **a** to all that 1Ki 22:53
So Ahaziah died **a** to the word of 2Ki 1:17
a to the word of Elisha which he 2Ki 2:22
over, **a** to the word of the LORD. 2Ki 4:44
a to the word of the man of God; 2Ki 5:14
blindness **a** to the word of Elisha. 2Ki 6:18
shekel, **a** to the word of the LORD. 2Ki 7:16
a to the word of the man of God, 2Ki 8:2
a to the word of the LORD." 2Ki 9:26
him, **a** to the word of the LORD which 2Ki 10:17
a to all that *was* in My heart, 2Ki 10:30
So the captains of hundreds did **a** 2Ki 11:9
by the pillar, **a** to the custom, 2Ki 11:14
he did **a** to all that Joash his 2Ki 14:3
a to what is written in the book 2Ki 14:6
Arabah, **a** to the word of the LORD, 2Ki 14:25
a to all that his father Amaziah 2Ki 15:3
he did **a** to all that his father 2Ki 15:34
a to the abominations of the 2Ki 16:3
model, **a** to all its workmanship. 2Ki 16:10
a to all that King Ahaz had sent 2Ki 16:11
So Urijah the priest did **a** to all 2Ki 16:16
My statutes **a** to all the law which 2Ki 17:13
served their own gods **a** to the custom 2Ki 17:33
they do **a** to the earlier customs: 2Ki 17:34
did **a** to their earlier custom. 2Ki 17:40
a to all that his father David had 2Ki 18:3
a to the abominations of the 2Ki 21:2
do **a** to all that I have commanded 2Ki 21:8
and **a** to all the law that My 2Ki 21:8
to do **a** to all that is written 2Ki 22:13
the altar and defiled it **a** to the word 2Ki 23:16
might, **a** to all the law of Moses; 2Ki 23:25
a to all that his fathers had done. 2Ki 23:32
the land, each **a** to his valuation, 2Ki 23:35
a to all that his fathers had done. 2Ki 23:37
it, **a** to the word of the LORD which 2Ki 24:2
a to all that he had done, 2Ki 24:3
a to all that his father had done. 2Ki 24:9
a to all that Jehoiakim had done. 2Ki 24:19
the genealogy **a** to the birthright. 1Ch 5:1
a to their fathers' *households.* 1Ch 6:19
in their office **a** to their order. 1Ch 6:32 5921
a to all that Moses the servant of 1Ch 6:49
Now these are their settlements **a** 1Ch 6:54
of Gershom, **a** to their families, 1Ch 6:62
given by lot, **a** to their families, 1Ch 6:63
by their generations **a** to their fathers' 1Ch 7:4
genealogy, **a** to their generations, 1Ch 7:9
a to the heads of their fathers' 1Ch 7:11
households **a** to their generations, 1Ch 8:28
relatives **a** to their generations, 1Ch 9:9
a to their fathers' houses. 1Ch 9:9
Levites **a** to their generations, 1Ch 9:34
a to the word of the LORD through 1Ch 11:3
a to the word of the LORD 1Ch 11:10
to him, **a** to the word of the LORD. 1Ch 12:23
not seek Him **a** to the ordinance." 1Ch 15:13
a to the word of the LORD. 1Ch 15:15
even **a** to all that is written in 1Ch 16:40
A to all these words and according 1Ch 17:15
words and **a** to all this vision, 1Ch 17:15
and have regarded me **a** to the 1Ch 17:17
sake, and **a** to Your own heart, 1Ch 17:19
a to all that we have heard with 1Ch 17:20
divisions **a** to the sons of Levi: 1Ch 23:6
a to their fathers' households, 1Ch 23:24
divided them **a** to their offices 1Ch 24:3
a to their fathers' households. 1Ch 24:4
house of the LORD **a** to the ordinance 1Ch 24:19
a to their fathers' households. 1Ch 24:30
exalt him **a** to the words of God, 1Ch 25:5
a to their fathers' households, 1Ch 26:13
Hebronites were investigated **a** to their 1Ch 26:31
a to the use of each lampstand; 1Ch 28:15
a to the old standard *was* sixty 2Ch 3:3
giving him **a** to his righteousness. 2Ch 6:23
render to each **a** to all his ways, 2Ch 6:30
and do **a** to all for which the 2Ch 6:33
David walked, even to do **a** to all that 2Ch 7:17
and *did so* **a** to the daily rule, 2Ch 8:13
up **a** to the commandment of Moses, 2Ch 8:13
Now **a** to the ordinance of his 2Ch 8:14
the priests **a** to the daily rule, 2Ch 8:14
He spoke to them **a** to the 2Ch 10:14
a to genealogical enrollment? 2Ch 12:15
a to their fathers' households: 2Ch 17:14
He also walked **a** to their counsel, 2Ch 22:5

all Judah did **a** to all that Jehoiada 2Ch 23:8
singing **a** to the order of David. 2Ch 23:18 5921
of God **a** to its specifications and 2Ch 24:13 5921
Judah and appointed them **a** to *their* 2Ch 25:5
did right in the sight of the LORD **a** 2Ch 26:4
a to the number of their muster, 2Ch 26:11
a to all that his father Uzziah 2Ch 27:2
a to the abominations of the 2Ch 28:3
a to all that his father David had 2Ch 29:2
a to the commandment of the king 2Ch 29:15
a to the command of David and of 2Ch 29:25
even **a** to the command of the king, 2Ch 30:6
a to the law of Moses the man of 2Ch 30:16
though not **a** to the purification 2Ch 30:19
divisions, each **a** to his service, 2Ch 31:2 6310
their duties **a** to their divisions; 2Ch 31:16
a to their fathers' households, 2Ch 31:17
He did evil in the sight of the LORD **a** 2Ch 33:2
commanded them **a** to all the law, 2Ch 33:8
to do **a** to all that is written in 2Ch 34:21
did **a** to the covenant of God, 2Ch 34:32
a to the writing of David king of 2Ch 35:4
a to the writing of his son Solomon. 2Ch 35:4
stand in the holy place **a** to the 2Ch 35:5
lay people, and **a** to the Levites, 2Ch 35:5
and prepare for your brethren to do **a** 2Ch 35:6
divisions **a** to the king's command. 2Ch 35:10
on the fire **a** to the ordinance, 2Ch 35:13
a to the command of David, 2Ch 35:15
a to the command of King Josiah. 2Ch 35:16
A to their ability they gave to Ezr 2:69
daily, **a** to the ordinance, Ezr 3:4
a to the permission they had from Ezr 3:7
to praise the LORD **a** to the Ezr 3:10 5921
And they finished building **a** to Ezr 6:14 4481
Judah and Jerusalem **a** to the law Ezr 7:14
may do **a** to the will of your God. Ezr 7:18
a to the wisdom of your God which Ezr 7:25
Thus I was strengthened **a** to the Ezr 7:28
A to the good hand of our God upon us Ezr 8:18
lands, **a** to their abominations, Ezr 9:1
a to the counsel of my lord and of Ezr 10:3
and let it be done **a** to the law. Ezr 10:3
they would do **a** to this proposal; Ezr 10:5
a to the counsel of the leaders Ezr 10:8
"We **a** to our ability have Ne 5:8
they would do **a** to this promise. Ne 5:12
the people did **a** to this promise. Ne 5:13
a *to* all that I have done for Ne 5:19
be their king, **a** to these reports. Ne 6:6
to the king **a** to these reports. Ne 6:7
a to these works of theirs, Ne 6:14
assembly **a** to the ordinance. Ne 8:18
and **a** to Your great compassion You Ne 9:27
rescued them **a** to Your compassion, Ne 9:28
God, **a** to our fathers' households, Ne 10:34
and have compassion on me **a** to the Ne 13:22
plentiful **a** to the king's bounty. Es 1:7
drinking was *done* **a** to the law, Es 1:8
a to the desires of each person. Es 1:8
"**A** to law, what is to be done Es 1:15
to each province **a** to its script Es 1:22
every people **a** to their language, Es 1:22
gave gifts **a** to the king's bounty. Es 2:18
each province **a** to its script, Es 3:12
each people **a** to its language, Es 3:12
king, which is not **a** to the law; Es 4:16
and it was written **a** to all that Es 8:9
to every province **a** to its script, Es 8:9
every people **a** to their language as Es 8:9
as well as to the Jews **a** to their Es 8:9
to do **a** to the edict of today; Es 9:13
two days **a** to their regulation and Es 9:27
and **a** to their appointed time Es 9:27
and offering burnt offerings **a** *to* Jb 1:5
"**A** to what I have seen, those who Jb 4:8
"**A** to Your knowledge I am indeed Jb 10:7 5921
"For He pays a man **a** to his work, Jb 34:11
makes him find it **a** to his way. Jb 34:11
"Do you think this is **a** to justice? Jb 35:2
him so that I may not do with you **a** Jb 42:8
a to my righteousness and my Ps 7:8
the LORD **a** to His righteousness And Ps 7:17
rewarded me **a** to my righteousness; Ps 18:20
A to the cleanness of my hands He Ps 18:20
me **a** to my righteousness, Ps 18:24
A to the cleanness of my hands in Ps 18:24
A to Your lovingkindness remember Ps 25:7
Requite them **a** to their work and Ps 28:4
and **a** to the evil of their practices; Ps 28:4
Requite them **a** to the deeds of Ps 28:4
us, **A** as we have hoped in You. Ps 33:22
my God, **a** to Your righteousness, Ps 35:24
O God, **a** to Your lovingkindness; Ps 51:1
A to the greatness of Your Ps 51:1
recompense a man **a** to his work. Ps 62:12
A to the greatness of Your Ps 69:16
By asking food **a** to their desire. Ps 78:18
a to the integrity of his heart, Ps 78:72
A to the greatness of Your power Ps 79:11
a to the fear that is due You? Ps 90:11
Make us glad **a** to the days You Ps 90:15
not dealt with us **a** to our sins, Ps 103:10
rewarded us **a** to our iniquities. Ps 103:10
And relented **a** to the greatness of Ps 106:45
Save me **a** to Your lovingkindness. Ps 109:26
A to the order of Melchizedek." Ps 110:4 5921
By keeping *it* **a** to Your word. Ps 119:9
Revive me **a** to Your word. Ps 119:25

Strengthen me a to Your word.	Ps 119:28	
LORD, Your salvation a to Your word;	Ps 119:41	
Be gracious to me a to Your word.	Ps 119:58	
servant, O LORD, a to Your word.	Ps 119:65	
me, A to Your word to Your servant.	Ps 119:76	
Revive me a to Your lovingkindness,	Ps 119:88	
this day a to Your ordinances,	Ps 119:91	
Revive me, O LORD, a to Your word.	Ps 119:107	
Sustain me a to Your word, that I	Ps 119:116	
servant a to Your lovingkindness And	Ps 119:124	
my voice a to Your lovingkindness;	Ps 119:149	
me, O LORD, a to Your ordinances.	Ps 119:149	
Revive me a to Your word.	Ps 119:154	
Revive me a to Your ordinances.	Ps 119:156	
O LORD, a to Your lovingkindness.	Ps 119:159	
me understanding a to Your word.	Ps 119:169	
Deliver me a to Your word.	Ps 119:170	
Your word a to all Your name.	Ps 138:2	5921
Him a to His excellent greatness.	Ps 150:2	
will be praised a to his insight,	Pr 12:8	6310
not render to man a to his work?	Pr 24:12	
render to the man a to his work."	Pr 24:29	
not answer a fool a to his folly,	Pr 26:4	
a to the deeds of the wicked.	Ec 8:14	
a to the deeds of the righteous.	Ec 8:14	
they do not speak a to this word,	Is 8:20	
A *to* the faithful mercies shown	Is 55:3	
A *to their* deeds, so He will	Is 59:18	5921
A to all that the LORD has granted	Is 63:7	5921
granted them a to His compassion And	Is 63:7	
And a to the abundance of His	Is 63:7	
For a *to* the number of your	Jer 2:28	
My voice nor walked a to it,	Jer 9:13	
do a to all which I command you;	Jer 11:4	
you are each one walking a to the	Jer 16:12	310
to give to each man a to his ways,	Jer 17:10	
A to the results of his deeds.	Jer 17:10	
and each of us will act a to the	Jer 18:12	
us a to all His wonderful acts,	Jer 21:2	
a to the results of your deeds,"	Jer 21:14	
recompense them a to their deeds and	Jer 25:14	
a to the work of their hands.)"	Jer 25:14	
guard a to the word of the LORD and	Jer 32:8	
giving to everyone a to his ways	Jer 32:19	
and a to the fruit of his deeds;	Jer 32:19	
had set free a to their desire,	Jer 34:16	
and have done a to all that	Jer 35:10	
a to all that he commanded you;	Jer 35:18	
Baruch the son of Neriah did a to all	Jer 36:8	
"And do a to all that I have	Jer 50:21	
Repay her a to her work;	Jer 50:29	
A to all that she has done, *so* do	Jer 50:29	
Then He will have compassion A to	La 3:32	
A to the work of their hands.	La 3:64	
you shall eat it a to the number	Ezk 4:9	
I will judge you a to your ways	Ezk 7:3	
you; judge you a to your ways	Ezk 7:8	
I will repay you a to your ways,	Ezk 7:9	
A to their conduct I will deal	Ezk 7:27	4480
but have acted a to the ordinances	Ezk 11:12	
or done a to their abominations;	Ezk 16:47	
and does a to all the abominations	Ezk 18:24	
Israel, each a to his conduct,"	Ezk 18:30	
not a to your evil ways or	Ezk 20:44	
ways or a to your corrupt deeds,	Ezk 20:44	
of Israel, each a to his power,	Ezk 22:6	
will judge you a to their customs.	Ezk 23:24	
a to your ways and according to	Ezk 24:14	
according to your ways and a to	Ezk 24:14	
a to all that he has done you will	Ezk 24:24	
they will act in Edom a to My	Ezk 25:14	
to My anger and a to My wrath;	Ezk 25:14	
A to its wickedness I have driven	Ezk 31:11	
judge each of you a to his ways."	Ezk 33:20	
"I will deal *with you* a to your	Ezk 35:11	
and a to your envy which you showed	Ezk 35:11	
A to their ways and their deeds I	Ezk 36:19	
"A to their uncleanness and	Ezk 39:24	
and a to their transgressions I dealt	Ezk 39:24	
a to those same measurements.	Ezk 40:24	
gate a to those same measurements.	Ezk 40:28	
were a to those same measurements.	Ezk 40:29	
gate a to those same measurements.	Ezk 40:32	
were a to those same measurements.	Ezk 40:33	
it a to those same measurements,	Ezk 40:35	
a to their length so was their	Ezk 42:11	
and all their exits *were* both a to	Ezk 42:11	
shall judge it a to My ordinances.	Ezk 44:24	
of Israel a to their tribes."	Ezk 45:8	
standard shall be a to the homer.	Ezk 45:11	413
fish will be a to their kinds,	Ezk 47:10	
a to the tribes of Israel.	Ezk 47:21	
your servants a to what you see."	Da 1:13	
a to the name of my god,	Da 4:8	
But He does a to His will in the	Da 4:35	4481
a to the law of the Medes and	Da 6:8	
a to the law of the Medes and	Da 6:12	
had spoken to me a to these words,	Da 10:15	
nor a to his authority which he	Da 11:4	
will punish Jacob a to his ways;	Hos 12:2	
He will repay him a to his deeds.	Hos 12:2	
Nineveh a to the word of the LORD.	Jon 3:3	
the prophet, a to Shigionoth.	Hab 3:1	5921
her dwelling will not be cut off A	Zph 3:7	
away a to the writing on one side,	Zch 5:3	
will be purged away a to the writing	Zch 5:3	
a to the time which he had	Mt 2:16	2596
be done to you a to your faith."	Mt 9:29	2596
EVERY MAN A TO HIS DEEDS.	Mt 16:27	2596
but do not do a to their deeds;	Mt 23:3	2596
one, each a to his own ability;	Mt 25:15	2596
"Why do Your disciples not walk a	Mk 7:5	2596
Him again, and, a to His custom,	Mk 10:1	5613
a to the custom of the priestly	Lk 1:9	2596
be done to me a to your word."	Lk 1:38	2596
days for their purification a to the law	Lk 2:22	2596
and to offer a sacrifice a to what	Lk 2:24	2596
A to Your word;	Lk 2:29	2596
a to the Law of the Lord,	Lk 2:39	2596
a to the custom of the Feast;	Lk 2:42	2596
they rested a to the commandment.	Lk 23:56	2596
"Do not judge a to appearance,	Jn 7:24	2596
"You judge a to the flesh;	Jn 8:15	2596
and judge Him a to your law."	Jn 18:31	2596
him to make it a to the pattern which	Ac 7:44	2596
of this man, a to promise,	Ac 13:23	2596
a to the custom of Moses,	Ac 15:1	
And a to Paul's custom, he went to	Ac 17:2	2596
nor to walk a to the customs.	Ac 21:21	
a to the law of our fathers,	Ac 22:3	2596
Do you sit to try me a to the Law,	Ac 23:3	2596
to judge him a to our own Law.	Ac 24:6	2596
that a to the Way which they call	Ac 24:14	2596
that I lived *as* a Pharisee a to	Ac 26:5	2596
of David a to the flesh,	Ro 1:3	2596
dead, a to the Spirit of holiness,	Ro 1:4	2596
TO EACH PERSON A TO HIS DEEDS:	Ro 2:6	2596
on the day when, a to my gospel,	Ro 2:16	2596
our forefather a to the flesh,	Ro 4:1	2596
a to that which had been spoken,	Ro 4:18	2596
who do not walk a to the flesh but	Ro 8:4	2596
to the flesh but a to the Spirit.	Ro 8:4	2596
For those who are a to the flesh	Ro 8:5	2596
but those who are a to the Spirit,	Ro 8:5	2596
the flesh, to live a to the flesh—	Ro 8:12	2596
if you are living a to the flesh,	Ro 8:13	2596
the saints a to *the will of* God.	Ro 8:27	2596
who are called a to *His* purpose.	Ro 8:28	2596
my kinsmen a to the flesh,	Ro 9:3	2596
whom is the Christ a to the flesh,	Ro 9:5	2596
a to *His* choice would stand,	Ro 9:11	2596
remnant a to *God's* gracious choice.	Ro 11:5	2596
differ a to the grace given to us,	Ro 12:6	2596
a to the proportion of his faith;	Ro 12:6	2596
are no longer walking a to love.	Ro 14:15	2596
one another a to Christ Jesus,	Ro 15:5	2596
able to establish you a to my gospel	Ro 16:25	2596
a to the revelation of the mystery	Ro 16:25	2596
a to the commandment of the	Ro 16:26	2596
were not many wise a to the flesh,	1Co 1:26	2596
his own reward a to his own labor.	1Co 3:8	2596
A to the grace of God which was	1Co 3:10	2596
these things a to human judgment,	1Co 9:8	2596
of knowledge a to the same Spirit;	1Co 12:8	2596
for our sins a to the Scriptures,	1Co 15:3	2596
the third day a to the Scriptures,	1Co 15:4	2596
do I purpose a to the flesh,	2Co 1:17	2596
of faith, a to what is written,	2Co 4:13	2596
the body, a to what he has done,	2Co 5:10	4314
recognize no one a to the flesh;	2Co 5:16	2596
have known Christ a to the flesh,	2Co 5:16	2596
sorrowful a to *the will of* God,	2Co 7:9	2596
For the sorrow that is a to *the*	2Co 7:10	2596
I testify that a to their ability,	2Co 8:3	2596
is acceptable a to what *a person* has,	2Co 8:12	2526
not a to what he does not have.	2Co 8:12	2526
us as if we walked a to the flesh.	2Co 10:2	2596
we do not war a to the flesh,	2Co 10:3	2596
end will be a to their deeds.	2Co 11:15	2596
Since many boast a to the flesh,	2Co 11:18	2596
a to the will of our God and	Ga 1:4	2596
preached by me is not a to man.	Ga 1:11	2596
descendants, heirs a to promise.	Ga 3:29	2596
bondwoman was born a to the flesh,	Ga 4:23	2596
who was born a to the flesh persecuted	Ga 4:29	2596
him *who was born* a to the Spirit,	Ga 4:29	2596
a to the kind intention of His	Eph 1:5	2596
a to the riches of His grace	Eph 1:7	2596
a to His kind intention which He	Eph 1:9	2596
having been predestined a to His	Eph 1:11	2596
a to the course of this world,	Eph 2:2	2596
a to the prince of the power of	Eph 2:2	2596
a to the gift of God's grace which	Eph 3:7	2596
me a to the working of His power.	Eph 3:7	2596
you, a to the riches of His glory,	Eph 3:16	2596
a to the power that works within	Eph 3:20	2596
grace was given a to the measure	Eph 4:7	2596
a to the proper working of each	Eph 4:16	2596
a to the need *of the moment,*	Eph 4:29	2596
are your masters a to the flesh,	Eph 6:5	2596
a to my earnest expectation and	Php 1:20	2596
a to the pattern you have in us.	Php 3:17	2531a
supply all your needs a to His riches	Php 4:19	2596
power, a to His glorious might,	Col 1:11	2596
made a minister a to the stewardship	Col 1:25	2596
I labor, striving a to His power,	Col 1:29	2596
a to the tradition of men,	Col 2:8	2596
a to the elementary principles of	Col 2:8	2596
world, rather than a to Christ.	Col 2:8	2596
knowledge a to the image of the One	Col 3:10	2596
a to the grace of our God and	2Th 1:12	2596
unruly life and not a to the tradition	2Th 3:6	2596
an apostle of Christ Jesus a to	1Tm 1:1	2596
a to the glorious gospel of the	1Tm 1:11	2596
a to the promise of life in Christ	2Tm 1:1	2596
the gospel a to the power of God,	2Tm 1:8	2596
holy calling, not a to our works,	2Tm 1:9	2596
but a to His own purpose and grace	2Tm 1:9	2596
unless he competes a to the rules.	2Tm 2:5	
of David, a to my gospel,	2Tm 2:8	2596
will repay him a to his deeds.	2Tm 4:14	2596
the truth which is a to godliness,	Ti 1:1	2596
entrusted a to the commandment	Ti 1:3	2596
righteousness, but a to His mercy,	Ti 3:5	2596
a to *the* hope of eternal life.	Ti 3:7	2596
the Holy Spirit a to His own will.	Heb 2:4	2596
A TO THE ORDER OF MELCHIZEDEK."	Heb 5:6	2596
a to the order of Melchizedek.	Heb 5:10	2596
a to the order of Melchizedek.	Heb 6:20	2596
a to the order of Melchizedek,	Heb 7:11	2596
a to the order of Aaron?	Heb 7:11	2596
if another priest arises a to the	Heb 7:15	2596
but a to the power of an	Heb 7:16	2596
A TO THE ORDER OF MELCHIZEDEK."	Heb 7:17	2596
who offer the gifts a to the Law;	Heb 8:4	2596
"THAT YOU MAKE all things A TO	Heb 8:5	2596
to all the people a to the Law,	Heb 9:19	2596
And a to the Law, *one may* almost	Heb 9:22	2596
(which are offered a to the Law),	Heb 10:8	2596
righteousness which is a to faith.	Heb 11:7	2596
the royal law a to the Scripture,	Jas 2:8	2596
a to the foreknowledge of God the	1Pe 1:2	2596
who a to His great mercy has	1Pe 1:3	2596
judges a to each one's work,	1Pe 1:17	2596
the spirit a to *the will of* God.	1Pe 4:6	2596
those also who suffer a to the	1Pe 4:19	2596
voluntarily, a to *the will of* God;	1Pe 5:2	2596
to them a to the true proverb,	2Pe 2:22	
But a to His promise we are	2Pe 3:13	2596
Paul, a to the wisdom given him,	2Pe 3:15	2596
if we ask anything a to His will,	1Jn 5:14	2596
we walk a to His commandments.	2Jn 1:6	2596
each one of you a to your deeds.	Rv 2:23	2596
back *to her* double a to her deeds;	Rv 18:6	2596
in the books, a to their deeds.	Rv 20:12	2596
one *of them* a to their deeds.	Rv 20:13	2596
a *to* human measurements, which	Rv 21:17	
every man a to what he has done.	Rv 22:12	5613

ACCORDINGLY

has done a as He spoke through me;	1Sa 28:17	3512c
Then we told them a what the names	Ezr 5:4	3660
frightened and act a and sin,	Ne 6:13	3651
pleased the king, and he did a.	Es 2:4	3651
who has heard and has not acted a,	Lk 6:49	
"A, whatever you have said in the	Lk 12:3	473
each of us is to exercise them a:	Ro 12:6	
A both gifts and sacrifices are	Heb 9:9	2596

ACCOUNT

This is the a of the heavens and	Gn 2:4	8435
curse the ground on a of man,	Gn 8:21	5668
and that I may live on a of you."	Gn 12:13	1558
the whole place on their a."	Gn 18:26	5668
not do *it* on a of the forty."	Gn 18:29	5668
destroy *it* on a of the twenty."	Gn 18:31	5668
not destroy *it* on a of the ten."	Gn 18:32	5668
might kill me on a of Rebekah,	Gn 26:7	5921
'I might die on a of her.'"	Gn 26:9	5921
LORD has blessed me on your a."	Gn 30:27	1558
Egyptian's house on a of Joseph;	Gn 39:5	1558
but they did not listen to Moses on a	Ex 6:9	4480
let him go free on a of his eye.	Ex 21:26	8478
let him go free on a of his tooth.	Ex 21:27	8478
be no bloodguiltiness on his a.	Ex 22:2	
will be bloodguiltiness on his a.	Ex 22:3	
beg you, do not a *this* sin to us,	Nu 12:11	7896
those who died on a of Korah.	Nu 16:49	
		5921, 1697
was angry with me also on your a,	Dt 1:37	1558
LORD was angry with me on your a,	Dt 3:26	4616
LORD was angry with me on your a,	Dt 4:21	
		5921, 1697
against a man on a of any iniquity	Dt 19:15	
on a of the evil of your deeds,	Dt 28:20	
		4480, 6440
cried to the LORD on a of Midian,	Jg 6:7	182
When Gideon heard the a of the dream	Jg 7:15	4557
His people on a of His great name,	1Sa 12:22	5668
no man's heart fail on a of him;	1Sa 17:32	5921
to destroy the city on my a.	1Sa 23:10	5668
he died on a of the blood of Asahel	2Sa 3:27	
to him, on a of the ark of God."	2Sa 6:12	5668
Now this is the a of the forced	1Ki 9:15	1697
on a of the sins of Jeroboam,	1Ki 14:16	1558
the a of the chronicles of King David.	1Ch 27:24	1697
made a refuse heap on a of this.	Ezr 6:11	5922
on a of the unfaithfulness of the exiles	Ezr 9:4	5921
and on a of our iniquities we,	Ezr 9:7	
anger of our God on a of this matter	Ezr 10:14	5704
a of the greatness of Mordecai to	Es 10:2	6575
arises? And when He calls me to a,	Jb 31:14	6485
not give an a of all His doings?	Jb 33:13	6030a
have taken a of my wanderings;	Ps 56:8	5608
On a *of* the sin of their mouth	Ps 59:12	
And on a of curses and lies which	Ps 59:12	4480
went hard with Moses on their a;	Ps 106:32	5668
For on a of a harlot *one is*	Pr 6:26	1157
Why should God be angry on a of	Ec 5:6	5921
On this a the anger of the LORD	Is 5:25	3651
on a of the fierce anger of Rezin	Is 7:4	
Behold, you are of no a,	Is 41:24	369
shut their mouths on a of Him;	Is 52:15	5921
and call their sins to a."	Jer 14:10	6485
King Asa had made on a of Baasha,	Jer 41:9	
		4480, 6440
On a of the day that is coming To	Jer 47:4	5921
will be stripped of its fullness on a of	Ezk 12:19	6440

the nations on **a** of your beauty, **Ezk 16:14**
the field wilted away on **a** of it. **Ezk 31:15** 5921
And on **a** of transgression the host **Da 8:12**
on **a** of any merits of our own, **Da 9:18** 5921
but on **a** of Your great compassion. **Da 9:18** 5921
On **a** of the sweet wine That is cut **Jl 1:5** 5921
a this calamity *has struck* us." **Jon 1:7** 7945
a *has* this calamity *struck* us? **Jon 1:8**
for I know that on **a** of me this **Jon 1:12** 7945
do not let us perish on **a** of this **Jon 1:14**
Therefore, on **a** of you Zion will **Mi 3:12** 1558
On **a** of the fruit of their deeds. **Mi 7:13** 4480
bound in prison on **a** of Herodias, **Mk 6:17** *1223*
have undertaken to compile an **a** **Lk 1:1** *1335*
they gave an **a** to Him of all that **Lk 9:10** *1334*
nor do you take into **a** that it is **Jn 11:50** *3049*
because on **a** of him many of the **Jn 12:11** *1223*
The first **a** I composed, **Ac 1:1** *3056*
on **a** of the people, because they **Ac 4:21** *1223*
a for this disorderly gathering." **Ac 19:40**
3056, 591
life of any **a** as dear to myself, **Ac 20:24** *3056*
THE LORD WILL NOT TAKE INTO **A**." **Ro 4:8** *3049*
us will give an **a** of himself to God. **Ro 14:12** *3056*
who are of no **a** in the church? **1Co 6:4** *1848*
not take into **a** a wrong *suffered*, **1Co 13:5** *3049*
by all, he is called to **a** by all; **1Co 14:24** *350*
profit which increases to your **a**. **Php 4:17** *3056*
rejoice before our God on your **a**, **1Th 3:9** *1223*
you anything, charge that to my **a**; **Phm 1:18** *1677*
as those who will give an **a**. **Heb 13:17** *3056*
an **a** for the hope that is in you, **1Pe 3:15** *3056*
but they will give **a** to Him who **1Pe 4:5** *3056*

ACCOUNTABLE
these satraps might be **a** to them, **Da 6:2** 2942
all the world may become **a** to God; **Ro 3:19** *5267*

ACCOUNTED
"I am **a** wicked, Why then should I **Jb 9:29**
of the earth are **a** as nothing, **Da 4:35** 2804

ACCOUNTING
they did not require an **a** from the **2Ki 12:15** 2803
"Only no **a** shall be made with **2Ki 22:7** 2803
they shall give an **a** for it in **Mt 12:36** *3056*
Give an **a** of your management, for **Lk 16:2** *3056*

ACCOUNTS
to settle **a** with his slaves. **Mt 18:23** *3056*
came and settled **a** with them. **Mt 25:19** *3056*

ACCUMULATE
they will **a** for themselves **2Tm 4:3** *2002*

ACCUMULATED
possessions which they had **a**, **Gn 12:5** 7408

ACCURATE
Let Him weigh me with **a** scales, **Jb 31:6** 6664

ACCURATELY
a the things concerning Jesus, **Ac 18:25** *199*
to him the way of God more **a**. **Ac 18:26** *199*
a handling the word of truth. **2Tm 2:15** *3718*

ACCURSED
(for he who is hanged is **a** of God), **Dt 21:23** 7045
Israel **a** and bring trouble on it. **Jos 6:18** 2764a
enemies, for they have become **a**. **Jos 7:12** 2764a
of one hundred Will be *thought* **a**. **Is 65:20** 7043
'Depart from Me, **a** ones, into the **Mt 25:41** *2672*
does not know the Law is **a**." **Jn 7:49** *1884a*
I could wish that I myself were **a**, **Ro 9:3** *331*
the Spirit of God says, "Jesus is **a**"; **1Co 12:3** *331*
not love the Lord, he is to be **a**. **1Co 16:22** *331*
preached to you, he is to be **a**! **Ga 1:8** *331*
what you received, he is to be **a**! **Ga 1:9** *331*
trained in greed, **a** children; **2Pe 2:14** *2671*

ACCUSATION
they wrote an **a** against the **Ezr 4:6** 7855
to find a ground of **a** against Daniel **Da 6:4** 5931
of **a** or *evidence of* corruption, **Da 6:4** 5931
any ground of **a** against this Daniel **Da 6:5** 5931
a do you bring against this Man?" **Jn 18:29** *2724*
but under no **a** deserving death or **Ac 23:29** *1462*
present before you and to make **a**, **Ac 24:19** *2723*
I had any **a** against my nation. **Ac 28:19** *2723*
Do not receive an **a** against an **1Tm 5:19** *2724*

ACCUSE
a man to **a** him of wrongdoing, **Dt 19:16** 6030a
at his right hand to **a** him. **Zch 3:1** 7853
so that they might **a** Him. **Mt 12:10** *2723*
so that they might **a** Him. **Mk 3:2** *2723*
priests *began* to **a** Him harshly. **Mk 15:3** *2723*
by force, or **a** *anyone* falsely, **Lk 3:14** *4811*
they might find *reason* to **a** Him. **Lk 6:7** *2723*
And they began to **a** Him, **Lk 23:2** *2723*
I will **a** you before the Father; **Jn 5:45** *2723*
Tertullus began to **a** him, **Ac 24:2** *2723*
the things of which we **a** him." **Ac 24:8** *2723*
charges of which they now **a** me. **Ac 24:13** *2723*
is *true* of which these men **a** me, **Ac 25:11** *2723*

ACCUSED
and he has **a** his brother falsely, **Dt 19:18** 6030a
men who had maliciously **a** Daniel, **Da 6:24**
399, 7170
And while He was being **a** by the **Mt 27:12** *2723*
we are in danger of being **a** of a riot **Ac 19:40** *1458*
why he had been **a** by the Jews, **Ac 22:30** *2723*
and I found him to be **a** over **Ac 23:29** *1458*
before the **a** meets his accusers face **Ac 25:16** *2723*
of which I am **a** by the Jews, **Ac 26:2** *1458*
O King, I am being **a** by Jews. **Ac 26:7** *1458*
not **a** of dissipation or rebellion. **Ti 1:6** *2724*

ACCUSER
let an **a** stand at his right hand. **Ps 109:6** 7854
for the **a** of our brethren has been **Rv 12:10** *2725b*

ACCUSERS
for my love they act as my **a**; **Ps 109:4** 7853
the reward of my **a** from the LORD, **Ps 109:20** 7853
Let my **a** be clothed with dishonor, **Ps 109:29** 7853
also instructing his **a** to bring **Ac 23:30** *2725a*
after your **a** arrive also," **Ac 23:35** *2725a*
his **a** to come before you.] **Ac 24:8** *2725a*
accused meets his **a** face to face and **Ac 25:16** *2725a*
"When the **a** stood up, they **Ac 25:18** *2725a*

ACCUSES
And every tongue that **a** you in **Is 54:17** 6965
the one who **a** you is Moses, in **Jn 5:45** *2723*
who **a** them before our God day and **Rv 12:10** *2723*

ACCUSING
standing there, **a** Him vehemently. **Lk 23:10** *2723*
they might have grounds for **a** Him. **Jn 8:6** *2723*
charge for which they were **a** him, **Ac 23:28** *1458*
a or else defending them, **Ro 2:15** *2723*
unjustly **a** us with wicked words; **3Jn 1:10** *5396*

ACCUSTOMED
I ever been **a** to do so to you?" **Nu 22:30** 5532a
and his men were **a** to go." **1Sa 30:31**
A wild donkey **a** to the wilderness, **Jer 2:24** 3928
can do good Who are **a** to doing evil. **Jer 13:23** 3928
feast the governor was **a** to release **Mt 27:15** *1486*
as he had been **a** to do for them. **Mk 15:8**
being **a** to the idol until now, **1Co 8:7** *4914*
not **a** to the word of righteousness, **Heb 5:13** *552*

ACHAIA
while Gallio was proconsul of **A**, **Ac 18:12** *882*
when he wanted to go across to **A**, **Ac 18:27** *882*
passed through Macedonia and **A**, **Ac 19:21** *882*
For Macedonia and **A** have been **Ro 15:26** *882*
they were the first fruits of **A**, **1Co 16:15** *882*
the saints who are throughout **A**: **2Co 1:1** *882*
that **A** has been prepared since **2Co 9:2** *882*
be stopped in the regions of **A**. **2Co 11:10** *882*
believers in Macedonia and in **A**. **1Th 1:7** *882*
you, not only in Macedonia and **A**, **1Th 1:8** *882*

ACHAICUS
of Stephanas and Fortunatus and **A**, **1Co 16:17** *883*

ACHAN
the things under the ban, for **A**, **Jos 7:1** 5912
and **A**, son of Carmi, son of Zabdi, **Jos 7:18** 5912
Then Joshua said to **A**, **Jos 7:19** 5912
So **A** answered Joshua and said, **Jos 7:20** 5912
with him, took **A** the son of Zerah, **Jos 7:24** 5912
'Did not **A** the son of Zerah act **Jos 22:20** 5912

ACHAR
The son of Carmi *was* **A**, **1Ch 2:7** 5917

ACHBOR
son of **A** became king in his place. **Gn 36:38** 5907
Then Baal-hanan the son of **A** died, **Gn 36:39** 5907
of Shaphan, **A** the son of Micaiah, **2Ki 22:12** 5907
So Hilkiah the priest, Ahikam, **A**, **2Ki 22:14** 5907
son of **A** became king in his place. **1Ch 1:49** 5907
Elnathan the son of **A** and *certain* **Jer 26:22** 5907
and Elnathan the son of **A**, **Jer 36:12** 5907

ACHIEVE
and may you **a** wealth in Ephrathah **Ru 4:11** 6213a
"His sons **a** honor, but he does **Jb 14:21** 3513
not **a** the righteousness of God. **Jas 1:20** *2038b*

ACHIEVEMENTS
trust in your own **a** and treasures, **Jer 48:7** 4639

ACHIM
Zadok the father of **A**, **Mt 1:14** *885*
A the father of Eliud. **Mt 1:14** *885*

ACHISH
Saul, and went to **A** king of Gath. **1Sa 21:10** 397
But the servants of **A** said to him, **1Sa 21:11** 397
and greatly feared **A** king of Gath. **1Sa 21:12** 397
Then **A** said to his servants, **1Sa 21:14** 397
with him, to **A** the son of Maoch, **1Sa 27:2** 397
And David lived with **A** at Gath, **1Sa 27:3** 397
Then David said to **A**, **1Sa 27:5** 397
So **A** gave him Ziklag that day; **1Sa 27:6** 397
Then he returned and came to **A**. **1Sa 27:9** 397
A said, "Where have you made a raid **1Sa 27:10** 397
So **A** believed David, saying, **1Sa 27:12** 397
And **A** said to David, **1Sa 28:1** 397
David said to **A**, **1Sa 28:2** 397
So **A** said to David, **1Sa 28:2** 397
proceeding on in the rear with **A**. **1Sa 29:2** 397
And **A** said to the commanders of **1Sa 29:3** 397
A called David and said to him, **1Sa 29:6** 397
David said to **A**, **1Sa 29:8** 397
But **A** replied to David, **1Sa 29:9** 397
ran away to **A** son of Maacah, **1Ki 2:39** 397
to **A** to look for his servants. **1Ki 2:40** 397

ACHOR
them up to the valley of **A**. **Jos 7:24** 5911
the valley of **A** to this day. **Jos 7:26** 5911
up to Debir from the valley of **A**, **Jos 15:7** 5911
of **A** a resting place for herds, **Is 65:10** 5911
the valley of **A** as a door of hope. **Hos 2:15** 5911

ACHSAH
him **A** my daughter as a wife." **Jos 15:16** 5915
gave him **A** his daughter as a wife. **Jos 15:17** 5915
him my daughter **A** for a wife." **Jg 1:12** 5915
him his daughter **A** for a wife. **Jg 1:13** 5915
and the daughter of Caleb *was* **A**. **1Ch 2:49** 5915

ACHSHAPH
of Shimron and to the king of **A**, **Jos 11:1** 407
the king of **A**, one; **Jos 12:20** 407
Helkath and Hali and Beten and **A**, **Jos 19:25** 407

ACHZIB
and Keilah and **A** and Mareshah; **Jos 15:44** 392
at the sea by the region of **A**. **Jos 19:29** 392
of Sidon, or of Ahlab, or of **A**, **Jg 1:31** 392
The houses of **A** *will* become a **Mi 1:14** 392

ACKNOWLEDGE
"But he shall **a** the firstborn, **Dt 21:17** 5234
And he did not **a** his brothers, Nor **Dt 33:9** 5234
evil which you **a** in your heart, **1Ki 2:44** 3045
In all your ways **a** Him, **Pr 3:6** 3045
you who are near, **a** My might." **Is 33:13** 3045
'Only **a** your iniquity, That you **Jer 3:13** 3045
great honor to those who **a** *him* **Da 11:39** 5234
a their guilt and seek My face; **Hos 5:15** 816
but the Pharisees **a** them all. **Ac 23:8** *3670*
we **a** *this* in every way and **Ac 24:3** *588*
not see fit to **a** God any longer, **Ro 1:28**
2192, 1922
Therefore **a** such men. **1Co 16:18** *1921*
those who do not **a** Jesus Christ *as* **2Jn 1:7** *3670*

ACKNOWLEDGED
Nor has He **a** transgression well, **Jb 35:15** 3045
I **a** my sin to You, And my **Ps 32:5** 3045
heard *this*, they **a** God's justice, **Lk 7:29** *1344*

ACKNOWLEDGES
And its place **a** it no longer. **Ps 103:16** 5234

ACQUAINTANCE
for themselves, each from his **a**; **2Ki 12:5** 4378

ACQUAINTANCES
men and his **a** and his priests, **2Ki 10:11** 3045
take no *more* money from your **a**, **2Ki 12:7** 4378
And my **a** are completely estranged **Jb 19:13** 3045
And an object of dread to my **a**; **Ps 31:11** 3045
have removed my **a** far from me; **Ps 88:8** 3045
My **a** are *in* darkness. **Ps 88:18** 3045
Him among their relatives and **a**. **Lk 2:44** *1110*
And all His **a** and the women who **Lk 23:49** *1110*

ACQUAINTED
are intimately **a** with all my ways. **Ps 139:3** 5532a
man of sorrows and **a** with grief; **Is 53:3** 3045
a only with the baptism of John; **Ac 18:25** *1987*
Jerusalem to become **a** with Cephas, **Ga 1:18** *2477*

ACQUIRE
in it and **a** property in it." **Gn 34:10** 270
you may **a** male and female slaves **Lv 25:44** 7069
must also **a** Ruth the Moabitess, **Ru 4:5** 7069
understanding will **a** wise counsel, **Pr 1:5** 7069
A wisdom! Acquire understanding! **Pr 4:5** 7069
Acquire wisdom! **A** understanding! **Pr 4:5** 7069
beginning of wisdom *is*: **A** wisdom; **Pr 4:7** 7069
"Do not **a** gold, or silver, or **Mt 10:9** *2932*

ACQUIRED
persons which they had **a** in Haran, **Gn 12:5** 6213a
his **a** livestock which he had **Gn 31:18** 7075
he had **a** in the land of Canaan, **Gn 36:6** 7408
they had **a** in the land of Canaan, **Gn 46:6** 7408
and they **a** property in it and were **Gn 47:27** 270
who is a slave **a** for *another* man, **Lv 19:20** 2778c
I have **a** Ruth the Moabitess, **Ru 4:10** 7069
a flocks and herds in abundance, **2Ch 32:29** 4735
the abundance *which* they have **a** and **Is 15:7** 6213a
your dishonest gain which you have **a** **Ezk 22:13** 6213a
You have **a** riches for yourself And **Ezk 28:4** 6213a
And have **a** gold and silver for **Ezk 28:4** 6213a
who have **a** cattle and goods, **Ezk 38:12** 6213a
(Now this man **a** a field with the **Ac 1:18** *2932*
"I **a** this citizenship with a **Ac 22:28** *2932*

ACQUIRES
to reproof **a** understanding. **Pr 15:32** 7069
mind of the prudent **a** knowledge, **Pr 18:15** 7069

ACQUIRING
And with all your **a**, **Pr 4:7** 7075

ACQUISITION
among you that you may gain **a**, **Lv 25:45** 7069
And the **a** of wisdom is above *that* **Jb 28:18** 4901
The **a** of treasures by a lying tongue **Pr 21:6** 6467

ACQUIT
for I will not **a** the guilty. **Ex 23:7** 6663
I know that You will not **a** me. **Jb 9:28** 5352
And would not **a** me of my guilt. **Jb 10:14** 5352
A me of hidden *faults*. **Ps 19:12** 5352

ACQUITTED
And a talkative man be **a**? **Jb 11:2** 6663
shall be **a** of great transgression. **Ps 19:13** 5352
the one who will be completely **a**? **Jer 49:12** 5352
You will not be **a**, but you will **Jer 49:12** 5352
myself, yet I am not by this **a**; **1Co 4:4** *1344*

ACRE
half a furrow in an **a** of land. **1Sa 14:14** 6776

ACRES
"For ten **a** of vineyard will yield **Is 5:10** 6776

ACROSS
them and sent them **a** the stream. **Gn 32:23** 5674a
And he sent **a** whatever he had. **Gn 32:23** 5674a
do not take us **a** the Jordan." **Nu 32:5** 5674a
remain with us **a** the Jordan." **Nu 32:32**
4480, 5676
a the Jordan opposite Jericho, **Nu 34:15**
4480, 5676
'You shall give three cities **a** the **Nu 35:14**
4480, 5676
a the Jordan in the wilderness, **Dt 1:1** 5676
A the Jordan in the land of Moab, **Dt 1:5** 5676
go **a** at the head of this people, **Dt 3:28** 5674a

cities **a** the Jordan to the east, Dt 4:41 5676
a the Jordan, in the valley Dt 4:46 5676
who were **a** the Jordan to the east, Dt 4:47 5676
Arabah **a** the Jordan to the east, Dt 4:49 5676
"Are they not **a** the Jordan, west Dt 11:30 5676
"Gilead remained **a** the Jordan; Jg 5:17 5676
Zeeb to Gideon from **a** the Jordan. Jg 7:25 5676
to bring the king **a** the Jordan. 2Sa 19:15 5674a
And he drew chains of gold **a** the 1Ki 6:21 5674a
length **a** the width of the house 2Ch 3:8 5921, 6440
a great wind came from **a** the Jb 1:19 5676
Your tendrils stretched **a** the sea, Jer 48:32 5674a
court and led me **a** to the four corners Ezk 46:21 5674a
when he wanted to go **a** to Achaia, Ac 18:27 *1330*
and girded **a** His chest with a Rv 1:13 *4314*

ACT

my brothers, do not **a** wickedly. Gn 19:7 7489a
are not to **a** as a creditor to him; Ex 22:25 1961
and you are not to **a** against the Lv 19:16 5975
have committed a detestable **a**; Lv 20:13 8441
you **a** with hostility against Me Lv 26:21 1980
but **a** with hostility against Me, Lv 26:23 1980
will **a** with hostility against you; Lv 26:24 1980
but **a** with hostility against Me, Lv 26:27 1980
then I will **a** with wrathful Lv 26:28 1980
she has not been caught in the **a**, Nu 5:13 8610
so that you do not **a** corruptly and make Dt 4:16 7843
long in the land, and **a** corruptly, Dt 4:25 7843
"You shall not **a** like this toward Dt 12:4 6213a
for every abominable **a** which the Dt 12:31 8441
will not **a** presumptuously again. Dt 17:13 2102
committed an **a** of folly in Israel by Dt 22:21 5039
after my death you will **a** corruptly Dt 31:29 7843
'What is this unfaithful **a** which Jos 22:16 4604
'Did not Achan the son of Zerah **a** Jos 22:20 4603
or if in an unfaithful **a** against Jos 22:22 4604
unfaithful **a** against the LORD; Jos 22:31 4604
turn back and **a** more corruptly Jg 2:19 7843
"Since you **a** like this, I will Jg 15:7 6213a
please do not **a** so wickedly; Jg 19:23 7489a
do not commit this **a** of folly. Jg 19:23 5039
an **a** of folly against this man." Jg 19:24 1697
lewd and disgraceful **a** in Israel. Jg 20:6 5039
to **a** the madman in my presence? 1Sa 21:15 7696
trees, then you shall **a** promptly, 2Sa 5:24 2782
"So **a** according to your wisdom, 1Ki 2:6 6213a
and **a** and judge Your servants, 1Ki 8:32 6213a
and forgive and **a** and render to 1Ki 8:39 6213a
be courageous and **a**." 1Ch 28:10 6213a
"Be strong and courageous, and **a**; 1Ch 28:20 6213a
and **a** and judge Your servants, 2Ch 6:23 6213a
and did not **a** as Israel did. 2Ch 17:4 4639
A resolutely, and the LORD be with 2Ch 19:11 6213a
But the Levites did not **a** quickly. 2Ch 24:5 4116
be courageous and **a**." Ezr 10:4 6213a
and **a** accordingly and sin, Ne 6:13 6213a
Why then do you **a** foolishly? Jb 27:12 1891
"Surely, God will not **a** wickedly, Jb 34:12 7561
for my love they **a** as my accusers; Ps 109:4 7853
It is time for the LORD to **a**, Ps 119:126 6213a
they refuse to **a** with justice. Pr 21:7 6213a
will bring every **a** to judgment, Ec 12:14 4639
evildoers, Sons who **a** corruptly! Is 1:4 7843
I **a** and who can reverse it?" Is 43:13 6466
sake, for My own sake, I will **a**; Is 48:11 6213a
a of violence is in their hands. Is 59:6 6467
So I will **a** on behalf of My Is 65:8 6213a
us, O LORD, **a** for Your name's sake! Jer 14:7 6213a
and each of us will **a** according to Jer 18:12 6213a
And He will reign as king and **a** Jer 23:5 7919a
if we do not **a** in accordance with Jer 42:5 6213a
unfaithful **a** which he has committed Ezk 17:20 4604
the LORD, have spoken and will **a**. Ezk 22:14 6213a
it is coming and I will **a**. Ezk 24:14 6213a
they will **a** in Edom according to Ezk 25:14 6213a
of Israel, that I am about to **a**, Ezk 36:22 6213a
a wickedly toward the covenant, Da 11:32 7561
but the wicked will **a** wickedly; Da 12:10 7561
known to Jacob his rebellious **a**, Mi 3:8 6588
over the rebellious **a** of the remnant Mi 7:18 6588
of Mine and does not **a** on them, Mt 7:26 *4160*
or **a** in accord with his will, Lk 12:47 *4160*
caught in adultery, in the very **a**. Jn 8:4 *849a*
and they all **a** contrary to the Ac 17:7 *4238*
even so through one **a** of Ro 5:18 *1345*
Nor let us **a** immorally, as some of 1Co 10:8 *4203*
does not **a** unbecomingly; 1Co 13:5 *807*
firm in the faith, **a** like men, 1Co 16:13 *407*
Therefore no one is to **a** as your Col 2:16 *2919*
because we did not **a** in an 2Th 3:7 *812*
So speak and so **a** as those who Jas 2:12 *4160*
A as free men, and do not use 1Pe 2:16
ever made by an **a** of human will, 2Pe 1:21
and authority to **a** for forty-two Rv 13:5 *4160*

ACTED

in which we have **a** foolishly and Nu 12:11 2973
and **a** presumptuously and went up Dt 1:43 2102
out of Egypt have **a** corruptly. Dt 9:12 7843
"They have **a** corruptly toward Dt 32:5 7843
But the sons of Israel **a** Jos 7:1 4603
they also **a** craftily and set out Jos 9:4 6213a
"You have **a** foolishly; 1Sa 13:13 5528
"You have **a** treacherously; 1Sa 14:33 898
He **a** valiantly and defeated 1Sa 14:48 6213a
and **a** insanely in their hands, 1Sa 21:13 1984b
not **a** wickedly against my God. 2Sa 22:22 7561
for I have **a** very foolishly." 2Sa 24:10 5528
iniquity, we have **a** wickedly'; 1Ki 8:47 7561
and **a** more wickedly than all who 1Ki 16:25 7489a
He **a** very abominably in 1Ki 21:26 8581
who **a** for them in the houses of 2Ki 17:32 6213a
But they **a** treacherously against 1Ch 5:25 4603
iniquity and have **a** wickedly'; 2Ch 6:37 7561
He **a** wisely and distributed 2Ch 11:23 995
You have **a** foolishly in this. 2Ch 16:9 5528
He **a** wickedly in so doing. 2Ch 20:35 7561
was so proud that he **a** corruptly, 2Ch 26:16 7843
"We have **a** very corruptly against Ne 1:7 2254b
they **a** arrogantly toward them, Ne 9:10 2102
they, our fathers, **a** arrogantly; Ne 9:16 2102
Yet they **a** arrogantly and did not Ne 9:29 2102
but we have **a** wickedly. Ne 9:33 7561
have **a** deceitfully like a wadi, Jb 6:15 898
O God, who have **a** on our behalf. Ps 68:28 6466
But turned back and **a** treacherously Ps 78:57 898
princes of Zoan have **a** foolishly, Is 19:13 2973
Suddenly I **a**, and they came to Is 48:3 6213a
they have **a** foolishly in Israel, Jer 29:23 6213a
these men have **a** wickedly in all Jer 38:9 7489a
but have **a** according to the Ezk 11:12 6213a
they have **a** unfaithfully,' " Ezk 15:8 4603
you **a** more corruptly in all your Ezk 16:47 7843
you **a** more abominably than they, Ezk 16:52 8581
"But I **a** for the sake of My name, Ezk 20:9 6213a
"But I **a** for the sake of My name, Ezk 20:14 6213a
and **a** for the sake of My name, Ezk 20:22 6213a
"Because Edom has **a** against the Ezk 25:12 6213a
"Because the Philistines have **a** Ezk 25:15 6213a
because they **a** for Me," Ezk 29:20 6213a
they **a** treacherously against Me, Ezk 39:23 4603
committed iniquity, **a** wickedly and Da 9:5 7561
conceived them has **a** shamefully. Hos 2:5 954
heard and has not **a** *accordingly,* Lk 6:49 *4160*
manager because he had **a** shrewdly; Lk 16:8 *4160*
a as though He were going farther. Lk 24:28 *4364*
I know that you **a** in ignorance, Ac 3:17 *4238*
I **a** ignorantly in unbelief; 1Tm 1:13 *4160*

ACTING

and already he is **a** like a judge; Gn 19:9 8199
their **a** with hostility against Me Lv 26:40 1980
was **a** with hostility against them, Lv 26:41 1980
a unfaithfully against the LORD, Nu 5:6 4603
the people continued **a** corruptly. 2Ch 27:2 7843
all this great evil by **a** unfaithfully Ne 13:27 4603
labored by **a** wisely under the sun. Ec 2:19 2449
Me by **a** treacherously against Me. Ezk 20:27 4603
man thinks that he is **a** unbecomingly 1Co 7:36 *807*
at all, but **a** like busybodies. 2Th 3:11 *4020*
you are **a** faithfully in whatever 3Jn 1:5 *4160*

ACTION

"Let Pharaoh take **a** to appoint Gn 41:34 6213a
sons of Reuben, took **a**, Nu 16:1
O Lord, listen and take **a**! Da 9:19 6213a
and he will take **a** and *then* return Da 11:28 6213a
at the holy covenant and take **a**; Da 11:30 6213a
will display strength and take **a**. Da 11:32 6213a
"He will take **a** against the Da 11:39 6213a
consented to their plan and **a**), Lk 23:51 *4234*
this plan or **a** is of men, Ac 5:38 *2041*
Therefore, prepare your minds for **a**, 1Pe 1:13

ACTIONS

And with Him **a** are weighed. 1Sa 2:3 5949
"Who will confront him with his **a**, Jb 21:31 1870
and their **a** are against the LORD, Is 3:8 4611
will eat the fruit of their **a**. Is 3:10 4611
you will see their conduct and **a**; Ezk 14:22 5949
when you see their conduct and **a**, Ezk 14:23 5949
the **a** of a bold-faced harlot. Ezk 16:30 4639

ACTIVE

No soldier in **a** service entangles 2Tm 2:4 *4754*
For the word of God is living and **a** Heb 4:12 *1756*

ACTIVITIES

Thus I considered all my **a** which Ec 2:11 4639
that man should be happy in his **a**, Ec 3:22 4639

ACTIVITY

go forth seeking food in their **a**, Jb 24:5 6467
evil **a** that is done under the sun. Ec 4:3 4639
for there is no **a** or planning or Ec 9:10 4639
the **a** of God who makes all things. Ec 11:5 4639
is in accord with the **a** of Satan, 2Th 2:9 *1753b*

ACTS

a man **a** presumptuously toward his Ex 21:14 2102
"If a person **a** unfaithfully and Lv 5:15 4603
a unfaithfully against the LORD, Lv 6:2 4603
such works and mighty **a** as Yours? Dt 3:24 1369
"The man who **a** presumptuously Dt 17:12 6213a
everyone who **a** unjustly is an Dt 25:16 6213a
punish *them* for all the disgraceful **a** Jg 20:10 5039
all the righteous **a** of the LORD 1Sa 12:7 6666
Now the rest of the **a** of Solomon 1Ki 11:41 1697
in the book of the **a** of Solomon? 1Ki 11:41 1697
Now the rest of the **a** of Jeroboam, 1Ki 14:19 1697
Now the rest of the **a** of Rehoboam 1Ki 14:29 1697
a of Abijam and all that he did, 1Ki 15:7 1697
Now the rest of all the **a** of Asa 1Ki 15:23 1697
a of Nadab and all that he did, 1Ki 15:31 1697
Now the rest of the **a** of Baasha 1Ki 16:5 1697
the **a** of Elah and all that he did, 1Ki 16:14 1697
Now the rest of the **a** of Zimri and 1Ki 16:20 1697
Now the rest of the **a** of Omri 1Ki 16:27 1697
Now the rest of the **a** of Ahab and 1Ki 22:39 1697
the rest of the **a** of Jehoshaphat, 1Ki 22:45 1697
of the **a** of Ahaziah which he did, 2Ki 1:18 1697
a of Joram and all that he did, 2Ki 8:23 1697
Now the rest of the **a** of Jehu and 2Ki 10:34 1697
a of Joash and all that he did, 2Ki 12:19 1697
Now the rest of the **a** of Jehoahaz, 2Ki 13:8 1697
Now the rest of the **a** of Joash and 2Ki 13:12 1697
of the **a** of Jehoash which he did, 2Ki 14:15 1697
Now the rest of the **a** of Amaziah, 2Ki 14:18 1697
Now the rest of the **a** of Jeroboam 2Ki 14:28 1697
Now the rest of the **a** of Azariah 2Ki 15:6 1697
the rest of the **a** of Zechariah, 2Ki 15:11 1697
Now the rest of the **a** of Shallum 2Ki 15:15 1697
Now the rest of the **a** of Menahem 2Ki 15:21 1697
Now the rest of the **a** of Pekahiah 2Ki 15:26 1697
a of Pekah and all that he did, 2Ki 15:31 1697
a of Jotham and all that he did, 2Ki 15:36 1697
of the **a** of Ahaz which he did, 2Ki 16:19 1697
a of Hezekiah and all his might, 2Ki 20:20 1697
Now the rest of the **a** of Manasseh 2Ki 21:17 1697
of the **a** of Amon which he did, 2Ki 21:25 1697
a of Josiah and all that he did, 2Ki 23:28 1697
Now the rest of the **a** of Jehoiakim 2Ki 24:5 1697
Now the **a** of King David, from 1Ch 29:29 1697
Now the rest of the **a** of Solomon, 2Ch 9:29 1697
Now the **a** of Rehoboam, from first 2Ch 12:15 1697
Now the rest of the **a** of Abijah, 2Ch 13:22 1697
the **a** of Asa from first to last, 2Ch 16:11 1697
the rest of the **a** of Jehoshaphat, 2Ch 20:34 1697
Now the rest of the **a** of Amaziah, 2Ch 25:26 1697
Now the rest of the **a** of Uzziah, 2Ch 26:22 1697
Now the rest of the **a** of Jotham, 2Ch 27:7 1697
even all his wars and his **a**, 2Ch 27:7 1870
rest of his **a** and all his ways, 2Ch 28:26 1697
After these **a** of faithfulness 2Ch 32:1 1697
Now the rest of the **a** of Hezekiah 2Ch 32:32 1697
Now the rest of the **a** of Manasseh 2Ch 33:18 1697
Now the rest of the **a** of Josiah 2Ch 35:26 1697
and his **a**, first to last, behold, 2Ch 35:27 1697
Now the rest of the **a** of Jehoiakim 2Ch 36:8 1697
When He **a** on the left, I cannot Jb 23:9 6213a
His **a** to the sons of Israel. Ps 103:7 5949
His wondrous **a** among them, Ps 105:27 1697
And shall declare Your mighty **a**. Ps 145:4 1369
of the power of Your awesome **a** Ps 145:6 3372a
to the sons of men Your mighty **a** And Ps 145:12 1369
in summer is a son who **a** wisely, Pr 10:5 7919a
harvest is a son who **a** shamefully. Pr 10:5 954
man **a** disgustingly and shamefully. Pr 13:5 887
prudent man **a** with knowledge, Pr 13:16 6213a
A quick-tempered man **a** foolishly, Pr 14:17 6213a
is toward a servant who **a** wisely, Pr 14:35 7919a
is toward him who **a** shamefully. Pr 14:35 954
for kings to commit wicked **a**, For a Pr 16:12 7562
A servant who **a** wisely will rule Pr 17:2 7919a
rule over a son who **a** shamefully, Pr 17:2 954
names, Who **a** with insolent pride. Pr 21:24 6213a
Then I looked again at all the **a** Ec 4:1 6217
Who **a** in behalf of the one who Is 64:4 6213a
according to all His wonderful **a**, Jer 21:2 6381
they have committed **a** of lewdness. Ezk 22:9 2154
with all Your righteous **a**, Da 9:16 6666
found The rebellious **a** of Israel. Mi 1:13 6588
the righteous **a** of the LORD." Mi 6:5 6666
my firstborn *for* my rebellious **a**, Mi 6:7 6588
words of Mine and **a** on them, Mt 7:24 *4160*
hears My words and **a** on them, Lk 6:47 *4160*
men with men committing indecent **a** Ro 1:27 *808*
performed **a** *of* righteousness, Heb 11:33
sacrificed to idols and to commit **a** Rv 2:14
astray so that they commit **a** *of* Rv 2:20
RIGHTEOUS **A** HAVE BEEN REVEALED." Rv 15:4 *1345*
the kings of the earth committed **a** Rv 17:2
kings of the earth have committed **a** Rv 18:3
who committed **a** *of* immorality Rv 18:9
is the righteous **a** of the saints. Rv 19:8 *1345*

ACTUALLY

"Besides, she **a** is my sister, the Gn 20:12 546
"Are you **a** going to reign over us? Gn 37:8 4427a
your mother and your brothers **a** come Gn 37:10 935
a found alive in his possession, Ex 22:4 4672
"But if it is **a** stolen from him, Ex 22:12 1589
'If a man **a** lies with her so Lv 15:24 7901
behold, you have **a** blessed them!" Nu 23:11 1288
that my grief were **a** weighed Jb 6:2 8254
was it **a** for Me that you fasted? Zch 7:5 6684
"But I was **a** born *a citizen.*" Ac 22:28 *2532*
It is **a** reported that there is 1Co 5:1 *3654*
But **a**, I wrote to you not to 1Co 5:11 *3568*
A, then, it is already a defeat 1Co 6:7 *3654*
A I should have been commended by 2Co 12:11 *1063*
A, it is in the sight of God 2Co 12:19
(just as you **a** do walk), 1Th 4:1 *2532*
But godliness **a** is a means of 1Tm 6:6

ADADAH

and Kinah and Dimonah and **A**, Jos 15:22 5735

ADAH

the name of the one was **A**, Gn 4:19 5711
A gave birth to Jabal; Gn 4:20 5711
"**A** and Zillah, Listen to my Gn 4:23 5711
A the daughter of Elon the Gn 36:2 5711
A bore Eliphaz to Esau, and Gn 36:4 5711
Eliphaz the son of Esau's wife **A**, Gn 36:10 5711
are the sons of Esau's wife **A**. Gn 36:12 5711
these are the sons of **A**. Gn 36:16 5711

ADAIAH

the daughter of **A** of Bozkath. 2Ki 22:1 5718
the son of Zerah, the son of **A**, 1Ch 6:41 5718
A, Beraiah and Shimrath *were* the 1Ch 8:21 5718
and **A** the son of Jeroham, *the* son 1Ch 9:12 5718
of Obed, Maaseiah the son of **A**, 2Ch 23:1 5718

Meshullam, Malluch and **A**, Ezr 10:29 5718
Shelemiah, Nathan, **A**, Ezr 10:39 5718
the son of Hazaiah, the son of **A**, Ne 11:5 5718
and **A** the son of Jeroham, the son Ne 11:12 5718

ADALIA
Poratha, **A**, Aridatha, Es 9:8 118

ADAM
but for **A** there was not found a Gn 2:20 121
Then to **A** He said, Gn 3:17 121
of skin for **A** and his wife, Gn 3:21 121
A had relations with his wife Gn 4:25 121
the book of the generations of **A**. Gn 5:1 121
When **A** had lived one hundred and Gn 5:3 121
Then the days of **A** after he became Gn 5:4 121
So all the days that **A** lived were Gn 5:5 121
heap, a great distance away at **A**, Jos 3:16 121
A, Seth, Enosh, 1Ch 1:1 121
covered my transgressions like **A**, Jb 31:33 121
But like **A** they have transgressed Hos 6:7 121
the son of Seth, the son of **A**, Lk 3:38 *76*
death reigned from **A** until Moses, Ro 5:14 *76*
the likeness of the offense of **A**, Ro 5:14 *76*
For as in **A** all die, so also in 1Co 15:22 *76*
"The first MAN, **A**, BECAME A 1Co 15:45 *76*
last **A** *became* a life-giving spirit. 1Co 15:45 *76*
it was **A** who was first created, 1Tm 2:13 *76*
And *it was* not **A** *who* was deceived, 1Tm 2:14 *76*
in the seventh *generation* from **A**, Jude 1:14 *76*

ADAMAH
and **A** and Ramah and Hazor, Jos 19:36 128

ADAMI-NEKEB
in Zaanannim and **A** and Jabneel, Jos 19:33 129

ADAR
on the third day of the month **A**; Ezr 6:15 144
month, that is the month **A**. Es 3:7 143
month, which is the month **A**, Es 3:13 143
month (that is, the month **A**), Es 8:12 143
month (that is, the month **A**), Es 9:1 143
the month **A** and killed three hundred Es 9:15 143
the thirteenth day of the month **A**, Es 9:17 143
month **A** *a* holiday for rejoicing Es 9:19 143
the fourteenth day of the month **A**, Es 9:21 143

ADBEEL
and Kedar and **A** and Mibsam Gn 25:13 110
was Nebaioth, then Kedar, **A**, 1Ch 1:29 110

ADD
shall **a** to it a fifth part of it and Lv 5:16 3254
full and **a** to it one-fifth more. Lv 6:5 3254
then he shall **a** to it a fifth of Lv 22:14 3254
then he shall **a** one-fifth of it to Lv 27:13 3254
then he shall **a** one-fifth of your Lv 27:15 3254
then he shall **a** one-fifth of your Lv 27:19 3254
and **a** to it one-fifth of it; Lv 27:27 3254
he shall **a** to it one-fifth of it. Lv 27:31 3254
wrong and **a** to it one-fifth of it, Nu 5:7 3254
to **a** still more to the burning Nu 32:14 5595
"You shall not **a** to the word Dt 4:2 3254
not **a** to nor take away from it. Dt 12:32 3254
then you shall **a** three more cities Dt 19:9 3254
"Now may the LORD your God **a** to 2Sa 24:3 3254
heavy yoke, I will **a** to your yoke; 1Ki 12:11 3254
heavy, but I will **a** to your yoke; 1Ki 12:14 3254
will **a** fifteen years to your life, 2Ki 20:6 3254
"May the LORD **a** to His people a 1Ch 21:3 3254
prepared, and you may **a** to them. 1Ch 22:14 3254
heavy yoke, I will **a** to your yoke; 2Ch 10:11 3254
yoke heavy, but I will **a** to it; 2Ch 10:14 3254
twice, and I will **a** nothing more." Jb 40:5 3254
A iniquity to their iniquity, Ps 69:27 5414
And peace they will **a** to you. Pr 3:2 3254
Do not **a** to His words Or He Pr 30:6 3254
there is nothing to **a** to it and Ec 3:14 3254
Woe to those who **a** house to house Is 5:8 5060
A year to year, observe *your* Is 29:1 3254
Spirit, In order to **a** sin to sin; Is 30:1 5595
will **a** fifteen years to your life. Is 38:5 3254
"**A** your burnt offerings to your Jer 7:21 3254
can **a** a *single* hour to his life? Mt 6:27 *4369*
by worrying can **a** a *single* hour Lk 12:25 *4369*
and we **a** our testimony, and you know 3Jn 1:12 *3140*
that he might **a** it to the prayers Rv 8:3 *1325*
God will **a** to him the plagues Rv 22:18 *2007*

ADDAN
Tel-melah, Tel-harsha, Cherub, **A** Ezr 2:59 135

ADDAR
up to **A** and turned about to Karka. Jos 15:3 146
A, Gera, Abihud, 1Ch 8:3 146

ADDED
shall be **a** to them in a vessel. Nu 19:17 5414
will be **a** to the inheritance of the tribe Nu 36:3 3254
then their inheritance will be **a** Nu 36:4 3254
a great voice, and He **a** no more. Dt 5:22 3254
for we have **a** to all our sins *this* 1Sa 12:19 3254
I would have **a** to you many more 2Sa 12:8 3254
an **a** burden to my lord the king? 2Sa 19:35 5750
years of life will be **a** to you. Pr 9:11 3254
I will bring **a** *woes* upon Dimon, Is 15:9 3254
many similar words were **a** to them. Jer 36:32 3254
the LORD has **a** sorrow to my pain; Jer 45:3 3254
upon disaster and rumor will be **a** Ezk 7:26
surpassing greatness was **a** to me. Da 4:36 3255
these things will be **a** to you. Mt 6:33 *4369*
but *to* wear sandals; and *He* **a** Mk 6:9
Herod also **a** this to them all: Lk 3:20 *4369*
these things will be **a** to you. Lk 12:31 *4369*
and he was **a** to the eleven apostles. Ac 1:26 *4785*
and that day there were **a** about Ac 2:41 *4369*
were constantly **a** to *their number*, Ac 5:14 *4369*
was **a** because of transgressions, Ga 3:19 *4369*

ADDERS
sending serpents against you, **A**, Jer 8:17 6848b

ADDERS'
They hatch **a** eggs and weave Is 59:5 6848b

ADDI
the son of Melchi, the son of **A**, Lk 3:28 *78*

ADDICTED
not **a** to wine or pugnacious, but 1Tm 3:3 *3943*
or **a** to much wine or fond of 1Tm 3:8 *4337*
not quick-tempered, not **a** to wine, Ti 1:7 *3943*

ADDING
LORD **a** to our sins and our guilt; 2Ch 28:13 3254
wives **a** to the guilt of Israel. Ezr 10:10 3254
Yet you are **a** to the wrath on Ne 13:18 3254
"**a** one thing to another to find Ec 7:27
And the Lord was **a** to their number Ac 2:47 *4369*

ADDITION
not marry a woman in **a** to her sister Lv 18:18 413
in **a** to what *else* he can afford; Nu 6:21
4480, 905
in **a** to the continual burnt offering Nu 28:10 5921
offered with its drink offering in **a** Nu 28:15 5921
be presented with its drink offering in **a** Nu 28:24 5921
and in **a** to them you shall give Nu 35:6 5921
and in **a** Abner went to speak in 2Sa 3:19 1571
and in **a** to them was Hanan the son Ne 13:13
5921, 3027
In **a** to being a wise man, the Ec 12:9 3148
in **a** to all your abominations. Ezk 44:7 413
in **a** to all, taking up the shield Eph 6:16

ADDON
Tel-melah, Tel-harsha, Cherub, **A** and Ne 7:61 114

ADDRESS
I **a** my verses to the King; Ps 45:1 559
and *began* delivering an **a** to them. Ac 12:21 *1215*
If you **a** as Father the One who 1Pe 1:17 *1941*

ADDRESSED
to release Jesus, **a** them again, Lk 23:20 *4377*
which is **a** to you as sons, Heb 12:5 *1256*

ADDRESSING
are You **a** this parable to us, Lk 12:41 *3004*
was **a** them in the Hebrew dialect, Ac 22:2 *4377*

ADDS
'For he **a** rebellion to his sin; Jb 34:37 3254
rich, And He **a** no sorrow to it. Pr 10:22 3254
And **a** persuasiveness to his lips. Pr 16:23 3254
Wealth **a** many friends, But a poor Pr 19:4 3254
it aside or **a** conditions to it. Ga 3:15 *1928*
if anyone **a** to them, God will add Rv 22:18 *2007*

ADEQUACY
ourselves, but our **a** is from God, 2Co 3:5 *2426*

ADEQUATE
And who is **a** for these things? 2Co 2:16 *2425*
Not that we are **a** in ourselves to 2Co 3:5 *2425*
a *as* servants of a new covenant, 2Co 3:6 *2427*
that the man of God may be **a**, 2Tm 3:17 *739*

ADHERE
they will not **a** to one another, Da 2:43 1693

ADIEL
Jaakobah, Jeshohaiah, Asaiah, **A**, 1Ch 4:36 5717
and Maasai the son of **A**, 1Ch 9:12 5717
Now Azmaveth the son of **A** had 1Ch 27:25 5717

ADIN
the sons of **A**, 454; Ezr 2:15 5720
and of the sons of **A**, Ezr 8:6 5720
the sons of **A**, 655; Ne 7:20 5720
Adonijah, Bigvai, **A**, Ne 10:16 5720

ADINA
A the son of Shiza the Reubenite, 1Ch 11:42 5721

ADINO
he was *called* **A** the Eznite, 2Sa 23:8 5722

ADITHAIM
and **A** and Gederah and Gederothaim; Jos 15:36 5723

ADJACENT
a to the holy allotment and the Ezk 45:7
413, 6440

ADJUDICATES
And ensnare him who **a** at the gate, Is 29:21 3198

ADJURATION
he hears a public **a** *to testify* when Lv 5:1 423

ADJURE
"How many times must I **a** you to 1Ki 22:16 7650
"How many times must I **a** you to 2Ch 18:15 7650
"I **a** you, O daughters of SS 2:7 7650
"I **a** you, O daughters of SS 3:5 7650
"I **a** you, O daughters of SS 5:8 7650
beloved, That thus you **a** us?" SS 5:9 7650
"I **a** You by the living God, that Mt 26:63 *1844*
"I **a** you by Jesus whom Paul Ac 19:13 *3726*
I **a** you by the Lord to have this 1Th 5:27 *1775a*

ADLAI
and Shaphat the son of **A** had 1Ch 27:29 5724

ADMAH
and Gomorrah and **A** and Zeboiim, Gn 10:19 126
of Gomorrah, Shinab king of **A**, Gn 14:2 126
king of Gomorrah and the king of **A** Gn 14:8 126
Sodom and Gomorrah, **A** and Zeboiim, Dt 29:23 126
How can I make you like **A**? Hos 11:8 126

ADMATHA
Carshena, Shethar, **A**, Es 1:14 133

ADMIN
son of Amminadab, the son of **A**, Lk 3:33 *96a*

ADMINISTER
of God was in him to **a** justice. 1Ki 3:28 6213a
"**A** justice every morning; Jer 21:12 1777

ADMINISTERED
and David **a** justice and 2Sa 8:15 6213a
and he **a** justice and righteousness 1Ch 18:14
1961, 6213a
which is being **a** by us for the 2Co 8:19 *1247*

ADMINISTRATION
the **a** of the province of Babylon, Da 2:49 5673
the **a** of the province of Babylon, Da 3:12 5673
us in our **a** of this generous gift; 2Co 8:20 *1247*
with a view to an **a** suitable to Eph 1:10 *3622*
to light what is the **a** of the mystery Eph 3:9 *3622*
the **a** of God which is by faith. 1Tm 1:4 *3622*

ADMINISTRATIONS
then gifts of healings, helps, **a**, 1Co 12:28 *2941*

ADMINISTRATORS
And I will make peace your **a** And Is 60:17 6486

ADMIT
"But this I **a** to you, that Ac 24:14 *3670*

ADMONISH
O My people, and I will **a** you; Ps 81:8 5749b
How shall I **a** you? La 2:13 5749b
cease to **a** each one with tears. Ac 20:31 *3560*
over, Paul *began* to **a** them, Ac 27:9 *3867*
and able also to **a** one another. Ro 15:14 *3560*
to **a** you as my beloved children. 1Co 4:14 *3560*
urge you, brethren, **a** the unruly, 1Th 5:14 *3560*
an enemy, but **a** him as a brother. 2Th 3:15 *3560*

ADMONISHED
killed Your prophets who had **a** them Ne 9:26 5749b
And **a** them in order to turn them Ne 9:29 5749b
And **a** them by Your Spirit through Ne 9:30 5749b
with which You have **a** them. Ne 9:34 5749b
So I **a** *them* on the day they sold Ne 13:15 5749b
"Behold you have **a** many, And you Jb 4:3 3256
that all women may be **a** and not Ezk 23:48 3256
angel of the LORD **a** Joshua, Zch 3:6 5749b

ADMONISHING
a every man and teaching every man Col 1:28 *3560*
with all wisdom teaching and **a** one Col 3:16 *3560*

ADMONITIONS
Your commandments and Your **a** Ne 9:34 5715

ADNA
A, Chelal, Benaiah, Maaseiah, Ezr 10:30 5733
of Harim, **A**; of Meraioth, Helkai; Ne 12:15 5733

ADNAH
A, Jozabad, Jediael, Michael, 1Ch 12:20 5734a
of thousands, **A** *was* the commander, 2Ch 17:14 5734a

ADONI-BEZEK
They found **A** in Bezek and Jg 1:5 137
But **A** fled; and they pursued him Jg 1:6 137
A said, "Seventy kings Jg 1:7 137

ADONIJAH
the fourth, **A** the son of Haggith; 2Sa 3:4 138
Now **A** the son of Haggith exalted 1Ki 1:5 138
and following **A** they helped him. 1Ki 1:7 138
to David, were not with **A**. 1Ki 1:8 138
A sacrificed sheep and oxen 1Ki 1:9 138
"Have you not heard that **A** the 1Ki 1:11 138
Why then has **A** become king?' 1Ki 1:13 138
"Now, behold, **A** is king; 1Ki 1:18 138
'**A** shall be king after me, and he 1Ki 1:24 138
'*Long* live King **A**!' 1Ki 1:25 138
Now **A** and all the guests who 1Ki 1:41 138
the priest came. Then **A** said, 1Ki 1:42 138
Jonathan replied to **A**, 1Ki 1:43 138
the guests of **A** were terrified; 1Ki 1:49 138
And **A** was afraid of Solomon, and 1Ki 1:50 138
A is afraid of King Solomon, 1Ki 1:51 138
Now **A** the son of Haggith came to 1Ki 2:13 138
Solomon to speak to him for **A**. 1Ki 2:19 138
to **A** your brother as a wife." 1Ki 2:21 138
Abishag the Shunammite for **A**? 1Ki 2:22 138
if **A** has not spoken this word 1Ki 2:23 138
A shall be put to death today." 1Ki 2:24 138
to Joab, for Joab had followed **A**, 1Ki 2:28 138
fourth *was* **A** the son of Haggith; 1Ch 3:2 138
Shemiramoth, Jehonathan, **A**, 2Ch 17:8 138
A, Bigvai, Adin, Ne 10:16 138

ADONIKAM
the sons of **A**, 666; Ezr 2:13 140
and of the sons of **A**, Ezr 8:13 140
the sons of **A**, 667; Ne 7:18 140

ADONIRAM
and **A** the son of Abda *was* over the 1Ki 4:6 141
A *was* over the forced laborers. 1Ki 5:14 141

ADONI-ZEDEK
Now it came about when **A** king of Jos 10:1 139
A king of Jerusalem sent *word* Jos 10:3 139

ADOPT
that you will **a** no other view; Ga 5:10 *5426*

ADOPTED
and **a** other gods and worshiped 1Ki 9:9 2388
and they **a** other gods and 2Ch 7:22 2388

ADOPTION
of **a** as sons by which we cry out, Ro 8:15 *5206*
waiting eagerly for *our* **a** as sons, Ro 8:23 *5206*
to whom belongs the **a** as sons, Ro 9:4 *5206*
we might receive the **a** as sons. Ga 4:5 *5206*
He predestined us to **a** as sons Eph 1:5 *5206*

ADORAIM
A, Lachish, Azekah, 2Ch 11:9 115

ADORAM
and **A** was over the forced labor, 2Sa 20:24 151
Then King Rehoboam sent **A**, 1Ki 12:18 151

ADORN
to **a** the house of the LORD which Ezr 7:27 6286
"**A** yourself with eminence and Jb 40:10 5710b
offer sacrifices to them And **a** herself Hos 2:13 5710b
a the monuments of the righteous, Mt 23:29 *2885*
I want women to **a** themselves with 1Tm 2:9 *2885*
will **a** the doctrine of God our Savior Ti 2:10 *2885*
in God, used to **a** themselves, 1Pe 3:5 *2885*

ADORNED
painted her eyes and **a** her head and 2Ki 9:30 3190
he **a** the house with precious 2Ch 3:6 6823
"I **a** you with ornaments, put Ezk 16:11 5710b
you were **a** with gold and silver, Ezk 16:13 5710b
that it was **a** with beautiful Lk 21:5 *2885*
and **a** with gold and precious Rv 17:4 *5558*
and **a** with gold and precious Rv 18:16 *5558*
as a bride **a** for her husband. Rv 21:2 *2885*
stones of the city wall were **a** Rv 21:19 *2885*

ADORNMENT
to your soul And **a** to your neck. Pr 3:22 2580
the **a** of the survivors of Israel. Is 4:2 8597
Your **a** must not be *merely* external 1Pe 3:3 *2889*

ADORNS
a bride **a** herself with her jewels. Is 61:10 5710b

ADRAMMELECH
burned their children in the fire to **A** 2Ki 17:31 152
that **A** and Sharezer killed him 2Ki 19:37 152
that **A** and Sharezer his sons Is 37:38 152

ADRAMYTTIAN
And embarking in an **A** ship, Ac 27:2 *98*

ADRIATIC
being driven about in the **A** Sea, Ac 27:27 *99*

ADRIEL
to **A** the Meholathite for a wife. 1Sa 18:19 5741
whom she had borne to **A** the son of 2Sa 21:8 5741

ADULLAM
the king of **A**, one; Jos 12:15 5725
Jarmuth and **A**, Socoh and Azekah, Jos 15:35 5725
and escaped to the cave of **A**; 1Sa 22:1 5725
the harvest time to the cave of **A**, 2Sa 23:13 5725
rock to David, into the cave of **A**, 1Ch 11:15 5725
Beth-zur, Soco, **A**, 2Ch 11:7 5725
Zanoah, **A**, and their villages, Ne 11:30 5725
The glory of Israel will enter **A**. Mi 1:15 5725

ADULLAMITE
brothers and visited a certain **A**, Gn 38:1 5726
he and his friend Hirah the **A**. Gn 38:12 5726
sent the young goat by his friend the **A**, Gn 38:20 5726

ADULTERATING
craftiness or **a** the word of God, 2Co 4:2 *1389*

ADULTERER
the **a** and the adulteress shall Lv 20:10 5003
of the **a** waits for the twilight, Jb 24:15 5003
of an **a** and a prostitute. Is 57:3 5003

ADULTERERS
him, And you associate with **a**. Ps 50:18 5003
For all of them are **a**, Jer 9:2 5003
For the land is full of **a**; Jer 23:10 5003
They are all **a**, Like an oven heated Hos 7:4 5003
against the sorcerers and against the **a** Mal 3:5 5003
swindlers, unjust, **a**, Lk 18:11 *3432*
fornicators, nor idolaters, nor **a**, 1Co 6:9 *3432*
fornicators and **a** God will judge. Heb 13:4 *3432*

ADULTERESS
a shall surely be put to death. Lv 20:10 5003
the **a** who flatters with her words; Pr 2:16 5237
For the lips of an **a** drip honey And Pr 5:3 2114a
my son, be exhilarated with an **a** And Pr 5:20 2114a
From the smooth tongue of the **a**. Pr 6:24 5237
an **a** hunts for the precious life. Pr 6:26 802, 376
That they may keep you from an **a**, Pr 7:5 802, 2114a
The mouth of an **a** is a deep pit; Pr 22:14 2114a
"You **a** wife, who takes strangers Ezk 16:32 5003
is loved by *her* husband, yet an **a**, Hos 3:1 5003
man, she shall be called an **a**; Ro 7:3 *3428*
the law, so that she is not an **a** though Ro 7:3 *3428*

ADULTERESSES
judge them with the judgment of **a** and Ezk 23:45 5003
are **a** and blood is on their hands. Ezk 23:45 5003
You **a**, do you not know that Jas 4:4 *3428*

ADULTERIES
for all the **a** of faithless Israel, Jer 3:8 5003
your **a** and your *lustful* neighings, Jer 13:27 5004
her who was worn out by **a**, Ezk 23:43 5004
come evil thoughts, murders, **a**, Mt 15:19 *3430*
fornications, thefts, murders, **a**, Mk 7:21 *3430*

ADULTEROUS
And an **a** woman is a narrow well. Pr 23:27 5237
for an **a** woman hold him in pledge. Pr 27:13 5237
This is the way of an **a** woman: Pr 30:20 5003
how I have been hurt by their **a** Ezk 6:9 2181
a generation craves for a sign; Mt 12:39 *3428*
a generation seeks after a sign; Mt 16:4 *3428*
in this **a** and sinful generation, Mk 8:38 *3428*

ADULTERY
"You shall not commit **a**. Ex 20:14 5003
commits **a** with another man's wife, Lv 20:10 5003
commits **a** with his friend's wife, Lv 20:10 5003
'You shall not commit **a**. Dt 5:18 5003
a with a woman is lacking sense; Pr 6:32 5003
committed **a** with stones and trees. Jer 3:9 5003
They committed **a** And trooped to Jer 5:7 5003
you steal, murder, and commit **a** and Jer 7:9 5003
of **a** and walking in falsehood; Jer 23:14 5003
a with their neighbors' wives and Jer 29:23 5003
commit **a** or shed blood are judged; Ezk 16:38 5003
"For they have committed **a**, Ezk 23:37 5003
Thus they have committed **a** with Ezk 23:37 5003
a with her when she is *thus?*' Ezk 23:43 2181
her **a** from between her breasts, Hos 2:2 5005
murder, stealing and **a**. Hos 4:2 5003
harlot And your brides commit **a**. Hos 4:13 5003
Or your brides when they commit **a**, Hos 4:14 5003
'YOU SHALL NOT COMMIT **A**' Mt 5:27 *3431*
a with her in his heart. Mt 5:28 *3431*
of unchastity, makes her commit **a**; Mt 5:32 *3431*
a divorced woman commits **a**. Mt 5:32 *3429*
marries another woman commits **a**." Mt 19:9 *3429*
YOU SHALL NOT COMMIT **A**; YOU SHALL Mt 19:18 *3431*
woman commits **a** against her; Mk 10:11 *3429*
man, she is committing **a**." Mk 10:12 *3429*
'DO NOT MURDER, DO NOT COMMIT **A**, Mk 10:19 *3431*
and marries another commits **a**, Lk 16:18 *3431*
divorced from a husband commits **a**. Lk 16:18 *3431*
'DO NOT COMMIT **A**, DO NOT MURDER, Lk 18:20 *3431*
brought a woman caught in **a**, Jn 8:3 *3430*
this woman has been caught in **a**, Jn 8:4 *3431*
say that one should not commit **a**, Ro 2:22 *3431*
commit adultery, do you commit **a**? Ro 2:22 *3431*
"YOU SHALL NOT COMMIT **A**, Ro 13:9 *3431*
"DO NOT COMMIT **A**," Jas 2:11 *3431*
Now if you do not commit **a**, Jas 2:11 *3431*
a that never cease from sin, 2Pe 2:14 *3428*
and those who commit **a** with her Rv 2:22 *3431*

ADUMMIM
which is opposite the ascent of **A**, Jos 15:7 131
which is opposite the ascent of **A**, Jos 18:17 131

ADVANCE
"Behold, I have told you in **a**. Mt 24:25 *4275b*
I have told you everything in **a**. Mk 13:23 *4275b*
and though now absent I say in **a** 2Co 13:2 *4302*
we *kept* telling you in **a** that we 1Th 3:4 *4302*

ADVANCED
and Sarah were old, **a** in age; Gn 18:11 935
Now Abraham was old, **a** in age; Gn 24:1 935
Now Joshua was old *and* **a** in years Jos 13:1 935
"You are old *and* **a** in years, and Jos 13:1 935
and Joshua was old, **a** in years, Jos 23:1 935
"I am old, **a** in years. Jos 23:2 935
of Saul, **a** *in years* among men. 1Sa 17:12 935
Now King David was old, **a** in age; 1Ki 1:1 935
and **a** him and established his Es 3:1 5375
Mordecai to which the king **a** him, Es 10:2 1431
beautiful and **a** to royalty. Ezk 16:13 6743b
and they were both **a** in years. Lk 1:7 *4260*
man and my wife is **a** in years." Lk 1:18 *4260*
She was **a** in years and had Lk 2:36 *4260*

ADVANCING
and I was **a** in Judaism beyond many Ga 1:14 *4298*

ADVANTAGE
'What **a** will it be to You? Jb 35:3 5532a
of the diligent *lead* surely to **a**, Pr 21:5 4195
What **a** does man have in all his Ec 1:3 3504
there is no **a** for man over beast, Ec 3:19 4195
the field is an **a** to the land. Ec 5:9 3504
So what is the **a** to their owners Ec 5:11 3788
a to him who toils for the wind? Ec 5:16 3504
For what **a** does the wise man have Ec 6:8 3148
What **a** does the poor man have, Ec 6:8
What *then* is the **a** to a man? Ec 6:11 3148
And an **a** to those who see the sun. Ec 7:11 3148
But the **a** of knowledge is that Ec 7:12 3504
has the **a** of giving success. Ec 10:10 3504
it is to your **a** that I go away; Jn 16:7 *4851a*
he who took shrewd **a** of our race and Ac 7:19 *2686*
Then what **a** has the Jew? Ro 3:1 *4053*
that no **a** would be taken of us by Satan 2Co 2:11 *4122*
no one, we took **a** of no one. 2Co 7:2 *4122*
matter, for this is to your **a**, 2Co 8:10 *4851a*
devours you, anyone takes **a** of you, 2Co 11:20
Certainly I have not taken **a** of 2Co 12:17 *4122*
Titus did not take any **a** of you, 2Co 12:18 *4122*
for the sake of *gaining an* **a**. Jude 1:16 *5622*

ADVERSARIES
and an adversary to your **a**. Ex 23:22 6887c
devour the nations *who are* his **a**, Nu 24:8 6862c
That their **a** would misjudge, Dt 32:27 6862c
I will render vengeance on My **a**, Dt 32:41 6862c
will render vengeance on His **a**, Dt 32:43 6862c
You be a help against his **a**." Dt 33:7 6862c
"Are you for us or for our **a**?" Jos 5:13 6862c
but if to betray me to my **a**, 1Ch 12:17 6862c
'Truly our **a** are cut off, And Jb 22:20 7009
O Lord, how my **a** have increased! Ps 3:1 6862c
become old because of all my **a**. Ps 6:7 6887c
Yourself against the rage of my **a**, Ps 7:6 6887c
strength Because of Your **a**, Ps 8:2 6887c
As for all his **a**, he snorts at Ps 10:5 6887c
my **a** will rejoice when I am shaken. Ps 13:4 6862c
my flesh, My **a** and my enemies, Ps 27:2 6862c
me over to the desire of my **a**, Ps 27:12 6862c
Because of all my **a**, Ps 31:11 6887c
of my bones, my **a** revile me, Ps 42:10 6887c
You we will push back our **a**; Ps 44:5 6862c
But You have saved us from our **a**, Ps 44:7 6862c
is He who will tread down our **a**. Ps 60:12 6862c
All my **a** are before You. Ps 69:19 6887c
Let those who are **a** of my soul be Ps 71:13 7853
Your **a** have roared in the midst Ps 74:4 6887c
not forget the voice of Your **a**, Ps 74:23 6887c
He drove His **a** backward; Ps 78:66 6862c
And turn My hand against their **a**. Ps 81:14 6862c
I shall crush his **a** before him, Ps 89:23 6862c
exalted the right hand of his **a**; Ps 89:42 6862c
And burns up His **a** round about. Ps 97:3 6862c
made them stronger than their **a**. Ps 105:24 6862c
The waters covered their **a**; Ps 106:11 6862c
is He who shall tread down our **a**. Ps 108:13 6862c
looks *with satisfaction* on his **a**. Ps 112:8 6862c
my **a** have forgotten Your words. Ps 119:139 6862c
Many are my persecutors and my **a**, Ps 119:157 6862c
And has rescued us from our **a**, Ps 136:24 6862c
"Ah, I will be relieved of My **a** And Is 1:24 6862c
raises against them **a** from Rezin And Is 9:11 6862c
so He will repay, Wrath to His **a**, Is 59:18 6862c
while, Our **a** have trodden *it* down. Is 63:18 6862c
To make Your name known to Your **a**, Is 64:2 6862c
And all your **a**, every one of them, Jer 30:16 6862c
And their **a** have said, Jer 50:7 6862c
Her **a** have become her masters, Her La 1:5 6862c
The **a** saw her, They mocked at her La 1:7 6862c
round about him should be his **a**; La 1:17 6862c
has exalted the might of your **a**. La 2:17 6862c
them into the hand of their **a**, Ezk 39:23 6862c
and its interpretation to your **a**! Da 4:19 6146
will be lifted up against your **a**, Mi 5:9 6862c
The LORD takes vengeance on His **a**, Na 1:2 6862c
to me, and there are many **a**. 1Co 16:9 *480*
A FIRE WHICH WILL CONSUME THE **A**. Heb 10:27 *5227*

ADVERSARY
and an **a** to your adversaries. Ex 23:22 6696b
against the **a** who attacks you, Nu 10:9 6862c
in the way as an **a** against him. Nu 22:22 7854
Behold, I have come out as an **a**, Nu 22:32 7854
from you and has become your **a**? 1Sa 28:16 6145
the battle he may become an **a** to us. 1Sa 29:4 7854
you should this day be an **a** to me? 2Sa 19:22 7854
there is neither **a** nor misfortune. 1Ki 5:4 7854
LORD raised up an **a** to Solomon, 1Ki 11:14 7854
also raised up *another* **a** to him, 1Ki 11:23 7854
So he was an **a** to Israel all the 1Ki 11:25 7854
Agagite, the **a** of all the Jews, Es 9:24 6887c
'Deliver me from the hand of the **a**,' Jb 6:23 6862c
My **a** glares at me. Jb 16:9 6862c
indictment which my **a** has written, Jb 31:35 7379
him who without cause was my **a**, Ps 7:4 6887c
cause us to turn back from the **a**; Ps 44:10 6862c
O give us help against the **a**, Ps 60:11 6862c
long, O God, will the **a** revile, Ps 74:10 6862c
when He redeemed them from the **a**, Ps 78:42 6862c
His glory into the hand of the **a**. Ps 78:61 6862c
redeemed from the hand of the **a** Ps 107:2 6862c
Oh give us help against the **a**, Ps 108:12 6862c
away As captives before the **a**. La 1:5 6862c
fell into the hand of the **a** And La 1:7 6862c
The **a** has stretched out his hand La 1:10 6862c
He has set His right hand like an **a** La 2:4 6862c
That the **a** and the enemy Could La 4:12 6862c
Your **a**, the devil, prowls around 1Pe 5:8 *476*

ADVERSITIES
him and comforted him for all the **a** Jb 42:11 7463a

ADVERSITY
of **a** in the hearing of the LORD; Nu 11:1 7451b
a from all the tribes of Israel, Dt 29:21 7463a
and prosperity, and death and **a**; Dt 30:15 7451b
brought all this **a** on them.' " 1Ki 9:9 7463a
brought all this **a** on them.' " 2Ch 7:22 7463a
good from God and not accept **a**?" Jb 2:10 7451b
all this **a** that had come upon him, Jb 2:11 7463a
generations I will not be in **a**." Ps 10:6 7451b
Why should I fear in days of **a**, Ps 49:5 7451b
him relief from the days of **a**, Ps 94:13 7451b
A wicked messenger falls into **a**, Pr 13:17 7451b
A pursues sinners, But the Pr 13:21 7463a
And a brother is born for **a**. Pr 17:17 7463a
But in the day of **a** consider—God Ec 7:14 7463a

ADVICE
give your **a** and counsel here." Jg 20:7 1697
said to Ahithophel, "Give your **a**. 2Sa 16:20 6098
The **a** of Ahithophel, which he 2Sa 16:23 6098
so was all the **a** of Ahithophel 2Sa 16:23 6098
"This time the **a** that Ahithophel 2Sa 17:7 6098
a first to bring back our king?" 2Sa 19:43 1697
'They will surely ask **a** at Abel,' 2Sa 20:18
for he forsook the **a** of the elders 1Ki 12:13 6098
to the **a** of the young men, 1Ki 12:14 6098
to the **a** of the young men, 2Ch 10:14 6098
And the **a** pleased Haman, so he had Es 5:14 1697
a of the cunning is quickly thwarted. Jb 5:13 6098
"Give *us* **a**, make a decision; Is 16:3 6098
The **a** of Pharaoh's wisest advisers Is 19:11 6098
Besides, if I give you **a**, Jer 38:15 3289
and give evil **a** in this city, Ezk 11:2 6098
king, may my **a** be pleasing to you: Da 4:27 4431
They took his **a**; Ac 5:40 *3982*
you ought to have followed my **a** Ac 27:21 *3980*

ADVISE
and I will **a** you what this people Nu 24:14 3289
I **a** you to buy from Me gold Rv 3:18 *4823*

ADVISED
who was in charge of the women, **a**. Es 2:15 559
Now Caiaphas was the one who had **a** Jn 18:14 *4823*

ADVISER
from Gerar with his **a** Ahuzzath and Gn 26:26 4828

ADVISERS
a who were found in the city; **2Ki 25:19** 582, 7200
wisest a has become stupid. **Is 19:11** 3289
a who were found in the city, **Jer 52:25** 582, 7200

ADVOCATE
is in heaven, And my a is on high. **Jb 16:19** 7717
men who forbid marriage *and* a **1Tm 4:3**
we have an A with the Father, **1Jn 2:1** *3875*

ADVOCATES
If anyone a a different doctrine and **1Tm 6:3** *2085*

AENEAS
he found a man named A, **Ac 9:33** *132*
"A, Jesus Christ heals you; **Ac 9:34** *132*

AENON
was baptizing in A near Salim, **Jn 3:23** *137*

AFAR
bring a nation against you from a, **Dt 28:49** 7350
Hence his fame spread a, **2Ch 26:15** 5704, 7350
joy of Jerusalem was heard from a. **Ne 12:43** 7350
"I will fetch my knowledge from a, **Jb 36:3** 7350
Man beholds from a. **Jb 36:25** 7350
And he scents the battle from a, **Jb 39:25** 7350
His eyes see *it* from a. **Jb 39:29** 7350
Why do You stand a off, **Ps 10:1** 7350
And my kinsmen stand a off. **Ps 38:11** 7350
But the haughty He knows from a. **Ps 138:6** 4801
You understand my thought from a. **Ps 139:2** 7350
She brings her food from a. **Pr 31:14** 4801
which will come from a? **Is 10:3** 4801
Bring My sons from a And **Is 43:6** 7350
pay attention, you peoples from a. **Is 49:1** 7350
"Behold, these will come from a; **Is 49:12** 7350
Your sons will come from a, **Is 60:4** 7350
first, To bring your sons from a, **Is 60:9** 7350
a nation against you from a, **Jer 5:15** 4801
behold, I will save you from a And **Jer 30:10** 7350
The LORD appeared to him from a, **Jer 31:3** 7350
declare in the coastlands a off, **Jer 31:10** 4801
I am going to save you from a, **Jer 46:27** 7350
Remember the LORD from a, **Jer 51:50** 7350
even sent for men who come from a, **Ezk 23:40** 4801
Their horsemen come from a; **Hab 1:8** 7350

AFFAIR
deceived you in the a of Peor and **Nu 25:18** 1697
of Peor and in the a of Cozbi, **Nu 25:18** 1697
nothing at all of this whole a." **1Sa 22:15** 1697

AFFAIRS
"Why do you still speak of your a? **2Sa 19:29** 1697
a of Israel west of the Jordan, **1Ch 26:30** 6486
all the a of God and of the king. **1Ch 26:32** 1697
the king in all the a of the divisions **1Ch 27:1** 1697
Daniel in regard to government a; **Da 6:4** 4437
As to all my a, Tychicus, *our* **Col 4:7**
himself in the a of everyday life, **2Tm 2:4** *4230*

AFFECTED
gift and not a by covetousness. **2Co 9:5** *5613*

AFFECTION
the LORD set His a to love them, **Dt 10:15** 2836a
His a abounds all the more **2Co 7:15** *4698*
all with the a of Christ Jesus. **Php 1:8** *4698*
Spirit, if any a and compassion, **Php 2:1** *4698*
Having so fond an a for you, **1Th 2:8** *3655b*

AFFECTIONS
you are restrained in your own a. **2Co 6:12** *4698*

AFFIRM
I a, brethren, by the boasting in **1Co 15:31** *3513*
and a together with the Lord, **Eph 4:17** *3143*

AFFLICT
them to a them with hard labor. **Ex 1:11** 6031a
shall not a any widow or orphan. **Ex 22:22** 6031a
"If you a him at all, *and if* he **Ex 22:23** 6031a
a Asshur and will afflict Eber; **Nu 24:24** 6031a
afflict Asshur and will a Eber; **Nu 24:24** 6031a
him that we may bind him to a him. **Jg 16:5** 6031a
how you may be bound to a you." **Jg 16:6** 6031a
Then she began to a him, **Jg 16:19** 6031a
a them any more as formerly, **2Sa 7:10** 6031a
their sin when You a them, **1Ki 8:35** 6031a
'Thus I will a the descendants of **1Ki 11:39** 6031a
their sin when You a them; **2Ch 6:26** 6031a
Nor the son of wickedness a him. **Ps 89:22** 6031a
O LORD, And a Your heritage. **Ps 94:5** 6031a
destroy all those who a my soul, **Ps 143:12** 6887c
Therefore the Lord will a the **Is 3:17** 8197c
silent and a us beyond measure? **Is 64:12** 6031a
For He does not a willingly Or **La 3:33** 6031a
"And they will a you from the **Am 6:14** 3905
you, I will a you no longer. **Na 1:12** 6031a
with affliction those who a you, **2Th 1:6** *2346*

AFFLICTED
But the more they a them, **Ex 1:12** 6031a
treated us harshly and a us, **Dt 26:6** 6031a
with which the LORD has a it, **Dt 29:22** 2470a
of those who oppressed and a them. **Jg 2:18** 1766
They a and crushed the sons of **Jg 10:8** 7492
for eighteen years they a all **Jg 10:8**
me and the Almighty has a me?" **Ru 1:21** 7489a
"And You save an a people; **2Sa 22:28** 6041
and because you were a in **1Ki 2:26** 6031a
with which my father was a." **1Ki 2:26** 6031a
the descendants of Israel and a them **2Ki 17:20** 6031a
for many disturbances a all the **2Ch 15:5** 5921
Assyria came against him and a him **2Ch 28:20** 6887a
has loosed His bowstring and a me, **Jb 30:11** 6031a
He might hear the cry of the a **Jb 34:28** 6041
alive, But gives justice to the a. **Jb 36:6** 6041
the a in their affliction, **Jb 36:15** 6041
does not forget the cry of the a. **Ps 9:12** 6035
the hope of the a perish forever. **Ps 9:18** 6041
the wicked hotly pursue the a; **Ps 10:2** 6041
He lurks to catch the a; **Ps 10:9** 6041
He catches the a when he draws him **Ps 10:9** 6041
Do not forget the a. **Ps 10:12** 6035
of the devastation of the a, **Ps 12:5** 6041
put to shame the counsel of the a, **Ps 14:6** 6041
For You save an a people **Ps 18:27** 6041
abhorred the affliction of the a; **Ps 22:24** 6041
The a will eat and be satisfied; **Ps 22:26** 6035
to me, For I am lonely and a. **Ps 25:16** 6041
Who delivers the a from him who is **Ps 35:10** 6041
And the a and the needy from him **Ps 35:10** 6041
To cast down the a and the needy, **Ps 37:14** 6041
Since I am a and needy, Let the **Ps 40:17** 6041
You a the peoples, Then You spread **Ps 44:2** 7489a
But I am a and in pain; **Ps 69:29** 6041
But I am a and needy; **Ps 70:5** 6041
And Your a with justice. **Ps 72:2** 6041
he vindicate the a of the people, **Ps 72:4** 6041
he cries for help, The a also, **Ps 72:12** 6041
the life of Your a forever. **Ps 74:19** 6041
the a and needy praise Your name. **Ps 74:21** 6041
Do justice to the a and destitute. **Ps 82:3** 6041
For I am a and needy. **Ps 86:1** 6041
You have a me with all Your waves. **Ps 88:7** 6031a
I was a and about to die from my **Ps 88:15** 6041
to the days You have a us, **Ps 90:15** 6031a
They a his feet with fetters, He **Ps 105:18** 6031a
of their iniquities, were a. **Ps 107:17** 6031a
persecuted the a and needy man, **Ps 109:16** 6041
For I am a and needy, And my heart **Ps 109:22** 6041
"I am greatly a." **Ps 116:10** 6031a
Before I was a I went astray, But **Ps 119:67** 6031a
It is good for me that I was a, **Ps 119:71** 6031a
in faithfulness You have a me. **Ps 119:75** 6031a
I am exceedingly a; **Ps 119:107** 6031a
will maintain the cause of the a And **Ps 140:12** 6031a
The LORD supports the a; **Ps 147:6** 6035
the a ones with salvation. **Ps 149:4** 6035
Yet He gives grace to the a. **Pr 3:34** 6035
All the days of the a are bad, **Pr 15:15** 6041
poor, Or crush the a at the gate; **Pr 22:22** 6041
To devour the a from the earth And **Pr 30:14** 6041
pervert the rights of all the a. **Pr 31:5** 1121, 6040a
the rights of the a and needy. **Pr 31:9** 6041
to the sons of men to be a with. **Ec 1:13** 6030b
fairness for the a of the earth; **Is 11:4** 6035
And the a of His people will seek **Is 14:32** 6041
and my a of the threshing floor! **Is 21:10** 1121
trample it, The feet of the a, **Is 26:6** 6041
The a also will increase their **Is 29:19** 6035
To destroy *the* a with slander, **Is 32:7** 6041
"The a and needy are seeking **Is 41:17** 6041
And will have compassion on His a. **Is 49:13** 6041
please hear this, you a, **Is 51:21** 6041
stricken, Smitten of God, and a. **Is 53:4** 6031a
He was oppressed and He was a, **Is 53:7** 6031a
"O a one, storm-tossed, *and* not **Is 54:11** 6041
And satisfy the desire of the a, **Is 58:10** 6031a
who a you will come bowing to you, **Is 60:14** 6031a
me To bring good news to the a; **Is 61:1** 6035
In all their affliction He was a, **Is 63:9** 6862b
pled the cause of the a and needy; **Jer 22:16** 6041
are groaning, Her virgins are a, **La 1:4** 3013
Even those whom I have a. **Mi 4:6** 7489a
Though I have a you, I will **Na 1:12** 6031a
wander like sheep, They are a, **Zch 10:2** 6031a
hence the a of the flock. **Zch 11:7** 6041
and thus the a of the flock who **Zch 11:11** 6041
disease with which he was a.] **Jn 5:4** *2722*
sick or a with unclean spirits, **Ac 5:16** *3791*
lying *in bed* a with *recurrent* fever **Ac 28:8** *4912*
But if we are a, it is for your **2Co 1:6** *2346*
we are a in every way, but not **2Co 4:8** *2346*
rest, but we were a on every side: **2Co 7:5** *2346*
and *to give* relief to you who are a **2Th 1:7** *2346*
in goatskins, being destitute, a, **Heb 11:37** *2346*

AFFLICTION
the LORD has given heed to your a. **Gn 16:11** 6040a
"Because the LORD has seen my a; **Gn 29:32** 6040a
my a and the toil of my hands, **Gn 31:42** 6040a
me fruitful in the land of my a." **Gn 41:52** 6040a
a of My people who are in Egypt, **Ex 3:7** 6040a
I will bring you up out of the a **Ex 3:17** 6040a
and that He had seen their a, **Ex 4:31** 6040a
unleavened bread, the bread of a **Dt 16:3** 6040a
LORD heard our voice and saw our a **Dt 26:7** 6040a
look on the a of Your maidservant **1Sa 1:11** 6040a
LORD will look on my a and return **2Sa 16:12** 6040a
knowing the a of his own heart, **1Ki 8:38** 5061
For the LORD saw the a of Israel, **2Ki 14:26** 6040a
his own a and his own pain, **2Ch 6:29** 5061
saw the a of our fathers in Egypt, **Ne 9:9** 6040a
"For a does not come from the **Jb 5:6** 205
Days of a have seized me. **Jb 30:16** 6040a
Days of a confront me. **Jb 30:27** 6040a
And are caught in the cords of a, **Jb 36:8** 6040a
delivers the afflicted in their a, **Jb 36:15** 6040a
For you have preferred this to a. **Jb 36:21** 6040a
my a from those who hate me, **Ps 9:13** 6040a
abhorred the a of the afflicted; **Ps 22:24** 6039
Look upon my a and my trouble, And **Ps 25:18** 6040a
Because You have seen my a; **Ps 31:7** 6040a
forget our a and our oppression? **Ps 44:24** 6040a
eye has wasted away because of a; **Ps 88:9** 6040a
securely on high away from a, **Ps 107:41** 6040a
This is my comfort in my a, **Ps 119:50** 6040a
I would have perished in my a. **Ps 119:92** 6040a
Look upon my a and rescue me, For **Ps 119:153** 6040a
LORD, on David's behalf, All his a; **Ps 132:1** 6031a
This is vanity and a severe a. **Ec 6:2** 2483
tested you in the furnace of a. **Is 48:10** 6040a
In all their a He was afflicted, **Is 63:9** 6869a
Judah has gone into exile under a And **La 1:3** 6040a
In the days of her a and **La 1:7** 6040a
"See, O LORD, my a, For the enemy **La 1:9** 6040a
I am the man who has seen a **La 3:1** 6040a
Remember my a and my wandering, **La 3:19** 6040a
a they will earnestly seek Me. **Hos 5:15** 6862b
and when a or persecution arises **Mt 13:21** *2347*
when a or persecution arises **Mk 4:17** *2347*
body that she was healed of her a. **Mk 5:29** *3148*
peace and be healed of your a." **Mk 5:34** *3148*
and Canaan, and great a *with it,* **Ac 7:11** *2347*
who comforts us in all our a so **2Co 1:4** *2347*
comfort those who are in any a with **2Co 1:4** *2347*
of our a which came *to us* in Asia, **2Co 1:8** *2347*
For out of much a and anguish of **2Co 2:4** *2347*
light a is producing for us an **2Co 4:17** *2347*
overflowing with joy in all our a. **2Co 7:4** *2347*
that in a great ordeal of a their **2Co 8:2** *2347*
the ease of others *and* for your a, **2Co 8:13** *2347*
well to share *with me* in my a. **Php 4:14** *2347*
that we were going to suffer a; **1Th 3:4** *2346*
in all our distress and a we were **1Th 3:7** *2347*
with a those who afflict you, **2Th 1:6** *2347*

AFFLICTIONS
Many are the a of the righteous, **Ps 34:19** 7463a
those who had a pressed around Him **Mk 3:10** *3148*
diseases and a and evil spirits; **Lk 7:21** *3148*
and rescued him from all his a, **Ac 7:10** *2347*
saying that bonds and a await me. **Ac 20:23** *2347*
of God, in much endurance, in a, **2Co 6:4** *2347*
what is lacking in Christ's a. **Col 1:24** *2347*
one would be disturbed by these a; **1Th 3:3** *2347*
and a which you endure. **2Th 1:4** *2347*

AFFORD
'But if he cannot a a lamb, **Lv 5:7** 5060, 3027
'But if she cannot a a lamb, **Lv 12:8** 4672, 3027
"*He shall offer* what he can a, **Lv 14:31** 5381, 3027
in addition to what *else* he can a; **Nu 6:21** 5381, 3027

AFIRE
a torrent of brimstone, sets it a. **Is 30:33** 1197a

AFLAME
Scorners set a city a, **Pr 29:8** 6315
sets the thickets of the forest a And **Is 9:18** 3341
in astonishment, Their faces a. **Is 13:8** 3857
And it set him a all around, Yet **Is 42:25** 3857
is set a by such a small fire! **Jas 3:5** *381*

AFORESAID
the a before the LORD at the doorway **Lv 14:11**

AFRAID
and I was a because I was naked; **Gn 3:10** 3372a
"I did not laugh"; for she was a. **Gn 18:15** 3372a
for he was a to stay in Zoar; **Gn 19:30** 3372a
is my sister," for he was a to say, **Gn 26:7** 3372a
He was a and said, **Gn 28:17** 3372a
"Because I was a, for I thought **Gn 31:31** 3372a
was greatly a and distressed; **Gn 32:7** 3372a
"*I am* a that he too may die like **Gn 38:11**
"I am a that harm may befall him." **Gn 42:4**
Now the men were a, **Gn 43:18** 3372a
"Be at ease, do not be a. **Gn 43:23** 3372a
do not be a to go down to Egypt, **Gn 46:3** 3372a
"Do not be a, for am I in God's **Gn 50:19** 3372a
"So therefore, do not be a; **Gn 50:21** 3372a
Then Moses was a and said, **Ex 2:14** 3372a
face, for he was a to look at God. **Ex 3:6** 3372a
said to the people, "Do not be a; **Ex 20:20** 3372a
and they were a to come near him. **Ex 34:30** 3372a
not a To speak against My servant, **Nu 12:8** 3372a
and they will be a of you. **Dt 2:4** 3372a
for you were a because of the fire **Dt 5:5** 3372a
you shall not be a of them; **Dt 7:18** 3372a
all the peoples of whom you are a. **Dt 7:19** 3372a
"For I was a of the anger and hot **Dt 9:19** 3025
all Israel will hear and be a, **Dt 13:11** 3372a
all the people will hear and be a, **Dt 17:13** 3372a
you shall not be a of him. **Dt 18:22** 1481c
"The rest will hear and be a, **Dt 19:20** 3372a
than you, do not be a of them; **Dt 20:1** 3372a
Do not be a, or panic, or tremble **Dt 20:3** 3372a
man that is a and fainthearted? **Dt 20:8** 3372a
and they will be a of you. **Dt 28:10** 3372a
of Egypt of which you were a, **Dt 28:60** 3025
do not be a or tremble at them, **Dt 31:6** 3372a
"Do not be a because of them, for **Jos 11:6** 3372a
turn aside to me! Do not be a." **Jg 4:18** 3372a
because he was too a of his **Jg 6:27** 3372a
'Whoever is a and trembling, let **Jg 7:3** 3372a
"But if you are a to go down, go **Jg 7:10** 3372a
not draw his sword, for he was a, **Jg 8:20** 3372a
was a to tell the vision to Eli. **1Sa 3:15** 3372a
The Philistines were a, **1Sa 4:7** 3372a
"Do not be a, for you have given **1Sa 4:20** 3372a
they were a of the Philistines. **1Sa 7:7** 3372a

they were dismayed and greatly **a**.	**1Sa 17:11**	3372a
fled from him and were greatly **a**.	**1Sa 17:24**	3372a
Now Saul was **a** of David, for the	**1Sa 18:12**	3372a
Saul was even more **a** of David.	**1Sa 18:29**	3372a
"Stay with me; do not be **a**,	**1Sa 22:23**	3372a
"Behold, we are **a** here in Judah.	**1Sa 23:3**	3372a
"Do not be **a**, because the hand of	**1Sa 23:17**	3372a
he was **a** and his heart trembled	**1Sa 28:5**	3372a
The king said to her, "Do not be **a**;	**1Sa 28:13**	3372a
a because of the words of Samuel;	**1Sa 28:20**	3372a
would not, for he was greatly **a**.	**1Sa 31:4**	3372a
"How is it you were not **a** to	**2Sa 1:14**	3372a
a word, because he was **a** of him.	**2Sa 3:11**	3372a
David was **a** of the LORD that day;	**2Sa 6:9**	3372a
And the servants of David were **a**	**2Sa 12:18**	3372a
that the people have made me **a**;	**2Sa 14:15**	3372a
And Adonijah was **a** of Solomon,	**1Ki 1:50**	3372a
Adonijah is **a** of King Solomon,	**1Ki 1:51**	3372a
And he was **a** and arose and ran for	**1Ki 19:3**	3372a
do not be **a** of him."	**2Ki 1:15**	3372a
"Do not be **a** because of the words	**2Ki 19:6**	3372a
"Do not be **a** of the servants of	**2Ki 25:24**	3372a
for they were **a** of the Chaldeans.	**2Ki 25:26**	3372a
would not, for he was greatly **a**.	**1Ch 10:4**	3372a
David was **a** of God that day,	**1Ch 13:12**	3372a
Jehoshaphat was **a** and turned	**2Ch 20:3**	3372a
Then I was very much **a**.	**Ne 2:2**	3372a
"Do not be **a** of them;	**Ne 4:14**	3372a
be **a** of violence when it comes.	**Jb 5:21**	3372a
will not be **a** of wild beasts.	**Jb 5:22**	3372a
such, You see a terror and are **a**.	**Jb 6:21**	3372a
I am **a** of all my pains, I know	**Jb 9:28**	3025
be **a** of the sword for yourselves,	**Jb 19:29**	1481c
and **a** to tell you what I think.	**Jb 32:6**	3372a
I will not be **a** of ten thousands	**Ps 3:6**	3372a
not be **a** when a man becomes rich,	**Ps 49:16**	3372a
When I am **a**, I will put my trust	**Ps 56:3**	3372a
I shall not be **a**.	**Ps 56:4**	3372a
put my trust, I shall not be **a**.	**Ps 56:11**	3372a
not be **a** of the terror by night,	**Ps 91:5**	3372a
You, And I am **a** of Your judgments.	**Ps 119:120**	3372a
you lie down, you will not be **a**;	**Pr 3:24**	6342
Do not be **a** of sudden fear Nor of	**Pr 3:25**	3372a
a of the snow for her household,	**Pr 31:21**	3372a
so is the one who is **a** to swear.	**Ec 9:2**	3372a
men are **a** of a high place and of	**Ec 12:5**	3372a
I will trust and not be **a**;	**Is 12:2**	6342
"Do not be **a** because of the words	**Is 37:6**	3372a
coastlands have seen and are **a**;	**Is 41:5**	3372a
'Do not tremble and do not be **a**;	**Is 44:8**	3385a
that you are **a** of man who dies And	**Is 51:12**	3372a
"Do not be **a** of them, For I am	**Jer 1:8**	3372a
and they will not be **a** any longer,	**Jer 23:4**	3372a
heard *it*, and he was **a** and fled and	**Jer 26:21**	3372a
ease, And no one will make him **a**.	**Jer 30:10**	2729
heard all these words were not **a**,	**Jer 36:24**	6342
not be **a** of serving the Chaldeans;	**Jer 40:9**	3372a
for they were **a** of them, since	**Jer 41:18**	3372a
not be **a** of the king of Babylon,	**Jer 42:11**	3372a
do not be **a** of him,' declares the	**Jer 42:11**	3372a
which you are **a** of, will overtake	**Jer 42:16**	3372a
And you are not **a** at the report that	**Jer 51:46**	3372a
Do not be **a** of them or be dismayed	**Ezk 3:9**	3372a
And their kings are horribly **a**;	**Ezk 27:35**	8175c
their kings will be horribly **a** of you	**Ezk 32:10**	8175c
and no one will make *them* **a**.	**Ezk 34:28**	2729
land with no one to make *them* **a**.	**Ezk 39:26**	2729
"I am **a** of my lord the king, who	**Da 1:10**	3372a
"Do not be **a**, Daniel, for from	**Da 10:12**	3372a
"O man of high esteem, do not be **a**.	**Da 10:19**	3372a
Then the sailors became **a** and	**Jon 1:5**	3372a
tree, With no one to make *them* **a**,	**Mi 4:4**	2729
And they will be **a** before You.	**Mi 7:17**	3372a
"Do not be **a**, O Zion;	**Zph 3:16**	3372a
Ashkelon will see it and be **a**.	**Zch 9:5**	3372a
be **a** to take Mary as your wife;	**Mt 1:20**	*5399*
Herod, he was **a** to go there.	**Mt 2:22**	*5399*
He said to them, "Why are you **a**,	**Mt 8:26**	*1169*
"Take courage, it is I; do not be **a**."	**Mt 14:27**	*5399*
"Get up, and do not be **a**."	**Mt 17:7**	*5399*
'And I was **a**, and went away and	**Mt 25:25**	*5399*
said to the women, "Do not be **a**;	**Mt 28:5**	*5399*
Jesus said to them, "Do not be **a**;	**Mt 28:10**	*5399*
And He said to them, "Why are you **a**?	**Mk 4:40**	*1169*
much **a** and said to one another,	**Mk 4:41**	*5399*
"Do not be **a** *any longer*, only	**Mk 5:36**	*5399*
for Herod was **a** of John, knowing	**Mk 6:20**	*5399*
it is I, do not be **a**."	**Mk 6:50**	*5399*
and they were **a** to ask Him.	**Mk 9:32**	*5399*
for they were **a** of Him, for the	**Mk 11:18**	*5399*
were **a** of the people, for everyone	**Mk 11:32**	*5399*
to anyone, for they were **a**.	**Mk 16:8**	*5399*
"Do not be **a**, Zacharias, for your	**Lk 1:13**	*5399*
"Do not be **a**, Mary;	**Lk 1:30**	*5399*
angel said to them, "Do not be **a**;	**Lk 2:10**	*5399*
"Do not be **a** *any longer*	**Lk 8:50**	*5399*
were **a** as they entered the cloud.	**Lk 9:34**	*5399*
and they were **a** to ask Him about	**Lk 9:45**	*5399*
be **a** of those who kill the body and	**Lk 12:4**	*5399*
"Do not be **a**, little flock, for	**Lk 12:32**	*5399*
for I was **a** of you, because you	**Lk 19:21**	*5399*
for they were **a** of the people.	**Lk 22:2**	*5399*
said to them, "It is I; do not be **a**."	**Jn 6:20**	*5399*
because they were **a** of the Jews;	**Jn 9:22**	*5399*
this statement, he was *even* more **a**;	**Jn 19:8**	*5399*
(for they were **a** of the people,	**Ac 5:26**	*5399*
but they were all **a** of him,	**Ac 9:26**	*5399*
They were **a** when they heard	**Ac 16:38**	*5399*
"Do not be **a** *any longer*, but go	**Ac 18:9**	*5399*
and the commander also was **a** when	**Ac 22:29**	*5399*
the commander was **a** Paul would be	**Ac 23:10**	*5399*
'Do not be **a**, Paul;	**Ac 27:24**	*5399*
But if you do what is evil, be **a**;	**Ro 13:4**	*5399*
is with you without cause to be **a**,	**1Co 16:10**	*870*
But I am **a** that, as the serpent	**2Co 11:3**	*5399*
For I am **a** that perhaps when I	**2Co 12:20**	*5399*
I am **a** that when I come again my	**2Co 12:21**	*5399*
were not **a** of the king's edict.	**Heb 11:23**	*5399*
IS MY HELPER, I WILL NOT BE **A**.	**Heb 13:6**	*5399*
"Do not be **a**; I am the first and the	**Rv 1:17**	*5399*

AFRESH

to kindle **a** the gift of God which is in	**2Tm 1:6**	*329*

AFTER

earth bearing fruit **a** their kind	**Gn 1:11**	
plants yielding seed **a** their kind,	**Gn 1:12**	
with seed in them, **a** their kind;	**Gn 1:12**	
the waters swarmed **a** their kind,	**Gn 1:21**	
and every winged bird **a** its kind;	**Gn 1:21**	
living creatures **a** their kind:	**Gn 1:24**	
of the earth **a** their kind";	**Gn 1:24**	
beasts of the earth **a** their kind,	**Gn 1:25**	
kind, and the cattle **a** their kind,	**Gn 1:25**	
creeps on the ground **a** its kind;	**Gn 1:25**	
city Enoch, **a** the name of his son.	**Gn 4:17**	
Then the days of Adam **a** he became	**Gn 5:4**	310
a he became the father of Enosh,	**Gn 5:7**	310
a he became the father of Kenan,	**Gn 5:10**	310
a he became the father of Mahalalel,	**Gn 5:13**	310
a he became the father of Jared,	**Gn 5:16**	310
a he became the father of Enoch,	**Gn 5:19**	310
a he became the father of Methuselah,	**Gn 5:22**	310
a he became the father of Lamech,	**Gn 5:26**	310
a he became the father of Noah,	**Gn 5:30**	310
"Of the birds **a** their kind, and	**Gn 6:20**	
and of the animals **a** their kind,	**Gn 6:20**	
thing of the ground **a** its kind,	**Gn 6:20**	
"For **a** seven more days, I will	**Gn 7:4**	
It came about **a** the seven days,	**Gn 7:10**	
they and every beast **a** its kind,	**Gn 7:14**	
and all the cattle **a** their kind,	**Gn 7:14**	
creeps on the earth **a** its kind,	**Gn 7:14**	
kind, and every bird **a** its kind,	**Gn 7:14**	
and with your descendants **a** you;	**Gn 9:9**	310
and fifty years **a** the flood.	**Gn 9:28**	310
were born to them **a** the flood.	**Gn 10:1**	310
on the earth **a** the flood.	**Gn 10:32**	310
Arpachshad two years **a** the flood;	**Gn 11:10**	310
Shem lived five hundred years **a** he	**Gn 11:11**	310
a he became the father of Shelah,	**Gn 11:13**	310
a he became the father of Eber,	**Gn 11:15**	310
a he became the father of Peleg,	**Gn 11:17**	310
a he became the father of Reu,	**Gn 11:19**	310
a he became the father of Serug,	**Gn 11:21**	310
a he became the father of Nahor,	**Gn 11:23**	310
a he became the father of Terah,	**Gn 11:25**	310
a Lot had separated from him,	**Gn 13:14**	310
Then **a** his return from the defeat	**Gn 14:17**	310
A these things the word of the	**Gn 15:1**	310
A Abram had lived ten years in	**Gn 16:3**	4480
alive here **a** seeing Him?"	**Gn 16:13**	310
Me and you and your descendants **a**	**Gn 17:7**	310
you and to your descendants **a** you.	**Gn 17:7**	310
you and to your descendants **a** you,	**Gn 17:8**	310
you and your descendants **a** you	**Gn 17:9**	310
you and your descendants **a** you:	**Gn 17:10**	310
for his descendants **a** him.	**Gn 17:19**	310
a that you may go on, since you	**Gn 18:5**	310
"**A** I have become old, shall I	**Gn 18:12**	310
his household **a** him to keep the way	**Gn 18:19**	310
to us **a** the manner of the earth.	**Gn 19:31**	
Now it came about **a** these things,	**Gn 22:1**	310
Now it came about **a** these things,	**Gn 22:20**	310
A this, Abraham buried Sarah his	**Gn 23:19**	310
was comforted **a** his mother's death.	**Gn 24:67**	310
came about **a** the death of Abraham,	**Gn 25:11**	310
them up **a** the death of Abraham;	**Gn 26:18**	310
"**A** this manner you shall speak to	**Gn 32:19**	
land to your descendants **a** you."	**Gn 35:12**	
So Joseph went **a** his brothers and	**Gn 37:17**	
Now **a** a considerable time Shua's	**Gn 38:12**	
A all, I sent this young goat, but you	**Gn 38:23**	2009
It came about **a** these events	**Gn 39:7**	310
As she spoke to Joseph day **a** day,	**Gn 39:10**	
Then it came about **a** these things	**Gn 40:1**	310
cows came up **a** them from the Nile,	**Gn 41:3**	310
the east wind, sprouted up **a** them.	**Gn 41:6**	310
seven other cows came up **a** them,	**Gn 41:19**	310
the east wind, sprouted up **a** them;	**Gn 41:23**	310
came up **a** them are seven years,	**Gn 41:27**	310
and **a** them seven years of famine	**Gn 41:30**	310
Now it came about **a** these things	**Gn 48:1**	310
descendants **a** you for an everlasting	**Gn 48:4**	310
been born **a** them shall be yours;	**Gn 48:6**	310
A he had buried his father, Joseph	**Gn 50:14**	310
and **a** that he will let you go.	**Ex 3:20**	310
a the LORD had struck the Nile.	**Ex 7:25**	310
a that he will let you go from	**Ex 11:1**	310
you,' and **a** that I will go out."	**Ex 11:8**	310
money, **a** you have circumcised him,	**Ex 12:44**	
heart, and he will chase **a** them;	**Ex 14:4**	310
and he chased **a** the sons of Israel	**Ex 14:8**	310
Then the Egyptians chased **a** them	**Ex 14:9**	310
Egyptians were marching **a** them,	**Ex 14:10**	310
so that they will go in **a** them;	**Ex 14:17**	310
in **a** them into the midst of the sea.	**Ex 14:23**	310
that had gone into the sea **a** them;	**Ex 14:28**	310
and all the women went out **a** her	**Ex 15:20**	310
second month **a** their departure	**Ex 16:1**	
Zipporah, **a** he had sent her away,	**Ex 18:2**	310
In the third month **a** the sons of	**Ex 19:1**	
to turn aside **a** a multitude in order	**Ex 23:2**	310
make *them* **a** the pattern for them,	**Ex 25:40**	
him and to his descendants **a** him.	**Ex 28:43**	310
Aaron shall be for his sons **a** him,	**Ex 29:29**	310
and gaze **a** Moses until he entered	**Ex 33:8**	310
a he hears a public adjuration *to*	**Lv 5:1**	
A he had washed the entrails and	**Lv 8:21**	
and he stepped down **a** making the	**Lv 9:22**	
and **a** putting fire in them,	**Lv 10:1**	
a he has shown himself to the	**Lv 13:7**	310
in the skin **a** his cleansing,	**Lv 13:35**	310
'**A** the article with the mark has	**Lv 13:55**	310
has faded **a** it has been washed,	**Lv 13:56**	310
a he has torn out the stones and	**Lv 14:43**	310
and **a** it has been replastered,	**Lv 14:43**	310
a the house has been replastered,	**Lv 14:48**	310
Now the LORD spoke to Moses **a** the	**Lv 16:1**	310
those who play the harlot **a** him,	**Lv 20:5**	310
by playing the harlot **a** Molech.	**Lv 20:5**	310
to play the harlot **a** them,	**Lv 20:6**	310
on the day **a** the sabbath the	**Lv 23:11**	4283
from the day **a** the sabbath,	**Lv 23:15**	4283
to the day **a** the seventh sabbath;	**Lv 23:16**	4283
the number of years **a** the jubilee,	**Lv 25:15**	310
bequeath them to your sons **a** you,	**Lv 25:46**	310
right **a** he has been sold.	**Lv 25:48**	310
'If also **a** these things you do	**Lv 26:18**	5704
and will draw out a sword **a** you,	**Lv 26:33**	310
a the shekel of the sanctuary.	**Lv 27:3**	
his field **a** the jubilee,	**Lv 27:18**	310
be **a** the shekel of the sanctuary.	**Lv 27:25**	
in the second year **a** they had come	**Nu 1:1**	
a that the sons of Kohath shall	**Nu 4:15**	310
hands of the Nazirite **a** he has shaved	**Nu 6:19**	310
for the altar **a** it was anointed.	**Nu 7:88**	310
"Then **a** that the Levites may go	**Nu 8:15**	310
Then **a** that the Levites went in to	**Nu 8:22**	310
the second year **a** they had come out	**Nu 9:1**	
do them and not follow **a** your own	**Nu 15:39**	310
a which you played the harlot,	**Nu 15:39**	310
A Moses had stripped Aaron of his	**Nu 20:28**	
and he went **a** the man of Israel	**Nu 25:8**	310
for him and his descendants **a** him,	**Nu 25:13**	310
Then it came about **a** the plague,	**Nu 26:1**	310
'**A** this manner you shall present	**Nu 28:24**	
annuls them **a** he has heard them,	**Nu 30:15**	310
called it Nobah **a** his own name.	**Nu 32:42**	
on the next day **a** the Passover the	**Nu 33:3**	4480
in the fortieth year **a** the sons of	**Nu 33:38**	
But **a** the death of the high priest	**Nu 35:28**	310
a he had defeated Sihon the king	**Dt 1:4**	310
and their descendants **a** them.'	**Dt 1:8**	310
that is, Bashan, **a** his own name,	**Dt 3:14**	5921
He chose their descendants **a** them.	**Dt 4:37**	310
you and with your children **a** you,	**Dt 4:40**	310
and go **a** other gods and serve them	**Dt 8:19**	310
He chose their descendants **a** them,	**Dt 10:15**	310
well with you and your sons **a** you,	**Dt 12:25**	310
you and your sons **a** you forever,	**Dt 12:28**	310
a they are destroyed before you,	**Dt 12:30**	310
you do not inquire **a** their gods,	**Dt 12:30**	
'Let us go **a** other gods	**Dt 13:2**	310
the Feast of Booths seven days **a** you	**Dt 16:13**	
and **a** that you may go in to her	**Dt 21:13**	310
to go **a** other gods to serve them.	**Dt 28:14**	310
your sons who rise up **a** you and	**Dt 29:22**	4480, 310
how much more, then, **a** my death?	**Dt 31:27**	310
"For I know that **a** my death you	**Dt 31:29**	310
Now it came about **a** the death of	**Jos 1:1**	310
out from your place and go **a** it.	**Jos 3:3**	310
the way **a** they came out of Egypt.	**Jos 5:4**	
On the day **a** the Passover, on	**Jos 5:11**	4283
The manna ceased on the day **a**	**Jos 5:12**	4283
and the rear guard came **a** the ark,	**Jos 6:9**	310
guard came **a** the ark of the LORD,	**Jos 6:13**	310
and they burned them with fire **a**	**Jos 7:25**	
"They will come out **a** us	**Jos 8:6**	310
who had not gone out **a** Israel,	**Jos 8:17**	310
days **a** they had made a covenant	**Jos 9:16**	310
day like that before it or **a** it,	**Jos 10:14**	310
a the name of Dan their father.	**Jos 19:47**	
and between our generations **a** us,	**Jos 22:27**	310
Now it came about **a** many days,	**Jos 23:1**	310
you **a** He has done good to you."	**Jos 24:20**	310
It came about **a** these things	**Jos 24:29**	310
Now it came about **a** the death of	**Jg 1:1**	310
generation **a** them who did not know	**Jg 2:10**	310
for they played the harlot **a** other	**Jg 2:17**	310
handle also went in **a** the blade,	**Jg 3:22**	310
So they went down **a** him and seized	**Jg 3:28**	310
A him came Shamgar the son of Anath,	**Jg 3:31**	310
sight of the LORD, **a** Ehud died.	**Jg 4:1**	
Now **a** Abimelech died, Tola the son	**Jg 10:1**	310
A him, Jair the Gileadite arose	**Jg 10:3**	310
It came about **a** a while that	**Jg 11:4**	4480
of Bethlehem judged Israel **a** him.	**Jg 12:8**	310
Zebulunite judged Israel **a** him;	**Jg 12:11**	310
Pirathonite judged Israel **a** him.	**Jg 12:13**	310
But **a** a while, in the time of	**Jg 15:1**	4480
on you, but **a** that I will quit."	**Jg 15:7**	310
A this it came about that he loved	**Jg 16:4**	310
to grow again **a** it was shaved off.	**Jg 16:22**	3512c
a the manner of the Sidonians,	**Jg 18:7**	
a the name of Dan their father who	**Jg 18:29**	
Then her husband arose and went **a**	**Jg 19:3**	310

return **a** your sister-in-law." Ru 1:15 310
glean among the ears of grain **a** one Ru 2:2 310
in the field **a** the reapers; Ru 2:3 310
a the reapers among the sheaves.' Ru 2:7 310
which they reap, and go **a** them. Ru 2:9 310
for your mother-in-law **a** the death Ru 2:11 310
she had left **a** she was satisfied. Ru 2:18 4480
first by not going **a** young men, Ru 3:10 310
to redeem *it,* and I am **a** you.' " Ru 4:4 310
It happened year **a** year, 1Sa 1:7 310
a eating and drinking in Shiloh. 1Sa 1:9 310
due time, **a** Hannah had conceived, 1Sa 1:20 310
A they had brought it around, 1Sa 5:9 310
of Israel lamented **a** the LORD. 1Sa 7:2 310
but turned aside **a** dishonest gain 1Sa 8:3 310
Now **a** Samuel had heard all the 1Sa 8:21 310
come out **a** Saul and after Samuel, 1Sa 11:7 310
come out after Saul and **a** Samuel, 1Sa 11:7 310
for *then you would go* **a** futile 1Sa 12:21 310
for Himself a man **a** His own heart, 1Sa 13:14 310
"Come up **a** me, for the LORD has 1Sa 14:12 310
bearer put some to death **a** him. 1Sa 14:13 310
"Let us go down **a** the Philistines 1Sa 14:36 310
"Shall I go down **a** the Philistines? 1Sa 14:37 310
had gone **a** Saul to the battle. 1Sa 17:13 310
I went out **a** him and attacked him, 1Sa 17:35 310
shot, Jonathan called **a** the lad and 1Sa 20:37 310
And Jonathan called **a** the lad, 1Sa 20:38 310
escaped and fled **a** David. 1Sa 22:20 310
out of the cave and called **a** Saul, 1Sa 24:8 310
"**A** whom has the king of Israel 1Sa 24:14 310
not cut off my descendants **a** me and 1Sa 24:21 310
behold, I am coming **a** you." 1Sa 25:19 310
came **a** him into the wilderness, 1Sa 26:3 310
it came about **a** the death of Saul, 2Sa 1:1 310
he could not live **a** he had fallen. 2Sa 1:10 310
David, he sent messengers **a** Abner, 2Sa 3:26 310
Jerusalem, **a** he came from Hebron; 2Sa 5:13 310
raise up your descendant **a** you, 2Sa 7:12 310
Now **a** this it came about that 2Sa 8:1 310
from the king was sent out **a** him. 2Sa 11:8 310
myself and it will be named **a** me." 2Sa 12:28 5921
Now it was **a** this that Absalom the 2Sa 13:1 310
so depressed morning **a** morning? 2Sa 13:4 310
Now it came about **a** two full years 2Sa 13:23 310
Now it came about **a** this that 2Sa 15:1
4480, 310
It came about **a** they had 2Sa 17:21 310
named the pillar **a** his own name, 2Sa 18:18 5921
let me also run **a** the Cushite." 2Sa 18:22 310
So Joab's men went out **a** him, 2Sa 20:7 310
all the men passed on **a** Joab to 2Sa 20:13 310
together and also went **a** him. 2Sa 20:14 310
for three years, year **a** year; 2Sa 21:1 310
and **a** that God was moved by 2Sa 21:14 310
Now it came about **a** this that 2Sa 21:18 310
earth, Through sunshine **a** rain.' 2Sa 23:4 4480
and **a** him was Eleazar the son of 2Sa 23:9 310
a him only to strip *the slain.* 2Sa 23:10 310
Now **a** him was Shammah the son of 2Sa 23:11 310
him **a** he had numbered the people. 2Sa 24:10
310, 3651
and he was born **a** Absalom. 1Ki 1:6 310
your son shall be king **a** me, 1Ki 1:13 310
in **a** you and confirm your words." 1Ki 1:14 310
your son Solomon shall be king **a** me 1Ki 1:17 310
throne of my lord the king **a** him. 1Ki 1:20 310
'Adonijah shall be king **a** me, 1Ki 1:24 310
of my lord the king **a** him?" 1Ki 1:27 310
son Solomon shall be king **a** me, 1Ki 1:30 310
"Then you shall come up **a** him, 1Ki 1:35 310
All the people went up **a** him, 1Ki 1:40 310
shall one like you arise **a** you. 1Ki 3:12 310
on the third day **a** I gave birth, 1Ki 3:18 310
four hundred and eightieth year **a** the 1Ki 6:1 310
their descendants who were left **a** 1Ki 9:21 310
your heart away **a** their gods." 1Ki 11:2 310
his heart away **a** other gods; 1Ki 11:4 310
For Solomon went **a** Ashtoreth the 1Ki 11:5 310
and **a** Milcom the detestable idol 1Ki 11:5 310
he should not go **a** other gods; 1Ki 11:10 310
band, **a** David slew them of *Zobah;* 1Ki 11:24 310
Now look **a** your own house, David!" 1Ki 12:16 310
So he went **a** the man of God and 1Ki 13:14 310
It came about **a** he had eaten 1Ki 13:23 310
eaten bread and **a** he had drunk, 1Ki 13:23 310
A he had buried him, he spoke to his 1Ki 13:31 310
A this event Jeroboam did not 1Ki 13:33 310
not to raise up his son **a** him and to 1Ki 15:4 310
Samaria, **a** the name of Shemer, 1Ki 16:24 5921
It happened **a** a while that 1Ki 17:7
4480, 7093
Now it came about **a** these things that 1Ki 17:17 310
Now it happened **a** many days that 1Ki 18:1 310
And **a** the wind an earthquake, *but* 1Ki 19:11 310
A the earthquake a fire, *but* 1Ki 19:12 310
and **a** the fire a sound of a gentle 1Ki 19:12 310
oxen and ran **a** Elijah and said, 1Ki 19:20 310
and **a** them he mustered all the 1Ki 20:15 310
Now it came about **a** these things that 1Ki 21:1 310
Israel **a** the death of Ahab. 2Ki 1:1 310
I will run **a** him and take 2Ki 5:20 310
When Naaman saw one running **a** him, 2Ki 5:21 310
Now it came about **a** this, 2Ki 6:24 310
sent **a** the army of the Arameans, 2Ki 7:14 310
They went **a** them to the Jordan, 2Ki 7:15 310
riding together **a** Ahab his father, 2Ki 9:25 310
fifteen years **a** the death of Jehoash 2Ki 14:17 310
but they sent **a** him to Lachish and 2Ki 14:19 310
a the king slept with his fathers. 2Ki 14:22 310
and *went* **a** the nations which 2Ki 17:15 310
so that **a** him there was none like 2Ki 18:5 310
the LORD, to walk **a** the LORD, 2Ki 23:3 310
nor did any like him arise **a** him. 2Ki 23:25 310
A the death of Hezron in 1Ch 2:24 310
and played the harlot **a** the gods 1Ch 5:25 310
the LORD, **a** the ark rested *there.* 1Ch 6:31 4480
a he had sent away Hushim and 1Ch 8:8 4480
A him was Eleazar the son of Dodo, 1Ch 11:12 310
a consultation sent him away, 1Ch 12:19 310
"You shall not go up **a** them; 1Ch 14:14 310
up *one of* your descendants **a** you, 1Ch 17:11 310
Now **a** this it came about that 1Ch 18:1 310
Now it came about **a** this, 1Ch 19:1 310
Now it came about **a** this, 1Ch 20:4 310
Joab, and Zebadiah his son **a** him; 1Ch 27:7 310
observe and seek **a** all the 1Ch 28:8 1875
it to your sons **a** you forever. 1Ch 28:8 310
nor those who will come **a** you." 2Ch 1:12 310
descendants who were left **a** them in 2Ch 8:8 310
Now look **a** your own house, David." 2Ch 10:16 310
A her he took Maacah the daughter of 2Ch 11:20 310
Now it came about **a** this that the 2Ch 20:1 310
A this Jehoshaphat king of Judah 2Ch 20:35 310
So **a** all this the LORD smote him 2Ch 21:18 310
a the death of his father, 2Ch 22:4 310
Now it came about **a** this that 2Ch 24:4 310
But **a** the death of Jehoiada the 2Ch 24:17 310
Now **a** Amaziah came 2Ch 25:14 310
years **a** the death of Joash, 2Ch 25:25 310
but they sent **a** him to Lachish and 2Ch 25:27 310
restored it to Judah **a** the king slept 2Ch 26:2 310
Then Azariah the priest entered **a** 2Ch 26:17 310
at their stations **a** their custom, 2Ch 30:16 310
priests praised the LORD day **a** day 2Ch 30:21 310
A these acts of faithfulness 2Ch 32:1 310
A this Sennacherib king of Assyria 2Ch 32:9 310
Now **a** this he built the outer wall 2Ch 33:14 310
the LORD to walk **a** the LORD, 2Ch 34:31 310
A all this, when Josiah had set 2Ch 35:20 310
Now **a** these things, in the reign Ezr 7:1 310
our God, what shall we say **a** this? Ezr 9:10 310
"**A** all that has come upon us for our Ezr 9:13 310
A him Nehemiah the son of Azbuk, Ne 3:16 310
A him the Levites carried out Ne 3:17 310
A him their brothers carried out Ne 3:18 310
A him Baruch the son of Zabbai Ne 3:20 310
A him Meremoth the son of Uriah Ne 3:21 310
A him the priests, the men of Ne 3:22 310
A them Benjamin and Hasshub Ne 3:23 310
A them Azariah the son of Ne 3:23 310
A him Binnui the son of Henadad Ne 3:24 310
A him Pedaiah the son of Parosh Ne 3:25 310
A them the Tekoites repaired Ne 3:27 310
A them Zadok the son of Immer Ne 3:29 310
And **a** him Shemaiah the son of Ne 3:29 310
A him Hananiah the son of Ne 3:30 310
A him Meshullam the son of Ne 3:30 310
A him Malchijah, one of the Ne 3:31 310
Gileadite, and was named **a** them. Ne 7:63 5921
and **a** him Gabbai *and* Sallai, 928. Ne 11:8 310
A some time, however, I asked Ne 13:6 7093
not open them until **a** the sabbath. Ne 13:19 310
A these things when the anger of Es 2:1 310
a the end of her twelve months Es 2:12 4480
A these events King Ahasuerus Es 3:1 310
days Purim **a** the name of Pur. Es 9:26 5921
for my guilt And search **a** my sin? Jb 10:6 310
Hardship **a** hardship is with me. Jb 10:17 310
through me with breach **a** breach; Jb 16:14
5921, 6440
"Even **a** my skin is destroyed, Yet Jb 19:26 310
Then **a** I have spoken, you may mock. Jb 21:3 310
he care for his household **a** him, Jb 21:21 310
all men will follow **a** him, Jb 21:33 310
"**A** my words they did not speak Jb 29:22 310
And my foot has hastened **a** deceit, Jb 31:5 5921
"**A** it, a voice roars; Jb 37:4 310
And searches **a** every green thing. Jb 39:8 310
will he harrow the valleys **a** you? Jb 39:10 310
It came about **a** the LORD had Jb 42:7 310
A this, Job lived 140 years, and saw Jb 42:16 310
who understand, Who seek **a** God. Ps 14:2
their lands **a** their own names. Ps 49:11
a them who approve their words. Ps 49:13 310
His glory will not descend **a** him. Ps 49:17 310
who understands, Who seeks **a** God. Ps 53:2
went on, the musicians **a** *them,* Ps 68:25 310
The young lions roar **a** their prey And Ps 104:21
A Your ordinances at all times. Ps 119:20 413
A Your manner with those who love Ps 119:132
who follow **a** wickedness draw near; Ps 119:150
does not plow **a** the autumn, Pr 20:4 4480
How blessed are his sons **a** him. Pr 20:7 310
And **a** the vows to make inquiry. Pr 20:25 310
with an evil eye hastens **a** wealth And Pr 28:22
A man who hardens *his* neck **a** much Pr 29:1
all is vanity and striving **a** wind. Ec 1:14
that this also is striving **a** wind. Ec 1:17
all was vanity and striving **a** wind Ec 2:11
the man *do* who will come **a** the king Ec 2:12 310
is futility and striving **a** wind. Ec 2:17
it to the man who will come **a** me. Ec 2:18 310
too is vanity and striving **a** wind. Ec 2:26
him to see what will occur **a** him? Ec 3:22 310
too is vanity and striving **a** wind. Ec 4:4
full of labor and striving **a** wind. Ec 4:6
too is vanity and striving **a** wind. Ec 4:16
A all, a king who cultivates the Ec 5:9
is futility and a striving **a** wind. Ec 6:9
what will be **a** him under the sun? Ec 6:12 310
anything *that will be* **a** him. Ec 7:14 310
can tell him what will come **a** him? Ec 10:14
4480, 310
for you will find it **a** many days. Ec 11:1
and clouds return **a** the rain; Ec 12:2 310
me **a** you *and* let us run *together!* SS 1:4 310
"On my bed night **a** night I sought SS 3:1
a bribe And chases **a** rewards. Is 1:23
A that you will be called the city Is 1:26 310
And **a** many days they *will be* Is 24:22 4480
a morning it will pass through, Is 28:19
Judah **a** his illness and recovery: Is 38:9
And there will be none **a** Me. Is 43:10 310
call themselves **a** the holy city And Is 48:2 4480
following **a** Me in the wilderness, Jer 2:2 310
a emptiness and became empty? Jer 2:5 310
a things that did not profit. Jer 2:8 310
I have not gone **a** the Baals'? Jer 2:23 310
And **a** them I will walk.' Jer 2:25 310
'**A** she has done all these things she Jer 3:7 310
give you shepherds **a** My own heart, Jer 3:15
nor will they walk anymore **a** the Jer 3:17 310
one neighing **a** his neighbor's wife. Jer 5:8 413
a other gods to your own ruin, Jer 7:6 310
and walk **a** other gods that you Jer 7:9 310
and which they have gone **a** and Jer 8:2 310
but have walked **a** the stubbornness Jer 9:14 310
of their heart and **a** the Baals, Jer 9:14 310
and I will send the sword **a** them Jer 9:16 310
And like the sheaf **a** the reaper, Jer 9:22
4480, 310
gone **a** other gods to serve them; Jer 11:10 310
Even they have cried aloud **a** you. Jer 12:6 310
about that **a** I have uprooted them, Jer 12:15 310
A many days the LORD said to me, Jer 13:6 4480
have gone **a** other gods to serve them Jer 13:10 310
away from *being* a shepherd **a** You, Jer 17:16 310
A Nebuchadnezzar king of Babylon Jer 24:1 310
and do not go **a** other gods to Jer 25:6 310
king of Sheshach shall drink **a** them. Jer 25:26 310
a Hananiah the prophet had broken Jer 28:12 310
(This was **a** King Jeconiah and the Jer 29:2 310
'For **a** I turned back, I repented; Jer 31:19 310
And **a** I was instructed, I smote on Jer 31:19 310
house of Israel **a** those days," Jer 31:33 310
"**A** I had given the deed of Jer 32:16 310
bosom of their children **a** them, Jer 32:18 310
the good of their children **a** them. Jer 32:39 310
a King Zedekiah had made a Jer 34:8 310
go **a** other gods to worship them. Jer 35:15 310
to Jeremiah **a** the king had burned the Jer 36:27 310
"Take him and look **a** him, Jer 39:12 5921
the LORD **a** Nebuzaradan captain of Jer 40:1 310
come *along,* and I will look **a** you; Jer 40:4 5921
day **a** the killing of Gedaliah, Jer 41:4
a he had struck down Gedaliah the Jer 41:16 310
closely **a** you there *in* Egypt, Jer 42:16 310
The sword will follow **a** you. Jer 48:2 310
'And I will send out the sword **a** Jer 49:37 310
And **a** that another report in Jer 51:46 310
played the harlot **a** their idols; Ezk 6:9 310
through the city **a** him and strike; Ezk 9:5 310
whose hearts go **a** their detestable Ezk 11:21
I will draw out a sword **a** them. Ezk 12:14 310
came about **a** all your wickedness Ezk 16:23 310
continually went **a** their idols. Ezk 20:16 310
"Will you defile yourselves **a** the Ezk 20:30
harlot **a** their detestable things? Ezk 20:30 310
and she lusted **a** her lovers, after Ezk 23:5 5921
after her lovers, **a** the Assyrians, Ezk 23:5 413
and with all whom she lusted **a**, Ezk 23:7
the Assyrians, **a** whom she lusted. Ezk 23:9 5921
"She lusted **a** the Assyrians, Ezk 23:12 413
When she saw them she lusted **a** them Ezk 23:16 5921
"She lusted **a** their Ezk 23:20 5921
Take out of it piece **a** piece, Ezk 24:6
and their heart goes **a** their gain. Ezk 33:31 310
"**A** many days you will be summoned; Ezk 38:8 4480
year **a** the city was taken, Ezk 40:1 310
went astray from Me **a** their idols, Ezk 44:10 310
"**A** he is cleansed, seven days shall Ezk 44:26 310
gate shall be shut **a** he goes out. Ezk 46:12 310
"**A** you there will arise another Da 2:39 870
kingdom will be assured to you **a** you Da 4:26
4481, 1768
"**A** this I kept looking, and Da 7:6 870
"**A** this I kept looking in the Da 7:7 870
and another will arise **a** them, Da 7:24 311
"Then **a** the sixty-two weeks the Da 9:26 310
"**A** some years they will form an Da 11:6 7093
and **a** an interval of some years he Da 11:13 7093
"**A** an alliance is made with him he Da 11:23 4480
'I will go **a** my lovers, Who give Hos 2:5 310
"He will revive us **a** two days; Hos 6:2 4480
They will walk **a** the LORD, He will Hos 11:10 310
It is I who answer and look **a** you. Hos 14:8
Nor will there be again **a** it To Jl 2:2 310
"It will come about **a** this Jl 2:28 310
a which their fathers walked. Am 2:4 310
"These who pant **a** the *very* dust Am 2:7 5921
among you **a** the manner of Egypt; Am 4:10
crop *was* **a** the king's mowing. Am 7:1 310
"If a man walking **a** wind and Mi 2:11
And plague comes **a** Him. Hab 3:5 7272
"**A** glory He has sent Me against Zch 2:8 310
going forth **a** standing before the Zch 6:5 4480

the white ones go forth **a** them, **Zch 6:6** 413, 310
A the deportation to Babylon: **Mt 1:12** *3326*
Now **a** Jesus was born in Bethlehem **Mt 2:1**
A hearing the king, they went their **Mt 2:9** *1161*
A coming into the house they saw **Mt 2:11** *2532*
Then **a** being warned *by God* in a **Mt 2:22**
is coming **a** me is mightier than I, **Mt 3:11** *3694*
A being baptized, Jesus came up **Mt 3:16**
And **a** He had fasted forty days and **Mt 4:2**
and **a** He sat down, His disciples **Mt 5:1**
A the demon was cast out, the mute **Mt 9:33**
Jesus sent out **a** instructing them: **Mt 10:5**
follow **a** Me is not worthy of Me. **Mt 10:38** *3694*
A He had sent the crowds away, He **Mt 14:23**
A Jesus called the crowd to Him, He **Mt 15:10**
generation seeks **a** a sign; **Mt 16:4** *1934*
"If anyone wishes to come **a** Me, **Mt 16:24** *3694*
A laying His hands on them, He **Mt 19:15**
"But immediately **a** the **Mt 24:29** *3326*
"Now **a** a long time the master of **Mt 25:19** *3326*
"You know that **a** two days the **Mt 26:2** *3326*
took *some* bread, and **a** a blessing, **Mt 26:26**
A singing a hymn, they went out to **Mt 26:30**
"But **a** I have been raised, I will **Mt 26:32** *3326*
but **a** having Jesus scourged, he **Mt 27:26**
a twisting together a crown of thorns, **Mt 27:29**
A they had mocked Him, they took **Mt 27:31** *3753*
and **a** tasting *it*, He was unwilling **Mt 27:34**
and coming out of the tombs **a** His **Mt 27:53** *3326*
the day **a** the preparation, **Mt 27:62** *3326*
'**A** three days I *am to* rise again.' **Mt 27:63** *3326*
Now **a** the Sabbath, as it began to **Mt 28:1** *3796*
"**A** me One is coming who is **Mk 1:7** *3694*
Now **a** John had been taken into **Mk 1:14** *3326*
And immediately **a** they came **Mk 1:29**
came, **a** the sun had set, **Mk 1:32** *3753*
A looking around at them with anger, **Mk 3:5**
"And **a** the sun had risen, it was **Mk 4:6** *3753*
a hearing about Jesus, she came up in **Mk 5:27**
A bidding them farewell, He left for **Mk 6:46**
A He called the crowd to Him again, **Mk 7:14**
But **a** hearing of Him, a woman **Mk 7:25**
into his ears, and **a** spitting, **Mk 7:33**
and **a** He had blessed them, He **Mk 8:7**
and **a** spitting on his eyes and **Mk 8:23**
and **a** three days rise again. **Mk 8:31** *3326*
"If anyone wishes to come **a** Me, **Mk 8:34** *3694*
of God **a** it has come with power." **Mk 9:1**
A crying out and throwing him into **Mk 9:26**
and **a** looking around at everything, **Mk 11:11**
A that, no one would venture to ask **Mk 12:34**
in those days, **a** that tribulation, **Mk 13:24** *3326*
and **a** a blessing He broke *it* **Mk 14:22**
A singing a hymn, they went out to **Mk 14:26**
"But **a** I have been raised, I will **Mk 14:28** *3326*
A coming, Judas immediately went to **Mk 14:45**
And **a** a little while the **Mk 14:70** *3326*
them, and **a** having Jesus scourged, **Mk 15:15**
and **a** twisting a crown of thorns, **Mk 15:17**
A they had mocked Him, they took **Mk 15:20** *3753*
[Now **a** He had risen early on the **Mk 16:9**
A that, He appeared in a different **Mk 16:12** *3326*
who had seen Him **a** He had risen. **Mk 16:14**
And **a** that, Jesus Himself sent out **Mk 16:20** *3326*
A these days Elizabeth his wife **Lk 1:24** *3326*
IS UPON GENERATION **A** GENERATION **Lk 1:50** *2532*
call him Zacharias, **a** his father. **Lk 1:59** *1909*
seven years **a** her marriage, **Lk 2:36** *575*
a spending the full number of **Lk 2:43**
Then, **a** three days **Lk 2:46** *3326*
A that He went out and noticed a tax **Lk 5:27** *3326*
a drinking old *wine* wishes for new; **Lk 5:39**
A looking around at them all, He **Lk 6:10**
a he has been fully trained, **Lk 6:40**
"Now no one **a** lighting a lamp **Lk 8:16**
"If anyone wishes to come **a** Me, **Lk 9:23** *3694*
Some eight days **a** these sayings, **Lk 9:28** *3326*
a putting his hand to the plow and **Lk 9:62**
Now **a** this the Lord appointed **Lk 10:1** *3326*
certain place, **a** He had finished, **Lk 11:1** *5613*
"No one, **a** lighting a lamp, puts **Lk 11:33**
a so many thousands of people **Lk 12:1**
and **a** that have no more that they **Lk 12:4** *3326*
fear the One who, **a** He has killed **Lk 12:5** *3326*
come **a** Me cannot be My disciple. **Lk 14:27** *3694*
and go **a** the one which is lost until **Lk 15:4** *1909*
go away, and do not run **a** *them.* **Lk 17:23** *1377*
and **a** they have scourged Him, they **Lk 18:33**
him and sent a delegation **a** him, **Lk 19:14** *3694*
returned, **a** receiving the kingdom, **Lk 19:15**
A He had said these things, He was **Lk 19:28**
Do not go **a** them. **Lk 21:8** *3694*
He took the cup **a** they had eaten, **Lk 22:20** *3326*
A they had kindled a fire in **Lk 22:55**
A about an hour had passed, another **Lk 22:59**
a treating Him with contempt and **Lk 23:11**
And they, **a** worshiping Him, **Lk 24:52**
a me has a higher rank than I, **Jn 1:15** *3694*
"*It is* He who comes **a** me, **Jn 1:27** *3694*
'**A** me comes a Man who has a higher **Jn 1:30** *3694*
A this He went down to Capernaum, **Jn 2:12** *3326*
A these things Jesus and His **Jn 3:22** *3326*
A the two days He went forth from **Jn 4:43** *3326*
A these things there was a feast **Jn 5:1** *3326*
a the stirring up of the water, **Jn 5:4** *3326*
A these things Jesus went away to **Jn 6:1** *3326*
and **a** getting into a boat, they **Jn 6:17**
bread **a** the Lord had given thanks. **Jn 6:23**
A these things Jesus was walking in **Jn 7:1** *3326*
a this He said to the disciples, **Jn 11:7** *3326*
said, and **a** that He said to them, **Jn 11:11** *3326*
look, the world has gone **a** Him." **Jn 12:19** *3694*
A the morsel, Satan then entered **Jn 13:27** *3326*
So **a** receiving the morsel he **Jn 13:30**
"**A** a little while the world will **Jn 14:19** *2089*
A this, Jesus, knowing that all **Jn 19:28** *3326*
A these things Joseph of Arimathea, **Jn 19:38** *3326*
A eight days His disciples were again **Jn 20:26** *3326*
A these things Jesus manifested **Jn 21:1** *3326*
a He was raised from the dead. **Jn 21:14**
a He had by the Holy Spirit given **Ac 1:2**
Himself alive **a** His suffering, **Ac 1:3** *3326*
And **a** He had said these things, He **Ac 1:9**
And **a** it was sold, was it not **Ac 5:4**
him up, and **a** carrying him out, **Ac 5:6**
"**A** this man, Judas of Galilee rose **Ac 5:37** *3326*
and drew away *some* people **a** him; **Ac 5:37** *3694*
and **a** calling the apostles in, **Ac 5:40**
and **a** praying, they laid their **Ac 6:6**
From there, **a** his father died, **Ac 7:4** *3326*
AND TO HIS DESCENDANTS **A** HIM. **Ac 7:5** *3326*
'AND **A** THAT THEY WILL COME OUT AND **Ac 7:7** *3326*
"And **a** he had been set **Ac 7:21**
"**A** forty years had passed, AN **Ac 7:30**
church, entering house **a** house, **Ac 8:3** *2596*
and **a** being baptized, he continued **Ac 8:13**
a laying his hands on him said, **Ac 9:17**
and **a** he had explained everything **Ac 10:8**
a the baptism which John **Ac 10:37** *3326*
with Him **a** He arose from the dead. **Ac 10:41** *3326*
gift as *He gave* to us also **a** believing **Ac 11:17**
intending **a** the Passover to bring **Ac 12:4** *3326*
A the reading of the Law **Ac 13:15** *3326*
"**A** these things He gave *them* **Ac 13:20** *3326*
"**A** He had removed him, He raised up **Ac 13:22** *2596*
son of Jesse, A MAN **A** MY HEART, **Ac 13:22** *2596*
a John had proclaimed before His **Ac 13:24**
one is coming **a** me the sandals of **Ac 13:25** *3326*
a he had served the purpose of God **Ac 13:36**
A they had preached the gospel to **Ac 14:21**
A there had been much debate, Peter **Ac 15:7**
A they had stopped speaking, James **Ac 15:13** *3326*
'**A** THESE THINGS I will return, AND **Ac 15:16** *3326*
A they had spent time *there,* **Ac 15:33**
A some days Paul said to Barnabas, **Ac 15:36** *3326*
and **a** they came to Mysia, they were **Ac 16:7**
Following **a** Paul and us, she kept **Ac 16:17** *2628*
and **a** he brought them out, he **Ac 16:30**
A these things he left Athens and **Ac 18:1** *3326*
own law, look **a** it yourselves; **Ac 18:15** *3708*
in Him who was coming **a** him, **Ac 19:4** *3326*
Now **a** these things were finished, **Ac 19:21** *5613*
a he had passed through Macedonia **Ac 19:21**
"**A** I have been there, I must also **Ac 19:21** *3326*
A quieting the crowd, the town clerk **Ac 19:35** *1063*
what man is there **a** all who does **Ac 19:35** *1063*
A saying this he dismissed **Ac 19:41**
A the uproar had ceased, Paul sent **Ac 20:1** *3326*
a the days of Unleavened Bread, **Ac 20:6** *3326*
fell upon him, and **a** embracing him, **Ac 20:10**
"I know that **a** my departure **Ac 20:29** *3326*
to draw away the disciples **a** them. **Ac 20:30** *3694*
A looking up the disciples, we **Ac 21:4**
A kneeling down on the beach **Ac 21:5**
and **a** greeting the brethren, we **Ac 21:7**
A these days we got ready and started **Ac 21:15** *3326*
A we arrived in Jerusalem, **Ac 21:17** *1161*
A he had greeted them, *he began* **Ac 21:19**
in one synagogue **a** another I used to **Ac 22:19** *2596*
a your accusers arrive also," **Ac 23:35** *3752*
A five days the high priest Ananias **Ac 24:1** *3326*
A *Paul* had been summoned, **Ac 24:2**
"Now **a** several years I came to **Ac 24:17** *1223*
But **a** two years had passed, Felix **Ac 24:27**
A he had spent not more than eight or **Ac 25:6**
A Paul arrived, the Jews who had **Ac 25:7**
"So **a** they had assembled **Ac 25:17**
so that **a** the investigation has **Ac 25:26**
A they had hoisted it up, they used **Ac 27:17**
But **a** they had waited a long time **Ac 28:6**
in *to see* him and **a** he had prayed, **Ac 28:8**
A this had happened, the rest of **Ac 28:9**
A we put in at Syracuse, we stayed **Ac 28:12**
A three days Paul called together **Ac 28:17** *3326*
they *began* leaving **a** Paul had **Ac 28:25**
a I have preached to others, **1Co 9:27**
He took the cup also **a** supper, **1Co 11:25** *3326*
A that He appeared to more than **1Co 15:6** *1899*
a that those who are Christ's at **1Co 15:23** *1899*
to you **a** I go through Macedonia, **1Co 16:5** *3752*
Then **a** an interval of fourteen **Ga 2:1** *1223*
things **a** the counsel of His will, **Eph 1:11** *2596*
a listening to the message of **Eph 1:13**
all seek **a** their own interests, **Php 2:21** *2212*
a I left Macedonia, **Php 4:15** *3753*
but **a** we had already suffered and **1Th 2:2**
but always seek **a** that which is **1Th 5:15** *1377*
For **a** all it is *only* just for God **2Th 1:6** *1512*
for others, their *sins* follow **a**. **1Tm 5:24** *1872*
man **a** a first and second warning, **Ti 3:10** *3326*
a He spoke long ago to the fathers **Heb 1:1**
A it was at the first spoken **Heb 2:3** *3748*
encourage one another day **a** day, **Heb 3:13** *2596*
saying through David **a** so long a **Heb 4:7** *3326*
have spoken of another day **a** that. **Heb 4:8** *3326*
of the oath, which came **a** the Law, **Heb 7:28** *3326*
THE HOUSE OF ISRAEL **A** THOSE DAYS, **Heb 8:10** *3326*
once and **a** this *comes* judgment, **Heb 9:27** *3326*
A saying above, "SACRIFICES AND **Heb 10:8**
time **a** time the same sacrifices, **Heb 10:11** *4178*
Spirit also testifies to us; for **a** **Heb 10:15** *3326*
WILL MAKE WITH THEM **A** THOSE DAYS, **Heb 10:16** *3326*
we go on sinning willfully **a** receiving **Heb 10:26** *3326*
days, when, **a** being enlightened, **Heb 10:32**
a they had been encircled for **Heb 11:30**
a she had welcomed the spies in **Heb 11:31**
a angels and authorities and **1Pe 3:22**
A you have suffered for a little **1Pe 5:10**
at any time **a** my departure you will **2Pe 1:15** *3326*
a day by *their* lawless deeds), **2Pe 2:8** *1537*
For if, **a** they have escaped the **2Pe 2:20**
"A sow, **a** washing, *returns* to **2Pe 2:22**
following **a** their own lusts, **2Pe 3:3** *2596*
a saving a people out of the land **Jude 1:5**
and went **a** strange flesh, **Jude 1:7** *3694*
following **a** their *own* lusts; **Jude 1:16** *2596*
a their own ungodly lusts." **Jude 1:18** *2596*
will take place **a** these things. **Rv 1:19** *3326*
A these things I looked, **Rv 4:1** *3326*
must take place **a** these things." **Rv 4:1** *3326*
A this I saw four angels standing **Rv 7:1** *3326*
A these things I looked, and **Rv 7:9** *3326*
are still coming **a** these things. **Rv 9:12** *3326*
But **a** the three and a half days **Rv 11:11** *3326*
out of his mouth **a** the woman, **Rv 12:15** *3694*
amazed *and followed* **a** the beast; **Rv 13:3** *3694*
A these things I looked, and the **Rv 15:5** *3326*
A these things I saw another angel **Rv 18:1** *3326*
A these things I heard something **Rv 19:1** *3326*
a these things he must be released **Rv 20:3** *3326*

AFTERBIRTH

and toward her **a** which issues from **Dt 28:57** 7988

AFTERGROWTH

harvest's **a** you shall not reap, **Lv 25:5** 5599b
you shall not sow, nor reap its **a**, **Lv 25:11** 5599b

AFTERNOON

yourself, and wait until **a**"; **Jg 19:8** 5186, 3117

AFTERWARD

earth in those days, and also **a**, **Gn 6:4** 310, 3651
and **a** the families of the **Gn 10:18** 310
and **a** they will come out with many **Gn 15:14** 310, 3651
a few days, say ten; **a** she may go." **Gn 24:55** 310
A his brother came forth with his **Gn 25:26** 310
A she bore a daughter and named her **Gn 30:21** 310
Then **a** I will see his face; **Gn 32:20** 310, 3651
a Joseph came near with Rachel, **Gn 33:7** 310
A his brother came out who had **Gn 38:30** 310
a his brothers talked with him. **Gn 45:15** 310, 3651
And **a** Moses and Aaron came and **Ex 5:1** 310
A all the sons of Israel came near, **Ex 34:32** 310
Now **a**, he may enter the camp, but **Lv 14:8** 310
Then **a**, he shall slaughter the **Lv 14:19** 310
and **a** the priest shall go in to **Lv 14:36** 310, 3651
and **a** she will be clean. **Lv 15:28** 310
a he shall come into the camp. **Lv 16:26** 310, 3651
a he shall come into the camp. **Lv 16:28** 310, 3651
and **a** he shall eat of the holy **Lv 22:7** 310
and **a** he shall make the woman **Nu 5:26** 310
a the Nazirite may drink wine.' **Nu 6:20** 310
a the sons of Israel would then **Nu 9:17** 310, 3651
and **a** she may be received again." **Nu 12:14** 310
A, however, the people moved out **Nu 12:16** 310
water, and **a** come into the camp, **Nu 19:7** 310
a you will be gathered to your **Nu 31:2** 310
and **a** you may enter the camp." **Nu 31:24** 310
then **a** you shall return and be **Nu 32:22** 310
and **a** the hand of all the people. **Dt 17:7** 314
Then **a** you may go on your way." **Jos 2:16** 310
Then **a** he read all the words of **Jos 8:34** 310, 3651
So **a** Joshua struck them and put **Jos 10:26** 310, 3651
and **a** I brought you out. **Jos 24:5** 310
A the sons of Judah went down to **Jg 1:9** 310
and **a** your hands will be **Jg 7:11** 310
of bread, and **a** you may go." **Jg 19:5** 310
a those who are invited will eat. **1Sa 9:13** 310, 3651
"**A** you will come to the hill of **1Sa 10:5** 310, 3651
It came about **a** that David's **1Sa 24:5** 310, 3651
Now **a** David arose and went out of **1Sa 24:8** 310, 3651
A when David heard it, he said, **2Sa 3:28** 310
and **a** you may make *one* for **1Ki 17:13** 314
A Hezron went in to the daughter **1Ch 2:21** 310
and **a** *there was* a continual burnt **Ezr 3:5** 310, 3651
A Job opened his mouth and cursed **Jb 3:1** 310, 3651
me, And **a** receive me to glory. **Ps 73:24** 310
But **a** his mouth will be filled **Pr 20:17** 310
He who rebukes a man will **a** find **Pr 28:23** 318a
things that are going to come **a**, **Is 41:23** 268
But **a** they turned around and took **Jer 34:11** 310, 3651
"But **a** I will restore The **Jer 49:6** 310, 3651
A the sons of Israel will return **Hos 3:5** 310

but **a** he regretted it and went. **Mt 21:29** *5305*
remorse **a** so as to believe him. **Mt 21:32** *5305*
"But **a** he sent his son to them, **Mt 21:37** *5305*
back to Capernaum several days **a**, **Mk 2:1** *1223*
able soon **a** to speak evil of Me. **Mk 9:39** *5035*
A He appeared to the eleven **Mk 16:14** *5305*
and **a** you may eat and drink'? **Lk 17:8** *3326, 3778*
but **a** he said to himself, **Lk 18:4** *3326, 3778*
A Jesus found him in the temple and **Jn 5:14** *3326, 3778*

AFTERWARDS
and **a** the hand of all the people. **Dt 13:9** 314
Then it came about **a** that David **2Sa 2:1** 310, 3651
Now it happened **a** that the king of **2Sa 10:1** 310, 3651
A they prepared for themselves **2Ch 35:14** 310
A, then, build your house. **Pr 24:27** 310
A they *go* to the dead. **Ec 9:3** 310
a I will send for many hunters, **Jer 16:16** 310, 3651
"Then **a**," declares the LORD, **Jer 21:7** 310, 3651
A, however, it will be inhabited **Jer 46:26** 310, 3651
Soon **a** He went **Lk 7:11** *1722, 1836*
Soon **a**, He *began* **Lk 8:1** *1722, 2517*
a it yields the peaceful fruit of **Heb 12:11** *5305*
For you know that even **a**, **Heb 12:17** *3347*

AGABUS
One of them named **A** stood up **Ac 11:28** *13*
named **A** came down from Judea. **Ac 21:10** *13*

AGAG
his king shall be higher than **A**, **Nu 24:7** 90
He captured **A** the king of the **1Sa 15:8** 90
A and the best of the sheep, **1Sa 15:9** 90
brought back **A** the king of Amalek, **1Sa 15:20** 90
"Bring me **A**, the king of the **1Sa 15:32** 90
And **A** came to him cheerfully. **1Sa 15:32** 90
And **A** said, "Surely the **1Sa 15:32** 90
And Samuel hewed **A** to pieces **1Sa 15:33** 90

AGAGITE
the son of Hammedatha the **A**, **Es 3:1** 91
the son of Hammedatha the **A**, **Es 3:10** 91
scheme of Haman the **A** and his plot **Es 8:3** 91
the son of Hammedatha the **A**, **Es 8:5** 91
the son of Hammedatha, the **A**, **Es 9:24** 91

AGAIN
A, she gave birth to his brother **Gn 4:2** 3254
had relations with his wife **a**; **Gn 4:25** 5750
and **a** he sent out the dove from **Gn 8:10** 3254
but she did not return to him **a**. **Gn 8:12** 3254
"I will never **a** curse the ground **Gn 8:21** 3254
and I will never **a** destroy every **Gn 8:21** 3254
and all flesh shall never **a** be cut **Gn 9:11** 5750
neither shall there **a** be a flood **Gn 9:11** 5750
and never **a** shall the water become **Gn 9:15** 5750
He spoke to Him yet **a** and said, **Gn 18:29** 3254
A she said to him, **Gn 24:25**
Then Isaac dug **a** the wells of **Gn 26:18** 7725
she conceived **a** and bore a son **Gn 29:33** 5750
She conceived **a** and bore a son **Gn 29:34** 5750
she conceived **a** and bore a son **Gn 29:35** 5750
a and bore Jacob a second son. **Gn 30:7** 5750
a and bore a sixth son to Jacob. **Gn 30:19** 5750
a pasture *and* keep your flock: **Gn 30:31** 7725
a when he came from Paddan-aram, **Gn 35:9** 5750
Then she conceived **a** and bore a **Gn 38:4** 5750
did not have relations with her **a**. **Gn 38:26** 3254, 5750
you, you will not see my face **a**.' **Gn 44:23** 3254
I will also surely bring you up **a**; **Gn 46:4** 3254
"Put your hand into your bosom **a**." **Ex 4:7** 7725
he put his hand into his bosom **a**, **Ex 4:7** 7725
A Pharaoh said, "Look, the people **Ex 5:5**
do not let Pharaoh deal deceitfully **a** **Ex 8:29** 3254
sinned **a** and hardened his heart, **Ex 9:34** 3254
nor would there be so *many* **a**. **Ex 10:14** 310
Beware, do not see my face **a**, **Ex 10:28** 3254
I shall never see your face **a**!" **Ex 10:29** 3254
and such as shall never be **a**. **Ex 11:6** 3254
you will never see them **a** forever. **Ex 14:13** 3254
"Go down and come up **a**, you **Ex 19:24**
spoke **a** to Moses and to Aaron, **Lv 11:1**
look at him **a** on the seventh day, **Lv 13:6** 8145
he shall appear **a** to the priest. **Lv 13:7** 8145
turns **a** and is changed to white, **Lv 13:16** 7725
washed, the priest shall **a** look, **Lv 13:55** 310
if it appears **a** in the garment, **Lv 13:57** 5750
mark breaks out **a** in the house after **Lv 14:43** 7725
The LORD spoke **a** to Moses, saying, **Lv 23:1**
A the LORD spoke to Moses, saying, **Lv 23:23**
A the LORD spoke to Moses, saying, **Lv 23:33**
A, the LORD spoke to Moses, **Lv 27:1**
'**A**, if a man consecrates to the **Lv 27:16**
A the LORD spoke to Moses, saying, **Nu 3:11**
A the LORD spoke to Moses, saying, **Nu 6:1**
A the LORD spoke to Moses, saying, **Nu 8:5**
sons of Israel wept **a** and said, **Nu 11:4** 7725
But they did not do *it* **a**. **Nu 11:25** 3254
afterward she may be received **a**." **Nu 12:14**
on until Miriam was received **a**. **Nu 12:15**
come near the tent of meeting **a**, **Nu 18:22** 5750
A, the sons of Israel said to him, **Nu 20:19**
Then Balak **a** sent leaders, more **Nu 22:15** 5750, 3254
the wall, so he struck her **a**. **Nu 22:25** 3254
"**A** at Taberah and at Massah and **Dt 9:22**
and will never **a** do such a wicked **Dt 13:11** 3254
and will not act presumptuously **a**. **Dt 17:13** 5750
shall never **a** return that way.' **Dt 17:16** 3254
a the voice of the LORD my God, **Dt 18:16** 3254
and will never **a** do such an evil **Dt 19:20** 5750, 3254
to take her **a** to be his wife, **Dt 24:4** 7725
shall not go over the boughs **a**; **Dt 24:20** 310
you shall not go over it **a**; **Dt 24:21** 310
'You will never see it **a**!' **Dt 28:68** 3254
and will gather you **a** from all the **Dt 30:3** 7725
"And you shall **a** obey the LORD, **Dt 30:8** 7725
will **a** rejoice over you for good, **Dt 30:9** 7725
so that they will not rise **a**." **Dt 33:11**
"Cross **a** to the ark of the LORD **Jos 4:5** 6440
and circumcise **a** the sons of Israel **Jos 5:2** 7725
Now the sons of Israel **a** did evil **Jg 3:12** 3254
Then the sons of Israel **a** did evil **Jg 4:1** 3254
that the sons of Israel **a** played **Jg 8:33** 7725
Gaal spoke **a** and said, **Jg 9:37** 5750, 3254
Then the sons of Israel **a** did evil **Jg 10:6** 3254
But Jephthah sent messengers **a** to **Jg 11:14** 5750, 3254
Now the sons of Israel **a** did evil **Jg 13:1** 3254
come to us **a** that he may teach us **Jg 13:8** 5750
and the angel of God came **a** to the **Jg 13:9** 5750
not appear to Manoah or his wife **a**. **Jg 13:21** 3254, 5750
to grow **a** after it was shaved off. **Jg 16:22**
that he spent the night there **a**. **Jg 19:7** 7725
and arrayed for battle **a** in the place **Jg 20:22** 3254
"Shall we **a** draw near for battle **Jg 20:23** 3254
felled to the ground **a** 18,000 men **Jg 20:25** 5750
"Shall I yet **a** go out to battle **Jg 20:28** 3254
lifted up their voices and wept **a**; **Ru 1:14** 5750
A Naomi said to her, **Ru 2:20**
A he said, "Give me the cloak that **Ru 3:15**
a to their house in Ramah. **1Sa 1:19** 7725
"I did not call, lie down **a**." **1Sa 3:5** 7725
The LORD called yet **a**, **1Sa 3:6** 3254
not call, my son, lie down **a**." **1Sa 3:6** 7725
Samuel **a** for the third time. **1Sa 3:8** 3254
And the LORD appeared **a** at Shiloh, **1Sa 3:21** 3254
Dagon and set him in his place **a**. **1Sa 5:3** 7725
servant answered Saul **a** and said, **1Sa 9:8** 3254
Saul **a** until the day of his death; **1Sa 15:35** 3254
A the Philistine said, **1Sa 17:10**
When there was war **a**, **1Sa 19:8** 3254
sent messengers **a** the third time, **1Sa 19:21** 3254
Yet David vowed **a**, saying, **1Sa 20:3** 5750
vow **a** because of his love for him, **1Sa 20:17** 3254
for I will not harm you **a** because **1Sa 26:21** 5750
Abner repeated **a** to Asahel, **2Sa 2:22** 5750
all the people wept **a** over him. **2Sa 3:34** 3254
Philistines came up once **a** and spread **2Sa 5:22** 3254
Now David **a** gathered all the **2Sa 6:1** 3254, 5750
own place and not be disturbed **a**, **2Sa 7:10** 5750
"**A** what more can David say to You? **2Sa 7:20** 5750
A he prostrated himself and said, **2Sa 9:8**
Can I bring him back **a**? **2Sa 12:23** 5750
which cannot be gathered up **a**. **2Sa 14:14**
So he sent **a** a second time, but he **2Sa 14:29** 5750
then He will bring me back **a** and **2Sa 15:25**
ground, and did not *strike* him **a**, **2Sa 20:10** 8138
were at war **a** with Israel, **2Sa 21:15** 5750
not go out **a** with us to battle, **2Sa 21:17** 5750
war **a** with the Philistines at Gob; **2Sa 21:18** 5750
war with the Philistines **a** at Gob, **2Sa 21:19** 5750
There was war at Gath **a**, **2Sa 21:20** 5750
Now **a** the anger of the LORD burned **2Sa 24:1** 3254
Benaiah brought the king word **a**, **1Ki 2:30** 7725
if they turn to You **a** and confess **1Ki 8:33** 7725
Never **a** did such abundance of **1Ki 10:10** 5750
such almug trees have not come in **a** **1Ki 10:12**
but **a** he made priests of the high **1Ki 13:33** 7725
have turned their heart back **a**." **1Ki 18:37** 322
he ate and drank and lay down **a**. **1Ki 19:6** 7725
The angel of the LORD came **a** a **1Ki 19:7** 7725
"Go back **a**, for what have I done **1Ki 19:20** 7725
departed and brought him word **a**. **1Ki 20:9** 7725
So he **a** sent to him another **2Ki 1:11** 7725
So he **a** sent the captain of a **2Ki 1:13** 7725
come **a** into the land of Israel. **2Ki 6:23** 5750, 3254
Jehoash the son of Jehoahaz took **a** **2Ki 13:25** 7725
messengers **a** to Hezekiah saying, **2Ki 19:9** 7725
the house of Judah will **a** take root **2Ki 19:30** 3254
did not come out of his land **a**, **2Ki 24:7** 5750, 3254
David inquired **a** of God, **1Ch 14:14** 5750
in their own place and not be moved **a**; **1Ch 17:9** 5750
was war with the Philistines **a**, **1Ch 20:5** 5750
A there was war at Gath, where there **1Ch 20:6** 5750
"Return to me **a** in three days." **2Ch 10:5** 5750
Jeroboam did not **a** recover **2Ch 13:20** 5750
LORD and **a** removed the high places **2Ch 17:6** 5750
and went out **a** among the people **2Ch 19:4** 7725
For **a** the Edomites had come and **2Ch 28:17** 5750
of the LORD was established **a**. **2Ch 29:35**
and I will not **a** remove the foot **2Ch 33:8** 3254
him **a** to Jerusalem to his kingdom. **2Ch 33:13** 7725
a and again by His messengers, **2Ch 36:15** 7925
again and **a** by His messengers, **2Ch 36:15** 7971
shall we **a** break Your commandments **Ezr 9:14** 7725
the Valley Gate **a** and returned. **Ne 2:15**
A I said, "The thing which you are **Ne 5:9**
rest, they did evil **a** before You; **Ne 9:28** 7725
When they cried **a** to You, You **Ne 9:28** 7725
If you do so **a**, I will use force **Ne 13:21** 8138
She would not **a** go in to the king **Es 2:14** 5750
Then Esther spoke **a** to the king, **Es 8:3** 3254
A there was a day when the sons of **Jb 2:1**
My eye will not **a** see good. **Jb 7:7** 7725
"He will not return **a** to his house, **Jb 7:10** 5750
would You turn me into dust **a**? **Jb 10:9** 7725
And **a** You would show Your power **Jb 10:16** 7725
cut down, that it will sprout **a**, **Jb 14:7** 5750
"If a man dies, will he live **a**? **Jb 14:14**
"But come **a** all of you now, For I **Jb 17:10** 7725
"He lies down rich, but never **a**; **Jb 27:19** 622
And Job **a** took up his discourse **Jb 29:1** 3254
my words they did not speak **a**, **Jb 29:22** 8138
I will not do it **a**'? **Jb 34:32** 3254
you will not do it **a**! **Jb 41:8** 3254
that I may smile **a** Before I **Ps 39:13**
down, he will not rise up **a**." **Ps 41:8** 3254
for I shall **a** praise Him *For* the **Ps 42:5** 5750
in God, for I shall **a** praise Him, **Ps 43:5** 5750
and distresses Will revive me **a**, **Ps 71:20** 7725
up **a** from the depths of the earth. **Ps 71:20** 7725
And will He never be favorable **a**? **Ps 77:7** 3254
A and again they tempted God, **Ps 78:41** 7725
Again and **a** they tempted God, **Ps 78:41**
O God *of* hosts, turn **a** now, **Ps 80:14** 7725
Will You not Yourself revive us **a**, **Ps 85:6** 7725
For judgment will **a** be righteous, **Ps 94:15** 7725
indeed come **a** with a shout of joy, **Ps 126:6**
None who go to her return **a**, **Pr 2:19**
you will only have to do it **a**. **Pr 19:19** 3254
falls seven times, and rises **a**, **Pr 24:16**
of bringing it to his mouth **a**. **Pr 26:15** 7725
to its place it rises there **a**. **Ec 1:5**
rivers flow, There they flow **a**. **Ec 1:7** 7725
Then I looked **a** at all the acts of **Ec 4:1** 7725
looked **a** at vanity under the sun. **Ec 4:7** 7725
I **a** saw under the sun that the **Ec 9:11** 7725
How can I put it on **a**? I have **SS 5:3**
How can I dirty them **a**? **SS 5:3**
Where will you be stricken **a**, **Is 1:5** 5750
And never **a** will they learn war. **Is 2:4** 5750
it will **a** be *subject* to burning, **Is 6:13** 7725
Then the LORD spoke **a** to Ahaz, **Is 7:10** 3254
A the LORD spoke to me further, **Is 8:5** 3254
will never **a** rely on the one who **Is 10:20** 3254
Lord Will **a** recover the second time **Is 11:11** 3254
on Jacob and **a** choose Israel, **Is 14:1** 5750
inquire, inquire; Come back **a**." **Is 21:12** 7725
And it will fall, never to rise **a**. **Is 24:20** 3254
I will once **a** deal marvelously **Is 29:14** 3254
the house of Judah will **a** take root **Is 37:31** 3254
lie down together *and* not rise **a**; **Is 43:17**
And I will raise up her ruins **a**. **Is 44:26**
anger; You will never drink it **a**. **Is 51:22** 3254
A the LORD declares, "Those **Is 52:5**
Noah Would not flood the earth **a** **Is 54:9** 5750
will not be heard **a** in your land, **Is 60:18** 5750
"I will never **a** give your grain **Is 62:8** 5750
miss *it*, nor will it be made **a**. **Jer 3:16** 5750
Pass your hand **a** like a grape **Jer 6:9** 7725
"Do *men* fall and not get up **a**? **Jer 8:4**
tent **a** Or to set up my curtains. **Jer 10:20** 5750
I will **a** have compassion on them; **Jer 12:15** 7725
which cannot **a** be repaired; **Jer 19:11** 5750
will die and not see this land **a**. **Jer 22:12** 5750
of David Or ruling **a** in Judah.' " **Jer 22:30** 5750
I will bring them **a** to this land; **Jer 24:6** 7725
I have spoken to you **a** and again, **Jer 25:3** 7925
I have spoken to you again and **a**, **Jer 25:3** 1696
servants the prophets **a** and again, **Jer 25:4** 7925
servants the prophets again and **a**, **Jer 25:4** 7971
been sending to you **a** and again, **Jer 26:5** 7925
been sending to you again and **a**, **Jer 26:5** 7971
be brought **a** from Babylon'; **Jer 27:16** 7725
'which I sent to them **a** and again **Jer 29:19** 7925
and **a** by My servants the prophets; **Jer 29:19** 7971
"**A** I will build you and you **Jer 31:4** 5750
A you will take up your **Jer 31:4** 5750
"**A** you will plant vineyards On **Jer 31:5** 5750
And they will never languish **a**. **Jer 31:12** 3254
"Once **a** they will speak this word **Jer 31:23** 5750
"In those days they will not say **a**, **Jer 31:29** 5750
"They will not teach **a**, **Jer 31:34** 5750
a be bought in this land." **Jer 32:15** 5750
taught them, teaching **a** and again, **Jer 32:33** 7925
taught them, teaching again and **a**, **Jer 32:33** 3925
'Yet **a** there will be heard in **Jer 33:10** 5750
'There will **a** be in this place **Jer 33:12** 5750
the flocks will **a** pass under the **Jer 33:13** 5750
I have spoken to you **a** and again; **Jer 35:14** 7925
I have spoken to you again and **a**; **Jer 35:14** 1696
sending *them* **a** and again, **Jer 35:15** 7925
sending *them* again and **a**, **Jer 35:15** 7971
"Take **a** another scroll and write **Jer 36:28** 7725
the prophets, **a** and again, **Jer 44:4** 7925
the prophets, again and **a**, **Jer 44:4** 7971
'never shall My name be invoked **a** **Jer 44:26** 5750
And it will never **a** be inhabited **Jer 50:39** 5750
Babylon sink down and not rise **a** **Jer 51:64**
"**A**, when a righteous man turns **Ezk 3:20**
"Take **a** some of them and **Ezk 5:4** 5750
like of which I will never do **a**. **Ezk 5:9** 5750
can it be raised from its roots **a**. **Ezk 17:9**

Context	Reference	Number
“**A**, when a wicked man turns away	**Ezk 18:27**	
not return *to its sheath* **a**.”	**Ezk 21:5**	5750
A the word of the LORD came to me	**Ezk 21:8**	
of the LORD came to me **a**,	**Ezk 23:1**	
“**A**, they have done this to Me:	**Ezk 23:38**	5750
cleansed from your filthiness **a** Until	**Ezk 24:13**	5750
you will never be found **a**,”	**Ezk 26:21**	5750
of the LORD came **a** to me,	**Ezk 28:1**	
A the word of the LORD came to me	**Ezk 28:11**	
and it will never **a** lift itself up	**Ezk 29:15**	5750
“And it will never **a** be the	**Ezk 29:16**	5750
of the LORD came **a** to me saying,	**Ezk 30:1**	
and they will not **a** be victims of	**Ezk 34:29**	5750
never **a** bereave them of children.’	**Ezk 36:12**	3254
that you will not receive **a** the	**Ezk 36:30**	5750
A He said to me,	**Ezk 37:4**	
of the LORD came **a** to me saying,	**Ezk 37:15**	
and then gathered them **a** to their	**Ezk 39:28**	
will not **a** defile My holy name,	**Ezk 43:7**	5750
A he measured a thousand and led	**Ezk 47:4**	
A he measured a thousand and led	**Ezk 47:4**	
A he measured a thousand;	**Ezk 47:5**	
Then I got up **a** and carried on	**Da 8:27**	
it will be built **a**,	**Da 9:25**	7725
touched me **a** and strengthened me.	**Da 10:18**	3254
that he may **a** wage war up to his	**Da 11:10**	7725
“For the king of the North will **a**	**Da 11:13**	7725
you will enter into rest and rise **a**	**Da 12:13**	
a and gave birth to a daughter.	**Hos 1:6**	5750
“Go **a**, love a woman *who* is loved	**Hos 3:1**	5750
I will not destroy Ephraim **a**.	**Hos 11:9**	7725
I will make you live in tents **a**,	**Hos 12:9**	5750
Nor will we say **a**,	**Hos 14:3**	5750
in his shadow Will **a** raise grain,	**Hos 14:7**	7725
Nor will there be **a** after it To	**Jl 2:2**	3254
And I will never **a** make you a	**Jl 2:19**	5750
will not rise **a**—The virgin Israel.	**Am 5:2**	3254
They will fall and not rise **a**.”	**Am 8:14**	5750
And they will not **a** be rooted out	**Am 9:15**	5750
look **a** toward Your holy temple.’	**Jon 2:4**	3254
never **a** will they train for war.	**Mi 4:3**	5750
He will **a** have compassion on us;	**Mi 7:19**	7725
For never **a** will the wicked one	**Na 1:15**	3254
And you will never **a** be haughty On	**Zph 3:11**	3254
“**A**, proclaim, saying,	**Zch 1:17**	5750
will **a** overflow with prosperity,	**Zch 1:17**	5750
and the LORD will **a** comfort Zion	**Zch 1:17**	5750
and **a** choose Jerusalem.	**Zch 1:17**	5750
land, and will **a** choose Jerusalem.	**Zch 2:12**	5750
A he said to him, “See, I have taken	**Zch 3:4**	
I lifted up my eyes **a** and looked,	**Zch 5:1**	7725
A he said, “This is their appearance	**Zch 5:6**	
I lifted up my eyes **a** and looked,	**Zch 6:1**	7725
‘Old men and old women will **a** sit	**Zch 8:4**	5750
so I have **a** purposed in these days	**Zch 8:15**	7725
“Take **a** for yourself the	**Zch 11:15**	5750
the inhabitants of Jerusalem **a** dwell	**Zch 12:6**	5750
So you will **a** distinguish between	**Mal 3:18**	7725
A, the devil took Him to a very	**Mt 4:8**	*3825*
how can it be made salty **a**?	**Mt 5:13**	
“**A**, you have heard that the	**Mt 5:33**	*3825*
which a man found and hid **a**;	**Mt 13:44**	
“**A**, the kingdom of heaven is like	**Mt 13:45**	*3825*
“**A**, the kingdom of heaven is like	**Mt 13:47**	*3825*
“**A** I say to you, that if two of	**Mt 18:19**	*3825*
“**A** I say to you, it is easier for a	**Mt 19:24**	*3825*
“**A** he went out about the sixth	**Mt 20:5**	*3825*
“**A** he sent another group of	**Mt 21:36**	*3825*
Jesus spoke to them **a** in parables,	**Mt 22:1**	*3825*
“**A** he sent out other slaves	**Mt 22:4**	*3825*
away **a** a second time and prayed,	**Mt 26:42**	*3825*
A He came and found them sleeping,	**Mt 26:43**	*3825*
And He left them **a**,	**Mt 26:44**	*3825*
And **a** he denied *it* with an oath,	**Mt 26:72**	*3825*
cried out **a** with a loud voice,	**Mt 27:50**	*3825*
‘After three days I *am to* rise **a**.’	**Mt 27:63**	*1453*
And He went out **a** by the seashore;	**Mk 2:13**	*3825*
He entered **a** into a synagogue;	**Mk 3:1**	*3825*
and the crowd gathered **a**,	**Mk 3:20**	*3825*
He began to teach **a** by the sea.	**Mk 4:1**	*3825*
When Jesus had crossed over **a**	**Mk 5:21**	*3825*
He called the crowd to Him **a**,	**Mk 7:14**	*3825*
A He went out from the region of Tyre,	**Mk 7:31**	*3825*
In those days, when there was **a** a	**Mk 8:1**	*3825*
He **a** embarked and went away to the	**Mk 8:13**	*3825*
Then **a** He laid His hands on his	**Mk 8:25**	*3825*
and after three days rise **a**.	**Mk 8:31**	*450*
of him and do not enter him **a**.”	**Mk 9:25**	*3371*
with what will you make it salty **a**?	**Mk 9:50**	
crowds gathered around Him **a**,	**Mk 10:1**	*3825*
questioning Him about this **a**.	**Mk 10:10**	*3825*
Jesus answered **a** and said to them,	**Mk 10:24**	*3825*
And **a** He took the twelve aside and	**Mk 10:32**	*3825*
three days later He will rise **a**.”	**Mk 10:34**	*450*
one ever eat fruit from you **a**!”	**Mk 11:14**	*3371*
They came **a** to Jerusalem.	**Mk 11:27**	*3825*
“**A** he sent them another slave,	**Mk 12:4**	*3825*
resurrection, when they rise **a**,	**Mk 12:23**	*450*
the fact that the dead rise **a**,	**Mk 12:26**	*1453*
I will never **a** drink of the fruit	**Mk 14:25**	*3765*
A He went away and prayed, saying	**Mk 14:39**	*3825*
And **a** He came and found them	**Mk 14:40**	*3825*
A the high priest was questioning	**Mk 14:61**	*3825*
But **a** he denied it.	**Mk 14:70**	*3825*
bystanders were **a** saying to Peter,	**Mk 14:70**	*3825*
Then Pilate questioned Him **a**,	**Mk 15:4**	*3825*
Answering **a**, Pilate said	**Mk 15:12**	*3825*
the prophets of old had risen **a**.	**Lk 9:8**	*450*
the prophets of old has risen **a**.”	**Lk 9:19**	*450*
immediately she was made erect **a** and	**Lk 13:13**	*461*
a He said, “To what shall I compare	**Lk 13:20**	*3825*
was dead and has come to life **a**;	**Lk 15:24**	*326*
the third day He will rise **a**.”	**Lk 18:33**	*450*
I shall never **a** eat it until it is	**Lk 22:16**	*3765*
you, when once you have turned **a**,	**Lk 22:32**	*1994*
release Jesus, addressed them **a**,	**Lk 23:20**	*3825*
and the third day rise **a**.”	**Lk 24:7**	*450*
a from the dead the third day,	**Lk 24:46**	*450*
A the next day John was standing	**Jn 1:35**	*3825*
say to you, unless one is born **a** he	**Jn 3:3**	*509*
‘You must be born **a**.’	**Jn 3:7**	*509*
and went away **a** into Galilee.	**Jn 4:3**	*3825*
of this water will thirst **a**;	**Jn 4:13**	*3825*
He came **a** to Cana of	**Jn 4:46**	*3825*
This is **a** a second sign that Jesus	**Jn 4:54**	*3825*
withdrew **a** to the mountain by	**Jn 6:15**	*3825*
morning He came **a** into the temple,	**Jn 8:2**	*3825*
A He stooped down and wrote on	**Jn 8:8**	*3825*
Then Jesus **a** spoke to them, saying,	**Jn 8:12**	*3825*
He said **a** to them,	**Jn 8:21**	*3825*
the Pharisees also were asking him **a**	**Jn 9:15**	*3825*
said to the blind man **a**,	**Jn 9:17**	*3825*
why do you want to hear *it* **a**?	**Jn 9:27**	*3825*
Jesus said to them **a**,	**Jn 10:7**	*3825*
down My life so that I may take it **a**.	**Jn 10:17**	*3825*
I have authority to take it up **a**.	**Jn 10:18**	*3825*
A division occurred **a** among the	**Jn 10:19**	*3825*
picked up stones **a** to stone Him.	**Jn 10:31**	*3825*
they were seeking **a** to seize Him,	**Jn 10:39**	*3825*
And He went away **a** beyond the	**Jn 10:40**	*3825*
“Let us go to Judea **a**.”	**Jn 11:7**	*3825*
You, and are You going there **a**?”	**Jn 11:8**	*3825*
“Your brother will rise **a**.”	**Jn 11:23**	*450*
“I know that he will rise **a** in	**Jn 11:24**	*450*
a being deeply moved within,	**Jn 11:38**	*3825*
it, and will glorify it **a**.”	**Jn 12:28**	*3825*
not believe, for Isaiah said **a**,	**Jn 12:39**	*3825*
and reclined *at the table* **a**,	**Jn 13:12**	*3825*
a place for you, I will come **a** and	**Jn 14:3**	*3825*
and **a** a little while, and you will	**Jn 16:16**	*3825*
and **a** a little while, and you will	**Jn 16:17**	*3825*
see Me, and **a** a little while,	**Jn 16:19**	*3825*
but I will see you **a**,	**Jn 16:22**	*3825*
I am leaving the world **a** and	**Jn 16:28**	*3825*
Therefore He **a** asked them, “Whom do	**Jn 18:7**	*3825*
Peter then denied *it* **a**	**Jn 18:27**	*3825*
entered **a** into the Praetorium,	**Jn 18:33**	*3825*
this, he went out **a** to the Jews and	**Jn 18:38**	*3825*
So they cried out **a**,	**Jn 18:40**	*3825*
Pilate came out **a** and	**Jn 19:4**	*3825*
he entered into the Praetorium **a** and	**Jn 19:9**	*3825*
And **a** another Scripture says,	**Jn 19:37**	*3825*
that He must rise **a** from the dead.	**Jn 20:9**	*450*
went away **a** to their own homes.	**Jn 20:10**	*3825*
Jesus said to them **a**,	**Jn 20:21**	*3825*
days His disciples were **a** inside,	**Jn 20:26**	*3825*
manifested Himself **a** to the disciples	**Jn 21:1**	*3825*
He said to him **a** a second time,	**Jn 21:16**	*3825*
“But God raised Him up **a**,	**Ac 2:24**	*450*
“This Jesus God raised up **a**,	**Ac 2:32**	*450*
A a voice *came* to him a second	**Ac 10:15**	*3825*
suffer and rise **a** from the dead,	**Ac 17:3**	*450*
hear you **a** concerning this.”	**Ac 17:32**	*2532, 3825*
return to you **a** if God wills,”	**Ac 18:21**	*3825*
that they would not see his face **a**.	**Ac 20:38**	*3765*
ship, and they returned home **a**.	**Ac 21:6**	
from the dead, is never to die **a**;	**Ro 6:9**	*3765*
of slavery leading to fear **a**,	**Ro 8:15**	*3825*
God is able to graft them in **a**.	**Ro 11:23**	*3825*
IT MIGHT BE PAID BACK TO HIM **A**?	**Ro 11:35**	
to this end Christ died and lived **a**,	**Ro 14:9**	
Or you **a**, why do you regard your	**Ro 14:10**	*2532*
A he says, “REJOICE, O	**Ro 15:10**	*3825*
And **a**, “PRAISE THE LORD	**Ro 15:11**	*3825*
A Isaiah says, “THERE SHALL COME	**Ro 15:12**	*3825*
points so as to remind you **a**,	**Ro 15:15**	*1878*
and **a**, “THE LORD KNOWS	**1Co 3:20**	*3825*
and come together **a** so that Satan	**1Co 7:5**	*3825*
stumble, I will never eat meat **a**,	**1Co 8:13**	
or **a** the head to the feet,	**1Co 12:21**	*3825*
a from Macedonia to come to you,	**2Co 1:16**	*3825*
that to spare you I did not come **a** to	**2Co 1:23**	*3765*
would not come to you in sorrow **a**.	**2Co 2:1**	*3825*
beginning to commend ourselves **a**?	**2Co 3:1**	*3825*
We are not **a** commending ourselves	**2Co 5:12**	*3825*
died and rose **a** on their behalf.	**2Co 5:15**	*1453*
consider this **a** within himself,	**2Co 10:7**	*3825*
A I say, let no one think me	**2Co 11:16**	*3825*
I am afraid that when I come **a** my	**2Co 12:21**	*3825*
rest *as well*, that if I come **a**	**2Co 13:2**	*3825*
have said before, so I say **a** now,	**Ga 1:9**	*3825*
up **a** to Jerusalem with Barnabas,	**Ga 2:1**	*3825*
how is it that you turn back **a** to	**Ga 4:9**	*3825*
desire to be enslaved all over **a**?	**Ga 4:9**	*3825*
with whom I am **a** in labor until	**Ga 4:19**	*3825*
be subject **a** to a yoke of slavery.	**Ga 5:1**	*3825*
And I testify **a** to every man who	**Ga 5:3**	*3825*
Jesus through my coming to you **a**.	**Php 1:26**	*3825*
when you see him **a** you may rejoice	**Php 2:28**	*3825*
To write the same things **a** is no	**Php 3:1**	
a I will say, rejoice!	**Php 4:4**	*3825*
that Jesus died and rose **a**,	**1Th 4:14**	*450*
And **a**, “I WILL BE A FATHER TO HIM	**Heb 1:5**	*3825*
And when He **a** brings the	**Heb 1:6**	*3825*
And **a**, “I WILL PUT MY TRUST	**Heb 2:13**	*3825*
And **a**, “BEHOLD, I AND THE	**Heb 2:13**	*3825*
and **a** in this *passage*,	**Heb 4:5**	*3825*
He **a** fixes a certain day,	**Heb 4:7**	*3825*
you have need **a** for someone to	**Heb 5:12**	*3825*
not laying **a** a foundation of	**Heb 6:1**	*3825*
to renew them **a** to repentance,	**Heb 6:6**	*3825*
since they **a** crucify to themselves	**Heb 6:6**	*388*
I WILL REPAY.” And **a**, “THE LORD	**Heb 10:30**	*3825*
Then he prayed **a**, and the sky	**Jas 5:18**	*3825*
caused us to be born **a** to a living hope	**1Pe 1:3**	*313*
for you have been born **a** not of	**1Pe 1:23**	*313*
they are **a** entangled in them and	**2Pe 2:20**	*3825*
I heard **a** speaking with me,	**Rv 10:8**	*3825*
“You must prophesy **a** concerning	**Rv 10:11**	*3825*

AGAINST

Context	Reference	Number
that Cain rose up **a** Abel his	**Gn 4:8**	*413*
and sinners **a** the LORD.	**Gn 13:13**	
a them in the valley of Siddim,	**Gn 14:8**	854
a Chedorlaomer king of Elam and	**Gn 14:9**	854
king of Ellasar—four kings **a** five.	**Gn 14:9**	854
his forces **a** them by night,	**Gn 14:15**	5921
man, His hand *will be* **a** everyone,	**Gn 16:12**	
And everyone’s hand *will be* **a** him;	**Gn 16:12**	
So they pressed hard **a** Lot and	**Gn 19:9**	
I also kept you from sinning **a** Me;	**Gn 20:6**	
And how have I sinned **a** you,	**Gn 20:9**	
stretch out your hand **a** the lad,	**Gn 22:12**	413
So Esau bore a grudge **a** Jacob	**Gn 27:41**	7852
brother’s anger **a** you subsides and	**Gn 27:45**	4480
Then Jacob’s anger burned **a** Rachel,	**Gn 30:2**	
that he had not prevailed **a** him,	**Gn 32:25**	
they will gather together **a** me and	**Gn 34:30**	5921
plotted **a** him to put him to death.	**Gn 37:18**	854
this great evil and sin **a** God?”	**Gn 39:9**	
‘Do not sin **a** the boy’;	**Gn 42:22**	
all these things are **a** me.”	**Gn 42:36**	5921
occasion **a** us and fall upon us,	**Gn 43:18**	5921
if Joseph bears a grudge **a** us	**Gn 50:15**	7852
As for you, you meant evil **a** me,	**Gn 50:20**	5921
those who hate us, and fight **a** us and	**Ex 1:10**	
anger of the LORD burned **a** Moses,	**Ex 4:14**	
“Still you exalt yourself **a** My	**Ex 9:17**	
“I have sinned **a** the LORD your	**Ex 10:16**	
the LORD your God and **a** you.	**Ex 10:16**	
‘But **a** any of the sons of Israel a	**Ex 11:7**	
even bark, whether **a** man or beast,	**Ex 11:7**	
and **a** all the gods of Egypt I will	**Ex 12:12**	
for them **a** the Egyptians.”	**Ex 14:25**	
the LORD had used **a** the Egyptians,	**Ex 14:31**	
those who rise up **a** You;	**Ex 15:7**	
desire shall be gratified **a** them;	**Ex 15:9**	
the sons of Israel grumbled **a** Moses	**Ex 16:2**	5921
hears your grumblings **a** the LORD;	**Ex 16:7**	5921
are we, that you grumble **a** us?”	**Ex 16:7**	5921
which you grumble **a** Him.	**Ex 16:8**	5921
not **a** us but against the LORD.”	**Ex 16:8**	5921
not against us but **a** the LORD.”	**Ex 16:8**	5921
they grumbled **a** Moses and said,	**Ex 17:3**	5921
and fought **a** Israel at Rephidim.	**Ex 17:8**	5973
us and go out, fight **a** Amalek.	**Ex 17:9**	
told him, and fought **a** Amalek;	**Ex 17:10**	
the LORD will have war **a** Amalek	**Ex 17:16**	
they dealt proudly **a** the people.”	**Ex 18:11**	5921
the LORD will break out **a** them.”	**Ex 19:22**	
false witness **a** your neighbor.	**Ex 20:16**	
they will make you sin **a** Me;	**Ex 23:33**	
not stretch out His hand **a** the nobles	**Ex 24:11**	413
that My anger may burn **a** them and	**Ex 32:10**	
why does Your anger burn **a** Your	**Ex 32:11**	
for every man has been **a** his son	**Ex 32:29**	
against his son and **a** his brother	**Ex 32:29**	
“Whoever has sinned **a** Me,	**Ex 32:33**	
a the LORD’s holy things,	**Lv 5:15**	4480
he has sinned **a** the holy thing,	**Lv 5:16**	4480
and acts unfaithfully **a** the LORD,	**Lv 6:2**	
wrathful **a** all the congregation.	**Lv 10:6**	5921
face **a** that person who eats blood and	**Lv 17:10**	
act **a** the life of your neighbor;	**Lv 19:16**	5921
grudge **a** the sons of your people,	**Lv 19:18**	854
‘I will also set My face **a** that	**Lv 20:3**	
then I Myself will set My face **a**	**Lv 20:5**	
against that man and **a** his family,	**Lv 20:5**	
I will also set My face **a** that	**Lv 20:6**	
‘I will set My face **a** you so	**Lv 26:17**	
you act with hostility **a** Me and	**Lv 26:21**	5973
Me, but act with hostility **a** Me,	**Lv 26:23**	5973
I will act with hostility **a** you;	**Lv 26:24**	5973
Me, but act with hostility **a** Me,	**Lv 26:27**	5973
act with wrathful hostility **a** you,	**Lv 26:28**	5973
which they committed **a** Me,	**Lv 26:40**	
their acting with hostility **a** Me	**Lv 26:40**	5973
was acting with hostility **a** them,	**Lv 26:41**	5973
acting unfaithfully **a** the LORD,	**Nu 5:6**	
and there is no witness **a** her and	**Nu 5:13**	
a the adversary who attacks you,	**Nu 10:9**	5921
the LORD was kindled **a** the people,	**Nu 11:33**	
Then Miriam and Aaron spoke **a**	**Nu 12:1**	
not afraid To speak **a** My servant,	**Nu 12:8**	
against My servant, **a** Moses?”	**Nu 12:8**	
burned **a** them and He departed.	**Nu 12:9**	
not able to go up **a** the people,	**Nu 13:31**	413
Israel grumbled **a** Moses and Aaron;	**Nu 14:2**	5921
“Only do not rebel **a** the LORD;	**Nu 14:9**	
who are grumbling **a** Me?	**Nu 14:27**	5921
which they are making **a** Me.	**Nu 14:27**	5921
upward, who have grumbled **a** Me.	**Nu 14:29**	5921
who are gathered together **a** Me.	**Nu 14:35**	5921
all the congregation grumble **a** him	**Nu 14:36**	5921
together **a** Moses and Aaron,	**Nu 16:3**	5921
are gathered together **a** the LORD;	**Nu 16:11**	5921
is he that you grumble **a** him?”	**Nu 16:11**	5921

assembled all the congregation **a** them Nu 16:19 5921
Israel grumbled **a** Moses and Aaron, Nu 16:41 5921
had assembled **a** Moses and Aaron, Nu 16:42 5921
Israel, who are grumbling **a** you." Nu 17:5 5921
to be kept as a sign **a** the rebels, Nu 17:10
an end to their grumblings **a** Me, Nu 17:10
4480, 5921
themselves **a** Moses and Aaron. Nu 20:2 5921
I will come out with the sword **a** you." Nu 20:18 7122
came out **a** him with a heavy force and Nu 20:20 7122
because you rebelled **a** My command Nu 20:24 854
Atharim, then he fought **a** Israel and Nu 21:1
The people spoke **a** God and Moses, Nu 21:5
we have spoken **a** the LORD and you; Nu 21:7
out **a** Israel in the wilderness, Nu 21:23 7122
came to Jahaz and fought **a** Israel. Nu 21:23
who had fought **a** the former king Nu 21:26
I may be able to fight **a** them and Nu 22:11
in the way as an adversary **a** him. Nu 22:22
pressed Balaam's foot **a** the wall, Nu 22:25 413
you were standing in the way **a** me. Nu 22:34 7122
"For there is no omen **a** Jacob, Nu 23:23
is there any divination **a** Israel; Nu 23:23
Then Balak's anger burned **a** Balaam, Nu 24:10 413
and the LORD was angry **a** Israel. Nu 25:3
who contended **a** Moses and against Nu 26:9 5921
a Aaron in the company of Korah, Nu 26:9 5921
when they contended **a** the LORD, Nu 26:9 5921
together **a** the LORD in the company Nu 27:3 5921
you rebelled **a** My command to treat Nu 27:14 854
bound herself, shall stand **a** her. Nu 30:9 5921
war, that they may go **a** Midian to Nu 31:3 5921
So they made war **a** Midian, Nu 31:7 5921
to trespass **a** the LORD in the Nu 31:16
the LORD's anger burned **a** Israel, Nu 32:13
anger of the LORD **a** Israel. Nu 32:14 413
you have sinned **a** the LORD, Nu 32:23
but rebelled **a** the command of the Dt 1:26 854
'We have sinned **a** the LORD; Dt 1:41
a the command of the LORD, Dt 1:43 854
that hill country came out **a** you and Dt 1:44 7122
the hand of the LORD was **a** them, Dt 2:15
image in the form of anything **a** Dt 4:23
and earth to witness **a** you today, Dt 4:26
false witness **a** your neighbor. Dt 5:20
your God will be kindled **a** you, Dt 6:15
wonders before our eyes **a** Egypt, Dt 6:22
of the LORD will be kindled **a** you and Dt 7:4
God will send the hornet **a** them, Dt 7:20
I testify **a** you today that you Dt 8:19
have been rebellious **a** the LORD. Dt 9:7 5973
indeed sinned **a** the LORD your God. Dt 9:16
a you in order to destroy you, Dt 9:19 5921
then you rebelled **a** the command of Dt 9:23 854
"You have been rebellious **a** the Dt 9:24 5973
of the LORD will be kindled **a** you, Dt 11:17
rebellion **a** the LORD your God who Dt 13:5 5921
first **a** him to put him to death, Dt 13:9
then he may cry to the LORD **a** you, Dt 15:9 5921
first **a** him to put him to death, Dt 17:7
and rises up **a** him Dt 19:11 5921
shall not rise up **a** a man on account Dt 19:15
a malicious witness rises up **a** a man Dt 19:16
"When you go out to battle **a** your Dt 20:1 5921
the battle **a** your enemies today. Dt 20:3 5921
to fight for you **a** your enemies, Dt 20:4 5973
you approach a city to fight **a** it, Dt 20:10 5921
with you, but makes war **a** you, Dt 20:12 5973
you would sin **a** the LORD your God. Dt 20:18
war **a** it in order to capture it, Dt 20:19 5921
trees by swinging an axe **a** them; Dt 20:19 5921
may construct siegeworks **a** the city Dt 20:20 5921
go out to battle **a** your enemies, Dt 21:10 5921
in to her and *then* turns **a** her, Dt 22:13 8130
for a wife, but he turned **a** her; Dt 22:16 8130
a his neighbor and murders him, Dt 22:26 5921
and because they hired **a** you Dt 23:4 5921
go out as an army **a** your enemies, Dt 23:9 5921
and if the latter husband turns **a** Dt 24:3 8130
careful **a** an infection of leprosy, Dt 24:8
so that he will not cry **a** you to Dt 24:15 5921
a you to be defeated before you; Dt 28:7 5921
they will come out **a** you one way Dt 28:7 413
you will go out one way **a** them, Dt 28:25 413
whom the LORD will send **a** you, Dt 28:48
bring a nation **a** you from afar, Dt 28:49 5921
His jealousy will burn **a** that man, Dt 29:20
of the LORD burned **a** that land, Dt 29:27
and earth to witness **a** you today, Dt 30:19
be kindled **a** them in that day, Dt 31:17
a witness for Me **a** the sons of Israel. Dt 31:19
remain there as a witness **a** you. Dt 31:26
have been rebellious **a** the LORD; Dt 31:27 5973
and the earth to witness **a** them. Dt 31:28
be a help **a** his adversaries." Dt 33:7 4480
loins of those who rise up **a** him, Dt 33:11
in the land of Egypt **a** Pharaoh, Dt 34:11
"Anyone who rebels **a** your command Jos 1:18 854
LORD burned **a** the sons of Israel. Jos 7:1
"Truly, I have sinned **a** the LORD, Jos 7:20
an ambush **a** him behind the city. Jos 8:14
wilderness turned **a** the pursuers. Jos 8:20 413
grumbled **a** the leaders. Jos 9:18 5921
camped by Gibeon and fought **a** it. Jos 10:5 5921
country have assembled **a** us." Jos 10:6 413
stones **a** the mouth of the cave, Jos 10:18 413
word **a** any of the sons of Israel. Jos 10:21
to Libnah, and fought **a** Libnah. Jos 10:29 5973
they camped by it and fought **a** it. Jos 10:31
they camped by it and fought **a** it. Jos 10:34 5921
to Hebron, and they fought **a** it. Jos 10:36 5921
to Debir, and they fought **a** it. Jos 10:38 5921
of Merom, to fight **a** Israel. Jos 11:5 5973
there **a** the inhabitants of Debir; Jos 15:15 413
with the territory over **a** Joppa. Jos 19:46 4136
at Shiloh to go up **a** them in war. Jos 22:12 5921
committed **a** the God of Israel, Jos 22:16
to rebel **a** the LORD this day? Jos 22:16
If you rebel **a** the LORD today, Jos 22:18
Only do not rebel **a** the LORD, Jos 22:19
or rebel **a** us by building an altar Jos 22:19 854
or if in an unfaithful act **a** the Jos 22:22
rebel **a** the LORD and turn away from Jos 22:29
this unfaithful act **a** the LORD; Jos 22:31
speak of going up **a** them in war to Jos 22:33 5921
anger of the LORD will burn **a** you, Jos 23:16
Moab, arose and fought **a** Israel, Jos 24:9
citizens of Jericho fought **a** you, Jos 24:11
"You are witnesses **a** yourselves Jos 24:22
stone shall be for a witness **a** us, Jos 24:27
it shall be for a witness **a** you, Jos 24:27
up first for us **a** the Canaanites, Jg 1:1 413
the Canaanites, to fight **a** them?" Jg 1:1
we may fight **a** the Canaanites; Jg 1:3
Adoni-bezek in Bezek and fought **a** Jg 1:5
Then the sons of Judah fought **a** Jg 1:8
went down to fight **a** the Canaanites Jg 1:9
So Judah went **a** the Canaanites who Jg 1:10 413
went **a** the inhabitants of Debir Jg 1:11 413
house of Joseph went up **a** Bethel, Jg 1:22
anger of the LORD burned **a** Israel, Jg 2:14
of the LORD was **a** them for evil, Jg 2:15
anger of the LORD burned **a** Israel, Jg 2:20
of the LORD was kindled **a** Israel, Jg 3:8
Eglon the king of Moab **a** Israel, Jg 3:12 5921
courses they fought **a** Sisera. Jg 5:20 5973
help of the LORD **a** the warriors.' Jg 5:23
power of Midian prevailed **a** Israel. Jg 6:2 5921
sons of the east and go **a** them. Jg 6:3 5921
So they would camp **a** them and Jg 6:4 5921
Joash said to all who stood **a** him, Jg 6:31 5921
"Let Baal contend **a** him," Jg 6:32
"Do not let Your anger burn **a** me Jg 6:39
"Arise, go down **a** the camp, for I Jg 7:9
that you may go down **a** the camp." Jg 7:11
the LORD set the sword of one **a** Jg 7:22
"Come down **a** Midian and take the Jg 7:24 7122
when you went to fight **a** Midian?" Jg 8:1
but you have risen **a** my father's Jg 9:18 5921
Shechem set men in ambush **a** him Jg 9:25
are stirring up the city **a** you. Jg 9:31 5921
who are with him come out **a** you, Jg 9:33 413
wait **a** Shechem in four companies. Jg 9:34 5921
he arose **a** them and slew them. Jg 9:43 5921
two companies then dashed **a** all who Jg 9:44 5921
fought **a** the city all that day, Jg 9:45
camped **a** Thebez and captured it. Jg 9:50
came to the tower and fought **a** it, Jg 9:52
anger of the LORD burned **a** Israel, Jg 10:7
the Jordan to fight also **a** Judah, Jg 10:9
"We have sinned **a** You, for Jg 10:10
to fight **a** the sons of Ammon? Jg 10:18
the sons of Ammon fought **a** Israel. Jg 11:4 5973
the sons of Ammon fought **a** Israel Jg 11:5 5973
may fight **a** the sons of Ammon." Jg 11:6
"If you take me back to fight **a** Jg 11:9
come to me to fight **a** my land?" Jg 11:12
or did he ever fight **a** them? Jg 11:25
'I therefore have not sinned **a** you, Jg 11:27
doing me wrong by making war **a** me; Jg 11:27
the sons of Ammon to fight **a** them; Jg 11:32
over to fight **a** the sons of Ammon Jg 12:1
crossed over **a** the sons of Ammon, Jg 12:3 413
to me this day to fight **a** me?" Jg 12:3
an occasion **a** the Philistines. Jg 14:4 4480
"Why have you come up **a** us?" Jg 15:10 5921
rests, that I may lean **a** them." Jg 16:26 5921
rested, and braced himself **a** them, Jg 16:29 5921
"Arise, and let us go up **a** them; Jg 18:9 5921
concubine played the harlot **a** him, Jg 19:2 5921
such an act of folly **a** this man." Jg 19:24
"But the men of Gibeah rose up **a** Jg 20:5 5921
we will go up **a** it by lot. Jg 20:9 5921
Israel were gathered **a** the city, Jg 20:11 413
to battle **a** the sons of Israel. Jg 20:14 5973
battle **a** the sons of Benjamin?" Jg 20:18 5973
the morning and camped **a** Gibeah. Jg 20:19 5921
went out to battle **a** Benjamin, Jg 20:20 5973
for battle **a** them at Gibeah. Jg 20:20 854
a the sons of my brother Benjamin?" Jg 20:23 5973
And the LORD said, "Go up **a** him." Jg 20:23 413
Then the sons of Israel came **a** the Jg 20:24 413
Benjamin went out **a** them from Jg 20:25 7122
out to battle **a** the sons of my brother Jg 20:28 5973
The sons of Israel went up **a** Jg 20:30 413
and arrayed themselves **a** Gibeah as Jg 20:30 413
The sons of Benjamin went out **a** the Jg 20:31 7122
men from all Israel came **a** Gibeah, Jg 20:34 5048
ambush whom they had set **a** Gibeah, Jg 20:36 413
hurried and rushed **a** Gibeah; Jg 20:37 413
turned back **a** the sons of Benjamin Jg 20:48 413
of the LORD has gone forth **a** me." Ru 1:13
since the LORD has witnessed **a** me Ru 1:21
mouth speaks boldly **a** my enemies, 1Sa 2:1 5921
A them He will thunder in the 1Sa 2:10 5921
"If one man sins **a** another, God 1Sa 2:25
but if a man sins **a** the LORD, 1Sa 2:25
"In that day I will carry out **a** 1Sa 3:12 413
the hand of the LORD was **a** the 1Sa 5:9
"We have sinned **a** the LORD." 1Sa 7:6
the Philistines went up **a** Israel. 1Sa 7:7 413
drew near to battle **a** Israel. 1Sa 7:10
thunder on that day **a** the Philistines 1Sa 7:10 5921
And the hand of the LORD was **a** the 1Sa 7:13
bear witness **a** me before the LORD 1Sa 12:3
"The LORD is witness **a** you, 1Sa 12:5
of Moab, and they fought **a** them. 1Sa 12:9
of the sons of Ammon came **a** you, 1Sa 12:12 5921
rebel **a** the command of the LORD, 1Sa 12:14 854
rebel **a** the command of the LORD, 1Sa 12:15 854
hand of the LORD will be **a** you, 1Sa 12:15
you, *as it was* **a** your fathers. 1Sa 12:15
sin **a** the LORD by ceasing to pray 1Sa 12:23
will come down **a** me at Gilgal, 1Sa 13:12 413
every man's sword was **a** his fellow, 1Sa 14:20
the people are sinning **a** the LORD 1Sa 14:33
and do not sin **a** the LORD by 1Sa 14:34
a all his enemies on every side, 1Sa 14:47
his enemies on every side, **a** Moab, 1Sa 14:47
Now the war **a** the Philistines was 1Sa 14:52 5921
how he set himself **a** him on the 1Sa 15:2
and fight **a** them until they are 1Sa 15:18
if I prevail **a** him and kill him, 1Sa 17:9
up in battle array, army **a** army. 1Sa 17:21 7122
anger burned **a** David and he said, 1Sa 17:28
"You are not able to go **a** this 1Sa 17:33 413
and when he rose up **a** me, 1Sa 17:35 5921
David going out **a** the Philistine, 1Sa 17:55 7122
"My hand shall not be **a** him, 1Sa 18:17
of the Philistines be **a** him." 1Sa 18:17
of the Philistines may be **a** him." 1Sa 18:21
the king sin **a** his servant David, 1Sa 19:4
since he has not sinned **a** you, 1Sa 19:4
will you sin **a** innocent blood by 1Sa 19:5
a Jonathan and he said to him, 1Sa 20:30
"For all of you have conspired **a** 1Sa 22:8 5921
my servant **a** me to lie in ambush, 1Sa 22:8 5921
the son of Jesse conspired **a** me, 1Sa 22:13 5921
that he would rise up **a** me by 1Sa 22:13 413
Philistines are fighting **a** Keilah and 1Sa 23:1
a the ranks of the Philistines?" 1Sa 23:3 413
that Saul was plotting evil **a** him; 1Sa 23:9 5921
to stretch out my hand **a** him, 1Sa 24:6
not allow them to rise up **a** Saul. 1Sa 24:7 413
not stretch out my hand **a** my lord, 1Sa 24:10
and I have not sinned **a** you, 1Sa 24:11
but my hand shall not be **a** you. 1Sa 24:12
but my hand shall not be **a** you. 1Sa 24:13
for evil is plotted **a** our master 1Sa 25:17 413
master and **a** all his household; 1Sa 25:17 5921
and those who seek evil **a** my lord, 1Sa 25:26 413
out his hand **a** the LORD's anointed 1Sa 26:9
out my hand **a** the LORD's anointed; 1Sa 26:11
the LORD has stirred you up **a** me, 1Sa 26:19
out my hand **a** the LORD's anointed. 1Sa 26:23
"**A** the Negev of Judah and against 1Sa 27:10 5921
"Against the Negev of Judah and **a** 1Sa 27:10 5921
and **a** the Negev of the Kenites." 1Sa 27:10 413
camps for war, to fight **a** Israel. 1Sa 28:1
Philistines are waging war **a** me, 1Sa 28:15
that I may not go and fight **a** the 1Sa 29:8
our hand the band that came **a** us. 1Sa 30:23 5921
were fighting **a** Israel, 1Sa 31:1
The battle went heavily **a** Saul, 1Sa 31:3 413
your mouth has testified **a** you, 2Sa 1:16
went to Jerusalem **a** the Jebusites, 2Sa 5:6 413
"Shall I go up **a** the Philistines? 2Sa 5:19 413
anger of the LORD burned **a** Uzzah, 2Sa 6:7
of the LORD's outburst **a** Uzzah, 2Sa 6:8
a Hadadezer and defeated him; 2Sa 8:10
a him in front and in the rear, 2Sa 10:9 413
and arrayed *them* **a** the Arameans. 2Sa 10:9 7122
arrayed *them* **a** the sons of Ammon. 2Sa 10:10 7122
near to the battle **a** the Arameans, 2Sa 10:13
Joab returned from *fighting* **a** the sons 2Sa 10:14 5921
to meet David and fought **a** him. 2Sa 10:17 5973
city went out and fought **a** Joab, 2Sa 11:17 854
"The men prevailed **a** us and came 2Sa 11:23 5921
us and came out **a** us in the field, 2Sa 11:23 413
make your battle **a** the city 2Sa 11:25 413
anger burned greatly **a** the man, 2Sa 12:5
a you from your own household; 2Sa 12:11 5921
"I have sinned **a** the LORD." 2Sa 12:13
a Rabbah of the sons of Ammon and 2Sa 12:26
"I have fought **a** Rabbah, I have 2Sa 12:27
camp **a** the city and capture it, 2Sa 12:28 5921
and went to Rabbah, fought **a** it and 2Sa 12:29
has risen **a** your maidservant, 2Sa 14:7 5921
such a thing **a** the people of God? 2Sa 14:13 5921
Ahithophel has counseled **a** you." 2Sa 17:21 5921
went out into the field **a** Israel, 2Sa 18:6 7122
put out my hand **a** the king's son; 2Sa 18:12 413
dealt treacherously **a** his life 2Sa 18:13
their hands **a** my lord the king." 2Sa 18:28
of all those who rose up **a** you." 2Sa 18:31 5921
all who rise up **a** you for evil, 2Sa 18:32 5921
But Amasa was not on guard **a** the 2Sa 20:10
they cast up a siege ramp **a** the city, 2Sa 20:15 413
lifted up his hand **a** King David. 2Sa 20:21
as they fought **a** the Philistines, 2Sa 21:15 854
have not acted wickedly **a** my God. 2Sa 22:22 4480
under me those who rose up **a** me. 2Sa 22:40
me above those who rise up **a** me; 2Sa 22:49
a three hundred and killed *them*, 2Sa 23:18 5921
anger of the LORD burned **a** Israel, 2Sa 24:1
it incited David **a** them to say, 2Sa 24:1
the king's word prevailed **a** Joab 2Sa 24:4 413

and **a** the commanders of the army. 2Sa 24:4 5921
Please let Your hand be **a** me and 2Sa 24:17
me and **a** my father's house." 2Sa 24:17
spoken this word **a** his own life. 1Ki 2:23
A the wall of the house he built 1Ki 6:5 5921
the stories **a** the whole house, 1Ki 6:10 5921
"If a man sins **a** his neighbor and 1Ki 8:31
because they have sinned **a** You, 1Ki 8:33
because they have sinned **a** You, 1Ki 8:35
go out to battle **a** their enemy, 1Ki 8:44 5921
"When they sin **a** You 1Ki 8:46
Your people who have sinned **a** You 1Ki 8:50
they have transgressed **a** You, 1Ki 8:50
a widow, also rebelled **a** the king. 1Ki 11:26
reason why he rebelled **a** the king: 1Ki 11:27
So Israel has been in rebellion **a** 1Ki 12:19
to fight **a** the house of Israel to 1Ki 12:21 5973
"You must not go up and fight **a** 1Ki 12:24 5973
He cried **a** the altar by the 1Ki 13:2 5921
he cried **a** the altar in Bethel, 1Ki 13:4 5921
he stretched out **a** him dried up, 1Ki 13:4 5921
word of the LORD **a** the altar in Bethel 1Ki 13:32 5921
a all the houses of the high places 1Ki 13:32 5921
king of Egypt came up **a** Jerusalem. 1Ki 14:25 5921
Baasha king of Israel went up **a** Judah 1Ki 15:17 5921
his armies **a** the cities of Israel, 1Ki 15:20 5921
house of Issachar conspired **a** him, 1Ki 15:27 5921
Jehu the son of Hanani **a** Baasha, 1Ki 16:1 5921
came **a** Baasha and his household, 1Ki 16:7 413
his chariots, conspired **a** him. 1Ki 16:9 5921
which He spoke **a** Baasha through 1Ki 16:12 413
people were camped **a** Gibbethon, 1Ki 16:15 5921
besieged Samaria and fought **a** it. 1Ki 20:1
stationed *themselves* **a** the city. 1Ki 20:12 5921
king of Aram will come up **a** you." 1Ki 20:22 5921
let us fight **a** them in the plain, 1Ki 20:23 854
we will fight **a** them in the plain, 1Ki 20:25 854
up to Aphek to fight **a** Israel. 1Ki 20:26 5973
one over **a** the other seven days. 1Ki 20:29 5227
him, and let them testify **a** him, 1Ki 21:10
the worthless men testified **a** him, 1Ki 21:13
against him, even **a** Naboth, 1Ki 21:13
"Shall I go **a** Ramoth-gilead to 1Ki 22:6 5921
has proclaimed disaster **a** you." 1Ki 22:23 5921
of Judah went up **a** Ramoth-gilead. 1Ki 22:29
they turned aside to fight **a** him, 1Ki 22:32 5921
Now Moab rebelled **a** Israel after 2Ki 1:1
rebelled **a** the king of Israel. 2Ki 3:5
king of Moab has rebelled **a** me. 2Ki 3:7
you go with me to fight **a** Moab?" 2Ki 3:7 413
kings had come up to fight **a** them. 2Ki 3:21
there came great wrath **a** Israel, 2Ki 3:27 5921
he is seeking a quarrel **a** me." 2Ki 5:7
king of Aram was warring **a** Israel; 2Ki 6:8
door and hold the door shut **a** him. 2Ki 6:32
the king of Israel has hired **a** us 2Ki 7:6 5921
Edom revolted **a** Judah to this day. 2Ki 8:22
4480, 8478, 3027
son of Ahab to war **a** Hazael king of 2Ki 8:28 5973
he fought **a** Hazael king of Aram. 2Ki 8:29 854
son of Nimshi conspired **a** Joram. 2Ki 9:14 413
a Hazael king of Aram, 2Ki 9:14
4480, 6440
the LORD laid this oracle **a** him: 2Ki 9:25 5921
a my master and killed him, 2Ki 10:9 5921
and fought **a** Gath and captured it, 2Ki 12:17 5921
of the LORD was kindled **a** Israel, 2Ki 13:3
he fought **a** Amaziah king of Judah, 2Ki 13:12 5973
They conspired **a** him in Jerusalem, 2Ki 14:19 5921
Shallum the son of Jabesh conspired **a** 2Ki 15:10 5921
king of Assyria, came **a** the land, 2Ki 15:19 5921
a him and struck him in Samaria, 2Ki 15:25 5921
a Pekah the son of Remaliah, 2Ki 15:30 5921
Pekah the son of Remaliah **a** Judah. 2Ki 15:37
Israel, who are rising up **a** me." 2Ki 16:7 5921
up **a** Damascus and captured it, 2Ki 16:9 413
king of Assyria came up **a** him, 2Ki 17:3 5921
had sinned **a** the LORD their God, 2Ki 17:7
not right **a** the LORD their God. 2Ki 17:9 5921
And he rebelled **a** the king of 2Ki 18:7
came up **a** Samaria and besieged it. 2Ki 18:9 5921
Sennacherib king of Assyria came up **a** 2Ki 18:13 5921
rely, that you have rebelled **a** me? 2Ki 18:20
a this place to destroy it? 2Ki 18:25 5921
'Go up **a** this land and destroy it.' 2Ki 18:25 5921
king of Assyria fighting **a** Libnah, 2Ki 19:8 5921
he has come out to fight **a** you," 2Ki 19:9 854
that the LORD has spoken **a** him: 2Ki 19:21 5921
And **a** whom have you raised *your* 2Ki 19:22 5921
A the Holy One of Israel! 2Ki 19:22 5921
coming in, And your raging **a** Me. 2Ki 19:27 413
'Because of your raging **a** Me, 2Ki 19:28 413
shield or throw up a siege ramp **a** it. 2Ki 19:32 5921
servants of Amon conspired **a** him 2Ki 21:23 5921
who had conspired **a** King Amon, 2Ki 21:24 5921
wrath of the LORD that burns **a** us, 2Ki 22:13
My wrath burns **a** this place, 2Ki 22:17
you heard what I spoke **a** this place 2Ki 22:19 5921
against this place and **a** its inhabitants 2Ki 22:19 5921
have done **a** the altar of Bethel." 2Ki 23:17 5921
which His anger burned **a** Judah, 2Ki 23:26
then he turned and rebelled **a** him. 2Ki 24:1
sent **a** him bands of Chaldeans, 2Ki 24:2
sent them **a** Judah to destroy it, 2Ki 24:2
rebelled **a** the king of Babylon. 2Ki 24:20
he and all his army, **a** Jerusalem, 2Ki 25:1 5921
against Jerusalem, camped **a** it and 2Ki 25:1 5921
They made war **a** the Hagrites, 1Ch 5:19 5973
They were helped **a** them, 1Ch 5:20 5921

a the God of their fathers and 1Ch 5:25
the Philistines fought **a** Israel; 1Ch 10:1
The battle became heavy **a** Saul, 1Ch 10:3 5921
which he committed **a** the LORD, 1Ch 10:13
he lifted up his spear **a** three 1Ch 11:11 5921
a three hundred and killed them; 1Ch 11:20 5921
with the Philistines **a** Saul. 1Ch 12:19 5921
David **a** the band of raiders, 1Ch 12:21 5921
anger of the LORD burned **a** Uzza, 1Ch 13:10
of the LORD's outburst **a** Uzza; 1Ch 13:11
heard of it and went out **a** them. 1Ch 14:8 6440
"Shall I go up **a** the Philistines? 1Ch 14:10 5921
because he had fought **a** Hadadezer 1Ch 18:10
a him in front and in the rear, 1Ch 19:10 413
arrayed themselves **a** the Arameans. 1Ch 19:10 7122
themselves **a** the sons of Ammon. 1Ch 19:11 7122
near to the battle **a** the Arameans, 1Ch 19:14 6440
and drew up in formation **a** them. 1Ch 19:17 413
up in battle array **a** the Arameans, 1Ch 19:17 7122
the Arameans, they fought **a** him. 1Ch 19:17 5973
Then Satan stood up **a** Israel and 1Ch 21:1 5921
the king's word prevailed **a** Joab. 1Ch 21:4 5921
be **a** me and my father's household, 1Ch 21:17
but not **a** Your people that they 1Ch 21:17
"If a man sins **a** his neighbor and 2Ch 6:22
because they have sinned **a** You, 2Ch 6:24
because they have sinned **a** You, 2Ch 6:26
go out to battle **a** their enemies, 2Ch 6:34 5921
"When they sin **a** You 2Ch 6:36
Your people who have sinned **a** You. 2Ch 6:39
So Israel has been in rebellion **a** 2Ch 10:19
to fight **a** Israel to restore the 2Ch 11:1 5973
go up or fight **a** your relatives; 2Ch 11:4 5973
returned from going **a** Jeroboam. 2Ch 11:4 413
king of Egypt came up **a** Jerusalem 2Ch 12:2 5921
king of Egypt came up **a** Jerusalem, 2Ch 12:9 5921
battle formation **a** him with 800,000 2Ch 13:3 5973
rose up and rebelled **a** his master, 2Ch 13:6 5921
and could not hold his own **a** them. 2Ch 13:7 6440
trumpets to sound the alarm **a** you. 2Ch 13:12 5921
a the LORD God of your fathers, 2Ch 13:12 5973
Zerah the Ethiopian came out **a** them 2Ch 14:9 413
name have come **a** this multitude. 2Ch 14:11 5921
let not man prevail **a** You." 2Ch 14:11 5973
Baasha king of Israel came up **a** Judah 2Ch 16:1 5921
his armies **a** the cities of Israel, 2Ch 16:4 413
did not make war **a** Jehoshaphat. 2Ch 17:10 5973
him to go up **a** Ramoth-gilead. 2Ch 18:2 413
"Will you go with me **a** 2Ch 18:3
we go **a** Ramoth-gilead to battle, 2Ch 18:5 413
has proclaimed disaster **a** you." 2Ch 18:22 5921
of Judah went up **a** Ramoth-gilead. 2Ch 18:28 413
they turned aside to fight **a** him. 2Ch 18:31 5921
came to make war **a** Jehoshaphat. 2Ch 20:1 5921
coming **a** you from beyond the sea, 2Ch 20:2 5921
so that no one can stand **a** You. 2Ch 20:6 5973
multitude who are coming **a** us; 2Ch 20:12 5921
'Tomorrow go down **a** them. 2Ch 20:16 5921
set ambushes **a** the sons of Ammon, 2Ch 20:22 5921
Mount Seir, who had come **a** Judah; 2Ch 20:22
up **a** the inhabitants of Mount Seir 2Ch 20:23 5921
fought **a** the enemies of Israel. 2Ch 20:29 5973
prophesied **a** Jehoshaphat saying, 2Ch 20:37 5921
Edom revolted **a** the rule of Judah and 2Ch 21:8
4480, 8478, 3027
Edom revolted **a** Judah to this day. 2Ch 21:10
4480, 8478, 3027
at the same time **a** his rule, 2Ch 21:10
4480, 8478
Then the LORD stirred up **a** Jehoram 2Ch 21:16 5921
they came **a** Judah and invaded it, 2Ch 21:17
to wage war **a** Hazael king of Aram 2Ch 22:5 5921
he fought **a** Hazael king of Aram. 2Ch 22:6 854
Jehoram **a** Jehu the son of Nimshi, 2Ch 22:7 413
though they testified **a** them, 2Ch 24:19
So they conspired **a** him and at the 2Ch 24:21 5921
of the Arameans came up **a** him; 2Ch 24:23 5921
his own servants conspired **a** him 2Ch 24:25 5921
are those who conspired **a** him: 2Ch 24:26 5921
many oracles **a** him and the rebuilding 2Ch 24:27 5921
so their anger burned **a** Judah and 2Ch 25:10
of the LORD burned **a** Amaziah, 2Ch 25:15
they conspired **a** him in Jerusalem, 2Ch 25:27 5921
out and warred **a** the Philistines, 2Ch 26:6
God helped him **a** the Philistines, 2Ch 26:7 5921
and **a** the Arabians who lived in 2Ch 26:7 5921
to help the king **a** the enemy. 2Ch 26:13 5921
of your own **a** the LORD your God? 2Ch 28:10
anger of the LORD is **a** you." 2Ch 28:11 5921
Amasa the son of Hadlai—arose **a** 2Ch 28:12 5921
guilt **a** the LORD adding to our sins 2Ch 28:13
His burning anger is **a** Israel." 2Ch 28:13 5921
of Assyria came **a** him and afflicted 2Ch 28:20 5921
LORD was **a** Judah and Jerusalem, 2Ch 29:8 5921
a Hezekiah king of Judah and 2Ch 32:9 5921
a all Judah who *were* at Jerusalem, 2Ch 32:9 5921
His servants spoke further **a** 2Ch 32:16 5921
God and **a** His servant Hezekiah. 2Ch 32:16 5921
God of Israel, and to speak **a** Him, 2Ch 32:17 5921
of the king of Assyria **a** them, 2Ch 33:11 5921
Finally his servants conspired **a** 2Ch 33:24 5921
all the conspirators **a** King Amon, 2Ch 33:25 5921
when you heard His words **a** this 2Ch 34:27 5921
this place and **a** its inhabitants, 2Ch 34:27 5921
I am not coming **a** you today but 2Ch 35:21 5921
a the house with which I am at war, 2Ch 35:21 413
king of Babylon came up **a** him 2Ch 36:6 5921
he did, and what was found **a** him, 2Ch 36:8 5921
He also rebelled **a** King 2Ch 36:13

his heart **a** turning to the LORD God 2Ch 36:13 4480
of the LORD arose **a** His people, 2Ch 36:16
Therefore He brought up **a** them the 2Ch 36:17 5921
and hired counselors **a** them to Ezr 4:5 5921
they wrote an accusation **a** the Ezr 4:6 5921
a Jerusalem to King Artaxerxes, Ezr 4:8 5922
risen up **a** the kings in past days, Ezr 4:19 5922
there will not be wrath **a** the kingdom Ezr 7:23 5922
are **a** all those who forsake Him." Ezr 8:22 5921
which we have sinned **a** You; Ne 1:6
"We have acted very corruptly **a** Ne 1:7
Are you rebelling **a** the king?" Ne 2:19 5921
to come *and* fight **a** Jerusalem Ne 4:8
up a guard **a** them day and night. Ne 4:9 5921
"They will come up **a** us from Ne 4:12 5921
wives **a** their Jewish brothers. Ne 5:1 413
I held a great assembly **a** them. Ne 5:7 5921
but he uttered *his* prophecy **a** me Ne 6:12 5921
signs and wonders **a** Pharaoh, Ne 9:10
A all his servants and all the Ne 9:10
disobedient and rebelled **a** You, Ne 9:26
but sinned **a** Your ordinances, Ne 9:29
hired Balaam **a** them to curse them. Ne 13:2 5921
again, I will use force **a** you." Ne 13:21
evil by acting unfaithfully **a** our God Ne 13:27
and what had been decreed **a** her. Es 2:1 5921
was filled with anger **a** Mordecai. Es 5:9 5921
been determined **a** him by the king. Es 7:7 413
which he had devised **a** the Jews. Es 8:3 5921
out his hands **a** the Jews. Es 8:7
a the Jews to destroy them and Es 9:24 5921
which he had devised **a** the Jews, Es 9:25 5921
although you incited Me **a** him to Jb 2:3
And **a** His angels He charges error. Jb 4:18
terrors of God are arrayed **a** me. Jb 6:4
"If your sons sinned **a** Him, Jb 8:4
You would show Your power **a** me. Jb 10:16
You renew Your witnesses **a** me Jb 10:17 5048
speak, And open His lips **a** you, Jb 11:5 5973
You write bitter things **a** me Jb 13:26 5921
And your own lips testify **a** you. Jb 15:6
you should turn your spirit **a** God And Jb 15:13 413
has stretched out his hand **a** God And Jb 15:25 413
himself arrogantly **a** the Almighty. Jb 15:25 413
I could compose words **a** you And Jb 16:4 5921
And my leanness rises up **a** me, Jb 16:8
They have massed themselves **a** me. Jb 16:10 5921
"He who informs **a** friends for a Jb 17:5
stir up himself **a** the godless. Jb 17:8 5921
indeed you vaunt yourselves **a** me And Jb 19:5 5921
has also kindled His anger **a** me And Jb 19:11 5921
And build up their way **a** me And Jb 19:12 5921
I rise up and they speak **a** me. Jb 19:18
And those I love have turned **a** me. Jb 19:19
for a case **a** him can we find?' Jb 19:28
of everyone who suffers will come **a** Jb 20:22
And the earth will rise up **a** him. Jb 20:27
He enters into judgment **a** you? Jb 22:4 5973
And have no covering **a** the cold. Jb 24:7
And **a** the poor they take a pledge. Jb 24:9 5921
with those who rebel **a** the light; Jb 24:13
shout **a** them as *against* a thief, Jb 30:5 5921
They shout against them as **a** Jb 30:5
up **a** me their ways of destruction. Jb 30:12 5921
"Terrors are turned **a** me; Jb 30:15 5921
You turn Your attention **a** me. Jb 30:20
When they filed a complaint **a** me, Jb 31:13 5973
lifted up my hand **a** the orphan, Jb 31:21 5921
"If my land cries out **a** me, Jb 31:38 5921
a Job his anger burned because he Jb 32:2
And his anger burned **a** his three Jb 32:3
has not arranged *his* words **a** me, Jb 32:14 413
'Behold, He invents pretexts **a** me; Jb 33:10 5921
"Why do you complain **a** Him That Jb 33:13 413
multiplies his words **a** God.'" Jb 34:37
what do you accomplish **a** Him? Jb 35:6
"The quiver rattles **a** him, Jb 39:23 5921
"My wrath is kindled **a** you and Jb 42:7
you and **a** your two friends, Jb 42:7
take counsel together **A** the LORD Ps 2:2 5921
the LORD and **a** His Anointed, Ps 2:2 5921
Many are rising up **a** me. Ps 3:1 5921
set themselves **a** me round about. Ps 3:6 5921
For they are rebellious **a** You. Ps 5:10
a the rage of my adversaries, Ps 7:6
takes up a reproach **a** his friend; Ps 15:3 5921
he take a bribe **a** the innocent. Ps 15:5 5921
right hand From those who rise up **a** Ps 17:7
under me those who rose up **a** me. Ps 18:39
me above those who rise up **a** me; Ps 18:48
Though they intended evil **a** You Ps 21:11 5921
Though a host encamp **a** me, Ps 27:3 5921
Though war arise **a** me, Ps 27:3 5921
false witnesses have risen **a** me, Ps 27:12
they took counsel together **a** me, Ps 31:13 5921
Which speak arrogantly **a** the Ps 31:18 5921
face of the LORD is **a** evildoers, Ps 34:16
a those who fight against me. Ps 35:1 854
against those who fight **a** me. Ps 35:1
humiliated who devise evil **a** me. Ps 35:4
not know gathered together **a** me, Ps 35:15 5921
deceitful words **a** those who are quiet Ps 35:20 5921
They opened their mouth wide **a** me; Ps 35:21 5921
The wicked plots **a** the righteous And Ps 37:12
would magnify themselves **a** me." Ps 38:16 5921
soul, for I have sinned **a** You." Ps 41:4
My enemies speak evil **a** me, Ps 41:5
who hate me whisper together **a** me; Ps 41:7 5921
A me they devise my hurt, *saying,* Ps 41:7 5921

Has lifted up his heel **a** me. **Ps 41:9** 5921
plead my case **a** an ungodly nation; **Ps 43:1** 4480
down those who rise up **a** us. **Ps 44:5**
O Israel, I will testify **a** you; **Ps 50:7**
"You sit and speak **a** your brother; **Ps 50:20**
A You, You only, I have sinned And **Ps 51:4**
bones of him who encamped **a** you; **Ps 53:5**
For strangers have risen **a** me And **Ps 54:3** 5921
in anger they bear a grudge **a** me. **Ps 55:3** 7852
me who has exalted himself **a** me, **Ps 55:12** 5921
from the battle *which is* **a** me, **Ps 55:18**
He has put forth his hands **a** those **Ps 55:20**
are many who fight proudly **a** me. **Ps 56:2**
their thoughts are **a** me for evil. **Ps 56:5** 5921
away from those who rise up **a** me. **Ps 59:1**
Fierce men launch an attack **a** me, **Ps 59:3** 5921
they run and set themselves **a** me. **Ps 59:4**
O give us help **a** the adversary, **Ps 60:11** 4480
A tower of strength **a** the enemy. **Ps 61:3**
4480, 6440
Their own tongue is **a** them; **Ps 64:8** 5921
Iniquities prevail **a** me; **Ps 65:3** 4480
For my enemies have spoken **a** me; **Ps 71:10**
set their mouth **a** the heavens, **Ps 73:9**
smoke **a** the sheep of Your pasture? **Ps 74:1**
The uproar of those who rise **a** **Ps 74:23**
they still continued to sin **a** Him, **Ps 78:17**
a the Most High in the desert. **Ps 78:17**
Then they spoke **a** God; **Ps 78:19**
And a fire was kindled **a** Jacob And **Ps 78:21**
And anger also mounted **a** Israel, **Ps 78:21**
The anger of God rose **a** them And **Ps 78:31**
rebelled **a** Him in the wilderness And **Ps 78:40**
and rebelled **a** the Most High God And **Ps 78:56** 854
the iniquities of *our* forefathers **a** us; **Ps 79:8**
turn My hand **a** their adversaries. **Ps 81:14** 5921
make shrewd plans **a** Your people, **Ps 83:3** 5921
together **a** Your treasured ones. **Ps 83:3** 5921
A You they make a covenant: **Ps 83:5** 5921
arrogant men have risen up **a** me, **Ps 86:14** 5921
full of wrath **a** Your anointed. **Ps 89:38** 5973
not strike your foot **a** a stone. **Ps 91:12**
of the evildoers who rise up **a** me. **Ps 92:11** 5921
will stand up for me **a** evildoers? **Ps 94:16** 5973
for me **a** those who do wickedness? **Ps 94:16** 5973
a the life of the righteous And **Ps 94:21** 5921
they did not rebel **a** His words. **Ps 105:28** 854
they were rebellious **a** His Spirit, **Ps 106:33** 854
the LORD was kindled **a** His people And **Ps 106:40**
had rebelled **a** the words of God And **Ps 107:11**
Oh give us help **a** the adversary, **Ps 108:12** 4480
wicked and deceitful mouth **a** me; **Ps 109:2** 5921
spoken **a** me with a lying tongue. **Ps 109:2** 854
And fought **a** me without cause. **Ps 109:3**
of those who speak evil **a** my soul. **Ps 109:20** 5921
heart, That I may not sin **a** You. **Ps 119:11**
though princes sit *and* talk **a** me, **Ps 119:23**
arrogant have forged a lie **a** me; **Ps 119:69** 5921
our side When men rose up **a** us **Ps 124:2** 5921
When their anger was kindled **a** us; **Ps 124:3**
Yet they have not prevailed **a** me. **Ps 129:2**
a weaned child *rests* **a** his mother, **Ps 131:2** 5921
a the sons of Edom The day of **Ps 137:7**
your little ones **A** the rock. **Ps 137:9** 413
hand **a** the wrath of my enemies, **Ps 138:7** 5921
For they speak **a** You wickedly, **Ps 139:20**
loathe those who rise up **a** You? **Ps 139:21**
my prayer is **a** their wicked deeds. **Ps 141:5**
not devise harm **a** your neighbor, **Pr 3:29** 5921
he who sins **a** me injures himself; **Pr 8:36**
messenger will be sent **a** him. **Pr 17:11**
He quarrels **a** all sound wisdom. **Pr 18:1**
And his heart rages **a** the LORD. **Pr 19:3** 5921
And no counsel **a** the LORD. **Pr 21:30** 5048
He will plead their case **a** you. **Pr 23:11** 854
a the dwelling of the righteous; **Pr 24:15**
a your neighbor without cause, **Pr 24:28**
false witness **a** his neighbor. **Pr 25:18**
Because the sentence **a** an evil **Ec 8:11**
constructed large siegeworks **a** it. **Ec 9:14** 5921
If the ruler's temper rises **a** you, **Ec 10:4** 5921
a the terrors of the night. **SS 3:8** 4480
up, But they have revolted **a** Me. **Is 1:2**
"I will also turn My hand **a** you, **Is 1:25** 5921
will not lift up sword **a** nation, **Is 2:4** 413
reckoning **A** everyone who is proud **Is 2:12** 5921
And **a** everyone who is lifted up, **Is 2:12** 5921
And *it will be* **a** all the cedars of **Is 2:13** 5921
up, **A** all the oaks of Bashan, **Is 2:13** 5921
A all the lofty mountains, Against **Is 2:14** 5921
A all the hills that are lifted **Is 2:14** 5921
A every high tower, Against every **Is 2:15** 5921
tower, **A** every fortified wall, **Is 2:15** 5921
A all the ships of Tarshish And **Is 2:16** 5921
And **a** all the beautiful craft. **Is 2:16** 5921
The youth will storm **a** the elder And **Is 3:5**
And the inferior **a** the honorable. **Is 3:5**
and their actions are **a** the LORD, **Is 3:8** 413
To rebel **a** His glorious presence. **Is 3:8**
their faces bears witness **a** them, **Is 3:9**
the LORD has burned **a** His people, **Is 5:25**
hand **a** them and struck them down. **Is 5:25** 5921
up to Jerusalem to *wage* war **a** it, **Is 7:1** 5921
Remaliah, has planned evil **a** you, **Is 7:5** 5921
us go up **a** Judah and terrorize it, **Is 7:6**
The Lord sends a message **a** Jacob, **Is 9:8**
a them adversaries from Rezin And **Is 9:11** 5921
And together they are **a** Judah. **Is 9:21** 5921
I send it **a** a godless nation And **Is 10:6**

commission it **a** the people of My fury **Is 10:6** 5921
rod and lifts up his staff **a** you, **Is 10:24** 5921
very little while My indignation **a** **Is 10:25**
LORD of hosts will arouse a scourge **a** **Is 10:26** 5921
He has come **a** Aiath, He has passed **Is 10:28** 5921
going to stir up the Medes **a** them, **Is 13:17** 5921
this taunt **a** the king of Babylon, **Is 14:4** 5921
no *tree* cutter comes up **a** us.' **Is 14:8** 5921
"I will rise up **a** them," **Is 14:22** 5921
plan devised **a** the whole earth; **Is 14:26** 5921
stretched out **a** all the nations. **Is 14:26** 5921
will incite Egyptians **a** Egyptians; **Is 19:2**
will each fight **a** his brother and **Is 19:2**
brother and each **a** his neighbor, **Is 19:2**
against his neighbor, City **a** city **Is 19:2**
city *and* kingdom **a** kingdom. **Is 19:2**
of hosts Has purposed **a** Egypt. **Is 19:12** 5921
which He is purposing **a** them. **Is 19:17** 5921
fought **a** Ashdod and captured it, **Is 20:1**
a sign and token **a** Egypt and Cush, **Is 20:3** 5921
Who has planned this **a** Tyre, **Is 23:8** 5921
ruthless Is like a *rain* storm **a** **Is 25:4**
I will camp **a** you encircling *you,* **Is 29:3** 5921
And I will set siegeworks **a** you, **Is 29:3** 5921
will raise up battle towers **a** you. **Is 29:3** 5921
the nations who wage war **a** Ariel, **Is 29:7** 5921
wage war **a** her and her stronghold, **Is 29:7**
be Who wage war **a** Mount Zion. **Is 29:8** 5921
arise **a** the house of evildoers And **Is 31:2** 5921
And **a** the help of the workers of **Is 31:2** 5921
A which a band of shepherds is **Is 31:4** 5921
and to speak error **a** the LORD, **Is 32:6** 413
indignation is **a** all the nations, **Is 34:2** 5921
And *His* wrath **a** all their armies; **Is 34:2** 5921
Assyria came up **a** all the fortified **Is 36:1** 5921
rely, that you have rebelled **a** me? **Is 36:5**
a this land to destroy it? **Is 36:10** 5921
'Go up **a** this land and destroy it.' **Is 36:10** 413
king of Assyria fighting **a** Libnah, **Is 37:8** 5921
"He has come out to fight **a** you," **Is 37:9** 854
that the LORD has spoken **a** him: **Is 37:22** 5921
And **a** whom have you raised *your* **Is 37:23** 5921
A the Holy One of Israel! **Is 37:23** 413
coming in And your raging **a** Me. **Is 37:28** 413
"Because of your raging **a** Me And **Is 37:29** 413
shield, or throw up a siege ramp **a** it. **Is 37:33** 5921
He will prevail **a** His enemies. **Is 42:13** 5921
the LORD, **a** whom we have sinned, **Is 42:24**
spokesmen have transgressed **a** Me. **Is 43:27**
And His arm *will be* **a** **Is 48:14**
Who has a case **a** Me? **Is 50:8**
is formed **a** you will prosper; **Is 54:17** 5921
"**A** whom do you jest? **Is 57:4** 5921
A whom do you open wide your mouth **Is 57:4** 5921
You, And our sins testify **a** us; **Is 59:12**
their enemy, He fought **a** them. **Is 63:10**
men Who have transgressed **a** Me. **Is 66:24**
and **a** all its walls round about and **Jer 1:15** 5921
and **a** all the cities of Judah. **Jer 1:15** 5921
walls of bronze **a** the whole land, **Jer 1:18** 5921
"They will fight **a** you, **Jer 1:19** 413
The rulers also transgressed **a** Me, **Jer 2:8**
You have all transgressed **a** Me," **Jer 2:29**
That you have transgressed **a** the **Jer 3:13**
we have sinned **a** the LORD our God, **Jer 3:25**
also pronounce judgments **a** them. **Jer 4:12**
voices **a** the cities of Judah. **Jer 4:16** 5921
field they are **a** her round about, **Jer 4:17** 5921
Because she has rebelled **a** Me,' **Jer 4:17**
bringing a nation **a** you from afar, **Jer 5:15** 5921
"Prepare war **a** her; **Jer 6:4** 5921
And cast up a siege **a** Jerusalem. **Jer 6:6** 5921
A the inhabitants of the land," **Jer 6:12** 5921
And they will stumble **a** them, **Jer 6:21**
as a man for the battle **A** you, **Jer 6:23** 5921
For we have sinned **a** the LORD. **Jer 8:14**
I am sending serpents **a** you, **Jer 8:17**
be on guard **a** his neighbor, **Jer 9:4** 4480
has pronounced evil **a** you because **Jer 11:17** 5921
that they had devised plots **a** me, **Jer 11:19** 5921
She has roared **a** Me; **Jer 12:8** 5921
birds of prey **a** her on every side? **Jer 12:9** 5921
"I will dash them **a** each other, **Jer 13:14** 413
our iniquities testify **a** us, **Jer 14:7**
been many, We have sinned **a** You. **Jer 14:7**
for we have sinned **a** You. **Jer 14:20**
out My hand **a** you and destroy you; **Jer 15:6** 5921
I will bring **a** them, against the **Jer 15:8**
them, **a** the mother of a young man, **Jer 15:8** 5921
And though they fight **a** you, **Jer 15:20** 413
all this great calamity **a** us? **Jer 16:10** 5921
committed **a** the LORD our God?' **Jer 16:10**
if that nation **a** which I have **Jer 18:8** 5921
speak to the men of Judah and **a** **Jer 18:11** 5921
I am fashioning calamity **a** you and **Jer 18:11** 5921
you and devising a plan **a** you. **Jer 18:11** 5921
let us devise plans **a** Jeremiah. **Jer 18:18** 5921
All their deadly designs **a** me; **Jer 18:23** 5921
that I have declared **a** it, **Jer 19:15** 5921
so that we may prevail **a** him And **Jer 20:10**
king of Babylon is warring **a** us; **Jer 21:2** 5921
with which you are warring **a** the **Jer 21:4** 854
"I Myself will war **a** you **Jer 21:5** 854
"For I have set My face **a** this **Jer 21:10**
"Behold, I am **a** you, O valley **Jer 21:13** 413
'Who will come down **a** us? **Jer 21:13** 5921
will set apart destroyers **a** you, **Jer 22:7** 5921
behold, I am **a** the prophets," **Jer 23:30** 5921
"Behold, I am **a** the prophets," **Jer 23:31** 5921

I am **a** those who have prophesied **Jer 23:32** 5921
and will bring them **a** this land and **Jer 25:9** 5921
this land and **a** its inhabitants **Jer 25:9** 5921
a all these nations round **Jer 25:9** 5921
which I have pronounced **a** it, **Jer 25:13** 5921
has prophesied **a** all the nations. **Jer 25:13** 5921
for I am summoning a sword **a** all **Jer 25:29** 5921
prophesy **a** them all these words, **Jer 25:30** 413
He will roar mightily **a** His fold. **Jer 25:30** 5921
A all the inhabitants of the earth. **Jer 25:30** 413
For he has prophesied **a** this city **Jer 26:11** 413
"The LORD sent me to prophesy **a** **Jer 26:12** 413
against this house and **a** this city all **Jer 26:12** 413
which He has pronounced **a** you. **Jer 26:13** 5921
which He had pronounced **a** them? **Jer 26:19** 5921
a great evil **a** ourselves." **Jer 26:19** 5921
and he prophesied **a** this city and **Jer 26:20** 5921
this city and **a** this land words similar **Jer 26:20** 5921
prophesied **a** many lands and against **Jer 28:8** 413
many lands and **a** great kingdoms, **Jer 28:8** 5921
rebellion **a** the LORD.' " **Jer 28:16** 413
rebellion **a** the LORD." ' " **Jer 29:32** 5921
as often as I have spoken **a** him, **Jer 31:20**
"If you fight **a** the Chaldeans, **Jer 32:5** 854
of the Chaldeans who fight **a** it, **Jer 32:24** 5921
Chaldeans who are fighting **a** this city **Jer 32:29** 5921
to make a defense **a** the siege ramps **Jer 33:4** 413
the siege ramps and **a** the sword, **Jer 33:4** 413
by which they have sinned **a** Me, **Jer 33:8**
by which they have sinned **a** Me **Jer 33:8**
which they have transgressed **a** Me. **Jer 33:8**
were fighting **a** Jerusalem and **Jer 34:1** 5921
Jerusalem and **a** all its cities, **Jer 34:1** 5921
Babylon was fighting **a** Jerusalem **Jer 34:7** 5921
a all the remaining cities of Judah, **Jer 34:7** 5921
and they will fight **a** it and take **Jer 34:22** 5921
of Babylon came up **a** the land, **Jer 35:11** 413
that I have pronounced **a** them; **Jer 35:17** 5921
has pronounced **a** this people." **Jer 36:7** 413
also return and fight **a** this city, **Jer 37:8** 5921
Chaldeans who were fighting **a** you, **Jer 37:10** 854
"*In what way* have I sinned **a** you, **Jer 37:18**
against you, or **a** your servants, **Jer 37:18**
your servants, or **a** this people, **Jer 37:18**
come **a** you or against this land'? **Jer 37:19** 5921
come against you or **a** this land'? **Jer 37:19** 5921
the king can *do* nothing **a** you." **Jer 38:5**
this calamity **a** this place; **Jer 40:2** 413
Because you *people* sinned **a** the **Jer 40:3**
a true and faithful witness **a** us if **Jer 42:5**
that today I have testified **a** you. **Jer 42:19**
the son of Neriah is inciting you **a** us **Jer 43:3**
to set My face **a** you for woe, **Jer 44:11**
sinned **a** the LORD and not obeyed **Jer 44:23**
will surely stand **a** you for harm.' **Jer 44:29** 5921
they have fallen one **a** another. **Jer 46:16** 413
A Ashkelon and against the **Jer 47:7** 413
Against Ashkelon and **a** the seacoast **Jer 47:7** 413
they have devised calamity **a** her: **Jer 48:2** 5921
of Moab has come up **a** you, **Jer 48:18**
Holon, Jahzah and **a** Mephaath, **Jer 48:21** 5921
a Dibon, Nebo and **Jer 48:22** 5921
a Kiriathaim, Beth-gamul and **Jer 48:23** 5921
a Kerioth, Bozrah and all the **Jer 48:24** 5921
And spread out his wings **a** Moab. **Jer 48:40** 413
A Rabbah of the sons of Ammon; **Jer 49:2** 413
'Who will come **a** me?' **Jer 49:4** 413
together and come **a** her, **Jer 49:14** 5921
a a perennially watered pasture; **Jer 49:19** 413
the shepherd who can stand **a** Me?" **Jer 49:19** 6440
LORD which He has planned **a** Edom, **Jer 49:20** 413
a the inhabitants of Teman: **Jer 49:20** 413
and spread out His wings **a** Bozrah; **Jer 49:22** 5921
Babylon has formed a plan **a** you **Jer 49:30** 5921
you And devised a scheme **a** you. **Jer 49:30** 5921
go up **a** a nation which is at ease, **Jer 49:31** 413
come up **a** her out of the north; **Jer 50:3** 5921
Inasmuch as they have sinned **a** the **Jer 50:7**
up **a** Babylon A horde of great nations **Jer 50:9** 5921
draw up *their* battle lines **a** her; **Jer 50:9**
lines **a** Babylon on every side, **Jer 50:14** 5921
For she has sinned **a** the LORD. **Jer 50:14**
battle cry **a** her on every side! **Jer 50:15** 5921
"**A** the land of Merathaim, go up **Jer 50:21** 5921
the land of Merathaim, go up **a** it, **Jer 50:21** 5921
And **a** the inhabitants of Pekod. **Jer 50:21** 413
"Summon many **a** Babylon, All those **Jer 50:29** 413
Encamp **a** her on every side, Let **Jer 50:29** 5921
has become arrogant **a** the LORD, **Jer 50:29** 413
LORD, **A** the Holy One of Israel. **Jer 50:29** 413
"Behold, I am **a** you, O arrogant **Jer 50:31** 413
"A sword **a** the Chaldeans," **Jer 50:35** 5921
"And **a** the inhabitants of **Jer 50:35** 413
And **a** her officials and her wise **Jer 50:35** 413
"A sword **a** the oracle priests, **Jer 50:36** 413
A sword **a** her mighty men, and they **Jer 50:36** 413
"A sword **a** their horses and **Jer 50:37** 413
their horses and **a** their chariots And **Jer 50:37** 413
And **a** all the foreigners who are **Jer 50:37** 413
A sword **a** her treasures, and they **Jer 50:37** 413
like a man for the battle **A** you, **Jer 50:42** 5921
which He has planned **a** Babylon, **Jer 50:45** 413
a the land of the Chaldeans: **Jer 50:45** 413
I am going to arouse **a** Babylon And **Jer 51:1** 5921
And **a** the inhabitants of Leb-kamai **Jer 51:1** 413
is **a** Babylon to destroy it; **Jer 51:11** 5921
a signal **a** the walls of Babylon; **Jer 51:12** 413
"Behold, I am **a** you, O destroying **Jer 51:25** 413
I will stretch out My hand **a** you, **Jer 51:25** 5921

Consecrate the nations **a** her,	Jer 51:27	5921
a her the kingdoms of Ararat,	Jer 51:27	5921
Appoint a marshal **a** her,	Jer 51:27	5921
Consecrate the nations **a** her,	Jer 51:28	5921
of the LORD **a** Babylon stand,	Jer 51:29	5921
will be in the land With ruler **a** ruler	Jer 51:46	5921
For the destroyer is coming **a** her,	Jer 51:56	5921
is coming against her, **a** Babylon,	Jer 51:56	5921
rebelled **a** the king of Babylon.	Jer 52:3	
he and all his army, **a** Jerusalem,	Jer 52:4	5921
against Jerusalem, camped **a** it and	Jer 52:4	5921
given me into the hands Of *those* **a**	La 1:14	
time **a** me To crush my young men;	La 1:15	5921
For I have rebelled **a** His command;	La 1:18	854
opened their mouths wide **a** you;	La 2:16	5921
Surely **a** me He has turned His hand	La 3:3	
have opened their mouths **a** us.	La 3:46	5921
vengeance, All their schemes **a** me.	La 3:60	
O LORD, All their schemes **a** me.	La 3:61	5921
whispering *Are* **a** me all day long.	La 3:62	5921
sons of Zion, Weighed **a** fine gold,	La 4:2	
people who have rebelled **a** Me;	Ezk 2:3	
a Me to this very day.	Ezk 2:3	
"Then lay siege **a** it, build a	Ezk 4:2	5921
battering rams **a** it all around.	Ezk 4:2	5921
your arm bared and prophesy **a** it.	Ezk 4:7	5921
'But she has rebelled **a** My	Ezk 5:6	854
a My statutes more than the lands	Ezk 5:6	854
'Behold, I, even I, am **a** you,	Ezk 5:8	5921
execute judgments **a** you in anger,	Ezk 5:15	
'When I send **a** them the deadly	Ezk 5:16	
of Israel, and prophesy **a** them	Ezk 6:2	413
I will stretch out My hand **a** them	Ezk 6:14	5921
and I will send My anger **a** you;	Ezk 7:3	
It has awakened **a** you;	Ezk 7:6	413
on you and spend My anger **a** you	Ezk 7:8	
wrath is **a** all their multitude.	Ezk 7:12	413
My wrath is **a** all their multitude.	Ezk 7:14	413
"Therefore, prophesy **a** them,	Ezk 11:4	5921
and execute judgments **a** you.	Ezk 11:9	
prophesy **a** the prophets of Israel	Ezk 13:2	413
therefore behold, I am **a** you,"	Ezk 13:8	413
"So My hand will be **a** the	Ezk 13:9	413
set your face **a** the daughters of	Ezk 13:17	413
Prophesy **a** them	Ezk 13:17	5921
I am **a** your *magic* bands by which	Ezk 13:20	413
"I will set My face **a** that	Ezk 14:8	
and I will stretch out My hand **a**	Ezk 14:9	5921
if a country sins **a** Me by	Ezk 14:13	
and I stretch out My hand **a** it,	Ezk 14:13	5921
supply of bread, send famine **a** it and	Ezk 14:13	
"Or *if* I should send a plague **a**	Ezk 14:19	413
four severe judgments **a** Jerusalem:	Ezk 14:21	413
which I have brought **a** Jerusalem	Ezk 14:22	5921
and I set My face **a** them.	Ezk 15:7	
LORD, when I set My face **a** them.	Ezk 15:7	
I have stretched out My hand **a** you	Ezk 16:27	5921
So I will gather them **a** you from	Ezk 16:37	5921
"They will incite a crowd **a** you and	Ezk 16:40	5921
"So I will calm My fury **a** you	Ezk 16:42	
'But he rebelled **a** him by sending	Ezk 17:15	
act which he has committed **a** Me.	Ezk 17:20	
will not be remembered **a** him;	Ezk 18:22	
'Then nations set **a** him On every	Ezk 19:8	5921
"But they rebelled **a** Me and were	Ezk 20:8	
to accomplish My anger **a** them in	Ezk 20:8	
rebelled **a** Me in the wilderness.	Ezk 20:13	
"But the children rebelled **a** Me;	Ezk 20:21	
My anger **a** them in the wilderness.	Ezk 20:21	
Me by acting treacherously **a** Me.	Ezk 20:27	
and those who transgress **a** Me;	Ezk 20:38	
Teman, and speak out **a** the south and	Ezk 20:46	413
a the forest land of the Negev,	Ezk 20:46	413
and speak **a** the sanctuaries and	Ezk 21:2	413
and prophesy **a** the land of Israel;	Ezk 21:2	413
"Behold, I am **a** you;	Ezk 21:3	413
a all flesh from south *to* north.	Ezk 21:4	413
for it is **a** My people, it is	Ezk 21:12	
is **a** all the officials of Israel.	Ezk 21:12	
to set battering rams **a** the gates,	Ezk 21:22	5921
I will arouse your lovers **a** you,	Ezk 23:22	5921
bring them **a** you from every side:	Ezk 23:22	5921
They will come **a** you with weapons,	Ezk 23:24	5921
They will set themselves **a** you on	Ezk 23:24	5921
'I will set My jealousy **a** you,	Ezk 23:25	
'Bring up a company **a** them and	Ezk 23:46	5921
of Ammon and prophesy **a** them,	Ezk 25:2	5921
a My sanctuary when it was	Ezk 25:3	413
and **a** the land of Israel when it	Ezk 25:3	413
and **a** the house of Judah when they	Ezk 25:3	413
of your soul **a** the land of Israel,	Ezk 25:6	413
have stretched out My hand **a** you and	Ezk 25:7	5921
"Because Edom has acted **a** the	Ezk 25:12	
also stretch out My hand **a** Edom	Ezk 25:13	5921
out My hand **a** the Philistines,	Ezk 25:16	5921
'Behold, I am **a** you, O Tyre, and I	Ezk 26:3	5921
will bring up many nations **a** you,	Ezk 26:3	5921
he will make siege walls **a** you,	Ezk 26:8	5921
you, cast up a ramp **a** you	Ezk 26:8	5921
and raise up a large shield **a** you.	Ezk 26:8	5921
rams he will direct **a** your walls,	Ezk 26:9	
swords **A** the beauty of your wisdom	Ezk 28:7	5921
face toward Sidon, prophesy **a** her	Ezk 28:21	5921
"Behold, I am **a** you, O Sidon, And I	Ezk 28:22	5921
of man, set your face **a** Pharaoh king	Ezk 29:2	5921
a him and against all Egypt.	Ezk 29:2	5921
against him and **a** all Egypt.	Ezk 29:2	5921
"Behold, I am **a** you, Pharaoh king	Ezk 29:3	5921
am **a** you and against your rivers,	Ezk 29:10	413

am against you and **a** your rivers,	Ezk 29:10	413
made his army labor hard **a** Tyre;	Ezk 29:18	413
that he had performed **a** it."	Ezk 29:18	5921
they will draw their swords **a** Egypt	Ezk 30:11	5921
I am **a** Pharaoh king of Egypt and	Ezk 30:22	413
it out **a** the land of Egypt.	Ezk 30:25	413
will be remembered **a** him.	Ezk 33:16	
a the shepherds of Israel.	Ezk 34:2	5921
"Behold, I am **a** the shepherds,	Ezk 34:10	413
man, set your face **a** Mount Seir,	Ezk 35:2	5921
Mount Seir, and prophesy **a** it	Ezk 35:2	5921
"Behold, I am **a** you, Mount Seir,	Ezk 35:3	413
I will stretch out My hand **a** you And	Ezk 35:3	
because of your hatred **a** them;	Ezk 35:11	
spoken **a** the mountains of Israel	Ezk 35:12	5921
"And you have spoken arrogantly **a**	Ezk 35:13	5921
have multiplied your words **a** Me;	Ezk 35:13	5921
the enemy has spoken **a** you,	Ezk 36:2	5921
spoken **a** the rest of the nations,	Ezk 36:5	5921
of the nations, and **a** all Edom,	Ezk 36:5	5921
and Tubal, and prophesy **a** him	Ezk 38:2	5921
"Behold, I am **a** you, O Gog,	Ezk 38:3	413
a the land of unwalled villages.	Ezk 38:11	5921
I will go **a** those who are at rest,	Ezk 38:11	
to turn your hand **a** the waste	Ezk 38:12	5921
and **a** the people who are gathered	Ezk 38:12	413
and you will come up **a** My people	Ezk 38:16	5921
that I will bring you **a** My land,	Ezk 38:16	5921
that I would bring you **a** them?	Ezk 38:17	5921
Gog comes **a** the land of Israel,"	Ezk 38:18	5921
sword **a** him on all My mountains,"	Ezk 38:21	5921
man's sword will be **a** his brother.	Ezk 38:21	
you, son of man, prophesy **a** Gog and	Ezk 39:1	5921
"Behold, I am **a** you, O Gog,	Ezk 39:1	413
you **a** the mountains of Israel.	Ezk 39:2	5921
they acted treacherously **a** Me,	Ezk 39:23	
which they perpetrated **a** Me,	Ezk 39:26	
therefore I have sworn **a** them,"	Ezk 44:12	5921
and brought charges **a** the Jews.	Da 3:8	1768
offensive **a** the God of Shadrach,	Da 3:29	5922
yourself **a** the Lord of heaven;	Da 5:23	5922
find a ground of accusation **a** Daniel	Da 6:4	
ground of accusation **a** this Daniel	Da 6:5	
find *it* **a** him with regard to the law	Da 6:5	5922
'He will speak out **a** the Most	Da 7:25	6655
which they have committed **a** You.	Da 9:7	
because we have sinned **a** You.	Da 9:8	
for we have rebelled **a** Him;	Da 9:9	
of God, for we have sinned **a** Him.	Da 9:11	
His words which He had spoken **a** us	Da 9:12	5921
us and **a** our rulers who ruled us,	Da 9:12	5921
to fight **a** the prince of Persia;	Da 10:20	5973
stands firmly with me **a** these *forces*	Da 10:21	5921
empire **a** the realm of Greece.	Da 11:2	
and he will come **a** *their* army and	Da 11:7	413
rise up **a** the king of the South;	Da 11:14	5921
comes **a** him will do as he pleases,	Da 11:16	413
put a stop to his scorn **a** him;	Da 11:18	
devise his schemes **a** strongholds,	Da 11:24	5921
his strength and courage **a** the king	Da 11:25	5921
for schemes will be devised **a** him.	Da 11:25	5921
will be *set* **a** the holy covenant,	Da 11:28	5921
ships of Kittim will come **a** him;	Da 11:30	
things **a** the God of gods;	Da 11:36	5921
"He will take action **a** the	Da 11:39	
will storm **a** him with chariots,	Da 11:40	5921
out his hand **a** *other* countries,	Da 11:42	
And I will build a wall **a** her so	Hos 2:6	
a the inhabitants of the land,	Hos 4:1	5973
the more they sinned **a** Me;	Hos 4:7	
pride of Israel testifies **a** him,	Hos 5:5	6440
dealt treacherously **a** the LORD,	Hos 5:7	
have dealt treacherously **a** Me.	Hos 6:7	
pride of Israel testifies **a** him,	Hos 7:10	6440
for they have rebelled **a** Me!	Hos 7:13	
them, but they speak lies **a** Me.	Hos 7:13	5921
arms, Yet they devise evil **a** Me.	Hos 7:15	413
comes **a** the house of the LORD,	Hos 8:1	5921
covenant And rebelled **a** My law.	Hos 8:1	5921
"My anger burns **a** them!"	Hos 8:5	
Will not the battle **a** the sons of	Hos 10:9	5921
the peoples will be gathered **a** them	Hos 10:10	5921
sword will whirl **a** their cities,	Hos 11:6	
Judah is also unruly **a** God,	Hos 11:12	5973
a the Holy One who is faithful.	Hos 11:12	5973
O Israel, That *you are* **a** Me,	Hos 13:9	
you are against Me, **a** your help.	Hos 13:9	
For she has rebelled **a** her God.	Hos 13:16	
which the LORD has spoken **a** you,	Am 3:1	5921
a the entire family which He	Am 3:1	5921
testify **a** the house of Jacob,"	Am 3:13	
home, leans his hand **a** the wall And	Am 5:19	5921
going to raise up a nation **a** you,	Am 6:14	5921
Then I will rise up **a** the house	Am 7:9	5921
"Amos has conspired **a** you in the	Am 7:10	5921
'You shall not prophesy **a** Israel	Am 7:16	5921
you speak **a** the house of Isaac.'	Am 7:16	5921
And I will set My eyes **a** them for	Am 9:4	5921
and let us go **a** her for battle"	Ob 1:1	5921
the great city and cry **a** it,	Jon 1:2	5921
was becoming *even* stormier **a** them.	Jon 1:13	5921
the Lord GOD be a witness **a** you,	Mi 1:2	
I am planning **a** this family a	Mi 2:3	5921
"On that day they will take up **a**	Mi 2:4	5921
But **a** him who puts nothing in	Mi 3:5	5921
will not lift up sword **a** nation,	Mi 4:3	413
have been assembled **a** you Who say,	Mi 4:11	5921
They have laid siege **a** us;	Mi 5:1	5921
Then we will raise **a** him Seven	Mi 5:5	5921

be lifted up **a** your adversaries,	Mi 5:9	5921
the LORD has a case **a** His people;	Mi 6:2	5973
Daughter rises up **a** her mother,	Mi 7:6	
Daughter-in-law **a** her mother-in-law;	Mi 7:6	
LORD Because I have sinned **a** Him,	Mi 7:9	
Whatever you devise **a** the LORD,	Na 1:9	413
One who plotted evil **a** the LORD,	Na 1:11	5921
who scatters has come up **a** you.	Na 2:1	5921
"Behold, I am **a** you,"	Na 2:13	413
"Behold, I am **a** you,"	Na 3:5	413
these take up a taunt-song **a** him,	Hab 2:6	5921
mockery *and* insinuations **a** him And	Hab 2:6	
So you are sinning **a** yourself.	Hab 2:10	
Did the LORD rage **a** the rivers,	Hab 3:8	
Or *was* Your anger **a** the rivers,	Hab 3:8	
Or *was* Your wrath **a** the sea,	Hab 3:8	
"So I will stretch out My hand **a**	Zph 1:4	5921
And **a** all the inhabitants of Jerusalem.	Zph 1:4	5921
A the fortified cities And the	Zph 1:16	5921
they have sinned **a** the LORD;	Zph 1:17	
The word of the LORD is **a** you,	Zph 2:5	5921
become arrogant **a** their territory.	Zph 2:8	5921
arrogant **a** the people of the LORD	Zph 2:10	5921
a the north And destroy Assyria,	Zph 2:13	5921
By which you have rebelled **a** Me;	Zph 3:11	
taken away *His* judgments **a** you,	Zph 3:15	
have lifted up *their* horns **a** the land	Zch 1:21	413
a the nations which plunder you,	Zch 2:8	413
in your hearts **a** one another.'	Zch 7:10	
and I set all men one **a** another.	Zch 8:10	
evil in your heart **a** another,	Zch 8:17	
the LORD is **a** the land of Hadrach,	Zch 9:1	
up your sons, O Zion, **a** your sons,	Zch 9:13	5921
anger is kindled **a** the shepherds,	Zch 10:3	5921
and when the siege is **a** Jerusalem,	Zch 12:2	5921
it will also be **a** Judah.	Zch 12:2	5921
the earth will be gathered **a** it.	Zch 12:3	5921
the nations that come **a** Jerusalem.	Zch 12:9	5921
"Awake, O sword, **a** My Shepherd,	Zch 13:7	5921
My Shepherd, And **a** the man,	Zch 13:7	5921
turn My hand **a** the little ones.	Zch 13:7	5921
the nations **a** Jerusalem to battle,	Zch 14:2	413
forth and fight **a** those nations,	Zch 14:3	
who have gone to war **a** Jerusalem;	Zch 14:12	5921
be lifted **a** the hand of another.	Zch 14:13	5921
all the nations that went **a** Jerusalem	Zch 14:16	5921
deal treacherously each **a** his brother	Mal 2:10	
a whom you have dealt	Mal 2:14	
a the wife of your youth.	Mal 2:15	
and I will be a swift witness **a**	Mal 3:5	
the sorcerers and **a** the adulterers	Mal 3:5	
and **a** those who swear falsely,	Mal 3:5	
and **a** those who oppress the wage	Mal 3:5	
words have been arrogant **a** Me,"	Mal 3:13	5921
'What have we spoken **a** You?'	Mal 3:13	5921
STRIKE YOUR FOOT **A** A STONE.' "	Mt 4:6	*4314*
all kinds of evil **a** you because	Mt 5:11	*2596*
your brother has something **a** you,	Mt 5:23	*2596*
blew and slammed **a** that house;	Mt 7:25	*4363*
blew and slammed **a** that house;	Mt 7:27	*4350*
children will rise up **a** parents and	Mt 10:21	*1909*
I came to SET A MAN **A** HIS FATHER,	Mt 10:35	*2596*
AND A DAUGHTER **A** HER MOTHER,	Mt 10:35	*2596*
A HER MOTHER-IN-LAW;	Mt 10:35	*2596*
out and conspired **a** Him,	Mt 12:14	*2596*
divided **a** itself is laid waste;	Mt 12:25	*2596*
divided **a** itself will not stand.	Mt 12:25	*2596*
Satan, he is divided **a** himself;	Mt 12:26	*1909*
"He who is not with Me is **a** Me;	Mt 12:30	*2596*
but blasphemy **a** the Spirit shall	Mt 12:31	
speaks a word **a** the Son of Man,	Mt 12:32	*2596*
speaks **a** the Holy Spirit,	Mt 12:32	*2596*
sin **a** me and I forgive him?	Mt 18:21	*1519*
you testify **a** yourselves,	Mt 23:31	
"For nation will rise **a** nation,	Mt 24:7	*1909*
nation, and kingdom **a** kingdom,	Mt 24:7	*1909*
to arrest Me as *you would* **a** a robber?	Mt 26:55	*1909*
to obtain false testimony **a** Jesus,	Mt 26:59	*2596*
these men are testifying **a** You?"	Mt 26:62	*2649*
a Jesus to put Him to death;	Mt 27:1	*2596*
many things they testify **a** You?"	Mt 27:13	*2649*
up the charge **a** Him which read,	Mt 27:37	*156*
and he rolled a large stone **a** the	Mt 27:60	
conspiring with the Herodians **a** Him,	Mk 3:6	*2596*
If a kingdom is divided **a** itself,	Mk 3:24	*1909*
If a house is divided **a** itself,	Mk 3:25	*1909*
risen up **a** himself and is divided,	Mk 3:26	*1909*
whoever blasphemes **a** the Holy Spirit	Mk 3:29	*1519*
feet for a testimony **a** them."	Mk 6:11	
Herodias had a grudge **a** him	Mk 6:19	*1758*
the oars, for the wind was **a** them,	Mk 6:48	*1727*
"For he who is not **a** us is for us.	Mk 9:40	*2596*
woman commits adultery **a** her;	Mk 10:11	*1909*
if you have anything **a** anyone,	Mk 11:25	*2596*
that He spoke the parable **a** them.	Mk 12:12	*4314*
"For nation will rise up **a** nation,	Mk 13:8	*1909*
nation, and kingdom **a** kingdom;	Mk 13:8	*1909*
and children will rise up **a**	Mk 13:12	*1909*
to arrest Me, as *you would* **a** a robber?	Mk 14:48	*1909*
a Jesus to put Him to death,	Mk 14:55	*2596*
were giving false testimony **a** Him,	Mk 14:56	*2596*
to give false testimony **a** Him,	Mk 14:57	*2596*
these men are testifying **a** You?"	Mk 14:60	*2649*
many charges they bring **a** You!"	Mk 15:4	*2723*
of the charge **a** Him read,	Mk 15:26	*156*
stone **a** the entrance of the tomb.	Mk 15:46	*1909*
STRIKE YOUR FOOT **A** A STONE.' "	Lk 4:11	*4314*
the torrent burst **a** that house and	Lk 6:48	*4366*
and the torrent burst **a** it and	Lk 6:49	*4366*

crowds were pressing **a** Him. Lk 8:42 *4846*
your feet as a testimony **a** them." Lk 9:5 *1909*
he who is not **a** you is for you." Lk 9:50 *2596*
we wipe off *in protest* **a** you; Lk 10:11
divided **a** itself is laid waste; Lk 11:17 *1909*
a house *divided* **a** itself falls. Lk 11:17 *1909*
Satan also is divided **a** himself, Lk 11:18 *1909*
"He who is not with Me is **a** Me; Lk 11:23 *2596*
may be charged **a** this generation, Lk 11:50 *575*
be charged **a** this generation.' Lk 11:51 *575*
plotting **a** Him to catch *Him* in Lk 11:54 *1748*
speaks a word **a** the Son of Man, Lk 12:10 *1519*
who blasphemes **a** the Holy Spirit, Lk 12:10 *1519*
your guard **a** every form of greed; Lk 12:15 *575*
will be divided, three **a** two and Lk 12:52 *1909*
against two and two **a** three. Lk 12:52 *1909*
will be divided, father **a** son and Lk 12:53 *1909*
against son and son **a** father Lk 12:53 *1909*
mother **a** daughter and daughter Lk 12:53 *1909*
daughter and daughter **a** mother Lk 12:53 *1909*
mother-in-law **a** daughter-in-law and Lk 12:53 *1909*
and daughter-in-law **a** mother-in-law." Lk 12:53 *1909*
coming **a** him with twenty thousand? Lk 14:31 *1909*
"Father, I have sinned **a** heaven, Lk 15:18 *1519*
sinned **a** heaven and in your sight; Lk 15:21 *1519*
he sins **a** you seven times a day, Lk 17:4 *1519*
enemies will throw up a barricade **a** Lk 19:43
that He spoke this parable **a** them. Lk 20:19 *4314*
"Nation will rise **a** nation and Lk 21:10 *1909*
nation and kingdom **a** kingdom, Lk 21:10 *1909*
and elders who had come **a** Him, Lk 22:52 *1909*
clubs as you would **a** a robber? Lk 22:52 *1909*
saying many other things **a** Him, Lk 22:65 *1519*
the charges which you make **a** Him. Lk 23:14 *2596*
cave, and a stone was lying **a** it. Jn 11:38 *1909*
HAS LIFTED UP HIS HEEL **A** ME.' Jn 13:18 *1909*
do you bring **a** this Man?" Jn 18:29
WERE GATHERED TOGETHER **A** THE LORD Ac 4:26 *2596*
THE LORD AND **A** HIS CHRIST.' Ac 4:26 *2596*
together **a** Your holy servant Jesus, Ac 4:27 *1909*
even be found fighting **a** God." Ac 5:39 *2314*
Jews **a** the *native* Hebrews, Ac 6:1 *4314*
words **a** Moses and *against* God." Ac 6:11 *1519*
words against Moses and **a** God." Ac 6:11
speaks **a** this holy place and Ac 6:13 *2596*
do not hold this sin **a** them!" Ac 7:60
began **a** the church in Jerusalem Ac 8:1 *1909*
a the disciples of the Lord, Ac 9:1 *1519*
a persecution **a** Paul and Barnabas, Ac 13:50 *1909*
a them and went to Iconium. Ac 13:51 *1909*
embittered them **a** the brethren. Ac 14:2 *2596*
The crowd rose up together **a** them, Ac 16:22 *2596*
Jews with one accord rose up **a** Paul Ac 18:12 *2721b*
him have a complaint **a** any man, Ac 19:38 *4314*
them bring charges **a** one another. Ac 19:38 *1458*
and when a plot was formed **a** him Ac 20:3 *1917*
all men everywhere **a** our people and Ac 21:28 *2596*
they were shouting **a** him that way. Ac 22:24
there would be a plot **a** the man, Ac 23:30 *1519*
bring charges **a** him before you." Ac 23:30 *4314*
charges to the governor **a** Paul. Ac 24:1 *2596*
if they should have anything **a** me. Ac 24:19 *4314*
the Jews brought charges **a** Paul, Ac 25:2 *2596*
requesting a concession **a** Paul, Ac 25:3 *2596*
and serious charges **a** him which they Ac 25:7 *2702*
committed no offense either **a** the Law Ac 25:8 *1519*
a the temple or against Caesar." Ac 25:8 *1519*
against the temple or **a** Caesar." Ac 25:8 *1519*
of the Jews brought charges **a** him, Ac 25:15 *4012*
for a sentence of condemnation **a** him. Ac 25:15 *4012*
to make his defense **a** the charges. Ac 25:16 *4012*
they *began* bringing charges **a** him Ac 25:18 *4012*
indicate also the charges **a** him." Ac 25:27 *2596*
to death I cast my vote **a** them. Ac 26:10 *2702*
hard for you to kick **a** the goads.' Ac 26:14 *4314*
I had done nothing **a** our people or Ac 28:17 *1727*
I had any accusation **a** my nation. Ac 28:19 *2723*
that it is spoken **a** everywhere." Ac 28:22 *483*
revealed from heaven **a** all ungodliness Ro 1:18 *1909*
In hope **a** hope he believed, so Ro 4:18 *1909*
waging war **a** the law of my mind and Ro 7:23 *497*
If God *is* for us, who *is* **a** us? Ro 8:31 *2596*
will bring a charge **a** God's elect? Ro 8:33 *2596*
how he pleads with God **a** Israel? Ro 11:2 *2596*
am conscious of nothing **a** myself, 1Co 4:4
in behalf of one **a** the other. 1Co 4:6 *2596*
when he has a case **a** his neighbor, 1Co 6:1 *4314*
immoral man sins **a** his own body. 1Co 6:18 *1519*
by sinning **a** the brethren and 1Co 8:12 *1519*
when it is weak, you sin **a** Christ. 1Co 8:12 *1519*
but if **a** my will, I have a 1Co 9:17 *210*
a God that He raised Christ, 1Co 15:15 *2596*
counting their trespasses **a** them, 2Co 5:19
I propose to be courageous **a** some, 2Co 10:2 *1909*
raised up **a** the knowledge of God, 2Co 10:5 *2596*
For we can do nothing **a** the truth, 2Co 13:8 *2596*
sets its desire **a** the Spirit, Ga 5:17 *2596*
and the Spirit **a** the flesh; Ga 5:17 *2596*
a such things there is no law. Ga 5:23 *2596*
firm **a** the schemes of the devil. Eph 6:11 *4314*
struggle is not **a** flesh and blood, Eph 6:12 *4314*
flesh and blood, but **a** the rulers, Eph 6:12 *4314*
against the rulers, **a** the powers, Eph 6:12 *4314*
a the world forces of this darkness, Eph 6:12 *4314*
a the spiritual *forces* of wickedness Eph 6:12 *4314*
of debt consisting of decrees **a** us Col 2:14 *2596*
of no value **a** fleshly indulgence. Col 2:23 *4314*
whoever has a complaint **a** anyone; Col 3:13 *4314*
and do not be embittered **a** them. Col 3:19 *4314*
Do not receive an accusation **a** an 1Tm 5:19 *2596*
our doctrine will not be spoken **a**. 1Tm 6:1 *987*
Be on guard **a** him yourself, for he 2Tm 4:15
may it not be counted **a** them. 2Tm 4:16
hostility by sinners **a** Himself, Heb 12:3 *1519*
blood in your striving **a** sin; Heb 12:4 *4314*
arrogant and *so* lie **a** the truth. Jas 3:14 *2596*
Do not speak **a** one another, Jas 4:11 *2635*
He who speaks **a** a brother or Jas 4:11 *2635*
his brother, speaks **a** the law and Jas 4:11 *2635*
their rust will be a witness **a** you and Jas 5:3
cries out **a** *you;* and the outcry Jas 5:4
complain, brethren, **a** one another, Jas 5:9 *2596*
lusts which wage war **a** the soul. 1Pe 2:11 *2596*
THE LORD IS **A** THOSE WHO DO EVIL." 1Pe 3:12 *1909*
judgment **a** them before the Lord. 2Pe 2:11 *2596*
need and closes his heart **a** him, 1Jn 3:17 *575*
a him a railing judgment, Jude 1:9 *2018*
sinners have spoken **a** Him." Jude 1:15 *2596*
'But I have *this* **a** you, that you Rv 2:4 *2596*
'But I have a few things **a** you, Rv 2:14 *2596*
and I will make war **a** them with Rv 2:16 *3326*
'But I have *this* **a** you, that you Rv 2:20 *2596*
his mouth in blasphemies **a** God, Rv 13:6 *4314*
"These will wage war **a** the Lamb, Rv 17:14 *3326*
judgment for you **a** her." Rv 18:20 *1537*
war **a** Him who sat on the horse Rv 19:19 *3326*
on the horse and **a** His army. Rv 19:19 *3326*

AGATE
a jacinth, an **a** and an amethyst; Ex 28:19 7618
the third row, a jacinth, an **a**, Ex 39:12 7618

AGE
will be buried at a good old **a**. Gn 15:15 7872
and Sarah were old, advanced in **a**; Gn 18:11 3117
a son to Abraham in his old **a**, Gn 21:2 2208
borne him a son in his old **a**." Gn 21:7 2208
Abraham was old, advanced in **a**; Gn 24:1 3117
a son to my master in her old **a**, Gn 24:36 2209
his last and died in a ripe old **a**, Gn 25:8 7872
his people, an old man of ripe **a**; Gn 35:29 3117
Joseph, when seventeen years of **a**, Gn 37:2 1121
he was the son of his old **a**; Gn 37:3 2208
and a little child of *his* old **a**. Gn 44:20 2208
dim from **a** *that* he could not see. Gn 48:10 2207
a of one hundred and ten years; Gn 50:26 1121
"But at the **a** of fifty years they Nu 8:25 1121
at the **a** of one hundred and ten. Jg 2:8 1121
the son of Joash died at a ripe old **a** Jg 8:32 7872
and a sustainer of your old **a**; Ru 4:15 7872
King David was old, advanced in **a**; 1Ki 1:1 3117
eyes were dim because of his **a**. 1Ki 14:4 7869
old **a** he was diseased in his feet. 1Ki 15:23 2209
Now when David reached old **a**, 1Ch 23:1 3117
those twenty years of **a** and under, 1Ch 27:23 1121
Then he died in a ripe old **a**, 1Ch 29:28 7872
reached a ripe old **a** he died; 2Ch 24:15 3117
"I thought **a** should speak, And Jb 32:7 3117
cast me off in the time of old **a**; Ps 71:9 2209
will still yield fruit in old **a**; Ps 92:14 7872
Even to *your* old **a** Is 46:4 2209
For the youth will die at the **a** of Is 65:20 1121
does not reach the **a** of one hundred Is 65:20 1121
reached the **a** for fine ornaments; Ezk 16:7 935
the youths who are your own **a**? Da 1:10 1524b
at about the **a** of sixty-two. Da 5:31 1247, 8140
portion at the end of the **a**." Da 12:13 3117
staff in his hand because of **a**. Zch 8:4 7230, 3117
be forgiven him, either in this **a** or Mt 12:32 *165*
either in this age or in the **a** to Mt 12:32
the harvest is the end of the **a**; Mt 13:39 *165*
shall it be at the end of the **a**. Mt 13:40 *165*
"So it will be at the end of the **a**; Mt 13:49 *165*
coming, and of the end of the **a**?" Mt 24:3 *165*
even to the end of the **a**." Mt 28:20 *165*
as much now in the present **a**, Mk 10:30 *2540*
and in the **a** to come, eternal life. Mk 10:30 *165*
also conceived a son in her old **a**; Lk 1:36 *1094*
as a widow to the **a** of eighty-four. Lk 2:37 *2094*
was about thirty years of **a**, Lk 3:23 *2094*
for the sons of this **a** are more Lk 16:8 *165*
at this time and in the **a** to come, Lk 18:30 *165*
"The sons of this **a** marry and are Lk 20:34 *165*
attain to that **a** and the resurrection Lk 20:35 *165*
he is of **a**, he will speak for Jn 9:21 *2244*
parents said, "He is of **a**; ask him." Jn 9:23 *2244*
he was approaching the **a** of forty, Ac 7:23 *5550*
Where is the debater of this **a**? 1Co 1:20 *165*
a wisdom, however, not of this **a** nor 1Co 2:6 *165*
age nor of the rulers of this **a**, 1Co 2:6 *165*
rulers of this **a** has understood; 1Co 2:8 *165*
thinks that he is wise in this **a**, 1Co 3:18 *165*
us from this present evil **a**, Ga 1:4 *165*
that is named, not only in this **a** but Eph 1:21 *165*
and godly in the present **a**, Ti 2:12 *165*
and the powers of the **a** to come, Heb 6:5 *165*

AGED
the grayheaded and honor the **a**, Lv 19:32 6440, 2205
"Wisdom is with **a** men, *With* long Jb 12:12 3453
gray-haired and the **a** are among us, Jb 15:10 3453
I understand more than the **a**, Ps 119:100 2205
A banquet of **a** wine, choice pieces Is 25:6 8105
with marrow, *And* refined, **a** wine. Is 25:6 8105
a you made your yoke very heavy. Is 47:6 2205
be taken, The **a** and the very old. Jer 6:11 2205
I am such a person as Paul, the **a**, Phm 1:9 *4246*

AGEE
Shammah the son of **A** a Hararite. 2Sa 23:11 89

AGENCY
he will be broken without human **a**. Da 8:25 3027
men nor through the **a** of man, Ga 1:1 *1223*
angels by the **a** of a mediator, Ga 3:19 *5495*

AGENT
the Lord has a strong and mighty **a**; Is 28:2

AGE-OLD
will raise up the **a** foundations; Is 58:12 1755

AGES
for **a** Which were before us. Ec 1:10 5769
forever, for all **a** to come.' Da 7:18 5957
been kept secret for long **a** past, Ro 16:25 *5550*
before the **a** to our glory; 1Co 2:7 *165*
whom the ends of the **a** have come. 1Co 10:11 *165*
so that in the **a** to come He Eph 2:7 *165*
for **a** has been hidden in God who Eph 3:9 *165*
from the *past* **a** and generations, Col 1:26 *165*
cannot lie, promised long **a** ago, Ti 1:2 *5550*
consummation of the **a** He has been Heb 9:26 *165*

AGGRESSOR
and a persecutor and a violent **a**. 1Tm 1:13 *5197*

AGILE
firm, And his arms were **a**, Gn 49:24 6339

AGITATING
a and stirring up the crowds. Ac 17:13 *4531*

AGITATION
Even because of my inward **a**. Jb 20:2 2363a
because of the **a** of my heart. Ps 38:8 5100

AGO
which were lost three days **a**, 1Sa 9:20 3117
when I fell sick three days **a**. 1Sa 30:13
Long **a** I did it; From ancient times 2Ki 19:25 7350
that was built many years **a**, Ezr 5:11 6928
days of old, The years of long **a**. Ps 77:5 5769
Him who planned it long **a**. Is 22:11 7350
wonders, Plans *formed* long **a**, Is 25:1 7350
Long **a** I did it, From ancient Is 37:26 7350
"I declared the former things long **a** Is 48:3 3975b
I declared *them* to you long **a**, Is 48:5 3975b
are created now and not long **a**; Is 48:7 3975b
long **a** your ear has not been open, Is 48:8 3975b
of old, the generations of long **a**. Is 51:9 5769
"For long **a** I broke your yoke *And* Jer 2:20 5769
His goings forth are from long **a**, Mi 5:2 6924a
long **a** in sackcloth and ashes. Mt 11:21 *3819*
they would have repented long **a**, Lk 10:13 *3819*
"For some time **a** Theudas rose up, Ac 5:36 *4253*
"Four days **a** to this hour, I was Ac 10:30 *575*
MAKES THESE THINGS KNOWN FROM LONG **A**. Ac 15:18 *165*
Egyptian who some time **a** stirred up Ac 21:38 *4253*
twelve days **a** I went up to Jerusalem Ac 24:11 *575*
a year **a** not only to do *this,* 2Co 8:10 *4070*
fourteen years **a**—whether in the body 2Co 12:2 *4253*
cannot lie, promised long ages **a**, Ti 1:2 *4253*
after He spoke long **a** to the Heb 1:1 *3819*
judgment from long **a** is not idle, 2Pe 2:3 *1597*
heavens existed long **a** and *the* earth 2Pe 3:5 *1597*

AGONY
for **a** has seized me because my 2Sa 1:9 7661
him, **A** like a woman in childbirth. Jer 50:43 2427
That **a** has gripped you like a Mi 4:9 2427
for I am in **a** in this flame.' Lk 16:24 *3600*
comforted here, and you are in **a**. Lk 16:25 *3600*
being in **a** He was praying very Lk 22:44 *74*
putting an end to the **a** of death, Ac 2:24 *5604*

AGREE
that if two of you **a** on earth Mt 18:19 *4856*
you not **a** with me for a denarius? Mt 20:13 *4856*
this the words of the Prophets **a**, Ac 15:15 *4856*
they did not **a** with one another, Ac 28:25 *800*
not want *to do,* I **a** with the Law, Ro 7:16 *4852*
Lord Jesus Christ, that you all **a** and 1Co 1:10 *846, 3004*
and does not **a** with sound words, 1Tm 6:3 *4334*

AGREEABLE
perhaps it will be **a** with God that Nu 23:27 3474
told Saul, the thing was **a** to him. 1Sa 18:20 3474

AGREED
of these kings having **a** to meet, Jos 11:5 3259
The Levite **a** to live with the man Jg 17:11 2974
So the priests **a** that they would 2Ki 12:8 225
For you have **a** together to speak Da 2:9 2164
"When he had **a** with the Mt 20:2 *4856*
glad and **a** to give him money. Lk 22:5 *4934*
for the Jews had already **a** that Jn 9:22 *4934*
"Why is it that you have **a** Ac 5:9 *4856*
"The Jews have **a** to ask you to Ac 23:20 *4934*

AGREEMENT
"As for the **a** of which you and I 1Sa 20:23 1697
We are making an **a** in writing; Ne 9:38 548
an **a** for yourself with them, Is 57:8
and satraps came by **a** to the king Da 6:6 7284
Then these men came by **a** and found Da 6:11 7284
Then these men came by **a** to the Da 6:15 7284
a with putting him to death. Ac 8:1 *4909*
except by **a** for a time, so that you 1Co 7:5 *4859*
Or what **a** has the temple of God 2Co 6:16 *4783*
and the three are in **a**. 1Jn 5:8 *1520*

AGREES
If it **a** to make peace with you and Dt 20:11 6030a

AGRICULTURAL
the **a** workers who tilled the soil. 1Ch 27:26 7704

AGRIPPA
King **A** and Bernice arrived at Ac 25:13 *67*

Then A *said* to Festus, Ac 25:22 *67*
on the next day when A came Ac 25:23 *67*
"King A, and all you gentlemen Ac 25:24 *67*
and especially before you, King A, Ac 25:26 *67*
A said to Paul, Ac 26:1 *67*
consider myself fortunate, King A, Ac 26:2 *67*
"So, King A, Ac 26:19 *67*
"King A, do you believe the Ac 26:27 *67*
A *replied* to Paul, Ac 26:28 *67*
And A said to Festus, Ac 26:32 *67*

AGROUND
run a on *the shallows* of Syrtis, Ac 27:17 *1601b*
must run a on a certain island." Ac 27:26 *1601b*
run a somewhere on the rocks, Ac 27:29 *1601b*
seas met, they ran the vessel a; Ac 27:41 *1946a*

AGUR
The words of A the son of Jakeh, Pr 30:1 94

AH
"A, I will be relieved of My Is 1:24 1945
"A, Lord GOD! Surely You have Jer 4:10 162
"A, woe is me, for I faint before Jer 4:31 4994
"A, Lord GOD!" I said, "Look, Jer 14:13 162
'A Lord GOD! Behold, You have Jer 32:17 162
"A, woe is me! For the LORD has Jer 45:3 4994
"A, sword of the LORD, How long Jer 47:6 1945
But I said, "A, Lord GOD! Behold, Ezk 4:14 162
Then I said, "A Lord GOD! They Ezk 20:49 162
given the glittering sword. A! Ezk 21:15 253

AHA
the trumpet *sounds* he says, 'A!' Jb 39:25 1889
"A, aha, our eyes have seen it!" Ps 35:21 1889
"Aha, a, our eyes have seen it!" Ps 35:21 1889
"A, our desire!" Ps 35:25 1889
Who say to me, "A, aha!" Ps 40:15 1889
shame Who say to me, "Aha, a!" Ps 40:15 1889
because of their shame Who say, "A, Ps 70:3 1889
of their shame Who say, "Aha, a!" Ps 70:3 1889
also warms himself and says, "A! Is 44:16 1889
"Because you said, 'A!' Ezk 25:3 1889
'A, the gateway of the peoples is Ezk 26:2 1889
enemy has spoken against you, 'A!' Ezk 36:2 1889

AHAB
and A his son became king in his 1Ki 16:28 256
Now A the son of Omri became king 1Ki 16:29 256
and A the son of Omri reigned over 1Ki 16:29 256
A the son of Omri did evil in 1Ki 16:30 256
A also made the Asherah. 1Ki 16:33 256
Thus A did more to provoke the 1Ki 16:33 256
the settlers of Gilead, said to A, 1Ki 17:1 256
"Go, show yourself to A, 1Ki 18:1 256
Elijah went to show himself to A. 1Ki 18:2 256
A called Obadiah who *was* over 1Ki 18:3 256
Then A said to Obadiah, 1Ki 18:5 256
A went one way by himself and 1Ki 18:6 256
your servant into the hand of A to 1Ki 18:9 256
and tell A and he cannot find you, 1Ki 18:12 256
So Obadiah went to meet A and 1Ki 18:16 256
and A went to meet Elijah. 1Ki 18:16 256
When A saw Elijah, Ahab said to him, 1Ki 18:17 256
saw Elijah, A said to him, 1Ki 18:17 256
So A sent *a message* among all the 1Ki 18:20 256
Now Elijah said to A, 1Ki 18:41 256
So A went up to eat and drink. 1Ki 18:42 256
"Go up, say to A, 1Ki 18:44 256
And A rode and went to Jezreel. 1Ki 18:45 256
his loins and outran A to Jezreel. 1Ki 18:46 256
Now A told Jezebel all that Elijah 1Ki 19:1 256
to the city to A king of Israel and 1Ki 20:2 256
A king of Israel and said, 1Ki 20:13 256
A said, "By whom?" So he said, 1Ki 20:14 256
A *said,* "And I will let you go 1Ki 20:34
the palace of A king of Samaria. 1Ki 21:1 256
A spoke to Naboth, saying, 1Ki 21:2 256
But Naboth said to A, 1Ki 21:3 256
So A came into his house sullen 1Ki 21:4 256
was dead, Jezebel said to A, 1Ki 21:15 256
When A heard that Naboth was dead, 1Ki 21:16 256
A arose to go down to the 1Ki 21:16 256
go down to meet A king of Israel, 1Ki 21:18 256
A said to Elijah, 1Ki 21:20 256
will cut off from A every male, 1Ki 21:21 256
"The one belonging to A, 1Ki 21:24 256
Surely there was no one like A who 1Ki 21:25 256
about when A heard these words, 1Ki 21:27 256
A has humbled himself before Me? 1Ki 21:29 256
'Who will entice A to go up and 1Ki 22:20 256
Now the rest of the acts of A and 1Ki 22:39 256
So A slept with his fathers, and 1Ki 22:40 256
fourth year of A king of Israel. 1Ki 22:41 256
the son of A said to Jehoshaphat, 1Ki 22:49 256
Ahaziah the son of A became king 1Ki 22:51 256
Israel after the death of A. 2Ki 1:1 256
Now Jehoram the son of A became 2Ki 3:1 256
But when A died, 2Ki 3:5 256
Joram the son of A king of Israel, 2Ki 8:16 256
just as the house of A had done, 2Ki 8:18 256
the daughter of A became his wife; 2Ki 8:18 256
Joram the son of A king of Israel, 2Ki 8:25 256
in the way of the house of A and 2Ki 8:27 256
like the house of A *had done,* 2Ki 8:27 256
was a son-in-law of the house of A. 2Ki 8:27 256
went with Joram the son of A to war 2Ki 8:28 256
went down to see Joram the son of A 2Ki 8:29 256
strike the house of A your master, 2Ki 9:7 256
the whole house of A shall perish, 2Ki 9:8 256
and I will cut off from A every 2Ki 9:8 256
'I will make the house of A 2Ki 9:9 256
together after A his father, 2Ki 9:25 256
eleventh year of Joram, the son of A, 2Ki 9:29 256
Now A had seventy sons in Samaria. 2Ki 10:1 256
guardians of *the children of* A, 2Ki 10:1 256
spoke concerning the house of A, 2Ki 10:10 256
of the house of A in Jezreel, 2Ki 10:11 256
all who remained to A in Samaria, 2Ki 10:17 256
"A served Baal a little; 2Ki 10:18 256
and have done to the house of A 2Ki 10:30 256
as A king of Israel had done, 2Ki 21:3 256
and the plummet of the house of A, 2Ki 21:13 256
allied himself by marriage with A. 2Ch 18:1 256
went down to *visit* A at Samaria. 2Ch 18:2 256
And A slaughtered many sheep and 2Ch 18:2 256
A king of Israel said to 2Ch 18:3 256
'Who will entice A king of Israel 2Ch 18:19 256
just as the house of A did 2Ch 21:6 256
the house of A played the harlot, 2Ch 21:13 256
in the ways of the house of A, 2Ch 22:3 256
of the LORD like the house of A, 2Ch 22:4 256
son of A king of Israel to wage war 2Ch 22:5 256
Jehoram the son of A in Jezreel, 2Ch 22:6 256
to cut off the house of A. 2Ch 22:7 256
judgment on the house of A, 2Ch 22:8 256
concerning A the son of Kolaiah Jer 29:21 256
make you like Zedekiah and like A, Jer 29:22 256
of the house of A are observed; Mi 6:16 256

AHAB'S
So she wrote letters in A name and 1Ki 21:8 256
(for A daughter was his wife), 2Ch 21:6 256

AHARAH
Ashbel the second, A the third, 1Ch 8:1 315

AHARHEL
families of A the son of Harum. 1Ch 4:8 316

AHASBAI
Eliphelet the son of A, 2Sa 23:34 308

AHASUERUS
Now in the reign of A, Ezr 4:6 325
it took place in the days of A, Es 1:1 325
the A who reigned from India to Es 1:1 325
in those days as King A sat on his Es 1:2 325
palace which belonged to King A. Es 1:9 325
served in the presence of King A, Es 1:10 325
King A *delivered* by the eunuchs?" Es 1:15 325
in all the provinces of King A. Es 1:16 325
'King A commanded Queen Vashti to Es 1:17 325
come into the presence of King A, Es 1:19 325
the anger of King A had subsided, Es 2:1 325
lady came to go in to King A, Es 2:12 325
So Esther was taken to King A to Es 2:16 325
and sought to lay hands on King A. Es 2:21 325
events King A promoted Haman, Es 3:1 325
throughout the whole kingdom of A. Es 3:6 325
in the twelfth year of King A, Es 3:7 325
Then Haman said to King A, Es 3:8 325
being written in the name of King A Es 3:12 325
had sought to lay hands on King A. Es 6:2 325
Then King A asked Queen Esther, Es 7:5 325
King A gave the house of Haman, Es 8:1 325
So King A said to Queen Esther and Es 8:7 325
He wrote in the name of King A, Es 8:10 325
in all the provinces of King A, Es 8:12 325
the provinces of King A to lay hands Es 9:2 325
in all the provinces of King A, Es 9:20 325
127 provinces of the kingdom of A, Es 9:30 325
Now King A laid a tribute on the Es 10:1 325
King A, and great among the Jews Es 10:3 325
first year of Darius the son of A, Da 9:1 325

AHAVA
them at the river that runs to A, Ezr 8:15 163
a fast there at the river of A, Ezr 8:21 163
Then we journeyed from the river A Ezr 8:31 163

AHAZ
and A his son became king in his 2Ki 15:38 271
of Remaliah, A the son of Jotham, 2Ki 16:1 271
A *was* twenty years old when he 2Ki 16:2 271
and they besieged A, 2Ki 16:5 271
So A sent messengers to 2Ki 16:7 271
A took the silver and gold 2Ki 16:8 271
Now King A went to Damascus to 2Ki 16:10 271
and King A sent to Urijah the 2Ki 16:10 271
King A had sent from Damascus, 2Ki 16:11 271
coming of King A from Damascus. 2Ki 16:11 271
A commanded Urijah the priest, 2Ki 16:15 271
to all that King A commanded. 2Ki 16:16 271
Then King A cut off the borders of 2Ki 16:17 271
of the acts of A which he did, 2Ki 16:19 271
So A slept with his fathers, and 2Ki 16:20 271
twelfth year of A king of Judah, 2Ki 17:1 271
son of A king of Judah became king. 2Ki 18:1 271
gone down on the stairway of A, 2Ki 20:11 271
the roof, the upper chamber of A, 2Ki 23:12 271
A his son, Hezekiah his son, 1Ch 3:13 271
were Pithon, Melech, Tarea and A. 1Ch 8:35 271
A became the father of 1Ch 8:36 271
Pithon, Melech, Tahrea *and* A. 1Ch 9:41
A became the father of Jarah, 1Ch 9:42 271
and A his son became king in his 2Ch 27:9 271
A *was* twenty years old when he 2Ch 28:1 271
At that time King A sent to the 2Ch 28:16 271
Judah because of A king of Israel, 2Ch 28:19 271
A took a portion out of the house 2Ch 28:21 271
King A became yet more unfaithful 2Ch 28:22 271
when A gathered together the 2Ch 28:24 271
So A slept with his fathers, and 2Ch 28:27 271
all the utensils which King A had 2Ch 29:19 271
the reigns of Uzziah, Jotham, A Is 1:1 271
it came about in the days of A, Is 7:1 271
"Go out now to meet A, Is 7:3 271
Then the LORD spoke again to A, Is 7:10 271
But A said, "I will not ask, nor will Is 7:12 271
that King A died this oracle came: Is 14:28 271
with the sun on the stairway of A, Is 38:8 271
the days of Uzziah, Jotham, A Hos 1:1 271
in the days of Jotham, A Mi 1:1 271
Jotham the father of A, Mt 1:9 *881*
and A the father of Hezekiah. Mt 1:9 *881*

AHAZIAH
and A his son became king in his 1Ki 22:40 274
Then A the son of Ahab said to 1Ki 22:49 274
A the son of Ahab became king over 1Ki 22:51 274
And A fell through the lattice in 2Ki 1:2 274
So A died according to the word of 2Ki 1:17
of the acts of A which he did, 2Ki 1:18 274
and A his son became king in his 2Ki 8:24 274
A the son of Jehoram king of Judah 2Ki 8:25 274
A *was* twenty-two years old when he 2Ki 8:26 274
Then A the son of Jehoram king of 2Ki 8:29 274
A king of Judah had come down 2Ki 9:16 274
and A king of Judah went out, 2Ki 9:21 274
about and fled and said to A, 2Ki 9:23 274
"*There is* treachery, O A!" 2Ki 9:23 274
When A the king of Judah saw *this,* 2Ki 9:27 274
of Ahab, A became king over Judah. 2Ki 9:29 274
of A king of Judah and said, 2Ki 10:13 274
"We are the relatives of A; 2Ki 10:13 274
mother of A saw that her son was 2Ki 11:1 274
of King Joram, sister of A, 2Ki 11:2 274
took Joash the son of A and stole 2Ki 11:2 274
Jehoshaphat and Jehoram and A, 2Ki 12:18 274
year of Joash the son of A, 2Ki 13:1 274
the son of Jehoash the son of A, 2Ki 14:13 274
Joram his son, A his son, Joash 1Ch 3:11 274
himself with A king of Israel. 2Ch 20:35 274
you have allied yourself with A, 2Ch 20:37 274
inhabitants of Jerusalem made A, 2Ch 22:1 274
So A the son of Jehoram king of 2Ch 22:1 274
A *was* twenty-two years old when he 2Ch 22:2 274
And A, the son of Jehoram king of 2Ch 22:6 274
the destruction of A was from God, 2Ch 22:7 274
brothers ministering to A, 2Ch 22:8 274
He also sought A, and they caught 2Ch 22:9 274
no one of the house of A to retain 2Ch 22:9 274
of A saw that her son was dead, 2Ch 22:10 274
daughter took Joash the son of A, 2Ch 22:11 274
(for she was the sister of A), 2Ch 22:11 274

AHAZIAH'S
Judah and the sons of A brothers 2Ch 22:8 274

AHBAN
and she bore him A and Molid. 1Ch 2:29 257

AHEAD
But he himself passed on a of them Gn 33:3 6440
"Go a." So the girl went Ex 2:8
"I will send My terror a of you, Ex 23:27 6440
"I will send hornets a of you so Ex 23:28 6440
on your journey a of the people, Dt 10:11 6440
your God who will cross a of you; Dt 31:3 6440
the one who will cross a of you, Dt 31:3 6440
LORD is the one who goes a of you; Dt 31:8 6440
and cross over a of the people." Jos 3:6 6440
covenant and went a of the people. Jos 3:6 6440
over a of you into the Jordan. Jos 3:11 6440
will go up every man straight a." Jos 6:5 5048
the city, every man straight a, Jos 6:20 5048
see, *he is* a of you. 1Sa 9:12 6440
he might go a of us and pass on, 1Sa 9:27 6440
drove a of the *other* livestock, 1Sa 30:20 6440
and Ahio was walking a of the ark. 2Sa 6:4 6440
Let your eyes look directly a And Pr 4:25 5227
straight a to the hill Gareb; Jer 31:39 5048
Go a and confirm your vows, and Jer 44:25 6965
Each one went straight a. Ezk 10:22 6440
I SEND MY MESSENGER A OF YOU, Mt 11:10
and go a of Him to the other side, Mt 14:22 *4254*
The crowds going a of Him, and those Mt 21:9 *4254*
I will go a of you to Galilee." Mt 26:32 *4254*
He is going a of you into Galilee, Mt 28:7 *4254*
I SEND MY MESSENGER A OF YOU, Mk 1:2 *4253*
cities, and got there a of them. Mk 6:33 *4281*
get into the boat and go a of *Him* Mk 6:45 *4254*
Jesus was walking on a of them; Mk 10:32 *4254*
I will go a of you to Galilee." Mk 14:28 *4254*
'He is going a of you to Galilee; Mk 16:7 *4254*
I SEND MY MESSENGER A OF YOU, Lk 7:27 *4253*
He sent messengers on a of Him, Lk 9:52
4253, 4383
and sent them in pairs a of Him Lk 10:1
4253, 4383
So he ran on a and climbed up Lk 19:4 *1715*
these things, He was going on a, Lk 19:28 *1715*
saying, "Go into the village a of Lk 19:30 *2713*
'I have been sent a of Him.' Jn 3:28 *1715*
he goes a of them, and the sheep Jn 10:4 *1715*
disciple ran a faster than Peter and Jn 20:4 *4390*
he looked a and spoke of the Ac 2:31 *4275a*
But these had gone on a and were Ac 20:5 *4281*
But we, going a to the ship, set Ac 20:13 *4281*
would go on a to you and arrange 2Co 9:5 *4281*
reaching forward to what *lies* a, Php 3:13 *1715*

AHER
Hushim *was* the son of A. 1Ch 7:12 313

AHI
A the son of Abdiel, the son of 1Ch 5:15 277
sons of Shemer *were* A and Rohgah, 1Ch 7:34 277

AHIAH
A, Hanan, Anan, Ne 10:26 281
AHIAM
A the son of Sharar the Ararite, 2Sa 23:33 279
A the son of Sacar the Hararite, 1Ch 11:35 279
AHIAN
The sons of Shemida were A and 1Ch 7:19 291
AHIEZER
of Dan, A the son of Ammishaddai; Nu 1:12 295
A the son of Ammishaddai, Nu 2:25 295
it was A the son of Ammishaddai, Nu 7:66 295
of A the son of Ammishaddai. Nu 7:71 295
with A the son of Ammishaddai over Nu 10:25 295
The chief was A, then Joash, the 1Ch 12:3 295
AHIHUD
a leader, A the son of Shelomi. Nu 34:27 282
became the father of Uzza and A. 1Ch 8:7 284
AHIJAH
and A, the son of Ahitub, 1Sa 14:3 281
Then Saul said to A, 1Sa 14:18 281
Elihoreph and A, the sons of 1Ki 4:3 281
that the prophet A the Shilonite 1Ki 11:29 281
Now A had clothed himself with a 1Ki 11:29 281
Then A took hold of the new cloak 1Ki 11:30 281
which the LORD spoke through A the 1Ki 12:15 281
behold, A the prophet is there, 1Ki 14:2 281
and came to the house of A. 1Ki 14:4 281
Now A could not see, for his eyes 1Ki 14:4 281
Now the LORD had said to A, 1Ki 14:5 281
When A heard the sound 1Ki 14:6 281
through His servant A the prophet. 1Ki 14:18 281
Then Baasha the son of A of the 1Ki 15:27 281
by His servant A the Shilonite, 1Ki 15:29 281
Baasha the son of A became king 1Ki 15:33 281
the house of Baasha the son of A, 1Ki 21:22 281
the house of Baasha the son of A, 2Ki 9:9 281
then Bunah, Oren, Ozem *and* A. 1Ch 2:25 281
namely, Naaman, A and Gera—he 1Ch 8:7 281
the Mecherathite, A the Pelonite, 1Ch 11:36 281
the prophecy of A the Shilonite, 2Ch 9:29 281
which He spoke through A the 2Ch 10:15 281
AHIKAM
the priest, A the son of Shaphan, 2Ki 22:12 296
So Hilkiah the priest, A, 2Ki 22:14 296
appointed Gedaliah the son of A, 2Ki 25:22 296
Hilkiah, A the son of Shaphan, 2Ch 34:20 296
But the hand of A the son of Jer 26:24 296
him to Gedaliah, the son of A, Jer 39:14 296
then to Gedaliah the son of A, Jer 40:5 296
to Gedaliah the son of A and stayed Jer 40:6 296
appointed Gedaliah the son of A Jer 40:7 296
Then Gedaliah the son of A, Jer 40:9 296
over them Gedaliah the son of A, Jer 40:11 296
the son of A did not believe them. Jer 40:14 296
But Gedaliah the son of A said to Jer 40:16 296
Mizpah to Gedaliah the son of A. Jer 41:1 296
struck down Gedaliah the son of A, Jer 41:2 296
"Come to Gedaliah the son of A!" Jer 41:6 296
charge of Gedaliah the son of A; Jer 41:10 296
struck down Gedaliah the son of A, Jer 41:16 296
struck down Gedaliah the son of A, Jer 41:18 296
son of A and grandson of Shaphan, Jer 43:6 296
AHILUD
the son of A *was* recorder. 2Sa 8:16 286
the son of A was the recorder; 2Sa 20:24 286
the son of A *was* the recorder; 1Ki 4:3 286
Baana the son of A, 1Ki 4:12 286
the son of A *was* recorder; 1Ch 18:15 286
AHIMAAZ
was Ahinoam the daughter of A. 1Sa 14:50 290
your son A and Jonathan the son of 2Sa 15:27 290
two sons are with them there, A, 2Sa 15:36 290
and A were staying at En-rogel, 2Sa 17:17 290
"Where are A and Jonathan?" 2Sa 17:20 290
Then A the son of Zadok said, 2Sa 18:19 290
Now A the son of Zadok said once 2Sa 18:22 290
Then A ran by way of the plain and 2Sa 18:23 290
running of A the son of Zadok." 2Sa 18:27 290
A called and said to the king, 2Sa 18:28 290
And A answered, "When Joab sent 2Sa 18:29 290
A, in Naphtali 1Ki 4:15 290
and Zadok became the father of A, 1Ch 6:8 290
A became the father of Azariah, 1Ch 6:9 290
Zadok his son, A his son. 1Ch 6:53 290
AHIMAN
they came to Hebron where A, Nu 13:22 289
Sheshai and A and Talmai, the Jos 15:14 289
struck Sheshai and A and Talmai. Jg 1:10 289
Talmon and A and their relatives 1Ch 9:17 289
AHIMELECH
David came to Nob to A the priest; 1Sa 21:1 288
A came trembling to meet David and 1Sa 21:1 288
David said to A the priest, 1Sa 21:2 288
David said to A, 1Sa 21:8 288
to Nob, to A the son of Ahitub. 1Sa 22:9 288
someone to summon A the priest, 1Sa 22:11 288
Then A answered the king and said, 1Sa 22:14 288
"You shall surely die, A, 1Sa 22:16 288
one son of A the son of Ahitub, 1Sa 22:20 288
son of A fled to David at Keilah, 1Sa 23:6 288
Then David said to A 1Sa 26:6 288
Abiathar the priest, the son of A, 1Sa 30:7 288
Zadok the son of Ahitub and A 2Sa 8:17 288
and A of the sons of Ithamar, 1Ch 24:3 288
the priest, A the son of Abiathar, 1Ch 24:6 288
of David the king, Zadok, A, 1Ch 24:31 288

AHIMOTH
sons of Elkanah *were* Amasai and A. 1Ch 6:25 287
AHINADAB
A the son of Iddo, *in* Mahanaim; 1Ki 4:14 292
AHINOAM
was A the daughter of Ahimaaz. 1Sa 14:50 293
David had also taken A of Jezreel, 1Sa 25:43 293
his two wives, A the Jezreelitess, 1Sa 27:3 293
A the Jezreelitess and Abigail the 1Sa 30:5 293
A the Jezreelitess and Abigail the 2Sa 2:2 293
was Amnon, by A the Jezreelitess; 2Sa 3:2 293
was Amnon, by A the Jezreelitess; 1Ch 3:1 293
AHIO
and Uzzah and A, the sons of 2Sa 6:3 283
A was walking ahead of the ark. 2Sa 6:4 283
and A, Shashak and Jeremoth. 1Ch 8:14 283
Gedor, A and Zecher. 1Ch 8:31 283
Gedor, A, Zechariah and Mikloth. 1Ch 9:37 283
and Uzza and A drove the cart. 1Ch 13:7 283
AHIRA
of Naphtali, A the son of Enan. Nu 1:15 299
A the son of Enan, Nu 2:29 299
day *it was* A the son of Enan, Nu 7:78 299
the offering of A the son of Enan. Nu 7:83 299
and A the son of Enan over the Nu 10:27 299
AHIRAM
of A, the family of the Ahiramites; Nu 26:38 297
AHIRAMITES
of Ahiram, the family of the A; Nu 26:38 298
AHISAMACH
with him Oholiab, the son of A, Ex 31:6 294
both he and Oholiab, the son of A, Ex 35:34 294
him *was* Oholiab the son of A, Ex 38:23 294
AHISHAHAR
Zethan, Tarshish and A. 1Ch 7:10 300
AHISHAR
and A was over the household; 1Ki 4:6 301
AHITHOPHEL
Absalom sent for A the Gilonite, 2Sa 15:12 302
"A is among the conspirators with 2Sa 15:31 302
the counsel of A foolishness." 2Sa 15:31 302
thwart the counsel of A for me. 2Sa 15:34 302
entered Jerusalem, and A with him. 2Sa 16:15 302
Then Absalom said to A, 2Sa 16:20 302
A said to Absalom, 2Sa 16:21 302
The advice of A, 2Sa 16:23 302
so was all the advice of A 2Sa 16:23 302
Furthermore, A said to Absalom, 2Sa 17:1 302
"A has spoken thus. 2Sa 17:6 302
that A has given is not good." 2Sa 17:7 302
is better than the counsel of A." 2Sa 17:14 302
to thwart the good counsel of A, 2Sa 17:14 302
"This is what A counseled Absalom 2Sa 17:15 302
A has counseled against you." 2Sa 17:21 302
Now when A saw that his counsel 2Sa 17:23 302
Eliam the son of A the Gilonite, 2Sa 23:34 302
A *was* counselor to the king; 1Ch 27:33 302
Benaiah, and Abiathar succeeded A; 1Ch 27:34 302
AHITUB
and Ahijah, the son of A, 1Sa 14:3 285
to Nob, to Ahimelech the son of A. 1Sa 22:9 285
the priest, the son of A, 1Sa 22:11 285
"Listen now, son of A." 1Sa 22:12 285
one son of Ahimelech the son of A, 1Sa 22:20 285
Zadok the son of A and 2Sa 8:17 285
Amariah became the father of A, 1Ch 6:7 285
and A became the father of Zadok, 1Ch 6:8 285
Amariah became the father of A, 1Ch 6:11 285
and A became the father of Zadok, 1Ch 6:12 285
son, Amariah his son, A his son, 1Ch 6:52 285
the son of Meraioth, the son of A, 1Ch 9:11 285
and Zadok the son of A and 1Ch 18:16 285
Shallum, son of Zadok, son of A, Ezr 7:2 285
the son of Meraioth, the son of A, Ne 11:11 285
AHLAB
the inhabitants of Sidon, or of A, Jg 1:31 303
AHLAI
And the son of Sheshan *was* A. 1Ch 2:31 304
the Hittite, Zabad the son of A, 1Ch 11:41 304
AHOAH
Abishua, Naaman, A, 1Ch 8:4 265
AHOHITE
was Eleazar the son of Dodo the A, 2Sa 23:9 266
Zalmon the A, Maharai the 2Sa 23:28 266
Eleazar the son of Dodo, the A, 1Ch 11:12 266
the Hushathite, Ilai the A, 1Ch 11:29 266
Dodai the A and his division had 1Ch 27:4 266
AHUMAI
became the father of A and Lahad. 1Ch 4:2 267
AHUZZAM
Naarah bore him A, 1Ch 4:6 275
AHUZZATH
him from Gerar with his adviser A and Gn 26:26 276
AHZAI
the son of Azarel, the son of A, Ne 11:13 273
AI
on the west and A on the east; Gn 12:8 5857
beginning, between Bethel and A, Gn 13:3 5857
Joshua sent men from Jericho to A, Jos 7:2 5857
the men went up and spied out A. Jos 7:2 5857
thousand men need go up to A; Jos 7:3 5857
but they fled from the men of A. Jos 7:4 5857
The men of A struck down about Jos 7:5 5857
with you and arise, go up to A; Jos 8:1 5857
into your hand the king of A, Jos 8:1 5857

"You shall do to A and its Jos 8:2 5857
the people of war to go up to A; Jos 8:3 5857
and remained between Bethel and A, Jos 8:9 5857
and Ai, on the west side of A; Jos 8:9 5857
of Israel before the people to A. Jos 8:10 5857
and camped on the north side of A. Jos 8:11 5857
was a valley between him and A. Jos 8:11 5857
in ambush between Bethel and A, Jos 8:12 5857
about when the king of A saw *it*, Jos 8:14 5857
So not a man was left in A or Jos 8:17 5857
that is in your hand toward A, Jos 8:18 5857
men of A turned back and looked, Jos 8:20 5857
turned back and slew the men of A. Jos 8:21 5857
But they took alive the king of A Jos 8:23 5857
killing all the inhabitants of A Jos 8:24 5857
then all Israel returned to A and Jos 8:24 5857
were 12,000—all the people of A. Jos 8:25 5857
all the inhabitants of A. Jos 8:26 5857
A and made it a heap forever, Jos 8:28 5857
king of A on a tree until evening; Jos 8:29 5857
had done to Jericho and to A, Jos 9:3 5857
heard that Joshua had captured A, Jos 10:1 5857
so he had done to A and its king), Jos 10:1 5857
and because it was greater than A, Jos 10:2 5857
the king of A, which is beside Jos 12:9 5857
the men of Bethel and A, Ezr 2:28 5857
the men of Bethel and A, Ne 7:32 5857
Heshbon, for A has been destroyed! Jer 49:3 5857
AIAH
A and Anah—he is the Anah who Gn 36:24 345
was Rizpah, the daughter of A; 2Sa 3:7 345
sons of Rizpah the daughter of A, 2Sa 21:8 345
And Rizpah the daughter of A took 2Sa 21:10 345
what Rizpah the daughter of A, 2Sa 21:11 345
sons of Zibeon *were* A and Anah. 1Ch 1:40 345
AIATH
He has come against A, Is 10:28 5857
AID
"Men of Israel, come to our a! Ac 21:28 *997*
to the a of those who are tempted. Heb 2:18 *997*
AIJA
Geba *onward,* at Michmash and A, Ne 11:31 5857
AIJALON
And O moon in the valley of A." Jos 10:12 357
and Shaalabbin and A and Ithlah, Jos 19:42 357
A with its pasture lands, Jos 21:24 357
Mount Heres, in A and in Shaalbim; Jg 1:35 357
at A in the land of Zebulun. Jg 12:12 357
that day from Michmash to A. 1Sa 14:31 357
A with its pasture lands and 1Ch 6:69 357
of the inhabitants of A, 1Ch 8:13 357
Zorah, A and Hebron, which are 2Ch 11:10 357
and had taken Beth-shemesh, A, 2Ch 28:18 357
AILMENTS
your stomach and your frequent a. 1Tm 5:23 *769*
AILS
What a you, O sea, that you flee? Ps 114:5
AIM
is worthless and a at deception? Ps 4:2 1245
You will a with Your bowstrings at Ps 21:12 3559
in such a way, as not without a; 1Co 9:26 *84*
AIMED
a bitter speech *as* their arrow, Ps 64:3 1869
AIMLESSLY
'They are wandering a in the land; Ex 14:3 943
The herds of cattle wander a Jl 1:18 943
AIMS
When he a his arrows, let them be Ps 58:7 1869
AIN
to Riblah on the east side of A; Nu 34:11 5871b
and Shilhim and A and Rimmon; Jos 15:32 5871b
A, Rimmon and Ether and Ashan; Jos 19:7 5871b
and A with its pasture lands and Jos 21:16 5871b
Their villages *were* Etam, A, 1Ch 4:32 5871b
AIR
That no a can come between them. Jb 41:16 7307
They pant for a like jackals, Jer 14:6 7307
"Look at the birds of the a, Mt 6:26 *3772*
and the birds of the a *have* nests, Mt 8:20 *3772*
THE BIRDS OF THE A come and NEST Mt 13:32 *3772*
THE BIRDS OF THE A can NEST Mk 4:32 *3772*
and the birds of the a ate it up. Lk 8:5 *3772*
and the birds of the a *have* nests, Lk 9:58 *3772*
THE BIRDS OF THE A NESTED IN ITS Lk 13:19 *3772*
of the earth and birds of the a. Ac 10:12 *3772*
creatures and the birds of the a. Ac 11:6 *3772*
and tossing dust into the a, Ac 22:23 *109*
such a way, as not beating the a; 1Co 9:26 *109*
you will be speaking into the a. 1Co 14:9 *109*
the prince of the power of the a, Eph 2:2 *109*
clouds to meet the Lord in the a, 1Th 4:17 *109*
and the sun and the a were Rv 9:2 *109*
poured out his bowl upon the a, Rv 16:17 *109*
AKAN
Bilhan and Zaavan and A. Gn 36:27 6130
AKKUB
Hodaviah, Eliashib, Pelaiah, A, 1Ch 3:24 6126
gatekeepers *were* Shallum and A 1Ch 9:17 6126
the sons of Talmon, the sons of A, Ezr 2:42 6126
sons of Hagabah, the sons of A, Ezr 2:45 6126
the sons of Talmon, the sons of A, Ne 7:45 6126
Jeshua, Bani, Sherebiah, Jamin, A, Ne 8:7 6126
Also the gatekeepers, A, Ne 11:19 6126
and A *were* gatekeepers keeping Ne 12:25 6126
AKRABBIM
from the south to the ascent of A and Nu 34:4 4610

ascent of **A** and continued to Zin, **Jos 15:3** 4610
Amorites ran from the ascent of **A**, **Jg 1:36** 4610

ALABASTER
stones and **a** in abundance. **1Ch 29:2** 7893
a Set on pedestals of pure gold; **SS 5:15** 8337b
an **a** vial of very costly perfume, **Mt 26:7** *211*
there came a woman with an **a** vial **Mk 14:3** *211*
she brought an **a** vial of perfume, **Lk 7:37** *211*

ALAMOTH
Benaiah, with harps *tuned* to **a**; **1Ch 15:20** 5961

ALARM
"But when you blow an **a**, **Nu 10:5** 8643
you blow an **a** the second time, **Nu 10:6** 8643
an **a** is to be blown for them to **Nu 10:6** 8643
shall blow without sounding an **a**. **Nu 10:7** 7321
sound an **a** with the trumpets, **Nu 10:9** 7321
trumpets for the **a** in his hand. **Nu 31:6** 8643
to sound the **a** against you. **2Ch 13:12** 7321
As for me, I said in my **a**, **Ps 31:22** 2648
were terrified, they fled in **a**. **Ps 48:5** 2648
I said in my **a**, "All men are liars." **Ps 116:11** 2648
of the trumpet, The **a** of war. **Jer 4:19** 8643
morning And a shout of **a** at noon; **Jer 20:16** 8643
or its interpretation **a** you.' **Da 4:19** 927
a you or your face be pale. **Da 5:10** 927
Sound an **a** at Beth-aven: **Hos 5:8** 7321
sound an **a** on My holy mountain! **Jl 2:1** 7321

ALARMED
"If a river rages, he is not **a**; **Jb 40:23** 2648
for a while as his thoughts **a** him. **Da 4:19** 927
grew pale and his thoughts **a** him **Da 5:6** 927
King Belshazzar was greatly **a**, **Da 5:9** 927
gaze on him and being much **a**, **Ac 10:4** *1719*
in no way **a** by *your* **Php 1:28** *4426*

ALARMING
the visions in my mind kept **a** me. **Da 4:5** 927
the visions in my mind kept **a** me. **Da 7:15** 927
a me and my face grew pale, **Da 7:28** 927

ALAS
"**A**, this people has committed a **Ex 32:31** 577
"**A**, who can live except God has **Nu 24:23** 188
"**A**, O Lord GOD, why did You **Jos 7:7** 162
the LORD, he said, "**A**, O Lord GOD! **Jg 6:22** 162
"**A**, my daughter! **Jg 11:35** 162
"**A**, my brother!" **1Ki 13:30** 1945
Then the king of Israel said, "**A**! **2Ki 3:10** 162
"**A**, my master! For it was borrowed." **2Ki 6:5** 162
"**A**, my master! What shall we do?" **2Ki 6:15** 162
A, sinful nation, People weighed **Is 1:4** 1945
A, the uproar of many peoples Who **Is 17:12** 1945
A, oh land of whirring wings Which **Is 18:1** 1945
"Woe to me! Woe to me! **A** for me! **Is 24:16** 188
Then I said, "**A**, Lord GOD! Behold, **Jer 1:6** 162
not lament for him: '**A**, my brother!' **Jer 22:18** 1945
or, '**A**, sister!' They will not lament **Jer 22:18** 1945
'**A** for the master!' **Jer 22:18** 1945
'**A** for his splendor!' **Jer 22:18** 1945
'**A**! for that day is great, **Jer 30:7** 1945
they will lament for you, "**A**, lord!" **Jer 34:5** 1945
"**A**, because of all the evil **Ezk 6:11** 253
"**A**, Lord GOD! Are You destroying **Ezk 9:8** 162
"**A**, Lord GOD! Will You bring the **Ezk 11:13** 162
Lord GOD, "Wail, '**A** for the day!' **Ezk 30:2** 1929
"**A**, O Lord, the great and awesome **Da 9:4** 577
A for the day! For the day of the **Jl 1:15** 162
in all the streets they say, '**A**! **Am 5:16** 1930
in all the streets they say, 'Alas! **A**!' **Am 5:16** 1930
A, you who are longing for the day **Am 5:18** 1945

ALEMETH
Jeremoth, Abijah, Anathoth and **A**. **1Ch 7:8** 5964
Jehoaddah became the father of **A**, **1Ch 8:36** 5964
and Jarah became the father of **A**, **1Ch 9:42** 5964

ALERT
"Therefore be on the **a**, **Mt 24:42** *1127*
he would have been on the **a** and **Mt 24:43** *1127*
"Be on the **a** then, for you do not **Mt 25:13** *1127*
"Take heed, keep on the **a**; **Mk 13:33** *69*
the doorkeeper to stay on the **a**. **Mk 13:34** *1127*
be on the **a**—for you do not know **Mk 13:35** *1127*
I say to all, 'Be on the **a**!' " **Mk 13:37** *1127*
will find on the **a** when he comes; **Lk 12:37** *1127*
"But keep on the **a** at all times, **Lk 21:36** *69*
"Therefore be on the **a**, **Ac 20:31** *1127*
Be on the **a**, stand firm in the **1Co 16:13** *1127*
be on the **a** with all perseverance **Eph 6:18** *69*
keeping **a** in it with *an attitude* **Col 4:2** *1127*
do, but let us be **a** and sober. **1Th 5:6** *1127*
Be of sober *spirit,* be on the **a**. **1Pe 5:8** *1127*

ALEXANDER
(the father of **A** and Rufus), **Mk 15:21** *223*
and Caiaphas and John and **A**, **Ac 4:6** *223*
of the crowd concluded *it was* **A**, **Ac 19:33** *223*
A was intending to make a defense **Ac 19:33** *223*
Among these are Hymenaeus and **A**, **1Tm 1:20** *223*
A the coppersmith did me much harm; **2Tm 4:14** *223*

ALEXANDRIAN
Jew named Apollos, an **A** by birth, **Ac 18:24** *221*
found an **A** ship sailing for Italy, **Ac 27:6** *222*
three months we set sail on an **A** ship **Ac 28:11** *222*

ALEXANDRIANS
including both Cyrenians and **A**, **Ac 6:9** *221*

ALGUM
cypress and **a** timber from Lebanon, **2Ch 2:8** 418
a trees and precious stones. **2Ch 9:10** 418
From the **a** trees the king made steps **2Ch 9:11** 418

ALIAH
chief Timna, chief **A**, **1Ch 1:51** 5933

ALIAN
The sons of Shobal *were* **A**, **1Ch 1:40** 5935

ALIEN
"This one came in as an **a**, **Gn 19:9** 1481a
is an **a** or a native of the land. **Ex 12:19** 1616
or the **a** who sojourns among you; **Lv 16:29** 1616
nor may any **a** who sojourns among **Lv 17:12** 1616
whether he is a native or an **a**, **Lv 17:15** 1616
nor the **a** who sojourns among you **Lv 18:26** 1616
them for the needy and the **a**. **Lv 23:22** 1616
The **a** as well as the native, when **Lv 24:16** 1616
'If an **a** sojourns among you **Nu 9:14** 1616
both for the **a** and for the native **Nu 9:14** 1616
'If an **a** sojourns with you, or **Nu 15:14** 1616
for the **a** who sojourns *with you,* **Nu 15:15** 1616
so shall the **a** be before the LORD. **Nu 15:15** 1616
the **a** who sojourns with you.' " **Nu 15:16** 1616
the **a** who sojourns among them, **Nu 15:26** 1616
for the **a** who sojourns among them. **Nu 15:29** 1616
whether he is native or an **a**, **Nu 15:30** 1616
to the **a** who sojourns among them. **Nu 19:10** 1616
and for the **a** and for the **Nu 35:15** 1616
or the **a** who is with him. **Dt 1:16** 1616
and shows His love for the **a** by **Dt 10:18** 1616
"So show your love for the **a**, **Dt 10:19** 1616
it to the **a** who is in your town, **Dt 14:21** 1616
inheritance among you, and the **a**, **Dt 14:29** 1616
because you were an **a** in his land. **Dt 23:7** 1616
the justice due an **a** *or* an orphan, **Dt 24:17** 1616
it shall be for the **a**, **Dt 24:19** 1616
it shall be for the **a**, **Dt 24:20** 1616
it shall be for the **a**, **Dt 24:21** 1616
and you and the Levite and the **a** **Dt 26:11** 1616
given it to the Levite and the **a**, **Dt 26:13** 1616
who distorts the justice due an **a**, **Dt 27:19** 1616
"The **a** who is among you shall **Dt 28:43** 1616
the **a** who is within your camps, **Dt 29:11** 1616
and the **a** who is in your town, **Dt 31:12** 1616
"I am the son of an **a**, **2Sa 1:13** 1616
given, And no **a** passed among them. **Jb 15:19** 2114a
"The **a** has not lodged outside, **Jb 31:32** 1616
And an **a** to my mother's sons. **Ps 69:8** 5237
goods *will go* to the house of an **a**; **Pr 5:10** 5237
if you do not oppress the **a**, **Jer 7:6** 1616
made this an **a** place and have burned **Jer 19:4** 5235a
The **a** they have oppressed in your **Ezk 22:7** 1616
"**A** tyrants of the nations have cut **Ezk 31:12** 2114a
the tribe with which the **a** stays, **Ezk 47:23** 1616
and those who turn aside the **a** and **Mal 3:5** 1616
BECAME AN **A** IN THE LAND OF MIDIAN, **Ac 7:29** *3941*
as an **a** in the land of promise, **Heb 11:9** *3939*

ALIENATE
or **a** this choice *portion* of land; **Ezk 48:14** 5674a

ALIENATED
O Jerusalem, Or I shall be **a** from you, **Jer 6:8** 3363
against you, from whom you were **a**, **Ezk 23:22** 5361
of those from whom you were **a**. **Ezk 23:28** 5361
formerly **a** and hostile in mind, **Col 1:21** *526*

ALIENS
from the **a** who sojourn among them, **Lv 17:8** 1616
from the **a** who sojourn among them, **Lv 17:10** 1616
from the **a** who sojourn among them, **Lv 17:13** 1616
you were **a** in the land of Egypt; **Lv 19:34** 1616
from the **a** sojourning in Israel who **Lv 20:2** 1616
a in Israel who presents his offering, **Lv 22:18** 1616
those who live as **a** with you. **Lv 25:6** 1481a
are *but* **a** and sojourners with Me. **Lv 25:23** 1616
sojourners who live as **a** among you **Lv 25:45** 1481a
you were **a** in the land of Egypt. **Dt 10:19** 1616
or one of your **a** who is in your land **Dt 24:14** 1616
have been **a** there until this day). **2Sa 4:3** 1481a
Solomon numbered all the **a** who **2Ch 2:17** 1616
waters, Out of the hand of **a** **Ps 144:7** 1121, 5236
deliver me out of the hand of **a**, **Ps 144:11** 1121, 5236
You subdue the uproar of **a**; **Is 25:5** 2114a
For **a** have entered The holy places **Jer 51:51** 2114a
to strangers, Our houses to **a**. **La 5:2** 5237
the **a** who stay in your midst, **Ezk 47:22** 1616
WOULD BE **A** IN A FOREIGN LAND, **Ac 7:6** *3941*
you are no longer strangers and **a**, **Eph 2:19** *3941*
Christ, To those who reside as **a**, **1Pe 1:1** *3927*
I urge you as **a** and strangers to **1Pe 2:11** *3941*

ALIGHT
a curse without cause does not **a**. **Pr 26:2** 935

ALIGHTED
So she **a** from the donkey, and **Jos 15:18** 6795
Then she **a** from her donkey, and **Jg 1:14** 6795
and Sisera **a** from *his* chariot and **Jg 4:15** 3381

ALIKE
and the wicked are *treated* **a**. **Gn 18:25**
all the sons of Aaron, to all **a**. **Lv 7:10** 251
hear the small and the great **a**. **Dt 1:17**
and the clean **a** may eat of it. **Dt 12:22** 3164a
and the clean **a** *may eat it,* **Dt 15:22** 3164a
they shall share **a**." **1Sa 30:24** 3164a
cast lots for their duties, all **a**, **1Ch 25:8** 5980
lots, the small and the great **a**, **1Ch 26:13**
stupid and the senseless **a** perish And **Ps 49:10** 3162
the green and the burning **a**. **Ps 58:9** 3644
Darkness and light are **a** *to You.* **Ps 139:12**
Both of them **a** are an abomination **Pr 17:15** 1571
And a contentious woman are **a**; **Pr 27:15** 7737a
the wise man and the fool **a** die! **Ec 2:16** 5973
both of them **a** will be good. **Ec 11:6** 259
compare Me, That we would be **a**? **Is 46:5** 1819
they all **a** began to make excuses. **Lk 14:18** *575, 1520*
being baptized, men and women **a**. **Ac 8:12** *5037*
another regards every day **a**. **Ro 14:5**

ALIVE
the ark, to keep *them* **a** with you; **Gn 6:19** 2421a
will come to you to keep *them* **a**. **Gn 6:20** 2421a
a on the face of all the earth. **Gn 7:3** 2421a
that is **a** shall be food for you; **Gn 9:3** 2416a
a here after seeing Him?" **Gn 16:13** 7200
and one is no longer **a**." **Gn 42:13**
one is no longer **a**, and the youngest **Gn 42:32**
'Is your father still **a**? **Gn 43:7** 2416a
of whom you spoke? Is he still **a**?" **Gn 43:27** 2416a
our father is well; he is still **a**." **Gn 43:28** 2416a
Is my father still **a**?" **Gn 45:3** 2416a
keep you **a** by a great deliverance. **Gn 45:7** 2421a
"Joseph is still **a**, and indeed he **Gn 45:26** 2416a
my son Joseph is still **a**. **Gn 45:28** 2416a
your face, that you are still **a**." **Gn 46:30** 2416a
result, to preserve many people **a**. **Gn 50:20** 2421a
daughter you are to keep **a**." **Ex 1:22** 2421a
and see if they are still **a**." **Ex 4:18** 2416a
found **a** in his possession, **Ex 22:4** 2416a
be presented **a** before the LORD, **Lv 16:10** 2416a
sister as a rival while she is **a**, **Lv 18:18** 2425b
a out of those men who went to spy **Nu 14:38** 2421a
and they descend **a** into Sheol, **Nu 16:30** 2416a
to them went down **a** to Sheol; **Nu 16:33** 2416a
to the LORD your God are **a** today, **Dt 4:4** 2416a
with all those of us **a** here today. **Dt 5:3** 2416a
leave **a** anything that breathes. **Dt 20:16** 2421a
while I am still **a** with you today, **Dt 31:27** 2416a
But they took **a** the king of Ai and **Jos 8:23** 2416a
women whom they had kept **a** from **Jg 21:14** 2421a
"The LORD kills and makes **a**; **1Sa 2:6** 2421a
Agag the king of the Amalekites **a**, **1Sa 15:8** 2416a
"If I am still **a**, **1Sa 20:14** 2416a
did not leave a man or a woman **a**, **1Sa 27:9** 2421a
did not leave a man or a woman **a** to **1Sa 27:11** 2421a
death and one full line to keep **a**. **2Sa 8:2** 2421a
while the child was *still* **a**, **2Sa 12:18** 2416a
While the child was **a**, **2Sa 12:21** 2416a
"While the child was *still* **a**, **2Sa 12:22** 2416a
was yet **a** in the midst of the oak. **2Sa 18:14** 2416a
a and all of us were dead today, **2Sa 19:6** 2416a
Solomon while he was still **a**, **1Ki 12:6** 2416a
leave to Jeroboam any persons **a**, **1Ki 15:29** 5397
"See, your son is **a**." **1Ki 17:23** 2416a
and keep the horses and mules **a**, **1Ki 18:5** 2421a
come out for peace, take them **a**; **1Ki 20:18** 2416a
come out for war, take them **a**." **1Ki 20:18** 2416a
"Is he still **a**? He is my brother." **1Ki 20:32** 2416a
for Naboth is not **a**, **1Ki 21:15** 2416a
"Am I God, to kill and to make **a**, **2Ki 5:7** 2421a
them **a** and get into the city.' " **2Ki 7:12** 2416a
"Take them **a**." So they took them **2Ki 10:14** 2416a
So they took them **a** and killed **2Ki 10:14** 2416a
Solomon while he was still **a**, **2Ch 10:6** 2416a
captured 10,000 **a** and brought them **2Ch 25:12** 2416a
"He does not keep the wicked **a**, **Jb 36:6** 2421a
he who cannot keep his soul **a**. **Ps 22:29** 2421a
You have kept me **a**, **Ps 30:3** 2421a
And to keep them **a** in famine. **Ps 33:19** 2421a
will protect him and keep him **a**, **Ps 41:2** 2421a
Let them go down **a** to Sheol, **Ps 55:15** 2416a
they would have swallowed us **a**, **Ps 124:3** 2416a
Let us swallow them **a** like Sheol, **Pr 1:12** 2416a
that day a man may keep **a** a heifer **Is 7:21** 2421a
his *own* life as booty and stay **a**.' **Jer 38:2** 2421a
behind, I will keep *them* **a**; **Jer 49:11** 2421a
keep others **a** who should not live, **Ezk 13:19** 2421a
breath in you that you may come **a**; **Ezk 37:6** 2421a
whomever he wished he spared **a**; **Da 5:19** 2418
which is **a** today and tomorrow is **Mt 6:30**
He was still **a** that deceiver said, **Mt 27:63** *2198*
When they heard that He was **a** and **Mk 16:11** *2198*
which is **a** today and tomorrow is **Lk 12:28**
of angels who said that He was **a**. **Lk 24:23** *2198*
these He also presented Himself **a** after **Ac 1:3** *2198*
and widows, he presented her **a**. **Ac 9:41** *2198*
They took away the boy **a**, **Ac 20:12** *2198*
Jesus, whom Paul asserted to be **a**. **Ac 25:19** *2198*
sin, but **a** to God in Christ Jesus. **Ro 6:11** *2198*
to God as those **a** from the dead, **Ro 6:13** *2198*
I was once **a** apart from the Law; **Ro 7:9** *2198*
commandment came, sin became **a** and **Ro 7:9** *326*
is **a** because of righteousness. **Ro 8:10** *2222*
in Christ all will be made **a**. **1Co 15:22** *2227*
made us **a** together with Christ **Eph 2:5** *4806*
He made you **a** together with Him, **Col 2:13** *4806*
of the Lord, that we who are **a** and **1Th 4:15** *2198*
Then we who are **a** and remain will **1Th 4:17** *2198*
flesh, but made **a** in the spirit; **1Pe 3:18** *2227*
and behold, I am **a** forevermore, **Rv 1:18** *2198*
you have a name that you are **a**, **Rv 3:1** *2198*
these two were thrown **a** into the **Rv 19:20** *2198*

ALL
the cattle and over **a** the earth, **Gn 1:26** 3605
is on the surface of **a** the earth, **Gn 1:29** 3605
God saw **a** that He had made, **Gn 1:31** 3605
were completed, and **a** their hosts. **Gn 2:1** 3605
from **a** His work which He had done. **Gn 2:2** 3605
because in it He rested from **a** His **Gn 2:3** 3605
man gave names to **a** the cattle, **Gn 2:20** 3605
Cursed are you more than **a** cattle, **Gn 3:14** 3605

Context	Reference	Number
you will eat **A** the days of your life;	Gn 3:14	3605
eat of it **A** the days of your life.	Gn 3:17	3605
was the mother of **a** *the* living.	Gn 3:20	3605
he was the father of **a** those who	Gn 4:21	3605
a implements of bronze and iron;	Gn 4:22	3605
So **a** the days that Adam lived were	Gn 5:5	3605
So **a** the days of Seth were nine	Gn 5:8	3605
So **a** the days of Enosh were nine	Gn 5:11	3605
So **a** the days of Kenan were nine	Gn 5:14	3605
So **a** the days of Mahalalel were	Gn 5:17	3605
So **a** the days of Jared were nine	Gn 5:20	3605
So **a** the days of Enoch were three	Gn 5:23	3605
So **a** the days of Methuselah were	Gn 5:27	3605
So **a** the days of Lamech were seven	Gn 5:31	3605
for **a** flesh had corrupted their	Gn 6:12	3605
end of **a** flesh has come before Me;	Gn 6:13	3605
to destroy **a** flesh in which is the	Gn 6:17	3605
of every living thing of **a** flesh,	Gn 6:19	3605
some of **a** food which is edible,	Gn 6:21	3605
to **a** that God had commanded him,	Gn 6:22	3605
the ark, you and **a** your household,	Gn 7:1	3605
alive on the face of **a** the earth.	Gn 7:3	3605
Noah did according to **a** that	Gn 7:5	3605
on the same day **a** the fountains of	Gn 7:11	3605
and **a** the cattle after their kind,	Gn 7:14	3605
after its kind, **a** sorts of birds.	Gn 7:14	3605
by twos of **a** flesh in which was	Gn 7:15	3605
male and female of **a** flesh,	Gn 7:16	3605
so that **a** the high mountains	Gn 7:19	3605
A flesh that moved on the earth	Gn 7:21	3605
upon the earth, and **a** mankind;	Gn 7:21	3605
of **a** that was on the dry land, all	Gn 7:22	3605
a in whose nostrils was the breath	Gn 7:22	3605
But God remembered Noah and **a** the	Gn 8:1	3605
the beasts and **a** the cattle that were	Gn 8:1	3605
was on the surface of **a** the earth.	Gn 8:9	3605
thing of **a** flesh that is with you,	Gn 8:17	3605
ground, and **a** the fish of the sea,	Gn 9:2	3605
I give **a** to you, as *I gave* the	Gn 9:3	3605
of **a** that comes out of the ark,	Gn 9:10	3605
and **a** flesh shall never again be	Gn 9:11	3605
you, for **a** successive generations;	Gn 9:12	5769
every living creature of **a** flesh;	Gn 9:15	3605
become a flood to destroy **a** flesh.	Gn 9:15	3605
of **a** flesh that is on the earth."	Gn 9:16	3605
a flesh that is on the earth."	Gn 9:17	3605
So **a** the days of Noah were nine	Gn 9:29	3605
father of **a** the children of Eber,	Gn 10:21	3605
a these were the sons of Joktan.	Gn 10:29	3605
and they **a** have the same language.	Gn 11:6	3605
And in you **a** the families of the	Gn 12:3	3605
and **a** their possessions which they	Gn 12:5	3605
wife and **a** that belonged to him.	Gn 12:20	3605
wife and **a** that belonged to him,	Gn 13:1	3605
saw **a** the valley of the Jordan,	Gn 13:10	3605
a the valley of the Jordan,	Gn 13:11	3605
for **a** the land which you see, I	Gn 13:15	3605
A these came as allies to the	Gn 14:3	3605
a the country of the Amalekites,	Gn 14:7	3605
Then they took **a** the goods of	Gn 14:11	3605
Gomorrah and **a** their food supply,	Gn 14:11	3605
He brought back **a** the goods,	Gn 14:16	3605
He gave him a tenth of **a**.	Gn 14:20	3605
Then he brought **a** these to Him and	Gn 15:10	3605
to the east of **a** his brothers."	Gn 16:12	3605
sojournings, **a** the land of Canaan,	Gn 17:8	3605
and **a** *the servants* who were born	Gn 17:23	3605
a who were bought with his money,	Gn 17:23	3605
A the men of his household, who were	Gn 17:27	3605
and in him **a** the nations of the	Gn 18:18	3605
of **a** the earth deal justly?"	Gn 18:25	3605
a the people from every quarter;	Gn 19:4	3605
those cities, and **a** the valley,	Gn 19:25	3605
and **a** the inhabitants of the cities,	Gn 19:25	3605
toward **a** the land of the valley,	Gn 19:28	3605
die, you and **a** who are yours."	Gn 20:7	3605
and called **a** his servants and told all	Gn 20:8	3605
a these things in their hearing;	Gn 20:8	3605
before **a** who are with you,	Gn 20:16	3605
before **a** men you are cleared."	Gn 20:16	3605
For the LORD had closed fast **a** the	Gn 20:18	3605
"God is with you in **a** that you do;	Gn 21:22	3605
"In your seed **a** the nations	Gn 22:18	3605
even of **a** who went in at the gate	Gn 23:10	3605
and **a** the trees which were in the	Gn 23:17	3605
a the confines of its border,	Gn 23:17	3605
before **a** who went in at the gate	Gn 23:18	3605
who had charge of **a** that he owned,	Gn 24:2	3605
and she drew for **a** his camels.	Gn 24:20	3605
he has given him **a** that he has.	Gn 24:36	3605
a the things that he had done.	Gn 24:66	3605
A these *were* the sons of Keturah.	Gn 25:4	3605
gave **a** that he had to Isaac;	Gn 25:5	3605
These are **a** the years of	Gn 25:7	3117
in defiance of **a** his relatives.	Gn 25:18	3605
red, **a** over like a hairy garment;	Gn 25:25	3605
I will give **a** these lands,	Gn 26:3	3605
your descendants **a** these lands;	Gn 26:4	3605
and by your descendants **a** the	Gn 26:4	3605
So Abimelech charged **a** the people,	Gn 26:11	3605
Now **a** the wells which his father's	Gn 26:15	3605
I ate of **a** *of it* before you came,	Gn 27:33	3605
and **a** his relatives I have given	Gn 27:37	3605
your descendants shall **a** the families	Gn 28:14	3605
and of **a** that You give me I	Gn 28:22	3605
When **a** the flocks were gathered	Gn 29:3	3605
until **a** the flocks are gathered,	Gn 29:8	3605
related to Laban **a** these things.	Gn 29:13	3605
gathered **a** the men of the place and	Gn 29:22	3605
and **a** the speckled and spotted female	Gn 30:35	3605
and **a** the black ones among the	Gn 30:35	3605
and **a** the black in the flock of Laban;	Gn 30:40	3605
taken away **a** that was our father's,	Gn 31:1	3605
he has made **a** this wealth."	Gn 31:1	3605
your father with **a** my strength.	Gn 31:6	3605
then **a** the flock brought forth	Gn 31:8	3605
then **a** the flock brought forth	Gn 31:8	3605
your eyes and see *that* **a** the male	Gn 31:12	3605
for I have seen **a** that Laban has	Gn 31:12	3605
"Surely **a** the wealth which God	Gn 31:16	3605
and he drove away **a** his livestock	Gn 31:18	3605
all his livestock and **a** his property	Gn 31:18	3605
So he fled with **a** that he had;	Gn 31:21	3605
And Laban felt through **a** the tent but	Gn 31:34	3605
you have felt through **a** my goods,	Gn 31:37	3605
found of **a** your household goods?	Gn 31:37	3605
and **a** that you see is mine.	Gn 31:43	3605
I am unworthy of **a** the	Gn 32:10	3605
and of **a** the faithfulness which You	Gn 32:10	3605
a those who followed the droves,	Gn 32:19	3605
a this company which I have met?"	Gn 33:8	3605
one day, **a** the flocks will die.	Gn 33:13	3605
a the household of his father.	Gn 34:19	3605
and **a** their animals be ours?	Gn 34:23	3605
A who went out of the gate of his	Gn 34:24	3605
a who went out of the gate of his	Gn 34:24	3605
and they captured and looted **a**	Gn 34:29	3605
looted all their wealth and **a** their	Gn 34:29	3605
even **a** that *was* in the houses.	Gn 34:29	3605
and to **a** who were with him,	Gn 35:2	3605
So they gave to Jacob **a** the	Gn 35:4	3605
a the people who were with him.	Gn 35:6	3605
his daughters and **a** his household,	Gn 36:6	3605
and his livestock and **a** his cattle	Gn 36:6	3605
a his goods which he had acquired	Gn 36:6	3605
loved Joseph more than **a** his sons,	Gn 37:3	3605
him more than **a** his brothers;	Gn 37:4	3605
Then **a** his sons and all his	Gn 37:35	3605
Then all his sons and **a** his	Gn 37:35	3605
After **a**, I sent this young goat, but you	Gn 38:23	2009
LORD caused **a** that he did to prosper	Gn 39:3	3605
and **a** that he owned he put in his	Gn 39:4	3605
house and over **a** that he owned,	Gn 39:5	3605
blessing was upon **a** that he owned,	Gn 39:5	3605
put **a** that he owns in my charge.	Gn 39:8	3605
to Joseph's charge **a** the prisoners	Gn 39:22	3605
of **a** sorts of baked food for Pharaoh,	Gn 40:17	3605
made a feast for **a** his servants;	Gn 40:20	3605
for **a** the magicians of Egypt,	Gn 41:8	3605
of Egypt, and **a** its wise men.	Gn 41:8	3605
ugliness in **a** the land of Egypt;	Gn 41:19	3605
are coming in **a** the land of Egypt;	Gn 41:29	3605
and **a** the abundance will be	Gn 41:30	3605
"Then let them gather **a** the food	Gn 41:35	3605
to Pharaoh and to **a** his servants.	Gn 41:37	3605
God has informed you of **a** this,	Gn 41:39	3605
a my people shall do homage;	Gn 41:40	3605
you over **a** the land of Egypt."	Gn 41:41	3605
set him over **a** the land of Egypt.	Gn 41:43	3605
or foot in **a** the land of Egypt."	Gn 41:44	3605
went through **a** the land of Egypt.	Gn 41:46	3605
So he gathered **a** the food of *these*	Gn 41:48	3605
"God has made me forget **a** my	Gn 41:51	3605
and **a** my father's household."	Gn 41:51	3605
there was famine in **a** the lands,	Gn 41:54	3605
but in **a** the land of Egypt there	Gn 41:54	3605
So when **a** the land of Egypt was	Gn 41:55	3605
Pharaoh said to **a** the Egyptians,	Gn 41:55	3605
over **a** the face of the earth,	Gn 41:56	3605
Joseph opened **a** the storehouses,	Gn 41:56	3605
The people of **a** the earth came	Gn 41:57	3605
famine was severe in **a** the earth.	Gn 41:57	3605
sold to **a** the people of the land.	Gn 42:6	3605
"We are **a** sons of one man;	Gn 42:11	3605
servants are twelve brothers *in* **a**,	Gn 42:13	
So he put them **a** together in	Gn 42:17	622
him **a** that had happened to them,	Gn 42:29	3605
a these things are against me."	Gn 42:36	3605
before **a** those who stood by him,	Gn 45:1	3605
Pharaoh and lord of **a** his household	Gn 45:8	3605
ruler over **a** the land of Egypt.	Gn 45:8	3605
"God has made me lord of **a** Egypt;	Gn 45:9	3605
your herds and **a** that you have.	Gn 45:10	3605
and **a** that you have would be	Gn 45:11	3605
father of **a** my splendor in Egypt,	Gn 45:13	3605
Egypt, and **a** that you have seen;	Gn 45:13	3605
a his brothers and wept on them,	Gn 45:15	3605
a the land of Egypt is yours.'"	Gn 45:20	3605
ruler over **a** the land of Egypt."	Gn 45:26	3605
When they told him **a** the words of	Gn 45:27	3605
Israel set out with **a** that he had,	Gn 46:1	3605
and **a** his descendants with him:	Gn 46:6	3605
and **a** his descendants he brought	Gn 46:7	3605
a his sons and his daughters	Gn 46:15	3605
there were fourteen persons in **a**.	Gn 46:22	3605
there were seven persons in **a**.	Gn 46:25	3605
A the persons belonging to Jacob,	Gn 46:26	3605
sons, *were* sixty-six persons in **a**,	Gn 46:26	3605
a the persons of the house of	Gn 46:27	3605
their herds and **a** that they have.'	Gn 46:32	3605
their herds and **a** that they have,	Gn 47:1	3605
a his father's household with food,	Gn 47:12	3605
there was no food in **a** the land,	Gn 47:13	3605
Joseph gathered **a** the money	Gn 47:14	3605
When the money was **a** spent in	Gn 47:15	8552
a the Egyptians came to Joseph and	Gn 47:15	3605
for **a** their livestock that year.	Gn 47:17	3605
my lord that our money is **a** spent,	Gn 47:18	8552
a the land of Egypt for Pharaoh,	Gn 47:20	3605
my shepherd **a** my life to this day,	Gn 48:15	4480, 5750
who has redeemed me from **a** evil,	Gn 48:16	3605
A these are the twelve tribes of	Gn 49:28	3605
went up **a** the servants of Pharaoh,	Gn 50:7	3605
and **a** the elders of the land of Egypt,	Gn 50:7	3605
and **a** the household of Joseph and	Gn 50:8	3605
and **a** who had gone up with him to	Gn 50:14	3605
a the wrong which we did to him!"	Gn 50:15	3605
A the persons who came from the loins	Ex 1:5	3605
and **a** his brothers and all that	Ex 1:6	3605
brothers and **a** that generation.	Ex 1:6	3605
at **a** *kinds* of labor in the field	Ex 1:14	3605
a their labors which they	Ex 1:14	3605
Pharaoh commanded **a** his people,	Ex 1:22	3605
My memorial-name to **a** generations.	Ex 3:15	1755
and strike Egypt with **a** My	Ex 3:20	3605
for **a** the men who were seeking	Ex 4:19	3605
perform before Pharaoh **a** the wonders	Ex 4:21	3605
Moses told Aaron **a** the words	Ex 4:28	3605
and **a** the signs that He had	Ex 4:28	3605
assembled **a** the elders of the sons of	Ex 4:29	3605
and Aaron spoke **a** the words which	Ex 4:30	3605
So the people scattered through **a**	Ex 5:12	3605
not delivered Your people at **a**."	Ex 5:23	5337
of Egypt **a** that I speak to you."	Ex 6:29	3605
shall speak **a** that I command you,	Ex 7:2	3605
over **a** their reservoirs of water,	Ex 7:19	3605
throughout **a** the land of Egypt,	Ex 7:19	3605
and **a** the water that *was* in the	Ex 7:20	3605
was through **a** the land of Egypt.	Ex 7:21	3605
So **a** the Egyptians dug around the	Ex 7:24	3605
people and **a** your servants.	Ex 8:4	3605
through **a** the land of Egypt.'"	Ex 8:16	3605
A the dust of the earth became	Ex 8:17	3605
gnats through **a** the land of Egypt.	Ex 8:17	3605
of insects in **a** the land of Egypt.	Ex 8:24	3605
so that nothing will die of **a** that	Ex 9:4	3605
and **a** the livestock of Egypt died;	Ex 9:6	3605
dust over **a** the land of Egypt,	Ex 9:9	3605
through **a** the land of Egypt."	Ex 9:9	3605
as well as on **a** the Egyptians.	Ex 9:11	3605
"For this time I will send **a** My	Ex 9:14	3605
is no one like Me in **a** the earth.	Ex 9:14	3605
My name through **a** the earth.	Ex 9:16	3605
may fall on **a** the land of Egypt,	Ex 9:22	3605
such as had not been in **a** the land	Ex 9:24	3605
The hail struck **a** that was in	Ex 9:25	3605
field through **a** the land of Egypt,	Ex 9:25	3605
and the houses of **a** your servants	Ex 10:6	3605
and the houses of **a** the Egyptians,	Ex 10:6	3605
even **a** that the hail has left."	Ex 10:12	3605
a that day and all that night;	Ex 10:13	3605
all that day and **a** that night;	Ex 10:13	3605
The locusts came up over **a** the	Ex 10:14	3605
in **a** the territory of Egypt;	Ex 10:14	3605
a the fruit of the trees that the hail	Ex 10:15	3605
field through **a** the land of Egypt.	Ex 10:15	3605
left in **a** the territory of Egypt.	Ex 10:19	3605
thick darkness in **a** the land of Egypt	Ex 10:22	3605
but **a** the sons of Israel had light	Ex 10:23	3605
and **a** the firstborn in the land	Ex 11:5	3605
a the firstborn of the cattle as	Ex 11:5	3605
great cry in **a** the land of Egypt,	Ex 11:6	3605
'**A** these your servants will come	Ex 11:8	3605
and **a** the people who follow you,'	Ex 11:8	3605
a these wonders before Pharaoh;	Ex 11:10	3605
to **a** the congregation of Israel,	Ex 12:3	3605
it raw or boiled at **a** with water,	Ex 12:9	1310
and will strike down **a** the	Ex 12:12	3605
and against **a** the gods of Egypt I	Ex 12:12	3605
work at **a** shall be done on them,	Ex 12:16	3605
in **a** your dwellings you shall eat	Ex 12:20	3605
called for **a** the elders of Israel and	Ex 12:21	3605
that the LORD struck **a** the firstborn	Ex 12:29	3605
and **a** the firstborn of cattle.	Ex 12:29	3605
he and **a** his servants and all the	Ex 12:30	3605
his servants and **a** the Egyptians,	Ex 12:30	3605
"We will **a** be dead."	Ex 12:33	3605
a the hosts of the LORD went	Ex 12:41	3605
to be observed by **a** the sons of	Ex 12:42	3605
"**A** the congregation of Israel are	Ex 12:47	3605
let **a** his males be circumcised,	Ex 12:48	3605
Then **a** the sons of Israel did *so;*	Ex 12:50	3605
seen among you in **a** your borders.	Ex 13:7	3605
through Pharaoh and **a** his army,	Ex 14:4	3605
and **a** the *other* chariots of Egypt	Ex 14:7	3605
with officers over **a** of them.	Ex 14:7	3605
Egyptians chased after them *with* **a**	Ex 14:9	3605
through Pharaoh and **a** his army,	Ex 14:17	3605
not come near the other **a** night.	Ex 14:20	3605
by a strong east wind **a** night and	Ex 14:21	3605
pursuit, and **a** Pharaoh's horses,	Ex 14:23	3605
A the inhabitants of Canaan have	Ex 15:15	3605
and **a** the women went out after her	Ex 15:20	3605
and keep **a** His statutes,	Ex 15:26	3605
and **a** the congregation of the sons	Ex 16:1	3605
said to **a** the sons of Israel,	Ex 16:6	3605
"Say to **a** the congregation of the	Ex 16:9	3605
When **a** the leaders of the	Ex 16:22	3605
and **a** that is left over put aside	Ex 16:23	3605
Then **a** the congregation of the	Ex 17:1	3605
heard of **a** that God had done for	Ex 18:1	3605
Moses told his father-in-law **a**	Ex 18:8	3605
a the hardship that had befallen	Ex 18:8	3605
Jethro rejoiced over **a** the	Ex 18:9	3605
LORD is greater than **a** the gods;	Ex 18:11	3605
and Aaron came with **a** the elders	Ex 18:12	3605

Moses' father-in-law saw **a** that he	**Ex 18:14**	3605
as judge and **a** the people stand about	**Ex 18:14**	3605
you shall select out of **a** the	**Ex 18:21**	3605
them judge the people at **a** times;	**Ex 18:22**	3605
and **a** these people also will go to	**Ex 18:23**	3605
and did **a** that he had said.	**Ex 18:24**	3605
chose able men out of **a** Israel and	**Ex 18:25**	3605
They judged the people at **a** times;	**Ex 18:26**	3605
possession among **a** the peoples,	**Ex 19:5**	3605
peoples, for **a** the earth is Mine;	**Ex 19:5**	3605
and set before them **a** these words	**Ex 19:7**	3605
A the people answered together	**Ex 19:8**	3605
"**A** that the LORD has spoken we	**Ex 19:8**	3605
in the sight of **a** the people.	**Ex 19:11**	3605
bounds for the people **a** around,	**Ex 19:12**	5439
so that **a** the people who *were* in	**Ex 19:16**	3605
Now Mount Sinai *was* **a** in smoke	**Ex 19:18**	3605
Then God spoke **a** these words,	**Ex 20:1**	3605
shall labor and do **a** your work,	**Ex 20:9**	3605
the sea and **a** that is in them,	**Ex 20:11**	3605
A the people perceived the thunder	**Ex 20:18**	3605
"If it is **a** torn to pieces, let	**Ex 22:13**	
"If you afflict him at **a**,	**Ex 22:23**	6031a
"Three times a year **a** your males	**Ex 23:17**	3605
his voice and do **a** that I say,	**Ex 23:22**	3605
and throw into confusion **a** the	**Ex 23:27**	3605
and I will make **a** your enemies	**Ex 23:27**	3605
recounted to the people **a** the words	**Ex 24:3**	3605
of the LORD and **a** the ordinances;	**Ex 24:3**	3605
and **a** the people answered with one	**Ex 24:3**	3605
"**A** the words which the LORD has	**Ex 24:3**	3605
down **a** the words of the LORD.	**Ex 24:4**	3605
"**A** that the LORD has spoken we	**Ex 24:7**	3605
accordance with **a** these words."	**Ex 24:8**	3605
to **a** that I am going to show you,	**Ex 25:9**	3605
the pattern of **a** its furniture,	**Ex 25:9**	3605
I will speak to you about **a** that I	**Ex 25:22**	3605
on the table before Me at **a** times.	**Ex 25:30**	8548
a of it shall be one piece of	**Ex 25:36**	3605
pure gold, with **a** these utensils.	**Ex 25:39**	3605
a the curtains shall have the same	**Ex 26:2**	3605
shall make eleven curtains in **a**.	**Ex 26:7**	
a the boards of the tabernacle.	**Ex 26:17**	3605
make **a** its utensils of bronze.	**Ex 27:3**	3605
"**A** the pillars around the court	**Ex 27:17**	3605
"**A** the utensils of the tabernacle	**Ex 27:19**	3605
tabernacle *used* in **a** its service,	**Ex 27:19**	3605
all its service, and **a** its pegs,	**Ex 27:19**	3605
pegs, and **a** the pegs of the court,	**Ex 27:19**	3605
"You shall speak to **a** the	**Ex 28:3**	3605
the robe of the ephod **a** of blue.	**Ex 28:31**	3632
material, **a** around on its hem,	**Ex 28:33**	5439
of gold between them **a** around:	**Ex 28:33**	5439
a around on the hem of the robe.	**Ex 28:34**	5439
with regard to **a** their holy gifts;	**Ex 28:38**	3605
and you shall pour out **a** the blood	**Ex 29:12**	3605
"You shall take **a** the fat	**Ex 29:13**	3605
and you shall put **a** these in the	**Ex 29:24**	3605
to **a** that I have commanded you;	**Ex 29:35**	3605
its top and its sides **a** around,	**Ex 30:3**	5439
a gold molding **a** around for it.	**Ex 30:3**	5439
and the table and **a** its utensils,	**Ex 30:27**	3605
burnt offering and **a** its utensils,	**Ex 30:28**	3605
and in **a** *kinds of* craftsmanship,	**Ex 31:3**	3605
work in **a** *kinds of* craftsmanship.	**Ex 31:5**	3605
and in the hearts of **a** who are	**Ex 31:6**	3605
make **a** that I have commanded you:	**Ex 31:6**	3605
and **a** the furniture of the tent,	**Ex 31:7**	3605
lampstand with **a** its utensils,	**Ex 31:8**	3605
offering also with **a** its utensils,	**Ex 31:9**	3605
to **a** that I have commanded you."	**Ex 31:11**	3605
Then **a** the people tore off the	**Ex 32:3**	3605
and **a** this land of which I have	**Ex 32:13**	3605
And **a** the sons of Levi gathered	**Ex 32:26**	3605
that **a** the people would arise and	**Ex 33:8**	3605
When **a** the people saw the pillar	**Ex 33:10**	3605
a the people would arise and	**Ex 33:10**	3605
may be distinguished from **a** the	**Ex 33:16**	3605
a My goodness pass before you,	**Ex 33:19**	3605
Before **a** your people I will	**Ex 34:10**	3605
not been produced in **a** the earth nor	**Ex 34:10**	3605
and **a** the people among whom you	**Ex 34:10**	3605
to Me, and **a** your male livestock,	**Ex 34:19**	3605
a the firstborn of your sons.	**Ex 34:20**	3605
"Three times a year **a** your males	**Ex 34:23**	3605
a the sons of Israel saw Moses,	**Ex 34:30**	3605
and Aaron and **a** the rulers in the	**Ex 34:31**	3605
a the sons of Israel came near,	**Ex 34:32**	3605
Then Moses assembled **a** the	**Ex 35:1**	3605
Moses spoke to **a** the	**Ex 35:4**	3605
a that the LORD has commanded:	**Ex 35:10**	3605
and its poles, and **a** its utensils,	**Ex 35:13**	3605
its poles, and **a** its utensils,	**Ex 35:16**	3605
Then **a** the congregation of the	**Ex 35:20**	3605
tent of meeting and for **a** its service	**Ex 35:21**	3605
Then **a** whose hearts moved them,	**Ex 35:22**	3605
and bracelets, **a** articles of gold;	**Ex 35:22**	3605
A the skilled women spun with their	**Ex 35:25**	3605
A the women whose heart stirred with	**Ex 35:26**	3605
Israelites, **a** the men and women,	**Ex 35:29**	3605
to bring *material* for **a** the work,	**Ex 35:29**	3605
knowledge and in **a** craftsmanship;	**Ex 35:31**	3605
perform **a** the work in the construction	**Ex 36:1**	3605
a that the LORD has commanded."	**Ex 36:1**	3605
They received from Moses **a** the	**Ex 36:3**	3605
And **a** the skillful men who were	**Ex 36:4**	3605
skillful men who were performing **a**	**Ex 36:4**	3605
more than enough for **a** the work,	**Ex 36:7**	3605
A the skillful men among those who	**Ex 36:8**	3605
a the curtains had the same	**Ex 36:9**	3605
he made eleven curtains in **a**.	**Ex 36:14**	
a the boards of the tabernacle.	**Ex 36:22**	3605
a gold molding for it **a** around.	**Ex 37:2**	5439
a gold molding for it **a** around.	**Ex 37:11**	5439
for it of a handbreadth **a** around,	**Ex 37:12**	5439
gold molding for its rim **a** around.	**Ex 37:12**	5439
He made it and **a** its utensils from	**Ex 37:24**	3605
its top and its sides **a** around,	**Ex 37:26**	5439
a gold molding for it **a** around.	**Ex 37:26**	5439
made **a** the utensils of the altar,	**Ex 38:3**	3605
he made **a** its utensils of bronze.	**Ex 38:3**	3605
A the hangings of the court all	**Ex 38:16**	3605
All the hangings of the court **a**	**Ex 38:16**	5439
and **a** the pillars of the court	**Ex 38:17**	3605
A the pegs of the tabernacle and of	**Ex 38:20**	3605
the court **a** around *were* of bronze.	**Ex 38:20**	5439
made **a** that the LORD had commanded	**Ex 38:22**	3605
A the gold that was used for the	**Ex 38:24**	3605
in **a** the work of the sanctuary,	**Ex 38:24**	3605
and **a** the utensils of the altar,	**Ex 38:30**	3605
and the sockets of the court **a** around	**Ex 38:31**	5439
and **a** the pegs of the tabernacle	**Ex 38:31**	3605
pegs of the tabernacle and **a** the pegs	**Ex 38:31**	3605
the pegs of the court **a** around.	**Ex 38:31**	5439
ephod of woven work, **a** of blue;	**Ex 39:22**	3632
a binding **a** around its opening,	**Ex 39:23**	5439
a around on the hem of the robe,	**Ex 39:25**	5439
a around on the hem of the robe for	**Ex 39:26**	5439
Thus **a** the work of the tabernacle	**Ex 39:32**	3605
to **a** that the LORD had commanded	**Ex 39:32**	3605
the tent and **a** its furnishings:	**Ex 39:33**	3605
the table, **a** its utensils, and the	**Ex 39:36**	3605
of lamps and **a** its utensils,	**Ex 39:37**	3605
its poles and **a** its utensils,	**Ex 39:39**	3605
its cords and its pegs and **a** the	**Ex 39:40**	3605
So the sons of Israel did **a** the	**Ex 39:42**	3605
work according to **a** that the LORD	**Ex 39:42**	3605
examined **a** the work and behold,	**Ex 39:43**	3605
"You shall set up the court **a**	**Ex 40:8**	5439
tabernacle and **a** that is in it,	**Ex 40:9**	3605
it and **a** its furnishings;	**Ex 40:9**	3605
burnt offering and **a** its utensils,	**Ex 40:10**	3605
according to **a** that the LORD had	**Ex 40:16**	3605
He erected the court **a** around	**Ex 40:33**	5439
Throughout **a** their journeys	**Ex 40:36**	3605
For throughout **a** their journeys,	**Ex 40:38**	3605
sight of **a** the house of Israel.	**Ex 40:38**	3605
offer up in smoke **a** of it on the altar	**Lv 1:9**	3605
the priest shall offer **a** of it,	**Lv 1:13**	3605
oil with **a** of its frankincense.	**Lv 2:2**	3605
with **a** your offerings you shall	**Lv 2:13**	3605
its grits and its oil with **a** its incense	**Lv 2:16**	3605
and **a** the fat that is on the entrails,	**Lv 3:3**	3605
that covers the entrails and **a** the fat	**Lv 3:9**	3605
covers the entrails and **a** the fat that	**Lv 3:14**	3605
a fat is the LORD's.	**Lv 3:16**	3605
generations in **a** your dwellings:	**Lv 3:17**	3605
and **a** the blood of the bull he	**Lv 4:7**	3605
'He shall remove from it **a** the	**Lv 4:8**	3605
and **a** the fat which is on the	**Lv 4:8**	3605
'But the hide of the bull and **a**	**Lv 4:11**	3605
that is, **a** *the rest of* the bull,	**Lv 4:12**	3605
and **a** the blood he shall pour out	**Lv 4:18**	3605
'He shall remove **a** its fat	**Lv 4:19**	3605
unintentionally does any one of **a** the	**Lv 4:22**	3605
'**A** its fat he shall offer up in	**Lv 4:26**	3605
and **a** *the rest of* its blood he	**Lv 4:30**	3605
'Then he shall remove **a** its fat,	**Lv 4:31**	3605
and **a** *the rest of* its blood he	**Lv 4:34**	3605
'Then he shall remove **a** its fat,	**Lv 4:35**	3605
altar **a** night until the morning,	**Lv 6:9**	3605
with its oil and **a** the incense	**Lv 6:15**	3605
he shall offer from it **a** its fat:	**Lv 7:3**	3605
belong to **a** the sons of Aaron,	**Lv 7:10**	3605
all the sons of Aaron, to **a** alike.	**Lv 7:10**	376
and assemble **a** the congregation at	**Lv 8:3**	3605
tabernacle and **a** that was in it,	**Lv 8:10**	3605
the altar and **a** its utensils,	**Lv 8:11**	3605
He also took **a** the fat that was on	**Lv 8:16**	3605
and **a** the fat that was on the	**Lv 8:25**	3605
He then put **a** *these* on the hands	**Lv 8:27**	3605
Thus Aaron and his sons did **a** the	**Lv 8:36**	3605
the LORD appeared to **a** the people.	**Lv 9:23**	3605
and when **a** the people saw *it,* they	**Lv 9:24**	3605
before **a** the people I will be honored.	**Lv 10:3**	3605
against **a** the congregation.	**Lv 10:6**	3605
teach the sons of Israel **a** the statutes	**Lv 10:11**	3605
which you may eat from **a** the animals	**Lv 11:2**	3605
a that have fins and scales, those	**Lv 11:9**	3605
scales among **a** the teeming life	**Lv 11:10**	3605
and among **a** the living creatures	**Lv 11:10**	3605
'**A** the winged insects that walk on	**Lv 11:20**	3605
the winged insects that walk on **a**	**Lv 11:20**	
'Yet these you may eat among **a** the	**Lv 11:21**	3605
the winged insects which walk on **a**	**Lv 11:21**	
'But **a** other winged insects which	**Lv 11:23**	3605
'Concerning **a** the animals which	**Lv 11:26**	3605
among **a** the creatures that walk on	**Lv 11:27**	3605
all the creatures that walk on **a**	**Lv 11:27**	
among **a** the swarming things;	**Lv 11:31**	3605
and whatever walks on **a** fours,	**Lv 11:42**	
and the leprosy covers **a** the skin	**Lv 13:12**	3605
leprosy has covered **a** his body,	**Lv 13:13**	3605
a turned white *and* he is clean.	**Lv 13:13**	3605
"He shall remain unclean **a** the	**Lv 13:46**	3605
clothes and shave off **a** his hair and	**Lv 14:8**	3605
he shall shave off **a** his hair:	**Lv 14:9**	3605
and his eyebrows, even **a** his hair.	**Lv 14:9**	3605
the house scraped **a** around inside,	**Lv 14:41**	5439
and **a** the plaster of the house,	**Lv 14:45**	3605
he shall bathe **a** his body in water	**Lv 15:16**	3605
a the days of her impure discharge	**Lv 15:25**	3605
'Any bed on which she lies **a** the	**Lv 15:26**	3605
in regard to **a** their sins;	**Lv 16:16**	3605
and for **a** the assembly of Israel.	**Lv 16:17**	3605
the horns of the altar on **a** sides.	**Lv 16:18**	5439
and confess over it **a** the	**Lv 16:21**	3605
and **a** their transgressions in	**Lv 16:21**	3605
in regard to **a** their sins;	**Lv 16:21**	3605
shall bear on itself **a** their iniquities	**Lv 16:22**	3605
from **a** your sins before the LORD.	**Lv 16:30**	3605
for **a** the people of the assembly.	**Lv 16:33**	3605
a their sins once every year."	**Lv 16:34**	3605
sons and to **a** the sons of Israel	**Lv 17:2**	3605
"For *as for the* life of **a** flesh,	**Lv 17:14**	3605
the life of **a** flesh is its blood;	**Lv 17:14**	3605
for by **a** these the nations which I	**Lv 18:24**	3605
have done **a** these abominations,	**Lv 18:27**	3605
"Speak to **a** the congregation of	**Lv 19:2**	3605
it is eaten at **a** on the third day,	**Lv 19:7**	398
with you **a** night until morning.	**Lv 19:13**	
plant **a** kinds of trees for food,	**Lv 19:23**	3605
year **a** its fruit shall be holy,	**Lv 19:24**	3605
shall thus observe **a** My statutes and	**Lv 19:37**	3605
My statutes and **a** My ordinances	**Lv 19:37**	3605
him and **a** those who play the harlot	**Lv 20:5**	3605
'You are therefore to keep **a** My	**Lv 20:22**	3605
and **a** My ordinances and do them,	**Lv 20:22**	3605
you, for they did **a** these things,	**Lv 20:23**	3605
sons and to **a** the sons of Israel.	**Lv 21:24**	3605
'If any man among **a** your	**Lv 22:3**	3605
sons and to **a** the sons of Israel and	**Lv 22:18**	3605
to the LORD in **a** your dwellings.	**Lv 23:3**	3605
in **a** your dwelling places.	**Lv 23:14**	3605
a perpetual statute in **a** your dwelling	**Lv 23:21**	3605
"You shall do no work at **a**.	**Lv 23:31**	3605
in **a** your dwelling places.	**Lv 23:31**	3605
and besides **a** your votive and	**Lv 23:38**	3605
a the native-born in Israel shall	**Lv 23:42**	3605
and let **a** who heard him lay their	**Lv 24:14**	3605
let **a** the congregation stone him.	**Lv 24:14**	3605
a the congregation shall certainly	**Lv 24:16**	3605
'**A** of you shall have the sabbath	**Lv 25:6**	
shall have **a** its crops to eat.	**Lv 25:7**	3605
sound a horn **a** through your land.	**Lv 25:9**	3605
the land to **a** its inhabitants.	**Lv 25:10**	3605
carry out **a** these commandments,	**Lv 26:14**	3605
to carry out **a** My commandments,	**Lv 26:15**	3605
a the days of the desolation,	**Lv 26:34**	3605
'**A** the days of *its* desolation it	**Lv 26:35**	3605
to the LORD out of **a** that he has,	**Lv 27:28**	3605
'Thus **a** the tithe of the land, of	**Lv 27:30**	3605
"Take a census of **a** the	**Nu 1:2**	3605
and they assembled **a** the	**Nu 1:18**	3605
So **a** the numbered men of the sons	**Nu 1:45**	3605
a the numbered men were 603,550.	**Nu 1:46**	3605
and over **a** its furnishings and	**Nu 1:50**	3605
and over **a** that belongs to it.	**Nu 1:50**	3605
tabernacle and **a** its furnishings,	**Nu 1:50**	3605
according to **a** which the LORD had	**Nu 1:54**	3605
a that the LORD commanded Moses,	**Nu 2:34**	3605
"They shall also keep **a** the	**Nu 3:8**	3605
"For **a** the firstborn are Mine;	**Nu 3:13**	3605
on the day that I struck down **a**	**Nu 3:13**	3605
Myself **a** the firstborn in Israel,	**Nu 3:13**	3605
to **a** the service concerning them.	**Nu 3:26**	3605
and **a** the service concerning them;	**Nu 3:31**	3605
its sockets, **a** its equipment,	**Nu 3:36**	3605
A the numbered men of the Levites,	**Nu 3:39**	3605
instead of **a** the firstborn among	**Nu 3:41**	3605
instead of **a** the firstborn among	**Nu 3:41**	3605
So Moses numbered **a** the firstborn	**Nu 3:42**	3605
and **a** the firstborn males by the	**Nu 3:43**	3605
"Take the Levites instead of **a**	**Nu 3:45**	3605
a who enter the service to do the	**Nu 4:3**	3605
its trays and **a** its oil vessels,	**Nu 4:9**	3605
and they shall put it and **a** its	**Nu 4:10**	3605
take **a** the utensils of service,	**Nu 4:12**	3605
"They shall also put on it **a** its	**Nu 4:14**	3605
a the utensils of the altar;	**Nu 4:14**	3605
the holy *objects* and **a** the furnishings	**Nu 4:15**	3605
the responsibility of **a** the tabernacle	**Nu 4:16**	3605
tabernacle and of **a** that is in it,	**Nu 4:16**	3605
a who enter to perform the service	**Nu 4:23**	3605
and their cords and **a** the	**Nu 4:26**	3605
and **a** that is to be done, they	**Nu 4:26**	3605
"**A** the service of the sons of the	**Nu 4:27**	3605
in **a** their loads and in all their	**Nu 4:27**	3605
their loads and in **a** their work,	**Nu 4:27**	3605
to them as a duty **a** their loads.	**Nu 4:27**	3605
for **a** their service in the tent of	**Nu 4:31**	3605
with **a** their equipment and with	**Nu 4:32**	3605
and with **a** their service;	**Nu 4:32**	3605
according to **a** their service in	**Nu 4:33**	3605
A the numbered men of the Levites,	**Nu 4:46**	3605
contribution pertaining to **a** the holy	**Nu 5:9**	3605
shall apply **a** this law to her.	**Nu 5:30**	3605
'**A** the days of his separation he	**Nu 6:4**	3605
'**A** the days of his vow of	**Nu 6:5**	3605
'**A** the days of his separation to	**Nu 6:6**	3605
'**A** the days of his separation he	**Nu 6:8**	3605
consecrated it with **a** its furnishings	**Nu 7:1**	3605
and the altar and **a** its utensils;	**Nu 7:1**	3605
a the silver of the utensils *was*	**Nu 7:85**	3605
a the gold of the pans 120 *shekels;*	**Nu 7:86**	3605
a the oxen for the burnt offering	**Nu 7:87**	3605
a the rams twelve, the male	**Nu 7:87**	

Context	Reference	Number
and **a** the oxen for the sacrifice	Nu 7:88	3605
a the rams 60, the male goats 60,	Nu 7:88	
firstborn of **a** the sons of Israel.	Nu 8:16	3605
on the day that I struck down **a**	Nu 8:17	3605
Thus did Moses and Aaron and **a** the	Nu 8:20	3605
according to **a** that the LORD had	Nu 8:20	3605
observe it according to **a** its statutes	Nu 9:3	3605
according to **a** its ordinances."	Nu 9:3	3605
according to **a** that the LORD had	Nu 9:5	3605
according to **a** the statute of the	Nu 9:12	3605
a the congregation shall gather	Nu 10:3	3605
the rear guard for **a** the camps,	Nu 10:25	3605
a to look at except this manna."	Nu 11:6	3605
the burden of **a** this people on me?	Nu 11:11	3605
it I who conceived **a** this people?	Nu 11:12	3605
get meat to give to **a** this people?	Nu 11:13	3605
not able to carry **a** this people,	Nu 11:14	3605
you will not bear *it* **a** alone.	Nu 11:17	
Or should **a** the fish of the sea be	Nu 11:22	3605
Would that **a** the LORD's people	Nu 11:29	3605
the other side, **a** around the camp and	Nu 11:31	5439
The people spent **a** day and all	Nu 11:32	3605
and **a** night and all the next day,	Nu 11:32	3605
and all night and **a** the next day,	Nu 11:32	3605
for themselves **a** around the camp.	Nu 11:32	5439
He is faithful in **a** My household;	Nu 12:7	3605
a of them men who were heads of	Nu 13:3	3605
and Aaron and to **a** the congregation	Nu 13:26	3605
to them and to **a** the congregation	Nu 13:26	3605
"We should by **a** means go up and	Nu 13:30	5927
and **a** the people whom we saw in it	Nu 13:32	3605
Then **a** the congregation lifted up	Nu 14:1	3605
A the sons of Israel grumbled against	Nu 14:2	3605
in the presence of **a** the assembly	Nu 14:5	3605
and they spoke to **a** the congregation	Nu 14:7	3605
But **a** the congregation said to stone	Nu 14:10	3605
meeting to **a** the sons of Israel.	Nu 14:10	3605
despite **a** the signs which I have	Nu 14:11	3605
a the earth will be filled with	Nu 14:21	3605
"Surely **a** the men who have seen	Nu 14:22	3605
even **a** your numbered men,	Nu 14:29	3605
surely this I will do to **a** this	Nu 14:35	3605
made **a** the congregation grumble	Nu 14:36	3605
words to **a** the sons of Israel,	Nu 14:39	3605
'**A** who are native shall do these	Nu 15:13	3605
not observe **a** these commandments,	Nu 15:22	3605
even **a** that the LORD has commanded	Nu 15:23	3605
that **a** the congregation shall	Nu 15:24	3605
atonement for **a** the congregation of	Nu 15:25	3605
'So **a** the congregation of the sons	Nu 15:26	3605
to **a** the people through error.	Nu 15:26	3605
Aaron and to **a** the congregation;	Nu 15:33	3605
a the congregation shall stone him	Nu 15:35	3605
So **a** the congregation brought him	Nu 15:36	3605
a the commandments of the LORD,	Nu 15:39	3605
remember to do **a** My commandments	Nu 15:40	3605
for **a** the congregation are holy,	Nu 16:3	3605
spoke to Korah and **a** his company,	Nu 16:5	3605
Korah and **a** your company,	Nu 16:6	3605
near, *Korah,* and **a** your brothers,	Nu 16:10	3605
"Therefore you and **a** your company	Nu 16:11	3605
"You and **a** your company be	Nu 16:16	3605
Thus Korah assembled **a** the	Nu 16:19	3605
appeared to **a** the congregation.	Nu 16:19	3605
God of the spirits of **a** flesh,	Nu 16:22	3605
be swept away in **a** their sin."	Nu 16:26	3605
has sent me to do **a** these deeds;	Nu 16:28	3605
these men die the death of **a** men or	Nu 16:29	3605
if they suffer the fate of **a** men,	Nu 16:29	3605
them up with **a** that is theirs,	Nu 16:30	3605
finished speaking **a** these words,	Nu 16:31	3605
a the men who belonged to Korah with	Nu 16:32	3605
So they and **a** that belonged to	Nu 16:33	3605
A Israel who *were* around them	Nu 16:34	3605
But on the next day **a** the	Nu 16:41	3605
from **a** their leaders according to	Nu 17:2	3605
and **a** their leaders gave him a rod	Nu 17:6	3605
Moses then brought out **a** the rods	Nu 17:9	3605
the LORD to **a** the sons of Israel;	Nu 17:9	3605
we are dying, we are **a** dying!	Nu 17:12	3605
and the obligation of **a** the tent,	Nu 18:3	3605
for **a** the service of the tent;	Nu 18:4	3605
even **a** the holy gifts of the sons	Nu 18:8	3605
even **a** the wave offerings of the	Nu 18:11	3605
"**A** the best of the fresh oil and	Nu 18:12	3605
oil and **a** the best of the fresh wine	Nu 18:12	3605
fruits of **a** that is in their land,	Nu 18:13	3605
issue of the womb of **a** flesh,	Nu 18:15	3605
"**A** the offerings of the holy	Nu 18:19	3605
I have given **a** the tithe in Israel	Nu 18:21	3605
'Out of **a** your gifts you shall	Nu 18:29	3605
the LORD, from **a** the best of them,	Nu 18:29	3605
on the tent and on **a** the furnishings	Nu 19:18	3605
'You know **a** the hardship that has	Nu 20:14	3605
the sight of **a** the congregation.	Nu 20:27	3605
When **a** the congregation saw	Nu 20:29	3605
a the house of Israel wept for	Nu 20:29	3605
So Sihon gathered **a** his people and	Nu 21:23	3605
Israel took **a** these cities and	Nu 21:25	3605
in **a** the cities of the Amorites,	Nu 21:25	3605
in Heshbon, and in **a** her villages.	Nu 21:25	3605
taken **a** his land out of his hand,	Nu 21:26	3605
Bashan went out with **a** his people,	Nu 21:33	3605
and **a** his people and his land;	Nu 21:34	3605
him and his sons and **a** his people,	Nu 21:35	3605
Now Balak the son of Zippor saw **a**	Nu 22:2	3605
will lick up **a** that is around us,	Nu 22:4	3605
ridden **a** your life to this day?	Nu 22:30	4480, 5750
he bowed **a** the way to the ground.	Nu 22:31	
Am I able to speak anything at **a**?	Nu 22:38	
he and **a** the leaders of Moab.	Nu 23:6	3605
them and will not see **a** of them;	Nu 23:13	3605
"Do not curse them at **a** nor bless	Nu 23:25	6895
them at all nor bless them at **a**!"	Nu 23:25	1288
And tear down **a** the sons of Sheth.	Nu 24:17	3605
"Take **a** the leaders of the people	Nu 25:4	3605
sight of **a** the congregation of the sons	Nu 25:6	3605
"Take a census of **a** the	Nu 26:2	3605
A the families of the Shuhamites,	Nu 26:43	3605
leaders and **a** the congregation,	Nu 27:2	3605
the God of the spirits of **a** flesh,	Nu 27:16	3605
and before **a** the congregation,	Nu 27:19	3605
in order that **a** the congregation	Nu 27:20	3605
him, even **a** the congregation."	Nu 27:21	3605
and before **a** the congregation.	Nu 27:22	3605
in accordance with **a** that the LORD	Nu 29:40	3605
he shall do according to **a** that	Nu 30:2	3605
her, then **a** her vows shall stand and	Nu 30:4	3605
her, then **a** her vows shall stand and	Nu 30:11	3605
then he confirms **a** her vows or all	Nu 30:14	3605
all her vows or **a** her obligations	Nu 30:14	3605
"A thousand from each tribe of **a**	Nu 31:4	3605
and **a** their cattle and all their	Nu 31:9	3605
and all their cattle and **a** their	Nu 31:9	3605
their flocks and **a** their goods they	Nu 31:9	3605
Then they burned **a** their cities	Nu 31:10	3605
lived and **a** their camps with fire.	Nu 31:10	3605
took **a** the spoil and all the prey,	Nu 31:11	3605
took all the spoil and **a** the prey,	Nu 31:11	3605
Eleazar the priest and **a** the leaders	Nu 31:13	3605
"Have you spared **a** the women?	Nu 31:15	3605
"But **a** the girls who have not	Nu 31:18	3605
and **a** the work of goats' *hair,*	Nu 31:20	3605
hair, and **a** articles of wood."	Nu 31:20	3605
to battle and **a** the congregation.	Nu 31:27	3605
of the sheep, from **a** the animals,	Nu 31:30	3605
a the persons were 32,000.	Nu 31:35	3605
them, **a** kinds of wrought articles.	Nu 31:51	3605
A the gold of the offering which they	Nu 31:52	3605
you will destroy **a** these people."	Nu 32:15	3605
and **a** of your armed men cross over	Nu 32:21	3605
our livestock and **a** our cattle	Nu 32:26	3605
in the sight of **a** the Egyptians,	Nu 33:3	3605
were burying **a** their firstborn whom	Nu 33:4	3605
then you shall drive out **a** the	Nu 33:52	3605
destroy **a** their figured stones,	Nu 33:52	3605
and destroy **a** their molten images	Nu 33:52	3605
and demolish **a** their high places;	Nu 33:52	3605
to its borders **a** around.' "	Nu 34:12	5439
herds and for **a** their beasts.	Nu 35:3	3605
"**A** the cities which you shall	Nu 35:7	3605
generations in **a** your dwellings.	Nu 35:29	3605
words which Moses spoke to **a** Israel	Dt 1:1	3605
according to **a** that the LORD had	Dt 1:3	3605
a their neighbors in the Arabah,	Dt 1:7	3605
a the things that you should do.	Dt 1:18	3605
and went through **a** that great and	Dt 1:19	3605
a of you approached me and said,	Dt 1:22	3605
a the way which you have walked until	Dt 1:31	3605
"But for **a** this, you did not	Dt 1:32	
you in **a** that you have done;	Dt 2:7	3605
until **a** the generation of the men	Dt 2:14	3605
the camp until they **a** perished.	Dt 2:15	
"So it came about when **a** the men	Dt 2:16	3605
"Then Sihon with **a** his people	Dt 2:32	3605
with his sons and **a** his people.	Dt 2:33	3605
a his cities at that time and	Dt 2:34	3605
our God delivered **a** over to us.	Dt 2:36	3605
a along the river Jabbok and the	Dt 2:37	3605
with **a** his people came out to meet	Dt 3:1	3605
for I have delivered him and **a** his	Dt 3:2	3605
with **a** his people into our hand,	Dt 3:3	3605
a his cities at that time;	Dt 3:4	3605
cities, **a** the region of Argob,	Dt 3:4	3605
"**A** these were cities fortified	Dt 3:5	3605
"But **a** the animals and the spoil	Dt 3:7	3605
a the cities of the plateau and	Dt 3:10	3605
and **a** Gilead and all Bashan,	Dt 3:10	3605
and all Gilead and **a** Bashan,	Dt 3:10	3605
"The rest of Gilead and **a** Bashan,	Dt 3:13	3605
Manasseh, **a** the region of Argob	Dt 3:13	3605
(concerning **a** Bashan, it is called	Dt 3:13	3605
Jair the son of Manasseh took **a**	Dt 3:14	3605
a you valiant men shall cross over	Dt 3:18	3605
'Your eyes have seen **a** that the	Dt 3:21	3605
so the LORD shall do to **a** the	Dt 3:21	3605
for **a** the men who followed	Dt 4:3	3605
hear **a** these statutes and say,	Dt 4:6	3605
heart **a** the days of your life;	Dt 4:9	3605
learn to fear Me **a** the days they live	Dt 4:10	3605
the stars, **a** the host of heaven,	Dt 4:19	3605
God has allotted to **a** the peoples	Dt 4:19	3605
a your heart and all your soul.	Dt 4:29	3605
all your heart and **a** your soul.	Dt 4:29	3605
"When you are in distress and **a**	Dt 4:30	3605
God is giving you for **a** time."	Dt 4:40	3605
with **a** the Arabah across the	Dt 4:49	3605
Then Moses summoned **a** Israel and	Dt 5:1	3605
a those of us alive here today.	Dt 5:3	3605
shall labor and do **a** your work,	Dt 5:13	3605
"These words the LORD spoke to **a**	Dt 5:22	3605
a the heads of your tribes and	Dt 5:23	3605
'For who is there of **a** flesh who	Dt 5:26	3605
hear **a** that the LORD our God says;	Dt 5:27	3605
then speak to us **a** that the LORD	Dt 5:27	3605
well in **a** that they have spoken.	Dt 5:28	3605
and keep **a** My commandments always,	Dt 5:29	3605
that I may speak to you **a** the	Dt 5:31	3605
"You shall walk in **a** the way	Dt 5:33	3605
to keep **a** His statutes and His	Dt 6:2	3605
you, **a** the days of your life,	Dt 6:2	3605
the LORD your God with **a** your heart	Dt 6:5	3605
all your heart and with **a** your soul	Dt 6:5	3605
your soul and with **a** your might.	Dt 6:5	3605
and houses full of **a** good things	Dt 6:11	3605
a your enemies from before you,	Dt 6:19	3605
Pharaoh and **a** his household;	Dt 6:22	3605
us to observe **a** these statutes,	Dt 6:24	3605
observe **a** this commandment before	Dt 6:25	3605
own possession out of **a** the peoples	Dt 7:6	3605
you were the fewest of **a** peoples,	Dt 7:7	3605
shall be blessed above **a** peoples;	Dt 7:14	3605
will remove from you **a** sickness;	Dt 7:15	3605
will lay them on **a** who hate you.	Dt 7:15	3605
"You shall consume **a** the	Dt 7:16	3605
God did to Pharaoh and to **a** Egypt:	Dt 7:18	3605
So shall the LORD your God do to **a**	Dt 7:19	3605
"**A** the commandments that I am	Dt 8:1	3605
"You shall remember **a** the way	Dt 8:2	3605
and **a** that you have multiplies,	Dt 8:13	3605
and on them *were* **a** the words which	Dt 9:10	3605
because of **a** your sin which you	Dt 9:18	3605
walk in **a** His ways and love Him,	Dt 10:12	3605
serve the LORD your God with **a** your	Dt 10:12	3605
your heart and with **a** your soul,	Dt 10:12	3605
the earth and **a** that is in it.	Dt 10:14	3605
them, *even* you above **a** peoples,	Dt 10:15	3605
down to Egypt seventy persons *in* **a**,	Dt 10:22	
king of Egypt and to **a** his land;	Dt 11:3	3605
followed them, among **a** Israel	Dt 11:6	3605
but your own eyes have seen **a** the	Dt 11:7	3605
a your heart and all your soul,	Dt 11:13	3605
all your heart and **a** your soul,	Dt 11:13	3605
"For if you are careful to keep **a**	Dt 11:22	3605
a His ways and hold fast to Him,	Dt 11:22	3605
a these nations from before you,	Dt 11:23	3605
fear of you on **a** the land on which	Dt 11:25	3605
and you shall be careful to do **a**	Dt 11:32	3605
"You shall utterly destroy **a** the	Dt 12:2	3605
will choose from **a** your tribes,	Dt 12:5	3605
and rejoice in **a** your undertakings	Dt 12:7	3605
at **a** what we are doing here today,	Dt 12:8	3605
and He gives you rest from **a** your	Dt 12:10	3605
shall bring **a** that I command you:	Dt 12:11	3605
and **a** your choice votive offerings	Dt 12:11	3605
you shall do **a** that I command you.	Dt 12:14	3605
your God in **a** your undertakings.	Dt 12:18	3605
"Be careful to listen to **a** these	Dt 12:28	3605
love the LORD your God with **a** your	Dt 13:3	3605
your heart and with **a** your soul.	Dt 13:3	3605
the hand of **a** the people.	Dt 13:9	3605
"Then **a** Israel will hear and be	Dt 13:11	3605
utterly destroying it and **a** that	Dt 13:15	3605
"Then you shall gather **a** its	Dt 13:16	3605
burn the city and **a** its booty with fire	Dt 13:16	3605
keeping **a** His commandments which I	Dt 13:18	3605
own possession out of **a** the peoples	Dt 14:2	3605
may eat of **a** that are in water:	Dt 14:9	3605
"And **a** the teeming life with	Dt 14:19	3605
a the produce from what you sow,	Dt 14:22	3605
third year you shall bring out **a** the	Dt 14:28	3605
God may bless you in **a** the work of	Dt 14:29	3605
to observe carefully **a** this	Dt 15:5	3605
God will bless you in **a** your work	Dt 15:10	3605
work and in **a** your undertakings.	Dt 15:10	3605
consecrate to the LORD your God **a**	Dt 15:19	3605
so that you may remember **a**	Dt 16:3	3605
seen with you in **a** your territory,	Dt 16:4	3605
God will bless you in **a** your produce	Dt 16:15	3605
and in **a** the work of your hands,	Dt 16:15	3605
"Three times in a year **a** your	Dt 16:16	3605
judges and officers in **a** your towns	Dt 16:18	3605
the hand of **a** the people.	Dt 17:7	3605
to **a** that they teach you.	Dt 17:10	3605
"Then **a** the people will hear and	Dt 17:13	3605
a the nations who are around me,'	Dt 17:14	3605
read it **a** the days of his life,	Dt 17:19	3605
by carefully observing **a** the words	Dt 17:19	3605
and his sons from **a** your tribes,	Dt 18:5	3605
like **a** his fellow Levites who	Dt 18:7	3605
"This is according to **a** that you	Dt 18:16	3605
to them **a** that I command him.	Dt 18:18	3605
and gives you **a** the land which He	Dt 19:8	3605
observe **a** this commandment which	Dt 19:9	3605
then **a** the people who are found in it	Dt 20:11	3605
you shall strike **a** the men in it	Dt 20:13	3605
animals and **a** that is in the city,	Dt 20:14	3605
that is in the city, **a** its spoil,	Dt 20:14	3605
"Thus you shall do to **a** the	Dt 20:15	3605
according to **a** their detestable things	Dt 20:18	3605
"**A** the elders of that city which is	Dt 21:6	3605
a double portion of **a** that he has,	Dt 21:17	3605
"Then **a** the men of his city shall	Dt 21:21	3605
and **a** Israel will hear *of it* and	Dt 21:21	3605
not hang **a** night on the tree,	Dt 21:23	
or **a** the produce of the seed	Dt 22:9	4395
he cannot divorce her **a** his days.	Dt 22:19	3605
he cannot divorce her **a** his days.	Dt 22:29	3605
or their prosperity **a** your days.	Dt 23:6	3605
bless you in **a** that you undertake	Dt 23:20	3605
do according to **a** that the Levitical	Dt 24:8	3605
you in **a** the work of your hands.	Dt 24:19	3605
attacked among you **a** the stragglers	Dt 25:18	3605
from **a** your surrounding enemies,	Dt 25:19	3605
first of **a** the produce of the ground	Dt 26:2	3605
rejoice in **a** the good which the LORD	Dt 26:11	3605

"When you have finished paying **a**	Dt 26:12	3605
according to **a** Your commandments	Dt 26:13	3605
to **a** that You have commanded me.	Dt 26:14	3605
careful to do them with **a** your heart	Dt 26:16	3605
your heart and with **a** your soul.	Dt 26:16	3605
should keep **a** His commandments;	Dt 26:18	3605
above **a** nations which He has made,	Dt 26:19	3605
"Keep **a** the commandments which I	Dt 27:1	3605
on them **a** the words of this law,	Dt 27:3	3605
shall write on the stones **a** the words	Dt 27:8	3605
priests spoke to **a** Israel,	Dt 27:9	3605
answer and say to **a** the men of Israel	Dt 27:14	3605
And **a** the people shall answer and	Dt 27:15	3605
And **a** the people shall say,	Dt 27:16	3605
And **a** the people shall say,	Dt 27:17	3605
And **a** the people shall say,	Dt 27:18	3605
And **a** the people shall say,	Dt 27:19	3605
And **a** the people shall say,	Dt 27:20	3605
And **a** the people shall say,	Dt 27:21	3605
And **a** the people shall say,	Dt 27:22	3605
And **a** the people shall say,	Dt 27:23	3605
And **a** the people shall say,	Dt 27:24	3605
And **a** the people shall say,	Dt 27:25	3605
And **a** the people shall say,	Dt 27:26	3605
being careful to do **a** His	Dt 28:1	3605
above **a** the nations of the earth.	Dt 28:1	3605
"**A** these blessings will come upon	Dt 28:2	3605
in **a** that you put your hand to,	Dt 28:8	3605
"So **a** the peoples of the earth	Dt 28:10	3605
to bless **a** the work of your hand;	Dt 28:12	3605
to observe to do **a** His	Dt 28:15	3605
that **a** these curses will come	Dt 28:15	3605
rebuke, in **a** you undertake to do,	Dt 28:20	3605
to **a** the kingdoms of the earth.	Dt 28:25	3605
carcasses will be food to **a** birds	Dt 28:26	3605
of your ground and **a** your labors,	Dt 28:33	3605
and a taunt among **a** the people	Dt 28:37	3605
"The cricket shall possess **a** your	Dt 28:42	3605
"So **a** these curses shall come on	Dt 28:45	3605
for the abundance of **a** things;	Dt 28:47	3605
and in the lack of **a** things;	Dt 28:48	3605
"It shall besiege you in **a**	Dt 28:52	3605
and it shall besiege you in **a** your	Dt 28:52	3605
will oppress you in **a** your towns.	Dt 28:55	3605
to observe **a** the words of this law	Dt 28:58	3605
"He will bring back on you **a**	Dt 28:60	3605
will scatter you among **a** peoples,	Dt 28:64	3605
a Israel and said to them,	Dt 29:2	3605
"You have seen **a** that the LORD	Dt 29:2	3605
a his servants and all his land;	Dt 29:2	3605
all his servants and **a** his land;	Dt 29:2	3605
you may prosper in **a** that you do.	Dt 29:9	3605
"You stand today, **a** of you,	Dt 29:10	3605
even **a** the men of Israel,	Dt 29:10	3605
from **a** the tribes of Israel,	Dt 29:21	3605
according to **a** the curses of the	Dt 29:21	3605
'**A** its land is brimstone and salt,	Dt 29:23	3605
"**A** the nations will say, 'Why has	Dt 29:24	3605
observe **a** the words of this law.	Dt 29:29	3605
"So it shall be when **a** of these	Dt 30:1	3605
and you call *them* to mind in **a**	Dt 30:1	3605
obey Him with **a** your heart and soul	Dt 30:2	3605
to **a** that I command you today,	Dt 30:2	3605
and will gather you again from **a**	Dt 30:3	3605
to love the LORD your God with **a**	Dt 30:6	3605
your heart and with **a** your soul,	Dt 30:6	3605
your God will inflict **a** these curses	Dt 30:7	3605
and observe **a** His commandments	Dt 30:8	3605
in **a** the work of your hand,	Dt 30:9	3605
God with **a** your heart and soul.	Dt 30:10	3605
and spoke these words to **a** Israel.	Dt 31:1	3605
according to **a** the commandments	Dt 31:5	3605
to him in the sight of **a** Israel,	Dt 31:7	3605
and to **a** the elders of Israel.	Dt 31:9	3605
when **a** Israel comes to appear	Dt 31:11	3605
of **a** Israel in their hearing.	Dt 31:11	3605
observe **a** the words of this law.	Dt 31:12	3605
of **a** the evil which they will do,	Dt 31:18	3605
"Assemble to me **a** the elders of	Dt 31:28	3605
hearing of **a** the assembly of Israel	Dt 31:30	3605
perfect, For **a** His ways are just;	Dt 32:4	3605
the years of **a** generations.	Dt 32:7	1755
the LORD has not done **a** this."	Dt 32:27	3605
Then Moses came and spoke **a** the	Dt 32:44	3605
a these words to all Israel,	Dt 32:45	3605
all these words to **a** Israel,	Dt 32:45	3605
"Take to your heart **a** the words	Dt 32:46	3605
even **a** the words of this law.	Dt 32:46	3605
A Your holy ones are in Your hand,	Dt 33:3	3605
by Him, Who shields him **a** the day,	Dt 33:12	3605
will push the peoples, **A** at once,	Dt 33:17	3164a
the LORD showed him **a** the land,	Dt 34:1	3605
and **a** Naphtali and the land of	Dt 34:2	3605
and **a** the land of Judah as far as	Dt 34:2	3605
for **a** the signs and wonders which	Dt 34:11	3605
against Pharaoh, **a** his servants,	Dt 34:11	3605
all his servants, and **a** his land,	Dt 34:11	3605
and for **a** the mighty power and for	Dt 34:12	3605
for **a** the great terror which Moses	Dt 34:12	3605
in the sight of **a** Israel.	Dt 34:12	3605
Jordan, you and **a** this people,	Jos 1:2	3605
a the land of the Hittites,	Jos 1:4	3605
you **a** the days of your life.	Jos 1:5	3605
be careful to do according to **a**	Jos 1:7	3605
to **a** that is written in it;	Jos 1:8	3605
array, **a** your valiant warriors,	Jos 1:14	3605
"**A** that you have commanded us we	Jos 1:16	3605
as we obeyed Moses in **a** things,	Jos 1:17	3605
words in **a** that you command him,	Jos 1:18	3605

come to search out **a** the land."	Jos 2:3	3605
and that **a** the inhabitants of the	Jos 2:9	3605
with **a** who belong to them,	Jos 2:13	3605
and **a** your father's household.	Jos 2:18	3605
had sought *them* **a** along the road,	Jos 2:22	3605
him **a** that had happened to them.	Jos 2:23	3605
given **a** the land into our hands;	Jos 2:24	3605
a the inhabitants of the land	Jos 2:24	3605
and he and **a** the sons of Israel	Jos 3:1	3605
you in the sight of **a** Israel,	Jos 3:7	3605
covenant of the Lord of **a** the earth	Jos 3:11	3605
the LORD, the Lord of **a** the earth,	Jos 3:13	3605
the Jordan overflows **a** its banks	Jos 3:15	3605
its banks **a** the days of harvest),	Jos 3:15	3605
a Israel crossed on dry ground,	Jos 3:17	3605
until **a** the nation had finished	Jos 3:17	3605
Now when **a** the nation	Jos 4:1	3605
according to **a** that Moses had	Jos 4:10	3605
and when **a** the people	Jos 4:11	3605
Joshua in the sight of **a** Israel;	Jos 4:14	3605
Moses **a** the days of his life.	Jos 4:14	3605
went over **a** its banks as before.	Jos 4:18	3605
that **a** the peoples of the earth	Jos 4:24	3605
Now it came about when **a** the kings	Jos 5:1	3605
and **a** the kings of the Canaanites	Jos 5:1	3605
a the people who came out of Egypt	Jos 5:4	3605
who were males, **a** the men of war,	Jos 5:4	3605
For **a** the people who came out were	Jos 5:5	3605
but **a** the people who were born in	Jos 5:5	3605
wilderness, until **a** the nation,	Jos 5:6	3605
circumcising **a** the nation,	Jos 5:8	3605
a the men of war circling the city	Jos 6:3	3605
a the people shall shout with a	Jos 6:5	3605
it and **a** that is in it belongs to	Jos 6:17	3605
only Rahab the harlot and **a** who	Jos 6:17	3605
"But **a** the silver and gold and	Jos 6:19	3605
woman and **a** she has out of there,	Jos 6:22	3605
and her brothers and **a** she had;	Jos 6:23	3605
also brought out **a** her relatives and	Jos 6:23	3605
with fire, and **a** that was in it.	Jos 6:24	3605
father's household and **a** she had,	Jos 6:25	3605
and his fame was in **a** the land.	Jos 6:27	3605
"Do not let **a** the people go up;	Jos 7:3	3605
make **a** the people toil up there,	Jos 7:3	3605
"For the Canaanites and **a** the	Jos 7:9	3605
he and **a** that belongs to him,	Jos 7:15	3605
and to **a** the sons of Israel,	Jos 7:23	3605
Then Joshua and **a** Israel with him,	Jos 7:24	3605
tent and **a** that belonged to him;	Jos 7:24	3605
And **a** Israel stoned them with	Jos 7:25	3605
Take **a** the people of war with you	Jos 8:1	3605
So Joshua rose with **a** the people	Jos 8:3	3605
the city, but **a** of you be ready.	Jos 8:4	3605
"Then I and **a** the people who are	Jos 8:5	3605
Then **a** the people of war who *were*	Jos 8:11	3605
a the army that was on the north	Jos 8:13	3605
he and **a** his people at the	Jos 8:14	3605
Joshua and **a** Israel pretended	Jos 8:15	3605
And **a** the people who were in the	Jos 8:16	3605
When Joshua and **a** Israel saw that	Jos 8:21	3605
finished killing **a** the inhabitants of Ai	Jos 8:24	3605
and **a** of them were fallen by the	Jos 8:24	3605
then **a** Israel returned to Ai and	Jos 8:24	3605
A who fell that day, both men	Jos 8:25	3605
were 12,000—**a** the people of Ai.	Jos 8:25	3605
destroyed **a** the inhabitants of Ai.	Jos 8:26	3605
A Israel with their elders	Jos 8:33	3605
he read **a** the words of the law,	Jos 8:34	3605
according to **a** that is written in	Jos 8:34	3605
There was not a word of **a** that	Jos 8:35	3605
which Joshua did not read before **a**	Jos 8:35	3605
Now it came about when **a** the kings	Jos 9:1	3605
and on **a** the coast of the Great Sea	Jos 9:1	3605
and **a** the bread of their provision	Jos 9:5	3605
of Him and **a** that He did in Egypt,	Jos 9:9	3605
and **a** that He did to the two kings	Jos 9:10	3605
"So our elders and **a** the	Jos 9:11	3605
But **a** the leaders said to the	Jos 9:19	3605
Moses to give you **a** the land,	Jos 9:24	3605
and to destroy **a** the inhabitants	Jos 9:24	3605
Ai, and **a** its men *were* mighty.	Jos 10:2	3605
went up, they with **a** their armies,	Jos 10:5	3605
for **a** the kings of the Amorites	Jos 10:6	3605
he and **a** the people of war with	Jos 10:7	3605
him and **a** the valiant warriors.	Jos 10:7	3605
by marching **a** night from Gilgal.	Jos 10:9	3605
Then Joshua and **a** Israel with him	Jos 10:15	3605
that **a** the people returned to the	Jos 10:21	3605
called for **a** the men of Israel,	Jos 10:24	3605
for thus the LORD will do to **a**	Jos 10:25	3605
Then Joshua and **a** Israel with him	Jos 10:29	3605
And Joshua and **a** Israel with him	Jos 10:31	3605
to **a** that he had done to Libnah.	Jos 10:32	3605
And Joshua and **a** Israel with him	Jos 10:34	3605
to **a** that he had done to Lachish.	Jos 10:35	3605
Then Joshua and **a** Israel with him	Jos 10:36	3605
struck it and its king and **a** its cities	Jos 10:37	3605
and all its cities and **a** the persons	Jos 10:37	3605
to **a** that he had done to Eglon.	Jos 10:37	3605
Then Joshua and **a** Israel with him	Jos 10:38	3605
it and its king and **a** its cities,	Jos 10:39	3605
Thus Joshua struck **a** the land,	Jos 10:40	3605
and the slopes and **a** their kings.	Jos 10:40	3605
utterly destroyed **a** who breathed,	Jos 10:40	3605
and **a** the country of Goshen even	Jos 10:41	3605
Joshua captured **a** these kings	Jos 10:42	3605
So Joshua and **a** Israel with him	Jos 10:43	3605
they and **a** their armies with them,	Jos 11:4	3605
So **a** of these kings having agreed	Jos 11:5	3605

a of them slain before Israel;	Jos 11:6	3605
So Joshua and **a** the people of war	Jos 11:7	3605
was the head of **a** these kingdoms.	Jos 11:10	3605
a the cities of these kings,	Jos 11:12	3605
of these kings, and **a** their kings,	Jos 11:12	3605
A the spoil of these cities	Jos 11:14	3605
he left nothing undone of **a** that	Jos 11:15	3605
Thus Joshua took **a** that land:	Jos 11:16	3605
the hill country and **a** the Negev,	Jos 11:16	3605
the Negev, **a** that land of Goshen,	Jos 11:16	3605
And he captured **a** their kings and	Jos 11:17	3605
a long time with **a** these kings.	Jos 11:18	3605
they took them **a** in battle.	Jos 11:19	3605
from Anab and from **a** the hill	Jos 11:21	3605
from **a** the hill country of Israel.	Jos 11:21	3605
according to **a** that the LORD had	Jos 11:23	3605
and **a** the Arabah to the east:	Jos 12:1	3605
Hermon and Salecah and **a** Bashan,	Jos 12:5	3605
in **a**, thirty-one kings.	Jos 12:24	3605
a the regions *of* the Philistines	Jos 13:2	3605
and **a** *those of* the Geshurites;	Jos 13:2	3605
a the land of the Canaanite,	Jos 13:4	3605
of the Gebalite, and **a** of Lebanon,	Jos 13:5	3605
"**A** the inhabitants of the hill	Jos 13:6	3605
Misrephoth-maim, **a** the Sidonians,	Jos 13:6	3605
valley, and **a** the plain of Medeba,	Jos 13:9	3605
and **a** the cities of Sihon king of	Jos 13:10	3605
Maacathites, and **a** Mount Hermon,	Jos 13:11	3605
and **a** Bashan as far as Salecah;	Jos 13:11	3605
a the kingdom of Og in Bashan, who	Jos 13:12	3605
valley and **a** the plain by Medeba;	Jos 13:16	3605
and **a** its cities which are on the	Jos 13:17	3605
even **a** the cities of the plain and	Jos 13:21	3605
cities of the plain and **a** the kingdom	Jos 13:21	3605
Jazer, and **a** the cities of Gilead,	Jos 13:25	3605
was from Mahanaim, **a** Bashan,	Jos 13:30	3605
a the kingdom of Og king of Bashan,	Jos 13:30	3605
Bashan, and **a** the towns of Jair,	Jos 13:30	3605
in **a**, twenty-nine cities with	Jos 15:32	3605
a that were by the side of Ashdod,	Jos 15:46	3605
a the cities with their villages.	Jos 16:9	3605
and **a** the Canaanites who live in	Jos 17:16	3605
according to its borders **a** around.	Jos 18:20	5439
and **a** the villages which *were*	Jos 19:8	3605
the appointed cities for **a** the sons of	Jos 20:9	3605
A the cities of the sons of Aaron,	Jos 21:19	3605
A the cities with their pasture	Jos 21:26	3605
A the cities of the Gershonites	Jos 21:33	3605
four cities in **a**.	Jos 21:39	3605
A *these were* the cities of the	Jos 21:40	3605
A the cities of the Levites in the	Jos 21:41	3605
thus *it was* with **a** these cities.	Jos 21:42	3605
So the LORD gave Israel **a** the land	Jos 21:43	3605
according to **a** that He had sworn	Jos 21:44	3605
and no one of **a** their enemies	Jos 21:44	3605
a their enemies into their hand.	Jos 21:44	3605
house of Israel failed; **a** came to pass.	Jos 21:45	3605
"You have kept **a** that Moses the	Jos 22:2	3605
voice in **a** that I commanded you.	Jos 22:2	3605
your God and walk in **a** His ways	Jos 22:5	3605
a your heart and with all	Jos 22:5	3605
your heart and with **a** your soul."	Jos 22:5	3605
on **a** the congregation of Israel?	Jos 22:20	3605
a their enemies on every side,	Jos 23:1	3605
that Joshua called for **a** Israel,	Jos 23:2	3605
"And you have seen **a** that the	Jos 23:3	3605
to **a** these nations because of you,	Jos 23:3	3605
with **a** the nations which I have	Jos 23:4	3605
to keep and do **a** that is written	Jos 23:6	3605
I am going the way of **a** the earth,	Jos 23:14	3605
and you know in **a** your hearts and	Jos 23:14	3605
in all your hearts and in **a** your souls	Jos 23:14	3605
not one word of **a** the good words	Jos 23:14	3605
a have been fulfilled for you, not	Jos 23:14	3605
as **a** the good words which the LORD	Jos 23:15	3605
will bring upon you **a** the threats,	Jos 23:15	3605
Then Joshua gathered **a** the tribes	Jos 24:1	3605
Joshua said to **a** the people,	Jos 24:2	3605
him through **a** the land of Canaan,	Jos 24:3	3605
and preserved us through **a** the way	Jos 24:17	3605
among **a** the peoples through whose	Jos 24:17	3605
out from before us **a** the peoples,	Jos 24:18	3605
Joshua said to **a** the people,	Jos 24:27	3605
for it has heard **a** the words of	Jos 24:27	3605
Israel served the LORD **a** the	Jos 24:31	3605
of Joshua and **a** the days of the elders	Jos 24:31	3605
and had known **a** the deeds of the	Jos 24:31	3605
the man and **a** his family go free.	Jg 1:25	3605
words to **a** the sons of Israel,	Jg 2:4	3605
the LORD **a** the days of Joshua,	Jg 2:7	3605
and **a** the days of the elders who	Jg 2:7	3605
who had seen **a** the great work of	Jg 2:7	3605
A that generation also were gathered	Jg 2:10	3605
enemies **a** the days of the judge;	Jg 2:18	3605
a who had not experienced any of	Jg 3:1	3605
the Philistines and **a** the Canaanites	Jg 3:3	3605
And **a** who attended him left him.	Jg 3:19	3605
a robust and valiant men;	Jg 3:29	3605
called together **a** his chariots,	Jg 4:13	3605
a the people who *were* with him,	Jg 4:13	3605
a *his* chariots and all *his* army with	Jg 4:15	3605
all *his* chariots and **a** *his* army with	Jg 4:15	3605
and **a** the army of Sisera fell by	Jg 4:16	3605
"Thus let **a** Your enemies perish,	Jg 5:31	3605
the hands of **a** your oppressors,	Jg 6:9	3605
then has **a** this happened to us?	Jg 6:13	3605
And where are **a** His miracles which	Jg 6:13	3605
said to **a** who stood against him,	Jg 6:31	3605
Then **a** the Midianites and the	Jg 6:33	3605

and it is dry on **a** the ground, Jg 6:37 3605
there be dew on **a** the ground." Jg 6:39 3605
and dew was on **a** the ground. Jg 6:40 3605
a the people who were with him, Jg 7:1 3605
but **a** the rest of the people Jg 7:6 3605
so let **a** the *other* people go, each Jg 7:7 3605
sent **a** the *other* men of Israel, Jg 7:8 3605
Amalekites and **a** the sons of the east Jg 7:12 3605
and **a** the camp into his hand." Jg 7:14 3605
into the hands of **a** of them, Jg 7:16 3605
"When I and **a** who are with me Jg 7:18 3605
the trumpets **a** around the camp and Jg 7:18 3605
and **a** the army ran, crying out as Jg 7:21 3605
Naphtali and Asher and **a** Manasseh, Jg 7:23 3605
a the hill country of Ephraim, Jg 7:24 3605
So **a** the men of Ephraim were Jg 7:24 3605
"**A** right, when the LORD has given Jg 8:7 3605
a who were left of the entire army Jg 8:10 3605
and **a** Israel played the harlot Jg 8:27 3605
of **a** their enemies on every side; Jg 8:34 3605
in accord with **a** the good that he Jg 8:35 3605
of **a** the leaders of Shechem, Jg 9:2 3605
men, **a** the sons of Jerubbaal, Jg 9:2 3605
And his mother's relatives spoke **a** Jg 9:3 3605
of **a** the leaders of Shechem; Jg 9:3 3605
A the men of Shechem and all Jg 9:6 3605
a Beth-millo assembled together, Jg 9:6 3605
a the trees said to the bramble, Jg 9:14 3605
and they robbed **a** who might pass Jg 9:25 3605
So Abimelech and **a** the people who Jg 9:34 3605
dashed against **a** who *were* in the field Jg 9:44 3605
against the city **a** that day, Jg 9:45 3605
When **a** the leaders of the tower of Jg 9:46 3605
It was told Abimelech that **a** Jg 9:47 3605
a the people who *were* with him; Jg 9:48 3605
A the people also cut down each one Jg 9:49 3605
so that **a** the men of the tower of Jg 9:49 3605
and **a** the men and women with all Jg 9:51 3605
and all the men and women with **a** Jg 9:51 3605
Also God returned **a** the wickedness Jg 9:57 3605
years they *afflicted* **a** the sons of Israel Jg 10:8 3605
a the inhabitants of Gilead. Jg 10:18 3605
a the inhabitants of Gilead." Jg 11:8 3605
and Jephthah spoke **a** his words Jg 11:11 3605
so Sihon gathered **a** his people and Jg 11:20 3605
gave Sihon and **a** his people into Jg 11:21 3605
a the land of the Amorites, Jg 11:21 3605
a the territory of the Amorites, Jg 11:22 3605
and in **a** the cities that are on Jg 11:26 3605
Then Jephthah gathered **a** the men Jg 12:4 3605
pay attention to **a** that I said. Jg 13:13 3605
her observe **a** that I commanded." Jg 13:14 3605
He have shown us **a** these things, Jg 13:23 3605
relatives, or among **a** our people, Jg 14:3 3605
a night at the gate of the city. Jg 16:2 3605
And they kept silent **a** night, Jg 16:2 3605
So he told her **a** *that was* in his Jg 16:17 3605
told her **a** *that was* in his heart, Jg 16:18 3605
told me **a** *that is* in his heart." Jg 16:18 3605
and **a** the lords of the Philistines Jg 16:27 3605
And he bent with **a** his might so Jg 16:30 3605
and **a** the people who were in it. Jg 16:30 3605
Then his brothers and **a** his Jg 16:31 3605
a the time that the house of God Jg 18:31 3605
let me *take care of* **a** your needs; Jg 19:20 3605
abused her **a** night until morning, Jg 19:25 3605
A who saw *it* said, "Nothing Jg 19:30 3605
Then **a** the sons of Israel from Dan Jg 20:1 3605
The chiefs of **a** the people, Jg 20:2 3605
even of **a** the tribes of Israel, Jg 20:2 3605
"Behold, **a** you sons of Israel, Jg 20:7 3605
a the people arose as one man, Jg 20:8 3605
they may punish *them* for **a** the Jg 20:10 3605
Thus **a** the men of Israel were Jg 20:11 3605
Out of **a** these people 700 choice Jg 20:16 3605
a these were men of war. Jg 20:17 3605
a these drew the sword. Jg 20:25 3605
Then **a** the sons of Israel and all Jg 20:26 3605
Then all the sons of Israel and **a** Jg 20:26 3605
Then **a** the men of Israel arose Jg 20:33 3605
from **a** Israel came against Gibeah, Jg 20:34 3605
that day, **a** who draw the sword. Jg 20:35 3605
also deployed and struck **a** the city Jg 20:37 3605
a these were valiant warriors. Jg 20:44 3605
So **a** of Benjamin who fell that day Jg 20:46 3605
a these were valiant warriors. Jg 20:46 3605
the cattle and **a** that they found; Jg 20:48 3605
a the cities which they found. Jg 20:48 3605
"Who is there among **a** the tribes Jg 21:5 3605
a the city was stirred Ru 1:19 3605
"**A** that you have done for your Ru 2:11 3605
have finished **a** my harvest.'" Ru 2:21 3605
"**A** that you say I will do." Ru 3:5 3605
according to **a** that her mother-in-law Ru 3:6 3605
for **a** my people in the city know Ru 3:11 3605
a that the man had done for her. Ru 3:16 3605
to the elders and **a** the people, Ru 4:9 3605
bought from the hand of Naomi **a** Ru 4:9 3605
to Elimelech and **a** that belonged to Ru 4:9 3605
A the people who were in the court, Ru 4:11 3605
to **a** her sons and her daughters; 1Sa 1:4 3605
the LORD **a** the days of his life, 1Sa 1:11 3605
Elkanah went up with **a** his household 1Sa 1:21 3605
a that the fork brought up the 1Sa 2:14 3605
a the Israelites who came there. 1Sa 2:14 3605
and he heard **a** that his sons were 1Sa 2:22 3605
his sons were doing to **a** Israel, 1Sa 2:22 3605
that I hear from **a** these people? 1Sa 2:23 3605
'Did I *not* choose them from **a** 1Sa 2:28 3605
house of your father **a** the fire *offerings* 1Sa 2:28 3605
of **a** the good that I do for Israel; 1Sa 2:32 3605
and **a** the increase of your house 1Sa 2:33 3605
out against Eli **a** that I have spoken 1Sa 3:12 3605
hide anything from me of **a** the words 1Sa 3:17 3605
A Israel from Dan even to Beersheba 1Sa 3:20 3605
word of Samuel came to **a** Israel. 1Sa 4:1 3605
a Israel shouted with a great 1Sa 4:5 3605
the Egyptians with **a** *kinds of* plagues 1Sa 4:8 3605
city, and **a** the city cried out. 1Sa 4:13 3605
the priests of Dagon nor **a** who enter 1Sa 5:5 3605
So they sent and gathered **a** the 1Sa 5:8 3605
gathered **a** the lords of the Philistines 1Sa 5:11 3605
was on **a** of you and on your lords. 1Sa 6:4 3605
according to the number of **a** the 1Sa 6:18 3605
He struck down of **a** the people, 1Sa 6:19 3605
and **a** the house of Israel lamented 1Sa 7:2 3605
spoke to **a** the house of Israel, 1Sa 7:3 3605
to the LORD with **a** your heart, 1Sa 7:3 3605
"Gather **a** Israel to Mizpah and I 1Sa 7:5 3605
Philistines **a** the days of Samuel. 1Sa 7:13 3605
Israel **a** the days of his life. 1Sa 7:15 3605
judged Israel in **a** these places. 1Sa 7:16 3605
Then **a** the elders of Israel 1Sa 8:4 3605
to judge us like **a** the nations." 1Sa 8:5 3605
regard to **a** that they say to you, 1Sa 8:7 3605
"Like **a** the deeds which they have 1Sa 8:8 3605
So Samuel spoke **a** the words of the 1Sa 8:10 3605
we also may be like **a** the nations, 1Sa 8:20 3605
heard **a** the words of the people, 1Sa 8:21 3605
a that he says surely comes true. 1Sa 9:6 3605
tell you **a** that is on your mind. 1Sa 9:19 3605
is **a** that is desirable in Israel? 1Sa 9:20 3605
for **a** your father's household?" 1Sa 9:20 3605
and my family the least of **a** the 1Sa 9:21 3605
and **a** those signs came about on 1Sa 10:9 3605
when **a** who knew him previously saw 1Sa 10:11 3605
and from the power of **a** the 1Sa 10:18 3605
who delivers you from **a** your 1Sa 10:19 3605
a the tribes of Israel near, 1Sa 10:20 3605
Samuel said to **a** the people, 1Sa 10:24 3605
one like him among **a** the people." 1Sa 10:24 3605
So **a** the people shouted and said, 1Sa 10:24 3605
And Samuel sent **a** the people away, 1Sa 10:25 3605
and **a** the men of Jabesh said to 1Sa 11:1 3605
make it a reproach on **a** Israel." 1Sa 11:2 3605
and **a** the people lifted up their 1Sa 11:4 3605
So **a** the people went to Gilgal, 1Sa 11:15 3605
and there Saul and **a** the men of 1Sa 11:15 3605
Then Samuel said to **a** Israel, 1Sa 12:1 3605
voice in **a** that you said to me and 1Sa 12:1 3605
LORD concerning **a** the righteous acts 1Sa 12:7 3605
hands of your enemies **a** around, 1Sa 12:11
4480, 5439
and **a** the people greatly feared 1Sa 12:18 3605
Then **a** the people said to Samuel, 1Sa 12:19 3605
for we have added to **a** our sins 1Sa 12:19 3605
You have committed **a** this evil, 1Sa 12:20 3605
serve the LORD with **a** your heart. 1Sa 12:20 3605
Him in truth with **a** your heart; 1Sa 12:24 3605
A Israel heard the news that Saul had 1Sa 13:4 3605
and **a** the people followed him 1Sa 13:7 3605
be found in **a** the land of Israel, 1Sa 13:19 3605
So **a** Israel went down to the 1Sa 13:20 3605
"Do **a** that is in your heart; 1Sa 14:7 3605
the field, and among **a** the people. 1Sa 14:15 3605
Then Saul and **a** the people who 1Sa 14:20 3605
up with them **a** around in the camp, 1Sa 14:21 5439
When **a** the men of Israel who had 1Sa 14:22 3605
A *the people of* the land entered 1Sa 14:25 3605
So **a** the people that night brought 1Sa 14:34 3605
here, **a** you chiefs of the people, 1Sa 14:38 3605
one of **a** the people answered him. 1Sa 14:39 3605
Then he said to **a** Israel, 1Sa 14:40 3605
a his enemies on every side, 1Sa 14:47 3605
was severe **a** the days of Saul; 1Sa 14:52 3605
and utterly destroy **a** that he has, 1Sa 15:3 3605
for you showed kindness to **a** the sons 1Sa 15:6 3605
and utterly destroyed **a** the people 1Sa 15:8 3605
the lambs, and **a** that was good, 1Sa 15:9 3605
and cried out to the LORD **a** night. 1Sa 15:11 3605
"Are these **a** the children?" 1Sa 16:11 8552
When Saul and **a** Israel heard these 1Sa 17:11 3605
"For Saul and they and **a** the men 1Sa 17:19 3605
a the men of Israel saw the man, 1Sa 17:24 3605
that **a** the earth may know that 1Sa 17:46 3605
and that **a** this assembly may know 1Sa 17:47 3605
pleasing in the sight of **a** the people 1Sa 18:5 3605
out of **a** the cities of Israel, 1Sa 18:6 3605
David was prospering in **a** his 1Sa 18:14 3605
a Israel and Judah loved David, 1Sa 18:16 3605
you, and **a** his servants love you; 1Sa 18:22 3605
than **a** the servants of Saul. 1Sa 18:30 3605
Jonathan his son and **a** his servants 1Sa 19:1 3605
a great deliverance for **a** Israel; 1Sa 19:5 3605
Jonathan told him **a** these words. 1Sa 19:7 3605
him **a** that Saul had done to him. 1Sa 19:18 3605
a that day and all that night. 1Sa 19:24 3605
all that day and **a** that night. 1Sa 19:24 3605
"If your father misses me at **a**, 1Sa 20:6 6485
and when his brothers and **a** his 1Sa 22:1 3605
and they stayed with him **a** the time 1Sa 22:4 3605
and **a** his servants were standing 1Sa 22:6 3605
to **a** of you fields and vineyards? 1Sa 22:7 3605
Will he make you **a** commanders of 1Sa 22:7 3605
"For **a** of you have conspired 1Sa 22:8 3605
and **a** his father's household, 1Sa 22:11 3605
and **a** of them came to the king. 1Sa 22:11 3605
"And who among **a** your servants is 1Sa 22:14 3605
servant knows nothing at **a** of this 1Sa 22:15
6996b, 1419
and **a** your father's household!" 1Sa 22:16 3605
summoned **a** the people for war, 1Sa 23:8 3605
come down according to **a** the 1Sa 23:20 3605
and learn about **a** the hiding 1Sa 23:23 3605
among **a** the thousands of Judah." 1Sa 23:23 3605
thousand chosen men from **a** Israel and 1Sa 24:2 3605
and **a** Israel gathered together and 1Sa 25:1 3605
and peace be to **a** that you have. 1Sa 25:6 3605
a the days they were in Carmel. 1Sa 25:7 3605
to **a** these words in David's name; 1Sa 25:9 3605
him according to **a** these words. 1Sa 25:12 3605
a the time we were with them 1Sa 25:16 3605
and against **a** his household; 1Sa 25:17 3605
"Surely in vain I have guarded **a** 1Sa 25:21 3605
missed of **a** that belonged to him; 1Sa 25:21 3605
not be found in you **a** your days. 1Sa 25:28 4480
according to **a** the good that He has 1Sa 25:30 3605
at **a** until the morning light. 1Sa 25:36
6996b, 1419
any awake, for they were **a** asleep, 1Sa 26:12 3605
a of you must surely die, 1Sa 26:16 3605
He deliver me from **a** distress." 1Sa 26:24 3605
in **a** the territory of Israel, 1Sa 27:1 3605
so *has been* his practice **a** the time 1Sa 27:11 3605
and **a** Israel had lamented him and 1Sa 28:3 3605
and Saul gathered **a** Israel 1Sa 28:4 3605
eaten no food **a** day and all night. 1Sa 28:20 3605
eaten no food all day and **a** night. 1Sa 28:20 3605
together **a** their armies to Aphek, 1Sa 29:1 3605
they took captive the women *and* **a** 1Sa 30:2 3605
for **a** the people were embittered, 1Sa 30:6 3605
and you will surely rescue **a**." 1Sa 30:8 3605
they were spread over **a** the land, 1Sa 30:16 3605
dancing because of **a** the great spoil 1Sa 30:16 3605
a that the Amalekites had taken, 1Sa 30:18 3605
David brought *it* **a** back. 1Sa 30:19 3605
So David had captured **a** the sheep 1Sa 30:20 3605
Then **a** the wicked and worthless 1Sa 30:22 3605
and to **a** the places where David 1Sa 30:31 3605
a his men on that day together. 1Sa 31:6 3605
a the valiant men rose and walked 1Sa 31:12 3605
men rose and walked **a** night, 1Sa 31:12 3605
did **a** the men who *were* with him. 2Sa 1:11 3605
over Benjamin, even over **a** Israel. 2Sa 2:9 3605
And it came about that **a** who came 2Sa 2:23 3605
and **a** the people halted and 2Sa 2:28 3605
through the Arabah **a** that night; 2Sa 2:29 3605
the Jordan, walked **a** morning, 2Sa 2:29 3605
gathered **a** the people together, 2Sa 2:30 3605
Then Joab and his men went **a** night 2Sa 2:32 3605
to bring **a** Israel over to you." 2Sa 3:12 3605
the hand of **a** their enemies.'" 2Sa 3:18 3605
David in Hebron **a** that seemed good 2Sa 3:19 3605
and gather **a** Israel to my lord the 2Sa 3:21 3605
over **a** that your soul desires." 2Sa 3:21 3605
When Joab and **a** the army that was 2Sa 3:23 3605
find out **a** that you are doing." 2Sa 3:25 3605
Joab and on **a** his father's house; 2Sa 3:29 3605
to **a** the people who were with him, 2Sa 3:31 3605
of Abner, and **a** the people wept. 2Sa 3:32 3605
And **a** the people wept again over 2Sa 3:34 3605
Then **a** the people came to persuade 2Sa 3:35 3605
Now **a** the people took note *of it,* 2Sa 3:36 3605
the king did pleased **a** the people. 2Sa 3:36 3605
So **a** the people and all Israel 2Sa 3:37 3605
So all the people and **a** Israel 2Sa 3:37 3605
and **a** Israel was disturbed. 2Sa 4:1 3605
by way of the Arabah **a** night. 2Sa 4:7 3605
redeemed my life from **a** distress, 2Sa 4:9 3605
Then **a** the tribes of Israel came 2Sa 5:1 3605
So **a** the elders of Israel came to 2Sa 5:3 3605
years over **a** Israel and Judah. 2Sa 5:5 3605
And David built **a** around from the 2Sa 5:9 5439
a the Philistines went up to seek 2Sa 5:17 3605
a the chosen men of Israel, 2Sa 6:1 3605
And David arose and went with **a** 2Sa 6:2 3605
David and **a** the house of Israel 2Sa 6:5 3605
celebrating before the LORD with **a** 2Sa 6:5 3605
Obed-edom and **a** his household. 2Sa 6:11 3605
and **a** that belongs to him, 2Sa 6:12 3605
before the LORD with **a** *his* might, 2Sa 6:14 3605
So David and **a** the house of Israel 2Sa 6:15 3605
he distributed to **a** the people, 2Sa 6:19 3605
to **a** the multitude of Israel, 2Sa 6:19 3605
Then **a** the people departed each to 2Sa 6:19 3605
your father and above **a** his house, 2Sa 6:21 3605
on every side from **a** his enemies, 2Sa 7:1 3605
"Go, do **a** that is in your mind, 2Sa 7:3 3605
gone with **a** the sons of Israel, 2Sa 7:7 3605
a your enemies from before you; 2Sa 7:9 3605
give you rest from **a** your enemies. 2Sa 7:11 3605
In accordance with **a** these words 2Sa 7:17 3605
all these words and **a** this vision, 2Sa 7:17 3605
You have done **a** this greatness to 2Sa 7:21 3605
according to **a** that we have heard 2Sa 7:22 3605
defeated **a** the army of Hadadezer, 2Sa 8:9 3605
gold that he had dedicated from **a** 2Sa 8:11 3605
In **a** Edom he put garrisons, and 2Sa 8:14 3605
and **a** the Edomites became servants 2Sa 8:14 3605
So David reigned over **a** Israel; 2Sa 8:15 3605
righteousness for **a** his people. 2Sa 8:15 3605
and will restore to you **a** the land 2Sa 9:7 3605
"**A** that belonged to Saul and to 2Sa 9:9 3605
belonged to Saul and to **a** his house 2Sa 9:9 3605
"According to **a** that my lord the 2Sa 9:11 3605
And **a** who lived in the house of 2Sa 9:12 3605
it, he sent Joab and **a** the army, 2Sa 10:7 3605

from **a** the choice men of Israel, 2Sa 10:9 3605
he gathered **a** Israel together and 2Sa 10:17 3605
When **a** the kings, servants of 2Sa 10:19 3605
servants with him and **a** Israel, 2Sa 11:1 3605
with **a** the servants of his lord, 2Sa 11:9 3605
to David **a** the events of the war. 2Sa 11:18 3605
"When you have finished telling **a** 2Sa 11:19 3605
reported to David **a** that Joab had 2Sa 11:22 3605
do this thing before **a** Israel, 2Sa 12:12 3605
and lay **a** night on the ground. 2Sa 12:16 3605
a the people and went to Rabbah, 2Sa 12:29 3605
And thus he did to **a** the cities of 2Sa 12:31 3605
Then David and **a** the people 2Sa 12:31 3605
David heard of **a** these matters, 2Sa 13:21 3605
Absalom invited **a** the king's sons. 2Sa 13:23 3605
"No, my son, we should not **a** go, 2Sa 13:25 3605
and **a** the king's sons go with him. 2Sa 13:27 3605
Then **a** the king's sons arose and 2Sa 13:29 3605
has struck down **a** the king's sons, 2Sa 13:30 3605
and **a** his servants were standing 2Sa 13:31 3605
have put to death **a** the young men, 2Sa 13:32 3605
'**a** the king's sons are dead,' for 2Sa 13:33 3605
and also the king and **a** his 2Sa 13:36 3605
hand of Joab with you in **a** this?" 2Sa 14:19 3605
and it was he who put **a** these 2Sa 14:19 3605
to know **a** that is in the earth." 2Sa 14:20 3605
Now in **a** Israel was no one as 2Sa 14:25 3605
Absalom dealt with **a** Israel who came 2Sa 15:6 3605
throughout **a** the tribes of Israel, 2Sa 15:10 3605
David said to **a** his servants 2Sa 15:14 3605
out and **a** his household with him. 2Sa 15:16 3605
out and **a** the people with him, 2Sa 15:17 3605
Now **a** his servants passed on 2Sa 15:18 3605
on beside him, **a** the Cherethites, 2Sa 15:18 3605
the Cherethites, **a** the Pelethites and 2Sa 15:18 3605
Pelethites and **a** the Gittites, 2Sa 15:18 3605
Ittai the Gittite passed over with **a** 2Sa 15:22 3605
with all his men and **a** the little ones 2Sa 15:22 3605
While **a** the country was weeping 2Sa 15:23 3605
voice, **a** the people passed over. 2Sa 15:23 3605
and **a** the people passed over 2Sa 15:23 3605
and **a** the Levites with him 2Sa 15:24 3605
and Abiathar came up until **a** the 2Sa 15:24 3605
Then **a** the people who were with 2Sa 15:30 3605
a that belongs to Mephibosheth is 2Sa 16:4 3605
at **a** the servants of King David; 2Sa 16:6 3605
and **a** the people and all the 2Sa 16:6 3605
and all the people and **a** the 2Sa 16:6 3605
"The LORD has returned upon you **a** 2Sa 16:8 3605
to Abishai and to **a** his servants, 2Sa 16:11 3605
The king and **a** the people who 2Sa 16:14 3605
Then Absalom and **a** the people, 2Sa 16:15 3605
a the men of Israel have chosen, 2Sa 16:18 3605
then **a** Israel will hear that you 2Sa 16:21 3605
The hands of **a** who are with you 2Sa 16:21 3605
in the sight of **a** Israel. 2Sa 16:22 3605
so was **a** the advice of Ahithophel 2Sa 16:23 3605
terrify him, so that **a** the people 2Sa 17:2 3605
bring back **a** the people to you. 2Sa 17:3 3605
a the people will be at peace." 2Sa 17:3 3605
and **a** the elders of Israel. 2Sa 17:4 3605
for **a** Israel knows that your 2Sa 17:10 3605
"But I counsel that **a** Israel be 2Sa 17:11 3605
and of **a** the men who are with him, 2Sa 17:12 3605
then **a** Israel shall bring ropes to 2Sa 17:13 3605
and **a** the men of Israel said, 2Sa 17:14 3605
but by **a** means cross over, 2Sa 17:16
1571, 5674
else the king and **a** the people who 2Sa 17:16 3605
Then David and **a** the people who 2Sa 17:22 3605
and **a** the men of Israel with him. 2Sa 17:24 3605
and **a** the people went out by 2Sa 18:4 3605
And **a** the people heard when the 2Sa 18:5 3605
the king charged **a** the commanders 2Sa 18:5 3605
And **a** Israel fled, each to his 2Sa 18:17 3605
and said to the king, "**A** is well." 2Sa 18:28 3605
a those who rose up against you." 2Sa 18:31 3605
and **a** who rise up against you for 2Sa 18:32 3605
to mourning for **a** the people, 2Sa 19:2 3605
the faces of **a** your servants, 2Sa 19:5 3605
alive and **a** of us were dead today, 2Sa 19:6 3605
will be worse for you than **a** the evil 2Sa 19:7 3605
When they told **a** the people, 2Sa 19:8 3605
then **a** the people came before the 2Sa 19:8 3605
A the people were quarreling 2Sa 19:9 3605
throughout **a** the tribes of Israel, 2Sa 19:9 3605
of **a** Israel has come to the king, 2Sa 19:11 3605
of **a** the men of Judah as one man, 2Sa 19:14 3605
"Return, you and **a** your servants." 2Sa 19:14 3605
the first of **a** the house of Joseph 2Sa 19:20 3605
"For **a** my father's household was 2Sa 19:28 3605
"Let him even take it **a**, 2Sa 19:30 3605
A the people crossed over the 2Sa 19:39 3605
and **a** the people of Judah and also 2Sa 19:40 3605
a the men of Israel came to the 2Sa 19:41 3605
his household and **a** David's men 2Sa 19:41 3605
Then **a** the men of Judah answered 2Sa 19:42 3605
eaten at **a** at the king's *expense,* 2Sa 19:42 398
So **a** the men of Israel withdrew 2Sa 20:2 3605
Pelethites and **a** the mighty men; 2Sa 20:7 3605
saw that **a** the people stood still, 2Sa 20:12 3605
a the men passed on after Joab to 2Sa 20:13 3605
Now he went through **a** the tribes 2Sa 20:14 3605
Beth-maacah, and **a** the Berites; 2Sa 20:14 3605
and **a** the people who were with 2Sa 20:15 3605
woman wisely came to **a** the people. 2Sa 20:22 3605
did **a** that the king commanded, 2Sa 21:14 3605
him from the hand of **a** his enemies 2Sa 22:1 3605
a His ordinances *were* before me, 2Sa 22:23 3605

to **a** who take refuge in Him. 2Sa 22:31 3605
with me, Ordered in **a** things, 2Sa 23:5 3605
For **a** my salvation and all *my* 2Sa 23:5 3605
all my salvation and **a** *my* desire, 2Sa 23:5 3605
thirty-seven in **a**. 2Sa 23:39 3605
through **a** the tribes of Israel, 2Sa 24:2 3605
the fortress of Tyre and to **a** the cities 2Sa 24:7 3605
a the territory of Israel, 1Ki 1:3 3605
and he invited **a** his brothers, the 1Ki 1:9 3605
sons, and **a** the men of Judah, 1Ki 1:9 3605
and has invited **a** the sons of the 1Ki 1:19 3605
the eyes of **a** Israel are on you, 1Ki 1:20 3605
and has invited **a** the king's sons 1Ki 1:25 3605
redeemed my life from **a** distress, 1Ki 1:29 3605
trumpet, and **a** the people said, 1Ki 1:39 3605
A the people went up after him, 1Ki 1:40 3605
Now Adonijah and **a** the guests who 1Ki 1:41 3605
Then **a** the guests of Adonijah were 1Ki 1:49 3605
"I am going the way of **a** the earth. 1Ki 2:2 3605
that you may succeed in **a** that you 1Ki 2:3 3605
to walk before Me in truth with **a** 1Ki 2:4 3605
their heart and with **a** their soul, 1Ki 2:4 3605
a Israel expected me to be king; 1Ki 2:15 3605
"You know **a** the evil which you 1Ki 2:44 3605
the kings like you **a** your days. 1Ki 3:13 3605
made a feast for **a** his servants. 1Ki 3:15 3605
When **a** Israel heard of the 1Ki 3:28 3605
Solomon was king over **a** Israel. 1Ki 4:1 3605
had twelve deputies over **a** Israel, 1Ki 4:7 3605
was his and **a** the land of Hepher); 1Ki 4:10 3605
in **a** the height of Dor 1Ki 4:11 3605
and **a** Beth-shean which is beside 1Ki 4:12 3605
Now Solomon ruled over **a** the 1Ki 4:21 3605
Solomon **a** the days of his life. 1Ki 4:21 3605
a the kings west of the River; 1Ki 4:24 3605
peace on **a** sides around about him. 1Ki 4:24 3605
Beersheba, **a** the days of Solomon. 1Ki 4:25 3605
provided for King Solomon and **a** 1Ki 4:27 3605
wisdom surpassed the wisdom of **a** 1Ki 4:30 3605
east and **a** the wisdom of Egypt. 1Ki 4:30 3605
For he was wiser than **a** men, 1Ki 4:31 3605
in **a** the surrounding nations. 1Ki 4:31 3605
Men came from **a** peoples to 1Ki 4:34 3605
from **a** the kings of the earth who 1Ki 4:34 3605
according to **a** that you say, 1Ki 5:6 3605
forced laborers from **a** Israel; 1Ki 5:13 3605
he made side chambers **a** around. 1Ki 6:5 5439
in the wall of the house **a** around 1Ki 6:6 5439
and keep **a** My commandments 1Ki 6:12 3605
a was cedar, there was no stone 1Ki 6:18 3605
until **a** the house was finished. 1Ki 6:22 3605
Then he carved **a** the walls of the 1Ki 6:29 3605
the house was finished throughout **a** 1Ki 6:38 3605
and according to **a** its plans. 1Ki 6:38 3605
and he finished **a** his house. 1Ki 7:1 3605
A the doorways and doorposts *had* 1Ki 7:5 3605
A these were of costly stones, of 1Ki 7:9 3605
So the great court **a** around *had* 1Ki 7:12 5439
Solomon and performed **a** his work. 1Ki 7:14 3605
and **a** their rear parts *turned* 1Ki 7:25 3605
and their hubs *were* **a** cast. 1Ki 7:33 3605
space on each, with wreaths **a** around. 1Ki 7:36 3605
a of them had one casting, one 1Ki 7:37 3605
So Hiram finished doing **a** the work 1Ki 7:40 3605
even **a** these utensils which Hiram 1Ki 7:45 3605
left **a** the utensils *unweighed,* 1Ki 7:47 3605
Solomon made **a** the furniture 1Ki 7:48 3605
Thus **a** the work that King Solomon 1Ki 7:51 3605
and **a** the heads of the tribes, 1Ki 8:1 3605
A the men of Israel assembled 1Ki 8:2 3605
Then **a** the elders of Israel came, 1Ki 8:3 3605
meeting and **a** the holy utensils, 1Ki 8:4 3605
and **a** the congregation of Israel, 1Ki 8:5 3605
blessed **a** the assembly of Israel, 1Ki 8:14 3605
while **a** the assembly of Israel was 1Ki 8:14 3605
I did not choose a city out of **a** 1Ki 8:16 3605
presence of **a** the assembly of Israel 1Ki 8:22 3605
before You with **a** their heart, 1Ki 8:23 3605
any man *or* by **a** Your people Israel, 1Ki 8:38 3605
to each according to **a** his ways, 1Ki 8:39 3605
the hearts of **a** the sons of men, 1Ki 8:39 3605
that they may fear You **a** the days 1Ki 8:40 3605
and do according to **a** for which 1Ki 8:43 3605
in order that **a** the peoples of the 1Ki 8:43 3605
if they return to You with **a** 1Ki 8:48 3605
all their heart and with **a** their soul 1Ki 8:48 3605
who have sinned against You and **a** 1Ki 8:50 3605
separated them from **a** the peoples 1Ki 8:53 3605
And he stood and blessed **a** the 1Ki 8:55 3605
according to **a** that He promised; 1Ki 8:56 3605
has failed of **a** His good promise, 1Ki 8:56 3605
to walk in **a** His ways and to keep 1Ki 8:58 3605
so that **a** the peoples of the earth 1Ki 8:60 3605
Now the king and **a** Israel with him 1Ki 8:62 3605
So the king and **a** the sons of 1Ki 8:63 3605
that time, and **a** Israel with him, 1Ki 8:65 3605
and glad of heart for **a** the goodness 1Ki 8:66 3605
and **a** that Solomon desired to do, 1Ki 9:1 3605
doing according to **a** that I have 1Ki 9:4 3605
and a byword among **a** peoples. 1Ki 9:7 3605
a this adversity on them.' " 1Ki 9:9 3605
gold according to **a** his desire), 1Ki 9:11 3605
and **a** the storage cities which 1Ki 9:19 3605
and **a** that it pleased Solomon to 1Ki 9:19 2837
and in **a** the land under his rule. 1Ki 9:19 3605
As for **a** the people who were left 1Ki 9:20 3605
him about **a** that was in her heart. 1Ki 10:2 3605
Solomon answered **a** her questions; 1Ki 10:3 3605
perceived **a** the wisdom of Solomon, 1Ki 10:4 3605

to the queen of Sheba **a** her desire 1Ki 10:13 3605
of the merchants and **a** the kings 1Ki 10:15 3605
A King Solomon's drinking vessels 1Ki 10:21 3605
and **a** the vessels of the house of 1Ki 10:21 3605
King Solomon became greater than **a** 1Ki 10:23 3605
A the earth was seeking the presence 1Ki 10:24 3605
they exported them to **a** the kings 1Ki 10:29 3605
he did for **a** his foreign wives, 1Ki 11:8 3605
will not tear away **a** the kingdom, 1Ki 11:13 3605
(for Joab and **a** Israel stayed 1Ki 11:16 3605
to Israel **a** the days of Solomon, 1Ki 11:25 3605
he appointed him over **a** the forced 1Ki 11:28 3605
from **a** the tribes of Israel), 1Ki 11:32 3605
him ruler **a** the days of his life, 1Ki 11:34 3605
that if you listen to **a** that I 1Ki 11:38 3605
over **a** Israel was forty years. 1Ki 11:42 3605
for **a** Israel had come to Shechem 1Ki 12:1 3605
and Jeroboam and **a** the assembly of 1Ki 12:3 3605
Then Jeroboam and **a** the people 1Ki 12:12 3605
When **a** Israel *saw* that the king 1Ki 12:16 3605
and **a** Israel stoned him to death. 1Ki 12:18 3605
It came about when **a** Israel 1Ki 12:20 3605
and made him king over **a** Israel. 1Ki 12:20 3605
he assembled **a** the house of Judah 1Ki 12:21 3605
and to **a** the house of Judah and 1Ki 12:23 3605
and made priests from among **a** the 1Ki 12:31 7098
and his sons came and told him **a** 1Ki 13:11 3605
against **a** the houses of the high places 1Ki 13:32 3605
places from among **a** the people; 1Ki 13:33 7098
who followed Me with **a** his heart, 1Ki 14:8 3605
evil than **a** who were before you, 1Ki 14:9 3605
away dung until it is **a** gone. 1Ki 14:10 8552
"**A** Israel shall mourn for him 1Ki 14:13 3605
A Israel buried him and mourned for 1Ki 14:18 3605
LORD had chosen from **a** the tribes 1Ki 14:21 3605
a that their fathers had done, 1Ki 14:22 3605
did according to **a** the abominations 1Ki 14:24 3605
even taking **a** the shields of gold 1Ki 14:26 3605
of Rehoboam and **a** that he did, 1Ki 14:29 3605
He walked in **a** the sins of his 1Ki 15:3 3605
him **a** the days of his life, 1Ki 15:5 3605
Jeroboam **a** the days of his life. 1Ki 15:6 3605
acts of Abijam and **a** that he did, 1Ki 15:7 3605
and removed **a** the idols which his 1Ki 15:12 3605
devoted to the LORD **a** his days. 1Ki 15:14 3605
king of Israel **a** their days. 1Ki 15:16 3605
Then Asa took **a** the silver and the 1Ki 15:18 3605
Abel-beth-maacah and **a** Chinneroth, 1Ki 15:20 3605
besides **a** the land of Naphtali. 1Ki 15:20 3605
Asa made a proclamation to **a** Judah 1Ki 15:22 3605
Now the rest of **a** the acts of Asa 1Ki 15:23 3605
all the acts of Asa and **a** his might 1Ki 15:23 3605
and all his might and **a** that he did 1Ki 15:23 3605
while Nadab and **a** Israel were 1Ki 15:27 3605
down **a** the household of Jeroboam. 1Ki 15:29 3605
acts of Nadab and **a** that he did, 1Ki 15:31 3605
king of Israel **a** their days. 1Ki 15:32 3605
king over **a** Israel at Tirzah, 1Ki 15:33 3605
both because of **a** the evil which 1Ki 16:7 3605
killed **a** the household of Baasha; 1Ki 16:11 3605
a the household of Baasha, 1Ki 16:12 3605
for **a** the sins of Baasha and the 1Ki 16:13 3605
acts of Elah and **a** that he did, 1Ki 16:14 3605
Therefore **a** Israel made Omri, the 1Ki 16:16 3605
Then Omri and **a** Israel with him 1Ki 16:17 3605
than **a** who *were* before him. 1Ki 16:25 3605
For he walked in **a** the way of 1Ki 16:26 3605
more than **a** who were before him. 1Ki 16:30 3605
LORD God of Israel than **a** the kings 1Ki 16:33 3605
"Go through the land to **a** the 1Ki 18:5 3605
of water and to **a** the valleys; 1Ki 18:5 3605
to me **a** Israel at Mount Carmel, 1Ki 18:19 3605
among **a** the sons of Israel and 1Ki 18:20 3605
near to **a** the people and said, 1Ki 18:21 3605
a the people said, 1Ki 18:24 3605
Then Elijah said to **a** the people, 1Ki 18:30 3605
So **a** the people came near to him. 1Ki 18:30 3605
done **a** these things at Your word. 1Ki 18:36 3605
When **a** the people saw it, they 1Ki 18:39 3605
Jezebel **a** that Elijah had done, 1Ki 19:1 3605
a the prophets with the sword. 1Ki 19:1 3605
a the knees that have not bowed to 1Ki 19:18 3605
king of Aram gathered **a** his army, 1Ki 20:1 3605
I am yours, and **a** that I have." 1Ki 20:4 3605
Then the king of Israel called **a** 1Ki 20:7 3605
A the elders and all the people said 1Ki 20:8 3605
and **a** the people said to him, 1Ki 20:8 3605
'**A** that you sent for to your 1Ki 20:9 3605
for **a** the people who follow me." 1Ki 20:10 3605
you seen **a** this great multitude? 1Ki 20:13 3605
them he mustered **a** the people, 1Ki 20:15 3605
people, *even* **a** the sons of Israel, 1Ki 20:15 3605
therefore I will give **a** this great 1Ki 20:28 3605
to **a** that the Amorites had done, 1Ki 21:26 3605
and **a** the prophets were 1Ki 22:10 3605
A the prophets were prophesying thus, 1Ki 22:12 3605
"I saw **a** Israel Scattered on the 1Ki 22:17 3605
and **a** the host of heaven standing 1Ki 22:19 3605
in the mouth of **a** his prophets.' 1Ki 22:22 3605
mouth of **a** these your prophets; 1Ki 22:23 3605
"Listen, **a** you people." 1Ki 22:28 3605
the acts of Ahab and **a** that he did 1Ki 22:39 3605
and **a** the cities which he built, 1Ki 22:39 3605
in **a** the way of Asa his father; 1Ki 22:43 3605
to **a** that his father had done. 1Ki 22:53 3605
that time and mustered **a** Israel. 2Ki 3:6 3605
tree and stop **a** springs of water, 2Ki 3:19 3605
Now **a** the Moabites heard that the 2Ki 3:21 3605
And **a** who were able to put on 2Ki 3:21 3605

So they stopped **a** the springs of	**2Ki 3:25**	3605
water and felled **a** the good trees,	**2Ki 3:25**	3605
yourself from **a** your neighbors,	**2Ki 4:3**	3605
and pour out into **a** these vessels,	**2Ki 4:4**	3605
careful for us with **a** this care;	**2Ki 4:13**	3605
than **a** the waters of Israel?	**2Ki 5:12**	3605
the man of God with **a** his company,	**2Ki 5:15**	3605
there is no God in **a** the earth,	**2Ki 5:15**	3605
to meet him and said, "Is **a** well?"	**2Ki 5:21**	
"**A** is well. My master has sent me,	**2Ki 5:22**	
chariots of fire **a** around Elisha.	**2Ki 6:17**	5439
Ben-hadad king of Aram gathered **a**	**2Ki 6:24**	3605
like **a** the multitude of Israel who are	**2Ki 7:13**	3605
like **a** the multitude of Israel who	**2Ki 7:13**	3605
a the way was full of clothes and	**2Ki 7:15**	3605
"Please relate to me **a** the great	**2Ki 8:4**	3605
"Restore **a** that was hers and all	**2Ki 8:6**	3605
"Restore all that was hers and **a**	**2Ki 8:6**	3605
Zair, and **a** his chariots with him.	**2Ki 8:21**	3605
acts of Joram and **a** that he did,	**2Ki 8:23**	3605
of **a** the servants of the LORD,	**2Ki 9:7**	3605
"Is **a** well? Why did this mad fellow	**2Ki 9:11**	
Now Joram with **a** Israel was	**2Ki 9:14**	3605
a that you say to us we will do,	**2Ki 10:5**	3605
stood and said to **a** the people,	**2Ki 10:9**	3605
him, but who killed **a** these?	**2Ki 10:9**	3605
So Jehu killed **a** who remained of	**2Ki 10:11**	3605
and **a** his great men and his	**2Ki 10:11**	3605
he killed **a** who remained to Ahab	**2Ki 10:17**	3605
a the people and said to them,	**2Ki 10:18**	3605
summon **a** the prophets of Baal,	**2Ki 10:19**	3605
a his worshipers and all his	**2Ki 10:19**	3605
his worshipers and **a** his priests;	**2Ki 10:19**	3605
and **a** the worshipers of Baal came,	**2Ki 10:21**	3605
for **a** the worshipers of Baal."	**2Ki 10:22**	3605
to **a** that *was* in My heart,	**2Ki 10:30**	3605
God of Israel, with **a** his heart;	**2Ki 10:31**	3605
eastward, **a** the land of Gilead,	**2Ki 10:33**	3605
a that he did and all his might,	**2Ki 10:34**	3605
all that he did and **a** his might,	**2Ki 10:34**	3605
destroyed **a** the royal offspring.	**2Ki 11:1**	3605
even **a** who go out on the sabbath,	**2Ki 11:7**	3605
did according to **a** that Jehoiada	**2Ki 11:9**	3605
and **a** the people of the land	**2Ki 11:14**	3605
A the people of the land went to	**2Ki 11:18**	3605
and **a** the people of the land;	**2Ki 11:19**	3605
So **a** the people of the land	**2Ki 11:20**	3605
did right in the sight of the LORD **a**	**2Ki 12:2**	3605
"**A** the money of the sacred things	**2Ki 12:4**	3605
man's assessment *and* **a** the money	**2Ki 12:4**	3605
put in it **a** the money which was	**2Ki 12:9**	3605
and for **a** that was laid out for	**2Ki 12:12**	3605
Jehoash king of Judah took **a**	**2Ki 12:18**	3605
and his own sacred things and **a**	**2Ki 12:18**	3605
acts of Joash and **a** that he did,	**2Ki 12:19**	3605
and **a** that he did and his might,	**2Ki 13:8**	3605
he did not turn away from **a** the	**2Ki 13:11**	3605
the acts of Joash and **a** that he did	**2Ki 13:12**	3605
Israel **a** the days of Jehoahaz.	**2Ki 13:22**	3605
he did according to **a** that Joash	**2Ki 14:3**	3605
He took **a** the gold and silver	**2Ki 14:14**	3605
the gold and silver and **a** the utensils	**2Ki 14:14**	3605
A the people of Judah took Azariah,	**2Ki 14:21**	3605
he did not depart from **a** the sins	**2Ki 14:24**	3605
and **a** that he did and his might,	**2Ki 14:28**	3605
according to **a** that his father	**2Ki 15:3**	3605
acts of Azariah and **a** that he did,	**2Ki 15:6**	3605
Then Menahem struck Tiphsah and **a**	**2Ki 15:16**	3605
a its women who were with child.	**2Ki 15:16**	3605
he did not depart **a** his days from	**2Ki 15:18**	3605
from **a** the mighty men of wealth,	**2Ki 15:20**	3605
acts of Menahem and **a** that he did,	**2Ki 15:21**	3605
of Pekahiah and **a** that he did,	**2Ki 15:26**	3605
Galilee, **a** the land of Naphtali;	**2Ki 15:29**	3605
acts of Pekah and **a** that he did,	**2Ki 15:31**	3605
he did according to **a** that his	**2Ki 15:34**	3605
acts of Jotham and **a** that he did,	**2Ki 15:36**	3605
according to **a** its workmanship.	**2Ki 16:10**	3605
according to **a** that King Ahaz had	**2Ki 16:11**	3605
with the burnt offering of **a** the	**2Ki 16:15**	3605
and sprinkle on it **a** the blood of	**2Ki 16:15**	3605
and **a** the blood of the sacrifice.	**2Ki 16:15**	3605
to **a** that King Ahaz commanded.	**2Ki 16:16**	3605
high places in **a** their towns,	**2Ki 17:9**	3605
burned incense on **a** the high places	**2Ki 17:11**	3605
a His prophets *and* every seer,	**2Ki 17:13**	3605
My statutes according to **a** the law	**2Ki 17:13**	3605
They forsook **a** the	**2Ki 17:16**	3605
and worshiped **a** the host of heaven	**2Ki 17:16**	3605
The LORD rejected **a** the	**2Ki 17:20**	3605
walked in **a** the sins of Jeroboam	**2Ki 17:22**	3605
a His servants the prophets.	**2Ki 17:23**	3605
from the hand of **a** your enemies."	**2Ki 17:39**	3605
according to **a** that his father	**2Ki 18:3**	3605
him among **a** the kings of Judah,	**2Ki 18:5**	3605
even **a** that Moses the servant of	**2Ki 18:12**	3605
king of Assyria came up against **a**	**2Ki 18:13**	3605
Hezekiah gave *him* **a** the silver	**2Ki 18:15**	3605
of Egypt to **a** who rely on him.	**2Ki 18:21**	3605
'Who among **a** the gods of the lands	**2Ki 18:35**	3605
hear **a** the words of Rabshakeh,	**2Ki 19:4**	3605
Assyria have done to **a** the lands,	**2Ki 19:11**	3605
of **a** the kingdoms of the earth.	**2Ki 19:15**	3605
deliver us from his hand that **a**	**2Ki 19:19**	3605
dried up **A** the rivers of Egypt."	**2Ki 19:24**	3605
behold, **a** of them were dead.	**2Ki 19:35**	3605
showed them **a** his treasure house,	**2Ki 20:13**	3605
and **a** that was found in his treasuries.	**2Ki 20:13**	3605
his house nor in **a** his dominion	**2Ki 20:13**	3605

have seen **a** that is in my house;	**2Ki 20:15**	3605
when **a** that is in your house,	**2Ki 20:17**	3605
and **a** that your fathers have laid	**2Ki 20:17**	
acts of Hezekiah and **a** his might,	**2Ki 20:20**	3605
and worshiped **a** the host of heaven	**2Ki 21:3**	3605
For he built altars for **a** the host	**2Ki 21:5**	3605
from **a** the tribes of Israel,	**2Ki 21:7**	3605
to **a** that I have commanded them,	**2Ki 21:8**	3605
and according to **a** the law that My	**2Ki 21:8**	3605
having done wickedly more than **a**	**2Ki 21:11**	3605
and spoil to **a** their enemies;	**2Ki 21:14**	3605
acts of Manasseh and **a** that he did	**2Ki 21:17**	3605
For he walked in **a** the way that	**2Ki 21:21**	3605
killed **a** those who had conspired	**2Ki 21:24**	3605
in **a** the way of his father David,	**2Ki 22:2**	3605
for me and the people and **a** Judah	**2Ki 22:13**	3605
a that is written concerning us."	**2Ki 22:13**	3605
even **a** the words of the book which	**2Ki 22:16**	3605
with **a** the work of their hands,	**2Ki 22:17**	3605
and your eyes will not see **a** the	**2Ki 22:20**	3605
and they gathered to him **a** the	**2Ki 23:1**	3605
up to the house of the LORD and **a**	**2Ki 23:2**	3605
and **a** the inhabitants of Jerusalem	**2Ki 23:2**	3605
and the prophets and **a** the people,	**2Ki 23:2**	3605
and he read in their hearing **a** the	**2Ki 23:2**	3605
with **a** *his* heart and all *his* soul,	**2Ki 23:3**	3605
with all *his* heart and **a** *his* soul,	**2Ki 23:3**	3605
And **a** the people entered into the	**2Ki 23:3**	3605
the temple of the LORD **a** the vessels	**2Ki 23:4**	3605
and for **a** the host of heaven;	**2Ki 23:4**	3605
and to **a** the host of heaven.	**2Ki 23:5**	3605
Then he brought **a** the priests from	**2Ki 23:8**	3605
Josiah also removed **a** the houses	**2Ki 23:19**	3605
A the priests of the high places who	**2Ki 23:20**	3605
commanded **a** the people saying,	**2Ki 23:21**	3605
nor in **a** the days of the kings of	**2Ki 23:22**	3605
and the idols and **a** the abominations	**2Ki 23:24**	3605
turned to the LORD with **a** his heart	**2Ki 23:25**	3605
with **a** his soul and with all his might,	**2Ki 23:25**	3605
all his soul and with **a** his might,	**2Ki 23:25**	3605
according to **a** the law of Moses;	**2Ki 23:25**	3605
because of **a** the provocations with	**2Ki 23:26**	3605
acts of Josiah and **a** that he did,	**2Ki 23:28**	3605
to **a** that his fathers had done.	**2Ki 23:32**	3605
to **a** that his fathers had done.	**2Ki 23:37**	3605
according to **a** that he had done,	**2Ki 24:3**	3605
of Jehoiakim and **a** that he did,	**2Ki 24:5**	3605
for the king of Babylon had taken **a**	**2Ki 24:7**	3605
to **a** that his father had done.	**2Ki 24:9**	3605
He carried out from there **a**	**2Ki 24:13**	3605
and cut in pieces **a** the vessels of	**2Ki 24:13**	3605
Then he led away into exile **a**	**2Ki 24:14**	3605
away into exile all Jerusalem and **a**	**2Ki 24:14**	3605
and **a** the mighty men of valor,	**2Ki 24:14**	3605
a the craftsmen and the smiths.	**2Ki 24:14**	3605
A the men of valor, seven thousand,	**2Ki 24:16**	3605
a strong and fit for war,	**2Ki 24:16**	3605
to **a** that Jehoiakim had done.	**2Ki 24:19**	3605
Babylon came, he and **a** his army,	**2Ki 25:1**	3605
built a siege wall **a** around it.	**2Ki 25:1**	5439
and **a** the men of war *fled* by night	**2Ki 25:4**	3605
Chaldeans were **a** around the city.	**2Ki 25:4**	5439
a his army was scattered from him.	**2Ki 25:5**	3605
and **a** the houses of Jerusalem;	**2Ki 25:9**	3605
So **a** the army of the Chaldeans who	**2Ki 25:10**	3605
and **a** the bronze vessels which	**2Ki 25:14**	3605
bronze of **a** these vessels was beyond	**2Ki 25:16**	3605
on the capital **a** around,	**2Ki 25:17**	5439
capital all around, **a** of bronze.	**2Ki 25:17**	3605
When **a** the captains of the forces,	**2Ki 25:23**	3605
Then **a** the people, both small and	**2Ki 25:26**	3605
regularly **a** the days of his life;	**2Ki 25:29**	3605
each day, **a** the days of his life.	**2Ki 25:30**	3605
a these *were* the sons of Joktan.	**1Ch 1:23**	3605
A these were the sons of Keturah.	**1Ch 1:33**	3605
Judah had five sons in **a**.	**1Ch 2:4**	3605
five of them in **a**.	**1Ch 2:6**	3605
A these were the sons of Machir,	**1Ch 2:23**	3605
A *these were* the sons of David,	**1Ch 3:9**	3605
nor did **a** their family multiply	**1Ch 4:27**	3605
and **a** their villages that *were*	**1Ch 4:33**	3605
a the land east of Gilead.	**1Ch 5:10**	3605
in **a** the pasture lands of Sharon,	**1Ch 5:16**	3605
A of these were enrolled in the	**1Ch 5:17**	3605
and the Hagrites and **a** who *were*	**1Ch 5:20**	3605
Levites were appointed for **a**	**1Ch 6:48**	3605
for **a** the work of the most holy	**1Ch 6:49**	3605
according to **a** that Moses the	**1Ch 6:49**	3605
A their cities throughout their	**1Ch 6:60**	3605
a five of them *were* chief men.	**1Ch 7:3**	3605
Their relatives among **a** the	**1Ch 7:5**	3605
by genealogy, in **a** 87,000.	**1Ch 7:5**	3605
A these *were* the sons of Becher.	**1Ch 7:8**	3605
A these *were* sons of Jediael,	**1Ch 7:11**	3605
A these *were* the sons of Asher,	**1Ch 7:40**	3605
A these *were* the sons of Azel.	**1Ch 8:38**	3605
A these *were* of the sons of	**1Ch 8:40**	3605
So **a** Israel was enrolled by	**1Ch 9:1**	3605
A these *were* heads of fathers'	**1Ch 9:9**	3605
A these who were chosen to be	**1Ch 9:22**	3605
over **a** the utensils of the sanctuary	**1Ch 9:29**	3605
and **a** *those* of his house died	**1Ch 10:6**	3605
When **a** the men of Israel who were	**1Ch 10:7**	3605
When **a** Jabesh-gilead heard all	**1Ch 10:11**	3605
When all Jabesh-gilead heard **a**	**1Ch 10:11**	3605
a the valiant men arose and took	**1Ch 10:12**	3605
Then **a** Israel gathered to David at	**1Ch 11:1**	3605
So **a** the elders of Israel came to	**1Ch 11:3**	3605
and **a** Israel went to Jerusalem	**1Ch 11:4**	3605

He built the city **a** around,	**1Ch 11:8**	5439
kingdom, together with **a** Israel,	**1Ch 11:10**	3605
when it was overflowing **a** its banks	**1Ch 12:15**	3605
to flight **a** those in the valleys,	**1Ch 12:15**	3605
they were **a** mighty men of valor,	**1Ch 12:21**	3605
and **a** their kinsmen *were* at their	**1Ch 12:32**	3605
formation with **a** kinds of weapons	**1Ch 12:33**	3605
there were 120,000 with **a** *kinds* of	**1Ch 12:37**	3605
A these, being men of war who	**1Ch 12:38**	3605
to make David king over **a** Israel;	**1Ch 12:38**	3605
and **a** the rest also of Israel were	**1Ch 12:38**	3605
said to **a** the assembly of Israel,	**1Ch 13:2**	3605
remain in **a** the land of Israel,	**1Ch 13:2**	3605
Then **a** the assembly said that they	**1Ch 13:4**	3605
right in the eyes of **a** the people.	**1Ch 13:4**	3605
David assembled **a** Israel together,	**1Ch 13:5**	3605
and **a** Israel went up to Baalah,	**1Ch 13:6**	3605
David and **a** Israel were	**1Ch 13:8**	3605
before God with **a** *their* might,	**1Ch 13:8**	3605
of Obed-edom with **a** that he had.	**1Ch 13:14**	3605
been anointed king over **a** Israel,	**1Ch 14:8**	3605
a the Philistines went up in	**1Ch 14:8**	3605
David went out into **a** the lands;	**1Ch 14:17**	3605
the fear of him on **a** the nations.	**1Ch 14:17**	3605
assembled **a** Israel at Jerusalem to	**1Ch 15:3**	3605
robe of fine linen with **a** the Levites	**1Ch 15:27**	3605
Thus **a** Israel brought up the ark	**1Ch 15:28**	3605
Speak of **a** His wonders.	**1Ch 16:9**	3605
His judgments are in **a** the earth.	**1Ch 16:14**	3605
Sing to the LORD, **a** the earth;	**1Ch 16:23**	3605
deeds among **a** the peoples.	**1Ch 16:24**	3605
also is to be feared above **a** gods.	**1Ch 16:25**	3605
For **a** the gods of the peoples are	**1Ch 16:26**	3605
Tremble before Him, **a** the earth;	**1Ch 16:30**	3605
the sea roar, and **a** it contains;	**1Ch 16:32**	4393
field exult, and **a** that is in it.	**1Ch 16:32**	3605
Then **a** the people said,	**1Ch 16:36**	3605
even according to **a** that is	**1Ch 16:40**	3605
Then **a** the people departed each to	**1Ch 16:43**	3605
"Do **a** that is in your heart, for	**1Ch 17:2**	3605
"In **a** places where I have walked	**1Ch 17:6**	3605
where I have walked with **a** Israel,	**1Ch 17:6**	3605
a your enemies from before you;	**1Ch 17:8**	3605
And I will subdue **a** your enemies.	**1Ch 17:10**	3605
According to **a** these words and	**1Ch 17:15**	3605
and according to **a** this vision,	**1Ch 17:15**	3605
have wrought **a** this greatness,	**1Ch 17:19**	3605
make known **a** these great things.	**1Ch 17:19**	3605
according to **a** that we have heard	**1Ch 17:20**	3605
hamstrung **a** the chariot horses,	**1Ch 18:4**	3605
defeated **a** the army of Hadadezer	**1Ch 18:9**	3605
And *Hadoram brought* **a** kinds of	**1Ch 18:10**	3605
carried away from **a** the nations:	**1Ch 18:11**	3605
and **a** the Edomites became servants	**1Ch 18:13**	3605
So David reigned over **a** Israel;	**1Ch 18:14**	3605
righteousness for **a** his people.	**1Ch 18:14**	3605
it, he sent Joab and **a** the army,	**1Ch 19:8**	3605
he selected from **a** the choice men	**1Ch 19:10**	3605
he gathered **a** Israel together and	**1Ch 19:17**	3605
And thus David did to **a** the cities	**1Ch 20:3**	3605
Then David and **a** the people	**1Ch 20:3**	3605
are they not **a** my lord's servants?	**1Ch 21:3**	3605
and went throughout **a** Israel,	**1Ch 21:4**	3605
gave the number of the census of **a**	**1Ch 21:5**	
And **a** Israel were 1,100,000 men	**1Ch 21:5**	3605
a the territory of Israel.'	**1Ch 21:12**	3605
I will give *it* **a**."	**1Ch 21:23**	3605
and glorious throughout **a** lands.	**1Ch 22:5**	3605
from **a** his enemies on every side;	**1Ch 22:9**	3605
and **a** men who are skillful in	**1Ch 22:15**	3605
David also commanded **a** the leaders	**1Ch 22:17**	3605
And he gathered together **a** the	**1Ch 23:2**	3605
a its utensils for its service."	**1Ch 23:26**	3605
in the purifying of **a** holy things,	**1Ch 23:28**	3605
and **a** measures of volume and size.	**1Ch 23:29**	3605
a burnt offerings to the LORD,	**1Ch 23:31**	3605
A these *were* the sons of Heman the	**1Ch 25:5**	3605
A these were under the direction	**1Ch 25:6**	3605
relatives, **a** who were skillful,	**1Ch 25:7**	3605
lots for their duties, **a** alike,	**1Ch 25:8**	5980
A these *were* of the sons of	**1Ch 26:8**	3605
a the sons and relatives of Hosah	**1Ch 26:11**	3605
relatives had charge of **a** the treasures	**1Ch 26:26**	3605
And **a** that Samuel the seer had	**1Ch 26:28**	3605
a *of this* was in the care of	**1Ch 26:28**	
for **a** the work of the LORD and the	**1Ch 26:30**	3605
concerning **a** the affairs of God	**1Ch 26:32**	3605
who served the king in **a** the affairs	**1Ch 27:1**	3605
a the months of the year,	**1Ch 27:1**	3605
and was chief of **a** the commanders	**1Ch 27:3**	3605
A these were overseers of the	**1Ch 27:31**	3605
a the officials of Israel,	**1Ch 28:1**	3605
and the overseers of **a** the	**1Ch 28:1**	3605
men, even **a** the valiant men.	**1Ch 28:1**	3605
chose me from **a** the house of my	**1Ch 28:4**	3605
me to make *me* king over **a** Israel.	**1Ch 28:4**	3605
"Of **a** my sons	**1Ch 28:5**	3605
"So now, in the sight of **a** Israel,	**1Ch 28:8**	3605
observe and seek after **a** the	**1Ch 28:8**	3605
for the LORD searches **a** hearts,	**1Ch 28:9**	3605
the plan of **a** that he had in mind,	**1Ch 28:12**	3605
and for **a** the surrounding rooms,	**1Ch 28:12**	3605
and for **a** the work of the service	**1Ch 28:13**	3605
and for **a** the utensils of service	**1Ch 28:13**	3605
the weight of gold for **a** utensils	**1Ch 28:14**	3605
the weight *of silver* for **a** utensils	**1Ch 28:14**	3605
A *this," said David,* "the LORD made	**1Ch 28:19**	3605
a the details of this pattern."	**1Ch 28:19**	3605
not fail you nor forsake you until **a**	**1Ch 28:20**	3605

for **a** the service of the house of God,	1Ch 28:21	3605
will be with you in **a** the work for all	1Ch 28:21	3605
the work for **a** kinds of service.	1Ch 28:21	3605
The officials also and **a** the	1Ch 28:21	3605
"Now with **a** my ability I have	1Ch 29:2	3605
and **a** kinds of precious stones and	1Ch 29:2	3605
over and above **a** that I have	1Ch 29:3	3605
for **a** the work done by the	1Ch 29:5	3605
in the sight of **a** the assembly;	1Ch 29:10	3605
You exalt Yourself as head over **a**.	1Ch 29:11	3605
You, and You rule over **a**,	1Ch 29:12	3605
For **a** things come from You, and	1Ch 29:14	3605
tenants, as **a** our fathers were;	1Ch 29:15	3605
a this abundance that we have	1Ch 29:16	3605
is from Your hand, and **a** is Yours.	1Ch 29:16	3605
willingly offered **a** these *things;*	1Ch 29:17	3605
Your statutes, and to do *them* **a**,	1Ch 29:19	3605
Then David said to **a** the assembly,	1Ch 29:20	3605
a the assembly blessed the LORD,	1Ch 29:20	3605
in abundance for **a** Israel.	1Ch 29:21	3605
and **a** Israel obeyed him.	1Ch 29:23	3605
A the officials, the mighty men,	1Ch 29:24	3605
and also **a** the sons of King David	1Ch 29:24	3605
Solomon in the sight of **a** Israel,	1Ch 29:25	3605
of Jesse reigned over **a** Israel.	1Ch 29:26	3605
with **a** his reign, his power, and	1Ch 29:30	3605
on **a** the kingdoms of the lands.	1Ch 29:30	3605
Solomon spoke to **a** Israel,	2Ch 1:2	3605
and to every leader in **a** Israel,	2Ch 1:2	3605
and **a** the assembly with him went	2Ch 1:3	3605
they exported them to **a** the kings	2Ch 1:17	3605
is our God than **a** the gods.	2Ch 2:5	3605
and *who knows how* to make **a** kinds	2Ch 2:14	3605
Solomon numbered **a** the aliens	2Ch 2:17	3605
were under it *and* **a** around it,	2Ch 4:3	5439
and **a** their hindquarters turned	2Ch 4:4	3605
the forks and **a** its utensils,	2Ch 4:16	3605
Thus Solomon made **a** these utensils	2Ch 4:18	3605
Solomon also made **a** the things	2Ch 4:19	3605
Thus **a** the work that Solomon	2Ch 5:1	3605
and the gold and **a** the utensils,	2Ch 5:1	3605
and **a** the heads of the tribes,	2Ch 5:2	3605
A the men of Israel assembled	2Ch 5:3	3605
Then **a** the elders of Israel came,	2Ch 5:4	3605
tent of meeting and **a** the holy utensils	2Ch 5:5	3605
And King Solomon and **a** the	2Ch 5:6	3605
for **a** the priests who were present	2Ch 5:11	3605
and **a** the Levitical singers,	2Ch 5:12	3605
blessed **a** the assembly of Israel,	2Ch 6:3	3605
while **a** the assembly of Israel was	2Ch 6:3	3605
I did not choose a city out of **a**	2Ch 6:5	3605
in the presence of **a** the assembly	2Ch 6:12	3605
of **a** the assembly of Israel and	2Ch 6:13	3605
before You with **a** their heart;	2Ch 6:14	3605
any man or by **a** Your people Israel,	2Ch 6:29	3605
to each according to **a** his ways,	2Ch 6:30	3605
and do according to **a** for which	2Ch 6:33	3605
in order that **a** the peoples of the	2Ch 6:33	3605
if they return to You with **a**	2Ch 6:38	3605
all their heart and with **a** their soul	2Ch 6:38	3605
A the sons of Israel, seeing	2Ch 7:3	3605
Then the king and **a** the people	2Ch 7:4	3605
Thus the king and **a** the people	2Ch 7:5	3605
and **a** Israel was standing.	2Ch 7:6	3605
seven days, and **a** Israel with him,	2Ch 7:8	3605
and successfully completed **a** that	2Ch 7:11	3605
even to do according to **a** that I have	2Ch 7:17	3605
and a byword among **a** peoples.	2Ch 7:20	3605
a this adversity on them.' "	2Ch 7:22	3605
built Tadmor in the wilderness and **a**	2Ch 8:4	3605
and Baalath and **a** the storage	2Ch 8:6	3605
and **a** the cities for his chariots	2Ch 8:6	3605
and **a** that it pleased Solomon to	2Ch 8:6	3605
and in **a** the land under his rule.	2Ch 8:6	3605
A of the people who were left of	2Ch 8:7	3605
Thus **a** the work of Solomon was	2Ch 8:16	3605
him about **a** that was on her heart.	2Ch 9:1	3605
Solomon answered **a** her questions;	2Ch 9:2	3605
to the queen of Sheba **a** her desire	2Ch 9:12	3605
and **a** the kings of Arabia and the	2Ch 9:14	3605
A King Solomon's drinking vessels	2Ch 9:20	3605
and **a** the vessels of the house of	2Ch 9:20	3605
King Solomon became greater than **a**	2Ch 9:22	3605
And **a** the kings of the earth were	2Ch 9:23	3605
He was the ruler over **a** the	2Ch 9:26	3605
from Egypt and from **a** countries.	2Ch 9:28	3605
years in Jerusalem over **a** Israel.	2Ch 9:30	3605
for **a** Israel had come to Shechem	2Ch 10:1	3605
When Jeroboam and **a** Israel came,	2Ch 10:3	3605
So Jeroboam and **a** the people came	2Ch 10:12	3605
When **a** Israel *saw* that the	2Ch 10:16	3605
So **a** Israel departed to their	2Ch 10:16	3605
to **a** Israel in Judah and Benjamin,	2Ch 11:3	3605
the Levites who were in **a** Israel stood	2Ch 11:13	3605
with him from **a** their districts.	2Ch 11:13	3605
Those from **a** the tribes of	2Ch 11:16	3605
daughter of Absalom more than **a** his	2Ch 11:21	3605
his sons through **a** the territories	2Ch 11:23	3605
to **a** the fortified cities,	2Ch 11:23	3605
and **a** Israel with him forsook the law	2Ch 12:1	3605
from **a** the tribes of Israel,	2Ch 12:13	3605
to me, Jeroboam and **a** Israel:	2Ch 13:4	3605
God routed Jeroboam and **a** Israel	2Ch 13:15	3605
altars from **a** the cities of Judah.	2Ch 14:5	3605
a of them were valiant warriors.	2Ch 14:8	3605
a the cities around Gerar,	2Ch 14:14	3605
and they despoiled **a** the cities,	2Ch 14:14	3605
me, Asa, and **a** Judah and Benjamin:	2Ch 15:2	3605
a the inhabitants of the lands.	2Ch 15:5	3605

removed the abominable idols from **a**	2Ch 15:8	3605
He gathered **a** Judah and	2Ch 15:9	3605
with **a** their heart and soul;	2Ch 15:12	3605
A Judah rejoiced concerning the oath,	2Ch 15:15	3605
heart was blameless **a** his days.	2Ch 15:17	3605
a the store cities of Naphtali.	2Ch 16:4	3605
Then King Asa brought **a** Judah,	2Ch 16:6	3605
a the fortified cities of Judah,	2Ch 17:2	3605
and **a** Judah brought tribute to	2Ch 17:5	3605
and they went throughout **a** the	2Ch 17:9	3605
Now the dread of the LORD was on **a**	2Ch 17:10	3605
fortified cities through **a** Judah.	2Ch 17:19	3605
and **a** the prophets were	2Ch 18:9	3605
A the prophets were prophesying thus,	2Ch 18:11	3605
"I saw **a** Israel Scattered on the	2Ch 18:16	3605
and **a** the host of heaven standing	2Ch 18:18	3605
in the mouth of **a** his prophets.'	2Ch 18:21	3605
"Listen, **a** you people."	2Ch 18:27	3605
a the fortified cities of Judah,	2Ch 19:5	3605
in **a** that pertains to the LORD,	2Ch 19:11	3605
in **a** that pertains to the king.	2Ch 19:11	3605
a fast throughout **a** Judah.	2Ch 20:3	3605
they even came from **a** the cities	2Ch 20:4	3605
a the kingdoms of the nations?	2Ch 20:6	3605
A Judah was standing before the	2Ch 20:13	3605
a Judah and the inhabitants of	2Ch 20:15	3605
and **a** Judah and the inhabitants of	2Ch 20:18	3605
And the dread of God was on **a** the	2Ch 20:29	3605
his God gave him rest on **a** sides.	2Ch 20:30	5439
A these *were* the sons of	2Ch 21:2	3605
a his brothers with the sword,	2Ch 21:4	3605
and **a** his chariots with him.	2Ch 21:9	3605
and **a** your possessions with a	2Ch 21:14	3605
and carried away **a** the possessions	2Ch 21:17	3605
So after **a** this the LORD smote him	2Ch 21:18	3605
camp had slain **a** the older *sons.*	2Ch 22:1	3605
the LORD with **a** his heart."	2Ch 22:9	3605
she rose and destroyed **a** the royal	2Ch 22:10	3605
from **a** the cities of Judah,	2Ch 23:2	3605
Then **a** the assembly made a	2Ch 23:3	3605
and **a** the people *shall be* in the	2Ch 23:5	3605
And let **a** the people keep the	2Ch 23:6	3605
So the Levites and **a** Judah did	2Ch 23:8	3605
did according to **a** that Jehoiada	2Ch 23:8	3605
He stationed **a** the people,	2Ch 23:10	3605
And **a** the people of the land	2Ch 23:13	3605
and **a** the people and the king,	2Ch 23:16	3605
And **a** the people went to the house	2Ch 23:17	3605
and **a** the people of the land,	2Ch 23:20	3605
So **a** of the people of the land	2Ch 23:21	3605
was right in the sight of the LORD **a**	2Ch 24:2	3605
and collect money from **a** Israel to	2Ch 24:5	3605
A the officers and all the people	2Ch 24:10	3605
All the officers and **a** the	2Ch 24:10	3605
a the days of Jehoiada.	2Ch 24:14	3605
destroyed **a** the officials of the	2Ch 24:23	3605
and sent **a** their spoil to the king	2Ch 24:23	3605
that they were **a** dashed to pieces.	2Ch 25:12	3605
He took **a** the gold and silver	2Ch 25:24	3605
and **a** the utensils which were	2Ch 25:24	3605
And **a** the people of Judah took	2Ch 26:1	3605
according to **a** that his father Amaziah	2Ch 26:4	3605
prepared for **a** the army shields,	2Ch 26:14	3605
and **a** the priests looked at him,	2Ch 26:20	3605
according to **a** that his father had	2Ch 27:2	3605
even **a** his wars and his acts,	2Ch 27:7	3605
120,000 in one day, **a** valiant men,	2Ch 28:6	3605
the officers and **a** the assembly.	2Ch 28:14	3605
and they clothed **a** their naked	2Ch 28:15	3605
a their feeble ones on donkeys,	2Ch 28:15	3605
the downfall of him and **a** Israel.	2Ch 28:23	3605
rest of his acts and **a** his ways,	2Ch 28:26	3605
according to **a** that his father	2Ch 29:2	3605
offering with **a** of its utensils,	2Ch 29:18	3605
showbread with **a** of its utensils.	2Ch 29:18	3605
a the utensils which King Ahaz had	2Ch 29:19	3605
their blood to atone for **a** Israel,	2Ch 29:24	3605
and the sin offering for **a** Israel.	2Ch 29:24	3605
a this *continued* until the burnt	2Ch 29:28	3605
the king and **a** who were present	2Ch 29:29	3605
and **a** those who were willing	2Ch 29:31	3605
a these were for a burnt offering	2Ch 29:32	3605
to skin **a** the burnt offerings;	2Ch 29:34	3605
Then Hezekiah and **a** the people	2Ch 29:36	3605
Now Hezekiah sent to **a** Israel and	2Ch 30:1	3605
For the king and his princes and **a**	2Ch 30:2	3605
of the king and **a** the assembly.	2Ch 30:4	3605
a proclamation throughout **a** Israel	2Ch 30:5	3605
couriers went throughout **a** Israel and	2Ch 30:6	3605
they also removed **a** the incense	2Ch 30:14	3605
Hezekiah spoke encouragingly to **a**	2Ch 30:22	3605
A the assembly of Judah rejoiced,	2Ch 30:25	3605
and **a** the assembly that came from	2Ch 30:25	3605
Now when **a** this was finished, all	2Ch 31:1	3605
a Israel who were present went out	2Ch 31:1	3605
throughout **a** Judah and Benjamin,	2Ch 31:1	3605
until they had destroyed them **a**.	2Ch 31:1	3615
Then **a** the sons of Israel returned	2Ch 31:1	3605
and of **a** the produce of the field;	2Ch 31:5	3605
in abundantly the tithe of **a**.	2Ch 31:5	3605
included **a** their little children,	2Ch 31:18	3605
Hezekiah did throughout **a** Judah;	2Ch 31:20	3605
with **a** his heart and prospered.	2Ch 31:21	3605
and stopped up **a** the springs	2Ch 32:4	3605
And he took courage and rebuilt **a**	2Ch 32:5	3605
nor because of **a** the horde	2Ch 32:7	3605
with **a** his forces with him,	2Ch 32:9	3605
a Judah who *were* at Jerusalem,	2Ch 32:9	3605
to **a** the peoples of the lands?	2Ch 32:13	3605

able at **a** to deliver their land from	2Ch 32:13	3201
'Who *was there* among **a** the gods of	2Ch 32:14	3605
and from the hand of **a** *others,*	2Ch 32:22	3605
the sight of **a** nations thereafter.	2Ch 32:23	3605
and **a** kinds of valuable articles,	2Ch 32:27	3605
pens for **a** kinds of cattle and	2Ch 32:28	3605
prospered in **a** that he did.	2Ch 32:30	3605
know **a** that was in his heart.	2Ch 32:31	3605
and **a** Judah and the inhabitants of	2Ch 32:33	3605
and worshiped **a** the host of heaven	2Ch 33:3	3605
For he built altars for **a** the host	2Ch 33:5	3605
from **a** the tribes of Israel,	2Ch 33:7	3605
if only they will observe to do **a** that	2Ch 33:8	3605
them according to **a** the law,	2Ch 33:8	3605
a the fortified cities of Judah.	2Ch 33:14	3605
as well as **a** the altars which he	2Ch 33:15	3605
entreated by him, and **a** his sin,	2Ch 33:19	3605
and Amon sacrificed to **a** the	2Ch 33:22	3605
killed **a** the conspirators against King	2Ch 33:25	3605
and chopped down **a** the incense	2Ch 34:7	3605
and from **a** the remnant of Israel,	2Ch 34:9	3605
and from **a** Judah and Benjamin and	2Ch 34:9	3605
a who were skillful with musical	2Ch 34:12	3605
a the workmen from job to job;	2Ch 34:13	3605
a that is written in this book."	2Ch 34:21	3605
even **a** the curses written in the	2Ch 34:24	3605
with **a** the works of their hands;	2Ch 34:25	3605
so your eyes will not see **a** the	2Ch 34:28	3605
Then the king sent and gathered **a**	2Ch 34:29	3605
the LORD and **a** the men of Judah,	2Ch 34:30	3605
the Levites and **a** the people,	2Ch 34:30	3605
and he read in their hearing **a** the	2Ch 34:30	3605
with **a** his heart and with all his soul,	2Ch 34:31	3605
all his heart and with **a** his soul,	2Ch 34:31	3605
he made **a** who were present in	2Ch 34:32	3605
Josiah removed **a** the	2Ch 34:33	3605
removed all the abominations from **a**	2Ch 34:33	3605
and made **a** who were present in	2Ch 34:33	3605
to the Levites who taught **a** Israel	2Ch 35:3	3605
lay people, to **a** who were present,	2Ch 35:7	3605
a for the Passover offerings,	2Ch 35:7	3605
them speedily to **a** the lay people.	2Ch 35:13	3605
So **a** the service of the LORD was	2Ch 35:16	3605
a Judah and Israel who were	2Ch 35:18	3605
After **a** this, when Josiah had set	2Ch 35:20	3605
A Judah and Jerusalem mourned for	2Ch 35:24	3605
And **a** the male and female singers	2Ch 35:25	3605
a the officials of the priests and	2Ch 36:14	3605
people were very unfaithful *following* **a**	2Ch 36:14	3605
He gave *them* **a** into his hand.	2Ch 36:17	3605
A the articles of the house of God,	2Ch 36:18	3605
he brought *them* **a** to Babylon.	2Ch 36:18	3605
and burned **a** its fortified buildings	2Ch 36:19	3605
destroyed **a** its valuable articles.	2Ch 36:19	3605
A the days of its desolation it	2Ch 36:21	3605
me **a** the kingdoms of the earth,	2Ch 36:23	3605
is among you of **a** His people,	2Ch 36:23	3605
throughout **a** his kingdom,	Ezr 1:1	3605
me **a** the kingdoms of the earth and	Ezr 1:2	3605
is among you of **a** His people,	Ezr 1:3	3605
A those about them encouraged them	Ezr 1:6	3605
aside from **a** that was given as a	Ezr 1:6	3605
A the articles of gold and silver	Ezr 1:11	3605
Sheshbazzar brought them **a** up with	Ezr 1:11	3605
the sons of Shobai, in **a** 139.	Ezr 2:42	3605
A the temple servants and the	Ezr 2:58	3605
and **a** Israel in their cities.	Ezr 2:70	3605
also for the new moons and for **a**	Ezr 3:5	3605
and **a** who came from the captivity	Ezr 3:8	3605
And **a** the people shouted with a	Ezr 3:11	3605
to frustrate their counsel **a** the days	Ezr 4:5	3605
governing **a** *the provinces* beyond	Ezr 4:20	3606
"To Darius the king, **a** peace.	Ezr 5:7	3606
be carried out with **a** diligence!"	Ezr 6:12	629
out *the decree* with **a** diligence,	Ezr 6:13	629
for **a** Israel 12 male goats,	Ezr 6:17	3606
a of them were pure.	Ezr 6:20	3605
Passover *lamb* for **a** the exiles,	Ezr 6:20	3605
who returned from exile and **a** those	Ezr 6:21	3605
and the king granted him **a** he	Ezr 7:6	3605
with **a** the silver and gold which	Ezr 7:16	3606
issue a decree to **a** the treasurers	Ezr 7:21	3606
that they may judge **a** the people	Ezr 7:25	3606
even **a** those who know the laws of	Ezr 7:25	3606
before **a** the king's mighty princes.	Ezr 7:28	3605
a of them designated by name.	Ezr 8:20	3605
ones, and **a** our possessions.	Ezr 8:21	3605
disposed to **a** those who seek Him,	Ezr 8:22	3605
against **a** those who forsake Him."	Ezr 8:22	3605
and **a** Israel present *there*	Ezr 8:25	3605
and **a** the weight was recorded at	Ezr 8:34	3605
12 bulls for **a** Israel, 96 rams, 77	Ezr 8:35	3605
a as a burnt offering to the LORD.	Ezr 8:35	3605
"After **a** that has come upon	Ezr 9:13	3605
a the wives and their children,	Ezr 10:3	3605
the Levites and **a** Israel,	Ezr 10:5	3605
and Jerusalem to **a** the exiles,	Ezr 10:7	3605
a his possessions should be	Ezr 10:8	3605
So **a** the men of Judah and Benjamin	Ezr 10:9	3605
and **a** the people sat in the open	Ezr 10:9	3605
Then **a** the assembly replied	Ezr 10:12	3605
assembly and let **a** those in our cities	Ezr 10:14	3605
households, **a** of them by name.	Ezr 10:16	3605
They finished *investigating* **a**	Ezr 10:17	3605
A these had married foreign wives,	Ezr 10:44	3605
A of them conspired together to come	Ne 4:8	3605
then **a** of us returned to the wall,	Ne 4:15	3605
And **a** the assembly said,	Ne 5:13	3605
and **a** my servants were gathered	Ne 5:16	3605

and once in ten days **a** sorts of	**Ne 5:18**	3605
Yet for **a** this I did not demand	**Ne 5:18**	
according to **a** that I have done	**Ne 5:19**	3605
For **a** of them were *trying* to	**Ne 6:9**	3605
When **a** our enemies heard *of it,*	**Ne 6:16**	3605
and **a** the nations surrounding us	**Ne 6:16**	3605
A the temple servants and the sons	**Ne 7:60**	3605
the temple servants and **a** Israel,	**Ne 7:73**	3605
And **a** the people gathered as one	**Ne 8:1**	3605
and **a** who *could* listen with	**Ne 8:2**	3605
and **a** the people were attentive to	**Ne 8:3**	3605
opened the book in the sight of **a**	**Ne 8:5**	3605
was standing above **a** the people;	**Ne 8:5**	3605
opened it, **a** the people stood up.	**Ne 8:5**	3605
And **a** the people answered,	**Ne 8:6**	3605
the people said to **a** the people,	**Ne 8:9**	3605
For **a** the people were weeping when	**Ne 8:9**	3605
the Levites calmed **a** the people,	**Ne 8:11**	3605
A the people went away to eat, to	**Ne 8:12**	3605
households of **a** the people,	**Ne 8:13**	3605
a their cities and in Jerusalem,	**Ne 8:15**	3605
themselves from **a** foreigners,	**Ne 9:2**	3605
above **a** blessing and praise!	**Ne 9:5**	3605
of heavens with **a** their host,	**Ne 9:6**	3605
The earth and **a** that is on it,	**Ne 9:6**	3605
The seas and **a** that is in them.	**Ne 9:6**	3605
You give life to **a** of them	**Ne 9:6**	3605
Against **a** his servants and all the	**Ne 9:10**	3605
and **a** the people of his land;	**Ne 9:10**	3605
Do not let **a** the hardship seem	**Ne 9:32**	3605
our fathers and on **a** Your people,	**Ne 9:32**	3605
just in **a** that has come upon us;	**Ne 9:33**	3605
"Now because of **a** this We are	**Ne 9:38**	3605
and **a** those who had separated	**Ne 10:28**	3605
a those who had knowledge and	**Ne 10:28**	3605
and to keep and to observe **a** the	**Ne 10:29**	3605
and **a** the work of the house of our	**Ne 10:33**	3605
first fruits of **a** the fruit of every tree	**Ne 10:35**	3605
the tithes in **a** the rural towns.	**Ne 10:37**	3605
And the people blessed **a** the men	**Ne 11:2**	3605
A the sons of Perez who lived in	**Ne 11:6**	3605
A the Levites in the holy city	**Ne 11:18**	3605
were in **a** the cities of Judah,	**Ne 11:20**	3605
a matters concerning the people.	**Ne 11:24**	3605
the Levites from **a** their places,	**Ne 12:27**	3605
So **a** Israel in the days of	**Ne 12:47**	3605
excluded **a** foreigners from Israel.	**Ne 13:3**	3605
But during **a** this *time* I was not	**Ne 13:6**	3605
so I threw **a** of Tobiah's household	**Ne 13:8**	3605
A Judah then brought the tithe of	**Ne 13:12**	3605
figs and **a** kinds of loads,	**Ne 13:15**	3605
fish and **a** kinds of merchandise,	**Ne 13:16**	3605
and on this city **a** this trouble?	**Ne 13:18**	3605
God made him king over **a** Israel;	**Ne 13:26**	3605
you have committed **a** this great evil	**Ne 13:27**	3605
for **a** his princes and attendants,	**Es 1:3**	3605
a banquet lasting seven days for **a**	**Es 1:5**	3605
before **a** who knew law and justice	**Es 1:13**	3605
the king but *also* **a** the princes and	**Es 1:16**	3605
and **a** the peoples who are in all	**Es 1:16**	3605
and all the peoples who are in **a**	**Es 1:16**	3605
known to **a** the women causing them	**Es 1:17**	3605
same way to **a** the king's princes,	**Es 1:18**	3605
is heard throughout **a** his kingdom,	**Es 1:20**	3605
then **a** women will give honor to	**Es 1:20**	3605
letters to **a** the king's provinces,	**Es 1:22**	3605
appoint overseers in **a** the provinces	**Es 2:3**	3605
in the eyes of **a** who saw her.	**Es 2:15**	3605
Esther more than **a** the women,	**Es 2:17**	3605
with him more than **a** the virgins,	**Es 2:17**	3605
a his princes and his servants;	**Es 2:18**	3605
a the princes who *were* with him.	**Es 3:1**	3605
A the king's servants who were at	**Es 3:2**	3605
sought to destroy **a** the Jews,	**Es 3:6**	3605
a the provinces of your kingdom;	**Es 3:8**	3605
from *those* of **a** *other* people and	**Es 3:8**	3605
by couriers to **a** the king's provinces	**Es 3:13**	3605
and to annihilate **a** the Jews,	**Es 3:13**	3605
was published to **a** the peoples	**Es 3:14**	3605
learned **a** that had been done,	**Es 4:1**	3605
him **a** that had happened to him,	**Es 4:7**	3605
"**A** the king's servants and the	**Es 4:11**	3605
escape any more than **a** the Jews.	**Es 4:13**	3605
assemble **a** the Jews who are found	**Es 4:16**	3605
"Yet **a** of this does not satisfy	**Es 5:13**	3605
and **a** his friends said to him,	**Es 5:14**	3605
of **a** that you have said."	**Es 6:10**	3605
to Zeresh his wife and **a** his friends	**Es 6:13**	3605
who are in **a** the king's provinces.	**Es 8:5**	3605
written according to **a** that Mordecai	**Es 8:9**	3605
on one day in **a** the provinces of	**Es 8:12**	3605
was published to **a** the peoples,	**Es 8:13**	3605
assembled in their cities throughout **a**	**Es 9:2**	3605
them had fallen on **a** the peoples.	**Es 9:2**	3605
a the princes of the provinces,	**Es 9:3**	3605
spread throughout **a** the provinces;	**Es 9:4**	3605
a their enemies with the sword,	**Es 9:5**	3605
and he sent letters to **a** the Jews	**Es 9:20**	3605
letters to all the Jews who were in **a**	**Es 9:20**	3605
the adversary of **a** the Jews,	**Es 9:24**	3605
and for **a** those who allied	**Es 9:27**	3605
He sent letters to **a** the Jews,	**Es 9:30**	3605
And **a** the accomplishments of his	**Es 10:2**	3605
greatest of **a** the men of the east.	**Jb 1:3**	3605
according to the number of them **a**;	**Jb 1:5**	3605
and his house and **a** that he has,	**Jb 1:10**	3605
hand now and touch **a** that he has;	**Jb 1:11**	3605
a that he has is in your power,	**Jb 1:12**	3605
Through **a** this Job did not sin nor	**Jb 1:22**	3605

a that a man has he will give for	**Jb 2:4**	3605
In **a** this Job did not sin with his	**Jb 2:10**	3605
Job's three friends heard of **a** this	**Jb 2:11**	3605
And made **a** my bones shake.	**Jb 4:14**	7230
are the paths of **a** who forget God;	**Jb 8:13**	3605
"It is **a** one; therefore I say,	**Jb 9:22**	
I am afraid of **a** my pains, I know	**Jb 9:28**	3605
"Who among **a** these does not know	**Jb 12:9**	3605
And the breath of **a** mankind?	**Jb 12:10**	3605
"Behold, my eye has seen **a** *this,*	**Jb 13:1**	3605
You are **a** worthless physicians.	**Jb 13:4**	3605
stocks And watch **a** my paths;	**Jb 13:27**	3605
A the days of my struggle I will	**Jb 14:14**	3605
man writhes in pain **a** *his* days,	**Jb 15:20**	3605
Sorry comforters are you **a**.	**Jb 16:2**	3605
You have laid waste **a** my company.	**Jb 16:7**	3605
And **a** my members are as a shadow.	**Jb 17:7**	3605
"But come again **a** of you now, For	**Jb 17:10**	3605
"**A** around terrors frighten him,	**Jb 18:11**	5439
"**A** my associates abhor me, And	**Jb 19:19**	3605
a men will follow after him,	**Jb 21:33**	3605
Will he call on God at **a** times?	**Jb 27:10**	3605
"Behold, **a** of you have seen *it;*	**Jb 27:12**	3605
hidden from the eyes of **a** living And	**Jb 28:21**	3605
And dew lies **a** night on my branch.	**Jb 29:19**	
the house of meeting for **a** living.	**Jb 30:23**	3605
my ways And number **a** my steps?	**Jb 31:4**	3605
And would uproot **a** my increase.	**Jb 31:12**	3605
speech, And listen to **a** my words.	**Jb 33:1**	3605
He watches **a** my paths.'	**Jb 33:11**	3605
give an account of **a** His doings?	**Jb 33:13**	3605
does **a** these oftentimes with men,	**Jb 33:29**	3605
A flesh would perish together, And	**Jb 34:15**	3605
they **a** are the work of His hands?	**Jb 34:19**	3605
of a man, And He sees **a** his steps.	**Jb 34:21**	3605
Or **a** the forces of *your* strength?	**Jb 36:19**	3605
"**A** men have seen it;	**Jb 36:25**	3605
man, That **a** men may know His work.	**Jb 37:7**	3605
And **a** the sons of God shouted for	**Jb 38:7**	3605
Tell *Me,* if you know **a** this.	**Jb 38:18**	3605
And **a** the beasts of the field play	**Jb 40:20**	3605
king over **a** the sons of pride."	**Jb 41:34**	3605
know that You can do **a** things,	**Jb 42:2**	3605
increased **a** that Job had twofold.	**Jb 42:10**	3605
Then **a** his brothers and all his	**Jb 42:11**	3605
his brothers and **a** his sisters	**Jb 42:11**	3605
and **a** who had known him before came	**Jb 42:11**	3605
comforted him for **a** the adversities	**Jb 42:11**	3605
In **a** the land no women were	**Jb 42:15**	3605
are **a** who take refuge in Him!	**Ps 2:12**	3605
smitten **a** my enemies on the cheek;	**Ps 3:7**	3605
You hate **a** who do iniquity.	**Ps 5:5**	3605
But let **a** who take refuge in You	**Ps 5:11**	3605
old because of **a** my adversaries.	**Ps 6:7**	3605
from me, **a** you who do iniquity,	**Ps 6:8**	3605
A my enemies will be ashamed and	**Ps 6:10**	3605
me from **a** those who pursue me,	**Ps 7:1**	3605
is Your name in **a** the earth,	**Ps 8:1**	3605
have put **a** things under his feet,	**Ps 8:6**	3605
A sheep and oxen, And also the	**Ps 8:7**	3605
is Your name in **a** the earth!	**Ps 8:9**	3605
to the LORD with **a** my heart;	**Ps 9:1**	3605
I will tell of **a** Your wonders.	**Ps 9:1**	3605
That I may tell of **a** Your praises,	**Ps 9:14**	3605
Even **a** the nations who forget God.	**Ps 9:17**	3605
A his thoughts are,	**Ps 10:4**	3605
His ways prosper at **a** times;	**Ps 10:5**	3605
As for **a** his adversaries, he	**Ps 10:5**	3605
Throughout **a** generations I will	**Ps 10:6**	1755
LORD cut off **a** flattering lips,	**Ps 12:3**	3605
sorrow in my heart **a** the day?	**Ps 13:2**	
They have **a** turned aside,	**Ps 14:3**	3605
Do **a** the workers of wickedness not	**Ps 14:4**	3605
ones in whom is **a** my delight.	**Ps 16:3**	3605
A His ordinances were before me,	**Ps 18:22**	3605
to **a** who take refuge in Him.	**Ps 18:30**	3605
has gone out through **a** the earth,	**Ps 19:4**	3605
He remember **a** your meal offerings	**Ps 20:3**	3605
And fulfill **a** your counsel!	**Ps 20:4**	3605
the LORD fulfill **a** your petitions.	**Ps 20:5**	3605
hand will find out **a** your enemies;	**Ps 21:8**	3605
A who see me sneer at me;	**Ps 22:7**	3605
And **a** my bones are out of joint;	**Ps 22:14**	3605
I can count **a** my bones.	**Ps 22:17**	3605
A you descendants of Jacob,	**Ps 22:23**	3605
Him, **a** you descendants of Israel.	**Ps 22:23**	3605
A the ends of the earth will	**Ps 22:27**	3605
And **a** the families of the nations	**Ps 22:27**	3605
A the prosperous of the earth will	**Ps 22:29**	3605
A those who go down to the dust	**Ps 22:29**	3605
follow me **a** the days of my life,	**Ps 23:6**	3605
is the LORD's, and **a** it contains,	**Ps 24:1**	4393
For You I wait **a** the day.	**Ps 25:5**	3605
A the paths of the LORD are	**Ps 25:10**	3605
my trouble, And forgive **a** my sins.	**Ps 25:18**	3605
O God, Out of **a** his troubles.	**Ps 25:22**	3605
And declare **a** Your wonders.	**Ps 26:7**	3605
of the LORD **a** the days of my life,	**Ps 27:4**	3605
Because of **a** my adversaries, I	**Ps 31:11**	3605
the LORD, **a** you His godly ones!	**Ps 31:23**	3605
A you who hope in the LORD.	**Ps 31:24**	3605
Through my groaning **a** day long.	**Ps 32:3**	3605
a you who are upright in heart.	**Ps 32:11**	3605
And **a** His work is *done* in	**Ps 33:4**	3605
breath of His mouth **a** their host.	**Ps 33:6**	3605
Let **a** the earth fear the LORD;	**Ps 33:8**	3605
Let **a** the inhabitants of the world	**Ps 33:8**	3605
He sees **a** the sons of men;	**Ps 33:13**	3605
On **a** the inhabitants of the earth,	**Ps 33:14**	3605

who fashions the hearts of them **a**,	**Ps 33:15**	3162
He who understands **a** their works.	**Ps 33:15**	3605
I will bless the LORD at **a** times;	**Ps 34:1**	3605
And delivered me from **a** my fears.	**Ps 34:4**	3605
saved him out of **a** his troubles.	**Ps 34:6**	3605
them out of **a** their troubles.	**Ps 34:17**	3605
LORD delivers him out of them **a**.	**Ps 34:19**	3605
He keeps **a** his bones,	**Ps 34:20**	3605
A my bones will say,	**Ps 35:10**	3605
And Your praise **a** day long.	**Ps 35:28**	3605
A day long he is gracious and	**Ps 37:26**	3605
I go mourning **a** day long.	**Ps 38:6**	3605
Lord, **a** my desire is before You;	**Ps 38:9**	3605
they devise treachery **a** day long.	**Ps 38:12**	3605
me from **a** my transgressions;	**Ps 39:8**	3605
A sojourner like **a** my fathers.	**Ps 39:12**	3605
Let **a** who seek You rejoice and be	**Ps 40:16**	3605
A who hate me whisper together	**Ps 41:7**	3605
While *they* say to me **a** day long,	**Ps 42:3**	3605
A Your breakers and Your waves have	**Ps 42:7**	3605
While they say to me **a** day long,	**Ps 42:10**	3605
In God we have boasted **a** day long,	**Ps 44:8**	3605
A day long my dishonor is before	**Ps 44:15**	3605
A this has come upon us, but we	**Ps 44:17**	3605
Your sake we are killed **a** day long;	**Ps 44:22**	3605
A Your garments are *fragrant with*	**Ps 45:8**	3605
daughter is **a** glorious within;	**Ps 45:13**	3605
make them princes in **a** the earth.	**Ps 45:16**	3605
to be remembered in **a** generations;	**Ps 45:17**	3605
O clap your hands, **a** peoples;	**Ps 47:1**	3605
A great King over **a** the earth.	**Ps 47:2**	3605
God is the King of **a** the earth;	**Ps 47:7**	3605
Hear this, **a** peoples;	**Ps 49:1**	3605
ear, **a** inhabitants of the world,	**Ps 49:1**	3605
dwelling places to **a** generations;	**Ps 49:11**	1755
world is Mine, and **a** it contains.	**Ps 50:12**	4393
And blot out **a** my iniquities.	**Ps 51:9**	3605
of God *endures* **a** day long.	**Ps 52:1**	3605
You love **a** words that devour, O	**Ps 52:4**	3605
has delivered me from **a** trouble,	**Ps 54:7**	3605
a day long he oppresses me.	**Ps 56:1**	3605
have trampled upon me **a** day long,	**Ps 56:2**	3605
A day long they distort my words;	**Ps 56:5**	3605
A their thoughts are against me	**Ps 56:5**	3605
To God who accomplishes **a** *things*	**Ps 57:2**	
Your glory *be* above **a** the earth.	**Ps 57:5**	3605
Your glory *be* above **a** the earth.	**Ps 57:11**	3605
Awake to punish **a** the nations;	**Ps 59:5**	3605
You scoff at **a** the nations.	**Ps 59:8**	3605
That you may murder *him,* **a** of you,	**Ps 62:3**	3605
Trust in Him at **a** times, O people;	**Ps 62:8**	3605
A who see them will shake the head.	**Ps 64:8**	3605
Then **a** men will fear, And they	**Ps 64:9**	3605
And **a** the upright in heart will	**Ps 64:10**	3605
hear prayer, To You **a** men come.	**Ps 65:2**	3605
You who are the trust of **a** the	**Ps 65:5**	3605
joyfully to God, **a** the earth;	**Ps 66:1**	3605
"**A** the earth will worship You,	**Ps 66:4**	3605
Come *and* hear, **a** who fear God, And	**Ps 66:16**	3605
Your salvation among **a** nations.	**Ps 67:2**	3605
Let **a** the peoples praise You.	**Ps 67:3**	3605
Let **a** the peoples praise You.	**Ps 67:5**	3605
That **a** the ends of the earth may	**Ps 67:7**	3605
A my adversaries are before You.	**Ps 69:19**	3605
Let **a** who seek You rejoice and be	**Ps 70:4**	3605
And with Your glory **a** day long.	**Ps 71:8**	3605
And of Your salvation **a** day long;	**Ps 71:15**	3605
Your power to **a** who are to come.	**Ps 71:18**	3605
Your righteousness **a** day long;	**Ps 71:24**	3605
moon, throughout **a** generations.	**Ps 72:5**	1755
let **a** kings bow down before him,	**Ps 72:11**	3605
before him, **A** nations serve him.	**Ps 72:11**	3605
Let them bless him **a** day long.	**Ps 72:15**	3605
Let **a** nations call him blessed.	**Ps 72:17**	3605
I have been stricken **a** day long And	**Ps 73:14**	3605
You have destroyed **a** those who	**Ps 73:27**	3605
That I may tell of **a** Your works.	**Ps 73:28**	3605
And now **a** its carved work They	**Ps 74:6**	3162
They have burned **a** the meeting	**Ps 74:8**	3605
a the boundaries of the earth;	**Ps 74:17**	3605
man reproaches You **a** day long.	**Ps 74:22**	3605
earth and **a** who dwell in it melt;	**Ps 75:3**	3605
Surely **a** the wicked of the earth	**Ps 75:8**	3605
And **a** the horns of the wicked He	**Ps 75:10**	3605
a the humble of the earth. Selah.	**Ps 76:9**	3605
Let **a** who are around Him bring	**Ps 76:11**	3605
I will meditate on **a** Your work And	**Ps 77:12**	3605
And **a** the night with a light of	**Ps 78:14**	3605
spite of **a** this they still sinned And	**Ps 78:32**	3605
And did not arouse **a** His wrath.	**Ps 78:38**	3605
smote **a** the firstborn in Egypt,	**Ps 78:51**	3605
To **a** generations we will tell of	**Ps 79:13**	1755
So that **a** who pass *that* way pick	**Ps 80:12**	3605
A the foundations of the earth are	**Ps 82:5**	3605
And **a** of you are sons of the Most	**Ps 82:6**	3605
who possesses **a** the nations.	**Ps 82:8**	3605
And **a** their princes like Zebah and	**Ps 83:11**	3605
the Most High over **a** the earth.	**Ps 83:18**	3605
You covered **a** their sin. Selah.	**Ps 85:2**	3605
You withdrew **a** Your fury;	**Ps 85:3**	3605
Your anger to **a** generations?	**Ps 85:5**	1755
For to You I cry **a** day long.	**Ps 86:3**	3605
to **a** who call upon You.	**Ps 86:5**	3605
A nations whom You have made	**Ps 86:9**	3605
O Lord my God, with **a** my heart,	**Ps 86:12**	3605
loves the gates of Zion More than **a**	**Ps 87:2**	3605
"**A** my springs *of joy* are in you."	**Ps 87:7**	3605
afflicted me with **a** Your waves.	**Ps 88:7**	3605
me like water **a** day long;	**Ps 88:17**	3605

To **a** generations I will make known Ps 89:1 1755
up your throne to **a** generations." Ps 89:4 1755
above **a** those who are around Him? Ps 89:7 3605
The world and **a** it contains, You Ps 89:11 4393
Your name they rejoice **a** the day, Ps 89:16 3605
You have broken down **a** his walls; Ps 89:40 3605
A who pass along the way plunder Ps 89:41 3605
have made **a** his enemies rejoice. Ps 89:42 3605
have created **a** the sons of men! Ps 89:47 3605
reproach of **a** the many peoples, Ps 89:50 3605
dwelling place in **a** generations. Ps 90:1 1755
For **a** our days have declined in Ps 90:9 3605
for joy and be glad **a** our days. Ps 90:14 3605
you, To guard you in **a** your ways. Ps 91:11 3605
And **a** who did iniquity flourished, Ps 92:7 3605
A who do iniquity will be Ps 92:9 3605
A who do wickedness vaunt Ps 94:4 3605
And **a** the upright in heart will Ps 94:15 3605
And a great King above **a** gods, Ps 95:3 3605
Sing to the LORD, **a** the earth. Ps 96:1 3605
deeds among **a** the peoples. Ps 96:3 3605
He is to be feared above **a** gods. Ps 96:4 3605
For **a** the gods of the peoples are Ps 96:5 3605
Tremble before Him, **a** the earth. Ps 96:9 3605
the sea roar, and **a** it contains; Ps 96:11 4393
field exult, and **a** that is in it. Ps 96:12 3605
Then **a** the trees of the forest Ps 96:12 3605
And **a** the peoples have seen His Ps 97:6 3605
Let **a** those be ashamed who serve Ps 97:7 3605
Worship Him, **a** you gods. Ps 97:7 3605
LORD Most High over **a** the earth; Ps 97:9 3605
You are exalted far above **a** gods. Ps 97:9 3605
A the ends of the earth have seen Ps 98:3 3605
joyfully to the LORD, **a** the earth; Ps 98:4 3605
the sea roar and **a** it contains, Ps 98:7 4393
He is exalted above **a** the peoples. Ps 99:2 3605
joyfully to the LORD, **a** the earth. Ps 100:1 3605
His faithfulness to **a** generations. Ps 100:5 1755
destroy **a** the wicked of the land, Ps 101:8 3605
the LORD **a** those who do iniquity. Ps 101:8 3605
have reproached me **a** day long; Ps 102:8 3605
And Your name to **a** generations. Ps 102:12 1755
And **a** the kings of the earth Your Ps 102:15 3605
are throughout **a** generations. Ps 102:24 1755
And **a** of them will wear out like a Ps 102:26 3605
And **a** that is within me, *bless* His Ps 103:1 3605
Who pardons **a** your iniquities, Ps 103:3 3605
Who heals **a** your diseases; Ps 103:3 3605
judgments for **a** who are oppressed. Ps 103:6 3605
And His sovereignty rules over **a**. Ps 103:19 3605
Bless the LORD, **a** you His hosts, Ps 103:21 3605
the LORD, **a** you works of His, Ps 103:22 3605
His, In **a** places of His dominion; Ps 103:22 3605
In which **a** the beasts of the Ps 104:20 3605
In wisdom You have made them **a**; Ps 104:24 3605
They **a** wait for You To give them Ps 104:27 3605
Speak of **a** His wonders. Ps 105:2 3605
His judgments are in **a** the earth. Ps 105:7 3605
And ruler over **a** his possessions, Ps 105:21 3605
And gnats in **a** their territory. Ps 105:31 3605
ate up **a** vegetation in their land, Ps 105:35 3605
a the firstborn in their land, Ps 105:36 3605
The first fruits of **a** their vigor. Ps 105:36 3605
Or can show forth **a** His praise? Ps 106:2 3605
practice righteousness at **a** times! Ps 106:3 3605
To **a** generations forever. Ps 106:31 1755
the presence of **a** their captors. Ps 106:46 3605
And let **a** the people say, "Amen." Ps 106:48 3605
soul abhorred **a** kinds of food, Ps 107:18 3605
But **a** unrighteousness shuts its Ps 107:42 3605
And Your glory above **a** the earth. Ps 108:5 3605
the creditor seize **a** that he has, Ps 109:11 3605
to the LORD with **a** *my* heart, Ps 111:1 3605
studied by **a** who delight in them. Ps 111:2 3605
A His precepts are sure. Ps 111:7 3605
a those who do *His commandments;* Ps 111:10 3605
The LORD is high above **a** nations; Ps 113:4 3605
"**A** men are liars." Ps 116:11 3605
LORD For **a** His benefits toward me? Ps 116:12 3605
in the presence of **a** His people. Ps 116:14 3605
in the presence of **a** His people, Ps 116:18 3605
Praise the LORD, **a** nations; Ps 117:1 3605
Laud Him, **a** peoples! Ps 117:1 3605
A nations surrounded me; Ps 118:10 3605
Who seek Him with **a** *their* heart. Ps 119:2 3605
I look upon **a** Your commandments. Ps 119:6 3605
a my heart I have sought You; Ps 119:10 3605
of **A** the ordinances of Your mouth. Ps 119:13 3605
As much as in **a** riches. Ps 119:14 3605
After Your ordinances at **a** times. Ps 119:20 3605
law And keep it with **a** *my* heart. Ps 119:34 3605
Your favor with **a** *my* heart; Ps 119:58 3605
of **a** those who fear You, Ps 119:63 3605
With **a** *my* heart I will observe Your Ps 119:69 3605
A Your commandments are faithful; Ps 119:86 3605
throughout **a** generations; Ps 119:90 1755
For **a** things are Your servants. Ps 119:91 3605
have seen a limit to **a** perfection; Ps 119:96 3605
It is my meditation **a** the day. Ps 119:97 3605
more insight than **a** my teachers, Ps 119:99 3605
You have rejected **a** those who Ps 119:118 3605
You have removed **a** the wicked of Ps 119:119 3605
Therefore I esteem right **a** *Your* Ps 119:128 3605
I cried with **a** my heart; Ps 119:145 3605
And **a** Your commandments are truth. Ps 119:151 3605
For **a** my ways are before You. Ps 119:168 3605
For **a** Your commandments are Ps 119:172 3605
LORD will protect you from **a** evil; Ps 121:7 3605
Jerusalem **a** the days of your life. Ps 128:5 3605

May **a** who hate Zion Be put to Ps 129:5 3605
Israel From **a** his iniquities. Ps 130:8 3605
David's behalf, **A** his affliction; Ps 132:1 3605
the LORD, **a** servants of the LORD, Ps 134:1 3605
And that our Lord is above **a** gods. Ps 135:5 3605
earth, in the seas and in **a** deeps. Ps 135:6 3605
Upon Pharaoh and **a** his servants. Ps 135:9 3605
And **a** the kingdoms of Canaan; Ps 135:11 3605
O LORD, throughout **a** generations. Ps 135:13 1755
any breath at **a** in their mouths. Ps 135:17 637
Who gives food to **a** flesh, Ps 136:25 3605
give You thanks with **a** my heart; Ps 138:1 3605
Your word according to **a** Your name. Ps 138:2 3605
A the kings of the earth will give Ps 138:4 3605
acquainted with **a** my ways. Ps 139:3 3605
O LORD, You know it **a**. Ps 139:4 3605
in Your book were **a** written Ps 139:16 3605
I meditate on **a** Your doings; Ps 143:5 3605
a those who afflict my soul, Ps 143:12 3605
The LORD is good to **a**, Ps 145:9 3605
His mercies are over **a** His works. Ps 145:9 3605
A Your works shall give thanks to Ps 145:10 3605
endures throughout **a** generations. Ps 145:13 3605
The LORD sustains **a** who fall And Ps 145:14 3605
raises up **a** who are bowed down. Ps 145:14 3605
The eyes of **a** look to You, And Ps 145:15 3605
LORD is righteous in **a** His ways And Ps 145:17 3605
His ways And kind in **a** His deeds. Ps 145:17 3605
is near to **a** who call upon Him, Ps 145:18 3605
To **a** who call upon Him in truth. Ps 145:18 3605
The LORD keeps **a** who love Him, Ps 145:20 3605
But **a** the wicked He will destroy. Ps 145:20 3605
And **a** flesh will bless His holy Ps 145:21 3605
The sea and **a** that is in them; Ps 146:6 3605
Your God, O Zion, to **a** generations. Ps 146:10 1755
He gives names to **a** of them. Ps 147:4 3605
Praise Him, **a** His angels; Ps 148:2 3605
Praise Him, **a** His hosts! Ps 148:2 3605
Praise Him, **a** stars of light! Ps 148:3 3605
earth, Sea monsters and **a** deeps; Ps 148:7 3605
Mountains and **a** hills; Ps 148:9 3605
Fruit trees and **a** cedars; Ps 148:9 3605
Beasts and **a** cattle; Ps 148:10 3605
Kings of the earth and **a** peoples; Ps 148:11 3605
Princes and **a** judges of the earth; Ps 148:11 3605
Praise for **a** His godly ones; Ps 148:14 3605
is an honor for **a** His godly ones. Ps 149:9 3605
find **a** *kinds* of precious wealth, Pr 1:13 3605
us, We shall **a** have one purse," Pr 1:14 3605
And you neglected **a** my counsel And Pr 1:25 3605
They spurned **a** my reproof. Pr 1:30 3605
in the LORD with **a** your heart And Pr 3:5 3605
In **a** your ways acknowledge Him, Pr 3:6 3605
from the first of **a** your produce; Pr 3:9 3605
ways And **a** her paths are peace. Pr 3:17 3605
And happy are **a** who hold her fast. Pr 3:18
And with **a** your acquiring, get Pr 4:7 3605
And health to **a** their body. Pr 4:22 3605
over your heart with **a** diligence, Pr 4:23 3605
a your ways will be established. Pr 4:26 3605
breasts satisfy you at **a** times; Pr 5:19 3605
LORD, And He watches **a** his paths. Pr 5:21 3605
give **a** the substance of his house. Pr 6:31 3605
And numerous are **a** her slain. Pr 7:26 3605
"**A** the utterances of my mouth are Pr 8:8 3605
"They are **a** straightforward to Pr 8:9 3605
And **a** desirable things cannot Pr 8:11 3605
and nobles, **A** who judge rightly. Pr 8:16 3605
A those who hate me love death." Pr 8:36 3605
But love covers **a** transgressions. Pr 10:12 3605
yet increases **a** the more, Pr 11:24 5750
In **a** labor there is profit, But Pr 14:23 3605
A the days of the afflicted are Pr 15:15 3605
A the ways of a man are clean in Pr 16:2 3605
A the weights of the bag are His Pr 16:11 3605
A friend loves at **a** times, Pr 17:17 3605
quarrels against **a** sound wisdom. Pr 18:1 3605
A the brothers of a poor man hate Pr 19:7 3605
Disperses **a** evil with his eyes. Pr 20:8 3605
Searching **a** the innermost parts of Pr 20:27 3605
A day long he is craving, While Pr 21:26 3605
The LORD is the maker of them **a**. Pr 22:2 3605
a precious and pleasant riches. Pr 24:4 3605
a crown *endure* to **a** generations. Pr 27:24 1755
seek the LORD understand **a** things. Pr 28:5 3605
is crooked will fall **a** at once. Pr 28:18 259
A his ministers *become* wicked. Pr 29:12 3605
a the ends of the earth? Pr 30:4 3605
Yet **a** of them go out in ranks; Pr 30:27 3605
the rights of **a** the afflicted. Pr 31:5 3605
the rights of **a** the unfortunate. Pr 31:8 3605
not evil **A** the days of her life. Pr 31:12 3605
For **a** her household are clothed Pr 31:21 3605
nobly, But you excel them **a**." Pr 31:29 3605
"Vanity of vanities! **A** is vanity." Ec 1:2 3605
What advantage does man have in **a** Ec 1:3 3605
A the rivers flow into the sea, Ec 1:7 3605
A things are wearisome; Ec 1:8 3605
and explore by wisdom concerning **a** Ec 1:13 3605
I have seen **a** the works which have Ec 1:14 3605
a is vanity and striving after Ec 1:14 3605
wisdom more than **a** who were over Ec 1:16 3605
in them **a** kinds of fruit trees; Ec 2:5 3605
a who preceded me in Jerusalem. Ec 2:7 3605
a who preceded me in Jerusalem. Ec 2:9 3605
A that my eyes desired I did not Ec 2:10 3605
was pleased because of **a** my labor Ec 2:10 3605
this was my reward for **a** my labor. Ec 2:10 3605
Thus I considered **a** my activities Ec 2:11 3605

and behold **a** was vanity and Ec 2:11 3605
coming days **a** will be forgotten. Ec 2:16 3605
Thus I hated **a** the fruit of my Ec 2:18 3605
Yet he will have control over **a** Ec 2:19 3605
despaired of **a** the fruit of my labor Ec 2:20 3605
For what does a man get in **a** his Ec 2:22 3605
Because **a** his days his task is Ec 2:23 3605
sees good in **a** his labor—it is the gift Ec 3:13 3605
they **a** have the same breath and Ec 3:19 3605
man over beast, for **a** is vanity. Ec 3:19 3605
A go to the same place. Ec 3:20 3605
A came from the dust and all Ec 3:20 3605
the dust and **a** return to the dust. Ec 3:20 3605
Then I looked again at **a** the acts Ec 4:1 3605
there was no end to **a** his labor. Ec 4:8 3605
I have seen **a** the living under the Ec 4:15 3605
There is no end to **a** the people, Ec 4:16 3605
people, to **a** who were before them, Ec 4:16 3605
After **a**, a king who cultivates the Ec 5:9 3605
to drink and enjoy oneself in **a**. Ec 5:18 3605
nothing of **a** that he desires; Ec 6:2 3605
things—do not **a** go to one place?" Ec 6:6 3605
A a man's labor is for his mouth Ec 6:7 3605
a words which are spoken, Ec 7:21 3605
I tested **a** this with wisdom, *and* I Ec 7:23 3605
not found a woman among **a** these. Ec 7:28 3605
A this I have seen and applied my Ec 8:9 3605
For I have taken **a** this to my Ec 9:1 3605
It is the same for **a**. Ec 9:2 3605
in **a** that is done under the sun, Ec 9:3 3605
that there is one fate for **a** men. Ec 9:3 3605
whoever is joined with **a** the living Ec 9:4 3605
in **a** that is done under the sun. Ec 9:6 3605
your clothes be white **a** the time, Ec 9:8 3605
the woman whom you love **a** the days Ec 9:9 3605
do *it* with **a** your might; Ec 9:10 3605
time and chance overtake them **a**. Ec 9:11 3605
of God who makes **a** things. Ec 11:5 3605
years, let him rejoice in them **a**, Ec 11:8 3605
to judgment for **a** these things. Ec 11:9 3605
and **a** the daughters of song will Ec 12:4 3605
says the Preacher, "**a** is vanity!" Ec 12:8 3605
conclusion, when **a** has been heard, Ec 12:13 3605
lies **a** night between my breasts. SS 1:13
With **a** scented powders of the SS 3:6 3605
"**A** of them are wielders of the SS 3:8 3605
washing, **A** of which bear twins, SS 4:2 3605
A the round shields of the mighty SS 4:4 3605
your oils Than **a** *kinds* of spices! SS 4:10 3605
With **a** the trees of frankincense, SS 4:14 3605
along with **a** the finest spices. SS 4:14 3605
washing, **A** of which bear twins, SS 6:6 3605
with **a** your charms! SS 7:6
our doors are **a** choice *fruits,* SS 7:13 3605
If a man were to give **a** the riches SS 8:7 3605
lye And will remove **a** your alloy. Is 1:25 3605
a the nations will stream to it. Is 2:2 3605
And *it will be* against **a** the Is 2:13 3605
up, Against **a** the oaks of Bashan, Is 2:13 3605
Against **a** the lofty mountains, Is 2:14 3605
Against **a** the hills that Is 2:14 3605
Against **a** the ships of Tarshish And Is 2:16 3605
And against **a** the beautiful craft. Is 2:16 3605
over **a** the glory will be a canopy. Is 4:5 3605
He dug it **a** around, removed Is 5:2
For **a** this His anger is not spent, Is 5:25 3605
sharp and **a** its bows are bent; Is 5:28 3605
They will **a** come and settle on Is 7:19 3605
the cliffs, on **a** the thorn bushes and Is 7:19 3605
and on **a** the watering places. Is 7:19 3605
a the land will be briars and thorns. Is 7:24 3605
As for **a** the hills which used Is 7:25 3605
king of Assyria and **a** his glory; Is 8:7 3605
And it will rise up over **a** its Is 8:7 3605
channels and go over **a** its banks. Is 8:7 3605
give ear, **a** remote places of the earth. Is 8:9 3605
In regard to **a** that this people Is 8:12 3605
And **a** the people know *it, That is,* Is 9:9 3605
In *spite of* **a** this, His anger does Is 9:12 3605
In *spite of* **a** this, His anger does Is 9:17 3605
In *spite of* **a** this, His anger does Is 9:21 3605
In *spite of* **a** this, His anger does Is 10:4 3605
"Are not my princes **a** kings? Is 10:8 3164a
the Lord has completed **a** His work Is 10:12 3605
eggs, I gathered **a** the earth; Is 10:14 3605
or destroy in **a** My holy mountain, Is 11:9 3605
Therefore **a** hands will fall limp, Is 13:7 3605
dead, **a** the leaders of the earth; Is 14:9 3605
It raises **a** the kings of the Is 14:9 3605
will **a** respond and say to you, Is 14:10 3605
"**A** the kings of the nations lie Is 14:18 3605
out against **a** the nations. Is 14:26 3605
rejoice, O Philistia, **a** of you, Is 14:29 3605
Melt away, O Philistia, **a** of you; Is 14:31 3605
voice is heard **a** the way to Jahaz; Is 15:4 5704
along with **a** *his* great population, Is 16:14 3605
A you inhabitants of the world and Is 18:3 3605
And **a** the beasts of the earth will Is 18:6 3605
by the edge of the Nile And **a** the Is 19:7 3605
And **a** those who cast a line into Is 19:8 3605
A the hired laborers will be Is 19:10 3605
Egypt astray in **a** that it does, Is 19:14 3605
of **a** the groaning she has caused. Is 21:2 3605
And **a** the images of her gods are Is 21:9 3605
a the splendor of Kedar will Is 21:16 3605
have **a** gone up to the housetops? Is 22:1 3605
A your rulers have fled together, Is 22:3 3605
A of you who were found were taken Is 22:3 3605
"So they will hang on him **a** the Is 22:24 3605

and issue, **a** the least of vessels,	**Is 22:24**	3605
vessels, from bowls to **a** the jars.	**Is 22:24**	3605
to defile the pride of **a** beauty,	**Is 23:9**	3605
a the honored of the earth.	**Is 23:9**	3605
and will play the harlot with **a**	**Is 23:17**	3605
decays, **A** the merry-hearted sigh.	**Is 24:7**	3605
A joy turns to gloom.	**Is 24:11**	3605
for **a** peoples on this mountain;	**Is 25:6**	3605
covering which is over **a** peoples,	**Is 25:7**	3605
which is stretched over **a** nations.	**Is 25:7**	3605
will swallow up death for **a** time,	**Is 25:8**	5331
will wipe tears away from **a** faces,	**Is 25:8**	3605
of His people from **a** the earth;	**Is 25:8**	3605
also performed for us **a** our works.	**Is 26:12**	3605
wiped out **a** remembrance of them.	**Is 26:14**	3605
a the borders of the land.	**Is 26:15**	3605
When he makes **a** the altar stones	**Is 27:9**	3605
For **a** the tables are full of	**Is 28:8**	3605
destruction on **a** the earth.	**Is 28:22**	3605
And the multitude of **a** the nations	**Is 29:7**	3605
Even **a** who wage war against her	**Is 29:7**	3605
of **a** the nations will be	**Is 29:8**	3605
Indeed **a** who are intent on doing	**Is 29:20**	3605
are **a** those who long for Him.	**Is 30:18**	3605
And **a** of them will come to an end	**Is 31:3**	3605
Yea, for **a** the joyful houses *and*	**Is 32:13**	3605
be, you who sow beside **a** waters,	**Is 32:20**	3605
the earth and **a** it contains hear,	**Is 34:1**	3605
world and **a** that springs from it.	**Is 34:1**	3605
is against **a** the nations,	**Is 34:2**	3605
His wrath against **a** their armies;	**Is 34:2**	3605
And **a** the host of heaven will wear	**Is 34:4**	3605
A their hosts will also wither	**Is 34:4**	3605
a its princes will be nothing.	**Is 34:12**	3605
king of Assyria came up against **a**	**Is 36:1**	3605
of Egypt to **a** who rely on him.	**Is 36:6**	3605
'Who among **a** the gods of these	**Is 36:20**	3605
Assyria have done to **a** the lands,	**Is 37:11**	3605
of **a** the kingdoms of the earth.	**Is 37:16**	3605
to **a** the words of Sennacherib,	**Is 37:17**	3605
a the countries and their lands,	**Is 37:18**	3605
deliver us from his hand that **a**	**Is 37:20**	3605
I dried up **A** the rivers of Egypt.'	**Is 37:25**	3605
behold, **a** of these were dead.	**Is 37:36**	3605
a lion—so He breaks **a** my bones,	**Is 38:13**	3605
I will wander about **a** my years	**Is 38:15**	3605
And in **a** these is the life of my	**Is 38:16**	3605
cast **a** my sins behind Your back.	**Is 38:17**	3605
on stringed instruments **A** *the* days	**Is 38:20**	3605
showed them **a** his treasure house,	**Is 39:2**	3605
and **a** that was found in his treasuries.	**Is 39:2**	3605
his house nor in **a** his dominion	**Is 39:2**	3605
have seen **a** that is in my house;	**Is 39:4**	3605
when **a** that is in your house and	**Is 39:6**	3605
and **a** that your fathers have laid	**Is 39:6**	3605
hand Double for **a** her sins."	**Is 40:2**	3605
And **a** flesh will see *it* together;	**Is 40:5**	3605
A flesh is grass, and all its loveliness	**Is 40:6**	3605
and **a** its loveliness is like the	**Is 40:6**	3605
A the nations are as nothing	**Is 40:17**	3605
number, He calls them **a** by name;	**Is 40:26**	3605
a those who are angered at you	**Is 41:11**	3605
"Behold, **a** of them are false;	**Is 41:29**	3605
to the sea, and **a** that is in it.	**Is 42:10**	4393
And wither **a** their vegetation;	**Is 42:15**	3605
A of them are trapped in caves, Or	**Is 42:22**	3605
And it set him aflame **a** around,	**Is 42:25**	4480, 5439
A the nations have gathered	**Is 43:9**	3605
bring them **a** down as fugitives,	**Is 43:14**	3605
graven image are **a** of them futile,	**Is 44:9**	3605
a his companions will be put to	**Is 44:11**	3605
Let them **a** assemble themselves,	**Is 44:11**	3605
LORD, am the maker of **a** things,	**Is 44:24**	3605
spreading out the earth **a** alone,	**Is 44:24**	4480, 854
And he will perform **a** My desire.'	**Is 44:28**	3605
I am the LORD who does **a** these.	**Is 45:7**	3605
And I ordained **a** their host.	**Is 45:12**	3605
And I will make **a** his ways smooth;	**Is 45:13**	3605
and even humiliated, **a** of them;	**Is 45:16**	3605
shame or humiliated To **a** eternity.	**Is 45:17**	5703
be saved, **a** the ends of the earth;	**Is 45:22**	3605
And **a** who were angry at Him will	**Is 45:24**	3605
"In the LORD **a** the offspring of	**Is 45:25**	3605
And **a** the remnant of the house of	**Is 46:3**	3605
accomplish **a** My good pleasure';	**Is 46:10**	3605
"You have heard; look at **a** this.	**Is 48:6**	3605
"Assemble, **a** of you, and listen!	**Is 48:14**	3605
pasture *will be* on **a** bare heights.	**Is 49:9**	3605
I will make **a** My mountains a road,	**Is 49:11**	3605
A of them gather together, they	**Is 49:18**	3605
surely put on **a** of them as jewels and	**Is 49:18**	3605
And **a** flesh will know that I, the	**Is 49:26**	3605
will **a** wear out like a garment;	**Is 50:9**	3605
Behold, **a** you who kindle a fire,	**Is 50:11**	3605
will comfort **a** her waste places.	**Is 51:3**	3605
My salvation to **a** generations."	**Is 51:8**	1755
That you fear continually **a** day	**Is 51:13**	3605
among **a** the sons she has borne,	**Is 51:18**	3605
among **a** the sons she has reared.	**Is 51:18**	3605
continually blasphemed **a** day long.	**Is 52:5**	3605
arm In the sight of **a** the nations,	**Is 52:10**	3605
That **a** the ends of the earth may	**Is 52:10**	3605
A of us like sheep have gone	**Is 53:6**	3605
iniquity of us **a** To fall on Him.	**Is 53:6**	3605
is called the God of **a** the earth.	**Is 54:5**	3605
"**A** your sons will be taught of the	**Is 54:13**	3605
And **a** the trees of the field will	**Is 55:12**	3605
of prayer for **a** the peoples."	**Is 56:7**	3605
A you beasts of the field, All you	**Is 56:9**	3605
field, **A** you beasts in the forest,	**Is 56:9**	3605
are blind, **A** of them know nothing.	**Is 56:10**	3605
A of them are mute dogs unable to	**Is 56:10**	3605
have **a** turned to their own way,	**Is 56:11**	3605
the wind will carry **a** of them up,	**Is 57:13**	3605
And drive hard **a** your workers.	**Is 58:3**	3605
A of us growl like bears, And moan	**Is 59:11**	3605
They **a** gather together, they come	**Is 60:4**	3605
A those from Sheba will come;	**Is 60:6**	3605
"**A** the flocks of Kedar will be	**Is 60:7**	3605
And **a** those who despised you will	**Is 60:14**	3605
a your people *will be* righteous;	**Is 60:21**	3605
To comfort **a** who mourn,	**Is 61:2**	3605
A who see them will recognize them	**Is 61:9**	3605
To spring up before **a** the nations.	**Is 61:11**	3605
And **a** kings your glory;	**Is 62:2**	3605
A day and all night they will	**Is 62:6**	3605
All day and **a** night they will	**Is 62:6**	3605
And I stained **a** My raiment.	**Is 63:3**	3605
to **a** that the LORD has granted us,	**Is 63:7**	3605
In **a** their affliction He was	**Is 63:9**	3605
carried them **a** the days of old.	**Is 63:9**	3605
For **a** of us have become like one	**Is 64:6**	3605
And **a** our righteous deeds are like	**Is 64:6**	3605
And **a** of us wither like a leaf,	**Is 64:6**	3605
And **a** of us are the work of Your	**Is 64:8**	3605
look now, **a** of us are Your people.	**Is 64:9**	3605
And **a** our precious things have	**Is 64:11**	3605
"I have spread out My hands **a** day	**Is 65:2**	3605
A fire that burns **a** the day.	**Is 65:5**	3605
In order not to destroy **a** of them.	**Is 65:8**	3605
And **a** of you will bow down to the	**Is 65:12**	3605
or harm in **a** My holy mountain,"	**Is 65:25**	3605
"For My hand made **a** these things,	**Is 66:2**	3605
a these things came into being,"	**Is 66:2**	3605
nation be brought forth **a** at once?	**Is 66:8**	6471
for her, **a** you who love her;	**Is 66:10**	3605
her, **a** you who mourn over her,	**Is 66:10**	3605
fire And by His sword on **a** flesh,	**Is 66:16**	3605
to gather **a** nations and tongues.	**Is 66:18**	3605
"Then they shall bring **a** your	**Is 66:20**	3605
brethren from **a** the nations as a grain	**Is 66:20**	3605
A mankind will come to bow down	**Is 66:23**	3605
be an abhorrence to **a** mankind."	**Is 66:24**	3605
go, And **a** that I command you,	**Jer 1:7**	3605
on **a** the inhabitants of the land.	**Jer 1:14**	3605
I am calling **a** the families of the	**Jer 1:15**	3605
against **a** its walls round about and	**Jer 1:15**	3605
and against **a** the cities of Judah.	**Jer 1:15**	3605
concerning **a** their wickedness,	**Jer 1:16**	3605
to them **a** which I command you.	**Jer 1:17**	3605
A who ate of it became guilty;	**Jer 2:3**	3605
and **a** the families of the house of	**Jer 2:4**	3605
A who seek her will not become	**Jer 2:24**	3605
have **a** transgressed against Me,"	**Jer 2:29**	3605
But in spite of **a** these things,	**Jer 2:34**	3605
'After she has done **a** these things she	**Jer 3:7**	3605
"And I saw that for **a** the	**Jer 3:8**	3605
"Yet in spite of **a** this her	**Jer 3:10**	3605
not return to Me with **a** her heart,	**Jer 3:10**	3605
and **a** the nations will be gathered	**Jer 3:17**	3605
And **a** the hills moved to and fro.	**Jer 4:24**	3605
And **a** the birds of the heavens had	**Jer 4:25**	3605
And **a** its cities were pulled down	**Jer 4:26**	3605
grave, **A** of them are mighty men.	**Jer 5:16**	3605
God done **a** these things to us?'	**Jer 5:19**	3605
They were not even ashamed at **a**;	**Jer 6:15**	954
A of them are stubbornly	**Jer 6:28**	3605
They, **a** of them, are corrupt.	**Jer 6:28**	3605
word of the LORD, **a** you of Judah,	**Jer 7:2**	3605
you may do **a** these abominations?	**Jer 7:10**	3605
you have done **a** these things,"	**Jer 7:13**	3605
I have cast out **a** your brothers,	**Jer 7:15**	3605
a the offspring of Ephraim.	**Jer 7:15**	3605
in **a** the way which I command you,	**Jer 7:23**	3605
you **a** My servants the prophets,	**Jer 7:25**	3605
shall speak **a** these words to them,	**Jer 7:27**	3605
moon and to **a** the host of heaven,	**Jer 8:2**	3605
will be chosen rather than life by **a**	**Jer 8:3**	3605
that remains in **a** the places to	**Jer 8:3**	3605
For **a** of them are adulterers, An	**Jer 9:2**	3605
"that I will punish **a** who are	**Jer 9:25**	3605
and **a** those inhabiting the desert	**Jer 9:26**	3605
a the nations are uncircumcised,	**Jer 9:26**	3605
and **a** the house of Israel are	**Jer 9:26**	3605
a the wise men of the nations And	**Jer 10:7**	3605
nations And in **a** their kingdoms,	**Jer 10:7**	3605
are **a** the work of skilled men.	**Jer 10:9**	3605
For the Maker of **a** is He,	**Jer 10:16**	3605
And **a** my ropes are broken;	**Jer 10:20**	3605
And **a** their flock is scattered.	**Jer 10:21**	3605
to **a** which I command you;	**Jer 11:4**	3605
"Proclaim **a** these words in the	**Jer 11:6**	3605
them **a** the words of this covenant,	**Jer 11:8**	3605
Why are **a** those who deal in	**Jer 12:1**	3605
gather **a** the beasts of the field,	**Jer 12:9**	3605
"On **a** the bare heights in the	**Jer 12:12**	3605
Thus says the LORD concerning **a** My	**Jer 12:14**	3605
"Behold I am about to fill **a** the	**Jer 13:13**	3605
the prophets and **a** the inhabitants	**Jer 13:13**	3605
A Judah has been carried into	**Jer 13:19**	3605
one who has done **a** these things.	**Jer 14:22**	3605
among **a** the kingdoms of the earth	**Jer 15:4**	3605
a man of contention to **a** the land!	**Jer 15:10**	3605
Even for **a** your sins And within	**Jer 15:13**	3605
sins And within **a** your borders.	**Jer 15:13**	3605
you tell this people **a** these words	**Jer 16:10**	3605
LORD declared **a** this great calamity	**Jer 16:10**	3605
of the north and from **a** the countries	**Jer 16:15**	3605
"For My eyes are on **a** their ways;	**Jer 16:17**	3605
and **a** your treasures for booty,	**Jer 17:3**	3605
heart is more deceitful than **a** else	**Jer 17:9**	3605
A who forsake You will be put to	**Jer 17:13**	3605
as in **a** the gates of Jerusalem;	**Jer 17:19**	3605
LORD, kings of Judah, and **a** Judah and	**Jer 17:20**	3605
and **a** inhabitants of Jerusalem who	**Jer 17:20**	3605
know **A** their deadly designs	**Jer 18:23**	3605
hiss because of **a** its disasters.	**Jer 19:8**	3605
because of **a** the houses on whose	**Jer 19:13**	3605
sacrifices to **a** the heavenly host	**Jer 19:13**	3605
house and said to **a** the people:	**Jer 19:14**	3605
to bring on this city and **a** its towns	**Jer 19:15**	3605
to yourself and to **a** your friends;	**Jer 20:4**	3605
So I will give over **a** Judah to	**Jer 20:4**	3605
over **a** the wealth of this city,	**Jer 20:5**	3605
of this city, **a** its produce and	**Jer 20:5**	3605
produce and **a** its costly things;	**Jer 20:5**	3605
even **a** the treasures of the kings	**Jer 20:5**	3605
and **a** who live in your house will	**Jer 20:6**	3605
you and **a** your friends to whom you	**Jer 20:6**	3605
become a laughingstock **a** day long;	**Jer 20:7**	3605
reproach and derision **a** day long.	**Jer 20:8**	3605
A my trusted friends,	**Jer 20:10**	3605
according to **a** His wonderful acts,	**Jer 21:2**	3605
may devour **a** its environs.	**Jer 21:14**	3605
a your lovers have been crushed.	**Jer 22:20**	3605
will sweep away **a** your shepherds,	**Jer 22:22**	3605
Because of **a** your wickedness.	**Jer 22:22**	3605
My flock out of **a** the countries	**Jer 23:3**	3605
north land and from **a** the countries	**Jer 23:8**	3605
within me, **A** my bones tremble;	**Jer 23:9**	3605
A of them have become to Me like	**Jer 23:14**	3605
gone forth into **a** the land.' "	**Jer 23:15**	3605
for **a** the kingdoms of the earth,	**Jer 24:9**	3605
a taunt and a curse in **a** places	**Jer 24:9**	3605
concerning **a** the people of Judah,	**Jer 25:1**	3605
the prophet spoke to **a** the people	**Jer 25:2**	3605
to **a** the inhabitants of Jerusalem,	**Jer 25:2**	3605
"And the LORD has sent to you **a**	**Jer 25:4**	3605
take **a** the families of the north,'	**Jer 25:9**	3605
a these nations round about;	**Jer 25:9**	3605
'I will bring upon that land **a**	**Jer 25:13**	3605
a that is written in this book which	**Jer 25:13**	3605
prophesied against **a** the nations.	**Jer 25:13**	3605
My hand and cause **a** the nations	**Jer 25:15**	3605
and made **a** the nations to	**Jer 25:17**	3605
his princes and **a** his people;	**Jer 25:19**	3605
and **a** the foreign people, all the	**Jer 25:20**	3605
a the kings of the land of Uz,	**Jer 25:20**	3605
a the kings of the land of the	**Jer 25:20**	3605
and **a** the kings of Tyre, all the	**Jer 25:22**	3605
of Tyre, **a** the kings of Sidon and	**Jer 25:22**	3605
and **a** who cut the corners *of their*	**Jer 25:23**	3605
and **a** the kings of Arabia and all	**Jer 25:24**	3605
and **a** the kings of the foreign people	**Jer 25:24**	3605
and **a** the kings of Zimri, all the	**Jer 25:25**	3605
of Zimri, **a** the kings of Elam and	**Jer 25:25**	3605
of Elam and **a** the kings of Media;	**Jer 25:25**	3605
and **a** the kings of the north, near	**Jer 25:26**	3605
and **a** the kingdoms of the earth	**Jer 25:26**	3605
a the inhabitants of the earth,"	**Jer 25:29**	3605
against them **a** these words,	**Jer 25:30**	3605
a the inhabitants of the earth.	**Jer 25:30**	3605
into judgment with **a** flesh;	**Jer 25:31**	3605
speak to **a** the cities of Judah who	**Jer 26:2**	3605
a the words that I have commanded	**Jer 26:2**	3605
a the nations of the earth.	**Jer 26:6**	3605
a the people heard Jeremiah speaking	**Jer 26:7**	3605
When Jeremiah finished speaking **a**	**Jer 26:8**	3605
him to speak to **a** the people,	**Jer 26:8**	3605
and **a** the people seized him,	**Jer 26:8**	3605
And **a** the people gathered about	**Jer 26:9**	3605
the officials and to **a** the people,	**Jer 26:11**	3605
Then Jeremiah spoke to **a** the	**Jer 26:12**	3605
the officials and to **a** the people,	**Jer 26:12**	3605
a the words that you have heard.	**Jer 26:12**	3605
a these words in your hearing."	**Jer 26:15**	3605
Then the officials and **a** the	**Jer 26:16**	3605
to **a** the assembly of the people,	**Jer 26:17**	3605
he spoke to **a** the people of Judah,	**Jer 26:18**	3605
and **a** Judah put him to death?	**Jer 26:19**	3605
similar to **a** those of Jeremiah.	**Jer 26:20**	3605
When King Jehoiakim and **a** his	**Jer 26:21**	3605
men and **a** the officials heard his words,	**Jer 26:21**	3605
"Now I have given **a** these	**Jer 27:6**	3605
"**A** the nations shall serve him	**Jer 27:7**	3605
I spoke words like **a** these to	**Jer 27:12**	3605
the priests and to **a** this people,	**Jer 27:16**	3605
and **a** the nobles of Judah and	**Jer 27:20**	3605
of the priests and **a** the people,	**Jer 28:1**	3605
bring back to this place **a** the vessels	**Jer 28:3**	3605
and **a** the exiles of Judah who went	**Jer 28:4**	3605
and in the presence of **a** the people	**Jer 28:5**	3605
the LORD's house and **a** the exiles,	**Jer 28:6**	3605
in the hearing of **a** the people!	**Jer 28:7**	3605
in the presence of **a** the people,	**Jer 28:11**	3605
the neck of **a** the nations.' "	**Jer 28:11**	3605
on the neck of **a** these nations,	**Jer 28:14**	3605
and **a** the people whom	**Jer 29:1**	3605
to **a** the exiles whom I have sent	**Jer 29:4**	3605
search for Me with **a** your heart.	**Jer 29:13**	3605
will gather you from **a** the nations	**Jer 29:14**	3605
from **a** the places where I have driven	**Jer 29:14**	3605
and concerning **a** the people who	**Jer 29:16**	3605
to **a** the kingdoms of the earth,	**Jer 29:18**	3605
and a reproach among **a** the nations	**Jer 29:18**	3605

Context	Reference	Number
word of the LORD, **a** you exiles,	Jer 29:20	3605
a curse will be used by **a** the exiles	Jer 29:22	3605
sent letters in your own name to **a**	Jer 29:25	3605
the priest, and to **a** the priests,	Jer 29:25	3605
"Send to **a** the exiles, saying,	Jer 29:31	3605
'Write **a** the words which I have	Jer 30:2	3605
And *why* have **a** faces turned pale?	Jer 30:6	3605
For I will destroy completely **a**	Jer 30:11	3605
'**A** your lovers have forgotten you,	Jer 30:14	3605
'Therefore **a** who devour you will	Jer 30:16	3605
And **a** your adversaries, every one	Jer 30:16	3605
And **a** who prey upon you I will	Jer 30:16	3605
I will punish **a** their oppressors.	Jer 30:20	3605
God of **a** the families of Israel,	Jer 31:1	3605
"Judah and **a** its cities will	Jer 31:24	3605
LORD,' for they will **a** know Me,	Jer 31:34	3605
Then I will also cast off **a** the	Jer 31:37	3605
For **a** that they have done,"	Jer 31:37	3605
and **a** the fields as far as the	Jer 31:40	3605
before **a** the Jews who were sitting	Jer 32:12	3605
to **a** the ways of the sons of men,	Jer 32:19	3605
they have done nothing of **a** that	Jer 32:23	3605
a this calamity come upon them.	Jer 32:23	3605
I am the LORD, the God of **a** flesh;	Jer 32:27	3605
because of **a** the evil of the sons	Jer 32:32	3605
I will gather them out of **a** the	Jer 32:37	3605
a My heart and with all My soul.	Jer 32:41	3605
all My heart and with **a** My soul.	Jer 32:41	3605
'Just as I brought **a** this great	Jer 32:42	3605
so I am going to bring on them **a**	Jer 32:42	3605
because of **a** their wickedness:	Jer 33:5	3605
'I will cleanse them from **a**	Jer 33:8	3605
and I will pardon **a** their	Jer 33:8	3605
before **a** the nations of the earth which	Jer 33:9	3605
of **a** the good that I do for them,	Jer 33:9	3605
and tremble because of **a** the good	Jer 33:9	3605
a the peace that I make for it.'	Jer 33:9	3605
man or beast, and in **a** its cities,	Jer 33:12	3605
king of Babylon and **a** his army,	Jer 34:1	3605
with **a** the kingdoms of the earth	Jer 34:1	3605
his dominion and **a** the peoples,	Jer 34:1	3605
and against **a** its cities,	Jer 34:1	3605
Then Jeremiah the prophet spoke **a**	Jer 34:6	3605
a the remaining cities of Judah,	Jer 34:7	3605
made a covenant with **a** the people	Jer 34:8	3605
And **a** the officials and all the	Jer 34:10	3605
officials and **a** the people obeyed who	Jer 34:10	3605
to **a** the kingdoms of the earth.	Jer 34:17	3605
and **a** the people of the land who	Jer 34:19	3605
and his brothers and **a** his sons	Jer 35:3	3605
tents you shall dwell **a** your days,	Jer 35:7	3605
father, in **a** that he commanded us,	Jer 35:8	3605
us, not to drink wine **a** our days,	Jer 35:8	3605
and have done according to **a** that	Jer 35:10	3605
to you **a** My servants the prophets,	Jer 35:15	3605
I am bringing on Judah and on **a**	Jer 35:17	3605
inhabitants of Jerusalem **a** the disaster	Jer 35:17	3605
your father, kept **a** his commands and	Jer 35:18	3605
to **a** that he commanded you;	Jer 35:18	3605
"Take a scroll and write on it **a**	Jer 36:2	3605
and concerning **a** the nations,	Jer 36:2	3605
Judah will hear **a** the calamity	Jer 36:3	3605
Jeremiah **a** the words of the LORD which	Jer 36:4	3605
read them to **a** *the people of* Judah	Jer 36:6	3605
did according to **a** that Jeremiah	Jer 36:8	3605
a the people in Jerusalem and	Jer 36:9	3605
people in Jerusalem and **a** the people	Jer 36:9	3605
the LORD's house, to **a** the people.	Jer 36:10	3605
had heard **a** the words of the LORD	Jer 36:11	3605
a the officials were sitting	Jer 36:12	3605
and **a** the *other* officials.	Jer 36:12	3605
a the words that he had heard when	Jer 36:13	3605
Then **a** the officials sent Jehudi	Jer 36:14	3605
When they had heard **a** the words,	Jer 36:16	3605
a these words to the king."	Jer 36:16	3605
how did you write **a** these words?	Jer 36:17	3605
"He dictated **a** these words to me,	Jer 36:18	3605
reported **a** the words to the king.	Jer 36:20	3605
read it to the king as well as to **a**	Jer 36:21	3605
until **a** the scroll was consumed in	Jer 36:23	3605
Yet the king and **a** his servants	Jer 36:24	3605
a these words were not afraid,	Jer 36:24	3605
and write on it **a** the former words	Jer 36:28	3605
and the men of Judah **a** the calamity	Jer 36:31	3605
the dictation of Jeremiah **a** the words	Jer 36:32	3605
until **a** the bread in the city was	Jer 37:21	3605
was speaking to **a** the people,	Jer 38:1	3605
in this city and **a** the people,	Jer 38:4	3605
have acted wickedly in **a** that they	Jer 38:9	3605
a of the women who have been left	Jer 38:22	3605
'They will also bring out **a** your	Jer 38:23	3605
Then **a** the officials came to	Jer 38:27	3605
in accordance with **a** these words	Jer 38:27	3605
king of Babylon and **a** his army came	Jer 39:1	3605
Then **a** the officials of the king	Jer 39:3	3605
and **a** the rest of the officials of	Jer 39:3	3605
and **a** the men of war saw them,	Jer 39:4	3605
also slew **a** the nobles of Judah.	Jer 39:6	3605
and **a** the leading officers of the	Jer 39:13	3605
among **a** the exiles of Jerusalem	Jer 40:1	3605
Now **a** the commanders of the forces	Jer 40:7	3605
Likewise, also **a** the Jews who were	Jer 40:11	3605
who were in **a** the *other* countries,	Jer 40:11	3605
Then **a** the Jews returned from all	Jer 40:12	3605
Then all the Jews returned from **a**	Jer 40:12	3605
Johanan the son of Kareah and **a**	Jer 40:13	3605
so that **a** the Jews who are	Jer 40:15	3605
down **a** the Jews who were with him,	Jer 41:3	3605
where Ishmael had cast **a** the corpses	Jer 41:9	3605
Then Ishmael took captive **a** the	Jer 41:10	3605
the king's daughters and **a** the	Jer 41:10	3605
But Johanan the son of Kareah and **a**	Jer 41:11	3605
heard of **a** the evil that Ishmael	Jer 41:11	3605
So they took **a** the men and went to	Jer 41:12	3605
as soon as **a** the people who were	Jer 41:13	3605
So **a** the people whom Ishmael had	Jer 41:14	3605
and **a** the commanders of the forces	Jer 41:16	3605
took from Mizpah **a** the remnant	Jer 41:16	3605
a the commanders of the forces,	Jer 42:1	3605
and **a** the people both small and	Jer 42:1	3605
God, *that is* for **a** this remnant;	Jer 42:2	3605
and **a** the commanders of the forces	Jer 42:8	3605
and for **a** the people both small	Jer 42:8	3605
"So **a** the men who set their mind	Jer 42:17	3605
had finished telling **a** the people	Jer 43:1	3605
the people **a** the words of the LORD	Jer 43:1	3605
their God—that is, **a** these words	Jer 43:1	3605
and **a** the arrogant men said to	Jer 43:2	3605
and **a** the commanders of the forces,	Jer 43:4	3605
of the forces, and **a** the people,	Jer 43:4	3605
But Johanan the son of Kareah and **a**	Jer 43:5	3605
who had returned from **a** the nations	Jer 43:5	3605
that came to Jeremiah for **a** the Jews	Jer 44:1	3605
'You yourselves have seen **a** the	Jer 44:2	3605
and **a** the cities of Judah;	Jer 44:2	3605
you **a** My servants the prophets,	Jer 44:4	3605
among **a** the nations of the earth?	Jer 44:8	3605
for woe, even to cut off **a** Judah.	Jer 44:11	3605
and they will **a** meet their end in	Jer 44:12	3605
Then **a** the men who were aware that	Jer 44:15	3605
along with **a** the women who were	Jer 44:15	3605
including **a** the people who were	Jer 44:15	3605
Jeremiah said to **a** the people,	Jer 44:20	3605
to the men and women—even to **a** the	Jer 44:20	3605
LORD remember them and did not **a**	Jer 44:21	
Jeremiah said to **a** the people,	Jer 44:24	3605
the people, including **a** the women,	Jer 44:24	3605
a Judah who are in the land of	Jer 44:24	3605
a Judah who are living in the land	Jer 44:26	3605
of Judah in **a** the land of Egypt,	Jer 44:26	3605
and **a** the men of Judah who are in	Jer 44:27	3605
Then **a** the remnant of Judah who	Jer 44:28	3605
to bring disaster on **a** flesh,'	Jer 45:5	3605
a the places where you may go.' "	Jer 45:5	3605
For I will make a full end of **a**	Jer 46:28	3605
the land and **a** its fullness,	Jer 47:2	4393
To destroy **a** the Philistines,	Jer 47:4	3605
him, **a** you who *live* around him,	Jer 48:17	3605
Even **a** of you who know his name;	Jer 48:17	3605
and **a** the cities of the land of	Jer 48:24	3605
Even for **a** Moab will I cry out;	Jer 48:31	3605
there are gashes on **a** the hands	Jer 48:37	3605
"On **a** the housetops of Moab and	Jer 48:38	3605
of terror to **a** around him."	Jer 48:39	3605
"From **a** *directions* around you;	Jer 49:5	3605
and **a** its cities will become	Jer 49:13	3605
and will hiss at **a** its wounds.	Jer 49:17	3605
And **a** the men of war will be	Jer 49:26	3605
tent curtains, **a** their goods and	Jer 49:29	3605
And I will scatter to **a** the winds	Jer 49:32	3605
scatter them to **a** these winds;	Jer 49:36	3605
"**A** who came upon them have	Jer 50:7	3605
A who plunder her will have	Jer 50:10	3605
will hiss because of **a** her wounds.	Jer 50:13	3605
side, **A** you who bend the bow;	Jer 50:14	3605
to **a** that I have commanded you.	Jer 50:21	3605
a her young bulls to the sword;	Jer 50:27	3605
Babylon, **A** those who bend the bow:	Jer 50:29	3605
According to **a** that she has done,	Jer 50:29	3605
And **a** her men of war will be	Jer 50:30	3605
it will devour **a** his environs."	Jer 50:32	3605
And **a** who took them captive have	Jer 50:33	3605
And against **a** the foreigners who	Jer 50:37	3605
Devote **a** her army to destruction.	Jer 51:3	3605
LORD, Intoxicating **a** the earth.	Jer 51:7	3605
A mankind is stupid, devoid of	Jer 51:17	3605
For the Maker of **a** is He,	Jer 51:19	3605
"But I will repay Babylon and **a**	Jer 51:24	3605
Chaldea for **a** their evil that they have	Jer 51:24	3605
governors and **a** their prefects,	Jer 51:28	3605
And **a** her slain will fall in her	Jer 51:47	3605
"Then heaven and earth and **a** that	Jer 51:48	3605
slain of **a** the earth have fallen.	Jer 51:49	3605
wrote in a single scroll **a** the calamity	Jer 51:60	3605
a these words which have been	Jer 51:60	3605
that you read **a** these words aloud,	Jer 51:61	3605
like **a** that Jehoiakim had done.	Jer 52:2	3605
Babylon came, he and **a** his army,	Jer 52:4	3605
built a siege wall **a** around it.	Jer 52:4	5439
and **a** the men of war fled and went	Jer 52:7	3605
Chaldeans were **a** around the city.	Jer 52:7	5439
and **a** his army was scattered from	Jer 52:8	3605
and he also slaughtered **a** the	Jer 52:10	3605
and **a** the houses of Jerusalem;	Jer 52:13	3605
So **a** the army of the Chaldeans who	Jer 52:14	3605
down **a** the walls around Jerusalem.	Jer 52:14	3605
carried **a** their bronze to Babylon.	Jer 52:17	3605
and **a** the bronze vessels which	Jer 52:18	3605
bronze of **a** these vessels was beyond	Jer 52:20	3605
upon the capital **a** around,	Jer 52:22	5439
capital all around, **a** of bronze.	Jer 52:22	3605
a the pomegranates *numbered* **a**	Jer 52:23	3605
a hundred on the network **a** around.	Jer 52:23	5439
there were 4,600 persons in **a**.	Jer 52:30	3605
regularly **a** the days of his life.	Jer 52:33	3605
a daily portion **a** the days of his	Jer 52:34	3605
to comfort her Among **a** her lovers.	La 1:2	3605
A her friends have dealt	La 1:2	3605
A her pursuers have overtaken her	La 1:3	3605
A her gates are desolate;	La 1:4	3605
A her majesty Has departed from	La 1:6	3605
Jerusalem remembers **a** her precious	La 1:7	3605
A who honored her despise her	La 1:8	3605
hand Over **a** her precious things,	La 1:10	3605
A her people groan seeking bread;	La 1:11	3605
to **a** you who pass this way?	La 1:12	3605
me desolate, Faint **a** day long.	La 1:13	3605
a my strong men In my midst;	La 1:15	3605
Hear now, **a** peoples, And behold my	La 1:18	3605
A my enemies have heard of my	La 1:21	3605
"Let **a** their wickedness come	La 1:22	3605
with me For **a** my transgressions;	La 1:22	3605
spared **A** the habitations of Jacob.	La 2:2	3605
cut off **A** the strength of Israel;	La 2:3	3605
a that were pleasant to the eye;	La 2:4	3605
He has swallowed up **a** its palaces,	La 2:5	3605
A who pass along the way Clap	La 2:15	3605
beauty, A joy to **a** the earth'?"	La 2:15	3605
A your enemies Have opened their	La 2:16	3605
His hand Repeatedly **a** the day.	La 3:3	3605
a laughingstock to **a** my people,	La 3:14	3605
Their *mocking* song **a** the day.	La 3:14	3605
feet **A** the prisoners of the land,	La 3:34	3605
A our enemies have opened their	La 3:46	3605
of **a** the daughters of my city.	La 3:51	3605
You have seen **a** their vengeance,	La 3:60	3605
A their schemes against me.	La 3:60	3605
LORD, **A** their schemes against me.	La 3:61	3605
Are against me **a** day long.	La 3:62	3605
a four had the face of a lion on	Ezk 1:10	
a four had the face of an eagle.	Ezk 1:10	
and **a** four of them had the same	Ezk 1:16	
and the rims of **a** four of them	Ezk 1:18	
like fire **a** around within it,	Ezk 1:27	5439
take into your heart **a** My words	Ezk 3:10	3605
rams against it **a** around.	Ezk 4:2	5439
with the sword **a** around the city,	Ezk 5:2	5439
spread to **a** the house of Israel.	Ezk 5:4	3605
because of **a** your abominations,	Ezk 5:9	3605
a your remnant to every wind.	Ezk 5:10	3605
defiled My sanctuary with **a** your	Ezk 5:11	3605
and with **a** your abominations,	Ezk 5:11	3605
in the sight of **a** who pass by.	Ezk 5:14	3605
"In **a** your dwellings, cities will	Ezk 6:6	3605
for **a** their abominations.	Ezk 6:9	3605
because of **a** the evil abominations	Ezk 6:11	3605
on **a** the tops of the mountains,	Ezk 6:13	3605
soothing aroma to **a** their idols.	Ezk 6:13	3605
"So throughout **a** their habitations	Ezk 6:14	3605
a your abominations upon you.	Ezk 7:3	3605
bring on you **a** your abominations.	Ezk 7:8	3605
is against **a** their multitude.	Ezk 7:12	3605
for the vision regarding **a** their	Ezk 7:13	3605
is against **a** their multitude.	Ezk 7:14	3605
the valleys, **a** of them mourning,	Ezk 7:16	3605
'**A** hands will hang limp and all	Ezk 7:17	3605
a knees will become *like* water.	Ezk 7:17	3605
and shame *will be* on **a** faces and	Ezk 7:18	3605
and baldness on **a** their heads.	Ezk 7:18	3605
with **a** the idols of the house of	Ezk 8:10	3605
were carved on the wall **a** around.	Ezk 8:10	5439
and groan over **a** the abominations	Ezk 9:4	3605
a four of them had the same	Ezk 10:10	
wheels were full of eyes **a** around,	Ezk 10:12	5439
belonging to **a** four of them.	Ezk 10:12	
whole house of Israel, **a** of them,	Ezk 11:15	3605
they will remove **a** its detestable	Ezk 11:18	3605
and **a** its abominations from it.	Ezk 11:18	3605
Then I told the exiles **a** the	Ezk 11:25	3605
as well as **a** the house of Israel	Ezk 12:10	3605
every wind **a** who are around him,	Ezk 12:14	3605
him, his helpers and **a** his troops;	Ezk 12:14	3605
they may tell **a** their abominations	Ezk 12:16	3605
the violence of **a** who live in it.	Ezk 12:19	3605
who sew *magic* bands on **a** wrists and	Ezk 13:18	3605
I be consulted by them at **a**?	Ezk 14:3	1875
from Me through **a** their idols."	Ezk 14:5	3605
away from **a** your abominations.	Ezk 14:6	3605
with **a** their transgressions.	Ezk 14:11	3605
"Besides **a** your abominations	Ezk 16:22	3605
about after **a** your wickedness	Ezk 16:23	3605
"while you do **a** these things, the	Ezk 16:30	3605
"Men give gifts to **a** harlots,	Ezk 16:33	3605
but you give your gifts to **a** your	Ezk 16:33	3605
and with **a** your detestable idols,	Ezk 16:36	3605
I will gather **a** your lovers with	Ezk 16:37	3605
even **a** those whom you loved *and*	Ezk 16:37	3605
loved *and* **a** those whom you hated.	Ezk 16:37	3605
they may see **a** your nakedness.	Ezk 16:37	3605
have enraged Me by **a** these things,	Ezk 16:43	3605
top of **a** your *other* abominations.	Ezk 16:43	3605
in **a** your conduct than they.	Ezk 16:47	3605
righteous by **a** your abominations	Ezk 16:51	3605
and feel ashamed for **a** that you	Ezk 16:54	3605
Edom and of **a** who are around her,	Ezk 16:57	3605
you for **a** that you have done,"	Ezk 16:63	3605
a its sprouting leaves wither?	Ezk 17:9	3605
yet did **a** these things;	Ezk 17:18	3605
"**A** the choice men in all his troops	Ezk 17:21	3605
"All the choice men in **a** his	Ezk 17:21	3605
"**A** the trees of the field will know	Ezk 17:24	3605
"Behold, **a** souls are Mine;	Ezk 18:4	3605
committed **a** these abominations,	Ezk 18:13	3605
he has a son who has observed **a**	Ezk 18:14	3605
a My statutes and done them,	Ezk 18:19	3605
the wicked man turns from **a** his sins	Ezk 18:21	3605
observes **a** My statutes and practices	Ezk 18:21	3605

"**A** his transgressions which he	Ezk 18:22	3605
and does according to **a** the	Ezk 18:24	3605
A his righteous deeds which he has	Ezk 18:24	3605
turned away from **a** his transgressions	Ezk 18:28	3605
away from **a** your transgressions,	Ezk 18:30	3605
"Cast away from you **a** your	Ezk 18:31	3605
which is the glory of **a** lands.	Ezk 20:6	3605
which is the glory of **a** lands,	Ezk 20:15	3605
in that they caused **a** their	Ezk 20:26	3605
with **a** your idols to this day.	Ezk 20:31	3605
whole house of Israel, **a** of them,	Ezk 20:40	3605
gifts, with **a** your holy things.	Ezk 20:40	3605
your ways and **a** your deeds with	Ezk 20:43	3605
a the evil things that you have done.	Ezk 20:43	3605
"**A** flesh will see that I, the	Ezk 20:48	3605
a flesh from south *to* north.	Ezk 21:4	3605
"Thus **a** flesh will know that I,	Ezk 21:5	3605
will melt, **a** hands will be feeble,	Ezk 21:7	3605
and **a** knees will be weak as water.	Ezk 21:7	3605
against **a** the officials of Israel.	Ezk 21:12	3605
and many fall at **a** their gates.	Ezk 21:15	3605
so that in **a** your deeds your sins	Ezk 21:24	3605
her to know **a** her abominations.	Ezk 22:2	3605
and a mocking to **a** the lands.	Ezk 22:4	3605
a of them are bronze and tin and	Ezk 22:18	3605
a of you have become dross,	Ezk 22:19	3605
a of them desirable young men,	Ezk 23:6	3605
a of whom *were* the choicest men of	Ezk 23:7	3605
and with **a** whom she lusted after,	Ezk 23:7	3605
with **a** their idols she defiled	Ezk 23:7	3605
a of them desirable young men.	Ezk 23:12	3605
a of them looking like officers,	Ezk 23:15	3605
Babylonians and **a** the Chaldeans,	Ezk 23:23	3605
and **a** the Assyrians with them;	Ezk 23:23	3605
governors and officials **a** of them,	Ezk 23:23	3605
a of them riding on horses.	Ezk 23:23	3605
in hatred, take **a** your property,	Ezk 23:29	3605
that **a** women may be admonished and	Ezk 23:48	3605
to **a** that he has done you will do;	Ezk 24:24	3605
rejoiced with **a** the scorn of your soul	Ezk 25:6	3605
of Judah is like **a** the nations,'	Ezk 25:8	3605
he will trample **a** your streets.	Ezk 26:11	3605
"Then **a** the princes of the sea	Ezk 26:16	3605
her terror On **a** her inhabitants!	Ezk 26:17	3605
"They have made **a** *your* planks of	Ezk 27:5	3605
A the ships of the sea and their	Ezk 27:9	3605
a around, and the Gammadim were	Ezk 27:11	
hung their shields on your walls **a**	Ezk 27:11	
abundance of **a** *kinds* of wealth;	Ezk 27:12	3605
abundance of **a** *kinds* of wealth,	Ezk 27:18	3605
"Arabia and **a** the princes of	Ezk 27:21	3605
the best of **a** *kinds* of spices,	Ezk 27:22	3605
with **a** *kinds* of precious stones and	Ezk 27:22	3605
And **a** your men of war who are in	Ezk 27:27	3605
With **a** your company that is in	Ezk 27:27	3605
"**A** who handle the oar, The sailors	Ezk 27:29	3605
and **a** the pilots of the sea Will	Ezk 27:29	3605
Your merchandise and **a** your	Ezk 27:34	3605
'**A** the inhabitants of the	Ezk 27:35	3605
In the eyes of **a** who see you.	Ezk 28:18	3605
"**A** who know you among the peoples	Ezk 28:19	3605
when I execute judgments upon **a**	Ezk 28:26	3605
against him and against **a** Egypt.	Ezk 29:2	3605
And **a** the fish of your rivers will	Ezk 29:4	3605
you and **a** the fish of your rivers;	Ezk 29:5	3605
"Then **a** the inhabitants of Egypt	Ezk 29:6	3605
You broke and tore **a** their hands;	Ezk 29:7	3605
and made **a** their loins quake."	Ezk 29:7	3605
"Ethiopia, Put, Lud, **a** Arabia,	Ezk 30:5	3605
And **a** her helpers are broken.	Ezk 30:8	3605
desolate And **a** that is in it,	Ezk 30:12	4393
a around its planting place,	Ezk 31:4	5439
to **a** the trees of the field.	Ezk 31:4	3605
its height was loftier than **a** the trees	Ezk 31:5	3605
'**A** the birds of the heavens nested	Ezk 31:6	3605
And under its branches **a** the	Ezk 31:6	3605
And **a** great nations lived under	Ezk 31:6	3605
branches, And **a** the trees of Eden,	Ezk 31:9	3605
on the mountains and in **a** the	Ezk 31:12	3605
in **a** the ravines of the land.	Ezk 31:12	3605
And **a** the peoples of the earth	Ezk 31:12	3605
"On its ruin **a** the birds of the	Ezk 31:13	3605
and **a** the beasts of the field will	Ezk 31:13	3605
so that **a** the trees by the	Ezk 31:14	3605
have **a** been given over to death,	Ezk 31:14	3605
and **a** the trees of the field	Ezk 31:15	3605
and **a** the well-watered trees of	Ezk 31:16	3605
Pharaoh and **a** his hordes!"	Ezk 31:18	3605
And I will cause **a** the birds of	Ezk 32:4	3605
"**A** the shining lights in the	Ezk 32:8	3605
a of them are tyrants of the	Ezk 32:12	3605
And **a** its hordes will be	Ezk 32:12	3605
"I will also destroy **a** its cattle	Ezk 32:13	3605
I smite **a** those who live in it,	Ezk 32:15	3605
Over Egypt and over **a** her	Ezk 32:16	3605
her and **a** her hordes away.	Ezk 32:20	3605
is there and **a** her company;	Ezk 32:22	3605
A of them are slain, fallen by the	Ezk 32:22	3605
A of them are slain, fallen by the	Ezk 32:23	3605
"Elam is there and **a** her	Ezk 32:24	3605
a of them slain, fallen by the	Ezk 32:24	3605
the slain with **a** her hordes.	Ezk 32:25	3605
it, they are **a** uncircumcised,	Ezk 32:25	3605
and **a** their hordes are there;	Ezk 32:26	3605
A of them were slain by the sword	Ezk 32:26	3605
its kings and **a** its princes,	Ezk 32:29	3605
who for **a** their might are laid	Ezk 32:29	
chiefs of the north, **a** of them,	Ezk 32:30	3605
all of them, and **a** the Sidonians,	Ezk 32:30	3605
and he will be comforted for **a** his	Ezk 32:31	3605
even Pharaoh and **a** his army,"	Ezk 32:31	3605
Pharaoh and **a** his hordes,"	Ezk 32:32	3605
waste because of **a** their abominations	Ezk 33:29	3605
"My flock wandered through **a** the	Ezk 34:6	3605
over **a** the surface of the earth,	Ezk 34:6	3605
has even become food for **a** the beasts	Ezk 34:8	3605
will deliver them from **a** the places	Ezk 34:12	3605
and in **a** the inhabited places of	Ezk 34:13	3605
at **a** the weak with your horns until	Ezk 34:21	3605
in your valleys and in **a** your ravines	Ezk 35:8	3605
have heard **a** your revilings which	Ezk 35:12	3605
"As **a** the earth rejoices, I will	Ezk 35:14	3605
O Mount Seir, and **a** Edom,	Ezk 35:15	3605
Mount Seir, and all Edom, **a** of it.	Ezk 35:15	3605
the nations, and against **a** Edom,	Ezk 36:5	3605
men on you, **a** the house of Israel,	Ezk 36:10	3605
all the house of Israel, **a** of it;	Ezk 36:10	3605
gather you from **a** the lands and	Ezk 36:24	3605
I will cleanse you from **a** your	Ezk 36:25	3605
filthiness and from **a** your idols.	Ezk 36:25	3605
save you from **a** your uncleanness;	Ezk 36:29	3605
you from **a** your iniquities,	Ezk 36:33	3605
Ephraim and **a** the house of Israel,	Ezk 37:16	3605
king will be king for **a** of them;	Ezk 37:22	3605
but I will deliver them from **a**	Ezk 37:23	3605
and they will **a** have one shepherd;	Ezk 37:24	3605
bring you out, and **a** your army,	Ezk 38:4	3605
a of them splendidly attired,	Ezk 38:4	3605
shield, **a** of them wielding swords;	Ezk 38:4	3605
a of them *with* shield and helmet;	Ezk 38:5	3605
Gomer with **a** its troops;	Ezk 38:6	3605
remote parts of the north with **a** its	Ezk 38:6	3605
you and **a** your companies that are	Ezk 38:7	3605
are living securely, **a** of them.	Ezk 38:8	3605
the land, you and **a** your troops,	Ezk 38:9	3605
a of them living without walls and	Ezk 38:11	3605
of Tarshish with **a** its villages	Ezk 38:13	3605
you, **a** of them riding on horses,	Ezk 38:15	3605
a the creeping things that creep	Ezk 38:20	3605
and **a** the men who are on the face	Ezk 38:20	3605
against him on **a** My mountains,"	Ezk 38:21	3605
of Israel, you and **a** your troops and	Ezk 39:4	3605
Gog there with **a** his horde,	Ezk 39:11	3605
"Even **a** the people of the land	Ezk 39:13	3605
a of them fatlings of Bashan.	Ezk 39:18	3605
mighty men and **a** the men of war,"	Ezk 39:20	3605
and **a** the nations will see My	Ezk 39:21	3605
and **a** of them fell by the sword.	Ezk 39:23	3605
their disgrace and **a** their treachery	Ezk 39:26	3605
to **a** that I am going to show you;	Ezk 40:4	3605
house of Israel **a** that you see."	Ezk 40:4	3605
outside of the temple **a** around,	Ezk 40:5	5439
pillars within the gate **a** around,	Ezk 40:16	5439
were windows **a** around inside;	Ezk 40:16	5439
made for the court **a** around;	Ezk 40:17	5439
its porches had windows **a** around	Ezk 40:25	5439
its porches had windows **a** around;	Ezk 40:29	5439
There were porches **a** around,	Ezk 40:30	5439
its porches had windows **a** around;	Ezk 40:33	5439
And the gate had windows **a** around;	Ezk 40:36	5439
installed in the house **a** around;	Ezk 40:43	5439
a around about the house on every	Ezk 41:5	5439
on their inward side **a** around,	Ezk 41:6	5439
stages on **a** sides of the temple,	Ezk 41:7	5439
had a raised platform **a** around;	Ezk 41:8	5439
was twenty cubits in width **a** around	Ezk 41:10	5439
space *was* five cubits **a** around.	Ezk 41:11	5439
was five cubits thick **a** around,	Ezk 41:12	5439
were paneled with wood **a** around,	Ezk 41:16	5439
and on **a** the wall all around	Ezk 41:17	3605
wall **a** around inside and outside,	Ezk 41:17	5439
carved on **a** the house all around.	Ezk 41:19	3605
carved on all the house **a** around.	Ezk 41:19	5439
and **a** their exits *were* both	Ezk 42:11	3605
east and measured it **a** around.	Ezk 42:15	5439
it had a wall **a** around, the length	Ezk 42:20	5439
ashamed of **a** that they have done,	Ezk 43:11	3605
its entrances, **a** its designs,	Ezk 43:11	3605
all its designs, **a** its statutes,	Ezk 43:11	3605
all its statutes, and **a** its laws.	Ezk 43:11	3605
whole design and **a** its statutes and	Ezk 43:11	3605
a around *shall be* most holy.	Ezk 43:12	5439
and hear with your ears **a** that I	Ezk 44:5	3605
I say to you concerning **a** the statutes	Ezk 44:5	3605
LORD and concerning **a** its laws;	Ezk 44:5	3605
with **a** exits of the sanctuary.	Ezk 44:5	3605
"Enough of **a** your abominations, O	Ezk 44:6	3605
addition to **a** your abominations.	Ezk 44:7	3605
of **a** the foreigners who are among	Ezk 44:9	3605
of the house, of **a** its service and	Ezk 44:14	3605
and of **a** that shall be done in it.	Ezk 44:14	3605
statutes in **a** My appointed feasts and	Ezk 44:24	3605
"The first of **a** the first fruits	Ezk 44:30	3605
kind, from **a** your contributions,	Ezk 44:30	3605
within **a** its boundary round about.	Ezk 45:1	3605
"**A** the people of the land shall	Ezk 45:16	3605
at **a** the appointed feasts of the	Ezk 45:17	3605
provide for himself and **a** the people	Ezk 45:22	3605
grow **a** *kinds of* trees for food.	Ezk 47:12	3605
out of **a** the tribes of Israel,	Ezk 48:19	3605
they were fatter than **a** the youths	Da 1:15	3605
a *kinds of* visions and dreams.	Da 1:17	3605
a not one was found like Daniel,	Da 1:19	3605
ten times better than **a** the magicians	Da 1:20	3605
conjurers who *were* in **a** his realm.	Da 1:20	3605
destroy **a** the wise men of Babylon.	Da 2:12	3606
were crushed **a** at the same time and	Da 2:35	3606
caused you to rule over them **a**.	Da 2:38	3606
which will rule over **a** the earth.	Da 2:39	3606
crushes and shatters **a** things,	Da 2:40	3606
crush and break **a** these in pieces.	Da 2:40	3606
put an end to **a** these kingdoms,	Da 2:44	3606
over **a** the wise men of Babylon.	Da 2:48	3606
the magistrates and **a** the rulers	Da 3:2	3606
the magistrates and **a** the rulers	Da 3:3	3606
bagpipe and **a** kinds of music,	Da 3:5	3606
when **a** the peoples heard the sound	Da 3:7	3606
bagpipe and **a** kinds of music,	Da 3:7	3606
all kinds of music, **a** the peoples,	Da 3:7	3606
and bagpipe and **a** kinds of music,	Da 3:10	3606
and bagpipe and **a** kinds of music,	Da 3:15	3606
the king to **a** the peoples,	Da 4:1	3606
language that live in **a** the earth:	Da 4:1	3606
a the wise men of Babylon,	Da 4:6	3606
And in it *was* food for **a**.	Da 4:12	3606
And **a** living creatures fed	Da 4:12	3606
and was visible to **a** the earth	Da 4:20	3606
and in which *was* food for **a**,	Da 4:21	3606
"**A** *this* happened to	Da 4:28	3606
"**A** the inhabitants of the earth are	Da 4:35	3606
for **a** His works are true and His	Da 4:37	3606
Then **a** the king's wise men came	Da 5:8	3606
He bestowed on him, **a** the peoples,	Da 5:19	3606
even though you knew **a** this,	Da 5:22	3606
"**A** the commissioners of the	Da 6:7	3606
them and crushed **a** their bones.	Da 6:24	3606
the king wrote to **a** the peoples,	Da 6:25	3606
who were living in **a** the land:	Da 6:25	3606
"I make a decree that in **a** the	Da 6:26	3606
and it was different from **a** the beasts	Da 7:7	3606
and a kingdom, That **a** the peoples,	Da 7:14	3606
him the exact meaning of **a** this.	Da 7:16	3606
forever, for **a** ages to come.'	Da 7:18	5957
was different from **a** the others,	Da 7:19	3606
from **a** the *other* kingdoms and	Da 7:23	3606
the dominion and the greatness of **a**	Da 7:27	
and **a** the dominions will serve and	Da 7:27	3606
and **a** the people of the land.	Da 9:6	3605
of Jerusalem and **a** Israel,	Da 9:7	3605
who are far away in **a** the countries	Da 9:7	3605
"Indeed **a** Israel has transgressed	Da 9:11	3605
a this calamity has come on us;	Da 9:13	3605
to **a** His deeds which He has done,	Da 9:14	3605
with **a** Your righteous acts,	Da 9:16	3605
a reproach to **a** those around us.	Da 9:16	3605
nor did I use any ointment at **a** until	Da 10:3	
far more riches than **a** *of them;*	Da 11:2	3605
will magnify himself above *them* **a**.	Da 11:37	3605
a the precious things of Egypt;	Da 11:43	3605
a these *events* will be completed.	Da 12:7	3605
also put an end to **a** her gaiety,	Hos 2:11	3605
And **a** her festal assemblies.	Hos 2:11	3605
But I will chastise **a** of them.	Hos 5:2	3605
I remember **a** their wickedness.	Hos 7:2	3605
Now their deeds are **a** around them;	Hos 7:2	5437
They are **a** adulterers, Like an oven	Hos 7:4	3605
Their anger smolders **a** night,	Hos 7:6	3605
A of them are hot like an oven,	Hos 7:7	3605
A their kings have fallen.	Hos 7:7	3605
have they sought Him, for **a** this.	Hos 7:10	3605
Like a wild donkey **a** alone;	Hos 8:9	
A who eat of it will be defiled,	Hos 9:4	3605
a bird catcher is in **a** his ways,	Hos 9:8	3605
A their evil is at Gilgal;	Hos 9:15	3605
A their princes are rebels.	Hos 9:15	3605
And **a** your fortresses will be	Hos 10:14	3605
One on high, None at **a** exalts *Him*.	Hos 11:7	3162
Me, **A** My compassions are kindled.	Hos 11:8	3162
In **a** my labors they will find in	Hos 12:8	3605
A of them the work of craftsmen.	Hos 13:2	3605
he may save you in **a** your cities,	Hos 13:10	3605
"Take away **a** iniquity And	Hos 14:2	3605
listen, **a** inhabitants of the land.	Jl 1:2	3605
And wail, **a** you wine drinkers, On	Jl 1:5	3605
A the trees of the field dry up.	Jl 1:12	3605
Gather the elders *And* **a** the	Jl 1:14	3605
up **a** the trees of the field.	Jl 1:19	3605
Let **a** the inhabitants of the land	Jl 2:1	3605
And nothing at **a** escapes them.	Jl 2:3	1571
A faces turn pale.	Jl 2:6	3605
"Return to Me with **a** your heart,	Jl 2:12	3605
pour out My Spirit on **a** mankind;	Jl 2:28	3605
I will gather **a** the nations And	Jl 3:2	3605
and **a** the regions of Philistia?	Jl 3:4	3605
Let **a** the soldiers draw near, let	Jl 3:9	3605
come, **a** you surrounding nations,	Jl 3:11	3605
judge **A** the surrounding nations.	Jl 3:12	3605
And **a** the brooks of Judah will	Jl 3:18	3605
And Jerusalem for **a** generations.	Jl 3:20	1755
And slay **a** her princes with him,"	Am 2:3	3605
among **a** the families of the earth;	Am 3:2	3605
you for **a** your iniquities."	Am 3:2	3605
when it captures nothing at **a**?	Am 3:5	3920
also cleanness of teeth in **a** your cities	Am 4:6	3605
lack of bread in **a** your places,	Am 4:6	3605
"There is wailing in **a** the plazas,	Am 5:16	3605
And in **a** the streets they say,	Am 5:16	3605
"And in **a** the vineyards *there is*	Am 5:17	3605
up *the* city and **a** it contains."	Am 6:8	4393
is unable to endure **a** his words.	Am 7:10	3605
a of it will rise up like the	Am 8:8	3605
And **a** your songs into lamentation;	Am 8:10	3605
break them on the heads of them **a**!	Am 9:1	3605
And **a** those who dwell in it mourn,	Am 9:5	3605
And **a** of it rises up like the Nile	Am 9:5	3605
the house of Israel among **a** nations	Am 9:9	3605
"**A** the sinners of My people will	Am 9:10	3605

remnant of Edom And **a** the nations	**Am 9:12**	3605
And **a** the hills will be dissolved.	**Am 9:13**	3605
"**A** the men allied with you Will	**Ob 1:7**	3605
LORD draws near on **a** the nations.	**Ob 1:15**	3605
A the nations will drink	**Ob 1:16**	3605
A Your breakers and billows passed	**Jon 2:3**	3605
he became faint and begged with **a**	**Jon 4:8**	
Hear, O peoples, **a** of you;	**Mi 1:2**	3605
Listen, O earth and **a** it contains,	**Mi 1:2**	4393
A this is for the rebellion of	**Mi 1:5**	3605
A of her idols will be smashed,	**Mi 1:7**	3605
A of her earnings will be burned	**Mi 1:7**	3605
And **a** of her images I will make	**Mi 1:7**	3605
it not in Gath, Weep not at **a**.	**Mi 1:10**	1058
"I will surely assemble **a** of you,	**Mi 2:12**	3605
they will **a** cover *their* mouths	**Mi 3:7**	3605
Though **a** the peoples walk Each in	**Mi 4:5**	3605
wealth to the Lord of **a** the earth.	**Mi 4:13**	3605
a your enemies will be cut off.	**Mi 5:9**	3605
tear down **a** your fortifications.	**Mi 5:11**	3605
"The statutes of Omri And **a** the	**Mi 6:16**	3605
A of them lie in wait for	**Mi 7:2**	3605
and be ashamed Of **a** their might.	**Mi 7:16**	3605
You will cast **a** their sins Into	**Mi 7:19**	3605
He dries up **a** the rivers.	**Na 1:4**	3605
world and **a** the inhabitants in it.	**Na 1:5**	3605
your back, summon **a** *your* strength.	**Na 2:1**	3966
And **a** their faces are grown pale!	**Na 2:10**	3605
A because of the many harlotries	**Na 3:4**	
"And it will come about that **a**	**Na 3:7**	3605
And **a** her great men were bound	**Na 3:10**	3605
A your fortifications are fig	**Na 3:12**	3605
A who hear about you Will clap	**Na 3:19**	3605
"**A** of them come for violence.	**Hab 1:9**	3605
bring **a** of them up with a hook,	**Hab 1:15**	3605
He also gathers to himself **a**	**Hab 2:5**	3605
And collects to himself **a** peoples.	**Hab 2:5**	3605
"Will not **a** of these take up a	**Hab 2:6**	3605
A the remainder of the peoples	**Hab 2:8**	3605
To the town and **a** its inhabitants.	**Hab 2:8**	3605
To the town and **a** its inhabitants.	**Hab 2:17**	3605
there is no breath at **a** inside it.	**Hab 2:19**	3605
Let **a** the earth be silent before	**Hab 2:20**	3605
"I will completely remove **a**	**Zph 1:2**	3605
a the inhabitants of Jerusalem.	**Zph 1:4**	3605
And **a** who clothe themselves with	**Zph 1:8**	3605
"And I will punish on that day **a**	**Zph 1:9**	3605
For **a** the people of Canaan will be	**Zph 1:11**	3605
A who weigh out silver will be cut	**Zph 1:11**	3605
And **a** the earth will be devoured	**Zph 1:18**	3605
Of **a** the inhabitants of the earth.	**Zph 1:18**	3605
A you humble of the earth Who have	**Zph 2:3**	3605
starve **a** the gods of the earth;	**Zph 2:11**	3605
and **a** the coastlands of the	**Zph 2:11**	3605
A beasts which range in herds;	**Zph 2:14**	3605
will not be cut off *According to* **a** that	**Zph 3:7**	3605
eager to corrupt **a** their deeds.	**Zph 3:7**	3605
indignation, **A** My burning anger;	**Zph 3:8**	3605
For **a** the earth will be devoured	**Zph 3:8**	3605
That **a** of them may call on the	**Zph 3:9**	3605
no shame Because of **a** your deeds	**Zph 3:11**	3605
and exult with **a** *your* heart,	**Zph 3:14**	3605
that time With **a** your oppressors,	**Zph 3:19**	3605
praise and renown In **a** the earth.	**Zph 3:19**	3605
Among **a** the peoples of the earth,	**Zph 3:20**	3605
on **a** the labor of your hands."	**Hg 1:11**	3605
with **a** the remnant of the people,	**Hg 1:12**	3605
of **a** the remnant of the people;	**Hg 1:14**	3605
and **a** you people of the land take	**Hg 2:4**	3605
'I will shake **a** the nations;	**Hg 2:7**	3605
come with the wealth of **a** nations,	**Hg 2:7**	3605
a the earth is peaceful and quiet."	**Zch 1:11**	3605
"Be silent, **a** flesh, before the	**Zch 2:13**	3605
a lampstand **a** of gold with its	**Zch 4:2**	3605
is their appearance in **a** the land	**Zch 5:6**	3605
before the Lord of **a** the earth,	**Zch 6:5**	3605
"Say to **a** the people of the land	**Zch 7:5**	3605
a storm wind among **a** the nations	**Zch 7:14**	3605
I set **a** men one against another.	**Zch 8:10**	3605
people to inherit **a** these *things*.	**Zch 8:12**	3605
for **a** these are what I hate,'	**Zch 8:17**	3605
'In those days ten men from **a** the	**Zch 8:23**	3605
of **a** the tribes of Israel,	**Zch 9:1**	3605
every ruler, **a** of them together.	**Zch 10:4**	
So that **a** the depths of the Nile	**Zch 10:11**	3605
I had made with **a** the peoples.	**Zch 11:10**	3605
reeling to **a** the peoples around;	**Zch 12:2**	3605
a heavy stone for **a** the peoples;	**Zch 12:3**	3605
a who lift it will be severely	**Zch 12:3**	3605
And **a** the nations of the earth	**Zch 12:3**	3605
left **a** the surrounding peoples,	**Zch 12:6**	3605
will set about to destroy **a** the nations	**Zch 12:9**	3605
a the families that remain, every	**Zch 12:14**	3605
will come about in **a** the land,"	**Zch 13:8**	3605
For I will gather **a** the nations	**Zch 14:2**	3605
and **a** the holy ones with Him!	**Zch 14:5**	3605
will be king over **a** the earth;	**Zch 14:9**	3605
A the land will be changed into a	**Zch 14:10**	3605
the LORD will strike **a** the peoples	**Zch 14:12**	3605
and the wealth of **a** the	**Zch 14:14**	3605
and **a** the cattle that will be in	**Zch 14:15**	3605
any who are left of **a** the nations	**Zch 14:16**	3605
and the punishment of **a** the	**Zch 14:19**	3605
and **a** who sacrifice will come and	**Zch 14:21**	3605
and abased before **a** the people,	**Mal 2:9**	3605
"Do we not **a** have one father?	**Mal 2:10**	3605
"**A** the nations will call you blessed,	**Mal 3:12**	3605
and **a** the arrogant and every	**Mal 4:1**	3605
him in Horeb for **a** Israel.	**Mal 4:4**	3605

So **a** the generations from	**Mt 1:17**	3956
Now **a** this took place	**Mt 1:22**	3650
and **a** Jerusalem with him.	**Mt 2:3**	3956
Gathering together **a** the chief	**Mt 2:4**	3956
and sent and slew **a** the male	**Mt 2:16**	3956
Bethlehem and **a** its vicinity,	**Mt 2:16**	3956
was going out to him, and **a** Judea and	**Mt 3:5**	3956
and **a** the district around the	**Mt 3:5**	3956
us to fulfill **a** righteousness."	**Mt 3:15**	3956
Him **a** the kingdoms of the world and	**Mt 4:8**	3956
"**A** these things I will give You,	**Mt 4:9**	3956
was going throughout **a** Galilee,	**Mt 4:23**	3650
about Him spread throughout **a** Syria;	**Mt 4:24**	3650
brought to Him **a** who were ill,	**Mt 4:24**	3956
and falsely say **a** kinds of evil against	**Mt 5:11**	3956
light to **a** who are in the house.	**Mt 5:15**	3956
the Law until **a** is accomplished.	**Mt 5:18**	3956
I say to you, make no oath at **a**,	**Mt 5:34**	3654
not even Solomon in **a** his glory clothed	**Mt 6:29**	3956
Gentiles eagerly seek **a** these things;	**Mt 6:32**	3956
that you need **a** these things.	**Mt 6:32**	537a
and **a** these things will be added	**Mt 6:33**	3956
a word, and healed **a** who were ill	**Mt 8:16**	3956
news spread throughout **a** that land.	**Mt 9:26**	3650
about Him throughout **a** that land.	**Mt 9:31**	3650
a the cities and villages,	**Mt 9:35**	3956
hated by **a** because of My name,	**Mt 10:22**	3956
hairs of your head are **a** numbered.	**Mt 10:30**	3956
"For **a** the prophets and the Law	**Mt 11:13**	3956
"**A** things have been handed over	**Mt 11:27**	3956
a who are weary and heavy-laden,	**Mt 11:28**	3956
Him, and He healed them **a**,	**Mt 12:15**	3956
A the crowds were amazed, and were	**Mt 12:23**	3956
is smaller than **a** *other* seeds,	**Mt 13:32**	3956
flour until it was **a** leavened."	**Mt 13:33**	3650
A these things Jesus spoke to the	**Mt 13:34**	3956
of His kingdom **a** stumbling blocks,	**Mt 13:41**	3956
he goes and sells **a** that he has and	**Mt 13:44**	3745
he went and sold **a** that he had and	**Mt 13:46**	3956
you understood **a** these things?"	**Mt 13:51**	3956
sisters, are they not **a** with us?	**Mt 13:56**	3956
did this man *get* **a** these things?"	**Mt 13:56**	3956
and they **a** ate and were satisfied.	**Mt 14:20**	3956
they sent *word* into **a** that surrounding	**Mt 14:35**	3650
brought to Him **a** who were sick;	**Mt 14:35**	3956
And they **a** ate and were	**Mt 15:37**	3956
coming and will restore **a** things;	**Mt 17:11**	3956
and children and **a** that he had,	**Mt 18:25**	3956
to their lord **a** that had happened.	**Mt 18:31**	3956
I forgave you **a** that debt because	**Mt 18:32**	3956
should repay **a** that was owed him.	**Mt 18:34**	3956
his wife for any reason at **a**?"	**Mt 19:3**	3956
a men *can* accept this statement,	**Mt 19:11**	3956
"**A** these things I have kept;	**Mt 19:20**	3956
with God **a** things are possible."	**Mt 19:26**	3956
standing here idle **a** day long?'	**Mt 20:6**	3650
but they cried out **a** the more,	**Mt 20:31**	3173
Jerusalem, **a** the city was stirred,	**Mt 21:10**	3956
drove out **a** those who were buying	**Mt 21:12**	3956
"How did the fig tree wither **a**	**Mt 21:20**	
"And **a** things you ask in prayer,	**Mt 21:22**	3956
a regard John as a prophet."	**Mt 21:26**	3956
and my fattened livestock are **a**	**Mt 22:4**	
gathered together **a** they found,	**Mt 22:10**	3956
"Last of **a**, the woman died.	**Mt 22:27**	3956
For they **a** had *married* her."	**Mt 22:28**	3956
LORD YOUR GOD WITH **A** YOUR HEART,	**Mt 22:37**	3650
YOUR HEART, AND WITH **A** YOUR SOUL,	**Mt 22:37**	3650
YOUR SOUL, AND WITH **A** YOUR MIND.'	**Mt 22:37**	3650
therefore **a** that they tell you, do	**Mt 23:3**	3956
"But they do **a** their deeds to be	**Mt 23:5**	3956
Teacher, and you are **a** brothers.	**Mt 23:8**	3956
dead men's bones and **a** uncleanness.	**Mt 23:27**	3956
fall *the guilt of* **a** the righteous blood	**Mt 23:35**	3956
a these things will come upon	**Mt 23:36**	3956
"Do you not see **a** these things?	**Mt 24:2**	3956
"But **a** these things are *merely*	**Mt 24:8**	3956
a nations because of My name.	**Mt 24:9**	3956
as a testimony to **a** the nations,	**Mt 24:14**	3956
and then **a** the tribes of the earth	**Mt 24:30**	3956
too, when you see **a** these things,	**Mt 24:33**	3956
until **a** these things take place.	**Mt 24:34**	3956
flood came and took them **a** away;	**Mt 24:39**	537a
in charge of **a** his possessions.	**Mt 24:47**	3956
a got drowsy and *began* to sleep.	**Mt 25:5**	3956
"Then **a** those virgins rose and	**Mt 25:7**	3956
glory, and **a** the angels with Him,	**Mt 25:31**	3956
"**A** the nations will be gathered	**Mt 25:32**	3956
Jesus had finished **a** these words,	**Mt 26:1**	3956
"Drink from it, **a** of you;	**Mt 26:27**	3956
"You will **a** fall away because of	**Mt 26:31**	3956
a may fall away because of You,	**Mt 26:33**	3956
A the disciples said the same	**Mt 26:35**	3956
for **a** those who take up the sword	**Mt 26:52**	3956
"But **a** this has taken place to	**Mt 26:56**	3650
Then **a** the disciples left Him and	**Mt 26:56**	3956
But he denied *it* before them **a**,	**Mt 26:70**	3956
a the chief priests and the elders	**Mt 27:1**	3956
They **a** said, "Crucify Him!"	**Mt 27:22**	3956
But they kept shouting **a** the more,	**Mt 27:23**	4057
a the people said,	**Mt 27:25**	3956
a the land until the ninth hour.	**Mt 27:45**	3956
chief priests **a** that had happened.	**Mt 28:11**	537a
"**A** authority has been given to Me	**Mt 28:18**	3956
make disciples of **a** the nations,	**Mt 28:19**	3956
to observe **a** that I commanded you;	**Mt 28:20**	3956
And **a** the country of Judea was	**Mk 1:5**	3956
and **a** the people of Jerusalem;	**Mk 1:5**	3956
They were **a** amazed, so that	**Mk 1:27**	537a

about Him spread everywhere into **a**	**Mk 1:28**	3650
they *began* bringing to Him **a** who	**Mk 1:32**	3956
synagogues throughout **a** Galilee,	**Mk 1:39**	3650
so that they were **a** amazed and	**Mk 2:12**	3956
and **a** the people were coming to	**Mk 2:13**	3956
a great number of people heard of **a** that	**Mk 3:8**	3745
with the result that **a** those who	**Mk 3:10**	3745
a sins shall be forgiven the sons	**Mk 3:28**	3956
you understand **a** the parables?	**Mk 4:13**	3956
though it is smaller than **a** the	**Mk 4:31**	3956
becomes larger than **a** the garden	**Mk 4:32**	3956
and **a** about the swine.	**Mk 5:16**	
and had spent **a** that she had *and*	**Mk 5:26**	3956
she had and was not helped at **a**,	**Mk 5:26**	3367
But putting them **a** out,	**Mk 5:40**	3956
a that they had done and taught.	**Mk 6:30**	3956
on foot from **a** the cities,	**Mk 6:33**	3956
And He commanded them **a** to sit	**Mk 6:39**	3956
up the two fish among them **a**.	**Mk 6:41**	3956
They **a** ate and were satisfied.	**Mk 6:42**	3956
a saw Him and were terrified.	**Mk 6:50**	3956
(For the Pharisees and **a** the Jews	**Mk 7:3**	3956
"Listen to Me, **a** of you, and	**Mk 7:14**	3956
(*Thus He* declared **a** foods clean.)	**Mk 7:19**	3956
"**A** these evil things proceed from	**Mk 7:23**	3956
"He has done **a** things well;	**Mk 7:37**	3956
A at once they looked around and saw	**Mk 9:8**	1819
first come and restore **a** things.	**Mk 9:12**	3956
A things are possible to him who	**Mk 9:23**	3956
be first, he shall be last of **a** and	**Mk 9:35**	3956
last of all and servant of **a**."	**Mk 9:35**	3956
a child will not enter it *at* **a**."	**Mk 10:15**	
a these things from my youth up."	**Mk 10:20**	3956
go and sell **a** you possess and	**Mk 10:21**	3745
a things are possible with God."	**Mk 10:27**	3956
among you shall be slave of **a**.	**Mk 10:44**	3956
but he kept crying out **a** the more,	**Mk 10:48**	4183
OF PRAYER FOR **A** THE NATIONS'?	**Mk 11:17**	3956
a things for which you pray and	**Mk 11:24**	3956
he sent him last *of* **a** to them,	**Mk 12:6**	
and *so* **a** seven left no children.	**Mk 12:22**	3588
Last of **a** the woman died also.	**Mk 12:22**	3956
For **a** seven had married her."	**Mk 12:23**	3588
is the foremost of **a**?"	**Mk 12:28**	3956
LORD YOUR GOD WITH **A** YOUR HEART,	**Mk 12:30**	3650
YOUR HEART, AND WITH **A** YOUR SOUL,	**Mk 12:30**	3650
YOUR SOUL, AND WITH **A** YOUR MIND,	**Mk 12:30**	3650
MIND, AND WITH **A** YOUR STRENGTH.'	**Mk 12:30**	3650
AND TO LOVE HIM WITH **A** THE HEART	**Mk 12:33**	3650
AND WITH **A** THE UNDERSTANDING	**Mk 12:33**	3650
AND WITH **A** THE STRENGTH,	**Mk 12:33**	3650
is much more than **a** burnt	**Mk 12:33**	3956
put in more than **a** the contributors	**Mk 12:43**	3956
a put in out of their surplus,	**Mk 12:44**	3956
her poverty, put in **a** she owned,	**Mk 12:44**	3956, 3745
she owned, **a** she had to live on."	**Mk 12:44**	3650
and what *will be* the sign when **a**	**Mk 13:4**	3956
be preached to **a** the nations.	**Mk 13:10**	3956
hated by **a** because of My name,	**Mk 13:13**	3956
until **a** these things take place.	**Mk 13:30**	3956
"What I say to you I say to **a**,	**Mk 13:37**	3956
and they **a** drank from it.	**Mk 14:23**	3956
"You will **a** fall away, because it	**Mk 14:27**	3956
"*Even* though **a** may fall away, yet	**Mk 14:29**	3956
they **a** were saying the same thing also	**Mk 14:31**	3956
A things are possible for You;	**Mk 14:36**	3956
And they **a** left Him and fled.	**Mk 14:50**	3956
and **a** the chief priests and the	**Mk 14:53**	3956
And they **a** condemned Him to be	**Mk 14:64**	3956
But they shouted **a** the more,	**Mk 15:14**	4057
"Go into **a** the world and preach	**Mk 16:15**	537a
preach the gospel to **a** creation.	**Mk 16:15**	3956
[*And they promptly reported* **a**	**Mk 16:20**	
walking blamelessly in **a** the	**Lk 1:6**	3956
from this time on **a** generations	**Lk 1:48**	3956
And they were **a** astonished.	**Lk 1:63**	3956
on **a** those living around them;	**Lk 1:65**	3956
and **a** these matters were being	**Lk 1:65**	3956
in **a** the hill country of Judea.	**Lk 1:65**	3650
A who heard them kept them in mind,	**Lk 1:66**	3956
FROM THE HAND OF **A** WHO HATE US;	**Lk 1:71**	3956
before Him **a** our days.	**Lk 1:75**	3956
be taken of **a** the inhabited earth.	**Lk 2:1**	3956
which will be for **a** the people;	**Lk 2:10**	3956
And **a** who heard it wondered at the	**Lk 2:18**	3956
Mary treasured **a** these things,	**Lk 2:19**	3956
a that they had heard and seen,	**Lk 2:20**	3956
in the presence of **a** peoples,	**Lk 2:31**	3956
continued to speak of Him to **a** those	**Lk 2:38**	3956
And **a** who heard Him were amazed at	**Lk 2:47**	3956
a *these* things in her heart.	**Lk 2:51**	3956
And he came into **a** the district	**Lk 3:3**	3956
AND **A** FLESH WILL SEE THE	**Lk 3:6**	3956
and **a** were wondering in their hearts	**Lk 3:15**	3956
John answered and said to them **a**,	**Lk 3:16**	3956
and because of **a** the wicked	**Lk 3:19**	3956
Herod also added this to them **a**:	**Lk 3:20**	3956
when **a** the people were baptized,	**Lk 3:21**	537a
and showed Him **a** the kingdoms	**Lk 4:5**	3956
You **a** this domain and its glory;	**Lk 4:6**	537a
before me, it shall **a** be Yours."	**Lk 4:7**	3956
a the surrounding district.	**Lk 4:14**	3650
synagogues and was praised by **a**.	**Lk 4:15**	3956
and the eyes of **a** in the synagogue	**Lk 4:20**	3956
And **a** were speaking well of Him,	**Lk 4:22**	3956
great famine came over **a** the land;	**Lk 4:25**	3956
And **a** *the people* in the synagogue	**Lk 4:28**	3956
And amazement came upon them **a**,	**Lk 4:36**	3956

a those who had any *who were* sick	Lk 4:40	537a
hard **a** night and caught nothing,	Lk 5:5	3650
amazement had seized him and **a** his	Lk 5:9	3956
They were **a** struck with	Lk 5:26	537a
After looking around at them **a**,	Lk 6:10	3956
people from **a** Judea and Jerusalem	Lk 6:17	3956
And **a** the people were trying to	Lk 6:19	3956
from Him and healing *them* **a**.	Lk 6:19	3956
you when **a** men speak well of you,	Lk 6:26	3956
When He had completed **a** His	Lk 7:1	3956
Fear gripped them **a**,	Lk 7:16	3956
Him went out **a** over Judea and	Lk 7:17	3650
and in **a** the surrounding district.	Lk 7:17	3956
to him about **a** these things.	Lk 7:18	3956
When **a** the people and the	Lk 7:29	3956
is vindicated by **a** her children."	Lk 7:35	3956
And **a** the people of the country of	Lk 8:37	537a
they had **a** been waiting for Him.	Lk 8:40	3956
And while they were **a** denying it,	Lk 8:45	3956
presence of **a** the people the reason	Lk 8:47	3956
a weeping and lamenting for her;	Lk 8:52	3956
and authority over **a** the demons and	Lk 9:1	3956
heard of **a** that was happening;	Lk 9:7	3956
to Him of **a** that they had done.	Lk 9:10	3745
and buy food for **a** these people."	Lk 9:13	3956
did so, and had them **a** sit down.	Lk 9:15	537a
And they **a** ate and were satisfied;	Lk 9:17	3956
And He was saying to *them* **a**,	Lk 9:23	3956
And they were **a** amazed at the	Lk 9:43	3956
marveling at **a** that He was doing,	Lk 9:43	3956
for the one who is least among **a** of	Lk 9:48	3956
and over **a** the power of the enemy,	Lk 10:19	3956
"**A** things have been handed over	Lk 10:22	3956
LORD YOUR GOD WITH **A** YOUR HEART,	Lk 10:27	3650
YOUR HEART, AND WITH **A** YOUR SOUL,	Lk 10:27	3650
SOUL, AND WITH **A** YOUR STRENGTH,	Lk 10:27	3650
STRENGTH, AND WITH **A** YOUR MIND;	Lk 10:27	3650
with **a** her preparations;	Lk 10:40	4183
left me to do **a** the serving alone?	Lk 10:40	
he takes away from him **a** his armor	Lk 11:22	3833
then **a** things are clean for you.	Lk 11:41	3956
that the blood of **a** the prophets,	Lk 11:50	3956
saying to His disciples first *of* **a**,	Lk 12:1	
hairs of your head are **a** numbered.	Lk 12:7	3956
store **a** my grain and my goods.	Lk 12:18	3956
even Solomon in **a** his glory clothed	Lk 12:27	3956
"For **a** these things the nations	Lk 12:30	3956
in charge of **a** his possessions.	Lk 12:44	3956
of him they will ask **a** the more.	Lk 12:48	4057
sinners than **a** *other* Galileans because	Lk 13:2	3956
you will **a** likewise perish.	Lk 13:3	3956
a the men who live in Jerusalem?	Lk 13:4	3956
you will **a** likewise perish."	Lk 13:5	3956
and could not straighten up at **a**.	Lk 13:11	3838
a His opponents were being	Lk 13:17	3956
rejoicing over **a** the glorious things	Lk 13:17	3956
flour until it was **a** leavened."	Lk 13:21	3650
DEPART FROM ME, **A** YOU EVILDOERS.'	Lk 13:27	3956
Isaac and Jacob and **a** the prophets	Lk 13:28	3956
a who are at the table with you.	Lk 14:10	3956
a alike began to make excuses.	Lk 14:18	3956
a who observe it begin to ridicule	Lk 14:29	3956
not give up **a** his own possessions.	Lk 14:33	3956
Now **a** the tax collectors and the	Lk 15:1	3956
me, and **a** that is mine is yours.	Lk 15:31	3956
were listening to **a** these things and	Lk 16:14	3956
'And besides **a** this, between us	Lk 16:26	3956
when you do **a** the things which are	Lk 17:10	3956
flood came and destroyed them **a**.	Lk 17:27	3956
from heaven and destroyed them **a**.	Lk 17:29	3956
at **a** times they ought to pray and not	Lk 18:1	3842
I pay tithes of **a** that I get.'	Lk 18:12	3956
a child will not enter it *at* **a**."	Lk 18:17	
"**A** these things I have kept from	Lk 18:21	3956
sell **a** that you possess and	Lk 18:22	3956
and **a** things which are written	Lk 18:31	3956
but he kept crying out **a** the more,	Lk 18:39	4183
and when **a** the people saw it, they	Lk 18:43	3956
saw it, they **a** *began* to grumble,	Lk 19:7	3956
for **a** the miracles which they had seen,	Lk 19:37	3956
for **a** the people were hanging on	Lk 19:48	537a
a the people will stone us to	Lk 20:6	537a
and in the same way **a** seven died,	Lk 20:31	3588
For **a** seven had married her."	Lk 20:33	3588
for **a** live to Him."	Lk 20:38	3956
while **a** the people were listening,	Lk 20:45	3956
widow put in more than **a** *of them;*	Lk 21:3	3956
for they **a** out of their surplus	Lk 21:4	3956
in **a** that she had to live on."	Lk 21:4	3956
"But before **a** these things, they	Lk 21:12	3956
hated by **a** because of My name.	Lk 21:17	3956
so that **a** things which are	Lk 21:22	3956
be led captive into **a** the nations;	Lk 21:24	3956
the fig tree and **a** the trees;	Lk 21:29	3956
away until **a** things take place.	Lk 21:32	3956
for it will come upon **a** those who	Lk 21:35	3956
dwell on the face of **a** the earth.	Lk 21:35	3956
"But keep on the alert at **a** times,	Lk 21:36	3956
have strength to escape **a** these things	Lk 21:36	3956
And **a** the people would get up	Lk 21:38	3956
And they **a** said,	Lk 22:70	3956
the people, teaching **a** over Judea,	Lk 23:5	3650
But they cried out **a** together,	Lk 23:18	3826
And **a** the crowds who came	Lk 23:48	3956
And **a** His acquaintances and the	Lk 23:49	3956
reported **a** these things to the eleven	Lk 24:9	3956
to the eleven and to **a** the rest.	Lk 24:9	3956
with each other about **a** these things	Lk 24:14	3956
the sight of God and **a** the people,	Lk 24:19	3956
Indeed, besides **a** this, it is the	Lk 24:21	3956
a that the prophets have spoken!	Lk 24:25	3956
Moses and with **a** the prophets,	Lk 24:27	3956
Himself in **a** the Scriptures.	Lk 24:27	3956
that **a** things which are written	Lk 24:44	3956
in His name to **a** the nations,	Lk 24:47	3956
A things came into being through Him,	Jn 1:3	3956
that **a** might believe through him.	Jn 1:7	3956
of His fullness we have **a** received,	Jn 1:16	3956
drove *them* **a** out of the temple,	Jn 2:15	3956
to them, for He knew **a** men,	Jn 2:24	3956
and **a** are coming to Him."	Jn 3:26	3956
who comes from above is above **a**,	Jn 3:31	3956
who comes from heaven is above **a**.	Jn 3:31	3956
has given **a** things into His hand.	Jn 3:35	3956
nor come **a** the way here to draw."	Jn 4:15	
He will declare **a** things to us."	Jn 4:25	537a
me **a** the things that I *have* done;	Jn 4:29	3956
a the things that I *have* done."	Jn 4:39	3956
having seen **a** the things that He	Jn 4:45	3956
seeking **a** the more to kill Him,	Jn 5:18	
and shows Him **a** things that He	Jn 5:20	3956
has given **a** judgment to the Son,	Jn 5:22	3956
so that **a** will honor the Son	Jn 5:23	3956
in which **a** who are in the tombs	Jn 5:28	3956
"**A** that the Father gives Me will	Jn 6:37	3956
that of **a** that He has given Me I	Jn 6:39	3956
THEY SHALL **A** BE TAUGHT OF GOD.'	Jn 6:45	3956
"I did one deed, and you **a** marvel.	Jn 7:21	3956
a the people were coming to Him;	Jn 8:2	3956
"When he puts forth **a** his own,	Jn 10:4	3956
"**A** who came before Me are thieves	Jn 10:8	3956
them to Me, is greater than **a**;	Jn 10:29	3956
this, **a** men will believe in Him,	Jn 11:48	3956
"You know nothing at **a**,	Jn 11:49	3762
will not come to the feast at **a**?"	Jn 11:56	3756, 3361
will draw **a** men to Myself."	Jn 12:32	3956
had given **a** things into His hands,	Jn 13:3	3956
you are clean, but not **a** *of you*."	Jn 13:10	3956
"Not **a** of you are clean."	Jn 13:11	3956
"I do not speak of **a** of you.	Jn 13:18	3956
"By this **a** men will know that you	Jn 13:35	3956
name, He will teach you **a** things,	Jn 14:26	3956
remembrance **a** that I said to you.	Jn 14:26	3956
for **a** things that I have heard	Jn 15:15	3956
"But **a** these things they will do	Jn 15:21	3956
will guide you into **a** the truth;	Jn 16:13	3956
"**A** things that the Father has are	Jn 16:15	3956
we know that You know **a** things,	Jn 16:30	3956
Him authority over **a** flesh,	Jn 17:2	3956
to **a** whom You have given Him,	Jn 17:2	3956
and **a** things that are Mine are	Jn 17:10	3956
that they may **a** be one;	Jn 17:21	3956
knowing **a** the things that were	Jn 18:4	3956
where **a** the Jews come together;	Jn 18:20	3956
knowing that **a** things had already	Jn 19:28	3956
"Lord, You know **a** things;	Jn 21:17	3956
about **a** that Jesus began to do and	Ac 1:1	3956
and in **a** Judea and Samaria,	Ac 1:8	3956
These **a** with one mind were	Ac 1:14	3956
and **a** his intestines gushed out.	Ac 1:18	3956
to **a** who were living in Jerusalem;	Ac 1:19	3956
a the time that the Lord Jesus went	Ac 1:21	3956
who know the hearts of **a** men,	Ac 1:24	3956
they were **a** together in one place.	Ac 2:1	3956
And they were **a** filled with the	Ac 2:4	3956
are not **a** these who are speaking	Ac 2:7	3956
they **a** continued in amazement	Ac 2:12	3956
and **a** you who live in Jerusalem,	Ac 2:14	3956
FORTH OF MY SPIRIT ON **A** MANKIND;	Ac 2:17	3956
to which we are **a** witnesses.	Ac 2:32	3956
"Therefore let **a** the house of Israel	Ac 2:36	3956
and for **a** who are far off,	Ac 2:39	3956
And **a** those who had believed were	Ac 2:44	3956
and had **a** things in common;	Ac 2:44	537a
and were sharing them with **a**,	Ac 2:45	3956
having favor with **a** the people.	Ac 2:47	3650
And **a** the people saw him walking	Ac 3:9	3956
a the people ran together to them	Ac 3:11	3956
health in the presence of you **a**.	Ac 3:16	3956
by the mouth of **a** the prophets,	Ac 3:18	3956
the period of restoration of **a** things	Ac 3:21	3956
a the prophets who have spoken,	Ac 3:24	3956
'AND IN YOUR SEED **A** THE FAMILIES	Ac 3:25	3956
and **a** who were of high-priestly	Ac 4:6	3745
let it be known to **a** of you and	Ac 4:10	3956
and to **a** the people of Israel,	Ac 4:10	3956
to **a** who live in Jerusalem,	Ac 4:16	3956
teach at **a** in the name of Jesus.	Ac 4:18	2527
because they were **a** glorifying God	Ac 4:21	3956
and reported **a** that the chief	Ac 4:23	3745
THE SEA, AND **A** THAT IS IN THEM,	Ac 4:24	3956
speak Your word with **a** confidence,	Ac 4:29	3956
a filled with the Holy Spirit and	Ac 4:31	537a
but **a** things were common property	Ac 4:32	3956
abundant grace was upon them **a**.	Ac 4:33	3956
for **a** who were owners of land or	Ac 4:34	3745
fear came over **a** who heard of it.	Ac 5:5	3956
over **a** who heard of these things.	Ac 5:11	3956
and they were **a** with one accord in	Ac 5:12	3956
And **a** the more believers in the	Ac 5:14	3123
and they were **a** being healed.	Ac 5:16	537a
up, along with **a** his associates	Ac 5:17	3956
even **a** the Senate of the sons of	Ac 5:21	3956
Law, respected by **a** the people,	Ac 5:34	3956
and **a** who followed him were	Ac 5:36	3956
and **a** those who followed him were	Ac 5:37	3956
a who were sitting in the Council	Ac 6:15	3956
him from **a** his afflictions,	Ac 7:10	3956
over Egypt and **a** his household.	Ac 7:10	3650
came over **a** Egypt and Canaan,	Ac 7:11	3650
a his relatives to come to him,	Ac 7:14	3956
seventy-five persons *in* **a**.	Ac 7:14	
a the learning of the Egyptians,	Ac 7:22	3956
HAND WHICH MADE **A** THESE THINGS?'	Ac 7:50	3956
and they were **a** scattered	Ac 8:1	3956
and they **a**, from smallest to	Ac 8:10	3956
was in charge of **a** her treasure;	Ac 8:27	3956
"If you believe with **a** your heart,	Ac 8:37	3650
the gospel to **a** the cities until	Ac 8:40	3956
bind **a** who call on Your name."	Ac 9:14	3956
A those hearing him continued to be	Ac 9:21	3956
but they were **a** afraid of him, not	Ac 9:26	3956
So the church throughout **a** Judea	Ac 9:31	3650
traveling through **a** *those regions,*	Ac 9:32	3956
And **a** who lived at Lydda and	Ac 9:35	3956
and **a** the widows stood beside him	Ac 9:39	3956
and showing **a** the tunics and	Ac 9:39	3745
a out and knelt down and prayed,	Ac 9:40	3956
It became known **a** over Joppa,	Ac 9:42	3650
feared God with **a** his household,	Ac 10:2	3956
a *kinds of* four-footed animals	Ac 10:12	3956
we are **a** here present before God	Ac 10:33	3956
present before God to hear **a** that	Ac 10:33	3956
Jesus Christ (He is Lord of **a**)	Ac 10:36	3956
took place throughout **a** Judea,	Ac 10:37	3650
and healing **a** who were oppressed	Ac 10:38	3956
"We are witnesses of **a** the	Ac 10:39	3956
not to **a** the people, but to	Ac 10:41	3956
"Of Him **a** the prophets bear	Ac 10:43	3956
the Holy Spirit fell upon **a** those	Ac 10:44	3956
A the circumcised believers who came	Ac 10:45	3745
saved, you and **a** your household.'	Ac 11:14	3956
encourage them **a** with resolute heart	Ac 11:23	3956
a great famine **a** over the world.	Ac 11:28	3650
from **a** that the Jewish people were	Ac 12:11	3956
are full of **a** deceit and fraud,	Ac 13:10	3956
you enemy of **a** righteousness,	Ac 13:10	3956
their land as an inheritance—**a**	Ac 13:19	
MY HEART, who will do **a** My will.'	Ac 13:22	3956
to **a** the people of Israel.	Ac 13:24	3956
"When they had carried out **a**	Ac 13:29	3956
believes is freed from **a** things,	Ac 13:39	3956
THE SEA AND **A** THAT IS IN THEM.	Ac 14:15	3956
He permitted **a** the nations to go their	Ac 14:16	3956
they *began* to report **a** things that	Ac 14:27	3745
great joy to **a** the brethren.	Ac 15:3	3956
a that God had done with them.	Ac 15:4	3745
A the people kept silent, and they	Ac 15:12	3956
AND **A** THE GENTILES WHO ARE CALLED	Ac 15:17	3956
for they **a** knew that his father	Ac 16:3	537a
a the doors were opened and	Ac 16:26	3956
not harm yourself, for we are **a** here!"	Ac 16:28	537a
with **a** who were in his house.	Ac 16:32	3956
baptized, he and **a** his *household.*	Ac 16:33	537a
and they **a** act contrary to the	Ac 17:7	3956
(Now **a** the Athenians and the	Ac 17:21	3956
are very religious in **a** respects.	Ac 17:22	3956
made the world and **a** things in it,	Ac 17:24	3956
since He Himself gives to **a**	Ac 17:25	3956
life and breath and **a** things;	Ac 17:25	3956
live on **a** the face of the earth,	Ac 17:26	3956
that **a** *people* everywhere should repent,	Ac 17:30	3956
having furnished proof to **a** men by	Ac 17:31	3956
a the Jews to leave Rome.	Ac 18:2	3956
in the Lord with **a** his household,	Ac 18:8	3650
And they **a** took hold of Sosthenes,	Ac 18:17	3956
strengthening **a** the disciples.	Ac 18:23	3956
There were in **a** about twelve men.	Ac 19:7	3956
so that **a** who lived in Asia heard	Ac 19:10	3956
a of them and overpowered them,	Ac 19:16	297
This became known to **a**,	Ac 19:17	3956
and fear fell upon them **a** and the	Ac 19:17	3956
Ephesus, but in almost **a** of Asia,	Ac 19:26	3956
made with hands are no gods *at* **a**.	Ac 19:26	
she whom **a** of Asia and the world	Ac 19:27	3650
a *single* outcry arose from them **a**	Ac 19:34	3956
what man is there after **a** who does	Ac 19:35	1063
serving the Lord with **a** humility	Ac 20:19	3956
now, behold, I know that **a** of you,	Ac 20:25	3956
am innocent of the blood of **a** men.	Ac 20:26	3956
yourselves and for **a** the flock,	Ac 20:28	3956
among **a** those who are sanctified.	Ac 20:32	3956
knelt down and prayed with them **a**.	Ac 20:36	3956
on our journey, while they **a**,	Ac 21:5	3956
and **a** the elders were present.	Ac 21:18	3956
they are **a** zealous for the Law;	Ac 21:20	3956
that you are teaching **a** the Jews	Ac 21:21	3956
and **a** will know that there is	Ac 21:24	3956
began to stir up **a** the crowd	Ac 21:27	3956
who preaches to **a** men everywhere	Ac 21:28	3956
Then **a** the city was provoked, and	Ac 21:30	3650
that **a** Jerusalem was in confusion.	Ac 21:31	3650
for God just as you **a** are today.	Ac 22:3	3956
also the high priest and **a** the Council	Ac 22:5	3956
flashed from heaven **a** around me,	Ac 22:6	4012
and there you will be told of **a**	Ac 22:10	3956
of by **a** the Jews who lived there,	Ac 22:12	3956
will be a witness for Him to **a** men	Ac 22:15	3956
and **a** the Council to assemble,	Ac 22:30	3956
the Pharisees acknowledge them **a**.	Ac 23:8	297
Felix, with **a** thankfulness.	Ac 24:3	3956
a the Jews throughout the world,	Ac 24:5	3956
concerning **a** these matters you	Ac 24:8	3956
and **a** you gentlemen here present	Ac 25:24	3956
you see this man about whom **a**	Ac 25:24	537a
I have brought him before you **a**	Ac 25:26	

"In regard to **a** the things of	**Ac 26:2**	*3956*
an expert in **a** customs and questions	**Ac 26:3**	*3956*
a Jews know my manner of life from	**Ac 26:4**	*3956*
them often in **a** the synagogues,	**Ac 26:11**	*3956*
shining **a** around me and those who	**Ac 26:13**	*3956*
we had **a** fallen to the ground,	**Ac 26:14**	*3956*
throughout **a** the region of Judea,	**Ac 26:20**	*3956*
but also **a** who hear me this day,	**Ac 26:29**	*3956*
from then on **a** hope of our being	**Ac 27:20**	*3956*
God has granted you **a** those who	**Ac 27:24**	*3956*
them **a** to take some food,	**Ac 27:33**	*537a*
to God in the presence of **a**,	**Ac 27:35**	*3956*
A of them were encouraged and they	**Ac 27:36**	*3956*
A of us in the ship were two hundred	**Ac 27:37**	*3956*
a were brought safely to land.	**Ac 27:44**	*3956*
kindled a fire and received us **a**.	**Ac 28:2**	*3956*
they supplied *us* with **a** we needed.	**Ac 28:10**	*3588*
was welcoming **a** who came to him,	**Ac 28:30**	*3956*
Lord Jesus Christ with **a** openness,	**Ac 28:31**	*3956*
of faith among **a** the Gentiles for	**Ro 1:5**	*3956*
to **a** who are beloved of God in	**Ro 1:7**	*3956*
through Jesus Christ for you **a**,	**Ro 1:8**	*3956*
from heaven against **a** ungodliness	**Ro 1:18**	*3956*
filled with **a** unrighteousness,	**Ro 1:29**	*3956*
For **a** who have sinned without the	**Ro 2:12**	*3745*
and **a** who have sinned under the	**Ro 2:12**	*3745*
First of **a**, that they were	**Ro 3:2**	*4413*
Are we better than they? Not at **a**;	**Ro 3:9**	*3843*
Jews and Greeks are **a** under sin;	**Ro 3:9**	*3956*
A HAVE TURNED ASIDE,	**Ro 3:12**	*3956*
and **a** the world may become	**Ro 3:19**	*3956*
Christ for **a** those who believe;	**Ro 3:22**	*3956*
for **a** have sinned and fall short	**Ro 3:23**	*3956*
that he might be the father of **a**	**Ro 4:11**	*3956*
be guaranteed to **a** the descendants,	**Ro 4:16**	*3956*
who is the father of us **a**,	**Ro 4:16**	*3956*
sin, and so death spread to **a** men,	**Ro 5:12**	*3956*
to all men, because **a** sinned	**Ro 5:12**	*3956*
resulted condemnation to **a** men,	**Ro 5:18**	*3956*
justification of life to **a** men.	**Ro 5:18**	*3956*
grace abounded **a** the more,	**Ro 5:20**	*5248*
Or do you not know that **a** of us	**Ro 6:3**	*3745*
died, He died to sin once for **a**;	**Ro 6:10**	*2178*
For **a** who are being led by the	**Ro 8:14**	*3745*
And we know that God causes **a**	**Ro 8:28**	*3956*
but delivered Him over for us **a**,	**Ro 8:32**	*3956*
with Him freely give us **a** things?	**Ro 8:32**	*3956*
ARE BEING PUT TO DEATH **A** DAY LONG;	**Ro 8:36**	*3650*
But in **a** these things we	**Ro 8:37**	*3956*
to the flesh, who is over **a**,	**Ro 9:5**	*3956*
For they are not **a** Israel who are	**Ro 9:6**	*3956*
nor are they **a** children	**Ro 9:7**	*3956*
for the same *Lord* is Lord of **a**,	**Ro 10:12**	*3956*
in riches for **a** who call on Him;	**Ro 10:12**	*3956*
did not **a** heed the good news;	**Ro 10:16**	*3956*
HAS GONE OUT INTO **A** THE EARTH,	**Ro 10:18**	*3956*
"**A** THE DAY LONG I HAVE STRETCHED	**Ro 10:21**	*3650*
and so **a** Israel will be saved;	**Ro 11:26**	*3956*
For God has shut up **a** in	**Ro 11:32**	*3956*
that He may show mercy to **a**.	**Ro 11:32**	*3956*
Him and to Him are **a** things.	**Ro 11:36**	*3956*
a the members do not have the same	**Ro 12:4**	*3956*
is right in the sight of **a** men.	**Ro 12:17**	*3956*
on you, be at peace with **a** men.	**Ro 12:18**	*3956*
Render to **a** what is due them:	**Ro 13:7**	*3956*
faith that he may eat **a** things,	**Ro 14:2**	*3956*
For we will **a** stand before the	**Ro 14:10**	*3956*
A things indeed are clean, but	**Ro 14:20**	*3956*
"PRAISE THE LORD **A** YOU GENTILES,	**Ro 15:11**	*3956*
LET **A** THE PEOPLES PRAISE HIM."	**Ro 15:11**	*3956*
with **a** joy and peace in believing,	**Ro 15:13**	*3956*
goodness, filled with **a** knowledge and	**Ro 15:14**	*3956*
the God of peace be with you **a**.	**Ro 15:33**	*3956*
a the churches of the Gentiles;	**Ro 16:4**	*3956*
a the saints who are with them.	**Ro 16:15**	*3956*
A the churches of Christ greet you.	**Ro 16:16**	*3956*
your obedience has reached to **a**;	**Ro 16:19**	*3956*
Lord Jesus Christ be with you **a**.	**Ro 16:24**	*3956*
been made known to **a** the nations,	**Ro 16:26**	*3956*
with **a** who in every place call	**1Co 1:2**	*3956*
in **a** speech and all knowledge,	**1Co 1:5**	*3956*
in all speech and **a** knowledge,	**1Co 1:5**	*3956*
Jesus Christ, that you **a** agree and	**1Co 1:10**	*3956*
A THAT GOD HAS PREPARED FOR THOSE WHO	**1Co 2:9**	*3745*
for the Spirit searches **a** things,	**1Co 2:10**	*3956*
is spiritual appraises **a** things,	**1Co 2:15**	*3956*
For **a** things belong to you,	**1Co 3:21**	*3956*
a things belong to you,	**1Co 3:22**	*3956*
exhibited us apostles last of **a**,	**1Co 4:9**	*2078*
the world, the dregs of **a** things,	**1Co 4:13**	*3956*
I *did* not at **a** *mean* with the	**1Co 5:10**	*3843*
A things are lawful for me, but	**1Co 6:12**	*3956*
but not **a** things are profitable.	**1Co 6:12**	*3956*
A things are lawful for me, but I	**1Co 6:12**	*3956*
a men were even as I myself am.	**1Co 7:7**	*3956*
so I direct in **a** the churches.	**1Co 7:17**	*3956*
we know that we **a** have knowledge.	**1Co 8:1**	*3956*
Father, from whom are **a** things and	**1Co 8:6**	*3956*
Christ, by whom are **a** things,	**1Co 8:6**	*3956*
not **a** men have this knowledge;	**1Co 8:7**	*3956*
right, but we endure **a** things so	**1Co 9:12**	*3956*
For though I am free from **a** *men,*	**1Co 9:19**	*3956*
I have made myself a slave to **a**,	**1Co 9:19**	*3956*
I have become **a** things to all men,	**1Co 9:22**	*3956*
I have become all things to **a** men,	**1Co 9:22**	*3956*
that I may by **a** means save some.	**1Co 9:22**	*3843*
I do **a** things for the sake of	**1Co 9:23**	*3956*
those who run in a race **a** run,	**1Co 9:24**	*3956*
exercises self-control in **a** things.	**1Co 9:25**	*3956*
fathers were **a** under the cloud and	**1Co 10:1**	*3956*
and **a** passed through the sea;	**1Co 10:1**	*3956*
and **a** were baptized into Moses in	**1Co 10:2**	*3956*
and **a** ate the same spiritual food;	**1Co 10:3**	*3956*
and **a** drank the same spiritual	**1Co 10:4**	*3956*
for we **a** partake of the one bread.	**1Co 10:17**	*3956*
A things are lawful, but not all	**1Co 10:23**	*3956*
but not **a** things are profitable.	**1Co 10:23**	*3956*
A things are lawful, but not all	**1Co 10:23**	*3956*
lawful, but not **a** things edify.	**1Co 10:23**	*3956*
IS THE LORD'S, AND **A** IT CONTAINS.	**1Co 10:26**	*4138*
you do, do **a** to the glory of God.	**1Co 10:31**	*3956*
I also please **a** men in all things,	**1Co 10:33**	*3956*
I also please all men in **a** things,	**1Co 10:33**	*3956*
and **a** things originate from God.	**1Co 11:12**	*3956*
who works **a** things in all *persons.*	**1Co 12:6**	*3956*
who works all things in **a** *persons.*	**1Co 12:6**	*3956*
same Spirit works **a** these things,	**1Co 12:11**	*3956*
and **a** the members of the body,	**1Co 12:12**	*3956*
we were **a** baptized into one body,	**1Co 12:13**	*3956*
we were **a** made to drink of	**1Co 12:13**	*3956*
If they were **a** one member,	**1Co 12:19**	*3956*
a the members suffer with it;	**1Co 12:26**	*3956*
a the members rejoice with it.	**1Co 12:26**	*3956*
A are not apostles, are they?	**1Co 12:29**	*3956*
A are not prophets, are they?	**1Co 12:29**	*3956*
A are not teachers, are they?	**1Co 12:29**	*3956*
A are not *workers of* miracles, are	**1Co 12:29**	*3956*
A do not have gifts of healings,	**1Co 12:30**	*3956*
A do not speak with tongues, do	**1Co 12:30**	*3956*
A do not interpret, do they?	**1Co 12:30**	*3956*
a mysteries and all knowledge;	**1Co 13:2**	*3956*
all mysteries and **a** knowledge;	**1Co 13:2**	*3956*
and if I have **a** faith, so as to	**1Co 13:2**	*3956*
And if I give **a** my possessions to	**1Co 13:3**	*3956*
bears **a** things, believes all	**1Co 13:7**	*3956*
all things, believes **a** things,	**1Co 13:7**	*3956*
all things, hopes **a** things,	**1Co 13:7**	*3956*
all things, endures **a** things.	**1Co 13:7**	*3956*
wish that you **a** spoke in tongues,	**1Co 14:5**	*3956*
speak in tongues more than you **a**;	**1Co 14:18**	*3956*
together and **a** speak in tongues,	**1Co 14:23**	*3956*
But if **a** prophesy, and an	**1Co 14:24**	*3956*
man enters, he is convicted by **a**,	**1Co 14:24**	*3956*
all, he is called to account by **a**;	**1Co 14:24**	*3956*
Let **a** things be done for	**1Co 14:26**	*3956*
For you can **a** prophesy one by one,	**1Co 14:31**	*3956*
so that **a** may learn and all may be	**1Co 14:31**	*3956*
may learn and **a** may be exhorted;	**1Co 14:31**	*3956*
in **a** the churches of the saints.	**1Co 14:33**	*3956*
But **a** things must be done properly	**1Co 14:40**	*3956*
to James, then to **a** the apostles;	**1Co 15:7**	*3956*
and last of **a**, as to one	**1Co 15:8**	*3956*
labored even more than **a** of them,	**1Co 15:10**	*3956*
we are of **a** men most to be pitied.	**1Co 15:19**	*3956*
For as in Adam **a** die, so also in	**1Co 15:22**	*3956*
in Christ **a** will be made alive.	**1Co 15:22**	*3956*
when He has abolished **a** rule and	**1Co 15:24**	*3956*
rule and **a** authority and power.	**1Co 15:24**	*3956*
put **a** His enemies under His feet.	**1Co 15:25**	*3956*
For HE HAS PUT **A** THINGS IN	**1Co 15:27**	*3956*
"**A** things are put in subjection,"	**1Co 15:27**	*3956*
put **a** things in subjection to Him.	**1Co 15:27**	*3956*
a things are subjected to Him,	**1Co 15:28**	*3956*
One who subjected **a** things to Him,	**1Co 15:28**	*3956*
to Him, so that God may be **a** in all.	**1Co 15:28**	*3956*
to Him, so that God may be all in **a**.	**1Co 15:28**	*3956*
If the dead are not raised at **a**,	**1Co 15:29**	*3654*
A flesh is not the same flesh, but	**1Co 15:39**	*3956*
we will not **a** sleep, but we will	**1Co 15:51**	*3956*
sleep, but we will **a** be changed,	**1Co 15:51**	*3956*
not at **a** *his* desire to come now,	**1Co 16:12**	*3843*
Let **a** that you do be done in love.	**1Co 16:14**	*3956*
A the brethren greet you.	**1Co 16:20**	*3956*
be with you **a** in Christ Jesus.	**1Co 16:24**	*3956*
which is at Corinth with **a** the saints	**2Co 1:1**	*3956*
of mercies and God of **a** comfort,	**2Co 1:3**	*3956*
who comforts us in **a** our affliction	**2Co 1:4**	*3956*
having confidence in you **a** that	**2Co 2:3**	*3956*
my joy would be *the joy* of you **a**.	**2Co 2:3**	*3956*
not to say too much—to **a** of you.	**2Co 2:5**	*3956*
you are obedient in **a** things.	**2Co 2:9**	*3956*
hearts, known and read by **a** men;	**2Co 3:2**	*3956*
But we **a**, with unveiled face	**2Co 3:18**	*3956*
For **a** things *are* for your sakes,	**2Co 4:15**	*3956*
of glory far beyond **a** comparison,	**2Co 4:17**	*5236*
For we must **a** appear before the	**2Co 5:10**	*3956*
this, that one died for **a**,	**2Co 5:14**	*3956*
died for all, therefore **a** died;	**2Co 5:14**	*3956*
and He died for **a**, so that they who	**2Co 5:15**	*3956*
Now **a** *these* things are from God,	**2Co 5:18**	*3956*
nothing yet possessing **a** things.	**2Co 6:10**	*3956*
let us cleanse ourselves from **a**	**2Co 7:1**	*3956*
with joy in **a** our affliction.	**2Co 7:4**	*3956*
has been refreshed by you **a**.	**2Co 7:13**	*3956*
we spoke **a** things to you in truth,	**2Co 7:14**	*3956*
abounds **a** the more toward you,	**2Co 7:15**	*4053*
remembers the obedience of you **a**,	**2Co 7:15**	*3956*
and in **a** earnestness and in the love	**2Co 8:7**	*3956*
has spread through **a** the churches;	**2Co 8:18**	*3956*
to make **a** grace abound to you,	**2Co 9:8**	*3956*
a sufficiency in everything,	**2Co 9:8**	*3956*
in everything for **a** liberality,	**2Co 9:11**	*3956*
contribution to them and to **a**,	**2Co 9:13**	*3956*
ready to punish **a** disobedience,	**2Co 10:6**	*3956*
this evident to you in **a** things.	**2Co 11:6**	*3956*
me *of* concern for **a** the churches.	**2Co 11:28**	*3956*
among you with **a** perseverance,	**2Co 12:12**	*3956*
A this time you have been thinking	**2Co 12:19**	*3819*
and **a** for your upbuilding, beloved.	**2Co 12:19**	*3956*
past and to **a** the rest *as well*	**2Co 13:2**	*3956*
A the saints greet you.	**2Co 13:13**	*3956*
of the Holy Spirit, be with you **a**.	**2Co 13:14**	*3956*
a the brethren who are with me,	**Ga 1:2**	*3956*
to Cephas in the presence of **a**,	**Ga 2:14**	*3956*
"**A** THE NATIONS WILL BE BLESSED	**Ga 3:8**	*3956*
DOES NOT ABIDE BY **A** THINGS WRITTEN	**Ga 3:10**	*3956*
For you are **a** sons of God through	**Ga 3:26**	*3956*
For **a** of you who were baptized	**Ga 3:27**	*3745*
for you are **a** one in Christ Jesus.	**Ga 3:28**	*3956*
he does not differ at **a** from a	**Ga 4:1**	*3761*
to be enslaved **a** over again?	**Ga 4:9**	*509*
who is taught the word is to share **a** good	**Ga 6:6**	*3956*
let us do good to **a** people,	**Ga 6:10**	*3956*
In **a** wisdom and insight	**Eph 1:8**	*3956*
summing up of **a** things in Christ,	**Eph 1:10**	*3956*
who works **a** things after the counsel	**Eph 1:11**	*3956*
and your love for **a** the saints,	**Eph 1:15**	*3956*
far above **a** rule and authority and	**Eph 1:21**	*3956*
And He put **a** things in subjection	**Eph 1:22**	*3956*
head over **a** things to the church,	**Eph 1:22**	*3956*
fullness of Him who fills **a** in all.	**Eph 1:23**	*3956*
fullness of Him who fills all in **a**.	**Eph 1:23**	*3956*
Among them we too **a** formerly lived	**Eph 2:3**	*3956*
To me, the very least of **a** saints,	**Eph 3:8**	*3956*
in God who created **a** things;	**Eph 3:9**	*3956*
may be able to comprehend with **a**	**Eph 3:18**	*3956*
filled up to **a** the fullness of God.	**Eph 3:19**	*3956*
beyond **a** that we ask or think,	**Eph 3:20**	*3956*
to **a** generations forever and ever.	**Eph 3:21**	*3956*
with **a** humility and gentleness,	**Eph 4:2**	*3956*
one God and Father of **a** who is	**Eph 4:6**	*3956*
over **a** and through all and in all.	**Eph 4:6**	*3956*
over all and through **a** and in all.	**Eph 4:6**	*3956*
over all and through all and in **a**.	**Eph 4:6**	*3956*
ascended far above **a** the heavens,	**Eph 4:10**	*3956*
that He might fill **a** things.)	**Eph 4:10**	*3956*
until we **a** attain to the unity of	**Eph 4:13**	*3956*
to grow up in **a** *aspects* into Him who	**Eph 4:15**	*3956*
Let **a** bitterness and wrath and	**Eph 4:31**	*3956*
from you, along with **a** malice.	**Eph 4:31**	*3956*
fruit of the Light *consists* in **a** goodness	**Eph 5:9**	*3956*
But **a** things become visible when	**Eph 5:13**	*3956*
always giving thanks for **a** things	**Eph 5:20**	*3956*
Himself the church in **a** her glory,	**Eph 5:27**	*1741*
in addition to **a**, taking up the	**Eph 6:16**	*3956*
to extinguish **a** the flaming arrows	**Eph 6:16**	*3956*
With **a** prayer and petition pray at	**Eph 6:18**	*3956*
pray at **a** times in the Spirit,	**Eph 6:18**	*3956*
with **a** perseverance and petition	**Eph 6:18**	*3956*
and petition for **a** the saints,	**Eph 6:18**	*3956*
Grace be with **a** those who love our	**Eph 6:24**	*3956*
To **a** the saints in Christ Jesus	**Php 1:1**	*3956*
my God in **a** my remembrance of you,	**Php 1:3**	*3956*
joy in my every prayer for you **a**,	**Php 1:4**	*3956*
me to feel this way about you **a**,	**Php 1:7**	*3956*
you **a** are partakers of grace with	**Php 1:7**	*3956*
how I long for you **a** with the	**Php 1:8**	*3956*
real knowledge and **a** discernment,	**Php 1:9**	*3956*
but *that* with **a** boldness,	**Php 1:20**	*3956*
continue with you **a** for your progress	**Php 1:25**	*3956*
Do **a** things without grumbling or	**Php 2:14**	*3956*
and share my joy with you **a**.	**Php 2:17**	*3956*
For they **a** seek after their own	**Php 2:21**	*3956*
because he was longing for you **a**	**Php 2:26**	*3956*
Therefore I have sent him **a** the	**Php 2:28**	*4709*
him then in the Lord with **a** joy,	**Php 2:29**	*3956*
I count **a** things to be loss in	**Php 3:8**	*3956*
suffered the loss of **a** things,	**Php 3:8**	*3956*
to subject **a** things to Himself.	**Php 3:21**	*3956*
spirit be known to **a** men.	**Php 4:5**	*3956*
which surpasses **a** comprehension,	**Php 4:7**	*3956*
I can do **a** things through Him who	**Php 4:13**	*3956*
And my God will supply **a** your	**Php 4:19**	*3956*
A the saints greet you, especially	**Php 4:22**	*3956*
which you have for **a** the saints;	**Col 1:4**	*3956*
just as in **a** the world also it is	**Col 1:6**	*3956*
of His will in **a** spiritual wisdom and	**Col 1:9**	*3956*
Lord, to please *Him* in **a** respects,	**Col 1:10**	*3956*
strengthened with **a** power,	**Col 1:11**	*3956*
of **a** steadfastness and patience;	**Col 1:11**	*3956*
God, the firstborn of **a** creation.	**Col 1:15**	*3956*
For by Him **a** things were	**Col 1:16**	*3956*
a things have been created through	**Col 1:16**	*3956*
He is before **a** things,	**Col 1:17**	*3956*
and in Him **a** things hold together.	**Col 1:17**	*3956*
for **a** the fullness to dwell in Him,	**Col 1:19**	*3956*
to reconcile **a** things to Himself,	**Col 1:20**	*3956*
in **a** creation under heaven,	**Col 1:23**	*3956*
teaching every man with **a** wisdom,	**Col 1:28**	*3956*
and for **a** those who have not	**Col 2:1**	*3745*
and *attaining* to **a** the wealth that	**Col 2:2**	*3956*
in whom are hidden **a** the treasures	**Col 2:3**	*3956*
For in Him **a** the fullness of Deity	**Col 2:9**	*3956*
head over **a** rule and authority;	**Col 2:10**	*3956*
forgiven us **a** our transgressions,	**Col 2:13**	*3956*
(which **a** *refer to* things destined	**Col 2:22**	*3956*
now you also, put them **a** aside:	**Col 3:8**	*3956*
and freeman, but Christ is **a**,	**Col 3:11**	*3956*
but Christ is all, and in **a**.	**Col 3:11**	*3956*
Beyond **a** these things *put on* love,	**Col 3:14**	*3956*
with **a** wisdom teaching and	**Col 3:16**	*3956*
a in the name of the Lord Jesus,	**Col 3:17**	*3956*
to your parents in **a** things,	**Col 3:20**	*3956*
in **a** things obey those who are	**Col 3:22**	*3956*
As to **a** my affairs, Tychicus, *our*	**Col 4:7**	*3956*
assured in **a** the will of God.	**Col 4:12**	*3956*
thanks to God always for **a** of you,	**1Th 1:2**	*3956*

became an example to a the believers 1Th 1:7 3956
to God, but hostile to a men, 1Th 2:15 3956
not in spirit—were a the more 1Th 2:17 4053
in a our distress and affliction 1Th 3:7 3956
for a the joy with which we rejoice 1Th 3:9 3956
for one another, and for a people, 1Th 3:12 3956
our Lord Jesus with a His saints. 1Th 3:13 3956
is *the* avenger in a these things, 1Th 4:6 3956
do practice it toward a the brethren 1Th 4:10 3956
brethren who are in a Macedonia. 1Th 4:10 3650
a sons of light and sons of day. 1Th 5:5 3956
for one another and for a people. 1Th 5:15 3956
a the brethren with a holy kiss. 1Th 5:26 3956
letter read to a the brethren. 1Th 5:27 3956
in the midst of a your persecutions 2Th 1:4 3956
For after a it is *only* just for 2Th 1:6 1512
and to be marveled at among a who 2Th 1:10 3956
with a power and signs and false 2Th 2:9 3956
and with a the deception of 2Th 2:10 3956
in order that they a may be judged 2Th 2:12 3956
for not a have faith. 2Th 3:2 3956
life, doing no work at a, 2Th 3:11 3367
The Lord be with you a! 2Th 3:16 3956
Lord Jesus Christ be with you a. 2Th 3:18 3956
among whom I am foremost *of* a. 1Tm 1:15
First of a, then, I urge that 1Tm 2:1 3956
be made on behalf of a men, 1Tm 2:1 3956
kings and a who are in authority, 1Tm 2:2 3956
life in a godliness and dignity. 1Tm 2:2 3956
who desires a men to be saved and 1Tm 2:4 3956
gave Himself as a ransom for a, 1Tm 2:6 3956
under control with a dignity 1Tm 3:4 3956
temperate, faithful in a things. 1Tm 3:11 3956
is profitable for a things, 1Tm 4:8 3956
God, who is the Savior of a men, 1Tm 4:10 3956
your progress will be evident to a. 1Tm 4:15 3956
women as sisters, in a purity. 1Tm 5:2 3956
sin, rebuke in the presence of a, 1Tm 5:20 3956
A who are under the yoke as 1Tm 6:1 3745
own masters as worthy of a honor 1Tm 6:1 3956
must serve them a the more, 1Tm 6:2 3123
is a root of a sorts of evil, 1Tm 6:10 3956
God, who gives life to a things, 1Tm 6:13 3956
us with a things to enjoy. 1Tm 6:17 3956
in Christ Jesus from a eternity, 2Tm 1:9 5550
You are aware of the fact that a 2Tm 1:15 3956
For this reason I endure a things 2Tm 2:10 3956
be quarrelsome, but be kind to a, 2Tm 2:24 3956
their folly will be obvious to a, 2Tm 3:9 3956
of them a the Lord rescued me! 2Tm 3:11 3956
a who desire to live godly in 2Tm 3:12 3956
A Scripture is inspired by God and 2Tm 3:16 3956
But you, be sober in a things, 2Tm 4:5 3956
to a who have loved His appearing. 2Tm 4:8 3956
supported me, but a deserted me; 2Tm 4:16 3956
that a the Gentiles might hear; 2Tm 4:17 3956
and Claudia and a the brethren. 2Tm 4:21 3956
To the pure, a things are pure; Ti 1:15 3956
in a things show yourself to be an Ti 2:7 3956
but showing a good faith so that they Ti 2:10 3956
bringing salvation to a men, Ti 2:11 3956
and reprove with a authority. Ti 2:15 3956
every consideration for a men. Ti 3:2 3956
A who are with me greet you. Ti 3:15 3956
Grace be with you a. Ti 3:15 3956
Jesus and toward a the saints; Phm 1:5 3956
He appointed heir of a things, Heb 1:2 3956
and upholds a things by the word Heb 1:3 3956
A THE ANGELS OF GOD WORSHIP HIM." Heb 1:6 3956
A WILL BECOME OLD LIKE A GARMENT, Heb 1:11 3956
they not a ministering spirits, Heb 1:14 3956
YOU HAVE PUT A THINGS IN Heb 2:8 3956
For in subjecting a things to him, Heb 2:8 3956
yet see a things subjected to him. Heb 2:8 3956
for Him, for whom are a things, Heb 2:10 3956
and through whom are a things, Heb 2:10 3956
sanctified are a from one *Father;* Heb 2:11 3956
subject to slavery a their lives. Heb 2:15 3956
like His brethren in a things, Heb 2:17 3956
as Moses also was in a His house. Heb 3:2 3650
the builder of a things is God. Heb 3:4 3956
in a His house as a servant, Heb 3:5 3650
did not a those who came out of Heb 3:16 3956
SEVENTH DAY FROM A HIS WORKS"; Heb 4:4 3956
but a things are open and laid Heb 4:13 3956
tempted in a things as *we are,* Heb 4:15 3956
He became to a those who obey Him Heb 5:9 3956
a tenth part of a *the spoils,* Heb 7:2 3956
of all *the spoils,* was first of a, Heb 7:2 4413
for a when He offered up Himself. Heb 7:27 2178
He would not be a priest at a, Heb 8:4 3761
"THAT YOU MAKE a things ACCORDING Heb 8:5 3956
THE LORD,' FOR A WILL KNOW ME, Heb 8:11 3956
covered on a sides with gold, Heb 9:4 3840
entered the holy place once for a, Heb 9:12 2178
been spoken by Moses to a the people Heb 9:19 3956
the book itself and a the people, Heb 9:19 3956
both the tabernacle and a the vessels Heb 9:21 3956
a things are cleansed with blood, Heb 9:22 3956
body of Jesus Christ once for a. Heb 10:10 2178
one sacrifice for sins for a time, Heb 10:12 1336
He has perfected for a time those Heb 10:14 1336
and a the more as you see the day Heb 10:25 5118
A these died in faith, without Heb 11:13 3956
And a these, having gained Heb 11:39 3956
of which a have become partakers, Heb 12:8 3956
A discipline for the moment seems Heb 12:11 3956
Pursue peace with a men, Heb 12:14 3956
and to God, the Judge of a, Heb 12:23 3956
Marriage *is to be held* in honor among a, Heb 13:4 3956
ourselves honorably in a things. Heb 13:18 3956
I urge *you* a the more to do this, Heb 13:19 4053
Greet a of your leaders and all Heb 13:24 3956
of your leaders and a the saints. Heb 13:24 3956
Grace be with you a. Heb 13:25 3956
Consider it a joy, my brethren, Jas 1:2 3956
who gives to a generously and Jas 1:5 3956
man, unstable in a his ways. Jas 1:8 3956
Therefore, putting aside a filthiness Jas 1:21 3956
putting aside all filthiness and a Jas 1:21
point, he has become guilty of a. Jas 2:10 3956
For we a stumble in many *ways.* Jas 3:2 537a
a such boasting is evil. Jas 4:16 3956
But above a, my brethren, do not Jas 5:12 3956
also in a *your* behavior; 1Pe 1:15 3956
"A FLESH IS LIKE GRASS, AND ALL 1Pe 1:24 3956
AND A ITS GLORY LIKE THE FLOWER OF 1Pe 1:24 3956
putting aside a malice and all 1Pe 2:1 3956
putting aside all malice and a 1Pe 2:1 3956
hypocrisy and envy and a slander, 1Pe 2:1 3956
Honor a people, love the brotherhood, 1Pe 2:17 3956
to your masters with a respect, 1Pe 2:18 3956
To sum up, a of you be harmonious, 1Pe 3:8 3956
also died for sins once for a, 1Pe 3:18 530
In a this, they are surprised 1Pe 4:4
The end of a things is near; 1Pe 4:7 3956
Above a, keep fervent in your love 1Pe 4:8 3956
so that in a things God may be 1Pe 4:11 3956
and a of you, clothe yourselves 1Pe 5:5 3956
casting a your anxiety on Him, 1Pe 5:7 3956
little while, the God of a grace, 1Pe 5:10 3956
be to you a who are in Christ. 1Pe 5:14 3956
reason also, applying a diligence, 2Pe 1:5 3956
be a the more diligent to make 2Pe 1:10 3123
But know this first of a, 2Pe 1:20
Know this first of a, 2Pe 3:3
a continues just as it was from 2Pe 3:4 3956
but for a to come to repentance. 2Pe 3:9 3956
Since a these things are to be 2Pe 3:11 3956
as also in a *his* letters, speaking 2Pe 3:16 3956
in Him there is no darkness at a. 1Jn 1:5 3762
His Son cleanses us from a sin. 1Jn 1:7 3956
cleanse us from a unrighteousness. 1Jn 1:9 3956
For a that is in the world, the 1Jn 2:16 3956
shown that they a are not of us. 1Jn 2:19 3956
from the Holy One, and you a know. 1Jn 2:20 3956
teaches you about a things, 1Jn 2:27 3956
our heart and knows a things. 1Jn 3:20 3956
A unrighteousness is sin, and 1Jn 5:17 3956
I, but also a who know the truth, 2Jn 1:1 3956
I pray that in a respects you may 3Jn 1:2 3956
for a handed down to the saints. Jude 1:3 530
you know a things once for all, Jude 1:5 3956
you know all things once for a, Jude 1:5 530
to execute judgment upon a, Jude 1:15 3956
and to convict a the ungodly of Jude 1:15 3956
the ungodly of a their ungodly deeds Jude 1:15 3956
and of a the harsh things which Jude 1:15 3956
before a time and now and forever. Jude 1:25 3956
Christ, *even* to a that he saw. Rv 1:2 3745
and a the tribes of the earth will Rv 1:7 3956
and a the churches will know that Rv 2:23 3956
for You created a things, Rv 4:11 3956
of God, sent out into a the earth. Rv 5:6 3956
on the sea, and a things in them, Rv 5:13 3956
from every nation and a tribes Rv 7:9
And a the angels were standing Rv 7:11 3956
add it to the prayers of a the saints Rv 8:3 3956
a the green grass was burned up. Rv 8:7 3956
who is to rule a the nations with Rv 12:5 3956
A who dwell on the earth will worship Rv 13:8 3956
He exercises a the authority Rv 13:12 3956
And he causes a, the small and the Rv 13:16 3956
she who has made a the nations Rv 14:8 3956
For A THE NATIONS WILL COME AND Rv 15:4 3956
"For a the nations have drunk of Rv 18:3 3956
and a things that were luxurious Rv 18:14 3956
in which a who had ships at sea Rv 18:19 3956
because a the nations were Rv 18:23 3956
a who have been slain on the earth." Rv 18:24 3956
our God, a you His bond-servants, Rv 19:5 3956
saying to a the birds which fly in Rv 19:17 3956
on them and the flesh of a men, Rv 19:18 3956
and a the birds were filled with Rv 19:21 3956
I am making a things new." Rv 21:5 3956
and idolaters and a liars, Rv 21:8 3956
grace of the Lord Jesus be with a. Rv 22:21 3956

ALLAMMELECH
and A and Amad and Mishal; Jos 19:26 487

ALLAYS
composure a great offenses. Ec 10:4 5117

ALLEGIANCE
kept their a to the house of Saul. 1Ch 12:29 4931
David pledged a to King Solomon. 1Ch 29:24 3027, 8478
who had made him swear a by God. 2Ch 36:13
language of Canaan and swearing a Is 19:18
every tongue will swear a. Is 45:23
and behold, he pledged his a, Ezk 17:18 3027

ALLEGORICALLY
This is a speaking, Ga 4:24 238

ALLEMETH
lands, A with its pasture lands, 1Ch 6:60 5964

ALLIANCE
a with Pharaoh king of Egypt, 1Ki 3:1 2859
plan, but not Mine, And make an a, Is 30:1 4541a
some years they will form an a, Da 11:6 2266
"After an a is made with him Da 11:23 2266

ALLIED
a himself by marriage with Ahab. 2Ch 18:1 2859
king of Judah a himself with Ahaziah 2Ch 20:35 2266
So he a himself with him to make 2Ch 20:36 2266
you have a yourself with Ahaziah, 2Ch 20:37 2266
those who a themselves with them, Es 9:27 3867a
of destruction be a with You, Ps 94:20 2266
"All the men a with you Will send Ob 1:7 1285

ALLIES
came as a to the valley of Siddim Gn 14:3 2266
Aner, and these were a with Abram. Gn 14:13 1167, 1285
Even though they hire a among Hos 8:10

ALLON
the son of Shiphi, the son of A, 1Ch 4:37 438

ALLON-BACUTH
under the oak; it was named A. Gn 35:8 439

ALLOT
only a it to Israel for an Jos 13:6 5307
a Him a portion with the great, Is 53:12 2505a

ALLOTMENT
the priests had an a from Pharaoh, Gn 47:22 2706
off the a which Pharaoh gave them. Gn 47:22 2706
and to your sons as a perpetual a. Nu 18:8 2706
with you as a perpetual a. Nu 18:11 2706
with you, as a perpetual a. Nu 18:19 2706
Jacob is the a of His inheritance. Dt 32:9 2256a
you shall offer an a to the LORD, Ezk 45:1 8641
the a of the holy portion; Ezk 45:6 8641
holy a and the property of the city, Ezk 45:7 8641
holy a and the property of the city, Ezk 45:7 8641
the a which you shall set apart, Ezk 48:8 8641
"The a that you shall set apart Ezk 48:9 8641
"The holy a shall be for Ezk 48:10 8641
"It shall be an a to them Ezk 48:12 8642
to them from the a of the land, Ezk 48:12 8641
the holy a shall be 10,000 *cubits* Ezk 48:18 8641
it shall be alongside the holy a. Ezk 48:18 8641
"The whole a *shall be* 25,000 by Ezk 48:20 8641
you shall set apart the holy a, Ezk 48:20 8641
holy a and of the property of the city; Ezk 48:21 8641
25,000 *cubits* of the a toward the east Ezk 48:21 8641
And the holy a and the sanctuary Ezk 48:21 8641

ALLOTTED
withdrawn from our a inheritance. Nu 36:3 1486
your God has a to all the peoples Dt 4:19 2505a
and whom He had not a to them. Dt 29:26 2505a
Gilead, were a Gilead and Bashan, Jos 17:1 1961
cities from the tribe of Ephraim were a Jos 21:20 1486
they a Taanach with its pasture Jos 21:25
with me into the territory a me, Jg 1:3 1486
you into the territory a you." Jg 1:3 1486
an inheritance had not been a to them Jg 18:1 5307
And a *them* to them as a boundary. Ne 9:22 2505a
So am I a months of vanity, And Jb 7:3 5157
they shall be a an inheritance Ezk 47:22 5307
a portion at the end of the age." Da 12:13 1486
has a to each a measure of faith. Ro 12:3 3307
it over those a to your charge, 1Pe 5:3 2819

ALLOW
God did not a him to hurt me. Gn 31:7 5414
and did not a me to kiss my sons Gn 31:28 5203
will not a the destroyer to come in Ex 12:23 5414
shall not a a sorceress to live. Ex 22:18
Thus Edom refused to a Israel to Nu 20:21 5414
not a them to enter their cities, Jos 10:19 5414
for they did not a them to come Jg 1:34 5414
and did not a anyone to cross. Jg 3:28 5414
did they not a the people to go, 1Sa 6:6
a them to rise up against Saul. 1Sa 24:7 5414
that they may a me to pass through Ne 2:7
"He will not a me to get my Jb 9:18 5414
And a *such* words to go out of your Jb 15:13
a Your Holy One to undergo decay. Ps 16:10 5414
a the righteous to be shaken. Ps 55:22 5414
And does not a our feet to slip. Ps 66:9 5414
He will not a your foot to slip; Ps 121:3 5414
not a the righteous to hunger, Pr 10:3
rich man does not a him to sleep. Ec 5:12 5117
not a his prisoners to *go* home? Is 14:17 6605a
so as to a both the holy place and Da 8:13 5414
not a them To return to their God. Hos 5:4 5414
and a the dead to bury their own Mt 8:22 863
'A both to grow together until the Mt 13:30 863
nor do you a those who are Mt 23:13 863
He would not a them to speak, Lk 4:41 1439
not a anyone to enter with Him, Lk 8:51 863
"A the dead to bury their own Lk 9:60 863
A YOUR HOLY ONE TO UNDERGO DECAY. Ac 2:27 1325
A YOUR HOLY ONE TO UNDERGO DECAY.' Ac 13:35 1325
a me to speak to the people." Ac 21:39 2010
who will not a you to be tempted 1Co 10:13 1439
But I do not a a woman to teach or 1Tm 2:12 2010

ALLOWANCE
and for his a, a regular allowance 2Ki 25:30 737
a was given him by the king, 2Ki 25:30 737
have eaten the governor's food a. Ne 5:14
not demand the governor's food a, Ne 5:18
For his a, a regular allowance Jer 52:34 737
a regular a was given him by the Jer 52:34 737

ALLOWED
this reason I have a you to remain, Ex 9:16
"You are not a to eat within your Dt 12:17 3201
"You are not a to sacrifice the Dt 16:5 3201
your God has not a you *to do* so. Dt 18:14 5414
You are not a to neglect *them.* Dt 22:3 3201

not **a** to take her again to be his wife, **Dt 24:4** 3201
LORD **a** those nations to remain, **Jg 2:23**
and she **a** neither the birds of the **2Sa 21:10** 5414
that it is not **a** to impose tax, **Ezr 7:24** 7990
I have not **a** my mouth to sin By **Jb 31:30** 5414
a his house to be broken into. **Mt 24:43** *1439*
He **a** no one to accompany Him, **Mk 5:37** *863*
a his house to be broken into. **Lk 12:39** *863*
for he should not be **a** to live!" **Ac 22:22** *2520*
treated Paul with consideration and **a** **Ac 27:3** *2010*
justice has not **a** him to live." **Ac 28:4** *1439*
Paul was **a** to stay by himself, **Ac 28:16** *2010*

ALLOWS
his body **a** its discharge to flow or **Lv 15:3**

ALLOY
lye And will remove all your **a**. **Is 1:25** 913

ALLURE
"Therefore, behold, I will **a** her, **Hos 2:14** 6601b

ALLY
and Sidon Every **a** that is left; **Jer 47:4** 5826

ALMIGHTY
"I am God **A**; Walk before Me, **Gn 17:1** 7706b
"May God **A** bless you and make **Gn 28:3** 7706b
God also said to him, "I am God **A**; **Gn 35:11** 7706b
and may God **A** grant you compassion **Gn 43:14** 7706b
"God **A** appeared to me at Luz in **Gn 48:3** 7706b
And by the **A** who blesses you *With* **Gn 49:25** 7706b
Isaac, and Jacob, as God **A**, **Ex 6:3** 7706b
God, Who sees the vision of the **A**, **Nu 24:4** 7706b
Who sees the vision of the **A**, **Nu 24:16** 7706b
for the **A** has dealt very bitterly **Ru 1:20** 7706b
me and the **A** has afflicted me?" **Ru 1:21** 7706b
despise the discipline of the **A**. **Jb 5:17** 7706b
the arrows of the **A** are within me, **Jb 6:4** 7706b
does not forsake the fear of the **A**. **Jb 6:14** 7706b
does the **A** pervert what is right? **Jb 8:3** 7706b
implore the compassion of the **A**, **Jb 8:5** 7706b
you discover the limits of the **A**? **Jb 11:7** 7706b
"But I would speak to the **A**, **Jb 13:3** 7706b
himself arrogantly against the **A**. **Jb 15:25** 7706b
'Who is the **A**, that we should **Jb 21:15** 7706b
him drink of the wrath of the **A**. **Jb 21:20** 7706b
to the **A** if you are righteous, **Jb 22:3** 7706b
'What can the **A** do to them?' **Jb 22:17** 7706b
"If you return to the **A**, **Jb 22:23** 7706b
Then the **A** will be your gold And **Jb 22:25** 7706b
then you will delight in the **A** And **Jb 22:26** 7706b
And the **A** *who* has dismayed me, **Jb 23:16** 7706b
are times not stored up by the **A**, **Jb 24:1** 7706b
taken away my right, And the **A**, **Jb 27:2** 7706b
"Will he take delight in the **A**? **Jb 27:10** 7706b
is with the **A** I will not conceal. **Jb 27:11** 7706b
which tyrants receive from the **A**. **Jb 27:13** 7706b
When the **A** was yet with me, *And* my **Jb 29:5** 7706b
heritage of the **A** from on high? **Jb 31:2** 7706b
Let the **A** answer me! **Jb 31:35** 7706b
of the **A** gives them understanding. **Jb 32:8** 7706b
the breath of the **A** gives me life. **Jb 33:4** 7706b
And from the **A** to do wrong. **Jb 34:10** 7706b
the **A** will not pervert justice. **Jb 34:12** 7706b
cry, Nor will the **A** regard it. **Jb 35:13** 7706b
"The **A**—we cannot find Him; **Jb 37:23** 7706b
faultfinder contend with the **A**? **Jb 40:2** 7706b
the **A** scattered the kings there, **Ps 68:14** 7706b
Will abide in the shadow of the **A**. **Ps 91:1** 7706b
come as destruction from the **A**. **Is 13:6** 7706b
went, like the voice of the **A**, **Ezk 1:24** 7706b
the voice of God **A** when He speaks. **Ezk 10:5** 7706b
come as destruction from the **A**. **Jl 1:15** 7706b
daughters to Me," Says the Lord **A**. **2Co 6:18** *3841*
was and who is to come, the **A**." **Rv 1:8** *3841*
THE **A**, WHO WAS AND WHO IS AND WHO IS **Rv 4:8** *3841*
You thanks, O Lord God, the **A**, **Rv 11:17** *3841*
are Your works, O Lord God, the **A**; **Rv 15:3** *3841*
"Yes, O Lord God, the **A**, **Rv 16:7** *3841*
of the great day of God, the **A**. **Rv 16:14** *3841*
For the Lord our God, the **A**, **Rv 19:6** *3841*
of the fierce wrath of God, the **A**. **Rv 19:15** *3841*
in it, for the Lord God the **A** **Rv 21:22** *3841*

ALMODAD
Joktan became the father of **A** **Gn 10:26** 486
Joktan became the father of **A**, **1Ch 1:20** 486

ALMON
and **A** with its pasture lands; **Jos 21:18** 5960

ALMOND
of poplar and **a** and plane trees, **Gn 30:37** 3869
like **a** *blossoms* in the one branch, **Ex 25:33** 8246
cups shaped like **a** *blossoms* **Ex 25:33** 8246
four cups shaped like **a** *blossoms,* **Ex 25:34** 8246
three cups shaped like **a** *blossoms,* **Ex 37:19** 8246
three cups shaped like **a** *blossoms,* **Ex 37:19** 8246
four cups shaped like **a** *blossoms,* **Ex 37:20** 8246
the **a** tree blossoms, the **Ec 12:5** 8247
"I see a rod of an **a** tree." **Jer 1:11** 8247

ALMON-DIBLATHAIM
from Dibon-gad and camped at **A**. **Nu 33:46** 5963
They journeyed from **A** and **Nu 33:47** 5963

ALMONDS
and myrrh, pistachio nuts and **a**. **Gn 43:11** 8247
blossoms, and it bore ripe **a**. **Nu 17:8** 8247

ALMOST
near Jebus, the day was **a** gone; **Jg 19:11** 3966
My steps had **a** slipped. **Ps 73:2** 369
They **a** destroyed me on earth, But **Ps 119:87** 4592
"I was **a** in utter ruin In the **Pr 5:14** 4592
in Ephesus, but in **a** all of Asia, **Ac 19:26** *4975*
When the seven days were **a** over, **Ac 21:27** *3195*
The night is **a** gone, and the day **Ro 13:12** *4298*
to the Law, *one may* **a** *say,* **Heb 9:22** *4975*

ALMS
in order to beg **a** of those who **Ac 3:2** *1654*
he *began* asking to receive **a**. **Ac 3:3** *1654*
Gate of the temple to *beg* **a**, **Ac 3:10** *1654*
gave many **a** to the *Jewish* people and **Ac 10:2** *1654*
"Your prayers and **a** have ascended **Ac 10:4** *1654*
a have been remembered before God. **Ac 10:31** *1654*
I came to bring **a** to my nation and **Ac 24:17** *1654*

ALMUG
of **a** trees and precious stones. **1Ki 10:11** 484
The king made of the **a** trees **1Ki 10:12** 484
a trees have not come in *again* **1Ki 10:12** 484

ALOES
river, Like **a** planted by the LORD, **Nu 24:6** 174
with myrrh and **a** *and* cassia; **Ps 45:8** 174
my bed With myrrh, **a** and cinnamon. **Pr 7:17** 174
of frankincense, Myrrh and **a**, **SS 4:14** 174
bringing a mixture of myrrh and **a**, **Jn 19:39** *250*

ALONE
is not good for the man to be **a**; **Gn 2:18** 905
for you **a** I have seen *to be* **Gn 7:1**
Then Jacob was left **a**, **Gn 32:24** 905
brother is dead, and he **a** is left. **Gn 42:38** 905
so he **a** is left of his mother, **Gn 44:20** 905
He let him **a**. At that time she said, **Ex 4:26** 7503
that **a** may be prepared by you. **Ex 12:16** 905
'Leave us **a** that we may serve the **Ex 14:12** 4480
Why do you **a** sit *as judge* and all **Ex 18:14** 905
you cannot do it **a**. **Ex 18:18** 905
"If he comes **a**, he shall go out **Ex 21:3** 1610
he comes alone, he shall go out **a**; **Ex 21:3** 1610
her master, and he shall go out **a**. **Ex 21:4** 1610
any god, other than to the LORD **a**, **Ex 22:20** 905
"Moses **a**, however, shall come **Ex 24:2** 905
"Now then let Me **a**, that My anger **Ex 32:10** 5117
he is unclean. He shall live **a**; **Lv 13:46** 910
"I **a** am not able to carry all **Nu 11:14** 905
that you will not bear *it* all **a**. **Nu 11:17** 905
able to bear *the burden* of you **a**. **Dt 1:9** 905
'How can I **a** bear the load and **Dt 1:12** 905
that man does not live by bread **a**, **Dt 8:3** 905
'Let Me **a**, that I may destroy them **Dt 9:14** 4480, 7503
"Now not with you **a** am I making **Dt 29:14** 905
"The LORD **a** guided him, And there **Dt 32:12** 910
on their mounds, except Hazor **a**, **Jos 11:13** 905
(he **a** was left of the remnant of the **Jos 13:12**
not perish **a** in his iniquity.' " **Jos 22:20** 259
a in his cool roof chamber. **Jg 3:20** 905
let me **a** two months, that I may go **Jg 11:37** 4480, 7503
to the LORD and serve Him **a**; **1Sa 7:3** 905
Ashtaroth and served the LORD **a**. **1Sa 7:4** 905
"Let us **a** for seven days, that we **1Sa 11:3** 7503
are you **a** and no one with you?" **1Sa 21:1** 905
"On me **a**, my lord, be the blame. **1Sa 25:24** 589
king's sons, for Amnon **a** is dead; **2Sa 13:32** 905
Let him **a** and let him curse, **2Sa 16:11** 5117
I will strike down the king **a**, **2Sa 17:2** 905
for You **a** know the hearts of **1Ki 8:39** 905
both of them were **a** in the field. **1Ki 11:29** 905
for he **a** of Jeroboam's *family* **1Ki 14:13** 905
"I **a** am left a prophet of the **1Ki 18:22** 905
I **a** am left; and they seek my life, **1Ki 19:10** 905
I **a** am left; and they seek my life, **1Ki 19:14** 905
but with the king of Israel **a**." **1Ki 22:31** 905
"Let her **a**, for her soul is **2Ki 4:27** 7503
You are the God, You **a**, **2Ki 19:15** 905
of the earth may know that You **a**, **2Ki 19:19** 905
"Let him **a**; let no one disturb his **2Ki 23:18** 5117
Solomon, whom **a** God has chosen, **1Ch 29:1** 259
for You **a** know the hearts of **2Ch 6:30** 905
but with the king of Israel **a**." **2Ch 18:30** 905
God left him **a** *only* to test him, **2Ch 32:31** 905
this work on the house of God **a**; **Ezr 6:7** 7662
"You **a** are the LORD. **Ne 9:6** 905
to lay hands on Mordecai **a**, **Es 3:6** 905
I **a** have escaped to tell you." **Jb 1:15** 905, 7534
I **a** have escaped to tell you." **Jb 1:16** 905, 7534
I **a** have escaped to tell you." **Jb 1:17** 905, 7534
I **a** have escaped to tell you." **Jb 1:19** 905, 7534
Leave me **a**, for my days are *but* a **Jb 7:16** 4480
me **a** until I swallow my spittle? **Jb 7:19** 7503
Who **a** stretches out the heavens And **Jb 9:8** 905
"Would He not let my few days **a**? **Jb 10:20** 2308
To whom **a** the land was given, And **Jb 15:19** 905
Or have eaten my morsel **a**, **Jb 31:17** 905
lie down and sleep, For You **a**, **Ps 4:8** 910
of Your righteousness, Yours **a**. **Ps 71:16** 905
of Israel, Who **a** works wonders. **Ps 72:18** 905
That they may know that You **a**, **Ps 83:18** 905
wondrous deeds; You **a** are God. **Ps 86:10** 905
To Him who **a** does great wonders, **Ps 136:4** 905
LORD, For His name **a** is exalted; **Ps 148:13** 905
Let them be yours **a** And **Pr 5:17** 905
if you scoff, you **a** will bear it. **Pr 9:12** 905
will not be instructed by words **a**; **Pr 29:19**
but how can one be warm **a**? **Ec 4:11**
if one can overpower him who is **a**, **Ec 4:12**
a will be exalted in that day. **Is 2:11** 905
a will be exalted in that day, **Is 2:17** 905
live **a** in the midst of the land! **Is 5:8** 905
You **a** we confess Your name. **Is 26:13** 905
You are the God, You **a**, **Is 37:16** 905
of the earth may know that You **a**, **Is 37:20** 905
And spreading out the earth all **a**, **Is 44:24** 4480, 854
Behold, I was left **a**; **Is 49:21** 905
"I have trodden the wine trough **a**, **Is 63:3** 905
of Your hand *upon me* I sat **a**, **Jer 15:17** 910
for they **a** remained as fortified **Jer 34:7**
has no gates or bars; They dwell **a**. **Jer 49:31** 910
Let him sit **a** and be silent Since **La 3:28** 910
striking *the people* and I **a** **Ezk 9:8**
They **a** would be delivered, but the **Ezk 14:16** 905
but they **a** would be delivered. **Ezk 14:18** 905
Now I, Daniel, **a** saw the vision, **Da 10:7** 905
left **a** and saw this great vision; **Da 10:8** 905
Ephraim is joined to idols; Let him **a**. **Hos 4:17** 5117
Assyria, *Like* a wild donkey all **a**; **Hos 8:9** 909
bread will be for themselves **a**; **Hos 9:4**
'MAN SHALL NOT LIVE ON BREAD **A**, **Mt 4:4** *3441*
with him, but for the priests **a**? **Mt 12:4** *3441*
it was evening, He was there **a**. **Mt 14:23** *3441*
"Let them **a**; they are blind guides **Mt 15:14** *863*
no one except Jesus Himself **a**. **Mt 17:8** *3441*
"Let the children **a**, **Mt 19:14** *863*
nor the Son, but the Father **a**. **Mt 24:36** *3441*
who can forgive sins but God **a**?" **Mk 2:7** *1520*
As soon as He was **a**, **Mk 4:10** *3441*
the sea, and He was **a** on the land. **Mk 6:47** *3441*
with them anymore, except Jesus **a**. **Mk 9:8** *3441*
No one is good except God **a**. **Mk 10:18** *1520*
the Son, but the Father **a**. **Mk 13:32**
"Let her **a**; why do you bother her? **Mk 14:6** *863*
'MAN SHALL NOT LIVE ON BREAD **A**.' " **Lk 4:4** *3441*
"Let us **a**! What business do we have **Lk 4:34** *1436*
Who can forgive sins, but God **a**?" **Lk 5:21** *3441*
any to eat except the priests **a**, **Lk 6:4** *3441*
happened that while He was praying **a**, **Lk 9:18** *3441*
had spoken, Jesus was found **a**. **Lk 9:36** *3441*
left me to do all the serving **a**? **Lk 10:40** *3441*
'Let it **a**, sir, for this year too, **Lk 13:8** *863*
No one is good except God **a**. **Lk 18:19** *1520*
"If I **a** testify about Myself, **Jn 5:31**
to the mountain by Himself **a**. **Jn 6:15** *3441*
His disciples had gone away **a**. **Jn 6:22** *3441*
the older ones, and He was left **a**, **Jn 8:9** *3441*
for I am not **a** *in it,* but I and the **Jn 8:16** *3441*
He has not left Me **a**, **Jn 8:29** *3441*
"Let her **a**, so that she may **Jn 12:7** *863*
and dies, it remains **a**; **Jn 12:24** *3441*
his own *home,* and to leave Me **a**; **Jn 16:32** *3441*
and *yet* I am not **a**, **Jn 16:32** *3441*
"I do not ask on behalf of these **a**, **Jn 17:20** *3441*
from these men and let them **a**, **Ac 5:38** *863*
word to no one except to Jews **a**. **Ac 11:19** *3441*
YOUR ALTARS, AND I **A** AM LEFT, **Ro 11:3** *3441*
boasting in regard to himself **a**, **Ga 6:4** *3441*
of giving and receiving but you **a**; **Php 4:15** *3441*
to be left behind at Athens **a**, **1Th 3:1** *3441*
left **a**, has fixed her hope on God **1Tm 5:5** *3443*
who **a** possesses immortality and **1Tm 6:16** *3441*
by works and not by faith **a**. **Jas 2:24** *3441*
For You **a** are holy; **Rv 15:4** *3441*

ALONG
a with the sons of Bilhah and the **Gn 37:2**
which Abraham bought **a** with the **Gn 49:30**
which Abraham had bought **a** with **Gn 50:13**
and its legs **a** with its entrails. **Ex 12:9** 5921
them, **a** with flocks and herds, **Ex 12:38**
was the cloud **a** with the darkness, **Ex 14:20**
before you to guard you **a** the way and **Ex 23:20**
a with the bull and the two rams. **Ex 29:3**
let the Lord go **a** in our midst, **Ex 34:9**
then **a** with the sacrifice of **Lv 7:12** 5921
they shall bring **a** with the offerings **Lv 10:15** 5921
a with the live bird and with the **Lv 14:52**
'**A** with the bread you shall **Lv 23:18** 5921
a with the duties of the sons of **Nu 3:8**
a with its lamps and its snuffers, **Nu 4:9**
a with their grain offering and **Nu 6:15**
both you and they **a** with Aaron. **Nu 16:16**
a with their wives and their sons **Nu 16:27**
We will go **a** the king's highway, **Nu 20:17**
went **a** with the leaders of Balak. **Nu 22:35**
swallowed them up **a** with Korah, **Nu 26:10**
a with the *rest of* their slain: **Nu 31:8** 5921
of Zin **a** the side of Edom, **Nu 34:3** 5921
all **a** the river Jabbok and the **Dt 2:37** 3027
when you walk **a** the road and when **Dt 11:19**
come upon a bird's nest **a** the way, **Dt 22:6**
what Amalek did to you **a** the way **Dt 25:17**
how he met you **a** the way and **Dt 25:18**
had sought *them* all **a** the road, **Jos 2:22**
died in the wilderness **a** the way after **Jos 5:4**
were born in the wilderness **a** the way **Jos 5:5**
not circumcised them **a** the way. **Jos 5:7**
who might pass by them **a** the road; **Jg 9:25**
a with the vineyards *and* groves. **Jg 15:5** 5704
pulled them up **a** with the bars; **Jg 16:3** 5973
When the man arose to go **a** with **Jg 19:9**
they passed **a** and went their way, **Jg 19:14** 5674a
they went **a** the highway, lowing as **1Sa 6:12**
lay **a** the way to Shaaraim, **1Sa 17:52**
so that he went **a** prophesying **1Sa 19:23**
LORD will also give over Israel **a** with **1Sa 28:19** 5973
and Shimei went **a** on the hillside **2Sa 16:13**
a with the Cherethites and the **2Sa 20:7**
and its depth **a** the front of the **1Ki 6:3** 5921
a with the servants of Solomon. **1Ki 9:27** 5973

a with the daughter of Pharaoh: 1Ki 11:1
a with the evil that Hadad *did;* 1Ki 11:25
As they were going **a** and talking, 2Ki 2:11
Gedaliah down so that he died **a** with 2Ki 25:25
and Jehozadak went **a** when the 1Ch 6:15
Rephah was his son **a** with Resheph, 1Ch 7:25
and **a** the borders of the sons of 1Ch 7:29 5921
a with the freewill offering of Ezr 7:16 5973
"The paths of their course wind **a**, Jb 6:18 3943
Do not take my soul away **a** with Ps 26:9
For I used to go **a** with the throng Ps 42:4 5674a
which melts away as it goes **a**, Ps 58:8
who pass **a** the way plunder him; Ps 89:41 5674a
There the ships move **a**, Ps 104:26
a pestle **a** with crushed grain, Pr 27:22 8432
The wind continues swirling **a**; Ec 1:6 1980
Wisdom **a** with an inheritance is Ec 7:11 5973
a the road, his sense is lacking Ec 10:3
the grasshopper drags himself **a**, Ec 12:5
my beautiful one, And come **a**. SS 2:10
my beautiful one, And come **a**!' " SS 2:13
a with all the finest spices. SS 4:14 5973
my myrrh **a** with my balsam. SS 5:1 5973
eyes, And go **a** with mincing steps And Is 3:16
a and bring them to their place, Is 14:2
a with all *his* great population, Is 16:14
A the roads they will feed, Is 49:9 5921
grope **a** the wall like blind men, Is 59:10
a with the city which I gave you Jer 23:39
a with Nebushazban the Rab-saris, Jer 39:13
come **a**, and I will look after Jer 40:4
a with Ishmael the son of Jer 40:8
of the king, **a** with ten men, Jer 41:1
to death **a** with their companions. Jer 41:8 8432
a with all the women who were Jer 44:15
"Its sound moves **a** like a serpent; Jer 46:22
a with her gods and her kings, Jer 46:25
offspring has been destroyed **a** with Jer 49:10
they will go **a** weeping as they go, Jer 50:4
They have gone **a** from mountain to Jer 50:6
live *there* **a** with the jackals; Jer 50:39 854
All who pass **a** the way Clap their La 2:15 5674a
a *with* the prophets of Israel who Ezk 13:16
a with them your own captivity, Ezk 16:53 8432
a with the sons of Ammon to Ezk 25:10 5921
down among *the* uncircumcised **a** Ezk 32:32
areas **a** the east *side totaled* a hundred Ezk 41:14
the length of the building **a** the front Ezk 41:15 413
A the length, *which was* a hundred Ezk 42:2 413, 6440
a with some of the vessels of the Da 1:2
seen, **a** with its interpretation. Da 4:9
horn **a** with the regular sacrifice; Da 8:12 5921
a with the oath which is written Da 9:11
a with *one* of his princes who will Da 11:5
a with those who brought her in and Da 11:6
lives in it languishes **A** with the beasts Hos 4:3
sword **a** with your captured horses, Am 4:10 5973
You also carried **a** Sikkuth your king Am 5:26
A *with* treasures of wickedness Mi 6:10
And the ruins **a** with the wicked; Zph 1:3 854
priests **a** with the priests. Zph 1:4 5973
was inhabited and prosperous **a** with Zch 7:7
and takes **a** with it seven other Mt 12:45 *3880*
went **a** by the Sea of Galilee, Mt 15:29 *3844*
a with his wife and children and Mt 18:25 *2532*
to Him, **a** with the Herodians, Mt 22:16
oil in flasks **a** with their lamps. Mt 25:4
a with the scribes and elders, Mt 27:41
and **a** with the guard they set a Mt 27:66
was going **a** by the Sea of Galilee, Mk 1:16 *3855*
disciples began to make their way **a** Mk 2:23
His followers, **a** with the twelve, Mk 4:10 *4862*
they took Him **a** with them in Mk 4:36 *3880*
He took **a** the child's father and Mk 5:40 *3880*
went out, **a** with His disciples, Mk 8:27 *2532*
appeared to them **a** with Moses; Mk 9:4 *4862*
and farms, **a** with persecutions; Mk 10:30
priests also, **a** with the scribes, Mk 15:31
they were walking **a** on their way Mk 16:12
in order to register **a** with Mary, Lk 2:5 *4862*
disciples were going **a** with Him, Lk 7:11 *4848*
were sailing **a** He fell asleep; Lk 8:23
took **a** Peter and John and James, Lk 9:28 *3880*
he does not follow **a** with us." Lk 9:49
As they were going **a** the road, Lk 9:57 *1722*
Now as they were traveling **a**, Lk 10:38
"Then it goes and takes **a** seven Lk 11:26
the highways and **a** the hedges, Lk 14:23
crowds were going **a** with Him; Lk 14:25 *4848*
whoever has a money belt is to take it **a**, Lk 22:36
to prayer, **a** with *the* women, Ac 1:14 *4862*
mother's womb was being carried **a**, Ac 3:2
But Peter, **a** with John, fixed his Ac 3:4 *4862*
a with the Gentiles and the Ac 4:27 *4862*
up, **a** with all his associates Ac 5:17 *2532*
Then the captain went **a** with the Ac 5:26 *565*
'YOU ALSO TOOK **A** THE TABERNACLE OF Ac 7:43
As they went **a** the road they Ac 8:36 *2596*
went out and went **a** one street, Ac 12:10 *4281*
mission, taking **a** with *them* John, Ac 12:25 *4838*
called Mark, **a** with them also. Ac 15:37 *4838*
not take him **a** who had deserted Ac 15:38 *4838*
a with a large number of the Ac 17:4 *5037*
becoming jealous and taking **a** some Ac 17:5 *4355*
a with a number of prominent Greek Ac 17:12 *2532*
dragging **a** Gaius and Aristarchus, Ac 19:29 *4884*
and purify yourself **a** with them, Ac 21:24 *4862*
purifying himself **a** with them, Ac 21:26 *4862*
a *some* soldiers and centurions and Ac 21:32 *3880*
"But Lysias the commander came **a**, Ac 24:7 *3928*
the regions **a** the coast of Asia, Ac 27:2 *2596*
through the sea **a** the coast of Cilicia Ac 27:5 *2596*
anchor and *began* sailing **a** Crete, Ac 27:13 *3881*
it and let ourselves be driven **a**. Ac 27:15
in this way let themselves be driven **a**. Ac 27:17
right to take **a** a believing wife, 1Co 9:5 *4013*
not be condemned **a** with the world. 1Co 11:32 *4862*
We have sent **a** with him the 2Co 8:18 *4842*
Barnabas, taking Titus **a** also. Ga 2:1 *4838*
away from you, **a** with all malice. Eph 4:31 *4862*
how to get **a** with humble means, Php 4:12 *5013*
Rahab the harlot did not perish **a** with Heb 11:31 *4881*
without water, carried **a** by winds; Jude 1:12 *3911*

ALONGSIDE

her maidens walking **a** the Nile; Ex 2:5 5921, 3027
a the allotment of the holy Ezk 45:6 5980
"**A** the border of the priests Ezk 48:13 5980
the length **a** the holy allotment shall Ezk 48:18 5980
it shall be **a** the holy allotment. Ezk 48:18 5980
the west border, **a** the portions, Ezk 48:21 5980

ALOOF

you yourself would have stood **a**." 2Sa 18:13 4480, 5048
"They abhor me *and* stand **a** from me, Jb 30:10 7368
my friends stand **a** from my plague; Ps 38:11 4480, 5048
"On the day that you stood **a**, Ob 1:11 4480, 5048
to withdraw and hold himself **a**, Ga 2:12 *873*

ALOUD

went away, crying **a** as she went. 2Sa 13:19 2199
to sound **a** cymbals of bronze; 1Ch 15:19
for those who should sound **a**, 1Ch 16:42
while many shouted **a** for joy, Ezr 3:12 7311
On that day they read **a** from the Ne 13:1
rises to God, and I will cry **a**; Ps 77:1 6817
Over Philistia I will shout **a**." Ps 108:9 7321
godly ones will sing **a** for joy. Ps 132:16 7442
I cry **a** with my voice to the LORD; Ps 142:1 2199
Cry **a** with your voice, O daughter Is 10:30 6670a
Cry **a** and shout for joy, O Is 12:6 6670a
the armed men of Moab cry **a**; Is 15:4 7321
the inhabitants of Sela sing **a**, Is 42:11 7442
into joyful shouting and cry **a**, Is 54:1 6670a
Cry **a** and say, 'Assemble yourselves, Jer 4:5 4390
Even they have cried **a** after you. Jer 12:6 4392
For each time I speak, I cry **a**; Jer 20:8 2199
"Sing **a** with gladness for Jacob, Jer 31:7 7442
that you read all these words **a**, Jer 51:61
cry **a** in the night At the La 2:19 7442
a to bring in the conjurers, Da 5:7 2429
began to weep **a** and embraced Paul, Ac 20:37 *2425*

ALPHA

"I am the **A** and the Omega," Rv 1:8 *256a*
I am the **A** and the Omega, the Rv 21:6 *256a*
"I am the **A** and the Omega, the Rv 22:13 *256a*

ALPHAEUS

James the son of **A**, Mt 10:3 *256b*
of **A** sitting in the tax booth, Mk 2:14 *256b*
Thomas, and James the son of **A**, Mk 3:18 *256b*
James *the son* of **A**, Lk 6:15 *256b*
and Matthew, James *the son* of **A**, Ac 1:13 *256b*

ALREADY

and **a** he is acting like a judge; Gn 19:9 8199
but Joseph was **a** in Egypt. Ex 1:5
and Zalmunna **a** in your hands, Jg 8:6 6258
Zebah and Zalmunna **a** in your hand, Jg 8:15 6258
jugs of wine and five sheep **a** prepared 1Sa 25:18
sent him away and he is **a** gone? 2Sa 3:24 1980
of Israel who have **a** perished, 2Ki 7:13
a provided for the holy temple, 1Ch 29:3
daughters are forced into bondage **a**, Ne 5:5
A it has existed for ages Which Ec 1:10 3528
king *except* what has **a** been done? Ec 2:12 3528
That which is has been **a** and Ec 3:15 3528
and that which will be has **a** been, Ec 3:15 3528
congratulated the dead who are **a** dead Ec 4:2 3528
Whatever exists has **a** been named, Ec 6:10 3528
and their zeal have **a** perished, Ec 9:6 3528
for God has **a** approved your works. Ec 9:7 3528
'The flowers have **a** appeared in SS 2:12
to those **a** gathered." Is 56:8
I have cursed them **a**, because Mal 2:2
a laid at the root of the trees; Mt 3:10 *2235*
at a woman with lust for her has **a** Mt 5:28 *2235*
desolate and the hour is **a** late; Mt 14:15 *2235*
But the boat was **a** a long distance Mt 14:24 *2235*
I say to you that Elijah **a** came, Mt 17:12 *2235*
its branch has **a** become tender and Mt 24:32 *2235*
that the boat was **a** filling up. Mk 4:37 *2235*
When it was **a** quite late, His Mk 6:35 *2235*
desolate and it is **a** quite late; Mk 6:35 *2235*
the twelve, since it was **a** late. Mk 11:11 *2235*
its branch has **a** become tender and Mk 13:28 *2235*
When evening had **a** come, Mk 15:42 *2235*
him as to whether He was **a** dead. Mk 15:44 *2235*
a laid at the root of the trees; Lk 3:9 *2235*
the door has **a** been shut and my Lk 11:7 *2235*
and how I wish it were **a** kindled! Lk 12:49 *2235*
he has ten minas **a**.' Lk 19:25 *2235*
not believe has been judged **a**, Jn 3:18 *2235*
"**A** he who reaps is receiving Jn 4:36 *2235*
and knew that he had **a** been a long Jn 5:6 *2235*
It had **a** become dark, and Jn 6:17 *2235*
for the Jews had **a** agreed that Jn 9:22 *2235*
"I told you **a** and you did not Jn 9:27 *2235*
had **a** been in the tomb four days. Jn 11:17 *2235*
the devil having **a** put into the Jn 13:2 *2235*
"You are **a** clean because of the Jn 15:3 *2235*
and has **a** come, for you to be Jn 16:32 *2235*
things had **a** been accomplished, Jn 19:28 *2235*
when they saw that He was **a** dead, Jn 19:33 *2235*
and saw the stone **a** taken away Jn 20:1
they saw a charcoal fire **a** laid Jn 21:9
next day, for it was **a** evening. Ac 4:3 *2235*
since even the fast was **a** over, Ac 27:9 *2235*
for we have **a** charged that both Ro 3:9 *4256*
for who hopes for what he **a** sees? Ro 8:24
that it is **a** the hour for you to Ro 13:11 *2235*
not where Christ was **a** named, so Ro 15:20
You are **a** filled, you have already 1Co 4:8 *2235*
filled, you have **a** become rich, 1Co 4:8 *2235*
have **a** judged him who has so 1Co 5:3 *2235*
then, it is **a** a defeat for you, 1Co 6:7 *2235*
Was any man called *when he was* **a** 1Co 7:18
Not that I have **a** obtained *it* or Php 3:12 *2235*
it or have **a** become perfect, Php 3:12 *2235*
but after we had **a** suffered and 1Th 2:2 *4310a*
of lawlessness is **a** at work; 2Th 2:7 *2235*
a turned aside to follow Satan. 1Tm 5:15 *2235*
resurrection has **a** taken place, 2Tm 2:18 *2235*
For I am **a** being poured out as a 2Tm 4:6 *2235*
For the time **a** past is sufficient 1Pe 4:3
even though you **a** know *them,* 2Pe 1:12
and the true Light is **a** shining. 1Jn 2:8 *2235*
and now it is **a** in the world. 1Jn 4:3 *2235*

ALSO

He made the stars **a**. Gn 1:16
life **a** in the midst of the garden, Gn 2:9
gave **a** to her husband with her, Gn 3:6 1571
and take **a** from the tree of life, Gn 3:22 1571
on his part **a** brought of the Gn 4:4 1571
she **a** gave birth to Tubal-cain, Gn 4:22 1571
To Seth, to him **a** a son was born; Gn 4:26 1571
forever, because he **a** is flesh; Gn 6:3 7683
in those days, and **a** afterward, Gn 6:4 1571
a of the birds of the sky, by Gn 7:3 1571
A the fountains of the deep and Gn 8:2
He **a** said, "Blessed be the LORD, Gn 9:26
A to Shem, the father of all Gn 10:21 1571
a had flocks and herds and tents. Gn 13:5 1571
descendants can **a** be numbered. Gn 13:16 1571
Amalekites, and **a** the Amorites, Gn 14:7 1571
They **a** took Lot, Abram's Gn 14:12
and **a** brought back his relative Gn 14:16 1571
his possessions, and **a** the women, Gn 14:16 1571
"But I will **a** judge the nation Gn 15:14 1571
Abraham **a** ran to the herd, and Gn 18:7
pleasure, my lord being old **a**?" Gn 18:12
I grant you this request **a**, Gn 19:21 1571
us make him drink wine tonight **a**; Gn 19:34 1571
father drink wine that night **a**, Gn 19:35 1571
for the younger, she **a** bore a son, Gn 19:38 1571
and I **a** kept you from sinning Gn 20:6 1571
the maid I will make a nation **a**, Gn 21:13 1571
Milcah **a** has borne children to Gn 22:20 1571
a bore Tebah and Gaham and Tahash Gn 22:24 1571
and I will water your camels **a**' Gn 24:14 1571
"I will draw **a** for your camels Gn 24:19 1571
I will draw for your camels **a**"; Gn 24:44 1571
and I will water your camels **a**' Gn 24:46 1571
and she watered the camels **a**. Gn 24:46 1571
he gave precious things to her Gn 24:53
She **a** gave the savory food and the Gn 27:17
a brought him wine and he drank. Gn 27:25
Then he **a** made savory food, and Gn 27:31 1571
"Bless me, *even* me **a**, Gn 27:34 1571
Bless me, *even* me **a**, Gn 27:38 1571
"May He **a** give you the blessing Gn 28:4
a be like the dust of the earth, Gn 28:14
Laban **a** gave his maid Zilpah to Gn 29:24
and we will give you the other **a** Gn 29:27 1571
Laban **a** gave his maid Bilhah to Gn 29:29
So *Jacob* went in to Rachel **a**, Gn 29:30 1571
therefore given me this *son* **a**." Gn 29:33 1571
you take my son's mandrakes **a**?" Gn 30:15 1571
provide for my own household **a**?" Gn 30:30 1571
and has **a** entirely consumed our Gn 31:15 1571
He **a** commanded them saying, Gn 32:4
And behold, he **a** is behind us.' " Gn 32:18 1571
a the second and the third, Gn 32:19 1571
servant Jacob **a** is behind us.' " Gn 32:20 1571
Shechem **a** said to her father and Gn 34:11
God **a** said to him, Gn 35:11
he **a** poured oil on it. Gn 35:14
a Basemath, Ishmael's daughter, Gn 36:3
sheaf rose up and **a** stood erect; Gn 37:7 1571
so He took his life **a**. Gn 38:10 1571
she is **a** with child by harlotry." Gn 38:24 1571
"I **a** *saw* in my dream, and behold, Gn 40:16 637
"I saw **a** in my dream, and behold, Gn 41:22
famine was in the land of Canaan **a**. Gn 42:5
"Take your brother **a**, Gn 43:13
"We have **a** brought down other Gn 43:22
we **a** will be my lord's slaves." Gn 44:9 1571
it **a** be according to your words; Gn 44:10 1571
If you take this one **a** from me, Gn 44:29 1571
"There I will **a** provide for you, Gn 45:11
will **a** surely bring you up again; Gn 46:4 1571
he **a** will become a people and he Gn 48:19 1571
a people and he **a** will be great. Gn 48:19 1571
There **a** went up with him both Gn 50:9
Then his brothers **a** came and fell Gn 50:18 1571
a the sons of Machir, the son of Gn 50:23 1571

they will **a** join themselves to those	**Ex 1:10**	1571
He said **a**, "I am the God of your	**Ex 3:6**	
Moses **a** took the staff of God in	**Ex 4:20**	
"I **a** established My covenant	**Ex 6:4**	1571
I will **a** redeem you with an	**Ex 6:6**	
Then Pharaoh **a** called for *the* wise	**Ex 7:11**	1571
men and *the* sorcerers, and they **a**,	**Ex 7:11**	1571
and **a** the ground on which they	**Ex 8:21**	1571
hardened his heart this time **a**,	**Ex 8:32**	1571
the hail **a** struck every plant of	**Ex 9:25**	
They will **a** eat the rest of what	**Ex 10:5**	
"You must **a** let us have	**Ex 10:25**	1571
'You shall **a** observe the *Feast of*	**Ex 12:17**	
said, and go, and bless me **a**."	**Ex 12:32**	1571
multitude **a** went up with them,	**Ex 12:38**	1571
and all these people **a** will go to	**Ex 18:23**	1571
may **a** believe in you forever."	**Ex 19:9**	1571
The LORD **a** said to Moses,	**Ex 19:10**	
"**A** let the priests who come near to	**Ex 19:22**	1571
its owner **a** shall be put to death.	**Ex 21:29**	1571
a they shall divide the dead *ox*.	**Ex 21:35**	1571
for you **a** were strangers in	**Ex 23:9**	
"**A** *you shall observe* the Feast of	**Ex 23:16**	
a the Feast of the Ingathering at	**Ex 23:16**	
their hooks **a** *being of* gold, on	**Ex 26:32**	1571
their hooks **a** *being of* gold;	**Ex 26:37**	
shall **a** make the ephod of gold,	**Ex 28:6**	
"You shall **a** make a plate of pure	**Ex 28:36**	
you shall **a** make sashes for them,	**Ex 28:40**	
"You shall **a** take the one ram,	**Ex 29:15**	
"You shall **a** take the fat from	**Ex 29:22**	
I will **a** consecrate Aaron and his	**Ex 29:44**	
The LORD **a** spoke to Moses, saying,	**Ex 30:11**	
shall **a** make a laver of bronze,	**Ex 30:18**	
"Take **a** for yourself the finest	**Ex 30:23**	
"You shall **a** consecrate them,	**Ex 30:29**	
the table **a** and its utensils, and	**Ex 31:8**	
offering **a** with all its utensils,	**Ex 31:9**	
the anointing oil **a**,	**Ex 31:11**	
have **a** found favor in My sight.'	**Ex 33:12**	1571
"I will **a** do this thing of which	**Ex 33:17**	1571
their gods and cause your sons **a**	**Ex 34:16**	
the lampstand **a** for the light and	**Ex 35:14**	
a has put in his heart to teach,	**Ex 35:34**	
They **a** made bells of pure gold,	**Ex 39:25**	
'He shall **a** take away its crop	**Lv 1:16**	
'**A** if you bring a grain offering	**Lv 2:14**	
'The priest shall **a** put some of	**Lv 4:7**	
'He shall **a** do with the bull just	**Lv 4:20**	
'He shall **a** bring his guilt	**Lv 5:6**	
'He shall **a** sprinkle some of the	**Lv 5:9**	
'**A** the earthenware vessel in which	**Lv 6:28**	
'**A** the priest who presents any	**Lv 7:8**	
'**A** the flesh that touches anything	**Lv 7:19**	
'**A** the fat of *an animal* which	**Lv 7:24**	
a placed the turban on his head,	**Lv 8:9**	
He **a** took all the fat that was on	**Lv 8:16**	
He **a** had Aaron's sons come near;	**Lv 8:24**	
Moses **a** took the breast and	**Lv 8:29**	
He **a** washed the entrails and the	**Lv 9:14**	
He **a** presented the burnt offering,	**Lv 9:16**	
called **a** to Mishael and Elzaphan,	**Lv 10:4**	
the rabbit **a**, for though it chews	**Lv 11:6**	
'**A** whatever walks on its paws,	**Lv 11:27**	
'**A** anything on which one of them	**Lv 11:32**	
'**A** if one of the animals dies	**Lv 11:39**	
"The priest shall **a** give orders	**Lv 14:5**	
a take some of the log of oil,	**Lv 14:15**	
"The priest shall **a** pour some of	**Lv 14:26**	
a spoke to Moses and to Aaron,	**Lv 15:1**	
'**A** whoever touches the person with	**Lv 15:7**	
'Everything **a** on which she lies	**Lv 15:20**	
a in front of the mercy seat he	**Lv 16:14**	
He shall **a** make atonement for the	**Lv 16:33**	
that man **a** shall be cut off from	**Lv 17:9**	
'**A** you shall not approach a woman	**Lv 18:19**	
'**A** you shall not have intercourse	**Lv 18:23**	
"The priest shall **a** make atonement	**Lv 19:22**	
shall **a** say to the sons of Israel:	**Lv 20:2**	
'I will **a** set My face against that	**Lv 20:3**	
I will **a** set My face against that	**Lv 20:6**	
you shall **a** kill the animal.	**Lv 20:15**	
'You shall **a** not uncover the	**Lv 20:19**	
a for his virgin sister, who is	**Lv 21:3**	
'**A** the daughter of any priest, if	**Lv 21:9**	
'**A** anything *with its testicles*	**Lv 22:24**	
'You shall **a** count for yourselves	**Lv 23:15**	
'You shall **a** offer one male goat	**Lv 23:19**	
'You are **a** to count off seven	**Lv 25:8**	
they **a** may become your possession.	**Lv 25:45**	
'I shall **a** grant peace in the	**Lv 26:6**	
I shall **a** eliminate harmful beasts	**Lv 26:6**	
'I will **a** walk among you and be	**Lv 26:12**	
a, you will sow your seed	**Lv 26:16**	
'If **a** after these things you do	**Lv 26:18**	
'I will **a** break down your	**Lv 26:19**	
I will **a** make your sky like iron	**Lv 26:19**	
'I will **a** bring upon you a sword	**Lv 26:25**	
I will **a** bring weakness into their	**Lv 26:36**	
and **a** because of the iniquities of	**Lv 26:39**	637
and **a** in their acting with	**Lv 26:40**	637
I **a** was acting with hostility	**Lv 26:41**	637
remember **a** My covenant with Isaac,	**Lv 26:42**	637
a camp around the tabernacle.	**Nu 1:50**	
"They shall **a** keep all the	**Nu 3:8**	
they shall **a** spread a cloth of blue	**Nu 4:7**	
"They shall **a** put on it all its	**Nu 4:14**	
a census of the sons of Gershon **a**,	**Nu 4:22**	1571
'**A** every contribution pertaining	**Nu 5:9**	
'He shall **a** offer the ram for a	**Nu 6:17**	
them and consecrated them **a**.	**Nu 7:1**	
You shall **a** assemble the whole	**Nu 8:9**	
Aaron **a** made atonement for them to	**Nu 8:21**	
"**A** in the day of your gladness	**Nu 10:10**	
and **a** the sons of Israel wept	**Nu 11:4**	1571
A, he gathered seventy men of the	**Nu 11:24**	
"There **a** we saw the Nephilim	**Nu 13:33**	
You **a** have forgiven this people,	**Nu 14:19**	
'**A** if one person sins	**Nu 15:27**	
The LORD **a** spoke to Moses, saying,	**Nu 15:37**	
you seeking for the priesthood **a**?	**Nu 16:10**	1571
but you would **a** lord it over us?	**Nu 16:13**	1571
a you and Aaron *shall* each *bring*	**Nu 16:17**	
Fire **a** came forth from the LORD	**Nu 16:35**	
bring with you **a** your brothers,	**Nu 18:2**	1571
"This **a** is yours, the offering of	**Nu 18:11**	
'So you shall **a** present an	**Nu 18:28**	1571
'The one who burns it shall **a** wash	**Nu 19:8**	
'**A**, anyone who in the open field	**Nu 19:16**	
please, you **a** stay here tonight,	**Nu 22:19**	1571
enemies, **a**, will be a possession,	**Nu 24:18**	
a *will come* to destruction."	**Nu 24:24**	1571
place, and Balak **a** went his way.	**Nu 24:25**	1571
a a tenth of an ephah of fine	**Nu 28:5**	
'**A** on the day of the first fruits,	**Nu 28:26**	
a one male goat to make atonement	**Nu 28:30**	
shall **a** have a holy convocation;	**Nu 29:1**	
a their grain offering, fine flour	**Nu 29:3**	
"**A** if a woman makes a vow to the	**Nu 30:3**	
they **a** killed Balaam the son of	**Nu 31:8**	
The LORD had **a** executed judgments	**Nu 33:4**	
shall **a** draw a line from Hazar-enan	**Nu 34:10**	
"You shall **a** measure outside the	**Nu 35:5**	
angry with me **a** on your account,	**Dt 1:37**	1571
and you shall **a** purchase water	**Dt 2:6**	1571
they are **a** regarded as Rephaim,	**Dt 2:11**	637
(It is **a** regarded as the land of	**Dt 2:20**	637
the LORD our God delivered Og **a**,	**Dt 3:3**	1571
the Arabah **a**, with the Jordan as *a*	**Dt 3:17**	
and they **a** possess the land which	**Dt 3:20**	1571
"I **a** pleaded with the LORD at	**Dt 3:23**	
He will **a** bless the fruit of your	**Dt 7:13**	
LORD listened to me that time **a**.	**Dt 9:19**	1571
so I **a** prayed for Aaron at the	**Dt 9:20**	1571
LORD listened to me that time **a**;	**Dt 10:10**	1571
"There **a** you and your households	**Dt 12:7**	
gods, that I **a** may do likewise?'	**Dt 12:30**	1571
"**A** you shall not neglect the	**Dt 14:27**	
A you shall do likewise to your	**Dt 15:17**	637
a shall speak to the people,	**Dt 20:5**	
"She shall **a** remove the clothes	**Dt 21:13**	
"You shall **a** have a place outside	**Dt 23:12**	
and **a** have given it to the Levite	**Dt 26:13**	1571
Moses **a** charged the people on that	**Dt 27:11**	
who **a** leaves you no grain,	**Dt 28:51**	
"**A** every sickness and every	**Dt 28:61**	1571
the arm, **a** the crown of the head.	**Dt 33:20**	637
His heavens **a** drop down dew.	**Dt 33:28**	637
and they **a** possess the land which	**Jos 1:15**	1571
that you **a** will deal kindly with	**Jos 2:12**	1571
"**A** seven priests shall carry	**Jos 6:4**	
a brought out all her relatives and	**Jos 6:23**	
and they have **a** transgressed My	**Jos 7:11**	1571
they have **a** put *them* among their	**Jos 7:11**	1571
they **a** acted craftily and set out	**Jos 9:4**	1571
The LORD gave it **a** with its	**Jos 10:30**	1571
had **a** done to Libnah and its king.	**Jos 10:39**	1571
a killed Balaam the son of Beor,	**Jos 13:22**	
Moses **a** gave *an inheritance* to the	**Jos 13:24**	
Moses **a** gave *an inheritance* to the	**Jos 13:29**	
a half of Gilead, with Ashtaroth	**Jos 13:31**	
give me **a** springs of water."	**Jos 15:19**	
half-tribe of Manasseh **a** have received	**Jos 18:7**	
Included **a** *were* Kattah and Nahalal	**Jos 19:15**	
Included **a** *were* Ummah, and Aphek	**Jos 19:30**	
'It shall **a** come about if they say	**Jos 22:28**	
We **a** will serve the LORD, for He	**Jos 24:18**	1571
give me **a** springs of water."	**Jg 1:15**	
"Therefore I **a** said,	**Jg 2:3**	1571
All that generation **a** were	**Jg 2:10**	1571
I **a** will no longer drive out	**Jg 2:21**	1571
handle **a** went in after the blade,	**Jg 3:22**	1571
and he **a** saved Israel.	**Jg 3:31**	1571
Deborah **a** went up with him.	**Jg 4:10**	
quaked, the heavens **a** dripped,	**Jg 5:4**	1571
even to death, And Naphtali **a**,	**Jg 5:18**	
and they **a** were called together to	**Jg 6:35**	1571
then you **a** blow the trumpets all	**Jg 7:18**	1571
he spoke **a** to the men of Penuel,	**Jg 8:9**	1571
you and your son, **a** your son's son,	**Jg 8:22**	1571
was in Shechem **a** bore him a son,	**Jg 8:31**	1571
A, remember that I am your bone	**Jg 9:2**	
and let him **a** rejoice in you.	**Jg 9:19**	1571
All the people **a** cut down each	**Jg 9:49**	1571
of the tower of Shechem **a** died,	**Jg 9:49**	1571
A God returned all the wickedness	**Jg 9:57**	
Jordan to fight **a** against Judah,	**Jg 10:9**	1571
"**A** when the Sidonians, the	**Jg 10:12**	
they **a** sent to the king of Moab,	**Jg 11:17**	1571
his concubine **a** was with him.	**Jg 19:10**	
and **a** bread and wine for me,	**Jg 19:19**	1571
the men in ambush **a** deployed and	**Jg 20:37**	
they **a** set on fire all the cities	**Jg 20:48**	1571
both Mahlon and Chilion **a** died,	**Ru 1:5**	1571
a husband tonight and **a** bear sons,	**Ru 1:12**	1571
"**A** you shall purposely pull out for	**Ru 2:16**	1571
She **a** took *it* out and gave Naomi	**Ru 2:18**	
must **a** acquire Ruth the Moabitess,	**Ru 4:5**	
"May he **a** be to you a restorer of	**Ru 4:15**	
have **a** dedicated him to the LORD;	**1Sa 1:28**	1571
He brings low, He **a** exalts.	**1Sa 2:7**	637
A, before they burned the fat, the	**1Sa 2:15**	1571
May God do so to you, and more **a**,	**1Sa 3:17**	3541
there has **a** been a great slaughter	**1Sa 4:17**	1571
the people, and your two sons **a**,	**1Sa 4:17**	1571
gods—so they are doing to you **a**.	**1Sa 8:8**	1571
"He will **a** take your daughters	**1Sa 8:13**	
"He will **a** take your male	**1Sa 8:16**	
we **a** may be like all the nations,	**1Sa 8:20**	1571
Is Saul **a** among the prophets?"	**1Sa 10:11**	1571
"Is Saul **a** among the prophets?"	**1Sa 10:12**	1571
a went to his house at Gibeah;	**1Sa 10:26**	1571
There they **a** offered sacrifices of	**1Sa 11:15**	
then both you and **a** the king who	**1Sa 12:14**	1571
and **a** that Israel had become	**1Sa 13:4**	1571
A *some of* the Hebrews crossed the	**1Sa 13:7**	
even they **a** *turned* to be with the	**1Sa 14:21**	1571
even they **a** pursued them closely	**1Sa 14:22**	1571
"May God do this *to me* and more **a**,	**1Sa 14:44**	3541
a rejected you from *being* king."	**1Sa 15:23**	
"**A** the Glory of Israel will not lie	**1Sa 15:29**	1571
He **a** consecrated Jesse and his	**1Sa 16:5**	
He **a** *had* bronze greaves on his	**1Sa 17:6**	
shield-carrier **a** walked before him.	**1Sa 17:7**	
"Bring **a** these ten cuts of cheese	**1Sa 17:18**	
The Philistine **a** said to David,	**1Sa 17:44**	
and **a** in the sight of Saul's servants.	**1Sa 18:5**	1571
and they **a** prophesied.	**1Sa 19:20**	1571
messengers, and they **a** prophesied.	**1Sa 19:21**	1571
third time, and they **a** prophesied.	**1Sa 19:21**	1571
the Spirit of God came upon him **a**,	**1Sa 19:23**	1571
He **a** stripped off his clothes,	**1Sa 19:24**	1571
"Is Saul **a** among the prophets?"	**1Sa 19:24**	1571
LORD do so to Jonathan and more **a**,	**1Sa 20:13**	3254
Will the son of Jesse **a** give to	**1Sa 22:7**	1571
because their hand **a** is with David	**1Sa 22:17**	1571
a oxen, donkeys, and sheep *he*	**1Sa 22:19**	
and Saul my father knows that **a**."	**1Sa 23:17**	1571
And David **a** girded on his sword,	**1Sa 25:13**	1571
the enemies of David, and more **a**,	**1Sa 25:22**	3541
The LORD has **a** returned the	**1Sa 25:39**	
had **a** taken Ahinoam of Jezreel,	**1Sa 25:43**	1571
David **a** said, "As the LORD lives,	**1Sa 26:10**	
He **a** said, "Why then is my lord	**1Sa 26:18**	
"Moreover the LORD will **a** give	**1Sa 28:19**	1571
a there was no strength in him,	**1Sa 28:20**	1571
"So now **a**, please listen to the	**1Sa 28:22**	1571
a been left at the brook Besor,	**1Sa 30:21**	
he **a** fell on his sword and died	**1Sa 31:5**	1571
and **a** many of the people have	**2Sa 1:4**	1571
and Jonathan his son are dead **a**."	**2Sa 1:4**	1571
and *so* **a** *did* all the men who *were*	**2Sa 1:11**	1571
up there, and his two wives **a**,	**2Sa 2:2**	1571
and I **a** will show this goodness to	**2Sa 2:6**	1571
and **a** the house of Judah has	**2Sa 2:7**	1571
God do so to Abner, and more **a**,	**2Sa 3:9**	3541
Abner **a** spoke in the hearing	**2Sa 3:19**	1571
"May God do so to me, and more **a**,	**2Sa 3:35**	3541
is **a** considered *part* of Benjamin,	**2Sa 4:2**	1571
"I will **a** appoint a place for My	**2Sa 7:10**	
The LORD **a** declares to you that	**2Sa 7:11**	
for You have spoken **a** of the	**2Sa 7:19**	1571
a dedicated these to the LORD,	**2Sa 8:11**	1571
they **a** fled before Abishai	**2Sa 10:14**	
"Stay here today **a**, and tomorrow	**2Sa 11:12**	1571
and Uriah the Hittite **a** died.	**2Sa 11:17**	1571
Uriah the Hittite is dead **a**.'"	**2Sa 11:21**	1571
Uriah the Hittite is **a** dead."	**2Sa 11:24**	1571
'I **a** gave you your master's house	**2Sa 12:8**	
LORD **a** has taken away your sin;	**2Sa 12:13**	1571
the child **a** that is born to you	**2Sa 12:14**	1571
He **a** brought out the people who	**2Sa 12:31**	
and **a** the king and all his	**2Sa 13:36**	1571
killed, and destroy the heir **a**.'	**2Sa 14:7**	1571
"Why will you **a** go with us?	**2Sa 15:19**	1571
are a foreigner and **a** an exile;	**2Sa 15:19**	1571
there **a** your servant will be."	**2Sa 15:21**	3588
a passed over the brook Kidron,	**2Sa 15:23**	
Now behold, Zadok **a** *came*,	**2Sa 15:24**	1571
king said **a** to Zadok the priest,	**2Sa 15:27**	
with you will **a** be strengthened."	**2Sa 16:21**	
"Now call Hushai the Archite **a**,	**2Sa 17:5**	1571
will surely go out with you **a**."	**2Sa 18:2**	1571
let me **a** run after the Cushite."	**2Sa 18:22**	1571
one **a** is bringing good news."	**2Sa 18:26**	1571
May God do so to me, and more **a**,	**2Sa 19:13**	3541
Judah and **a** half the people of Israel	**2Sa 19:40**	1571
therefore we **a** have more *claim* on	**2Sa 19:43**	1571
together and **a** went after him.	**2Sa 20:14**	637
Joab **a** returned to the king at	**2Sa 20:22**	
Jairite was **a** a priest to David.	**2Sa 20:26**	1571
he **a** had been born to the giant.	**2Sa 21:20**	1571
"He bowed the heavens **a**,	**2Sa 22:10**	
"He **a** brought me forth into a	**2Sa 22:20**	
"I was **a** blameless toward Him,	**2Sa 22:24**	
"You have **a** given me the shield	**2Sa 22:36**	
"You have **a** made my enemies turn	**2Sa 22:41**	
"You have **a** delivered me from	**2Sa 22:44**	
a brings me out from my enemies;	**2Sa 22:49**	
He **a** went down and killed a lion	**2Sa 23:20**	
And he was **a** a very handsome man,	**1Ki 1:6**	1571
"The king has **a** sent with him	**1Ki 1:44**	
"The king has **a** said thus,	**1Ki 1:48**	1571
"Now you **a** know what Joab the son	**1Ki 2:5**	1571
he **a** shed the blood of war in	**1Ki 2:5**	
Ask for him **a** the kingdom—for he	**1Ki 2:22**	
"May God do so to me and more **a**,	**1Ki 2:23**	3541

The king a said to Shimei, 1Ki 2:44
"I have a given you what you 1Ki 3:13 1571
woman a gave birth to a child, 1Ki 3:18 1571
(he a married Basemath the daughter 1Ki 4:15 1571
They a brought barley and straw 1Ki 4:28
He a spoke 3,000 proverbs, and his 1Ki 4:32
he spoke a of animals and birds 1Ki 4:33
A for the house he made windows 1Ki 6:4
He a built the stories against the 1Ki 6:10
a overlaid the altar with cedar. 1Ki 6:20
A the whole altar which was by the 1Ki 6:22
A in the inner sanctuary he made 1Ki 6:23
He a overlaid the cherubim with 1Ki 6:28
So a he made for the entrance of 1Ki 6:33
He a made a house like this hall 1Ki 7:8
He a made two capitals of molten 1Ki 7:16
and a on its opening *there were* 1Ki 7:31 1571
"A concerning the foreigner who 1Ki 8:41 1571
King Solomon a built a fleet of 1Ki 9:26
A the ships of Hiram, which brought 1Ki 10:11 1571
a lyres and harps for the singers; 1Ki 10:12
A Solomon's import of horses was 1Ki 10:28
Thus a he did for all his foreign 1Ki 11:8
God a raised up *another* adversary 1Ki 11:23
a rebelled against the king. 1Ki 11:26
The altar a was split apart and 1Ki 13:5
a they related to their father. 1Ki 13:11
"I a am a prophet like you, and 1Ki 13:18 1571
a was standing beside the body. 1Ki 13:24
you a have done more evil than all 1Ki 14:9
For they a built for themselves 1Ki 14:23 1571
There were a male cult 1Ki 14:24 1571
He a put away the male cult 1Ki 15:12
He a removed Maacah his mother 1Ki 15:13 1571
son of Hanani a came against Baasha 1Ki 16:7 1571
and has a struck down the king." 1Ki 16:16 1571
Ahab a made the Asherah. 1Ki 16:33
have You a brought calamity to 1Ki 17:20 1571
he a filled the trench with water. 1Ki 18:35 1571
wives and children are a mine.'" 1Ki 20:3
the gods do so to me and more a, 1Ki 20:10 3541
and a taken possession?" 1Ki 21:19 1571
Of Jezebel a has the LORD spoken, 1Ki 21:23 1571
are to entice *him* and a prevail. 1Ki 22:22 1571
Jehoshaphat a made peace with the 1Ki 22:44
He a took up the mantle of Elijah 2Ki 2:13
when he a had struck the waters, 2Ki 2:14 637
He will a give the Moabites into 2Ki 3:18
The man was a a valiant warrior, 2Ki 5:1
"May God do so to me and more a, 2Ki 6:31 3541
and if we sit here, we die a. 2Ki 7:4
tent and carried from there a, 2Ki 7:8
They a broke down the *sacred* 2Ki 10:27
third a *shall be* at the gate Sur, 2Ki 11:6
shall a keep watch over the house 2Ki 11:7
a between the king and the people. 2Ki 11:17
a remained standing in Samaria. 2Ki 13:6 1571
the king's house, the hostages a, 2Ki 14:14
he a took down the sea from the 2Ki 16:17
A Judah did not keep the 2Ki 17:19 1571
They a feared the LORD and 2Ki 17:32
LORD, they a served their idols; 2Ki 17:41
He a broke in pieces the bronze 2Ki 18:4
a made Judah sin with his idols; 2Ki 21:11 1571
a those who burned incense to 2Ki 23:5
He a broke down the houses of the 2Ki 23:7
He a defiled Topheth, which is in 2Ki 23:10
Josiah a removed all the 2Ki 23:19 1571
will remove Judah a from My sight, 2Ki 23:27 1571
and a for the innocent blood which 2Ki 24:4 1571
a the king's mother and the king's 2Ki 24:15
The captain of the guard a took 2Ki 25:15
She a bore Shaaph the father of 1Ch 2:49
Libnah a with its pasture lands, 1Ch 6:57
Gezer a with its pasture lands, 1Ch 6:67
upper Beth-horon, a Uzzen-sheerah. 1Ch 7:24
And they a lived with their 1Ch 8:32 637
Some of them a were appointed over 1Ch 9:29
And they a lived with their 1Ch 9:38 637
and a because he asked counsel of 1Ch 10:13 1571
He a went down and killed a lion 1Ch 11:22
Manasseh a some defected to David 1Ch 12:19
a Zadok, a young man mighty of 1Ch 12:28
and all the rest a of Israel were 1Ch 12:38 1571
a to the priests and Levites who 1Ch 13:2
a *were* gatekeepers for the ark. 1Ch 15:24
David a wore an ephod of linen. 1Ch 15:27
a Asaph *played* loud-sounding 1Ch 16:5
He a confirmed it to Jacob for a 1Ch 16:17
He a is to be feared above all 1Ch 16:25
Obed-edom, a the son of Jeduthun, 1Ch 16:38
David a defeated Hadadezer king of 1Ch 18:3
A from Tibhath and from Cun, 1Ch 18:8
King David a dedicated these to 1Ch 18:11 1571
they a fled before Abshai his 1Ch 19:15 1571
a was descended from the giants. 1Ch 20:6 1571
a timber and stone I have 1Ch 22:14
David a commanded all the leaders 1Ch 22:17
"A, the Levites will no longer need 1Ch 23:26 1571
These a cast lots just as their 1Ch 24:31 1571
A to his son Shemaiah sons were 1Ch 26:6
A Hosah, *one* of the sons of Merari 1Ch 26:10
A Jonathan, David's uncle, *was* a 1Ch 27:32
a for the divisions of the priests 1Ch 28:13
The officials a and all the people 1Ch 28:21
and King David a rejoiced greatly. 1Ch 29:9 1571
and a all the sons of King David 1Ch 29:24 1571
"Send me a cedar, cypress and 2Ch 2:8
He a overlaid the house with 2Ch 3:7

He a overlaid the upper rooms with 2Ch 3:9
He a made two pillars for the 2Ch 3:15
A he made the cast *metal* sea, ten 2Ch 4:2
He a made ten basins in which to 2Ch 4:6
He a made ten tables and placed 2Ch 4:8
Huram a made the pails, the 2Ch 4:11
He a made the stands and he made 2Ch 4:14
Solomon a made all the things that 2Ch 4:19
"A concerning the foreigner who 2Ch 6:32 1571
and the Levites a, with 2Ch 7:6
He a built upper Beth-horon and 2Ch 8:5
a brought algum trees and precious 2Ch 9:10 1571
He a strengthened the fortresses 2Ch 11:11
so I a have forsaken you to Shishak.'" 2Ch 12:5 637
a conditions were good in Judah. 2Ch 12:12 1571
He a removed the high places and 2Ch 14:5
They a struck down those who owned 2Ch 14:15 1571
He a removed Maacah, the 2Ch 15:16 1571
the Arabians a brought him flocks, 2Ch 17:11 1571
are to entice *him* and prevail a. 2Ch 18:21 1571
In Jerusalem a Jehoshaphat 2Ch 19:8 1571
A the Levites shall be officers 2Ch 19:11
some of the rulers of Israel a. 2Ch 21:4 1571
you have a killed your brothers, 2Ch 21:13 1571
He a walked in the ways of the 2Ch 22:3 1571
He a walked according to their 2Ch 22:5 1571
He a sought Ahaziah, and they 2Ch 22:9
and a workers in iron and bronze 2Ch 24:12 1571
LORD, He has a forsaken you.'" 2Ch 24:20
He hired a 100,000 valiant 2Ch 25:6
The sons of Judah a captured 2Ch 25:12
the king's house, the hostages a, 2Ch 25:24
a gave tribute to Uzziah, 2Ch 26:8
He a *had* plowmen and vinedressers 2Ch 26:10
and he himself a hastened to get 2Ch 26:20 1571
He fought a with the king of the 2Ch 27:5
The Ammonites a paid him this 2Ch 27:5
he a made molten images for the 2Ch 28:2 1571
And he was a delivered into the 2Ch 28:5 1571
and they took a a great deal of spoil 2Ch 28:8 1571
The Philistines a had invaded the 2Ch 28:18
"They have a shut the doors of 2Ch 29:7 1571
They a slaughtered the rams and 2Ch 29:22
they slaughtered the lambs a and 2Ch 29:22
LORD a began with the trumpets, 2Ch 29:27
a sang and the trumpets sounded; 2Ch 29:28
There *were* a many burnt 2Ch 29:35 1571
letters a to Ephraim and Manasseh, 2Ch 30:1 1571
The hand of God was a on Judah to 2Ch 30:12 1571
they a removed all the incense 2Ch 30:14
He a *appointed* the king's portion 2Ch 31:3
A he commanded the people who 2Ch 31:4
a brought in the tithe of oxen and 2Ch 31:6 1571
A for the sons of Aaron the 2Ch 31:19
He a wrote letters to insult the 2Ch 32:17
a for the produce of grain, 2Ch 32:28
he a erected altars for the Baals 2Ch 33:3
He a removed the foreign gods and 2Ch 33:15
His prayer a and *how God* was 2Ch 33:19
a the Asherim, the carved images and 2Ch 34:4
he a tore down the altars and beat 2Ch 34:7
were a over the burden bearers, 2Ch 34:13
"They have a emptied out the 2Ch 34:17
He a said to the Levites who 2Ch 35:3
His officers a contributed a 2Ch 35:8
Conaniah a, and Shemaiah and 2Ch 35:9
They did this a with the bulls. 2Ch 35:12
were a at their stations according 2Ch 35:15
are a written in the Lamentations. 2Ch 35:25
Nebuchadnezzar a brought *some* of 2Ch 36:7
He a rebelled against King 2Ch 36:13 1571
kingdom, and a *put it* in writing, 2Ch 36:22 1571
kingdom, and a *put it* in writing, Ezr 1:1 1571
A King Cyrus brought out the Ezr 1:7
a for the new moons and for all Ezr 3:5
"We a asked them their names so Ezr 5:10 638
'A the gold and silver utensils of Ezr 5:14 638
'A let the gold and silver utensils Ezr 6:5 638
"A the utensils which are given Ezr 7:19
"We a inform you that it is not Ezr 7:24
and a about the king's words which Ne 2:18 637
the son of Baana a made repairs. Ne 3:4
a made repairs for the official Ne 3:7
that time I a said to the people, Ne 4:22 1571
A there were those who said, Ne 5:4
a the hundredth *part* of the money Ne 5:11
I a shook out the front of my Ne 5:13 1571
I a applied myself to the work Ne 5:16 1571
a birds were prepared for me; Ne 5:18
"You have a appointed Ne 6:7 1571
and a Noadiah the prophetess and Ne 6:14 1571
A in those days many letters went Ne 6:17 1571
A appoint guards from the Ne 7:3
A Jeshua, Bani, Sherebiah, Jamin, Ne 8:7
"You a gave them kingdoms Ne 9:22
They a rule over our bodies And Ne 9:37
a their brothers Shebaniah, Ne 10:10
We a placed ourselves under Ne 10:32
a bring the first of our dough, Ne 10:37
A the gatekeepers, Akkub, Talmon and Ne 11:19
Benjamin a *lived* from Geba *onward,* Ne 11:31
A Bakbukiah and Unni, their Ne 12:9
they a purified the people, the Ne 12:30
On that day men were a appointed Ne 12:44
I a discovered that the portions Ne 13:10
A men of Tyre were living there Ne 13:16
For this a remember me, O my God, Ne 13:22 1571
In those days I a saw that the Ne 13:23 1571
Queen Vashti a gave a banquet for Es 1:9 1571

has wronged not only the king but a Es 1:16
he a made a holiday for the Es 2:18
and the people a, to do with Es 3:11
He a gave him a copy of the text Es 4:8
a will fast in the same way. Es 4:16 1571
Haman a said, "Even Esther the Es 5:12 637
and tomorrow a I am invited by her Es 5:12 1571
said to Esther on the second day a as Es 7:2 1571
It shall a be done." Es 9:12
let tomorrow a be granted to the Es 9:13 1571
Jews who were in Susa assembled a Es 9:15 1571
possessions a were 7,000 sheep, Jb 1:3
LORD, and Satan a came among them. Jb 1:6 1571
They a slew the servants with the Jb 1:15
speaking, another a came and said, Jb 1:16
speaking, another a came and said, Jb 1:17
speaking, another a came and said, Jb 1:18
and Satan a came among them to Jb 2:1 1571
and His hands a heal. Jb 5:18
"You will know a that your Jb 5:25
"What you know I a know; Jb 13:2 1571
"This a will be my salvation, For Jb 13:16 1571
He a flees like a shadow and does Jb 14:2
a open Your eyes on him Jb 14:3 637
what I have seen I will a declare; Jb 15:17
He has a set me up as His target. Jb 16:12
of his children a will languish. Jb 17:5
has a grown dim because of grief, Jb 17:7
a kindled His anger against me And Jb 19:11
on, a become very powerful? Jb 21:7 1571
Look a at the distant stars, how Jb 22:12
"You will a decree a thing, and Jb 22:28
it and a searched it out. Jb 28:27 1571
share, I a will tell my opinion. Jb 32:17 637
"Man is a chastened with pain on Jb 33:19
The cattle a, concerning what is Jb 36:33 637
"At this a my heart trembles, And Jb 37:1 637
"A with moisture He loads the Jb 37:11 637
"His young ones a suck up blood; Jb 39:30
"Then I will a confess to you, Jb 40:14 1571
He has a prepared for Himself Ps 7:13
And a the beasts of the field, Ps 8:7 1571
The LORD a will be a stronghold Ps 9:9
My flesh a will dwell securely. Ps 16:9 637
He bowed the heavens a, Ps 18:9
LORD a thundered in the heavens, Ps 18:13
me forth a into a broad place; Ps 18:19
I was a blameless with Him, And I Ps 18:23
You have a given me the shield of Ps 18:35
You have a made my enemies turn Ps 18:40
Sweeter a than honey and the Ps 19:10
A keep back Your servant from Ps 19:13 1571
Be their shepherd a, Ps 28:9
my soul and my body a. Ps 31:9
Draw a the spear and the Ps 35:3
way to the LORD, Trust a in Him, Ps 37:5
a is the helmet of My head; Ps 60:7
The heavens a dropped *rain* at the Ps 68:8 637
men, Even *among* the rebellious a, Ps 68:18 637
They a gave me gall for my food And Ps 69:21
I will a praise You with a harp, Ps 71:22 1571
My tongue a will utter Your Ps 71:24 1571
May he a rule from sea to sea And Ps 72:8
cries for help, The afflicted a, Ps 72:12
Yours a is the night Ps 74:16 637
His dwelling place a is in Zion. Ps 76:2
The deeps a trembled. Ps 77:16 637
forth streams a from the rock And Ps 78:16
Can He give bread a? Ps 78:20 1571
anger a mounted against Israel, Ps 78:21 1571
He gave a their crops to the Ps 78:46
their cattle a to the hailstones And Ps 78:48
He a drove out the nations before Ps 78:55
He a delivered His people to the Ps 78:62
He a rejected the tent of Joseph, Ps 78:67
He a chose David His servant And Ps 78:70
Assyria a has joined with them; Ps 83:8 1571
The bird a has found a house, And Ps 84:3 1571
rain a covers it with blessings. Ps 84:6 1571
Your faithfulness a in the assembly Ps 89:5 637
Your faithfulness a surrounds You. Ps 89:8
are Yours, the earth a is Yours; Ps 89:11 637
My arm a will strengthen him. Ps 89:21 637
"I shall a set his hand on the Ps 89:25
"I a shall make him *My* Ps 89:27 637
You a turn back the edge of Ps 89:43 637
peaks of the mountains are His a. Ps 95:4
Israel a came into Egypt; Ps 105:23
their vines a and their fig trees, Ps 105:33
He a struck down all the Ps 105:36
them a the lands of the nations, Ps 105:44
joined themselves a to Baal-peor, Ps 106:28
They a provoked *Him* to wrath at Ps 106:32
Their enemies a oppressed them, Ps 106:42
He a made them *objects* of Ps 106:46
He led them a by a straight way, Ps 107:7
Let them a offer sacrifices of Ps 107:22
Let them extol Him a in the Ps 107:32
A He blesses them and they Ps 107:38
a is the helmet of My head; Ps 108:8
They have a surrounded me with Ps 109:3
He a loved cursing, so it came to Ps 109:17
I a have become a reproach to them; Ps 109:25
They a do no unrighteousness; Ps 119:3 637
Your testimonies a are my delight; Ps 119:24 1571
Your lovingkindnesses a come to me, Ps 119:41
I will a speak of Your testimonies Ps 119:46
Their sons a shall sit upon your Ps 132:12 1571
a I will clothe with salvation, Ps 132:16

precious **a** are Your thoughts to me, Ps 139:17
He will **a** hear their cry and will Ps 145:19
He has **a** established them forever Ps 148:6
I will **a** laugh at your calamity; Pr 1:26 1571
She has **a** set her table; Pr 9:2 637
It is **a** not good to fine the Pr 17:26 1571
man comes, contempt **a** comes, Pr 18:3 1571
He **a** who is slack in his work Is Pr 18:9 1571
A it is not good for a person to Pr 19:2 1571
the cry of the poor Will **a** cry himself Pr 21:13 1571
wise, My own heart **a** will be glad; Pr 23:15 1571
These **a** are sayings of the wise. Pr 24:23 1571
These **a** are proverbs of Solomon Pr 25:1 1571
his folly, Or you will **a** be like him. Pr 26:4 1571
He will **a** delight your soul. Pr 29:17
strutting rooster, the male goat **a**, Pr 30:31 176
rises **a** while it is still night And Pr 31:15
Her husband **a**, and he praises Pr 31:28
A, the sun rises and the sun sets; Ec 1:5
And **a** of the later things which Ec 1:11 1571
this **a** is striving after wind. Ec 1:17 1571
A I possessed flocks and herds Ec 2:7 1571
A, I collected for myself silver Ec 2:8 1571
My wisdom **a** stood by me. Ec 2:9 637
of the fool, it will **a** befall me. Ec 2:15 1571
This **a** I have seen that it is Ec 2:24 1571
has **a** set eternity in their heart, Ec 3:11 1571
This **a** is a grievous Ec 5:16 1571
Throughout his life *he* **a** eats in Ec 5:17 1571
He has **a** empowered him to eat from Ec 5:19
and **a** not let go of the other; Ec 7:18 1571
A, do not take seriously all words Ec 7:21 1571
For you **a** have realized that you Ec 7:22 1571
A this I came to see as wisdom Ec 9:13 1571
Remember **a** your Creator in the Ec 12:1
a taught the people knowledge; Ec 12:9 5750
The queens and the concubines **a**, SS 6:9
"I will **a** turn My hand against Is 1:25
become tinder, His work **a** a spark. Is 1:31
Their land has **a** been filled with Is 2:7
Their land has **a** been filled with Is 2:7
land has **a** been filled with idols; Is 2:8
a tower in the middle of it And **a** Is 5:2 1571
I will **a** charge the clouds to rain Is 5:6
of the proud **a** will be abased. Is 5:15
He will **a** lift up a standard to Is 5:26
and it will **a** remove the beard. Is 7:20 1571
Those **a** who are tall in stature Is 10:33
A righteousness will be the belt Is 11:5
A the cow and the bear will graze, Is 11:7
I will **a** put an end to the Is 13:11
Their little ones **a** will be dashed Is 13:16
owls; Ostriches **a** will live there, Is 13:21
Her *fateful* time **a** will soon come Is 13:22
"I will **a** make it a possession Is 14:23
Heshbon and Elealeh **a** cry out, Is 15:4
In the vineyards **a** there will be Is 16:10
"Morning comes but **a** night. Is 21:12 1571
is **a** polluted by its inhabitants, Is 24:5
Since You have **a** performed for us Is 26:12 1571
It will come about **a** in that day Is 27:13
And these **a** reel with wine and Is 28:7 1571
a comes from the LORD of hosts, Is 28:29 1571
Your voice will **a** be like that of Is 29:4
The afflicted **a** will increase Is 29:19
for shame and **a** for reproach." Is 30:5 1571
A the oxen and the donkeys which Is 30:24
Yet He **a** is wise and will bring Is 31:2 1571
a in the time of distress. Is 33:2 637
All their hosts will **a** wither away Is 34:4
Wild oxen will **a** fall with them Is 34:7
It will **a** be a haunt of jackals Is 34:13
goat **a** will cry to its kind; Is 34:14
I will **a** hold you by the hand and Is 42:6
He **a** gets hungry and his strength Is 44:12 1571
he **a** makes a fire to bake bread. Is 44:15 637
He **a** makes a god and worships it; Is 44:15 637
He **a** warms himself and says, Is 44:16 637
he **a** prays to it and says, Is 44:17
and **a** have baked bread over its Is 44:19 637
I have **a** called you by your name; Is 45:4
Your shame **a** will be exposed; Is 47:3 1571
I am the first, I am **a** the last. Is 48:12 637
He has **a** made Me a select arrow, Is 49:2
I will **a** make You a light of the Is 49:6
arise, Princes will **a** bow down Is 49:7
"**A** the foreigners who join Is 56:6
You **a** went up there to offer Is 57:7 1571
And **a** with the contrite and lowly Is 57:15
will **a** suck the milk of nations And Is 60:16
You will **a** be a crown of beauty in Is 62:3
I **a** trod them in My anger And Is 63:3
"I will **a** rejoice in Jerusalem and Is 65:19
They will **a** plant vineyards and Is 65:21
"It will **a** come to pass that Is 65:24
she **a** brought forth her sons. Is 66:8 1571
"I will **a** take some of them for Is 66:21 1571
came **a** in the days of Jehoiakim the Jer 1:3
rulers **a** transgressed against Me, Jer 2:8
"**A** the men of Memphis and Jer 2:16 1571
"**A** on your skirts is found The Jer 2:34 1571
A, you will be put to shame by Jer 2:36 1571
"From this *place* **a** you will go Jer 2:37 1571
but she went and was a harlot **a**. Jer 3:8 1571
now I will **a** pronounce judgments Jer 4:12 1571
a excel in deeds of wickedness; Jer 5:28 1571
My law, they have rejected it **a**. Jer 6:19
them, they have **a** taken root; Jer 12:2 1571
Then you **a** can do good Who are Jer 13:23 1571

"So I Myself have **a** stripped your Jer 13:26 1571
"The people **a** to whom they are Jer 14:16
of the LORD **a** came to me saying, Jer 16:1
their men **a** be smitten to death, Jer 18:21
"I will **a** make this city a Jer 19:8
"I will **a** give over all the Jer 20:5
"I will **a** strike down the Jer 21:6
"You shall **a** say to this people, Jer 21:8
A do not mistreat *or* do violence Jer 22:3
Cry out **a** from Abarim, For all Jer 22:20
"I will **a** raise up shepherds Jer 23:4
Their course **a** is evil And their Jer 23:10
"**A** among the prophets of Jer 23:14
I have **a** sent to you, saying, Jer 23:38
there was **a** a man who prophesied Jer 26:20 1571
and I have given him **a** the wild Jer 27:6 1571
'I am **a** going to bring back to Jer 28:4
And I have **a** given him the beasts Jer 28:14 1571
'I will **a** bring them back to the Jer 30:3
I will **a** honor them and they Jer 30:19
children **a** will be as formerly, Jer 30:20
I was ashamed and **a** humiliated Jer 31:19 1571
"Then the offspring of Israel **a** Jer 31:36 1571
Then I will **a** cast off all the Jer 31:37 1571
then My covenant may **a** be broken Jer 33:21 1571
"**A** I have sent to you all My Jer 35:15
And **a** you shall read them to all Jer 36:6 1571
"I will **a** punish him and his Jer 36:31
"The Chaldeans will **a** return and Jer 37:8
"They will **a** bring out all your Jer 38:23
a slew all the nobles of Judah. Jer 39:6
The Chaldeans **a** burned with fire Jer 39:8
Likewise, **a** all the Jews who were Jer 40:11 1571
Ishmael **a** struck down all the Jews Jer 41:3
'I will **a** show you compassion, so Jer 42:12
"He will **a** come and strike the Jer 43:11
"He will **a** shatter the obelisks Jer 43:13
a in Memphis and Tahpanhes; Jer 46:14
"**A** her mercenaries in her midst Jer 46:21 1571
The valley **a** will be ruined And Jer 48:8
a been undisturbed, *like wine* Jer 48:11
a gone down to the slaughter," Jer 48:15
has **a** come upon the plain, Jer 48:21
he **a** will become a laughingstock. Jer 48:26 1571
My heart **a** wails like flutes for Jer 48:36
Be **a** like male goats at the head Jer 50:8
for you and you were **a** caught, Jer 50:24 1571
You have been found and **a** seized Jer 50:24 1571
The ostriches **a** will live in it, Jer 50:39
The fords **a** have been seized, And Jer 51:32
As **a** for Babylon the slain of all Jer 51:49 1571
and he **a** slaughtered all the Jer 52:10 1571
They **a** took away the pots, the Jer 52:18
the guard **a** took away the bowls, Jer 52:19
He **a** took from the city one Jer 52:25
A, her prophets find No vision La 2:9 1571
the wheels rose **a**. Ezk 1:19
each one **a** had two wings covering Ezk 1:23
I **a** heard the sound of their wings Ezk 1:24
"Take **a** a few in number from them Ezk 5:3
therefore I will **a** withdraw, Ezk 5:11 1571
a intensify the famine upon you and Ezk 5:16
bloodshed **a** will pass through you, Ezk 5:17
"I will **a** lay the dead bodies of Ezk 6:5
will **a** consume those in the city. Ezk 7:15
"I will **a** turn My face from them, Ezk 7:22
I will **a** make the pride of the Ezk 7:24
a when the cherubim lifted up Ezk 10:16
"I will **a** spread My net over Ezk 12:13
There will **a** be in My anger a Ezk 13:13
"I will **a** tear off your veils and Ezk 13:21
I **a** swore to you and entered into Ezk 16:8
"I **a** clothed you with embroidered Ezk 16:10
"I **a** put a ring in your nostril, Ezk 16:12
"You **a** took your beautiful jewels Ezk 16:17
"**A** My bread which I gave you, Ezk 16:19
"You **a** played the harlot with the Ezk 16:26
"You **a** multiplied your harlotry Ezk 16:29
"I will **a** give you into the Ezk 16:39
will **a** no longer pay your lovers. Ezk 16:41 1571
are **a** the sister of your sisters, Ezk 16:45
"**A** bear your disgrace in that you Ezk 16:52 1571
be **a** ashamed and bear your Ezk 16:52 1571
and you with your daughters will **a** Ezk 16:55
a do with you as you have done, Ezk 16:59
"He **a** took some of the seed of Ezk 17:5
He **a** took away the mighty of the Ezk 17:13
"I will **a** take *a sprig* from the Ezk 17:22
"**A** I gave them My sabbaths to be a Ezk 20:12 1571
"**A** I swore to them in the wilderness Ezk 20:15 1571
"**A** I swore to them in the Ezk 20:23 1571
"I **a** gave them statutes that Ezk 20:25 1571
There **a** they made their soothing Ezk 20:28
a sword sharpened And **a** polished! Ezk 21:9
"I will **a** clap My hands Ezk 21:17 1571
This **a** will be no more until He Ezk 21:27 1571
'They will **a** strip you of your Ezk 23:26
put *it* on and **a** pour water in it; Ezk 24:3 1571
And **a** pile wood under the pot. Ezk 24:5 1571
A seethe its bones in it." Ezk 24:5 1571
I **a** will make the pile great. Ezk 24:9 1571
"I will **a** stretch out My hand Ezk 25:13
'**A** her daughters who are on the Ezk 26:6
"**A** they will make a spoil of your Ezk 26:12
"**A** they will make themselves bald Ezk 27:31
"I will **a** make the hordes of Ezk 30:10
"I will **a** destroy the idols And Ezk 30:13
I will **a** cut off the hordes of Ezk 30:15
"They **a** went down with it to Ezk 31:17 1571

"I will **a** make the land drink the Ezk 32:6
"I will **a** trouble the hearts of Ezk 32:9
"I will **a** destroy all its cattle Ezk 32:13
"There **a** is Edom, its kings and Ezk 32:29
a are the chiefs of the north, Ezk 32:30
"**A** the tree of the field will Ezk 34:27
"**A** I scattered them among the Ezk 36:19
"This **a** I will let the house of Ezk 36:37 5750
place **a** will be with them; Ezk 37:27
mountains **a** will be thrown down, Ezk 38:20
The side pillars **a** had the same Ezk 40:10
Its guardrooms **a**, its side Ezk 40:29
Its guardrooms **a**, its side Ezk 40:33
I saw **a** that the house had a Ezk 41:8
were **a** a hundred cubits long. Ezk 41:13
A the width of the front of the Ezk 41:14
he **a** *measured* the inner nave and Ezk 41:15
A there were carved on them, on Ezk 41:25
'You shall **a** take the bull for the Ezk 43:21
a a young bull and a ram from the Ezk 43:25
"**A** they shall not shave their Ezk 44:20
They shall **a** keep My laws and My Ezk 44:24
you shall **a** give to the priest the Ezk 44:30
"The people of the land shall **a** Ezk 45:16
blemish, **a** six lambs and a ram, Ezk 46:6
"**A** you shall provide a grain Ezk 46:14
"He was **a** driven away from Da 5:21
and **a** toward you, O king, I have Da 6:22 638
Who has **a** delivered Daniel from Da 6:27
a human mind **a** was given to it. Da 7:4
the beast **a** had four heads, and Da 7:6
His body **a** *was* like beryl, his Da 10:6
"**A** their gods with their metal Da 11:8 1571
your people will **a** lift themselves up Da 11:14
he will **a** stay *for a time* in the Da 11:16
he will **a** give him the daughter of Da 11:17
and **a** the prince of the covenant. Da 11:22 1571
will **a** enter the Beautiful Land, Da 11:41
will **a** make her like a wilderness, Hos 2:3
"**A**, I will have no compassion on Hos 2:4
I will **a** take away My wool and My Hos 2:9
I will **a** put an end to all her gaiety, Hos 2:11
"In that day I will **a** make a Hos 2:18
I will **a** have compassion on her Hos 2:23
so I will **a** be toward you." Hos 3:3 1571
a the fish of the sea disappear. Hos 4:3 1571
And the prophet **a** will stumble Hos 4:5 1571
I **a** will reject you from being My Hos 4:6
I **a** will forget your children. Hos 4:6 1571
A do not go to Gilgal, Or go up to Hos 4:15
Judah **a** has stumbled with them. Hos 5:5 1571
A, O Judah, there is a harvest Hos 6:11 1571
Gray hairs **a** are sprinkled on him, Hos 7:9 1571
A the high places of Aven, the sin Hos 10:8
Judah is **a** unruly against God, Hos 11:12 5750
LORD **a** has a dispute with Judah, Hos 12:2
I have **a** spoken to the prophets, Hos 12:10
will **a** devour them like a lioness, Hos 13:8
The pomegranate, the palm **a**, Jl 1:12 1571
have **a** cast lots for My people, Jl 3:3
"**A** I will sell your sons and your Jl 3:8
"I will **a** break the *gate* bar of Am 1:5
"I will **a** cut off the inhabitant Am 1:8
His anger **a** tore continually, And Am 1:11
"I will **a** cut off the judge from Am 2:3
Their lies **a** have led them astray, Am 2:4
A turn aside the way of the humble; Am 2:7
a punish the altars of Bethel; Am 3:14
"I will **a** smite the winter house Am 3:15
The houses of ivory will **a** perish Am 3:15
a from that which is leavened, Am 4:5
"But I gave you **a** cleanness of Am 4:6 1571
Who **a** darkens day *into* night, Am 5:8
They **a** call the farmer to mourning Am 5:16
"You **a** carried along Sikkuth your Am 5:26
I will **a** raise up its ruins And Am 9:11
"**A** I will restore the captivity Am 9:14
They will **a** plant vineyards and Am 9:14
"I will **a** plant them on their Am 9:15
A, possess the territory Ob 1:19
"I will **a** cut off the cities of Mi 5:11
"So **a** I will make *you* sick, Mi 6:13 1571
The prince asks, **a** the judge, Mi 7:3
A anguish is in the whole body And Na 2:10
A her small children were dashed Na 3:10 1571
He **a** gathers to himself all Hab 2:5
"You **a**, O Ethiopians, will be Zph 2:12 1571
'take courage **a**, Joshua son of Hg 2:4
earth, the sea **a** and the dry land. Hg 2:6
then you will **a** govern My house Zch 3:7 1571
and **a** have charge of My courts, Zch 3:7 1571
a two olive trees by it, one on Zch 4:3
A the word of the LORD came to me Zch 4:8
of the LORD **a** came to me, Zch 6:9
a be too difficult in My sight?' Zch 8:6 1571
'**A** let none of you devise evil in Zch 8:17
seek the LORD of hosts; I will **a** go." Zch 8:21 1571
And Hamath **a**, which borders on it; Zch 9:2 1571
A Ekron, for her expectation has Zch 9:5
a will be a remnant for our God, Zch 9:7 1571
As for you **a**, because of the blood Zch 9:11 1571
and their soul **a** was weary of me. Zch 11:8 1571
it will **a** be against Judah. Zch 12:2 1571
"The LORD **a** will save the tents Zch 12:7
and I will **a** remove the prophets Zch 13:2 1571
"**A** it will come about in that day Zch 13:4
Judah **a** will fight at Jerusalem; Zch 14:14 1571
So **a** like this plague will be the Zch 14:15
"You **a** say, 'My, how tiresome it is!' Mal 1:13

"So I **a** have made you despised	Mal 2:9	1571
they **a** test God and escape.' "	Mal 3:15	1571
cheek, turn the other to him **a**.	Mt 5:39	2532
shirt, let him have your coat **a**.	Mt 5:40	2532
as we **a** have forgiven our debtors.	Mt 6:12	2532
Father will **a** forgive you.	Mt 6:14	2532
is, there your heart will be **a**.	Mt 6:21	2532
"For I **a** am a man under authority,	Mt 8:9	2532
I will **a** confess him before My	Mt 10:32	2532
I will **a** deny him before My Father	Mt 10:33	2532
a be with this evil generation."	Mt 12:45	2532
then the tares became evident **a**.	Mt 13:26	2532
still lacking in understanding **a**?	Mt 15:16	2532
I **a** say to you that you are Peter,	Mt 16:18	2532
So **a** the Son of Man is going to	Mt 17:12	2532
'Should you not **a** have had mercy	Mt 18:33	2532
"My heavenly Father will **a** do	Mt 18:35	2532
and there are **a** eunuchs who made	Mt 19:12	2532
a shall sit upon twelve thrones,	Mt 19:28	2532
and to those he said, 'You **a** go	Mt 20:4	2532
each of them **a** received a denarius.	Mt 20:10	2532
Jesus said to them, "I will **a** ask	Mt 21:24	2532
I will **a** tell you by what	Mt 21:24	2532
He **a** said to them,	Mt 21:27	2532
so **a** the second, and the third,	Mt 22:26	2532
outside of it may become clean **a**.	Mt 23:26	2532
"For this reason you **a** must be ready;	Mt 24:44	2532
Later the other virgins **a** came,	Mt 25:11	2532
"**A** the one who *had received*	Mt 25:22	2532
"And the one **a** who had received	Mt 25:24	2532
will **a** say to those on His left,	Mt 25:41	2532
they themselves **a** will answer,	Mt 25:44	2532
a be spoken of in memory of her."	Mt 26:13	2532
the same way the chief priests **a**,	Mt 27:41	2532
had been crucified with Him were **a**	Mt 27:44	2532
had **a** become a disciple of Jesus.	Mt 27:57	2532
a in the boat mending the nets.	Mk 1:19	2532
so that I may preach there **a**;	Mk 1:38	2532
a gave it to those who were with him?"	Mk 2:26	2532
Galilee followed; and **a** from Judea,	Mk 3:7	
broken pieces, and **a** of the fish.	Mk 6:43	
He was **a** saying to them,	Mk 7:9	2532
you so lacking in understanding **a**?	Mk 7:18	2532
They **a** had a few small fish;	Mk 8:7	2532
the Son of Man will **a** be ashamed	Mk 8:38	2532
your Father who is in heaven will **a**	Mk 11:25	2532
Last of all the woman died **a**.	Mk 12:22	2532
there will **a** be famines. These	Mk 13:8	
a commanded the doorkeeper to stay	Mk 13:34	2532
what this woman has done will **a**	Mk 14:9	2532
they all were saying the same thing **a**.	Mk 14:31	2532
"You **a** were with Jesus the Nazarene."	Mk 14:67	2532
the same way the chief priests **a**,	Mk 15:31	2532
who were crucified with Him were **a**	Mk 15:32	2532
There were **a** *some* women	Mk 15:40	2532
relative Elizabeth has **a** conceived a	Lk 1:36	2532
Joseph **a** went up from Galilee,	Lk 2:4	2532
a came to be baptized,	Lk 3:12	2532
Herod **a** added this to them all:	Lk 3:20	2532
Jesus was **a** baptized,	Lk 3:21	2532
Demons **a** were coming out of many,	Lk 4:41	2532
of God to the other cities **a**,	Lk 4:43	2532
and so **a** *were* James and John, sons of	Lk 5:10	2532
of the Pharisees **a** do the same,	Lk 5:33	2532
He was **a** telling them a parable:	Lk 5:36	2532
them, whom He **a** named as apostles:	Lk 6:13	2532
Simon, whom He **a** named Peter, and	Lk 6:14	2532
the cheek, offer him the other **a**;	Lk 6:29	2532
And He **a** spoke a parable to them:	Lk 6:39	2532
"For I **a** am a man placed under	Lk 7:8	2532
and **a** some women who had been	Lk 8:2	2532
Another **a** said,	Lk 9:61	2532
"Likewise a Levite **a**,	Lk 10:32	2532
as John **a** taught his disciples."	Lk 11:1	2532
For we ourselves **a** forgive	Lk 11:4	2532
a is divided against himself,	Lk 11:18	2532
whole body **a** is full of light;	Lk 11:34	2532
your body **a** is full of darkness.	Lk 11:34	2532
the outside make the inside **a**?	Lk 11:40	2532
reason **a** the wisdom of God said,	Lk 11:49	2532
him **a** before the angels of God;	Lk 12:8	2532
is, there your heart will be **a**.	Lk 12:34	2532
He was **a** saying to the crowds,	Lk 12:54	2532
And He **a** went on to say to the one	Lk 14:12	2532
they may **a** invite you in return	Lk 14:12	2532
He was **a** saying to the disciples,	Lk 16:1	2532
thing is faithful **a** in much;	Lk 16:10	2532
thing is unrighteous **a** in much.	Lk 16:10	2532
rich man **a** died and was buried.	Lk 16:22	2532
a come to this place of torment.'	Lk 16:28	2532
a in the days of the Son of Man:	Lk 17:26	2532
a the vultures will be gathered."	Lk 17:37	2532
And He **a** told this parable to	Lk 18:9	2532
"And he said to him **a**,	Lk 19:19	2532
"I will **a** ask you a question,	Lk 20:3	2532
him **a** and treated him shamefully and	Lk 20:11	2548
one **a** they wounded and cast out.	Lk 20:12	2532
"Finally the woman died **a**.	Lk 20:32	2532
"So you **a**, when you see these	Lk 21:31	2532
And there arose **a** a dispute among	Lk 22:24	2532
take it along, likewise **a** a bag,	Lk 22:36	2532
and the disciples **a** followed Him.	Lk 22:39	2532
"Certainly this man **a** was with Him,	Lk 22:59	2532
a was in Jerusalem at that time.	Lk 23:7	2532
Two others **a**, who were	Lk 23:32	2532
The soldiers **a** mocked Him,	Lk 23:36	2532
was **a** an inscription above Him,	Lk 23:38	2532
a the other women with them were	Lk 24:10	2532
a some women among us amazed us.	Lk 24:22	2532
had **a** seen a vision of angels who	Lk 24:23	2532
exactly as the women **a** had said;	Lk 24:24	2532
Him of whom Moses in the Law and **a**	Jn 1:45	2532
John **a** was baptizing in Aenon	Jn 3:23	2532
themselves **a** went to the feast.	Jn 4:45	2532
but **a** was calling God His own	Jn 5:18	2532
the Son **a** does in like manner.	Jn 5:19	2532
a gives life to whom He wishes.	Jn 5:21	2532
the Son **a** to have life in Himself;	Jn 5:26	2532
likewise **a** of the fish as much as	Jn 6:11	2532
and the bread **a** which I will give	Jn 6:51	2532
Me, he **a** will live because of Me.	Jn 6:57	2548
"You do not want to go away **a**,	Jn 6:67	2532
that Your disciples **a** may see	Jn 7:3	2532
feast, then He Himself **a** went up,	Jn 7:10	2532
"You have not **a** been led astray,	Jn 7:47	2532
"You are not **a** from Galilee, are	Jn 7:52	2532
Me, you would know My Father **a**."	Jn 8:19	2532
therefore you **a** do the things	Jn 8:38	2532
and the prophets **a**; and You say,	Jn 8:52	2532
the Pharisees **a** were asking him	Jn 9:15	2532
I must bring them **a**,	Jn 10:16	2548
"Let us **a** go, so that we may die	Jn 11:16	2532
and the Jews who came with her **a**	Jn 11:33	
have kept this man **a** from dying?"	Jn 11:37	2532
order that He might **a** gather	Jn 11:52	2532
but that they might **a** see Lazarus,	Jn 12:9	2532
to put Lazarus to death **a**;	Jn 12:10	2532
For this reason **a** the people	Jn 12:18	2532
I am, there My servant will be **a**;	Jn 12:26	2532
but **a** my hands and my head."	Jn 13:9	2532
you **a** ought to wash one another's	Jn 13:14	2532
you **a** should do as I did to you.	Jn 13:15	2532
God will **a** glorify Him in Himself,	Jn 13:32	2532
to the Jews, now I **a** say to you,	Jn 13:33	2532
you, that you **a** love one another.	Jn 13:34	2532
believe in God, believe **a** in Me.	Jn 14:1	2532
where I am, *there* you may be **a**.	Jn 14:3	2532
you would have known My Father **a**;	Jn 14:7	2532
the works that I do, he will do **a**;	Jn 14:12	2548
because I live, you will live **a**.	Jn 14:19	2532
has loved Me, I have **a** loved you;	Jn 15:9	2532
Me, they will **a** persecute you;	Jn 15:20	2532
My word, they will keep yours **a**.	Jn 15:20	2532
"He who hates Me hates My Father **a**.	Jn 15:23	2532
and you *will* testify **a**,	Jn 15:27	2532
I **a** have sent them into the world.	Jn 17:18	2532
a may be sanctified in truth.	Jn 17:19	2532
but for those **a** who believe in Me	Jn 17:20	2532
in You, that they **a** may be in Us,	Jn 17:21	2532
"Father, I desire that they **a**,	Jn 17:24	2548
Now Judas **a**, who was betraying	Jn 18:2	2532
And Judas **a**, who was betraying Him,	Jn 18:5	2532
not **a** *one* of this man's disciples,	Jn 18:17	2532
and Peter was **a** with them,	Jn 18:18	2532
are not **a** *one* of His disciples,	Jn 18:25	2532
Pilate **a** wrote an inscription	Jn 19:19	2532
a part to every soldier and **a**	Jn 19:23	2532
truth, so that you **a** may believe.	Jn 19:35	2532
first come to Him by night, **a** came,	Jn 19:39	2532
Simon Peter **a** came,	Jn 20:6	2532
come to the tomb then **a**	Jn 20:8	2532
has sent Me, I **a** send you."	Jn 20:21	2532
signs Jesus **a** performed in	Jn 20:30	2532
"We will **a** come with you."	Jn 21:3	2532
the one who **a** had leaned back on	Jn 21:20	2532
And there are **a** many other things	Jn 21:25	2532
He **a** presented Himself alive after	Ac 1:3	2532
They **a** said,	Ac 1:11	2532
(who was **a** called Justus),	Ac 1:23	2532
MY FLESH **A** WILL LIVE IN HOPE;	Ac 2:26	2532
just as your rulers did **a**.	Ac 3:17	2532
onward, **a** announced these days.	Ac 3:24	2532
who was **a** called Barnabas by the	Ac 4:36	
A the people from the cities in	Ac 5:16	2532
'YOU **A** TOOK ALONG THE TABERNACLE	Ac 7:43	2532
I **A** WILL REMOVE YOU BEYOND BABYLON.'	Ac 7:43	2532
They were **a** watching the gates	Ac 9:24	2532
he came down **a** to the saints who	Ac 9:32	2532
Simon, who is **a** called Peter;	Ac 10:5	
Simon, who is **a** called Peter,	Ac 10:18	
Simon, who is **a** called Peter,	Ac 10:32	
They **a** put Him to death by	Ac 10:39	2532
poured out on the Gentiles **a**.	Ac 10:45	2532
a had received the word of God.	Ac 11:1	2532
I **a** heard a voice saying to me,	Ac 11:7	2532
These six brethren **a** went with me	Ac 11:12	2532
have Simon, who is **a** called Peter,	Ac 11:13	
the same gift as *He gave* to us **a** after	Ac 11:17	2532
God has granted to the Gentiles **a**	Ac 11:18	2532
began speaking to the Greeks **a**,	Ac 11:20	2532
he proceeded to arrest Peter **a**.	Ac 12:3	2532
of John who was **a** called Mark,	Ac 12:12	
them John, who was **a** called Mark.	Ac 12:25	
they **a** had John as their helper.	Ac 13:5	2532
But Saul, who was **a** *known as* Paul,	Ac 13:9	2532
whom He **a** testified and said,	Ac 13:22	2532
is **a** written in the second Psalm,	Ac 13:33	2532
He **a** says in another *Psalm*,	Ac 13:35	2532
a men of the same nature as you,	Ac 14:15	2532
Spirit, just as He **a** did to us;	Ac 15:8	2532
in the same way as they **a** are."	Ac 15:11	2548
who themselves will **a** report the	Ac 15:27	2532
a being prophets themselves,	Ac 15:32	2532
and preaching with many others **a**,	Ac 15:35	2532
called Mark, along with them **a**.	Ac 15:37	2532
Paul came **a** to Derbe and to Lystra.	Ac 16:1	2532
upset the world have come here **a**;	Ac 17:6	2532
proclaimed by Paul in Berea **a**,	Ac 17:13	2532
And **a** some of the Epicurean and	Ac 17:18	2532
I **a** found an altar with this	Ac 17:23	2532
'For we **a** are His children.'	Ac 17:28	2532
among whom **a** were Dionysius the	Ac 17:34	2532
a some of the Jewish exorcists,	Ac 19:13	2532
Many **a** of those who had believed	Ac 19:18	5037
been there, I must **a** see Rome."	Ac 19:21	2532
but **a** that the temple of the great	Ac 19:27	2532
A some of the Asiarchs who were	Ac 19:31	2532
from Caesarea **a** came with us,	Ac 21:16	2532
that you yourself **a** walk orderly,	Ac 21:24	2532
as **a** the high priest and all the	Ac 22:5	2532
From them I **a** received letters to	Ac 22:5	2532
I **a** was standing by approving,	Ac 22:20	2532
and the commander **a** was afraid	Ac 22:29	2532
so you must witness at Rome **a**."	Ac 23:11	2532
They were **a** to provide mounts to	Ac 23:24	5037
a instructing his accusers to	Ac 23:30	2532
they **a** presented Paul to him.	Ac 23:33	2532
after your accusers arrive **a**,"	Ac 23:35	2532
The Jews **a** joined in the attack,	Ac 24:9	2532
I **a** do my best to maintain always	Ac 24:16	2532
therefore he **a** used to send for	Ac 24:26	2532
the Jews, as you **a** very well know.	Ac 25:10	2532
"I **a** would like to hear the man	Ac 25:22	2532
a the charges against him."	Ac 25:27	2532
but **a** when they were being put to	Ac 26:10	5037
but **a** to the things in which I	Ac 26:16	5037
and **a** at Jerusalem and *then*	Ac 26:20	
I speak to him **a** with confidence,	Ac 26:26	2532
but **a** all who hear me this day,	Ac 26:29	2532
the ship, but **a** of our lives."	Ac 27:10	2532
and they themselves **a** took food.	Ac 27:36	2532
They **a** honored us with many	Ac 28:10	2532
they will **a** listen."	Ac 28:28	2532
among whom you **a** are the called of	Ro 1:6	2532
obtain some fruit among you **a**,	Ro 1:13	2532
gospel to you **a** who are in Rome.	Ro 1:15	2532
the Jew first and **a** to the Greek.	Ro 1:16	5037
and in the same way **a** the men	Ro 1:27	2532
but **a** give hearty approval to	Ro 1:32	2532
the Jew first and **a** of the Greek,	Ro 2:9	5037
the Jew first and **a** to the Greek.	Ro 2:10	5037
Law will **a** perish without the Law,	Ro 2:12	2532
why am I **a** still being judged as a	Ro 3:7	2532
Is He not *the God* of Gentiles **a**?	Ro 3:29	2532
Yes, of Gentiles **a**,	Ro 3:29	2532
just as David **a** speaks of the	Ro 4:6	2532
or on the uncircumcised **a**?	Ro 4:9	2532
but who **a** follow in the steps of	Ro 4:12	2532
there **a** is no violation.	Ro 4:15	
but **a** to those who are of the	Ro 4:16	2532
He was able **a** to perform.	Ro 4:21	2532
Therefore IT WAS **A** CREDITED TO HIM	Ro 4:22	2532
but for our sake **a**,	Ro 4:24	2532
through whom **a** we have obtained	Ro 5:2	2532
we **a** exult in our tribulations,	Ro 5:3	2532
but we **a** exult in God through our	Ro 5:11	2532
certainly we shall **a** be *in the*	Ro 6:5	2532
that we shall **a** live with Him,	Ro 6:8	2532
you **a** were made to die to the Law	Ro 7:4	2532
Jesus from the dead will **a** give life to	Ro 8:11	2532
and if children, heirs **a**,	Ro 8:17	2532
we may **a** be glorified with *Him*.	Ro 8:17	2532
that the creation itself **a** will be	Ro 8:21	2532
not only this, but **a** we ourselves,	Ro 8:23	2532
the Spirit **a** helps our weakness;	Ro 8:26	2532
He **a** predestined *to become*	Ro 8:29	2532
He predestined, He **a** called;	Ro 8:30	2532
He called, He **a** justified;	Ro 8:30	2532
justified, He **a** glorified.	Ro 8:30	2532
how will He not **a** with Him freely	Ro 8:32	2532
of God, who **a** intercedes for us.	Ro 8:34	2532
this, but there was Rebekah **a**,	Ro 9:10	2532
even us, whom He **a** called,	Ro 9:24	2532
only, but **a** from among Gentiles.	Ro 9:24	2532
As He says **a** in Hosea,	Ro 9:25	2532
there has **a** come to be at the	Ro 11:5	2532
of dough is holy, the lump is **a**;	Ro 11:16	2532
otherwise you **a** will be cut off.	Ro 11:22	2532
And they **a**, if they do not	Ro 11:23	2548
these **a** now have been disobedient,	Ro 11:31	2532
you they **a** may now be shown mercy.	Ro 11:31	2532
wrath, but **a** for conscience' sake.	Ro 13:5	2532
because of this you **a** pay taxes,	Ro 13:6	2532
just as Christ **a** accepted us to	Ro 15:7	2532
I myself **a** am convinced that you	Ro 15:14	2532
able **a** to admonish one another.	Ro 15:14	2532
to them **a** in material things.	Ro 15:27	2532
has **a** been a helper of many,	Ro 16:2	2532
but **a** all the churches of the	Ro 16:4	2532
a *greet* the church that is in	Ro 16:5	2532
who **a** were in Christ before me.	Ro 16:7	2532
the Lord, **a** his mother and mine.	Ro 16:13	2532
will **a** confirm you to the end,	1Co 1:8	2532
a the household of Stephanas;	1Co 1:16	2532
which things we **a** speak, not in	1Co 2:13	2532
so that we **a** might reign with you.	1Co 4:8	2532
Passover **a** has been sacrificed.	1Co 5:7	2532
a raise us up through His power.	1Co 6:14	2532
a the wife to her husband.	1Co 7:3	2532
and likewise **a** the husband does	1Co 7:4	2532
if you are able **a** to become free,	1Co 7:21	2532
that I **a** have the Spirit of God.	1Co 7:40	2532
not the Law **a** say these things?	1Co 9:8	2532
So **a** the Lord directed those who	1Co 9:14	2532
evil things as they **a** craved.	1Co 10:6	2548
will provide the way of escape **a**,	1Co 10:13	2532
I **a** please all men in all things,	1Co 10:33	2532

of me, just as I **a** am of Christ. **1Co 11:1** *2532*
let her **a** have her hair cut off; **1Co 11:6** *2532*
so **a** the man *has his birth* through **1Co 11:12** *2532*
must **a** be factions among you, **1Co 11:19** *2532*
that which I **a** delivered to you, **1Co 11:23** *2532*
In the same way *He took* the cup **a** after **1Co 11:25** *2532*
are one body, so **a** is Christ. **1Co 12:12** *2532*
just as I **a** have been fully known. **1Co 13:12** *2532*
So **a** you, unless you utter by the **1Co 14:9** *2532*
So **a** you, since you are zealous of **1Co 14:12** *2532*
and I will pray with the mind **a**; **1Co 14:15** *2532*
and I will sing with the mind **a**. **1Co 14:15** *2532*
that I may instruct others **a**, **1Co 14:19** *2532*
just as the Law **a** says. **1Co 14:34** *2532*
to you, which **a** you received, **1Co 15:1** *2532*
received, in which **a** you stand, **1Co 15:1** *2532*
by which **a** you are saved, if you **1Co 15:2** *2532*
importance what I **a** received, **1Co 15:3** *2532*
born, He appeared to me **a**. **1Co 15:8** *2532*
is vain, your faith **a** is vain. **1Co 15:14** *2532*
Then those **a** who have fallen **1Co 15:18** *2532*
by a man **a** *came* the resurrection **1Co 15:21** *2532*
so **a** in Christ all will be made **1Co 15:22** *2532*
then the Son Himself **a** will be **1Co 15:28** *2532*
Why are we **a** in danger every hour? **1Co 15:30** *2532*
There are **a** heavenly bodies and **1Co 15:40** *2532*
So **a** is the resurrection of the **1Co 15:42** *2532*
body, there is **a** a spiritual *body*. **1Co 15:44** *2532*
So **a** it is written, **1Co 15:45** *2532*
so **a** are those who are earthy; **1Co 15:48** *2532*
so **a** are those who are heavenly. **1Co 15:48** *2532*
we will **a** bear the image of the **1Co 15:49** *2532*
churches of Galatia, so do you **a**. **1Co 16:1** *2532*
if it is fitting for me to go **a**, **1Co 16:4** *2532*
doing the Lord's work, as I **a** am. **1Co 16:10** *2532*
that you **a** be in subjection to **1Co 16:16** *2532*
so **a** our comfort is abundant **2Co 1:5** *2532*
same sufferings which we **a** suffer; **2Co 1:6** *2532*
so **a** you are *sharers* of our **2Co 1:7** *2532*
you **a** joining in helping us **2Co 1:11** *2532*
you **a** partially did understand us, **2Co 1:14** *2532*
to be proud as you **a** are ours, **2Co 1:14** *2532*
therefore **a** through Him is our Amen to **2Co 1:20** *2532*
who **a** sealed us and gave *us* the **2Co 1:22** *2532*
For to this end **a** I wrote, so that I **2Co 2:9** *2532*
you forgive anything, I *forgive* **a**; **2Co 2:10** *2532*
who **a** made us adequate *as* servants **2Co 3:6** *2532*
a may be manifested in our body. **2Co 4:10** *2532*
that the life of Jesus **a** may be **2Co 4:11** *2532*
THEREFORE I SPOKE," we **a** believe, **2Co 4:13** *2532*
believe, therefore we **a** speak, **2Co 4:13** *2532*
Lord Jesus will raise us **a** with Jesus **2Co 4:14** *2532*
a have as our ambition, **2Co 5:9** *2532*
manifest **a** in your consciences. **2Co 5:11** *2532*
we **a** urge you not to receive the **2Co 6:1** *2532*
as to children—open wide *to us* **a**. **2Co 6:13** *2532*
but **a** by the comfort with which he **2Co 7:7** *2532*
so **a** our boasting before Titus **2Co 7:14** *2532*
so he would **a** complete in you this **2Co 8:6** *2532*
abound in this gracious work **a**. **2Co 8:7** *2532*
the sincerity of your love **a**. **2Co 8:8** *2532*
do *this*, but **a** to desire *to do it*. **2Co 8:10** *2532*
But now finish doing it **a**, **2Co 8:11** *2532*
so *there may be* **a** the completion **2Co 8:11** *2532*
that their abundance **a** may become **2Co 8:14** *2532*
but he has **a** been appointed by the **2Co 8:19** *2532*
Lord, but **a** in the sight of men. **2Co 8:21** *2532*
sparingly will **a** reap sparingly **2Co 9:6** *2532*
will **a** reap bountifully. **2Co 9:6** *2532*
but is **a** overflowing through many **2Co 9:12** *2532*
while they **a**, by prayer on your **2Co 9:14** *2532*
as he is Christ's, so **a** are we. **2Co 10:7** *2532*
we are **a** in deed when present. **2Co 10:11** *2532*
if his servants **a** disguise themselves **2Co 11:15** *2532*
that I **a** may boast a little. **2Co 11:16** *2532*
to the flesh, I will boast **a**. **2Co 11:18** *2532*
For we **a** are weak in Him, yet we **2Co 13:4** *2532*
this we **a** pray for, that you be **2Co 13:9** *2532*
Barnabas, taking Titus along **a**. **Ga 2:1** *2532*
worked for me **a** to the Gentiles), **Ga 2:8** *2532*
very thing I **a** was eager to do. **Ga 2:10** *2532*
have **a** been found sinners, **Ga 2:17** *2532*
So **a** we, while we were children, **Ga 4:3** *2532*
for I **a** *have become* as you *are*. **Ga 4:12** *2532*
to the Spirit, so it is now **a**. **Ga 4:29** *2532*
let us **a** walk by the Spirit. **Ga 5:25** *2532*
a man sows, this he will **a** reap. **Ga 6:7** *2532*
a we have obtained an inheritance, **Eph 1:11** *2532*
In Him, you **a**, after listening to **Eph 1:13** *2532*
your salvation—having **a** believed, **Eph 1:13** *2532*
age but **a** in the one to come. **Eph 1:21** *2532*
in whom you **a** are being built **Eph 2:22** *2532*
just as **a** you were called in one **Eph 4:4** *2532*
He **a** had descended into the lower **Eph 4:9** *2532*
He who descended is Himself **a** He **Eph 4:10** *2532*
just as the Gentiles **a** walk, **Eph 4:17** *2532*
God in Christ **a** has forgiven you. **Eph 4:32** *2532*
love, just as Christ **a** loved you and **Eph 5:2** *2532*
a is the head of the church, **Eph 5:23** *2532*
so **a** the wives *ought to be* to **Eph 5:24** *2532*
just as Christ **a** loved the church **Eph 5:25** *2532*
So husbands ought **a** to love their **Eph 5:28** *2532*
just as Christ **a** *does* the church, **Eph 5:29** *2532*
each individual among you **a** is to **Eph 5:33** *2532*
But that you **a** may know about my **Eph 6:21** *2532*
strife, but some **a** from good will; **Php 1:15** *2532*
Him, but **a** to suffer for His sake, **Php 1:29** *2532*
but **a** for the interests of others. **Php 2:4** *2532*
which was **a** in Christ Jesus, **Php 2:5** *2532*

a, God highly exalted Him, **Php 2:9** *2532*
so that I **a** may be encouraged when **Php 2:19** *2532*
myself **a** will be coming shortly. **Php 2:24** *2532*
who is **a** your messenger and **Php 2:25** *1161*
and not on him only but **a** on me, **Php 2:27** *2532*
a I was laid hold of by Christ Jesus. **Php 3:12** *2532*
God will reveal that **a** to you; **Php 3:15** *2532*
a we eagerly wait for a Savior, **Php 3:20** *2532*
I ask you **a** to help these women **Php 4:3** *2532*
gospel, together with Clement **a** and **Php 4:3** *2532*
and I **a** know how to live in **Php 4:12** *2532*
You yourselves **a** know, **Php 4:15** *2532*
just as in all the world **a** it is **Col 1:6** *2532*
even as *it has been doing* in you **a** **Col 1:6** *2532*
and he **a** informed us of your love **Col 1:8** *2532*
For this reason **a**, since the day **Col 1:9** *2532*
He is **a** head of the body, the **Col 1:18** *2532*
For this purpose **a** I labor, **Col 1:29** *2532*
and in Him you were **a** circumcised **Col 2:11** *2532*
in which you were **a** raised up with **Col 2:12** *2532*
then you **a** will be revealed with **Col 3:4** *2532*
and in them you **a** once walked, **Col 3:7** *2532*
But now you **a**, put them all aside: **Col 3:8** *2532*
Lord forgave you, so **a** should you. **Col 3:13** *2532*
which I have **a** been imprisoned; **Col 4:3** *2532*
and **a** Barnabas's cousin Mark **Col 4:10**
and **a** Jesus who is called Justus; **Col 4:11**
you his greetings, and **a** Demas. **Col 4:14**
who are in Laodicea and **a** Nympha **Col 4:15**
have it **a** read in the church of **Col 4:16** *2532*
but **a** in power and in the Holy **1Th 1:5** *2532*
You **a** became imitators of us and **1Th 1:6** *2532*
but **a** in every place your faith **1Th 1:8**
gospel of God but **a** our own lives, **1Th 2:8** *2532*
For this reason we **a** **1Th 2:13** *2532*
which **a** performs its work in you **1Th 2:13** *2532*
for you **a** endured the same **1Th 2:14** *2532*
I **a** sent to find out about your **1Th 3:5** *2532*
us just as we **a** long to see you, **1Th 3:6** *2532*
all people, just as we **a** *do* for you; **1Th 3:12** *2532*
just as we **a** told you before and **1Th 4:6** *2532*
another, just as you **a** are doing. **1Th 5:11** *2532*
and He **a** will bring it to pass. **1Th 5:24** *2532*
To this end **a** we pray for you **2Th 1:11** *2532*
just as *it did* **a** with you; **2Th 3:1** *2532*
mediator **a** between God and men, **1Tm 2:5** *2532*
These men must **a** first be tested; **1Tm 3:10** *2532*
promise for the present life and **a** **1Tm 4:8**
same time they **a** learn *to be* idle, **1Tm 5:13** *2532*
but **a** gossips and busybodies, **1Tm 5:13** *2532*
rest **a** will be fearful *of sinning*. **1Tm 5:20** *2532*
Likewise **a**, deeds that are good **1Tm 5:25** *2532*
reason I **a** suffer these things, **2Tm 1:12** *2532*
will be able to teach others **a**. **2Tm 2:2** *2532*
A if anyone competes as an athlete, **2Tm 2:5** *2532*
that they **a** may obtain the **2Tm 2:10** *2532*
Him, we will **a** live with Him; **2Tm 2:11** *2532*
endure, we will **a** reign with Him; **2Tm 2:12** *2532*
If we deny Him, He **a** will deny us; **2Tm 2:12** *2548*
but **a** vessels of wood and of **2Tm 2:20** *2532*
so these *men* **a** oppose the truth, **2Tm 3:8** *2532*
as Jannes's and Jambres's folly was **a**. **2Tm 3:9** *2532*
but **a** to all who have loved His **2Tm 4:8** *2532*
a Pudens and Linus and Claudia and **2Tm 4:21** *2532*
we **a** once were foolish ourselves, **Ti 3:3** *2532*
Our people must **a** learn to **Ti 3:14** *2532*
now **a** a prisoner of Christ Jesus **Phm 1:9** *2532*
same time **a** prepare me a lodging, **Phm 1:22** *2532*
through whom **a** He made the world. **Heb 1:2** *2532*
A GARMENT THEY WILL **A** BE CHANGED. **Heb 1:12** *2532*
God **a** testifying with them, **Heb 2:4**
likewise **a** partook of the same, **Heb 2:14** *2532*
as Moses **a** was in all His house. **Heb 3:2** *2532*
preached to us, just as they **a**; **Heb 4:2** *2548*
himself **a** rested from his works, **Heb 4:10** *2532*
himself **a** is beset with weakness; **Heb 5:2** *2532*
for the people, so **a** for himself. **Heb 5:3** *2532*
So **a** Christ did not glorify **Heb 5:5** *2532*
as He says **a** in another *passage*, **Heb 5:6** *2532*
for whose sake it is **a** tilled, **Heb 6:7** *2532*
to whom **a** Abraham apportioned a **Heb 7:2** *2532*
and then **a** king of Salem, **Heb 7:2** *2532*
takes place a change of law **a**. **Heb 7:12** *2532*
so much the more **a** Jesus has **Heb 7:22** *2532*
Therefore He is able **a** to save **Heb 7:25** *2532*
priest **a** have something to offer. **Heb 8:3** *2532*
by as much as He is **a** the mediator **Heb 8:6** *2532*
so Christ **a**, having been offered **Heb 9:28** *2532*
Holy Spirit **a** testifies to us; **Heb 10:15** *2532*
he **a** received him back as a type. **Heb 11:19** *2532*
yes, **a** chains and imprisonment. **Heb 11:36** *1161*
us **a** lay aside every encumbrance and **Heb 12:1** *2532*
THE EARTH, BUT **A** THE HEAVEN." **Heb 12:26** *2532*
you yourselves **a** are in the body. **Heb 13:3** *2532*
Therefore Jesus **a**, that He might **Heb 13:12** *2532*
and there **a** comes in a poor man in **Jas 2:2** *2532*
"DO NOT COMMIT ADULTERY," **a** said, **Jas 2:11** *2532*
the demons **a** believe, and shudder. **Jas 2:19** *2532*
the harlot **a** justified by works when **Jas 2:25** *2532*
so **a** faith without works is dead. **Jas 2:26** *2532*
Look at the ships **a**, **Jas 3:4** *2532*
So **a** the tongue is a small part of **Jas 3:5** *2532*
live and **a** do this or that." **Jas 4:15** *2532*
yourselves **a** in all *your* behavior; **1Pe 1:15** *2532*
you **a**, as living stones, are being **1Pe 2:5** *2532*
this *doom* they were **a** appointed. **1Pe 2:8** *2532*
a to those who are unreasonable. **1Pe 2:18** *2532*
since Christ **a** suffered for you, **1Pe 2:21** *2532*
in former times the holy women **a**, **1Pe 3:5** *2532*

a died for sins once for all, **1Pe 3:18** *2532*
in which **a** He went and made **1Pe 3:19** *2532*
a with the same purpose, **1Pe 4:1** *2532*
so that **a** at the revelation of His **1Pe 4:13** *2532*
those **a** who suffer according **1Pe 4:19** *2532*
and a partaker **a** of the glory that **1Pe 5:1** *2532*
Now for this very reason **a**, **2Pe 1:5** *2532*
as **a** our Lord Jesus Christ has **2Pe 1:14** *2532*
And I will **a** be diligent that at **2Pe 1:15** *2532*
prophets **a** arose among the people, **2Pe 2:1** *2532*
a be false teachers among you, **2Pe 2:1** *2532*
of those creatures **a** be destroyed, **2Pe 2:12** *2532*
as **a** our beloved brother Paul, **2Pe 3:15** *2532*
as **a** in all *his* letters, speaking **2Pe 3:16** *2532*
do **a** the rest of the Scriptures, **2Pe 3:16** *2532*
and heard we proclaim to you **a**, **1Jn 1:3** *2532*
a for *those of* the whole world. **1Jn 2:2** *2532*
The world is passing away, and **a** **1Jn 2:17**
the Son has the Father **a**. **1Jn 2:23** *2532*
you **a** will abide in the Son and in **1Jn 2:24** *2532*
you know that everyone **a** who **1Jn 2:29** *2532*
sin **a** practices lawlessness; **1Jn 3:4** *2532*
we **a** ought to love one another. **1Jn 4:11** *2532*
He is, so **a** are we in this world. **1Jn 4:17** *2532*
God should love his brother **a**. **1Jn 4:21** *2532*
I, but **a** all who know the truth, **2Jn 1:1** *2532*
way these men, **a** by dreaming, **Jude 1:8** *2532*
It was **a** about these men *that* Enoch, **Jude 1:14** *2532*
the Nicolaitans, which I **a** hate. **Rv 2:6** *2532*
'So you **a** have some who in the **Rv 2:15** *2532*
as I **a** have received *authority* **Rv 2:27** *2532*
I **a** will keep you from the hour of **Rv 3:10** *2532*
as I **a** overcame and sat down with **Rv 3:21** *2532*
had been, would be completed **a**. **Rv 6:11** *2532*
where **a** their Lord was crucified. **Rv 11:8** *2532*
It was **a** given to him to make war **Rv 13:7** *2532*
he **a** will drink of the wine of the **Rv 14:10** *2532*
and he **a** had a sharp sickle. **Rv 14:17** *2532*
is not, is himself **a** an eighth and **Rv 17:11** *2532*
beast and the false prophet are **a**; **Rv 20:10** *2532*
which are **a** angelic **Rv 21:17**

ALTAR

Then Noah built an **a** to the LORD, **Gn 8:20** 4196
offered burnt offerings on the **a**. **Gn 8:20** 4196
So he built an **a** there to the LORD **Gn 12:7** 4196
and there he built an **a** to the **Gn 12:8** 4196
to the place of the **a** which **Gn 13:4** 4196
there he built an **a** to the LORD. **Gn 13:18** 4196
and Abraham built the **a** there and **Gn 22:9** 4196
him on the **a**, on top of the wood. **Gn 22:9** 4196
So he built an **a** there and called **Gn 26:25** 4196
Then he erected there an **a** and **Gn 33:20** 4196
and make an **a** there to God, who **Gn 35:1** 4196
and I will make an **a** there to God, **Gn 35:3** 4196
He built an **a** there, and **Gn 35:7** 4196
Moses built an **a** and **Ex 17:15** 4196
shall make an **a** of earth for Me, **Ex 20:24** 4196
If you make an **a** of stone for Me, **Ex 20:25** 4196
shall not go up by steps to My **a**, **Ex 20:26** 4196
are to take him *even* from My **a**, **Ex 21:14** 4196
and built an **a** at the foot of the **Ex 24:4** 4196
the blood he sprinkled on the **a**. **Ex 24:6** 4196
shall make the **a** of acacia wood, **Ex 27:1** 4196
the **a** shall be square, and its **Ex 27:1** 4196
beneath, under the ledge of the **a**, **Ex 27:5** 4196
net will reach halfway up the **a**. **Ex 27:5** 4196
You shall make poles for the **a**, **Ex 27:6** 4196
sides of the **a** when it is carried. **Ex 27:7** 4196
a to minister in the holy place, **Ex 28:43** 4196
horns of the **a** with your finger; **Ex 29:12** 4196
the blood at the base of the **a**. **Ex 29:12** 4196
offer them up in smoke on the **a**. **Ex 29:13** 4196
and sprinkle it around on the **a**. **Ex 29:16** 4196
in smoke the whole ram on the **a**; **Ex 29:18** 4196
rest of the blood around on the **a**. **Ex 29:20** 4196
a and some of the anointing oil, **Ex 29:21** 4196
offer them up in smoke on the **a** on **Ex 29:25** 4196
and you shall purify the **a** when **Ex 29:36** 4196
for the **a** and consecrate it; **Ex 29:37** 4196
then the **a** shall be most holy, *and* **Ex 29:37** 4196
touches the **a** shall be holy. **Ex 29:37** 4196
is what you shall offer on the **a**: **Ex 29:38** 4196
the tent of meeting and the **a**; **Ex 29:44** 4196
you shall make an **a** as a place for **Ex 30:1** 4196
"You shall put this **a** in **Ex 30:6**
any strange incense on this **a**, **Ex 30:9**
the tent of meeting and the **a**, **Ex 30:18** 4196
they approach the **a** to minister, **Ex 30:20** 4196
utensils, and the **a** of incense, **Ex 30:27** 4196
and the **a** of burnt offering and **Ex 30:28** 4196
utensils, and the **a** of incense, **Ex 31:8** 4196
the **a** of burnt offering also with **Ex 31:9** 4196
saw *this*, he built an **a** before it; **Ex 32:5** 4196
the **a** of incense and its poles, **Ex 35:15** 4196
the **a** of burnt offering with its **Ex 35:16** 4196
the **a** of incense of acacia wood: **Ex 37:25** 4196
Then he made the **a** of burnt offering **Ex 38:1** 4196
He made all the utensils of the **a**, **Ex 38:3** 4196
He made for the **a** a grating of **Ex 38:4** 4196
the rings on the sides of the **a**, **Ex 38:7** 4196
bronze **a** and its bronze grating, **Ex 38:30** 4196
and all the utensils of the **a**, **Ex 38:30** 4196
and the gold **a**, and the anointing **Ex 39:38** 4196
bronze **a** and its bronze grating, **Ex 39:39** 4196
you shall set the gold **a** of **Ex 40:5** 4196
You shall set the **a** of burnt offering **Ex 40:6** 4196
the tent of meeting and the **a** and **Ex 40:7** 4196
shall anoint the **a** of burnt offering **Ex 40:10** 4196
utensils, and consecrate the **a**, **Ex 40:10** 4196

and the **a** shall be most holy.	**Ex 40:10**	4196
Then he placed the gold **a** in the	**Ex 40:26**	4196
He set the **a** of burnt offering	**Ex 40:29**	4196
the tent of meeting and the **a** and	**Ex 40:30**	4196
and when they approached the **a**,	**Ex 40:32**	4196
around the tabernacle and the **a**,	**Ex 40:33**	4196
sprinkle the blood around on the **a**	**Lv 1:5**	4196
Aaron the priest shall put fire on the **a**	**Lv 1:7**	4196
is on the fire that is on the **a**.	**Lv 1:8**	4196
it on the **a** for a burnt offering,	**Lv 1:9**	4196
the **a** northward before the LORD,	**Lv 1:11**	4196
its blood around on the **a**.	**Lv 1:11**	4196
is on the fire that is on the **a**.	**Lv 1:12**	4196
and offer it up in smoke on the **a**;	**Lv 1:13**	4196
to the **a**, and wring off its head	**Lv 1:15**	4196
and offer it up in smoke on the **a**;	**Lv 1:15**	4196
drained out on the side of the **a**.	**Lv 1:15**	4196
and cast it beside the **a** eastward,	**Lv 1:16**	4196
shall offer it up in smoke on the **a** on	**Lv 1:17**	4196
as its memorial portion on the **a**,	**Lv 2:2**	4196
and he shall bring it to the **a**.	**Lv 2:8**	4196
it up in smoke on the **a** *as* an offering	**Lv 2:9**	4196
for a soothing aroma on the **a**.	**Lv 2:12**	4196
the blood around on the **a**.	**Lv 3:2**	4196
on the **a** on the burnt offering,	**Lv 3:5**	4196
its blood around on the **a**.	**Lv 3:8**	4196
offer *it* up in smoke on the **a**	**Lv 3:11**	4196
its blood around on the **a**.	**Lv 3:13**	4196
them up in smoke on the **a** *as* food,	**Lv 3:16**	4196
the horns of the **a** of fragrant incense	**Lv 4:7**	4196
pour out at the base of the **a** of burnt	**Lv 4:7**	4196
smoke on the **a** of burnt offering.	**Lv 4:10**	4196
blood on the horns of the **a** which is	**Lv 4:18**	4196
at the base of the **a** of burnt offering	**Lv 4:18**	4196
and offer it up in smoke on the **a**.	**Lv 4:19**	4196
horns of the **a** of burnt offering;	**Lv 4:25**	4196
base of the **a** of burnt offering.	**Lv 4:25**	4196
fat he shall offer up in smoke on the **a**	**Lv 4:26**	4196
horns of the **a** of burnt offering;	**Lv 4:30**	4196
pour out at the base of the **a**.	**Lv 4:30**	4196
a for a soothing aroma to the LORD.	**Lv 4:31**	4196
horns of the **a** of burnt offering,	**Lv 4:34**	4196
pour out at the base of the **a**.	**Lv 4:34**	4196
offer them up in smoke on the **a**,	**Lv 4:35**	4196
sin offering on the side of the **a**,	**Lv 5:9**	4196
drained out at the base of the **a**:	**Lv 5:9**	4196
and offer *it* up in smoke on the **a**,	**Lv 5:12**	4196
the **a** all night until the morning,	**Lv 6:9**	4196
the **a** is to be kept burning on it.	**Lv 6:9**	4196
the burnt offering on the **a** and	**Lv 6:10**	4196
and place them beside the **a**.	**Lv 6:10**	4196
the **a** shall be kept burning on it.	**Lv 6:12**	4196
kept burning continually on the **a**;	**Lv 6:13**	4196
before the LORD in front of the **a**.	**Lv 6:14**	4196
offer *it* up in smoke on the **a**,	**Lv 6:15**	4196
its blood around on the **a**.	**Lv 7:2**	4196
a as an offering by fire to the LORD;	**Lv 7:5**	4196
up the fat in smoke on the **a**,	**Lv 7:31**	4196
He sprinkled some of it on the **a** seven	**Lv 8:11**	4196
anointed the **a** and all its utensils,	**Lv 8:11**	4196
it around on the horns of the **a**,	**Lv 8:15**	4196
of the altar, and purified the **a**.	**Lv 8:15**	4196
base of the **a** and consecrated it,	**Lv 8:15**	4196
offered it up in smoke on the **a**.	**Lv 8:16**	4196
the blood around on the **a**.	**Lv 8:19**	4196
the whole ram in smoke on the **a**.	**Lv 8:21**	4196
rest of the blood around on the **a**.	**Lv 8:24**	4196
on the **a** with the burnt offering.	**Lv 8:28**	4196
of the blood which was on the **a** and	**Lv 8:30**	4196
"Come near to the **a** and offer	**Lv 9:7**	4196
So Aaron came near to the **a** and	**Lv 9:8**	4196
put *some* on the horns of the **a**,	**Lv 9:9**	4196
of the blood at the base of the **a**.	**Lv 9:9**	4196
he then offered up in smoke on the **a**	**Lv 9:10**	4196
he sprinkled it around on the **a**.	**Lv 9:12**	4196
offered *them* up in smoke on the **a**.	**Lv 9:13**	4196
with the burnt offering on the **a**.	**Lv 9:14**	4196
offered *it* up in smoke on the **a**,	**Lv 9:17**	4196
he sprinkled it around on the **a**.	**Lv 9:18**	4196
offered them up in smoke on the **a**.	**Lv 9:20**	4196
and the portions of fat on the **a**;	**Lv 9:24**	4196
eat it unleavened beside the **a**,	**Lv 10:12**	4196
and the grain offering on the **a**.	**Lv 14:20**	4196
from upon the **a** before the LORD and	**Lv 16:12**	4196
"Then he shall go out to the **a**	**Lv 16:18**	4196
the horns of the **a** on all sides.	**Lv 16:18**	4196
and the tent of meeting and the **a**,	**Lv 16:20**	4196
fat of the sin offering on the **a**.	**Lv 16:25**	4196
the tent of meeting and for the **a**.	**Lv 16:33**	4196
on the **a** of the LORD at the doorway	**Lv 17:6**	4196
I have given it to you on the **a**	**Lv 17:11**	4196
the **a** because he has a defect,	**Lv 21:23**	4196
by fire on the **a** to the LORD.	**Lv 22:22**	4196
around the tabernacle and the **a**,	**Nu 3:26**	4196
"Over the golden **a** they shall	**Nu 4:11**	4196
take away the ashes from the **a**,	**Nu 4:13**	4196
basins, all the utensils of the **a**;	**Nu 4:14**	4196
around the tabernacle and the **a**,	**Nu 4:26**	4196
the LORD and bring it to the **a**;	**Nu 5:25**	4196
and offer *it* up in smoke on the **a**,	**Nu 5:26**	4196
and the **a** and all its utensils;	**Nu 7:1**	4196
for the **a** when it was anointed,	**Nu 7:10**	4196
their offering before the **a**.	**Nu 7:10**	4196
for the dedication of the **a**."	**Nu 7:11**	4196
offering for the **a** from the leaders	**Nu 7:84**	4196
for the **a** after it was anointed.	**Nu 7:88**	4196
sheets for a plating of the **a**,	**Nu 16:38**	4196
them out as a plating for the **a**,	**Nu 16:39**	4196
and put in it fire from the **a**,	**Nu 16:46**	4196
of the sanctuary and the **a**,	**Nu 18:3**	4196
and the obligations of the **a**,	**Nu 18:5**	4196
the **a** and inside the veil,	**Nu 18:7**	4196
shall sprinkle their blood on the **a** and	**Nu 18:17**	4196
up a bull and a ram on each **a**.	**Nu 23:2**	4196
up a bull and a ram on each **a**."	**Nu 23:4**	4196
a bull and a ram on *each* **a**.	**Nu 23:14**	4196
up a bull and a ram on *each* **a**.	**Nu 23:30**	4196
on the **a** of the LORD your God;	**Dt 12:27**	4196
out on the **a** of the LORD your God,	**Dt 12:27**	4196
beside the **a** of the LORD your God,	**Dt 16:21**	4196
before the **a** of the LORD your God.	**Dt 26:4**	4196
there an **a** to the LORD your God,	**Dt 27:5**	4196
the LORD your God, an **a** of stones;	**Dt 27:5**	4196
"You shall build the **a** of the LORD	**Dt 27:6**	4196
whole burnt offerings on Your **a**.	**Dt 33:10**	4196
Joshua built an **a** to the LORD,	**Jos 8:30**	4196
of Moses, an **a** of uncut stones on	**Jos 8:31**	4196
and for the **a** of the LORD,	**Jos 9:27**	4196
built an **a** there by the Jordan,	**Jos 22:10**	4196
Jordan, a large **a** in appearance.	**Jos 22:10**	4196
half-tribe of Manasseh have built an **a**	**Jos 22:11**	4196
day, by building yourselves an **a**,	**Jos 22:16**	4196
by building an **a** for yourselves,	**Jos 22:19**	4196
besides the **a** of the LORD our God.	**Jos 22:19**	4196
"If we have built us an **a** to turn	**Jos 22:23**	4196
'Let us build an **a**, not for burnt	**Jos 22:26**	4196
"See the copy of the **a** of the	**Jos 22:28**	4196
building an **a** for burnt offering,	**Jos 22:29**	4196
besides the **a** of the LORD our God	**Jos 22:29**	4196
sons of Gad called the **a** *Witness;*	**Jos 22:34**	4196
Then Gideon built an **a** there to	**Jg 6:24**	4196
and pull down the **a** of Baal which	**Jg 6:25**	4196
and build an **a** to the LORD your	**Jg 6:26**	4196
the **a** of Baal was torn down,	**Jg 6:28**	4196
on the **a** which had been built.	**Jg 6:28**	4196
he has torn down the **a** of Baal,	**Jg 6:30**	4196
someone has torn down his **a**."	**Jg 6:31**	4196
because he had torn down his **a**.	**Jg 6:32**	4196
went up from the **a** toward heaven,	**Jg 13:20**	4196
ascended in the flame of the **a**.	**Jg 13:20**	4196
arose early and built an **a** there and	**Jg 21:4**	4196
be My priests, to go up to My **a**,	**1Sa 2:28**	4196
cut off every man of yours from My **a**	**1Sa 2:33**	4196
he built there an **a** to the LORD.	**1Sa 7:17**	4196
And Saul built an **a** to the LORD;	**1Sa 14:35**	4196
first **a** that he built to the LORD.	**1Sa 14:35**	4196
erect an **a** to the LORD on the	**2Sa 24:18**	4196
order to build an **a** to the LORD,	**2Sa 24:21**	4196
built there an **a** to the LORD and	**2Sa 24:25**	4196
took hold of the horns of the **a**.	**1Ki 1:50**	4196
taken hold of the horns of the **a**,	**1Ki 1:51**	4196
they brought him down from the **a**.	**1Ki 1:53**	4196
took hold of the horns of the **a**.	**1Ki 2:28**	4196
and behold, he is beside the **a**.	**1Ki 2:29**	4196
burnt offerings on that **a**.	**1Ki 3:4**	4196
He also overlaid the **a** with cedar.	**1Ki 6:20**	4196
Also the whole **a** which was by the	**1Ki 6:22**	4196
the golden **a** and the golden table	**1Ki 7:48**	4196
Then Solomon stood before the **a** of	**1Ki 8:22**	4196
oath before Your **a** in this house,	**1Ki 8:31**	4196
from before the **a** of the LORD,	**1Ki 8:54**	4196
for the bronze **a** that *was* before	**1Ki 8:64**	4196
the **a** which he built to the LORD,	**1Ki 9:25**	4196
burning incense with them *on the* **a**	**1Ki 9:25**	4196
in Judah, and he went up to the **a**;	**1Ki 12:32**	4196
Then he went up to the **a** which he	**1Ki 12:33**	4196
went up to the **a** to burn incense.	**1Ki 12:33**	4196
standing by the **a** to burn incense.	**1Ki 13:1**	4196
the **a** by the word of the LORD,	**1Ki 13:2**	4196
"O **a**, altar, thus says the LORD,	**1Ki 13:2**	4196
"O altar, **a**, thus says the LORD,	**1Ki 13:2**	4196
the **a** shall be split apart and the	**1Ki 13:3**	4196
he cried against the **a** in Bethel,	**1Ki 13:4**	4196
stretched out his hand from the **a**,	**1Ki 13:4**	4196
The **a** also was split apart and the	**1Ki 13:5**	4196
ashes were poured out from the **a**,	**1Ki 13:5**	4196
of the LORD against the **a** in Bethel	**1Ki 13:32**	4196
a for Baal in the house of Baal which	**1Ki 16:32**	4196
about the **a** which they made.	**1Ki 18:26**	4196
And he repaired the **a** of the LORD	**1Ki 18:30**	4196
an **a** in the name of the LORD,	**1Ki 18:32**	4196
and he made a trench around the **a**,	**1Ki 18:32**	4196
The water flowed around the **a** and	**1Ki 18:35**	4196
house, by the **a** and by the house,	**2Ki 11:11**	4196
its lid and put it beside the **a**,	**2Ki 12:9**	4196
saw the **a** which *was* at Damascus;	**2Ki 16:10**	4196
pattern of the **a** and its model,	**2Ki 16:10**	4196
So Urijah the priest built an **a**;	**2Ki 16:11**	4196
from Damascus, the king saw the **a**;	**2Ki 16:12**	4196
then the king approached the **a**	**2Ki 16:12**	4196
of his peace offerings on the **a**.	**2Ki 16:13**	4196
The bronze **a**, which *was* before	**2Ki 16:14**	4196
his **a** and the house of the LORD,	**2Ki 16:14**	4196
put it on the north side of *his* **a**.	**2Ki 16:14**	4196
"Upon the great **a** burn the	**2Ki 16:15**	4196
a shall be for me to inquire *by*."	**2Ki 16:15**	4196
before this **a** in Jerusalem'?	**2Ki 18:22**	4196
to the **a** of the LORD in Jerusalem,	**2Ki 23:9**	4196
the **a** that *was* at Bethel *and* the	**2Ki 23:15**	4196
even that **a** and the high place he	**2Ki 23:15**	4196
burned *them* on the **a** and defiled it	**2Ki 23:16**	4196
done against the **a** of Bethel."	**2Ki 23:17**	4196
Aaron and his sons offered on the **a**	**1Ch 6:49**	4196
offering and on the **a** of incense,	**1Ch 6:49**	4196
burnt offerings to the LORD on the **a**	**1Ch 16:40**	4196
a to the LORD on the threshing floor	**1Ch 21:18**	4196
may build on it an **a** to the LORD;	**1Ch 21:22**	4196
built an **a** to the LORD there and	**1Ch 21:26**	4196
heaven on the **a** of burnt offering.	**1Ch 21:26**	4196
and the **a** of burnt offering *were*	**1Ch 21:29**	4196
a of burnt offering for Israel."	**1Ch 22:1**	4196
and for the **a** of incense refined	**1Ch 28:18**	4196
Now the bronze **a**, which Bezalel	**2Ch 1:5**	4196
the bronze **a** which *was* at the tent of	**2Ch 1:6**	4196
Then he made a bronze **a**,	**2Ch 4:1**	4196
even the golden **a**, the tables with	**2Ch 4:19**	4196
and lyres, standing east of the **a**,	**2Ch 5:12**	4196
Then he stood before the **a** of the	**2Ch 6:12**	4196
oath before Your **a** in this house,	**2Ch 6:22**	4196
because the bronze **a** which Solomon	**2Ch 7:7**	4196
of the **a** they observed seven days and	**2Ch 7:9**	4196
burnt offerings to the LORD on the **a**	**2Ch 8:12**	4196
He then restored the **a** of the LORD	**2Ch 15:8**	4196
house, by the **a** and by the house,	**2Ch 23:10**	4196
burn incense on the **a** of incense.	**2Ch 26:16**	4196
the LORD, beside the **a** of incense.	**2Ch 26:19**	4196
the **a** of burnt offering with all	**2Ch 29:18**	4196
are before the **a** of the LORD."	**2Ch 29:19**	4196
offer *them* on the **a** of the LORD.	**2Ch 29:21**	4196
blood and sprinkled it on the **a**.	**2Ch 29:22**	4196
and sprinkled the blood on the **a**;	**2Ch 29:22**	4196
and sprinkled the blood on the **a**.	**2Ch 29:22**	4196
purged the **a** with their blood to atone	**2Ch 29:24**	4196
offer the burnt offering on the **a**.	**2Ch 29:27**	4196
"You shall worship before one **a**,	**2Ch 32:12**	4196
He set up the **a** of the LORD	**2Ch 33:16**	4196
burnt offerings on the **a** of the LORD	**2Ch 35:16**	4196
built the **a** of the God of Israel to	**Ezr 3:2**	4196
set up the **a** on its foundation,	**Ezr 3:3**	4196
offerings and offer them on the **a** of	**Ezr 7:17**	4056
to burn on the **a** of the LORD our	**Ne 10:34**	4196
And I will go about Your **a**,	**Ps 26:6**	4196
Then I will go to the **a** of God,	**Ps 43:4**	4196
bulls will be offered on Your **a**.	**Ps 51:19**	4196
with cords to the horns of the **a**.	**Ps 118:27**	4196
had taken from the **a** with tongs.	**Is 6:6**	4196
In that day there will be an **a** to	**Is 19:19**	4196
When he makes all the **a** stones	**Is 27:9**	4196
'You shall worship before this **a**'?	**Is 36:7**	4196
will be acceptable on My **a**;	**Is 56:7**	4196
go up with acceptance on My **a**,	**Is 60:7**	4196
The Lord has rejected His **a**,	**La 2:7**	4196
to the north of the **a** gate *was*	**Ezk 8:5**	4196
LORD, between the porch and the **a**,	**Ezk 8:16**	4196
in and stood beside the bronze **a**.	**Ezk 9:2**	4196
priests who keep charge of the **a**.	**Ezk 40:46**	4196
the **a** was in front of the temple.	**Ezk 40:47**	4196
The **a** *was* of wood, three cubits	**Ezk 41:22**	4196
measurements of the **a** by cubits	**Ezk 43:13**	4196
the *height* of the base of the **a**.	**Ezk 43:13**	4196
The **a** hearth *shall be* four cubits;	**Ezk 43:15**	741
and from the **a** hearth shall extend	**Ezk 43:15**	741
"Now the **a** hearth *shall be* twelve	**Ezk 43:16**	741
for the **a** on the day it is built,	**Ezk 43:18**	4196
and they shall cleanse the **a** as	**Ezk 43:22**	4196
atonement for the **a** and purify it;	**Ezk 43:26**	4196
your burnt offerings on the **a**,	**Ezk 43:27**	4196
corners of the ledge of the **a** and	**Ezk 45:19**	4196
of the house, from south of the **a**.	**Ezk 47:1**	4196
Wail, O ministers of the **a**!	**Jl 1:13**	4196
Weep between the porch and the **a**,	**Jl 2:17**	4196
they stretch out beside every **a**,	**Am 2:8**	4196
horns of the **a** will be cut off And	**Am 3:14**	4196
the Lord standing beside the **a**,	**Am 9:1**	4196
like the corners of the **a**.	**Zch 9:15**	4196
be like the bowls before the **a**.	**Zch 14:20**	4196
presenting defiled food upon My **a**.	**Mal 1:7**	4196
not uselessly kindle *fire on* My **a**!	**Mal 1:10**	4196
the **a** of the LORD with tears,	**Mal 2:13**	4196
presenting your offering at the **a**,	**Mt 5:23**	*2379*
your offering there before the **a** and	**Mt 5:24**	*2379*
'Whoever swears by the **a**,	**Mt 23:18**	*2379*
a that sanctifies the offering?	**Mt 23:19**	*2379*
"Therefore, whoever swears by the **a**,	**Mt 23:20**	*2379*
by the **a** and by everything on it.	**Mt 23:20**	*2379*
between the temple and the **a**.	**Mt 23:35**	*2379*
to the right of the **a** of incense.	**Lk 1:11**	*2379*
the **a** and the house *of God*	**Lk 11:51**	*2379*
found an **a** with this inscription,	**Ac 17:23**	*1041*
those who attend regularly to the **a**	**1Co 9:13**	*2379*
altar have their share from the **a**?	**1Co 9:13**	*2379*
the sacrifices sharers in the **a**?	**1Co 10:18**	*2379*
no one has officiated at the **a**.	**Heb 7:13**	*2379*
having a golden **a** of incense and	**Heb 9:4**	*2369*
We have an **a** from which those who	**Heb 13:10**	*2379*
offered up Isaac his son on the **a**?	**Jas 2:21**	*2379*
I saw underneath the **a** the souls	**Rv 6:9**	*2379*
angel came and stood at the **a**,	**Rv 8:3**	*2379*
a which was before the throne.	**Rv 8:3**	*2379*
the **a**, and threw it to the earth;	**Rv 8:5**	*2379*
the golden **a** which is before God,	**Rv 9:13**	*2379*
the temple of God and the **a**,	**Rv 11:1**	*2379*
over fire, came out from the **a**;	**Rv 14:18**	*2379*
And I heard the **a** saying,	**Rv 16:7**	*2379*

ALTARS

you are to tear down their **a** and	**Ex 34:13**	4196
and cut down your incense **a**,	**Lv 26:30**	2553
the table, the lampstand, the **a**,	**Nu 3:31**	4196
"Build seven **a** for me here, and	**Nu 23:1**	4196
"I have set up the seven **a**,	**Nu 23:4**	4196
and built seven **a** and offered a	**Nu 23:14**	4196
"Build seven **a** for me here and	**Nu 23:29**	4196
you shall tear down their **a**,	**Dt 7:5**	4196
'You shall tear down their **a**	**Dt 12:3**	4196
you shall tear down their **a**.'	**Jg 2:2**	4196
torn down Your **a** and killed Your	**1Ki 19:10**	4196
torn down Your **a** and killed Your	**1Ki 19:14**	4196

his a and his images they broke in 2Ki 11:18 4196
the priest of Baal before the a. 2Ki 11:18 4196
whose a Hezekiah has taken away, 2Ki 18:22 4196
a for Baal and made an Asherah, 2Ki 21:3 4196
built a in the house of the LORD, 2Ki 21:4 4196
For he built a for all the host of 2Ki 21:5 4196
The a which *were* on the roof, 2Ki 23:12 4196
and the a which Manasseh had made 2Ki 23:12 4196
on the a and burned human bones 2Ki 23:20 4196
the foreign a and high places, 2Ch 14:3 4196
a from all the cities of Judah. 2Ch 14:5 2553
in pieces his a and his images, 2Ch 23:17 4196
the priest of Baal before the a. 2Ch 23:17 4196
and made a for himself in every 2Ch 28:24 4196
the a which *were* in Jerusalem; 2Ch 30:14 4196
they also removed all the incense a 2Ch 30:14 4729c
pulled down the high places and the a 2Ch 31:1 4196
away His high places and His a, 2Ch 32:12 4196
he also erected a for the Baals 2Ch 33:3 4196
He built a in the house of the 2Ch 33:4 4196
For he built a for all the host of 2Ch 33:5 4196
as well as all the a which he had 2Ch 33:15 4196
a of the Baals in his presence, 2Ch 34:4 4196
and the incense a that were high 2Ch 34:4 2553
bones of the priests on their a and 2Ch 34:5 4196
he also tore down the a and beat 2Ch 34:7 4196
a throughout the land of Israel. 2Ch 34:7 2553
may lay her young, Even Your a, Ps 84:3 4196
He will not have regard for the a, Is 17:8 4196
and incense a will not stand. Is 27:9 2553
whose a Hezekiah has taken away and Is 36:7 4196
the a you have set up to the shameful Jer 11:13 4196
thing, a to burn incense to Baal. Jer 11:13 4196
And on the horns of their a, Jer 17:1 4196
So they *remember* their a and their Jer 17:2 4196
"So your a will become desolate and Ezk 6:4 4196
your incense a will be smashed; Ezk 6:4 2553
scatter your bones around your a. Ezk 6:5 4196
a may become waste and desolate, Ezk 6:6 4196
your incense a may be cut down, Ezk 6:6 2553
among their idols around their a, Ezk 6:13 4196
Ephraim has multiplied a for sin, Hos 8:11 4196
have become a of sinning for him. Hos 8:11 4196
his fruit, The more a he made; Hos 10:1 4196
The LORD will break down their a Hos 10:2 4196
and thistle will grow on their a; Hos 10:8 4196
their a are like the stone heaps Hos 12:11 4196
will also punish the a of Bethel; Am 3:14 4196
THEY HAVE TORN DOWN YOUR A, Ro 11:3 *2379*

ALTER
will I a the utterance of My lips. Ps 89:34 8132
a the customs which Moses handed Ac 6:14 *236*

ALTERATIONS
to make a in times and in law; Da 7:25 8133

ALTERED
expression was a toward Shadrach, Da 3:19 8133

ALTERNATELY
and their thoughts a accusing or Ro 2:15 *3342*

ALTERNATING
a a bell and a pomegranate all Ex 39:26

ALTHOUGH
Lord, a I am *but* dust and ashes. Gn 18:27
a no man is with us, see, God Gn 31:50
a they did not recognize him. Gn 42:8
a Manasseh was the firstborn. Gn 48:14 3588
the sword, a no one is pursuing; Lv 26:37
a she has defiled herself, Nu 5:13
a you will only see the extreme Nu 23:13
A Moses was one hundred and twenty Dt 34:7
a a plague came on the Jos 22:17
in Shiloh, a the child was young. 1Sa 1:24
a the LORD your God *was* your king. 1Sa 12:12
A he urged him, he would not go, 2Sa 13:25
a he had not followed Absalom. 1Ki 2:28
a *I* your servant have feared the 1Ki 18:12
a he was not the firstborn, 1Ch 26:10 3588
A Ahaz took a portion out 2Ch 28:21 3588
a only to the LORD their God. 2Ch 33:17
A he went there, he did not eat Ezr 10:6
a at that time I had not set up Ne 6:1 1571
a you incited Me against him to Jb 2:3
A there is no violence in my Jb 16:17 5921
A you strike him with the rod, Pr 23:13 3588
A a sinner does evil a hundred Ec 8:12 834
For a You were angry with me, Is 12:1
A the Lord has given you bread of Is 30:20
"A you wash yourself with lye And Jer 2:22
3588, 518
A you dress in scarlet, Although Jer 4:30 3588
A you decorate *yourself with* Jer 4:30 3588
A you enlarge your eyes with Jer 4:30 3588
"And a they say, 'As the LORD lives,' Jer 5:2 518
A the nations are terrified by them; Jer 10:2 3588
a they may say nice things to you." Jer 12:6 3588
"A our iniquities testify against Jer 14:7 518
a it was not I who sent them—yet Jer 14:15
to you, a I did not send him, Jer 29:31
a I was a husband to them," Jer 31:32
a the city is given into the hand Jer 32:25
"A recently you *had* turned and Jer 34:15
A their land is full of guilt Jer 51:5 3588
A you make your heart like the Ezk 28:2
(a their terror was instilled in the land Ezk 32:25 3588
them,' a the LORD was there, Ezk 35:10
his nation, a not with his power. Da 8:22
A I trained *and* strengthened their Hos 7:15
A Herod wanted to put him to death, Mt 14:5
A he was grieved, the king commanded Mt 14:9
And a the king was very sorry, *yet* Mk 6:26
away, a it was extremely large. Mk 16:4 *1063*
(a Jesus Himself was not baptizing, Jn 4:2 *2544*
a the world has not known You, Jn 17:25 *2532*
and a there were so many, the net Jn 21:11
a they know the ordinance of God, Ro 1:32
a willing to demonstrate His wrath Ro 9:22
So a I wrote to you, *it was* not for 2Co 7:12
1487, 2532
slave a he is owner of everything, Ga 4:1
a He existed in the form of God, Php 2:6
a I myself might have confidence Php 3:4 *2539*
And a you were formerly alienated Col 1:21
a they have denied its power; 2Tm 3:5
a His works were finished from the Heb 4:3 *2543*
A He was a Son, He learned Heb 5:8 *2539*
a these are descended from Abraham. Heb 7:5 *2539*

ALTOGETHER
so that you will be a joyful. Dt 16:15 389
'Your hands fashioned and made me a, Jb 10:8
3162, 5439
are made to hide themselves a. Jb 24:4 3162
they are righteous a. Ps 19:9 3164a
a who rejoice at my distress; Ps 35:26 3164a
transgressors will be a destroyed; Ps 37:38 3164a
They have encompassed me a. Ps 88:17 3162
"You are a beautiful, my darling, SS 4:7 3605
mice, Will come to an end a," Is 66:17 3164a
But they are a stupid and foolish Jer 10:8 259
Or is He speaking a for our sake? 1Co 9:10 *3843*

ALUSH
from Dophkah and camped at A. Nu 33:13 442
They journeyed from A and Nu 33:14 442

ALVAH
chief Timna, chief A, Gn 36:40 5933

ALVAN
A and Manahath and Ebal, Shepho Gn 36:23 5935

ALWAYS
and it shall a be on his forehead, Ex 28:38 8548
and keep all My commandments a, Dt 5:29
3605, 3117
our good a and for our survival, Dt 6:24
3605, 3117
your God, and a keep His charge, Dt 11:1
3605, 3117
of the LORD your God are a on it, Dt 11:12 8548
learn to fear the LORD your God a. Dt 14:23
3605, 3117
and to walk in His ways a—then you Dt 19:9
3605, 3117
he will walk before My anointed a. 1Sa 2:35
3605, 3117
had a been a friend of David. 1Ki 5:1
3605, 3117
a lamp a before Me in Jerusalem, 1Ki 11:36
3605, 3117
of David for this, but not a.' " 1Ki 11:39
3605, 3117
a lamp to him through his sons a. 2Ki 8:19
3605, 3117
good concerning me but a evil. 2Ch 18:7
3605, 3117
the needy will not a be forgotten, Ps 9:18 5331
And a at ease, they have increased Ps 73:12 5769
He will not a strive *with us,* Ps 103:9 5331
Be exhilarated a with her love. Pr 5:19 8548
delight, Rejoicing a before Him, Pr 8:30
3605, 6256
live in the fear of the LORD a. Pr 23:17
3605, 3117
blessed is the man who fears a, Pr 28:14 8548
A fool a loses his temper, But a Pr 29:11
Nor will I a be angry; Is 57:16 5331
one way, that they may fear Me a, Jer 32:39
3605, 3117
a man to stand before Me a. Jer 35:19
3605, 3117
"For you a have the poor with you; Mt 26:11 *3842*
but you do not a have Me. Mt 26:11 *3842*
and lo, I am with you a, Mt 28:20
3956, 2250
"For you a have the poor with you, Mk 14:7 *3842*
but you do not a have Me. Mk 14:7 *3842*
'Son, you have a been with me, Lk 15:31 *3842*
Then they said to Him, "Lord, a Jn 6:34 *3842*
but your time is a opportune. Jn 7:6 *3842*
for I a do the things that are Jn 8:29 *3842*
"I knew that You a hear Me; Jn 11:42 *3842*
"For you a have the poor with you, Jn 12:8 *3842*
you, but you do not a have Me." Jn 12:8 *3842*
I a taught in synagogues and in Jn 18:20 *3842*
I SAW THE LORD A IN MY Ac 2:25
1223, 3956
are a resisting the Holy Spirit; Ac 7:51 *104*
I also do my best to maintain a a Ac 24:16
1223, 3956
a in my prayers making request, if Ro 1:10 *3842*
I thank my God a concerning you for 1Co 1:4 *3842*
a abounding in the work of the 1Co 15:58 *3842*
who a leads us in triumph in 2Co 2:14 *3842*
a carrying about in the body the 2Co 4:10 *3842*
being a of good courage, 2Co 5:6 *3842*
as sorrowful yet a rejoicing, 2Co 6:10 *104*
that a having all sufficiency in 2Co 9:8 *3842*
But it is good a to be eagerly Ga 4:18 *3842*
a giving thanks for all things in Eph 5:20 *3842*
a offering prayer with joy in my Php 1:4 *3842*
Christ will even now, as a, Php 1:20 *3842*
just as you have a obeyed, Php 2:12 *3842*
Rejoice in the Lord a; Php 4:4 *3842*
Jesus Christ, praying a for you, Col 1:3 *3842*
Let your speech a be with grace, Col 4:6 *3842*
a laboring earnestly for you in Col 4:12 *3842*
thanks to God a for all of you, 1Th 1:2 *3842*
with the result that they a fill 1Th 2:16 *3842*
and that you a think kindly of us, 1Th 3:6 *3842*
so we shall a be with the Lord. 1Th 4:17 *3842*
but a seek after that which is 1Th 5:15 *3842*
Rejoice a; 1Th 5:16 *3842*
a to give thanks to God for you, 2Th 1:3 *3842*
To this end also we pray for you a 2Th 1:11 *3842*
a give thanks to God for you, 2Th 2:13 *3842*
a learning and never able to come 2Tm 3:7 *3842*
"Cretans are a liars, evil Ti 1:12 *104*
I thank my God a, making mention Phm 1:4 *3842*
'THEY A GO ASTRAY IN THEIR HEART, Heb 3:10 *104*
since He a lives to make Heb 7:25 *3842*
a *being* ready to make a defense to 1Pe 3:15 *104*
I will a be ready to remind you 2Pe 1:12 *104*

AM
A I my brother's keeper?" Gn 4:9
I a sorry that I have made them." Gn 6:7 5162
I a about to destroy them with the Gn 6:13
even I a bringing the flood of Gn 6:17
covenant which I a making between Gn 9:12
fear, Abram, I a a shield to you; Gn 15:1
You give me, since I a childless, Gn 15:2 1980
"I a the LORD who brought you out Gn 15:7
"I a fleeing from the presence of Gn 16:8
"I a God Almighty; Gn 17:1
bear *a child,* when I a *so* old?' Gn 18:13 2204
from Abraham what I a about to do, Gn 18:17
although I a *but* dust and ashes. Gn 18:27
"Abraham!" And he said, "Here I a." Gn 22:1
And he said, "Here I a, my son." Gn 22:7
Abraham!" And he said, "Here I a." Gn 22:11
"I a a stranger and a sojourner Gn 23:4
I a standing by the spring, Gn 24:13
"I a the daughter of Bethuel, the Gn 24:24
"I a Abraham's servant. Gn 24:34
I a standing by the spring, Gn 24:43
is so, why then a I *this way?*" Gn 25:22
red stuff there, for I a famished." Gn 25:30
"Behold, I a about to die; Gn 25:32 1980
"I a the God of your father Gn 26:24
Do not fear, for I a with you. Gn 26:24
And he said to him, "Here I a." Gn 27:1
I a old *and* I do not know the day Gn 27:2 2204
a hairy man and I a a smooth man. Gn 27:11
"My father." And he said, "Here I a. Gn 27:18
"I a Esau your firstborn; Gn 27:19
my son Esau?" And he said, "I a." Gn 27:24
"I a your son, your firstborn, Gn 27:32
"I a tired of living because of Gn 27:46
"I a the LORD, the God of your Gn 28:13
"Behold, I a with you and Gn 28:15
LORD has heard that I a unloved, Gn 29:33
"A I in the place of God, who has Gn 30:2
Leah said, "Happy a I! For women Gn 30:13
dream, 'Jacob,' and I said, 'Here I a.' Gn 31:11
'I a the God *of* Bethel, where you Gn 31:13
I a unworthy of all the Gn 32:10
"I a God Almighty; Gn 35:11
"I a looking for my brothers; Gn 37:16
as for me, where a I to go?" Gn 37:30
"*I a afraid* that he too may die Gn 38:11
"I a with child by the man to Gn 38:25
"*Though* I a Pharaoh, yet without Gn 41:44
"I a afraid that harm may befall Gn 42:4
if I a bereaved of my children, Gn 43:14
of my children, I a bereaved." Gn 43:14
said to his brothers, "I a Joseph! Gn 45:3
"I a your brother Joseph, whom Gn 45:4
Jacob." And he said, "Here I a." Gn 46:2
"I a God, the God of your father; Gn 46:3
"Behold, I a about to die, but Gn 48:21
"I a about to be gathered to my Gn 49:29
"Behold, I a about to die; Gn 50:5
be afraid, for a I in God's place? Gn 50:19
"I a about to die, but God will Gn 50:24
Moses!" And he said, "Here I a." Ex 3:4
"I a the God of your father, the Ex 3:6
for I a aware of their sufferings. Ex 3:7
"Who a I, that I should go to Ex 3:11
I a going to the sons of Israel, Ex 3:13
God said to Moses, "I AM WHO I AM"; Ex 3:14 1961
God said to Moses, "I AM WHO I A"; Ex 3:14 1961
'I A has sent me to you.' " Ex 3:14 1961
"I a indeed concerned about you Ex 3:16 6485
for I a slow of speech and slow of Ex 4:10
'I a not going to give you *any* Ex 5:10
Moses and said to him, "I a the LORD; Ex 6:2
'I a the LORD, and I will bring Ex 6:6
know that I a the LORD your God, Ex 6:7
I a the LORD.' " Ex 6:8
me, for I a unskilled in speech?" Ex 6:12
to Moses, saying, "I a the LORD; Ex 6:29
"Behold, I a unskilled in speech; Ex 6:30
shall know that I a the LORD, Ex 7:5
you shall know that I a the LORD: Ex 7:17
LORD, a in the midst of the land. Ex 8:22
"Behold, I a going out from you, Ex 8:29
you may know that I a the LORD." Ex 10:2
'About midnight I a going out into Ex 11:4
execute judgments—I a the LORD. Ex 12:12
will know that I a the LORD." Ex 14:4
will know that I a the LORD, Ex 14:18

when I **a** honored through Pharaoh, **Ex 14:18**
for I, the LORD, **a** your healer." **Ex 15:26**
that I **a** the LORD your God.' " **Ex 16:12**
a coming to you with your wife and **Ex 18:6**
"I **a** the LORD your God, who **Ex 20:2**
LORD your God, **a** a jealous God, **Ex 20:5**
I will hear *him,* for I **a** gracious. **Ex 22:27**
I **a** going to send an angel before **Ex 23:20**
to all that I **a** going to show you, **Ex 25:9**
"They shall know that I **a** the **Ex 29:46**
I **a** the LORD their God. **Ex 29:46**
I **a** the LORD who sanctifies you. **Ex 31:13**
and now I **a** going up to the LORD, **Ex 32:30**
I **a** going to make a covenant. **Ex 34:10**
I **a** going to perform with you. **Ex 34:10**
what I **a** commanding you this day: **Ex 34:11**
I **a** going to drive out the Amorite **Ex 34:11**
'For I **a** the LORD your God. **Lv 11:44**
therefore, and be holy, for I **a** holy. **Lv 11:44**
'For I **a** the LORD who brought you **Lv 11:45**
shall be holy, for I **a** holy.' " **Lv 11:45**
'I **a** the LORD your God. **Lv 18:2**
of Canaan where I **a** bringing you; **Lv 18:3**
I **a** the LORD your God. **Lv 18:4**
live if he does them; I **a** the LORD. **Lv 18:5**
to uncover nakedness; I **a** the LORD. **Lv 18:6**
name of your God; I **a** the LORD. **Lv 18:21**
the nations which I **a** casting out **Lv 18:24**
I **a** the LORD your God.' " **Lv 18:30**
for I the LORD your God **a** holy. **Lv 19:2**
I **a** the LORD your God. **Lv 19:3**
I **a** the LORD your God. **Lv 19:4**
I **a** the LORD your God. **Lv 19:10**
name of your God; I **a** the LORD. **Lv 19:12**
revere your God; I **a** the LORD. **Lv 19:14**
life of your neighbor; I **a** the LORD. **Lv 19:16**
neighbor as yourself; I **a** the LORD. **Lv 19:18**
I **a** the LORD your God. **Lv 19:25**
marks on yourselves: I **a** the LORD. **Lv 19:28**
revere My sanctuary; I **a** the LORD. **Lv 19:30**
I **a** the LORD your God. **Lv 19:31**
shall revere your God; I **a** the LORD. **Lv 19:32**
I **a** the LORD your God. **Lv 19:34**
I **a** the LORD your God, who brought **Lv 19:36**
I **a** the LORD.' " **Lv 19:37**
holy, for I **a** the LORD your God. **Lv 20:7**
I **a** the LORD who sanctifies you. **Lv 20:8**
so that the land to which I **a** **Lv 20:22**
I **a** the LORD your God, who has **Lv 20:24**
holy to Me, for I the LORD **a** holy; **Lv 20:26**
LORD, who sanctifies you, **a** holy. **Lv 21:8**
of his God is on him; I **a** the LORD. **Lv 21:12**
a the LORD who sanctifies him.' " **Lv 21:15**
For I the LORD who sanctifies them.' **Lv 21:23**
My holy name; I **a** the LORD. **Lv 22:2**
cut off from before Me; I **a** the LORD. **Lv 22:3**
unclean by it; I **a** the LORD. **Lv 22:8**
I **a** the LORD who sanctifies them. **Lv 22:9**
for I **a** the LORD who sanctifies them.' " **Lv 22:16**
of it until morning; I **a** the LORD. **Lv 22:30**
and do them; I **a** the LORD. **Lv 22:31**
I **a** the LORD who sanctifies you, **Lv 22:32**
to be your God; I **a** the LORD." **Lv 22:33**
'When you enter the land which I **a** **Lv 23:10**
I **a** the LORD your God.' " **Lv 23:22**
I **a** the LORD your God.' " **Lv 23:43**
for I **a** the LORD your God.' " **Lv 24:22**
for I **a** the LORD your God. **Lv 25:17**
'I **a** the LORD your God, who **Lv 25:38**
I **a** the LORD your God. **Lv 25:55**
for I **a** the LORD your God. **Lv 26:1**
My sanctuary; I **a** the LORD. **Lv 26:2**
'I **a** the LORD your God, who **Lv 26:13**
for I **a** the LORD their God. **Lv 26:44**
I **a** the LORD.' " **Lv 26:45**
They shall be Mine; I **a** the LORD." **Nu 3:13**
the Levites for Me, I **a** the LORD, **Nu 3:41**
Levites shall be Mine; I **a** the LORD. **Nu 3:45**
I **a** the LORD your God." **Nu 10:10**
"Where **a** I to get meat to give to **Nu 11:13**
"I alone **a** not able to carry all **Nu 11:14**
"The people, among whom I **a**, **Nu 11:21**
which I **a** going to give to the **Nu 13:2**
are to live, which I **a** giving you, **Nu 15:2**
"I **a** the LORD your God who **Nu 15:41**
I **a** the LORD your God." **Nu 15:41**
I **a** giving you the priesthood as a **Nu 18:7**
I **a** your portion and your **Nu 18:20**
"**A** I not your donkey on which you **Nu 22:30**
A I really unable to honor you?" **Nu 22:37**
A I able to speak anything at all? **Nu 22:38**
behold, I **a** going to my people; **Nu 24:14**
for I the LORD **a** dwelling in the **Nu 35:34**
'I **a** not able to bear *the burden* **Dt 1:9**
nor fight, for I **a** not among you; **Dt 1:42**
which I **a** teaching you to perform, **Dt 4:1**
the word which I **a** commanding you, **Dt 4:2**
I **a** setting before you today? **Dt 4:8**
which I **a** giving you today, **Dt 4:40**
ordinances which I **a** speaking today **Dt 5:1**
'I **a** the LORD your God who **Dt 5:6**
LORD your God, **a** a jealous God, **Dt 5:9**
which I **a** commanding you today, **Dt 6:6**
which I **a** commanding you today, **Dt 7:11**
"All the commandments that I **a** **Dt 8:1**
which I **a** commanding you today; **Dt 8:11**
His statutes which I **a** commanding **Dt 10:13**
"Know this day that I **a** not **Dt 11:2**
which I **a** commanding you today, **Dt 11:8**

which I **a** commanding you today, **Dt 11:13**
which I **a** commanding you to **Dt 11:22**
I **a** setting before you today a **Dt 11:26**
which I **a** commanding you today; **Dt 11:27**
which I **a** commanding you today, **Dt 11:28**
I **a** setting before you today. **Dt 11:32**
which I **a** commanding you today, **Dt 13:18**
which I **a** commanding you today. **Dt 15:5**
therefore I **a** commanding you to do **Dt 24:18**
therefore I **a** commanding you to do **Dt 24:22**
as I **a** commanding you today, **Dt 27:4**
know that I **a** the LORD your God. **Dt 29:6**
"Now not with you alone **a** I **Dt 29:14**
"I **a** a hundred and twenty years **Dt 31:2**
I **a** no longer able to come and go, **Dt 31:2**
I **a** still alive with you today, **Dt 31:27**
'See now that I, I **a** He, **Dt 32:39**
with which I **a** warning you today, **Dt 32:46**
which I **a** giving to the sons of **Dt 32:49**
I **a** giving the sons of Israel." **Dt 32:52**
the land which I **a** giving to them, **Jos 1:2**
I **a** eighty-five years old today. **Jos 14:10**
"I **a** still as strong today as I **Jos 14:11**
since I **a** a numerous people whom **Jos 17:14**
"I **a** old, advanced in years. **Jos 23:2** 2204
today I **a** going the way of all the **Jos 23:14**
water to drink, for I **a** thirsty." **Jg 4:19**
"I **a** the LORD your God; **Jg 6:10**
and I **a** the youngest in my **Jg 6:15**
I **a** pursuing Zebah and Zalmunna, **Jg 8:5**
I **a** your bone and your flesh." **Jg 9:2**
to the woman?" And he said, "I **a**." **Jg 13:11**
If I **a** shaved, then my strength **Jg 16:17**
"I **a** a Levite from Bethlehem in **Jg 17:9**
and I **a** going to stay wherever I **Jg 17:9**
of Ephraim, *for* I **a** from there, **Jg 19:18**
But I **a** *now* going to my house, and **Jg 19:18**
for I **a** too old to have a husband. **Ru 1:12** 2204
of me, since I **a** a foreigner?" **Ru 2:10**
though I **a** not like one of your **Ru 2:13** 1961
"I **a** Ruth your maid. **Ru 3:9**
it is true I **a** a close relative; **Ru 3:12**
redeem *it,* and I **a** after you.' " **Ru 4:4**
A I not better to you than ten **1Sa 1:8**
I **a** a woman oppressed in spirit; **1Sa 1:15**
I **a** the woman who stood here **1Sa 1:26**
Samuel; and he said, "Here I **a**." **1Sa 3:4**
"Here I **a**, for you called me." **1Sa 3:5**
"Here I **a**, for you called me." **1Sa 3:6**
"Here I **a**, for you called me." **1Sa 3:8**
I **a** about to do a thing in Israel **1Sa 3:11**
"For I have told him that I **a** **1Sa 3:13**
my son." And he said, "Here I **a**." **1Sa 3:16**
"I **a** the one who came from the **1Sa 4:16**
"I **a** the seer. Go up before me **1Sa 9:19**
"**A** I not a Benjamite, of the **1Sa 9:21**
before you, but I **a** old and gray, **1Sa 12:2** 2204
"Here I **a**; bear witness against me **1Sa 12:3**
and here I **a** with you according to **1Sa 14:7**
Here I **a**, I must die!" **1Sa 14:43**
A I not the Philistine and you **1Sa 17:8**
"**A** I a dog, that you come to me **1Sa 17:43**
"*I* **a** the son of your servant **1Sa 17:58**
"Who **a** I, and what is my life *or* **1Sa 18:18**
since I **a** a poor man and lightly **1Sa 18:23** 7326
"If I **a** still alive, will you **1Sa 20:14**
arrows which I **a** about to shoot." **1Sa 20:36**
the matter on which I **a** sending you **1Sa 21:2**
"Here I **a**, my lord." **1Sa 22:12**
I **a** told that he is very cunning. **1Sa 23:22**
I **a** about to give your enemy into **1Sa 24:4**
behold, I **a** coming after you." **1Sa 25:19**
"I **a** greatly distressed; **1Sa 28:15**
"I **a** a young man of Egypt, a **1Sa 30:13**
called to me. And I said, 'Here I **a**.' **2Sa 1:7**
'I **a** an Amalekite.' **2Sa 1:8**
"I **a** the son of an alien, an **2Sa 1:13**
"I **a** distressed for you, my **2Sa 1:26**
"**A** I a dog's head that belongs to **2Sa 3:8**
"I **a** weak today, though **2Sa 3:39**
"Who **a** I, O Lord GOD, and what is **2Sa 7:18**
"*I* **a** your servant." **2Sa 9:2**
told David, and said, "I **a** pregnant." **2Sa 11:5** 2029
"I **a** in love with Tamar, the **2Sa 13:4**
"Truly I **a** a widow, for my **2Sa 14:5**
me that I **a** about to ask you." **2Sa 14:18**
delight in you,' behold, here I **a**, **2Sa 15:26**
I **a** going to wait at the fords of **2Sa 15:28**
that I **a** king over Israel today?" **2Sa 19:22**
"I **a** now eighty years old. **2Sa 19:35**
you Joab?" And he answered, "I **a**." **2Sa 20:17**
And he answered, "I **a** listening." **2Sa 20:17**
"I **a** of those who are peaceable **2Sa 20:19**
And I **a** saved from my enemies. **2Sa 22:4**
"I **a** offering you three things; **2Sa 24:12**
"I **a** in great distress. **2Sa 24:14**
"I **a** going the way of all the **1Ki 2:2**
Now I **a** making one request of you; **1Ki 2:16**
"I **a** making one small request of **1Ki 2:20**
David, yet I **a** but a little child; **1Ki 3:7**
from Judah?" And he said, "I **a**." **1Ki 13:14**
"I also **a** a prophet like you, and **1Ki 13:18**
For I **a** sent to you *with* a harsh **1Ki 14:6**
I **a** bringing calamity on the house **1Ki 14:10**
I **a** gathering a few sticks that I **1Ki 17:12**
the widow with whom I **a** staying, **1Ki 17:20**
a left a prophet of the LORD, **1Ki 18:22**
Israel and that I **a** Your servant **1Ki 18:36**
I **a** not better than my fathers." **1Ki 19:4**

And I alone **a** left; **1Ki 19:10**
And I alone **a** left; **1Ki 19:14**
I **a** yours, and all that I have." **1Ki 20:4**
shall know that I **a** the LORD.' " **1Ki 20:13**
shall know that I **a** the LORD.' " **1Ki 20:28**
"I **a** as you are, my people as **1Ki 22:4**
for I **a** severely wounded." **1Ki 22:34** 2470a
"If I **a** a man of God, let fire **2Ki 1:10**
"If I **a** a man of God, let fire **2Ki 1:12**
you before I **a** taken from you." **2Ki 2:9**
see me when I **a** taken from you, **2Ki 2:10**
I **a** as you are, my people as your **2Ki 3:7**
"**A** I God, to kill and to make **2Ki 5:7**
"I **a** your servant and your son; **2Ki 16:7**
I **a** bringing *such* calamity on **2Ki 21:12**
I **a** dwelling in a house of cedar, **1Ch 17:1**
"Who **a** I, O LORD God, and what is **1Ch 17:16**
"I **a** in great distress; **1Ch 21:13**
I **a** the one who has sinned and **1Ch 21:17**
"But who **a** I and who are my **1Ch 29:14**
I **a** about to build a house for the **2Ch 2:4**
I **a** about to build *will be* great, **2Ch 2:5**
So who **a** I, that I should build a **2Ch 2:6**
for the house which I **a** about to **2Ch 2:9**
"Now I **a** sending Huram-abi, a **2Ch 2:13**
"I **a** as you are, and my people as **2Ch 18:3**
for I **a** severely wounded." **2Ch 18:33** 2470a
I **a** bringing evil on this place **2Ch 34:24**
I **a** not *coming* against you **2Ch 35:21**
the house with which I **a** at war, **2Ch 35:21**
me away, for I **a** badly wounded." **2Ch 35:23**
I **a** ashamed and embarrassed to **Ezr 9:6**
which I **a** praying before You now, **Ne 1:6**
"I **a** doing a great work and I **Ne 6:3**
I **a** invited by her with the king. **Es 5:12**
and I **a** pleasing in his sight, **Es 8:5**
"I **a** not at ease, nor am I quiet, **Jb 3:26**
"I am not at ease, nor **a** I quiet, **Jb 3:26**
am I quiet, And I **a** not at rest, **Jb 3:26**
So I **a** allotted months of vanity, **Jb 7:3**
And I **a** continually tossing until **Jb 7:4**
"**A** I the sea, or the sea monster, **Jb 7:12**
So that I **a** a burden to myself? **Jb 7:20** 1961
"Though I **a** righteous, my mouth **Jb 9:20**
Though I **a** guiltless, He will **Jb 9:20**
"I **a** guiltless; I do not take notice **Jb 9:21**
I **a** afraid of all my pains, I know **Jb 9:28**
"I **a** accounted wicked, Why then **Jb 9:29**
man as I **a** that I may answer Him, **Jb 9:32**
But I **a** not like that in myself. **Jb 9:35**
knowledge I **a** indeed not guilty, **Jb 10:7**
'If I **a** wicked, woe to me! **Jb 10:15**
And if I **a** righteous, I dare not **Jb 10:15**
I **a** sated with disgrace **Jb 10:15**
And I **a** innocent in your eyes.' **Jb 11:4** 1961
I **a** not inferior to you. **Jb 12:3**
"I **a** a joke to my friends, **Jb 12:4** 1961
I **a** not inferior to you. **Jb 13:2**
I **a** decaying like a rotten thing, **Jb 13:28**
And I **a** one at whom men spit. **Jb 17:6** 1961
down on every side, and I **a** gone; **Jb 19:10**
I **a** a foreigner in their sight. **Jb 19:15** 1961
I **a** loathsome to my own brothers. **Jb 19:17**
when I remember, I **a** disturbed, **Jb 21:6**
I consider, I **a** terrified of Him. **Jb 23:15**
I **a** not silenced by the darkness, **Jb 23:17**
"I **a** seething within and cannot **Jb 30:27**
"I **a** young in years and you are **Jb 32:6**
"For I **a** full of words; **Jb 32:18**
'I **a** pure, without transgression; **Jb 33:9**
I **a** innocent and there is no guilt **Jb 33:9**
'I **a** righteous, But God has taken **Jb 34:5**
though I **a** without transgression.' **Jb 36:6**
"Behold, I **a** insignificant; **Jb 40:4**
for I **a** pining away; Heal me, **Ps 6:2**
I **a** weary with my sighing; **Ps 6:6**
rejoice when I **a** shaken. **Ps 13:4**
And I **a** saved from my enemies. **Ps 18:3**
But I **a** a worm and not a man, A **Ps 22:6**
I **a** poured out like water, And all **Ps 22:14**
me, For I **a** lonely and afflicted. **Ps 25:16**
trusts in Him, and I **a** helped; **Ps 28:7**
me, O LORD, for I **a** in distress; **Ps 31:9**
I **a** forgotten as a dead man, out **Ps 31:12**
of mind; I **a** like a broken vessel. **Ps 31:12** 1961
"I **a** cut off from before Your **Ps 31:22**
"I **a** your salvation." **Ps 35:3**
have been young and now I **a** old **Ps 37:25**
I **a** bent over and greatly bowed **Ps 38:6**
I **a** benumbed and badly crushed; **Ps 38:8**
And *I* **a** like a mute man who does **Ps 38:13**
I **a** like a man who does not hear, **Ps 38:14**
For I **a** ready to fall, And my **Ps 38:17**
I **a** full of anxiety because of my **Ps 38:18**
Let me know how transient I **a**. **Ps 39:4**
of Your hand I **a** perishing. **Ps 39:10**
For I **a** a stranger with You, A **Ps 39:12**
Before I depart and **a** no more." **Ps 39:13**
me, so that I **a** not able to see; **Ps 40:12**
Since I **a** afflicted and needy, Let **Ps 40:17**
striving and know that I **a** God; **Ps 46:10**
I **a** God, your God. **Ps 50:7**
I **a** like a green olive tree in the **Ps 52:8**
I **a** restless in my complaint and **Ps 55:2**
complaint and **a** surely distracted, **Ps 55:2**
When I **a** afraid, I will put my **Ps 56:3**
I **a** weary with my crying; **Ps 69:3**
And I **a** the song of the drunkards. **Ps 69:12**
Your servant, For I **a** in distress; **Ps 69:17**

broken my heart and I a so sick. Ps 69:20
But I a afflicted and in pain; Ps 69:29
But I a afflicted and needy; Ps 70:5
And even when *I* a old and gray, Ps 71:18
I a continually with You; Ps 73:23
remember God, then I a disturbed; Ps 77:3
I a so troubled that I cannot Ps 77:4
"I, the LORD, a your God, Who Ps 81:10
For I a afflicted and needy. Ps 86:1
my soul, for I a a godly man; Ps 86:2
I a reckoned among those who go Ps 88:4
I a shut up and cannot go out. Ps 88:8
I suffer Your terrors; I a overcome. Ps 88:15
But I a *in* prayer. Ps 109:4
For I a afflicted and needy, And Ps 109:22
I a passing like a shadow when it Ps 109:23
I a shaken off like the locust. Ps 109:23
"I a greatly afflicted." Ps 116:10
O LORD, surely I a Your servant, Ps 116:16
I am Your servant, I a Your servant, Ps 116:16
I a a stranger in the earth; Ps 119:19
I a a companion of all those who Ps 119:63
I a Yours, save me; Ps 119:94
I a exceedingly afflicted; Ps 119:107
And I a afraid of Your judgments. Ps 119:120
I a Your servant; Ps 119:125
I a small and despised, *Yet* I do Ps 119:141
I a *for* peace, but when I speak, Ps 120:7
for I a fearfully and wonderfully Ps 139:14
When I awake, I a still with You. Ps 139:18
my cry, For I a brought very low; Ps 142:6
For I a Your servant. Ps 143:12
I a understanding, power is mine. Pr 8:14
my heart, I a pure from my sin"? Pr 20:9
I a more stupid than any man, Pr 30:2
"And for whom a I laboring and Ec 4:8
which I a still seeking but have Ec 7:28
"I a black but lovely, O SS 1:5
stare at me because I a swarthy, SS 1:6
"I a the rose of Sharon, The lily SS 2:1
with apples, Because I a lovesick. SS 2:5
"My beloved is mine, and I a his; SS 2:16
For I a lovesick." SS 5:8
"I a my beloved's and my beloved SS 6:3
"I a my beloved's, And his desire SS 7:10
I a weary of bearing *them*. Is 1:14
I a going to do to My vineyard: Is 5:5
"Woe is me, for I a ruined! Is 6:5
Because I a a man of unclean lips, Is 6:5
Then I said, "Here a I. Send me!" Is 6:8
I a going to stir up the Medes Is 13:17
"I a a son of the wise, a son of Is 19:11
I a so bewildered I cannot hear, Is 21:3
And I a stationed every night at Is 21:8
"I, the LORD, a its keeper; Is 27:3
I a laying in Zion a stone, Is 28:16
And no resident will say, "I a sick"; Is 33:24
I a to enter the gates of Sheol; Is 38:10
I a to be deprived of the rest of Is 38:10
O Lord, I a oppressed, be my Is 38:14
"I, the LORD, a the first, and Is 41:4
the first, and with the last. I a He.' Is 41:4
'Do not fear, for I a with you; Is 41:10
look about you, for I a your God. Is 41:10
"For I a the LORD your God, who Is 41:13
"I a the LORD, I have called you Is 42:6
"I a the LORD, that is My name; Is 42:8
"For I a the LORD your God, The Is 43:3
"Do not fear, for I a with you; Is 43:5
Me And understand that I a He. Is 43:10
"I, even I, a the LORD, Is 43:11
declares the LORD, "And I a God. Is 43:12
"Even from eternity I a He, Is 43:13
"I a the LORD, your Holy One, The Is 43:15
a the one who wipes out your Is 43:25
'This one will say, 'I a the LORD's'; Is 44:5
'I a the first and I am the last, Is 44:6
'I am the first and I a the last, Is 44:6
I a warm, I have seen the fire." Is 44:16
LORD, a the maker of all things, Is 44:24
"I a the LORD, and there is no Is 45:5
I a the LORD, and there is no Is 45:6
I a the LORD who does all these. Is 45:7
"I a the LORD, and there is none Is 45:18
For I a God, and there is no other. Is 45:22
things long past, For I a God, Is 46:9
I a God, and there is no one Is 46:9
'I a, and there is no one besides Is 47:8
'I a, and there is no one besides Is 47:10
I a He, I am the first, I am also Is 48:12
I am He, I a the first, I am also Is 48:12
I am the first, I a also the last. Is 48:12
"I a the LORD your God, who Is 48:17
I a honored in the sight of the LORD, Is 49:5
of my children And a barren, Is 49:21
you will know that I a the LORD; Is 49:23
that I, the LORD, a your Savior And Is 49:26
Me, Therefore, I a not disgraced; Is 50:7
"I, even I, a He who comforts you. Is 51:12
"For I a the LORD your God, who Is 51:15
day I a the one who is speaking, Is 52:6
one who is speaking, 'Here I a.'" Is 52:6
"Behold, I a a dry tree." Is 56:3
will cry, and He will say, 'Here I a.' Is 58:9
that I, the LORD, a your Savior And Is 60:16
'Here a I, here am I,' To a nation Is 65:1
'Here am I, here a I,' To a nation Is 65:1
near me, For I a holier than you!' Is 65:5
to speak, Because I a a youth." Jer 1:6

"Do not say, 'I a a youth,' Jer 1:7
For I a with you to deliver you," Jer 1:8
For I a watching over My word to Jer 1:12
I a calling all the families of Jer 1:15
For I a with you to deliver you," Jer 1:19
'I a not defiled, I have not gone Jer 2:23
said, 'I a innocent; Surely His anger Jer 2:35
For I a gracious,' declares the Jer 3:12
'For I a a master to you, And I Jer 3:14
I a bringing evil from the north, Jer 4:6
My soul, my soul! I a in anguish! Jer 4:19
I a making My words in your mouth Jer 5:14
I a bringing a nation against you Jer 5:15
I a full of the wrath of the LORD; Jer 6:11
I a weary with holding *it* in. Jer 6:11
I a bringing disaster on this Jer 6:19
I a laying stumbling blocks before Jer 6:21
I a sending serpents against you, Jer 8:17
daughter of my people I a broken; Jer 8:21
that I a the LORD who exercises Jer 9:24
I a slinging out the inhabitants Jer 10:18
"Behold I a bringing disaster on Jer 11:11
"Behold, I a about to punish them! Jer 11:22
"Behold I a about to uproot them Jer 12:14
"Behold I a about to fill all the Jer 13:13
I a not going to listen to their Jer 14:12
I a not going to accept them. Jer 14:12
Rather I a going to make an end of Jer 14:12
I a tired of relenting! Jer 15:6
For I a with you to save you And Jer 15:20
I a going to eliminate from this Jer 16:9
I a going to send for many Jer 16:16
I a going to make them know—This Jer 16:21
I a fashioning calamity against Jer 18:11
"Behold I a about to bring a Jer 19:3
I a about to bring on this city Jer 19:15
I a going to make you a terror to Jer 20:4
And I a weary of holding *it* in, Jer 20:9
I a about to turn back the weapons Jer 21:4
"Behold, I a against you, O Jer 21:13
I a about to attend to you for the Jer 23:2
I a going to feed them wormwood Jer 23:15
"A I a God who is near," Jer 23:23
I a against the prophets," Jer 23:30
I a against the prophets," Jer 23:31
I a against those who have Jer 23:32
to know Me, for I a the LORD; Jer 24:7
I a beginning to work calamity in Jer 25:29
for I a summoning a sword against Jer 25:29
may repent of the calamity which I a Jer 26:3
for me, behold, I a in your hands; Jer 26:14
'Within two years I a going to Jer 28:3
'I a also going to bring back to Jer 28:4
"Yet hear now this word which I a Jer 28:7
I a about to remove you from the Jer 28:16
I a sending upon them the sword, Jer 29:17
and I a He who knows and am a Jer 29:23
He who knows and a a witness," Jer 29:23
I a about to punish Shemaiah the Jer 29:32
I a about to do to My people," Jer 29:32
'For I a with you,' declares the Jer 30:11
I a bringing them from the north Jer 31:8
For I a a father to Israel, And Jer 31:9 1961
I a about to give this city into Jer 32:3
"Behold, I a the LORD, the God of Jer 32:27
I a about to give this city into Jer 32:28
so I a going to bring on them all Jer 32:42
the good that I a promising them. Jer 32:42
I a giving this city into the hand Jer 34:2
I a proclaiming a release to you,' Jer 34:17
'Behold, I a going to command,' Jer 34:22
I a bringing on Judah and on all Jer 35:17
Baruch, saying, "I a restricted; Jer 36:5
I a not going over to the Jer 37:14
"I a going to ask you something; Jer 38:14
LORD in what I a saying to you, Jer 38:20
I a about to bring My words on Jer 39:16
I a freeing you today from the Jer 40:4
I a going to stay at Mizpah to Jer 40:10
I a going to pray to the LORD your Jer 42:4
'for I a with you to save you and Jer 42:11
I a going to bring on them. Jer 42:17
I a going to send and get Jer 43:10
and I a going to set his throne Jer 43:10
I a going to set My face against Jer 44:11
I a watching over them for harm Jer 44:27
'that I a going to punish you in Jer 44:29
I a going to give over Pharaoh Jer 44:30
I a weary with my groaning and Jer 45:3
have built I a about to tear down, Jer 45:4
have planted I a about to uproot, Jer 45:4
I a going to bring disaster on all Jer 45:5
I a going to punish Amon of Jer 46:25
I a going to save you from afar, Jer 46:27
"For I a with you. Jer 46:28
I a going to bring terror upon Jer 49:5
I a going to break the bow of Jer 49:35
I a going to arouse and bring up Jer 50:9
I a going to punish the king of Jer 50:18
"Behold, I a against you, O Jer 50:31
I a going to arouse against Jer 51:1
"Behold, I a against you, O Jer 51:25
I a going to plead your case And Jer 51:36
that I a going to bring upon her; Jer 51:64
and look, For I a despised." La 1:11 1961
whom I a not able to stand. La 1:14
"See, O LORD, for I a in distress; La 1:20
I a the man who has seen La 3:1
over my head; I said, "I a cut off!" La 3:54

I a their mocking song. La 3:63
I a sending you to the sons of Ezk 2:3
"I a sending you to them who Ezk 2:4
to what I a speaking to you; Ezk 2:8
and eat what I a giving you." Ezk 2:8
scroll which I a giving you." Ezk 3:3
I a going to break the staff of Ezk 4:16
'Behold, I, even I, a against you, Ezk 5:8
a going to bring a sword on you, Ezk 6:3
you will know that I a the LORD. Ezk 6:7
they will know that I a the LORD; Ezk 6:10
you will know that I a the LORD, Ezk 6:13
know that I a the LORD. Ezk 6:14
you will know that I a the LORD!' Ezk 7:4
will know that I a the LORD.'" Ezk 7:27
you shall know that I a the LORD. Ezk 11:10
you will know that I a the LORD; Ezk 11:12
"I a a sign to you. Ezk 12:11
"So they will know that I a the LORD Ezk 12:15
and may know that I a the LORD." Ezk 12:16
know that I a the LORD. Ezk 12:20
behold, I a against you," Ezk 13:8
may know that I a the Lord GOD. Ezk 13:9
you will know that I a the LORD. Ezk 13:14
I a against your *magic* bands by Ezk 13:20
you will know that I a the LORD. Ezk 13:21
you will know that I a the LORD." Ezk 13:23
you will know that I a the LORD. Ezk 14:8
you will know that I a the LORD, Ezk 15:7
you shall know that I a the LORD, Ezk 16:62
field will know that I a the LORD; Ezk 17:24
I a the LORD; I have spoken, and I Ezk 17:24
saying, I a the LORD your God, Ezk 20:5
I a the LORD your God.' Ezk 20:7
I a the LORD who sanctifies them. Ezk 20:12
'I a the LORD your God; Ezk 20:19
know that I a the LORD your God.' Ezk 20:20
might know that I a the LORD."' Ezk 20:26
you will know that I a the LORD. Ezk 20:38
you will know that I a the LORD, Ezk 20:42
you will know that I a the LORD Ezk 20:44
I a about to kindle a fire in you, Ezk 20:47
"Behold, I a against you; Ezk 21:3
know that I a the LORD. Ezk 22:16
I a going to gather you into the Ezk 22:19
and I a profaned among them. Ezk 22:26
know that I a the Lord GOD.'" Ezk 23:49
I a about to take from you the Ezk 24:16
I a about to profane My sanctuary, Ezk 24:21
know that I a the Lord GOD.'" Ezk 24:24
will know that I a the LORD.'" Ezk 24:27
I a going to give you to the sons Ezk 25:4
you will know that I a the LORD. Ezk 25:5
you will know that I a the LORD." Ezk 25:7
I a going to deprive the flank of Ezk 25:9
will know that I a the LORD." Ezk 25:11
they will know that I a the LORD Ezk 25:17
'Behold, I a against you, O Tyre, Ezk 26:3
will know that I a the LORD.'" Ezk 26:6
'I a perfect in beauty.' Ezk 27:3
'I a a god, I sit in the seat of Ezk 28:2
'Will you still say, "I a a god," Ezk 28:9
"Behold, I a against you, O Ezk 28:22
they will know that I a the LORD when Ezk 28:22
they will know that I a the LORD. Ezk 28:23
will know that I a the Lord GOD." Ezk 28:24
I a the LORD their God. Ezk 28:26
"Behold, I a against you, Ezk 29:3
Egypt will know that I a the LORD, Ezk 29:6
they will know that I a the LORD. Ezk 29:9
I a against you and against your Ezk 29:10
know that I a the Lord GOD. Ezk 29:16
will know that I a the LORD." Ezk 29:21
they will know that I a the LORD, Ezk 30:8
know that I a the LORD. Ezk 30:19
I a against Pharaoh king of Egypt Ezk 30:22
they will know that I a the LORD, Ezk 30:25
will know that I a the LORD.'" Ezk 30:26
they shall know that I a the LORD. Ezk 32:15
they will know that I a the LORD, Ezk 33:29
"Behold, I a against the Ezk 34:10
they will know that I a the LORD, Ezk 34:27
the LORD their God, a with them, Ezk 34:30
you are men, and I a your God," Ezk 34:31
"Behold, I a against you, Mount Ezk 35:3
you will know that I a the LORD. Ezk 35:4
you will know that I a the LORD. Ezk 35:9
will know that I a the LORD." Ezk 35:15
'For, behold, I a for you, and I Ezk 36:9
you will know that I a the LORD. Ezk 36:11
of Israel, that I a about to act, Ezk 36:22
will know that I a the LORD," Ezk 36:23
a not doing *this* for your sake," Ezk 36:32
know that I a the LORD. Ezk 36:38
will know that I a the LORD.'" Ezk 37:6
you will know that I a the LORD, Ezk 37:13
nations will know that I a the LORD Ezk 37:28
"Behold, I a against you, O Gog, Ezk 38:3
that the nations may know Me when I a Ezk 38:16
will know that I a the LORD." Ezk 38:23
"Behold, I a against you, O Gog, Ezk 39:1
they will know that I a the LORD. Ezk 39:6
will know that I a the LORD, Ezk 39:7
I a going to sacrifice for you, Ezk 39:17
Israel will know that I a the LORD Ezk 39:22
they will know that I a the LORD Ezk 39:28
to all that I a going to show you; Ezk 40:4
them, *that* I a their inheritance; Ezk 44:28
in Israel—I a their possession. Ezk 44:28

"I **a** afraid of my lord the king,	Da 1:10	
I **a** going to let you know what	Da 8:19	
understand the words that I **a**	Da 10:11	
so I **a** going forth, and behold,	Da 10:20	
My people and I **a** not your God."	Hos 1:9	
my wife, and I **a** not her husband;	Hos 2:2	
I **a** like a moth to Ephraim And	Hos 5:12	
For I **a** God and not man, the Holy	Hos 11:9	
I **a** like a luxuriant cypress;	Hos 14:8	
I **a** going to send you grain,	Jl 2:19	
that I **a** in the midst of Israel,	Jl 2:27	
And that I **a** the LORD your God,	Jl 2:27	
I **a** going to arouse them from the	Jl 3:7	
"I **a** a mighty man."	Jl 3:10	
know that I **a** the LORD your God,	Jl 3:17	
I **a** weighted down beneath you As a	Am 2:13	
I **a** going to raise up a nation	Am 6:14	
"Behold I **a** about to put a plumb	Am 7:8	
"I **a** not a prophet, nor am I the	Am 7:14	
nor **a** I the son of a prophet;	Am 7:14	
for I **a** a herdsman and a grower of	Am 7:14	
"For behold, I **a** commanding, And	Am 9:9	
"I **a** a Hebrew, and I fear the	Jon 1:9	
which I **a** going to tell you."	Jon 3:2	
I **a** planning against this family a	Mi 2:3	
On the other hand I **a** filled with	Mi 3:8	
For I **a** Like the fruit pickers,	Mi 7:1	1961
"Behold, I **a** against you,"	Na 2:13	
"Behold, I **a** against you,"	Na 3:5	
Because *I* **a** doing something in	Hab 1:5	
I **a** raising up the Chaldeans,	Hab 1:6	
how I may reply when I **a** reproved.	Hab 2:1	
"I **a**, and there is no one besides	Zph 2:15	
I **a** going to deal at that time	Zph 3:19	
"'I **a** with you,' declares the	Hg 1:13	
for I **a** with you,' declares the LORD	Hg 2:4	
I **a** going to shake the heavens and	Hg 2:6	
'I **a** going to shake the heavens	Hg 2:21	
"I **a** exceedingly jealous for	Zch 1:14	
"But I **a** very angry with the	Zch 1:15	
for behold I **a** coming and I will	Zch 2:10	
I **a** going to bring in My servant	Zch 3:8	
'I **a** exceedingly jealous for Zion,	Zch 8:2	
great wrath I **a** jealous for her.'	Zch 8:2	
I **a** going to save My people from	Zch 8:7	
This very day I **a** declaring that I	Zch 9:12	
them, For I **a** the LORD their God and	Zch 10:6	
I **a** going to raise up a shepherd	Zch 11:16	
I **a** going to make Jerusalem a cup	Zch 12:2	
'I **a** not a prophet;	Zch 13:5	
I **a** a tiller of the ground, for a	Zch 13:5	
Then if I **a** a father, where is My	Mal 1:6	
And if I **a** a master, where is My	Mal 1:6	
I **a** not pleased with you,"	Mal 1:10	
the Lord, for I **a** a great King,"	Mal 1:14	
I **a** going to rebuke your	Mal 2:3	
I **a** going to send My messenger,	Mal 3:1	
on the day which I **a** preparing,"	Mal 4:3	
I **a** going to send you Elijah the	Mal 4:5	
I **a** not fit to remove His sandals;	Mt 3:11	1510
Son, in whom I **a** well-pleased."	Mt 3:17	2106
saying, "I **a** willing; be cleansed."	Mt 8:3	2309
I **a** not worthy for You to come	Mt 8:8	1510
I also **a** a man under authority,	Mt 8:9	1510
that I **a** able to do this?"	Mt 9:28	1410
I **a** gentle and humble in heart,	Mt 11:29	1510
"But who do you say that I **a**?"	Mt 16:15	1510
Son, with whom I **a** well-pleased;	Mt 17:5	2106
I **a** there in their midst."	Mt 18:20	1510
what **a** I still lacking?"	Mt 19:20	5302
'Friend, I **a** doing you no wrong;	Mt 20:13	
eye envious because I **a** generous?'	Mt 20:15	1510
the cup that I **a** about to drink?"	Mt 20:22	3195
'I **A** THE GOD OF ABRAHAM, AND THE	Mt 22:32	1510
I **a** sending you prophets and wise	Mt 23:34	
'I **a** the Christ,' and will mislead	Mt 24:5	1510
I **a** *to* keep the Passover at your	Mt 26:18	
'I **a** able to destroy the temple of	Mt 26:61	1410
"I **a** innocent of this Man's blood;	Mt 27:24	1510
'I **a** the Son of God.' "	Mt 27:43	1510
'After three days I **a** *to* rise	Mt 27:63	
and lo, I **a** with you always, even	Mt 28:20	1510
and I **a** not fit to stoop down and	Mk 1:7	1510
Son, in You I **a** well-pleased."	Mk 1:11	2106
"I **a** willing; be cleansed."	Mk 1:41	2309
"Who do people say that I **a**?"	Mk 8:27	1510
"But who do you say that I **a**?"	Mk 8:29	1510
baptism with which I **a** baptized?"	Mk 10:38	
baptism with which I **a** baptized.	Mk 10:39	
'I **A** THE GOD OF ABRAHAM, AND THE	Mk 12:26	
come in My name, saying, 'I **a** *He!*'	Mk 13:6	1510
"I **a**; and you shall see THE SON OF	Mk 14:62	1510
For I **a** an old man and my wife is	Lk 1:18	1510
"I **a** Gabriel, who stands in the	Lk 1:19	1510
can this be, since I **a** a virgin?"	Lk 1:34	
and I **a** not fit to untie the thong	Lk 3:16	1510
Son, in You I **a** well-pleased."	Lk 3:22	2106
from me Lord, for I **a** a sinful man,	Lk 5:8	1510
saying, "I **a** willing; be cleansed."	Lk 5:13	2309
for I **a** not worthy for You to come	Lk 7:6	1510
I also **a** a man placed under authority,	Lk 7:8	1510
do the people say that I **a**?"	Lk 9:18	1510
"But who do you say that I **a**?"	Lk 9:20	1510
I **a** until it is accomplished!	Lk 12:50	
and I **a** going to try them out;	Lk 14:19	
but I **a** dying here with hunger!	Lk 15:17	
I **a** no longer worthy to be	Lk 15:19	1510
I **a** no longer worthy to be called	Lk 15:21	1510
I **a** not strong enough to dig;	Lk 16:3	2480
I **a** ashamed to beg.	Lk 16:3	
I **a** removed from the management	Lk 16:4	
for I **a** in agony in this flame.'	Lk 16:24	3600
that I **a** not like other people:	Lk 18:11	1510
you know that I **a** an exacting man,	Lk 19:22	1510
'I **a** *He*,' and, 'The time is near.'	Lk 21:8	1510
But I **a** among you as the one who	Lk 22:27	1510
with You I **a** ready to go both to	Lk 22:33	1510
But Peter said, "Man, I **a** not!"	Lk 22:58	1510
And He said to them, "Yes, I **a**."	Lk 22:70	1510
I **a** sending forth the promise of	Lk 24:49	
"I **a** not the Christ."	Jn 1:20	1510
you Elijah?" And he said, "I **a** not."	Jn 1:21	1510
"I **a** A VOICE OF ONE CRYING IN THE	Jn 1:23	
sandal I **a** not worthy to untie."	Jn 1:27	1510
'I **a** not the Christ,' but,	Jn 3:28	1510
since I **a** a Samaritan woman?"	Jn 4:9	1510
"I who speak to you **a** *He*."	Jn 4:26	1510
stirred up, but while I **a** coming,	Jn 5:7	
now, and I Myself **a** working."	Jn 5:17	
"I **a** the bread of life;	Jn 6:35	1510
"I **a** the bread that came down out	Jn 6:41	1510
"I **a** the bread of life.	Jn 6:48	1510
"I **a** the living bread that came	Jn 6:51	1510
know Me and know where I **a** from;	Jn 7:28	1510
because I **a** from Him, and He sent	Jn 7:29	1510
little while longer I **a** with you,	Jn 7:33	1510
and where I **a**, you cannot come."	Jn 7:34	1510
and where I **a**, you cannot come'?"	Jn 7:36	1510
"I **a** the Light of the world;	Jn 8:12	1510
I came from and where I **a** going;	Jn 8:14	
I come from or where I **a** going.	Jn 8:14	
I **a** not judging anyone.	Jn 8:15	
for I **a** not alone *in it*, but I and	Jn 8:16	1510
"I **a** He who testifies about	Jn 8:18	1510
where I **a** going, you cannot come."	Jn 8:21	
'Where I **a** going, you cannot come'?"	Jn 8:22	
are from below, I **a** from above;	Jn 8:23	1510
this world, I **a** not of this world.	Jn 8:23	1510
unless you believe that I **a** *He*	Jn 8:24	1510
then you will know that I **a** *He*,	Jn 8:28	1510
not understand what I **a** saying?	Jn 8:43	
before Abraham was born, I **a**."	Jn 8:58	1510
"While I **a** in the world, I am the	Jn 9:5	1510
I **a** the Light of the world."	Jn 9:5	1510
He kept saying, "I **a** the one."	Jn 9:9	1510
to you, I **a** the door of the sheep.	Jn 10:7	1510
"I **a** the door; if anyone enters	Jn 10:9	1510
"I **a** the good shepherd;	Jn 10:11	1510
"I **a** the good shepherd,	Jn 10:14	1510
'I **a** the Son of God'?	Jn 10:36	1510
and I **a** glad for your sakes that I	Jn 11:15	5463
"I **a** the resurrection and the life;	Jn 11:25	1510
and where I **a**, there My	Jn 12:26	1510
"And I, if I **a** lifted up from	Jn 12:32	
and you are right, for *so* I **a**.	Jn 13:13	1510
"From now on I **a** telling you	Jn 13:19	
you may believe that I **a** *He*.	Jn 13:19	1510
I **a** with you a little while longer.	Jn 13:33	1510
'Where I **a** going, you cannot come.'	Jn 13:33	
that where I **a**, *there* you may be	Jn 14:3	1510
know the way where I **a** going."	Jn 14:4	
"I **a** the way, and the truth, and	Jn 14:6	1510
believe that I **a** in the Father,	Jn 14:10	
"Believe Me that I **a** in the Father and	Jn 14:11	
will know that I **a** in My Father,	Jn 14:20	
"I **a** the true vine, and My Father	Jn 15:1	1510
"I **a** the vine, you are the	Jn 15:5	1510
now I **a** going to Him who sent Me;	Jn 16:5	
I **a** leaving the world again and	Jn 16:28	
and *yet* I **a** not alone, because the	Jn 16:32	1510
"I **a** no longer in the world;	Jn 17:11	1510
even as I **a** not of the world.	Jn 17:14	1510
even as I **a** not of the world.	Jn 17:16	1510
given Me, be with Me where I **a**,	Jn 17:24	1510
"I **a** *He*." And Judas also, who was	Jn 18:5	1510
"I **a** *He*," they drew back and fell	Jn 18:6	1510
"I told you that I **a** *He*;	Jn 18:8	1510
are you?" He said, "I **a** not."	Jn 18:17	1510
He denied *it*, and said, "I **a** not."	Jn 18:25	1510
"I **a** not a Jew, am I?	Jn 18:35	1510
"I am not a Jew, **a** I?	Jn 18:35	
"You say *correctly* that I **a** a king.	Jn 18:37	1510
I **a** bringing Him out to you so	Jn 19:4	
'I **a** King of the Jews.' "	Jn 19:21	1510
fulfill the Scripture, said, "I **a** thirsty."	Jn 19:28	1372
"I **a** going fishing."	Jn 21:3	
'I **A** THE GOD OF YOUR FATHERS, THE	Ac 7:32	
"I **a** Jesus whom you are	Ac 9:5	1510
"Here I **a**, Lord."	Ac 9:10	
I **a** the one you are looking for;	Ac 10:21	1510
I too **a** *just* a man."	Ac 10:26	1510
'What do you suppose that I **a**?	Ac 13:25	1510
I **a** not *He*. But behold, one is coming	Ac 13:25	1510
feet I **a** not worthy to untie.'	Ac 13:25	1510
FOR I **A** ACCOMPLISHING A WORK IN	Ac 13:41	
"This Jesus whom I **a** proclaiming	Ac 17:3	
be on your own heads! I **a** clean.	Ac 18:6	
for I **a** with you, and no man will	Ac 18:10	1510
I **a** unwilling to be a judge of	Ac 18:15	1014
I **a** on my way to Jerusalem,	Ac 20:22	4198
that I **a** innocent of the blood of	Ac 20:26	1510
I **a** ready not only to be bound,	Ac 21:13	2192
"I **a** a Jew of Tarsus in Cilicia,	Ac 21:39	1510
"I **a** a Jew, born in Tarsus of	Ac 22:3	1510
'I **a** Jesus the Nazarene, whom you	Ac 22:8	1510
"Brethren, I **a** a Pharisee, a son	Ac 23:6	1510
I **a** on trial for the hope and	Ac 23:6	
I **a** on trial before you today.' "	Ac 24:21	
"I **a** standing before Caesar's	Ac 25:10	1510
"If, then, I **a** a wrongdoer and	Ac 25:11	91
of which I **a** accused by the Jews,	Ac 26:2	
that I **a** about to make my defense	Ac 26:2	3195
"And now I **a** standing trial for	Ac 26:6	
O King, I **a** being accused by Jews.	Ac 26:7	
'I **a** Jesus whom you are	Ac 26:15	1510
Gentiles, to whom I **a** sending you,	Ac 26:17	
"I **a** not out of my mind, most	Ac 26:25	3105
since I **a** persuaded that none of	Ac 26:26	
day, might become such as I **a**,	Ac 26:29	1510
for I **a** wearing this chain for the	Ac 28:20	
I **a** under obligation both to	Ro 1:14	1510
I **a** eager to preach the gospel to	Ro 1:15	
For I **a** not ashamed of the gospel,	Ro 1:16	1870
(I **a** speaking in human terms.)	Ro 3:5	
why **a** I also still being judged as	Ro 3:7	
I **a** speaking in human terms	Ro 6:19	
(for I **a** speaking to those who know	Ro 7:1	
but I **a** of flesh, sold into	Ro 7:14	1510
For what I **a** doing,	Ro 7:15	
for I **a** not practicing what I	Ro 7:15	
I **a** doing the very thing I hate.	Ro 7:15	
no longer **a** I the one doing it,	Ro 7:17	
But if I **a** doing the very thing I	Ro 7:20	
I **a** no longer the one doing it,	Ro 7:20	
Wretched man that I **a**!	Ro 7:24	
my mind **a** serving the law of God,	Ro 7:25	
I **a** convinced that neither death,	Ro 8:38	
I **a** telling the truth in Christ, I	Ro 9:1	
truth in Christ, I **a** not lying,	Ro 9:1	
For I too **a** an Israelite, a	Ro 11:1	1510
YOUR ALTARS, AND I ALONE **A** LEFT,	Ro 11:3	
But I **a** speaking to you who are	Ro 11:13	
as I **a** an apostle of Gentiles,	Ro 11:13	1510
I know and **a** convinced in the Lord	Ro 14:14	
I myself also **a** convinced that you	Ro 15:14	
I **a** going to Jerusalem serving the	Ro 15:25	
therefore I **a** rejoicing over you,	Ro 16:19	
"I **a** of Paul," and "I of Apollos,"	1Co 1:12	1510
For when one says, "I **a** of Paul,"	1Co 3:4	1510
"I **a** of Apollos,"	1Co 3:4	
I **a** conscious of nothing against	1Co 4:4	4924a
yet I **a** not by this acquitted;	1Co 4:4	
all men were even as I myself **a**.	1Co 7:7	
life, and I **a** trying to spare you.	1Co 7:28	
A I not free? Am I not an apostle?	1Co 9:1	1510
A I not an apostle?	1Co 9:1	1510
If to others I **a** not an apostle,	1Co 9:2	1510
an apostle, at least I **a** to you;	1Co 9:2	1510
I **a** not speaking these things	1Co 9:8	
according to human judgment, **a** I?	1Co 9:8	
And I **a** not writing these things	1Co 9:15	
of, for I **a** under compulsion;	1Co 9:16	1945
For though I **a** free from all *men*,	1Co 9:19	1510
why **a** I slandered concerning that	1Co 10:30	
of me, just as I also **a** of Christ.	1Co 11:1	
"Because I **a** not a hand, I am not	1Co 12:15	1510
I **a** not *a part* of the body,"	1Co 12:15	1510
"Because I **a** not an eye, I am not	1Co 12:16	1510
eye, I **a** not *a part* of the body,"	1Co 12:16	1510
but do not have love, I **a** nothing.	1Co 13:2	1510
For I **a** the least of the apostles,	1Co 15:9	1510
by the grace of God I **a** what I am,	1Co 15:10	1510
by the grace of God I am what I **a**,	1Co 15:10	1510
for I **a** going through Macedonia;	1Co 16:5	
doing the Lord's work, as I also **a**.	1Co 16:10	
I **a** filled with comfort;	2Co 7:4	
I **a** overflowing with joy in all	2Co 7:4	
I **a** not speaking *this* as a	2Co 8:8	
I who **a** meek when face to face with	2Co 10:1	
I ask that when I **a** present I	2Co 10:2	
For I **a** jealous for you with a	2Co 11:2	2206
But I **a** afraid that, as the	2Co 11:3	5399
even if I **a** unskilled in speech,	2Co 11:6	
yet I **a** not *so* in knowledge;	2Co 11:6	
But what I **a** doing I will	2Co 11:12	
What I **a** saying, I am not saying as	2Co 11:17	
I **a** not saying as the Lord	2Co 11:17	
I **a** just as bold myself.	2Co 11:21	5111
Are they Hebrews? So **a** I. Are they	2Co 11:22	
Are they Israelites? So **a** I. Are they	2Co 11:22	
descendants of Abraham? So **a** I.	2Co 11:22	
forever, knows that I **a** not lying.	2Co 11:31	
I **a** well content with weaknesses,	2Co 12:10	2106
for when I **a** weak, then I am	2Co 12:10	770
when I am weak, then I **a** strong.	2Co 12:10	1510
even though I **a** a nobody.	2Co 12:11	1510
time I **a** ready to come to you,	2Co 12:14	2192
more, **a** I to be loved less?	2Co 12:15	
crafty fellow that I **a**,	2Co 12:16	
For I **a** afraid that perhaps when I	2Co 12:20	5399
I **a** afraid that when I come again	2Co 12:21	
the third time I **a** coming to you.	2Co 13:1	
For this reason I **a** writing these	2Co 13:10	
I **a** amazed that you are so quickly	Ga 1:6	2296
For **a** I now seeking the favor of	Ga 1:10	
Or **a** I striving to please men?	Ga 1:10	
(Now in what I **a** writing to you, I	Ga 1:20	
before God that I **a** not lying.)	Ga 1:20	
What I **a** saying is this:	Ga 3:17	
become as I **a**, for I also *have*	Ga 4:12	
only when I **a** present with you.	Ga 4:18	3918b
with whom I **a** again in labor until	Ga 4:19	5605
tone, for I **a** perplexed about you.	Ga 4:20	639
why **a** I still persecuted?	Ga 5:11	
See with what large letters I **a**	Ga 6:11	
but I **a** speaking with reference to	Eph 5:32	
which I **a** an ambassador in chains;	Eph 6:20	4243

my circumstances, how I **a** doing, **Eph 6:21**
For I **a** confident of this very **Php 1:6**
knowing that I **a** appointed for the **Php 1:16**
But if *I* **a** to live *on* in **Php 1:22**
But I **a** hard-pressed from both **Php 1:23**
But even if I **a** being poured out **Php 2:17**
in whatever circumstances I **a**. **Php 4:11** *1510*
I **a** amply supplied, having **Php 4:18**
even though I **a** absent in body, **Col 2:5** *548*
I **a** with you in spirit, **Col 2:5** *1510*
among whom I **a** foremost *of all.* **1Tm 1:15** *1510*
(I **a** telling the truth, I am not lying) **1Tm 2:7**
telling the truth, I **a** not lying) **1Tm 2:7**
I **a** writing these things to you, **1Tm 3:14**
but in case I **a** delayed, *I write* **1Tm 3:15** *1019*
For I **a** mindful of the sincere **2Tm 1:3**
and I **a** sure that *it is* in you as **2Tm 1:5**
these things, but I **a** not ashamed; **2Tm 1:12** *1870*
I **a** convinced that He is able to guard **2Tm 1:12**
For I **a** already being poured out **2Tm 4:6**
I **a** such a person as Paul, **Phm 1:9** *1510*
a writing this with my own hand, **Phm 1:19**
"I A FULL OF FEAR and trembling." **Heb 12:21** *1510*
"I **a** being tempted by God"; **Jas 1:13**
"YOU SHALL BE HOLY, FOR I A HOLY." **1Pe 1:16**
as I **a** in this *earthly* dwelling, **2Pe 1:13** *1510*
Son with whom I **a** well-pleased" **2Pe 1:17** *2106*
the second letter I **a** writing to **2Pe 3:1**
I **a** stirring up your sincere mind by **2Pe 3:1**
I **a** writing these things to you **1Jn 2:1**
I **a** not writing a new commandment **1Jn 2:7**
I **a** writing a new commandment to **1Jn 2:8**
I **a** writing to you, little **1Jn 2:12**
I **a** writing to you, fathers, **1Jn 2:13**
I **a** writing to you, young men, **1Jn 2:13**
but I **a** not willing to write *them* **3Jn 1:13** *2309*
"I **a** the Alpha and the Omega," **Rv 1:8** *1510*
I **a** the first and the last, **Rv 1:17** *1510*
and behold, I **a** alive forevermore, **Rv 1:18** *1510*
or else I **a** coming to you and **Rv 2:5**
or else I **a** coming to you quickly, **Rv 2:16**
that I **a** He who searches the minds **Rv 2:23** *1510*
'I **a** coming quickly; hold fast what **Rv 3:11**
"I **a** rich, and have become **Rv 3:17** *1510*
("Behold, I **a** coming like a thief. **Rv 16:15**
'I SIT *as* A QUEEN AND I **A** **Rv 18:7** *1510*
I **a** a fellow servant of yours and **Rv 19:10** *1510*
I **a** making all things new." **Rv 21:5**
I **a** the Alpha and the Omega, the **Rv 21:6**
"And behold, I **a** coming quickly. **Rv 22:7**
a the one who heard and saw these **Rv 22:8**
I **a** a fellow servant of yours and **Rv 22:9** *1510*
"Behold, I **a** coming quickly, and **Rv 22:12**
"I **a** the Alpha and the Omega, the **Rv 22:13**
I **a** the root and the descendant of **Rv 22:16** *1510*
"Yes, I **a** coming quickly." **Rv 22:20**

AMAD
and Allammelech and **A** and Mishal; **Jos 19:26** 6008

AMAL
were Zophah, Imna, Shelesh and **A**. **1Ch 7:35** 6000

AMALEK
Eliphaz and she bore **A** to Eliphaz. **Gn 36:12** 6002
chief Korah, chief Gatam, chief **A**. **Gn 36:16** 6002
Then **A** came and fought against **Ex 17:8** 6002
us and go out, fight against **A**. **Ex 17:9** 6002
told him, and fought against **A**; **Ex 17:10** 6002
he let his hand down, **A** prevailed. **Ex 17:11** 6002
So Joshua overwhelmed **A** and his **Ex 17:13** 6002
memory of **A** from under heaven." **Ex 17:14** 6002
A from generation to generation." **Ex 17:16** 6002
"**A** is living in the land of the **Nu 13:29** 6002
And he looked at **A** and took up his **Nu 24:20** 6002
"**A** was the first of the nations, **Nu 24:20** 6002
"Remember what **A** did to you along **Dt 25:17** 6002
the memory of **A** from under heaven; **Dt 25:19** 6002
himself the sons of Ammon and **A**; **Jg 3:13** 6002
whose root is in **A** *came down,* **Jg 5:14** 6002
A *for* what he did to Israel, **1Sa 15:2** 6002
'Now go and strike **A** and utterly **1Sa 15:3** 6002
Saul came to the city of **A** and **1Sa 15:5** 6002
brought back Agag the king of **A**, **1Sa 15:20** 6002
not execute His fierce wrath on **A**, **1Sa 28:18** 6002
Ammon and the Philistines and **A**, **2Sa 8:12** 6002
Zephi, Gatam, Kenaz, Timna and **A**. **1Ch 1:36** 6002
the Philistines, and from **A**. **1Ch 18:11** 6002
Gebal and Ammon and **A**, **Ps 83:7** 6002

AMALEKITE
man of Egypt, a servant of an **A**; **1Sa 30:13** 6003
And I answered him, 'I am an **A**.' **2Sa 1:8** 6003
"I am the son of an alien, an **A**." **2Sa 1:13** 6003

AMALEKITES
all the country of the **A**, **Gn 14:7** 6003
"Now the **A** and the Canaanites **Nu 14:25** 6003
"For the **A** and the Canaanites **Nu 14:43** 6003
Then the **A** and the Canaanites who **Nu 14:45** 6003
Midianites would come up with the **A** **Jg 6:3** 6002
Then all the Midianites and the **A** **Jg 6:33** 6002
Now the Midianites and the **A** and **Jg 7:12** 6002
the **A** and the Maonites oppressed **Jg 10:12** 6002
in the hill country of the **A**. **Jg 12:15** 6003
valiantly and defeated the **A**, **1Sa 14:48** 6002
depart, go down from among the **A**, **1Sa 15:6** 6003
Kenites departed from among the **A**. **1Sa 15:6** 6002
So Saul defeated the **A**, **1Sa 15:7** 6002
Agag the king of the **A** alive, **1Sa 15:8** 6002
"They have brought them from the **A**, **1Sa 15:15** 6003
destroy the sinners, the **A**, **1Sa 15:18** 6003
and have utterly destroyed the **A**. **1Sa 15:20** 6002
me Agag, the king of the **A**." **1Sa 15:32** 6002
and the Girzites and the **A**; **1Sa 27:8** 6003
that the **A** had made a raid on the **1Sa 30:1** 6003
all that the **A** had taken, **1Sa 30:18** 6002
from the slaughter of the **A**, **2Sa 1:1** 6002
the remnant of the **A** who escaped, **1Ch 4:43** 6002

AMAM
A and Shema and Moladah, **Jos 15:26** 538

AMANA
Journey down from the summit of **A**, **SS 4:8** 549

AMARIAH
Meraioth became the father of **A**, **1Ch 6:7** 568
and **A** became the father of Ahitub, **1Ch 6:7** 568
Azariah became the father of **A**, **1Ch 6:11** 568
and **A** became the father of Ahitub, **1Ch 6:11** 568
Meraioth his son, **A** his son, **1Ch 6:52** 568
Jeriah the first, **A** the second, **1Ch 23:19** 568
Jeriah *the first,* **A** the second, **1Ch 24:23** 568
A the chief priest will be over **2Ch 19:11** 568
Miniamin, Jeshua, Shemaiah, **A** and **2Ch 31:15** 568
son of **A**, son of Azariah, son of **Ezr 7:3** 568
Shallum, **A** *and* Joseph. **Ezr 10:42** 568
Pashhur, **A**, Malchijah, **Ne 10:3** 568
son of Zechariah, the son of **A**, **Ne 11:4** 568
A, Malluch, Hattush, **Ne 12:2** 568
Ezra, Meshullam; of **A**, Jehohanan; **Ne 12:13** 568
Cushi, son of Gedaliah, son of **A**, **Zph 1:1** 568

AMASA
Absalom set **A** over the army in **2Sa 17:25** 6021
Now **A** was the son of a man whose **2Sa 17:25** 6021
Say to **A**, 'Are you not my bone and **2Sa 19:13** 6021
Then the king said to **A**, **2Sa 20:4** 6021
So **A** went to call out *the men of* **2Sa 20:5** 6021
is in Gibeon, **A** came to meet them. **2Sa 20:8** 6021
Joab said to **A**, **2Sa 20:9** 6021
And Joab took **A** by the beard with **2Sa 20:9** 6021
But **A** was not on guard against the **2Sa 20:10** 6021
But **A** lay wallowing in *his* blood **2Sa 20:12** 6021
he removed **A** from the highway into **2Sa 20:12** 6021
Ner, and to **A** the son of Jether, **1Ki 2:5** 6021
Israel, and **A** the son of Jether, **1Ki 2:32** 6021
Abigail bore **A**, **1Ch 2:17** 6021
of **A** was Jether the Ishmaelite. **1Ch 2:17** 6021
and **A** the son of Hadlai—arose **2Ch 28:12** 6021

AMASAI
of Elkanah *were* **A** and Ahimoth. **1Ch 6:25** 6022
the son of Mahath, the son of **A**, **1Ch 6:35** 6022
Then the Spirit came upon **A**, **1Ch 12:18** 6022
Shebaniah, Joshaphat, Nethanel, **A**, **1Ch 15:24** 6022
of **A** and Joel the son of Azariah, **2Ch 29:12** 6022

AMASHSAI
and **A** the son of Azarel, the son **Ne 11:13** 6023

AMASIAH
next to him **A** the son of Zichri, **2Ch 17:16** 6007

AMASSED
Solomon **a** chariots and horsemen. **2Ch 1:14** 622

AMASSES
He **a** *riches* and does not know who **Ps 39:6** 6651

AMAZED
tremble And are **a** at His rebuke. **Jb 26:11** 8539
They saw *it,* then they were **a**; **Ps 48:5** 8539
crowds were **a** at His teaching; **Mt 7:28** *1605*
The men were **a**, and said, "What **Mt 8:27** *2296*
and the crowds were **a**, *and were* **Mt 9:33** *2296*
All the crowds were **a**, **Mt 12:23** *1839*
the disciples were **a** and asked, **Mt 21:20** *2296*
And hearing *this,* they were **a**, **Mt 22:22** *2296*
so the governor was quite **a**. **Mt 27:14** *2296*
They were **a** at His teaching; **Mk 1:22** *1605*
They were all **a**, **Mk 1:27** *2284*
all **a** and were glorifying God, **Mk 2:12** *1839*
and everyone was **a**. **Mk 5:20** *2296*
entire crowd saw Him, they were **a** and **Mk 9:15** *1568*
The disciples were **a** at His words. **Mk 10:24** *2284*
and they were **a**, and those who **Mk 10:32** *2284*
And they were **a** at Him. **Mk 12:17** *1569b*
so Pilate was **a**. **Mk 15:5** *2296*
a white robe; and they were **a**. **Mk 16:5** *1568*
not be **a**; you are looking for Jesus **Mk 16:6** *1568*
And His father and mother were **a** **Lk 2:33** *2296*
And all who heard Him were **a** at **Lk 2:47** *1839*
and they were **a** at His teaching, **Lk 4:32** *1605*
They were fearful and **a**, **Lk 8:25** *2296*
Her parents were **a**; **Lk 8:56** *1839*
all **a** at the greatness of God. **Lk 9:43** *1605*
and the crowds were **a**. **Lk 11:14** *2296*
and being **a** at His answer, they **Lk 20:26** *2296*
"But also some women among us **a** us. **Lk 24:22** *1839*
"Do not be **a** that I said to you, **Jn 3:7** *2296*
and they were **a** that He had been **Jn 4:27** *2296*
They were **a** and astonished, **Ac 2:7** *1839*
why are you **a** at this, or why do you **Ac 3:12** *2296*
they were **a**, and *began* to **Ac 4:13** *2296*
taking place, he was constantly **a**. **Ac 8:13** *1839*
hearing him continued to be **a**, **Ac 9:21** *1839*
who came with Peter were **a**, **Ac 10:45** *1839*
the door, they saw him and were **a**. **Ac 12:16** *1839*
a at the teaching of the Lord. **Ac 13:12** *1605*
I am **a** that you are so quickly **Ga 1:6** *2296*
a *and followed* after the beast; **Rv 13:3** *2296*

AMAZEMENT
And **a** came upon them all, and they **Lk 4:36** *2285*
For **a** had seized him and all his **Lk 5:9** *2285*
it because of their joy and **a**, **Lk 24:41** *2296*
in **a** and great perplexity, **Ac 2:12** *1839*
and **a** at what had happened to him. **Ac 3:10** *1611*
portico of Solomon, full of **a**. **Ac 3:11** *1569a*

AMAZIAH
and **A** his son became king in his **2Ki 12:21** 558
he fought against **A** king of Judah, **2Ki 13:12** 558
A the son of Joash king of Judah **2Ki 14:1** 558
Then **A** sent messengers to Jehoash, **2Ki 14:8** 558
of Israel sent to **A** king of Judah, **2Ki 14:9** 558
But **A** would not listen. **2Ki 14:11** 558
and he and **A** king of Judah faced **2Ki 14:11** 558
Israel captured **A** king of Judah, **2Ki 14:13** 558
he fought with **A** king of Judah, **2Ki 14:15** 558
A the son of Joash king of **2Ki 14:17** 558
Now the rest of the acts of **A**, **2Ki 14:18** 558
king in the place of his father **A**. **2Ki 14:21** 558
In the fifteenth year of **A** the son **2Ki 14:23** 558
of **A** king of Judah became king. **2Ki 15:1** 558
to all that his father **A** had done. **2Ki 15:3** 558
A his son, Azariah his son, Jotham **1Ch 3:12** 558
Jamlech and Joshah the son of **A**, **1Ch 4:34** 558
son of Hashabiah, the son of **A**, **1Ch 6:45** 558
Then **A** his son became king in his **2Ch 24:27** 558
A was twenty-five years old when **2Ch 25:1** 558
A assembled Judah and appointed **2Ch 25:5** 558
A said to the man of God, **2Ch 25:9** 558
Then **A** dismissed them, the troops **2Ch 25:10** 558
Now **A** strengthened himself and **2Ch 25:11** 558
But the troops whom **A** sent back **2Ch 25:13** 558
Now after **A** came **2Ch 25:14** 558
of the LORD burned against **A**, **2Ch 25:15** 558
Then **A** king of Judah took counsel **2Ch 25:17** 558
of Israel sent to **A** king of Judah, **2Ch 25:18** 558
But **A** would not listen, for it was **2Ch 25:20** 558
and he and **A** king of Judah faced **2Ch 25:21** 558
Israel captured **A** king of Judah, **2Ch 25:23** 558
And **A**, the son of Joash king of **2Ch 25:25** 558
Now the rest of the acts of **A**, **2Ch 25:26** 558
From the time that **A** turned **2Ch 25:27** 558
king in the place of his father **A**. **2Ch 26:1** 558
to all that his father **A** had done. **2Ch 26:4** 558
Then **A**, the priest of Bethel, sent **Am 7:10** 558
Then **A** said to Amos, **Am 7:12** 558
Then Amos replied to **A**, **Am 7:14** 558

AMAZING
"Well, here is an **a** thing, **Jn 9:30** *2298*

AMBASSADOR
for which I am an **a** in chains; **Eph 6:20** *4243*

AMBASSADORS
Zoan And their **a** arrive at Hanes. **Is 30:4** 4397
The **a** of peace weep bitterly. **Is 33:7** 4397
Therefore, we are **a** for Christ, **2Co 5:20** *4243*

AMBITION
Therefore we also have as our **a**, **2Co 5:9** *5389*
proclaim Christ out of selfish **a** rather **Php 1:17** *2052*
and to make it your **a** to lead a **1Th 4:11** *5389*
and selfish **a** in your heart, **Jas 3:14** *2052*
jealousy and selfish **a** exist, **Jas 3:16** *2052*

AMBITIOUS
a and do not obey the truth, **Ro 2:8** *2052*

AMBUSH
Set an **a** for the city behind it." **Jos 8:2** 693
to **a** the city from behind it. **Jos 8:4** 693
"And you shall rise from *your* **a** **Jos 8:7** 693
and they went to the place of **a** **Jos 8:9** 3993
them in **a** between Bethel and Ai, **Jos 8:12** 693
an **a** against him behind the city. **Jos 8:14** 693
a rose quickly from their place, **Jos 8:19** 693
the *men in* **a** had captured the city **Jos 8:21** 693
men of Shechem set men in **a** against **Jg 9:25** 693
were with him arose from the **a**. **Jg 9:35** 3993
Israel set men in **a** around Gibeah. **Jg 20:29** 693
in **a** broke out of their place, **Jg 20:33** 693
they relied on the men in **a** whom **Jg 20:36** 693
the men in **a** hurried and rushed **Jg 20:37** 693
the men in **a** also deployed and **Jg 20:37** 693
the men of Israel and the men in **a** **Jg 20:38** 693
and set an **a** in the valley. **1Sa 15:5** 693
my servant against me to lie in **a**, **1Sa 22:8** 693
by lying in **a** as *it is* this day?" **1Sa 22:13** 693
set an **a** to come from the rear, **2Ch 13:13** 3993
Judah and the **a** was behind them. **2Ch 13:13** 3993
they have set an **a** for my life; **Ps 59:3** 693
us **a** the innocent without cause; **Pr 1:11** 6845
They **a** their own lives. **Pr 1:18** 6845
But inwardly he sets an **a** for him. **Jer 9:8** 696
Station sentries, Place men in **a**! **Jer 51:12** 693
in **a** for us in the wilderness. **La 4:19** 693
your bread Will set an **a** for you. **Ob 1:7** 4204
of Paul's sister heard of their **a**, **Ac 23:16** *1747*
an **a** to kill him on the way). **Ac 25:3** *1747*

AMBUSHES
set **a** against the sons of Ammon, **2Ch 20:22** 693
of the enemy and the **a** by the way. **Ezr 8:31** 693

AMEN
And the woman shall say, "**A**. **Nu 5:22** 543
the woman shall say, "Amen. **A**." **Nu 5:22** 543
people shall answer and say, '**A**.' **Dt 27:15** 543
And all the people shall say, '**A**.' **Dt 27:16** 543
And all the people shall say, '**A**.' **Dt 27:17** 543
And all the people shall say, '**A**.' **Dt 27:18** 543
And all the people shall say, '**A**.' **Dt 27:19** 543
And all the people shall say, '**A**.' **Dt 27:20** 543
And all the people shall say, '**A**.' **Dt 27:21** 543
And all the people shall say, '**A**.' **Dt 27:22** 543
And all the people shall say, '**A**.' **Dt 27:23** 543
And all the people shall say, '**A**.' **Dt 27:24** 543
And all the people shall say, '**A**.' **Dt 27:25** 543
And all the people shall say, '**A**.' **Dt 27:26** 543
answered the king and said, "**A**! **1Ki 1:36** 543

Then all the people said, "A," 1Ch 16:36 543
And all the assembly said, "A!" Ne 5:13 543
all the people answered, "A, Amen!" Ne 8:6 543
A!" while lifting up their hands; Ne 8:6 543
to everlasting. A and Amen. Ps 41:13 543
to everlasting. Amen and A. Ps 41:13 543
filled with His glory. A, and Amen. Ps 72:19 543
filled with His glory. Amen, and A. Ps 72:19 543
Blessed be the LORD forever! A Ps 89:52 543
the LORD forever! Amen and A. Ps 89:52 543
And let all the people say, "A." Ps 106:48 543
I said, "A, O LORD." Jer 11:5 543
the prophet Jeremiah said, "A! Jer 28:6 543
and the glory forever. A.]' Mt 6:13 *281*
who is blessed forever. A. Ro 1:25 *281*
over all, God blessed forever. A. Ro 9:5 *281*
To Him *be* the glory forever. A. Ro 11:36 *281*
God of peace be with you all. A. Ro 15:33 *281*
Jesus Christ be with you all. A.] Ro 16:24 *281*
Christ, be the glory forever. A. Ro 16:27 *281*
of the ungifted say the "A" 1Co 14:16 *281*
with you all in Christ Jesus. A. 1Co 16:24 *281*
therefore also through Him is our A to 2Co 1:20 *281*
whom *be* the glory forevermore. A. Ga 1:5 *281*
be with your spirit, brethren. A. Ga 6:18 *281*
generations forever and ever. A. Eph 3:21 *281*
be the glory forever and ever. A. Php 4:20 *281*
and glory forever and ever. A. 1Tm 1:17 *281*
be honor and eternal dominion! A. 1Tm 6:16 *281*
be the glory forever and ever. A. 2Tm 4:18 *281*
be the glory forever and ever. A. Heb 13:21 *281*
and dominion forever and ever. A. 1Pe 4:11 *281*
be dominion forever and ever. A. 1Pe 5:11 *281*
now and to the day of eternity. A. 2Pe 3:18 *281*
all time and now and forever. A. Jude 1:25 *281*
the dominion forever and ever. A. Rv 1:6 *281*
will mourn over Him. So it is to be. A. Rv 1:7 *281*
The A, the faithful and true Rv 3:14 *281*
creatures kept saying, "A." Rv 5:14 *281*
"A, blessing and glory and wisdom Rv 7:12 *281*
to our God forever and ever. A." Rv 7:12 *281*
sits on the throne saying, "A. Rv 19:4 *281*
"Yes, I am coming quickly." A. Rv 22:20 *281*

AMEND
"A your ways and your deeds, and Jer 7:3 3190
truly a your ways and your deeds, Jer 7:5 3190
a your ways and your deeds and Jer 26:13 3190
his evil way and a your deeds, Jer 35:15 3190

AMENDS
then make a for their iniquity, Lv 26:41 7521
be making a for their iniquity, Lv 26:43 7521

AMETHYST
row a jacinth, an agate and an a; Ex 28:19 306
a jacinth, an agate, and an a; Ex 39:12 306
the eleventh, jacinth; the twelfth, a. Rv 21:20 *271*

AMI
Pochereth-hazzebaim, the sons of A. Ezr 2:57 532a

AMID
"A disquieting thoughts from the Jb 4:13
come, A the tempest they roll on. Jb 30:14 8478
consume her citadels A war cries on Am 1:14
And Moab will die a tumult, Am 2:2
with Bernice a great pomp, Ac 25:23 *3326*
gospel of God a much opposition. 1Th 2:2 *1722*

AMITTAI
His servant Jonah the son of A, 2Ki 14:25 573
came to Jonah the son of A saying, Jon 1:1 573

AMMAH
down, they came to the hill of A, 2Sa 2:24 522a

AMMI
Say to your brothers, "A," Hos 2:1 5971a

AMMIEL
of Dan, A the son of Gemalli; Nu 13:12 5988
Machir the son of A in Lo-debar." 2Sa 9:4 5988
the house of Machir the son of A 2Sa 9:5 5988
Machir the son of A from Lo-debar, 2Sa 17:27 5988
by Bath-shua the daughter of A; 1Ch 3:5 5988
A the sixth, Issachar the seventh 1Ch 26:5 5988

AMMIHUD
of Ephraim, Elishama the son of A; Nu 1:10 5989
shall be Elishama the son of A, Nu 2:18 5989
day *it was* Elishama the son of A, Nu 7:48 5989
offering of Elishama the son of A. Nu 7:53 5989
the son of A over its army, Nu 10:22 5989
of Simeon, Samuel the son of A. Nu 34:20 5989
a leader, Pedahel the son of A." Nu 34:28 5989
and went to Talmai the son of A, 2Sa 13:37 5989
Ladan his son, A his son, Elishama 1Ch 7:26 5989
Uthai the son of A, 1Ch 9:4 5989

AMMINADAB
Elisheba, the daughter of A, Ex 6:23 5992
of Judah, Nahshon the son of A; Nu 1:7 5992
Nahshon the son of A, Nu 2:3 5992
day was Nahshon the son of A, Nu 7:12 5992
offering of Nahshon the son of A. Nu 7:17 5992
first, with Nahshon the son of A, Nu 10:14 5992
was born Ram, and to Ram, A, Ru 4:19 5992
and to A was born Nahshon, and to Ru 4:20 5992
Ram became the father of A, 1Ch 2:10 5992
A became the father of Nahshon, 1Ch 2:10 5992
The sons of Kohath *were* A his son, 1Ch 6:22 5992
the sons of Uzziel, A the chief, 1Ch 15:10 5992
Joel, Shemaiah, Eliel and A, 1Ch 15:11 5992
Ram was the father of A, Mt 1:4 *284*
A the father of Nahshon, Mt 1:4 *284*
the son of A, the son of Admin, Lk 3:33 *284*

AMMISHADDAI
of Dan, Ahiezer the son of A; Nu 1:12 5996
Ahiezer the son of A, Nu 2:25 5996
day *it was* Ahiezer the son of A, Nu 7:66 5996
offering of Ahiezer the son of A. Nu 7:71 5996
the son of A over its army, Nu 10:25 5996

AMMIZABAD
over his division was A his son. 1Ch 27:6 5990

AMMON
of the sons of A to this day. Gn 19:38 5983
Jabbok, as far as the sons of A; Nu 21:24 5983
border of the sons of A *was* Jazer. Nu 21:24 5983
you come opposite the sons of A, Dt 2:19 5983
of the sons of A as a possession, Dt 2:19 5983
near to the land of the sons of A, Dt 2:37 5983
it is in Rabbah of the sons of A. Dt 3:11 5983
the border of the sons of A; Dt 3:16 5983
the border of the sons of A; Jos 12:2 5983
as the border of the sons of A; Jos 13:10 5983
half the land of the sons of A, Jos 13:25 5983
himself the sons of A and Amalek; Jg 3:13 5983
Moab, the gods of the sons of A, Jg 10:6 5983
into the hands of the sons of A. Jg 10:7 5983
The sons of A crossed the Jg 10:9 5983
the Amorites, the sons of A, Jg 10:11 5983
Then the sons of A were summoned and Jg 10:17 5983
to fight against the sons of A? Jg 10:18 5983
sons of A fought against Israel. Jg 11:4 5983
the sons of A fought against Israel Jg 11:5 5983
may fight against the sons of A." Jg 11:6 5983
with us and fight with the sons of A Jg 11:8 5983
against the sons of A and the LORD Jg 11:9 5983
to the king of the sons of A, Jg 11:12 5983
The king of the sons of A said Jg 11:13 5983
to the king of the sons of A, Jg 11:14 5983
nor the land of the sons of A. Jg 11:15 5983
of Israel and the sons of A.'" Jg 11:27 5983
But the king of the sons of A Jg 11:28 5983
he went on to the sons of A. Jg 11:29 5983
give the sons of A into my hand, Jg 11:30 5983
in peace from the sons of A, Jg 11:31 5983
sons of A to fight against them; Jg 11:32 5983
So the sons of A were subdued Jg 11:33 5983
of your enemies, the sons of A." Jg 11:36 5983
cross over to fight against the sons of A Jg 12:1 5983
great strife with the sons of A; Jg 12:2 5983
over against the sons of A, Jg 12:3 5983
king of the sons of A came against 1Sa 12:12 5983
side, against Moab, the sons of A, 1Sa 14:47 5983
the sons of A and the Philistines and 2Sa 8:12 5983
Now when the sons of A saw that 2Sa 10:6 5983
the sons of A sent and hired the 2Sa 10:6 5983
The sons of A came out and 2Sa 10:8 5983
them against the sons of A. 2Sa 10:10 5983
sons of A are too strong for you, 2Sa 10:11 5983
of A saw that the Arameans fled, 2Sa 10:14 5983
sons of A and came to Jerusalem. 2Sa 10:14 5983
to help the sons of A anymore. 2Sa 10:19 5983
the sons of A and besieged Rabbah. 2Sa 11:1 5983
with the sword of the sons of A. 2Sa 12:9 5983
against Rabbah of the sons of A and 2Sa 12:26 5983
all the cities of the sons of A. 2Sa 12:31 5983
from Rabbah of the sons of A, 2Sa 17:27 5983
detestable idol of the sons of A. 1Ki 11:7 5983
Milcom the god of the sons of A; 1Ki 11:33 5983
the abomination of the sons of A, 2Ki 23:13 5983
from Edom, Moab, the sons of A, 1Ch 18:11 5983
the king of the sons of A died, 1Ch 19:1 5983
land of the sons of A to Hanun to 1Ch 19:2 5983
of the sons of A said to Hanun, 1Ch 19:3 5983
When the sons of A saw that they 1Ch 19:6 5983
Hanun and the sons of A sent 1,000 1Ch 19:6 5983
And the sons of A gathered 1Ch 19:7 5983
The sons of A came out and 1Ch 19:9 5983
themselves against the sons of A. 1Ch 19:11 5983
sons of A are too strong for you, 1Ch 19:12 5983
of A saw that the Arameans fled, 1Ch 19:15 5983
to help the sons of A anymore. 1Ch 19:19 5983
ravaged the land of the sons of A, 1Ch 20:1 5983
all the cities of the sons of A. 1Ch 20:3 5983
sons of Moab and the sons of A, 2Ch 20:1 5983
sons of A and Moab and Mount Seir, 2Ch 20:10 5983
ambushes against the sons of A, 2Ch 20:22 5983
For the sons of A and Moab rose up 2Ch 20:23 5983
had married women from Ashdod, A Ne 13:23 5985
Gebal and A and Amalek, Ps 83:7 5983
sons of A will be subject to them. Is 11:14 5983
and Edom and the sons of A, Jer 9:26 5983
Edom, Moab and the sons of A; Jer 25:21 5983
to the king of the sons of A, Jer 27:3 5983
among the sons of A and in Edom and Jer 40:11 5983
sons of A has sent Ishmael the son Jer 40:14 5983
to cross over to the sons of A. Jer 41:10 5983
men and went to the sons of A. Jer 41:15 5983
Concerning the sons of A. Jer 49:1 5983
Against Rabbah of the sons of A; Jer 49:2 5983
The fortunes of the sons of A," Jer 49:6 5983
come to Rabbah of the sons of A, Ezk 21:20 5983
A and concerning their reproach,' Ezk 21:28 5983
your face toward the sons of A and Ezk 25:2 5983
and say to the sons of A, Ezk 25:3 5983
of A a resting place for flocks. Ezk 25:5 5983
along with the sons of A to Ezk 25:10 5983
that the sons of A will not be Ezk 25:10 5983
and the foremost of the sons of A. Da 11:41 5983
three transgressions of the sons of A Am 1:13 5983
the revilings of the sons of A, Zph 2:8 5983
And the sons of A like Gomorrah Zph 2:9 5983

AMMONITE
"No A or Moabite shall enter the Dt 23:3 5984
Now Nahash the A came up and 1Sa 11:1 5984
But Nahash the A said to them, 1Sa 11:2 5984
Zelek the A, Naharai the 2Sa 23:37 5984
Moabite, A, Edomite, Sidonian, and 1Ki 11:1 5984
Zelek the A, Naharai the 1Ch 11:39 5984
the A official heard *about it,* Ne 2:10 5984
and Tobiah the A official, Ne 2:19 5984
the A *was* near him and he said, Ne 4:3 5984
no A or Moabite should ever enter Ne 13:1 5984

AMMONITES
it, but the A call them Zamzummin, Dt 2:20 5984
the A until the heat of the day. 1Sa 11:11 5983
that the king of the A died, 2Sa 10:1 1121, 5983
came to the land of the A, 2Sa 10:2 1121, 5983
of the A said to Hanun their lord, 2Sa 10:3 1121, 5983
the detestable idol of the A. 1Ki 11:5 5984
bands of Moabites, and bands of A. 2Ki 24:2 1121, 5983
The A also gave tribute to Uzziah, 2Ch 26:8 5984
fought also with the king of the A 2Ch 27:5 1121, 5983
prevailed over them so that the A 2Ch 27:5 1121, 5983
The A also paid him this *amount* in 2Ch 27:5 1121, 5983
Perizzites, the Jebusites, the A, Ezr 9:1 5984
Tobiah, the Arabs, the A and Ne 4:7 5984

AMMONITESS
his mother's name was Naamah the A. 1Ki 14:21 5985
his mother's name was Naamah the A. 1Ki 14:31 5985
his mother's name was Naamah the A. 2Ch 12:13 5985
Zabad the son of Shimeath the A, 2Ch 24:26 5985

AMNON
his firstborn was A, 2Sa 3:2 550
and A the son of David loved her. 2Sa 13:1 550
A was so frustrated because of 2Sa 13:2 550
hard to A to do anything to her. 2Sa 13:2 550
But A had a friend whose name was 2Sa 13:3 550
Then A said to him, 2Sa 13:4 550
So A lay down and pretended to be 2Sa 13:6 550
to see him, A said to the king, 2Sa 13:6 550
And A said, "Have everyone go out 2Sa 13:9 550
Then A said to Tamar, 2Sa 13:10 550
into the bedroom to her brother A. 2Sa 13:10 550
Then A hated her with a very great 2Sa 13:15 550
And A said to her, 2Sa 13:15 550
"Has A your brother been with you? 2Sa 13:20 550
not speak to A either good or bad; 2Sa 13:22 550
for Absalom hated A because he had 2Sa 13:22 550
let my brother A go with us." 2Sa 13:26 550
he let A and all the king's sons 2Sa 13:27 550
'Strike A,' then put him to death. 2Sa 13:28 550
A just as Absalom had commanded. 2Sa 13:29 550
king's sons, for A alone is dead; 2Sa 13:32 550
are dead,' for only A is dead." 2Sa 13:33 550
for he was comforted concerning A, 2Sa 13:39 550
the firstborn *was* A, 1Ch 3:1 550
sons of Shimon *were* A and Rinnah, 1Ch 4:20 550

AMNON'S
"Go now to your brother A house, 2Sa 13:7 550
Tamar went to her brother A house, 2Sa 13:8 550
when A heart is merry with wine, 2Sa 13:28 550

AMOK
Sallu, A, Hilkiah and Jedaiah. Ne 12:7 5987
of Sallai, Kallai; of A, Eber; Ne 12:20 5987

AMON
"Take Micaiah and return him to A 1Ki 22:26 526
and A his son became king in his 2Ki 21:18 526
A was twenty-two years old when he 2Ki 21:19 526
The servants of A conspired 2Ki 21:23 526
who had conspired against King A, 2Ki 21:24 526
of the acts of A which he did, 2Ki 21:25 526
A his son, Josiah his son. 1Ch 3:14 526
him to A the governor of the city and 2Ch 18:25 526
And A his son became king in his 2Ch 33:20 526
A *was* twenty-two years old when he 2Ch 33:21 526
and A sacrificed to all the carved 2Ch 33:22 526
had done, but A multiplied guilt. 2Ch 33:23 526
the conspirators against King A, 2Ch 33:25 526
Pochereth-hazzebaim, the sons of A. Ne 7:59 526
the days of Josiah the son of A, Jer 1:2 526
year of Josiah the son of A, Jer 25:3 526
I am going to punish A of Thebes, Jer 46:25 528
in the days of Josiah son of A, Zph 1:1 526
Manasseh the father of A, Mt 1:10 *300*
and A the father of Josiah. Mt 1:10 *300*

AMONG
God a the trees of the garden. Gn 3:8 8432
male a you shall be circumcised. Gn 17:10
"And every male a you who is Gn 17:12
every male a the men of Abraham's Gn 17:23
a stranger and a sojourner a you; Gn 23:4 5973
give me a burial site a you that Gn 23:4 5973
you are a mighty prince a us; Gn 23:6 8432
was sitting a the sons of Heth; Gn 23:10 8432
of the Canaanites, a whom I live, Gn 24:3 7130
and every black one a the lambs and Gn 30:32
spotted and speckled a the goats; Gn 30:32
spotted a the goats and black among Gn 30:33
the goats and black a the lambs, Gn 30:33
all the black ones a the sheep, Gn 30:35
kinsmen point out what is yours a my Gn 31:32 5973

So he divided the children **a** Leah Gn 33:1 5921
that every male **a** us be Gn 34:22
a the inhabitants of the land, Gn 34:30
a the Canaanites and the Gn 34:30
the foreign gods which are **a** you, Gn 35:2 8432
of the chief baker **a** his servants. Gn 40:20 8432
buy grain **a** those who were coming, Gn 42:5 8432
took five men from **a** his brothers and Gn 47:2 7097a
you know any capable men **a** them, Gn 47:6
one distinguished **a** his brothers. Gn 49:26
and set *it* **a** the reeds by the bank Ex 2:3
a the reeds and sent her maid, Ex 2:5 8432
The one **a** the servants of Pharaoh Ex 9:20
these signs of Mine **a** them, Ex 10:1 7130
how I performed My signs **a** them, Ex 10:2
"Not so! Go now, the men **a** *you,* Ex 10:11
"Rise up, get out from **a** my people, Ex 12:31 8432
the stranger who sojourns **a** you." Ex 12:49 8432
every womb **a** the sons of Israel, Ex 13:2
leavened shall be seen **a** you, Ex 13:7
be seen **a** you in all your borders. Ex 13:7
man **a** your sons you shall redeem. Ex 13:13
"Who is like You **a** the gods, Ex 15:11
"Is the LORD **a** us, or not?" Ex 17:7 7130
own possession **a** all the peoples, Ex 19:5 4480
to My people, to the poor **a** you, Ex 22:25 5973
all the people **a** whom you come, Ex 23:27
for Me, that I may dwell **a** them. Ex 25:8 8432
him, from **a** the sons of Israel, Ex 28:1 8432
"I will dwell **a** the sons of Ex 29:45 8432
Egypt, that I might dwell **a** them; Ex 29:46 8432
a them when you number them. Ex 30:12
be cut off from **a** his people. Ex 31:14 7130
to be a derision **a** their enemies Ex 32:25
earth nor **a** any of the nations; Ex 34:10
and all the people **a** whom you live Ex 34:10 7130
'Take from **a** you a contribution to Ex 35:5
Let every skillful man **a** you come, Ex 35:10
All the skillful men **a** those Ex 36:8
a the sons of Aaron may eat it; Lv 6:18
place **a** his sons shall offer it. Lv 6:22 4480
male **a** the priests may eat of it; Lv 6:29
male **a** the priests may eat of it. Lv 7:6
'The one **a** the sons of Aaron who Lv 7:33 4480
and chews the cud, **a** the animals, Lv 11:3
these, **a** those which chew the cud, Lv 11:4
or **a** those which divide the hoof: Lv 11:4
fins and scales **a** all the teeming life Lv 11:10 4480
and **a** all the living creatures Lv 11:10 4480
you shall detest **a** the birds; Lv 11:13 4480
'Yet these you may eat **a** all the Lv 11:21 4480
a all the creatures that walk on Lv 11:27
the unclean **a** the swarming things Lv 11:29
unclean **a** all the swarming things; Lv 11:31
My tabernacle that is **a** them." Lv 15:31 8432
or the alien who sojourns **a** you; Lv 16:29 8432
be cut off from **a** his people. Lv 17:4 7130
the aliens who sojourn **a** them, Lv 17:8 8432
the aliens who sojourn **a** them, Lv 17:10 8432
cut him off from **a** his people. Lv 17:10 7130
'No person **a** you may eat blood, Lv 17:12 4480
who sojourns **a** you eat blood.' Lv 17:12 8432
the aliens who sojourn **a** them, Lv 17:13 8432
nor the alien who sojourns **a** you Lv 18:26 8432
be cut off from **a** their people. Lv 18:29 7130
as a slanderer **a** your people, Lv 19:16
be to you as the native **a** you, Lv 19:34 854
cut him off from **a** his people, Lv 20:3 7130
and I will cut off from **a** their Lv 20:5 7130
cut him off from **a** his people. Lv 20:6 7130
be cut off from **a** their people. Lv 20:18 7130
for a *dead* person **a** his people, Lv 21:1
relative by marriage **a** his people, Lv 21:4
who is the highest **a** his brothers, Lv 21:10 4480
his offspring **a** his people; Lv 21:15
'No man **a** the descendants of Aaron Lv 21:21 4480
'If any man **a** all your descendants Lv 22:3 4480
sanctified **a** the sons of Israel; Lv 22:32 8432
I will destroy from **a** his people. Lv 23:30 7130
went out **a** the sons of Israel; Lv 24:10 8432
possession **a** the sons of Israel. Lv 25:33 8432
sojourners who live as aliens **a** you Lv 25:45 5973
I will make My dwelling **a** you, Lv 26:11 8432
also walk **a** you and be your God, Lv 26:12 8432
a you the beasts of the field, Lv 26:22
I will send pestilence **a** you, Lv 26:25 8432
I will scatter **a** the nations and Lv 26:33
'But you will perish **a** the nations, Lv 26:38
'However, a firstborn **a** animals, Lv 27:26
if *it is* **a** the unclean animals, Lv 27:27
set apart **a** men shall be ransomed; Lv 27:29 4480
a them by their fathers' tribe. Nu 1:47 8432
their census **a** the sons of Israel. Nu 1:49 8432
not numbered **a** the sons of Israel, Nu 2:33 8432
to him from **a** the sons of Israel. Nu 3:9
I have taken the Levites from **a** Nu 3:12 8432
of the womb **a** the sons of Israel. Nu 3:12 4480
firstborn **a** the sons of Israel, Nu 3:41
Levites instead of all the firstborn **a** Nu 3:41
firstborn **a** the sons of Israel, Nu 3:42
all the firstborn **a** the sons of Israel Nu 3:45
of those who are in excess **a** them, Nu 3:48
of Kohath from **a** the sons of Levi, Nu 4:2 8432
be cut off from **a** the Levites. Nu 4:18 8432
you a curse and an oath **a** your people Nu 5:21 8432
will become a curse **a** her people. Nu 5:27 7130
"Take the Levites from **a** the sons Nu 8:6 8432
Levites from **a** the sons of Israel, Nu 8:14 8432
to Me from **a** the sons of Israel. Nu 8:16 8432
a the sons of Israel is Mine, Nu 8:17
a the men and among the animals; Nu 8:17
among the men and **a** the animals; Nu 8:17
firstborn **a** the sons of Israel. Nu 8:18
sons from **a** the sons of Israel, Nu 8:19 8432
that there will be no plague **a** the Nu 8:19
time **a** the sons of Israel?" Nu 9:7 8432
'If an alien sojourns **a** you Nu 9:14 854
the fire of the LORD burned **a** them Nu 11:1
fire of the LORD burned **a** them. Nu 11:3
were **a** them had greedy desires; Nu 11:4 7130
is **a** you and have wept before Him, Nu 11:20 7130
"The people, **a** whom I am, are Nu 11:21 7130
a those who had been registered, Nu 11:26
If there is a prophet **a** you, Nu 12:6
every one a leader **a** them." Nu 13:2
for the LORD is not **a** you. Nu 14:42 7130
or one who may be **a** you throughout Nu 15:14 8432
the alien who sojourns **a** them, Nu 15:26 8432
for him who is native **a** the sons Nu 15:29
for the alien who sojourns **a** them. Nu 15:29 8432
be cut off from **a** his people. Nu 15:30 7130
from **a** this congregation, Nu 16:21 8432
"Get away from **a** this Nu 16:45 8432
the plague had begun **a** the people. Nu 16:47
the rod of Aaron **a** their rods. Nu 17:6 8432
Levites from **a** the sons of Israel; Nu 18:6 8432
land nor own any portion **a** them; Nu 18:20 8432
inheritance **a** the sons of Israel. Nu 18:20 8432
and **a** the sons of Israel they Nu 18:23 8432
a the sons of Israel.' " Nu 18:24 8432
to the alien who sojourns **a** them. Nu 19:10 8432
and He proved Himself holy **a** them. Nu 20:13
LORD sent fiery serpents **a** the people Nu 21:6
not be reckoned **a** the nations. Nu 23:9
And the shout of a king is **a** them. Nu 23:21
jealous with My jealousy **a** them, Nu 25:11 8432
household **a** the Simeonites. Nu 25:14
"**A** these the land shall be Nu 26:53
for they were not numbered **a** the Nu 26:62 8432
to them **a** the sons of Israel. Nu 26:62 8432
But **a** these there was not a man of Nu 26:64
yet he was not **a** the company of Nu 27:3 8432
father be withdrawn from **a** his family Nu 27:4 8432
a our father's brothers." Nu 27:4 8432
a their father's brothers, Nu 27:7 8432
"Arm men from **a** you for the war, Nu 31:3 854
a the congregation of the LORD. Nu 31:16
kill every male **a** the little ones, Nu 31:17
a you in the land of Canaan." Nu 32:30 8432
the LORD had struck down **a** them. Nu 33:4
by lot **a** you as a possession, Nu 34:13
and for the sojourner **a** them; Nu 35:15 8432
up nor fight, for I am not **a** you; Dt 1:42 7130
perished from **a** the people, Dt 2:16 7130
God has destroyed them from **a** you. Dt 4:3 7130
will scatter you **a** the peoples, Dt 4:27
left few in number **a** the nations where Dt 4:27
barren **a** you or among your cattle. Dt 7:14
barren among you or **a** your cattle. Dt 7:14
that followed them, **a** all Israel Dt 11:6 7130
dreamer of dreams arises **a** you and Dt 13:1 7130
shall purge the evil from **a** you. Dt 13:5 7130
do such a wicked thing **a** you. Dt 13:11 7130
worthless men have gone out from **a** Dt 13:13 7130
abomination has been done **a** you, Dt 13:14 7130
and chews the cud, **a** the animals, Dt 14:6
these **a** those which chew the cud, Dt 14:7 4480
or **a** those that divide the hoof in Dt 14:7 4480
no portion or inheritance **a** you. Dt 14:27 5973
no portion or inheritance **a** you, Dt 14:29 5973
there will be no poor **a** you, Dt 15:4
one from **a** your countrymen you Dt 17:15 7130
no inheritance **a** their countrymen; Dt 18:2 7130
"There shall not be found **a** you Dt 18:10
you a prophet like me from **a** you, Dt 18:15 7130
from **a** their countrymen like you, Dt 18:18 7130
shall purge the evil from **a** you. Dt 19:19 7130
again do such an evil thing **a** you. Dt 19:20 7130
and see **a** the captives a beautiful Dt 21:11
shall purge the evil from **a** you. Dt 22:21 7130
shall purge the evil from **a** you. Dt 22:24 7130
"If there is **a** you any man who is Dt 23:10
shall have a spade **a** your tools, Dt 23:13 5921
He must not see anything indecent **a** Dt 23:14
shall purge the evil from **a** you. Dt 24:7 7130
and attacked **a** you all the stragglers Dt 25:18
the Levite and the alien who is **a** you Dt 26:11 7130
and a taunt **a** all the people where Dt 28:37
"The alien who is **a** you shall Dt 28:43 7130
who is refined and very delicate **a** you Dt 28:54
refined and delicate woman **a** you, Dt 28:56
will scatter you **a** all peoples, Dt 28:64
"**A** those nations you shall find no Dt 28:65
not be **a** you a man or woman, Dt 29:18
there will not be **a** you a root Dt 29:18
our God is not **a** us that these evils Dt 31:17 7130
one distinguished **a** his brothers. Dt 33:16
the LORD will do wonders **a** you." Jos 3:5 7130
know that the living God is **a** you, Jos 3:10 7130
"Let this be a sign **a** you, Jos 4:6 7130
also put *them* **a** their own things. Jos 7:11
when I saw **a** the spoil a beautiful Jos 7:21
spent that night **a** the people. Jos 8:9 8432
strangers who were living **a** them. Jos 8:35 7130
live **a** Israel until this day. Jos 13:13 7130
sword **a** *the rest of* their slain. Jos 13:22 413
inheritance to the Levites **a** them. Jos 14:3 8432
was the greatest man **a** the Anakim. Jos 14:15
a portion **a** the sons of Judah, Jos 15:13 8432
an inheritance **a** our brothers." Jos 17:4 8432
a their father's brothers. Jos 17:4 8432
an inheritance **a** his sons. Jos 17:6 8432
Ephraim **a** the cities of Manasseh), Jos 17:9 8432
There remained **a** the sons of Jos 18:2
the Levites have no portion **a** you, Jos 18:7 7130
so that he may dwell **a** them. Jos 20:4 5973
the stranger who sojourns **a** them, Jos 20:9 8432
possession **a** their brothers westward Jos 22:7 5973
a the thousands of Israel. Jos 22:14
stands, and take possession **a** us. Jos 22:19 8432
nations, these which remain **a** you, Jos 23:7 854
nations, these which remain **a** you, Jos 23:12 854
which we went and **a** all the peoples Jos 24:17
Canaanites lived in Gezer **a** them. Jg 1:29 7130
so the Canaanites lived **a** them and Jg 1:30 7130
Asherites lived **a** the Canaanites, Jg 1:32 7130
but lived **a** the Canaanites, Jg 1:33 7130
and followed other gods from **a** Jg 2:12
of Israel lived **a** the Canaanites, Jg 3:5 7130
seen **A** forty thousand in Israel. Jg 5:8
The volunteers **a** the people; Jg 5:9
flocks **a** the watering places, Jg 5:11 996
A the divisions of Reuben *There* Jg 5:15
"Why did you sit **a** the sheepfolds, Jg 5:16 996
A the divisions of Reuben *There* Jg 5:16
away the foreign gods from **a** them and Jg 10:16 7130
you are **a** those who trouble me; Jg 11:35
"Is there no woman **a** the Jg 14:3
relatives, or **a** all our people, Jg 14:3
possession **a** the tribes of Israel. Jg 18:1 8432
image and went **a** the people. Jg 18:20 7130
not let your voice be heard **a** us, Jg 18:25 5973
that has taken place **a** you? Jg 20:12
"Who is there **a** all the tribes of Jg 21:5 4480
And they found **a** the inhabitants Jg 21:12 4480
the field and glean **a** the ears of grain Ru 2:2
after the reapers **a** the sheaves.' Ru 2:7
"Let her glean even **a** the sheaves, Ru 2:15 996
that it may come **a** us and deliver 1Sa 4:3 7130
a great slaughter **a** the people, 1Sa 4:17
gods and the Ashtaroth from **a** you 1Sa 7:3 8432
in his chariots and **a** his horsemen 1Sa 8:11
than he **a** the sons of Israel; 1Sa 9:2 4480
so that he prophesied **a** them. 1Sa 10:10 8432
Is Saul also **a** the prophets?" 1Sa 10:11
"Is Saul also **a** the prophets?" 1Sa 10:12
and when he stood **a** the people, 1Sa 10:23 8432
one like him **a** all the people." 1Sa 10:24
the field, and **a** all the people. 1Sa 14:15
For now the slaughter **a** the 1Sa 14:30
They struck **a** the Philistines 1Sa 14:31
a the people and say to them, 1Sa 14:34
a them until the morning light, 1Sa 14:36
go down from **a** the Amalekites, 1Sa 15:6 8432
departed from **a** the Amalekites. 1Sa 15:6 8432
mother be childless **a** women." 1Sa 15:33 4480
a king for Myself **a** his sons." 1Sa 16:1
of Saul, advanced *in years* **a** men. 1Sa 17:12
two hundred men **a** the Philistines. 1Sa 18:27
"Is Saul also **a** the prophets?" 1Sa 19:24
"And who **a** all your servants is 1Sa 22:14
a all the thousands of Judah." 1Sa 23:23
odious **a** his people Israel; 1Sa 27:12
men **a** those who went with David 1Sa 30:22 4480
a the Arameans of Damascus, 2Sa 8:6
the people **a** David's servants fell; 2Sa 11:17 4480
a the conspirators with Absalom." 2Sa 15:31
a the people who follow Absalom.' 2Sa 17:9
yet you set your servant **a** those 2Sa 19:28
a the descendants of the giant, 2Sa 21:16
a the descendants of the giant. 2Sa 21:18
to You, O LORD, **a** the nations, 2Sa 22:50
He was honored **a** the thirty, but 2Sa 23:23 4480
brother of Joab was **a** the thirty; 2Sa 23:24
be **a** those who eat at your table; 1Ki 2:7
there will not be any **a** the kings 1Ki 3:13
no one **a** us who knows how to cut 1Ki 5:6
I will dwell **a** the sons of Israel, 1Ki 6:13 8432
and a byword **a** all peoples. 1Ki 9:7
house **a** the sons of Pharaoh. 1Ki 11:20 8432
and made priests from **a** all the 1Ki 12:31
high places from **a** all the people; 1Ki 13:33
"Because I exalted you from **a** the 1Ki 14:7 8432
message **a** all the sons of Israel 1Ki 18:20
"I live **a** my own people." 2Ki 4:13 8432
bid him arise from **a** his brothers, 2Ki 9:2 8432
stole him from **a** the king's sons 2Ki 11:2 8432
gold that was found **a** the treasuries 2Ki 12:18
therefore the LORD sent lions **a** 2Ki 17:25
so he has sent lions **a** them, 2Ki 17:26
appointed from **a** themselves priests 2Ki 17:32 7098
custom of the nations from **a** whom 2Ki 17:33
like him **a** all the kings of Judah, 2Ki 18:5
nor **a** *those* who were before him. 2Ki 18:5
'Who **a** all the gods of the lands 2Ki 18:35
there is nothing **a** my treasuries 2Ki 20:15
unleavened bread **a** their brothers. 2Ki 23:9 8432
Their relatives **a** all the 1Ch 7:5
he was honored **a** the thirty, 1Ch 11:25 4480
and they were **a** the mighty men who 1Ch 12:1
a mighty man **a** the thirty, 1Ch 12:4
known His deeds **a** the peoples. 1Ch 16:8
Tell of His glory **a** the nations, 1Ch 16:24
wonderful deeds **a** all the peoples. 1Ch 16:24
And let them say **a** the nations, 1Ch 16:31
a the Arameans of Damascus; 1Ch 18:6
number Levi and Benjamin **a** them, 1Ch 21:6 8432

were named **a** the tribe of Levi. 1Ch 23:14 5921
found **a** them at Jazer of Gilead) 1Ch 26:31
and **a** the sons of my father He 1Ch 28:4
if I send pestilence **a** My people, 2Ch 7:13
and a byword **a** all peoples. 2Ch 7:20
as head and leader **a** his brothers, 2Ch 11:22
of Judah and taught **a** the people. 2Ch 17:9
out again **a** the people from Beersheba 2Ch 19:4
a the inhabitants of Jerusalem. 2Ch 19:8
spoil, they found much **a** them, 2Ch 20:25
and stole him from **a** the king's 2Ch 22:11 8432
in the city of David **a** the kings, 2Ch 24:16 5973
of the people from **a** the people, 2Ch 24:23
of Ashdod and **a** the Philistines. 2Ch 26:6
portions to every male **a** the priests 2Ch 31:19
enrolled **a** the Levites. 2Ch 31:19
'Who *was there* **a** all the gods of 2Ch 32:14
they are **a** the records of the 2Ch 33:18 5921
there is **a** you of all His people, 2Ch 36:23
there is **a** you of all His people, Ezr 1:3
These searched **a** their ancestral Ezr 2:62
A the sons of the priests who had Ezr 10:18 4480
I will scatter you **a** the peoples; Ne 1:8
know or see until we come **a** them, Ne 4:11
413, 8432
"It is reported **a** the nations, Ne 6:6
These searched **a** their ancestral Ne 7:64
Some from **a** the heads of Ne 7:70
which You had performed **a** them; Ne 9:17 5973
cast lots for the supply of wood **a** Ne 10:34
the second **a** his brethren; Ne 11:17 4480
Yet **a** the many nations there was Ne 13:26
scattered and dispersed **a** the peoples Es 3:8 996
was great mourning **a** the Jews, Es 4:3
And many **a** the peoples of the land Es 8:17 4480
were not to fail from **a** the Jews, Es 9:28 8432
Ahasuerus, and great **a** the Jews Es 10:3
LORD, and Satan also came **a** them. Jb 1:6 8432
and Satan also came **a** them to Jb 2:1 8432
while he was sitting **a** the ashes. Jb 2:8 8432
rejoice **a** the days of the year; Jb 3:6
"Who **a** all these does not know Jb 12:9
gray-haired and the aged are **a** us, Jb 15:10
given, And no alien passed **a** them. Jb 15:19 8432
I do not find a wise man **a** you. Jb 17:10
or posterity **a** his people, Jb 18:19
Ophir **a** the stones of the brooks, Jb 22:24
And dwelt as a king **a** the troops, Jb 29:25
"**A** the bushes they cry out; Jb 30:7 996
us know **a** ourselves what is good. Jb 34:4 996
He claps his hands **a** us, Jb 34:37 996
perishes **a** the cult prostitutes. Jb 36:14
they divide him **a** the merchants? Jb 41:6 996
them inheritance **a** their brothers. Jb 42:15 8432
Declare **a** the peoples His deeds. Ps 9:11
disappear from **a** the sons of men. Ps 12:1
is exalted **a** the sons of men. Ps 12:8
give thanks to You **a** the nations, Ps 18:49
from **a** the sons of men. Ps 21:10
They divide my garments **a** them, Ps 22:18
praise You **a** a mighty throng. Ps 35:18
have scattered us **a** the nations. Ps 44:11
make us a byword **a** the nations, Ps 44:14
A laughingstock **a** the peoples. Ps 44:14
daughters are **a** Your noble ladies; Ps 45:9
The rich **a** the people will seek Ps 45:12
I will be exalted **a** the nations, Ps 46:10
My soul is **a** lions; Ps 57:4 8432
a those who breathe forth fire, Ps 57:4
to You, O Lord, **a** the peoples; Ps 57:9
praises to You **a** the nations. Ps 57:9
Your salvation **a** all nations. Ps 67:2
you lie down **a** the sheepfolds, Ps 68:13 996
The Lord is **a** them *as at* Sinai, in Ps 68:17
You have received gifts **a** men, Ps 68:18
Even **a** the rebellious also, that Ps 68:18
there any **a** us who knows how long. Ps 74:9 854
known Your strength **a** the peoples. Ps 77:14
He sent **a** them swarms of flies which Ps 78:45
tent which He had pitched **a** men, Ps 78:60
known **a** the nations in our sight, Ps 79:10
our enemies laugh **a** themselves. Ps 80:6
"Let there be no strange god **a** you; Ps 81:9
is no one like You **a** the gods, Ps 86:8
and Babylon **a** those who know Me; Ps 87:4
a those who go down to the pit; Ps 88:4 5973
Forsaken **a** the dead, Like the Ps 88:5
Who **a** the sons of the mighty is Ps 89:6
heed, you senseless **a** the people; Ps 94:8
Tell of His glory **a** the nations, Ps 96:3
wonderful deeds **a** all the peoples. Ps 96:3
Say **a** the nations, Ps 96:10
and Aaron were **a** His priests, Ps 99:6
a those who called on His name; Ps 99:6
up *their* voices **a** the branches. Ps 104:12
4480, 996
known His deeds **a** the peoples. Ps 105:1
His wondrous acts **a** them, Ps 105:27
And **a** His tribes there was not one Ps 105:37
But sent a wasting disease **a** them. Ps 106:15
cast their seed **a** the nations And Ps 106:27
And the plague broke out **a** them. Ps 106:29
And gather us from **a** the nations, Ps 106:47
to You, O LORD, **a** the peoples, Ps 108:3
praises to You **a** the nations. Ps 108:3
He will judge **a** the nations, He Ps 110:6
is for me **a** those who help me; Ps 118:7
For I dwell **a** the tents of Kedar! Ps 120:5 5973
Then they said **a** the nations, Ps 126:2

one who spreads strife **a** brothers. Pr 6:19 996
And I saw **a** the naive, *And* discerned Pr 7:7
naive, *And* discerned **a** the youths Pr 7:7
But **a** the upright there is good Pr 14:9 996
reproof Will dwell **a** the wise. Pr 15:31 7130
in the inheritance **a** the brothers. Pr 17:2 8432
not be **a** those who give pledges, Pr 22:26
A those who become guarantors for Pr 22:26
And increases the faithless **a** men. Pr 23:28
earth And the needy from **a** men. Pr 30:14
The lion *which is* mighty **a** beasts Pr 30:30
he sits **a** the elders of the land. Pr 31:23 5973
no remembrance **A** those who will Ec 1:11 5973
the sun and it is prevalent **a** men Ec 6:1 5921
I have found one man **a** a thousand, Ec 7:28 4480
not found a woman **a** all these. Ec 7:28
men **a** them are given fully to do evil. Ec 8:11
the shouting of a ruler **a** fools. Ec 9:17
not know, Most beautiful **a** women, SS 1:8
My mare **a** the chariots of Pharaoh. SS 1:9
"Like a lily **a** the thorns, So is SS 2:2 996
So is my darling **a** the maidens." SS 2:2 996
tree **a** the trees of the forest, SS 2:3
So is my beloved **a** the young men. SS 2:3 996
pastures *his flock* **a** the lilies. SS 2:16
not one **a** them has lost her young. SS 4:2
gazelle Which feed **a** the lilies. SS 4:5
beloved, O most beautiful **a** women? SS 5:9
ruddy, Outstanding **a** ten thousand. SS 5:10 4480
gone, O most beautiful **a** women? SS 6:1
pastures *his flock* **a** the lilies." SS 6:3
not one **a** them has lost her young. SS 6:6
I live **a** a people of unclean lips; Is 6:5 8432
seal the law **a** my disciples. Is 8:16
Nothing *remains* but to crouch **a** Is 10:4 8478
the captives Or fall **a** the slain. Is 10:4 8478
disease **a** his stout warriors; Is 10:16
known His deeds **a** the peoples; Is 12:4
midst of the earth **a** the peoples, Is 24:13 8432
a sherd will not be found **a** its pieces Is 30:14
"Who **a** us can live with the Is 33:14
Who **a** us can live with continual Is 33:14
'Who **a** all the gods of these lands Is 36:20
a the inhabitants of the world. Is 38:11 5973
there is nothing **a** my treasuries Is 39:4
there is no counselor **a** them Who, Is 41:28 4480
Who **a** you will give ear to this? Is 42:23
Who **a** them can declare this And Is 43:9
there was no strange *god* **a** you; Is 43:12
And they will spring up **a** the Is 44:4 996
himself **a** the trees of the forest. Is 44:14
vessel **a** the vessels of earth! Is 45:9 854
Who **a** them has declared these Is 48:14
Who is **a** you that fears the LORD, Is 50:10
And **a** the brands you have set ablaze. Is 50:11
her **a** all the sons she has borne, Is 51:18 4480
a all the sons she has reared. Is 51:18 4480
Who inflame yourselves **a** the oaks, Is 57:5
"**A** the smooth *stones* of the Is 57:6
"Those from **a** you will Is 58:12
A those who are vigorous *we are* Is 59:10
will be known **a** the nations, Is 61:9
Who sit **a** graves and spend the Is 65:4
"I will set a sign **a** them and Is 66:19
declare My glory **a** the nations. Is 66:19
'How I would set you **a** My sons And Jer 3:19
ground, And do not sow **a** thorns. Jer 4:3 413
thickets and climb **a** the rocks; Jer 4:29
wicked men are found **a** My people, Jer 5:26
they shall fall **a** those who fall; Jer 6:15
O congregation, what is **a** them. Jer 6:18
assayer *and* a tester **a** My people, Jer 6:27
they shall fall **a** those who fall; Jer 8:12
I will scatter them **a** the nations, Jer 9:16
For **a** all the wise men of the Jer 10:7
"A conspiracy has been found **a** Jer 11:9
a the inhabitants of Jerusalem. Jer 11:9
the house of Judah from **a** them. Jer 12:14 8432
Are there any **a** the idols of the Jer 14:22
object of horror **a** all the kingdoms Jer 15:4
'Ask now **a** the nations, Who ever Jer 18:13
a the prophets of Samaria I saw an Jer 23:13
"Also **a** the prophets of Jerusalem Jer 23:14
sword that I will send **a** them." Jer 25:16 996
sword which I will send **a** you." Jer 25:27 996
and a reproach **a** all the nations Jer 29:18
have anyone living **a** this people, Jer 29:32 8432
shout **a** the chief of the nations; Jer 31:7
A them the blind and the lame, Jer 31:8
day both in Israel and **a** mankind; Jer 32:20
cities **a** the cities of Judah. Jer 34:7
in and going out **a** the people, Jer 37:4 8432
were *only* wounded men left **a** them, Jer 37:10
some property there **a** the people. Jer 37:12 8432
So he stayed **a** the people. Jer 39:14 8432
a all the exiles of Jerusalem and Jer 40:1 8432
and stay with him **a** the people; Jer 40:5 8432
and stayed with him **a** the people Jer 40:6 8432
a the sons of Ammon and in Edom and Jer 40:11
were found **a** them said to Ishmael, Jer 41:8
child and infant, from **a** Judah, Jer 44:7 8432
a all the nations of the earth? Jer 44:8
up like Tabor **a** the mountains, Jer 46:18
Or was he caught **a** thieves? Jer 48:27
the cities and dwell **a** the crags, Jer 48:28
an envoy is sent **a** the nations, Jer 49:14
have made you small **a** the nations, Jer 49:15
among the nations, Despised **a** men. Jer 49:15
and proclaim **a** the nations. Jer 50:2

An object of horror **a** the nations! Jer 50:23
an outcry is heard **a** the nations. Jer 50:46
Blow a trumpet **a** the nations! Jer 51:27
an object of horror **a** the nations! Jer 51:41
Who was *once* great **a** the nations! La 1:1
She who was a princess **a** the La 1:1
to comfort her **A** all her lovers. La 1:2 4480
She dwells **a** the nations, *But* she La 1:3
become an unclean thing **a** them. La 1:17 996
and her princes are **a** the nations; La 2:9
Men **a** the nations said, La 4:15
We shall live **a** the nations." La 4:20
by the river Chebar **a** the exiles, Ezk 1:1 8432
and forth **a** the living beings. Ezk 1:13 996
that a prophet has been **a** them. Ezk 2:5 8432
causing consternation **a** them. Ezk 3:15 8432
so that you cannot go out **a** them. Ezk 3:25 8432
eat their bread unclean **a** the nations Ezk 4:13
and I will execute judgments **a** you Ezk 5:8 8432
do **a** you what I have not done, Ezk 5:9
fathers will eat *their* sons **a** you, Ezk 5:10 8432
or be consumed by famine **a** you, Ezk 5:12 8432
a desolation and a reproach **a** the Ezk 5:14
"The slain will fall **a** you, Ezk 6:7 8432
who escaped the sword **a** the nations Ezk 6:8
you are scattered **a** the countries. Ezk 6:8
you who escape will remember Me **a** Ezk 6:9
when their slain are **a** their idols Ezk 6:13 8432
your abominations will be **a** you; Ezk 7:4 8432
nor anything eminent **a** them. Ezk 7:11
son of Shaphan standing **a** them, Ezk 8:11 8432
and **a** them was a certain man Ezk 9:2 8432
and **a** them I saw Jaazaniah son of Ezk 11:1 8432
them far away **a** the nations and Ezk 11:16
scattered them **a** the countries, Ezk 11:16
a which you have been scattered, Ezk 11:17
"The prince who is **a** them Ezk 12:12 8432
when I scatter them **a** the nations and Ezk 12:15
and spread them **a** the countries. Ezk 12:15
a the nations where they go, Ezk 12:16
have been like foxes **a** ruins. Ezk 13:4
cut him off from **a** My people. Ezk 14:8 8432
him from **a** My people Israel. Ezk 14:9 8432
is **a** the trees of the forest? Ezk 15:2
vine **a** the trees of the forest, Ezk 15:6
"Then your fame went forth **a** the Ezk 16:14
what was not good **a** his people, Ezk 18:18 8432
A lioness **a** lions! Ezk 19:2 996
She lay down **a** young lions, She Ezk 19:2 8432
'And he walked about **a** the lions; Ezk 19:6 8432
of the nations **a** whom they *lived*, Ezk 20:9 8432
I would scatter them **a** the nations Ezk 20:23
and disperse them **a** the lands, Ezk 20:23
and I will prove Myself holy **a** Ezk 20:41
at the bloodshed which is **a** you. Ezk 22:13 8432
I will scatter you **a** the nations Ezk 22:15
and I am profaned **a** them. Ezk 22:26 8432
"I searched for a man **a** them Ezk 22:30 4480
Thus she became a byword **a** women, Ezk 23:10
they will set their encampments **a** you Ezk 25:4
and make their dwellings **a** you; Ezk 25:4
not be remembered **a** the nations. Ezk 25:10
cane were **a** your merchandise. Ezk 27:19
which were **a** your merchandise. Ezk 27:24
merchants **a** the peoples hiss at you; Ezk 27:36
"All who know you **a** the peoples Ezk 28:19
peoples **a** whom they are scattered, Ezk 28:25
scatter the Egyptians **a** the nations Ezk 29:12
and disperse them **a** the lands." Ezk 29:12
a whom they were scattered. Ezk 29:13
scatter the Egyptians **a** the nations Ezk 30:23
and disperse them **a** the lands. Ezk 30:23
'When I scatter the Egyptians **a** Ezk 30:26
and disperse them **a** the lands, Ezk 30:26
And its top was **a** the clouds. Ezk 31:3 996
and has set its top **a** the clouds, Ezk 31:10 996
nor set their top **a** the clouds, Ezk 31:14 996
earth beneath, **a** the sons of men, Ezk 31:14 8432
under its shade **a** the nations. Ezk 31:17 8432
"To which **a** the trees of Eden are Ezk 31:18
your destruction **a** the nations, Ezk 32:9
"The strong **a** the mighty ones Ezk 32:21
"They have made a bed for her **a** Ezk 32:25 8432
made to lie down **a** *the* uncircumcised Ezk 32:32 8432
take one man from **a** them and make Ezk 33:2 7097a
when he is **a** his scattered sheep, Ezk 34:12 8432
David will be prince **a** them; Ezk 34:24 8432
known **a** them when I judge you. Ezk 35:11
I scattered them **a** the nations and Ezk 36:19
a the nations where they went. Ezk 36:21
a the nations where you went. Ezk 36:22
has been profaned **a** the nations, Ezk 36:23
Myself holy **a** you in their sight. Ezk 36:23
disgrace of famine **a** the nations. Ezk 36:30
me to pass **a** them round about, Ezk 37:2 5921
take the sons of Israel from **a** the Ezk 37:21 996
will set My glory **a** the nations; Ezk 39:21
them go into exile **a** the nations, Ezk 39:28 413
a the sons of Israel forever. Ezk 43:7 8432
and I will dwell **a** them forever. Ezk 43:9 8432
who are **a** the sons of Israel, Ezk 44:9 8432
in, the prince shall go in **a** them; Ezk 46:10 8432
a the twelve tribes of Israel; Ezk 47:13
"So you shall divide this land **a** Ezk 47:21
by lot for an inheritance **a** yourselves Ezk 47:22
among yourselves and **a** the aliens Ezk 47:22
native-born **a** the sons of Israel; Ezk 47:22
with you **a** the tribes of Israel. Ezk 47:22 8432
Now **a** them from the sons of Judah Da 1:6

"I have found a man a the exiles Da 2:25
4481, 1123
will in the host of heaven And a Da 4:35
Daniel began distinguishing himself a Da 6:3 5922
a little one, came up a them, Da 7:8 997
the violent ones a your people Da 11:14
booty and possessions a them, Da 11:24
"Those who have insight a the Da 11:33
A the tribes of Israel I declare Hos 5:9
They are now a the nations Like a Hos 8:8
they hire *allies* a the nations, Hos 8:10
will be wanderers a the nations. Hos 9:17
a tumult will arise a your people, Hos 10:14
Though he flourishes a the reeds, Hos 13:15 996
reproach, A byword a the nations. Jl 2:17
Why should they a the peoples say, Jl 2:17
make you a reproach a the nations. Jl 2:19
My great army which I sent a you. Jl 2:25
Even a the survivors whom the LORD Jl 2:32
they have scattered a the nations; Jl 3:2
Proclaim this a the nations: Jl 3:9
was a the sheepherders from Tekoa, Am 1:1
"Even the bravest a the warriors Am 2:16
a all the families of the earth; Am 3:2 4480
a you after the manner of Egypt; Am 4:10
shake the house of Israel a all nations Am 9:9
been sent a the nations *saying,* Ob 1:1
will make you small a the nations; Ob 1:2
you set your nest a the stars, Ob 1:4 996
Who are a the Canaanites as far Ob 1:20
Is there no king a you, Mi 4:9
little to be a the clans of Judah, Mi 5:2
the remnant of Jacob Will be a many Mi 5:7 7130
of Jacob Will be a the nations, Mi 5:8
A many peoples Like a lion among Mi 5:8 7130
a lion a the beasts of the forest, Mi 5:8
a young lion a flocks of sheep, Mi 5:8
a you And destroy your chariots. Mi 5:10 7130
your *sacred* pillars from a you, Mi 5:13 7130
a you And destroy your cities. Mi 5:14 7130
there is no upright *person* a men. Mi 7:2
Put and Lubim were a her helpers. Na 3:9
"Look a the nations! Hab 1:5
a you A humble and lowly people, Zph 3:12 7130
A all the peoples of the earth, Zph 3:20
'Who is left a you who saw this Hg 2:3
and he was standing a the myrtle Zch 1:8 996
And the man who was standing a the Zch 1:10 996
was standing a the myrtle trees and Zch 1:11 996
a these who are standing *here.* Zch 3:7 996
I scattered them with a storm wind a Zch 7:14 5921
as you were a curse a the nations; Zch 8:13
"When I scatter them a the peoples, Zch 10:9
Judah like a firepot a pieces of wood Zch 12:6
and a flaming torch a sheaves, Zch 12:6
and the one who is feeble a them Zch 12:8
from you will be divided a you. Zch 14:1 7130
a you who would shut the gates, Mal 1:10
name *will be* great a the nations, Mal 1:11
will be great a the nations," Mal 1:11
My name is feared a the nations." Mal 1:14
LEAST A THE LEADERS OF JUDAH; Mt 2:6 1722
kind of sickness a the people. Mt 4:23 1722
what man is there a you who, Mt 7:9 1537
a those born of women there has Mt 11:11 1722
"What man is there a you Mt 12:11 1537
"Others fell a the thorns, Mt 13:7 1909
whom seed was sown a the thorns, Mt 13:22 1519
and sowed tares a the wheat, Mt 13:25
303, 3319
the wicked from a the righteous, Mt 13:49 3319
began to discuss *this* a themselves, Mt 16:7 1722
why do you discuss a yourselves Mt 16:8 1722
"It is not this way a you, but whoever Mt 20:26 1722
great a you shall be your servant, Mt 20:26 1722
first a you shall be your slave; Mt 20:27 1722
they *began* reasoning a themselves, Mt 21:25 1722
the son, they said a themselves, Mt 21:38 1722
a you shall be your servant. Mt 23:11
a riot might occur a the people." Mt 26:5 1722
up His garments a themselves by Mt 27:35 1266
A them was Mary Magdalene, and Mary Mt 27:56 1722
was widely spread a the Jews, Mt 28:15 3844
so that they debated a themselves, Mk 1:27
"Other *seed* fell a the thorns, Mk 4:7 1519
whom seed was sown a the thorns; Mk 4:18 1519
he had his dwelling a the tombs. Mk 5:3 1722
a the tombs and in the mountains, Mk 5:5 1722
his hometown and a his *own* relatives Mk 6:4 1722
up the two fish a them all. Mk 6:41
"But it is not this way a you, Mk 10:43 1722
great a you shall be your servant; Mk 10:43 1722
first a you shall be slave of all. Mk 10:44 1722
They *began* reasoning a themselves, Mk 11:31 4314
up His garments a themselves, Mk 15:24 1266
were mocking *Him* a themselves Mk 15:31 4314
a whom *were* Mary Magdalene, Mk 15:40 1722
of the things accomplished a us, Lk 1:1 1722
to take away my disgrace a men." Lk 1:25 1722
"Blessed *are* you a women, and Lk 1:42 1722
"There is no one a your relatives Lk 1:61 1537
a men with whom He is pleased." Lk 2:14 1722
and they *began* looking for Him a Lk 2:44 1722
"A great prophet has arisen a us!" Lk 7:16 1722
say to you, a those born of women there Lk 7:28 1722
"Other *seed* fell a the thorns; Lk 8:7
1722, 3319
The *seed* which fell a the thorns, Lk 8:14 1519
An argument started a them as to Lk 9:46 1722
for the one who is least a all Lk 9:48 1722
and fell a robbers, and they Lk 10:30 4045
"What man a you, if he has a Lk 15:4 1537
that which is highly esteemed a men Lk 16:15 1722
leading men a the people were trying Lk 19:47
They reasoned a themselves, Lk 20:5 4314
on the earth dismay a nations, Lk 21:25
this and share it a yourselves; Lk 22:17 1519
And they began to discuss a Lk 22:23 4314
And there arose also a dispute a Lk 22:24 1722
a you must become like the youngest, Lk 22:26 1722
I am a you as the one who serves. Lk 22:27
1722, 3319
Peter was sitting a them. Lk 22:55 3319
up His garments a themselves. Lk 23:34 1266
seek the living One a the dead? Lk 24:5 3326
also some women a us amazed us. Lk 24:22 1537
Word became flesh, and dwelt a us, Jn 1:14 1722
but a you stands One whom you do Jn 1:26 3319
"Do not grumble a yourselves. Jn 6:43 3326
a the crowds concerning Him; Jn 7:12 1722
go to the Dispersion a the Greeks, Jn 7:35
"He who is without sin a you, Jn 8:7
And there was a division a them. Jn 9:16 1722
A division occurred again a the Jn 10:19 1722
to walk publicly a the Jews, Jn 11:54 1722
Now there were some Greeks a Jn 12:20 1537
while longer the Light is a you. Jn 12:35 1722
"If I had not done a them the Jn 15:24 1722
DIVIDED MY OUTER GARMENTS A THEM, Jn 19:24 1266
Therefore this saying went out a Jn 21:23 1519
"For he was counted a us and Ac 1:17 1722
Lord Jesus went in and out a us Ac 1:21 1909
destroyed from a the people.' Ac 3:23 1537
heaven that has been given a men by Ac 4:12 1722
spread any further a the people, Ac 4:17 1519
was not a needy person a them, Ac 4:34 1722
were taking place a the people; Ac 5:12 1722
"Therefore, brethren, select from a you Ac 6:3 1537
wonders and signs a the people. Ac 6:8 1722
there was no small disturbance a Ac 12:18 1722
and those a you who fear God, Ac 13:26 1722
and was laid a his fathers and Ac 13:36 4314
days God made a choice a you, Ac 15:7 1722
done through them a the Gentiles. Ac 15:12 1722
taking from a the Gentiles a people Ac 15:14 1537
to God from a the Gentiles, Ac 15:19 575
to choose men from a them to send Ac 15:22 1537
Silas, leading men a the brethren, Ac 15:22 1722
a whom also were Dionysius the Ac 17:34 1722
teaching the word of God a them. Ac 18:11 1722
a whom I went about preaching the Ac 20:25 1722
a which the Holy Spirit has made Ac 20:28 1722
savage wolves will come in a you, Ac 20:29 1519
and from a your own selves men Ac 20:30 1537
a all those who are sanctified. Ac 20:32 1722
which God had done a the Gentiles Ac 21:19 1722
how many thousands there are a the Ac 21:20 1722
a the Gentiles to forsake Moses, Ac 21:21 2596
But a the crowd some were shouting Ac 21:34 1722
who stirs up dissension a all the Jews Ac 24:5
shouted out while standing a them, Ac 24:21 1722
men a you go there with me, Ac 25:5 1722
than eight or ten days a them, Ac 25:6 1722
customs and questions a *the* Jews; Ac 26:3 2596
beginning was spent a my *own* nation Ac 26:4 1722
Why is it considered incredible a you Ac 26:8 3844
an inheritance a those who have been Ac 26:18 1722
will be no loss of life a you, Ac 27:22 1537
a great dispute a themselves.] Ac 28:29 1722
of faith a all the Gentiles for Ro 1:5 1722
a whom you also are the called of Ro 1:6 1722
together with you *while* a you, Ro 1:12 1722
obtain some fruit a you also, Ro 1:13 1722
as a the rest of the Gentiles. Ro 1:13 1722
bodies would be dishonored a them. Ro 1:24 1722
A THE GENTILES BECAUSE OF YOU," Ro 2:24 1722
be the firstborn a many brethren; Ro 8:29 1722
also called, not from a Jews only, Ro 9:24 1537
only, but also from a Gentiles. Ro 9:24 1537
were grafted in a them and became Ro 11:17 1722
I say to everyone a you not to think Ro 12:3 1722
PRAISE TO YOU A THE GENTILES, Ro 15:9 1722
poor a the saints in Jerusalem. Ro 15:26
are outstanding a the apostles, Ro 16:7 1722
and that there be no divisions a you, 1Co 1:10 1722
that there are quarrels a you. 1Co 1:11 1722
nothing a you except Jesus Christ, 1Co 2:2 1722
wisdom a those who are mature; 1Co 2:6 1722
For who a men knows the *thoughts* 1Co 2:11
is jealousy and strife a you, 1Co 3:3 1722
If any man a you thinks that he is 1Co 3:18 1722
that there is immorality a you, 1Co 5:1 1722
not exist even a the Gentiles, 1Co 5:1 1722
THE WICKED MAN FROM A YOURSELVES. 1Co 5:13 1537
that there is not a you one wise 1Co 6:5 1722
I hear that divisions exist a you; 1Co 11:18 1722
there must also be factions a you, 1Co 11:19 1722
may become evident a you. 1Co 11:19 1722
many a you are weak and sick, 1Co 11:30 1722
that God is certainly a you. 1Co 14:25 1722
how do some a you say that there 1Co 15:12 1722
who was preached a you by us—by me 2Co 1:19 1722
a fragrance of Christ to God a those 2Co 2:15 1722
and a those who are perishing; 2Co 2:15 1722
DWELL IN THEM AND WALK A THEM; 2Co 6:16 1704
partner and fellow worker a you; 2Co 8:23 1519
the sea, dangers a false brethren; 2Co 11:26 1722
a you with all perseverance, 2Co 12:12 1722
my contemporaries a my countrymen, Ga 1:14 1722
I might preach Him a the Gentiles, Ga 1:16 1722
which I preach a the Gentiles, Ga 2:2 1722
not sinners from a the Gentiles; Ga 2:15 1537
Spirit and works miracles a you, Ga 3:5 1722
the Lord Jesus which *exists* a you and Eph 1:15 2596
A them we too all formerly lived Eph 2:3 1722
or greed must not even be named a you, Eph 5:3 1722
among you, as is proper a saints; Eph 5:3
each individual a you also is to love his Eph 5:33
a whom you appear as lights in the Php 2:15 1722
of this mystery a the Gentiles, Col 1:27 1722
When this letter is read a you, Col 4:16 3844
proved to be a you for your sake. 1Th 1:5 1722
But we proved to be gentle a you, 1Th 2:7
1722, 3319
those who diligently labor a you, 1Th 5:12 1722
speak proudly of you a the churches 2Th 1:4 1722
and to be marveled at a all who 2Th 1:10 1722
in an undisciplined manner a you, 2Th 3:7 1722
For we hear that some a you are 2Th 3:11 1722
a whom I am foremost *of all.* 1Tm 1:15
A these are Hymenaeus and 1Tm 1:20
angels, Proclaimed a the nations, 1Tm 3:16 1722
a whom are Phygelus and Hermogenes. 2Tm 1:15
A them are Hymenaeus and Philetus, 2Tm 2:17
For a them are those who enter 2Tm 3:6 1537
every high priest taken from a men Heb 5:1 1537
Marriage *is to be held* in honor a all, Heb 13:4 1722
of first fruits a His creatures. Jas 1:18
made distinctions a yourselves, Jas 2:4 1722
the tongue is set a our members as Jas 3:6 1722
a you is wise and understanding? Jas 3:13 1722
of quarrels and conflicts a you? Jas 4:1 1722
Is anyone a you suffering? Jas 5:13 1722
Is anyone a you sick? Jas 5:14 1722
any a you strays from the truth and Jas 5:19 1722
behavior excellent a the Gentiles, 1Pe 2:12 1722
at the fiery ordeal a you, 1Pe 4:12 1722
I exhort the elders a you, 1Pe 5:1 1722
shepherd the flock of God a you, 1Pe 5:2 1722
prophets also arose a the people, 2Pe 2:1 1722
will also be false teachers a you, 2Pe 2:1 1722
man, while living a them, 2Pe 2:8 1722
who loves to be first a them, 3Jn 1:9
a the seven golden lampstands, Rv 2:1
1722, 3319
one, who was killed a you, Rv 2:13 3844
and a the rocks of the mountains; Rv 6:15 1519
These have been purchased from a Rv 14:4 575
the tabernacle of God is a men, Rv 21:3 3326
men, and He will dwell a them, Rv 21:3 3326
and God Himself will be a them, Rv 21:3 3326

AMORITE

and the A and the Girgashite Gn 10:16 567
living by the oaks of Mamre the A, Gn 14:13 567
of the A is not yet complete." Gn 15:16 567
and the A and the Canaanite and Gn 15:21 567
the A with my sword and my bow." Gn 48:22 567
Hittite and the A and the Perizzite Ex 3:8 567
Canaanite and the Hittite and the A Ex 3:17 567
the Canaanite, the Hittite, the A, Ex 13:5 567
drive out the Canaanite, the A, Ex 33:2 567
to drive out the A before you, Ex 34:11 567
into captivity, To an A king, Nu 21:29 567
I have given Sihon the A, Dt 2:24 567
them, the Hittite and the A, Dt 20:17 567
Perizzite, the Girgashite, the A, Jos 3:10 567
Lebanon, the Hittite and the A, Jos 9:1 567
and the A and the Hittite and the Jos 11:3 567
Hittite, the A and the Canaanite, Jos 12:8 567
as Aphek, to the border of the A; Jos 13:4 567
and the A and the Perizzite and Jos 24:11 567
Of the Hittite and the A, Ne 9:8 567
an A and your mother a Hittite. Ezk 16:3 567
a Hittite and your father an A. Ezk 16:45 567
I who destroyed the A before them, Am 2:9 567
possession of the land of the A. Am 2:10 567

AMORITES

of the Amalekites, and also the A, Gn 14:7 567
bring you in to *the land of* the A, Ex 23:23 567
and the Jebusites and the A are living Nu 13:29 567
comes out of the border of the A, Nu 21:13 567
of Moab, between Moab and the A. Nu 21:13 567
to Sihon, king of the A, Nu 21:21 567
lived in all the cities of the A, Nu 21:25 567
the city of Sihon, king of the A, Nu 21:26 567
Israel lived in the land of the A. Nu 21:31 567
dispossessed the A who *were* there. Nu 21:32 567
you did to Sihon, king of the A, Nu 21:34 567
all that Israel had done to the A. Nu 22:2 567
of the A and the kingdom of Og, Nu 32:33 567
dispossessed the A who were in it. Nu 32:39 567
defeated Sihon the king of the A, Dt 1:4 567
go to the hill country of the A, Dt 1:7 567
way to the hill country of the A, Dt 1:19 567
hill country of the A which the LORD Dt 1:20 567
the hand of the A to destroy us. Dt 1:27 567
"The A who lived in that hill Dt 1:44 567
as you did to Sihon king of the A, Dt 3:2 567
the A who were beyond the Jordan, Dt 3:8 567
Sirion, and the A call it Senir): Dt 3:9 567
of the A who lived at Heshbon, Dt 4:46 567
of Bashan, the two kings of the A, Dt 4:47 567
and the A and the Canaanites and Dt 7:1 567
Sihon and Og, the kings of the A, Dt 31:4 567
the A who were beyond the Jordan, Jos 2:10 567
the kings of the A who *were* beyond Jos 5:1 567

deliver us into the hand of the A,	Jos 7:7	567
the A who were beyond the Jordan,	Jos 9:10	567
So the five kings of the A,	Jos 10:5	567
for all the kings of the A that	Jos 10:6	567
the A before the sons of Israel,	Jos 10:12	567
Sihon king of the A,	Jos 12:2	567
the cities of Sihon king of the A,	Jos 13:10	567
of the A who reigned in Heshbon,	Jos 13:21	567
the A who lived beyond the Jordan,	Jos 24:8	567
kings of the A from before you,	Jos 24:12	567
A in whose land you are living;	Jos 24:15	567
even the A who lived in the land.	Jos 24:18	567
Then the A forced the sons of Dan	Jg 1:34	567
yet the A persisted in living in	Jg 1:35	567
The border of the A ran from	Jg 1:36	567
Canaanites, the Hittites, the A,	Jg 3:5	567
of the A in whose land you live.	Jg 6:10	567
in Gilead in the land of the A.	Jg 10:8	567
you from the Egyptians, the A,	Jg 10:11	567
messengers to Sihon king of the A,	Jg 11:19	567
possessed all the land of the A,	Jg 11:21	567
all the territory of the A,	Jg 11:22	567
A from before His people Israel,	Jg 11:23	567
peace between Israel and the A.	1Sa 7:14	567
but of the remnant of the A,	2Sa 21:2	567
of the A and of Og king of Bashan;	1Ki 4:19	567
the people who were left of the A,	1Ki 9:20	567
to all that the A had done,	1Ki 21:26	567
all the A did who *were* before him,	2Ki 21:11	567
and the Jebusites, the A,	1Ch 1:14	567
were left of the Hittites, the A,	2Ch 8:7	567
the Egyptians and the A.	Ezr 9:1	567
Sihon, king of the A,	Ps 135:11	567
Sihon, king of the A,	Ps 136:19	567
AMOS		
The words of A, who was among the	Am 1:1	5986
"What do you see, A?"	Am 7:8	5986
"A has conspired against you in	Am 7:10	5986
"For thus A says,	Am 7:11	5986
Then Amaziah said to A,	Am 7:12	5986
A replied to Amaziah,	Am 7:14	5986
"What do you see, A?"	Am 8:2	5986
son of Mattathias, the son of A,	Lk 3:25	*301*
AMOUNT		
your work quota, *your* daily a,	Ex 5:13	1697, 3117
you not completed your required a	Ex 5:14	2706
reduce *your* daily a of bricks."	Ex 5:19	1697, 3117
to his years he is to refund *the* a	Lv 25:52	
priest shall calculate for him the a of	Lv 27:23	4373
took a very large a of bronze.	2Sa 8:8	
and a very great a of spices	1Ki 10:10	
took a very large a of bronze,	1Ch 18:8	
spoil of the city, a very great a.	1Ch 20:2	
a of gold and precious stones;	2Ch 9:1	7230
talents of gold and a very great a	2Ch 9:9	
The Ammonites also paid him this a	2Ch 27:5	
and the exact a of money that	Es 4:7	6575
copper coins, which a to a cent.	Mk 12:42	*1510*
in order to receive back the same a.	Lk 6:34	
AMOUNTING		
a to 600 talents.	2Ch 3:8	
AMOUNTS		
back your bread in rationed a,	Lv 26:26	4948
the spoil of the city in great a.	2Sa 12:30	7235a
And your work a to nothing;	Is 41:24	
and greed, which a to idolatry.	Col 3:5	*1510*
AMOZ		
Isaiah the prophet the son of A.	2Ki 19:2	531
son of A sent to Hezekiah saying,	2Ki 19:20	531
of A came to him and said to him,	2Ki 20:1	531
the prophet Isaiah, the son of A,	2Ch 26:22	531
Isaiah the prophet, the son of A,	2Ch 32:20	531
Isaiah the prophet, the son of A,	2Ch 32:32	531
The vision of Isaiah the son of A	Is 1:1	531
word which Isaiah the son of A saw	Is 2:1	531
which Isaiah the son of A saw.	Is 13:1	531
spoke through Isaiah the son of A,	Is 20:2	531
Isaiah the prophet, the son of A.	Is 37:2	531
son of A sent *word* to Hezekiah,	Is 37:21	531
of A came to him and said to him,	Is 38:1	531
AMPHIPOLIS		
traveled through A and Apollonia,	Ac 17:1	*295*
AMPLE		
a preparations before his death.	1Ch 22:5	7230
AMPLIATUS		
Greet A, my beloved in the Lord.	Ro 16:8	*291*
AMPLY		
I am a supplied, having received	Php 4:18	*4137*
AMRAM		
A and Izhar and Hebron and Uzziel;	Ex 6:18	6019
A married his father's sister	Ex 6:20	6019
A and Izhar, Hebron and Uzziel;	Nu 3:19	6019
Kohath became the father of A.	Nu 26:58	6019
and she bore to A:	Nu 26:59	6019
The sons of Kohath *were* A,	1Ch 6:2	6019
The children of A *were* Aaron,	1Ch 6:3	6019
The sons of Kohath *were* A,	1Ch 6:18	6019
A, Izhar, Hebron and Uzziel.	1Ch 23:12	6019
sons of A were Aaron and Moses.	1Ch 23:13	6019
of the sons of A, Shubael;	1Ch 24:20	6019
of the sons of Bani: Maadai, A, Uel,	Ezr 10:34	6019
AMRAMITES		
Of Kohath *was* the family of the A	Nu 3:27	6020
As for the A, the Izharites, the	1Ch 26:23	6020
AMRAM'S		
and the length of A life was one	Ex 6:20	6019
The name of A wife was Jochebed,	Nu 26:59	6019
AMRAPHEL		
in the days of A king of Shinar,	Gn 14:1	569
king of Goiim and A king of Shinar	Gn 14:9	569
AMULETS		
chains, sashes, perfume boxes, a,	Is 3:20	3908
AMUSE		
for Samson, that he may a us."	Jg 16:25	7832
AMUSING		
on while Samson was a *them.*	Jg 16:27	7832
AMZI		
the son of A, the son of Bani, the	1Ch 6:46	557
the son of Pelaliah, the son of A,	Ne 11:12	557
ANAB		
from A and from all the hill	Jos 11:21	6024
and A and Eshtemoh and Anim,	Jos 15:50	6024
ANAH		
and Oholibamah the daughter of A	Gn 36:2	6034
the daughter of A and the	Gn 36:14	6034
Oholibamah, the daughter of A.	Gn 36:18	6034
Lotan and Shobal and Zibeon and A,	Gn 36:20	6034
Aiah and A—he is the Anah who	Gn 36:24	6034
Aiah and Anah—he is the A who	Gn 36:24	6034
These are the children of A:	Gn 36:25	6034
and Oholibamah, the daughter of A.	Gn 36:25	6034
Shobal, chief Zibeon, chief A,	Gn 36:29	6034
were Lotan, Shobal, Zibeon, A,	1Ch 1:38	6034
sons of Zibeon *were* Aiah and A.	1Ch 1:40	6034
The son of A *was* Dishon.	1Ch 1:41	6034
ANAHARATH		
and Hapharaim and Shion and A,	Jos 19:19	588
ANAIAH		
him stood Mattithiah, Shema, A,	Ne 8:4	6043
Pelatiah, Hanan, A,	Ne 10:22	6043
ANAK		
Talmai, the descendants of A were.	Nu 13:22	6061
we saw the descendants of A there.	Nu 13:28	6061
of A are part of the Nephilim);	Nu 13:33	6061
can stand before the sons of A?'	Dt 9:2	6061
Arba being the father of A	Jos 15:13	6061
from there the three sons of A:	Jos 15:14	6061
and Talmai, the children of A.	Jos 15:14	6061
Arba being the father of A	Jos 21:11	6061
from there the three sons of A.	Jg 1:20	6061
ANAKIM		
saw the sons of the A there."	Dt 1:28	6062
numerous, and tall as the A.	Dt 2:10	6062
Like the A, they are also regarded	Dt 2:11	6062
numerous, and tall as the A,	Dt 2:21	6062
great and tall, the sons of the A,	Dt 9:2	6062
off the A from the hill country,	Jos 11:21	6062
There were no A left in the land	Jos 11:22	6062
on that day that A *were* there,	Jos 14:12	6062
was the greatest man among the A.	Jos 14:15	6062
ANALYZE		
You know how to a the appearance	Lk 12:56	*1381a*
do you not a this present time?	Lk 12:56	*1381a*
ANAM		
father of the people of Lud, A,	1Ch 1:11	6047
ANAMIM		
and A and Lehabim and Naphtuhim	Gn 10:13	6047
ANAMMELECH		
and A the gods of Sepharvaim.	2Ki 17:31	6048
ANAN		
Ahiah, Hanan, A,	Ne 10:26	6052
ANANI		
Akkub, Johanan, Delaiah and A,	1Ch 3:24	6054
ANANIAH		
son of A, carried out repairs	Ne 3:23	6055
at Anathoth, Nob, A,	Ne 11:32	6055
ANANIAS		
But a man named A,	Ac 5:1	*367*
"A, why has Satan filled your	Ac 5:3	*367*
A fell down and breathed his last;	Ac 5:5	*367*
disciple at Damascus named A;	Ac 9:10	*367*
said to him in a vision, "A."	Ac 9:10	*367*
seen in a vision a man named A come	Ac 9:12	*367*
But A answered, "Lord, I have heard	Ac 9:13	*367*
So A departed and entered the	Ac 9:17	*367*
"A certain A, a man who was	Ac 22:12	*367*
The high priest A commanded	Ac 23:2	*367*
A came down with some elders,	Ac 24:1	*367*
ANATH		
him came Shamgar the son of A,	Jg 3:31	6067
the days of Shamgar the son of A,	Jg 5:6	6067
ANATHOTH		
A with its pasture lands and Almon	Jos 21:18	6068
"Go to A to your own field, for	1Ki 2:26	6068
and A with its pasture lands.	1Ch 6:60	6068
Omri, Jeremoth, Abijah, A and	1Ch 7:8	6068
the men of A, 128;	Ezr 2:23	6068
the men of A, 128;	Ne 7:27	6068
Hariph, A, Nebai,	Ne 10:19	6068
at A, Nob, Ananiah,	Ne 11:32	6068
attention, Laishah *and* wretched A!	Is 10:30	6068
were in A in the land of Benjamin,	Jer 1:1	6068
the LORD concerning the men of A,	Jer 11:21	6068
A—the year of their punishment."	Jer 11:23	6068
of A who prophesies to you?	Jer 29:27	6069
yourself my field which is at A,	Jer 32:7	6068
my field, please, that is at A,	Jer 32:8	6068
at A from Hanamel my uncle's son,	Jer 32:9	6068
ANATHOTHITE		
Abiezer the A, Mebunnai the	2Sa 23:27	6069
Ikkesh the Tekoite, Abiezer the A,	1Ch 11:28	6069
and Beracah and Jehu the A,	1Ch 12:3	6069
Abiezer the A of the Benjamites;	1Ch 27:12	6069
ANCESTORS		
Have surpassed the blessings of my a	Gn 49:26	2029
them the covenant with their a,	Lv 26:45	7223
mark, which the a have set,	Dt 19:14	7223
a who refused to hear My words,	Jer 11:10	7223
his fathers never did, nor his a;	Da 11:24	1
ANCESTRAL		
among their a registration,	Ezr 2:62	3187
among their a registration,	Ne 7:64	3187
zealous for my a traditions.	Ga 1:14	*3967*
ANCESTRY		
registered by a in their families,	Nu 1:18	3205
ANCHOR		
a and *began* sailing along Crete,	Ac 27:13	*142*
Syrtis, they let down the sea a and	Ac 27:17	*4632*
hope we have as an a of the soul,	Heb 6:19	*45*
ANCHORS		
they cast four a from the stern	Ac 27:29	*45*
to lay out a from the bow,	Ac 27:30	*45*
And casting off the a,	Ac 27:40	*45*
ANCIENT		
best things of the a mountains,	Dt 33:15	6924a
'From a times your fathers lived	Jos 24:2	5769
swept them away, The a torrent,	Jg 5:21	6917
of the land from a times,	1Sa 27:8	5769
From a times I planned it.	2Ki 19:25	6924a
And the records are a.	1Ch 4:22	6267
of David and Asaph, in a times,	Ne 12:46	6924a
"Will you keep to the a path	Jb 22:15	5769
And be lifted up, O a doors,	Ps 24:7	5769
And lift *them* up, O a doors,	Ps 24:9	5769
heavens, which are from a times;	Ps 68:33	6924a
Do not move the a boundary Which	Pr 22:28	5769
Do not move the a boundary Or go	Pr 23:10	5769
of the wise, a son of a kings'?	Is 19:11	6924a
did it, From a times I planned it.	Is 37:26	6924a
that I established the a nation.	Is 44:7	5769
from the beginning, And from a times	Is 46:10	6924a
you will rebuild the a ruins;	Is 58:12	5769
they will rebuild the a ruins,	Is 61:4	5769
nation, It is an a nation,	Jer 5:15	5769
and see and ask for the a paths,	Jer 6:16	5769
from their ways, From the a paths,	Jer 18:15	5769
from a times prophesied against many	Jer 28:8	5769
earth, like the a waste places,	Ezk 26:20	5769
And the A of Days took *His* seat;	Da 7:9	6268
And He came up to the A of Days	Da 7:13	6268
until the A of Days came and	Da 7:22	6268
shattered, The a hills collapsed.	Hab 3:6	5769
of His holy prophets from a time.	Ac 3:21	*165*
"For Moses from a generations has	Ac 15:21	*744*
and did not spare the a world,	2Pe 2:5	*744*
ANCIENTS		
"As the proverb of the a says,	1Sa 24:13	6931
have heard that the a were told,	Mt 5:21	*744*
have heard that the a were told,	Mt 5:33	*744*
ANDREW		
called Peter, and A his brother,	Mt 4:18	*406*
called Peter, and A his brother;	Mt 10:2	*406*
of Galilee, He saw Simon and A,	Mk 1:16	*406*
into the house of Simon and A,	Mk 1:29	*406*
and A, and Philip, and	Mk 3:18	*406*
Peter and James and John and A	Mk 13:3	*406*
named Peter, and A his brother;	Lk 6:14	*406*
speak and followed Him, was A,	Jn 1:40	*406*
of the city of A and Peter.	Jn 1:44	*406*
One of His disciples, A,	Jn 6:8	*406*
Philip came and told A;	Jn 12:22	*406*
A and Philip came and told	Jn 12:22	*406*
Peter and John and James and A,	Ac 1:13	*406*
ANDRONICUS		
Greet A and Junias, my kinsmen and	Ro 16:7	*408*
ANEM		
lands, A with its pasture lands;	1Ch 6:73	6046
ANER		
of Eshcol and brother of A,	Gn 14:13	6063
of the men who went with me, A,	Gn 14:24	6063
A with its pasture lands and	1Ch 6:70	6063
ANEW		
are like grass which sprouts a.	Ps 90:5	2498
it flourishes and sprouts a;	Ps 90:6	2498
ANGEL		
Now the a of the LORD found her by	Gn 16:7	4397
the a of the LORD said to her,	Gn 16:9	4397
the a of the LORD said to her,	Gn 16:10	4397
The a of the LORD said to her	Gn 16:11	4397
and the a of God called to Hagar	Gn 21:17	4397
But the a of the LORD called to	Gn 22:11	4397
Then the a of the LORD called to	Gn 22:15	4397
He will send His a before you,	Gn 24:7	4397
will send His a with you to make	Gn 24:40	4397
"Then the a of God said to me in	Gn 31:11	4397
The a who has redeemed me from all	Gn 48:16	4397
The a of the LORD appeared to	Ex 3:2	4397
The a of God, who had been	Ex 14:19	4397
I am going to send an a before you	Ex 23:20	4397

"For My **a** will go before you and	Ex 23:23	4397
Behold, My **a** shall go before you;	Ex 32:34	4397
"I will send an **a** before you	Ex 33:2	4397
a and brought us out from Egypt;	Nu 20:16	4397
and the **a** of the LORD took his	Nu 22:22	4397
When the donkey saw the **a** of the	Nu 22:23	4397
Then the **a** of the LORD stood in a	Nu 22:24	4397
the donkey saw the **a** of the LORD,	Nu 22:25	4397
The **a** of the LORD went further,	Nu 22:26	4397
the donkey saw the **a** of the LORD,	Nu 22:27	4397
and he saw the **a** of the LORD	Nu 22:31	4397
The **a** of the LORD said to him,	Nu 22:32	4397
Balaam said to the **a** of the LORD,	Nu 22:34	4397
the **a** of the LORD said to Balaam,	Nu 22:35	4397
Now the **a** of the LORD came up from	Jg 2:1	4397
When the **a** of the LORD spoke	Jg 2:4	4397
Meroz,' said the **a** of the LORD,	Jg 5:23	4397
Then the **a** of the LORD came and	Jg 6:11	4397
The **a** of the LORD appeared to	Jg 6:12	4397
The **a** of God said to him,	Jg 6:20	4397
Then the **a** of the LORD put out the	Jg 6:21	4397
Then the **a** of the LORD vanished	Jg 6:21	4397
saw that he was the **a** of the LORD,	Jg 6:22	4397
the **a** of the LORD face to face."	Jg 6:22	4397
Then the **a** of the LORD appeared to	Jg 13:3	4397
the appearance of the **a** of God,	Jg 13:6	4397
and the **a** of God came again to the	Jg 13:9	4397
the **a** of the LORD said to Manoah,	Jg 13:13	4397
Manoah said to the **a** of the LORD,	Jg 13:15	4397
The **a** of the LORD said to Manoah,	Jg 13:16	4397
that he was the **a** of the LORD.	Jg 13:16	4397
Manoah said to the **a** of the LORD,	Jg 13:17	4397
But the **a** of the LORD said to him,	Jg 13:18	4397
that the **a** of the LORD ascended in	Jg 13:20	4397
Now the **a** of the LORD did not appear	Jg 13:21	4397
that he was the **a** of the LORD.	Jg 13:21	4397
in my sight, like an **a** of God;	1Sa 29:9	4397
comforting, for as the **a** of God,	2Sa 14:17	4397
like the wisdom of the **a** of God,	2Sa 14:20	4397
the king is like the **a** of God,	2Sa 19:27	4397
When the **a** stretched out his hand	2Sa 24:16	4397
to the **a** who destroyed the people,	2Sa 24:16	4397
And the **a** of the LORD was by the	2Sa 24:16	4397
he saw the **a** who was striking down	2Sa 24:17	4397
and an **a** spoke to me by the word	1Ki 13:18	4397
there was an **a** touching him,	1Ki 19:5	4397
The **a** of the LORD came again a	1Ki 19:7	4397
But the **a** of the LORD said to	2Ki 1:3	4397
The **a** of the LORD said to Elijah,	2Ki 1:15	4397
that the **a** of the LORD went out and	2Ki 19:35	4397
and the **a** of the LORD destroying	1Ch 21:12	4397
an **a** to Jerusalem to destroy it;	1Ch 21:15	4397
and said to the destroying **a**,	1Ch 21:15	4397
And the **a** of the LORD was standing	1Ch 21:15	4397
David lifted up his eyes and saw the **a**	1Ch 21:16	4397
Then the **a** of the LORD commanded	1Ch 21:18	4397
Ornan turned back and saw the **a**,	1Ch 21:20	4397
The LORD commanded the **a**,	1Ch 21:27	4397
by the sword of the **a** of the LORD.	1Ch 21:30	4397
And the LORD sent an **a** who	2Ch 32:21	4397
there is an **a** *as* mediator for him,	Jb 33:23	4397
The **a** of the LORD encamps around	Ps 34:7	4397
the **a** of the LORD driving *them* on.	Ps 35:5	4397
the **a** of the LORD pursuing them.	Ps 35:6	4397
Then the **a** of the LORD went out and	Is 37:36	4397
the **a** of His presence saved them;	Is 63:9	4397
who has sent His **a** and delivered	Da 3:28	4398
His **a** and shut the lions' mouths and	Da 6:22	4398
wrestled with the **a** and prevailed;	Hos 12:4	4397
And the **a** who was speaking with me	Zch 1:9	4397
So they answered the **a** of the LORD	Zch 1:11	4397
Then the **a** of the LORD said,	Zch 1:12	4397
The LORD answered the **a** who	Zch 1:13	4397
So the **a** who was speaking with me	Zch 1:14	4397
to the **a** who was speaking with me,	Zch 1:19	4397
the **a** who was speaking with me was	Zch 2:3	4397
a was coming out to meet him,	Zch 2:3	4397
standing before the **a** of the LORD,	Zch 3:1	4397
and standing before the **a**.	Zch 3:3	4397
the **a** of the LORD was standing by.	Zch 3:5	4397
And the **a** of the LORD admonished	Zch 3:6	4397
Then the **a** who was speaking with	Zch 4:1	4397
Then I said to the **a**	Zch 4:4	4397
So the **a** who was speaking with me	Zch 4:5	4397
Then the **a** who was speaking with	Zch 5:5	4397
to the **a** who was speaking with me,	Zch 5:10	4397
to the **a** who was speaking with me,	Zch 6:4	4397
The **a** replied to me,	Zch 6:5	4397
the **a** of the LORD before them.	Zch 12:8	4397
an **a** of the Lord appeared to him	Mt 1:20	32a
the **a** of the Lord commanded him,	Mt 1:24	32a
an **a** of the Lord appeared to	Mt 2:13	32a
an **a** of the Lord appeared in a	Mt 2:19	32a
for an **a** of the Lord descended	Mt 28:2	32a
The **a** said to the women,	Mt 28:5	32a
an **a** of the Lord appeared to him,	Lk 1:11	32a
was troubled when he saw *the* **a**,	Lk 1:12	
But the **a** said to him,	Lk 1:13	32a
Zacharias said to the **a**,	Lk 1:18	32a
The **a** answered and said to him,	Lk 1:19	32a
Now in the sixth month the **a**	Lk 1:26	32a
The **a** said to her,	Lk 1:30	32a
Mary said to the **a**,	Lk 1:34	32a
The **a** answered and said to her,	Lk 1:35	32a
And the **a** departed from her.	Lk 1:38	32a
And an **a** of the Lord suddenly	Lk 2:9	32a
But the **a** said to them,	Lk 2:10	32a
suddenly there appeared with the **a**	Lk 2:13	32a
the name given by the **a** before He	Lk 2:21	32a
an **a** from heaven appeared to Him,	Lk 22:43	32a
for an **a** of the Lord went down at	Jn 5:4	32a
"An **a** has spoken to Him."	Jn 12:29	32a
during the night an **a** of the Lord	Ac 5:19	32a
his face like the face of an **a**.	Ac 6:15	32a
AN A APPEARED TO HIM IN THE	Ac 7:30	32a
with the help of the **a** who appeared	Ac 7:35	32a
with the **a** who was speaking to him	Ac 7:38	32a
But an **a** of the Lord spoke to	Ac 8:26	32a
he clearly saw in a vision an **a** of God	Ac 10:3	32a
When the **a** who was speaking to	Ac 10:7	32a
directed by a holy **a** to send for you	Ac 10:22	32a
seen the **a** standing in his house,	Ac 11:13	32a
a of the Lord suddenly appeared and	Ac 12:7	32a
And the **a** said to him,	Ac 12:8	32a
was being done by the **a** was real,	Ac 12:9	32a
the **a** departed from him.	Ac 12:10	32a
has sent forth His **a** and rescued me	Ac 12:11	32a
They kept saying, "It is his **a**."	Ac 12:15	32a
And immediately an **a** of the Lord	Ac 12:23	32a
is no resurrection, nor an **a**,	Ac 23:8	32a
or an **a** has spoken to him?"	Ac 23:9	32a
"For this very night an **a** of the	Ac 27:23	32a
himself as an **a** of light.	2Co 11:14	32a
if we, or an **a** from heaven,	Ga 1:8	32a
you received me as an **a** of God,	Ga 4:14	32a
by His **a** to His bond-servant John,	Rv 1:1	32a
"To the **a** of the church in	Rv 2:1	32a
a of the church in Smyrna write:	Rv 2:8	32a
"And to the **a** of the church in	Rv 2:12	32a
"And to the **a** of the church in	Rv 2:18	32a
a of the church in Sardis write:	Rv 3:1	32a
"And to the **a** of the church in	Rv 3:7	32a
"To the **a** of the church in	Rv 3:14	32a
a proclaiming with a loud voice,	Rv 5:2	32a
And I saw another **a** ascending from	Rv 7:2	32a
a came and stood at the altar,	Rv 8:3	32a
Then the **a** took the censer	Rv 8:5	32a
The second **a** sounded, and	Rv 8:8	32a
The third **a** sounded, and a	Rv 8:10	32a
The fourth **a** sounded, and a	Rv 8:12	32a
Then the fifth **a** sounded, and I saw	Rv 9:1	32a
over them, the **a** of the abyss;	Rv 9:11	32a
Then the sixth **a** sounded, and I	Rv 9:13	32a
the sixth **a** who had the trumpet,	Rv 9:14	32a
a coming down out of heaven,	Rv 10:1	32a
Then the **a** whom I saw standing on	Rv 10:5	32a
of the voice of the seventh **a**,	Rv 10:7	32a
hand of the **a** who stands on the sea	Rv 10:8	32a
So I went to the **a**,	Rv 10:9	32a
Then the seventh **a** sounded;	Rv 11:15	32a
saw another **a** flying in midheaven,	Rv 14:6	32a
And another **a**, a second one,	Rv 14:8	32a
Then another **a**, a third one,	Rv 14:9	32a
another **a** came out of the temple,	Rv 14:15	32a
And another **a** came out of the	Rv 14:17	32a
Then another **a**, the one who has	Rv 14:18	32a
a swung his sickle to the earth and	Rv 14:19	32a
So the first **a** went and poured	Rv 16:2	
The second **a** poured out his bowl	Rv 16:3	
Then the third **a** poured out his	Rv 16:4	
heard the **a** of the waters saying,	Rv 16:5	32a
The fourth **a** poured out his bowl	Rv 16:8	
Then the fifth **a** poured out his	Rv 16:10	
The sixth **a** poured out his bowl	Rv 16:12	
Then the seventh **a** poured out his	Rv 16:17	
And the **a** said to me,	Rv 17:7	32a
another **a** coming down from heaven,	Rv 18:1	32a
Then a strong **a** took up a stone	Rv 18:21	32a
I saw an **a** standing in the sun,	Rv 19:17	32a
saw an **a** coming down from heaven,	Rv 20:1	32a
sent His **a** to show to His	Rv 22:6	32a
the **a** who showed me these things.	Rv 22:8	32a
have sent My **a** to testify to you	Rv 22:16	32a

ANGELIC

an **a** watcher, a holy one,	Da 4:13	
sentence is by the decree of the **a**	Da 4:17	
'In that the king saw an **a**	Da 4:23	
when they revile **a** majesties,	2Pe 2:10	
authority, and revile **a** majesties.	Jude 1:8	
which are *also* **a** *measurements*.	Rv 21:17	32a

ANGEL'S

up before God out of the **a** hand.	Rv 8:4	32a
book out of the **a** hand and ate it,	Rv 10:10	32a

ANGELS

Now the two **a** came to Sodom in the	Gn 19:1	4397
morning dawned, the **a** urged Lot,	Gn 19:15	4397
the **a** of God were ascending and	Gn 28:12	4397
on his way, the **a** of God met him.	Gn 32:1	4397
against His **a** He charges error.	Jb 4:18	4397
Man did eat the bread of **a**;	Ps 78:25	47
trouble, A band of destroying **a**.	Ps 78:49	4397
give His **a** charge concerning you,	Ps 91:11	4397
Bless the LORD, you His **a**,	Ps 103:20	4397
Praise Him, all His **a**;	Ps 148:2	4397
COMMAND HIS A CONCERNING YOU';	Mt 4:6	32a
a came and *began* to minister to	Mt 4:11	32a
and the reapers are **a**.	Mt 13:39	32a
Son of Man will send forth His **a**,	Mt 13:41	32a
the **a** will come forth and take	Mt 13:49	32a
glory of His Father with His **a**,	Mt 16:27	32a
that their **a** in heaven continually	Mt 18:10	32a
but are like **a** in heaven.	Mt 22:30	32a
"And He will send forth His **a**	Mt 24:31	32a
knows, not even the **a** of heaven,	Mt 24:36	32a
His glory, and all the **a** with Him,	Mt 25:31	32a
prepared for the devil and his **a**;	Mt 25:41	32a
more than twelve legions of **a**?	Mt 26:53	32a
and the **a** were ministering to Him.	Mk 1:13	32a
of His Father with the holy **a**."	Mk 8:38	32a
but are like **a** in heaven.	Mk 12:25	32a
"And then He will send forth the **a**,	Mk 13:27	32a
knows, not even the **a** in heaven,	Mk 13:32	32a
When the **a** had gone away	Lk 2:15	32a
'HE WILL COMMAND HIS A	Lk 4:10	32a
of the Father and of the holy **a**.	Lk 9:26	32a
him also before the **a** of God;	Lk 12:8	32a
be denied before the **a** of God.	Lk 12:9	32a
joy in the presence of the **a** of God	Lk 15:10	32a
away by the **a** to Abraham's bosom;	Lk 16:22	32a
die anymore, because they are like **a**,	Lk 20:36	2465
they had also seen a vision of **a** who	Lk 24:23	32a
and the **a** of God ascending and	Jn 1:51	32a
she saw two **a** in white sitting,	Jn 20:12	32a
received the law as ordained by **a**,	Ac 7:53	32a
neither death, nor life, nor **a**,	Ro 8:38	32a
the world, both to **a** and to men.	1Co 4:9	32a
not know that we will judge **a**?	1Co 6:3	32a
on her head, because of the **a**.	1Co 11:10	32a
with the tongues of men and of **a**,	1Co 13:1	32a
a by the agency of a mediator,	Ga 3:19	32a
and the worship of the **a**,	Col 2:18	32a
with His mighty **a** in flaming fire,	2Th 1:7	32a
in the Spirit, Seen by **a**,	1Tm 3:16	32a
Christ Jesus and of *His* chosen **a**,	1Tm 5:21	32a
become as much better than the **a**,	Heb 1:4	32a
to which of the **a** did He ever say,	Heb 1:5	32a
ALL THE A OF GOD WORSHIP HIM."	Heb 1:6	32a
And of the **a** He says,	Heb 1:7	32a
"WHO MAKES HIS A WINDS, AND HIS	Heb 1:7	32a
which of the **a** has He ever said,	Heb 1:13	32a
through **a** proved unalterable,	Heb 2:2	32a
subject to **a** the world to come,	Heb 2:5	32a
A LITTLE WHILE LOWER THAN THE A;	Heb 2:7	32a
a little while lower than the **a**,	Heb 2:9	32a
He does not give help to **a**,	Heb 2:16	32a
Jerusalem, and to myriads of **a**,	Heb 12:22	32a
entertained **a** without knowing it.	Heb 13:2	32a
into which **a** long to look.	1Pe 1:12	32a
after **a** and authorities and powers	1Pe 3:22	32a
did not spare **a** when they sinned,	2Pe 2:4	32a
whereas **a** who are greater in might	2Pe 2:11	32a
And **a** who did not keep their own	Jude 1:6	32a
are the **a** of the seven churches,	Rv 1:20	32a
My Father and before His **a**.	Rv 3:5	32a
and I heard the voice of many **a**	Rv 5:11	32a
After this I saw four **a** standing	Rv 7:1	32a
out with a loud voice to the four **a**	Rv 7:2	32a
And all the **a** were standing around	Rv 7:11	32a
the seven **a** who stand before God,	Rv 8:2	32a
And the seven **a** who had the seven	Rv 8:6	32a
three **a** who are about to sound!"	Rv 8:13	32a
"Release the four **a** who are bound	Rv 9:14	32a
And the four **a**, who had been	Rv 9:15	32a
his **a** waging war with the dragon.	Rv 12:7	32a
The dragon and his **a** waged war,	Rv 12:7	32a
his **a** were thrown down with him.	Rv 12:9	32a
a and in the presence of the Lamb.	Rv 14:10	32a
seven **a** who had seven plagues,	Rv 15:1	32a
and the seven **a** who had the seven	Rv 15:6	32a
gave to the seven **a** seven golden	Rv 15:7	32a
of the seven **a** were finished.	Rv 15:8	32a
the temple, saying to the seven **a**,	Rv 16:1	32a
Then one of the seven **a** who had the	Rv 17:1	32a
Then one of the seven **a** who had the	Rv 21:9	32a
gates, and at the gates twelve **a**;	Rv 21:12	32a

ANGER

brother's **a** against you subsides and	Gn 27:45	639
Jacob's **a** burned against Rachel,	Gn 30:2	639
did to me," his **a** burned.	Gn 39:19	639
Because in their **a** they slew men,	Gn 49:6	639
"Cursed be their **a**, for it is	Gn 49:7	639
Then the **a** of the LORD burned	Ex 4:14	639
he went out from Pharaoh in hot **a**.	Ex 11:8	639
You send forth Your burning **a**,	Ex 15:7	2740
and My **a** will be kindled, and I	Ex 22:24	639
that My **a** may burn against them and	Ex 32:10	639
why does Your **a** burn against Your	Ex 32:11	639
Turn from Your burning **a** and change	Ex 32:12	639
and Moses' **a** burned, and he threw	Ex 32:19	639
"Do not let the **a** of my lord burn;	Ex 32:22	639
and gracious, slow to **a**,	Ex 34:6	639
LORD heard *it*, His **a** was kindled,	Nu 11:1	639
and the **a** of the LORD was kindled	Nu 11:10	639
the **a** of the LORD was kindled	Nu 11:33	639
So the **a** of the LORD burned	Nu 12:9	639
'The LORD is slow to **a** and	Nu 14:18	639
Balak's **a** burned against Balaam,	Nu 24:10	639
so that the fierce **a** of the LORD	Nu 25:4	639
"So the LORD's **a** burned in that	Nu 32:10	639
the LORD's **a** burned against Israel,	Nu 32:13	639
a of the LORD against Israel.	Nu 32:14	639
God *so as* to provoke Him to **a**,	Dt 4:25	3707
otherwise the **a** of the LORD your	Dt 6:15	639
then the **a** of the LORD will be	Dt 7:4	639
of the LORD to provoke Him to **a**.	Dt 9:18	3707
"For I was afraid of the **a** and	Dt 9:19	639
"Or the **a** of the LORD will be	Dt 11:17	639
burning **a** and show mercy to you,	Dt 13:17	639
manslayer in the heat of his **a**,	Dt 19:6	3824
but rather the **a** of the LORD and	Dt 29:20	639
in His **a** and in His wrath.'	Dt 29:23	639
Why this great outburst of **a**?'	Dt 29:24	639
the **a** of the LORD burned against	Dt 29:27	639
uprooted them from their land in **a**	Dt 29:28	639
"Then My **a** will be kindled	Dt 31:17	639
a with the work of your hands."	Dt 31:29	3707

they provoked Him to **a**.	Dt 32:16	3707
provoked Me to **a** with their idols.	Dt 32:21	3707
them to **a** with a foolish nation,	Dt 32:21	3707
For a fire is kindled in My **a**,	Dt 32:22	639
therefore the **a** of the LORD burned	Jos 7:1	639
from the fierceness of His **a**.	Jos 7:26	639
then the **a** of the LORD will burn	Jos 23:16	639
thus they provoked the LORD to **a**.	Jg 2:12	3707
The **a** of the LORD burned	Jg 2:14	639
So the **a** of the LORD burned	Jg 2:20	639
Then the **a** of the LORD was kindled	Jg 3:8	639
"Do not let Your **a** burn against	Jg 6:39	639
Then their **a** toward him subsided	Jg 8:3	7307
the son of Ebed, his **a** burned.	Jg 9:30	639
The **a** of the LORD burned	Jg 10:7	639
And his **a** burned, and he went up	Jg 14:19	639
and Eliab's **a** burned against David	1Sa 17:28	639
Then Saul's **a** burned against	1Sa 20:30	639
arose from the table in fierce **a**,	1Sa 20:34	639
And the **a** of the LORD burned	2Sa 6:7	639
Then David's **a** burned greatly	2Sa 12:5	639
Now again the **a** of the LORD burned	2Sa 24:1	639
molten images to provoke Me to **a**,	1Ki 14:9	3707
Asherim, provoking the LORD to **a**.	1Ki 14:15	3707
the LORD God of Israel to **a**.	1Ki 15:30	3708a
provoking Me to **a** with their sins,	1Ki 16:2	3707
to **a** with the work of his hands,	1Ki 16:7	3707
of Israel to **a** with their idols.	1Ki 16:13	3707
which you have provoked *Me* to **a**,	1Ki 21:22	3707
provoked the LORD God of Israel to **a**	1Ki 22:53	3707
So the **a** of the LORD was kindled	2Ki 13:3	639
of the LORD provoking *Him to* **a**.	2Ki 21:6	
and have been provoking Me to **a** since	2Ki 21:15	3707
gods that they might provoke Me to **a**	2Ki 22:17	3707
which His **a** burned against Judah,	2Ki 23:26	639
For through the **a** of the LORD *this*	2Ki 24:20	639
The **a** of the LORD burned	1Ch 13:10	639
the **a** of the LORD turned away from	2Ch 12:12	639
so their **a** burned against Judah	2Ch 25:10	639
they returned home in fierce **a**.	2Ch 25:10	639
Then the **a** of the LORD burned	2Ch 25:15	639
a of the LORD is against you."	2Ch 28:11	639
His burning **a** is against Israel."	2Ch 28:13	639
the God of his fathers, to **a**.	2Ch 28:25	3707
burning **a** may turn away from us.	2Ch 29:10	639
burning **a** may turn away from you.	2Ch 30:8	639
provoking Him *to* **a**.	2Ch 33:6	
that they might provoke Me to **a**	2Ch 34:25	3707
but His power and His **a** are	Ezr 8:22	639
until the fierce **a** of our God on	Ezr 10:14	639
and compassionate, Slow to **a** and	Ne 9:17	639
will be plenty of contempt and **a**.	Es 1:18	7110a
when the **a** of King Ahasuerus had	Es 2:1	2534
filled with **a** against Mordecai.	Es 5:9	2534
The king arose in his **a** from	Es 7:7	2534
and the king's **a** subsided.	Es 7:10	2534
of His **a** they come to an end.	Jb 4:9	639
"For **a** slays the foolish man,	Jb 5:2	7068
When He overturns them in His **a**;	Jb 9:5	639
"God will not turn back His **a**;	Jb 9:13	639
And increase Your **a** toward me	Jb 10:17	3708b
"His **a** has torn me and hunted me	Jb 16:9	639
"O you who tear yourself in your **a**	Jb 18:4	639
has also kindled His **a** against me And	Jb 19:11	639
God will send His fierce **a** on him	Jb 20:23	639
flow away in the day of His **a**.	Jb 20:28	639
apportion destruction in His **a**?	Jb 21:17	639
But the **a** of Elihu the son of	Jb 32:2	639
against Job his **a** burned because	Jb 32:2	639
And his **a** burned against his three	Jb 32:3	639
of the three men his **a** burned.	Jb 32:5	639
He has not visited *in* His **a**,	Jb 35:15	639
"But the godless in heart lay up **a**;	Jb 36:13	639
out the overflowings of your **a**,	Jb 40:11	639
Then He will speak to them in His **a**	Ps 2:5	639
Lord, do not rebuke me in Your **a**,	Ps 6:1	639
Arise, O LORD, in Your **a**;	Ps 7:6	639
fiery oven in the time of your **a**;	Ps 21:9	6440
Do not turn Your servant away in **a**;	Ps 27:9	639
For His **a** is but for a moment, His	Ps 30:5	639
Cease from **a** and forsake wrath;	Ps 37:8	639
chasten me not in Your burning **a**.	Ps 38:1	2534
a they bear a grudge against me.	Ps 55:3	639
forth, In **a** put down the peoples,	Ps 56:7	639
may Your burning **a** overtake them.	Ps 69:24	639
Why does Your **a** smoke against the	Ps 74:1	639
He in **a** withdrawn His compassion?	Ps 77:9	639
And **a** also mounted against Israel,	Ps 78:21	639
The **a** of God rose against them And	Ps 78:31	639
And often He restrained His **a** And	Ps 78:38	639
He sent upon them His burning **a**,	Ps 78:49	639
He leveled a path for His **a**;	Ps 78:50	639
turned away from Your burning **a**.	Ps 85:3	639
Your **a** to all generations?	Ps 85:5	639
Slow to **a** and abundant in	Ps 86:15	639
Your burning **a** has passed over me;	Ps 88:16	2740
we have been consumed by Your **a**	Ps 90:7	639
understands the power of Your **a**	Ps 90:11	639
"Therefore I swore in My **a**,	Ps 95:11	639
Slow to **a** and abounding in	Ps 103:8	639
Nor will He keep *His* **a** forever.	Ps 103:9	
Him to **a** with their deeds,	Ps 106:29	3707
Therefore the **a** of the LORD was	Ps 106:40	639
their **a** was kindled against us;	Ps 124:3	639
to **a** and great in lovingkindness.	Ps 145:8	639
A fool's **a** is known at once,	Pr 12:16	3708a
slow to **a** has great understanding,	Pr 14:29	639
But his **a** is toward him who acts	Pr 14:35	5678
But a harsh word stirs up **a**.	Pr 15:1	639
the slow to **a** calms a dispute.	Pr 15:18	639
to **a** is better than the mighty,	Pr 16:32	639
discretion makes him slow to **a**,	Pr 19:11	639
of great **a** will bear the penalty,	Pr 19:19	2534
He who provokes him to **a** forfeits	Pr 20:2	5674b
A gift in secret subdues **a**,	Pr 21:14	639
associate with a man *given* to **a**;	Pr 22:24	639
And turn His **a** away from him.	Pr 24:18	639
Wrath is fierce and **a** is a flood,	Pr 27:4	639
aflame, But wise men turn away **a**.	Pr 29:8	639
the churning of **a** produces strife.	Pr 30:33	639
great vexation, sickness and **a**.	Ec 5:17	7110a
a resides in the bosom of fools.	Ec 7:9	3708a
So, remove grief and **a** from your	Ec 11:10	3708a
On this account the **a** of the LORD	Is 5:25	639
For all this His **a** is not spent,	Is 5:25	639
of the fierce **a** of Rezin and Aram and	Is 7:4	639
all this, His **a** does not turn away	Is 9:12	639
all this, His **a** does not turn away	Is 9:17	639
all this, His **a** does not turn away	Is 9:21	639
all this, His **a** does not turn away	Is 10:4	639
the rod of My **a** And the staff in	Is 10:5	639
and My **a** *will be directed* to their	Is 10:25	639
with me, Your **a** is turned away,	Is 12:1	639
exulting ones, To *execute* My **a**.	Is 13:3	639
Cruel, with fury and burning **a**,	Is 13:9	639
hosts In the day of His burning **a**.	Is 13:13	639
a with unrestrained persecution.	Is 14:6	639
Burning is His **a** and dense is *His*	Is 30:27	639
of His arm to be seen in fierce **a**,	Is 30:30	639
poured out on him the heat of His **a**	Is 42:25	639
the LORD's hand the cup of His **a**;	Is 51:17	2534
The chalice of My **a**;	Is 51:22	2534
"In an outburst of **a** I hid My	Is 54:8	7110a
I also trod them in My **a** And	Is 63:3	639
I trod down the peoples in My **a** And	Is 63:6	639
To render His **a** with fury,	Is 66:15	639
His **a** is turned away from me.'	Jer 2:35	639
'I will not look upon you in **a**.	Jer 3:12	
For the fierce **a** of the LORD Has	Jer 4:8	639
the LORD, before His fierce **a**.	Jer 4:26	639
My **a** and My wrath will be poured	Jer 7:20	639
Not with Your **a**, or You will bring	Jer 10:24	639
of the fierce **a** of the LORD."	Jer 12:13	639
a fire has been kindled in My **a**,	Jer 15:14	639
in My **a** Which will burn forever.	Jer 17:4	639
with them in the time of Your **a**!	Jer 18:23	639
even in **a** and wrath and great	Jer 21:5	639
"The **a** of the LORD will not turn	Jer 23:20	639
do not provoke Me to **a** with the	Jer 25:6	3707
order that you might provoke Me to **a**	Jer 25:7	3707
of the fierce **a** of the LORD.	Jer 25:37	639
And because of His fierce **a**."	Jer 25:38	639
The fierce **a** of the LORD will not	Jer 30:24	639
to other gods to provoke Me to **a**.	Jer 32:29	3707
to **a** by the work of their hands,"	Jer 32:30	3707
has been to Me *a provocation of* My **a**	Jer 32:31	639
have done to provoke Me to **a**—they,	Jer 32:32	3707
which I have driven them in My **a**,	Jer 32:37	639
slain in My **a** and in My wrath,	Jer 33:5	639
for great is the **a** and the wrath	Jer 36:7	639
"As My **a** and wrath have been	Jer 42:18	639
committed so as to provoke Me to **a**	Jer 44:3	3707
'Therefore My wrath and My **a** were	Jer 44:6	639
to **a** with the works of your hands,	Jer 44:8	3707
upon them, Even My fierce **a**,'	Jer 49:37	639
From the fierce **a** of the LORD.	Jer 51:45	639
For through the **a** of the LORD *this*	Jer 52:3	639
on the day of His fierce **a**.	La 1:12	639
of Zion With a cloud in His **a**!	La 2:1	639
His footstool In the day of His **a**.	La 2:1	639
In fierce **a** He has cut off All the	La 2:3	639
In the indignation of His **a**.	La 2:6	639
slain *them* in the day of Your **a**,	La 2:21	639
In the day of the LORD's **a**.	La 2:22	639
Yourself with **a** And pursued us;	La 3:43	639
You will pursue them in **a** and	La 3:66	639
He has poured out His fierce **a**;	La 4:11	639
'Thus My **a** will be spent and I	Ezk 5:13	639
judgments against you in **a**,	Ezk 5:15	639
and I will send My **a** against you;	Ezk 7:3	639
you and spend My **a** against you	Ezk 7:8	639
There will also be in My **a** a	Ezk 13:13	639
to accomplish My **a** against them in	Ezk 20:8	639
to accomplish My **a** against them in	Ezk 20:21	639
you in My **a** and in My wrath and	Ezk 22:20	639
to My **a** and according to My wrath;	Ezk 25:14	639
will deal *with you* according to your **a**	Ezk 35:11	639
My fury will mount up in My **a**.	Ezk 38:18	639
So I have consumed them in My **a**.	Ezk 43:8	639
a gave orders to bring Shadrach,	Da 3:13	2528
let now Your **a** and Your wrath turn	Da 9:16	639
though not in **a** nor in battle.	Da 11:20	639
Their **a** smolders all night, In the	Hos 7:6	644
"My **a** burns against them!"	Hos 8:5	639
I will not execute My fierce **a**;	Hos 11:9	639
Ephraim has provoked to bitter **a**;	Hos 12:14	3707
I gave you a king in My **a** And	Hos 13:11	639
My **a** has turned away from them.	Hos 14:4	639
and compassionate, Slow to **a**,	Jl 2:13	639
His **a** also tore continually, And	Am 1:11	639
withdraw His burning **a** so that we	Jon 3:9	639
slow to **a** and abundant in	Jon 4:2	639
"And I will execute vengeance in **a**	Mi 5:15	639
He does not retain His **a** forever,	Mi 7:18	639
is slow to **a** and great in power,	Na 1:3	639
can endure the burning of His **a**?	Na 1:6	639
Or *was* Your **a** against the rivers,	Hab 3:8	639
In **a** You trampled the	Hab 3:12	639
a of the LORD comes upon you,	Zph 2:2	639
day of the LORD's **a** comes upon you.	Zph 2:2	639
hidden In the day of the LORD's **a**.	Zph 2:3	639
My indignation, All My burning **a**;	Zph 3:8	639
"My **a** is kindled against the	Zch 10:3	639
"And his lord, moved with **a**,	Mt 18:34	*3710*
looking around at them with **a**,	Mk 3:5	*3709*
UNDERSTANDING WILL I **A** YOU."	Ro 10:19	*3949*
strife, jealousy, outbursts of **a**,	Ga 5:20	*2372*
not let the sun go down on your **a**,	Eph 4:26	*3950*
Let all bitterness and wrath and **a**	Eph 4:31	*3709*
do not provoke your children to **a**,	Eph 6:4	*3949*
a, wrath, malice, slander, *and*	Col 3:8	*3709*
hear, slow to speak *and* slow to **a**;	Jas 1:19	*3709*
for the **a** of man does not achieve	Jas 1:20	*3709*
full strength in the cup of His **a**;	Rv 14:10	*3709*

ANGERED

all those who are **a** at you will be	Is 41:11	2734

ANGLE

the ascent of the armory at the **A**.	Ne 3:19	4740
from the **A** to the doorway of the	Ne 3:20	4740
as the **A** and as far as the corner.	Ne 3:24	4740
of Uzai *made repairs* in front of the **A**	Ne 3:25	4740

ANGRY

very **a** and his countenance fell.	Gn 4:5	2734
LORD said to Cain, "Why are you **a**?	Gn 4:6	2734
"Oh may the Lord not be **a**,	Gn 18:30	2734
"Oh may the Lord not be **a**,	Gn 18:32	2734
a that I cannot rise before you,	Gn 31:35	2734
became **a** and contended with Laban;	Gn 31:36	2734
and they were very **a** because he	Gn 34:7	2734
and do not be **a** with your servant;	Gn 44:18	639, 2734
be grieved or **a** with yourselves,	Gn 45:5	2734
and Moses was **a** with them.	Ex 16:20	7107
So he was **a** with Aaron's surviving	Lv 10:16	7107
very **a** and said to the LORD,	Nu 16:15	2734
a with the entire congregation?"	Nu 16:22	7107
God was **a** because he was going,	Nu 22:22	639, 2734
so Balaam was **a** and struck the	Nu 22:27	639, 2734
and the LORD was **a** against Israel.	Nu 25:3	639, 2734
a with the officers of the army,	Nu 31:14	7107
and He was **a** and took an oath,	Dt 1:34	7107
a with me also on your account,	Dt 1:37	599
was **a** with me on your account,	Dt 3:26	5674b
was **a** with me on your account,	Dt 4:21	599
and the LORD was so **a** with you	Dt 9:8	599
"The LORD was **a** enough with	Dt 9:20	599
He will be **a** with the whole	Jos 22:18	7107
these words, and he became very **a**.	1Sa 11:6	639, 2734
Then Saul became very **a**,	1Sa 18:8	2734
but if he is very **a**,	1Sa 20:7	2734
the Philistines were **a** with him,	1Sa 29:4	7107
Then Abner was very **a** over the	2Sa 3:8	2734
David became **a** because of the	2Sa 6:8	2734
all these matters, he was very **a**.	2Sa 13:21	2734
then are you **a** about this matter?	2Sa 19:42	2734
And were shaken, because He was **a**.	2Sa 22:8	2734
and You are **a** with them and deliver	1Ki 8:46	599
Now the LORD was **a** with Solomon	1Ki 11:9	599
of God was **a** with him and said,	2Ki 13:19	7107
the LORD was very **a** with Israel and	2Ki 17:18	599
Then David became **a** because of the	1Ch 13:11	2734
and You are **a** with them and deliver	2Ch 6:36	599
Then Asa was **a** with the seer and	2Ch 16:10	3707
of your fathers, was **a** with Judah,	2Ch 28:9	2534
Would You not be **a** with us to	Ezr 9:14	599
and very **a** and mocked the Jews.	Ne 4:1	3707
to be closed, they were very **a**.	Ne 4:7	2734
Then I was very **a** when I had heard	Ne 5:6	2734
Then the king became very **a** and	Es 1:12	7107
became **a** and sought to lay hands	Es 2:21	7107
to the Son, that He not become **a**,	Ps 2:12	599
And were shaken, because He was **a**.	Ps 18:7	2734
You have been **a**;	Ps 60:1	599
Your presence when once You are **a**?	Ps 76:7	639
Will You be **a** forever?	Ps 79:5	599
a with the prayer of Your people?	Ps 80:4	6225
Will You be **a** with us forever?	Ps 85:5	599
tongue, an **a** countenance.	Pr 25:23	2194
An **a** man stirs up strife, And a	Pr 29:22	639
Why should God be **a** on account of	Ec 5:6	7107
Do not be eager in your heart to be **a**,	Ec 7:9	3707
My mother's sons were **a** with me;	SS 1:6	2734
For although You were **a** with me,	Is 12:1	599
a at Him will be put to shame.	Is 45:24	2734
"I was **a** with My people, I	Is 47:6	7107
that I will not be **a** with you Nor	Is 54:9	7107
Nor will I always be **a**;	Is 57:16	7107
gain I was **a** and struck him;	Is 57:17	7107
I hid *My face* and was **a**,	Is 57:17	7107
Behold, You were **a**,	Is 64:5	7107
Do not be **a** beyond measure, O	Is 64:9	7107
'Will He be **a** forever?	Jer 3:5	5201
'I will not be **a** forever.	Jer 3:12	5201
were **a** at Jeremiah and beat him,	Jer 37:15	7107
us *And* are exceedingly **a** with us.	La 5:22	7107
your harlotry to make Me **a**.	Ezk 16:26	3707
I will be pacified and **a** no more.	Ezk 16:42	3707
displeased Jonah and he became **a**.	Jon 4:1	2734
"Do you have good reason to be **a**?"	Jon 4:4	2734
reason to be **a** about the plant?"	Jon 4:9	2734
"I have good reason to be **a**,	Jon 4:9	2734
LORD was very **a** with your fathers.	Zch 1:2	7107

“But I am very **a** with the nations Zch 1:15 7107
for while I was only a little **a**, Zch 1:15 7107
everyone who is **a** with his brother Mt 5:22 *3710*
became **a** and said to his slave, Lk 14:21 *3710*
“But he became **a** and was not Lk 15:28 *3710*
are you **a** with Me because I made Jn 7:23 *5520*
Now he was very **a** with the people Ac 12:20 *2371*
be strife, jealousy, **a** tempers, 2Co 12:20 *2372*
BE **A**, AND *yet* DO NOT SIN; Eph 4:26 *3710*
I WAS **A** WITH THIS GENERATION, Heb 3:10 *4360*
whom was He **a** for forty years? Heb 3:17 *4360*

ANGUISH
A has gripped the inhabitants of Ex 15:14 2427
and be in **a** because of you.’ Dt 2:25 2342a
and the queen writhed in great **a**. Es 4:4
will speak in the **a** of my spirit, Jb 7:11 6862b
“Distress and **a** terrify him, They Jb 15:24 4691
Panic seized them there, **A**, Ps 48:6 2427
My heart is in **a** within me, And Ps 55:4 2342a
waters saw You, they were in **a**; Ps 77:16 2342a
Trouble and **a** have come upon me, Ps 119:143 4689
When distress and **a** come upon you. Pr 1:27 6695b
and darkness, the gloom of **a**; Is 8:22 6695b
more gloom for her who was in **a**; Is 9:1 4164
and **a** will take hold of *them;* Is 13:8 2256b
reason my loins are full of **a**; Is 21:3 2479
be in **a** at the report of Tyre. Is 23:5 2342a
Through a land of distress and **a**, Is 30:6 6695b
As a result of the **a** of His soul, Is 53:11 5999
I am in **a**! Oh, my heart! My heart Jer 4:19 2342a
The **a** as of one giving birth to Jer 4:31 6869a
A has seized us, Pain as of a Jer 6:24 6869a
bring down on her **A** and dismay. Jer 15:8 5892a
‘When **a** comes, they will seek Ezk 7:25 7089
Egypt, And **a** will be in Ethiopia; Ezk 30:4 2479
and **a** will be on them as on the Ezk 30:9 2479
Sin will writhe in **a**, Ezk 30:16 2342a
of the vision **a** has come upon me, Da 10:16 6735c
Before them the people are in **a**; Jl 2:6 2342a
Also **a** is in the whole body And Na 2:10 2479
she no longer remembers the **a** Jn 16:21 *2347*
For out of much affliction and **a** 2Co 2:4 *4928*

ANGUISHED
heard the **a** cry of destruction. Jer 48:5 6862b

ANIAM
Ahian and Shechem and Likhi and **A**. 1Ch 7:19 593

ANIM
and Anab and Eshtemoh and **A**, Jos 15:50 6044

ANIMAL
you of every clean **a** by sevens, Gn 7:2 929
and took of every clean **a** and of Gn 8:20 929
and slay an **a** and make ready; for Gn 43:16 2874
and the dead **a** shall become his. Ex 21:34
and the dead **a** shall become his. Ex 21:36
lets his **a** loose so that it grazes in Ex 22:5 1165
a sheep, or any **a** to keep *for him,* Ex 22:10 929
an **a** shall surely be put to death. Ex 22:19 929
uncleanness, or an unclean **a**, Lv 7:21 929
‘Also the fat of *an* **a** which dies Lv 7:24
the fat of an **a** torn *by beasts* may Lv 7:24 2966
‘For whoever eats the fat of the **a** Lv 7:25 929
any blood, either of bird or **a**, Lv 7:26 929
This is the law regarding the **a** and Lv 11:46 929
“When any person eats *an* **a** which Lv 17:15
not have intercourse with any **a** Lv 18:23 929
stand before an **a** to mate with it; Lv 18:23 929
there is a man who lies with an **a**, Lv 20:15 929
you shall also kill the **a**. Lv 20:15 929
approaches any **a** to mate with it, Lv 20:16 929
shall kill the woman and the **a**; Lv 20:16 929
the clean **a** and the unclean, Lv 20:25 929
not make yourselves detestable by **a** Lv 20:25 929
‘He shall not eat *an* **a** which Lv 22:8
life of an **a** shall make it good, Lv 24:18 929
who kills an **a** shall make it good, Lv 24:21 929
‘Now if it is an **a** of the kind Lv 27:9 929
if he does exchange **a** for animal, Lv 27:10 929
if he does exchange animal for **a**, Lv 27:10 929
it is any unclean **a** of the kind Lv 27:11 929
place the **a** before the priest. Lv 27:11 929
of man or **a** or of the fields of Lv 27:28 929
of all flesh, whether man or **a**, Nu 18:15 929
captured, both of man and of **a**; Nu 31:26 929
of any **a** that is on the earth, Dt 4:17 929
“Any **a** that divides the hoof Dt 14:6 929
‘Cursed is he who lies with any **a**.’ Dt 27:21 929
and there was no **a** with me except Ne 2:12 929
the **a** on which I was riding. Ne 2:12 929
man has regard for the life of his **a**, Pr 12:10 929
no wage for man or any wage for **a**; Zch 8:10 929
a blemished **a** to the Lord, Mal 1:14 7843

ANIMALS
from man to **a** to creeping things Gn 6:7 929
and of the **a** after their kind, Gn 6:20 929
of the **a** that are not clean two, Gn 7:2 929
Of clean **a** and animals that are Gn 7:8 929
Of clean animals and **a** that are Gn 7:8 929
from man to **a** to creeping things Gn 7:23 929
birds and **a** and every creeping Gn 8:17 929
and to whom do these **a** in front Gn 32:17
property and all their **a** be ours? Gn 34:23 929
of **a** from the herd or the flock. Lv 1:2 929
all the **a** that are on the earth. Lv 11:2 929
and chews the cud, among the **a**, Lv 11:3 929
all the **a** which divide the hoof but Lv 11:26 929
if one of the **a** dies which you have Lv 11:39 929
‘Even your cattle and the **a** that Lv 25:7 2421b
‘However, a firstborn among **a**, Lv 27:26 929
‘But if *it is* among the unclean **a**, Lv 27:27 929
among the men and among the **a**; Nu 8:17 929
of unclean **a** you shall redeem. Nu 18:15 929
and of the sheep, from all the **a**, Nu 31:30 929
every fifty, both of man and of **a**, Nu 31:47 929
“We took only the **a** as our booty Dt 2:35 929
“But all the **a** and the spoil of Dt 3:7 929
“These are the **a** which you may eat: Dt 14:4 929
and chews the cud, among the **a**, Dt 14:6 929
the **a** and all that is in the city, Dt 20:14 929
he spoke also of **a** and birds and 1Ki 4:33 929
and they slaughtered the Passover **a** 2Ch 35:1
“Now slaughter the Passover **a**, 2Ch 35:6
They slaughtered the Passover **a**, 2Ch 35:11
So they roasted the Passover **a** on 2Ch 35:13
number, **A** both small and great. Ps 104:25 2421b
A and birds have been snatched Jer 12:4 929
wild **a** of the field to serve him. Jer 27:6 2421b
left hand, as well as many **a**?” Jon 4:11 929
were in it all *kinds of* four-footed **a** Ac 10:12 *5074*
I saw the four-footed **a** of the earth Ac 11:6 *5074*
and of birds and four-footed **a** Ro 1:23 *5074*
For the bodies of those **a** whose Heb 13:11 *2226*
But these, like unreasoning **a**, 2Pe 2:12 *2226*
by instinct, like unreasoning **a**, Jude 1:10 *2226*

ANKLE
headdresses, **a** chains, sashes, Is 3:20 6807b

ANKLES
the water, water *reaching* the **a**. Ezk 47:3 658a
feet and his **a** were strengthened. Ac 3:7 *4974*

ANKLETS
take away the beauty of *their* **a**, Is 3:18 5914

ANNA
A the daughter of Phanuel, Lk 2:36 *451*

ANNALS
the **a** of Jehu the son of Hanani, 2Ch 20:34 1697

ANNAS
high priesthood of **A** and Caiaphas, Lk 3:2 *452*
and led Him to **A** first; Jn 18:13 *452*
A sent Him bound to Jn 18:24 *452*
and **A** the high priest *was there,* Ac 4:6 *452*

ANNIHILATE
to kill and to **a** all the Jews, Es 3:13 6
and to **a** the entire army of any Es 8:11 6
them in the wilderness, to **a** them. Ezk 20:13 3615
great wrath to destroy and **a** many. Da 11:44 2763a

ANNIHILATED
to be killed and to be **a**. Es 7:4 6
after them until I have **a** them.” Jer 9:16 3615
bore and reared, My enemy **a** them. La 2:22 3615
away, **a** and destroyed forever. Da 7:26 8046a
Then I **a** the three shepherds in Zch 11:8 3582
let it die, and what is to be **a**, Zch 11:9 3582
is to be annihilated, let it be **a**; Zch 11:9 3582

ANNIHILATION
cause their **a** in the wilderness. Ezk 20:17 3617

ANNOUNCE
Or **a** to us what is coming; Is 41:22 8085
there I will **a** My words to you.” Jer 18:2 8085
have heard from Him and **a** to you, 1Jn 1:5 *312*

ANNOUNCED
since **a** *it* to you and declared *it?* Is 44:8 8085
Who has **a** this from of old? Is 45:21 8085
have **a** My words to My people, Jer 23:22 8085
“But the things which God **a** Ac 3:18 *4293*
onward, also **a** these days. Ac 3:24 *2605*
killed those who had previously **a** Ac 7:52 *4293*
but ran in and **a** that Peter was Ac 12:14 *518*
things which now have been **a** to you 1Pe 1:12 *312*

ANNOUNCES
Who **a** peace And brings good news Is 52:7 8085
of happiness, Who **a** salvation, Is 52:7 8085
who brings good news, Who **a** peace! Na 1:15 8085

ANNOUNCING
came, **a** to the disciples, Jn 20:18 *31b*

ANNOYANCE
with the **a** to the king.” Es 7:4 5143

ANNOYED
him, that his soul was **a** to death. Jg 16:16 7114a
But Paul was greatly **a**, Ac 16:18 *1278*

ANNUAL
and the three **a** feasts—the Feast 2Ch 8:13
6471, 8141

ANNUALLY
He used to go **a** on circuit to 1Sa 7:16
1767, 8141
to repair the house of your God **a**, 2Ch 24:5
1767, 8141
households, at fixed times **a**, Ne 10:34 8141
tree to the house of the LORD **a**, Ne 10:35 8141
day of the same month, **a**, Es 9:21
3605, 8141
to their appointed time **a**. Es 9:27
3605, 8141

ANNUL
then he shall **a** her vow which she Nu 30:8 6565a
it or her husband may **a** it. Nu 30:13 6565a
“Will you really **a** My judgment? Jb 40:8 6565a
and do not **a** Your covenant with us. Jer 14:21 6565a

ANNULLED
her husband has **a** them, and the Nu 30:12 6565a

ANNULS
a them on the day he hears *them,* Nu 30:12 6565a
a them after he has heard them, Nu 30:15 6565a
“Whoever then **a** one of the least Mt 5:19 *3089*

ANOINT
and you shall **a** them and ordain Ex 28:41 4886
and pour it on his head and **a** him. Ex 29:7 4886
you shall **a** it to consecrate it. Ex 29:36 4886
“With it you shall **a** the tent Ex 30:26 4886
You shall **a** Aaron and his sons, Ex 30:30 4886
a the tabernacle and all that is in it, Ex 40:9 4886
“You shall **a** the altar of Ex 40:10 4886
shall **a** the laver and its stand, Ex 40:11 4886
and **a** him and consecrate him, Ex 40:13 4886
and you shall **a** them even as you Ex 40:15 4886
will not **a** yourself with the oil, Dt 28:40 5480a
went forth to **a** a king over them, Jg 9:8 4886
and **a** yourself and put on your Ru 3:3 5480a
and you shall **a** him to be prince 1Sa 9:16 4886
to **a** you as king over His people, 1Sa 15:1 4886
and you shall **a** for Me the one 1Sa 16:3 4886
LORD said, “Arise, **a** him; for this is 1Sa 16:12 4886
and do not **a** yourself with oil, 2Sa 14:2 5480a
a him there as king over Israel, 1Ki 1:34 4886
you shall **a** Hazael king over Aram; 1Ki 19:15 4886
you shall **a** king over Israel; 1Ki 19:16 4886
shall **a** as prophet in your place. 1Ki 19:16 4886
and to **a** the most holy *place.* Da 9:24 4886
a themselves with the finest of oils, Am 6:6 4886
but will not **a** yourself with oil; Mi 6:15 5480a
you, when you fast, **a** your head and Mt 6:17 *218b*
that they might come and **a** Him. Mk 16:1 *218b*
“You did not **a** My head with oil, Lk 7:46 *218b*
and eye salve to **a** your eyes so that Rv 3:18 *1472*

ANOINTED
of Bethel, where you **a** a pillar, Gn 31:13 4886
them they may be **a** and ordained. Ex 29:29 4886
even as you have **a** their father, Ex 40:15 4886
if the **a** priest sins so as to Lv 4:3 4899
‘Then the **a** priest is to take some Lv 4:5 4899
‘Then the **a** priest is to bring Lv 4:16 4899
the LORD on the day when he is **a**; Lv 6:20 4886
“The **a** priest who will be in Lv 6:22 4899
Israel in the day that He **a** them. Lv 7:36 4886
then took the anointing oil and **a** Lv 8:10 4886
and **a** the altar and all its utensils, Lv 8:11 4886
oil on Aaron’s head and **a** him, Lv 8:12 4886
“So the priest who is **a** and Lv 16:32 4886
the sons of Aaron, the **a** priests, Nu 3:3 4886
he **a** it and consecrated it with Nu 7:1 4886
he **a** them and consecrated them Nu 7:1 4886
for the altar when it was **a**, Nu 7:10 4886
leaders of Israel when it was **a**: Nu 7:84 4886
for the altar after it was **a**. Nu 7:88 4886
who was **a** with the holy oil. Nu 35:25 4886
will exalt the horn of His **a**.” 1Sa 2:10 4899
he will walk before My **a** always. 1Sa 2:35 4899
“Has not the LORD **a** you a ruler 1Sa 10:1 4886
me before the LORD and His **a**. 1Sa 12:3 4899
and His **a** is witness this day that 1Sa 12:5 4899
the LORD **a** you king over Israel, 1Sa 15:17 4886
the LORD’s **a** is before Him.” 1Sa 16:6 4899
Samuel took the horn of oil and **a** him 1Sa 16:13 4886
thing to my lord, the LORD’s **a**, 1Sa 24:6 4899
him, since he is the LORD’s **a**.” 1Sa 24:6 4899
my lord, for he is the LORD’s **a**.’ 1Sa 24:10 4899
LORD’s **a** and be without guilt?” 1Sa 26:9 4899
out my hand against the LORD’s **a**; 1Sa 26:11 4899
not guard your lord, the LORD’s **a**. 1Sa 26:16 4899
out my hand against the LORD’s **a**. 1Sa 26:23 4899
hand to destroy the LORD’s **a**?” 2Sa 1:14 4899
‘I have killed the LORD’s **a**.’ ” 2Sa 1:16 4899
shield of Saul, not **a** with oil. 2Sa 1:21 4899
Judah came and there **a** David king 2Sa 2:4 4886
Judah has **a** me king over them.” 2Sa 2:7 4886
I am weak today, though **a** king; 2Sa 3:39 4886
they **a** David king over Israel. 2Sa 5:3 4886
they had **a** David king over Israel, 2Sa 5:17 4886
‘It is I who **a** you king over 2Sa 12:7 4886
the ground, washed, **a** *himself,* 2Sa 12:20 5480a
Absalom, whom we **a** over us, 2Sa 19:10 4886
because he cursed the LORD’s **a**?” 2Sa 19:21 4899
And shows lovingkindness to His **a**, 2Sa 22:51 4899
The **a** of the God of Jacob, 2Sa 23:1 4899
oil from the tent and **a** Solomon. 1Ki 1:39 4886
prophet have **a** him king in Gihon, 1Ki 1:45 4886
when he heard that they had **a** him 1Ki 5:1 4886
“I have **a** you king over Israel.” 2Ki 9:3 4886
‘I have **a** you king over the people 2Ki 9:6 4886
a you king over Israel.’ 2Ki 9:12 4886
and they made him king and **a** him, 2Ki 11:12 4886
Jehoahaz the son of Josiah and **a** him 2Ki 23:30 4886
and they **a** David king over Israel, 1Ch 11:3 4886
had been **a** king over all Israel, 1Ch 14:8 4886
“Do not touch My **a** ones, And do 1Ch 16:22 4899
and they **a** *him* as ruler for the 1Ch 29:22 4886
not turn away the face of Your **a**; 2Ch 6:42 4899
a to cut off the house of Ahab. 2Ch 22:7 4886
and his sons **a** him and said, 2Ch 23:11 4886
gave them drink, **a** them *with oil,* 2Ch 28:15 5480a
the LORD and against His **A**, Ps 2:2 4899
And shows lovingkindness to His **a**, Ps 18:50 4899
I know that the LORD saves His **a**; Ps 20:6 4899
You have **a** my head with oil; Ps 23:5 1878
He is a saving defense to His **a**. Ps 28:8 4899
has **a** You With the oil of joy Ps 45:7 4886
And look upon the face of Your **a**. Ps 84:9 4899
With My holy oil I have **a** him, Ps 89:20 4886
full of wrath against Your **a**. Ps 89:38 4899
the footsteps of Your **a**. Ps 89:51 4899
I have been **a** with fresh oil. Ps 92:10 1101a
“Do not touch My **a** ones, And do Ps 105:15 4899
not turn away the face of Your **a**. Ps 132:10 4899

I have prepared a lamp for Mine **a**. Ps 132:17 4899
Thus says the LORD to Cyrus His **a**, Is 45:1 4899
Because the LORD has **a** me To bring Is 61:1 4886
of our nostrils, the LORD's **a**, La 4:20 4899
from you and **a** you with oil. Ezk 16:9 5480a
"You were the **a** cherub who Ezk 28:14 4473
For the salvation of Your **a**. Hab 3:13 4899
"These are the two **a** ones who Zch 4:14 1121, 3323
she has **a** My body beforehand for Mk 14:8 *3462*
BECAUSE HE **A** ME TO PREACH THE Lk 4:18 *5548*
but she **a** My feet with perfume. Lk 7:46 *218b*
Jesus made clay, and **a** my eyes, Jn 9:11 *2025*
Mary who **a** the Lord with ointment, Jn 11:2 *218b*
nard, and **a** the feet of Jesus and Jn 12:3 *218b*
whom You **a**, both Herod and Pontius Ac 4:27 *5548*
how God **a** Him with the Holy Spirit Ac 10:38 *5548*
you in Christ and **a** us is God, 2Co 1:21 *5548*
HAS **A** YOU WITH THE OIL OF Heb 1:9 *5548*

ANOINTING

spices for the **a** oil and for the Ex 25:6 4888b
"Then you shall take the **a** oil and Ex 29:7 4888b
the altar and some of the **a** oil, Ex 29:21 4888b
shall make of these a holy **a** oil, Ex 30:25 4888b
it shall be a holy **a** oil. Ex 30:25 4888b
'This shall be a holy **a** oil to Me Ex 30:31 4888b
the **a** oil also, and the fragrant Ex 31:11 4888b
and spices for the **a** oil, Ex 35:8 4888b
a oil and the fragrant incense, Ex 35:15 4888b
the oil for the light and for the **a** oil Ex 35:28 4888b
made the holy **a** oil and the pure, Ex 37:29 4888b
a oil and the fragrant incense, Ex 39:38 4888b
"Then you shall take the **a** oil Ex 40:9 4888b
and their **a** will qualify them for Ex 40:15 4888b
and the garments and the **a** oil and Lv 8:2 4888b
Moses then took the **a** oil and Lv 8:10 4888b
Then he poured some of the **a** oil Lv 8:12 4888b
So Moses took some of the **a** oil Lv 8:30 4888b
for the LORD's **a** oil is upon you." Lv 10:7 4888b
head the **a** oil has been poured and Lv 21:10 4888b
of the **a** oil of his God is on him; Lv 21:12 4888b
continual grain offering and the **a** oil Nu 4:16 4888b
you are **a** me as king over you, Jg 9:15 4886
and wheat, salt, wine and **a** oil, Ezr 6:9 4887
casting out many demons and were **a** Mk 6:13 *218b*
feet and **a** them with the perfume. Lk 7:38 *218b*
a him with oil in the name of the Jas 5:14 *218b*
you have an **a** from the Holy One, 1Jn 2:20 *5545*
the **a** which you received from Him 1Jn 2:27 *5545*
a teaches you about all things, 1Jn 2:27 *5545*

ANOTHER

me **a** offspring in place of Abel, Gn 4:25 312
So he waited yet **a** seven days; Gn 8:10 312
Then he waited yet **a** seven days, Gn 8:12 312
They said to one **a**, Gn 11:3 7453
Now Abraham took **a** wife, Gn 25:1 3254
Then they dug **a** well, and they Gn 26:21 312
away from there and dug **a** well, Gn 26:22 312
to give her to **a** man; Gn 29:19 312
serve with me for **a** seven years." Gn 29:27 312
with Laban for **a** seven years. Gn 29:30 312
"May the LORD give me **a** son." Gn 30:24 312
for now you have **a** son." Gn 35:17
and went to **a** land away from his Gn 36:6
Now he had still **a** dream, Gn 37:9 312
"Lo, I have had still **a** dream; Gn 37:9
They said to one **a**, Gn 37:19 251
still **a** son and named him Shelah; Gn 38:5 3254
"Why are you staring at one **a**?" Gn 42:1
Then they said to one **a**, Gn 42:21 251
they *turned* trembling to one **a**, Gn 42:28 251
the man whether you still had **a** Gn 43:6
Have you **a** brother?' So we Gn 43:7
looked at one **a** in astonishment. Gn 43:33 7453
They did not see one **a**, Ex 10:23 251
and **a** holy assembly on Ex 12:16
Israel saw *it,* they said to one **a**, Ex 16:15 251
"If he takes to himself **a** woman, Ex 21:10 312
so that it grazes in **a** man's field, Ex 22:5 312
with their wings and facing one **a**; Ex 25:20 251
curtains shall be joined to one **a**, Ex 26:3 259
curtains *shall be* joined to one **a**. Ex 26:3 259
curtains to one **a** with the clasps so Ex 26:6 259
for each board, fitted to one **a**; Ex 26:17 259
under **a** board for its two tenons; Ex 26:19 259
and two sockets under **a** board. Ex 26:21 259
and two sockets under **a** board. Ex 26:25 259
He joined five curtains to one **a** Ex 36:10 259
five curtains he joined to one **a**. Ex 36:10 259
curtains to one **a** with the clasps, Ex 36:13 259
for each board, fitted to one **a**; Ex 36:22 259
under **a** board for its two tenons. Ex 36:24 259
and two sockets under **a** board. Ex 36:26 259
deal falsely, nor lie to one **a**. Lv 19:11 5997
woman who is a slave acquired for **a** Lv 19:20
commits adultery with **a** man's wife, Lv 20:10
hand, you shall not wrong one **a**. Lv 25:14 251
'So you shall not wrong one **a**, Lv 25:17 5997
not rule with severity over one **a**. Lv 25:46 251
but has sold the field to **a** man, Lv 27:20 312
So they said to one **a**, Nu 14:4 251
"Please come with me to **a** place Nu 23:13 312
come, I will take you to **a** place; Nu 23:27 312
from one tribe to **a** tribe, Nu 36:9 312
for himself a nation from within **a** Dt 4:34
between one kind of homicide or **a**, Dt 17:8 1818
between one kind of lawsuit or **a**, Dt 17:8 1779
between one kind of assault or **a**, Dt 17:8 5061
the battle and **a** man would dedicate it. Dt 20:5 312
and **a** man would begin to use its fruit. Dt 20:6 312
the battle and **a** man would marry her.' Dt 20:7 312
and **a** man finds her in the city Dt 22:23
and goes and becomes **a** man's *wife,* Dt 24:2 312
wife, but **a** man will violate her; Dt 28:30 312
shall be given to **a** people, Dt 28:32 312
wrath, and cast them into **a** land, Dt 29:28 312
and there arose **a** generation after Jg 2:10 312
They said to one **a**, Jg 6:29 7453
LORD set the sword of one against **a** Jg 7:22 7453
leaders of Gilead, said to one **a**, Jg 10:18 7453
for you are the son of **a** woman." Jg 11:2 312
Do not go to glean in **a** field; Ru 2:8 312
others do not fall upon you in **a** field." Ru 2:22 312
rose before one could recognize **a**; Ru 3:14 7453
his sandal and gave it to **a**; Ru 4:7 7453
"If one man sins against **a**, 1Sa 2:25 376
a carrying three loaves of bread, 1Sa 10:3 259
and **a** carrying a jug of wine; 1Sa 10:3 259
them and be changed into **a** man. 1Sa 10:6 312
that the people said to one **a**, 1Sa 10:11 7453
and **a** company turned toward 1Sa 13:18 259
and **a** company turned toward the 1Sa 13:18 259
him to **a** and said the same thing; 1Sa 17:30 312
sword devours one as well as **a**; 2Sa 11:25 2088
in one of the caves or in **a** place; 2Sa 17:9 259
but you shall carry news **a** day; 2Sa 18:20 312
the watchman saw **a** man running; 2Sa 18:26 312
a man running by himself." 2Sa 18:26
God also raised up **a** adversary to 1Ki 11:23
So he went **a** way and did not 1Ki 13:10 312
she will pretend to be **a** woman." 1Ki 14:5 5235a
why do you pretend to be **a** woman? 1Ki 14:6 5235a
and Obadiah went **a** way by himself. 1Ki 18:6 259
said to **a** by the word of the LORD, 1Ki 20:35 7453
Then he found **a** man and said, 1Ki 20:37 312
one said this while **a** said that. 1Ki 22:20 2088
So he again sent to him **a** captain 2Ki 1:11 312
and they have slain one **a**. 2Ki 3:23 7453
"Bring me **a** vessel." 2Ki 4:6 5750
and they said to one **a**, 2Ki 7:3 7453
army, so that they said to one **a**, 2Ki 7:6 251
and they returned and entered **a** 2Ki 7:8 312
Then they said to one **a**, 2Ki 7:9 7453
Jerusalem from one end to **a**; 2Ki 21:16 6310
Jerahmeel had **a** wife, 1Ch 2:26 312
made yet **a** raid in the valley. 1Ch 14:13 3254
And from *one* kingdom to **a** people, 1Ch 16:20 312
from *one* dwelling place *to* **a**. 1Ch 17:5
one said this while **a** said that. 2Ch 18:19 2088
they helped to destroy one **a**. 2Ch 20:23 7453
celebrate *the feast* **a** seven days, 2Ch 30:23 312
on it, and *built* **a** outside wall and 2Ch 32:5 312
son of Pahath-moab repaired **a** section Ne 3:11 8145
of Mizpah, repaired **a** section in Ne 3:19 8145
zealously repaired **a** section, Ne 3:20 8145
son of Hakkoz repaired **a** section, Ne 3:21 8145
son of Henadad repaired **a** section, Ne 3:24 8145
After them the Tekoites repaired **a** Ne 3:27 8145
son of Zalaph, repaired **a** section. Ne 3:30 8145
on the wall far from one **a**. Ne 4:19 251
and for **a** fourth they confessed Ne 9:3
to **a** who is more worthy than she. Es 1:19 7468
will arise for the Jews from **a** place Es 4:14 312
sending portions *of food* to one **a**. Es 9:19 7453
to one **a** and gifts to the poor. Es 9:22 7453
speaking, **a** also came and said, Jb 1:16 2088
speaking, **a** also came and said, Jb 1:17 2088
speaking, **a** also came and said, Jb 1:18 2088
whom my eyes will see and not **a**. Jb 19:27 2114a
While **a** dies with a bitter soul, Jb 21:25 2088
Let me sow and **a** eat, And let my Jb 31:8 312
May my wife grind for **a**, Jb 31:10 312
"One is so near to **a** That Jb 41:16 259
"They are joined one to **a**; Jb 41:17 251
They speak falsehood to one **a**; Ps 12:2 7453
for **a** *god* will be multiplied; Ps 16:4 312
He puts down one and exalts **a**. Ps 75:7 2088
From *one* kingdom to **a** people. Ps 105:13 312
Let **a** take his office. Ps 109:8 312
shall praise Your works to **a**, Ps 145:4 1755
A pretends to be poor, but has Pr 13:7
Until **a** comes and examines him. Pr 18:17 7453
I will seek **a** drink." Pr 23:35 5750, 3254
And do not reveal the secret of **a**, Pr 25:9 312
Let **a** praise you, and not your own Pr 27:2 2114a
iron, So one man sharpens **a**. Pr 27:17 6440, 7453
there is not **a** to lift him up. Ec 4:10 8145
official watches over **a** official, Ec 5:8
thing to **a** to find an explanation, Ec 7:27 259
man has exercised authority over **a** Ec 8:9
will be oppressed, Each one by **a**, Is 3:5 376
And one called out to **a** and said, Is 6:3 2088
a 65 years Ephraim will be shattered, Is 7:8 5750
look at one **a** in astonishment, Is 13:8 7453
I will not give My glory to **a**, Is 42:8 312
And **a** will write *on* his hand, Is 44:5 2088
A shapes wood, he extends a Is 44:13
And My glory I will not give to **a**. Is 48:11 312
servants will be called by **a** name. Is 65:15 312
will not build and **a** inhabit, Is 65:22 312
They will not plant and **a** eat; Is 65:22 312
from him And belongs to **a** man, Jer 3:1 312
so he remade it into **a** vessel, Jer 18:4 312
"Or at **a** moment I might speak Jer 18:9
and they will say to one **a**, Jer 22:8 7453
mother who bore you into **a** country Jer 22:26 312
dreams which they relate to one **a**, Jer 23:27 7453
north, near and far, one with **a**; Jer 25:26 251
fear one to **a** and said to Baruch, Jer 36:16 7453
"Take again **a** scroll and write on Jer 36:28 312
Then Jeremiah took **a** scroll and Jer 36:32 312
one warrior has stumbled over **a**, Jer 46:12 1368
they have fallen one against **a**. Jer 46:16 7453
And they will call out to one **a**, Jer 49:29
One courier runs to meet **a**, Jer 51:31 7323
And one messenger to meet **a**, Jer 51:31 5046
that **a** report in another year, Jer 51:46
that another report in **a** year, Jer 51:46
their wings touched one **a**; Ezk 1:9 269
each had two touching **a** *being,* Ezk 1:11 376
as if one wheel were within **a**. Ezk 1:16 212
the living beings touching one **a** and Ezk 3:13 269
will be appalled with one **a** and waste Ezk 4:17 251
if one wheel were within **a** wheel. Ezk 10:10
place to **a** place in their sight. Ezk 12:3 312
"But there was **a** great eagle with Ezk 17:7 259
She took **a** of her cubs And made Ezk 19:5 259
and **a** has lewdly defiled his Ezk 22:11 376
a in you has humbled his sister, Ezk 22:11 376
and you will groan to one **a**. Ezk 24:23 251
of the houses, speak to one **a**, Ezk 33:30 259
judge between one sheep and **a**, Ezk 34:17 7716
judge between one sheep and **a**. Ezk 34:22 7716
then take **a** stick and write on it, Ezk 37:16 259
yourself one to **a** into one stick, Ezk 37:17 259
in three stories, one above **a**, Ezk 41:6 6763
and **a** doorway toward the south; Ezk 41:11 259
arise **a** kingdom inferior to you, Da 2:39 321
then **a** third kingdom of bronze, Da 2:39 321
with one **a** in the seed of men; Da 2:43
but they will not adhere to one **a**, Da 2:43 1836, 5974
will not be left for **a** people; Da 2:44 312
the sea, different from one **a**. Da 7:3 1668
"And behold, **a** beast, a second Da 7:5 321
I kept looking, and behold, **a** one, Da 7:6 321
the horns, behold, **a** horn, Da 7:8 321
and **a** will arise after them, and Da 7:24 321
and **a** holy one said to that Da 8:13 259
on **a** city I would not send rain; Am 4:7 259
stagger to **a** city to drink water, Am 4:8 259
on **a** in the temple of the LORD, Hg 2:15 68
down, everyone by the sword of **a**.' Hg 2:22 251
and **a** angel was coming out to meet Zch 2:3 312
in your hearts against one **a**.' Zch 7:10 312
and I set all men one against **a**. Zch 8:10 7453
speak the truth to one **a**; Zch 8:16 7453
evil in your heart against **a**, Zch 8:17 7453
of one will go to **a**, Zch 8:21 259
be lifted against the hand of **a**. Zch 14:13 7453
"This is **a** thing you do: Mal 2:13 8145
feared the LORD spoke to one **a**, Mal 3:16 7453
for their own country by **a** way. Mt 2:12 *243*
and to **a**, 'Come!' and he comes, Mt 8:9 *243*
A of the disciples said to Him, Mt 8:21 *2087*
Jesus presented **a** parable to them, Mt 13:24 *243*
He presented **a** parable to them, Mt 13:31 *243*
He spoke **a** parable to them, Mt 13:33 *243*
a woman commits adultery." Mt 19:9 *243*
"Listen to **a** parable. Mt 21:33 *243*
slaves and beat one, and killed **a**, Mt 21:35 *3739, 1161*
"Again he sent **a** group of slaves Mt 21:36 *243*
his own farm, **a** to his business, Mt 22:5 *3739, 1161*
that day on to ask Him **a** question. Mt 22:46 *3765*
stone here will be left upon **a**, Mt 24:2 *3037*
betray one **a** and hate one another. Mt 24:10 *240*
betray one another and hate one **a**. Mt 24:10 *240*
To one he gave five talents, to **a**, Mt 25:15 *3739, 1161*
to another, two, and to **a**, Mt 25:15 *3739, 1161*
He will separate them from one **a**, Mt 25:32 *240*
a *servant-girl* saw him and said to Mt 26:71 *243*
much afraid and said to one **a**, Mk 4:41 *240*
began to discuss with one **a** *the fact* Mk 8:16 *240*
discussing with one **a** what rising Mk 9:10 *1438*
discussed with one **a** which *of them* Mk 9:34 *240*
and be at peace with one **a**." Mk 9:50 *240*
marries **a** woman commits adultery Mk 10:11 *243*
her husband and marries **a** man, Mk 10:12 *243*
"Again he sent them **a** slave, Mk 12:4 *243*
"And he sent **a**, and that one they Mk 12:5 *243*
those vine-growers said to one **a**, Mk 12:7 *1438*
a which will not be torn down." Mk 13:2 *3037*
indignantly *remarking* to one **a**, Mk 14:4 *1438*
build **a** made without hands.'" Mk 14:58 *243*
They were saying to one **a**, Mk 16:3 *1438*
shepherds *began* saying to one **a**, Lk 2:15 *240*
talking with one **a** saying, Lk 4:36 *240*
On **a** Sabbath He entered Lk 6:6 *2087*
'Go!' and he goes, and to **a**, 'Come!' Lk 7:8 *243*
market place and call to one **a**, Lk 7:32 *240*
from one city and village to **a**, Lk 8:1 *2596*
and amazed, saying to one **a**, Lk 8:25 *240*
And they went on to **a** village. Lk 9:56 *2087*
And He said to **a**, Lk 9:59 *2087*
A also said, "I will follow You, Lk 9:61 *2087*
that they were stepping on one **a**, Lk 12:1 *240*
from one city and village to **a**, Lk 13:22 *2596*
"**A** one said, 'I have bought five Lk 14:19 *2087*
"**A** one said, 'I have married a Lk 14:20 *2087*
sets out to meet **a** king in battle, Lk 14:31 *2087*

“Then he said to **a**, Lk 16:7 *2087*
and marries **a** commits adultery, Lk 16:18 *2087*
“**A** came, saying, ‘Master, here Lk 19:20 *2087*
not leave in you one stone upon **a**, Lk 19:44 *3037*
“And he proceeded to send **a** slave; Lk 20:11 *2087*
saw him, they reasoned with one **a**, Lk 20:14 *240*
a which will not be torn down.” Lk 21:6 *3037*
little later, **a** saw him and said, Lk 22:58 *2087*
had passed, **a** man *began* to insist, Lk 22:59 *243*
friends with one **a** that very day; Lk 23:12 *240*
with one **a** as you are walking?” Lk 24:17 *240*
They said to one **a**, Lk 24:32 *240*
disciples were saying to one **a**, Jn 4:33 *240*
‘One sows and **a** reaps.’ Jn 4:37 *243*
coming, **a** steps down before me.” Jn 5:7 *243*
is **a** who testifies of Me, Jn 5:32 *243*
if **a** comes in his own name, Jn 5:43 *243*
when you receive glory from one **a** and Jn 5:44 *240*
began to argue with one **a**, Jn 6:52 *240*
The Jews then said to one **a**, Jn 7:35 *1438*
Jesus, and were saying to one **a** as Jn 11:56 *240*
Pharisees said to one **a**, Jn 12:19 *1438*
disciples *began* looking at one **a**, Jn 13:22 *240*
give to you, that you love one **a**, Jn 13:34 *240*
you, that you also love one **a**. Jn 13:34 *240*
if you have love for one **a**.” Jn 13:35 *240*
and He will give you **a** Helper, Jn 14:16 *243*
commandment, that you love one **a**, Jn 15:12 *240*
command you, that you love one **a**. Jn 15:17 *240*
disciples then said to one **a**, Jn 16:17 *240*
Jesus, and *so was* **a** disciple. Jn 18:15 *243*
So they said to one **a**, Jn 19:24 *240*
And again **a** Scripture says, Jn 19:37 *2087*
‘LET A MAN TAKE HIS OFFICE.’ Ac 1:20 *2087*
great perplexity, saying to one **a**, Ac 2:12 *243*
they *began* to confer with one **a**, Ac 4:15 *240*
until THERE AROSE A KING OVER Ac 7:18 *2087*
why do you injure one **a**?’ Ac 7:26 *240*
he left and went to **a** place. Ac 12:17 *2087*
“Therefore He also says in **a** *Psalm*, Ac 13:35 *2087*
that they separated from one **a**, Ac 15:39 *240*
saying that there is **a** king, Ac 17:7 *2087*
shouting one thing and some **a**, Ac 19:32 *243*
them bring charges against one **a**. Ac 19:38 *240*
we said farewell to one **a**. Ac 21:5 *240*
shouting one thing *and* some **a**, Ac 21:34 *243*
synagogue after **a** I used to imprison Ac 22:19 *2596*
they *began* talking to one **a**, Ac 26:31 *240*
little farther on they took **a** sounding Ac 27:28 *3825*
hand, they *began* saying to one **a**, Ac 28:4 *240*
they did not agree with one **a**, Ac 28:25 *240*
in their desire toward one **a**, Ro 1:27 *240*
judgment, for in that which you judge **a**, Ro 2:1 *2087*
you, therefore, who teach **a**, Ro 2:21 *2087*
is living she is joined to **a** man, Ro 7:3 *2087*
though she is joined to **a** man. Ro 7:3 *2087*
that you might be joined to **a**, Ro 7:4 *2087*
use and **a** for common use? Ro 9:21 *3739, 1161*
and individually members one of **a**. Ro 12:5 *240*
to one **a** in brotherly love; Ro 12:10 *240*
give preference to one **a** in honor; Ro 12:10 *240*
Be of the same mind toward one **a**; Ro 12:16 *240*
to anyone except to love one **a**; Ro 13:8 *240*
are you to judge the servant of **a**? Ro 14:4 *245*
One person regards one day above **a**, Ro 14:5 *2250*
a regards every day *alike*. Ro 14:5 *3739, 1161*
let us not judge one **a** anymore, Ro 14:13 *240*
and the building up of one **a**. Ro 14:19 *240*
one **a** according to Christ Jesus, Ro 15:5 *240*
Therefore, accept one **a**, Ro 15:7 *240*
and able also to admonish one **a**. Ro 15:14 *240*
not build on **a** man's foundation; Ro 15:20 *245*
Greet one **a** with a holy kiss. Ro 16:16 *240*
“I am of Paul,” and **a**, 1Co 3:4 *2087*
and **a** is building on it. 1Co 3:10 *243*
that you have lawsuits with one **a**. 1Co 6:7 *1438*
Stop depriving one **a**, 1Co 7:5 *240*
one in this manner, and **a** in that. 1Co 7:7 *3739, 1161*
and one is hungry and **a** is drunk. 1Co 11:21 *3739, 1161*
together to eat, wait for one **a**. 1Co 11:33 *240*
and to **a** the word of knowledge 1Co 12:8 *243*
to **a** faith by the same Spirit, and 1Co 12:9 *2087*
and to **a** gifts of healing by the 1Co 12:9 *243*
to **a** the effecting of miracles, 1Co 12:10 *243*
of miracles, and to **a** prophecy, 1Co 12:10 *243*
a the distinguishing of spirits, 1Co 12:10 *243*
to **a** *various* kinds of tongues, 1Co 12:10 *2087*
a the interpretation of tongues. 1Co 12:10 *243*
have the same care for one **a**. 1Co 12:25 *240*
is made to **a** who is seated, 1Co 14:30 *243*
of men, and **a** flesh of beasts, 1Co 15:39 *243*
of beasts, and **a** flesh of birds, 1Co 15:39 *243*
flesh of birds, and **a** of fish. 1Co 15:39 *243*
and the *glory* of the earthly is **a**. 1Co 15:40 *2087*
the sun, and **a** glory of the moon, 1Co 15:41 *243*
moon, and **a** glory of the stars; 1Co 15:41 *243*
Greet one **a** with a holy kiss. 1Co 16:20 *240*
accomplished in the sphere of **a**. 2Co 10:16 *245*
For if one comes and preaches **a** 2Co 11:4 *243*
Greet one **a** with a holy kiss. 2Co 13:12 *240*
which is *really* not **a**; Ga 1:7 *243*
but through love serve one **a**. Ga 5:13 *240*
But if you bite and devour one **a**, Ga 5:15 *240*
that you are not consumed by one **a**. Ga 5:15 *240*
these are in opposition to one **a**, Ga 5:17 *240*
boastful, challenging one **a**, Ga 5:26 *240*
one another, envying one **a**. Ga 5:26 *240*
alone, and not in regard to **a**. Ga 6:4 *2087*
tolerance for one **a** in love, Eph 4:2 *240*
for we are members of one **a**. Eph 4:25 *240*
Be kind to one **a**, Eph 4:32 *240*
speaking to one **a** in psalms and Eph 5:19 *1438*
to one **a** in the fear of Christ. Eph 5:21 *240*
regard one **a** as more important than Php 2:3 *240*
Do not lie to one **a**, Col 3:9 *240*
bearing with one **a**, Col 3:13 *240*
and admonishing one **a** with psalms Col 3:16 *1438*
and abound in love for one **a**, 1Th 3:12 *240*
are taught by God to love one **a**; 1Th 4:9 *240*
comfort one **a** with these words. 1Th 4:18 *240*
Therefore encourage one **a** and 1Th 5:11 *240*
one another and build up one **a**, 1Th 5:11 *1520*
Live in peace with one **a**. 1Th 5:13 *1438*
one repays **a** with evil for evil, 1Th 5:15 *5100*
is good for one **a** and for all people. 1Th 5:15 *240*
toward one **a** grows *ever* greater; 2Th 1:3 *240*
and envy, hateful, hating one **a**. Ti 3:3 *240*
But encourage one **a** day after day, Heb 3:13 *1438*
have spoken of **a** day after that. Heb 4:8 *243*
just as He says also in **a** *passage*, Heb 5:6 *2087*
further need *was there* for **a** priest Heb 7:11 *2087*
are spoken belongs to **a** tribe, Heb 7:13 *2087*
if **a** priest arises according to Heb 7:15 *2087*
one **a** to love and good deeds, Heb 10:24 *240*
but encouraging *one* **a**; and all Heb 10:25 *240*
and sent them out by **a** way? Jas 2:25 *2087*
Do not speak against one **a**, Jas 4:11 *240*
complain, brethren, against one **a**, Jas 5:9 *240*
confess your sins to one **a**, Jas 5:16 *240*
one another, and pray for one **a** so Jas 5:16 *240*
love one **a** from the heart, 1Pe 1:22 *240*
fervent in your love for one **a**, 1Pe 4:8 *1438*
to one **a** without complaint. 1Pe 4:9 *240*
gift, employ it in serving one **a** as 1Pe 4:10 *1438*
with humility toward one **a**, 1Pe 5:5 *240*
Greet one **a** with a kiss of love. 1Pe 5:14 *240*
we have fellowship with one **a**, 1Jn 1:7 *240*
that we should love one **a**; 1Jn 3:11 *240*
Son Jesus Christ, and love one **a**, 1Jn 3:23 *240*
Beloved, let us love one **a**, 1Jn 4:7 *240*
us, we also ought to love one **a**. 1Jn 4:11 *240*
if we love one **a**, God abides in 1Jn 4:12 *240*
the beginning, that we love one **a**. 2Jn 1:5 *240*
And **a**, a red horse, went out; Rv 6:4 *243*
and that *men* would slay one **a**; Rv 6:4 *240*
And I saw **a** angel ascending from Rv 7:2 *243*
A angel came and stood at the altar, Rv 8:3 *243*
I saw **a** strong angel coming Rv 10:1 *243*
and they will send gifts to one **a**, Rv 11:10 *240*
Then **a** sign appeared in heaven: Rv 12:3 *243*
Then I saw **a** beast coming up out of Rv 13:11 *243*
I saw **a** angel flying in midheaven, Rv 14:6 *243*
And **a** angel, a second one, Rv 14:8 *243*
Then **a** angel, a third one, followed Rv 14:9 *243*
a angel came out of the temple, Rv 14:15 *243*
And **a** angel came out of the temple Rv 14:17 *243*
Then **a** angel, the one who has power Rv 14:18 *243*
Then I saw **a** sign in heaven, great Rv 15:1 *243*
a angel coming down from heaven, Rv 18:1 *243*
I heard **a** voice from heaven, Rv 18:4 *243*
and **a** book was opened, which is Rv 20:12 *243*

ANOTHER'S

will not understand one **a** speech.” Gn 11:7 7453
man's ox hurts **a** so that it dies, Ex 21:35 7453
and they will eat one **a** flesh in Jer 19:9 7453
each into **a** power and into the Zch 11:6 7453
who are left eat one **a** flesh.” Zch 11:9 7468
and they will seize one **a** hand, Zch 14:13 7453
in *the use of* that which is **a**, Lk 16:12 *245*
you also ought to wash one **a** feet. Jn 13:14 *240*
my freedom judged by **a** conscience? 1Co 10:29 *243*
Bear one **a** burdens, and thereby Ga 6:2 *240*

ANSWER

“So my honesty will **a** for me later, Gn 30:33 6030a
will give Pharaoh a favorable **a**.” Gn 41:16 6030a
But his brothers could not **a** him, Gn 45:3 6030a
and they shall **a** and say, Dt 21:7 6030a
“You shall **a** and say before Dt 26:5 6030a
“The Levites shall then **a** and say Dt 27:14 6030a
all the people shall **a** and say, Dt 27:15 6030a
“Her wise princesses would **a** her, Jg 5:29 6030a
and let us go,” but there was no **a**. Jg 19:28 6030a
she did not **a** or pay attention. 1Sa 4:20 6030a
LORD will not **a** you in that day.” 1Sa 8:18 6030a
But He did not **a** him on that day. 1Sa 14:37 6030a
“Will you not **a**, Abner?” 1Sa 26:14 6030a
the LORD, the LORD did not **a** him, 1Sa 28:6 6030a
he could no longer **a** Abner a word, 2Sa 3:11 7725
the LORD, but He did not **a** them. 2Sa 22:42 6030a
Now consider and see what **a** I 2Sa 24:13 1697
you counsel *me* to **a** this people?” 1Ki 12:6 7725, 1697
counsel do you give that we may **a** 1Ki 12:9 7725, 1697
the people did not **a** him a word. 1Ki 18:21 6030a
Baal, **a** us.” But there was no voice 1Ki 18:26 6030a
“**A** me, O LORD, answer me, that 1Ki 18:37 6030a
“Answer me, O LORD, **a** me, 1Ki 18:37 6030a
anyone salutes you, do not **a** him; 2Ki 4:29 6030a
commandment was, “Do not **a** him.” 2Ki 18:36 6030a
consider what **a** I shall return to 1Ch 21:12 1697
you counsel *me* to **a** this people?” 2Ch 10:6 7725, 1697
give that we may **a** this people, 2Ch 10:9 7725, 1697
sent an **a** to Rehum the commander, Ezr 4:17 6600
is there anyone who will **a** you? Jb 5:1 6030a
a Him once in a thousand *times*. Jb 9:3 6030a
“How then can I **a** Him, *And* choose Jb 9:14 6030a
I were right, I could not **a**; Jb 9:15 6030a
a man as I am that I may **a** Him, Jb 9:32 6030a
“Then call, and I will **a**; Jb 13:22 6030a
“You will call, and I will **a** You; Jb 14:15 6030a
a wise man **a** with windy knowledge Jb 15:2 6030a
Or what plagues you that you **a**? Jb 16:3 6030a
I cry, ‘Violence!’ but I get no **a**; Jb 19:7 6030a
to my servant, but he does not **a**; Jb 19:16 6030a
of my understanding makes me **a**. Jb 20:3 6030a
learn the words *which* He would **a**, Jb 23:5 6030a
for help, but You do not **a** me; Jb 30:20 6030a
me to account, what will I **a** Him? Jb 31:14 7725
Let the Almighty **a** me! Jb 31:35 6030a
because they had found no **a**, Jb 32:3 4617
when Elihu saw that there was no **a** Jb 32:5 4617
“They are dismayed, they no longer **a**; Jb 32:15 6030a
Because they stop *and* no longer **a**? Jb 32:16 6030a
“I too will **a** my share, I also Jb 32:17 6030a
Let me open my lips and **a**. Jb 32:20 6030a
if you have anything to say, **a** me; Jb 33:32 7725
“I will **a** you, And your friends Jb 35:4 7725, 4405
but He does not **a** Because of the Jb 35:12 6030a
Let him who reproves God **a** it.” Jb 40:2 6030a
I have spoken, and I will not **a**; Jb 40:5 6030a
A me when I call, O God of my Ps 4:1 6030a
Consider *and* **a** me, O LORD my God; Ps 13:3 6030a
upon You, for You will **a** me, Ps 17:6 6030a
the LORD, but He did not **a** them. Ps 18:41 6030a
LORD **a** you in the day of trouble! Ps 20:1 6030a
will **a** him from His holy heaven With Ps 20:6 6030a
the King **a** us in the day we call. Ps 20:9 6030a
I cry by day, but You do not **a**; Ps 22:2 6030a
of the wild oxen You **a** me. Ps 22:21 6030a
And be gracious to me and **a** me. Ps 27:7 6030a
You will **a**, O Lord my God. Ps 38:15 6030a
Give heed to me and **a** me; Ps 55:2 6030a
God will hear and **a** them—Even the Ps 55:19 6030a
with Your right hand, and **a** us! Ps 60:5 6030a
You **a** us in righteousness, Ps 65:5 6030a
A me with Your saving truth. Ps 69:13 6030a
A me, O LORD, for Your Ps 69:16 6030a
For I am in distress; **a** me quickly. Ps 69:17 6030a
Your ear, O LORD, *and* **a** me; Ps 86:1 6030a
upon You, For You will **a** me. Ps 86:7 6030a
call upon Me, and I will **a** him; Ps 91:15 6030a
the day when I call **a** me quickly. Ps 102:2 6030a
with Your right hand, and **a** me! Ps 108:6 6030a
an **a** for him who reproaches me, Ps 119:42 6030a, 1697
with all my heart; **a** me, O LORD! Ps 119:145 6030a
A me in Your faithfulness, in Your Ps 143:1 6030a
A me quickly, O LORD, my spirit Ps 143:7 6030a
will call on me, but I will not **a**; Pr 1:28 6030a
A gentle **a** turns away wrath, But a Pr 15:1 4617
A man has joy in an apt **a**, Pr 15:23 4617
of the righteous ponders how to **a**, Pr 15:28 6030a
But the **a** of the tongue is from Pr 16:1 4617
He who gives an **a** before he hears, Pr 18:13 1697
correctly **a** him who sent you? Pr 22:21 7725
the lips Who gives a right **a**. Pr 24:26 1697
a a fool according to his folly, Pr 26:4 6030a
A a fool as his folly *deserves*, Pr 26:5 6030a
men who can give a discreet **a**. Pr 26:16 7725
and money is the **a** to everything. Ec 10:19 6030a
I called him but he did not **a** me. SS 5:6 6030a
a the messengers of the nation? Is 14:32 6030a
when He hears it, He will **a** you. Is 30:19 6030a
king's commandment was, “Do not **a** Is 36:21 6030a
I, the LORD, will **a** them Myself, Is 41:17 6030a
them Who, if I ask, can give an **a**. Is 41:28 1697
one may cry to it, it cannot **a**; Is 46:7 6030a
I called, *why* was there none to **a**? Is 50:2 6030a
will call, and the LORD will **a**; Is 58:9 6030a
I called, but you did not **a**; Is 65:12 6030a
that before they call, I will **a**; Is 65:24 6030a
I called you but you did not **a**, Jer 7:13 6030a
to them, but they will not **a** you. Jer 7:27 6030a
“Then they will **a**, Jer 22:9 559
‘Call to Me and I will **a** you, Jer 33:3 6030a
them but they did not **a**.’ ” Jer 35:17 6030a
message which the LORD will **a** you. Jer 42:4 6030a
were giving him *such* an **a**—saying, Jer 44:20 1697
LORD will be brought to give him an **a** Ezk 14:4 6030a
brought to **a** him in My own person. Ezk 14:7 6030a
you an **a** concerning this matter. Da 3:16 6600
It is I who **a** and look after you. Hos 14:8 6030a
LORD will **a** and say to His people, Jl 2:19 6030a
Then he will **a**, “Keep quiet. Am 6:10 559
the LORD, but He will not **a** them. Mi 3:4 6030a
Because there is no **a** from God. Mi 3:7 4617
And how have I wearied you? **A** Me. Mi 6:3 6030a
will **a** it from the framework. Hab 2:11 6030a
LORD their God and I will **a** them. Zch 10:6 6030a
on My name, And I will **a** them; Zch 13:9 6030a
But He did not **a** her a word. Mt 15:23 *611*
No one was able to **a** Him a word, Mt 22:46 *611*
“Then the righteous will **a** Him, Mt 25:37 *611*
The King will **a** and say to them, Mt 25:40 *611*
“Then they themselves also will **a**, Mt 25:44 *611*
“Then He will **a** them, Mt 25:45 *611*
“Do You not **a**? Mt 26:62 *611*
priests and elders, He did not **a**. Mt 27:12 *611*

And He did not **a** him with regard	**Mt 27:14**	*611*
"Because of this **a** go;	**Mk 7:29**	*3056*
For he did not know what to **a**;	**Mk 9:6**	*611*
you one question, and you **a** Me,	**Mk 11:29**	*611*
from heaven, or from men? **A** Me."	**Mk 11:30**	*611*
they did not know what to **a** Him.	**Mk 14:40**	*611*
"Do You not **a**?	**Mk 14:60**	*611*
But He kept silent and did not **a**.	**Mk 14:61**	*611*
"Do You not **a**?	**Mk 15:4**	*611*
But Jesus made no further **a**;	**Mk 15:5**	*611*
And he would **a** and say to them,	**Lk 3:11**	*611*
then He will **a** and say to you,	**Lk 13:25**	*611*
and being amazed at His **a**,	**Lk 20:26**	*612*
I ask a question, you will not **a**.	**Lk 22:68**	*611*
give an **a** to those who sent us?	**Jn 1:22**	*612*
the way You **a** the high priest?"	**Jn 18:22**	*611*
But Jesus gave him no **a**.	**Jn 19:9**	*612*
servant-girl named Rhoda came to **a**.	**Ac 12:13**	*5219*
so that you will have *an* **a** for	**2Co 5:12**	

ANSWERED

The sons of Heth **a** Abraham,	**Gn 23:5**	6030a
and Ephron the Hittite **a** Abraham	**Gn 23:10**	6030a
Then Ephron **a** Abraham, saying to	**Gn 23:14**	6030a
and the LORD **a** him and Rebekah his	**Gn 25:21**	6279
Jacob **a** his mother Rebekah,	**Gn 27:11**	559
his father **a** and said to him,	**Gn 27:39**	6030a
a Shechem and his father Hamor with	**Gn 34:13**	6030a
a me in the day of my distress and	**Gn 35:3**	6030a
Then Joseph **a** and said,	**Gn 40:18**	6030a
Joseph then **a** Pharaoh, saying,	**Gn 41:16**	6030a
Reuben **a** them, saying,	**Gn 42:22**	6030a
So we **a** his questions.	**Gn 43:7**	5046
Miriam **a** them,	**Ex 15:21**	6030a
the people **a** together and said,	**Ex 19:8**	6030a
spoke and God **a** him with thunder.	**Ex 19:19**	6030a
all the people **a** with one voice and	**Ex 24:3**	6030a
of Gad and the sons of Reuben **a**,	**Nu 32:31**	6030a
"You **a** me and said,	**Dt 1:14**	6030a
They **a** Joshua, saying,	**Jos 1:16**	6030a
So Achan **a** Joshua and said,	**Jos 7:20**	6030a
So they **a** Joshua and said,	**Jos 9:24**	6030a
and the half-tribe of Manasseh **a** and	**Jos 22:21**	6030a
The people **a** and said,	**Jos 24:16**	6030a
and the men of Penuel **a** him just	**Jg 8:8**	6030a
just as the men of Succoth had **a**.	**Jg 8:8**	6030a
who was murdered, **a** and said,	**Jg 20:4**	6030a
And she **a**, "I am Ruth your maid.	**Ru 3:9**	559
Then Eli **a** and said,	**1Sa 1:17**	6030a
you called me." But he **a**, "I did not	**1Sa 3:6**	559
for Israel and the LORD **a** him.	**1Sa 7:9**	6030a
The servant **a** Saul again and said,	**1Sa 9:8**	6030a
They **a** them and said,	**1Sa 9:12**	6030a
Samuel **a** Saul and said,	**1Sa 9:19**	6030a
not one of all the people **a** him.	**1Sa 14:39**	6030a
a him in accord with this word,	**1Sa 17:27**	559
people **a** the same thing as before.	**1Sa 17:30**	7725
And David **a**, "*I am* the son of your	**1Sa 17:58**	559
Jonathan then **a** Saul,	**1Sa 20:28**	6030a
But Jonathan **a** Saul his father and	**1Sa 20:32**	6030a
The priest **a** David and said,	**1Sa 21:4**	6030a
a the priest and said to him,	**1Sa 21:5**	6030a
Listen now, son of Ahitub." And he **a**,	**1Sa 22:12**	559
Ahimelech **a** the king and said,	**1Sa 22:14**	6030a
And the LORD **a** him and said,	**1Sa 23:4**	6030a
But Nabal **a** David's servants and	**1Sa 25:10**	6030a
And Saul **a**, "I am greatly distressed;	**1Sa 28:15**	559
And I **a** him, 'I am an Amalekite.'	**2Sa 1:8**	559
And he **a**, "I am the son of an alien,	**2Sa 1:13**	559
"Is that you, Asahel?" And he **a**,	**2Sa 2:20**	559
a Rechab and Baanah his brother,	**2Sa 4:9**	6030a
she **a** him, "No, my brother, do not	**2Sa 13:12**	559
And she **a**, "Truly I am a widow,	**2Sa 14:5**	559
the king **a** and said to the woman,	**2Sa 14:18**	6030a
Absalom **a** Joab,	**2Sa 14:32**	559
But Ittai **a** the king and said,	**2Sa 15:21**	6030a
And Ahimaaz **a**, "When Joab sent	**2Sa 18:29**	559
And the Cushite **a**,	**2Sa 18:32**	559
So he **a**, "O my lord, the king, my	**2Sa 19:26**	559
king **a**, "Chimham shall cross over	**2Sa 19:38**	559
men of Judah **a** the men of Israel,	**2Sa 19:42**	6030a
a the men of Judah and said,	**2Sa 19:43**	6030a
"Are you Joab?" And he **a**, "I am."	**2Sa 20:17**	559
And he **a**, "I am listening."	**2Sa 20:17**	559
of Jehoiada **a** the king and said,	**1Ki 1:36**	6030a
Solomon **a** and said to his mother,	**1Ki 2:22**	6030a
spoke Joab, and thus he **a** me."	**1Ki 2:30**	6030a
Solomon **a** all her questions;	**1Ki 10:3**	5046
go to your own country?" And he **a**,	**1Ki 11:22**	559
The king **a** the people harshly,	**1Ki 12:13**	6030a
to them, the people **a** the king,	**1Ki 12:16**	7725
there was no voice and no one **a**.	**1Ki 18:26**	6030a
but there was no voice, no one **a**,	**1Ki 18:29**	6030a
shall begin the battle?" And he **a**,	**1Ki 20:14**	559
found me, O my enemy?" And he **a**,	**1Ki 21:20**	559
And he **a** him, "Go up and succeed,	**1Ki 22:15**	559
They **a** him, "*He was* a hairy man	**2Ki 1:8**	559
And he **a**, "Yes, I know; be still."	**2Ki 2:5**	559
way shall we go up?" And he **a**,	**2Ki 3:8**	559
of Israel's servants **a** and said,	**2Ki 3:11**	6030a
she **a**, "I live among my own people.	**2Ki 4:13**	559
And Gehazi **a**, "Truly she has no son	**2Ki 4:14**	559
it well with the child?' " And she **a**,	**2Ki 4:26**	559
servants." And he **a**, "I shall go."	**2Ki 6:3**	559
So he **a**, "Do not fear, for those who	**2Ki 6:16**	559
He **a**, "You shall not kill *them.*	**2Ki 6:22**	559
is the matter with you?" And she **a**,	**2Ki 6:28**	559
leaning **a** the man of God and said,	**2Ki 7:2**	6030a
officer **a** the man of God and said,	**2Ki 7:19**	6030a
Why does my lord weep?" Then he **a**,	**2Ki 8:12**	559
Elisha **a**, "The LORD has shown me	**2Ki 8:13**	559
did Elisha say to you?" And he **a**,	**2Ki 8:14**	559
the king, 'Is it peace?' " And Jehu **a**,	**2Ki 9:19**	559
Jehu?" And he **a**, "What peace,	**2Ki 9:22**	559
a, "We are the relatives of Ahaziah;	**2Ki 10:13**	559
And Jehonadab **a**,	**2Ki 10:15**	559
were silent and **a** him not a word,	**2Ki 18:36**	6030a
Hezekiah **a**, "It is easy for the shadow	**2Ki 20:10**	559
So Hezekiah **a**, "They have seen all	**2Ki 20:15**	559
and He **a** their prayers because they	**1Ch 5:20**	6279
he called to the LORD and He **a** him	**1Ch 21:26**	6030a
when David saw that the LORD had **a**	**1Ch 21:28**	6030a
a in a letter sent to Solomon:	**2Ch 2:11**	559
Solomon **a** all her questions;	**2Ch 9:2**	5046
The king **a** them harshly, and	**2Ch 10:13**	6030a
to them the people **a** the king,	**2Ch 10:16**	7725
And the man of God **a**,	**2Ch 25:9**	559
"Thus they **a** us, saying,	**Ezr 5:11**	8421, 6600
So I **a** them and said to them,	**Ne 2:20**	7725
and I **a** them in the same way.	**Ne 6:4**	7725
And all the people **a**,	**Ne 8:6**	6030a
Then Satan **a** the LORD and said,	**Jb 1:7**	6030a
Then Satan **a** the LORD,	**Jb 1:9**	6030a
Then Satan **a** the LORD and said,	**Jb 2:2**	6030a
Satan **a** the LORD and said,	**Jb 2:4**	6030a
Then Eliphaz the Temanite **a**,	**Jb 4:1**	6030a
Then Job **a**,	**Jb 6:1**	6030a
Then Bildad the Shuhite **a**,	**Jb 8:1**	6030a
Then Job **a**,	**Jb 9:1**	6030a
"If I called and He **a** me,	**Jb 9:16**	6030a
Then Zophar the Naamathite **a**,	**Jb 11:1**	6030a
who called on God and He **a** him;	**Jb 12:4**	6030a
Then Job **a**,	**Jb 16:1**	6030a
Then Zophar the Naamathite **a**,	**Jb 20:1**	6030a
Then Job **a**,	**Jb 21:1**	6030a
Then Bildad the Shuhite **a**,	**Jb 25:1**	6030a
Not one of you who **a** his words.	**Jb 32:12**	6030a
Then the LORD **a** Job out of the	**Jb 38:1**	6030a
Then Job **a** the LORD and said,	**Jb 40:3**	6030a
the LORD **a** Job out of the storm and	**Jb 40:6**	6030a
Then Job **a** the LORD and said,	**Jb 42:1**	6030a
And He **a** me from His holy mountain	**Ps 3:4**	6030a
I sought the LORD, and He **a** me,	**Ps 34:4**	6030a
I **a** you in the hiding place of	**Ps 81:7**	6030a
upon the LORD and He **a** them.	**Ps 99:6**	6030a
O LORD our God, You **a** them; You	**Ps 99:8**	6030a
The LORD **a** me *and set me* in a	**Ps 118:5**	6030a
to You, for You have **a** me,	**Ps 118:21**	6030a
of my ways, and You have **a** me;	**Ps 119:26**	6030a
I cried to the LORD, And He **a** me.	**Ps 120:1**	6030a
On the day I called, You **a** me;	**Ps 138:3**	6030a
also cry himself and not be **a**.	**Pr 21:13**	6030a
I said, "Lord, how long?" And He **a**,	**Is 6:11**	559
were silent and **a** him not a word;	**Is 36:21**	6030a
So Hezekiah **a**, "They have seen all	**Is 39:4**	559
A voice says, "Call out." Then he **a**,	**Is 40:6**	559
"In a favorable time I have **a** You,	**Is 49:8**	6030a
Because I called, but no one **a**;	**Is 66:4**	6030a
'What has the LORD **a**?'	**Jer 23:35**	6030a
'What has the LORD **a** you?'	**Jer 23:37**	6030a
man, can these bones live?" And I **a**,	**Ezk 37:3**	559
They **a** a second time and said,	**Da 2:7**	6032
The Chaldeans **a** the king and said,	**Da 2:10**	6032
Daniel **a** before the king and said,	**Da 2:27**	6032
The king **a** Daniel and said,	**Da 2:47**	6032
He **a** by giving orders to heat the	**Da 3:19**	6032
Daniel **a** and said before the king,	**Da 5:17**	6032
they **a** and spoke before the king,	**Da 6:13**	6032
distress to the LORD, And He **a** me.	**Jon 2:2**	6030a
And what Balaam son of Beor **a** him,	**Mi 6:5**	6030a
Then the LORD **a** me and said,	**Hab 2:2**	6030a
And the priests **a**,	**Hg 2:12**	6030a
And the priests **a**,	**Hg 2:13**	6030a
among the myrtle trees **a** and said,	**Zch 1:10**	6030a
So they **a** the angel of the LORD	**Zch 1:11**	6030a
The LORD **a** the angel who was	**Zch 1:13**	6030a
And he **a** me, "These are the horns	**Zch 1:19**	559
speaking with me **a** and said to me,	**Zch 4:5**	6030a
And I **a** the second time and said	**Zch 4:12**	6030a
So he **a** me,	**Zch 4:13**	559
see?" And I **a**, "I see a flying scroll;	**Zch 5:2**	559
But He **a** and said,	**Mt 4:4**	*611*
Jesus **a** and said to them,	**Mt 11:4**	*611*
But He **a** and said to them,	**Mt 12:39**	*611*
But Jesus **a** the one who was telling	**Mt 12:48**	*611*
Jesus **a** them,	**Mt 13:11**	*611*
And He **a** and said to them,	**Mt 15:3**	*611*
But He **a** and said,	**Mt 15:13**	*611*
But He **a** and said,	**Mt 15:24**	*611*
And He **a** and said,	**Mt 15:26**	*611*
Simon Peter **a**,	**Mt 16:16**	*611*
And He **a** and said,	**Mt 17:11**	*611*
And Jesus **a** and said,	**Mt 17:17**	*611*
And He **a** and said,	**Mt 19:4**	*611*
"But he **a** and said to one of	**Mt 20:13**	*611*
But Jesus **a**,	**Mt 20:22**	*611*
And Jesus **a** and said to them,	**Mt 21:21**	*611*
"And he **a**,	**Mt 21:29**	*611*
and he **a**, 'I *will*, sir';	**Mt 21:30**	*611*
But Jesus **a** and said to them,	**Mt 22:29**	*611*
And Jesus **a** and said to them,	**Mt 24:4**	*611*
"But the prudent **a**, '	**Mt 25:9**	*611*
"But he **a**, 'Truly I say to you,	**Mt 25:12**	*611*
"But his master **a** and said to	**Mt 25:26**	*611*
And He **a**, "He who dipped	**Mt 26:23**	*611*
They **a**, "He deserves death!"	**Mt 26:66**	*611*
But He **a** them, "You give them	**Mk 6:37**	*611*
But she **a** and said to Him,	**Mk 7:28**	*611*
And His disciples **a** Him,	**Mk 8:4**	*611*
Peter **a** and said to Him,	**Mk 8:29**	*611*
And one of the crowd **a** Him,	**Mk 9:17**	*611*
And He **a** them and said,	**Mk 9:19**	*611*
And He **a** and said to them,	**Mk 10:3**	*611*
Jesus **a** again and said to them,	**Mk 10:24**	*611*
And Jesus **a** saying to them,	**Mk 11:22**	*611*
that He had **a** them well,	**Mk 12:28**	*611*
Jesus **a**, "The foremost is, 'HEAR,	**Mk 12:29**	*611*
saw that he had **a** intelligently,	**Mk 12:34**	*611*
And He **a** him, "*It is as* you say."	**Mk 15:2**	*611*
Pilate **a** them, saying,	**Mk 15:9**	*611*
The angel **a** and said to him,	**Lk 1:19**	*611*
The angel **a** and said to her,	**Lk 1:35**	*611*
But his mother **a** and said,	**Lk 1:60**	*611*
John **a** and said to them all,	**Lk 3:16**	*611*
And Jesus **a** him,	**Lk 4:4**	*611*
Jesus **a** him,	**Lk 4:8**	*611*
And Jesus **a** and said to him,	**Lk 4:12**	*611*
Simon **a** and said,	**Lk 5:5**	*611*
reasonings, **a** and said to them,	**Lk 5:22**	*611*
And Jesus **a** and said to them,	**Lk 5:31**	*611*
And He **a** and said to them,	**Lk 7:22**	*611*
And Jesus **a** him, "Simon,	**Lk 7:40**	*611*
Simon **a** and said,	**Lk 7:43**	*611*
But He **a** and said to them,	**Lk 8:21**	*611*
when Jesus heard *this*, He **a** him,	**Lk 8:50**	*611*
They **a** and said,	**Lk 9:19**	*611*
And Peter **a** and said,	**Lk 9:20**	*611*
And Jesus **a** and said,	**Lk 9:41**	*611*
John **a** and said,	**Lk 9:49**	*611*
And he **a**, "YOU SHALL LOVE	**Lk 10:27**	*611*
"You have **a** correctly;	**Lk 10:28**	*611*
But the Lord **a** and said to her,	**Lk 10:41**	*611*
"And he **a** and said to him,	**Lk 13:8**	*611*
But the Lord **a** him and said,	**Lk 13:15**	*611*
And Jesus **a** and spoke to the	**Lk 14:3**	*611*
"But he **a** and said to his father,	**Lk 15:29**	*611*
Then Jesus **a** and said,	**Lk 17:17**	*611*
was coming, He **a** them and said,	**Lk 17:20**	*611*
But Jesus **a**, "I tell you, if	**Lk 19:40**	*611*
Jesus **a** and said to them,	**Lk 20:3**	*611*
So they **a** that they did not know	**Lk 20:7**	*611*
Some of the scribes **a** and said,	**Lk 20:39**	*611*
But Jesus **a** and said,	**Lk 22:51**	*611*
And He **a** him and said,	**Lk 23:3**	*611*
but He **a** him nothing.	**Lk 23:9**	*611*
But the other **a**, and rebuking him	**Lk 23:40**	*611*
named Cleopas, **a** and said to Him,	**Lk 24:18**	*611*
you the Prophet?" And he **a**, "No."	**Jn 1:21**	*611*
John **a** them saying,	**Jn 1:26**	*611*
Jesus **a** and said to him,	**Jn 1:48**	*611*
Nathanael **a** Him,	**Jn 1:49**	*611*
Jesus **a** and said to him,	**Jn 1:50**	*611*
Jesus **a** them, "Destroy this temple, and	**Jn 2:19**	*611*
Jesus **a** and said to him,	**Jn 3:3**	*611*
Jesus **a**, "Truly, truly, I say to you,	**Jn 3:5**	*611*
Jesus **a** and said to him,	**Jn 3:10**	*611*
John **a** and said,	**Jn 3:27**	*611*
Jesus **a** and said to her,	**Jn 4:10**	*611*
Jesus **a** and said to her,	**Jn 4:13**	*611*
The woman **a** and said,	**Jn 4:17**	*611*
The sick man **a** Him,	**Jn 5:7**	*611*
he **a** them, "He who made me well	**Jn 5:11**	*611*
He **a** them, "My Father is working	**Jn 5:17**	*611*
a and was saying to them,	**Jn 5:19**	*611*
Philip **a** Him, "Two hundred denarii	**Jn 6:7**	*611*
Jesus **a** them and said,	**Jn 6:26**	*611*
Jesus **a** and said to them,	**Jn 6:29**	*611*
Jesus **a** and said to them,	**Jn 6:43**	*611*
Simon Peter **a** Him,	**Jn 6:68**	*611*
Jesus **a** them, "Did I Myself not	**Jn 6:70**	*611*
So Jesus **a** them and said,	**Jn 7:16**	*611*
The crowd **a**,	**Jn 7:20**	*611*
Jesus **a** them, "I did one deed,	**Jn 7:21**	*611*
officers **a**, "Never has a man spoken	**Jn 7:46**	*611*
The Pharisees then **a** them,	**Jn 7:47**	*611*
They **a** him,	**Jn 7:52**	*611*
Jesus **a** and said to them,	**Jn 8:14**	*611*
Jesus **a**, "You know neither Me nor	**Jn 8:19**	*611*
They **a** Him, "We are Abraham's	**Jn 8:33**	*611*
Jesus **a** them, "Truly, truly, I say	**Jn 8:34**	*611*
They **a** and said to Him,	**Jn 8:39**	*611*
The Jews **a** and said to Him,	**Jn 8:48**	*611*
Jesus **a**, "I do not have a demon;	**Jn 8:49**	*611*
Jesus **a**, "If I glorify Myself, My	**Jn 8:54**	*611*
Jesus **a**, "*It was* neither *that* this man	**Jn 9:3**	*611*
He **a**, "The man who is called Jesus	**Jn 9:11**	*611*
His parents **a** them and said,	**Jn 9:20**	*611*
then **a**, "Whether He is a sinner,	**Jn 9:25**	*611*
He **a** them, "I told you already and	**Jn 9:27**	*611*
The man **a** and said to them,	**Jn 9:30**	*611*
They **a** him, "You were born entirely	**Jn 9:34**	*611*
a, "Who is He, Lord,	**Jn 9:36**	*611*
Jesus **a** them, "I told you, and you do	**Jn 10:25**	*611*
Jesus **a** them, "I showed you many	**Jn 10:32**	*611*
Jews **a** Him, "For a good work we	**Jn 10:33**	*611*
Jesus **a** them, "Has it not been	**Jn 10:34**	*611*
Jesus **a**, "Are there not twelve hours	**Jn 11:9**	*611*
And Jesus **a** them, saying,	**Jn 12:23**	*611*
Jesus **a** and said,	**Jn 12:30**	*611*
The crowd then **a** Him,	**Jn 12:34**	*611*
Jesus **a** and said to him,	**Jn 13:7**	*611*
Jesus **a** him, "If I do not wash you,	**Jn 13:8**	*611*
Jesus then **a**,	**Jn 13:26**	*611*
Jesus **a**, "Where I go, you cannot	**Jn 13:36**	*611*
Jesus **a**, "Will you lay down your life	**Jn 13:38**	*611*
Jesus **a** and said to him,	**Jn 14:23**	*611*
Jesus **a** them, "Do you now believe?	**Jn 16:31**	*611*

They **a** Him, "Jesus the Nazarene." **Jn 18:5** *611*
Jesus **a**, "I told you that I am *He;* **Jn 18:8** *611*
Jesus **a** him, "I have spoken openly **Jn 18:20** *611*
Jesus **a** him, "If I have spoken **Jn 18:23** *611*
They **a** and said to him, **Jn 18:30** *611*
Jesus **a**, "Are you saying this on your **Jn 18:34** *611*
Pilate **a**, "I am not a Jew, am I? **Jn 18:35** *611*
Jesus **a**, "My kingdom is not of this **Jn 18:36** *611*
Him, "So You are a king?" Jesus **a**, **Jn 18:37** *611*
The Jews **a** him, "We have a law, **Jn 19:7** *611*
Jesus **a**, "You would have no **Jn 19:11** *611*
The chief priests **a**, **Jn 19:15** *611*
Pilate **a**, "What I have written I have **Jn 19:22** *611*
Thomas **a** and said to Him, **Jn 20:28** *611*
have any fish, do you?" They **a** Him, **Jn 21:5** *611*
Peter and John **a** and said to them, **Ac 4:19** *611*
Peter and the apostles **a**, **Ac 5:29** *611*
But Simon **a** and said, **Ac 8:24** *611*
The eunuch **a** Philip and said, **Ac 8:34** *611*
And he **a** and said, **Ac 8:37** *611*
But Ananias **a**, "Lord, I have heard **Ac 9:13** *611*
and exalting God. Then Peter **a**, **Ac 10:46** *611*
voice from heaven **a** a second time, **Ac 11:9** *611*
had stopped speaking, James **a**, **Ac 15:13** *611*
evil spirit **a** and said to them, **Ac 19:15** *611*
Then Paul **a**, "What are you doing, **Ac 21:13** *611*
"And I **a**, 'Who are You, Lord?' **Ac 22:8** *611*
The commander **a**, **Ac 22:28** *611*
Festus then **a** that Paul was being **Ac 25:4** *611*
the Jews a favor, **a** Paul and said, **Ac 25:9** *611*
conferred with his council, he **a**, **Ac 25:12** *611*
"I **a** them that it is not the **Ac 25:16** *611*
Then one of the elders **a**, **Rv 7:13** *611*

ANSWERING
Then these three men ceased **a** Job, **Jb 32:1** 6030a
But Jesus **a** said to him, **Mt 3:15** *611*
And **a** Jesus, they said, **Mt 21:27** *611*
A them, He said, "Who are My **Mk 3:33** *611*
And **a** him, Jesus said, **Mk 10:51** *611*
A Jesus, they said, "We do not **Mk 11:33** *611*
A again, Pilate said to them, **Mk 15:12** *611*
And Jesus **a** them said, **Lk 6:3** *611*
And **a** they said to Him, **Lk 17:37** *611*

ANSWERS
so that I may drink,' and who **a**, **Gn 24:14** 559
me if your father **a** you harshly?" **1Sa 20:10** 6030a
departed from me and no longer **a** me, **1Sa 28:15** 6030a
LORD, and the God who **a** by fire, **1Ki 18:24** 6030a
your **a** remain *full of* falsehood?" **Jb 21:34** 8666
Because he **a** like wicked men. **Jb 34:36** 8666
But the rich man **a** roughly. **Pr 18:23** 6030a
Jacob *everyone* who awakes and **a**, **Mal 2:12** 6030a
at His understanding and His **a**. **Lk 2:47** *612*
and from inside he **a** and says, 'Do **Lk 11:7** *611*
are you, O man, who **a** back to God? **Ro 9:20** *470*

ANT
Go to the **a**, O sluggard, Observe **Pr 6:6** 5244

ANTELOPE
the **a** and the mountain sheep. **Dt 14:5** 8377
every street, Like an **a** in a net, **Is 51:20** 8377

ANTHOTHIJAH
Hananiah, Elam, **A**, **1Ch 8:24** 6070

ANTICHRIST
as you heard that **a** is coming, **1Jn 2:18** *500*
This is the **a**, the one who denies **1Jn 2:22** *500*
this is the *spirit* of the **a**, **1Jn 4:3** *500*
This is the deceiver and the **a**. **2Jn 1:7** *500*

ANTICHRISTS
even now many **a** have appeared; **1Jn 2:18** *500*

ANTICIPATE
My eyes **a** the night watches, That **Ps 119:148** 6923

ANTIMONY
and inlaid *stones,* stones of **a** and **1Ch 29:2** 6320
I will set your stones in **a**, **Is 54:11** 6320

ANTIOCH
and Nicolas, a proselyte from **A**. **Ac 6:5** *491*
way to Phoenicia and Cyprus and **A**, **Ac 11:19** *490*
who came to **A** and *began* speaking **Ac 11:20** *490*
and they sent Barnabas off to **A**. **Ac 11:22** *490*
found him, he brought him to **A**. **Ac 11:26** *490*
were first called Christians in **A**. **Ac 11:26** *490*
came down from Jerusalem to **A**. **Ac 11:27** *490*
Now there were at **A**, **Ac 13:1** *490*
Perga, they arrived at Pisidian **A**, **Ac 13:14** *490*
But Jews came from **A** and Iconium, **Ac 14:19** *490*
to Lystra and to Iconium and to **A**, **Ac 14:21** *490*
From there they sailed to **A**, **Ac 14:26** *490*
to send to **A** with Paul and Barnabas **Ac 15:22** *490*
to the brethren in **A** and Syria and **Ac 15:23** *490*
sent away, they went down to **A**; **Ac 15:30** *490*
But Paul and Barnabas stayed in **A**, **Ac 15:35** *490*
the church, and went down to **A**. **Ac 18:22** *490*
But when Cephas came to **A**, **Ga 2:11** *490*
such as happened to me at **A**, **2Tm 3:11** *490*

ANTIPAS
My faith even in the days of **A**, **Rv 2:13** *493*

ANTIPATRIS
and brought him by night to **A**. **Ac 23:31** *494*

ANTIQUITY
city, Whose origin is from **a**, **Is 23:7** 6927

ANTS
The **a** are not a strong people, But **Pr 30:25** 5244

ANUB
the father of **A** and Zobebah, **1Ch 4:8** 6036

ANVIL
encourages him who beats the **a**, **Is 41:7** 6471

ANXIETY
I am full of **a** because of my sin. **Ps 38:18** 1672
A in a man's heart weighs it **Pr 12:25** 1674
There is **a** by the sea, It cannot **Jer 49:23** 1674
eat bread by weight and with **a**, **Ezk 4:16** 1674
your water with quivering and **a**. **Ezk 12:18** 1674
"They will eat their bread with **a** **Ezk 12:19** 1674
casting all your **a** on Him, **1Pe 5:7** *3308*

ANXIOUS
They waited until they became **a**; **Jg 3:25** 954
the donkeys and will become **a** for us." **1Sa 9:5** 1672
the donkeys and is **a** for you, **1Sa 10:2** 1672
my **a** thoughts multiply within me, **Ps 94:19** 8312
Try me and know my **a** thoughts; **Ps 139:23** 8312
Say to those with **a** heart, **Is 35:4** 4116
And it will not be **a** in a year of **Jer 17:8** 1672
the famine, about which you are **a**, **Jer 42:16** 1672
is **a** to understand the dream." **Da 2:3** 6470
For the **a** longing of the creation **Ro 8:19** *603*
Be **a** for nothing, but in **Php 4:6** *3309*

ANXIOUSLY
Do not **a** look about you, for I am **Is 41:10**
that we may **a** look about us and **Is 41:23**
I have been **a** looking for You." **Lk 2:48** *3600*
waiting **a** for the mercy of our **Jude 1:21** *4327*

ANY
"From **a** tree of the garden you **Gn 2:16** 3605
serpent was more crafty than **a** beast **Gn 3:1** 3605
from **a** tree of the garden'?" **Gn 3:1** 3605
with money from **a** foreigner, **Gn 17:12** 3605
"Do we still have **a** portion or **Gn 31:14**
before **a** king reigned over the sons **Gn 36:31**
was empty, without **a** water in it. **Gn 37:24**
five times as much as **a** of theirs. **Gn 43:34** 3605
you know **a** capable men among them, **Gn 47:6** 3426
you are not to reduce **a** of it. **Ex 5:8** 4480
'I am not going to give you **a** **Ex 5:10**
'But against **a** of the sons of **Ex 11:7** 3605
'Do not eat **a** of it raw or boiled **Ex 12:9** 4480
leave **a** of it over until morning, **Ex 12:10** 4480
a provisions for themselves. **Ex 12:39** 1571
you are not to bring forth **a** of **Ex 12:46** 4480
nor are you to break **a** bone of it. **Ex 12:46**
nor shall **a** leaven be seen among **Ex 13:7**
man leave **a** of it until morning." **Ex 16:19** 4480
foul nor was there **a** worm in it. **Ex 16:24**
or **a** likeness of what is in heaven **Ex 20:4** 3605
in it you shall not do **a** work, **Ex 20:10** 3605
"But if there is **a** *further* **Ex 21:23**
or for **a** lost thing about which **Ex 22:9** 3605
or **a** animal to keep *for him,* **Ex 22:10** 3605
"He who sacrifices to **a** god, **Ex 22:20**
not afflict **a** widow or orphan. **Ex 22:22** 3605
therefore you shall not eat **a** **Ex 22:31**
"If **a** of the flesh of **Ex 29:34** 4480
a of the bread remains until morning, **Ex 29:34** 4480
a strange incense on this altar, **Ex 30:9**
nor shall you make **a** like it in **Ex 30:32**
'Whoever shall mix **a** like it or **Ex 30:33**
whoever puts **a** of it on a layman shall **Ex 30:33** 4480
"Whoever shall make **a** like it, **Ex 30:38**
for whoever does **a** work on it, **Ex 31:14** 3605
whoever does **a** work on the sabbath **Ex 31:15** 3605
'Whoever has **a** gold, let them tear **Ex 32:24**
nor let **a** man be seen anywhere on **Ex 34:3** 1571
earth nor among **a** of the nations; **Ex 34:10** 3605
you shall not worship **a** other god, **Ex 34:14** 312
whoever does **a** work on it shall be **Ex 35:2**
"You shall not kindle a fire in **a** **Ex 35:3** 3605
wood for **a** work of the service brought **Ex 35:24** 3605
"Let no man or woman **a** **Ex 36:6** 5750
were restrained from bringing **a** **Ex 36:6**
'When **a** man of you brings an **Lv 1:2** 120
shall not offer up in smoke **a** leaven **Lv 2:11** 3605
any leaven or **a** honey as an offering **Lv 2:11** 3605
not eat **a** fat or any blood.' " **Lv 3:17** 3605
not eat any fat or **a** blood.' " **Lv 3:17** 3605
sins unintentionally in **a** of the things **Lv 4:2** 3605
to be done, and commits **a** of them, **Lv 4:2** 259
and they commit **a** of the things **Lv 4:13** 259
leader sins and unintentionally does **a** **Lv 4:22** 259
sins unintentionally in doing **a** of the **Lv 4:27** 259
a person touches **a** unclean thing, **Lv 5:2** 3605
"Now if a person sins and does **a** **Lv 5:17** 259
so that he sins in regard to **a** one **Lv 6:3** 259
and he will be forgiven for **a** one **Lv 6:7** 259
and when **a** of its blood splashes **Lv 6:27** 4480
'But no sin offering of which **a** of **Lv 6:30** 4480
presents **a** man's burnt offering, **Lv 7:8** 376
leave **a** of it over until morning. **Lv 7:15** 4480
'So if **a** of the flesh of the **Lv 7:18** 4480
or **a** unclean detestable thing, **Lv 7:21** 3605
shall not eat **a** fat *from* an ox, **Lv 7:23** 3605
beasts may be put to **a** other use, **Lv 7:24** 3605
'You are not to eat **a** blood, **Lv 7:26** 3605
or animal, in **a** of your dwellings. **Lv 7:26** 3605
'**A** person who eats any blood, even **Lv 7:27** 3605
'Any person who eats **a** blood, **Lv 7:27** 3605
and whoever picks up **a** of their **Lv 11:25** 4480
including **a** wooden article, **Lv 11:32** 3605
or a sack—**a** article of which use **Lv 11:32** 3605
'As for **a** earthenware vessel into **Lv 11:33** 3605
'**A** of the food which may be eaten, **Lv 11:34**
4480, 3605
and **a** liquid which may be drunk in **Lv 11:34** 3605
a part of their carcass falls on **a** seed **Lv 11:37** 3605
a of the swarming things that swarm **Lv 11:43** 3605
not make yourselves unclean with **a** **Lv 11:44** 3605
not touch **a** consecrated thing, **Lv 12:4** 3605
or in **a** article made of leather, **Lv 13:48** 3605
woof, or in **a** article of leather, **Lv 13:49** 3605
or **a** article of leather in which **Lv 13:52** 3605
woof, or in **a** article of leather, **Lv 13:53** 3605
woof, or in **a** article of leather, **Lv 13:57** 3605
or **a** article of leather from which **Lv 13:58** 3605
woof, or in **a** article of leather, **Lv 13:59** 3605
This is the law for **a** mark of **Lv 14:54** 3605
'When **a** man has a discharge from **Lv 15:2** 376
'Whoever then touches **a** of the **Lv 15:10** 3605
'As for **a** garment or any leather **Lv 15:17** 3605
'As for any garment or **a** leather **Lv 15:17** 3605
'Whoever touches **a** thing on **Lv 15:22** 3605
'**A** bed on which she lies all the **Lv 15:26** 3605
shall not enter at **a** time into the holy **Lv 16:2** 3605
your souls and not do **a** work, **Lv 16:29** 3605
"**A** man from the house of Israel **Lv 17:3** 376
'**A** man from the house of Israel, **Lv 17:8** 376
a man from the house of Israel, **Lv 17:10** 376
among them, who eats **a** blood, **Lv 17:10** 3605
nor may **a** alien who sojourns among **Lv 17:12**
a man from the sons of Israel, **Lv 17:13** 376
not to eat the blood of **a** flesh, **Lv 17:14** 3605
"When **a** person eats *an animal* **Lv 17:15** 3605
'None of you shall approach **a** **Lv 18:6** 3605
'You shall not give **a** of your **Lv 18:21** 4480
a animal to be defiled with it, **Lv 18:23** 3605
nor shall **a** woman stand before an **Lv 18:23** 802
yourselves by **a** of these things; **Lv 18:24** 3605
not do **a** of these abominations, **Lv 18:26**
4480, 3605
does **a** of these abominations, **Lv 18:29**
4480, 3605
that you do not practice **a** of the **Lv 18:30** 4480
nor bear **a** grudge against the sons **Lv 19:18**
'You shall not make **a** cuts in your **Lv 19:28**
make **a** tattoo marks on yourselves: **Lv 19:28**
'**A** man from the sons of Israel or **Lv 20:2** 376
a of his offspring to Molech, **Lv 20:2** 4480
a of his offspring to Molech, **Lv 20:4** 4480
a animal to mate with it, **Lv 20:16** 3605
make **a** baldness on their heads, **Lv 21:5**
nor make **a** cuts in their flesh. **Lv 21:5**
'Also the daughter of **a** priest, **Lv 21:9** 376
shall he approach **a** dead person, **Lv 21:11**
face, or **a** deformed *limb,* **Lv 21:18**
'If **a** man among all your **Lv 22:3** 3605
if a man touches **a** teeming things by **Lv 22:5** 3605
or **a** man by whom he is made **Lv 22:5** 120
a person who touches **a** such shall **Lv 22:6**
'**A** man of the house of Israel or **Lv 22:18** 376
whether it is **a** of their votive or **Lv 22:18** 3605
or **a** of their freewill offerings, **Lv 22:18** 3605
nor shall you accept **a** such from **Lv 22:25**
4480, 3605
You shall not do **a** work; **Lv 23:3** 3605
you shall not do **a** laborious work. **Lv 23:7** 3605
shall not do **a** laborious work.' " **Lv 23:8** 3605
'You shall not do **a** laborious work, **Lv 23:25** 3605
not do **a** work on this same day, **Lv 23:28** 3605
"If there is a person who will **Lv 23:29** 3605
"As for **a** person who does any **Lv 23:30** 3605
who does **a** work on this same day, **Lv 23:30** 3605
do no laborious work of **a** kind. **Lv 23:35** 3605
takes the life of **a** human being, **Lv 24:17** 3605
a such that one gives to the LORD **Lv 27:9** 3605
it is **a** unclean animal of the kind **Lv 27:11** 3605
commits **a** of the sins of mankind, **Nu 5:6**
4480, 3605
a man gives to the priest, **Nu 5:10** 376
'If **a** man's wife goes astray and **Nu 5:12** 376
shall he drink **a** grape juice nor **Nu 6:3** 3605
But he did not give **a** to the sons **Nu 7:9**
in the work and not work **a** more. **Nu 8:25** 5750
'If **a** one of you or of your **Nu 9:10** 376
more than **a** man who was on the **Nu 12:3** 3605
nor shall **a** of those who spurned **Nu 14:23** 3605
have I done harm to **a** of them." **Nu 16:15** 259
nor own **a** portion among them; **Nu 18:20**
who touches the corpse of **a** person **Nu 19:11** 3605
do drink **a** of your water, **Nu 20:19**
that if a serpent bit **a** man, **Nu 21:9** 376
there **a** divination against Israel; **Nu 23:23**
you shall not do **a** work. **Nu 29:7** 3605
whoever has killed **a** person and **Nu 31:19**
and whoever has touched **a** slain, **Nu 31:19**
manslayer who has killed **a** person **Nu 35:11**
or with **a** deadly object of stone, **Nu 35:23** 3605
'But if the manslayer at **a** **Nu 35:26** 3318
of **a** tribe of the sons of Israel shall **Nu 36:8** 4480
will not give you **a** of their land, **Dt 2:5** 4480
a of their land as a possession, **Dt 2:9** 4480
for I will not give you **a** of the **Dt 2:19** 4480
since you did not see **a** form on **Dt 4:15** 3605
in the form of **a** figure, **Dt 4:16** 3605
of **a** animal that is on the earth, **Dt 4:17** 3605
the likeness of **a** winged bird that **Dt 4:17** 3605
the likeness of **a** fish that is in **Dt 4:18** 3605
"Has **a** people heard the voice of **Dt 4:33**
or **a** likeness *of* what is in heaven **Dt 5:8** 3605
in it you shall not do **a** work, **Dt 5:14** 3605
ox or your donkey or **a** of your cattle **Dt 5:14** 3605
of the LORD our God **a** longer, **Dt 5:25** 5750
a of the gods of the peoples who **Dt 6:14** 312
in number than **a** of the peoples, **Dt 7:7** 3605
and He will not put on you **a** of **Dt 7:15** 3605
eat meat within **a** of your gates, **Dt 12:15** 3605
or **a** of your votive offerings **Dt 12:17** 3605

shall not eat **a** detestable thing.	Dt 14:3	3605
"**A** animal that divides the hoof	Dt 14:6	3605
You shall not eat **a** of their flesh	Dt 14:8	4480
"You may eat **a** clean bird.	Dt 14:11	3605
"You may eat **a** clean bird.	Dt 14:20	3605
in **a** of your towns in your land	Dt 15:7	259
"But if it has **a** defect, *such as*	Dt 15:21	
or blindness, *or* **a** serious defect,	Dt 15:21	3605
to sacrifice the Passover in **a** of your	Dt 16:5	259
for yourself an Asherah of **a** kind of	Dt 16:21	3605
which has a blemish *or* **a** defect,	Dt 17:1	3605
in your midst, in **a** of your towns,	Dt 17:2	259
moon or **a** of the heavenly host,	Dt 17:3	3605
"If **a** case is too difficult for	Dt 17:8	
"Now if a Levite comes from **a** of	Dt 18:6	259
that **a** manslayer may flee there.	Dt 19:3	3605
on account of **a** iniquity or any sin	Dt 19:15	3605
or **a** sin which he has committed;	Dt 19:15	3605
"If **a** man has a stubborn and	Dt 21:18	376
way, in **a** tree or on the ground,	Dt 22:6	3605
"If **a** man takes a wife and goes	Dt 22:13	376
"If there is among you **a** man who	Dt 23:10	376
nor shall **a** of the sons of Israel	Dt 23:17	4480
your God for **a** votive offering,	Dt 23:18	3605
shall not put **a** in your basket.	Dt 23:24	
army nor be charged with **a** duty;	Dt 24:5	3605
"If **a** man is caught kidnapping a	Dt 24:7	5315
your neighbor a loan of **a** sort,	Dt 24:10	3972
forgotten **a** of Your commandments.	Dt 26:13	4480
a of it while I was unclean,	Dt 26:14	4480
nor offered **a** of it to the dead.	Dt 26:14	4480
is he who lies with **a** animal.'	Dt 27:21	3605
and do not turn aside from **a** of	Dt 28:14	3605
he will not give *even* one of them **a**	Dt 28:55	4480
a man any longer because of you;	Jos 2:11	
any man **a** longer because of you;	Jos 2:11	5750
was no spirit in them **a** longer because	Jos 5:1	5750
against **a** of the sons of Israel.	Jos 10:21	
Israel did not burn **a** cities that	Jos 11:13	3605
kills **a** person unintentionally,	Jos 20:3	
that whoever kills **a** person	Jos 20:9	
a of the nations which Joshua left	Jg 2:21	376
a of the wars of Canaan;	Jg 3:1	3605
'Now are you **a** better than	Jg 11:25	2895
And it happened when **a** *of*	Jg 12:5	
drink, nor eat **a** unclean thing.	Jg 13:4	3605
drink nor eat **a** unclean thing,	Jg 13:7	3605
drink, nor eat **a** unclean thing;	Jg 13:14	3605
weak and be like **a** *other* man."	Jg 16:7	259
weak and be like **a** *other* man."	Jg 16:11	259
weak and be like **a** other man."	Jg 16:13	259
weak and be like **a** *other* man."	Jg 16:17	3605
will **a** of us return to his house.	Jg 20:8	376
a of our daughters in marriage?"	Jg 21:7	4480
of land to confirm **a** matter:	Ru 4:7	3605
Nor is there **a** rock like our God.	1Sa 2:2	
a man was offering a sacrifice,	1Sa 2:13	3605
was taller than **a** of the people.	1Sa 9:2	3605
he was taller than **a** of the people	1Sa 10:23	3605
and did not bring him **a** present.	1Sa 10:27	
taken anything from **a** man's hand."	1Sa 12:4	376
a of the people who *were* with Saul	1Sa 13:22	3605
a mighty man or any valiant man,	1Sa 14:52	3605
any mighty man or **a** valiant man,	1Sa 14:52	3605
'The king does not desire **a** dowry	1Sa 18:25	
a of the household of my father,	1Sa 22:15	3605
one male of **a** who belong to him."	1Sa 25:22	3605
saw or knew *it,* nor did **a** awake,	1Sa 26:12	
we will not give them **a** of the	1Sa 30:22	4480
afflict them **a** more as formerly,	2Sa 7:10	3254
and when **a** man had a suit	2Sa 15:2	3605
then every man who has **a** suit or	2Sa 15:4	
Should **a** man be put to death in	2Sa 19:22	376
to put **a** man to death in Israel."	2Sa 21:4	376
within **a** border of Israel,	2Sa 21:5	3605
crossed him at **a** time by asking,	1Ki 1:6	4480
not go out from there to **a** place.	1Ki 2:36	575
so that there will not be **a** among	1Ki 3:13	376
nor **a** iron tool heard in the house	1Ki 6:7	3605
skill for doing **a** work in bronze.	1Ki 7:14	3605
or supplication is made by **a** man	1Ki 8:38	3605
it was made for **a** other kingdom.	1Ki 10:20	3605
a who would, he ordained, to be	1Ki 13:33	
leave to Jeroboam **a** persons alive,	1Ki 15:29	3605
if for **a** reason he is missing,	1Ki 20:39	6485
or unfruitfulness **a** longer.'"	2Ki 2:21	5750
if you meet **a** man, do not salute	2Ki 4:29	376
I wait for the LORD **a** longer?"	2Ki 6:33	5750
they *will be in* **a** *case* like all	2Ki 7:13	
they *will be in* **a** *case* like all	2Ki 7:13	
do, we will not make **a** man king;	2Ki 10:5	376
"The one who permits **a** of the men	2Ki 10:24	4480
money which **a** man's heart prompts	2Ki 12:4	376
wherever **a** damage may be found.	2Ki 12:5	
trumpets, **a** vessels of gold,	2Ki 12:13	3605
nor was there **a** helper for Israel.	2Ki 14:26	
'Has **a** one of the gods of the	2Ki 18:33	376
did **a** like him arise after him.	2Ki 23:25	
before **a** king of the sons of Israel	1Ch 1:43	
with **a** of the judges of Israel,	1Ch 17:6	259
is there **a** God besides You,	1Ch 17:20	
and every willing man of **a** skill	1Ch 28:21	3605
on **a** king before him in Israel.	1Ch 29:25	3605
to execute **a** design which may be	2Ch 2:14	3605
nor did I choose **a** man for a	2Ch 6:5	376
or supplication is made by **a** man	2Ch 6:29	3605
the priests and Levites in **a** manner	2Ch 8:15	3605
it was made for **a** *other* kingdom.	2Ch 9:19	3605
"Whenever **a** dispute comes to	2Ch 19:10	3605
the priest did not dismiss **a** *of*	2Ch 23:8	
enter *who was* in **a** way unclean.	2Ch 23:19	3605
nor with **a** of the sons of Ephraim.	2Ch 25:7	3605
for no god of **a** nation or kingdom	2Ch 32:15	3605
nor had **a** of the kings of Israel	2Ch 35:18	3605
a man who violates this edict,	Ezr 6:11	3606
overthrow **a** king or people who	Ezr 6:12	3606
I have issued a decree that **a** of	Ezr 7:13	3606
or toll *on* **a** of the priests,	Ezr 7:24	3606
I did not find **a** Levites there.	Ezr 8:15	4480
is no remnant nor **a** who escape?	Ezr 9:14	
we did not buy **a** land, and all my	Ne 5:16	
or **a** grain on the sabbath day to sell	Ne 10:31	3605
for **a** man or woman who comes to	Es 4:11	3605
escape **a** more than all the Jews.	Es 4:13	
annihilate the entire army of **a** people	Es 8:11	
a taste in the white of an egg?	Jb 6:6	3426
it withers before **a** *other* plant.	Jb 8:12	3605
Nor **a** survivor where he sojourned.	Jb 18:19	
"Is there **a** pleasure to the	Jb 22:3	
"Is there **a** number to His troops?	Jb 25:3	3426
does not reproach **a** of my days.	Jb 27:6	4480
if **a** spot has stuck to my hands,	Jb 31:7	
Nor flatter **a** man.	Jb 32:21	
had no regard for **a** of His ways;	Jb 34:27	3605
is mighty but does not despise **a**;	Jb 36:5	
regard **a** who are wise of heart."	Jb 37:24	3605
"Who will show us **a** good?"	Ps 4:6	
see if there are **a** who understand,	Ps 14:2	3426
not be in want of **a** good thing.	Ps 34:10	3605
can by **a** means redeem *his* brother Or	Ps 49:7	6299
Do not be gracious to **a** *who are*	Ps 59:5	3605
There is no longer **a** prophet,	Ps 74:9	
a among us who knows how long.	Ps 74:9	
shall you worship **a** foreign god.	Ps 81:9	
will die like men And fall like **a**	Ps 82:7	
Nor are there **a** works like Yours.	Ps 86:8	
will **a** plague come near your tent.	Ps 91:10	
Nor **a** to be gracious to his	Ps 109:12	
Nor *do* **a** who go down into silence;	Ps 115:17	3605
And do not let **a** iniquity have	Ps 119:133	3605
a breath at all in their mouths.	Ps 135:17	3426
if there be **a** hurtful way in me,	Ps 139:24	
incline my heart to **a** evil thing,	Ps 141:4	
has not dealt thus with **a** nation;	Ps 147:20	3605
baited net In the sight of **a** bird;	Pr 1:17	3605
And do not choose **a** of his ways.	Pr 3:31	3605
He will not accept **a** ransom,	Pr 6:35	3605
But sin is a disgrace to **a** people.	Pr 14:34	
a man, But **a** fool will quarrel.	Pr 20:3	3605
man **a** bitter thing is sweet.	Pr 27:7	3605
I am more stupid than **a** man,	Pr 30:2	376
And does not retreat before **a**,	Pr 30:30	3605
withhold my heart from **a** pleasure,	Ec 2:10	3605
nor have they **a** longer a reward,	Ec 9:5	5750
Nor **a** of its cords be torn apart.	Is 33:20	3605
will **a** vicious beast go up on it;	Is 35:9	
Has **a** one of the gods of the	Is 36:18	376
Is there **a** God besides Me, Or is	Is 44:8	3426
Me, Or is there **a** *other* Rock?	Is 44:8	
Without **a** payment or reward,"	Is 45:13	
was marred more than **a** man And	Is 52:14	376
was there **a** deceit in His mouth.	Is 53:9	
his hand from doing **a** evil."	Is 56:2	3605
land will it **a** longer be said,	Is 62:4	5750
And do not trust **a** brother;	Jer 9:4	3605
no harm, Nor can they do **a** good."	Jer 10:5	1571
Are there **a** among the idols of the	Jer 14:22	3426
and do not carry **a** load on the	Jer 17:21	
on the sabbath day nor do **a** work,	Jer 17:22	3605
give no heed to **a** of his words."	Jer 18:18	3605
they will not be afraid **a** longer,	Jer 23:4	5750
nor will **a** be missing,"	Jer 23:4	
keep them **a** longer in bondage;	Jer 34:10	5750
by the mouth of **a** man of Judah in	Jer 44:26	3605
there no longer **a** wisdom in Teman?	Jer 49:7	5750
Nor will **a** son of man reside in	Jer 50:40	
Look and see if there is **a** pain	La 1:12	3426
Why should **a** living mortal, or	La 3:39	
or **a** man, Offer complaint in	La 3:39	
Nor *did* **a** of the inhabitants of	La 4:12	3605
in **a** of their four directions without	Ezk 1:17	702
nor has **a** unclean meat ever	Ezk 4:14	
nor will **a** of them maintain his	Ezk 7:13	376
touch **a** man on whom is the mark;	Ezk 9:6	3605
When they moved, they went in **a** *of*	Ezk 10:11	
"For there will no longer be **a**	Ezk 12:24	3605
My words will be delayed **a** longer.	Ezk 12:28	5750
"**A** man of the house of Israel who	Ezk 14:4	376
wood of the vine *better* than **a** wood	Ezk 15:2	3605
from it on which to hang **a** vessel?	Ezk 15:3	3605
to do **a** of these things for you,	Ezk 16:5	259
a of these things to a brother	Ezk 18:10	4480, 259
did not do **a** of these things),	Ezk 18:11	3605
"Do I have **a** pleasure in the	Ezk 18:23	2654a
thorn from **a** round about them who	Ezk 28:24	3605
from the peoples **a** longer,	Ezk 36:15	5750
your nation to stumble **a** longer,"	Ezk 36:15	5750
or with **a** of their transgressions;	Ezk 37:23	3605
leave none of them there **a** longer.	Ezk 39:28	5750
hide My face from them **a** longer,	Ezk 39:29	5750
come near to **a** of My holy things,	Ezk 44:13	3605
"Nor shall **a** of the priests drink	Ezk 44:21	3605
"The priests shall not eat **a** bird	Ezk 44:31	3605
his inheritance to **a** of his sons,	Ezk 46:16	376
not sell or exchange **a** of it,	Ezk 48:14	4480
anything like this of **a** magician,	Da 2:10	3606
for **a** wisdom residing in me more	Da 2:30	
more than *in* **a** *other* living man,	Da 2:30	3606
a god except their own God.	Da 3:28	3606
I make a decree that **a** people,	Da 3:29	3606
"**A** man who can read this	Da 5:7	3606
"We will not find **a** ground of	Da 6:5	3606
to **a** god or man besides you,	Da 6:7	3606
an injunction that **a** man who makes	Da 6:12	3606
to **a** god or man besides you,	Da 6:12	3606
on account of **a** merits of our own,	Da 9:18	
I did not eat **a** tasty food, nor	Da 10:3	
nor did I use **a** ointment at all until	Da 10:3	
has **a** breath been left in me."	Da 10:17	
he show regard for **a** *other* god;	Da 11:37	3605
were not to know **a** god except Me,	Hos 13:4	
never forget **a** of their deeds.	Am 8:7	3605
food, wine, oil, or **a** *other* food,	Hg 2:12	3605
from a corpse touches **a** of these,	Hg 2:13	3605
wage for man or **a** wage for animal;	Zch 8:10	
Then it will come about that **a** who	Zch 14:16	3605
will He receive **a** of you kindly?"	Mal 1:9	4480
and do not enter **a** city of	Mt 10:5	
"**A** kingdom divided against itself	Mt 12:25	*3956*
and **a** city or house divided	Mt 12:25	*3956*
a sin and blasphemy shall be	Mt 12:31	*3956*
had forgotten to bring **a** bread.	Mt 16:5	
because we did not bring **a** bread."	Mt 16:7	
If **a** man has a hundred sheep, and	Mt 18:12	*5100*
his wife for **a** reason at all?"	Mt 19:3	*3956*
"No longer shall there ever be **a**	Mt 21:19	
for You are not partial to **a**.	Mt 22:16	*3762*
They did not find **a**, even though	Mt 26:60	
to release for the people **a** one	Mt 27:15	
"Do not be afraid **a** *longer,*	Mk 5:36	
"**A** place that does not receive you	Mk 6:11	*3739*
for they had not gained **a** insight	Mk 6:52	
for You are not partial to **a**,	Mk 12:14	*444*
to ask Him **a** more questions.	Mk 12:34	*3765*
and they were not finding **a**.	Mk 14:55	
feast he used to release for them **a**	Mk 15:6	
and if they drink **a** deadly *poison,*	Mk 16:18	*5100*
of him without doing him **a** harm.	Lk 4:35	*3367*
all those who had **a** *who were* sick	Lk 4:40	
But not finding **a** *way* to bring him	Lk 5:19	*4169*
bread which is not lawful for **a** to eat	Lk 6:4	
the ground without **a** foundation;	Lk 6:49	
put on **a** clothing for a long time,	Lk 8:27	
"Do not be afraid **a** *longer;*	Lk 8:50	
a of the things which they had seen.	Lk 9:36	*3762*
"**A** kingdom divided against itself	Lk 11:17	*3956*
seeking rest, and not finding **a**,	Lk 11:24	
fruit on it and did not find **a**.	Lk 13:6	
this fig tree without finding **a**.	Lk 13:7	
and You are not partial to **a**,	Lk 20:21	
Him **a** longer about anything.	Lk 20:40	*3765*
No one has seen God at **a** time;	Jn 1:18	*4455*
"Can **a** good thing come out of	Jn 1:46	*5100*
neither heard His voice at **a** time nor	Jn 5:37	*4455*
see that you are not doing **a** good;	Jn 12:19	*3762*
"If you forgive the sins of **a**,	Jn 20:23	*5100*
if you retain the *sins* of **a**,	Jn 20:23	*5100*
"Children, you do not have **a** fish,	Jn 21:5	*5100*
spread **a** further among the people,	Ac 4:17	*1909*
no longer to **a** man in this name."	Ac 4:17	*3367*
to each as **a** had need.	Ac 4:35	*5100*
might fall on **a** one of them.	Ac 5:15	*5100*
had not yet fallen upon **a** of them;	Ac 8:16	*3762*
he found **a** belonging to the Way,	Ac 9:2	*5100*
not call **a** man unholy or unclean.	Ac 10:28	*3367*
a objection when I was sent for.	Ac 10:29	
that **a** of the disciples had means,	Ac 11:29	*5100*
if you have **a** word of exhortation	Ac 13:15	*5100*
"Do not be afraid **a** *longer,* but	Ac 18:9	
concerned about **a** of these things.	Ac 18:17	*3762*
have a complaint against **a** man,	Ac 19:38	*5100*
of **a** account as dear to myself,	Ac 20:24	*3762*
I may not weary you **a** further,	Ac 24:4	*1909*
without **a** crowd or uproar. But	Ac 24:18	
and not to prevent **a** of his	Ac 24:23	*3367*
of the Romans to hand over **a** man	Ac 25:16	*5100*
he ought not to live **a** longer.	Ac 25:24	*3371*
head of **a** of you will perish."	Ac 27:34	*3762*
a accusation against my nation.	Ac 28:19	*5100*
nor have **a** of the brethren come	Ac 28:21	*5100*
fit to acknowledge God **a** longer,	Ro 1:28	
depth, nor **a** other created thing,	Ro 8:39	*5100*
if there is **a** other commandment,	Ro 13:9	*5100*
you are not lacking in **a** gift,	1Co 1:7	*3367*
know whether I baptized **a** other.	1Co 1:16	*5100*
Now if **a** man builds on the	1Co 3:12	*5100*
If **a** man's work which he has built	1Co 3:14	*5100*
If **a** man's work is burned up, he	1Co 3:15	*5100*
If **a** man destroys the temple of	1Co 3:17	*5100*
If **a** man among you thinks that he	1Co 3:18	*5100*
or by **a** human court; in fact, I	1Co 4:3	
to associate with **a** so-called brother	1Co 5:11	*5100*
Does **a** one of you, when he has a	1Co 6:1	*5100*
that if **a** brother has a wife who	1Co 7:12	*5100*
Was **a** man called *when*	1Co 7:18	*5100*
But if **a** man thinks that he is	1Co 7:36	*5100*
Who at **a** time serves as a soldier	1Co 9:7	*4218*
a man make my boast an empty one.	1Co 9:15	*5100*
a the less *a part* of the body.	1Co 12:15	*3756*
a the less *a part* of the body.	1Co 12:16	*3756*
comfort those who are in **a** affliction	2Co 1:4	*3956*
But if **a** has caused sorrow, he has	2Co 2:5	*5100*
if **a** Macedonians come with me	2Co 9:4	
through **a** of those whom I have sent	2Co 12:17	*5100*
did not take **a** advantage of you,	2Co 12:18	*4122*
if **a** man is preaching to you a	Ga 1:9	*5100*

But I did not see **a** other of the Ga 1:19 *2087*
even if anyone is caught in **a** Ga 6:1 *5100*
But immorality or **a** Eph 5:3 *3956*
spot or wrinkle or **a** such thing; Eph 5:27 *5100*
is **a** encouragement in Christ, Php 2:1 *5100*
if there is **a** consolation of love, Php 2:1 *5100*
is **a** fellowship of the Spirit, Php 2:1 *5100*
if **a** affection and compassion, Php 2:1 *5100*
if there is **a** excellence and if Php 4:8 *5100*
in **a** and every circumstance I have Php 4:12 *3956*
as not to be a burden to **a** of you, 1Th 2:9 *5100*
outsiders and not be in **a** need. 1Th 4:12 *3367*
Let no one in **a** way deceive you, 2Th 2:3 *3367*
would not be a burden to **a** of you; 2Th 3:8 *5100*
if a man aspires to the office of 1Tm 3:1 *5100*
but if **a** widow has children or 1Tm 5:4 *5100*
If **a** woman who is a believer has 1Tm 5:16 *5100*
if **a** man is above reproach, Ti 1:6 *5100*
and worthless for **a** good deed. Ti 1:16 *3956*
if he has wronged you in **a** way or Phm 1:18 *5100*
not be in **a** one of you an evil, Heb 3:12 *5100*
a one of you may seem to have Heb 4:1 *5100*
and sharper than **a** two-edged sword, Heb 4:12 *3956*
But without **a** dispute the lesser Heb 7:7 *3956*
there is no longer **a** offering for Heb 10:18
But if **a** of you lacks wisdom, let Jas 1:5 *5100*
ask in faith without **a** doubting, Jas 1:6 *3367*
or by earth or with **a** other oath; Jas 5:12 *5100*
if **a** among you strays from the Jas 5:19 *5100*
WAS A DECEIT FOUND IN HIS MOUTH; 1Pe 2:22
even if **a** *of them* are disobedient to 1Pe 3:1 *5100*
being frightened by **a** fear. 1Pe 3:6 *3367*
at **a** time after my departure you will 2Pe 1:15 *1539*
not wishing for **a** to perish but 2Pe 3:9 *5100*
No one has seen God at **a** time; 1Jn 4:12 *4455*
earth or on the sea or on **a** tree. Rv 7:1 *3956*
sun beat down on them, nor **a** heat; Rv 7:16 *3956*
of the earth, nor **a** green thing, Rv 9:4 *3956*
nor any green thing, nor **a** tree, Rv 9:4 *3956*
no one buys their cargoes **a** more Rv 18:11 *3765*
and will not be found **a** longer. Rv 18:21 *2089*
will not be heard in you **a** longer; Rv 18:22 *2089*
and no craftsman of **a** craft will Rv 18:22 *3956*
will be found in you **a** longer; Rv 18:22 *2089*
will not be heard in you **a** longer; Rv 18:22 *2089*
will not shine in you **a** longer; Rv 18:23 *2089*
will not be heard in you **a** longer; Rv 18:23 *2089*
not deceive the nations **a** longer, Rv 20:3 *2089*
and there is no longer **a** sea. Rv 21:1
will no longer be **a** death; Rv 21:4
will no longer be **a** mourning, Rv 21:4
There will no longer be **a** curse; Rv 22:3 *3956*
will no longer be **a** night; Rv 22:5

ANYMORE

let me not see this great fire **a**, Dt 18:16 5750
I will not be with you **a** unless Jos 7:12 3254
did not lift up their heads **a**. Jg 8:28 3254
a within the border of Israel. 1Sa 7:13 5750
will despair of searching for me **a** in 1Sa 27:1 5750
nor did they continue to fight **a**. 2Sa 2:28 5750
to help the sons of Ammon **a**. 2Sa 10:19 5750
me, and he will not touch you **a**." 2Sa 14:10 3254, 5750
I should complain **a** to the king?" 2Sa 19:28 5750
Or can I hear **a** the voice of 2Sa 19:35 5750
not make the feet of Israel wander **a** 2Ki 21:8 3254
not waste them **a** as formerly, 1Ch 17:9 3254
to help the sons of Ammon **a**. 1Ch 19:19 5750
Nor will his place know him **a**. Jb 7:10 5750
I will not offend **a**; Jb 34:31
nor will they walk **a** after the Jer 3:17 5750
Him Or speak **a** in His name," Jer 20:9 5750
up or overthrown **a** forever." Jer 31:40 5750
a because of your humiliation, Ezk 16:63 5750
to use this proverb in Israel **a**. Ezk 18:3 5750
eyes to them or remember Egypt **a**.' Ezk 23:27 5750
of man will not muddy them **a** Ezk 32:13 5750
will not feed themselves **a**, Ezk 34:10 5750
the insults of the nations **a**. Ezk 34:29 5750
hear insults from the nations **a**, Ezk 36:15 5750
let My holy name be profaned **a**. Ezk 39:7 5750
oppressor will pass over them **a**, Zch 9:8 5750
And no one was able to bind him **a**, Mk 5:3 *3765*
why trouble the Teacher **a**?" Mk 5:35 *2089*
around and saw no one with them **a**, Mk 9:8 *3765*
do not trouble the Teacher **a**." Lk 8:49 *3371*
for they cannot even die **a**, Lk 20:36 *2089*
do not sin **a**, so that nothing Jn 5:14 *3371*
and were not walking with Him **a**. Jn 6:66 *3765*
let us not judge one another **a**, Ro 14:13 *3371*
and he will not go out from it **a**; Rv 3:12 *2089*
hunger no longer, nor thirst **a**; Rv 7:16 *2089*

ANYONE

so that if **a** can number the dust Gn 13:16 376
nor did **a** rise from his place for Ex 10:23 376
'Now when **a** presents a grain Lv 2:1 5315
'Now if **a** of the common people Lv 4:27 5315, 259
'**A** who touches its flesh will Lv 6:27 3605
a who is clean may eat *such* flesh. Lv 7:19 3605
When **a** touches anything unclean, Lv 7:21 5315
'**A**, moreover, who touches his bed Lv 15:5 376
'**A** who touches her bed shall wash Lv 15:21 3605
'If *there is* **a** who curses his Lv 20:9 376
'If **a** curses his God, then he Lv 24:15 376
'**A** who touches a corpse, the body Nu 19:13 3605
a who in the open field touches Nu 19:16 3605
Wherever the lot falls to **a**, Nu 33:54
that **a** who kills a person Nu 35:15 3605
'If **a** kills a person, the murderer Nu 35:30 3605
to live in, **a** saying *that* Dt 13:12
shall not be found among you **a** who Dt 18:10
on your house if **a** falls from it. Dt 22:8 5307
"**A** who rebels against your Jos 1:18 3605, 376
"It shall come about that **a** Jos 2:19 3605
a who is with you in the house, Jos 2:19 3605
or make **a** swear *by them*, or Jos 23:7
and did not allow **a** to cross. Jg 3:28 376
be if **a** comes and inquires of you, Jg 4:20 376
'Is there **a** here?' Jg 4:20 376
and had no dealings with **a**. Jg 18:7 120
and they had no dealings with **a**, Jg 18:28 120
"Should **a** rise up to pursue 1Sa 25:29 120
and great, without killing **a**, 1Sa 30:2 376
yet **a** left of the house of Saul, 2Sa 9:1 834
"Is there not yet **a** of the house 2Sa 9:3 376
"**A** belonging to Jeroboam who dies 1Ki 14:11
Ramah in order to prevent **a** from 1Ki 15:17
"**A** of Baasha who dies in the city 1Ki 16:4
and **a** of his who dies in the field 1Ki 16:4
salute him, and if **a** salutes you, 2Ki 4:29 376
Ramah in order to prevent **a** from 2Ch 16:1
teach **a** who is ignorant *of them*. Ezr 7:25
I did not tell **a** what my God was Ne 2:12 120
is there **a** who will answer you? Jb 5:1
"Can **a** teach God knowledge, In Jb 21:22
a perish for lack of clothing, Jb 31:19
"For has **a** said to God, Jb 34:31
"Can **a** understand the spreading Jb 36:29
"Can **a** capture him when he is on Jb 40:24
With barbs can **a** pierce *his* nose? Jb 40:24
deliver **a** by its great strength. Ps 33:17
see if there is **a** who understands, Ps 53:2
A who is found will be thrust Is 13:15 3605
And **a** who is captured will fall by Is 13:15 3605
"If **a** fiercely assails *you* it Is 54:15
There is no peace for **a**. Jer 12:12 3605, 1320
"Can **a** smash iron, Iron from the Jer 15:12
nor will **a** gash himself or shave Jer 16:6
them, to comfort **a** for the dead, Jer 16:7
have **a** living among this people, Jer 29:32 376
do not let **a** know where you are." Jer 36:19
And when **a** builds a wall, behold, Ezk 13:10 1931
"For **a** of the house of Israel or Ezk 14:7 376
if a man does not oppress **a**, Ezk 18:7
or oppress **a**, or retain a pledge, Ezk 18:16 376
in the death of **a** who dies," Ezk 18:32
through and **a** sees a man's bone, Ezk 39:15
a from his possession. Ezk 46:18 376
an injunction that **a** who makes a Da 6:7 3605
there **a** to rescue from his power, Da 8:4
"Is **a** else with you?" Am 6:10
"And if **a** still prophesies, Zch 13:3 376
nor does **a** light a lamp and put Mt 5:15
"If **a** wants to sue you and Mt 5:40
such great faith with **a** in Israel. Mt 8:10 *3762*
of women there has not arisen **a** Mt 11:11
nor does **a** know the Father except Mt 11:27 *5100*
and **a** to whom the Son wills to Mt 11:27
A HEAR HIS VOICE IN THE STREETS. Mt 12:19 *5100*
"Or how can **a** enter the strong Mt 12:29 *5100*
a hears the word of the kingdom and Mt 13:19 *3956*
"If **a** wishes to come after Me, Mt 16:24 *5100*
"If **a** says anything to you, Mt 21:3 *5100*
nor did **a** dare from that day on to Mt 22:46 *5100*
"Do not call **a** on earth your Mt 23:9
"Then if **a** says to you, Mt 24:23 *5100*
"See that you say nothing to **a**; Mk 1:44 *3367*
which is not lawful for **a** to eat Mk 2:26
"If **a** has ears to hear, let him Mk 4:23 *5100*
["If **a** has ears to hear, let him Mk 7:16 *5100*
He gave them orders not to tell **a**; Mk 7:36 *3367*
"Where will **a** be able *to find* Mk 8:4 *5100*
"If **a** wishes to come after Me, Mk 8:34 *5100*
to relate to **a** what they had seen, Mk 9:9 *3367*
not want **a** to know *about it*. Mk 9:30 *5100*
"If **a** wants to be first, he shall Mk 9:35 *5100*
"If **a** says to you, Mk 11:3 *5100*
and He would not permit **a** to carry Mk 11:16 *5100*
if you have anything against **a**, Mk 11:25 *5100*
"And then if **a** says to you, Mk 13:21 *5100*
and they said nothing to **a**, Mk 16:8 *3762*
"Do not take money from **a** by force, Lk 3:14 *3367*
or accuse **a** falsely, and be Lk 3:14
and could not be healed by **a**, Lk 8:43 *3762*
did not allow **a** to enter with Him, Lk 8:51 *5100*
them not to tell this to **a**, Lk 9:21 *3367*
"If **a** wishes to come after Me, Lk 9:23 *5100*
and **a** to whom the Son wills to Lk 10:22
"If **a** comes to Me, and does not Lk 14:26 *5100*
if I have defrauded **a** of anything, Lk 19:8 *5100*
"If **a** asks you, Lk 19:31 *5100*
and because He did not need **a** to Jn 2:25 *5100*
"For not even the Father judges **a**, Jn 5:22 *3762*
"Not that **a** has seen the Father, Jn 6:46 *5100*
if **a** eats of this bread, he will Jn 6:51 *5100*
"If **a** is willing to do His will, he Jn 7:17 *5100*
"If **a** is thirsty, let him come to Jn 7:37 *5100*
I am not judging **a**. Jn 8:15 *3762*
have never yet been enslaved to **a**; Jn 8:33 *3762*
if **a** keeps My word he will never Jn 8:51 *5100*
'If **a** keeps My word, he will Jn 8:52 *5100*
that if **a** confessed Him to be Jn 9:22 *5100*
but if **a** is God-fearing and does Jn 9:31 *5100*
has never been heard that **a** opened Jn 9:32 *5100*
if **a** enters through Me, he will Jn 10:9 *5100*
If **a** walks in the day, he does not Jn 11:9 *5100*
"But if **a** walks in the night, he Jn 11:10 *5100*
that if **a** knew where He was, Jn 11:57 *5100*
"If **a** serves Me, he must follow Jn 12:26 *5100*
if **a** serves Me, the Father will Jn 12:26 *5100*
"If **a** hears My sayings and Jn 12:47 *5100*
"If **a** loves Me, he will keep My Jn 14:23 *5100*
"If **a** does not abide in Me, he is Jn 15:6 *5100*
no need for **a** to question You; Jn 16:30 *5100*
not permitted to put **a** to death," Jn 18:31 *3762*
with all, as **a** might have need. Ac 2:45 *5100*
with **a** or causing a riot. Ac 24:12 *5100*
But if **a** does not have the Spirit Ro 8:9 *5100*
Never pay back evil for evil to **a**. Ro 12:17 *3367*
to **a** except to love one another; Ro 13:8 *3367*
a been called in uncircumcision? 1Co 7:18 *5100*
If **a** supposes that he knows 1Co 8:2 *5100*
but if **a** loves God, he is known by 1Co 8:3 *5100*
But if **a** says to you, 1Co 10:28 *5100*
If **a** is hungry, let him eat at 1Co 11:34 *5100*
If **a** speaks in a tongue, *it should* 1Co 14:27 *5100*
If **a** thinks he is a prophet or 1Co 14:37 *5100*
But if **a** does not recognize *this*, 1Co 14:38 *5100*
If **a** does not love the Lord, he 1Co 16:22 *5100*
Therefore if **a** is in Christ, *he is* 2Co 5:17 *5100*
If **a** is confident in himself that 2Co 10:7 *5100*
in need, I was not a burden to **a**; 2Co 11:9 *3762*
tolerate it if **a** enslaves you, 2Co 11:20 *5100*
a devours you, anyone takes 2Co 11:20 *5100*
a takes advantage of you, anyone 2Co 11:20 *5100*
a exalts himself, anyone *hits you in* 2Co 11:20 *5100*
a hits you in the face. 2Co 11:20 *5100*
whatever respect **a** *else* is bold 2Co 11:21 *5100*
if I come again I will not spare **a**, 2Co 13:2
Brethren, even if **a** is caught in any Ga 6:1 *444*
For if **a** thinks he is something Ga 6:3 *5100*
If **a** else has a mind to put Php 3:4 *5100*
whoever has a complaint against **a**; Col 3:13 *5100*
you have no need for **a** to write 1Th 4:9
if **a** is not willing to work, then 2Th 3:10 *5100*
If **a** does not obey our 2Th 3:14 *5100*
if **a** does not provide for his own, 1Tm 5:8 *5100*
Do not lay hands upon **a** *too* 1Tm 5:22 *3367*
If **a** advocates a different 1Tm 6:3 *5100*
Also if **a** competes as an athlete, 2Tm 2:5 *5100*
Therefore, if **a** cleanses himself 2Tm 2:21 *5100*
A who has set aside the Law of Heb 10:28 *5100*
and He Himself does not tempt **a**. Jas 1:13 *3762*
For if **a** is a hearer of the word Jas 1:23 *5100*
If **a** thinks himself to be Jas 1:26 *5100*
If **a** does not stumble in what he Jas 3:2 *5100*
Is **a** among you suffering? Jas 5:13 *5100*
Is **a** cheerful? He is to sing praises. Jas 5:13 *5100*
Is **a** among you sick? Jas 5:14 *5100*
but if **a** *suffers* as a Christian, 1Pe 4:16
And if **a** sins, we have an Advocate 1Jn 2:1 *5100*
If **a** loves the world, the love of 1Jn 2:15 *5100*
have no need for **a** to teach you; 1Jn 2:27 *5100*
a who does not practice 1Jn 3:10 *3956*
If **a** sees his brother committing a 1Jn 5:16 *5100*
A who goes too far and does not 2Jn 1:9 *3956*
If **a** comes to you and does not 2Jn 1:10 *5100*
if **a** hears My voice and opens the Rv 3:20 *5100*
they were not permitted to kill **a**, Rv 9:5 *846*
And if **a** wants to harm them, Rv 11:5 *5100*
if **a** wants to harm them, Rv 11:5 *5100*
If **a** has an ear, let him hear. Rv 13:9 *5100*
If **a** *is destined* for captivity, to Rv 13:10 *5100*
if **a** kills with the sword, with Rv 13:10 *5100*
"If **a** worships the beast and his Rv 14:9 *5100*
if **a** adds to them, God will add Rv 22:18 *5100*
and if **a** takes away from the words Rv 22:19 *5100*

ANYONE'S

'It shall not be poured on **a** body, Ex 30:32 120
to drink for **a** father or mother. Jer 16:7
eat **a** bread without paying for it, 2Th 3:8 *3844, 5100*
And if **a** name was not found Rv 20:15 *5100*

ANYTHING

a sandal thong or **a** that is yours, Gn 14:23 3605
"Is **a** too difficult for the LORD? Gn 18:14 1697
do **a** until you arrive there." Gn 19:22 1697
"You shall not give me **a**. Gn 30:31 3972
a except the food which he ate. Gn 39:6 3972
himself with **a** in the house, Gn 39:8 4100
not supervise **a** under Joseph's charge Gn 39:23 3605, 3972
for whoever eats **a** leavened from Ex 12:15
'You shall not eat **a** leavened; Ex 12:20 3605
a that belongs to your neighbor." Ex 20:17 3605
"If a man borrows **a** from his Ex 22:14
or **a** about which he swore falsely; Lv 6:5 3605
a unclean shall not be eaten; Lv 7:19 3605
'When anyone touches **a** unclean, Lv 7:21 3605
'Also **a** on which one of them may Lv 11:32 3605
'You shall not eat **a** with Lv 19:26
or by **a** that creeps on the ground, Lv 20:25 3605
And if one touches **a** made unclean Lv 22:4 3605
'Also **a** *with its testicles* bruised Lv 22:24
a which a man sets apart to the Lv 27:28 3605
A devoted to destruction is most Lv 27:28 3605
he shall not eat **a** that is produced by Nu 6:4 4480, 3605
have one law for him who does **a** Nu 15:29
'But the person who does **a** Nu 15:30
a that the unclean *person* touches Nu 19:22 3605
silver and gold, I could not do **a**, Nu 22:18

Am I able to speak **a** at all? **Nu 22:38** 3972
I could not do **a** contrary to the **Nu 24:13**
of **a** that creeps on the ground, **Dt 4:18** 3605
graven image in the form of **a** *against* **Dt 4:23** 3605
and make an idol in the form of **a**, **Dt 4:25** 3605
Has **a** been done like this great **Dt 4:32**
or has **a** been heard like it? **Dt 4:32**
a that belongs to your neighbor.' **Dt 5:21** 3605
in which you will not lack **a**; **Dt 8:9** 3605
a that has fins and scales you may **Dt 14:9** 3605
but **a** that does not have fins and **Dt 14:10** 3605
not eat **a** which dies *of itself.* **Dt 14:21** 3605
not leave alive **a** that breathes. **Dt 20:16** 3605
with **a** lost by your countryman, **Dt 22:3** 3605
and He must not see **a** indecent **Dt 23:14** 1697
or **a** that may be loaned at **Dt 23:19** 3605
and you will never be **a** but **Dt 28:33** 7534
them secretly for lack of **a** *else,* **Dt 28:57** 3605
"She should not eat **a** that comes **Jg 13:14** 3605
them for **a** in the land, **Jg 18:7** 1697
lack of **a** that is on the earth." **Jg 18:10** 3605, 1697
there is no lack of **a**." **Jg 19:19** 3605, 1697
if **a** *but* death parts you and me." **Ru 1:17**
if you hide **a** from me of all the **1Sa 3:17** 1697
or taken **a** from any man's hand." **1Sa 12:4** 3972
if I find out **a**, then I will tell **1Sa 19:3** 4100
Saul did not speak **a** that day, **1Sa 20:26** 3972
But the lad was not aware of **a**; **1Sa 20:39** 3972
'Let no one know **a** about the **1Sa 21:2** 3972
Do not let the king impute **a** to **1Sa 22:15** 1697
nor have they missed **a** all the **1Sa 25:7** 3972
nor did we miss **a** as long as we **1Sa 25:15** 3972
so she did not tell him **a** at all **1Sa 25:36** 1697
spoil or **a** that they had taken for **1Sa 30:19** 3605
a else before the sun goes down." **2Sa 3:35** 3972
hard to Amnon to do **a** to her. **2Sa 13:2** 3972
"Please do not hide **a** from me **2Sa 14:18** 1697
a that my lord the king has spoken **2Sa 14:19** 3605
and they did not know **a**. **2Sa 15:11** 3605, 1697
or has **a** been taken for us?" **2Sa 19:42** 5375
and had not turned aside from **a** **1Ki 15:5** 3605
everyone who had dedicated **a**, *all* **1Ch 26:28**
a that she desired was given her **Es 2:13** 3605
not request **a** except what Hegai, **Es 2:15** 1697
in **a** of all that you have said." **Es 6:10** 1697
He does not retain **a** he desires. **Jb 20:20**
Never even tasting **a** good. **Jb 21:25**
And his eye sees **a** precious. **Jb 28:10** 3605
"*Then* if you have **a** to say, **Jb 33:32** 4405
Is there **a** of which one might say, **Ec 1:10** 1697
sees the sun and it never knows **a**; **Ec 6:5**
discover **a** *that will be* after him. **Ec 7:14** 3972
will be love or hatred; **a** awaits him. **Ec 9:1** 3605
but the dead do not know **a**, **Ec 9:5** 3972
or bring **a** in through the gates of **Jer 17:21**
"How long? Is there **a** in **Jer 23:26**
is **a** too difficult for Me?" **Jer 32:27** 3605, 1697
do not hide **a** from me." **Jer 38:14** 1697
wealth, nor **a** eminent among them. **Ezk 7:11**
wood be taken from it to make **a**, **Ezk 15:3** 4399
charred, is it *then* useful for **a**? **Ezk 15:4** 4399
is intact, it is not made into **a**. **Ezk 15:5** 4399
can it still be made into **a**! **Ezk 15:5** 4399
shall not gird themselves with **a** **Ezk 44:18**
asked **a** like this of any magician, **Da 2:10** 4406
nation or tongue that speaks **a** **Da 3:29**
heaven there has not been done **a** **Da 9:12**
Has **a** *like* this happened in your **Jl 1:2**
There has never been **a** like it, **Jl 2:2**
But you will not preserve **a**, **Mi 6:14**
It is no longer good for **a**, except **Mt 5:13** *3762*
a beyond these is of evil. **Mt 5:37**
earth about **a** that they may ask, **Mt 18:19** *3956, 4229*
"If anyone says **a** to you, you shall **Mt 21:3** *5100*
"We have never seen **a** like this." **Mk 2:12**
nor has **a** been secret, but that **Mk 4:22**
do **a** for *his* father or *his* mother; **Mk 7:12** *3762*
He asked him, "Do you see **a**?" **Mk 8:23** *5100*
But if You can do **a**, **Mk 9:22** *5100*
cannot come out by **a** but prayer." **Mk 9:29** *3762*
if perhaps He would find **a** on it; **Mk 11:13** *5100*
if you have **a** against anyone, **Mk 11:25** *5100*
in to get **a** out of his house; **Mk 13:15** *5100*
nor **a** secret that will not be **Lk 8:17**
I cannot get up and give you **a**.' **Lk 11:7**
he will not get up and give him **a** **Lk 11:8**
and no one was giving **a** to him. **Lk 15:16**
if I have defrauded anyone of **a**, **Lk 19:8** *5100*
not find **a** that they might do, **Lk 19:48** *5101*
question Him any longer about **a**. **Lk 20:40** *3762*
and sandals, you did not lack **a**, **Lk 22:35** *5100*
"Have you **a** here to eat?" **Lk 24:41** *5100*
"No one brought Him **a** to eat, **Jn 4:33**
"For no one does **a** in secret when **Jn 7:4** *5100*
"If you ask Me **a** in My name, I **Jn 14:14** *5100*
day you will not question Me about **a**. **Jn 16:23** *5100*
if you ask the Father for **a** **Jn 16:23** *5100*
a belonging to him was his own, **Ac 4:32** *5100*
eaten **a** unholy and unclean." **Ac 10:14** *3956*
hands, as though He needed **a**, **Ac 17:25** *5100*
"But if you want **a** beyond this, **Ac 19:39** *5100*
to you **a** that was profitable, **Ac 20:20** *3762*
if they should have **a** against me. **Ac 24:19** *5100*
if there is **a** wrong about the man, **Ac 25:5** *5100*
have committed **a** worthy of death, **Ac 25:11** *5100*
"This man is not doing **a** worthy **Ac 26:31** *3762*
or spoken **a** bad about you. **Ac 28:21** *5100*
and had not done **a** good or bad, **Ro 9:11** *5100*
to him who thinks **a** to be unclean, **Ro 14:14** *5100*
or *to do* **a** by which your brother **Ro 14:21**
For I will not presume to speak of **a** **Ro 15:18** *5100*
nor the one who waters is **a**, **1Co 3:7** *5100*
but I will not be mastered by **a**. **1Co 6:12** *5100*
anyone supposes that he knows **a**, **1Co 8:2** *5100*
a thing sacrificed to idols is **a**, **1Co 10:19** *5100*
is anything, or that an idol is **a**? **1Co 10:19** *5100*
Eat **a** that is sold in the meat **1Co 10:25** *3956*
go, eat **a** that is set before you without **1Co 10:27** *3956*
If they desire to learn **a**, **1Co 14:35** *5100*
But one whom you forgive **a**, **2Co 2:10** *5100*
forgiven, if I have forgiven **a**, **2Co 2:10** *5100*
a as *coming* from ourselves, **2Co 3:5** *5100*
giving no cause for offense in **a**, **2Co 6:3** *3367*
not suffer loss in **a** through us. **2Co 7:9** *3367*
For if in **a** I have boasted to him **2Co 7:14** *5100*
nor uncircumcision means **a**, **Ga 5:6** *5100*
For neither is circumcision **a**, **Ga 6:15** *5100*
I will not be put to shame in **a**, **Php 1:20** *3762*
a you have a different attitude, **Php 3:15** *5100*
and if **a** worthy of praise, **Php 4:8** *5100*
so that we have no need to say **a**. **1Th 1:8** *5100*
no need of **a** to be written to you. **1Th 5:1**
we cannot take **a** out of it either. **1Tm 6:7** *5100*
consent I did not want to do **a**, **Phm 1:14** *3762*
you in any way or owes you **a**, **Phm 1:18** *5100*
he will receive **a** from the Lord, **Jas 1:7** *5100*
if we ask **a** according to His will, **1Jn 5:14** *5100*

ANYTIME
a during the day or night, **Is 28:19**

ANYWHERE
and do not stay **a** in the valley; **Gn 19:17** 3605
any man be seen **a** on the mountain; **Ex 34:3** 3605
'You may eat it **a**, **Nu 18:31** 3605, 4725
on the day you depart and go **a**, **1Ki 2:42** 575
a it seems right for you to go." **Jer 40:5** 3605

APART
and he put his own herds **a**, **Gn 30:40** 905
I will set **a** the land of Goshen, **Ex 8:22** 6395
you **a** from the peoples to be Mine. **Lv 20:26** 914
to the LORD, like a field set **a**; **Lv 27:21** 2764a
anything which a man sets **a** to the **Lv 27:28** 2763a
set **a** among men shall be ransomed; **Lv 27:29** 2763a
Behold, a people *who* dwells **a**, **Nu 23:9** 910
Then Moses set **a** three cities **Dt 4:41** 914
At that time the LORD set **a** the **Dt 10:8** 914
cities which were set **a** for the sons of **Jos 16:9** 3995
So they set **a** Kedesh in Galilee in **Jos 20:7** 6942
the altar shall be split **a** and the **1Ki 13:3** 7167
The altar also was split **a** and the **1Ki 13:5** 7167
a to sanctify him as most holy, **1Ch 23:13** 914
set **a** for the service *some* of the sons **1Ch 25:1** 914
a from those whom the king put in **2Ch 17:19** 905
I set **a** twelve of the leading priests, **Ezr 8:24** 914
and set **a** the consecrated *portion* **Ne 12:47** 6942
and the Levites set **a** the **Ne 12:47** 6942
are past, my plans are torn **a**, **Jb 17:11** 5423
"Let us tear their fetters **a** And **Ps 2:3** 5423
set **a** the godly man for Himself; **Ps 4:3** 6395
of death And broke their bands **a**. **Ps 107:14** 5423
A time to tear **a** and a time to **Ec 3:7** 7167
strands is not quickly torn **a**. **Ec 4:12** 5423
wages will be set **a** to the LORD; **Is 23:18** 6944
up, Nor any of its cords be torn **a**. **Is 33:20** 5423
set them **a** for a day of carnage! **Jer 12:3** 6942
set **a** destroyers against you, **Jer 22:7** 6942
"They will set **a** men who will **Ezk 39:14** 914
allotment which you shall set **a**, **Ezk 48:8** 7311
"The allotment that you shall set **a** to **Ezk 48:9** 7311
shall set **a** the holy allotment, **Ezk 48:20** 7311
For *the men* themselves go **a** with **Hos 4:14** 6504
to the ground **a** from your Father. **Mt 10:29** *427*
the chains had been torn **a** by him and **Mk 5:4** *1288*
Him to them **a** from the crowd. **Lk 22:6** *817*
and **a** from Him nothing came into **Jn 1:3** *5565*
for **a** from Me you can do nothing. **Jn 15:5** *5565*
"Set **a** for Me Barnabas and Saul **Ac 13:2** *873*
set **a** for the gospel of God, **Ro 1:1** *873*
But now **a** from the Law *the* **Ro 3:21** *5565*
by faith **a** from works of the Law. **Ro 3:28** *5565*
righteousness **a** from works: **Ro 4:6** *5565*
for **a** from the Law sin *is* dead. **Ro 7:8** *5565*
I was once alive **a** from the Law; **Ro 7:9** *5565*
A from *such* external things, there **2Co 11:28** *5565*
or **a** from the body I do not know, **2Co 12:3** *5565*
But when God, who had set me **a** **Ga 1:15** *873*
so that **a** from us they would not **Heb 11:40** *5565*
The sky was split **a** like a **Rv 6:14** *673*

APELLES
Greet **A**, the approved in Christ. **Ro 16:10** *559*

APES
silver, ivory and **a** and peacocks. **1Ki 10:22** 6971
silver, ivory and **a** and peacocks. **2Ch 9:21** 6971

APHEK
the king of **A**, one; **Jos 12:18** 663
to the Sidonians, as far as **A**, **Jos 13:4** 663
also *were* Ummah, and **A** and Rehob; **Jos 19:30** 663
while the Philistines camped in **A**. **1Sa 4:1** 663
together all their armies to **A**, **1Sa 29:1** 663
up to **A** to fight against Israel. **1Ki 20:26** 663
the rest fled to **A** into the city, **1Ki 20:30** 663
A until you have destroyed *them*." **2Ki 13:17** 663

APHEKAH
and Janum and Beth-tappuah and **A**, **Jos 15:53** 664

APHIAH
the son of Becorath, the son of **A**, **1Sa 9:1** 647b

APHIK
of Achzib, or of Helbah, or of **A**, **Jg 1:31** 663

APIECE
you shall take an omer **a** according **Ex 16:16** 1538
you shall take five shekels **a**, **Nu 3:47** 2568
incense, *weighing* ten *shekels* **a**, **Nu 7:86** 6235
their leaders gave him a rod **a**, **Nu 17:6** 259
Egypt for 600 *shekels* of silver **a** and **2Ch 1:17**
apiece and horses for 150 **a**, **2Ch 1:17**
and do not *even* have two tunics **a**. **Lk 9:3** *303*

APOLLONIA
traveled through Amphipolis and **A**, **Ac 17:1** *624*

APOLLOS
Now a Jew named **A**, **Ac 18:24** *625*
happened that while **A** was at Corinth, **Ac 19:1** *625*
I am of Paul," and "I of **A**," **1Co 1:12** *625*
of Paul," and another, "I am of **A**," **1Co 3:4** *625*
What then is **A**? And what is Paul? **1Co 3:5** *625*
I planted, **A** watered, but God was **1Co 3:6** *625*
whether Paul or **A** or Cephas or the **1Co 3:22** *625*
to myself and **A** for your sakes, **1Co 4:6** *625*
But concerning **A** our brother, I **1Co 16:12** *625*
help Zenas the lawyer and **A** on their **Ti 3:13** *625*

APOLLYON
in the Greek he has the name **A**. **Rv 9:11** *623*

APOSTASIES
you, And your **a** will reprove you; **Jer 2:19** 4878
are many, Their **a** are numerous. **Jer 5:6** 4878
Truly our **a** have been many, We **Jer 14:7** 4878

APOSTASY
Turned away in continual **a**? **Jer 8:5** 4878
I will heal their **a**, **Hos 14:4** 4878
not come unless the **a** comes first, **2Th 2:3** *646*

APOSTATE
the **a** He apportions our fields.' **Mi 2:4** 7728

APOSTLE
of Christ Jesus, called *as* an **a**, **Ro 1:1** *652*
then as I am an **a** of Gentiles, **Ro 11:13** *652*
called *as* an **a** of Jesus Christ by **1Co 1:1** *652*
Am I not free? Am I not an **a**? **1Co 9:1** *652*
If to others I am not an **a**, **1Co 9:2** *652*
and not fit to be called an **a**, **1Co 15:9** *652*
an **a** of Christ Jesus by the will **2Co 1:1** *652*
The signs of a true **a** were **2Co 12:12** *652*
Paul, an **a** **Ga 1:1** *652*
an **a** of Christ Jesus by the will **Eph 1:1** *652*
an **a** of Jesus Christ by the will **Col 1:1** *652*
an **a** of Christ Jesus according to **1Tm 1:1** *652*
was appointed a preacher and an **a** **1Tm 2:7** *652*
an **a** of Christ Jesus by the will **2Tm 1:1** *652*
a preacher and an **a** and a teacher. **2Tm 1:11** *652*
of God and an **a** of Jesus Christ, **Ti 1:1** *652*
the **A** and High Priest of our **Heb 3:1** *652*
Peter, an **a** of Jesus Christ, To **1Pe 1:1** *652*
bond-servant and **a** of Jesus Christ, **2Pe 1:1** *652*

APOSTLES
names of the twelve **a** are these: **Mt 10:2** *652*
a gathered together with Jesus; **Mk 6:30** *652*
of them, whom He also named as **a**: **Lk 6:13** *652*
When the **a** returned, they gave **Lk 9:10** *652*
will send to them prophets and **a**, **Lk 11:49** *652*
The **a** said to the Lord, **Lk 17:5** *652*
at the table, and the **a** with Him. **Lk 22:14** *652*
telling these things to the **a**. **Lk 24:10** *652*
to the **a** whom He had chosen. **Ac 1:2** *652*
he was added to the eleven **a**. **Ac 1:26** *652*
to Peter and the rest of the **a**, **Ac 2:37** *652*
were taking place through the **a**. **Ac 2:43** *652*
And with great power the **a** were **Ac 4:33** *652*
was also called Barnabas by the **a** **Ac 4:36** *652*
At the hands of the **a** many **Ac 5:12** *652*
They laid hands on the **a** **Ac 5:18** *652*
Peter and the **a** answered, **Ac 5:29** *652*
and after calling the **a** in, **Ac 5:40** *652*
these they brought before the **a**; **Ac 6:6** *652*
Judea and Samaria, except the **a**. **Ac 8:1** *652*
Now when the **a** in Jerusalem heard **Ac 8:14** *652*
brought him to the **a** and described **Ac 9:27** *652*
Now the **a** and the brethren who **Ac 11:1** *652*
the Jews, and some with the **a**. **Ac 14:4** *652*
But when the **a** Barnabas and Paul **Ac 14:14** *652*
go up to Jerusalem to the **a** and **Ac 15:2** *652*
church and the **a** and the elders, **Ac 15:4** *652*
The **a** and the elders came **Ac 15:6** *652*
good to the **a** and the elders, **Ac 15:22** *652*
"The **a** and the brethren who are **Ac 15:23** *652*
decided upon by the **a** and elders **Ac 16:4** *652*
who are outstanding among the **a**, **Ro 16:7** *652*
has exhibited us **a** last of all, **1Co 4:9** *652*
wife, even as the rest of the **a** and **1Co 9:5** *652*
appointed in the church, first **a**, **1Co 12:28** *652*
All are not **a**, are they? **1Co 12:29** *652*
to James, then to all the **a**; **1Co 15:7** *652*
For I am the least of the **a**, **1Co 15:9** *652*
inferior to the most eminent **a**. **2Co 11:5** *652*
For such men are false **a**, **2Co 11:13** *5570*
themselves as **a** of Christ. **2Co 11:13** *652*
I inferior to the most eminent **a**, **2Co 12:11** *652*
to those who were **a** before me; **Ga 1:17** *652*
any other of the **a** except James, **Ga 1:19** *652*
foundation of the **a** and prophets, **Eph 2:20** *652*
holy **a** and prophets in the Spirit; **Eph 3:5** *652*
And He gave some *as* **a**, **Eph 4:11** *652*

even though as a of Christ we **1Th 2:6** *652*
Lord and Savior *spoken* by your a. **2Pe 3:2** *652*
by the a of our Lord Jesus Christ, **Jude 1:17** *652*
test those who call themselves a, **Rv 2:2** *652*
and you saints and a and prophets, **Rv 18:20** *652*
names of the twelve a of the Lamb. **Rv 21:14** *652*
APOSTLES'
themselves to the a teaching **Ac 2:42** *652*
and lay them at the a feet, **Ac 4:35** *652*
the money and laid it at the a feet. **Ac 4:37** *652*
he laid it at the a feet. **Ac 5:2** *652*
laying on of the a hands, **Ac 8:18** *652*
APOSTLESHIP
to occupy this ministry and a from **Ac 1:25** *651*
we have received grace and a to **Ro 1:5** *651*
are the seal of my a in the Lord. **1Co 9:2** *651*
effectually worked for Peter in *his* a **Ga 2:8** *651*
APPAIM
sons of Nadab *were* Seled and A, **1Ch 2:30** 649
The son of A *was* Ishi. **1Ch 2:31** 649
APPALLED
settle in it will be a over it. **Lv 26:32** 8074
head and my beard, and sat down a. **Ezr 9:3** 8074
sat a until the evening offering. **Ezr 9:4** 8074
"The upright will be a at this, **Jb 17:8** 8074
in the west are a at his fate, **Jb 18:20** 8074
Let those be a because of their **Ps 40:15** 8074
My heart is a within me. **Ps 143:4** 8074
"Be a, O heavens, at this, And **Jer 2:12** 8074
and the priests will be a and **Jer 4:9** 8074
and they will be a with one **Ezk 4:17** 8074
And the land and its fullness were a **Ezk 19:7** 3456
every moment and be a at you. **Ezk 26:16** 8074
of the coastlands Are a at you, **Ezk 27:35** 8074
among the peoples Are a at you; **Ezk 28:19** 8074
I will make many peoples a at you, **Ezk 32:10** 8074
was a for a while as his thoughts **Da 4:19** 8075
APPALLING
"An a and horrible thing Has **Jer 5:30** 8047
of Israel Has done a most a thing. **Jer 18:13** 8186b
APPAREL
put ornaments of gold on your a. **2Sa 1:24** 3830
stood in their a with trumpets, **Ezr 3:10** 3847
This One who is majestic in His a, **Is 63:1** 3830
Why is Your a red, And Your **Is 63:2** 3830
Herod, having put on his royal a, **Ac 12:21** *2066*
APPARENT
is a to all who live in Jerusalem, **Ac 4:16** *5318*
APPEAL
and she went out to a to the king **2Ki 8:3** 6817
that I cannot a to My Father, **Mt 26:53** *3870*
over to them. I a to Caesar." **Ac 25:11** *1941*
I was forced to a to Caesar, **Ac 28:19** *1941*
as though God were making an a **2Co 5:20** *3870*
For he not only accepted our a, **2Co 8:17** *3874*
but *rather* a to *him* as a father, **1Tm 5:1** *3870*
yet for love's sake I rather a *to* **Phm 1:9** *3870*
I a to you for my child Onesimus, **Phm 1:10** *3870*
but an a to God for a good **1Pe 3:21** *1906*
APPEALED
a to the king for her house and **2Ki 8:5** 6817
and they came and a to them, **Ac 16:39** *3870*
"You have a to Caesar, to Caesar **Ac 25:12** *1941*
"But when Paul a to be held in **Ac 25:21** *1941*
the people of the Jews a to me, **Ac 25:24** *1793*
since he himself a to the Emperor, **Ac 25:25** *1941*
free if he had not a to Caesar." **Ac 26:32** *1941*
APPEALING
was standing and a to him, **Ac 16:9** *3870*
to write to you a that you contend **Jude 1:3** *3870*
APPEAR
place, and let the dry land a"; **Gn 1:9** 7200
house shall a before the judges, **Ex 22:8** 7126
shall a before Me empty-handed. **Ex 23:15** 7200
males shall a before the Lord GOD. **Ex 23:17** 7200
shall a before Me empty-handed. **Ex 34:20** 7200
are to a before the Lord GOD, **Ex 34:23** 7200
to a before the LORD your God, **Ex 34:24** 7200
today the LORD will a to you.' " **Lv 9:4** 7200
glory of the LORD may a to you." **Lv 9:6** 7200
not a to be deeper than the skin, **Lv 13:4** 4758
he shall a again to the priest. **Lv 13:7** 7200
for I will a in the cloud over the **Lv 16:2** 7200
your males shall a before the LORD **Dt 16:16** 7200
not a before the LORD empty-handed. **Dt 16:16** 7200
when all Israel comes to a before **Dt 31:11** 7200
the angel of the LORD did not a **Jg 13:21** 7200
that he may a before the LORD and **1Sa 1:22** 7200
shall I come and a before God? **Ps 42:2** 7200
Let Your work a to Your servants **Ps 90:16** 7200
"When you come to a before Me, **Is 1:12** 7200
And His glory will a upon you. **Is 60:2** 7200
have made your sisters a righteous by **Ezk 16:51**
you made your sisters a righteous. **Ezk 16:52**
so that in all your deeds your sins a **Ezk 21:24** 7200
Then the LORD will a over them, **Zch 9:14** 7200
which on the outside a beautiful, **Mt 23:27** *5316*
too, outwardly a righteous to men, **Mt 23:28** *5316*
the Son of Man will a in the sky, **Mt 24:30** *5316*
to a before the magistrate, **Lk 12:58**
of God was going to a immediately. **Lk 19:11** *398*
things in which I will a to you; **Ac 26:16** *3708*
For we must all a before the **2Co 5:10** *5319*
that we ourselves may a approved, **2Co 13:7** *5316*
though we may a unapproved. **2Co 13:7**
1510, 5613
whom you a as lights in the world, **Php 2:15** *5316*

a in the presence of God for us; **Heb 9:24** *1718*
will a a second time for **Heb 9:28** *3708*
APPEARANCE
Joseph was handsome in form and a. **Gn 39:6** 4758
the a of the glory of the LORD was **Ex 24:17** 4758
and the a of the scale is no **Lv 13:32** 4758
like the a of leprosy in the skin **Lv 13:43** 4758
if the mark has not changed its a, **Lv 13:55** 5869
the a of fire over the tabernacle, **Nu 9:15** 4758
day, and the a of fire by night. **Nu 9:16** 4758
and its a like that of bdellium. **Nu 11:7** 5869
by the Jordan, a large altar in a. **Jos 22:10** 4758
A man of God came to me and his a **Jg 13:6** 4758
like the a of the angel of God, **Jg 13:6** 4758
"Do not look at his a or at the **1Sa 16:7** 4758
for man looks at the outward a, **1Sa 16:7** 5869
beautiful eyes and a handsome a. **1Sa 16:12** 7210
and ruddy, with a handsome a. **1Sa 17:42** 4758
intelligent and beautiful in a, **1Sa 25:3** 8389
the woman was very beautiful in a. **2Sa 11:2** 4758
in order to change the a of things **2Sa 14:20** 6440
she was a woman of beautiful a. **2Sa 14:27** 4758
but I could not discern its a; **Jb 4:16** 4758
change his a and send him away. **Jb 14:20** 6440
His a is like Lebanon Choice as **SS 5:15** 4758
a was marred more than any man And **Is 52:14** 4758
Nor a that we should be attracted **Is 53:2** 4758
Their a is blacker than soot, They **La 4:8** 8389
And this was their a: **Ezk 1:5** 4758
The a of the wheels and their **Ezk 1:16** 4758
their a and workmanship *being* as **Ezk 1:16** 4758
a throne, like lapis lazuli in a; **Ezk 1:26** 4758
was a figure with the a of a man. **Ezk 1:26** 4758
Then I noticed from the a of His **Ezk 1:27** 4758
and from the a of His loins and **Ezk 1:27** 4758
As the a of the rainbow in the **Ezk 1:28** 4758
the a of the surrounding radiance. **Ezk 1:28** 4758
Such *was* the a of the likeness of **Ezk 1:28** 4758
a likeness as the a of a man; **Ezk 8:2** 4758
downward *there was* the a of fire, **Ezk 8:2** 4758
and upward the a of brightness, **Ezk 8:2** 4758
like the a of glowing metal. **Ezk 8:2** 5869
the a which I saw in the plain. **Ezk 8:4** 4758
stone, in a resembling a throne, **Ezk 10:1** 4758
and the a of the wheels *was* like **Ezk 10:9** 4758
As for their a, **Ezk 10:10** 4758
they were the same faces whose a I **Ezk 10:22** 4758
there was a man whose a was like **Ezk 40:3** 4758
was like the a of bronze, **Ezk 40:3** 4758
the a of one doorpost was like **Ezk 41:21** 4758
was like the a of the chambers which **Ezk 42:11** 4758
the a of the vision which I saw, **Ezk 43:3** 4758
a be observed in your presence and **Da 1:13** 4758
and the a of the youths who are **Da 1:13** 4758
At the end of ten days their a **Da 1:15** 4758
of you, and its a was awesome. **Da 2:31** 7299
and the a of the fourth is like a **Da 3:25** 7299
larger in a than its associates. **Da 7:20** 2376
his face had the a of lightning, **Da 10:6** 4758
Then *this* one with human a touched **Da 10:18** 4758
Their a is like the appearance of **Jl 2:4** 4758
is like the a of horses; **Jl 2:4** 4758
squares, Their a is like torches, **Na 2:4** 4758
"This is their a in all the land **Zch 5:6** 5869
for they neglect their a so that **Mt 6:16** *4383*
how to discern the a of the sky, **Mt 16:3** *4383*
And his a was like lightning, and **Mt 28:3** *1490a*
the day of his public a to Israel. **Lk 1:80** *323*
a of His face became different, **Lk 9:29** *1491b*
the a of the earth and the sky, **Lk 12:56** *4383*
"Do not judge according to a, **Jn 7:24** *3799*
for those who take pride in a and **2Co 5:12** *4383*
Being found in a as a man, **Php 2:8** *4976*
the a of wisdom in self-made **Col 2:23** *3056*
to an end by the a of His coming; **2Th 2:8** *2015*
the beauty of its a is destroyed; **Jas 1:11** *4383*
a jasper stone and a sardius in a; **Rv 4:3** *3706*
the throne, like an emerald in a. **Rv 4:3** *3706*
The a of the locusts was like **Rv 9:7** *3667*
APPEARANCE'S
and for a sake offer long prayers; **Mk 12:40** *4392*
and for a sake offer long prayers. **Lk 20:47** *4392*
APPEARED
The LORD a to Abram and said, **Gn 12:7** 7200
to the LORD who had a to him. **Gn 12:7** 7200
there a a smoking oven and a **Gn 15:17**
LORD a to Abram and said to him, **Gn 17:1** 7200
a to him by the oaks of Mamre, **Gn 18:1** 7200
But he a to his sons-in-law to be **Gn 19:14**
1961, 5869
The LORD a to him and said, **Gn 26:2** 7200
The LORD a to him the same **Gn 26:24** 7200
who a to you when you fled from **Gn 35:1** 7200
Then God a to Jacob again when he **Gn 35:9** 7200
as soon as he a before him, he **Gn 46:29** 7200
"God Almighty a to me at Luz in **Gn 48:3** 7200
The angel of the LORD a to him **Ex 3:2** 7200
Isaac and Jacob, has a to me, **Ex 3:16** 7200
'The LORD has not a to you.' " **Ex 4:1** 7200
the God of Jacob, has a to you." **Ex 4:5** 7200
and I a to Abraham, Isaac, and **Ex 6:3** 7200
glory of the LORD a in the cloud. **Ex 16:10** 7200
a to be a pavement of sapphire, **Ex 24:10**
of the LORD a to all the people. **Lv 9:23** 7200
Then the glory of the LORD a in **Nu 14:10** 7200
LORD a to all the congregation. **Nu 16:19** 7200
it and the glory of the LORD a. **Nu 16:42** 7200
the glory of the LORD a to them; **Nu 20:6** 7200

The LORD a in the tent in a **Dt 31:15** 7200
the LORD a to him and said to him, **Jg 6:12** 7200
angel of the LORD a to the woman and **Jg 13:3** 7200
came the *other* day has a to me." **Jg 13:10** 7200
And the LORD a again at Shiloh, **1Sa 3:21** 7200
And He a on the wings of the wind. **2Sa 22:11** 7200
"Then the channels of the sea a, **2Sa 22:16** 7200
In Gibeon the LORD a to Solomon in **1Ki 3:5** 7200
LORD a to Solomon a second time, **1Ki 9:2** 7200
as He had a to him at Gibeon. **1Ki 9:2** 7200
of Israel, who had a to him twice, **1Ki 11:9** 7200
there a a chariot of fire **2Ki 2:11**
God a to Solomon and said to him, **2Ch 1:7** 7200
where *the LORD* had a to his **2Ch 3:1** 7200
Then the LORD a to Solomon at **2Ch 7:12** 7200
from dawn until the stars a. **Ne 4:21** 3318
Then the channels of water a, **Ps 18:15** 7200
He has a in His glory. **Ps 102:16** 7200
have *already* a in the land; **SS 2:12** 7200
The LORD a to him from afar, **Jer 31:3** 7200
resembling a throne, a above them. **Ezk 10:1** 7200
The cherubim a to have the **Ezk 10:8** 7200
the king a vision a to me, **Da 8:1** 7200
the one which a to me previously. **Da 8:1** 7200
of the Lord a to him in a dream, **Mt 1:20** *5316*
from them the exact time the star a. **Mt 2:7** *5316*
the Lord a to Joseph in a dream and **Mt 2:13** *5316*
a in a dream to Joseph in Egypt, **Mt 2:19** *5316*
Moses and Elijah a to them, **Mt 17:3** *3708*
the holy city and a to many. **Mt 27:53** *1718*
John the Baptist a in the **Mk 1:4** *1096*
Elijah a to them along with Moses; **Mk 9:4** *3708*
He first a to Mary Magdalene, **Mk 16:9** *5316*
He a in a different form to two of **Mk 16:12** *5319*
Afterward He a to the eleven **Mk 16:14** *5319*
And an angel of the Lord a to him, **Lk 1:11** *3708*
And suddenly there a with the **Lk 2:13** *1096*
and by some that Elijah had a, **Lk 9:8** *5316*
"The first a, saying, **Lk 19:16** *3854*
Now an angel from heaven a to Him, **Lk 22:43** *3708*
these words a to them as nonsense, **Lk 24:11** *5316*
risen and has a to Simon." **Lk 24:34** *3708*
And there a to them tongues as of **Ac 2:3** *3708*
The God of glory a to our father **Ac 7:2** *3708*
"On the following day he a to **Ac 7:26** *3708*
AN ANGEL A TO HIM IN THE **Ac 7:30** *3708*
who a to him in the thorn bush. **Ac 7:35** *3708*
who a to you on the road by which **Ac 9:17** *3708*
for Simon's house, a at the gate; **Ac 10:17** *2186*
at that moment three men a at **Ac 11:11** *2186*
an angel of the Lord suddenly a and **Ac 12:7** *2186*
and for many days He a to those **Ac 13:31** *3708*
A vision a to Paul in the night: **Ac 16:9** *3708*
for this purpose I have a to you, **Ac 26:16** *3708*
sun nor stars a for many days, **Ac 27:20** *2014*
and that He a to Cephas, then to **1Co 15:5** *3708*
After that He a to more than five **1Co 15:6** *3708*
then He a to James, then to all **1Co 15:7** *3708*
untimely born, He a to me also. **1Co 15:8** *3708*
For the grace of God has a, **Ti 2:11** *2014*
Savior and *His* love for mankind a, **Ti 3:4** *2014*
But when Christ a *as* a high priest **Heb 9:11** *3854*
but has a in these last times for **1Pe 1:20** *5319*
even now many antichrists have a; **1Jn 2:18** *1096*
has not a as yet what we will be. **1Jn 3:2** *5319*
He a in order to take away sins; **1Jn 3:5** *5319*
The Son of God a for this purpose, **1Jn 3:8** *5319*
and on their heads a to be crowns **Rv 9:7** *5613*
of His covenant a in His temple, **Rv 11:19** *3708*
A great sign a in heaven: **Rv 12:1** *3708*
Then another sign a in heaven: **Rv 12:3** *3708*
APPEARING
who, a in glory, were speaking of **Lk 9:31** *3708*
a to them over *a period of* forty **Ac 1:3** *3700*
the a of our Lord Jesus Christ, **1Tm 6:14** *2015*
the a of our Savior Christ Jesus, **2Tm 1:10** *2015*
and by His a and His kingdom: **2Tm 4:1** *2015*
also to all who have loved His a. **2Tm 4:8** *2015*
the a of the glory of our great God **Ti 2:13** *2015*
APPEARS
the infection a to be deeper than the **Lv 13:3** 4758
"But whenever raw flesh a on him, **Lv 13:14** 7200
if it a to be lower than the skin, **Lv 13:20** 4758
it a to be deeper than the skin, **Lv 13:25** 4758
it a to be deeper than the skin and **Lv 13:30** 4758
a to be no deeper than the skin and **Lv 13:31** 4758
a to be no deeper than the skin, **Lv 13:34** 4758
and if it a again in the garment, **Lv 13:57** 7200
and a deeper than the surface, **Lv 14:37** 4758
one of them a before God in Zion. **Ps 84:7** 7200
And who can stand when He a? **Mal 3:2** 7200
You are *just* a vapor that a for a **Jas 4:14** *5316*
And when the Chief Shepherd a, **1Pe 5:4** *5319*
abide in Him, so that when He a, **1Jn 2:28** *5319*
We know that when He a, **1Jn 3:2** *5319*
APPEASE
"I will a him with the present **Gn 32:20**
3722a, 6440
death, But a wise man will a it. **Pr 16:14** 3722a
together, and I will a My wrath; **Ezk 21:17** 5117
APPEASED
wrath on them, and I will be a; **Ezk 5:13** 5162
a My wrath in the land of the north." **Zch 6:8** 5117
APPETITE
but now our a is gone. **Nu 11:6** 5315
satisfy the a of the young lions, **Jb 38:39** 2421b
has enough to satisfy his a, **Pr 13:25** 5315
A worker's a works for him, For **Pr 16:26** 5315

If you are a man of *great* **a**. Pr 23:2 5315
and yet the **a** is not satisfied. Ec 6:7 5315
They cannot satisfy their **a** nor Ezk 7:19 5315
He enlarges his **a** like Sheol, And Hab 2:5 5315
destruction, whose god is *their* **a**, Php 3:19 *2836*

APPETITES
Lord Christ but of their own **a**; Ro 16:18 *2836*

APPHIA
and to **A** our sister, and to Phm 1:2 *682*

APPIUS
of **A** and Three Inns to meet us; Ac 28:15 *675*

APPLE
Keep me as the **a** of the eye; Ps 17:8 380
my teaching as the **a** of your eye. Pr 7:2 380
"Like an **a** tree among the trees SS 2:3 8598
"Beneath the **a** tree I awakened you; SS 8:5 8598
the palm also, and the **a** tree, Jl 1:12 8598
you, touches the **a** of His eye. Zch 2:8 892

APPLES
Like **a** of gold in settings of Pr 25:11 8598
raisin cakes, Refresh me with **a**, SS 2:5 8598
fragrance of your breath like **a**, SS 7:8 8598

APPLIED
evenly **a** on the engraved work. 1Ki 6:35 3474
I also **a** myself to the work on Ne 5:16 2388
All this I have seen and **a** my mind Ec 8:9 5414
We **a** healing to Babylon, but she Jer 51:9
the dream **a** to those who hate you and Da 4:19
and **a** the clay to his eyes, Jn 9:6 *2007*
"He **a** clay to my eyes, and I Jn 9:15 *2007*
I have figuratively **a** to myself 1Co 4:6 *3345*

APPLIES
"This is what **a** to the Levites: Nu 8:24
because this **a** *to* every person. Ec 12:13
For the judgment **a** to you, Hos 5:1

APPLY
and **a** some of the blood that is in Ex 12:22 5060
"The same law shall **a** to the Ex 12:49 1961
shall **a** all this law to her. Nu 5:30 6213a
And **a** your mind to my knowledge; Pr 22:17 7896
A your heart to discipline And Pr 23:12 935
of figs and **a** it to the boil, Is 38:21 4799
about the regular sacrifice **a**, Da 8:13

APPLYING
very reason also, **a** all diligence, 2Pe 1:5 *3923*

APPOINT
"Let Pharaoh take action to **a** Gn 41:34 6485
then I will **a** you a place to which Ex 21:13 7760
a *as a penalty* life for life, Ex 21:23 5414
I will **a** over you a sudden terror, Lv 26:16 6485
"But you shall **a** the Levites over Nu 1:50 6485
"So you shall **a** Aaron and his Nu 3:10 6485
a a leader and return to Egypt." Nu 14:4 5414
a a man over the congregation, Nu 27:16 6485
and I will **a** them as your heads.' Dt 1:13 7760
"You shall **a** for yourself judges Dt 16:18 5414
they shall **a** commanders of armies Dt 20:9 6485
Now **a** a king for us to judge us 1Sa 8:5 7760
"He will **a** for himself 1Sa 8:12 7760
their voice and **a** them a king." 1Sa 8:22 4427a
to **a** me ruler over the people of 2Sa 6:21 6680
"I will also **a** a place for My 2Sa 7:10 7760
one would **a** me judge in the land, 2Sa 15:4 7760
to **a** their relatives the singers, 1Ch 15:16 5975
a a place for My people Israel, 1Ch 17:9 7760
a magistrates and judges that they Ezr 7:25 4483
Also **a** guards from the inhabitants Ne 7:3 5975
"Let the king **a** overseers in Es 2:3 6485
A lovingkindness and truth that Ps 61:7 4487
a darkness and it becomes night, Ps 104:20 7896
A a wicked man over him, Ps 109:6 6485
not **a** me ruler of the people." Is 3:7 7760
And I will **a** you as a covenant to Is 42:6 5414
a over them four kinds *of doom*," Jer 15:3 6485
is chosen I shall **a** over it. Jer 49:19 6485
is chosen I will **a** over it. Jer 50:44 6485
A a marshal against her, Bring up Jer 51:27 6485
"Yet I will **a** them to keep charge Ezk 44:14 5414
to **a** 120 satraps over the kingdom, Da 6:1 6966
to **a** him over the entire kingdom. Da 6:3 6966
will **a** for themselves one leader, Hos 1:11 7760
to **a** you a minister and a witness Ac 26:16 *4400*
do you **a** them as judges who are of 1Co 6:4 *2523*
and **a** elders in every city as I Ti 1:5 *2525*

APPOINTED
And the LORD **a** a sign for Cain, Gn 4:15 7760
"God has **a** me another offspring Gn 4:25 7896
the **a** time I will return to you, Gn 18:14 4150
at the **a** time of which God had Gn 21:2 4150
You have **a** for Your servant Isaac; Gn 24:14 3198
LORD has **a** for my master's son.' Gn 24:44 3198
So they **a** taskmasters over them to Ex 1:11 7760
at its **a** time from year to year. Ex 13:10 4150
at the **a** time in the month Abib, Ex 23:15 4150
I Myself have **a** with him Oholiab, Ex 31:6 5414
the **a** time in the month of Abib, Ex 34:18 4150
'The LORD's **a** times which you Lv 23:2 4150
convocations—My **a** times are these: Lv 23:2 4150
'These are the **a** times of the Lv 23:4 4150
proclaim at the times **a** for them. Lv 23:4 4150
'These are the **a** times of the LORD Lv 23:37 4150
of Israel the **a** times of the LORD. Lv 23:44 4150
Now the **a** duties of the sons of Nu 3:36 6486
the Passover at its **a** time. Nu 9:2 4150
shall observe it at its **a** time; Nu 9:3 4150
a time among the sons of Israel?" Nu 9:7 4150
of the LORD at its **a** time. Nu 9:13 4150
gladness and in your **a** feasts, Nu 10:10 4150
offering or in your **a** times, Nu 15:3 4150
aroma to Me, at their **a** time.' Nu 28:2 4150
these to the LORD at your **a** times, Nu 29:39 4150
men, and **a** them heads over you, Dt 1:15 5414
he had **a** from the sons of Israel, Jos 4:4 3559
a place before the desert plain. Jos 8:14 4150
These were the **a** cities for all Jos 20:9 4152
Now the **a** sign between the men of Jg 20:38 4150
he **a** his sons judges over Israel. 1Sa 8:1 7760
kept for you until the **a** time, 1Sa 9:24 4150
me and I have **a** a king over you. 1Sa 12:1 4427a
"It is the LORD who **a** Moses and 1Sa 12:6 6213a
to the **a** time set by Samuel, 1Sa 13:8 4150
did not come within the **a** days, 1Sa 13:11 4150
a him as ruler over His people, 1Sa 13:14 6680
and **a** him as his commander of a 1Sa 18:13 7760
the set time which he had **a** him. 2Sa 20:5 3259
And David **a** him over his guard. 2Sa 23:23 7760
from the morning until the **a** time, 2Sa 24:15 4150
for I have **a** him to be ruler over 1Ki 1:35 6680
The king **a** Benaiah the son of 1Ki 2:35 5414
and the king **a** Zadok the priest in 1Ki 2:35 5414
he **a** him over all the forced labor 1Ki 11:28 6485
Now the king **a** the royal officer 2Ki 7:17 6485
king **a** for her a certain officer, 2Ki 8:6 5414
hundreds who were **a** over the army and 2Ki 11:15 6485
And the priest **a** officers over the 2Ki 11:18 7760
They also feared the LORD and **a** 2Ki 17:32 6213a
whom the kings of Judah had **a** to 2Ki 23:5 5414
he **a** Gedaliah the son of Ahikam, 2Ki 25:22 6485
Babylon had **a** Gedaliah *governor*, 2Ki 25:23 6485
Now these are those whom David **a** 1Ch 6:31 5975
Their kinsmen the Levites were **a** 1Ch 6:48 5414
seer **a** in their office of trust. 1Ch 9:22 3245
Some of them also were **a** over the 1Ch 9:29 4487
and David **a** him over his guard. 1Ch 11:25 7760
Levites **a** Heman the son of Joel, 1Ch 15:17 5975
Asaph and Ethan *were* **a** to sound 1Ch 15:19
He **a** some of the Levites *as* 1Ch 16:4 5414
the **a** feasts of the LORD our God, 2Ch 2:4 4150
a 70,000 of them to carry loads and 2Ch 2:18 6213a
he **a** the divisions of the priests 2Ch 8:14 5975
Rehoboam **a** Abijah the son of 2Ch 11:22 5975
He **a** judges in the land in all 2Ch 19:5 5975
Jehoshaphat **a** some of the Levites 2Ch 19:8 5975
he **a** those who sang to the LORD 2Ch 20:21 5975
hundreds who were **a** over the army and 2Ch 23:14 6485
Amaziah assembled Judah and **a** them 2Ch 25:5 5975
"Have we **a** you a royal counselor? 2Ch 25:16 5414
So they ate for the **a** seven days, 2Ch 30:22 4150
And Hezekiah **a** the divisions of 2Ch 31:2 5975
He also **a** the king's portion 2Ch 31:3
He **a** military officers over 2Ch 32:6 5414
which I have **a** for your fathers, 2Ch 33:8 5975
and He has **a** me to build Him a 2Ch 36:23 6485
and He has **a** me to build Him a Ezr 1:2 6485
began *the work* and **a** the Levites Ezr 3:8 5975
whom he had **a** governor. Ezr 5:14 7761
Then they **a** the priests to their Ezr 6:18 6966
foreign wives come at **a** times, Ezr 10:14 2163
from the day that I was **a** to be Ne 5:14 6680
"You have also **a** prophets to Ne 6:7 5975
singers and the Levites were **a**, Ne 7:1 6485
So they became stubborn and **a** a Ne 9:17 5414
the new moon, for the **a** times, Ne 10:33 4150
wall, and I **a** two great choirs, Ne 12:31 5975
On that day men were also **a** over Ne 12:44 6485
who was **a** over the chambers of the Ne 13:4 5414
I **a** Shelemiah the priest, Ne 13:13 686
foreign and **a** duties for the priests Ne 13:30 5975
for the supply of wood at **a** times Ne 13:31 2163
whom the king had **a** to attend her, Es 4:5 5975
to their **a** time annually. Es 9:27 2163
days of Purim at their **a** times, Es 9:31 2163
And nights of trouble are **a** me. Jb 7:3 4487
"For He performs what is **a** for me, Jb 23:14 2706
"Who has **a** Him His way, And who Jb 36:23 6485
You have **a** judgment. Ps 7:6 6680
As sheep they are **a** for Sheol; Ps 49:14 8371
"When I select an **a** time, Ps 75:2 4150
in Jacob And **a** a law in Israel, Ps 78:5 7760
to her, For the **a** time has come. Ps 102:13 4150
There is an **a** time for everything. Ec 3:1 2165
moon *festivals* and your **a** feasts, Is 1:14 4150
Assyria **a** it for desert Is 23:13 3245
Zion, the city of our **a** feasts; Is 33:20 4150
O Jerusalem, I have **a** watchmen; Is 62:6 6485
a you a prophet to the nations." Jer 1:5 5414
I have **a** you this day over the Jer 1:10 6485
us The **a** weeks of the harvest." Jer 5:24 2708
night will not be at their **a** time, Jer 33:20 6256
has **a** over the cities of Judah, Jer 40:5 6485
the king of Babylon had **a** Gedaliah Jer 40:7 6485
he had **a** over them Gedaliah the son Jer 40:11 6485
of Babylon had **a** over the land. Jer 41:2 6485
of Babylon had **a** over the land. Jer 41:18 6485
He has let the **a** time pass by!' Jer 46:17 4150
no one comes to the **a** feasts. La 1:4 4150
He has called an **a** time against me La 1:15 4150
has destroyed His **a** meeting place. La 2:6 4150
The **a** feast and sabbath in Zion, La 2:6 4150
LORD As in the day of an **a** feast. La 2:7 4150
in the day of an **a** feast My terrors La 2:22 4150
I have **a** you a watchman to the Ezk 3:17 5414
the left, wherever your edge is **a**. Ezk 21:16 3259
I have **a** you a watchman for the Ezk 33:7 5414
at Jerusalem during her **a** feasts, Ezk 36:38 4150
in the **a** place of the house, Ezk 43:21 4662
My statutes in all My **a** feasts and Ezk 44:24 4150
a feasts of the house of Israel; Ezk 45:17 4150
before the LORD at the **a** feasts, Ezk 46:9 4150
"At the festivals and the **a** Ezk 46:11 4150
The king **a** for them a daily Da 1:5 4487
and **a** that they should be Da 1:5
has **a** your food and your drink; Da 1:10 4487
the officials had **a** over Daniel, Da 1:11 4487
whom the king had **a** to destroy the Da 2:24 4483
of the king, and he **a** Shadrach, Da 2:49 4483
certain Jews whom you have **a** over Da 3:12 4483
a him chief of the magicians, Da 5:11 6966
to them for an **a** period of time. Da 7:12 2166
pertains to the **a** time of the end. Da 8:19 4150
is still *to come* at the **a** time. Da 11:27 4150
"At the **a** time he will return and Da 11:29 4150
it is still *to come* at the **a** time. Da 11:35 4150
there is a harvest **a** for you, Hos 6:11
They have **a** princes, but I did not Hos 8:4 8323
you do on the day of the **a** festival Hos 9:5 4150
As in the days of the **a** festival. Hos 12:9 4150
a a great fish to swallow Jonah, Jon 1:17 4487
So the LORD God **a** a plant and it Jon 4:6 4487
But God **a** a worm when dawn came Jon 4:7 4487
up God **a** a scorching east wind, Jon 4:8 4487
Who has **a** its time? Mi 6:9 3259
O LORD, have **a** them to judge; Hab 1:12 7760
the vision is yet for the **a** time; Hab 2:3 4150
all that I have **a** concerning her. Zph 3:7 6485
the **a** feasts—They came from you, Zph 3:18 4150
his mountains a desolation and **a** Mal 1:3
And He **a** twelve, so that they would Mk 3:14 *4160*
And He **a** the twelve: Mk 3:16 *4160*
do not know when the **a** time Mk 13:33
service before God in the **a** order Lk 1:8
this *Child* is **a** for the fall and Lk 2:34 *2749*
this the Lord **a** seventy others, Lk 10:1 *322*
who **a** Me a judge or arbitrator over Lk 12:14 *2525*
Me but I chose you, and **a** you Jn 15:16 *5087*
send Jesus, the Christ **a** for you, Ac 3:20 *4400*
One who has been **a** by God Ac 10:42 *3724*
On an **a** day Herod, having put Ac 12:21 *5002*
been **a** to eternal life believed. Ac 13:48 *5021*
When they had **a** elders for Ac 14:23 *5500*
having determined *their* **a** times and Ac 17:26 *4367*
through a Man whom He has **a**, Ac 17:31 *3724*
that has been **a** for you to do.' Ac 22:10 *5021*
has **a** you to know His will and Ac 22:14 *4400*
And God has **a** in the church, first 1Co 12:28 *5087*
but he has also been **a** by the 2Co 8:19 *5500*
a for the defense of the gospel; Php 1:16 *2749*
I was **a** a preacher and an apostle 1Tm 2:7 *5087*
for which I was **a** a preacher and 2Tm 1:11 *5087*
Son, whom He **a** heir of all things, Heb 1:2 *5087*
AND HAVE **A** HIM OVER THE WORKS OF Heb 2:7 *2525*
He was faithful to Him who **a** Him, Heb 3:2 *4160*
priest taken from among men is **a** on Heb 5:1 *2525*
For every high priest is **a** to Heb 8:3 *2525*
And inasmuch as it is **a** for men to Heb 9:27 *606*
and to this *doom* they were also **a**. 1Pe 2:8 *5087*

APPOINTMENT
the field for the **a** with David, 1Sa 20:35 4150
brother by the **a** of King Hezekiah, 2Ch 31:13 4662
and they made an **a** together to Jb 2:11 3259
unless they have made an **a**? Am 3:3 3259

APPOINTS
and **a** you ruler over Israel, 1Sa 25:30 6680
"What will you say when He **a** over Jer 13:21 6485
For the Law **a** men as high priests Heb 7:28 *2525*
a a Son, made perfect forever. Heb 7:28

APPORTION
the land that you are to **a** by lot Nu 34:13 5157
men who shall **a** the land to you Nu 34:17 5157
to **a** the land for inheritance. Nu 34:18 5157
whom the LORD commanded to **a** the Nu 34:29 5157
a this land for an inheritance to Jos 13:7 2505a
to **a** the contributions for the 2Ch 31:14 5414
God **a** destruction in His anger? Jb 21:17 2505a

APPORTIONED
which Moses **a** for an inheritance Jos 13:32 5157
a to them for an inheritance, Jos 14:1 5157
I have **a** to you these nations Jos 23:4 5307
And **a** them for an inheritance Ps 78:55 5307
which God **a** to us as a measure, 2Co 10:13 *3307*
to whom also Abraham **a** a tenth Heb 7:2 *3307*

APPORTIONING
When they finished **a** the land for Jos 19:49 5157

APPORTIONS
To the apostate He **a** our fields.' Mi 2:4 2505a

APPRAISED
because they are spiritually **a**. 1Co 2:14 *350*
yet he himself is **a** by no one. 1Co 2:15 *350*

APPRAISES
he who is spiritual **a** all things, 1Co 2:15 *350*

APPRECIATE
that you **a** those who diligently 1Th 5:12 *3609a*

APPROACH
and **a** Ephron the son of Zohar for Gn 23:8 6293
a legal matter, let him **a** them." Ex 24:14 5066
or when they **a** the altar to Ex 28:43 5066
when they **a** the altar to minister, Ex 30:20 5066
'None of you shall **a** any blood Lv 18:6 7126
you shall not **a** his wife, she is Lv 18:14 7126
'Also you shall not **a** a woman to Lv 18:19 7126
nor shall he **a** any dead person, Lv 21:11 935
a to offer the food of his God. Lv 21:17 7126
no one who has a defect shall **a**: Lv 21:18 7126

when they **a** the most holy *objects:* Nu 4:19 5066
you **a** a city to fight against it, Dt 20:10 7126
who are with me will **a** the city. Jos 8:5 7126
and let us **a** one of these places; Jg 19:13 7126
then let her go at the **a** of dawn. Jg 19:25 5927
Like a prince I would **a** Him. Jb 31:37 7126
But it shall not **a** you. Ps 91:7 5066
bring him near and he shall **a** Me; Jer 30:21 5066
dare to risk his life to **a** Me?" Jer 30:21 5066
or **a** a woman during her menstrual Ezk 18:6 7126
a that which is for the people." Ezk 42:14 7126
an oven *As* they **a** their plotting; Hos 7:6 7126

APPROACHED
Then Judah **a** him, and said, Gn 44:18 5066
a the thick cloud where God *was.* Ex 20:21 5066
and when they **a** the altar, Ex 40:32 7126
when they had **a** the presence of Lv 16:1 7126
the captains of hundreds, **a** Moses, Nu 31:48 7126
"Then all of you **a** me and said, Dt 1:22 7126
the Levites **a** Eleazar the priest, Jos 21:1 5066
and **a** the entrance of the tower to Jg 9:52 5066
Then Saul **a** Samuel in the gate and 1Sa 9:18 5066
and he **a** the Philistine. 1Sa 17:40 5066
Philistine came on and **a** David, 1Sa 17:41 7126
a the people and greeted them. 1Sa 30:21 5066
So he **a** her, and the woman said, 2Sa 20:17 7126
a Ahab king of Israel and said, 1Ki 20:13 5066
Jericho **a** Elisha and said to him, 2Ki 2:5 5066
a the altar and went up to it, 2Ki 16:12 7126
they **a** Zerubbabel and the heads of Ezr 4:2 5066
been completed, the princes **a** me, Ezr 9:1 5066
So I **a** the prophetess, and she Is 8:3 7126
people both small and great **a** Jer 42:1 5066
Then they **a** and spoke before the Da 6:12 7127
"I **a** one of those who were Da 7:16 7127
So the captain **a** him and said, Jon 1:6 7126
When they had **a** Jerusalem and Mt 21:1 *1448*
"When the harvest time **a**, Mt 21:34 *1448*
As they **a** Jerusalem, at Mk 11:1 *1448*
Now as He **a** the gate of the city, Lk 7:12 *1448*
Just at that time some Pharisees **a**, Lk 13:31 *4334*
and when he came and **a** the house, Lk 15:25 *1448*
When He **a** Bethphage and Bethany, Lk 19:29 *1448*
When He **a** *Jerusalem,* He saw the city Lk 19:41 *1448*
and he **a** Jesus to kiss Him. Lk 22:47 *1448*
and discussing, Jesus Himself **a** and Lk 24:15 *1448*
And they **a** the village where they Lk 24:28 *1448*
and as he **a** to look *more* closely, Ac 7:31 *4334*

APPROACHES
who **a** any animal to mate with it, Lv 20:16 7126
your generations **a** the holy *gifts* Lv 22:3 7126
"But it shall be when evening **a**, Dt 23:11 6437
woman **a** *the time* to give birth, Is 26:17 7126

APPROACHING
"When you are **a** the battle, Dt 20:2 7126
you are **a** the battle against your Dt 20:3 7126
While he was still **a**, Lk 9:42 *4334*
the days were **a** for His ascension, Lk 9:51 *4845*
As Jesus was **a** Jericho, Lk 18:35 *1448*
As soon as He was **a**, Lk 19:37 *1448*
is called the Passover, was **a**. Lk 22:1 *1448*
time of the promise was **a** which God Ac 7:17 *1448*
when he was **a** the age of forty, Ac 7:23 *4137*
he was **a** Damascus, Ac 9:3 *1448*
were on their way and **a** the city, Ac 10:9 *1448*
my way, **a** Damascus about noontime, Ac 22:6 *1448*
that they were **a** some land. Ac 27:27 *4317*

APPROPRIATE
one with the blessing **a** to him. Gn 49:28
has made everything **a** in its time. Ec 3:11 3303
eat at the **a** time—for strength and Ec 10:17
performing deeds **a** to repentance. Ac 26:20 *514*
but to promote what is **a** and *to* 1Co 7:35 *2158*

APPROPRIATED
who **a** My land for themselves as a Ezk 36:5 5414

APPROVAL
you are going has the LORD's **a**." Jg 18:6 5227
without the LORD's **a** against this 2Ki 18:25
without the LORD's **a** against this Is 36:10
for they loved the **a** of men rather Jn 12:43 *1391*
of men rather than the **a** of God. Jn 12:43 *1391*
a with the whole congregation; Ac 6:5 *700*
a to those who practice them. Ro 1:32 *4909*
For by it the men of old gained **a**. Heb 11:2 *3140*
gained **a** through their faith, Heb 11:39 *3140*

APPROVE
after them who **a** their words. Ps 49:13 7521
these things the Lord does not **a**. La 3:36 7200
Your eyes are too pure to **a** evil, Hab 1:13 7200
and **a** the deeds of your fathers; Lk 11:48 *4909*
a the things that are essential, Ro 2:18 *1381a*
When I arrive, whomever you may **a**, 1Co 16:3 *1381a*
a the things that are excellent, Php 1:10 *1381a*

APPROVED
for God has already **a** your works. Ec 9:7 7521
is acceptable to God and **a** by men. Ro 14:18 *1384*
Greet Apelles, the **a** in Christ. Ro 16:10 *1384*
so that those who are **a** may 1Co 11:19 *1384*
not he who commends himself that is **a**, 2Co 10:18 *1384*
that we ourselves may appear **a**, 2Co 13:7 *1384*
but just as we have been **a** by God 1Th 2:4 *1381a*
Be diligent to present yourself **a** 2Tm 2:15 *1384*
for once he has been **a**, Jas 1:12 *1384*

APPROVES
not condemn himself in what he **a**. Ro 14:22 *1381a*

APPROVING
shed, I also was standing by **a**, Ac 22:20 *4909*

APRONS
so that handkerchiefs or **a** were Ac 19:12 *4612*

APT
A man has joy in an **a** answer, Pr 15:23 6310

AQUILA
he found a Jew named **A**, Ac 18:2 *207*
and with him were Priscilla and **A**. Ac 18:18 *207*
when Priscilla and **A** heard him, Ac 18:26 *207*
Greet Prisca and **A**, Ro 16:3 *207*
A and Prisca greet you heartily in 1Co 16:19 *207*
Greet Prisca and **A**, 2Tm 4:19 *207*

AR
That extends to the site of **A**, Nu 21:15 6144
It devoured **A** of Moab, The Nu 21:28 6144
because I have given **A** to the sons Dt 2:9 6144
you shall cross over **A**, Dt 2:18 6144
Moabites who live in **A** did for me, Dt 2:29 6144
Surely in a night **A** of Moab is Is 15:1 6144

ARA
were Jephunneh, Pispa and **A**. 1Ch 7:38 690

ARAB
A and Dumah and Eshan, Jos 15:52 694
and Geshem the **A** heard *it,* Ne 2:19 6163a
Tobiah, to Geshem the **A** and Ne 6:1 6163a
will the **A** pitch *his* tent there, Is 13:20 6163b
for them Like an **A** in the desert, Jer 3:2 6163b

ARABAH
in the **A** opposite Suph, Dt 1:1 6160
to all their neighbors in the **A**, Dt 1:7 6160
in Seir, away from the **A** road, Dt 2:8 6160
the **A** also, with the Jordan as *a* Dt 3:17 6160
even as far as the sea of the **A**, Dt 3:17 6160
with all the **A** across the Dt 4:49 6160
even as far as the sea of the **A**, Dt 4:49 6160
the Canaanites who live in the **A**, Dt 11:30 6160
down toward the sea of the **A**, Jos 3:16 6160
and in the **A**—south of Chinneroth Jos 11:2 6160
of Goshen, the lowland, the **A**, Jos 11:16 6160
Hermon, and all the **A** to the east: Jos 12:1 6160
and the **A** as far as the Sea of Jos 12:3 6160
and as far as the sea of the **A**, Jos 12:3 6160
country, in the lowland, in the **A**, Jos 12:8 6160
side in front of the **A** northward and Jos 18:18 6160
northward and went down to the **A**. Jos 18:18 6160
in the **A** to the south of Jeshimon. 1Sa 23:24 6160
went through the **A** all that night; 2Sa 2:29 6160
by way of the **A** all night. 2Sa 4:7 6160
Hamath as far as the Sea of the **A**, 2Ki 14:25 6160
And they went by way of the **A**. 2Ki 25:4 6160
the **A** will rejoice and blossom; Is 35:1 6160
wilderness And streams in the **A**. Is 35:6 6160
and he went out toward the **A**. Jer 39:4 6160
And they went by way of the **A**. Jer 52:7 6160
region and go down into the **A**; Ezk 47:8 6160
of Hamath To the brook of the **A**. Am 6:14 6160

ARABIA
and all the kings of **A** and the 2Ch 9:14 6152a
The oracle about **A**. Is 21:13 6152b
of **A** you must spend the night, Is 21:13 6152b
and all the kings of **A** and all the Jer 25:24 6152a
"**A** and all the princes of Kedar, Ezk 27:21 6152a
"Ethiopia, Put, Lud, all **A**, Ezk 30:5 6152a
but I went away to **A**, Ga 1:17 *688*
this Hagar is Mount Sinai in **A** and Ga 4:25 *688*

ARABIANS
the **A** also brought him flocks, 2Ch 17:11 6163a
the **A** who lived in Gur-baal, 2Ch 26:7 6163a

ARABIM
carry off over the brook of **A**. Is 15:7 6155

ARABS
merchants and all the kings of the **A** 1Ki 10:15 6152a
the **A** who bordered the Ethiopians; 2Ch 21:16 6163a
band of men who came with the **A** 2Ch 22:1 6163a
when Sanballat, Tobiah, the **A**, Ne 4:7 6163a
Cretans and **A**—we hear them in our Ac 2:11 *690b*

ARAD
When the Canaanite, the king of **A**, Nu 21:1 6166a
the king of **A** who lived in the Nu 33:40 6166a
the king of **A**, one; Jos 12:14 6166a
Judah which is in the south of **A**; Jg 1:16 6166a
Zebadiah, **A**, Eder, 1Ch 8:15 6166b

ARAH
The sons of Ulla *were* **A**, 1Ch 7:39 733
the sons of **A**, 775; Ezr 2:5 733
of Shecaniah the son of **A**, Ne 6:18 733
the sons of **A**, 652; Ne 7:10 733

ARAM
and Arpachshad and Lud and **A**. Gn 10:22 758
The sons of **A** *were* Uz and Hul Gn 10:23 758
and Kemuel the father of **A** Gn 22:21 758
"From **A** Balak has brought me, Nu 23:7 6307
and the Ashtaroth, the gods of **A**, Jg 10:6 758
from **A** and Moab and the sons of 2Sa 8:12 758
while I was living at Geshur in **A**, 2Sa 15:8 758
Israel and reigned over **A**. 1Ki 11:25 758
the son of Hezion, king of **A**, 1Ki 15:18 758
shall anoint Hazael king over **A**; 1Ki 19:15 758
king of **A** gathered all his army, 1Ki 20:1 758
and Ben-hadad king of **A** escaped on 1Ki 20:20 758
of **A** will come up against you." 1Ki 20:22 758
of the king of **A** said to him, 1Ki 20:23 758
without war between **A** and Israel. 1Ki 22:1 758
of the hand of the king of **A**?" 1Ki 22:3 758
Now the king of **A** had commanded 1Ki 22:31 758
of the army of the king of **A**, 2Ki 5:1 758
the LORD had given victory to **A**. 2Ki 5:1 758
Then the king of **A** said, 2Ki 5:5 758
of **A** was warring against Israel; 2Ki 6:8 758
of **A** was enraged over this thing; 2Ki 6:11 758
that Ben-hadad king of **A** gathered 2Ki 6:24 758
Now Ben-hadad king of **A** was sick, 2Ki 8:7 758
king of **A** has sent me to you, 2Ki 8:9 758
me that you will be king over **A**." 2Ki 8:13 758
Hazael king of **A** at Ramoth-gilead, 2Ki 8:28 758
fought against Hazael king of **A**. 2Ki 8:29 758
against Hazael king of **A**, 2Ki 9:14 758
he fought with Hazael king of **A**. 2Ki 9:15 758
Then Hazael king of **A** went up and 2Ki 12:17 758
and sent *them* to Hazael king of **A**, 2Ki 12:18 758
into the hand of Hazael king of **A**, 2Ki 13:3 758
how the king of **A** oppressed them. 2Ki 13:4 758
for the king of **A** had destroyed 2Ki 13:7 758
even the arrow of victory over **A**; 2Ki 13:17 758
then you would have struck **A** until 2Ki 13:19 758
shall strike **A** *only* three times." 2Ki 13:19 758
Now Hazael king of **A** had oppressed 2Ki 13:22 758
When Hazael king of **A** died, 2Ki 13:24 758
LORD began to send Rezin king of **A** 2Ki 15:37 758
of **A** and Pekah son of Remaliah, 2Ki 16:5 758
of **A** recovered Elath for Aram, 2Ki 16:6 758
of Aram recovered Elath for **A**, 2Ki 16:6 758
me from the hand of the king of **A** and 2Ki 16:7 758
Elam, Asshur, Arpachshad, Lud, **A**, 1Ch 1:17 758
But Geshur and **A** took the towns of 1Ch 2:23 758
Ahi and Rohgah, Jehubbah and **A**. 1Ch 7:34 758
the Hittites and the kings of **A**. 2Ch 1:17 758
sent them to Ben-hadad king of **A**, 2Ch 16:2 758
relied on the king of **A** and have not 2Ch 16:7 758
of **A** has escaped out of your hand. 2Ch 16:7 758
Now the king of **A** had commanded 2Ch 18:30 758
the sea, out of **A** and behold, 2Ch 20:2 758
Hazael king of **A** at Ramoth-gilead. 2Ch 22:5 758
fought against Hazael king of **A**. 2Ch 22:6 758
into the hand of the king of **A**; 2Ch 28:5 758
of the kings of **A** helped them, 2Ch 28:23 758
A and Pekah the son of Remaliah, Is 7:1 758
the fierce anger of Rezin and **A** and Is 7:4 758
"Because **A**, *with* Ephraim and the Is 7:5 758
"For the head of **A** is Damascus Is 7:8 758
Damascus And the remnant of **A**; Is 17:3 758
"**A** was your customer because of Ezk 27:16 758
Now Jacob fled to the land of **A**, Hos 12:12 758
of **A** will go exiled to Kir," Am 1:5 758

ARAMAIC
"Speak now to your servants in **A**, 2Ki 18:26 762
in **A** and translated *from* Aramaic. Ezr 4:7 762
in Aramaic and translated *from* **A**. Ezr 4:7 762
"Speak now to your servants in **A**, Is 36:11 762
Chaldeans spoke to the king in **A**: Da 2:4 762

ARAMEAN
of Bethuel the **A** of Paddan-aram, Gn 25:20 761
the sister of Laban the **A**, Gn 25:20 761
to Laban, son of Bethuel the **A**, Gn 28:5 761
And Jacob deceived Laban the **A** by Gn 31:20 761
the **A** in a dream of the night and Gn 31:24 761
'My father was a wandering **A**, Dt 26:5 761
has spared this Naaman the **A**, 2Ki 5:20 761
Asriel, whom his **A** concubine bore; 1Ch 7:14 761

ARAMEANS
When the **A** of Damascus came to 2Sa 8:5 758
of Zobah, David killed 22,000 **A**. 2Sa 8:5 758
garrisons among the **A** of Damascus, 2Sa 8:6 758
the **A** became servants to David, 2Sa 8:6 758
18,000 **A** in the Valley of Salt. 2Sa 8:13 758
hired the **A** of Beth-rehob and the 2Sa 10:6 758
of Beth-rehob and the **A** of Zobah, 2Sa 10:6 758
while the **A** of Zobah and of Rehob 2Sa 10:8 758
and arrayed *them* against the **A**. 2Sa 10:9 758
"If the **A** are too strong for me, 2Sa 10:11 758
near to the battle against the **A**, 2Sa 10:13 758
sons of Ammon saw that the **A** fled, 2Sa 10:14 758
When the **A** saw that they had been 2Sa 10:15 758
the **A** who were beyond the River, 2Sa 10:16 758
And the **A** arrayed themselves to 2Sa 10:17 758
But the **A** fled before Israel, and 2Sa 10:18 758
David killed 700 charioteers of the **A** 2Sa 10:18 758
So the **A** feared to help the sons 2Sa 10:19 758
and to the kings of the **A**. 1Ki 10:29 758
and the **A** fled and Israel pursued 1Ki 20:20 758
the **A** with a great slaughter. 1Ki 20:21 758
Ben-hadad mustered the **A** and 1Ki 20:26 758
but the **A** filled the country. 1Ki 20:27 758
'Because the **A** have said, 1Ki 20:28 758
sons of Israel killed *of* the **A** 100,000 1Ki 20:29 758
the **A** until they are consumed.'" 1Ki 22:11 758
in his chariot in front of the **A**, 1Ki 22:35 758
Now the **A** had gone out in bands and 2Ki 5:2 758
for the **A** are coming down there." 2Ki 6:9 758
And the marauding bands of **A** did 2Ki 6:23 758
us go over to the camp of the **A**. 2Ki 7:4 758
to go to the camp of the **A**; 2Ki 7:5 758
outskirts of the camp of the **A**, 2Ki 7:5 758
Lord had caused the army of the **A** 2Ki 7:6 758
"We came to the camp of the **A**, 2Ki 7:10 758
you what the **A** have done to us. 2Ki 7:12 758
king sent after the army of the **A**, 2Ki 7:14 758
which the **A** had thrown away in 2Ki 7:15 758
and plundered the camp of the **A** 2Ki 7:16 758
and the **A** wounded Joram. 2Ki 8:28 761
A had inflicted on him at Ramah when 2Ki 8:29 761
healed of the wounds which the **A** 2Ki 9:15 761
from under the hand of the **A**; 2Ki 13:5 758
for you will defeat the **A** at 2Ki 13:17 758
and the **A** came to Elath and have 2Ki 16:6 130

bands of Chaldeans, bands of A, 2Ki 24:2 758
When the A of Damascus came to 1Ch 18:5 758
David killed 22,000 men of the A. 1Ch 18:5 758
garrisons among the A of Damascus; 1Ch 18:6 758
the A became servants to David, 1Ch 18:6 758
arrayed themselves against the A. 1Ch 19:10 758
"If the A are too strong for me, 1Ch 19:12 758
near to the battle against the A, 1Ch 19:14 758
sons of Ammon saw that the A fled, 1Ch 19:15 758
When the A saw that they had been 1Ch 19:16 758
the A who were beyond the River, 1Ch 19:16 758
up in battle array against the A, 1Ch 19:17 758
The A fled before Israel, and 1Ch 19:18 758
and David killed of the A 7,000 1Ch 19:18 758
Thus the A were not willing to 1Ch 19:19 758
'With these you shall gore the A until 2Ch 18:10 758
front of the A until the evening; 2Ch 18:34 758
But the A wounded Joram. 2Ch 22:5 761
army of the A came up against him; 2Ch 24:23 758
Indeed the army of the A came with 2Ch 24:24 758
"The A have camped in Ephraim," Is 7:2 758
The A on the east and the Is 9:12 758
and before the army of the A.' Jer 35:11 758
from Caphtor and the A from Kir? Am 9:7 758

ARAM-MAACAH
horsemen from Mesopotamia, from A 1Ch 19:6 758, 4601

ARAN
the sons of Dishan: Uz and A. Gn 36:28 765
The sons of Dishan were Uz and A. 1Ch 1:42 765

ARARAT
rested upon the mountains of A. Gn 8:4 780
they escaped into the land of A. 2Ki 19:37 780
they escaped into the land of A. Is 37:38 780
against her the kingdoms of A, Jer 51:27 780

ARARITE
Ahiam the son of Sharar the A, 2Sa 23:33 2043

ARAUNAH
threshing floor of A the Jebusite. 2Sa 24:16 728
floor of A the Jebusite." 2Sa 24:18 728
A looked down and saw the king 2Sa 24:20 728
and A went out and bowed his face 2Sa 24:20 728
A said, "Why has my lord the king 2Sa 24:21 728
A said to David, 2Sa 24:22 728
O king, A gives to the king." 2Sa 24:23 728
And A said to the king, 2Sa 24:23 728
However, the king said to A, 2Sa 24:24 728

ARBA
for A was the greatest man among Jos 14:15
A being the father of Anak Jos 15:13
A being the father of Anak Jos 21:11

ARBATHITE
Abi-albon the A, Azmaveth the 2Sa 23:31 6164
the brooks of Gaash, Abiel the A, 1Ch 11:32 6164

ARBITE
Hezro the Carmelite, Paarai the A, 2Sa 23:35 701

ARBITRATOR
who appointed Me a judge or a over Lk 12:14 3312

ARCHANGEL
a shout, with the voice of the a and 1Th 4:16 743
But Michael the a, when he Jude 1:9 743

ARCHELAUS
But when he heard that A was Mt 2:22 745

ARCHER
the wilderness and became an a. Gn 21:20 7235b, 7199
Like an a who wounds everyone, So Pr 26:10 7228

ARCHERS
"The a bitterly attacked him, And Gn 49:23 1167, 2671
against Saul, and the a hit him; 1Sa 31:3 3384, 376, 7198
and he was badly wounded by the a. 1Sa 31:3 3384
the a shot at your servants from 2Sa 11:24 3372b
Ulam were mighty men of valor, a, 1Ch 8:40 1869, 7198
Saul, and the a overtook him; 1Ch 10:3 3384, 7198
and he was wounded by the a. 1Ch 10:3 3384
The a shot King Josiah, and 2Ch 35:23 3384
Ephraim were a equipped with bows, Ps 78:9 7411a

ARCHIPPUS
Say to A, "Take heed to the ministry Col 4:17 751
and to A our fellow soldier, Phm 1:2 751

ARCHITE
the A met him with his coat torn and 2Sa 15:32 757
it came about when Hushai the A, 2Sa 16:16 757
"Now call Hushai the A also, 2Sa 17:5 757
"The counsel of Hushai the A is 2Sa 17:14 757
Hushai the A was the king's friend. 1Ch 27:33 757

ARCHITECT
whose a and builder is God. Heb 11:10 5079

ARCHITES
to the border of the A at Ataroth. Jos 16:2 757

ARCHIVES
and search was made in the a, Ezr 6:1 1005, 5609

ARD
Rosh, Muppim and Huppim and A. Gn 46:21 714
sons of Bela were A and Naaman: Nu 26:40 714
of A, the family of the Ardites; Nu 26:40

ARDITES
of Ard, the family of the A; Nu 26:40 716

ARDON
Jesher, Shobab, and A. 1Ch 2:18 715

AREA
with a large a between them. 1Sa 26:13 4725
in the surrounding a of Jerusalem, 2Ki 23:5 4524
Millo even to the surrounding a; 1Ch 11:8 5439
and he built cities in the a of 2Ch 26:6
LORD will create over the whole a of Is 4:5 4349
its place and rye within its a? Is 28:25 1367
in front of the separate a at the side Ezk 41:12 1508
the separate a with the building Ezk 41:13 1508
front of the separate a behind it, Ezk 41:15 1508
opposite the separate a and opposite Ezk 42:1 1508
a and facing the building, Ezk 42:10 1508
which are opposite the separate a, Ezk 42:13 1508
its entire a on the top of the Ezk 43:12 1366
"From this a you shall Ezk 45:3 4060a
"An a 25,000 cubits in Ezk 45:5
give the city possession of an a Ezk 45:6

AREAS
Therefore the Jews of the rural a, Es 9:19 6521
the temple and that of the separate a Ezk 41:14 1508
but stayed out in unpopulated a; Mk 1:45 5117

ARELI
and Ezbon, Eri and Arodi and A. Gn 46:16 692
of A, the family of the Arelites. Nu 26:17 692

ARELITES
of Areli, the family of the A. Nu 26:17 692

AREOPAGITE
whom also were Dionysius the A and Ac 17:34 698

AREOPAGUS
took him and brought him to the A, Ac 17:19 697
in the midst of the A and said, Ac 17:22 697

ARETAS
In Damascus the ethnarch under A 2Co 11:32 702

ARGOB
sixty cities, all the region of A, Dt 3:4 709b
of Manasseh, all the region of A Dt 3:13 709b
of Manasseh took all the region of A Dt 3:14 709b
the region of A, which is in 1Ki 4:13 709b
the king's house with A and Arieh; 2Ki 15:25 709b

ARGUE
And I desire to a with God. Jb 13:3 3198
I will a my ways before Him. Jb 13:15 3198
"Should he a with useless talk, Jb 15:3 3198
not go out hastily to a your case; Pr 25:8 7378
A your case with your neighbor, Pr 25:9 7378
let us a our case together; State Is 43:26 8199
came out and began to a with Him, Mk 8:11 4802
began to a with one another, Jn 6:52 3164
stood up and began to a heatedly, Ac 23:9 1264

ARGUED
Asia, rose up and a with Stephen. Ac 6:9 4802
and a about the body of Moses, Jude 1:9 1256

ARGUING
and some scribes a with them. Mk 9:14 4802
the scribes came and heard them a, Mk 12:28 4802
and a with the Hellenistic Jews Ac 9:29 4802

ARGUMENT
But what does your a prove? Jb 6:25 3198
"Please hear my a And listen to Jb 13:6 8433b
An a started among them as to Lk 9:46 1261
will delude you with persuasive a. Col 2:4 4086

ARGUMENTATIVE
to be well-pleasing, not a, Ti 2:9 483

ARGUMENTS
Him And fill my mouth with a. Jb 23:4 8433b
will I reply to him with your a. Jb 32:14 561
hear, And in whose mouth are no a. Ps 38:14 8433b
in the right with meaningless a. Is 29:21 8414
"Bring forward your strong a," Is 41:21
a of what is falsely called 1Tm 6:20 477

ARIDAI
Parmashta, Arisai, A and Es 9:9 742

ARIDATHA
Poratha, Adalia, A, Es 9:8 743a

ARIEH
the king's house with Argob and A; 2Ki 15:25 745a

ARIEL
killed the two sons of A of Moab. 2Sa 23:20 739
down the two sons of A of Moab. 1Ch 11:22 739
So I sent for Eliezer, A, Ezr 8:16 739
Woe, O A, Ariel the city where Is 29:1 740
A the city where David once camped! Is 29:1 740
I will bring distress to A, Is 29:2 740
And she will be like an A to me. Is 29:2 740
nations who wage war against A, Is 29:7 740

ARIGHT
And to him who orders his way a Ps 50:23

ARIMATHEA
there came a rich man from A, Mt 27:57 707
Joseph of A came, a prominent Mk 15:43 707
a man from A, a city of the Jews, Lk 23:51 707
After these things Joseph of A, Jn 19:38 707

ARIOCH
king of Shinar, A king of Ellasar, Gn 14:1 746a
king of Shinar and A king of Ellasar Gn 14:9 746a
discretion and discernment to A, Da 2:14 746b
he said to A, Da 2:15 746b
Then A informed Daniel about the Da 2:15 746b
Therefore, Daniel went in to A, Da 2:24 746b
Then A hurriedly brought Daniel Da 2:25 746b

ARISAI
Parmashta, A, Aridai and Es 9:9 747b

ARISE
"A, walk about the land through Gn 13:17 6965
"A, lift up the lad, and hold him Gn 21:18 6965
"Let my father a and eat of his Gn 27:31 6965
my son, obey my voice, and a, Gn 27:43 6965
"A, go to Paddan-aram, to the Gn 28:2 6965
now a, leave this land, and return Gn 31:13 6965
"A, go up to Bethel and live Gn 35:1 6965
and let us a and go up to Bethel, Gn 35:3 6965
lad with me and we will a and go, Gn 43:8 6965
"Take your brother also, and a, Gn 43:13 6965
all the people would a and stand, Ex 33:8 6965
the people would a and worship, Ex 33:10 6965
"A, O Balak, and hear; Nu 23:18 6965
'Now a and cross over the brook Dt 2:13 6965
'A, set out, and pass through the Dt 2:24 6965
'A, go down from here quickly, for Dt 9:12 6965
'A, proceed on your journey ahead Dt 10:11 6965
then you shall a and go up to the Dt 17:8 6965
and this people will a and play Dt 31:16 6965
now therefore a, cross this Jos 1:2 6965
the people of war with you and a, Jos 8:1 6965
and that they may a and walk Jos 18:4 6965
Deborah said to Barak, "A! Jg 4:14 6965
A, Barak, and take away your Jg 5:12 6965
"A, go down against the camp, for Jg 7:9 6965
"A, for the LORD has given the Jg 7:15 6965
"Now therefore, a by night, you Jg 9:32 6965
"A, and let us go up against them; Jg 18:9 6965
Then tomorrow you may a early for Jg 19:9 7925
you one of the servants, and a, 1Sa 9:3 6965
"A, anoint him; for this is he. 1Sa 16:12 6965
"A, go down to Keilah, for I will 1Sa 23:4 6965
"Now then a early in the morning 1Sa 29:10 7925
a and hold a contest before us." 2Sa 2:14 6965
And Joab said, "Let them a." 2Sa 2:14 6965
"Let me a and go and gather all 2Sa 3:21 6965
"A and let us flee, for otherwise 2Sa 15:14 6965
I may a and pursue David tonight. 2Sa 17:1 6965
"A and cross over the water 2Sa 17:21 6965
"Now therefore a, go out and 2Sa 19:7 6965
shall one like you a after you. 1Ki 3:12 6965
"A now, and disguise yourself so 1Ki 14:2 6965
"Now you, a, go to your house. 1Ki 14:12 6965
"A, go to Zarephath, which 1Ki 17:9 6965
and he said to him, "A, eat." 1Ki 19:5 6965
"A, eat, because the journey is 1Ki 19:7 6965
A, eat bread, and let your heart 1Ki 21:7 6965
"A, take possession of the 1Ki 21:15 6965
"A, go down to meet Ahab king of 1Ki 21:18 6965
"A, go up to meet the messengers 2Ki 1:3 6965
"A and go with your household, 2Ki 8:1 6965
bid him a from among his brothers, 2Ki 9:2 6965
nor did any like him a after him. 2Ki 23:25 6965
A and work, and may the LORD be 1Ch 22:16 6965
a, therefore, and build the 1Ch 22:19 6965
"Now therefore a, O LORD God, to 2Ch 6:41 6965
"A! For this matter is your Ezr 10:4 6965
"Let us a and build." Ne 2:18 6965
we His servants will a and build, Ne 2:20 6965
"A, bless the LORD your God Ne 9:5 6965
relief and deliverance will a for Es 4:14 5975
I lie down I say, 'When shall I a?' Jb 7:4 6965
A, O LORD; save me, O my God! Ps 3:7 6965
A, O LORD, in Your anger; Ps 7:6 6965
A, O LORD, do not let man prevail; Ps 9:19 6965
A, O LORD; O God, lift up Your hand. Ps 10:12 6965
of the needy, Now I will a," Ps 12:5 6965
A, O LORD, confront him, bring him Ps 17:13 6965
Though war a against me, In spite Ps 27:3 6965
Let God a, let His enemies be Ps 68:1 6965
A, O God, and plead Your own Ps 74:22 6965
That they may a and tell them to Ps 78:6 6965
A, O God, judge the earth! Ps 82:8 6965
a and have compassion on Zion; Ps 102:13 6965
When they a, they shall be Ps 109:28 6965
A, O LORD, to Your resting place, Ps 132:8 6965
When will you a from your sleep? Pr 6:9 6965
will a at the sound of the bird, Ec 12:4 6965
'A, my darling, my beautiful one, SS 2:10 6965
A, my darling, my beautiful one, SS 2:13 6965
must a now and go about the city; SS 3:2 6965
They must not a and take Is 14:21 6965
A, pass over to Cyprus; Is 23:12 6965
But will a against the house of Is 31:2 6965
"Now I will a," says the LORD, Is 33:10 6965
"Kings will see and a, Is 49:7 6965
A, O Jerusalem, You who have drunk Is 51:17 6965
"A, shine; for your light has come, Is 60:1 6965
"Now, gird up your loins and a, Jer 1:17 6965
they will say, 'A and save us.' Jer 2:27 6965
Let them a, if they can save you Jer 2:28 6965
A, and let us attack at noon. Jer 6:4 6965
'A, and let us attack by night Jer 6:5 6965
which is around your waist, and a, Jer 13:4 6965
"A, go to the Euphrates and take Jer 13:6 6965
"A and go down to the potter's Jer 18:2 6965
'A, and let us go up to Zion, To Jer 31:6 6965
"A, go up to Kedar And devastate Jer 49:28 6965
"A, go up against a nation which Jer 49:31 6965
"A, cry aloud in the night At the La 2:19 6965
"After you there will a Da 2:39 6966
'A, devour much meat!' Da 7:5 6966
kings who will a from the earth. Da 7:17 6966
of this kingdom ten kings will a; Da 7:24 6966
and another will a after them, Da 7:24 6966
which will a from his nation, Da 8:22 5975
A king will a, Insolent and skilled Da 8:23 5975
kings are going to a in Persia. Da 11:2 5975
"And a mighty king will a, Da 11:3 5975
of her line will a in his place, Da 11:7 5975
"Then in his place one will a who Da 11:20 5975

place a despicable person will **a**, Da 11:21 5975
"Forces from him will **a**, Da 11:31 5975
the sons of your people, will **a**. Da 12:1 5975
a tumult will **a** among your people, Hos 10:14 6965
And its stench will **a** and its foul Jl 2:20 5927
"**A** and let us go against her for Ob 1:1 6965
"**A**, go to Nineveh the great city and Jon 1:2 6965
"**A**, go to Nineveh the great city Jon 3:2 6965
"**A** and go, For this is no place Mi 2:10 6965
"**A** and thresh, daughter of Zion, Mi 4:13 6965
And He will **a** and shepherd *His* Mi 5:4 5975
"**A**, plead your case before the Mi 6:1 6965
To a mute stone, '**A**!' Hab 2:19 5782
people to **a** *who* will invade us. Hab 3:16 5927
"Many false prophets will **a** and Mt 24:11 *1453*
false Christs and false prophets will **a** Mt 24:24 *1453*
Christs and false prophets will **a**, Mk 13:22 *1453*
"Young man, I say to you, **a**!" Lk 7:14 *1453*
hand and called, saying, "Child, **a**!" Lk 8:54 *1453*
why do doubts **a** in your hearts? Lk 24:38 *305*
"Tabitha, **a**." And she opened her Ac 9:40 *450*
among your own selves men will **a**, Ac 20:30 *450*
sleeper, And **a** from the dead, Eph 5:14 *450*
about words, out of which **a** envy, 1Tm 6:4 *1096*
need *was there* for another priest to **a** Heb 7:11 *450*

ARISEN

and as soon as you have **a** early in 1Sa 29:10 7925
"But as soon as he has **a**, Da 11:4 5975
"Recently My people have **a** as an Mi 2:8 6965
has not **a** *anyone* greater than John Mt 11:11 *1453*
"A great prophet has **a** among us!" Lk 7:16 *1453*

ARISES

or a dreamer of dreams **a** among you Dt 13:1 6965
"The murderer **a** at dawn; Jb 24:14 6965
"On the right hand their brood **a**; Jb 30:12 6965
What then could I do when God **a**? Jb 31:14 6965
Light **a** in the darkness for the Ps 112:4 2224
He **a** to make the earth tremble. Is 2:19 6965
He **a** to make the earth tremble. Is 2:21 6965
The LORD **a** to contend, And stands Is 3:13 5324
Strife exists and contention **a**. Hab 1:3 5375
persecution **a** because of the word, Mt 13:21 *1096*
persecution **a** because of the word, Mk 4:17 *1096*
no prophet **a** out of Galilee." Jn 7:52 *1453*
WHO **A** TO RULE OVER THE GENTILES, Ro 15:12 *450*
if another priest **a** according to Heb 7:15 *450*
the morning star **a** in your hearts. 2Pe 1:19 *393*

ARISING

and from the toil of our hands **a** Gn 5:29

ARISTARCHUS

dragging along Gaius and **A**, Ac 19:29 *708*
and by **A** and Secundus of the Ac 20:4 *708*
put out to sea accompanied by **A**, Ac 27:2 *708*
A, my fellow prisoner, sends you Col 4:10 *708*
as do Mark, **A**, Demas, Luke, my Phm 1:24 *708*

ARISTOBULUS

who are of the *household* of **A**. Ro 16:10 *711*

ARK

for yourself an **a** of gopher wood; Gn 6:14 8392
you shall make the **a** with rooms, Gn 6:14 8392
of the **a** three hundred cubits, Gn 6:15 8392
"You shall make a window for the **a**, Gn 6:16 8392
door of the **a** in the side of it; Gn 6:16 8392
and you shall enter the **a**—you and Gn 6:18 8392
two of every *kind* into the **a**, Gn 6:19 8392
"Enter the **a**, you and all your Gn 7:1 8392
his sons' wives with him entered the **a** Gn 7:7 8392
went into the **a** to Noah by twos, Gn 7:9 8392
his sons with them, entered the **a**, Gn 7:13 8392
So they went into the **a** to Noah, Gn 7:15 8392
increased and lifted up the **a**, Gn 7:17 8392
and the **a** floated on the surface Gn 7:18 8392
those that were with him in the **a**. Gn 7:23 8392
that were with him in the **a**; Gn 8:1 8392
the **a** rested upon the mountains of Gn 8:4 8392
window of the **a** which he had made; Gn 8:6 8392
so she returned to him into the **a**, Gn 8:9 8392
brought her into the **a** to himself. Gn 8:9 8392
he sent out the dove from the **a**. Gn 8:10 8392
removed the covering of the **a**, Gn 8:13 8392
"Go out of the **a**, you and your Gn 8:16 8392
out by their families from the **a**. Gn 8:19 8392
of all that comes out of the **a**, Gn 9:10 8392
a were Shem and Ham and Japheth; Gn 9:18 8392
"They shall construct an **a** of Ex 25:10 727
the rings on the sides of the **a**, Ex 25:14 727
the ark, to carry the **a** with them. Ex 25:14 727
remain in the rings of the **a**; Ex 25:15 727
"You shall put into the **a** the Ex 25:16 727
the mercy seat on top of the **a**, Ex 25:21 727
and in the **a** you shall put the Ex 25:21 727
are upon the **a** of the testimony, Ex 25:22 727
and shall bring in the **a** of the Ex 26:33 727
mercy seat on the **a** of the testimony Ex 26:34 727
is near the **a** of the testimony, Ex 30:6 727
the mercy seat that is over *the* **a** Ex 30:6 727
and the **a** of the testimony, Ex 30:26 727
meeting, and the **a** of testimony, Ex 31:7 727
the **a** and its poles, the mercy Ex 35:12 727
Bezalel made the **a** of acacia wood; Ex 37:1 727
the rings on the sides of the **a**, Ex 37:5 727
the **a** of the testimony and its Ex 39:35 727
the **a** of the testimony there, Ex 40:3 727
shall screen the **a** with the veil. Ex 40:3 727
before the **a** of the testimony, Ex 40:5 727
testimony and put *it* into the **a**, Ex 40:20 727
and attached the poles to the **a**, Ex 40:20 727
the mercy seat on top of the **a**. Ex 40:20 727
brought the **a** into the tabernacle, Ex 40:21 727
off the **a** of the testimony, Ex 40:21 727
the mercy seat which is on the **a**, Lv 16:2 727
the mercy seat that is on *the* **a** *of* Lv 16:13 727
Now their duties *involved* the **a**, Nu 3:31 727
the **a** of the testimony with it; Nu 4:5 727
was on the **a** of the testimony, Nu 7:89 727
with the **a** of the covenant of the Nu 10:33 727
the **a** set out that Moses said, Nu 10:35 727
neither the **a** of the covenant of Nu 14:44 727
make an **a** of wood for yourself. Dt 10:1 727
and you shall put them in the **a**.' Dt 10:2 727
"So I made an **a** of acacia wood Dt 10:3 727
tablets in the **a** which I had made; Dt 10:5 727
the **a** of the covenant of the LORD, Dt 10:8 727
the **a** of the covenant of the LORD, Dt 31:9 727
the **a** of the covenant of the LORD, Dt 31:25 727
place it beside the **a** of the covenant Dt 31:26 727
"When you see the **a** of the Jos 3:3 727
"Take up the **a** of the covenant Jos 3:6 727
So they took up the **a** of the Jos 3:6 727
carrying the **a** of the covenant, Jos 3:8 727
the **a** of the covenant of the Lord Jos 3:11 727
who carry the **a** of the LORD, Jos 3:13 727
Jordan with the priests carrying the **a** Jos 3:14 727
the **a** came into the Jordan, Jos 3:15 727
the feet of the priests carrying the **a** Jos 3:15 727
And the priests who carried the **a** Jos 3:17 727
"Cross again to the **a** of the LORD Jos 4:5 727
the **a** of the covenant of the LORD; Jos 4:7 727
a of the covenant were standing, Jos 4:9 727
For the priests who carried the **a** Jos 4:10 727
the **a** of the LORD and the Jos 4:11 727
the priests who carry the **a** of the Jos 4:16 727
the priests who carried the **a** of the Jos 4:18 727
of rams' horns before the **a**; Jos 6:4 727
"Take up the **a** of the covenant, Jos 6:6 727
horns before the **a** of the LORD." Jos 6:6 727
go on before the **a** of the LORD." Jos 6:7 727
and the **a** of the covenant of the Jos 6:8 727
the rear guard came after the **a**, Jos 6:9 727
So he had the **a** of the LORD taken Jos 6:11 727
priests took up the **a** of the LORD. Jos 6:12 727
trumpets of rams' horns before the **a** Jos 6:13 727
came after the **a** of the LORD, Jos 6:13 727
a of the LORD until the evening, Jos 7:6 727
were standing on both sides of the **a** Jos 8:33 727
the **a** of the covenant of the LORD, Jos 8:33 727
(for the **a** of the covenant of God Jg 20:27 727
the LORD where the **a** of God *was*, 1Sa 3:3 727
the **a** of the covenant of the LORD, 1Sa 4:3 727
they carried the **a** of the covenant of 1Sa 4:4 727
with the **a** of the covenant of God. 1Sa 4:4 727
As the **a** of the covenant 1Sa 4:5 727
Then they understood that the **a** of 1Sa 4:6 727
And the **a** of God was taken; 1Sa 4:11 727
was trembling for the **a** of God. 1Sa 4:13 727
and the **a** of God has been taken." 1Sa 4:17 727
When he mentioned the **a** of God 1Sa 4:18 727
news that the **a** of God was taken 1Sa 4:19 727
because the **a** of God was taken and 1Sa 4:21 727
for the **a** of God was taken." 1Sa 4:22 727
Now the Philistines took the **a** of 1Sa 5:1 727
Then the Philistines took the **a** of 1Sa 5:2 727
ground before the **a** of the LORD. 1Sa 5:3 727
ground before the **a** of the LORD. 1Sa 5:4 727
"The **a** of the God of Israel must 1Sa 5:7 727
with the **a** of the God of Israel?" 1Sa 5:8 727
"Let the **a** of the God of Israel 1Sa 5:8 727
the **a** of the God of Israel *around*. 1Sa 5:8 727
they sent the **a** of God to Ekron. 1Sa 5:10 727
And as the **a** of God came to Ekron 1Sa 5:10 727
"They have brought the **a** of the 1Sa 5:10 727
away the **a** of the God of Israel, 1Sa 5:11 727
Now the **a** of the LORD had been in 1Sa 6:1 727
we do with the **a** of the LORD? 1Sa 6:2 727
away the **a** of the God of Israel, 1Sa 6:3 727
"Take the **a** of the LORD and 1Sa 6:8 727
put the **a** of the LORD on the cart, 1Sa 6:11 727
saw the **a** and were glad to see *it*. 1Sa 6:13 727
The Levites took down the **a** of 1Sa 6:15 727
large stone on which they set the **a** 1Sa 6:18 727
had looked into the **a** of the LORD. 1Sa 6:19 727
brought back the **a** of the LORD; 1Sa 6:21 727
took the **a** of the LORD and brought 1Sa 7:1 727
his son to keep the **a** of the LORD. 1Sa 7:1 727
From the day that the **a** remained at 1Sa 7:2 727
"Bring the **a** of God here." 1Sa 14:18 727
For the **a** of God was at that time 1Sa 14:18 727
to bring up from there the **a** of 2Sa 6:2 727
They placed the **a** of God on a 2Sa 6:3 727
So they brought it with the **a** of 2Sa 6:4 727
Ahio was walking ahead of the **a**. 2Sa 6:4 727
the **a** of God and took hold of it, 2Sa 6:6 727
and he died there by the **a** of God. 2Sa 6:7 727
the **a** of the LORD come to me?" 2Sa 6:9 727
David was unwilling to move the **a** 2Sa 6:10 727
Thus the **a** of the LORD remained in 2Sa 6:11 727
him, on account of the **a** of God." 2Sa 6:12 727
David went and brought up the **a** of 2Sa 6:12 727
that when the bearers of the **a** of 2Sa 6:13 727
house of Israel were bringing up the **a** 2Sa 6:15 727
Then it happened *as* the **a** of the 2Sa 6:16 727
So they brought in the **a** of the 2Sa 6:17 727
but the **a** of God dwells within 2Sa 7:2 727
"The **a** and Israel and Judah are 2Sa 11:11 727
the **a** of the covenant of God. 2Sa 15:24 727
And they set down the **a** of God, 2Sa 15:24 727
"Return the **a** of God to the city. 2Sa 15:25 727
Zadok and Abiathar returned the **a** 2Sa 15:29 727
because you carried the **a** of the 1Ki 2:26 727
the **a** of the covenant of the Lord, 1Ki 3:15 727
the **a** of the covenant of the LORD. 1Ki 6:19 727
to bring up the **a** of the covenant 1Ki 8:1 727
and the priests took up the **a**. 1Ki 8:3 727
They brought up the **a** of the 1Ki 8:4 727
him, were with him before the **a**, 1Ki 8:5 727
Then the priests brought the **a** of 1Ki 8:6 727
wings over the place of the **a**, 1Ki 8:7 727
the **a** and its poles from above. 1Ki 8:7 727
There was nothing in the **a** except 1Ki 8:9 727
I have set a place for the **a**, 1Ki 8:21 727
LORD, after the **a** rested *there*. 1Ch 6:31 727
bring back the **a** of our God to us, 1Ch 13:3 727
the **a** of God from Kiriath-jearim. 1Ch 13:5 727
bring up from there the **a** of God, 1Ch 13:6 727
They carried the **a** of God on a 1Ch 13:7 727
put out his hand to hold the **a**, 1Ch 13:9 727
he put out his hand to the **a**; 1Ch 13:10 727
I bring the **a** of God *home* to me?" 1Ch 13:12 727
a with him to the city of David, 1Ch 13:13 727
Thus the **a** of God remained with 1Ch 13:14 727
prepared a place for the **a** of God and 1Ch 15:1 727
the **a** of God but the Levites; 1Ch 15:2 727
chose them to carry the **a** of God and 1Ch 15:2 727
up the **a** of the LORD to its place which 1Ch 15:3 727
the **a** of the LORD God of Israel to 1Ch 15:12 727
the **a** of the LORD God of Israel. 1Ch 15:14 727
the **a** of God on their shoulders with 1Ch 15:15 727
were gatekeepers for the **a**. 1Ch 15:23 727
the trumpets before the **a** of God. 1Ch 15:24 727
also *were* gatekeepers for the **a**. 1Ch 15:24 727
who went to bring up the **a** of the 1Ch 15:25 727
the **a** of the covenant of the LORD, 1Ch 15:26 727
Levites who were carrying the **a**, 1Ch 15:27 727
Thus all Israel brought up the **a** 1Ch 15:28 727
It happened when the **a** of the 1Ch 15:29 727
And they brought in the **a** of God 1Ch 16:1 727
before the **a** of the LORD, 1Ch 16:4 727
the **a** of the covenant of God. 1Ch 16:6 727
the **a** of the covenant of the LORD to 1Ch 16:37 727
minister before the **a** continually, 1Ch 16:37 727
but the **a** of the covenant of the 1Ch 17:1 727
the **a** of the covenant of the LORD and 1Ch 22:19 727
build a permanent home for the **a** of 1Ch 28:2 727
the **a** of the covenant of the LORD. 1Ch 28:18 727
David had brought up the **a** of God 2Ch 1:4 727
to bring up the **a** of the covenant 2Ch 5:2 727
and the Levites took up the **a**. 2Ch 5:4 727
They brought up the **a** and the 2Ch 5:5 727
were assembled with him before the **a** 2Ch 5:6 727
Then the priests brought the **a** of 2Ch 5:7 727
wings over the place of the **a**, 2Ch 5:8 727
covering over the **a** and its poles. 2Ch 5:8 727
poles of the **a** could be seen in front 2Ch 5:9 727
There was nothing in the **a** except 2Ch 5:10 727
"There I have set the **a** in 2Ch 6:11 727
You and the **a** of Your might; 2Ch 6:41 727
the **a** of the LORD has entered." 2Ch 8:11 727
"Put the holy **a** in the house 2Ch 35:3 727
You and the **a** of Your strength. Ps 132:8 727
a of the covenant of the LORD.' Jer 3:16 727
the day that Noah entered the **a**, Mt 24:38 *2787*
the day that Noah entered the **a**, Lk 17:27 *2787*
the **a** of the covenant covered on all Heb 9:4 *2787*
in reverence prepared an **a** for the Heb 11:7 *2787*
during the construction of the **a**, 1Pe 3:20 *2787*
and the **a** of His covenant appeared Rv 11:19 *2787*

ARKITE

Hivite and the **A** and the Sinite Gn 10:17 6208

ARKITES

the Hivites, the **A**, 1Ch 1:15 6208

ARM

a and with great judgments. Ex 6:6 2220
a they are motionless as stone; Ex 15:16 2220
"**A** men from among you for the Nu 31:3 2502b
if you will **a** yourselves before Nu 32:20 2502b
a and by great terrors, Dt 4:34 2220
hand and by an outstretched **a**; Dt 5:15 2220
outstretched **a** by which the LORD Dt 7:19 2220
power and Your outstretched **a**.' Dt 9:29 2220
hand and His outstretched **a**, Dt 11:2 2220
mighty hand and an outstretched **a** Dt 26:8 2220
down as a lion, And tears the **a**, Dt 33:20 2220
the bracelet which *was* on his **a**, 2Sa 1:10 2220
and of Your outstretched **a**); 1Ki 8:42 2220
power and with an outstretched **a**, 2Ki 17:36 2220
hand and Your outstretched **a**, 2Ch 6:32 2220
"With him is *only* an **a** of flesh, 2Ch 32:8 2220
have saved the **a** without strength! Jb 26:2 2220
my **a** be broken off at the elbow. Jb 31:22 248
because of the **a** of the mighty. Jb 35:9 2220
And the uplifted **a** is broken. Jb 38:15 2220
"Or do you have an **a** like God, Jb 40:9 2220
Break the **a** of the wicked and the Ps 10:15 2220
And their own **a** did not save them, Ps 44:3 2220
But Your right hand and Your **a** Ps 44:3 2220
Your enemies with Your mighty **a**. Ps 89:10 2220
You have a strong **a**; Ps 89:13 2220
My **a** also will strengthen him. Ps 89:21 2220
His right hand and His holy **a** have Ps 98:1 2220
strong hand and an outstretched **a**, Ps 136:12 2220
your heart, Like a seal on your **a**. SS 8:6 2220
them eats the flesh of his own **a**. Is 9:20 2220
grain, As his **a** harvests the ears, Is 17:5 2220
His **a** to be seen in fierce anger, Is 30:30 2220
might, With His **a** ruling for Him. Is 40:10 2220

In His **a** He will gather the lambs And **Is 40:11** 2220
and working it with his strong **a**. **Is 44:12** 2220
And His **a** *will be against* the **Is 48:14** 2220
My **a** they will wait expectantly. **Is 51:5** 2220
put on strength, O **a** of the LORD; **Is 51:9** 2220
The LORD has bared His holy **a** In **Is 52:10** 2220
the **a** of the LORD been revealed? **Is 53:1** 2220
own **a** brought salvation to Him, **Is 59:16** 2220
right hand and by His strong **a**, **Is 62:8** 2220
My own **a** brought salvation to Me, **Is 63:5** 2220
Who caused His glorious **a** to go at **Is 63:12** 2220
outstretched hand and a mighty **a**, **Jer 21:5** 2220
power and by My outstretched **a**, **Jer 27:5** 2220
power and by Your outstretched **a**! **Jer 32:17** 2220
hand and with an outstretched **a** and **Jer 32:21** 2220
been cut off and his **a** broken," **Jer 48:25** 2220
of Jerusalem with your **a** bared and **Ezk 4:7** 2220
a and with wrath poured out, **Ezk 20:33** 2220
a and with wrath poured out; **Ezk 20:34** 2220
the **a** of Pharaoh king of Egypt; **Ezk 30:21** 2220
be on his **a** And on his right eye! **Zch 11:17** 2220
His **a** will be totally withered And **Zch 11:17** 2220
has done mighty deeds with His **a**; **Lk 1:51** *1023*
THE **A** OF THE LORD BEEN REVEALED?" **Jn 12:38** *1023*
a He led them out from it. **Ac 13:17** *1023*
a yourselves also with the same **1Pe 4:1** *3695*

ARMED

tribe, twelve thousand **a** for war. **Nu 31:5** 2502b
but we ourselves will be **a** ready **Nu 32:17** 2502b
and all of you **a** men cross over **Nu 32:21** 2502b
everyone who is **a** for war, **Nu 32:27** 2502b
everyone who is **a** for battle, **Nu 32:29** 2502b
will not cross over with you **a**, **Nu 32:30** 2502b
"We ourselves will cross over **a** **Nu 32:32** 2502b
cross over **a** before your brothers, **Dt 3:18** 2502b
and let the **a** men go on before the **Jos 6:7** 2502b
The **a** men went before the **Jos 6:9** 2502b
and the **a** men went before them and **Jos 6:13** 2502b
men **a** with weapons of war set out. **Jg 18:11** 2296
men **a** with their weapons of war, **Jg 18:16** 2296
hundred men **a** with weapons of war. **Jg 18:17** 2296
gathered their **a** camps for war, **1Sa 28:1**
Must be **a** with iron and the shaft of **2Sa 23:7** 4390
him 200,000 **a** with bow and shield; **2Ch 17:17** 5401b
So the **a** men left the captives and **2Ch 28:14** 2502b
And your need like an **a** man. **Pr 6:11** 4043
And your want like an **a** man. **Pr 24:34** 4043
the **a** men of Moab cry aloud; **Is 15:4** 2502b
"When a strong *man*, fully **a**, **Lk 11:21** *2528*

ARMIES

shall number them by their **a**. **Nu 1:3** 6635
standard, according to their **a**. **Nu 1:52** 6635
of the camp of Judah, by their **a**, **Nu 2:3** 6635
186,400, by their **a**. **Nu 2:9** 6635
of the camp of Reuben by their **a**, **Nu 2:10** 6635
151,450 by their **a**. **Nu 2:16** 6635
of the camp of Ephraim by their **a**, **Nu 2:18** 6635
108,100, by their **a**. **Nu 2:24** 6635
of the camp of Dan by their **a**, **Nu 2:25** 6635
men of the camps by their **a**, **Nu 2:32** 6635
of Judah, according to their **a**, **Nu 10:14** 6635
of Reuben, according to their **a**, **Nu 10:18** 6635
of Ephraim, according to their **a**, **Nu 10:22** 6635
sons of Dan, according to their **a**, **Nu 10:25** 6635
Israel by their **a** as they set out. **Nu 10:28** 6635
from the land of Egypt by their **a**, **Nu 33:1** 6635
of **a** at the head of the people. **Dt 20:9** 6635
went up, they with all their **a**, **Jos 10:5** 4264
they and all their **a** with them, **Jos 11:4** 4264
in Karkor, and their **a** with them, **Jg 8:10** 4264
gathered their **a** for battle; **1Sa 17:1** 4264
a champion came out from the **a** of **1Sa 17:4** 4264
taunt the **a** of the living God?" **1Sa 17:26** 4634
taunted the **a** of the living God." **1Sa 17:36** 4634
hosts, the God of the **a** of Israel, **1Sa 17:45** 4634
together all their **a** to Aphek, **1Sa 29:1** 4264
two commanders of the **a** of Israel, **1Ki 2:5** 6635
a against the cities of Israel, **1Ki 15:20** 2428
Now the mighty men of the **a** *were* **1Ch 11:26** 2428
a against the cities of Israel, **2Ch 16:4** 2428
And do not go out with our **a**. **Ps 44:9** 6635
will You not go forth with our **a**, **Ps 60:10** 6635
"Kings of **a** flee, they flee, And **Ps 68:12** 6635
will You not go forth with our **a**, **Ps 108:11** 6635
And *His* wrath against all their **a**; **Is 34:2** 6635
king was enraged, and he sent his **a** **Mt 22:7** *4753*
you see Jerusalem surrounded by **a**, **Lk 21:20** *4760*
in war, put foreign **a** to flight. **Heb 11:34** *3925b*
The number of the **a** of the **Rv 9:16** *4753*
And the **a** which are in heaven, **Rv 19:14** *4753*
kings of the earth and their **a** assembled **Rv 19:19** *4753*

ARMLETS

articles of gold, **a** and bracelets, **Nu 31:50** 685

ARMONI

A and Mephibosheth whom she had **2Sa 21:8** 764

ARMOR

to the young man, his **a** bearer, **Jg 9:54** 3627
young man who was carrying his **a**, **1Sa 14:1** 3627
young man who was carrying his **a**, **1Sa 14:6** 3627
His **a** bearer said to him, **1Sa 14:7** 3627
and his **a** bearer and said, **1Sa 14:12** 3627
And Jonathan said to his **a** bearer, **1Sa 14:12** 3627
with his **a** bearer behind him; **1Sa 14:13** 3627
and his **a** bearer put some to death **1Sa 14:13** 3627
which Jonathan and his **a** bearer **1Sa 14:14** 3627
and his **a** bearer were not *there*. **1Sa 14:17** 3627
and he became his **a** bearer. **1Sa 16:21** 3627
head, and he clothed him with **a**. **1Sa 17:38** 8302
over his **a** and tried to walk, **1Sa 17:39** 4055
and gave it to David, with his **a**, **1Sa 18:4** 4055
Then Saul said to his **a** bearer, **1Sa 31:4** 3627
But his **a** bearer would not, for he **1Sa 31:4** 3627
a bearer saw that Saul was dead, **1Sa 31:5** 3627
with his three sons, his **a** bearer, **1Sa 31:6** 3627
ten young men who carried Joab's **a** **2Sa 18:15** 3627
a bearers of Joab the son of **2Sa 23:37** 3627
'Let not him who girds on *his* **a** **1Ki 20:11** 3627
of Israel in a joint of the **a**. **1Ki 22:34** 8302
put on **a** and older were summoned and **2Ki 3:21** 2290b
his **a** and all that was found in his **2Ki 20:13** 3627
Then Saul said to his **a** bearer, **1Ch 10:4** 3627
But his **a** bearer would not, for he **1Ch 10:4** 3627
a bearer saw that Saul was dead, **1Ch 10:5** 3627
and took his head and his **a** and sent **1Ch 10:9** 3627
They put his **a** in the house of **1Ch 10:10** 3627
the **a** bearer of Joab the son of **1Ch 11:39** 3627
of Israel in a joint of the **a**. **2Ch 18:33** 8302
shields, spears, helmets, body **a**, **2Ch 26:14** 8302
"Who can strip off his outer **a**? **Jb 41:13** 3830
all his **a** on which he had relied and **Lk 11:22** *3833*
and put on the **a** of light. **Ro 13:12** *3696*
Put on the full **a** of God, so that you **Eph 6:11** *3833*
take up the full **a** of God, **Eph 6:13** *3833*

ARMORY

the ascent of the **a** at the Angle. **Ne 3:19** 5402
and the precious oil and his whole **a** **Is 39:2** 1004, 3627
The LORD has opened His **a** And has **Jer 50:25** 214

ARMPITS

under your **a** under the ropes"; **Jer 38:12** 679, 3027

ARMS

I gave my maid into your **a**, **Gn 16:5** 2436
firm, And his **a** were agile, **Gn 49:24** 2220
underneath are the everlasting **a**; **Dt 33:27** 2220
ropes that were on his **a** were as flax **Jg 15:14** 2220
ropes from his **a** like a thread. **Jg 16:12** 2220
my **a** can bend a bow of bronze. **2Sa 22:35** 2220
and **a** on each side of the seat, **1Ki 10:19** 3027
two lions standing beside the **a**. **1Ki 10:19** 3027
and shot Joram between his **a**; **2Ki 9:24** 2220
and **a** on each side of the seat, **2Ch 9:18** 3027
two lions standing beside the **a**. **2Ch 9:18** 3027
and stopped them by force of **a**. **Ezr 4:23** 2429
my **a** can bend a bow of bronze. **Ps 18:34** 2220
a of the wicked will be broken, **Ps 37:17** 2220
strength And makes her **a** strong. **Pr 31:17** 2220
And My **a** will judge the peoples; **Is 51:5** 2220
will be carried in the **a**. **Is 60:4** 6654
and I will tear them from your **a**; **Ezk 13:20** 2220
of Egypt and will break his **a**, **Ezk 30:22** 2220
'For I will strengthen the **a** of **Ezk 30:24** 2220
and I will break the **a** of Pharaoh, **Ezk 30:24** 2220
the **a** of the king of Babylon, **Ezk 30:25** 2220
but the **a** of Pharaoh will fall. **Ezk 30:25** 2220
its breast and its **a** of silver, **Da 2:32** 1872
his **a** and feet like the gleam of **Da 10:6** 2220
trained *and* strengthened their **a**, **Hos 7:15** 2220
to walk, I took them in My **a**; **Hos 11:3** 2220
are these wounds between your **a**?' **Zch 13:6** 3027
them, and taking him in His **a**, **Mk 9:36** *1723*
in His **a** and *began* blessing them, **Mk 10:16** *1723*
then he took Him into his **a**, **Lk 2:28** *43*

ARMY

Phicol, the commander of his **a**, **Gn 21:22** 6635
Phicol, the commander of his **a**, **Gn 21:32** 6635
and Phicol the commander of his **a**. **Gn 26:26** 6635
through Pharaoh and all his **a**, **Ex 14:4** 2428
Pharaoh, his horsemen and his **a**, **Ex 14:9** 2428
through Pharaoh and all his **a**, **Ex 14:17** 2428
the LORD looked down on the **a** of **Ex 14:24** 4264
the **a** of the Egyptians into confusion. **Ex 14:24** 4264
even Pharaoh's entire **a** that had **Ex 14:28** 2428
his **a** He has cast into the sea; **Ex 15:4** 2428
and his **a**, even their numbered **Nu 2:4** 6635
and his **a**, even their numbered **Nu 2:6** 6635
and his **a**, even his numbered men, **Nu 2:8** 6635
and his **a**, even their numbered **Nu 2:11** 6635
and his **a**, even their numbered **Nu 2:13** 6635
and his **a**, even their numbered **Nu 2:15** 6635
and his **a**, even their numbered **Nu 2:19** 6635
and his **a**, even their numbered **Nu 2:21** 6635
and his **a**, even their numbered **Nu 2:23** 6635
and his **a**, even their numbered **Nu 2:26** 6635
and his **a**, even their numbered **Nu 2:28** 6635
and his **a**, even their numbered **Nu 2:30** 6635
the son of Amminadab, over its **a**, **Nu 10:14** 6635
tribal **a** of the sons of Issachar; **Nu 10:15** 6635
tribal **a** of the sons of Zebulun. **Nu 10:16** 6635
the son of Shedeur, over its **a**, **Nu 10:18** 6635
tribal **a** of the sons of Simeon, **Nu 10:19** 6635
the tribal **a** of the sons of Gad. **Nu 10:20** 6635
the son of Ammihud over its **a**, **Nu 10:22** 6635
tribal **a** of the sons of Manasseh; **Nu 10:23** 6635
tribal **a** of the sons of Benjamin. **Nu 10:24** 6635
the son of Ammishaddai over its **a**, **Nu 10:25** 6635
the tribal **a** of the sons of Asher; **Nu 10:26** 6635
tribal **a** of the sons of Naphtali. **Nu 10:27** 6635
angry with the officers of the **a**, **Nu 31:14** 2428
were over the thousands of the **a**, **Nu 31:48** 6635
and what He did to Egypt's **a**, **Dt 11:4** 2428
out as an **a** against your enemies, **Dt 23:9** 4264
he shall not go out with the **a** nor **Dt 24:5** 6635
all the **a** that was on the north **Jos 8:13** 4264
the commander of his **a** was Sisera, **Jg 4:2** 6635
Sisera, the commander of Jabin's **a**, **Jg 4:7** 6635
all *his* chariots and all *his* **a** with **Jg 4:15** 4264
the **a** as far as Harosheth-hagoyim, **Jg 4:16** 4264
and all the **a** of Sisera fell by **Jg 4:16** 4264
of the **a** that was in the camp. **Jg 7:11** 2571
and all the **a** ran, crying out as **Jg 7:21** 4264
even throughout the whole **a**; **Jg 7:22** 4264
and the **a** fled as far as **Jg 7:22** 4264
we should give bread to your **a**?" **Jg 8:6** 6635
entire **a** of the sons of the east; **Jg 8:10** 4264
Zalmunna, and routed the whole **a**. **Jg 8:12** 4264
"Increase your **a** and come out." **Jg 9:29** 6635
Sisera, captain of the **a** of Hazor, **1Sa 12:9** 6635
of his **a** was Abner the son of Ner, **1Sa 14:50** 6635
the **a** was going out in battle array **1Sa 17:20** 2428
in battle array, **a** against army. **1Sa 17:21** 4634
in battle array, army against **a**. **1Sa 17:21** 4634
up from the **a** of the Philistines, **1Sa 17:23** 4634
dead bodies of the **a** of the Philistines **1Sa 17:46** 4264
to Abner the commander of the **a**, **1Sa 17:55** 6635
of Ner, the commander of his **a**; **1Sa 26:5** 6635
LORD will give over the **a** of Israel **1Sa 28:19** 4264
in the **a** are pleasing in my sight; **1Sa 29:6** 4264
son of Ner, commander of Saul's **a**, **2Sa 2:8** 6635
the **a** that was with him arrived, **2Sa 3:23** 6635
strike the **a** of the Philistines." **2Sa 5:24** 4264
defeated all the **a** of Hadadezer, **2Sa 8:9** 2428
the son of Zeruiah *was* over the **a**, **2Sa 8:16** 6635
of it, he sent Joab and all the **a**, **2Sa 10:7** 6635
of the **a** of Hadadezer led them. **2Sa 10:16** 6635
Shobach the commander of their **a**, **2Sa 10:18** 6635
Amasa over the **a** in place of Joab. **2Sa 17:25** 6635
not be commander of the **a** before me **2Sa 19:13** 6635
was over the whole **a** of Israel, **2Sa 20:23** 6635
of the **a** who was with him, **2Sa 24:2** 2428
against the commanders of the **a**. **2Sa 24:4** 2428
Joab and the commanders of the **a** **2Sa 24:4** 2428
and Joab the commander of the **a**, **1Ki 1:19** 6635
of the **a** and Abiathar the priest, **1Ki 1:25** 6635
Ner, commander of the **a** of Israel, **1Ki 2:32** 6635
commander of the **a** of Judah. **1Ki 2:32** 6635
Jehoiada over the **a** in his place, **1Ki 2:35** 6635
son of Jehoiada *was* over the **a**; **1Ki 4:4** 6635
a had gone up to bury the slain, **1Ki 11:15** 6635
the commander of the **a** was dead, **1Ki 11:21** 6635
made Omri, the commander of the **a**, **1Ki 16:16** 6635
king of Aram gathered all his **a**, **1Ki 20:1** 2428
and the **a** which followed them. **1Ki 20:19** 2428
and muster an **a** like the army that **1Ki 20:25** 2428
like the **a** that you have lost, **1Ki 20:25** 2428
throughout the **a** close to sunset, **1Ki 22:36** 4264
and there was no water for the **a** **2Ki 3:9** 4264
or to the captain of the **a**?' " **2Ki 4:13** 6635
of the **a** of the king of Aram, **2Ki 5:1** 6635
and chariots and a great **a** there, **2Ki 6:14** 2428
an **a** with horses and chariots was **2Ki 6:15** 2428
king of Aram gathered all his **a** **2Ki 6:24** 4264
For the Lord had caused the **a** of **2Ki 7:6** 4264
even the sound of a great **a**, **2Ki 7:6** 2428
sent after the **a** of the Arameans, **2Ki 7:14** 4264
but *his* **a** fled to their tents. **2Ki 8:21** 5971a
captains of the **a** were sitting, **2Ki 9:5** 2428
who were appointed over the **a** and **2Ki 11:15** 2428
For he left to Jehoahaz of the **a** **2Ki 13:7** 5971a
with a large **a** to Jerusalem. **2Ki 18:17** 2428
of Babylon came, he and all his **a**, **2Ki 25:1** 2428
But the **a** of the Chaldeans pursued **2Ki 25:5** 2428
all his **a** was scattered from him. **2Ki 25:5** 2428
So all the **a** of the Chaldeans who **2Ki 25:10** 2428
scribe of the captain of the **a** who **2Ki 25:19** 6635
36,000 troops of the **a** for war, **1Ch 7:4** 6635
ready to go out with the **a** to war. **1Ch 7:11** 6635
while the **a** of the Philistines was **1Ch 11:15** 4264
of Gad were captains of the **a**; **1Ch 12:14** 6635
valor, and were captains in the **a**. **1Ch 12:21** 6635
a great **a** like the army of God. **1Ch 12:22** 4264
a great army like the **a** of God. **1Ch 12:22** 4264
were 50,000 who went out in the **a**, **1Ch 12:33** 6635
40,000 who went out in the **a** to **1Ch 12:36** 6635
strike the **a** of the Philistines." **1Ch 14:15** 4264
and they struck down the **a** of the **1Ch 14:16** 4264
the **a** of Hadadezer king of Zobah, **1Ch 18:9** 2428
the son of Zeruiah *was* over the **a**, **1Ch 18:15** 6635
of it, he sent Joab and all the **a**, **1Ch 19:8** 6635
the **a** of Hadadezer leading them. **1Ch 19:16** 6635
Shophach the commander of the **a**. **1Ch 19:18** 6635
that Joab led out the **a** and **1Ch 20:1** 6635, 2428
David and the commanders of the **a** **1Ch 25:1** 6635
hundreds, and the commanders of the **a**, **1Ch 26:26** 6635
of the **a** for the first month. **1Ch 27:3** 6635
The third commander of the **a** for **1Ch 27:5** 6635
was the commander of the king's **a**. **1Ch 27:34** 6635
with an **a** of valiant warriors, **2Ch 13:3** 2428
had an **a** of 300,000 from Judah, **2Ch 14:8** 2428
came out against them with an **a** of **2Ch 14:9** 2428
before the LORD and before His **a**. **2Ch 14:13** 4264
therefore the **a** of the king of **2Ch 16:7** 2428
and the Lubim an immense **a** with **2Ch 16:8** 2428
went out before the **a** and said, **2Ch 20:21** 2502b
who were appointed over the **a** and **2Ch 23:14** 2428
a of the Arameans came up against **2Ch 24:23** 2428
Indeed the **a** of the Arameans came **2Ch 24:24** 2428
a very great **a** into their hands, **2Ch 24:24** 2428
let the **a** of Israel go with you, **2Ch 25:7** 6635
Uzziah had an **a** ready for battle, **2Ch 26:11** 2428
was an elite **a** of 307,500, **2Ch 26:13** 2428
prepared for all the **a** shields, **2Ch 26:14** 6635
and he went out to meet the **a** **2Ch 28:9** 6635
the commanders of the **a** of the king **2Ch 33:11** 6635

Then he put **a** commanders in all **2Ch 33:14** 2428
me officers of the **a** and horsemen. **Ne 2:9** 2428
a *officers* of Persia and Media, **Es 1:3** 2428
and to annihilate the entire **a** of **Es 8:11** 2428
king is not saved by a mighty **a**; **Ps 33:16** 2428
Pharaoh and his **a** in the Red Sea, **Ps 136:15** 2428
And a king *when his* **a** is with him. **Pr 30:31** 510
As awesome as an **a** with banners. **SS 6:4** 1713b
As awesome as an **a** with banners?' **SS 6:10** 1713b
is mustering the **a** for battle. **Is 13:4** 6635
to King Hezekiah with a large **a**. **Is 36:2** 2428
horse, The **a** and the mighty man **Is 43:17** 2428
Now at that time the **a** of the king **Jer 32:2** 2428
king of Babylon and all his **a**, **Jer 34:1** 2428
when the **a** of the king of Babylon **Jer 34:7** 2428
and into the hand of the **a** of the **Jer 34:21** 2428
let us go to Jerusalem before the **a** of **Jer 35:11** 2428
and before the **a** of the Arameans.' **Jer 35:11** 2428
Pharaoh's **a** had set out from Egypt; **Jer 37:5** 2428
Pharaoh's **a** which has come out for **Jer 37:7** 2428
defeated the entire **a** of Chaldeans **Jer 37:10** 2428
when the **a** of the Chaldeans had **Jer 37:11** 2428
Jerusalem because of Pharaoh's **a**, **Jer 37:11** 2428
of the **a** of the king of Babylon and **Jer 38:3** 2428
king of Babylon and all his **a** came to **Jer 39:1** 2428
But the **a** of the Chaldeans pursued **Jer 39:5** 2428
a of Pharaoh Neco king of Egypt, **Jer 46:2** 2428
For they move on like an **a** And **Jer 46:22** 2428
Devote all her **a** to destruction. **Jer 51:3** 6635
of Babylon came, he and all his **a**, **Jer 52:4** 2428
But the **a** of the Chaldeans pursued **Jer 52:8** 2428
all his **a** was scattered from him. **Jer 52:8** 2428
So all the **a** of the Chaldeans who **Jer 52:14** 2428
the scribe of the commander of the **a** **Jer 52:25** 6635
like the sound of an **a** camp; **Ezk 1:24** 4264
'Pharaoh with *his* mighty **a** and **Ezk 17:17** 2428
chariots, cavalry and a great **a**. **Ezk 26:7**
5971a, 6951
and Lud and Put were in your **a**, **Ezk 27:10** 2428
and your **a** were on your walls, **Ezk 27:11** 2428
his **a** labor hard against Tyre; **Ezk 29:18** 2428
But he and his **a** had no wages from **Ezk 29:18** 2428
and it will be wages for his **a**. **Ezk 29:19** 2428
even Pharaoh and all his **a**," **Ezk 32:31** 2428
feet, an exceedingly great **a**. **Ezk 37:10** 2428
bring you out, and all your **a**, **Ezk 38:4** 2428
a great assembly and a mighty **a**; **Ezk 38:15** 2428
were in his **a** to tie up Shadrach, **Da 3:20** 2429
and he will come against *their* **a** **Da 11:7** 2428
with a great **a** and much equipment. **Da 11:13** 2428
king of the South with a large **a**; **Da 11:25** 2428
large and mighty **a** for war; **Da 11:25** 2428
him, and his **a** will overflow, **Da 11:26** 2428
utters His voice before His **a**; **Jl 2:11** 2428
"But I will remove the northern **a** **Jl 2:20**
My great **a** which I sent among you. **Jl 2:25** 2428
around My house because of an **a**, **Zch 9:8** 4675
on the horse and against His **a**. **Rv 19:19** *4753*

ARNAN
sons of Rephaiah, the sons of **A**, **1Ch 3:21** 770

ARNON
camped on the other side of the **A**, **Nu 21:13** 769
for the **A** is the border of Moab, **Nu 21:13** 769
in Suphah, And the wadis of the **A**, **Nu 21:14** 769
his land from the **A** to the Jabbok, **Nu 21:24** 769
out of his hand, as far as the **A**. **Nu 21:26** 769
The dominant heights of the **A**, **Nu 21:28** 769
of Moab, which is on the **A** border, **Nu 22:36** 769
and pass through the valley of **A**. **Dt 2:24** 769
is on the edge of the valley of **A**, **Dt 2:36** 769
the valley of **A** to Mount Hermon **Dt 3:8** 769
which is by the valley of **A**, **Dt 3:12** 769
even as far as the valley of **A**, **Dt 3:16** 769
is on the edge of the valley of **A**, **Dt 4:48** 769
of the **A** as far as Mount Hermon, **Jos 12:1** 769
the edge of the valley of the **A**, **Jos 12:2** 769
the edge of the valley of the **A**, **Jos 13:9** 769
the edge of the valley of the **A**, **Jos 13:16** 769
from the **A** as far as the Jabbok **Jg 11:13** 769
and they camped beyond the **A**; **Jg 11:18** 769
for the **A** *was* the border of Moab. **Jg 11:18** 769
from the **A** as far as the Jabbok, **Jg 11:22** 769
that are on the banks of the **A**, **Jg 11:26** 769
which is by the valley of the **A**, **2Ki 10:33** 769
will be at the fords of the **A**. **Is 16:2** 769
A That Moab has been destroyed. **Jer 48:20** 769

AROD
of **A**, the family of the Arodites; **Nu 26:17** 720

ARODI
and Ezbon, Eri and **A** and Areli. **Gn 46:16** 722

ARODITES
of Arod, the family of the **A**; **Nu 26:17** 722

AROER
Gad built Dibon and Ataroth and **A**, **Nu 32:34** 6177
"From **A** which is on the edge of **Dt 2:36** 6177
From **A**, which is by the valley of **Dt 3:12** 6177
from **A**, which is on the edge of **Dt 4:48** 6177
in Heshbon, *and* ruled from **A**, **Jos 12:2** 6177
from **A**, which is on the edge of **Jos 13:9** 6177
Their territory was from **A**, **Jos 13:16** 6177
far as **A** which is before Rabbah; **Jos 13:25** 6177
and in **A** and its villages, **Jg 11:26** 6177
from **A** to the entrance of Minnith, **Jg 11:33** 6177
and to those who were in **A**, **1Sa 30:28** 6177
the Jordan and camped in **A**, **2Sa 24:5** 6177
and the Manassites, from **A**, **2Ki 10:33** 6177
the son of Joel, who lived in **A**, **1Ch 5:8** 6177
"The cities of **A** are forsaken; **Is 17:2** 6177
and keep watch, O inhabitant of **A**; **Jer 48:19** 6177

AROERITE
Jeiel the sons of Hotham the **A**, **1Ch 11:44** 6200

AROMA
The LORD smelled the soothing **a**; **Gn 8:21** 7381b
it is a soothing **a**, **Ex 29:18** 7381b
for a soothing **a** before the LORD; **Ex 29:25** 7381b
as in the morning, for a soothing **a**, **Ex 29:41** 7381b
fire of a soothing **a** to the LORD. **Lv 1:9** 7381b
fire of a soothing **a** to the LORD. **Lv 1:13** 7381b
fire of a soothing **a** to the LORD. **Lv 1:17** 7381b
fire of a soothing **a** to the LORD. **Lv 2:2** 7381b
fire of a soothing **a** to the LORD. **Lv 2:9** 7381b
for a soothing **a** on the altar. **Lv 2:12** 7381b
fire of a soothing **a** to the LORD. **Lv 3:5** 7381b
offering by fire for a soothing **a**; **Lv 3:16** 7381b
for a soothing **a** to the LORD. **Lv 4:31** 7381b
smoke on the altar, a soothing **a**, **Lv 6:15** 7381b
as a soothing **a** to the LORD. **Lv 6:21** 7381b
a burnt offering for a soothing **a**; **Lv 8:21** 7381b
offering for a soothing **a**; **Lv 8:28** 7381b
smoke as a soothing **a** to the LORD. **Lv 17:6** 7381b
fire to the LORD *for* a soothing **a**, **Lv 23:13** 7381b
fire of a soothing **a** to the LORD. **Lv 23:18** 7381b
to make a soothing **a** to the LORD, **Nu 15:3** 7381b
wine as a soothing **a** to the LORD. **Nu 15:7** 7381b
fire, as a soothing **a** to the LORD. **Nu 15:10** 7381b
fire, as a soothing **a** to the LORD. **Nu 15:13** 7381b
fire, as a soothing **a** to the LORD, **Nu 15:14** 7381b
as a soothing **a** to the LORD, **Nu 15:24** 7381b
for a soothing **a** to the LORD. **Nu 18:17** 7381b
by fire, of a soothing **a** to Me, **Nu 28:2** 7381b
in Mount Sinai as a soothing **a**, **Nu 28:6** 7381b
by fire, a soothing **a** to the LORD. **Nu 28:8** 7381b
a burnt offering of a soothing **a**, **Nu 28:13** 7381b
fire, of a soothing **a** to the LORD; **Nu 28:24** 7381b
for a soothing **a** to the LORD: **Nu 28:27** 7381b
as a soothing **a** to the LORD: **Nu 29:2** 7381b
their ordinance, for a soothing **a**, **Nu 29:6** 7381b
to the LORD *as* a soothing **a**: **Nu 29:8** 7381b
fire as a soothing **a** to the LORD: **Nu 29:13** 7381b
fire as a soothing **a** to the LORD: **Nu 29:36** 7381b
flavor, And his **a** has not changed. **Jer 48:11** 7381b
soothing **a** to all their idols. **Ezk 6:13** 7381b
before them for a soothing **a**; **Ezk 16:19** 7381b
also they made their soothing **a** and **Ezk 20:28** 7381b
a soothing **a** I will accept you **Ezk 20:41** 7381b
the sweet **a** of the knowledge of Him **2Co 2:14** *3744*
the one an **a** from death to death, **2Co 2:16** *3744*
the other an **a** from life to life. **2Co 2:16** *3744*
sacrifice to God as a fragrant **a**. **Eph 5:2** *3744*
what you have sent, a fragrant **a**, **Php 4:18** *3744*

AROMAS
I will not smell your soothing **a**. **Lv 26:31** 7381b

AROMATIC
bearing **a** gum and balm and myrrh, **Gn 37:25** 5219
a little honey, **a** gum and myrrh, **Gn 43:11** 5219

AROSE
Now Abraham **a** early in the morning **Gn 19:27** 7925
when she lay down or when she **a**. **Gn 19:33** 6965
the younger **a** and lay with him; **Gn 19:35** 6965
when she lay down or when she **a**. **Gn 19:35** 6965
So Abimelech **a** early in the **Gn 20:8** 7925
a and returned to the land of the **Gn 21:32** 6965
and **a** and went to the place of **Gn 22:3** 6965
and they **a** and went together to **Gn 22:19** 6965
and he **a** and went to Mesopotamia, **Gn 24:10** 6965
When they **a** in the morning, he **Gn 24:54** 6965
Then Rebekah **a** with her maids, and **Gn 24:61** 6965
they **a** early and exchanged oaths; **Gn 26:31** 7925
Then Jacob **a** and put his children **Gn 31:17** 6965
and he **a** and crossed the *Euphrates* **Gn 31:21** 6965
Early in the morning Laban **a**, **Gn 31:55** 7925
Now he **a** that same night and took **Gn 32:22** 6965
his daughters **a** to comfort him, **Gn 37:35** 6965
Then she **a** and departed, and **Gn 38:19** 6965
then they **a** and went down to Egypt **Gn 43:15** 6965
Then Jacob **a** from Beersheba; **Gn 46:5** 6965
Now a new king **a** over Egypt, who **Ex 1:8** 6965
Pharaoh **a** in the night, he and **Ex 12:30** 6965
Then he **a** early in the morning, **Ex 24:4** 7925
Moses **a** with Joshua his servant, **Ex 24:13** 6965
a and went to Dathan and Abiram, **Nu 16:25** 6965
So Balaam **a** in the morning and **Nu 22:13** 6965
of Moab **a** and went to Balak and **Nu 22:14** 6965
So Balaam **a** in the morning, and **Nu 22:21** 6965
Then Balaam **a** and departed and **Nu 24:25** 6965
he **a** from the midst of the **Nu 25:7** 6965
So Joshua **a** early in the morning **Jos 7:16** 7925
Then the men **a** and went, and **Jos 18:8** 6965
Moab, **a** and fought against Israel, **Jos 24:9** 6965
and there **a** another generation **Jg 2:10** 6965
And he **a** from his seat. **Jg 3:20** 6965
a and went with Barak to Kedesh. **Jg 4:9** 6965
in Israel, Until I, Deborah, **a**, **Jg 5:7** 6965
I, Deborah, arose, Until I **a**, **Jg 5:7** 6965
the city **a** early in the morning, **Jg 6:28** 7925
When he **a** early the next morning **Jg 6:38** 7925
a and killed Zebah and Zalmunna, **Jg 8:21** 6965
people who *were* with him **a** by night **Jg 9:34** 6965
were with him **a** from the ambush. **Jg 9:35** 6965
he **a** against them and slew them. **Jg 9:43** 6965
man of Issachar, **a** to save Israel; **Jg 10:1** 6965
After him, Jair the Gileadite **a** **Jg 10:3** 6965
Manoah **a** and followed his wife, **Jg 13:11** 6965
and at midnight he **a** and took hold **Jg 16:3** 6965
Then her husband **a** and went after **Jg 19:3** 6965
Then the man **a** to go, but his **Jg 19:7** 6965
he **a** to go early in the morning, **Jg 19:8** 7925
When the man **a** to go along with **Jg 19:9** 6965
so he **a** and departed and came to *a* **Jg 19:10** 6965
When her master **a** in the morning **Jg 19:27** 6965
the man **a** and went to his home. **Jg 19:28** 6965
Then all the people **a** as one man, **Jg 20:8** 6965
Now the sons of Israel **a**, **Jg 20:18** 6965
So the sons of Israel **a** in the **Jg 20:19** 6965
Then all the men of Israel **a** from **Jg 20:33** 6965
the people **a** early and built an altar **Jg 21:4** 7925
Then she **a** with her **Ru 1:6** 6965
Then they **a** early in the morning **1Sa 1:19** 7925
So Samuel **a** and went to Eli and **1Sa 3:6** 6965
And he **a** and went to Eli and **1Sa 3:8** 6965
a early the next morning, **1Sa 5:3** 7925
they **a** early the next morning, **1Sa 5:4** 7925
And they **a** early; **1Sa 9:26** 7925
So Saul **a**, and both he and Samuel **1Sa 9:26** 6965
Then Samuel **a** and went up from **1Sa 13:15** 6965
And Samuel **a** and went to Ramah. **1Sa 16:13** 6965
So David **a** early in the morning **1Sa 17:20** 7925
The men of Israel and Judah **a** **1Sa 17:52** 6965
Then Jonathan **a** from the table in **1Sa 20:34** 6965
a and fled that day from Saul, **1Sa 21:10** 6965
a and departed from Keilah, **1Sa 23:13** 6965
a and went to David at Horesh, **1Sa 23:16** 6965
a and went to Ziph before Saul. **1Sa 23:24** 6965
Then David **a** and cut off the edge **1Sa 24:4** 6965
And Saul **a**, left the cave, and **1Sa 24:7** 6965
Now afterward David **a** and went out **1Sa 24:8** 6965
And David **a** and went down to the **1Sa 25:1** 6965
She **a** and bowed with her face **1Sa 25:41** 6965
Then Abigail quickly **a**, **1Sa 25:42** 6965
So Saul **a** and went down to the **1Sa 26:2** 6965
David then **a** and came to the place **1Sa 26:5** 6965
So David **a** and crossed over, he **1Sa 27:2** 6965
So he **a** from the ground and sat on **1Sa 28:23** 6965
they **a** and went away that night. **1Sa 28:25** 6965
So David **a** early, he and his men, **1Sa 29:11** 7925
So they **a** and went over by count, **2Sa 2:15** 6965
And David **a** and went with all the **2Sa 6:2** 6965
Now when evening came David **a** from **2Sa 11:2** 6965
So David **a** from the ground, **2Sa 12:20** 6965
child died, you **a** and ate food." **2Sa 12:21** 6965
Then all the king's sons **a** and **2Sa 13:29** 6965
Then the king **a**, tore his clothes **2Sa 13:31** 6965
So Joab **a** and went to Geshur and **2Sa 14:23** 6965
Then Joab **a**, came to Absalom at **2Sa 14:31** 6965
So he **a** and went to Hebron. **2Sa 15:9** 6965
with him **a** and crossed the Jordan; **2Sa 17:22** 6965
donkey and **a** and went to his home, **2Sa 17:23** 6965
So the king **a** and sat in the gate. **2Sa 19:8** 6965
He **a** and struck the Philistines **2Sa 23:10** 6965
When David **a** in the morning, the **2Sa 24:11** 6965
they **a** and each went on his way. **1Ki 1:49** 6965
was afraid of Solomon, and he **a**, **1Ki 1:50** 6965
And the king **a** to meet her, bowed **1Ki 2:19** 6965
Shimei **a** and saddled his donkey, **1Ki 2:40** 6965
"So she **a** in the middle of the **1Ki 3:20** 6965
he **a** from before the altar of the **1Ki 8:54** 6965
a from Midian and came to Paran; **1Ki 11:18** 6965
but Jeroboam **a** and fled to Egypt **1Ki 11:40** 6965
did so, and **a** and went to Shiloh, **1Ki 14:4** 6965
Then Jeroboam's wife **a** and **1Ki 14:17** 6965
So he **a** and went to Zarephath, and **1Ki 17:10** 6965
And he was afraid and **a** and ran **1Ki 19:3** 6965
So he **a** and ate and drank, and **1Ki 19:8** 6965
Then he **a** and followed Elijah and **1Ki 19:21** 6965
Ahab **a** to go down to the **1Ki 21:16** 6965
So he **a** and went down with him to **2Ki 1:15** 6965
a and struck the Moabites, **2Ki 3:24** 6965
And he **a** and followed her. **2Ki 4:30** 6965
They **a** at twilight to go to **2Ki 7:5** 6965
they **a** and fled in the twilight, **2Ki 7:7** 6965
Then the king **a** in the night and **2Ki 7:12** 6965
So the woman **a** and did according **2Ki 8:2** 6965
And he **a** by night and **2Ki 8:21** 6965
He **a** and went into the house, **2Ki 9:6** 6965
Then he **a** and departed and went **2Ki 10:12** 6965
servants **a** and made a conspiracy and **2Ki 12:20** 6965
of the forces **a** and went to Egypt; **2Ki 25:26** 6965
all the valiant men **a** and took **1Ch 10:12** 6965
And he **a** by night and **2Ch 21:9** 6965
a against those who were coming **2Ch 28:12** 6965
men who were designated by name **a**, **2Ch 28:15** 6965
Then the Levites **a**: **2Ch 29:12** 6965
Then King Hezekiah **a** early and **2Ch 29:20** 7925
They **a** and removed the altars **2Ch 30:14** 6965
priests **a** and blessed the people; **2Ch 30:27** 6965
of the LORD **a** against His people, **2Ch 36:16** 5927
and the priests and the Levites **a**, **Ezr 1:5** 6965
and his brothers **a** and built the **Ezr 3:2** 6965
Jeshua the son of Jozadak **a** and **Ezr 5:2** 6966
offering I **a** from my humiliation, **Ezr 9:5** 6965
And I **a** in the night, I and a few **Ne 2:12** 6965
Then Eliashib the high priest **a** **Ne 3:1** 6965
a priest **a** with Urim and Thummim. **Ne 7:65** 5975
The king **a** in his anger from **Es 7:7** 6965
a and stood before the king. **Es 8:4** 6965
Then Job **a** and tore his robe and **Jb 1:20** 6965
And the old men **a** *and* stood. **Jb 29:8** 6965
When God **a** to judgment, To save **Ps 76:9** 6965
"I **a** to open to my beloved; **SS 5:5** 6965
when men **a** early in the morning, **Is 37:36** 7925
a and struck down Gedaliah the son **Jer 41:2** 6965
Then the king **a** at dawn, at **Da 6:19** 6966
and the four *horns that* **a** in its place **Da 8:22** 5975
I **a** to be an encouragement and a **Da 11:1** 5975
So Jonah **a** and went to Nineveh **Jon 3:3** 6965

of Nineveh, he **a** from his throne,	Jon 3:6	6965
there **a** a great storm on the sea,	Mt 8:24	*1096*
And there **a** a fierce gale of wind,	Mk 4:37	*1096*
Now at this time Mary **a** and went	Lk 1:39	*450*
And there **a** also a dispute among	Lk 22:24	*1096*
Therefore there **a** a discussion on	Jn 3:25	*1096*
a complaint **a** on the part of the	Ac 6:1	*1096*
until THERE A ANOTHER KING OVER	Ac 7:18	*450*
So Peter **a** and went with them.	Ac 9:39	*450*
with Him after He **a** from the dead.	Ac 10:41	*450*
a *single* outcry **a** from them all as	Ac 19:34	*1096*
for on the one hand the judgment **a**	Ro 5:16	
on the other hand the free gift **a**	Ro 5:16	
prophets also **a** among the people,	2Pe 2:1	*1096*

AROUND

flows **a** the whole land of Havilah,	Gn 2:11	5437
it flows **a** the whole land of Cush.	Gn 2:13	5437
upon the cities which were **a** them,	Gn 35:5	5439
a and bowed down to my sheaf."	Gn 37:7	5437
put the gold necklace **a** his neck.	Gn 41:42	5921
and when he saw there was no one **a**,	Ex 2:12	
dug **a** the Nile for water to drink,	Ex 7:24	5439
Hence God led the people **a** by the	Ex 13:18	5437
was a layer of dew **a** the camp.	Ex 16:13	5439
set bounds for the people all **a**,	Ex 19:12	5439
and walks **a** outside on his staff,	Ex 21:19	1980
shall make a gold molding **a** it.	Ex 25:11	5439
gold and make a gold border **a** it.	Ex 25:24	5439
it a rim of a handbreadth **a** *it;*	Ex 25:25	5439
a gold border for the rim **a** it.	Ex 25:25	5439
"All the pillars **a** the court	Ex 27:17	5439
a its opening there shall be a	Ex 28:32	5439
material, all **a** on its hem,	Ex 28:33	5439
bells of gold between them all **a**:	Ex 28:33	5439
all **a** on the hem of the robe.	Ex 28:34	5439
and sprinkle it **a** on the altar.	Ex 29:16	5439
rest of the blood **a** on the altar.	Ex 29:20	5439
gold, its top and its sides all **a**,	Ex 30:3	5439
make a gold molding all **a** for it.	Ex 30:3	5439
made a gold molding for it all **a**.	Ex 37:2	5439
made a gold molding for it all **a**.	Ex 37:11	5439
rim for it of a handbreadth all **a**,	Ex 37:12	5439
a gold molding for its rim all **a**.	Ex 37:12	5439
gold, its top and its sides all **a**,	Ex 37:26	5439
made a gold molding for it all **a**.	Ex 37:26	5439
all **a** *were* of fine twisted linen.	Ex 38:16	5439
of the court all **a** *were* of bronze.	Ex 38:20	5439
and the sockets of the court all **a** and	Ex 38:31	5439
all the pegs of the court all **a**.	Ex 38:31	5439
with a binding all **a** its opening,	Ex 39:23	5439
all **a** on the hem of the robe,	Ex 39:25	5439
all **a** on the hem of the robe for	Ex 39:26	5439
"You shall set up the court all **a**	Ex 40:8	5439
a the tabernacle and the altar,	Ex 40:33	5439
sprinkle the blood **a** on the altar	Lv 1:5	5439
sprinkle its blood **a** on the altar.	Lv 1:11	5439
sprinkle the blood **a** on the altar.	Lv 3:2	5439
sprinkle its blood **a** on the altar.	Lv 3:8	5439
sprinkle its blood **a** on the altar.	Lv 3:13	5439
sprinkle its blood **a** on the altar.	Lv 7:2	5439
of it **a** on the horns of the altar,	Lv 8:15	5439
the blood **a** on the altar.	Lv 8:19	5439
rest of the blood **a** on the altar.	Lv 8:24	5439
he sprinkled it **a** on the altar.	Lv 9:12	5439
he sprinkled it **a** on the altar.	Lv 9:18	5439
the house scraped all **a** inside,	Lv 14:41	5439
the pagan nations that are **a** you.	Lv 25:44	5439
shall also camp **a** the tabernacle.	Nu 1:50	5439
"But the Levites shall camp **a** the	Nu 1:53	5439
they shall camp **a** the tent of	Nu 2:2	5439
is **a** the tabernacle and the altar,	Nu 3:26	5439
and the pillars **a** the court with	Nu 3:37	5439
is **a** the tabernacle and the altar,	Nu 4:26	5439
and the pillars **a** the court and	Nu 4:32	5439
and stationed them **a** the tent.	Nu 11:24	5439
on the other side, all **a** the camp and	Nu 11:31	5439
out for themselves all **a** the camp.	Nu 11:32	5439
from **a** the dwellings of Korah,	Nu 16:24	5439
from **a** the dwellings of Korah,	Nu 16:27	5439
were **a** them fled at their outcry,	Nu 16:34	5439
Red Sea, to go **a** the land of Edom;	Nu 21:4	5437
will lick up all that is **a** us,	Nu 22:4	5439
to its borders all **a**.' "	Nu 34:12	5439
pasture lands **a** the cities.	Nu 35:2	5439
city outward a thousand cubits **a**.	Nu 35:4	5439
turn **a** and set out for the	Dt 1:40	
rest from all your enemies **a** *you* so	Dt 12:10	5439
gods of the peoples who are **a** you,	Dt 13:7	5439
like all the nations who are **a** me,'	Dt 17:14	5439
cities which are **a** the slain one.	Dt 21:2	5439
"You shall march **a** the city,	Jos 6:3	5437
march **a** the city seven times,	Jos 6:4	5437
"Go forward, and march **a** the city,	Jos 6:7	5437
ark of the LORD taken **a** the city,	Jos 6:11	5437
second day they marched **a** the city	Jos 6:14	5437
marched **a** the city in the same	Jos 6:15	5437
marched **a** the city seven times.	Jos 6:15	5437
This is the border **a** the sons of	Jos 15:12	5439
according to its borders all **a**.	Jos 18:20	5439
and all the villages which *were* **a**	Jos 19:8	5439
a it on the north to Hannathon,	Jos 19:14	5437
of the peoples who were **a** them,	Jg 2:12	5439
the hands of their enemies **a** *them,*	Jg 2:14	5439
blow the trumpets all **a** the camp and	Jg 7:18	5439
stood in his place **a** the camp;	Jg 7:21	5439
and **a** the land of Edom and the land	Jg 11:18	5437
who turned **a** and said to Micah,	Jg 18:23	6440
Israel set men in ambush **a** Gibeah.	Jg 20:29	5439
of Israel be brought **a** to Gath."	1Sa 5:8	5437
the ark of the God of Israel **a**.	1Sa 5:8	
After they had brought it **a**,	1Sa 5:9	5437
ark of the God of Israel **a** to us,	1Sa 5:10	5437
the hands of your enemies all **a**,	1Sa 12:11	5439
up with them all **a** in the camp,	1Sa 14:21	5439
his servants were standing **a** him.	1Sa 22:6	5921
to his servants who stood **a** him,	1Sa 22:7	5921
"Turn **a** and put the priests of	1Sa 22:17	5437
turn **a** and attack the priests."	1Sa 22:18	5437
turned **a** and attacked the priests,	1Sa 22:18	5437
and the people were camped **a** him.	1Sa 26:5	5439
and the people were lying **a** him.	1Sa 26:7	5439
all **a** from the Millo and inward.	2Sa 5:9	5439
circle **a** behind them and come at	2Sa 5:23	5437
walked **a** on the roof of the king's	2Sa 11:2	1980
gathered **a** and struck Absalom and	2Sa 18:15	5437
He made darkness canopies **a** Him,	2Sa 22:12	5439
came to Dan-jaan and **a** to Sidon,	2Sa 24:6	5439
the LORD and the wall **a** Jerusalem.	1Ki 3:1	5439
peace on all sides **a** about him.	1Ki 4:24	5439
walls of the house **a** both the nave	1Ki 6:5	5439
thus he made side chambers all **a**.	1Ki 6:5	5439
offsets *in the wall* of the house all **a**	1Ki 6:6	5439
So the great court all **a** *had* three	1Ki 7:12	5439
and two rows **a** on the one network	1Ki 7:18	5439
hundred in rows **a** both capitals.	1Ki 7:20	5439
a encircling it ten to a cubit,	1Ki 7:24	5439
space on each, with wreaths *all* **a**.	1Ki 7:36	5439
and he made a trench **a** the altar,	1Ki 18:32	5439
The water flowed **a** the altar and	1Ki 18:35	5439
"Turn **a** and take me out of the	1Ki 22:34	3027
and chariots of fire all **a** Elisha.	2Ki 6:17	5439
and by the house, **a** the king.	2Ki 11:11	5439
and built a siege wall all **a** it.	2Ki 25:1	5439
the Chaldeans were all **a** the city.	2Ki 25:4	5439
broke down the walls **a** Jerusalem.	2Ki 25:10	5439
pomegranates on the capital all **a**,	2Ki 25:17	5439
were **a** the same cities as far as Baal.	1Ch 4:33	5439
Judah and its pasture lands **a** it;	1Ch 6:55	5439
the night **a** the house of God,	1Ch 9:27	5439
a the land of the Philistines to	1Ch 10:9	5439
He built the city all **a**,	1Ch 11:8	5439
circle **a** behind them and come at	1Ch 14:14	5437
oxen *were* under it *and* all **a** it,	2Ch 4:3	
		5439, 5437
When Judah turned **a**,	2Ch 13:14	6437
destroyed all the cities **a** Gerar,	2Ch 14:14	5439
of the lands which *were* **a** Judah,	2Ch 17:10	5439
"Turn **a** and take me out of the	2Ch 18:33	3027
and by the house, **a** the king.	2Ch 23:10	5439
from the nations that were **a** us.	Ne 5:17	5439
from the district **a** Jerusalem,	Ne 12:28	5439
themselves villages **a** Jerusalem.	Ne 12:29	5439
the earth and walking **a** on it."	Jb 1:7	1980
the earth and walking **a** on it."	Jb 2:2	1980
"His roots wrap **a** a rock pile, He	Jb 8:17	5440
would look **a** and rest securely.	Jb 11:18	2658
"All **a** terrors frighten him, And	Jb 18:11	5439
me And has closed His net **a** me.	Jb 19:6	5362b
against me And camp **a** my tent.	Jb 19:12	5439
me, *And* my children were **a** me;	Jb 29:5	5439
turning **a** by His guidance,	Jb 37:12	2015
A God is awesome majesty.	Jb 37:22	5921
A his teeth there is terror.	Jb 41:14	5439
hiding place, His canopy **a** Him,	Ps 18:11	5439
lifted up above my enemies **a** me,	Ps 27:6	5439
LORD encamps **a** those who fear Him,	Ps 34:7	5439
and a derision to those **a** us.	Ps 44:13	5439
Walk about Zion and go **a** her;	Ps 48:12	5362b
And it is very tempestuous **a** Him.	Ps 50:3	5439
they go **a** her upon her walls,	Ps 55:10	5437
like a dog, And go **a** the city.	Ps 59:6	5437
like a dog, And go **a** the city.	Ps 59:14	5437
Let all who are **a** Him bring gifts	Ps 76:11	5439
and derision to those **a** us.	Ps 79:4	5439
above all those who are **a** Him?	Ps 89:7	5439
like olive plants **A** your table.	Ps 128:3	5439
the light **a** me will be night,"	Ps 139:11	1157
Bind them **a** your neck, Write them	Pr 3:3	5921
Tie them **a** your neck.	Pr 6:21	5921
Sixty mighty men **a** it,	SS 3:7	5439
He dug it all **a**,	Is 5:2	5823
has gone **a** the territory of Moab,	Is 15:8	5362b
You turn *things* **a**!	Is 29:16	2016
And it set him aflame all **a**,	Is 42:25	5439
"Lift up your eyes and look **a**;	Is 49:18	5439
from the chains **a** your neck,	Is 52:2	
go **a** so much Changing your way?	Jer 2:36	
They will pitch *their* tents **a** her,	Jer 6:3	5439
and put it **a** your waist,	Jer 13:1	5921
of the LORD and put it **a** my waist.	Jer 13:2	5921
bought, which is **a** your waist,	Jer 13:4	5921
But afterward they turned **a** and	Jer 34:11	7725
Mizpah turned **a** and came back,	Jer 41:14	5437
sword has devoured those **a** you.'	Jer 46:14	5439
for him, all you who *live* **a** him,	Jer 48:17	5439
object of terror to all **a** him."	Jer 48:39	5439
"From all *directions* **a** you;	Jer 49:5	5439
and built a siege wall all **a** it.	Jer 52:4	5439
the Chaldeans were all **a** the city.	Jer 52:7	5439
down all the walls **a** Jerusalem.	Jer 52:14	5439
upon the capital all **a**,	Jer 52:22	5439
a hundred on the network all **a**.	Jer 52:23	5439
cup will come **a** to you as well,	La 4:21	5674a
and a bright light **a** it,	Ezk 1:4	5439
looked like fire all **a** within it,	Ezk 1:27	5439
and *there was* a radiance **a** Him.	Ezk 1:27	5439
battering rams against it all **a**.	Ezk 4:2	5439
it with the sword all **a** the city,	Ezk 5:2	5439
of the nations, with lands **a** her.	Ezk 5:5	5439
will fall by the sword **a** you,	Ezk 5:12	5439
scatter your bones **a** your altars.	Ezk 6:5	5439
among their idols **a** their altars,	Ezk 6:13	5439
were carved on the wall all **a**.	Ezk 8:10	5439
wheels were full of eyes all **a**,	Ezk 10:12	5439
the ordinances of the nations **a** you.	Ezk 11:12	5439
to every wind all who are **a** him,	Ezk 12:14	5439
nor did you build the wall **a** the	Ezk 13:5	5921
hands and a necklace **a** your neck.	Ezk 16:11	5921
of Edom and of all who are **a** her,	Ezk 16:57	5439
army were on your walls, *all* **a**,	Ezk 27:11	5439
shields on your walls *all* **a**;	Ezk 27:11	5439
extended all **a** its planting place,	Ezk 31:4	5439
and all her hordes **a** her grave;	Ezk 32:24	5439
Her graves are **a** it, they are all	Ezk 32:25	5439
the places **a** My hill a blessing.	Ezk 34:26	5439
surely the nations which are **a** you	Ezk 36:7	5439
and I will turn you **a**,	Ezk 39:2	7725
the outside of the temple all **a**,	Ezk 40:5	5439
pillars within the gate all **a**,	Ezk 40:16	5439
there were windows all **a** inside;	Ezk 40:16	5439
made for the court all **a**,	Ezk 40:17	5439
all **a** like those other windows;	Ezk 40:25	5439
and its porches had windows all **a**;	Ezk 40:29	5439
There were porches all **a**,	Ezk 40:30	5439
and its porches had windows all **a**;	Ezk 40:33	5439
And the gate had windows all **a**;	Ezk 40:36	5439
were installed in the house all **a**;	Ezk 40:43	5439
a about the house on every side.	Ezk 41:5	5439
stood on their inward side all **a**.	Ezk 41:6	5439
house had a raised platform all **a**;	Ezk 41:8	5439
all **a** the temple on every side.	Ezk 41:10	5439
free space *was* five cubits all **a**.	Ezk 41:11	5439
was five cubits thick all **a**,	Ezk 41:12	5439
were paneled with wood all **a**,	Ezk 41:16	5439
the wall all **a** inside and outside,	Ezk 41:17	5439
carved on all the house all **a**.	Ezk 41:19	5439
the east and measured it all **a**.	Ezk 42:15	5439
it had a wall all **a**,	Ezk 42:20	5439
mountain all **a** *shall be* most holy.	Ezk 43:12	5439
border **a** it *shall be* half a cubit and	Ezk 43:17	5439
about in them, **a** the four of them,	Ezk 46:23	5439
led me **a** on the outside to the outer	Ezk 47:2	5437
the king's high officials gathered **a**	Da 3:27	3673
with a band of iron and bronze **a** *it*	Da 4:15	
with a band of iron and bronze **a** *it*	Da 4:23	
a necklace of gold **a** his neck,	Da 5:7	5922
a necklace of gold **a** your neck,	Da 5:16	5922
put a necklace of gold **a** his neck,	Da 5:29	5922
a reproach to all those **a** us.	Da 9:16	5439
Now their deeds are all **a** them;	Hos 7:2	5437
me, Weeds were wrapped **a** my head.	Jon 2:5	
with its bars *was* **a** me forever,	Jon 2:6	1157
right hand will come **a** to you,	Hab 2:16	5437
'will be a wall of fire **a** her,	Zch 2:5	5439
prosperous along with its cities **a** it,	Zch 7:7	5439
a My house because of an army,	Zch 9:8	
reeling to all the peoples **a**;	Zch 12:2	5439
of camel's hair and a leather belt **a**	Mt 3:4	*4012*
and all the district **a** the Jordan;	Mt 3:5	*4066*
Now when Jesus saw a crowd **a** Him,	Mt 8:18	*4012*
millstone hung **a** his neck,	Mt 18:6	*4012*
out and found others standing **a**;	Mt 20:6	
A IT AND DUG A WINE PRESS IN IT,	Mt 21:33	*4060*
because you travel **a** on sea and land	Mt 23:15	*4013*
the whole *Roman* cohort **a** Him.	Mt 27:27	*1909*
wore a leather belt **a** his waist,	Mk 1:6	*4012*
it freely and to spread the news **a**,	Mk 1:45	*1310*
looking **a** at them with anger,	Mk 3:5	*4017*
those who had afflictions pressed **a**	Mk 3:10	*1968*
A crowd was sitting **a** Him,	Mk 3:32	*4012*
at those who were sitting **a** Him,	Mk 3:34	
		4012, 2945
a large crowd gathered **a** Him; and so	Mk 5:21	*1909*
turned **a** in the crowd and said,	Mk 5:30	*1994*
And He looked **a** to see the woman	Mk 5:32	*4017*
was going **a** the villages teaching.	Mk 6:6	
		4013, 2945
the scribes gathered **a** Him	Mk 7:1	*4314*
like trees, walking **a**."	Mk 8:24	*4043*
a and seeing His disciples,	Mk 8:33	*1994*
All at once they looked **a** and	Mk 9:8	*4017*
they saw a large crowd **a** them,	Mk 9:14	*4012*
he *began* rolling **a** and foaming	Mk 9:20	*2947*
a heavy millstone hung **a** his neck,	Mk 9:42	*4012*
crowds gathered **a** Him again,	Mk 10:1	*4314*
And Jesus, looking **a**,	Mk 10:23	*4017*
and after looking **a**	Mk 11:11	*4017*
A VINEYARD AND PUT A WALL A IT,	Mk 12:1	*4060*
who like to walk **a** in long robes,	Mk 12:38	*4043*
came on all those living **a** them;	Lk 1:65	*4039*
glory of the Lord shone **a** them;	Lk 2:9	*4034*
all the district **a** the Jordan,	Lk 3:3	*4066*
from the Jordan and was led **a** by	Lk 4:1	
the crowd was pressing **a** Him	Lk 5:1	*1945*
After looking **a** at them all,	Lk 6:10	*4017*
He *began* going **a** from one city	Lk 8:1	*1353*
I dig **a** it and put in fertilizer;	Lk 13:8	*4012*
if a millstone were hung **a** his neck	Lk 17:2	*4012*
who like to walk **a** in long robes,	Lk 20:46	*4043*
When those who were **a** Him saw	Lk 22:49	*4012*
The Jews then gathered **a** Him,	Jn 10:24	*2944*
the people standing **a** I said it,	Jn 11:42	*4026*
face was wrapped **a** with a cloth.	Jn 11:44	*4019*
she had said this, she turned **a** and	Jn 20:14	*3694*
Peter, turning **a**, saw the disciple	Jn 21:20	*1994*
the districts of Libya **a** Cyrene,	Ac 2:10	*2596*
a light from heaven flashed **a** him;	Ac 9:3	*4015b*

your cloak **a** you and follow me." Ac 12:8 *4016*
while the disciples stood **a** him, Ac 14:20 *2944*
flashed from heaven all **a** me, Ac 22:6 *4012*
down from Jerusalem stood **a** him, Ac 25:7 *4026*
shining all **a** me and those who Ac 26:13 *4034*
sailed **a** and arrived at Rhegium, Ac 28:13 *4022*
as they go **a** from house to house; 1Tm 5:13 *4022*
prowls **a** like a roaring lion, 1Pe 5:8 *4043*
Gomorrah and the cities **a** them, Jude 1:7 *4012*
there was a rainbow **a** the throne, Rv 4:3 *2943b*
A the throne *were* twenty-four Rv 4:4 *2943b*
in the center and **a** the throne, Rv 4:6 *2945*
are full of eyes **a** and within; Rv 4:8 *2943b*
the voice of many angels **a** the throne Rv 5:11 *2945*
the angels were standing **a** the throne Rv 7:11 *2945*
standing around the throne and **a** Rv 7:11
and girded **a** their chests with Rv 15:6 *4012*

AROUSE
so fierce that he dares to **a** him; Jb 41:10 5782
adversaries, And **a** Yourself for me; Ps 7:6 5782
A Yourself, why do You sleep, O Ps 44:23 5782
A Yourself to help me, and see! Ps 59:4 5782
And did not **a** all His wrath. Ps 78:38 5782
you do not **a** or awaken *my* love SS 2:7 5782
you will not **a** or awaken *my* love Until SS 3:5 5782
Do not **a** or awaken *my* love Until SS 8:4 5782
The LORD of hosts will **a** a Is 10:26 5782
will **a** *His* zeal like a man of war. Is 42:13 5782
I am going to **a** and bring up Jer 50:9 5782
I am going to **a** against Babylon Jer 51:1 5782
I will **a** your lovers against you, Ezk 23:22 5782
he will **a** the whole *empire* against Da 11:2 5782
I am going to **a** them from the Jl 3:7 5782

AROUSED
awake nor be **a** out of his sleep. Jb 14:12 5782
when one awakes, O Lord, when **a**, Ps 73:20 5782
And **a** His jealousy with their Ps 78:58
And my feelings were **a** for him. SS 5:4 1993
"Who has **a** one from the east Whom Is 41:2 5782
"I have **a** one from the north, and Is 41:25 5782
"I have **a** him in righteousness And Is 45:13 5782
And a great nation will be **a** from Jer 6:22 5782
and many kings Will be **a** from the Jer 50:41 5782
The LORD has **a** the spirit of the Jer 51:11 5782
Let the nations be **a** And come up Jl 3:12 5782
is **a** from His holy habitation." Zch 2:13 5782
which were **a** by the Law, were at Ro 7:5

AROUSES
It **a** for you the spirits of the Is 14:9 5782
a himself to take hold of You; Is 64:7 5782

ARPACHSHAD
and Asshur and **A** and Lud and Aram. Gn 10:22 775
A became the father of Shelah; Gn 10:24 775
of **A** two years after the flood; Gn 11:10 775
after he became the father of **A**, Gn 11:11 775
A lived thirty-five years, and Gn 11:12 775
and **A** lived four hundred and three Gn 11:13 775
sons of Shem *were* Elam, Asshur, **A**, 1Ch 1:17 775
A became the father of Shelah 1Ch 1:18 775
Shem, **A**, Shelah, 1Ch 1:24 775

ARPAD
are the gods of Hamath and **A**? 2Ki 18:34 774
the king of Hamath, the king of **A**, 2Ki 19:13 774
like Carchemish, Or Hamath like **A**, Is 10:9 774
are the gods of Hamath and **A**? Is 36:19 774
the king of Hamath, the king of **A**, Is 37:13 774
"Hamath and **A** are put to shame, Jer 49:23 774

ARPHAXAD
the son of Cainan, the son of **A**, Lk 3:36 *742*

ARRANGE
table and **a** what belongs on it; Ex 40:4 6186a
the altar and **a** wood on the fire. Lv 1:7 6186a
the priests shall **a** the pieces, Lv 1:8 6186a
and the priest shall **a** them on the Lv 1:12 6186a
a *our case* because of darkness. Jb 37:19 6186a
matters I will **a** when I come. 1Co 11:34 *1299*
they would go on ahead to you and **a** 2Co 9:5 *4294*

ARRANGED
the altar there and **a** the wood, Gn 22:9 6186a
Then he **a** the wood and cut the ox 1Ki 18:33 6186a
and *I* **a** for the supply of wood at Ne 13:31
he has not **a** *his* words against me, Jb 32:14 6186a
searched out and **a** many proverbs. Ec 12:9 8626
couch with a table **a** before it on Ezk 23:41 6186a
Like a mighty people **a** for battle. Jl 2:5 6186a
for so he had **a** it, intending Ac 20:13 *1299*

ARRANGEMENT
a of lamps and all its utensils, Ex 39:37 4634
He set the **a** of bread in order Ex 40:23 6187
North to carry out a peaceful **a**. Da 11:6 4339

ARRANGEMENTS
according to their **a** and openings. Ezk 42:11 4941
the Samaritans to make **a** for Him. Lk 9:52 *2090*

ARRAY
martial **a** from the land of Egypt. Ex 13:18 2571
before your brothers in battle **a**, Jos 1:14 2571
a before the sons of Israel, Jos 4:12 2571
up in battle **a** to meet Israel. 1Sa 4:2
a to encounter the Philistines. 1Sa 17:2
come out to draw up in battle **a**? 1Sa 17:8
in battle **a** shouting the war cry. 1Sa 17:20 4634
Philistines drew up in battle **a**, 1Sa 17:21
a at the entrance of the city, 2Sa 10:8
Worship the LORD in holy **a**. 1Ch 16:29 1927a
a at the entrance of the city, 1Ch 19:9
in battle **a** against the Arameans, 1Ch 19:17
a the man whom the king desires to Es 6:9 3847
A yourselves before me, take your Jb 33:5 6186a
Worship the LORD in holy **a**. Ps 29:2 1927a
In holy **a**, from the womb of the Ps 110:3 1926

ARRAYED
and they **a** for battle against them Gn 14:8 6186a
and the men of Israel **a** for battle Jg 20:20 6186a
encouraged themselves and **a** for Jg 20:22 6186a
had **a** themselves the first day. Jg 20:22 6186a
and **a** themselves against Gibeah as Jg 20:30 6186a
and **a** themselves at Baal-tamar; Jg 20:33 6186a
and **a** *them* against the Arameans. 2Sa 10:9 6186a
and he **a** *them* against the sons of 2Sa 10:10 6186a
And the Arameans **a** themselves to 2Sa 10:17 6186a
on his throne, **a** in *their* robes, 1Ki 22:10 3847
a themselves against the Arameans. 1Ch 19:10 6186a
and they **a** themselves against the 1Ch 19:11 6186a
on his throne, **a** in *their* robes, 2Ch 18:9 3847
and the horse, and **a** Mordecai, Es 6:11 3847
terrors of God are **a** against me. Jb 6:4 6186a
A as a man for the battle Against Jer 6:23 6186a

ARREST
clubs to **a** Me as *you would* against Mt 26:55 *4815*
they **a** you and hand you over, Mk 13:11 *71*
out with swords and clubs to **a** Me, Mk 14:48 *4815*
he proceeded to **a** Peter also. Ac 12:3 *4815*

ARRESTED
and he **a** Jeremiah the prophet, Jer 37:13 8610
So Irijah **a** Jeremiah and brought Jer 37:14 8610
For when Herod had John **a**, Mt 14:3 *2902*
and had John **a** and bound in prison Mk 6:17 *2902*
Having **a** Him, they led Him Lk 22:54 *4815*
the Jews, **a** Jesus and bound Him, Jn 18:12 *4815*
a guide to those who **a** Jesus. Ac 1:16 *4815*
"When this man was **a** by the Jews Ac 23:27 *4815*
and then we **a** him. Ac 24:6 *2902*

ARRIVAL
was set up before their **a**. Nu 10:21 935
and on my **a** I would have received Mt 25:27 *2064*

ARRIVE
do anything until you **a** there." Gn 19:22 935
And until we **a** there, we ourselves Ex 10:26 935
"When you **a** there, search out 2Ki 9:2 935
And their ambassadors **a** at Hanes. Is 30:4 5060
after your accusers **a** also," Ac 23:35 *3854*
did not **a** at *that* law. Ro 9:31 *5348*
When I **a**, whomever you may 1Co 16:3 *3854*

ARRIVED
Egypt until you **a** at this place, Dt 9:7 935
near and **a** in front of the city, Jos 8:11 935
It came about when he had **a**, Jg 3:27 935
all the army that was with him **a**, 2Sa 3:23 935
people who were with him **a** weary 2Sa 16:14 935
Behold, the Cushite **a**, 2Sa 18:31 935
of Damascus, and when you have **a**, 1Ki 19:15 935
and when she **a** at the horses' 2Ki 11:16 935
and when she **a** at the entrance of 2Ch 23:15 935
when they **a** at the house of the Ezr 2:68 935
the king's eunuchs **a** and hastily Es 6:14 5060
commandment and his decree **a**, Es 8:17 5060
time has **a** for pruning *the vines,* SS 2:12 5060
'The time has come, the day has **a**. Ezk 7:12 5060
and the time **a** when the saints Da 7:22 4291
where they have **a** from Babylon. Zch 6:10 935
magi from the east **a** in Jerusalem, Mt 2:1 *3854*
Then Jesus **a** from Galilee at the Mt 3:13 *3854*
Then His mother and His brothers **a**, Mk 3:31 *2064*
When He **a** at the place, He Lk 22:40 *1096*
When he **a**, they brought him into Ac 9:39 *3854*
Then when he **a** and witnessed Ac 11:23 *3854*
Perga, they **a** at Pisidian Antioch, Ac 13:14 *3854*
When they had **a** and gathered Ac 14:27 *3854*
When they **a** at Jerusalem, they Ac 15:4 *3854*
and when they **a**, they went into Ac 17:10 *3854*
and when he had **a**, he greatly Ac 18:27 *3854*
we **a** the following day opposite Ac 20:15 *2658*
from Tyre, we **a** at Ptolemais, Ac 21:7 *2658*
After we **a** in Jerusalem, Ac 21:17 *1096*
days later Felix **a** with Drusilla, Ac 24:24 *3854*
having **a** in the province, Ac 25:1 *1910*
After Paul **a**, Ac 25:7 *3854*
Agrippa and Bernice **a** at Caesarea and Ac 25:13 *2658*
with difficulty had **a** off Cnidus, Ac 27:7 *1096*
we sailed around and **a** at Rhegium, Ac 28:13 *2658*

ARRIVES
for it will be when she **a** that she 1Ki 14:5 935

ARROGANCE
not let **a** come out of your mouth; 1Sa 2:3 6277
your **a** has come up to My ears, 2Ki 19:28 7600
Pride and **a** and the evil way And Pr 8:13 1344
And his eyelids are raised *in* **a**. Pr 30:13
in pride and in **a** of heart: Is 9:9 1433
put an end to the **a** of the proud And Is 13:11 1347b
Even of his **a**, pride, and fury; Is 16:6 1346
your **a** has come up to My ears, Is 37:29 7600
his **a** and his self-exaltation. Jer 48:29 1346
The **a** of your heart has deceived Jer 49:16 2087
rod has budded, **a** has blossomed. Ezk 7:10 2087
she and her daughters had **a**, Ezk 16:49 1347b
"I loathe the **a** of Jacob, And detest Am 6:8 1347b
"The **a** of your heart has deceived Ob 1:3 2087
disputes, slanders, gossip, **a**, 2Co 12:20 *5450*
But as it is, you boast in your **a**; Jas 4:16 *212*

ARROGANT
For I was envious of the **a** Ps 73:3 1984b
a men have risen up against me, Ps 86:14 2086
look and an **a** heart will I endure. Ps 101:5 7342
You rebuke the **a**, Ps 119:21 2086
The **a** utterly deride me, *Yet* I do Ps 119:51 2086
a have forged a lie against me; Ps 119:69 2086
May the **a** be ashamed, for they Ps 119:78 2086
The **a** have dug pits for me, *Men* Ps 119:85 2086
Do not let the **a** oppress me. Ps 119:122 2086
But a fool is **a** and careless. Pr 14:16 5674b
An **a** man stirs up strife, But he Pr 28:25 7342
"I will punish the fruit of the **a** Is 10:12 1433
all the **a** men said to Jeremiah, Jer 43:2 2086
he has become **a** toward the LORD; Jer 48:26 1431
he has become **a** toward the LORD. Jer 48:42 1431
she has become **a** against the LORD, Jer 50:29 2102
I am against you, O **a** one," Jer 50:31 2087
"The **a** one will stumble and Jer 50:32 2087
become **a** against their territory. Zph 2:8 1431
a against the people of the LORD Zph 2:10 1431
words have been **a** against Me," Mal 3:13 2388
'So now we call the **a** blessed; Mal 3:15 2086
and all the **a** and every evildoer Mal 4:1 2086
haters of God, insolent, **a**, Ro 1:30 *5244a*
do not be **a** toward the branches; Ro 11:18 *2620*
but if you are **a**, *remember that* it Ro 11:18 *2620*
that no one of you will become **a** 1Co 4:6 *5448*
Now some have become **a**, 1Co 4:18 *5448*
not the words of those who are **a** but 1Co 4:19 *5448*
You have become **a** and 1Co 5:2 *5448*
Knowledge makes **a**, but love 1Co 8:1 *5448*
love does not brag *and* is not **a**, 1Co 13:4 *5448*
lovers of money, boastful, **a**, 2Tm 3:2 *5244a*
be **a** and *so* lie against the truth. Jas 3:14 *2620*
For speaking out **a** *words* of vanity 2Pe 2:18 *5246*
speaking **a** words and blasphemies, Rv 13:5 *3173*

ARROGANTLY
that they acted **a** toward them, Ne 9:10 2102
"But they, our fathers, acted **a**; Ne 9:16 2102
Yet they acted **a** and did not Ne 9:29 2102
himself **a** against the Almighty. Jb 15:25 1396
Which speak **a** against the Ps 31:18 6277
pour forth *words,* they speak **a**; Ps 94:4 6277
"And you have spoken **a** against Me Ezk 35:13 1431
became so proud that he behaved **a**, Da 5:20 2103
they speak **a**, flattering people Jude 1:16 *5246*

ARROW
running, he shot an **a** past him. 1Sa 20:36 2678
of the **a** which Jonathan had shot, 1Sa 20:37 2678
"Is not the **a** beyond you?" 1Sa 20:37 2678
up the **a** and came to his master. 1Sa 20:38 2678
and the **a** went through his heart and 2Ki 9:24 2678
"The LORD's **a** of victory, even 2Ki 13:17 2671
even the **a** of victory over Aram; 2Ki 13:17 2671
to this city or shoot an **a** there; 2Ki 19:32 2671
"The **a** cannot make him flee; Jb 41:28 1121
ready their **a** upon the string To Ps 11:2 2671
aimed bitter speech *as* their **a**, Ps 64:3 2671
God will shoot at them with an **a**; Ps 64:7 2671
Or of the **a** that flies by day; Ps 91:5 2671
an **a** pierces through his liver; Pr 7:23 2671
and a sharp **a** Is a man who bears Pr 25:18 2671
to this city or shoot an **a** there; Is 37:33 2671
He has also made Me a select **a**, Is 49:2 2671
"Their tongue is a deadly **a**; Jer 9:8 2671
And set me as a target for the **a**. La 3:12 2671
a will go forth like lightning; Zch 9:14 2671

ARROWS
And shatter *them* with his **a**. Nu 24:8 2671
I will use My **a** on them. Dt 32:23 2671
'I will make My **a** drunk with Dt 32:42 2671
I will shoot three **a** to the side, 1Sa 20:20 2671
send the lad, *saying,* 'Go, find the **a**.' 1Sa 20:21 2671
the **a** are on this side of you, 1Sa 20:21 2671
'Behold, the **a** are beyond you,' 1Sa 20:22 2671
the **a** which I am about to shoot." 1Sa 20:36 2671
"And He sent out **a**, and scattered 2Sa 22:15 2671
"Take a bow and **a**." 2Ki 13:15 2671
So he took a bow and **a**. 2Ki 13:15 2671
"Take the **a**," and he took them. 2Ki 13:18 2671
and *to shoot* **a** from the bow; 1Ch 12:2 2671
of shooting **a** and great stones. 2Ch 26:15 2671
a of the Almighty are within me, Jb 6:4 2671
"His **a** surround me. Jb 16:13 7228
He makes His **a** fiery shafts. Ps 7:13 2671
He sent out His **a**, Ps 18:14 2671
Your **a** have sunk deep into me, Ps 38:2 2671
Your **a** are sharp; Ps 45:5 2671
Your **a** *are* in the heart of Ps 45:5
men, whose teeth are spears and **a** And Ps 57:4 2671
When he aims his **a**, Ps 58:7 2671
There He broke the flaming **a**, Ps 76:3 7198
Your **a** flashed here and there. Ps 77:17 2671
Sharp **a** of the warrior, With the Ps 120:4 2671
Like **a** in the hand of a warrior, Ps 127:4 2671
Send out Your **a** and confuse them. Ps 144:6 2671
throws Firebrands, **a**, and death, Pr 26:18 2671
Its **a** are sharp and all its bows Is 5:28 2671
with bows and **a** because all the land Is 7:24 2671
Their **a** will be like an expert Jer 50:9 2671
do not be sparing with *your* **a**, Jer 50:14 2671
Sharpen the **a**, fill the quivers! Jer 51:11 2671
He made the **a** of His quiver To La 3:13 1121
the deadly **a** of famine which were Ezk 5:16 2671
he shakes the **a**, he consults the Ezk 21:21 2671
down your **a** from your right hand. Ezk 39:3 2671
shields and bucklers, bows and **a**, Ezk 39:9 2671
went away at the light of Your **a**, Hab 3:11 2671
able to extinguish all the flaming **a** Eph 6:16 *956b*

ART
kinds blended by the perfumers' **a**; 2Ch 16:14 4639
an image formed by the **a** and thought Ac 17:29 *5078*

ARTAXERXES
And in the days of **A**, Bishlam, Ezr 4:7 783a
the rest of his colleagues wrote to **A** Ezr 4:7 783a
a letter against Jerusalem to King **A**, Ezr 4:8 783b
"To King **A**: Your servants, the men Ezr 4:11 783b
and **A** king of Persia. Ezr 6:14 783b
in the reign of **A** king of Persia, Ezr 7:1 783a
in the seventh year of King **A**. Ezr 7:7 783a
the copy of the decree which King **A** Ezr 7:11 783a
"**A**, king of kings, to Ezra Ezr 7:12 783b
"I, even I, King **A**, issue a Ezr 7:21 783b
from Babylon in the reign of King **A**: Ezr 8:1 783a
in the twentieth year of King **A**, Ne 2:1 783a
to the thirty-second year of King **A**, Ne 5:14 783a
for in the thirty-second year of **A** Ne 13:6 783a

ARTAXERXES'
as the copy of King **A** document Ezr 4:23 783b

ARTEMAS
When I send **A** or Tychicus to you, Ti 3:12 *734*

ARTEMIS
who made silver shrines of **A**, was Ac 19:24 *735*
the temple of the great goddess **A** be Ac 19:27 *735*
"Great is **A** of the Ephesians!" Ac 19:28 *735*
"Great is **A** of the Ephesians!" Ac 19:34 *735*
guardian of the temple of the great **A** Ac 19:35 *735*

ARTICLE
unclean, including any wooden **a**, Lv 11:32 3627
or a sack—any **a** of which use is Lv 11:32 3627
or in any **a** made of leather, Lv 13:48 4399
the woof, or in any **a** of leather, Lv 13:49 3627
a with the mark for seven days. Lv 13:50
or any **a** of leather in which the Lv 13:52 3627
the woof, or in any **a** of leather, Lv 13:53 3627
a with the mark has been washed, Lv 13:55
the woof, or in any **a** of leather, Lv 13:57 3627
the **a** with the mark shall be Lv 13:57
or any **a** of leather from which the Lv 13:58 3627
the woof, or in any **a** of leather, Lv 13:59 3627
every garment and every **a** of leather Nu 31:20 3627
his treasury of every precious **a**. Hos 13:15 3627
every **a** of ivory and every article Rv 18:12 *4632*
every article of ivory and every **a** Rv 18:12 *4632*

ARTICLES
The servant brought out **a** of Gn 24:53 3627
articles of silver and **a** of gold, Gn 24:53 3627
a of silver and articles of gold, Ex 3:22 3627
articles of silver and **a** of gold, Ex 3:22 3627
from her neighbor for **a** of silver and Ex 11:2 3627
of silver and **a** of gold." Ex 11:2 3627
from the Egyptians **a** of silver and Ex 12:35 3627
articles of silver and **a** of gold, Ex 12:35 3627
and bracelets, all **a** of gold; Ex 35:22 3627
goats' *hair*, and all **a** of wood." Nu 31:20 3627
what each man found, **a** of gold, Nu 31:50 3627
from them, all kinds of wrought **a**. Nu 31:51 3627
the silver and gold and **a** of bronze Jos 6:19 3627
and gold, and **a** of bronze and iron, Jos 6:24 3627
and put the **a** of gold which you 1Sa 6:8 3627
it, in which were the **a** of gold, 1Sa 6:15 3627
brought with him **a** of silver, 2Sa 8:10 3627
his gift, **a** of silver and gold, 1Ki 10:25 3627
a of gold and silver and bronze. 1Ch 18:10 3627
his gift, **a** of silver and gold, 2Ch 9:24 3627
and all kinds of valuable **a**, 2Ch 32:27 3627
of the **a** of the house of the LORD to 2Ch 36:7 3627
a of the house of the LORD, 2Ch 36:10 3627
All the **a** of the house of God, 2Ch 36:18 3627
and destroyed all its valuable **a**. 2Ch 36:19 3627
encouraged them with **a** of silver, Ezr 1:6 3627
the **a** of the house of the LORD, Ezr 1:7 3627
a second *kind and* 1,000 other **a**. Ezr 1:10 3627
All the **a** of gold and silver Ezr 1:11 3627
be exchanged for **a** of fine gold. Jb 28:17 3627

ARTIFICIAL
and as far as the **a** pool and the Ne 3:16 6213a

ARTISAN
The counselor and the expert **a**, Is 3:3 2796

ARTISANS
of Babylon and the rest of the **a**. Jer 52:15 525

ARTIST
The work of the hands of an **a**. SS 7:1 542

ARTISTIC
make **a** designs for work in gold, Ex 31:4
him with the **a** band of the ephod, Lv 8:7 2805
the house he made windows with **a** 1Ki 6:4
There were **a** *window* frames in 1Ki 7:4
and doorposts *had* squared **a** 1Ki 7:5

ARTS
did the same with their secret **a**. Ex 7:11 3909
did the same with their secret **a**; Ex 7:22 3909
did the same with their secret **a**, Ex 8:7 3909
secret **a** to bring forth gnats, Ex 8:18 3909
astonished them with his magic **a**. Ac 8:11 *3095*

ARUBBOTH
Ben-hesed, in **A** 1Ki 4:10 700

ARUMAH
Then Abimelech remained at **A**, Jg 9:41 725

ARVAD
of Sidon and **A** were your rowers; Ezk 27:8 719
"The sons of **A** and your army were Ezk 27:11 719

ARVADITE
and the **A** and the Zemarite and the Gn 10:18 721

ARVADITES
the **A**, the Zemarites and the 1Ch 1:16 721

ARZA
himself drunk in the house of **A**, 1Ki 16:9 777

ASA
and **A** his son became king in his 1Ki 15:8 609
A began to reign as king of Judah. 1Ki 15:9 609
A did what was right in the 1Ki 15:11 609
and **A** cut down her horrid image 1Ki 15:13 609
nevertheless the heart of **A** was 1Ki 15:14 609
Now there was war between **A** and 1Ki 15:16 609
or coming in to **A** king of Judah. 1Ki 15:17 609
Then **A** took all the silver and the 1Ki 15:18 609
And King **A** sent them to Ben-hadad 1Ki 15:18 609
So Ben-hadad listened to King **A** 1Ki 15:20 609
Then King **A** made a proclamation to 1Ki 15:22 609
And King **A** built with them Geba of 1Ki 15:22 609
Now the rest of all the acts of **A** 1Ki 15:23 609
And **A** slept with his fathers and 1Ki 15:24 609
second year of **A** king of Judah, 1Ki 15:25 609
the third year of **A** king of Judah and 1Ki 15:28 609
There was war between **A** and 1Ki 15:32 609
the third year of **A** king of Judah, 1Ki 15:33 609
year of **A** king of Judah, 1Ki 16:8 609
year of **A** king of Judah, 1Ki 16:10 609
year of **A** king of Judah, 1Ki 16:15 609
year of **A** king of Judah, 1Ki 16:23 609
year of **A** king of Judah, 1Ki 16:29 609
Now Jehoshaphat the son of **A** 1Ki 22:41 609
in all the way of **A** his father; 1Ki 22:43 609
in the days of his father **A**, 1Ki 22:46 609
Abijah *was* his son, **A** his son, 1Ch 3:10 609
and Berechiah the son of **A**, 1Ch 9:16 609
son **A** became king in his place. 2Ch 14:1 609
A did good and right in the 2Ch 14:2 609
Now **A** had an army of 300,000 from 2Ch 14:8 609
So **A** went out to meet him, and 2Ch 14:10 609
Then **A** called to the LORD his God and 2Ch 14:11 609
before **A** and before Judah, 2Ch 14:12 609
A and the people who *were* with 2Ch 14:13 609
out to meet **A** and said to him, 2Ch 15:2 609
"Listen to me, **A**, and all Judah 2Ch 15:2 609
Now when **A** heard these words and 2Ch 15:8 609
Maacah, the mother of King **A**, 2Ch 15:16 609
and **A** cut down her horrid image, 2Ch 15:16 609
or coming in to **A** king of Judah. 2Ch 16:1 609
Then **A** brought out silver and gold 2Ch 16:2 609
So Ben-hadad listened to King **A** 2Ch 16:4 609
Then King **A** brought all Judah, and 2Ch 16:6 609
A king of Judah and said to him, 2Ch 16:7 609
Then **A** was angry with the seer and 2Ch 16:10 609
And **A** oppressed some of the people 2Ch 16:10 609
the acts of **A** from first to last, 2Ch 16:11 609
A became diseased in his feet. 2Ch 16:12 609
So **A** slept with his fathers, 2Ch 16:13 609
which **A** his father had captured. 2Ch 17:2 609
A and did not depart from it, 2Ch 20:32 609
and the ways of **A** king of Judah, 2Ch 21:12 609
A had made on account of Baasha, Jer 41:9 609
and Abijah the father of **A**. Mt 1:7 *760*
A was the father of Jehoshaphat, Mt 1:8 *760*

ASAHEL
there, Joab and Abishai and **A**; 2Sa 2:18 6214
and **A** *was as* swift-footed as one 2Sa 2:18 6214
A pursued Abner and did not 2Sa 2:19 6214
"Is that you, **A**?" 2Sa 2:20 6214
But **A** was not willing to turn 2Sa 2:21 6214
Abner repeated again to **A**, 2Sa 2:22 6214
place where **A** had fallen and died, 2Sa 2:23 6214
servants besides **A** were missing. 2Sa 2:30 6214
And they took up **A** and buried him 2Sa 2:32 6214
of the blood of **A** his brother. 2Sa 3:27 6214
he had put their brother **A** to death 2Sa 3:30 6214
A the brother of Joab was among 2Sa 23:24 6214
Zeruiah *were* Abshai, Joab and **A**. 1Ch 2:16 6214
armies *were* **A** the brother of Joab, 1Ch 11:26 6214
month *was* **A** the brother of Joab, 1Ch 27:7 6214
Shemaiah, Nethaniah, Zebadiah, **A**, 2Ch 17:8 6214
Jehiel, Azaziah, Nahath, **A**, 2Ch 31:13 6214
Only Jonathan the son of **A** and Ezr 10:15 6214

ASAIAH
and **A** the king's servant saying, 2Ki 22:12 6222
A went to Huldah the prophetess, 2Ki 22:14 6222
Elioenai, Jaakobah, Jeshohaiah, **A**, 1Ch 4:36 6222
son, Haggiah his son, **A** his son. 1Ch 6:30 6222
were **A** the firstborn and his sons. 1Ch 9:5 6222
the sons of Merari, **A** the chief, 1Ch 15:6 6222
and for the Levites, for Uriel, **A**, 1Ch 15:11 6222
scribe, and **A** the king's servant, 2Ch 34:20 6222

ASAPH
Joah the son of **A** the recorder, 2Ki 18:18 623
the scribe and Joah the son of **A**, 2Ki 18:37 623
brother **A** stood at his right hand, 1Ch 6:39 623
hand, even **A** the son of Berechiah, 1Ch 6:39 623
the son of Zichri, the son of **A**, 1Ch 9:15 623
relatives, **A** the son of Berechiah; 1Ch 15:17 623
So the singers, Heman, **A** and 1Ch 15:19 623
A the chief, and second to him 1Ch 16:5 623
A *played* loud-sounding cymbals, 1Ch 16:5 623
on that day David first assigned **A** 1Ch 16:7 623
So he left **A** and his relatives 1Ch 16:37 623
of **A** and of Heman and of Jeduthun, 1Ch 25:1 623
Of the sons of **A**: 1Ch 25:2 623
the sons of **A** *were* under the 1Ch 25:2 623
were under the direction of **A**, 1Ch 25:2 623
A, Jeduthun and Heman *were* under 1Ch 25:6 623
lot came out for **A** to Joseph, 1Ch 25:9 623
the son of Kore, of the sons of **A**. 1Ch 26:1 623
and all the Levitical singers, **A**, 2Ch 5:12 623
the Levite of the sons of **A**; 2Ch 20:14 623
and from the sons of **A**, 2Ch 29:13 623
the words of David and **A** the seer. 2Ch 29:30 623
The singers, the sons of **A**, 2Ch 35:15 623
to the command of David, **A**, 2Ch 35:15 623
the sons of **A**, 128. Ezr 2:41 623
and the Levites, the sons of **A**, Ezr 3:10 623
and a letter to **A** the keeper of Ne 2:8 623
the sons of **A**, 148. Ne 7:44 623
the son of Zabdi, the son of **A**, Ne 11:17 623
son of Mica, from the sons of **A**, Ne 11:22 623
the son of Zaccur, the son of **A**, Ne 12:35 623
For in the days of David and **A**, Ne 12:46 623
the scribe, and Joah the son of **A**, Is 36:3 623
the scribe and Joah the son of **A**, Is 36:22 623

ASAREL
were Ziph and Ziphah, Tiria and **A**. 1Ch 4:16 840

ASA'S
of the fifteenth year of **A** reign. 2Ch 15:10 609
nevertheless **A** heart was blameless 2Ch 15:17 609
the thirty-fifth year of **A** reign. 2Ch 15:19 609
In the thirty-sixth year of **A** 2Ch 16:1 609

ASCEND
but they shall not **a** for a Lv 2:12 5927
die on the mountain where you **a**, Dt 32:50 5927
may **a** into the hill of the LORD? Ps 24:3 5927
to **a** from the ends of the earth; Ps 135:7 5927
If I **a** to heaven, You are there; Ps 139:8 5559a
'I will **a** to heaven; Is 14:13 5927
'I will **a** above the heights of the Is 14:14 5927
to **a** from the end of the earth; Jer 10:13 5927
will **a** with continual weeping; Jer 48:5 5927
to **a** from the end of the earth; Jer 51:16 5927
Babylon should **a** to the heavens, Jer 51:53 5927
And though they **a** to heaven, From Am 9:2 5927
The deliverers will **a** Mount Zion Ob 1:21 5927
'I **a** to My Father and your Father, Jn 20:17 *305*
'WHO WILL **A** INTO HEAVEN?' Ro 10:6 *305*

ASCENDANCY
a over him and obtain dominion; Da 11:5 2388

ASCENDED
a like the smoke of a furnace. Gn 19:28 5927
a like the smoke of a furnace, Ex 19:18 5927
smoke of the city **a** to the sky, Jos 8:20 5927
and that the smoke of the city **a**, Jos 8:21 5927
LORD **a** in the flame of the altar. Jg 13:20 5927
God has **a** with a shout, The LORD, Ps 47:5 5927
You have **a** on high, You have led Ps 68:18 5927
has **a** into heaven and descended? Pr 30:4 5927
And the cry of Jerusalem has **a**. Jer 14:2 5927
at the stairway by which it was **a** Ezk 40:49 5927
"No one has **a** into heaven, Jn 3:13 *305*
I have not yet **a** to the Father; Jn 20:17 *305*
was not David who **a** into heaven, Ac 2:34 *305*
have **a** as a memorial before God. Ac 10:4 *305*
"WHEN HE **A** ON HIGH, HE LED Eph 4:8 *305*
"He **a**," what does it mean except Eph 4:9 *305*
who **a** far above all the heavens, Eph 4:10 *305*

ASCENDING
God were **a** and descending on it. Gn 28:12 5927
of Shallecheth, on the **a** highway. 1Ch 26:16 5927
and the angels of God **a** and Jn 1:51 *305*
Son of Man **a** to where He was before? Jn 6:62 *305*
a from the rising of the sun, Rv 7:2 *305*

ASCENDS
against You which **a** continually. Ps 74:23 5927
Who knows that the breath of man **a** Ec 3:21 5927

ASCENSION
days were approaching for His **a**, Lk 9:51 *354*

ASCENT
the south to the **a** of Akrabbim and Nu 34:4 4610
by the way of the **a** of Beth-horon and Jos 10:10 4608
southward to the **a** of Akrabbim Jos 15:3 4610
is opposite the **a** of Adummim, Jos 15:7 4608
is opposite the **a** of Adummim, Jos 18:17 4608
ran from the **a** of Akrabbim, Jg 1:36 4610
from the battle by the **a** of Heres. Jg 8:13 4608
up the **a** of the *Mount of* Olives, 2Sa 15:30 4608
So they shot him at the **a** of Gur, 2Ki 9:27 4608
they will come up by the **a** of Ziz, 2Ch 20:16 4608
the **a** of the armory at the Angle. Ne 3:19 5927
go up the **a** of Luhith weeping; Is 15:5 4608
"For by the **a** of Luhith They will Jer 48:5 4608

ASCERTAIN
"And wanting to **a** the charge for Ac 23:28 *1921*
you will be able to **a** the things Ac 24:8 *1921*

ASCERTAINED
of the bronze could not be **a**. 1Ki 7:47 2713

ASCERTAINING
And **a** this from the centurion, he Mk 15:45 *1097*

ASCRIBE
A greatness to our God! Dt 32:3 3051
A to the LORD, O families of the 1Ch 16:28 3051
A to the LORD glory and strength. 1Ch 16:28 3051
A to the LORD the glory due His 1Ch 16:29 3051
will **a** righteousness to my Maker. Jb 36:3 5414
A to the LORD, O sons of the Ps 29:1 3051
A to the LORD glory and strength. Ps 29:1 3051
A to the LORD the glory due to His Ps 29:2 3051
A strength to God; Ps 68:34 5414
A to the LORD, O families of the Ps 96:7 3051
A to the LORD glory and strength. Ps 96:7 3051
A to the LORD the glory of His Ps 96:8 3051

ASCRIBED
have **a** to David ten thousands, 1Sa 18:8 5414
but to me they have **a** thousands. 1Sa 18:8 5414

ASENATH
and he gave him **A**, the daughter of Gn 41:45 621
sons were born to Joseph, whom **A**, Gn 41:50 621

born Manasseh and Ephraim, whom A, Gn 46:20 621
ASH
He lifts the needy from the a heap 1Sa 2:8 830
lifts the needy from the a heap, Ps 113:7 830
reared in purple Embrace a pits. La 4:5 830
ASHAMED
were both naked and were not a. Gn 2:25 954
they urged him until he was a, 2Ki 2:17 954
steadily *on him* until he was a, 2Ki 8:11 954
And the priests and Levites were a 2Ch 30:15 3637
For I was a to request from the Ezr 8:22 954
I am a and embarrassed to lift up Ezr 9:6 954
me; You are not a to wrong me. Jb 19:3 954
will be a and greatly dismayed; Ps 6:10 954
back, they will suddenly be a. Ps 6:10 954
You I trust, Do not let me be a; Ps 25:2 954
those who wait for You will be a; Ps 25:3 954
without cause will be a. Ps 25:3 954
Do not let me be a, Ps 25:20 954
Let me never be a; Ps 31:1 954
And their faces will never be a. Ps 34:5 2659
Let those be a and dishonored who Ps 35:4 954
Let those be a and humiliated Ps 35:26 954
will not be a in the time of evil, Ps 37:19 954
Let those be a and humiliated Ps 40:14 954
wait for You not be a through me, Ps 69:6 954
Let those be a and humiliated Who Ps 70:2 954
Let me never be a. Ps 71:1 954
of my soul be a *and* consumed; Ps 71:13 954
For they are a, for they are Ps 71:24 954
them be a and dismayed forever, Ps 83:17 954
who hate me may see *it* and be a, Ps 86:17 954
be a who serve graven images, Ps 97:7 954
When they arise, they shall be a, Ps 109:28 954
Then I shall not be a When I look Ps 119:6 954
before kings And shall not be a. Ps 119:46 954
May the arrogant be a, Ps 119:78 954
So that I will not be a. Ps 119:80 954
And do not let me be a of my hope. Ps 119:116 954
They will not be a Ps 127:5 954
you will be a of the oaks which Is 1:29 954
"Then they will be dismayed and a Is 20:5 954
Be a, O Sidon; For the sea speaks, Is 23:4 954
will be abashed and the sun a, Is 24:23 954
"Jacob shall not now be a, Is 29:22 954
"Everyone will be a because of a Is 30:5 954
And I know that I will not be a. Is 50:7 954
You refused to be a. Jer 3:3 3637
"Were they a because of the Jer 6:15 954
They were not even a at all; Jer 6:15 954
"Were they a because of the Jer 8:12 954
They certainly were not a, Jer 8:12 954
But be a of your harvest Because Jer 12:13 954
They will be utterly a, Jer 20:11 954
Then you will surely be a and Jer 22:22 954
I was a and also humiliated Jer 31:19 954
"And Moab will be a of Chemosh, Jer 48:13 954
house of Israel was a of Bethel, Jer 48:13 954
Moab has turned his back—he is a! Jer 48:39 954
Your mother will be greatly a, Jer 50:12 954
We are a because we have heard Jer 51:51 954
who are a of your lewd conduct. Ezk 16:27 3637
be also a and bear your disgrace, Ezk 16:52 954
and feel a for all that you have Ezk 16:54 3637
a when you receive your sisters, Ezk 16:61 3637
that you may remember and be a and Ezk 16:63 954
Be a and confounded for your ways, Ezk 36:32 954
they may be a of their iniquities; Ezk 43:10 3637
are a of all that they have done, Ezk 43:11 3637
be a because of their sacrifices. Hos 4:19 954
will be a of its own counsel. Hos 10:6 954
Be a, O farmers, Wail, O Jl 1:11 954
The seers will be a And the Mi 3:7 954
see and be a Of all their might. Mi 7:16 954
will each be a of his vision when he Zch 13:4 954
"For whoever is a of Me and My Mk 8:38 *1870*
the Son of Man will also be a of Mk 8:38 *1870*
whoever is a of Me and My words, Lk 9:26 *1870*
a of him when He comes in His glory, Lk 9:26 *1870*
strong enough to dig; I am a to beg. Lk 16:3 *153*
For I am not a of the gospel, for Ro 1:16 *1870*
the things of which you are now a? Ro 6:21 *1870*
be a of the testimony of our Lord or 2Tm 1:8 *1870*
these things, but I am not a; 2Tm 1:12 *1870*
me and was not a of my chains; 2Tm 1:16 *1870*
workman who does not need to be a, 2Tm 2:15 *422*
He is not a to call them brethren, Heb 2:11 *1870*
is not a to be called their God; Heb 11:16 *1870*
a Christian, he is not to be a, 1Pe 4:16 *153*
ASHAN
Libnah and Ether and A, Jos 15:42 6228
Ain, Rimmon and Ether and A; Jos 19:7 6228
Etam, Ain, Rimmon, Tochen and A, 1Ch 4:32 6228
A with its pasture lands and 1Ch 6:59 6228
ASHARELAH
Zaccur, Joseph, Nethaniah and A; 1Ch 25:2 841
ASHBEL
Bela and Becher and A, Gn 46:21 788
of A, the family of the Ashbelites; Nu 26:38 788
Bela his firstborn, A the second, 1Ch 8:1 788
ASHBELITES
of Ashbel, the family of the A; Nu 26:38 789
ASHDOD
in Gath, and in A some remained. Jos 11:22 795
all that were by the side of A, Jos 15:46 795
A, its towns and its villages; Jos 15:47 795
and brought it from Ebenezer to A. 1Sa 5:1 795
of Dagon in A to this day. 1Sa 5:5 795
both A and its territories. 1Sa 5:6 795
the men of A saw that it was so, 1Sa 5:7 795
one for A, one for Gaza, one for 1Sa 6:17 795
wall of Jabneh and the wall of A; 2Ch 26:6 795
of A and among the Philistines. 2Ch 26:6 795
the Jews had married women from A, Ne 13:23 796
half spoke in the language of A, Ne 13:24 797
year that the commander came to A, Is 20:1 795
fought against A and captured it, Is 20:1 795
Ekron and the remnant of A); Jer 25:20 795
cut off the inhabitant from A, Am 1:8 795
Proclaim on the citadels in A and Am 3:9 795
A will be driven out at noon And Zph 2:4 795
a mongrel race will dwell in A, Zch 9:6 795
ASHDODITE
the Gazite, the A, the Jos 13:3 796
ASHDODITES
A arose early the next morning, 1Sa 5:3 796
of the LORD was heavy on the A, 1Sa 5:6 796
and the A heard that the repair of Ne 4:7 796
ASHEN
I looked, and behold, an a horse; Rv 6:8 *5515*
ASHER
So she named him A. Gn 30:13 836
Gad and A. These are the sons of Gn 35:26 836
The sons of A: Imnah and Ishvah Gn 46:17 836
"As for A, his food shall be Gn 49:20 836
Dan and Naphtali, Gad and A. Ex 1:4 836
of A, Pagiel the son of Ochran; Nu 1:13 836
Of the sons of A, their Nu 1:40 836
numbered men of the tribe of A Nu 1:41 836
to him *shall be* the tribe of A, Nu 2:27 836
and the leader of the sons of A: Nu 2:27 836
Ochran, leader of the sons of A; Nu 7:72 836
the tribal army of the sons of A; Nu 10:26 836
from the tribe of A, Nu 13:13 836
of A according to their families: Nu 26:44 836
of the daughter of A *was* Serah. Nu 26:46 836
families of the sons of A according Nu 26:47 836
tribe of the sons of A a leader, Nu 34:27 836
Reuben, Gad, A, Zebulun, Dan, and Dt 27:13 836
Of A he said, Dt 33:24 836
"More blessed than sons is A; Dt 33:24 836
border of Manasseh ran from A to Jos 17:7 836
and they reached to A on the north Jos 17:10 836
In Issachar and in A, Jos 17:11 836
of A according to their families. Jos 19:24 836
of A according to their families, Jos 19:31 836
south and touched A on the west, Jos 19:34 836
of Issachar and from the tribe of A Jos 21:6 836
From the tribe of A, Jos 21:30 836
A did not drive out the Jg 1:31 836
A sat at the seashore, And Jg 5:17 836
and he sent messengers to A, Jg 6:35 836
Naphtali and A and all Manasseh, Jg 7:23 836
son of Hushai, in A and Bealoth; 1Ki 4:16 836
Benjamin, Naphtali, Gad and A. 1Ch 2:2 836
Issachar and from the tribe of A, 1Ch 6:62 836
and from the tribe of A: 1Ch 6:74 836
The sons of A *were* Imnah, Ishvah, 1Ch 7:30 836
All these *were* the sons of A, 1Ch 7:40 836
Of A *there were* 40,000 who 1Ch 12:36 836
Nevertheless some men of A, 2Ch 30:11 836
the east side to the west side, A, Ezk 48:2 836
"Beside the border of A, Ezk 48:3 836
the gate of A, one; Ezk 48:34 836
of Phanuel, of the tribe of A. Lk 2:36 *768*
the tribe of A twelve thousand, Rv 7:6 *768*
ASHERAH
shall not plant for yourself an A Dt 16:21 842
cut down the A that is beside it; Jg 6:25 842
the A which you shall cut down." Jg 6:26 842
and the A which was beside it was Jg 6:28 842
down the A which was beside it." Jg 6:30 842
had made a horrid image as an A; 1Ki 15:13 842
Ahab also made the A. 1Ki 16:33 842
of Baal and 400 prophets of the A, 1Ki 18:19 842
and the A also remained standing 2Ki 13:6 842
and made an A and worshiped all 2Ki 17:16 842
sacred pillars and cut down the A. 2Ki 18:4 842
altars for Baal and made an A, 2Ki 21:3 842
image of A that he had made, 2Ki 21:7 842
that were made for Baal, for A, 2Ki 23:4 842
He brought out the A from the 2Ki 23:6 842
were weaving hangings for the A. 2Ki 23:7 842
them to dust, and burned the A. 2Ki 23:15 842
had made a horrid image as an A, 2Ch 15:16 842
ASHERIM
pillars and cut down their A Ex 34:13 842
pillars, and hew down their A, Dt 7:5 842
and burn their A with fire, Dt 12:3 842
because they have made their A, 1Ki 14:15 842
sacred pillars and A on every high 1Ki 14:23 842
sacred pillars and A on every high 2Ki 17:10 842
the *sacred* pillars and cut down the A 2Ki 23:14 842
sacred pillars, cut down the A, 2Ch 14:3 842
high places and the A from Judah. 2Ch 17:6 842
and served the A and the idols; 2Ch 24:18 842
pillars in pieces, cut down the A and 2Ch 31:1 842
altars for the Baals and made A, 2Ch 33:3 842
the A and the carved images, 2Ch 33:19 842
of the high places, the A, 2Ch 34:3 842
also the A, the carved images and 2Ch 34:4 842
tore down the altars and beat the A 2Ch 34:7 842
Even the A and incense stands. Is 17:8 842
When A and incense altars will not Is 27:9 842
remember their altars and their A Jer 17:2 842
"I will root out your A from Mi 5:14 842
ASHERITES
the A lived among the Canaanites, Jg 1:32 843
ASHEROTH
and served the Baals and the A. Jg 3:7 842
for you have removed the A from 2Ch 19:3 842
ASHES
although I am *but* dust and a. Gn 18:27 665
make its pails for removing its a, Ex 27:3 1878
eastward, to the place of the a. Lv 1:16 1880
camp where the a are poured out, Lv 4:12 1880
where the a are poured out it Lv 4:12 1880
and he shall take up the a *to* Lv 6:10 1880
and carry the a outside the camp Lv 6:11 1880
take away the a from the altar, Nu 4:13 1878
shall gather up the a of the heifer Nu 19:9 665
'The one who gathers the a of Nu 19:10 665
a of the burnt purification from sin Nu 19:17 6083
Tamar put a on her head and 2Sa 13:19 665
altar shall be split apart and the a 1Ki 13:3 1880
the a were poured out from the altar 1Ki 13:5 1880
and carried their a to Bethel. 2Ki 23:4 6083
clothes, put on sackcloth and a, Es 4:1 665
and many lay on sackcloth and a. Es 4:3 665
while he was sitting among the a. Jb 2:8 665
sayings are proverbs of a, Jb 13:12 665
And I have become like dust and a. Jb 30:19 665
And I repent in dust and a." Jb 42:6 665
For I have eaten a like bread And Ps 102:9 665
He scatters the frost like a. Ps 147:16 665
He feeds on a; a deceived heart has Is 44:20 665
out sackcloth and a as a bed? Is 58:5 665
them a garland instead of a, Is 61:3 665
put on sackcloth And roll in a; Jer 6:26 665
And wallow *in* a, you masters of Jer 25:34
of the dead bodies and of the a, Jer 31:40 1880
heads, They will wallow in a. Ezk 27:30 665
And I have turned you to a on the Ezk 28:18 665
with fasting, sackcloth and a. Da 9:3 665
with sackcloth and sat on the a. Jon 3:6 665
for they will be a under the Mal 4:3 665
long ago in sackcloth and a. Mt 11:21 *4700*
ago, sitting in sackcloth and a. Lk 10:13 *4700*
blood of goats and bulls and the a of Heb 9:13 *4700*
destruction by reducing *them* to a, 2Pe 2:6 *5077*
ASHHUR
bore him A the father of Tekoa. 1Ch 2:24 806a
A, the father of Tekoa, had 1Ch 4:5 806a
ASHIMA
Nergal, the men of Hamath made A, 2Ki 17:30 807
ASHKELON
Gaza with its territory and A with its Jg 1:18 831
and he went down to A and killed Jg 14:19 831
Ashdod, one for Gaza, one for A, 1Sa 6:17 831
it not in the streets of A, 2Sa 1:20 831
land of the Philistines (even A, Jer 25:20 831
A has been ruined. Jer 47:5 831
Against A and against the Jer 47:7 831
him who holds the scepter, from A; Am 1:8 831
be abandoned And A a desolation; Zph 2:4 831
A they will lie down at evening; Zph 2:7 831
A will see *it* and be afraid. Zch 9:5 831
Gaza, And A will not be inhabited. Zch 9:5 831
ASHKELONITE
the Gazite, the Ashdodite, the A, Jos 13:3 832
ASHKENAZ
were A and Riphath and Togarmah. Gn 10:3 813
The sons of Gomer *were* A, 1Ch 1:6 813
kingdoms of Ararat, Minni and A; Jer 51:27 813
ASHNAH
Eshtaol and Zorah and A, Jos 15:33 823
and Iphtah and A and Nezib, Jos 15:43 823
ASHORE
When He went a, Mt 14:14 *1831*
When Jesus went a, Mk 6:34 *1831*
ASHPENAZ
Then the king ordered A, Da 1:3 828
ASHTAROTH
Bashan, who lived in A and Edrei. Dt 1:4 6252a
to Og king of Bashan who was at A. Jos 9:10 6252a
who lived at A and at Edrei, Jos 12:4 6252a
who reigned in A and in Edrei Jos 13:12 6252a
half of Gilead, with A and Edrei, Jos 13:31 6252a
LORD and served Baal and the A. Jg 2:13 6252b
LORD, served the Baals and the A, Jg 10:6 6252b
remove the foreign gods and the A 1Sa 7:3 6252b
the A and served the LORD alone. 1Sa 7:4 6252b
have served the Baals and the A; 1Sa 12:10 6252b
his weapons in the temple of A, 1Sa 31:10 6252b
and A with its pasture lands; 1Ch 6:71 6252a
ASHTERATHITE
Uzzia the A, Shama and Jeiel the 1Ch 11:44 6254
ASHTEROTH-KARNAIM
came and defeated the Rephaim in A Gn 14:5 6255
ASHTORETH
For Solomon went after A the 1Ki 11:5 6252b
A the goddess of the Sidonians, 1Ki 11:33 6252b
A the abomination of the Sidonians, 2Ki 23:13 6252b
ASHURITES
him king over Gilead, over the A, 2Sa 2:9 805a
ASHVATH
were Pasach, Bimhal and A. 1Ch 7:33 6220
ASIA
and Cappadocia, Pontus and A, Ac 2:9 *773*
and some from Cilicia and A, Ac 6:9 *773*

Spirit to speak the word in **A**;	**Ac 16:6**	*773*
in **A** heard the word of the Lord,	**Ac 19:10**	*773*
himself stayed in **A** for a while.	**Ac 19:22**	*773*
Ephesus, but in almost all of **A**,	**Ac 19:26**	*773*
worthless and that she whom all of **A**	**Ac 19:27**	*773*
and Tychicus and Trophimus of **A**.	**Ac 20:4**	*774*
would not have to spend time in **A**;	**Ac 20:16**	*773*
first day that I set foot in **A**,	**Ac 20:18**	*773*
were almost over, the Jews from **A**,	**Ac 21:27**	*773*
there were some Jews from **A**	**Ac 24:18**	*773*
the regions along the coast of **A**,	**Ac 27:2**	*773*
first convert to Christ from **A**.	**Ro 16:5**	*773*
The churches of **A** greet you.	**1Co 16:19**	*773*
affliction which came *to us* in **A**,	**2Co 1:8**	*773*
who are in **A** turned away from me,	**2Tm 1:15**	*773*
Pontus, Galatia, Cappadocia, **A**,	**1Pe 1:1**	*773*
the seven churches that are in **A**:	**Rv 1:4**	*773*

ASIARCHS

Also some of the **A** who were	**Ac 19:31**	*775*

ASIDE

turn **a** into your servant's house,	**Gn 19:2**	5493
a to him and entered his house;	**Gn 19:3**	5493
But they said, "Stand **a**."	**Gn 19:9**	1973
So he turned **a** to her by the road,	**Gn 38:16**	5186
"I must turn **a** now and see this	**Ex 3:3**	5493
LORD saw that he turned **a** to look,	**Ex 3:4**	5493
men on foot, **a** from children.	**Ex 12:37**	905
put **a** to be kept until morning."	**Ex 16:23**	5117
So they put it **a** until morning, as	**Ex 16:24**	5117
testify in a dispute so as to turn **a**	**Ex 23:2**	5186
"They have quickly turned **a** from	**Ex 32:8**	5493
"But the donkey saw me and turned **a**	**Nu 22:33**	5186
If she had not turned **a** from me,	**Nu 22:33**	5186
a to the right or to the left.	**Dt 2:27**	5493
a to the right or to the left.	**Dt 5:32**	5493
They have quickly turned **a** from	**Dt 9:12**	5493
you had turned **a** quickly from the	**Dt 9:16**	5493
but turn **a** from the way which I am	**Dt 11:28**	5493
you shall not turn **a** from the word	**Dt 17:11**	5493
not turn **a** from the commandment,	**Dt 17:20**	5493
you shall set **a** three cities for	**Dt 19:2**	914
set **a** three cities for yourself.'	**Dt 19:7**	914
and do not turn **a** from any of the	**Dt 28:14**	5493
so that you may not turn **a** from it	**Jos 23:6**	5493
They turned **a** quickly from the way	**Jg 2:17**	5493
"Turn **a**, my master, turn aside to	**Jg 4:18**	5493
aside, my master, turn **a** to me!	**Jg 4:18**	5493
he turned **a** to her into the tent,	**Jg 4:18**	5493
he turned **a** to look at the carcass	**Jg 14:8**	5493
and they turned **a** there and said	**Jg 18:3**	5493
They turned **a** there and came	**Jg 18:15**	5493
and let us turn **a** into this city	**Jg 19:11**	5493
"We will not turn **a** into the city	**Jg 19:12**	5493
They turned **a** there in order	**Jg 19:15**	5493
"Turn **a**, friend, sit down here."	**Ru 4:1**	5493
And he turned **a** and sat down.	**Ru 4:1**	5493
a to the right or to the left.	**1Sa 6:12**	5493
but turned **a** after dishonest gain	**1Sa 8:3**	5186
which I said to you, 'Set it **a**.' "	**1Sa 9:23**	5973
turn **a** from following the LORD,	**1Sa 12:20**	5493
"You must not turn **a**,	**1Sa 12:21**	5493
to turn **a** from following him.	**2Sa 2:21**	5493
"Turn **a** from following me.	**2Sa 2:22**	5493
However, he refused to turn **a**;	**2Sa 2:23**	5493
Joab took him **a** into the middle of	**2Sa 3:27**	5186
but David took it **a** to the house	**2Sa 6:10**	5186
"Turn **a** and stand here."	**2Sa 18:30**	5437
So he turned **a** and stood still.	**2Sa 18:30**	5437
and had not turned **a** from anything	**1Ki 15:5**	5493
either he is occupied or gone **a**,	**1Ki 18:27**	5509
a man turned **a** and brought a man	**1Ki 20:39**	5493
turned **a** to fight against him,	**1Ki 22:32**	5493
he did not turn **a** from it, doing	**1Ki 22:43**	5493
you shall set **a** what is full."	**2Ki 4:4**	5265
a to the right or to the left.	**2Ki 22:2**	5493
but took it **a** to the house of	**1Ch 13:13**	5186
turned **a** to fight against him.	**2Ch 18:31**	5437
they turned **a** from them and did not	**2Ch 20:10**	5493
a to the right or to the left.	**2Ch 34:2**	5493
a from all that was given as a	**Ezr 1:6**	905
kept His way and not turned **a**.	**Jb 23:11**	5186
push the needy **a** from the road;	**Jb 24:4**	5186
They thrust **a** my feet and build up	**Jb 30:12**	
may turn man **a** *from his* conduct,	**Jb 33:17**	5493
they turned **a** from following Him,	**Jb 34:27**	5493
of the ransom turn you **a**.	**Jb 36:18**	5186
They have all turned **a**,	**Ps 14:3**	5493
Every one of them has turned **a**;	**Ps 53:3**	5472
turned **a** like a treacherous bow.	**Ps 78:57**	2015
Yet I do not turn **a** from Your law.	**Ps 119:51**	5186
turned **a** from Your ordinances,	**Ps 119:102**	5493
not turn **a** from Your testimonies.	**Ps 119:157**	5186
who turn **a** to their crooked ways,	**Ps 125:5**	5186
let your heart turn **a** to her ways,	**Pr 7:25**	7847
turn **a** from the snares of death.	**Pr 13:14**	5493
thrust **a** the righteous in judgment.	**Pr 18:5**	5186
of the way, turn **a** from the path,	**Is 30:11**	5186
a deceived heart has turned him **a**.	**Is 44:20**	5186
And he who turns **a** from evil makes	**Is 59:15**	5493
They have turned **a** and departed.	**Jer 5:23**	5493
turn **a** to ask about your welfare?	**Jer 15:5**	5493
made them turn **a** *on* the mountains;	**Jer 50:6**	7725
a my ways and torn me to pieces;	**La 3:11**	5493
even turning **a** from Your	**Da 9:5**	5493
transgressed Your law and turned **a**,	**Da 9:11**	5493
Also turn **a** the way of the humble;	**Am 2:7**	5186
And turn **a** the poor in the gate.	**Am 5:12**	5186
throne, laid **a** his robe from him,	**Jon 3:6**	5674a
you have turned **a** from the way;	**Mal 2:8**	5493
and those who turn **a** the alien and	**Mal 3:5**	5186
have turned **a** from My statutes and	**Mal 3:7**	5493
Him **a** and began to rebuke Him,	**Mt 16:22**	*4355*
twelve *disciples* **a** by themselves,	**Mt 20:17**	
experts at setting **a** the commandment	**Mk 7:9**	*114*
a from the crowd, by himself,	**Mk 7:33**	*618*
Him **a** and began to rebuke Him.	**Mk 8:32**	*4355*
And again He took the twelve **a** and	**Mk 10:32**	*3880*
Throwing **a** his cloak, he jumped	**Mk 10:50**	*577*
the twelve **a** and said to them,	**Lk 18:31**	*3880*
supper, and laid **a** His garments;	**Jn 13:4**	*5087*
turned **a** to go to his own place."	**Ac 1:25**	*3845*
and the witnesses laid **a** their	**Ac 7:58**	*659*
they took him **a** and explained to	**Ac 18:26**	*4355*
him by the hand and stepping **a**,	**Ac 23:19**	*402*
and when they had gone **a**,	**Ac 26:31**	*402*
ALL HAVE TURNED A, TOGETHER THEY	**Ro 3:12**	*1578*
Therefore let us lay **a** the deeds	**Ro 13:12**	*659*
OF THE CLEVER I WILL SET A."	**1Co 1:19**	*114*
each one of you is to put **a** and save,	**1Co 16:2**	*3844, 1438*
it **a** or adds conditions to it.	**Ga 3:15**	*114*
of life, you lay **a** the old self,	**Eph 4:22**	*659*
Therefore, laying **a** falsehood,	**Eph 4:25**	*659*
But now you also, put them all **a**:	**Col 3:8**	*659*
since you laid **a** the old self with	**Col 3:9**	*554*
turned **a** to fruitless discussion,	**1Tm 1:6**	*1624*
have set **a** their previous pledge.	**1Tm 5:12**	*114*
already turned **a** to follow Satan.	**1Tm 5:15**	*1624*
truth and will turn **a** to myths.	**2Tm 4:4**	*1624*
there is a setting **a** of a former	**Heb 7:18**	*115*
Anyone who has set **a** the Law of	**Heb 10:28**	*114*
us also lay **a** every encumbrance and	**Heb 12:1**	*659*
Therefore, putting **a** all filthiness	**Jas 1:21**	*659*
putting **a** all malice and all deceit	**1Pe 2:1**	*659*
knowing that the laying **a** of my	**2Pe 1:14**	*595*

ASIEL

the son of Seraiah, the son of **A**,	**1Ch 4:35**	6221

ASK

"Why is it that you **a** my name?"	**Gn 32:29**	7592
"**A** me ever so much bridal payment	**Gn 34:12**	7235a
"But every woman shall **a** of her	**Ex 3:22**	7592
that each man **a** from his neighbor	**Ex 11:2**	7592
a now concerning the former days	**Dt 4:32**	7592
A your father, and he will inform	**Dt 32:7**	7592
that when your children **a** later,	**Jos 4:6**	7592
a their fathers in time to come,	**Jos 4:21**	7592
not **a** for the counsel of the LORD.	**Jos 9:14**	7592
him to **a** her father for a field.	**Jos 15:18**	7592
him to **a** her father for a field.	**Jg 1:14**	7592
did not **a** him where he *came* from,	**Jg 13:6**	7592
"Why do you **a** my name, seeing it	**Jg 13:18**	7592
I will do for you whatever you **a**,	**Ru 3:11**	559
'**A** your young men and they will	**1Sa 25:8**	7592
"Why then do you **a** me, since the	**1Sa 28:16**	7592
me that I am about to **a** you."	**2Sa 14:18**	7592
'They will surely **a** *advice* at Abel,'	**2Sa 20:18**	7592
"**A**, my mother, for I will not	**1Ki 2:20**	7592
A for him also the kingdom—for he	**1Ki 2:22**	7592
"**A** what *you wish* me to give you."	**1Ki 3:5**	7592
"**A** what I shall do for you before	**2Ki 2:9**	7592
"Did I **a** for a son from my lord?	**2Ki 4:28**	7592
"**A** what I shall give you."	**2Ch 1:7**	7592
in mind, and did not **a** for riches,	**2Ch 1:11**	7592
a the king to have Mordecai hanged	**Es 5:14**	559
"But now **a** the beasts, and let	**Jb 12:7**	7592
like a man, And I will **a** you,	**Jb 38:3**	7592
I will **a** you, and you instruct Me.	**Jb 40:7**	7592
I will **a** You, and You	**Jb 42:4**	7592
'**A** of Me, and I will surely give	**Ps 2:8**	7592
They **a** me of things that I do not	**Ps 35:11**	7592
from wisdom that you **a** about this.	**Ec 7:10**	7592
"**A** a sign for yourself from the	**Is 7:11**	7592
"I will not **a**, nor will I test	**Is 7:12**	7592
counselor among them Who, if I **a**,	**Is 41:28**	7592
"**A** Me about the things to come	**Is 45:11**	7592
They **a** Me *for* just decisions, They	**Is 58:2**	7592
by those who did not **a** *for Me;*	**Is 65:1**	7592
see and **a** for the ancient paths,	**Jer 6:16**	7592
aside to **a** about your welfare?	**Jer 15:5**	7592
'**A** now among the nations, Who ever	**Jer 18:13**	7592
'**A** now, and see If a male can	**Jer 30:6**	7592
"I am going to **a** you something;	**Jer 38:14**	7592
A him who flees and her who	**Jer 48:19**	7592
"They will **a** for the way to Zion,	**Jer 50:5**	7592
The little ones **a** for bread, *But*	**La 4:4**	7592
of Israel **a** Me to do for them:	**Ezk 36:37**	1875
'**A** now the priests *for* a ruling:	**Hg 2:11**	7592
A rain from the LORD at the time	**Zch 10:1**	7592
what you need before you **a** Him.	**Mt 6:8**	*154*
"**A**, and it will be given to you;	**Mt 7:7**	*154*
what is good to those who **a** Him!	**Mt 7:11**	*154*
about anything that they may **a**,	**Mt 18:19**	*154*
"And all things you **a** in prayer,	**Mt 21:22**	*154*
"I will also **a** you one thing,	**Mt 21:24**	*2065*
day on to **a** Him another question.	**Mt 22:46**	*1905*
the crowds to **a** for Barabbas	**Mt 27:20**	*154*
"**A** me for whatever you want and I	**Mk 6:22**	*154*
"Whatever you **a** of me, I will	**Mk 6:23**	*154*
"What shall I **a** for?"	**Mk 6:24**	*154*
and they were afraid to **a** Him.	**Mk 9:32**	*1905*
do for us whatever we **a** of You."	**Mk 10:35**	*154*
things for which you pray and **a**,	**Mk 11:24**	*154*
"I will **a** you one question, and	**Mk 11:29**	*1905*
to **a** Him any more questions.	**Mk 12:34**	*1905*
priests stirred up the crowd *to* **a**	**Mk 15:11**	
"I **a** you, is it lawful	**Lk 6:9**	*1905*
to **a**, 'Are You the Expected One,	**Lk 7:20**	*3004*
to **a** Him about this statement.	**Lk 9:45**	*2065*
"So I say to you, **a**,	**Lk 11:9**	*154*
Holy Spirit to those who **a** Him?"	**Lk 11:13**	*154*
of him they will **a** all the more.	**Lk 12:48**	*154*
"I will also **a** you a question,	**Lk 20:3**	*2065*
and if I **a** a question, you will	**Lk 22:68**	*2065*
Levites from Jerusalem to **a** him,	**Jn 1:19**	*2065*
a me for a drink since I am a	**Jn 4:9**	*154*
A him; he is of age, he will speak	**Jn 9:21**	*2065*
"He is of age; **a** him."	**Jn 9:23**	*2065*
I know that whatever You **a** of God,	**Jn 11:22**	*154*
of Galilee, and *began to* **a** him,	**Jn 12:21**	*2065*
"Whatever you **a** in My name,	**Jn 14:13**	*154*
"If you **a** Me anything in My name,	**Jn 14:14**	*154*
"I will **a** the Father, and He	**Jn 14:16**	*2065*
abide in you, **a** whatever you wish,	**Jn 15:7**	*154*
you **a** of the Father in My name He	**Jn 15:16**	*154*
you **a** the Father for anything	**Jn 16:23**	*154*
a and you will receive, so that your	**Jn 16:24**	*154*
"In that day you will **a** in My name,	**Jn 16:26**	*154*
"I **a** on their behalf;	**Jn 17:9**	*2065*
I do not **a** on behalf of the world,	**Jn 17:9**	*2065*
I do not **a** You to take them out	**Jn 17:15**	*2065*
do not **a** on behalf of these alone,	**Jn 17:20**	*2065*
So I **a** for what reason you	**Ac 10:29**	*4441*
"The Jews have agreed to **a** you to	**Ac 23:20**	*2065*
TO THOSE WHO DID NOT A FOR ME."	**Ro 10:20**	*1905*
For indeed Jews **a** for signs and	**1Co 1:22**	*154*
them **a** their own husbands at home;	**1Co 14:35**	*1905*
I **a** that when I am present I	**2Co 10:2**	*1189a*
Therefore I **a** you not to lose	**Eph 3:13**	*154*
beyond all that we **a** or think,	**Eph 3:20**	*154*
I **a** you also to help these women	**Php 4:3**	*2065*
not ceased to pray for you and to **a**	**Col 1:9**	*154*
lacks wisdom, let him **a** of God,	**Jas 1:5**	*154*
a in faith without any doubting,	**Jas 1:6**	*154*
do not have because you do not **a**.	**Jas 4:2**	*154*
You **a** and do not receive, because	**Jas 4:3**	*154*
because you **a** with wrong motives,	**Jas 4:3**	*154*
whatever we **a** we receive from Him,	**1Jn 3:22**	*154*
if we **a** anything according to His	**1Jn 5:14**	*154*
that He hears us *in* whatever we **a**,	**1Jn 5:15**	*154*
he shall **a** and *God* will for him	**1Jn 5:16**	*154*
Now I **a** you, lady, not as	**2Jn 1:5**	*2065*

ASKED

"Then I **a** her, and said,	**Gn 24:47**	7592
men of the place **a** about his wife,	**Gn 26:7**	7592
Then Jacob **a** him and said,	**Gn 32:29**	7592
and the man **a** him,	**Gn 37:15**	7592
He **a** the men of her place,	**Gn 38:21**	7592
He **a** Pharaoh's officials who	**Gn 40:7**	7592
he **a** them about their welfare,	**Gn 43:27**	7592
"My lord **a** his servants, saying,	**Gn 44:19**	7592
over them, were beaten and were **a**,	**Ex 5:14**	559
The LORD did as Moses **a**,	**Ex 8:31**	1697
a each other of their welfare and	**Ex 18:7**	7592
"This is according to all that you **a**	**Dt 18:16**	7592
gave him the city for which he **a**,	**Jos 19:50**	7592
"He **a** for water *and* she gave him	**Jg 5:25**	7592
Micah, and **a** him of his welfare.	**Jg 18:15**	7592
petition that you have **a** of Him."	**1Sa 1:17**	7592
I have **a** him of the LORD."	**1Sa 1:20**	7592
me my petition which I **a** of Him.	**1Sa 1:27**	7592
people who had **a** of him a king.	**1Sa 8:10**	7592
have chosen, whom you have **a** for,	**1Sa 12:13**	7592
have not **a** the favor of the LORD.'	**1Sa 13:12**	2470b
and he **a** and said,	**1Sa 19:22**	7592
'David earnestly **a** *leave* of me to	**1Sa 20:6**	7592
"David earnestly **a** leave of me *to*	**1Sa 20:28**	7592
David **a** concerning the welfare of	**2Sa 11:7**	7592
that Solomon had **a** this thing.	**1Ki 3:10**	7592
"Because you have **a** this thing	**1Ki 3:11**	7592
have not **a** for yourself long life,	**1Ki 3:11**	7592
nor have **a** riches for yourself,	**1Ki 3:11**	7592
a for the life of your enemies,	**1Ki 3:11**	7592
but have **a** for yourself	**1Ki 3:11**	7592
given you what you have not **a**,	**1Ki 3:13**	7592
"You have **a** a hard thing.	**2Ki 2:10**	7592
When the king **a** the woman, she	**2Ki 8:6**	7592
because he **a** counsel of a medium,	**1Ch 10:13**	7592
nor have you even **a** for long life,	**2Ch 1:11**	7592
but you have **a** for yourself wisdom	**2Ch 1:11**	7592
"Then we **a** those elders and said	**Ezr 5:9**	7593
"We also **a** them their names so as	**Ezr 5:10**	7593
and I **a** them concerning the Jews	**Ne 1:2**	7592
and they **a** Ezra the scribe to	**Ne 8:1**	559
however, I **a** leave from the king,	**Ne 13:6**	7592
King Ahasuerus **a** Queen Esther,	**Es 7:5**	559
"Have you not **a** wayfaring men,	**Jb 21:29**	7592
He **a** life of You, You gave	**Ps 21:4**	7592
One thing I have **a** from the LORD,	**Ps 27:4**	7592
They **a**, and He brought quail, And	**Ps 105:40**	7592
Two things I **a** of You, Do not	**Pr 30:7**	7592
with riches *and he never* **a**,	**Ec 4:8**	
And they **a** Baruch, saying,	**Jer 36:17**	7592
the king secretly **a** him and said,	**Jer 37:17**	7592
has fallen, will you not be **a**,	**Ezk 13:12**	559
as no great king or ruler has *ever* **a**	**Da 2:10**	7593
oath to give her whatever she **a**.	**Mt 14:7**	*154*
testing Jesus, they **a** Him to show them	**Mt 16:1**	*1905*
And His disciples **a** Him,	**Mt 17:10**	*1905*
the disciples were amazed and **a**,	**Mt 21:20**	*3004*
them, a lawyer, **a** Him *a question,*	**Mt 22:35**	*1905*
together, Jesus **a** them a question:	**Mt 22:41**	*1905*
the disciples came to Jesus and **a**,	**Mt 26:17**	*3004*
and **a** for the body of Jesus.	**Mt 27:58**	*154*
in a hurry to the king and **a**,	**Mk 6:25**	*154*
Pharisees and the scribes **a** Him,	**Mk 7:5**	*1905*

His hands on him, He **a** him, Mk 8:23 1905
They **a** Him, saying, Mk 9:11 1905
And He **a** them, "What are you Mk 9:16 1905
And He **a** his father, Mk 9:21 1905
and **a** Him, "Good Teacher, what Mk 10:17 1905
He had answered them well, **a** Him, Mk 12:28 1905
and **a** for the body of Jesus. Mk 15:43 154
And he **a** for a tablet and wrote Lk 1:63 154
and they **a** Him to help her. Lk 4:38 2065
and **a** him to put out a little way Lk 5:3 2065
And Jesus **a** him, Lk 8:30 1905
a Him to leave them, Lk 8:37 2065
is **a** by his son for a fish; Lk 11:11 154
"Or *if* he is **a** for an egg, he Lk 11:12 154
a Him to have lunch with him; Lk 11:37 2065
So Pilate **a** Him, saying, Lk 23:3 2065
he **a** whether the man was a Lk 23:6 1905
and **a** for the body of Jesus. Lk 23:52 154
They **a** him, "What then? Jn 1:21 2065
They **a** him, and said to him, Jn 1:25 2065
Me a drink,' you would have **a** Him, Jn 4:10 154
They **a** him, "Who is the man who Jn 5:12 2065
And His disciples **a** Him, Jn 9:2 2065
you have **a** for nothing in My name; Jn 16:24 154
Therefore He again **a** them, Jn 18:7 1905
a Pilate that their legs might be Jn 19:31 2065
a Pilate that he might take away Jn 19:38 2065
and **a** for a murderer to be granted Ac 3:14 154
and **a** that he might find a Ac 7:46 154
and **a** for letters from him to the Ac 9:2 154
a directions for Simon's house, Ac 10:17 1331
a him to stay on for a few days. Ac 10:48 2065
"Then they **a** for a king, and Ac 13:21 154
they **a** Pilate that He be executed. Ac 13:28 154
a him to stay for a longer time, Ac 18:20 2065
prisoner called me to him and **a** me Ac 23:18 2065
he **a** from what province he was, Ac 23:34 1905
I **a** whether he was willing to go Ac 25:20 3004
They only **a** us to remember Ga 2:10 3421
requests which we have **a** from Him. 1Jn 5:15 154

ASKING

LORD by **a** for yourselves a king." 1Sa 12:17 7592
evil by **a** for ourselves a king." 1Sa 12:19 7592
crossed him at any time by **a**, 1Ki 1:6 559
"And why are you **a** Abishag the 1Ki 2:22 7592
sin By **a** for his life in a curse. Jb 31:30 7592
By **a** food according to their desire. Ps 78:18 7592
a him the exact meaning of all this. Da 7:16 1156
a, "Why do we and the Pharisees Mt 9:14 3004
a, "Is it lawful to heal on Mt 12:10 3004
He was **a** His disciples, Mt 16:13 2065
testing Him and **a**, "Is it lawful Mt 19:3 3004
are you **a** Me about what is good? Mt 19:17 2065
do not know what you are **a**. Mt 20:22 154
a, "Teacher, Moses said, 'IF A Mt 22:24 3004
began **a** Him *about* the parables. Mk 4:10 2065
And He was **a** him, Mk 5:9 1905
And she kept **a** Him to cast the Mk 7:26 2065
And He was **a** them, Mk 8:5 2065
do not know what you are **a**. Mk 10:38 154
crowd went up and began **a** him Mk 15:8 154
to them and **a** them questions. Lk 2:46 1905
he sent some Jewish elders **a** Him Lk 7:3 2065
blindfolded Him and were **a** Him, Lk 22:64 1905
voices **a** that He be crucified. Lk 23:23 154
he released the man they were **a** for Lk 23:25 154
they were **a** Him to stay with them; Jn 4:40 2065
But when they persisted in **a** Him, Jn 8:7 2065
a him again how he received his sight. Jn 9:15 2065
come together, they were **a** Him, Ac 1:6 2065
he *began* **a** to receive alms. Ac 3:3 2065
out, they were **a** whether Simon, Ac 10:18 4441
they were **a** for peace, Ac 12:20 154
and he *began* **a** who he was and what Ac 21:33 4441
a for a sentence of condemnation Ac 25:15 154
without **a** questions for 1Co 10:25 350
without **a** questions for 1Co 10:27 350

ASKS

brother Esau meets you and **a** you, Gn 32:17 7592
your son **a** you in time to come, Ex 13:14 7592
your son **a** you in time to come, Dt 6:20 7592
prophet or a priest **a** you saying, Jer 23:33 7592
The prince **a**, also the judge, for Mi 7:3 7592
"Give to him who **a** of you, and do Mt 5:42 154
"For everyone who **a** receives, Mt 7:8 154
when his son **a** for a loaf, will give Mt 7:9 154
"Or if he **a** for a fish, he will not Mt 7:10 154
"Give to everyone who **a** of you, Lk 6:30 154
"For everyone who **a**, receives; Lk 11:10 154
a delegation and **a** for terms of peace. Lk 14:32 2065
"If anyone **a** you, Lk 19:31 2065
and none of you **a** Me, Jn 16:5 2065
a defense to everyone who **a** you to 1Pe 3:15 154

ASLEEP

fell **a** and dreamed a second time; Gn 41:5 3462
for he was sound **a** and exhausted. Jg 4:21 7290a
any awake, for they were all **a**, 1Sa 26:12 3463
is **a** and needs to be awakened." 1Ki 18:27 3463
away like a flood, they fall **a**; Ps 90:5 8142
"I was **a** but my heart was awake. SS 5:2 3463
the lips of those who fall **a**. SS 7:9 3463
lain down and fallen sound **a**. Jon 1:5 7290a
but Jesus Himself was **a**. Mt 8:24 2518
the girl has not died, but is **a**." Mt 9:24 2518
who had fallen **a** were raised; Mt 27:52 2837
stole Him away while we were **a**.' Mt 28:13 2837
in the stern, **a** on the cushion; Mk 4:38 2518
child has not died, but is **a**." Mk 5:39 2518
he should come suddenly and find you **a**. Mk 13:36 2518
"Simon, are you **a**? Mk 14:37 2518
they were sailing along He fell **a**; Lk 8:23 879a
for she has not died, but is **a**." Lk 8:52 2518
"Our friend Lazarus has fallen **a**; Jn 11:11 2837
"Lord, if he has fallen **a**, Jn 11:12 2837
Having said this, he fell **a**. Ac 7:60 2837
God in his own generation, fell **a**, Ac 13:36 2837
until now, but some have fallen **a**; 1Co 15:6 2837
fallen **a** in Christ have perished. 1Co 15:18 2837
first fruits of those who are **a**. 1Co 15:20 2837
brethren, about those who are **a**, 1Th 4:13 2837
those who have fallen **a** in Jesus. 1Th 4:14 2837
precede those who have fallen **a**. 1Th 4:15 2837
that whether we are awake or **a**, 1Th 5:10 2518
and their destruction is not **a**. 2Pe 2:3 3573
For *ever* since the fathers fell **a**, 2Pe 3:4 2837

ASNAH

the sons of **A**, the sons of Meunim, Ezr 2:50 619

ASPATHA

and Parshandatha, Dalphon, **A**, Es 9:7 630

ASPECTS

we are to grow up in all **a** into Eph 4:15

ASPIRED

And thus I **a** to preach the gospel, Ro 15:20 5389

ASPIRES

man **a** to the office of overseer, 1Tm 3:1 3713

ASPS

POISON OF A IS UNDER THEIR LIPS"; Ro 3:13 785

ASRIEL

and *of* **A**, the family of the Nu 26:31 844
sons of Helek and for the sons of **A** Jos 17:2 844
The sons of Manasseh *were* **A**, 1Ch 7:14 844

ASRIELITES

of Asriel, the family of the **A**; Nu 26:31 845

ASSAIL

How long will you **a** a man, Ps 62:3 1956a

ASSAILANTS

The lips of my **a** and their La 3:62 6965

ASSAILING

days, and no small storm was **a** *us*, Ac 27:20 1945

ASSAILS

a *you* it will not be from Me. Is 54:15 1481b
a you will fall because of you. Is 54:15 1481b

ASSASSINS

the **A** out into the wilderness?" Ac 21:38 4607

ASSAULT

between one kind of **a** or another, Dt 17:8 5061
every **a** shall be settled by them. Dt 21:5 5061
"Will he even **a** the queen with me Es 7:8 3533

ASSAULTS

He who **a** *his* father *and* drives *his* Pr 19:26 7703

ASSAY

you may know and **a** their way." Jer 6:27 974
I will refine them and **a** them; Jer 9:7 974

ASSAYER

an **a** *and* a tester among My people, Jer 6:27 969b

ASSEMBLE

"**A** yourselves that I may tell you Gn 49:1 622
and **a** all the congregation at the Lv 8:3 6950
You shall also **a** the whole Nu 8:9 6950
of Israel, shall **a** before you. Nu 10:4 3259
and you and your brother Aaron **a** Nu 20:8 6950
"**A** the people, that I may give Nu 21:16 622
'**A** the people to Me, that I may Dt 4:10 6950
"**A** the people, the men and the Dt 31:12 6950
"**A** to me all the elders of your Dt 31:28 6950
that they should **a** at Jerusalem, Ezr 10:7 6908
it into my heart to **a** the nobles, Ne 7:5 6908
a all the Jews who are found in Es 4:16 3664
to **a** and to defend their lives, Es 8:11 6950
a the banished ones of Israel, Is 11:12 622
Let them all **a** themselves, let Is 44:11 6908
"**A**, all of you, and listen! Is 48:14 6908
'**A** yourselves, and let us go Into Jer 4:5 622
A yourselves, and let us go into Jer 8:14 622
gather you from the peoples and **a** Ezk 11:17 622
"**A** and come, gather from every Ezk 39:17 6908
king sent *word* to **a** the satraps, Da 3:2 3673
and **a** a multitude of great forces; Da 11:10 622
and new wine they **a** themselves, Hos 7:14 1481a
the congregation, **A** the elders, Jl 2:16 6908
"**A** yourselves on the mountains of Am 3:9 622
"I will surely **a** all of you, Mi 2:12 622
"I will **a** the lame And gather Mi 4:6 622
to gather nations, To **a** kingdoms, Zph 3:8 6908
priests and all the Council to **a**, Ac 22:30 4905
When you **a**, each one has a psalm, 1Co 14:26 4905
a for the great supper of God, Rv 19:17 4863

ASSEMBLED

Then Moses and Aaron went and **a** Ex 4:29 622
the people **a** about Aaron and Ex 32:1 6950
Then Moses **a** all the congregation Ex 35:1 6950
When the congregation was **a** at the Lv 8:4 6950
and they **a** all the congregation Nu 1:18 6950
They **a** together against Moses Nu 16:3 6950
Thus Korah **a** all the congregation Nu 16:19 6950
had **a** against Moses and Aaron, Nu 16:42 6950
and they **a** themselves against Nu 20:2 6950
hill country have **a** against us." Jos 10:6 6908
of Israel **a** themselves at Shiloh, Jos 18:1 6950
the sons of the east **a** themselves; Jg 6:33 622
and all Beth-millo **a** together, Jg 9:6 622
a to offer a great sacrifice to Dagon Jg 16:23 622
a and overtook the sons of Dan. Jg 18:22 2199
you, that you have **a** together?" Jg 18:23 2199
and the congregation **a** as one man Jg 20:1 6950
a to fight with Israel, 1Sa 13:5 622
Then Solomon **a** the elders of 1Ki 8:1 6950
All the men of Israel **a** 1Ki 8:2 6950
of Israel, who were **a** to him, 1Ki 8:5 3259
he **a** all the house of Judah and 1Ki 12:21 6950
So David **a** all Israel together, 1Ch 13:5 6950
David **a** all Israel at Jerusalem to 1Ch 15:3 6950
Now David **a** at Jerusalem all the 1Ch 28:1 6950
Then Solomon **a** to Jerusalem the 2Ch 5:2 6950
All the men of Israel **a** 2Ch 5:3 6950
the congregation of Israel who were **a** 2Ch 5:6 3259
he **a** the house of Judah and 2Ch 11:1 6950
So they **a** at Jerusalem in the 2Ch 15:10 6908
the king of Israel **a** the prophets, 2Ch 18:5 6908
they **a** in the valley of Beracah, 2Ch 20:26 6950
Amaziah **a** Judah and appointed them 2Ch 25:5 6908
They **a** their brothers, 2Ch 29:15 622
Then King Hezekiah arose early and **a** 2Ch 29:20 622
So many people **a** and stopped up 2Ch 32:4 6908
Now I **a** them at the river that Ezr 8:15 6908
Judah and Benjamin **a** at Jerusalem Ezr 10:9 6908
the sons of Israel **a** with fasting, Ne 9:1 622
So the sons of the singers were **a** Ne 12:28 622
The Jews **a** in their cities Es 9:2 6950
The Jews who were in Susa **a** Es 9:15 6950
who *were* in the king's provinces **a**, Es 9:16 6950
But the Jews who were in Susa **a** on Es 9:18 6950
The princes of the people have **a** Ps 47:9 622
For, lo, the kings **a** themselves, Ps 48:4 3259
So that the peoples may be **a**. Is 43:9 622
companies that are **a** about you, Ezk 38:7 6950
a your company to seize plunder, Ezk 38:13 6950
all the rulers of the provinces were **a** Da 3:3 3673
have been **a** against you Who say, Mi 4:11 622
And when they had **a** with the Mt 28:12 4863
Council of elders of the people **a**, Lk 22:66 4863
entered and found many people **a**. Ac 10:27 4905
a to hear the word of the Lord. Ac 13:44 4863
speaking to the women who had **a**. Ac 16:13 4905
"So after they had **a** here, Ac 25:17 4905
of our Lord Jesus, when you are **a**, 1Co 5:4 4863
a to make war against Him who sat Rv 19:19 4863

ASSEMBLES

Therefore if the whole church **a** 1Co 14:23 4905

ASSEMBLIES

the calling of **a**—I cannot endure Is 1:13 4744
and over her **a** a cloud by day, Is 4:5 4744
sabbaths And all her festal **a**. Hos 2:11 4150
Nor do I delight in your solemn **a**. Am 5:21 6116

ASSEMBLING

Philistines were **a** at Michmash, 1Sa 13:11 622
not forsaking our own **a** together, Heb 10:25 1997

ASSEMBLY

my glory be united with their **a**; Gn 49:6 6951
then the whole **a** of the Ex 12:6 6951
first day you shall have a holy **a**, Ex 12:16 4744
another holy **a** on the seventh day; Ex 12:16 4744
kill this whole **a** with hunger." Ex 16:3 6951
escapes the notice of the **a**, Lv 4:13 6951
then the **a** shall offer a bull of Lv 4:14 6951
it is the sin offering for the **a**. Lv 4:21 6951
and for all the **a** of Israel. Lv 16:17 6951
and for all the people of the **a**. Lv 16:33 6951
it is an **a**. You shall do no laborious Lv 23:36 6116
"When convening the **a**, Nu 10:7 6951
the **a** of the congregation of the sons Nu 14:5 6951
'*As for* the **a**, there shall be one Nu 15:15 6951
the congregation, chosen in the **a**, Nu 16:2 4150
above the **a** of the LORD?" Nu 16:3 6951
perished from the midst of the **a**. Nu 16:33 6951
and ran into the midst of the **a**, Nu 16:47 6951
cut off from the midst of the **a**, Nu 19:20 6951
the LORD'S **a** into this wilderness, Nu 20:4 6951
came in from the presence of the **a** Nu 20:6 6951
gathered the **a** before the rock. Nu 20:10 6951
shall not bring this **a** into the land Nu 20:12 6951
day you shall have a solemn **a**; Nu 29:35 6116
words the LORD spoke to all your **a** Dt 5:22 6951
of the fire on the day of the **a**. Dt 9:10 6951
of the fire on the day of the **a**; Dt 10:4 6951
a solemn **a** to the LORD your God; Dt 16:8 6116
God in Horeb on the day of the **a**, Dt 18:16 6951
shall enter the **a** of the LORD. Dt 23:1 6951
shall enter the **a** of the LORD; Dt 23:2 6951
shall enter the **a** of the LORD. Dt 23:2 6951
shall enter the **a** of the LORD; Dt 23:3 6951
ever enter the **a** of the LORD, Dt 23:3 6951
them may enter the **a** of the LORD. Dt 23:8 6951
Moses spoke in the hearing of all the **a** Dt 31:30 6951
A possession for the **a** of Jacob. Dt 33:4 6952
Joshua did not read before all the **a** Jos 8:35 6951
in the **a** of the people of God, Jg 20:2 6951
come up in the **a** to the LORD?" Jg 21:5 6951
camp from Jabesh-gilead to the **a**. Jg 21:8 6951
and that all this **a** may know that 1Sa 17:47 6951
and blessed all the **a** of Israel, 1Ki 8:14 6951
all the **a** of Israel was standing. 1Ki 8:14 6951
the LORD in the presence of all the **a** 1Ki 8:22 6951
the **a** of Israel with a loud voice, 1Ki 8:55 6951
a great **a** from the entrance of 1Ki 8:65 6951
and Jeroboam and all the **a** of 1Ki 12:3 6951
to the **a** and made him king over all 1Ki 12:20 5712
"Sanctify a solemn **a** for Baal." 2Ki 10:20 6116
David said to all the **a** of Israel, 1Ch 13:2 6951
the **a** said that they would do so, 1Ch 13:4 6951
of all Israel, the **a** of the LORD, 1Ch 28:8 6951

King David said to the entire **a**, **1Ch 29:1** 6951
LORD in the sight of all the **a**; **1Ch 29:10** 6951
Then David said to all the **a**, **1Ch 29:20** 6951
And all the **a** blessed the LORD, **1Ch 29:20** 6951
Solomon and all the **a** with him **2Ch 1:3** 6951
Solomon and the **a** sought it out. **2Ch 1:5** 6951
and blessed all the **a** of Israel, **2Ch 6:3** 6951
all the **a** of Israel was standing. **2Ch 6:3** 6951
the LORD in the presence of all the **a** **2Ch 6:12** 6951
presence of all the **a** of Israel and **2Ch 6:13** 6951
Israel with him, a very great **a** **2Ch 7:8** 6951
eighth day they held a solemn **a**, **2Ch 7:9** 6116
in the **a** of Judah and Jerusalem, **2Ch 20:5** 6951
Then in the midst of the **a** the **2Ch 20:14** 6951
Then all the **a** made a covenant **2Ch 23:3** 6951
before the officers and all the **a**. **2Ch 28:14** 6951
before the king and the **a**, **2Ch 29:23** 6951
While the whole **a** worshiped, the **2Ch 29:28** 6951
And the **a** brought sacrifices and **2Ch 29:31** 6951
which the **a** brought was 70 bulls, **2Ch 29:32** 6951
the king and his princes and all the **a** **2Ch 30:2** 6951
sight of the king and all the **a**. **2Ch 30:4** 6951
the second month, a very large **a**. **2Ch 30:13** 6951
For *there were* many in the **a** who **2Ch 30:17** 6951
Then the whole **a** decided to **2Ch 30:23** 6951
the **a** 1,000 bulls and 7,000 sheep, **2Ch 30:24** 6951
contributed to the **a** 1,000 bulls **2Ch 30:24** 6951
All the **a** of Judah rejoiced, **2Ch 30:25** 6951
all the **a** that came from Israel, **2Ch 30:25** 6951
their daughters, for the whole **a**, **2Ch 31:18** 6951
The whole **a** numbered 42,360, **Ezr 2:64** 6951
the house of God, a very large **a**, **Ezr 10:1** 6951
excluded from the **a** of the exiles. **Ezr 10:8** 6951
Then all the **a** replied **Ezr 10:12** 6951
"Let our leaders represent the whole **a** **Ezr 10:14** 6951
I held a great **a** against them. **Ne 5:7** 6952
And all the **a** said, **Ne 5:13** 6951
The whole **a** together *was* 42,360, **Ne 7:66** 6951
the law before the **a** of men, **Ne 8:2** 6951
The entire **a** of those who had **Ne 8:17** 6951
a according to the ordinance. **Ne 8:18** 6116
should ever enter the **a** of God, **Ne 13:1** 6951
by or shuts up, Or calls an **a**, **Jb 11:10** 6950
up in the **a** *and* cry out for help. **Jb 30:28** 6951
sinners in the **a** of the righteous. **Ps 1:5** 5712
a of the peoples encompass You, **Ps 7:7** 5712
midst of the **a** I will praise You. **Ps 22:22** 6951
comes my praise in the great **a**; **Ps 22:25** 6951
I hate the **a** of evildoers, And I **Ps 26:5** 6951
also in the **a** of the holy ones. **Ps 89:5** 6951
of the upright and in the **a**. **Ps 111:1** 5712
midst of the **a** and congregation." **Pr 5:14** 6951
Will rest in the **a** of the dead. **Pr 21:16** 6951
will be revealed before the **a**. **Pr 26:26** 6951
endure iniquity and the solemn **a**. **Is 1:13** 6116
of **a** In the recesses of the north. **Is 14:13** 4150
An **a** of treacherous men. **Jer 9:2** 6116
spoke to all the **a** of the people, **Jer 26:17** 6951
were standing by, *as* a large **a**, **Jer 44:15** 6951
a great **a** and a mighty army; **Ezk 38:15** 6951
with the proclamation to their **a**. **Hos 7:12** 5712
a fast, Proclaim a solemn **a**; **Jl 1:14** 6116
a fast, proclaim a solemn **a**; **Jl 2:15** 6116
you by lot in the **a** of the LORD. **Mi 2:5** 6951
when Paul wanted to go into the **a**, **Ac 19:30** *1218*
for the **a** was in confusion and **Ac 19:32** *1577*
to make a defense to the **a**. **Ac 19:33** *1218*
shall be settled in the lawful **a**. **Ac 19:39** *1577*
saying this he dismissed the **a**. **Ac 19:41** *1577*
and the **a** was divided. **Ac 23:7** *4128*
to the general **a** and church of the **Heb 12:23** *3831*
For if a man comes into your **a** **Jas 2:2** *4864*

ASSERT
Why do you say, O Jacob, and **a**, **Is 40:27** 1696

ASSERTED
Jesus, whom Paul **a** to be alive. **Ac 25:19** *5335*
we might have **a** our authority. **1Th 2:6** *1510, 922*

ASSERTING
A in pride and in arrogance of **Is 9:9** 559
a that these things were so. **Ac 24:9** *5335*

ASSERTIONS
about which they make confident **a**. **1Tm 1:7** *1226*

ASSESSMENT
both the money of each man's **a** *and* **2Ki 12:4** 6187

ASSHUR
The sons of Shem *were* Elam and **A** **Gn 10:22** 804b
long will **A** keep you captive?" **Nu 24:22** 804b
afflict **A** and will afflict Eber; **Nu 24:24** 804b
The sons of Shem *were* Elam, **A**, **1Ch 1:17** 804b
Eden, the traders of Sheba, **A** **Ezk 27:23** 804b

ASSHURIM
were **A** and Letushim and Leummim. **Gn 25:3** 805b

ASSIGN
and **a** each of them to his work and **Nu 4:19** 7760
and you shall **a** to them as a duty **Nu 4:27** 6485
and you shall **a** *each man* by name **Nu 4:32** 6485
and **a** men by it to guard them, **Jos 10:18** 6485
"Please **a** me to one of the **1Sa 2:36** 5596
and will cut him in pieces and **a** **Mt 24:51** *5087*
and **a** him a place with the **Lk 12:46** *5087*

ASSIGNED
to his place where you have **a** him, **1Sa 29:4** 6485
and **a** him food and gave him land. **1Ki 11:18** 559
Then on that day David first **a** **1Ch 16:7** 5414
Chenaniah and his sons were **a** to **1Ch 26:29**
a 70,000 men to carry loads and **2Ch 2:2** 5608
any design which may be **a** to him, **2Ch 2:14** 5414
had **a** over the house of the LORD, **2Ch 23:18** 2505a
His grave was **a** with wicked men, **Is 53:9** 5414
the seacoast—There He has **a** it." **Jer 47:7** 3259
"For I have **a** you a number of **Ezk 4:5** 5414
I have **a** it to you for forty days, **Ezk 4:6** 5414
the officials **a** *new* names to them; **Da 1:7** 7760
Daniel he **a** *the name* Belteshazzar, **Da 1:7** 7760
as the Lord has **a** to each one, **1Co 7:17** *3307*

ASSIGNING
a to each one his task, also **Mk 13:34**

ASSIR
A and Elkanah and Abiasaph; **Ex 6:24** 617
his son, Korah his son, **A** his son, **1Ch 6:22** 617
Ebiasaph his son and **A** his son, **1Ch 6:23** 617
the son of Tahath, the son of **A**, **1Ch 6:37** 617

ASSIST
a their brothers in the tent of **Nu 8:26** 8334
For their office is to **a** the sons **1Ch 23:28** 3027
dependent widows, she must **a** them **1Tm 5:16** *1884b*
may **a** those who are widows indeed. **1Tm 5:16** *1884b*

ASSISTANCE
O You my help, hasten to my **a**. **Ps 22:19** 5833
army which has come out for your **a** **Jer 37:7** 5833

ASSISTED
for they **a** me when I fled from **1Ki 2:7** 7126
the king's business **a** the Jews, **Es 9:3** 5375
if she has **a** those in distress, **1Tm 5:10** *1884b*

ASSOCIATE
you will not **a** with these nations, **Jos 23:7** 935
you **a** with them and they with you, **Jos 23:12** 935
"You shall not **a** with them, **1Ki 11:2** 935
nor shall they **a** with you, **1Ki 11:2** 935
him, And you **a** with adulterers. **Ps 50:18** 2506
Therefore do not **a** with a gossip. **Pr 20:19** 6148
not **a** with a man *given* to anger; **Pr 22:24** 7462b
Do not **a** with those who are given **Pr 24:21** 6148
And against the man, My **A**," **Zch 13:7** 5997
of the rest dared to **a** with them; **Ac 5:13** *2853*
trying to **a** with the disciples; **Ac 9:26** *2853*
who is a Jew to **a** with a foreigner **Ac 10:28** *2853*
in mind, but **a** with the lowly. **Ro 12:16** *4879*
not to **a** with immoral people; **1Co 5:9** *4874*
I wrote to you not to **a** with any **1Co 5:11** *4874*
of that person and do not **a** with him, **2Th 3:14** *4874*

ASSOCIATES
"All my **a** abhor me, And those I **Jb 19:19** 4962
larger in appearance than its **a**. **Da 7:20** 2273
rose up, along with all his **a** **Ac 5:17** *4862*
high priest and his **a** came, **Ac 5:21** *4862*

ASSOS
ahead to the ship, set sail for **A**, **Ac 20:13** *789*
And when he met us at **A**, **Ac 20:14** *789*

ASSUME
a the name of his dead brother, **Dt 25:6** 6965

ASSURANCE
and shall have no **a** of your life. **Dt 28:66** 539
rises, but no one has **a** of life. **Jb 24:22** 539
from the full **a** of understanding, **Col 2:2** *4136*
of our **a** firm until the end, **Heb 3:14** *5287*
the full **a** of hope until the end, **Heb 6:11** *4136*
sincere heart in full **a** of faith, **Heb 10:22** *4136*
is the **a** of *things* hoped for, **Heb 11:1** *5287*

ASSURE
I **a** you before God that I am not **Ga 1:20** *2400*
and will **a** our heart before Him **1Jn 3:19** *3982*

ASSURED
"Remember this, and be **a**; **Is 46:8** 847a
your kingdom will be **a** to you **Da 4:26** 7011
which God had **a** to Abraham, **Ac 7:17** *3670*
fully **a** that what God had promised, **Ro 4:21** *4135*
fully **a** in all the will of God. **Col 4:12** *4135*

ASSUREDLY
and that He will **a** dispossess from **Jos 3:10** 3423
"Know **a** that you will go out with **1Sa 28:1** 3045
A, the evil man will not go **Pr 11:21** 3027
A, he will not be unpunished. **Pr 16:5** 3027
Yet most **a** I will make you like a **Jer 22:6** 518, 3808
For **a** He does not give help to **Heb 2:16** *1222*

ASSYRIA
it flows east of **A**. **Gn 2:14** 804b
that land he went forth into **A**, **Gn 10:11** 804b
of Egypt as one goes toward **A**; **Gn 25:18** 804b
Pul, king of **A**, came against the **2Ki 15:19** 804b
of silver to pay the king of **A**. **2Ki 15:20** 804b
So the king of **A** returned and did **2Ki 15:20** 804b
Tiglath-pileser king of **A** came and **2Ki 15:29** 804b
and he carried them captive to **A**. **2Ki 15:29** 804b
to Tiglath-pileser king of **A**, **2Ki 16:7** 804b
sent a present to the king of **A**. **2Ki 16:8** 804b
So the king of **A** listened to him; **2Ki 16:9** 804b
and the king of **A** went up against **2Ki 16:9** 804b
to meet Tiglath-pileser king of **A**, **2Ki 16:10** 804b
the LORD because of the king of **A**. **2Ki 16:18** 804b
king of **A** came up against him, **2Ki 17:3** 804b
of **A** found conspiracy in Hoshea, **2Ki 17:4** 804b
no tribute to the king of **A**, **2Ki 17:4** 804b
so the king of **A** shut him up and **2Ki 17:4** 804b
Then the king of **A** invaded the **2Ki 17:5** 804b
the king of **A** captured Samaria and **2Ki 17:6** 804b
Israel away into exile to **A**, **2Ki 17:6** 804b
own land to **A** until this day. **2Ki 17:23** 804b
The king of **A** brought *men* from **2Ki 17:24** 804b
So they spoke to the king of **A**, **2Ki 17:26** 804b
Then the king of **A** commanded, **2Ki 17:27** 804b
king of **A** and did not serve him. **2Ki 18:7** 804b
Shalmaneser king of **A** came up **2Ki 18:9** 804b
Then the king of **A** carried Israel **2Ki 18:11** 804b
Israel away into exile to **A**, **2Ki 18:11** 804b
Sennacherib king of **A** came up **2Ki 18:13** 804b
sent to the king of **A** at Lachish, **2Ki 18:14** 804b
So the king of **A** required of **2Ki 18:14** 804b
and gave it to the king of **A**. **2Ki 18:16** 804b
Then the king of **A** sent Tartan and **2Ki 18:17** 804b
the great king, the king of **A**, **2Ki 18:19** 804b
with my master the king of **A**, **2Ki 18:23** 804b
of the great king, the king of **A**. **2Ki 18:28** 804b
into the hand of the king of **A**." **2Ki 18:30** 804b
for thus says the king of **A**, **2Ki 18:31** 804b
from the hand of the king of **A**? **2Ki 18:33** 804b
whom his master the king of **A** has **2Ki 19:4** 804b
the king of **A** have blasphemed Me. **2Ki 19:6** 804b
king of **A** fighting against Libnah, **2Ki 19:8** 804b
into the hand of the king of **A**." **2Ki 19:10** 804b
of **A** have done to all the lands, **2Ki 19:11** 804b
the kings of **A** have devastated the **2Ki 19:17** 804b
to Me about Sennacherib king of **A**, **2Ki 19:20** 804b
the LORD concerning the king of **A**, **2Ki 19:32** 804b
of **A** departed and returned *home*, **2Ki 19:36** 804b
from the hand of the king of **A**; **2Ki 20:6** 804b
king of **A** to the river Euphrates. **2Ki 23:29** 804b
king of **A** carried away into exile; **1Ch 5:6** 804b
up the spirit of Pul, king of **A**, **1Ch 5:26** 804b
of Tilgath-pilneser king of **A**, **1Ch 5:26** 804b
sent to the kings of **A** for help. **2Ch 28:16** 804b
So Tilgath-pilneser king of **A** came **2Ch 28:20** 804b
and gave *it* to the king of **A** **2Ch 28:21** 804b
from the hand of the kings of **A**. **2Ch 30:6** 804b
Sennacherib king of **A** came **2Ch 32:1** 804b
A come and find abundant water?" **2Ch 32:4** 804b
dismayed because of the king of **A** nor **2Ch 32:7** 804b
After this Sennacherib king of **A** **2Ch 32:9** 804b
"Thus says Sennacherib king of **A**, **2Ch 32:10** 804b
from the hand of the king of **A**"? **2Ch 32:11** 804b
in the camp of the king of **A**. **2Ch 32:21** 804b
hand of Sennacherib the king of **A** and **2Ch 32:22** 804b
of the king of **A** against them, **2Ch 33:11** 804b
the days of Esarhaddon king of **A**, **Ezr 4:2** 804b
had turned the heart of the king of **A** **Ezr 6:22** 804b
of the kings of **A** to this day. **Ne 9:32** 804b
A also has joined with them; **Ps 83:8** 804b
from Judah, the king of **A**." **Is 7:17** 804b
the bee that is in the land of **A**. **Is 7:18** 804b
(*that is*, with the king of **A**), **Is 7:20** 804b
away before the king of **A**." **Is 8:4** 804b
the king of **A** and all his glory; **Is 8:7** 804b
Woe to **A**, the rod of My anger And **Is 10:5** 804b
of the arrogant heart of the king of **A** **Is 10:12** 804b
people, who will remain, From **A**, **Is 11:11** 804b
And there will be a highway from **A** **Is 11:16** 804b
to break **A** in My land, and I will **Is 14:25** 804b
will be a highway from Egypt to **A**, **Is 19:23** 804b
Egypt and the Egyptians into **A**, **Is 19:23** 804b
the third *party* with Egypt and **A**, **Is 19:24** 804b
and **A** the work of My hands, **Is 19:25** 804b
when Sargon the king of **A** sent him **Is 20:1** 804b
so the king of **A** will lead away **Is 20:4** 804b
be delivered from the king of **A**; **Is 20:6** 804b
A appointed it for desert **Is 23:13** 804b
who were perishing in the land of **A** **Is 27:13** 804b
of the LORD **A** will be terrified, **Is 30:31** 804b
Sennacherib king of **A** came up **Is 36:1** 804b
And the king of **A** sent Rabshakeh **Is 36:2** 804b
the great king, the king of **A**, **Is 36:4** 804b
with my master the king of **A**, **Is 36:8** 804b
of the great king, the king of **A**. **Is 36:13** 804b
into the hand of the king of **A**." **Is 36:15** 804b
for thus says the king of **A**, **Is 36:16** 804b
from the hand of the king of **A**? **Is 36:18** 804b
whom his master the king of **A** has **Is 37:4** 804b
the king of **A** have blasphemed Me. **Is 37:6** 804b
king of **A** fighting against Libnah, **Is 37:8** 804b
into the hand of the king of **A**." **Is 37:10** 804b
of **A** have done to all the lands, **Is 37:11** 804b
the kings of **A** have devastated all **Is 37:18** 804b
to Me about Sennacherib king of **A**, **Is 37:21** 804b
the LORD concerning the king of **A**, **Is 37:33** 804b
So Sennacherib king of **A** **Is 37:37** 804b
from the hand of the king of **A**; **Is 38:6** 804b
are you doing on the road to **A**, **Jer 2:18** 804b
As you were put to shame by **A**. **Jer 2:36** 804b
devoured him was the king of **A**, **Jer 50:17** 804b
just as I punished the king of **A**. **Jer 50:18** 804b
Egypt *and* **A** to get enough bread. **La 5:6** 804b
whom *were* the choicest men of **A**; **Ezk 23:7** 804b
A *was* a cedar in Lebanon With **Ezk 31:3** 804b
"**A** is there and all her company; **Ezk 32:22** 804b
went to **A** And sent to King Jareb. **Hos 5:13** 804b
They call to Egypt, they go to **A**. **Hos 7:11** 804b
For they have gone up to **A**, **Hos 8:9** 804b
in **A** they will eat unclean *food*. **Hos 9:3** 804b
to **A** As tribute to King Jareb; **Hos 10:6** 804b
But **A**—he will be their king Because **Hos 11:5** 804b
And like doves from the land of **A**; **Hos 11:11** 804b
he makes a covenant with **A**, **Hos 12:1** 804b
"**A** will not save us, We will not **Hos 14:3** 804b
the land of **A** with the sword, **Mi 5:6** 804b
From **A** and the cities of Egypt, **Mi 7:12** 804b
are sleeping, O king of **A**; **Na 3:18** 804b
against the north And destroy **A**, **Zph 2:13** 804b
of Egypt And gather them from **A**; **Zch 10:10** 804b
pride of **A** will be brought down And **Zch 10:11** 804b

ASSYRIAN
do not fear the **A** who strikes you **Is 10:24** 804b
And the **A** will fall by a sword not **Is 31:8** 804b

A oppressed them without cause. Is 52:4 804b
When the A invades our land, When Mi 5:5 804b
And He will deliver *us* from the A Mi 5:6 804b

ASSYRIANS
185,000 in the camp of the A; 2Ki 19:35 804b
and the A will come into Egypt and Is 19:23 804b
Egyptians will worship with the A. Is 19:23 804b
185,000 in the camp of the A; Is 37:36 804b
you played the harlot with the A Ezk 16:28 804b
after her lovers, after the A, Ezk 23:5 804b
lovers, into the hand of the A, Ezk 23:9 1121, 804b
"She lusted after the A, Ezk 23:12 1121, 804b
and Koa, *and* all the A with them; Ezk 23:23 1121, 804b

ASTONISHED
by will be a and hiss and say, 1Ki 9:8 8074
passes by it will be a and say, 2Ch 7:21 8074
"Look at me, and be a, Jb 21:5 8074
Just as many were a at you, Is 52:14 8074
And was a that there was no one to Is 59:16 8074
And I was a and there was no one Is 63:5 8074
it will be a And shake his head. Jer 18:16 8074
everyone who passes by it will be a Jer 19:8 8074
Be a! Wonder! Because *I am* doing Hab 1:5 8539
synagogue, so that they were a, Mt 13:54 *1605*
this, they were very a and said, Mt 19:25 *1605*
this, they were a at His teaching. Mt 22:33 *1605*
and the many listeners were a, Mk 6:2 *1605*
and they were utterly a, Mk 6:51 *1839*
They were utterly a, Mk 7:37 *1605*
were even more a and said to Him, Mk 10:26 *1605*
crowd was a at His teaching. Mk 11:18 *1605*
And they were all a. Lk 1:63 *2296*
When they saw Him, they were a; Lk 2:48 *1605*
The Jews then were a, saying, "How Jn 7:15 *2296*
They were amazed and a, saying, Ac 2:7 *2296*
time a them with his magic arts. Ac 8:11 *1839*

ASTONISHING
city and a the people of Samaria, Ac 8:9 *1839*

ASTONISHINGLY
Therefore she has fallen a; La 1:9 6382

ASTONISHMENT
men looked at one another in a. Gn 43:33 8539
will look at one another in a, Is 13:8 8539
trembling and a had gripped them; Mk 16:8 *1611*
with a and *began* glorifying God; Lk 5:26 *1611*

ASTOUNDED
and the prophets will be a." Jer 4:9 8539
king was a and stood up in haste; Da 3:24 8429
but I was a at the vision, and Da 8:27 8074
they were completely a. Mk 5:42 *1839*

ASTRAY
goes a and is unfaithful to him, Nu 5:12 7847
have not gone a into uncleanness, Nu 5:19 7847
if you, however, have gone a, Nu 5:20 7847
goes a and defiles herself, Nu 5:29 7847
a when he sins unintentionally, Nu 15:28 7683
play the harlot and led Judah a. 2Ch 21:11 5080
who speak lies go a from birth. Ps 58:3 8582
Before I was afflicted I went a, Ps 119:67 7683
have not gone a from Your precepts. Ps 119:110 8582
I have gone a like a lost sheep; Ps 119:176 8582
of his folly he will go a. Pr 5:23 7686
he who ignores reproof goes a. Pr 10:17 8582
way of the wicked leads them a. Pr 12:26 8582
they not go a who devise evil? Pr 14:22 8582
He who leads the upright a in an Pr 28:10 7686
Those who guide you lead *you* a And Is 3:12 8582
this people are leading *them* a; Is 9:16 8582
of her tribes Have led Egypt a. Is 19:13 8582
led Egypt a in all that it does, Is 19:14 8582
All of us like sheep have gone a, Is 53:6 8582
Baal and led My people Israel a. Jer 23:13 8582
and led My people a by their Jer 23:32 8582
Their shepherds have led them a. Jer 50:6 8582
far from Me when Israel went a, Ezk 44:10 8582
went a from Me after their idols, Ezk 44:10 8582
the sons of Israel went a from Me, Ezk 44:15 8582
everyone who goes a or is naive; Ezk 45:20 7686
who did not go a when the sons of Ezk 48:11 8582
when the sons of Israel went a as Ezk 48:11 8582
astray as the Levites went a. Ezk 48:11 8582
spirit of harlotry has led *them* a, Hos 4:12 8582
Their lies also have led them a, Am 2:4 8582
the prophets who lead my people a; Mi 3:5 8582
sheep, and one of them has gone a, Mt 18:12 *4105*
ninety-nine which have not gone a. Mt 18:13 *4105*
to lead a, if possible, the elect. Mk 13:22 *635*
He leads the people a." Jn 7:12 *4105*
"You have not also been led a, Jn 7:47 *4105*
you were led a to the mute idols, 1Co 12:2 *520*
your minds will be led a from 2Co 11:3 *5351*
and thus gone a from the faith. 1Tm 6:21 *795*
men who have gone a from the truth 2Tm 2:18 *795*
'THEY ALWAYS GO A IN THEIR HEART, Heb 3:10 *4105*
the right way, they have gone a, 2Pe 2:15 *4105*
and leads My bond-servants a so Rv 2:20 *4105*

ASTROLOGERS
Let now the a, Those who prophesy Is 47:13 1895, 8064

ASTUTE
You show Yourself a. 2Sa 22:27 6617
crooked You show Yourself a. Ps 18:26 6617

ASUNDER
of bronze And cut bars of iron a. Ps 107:16 1438
To Him who divided the Red Sea a, Ps 136:13 1506
The earth is broken a, Is 24:19 7489b

ASYNCRITUS
Greet A, Phlegon, Hermes, Ro 16:14 *799*

ATAD
came to the threshing floor of A, Gn 50:10 329
at the threshing floor of A, Gn 50:11 329

ATARAH
another wife, whose name was A; 1Ch 2:26 5851

ATAROTH
"A, Dibon, Jazer, Nimrah, Nu 32:3 5852
Gad built Dibon and A and Aroer, Nu 32:34 5852
the border of the Archites at A. Jos 16:2 5852
from Janoah to A and to Naarah, Jos 16:7 5852

ATAROTH-ADDAR
their inheritance eastward was A, Jos 16:5 5853
and the border went down to A, Jos 18:13 5853

ATE
she took from its fruit and a; Gn 3:6 398
to her husband with her, and he a. Gn 3:6 398
gave me from the tree, and I a." Gn 3:12 398
serpent deceived me, and I a." Gn 3:13 398
by them under the tree as they a. Gn 18:8 398
unleavened bread, and they a. Gn 19:3 398
a and drank and spent the night. Gn 24:54 398
and he a and drank, and rose and Gn 25:34 398
a feast, and they a and drank. Gn 26:30 398
he brought *it* to him, and he a; Gn 27:25 398
I a of all *of it* before you came, Gn 27:33 398
and they a there by the heap. Gn 31:46 398
and they a the meal and spent the Gn 31:54 398
except the food which he a. Gn 39:6 398
The ugly and gaunt cows a up Gn 41:4 398
a up the first seven fat cows. Gn 41:20 398
and the Egyptians who a with him Gn 43:32 398
and they a every plant of the land Ex 10:15 398
meat, when we a bread to the full; Ex 16:3 398
of Israel a the manna forty years, Ex 16:35 398
they a the manna until they came Ex 16:35 398
saw God, and they a and drank. Ex 24:11 398
a and bowed down to their gods. Nu 25:2 398
I neither a bread nor drank water. Dt 9:9 398
I neither a bread nor drank water, Dt 9:18 398
And he a the produce of the field; Dt 32:13 398
'Who a the fat of their Dt 32:38 398
they a some of the produce of the Jos 5:11 398
but they a some of the yield of Jos 5:12 398
and a and drank and cursed Jg 9:27 398
gave *some* to them and they a *it;* Jg 14:9 398
they a and drank and lodged there. Jg 19:4 398
sat down and a and drank together; Jg 19:6 398
so both of them a. Jg 19:8 398
washed their feet and a and drank. Jg 19:21 398
and she a and was satisfied and Ru 2:14 398
So the woman went her way and a, 1Sa 1:18 398
So Saul a with Samuel that day. 1Sa 9:24 398
the people a *them* with the blood. 1Sa 14:32 398
Saul and his servants, and they a. 1Sa 28:25 398
and gave him bread and he a, 1Sa 30:11 398
two clusters of raisins, and he a; 1Sa 30:12 398
So Mephibosheth a at David's table 2Sa 9:11 398
and he a at the king's table regularly. 2Sa 9:13 398
and he a and drank before him, 2Sa 11:13 398
they set food before him and he a. 2Sa 12:20 398
died, you arose and a food." 2Sa 12:21 398
those who a at your own table. 2Sa 19:28 398
and a bread in his house and drank 1Ki 13:19 398
and her household a for *many* days. 1Ki 17:15 398
he a and drank and lay down again. 1Ki 19:6 398
So he arose and a and drank, and 1Ki 19:8 398
gave *it* to the people and they a. 1Ki 19:21 398
away his face and a no food. 1Ki 21:4 398
and they a and had *some* left over, 2Ki 4:44 398
"So we boiled my son and a him; 2Ki 6:29 398
entered one tent and a and drank, 2Ki 7:8 398
When he came in, he a and drank; 2Ki 9:34 398
but they a unleavened bread among 2Ki 23:9 398
So they a and drank that day 1Ch 29:22 398
yet they a the Passover otherwise 2Ch 30:18 398
a for the appointed seven days, 2Ch 30:22 398
God of Israel, a *the Passover.* Ezr 6:21 398
So they a, were filled and grew Ne 9:25 398
a bread with him in his house; Jb 42:11 398
in whom I trusted, Who a my bread, Ps 41:9 398
My people *as though* they a bread And Ps 53:4 398
So they a and were well filled, Ps 78:29 398
And a up all vegetation in their Ps 105:35 398
And a up the fruit of their Ps 105:35 398
And a sacrifices offered to the Ps 106:28 398
All who a of it became guilty; Jer 2:3 398
Your words were found and I a them, Jer 15:16 398
Those who a delicacies Are La 4:5 398
Then I a it, and it was sweet as Ezk 3:3 398
You a fine flour, honey and oil; Ezk 16:13 398
and they a the consecrated bread, Mt 12:4 *2068*
and the birds came and a them up. Mt 13:4 *2719*
and they all a and were satisfied. Mt 14:20 *2068*
about five thousand men who a, Mt 14:21 *2068*
And they all a and were Mt 15:37 *2068*
who a were four thousand men, Mt 15:38 *2068*
and a the consecrated bread, Mk 2:26 *2068*
and the birds came and a it up. Mk 4:4 *2719*
They all a and were satisfied, Mk 6:42 *2068*
thousand men who a the loaves. Mk 6:44 *2068*
And they a and were satisfied; Mk 8:8 *2068*
He a nothing during those days, Lk 4:2 *2068*
and took and a the consecrated Lk 6:4 *2068*
and the birds of the air a it up. Lk 8:5 *2719*
And they all a and were satisfied; Lk 9:17 *2068*
'We a and drank in Your presence, Lk 13:26 *2068*
He took it and a *it* before them. Lk 24:43 *2068*
where they a the bread after the Lord Jn 6:23 *2068*
but because you a of the loaves and Jn 6:26 *2068*
a the manna in the wilderness; Jn 6:31 *2068*
a the manna in the wilderness, Jn 6:49 *2068*
not as the fathers a and Jn 6:58 *2068*
sight, and neither a nor drank. Ac 9:9 *2068*
who a and drank with Him after He Ac 10:41 *4906*
men and a with them." Ac 11:3 *4906*
and all a the same spiritual food; 1Co 10:3 *2068*
out of the angel's hand and a it, Rv 10:10 *2719*

ATER
the sons of A of Hezekiah, 98; Ezr 2:16 333
sons of Shallum, the sons of A, Ezr 2:42 333
the sons of A, of Hezekiah, 98; Ne 7:21 333
sons of Shallum, the sons of A, Ne 7:45 333
A, Hezekiah, Azzur, Ne 10:17 333

ATHACH
and to those who were in A, 1Sa 30:30 6269

ATHAIAH
A the son of Uzziah, the son of Ne 11:4 6265

ATHALIAH
And his mother's name *was* A the 2Ki 8:26 6271
When A the mother of Ahaziah saw 2Ki 11:1 6271
So they hid him from A, 2Ki 11:2 6271
A was reigning over the land. 2Ki 11:3 6271
When A heard the noise of the 2Ki 11:13 6271
Then A tore her clothes and cried, 2Ki 11:14 6271
For they had put A to death with 2Ki 11:20 6271
Shamsherai, Shehariah, A, 1Ch 8:26 6271
And his mother's name was A, 2Ch 22:2 6271
Now when A the mother of Ahaziah 2Ch 22:10 6271
hid him from A so that she would 2Ch 22:11 6271
while A reigned over the land. 2Ch 22:12 6271
When A heard the noise of the 2Ch 23:12 6271
Then A tore her clothes and said, 2Ch 23:13 6271
had put A to death with the sword. 2Ch 23:21 6271
For the sons of the wicked A had 2Ch 24:7 6271
son of A and 70 males with him; Ezr 8:7 6271

ATHARIM
Israel was coming by the way of A, Nu 21:1 871

ATHENIANS
(Now all the A and the strangers Ac 17:21 *117*

ATHENS
Paul brought him as far as A; Ac 17:15 *116*
Paul was waiting for them at A, Ac 17:16 *116*
"Men of A, I observe that you are Ac 17:22 *117*
he left A and went to Corinth. Ac 18:1 *116*
best to be left behind at A alone, 1Th 3:1 *116*

ATHLAI
Hananiah, Zabbai *and* A; Ezr 10:28 6271

ATHLETE
Also if anyone competes as an a, 2Tm 2:5 *118*

ATONE
a for His land *and* His people." Dt 32:43 3722a
their blood to a for all Israel, 2Ch 29:24 3722a
on you For which you cannot a; Is 47:11 3722a

ATONED
iniquity of Eli's house shall not be a 1Sa 3:14 3722a
and truth iniquity is a for, Pr 16:6 3722a

ATONEMENT
eat those things by which a was made Ex 29:33 3722a
a bull as a sin offering for a, Ex 29:36 3725
the altar when you make a for it, Ex 29:36 3722a
"For seven days you shall make a Ex 29:37 3722a
make a on its horns once a year; Ex 30:10 3722a
he shall make a on it with the Ex 30:10 3722a
with the blood of the sin offering of a Ex 30:10 3725
the LORD to make a for yourselves. Ex 30:15 3722a
a money from the sons of Israel and Ex 30:16 3725
LORD, to make a for yourselves." Ex 30:16 3722a
I can make a for your sin." Ex 32:30 3722a
for him to make a on his behalf. Lv 1:4 3722a
the priest shall make a for them, Lv 4:20 3722a
a for him in regard to his sin, Lv 4:26 3722a
the priest shall make a for him, Lv 4:31 3722a
Thus the priest shall make a for Lv 4:35 3722a
make a on his behalf for his sin. Lv 5:6 3722a
So the priest shall make a on his Lv 5:10 3722a
'So the priest shall make a for Lv 5:13 3722a
The priest shall then make a for Lv 5:16 3722a
So the priest shall make a for him Lv 5:18 3722a
make a for him before the LORD, Lv 6:7 3722a
into the tent of meeting to make a Lv 6:30 3722a
who makes a with it shall have it. Lv 7:7 3722a
consecrated it, to make a for it. Lv 8:15 3722a
day, to make a on your behalf. Lv 8:34 3722a
that you may make a for yourself Lv 9:7 3722a
that you may make a for them, Lv 9:7 3722a
make a for them before the LORD. Lv 10:17 3722a
the LORD and make a for her, Lv 12:7 3722a
the priest shall make a for her, Lv 12:8 3722a
a on his behalf before the LORD. Lv 14:18 3722a
next offer the sin offering and make a Lv 14:19 3722a
the priest shall make a for him, Lv 14:20 3722a
a wave offering to make a for him, Lv 14:21 3722a
a on his behalf before the LORD. Lv 14:29 3722a
So the priest shall make a before Lv 14:31 3722a
So he shall make a for the house, Lv 14:53 3722a
So the priest shall make a on his Lv 15:15 3722a
So the priest shall make a on her Lv 15:30 3722a
that he may make a for himself and Lv 16:6 3722a
the LORD, to make a upon it, Lv 16:10 3722a
and make a for himself and for his Lv 16:11 3722a
shall make a for the holy place, Lv 16:16 3722a

in to make **a** in the holy place, Lv 16:17 3722a
that he may make **a** for himself and Lv 16:17 3722a
before the LORD and make **a** for it, Lv 16:18 3722a
and make **a** for himself and for the Lv 16:24 3722a
in to make **a** in the holy place, Lv 16:27 3722a
for it is on this day that **a** shall Lv 16:30 3722a
in his father's place shall make **a**: Lv 16:32 3722a
and make **a** for the holy sanctuary, Lv 16:33 3722a
and he shall make **a** for the tent Lv 16:33 3722a
He shall also make **a** for the Lv 16:33 3722a
to make **a** for the sons of Israel Lv 16:34 3722a
altar to make **a** for your souls; Lv 17:11 3722a
reason of the life that makes **a**.' Lv 17:11 3722a
'The priest shall also make **a** for Lv 19:22 3722a
seventh month is the day of **a**; Lv 23:27 3725
same day, for it is a day of **a**, Lv 23:28 3725
to make **a** on your behalf before Lv 23:28 3722a
on the day of **a** you shall sound a Lv 25:9 3725
the priest, besides the ram of **a**, Nu 5:8 3725
by which **a** is made for him. Nu 5:8 3722a
and make **a** for him concerning his Nu 6:11 3722a
LORD, to make **a** for the Levites. Nu 8:12 3722a
and to make **a** on behalf of the Nu 8:19 3722a
made **a** for them to cleanse them. Nu 8:21 3722a
'Then the priest shall make **a** for Nu 15:25 3722a
'The priest shall make **a** Nu 15:28 3722a
making **a** for him that he may be Nu 15:28 3722a
congregation and make **a** for them, Nu 16:46 3722a
incense and made **a** for the people. Nu 16:47 3722a
made **a** for the sons of Israel.'' Nu 25:13 3722a
a sin offering to make **a** for you. Nu 28:22 3722a
one male goat to make **a** for you. Nu 28:30 3722a
a sin offering, to make **a** for you, Nu 29:5 3722a
besides the sin offering of **a** and Nu 29:11 3725
a for ourselves before the LORD.'' Nu 31:50 3722a
And how can I make **a** that you may 2Sa 21:3 3722a
place, and to make **a** for Israel, 1Ch 6:49 3722a
offerings to make **a** for Israel, Ne 10:33 3722a
cleanse it and make **a** for it. Ezk 43:20 3722a
a for the altar and purify it; Ezk 43:26 3722a
offerings, to make **a** for them,'' Ezk 45:15 3722a
make **a** for the house of Israel.'' Ezk 45:17 3722a
so you shall make **a** for the house. Ezk 45:20 3722a
of sin, to make **a** for iniquity, Da 9:24 3722a

ATONING
he finishes **a** for the holy place and Lv 16:20 3722a

ATROTH-BETH-JOAB
A and half of the Manahathites, 1Ch 2:54 5854

ATROTH-SHOPHAN
and **A** and Jazer and Jogbehah, Nu 32:35 5855

ATTACH
then strangers will join them and **a** Is 14:1 5596

ATTACHED
my husband will become **a** to me, Gn 29:34 3867a
it was **a** at its two *upper* ends. Ex 39:4 2266
ark, and **a** the poles to the ark, Ex 40:20 7760
man, he **a** him to his staff. 1Sa 14:52 622
was **a** to the wing of the first 2Ch 3:12 1695
footstool in gold **a** to the throne, 2Ch 9:18 270

ATTACHING
a shoulder pieces for the ephod; Ex 39:4 2266

ATTACHMENT
would have no **a** with the inheritance 1Sa 26:19 5596

ATTACK
I fear him, that he will come and **a** Gn 32:11 5221
and **a** me and I will be destroyed, Gn 34:30 5221
and help me, and let us **a** Gibeon, Jos 10:4 5221
enemies and **a** them in the rear. Jos 10:19 2179
to **a** the priests of the LORD. 1Sa 22:17 6293
turn around and **a** the priests.'' 1Sa 22:18 6293
I go and **a** these Philistines?'' 1Sa 23:2 5221
''Go and **a** the Philistines and 1Sa 23:2 5221
he falls on them at the first **a**, 2Sa 17:9 5221
or province which might **a** them, Es 8:11 6696b
him like a king ready for the **a**, Jb 15:24 3593
They **a**, they lurk, They watch my Ps 56:6 1481b
Fierce men launch an **a** against me, Ps 59:3 1481b
Arise, and let us **a** at noon. Jer 6:4 5927
and let us **a** by night And destroy Jer 6:5 5927
will **a** you in order to harm you, Ac 18:10 *2007*
The Jews also joined in the **a**, Ac 24:9 *4902a*

ATTACKED
''The archers bitterly **a** him, Gn 49:23
how he met you along the way and **a** Dt 25:18 2179
the waters of Merom, and **a** them. Jos 11:7 5307
and Jogbehah, and **a** the camp when Jg 8:11 5221
I went out after him and **a** him, 1Sa 17:35 5221
turned around and **a** the priests, 1Sa 22:18 6293
David **a** the land and did not 1Sa 27:9 5221
king of Judah, and **a** their tents and 1Ch 4:41 5221
they were **a** both front and rear; 2Ch 13:14 4421
the Edomites had come and **a** Judah and 2Ch 28:17 5221
and the Sabeans **a** and took them. Jb 1:15 5307
it **a** the plant and it withered. Jon 4:7 5221

ATTACKING
he on his part will refrain from **a** Da 11:8
and **a** the house of Jason, they were Ac 17:5 *2186*

ATTACKS
comes to the one company and **a** it, Gn 32:8 5221
against the adversary who **a** you, Nu 10:9 6887c
''The one who **a** Kiriath-sepher and Jos 15:16 5221
''The one who **a** Kiriath-sepher and Jg 1:12 5221
the Assyrian When he **a** our land Mi 5:6 935
than he **a** him and overpowers him, Lk 11:22 *1904*

ATTAI
in marriage, and she bore him **A**. 1Ch 2:35 6262
A became the father of Nathan, 1Ch 2:36 6262
A the sixth, Eliel the seventh, 1Ch 12:11 6262
and she bore him Abijah, **A**, 2Ch 11:20 6262

ATTAIN
he did not **a** to the three. 2Sa 23:19 935
but he did not **a** to the three. 2Sa 23:23 935
he did not **a** to the *first* three. 1Ch 11:21 935
but he did not **a** to the three; 1Ch 11:25 935
that their hands cannot **a** success. Jb 5:12 6213a
It is *too* high, I cannot **a** to it. Ps 139:6
honor, And ruthless men **a** riches. Pr 11:16 8551
steadfast in righteousness *will* **a** Pr 11:19
considered worthy to **a** to that age Lk 20:35 *5177*
which our twelve tribes hope to **a**, Ac 26:7 *2658*
all **a** to the unity of the faith, Eph 4:13 *2658*
in order that I may **a** to the Php 3:11 *2658*

ATTAINED
nor have they **a** the years that my Gn 47:9 5381
not **a** royalty for such a time as this?'' Es 4:14 5060
he has **a** And cannot swallow *it;* Jb 20:18 3022
we have through you **a** much peace, Ac 24:2 *5177*
supposing that they had **a** their Ac 27:13 *2902*
righteousness, **a** righteousness, Ro 9:30 *2638*
same *standard* to which we have **a**. Php 3:16 *5348*

ATTAINING
for the **a** of all steadfastness and Col 1:11
and **a** to all the wealth that Col 2:2

ATTAINS
A gracious woman **a** honor, Pr 11:16 8551
waiting and **a** to the 1,335 days! Da 12:12 5060

ATTALIA
in Perga, they went down to **A**. Ac 14:25 *825*

ATTEMPT
And when an **a** was made by both the Ac 14:5 *3730*

ATTEMPTED
a to name over those who had the Ac 19:13 *2021*
and the Egyptians, when they **a** it, Heb 11:29 *3984, 2983*

ATTEMPTING
they were **a** to put him to death. Ac 9:29 *2021*

ATTEMPTS
king or people who **a** to change *it,* Ezr 6:12 7972, 3028

ATTEND
''And they shall thus **a** to your Nu 18:3 8104
and **a** to the obligations of the tent Nu 18:4 8104
''So you shall **a** to the Nu 18:5 8104
you and your sons with you shall **a** Nu 18:7 8104
my brother has commanded me to **a**. 1Sa 20:29
a the king and become his nurse; 1Ki 1:2 5975, 6440
and the Levites **a** to their work. 2Ch 13:10
the king had appointed to **a** her, Es 4:5 6440
I am about to **a** to you for the Jer 23:2 6485
and those who **a** regularly to the 1Co 9:13 *3918a*
quiet life and **a** to your own business 1Th 4:11 *4238*
AND HIS EARS **A** TO THEIR PRAYER, 1Pe 3:12

ATTENDANCE
the **a** of his waiters and their 1Ki 10:5 4612
the **a** of his ministers and their 2Ch 9:4 4612

ATTENDANT
the **a** of Moses from his youth, Nu 11:28 8334
Then his **a** took her out and locked 2Sa 13:18 8334
His **a** said, ''What, will I set this 2Ki 4:43 8334
Now when the **a** of the man of God 2Ki 6:15 8334
book, gave it back to the **a** Lk 4:20 *5257*

ATTENDANTS
banquet for all his princes and **a**, Es 1:3 5650
Then the king's **a**, who served him, Es 2:2 5288
''The **a** of the bridegroom cannot Mt 9:15 *5207*
a of the bridegroom cannot fast, Mk 2:19 *5207*
''You cannot make the **a** of the Lk 5:34 *5207*
of those who were his personal **a**, Ac 10:7 *4342*

ATTENDED
And all who **a** him left him. Jg 3:19 5975
Then David came to Saul and **a** him; 1Sa 16:21 6440
with her five maidens who **a** her; 1Sa 25:42 1980, 7272
his young man who **a** him and said, 2Sa 13:17 8334
the king's servants who **a** him said, Es 6:3 8334
them away, and have not **a** to them; Jer 23:2 6485

ATTENDING
said to the guards who were **a** him, 1Sa 22:17 5324
upon thousands were **a** Him, Da 7:10 8120

ATTENTION
will pay no **a** to false words.'' Ex 5:9 8159
away, and pay no **a** to them; Dt 22:1 5956
on the way, and pay no **a** to them; Dt 22:4 5956
woman pay **a** to all that I said. Jg 13:13 8104
But she did not answer or pay **a**. 1Sa 4:20 3820
lord pay **a** to this worthless man, 1Sa 25:25 3820
one answered, and no one paid **a**. 1Ki 18:29 7182
and turned his **a** to seek the LORD, 2Ch 20:3 6440
his people, but they paid no **a**. 2Ch 33:10 7181
Or paid **a** to Your commandments Ne 9:34 7181
But when it came to the king's **a**, Es 9:25 6440
No, surely He would pay **a** to me. Jb 23:6 7760
Yet God does not pay **a** to folly. Jb 24:12 7760
You turn Your **a** against me. Jb 30:20 995
''I even paid close **a** to you; Jb 32:12 995
''Pay **a**, O Job, listen to me; Jb 33:31 7181
give **a** and incline your ear: Ps 45:10 7200
out my hand and no one paid **a**; Pr 1:24 7181
And give **a** that you may gain Pr 4:1 7181
My son, give **a** to my words; Pr 4:20 7181
My son, give **a** to my wisdom, Pr 5:1 7181
pay **a** to the words of my mouth. Pr 7:24 7181
a to the word will find good, Pr 16:20 7919a
pays **a** to a destructive tongue. Pr 17:4 238
flocks, *And* pay **a** to your herds; Pr 27:23 3820
If a ruler pays **a** to falsehood, Pr 29:12 7181
pay **a** to the deeds of the LORD, Is 5:12 5027
Pay **a**, Laishah *and* wretched Is 10:30 7181
of camels, Let him pay close **a**, Is 21:7 7181
close attention, very close **a**.'' Is 21:7 7182
it burned him, but he paid no **a**. Is 42:25 5921, 3820
you had paid **a** to My commandments! Is 48:18 7181
to Me, O islands, And pay **a**, Is 49:1 7181
''Pay **a** to Me, O My people, Is 51:4 7181
and give **a** to all that I am going Ezk 40:4 3820
from Judah, pays no **a** to you, Da 6:13 7761
So I gave my **a** to the Lord God to Da 9:3 6440
and giving **a** to Your truth. Da 9:13 7919a
''But they refused to pay **a** and Zch 7:11 7181
and the LORD gave **a** and heard *it,* Mal 3:16 7181
they paid no **a** and went their way, Mt 22:5 *272*
And he *began* to give them his **a**, Ac 3:5 *1907*
a to what was said by Philip, Ac 8:6 *4337*
to greatest, were giving **a** to him, Ac 8:10 *4337*
And they were giving him **a** because Ac 8:11 *4337*
nor to pay **a** to myths and endless 1Tm 1:4 *4337*
paying **a** to deceitful spirits and 1Tm 4:1 *4337*
give **a** to the *public* reading *of* 1Tm 4:13 *4337*
Pay close **a** to yourself and to 1Tm 4:16 *1907*
not paying **a** to Jewish myths and Ti 1:14 *4337*
closer **a** to what we have heard, Heb 2:1 *4337*
and you pay special **a** to the one Jas 2:3 *1914*
to which you do well to pay **a** as 2Pe 1:19 *4337*
call **a** to his deeds which he does, 3Jn 1:10 *5279*

ATTENTIVE
and Your ears **a** to the prayer 2Ch 6:40 7183b
and My ears **a** to the prayer *offered* 2Ch 7:15 7183b
let Your ear now be **a** and Your Ne 1:6 7183a
may Your ear be **a** to the prayer Ne 1:11 7183a
were **a** to the book of the law. Ne 8:3 241
Let Your ears be **a** To the voice Ps 130:2 7183b
Make your ear **a** to wisdom, Incline Pr 2:2 7181

ATTENTIVELY
about, if you listen **a** to Me,'' Jer 17:24 8085

ATTESTATION
was the *manner of* **a** in Israel. Ru 4:7 8584

ATTESTED
a man **a** to you by God with Ac 2:22 *584*
For it is **a** *of Him,* ''YOU ARE Heb 7:17 *3140*

ATTIRE
was dressed in his military **a**, 2Sa 20:8 3830, 4055
of his waiters and their **a**, 1Ki 10:5 4403
of his ministers and their **a**, 2Ch 9:4 4403
his cupbearers and their **a**, 2Ch 9:4 4403
those who praised *Him* in holy **a**, 2Ch 20:21 1927a
Worship the LORD in holy **a**; Ps 96:9 1927a
become sufficient food and choice **a** Is 23:18 4374
her ornaments, Or a bride her **a**? Jer 2:32 7196

ATTIRED
sash and **a** with the linen turban Lv 16:4 6801
all of them splendidly **a**, Ezk 38:4 3847

ATTITUDE
Jacob saw the **a** of Laban, Gn 31:2 6440
''I see your father's **a**, Gn 31:5 6440
And You examine my heart's **a** Jer 12:3
to the **a** of the righteous, Lk 1:17 *5428*
Have this **a** in yourselves which Php 2:5 *5426*
many as are perfect, have this **a**; Php 3:15 *5426*
anything you have a different **a**, Php 3:15 *5426*
keeping alert in it with *an* **a** *of* Col 4:2
Lord Jesus Christ with *an* **a** *of* Jas 2:1

ATTORNEY
with an **a** *named* Tertullus, Ac 24:1 *4489*

ATTRACTED
He was deeply **a** to Dinah the Gn 34:3 1692
that we should be **a** to Him. Is 53:2 2530

ATTRIBUTES
of the world His invisible **a**, Ro 1:20

AUDITORIUM
and entered the **a** accompanied Ac 25:23 *201*

AUGUSTAN
of the **A** cohort named Julius. Ac 27:1 *4575*

AUGUSTUS
a decree went out from Caesar **A**, Lk 2:1 *828*

AUNT
approach his wife, she is your **a**. Lv 18:14 1733

AUTHOR
to perfect the **a** of their Heb 2:10 *747*
the **a** and perfecter of faith, Heb 12:2 *747*

AUTHORITATIVE
Since the word of the king is **a**, Ec 8:4 7983

AUTHORITIES
and the rulers and the **a**, Lk 12:11 *1849*
the market place before the **a**, Ac 16:19 *758*
some brethren before the city **a**, Ac 17:6 *4173*
the city **a** who heard these things. Ac 17:8 *4173*
in subjection to the governing **a**. Ro 13:1 *1849*
and the **a** in the heavenly *places.* Eph 3:10 *1849*
thrones or dominions or rulers or **a** Col 1:16 *1849*
He had disarmed the rulers and **a**, Col 2:15 *1849*
to be subject to rulers, to **a**, Ti 3:1 *1849*
after angels and **a** and powers had 1Pe 3:22 *1849*

AUTHORITY
and submit yourself to her **a**.'' Gn 16:9 3027
in the cities under Pharaoh's **a**, Gn 41:35 3027

He does not have **a** to sell her to Ex 21:8 4910
being under *the* **a** *of* your Nu 5:19
being under *the* **a** *of* your Nu 5:20
being under *the* **a** *of* her Nu 5:29
shall put some of your **a** on him, Nu 27:20 1935
that this people were under my **a**! Jg 9:29 3027
the **a** of the Levitical priests, 2Ch 23:18 3027
overseers under the **a** of Conaniah 2Ch 31:13 3027
Under his **a** *were* Eden, 2Ch 31:15 3027
established his **a** over all the princes Es 3:1 3678
wrote with full **a** to confirm this Es 9:29 8633
of his **a** and strength, Es 10:2 8633
"Who gave Him **a** over the earth? Jb 34:13 6845
No man has **a** to restrain the wind Ec 8:8 7989
wind, or **a** over the day of death; Ec 8:8 7983
a over *another* man to his hurt. Ec 8:9 7980
I will entrust him with your **a**, Is 22:21 4475
cause His voice of **a** to be heard, Is 30:30 1935
the priests rule on their *own* **a**; Jer 5:31 3027
thirty men from here under your **a** and Jer 38:10 3027
Ebed-melech took the men under his **a** Jer 38:11 3027
a as third *ruler* in the kingdom." Da 5:7 7981
and you will have **a** as the third Da 5:16 7981
he *now* had **a** as the third *ruler* Da 5:29 7990
with great **a** and do as he pleases. Da 11:3 4474
to his **a** which he wielded, Da 11:4 4915a
and **a** originate with themselves. Hab 1:7 7613
was teaching them as *one* having **a**, Mt 7:29 *1849*
"For I also am a man under **a**, Mt 8:9 *1849*
has **a** on earth to forgive sins"—then Mt 9:6 *1849*
God, who had given such **a** to men. Mt 9:8 *1849*
gave them **a** over unclean spirits, Mt 10:1 *1849*
great men exercise **a** over them. Mt 20:25 *2715*
what **a** are You doing these things, Mt 21:23 *1849*
things, and who gave You this **a**?" Mt 21:23 *1849*
you by what **a** I do these things. Mt 21:24 *1849*
you by what **a** I do these things. Mt 21:27 *1849*
"All **a** has been given to Me in Mt 28:18 *1849*
was teaching them as *one* having **a**, Mk 1:22 *1849*
A new teaching with **a**! Mk 1:27 *1849*
has **a** on earth to forgive sins"—He Mk 2:10 *1849*
to have **a** to cast out the demons. Mk 3:15 *1849*
them **a** over the unclean spirits; Mk 6:7 *1849*
great men exercise **a** over them. Mk 10:42 *2715*
what **a** are You doing these things, Mk 11:28 *1849*
You this **a** to do these things?" Mk 11:28 *1849*
you by what **a** I do these things. Mk 11:29 *1849*
you by what **a** I do these things." Mk 11:33 *1849*
for His message was with **a**. Lk 4:32 *1849*
For with **a** and power He commands Lk 4:36 *1849*
has **a** on earth to forgive sins,"—He Lk 5:24 *1849*
"For I also am a man placed under **a**, Lk 7:8 *1849*
power and **a** over all the demons and Lk 9:1 *1849*
I have given you **a** to tread on Lk 10:19 *1849*
killed, has **a** to cast into hell; Lk 12:5 *1849*
you are to be in **a** over ten cities.' Lk 19:17 *1849*
what **a** You are doing these things, Lk 20:2 *1849*
is the one who gave You this **a**?" Lk 20:2 *1849*
you by what **a** I do these things." Lk 20:8 *1849*
rule and the **a** of the governor. Lk 20:20 *1849*
who have **a** over them are called Lk 22:25 *1850*
"What sign do You show us as your **a** Jn 2:18
He gave Him **a** to execute judgment, Jn 5:27 *1849*
I have **a** to lay it down, and I Jn 10:18 *1849*
and I have **a** to take it up again. Jn 10:18 *1849*
gave Him **a** over all flesh, Jn 17:2 *1849*
know that I have **a** to release You, Jn 19:10 *1849*
and I have **a** to crucify You?" Jn 19:10 *1849*
"You would have no **a** over Me, Jn 19:11 *1849*
the Father has fixed by His own **a**; Ac 1:7 *1849*
"Give this **a** to me as well, so Ac 8:19 *1849*
and here he has **a** from the chief Ac 9:14 *1849*
received **a** from the chief priests, Ac 26:10 *1849*
journeying to Damascus with the **a** Ac 26:12 *1849*
For there is no **a** except from God, Ro 13:1 *1849*
Therefore whoever resists **a** has Ro 13:2 *1849*
Do you want to have no fear of **a**? Ro 13:3 *1849*
does not have **a** over her own body, 1Co 7:4 *1850*
does not have **a** over his own body, 1Co 7:4 *1850*
but has **a** over his own will, 1Co 7:37 *1849*
to have *a symbol of* **a** on her head, 1Co 11:10 *1849*
all rule and all **a** and power. 1Co 15:24 *1849*
somewhat further about our **a**, 2Co 10:8 *1849*
with the **a** which the Lord gave me for 2Co 13:10 *1849*
rule and **a** and power and dominion, Eph 1:21 *1849*
is the head over all rule and **a**; Col 2:10 *1849*
we might have asserted our **a**. 1Th 2:6 *922*
commandments we gave you by *the* **a** 1Th 4:2
for kings and all who are in **a**, 1Tm 2:2 *5247*
to teach or exercise **a** over a man, 1Tm 2:12 *831*
and exhort and reprove with all **a**. Ti 2:15 *2003*
whether to a king as the one in **a**, 1Pe 2:13 *5242*
its corrupt desires and despise **a**. 2Pe 2:10 *2963*
defile the flesh, and reject **a**, Jude 1:8 *2963*
be glory, majesty, dominion and **a**, Jude 1:25 *1849*
I WILL GIVE **A** OVER THE NATIONS; Rv 2:26 *1849*
as I also have received **a** from Rv 2:27
A was given to them over a fourth of Rv 6:8 *1849*
"And I will grant **a** to my two Rv 11:3
and the **a** of His Christ have come, Rv 12:10 *1849*
power and his throne and great **a**. Rv 13:2 *1849*
he gave his **a** to the beast; Rv 13:4 *1849*
and **a** to act for forty-two months Rv 13:5 *1849*
and **a** over every tribe and people Rv 13:7 *1849*
He exercises all the **a** of the Rv 13:12 *1849*
but they receive **a** as kings with Rv 17:12 *1849*
their power and **a** to the beast. Rv 17:13 *1849*
down from heaven, having great **a**, Rv 18:1 *1849*

AUTUMN
does not plow after the **a**, Pr 20:4 2779
the **a** rain and the spring rain, Jer 5:24 3138
a trees without fruit, doubly Jude 1:12 *5352*

AVAIL
sword that reaches him cannot **a**, Jb 41:26 6965
in deceptive words to no **a**. Jer 7:8 3276

AVAILABLE
in session and proconsuls are **a**; Ac 19:38

AVEN
Also the high places of **A**, Hos 10:8 206
inhabitant from the valley of **A**, Am 1:5 206

AVENGE
will **a** the blood of His servants, Dt 32:43 5358
me, and may the LORD **a** me on you; 1Sa 24:12 5358
that I may **a** the blood of My 2Ki 9:7 5358
"May the LORD see and **a**!" 2Ch 24:22 1875
to **a** themselves on their enemies. Es 8:13 5358
And **a** Myself on My foes. Is 1:24 5358
as this Shall I not **a** Myself? Jer 5:9 5358
as this Shall I not **a** Myself?' Jer 5:29 5358
as this Shall I not **a** Myself? Jer 9:9 5358
so as to **a** Himself on His foes; Jer 46:10 5358
And I will **a** their blood which I Jl 3:21 5352

AVENGED
If Cain is **a** sevenfold, Then Gn 4:24 5358
a themselves of their enemies. Jos 10:13 5358
LORD has **a** you of your enemies, Jg 11:36 5360
that I may at once be **a** of the Jg 16:28 5358
I have **a** myself on my enemies." 1Sa 14:24 5358
and by my lord having **a** himself. 1Sa 25:31 3467
and **a** themselves upon them," Ezk 25:12 5358
their blood which I have not **a**, Jl 3:21 5352
and HE HAS **A** THE BLOOD OF HIS Rv 19:2 *1556*

AVENGER
be to you as a refuge from the **a**, Nu 35:12 1350
'The blood **a** himself shall put the Nu 35:19 1350
the blood **a** shall put the murderer Nu 35:21 1350
a according to these ordinances. Nu 35:24 1350
from the hand of the blood **a**, Nu 35:25 1350
and the blood **a** finds him outside Nu 35:27 1350
the blood **a** kills the manslayer, Nu 35:27 1350
otherwise the **a** of blood might pursue Dt 19:6 1350
into the hand of the **a** of blood, Dt 19:12 1350
your refuge from the **a** of blood. Jos 20:3 1350
'Now if the **a** of blood pursues Jos 20:5 1350
and not die by the hand of the **a** Jos 20:9 1350
so that the **a** of blood will not 2Sa 14:11 1350
presence of the enemy and the **a**. Ps 44:16 5358
And *yet* an **a** of their *evil* deeds. Ps 99:8 5358
an **a** who brings wrath on the one Ro 13:4 *1558*
Lord is *the* **a** in all these things, 1Th 4:6 *1558*

AVENGING
from **a** yourself by your own hand, 1Sa 25:26 3467
and from **a** myself by my own hand. 1Sa 25:33 3467
A jealous and **a** God is the LORD; Na 1:2 5358
The LORD is **a** and wrathful. Na 1:2 5358
what zeal, what **a** of wrong! 2Co 7:11 *1557*
refrain from judging and **a** our blood Rv 6:10 *1556*

AVERT
and implored him to **a** the evil Es 8:3 5674a

AVERTED
all their multitude will not be **a**, Ezk 7:13 7725

AVITH
and the name of his city was **A**. Gn 36:35 5762
and the name of his city *was* **A**. 1Ch 1:46 5762

AVOID
A it, do not pass by it; Pr 4:15 6544a
one may **a** the snares of death. Pr 14:27 5493
But **a** worldly *and* empty chatter, 2Tm 2:16 *4026*
A such men as these. 2Tm 3:5 *665*
But **a** foolish controversies Ti 3:9 *4026*

AVOIDING
a worldly *and* empty chatter *and* 1Tm 6:20 *1624*

AVVA
Cuthah and from **A** and from Hamath 2Ki 17:24 5755

AVVIM
And the **A**, who lived in villages Dt 2:23 5761
and **A** and Parah and Ophrah, Jos 18:23 5761

AVVITE
the Gittite, the Ekronite; and the **A** Jos 13:3 5761

AVVITES
and the **A** made Nibhaz and Tartak; 2Ki 17:31 5757

AWAIT
that bonds and afflictions **a** me. Ac 20:23 *3306*
sin, to those who eagerly **a** Him. Heb 9:28 *553*

AWAITING
a eagerly the revelation of our 1Co 1:7 *553*

AWAITS
love or hatred; anything **a** him. Ec 9:1 6440

AWAKE
"**A**, awake, Deborah; Jg 5:12 5782
"Awake, **a**, Deborah; Jg 5:12 5782
A, awake, sing a song! Jg 5:12 5782
Awake, **a**, sing a song! Jg 5:12 5782
one saw or knew *it*, nor did any **a**, 1Sa 26:12 7019a
He will not **a** nor be aroused out Jb 14:12 7019a
with Your likeness when I **a**. Ps 17:15 7019a
up Yourself, and **a** to my right And Ps 35:23 7019a
A, do not reject us forever. Ps 44:23 7019a
A, my glory! Awake, harp and lyre Ps 57:8 5782
A, harp and lyre! I will awaken Ps 57:8 5782
A to punish all the nations; Ps 59:5 7019a
I lie **a**, I have become like a Ps 102:7 8245
A, harp and lyre; Ps 108:2 5782
The watchman keeps **a** in vain. Ps 127:1 8245
When I **a**, I am still with You. Ps 139:18 7019a
And when you **a**, they will talk to Pr 6:22 7019a
I did not know *it*. When shall I **a**? Pr 23:35 7019a
"**A**, O north *wind*, And come, *wind* SS 4:16 5782
"I was asleep but my heart was **a**. SS 5:2 5782
in the dust, **a** and shout for joy, Is 26:19 7019a
A, awake, put on strength, O arm Is 51:9 5782
Awake, **a**, put on strength, O arm Is 51:9 5782
A as in the days of old, the Is 51:9 5782
A, awake, Clothe yourself in your Is 52:1 5782
Awake, **a**, Clothe yourself in your Is 52:1 5782
in the dust of the ground will **a**, Da 12:2 7019a
A, drunkards, and weep; Jl 1:5 7019a
who says to a *piece of* wood, '**A**!' Hab 2:19 7019a
"**A**, O sword, against My Shepherd, Zch 13:7 5782
but when they were fully **a**, Lk 9:32 *1235*
"**A**, sleeper, And arise from the Eph 5:14 *1453*
that whether we are **a** or asleep, 1Th 5:10 *1127*
stays **a** and keeps his clothes, Rv 16:15 *1127*

AWAKEN
harp and lyre! I will **a** the dawn. Ps 57:8 5782
I will **a** the dawn! Ps 108:2 5782
you do not arouse or **a** *my* love SS 2:7 5782
you will not arouse or **a** *my* love Until SS 3:5 5782
Do not arouse or **a** *my* love Until SS 8:4 5782
And those who collect from you **a**? Hab 2:7 3364
that I may **a** him out of sleep." Jn 11:11 *1852*
the hour for you to **a** from sleep; Ro 13:11 *1453*

AWAKENED
he is asleep and needs to be **a**." 1Ki 18:27 3364
"The lad has not **a**." 2Ki 4:31 7019a
"Beneath the apple tree I **a** you; SS 8:5 5782
It has **a** against you; Ezk 7:6 7019a
as a man who is **a** from his sleep. Zch 4:1 5782

AWAKENS
But when he **a**, his hunger is not Is 29:8 7019a
he is drinking, But when he **a**, Is 29:8 7019a
He **a** *Me* morning by morning, He Is 50:4 5782
He **a** My ear to listen as a Is 50:4 5782

AWAKES
Like a dream when one **a**, Ps 73:20 7019a
Jacob *everyone* who **a** and answers, Mal 2:12 5782

AWARD
Judge, will **a** to me on that day; 2Tm 4:8 *591*

AWARE
for I am **a** of their sufferings. Ex 3:7 3045
But the lad was not **a** of anything; 1Sa 20:39 3045
Now David became **a** that Saul had 1Sa 23:15 7200
"Before I was **a**, my soul set me SS 6:12 3045
Will you not be **a** of it? Is 43:19 3045
"Are you well **a** that Baalis the Jer 40:14 3045
Then all the men who were **a** that Jer 44:15 3045
While you yourself were not **a**; Jer 50:24 3045
But Jesus, **a** of *this*, withdrew Mt 12:15 *1097*
But Jesus, **a** of this, said, Mt 16:8 *1097*
But Jesus, **a** of this, said to Mt 26:10 *1097*
a in His spirit that they were Mk 2:8 *1921*
a of what had happened to her, Mk 5:33 *3609a*
And Jesus, **a** of this, said to Mk 8:17 *1097*
For he was **a** that the chief Mk 15:10 *1097*
But Jesus, **a** of their reasonings, Lk 5:22 *1921*
a that power had gone out of Me." Lk 8:46 *1097*
were **a** of this and followed Him; Lk 9:11 *1097*
they became **a** of it and fled to Ac 14:6 *4894*
"I was not **a**, brethren, that he Ac 23:5 *3609a*
You are **a** of the fact that all who 2Tm 1:15 *3609a*

AWAY
and their faces were turned **a**, Gn 9:23 322
and they escorted him **a**, Gn 12:20 7971
carcasses, and Abram drove them **a**. Gn 15:11 5380
Then the men turned **a** from there Gn 18:22 6437
a the righteous with the wicked? Gn 18:23 5595
will You indeed sweep *it* **a** and Gn 18:24 5595
a in the punishment of the city." Gn 19:15 5595
mountains, or you will be swept **a**." Gn 19:17 5595
gave her the boy, and sent her **a**. Gn 21:14 7971
opposite him, about a bowshot **a**, Gn 21:16 7368
"Send me **a** to my master." Gn 24:54 7971
me **a** that I may go to my master." Gn 24:56 7971
Thus they sent **a** their sister Gn 24:59 7971
a from his son Isaac eastward, Gn 25:6 7971
"Go **a** from us, for you are too Gn 26:16
He moved **a** from there and dug Gn 26:22 6275
me and have sent me **a** from you?" Gn 26:27 7971
and have sent you **a** in peace. Gn 26:29 7971
then Isaac sent them **a** and they Gn 26:31 7971
and has taken **a** your blessing." Gn 27:35
He took **a** my birthright, and Gn 27:36
now he has taken **a** my blessing." Gn 27:36
a from the fertility of the earth Gn 27:39
And **a** from the dew of heaven from Gn 27:39
Then Isaac sent Jacob **a**, Gn 28:5 7971
and sent him **a** to Paddan-aram to Gn 28:6 7971
"God has taken **a** my reproach." Gn 30:23 622
"Send me **a**, that I may go to my Gn 30:25 7971
taken **a** all that was our father's, Gn 31:1
"Thus God has taken **a** your Gn 31:9 5337
all the wealth which God has taken **a** Gn 31:16 5337
and he drove **a** all his livestock Gn 31:18 5090a
carrying **a** my daughters like captives Gn 31:26 5090a
you **a** with joy and with songs, Gn 31:27 7971
"Now you have indeed gone **a** Gn 31:30
would have sent me **a** empty-handed. Gn 31:42 7971
"Put **a** the foreign gods which are Gn 35:2 5493
land **a** from his brother Jacob. Gn 36:6
He turned **a** from them and wept. Gn 42:24 5437

Context	Reference	Number
it was light, the men were sent **a**,	Gn 44:3	7971
So he sent his brothers **a**,	Gn 45:24	7971
"Take this child **a** and nurse him	Ex 2:9	
shepherds came and drove them **a**,	Ex 2:17	1644
draw the people **a** from their work?	Ex 5:4	6544a
only you shall not go very far **a**.	Ex 8:28	
Pharaoh said to him, "Get **a** from me	Ex 10:28	1980
take **a** the pillar of cloud by day,	Ex 13:22	4185
us **a** to die in the wilderness?	Ex 14:11	
of Canaan have melted **a**.	Ex 15:15	4127
Zipporah, after he had sent her **a**,	Ex 18:2	7971
driven **a** while no one is looking,	Ex 22:10	7617
ox or his donkey wandering **a**,	Ex 23:4	8582
and Aaron shall take **a** the	Ex 28:38	
hand **a** and you shall see My back,	Ex 33:23	5493
take **a** its crop with its feathers and	Lv 1:16	5493
carry your relatives **a** from the	Lv 10:4	5375
a the guilt of the congregation,	Lv 10:17	
whether an eating **a** has produced	Lv 13:55	6356
throw them **a** at an unclean place	Lv 14:40	7993
on the head of the goat and send *it* **a**	Lv 16:21	7971
fever that will waste **a** the eyes	Lv 26:16	3615
eyes and cause the soul to pine **a**;	Lv 26:16	1727
will rot **a** because of their iniquity	Lv 26:39	4743
they will rot **a** with them.	Lv 26:39	4743
take **a** the ashes from the altar,	Nu 4:13	1878
send **a** from the camp every leper	Nu 5:2	7971
shall send **a** both male and female;	Nu 5:3	7971
waste **a** and your abdomen swell;	Nu 5:21	5307
swell and your thigh waste **a**."	Nu 5:22	5307
swell and her thigh will waste **a**,	Nu 5:27	5307
whose flesh is half eaten **a** when	Nu 12:12	
you will be swept **a** in all their sin."	Nu 16:26	5595
a from among this congregation,	Nu 16:45	7426a
so Israel turned **a** from him.	Nu 20:21	5186
the LORD may turn **a** from Israel."	Nu 25:4	7725
has turned **a** My wrath from the	Nu 25:11	7725
if you turn **a** from following Him,	Nu 32:15	7725
in Seir, **a** from the Arabah road,	Dt 2:8	4480
a from Elath and from Ezion-geber.	Dt 2:8	4480
you, nor take **a** from it,	Dt 4:2	1639
and be drawn **a** and worship them	Dt 4:19	5080
clears **a** many nations before you,	Dt 7:1	5394
"For they will turn your sons **a**	Dt 7:4	5493
your God will clear **a** these nations	Dt 7:22	5394
not turn **a** and serve other gods	Dt 11:16	5493
not add to nor take **a** from it.	Dt 12:32	1639
too far **a** from you when the LORD	Dt 14:24	
shall not send him **a** empty-handed.	Dt 15:13	7971
himself, or else his heart will turn **a**;	Dt 17:17	5493
and you take them **a** captive,	Dt 21:10	
ox or his sheep straying **a**,	Dt 22:1	5080
among you or He will turn **a** from you.	Dt 23:14	7725
husband who sent her **a** is not allowed	Dt 24:4	7971
be no one to frighten *them* **a**.	Dt 28:26	2729
donkey shall be torn **a** from you,	Dt 28:31	1497
a today from the LORD our God,	Dt 29:18	6437
turns **a** and you will not obey,	Dt 30:17	6437
but are drawn **a** and worship other	Dt 30:17	5080
the land have melted **a** before you.	Jos 2:9	4127
So she sent them **a**, and they	Jos 2:21	7971
have melted **a** before us."	Jos 2:24	4127
heap, a great distance **a** at Adam,	Jos 3:16	
"Today I have rolled **a** the	Jos 5:9	1556
have drawn them **a** from the city,	Jos 8:6	5423
So Joshua sent them **a**,	Jos 8:9	7971
and were drawn **a** from the city.	Jos 8:16	5423
blessed them and sent them **a**,	Jos 22:6	7971
Joshua sent them **a** to their tents,	Jos 22:7	7971
turning **a** from following the LORD	Jos 22:16	7725
that you must turn **a** this day from	Jos 22:18	7725
to turn **a** from following the LORD,	Jos 22:23	7725
rebel against the LORD and turn **a**	Jos 22:29	7725
and put **a** the gods which your	Jos 24:14	5493
put **a** the foreign gods which are	Jos 24:23	5493
that he sent **a** the people who had	Jg 3:18	7971
as far **a** as the oak in Zaanannim,	Jg 4:11	
his chariot and fled **a** on foot.	Jg 4:15	
Now Sisera fled **a** on foot to the	Jg 4:17	
Barak, and take **a** your captives,	Jg 5:12	
torrent of Kishon swept them **a**,	Jg 5:21	1640
So they put **a** the foreign gods	Jg 10:16	5493
"Because Israel took **a** my land	Jg 11:13	
did not take **a** the land of Moab nor	Jg 11:15	
So he sent her **a** for two months;	Jg 11:38	7971
have taken **a** my gods which I made,	Jg 18:24	
and the priest, and have gone **a**,	Jg 18:24	
and she went **a** from him to her	Jg 19:2	
and were drawn **a** from the city,	Jg 20:31	5423
a from the city to the highways."	Jg 20:32	5423
who danced, whom they carried **a**.	Jg 21:23	1497
Put **a** your wine from you."	1Sa 1:14	5493
a the ark of the God of Israel,	1Sa 5:11	7971
a the ark of the God of Israel,	1Sa 6:3	7971
their calves home, **a** from them.	1Sa 6:7	310
Then send it **a** that it may go.	1Sa 6:8	7971
"Get up, that I may send you **a**."	1Sa 9:26	7971
And Samuel sent all the people **a**,	1Sa 10:25	7971
and your king will be swept **a**."	1Sa 12:25	5595
he sent **a** the rest of the people,	1Sa 13:2	7971
behold, the multitude melted **a**;	1Sa 14:16	4127
takes **a** the reproach from Israel?	1Sa 17:26	5493
Then he turned **a** from him to	1Sa 17:30	5437, 681
slipped **a** out of Saul's presence,	1Sa 19:10	6362
it known to you and send you **a**,	1Sa 20:13	7971
go, for the LORD has sent you **a**.	1Sa 20:22	7971
get **a** that I may see my brothers.'	1Sa 20:29	4422
in its place when it was taken **a**.	1Sa 21:6	
and he led **a** their livestock and	1Sa 23:5	5090a
was hurrying to get **a** from Saul,	1Sa 23:26	1980
will he let him go **a** safely?	1Sa 24:19	7971
each breaking **a** from his master.	1Sa 25:10	6555
Saul's head, and they went **a**,	1Sa 26:12	
a from the presence of the LORD;	1Sa 26:20	5048
alive, and he took **a** the sheep,	1Sa 27:9	
they arose and went **a** that night.	1Sa 28:25	
they may lead *them* **a** and depart."	1Sa 30:22	5090a
would have gone **a** in the morning,	2Sa 2:27	5927
So David sent Abner **a**,	2Sa 3:21	7971
in Hebron, for he had sent him **a**,	2Sa 3:22	7971
the king, and he has sent him **a**,	2Sa 3:23	7971
sent him **a** and he is already gone?	2Sa 3:24	7971
blind and lame will turn you **a**";	2Sa 5:6	5493
David and his men carried them **a**.	2Sa 5:21	5375
him, as I took *it* **a** from Saul,	2Sa 7:15	5493
as their hips, and sent them **a**.	2Sa 10:4	7971
LORD also has taken **a** your sin;	2Sa 12:13	5674a
Amnon said to her, "Get up, go **a**!"	2Sa 13:15	
this wrong in sending me **a** is greater	2Sa 13:16	7971
her hand on her head and went **a**,	2Sa 13:19	
Yet God does not take **a** life,	2Sa 14:14	
so Absalom stole **a** the hearts of	2Sa 15:6	1589
steal **a** when they flee in battle.	2Sa 19:3	1589
the men of Judah stolen you **a**,	2Sa 19:41	1589
them will be thrust **a** like thorns,	2Sa 23:6	5074
a the iniquity of Your servant,	2Sa 24:10	5674a
ran **a** to Achish son of Maacah,	1Ki 2:39	1272
there, and you shall carry *them* **a**.	1Ki 5:9	
so that they take them **a** captive	1Ki 8:46	
a and they blessed the king.	1Ki 8:66	7971
indeed turn **a** from following Me,	1Ki 9:6	7725
your heart **a** after their gods."	1Ki 11:2	5186
and his wives turned his heart **a**.	1Ki 11:3	5186
his heart **a** after other gods;	1Ki 11:4	5186
heart was turned **a** from the LORD,	1Ki 11:9	5186
I will not tear **a** all the kingdom,	1Ki 11:13	7167
"Send me **a**, that I may go to my	1Ki 11:21	7971
for him and he rode **a** on it.	1Ki 13:13	
and tore the kingdom **a** from the	1Ki 14:8	7167
one sweeps **a** dung until it is all gone.	1Ki 14:10	1197a
He took **a** the treasures of the	1Ki 14:26	
He also put **a** the male cult	1Ki 15:12	5674a
the high places were not taken **a**;	1Ki 15:14	5493
they carried **a** the stones of Ramah	1Ki 15:22	
"Go **a** from here and turn	1Ki 17:3	
they seek my life, to take it **a**."	1Ki 19:10	
they seek my life, to take it **a**."	1Ki 19:14	
in their hand and carry **a**.' "	1Ki 20:6	
took the bandage **a** from his eyes,	1Ki 20:41	5493
turned **a** his face and ate no food.	1Ki 21:4	5437
you, and will utterly sweep you **a**,	1Ki 21:21	1197a
the high places were not taken **a**;	1Ki 22:43	5493
the LORD will take **a** your master	2Ki 2:3	
that the LORD will take **a** your master	2Ki 2:5	
for he put **a** the *sacred* pillar of	2Ki 3:2	5493
Gehazi came near to push her **a**;	2Ki 4:27	1920
was furious and went **a** and said,	2Ki 5:11	
So he turned and went **a** in a rage.	2Ki 5:12	
the house, and he sent the men **a**,	2Ki 5:24	7971
eaten and drunk he sent them **a**,	2Ki 6:23	7971
has sent to take **a** my head?	2Ki 6:32	5493
had thrown **a** in their haste.	2Ki 7:15	7993
the high places were not taken **a**;	2Ki 12:3	5493
Then he went **a** from Jerusalem.	2Ki 12:18	5927
Nevertheless they did not turn **a**	2Ki 13:6	5493
he did not turn **a** from all the	2Ki 13:11	5493
the high places were not taken **a**;	2Ki 14:4	5493
the high places were not taken **a**;	2Ki 15:4	5493
the high places were not taken **a**;	2Ki 15:35	5493
people of it **a** into exile to Kir,	2Ki 16:9	1540
Israel **a** into exile to Assyria,	2Ki 17:6	1540
carried **a** to exile before them;	2Ki 17:11	1540
Israel **a** from following the LORD and	2Ki 17:21	5067b
So Israel was carried **a** into exile	2Ki 17:23	1540
a into exile in the cities of Samaria	2Ki 17:26	1540
whom you carried **a** into exile and	2Ki 17:27	1540
the priests whom they had carried **a**	2Ki 17:28	1540
had been carried **a** into exile.	2Ki 17:33	1540
Israel **a** into exile to Assyria,	2Ki 18:11	1540
whose altars Hezekiah has taken **a**,	2Ki 18:22	5493
a to a land like your own land,	2Ki 18:32	
you will beget, will be taken **a**;	2Ki 20:18	
He did **a** with the idolatrous	2Ki 23:5	7673a
He did **a** with the horses which	2Ki 23:11	7673a
a and brought *him* to Egypt,	2Ki 23:34	
Then he led **a** into exile all	2Ki 24:14	1540
a into exile to Babylon;	2Ki 24:15	1540
he led **a** into exile from Jerusalem	2Ki 24:15	
of the guard carried **a** into exile.	2Ki 25:11	1540
They took **a** the pots, the	2Ki 25:14	
a the firepans and the basins,	2Ki 25:15	
led **a** into exile from its land.	2Ki 25:21	1540
of Assyria carried **a** into exile;	1Ch 5:6	1540
They took **a** their cattle:	1Ch 5:21	7617
and he carried them **a** into exile,	1Ch 5:26	1540
a into exile by Nebuchadnezzar.	1Ch 6:15	1540
sent **a** Hushim and Baara his wives.	1Ch 8:8	7971
And Judah was carried **a** into exile	1Ch 9:1	1540
arose and took **a** the body of Saul	1Ch 10:12	
after consultation sent him **a**,	1Ch 12:19	7971
take My lovingkindness **a** from him,	1Ch 17:13	5493
carried **a** from all the nations:	1Ch 18:11	
as their hips, and sent them **a**.	1Ch 19:4	7971
a the iniquity of Your servant,	1Ch 21:8	5674a
to be swept **a** before your foes,	1Ch 21:12	5595
so that they take them **a** captive	2Ch 6:36	
turn **a** the face of Your anointed;	2Ch 6:42	7725
"But if you turn **a** and forsake My	2Ch 7:19	7725
of the LORD turned **a** from him,	2Ch 12:12	7725
they carried **a** very much plunder.	2Ch 14:13	
and they carried **a** large numbers	2Ch 14:15	
and they carried **a** the stones of	2Ch 16:6	
and carried **a** all the possessions	2Ch 21:17	
Amaziah turned **a** from following	2Ch 25:27	5493
defeated him and carried **a** from him	2Ch 28:5	
The sons of Israel carried **a**	2Ch 28:8	
Judah and carried **a** captives.	2Ch 28:17	
forsaken Him and turned their faces **a**	2Ch 29:6	5437
burning anger may turn **a** from us.	2Ch 29:10	7725
burning anger may turn **a** from you.	2Ch 30:8	7725
a from you if you return to Him."	2Ch 30:9	5493
'Has not the same Hezekiah taken **a**	2Ch 32:12	5493
Josiah would not turn **a** from him,	2Ch 35:22	5437
"Take me **a**, for I am badly	2Ch 35:23	5674a
the sword he carried **a** to Babylon;	2Ch 36:20	1540
which Nebuchadnezzar had carried **a**	Ezr 1:7	3318
Babylon had carried **a** to Babylon,	Ezr 2:1	1540
and the sound was heard far **a**.	Ezr 3:13	4480
the River, keep **a** from there.	Ezr 6:6	7352
put **a** all the wives and their children,	Ezr 10:3	3318
this matter is turned **a** from us."	Ezr 10:14	7725
They pledged to put **a** their wives,	Ezr 10:19	3318
the king of Babylon had carried **a**,	Ne 7:6	1540
All the people went **a** to eat,	Ne 8:12	
performed the service had gone **a**,	Ne 13:10	1272
so I drove him **a** from me.	Ne 13:28	1272
So Mordecai went **a** and did just as	Es 4:17	5674a
which he had taken **a** from Haman,	Es 8:2	5674a
God and turning **a** from evil.	Jb 1:1	5493
God and turning **a** from evil."	Jb 1:8	5493
gave and the LORD has taken **a**.	Jb 1:21	
God and turning **a** from evil.	Jb 2:3	5493
"I waste **a**; I will not live forever.	Jb 7:16	3988a
never turn Your gaze **a** from me,	Jb 7:19	
And take **a** my iniquity?	Jb 7:21	5674a
"Were He to snatch **a**,	Jb 9:12	2862
They flee **a**, they see no good.	Jb 9:25	1272
is in your hand, put it far **a**,	Jb 11:14	7368
a the discernment of the elders.	Jb 12:20	
the nations, then leads them **a**.	Jb 12:23	
the falling mountain crumbles **a**,	Jb 14:18	5034b
Water wears **a** stones, Its torrents	Jb 14:19	7833
wash **a** the dust of the earth;	Jb 14:19	7857
his appearance and send him **a**.	Jb 14:20	7971
"Indeed, you do **a** with reverence And	Jb 15:4	6565a
"Why does your heart carry you **a**?	Jb 15:12	
breath of His mouth he will go **a**.	Jb 15:30	5493
"He flies **a** like a dream, and	Jb 20:8	5774a
of the night he is chased **a**.	Jb 20:8	5074
flow **a** in the day of His anger.	Jb 20:28	
chaff which the storm carries **a**?	Jb 21:18	1589
a a man's iniquity for his sons.'	Jb 21:19	6845
"You have sent widows **a** empty,	Jb 22:9	7971
were snatched **a** before their time,	Jb 22:16	7059
were washed **a** by a river?	Jb 22:16	3332
a the donkeys of the orphans;	Jb 24:3	5090a
a the sheaves from the hungry.	Jb 24:10	5375
lives, who has taken **a** my right,	Jb 27:2	5493
not put **a** my integrity from me.	Jb 27:5	5493
tempest steals him **a** in the night.	Jb 27:20	1589
"The east wind carries him **a**,	Jb 27:21	
it whirls him **a** from his place.	Jb 27:21	8175a
has passed **a** like a cloud.	Jb 30:15	5674a
my Maker would soon take me **a**.	Jb 32:22	
"His flesh wastes **a** from sight,	Jb 33:21	3615
But God has taken **a** my right;	Jb 34:5	5493
People are shaken and pass **a**,	Jb 34:20	5674a
mighty are taken **a** without a hand.	Jb 34:20	5493
chaff which the wind drives **a**.	Ps 1:4	5086
And cast **a** their cords from us!"	Ps 2:3	7993
to me, O LORD, for I *am* pining **a**;	Ps 6:2	536
My eye has wasted **a** with grief;	Ps 6:7	6244
soul like a lion, Dragging me **a**,	Ps 7:2	6561
not put **a** His statutes from me.	Ps 18:22	5493
Foreigners fade **a**, And come	Ps 18:45	5034b
take my soul **a** *along* with sinners,	Ps 26:9	622
not turn Your servant **a** in anger;	Ps 27:9	5186
Do not drag me **a** with the wicked	Ps 28:3	4900
My eye is wasted **a** from grief,	Ps 31:9	6244
And my body has wasted **a**.	Ps 31:10	6244
They schemed to take **a** my life.	Ps 31:13	
my body wasted **a** Through my	Ps 32:3	1086
My vitality was drained **a** *as* with	Ps 32:4	
not the hand of the wicked drive me **a**.	Ps 36:11	5110
vanish—like smoke they vanish **a**.	Ps 37:20	
Then he passed **a**, and lo, he was	Ps 37:36	5674a
"Turn Your gaze **a** from me, that I	Ps 39:13	8159
he dies he will carry nothing **a**;	Ps 49:17	
not cast me **a** from Your presence And	Ps 51:11	7993
up and tear you **a** from *your* tent,	Ps 52:5	5255
I would fly **a** and be at rest.	Ps 55:6	5774a
"Behold, I would wander far **a**,	Ps 55:7	
flow **a** like water that runs off;	Ps 58:7	
which melts **a** as it goes along,	Ps 58:8	8557
sweep them **a** with a whirlwind,	Ps 58:9	8175a
Set me *securely* on high **a** from	Ps 59:1	
Who has not turned **a** my prayer Nor	Ps 66:20	5493
As smoke is driven **a**,	Ps 68:2	5086
is driven away, *so* drive *them* **a**;	Ps 68:2	5086
utterly swept **a** by sudden terrors!	Ps 73:19	5486
A boar from the forest eats it **a** And	Ps 80:13	3765
turned **a** from Your burning anger.	Ps 85:3	7725
wasted **a** because of affliction;	Ps 88:9	1669
have swept them **a** like a flood,	Ps 90:5	2229
evening it fades and withers **a**.	Ps 90:6	
For soon it is gone and we fly **a**.	Ps 90:10	5774a

hate the work of those who fall **a**;	**Ps 101:3**	7846
like grass and has withered **a**,	**Ps 102:4**	
have lifted me up and cast me **a**.	**Ps 102:10**	7993
And I wither **a** like grass.	**Ps 102:11**	
take me **a** in the midst of my days,	**Ps 102:24**	5927
of Your thunder they hurried **a**.	**Ps 104:7**	2648
You take **a** their spirit,	**Ps 104:29**	622
To turn **a** His wrath from	**Ps 106:23**	7725
soul melted **a** in *their* misery.	**Ps 107:26**	
on high **a** from affliction,	**Ps 107:41**	
will gnash his teeth and melt **a**;	**Ps 112:10**	4549
a reproach and contempt from me,	**Ps 119:22**	1556
Turn **a** my eyes from looking at	**Ps 119:37**	5674a
Turn **a** my reproach which I dread,	**Ps 119:39**	5674a
them **a** with the doers of iniquity.	**Ps 125:5**	
turn **a** the face of Your anointed.	**Ps 132:10**	7725
a decree which will not pass **a**.	**Ps 148:6**	5674a
a the life of its possessors.	**Pr 1:19**	
the LORD and turn **a** from evil.	**Pr 3:7**	5493
turn **a** from the words of my mouth.	**Pr 4:5**	5186
Turn **a** from it and pass on.	**Pr 4:15**	7847
Put **a** from you a deceitful mouth And	**Pr 4:24**	5493
is an abomination to fools to turn **a**	**Pr 13:19**	5493
But it is swept **a** by injustice.	**Pr 13:23**	5595
is cautious and turns **a** from evil,	**Pr 14:16**	5493
A gentle answer turns **a** wrath,	**Pr 15:1**	7725
he may keep **a** from Sheol below.	**Pr 15:24**	5493
of the LORD one keeps **a** from evil.	**Pr 16:6**	5493
and drives *his* mother **a** Is a shameful	**Pr 19:26**	1272
Keeping **a** from strife is an honor	**Pr 20:3**	7674
Stripes that wound scour **a** evil,	**Pr 20:30**	
of the wicked will drag them **a**,	**Pr 21:7**	1641
who are being taken **a** to death,	**Pr 24:11**	
And turn His anger **a** from him.	**Pr 24:18**	7725
Take **a** the dross from the silver,	**Pr 25:4**	1898
Take **a** the wicked before the	**Pr 25:5**	1898
evil report about you will not pass **a**.	**Pr 25:10**	7725
who is near than a brother far **a**.	**Pr 27:10**	
He who turns **a** his ear from	**Pr 28:9**	5493
aflame, But wise men turn **a** anger.	**Pr 29:8**	7725
to keep and a time to throw **a**.	**Ec 3:6**	7993
and put **a** pain from your body,	**Ec 11:10**	5674a
the day when the shadows flee **a**,	**SS 2:17**	
the day When the shadows flee **a**,	**SS 4:6**	
beloved had turned **a** *and* had gone!	**SS 5:6**	2559
the walls took **a** my shawl from me.	**SS 5:7**	
"Turn your eyes **a** from me, For	**SS 6:5**	5437
They have turned **a** from Him.	**Is 1:4**	2114a
smelt **a** your dross as with lye And	**Is 1:25**	
be like an oak whose leaf fades **a** Or	**Is 1:30**	5034b
In that day men will cast **a** to the	**Is 2:20**	7993
a the beauty of *their* anklets,	**Is 3:18**	5493
take **a** our reproach!"	**Is 4:1**	622
When the Lord has washed **a** the	**Is 4:4**	7364
And take **a** the rights of the ones	**Is 5:23**	5493
and their blossom blow **a** as dust;	**Is 5:24**	5927
and your iniquity is taken **a** and	**Is 6:7**	5493
"The LORD has removed men far **a**,	**Is 6:12**	
a before the king of Assyria."	**Is 8:4**	
will be driven **a** into darkness.	**Is 8:22**	5080
this, His anger does not turn **a**	**Is 9:12**	7725
this, His anger does not turn **a**	**Is 9:17**	7725
this, His anger does not turn **a**	**Is 9:21**	7725
this, His anger does not turn **a**	**Is 10:4**	7725
be as when a sick man wastes **a**.	**Is 10:18**	4549
and Gibeah of Saul has fled **a**.	**Is 10:29**	
with me, Your anger is turned **a**,	**Is 12:1**	7725
Melt **a**, O Philistia, all of you;	**Is 14:31**	
and your harvest has fallen **a**.	**Is 16:9**	5307
taken **a** from the fruitful field;	**Is 16:10**	622
them and they will flee far **a**,	**Is 17:13**	4801
and cut **a** the spreading branches.	**Is 18:5**	8456
The reeds and rushes will rot **a**.	**Is 19:6**	7060
Nile Will become dry, be driven **a**,	**Is 19:7**	5086
nets on the waters will pine **a**.	**Is 19:8**	535
king of Assyria will lead **a** the captives	**Is 20:4**	5090a
Though they had fled far **a**.	**Is 22:3**	
"Turn your eyes **a** from me, Let me	**Is 22:4**	4480
of the people of the earth fade **a**.	**Is 24:4**	535
will wipe tears **a** from all faces,	**Is 25:8**	4229a
banishing them, by driving them **a**.	**Is 27:8**	7971
will sweep **a** the refuge of lies	**Is 28:17**	3261
ones like the chaff which blows **a**;	**Is 29:5**	5674a
every man will cast **a** his silver idols	**Is 31:7**	3988a
rock will pass **a** because of panic,	**Is 31:9**	5674a
The land mourns *and* pines **a**,	**Is 33:9**	535
"You who are far **a**, hear what I	**Is 33:13**	7350
the host of heaven will wear **a**,	**Is 34:4**	4743
will also wither **a** As a leaf withers	**Is 34:4**	5034b
sorrow and sighing will flee **a**.	**Is 35:10**	5127
whose altars Hezekiah has taken **a** and	**Is 36:7**	5493
a to a land like your own land,	**Is 36:17**	
you will beget, will be taken **a**,	**Is 39:7**	
storm carries them **a** like stubble.	**Is 40:24**	
and the wind will carry them **a**,	**Is 41:16**	
caves, Or are hidden **a** in prisons;	**Is 42:22**	
will go **a** together in humiliation.	**Is 45:16**	
you will not know how to charm **a**;	**Is 47:11**	7837
who swallowed you will be far **a**.	**Is 49:19**	
of the mighty man will be taken **a**,	**Is 49:25**	
which I have sent your mother **a**?	**Is 50:1**	7971
your mother was sent **a**.	**Is 50:1**	7971
sorrow and sighing will flee **a**.	**Is 51:11**	
have been taken **a** without cause?"	**Is 52:5**	
and judgment He was taken **a**;	**Is 53:8**	
And devout men are taken **a**,	**Is 57:1**	622
man is taken **a** from evil,	**Is 57:1**	622
And a breath will take *them* **a**.	**Is 57:13**	
angry, And he went on turning **a**,	**Is 57:17**	7726
LORD, And turning **a** from our God,	**Is 59:13**	5472
And righteousness stands far **a**;	**Is 59:14**	4480
like the wind, take us **a**.	**Is 64:6**	
pot, facing **a** from the north."	**Jer 1:13**	
of her heat who can turn her **a**?	**Jer 2:24**	7725
His anger is turned **a** from me.'	**Jer 2:35**	7725
I had sent her **a** and given her a	**Jer 3:8**	7971
And not turn **a** from following Me.'	**Jer 3:19**	7725
And if you will put **a** your	**Jer 4:1**	5493
Strip **a** her branches, For they are	**Jer 5:10**	5493
iniquities have turned these **a**,	**Jer 5:25**	5186
'Cut off your hair and cast *it* **a**,	**Jer 7:29**	7993
and no one will frighten *them* **a**.	**Jer 7:33**	
Does one turn **a** and not repent?	**Jer 8:4**	7725
Turned **a** in continual apostasy?	**Jer 8:5**	7725
"I will surely snatch them **a**,"	**Jer 8:13**	5486
given them will pass **a**.	**Jer 8:13**	5674a
take **a** from you your disaster,	**Jer 11:15**	5674a
and birds have been snatched **a**,	**Jer 12:4**	5595
send them **a** from My presence and	**Jer 15:1**	7971
"She who bore seven *sons* pines **a**;	**Jer 15:9**	535
view of Your patience, take me **a**;	**Jer 15:15**	
whose heart turns **a** from the LORD.	**Jer 17:5**	5493
a on earth will be written down,	**Jer 17:13**	5493
I have not hurried **a** from *being* a	**Jer 17:16**	
a foreign *land* ever snatched **a**?	**Jer 18:14**	5428
as to turn **a** Your wrath from them.	**Jer 18:20**	7725
and he will carry them **a** as exiles	**Jer 20:4**	1540
will plunder them, take them **a** and	**Jer 20:5**	
but he who goes out and falls **a** to	**Jer 21:9**	5307
for the one who goes **a**;	**Jer 22:10**	
will sweep **a** all your shepherds,	**Jer 22:22**	7462a
My flock and driven them **a**,	**Jer 23:2**	5080
They will be driven **a** into the	**Jer 23:12**	1760
and cast you **a** from My presence,	**Jer 23:39**	5203
had carried **a** captive Jeconiah the son	**Jer 24:1**	1540
king of Babylon took **a** from this	**Jer 28:3**	3947
sent **a** from Jerusalem to Babylon.	**Jer 29:20**	7971
that I will not turn **a** from them,	**Jer 32:40**	7725
that they will not turn **a** from Me.	**Jer 32:40**	5493
Babylon which has gone **a** from you.	**Jer 34:21**	5927
will surely go **a** from us,"	**Jer 37:9**	
a and came to the land of Judah,	**Jer 40:12**	5080
to which they had been driven **a**,	**Jer 43:5**	5080
'And I will take **a** the remnant of	**Jer 44:12**	
A from the sword of the oppressor.'	**Jer 46:16**	
back *and* have fled **a** together;	**Jer 46:21**	
to Moab, For she will flee **a**;	**Jer 48:9**	3318
taken **a** From the fruitful field,	**Jer 48:33**	622
sons have been taken **a** captive And	**Jer 48:46**	
Your valley is flowing **a**, O	**Jer 49:4**	
"Flee **a**, turn back, dwell in the	**Jer 49:8**	
I will make him run **a** from it,	**Jer 49:19**	
She has turned **a** to flee, And	**Jer 49:24**	
a their tents and their flocks;	**Jer 49:29**	
"Run **a**, flee! Dwell in the depths,	**Jer 49:30**	5127
wandered off, they have gone **a**!	**Jer 50:3**	
a from the midst of Babylon And	**Jer 50:8**	
the lions have driven *them* **a**.	**Jer 50:17**	5080
I will make them run **a** from it,	**Jer 50:44**	4480
He has washed me **a**.	**Jer 51:34**	1740
the guard carried **a** into exile some	**Jer 52:15**	1540
They also took **a** the pots,	**Jer 52:18**	
the guard also took **a** the bowls,	**Jer 52:19**	
led **a** into exile from its land.	**Jer 52:27**	1540
carried **a** into exile:	**Jer 52:28**	1540
Her little ones have gone **a** As	**La 1:5**	
she herself groans and turns **a**.	**La 1:8**	268
my flesh and my skin to waste **a**,	**La 3:4**	1086
For they pine **a**, being stricken	**La 4:9**	2100
Spirit lifted me up and took me **a**;	**Ezk 3:14**	
when a righteous man turns **a** from	**Ezk 3:20**	7725
and waste **a** in their iniquity.	**Ezk 4:17**	4743
hearts which turned **a** from Me,	**Ezk 6:9**	5493
them far **a** among the nations and	**Ezk 11:16**	
"Repent and turn **a** from your	**Ezk 14:6**	7725
a from all your abominations.	**Ezk 14:6**	7725
your clothing, take **a** your jewels,	**Ezk 16:39**	
and took **a** the top of the cedar.	**Ezk 17:3**	
took **a** the mighty of the land,	**Ezk 17:13**	
turns **a** from his righteousness,	**Ezk 18:24**	7725
turns **a** from his righteousness,	**Ezk 18:26**	7725
when a wicked man turns **a** from his	**Ezk 18:27**	7725
turned **a** from all his transgressions	**Ezk 18:28**	7725
a from all your transgressions,	**Ezk 18:30**	7725
"Cast **a** from you all your	**Ezk 18:31**	7993
'Cast **a**, each of you, the	**Ezk 20:7**	7993
they did not cast **a** the detestable	**Ezk 20:8**	7993
and take **a** your beautiful jewels.	**Ezk 23:26**	
you will rot **a** in your iniquities and	**Ezk 24:23**	4743
in Egypt, They take **a** her wealth,	**Ezk 30:4**	
its wickedness I have driven it **a**.	**Ezk 31:11**	1644
field wilted **a** on account of it.	**Ezk 31:15**	5968
her and all her hordes **a**.	**Ezk 32:20**	4900
and a sword comes and takes him **a**,	**Ezk 33:4**	
he is taken **a** in his iniquity;	**Ezk 33:6**	
us, and we are rotting **a** in them;	**Ezk 33:10**	4743
to carry **a** silver and gold,	**Ezk 38:13**	
gold, to take **a** cattle and goods,	**Ezk 38:13**	
galleries took more *space* **a** from them	**Ezk 42:5**	398
"Now let them put **a** their	**Ezk 43:9**	7368
put **a** violence and destruction,	**Ezk 45:9**	5493
and the wind carried them **a** so	**Da 2:35**	
that you be driven **a** from mankind and	**Da 4:25**	2957
break **a** now from your sins by	**Da 4:27**	6562
you will be driven **a** from mankind,	**Da 4:32**	2957
and he was driven **a** from mankind	**Da 4:33**	2957
his glory was taken **a** from him.	**Da 5:20**	5709
"He was also driven **a** from mankind,	**Da 5:21**	2957
their dominion was taken **a**,	**Da 7:12**	5709
dominion Which will not pass **a**;	**Da 7:14**	5709
and his dominion will be taken **a**,	**Da 7:26**	5709
who are far **a** in all the countries	**Da 9:7**	
turn **a** from Your city Jerusalem,	**Da 9:16**	7725
and they ran **a** to hide themselves.	**Da 10:7**	1272
"When the multitude is carried **a**,	**Da 11:12**	
a before him and shattered,	**Da 11:22**	7857
do **a** with the regular sacrifice.	**Da 11:31**	5493
put **a** her harlotry from her face And	**Hos 2:2**	5493
I will also take **a** My wool and My	**Hos 2:9**	5337
new wine take **a** the understanding.	**Hos 4:11**	
I, will tear to pieces and go **a**,	**Hos 5:14**	
and go away, I will carry **a**,	**Hos 5:14**	
I will go **a** *and* return to My place	**Hos 5:15**	
like the dew which goes **a** early.	**Hos 6:4**	
themselves, They turn **a** from Me.	**Hos 7:14**	5493
will fly **a** like a bird—No birth,	**Hos 9:11**	5774a
My God will cast them **a** Because	**Hos 9:17**	3988a
blown **a** from the threshing floor And	**Hos 13:3**	5590
anger And took him **a** in My wrath.	**Hos 13:11**	
"Take **a** all iniquity And receive	**Hos 14:2**	
My anger has turned **a** from them.	**Hos 14:4**	7725
them bare and cast *them* **a**;	**Jl 1:7**	7993
dwelling in Samaria be snatched **a**	**Am 3:12**	5337
will take you **a** with meat hooks,	**Am 4:2**	
"Take **a** from Me the noise of your	**Am 5:23**	5493
sprawlers' banqueting will pass **a**.	**Am 6:7**	5493
seer, flee **a** to the land of Judah and	**Am 7:12**	
do **a** with the humble of the land,	**Am 8:4**	7673a
"While I was fainting **a**,	**Jon 2:7**	5848c
them, And houses, and take *them* **a**.	**Mi 2:2**	
they will be cut off and pass **a**.	**Na 1:12**	5674a
She is stripped, she is carried **a**,	**Na 2:7**	5927
locust strips and flies **a**.	**Na 3:16**	5774a
hook, Drag them **a** with their net,	**Hab 1:15**	1641
a at the light of Your arrows,	**Hab 3:11**	
taken **a** *His* judgments against you,	**Zph 3:15**	5493
He has cleared **a** your enemies.	**Zph 3:15**	6437
I blow it **a**. Why?" declares	**Hg 1:9**	
I have taken your iniquity **a** from	**Zch 3:4**	5674a
everyone who steals will be purged **a**	**Zch 5:3**	
everyone who swears will be purged **a**	**Zch 5:3**	
and you will be taken **a** with it.	**Mal 2:3**	
planned to send her **a** secretly.	**Mt 1:19**	*630*
until heaven and earth pass **a**,	**Mt 5:18**	*3928*
WHOEVER SENDS HIS WIFE **A**, LET HIM GIVE	**Mt 5:31**	*630*
and do not turn **a** from him who	**Mt 5:42**	*654*
AND CARRIED **A** OUR DISEASES."	**Mt 8:17**	*941*
The herdsmen ran **a**,	**Mt 8:33**	*5343*
bridegroom is taken **a** from them,	**Mt 9:15**	*522*
patch pulls **a** from the garment,	**Mt 9:16**	*142*
As these men were going **a**, Jesus	**Mt 11:7**	
they had no root, they withered **a**.	**Mt 13:6**	*3583*
he has shall be taken **a** from him.	**Mt 13:12**	*142*
the evil *one* comes and snatches **a**	**Mt 13:19**	*726*
the word, immediately he falls **a**.	**Mt 13:21**	*4624*
tares among the wheat, and went **a**.	**Mt 13:25**	*565*
but the bad they threw **a**.	**Mt 13:48**	*1854*
and took **a** the body and buried it;	**Mt 14:12**	*142*
so send the crowds **a**,	**Mt 14:15**	*630*
"They do not need to go **a**;	**Mt 14:16**	*565*
while He sent the crowds **a**.	**Mt 14:22**	*630*
He had sent the crowds **a**,	**Mt 14:23**	*630*
BUT THEIR HEART IS FAR **A** FROM ME.	**Mt 15:8**	*568*
Jesus went **a** from there, and	**Mt 15:21**	*1831*
"Send her **a**, because she keeps shouting	**Mt 15:23**	*630*
do not want to send them **a** hungry,	**Mt 15:32**	*630*
And sending **a** the crowds, Jesus	**Mt 15:39**	*630*
And He left them and went **a**.	**Mt 16:4**	*565*
OF DIVORCE AND SEND *her* **A**?"	**Mt 19:7**	*630*
this statement, he went **a** grieving;	**Mt 19:22**	*565*
of God will be taken **a** from you and	**Mt 21:43**	*142*
and leaving Him, they went **a**.	**Mt 22:22**	*565*
was going **a** when His disciples came	**Mt 24:1**	*4198*
"At that time many will fall **a**	**Mt 24:10**	*4624*
this generation will not pass **a**	**Mt 24:34**	*3928*
"Heaven and earth will pass **a**,	**Mt 24:35**	*3928*
but My words will not pass **a**.	**Mt 24:35**	*3928*
flood came and took them all **a**;	**Mt 24:39**	*142*
were going **a** to make the purchase,	**Mt 25:10**	*565*
went **a**, and dug *a hole*	**Mt 25:18**	*565*
and went **a** and hid your talent in	**Mt 25:25**	*565*
take **a** the talent from him,	**Mt 25:28**	*142*
he does have shall be taken **a**.	**Mt 25:29**	*142*
will go **a** into eternal punishment,	**Mt 25:46**	*565*
fall **a** because of Me this night,	**Mt 26:31**	*4624*
all may fall **a** because of You,	**Mt 26:33**	*4624*
of You, I will never fall **a**."	**Mt 26:33**	*4624*
He went **a** again a second time and	**Mt 26:42**	*565*
cannot pass **a** unless I drink it,	**Mt 26:42**	*3928*
went **a** and prayed a third time,	**Mt 26:44**	*565*
Jesus led Him **a** to Caiaphas,	**Mt 26:57**	*520*
the way you talk gives you **a**."	**Mt 26:73**	*1212, 4160*
and they bound Him, and led Him **a** and	**Mt 27:2**	*520*
and he went **a** and hanged himself.	**Mt 27:5**	*565*
Him, and led Him **a** to crucify Him.	**Mt 27:31**	*520*
entrance of the tomb and went **a**.	**Mt 27:60**	*565*
steal Him **a** and say to the people,	**Mt 27:64**	*2813*
a the stone and sat upon it.	**Mt 28:2**	*617*
stole Him **a** while we were asleep.'	**Mt 28:13**	*2813*
and went **a** to follow Him.	**Mk 1:20**	*565*
and went **a** to a secluded place,	**Mk 1:35**	*565*
him and immediately sent him **a**,	**Mk 1:43**	*1544b*
bridegroom is taken **a** from them,	**Mk 2:20**	*522*
the patch pulls **a** from it,	**Mk 2:21**	*142*
it had no root, it withered **a**.	**Mk 4:6**	*3583*
Satan comes and takes **a** the word	**Mk 4:15**	*142*

the word, immediately they fall **a**.	Mk 4:17	4624
has shall be taken **a** from him."	Mk 4:25	142
Their herdsmen ran **a** and	Mk 5:14	5343
And he went **a** and began to	Mk 5:20	565
they came and took **a** his body and	Mk 6:29	142
"Come **a** by yourselves to a secluded	Mk 6:31	1205
They went **a** in the boat to a	Mk 6:32	565
send them **a** so that they may go	Mk 6:36	630
was sending the crowd **a**.	Mk 6:45	630
BUT THEIR HEART IS FAR A FROM ME.	Mk 7:6	568, 4206
went **a** from there to the region of Tyre.	Mk 7:24	565
send them **a** hungry to their homes,	Mk 8:3	630
And He sent them **a**.	Mk 8:9	630
and went **a** to the other side.	Mk 8:13	565
OF DIVORCE AND SEND *her* A."	Mk 10:4	630
was saddened, and he went **a** grieving,	Mk 10:22	565
They went **a** and found a colt	Mk 11:4	565
him and sent him **a** empty-handed.	Mk 12:3	649
And *so* they left Him and went **a**.	Mk 12:12	565
this generation will not pass **a**	Mk 13:30	3928
"Heaven and earth will pass **a**,	Mk 13:31	3928
but My words will not pass **a**.	Mk 13:31	3928
"*It is* like a man **a** on a journey,	Mk 13:34	590
Unleavened Bread were two days **a**;	Mk 14:1	3326
"You will all fall **a**,	Mk 14:27	4624
"*Even* though all may fall **a**,	Mk 14:29	4624
Again He went **a** and prayed,	Mk 14:39	565
Him and lead Him **a** under guard."	Mk 14:44	520
led Jesus **a** to the high priest;	Mk 14:53	520
and binding Jesus, they led Him **a** and	Mk 15:1	667
took Him **a** into the palace	Mk 15:16	520
"Who will roll **a** the stone for us	Mk 16:3	617
that the stone had been rolled **a**,	Mk 16:4	352a
a and reported it to the others,	Mk 16:13	565
to take **a** my disgrace among men."	Lk 1:25	851
And sent **a** the rich empty-handed.	Lk 1:53	1821
had gone **a** from them into heaven,	Lk 2:15	565
keep Him from going **a** from them.	Lk 4:42	4198
"Go **a** from me Lord, for I am a	Lk 5:8	1831
slip **a** to the wilderness and pray.	Lk 5:16	5298
bridegroom is taken **a** from them,	Lk 5:35	522
and whoever takes **a** your coat,	Lk 6:29	142
and whoever takes **a** what is yours,	Lk 6:30	142
soon as it grew up, it withered **a**,	Lk 8:6	3583
takes **a** the word from their heart,	Lk 8:12	142
and in time of temptation fall **a**.	Lk 8:13	868
has shall be taken **a** from him."	Lk 8:18	142
Him not to command them to go **a** into	Lk 8:31	565
they ran **a** and reported it in the	Lk 8:34	5343
but He sent him **a**, saying,	Lk 8:38	630
So he went **a**, proclaiming	Lk 8:39	565
"Send the crowd **a**,	Lk 9:12	630
and went **a** leaving him half dead.	Lk 10:30	565
shall not be taken **a** from her."	Lk 10:42	851
he takes **a** from him all his armor	Lk 11:22	142
a lamp, puts it **a** in a cellar nor	Lk 11:33	5087
have taken **a** the key of knowledge;	Lk 11:52	142
and lead him **a** to water *him?*	Lk 13:15	520
"Go **a**, leave here, for	Lk 13:31	1831
and healed him, and sent him **a**.	Lk 14:4	630
while the other is still far **a**,	Lk 14:32	4206
taking the management **a** from me?	Lk 16:3	851
easier for heaven and earth to pass **a**	Lk 16:17	3928
and was carried **a** by the angels	Lk 16:22	667
in torment, and saw Abraham far **a** and	Lk 16:23	575, 3113
Do not go **a**, and do not run after	Lk 17:23	565
standing some distance **a**,	Lk 18:13	3113
I kept put **a** in a handkerchief;	Lk 19:20	606
'Take the mina **a** from him and	Lk 19:24	142
he does have shall be taken **a**.	Lk 19:26	142
So those who were sent went **a** and	Lk 19:32	565
him and sent him **a** empty-handed.	Lk 20:10	1821
and sent him **a** empty-handed.	Lk 20:11	1821
will not pass **a** until all things take	Lk 21:32	3928
"Heaven and earth will pass **a**,	Lk 21:33	3928
but My words will not pass **a**.	Lk 21:33	3928
And he went **a** and discussed with	Lk 22:4	565
they led Him **a** and brought Him to	Lk 22:54	
Him **a** to their council *chamber,*	Lk 22:66	520
"**A** with this man, and release for	Lk 23:18	142
When they led Him **a**,	Lk 23:26	520
led **a** to be put to death with Him.	Lk 23:32	71
the stone rolled **a** from the tomb,	Lk 24:2	617
and he went **a** to his home,	Lk 24:12	565
who takes **a** the sin of the world!	Jn 1:29	142
"Take these things **a**;	Jn 2:16	142
He left Judea and went **a** again into	Jn 4:3	565
gone **a** into the city to buy food.	Jn 4:8	565
for Jesus had slipped **a** while	Jn 5:13	1593
The man went **a**, and told the Jews	Jn 5:15	565
After these things Jesus went **a** to	Jn 6:1	565
His disciples had gone **a** alone.	Jn 6:22	565
"You do not want to go **a** also,	Jn 6:67	5217
"I go **a**, and you will seek Me,	Jn 8:21	5217
So he went **a** and washed, and	Jn 9:7	565
so I went **a** and washed, and I	Jn 9:11	565
"No one has taken it **a** from Me,	Jn 10:18	142
And He went **a** again beyond the	Jn 10:40	565
she had said this, she went **a** and	Jn 11:28	565
a both our place and our nation."	Jn 11:48	142
but went **a** from there to the	Jn 11:54	565
him many of the Jews were going **a** and	Jn 12:11	5217
and He went **a** and hid Himself from	Jn 12:36	565
'I go **a**, and I will come to you.'	Jn 14:28	5217
does not bear fruit, He takes **a**;	Jn 15:2	142
in Me, he is thrown **a** as a branch and	Jn 15:6	1854
is to your advantage that I go **a**;	Jn 16:7	565
for if I do not go **a**,	Jn 16:7	565
no one *will* take your joy **a** from you.	Jn 16:22	142
So they cried out, "**A** with *Him,*	Jn 19:15	142
a with *Him,* crucify Him!"	Jn 19:15	142
and *that* they might be taken **a**.	Jn 19:31	142
he might take **a** the body of Jesus;	Jn 19:38	142
So he came and took **a** His body.	Jn 19:38	142
already taken **a** from the tomb.	Jn 20:1	142
taken **a** the Lord out of the tomb,	Jn 20:2	142
went **a** again to their own homes.	Jn 20:10	565
"Because they have taken **a** my Lord,	Jn 20:13	142
"Sir, if you have carried Him **a**,	Jn 20:15	941
laid Him, and I will take Him **a**."	Jn 20:15	142
but about one hundred yards **a**,	Jn 21:8	575
a Sabbath day's journey **a**.	Ac 1:12	
that your sins may be wiped **a**,	Ac 3:19	1813
and drew **a** *some* people after him;	Ac 5:37	868
stay **a** from these men and let them	Ac 5:38	868
came up to him and dragged him **a**	Ac 6:12	4884
Pharaoh's daughter took him **a** and	Ac 7:21	337
his neighbor pushed him **a**,	Ac 7:27	683
"But God turned **a** and delivered	Ac 7:42	4762
HIS JUDGMENT WAS TAKEN A;	Ac 8:33	142
of the Lord snatched Philip **a**;	Ac 8:39	726
plotted together to do **a** with him,	Ac 9:23	337
Caesarea and sent him **a** to Tarsus.	Ac 9:30	1821
day he got up and went **a** with them,	Ac 10:23	1831
that they be led **a** *to execution.*	Ac 12:19	520
hands on them, they sent them **a**.	Ac 13:3	630
the proconsul **a** from the faith.	Ac 13:8	1294
he went **a** with Barnabas to Derbe.	Ac 14:20	1831
So when they were sent **a**,	Ac 15:30	630
they were sent **a** from the brethren	Ac 15:33	630
with him and sailed **a** to Cyprus.	Ac 15:39	1602
are they sending us **a** secretly?	Ac 16:37	1544b
and Silas **a** by night to Berea,	Ac 17:10	1599
them **a** from the judgment seat.	Ac 18:16	556
them and took **a** the disciples,	Ac 19:9	873
this Paul has persuaded and turned **a**	Ac 19:26	3179
They took **a** the boy alive, and	Ac 20:12	71
draw **a** the disciples after them.	Ac 20:30	645
shouting, "**A** with him!"	Ac 21:36	142
be baptized, and wash **a** your sins,	Ac 22:16	628
you far **a** to the Gentiles.'"	Ac 22:21	1821
"**A** with such a fellow from the	Ac 22:22	142
and take him **a** from them by force,	Ac 23:10	726
"Go **a** for the present, and when I	Ac 24:25	4198
cut **a** the ropes of the *ship's* boat and	Ac 27:32	609
the *ship's* boat and let it fall **a**.	Ac 27:32	1601b
of them would swim **a** and escape;	Ac 27:42	1579
body of sin might be done **a** with,	Ro 6:6	2673
THEM, WHEN I TAKE A THEIR SINS."	Ro 11:27	851
you learned, and turn **a** from them.	Ro 16:17	1578
of this age, who are passing **a**;	1Co 2:6	2673
God will do **a** with both of them.	1Co 6:13	2673
Shall I then take **a** the members of	1Co 6:15	142
she must not send her husband **a**.	1Co 7:13	863
form of this world is passing **a**.	1Co 7:31	3855
of prophecy, they will be done **a**;	1Co 13:8	2673
is knowledge, it will be done **a**.	1Co 13:8	2673
comes, the partial will be done **a**.	1Co 13:10	2673
man, I did **a** with childish things.	1Co 13:11	2673
that which fades **a** *was* with glory,	2Co 3:11	2673
at the end of what was fading **a**.	2Co 3:13	2673
to the Lord, the veil is taken **a**.	2Co 3:16	4014
the old things passed **a**;	2Co 5:17	3928
but I went **a** to Arabia, and	Ga 1:17	565
was carried **a** by their hypocrisy.	Ga 2:13	4879
PEACE TO YOU WHO WERE FAR A,	Eph 2:17	3112
and slander be put **a** from you,	Eph 4:31	142
and not moved **a** from the hope of	Col 1:23	3334
having been taken **a** from you for a	1Th 2:17	642
a from the presence of the Lord	2Th 1:9	575
that you keep **a** from every brother	2Th 3:6	4724
some will fall **a** from the faith,	1Tm 4:1	868
it have wandered **a** from the faith and	1Tm 6:10	635
who are in Asia turned **a** from me,	2Tm 1:15	654
turn **a** their ears from the truth and	2Tm 4:4	654
of men who turn **a** from the truth.	Ti 1:14	654
we do not drift **a** *from it.*	Heb 2:1	3901
that falls **a** from the living God.	Heb 3:12	868
and *then* have fallen **a**,	Heb 6:6	3895
put **a** sin by the sacrifice of Himself.	Heb 9:26	115
of bulls and goats to take **a** sins.	Heb 10:4	851
He takes **a** the first in order to	Heb 10:9	337
which can never take **a** sins;	Heb 10:11	4014
do not throw **a** your confidence,	Heb 10:35	577
will we *escape* who turn **a** from Him	Heb 12:25	654
Do not be carried **a** by varied and	Heb 13:9	3911
flowering grass he will pass **a**.	Jas 1:10	3928
midst of his pursuits will fade **a**.	Jas 1:11	3133
a and enticed by his own lust.	Jas 1:14	1828
has looked at himself and gone **a**,	Jas 1:24	565
little while and then vanishes **a**.	Jas 4:14	853
and undefiled and will not fade **a**,	1Pe 1:4	263
TURN A FROM EVIL AND DO GOOD;	1Pe 3:11	1578
to turn **a** from the holy	2Pe 2:21	5290
in which the heavens will pass **a**	2Pe 3:10	3928
not carried **a** by the error of	2Pe 3:17	4879
because the darkness is passing **a** and	1Jn 2:8	3855
The world is passing **a**,	1Jn 2:17	3855
not shrink **a** from Him in shame	1Jn 2:28	575
appeared in order to take **a** sins;	1Jn 3:5	142
And his tail swept **a** a third of	Rv 12:4	4951
her to be swept **a** with the flood.	Rv 12:15	4216
And every island fled **a**,	Rv 16:20	5343
And he carried me **a** in the Spirit	Rv 17:3	667
and splendid have passed **a** from you	Rv 18:14	622
presence earth and heaven fled **a**,	Rv 20:11	5343
and the first earth passed **a**,	Rv 21:1	565
wipe **a** every tear from their eyes;	Rv 21:4	1813
the first things have passed **a**."	Rv 21:4	565
And he carried me **a** in the Spirit	Rv 21:10	667
and if anyone takes **a** from the	Rv 22:19	851
God will take **a** his part from the	Rv 22:19	851

AWE

"Dominion and **a** belong to Him Who	Jb 25:2	6343
Him, And stand in **a** of Him,	Ps 22:23	1481c
of the world stand in **a** of Him.	Ps 33:8	1481c
the earth stand in **a** of Your signs;	Ps 65:8	3372a
my heart stands in **a** of Your words.	Ps 119:161	6342
stand in **a** of the God of Israel.	Is 29:23	6206
Me and stood in **a** of My name.	Mal 2:5	2865
kept feeling a sense of **a**;	Ac 2:43	5401
service with reverence and **a**;	Heb 12:28	1190a

AWESOME

"How **a** is this place!	Gn 28:17	3372a
in holiness, **A** in praises,	Ex 15:11	3372a
in your midst, a great and **a** God.	Dt 7:21	3372a
and the **a** God who does not show	Dt 10:17	3372a
who has done these great and **a**	Dt 10:21	3372a
to fear this honored and **a** name,	Dt 28:58	3372a
of the angel of God, very **a**.	Jg 13:6	3372a
You and **a** things for Your land,	2Sa 7:23	3372a
of heaven, the great and **a** God,	Ne 1:5	3372a
the Lord who is great and **a**,	Ne 4:14	3372a
great, the mighty, and the **a** God,	Ne 9:32	3372a
Around God is **a** majesty.	Jb 37:22	3372a
right hand teach You **a** things.	Ps 45:4	3372a
By **a** *deeds* You answer us in	Ps 65:5	3372a
"How **a** are Your works!	Ps 66:3	3372a
Who is **a** in *His* deeds toward the	Ps 66:5	3372a
You are **a** from Your sanctuary.	Ps 68:35	3372a
And **a** above all those who are	Ps 89:7	3372a
them praise Your great and **a** name;	Ps 99:3	3372a
Ham *And* **a** things by the Red Sea.	Ps 106:22	3372a
Holy and **a** is His name.	Ps 111:9	3372a
of the power of Your **a** acts	Ps 145:6	3372a
As **a** as an army with banners.	SS 6:4	366
As **a** as an army with banners?'	SS 6:10	366
When You did **a** things which we	Is 64:3	3372a
their rims they were lofty and **a**,	Ezk 1:18	3374
like the **a** gleam of crystal,	Ezk 1:22	3372a
of you, and its appearance was **a**.	Da 2:31	1763
"Alas, O Lord, the great and **a** God,	Da 9:4	3372a
LORD is indeed great and very **a**,	Jl 2:11	3372a
great and **a** day of the LORD comes.	Jl 2:31	3372a

AWESTRUCK

they were **a**, and glorified God,	Mt 9:8	5399

AWL

shall pierce his ear with an **a**;	Ex 21:6	4836
then you shall take an **a** and	Dt 15:17	4836

AWNING

Your **a** was blue and purple from	Ezk 27:7	4374

AWOKE

When Noah **a** from his wine, he knew	Gn 9:24	3364
Jacob **a** from his sleep and said,	Gn 28:16	3364
sleek and fat cows. Then Pharaoh **a**.	Gn 41:4	3364
Then Pharaoh **a**, and behold, *it was*	Gn 41:7	3364
were just as ugly as before. Then I **a**.	Gn 41:21	3364
But he **a** from his sleep and pulled	Jg 16:14	3364
And he **a** from his sleep and said,	Jg 16:20	3364
Then Solomon **a**, and behold, it was	1Ki 3:15	3364
I **a**, for the LORD sustains me.	Ps 3:5	7019a
Then the Lord **a** as *if from* sleep,	Ps 78:65	3364
At this I **a** and looked, and my	Jer 31:26	7019a
And Joseph **a** from his sleep and did	Mt 1:24	1453
When the jailer **a** and saw the prison	Ac 16:27	1853

AXE

swings the **a** to cut down the tree,	Dt 19:5	1631
by swinging an **a** against them;	Dt 20:19	1631
and Abimelech took an **a** in his	Jg 9:48	7134
his plowshare, his mattock, his **a**,	1Sa 13:20	7134
hammer nor **a** nor any iron tool heard	1Ki 6:7	1631
the **a** head fell into the water;	2Ki 6:5	1270
up *His* **a** in a forest of trees.	Ps 74:5	7134
If the **a** is dull and he does not	Ec 10:10	1270
Is the **a** to boast itself over the	Is 10:15	1631
of the forest with an iron **a**,	Is 10:34	
"The **a** is already laid at the	Mt 3:10	513
"Indeed the **a** is already laid	Lk 3:9	513

AXES

mattocks, the forks, and the **a**,	1Sa 13:21	7134
iron instruments, and iron **a**,	2Sa 12:31	4037
with sharp instruments and with **a**.	1Ch 20:3	4050
come to her as woodcutters with **a**.	Jer 46:22	7134
and with his **a** he will break down	Ezk 26:9	2719

AXLES

four bronze wheels with bronze **a**,	1Ki 7:30	5633b
and the **a** of the wheels *were* on	1Ki 7:32	3027
Their **a**, their rims, their spokes,	1Ki 7:33	3027

AYYAH

towns as far as **A** with its towns,	1Ch 7:28	5857

AZALIAH

the son of **A** the son of Meshullam	2Ki 22:3	683
he sent Shaphan the son of **A**,	2Ch 34:8	683

AZANIAH

Jeshua the son of **A**,	Ne 10:9	245

AZAREL

Elkanah, Isshiah, **A**,	1Ch 12:6	5832
the eleventh to **A**, his sons and	1Ch 25:18	5832
for Dan, **A** the son of Jeroham.	1Ch 27:22	5832
A, Shelemiah, Shemariah,	Ezr 10:41	5832
and Amashsai the son of **A**,	Ne 11:13	5832
and his kinsmen, Shemaiah, **A**,	Ne 12:36	5832

AZARIAH
A the son of Zadok *was* the priest; 1Ki 4:2 5838
and **A** the son of Nathan *was* over 1Ki 4:5 5838
All the people of Judah took **A**, 2Ki 14:21 5838
A son of Amaziah king of Judah 2Ki 15:1 5838
the acts of **A** and all that he did, 2Ki 15:6 5838
And **A** slept with his fathers, and 2Ki 15:7 5838
year of **A** king of Judah, 2Ki 15:8 5838
year of **A** king of Judah, 2Ki 15:17 5838
fiftieth year of **A** king of Judah, 2Ki 15:23 5838
year of **A** king of Judah, 2Ki 15:27 5838
The son of Ethan *was* **A**. 1Ch 2:8 5838
and Jehu became the father of **A**, 1Ch 2:38 5838
and **A** became the father of Helez, 1Ch 2:39 5838
Amaziah his son, **A** his son, 1Ch 3:12 5838
Ahimaaz became the father of **A**, 1Ch 6:9 5838
A became the father of Johanan, 1Ch 6:9 5838
Johanan became the father of **A** 1Ch 6:10 5838
A became the father of Amariah, 1Ch 6:11 5838
Hilkiah became the father of **A**, 1Ch 6:13 5838
A became the father of Seraiah, 1Ch 6:14 5838
the son of Joel, the son of **A**, 1Ch 6:36 5838
and **A** the son of Hilkiah, the son 1Ch 9:11 5838
of God came on **A** the son of Oded, 2Ch 15:1 5838
prophecy which **A** the son of Oded 2Ch 15:8 5838
A, Jehiel, Zechariah, Azaryahu, 2Ch 21:2 5838
A the son of Jeroham, Ishmael the 2Ch 23:1 5838
son of Johanan, **A** the son of Obed, 2Ch 23:1 5838
Then **A** the priest entered after 2Ch 26:17 5838
A the chief priest and all the 2Ch 26:20 5838
of Ephraim—**A** the son of Johanan, 2Ch 28:12 5838
of Amasai and Joel the son of **A**, 2Ch 29:12 5838
Abdi and **A** the son of Jehallelel; 2Ch 29:12 5838
A the chief priest of the 2Ch 31:10 5838
and **A** *was* the *chief* officer of the 2Ch 31:13 5838
up Ezra son of Seraiah, son of **A**, Ezr 7:1 5838
son of Amariah, son of **A**, Ezr 7:3 5838
After them **A** the son of Maaseiah, Ne 3:23 5838
from the house of **A** as far as the Ne 3:24 5838
Zerubbabel, Jeshua, Nehemiah, **A**, Ne 7:7 5838
Hodiah, Maaseiah, Kelita, **A**, Ne 8:7 5838
Seraiah, **A**, Jeremiah, Ne 10:2 5838
with **A**, Ezra, Meshullam, Ne 12:33 5838
A the son of Hoshaiah, and Jer 43:2 5838
Daniel, Hananiah, Mishael and **A**. Da 1:6 5838
Meshach and to **A** Abed-nego. Da 1:7 5838
Daniel, Hananiah, Mishael and **A**, Da 1:11 5838
Daniel, Hananiah, Mishael and **A**; Da 1:19 5838
friends, Hananiah, Mishael and **A**, Da 2:17 5839

AZARYAHU
Azariah, Jehiel, Zechariah, **A**, 2Ch 21:2 5838

AZAZ
and Bela the son of **A**, 1Ch 5:8 5811

AZAZIAH
Mikneiah, Obed-edom, Jeiel and **A**, 1Ch 15:21 5812
of Ephraim, Hoshea the son of **A**; 1Ch 27:20 5812
Jehiel, **A**, Nahath, Asahel, 2Ch 31:13 5812

AZBUK
After him Nehemiah the son of **A**, Ne 3:16 5802

AZEKAH
them as far as **A** and Makkedah. Jos 10:10 5825
from heaven on them as far as **A**, Jos 10:11 5825
Jarmuth and Adullam, Socoh and **A**, Jos 15:35 5825
they camped between Socoh and **A**, 1Sa 17:1 5825
Adoraim, Lachish, **A**, 2Ch 11:9 5825
and its fields, **A** and its towns. Ne 11:30 5825
of Judah, *that is,* Lachish and **A**, Jer 34:7 5825

AZEL
son, Eleasah his son, **A** his son. 1Ch 8:37 682a
A had six sons, and these *were* 1Ch 8:38 682a
All these *were* the sons of **A**. 1Ch 8:38 682a
son, Eleasah his son, **A** his son. 1Ch 9:43 682a
A had six sons whose names are 1Ch 9:44 682a
These were the sons of **A**. 1Ch 9:44 682a
of the mountains will reach to **A**; Zch 14:5 682b

AZGAD
the sons of **A**, 1,222; Ezr 2:12 5803
and of the sons of **A**, Ezr 8:12 5803
the sons of **A**, 2,322; Ne 7:17 5803
Bunni, **A**, Bebai, Ne 10:15 5803

AZIEL
and Zechariah, **A**, Shemiramoth, 1Ch 15:20 5815

AZIZA
Mattaniah, Jeremoth, Zabad and **A**; Ezr 10:27 5819

AZMAVETH
the Arbathite, **A** the Barhumite, 2Sa 23:31 5820a
became the father of Alemeth, **A** and 1Ch 8:36 5820a
became the father of Alemeth, **A** and 1Ch 9:42 5820a
A the Baharumite, Eliahba the 1Ch 11:33 5820a
Jeziel and Pelet, the sons of **A**, 1Ch 12:3 5820a
Now **A** the son of Adiel had charge 1Ch 27:25 5820a
the sons of **A**, 42; Ezr 2:24 5820b
from *their* fields in Geba and **A**, Ne 12:29 5820b

AZMON
Hazaraddar and continue to **A**. Nu 34:4 6111
from **A** to the brook of Egypt, Nu 34:5 6111
It continued to **A** and Jos 15:4 6111

AZNOTH-TABOR
the border turned westward to **A** and Jos 19:34 243

AZOR
and Eliakim the father of **A**. Mt 1:13 *107*
A was the father of Zadok, Mt 1:14 *107*

AZOTUS
But Philip found himself at **A**, Ac 8:40 *108*

AZRIEL
even Epher, Ishi, Eliel, **A**, 1Ch 5:24 5837
Naphtali, Jeremoth the son of **A**; 1Ch 27:19 5837
king's son, Seraiah the son of **A**, Jer 36:26 5837

AZRIKAM
were Elioenai, Hizkiah and **A**, 1Ch 3:23 5840
A, Bocheru, Ishmael, Sheariah, 1Ch 8:38 5840
the son of Hasshub, the son of **A**, 1Ch 9:14 5840
A, Bocheru and Ishmael and 1Ch 9:44 5840
and **A** the ruler of the house and 2Ch 28:7 5840
the son of Hasshub, the son of **A**, Ne 11:15 5840

AZUBAH
name was **A** the daughter of Shilhi. 1Ki 22:42 5806
of Hezron had sons by **A** *his* wife, 1Ch 2:18 5806
When **A** died, Caleb married 1Ch 2:19 5806
name *was* **A** the daughter of Shilhi. 2Ch 20:31 5806

AZZAN
a leader, Paltiel the son of **A**. Nu 34:26 5821

AZZUR
Ater, Hezekiah, **A**, Ne 10:17 5809
month, Hananiah the son of **A**, Jer 28:1 5809
of **A** and Pelatiah son of Benaiah, Ezk 11:1 5809

B

BAAL
him up to the high places of **B**, Nu 22:41 1168a
joined themselves to **B** of Peor, Nu 25:3 1187
joined themselves to **B** of Peor." Nu 25:5 1187
and served **B** and the Ashtaroth. Jg 2:13 1168a
of **B** which belongs to your father, Jg 6:25 1168a
the altar of **B** was torn down, Jg 6:28 1168a
he has torn down the altar of **B**, Jg 6:30 1168a
"Will you contend for **B**, Jg 6:31 1168a
"Let **B** contend against him," Jg 6:32 1168a
went to serve **B** and worshiped him. 1Ki 16:31 1168a
altar for **B** in the house of Baal which 1Ki 16:32 1168a
altar for Baal in the house of **B** which 1Ki 16:32 1168a
together with 450 prophets of **B** 1Ki 18:19 1168a
but if **B**, follow him." 1Ki 18:21 1168a
Elijah said to the prophets of **B**, 1Ki 18:25 1168a
called on the name of **B** from morning 1Ki 18:26 1168a
"O **B**, answer us." 1Ki 18:26 1168a
"Seize the prophets of **B**; 1Ki 18:40 1168a
knees that have not bowed to **B** 1Ki 19:18 1168a
So he served **B** and worshiped him 1Ki 22:53 1168a
pillar of **B** which his father had made. 2Ki 3:2 1168a
"Ahab served **B** a little; 2Ki 10:18 1168a
Now, summon all the prophets of **B**, 2Ki 10:19 1168a
I have a great sacrifice for **B**; 2Ki 10:19 1168a
might destroy the worshipers of **B**. 2Ki 10:19 1168a
"Sanctify a solemn assembly for **B**." 2Ki 10:20 1168a
and all the worshipers of **B** came, 2Ki 10:21 1168a
they went into the house of **B**, 2Ki 10:21 1168a
the house of **B** was filled from one 2Ki 10:21 1168a
for all the worshipers of **B**." 2Ki 10:22 1168a
Jehu went into the house of **B** 2Ki 10:23 1168a
he said to the worshipers of **B**, 2Ki 10:23 1168a
but only the worshipers of **B**." 2Ki 10:23 1168a
the inner room of the house of **B**. 2Ki 10:25 1168a
sacred pillars of the house of **B** and 2Ki 10:26 1168a
broke down the *sacred* pillar of **B** 2Ki 10:27 1168a
and broke down the house of **B**, 2Ki 10:27 1168a
Jehu eradicated **B** out of Israel. 2Ki 10:28 1168a
the land went to the house of **B**, 2Ki 11:18 1168a
the priest of **B** before the altars. 2Ki 11:18 1168a
the host of heaven and served **B**. 2Ki 17:16 1168a
altars for **B** and made an Asherah, 2Ki 21:3 1168a
the vessels that were made for **B**, 2Ki 23:4 1168a
those who burned incense to **B**, 2Ki 23:5 1168a
the same cities as far as **B**. 1Ch 4:33 1168b
son, Reaiah his son, **B** his son, 1Ch 5:5 1168a
son *was* Abdon, then Zur, Kish, **B**, 1Ch 8:30 1168b
son *was* Abdon, then Zur, Kish, **B**, 1Ch 9:36 1168b
the people went to the house of **B** and 2Ch 23:17 1168a
the priest of **B** before the altars. 2Ch 23:17 1168a
And the prophets prophesied by **B** Jer 2:8 1168a
and offer sacrifices to **B** and Jer 7:9 1168a
altars to burn incense to **B**. Jer 11:13 1168a
Me by offering up sacrifices to **B**. Jer 11:17 1168a
taught My people to swear by **B**, Jer 12:16 1168a
have built the high places of **B** Jer 19:5 1168a
the fire as burnt offerings to **B**, Jer 19:5 1168a
They prophesied by **B** and led My Jer 23:13 1168a
forgot My name because of **B**? Jer 23:27 1168a
offered incense to **B** on their roofs Jer 32:29 1168a
"They built the high places of **B** Jer 32:35 1168a
and gold, *Which* they used for **B**. Hos 2:8 1168a
through **B** he did wrong and died. Hos 13:1 1168a
the remnant of **B** from this place, Zph 1:4 1168a
HAVE NOT BOWED THE KNEE TO **B**." Ro 11:4 *896*

BAALAH
then the border curved to **B** Jos 15:9 1173
from **B** westward to Mount Seir, Jos 15:10 1173
Mount **B** and proceeded to Jabneel, Jos 15:11 1173
B and Iim and Ezem, Jos 15:29 1173
David and all Israel went up to **B**, 1Ch 13:6 1173

BAALATH
and Eltekeh and Gibbethon and **B**, Jos 19:44 1191
and **B** and Tamar in the wilderness, 1Ki 9:18 1191
and **B** and all the storage cities 2Ch 8:6 1191

BAALATH-BEER
around these cities as far as **B**, Jos 19:8 1192

BAAL-BERITH
the Baals, and made **B** their god. Jg 8:33 1170
pieces of silver from the house of **B** Jg 9:4 1170

BAALE-JUDAH
the people who were with him to **B**, 2Sa 6:2 1184

BAAL-GAD
even as far as **B** in the valley of Jos 11:17 1171
from **B** in the valley of Lebanon Jos 12:7 1171
from **B** below Mount Hermon as far Jos 13:5 1171

BAAL-HAMON
"Solomon had a vineyard at **B**; SS 8:11 1174

BAAL-HANAN
and **B** the son of Achbor became Gn 36:38 1177
Then **B** the son of Achbor died, and Gn 36:39 1177
B the son of Achbor became king in 1Ch 1:49 1177
When **B** died, Hadad became king in 1Ch 1:50 1177
B the Gederite had charge of 1Ch 27:28 1177

BAAL-HAZOR
Absalom had sheepshearers in **B**, 2Sa 13:23 1178

BAAL-HERMON
from Mount **B** as far as Lebo-hamath. Jg 3:3 1179
from Bashan to **B** and Senir and 1Ch 5:23 1179

BAALI
Ishi And will no longer call Me **B**. Hos 2:16 1180

BAALIS
"Are you well aware that **B** the Jer 40:14 1185

BAAL-MEON
and Nebo and **B**—*their* names being Nu 32:38 1186
in Aroer, even to Nebo and **B**. 1Ch 5:8 1186
of the land, Beth-jeshimoth, **B** and Ezk 25:9 1186

BAAL-PEOR
LORD has done in the case of **B**, Dt 4:3 1187
for all the men who followed **B**, Dt 4:3 1187
They joined themselves also to **B**, Ps 106:28 1187
But they came to **B** and devoted Hos 9:10 1187

BAAL-PERAZIM
So David came to **B** and 2Sa 5:20 1188
Therefore he named that place **B**. 2Sa 5:20 1188
So they came up to **B**, 1Ch 14:11 1188
Therefore they named that place **B**. 1Ch 14:11 1188

BAAL'S
LORD, but **B** prophets are 450 men. 1Ki 18:22 1168a

BAALS
of the LORD and served the **B**, Jg 2:11 1168a
and served the **B** and the Asheroth. Jg 3:7 1168a
played the harlot with the **B**, Jg 8:33 1168a
served the **B** and the Ashtaroth, Jg 10:6 1168a
our God and served the **B**." Jg 10:10 1168a
So the sons of Israel removed the **B** 1Sa 7:4 1168a
served the **B** and the Ashtaroth; 1Sa 12:10 1168a
LORD and you have followed the **B**. 1Ki 18:18 1168a
days and did not seek the **B**, 2Ch 17:3 1168a
the house of the LORD for the **B**. 2Ch 24:7 1168a
also made molten images for the **B**. 2Ch 28:2 1168a
altars for the **B** and made Asherim, 2Ch 33:3 1168a
altars of the **B** in his presence, 2Ch 34:4 1168a
I have not gone after the **B**'? Jer 2:23 1168a
of their heart and after the **B**, Jer 9:14 1168a
will punish her for the days of the **B** Hos 2:13 1168a
the names of the **B** from her mouth, Hos 2:17 1168a
B And burning incense to idols. Hos 11:2 1168a

BAAL-SHALISHAH
Now a man came from **B**, 2Ki 4:42 1190

BAAL-TAMAR
place and arrayed themselves at **B**; Jg 20:33 1193

BAAL-ZEBUB
"Go, inquire of **B**, the god of 2Ki 1:2 1176
you are going to inquire of **B**, 2Ki 1:3 1176
you are sending to inquire of **B**, 2Ki 1:6 1176
sent messengers to inquire of **B**, 2Ki 1:16 1176

BAAL-ZEPHON
you shall camp in front of **B**, Ex 14:2 1189
beside Pi-hahiroth, in front of **B**. Ex 14:9 1189
back to Pi-hahiroth, which faces **B**, Nu 33:7 1189

BAANA
B the son of Ahilud, *in* Taanach 1Ki 4:12 1195
B the son of Hushai, in Asher and 1Ki 4:16 1195
the son of **B** *also* made repairs. Ne 3:4 1195

BAANAH
the name of the one was **B** and the 2Sa 4:2 1196
the Beerothite, Rechab and **B**, 2Sa 4:5 1196
Rechab and **B** his brother escaped. 2Sa 4:6 1196
answered Rechab and **B** his brother, 2Sa 4:9 1196
the son of **B** the Netophathite, 2Sa 23:29 1196
the son of **B** the Netophathite, 1Ch 11:30 1196
Mispar, Bigvai, Rehum *and* **B**. Ezr 2:2 1196
Mispereth, Bigvai, Nehum, **B**. Ne 7:7 1196
Malluch, Harim, **B**. Ne 10:27 1196

BAARA
sent away Hushim and **B** his wives. 1Ch 8:8 1199

BAASEIAH
the son of Michael, the son of **B**, 1Ch 6:40 1202

BAASHA
B king of Israel all their days. 1Ki 15:16 1201
B king of Israel went up 1Ki 15:17 1201
break your treaty with **B** king of 1Ki 15:19 1201
When **B** heard *of it,* 1Ki 15:21 1201
its timber with which **B** had built. 1Ki 15:22 1201
Then **B** the son of Ahijah of the 1Ki 15:27 1201
B struck him down at Gibbethon, 1Ki 15:27 1201
So **B** killed him in the third year 1Ki 15:28 1201
B king of Israel all their days. 1Ki 15:32 1201
B the son of Ahijah became king 1Ki 15:33 1201
Jehu the son of Hanani against **B**, 1Ki 16:1 1201
I will consume **B** and his house, 1Ki 16:3 1201
"Anyone of **B** who dies in the city 1Ki 16:4 1201
B and what he did and his might, 1Ki 16:5 1201
And **B** slept with his fathers and 1Ki 16:6 1201

came against **B** and his household, **1Ki 16:7** 1201
Elah the son of **B** became king over **1Ki 16:8** 1201
he killed all the household of **B**; **1Ki 16:11** 1201
destroyed all the household of **B**, **1Ki 16:12** 1201
B through Jehu the prophet, **1Ki 16:12** 1201
of **B** and the sins of Elah his son, **1Ki 16:13** 1201
the house of **B** the son of Ahijah, **1Ki 21:22** 1201
the house of **B** the son of Ahijah. **2Ki 9:9** 1201
B king of Israel came up against Judah **2Ch 16:1** 1201
break your treaty with **B** king of **2Ch 16:3** 1201
When **B** heard *of it,* **2Ch 16:5** 1201
with which **B** had been building, **2Ch 16:6** 1201
King Asa had made on account of **B**, **Jer 41:9** 1201

BABBLER
would this idle **b** wish to say?" **Ac 17:18** *4691*

BABBLING
But a **b** fool will be ruined. **Pr 10:8** 8193
And a **b** fool will be ruined. **Pr 10:10** 8193

BABEL
The beginning of his kingdom was **B** **Gn 10:10** 894
Therefore its name was called **B**, **Gn 11:9** 894

BABES
the mouth of infants and nursing **b** **Ps 8:2** 3243
leave their abundance to their **b**. **Ps 17:14** 5768

BABIES
OF THE MOUTH OF INFANTS AND NURSING **B** **Mt 21:16** *2337*
and to those who are nursing **b** in **Mt 24:19** *2337*
and to those who are nursing **b** in **Mk 13:17** *2337*
And they were bringing even their **b** **Lk 18:15** *1025*
and to those who are nursing **b** in **Lk 21:23** *2337*
like newborn **b**, long for the pure **1Pe 2:2** *1025*

BABY
"A **b** boy has been born to you!" **Jer 20:15** 1121
the **b** leaped in her womb; **Lk 1:41** *1025*
the **b** leaped in my womb for joy. **Lk 1:44** *1025*
will find a **b** wrapped in cloths and **Lk 2:12** *1025*
and the **b** as He lay in the manger. **Lk 2:16** *1025*

BABYLON
king of Assyria brought *men* from **B** **2Ki 17:24** 894
The men of **B** made Succoth-benoth, **2Ki 17:30** 894
a son of Baladan, king of **B**, **2Ki 20:12** 894
come from a far country, from **B**." **2Ki 20:14** 894
to this day will be carried to **B**; **2Ki 20:17** 894
the palace of the king of **B**.' " **2Ki 20:18** 894
Nebuchadnezzar king of **B** came up, **2Ki 24:1** 894
for the king of **B** had taken all **2Ki 24:7** 894
king of **B** went up to Jerusalem, **2Ki 24:10** 894
the king of **B** came to the city, **2Ki 24:11** 894
Judah went out to the king of **B**, **2Ki 24:12** 894
So the king of **B** took him captive **2Ki 24:12** 894
Jehoiachin away into exile to **B**; **2Ki 24:15** 894
into exile from Jerusalem to **B**. **2Ki 24:15** 894
B brought into exile to Babylon. **2Ki 24:16** 894
Babylon brought into exile to **B**. **2Ki 24:16** 894
of **B** made his uncle Mattaniah king **2Ki 24:17** 894
rebelled against the king of **B**. **2Ki 24:20** 894
Nebuchadnezzar king of **B** came, **2Ki 25:1** 894
him to the king of **B** at Riblah, **2Ki 25:6** 894
fetters and brought him to **B**. **2Ki 25:7** 894
of King Nebuchadnezzar, king of **B**, **2Ki 25:8** 894
guard, a servant of the king of **B**, **2Ki 25:8** 894
B and the rest of the people, **2Ki 25:11** 894
and carried the bronze to **B**. **2Ki 25:13** 894
them to the king of **B** at Riblah. **2Ki 25:20** 894
Then the king of **B** struck them **2Ki 25:21** 894
Nebuchadnezzar king of **B** had left, **2Ki 25:22** 894
heard that the king of **B** had **2Ki 25:23** 894
the land and serve the king of **B**, **2Ki 25:24** 894
that Evil-merodach king of **B**, **2Ki 25:27** 894
the kings who *were* with him in **B**. **2Ki 25:28** 894
to **B** for their unfaithfulness. **1Ch 9:1** 894
of the envoys of the rulers of **B**, **2Ch 32:31** 894
bronze *chains* and took him to **B**. **2Ch 33:11** 894
Nebuchadnezzar king of **B** came up **2Ch 36:6** 894
bronze *chains* to take him to **B**. **2Ch 36:6** 894
to **B** and put them in his temple at **2Ch 36:7** 894
and put them in his temple at **B**. **2Ch 36:7** 894
sent and brought him to **B** with the **2Ch 36:10** 894
he brought *them* all to **B**. **2Ch 36:18** 894
the sword he carried away to **B**; **2Ch 36:20** 894
who went up from **B** to Jerusalem. **Ezr 1:11** 894
the king of **B** had carried away **Ezr 2:1** 894
of Babylon had carried away to **B**, **Ezr 2:1** 894
hand of Nebuchadnezzar king of **B**, **Ezr 5:12** 895
and deported the people to **B**. **Ezr 5:12** 895
the first year of Cyrus king of **B**, **Ezr 5:13** 895
brought them to the temple of **B**, **Ezr 5:14** 895
Cyrus took from the temple of **B** and **Ezr 5:14** 895
house, which is there in **B**, **Ezr 5:17** 895
the treasures were stored in **B**. **Ezr 6:1** 895
in Jerusalem and brought to **B**, **Ezr 6:5** 895
This Ezra went up from **B**, **Ezr 7:6** 894
month he began to go up from **B**; **Ezr 7:9** 894
find in the whole province of **B**, **Ezr 7:16** 895
B in the reign of King Artaxerxes **Ezr 8:1** 894
the king of **B** had carried away, **Ne 7:6** 894
king of **B** I had gone to the king. **Ne 13:6** 894
the king of **B** had exiled. **Es 2:6** 894
and **B** among those who know Me; **Ps 87:4** 894
By the rivers of **B**, **Ps 137:1** 894
O daughter of **B**, you devastated **Ps 137:8** 894
The oracle concerning **B** which **Is 13:1** 894
And **B**, the beauty of kingdoms, the **Is 13:19** 894
this taunt against the king of **B**, **Is 14:4** 894
cut off from **B** name and survivors, **Is 14:22** 894
"Fallen, fallen is **B**; **Is 21:9** 894
son of Baladan, king of **B**, **Is 39:1** 894
me from a far country, from **B**." **Is 39:3** 894
to this day will be carried to **B**; **Is 39:6** 894
the palace of the king of **B**.' " **Is 39:7** 894
"For your sake I have sent to **B**, **Is 43:14** 894
the dust, O virgin daughter of **B**; **Is 47:1** 894
carry out His good pleasure on **B**, **Is 48:14** 894
Go forth from **B**! **Is 48:20** 894
to the hand of the king of **B**, **Jer 20:4** 894
he will carry them away as exiles to **B** **Jer 20:4** 894
them away and bring them to **B**. **Jer 20:5** 894
and you will enter **B**, **Jer 20:6** 894
king of **B** is warring against us; **Jer 21:2** 894
you are warring against the king of **B** **Jer 21:4** 894
hand of Nebuchadnezzar king of **B**, **Jer 21:7** 894
into the hand of the king of **B** and **Jer 21:10** 894
hand of Nebuchadnezzar king of **B** and **Jer 22:25** 894
After Nebuchadnezzar king of **B** had **Jer 24:1** 894
and had brought them to **B**, **Jer 24:1** 894
year of Nebuchadnezzar king of **B**), **Jer 25:1** 894
send to Nebuchadnezzar king of **B**, **Jer 25:9** 894
serve the king of **B** seventy years. **Jer 25:11** 894
the king of **B** and that nation,' **Jer 25:12** 894
hand of Nebuchadnezzar king of **B**, **Jer 27:6** 894
him, Nebuchadnezzar king of **B**, **Jer 27:8** 894
under the yoke of the king of **B**, **Jer 27:8** 894
will not serve the king of **B**.' **Jer 27:9** 894
of the king of **B** and serve him, **Jer 27:11** 894
under the yoke of the king of **B** and **Jer 27:12** 894
will not serve the king of **B**? **Jer 27:13** 894
'You will not serve the king of **B**,' **Jer 27:14** 894
shortly be brought again from **B**' **Jer 27:16** 894
serve the king of **B**, **Jer 27:17** 894
and in Jerusalem may not go to **B**. **Jer 27:18** 894
which Nebuchadnezzar king of **B** did **Jer 27:20** 894
of Judah, from Jerusalem to **B**, **Jer 27:20** 894
'They will be carried to **B** **Jer 27:22** 894
broken the yoke of the king of **B**. **Jer 28:2** 894
which Nebuchadnezzar king of **B** **Jer 28:3** 894
from this place and carried to **B**. **Jer 28:3** 894
the exiles of Judah who went to **B**,' **Jer 28:4** 894
the yoke of the king of **B**.' " **Jer 28:4** 894
the exiles, from **B** to this place. **Jer 28:6** 894
yoke of Nebuchadnezzar king of **B** **Jer 28:11** 894
serve Nebuchadnezzar king of **B**; **Jer 28:14** 894
into exile from Jerusalem to **B**. **Jer 29:1** 894
Zedekiah king of Judah sent to **B** **Jer 29:3** 894
to Nebuchadnezzar king of **B**, **Jer 29:3** 894
into exile from Jerusalem to **B**, **Jer 29:4** 894
years have been completed for **B**, **Jer 29:10** 894
raised up prophets for us in **B**' **Jer 29:15** 894
sent away from Jerusalem to **B**. **Jer 29:20** 894
hand of Nebuchadnezzar king of **B**, **Jer 29:21** 894
exiles from Judah who are in **B**, **Jer 29:22** 894
the king of **B** roasted in the fire, **Jer 29:22** 894
'For he has sent to us in **B**, **Jer 29:28** 894
king of **B** was besieging Jerusalem, **Jer 32:2** 894
into the hand of the king of **B**, **Jer 32:3** 894
into the hand of the king of **B**, **Jer 32:4** 894
and he will take Zedekiah to **B**, **Jer 32:5** 894
hand of Nebuchadnezzar king of **B**, **Jer 32:28** 894
hand of the king of **B** by sword, **Jer 32:36** 894
king of **B** and all his army, **Jer 34:1** 894
into the hand of the king of **B**, **Jer 34:2** 894
will see the king of **B** eye to eye, **Jer 34:3** 894
face, and you will go to **B**.' " **Jer 34:3** 894
when the army of the king of **B** was **Jer 34:7** 894
of **B** which has gone away from you. **Jer 34:21** 894
of **B** came up against the land, **Jer 35:11** 894
the king of **B** will certainly come **Jer 36:29** 894
whom Nebuchadnezzar king of **B** had **Jer 37:1** 894
into the hand of the king of **B**!" **Jer 37:17** 894
'The king of **B** will not come **Jer 37:19** 894
hand of the army of the king of **B** and **Jer 38:3** 894
to the officers of the king of **B**, **Jer 38:17** 894
to the officers of the king of **B**, **Jer 38:18** 894
to the officers of the king of **B**; **Jer 38:22** 894
by the hand of the king of **B**, **Jer 38:23** 894
Nebuchadnezzar king of **B** and all **Jer 39:1** 894
all the officials of the king of **B** came **Jer 39:3** 894
of the officials of the king of **B**. **Jer 39:3** 894
up to Nebuchadnezzar king of **B** **Jer 39:5** 894
Then the king of **B** slew the sons **Jer 39:6** 894
the king of **B** also slew all the **Jer 39:6** 894
of bronze to bring him to **B**. **Jer 39:7** 894
carried *them* into exile in **B**. **Jer 39:9** 894
Now Nebuchadnezzar king of **B** gave **Jer 39:11** 894
leading officers of the king of **B**; **Jer 39:13** 894
Judah who were being exiled to **B**. **Jer 40:1** 894
would prefer to come with me to **B**, **Jer 40:4** 894
prefer not to come with me to **B**, **Jer 40:4** 894
whom the king of **B** has appointed **Jer 40:5** 894
heard that the king of **B** had **Jer 40:7** 894
land who had not been exiled to **B**. **Jer 40:7** 894
the land and serve the king of **B**, **Jer 40:9** 894
heard that the king of **B** had left **Jer 40:11** 894
of **B** had appointed over the land. **Jer 41:2** 894
of **B** had appointed over the land. **Jer 41:18** 894
'Do not be afraid of the king of **B**, **Jer 42:11** 894
us to death or exile us to **B**." **Jer 43:3** 894
get Nebuchadnezzar the king of **B**, **Jer 43:10** 894
hand of Nebuchadnezzar king of **B**, **Jer 44:30** 894
which Nebuchadnezzar king of **B** **Jer 46:2** 894
of **B** to smite the land of Egypt: **Jer 46:13** 894
hand of Nebuchadnezzar king of **B** **Jer 46:26** 894
Nebuchadnezzar king of **B** defeated. **Jer 49:28** 894
"For Nebuchadnezzar king of **B** has **Jer 49:30** 894
which the LORD spoke concerning **B**, **Jer 50:1** 894
'**B** has been captured, Bel has been **Jer 50:2** 894
"Wander away from the midst of **B** **Jer 50:8** 894
to arouse and bring up against **B** **Jer 50:9** 894
Everyone who passes by **B** will be **Jer 50:13** 894
lines against **B** on every side, **Jer 50:14** 894
"Cut off the sower from **B** And **Jer 50:16** 894
bones is Nebuchadnezzar king of **B**. **Jer 50:17** 894
punish the king of **B** and his land, **Jer 50:18** 894
How **B** has become An object of **Jer 50:23** 894
and you were also caught, O **B**, **Jer 50:24** 894
and refugees from the land of **B**, **Jer 50:28** 894
"Summon many against **B**, **Jer 50:29** 894
turmoil to the inhabitants of **B**. **Jer 50:34** 894
"And against the inhabitants of **B** And **Jer 50:35** 894
Against you, O daughter of **B**. **Jer 50:42** 894
"The king of **B** has heard the **Jer 50:43** 894
which He has planned against **B**, **Jer 50:45** 894
"**B** has been seized!" **Jer 50:46** 894
I am going to arouse against **B** And **Jer 51:1** 894
"I will dispatch foreigners to **B** **Jer 51:2** 894
Flee from the midst of **B**, **Jer 51:6** 894
B has been a golden cup in the **Jer 51:7** 894
B has fallen and been broken; **Jer 51:8** 894
We applied healing to **B**, **Jer 51:9** 894
is against **B** to destroy it; **Jer 51:11** 894
a signal against the walls of **B**; **Jer 51:12** 894
concerning the inhabitants of **B**. **Jer 51:12** 894
"But I will repay **B** and all the **Jer 51:24** 894
of the LORD against **B** stand, **Jer 51:29** 894
To make the land of **B** A desolation **Jer 51:29** 894
men of **B** have ceased fighting, **Jer 51:30** 894
To tell the king of **B** That his **Jer 51:31** 894
"The daughter of **B** is like a **Jer 51:33** 894
"Nebuchadnezzar king of **B** has **Jer 51:34** 894
to me and to my flesh be upon **B**," **Jer 51:35** 894
"**B** will become a heap *of ruins,* **Jer 51:37** 894
How **B** has become an object of **Jer 51:41** 894
"The sea has come up over **B**; **Jer 51:42** 894
"I will punish Bel in **B**, **Jer 51:44** 894
the wall of **B** has fallen down! **Jer 51:44** 894
I will punish the idols of **B**; **Jer 51:47** 894
in them Will shout for joy over **B**, **Jer 51:48** 894
Indeed **B** is to fall *for* the slain **Jer 51:49** 894
As also for **B** the slain of all the **Jer 51:49** 894
B should ascend to the heavens, **Jer 51:53** 894
The sound of an outcry from **B**, **Jer 51:54** 894
the LORD is going to destroy **B**, **Jer 51:55** 894
is coming against her, against **B**, **Jer 51:56** 894
of **B** will be completely razed And **Jer 51:58** 894
with Zedekiah the king of Judah to **B** **Jer 51:59** 894
calamity which would come upon **B**, **Jer 51:60** 894
have been written concerning **B**. **Jer 51:60** 894
"As soon as you come to **B**, **Jer 51:61** 894
B sink down and not rise again because **Jer 51:64** 894
rebelled against the king of **B**. **Jer 52:3** 894
Nebuchadnezzar king of **B** came, **Jer 52:4** 894
brought him up to the king of **B** **Jer 52:9** 894
The king of **B** slaughtered the **Jer 52:10** 894
and the king of **B** bound him with **Jer 52:11** 894
fetters and brought him to **B** and **Jer 52:11** 894
of King Nebuchadnezzar, king of **B**, **Jer 52:12** 894
in the service of the king of **B**, **Jer 52:12** 894
who had deserted to the king of **B** and **Jer 52:15** 894
and carried all their bronze to **B**. **Jer 52:17** 894
them to the king of **B** at Riblah. **Jer 52:26** 894
Then the king of **B** struck them **Jer 52:27** 894
that Evil-merodach king of **B**, **Jer 52:31** 894
the kings who *were* with him in **B**. **Jer 52:32** 894
was given him by the king of **B**, **Jer 52:34** 894
to **B** in the land of the Chaldeans; **Ezk 12:13** 894
the king of **B** came to Jerusalem, **Ezk 17:12** 894
and brought them to him in **B**. **Ezk 17:12** 894
he broke, in **B** he shall die. **Ezk 17:16** 894
Then I will bring him to **B** and **Ezk 17:20** 894
And brought him to the king of **B**; **Ezk 19:9** 894
sword of the king of **B** to come; **Ezk 21:19** 894
"For the king of **B** stands at the **Ezk 21:21** 894
The king of **B** has laid siege to **Ezk 24:2** 894
north Nebuchadnezzar king of **B**, **Ezk 26:7** 894
Nebuchadnezzar king of **B** made his **Ezk 29:18** 894
Egypt to Nebuchadnezzar king of **B**. **Ezk 29:19** 894
hand of Nebuchadnezzar king of **B**. **Ezk 30:10** 894
of **B** and put My sword in his hand; **Ezk 30:24** 894
the arms of the king of **B**, **Ezk 30:25** 894
sword into the hand of the king of **B** **Ezk 30:25** 894
the king of **B** will come upon you. **Ezk 32:11** 894
Nebuchadnezzar king of **B** came to **Da 1:1** 894
to destroy all the wise men of **B**. **Da 2:12** 895
forth to slay the wise men of **B**; **Da 2:14** 895
the rest of the wise men of **B**. **Da 2:18** 895
to destroy the wise men of **B**; **Da 2:24** 895
"Do not destroy the wise men of **B**! **Da 2:24** 895
ruler over the whole province of **B** **Da 2:48** 895
over all the wise men of **B**. **Da 2:48** 895
of the province of **B**, **Da 2:49** 895
of Dura in the province of **B**. **Da 3:1** 895
of the province of **B**, **Da 3:12** 895
to prosper in the province of **B**. **Da 3:30** 895
my presence all the wise men of **B**, **Da 4:6** 895
the *roof of* the royal palace of **B**. **Da 4:29** 895
'Is this not **B** the great, which I **Da 4:30** 895
and said to the wise men of **B**, **Da 5:7** 895
the first year of Belshazzar king of **B** **Da 7:1** 895
Dwell in the field, And go to **B**. **Mi 4:10** 894
living with the daughter of **B**." **Zch 2:7** 894
where they have arrived from **B**. **Zch 6:10** 894
the time of the deportation to **B**. **Mt 1:11** *897*
After the deportation to **B**: **Mt 1:12** *897*
to **B**, fourteen generations; **Mt 1:17** *897*
and from the deportation to **B** to **Mt 1:17** *897*
I ALSO WILL REMOVE YOU BEYOND **B**.' **Ac 7:43** *897*

She who is in **B**, chosen together **1Pe 5:13** *897*
"Fallen, fallen is **B** the great, **Rv 14:8** *897*
B the great was remembered **Rv 16:19** *897*
"**B** THE GREAT, THE MOTHER **Rv 17:5** *897*
"Fallen, fallen is **B** the great! **Rv 18:2** *897*
'Woe, woe, the great city, **B**, **Rv 18:10** *897*
"So will **B**, the great city, be **Rv 18:21** *897*

BABYLONIANS
the men of Erech, the **B**, **Ezr 4:9** 896
officers, like the **B** *in* Chaldea, **Ezk 23:15** 1121, 894
"The **B** came to her to the bed **Ezk 23:17** 1121, 894
the **B** and all the Chaldeans, Pekod **Ezk 23:23** 1121, 894

BACA
Passing through the valley of **B** they **Ps 84:6** 1056

BACK
turned **b** and came to En-mishpat **Gn 14:7** 7725
He brought **b** all the goods, **Gn 14:16** 7725
and also brought **b** his relative **Gn 14:16** 7725
looked **b**, and she became a **Gn 19:26**
should I take your son **b** to the **Gn 24:5** 7725
do not take my son **b** there! **Gn 24:6** 7725
only do not take my son **b** there." **Gn 24:8** 7725
and ran **b** to the well to draw, **Gn 24:20** 5750
and will bring you **b** to this land; **Gn 28:15** 7725
and put the stone **b** in its place **Gn 29:3** 7725
And Joseph brought **b** a bad report **Gn 37:2**
and bring word **b** to me." **Gn 37:14** 7725
came about as he drew **b** his hand, **Gn 38:29** 7725
to death if I do not bring him **b** **Gn 42:37**
"Go **b**, buy us a little food." **Gn 43:2** 7725
If I do not bring him **b** to you **Gn 43:9**
and take **b** in your hand the money **Gn 43:12** 7725
we have brought it **b** in our hand. **Gn 43:21** 7725
our sacks we have brought **b** to you **Gn 44:8** 7725
'Go **b**, buy us a little food.' **Gn 44:25** 7725
'If I do not bring him **b** to you, **Gn 44:32**
you **b** to the land of your fathers. **Gn 48:21** 7725
and pays us **b** in full for all the wrong **Gn 50:15** 7725
"Why have you come **b** so soon **Ex 2:18**
"Go **b** to Egypt, for all the men **Ex 4:19** 7725
"When you go **b** to Egypt see that **Ex 4:21** 7725
Get **b** to your labors!" **Ex 5:4**
Aaron were brought **b** to Pharaoh, **Ex 10:8** 7725
turn **b** and camp before Pi-hahiroth, **Ex 14:2** 7725
and the LORD swept the sea **b** **Ex 14:21**
may come **b** over the Egyptians, **Ex 14:26** 7725
LORD brought **b** the waters of the sea **Ex 15:19** 7725
And Moses brought **b** the words of **Ex 19:8** 7725
lap over the **b** of the tabernacle. **Ex 26:12** 268
and go **b** and forth from gate to **Ex 32:27** 7725
hand away and you shall see My **b**, **Ex 33:23** 268
buy **b** what his relative has sold. **Lv 25:25** 1350
means to get it **b** for himself, **Lv 25:28** 7725
'But if it is not bought **b** for him **Lv 25:30** 1350
him, and shall go **b** to his family, **Lv 25:41** 7725
and they will bring **b** your bread **Lv 26:26** 7725
and they brought **b** word to them **Nu 13:26** 7725
turned **b** from following the LORD. **Nu 14:43** 7725
'Get **b** from around the dwellings **Nu 16:24** 5927
So they got **b** from around the **Nu 16:27** 5927
"Put **b** the rod of Aaron before **Nu 17:10** 7725
and I will bring word **b** to you as **Nu 22:8** 7725
"Go **b** to your land, for the LORD **Nu 22:13** 1980
donkey to turn her **b** into the way. **Nu 22:23** 5186
to you, I will turn **b**." **Nu 22:34** 7725
LORD has held you **b** from honor." **Nu 24:11** 4513
Etham and turned **b** to Pi-hahiroth, **Nu 33:7** 7725
and bring **b** to us word of the way **Dt 1:22** 7725
brought us **b** a report and said, **Dt 1:25** 7725
bring them **b** to your countryman. **Dt 22:1** 7725
you shall not go **b** to get it; **Dt 24:19** 7725
"He will bring **b** on you all **Dt 28:60** 7725
bring you **b** to Egypt in ships, **Dt 28:68** 7725
from there He will bring you **b**. **Dt 30:4**
their **b** before their enemies? **Jos 7:8** 6203
the men of Ai turned **b** and looked, **Jos 8:20** 310
turned **b** and slew the men of Ai. **Jos 8:21** 7725
Then Joshua turned **b** at that time, **Jos 11:10** 7725
b to him as *it was* in my heart. **Jos 14:7** 7725
and brought **b** word to them. **Jos 22:32** 7725
"For if you ever go **b** and cling **Jos 23:12** 7725
that they would turn **b** and act **Jg 2:19** 7725
But he himself turned **b** from the **Jg 3:19** 7725
until I come **b** to You, and bring **Jg 6:18**
"If you take me **b** to fight **Jg 11:9** 7725
LORD, and I cannot take *it* **b**." **Jg 11:35** 7725
So he came **b** and told his father **Jg 14:2** 5927
When they came **b** to their brothers **Jg 18:8**
he turned and went **b** to his house. **Jg 18:26** 7725
to her in order to bring her **b**, **Jg 19:3** 7725
The men of Israel then turned **b** **Jg 20:48** 7725
gone **b** to her people and her gods; **Ru 1:15** 7725
you *or* turn **b** from following you; **Ru 1:16** 7725
the LORD has brought me **b** empty. **Ru 1:21** 7725
has come **b** from the land of Moab, **Ru 4:3** 7725
brought **b** the ark of the LORD; **1Sa 6:21** 7725
he turned his **b** to leave Samuel, **1Sa 10:9** 7926
he has turned **b** from following Me and **1Sa 15:11** 7725
brought **b** Agag the king of Amalek, **1Sa 15:20**
before Israel, and go **b** with me, **1Sa 15:30** 7725
So Samuel went **b** following Saul, **1Sa 15:31** 7725
but David went **b** and forth from **1Sa 17:15** 7725
and bring **b** news of them. **1Sa 17:18**
men retraced their way and went **b**; **1Sa 25:12** 7725
has kept **b** His servant from evil. **1Sa 25:39** 2820
"Make the man go **b**, that he may **1Sa 29:4** 7725
David brought *it* all **b**. **1Sa 30:19** 7725
bow of Jonathan did not turn **b**, **2Sa 1:22** 268
that the spear came out at his **b**. **2Sa 2:23** 310
b from following their brothers?" **2Sa 2:26** 7725
him **b** from the well of Sirah; **2Sa 3:26** 7725
Can I bring him **b** again? **2Sa 12:23** 7725
does not bring **b** his banished one. **2Sa 14:13** 7725
bring **b** the young man Absalom." **2Sa 14:21** 7725
indeed bring me **b** to Jerusalem, **2Sa 15:8** 7725
Return and take **b** your brothers; **2Sa 15:20** 7725
then He will bring me **b** again and **2Sa 15:25** 7725
bring **b** all the people to you. **2Sa 17:3** 7725
about bringing the king **b**?" **2Sa 19:10** 7725
to bring the king **b** to his house, **2Sa 19:11** 7725
be the last to bring **b** the king?' **2Sa 19:12** 7725
first to bring **b** our king?" **2Sa 19:43** 7725
turn **b** until they were consumed. **2Sa 22:38** 7725
may be held **b** from the people." **2Sa 24:21** 6113
the plague was held **b** from Israel. **2Sa 24:25** 6113
and bring them **b** to the land which **1Ki 8:34** 7725
he could not draw it **b** to himself. **1Ki 13:4** 7725
'Bring him **b** with you to your house, **1Ki 13:18** 7725
So he went **b** with him, and ate **1Ki 13:19** 7725
the prophet who had brought him **b**; **1Ki 13:20** 7725
the prophet whom he had brought **b**. **1Ki 13:23** 7725
him **b** from the way heard *it*, **1Ki 13:26** 7725
and brought it **b**, and he came to **1Ki 13:29** 7725
and have cast Me behind your **b** **1Ki 14:9** 1458
bring them **b** into the guards' room. **1Ki 14:28** 7725
have turned their heart **b** again." **1Ki 18:37** 322
And he said, "Go **b**" seven times. **1Ki 18:43** 7725
"Go **b** again, for what have I done **1Ki 19:20** 7725
they turned **b** from pursuing him. **1Ki 22:33** 7725
in the house once **b** and forth, **2Ki 4:35** 2008
you **b** by the way which you came. **2Ki 19:28** 7725
ten steps or go **b** ten steps?" **2Ki 20:9** 7725
brought the shadow on the stairway **b** **2Ki 20:11** 322
b word to the king and said, **2Ki 22:9** 7725
they brought **b** word to the king. **2Ki 22:20** 7725
bring **b** the ark of our God to us, **1Ch 13:3** 5437
Ornan turned **b** and saw the angel, **1Ch 21:20** 7725
he put his sword **b** in its sheath. **1Ch 21:27** 7725
and bring them **b** to the land which **2Ch 6:25** 7725
them **b** into the guards' room. **2Ch 12:11** 7725
they turned **b** from pursuing him. **2Ch 18:32** 7725
and brought them **b** to the LORD, **2Ch 19:4** 7725
them to bring them **b** to the LORD; **2Ch 24:19** 7725
b from going with him to battle, **2Ch 25:13** 7725
they brought **b** word to the king. **2Ch 34:28** 7725
give **b** to them this very day their **Ne 5:11** 7725
"We will give *it* **b** and will **Ne 5:12** 7725
order to turn them **b** to Your law. **Ne 9:29** 7725
Every day Mordecai walked **b** **Es 2:11** 1980
Hathach came **b** and related **Es 4:9**
"God will not turn **b** His anger; **Jb 9:13** 7725
is not lessened, And if I hold **b**, **Jb 16:6** 2308
And his hands give **b** his wealth. **Jb 20:10** 7725
forth and comes out of his **b**, **Jb 20:25** 1465
He keeps **b** his soul from the pit, **Jb 33:18** 2820
To bring **b** his soul from the pit, **Jb 33:30** 7725
he does not turn **b** from the sword. **Jb 39:22** 7725
They shall turn **b**, they will **Ps 6:10** 7725
When my enemies turn **b**, **Ps 9:3** 268
turn **b** until they were consumed. **Ps 18:37** 7725
Also keep **b** Your servant from **Ps 19:13** 2820
You will make them turn their **b**; **Ps 21:12** 7926
Let those be turned **b** and **Ps 35:4** 268
wicked borrows and does not pay **b**, **Ps 37:21** 7999a
Let those be turned **b** and **Ps 40:14** 268
we will push **b** our adversaries; **Ps 44:5** 5055
us to turn **b** from the adversary; **Ps 44:10** 268
Our heart has not turned **b**, **Ps 44:18** 268
turn **b** in the day when I call; **Ps 56:9** 268
"I will bring *them* **b** from Bashan. **Ps 68:22** 7725
them **b** from the depths of the sea; **Ps 68:22** 7725
Let those be turned **b** and **Ps 70:2** 268
Let those be turned **b** because of **Ps 70:3** 7725
turned **b** in the day of battle. **Ps 78:9** 2015
But turned **b** and acted treacherously **Ps 78:57** 5472
we shall not turn **b** from You; **Ps 80:18** 5472
But let them not turn **b** to folly. **Ps 85:8** 7725
also turn **b** the edge of his sword And **Ps 89:43** 7725
You turn man **b** into dust **Ps 90:3** 7725
b their wickedness upon them And **Ps 94:23** 7725
The Jordan turned **b**. **Ps 114:3** 268
O Jordan, that you turn **b**? **Ps 114:5** 268
b the captive ones of Zion, **Ps 126:1** 7725
"The plowers plowed upon my **b**; **Ps 129:3** 1354
from which He will not turn **b**: **Ps 132:11** 7725
"Go, and come **b**, And tomorrow I **Pr 3:28** 7725
But a rod is for the **b** of him who **Pr 10:13** 1460a
of the foolish is a rod for *his* **b**, **Pr 14:3** 1346
not even bring it **b** to his mouth. **Pr 19:24** 7725
And blows for the **b** of fools. **Pr 19:29** 1460a
gives and does not hold **b**. **Pr 21:26** 2820
hold **b** discipline from the child, **Pr 23:13** 4513
to slaughter, Oh hold *them* **b**. **Pr 24:11** 2820
And a rod for the **b** of fools. **Pr 26:3** 1460a
a stone, it will come **b** on him. **Pr 26:27** 7725
temper, But a wise man holds it **b**. **Pr 29:11** 268
Its **b** of gold *And* its seat of **SS 3:10** 7507
"Come **b**, come back, O Shulammite; **SS 6:13** 7725
"Come back, come **b**, O Shulammite; **SS 6:13** 7725
Come **b**, come back, that we may **SS 6:13** 7725
Come back, come **b**, that we may **SS 6:13** 7725
not turn **b** to Him who struck them, **Is 9:13** 7725
hand, who can turn it **b**?" **Is 14:27** 7725
Come **b** again." **Is 21:12** 7725
will go **b** to her harlot's wages and **Is 23:17** 7725
nations **b** and forth in a sieve, **Is 30:28** 5130
you **b** by the way which you came. **Is 37:29** 7725
of Ahaz, to go **b** ten steps." **Is 38:8** 322
So the sun's *shadow* went **b** ten **Is 38:8** 7725
cast all my sins behind Your **b**. **Is 38:17** 1460a
b *and* be utterly put to shame, **Is 42:17** 268
with none to say, "Give *them* **b**!" **Is 42:22** 7725
'Do not hold *them* **b**.' **Is 43:6** 3607
Causing wise men to draw **b** And **Is 44:25** 268
righteousness And will not turn **b**, **Is 45:23** 7725
Servant, To bring Jacob **b** to Him, **Is 49:5** 7725
not disobedient Nor did I turn **b**. **Is 50:5** 268
gave My **b** to those who strike *Me*, **Is 50:6** 1460a
even made your **b** like the ground And **Is 51:23** 1460a
"Cry loudly, do not hold **b**; **Is 58:1** 2820
Justice is turned **b**, **Is 59:14** 268
they have turned *their* **b** to Me, **Jer 2:27** 6203
LORD Has not turned **b** from us." **Jer 4:8** 7725
"They have turned **b** to the **Jer 11:10** 7725
and I will bring them **b**, **Jer 12:15** 7725
Oh turn **b**, each of you from his **Jer 18:11** 7725
I will show them My **b** and not *My* **Jer 18:17** 6203
I am about to turn **b** the weapons **Jer 21:4** 5437
bring them **b** to their pasture, **Jer 23:3** 7725
who brought up and led **b** the **Jer 23:8**
has turned **b** from his wickedness. **Jer 23:14** 7725
The anger of the LORD will not turn **b** **Jer 23:20** 7725
And would have turned them **b** from **Jer 23:22** 7725
'Then I will bring them **b** and **Jer 27:22** 5927
bring **b** to this place all the vessels **Jer 28:3** 7725
'I am also going to bring **b** to **Jer 28:4** 7725
prophesied to bring **b** the vessels **Jer 28:6** 7725
you, to bring you **b** to this place. **Jer 29:10** 7725
'and I will bring you **b** to the **Jer 29:14** 7725
'I will also bring them **b** to the **Jer 30:3** 7725
anger of the LORD will not turn **b** Until **Jer 30:24** 7725
Bring me **b** that I may be restored, **Jer 31:18** 7725
'For after I turned **b**, **Jer 31:19** 7725
They have turned *their* **b** to Me **Jer 32:33** 6203
and I will bring them **b** to this **Jer 32:37** 7725
took **b** the male servants **Jer 34:11** 7725
each man took **b** his male servant **Jer 34:16** 7725
I will bring them **b** to this city; **Jer 34:22** 7725
sunk in the mire, They turned **b**." **Jer 38:22** 268
As Jeremiah was still not going **b**, **Jer 40:5** 7725
"Go on **b** then to Gedaliah the son **Jer 40:5** 7725
Mizpah turned around and came **b**, **Jer 41:14** 7725
whom he had brought **b** from Gibeon. **Jer 41:16** 7725
will not keep **b** a word from you." **Jer 42:4** 4513
are terrified, They are drawing **b**, **Jer 46:5** 268
in flight, Without facing **b**; **Jer 46:5** 6437
And let us go **b** To our own people **Jer 46:16** 7725
they too have turned **b** *and* have fled **Jer 46:21** 6437
not turned **b** for *their* children, **Jer 47:3** 6437
How Moab has turned his **b** **Jer 48:39** 6203
rush **b** and forth inside the walls; **Jer 49:3** 7751a
"Flee away, turn **b**, dwell in the **Jer 49:8** 6437
each turn **b** to his own people And **Jer 50:16** 6437
bring Israel **b** to his pasture and **Jer 50:19** 7725
He has turned me **b**; **La 1:13** 268
He has drawn **b** His right hand From **La 2:3** 268
like torches darting **b** and forth **Ezk 1:13** 1980
it was written on the front and **b**, **Ezk 2:10** 268
Me and cast Me behind your **b**, **Ezk 23:35** 1458
over it and held **b** its rivers. **Ezk 31:15** 4513
Turn **b**, turn back from your evil **Ezk 33:11** 7725
back, turn **b** from your evil ways! **Ezk 33:11** 7725
b what he has taken by robbery, **Ezk 33:15** 7999a
scattered you have not brought **b**, **Ezk 34:4** 7725
the lost, bring **b** the scattered, **Ezk 34:16** 7725
on you, make flesh grow **b** on you, **Ezk 37:6** 5927
"When I bring them **b** from the **Ezk 39:27** 7725
were set **b** from the ground upward, **Ezk 42:6** 680
Then He brought me **b** by the way of **Ezk 44:1** 7725
me **b** to the door of the house; **Ezk 47:1** 7725
me **b** to the bank of the river. **Ezk 47:6** 7725
and the king saw the **b** of the hand **Da 5:5** 6447
had on its **b** four wings of a bird; **Da 7:6** 1355
so he will come **b** and show regard **Da 11:30** 7725
many will go **b** and forth, and **Da 12:4** 7751a
'I will go **b** to my first husband, **Hos 2:7** 7725
I will take **b** My grain at harvest **Hos 2:9** 7725
And bring **b** his reproach to him. **Hos 12:14** 7725
Reproaches will not be turned **b**. **Mi 2:6** 5472
Strengthen your **b**, summon all *your* **Na 2:1** 4975
"Stop, stop," But no one turns **b**. **Na 2:8** 6437
turned **b** from following the LORD, **Zph 1:6** 5472
yet you *did* not *come* **b** to **Hg 2:17**
so that no one went **b** and forth, **Zch 7:14** 7725
and I will bring them **b** and they **Zch 8:8**
Joseph, And I will bring them **b**, **Zch 10:6** 7725
children will live and come **b**. **Zch 10:9** 7725
them **b** from the land of Egypt And **Zch 10:10** 7725
he turned many **b** from iniquity. **Mal 2:6** 7725
take **b** your *blessing of* peace. **Mt 10:13** *1994*
'Pay **b** what you owe.' **Mt 18:28** *591*
he should pay **b** what was owed. **Mt 18:30** *591*
field must not turn **b** to get his cloak. **Mt 24:18** *3694, 1994*
received my *money* **b** with interest. **Mt 25:27** *2865*
"Put your sword **b** into its place; **Mt 26:52** *654*
Him and put His *own* garments **b** on **Mt 27:31**
When He had come **b** to **Mk 2:1** *3825*
and commanded *him* to bring **b** **Mk 6:27**
And going **b** to her home, she found **Mk 7:30** *565*
When they came **b** to the disciples, **Mk 9:14**
he will send it **b** here." **Mk 11:3** *3825*

must not turn **b** to get his coat. Mk 13:16 3694, 1994
They shouted **b**, Mk 15:13 3825
turn many of the sons of Israel **b** to Lk 1:16 1994
OF THE FATHERS **B** TO THE CHILDREN, Lk 1:17 1994
were ended, he went **b** home. Lk 1:23 565
The shepherds went **b**, Lk 2:20 5290
gave it **b** to the attendant Lk 4:20 591
what is yours, do not demand it **b**. Lk 6:30 523
to receive **b** the same *amount*. Lk 6:34 618
Jesus gave him **b** to his mother. Lk 7:15
boy and gave him **b** to his father. Lk 9:42 591
hand to the plow and looking **b**, Lk 9:62 3694
"And the slave came **b** Lk 14:21
received him **b** safe and sound.' Lk 15:27 618
that he had been healed, turned **b**, Lk 17:15 5290
in the field must not turn **b**. Lk 17:31 3694, 1994
will give **b** four times as much." Lk 19:8 591
with this until I come **b**.' Lk 19:13
robe and sent Him **b** to Pilate. Lk 23:11 375
Herod, for he sent Him **b** to us; Lk 23:15 375
and came **b** seeing. Jn 9:7
from God and was going **b** to God, Jn 13:3 5217
leaning **b** thus on Jesus' bosom, Jn 13:25 377
"I am *He*," they drew **b** Jn 18:6 3694
who also had leaned **b** on His bosom Jn 21:20 377
b *some* of the price for himself, Ac 5:2 3557
b *some* of the price of the land? Ac 5:3 3557
and they returned and reported **b**, Ac 5:22
and *proceeded* to bring them **b** Ac 5:26
in their hearts turned **b** to Egypt, Ac 7:39 4762
Lord, they started **b** to Jerusalem, Ac 8:25 5290
was drawn **b** up into the sky. Ac 11:10 3825
When he had gone **b** up and had Ac 20:11
you, O man, who answers **b** to God? Ro 9:20 470
IT MIGHT BE PAID **B** TO HIM AGAIN? Ro 11:35 467
Never pay **b** evil for evil to anyone. Ro 12:17 591
how is it that you turn **b** again to Ga 4:9 1994
he will receive **b** from the Lord, Eph 6:8 2865
have sent him **b** to you in person, Phm 1:12 375
you would have him **b** forever, Phm 1:15 568
AND IF HE SHRINKS **B**, Heb 10:38 5288
those who shrink **b** to destruction, Heb 10:39 5289
he also received him **b** as a type. Heb 11:19 2865
Women received **b** their dead by Heb 11:35
the truth and one turns him **b**, Jas 5:19 1994
book written inside and on the **b**, Rv 5:1 3693
holding **b** the four winds of the earth, Rv 7:1 2902
"Pay her **b** even as she has paid, Rv 18:6 591
and give **b** *to her* double according Rv 18:6 1363

BACKBITING
a **b** tongue, an angry countenance. Pr 25:23 5643a

BACKBONE
he shall remove close to the **b**, Lv 3:9 6096

BACKS
your enemies turn *their* **b** to you. Ex 23:27 6203
turn *their* **b** before their enemies, Jos 7:12 6203
they turned their **b** before the men Jg 20:42
my enemies turn *their* **b** to me, 2Sa 22:41 6203
the LORD, and have turned *their* **b**. 2Ch 29:6 6203
And cast Your law behind their **b** Ne 9:26 1458
my enemies turn their **b** to me, Ps 18:40 6203
They carry their riches on the **b** Is 30:6 3802
men with their **b** to the temple of the Ezk 8:16 268
Their whole body, their **b**, Ezk 10:12 1354
NOT, AND BEND THEIR **B** FOREVER." Ro 11:10 3577

BACKSLIDER
The **b** in heart will have his fill Pr 14:14 5472

BACKSLIDING
O **b** daughter Who trusts in her Jer 49:4 7728

BACKWARD
walked **b** and covered the nakedness Gn 9:23 322
heels, So that his rider falls **b**. Gn 49:17 268
Eli fell off the seat **b** beside the gate, 1Sa 4:18 322
let the shadow turn **b** ten steps." 2Ki 20:10 322
but He is not *there,* And **b**, Jb 23:8 268
He drove His adversaries **b**; Ps 78:66 268
Be put to shame and turned **b**; Ps 129:5 268
That they may go and stumble **b**, Is 28:13 268
heart, and went **b** and not forward. Jer 7:24 268
"You keep going **b**. Jer 15:6 268

BAD
we cannot speak to you **b** or good. Gn 24:50 7451a
speak to Jacob either good or **b**." Gn 31:24 7451a
speak either good or **b** to Jacob.' Gn 31:29 7451a
And Joseph brought back a **b** report Gn 37:2 1681, 7451a
it or exchange it, a good for a **b**, Lv 27:10 7451a
good for a bad, or a **b** for a good; Lv 27:10 7451a
value it as either good or **b**; Lv 27:12 7451a
value it as either good or **b**; Lv 27:14 7451a
concerned whether *it is* good or **b**, Lv 27:33 7451a
which they live, is it good or **b**? Nu 13:19 7451a
sons of Israel a **b** report of the land Nu 13:32 1681
a **b** report concerning the land, Nu 14:36 1681
the very **b** report of the land Nu 14:37 1681, 7451a
of the LORD, either good or **b**, Nu 24:13 7451a
speak to Amnon either good or **b**; 2Sa 13:22 7451a
I distinguish between good and **b**? 2Sa 19:35 7451a
but the water is **b** and 2Ki 2:19 7451a
"You see the **b** situation we are Ne 2:17 7451a
the days of the afflicted are **b**, Pr 15:15 7451a
"**B**, bad," says the buyer, Pr 20:14 7451a
"Bad, **b**," says the buyer, But when Pr 20:14 7451a
Like a **b** tooth and an unsteady Pr 25:19 7489b
were lost through a **b** investment Ec 5:14 7451a
the other basket had very **b** figs which Jer 24:2 7451a
and the **b** *figs*, very bad, which Jer 24:3 7451a
and the bad *figs*, very **b**, Jer 24:3 7451a
'But like the **b** figs which cannot Jer 24:8 7451a
shame, For they have heard **b** news; Jer 49:23 7451a
"But if your eye is **b**, Mt 6:23 4190
but the **b** tree bears bad fruit. Mt 7:17 4550
but the bad tree bears **b** fruit. Mt 7:17 4190
good tree cannot produce **b** fruit, Mt 7:18 4190
can a **b** tree produce good fruit. Mt 7:18 4550
or make the tree **b** and Mt 12:33 4550
the tree bad and its fruit **b**; Mt 12:33 4550
but the **b** they threw away. Mt 13:48 4550
good tree which produces **b** fruit, Lk 6:43 4550
a **b** tree which produces good fruit. Lk 6:43 4550
but when it is **b**, your body also Lk 11:34 4190
and likewise Lazarus **b** things; Lk 16:25 2556
or spoken anything **b** about you. Ac 28:21 4190
had not done anything good or **b**, Ro 9:11 5337
"**B** company corrupts good morals." 1Co 15:33 2556
he has done, whether good or **b**. 2Co 5:10 5337
and impostors will proceed *from* **b** 2Tm 3:13
having nothing **b** to say about us. Ti 2:8 5337

BADE
Moses **b** his father-in-law farewell, Ex 18:27 7971

BADLY
"Why did you treat me so **b** by Gn 43:6 7489a
treated us and our fathers **b**. Nu 20:15 7489a
he was **b** wounded by the archers. 1Sa 31:3 3966
me away, for I am **b** wounded." 2Ch 35:23 3966
I am benumbed and **b** crushed; Ps 38:8 3966
It will go **b** *with him,* For what he Is 3:11 7451a
And vigorous young men stumble **b**, Is 40:30 3782

BAFFLES
is in you and no mystery **b** you, Da 4:9 598

BAG
have in your **b** differing weights, Dt 25:13 3599
in the shepherd's **b** which he had, 1Sa 17:40 3627
And David put his hand into his **b** 1Sa 17:49 3627
transgression is sealed up in a **b**, Jb 14:17 6872a
weeping, carrying *his* **b** of seed, Ps 126:6 4901
has taken a **b** of money with him, Pr 7:20 6872a
weights of the **b** are His concern. Pr 16:11 3599
And a **b** of deceptive weights? Mi 6:11 3599
or a **b** for *your* journey, or even Mt 10:10 4082
no bread, no **b**, no money in their Mk 6:8 4082
journey, neither a staff, nor a **b**, Lk 9:3 4082
"Carry no money belt, no **b**, Lk 10:4 4082
without money belt and **b** and sandals, Lk 22:35 4082
take it along, likewise also a **b**, Lk 22:36 4082

BAGGAGE
he is hiding himself by the **b**." 1Sa 10:22 3627
Then David left his **b** in the care 1Sa 17:22 3627
in the care of the **b** keeper, 1Sa 17:22 3627
two hundred stayed with the **b**. 1Sa 25:13 3627
his share be who stays by the **b**; 1Sa 30:24 3627
At Michmash he deposited his **b**. Is 10:28 3627
"Make your **b** ready for exile, O Jer 46:19 3627
prepare for yourself **b** for exile Ezk 12:3 3627
your **b** out by day in their sight, Ezk 12:4 3627
in their sight, as **b** for exile. Ezk 12:4 3627
"Load *the* **b** on *your* shoulder Ezk 12:6
my **b** like the baggage of an exile. Ezk 12:7 3627
my baggage like the **b** of an exile. Ezk 12:7 3627
in the dark *and* carried *the* **b** Ezk 12:7
who is among them will load *his* **b** Ezk 12:12

BAGPIPE
flute, lyre, trigon, psaltery, **b** and Da 3:5 5481
flute, lyre, trigon, psaltery, **b** and Da 3:7 5481
lyre, trigon, psaltery, and **b** and Da 3:10 5481
lyre, trigon, psaltery and **b** Da 3:15 5481

BAGS
Joseph gave orders to fill their **b** Gn 42:25 3627
products of the land in your **b**, Gn 43:11 3627
two **b** with two changes of clothes and 2Ki 5:23 2754
high priest came up and tied *it* in **b** 2Ki 12:10

BAHARUMITE
Azmaveth the **B**, Eliahba the 1Ch 11:33 978

BAHURIM
and followed her as far as **B**. 2Sa 3:16 980
When King David came to **B**, 2Sa 16:5 980
came to the house of a man in **B**, 2Sa 17:18 980
the Benjamite who was from **B**, 2Sa 19:16 980
son of Gera the Benjamite, of **B**; 1Ki 2:8 980

BAIT
ground when there is no **b** in it? Am 3:5 4170

BAITED
it is useless to spread the **b** net Pr 1:17

BAKBAKKAR
and **B**, Heresh and Galal and 1Ch 9:15 1230

BAKBUK
the sons of **B**, the sons of Ezr 2:51 1227
the sons of **B**, the sons of Ne 7:53 1227

BAKBUKIAH
B, the second among his brethren; Ne 11:17 1229
Also **B** and Unni, their brothers, Ne 12:9 1229
Mattaniah, **B**, Obadiah, Ne 12:25 1229

BAKE
B what you will bake and boil what Ex 16:23 644
b and boil what you will boil, Ex 16:23 644
flour and **b** twelve cakes with it; Lv 24:5 644
will **b** your bread in one oven, Lv 26:26 644
he also makes a fire to **b** bread. Is 44:15 644
they shall **b** the grain offering, Ezk 46:20 644

BAKED
for them, and **b** unleavened bread, Gn 19:3 644
all sorts of **b** food for Pharaoh, Gn 40:17 644
They **b** the dough which they Ex 12:39 644
of a grain offering **b** in an oven, Lv 2:4 3989
'It shall not be **b** with leaven. Lv 6:17 644
present the grain offering in **b** pieces Lv 6:21 8601
offering that is **b** in the oven and Lv 7:9 644
b with leaven as first fruits to Lv 23:17 644
as the taste of cakes **b** with oil. Nu 11:8 3955
and **b** unleavened bread from it. 1Sa 28:24 644
in his sight, and **b** the cakes. 2Sa 13:8 1310
was at his head a bread cake **b** *on* 1Ki 19:6
the things which were **b** in pans. 1Ch 9:31 2281
or *what is* **b** *in* the pan or what 1Ch 23:29
also have **b** bread over its coals. Is 44:19 644
having **b** *it* in their sight over Ezk 4:12 5746

BAKER
the **b** for the king of Egypt offended Gn 40:1 644
chief cupbearer and the chief **b**. Gn 40:2 644
and the **b** for the king of Egypt, Gn 40:5 644
When the chief **b** saw that he had Gn 40:16 644
of the chief **b** among his servants. Gn 40:20 644
but he hanged the chief **b**, Gn 40:22 644
both me and the chief **b**. Gn 41:10 644
Like an oven heated by the **b** Who Hos 7:4 644

BAKERS
for perfumers and cooks and **b**. 1Sa 8:13 644

BAKERS'
loaf of bread daily from the **b** street, Jer 37:21 644

BALAAM
messengers to **B** the son of Beor, Nu 22:5 1109a
and they came to **B** and repeated Nu 22:7 1109a
the leaders of Moab stayed with **B**. Nu 22:8 1109a
Then God came to **B** and said, Nu 22:9 1109a
B said to God, Nu 22:10 1109a
God said to **B**, Nu 22:12 1109a
So **B** arose in the morning and said Nu 22:13 1109a
"**B** refused to come with us." Nu 22:14 1109a
They came to **B** and said to him, Nu 22:16 1109a
B replied to the servants Nu 22:18 1109a
God came to **B** at night and said Nu 22:20 1109a
So **B** arose in the morning, and Nu 22:21 1109a
but **B** struck the donkey to turn Nu 22:23 1109a
of the LORD, she lay down under **B**; Nu 22:27 1109a
so **B** was angry and struck the Nu 22:27 1109a
of the donkey, and she said to **B**, Nu 22:28 1109a
Then **B** said to the donkey, Nu 22:29 1109a
The donkey said to **B**, Nu 22:30 1109a
the LORD opened the eyes of **B**, Nu 22:31 1109a
B said to the angel of the LORD, Nu 22:34 1109a
the angel of the LORD said to **B**, Nu 22:35 1109a
So **B** went along with the leaders Nu 22:35 1109a
Balak heard that **B** was coming, Nu 22:36 1109a
Then Balak said to **B**, Nu 22:37 1109a
So **B** said to Balak, Nu 22:38 1109a
And **B** went with Balak, and they Nu 22:39 1109a
and sent *some* to **B** and the leaders Nu 22:40 1109a
in the morning that Balak took **B** and Nu 22:41 1109a
Then **B** said to Balak, Nu 23:1 1109a
Balak did just as **B** had spoken, Nu 23:2 1109a
and Balak and **B** offered up a bull Nu 23:2 1109a
Then **B** said to Balak, Nu 23:3 1109a
Now God met **B**, and he said to Him, Nu 23:4 1109a
Then Balak said to **B**, Nu 23:11 1109a
Then the LORD met **B** and put a word Nu 23:16 1109a
Then Balak said to **B**, Nu 23:25 1109a
But **B** replied to Balak, Nu 23:26 1109a
Then Balak said to **B**, Nu 23:27 1109a
So Balak took **B** to the top of Peor Nu 23:28 1109a
B said to Balak, Nu 23:29 1109a
Balak did just as **B** had said, Nu 23:30 1109a
When **B** saw that it pleased the Nu 24:1 1109a
And **B** lifted up his eyes and saw Nu 24:2 1109a
"The oracle of **B** the son of Beor, Nu 24:3 1109a
Balak's anger burned against **B**, Nu 24:10 1109a
and Balak said to **B**, Nu 24:10 1109a
B said to Balak, Nu 24:12 1109a
"The oracle of **B** the son of Beor, Nu 24:15 1109a
Then **B** arose and departed and Nu 24:25 1109a
they also killed **B** the son of Beor Nu 31:8 1109a
Israel, through the counsel of **B**, Nu 31:16 1109a
hired against you **B** the son of Beor Dt 23:4 1109a
was not willing to listen to **B**, Dt 23:5 1109a
also killed **B** the son of Beor, Jos 13:22 1109a
B the son of Beor to curse you. Jos 24:9 1109a
I was not willing to listen to **B**. Jos 24:10 1109a
B against them to curse them. Ne 13:2 1109a
what **B** son of Beor answered him, Mi 6:5 1109a
having followed the way of **B**, 2Pe 2:15 903
headlong into the error of **B**, Jude 1:11 903
some who hold the teaching of **B**, Rv 2:14 903

BALAAM'S
pressed **B** foot against the wall, Nu 22:25 1109a
put a word in **B** mouth and said, Nu 23:5 1109a

BALADAN
time Berodach-baladan a son of **B**, 2Ki 20:12 1081
time Merodach-baladan son of **B**, Is 39:1 1081

BALAH
and Hazar-shual and **B** and Ezem, Jos 19:3 1088

BALAK
Now **B** the son of Zippor saw all Nu 22:2 1111
And **B** the son of Zippor was king Nu 22:4 1111
"**B** the son of Zippor, king of Nu 22:10 1111
of Moab arose and went home, Nu 22:14 1111
Then **B** again sent leaders, more Nu 22:15 1111
"Thus says **B** the son of Zippor, Nu 22:16 1111

replied to the servants of **B**, Nu 22:18 1111
"Though **B** were to give me his Nu 22:18 1111
went along with the leaders of **B**. Nu 22:35 1111
B heard that Balaam was coming, Nu 22:36 1111
Then **B** said to Balaam, Nu 22:37 1111
So Balaam said to **B**, Nu 22:38 1111
And Balaam went with **B**, Nu 22:39 1111
B sacrificed oxen and sheep, Nu 22:40 1111
in the morning that **B** took Balaam and Nu 22:41 1111
Then Balaam said to **B**, Nu 23:1 1111
B did just as Balaam had spoken, Nu 23:2 1111
and **B** and Balaam offered up a bull Nu 23:2 1111
Then Balaam said to **B**, Nu 23:3 1111
"Return to **B**, and you shall speak Nu 23:5 1111
"From Aram **B** has brought me, Nu 23:7 1111
Then **B** said to Balaam, Nu 23:11 1111
Then **B** said to him, Nu 23:13 1111
And he said to **B**, Nu 23:15 1111
"Return to **B**, and thus you shall Nu 23:16 1111
And **B** said to him, Nu 23:17 1111
"Arise, O **B**, and hear; Nu 23:18 1111
Then **B** said to Balaam, Nu 23:25 1111
But Balaam replied to **B**, Nu 23:26 1111
Then **B** said to Balaam, Nu 23:27 1111
So **B** took Balaam to the top of Nu 23:28 1111
Balaam said to **B**, Nu 23:29 1111
B did just as Balaam had said, Nu 23:30 1111
and **B** said to Balaam, Nu 24:10 1111
Balaam said to **B**, Nu 24:12 1111
'Though **B** were to give me his Nu 24:13 1111
place, and **B** also went his way. Nu 24:25 1111
'Then **B** the son of Zippor, king of Jos 24:9 1111
better than **B** the son of Zippor, Jg 11:25 1111
remember now What **B** king of Moab Mi 6:5 1111
who kept teaching **B** to put a Rv 2:14 *904*

BALAK'S
and repeated **B** words to him. Nu 22:7 1111
the morning and said to **B** leaders, Nu 22:13 1111
B anger burned against Balaam, Nu 24:10 1111

BALANCE
b to the man to whom he sold it, Lv 25:27 5736
b is an abomination to the LORD, Pr 11:1 3976
b and scales belong to the LORD; Pr 16:11 6425
And weighed the mountains in a **b** And Is 40:12 6425

BALANCES
'You shall have just **b**, Lv 19:36 3976
the **b** together with my calamity! Jb 6:2 3976
In the **b** they go up; Ps 62:9 3976
"You shall have just **b**, Ezk 45:10 3976
in whose hands are false **b**, Hos 12:7 3976

BALD
the hair of his head, he is **b**; Lv 13:40 7142
becomes **b** at the front and sides, Lv 13:41 4803
sides, he is **b** on the forehead; Lv 13:41 1371
the **b** head or the bald forehead, Lv 13:42 7146
the bald head or the **b** forehead, Lv 13:42 1372
leprosy breaking out on his **b** head Lv 13:42 7146
bald head or on his **b** forehead. Lv 13:42 1372
b head or on his bald forehead, Lv 13:43 1372
bald head or on his **b** forehead, Lv 13:43 1372
is **b** *and* every beard is cut off. Is 15:2 7144
is **b** and every beard cut short; Jer 48:37 7144
"Also they will make themselves **b** Ezk 27:31 7139, 7144
every head was made **b** and Ezk 29:18 7139
yourself **b** and cut off your hair, Mi 1:16 7139

BALDHEAD
and said to him, "Go up, you **b**; 2Ki 2:23 7142
"Go up, you baldhead; go up, you **b**!" 2Ki 2:23 7142

BALDNESS
not make any **b** on their heads, Lv 21:5 7139, 7144
"**B** has come upon Gaza; Jer 47:5 7144
faces and **b** on all their heads. Ezk 7:18 7144
loins And **b** on every head. Am 8:10 7144
Extend your **b** like the eagle, For Mi 1:16 7144

BALL
And roll you tightly like a **b**, Is 22:18 1754

BALM
aromatic gum and **b** and myrrh, Gn 37:25 6875
a little **b** and a little honey, Gn 43:11 6875
Is there no **b** in Gilead? Jer 8:22 6875
Go up to Gilead and obtain **b**, Jer 46:11 6875
Bring **b** for her pain; Jer 51:8 6875
and **b** they paid for your Ezk 27:17 6875

BALSAM
at them in front of the **b** trees. 2Sa 5:23 1057
in the tops of the **b** trees, 2Sa 5:24 1057
at them in front of the **b** trees. 1Ch 14:14 1057
in the tops of the **b** trees, 1Ch 14:15 1057
gathered my myrrh along with my **b**. SS 5:1 1314
"His cheeks are like a bed of **b**, SS 5:13 1314
to his garden, To the beds of **b**, SS 6:2 1314

BAMAH
name is called **B** to this day." Ezk 20:29 1117

BAMOTH
Nahaliel, and from Nahaliel to **B**, Nu 21:19 1120
and from **B** to the valley that is Nu 21:20 1120

BAMOTH-BAAL
Dibon and **B** and Beth-baal-meon, Jos 13:17 1120, 1168a

BAN
and like it come under the **b**; Dt 7:26 2764a
the **b** shall cling to your hand, Dt 13:17 2764a
"The city shall be under the **b**, Jos 6:17 2764a
from the things under the **b**, Jos 6:18 2764a
some of the things under the **b**, Jos 6:18 2764a
regard to the things under the **b**, Jos 7:1 2764a
some of the things under the **b**, Jos 7:1 2764a
taken some of the things under the **b** Jos 7:11 2764a
you destroy the things under the **b** Jos 7:12 2764a
things under the **b** in your midst, Jos 7:13 2764a
under the **b** from your midst." Jos 7:13 2764a
the **b** shall be burned with fire, Jos 7:15 2764a
in the things under the **b**, Jos 22:20 2764a
of Israel, who violated the **b**. 1Ch 2:7 2764a
And I will consign Jacob to the **b** and Is 43:28 2764a

BAND
"The skillfully woven **b**, Ex 28:8 2805
skillfully woven **b** of the ephod. Ex 28:27 2805
skillfully woven **b** of the ephod, Ex 28:28 2805
skillfully woven **b** of the ephod; Ex 29:5 2805
The skillfully woven **b** which Ex 39:5 2805
above the woven **b** of the ephod. Ex 39:20 2805
be on the woven **b** of the ephod, Ex 39:21 2805
with the artistic **b** of the ephod, Lv 8:7 2805
"Shall I pursue this **b**? 1Sa 30:8 1416
you bring me down to this **b**?" 1Sa 30:15 1416
I will bring you down to this **b**." 1Sa 30:15 1416
hand the **b** that came against us. 1Sa 30:23 1416
behind Abner and became one **b**, 2Sa 2:25 92
became leader of a marauding **b**, 1Ki 11:24 1416
behold, they saw a marauding **b**; 2Ki 13:21 1416
and made them captains of the **b**. 1Ch 12:18 1416
David against the **b** of raiders, 1Ch 12:21 1416
for the **b** of men who came with the 2Ch 22:1 1416
thick darkness its swaddling **b**, Jb 38:9 2854
A **b** of evildoers has encompassed Ps 22:16 5712
trouble, A **b** of destroying angels. Ps 78:49 4917
And a **b** of violent men have sought Ps 86:14 5712
They **b** themselves together against Ps 94:21 1481b
a **b** of shepherds is called out, Is 31:4 4393
But with a **b** of iron and bronze Da 4:15 613
but with a **b** of iron and bronze Da 4:23 613
So a **b** of priests murder on the Hos 6:9 2267

BANDAGE
himself with a **b** over his eyes. 1Ki 20:38 666
took the **b** away from his eyes, 1Ki 20:41 666
for healing or wrapped with a **b**, Ezk 30:21 2848
has wounded *us,* but He will **b** us. Hos 6:1 2280

BANDAGED
raw wounds, Not pressed out or **b**, Is 1:6 2280
came to him and **b** up his wounds, Lk 10:34 *2611*

BANDITS
thief enters in, **B** raid outside, Hos 7:1 1416

BANDS
and their **b** *shall be* of silver. Ex 27:10 2838
and their **b** *shall be* of silver. Ex 27:11 2838
court shall be furnished with silver **b** Ex 27:17 2836b
their tops and their **b** with gold; Ex 36:38 2838
and their **b** *were* of silver. Ex 38:10 2838
and their **b** *were* of silver. Ex 38:11 2838
and their **b** *were* of silver. Ex 38:12 2838
hooks of the pillars and their **b**, Ex 38:17 2838
were furnished with silver **b**. Ex 38:17 2836b
tops and their **b** *were* of silver. Ex 38:19 2838
their tops and made **b** for them. Ex 38:28 2836b
and besides the neck **b** that *were* Jg 8:26 6060
two men who were commanders of **b**: 2Sa 4:2 1416
the Arameans had gone out in **b** and 2Ki 5:2 1416
And the marauding **b** of Arameans 2Ki 6:23 1416
Now the **b** of the Moabites would 2Ki 13:20 1416
sent against him **b** of Chaldeans, 2Ki 24:2 1416
bands of Chaldeans, **b** of Arameans, 2Ki 24:2 1416
bands of Arameans, **b** of Moabites, 2Ki 24:2 1416
of Moabites, and **b** of Ammonites. 2Ki 24:2 1416
"The Chaldeans formed three **b** and Jb 1:17 7218
of death And broke their **b** apart. Ps 107:14 4147
To undo the **b** of the yoke, Is 58:6 92
who sew *magic* **b** on all wrists and Ezk 13:18 3704
I am against your *magic* **b** by which Ezk 13:20 3704

BANGLES
And tinkle the **b** on their feet, Is 3:16 5913

BANI
of Nathan of Zobah, **B** the Gadite, 2Sa 23:36 1137
the son of Amzi, the son of **B**, 1Ch 6:46 1137
the son of Imri, the son of **B**, 1Ch 9:4 1137
the sons of **B**, 642; Ezr 2:10 1137
and of the sons of **B**, Shelomith, Ezr 8:10 1137
and of the sons of **B**: Ezr 10:29 1137
of the sons of **B**: Ezr 10:34 1137
B, Binnui, Shimei, Ezr 10:38 1137
repairs *under* Rehum the son of **B**. Ne 3:17 1137
Also Jeshua, **B**, Sherebiah, Jamin, Ne 8:7 1137
Levites' platform stood Jeshua, **B**, Ne 9:4 1137
Shebaniah, Bunni, Sherebiah, **B** Ne 9:4 1137
the Levites, Jeshua, Kadmiel, **B**, Ne 9:5 1137
Hodiah, **B**, Beninu. Ne 10:13 1137
Pahath-moab, Elam, Zattu, **B**, Ne 10:14 1137
Jerusalem was Uzzi the son of **B**, Ne 11:22 1137

BANISH
nations where I will **b** them." Ezk 4:13 5080

BANISHED
where the LORD your God has **b** you, Dt 30:1 5080
does not bring back his **b** one. 2Sa 14:13 5080
but plans ways so that the **b** one 2Sa 14:14 5080
assemble the **b** ones of Israel, Is 11:12 5080
The gaiety of the earth is **b**. Is 24:11 1540
countries where He had **b** them.' Jer 16:15 5080

BANISHING
contended with them by **b** them, Is 27:8 5432

BANISHMENT
whether for death or for **b** or for Ezr 7:26 8332

BANK
other cows on the **b** of the Nile. Gn 41:3 8193
was standing on the **b** of the Nile; Gn 41:17 8193
the reeds by the **b** of the Nile. Ex 2:3 8193
to meet him on the **b** of the Nile; Ex 7:15 8193
and stood by the **b** of the Jordan. 2Ki 2:13 8193
me back to the **b** of the river. Ezk 47:6 8193
on the **b** of the river there *were* Ezk 47:7 8193
"By the river on its **b**, Ezk 47:12 8193
I was by the **b** of the great river, Da 10:4 3027
one on this **b** of the river and Da 12:5 8193
the other on that **b** of the river. Da 12:5 8193
rushed down the steep **b** into the sea Mt 8:32 *2911*
to have put my money in the **b**, Mt 25:27 *5133*
down the steep **b** into the sea, Mk 5:13 *2911*
down the steep **b** into the lake and Lk 8:33 *2911*
did you not put my money in the **b**, Lk 19:23 *5132*

BANKS
for the Jordan overflows all its **b** Jos 3:15 1415
and went over all its **b** as before. Jos 4:18 1415
that are on the **b** of the Arnon, Jg 11:26 3027
when it was overflowing all its **b** and 1Ch 12:15 1415
balsam, **B** of sweet-scented herbs; SS 5:13 4026
channels and go over all its **b**. Is 8:7 1415
of a man between *the* **b** *of* Ulai, Da 8:16

BANNED
abhor it, for it is something **b**. Dt 7:26 2764a

BANNER
and named it The LORD is My **B**; Ex 17:15 5251
given a **b** to those who fear You, Ps 60:4 5251
hall, And his **b** over me is love. SS 2:4 1714

BANNERS
the **b** of their fathers' households; Nu 2:2 226
of our God we will set up our **b**. Ps 20:5 1713b
As awesome as an army with **b**. SS 6:4 1713b
As awesome as an army with **b**?' SS 6:10 1713b

BANQUET
he gave a **b** for all his princes Es 1:3 4960
the king gave a **b** lasting seven Es 1:5 4960
Queen Vashti also gave a **b** for the Es 1:9 4960
Then the king gave a great **b**, Es 2:18 4960
gave a great banquet, Esther's **b**; Es 2:18 4960
b that I have prepared for him." Es 5:4 4960
the **b** which Esther had prepared. Es 5:5 4960
As they drank their wine at the **b**, Es 5:6 4960
the king and Haman come to the **b** Es 5:8 4960
to the **b** which she had prepared; Es 5:12 4960
joyfully with the king to the **b**." Es 5:14 4960
the **b** which Esther had prepared. Es 6:14 4960
as they drank their wine at the **b**, Es 7:2 4960
"He has brought me to *his* **b** hall, SS 2:4 3196
LORD of hosts will prepare a lavish **b** Is 25:6 4960
A **b** of aged wine, choice pieces Is 25:6 4960
them their **b** And make them drunk, Jer 51:39 4960
The queen entered the **b** hall Da 5:10 4961
Herod on his birthday gave a **b** for Mk 6:21 *1173*

BANQUETING
the sprawlers' **b** will pass away. Am 6:7 4798

BANQUETS
Their **b** are *accompanied* by Is 5:12 4960
They love the place of honor at **b** Mt 23:6 *1173*
and places of honor at **b**, Mk 12:39 *1173*
and places of honor at **b**, Lk 20:46 *1173*

BAPTISM
and Sadducees coming for **b**, Mt 3:7 *908*
b of John was from what *source,* Mt 21:25 *908*
wilderness preaching a **b** of repentance Mk 1:4 *908*
the **b** with which I am baptized?" Mk 10:38 *908*
the **b** with which I am baptized. Mk 10:39 *908*
"Was the **b** of John from heaven, Mk 11:30 *908*
preaching a **b** of repentance for Lk 3:3 *908*
been baptized with the **b** of John. Lk 7:29 *908*
"But I have a **b** to undergo, and Lk 12:50 *908*
"Was the **b** of John from heaven or Lk 20:4 *908*
beginning with the **b** of John until Ac 1:22 *908*
after the **b** which John proclaimed. Ac 10:37 *908*
b of repentance to all the people Ac 13:24 *908*
only with the **b** of John; Ac 18:25 *908*
And they said, "Into John's **b**." Ac 19:3 *908*
baptized with the **b** of repentance, Ac 19:4 *908*
with Him through **b** into death, Ro 6:4 *908*
one Lord, one faith, one **b**, Eph 4:5 *908*
having been buried with Him in **b**, Col 2:12 *908*
Corresponding to that, **b** now saves 1Pe 3:21 *908*

BAPTIST
Now in those days John the **B** came, Mt 3:1 *910*
anyone greater than John the **B**! Mt 11:11 *910*
"From the days of John the **B** Mt 11:12 *910*
"This is John the **B**; Mt 14:2 *910*
on a platter the head of John the **B**." Mt 14:8 *910*
"Some *say* John the **B**; Mt 16:14 *910*
spoken to them about John the **B**. Mt 17:13 *910*
John the **B** appeared in the Mk 1:4 *907*
the **B** has risen from the dead, Mk 6:14 *907*
"The head of John the **B**." Mk 6:24 *907*
head of John the **B** on a platter." Mk 6:25 *910*
"John the **B**; and others *say* Elijah; Mk 8:28 *910*
"John the **B** has sent us to You, Lk 7:20 *910*
"For John the **B** has come eating Lk 7:33 *910*
"John the **B**, and others *say* Lk 9:19 *910*

BAPTIZE
I **b** you with water for repentance, Mt 3:11 *907*
He will **b** you with the Holy Spirit Mt 3:11 *907*
will **b** you with the Holy Spirit." Mk 1:8 *907*
"As for me, I **b** you with water; Lk 3:16 *907*
He will **b** you with the Holy Spirit Lk 3:16 *907*
"I **b** in water, *but* among you Jn 1:26 *907*

He who sent me to **b** in water Jn 1:33 *907*
Now I did **b** also the household of 1Co 1:16 *907*
For Christ did not send me to **b**, 1Co 1:17 *907*

BAPTIZED
b by him in the Jordan River, Mt 3:6 *907*
coming to John, to be **b** by him. Mt 3:13 *907*
"I have need to be **b** by You, Mt 3:14 *907*
After being **b**, Jesus came up Mt 3:16 *907*
b by him in the Jordan River, Mk 1:5 *907*
"I **b** you with water; Mk 1:8 *907*
and was **b** by John in the Jordan. Mk 1:9 *907*
or to be **b** with the baptism with Mk 10:38 *907*
the baptism with which I am **b**?" Mk 10:38 *907*
and you shall be **b** with the Mk 10:39 *907*
the baptism with which I am **b**. Mk 10:39 *907*
and has been **b** shall be saved; Mk 16:16 *907*
who were going out to be **b** by him, Lk 3:7 *907*
tax collectors also came to be **b**, Lk 3:12 *907*
Now when all the people were **b**, Lk 3:21 *907*
Jesus was also **b**, and while He was Lk 3:21 *907*
been **b** with the baptism of John. Lk 7:29 *907*
not having been **b** by John. Lk 7:30 *907*
people were coming and were being **b** Jn 3:23 *907*
for John **b** with water, but you Ac 1:5 *907*
you will be **b** with the Holy Spirit Ac 1:5 *907*
and each of you be **b** in the Ac 2:38 *907*
who had received his word were **b**; Ac 2:41 *907*
they were being **b**, men and women Ac 8:12 *907*
and after being **b**, he continued on Ac 8:13 *907*
b in the name of the Lord Jesus. Ac 8:16 *907*
What prevents me from being **b**?" Ac 8:36 *907*
as well as the eunuch, and he **b** him. Ac 8:38 *907*
his sight, and he got up and was **b**; Ac 9:18 *907*
can refuse the water for these to be **b** Ac 10:47 *907*
be **b** in the name of Jesus Christ. Ac 10:48 *907*
'John **b** with water, but you Ac 11:16 *907*
will be **b** with the Holy Spirit.' Ac 11:16 *907*
she and her household had been **b**, Ac 16:15 *907*
wounds, and immediately he was **b**, Ac 16:33 *907*
heard were believing and being **b**. Ac 18:8 *907*
"Into what then were you **b**?" Ac 19:3 *907*
"John **b** with the baptism of Ac 19:4 *907*
b in the name of the Lord Jesus. Ac 19:5 *907*
Get up and be **b**, and wash away Ac 22:16 *907*
all of us who have been **b** into Christ Ro 6:3 *907*
Jesus have been **b** into His death? Ro 6:3 *907*
Or were you **b** in the name of Paul? 1Co 1:13 *907*
I thank God that I **b** none of you 1Co 1:14 *907*
would say you were **b** in my name. 1Co 1:15 *907*
do not know whether I **b** any other. 1Co 1:16 *907*
and all were **b** into Moses in the 1Co 10:2 *907*
we were all **b** into one body, 1Co 12:13 *907*
those do who are **b** for the dead? 1Co 15:29 *907*
all, why then are they **b** for them? 1Co 15:29 *907*
all of you who were **b** into Christ Ga 3:27 *907*

BAPTIZES
the One who **b** in the Holy Spirit.' Jn 1:33 *907*

BAPTIZING
b them in the name of the Father Mt 28:19 *907*
"Why then are you **b**, Jn 1:25 *907*
the Jordan, where John was **b**. Jn 1:28 *907*
to Israel, I came **b** in water." Jn 1:31 *907*
was spending time with them and **b**. Jn 3:22 *907*
also was **b** in Aenon near Salim, Jn 3:23 *907*
testified, behold, He is **b** Jn 3:26 *907*
and **b** more disciples than John Jn 4:1 *907*
(although Jesus Himself was not **b**, Jn 4:2 *907*
the place where John was first **b**, Jn 10:40 *907*

BAR
"The middle **b** in the center Ex 26:28 1280
He made the middle **b** to pass Ex 36:33 1280
a **b** of gold fifty shekels in weight, Jos 7:21 3956
silver, the mantle, the **b** of gold, Jos 7:24 3956
also break the *gate* **b** of Damascus, Am 1:5 1280
break his yoke **b** from upon you, Na 1:13 4132

BARABBAS
a notorious prisoner, called **B**. Mt 27:16 *912*
B, or Jesus who is called Christ?" Mt 27:17 *912*
the crowds to ask for **B** Mt 27:20 *912*
And they said, "**B**." Mt 27:21 *912*
Then he released **B** for them; Mt 27:26 *912*
The man named **B** had been Mk 15:7 *912*
him to release **B** for them instead. Mk 15:11 *912*
Pilate released **B** for them, Mk 15:15 *912*
this man, and release for us **B**!" Lk 23:18 *912*
"Not this Man, but **B**." Jn 18:40 *912*
Now **B** was a robber. Jn 18:40 *912*

BARACHEL
of Elihu the son of **B** the Buzite, Jb 32:2 1292
B the Buzite spoke out and said, Jb 32:6 1292

BARAK
Now she sent and summoned **B** the Jg 4:6 1301
Then **B** said to her, Jg 4:8 1301
arose and went with **B** to Kedesh. Jg 4:9 1301
B called Zebulun and Naphtali Jg 4:10 1301
Then they told Sisera that **B** the Jg 4:12 1301
Deborah said to **B**, Jg 4:14 1301
So **B** went down from Mount Tabor Jg 4:14 1301
the edge of the sword before **B**; Jg 4:15 1301
But **B** pursued the chariots and the Jg 4:16 1301
And behold, as **B** pursued Sisera, Jg 4:22 1301
Then Deborah and **B** the son of Jg 5:1 1301
Arise, **B**, and take away your Jg 5:12 1301
As *was* Issachar, so *was* **B**; Jg 5:15 1301
fail me if I tell of Gideon, **B**, Heb 11:32 *913*

BARBARIAN
be to the one who speaks a **b**, 1Co 14:11 *915*
one who speaks will be a **b** to me. 1Co 14:11 *915*
circumcised and uncircumcised, **b**, Col 3:11 *915*

BARBARIANS
both to Greeks and to **b**, Ro 1:14 *915*

BARBER'S
a **b** razor on your head and beard. Ezk 5:1 1532

BARBS
With **b** can anyone pierce *his* nose? Jb 40:24 4170

BARE
a field or vineyard be grazed **b** Ex 22:5
breeches to cover *their* **b** flesh; Ex 28:42 6172
nakedness, he has laid **b** her flow, Lv 20:18 6168
So he went to a **b** hill. Nu 23:3 8205
of the world were laid **b** By 2Sa 22:16 1540
it under him on the **b** steps, 2Ki 9:13 1634
world were laid **b** At Your rebuke, Ps 18:15 1540
calve And strips the forests **b** Ps 29:9 2834
will make their foreheads **b**." Is 3:17 6168
Lift up a standard on the **b** hill, Is 13:2 8192
will open rivers on the **b** heights And Is 41:18 8205
pasture *will be* on all **b** heights. Is 49:9 8205
eyes to the **b** heights and see; Jer 3:2 8205
A voice is heard on the **b** heights, Jer 3:21 8205
"A scorching wind from the **b** Jer 4:11 8205
up a lamentation on the **b** heights; Jer 7:29 8205
"On all the **b** heights in the Jer 12:12 8205
donkeys stand on the **b** heights; Jer 14:6 8205
"But I have stripped Esau **b**, Jer 49:10 2834
so that its foundation is laid **b**; Ezk 13:14 1540
Yet you were naked and **b**. Ezk 16:7 6181
and **b** and squirming in your blood. Ezk 16:22 6181
and will leave you naked and **b**. Ezk 16:39 6181
and leave you naked and **b**. Ezk 23:29 6181
She placed it on the **b** rock; Ezk 24:7 6706
have put her blood on the **b** rock, Ezk 24:8 6706
from her and make her a **b** rock. Ezk 26:4 6706
"I will make you a **b** rock; Ezk 26:14 6706
and every shoulder was rubbed **b**. Ezk 29:18 4803
them **b** and cast *them* away; Jl 1:7 2834
And will lay **b** her foundations. Mi 1:6 1540
Your bow was made **b**, Hab 3:9 6181, 5783
For He has laid **b** the cedar work. Zph 2:14 6168
which is to be, but a **b** grain, 1Co 15:37 *1131*
but all things are open and laid **b** Heb 4:13 *5136*

BARED
The LORD has **b** His holy arm In the Is 52:10 2834
of Jerusalem with your arm **b** and Ezk 4:7 2834

BAREFOOT
head was covered and he walked **b**. 2Sa 15:30 3182
"He makes counselors walk **b** And Jb 12:17 7758
"He makes priests walk **b** And Jb 12:19 7758
And he did so, going naked and **b**. Is 20:2 3182
Isaiah has gone naked and **b** three Is 20:3 3182
and **b** with buttocks uncovered, Is 20:4 3182
and wail, I must go **b** and naked; Mi 1:8 7758

BARELY
those who **b** escape from the ones 2Pe 2:18 *3643b*

BARENESS
an eating away has produced **b** on the Lv 13:55 7146, 1372

BARGAIN
make a **b** with my master the king 2Ki 18:23 6148
"Will the traders **b** over him? Jb 41:6 3739
come make a **b** with my master the Is 36:8 6148

BARGAINING
certain that you are **b** for time, Da 2:8 2084

BARGAINS
And they strike **b** with Is 2:6

BARHUMITE
the Arbathite, Azmaveth the **B**, 2Sa 23:31 978

BARIAH
of Shemaiah: Hattush, Igal, **B**, 1Ch 3:22 1282

BAR-JESUS
false prophet whose name was **B**, Ac 13:6 *919*

BARJONA
"Blessed are you, Simon **B**, Mt 16:17 *920*

BARK
of Israel a dog will not *even* **b**, Ex 11:7 2782, 3956
of them are mute dogs unable to **b**, Is 56:10 5024

BARKOS
the sons of **B**, the sons of Sisera, Ezr 2:53 1302
the sons of **B**, the sons of Sisera, Ne 7:55 1302

BARLEY
the flax and the **b** were ruined, Ex 9:31 8184
for the **b** was in the ear and the Ex 9:31 8184
a homer of **b** seed at fifty shekels Lv 27:16 8184
one-tenth of an ephah of **b** meal; Nu 5:15 8184
a land of wheat and **b**, Dt 8:8 8184
a loaf of **b** bread was tumbling Jg 7:13 8184
at the beginning of **b** harvest. Ru 1:22 8184
and it was about an ephah of **b**. Ru 2:17 8184
b harvest and the wheat harvest. Ru 2:23 8184
he winnows **b** at the threshing Ru 3:2 8184
measures of **b** and laid *it* on her. Ru 3:15 8184
six *measures* of **b** he gave to me, Ru 3:17 8184
next to mine, and he has **b** there; 2Sa 14:30 8184
beds, basins, pottery, wheat, **b**, 2Sa 17:28 8184
at the beginning of **b** harvest. 2Sa 21:9 8184
They also brought **b** and straw for 1Ki 4:28 8184
twenty loaves of **b** and fresh ears 2Ki 4:42 8184
two measures of **b** for a shekel, 2Ki 7:1 8184
two measures of **b** for a shekel, 2Ki 7:16 8184
"Two measures of **b** for a shekel 2Ki 7:18 8184
was a plot of ground full of **b**; 1Ch 11:13 8184
wheat and 20,000 kors of **b**, 2Ch 2:10 8184
send to his servants wheat and **b**, 2Ch 2:15 8184
of wheat and ten thousand of **b**. 2Ch 27:5 8184
And stinkweed instead of **b**." Jb 31:40 8184
wheat in rows, **B** in its place and Is 28:25 8184
for we have stores of wheat, **b**, Jer 41:8 8184
"But as for you, take wheat, **b**, Ezk 4:9 8184
"You shall eat it as a **b** cake, Ezk 4:12 8184
of **b** and fragments of bread, Ezk 13:19 8184
of an ephah from a homer of **b**; Ezk 45:13 8184
and a homer and a half of **b**. Hos 3:2 8184
For the wheat and the **b**; Jl 1:11 8184
has five **b** loaves and two fish, Jn 6:9 *2916*
fragments from the five **b** loaves which Jn 6:13 *2916*
three quarts of **b** for a denarius; Rv 6:6 *2915*

BARN
'Is the seed still in the **b**? Hg 2:19 4035
will gather His wheat into the **b**, Mt 3:12 *596*
gather the wheat into my **b**. Mt 13:30 *596*
to gather the wheat into His **b**; Lk 3:17 *596*
they have no storeroom nor **b** Lk 12:24 *596*

BARNABAS
was also called **B** by the apostles Ac 4:36 *921*
But **B** took hold of him and brought Ac 9:27 *921*
and they sent **B** off to Antioch. Ac 11:22 *921*
of **B** and Saul to the elders. Ac 11:30 *921*
And **B** and Saul returned from Ac 12:25 *921*
B, and Simeon who was called Ac 13:1 *921*
"Set apart for Me **B** and Saul for Ac 13:2 *921*
This man summoned **B** and Saul and Ac 13:7 *921*
As Paul and **B** were going out, Ac 13:42
proselytes followed Paul and **B**, Ac 13:43 *921*
and **B** spoke out boldly and said, Ac 13:46 *921*
a persecution against Paul and **B**, Ac 13:50 *921*
And they *began* calling **B**, Ac 14:12 *921*
But when the apostles **B** and Paul Ac 14:14 *921*
day he went away with **B** to Derbe. Ac 14:20 *921*
And when Paul and **B** had great Ac 15:2 *921*
brethren determined that Paul and **B** Ac 15:2 *921*
and they were listening to **B** and Ac 15:12 *921*
to send to Antioch with Paul and **B** Ac 15:22 *921*
you with our beloved **B** and Paul, Ac 15:25 *921*
But Paul and **B** stayed in Antioch, Ac 15:35 *921*
After some days Paul said to **B**, Ac 15:36 *921*
B wanted to take John, Ac 15:37 *921*
and **B** took Mark with him and Ac 15:39 *921*
Or do only **B** and I not have a 1Co 9:6 *921*
went up again to Jerusalem with **B**, Ga 2:1 *921*
B the right hand of fellowship, Ga 2:9 *921*
with the result that even **B** was Ga 2:13 *921*

BARNABAS'S
and *also* **B** cousin Mark (about Col 4:10 *921*

BARNS
blessing upon you in your **b** and in all Dt 28:8 618
your **b** will be filled with plenty And Pr 3:10 618
Open up her **b**, Pile her up like Jer 50:26 3965
are desolate, The **b** are torn down, Jl 1:17 4460
reap nor gather into **b**, Mt 6:26 *596*
down my **b** and build larger ones, Lk 12:18 *596*

BARRACKS
him to be brought into the **b**. Ac 21:34 *3925b*
about to be brought into the **b**, Ac 21:37 *3925b*
him to be brought into the **b**, Ac 22:24 *3925b*
force, and bring him into the **b**. Ac 23:10 *3925b*
and entered the **b** and told Paul. Ac 23:16 *3925b*
with him, they returned to the **b**. Ac 23:32 *3925b*

BARREN
Sarai was **b**; she had no child. Gn 11:30 6135
of his wife, because she was **b**; Gn 25:21 6135
opened her womb, but Rachel was **b**. Gn 29:31 6135
one miscarrying or **b** in your land; Ex 23:26 6135
there will be no male or female **b** Dt 7:14 6135
was **b** and had borne no *children*. Jg 13:2 6135
are **b** and have borne no *children*, Jg 13:3 6135
Even the **b** gives birth to seven, 1Sa 2:5 6135
"Behold, let that night be **b**; Jb 3:7 1565
the company of the godless is **b**, Jb 15:34 1565
"He wrongs the **b** woman And does Jb 24:21 6135
He makes the **b** woman abide in the Ps 113:9 6135
Sheol, and the **b** womb, Earth that Pr 30:16 6115
bereaved of my children And am **b**, Is 49:21 1565
"Shout for joy, O **b** one, Is 54:1 6135
no child, because Elizabeth was **b**, Lk 1:7 *4723*
b is now in her sixth month. Lk 1:36 *4723*
'Blessed are the **b**, and the wombs Lk 23:29 *4723*
B WOMAN WHO DOES NOT BEAR; Ga 4:27 *4723*

BARRICADE
b her with planks of cedar." SS 8:9 6696a
when your enemies will throw up a **b** Lk 19:43 *5482*

BARRIER
There was a **b** *wall* one cubit Ezk 40:12 1366
down the **b** of the dividing wall, Eph 2:14 *5418*

BARS
you shall make **b** of acacia wood, Ex 26:26 1280
and five **b** for the boards of the Ex 26:27 1280
and five **b** for the boards of the Ex 26:27 1280
of gold *as* holders for the **b**; Ex 26:29 1280
you shall overlay the **b** with gold. Ex 26:29 1280
its hooks and its boards, its **b**, Ex 35:11 1280
Then he made **b** of acacia wood, Ex 36:31 1280
and five **b** for the boards of the Ex 36:32 1280
and five **b** for the boards of the Ex 36:32 1280
of gold *as* holders for the **b**, Ex 36:34 1280
and overlaid the **b** with gold. Ex 36:34 1280
its clasps, its boards, its **b**, Ex 39:33 1280
its **b** and erected its pillars. Ex 40:18 1280

and I broke the **b** of your yoke and **Lv 26:13** 4133
frames of the tabernacle, its **b**, **Nu 3:36** 1280
shall put it on the carrying **b**. **Nu 4:10** 4132
and put them on the carrying **b**. **Nu 4:12** 4132
the boards of the tabernacle and its **b** **Nu 4:31** 1280
with high walls, gates and **b**, **Dt 3:5** 1280
pulled them up along with the **b**; **Jg 16:3** 1280
a city with double gates and **b**." **1Sa 23:7** 1280
with walls and bronze **b** *were* his); **1Ki 4:13** 1280
cities *with* walls, gates and **b**; **2Ch 8:5** 1280
walls and towers, gates and **b**. **2Ch 14:7** 1280
its doors with its bolts and **b**. **Ne 3:3** 1280
doors with its bolts and its **b**. **Ne 3:6** 1280
doors with its bolts and its **b**, **Ne 3:13** 1280
doors with its bolts and its **b**. **Ne 3:14** 1280
doors with its bolts and its **b**, **Ne 3:15** 1280
His limbs are like **b** of iron. **Jb 40:18** 4300
bronze And cut **b** of iron asunder. **Ps 107:16** 1280
strengthened the **b** of your gates; **Ps 147:13** 1280
are like the **b** of a citadel. **Pr 18:19** 1280
and cut through their iron **b**. **Is 45:2** 1280
"It has no gates or **b**; **Jer 49:31** 1280
The **b** of her *gates* are broken. **Jer 51:30** 1280
He has destroyed and broken her **b**. **La 2:9** 1280
I break there the yoke **b** of Egypt. **Ezk 30:18** 4133
when I have broken the **b** of their **Ezk 34:27** 4133
walls and having no **b** or gates, **Ezk 38:11** 1280
And will demolish their gate **b** And **Hos 11:6** 905
with its **b** *was* around me forever, **Jon 2:6** 1280
Fire consumes your gate **b**. **Na 3:13** 1280

BARSABBAS
forward two men, Joseph called **B** **Ac 1:23** *923*
Judas called **B**, and Silas, leading **Ac 15:22** *923*

BARTER
orphans And **b** over your friend. **Jb 6:27** 3739

BARTERED
The sorrows of those who have **b** **Ps 16:4** 4117

BARTHOLOMEW
Philip and **B**; Thomas and Matthew **Mt 10:3** *918*
and Andrew, and Philip, and **B**, **Mk 3:18** *918*
and Philip and **B**; **Lk 6:14** *918*
Philip and Thomas, **B** and Matthew, **Ac 1:13** *918*

BARTIMAEUS
crowd, a blind beggar *named* **B**, **Mk 10:46** *924*

BARUCH
After him **B** the son of Zabbai **Ne 3:20** 1263
Daniel, Ginnethon, **B**, **Ne 10:6** 1263
and Maaseiah the son of **B**, **Ne 11:5** 1263
purchase to **B** the son of Neriah, **Jer 32:12** 1263
I commanded **B** in their presence, **Jer 32:13** 1263
purchase to **B** the son of Neriah, **Jer 32:16** 1263
called **B** the son of Neriah, **Jer 36:4** 1263
B wrote on a scroll at the dictation **Jer 36:4** 1263
Jeremiah commanded **B**, **Jer 36:5** 1263
B the son of Neriah did **Jer 36:8** 1263
Then **B** read from the book the **Jer 36:10** 1263
when **B** read from the book to the **Jer 36:13** 1263
Shelemiah, the son of Cushi, to **B**, **Jer 36:14** 1263
So **B** the son of Neriah took the **Jer 36:14** 1263
So **B** read it to them. **Jer 36:15** 1263
fear one to another and said to **B**, **Jer 36:16** 1263
And they asked **B**, saying, **Jer 36:17** 1263
Then **B** said to them, **Jer 36:18** 1263
Then the officials said to **B**, **Jer 36:19** 1263
the son of Abdeel to seize **B** the scribe **Jer 36:26** 1263
the words which **B** had written at the **Jer 36:27** 1263
gave it to **B** the son of Neraiah, **Jer 36:32** 1263
but **B** the son of Neriah is **Jer 43:3** 1263
prophet and **B** the son of Neriah **Jer 43:6** 1263
spoke to **B** the son of Neriah, **Jer 45:1** 1263
the God of Israel to you, O **B**: **Jer 45:2** 1263

BARZILLAI
and **B** the Gileadite from Rogelim, **2Sa 17:27** 1271
Now **B** the Gileadite had come down **2Sa 19:31** 1271
Now **B** was very old, being eighty **2Sa 19:32** 1271
The king said to **B**, **2Sa 19:33** 1271
But **B** said to the king, **2Sa 19:34** 1271
then kissed **B** and blessed him, **2Sa 19:39** 1271
the son of **B** the Meholathite. **2Sa 21:8** 1271
to the sons of **B** the Gileadite, **1Ki 2:7** 1271
the sons of Hakkoz, the sons of **B**, **Ezr 2:61** 1271
the daughters of **B** the Gileadite, **Ezr 2:61** 1271
the sons of Hakkoz, the sons of **B**, **Ne 7:63** 1271
took a wife of the daughters of **B**, **Ne 7:63** 1271

BASE
The lampstand *and* its **b** and its **Ex 25:31** 3409
the blood at the **b** of the altar. **Ex 29:12** 3247
of bronze, with its **b** of bronze, **Ex 30:18** 3653b
work, its **b** and its shaft; **Ex 37:17** 3409
of bronze with its **b** of bronze, **Ex 38:8** 3653b
he shall pour out at the **b** of the altar **Lv 4:7** 3247
the blood he shall pour out at the **b** **Lv 4:18** 3247
its blood he shall pour out at the **b** **Lv 4:25** 3247
pour out at the **b** of the altar. **Lv 4:30** 3247
pour out at the **b** of the altar. **Lv 4:34** 3247
drained out at the **b** of the altar: **Lv 5:9** 3247
the blood at the **b** of the altar **Lv 8:15** 3247
the blood at the **b** of the altar. **Lv 9:9** 3247
from its **b** to its flowers it was **Nu 8:4** 3409
is no **b** thought in your heart, **Dt 15:9** 1100
overturns the mountains at the **b**. **Jb 28:9** 8328
hold the **b** of its mast firmly, **Is 33:23** 3653b
its corners, its **b** and **Ezk 41:22** 753
the **b** *shall be* a cubit and the **Ezk 43:13** 2436
the *height* of the **b** of the altar. **Ezk 43:13** 1354
"From the **b** on the ground to **Ezk 43:14** 2436
b *shall be* a cubit round about; **Ezk 43:17** 2436
and the **b** things of the world and **1Co 1:28** *36*

BASED
the righteousness which is **b** on law **Ro 10:5** *1537*
b on faith speaks as **Ro 10:6** *1537*
if the inheritance is **b** on law, **Ga 3:18** *1537*
it is no longer **b** on a promise; **Ga 3:18** *1537*
would indeed have been **b** on law. **Ga 3:21** *1537*

BASEMATH
and **B** the daughter of Elon the **Gn 26:34** 1315
also **B**, Ishmael's daughter, the **Gn 36:3** 1315
Eliphaz to Esau, and **B** bore Reuel, **Gn 36:4** 1315
Reuel the son of Esau's wife **B**. **Gn 36:10** 1315
were the sons of Esau's wife **B**. **Gn 36:13** 1315
are the sons of Esau's wife **B**. **Gn 36:17** 1315
B the daughter of Solomon); **1Ki 4:15** 1315

BASES
"On what were its **b** sunk? **Jb 38:6** 134

BASHAN
and went up by the way of **B**, **Nu 21:33** 1316
of **B** went out with all his people, **Nu 21:33** 1316
the kingdom of Og, the king of **B**, **Nu 32:33** 1316
in Heshbon, and Og the king of **B**, **Dt 1:4** 1316
turned and went up the road to **B**, **Dt 3:1** 1316
road to Bashan, and Og, king of **B**, **Dt 3:1** 1316
God delivered Og also, king of **B**, **Dt 3:3** 1316
of Argob, the kingdom of Og in **B**. **Dt 3:4** 1316
and all Gilead and all **B**, **Dt 3:10** 1316
cities of the kingdom of Og in **B**. **Dt 3:10** 1316
(For only Og king of **B** was left of **Dt 3:11** 1316
"The rest of Gilead and all **B**, **Dt 3:13** 1316
(concerning all **B**, it is called the land **Dt 3:13** 1316
and called it, *that is*, **B**, **Dt 3:14** 1316
and Golan in **B** for the Manassites. **Dt 4:43** 1316
land and the land of Og king of **B**, **Dt 4:47** 1316
Og the king of **B** came out to meet us **Dt 29:7** 1316
lambs, And rams, the breed of **B**, **Dt 32:14** 1316
whelp, That leaps forth from **B**." **Dt 33:22** 1316
Og king of **B** who was at Ashtaroth. **Jos 9:10** 1316
and the territory of Og king of **B**, **Jos 12:4** 1316
Hermon and Salecah and all **B**, **Jos 12:5** 1316
and all **B** as far as Salecah; **Jos 13:11** 1316
all the kingdom of Og in **B**, **Jos 13:12** 1316
was from Mahanaim, all **B**, **Jos 13:30** 1316
all the kingdom of Og king of **B**, **Jos 13:30** 1316
the towns of Jair, which are in **B**, **Jos 13:30** 1316
cities of the kingdom of Og in **B**, **Jos 13:31** 1316
Gilead, were allotted Gilead and **B**, **Jos 17:1** 1316
besides the land of Gilead and **B**, **Jos 17:5** 1316
in **B** from the tribe of Manasseh. **Jos 20:8** 1316
the half-tribe of Manasseh in **B**, **Jos 21:6** 1316
of Manasseh, *they gave* Golan in **B**, **Jos 21:27** 1316
Moses had given *a possession* in **B**, **Jos 22:7** 1316
region of Argob, which is in **B**, **1Ki 4:13** 1316
the Amorites and of Og king of **B**; **1Ki 4:19** 1316
of the Arnon, even Gilead and **B**. **2Ki 10:33** 1316
the land of **B** as far as Salecah. **1Ch 5:11** 1316
then Janai and Shaphat in **B**. **1Ch 5:12** 1316
in Gilead, in **B** and in its towns, **1Ch 5:16** 1316
from **B** to Baal-hermon and Senir **1Ch 5:23** 1316
of Manasseh, thirteen cities in **B**. **1Ch 6:62** 1316
Golan in **B** with its pasture lands **1Ch 6:71** 1316
And the land of Og the king of **B**. **Ne 9:22** 1316
bulls of **B** have encircled me. **Ps 22:12** 1316
of God is the mountain of **B**; **Ps 68:15** 1316
many peaks is the mountain of **B**. **Ps 68:15** 1316
"I will bring *them* back from **B**. **Ps 68:22** 1316
the Amorites, And Og, king of **B**, **Ps 135:11** 1316
And Og, king of **B**, For His **Ps 136:20** 1316
up, Against all the oaks of **B**, **Is 2:13** 1316
B and Carmel lose *their foliage*. **Is 33:9** 1316
out, And lift up your voice in **B**; **Jer 22:20** 1316
and he will graze on Carmel and **B**, **Jer 50:19** 1316
from **B** they have made your oars; **Ezk 27:6** 1316
bulls, all of them fatlings of **B**. **Ezk 39:18** 1316
you cows of **B** who are on the **Am 4:1** 1316
Let them feed in **B** and Gilead As **Mi 7:14** 1316
B and Carmel wither; **Na 1:4** 1316
Wail, O oaks of **B**, For the **Zch 11:2** 1316

BASIN
it in the blood which is in the **b**, **Ex 12:22** 5592a
some of the blood that is in the **b** **Ex 12:22** 5592a
its utensils, the **b** and its stand; **Ex 35:16** 3595
utensils, and the **b** and its stand, **Lv 8:11** 3595
beneath the **b** *were* cast supports **1Ki 7:30** 3595
of bronze, one **b** held forty baths; **1Ki 7:38** 3595
each **b** *was* four cubits, *and* on **1Ki 7:38** 3595
each of the ten stands *was* one **b**. **1Ki 7:38** 3595
be filled like a *sacrificial* **b**, **Zch 9:15** 4219
Then He poured water into the **b**, **Jn 13:5** *3537*

BASINS
half of the blood and put *it* in **b**, **Ex 24:6** 101
and its shovels and its **b** and its **Ex 27:3** 4219
pails and the shovels and the **b**, **Ex 38:3** 4219
the forks and shovels and the **b**, **Nu 4:14** 4219
brought beds, **b**, pottery, wheat, **2Sa 17:28** 5592a
He made ten **b** of bronze, one **1Ki 7:38** 3595
b and the shovels and the bowls. **1Ki 7:40** 3595
with the ten **b** on the stands; **1Ki 7:43** 3595
took away the firepans and the **b**, **2Ki 25:15** 4219
and the forks, the **b**, **1Ch 28:17** 4219
also made ten **b** in which to wash, **2Ch 4:6** 3595
and he made the **b** on the stands, **2Ch 4:14** 3595
1,000 gold drachmas, 50 **b**, **Ne 7:70** 4219
the shovels, the snuffers, the **b**, **Jer 52:18** 4219
the bowls, the firepans, the **b**, **Jer 52:19** 4219

BASIS
"And on the **b** of faith in His **Ac 3:16** *1909*
no **b** on which to punish **Ac 4:21** *3367*
it is no longer on the **b** of works, **Ro 11:6** *1537*
comes from God on the **b** of faith, **Php 3:9** *1909*
the **b** of two or three witnesses. **1Tm 5:19** *1909*
not on the **b** of deeds which we **Ti 3:5** *1537*
on the **b** of it the people received **Heb 7:11** *1909*
who has become *such* not on the **b** **Heb 7:16** *2596*

BASKET
and in the top **b** *there were* some **Gn 40:17** 5536
them out of the **b** on my head." **Gn 40:17** 5536
she got him a wicker **b** and covered **Ex 2:3** 8392
and she saw the **b** among the reeds **Ex 2:5** 8392
"You shall put them in one **b**, **Ex 29:3** 5536
and present them in the **b** along **Ex 29:3** 5536
wafer from the **b** of unleavened bread **Ex 29:23** 5536
and the bread that is in the **b**, **Ex 29:32** 5536
and the **b** of unleavened bread, **Lv 8:2** 5536
From the **b** of unleavened bread **Lv 8:26** 5536
the **b** of the ordination offering, **Lv 8:31** 5536
and a **b** of unleavened cakes of **Nu 6:15** 5536
with the **b** of unleavened cakes; **Nu 6:17** 5536
one unleavened cake out of the **b** and **Nu 6:19** 5536
you shall not put any in your **b**. **Dt 23:24** 3627
and you shall put *it* in a **b** and go **Dt 26:2** 2935
"Then the priest shall take the **b** **Dt 26:4** 2935
be your **b** and your kneading bowl. **Dt 28:5** 2935
be your **b** and your kneading bowl. **Dt 28:17** 2935
in a **b** and the broth in a pot, **Jg 6:19** 5536
His hands were freed from the **b**. **Ps 81:6** 1731
One **b** had very good figs, like **Jer 24:2** 1731
and the other **b** had very bad figs which **Jer 24:2** 1731
there was a **b** of summer fruit. **Am 8:1** 3619
"A **b** of summer fruit." **Am 8:2** 3619
light a lamp and put it under a **b**, **Mt 5:15** *3426*
is not brought to be put under a **b**, **Mk 4:21** *3426*
it away in a cellar nor under a **b**, **Lk 11:33** *3426*
wall, lowering him in a large **b**. **Ac 9:25** *4711*
a **b** through a window in the wall, **2Co 11:33** *4553*

BASKETS
three **b** of white bread on my head; **Gn 40:16** 5536
the three **b** are three days; **Gn 40:18** 5536
persons, and put their heads in **b**, **2Ki 10:7** 1731
two **b** of figs set before the **Jer 24:1** 1731
the broken pieces, twelve full **b**. **Mt 14:20** *2894*
broken pieces, seven large **b** full. **Mt 15:37** *4711*
and how many **b** *full* you picked up? **Mt 16:9** *2894*
how many large **b** *full* you picked up? **Mt 16:10** *4711*
full **b** of the broken pieces, **Mk 6:43** *2894*
and they picked up seven large **b** **Mk 8:8** *4711*
how many **b** full of broken pieces **Mk 8:19** *2894*
how many large **b** full of broken **Mk 8:20** *4711*
were picked up, twelve **b** *full*. **Lk 9:17** *2894*
and filled twelve **b** with fragments **Jn 6:13** *2894*

BAT
kinds, and the hoopoe, and the **b**. **Lv 11:19** 5847
kinds, and the hoopoe and the **b**. **Dt 14:18** 5847

BATH
will yield *only* one **b** *of wine*, **Is 5:10** 1324
a just ephah and a just **b**. **Ezk 45:10** 1324
the **b** shall be the same quantity, **Ezk 45:11** 1324
so that the **b** will contain a tenth **Ezk 45:11** 1324
(*namely*, the **b** of oil), **Ezk 45:14** 1324
a tenth of a **b** from *each* kor **Ezk 45:14** 1324

BATHE
came down to **b** at the Nile, **Ex 2:5** 7364
hair and **b** in water and be clean. **Lv 14:8** 7364
He shall then wash his clothes and **b** **Lv 14:9** 7364
shall wash his clothes and **b** in water **Lv 15:5** 7364
shall wash his clothes and **b** in **Lv 15:6** 7364
discharge shall wash his clothes and **b** **Lv 15:7** 7364
he too shall wash his clothes and **b** **Lv 15:8** 7364
shall wash his clothes and **b** in water **Lv 15:10** 7364
in water shall wash his clothes and **b** **Lv 15:11** 7364
he shall then wash his clothes and **b** **Lv 15:13** 7364
he shall **b** all his body in water **Lv 15:16** 7364
they shall both **b** in water and be **Lv 15:18** 7364
her bed shall wash his clothes and **b** **Lv 15:21** 7364
she sits shall wash his clothes and **b** **Lv 15:22** 7364
shall wash his clothes and **b** in water **Lv 15:27** 7364
Then he shall **b** his body in water **Lv 16:4** 7364
"He shall **b** his body with **Lv 16:24** 7364
clothes and **b** his body with water; **Lv 16:26** 7364
clothes and **b** his body with water, **Lv 16:28** 7364
wash his clothes and **b** in water, **Lv 17:15** 7364
does not wash *them* or **b** his body, **Lv 17:16** 7364
clothes and **b** his body in water, **Nu 19:7** 7364
in water and **b** his body in water, **Nu 19:8** 7364
shall wash his clothes and **b** *himself* **Nu 19:19** 7364
he shall **b** himself with water, **Dt 23:11** 7364

BATHED
unless he has **b** his body in water. **Lv 22:6** 7364
the harlots **b** themselves *there*), **1Ki 22:38** 7364
When my steps were **b** in butter, **Jb 29:6** 7364
streams of water, **B** in milk, **SS 5:12** 7364
"Then I **b** you with water, washed **Ezk 16:9** 7364
for whom you **b**, painted your eyes and **Ezk 23:40** 7364
has **b** needs only to wash his feet, **Jn 13:10** *3068*

BATHING
from the roof he saw a woman **b**; **2Sa 11:2** 7364

BATH-RABBIM
pools in Heshbon By the gate of **B**; **SS 7:4** 1337

BATHS
it could hold two thousand **b**. **1Ki 7:26** 1324
of bronze, one basin held forty **b**; **1Ki 7:38** 1324
of barley, and 20,000 **b** of wine and **2Ch 2:10** 1324
of wine and 20,000 **b** of oil." **2Ch 2:10** 1324
it could hold 3,000 **b**. **2Ch 4:5** 1324

100 kors of wheat, 100 **b** of wine, Ezr 7:22 1325
100 baths of wine, 100 **b** of oil, Ezr 7:22 1325
kor (*which is* ten **b** *or* a homer, Ezk 45:14 1324
a homer, for ten **b** are a homer); Ezk 45:14 1324

BATHSHEBA
"Is this not **B**, the daughter of 2Sa 11:3 1339
Then David comforted his wife **B**, 2Sa 12:24 1339
spoke to **B** the mother of Solomon, 1Ki 1:11 1339
So **B** went in to the king in the 1Ki 1:15 1339
Then **B** bowed and prostrated 1Ki 1:16 1339
"Call **B** to me." And she came into 1Ki 1:28 1339
Then **B** bowed with her face to the 1Ki 1:31 1339
came to **B** the mother of Solomon. 1Ki 2:13 1339
B said, "Very well; I will speak 1Ki 2:18 1339
So **B** went to King Solomon to speak 1Ki 2:19 1339
David was the father of Solomon by **B** Mt 1:6

BATH-SHUA
born to him by **B** the Canaanitess. 1Ch 2:3 1340
four, by **B** the daughter of Ammiel; 1Ch 3:5 1340

BATS
will cast away to the moles and the **b** Is 2:20 5847

BATTERED
city And the gate is **b** to ruins. Is 24:12 3807
"A **B** REED HE WILL NOT BREAK OFF, Mt 12:20 *4937*
from the land, **b** by the waves; Mt 14:24 *928*

BATTERING
b rams against it all around. Ezk 4:2 3733c
'Jerusalem,' to set **b** rams, Ezk 21:22 3733c
to set **b** rams against the gates, Ezk 21:22 3733c
"The blow of his **b** rams he Ezk 26:9 6904

BATTLE
and they arrayed for **b** against Gn 14:8 4421
all his people, for **b** at Edrei. Nu 21:33 4421
the men of war who had gone to **b**, Nu 31:21 4421
out to **b** and all the congregation. Nu 31:27 4421
the men of war who went out to **b**, Nu 31:28 4421
in the presence of the LORD to **b**, Nu 32:27 4421
everyone who is armed for **b**, Nu 32:29 4421
and contend with him in **b**. Dt 2:24 4421
came out to meet us in **b** at Jahaz. Dt 2:32 4421
came out to meet us in **b** at Edrei. Dt 3:1 4421
"When you go out to **b** against Dt 20:1 4421
When you are approaching the **b**, Dt 20:2 4421
the **b** against your enemies today. Dt 20:3 4421
the **b** and another man would dedicate Dt 20:5 4421
otherwise he might die in the **b** Dt 20:6 4421
the **b** and another man would marry Dt 20:7 4421
go out to **b** against your enemies, Dt 21:10 4421
Bashan came out to meet us for **b**, Dt 29:7 4421
before your brothers in **b** array, Jos 1:14 2571
Manasseh crossed over in **b** array Jos 4:12 2571
crossed for **b** before the LORD to Jos 4:13 4421
and went out to meet Israel in **b** Jos 8:14 4421
they took them all in **b**. Jos 11:19 4421
to meet Israel in **b** in order that Jos 11:20 4421
from the **b** by the ascent of Heres. Jg 8:13 4421
to **b** against the sons of Israel. Jg 20:14 4421
b against the sons of Benjamin?" Jg 20:18 4421
went out to **b** against Benjamin, Jg 20:20 4421
for **b** against them at Gibeah. Jg 20:20 4421
arrayed for **b** again in the place where Jg 20:22 4421
"Shall we again draw near for **b** Jg 20:23 4421
"Shall I yet again go out to **b** Jg 20:28 4421
Gibeah, the **b** became fierce; Jg 20:34 4421
the men of Israel turned in the **b**, Jg 20:39 4421
before us, as in the first **b**." Jg 20:39 4421
but the **b** overtook them while Jg 20:42 4421
each man *of Benjamin* a wife in **b**, Jg 21:22 4421
went out to meet the Philistines in **b** 1Sa 4:1 4421
drew up in **b** array to meet Israel. 1Sa 4:2 6186a
When the **b** spread, Israel was 1Sa 4:2 4421
a man of Benjamin ran from the **b** 1Sa 4:12 4634
the one who came from the **b** line. 1Sa 4:16 4634
I escaped from the **b** line today." 1Sa 4:16 4634
drew near to **b** against Israel. 1Sa 7:10 4421
So it came about on the day of **b** 1Sa 13:22 4421
him rallied and came to the **b**; 1Sa 14:20 4421
pursued them closely in the **b**. 1Sa 14:22 4421
and the **b** spread beyond Beth-aven. 1Sa 14:23 4421
gathered their armies for **b**; 1Sa 17:1 4421
and drew up in **b** array to 1Sa 17:2 4421
come out to draw up in **b** array? 1Sa 17:8 4421
had gone after Saul to the **b**. 1Sa 17:13 4421
to the **b** were Eliab the firstborn, 1Sa 17:13 4421
in **b** array shouting the war cry. 1Sa 17:20 4634
Philistines drew up in **b** array, 1Sa 17:21 6186a
and ran to the **b** line and entered 1Sa 17:22 4634
come down in order to see the **b**." 1Sa 17:28 4421
for the **b** is the LORD's and He 1Sa 17:47 4421
the **b** line to meet the Philistine. 1Sa 17:48 4634
of the Philistines went out *to* **b**, 1Sa 18:30
he will go down into **b** and perish. 1Sa 26:10 4421
not let him go down to **b** with us, 1Sa 29:4 4421
b he may become an adversary to us. 1Sa 29:4 4421
must not go up with us to the **b**.' 1Sa 29:9 4421
share is who goes down to the **b**, 1Sa 30:24 4421
The **b** went heavily against Saul, 1Sa 31:3 4421
"The people have fled from the **b**, 2Sa 1:4 4421
fallen in the midst of the **b**! 2Sa 1:25 4421
That day the **b** was very severe, 2Sa 2:17 4421
to death in the **b** at Gibeon. 2Sa 3:30 4421
Ammon came out and drew up in **b** 2Sa 10:8 4421
Now when Joab saw that the **b** was 2Sa 10:9 6440, 4421
to the **b** against the Arameans, 2Sa 10:13 4421
at the time when kings go out *to* **b**, 2Sa 11:1
fiercest **b** and withdraw from him, 2Sa 11:15 4421
make your **b** against the city 2Sa 11:25 4421
and that you personally go into **b**. 2Sa 17:11 7128
and the **b** took place in the forest 2Sa 18:6 4421
For the **b** there was spread over 2Sa 18:8 4421
steal away when they flee in **b**. 2Sa 19:3 4421
anointed over us, has died in **b**. 2Sa 19:10 4421
not go out again with us to **b**, 2Sa 21:17 4421
"He trains my hands for **b**, 2Sa 22:35 4421
girded me with strength for **b**; 2Sa 22:40 4421
gathered there to **b** and the men of 2Sa 23:9 4421
go out to **b** against their enemy, 1Ki 8:44 4421
"Who shall begin the **b**?" 1Ki 20:14 4421
the seventh day the **b** was joined, 1Ki 20:29 4421
went out into the midst of the **b**; 1Ki 20:39 4421
go with me to **b** at Ramoth-gilead?" 1Ki 22:4 4421
to **b** or shall I refrain?" 1Ki 22:6 4421
shall we go to Ramoth-gilead to **b**, 1Ki 22:15 4421
disguise myself and go into the **b**, 1Ki 22:30 4421
himself and went into the **b**. 1Ki 22:30 4421
The **b** raged that day, and the 1Ki 22:35 4421
that the **b** was too fierce for him, 2Ki 3:26 4421
with bow and *were* skillful in **b**, 1Ch 5:18 4421
they cried out to God in the **b**, 1Ch 5:20 4421
The **b** became heavy against Saul, 1Ch 10:3 4421
were gathered together there to **b**, 1Ch 11:13 4421
when he was about to go to **b** with 1Ch 12:19 4421
who could draw up in **b** formation 1Ch 12:33 4421
who could draw up in **b** formation, 1Ch 12:35 4421
army to draw up in **b** formation. 1Ch 12:36 4421
kinds of weapons of war for the **b**. 1Ch 12:37 4421
who could draw up in **b** formation, 1Ch 12:38 4634
trees, then you shall go out to **b**, 1Ch 14:15 4421
from their cities and came to **b**. 1Ch 19:7 4421
Ammon came out and drew up in **b** 1Ch 19:9 4421
Now when Joab saw that the **b** was 1Ch 19:10 4421
to the **b** against the Arameans, 1Ch 19:14 4421
in **b** array against the Arameans, 1Ch 19:17 4421
at the time when kings go out *to* **b**, 1Ch 20:1
go out to **b** against their enemies, 2Ch 6:34 4421
Abijah began the **b** with an 2Ch 13:3 4421
while Jeroboam drew up in **b** 2Ch 13:3 4421
and they drew up in **b** formation in 2Ch 14:10 4421
no one besides You to help *in the* **b** 2Ch 14:11
we will be with you in the **b**." 2Ch 18:3 4421
we go against Ramoth-gilead to **b**, 2Ch 18:5 4421
shall we go to Ramoth-gilead to **b**, 2Ch 18:14 4421
disguise myself and go into **b**, 2Ch 18:29 4421
himself, and they went into **b**. 2Ch 18:29 4421
The **b** raged that day, and the 2Ch 18:34 4421
for the **b** is not yours but God's. 2Ch 20:15 4421
'You *need* not fight in this **b**; 2Ch 20:17
do go, do *it*, be strong for the **b**; 2Ch 25:8 4421
back from going with him to **b**, 2Ch 25:13 4421
Uzziah had an army ready for **b**, 2Ch 26:11 4421
those who were coming from the **b**, 2Ch 28:12 6635
For the day of war and **b**? Jb 38:23 4421
And he scents the **b** from afar, Jb 39:25 4421
Remember the **b**; you will not do it Jb 41:8 4421
He trains my hands for **b**, Ps 18:34 4421
girded me with strength for **b**; Ps 18:39 4421
and mighty, The LORD mighty in **b**. Ps 24:8 4421
from the **b** *which is* against me, Ps 55:18 7128
they turned back in the day of **b**. Ps 78:9 7128
And have not made him stand in **b**. Ps 89:43 4421
covered my head in the day of **b**. Ps 140:7 5402
for war, *And* my fingers for **b**; Ps 144:1 4421
is prepared for the day of **b**, Pr 21:31 4421
and the **b** is not to the warriors, Ec 9:11 4421
sword And your mighty ones in **b**. Is 3:25 4421
oppressor, as at the **b** of Midian. Is 9:4 3117
boot of the booted warrior in the **b** Is 9:5
hosts is mustering the army for **b**. Is 13:4 4421
bent bow And from the press of **b**. Is 21:15 4421
the sword, Nor did they die in **b**. Is 22:2 4421
give Me briars *and* thorns in **b**, Is 27:4 4421
raise up **b** towers against you. Is 29:3 4694
His anger And the fierceness of **b**; Is 42:25 4421
as a man for the **b** Against you, Jer 6:23 4421
Like a horse charging into the **b**. Jer 8:6 4421
men struck down by the sword in **b**. Jer 18:21 4421
buckler, And draw near for the **b**! Jer 46:3 4421
warriors, And men valiant for **b**'? Jer 48:14 4421
against her, And rise up for **b**!" Jer 49:14 4421
draw up *their* **b** lines against her; Jer 50:9 6186a
"Draw up your **b** lines against Jer 50:14 6186a
b cry against her on every side! Jer 50:15 7321
"The noise of **b** is in the land, Jer 50:22 4421
like a man for the **b** Against you, Jer 50:42 4421
but no one is going to the **b**, Ezk 7:14 4421
in the **b** on the day of the LORD. Ezk 13:5 4421
to lift up the voice with a **b** cry, Ezk 21:22 8643
though not in anger nor in **b**. Da 11:20 4421
not deliver them by bow, sword, **b**, Hos 1:7 4421
Will not the **b** against the sons of Hos 10:9 4421
Beth-arbel on the day of **b**, Hos 10:14 4421
a mighty people arranged for **b**. Jl 2:5 4421
Amid war cries on the day of **b** Am 1:14 4421
and let us go against her for **b**" Ob 1:1 4421
A day of trumpet and **b** cry Against Zph 1:16 8643
them like His majestic horse in **b**. Zch 10:3 4421
tent peg, From them the bow of **b**, Zch 10:4 4421
in the mire of the streets in **b**; Zch 10:5 4421
nations against Jerusalem to **b**, Zch 14:2 4421
as when He fights on a day of **b**. Zch 14:3 7128
out to meet another king in **b**, Lk 14:31 *4171*
who will prepare himself for **b**? 1Co 14:8 *4171*
was like horses prepared for **b**; Rv 9:7 *4171*
of many horses rushing to **b**. Rv 9:9 *4171*

BATTLE-AXE
the **b** to meet those who pursue me; Ps 35:3 5462

BATTLEFIELD
about four thousand men on the **b**. 1Sa 4:2 4634, 7704

BATTLEMENT
will build on her a **b** of silver; SS 8:9 2918

BATTLEMENTS
I will make your **b** of rubies, Is 54:12 8121

BATTLES
out before us and fight our **b**." 1Sa 8:20 4421
for me and fight the LORD's **b**." 1Sa 18:17 4421
is fighting the **b** of the LORD, 1Sa 25:28 4421
the spoil won in **b** to repair the house 1Ch 26:27 4421
to help us and to fight our **b**." 2Ch 32:8 4421
And in **b**, brandishing weapons, He Is 30:32 4421

BAVVAI
under **B** the son of Henadad, Ne 3:18 942

BAY
the **b** that turns to the south. Jos 15:2 3956
the north side was from the **b** Jos 15:5 3956
at the north **b** of the Salt Sea, Jos 18:19 3956
observe a **b** with a beach, Ac 27:39 *2859*

BAZLITH
the sons of **B**, the sons of Mehida, Ne 7:54 1213

BAZLUTH
the sons of **B**, the sons of Mehida, Ezr 2:52 1213

BDELLIUM
b and the onyx stone are there. Gn 2:12 916
and its appearance like that of **b**. Nu 11:7 916

BEACH
crowd was standing on the **b**. Mt 13:2 *123*
filled, they drew it up on the **b**; Mt 13:48 *123*
breaking, Jesus stood on the **b**; Jn 21:4 *123*
down on the **b** and praying, Ac 21:5 *123*
observe a bay with a **b**, Ac 27:39 *123*
wind, they were heading for the **b**. Ac 27:40 *123*

BEADS
Your neck with strings of **b**." SS 1:10 2737
of gold With **b** of silver." SS 1:11 5351

BEAK
in her **b** was a freshly picked Gn 8:11 6310
wing or opened *its* **b** or chirped." Is 10:14 6310

BEALIAH
Eluzai, Jerimoth, **B**, 1Ch 12:5 1183

BEALOTH
Ziph and Telem and **B**, Jos 15:24 1175
the son of Hushai, in Asher and **B**; 1Ki 4:16 1175

BEAM
of his spear was like a weaver's **b**, 1Sa 17:7 4500
whose spear was like a weaver's **b**. 2Sa 21:19 4500
each of us take from there a **b**, 2Ki 6:2 6982
But as one was felling a **b**, 2Ki 6:5 6982
hand *was* a spear like a weaver's **b**, 1Ch 11:23 4500
whose spear *was* like a weaver's **b**. 1Ch 20:5 4500
and causes his stern face to **b**. Ec 8:1 8132

BEAMS
all around in order that *the* **b** 1Ki 6:6
house with **b** and planks of cedar. 1Ki 6:9 1356b
of cut stone and a row of cedar **b**. 1Ki 6:36 3772
with cedar **b** on the pillars. 1Ki 7:2 3772
row of cedar **b** even as the inner court 1Ki 7:12 3772
the **b**, the thresholds and its walls 2Ch 3:7 6982
make **b** for the houses which the kings 2Ch 34:11 7136b
and **b** are being laid in the walls; Ezr 5:8 636
make **b** for the gates of the fortress Ne 2:8 7136b
they laid its **b** and hung its doors Ne 3:3 7136b
laid its **b** and hung its doors with Ne 3:6 7136b
He lays the **b** of His upper Ps 104:3 7136b
"The **b** of our houses are cedars, SS 1:17 6982

BEANS
barley, flour, parched *grain*, **b**, 2Sa 17:28 6321
as for you, take wheat, barley, **b**, Ezk 4:9 6321

BEAR
"My punishment is too great to **b**! Gn 4:13 5375
with child, And you will **b** a son; Gn 16:11 3205
is ninety years old, **b** *a child?*" Gn 17:17 3205
Sarah your wife will **b** you a son, Gn 17:19 3205
whom Sarah will **b** to you at this Gn 17:21 3205
'Shall I indeed **b** *a child*, when I Gn 18:13 3205
her that she may **b** on my knees, Gn 30:3 3205
me **b** the blame before you forever. Gn 43:9 2398
then let me **b** the blame before my Gn 44:32 2398
bowed his shoulder to **b** *burdens*, Gn 49:15 5445
they will **b** *the burden* with you. Ex 18:22 5375
"You shall not **b** false witness Ex 20:16 6030a
"You shall not **b** a false report; Ex 23:1 5375
and Aaron shall **b** their names Ex 28:12 5375
tell *it*, then he will **b** his guilt. Lv 5:1 5375
and shall **b** his punishment. Lv 5:17 5375
of it will **b** his *own* iniquity. Lv 7:18 5375
and He gave it to you to **b** away Lv 10:17 5375
"The goat shall **b** on itself Lv 16:22 5375
body, then he shall **b** his guilt." Lv 17:16 5375
who eats it will **b** his iniquity, Lv 19:8 5375
nor **b** any grudge against the sons Lv 19:18 5201
they will **b** their guilt. Lv 20:19 5375
they will **b** their sin. Lv 20:20 5375
they will not **b** sin because of it Lv 22:9 5375
and *so* cause them to **b** punishment Lv 22:16 5375
his God, then he will **b** his sin. Lv 24:15 5375
of the field will **b** their fruit. Lv 26:4 5414
that woman shall **b** her guilt.' " Nu 5:31 5375
That man will **b** his sin. Nu 9:13 5375
and they shall **b** the burden of the Nu 11:17 5375
that you will not **b** *it* all alone. Nu 11:17 5375
not **b** her shame for seven days? Nu 12:14 3637
"How long *shall I* **b** with this Nu 14:27

day you shall **b** your guilt a year, **Nu 14:34** 5375
you shall **b** the guilt in connection **Nu 18:1** 5375
your sons with you shall **b** the guilt **Nu 18:1** 5375
again, or they will **b** sin and die. **Nu 18:22** 5375
and they shall **b** their iniquity; **Nu 18:23** 5375
will **b** no sin by reason of it **Nu 18:32** 5375
them, then he shall **b** her guilt." **Nu 30:15** 5375
able to **b** *the burden* of you alone. **Dt 1:9** 5375
'How can I alone **b** the load and **Dt 1:12** 5375
'You shall not **b** false witness **Dt 5:20** 6030a
and He could **b** the misery of **Jg 10:16** 7114a
a husband tonight and also **b** sons, **Ru 1:12** 3205
b witness against me before the **1Sa 12:3** 6030a
When a lion or a **b** came and took a **1Sa 17:34** 1677
killed both the lion and the **b**; **1Sa 17:36** 1677
lion and from the paw of the **b**, **1Sa 17:37** 1677
like a **b** robbed of her cubs in the **2Sa 17:8** 1677
you impose on me I will **b**." **2Ki 18:14** 5375
root downward and **b** fruit upward. **2Ki 19:30** 6213a
Who makes the **B**, Orion and the **Jb 9:9** 5906
"**B** with me that I may speak; **Jb 21:3** 5375
guide the **B** with her satellites? **Jb 38:32** 5906
anger they **b** a grudge against me. **Ps 55:3** 7852
reproaches me, Then I could **b** *it;* **Ps 55:12** 5375
How I **b** in my bosom *the* **Ps 89:50** 5375
They will **b** you up in their hands, **Ps 91:12** 5375
Let our cattle **b** Without mishap **Ps 144:14** 5445
if you scoff, you alone will **b** it. **Pr 9:12** 5375
a man meet a **b** robbed of her cubs, **Pr 17:12** 1677
as for a broken spirit who can **b** **Pr 18:14** 5375
great anger will **b** the penalty, **Pr 19:19** 5375
Like a roaring lion and a rushing **b** **Pr 28:15** 1677
And under four, it cannot **b** up: **Pr 30:21** 5375
washing, All of which **b** twins, **SS 4:2** 8382
washing, All of which **b** twins, **SS 6:6** 8382
will be with child and **b** a son, **Is 7:14** 3205
from his roots will **b** fruit. **Is 11:1** 6509
Also the cow and the **b** will graze, **Is 11:7** 1677
root downward and **b** fruit upward. **Is 37:31** 6213a
open up and salvation **b** fruit, **Is 45:8** 6509
your graying years I will **b** *you!* **Is 46:4** 5445
And I will **b** *you* and I will **Is 46:4** 5445
As He will **b** their iniquities. **Is 53:11** 5445
earth And making it **b** and sprout, **Is 55:10** 3205
And will **b** good news of the **Is 60:6** 1319
vain, Or **b** *children* for calamity; **Is 65:23** 3205
is a sickness, And I must **b** it." **Jer 10:19** 5375
their mothers who **b** them, **Jer 16:3** 3205
they may **b** sons and daughters; **Jer 29:6** 3205
is to me like a **b** lying in wait, **La 3:10** 1677
he should **b** The yoke in his youth. **La 3:27** 5375
you shall **b** their iniquity for the **Ezk 4:4** 5375
thus you shall **b** the iniquity of **Ezk 4:5** 5375
and **b** the iniquity of the house of **Ezk 4:6** 5375
"They will **b** *the punishment* **Ezk 14:10** 5375
"Also **b** your disgrace in that you **Ezk 16:52** 5375
also ashamed and **b** your disgrace, **Ezk 16:52** 5375
that you may **b** your humiliation and **Ezk 16:54** 5375
might yield branches and **b** fruit **Ezk 17:8** 5375
bring forth boughs and **b** fruit and **Ezk 17:23** 6213a
'Why should the son not **b** the **Ezk 18:19** 5375
The son will not **b** the punishment **Ezk 18:20** 5375
nor will the father **b** the **Ezk 18:20** 5375
b now the *punishment* of your **Ezk 23:35** 5375
and you will **b** the penalty of **Ezk 23:49** 5375
put forth your branches and **b** **Ezk 36:8** 5375
nor will you **b** disgrace from the **Ezk 36:15** 5375
shall **b** the punishment for their **Ezk 44:10** 5375
"that they shall **b** *the punishment* **Ezk 44:12** 5375
but they will **b** their shame and **Ezk 44:13** 5375
They will **b** every month because **Ezk 47:12** 1069
a second one, resembling a **b**. **Da 7:5** 1678
is dried up, They will **b** no fruit. **Hos 9:16** 6213a
Even though they **b** children, **Hos 9:16** 3205
Now they must **b** their guilt. **Hos 10:2** 816
them like a **b** robbed of her cubs, **Hos 13:8** 1677
from a lion And a **b** meets him, **Am 5:19** 1677
b the reproach of My people." **Mi 6:16** 5375
I will **b** the indignation of the **Mi 7:9** 5375
and He who will **b** the honor and **Zch 6:13** 5375
"She will **b** a Son; **Mt 1:21** *5088*
BE WITH CHILD AND SHALL **B** A SON, **Mt 1:23** *5088*
"Therefore **b** fruit in keeping with **Mt 3:8** *4160*
every tree that does not **b** **Mt 3:10** *4160*
ON *their* HANDS THEY WILL **B** YOU UP **Mt 4:6** *142*
"Every tree that does not **b** good **Mt 7:19** *4160*
YOU SHALL NOT **B** FALSE WITNESS; **Mt 19:18** *5576*
into service to **b** His cross. **Mt 27:32** *142*
word and accept it and **b** fruit, **Mk 4:20** *2592*
NOT STEAL, DO NOT **B** FALSE WITNESS, **Mk 10:19** *5576*
to **b** His cross. **Mk 15:21** *142*
wife Elizabeth will **b** you a son, **Lk 1:13** *1080*
in your womb and **b** a son, **Lk 1:31** *5088*
"Therefore **b** fruits in keeping with **Lk 3:8** *4160*
every tree that does not **b** **Lk 3:9** *4160*
ON *their* HANDS THEY WILL **B** YOU UP **Lk 4:11** *142*
and **b** fruit with perseverance. **Lk 8:15** *2592*
men down with burdens hard to **b**, **Lk 11:46** *1419*
NOT STEAL, DO NOT **B** FALSE WITNESS, **Lk 18:20** *5576*
in Me that does not **b** fruit, **Jn 15:2** *5342*
it so that it may **b** more fruit. **Jn 15:2** *5342*
branch cannot **b** fruit of itself unless **Jn 15:4** *5342*
this, that you **b** much fruit, **Jn 15:8** *5342*
that you would go and **b** fruit, **Jn 15:16** *5342*
to you, but you cannot **b** *them* now. **Jn 16:12** *941*
to **b** My name before the Gentiles **Ac 9:15** *941*
"Of Him all the prophets **b** **Ac 10:43** *3140*
nor we have been able to **b**? **Ac 15:10** *941*
But if you **b** the name **Ro 2:17** *2028*
that we might **b** fruit for God. **Ro 7:4** *2592*
of our body to **b** fruit for death. **Ro 7:5** *2592*
does not **b** the sword for nothing; **Ro 13:4** *5409*
Now we who are strong ought to **b** **Ro 15:1** *941*
also **b** the image of the heavenly. **1Co 15:49** *5409*
I wish that you would **b** with me in **2Co 11:1** *430*
accepted, you **b** *this* beautifully. **2Co 11:4** *430*
For I **b** you witness that, if **Ga 4:15** *3140*
BARREN WOMAN WHO DOES NOT **B**; **Ga 4:27** *5088*
you will **b** his judgment, **Ga 5:10** *941*
B one another's burdens, and thereby **Ga 6:2** *941*
For each one will **b** his own load. **Ga 6:5** *941*
for I **b** on my body the brand-marks **Ga 6:17** *941*
widows to get married, **b** children, **1Tm 5:14** *5041*
once to **b** the sins of many, **Heb 9:28** *399*
For they could not **b** the command, **Heb 12:20** *5342*
b with this word of exhortation, **Heb 13:22** *430*
his feet were like *those* of a **b**, **Rv 13:2** *715*

BEARD

infection on the head or on the **b**, **Lv 13:29** 2206
leprosy of the head or of the **b**. **Lv 13:30** 2206
head and his **b** and his eyebrows, **Lv 14:9** 2206
nor harm the edges of your **b**. **Lv 19:27** 2206
b and struck him and killed him. **1Sa 17:35** 2206
his saliva run down into his **b**. **1Sa 21:13** 2206
And Joab took Amasa by the **b** with **2Sa 20:9** 2206
of the hair from my head and my **b**, **Ezr 9:3** 2206
the head, Coming down upon the **b**, **Ps 133:2** 2206
upon the beard, *Even* Aaron's **b**, **Ps 133:2** 2206
and it will also remove the **b**. **Is 7:20** 2206
is bald *and* every **b** is cut off. **Is 15:2** 2206
to those who pluck out the **b**; **Is 50:6** 4803
is bald and every **b** cut short; **Jer 48:37** 2206
barber's razor on your head and **b**. **Ezk 5:1** 2206

BEARDS

shave off the edges of their **b**, **Lv 21:5** 2206
and shaved off half of their **b**, **2Sa 10:4** 2206
"Stay at Jericho until your **b** grow, **2Sa 10:5** 2206
"Stay at Jericho until your **b** grow, **1Ch 19:5** 2206
and from Samaria with their **b** **Jer 41:5** 2206

BEARER

to the young man, his armor **b**, **Jg 9:54** 5375
His armor **b** said to him, **1Sa 14:7** 5375
Jonathan and his armor **b** and said, **1Sa 14:12** 5375
And Jonathan said to his armor **b**, **1Sa 14:12** 5375
feet, with his armor **b** behind him; **1Sa 14:13** 5375
and his armor **b** put some to death **1Sa 14:13** 5375
which Jonathan and his armor **b** made **1Sa 14:14** 5375
and his armor **b** were not *there.* **1Sa 14:17** 5375
and he became his armor **b**. **1Sa 16:21** 5375
Then Saul said to his armor **b**, **1Sa 31:4** 5375
But his armor **b** would not, for he **1Sa 31:4** 5375
armor **b** saw that Saul was dead, **1Sa 31:5** 5375
with his three sons, his armor **b**, **1Sa 31:6** 5375
Then Saul said to his armor **b**, **1Ch 10:4** 5375
But his armor **b** would not, for he **1Ch 10:4** 5375
armor **b** saw that Saul was dead, **1Ch 10:5** 5375
b of Joab the son of Zeruiah, **1Ch 11:39** 5375
mountain, O Zion, **b** of good news, **Is 40:9** 1319
O Jerusalem, **b** of good news; **Is 40:9** 1319

BEARERS

that when the **b** of the ark of the **2Sa 6:13** 5375
b of Joab the son of Zeruiah, **2Sa 23:37** 5375
They were also over the burden **b**, **2Ch 34:13** 5449
of the burden **b** is failing, **Ne 4:10** 5449
and the **b** came to a halt. **Lk 7:14** *941*

BEARING

earth **b** fruit after their kind **Gn 1:11** 6213a
their kind, and trees **b** fruit with **Gn 1:12** 6213a
has prevented me from **b** *children.* **Gn 16:2** 3205
Then she stopped **b**. **Gn 29:35** 3205
Leah saw that she had stopped **b**, **Gn 30:9** 3205
with their camels **b** aromatic gum **Gn 37:25** 5375
b poisonous fruit and wormwood. **Dt 29:18** 6509
Judah, **b** large shields and spears, **2Ch 14:8** 5375
b shields and wielding bows; **2Ch 14:8** 5375
I am weary of **b** *them.* **Is 1:14** 5375
and He went out, **b** His own cross, **Jn 19:17** *941*
their conscience **b** witness and **Ro 2:15** *4828*
but indeed you are **b** with me. **2Co 11:1** *430*
b children who are to be slaves; **Ga 4:24** *1080*
constantly **b** fruit and increasing, **Col 1:6** *2592*
b fruit in every good work and **Col 1:10** *2592*
b with one another, and forgiving **Col 3:13** *430*
constantly **b** in mind your work of **1Th 1:3** *3421*
be preserved through the **b** of children **1Tm 2:15** *5042*
outside the camp, **b** His reproach. **Heb 13:13** *5342*
of life, **b** twelve *kinds of* fruit, **Rv 22:2** *4160*

BEARS

"What if Joseph **b** a grudge against **Gn 50:15** 7852
and she **b** him sons or daughters, **Ex 21:4** 3205
gives birth and **b** a male *child,* **Lv 12:2** 3205
'But if she **b** a female *child,* then **Lv 12:5** 3205
is the law for her who **b** *a child,* **Lv 12:7** 3205
his sister's nakedness; he **b** his guilt. **Lv 20:17** 5375
firstborn whom she **b** shall assume **Dt 25:6** 3205
toward her children whom she **b**; **Dt 28:57** 3205
Then two female **b** came out of the **2Ki 2:24** 1677
the Lord, who daily **b** our burden, **Ps 68:19** 6006
Is a man who **b** false witness against **Pr 25:18** 6030a
faces **b** witness against them, **Is 3:9** 6030a
All of us growl like **b**, **Is 59:11** 1677
"So every good tree **b** good fruit, **Mt 7:17** *4160*
but the bad tree **b** bad fruit. **Mt 7:17** *4160*
who indeed **b** fruit and brings **Mt 13:23** *2592*
and if it **b** fruit next year, *fine* **Lk 13:9** *4160*
but if it dies, it **b** much fruit. **Jn 12:24** *5342*
and every *branch* that **b** fruit, **Jn 15:2** *5342*
Me and I in him, he **b** much fruit **Jn 15:5** *5342*
b all things, believes all things, **1Co 13:7** *4722*
a person **b** up under sorrows when **1Pe 2:19** *5297*

BEAST

and to every **b** of the earth and to **Gn 1:30** 2421b
LORD God formed every **b** of the field **Gn 2:19** 2421b
sky, and to every **b** of the field, **Gn 2:20** 2421b
serpent was more crafty than any **b** **Gn 3:1** 2421b
more than every **b** of the field; **Gn 3:14** 2421b
they and every **b** after its kind, **Gn 7:14** 2421b
Every **b**, every creeping thing, and **Gn 8:19** 2421b
the terror of you will be on every **b** **Gn 9:2** 2421b
from every **b** I will require it. **Gn 9:5** 2421b
and every **b** of the earth with you; **Gn 9:10** 2421b
ark, even every **b** of the earth. **Gn 9:10** 2421b
'A wild **b** devoured him.' **Gn 37:20** 2421b
A wild **b** has devoured him; **Gn 37:33** 2421b
and there were gnats on man and **b**. **Ex 8:17** 929
so there were gnats on man and **b**. **Ex 8:18** 929
b through all the land of Egypt." **Ex 9:9** 929
out with sores on man and **b**. **Ex 9:10** 929
Every man and **b** that is found in **Ex 9:19** 929
on man and on **b** and on every plant **Ex 9:22** 929
the land of Egypt, both man and **b**; **Ex 9:25** 929
bark, whether against man or **b**, **Ex 11:7** 929
the land of Egypt, both man and **b**; **Ex 12:12** 929
sons of Israel, both of man and **b**; **Ex 13:2** 929
offspring of every **b** that you own; **Ex 13:12** 929
of man and the firstborn of **b**. **Ex 13:15** 929
whether **b** or man, he shall not **Ex 19:13** 929
leave the **b** of the field may eat. **Ex 23:11** 2421b
whether a carcass of an unclean **b** or **Lv 5:2** 2421b
a **b** or a bird which may be eaten, **Lv 17:13** 2421b
in Israel, from man to **b**. **Nu 3:13** 929
the prey, both of man and of **b**. **Nu 31:11** 929
and in the offspring of your **b** **Dt 28:11** 929
by a wild **b** that was in Lebanon, **2Ki 14:9** 2421b
by a wild **b** that was in Lebanon and **2Ch 25:18** 2421b
"Then the **b** goes into its lair And **Jb 37:8** 2421b
Or that a wild **b** may trample them. **Jb 39:15** 2421b
O LORD, You preserve man and **b**. **Ps 36:6** 929
"For every **b** of the forest is **Ps 50:10** 2421b
I was *like* a **b** before You. **Ps 73:22** 929
of Your turtledove to the wild **b**; **Ps 74:19** 2421b
drink to every **b** of the field; **Ps 104:11** 2421b
of Egypt, Both of man and **b**. **Ps 135:8** 929
He gives to the **b** its food, *And* to **Ps 147:9** 929
is no advantage for man over **b**, **Ec 3:19** 929
breath of the **b** descends downward **Ec 3:21** 929
will any vicious **b** go up on it; **Is 35:9** 2421b
A load for the weary **b**. **Is 46:1**
on man and on **b** and on the trees **Jer 7:20** 929
of this city, both man and **b**; **Jer 21:6** 929
of man and with the seed of **b**. **Jer 31:27** 929
is a desolation, without man or **b**; **Jer 32:43** 929
without man and without **b**," **Jer 33:10** 929
without inhabitant and without **b**, **Jer 33:10** 929
which is waste, without man or **b**, **Jer 33:12** 929
man and **b** to cease from it?' " **Jer 36:29** 929
Both man and **b** have wandered off, **Jer 50:3** 929
dwelling in it, whether man or **b**, **Jer 51:62** 929
cut off from it both man and **b**, **Ezk 14:13** 929
and cut off man and **b** from it,' **Ezk 14:17** 929
it to cut off man and **b** from it, **Ezk 14:19** 929
to cut off man and **b** from it! **Ezk 14:21** 929
and cut off man and **b** from it. **Ezk 25:13** 929
will cut off from you man and **b**. **Ezk 29:8** 929
of a **b** will not pass through it, **Ezk 29:11** 929
and they became food for every **b** **Ezk 34:5** 2421b
I will multiply on you man and **b**; **Ezk 36:11** 929
predatory bird and **b** of the field. **Ezk 39:4** 2421b
bird and to every **b** of the field, **Ezk 39:17** 2421b
The priests shall not eat any bird or **b** **Ezk 44:31** 929
"And behold, another **b**, **Da 7:5** 2423
the **b** also had four heads, and **Da 7:6** 2423
visions, and behold, a fourth **b**, **Da 7:7** 2423
looking until the **b** was slain, **Da 7:11** 2423
the exact meaning of the fourth **b**, **Da 7:19** 2423
'The fourth **b** will be a fourth **Da 7:23** 2423
As a wild **b** would tear them. **Hos 13:8** 2421b
Do not let man, **b**, herd, or flock **Jon 3:7** 929
"But both man and **b** must be **Jon 3:8** 929
"I will remove man and **b**; **Zph 1:3** 929
THE FOAL OF A **B** OF BURDEN.' " **Mt 21:5** *5268*
and he put him on his own **b**, **Lk 10:34** *2934*
"IF EVEN A **B** TOUCHES THE **Heb 12:20** *2342*
the **b** that comes up out of the **Rv 11:7** *2342*
saw a **b** coming up out of the sea, **Rv 13:1** *2342*
And the **b** which I saw was like a **Rv 13:2** *2342*
amazed *and followed* after the **b**; **Rv 13:3** *2342*
he gave his authority to the **b**; **Rv 13:4** *2342*
and they worshiped the **b**, **Rv 13:4** *2342*
"Who is like the **b**, and who is **Rv 13:4** *2342*
b coming up out of the earth; **Rv 13:11** *2342*
of the first **b** in his presence. **Rv 13:12** *2342*
in it to worship the first **b**, **Rv 13:12** *2342*
perform in the presence of the **b**, **Rv 13:14** *2342*
an image to the **b** who had the wound **Rv 13:14** *2342*
give breath to the image of the **b**, **Rv 13:15** *2342*
that the image of the **b** would even **Rv 13:15** *2342*
the image of the **b** to be killed. **Rv 13:15** *2342*
the **b** or the number of his name. **Rv 13:17** *2342*
calculate the number of the **b**, **Rv 13:18** *2342*
worships the **b** and his image, **Rv 14:9** *2342*
who worship the **b** and his image, **Rv 14:11** *2342*
been victorious over the **b** and **Rv 15:2** *2342*
the people who had the mark of the **b** **Rv 16:2** *2342*
his bowl on the throne of the **b** **Rv 16:10** *2342*
dragon and out of the mouth of the **b** **Rv 16:13** *2342*

a woman sitting on a scarlet **b**, Rv 17:3 2342
and of the **b** that carries her, Rv 17:7 2342
"The **b** that you saw was, and is not, Rv 17:8 2342
will wonder when they see the **b**, Rv 17:8 2342
"The **b** which was and is not, Rv 17:11 2342
as kings with the **b** for one hour. Rv 17:12 2342
power and authority to the **b**. Rv 17:13 2342
horns which you saw, and the **b**, Rv 17:16 2342
by giving their kingdom to the **b**, Rv 17:17 2342
And I saw the **b** and the kings of Rv 19:19 2342
And the **b** was seized, and with him Rv 19:20 2342
who had received the mark of the **b** Rv 19:20 2342
not worshiped the **b** or his image, Rv 20:4 2342
where the **b** and the false prophet Rv 20:10 2342

BEAST'S
And let a **b** mind be given to him, Da 4:16 2423

BEASTS
b of the earth after their kind"; Gn 1:24 2421b
b of the earth after their kind, Gn 1:25 2421b
birds and cattle and **b** and every Gn 7:21 2421b
God remembered Noah and all the **b** Gn 8:1 2421b
"That which was torn *of* **b** I did Gn 31:39
b and go to the land of Canaan, Gn 45:17 1165
and the **b** of the field become too Ex 23:29 2421b
and the fat of an animal torn *by* **b**, Lv 7:24
animal which dies or is torn *by* **b**, Lv 17:15
animal which dies or is torn *by* **b**, Lv 22:8
eliminate harmful **b** from the land, Lv 26:6 2421b
among you the **b** of the field, Lv 26:22 2421b
for us and our **b** to die here? Nu 20:4 1165
congregation and their **b** drink." Nu 20:8 1165
congregation and their **b** drank. Nu 20:11 1165
their herds and for all their **b**. Nu 35:3 2421b
wild **b** would grow too numerous Dt 7:22 2421b
and the offspring of your **b**, Dt 28:4 929
the sky and to the **b** of the earth, Dt 28:26 929
teeth of **b** I will send upon them, Dt 32:24 929
the sky and the **b** of the field." 1Sa 17:44 929
sky and the wild **b** of the earth, 1Sa 17:46 2421b
nor the **b** of the field by night. 2Sa 21:10 2421b
you and your cattle and your **b**. 2Ki 3:17 929
will not be afraid of wild **b**. Jb 5:22 2421b
And the **b** of the field will be at Jb 5:23 2421b
"But now ask the **b**, and let them Jb 12:7 929
"Why are we regarded as **b**, Jb 18:3 929
"The proud **b** have not trodden it, Jb 28:8 1121
us more than the **b** of the earth And Jb 35:11 929
all the **b** of the field play there. Jb 40:20 2421b
oxen, And also the **b** of the field, Ps 8:7 929
He is like the **b** that perish. Ps 49:12 929
Is like the **b** that perish. Ps 49:20 929
to You burnt offerings of fat **b**, Ps 66:15 4220
Rebuke the **b** in the reeds, The Ps 68:30 2421b
godly ones to the **b** of the earth. Ps 79:2 2421b
the **b** of the forest prowl about. Ps 104:20 2421b
B and all cattle; Ps 148:10 2421b
The lion *which* is mighty among **b** Pr 30:30 929
them to see that they are but **b**." Ec 3:18 929
men and the fate of **b** is the same. Ec 3:19 929
prey, And for the **b** of the earth; Is 18:6 929
And all the **b** of the earth will Is 18:6 929
concerning the **b** of the Negev. Is 30:6 929
its **b** enough for a burnt offering. Is 40:16 2421b
b of the field will glorify Me, Is 43:20 2421b
consigned to the **b** and the cattle. Is 46:1 2421b
All you **b** of the field, All you Is 56:9 2421b
field, All you **b** in the forest, Is 56:9 2421b
sky and for the **b** of the earth; Jer 7:33 929
of the sky and the **b** have fled; Jer 9:10 929
Go, gather all the **b** of the field, Jer 12:9 2421b
b of the earth to devour and destroy. Jer 15:3 929
sky and for the **b** of the earth." Jer 16:4 929
of the sky and the **b** of the earth. Jer 19:7 929
the men and the **b** which are on the Jer 27:5 929
him the **b** of the field. Jer 28:14 2421b
of the sky and the **b** of the earth. Jer 34:20 929
died of itself or was torn by **b**, Ezk 4:14 2966
send on you famine and wild **b**, Ezk 5:17 2421b
and **b** *and* detestable things, Ezk 8:10 929
wild **b** to pass through the land and Ezk 14:15 2421b
pass through it because of the **b**, Ezk 14:15 2421b
sword, famine, wild **b** and Ezk 14:21 2421b
given you for food to the **b** of the earth Ezk 29:5 2421b
all the **b** of the field gave birth, Ezk 31:6 2421b
and all the **b** of the field will be Ezk 31:13 2421b
the **b** of the whole earth with you. Ezk 32:4 2421b
hoofs of **b** will not muddy them. Ezk 32:13 929
will give to the **b** to be devoured, Ezk 33:27 2421b
become food for all the **b** of the field Ezk 34:8 2421b
eliminate harmful **b** from the land so Ezk 34:25 2421b
and the **b** of the earth will not Ezk 34:28 2421b
the heavens, the **b** of the field, Ezk 38:20 2421b
men dwell, *or* the **b** of the field, Da 2:38 2423
The **b** of the field found shade Da 4:12 2423
Let the **b** flee from under it And Da 4:14 2423
the **b** in the grass of the earth. Da 4:15 2423
under which the **b** of the field Da 4:21 2423
and let him share with the **b** of Da 4:23 2423
place be with the **b** of the field, Da 4:25 2423
will be with the **b** of the field. Da 4:32 2423
his heart was made like *that of* **b**, Da 5:21 2423
b were coming up from the sea, Da 7:3 2423
all the **b** that were before it, Da 7:7 2423
"As for the rest of the **b**, Da 7:12 2423
'These great **b**, which are four *in* Da 7:17 2423
no *other* **b** could stand before him nor Da 8:4 2421b
b of the field will devour them. Hos 2:12 2421b
for them With the **b** of the field, Hos 2:18 2421b
Along with the **b** of the field and Hos 4:3 2421b
b groan! The herds of cattle wander Jl 1:18 929
the **b** of the field pant for You; Jl 1:20 929
Do not fear, **b** of the field, For Jl 2:22 929
a lion among the **b** of the forest, Mi 5:8 929
its **b** by which you terrified them, Hab 2:17 929
midst, All **b** which range in herds; Zph 2:14 2421b
desolation, A resting place for **b**! Zph 2:15 2421b
And He was with the wild **b**, Mk 1:13 2342
wild **b** and the crawling creatures Ac 11:6 2342
I fought with wild **b** at Ephesus, 1Co 15:32 2341
of men, and another flesh of **b**, 1Co 15:39 2934
"Cretans are always liars, evil **b**, Ti 1:12 2342
For every species of **b** and birds, Jas 3:7 2342
and by the wild **b** of the earth. Rv 6:8 2342

BEAT
You shall **b** some of it very fine, Ex 30:36 7833
millstones or **b** *it* in the mortar, Nu 11:8 1743
and **b** them down as far as Hormah. Nu 14:45 3807
"When you **b** your olive tree, you Dt 24:20 2251
may **b** him forty times *but* no more, Dt 25:3 5221
he does not **b** him with many more Dt 25:3 5221
horses' hoofs **b** From the dashing, Jg 5:22 1986
she **b** out what she had gleaned, Ru 2:17 2251
b the Asherim and the carved images 2Ch 34:7 3807
Then I **b** them fine as the dust Ps 18:42 7833
"They **b** me, *but* I did not know *it*. Pr 23:35 1986
"You have made my heart **b** faster, SS 4:9 3823a
You have made my heart **b** faster SS 4:9 3823a
B your breasts for the pleasant Is 32:12 5594
were angry at Jeremiah and **b** him, Jer 37:15 5221
B your plowshares into swords And Jl 3:10 3807
and the sun **b** down on Jonah's head Jon 4:8 5221
took his slaves and **b** one, Mt 21:35 1194
and begins to **b** his fellow Mt 24:49 5180
face and **b** Him with their fists; Mt 26:67 2852
and *began* to **b** Him on the head. Mt 27:30 5180
"They took him, and **b** him and Mk 12:3 1194
and to **b** Him with their fists, Mk 14:65 2852
and they stripped him and **b** him, Lk 10:30
2007, 4127
and begins to **b** the slaves, Lk 12:45 5180
but the vine-growers **b** him and Lk 20:10 1194
and they **b** him also and treated Lk 20:11 1194
and **b** those who believed in You. Ac 22:19 1194
will the sun **b** down on them, Rv 7:16 4098

BEATEN
over them, were **b** and were asked, Ex 5:14 5221
behold, your servants are being **b**; Ex 5:16 5221
oil of **b** olives for the light, Ex 27:20 3795
with one-fourth of a hin of **b** oil, Ex 29:40 3795
oil from **b** olives for the light, Lv 24:2 3795
with a fourth of a hin of **b** oil. Nu 28:5 3795
the wicked man deserves to be **b**, Dt 25:2 5221
lie down and be **b** in his presence Dt 25:2 5221
pretended to be **b** before them, Jos 8:15 5060
b before the servants of David. 2Sa 2:17 5062
and twenty kors of **b** oil; 1Ki 5:11 3795
made 200 large shields of **b** gold, 1Ki 10:16 7819
He made 300 shields of **b** gold, 1Ki 10:17 7819
made 200 large shields of **b** gold, 2Ch 9:15 7819
of **b** gold on each large shield. 2Ch 9:15 7819
He made 300 shields of **b** gold, 2Ch 9:16 7819
But dill is **b** out with a rod, and Is 28:27 2251
B silver is brought from Tarshish, Jer 10:9 7554
had Jeremiah the prophet **b** and Jer 20:2 5221
"We have been **b** down, but we will Mal 1:4 7567
to order *them* to be **b** with rods. Ac 16:22 4463
have **b** us in public without trial, Ac 16:37 1194
b times without number, 2Co 11:23 4127
Three times I was **b** with rods, 2Co 11:25 4463

BEATING
and he saw an Egyptian **b** a Hebrew, Ex 2:11 5221
his son Gideon was **b** out wheat Jg 6:11 2251
of the maidens **b** tambourines. Ps 68:25 8608
of doves, **B** on their breasts. Na 2:7 8608
and *so with* many others, **b** some and Mk 12:5 1194
They kept **b** His head with a reed, Mk 15:19 5180
to heaven, but was **b** his breast, Lk 18:13 5180
were mocking Him and **b** Him, Lk 22:63 1194
began to return, **b** their breasts. Lk 23:48 5180
and *began* **b** him in front of the Ac 18:17 5180
the soldiers, they stopped **b** Paul. Ac 21:32 5180
in such a way, as not **b** the air; 1Co 9:26 1194

BEATINGS
in **b**, in imprisonments, in 2Co 6:5 4127

BEATS
encourages him who **b** the anvil, Is 41:7 1986

BEAUTIFICATION
their **b** were completed as follows: Es 2:12 4795

BEAUTIFUL
that the daughters of men were **b**; Gn 6:2 2896a
I know that you are a **b** woman; Gn 12:11 3303
saw that the woman was very **b**. Gn 12:14 3303
The girl was very **b**, Gn 24:16 2896a
of Rebekah, for she is **b**." Gn 26:7 2896a
but Rachel was **b** of form and face. Gn 29:17 3303
a doe let loose, He gives **b** words. Gn 49:21 8233
and when she saw that he was **b**, Ex 2:2 2896a
yourselves the foliage of **b** trees, Lv 23:40 1926
see among the captives a **b** woman, Dt 21:11 3303
when I saw among the spoil a **b** Jos 7:21 2896a
younger sister more **b** than she? Jg 15:2 2896a
with **b** eyes and a handsome 1Sa 16:12 3303
intelligent and **b** in appearance, 1Sa 25:3 3303
woman was very **b** in appearance. 2Sa 11:2 2896a
a **b** sister whose name was Tamar, 2Sa 13:1 3303
she was a woman of **b** appearance. 2Sa 14:27 3303
So they searched for a **b** girl 1Ki 1:3 3303
The girl was very **b**; 1Ki 1:4 3303
your most **b** wives and children are 1Ki 20:3 2896a
and the princes, for she was **b**. Es 1:11 2896a
"Let **b** young virgins be sought Es 2:2 2896a
may gather every **b** young virgin Es 2:3 2896a
young lady was **b** of form and face, Es 2:7 3303
Indeed, my heritage is **b** to me. Ps 16:6 8231b
B in elevation, the joy of the Ps 48:2 3303
is a **b** woman who lacks discretion. Pr 11:22 3303
do not know, Most **b** among women, SS 1:8 3303
"How **b** you are, my darling, How SS 1:15 3303
are, my darling, How **b** you are! SS 1:15 3303
'Arise, my darling, my **b** one, SS 2:10 3303
Arise, my darling, my **b** one, SS 2:13 3303
"How **b** you are, my darling, How SS 4:1 3303
are, my darling, How **b** you are! SS 4:1 3303
"You are altogether **b**, SS 4:7 3303
"How **b** is your love, my sister, SS 4:10 3302
beloved, O most **b** among women? SS 5:9 3303
gone, O most **b** among women? SS 6:1 3303
"You are as **b** as Tirzah, my SS 6:4 3303
the dawn, As **b** as the full moon, SS 6:10 3303
"How **b** are your feet in sandals, SS 7:1 3302
"How **b** and how delightful you SS 7:6 3302
And against all the **b** craft. Is 2:16 2532
the LORD will be **b** and glorious, Is 4:2 6643a
LORD of hosts will become a **b** crown Is 28:5 6643a
yourself in your **b** garments, Is 52:1 8597
Our holy and **b** house, Where our Is 64:11 8597
b inheritance of the nations!' Jer 3:19 6643a
In vain you make yourself **b**. Jer 4:30 3302
olive tree, **b** in fruit and form"; Jer 11:16 3303
For your **b** crown Has come down Jer 13:18 8597
that was given you, Your **b** sheep? Jer 13:20 8597
ears and a **b** crown on your head. Ezk 16:12 8597
b and advanced to royalty. Ezk 16:13 3302
"You also took your **b** jewels *made* Ezk 16:17 8597
and take away your **b** jewels. Ezk 23:26 8597
women and **b** crowns on their heads. Ezk 23:42 8597
With **b** branches and forest shade, Ezk 31:3 3303
'So it was **b** in its greatness, in Ezk 31:7 3302
'I made it **b** with the multitude of Ezk 31:9 3303
who has a **b** voice and plays well Ezk 33:32 3303
was **b** and its fruit abundant, Da 4:12 8209
was **b** and its fruit abundant, Da 4:21 8209
the east, and toward the **B** *Land*. Da 8:9 6643a
stay *for a time* in the **B** Land, Da 11:16 6643a
"He will also enter the **B** Land, Da 11:41 6643a
the seas and the **b** Holy Mountain; Da 11:45 6643a
"In that day the **b** virgins And Am 8:13 3303
which on the outside appear **b**, Mt 23:27 5611
with **b** stones and votive gifts, Lk 21:5 2570
of the temple which is called **B**, Ac 3:2 5611
one who used to sit at the **B** Gate Ac 3:10 5611
HOW **B** ARE THE FEET OF THOSE WHO Ro 10:15 5611
because they saw he was a **b** child; Heb 11:23 791

BEAUTIFULLY
not accepted, you bear *this* **b**. 2Co 11:4 2573

BEAUTIFY
He will **b** the afflicted ones with Ps 149:4 6286
To **b** the place of My sanctuary; Is 60:13 6286

BEAUTY
your brother, for glory and for **b**. Ex 28:2 8597
for them, for glory and for **b**. Ex 28:40 8597
"Your **b**, O Israel, is slain on 2Sa 1:19 6643a
b to the people and the princes, Es 1:11 3308
life, To behold the **b** of the LORD And Ps 27:4 5278
Then the King will desire your **b**. Ps 45:11 3308
Out of Zion, the perfection of **b**, Ps 50:2 3308
and **b** are in His sanctuary. Ps 96:6 8597
present you with a crown of **b**." Pr 4:9 8597
Do not desire her **b** in your heart, Pr 6:25 3308
Charm is deceitful and **b** is vain, Pr 31:30 3308
take away the **b** of *their* anklets, Is 3:18 8597
And branding instead of **b**. Is 3:24 3308
And Babylon, the **b** of kingdoms, Is 13:19 6643a
it, to defile the pride of all **b**, Is 23:9 6643a
fading flower of its glorious **b**, Is 28:1 6643a
fading flower of its glorious **b**, Is 28:4 6643a
eyes will see the King in His **b**; Is 33:17 3308
form of a man, like the **b** of man, Is 44:13 8597
of **b** in the hand of the LORD, Is 62:3 8597
'The perfection of **b**, La 2:15 3308
the **b** of His ornaments into pride, Ezk 7:20 6643a
the nations on account of your **b**, Ezk 16:14 3308
"But you trusted in your **b** and Ezk 16:15 3308
and made your **b** abominable, Ezk 16:25 3308
'I am perfect in **b**.' Ezk 27:3 3308
builders have perfected your **b**. Ezk 27:4 3308
they perfected your **b**. Ezk 27:11 3308
swords Against the **b** of your wisdom Ezk 28:7 3308
Full of wisdom and perfect in **b**. Ezk 28:12 3308
was lifted up because of your **b**; Ezk 28:17 3308
could compare with it in its **b**. Ezk 31:8 3308
'Whom do you surpass in **b**? Ezk 32:19 5276
his **b** will be like the olive tree And Hos 14:6 1935
comeliness and **b** *will be* theirs! Zch 9:17 3308
and the **b** of its appearance is Jas 1:11 2143

BEBAI
the sons of **B**, 623; Ezr 2:11 893
and of the sons of **B**, Ezr 8:11 893
son of **B** and 28 males with him; Ezr 8:11 893
and of the sons of **B**: Ezr 10:28 893
the sons of **B**, 628; Ne 7:16 893
Bunni, Azgad, **B**, Ne 10:15 893

BECAME

and man **b** a living being.	**Gn 2:7**	1961
it divided and **b** four rivers.	**Gn 2:10**	1961
So Cain **b** very angry and his	**Gn 4:5**	2734
and Irad **b** the father of Mehujael,	**Gn 4:18**	3205
Mehujael **b** the father of Methushael,	**Gn 4:18**	3205
Methushael **b** the father of Lamech.	**Gn 4:18**	3205
he **b** the father of *a son* in his	**Gn 5:3**	3205
Then the days of Adam after he **b**	**Gn 5:4**	3205
years, and **b** the father of Enosh.	**Gn 5:6**	3205
after he **b** the father of Enosh,	**Gn 5:7**	3205
years, and **b** the father of Kenan.	**Gn 5:9**	3205
after he **b** the father of Kenan,	**Gn 5:10**	3205
and **b** the father of Mahalalel.	**Gn 5:12**	3205
he **b** the father of Mahalalel,	**Gn 5:13**	3205
years, and **b** the father of Jared.	**Gn 5:15**	3205
after he **b** the father of Jared,	**Gn 5:16**	3205
years, and **b** the father of Enoch.	**Gn 5:18**	3205
after he **b** the father of Enoch,	**Gn 5:19**	3205
and **b** the father of Methuselah.	**Gn 5:21**	3205
he **b** the father of Methuselah,	**Gn 5:22**	3205
years, and **b** the father of Lamech.	**Gn 5:25**	3205
after he **b** the father of Lamech,	**Gn 5:26**	3205
years, and **b** the father of a son.	**Gn 5:28**	3205
after he **b** the father of Noah,	**Gn 5:30**	3205
and Noah **b** the father of Shem,	**Gn 5:32**	3205
Noah **b** the father of three sons:	**Gn 6:10**	3205
tops of the mountains **b** visible.	**Gn 8:5**	7200
He drank of the wine and **b** drunk,	**Gn 9:21**	7937
Now Cush **b** the father of Nimrod;	**Gn 10:8**	3205
he **b** a mighty one on the earth.	**Gn 10:8**	2490c, 1961
Mizraim **b** the father of Ludim	**Gn 10:13**	3205
Canaan **b** the father of Sidon,	**Gn 10:15**	3205
Arpachshad **b** the father of Shelah;	**Gn 10:24**	3205
and Shelah **b** the father of Eber.	**Gn 10:24**	3205
Joktan **b** the father of Almodad	**Gn 10:26**	3205
and **b** the father of Arpachshad two	**Gn 11:10**	3205
he **b** the father of Arpachshad,	**Gn 11:11**	3205
years, and **b** the father of Shelah;	**Gn 11:12**	3205
after he **b** the father of Shelah,	**Gn 11:13**	3205
years, and **b** the father of Eber;	**Gn 11:14**	3205
after he **b** the father of Eber,	**Gn 11:15**	3205
years, and **b** the father of Peleg;	**Gn 11:16**	3205
after he **b** the father of Peleg,	**Gn 11:17**	3205
years, and **b** the father of Reu;	**Gn 11:18**	3205
after he **b** the father of Reu,	**Gn 11:19**	3205
years, and **b** the father of Serug;	**Gn 11:20**	3205
after he **b** the father of Serug,	**Gn 11:21**	3205
years, and **b** the father of Nahor;	**Gn 11:22**	3205
after he **b** the father of Nahor,	**Gn 11:23**	3205
years, and **b** the father of Terah;	**Gn 11:24**	3205
after he **b** the father of Terah,	**Gn 11:25**	3205
years, and **b** the father of Abram,	**Gn 11:26**	3205
Terah **b** the father of Abram, Nahor	**Gn 11:27**	3205
and Haran **b** the father of Lot.	**Gn 11:27**	3205
and she **b** a pillar of salt.	**Gn 19:26**	1961
of my mother, and she **b** my wife;	**Gn 20:12**	1961
the wilderness and **b** an archer.	**Gn 21:20**	1961
Bethuel **b** the father of Rebekah;	**Gn 22:23**	3205
took Rebekah, and she **b** his wife,	**Gn 24:67**	1961
b the father of Sheba and Dedan.	**Gn 25:3**	3205
Abraham **b** the father of Isaac;	**Gn 25:19**	3205
grew up, Esau **b** a skillful hunter,	**Gn 25:27**	1961
and the man **b** rich, and continued	**Gn 26:13**	1431
richer until he **b** very wealthy;	**Gn 26:13**	1431
she **b** jealous of her sister;	**Gn 30:1**	7065
the man **b** exceedingly prosperous,	**Gn 30:43**	6555
Then Jacob **b** angry and contended	**Gn 31:36**	2734
of Bozrah **b** king in his place.	**Gn 36:33**	4427a
the Temanites **b** king in his place.	**Gn 36:34**	4427a
of Moab, **b** king in his place;	**Gn 36:35**	4427a
of Masrekah **b** king in his place.	**Gn 36:36**	4427a
River **b** king in his place.	**Gn 36:37**	4427a
son of Achbor **b** king in his place.	**Gn 36:38**	4427a
and Hadar **b** king in his place;	**Gn 36:39**	4427a
Joseph, so he **b** a successful man.	**Gn 39:2**	1961
sight and **b** his personal servant;	**Gn 39:4**	8334
"For your servant **b** surety for	**Gn 44:32**	6148
Thus the land **b** Pharaoh's.	**Gn 47:20**	1961
were fruitful and **b** very numerous.	**Gn 47:27**	7235a
And **b** a slave at forced labor.	**Gn 49:15**	1961
and **b** exceedingly mighty,	**Ex 1:7**	6105a
multiplied, and **b** very mighty.	**Ex 1:20**	6105a
daughter and he **b** her son.	**Ex 2:10**	1961
on the ground, and it **b** a serpent;	**Ex 4:3**	1961
it, and it **b** a staff in his hand	**Ex 4:4**	1961
his servants, and it **b** a serpent.	**Ex 7:10**	1961
Nile died, and the Nile **b** foul,	**Ex 7:21**	887
in heaps, and the land **b** foul.	**Ex 8:14**	887
All the dust of the earth **b** gnats	**Ex 8:17**	1961
and it **b** boils breaking out with	**Ex 9:10**	1961
land of Egypt since it **b** a nation.	**Ex 9:24**	1961
them, and they **b** very frightened;	**Ex 14:10**	3372a
waters, and the waters **b** sweet.	**Ex 15:25**	4985
and it bred worms and **b** foul;	**Ex 16:20**	887
Now the people **b** like those who	**Nu 11:1**	1961
and we **b** like grasshoppers in our	**Nu 13:33**	1961
Then Moses **b** very angry and said	**Nu 16:15**	2734
and the people **b** impatient because	**Nu 21:4**	7114a
250 men, so that they **b** a warning.	**Nu 26:10**	1961
and Machir **b** the father of Gilead:	**Nu 26:29**	3205
Kohath **b** the father of Amram.	**Nu 26:58**	3205
but there he **b** a great, mighty and	**Dt 26:5**	1961
the people melted and **b** as water.	**Jos 7:5**	1961
So they **b** hewers of wood and	**Jos 9:21**	1961
Hebron **b** the inheritance of Caleb	**Jos 14:14**	1961
day, and they **b** forced laborers.	**Jos 16:10**	1961
when the sons of Israel **b** strong,	**Jos 17:13**	2388
and they **b** the inheritance of	**Jos 24:32**	1961
came about when Israel **b** strong,	**Jg 1:28**	2388
and **b** subject to forced labor.	**Jg 1:30**	1961
Beth-anath **b** forced labor for them.	**Jg 1:33**	1961
grew strong, they **b** forced labor.	**Jg 1:35**	1961
They waited until they **b** anxious;	**Jg 3:25**	954
so that it **b** a snare to Gideon and	**Jg 8:27**	1961
Thus it **b** a custom in Israel,	**Jg 11:39**	1961
Then he **b** very thirsty, and he	**Jg 15:18**	6770
man **b** to him like one of his sons.	**Jg 17:11**	1961
and the young man **b** his priest and	**Jg 17:12**	1961
Gibeah, the battle **b** fierce;	**Jg 20:34**	3513
took Ruth, and she **b** his wife,	**Ru 4:13**	1961
him in her lap, and **b** his nurse.	**Ru 4:16**	1961
Therefore it **b** a proverb:	**1Sa 10:12**	1961
these words, and he **b** very angry.	**1Sa 11:6**	2734
so that it **b** a great trembling.	**1Sa 14:15**	1961
and he **b** his armor bearer.	**1Sa 16:21**	1961
Then Saul **b** very angry, for this	**1Sa 18:8**	2734
and he **b** captain over them.	**1Sa 22:2**	1961
Now David **b** aware that Saul had	**1Sa 23:15**	7200
him so that he **b** *as* a stone.	**1Sa 25:37**	1961
of David and **b** his wife.	**1Sa 25:42**	1961
and they both **b** his wives.	**1Sa 25:43**	1961
old when he **b** king over Israel,	**2Sa 2:10**	4427a
behind Abner and **b** one band,	**2Sa 2:25**	1961
hurry to flee, he fell and **b** lame.	**2Sa 4:4**	6452b
thirty years old when he **b** king,	**2Sa 5:4**	4427a
David **b** greater and greater,	**2Sa 5:10**	1980
David **b** angry because of the	**2Sa 6:8**	2734
the Moabites **b** servants to David,	**2Sa 8:2**	1961
the Arameans **b** servants to David,	**2Sa 8:6**	1961
the Edomites **b** servants to David.	**2Sa 8:14**	1961
Hanun his son **b** king in his place.	**2Sa 10:1**	4427a
to his house and she **b** his wife;	**2Sa 11:27**	1961
the Philistines, David **b** weary.	**2Sa 21:15**	5888
therefore he **b** their commander;	**2Sa 23:19**	1961
and she **b** the king's nurse and	**1Ki 1:4**	1961
So King Solomon **b** greater than all	**1Ki 10:23**	1431
and **b** leader of a marauding band,	**1Ki 11:24**	1961
Now this thing **b** a sin, for the	**1Ki 12:30**	1961
to him, and it **b** as it was before.	**1Ki 13:6**	1961
b sin to the house of Jeroboam,	**1Ki 13:34**	1961
Abijah the son of Jeroboam **b** sick.	**1Ki 14:1**	2470a
forty-one years old when he **b** king,	**1Ki 14:21**	4427a
his son **b** king in his place.	**1Ki 14:31**	4427a
Nebat, Abijam **b** king over Judah.	**1Ki 15:1**	4427a
Asa his son **b** king in his place.	**1Ki 15:8**	4427a
Now Nadab the son of Jeroboam **b**	**1Ki 15:25**	4427a
Baasha the son of Ahijah **b** king	**1Ki 15:33**	4427a
Elah his son **b** king in his place.	**1Ki 16:6**	4427a
b king over Israel at Tirzah,	**1Ki 16:8**	4427a
of Judah, and **b** king in his place.	**1Ki 16:10**	4427a
It came about when he **b** king,	**1Ki 16:11**	4427a
And Tibni died and Omri **b** king.	**1Ki 16:22**	4427a
of Judah, Omri **b** king over Israel	**1Ki 16:23**	4427a
Ahab his son **b** king in his place.	**1Ki 16:28**	4427a
Now Ahab the son of Omri **b** king	**1Ki 16:29**	4427a
the mistress of the house, **b** sick;	**1Ki 17:17**	2470a
his son **b** king in his place.	**1Ki 22:40**	4427a
Now Jehoshaphat the son of Asa **b**	**1Ki 22:41**	4427a
years old when he **b** king,	**1Ki 22:42**	4427a
his son **b** king in his place.	**1Ki 22:50**	4427a
Ahaziah the son of Ahab **b** king	**1Ki 22:51**	4427a
which *was* in Samaria, and **b** ill.	**2Ki 1:2**	2470a
Jehoram **b** king in his place in the	**2Ki 1:17**	4427a
Now Jehoram the son of Ahab **b** king	**2Ki 3:1**	4427a
and the flesh of the child **b** warm.	**2Ki 4:34**	2552
And Hazael **b** king in his place.	**2Ki 8:15**	4427a
Jehoshaphat king of Judah **b** king.	**2Ki 8:16**	4427a
years old when he **b** king,	**2Ki 8:17**	4427a
the daughter of Ahab **b** his wife;	**2Ki 8:18**	1961
his son **b** king in his place.	**2Ki 8:24**	4427a
years old when he **b** king,	**2Ki 8:26**	4427a
Ahab, Ahaziah **b** king over Judah.	**2Ki 9:29**	4427a
his son **b** king in his place.	**2Ki 10:35**	4427a
seven years old when he **b** king.	**2Ki 11:21**	4427a
year of Jehu, Jehoash **b** king,	**2Ki 12:1**	4427a
his son **b** king in his place.	**2Ki 12:21**	4427a
b king over Israel at Samaria,	**2Ki 13:1**	4427a
Joash his son **b** king in his place.	**2Ki 13:9**	4427a
b king over Israel in Samaria,	**2Ki 13:10**	4427a
When Elisha **b** sick with the	**2Ki 13:14**	2470a
his son **b** king in his place.	**2Ki 13:24**	4427a
son of Joash king of Judah **b** king.	**2Ki 14:1**	4427a
years old when he **b** king,	**2Ki 14:2**	4427a
his son **b** king in his place.	**2Ki 14:16**	4427a
king of Israel **b** king in Samaria,	**2Ki 14:23**	4427a
his son **b** king in his place.	**2Ki 14:29**	4427a
of Amaziah king of Judah **b** king.	**2Ki 15:1**	4427a
sixteen years old when he **b** king,	**2Ki 15:2**	4427a
his son **b** king in his place.	**2Ki 15:7**	4427a
Zechariah the son of Jeroboam **b**	**2Ki 15:8**	4427a
Shallum son of Jabesh **b** king in	**2Ki 15:13**	4427a
him and **b** king in his place.	**2Ki 15:14**	4427a
Menahem son of Gadi **b** king over	**2Ki 15:17**	4427a
his son **b** king in his place.	**2Ki 15:22**	4427a
b king over Israel in Samaria,	**2Ki 15:23**	4427a
him and **b** king in his place.	**2Ki 15:25**	4427a
b king over Israel in Samaria,	**2Ki 15:27**	4427a
to death and **b** king in his place,	**2Ki 15:30**	4427a
of Uzziah king of Judah **b** king.	**2Ki 15:32**	4427a
years old when he **b** king,	**2Ki 15:33**	4427a
Ahaz his son **b** king in his place.	**2Ki 15:38**	4427a
of Jotham, king of Judah, **b** king.	**2Ki 16:1**	4427a
twenty years old when he **b** king,	**2Ki 16:2**	4427a
b king over Israel in Samaria,	**2Ki 17:1**	4427a
and Hoshea **b** his servant and paid	**2Ki 17:3**	1961
they followed vanity and **b** vain,	**2Ki 17:15**	1891
son of Ahaz king of Judah **b** king.	**2Ki 18:1**	4427a
years old when he **b** king,	**2Ki 18:2**	4427a
his son **b** king in his place.	**2Ki 19:37**	4427a
days Hezekiah **b** mortally ill.	**2Ki 20:1**	2470a
his son **b** king in his place.	**2Ki 20:21**	4427a
twelve years old when he **b** king,	**2Ki 21:1**	4427a
Amon his son **b** king in his place.	**2Ki 21:18**	4427a
years old when he **b** king,	**2Ki 21:19**	4427a
his son **b** king in his place.	**2Ki 21:26**	4427a
eight years old when he **b** king,	**2Ki 22:1**	4427a
years old when he **b** king,	**2Ki 23:31**	4427a
years old when he **b** king,	**2Ki 23:36**	4427a
b his servant *for* three years;	**2Ki 24:1**	1961
his son **b** king in his place.	**2Ki 24:6**	4427a
eighteen years old when he **b** king,	**2Ki 24:8**	4427a
years old when he **b** king,	**2Ki 24:18**	4427a
in the year that he **b** king,	**2Ki 25:27**	4427a
Cush **b** the father of Nimrod;	**1Ch 1:10**	3205
Mizraim **b** the father of the	**1Ch 1:11**	3205
Canaan **b** the father of Sidon,	**1Ch 1:13**	3205
Arpachshad **b** the father of	**1Ch 1:18**	3205
and Shelah **b** the father of Eber.	**1Ch 1:18**	3205
Joktan **b** the father of Almodad,	**1Ch 1:20**	3205
Abraham **b** the father of Isaac.	**1Ch 1:34**	3205
of Bozrah **b** king in his place.	**1Ch 1:44**	4427a
the Temanites **b** king in his place.	**1Ch 1:45**	4427a
of Moab, **b** king in his place;	**1Ch 1:46**	4427a
of Masrekah **b** king in his place.	**1Ch 1:47**	4427a
by the River **b** king in his place.	**1Ch 1:48**	4427a
son of Achbor **b** king in his place.	**1Ch 1:49**	4427a
died, Hadad **b** king in his place;	**1Ch 1:50**	4427a
Ram **b** the father of Amminadab,	**1Ch 2:10**	3205
Amminadab **b** the father of Nahshon,	**1Ch 2:10**	3205
Nahshon **b** the father of Salma,	**1Ch 2:11**	3205
Salma, Salma **b** the father of Boaz,	**1Ch 2:11**	3205
Boaz **b** the father of Obed, and	**1Ch 2:12**	3205
and Obed **b** the father of Jesse;	**1Ch 2:12**	3205
and Jesse **b** the father of Eliab	**1Ch 2:13**	3205
Hur **b** the father of Uri, and	**1Ch 2:20**	3205
and Uri **b** the father of Bezalel.	**1Ch 2:20**	3205
Segub **b** the father of Jair,	**1Ch 2:22**	3205
Attai **b** the father of Nathan,	**1Ch 2:36**	3205
and Nathan **b** the father of Zabad,	**1Ch 2:36**	3205
and Zabad **b** the father of Ephlal,	**1Ch 2:37**	3205
and Ephlal **b** the father of Obed,	**1Ch 2:37**	3205
and Obed **b** the father of Jehu, and	**1Ch 2:38**	3205
and Jehu **b** the father of Azariah,	**1Ch 2:38**	3205
and Azariah **b** the father of Helez,	**1Ch 2:39**	3205
and Helez **b** the father of Eleasah,	**1Ch 2:39**	3205
Eleasah **b** the father of Sismai,	**1Ch 2:40**	3205
Sismai **b** the father of Shallum,	**1Ch 2:40**	3205
Shallum **b** the father of Jekamiah,	**1Ch 2:41**	3205
Jekamiah **b** the father of Elishama.	**1Ch 2:41**	3205
Shema **b** the father of Raham,	**1Ch 2:44**	3205
and Rekem **b** the father of Shammai.	**1Ch 2:44**	3205
and Haran **b** the father of Gazez.	**1Ch 2:46**	3205
of Shobal **b** the father of Jahath,	**1Ch 4:2**	3205
and Jahath **b** the father of Ahumai	**1Ch 4:2**	3205
Koz **b** the father of Anub and	**1Ch 4:8**	3205
of Shuhah **b** the father of Mehir,	**1Ch 4:11**	3205
Eshton **b** the father of	**1Ch 4:12**	3205
Meonothai **b** the father of Ophrah,	**1Ch 4:14**	3205
and Seraiah **b** the father of Joab	**1Ch 4:14**	3205
Eleazar **b** the father of Phinehas,	**1Ch 6:4**	3205
Phinehas **b** the father of Abishua,	**1Ch 6:4**	3205
and Abishua **b** the father of Bukki,	**1Ch 6:5**	3205
and Bukki **b** the father of Uzzi,	**1Ch 6:5**	3205
and Uzzi **b** the father of Zerahiah,	**1Ch 6:6**	3205
Zerahiah **b** the father of Meraioth,	**1Ch 6:6**	3205
Meraioth **b** the father of Amariah,	**1Ch 6:7**	3205
Amariah **b** the father of Ahitub,	**1Ch 6:7**	3205
and Ahitub **b** the father of Zadok,	**1Ch 6:8**	3205
and Zadok **b** the father of Ahimaaz,	**1Ch 6:8**	3205
Ahimaaz **b** the father of Azariah,	**1Ch 6:9**	3205
Azariah **b** the father of Johanan,	**1Ch 6:9**	3205
Johanan **b** the father of Azariah	**1Ch 6:10**	3205
Azariah **b** the father of Amariah,	**1Ch 6:11**	3205
Amariah **b** the father of Ahitub,	**1Ch 6:11**	3205
and Ahitub **b** the father of Zadok,	**1Ch 6:12**	3205
and Zadok **b** the father of Shallum,	**1Ch 6:12**	3205
Shallum **b** the father of Hilkiah,	**1Ch 6:13**	3205
Hilkiah **b** the father of Azariah,	**1Ch 6:13**	3205
Azariah **b** the father of Seraiah,	**1Ch 6:14**	3205
Seraiah **b** the father of Jehozadak;	**1Ch 6:14**	3205
Heber **b** the father of Japhlet,	**1Ch 7:32**	3205
And Benjamin **b** the father of Bela	**1Ch 8:1**	3205
b the father of Uzza and Ahihud.	**1Ch 8:7**	3205
Shaharaim **b** the father of	**1Ch 8:8**	3205
his wife he **b** the father of Jobab,	**1Ch 8:9**	3205
By Hushim he **b** the father of	**1Ch 8:11**	3205
Mikloth **b** the father of Shimeah.	**1Ch 8:32**	3205
Ner **b** the father of Kish, and	**1Ch 8:33**	3205
and Kish **b** the father of Saul,	**1Ch 8:33**	3205
and Saul **b** the father of Jonathan,	**1Ch 8:33**	3205
Merib-baal **b** the father of Micah.	**1Ch 8:34**	3205
Ahaz **b** the father of Jehoaddah,	**1Ch 8:36**	3205
Jehoaddah **b** the father of Alemeth,	**1Ch 8:36**	3205
and Zimri **b** the father of Moza.	**1Ch 8:36**	3205
Moza **b** the father of Binea;	**1Ch 8:37**	3205
Mikloth **b** the father of Shimeam.	**1Ch 9:38**	3205
Ner **b** the father of Kish, and	**1Ch 9:39**	3205
and Kish **b** the father of Saul,	**1Ch 9:39**	3205
and Saul **b** the father of Jonathan,	**1Ch 9:39**	3205
Merib-baal **b** the father of Micah.	**1Ch 9:40**	3205
Ahaz **b** the father of Jarah,	**1Ch 9:42**	3205
and Jarah **b** the father of Alemeth,	**1Ch 9:42**	3205
and Zimri **b** the father of Moza,	**1Ch 9:42**	3205
and Moza **b** the father of Binea and	**1Ch 9:43**	3205
The battle **b** heavy against Saul,	**1Ch 10:3**	3513

went up first, so he **b** chief.	1Ch 11:6	1961
David **b** greater and greater,	1Ch 11:9	1980
honored and **b** their commander;	1Ch 11:21	1961
Then David **b** angry because of the	1Ch 13:11	2734
and David **b** the father of more	1Ch 14:3	3205
O LORD, **b** their God.	1Ch 17:22	1961
the Moabites **b** servants to David,	1Ch 18:2	1961
the Arameans **b** servants to David,	1Ch 18:6	1961
the Edomites **b** servants to David.	1Ch 18:13	1961
and his son **b** king in his place.	1Ch 19:1	4427a
so they **b** a father's household,	1Ch 23:11	1961
So King Solomon **b** greater than all	2Ch 9:22	1431
son Abijah **b** king in his place.	2Ch 12:16	4427a
Abijah **b** king over Judah.	2Ch 13:1	4427a
But Abijah **b** powerful; and took	2Ch 13:21	2388
and **b** the father of twenty-two	2Ch 13:21	3205
his son Asa **b** king in his place.	2Ch 14:1	4427a
reign Asa **b** diseased in his feet.	2Ch 16:12	2456
his son then **b** king in his place,	2Ch 17:1	4427a
years old when he **b** king,	2Ch 20:31	4427a
his son **b** king in his place.	2Ch 21:1	4427a
years old when he **b** king,	2Ch 21:5	4427a
years old when he **b** king,	2Ch 21:20	4427a
years old when he **b** king,	2Ch 22:2	4427a
seven years old when he **b** king,	2Ch 24:1	4427a
and he **b** the father of sons and	2Ch 24:3	3205
his son **b** king in his place.	2Ch 24:27	4427a
years old when he **b** king,	2Ch 25:1	4427a
sixteen years old when he **b** king,	2Ch 26:3	4427a
of Egypt, for he **b** very strong.	2Ch 26:8	2388
But when he **b** strong, his heart	2Ch 26:16	2388
his son **b** king in his place.	2Ch 26:23	4427a
years old when he **b** king,	2Ch 27:1	4427a
So Jotham **b** mighty because he	2Ch 27:6	2388
years old when he **b** king,	2Ch 27:8	4427a
Ahaz his son **b** king in his place.	2Ch 27:9	4427a
twenty years old when he **b** king,	2Ch 28:1	4427a
King Ahaz **b** yet more unfaithful	2Ch 28:22	4603
But they **b** the downfall of him and	2Ch 28:23	1961
Hezekiah **b** king *when he was*	2Ch 29:1	4427a
days Hezekiah **b** mortally ill;	2Ch 32:24	2470a
son Manasseh **b** king in his place.	2Ch 32:33	4427a
twelve years old when he **b** king,	2Ch 33:1	4427a
Amon his son **b** king in his place.	2Ch 33:20	4427a
years old when he **b** king,	2Ch 33:21	4427a
eight years old when he **b** king,	2Ch 34:1	4427a
years old when he **b** king,	2Ch 36:2	4427a
years old when he **b** king,	2Ch 36:5	4427a
his son **b** king in his place.	2Ch 36:8	4427a
eight years old when he **b** king,	2Ch 36:9	4427a
years old when he **b** king,	2Ch 36:11	4427a
he **b** furious and very angry and	Ne 4:1	2734
They **b** stubborn and would not	Ne 9:16	7185, 6203
So they **b** stubborn and appointed a	Ne 9:17	7185, 6203
"But they **b** disobedient and	Ne 9:26	4784
Jeshua **b** the father of Joiakim,	Ne 12:10	3205
Joiakim **b** the father of Eliashib,	Ne 12:10	3205
Eliashib **b** the father of Joiada,	Ne 12:10	3205
Joiada **b** the father of Jonathan,	Ne 12:11	3205
Jonathan **b** the father of Jaddua.	Ne 12:11	3205
Then the king **b** very angry and his	Es 1:12	7107
b angry and sought to lay hands on	Es 2:21	7107
But the plot **b** known to Mordecai and	Es 2:22	
Then Haman **b** terrified before the	Es 7:6	
the peoples of the land **b** Jews,	Es 8:17	3054
Mordecai **b** greater and greater.	Es 9:4	1980
And my heart **b** secretly enticed,	Jb 31:27	6601b
with fasting, It **b** my reproach.	Ps 69:10	1961
my clothing, I **b** a byword to them.	Ps 69:11	1961
Who **b** as dung for the ground.	Ps 83:10	1961
b envious of Moses in the camp,	Ps 106:16	7065
idols, Which **b** a snare to them.	Ps 106:36	1961
they **b** unclean in their practices,	Ps 106:39	2930
Judah **b** His sanctuary, Israel, His	Ps 114:2	1961
the springs of the deep **b** fixed,	Pr 8:28	5810
Then I **b** great and increased more	Ec 2:9	1431
Then I **b** in his eyes as one who	SS 8:10	1961
his son **b** king in his place.	Is 37:38	4427a
days Hezekiah **b** mortally ill.	Is 38:1	2470a
So He **b** their Savior.	Is 63:8	1961
All who ate of it **b** guilty;	Jer 2:3	816
after emptiness and **b** empty?	Jer 2:5	1891
And Your words **b** for me a joy and	Jer 15:16	1961
who **b** king in the place of Josiah	Jer 22:11	4427a
years old when he **b** king,	Jer 52:1	4427a
They **b** food for them Because of	La 4:10	1961
and it **b** desolate so that no one	Ezk 14:15	1961
Then you grew up, **b** tall and	Ezk 16:7	1431
with you so that you **b** Mine,"	Ezk 16:8	1961
"Then it sprouted and **b** a low,	Ezk 17:6	1961
So it **b** a vine and yielded shoots	Ezk 17:6	1961
up one of her cubs, He **b** a lion,	Ezk 19:3	1961
He **b** a young lion, He learned to	Ezk 19:6	1961
And they **b** Mine, and they bore	Ezk 23:4	1961
Thus she **b** a byword among women,	Ezk 23:10	1961
them, she **b** disgusted with them.	Ezk 23:17	3363
then I **b** disgusted with her, as I	Ezk 23:18	3363
it **b** your distinguishing mark;	Ezk 27:7	1961
its boughs **b** many and its branches	Ezk 31:5	7235a
and they **b** food for every beast of	Ezk 34:5	1961
b a stumbling block of iniquity to	Ezk 44:12	1961
king **b** indignant and very furious and	Da 2:12	1149
and **b** like chaff from the summer	Da 2:35	1934
stone that struck the statue **b** a great	Da 2:35	1934
'The tree grew large and **b** strong And	Da 4:11	8631
which **b** large and grew strong,	Da 4:20	7236
lifted up and his spirit **b** so proud	Da 5:20	8631
the ground and **b** speechless.	Da 10:15	481
b sick with the heat of wine;	Hos 7:5	2470a
And they **b** as detestable as that	Hos 9:10	1961
And I **b** to them as one who lifts	Hos 11:4	1961
their pasture, they **b** satisfied,	Hos 13:6	7646
satisfied, their heart **b** proud;	Hos 13:6	7311
Then the sailors **b** afraid and	Jon 1:5	3372a
Then the men **b** extremely	Jon 1:10	3372a
displeased Jonah and he **b** angry.	Jon 4:1	2734
so that he **b** faint and begged	Jon 4:8	5968
Yet she **b** an exile, She went into	Na 3:10	
Josiah **b** the father of Jeconiah and	Mt 1:11	*1080*
Jeconiah **b** the father of Shealtiel,	Mt 1:12	*1080*
by the magi, he **b** very enraged,	Mt 2:16	
forty nights, He then **b** hungry.	Mt 4:2	
and it **b** perfectly calm.	Mt 8:26	*1096*
and His disciples **b** hungry and	Mt 12:1	
what David did when he **b** hungry,	Mt 12:3	
then the tares **b** evident also.	Mt 13:26	*5316*
But seeing the wind, he **b** frightened,	Mt 14:30	
His garments **b** as white as light.	Mt 17:2	*1096*
the ten **b** indignant with the two	Mt 20:24	
Son of David," they **b** indignant	Mt 21:15	
returning to the city, He **b** hungry.	Mt 21:18	
THIS **B** THE CHIEF CORNER *stone;*	Mt 21:42	*1096*
b very frightened and said,	Mt 27:54	
fear of him and **b** like dead men.	Mt 28:4	*1096*
he and his companions **b** hungry;	Mk 2:25	
died down and it **b** perfectly calm.	Mk 4:39	*1096*
They **b** very much afraid and	Mk 4:41	
and they **b** frightened.	Mk 5:15	
b radiant and exceedingly white,	Mk 9:3	*1096*
for they **b** terrified.	Mk 9:6	*1096*
and *the boy* **b** so much like a	Mk 9:26	*1096*
left Bethany, He **b** hungry.	Mk 11:12	
THIS **B** THE CHIEF CORNER *stone*	Mk 12:10	*1096*
Elizabeth his wife **b** pregnant,	Lk 1:24	*4815*
And when He **b** twelve, they went up	Lk 2:42	*1096*
when they had ended, He **b** hungry.	Lk 4:2	
Judas Iscariot, who **b** a traitor.	Lk 6:16	*1096*
and they stopped, and it **b** calm.	Lk 8:24	*1096*
and they **b** frightened.	Lk 8:35	
of His face **b** different,	Lk 9:29	*1096*
and His clothing **b** white *and*	Lk 9:29	
Jonah **b** a sign to the Ninevites,	Lk 11:30	*1096*
and it grew and **b** a tree,	Lk 13:19	*1096*
b angry and said to his slave,	Lk 14:21	
"But he **b** angry and was not	Lk 15:28	
heard these things, he **b** very sad,	Lk 18:23	*1096*
THIS **B** THE CHIEF CORNER *stone*'?	Lk 20:17	*1096*
at His answer, they **b** silent.	Lk 20:26	*4601*
His sweat **b** like drops of blood,	Lk 22:44	*1096*
Now Herod and Pilate **b** friends	Lk 23:12	*1096*
And the Word **b** flesh, and dwelt	Jn 1:14	*1096*
Immediately the man **b** well,	Jn 5:9	*1096*
this, He **b** troubled in spirit,	Jn 13:21	
who **b** a guide to those who	Ac 1:16	*1096*
And it **b** known to all who were	Ac 1:19	*1096*
but WHICH **B** THE CHIEF CORNER *stone.*	Ac 4:11	*1096*
so *Abraham* **b** the father of Isaac,	Ac 7:8	*1080*
and Isaac **b** *the father of* Jacob,	Ac 7:8	
"The patriarchs **b** jealous of	Ac 7:9	
AND **B** AN ALIEN IN THE LAND OF	Ac 7:29	*1096*
where he **b** the father of two sons.	Ac 7:29	*1080*
but their plot **b** known to Saul.	Ac 9:24	
It **b** known all over Joppa, and	Ac 9:42	*1096*
But he **b** hungry and was desiring	Ac 10:10	*1096*
they **b** aware of it and fled to the	Ac 14:6	
This **b** known to all, both Jews	Ac 19:17	*1096*
dialect, they **b** even more quiet;	Ac 22:2	*3930*
come, Felix **b** frightened and said,	Ac 24:25	*1096*
b futile in their speculations,	Ro 1:21	*3154*
Professing to be wise, they **b** fools,	Ro 1:22	*3471*
you **b** obedient from the heart to	Ro 6:17	*5219*
you **b** slaves of righteousness.	Ro 6:18	*1402*
the commandment came, sin **b** alive and	Ro 7:9	*326*
I **B** MANIFEST TO THOSE WHO DID NOT	Ro 10:20	*1096*
were grafted in among them and **b**	Ro 11:17	*1096*
THE LORD, OR WHO **B** HIS COUNSELOR?	Ro 11:34	*1096*
who **b** to us wisdom from God,	1Co 1:30	*1096*
for in Christ Jesus I **b** your	1Co 4:15	*1080*
To the Jews I **b** as a Jew,	1Co 9:20	*1096*
To the weak I **b** weak, that I might	1Co 9:22	*1096*
when I **b** a man, I did away with	1Co 13:11	*1096*
MAN, Adam, **B** A LIVING SOUL."	1Co 15:45	*1096*
The last Adam **b** a life-giving	1Co 15:45	
rich, yet for your sake He **b** poor,	2Co 8:9	*4433*
You also **b** imitators of us and of	1Th 1:6	*1096*
so that you **b** an example to all	1Th 1:7	*1096*
b imitators of the churches of God	1Th 2:14	*1096*
He **b** to all those who obey Him the	Heb 5:9	*1096*
indeed **b** priests without an oath,	Heb 7:21	*1096*
and **b** an heir of the righteousness	Heb 11:7	*1096*
were made strong, **b** mighty in war,	Heb 11:34	*1096*
THIS **B** THE VERY CORNER *stone,*"	1Pe 2:7	*1096*
and the sun **b** black as sackcloth	Rv 6:12	*1096*
and the whole moon **b** like blood;	Rv 6:12	*1096*
and a third of the sea **b** blood,	Rv 8:8	*1096*
a third of the waters **b** wormwood,	Rv 8:11	*1096*
and it **b** a loathsome and malignant	Rv 16:2	*1096*
b blood like *that* of a dead man;	Rv 16:3	*1096*
and they **b** blood.	Rv 16:4	*1096*
and his kingdom **b** darkened;	Rv 16:10	*1096*
these things, who **b** rich from her,	Rv 18:15	
ships at sea **b** rich by her wealth,	Rv 18:19	

BECAUSE

b in it He rested from all His	Gn 2:3	3588
B she was taken out of Man."	Gn 2:23	3588
and I was afraid **b** I was naked;	Gn 3:10	3588
"**B** you have done this, Cursed are	Gn 3:14	3588
"**B** you have listened to the voice	Gn 3:17	3588
Cursed is the ground **b** of you;	Gn 3:17	5668
ground, **B** from it you were taken;	Gn 3:19	3588
b she was the mother of all *the*	Gn 3:20	3588
man forever, **b** he also is flesh;	Gn 6:3	7683
is filled with violence **b** of them;	Gn 6:13	4480, 6440
ark **b** of the water of the flood.	Gn 7:7	4480, 6440
b there the LORD confused the	Gn 11:9	3588
it may go well with me **b** of you,	Gn 12:13	5668
with great plagues **b** of Sarai,	Gn 12:17	5921, 1697
B the LORD has given heed to your	Gn 16:11	3588
the whole city **b** of five?"	Gn 18:28	
b their outcry has become so great	Gn 19:13	3588
you are a dead man **b** of the woman	Gn 20:3	5921
"**B** I thought, surely there is no	Gn 20:11	3588
they will kill me **b** of my wife.	Gn 20:11	5921, 1697
household of Abimelech **b** of Sarah,	Gn 20:18	5921, 1697
Abraham greatly **b** of his son.	Gn 21:11	5921, 182
b of the lad and your maid;	Gn 21:12	5921
also, **b** he is your descendant."	Gn 21:13	3588
Abraham complained to Abimelech **b**	Gn 21:25	5921, 182
b there the two of them took an	Gn 21:31	3588
LORD, **b** you have done this thing and	Gn 22:16	3588, 3282
b you have obeyed My voice."	Gn 22:18	6118, 834
of his wife, **b** she was barren;	Gn 25:21	3588
Esau, **b** he had a taste for game,	Gn 25:28	3588
b Abraham obeyed Me and kept My	Gn 26:5	6118, 834
"**B** I said, 'I might die on account	Gn 26:9	3588
Esek, **b** they contended with him.	Gn 26:20	3588
"**B** the LORD your God caused *it* to	Gn 27:20	3588
b his hands were hairy like his	Gn 27:23	3588
grudge against Jacob **b** of the blessing	Gn 27:41	5921
living **b** of the daughters of Heth;	Gn 27:46	4480, 6440
night there, **b** the sun had set;	Gn 28:11	3588
"**B** you are my relative, should	Gn 29:15	3588
a few days **b** of his love for her.	Gn 29:20	
"**B** the LORD has seen my	Gn 29:32	3588
"**B** the LORD has heard that I am	Gn 29:33	3588
b I have borne him three sons."	Gn 29:34	3588
b I gave my maid to my husband."	Gn 30:18	834
me, **b** I have borne him six sons."	Gn 30:20	3588
gone away **b** you longed greatly for	Gn 31:30	3588
"**B** I was afraid, for I thought	Gn 31:31	3588
b he touched the socket of Jacob's	Gn 32:32	3588
b God has dealt graciously with	Gn 33:11	3588
with me and **b** I have plenty."	Gn 33:11	3588
and they were very angry **b** he had	Gn 34:7	3588
b he had defiled Dinah their	Gn 34:13	834
b he was delighted with Jacob's	Gn 34:19	3588
b they had defiled their sister.	Gn 34:27	834
b there God had revealed Himself	Gn 35:7	3588
sustain them **b** of their livestock.	Gn 36:7	4480, 6440
b he was the son of his old age;	Gn 37:3	3588
me except you, **b** you are his wife.	Gn 39:9	834
charge **b** the LORD was with him;	Gn 39:23	834
land **b** of that subsequent famine;	Gn 41:31	4480, 6440
b the famine was severe in all the	Gn 41:57	3588
b we saw the distress of his soul	Gn 42:21	834
b they were brought to Joseph's	Gn 43:18	3588
"*It is* **b** of the money that was	Gn 43:18	5921, 1697
b the Egyptians could not eat	Gn 43:32	3588
yourselves, **b** you sold me here,	Gn 45:5	3588
b the famine was very severe,	Gn 47:13	3588
Canaan languished **b** of the famine.	Gn 47:13	4480, 6440
b the famine was severe upon them.	Gn 47:20	3588
B you went up to your father's bed;	Gn 49:4	3588
B in their anger they slew men,	Gn 49:6	3588
"**B** the Hebrew women are not as	Ex 1:19	3588
B the midwives feared God, He	Ex 1:21	3588
"**B** I drew him out of the water."	Ex 2:10	3588
of Israel sighed **b** of the bondage,	Ex 2:23	4480
and their cry for help **b** of *their*	Ex 2:23	4480
their cry **b** of their taskmasters,	Ex 3:7	4480, 6440
of blood"—**b** of the circumcision.	Ex 4:26	
B they are lazy, therefore they	Ex 5:8	3588
were in trouble **b** they were told,	Ex 5:19	
b the Egyptians are holding them	Ex 6:5	834
laid waste **b** of the swarms of insects	Ex 8:24	4480, 6440
stand before Moses **b** of the boils,	Ex 9:11	4480, 6440
'It is **b** of what the LORD did for	Ex 13:8	5668
"Is it **b** there were no graves in	Ex 14:11	4480, 1097
Massah and Meribah **b** of the quarrel	Ex 17:7	5921
and **b** they tested the LORD,	Ex 17:7	5921
"**B** the people come to me to	Ex 18:15	3588
all in smoke **b** the LORD descended	Ex 19:18	4480, 6440, 834
people **b** of his unfairness to her.	Ex 21:8	
b they will make you sin against Me;	Ex 23:33	6435
not eat *them,* **b** they are holy.	Ex 29:33	3588

shall not be eaten, **b** it is holy. **Ex 29:34** 3588
b of what they did with the calf **Ex 32:35**
5921, 834
b you are an obstinate people, **Ex 33:3** 3588
shone **b** of his speaking with Him. **Ex 34:29**
b the cloud had settled on it, **Ex 40:35** 3588
b it is your due and your sons' **Lv 10:13** 3588
b the mark has not reappeared. **Lv 14:48** 3588
the LORD **b** of his discharge. **Lv 15:15** 4480
LORD **b** of her impure discharge.' **Lv 15:30** 4480
is ill **b** of menstrual impurity, **Lv 15:33**
b of the impurities of the sons of **Lv 16:16** 4480
and **b** of their transgressions in **Lv 16:16** 4480
but shall not incur sin **b** of him. **Lv 19:17** 5921
put to death, **b** she was not free. **Lv 19:20** 3588
b he has given some of his **Lv 20:3** 3588
to him **b** she has had no husband; **Lv 21:3** 834
near the altar **b** he has a defect, **Lv 21:23** 3588
they will not bear sin **b** of it **Lv 22:9** 5921
and die thereby **b** they profane it; **Lv 22:9** 3588
clear out the old **b** of the new. **Lv 26:10**
4480, 6440
will rot away **b** of their iniquity **Lv 26:39**
and also **b** of the iniquities of **Lv 26:39**
b they rejected My ordinances and **Lv 26:43** 3282
who is unclean **b** of a *dead* person. **Nu 5:2**
b his separation to God is on his **Nu 6:7** 3588
his sin **b** of the *dead* person. **Nu 6:11** 5921
void **b** his separation was defiled. **Nu 6:12** 3588
sons of Kohath **b** theirs *was* the service **Nu 7:9** 3588
were unclean **b** of *the* dead person, **Nu 9:6**
are unclean **b** of *the* dead person, **Nu 9:7**
unclean **b** of a *dead* person, **Nu 9:10**
b the fire of the LORD burned **Nu 11:3** 3588
b it is too burdensome for me. **Nu 11:14** 3588
b you have rejected the LORD who **Nu 11:20**
3282, 3588
b there they buried the people who **Nu 11:34** 3588
against Moses **b** of the Cushite woman **Nu 12:1**
5921, 182
b of the cluster which the sons of **Nu 13:24**
5921, 182
'**B** the LORD could not bring this **Nu 14:16** 4480
b he has had a different spirit **Nu 14:24** 6118
'**B** he has despised the word of the **Nu 15:31** 3588
and they put him in custody **b** it **Nu 15:34** 3588
B the water for impurity was not **Nu 19:13** 3588
b he has defiled the sanctuary of **Nu 19:20** 3588
"**B** you have not believed Me, to **Nu 20:12** 3282
b the sons of Israel contended **Nu 20:13** 834
b you rebelled against My command **Nu 20:24**
5921, 834
became impatient **b** of the journey. **Nu 21:4**
b we have spoken against the LORD **Nu 21:7** 3588
was in great fear **b** of the people, **Nu 22:3**
4480, 6440
But God was angry **b** he was going, **Nu 22:22** 3588
"**B** you have made a mockery of me! **Nu 22:29** 3588
b your way was contrary to me. **Nu 22:32** 3588
b he was jealous for his God and **Nu 25:13**
834, 8478
the day of the plague **b** of Peor." **Nu 25:18**
5921, 1697
among his family **b** he had no son? **Nu 27:4** 3588
b her father had forbidden her. **Nu 30:5** 3588
b he said nothing to her on the **Nu 30:14** 3588
b of the inhabitants of the land. **Nu 32:17**
4480, 6440
b our inheritance has fallen to us **Nu 32:19** 3588
b he should have remained in his **Nu 35:28** 3588
'**B** the LORD hates us, He has **Dt 1:27**
b he has followed the LORD fully.' **Dt 1:36**
3282, 834
even *as little as* a footstep **b** I **Dt 2:5** 3588
b I have given Ar to the sons of **Dt 2:9** 3588
b I have given it to the sons of **Dt 2:19** 3588
and be in anguish **b** of you.' **Dt 2:25**
4480, 6440
"**B** He loved your fathers, **Dt 4:37**
8478, 3588
for you were afraid **b** of the fire **Dt 5:5**
4480, 6440
choose you **b** you were more in **Dt 7:7** 3588
but **b** the LORD loved you and kept **Dt 7:8** 3588
b you listen to these judgments **Dt 7:12** 6118
b you would not listen to the **Dt 8:20** 6118
'**B** of my righteousness the LORD **Dt 9:4**
but *it is* **b** of the wickedness of **Dt 9:4**
but *it is* **b** of the wickedness of **Dt 9:5** 3588
it is not **b** of your righteousness **Dt 9:6**
b of all your sin which you had **Dt 9:18** 5921
which I did **b** the LORD had said He **Dt 9:25** 3588
"**B** the LORD was not able to bring **Dt 9:28**
4480, 1097
b He hated them He has brought **Dt 9:28** 4480
meat,' **b** you desire to eat meat, **Dt 12:20** 3588
b he has counseled rebellion **Dt 13:5** 3588
stone him to death **b** he has sought **Dt 13:10** 3588
b it divides the hoof but *does* not **Dt 14:8** 3588
b he has no portion or inheritance **Dt 14:29** 3588
b the LORD's remission has been **Dt 15:2** 3588
b for this thing the LORD your God **Dt 15:10**
3588, 1558
b he loves you and your household, **Dt 15:16** 3588
b the LORD your God will bless you **Dt 16:15** 3588
and **b** of these detestable things **Dt 18:12** 1558
overtake him, **b** the way is long, **Dt 19:6** 3588
her, **b** you have humbled her. **Dt 21:14**
8478, 834

b he publicly defamed a virgin of **Dt 22:19** 3588
b she has committed an act of folly **Dt 22:21** 3588
b she did not cry out in the city, **Dt 22:24**
5921, 1697, 834
b he has violated his neighbor's **Dt 22:24**
5921, 1697, 834
his wife **b** he has violated her; **Dt 22:29**
8478, 834
b they did not meet you with food **Dt 23:4**
5921, 1697, 834
and **b** they hired against you **Dt 23:4** 834
you **b** the LORD your God loves you. **Dt 23:5** 3588
b you were an alien in his land. **Dt 23:7** 3588
unclean **b** of a nocturnal emission, **Dt 23:10** 4480
finds no favor in his eyes **b** he has **Dt 24:1** 3588
b he has uncovered his father's **Dt 27:20** 3588
deeds, **b** you have forsaken Me. **Dt 28:20** 834
b you would not obey the LORD your **Dt 28:45** 3588
"**B** you did not serve the LORD **Dt 28:47**
8478, 834
b you did not obey the LORD your **Dt 28:62** 3588
b of the dread of your heart which **Dt 28:67** 4480
'**B** they forsook the covenant of **Dt 29:25**
5921, 834
'Is it not **b** our God is not among **Dt 31:17**
5921, 3588
b of all the evil which they will do, **Dt 31:18** 5921
His children, **b** of their defect; **Dt 32:5**
spurned *them* **B** of the provocation **Dt 32:19** 4480
b you broke faith with Me in the **Dt 32:51**
5921, 834
b you did not treat Me as holy in **Dt 32:51**
5921, 834
in any man any longer **b** of you; **Jos 2:11**
4480, 6440
'**B** the waters of the Jordan were **Jos 4:7** 834
longer **b** of the sons of Israel. **Jos 5:1**
4480, 6440
perished **b** they did not listen to **Jos 5:6** 834
b they had not circumcised them **Jos 5:7** 3588
shut **b** of the sons of Israel; **Jos 6:1**
4480, 6440
b she hid the messengers whom we **Jos 6:17** 3588
b he has transgressed the covenant **Jos 7:15** 3588
and **b** he has committed a **Jos 7:15** 3588
far country **b** of the fame of the LORD **Jos 9:9**
out **b** of the very long journey." **Jos 9:13** 4480
did not strike them **b** the leaders **Jos 9:18** 3588
"**B** it was certainly told your **Jos 9:24** 3588
greatly for our lives **b** of you, **Jos 9:24**
4480, 6440
b Gibeon *was* a great city, **Jos 10:2** 3588
and **b** it was greater than Ai, **Jos 10:2** 3588
lands at one time, **b** the LORD, **Jos 10:42** 3588
"Do not be afraid **b** of them, **Jos 11:6**
4480, 6440
b you have followed the LORD my **Jos 14:9** 3588
b he followed the LORD God of **Jos 14:14**
3282, 834
and Bashan, **b** he was a man of war. **Jos 17:1** 3588
b the daughters of Manasseh **Jos 17:6** 3588
b the Canaanites persisted in **Jos 17:12**
b the priesthood of the LORD is **Jos 18:7** 3588
b he struck his neighbor without **Jos 20:5** 3588
b you have not committed this **Jos 22:31** 834
to all these nations **b** of you, **Jos 23:3**
4480, 6440
valley **b** they had iron chariots. **Jg 1:19** 3588
groaning **b** of those who oppressed **Jg 2:18**
4480, 6440
"**B** this nation has transgressed **Jg 2:20**
3282, 834
b they had done evil in the sight **Jg 3:12**
5921, 3588
B they did not come to the help of **Jg 5:23** 3588
B of Midian the sons of Israel **Jg 6:2**
4480, 6440
was brought very low **b** of Midian, **Jg 6:6**
4480, 6440
b he was too afraid of his **Jg 6:27** 834
b someone has torn down his altar." **Jg 6:31** 3588
him," **b** he had torn down his altar. **Jg 6:32** 3588
afraid, **b** he was still a youth. **Jg 8:20** 3588
b they were Ishmaelites.) **Jg 8:24** 3588
of Shechem, **b** he is your relative **Jg 9:18** 3588
there **b** of Abimelech his brother. **Jg 9:21**
4480, 6440
"**B** Israel took away my land when **Jg 11:13** 3588
and weep **b** of my virginity, **Jg 11:37** 5921
the mountains **b** of her virginity. **Jg 11:38** 5921
defeated Ephraim, **b** they said, **Jg 12:4** 3588
her **b** she pressed him so hard. **Jg 14:17** 3588
b he took his wife and gave her to **Jg 15:6** 3588
b it was far from Sidon and they **Jg 18:28** 3588
the house at night **b** of me. **Jg 20:5** 5921
Israel gave ground to Benjamin **b** **Jg 20:36** 3588
sorry for Benjamin **b** the LORD **Jg 21:15** 3588
b we did not take for each man *of* **Jg 21:22** 3588
the city was stirred **b** of them, **Ru 1:19** 5921
b I would jeopardize my own **Ru 4:6** 6435
b the LORD had closed her womb. **1Sa 1:6** 3588
"**B** I have asked him of the LORD." **1Sa 1:20** 3588
B I rejoice in Your salvation. **1Sa 2:1** 3588
b his sons brought a curse on **1Sa 3:13** 3588
b the LORD revealed Himself to **1Sa 3:21** 3588
b his heart was trembling for the **1Sa 4:13** 3588
b the ark of God was taken and **1Sa 4:21** 413
b of her father-in-law and her **1Sa 4:21** 413
Beth-shemesh **b** they had looked **1Sa 6:19** 3588

and the people mourned **b** the LORD **1Sa 6:19** 3588
cry out in that day **b** of your king **1Sa 8:18**
4480, 6440
b he must bless the sacrifice; **1Sa 9:13** 3588
b their cry has come to Me." **1Sa 9:16** 3588
b it has been kept for you until **1Sa 9:24** 3588
'We have sinned **b** we have forsaken **1Sa 12:10** 3588
or deliver, **b** they are futile. **1Sa 12:21** 3588
b the LORD has been pleased to **1Sa 12:22** 3588
"**B** I saw that the people were **1Sa 13:11** 3588
b you have not kept what the LORD **1Sa 13:14** 3588
how my eyes have brightened **b** I **1Sa 14:29** 3588
B you have rejected the word of **1Sa 15:23** 3282
b I feared the people and listened **1Sa 15:24** 3588
stature, **b** I have rejected him; **1Sa 16:7** 3588
David **b** he loved him as himself. **1Sa 18:3**
b it is the yearly sacrifice there **1Sa 20:6** 3588
vow again **b** of his love for him, **1Sa 20:17**
b he loved him as he loved his own **1Sa 20:17** 3588
missed **b** your seat will be empty. **1Sa 20:18** 3588
b his father had dishonored him. **1Sa 20:34** 3588
b the king's matter was urgent." **1Sa 21:8** 3588
b their hand also is with David **1Sa 22:17** 3588
b they knew that he was fleeing **1Sa 22:17** 3588
b the hand of Saul my father will **1Sa 23:17** 3588
David's conscience bothered him **b** he **1Sa 24:5**
5921, 834
"Far be it from me **b** of the LORD **1Sa 24:6** 4480
b my lord is fighting the battles **1Sa 25:28** 3588
b a sound sleep from the LORD had **1Sa 26:12** 3588
b you did not guard your lord, **1Sa 26:16** 834
for I will not harm you again **b** my **1Sa 26:21**
8478, 834
afraid **b** of the words of Samuel; **1Sa 28:20** 4480
David was greatly distressed **b** the **1Sa 30:6** 3588
b of his sons and his daughters. **1Sa 30:6** 5921
dancing **b** of all the great spoil that **1Sa 30:16**
"**B** they did not go with us, we **1Sa 30:22**
3282, 834
me **b** my life still lingers in me.' **2Sa 1:9** 3588
b I knew that he could not live **2Sa 1:10** 3588
b they had fallen by the sword. **2Sa 1:12** 3588
"May you be blessed of the LORD **b** **2Sa 2:5** 834
you, **b** you have done this thing. **2Sa 2:6** 834
a word, **b** he was afraid of him. **2Sa 3:11** 4480
Abishai his brother killed Abner **b** he **2Sa 3:30**
5921, 834
David became angry **b** of the **2Sa 6:8** 5921, 834
b he had fought against Hadadezer **2Sa 8:10**
5921, 834
b he has sent consolers to you? **2Sa 10:3** 3588
b he did this thing and had no **2Sa 12:6**
6118, 834
b you have despised Me and have **2Sa 12:10**
6118, 3588
b by this deed you have given **2Sa 12:14** 3588
Amnon was so frustrated **b** of **2Sa 13:2** 5668
b this wrong in sending me away is **2Sa 13:16** 182
for Absalom hated Amnon **b** he had **2Sa 13:22**
5921, 1697, 834
b by the intent of Absalom this **2Sa 13:32** 3588
today **b** the king's son is dead." **2Sa 18:20**
3588, 5921
b he cursed the LORD's anointed?" **2Sa 19:21** 3588
the king,' **b** your servant is lame. **2Sa 19:26** 3588
"**B** the king is a close relative **2Sa 19:42** 3588
b he put the Gibeonites to death." **2Sa 21:1**
5921, 834
b of the oath of the LORD which **2Sa 21:7** 5921
And were shaken, **b** He was angry. **2Sa 22:8** 3588
rescued me, **b** He delighted in me. **2Sa 22:20** 3588
B they cannot be taken in hand; **2Sa 23:6** 3588
b of eight hundred slain *by him* at **2Sa 23:8** 5921
b you carried the ark of the Lord **1Ki 2:26** 3588
and **b** you were afflicted in **1Ki 2:26** 3588
b he fell upon two men more **1Ki 2:32** 834
b there was no house built for the **1Ki 3:2** 3588
"**B** you have asked this thing and **1Ki 3:11**
3282, 834
in the night, **b** she lay on it. **1Ki 3:19** 834
the LORD his God **b** of the wars **1Ki 5:3**
4480, 6440
unweighed, **b** *they were* too many; **1Ki 7:47** 4480
stand to minister **b** of the cloud, **1Ki 8:11**
4480, 6440
'**B** it was in your heart to build a **1Ki 8:18**
3282, 834
b they have sinned against You, **1Ki 8:33** 834
b they have sinned against You, **1Ki 8:35** 3588
b there he offered the burnt **1Ki 8:64** 3588
'**B** they forsook the LORD their **1Ki 9:9** 5921, 834
b the LORD loved Israel forever, **1Ki 10:9**
angry with Solomon **b** his heart **1Ki 11:9** 3588
"**B** you have done this, and you **1Ki 11:11**
3282, 834
b they have forsaken Me, and have **1Ki 11:33**
3282, 834
'**B** you have disobeyed the command **1Ki 13:21**
3282, 3588
his eyes were dim **b** of his age. **1Ki 14:4** 4480
"**B** I exalted you from among the **1Ki 14:7**
3282, 834
b in him something good was found **1Ki 14:13** 3282
b they have made their Asherim, **1Ki 14:15**
3282, 834
b David did what was right in the **1Ki 15:5** 834
b she had made a horrid image as **1Ki 15:13** 834
and **b** of the sins of Jeroboam **1Ki 15:30** 5921
b of his provocation with which he **1Ki 15:30**

both **b** of all the evil which he **1Ki 16:7** 5921
of Jeroboam, and **b** he struck it. **1Ki 16:7**
5921, 834
b of his sins which he sinned, **1Ki 16:19** 5921
b there was no rain in the land. **1Ki 17:7** 3588
b you have forsaken the **1Ki 18:18**
b the journey is too great for you." **1Ki 19:7** 3588
'**B** the Arameans have said, **1Ki 20:28**
3282, 834
"**B** you have not listened to the **1Ki 20:36**
3282, 834
'**B** you have let go out of *your* **1Ki 20:42** 3282
b it is close beside my house, **1Ki 21:2** 3588
sullen and vexed **b** of the word **1Ki 21:4** 5921
"**B** I spoke to Naboth the **1Ki 21:6** 3588
b you have sold yourself to do **1Ki 21:20** 3282
b of the provocation with which **1Ki 21:22** 413
and **b** you have made Israel sin. **1Ki 21:22**
b Jezebel his wife incited him. **1Ki 21:25** 834
B he has humbled himself before **1Ki 21:29**
3282, 3588
b he does not prophesy good **1Ki 22:8** 3588
'Is it **b** there is no God in Israel **2Ki 1:3**
4480, 1097
'Is it **b** there is no God in Israel **2Ki 1:6**
4480, 1097
'**B** you have sent messengers to **2Ki 1:16**
3282, 834
is it **b** there is no God in Israel **2Ki 1:16**
4480, 1097
And **b** he had no son, Jehoram **2Ki 1:17** 3588
b by him the LORD had given **2Ki 5:1** 3588
"**B** I know the evil that you will **2Ki 8:12** 3588
b he was a son-in-law of the house **2Ki 8:27** 3588
of Ahab in Jezreel **b** he was sick. **2Ki 8:29** 3588
"**B** you have done well in **2Ki 10:30**
3282, 834
b of His covenant with Abraham, **2Ki 13:23** 4616
b they did not open *to him;* **2Ki 15:16** 3588
the LORD **b** of the king of Assyria. **2Ki 16:18**
4480, 6440
b the sons of Israel had sinned **2Ki 17:7** 3588
they kill them **b** they do not know **2Ki 17:26** 834
b they did not obey the voice of **2Ki 18:12**
5921, 834
"Do not be afraid **b** of the words **2Ki 19:6**
4480, 6440
'**B** you have prayed to Me about **2Ki 19:20** 834
'**B** of your raging against Me, And **2Ki 19:28** 3282
And **b** your arrogance has come up **2Ki 19:28**
"**B** Manasseh king of Judah has **2Ki 21:11**
3282, 834
b they have done evil in My sight, **2Ki 21:15**
3282, 834
b our fathers have not listened to **2Ki 22:13**
5921, 834
"**B** they have forsaken Me and have **2Ki 22:17**
8478, 834
b your heart was tender and you **2Ki 22:19** 3282
b of all the provocations with **2Ki 23:26** 5921
sight **b** of the sins of Manasseh, **2Ki 24:3**
"**B** I bore *him* with pain." **1Ch 4:9** 3588
b there was pasture there for **1Ch 4:41** 3588
but **b** he defiled his father's bed, **1Ch 5:1**
b their cattle had increased in **1Ch 5:9** 3588
He answered their prayers **b** they trusted **1Ch 5:20** 3588
fell slain, **b** the war *was* of God. **1Ch 5:22** 3588
b they came down to take their **1Ch 7:21** 3588
b misfortune had come upon his **1Ch 7:23** 3588
b the watch was committed to them; **1Ch 9:27** 3588
b of the word of the LORD which he **1Ch 10:13** 5921
b he asked counsel of a medium, **1Ch 10:13**
b of Saul the son of Kish; **1Ch 12:1**
4480, 6440
ark, **b** the oxen nearly upset *it.* **1Ch 13:9** 3588
b he put out his hand to the ark; **1Ch 13:10**
5921, 834
Then David became angry **b** of the **1Ch 13:11** 3588
"**B** you did not *carry it* at the **1Ch 15:13** 3588
in singing **b** he was skillful. **1Ch 15:22** 3588
B God was helping the Levites who **1Ch 15:26**
b His lovingkindness is **1Ch 16:41** 3588
b he had fought against Hadadezer **1Ch 18:10**
5921, 834
b his father showed kindness to me." **1Ch 19:2** 3588
b you have shed *so* much blood on **1Ch 22:8** 3588
b the LORD had said He would **1Ch 27:23** 3588
and **b** of this, wrath came upon **1Ch 27:24**
not build a house for My name **b** **1Ch 28:3** 3588
b they had offered so willingly, **1Ch 29:9** 5921
"**B** you had this in mind, and did **2Ch 1:11**
3282, 834
"**B** the LORD loves His people, He **2Ch 2:11**
stand to minister **b** of the cloud, **2Ch 5:14**
4480, 6440
'**B** it was in your heart to build a **2Ch 6:8** 3282, 834
b they have sinned against You, **2Ch 6:24** 3588
b they have sinned against You, **2Ch 6:26** 3588
b the glory of the LORD filled the **2Ch 7:2** 3588
b the bronze altar which Solomon **2Ch 7:7** 3588
rejoicing and happy of heart **b** of **2Ch 7:10** 5921
'**B** they forsook the LORD, the God **2Ch 7:22**
5921, 834
b the places are holy where the **2Ch 8:11** 3588
b your God loved Israel **2Ch 9:8**
b they had been unfaithful to the **2Ch 12:2** 3588
at Jerusalem **b** of Shishak, **2Ch 12:5**
4480, 6440
He did evil **b** he did not set **2Ch 12:14** 3588

b they trusted in the LORD, **2Ch 13:18** 3588
b the LORD had given him rest. **2Ch 14:6** 3588
b we have sought the LORD our God; **2Ch 14:7** 3588
b she had made a horrid image as **2Ch 15:16** 834
"**B** you have relied on the king of **2Ch 16:7**
Yet **b** you relied on the LORD, He **2Ch 16:8**
LORD was with Jehoshaphat **b** he **2Ch 17:3** 3588
b of this great multitude, **2Ch 20:15**
4480, 6440
the spoil **b** there was so much. **2Ch 20:25** 3588
"**B** you have allied yourself with **2Ch 20:37**
to Jehoram **b** he was the firstborn. **2Ch 21:3** 3588
destroy the house of David **b** of the **2Ch 21:7** 4616
b he had forsaken the LORD God of **2Ch 21:10** 3588
'**B** you have not walked in the ways **2Ch 21:12**
8478, 834
bowels come out **b** of the sickness, **2Ch 21:15** 4480
that his bowels came out **b** of his **2Ch 21:19** 5973
of Ahab in Jezreel, **b** he was sick. **2Ch 22:6** 3588
b he had done well in Israel and **2Ch 24:16** 3588
B you have forsaken the LORD, He **2Ch 24:20** 3588
b they had forsaken the LORD, **2Ch 24:24** 3588
conspired against him **b** of the blood **2Ch 24:25**
destroy you, **b** you have done this and **2Ch 25:16** 3588
into the hand *of Joash* **b** they had **2Ch 25:20** 3588
out **b** the LORD had smitten him. **2Ch 26:20** 3588
So Jotham became mighty **b** he **2Ch 27:6** 3588
b they had forsaken the LORD God **2Ch 28:6**
"Behold, **b** the LORD, the God of **2Ch 28:9**
Judah **b** of Ahaz king of Israel, **2Ch 28:19** 5668
"**B** the gods of the kings of Aram **2Ch 28:23** 3588
b the thing came about suddenly. **2Ch 29:36** 3588
b the priests had not consecrated **2Ch 30:3** 3588
b there was nothing like this in **2Ch 30:26** 3588
dismayed **b** of the king of Assyria nor **2Ch 32:7**
4480, 6440
nor **b** of all the horde that **2Ch 32:7**
4480, 6440
received, **b** his heart was proud; **2Ch 32:25** 3588
poured out on us **b** our fathers **2Ch 34:21**
5921, 834
"**B** they have forsaken Me and have **2Ch 34:25**
8478, 834
"**B** your heart was tender and you **2Ch 34:27** 3282
and **b** you humbled yourself before **2Ch 34:27**
for the priests, **b** the priests, **2Ch 35:14** 3588
b the Levites their brethren **2Ch 35:15** 3588
b He had compassion on His people **2Ch 36:15** 3588
b of the peoples of the lands; **Ezr 3:3** 4480
praised the LORD **b** the foundation **Ezr 3:11** 5921
"Now **b** we are in the service of **Ezr 4:14**
3606, 6903, 1768
'But **b** our fathers had provoked **Ezr 5:12**
4481, 1768
granted him all he requested **b** the **Ezr 7:6**
b the good hand of his God *was* **Ezr 7:9**
way, **b** we had said to the king, **Ezr 8:22** 3588
can stand before You **b** of this." **Ezr 9:15** 5921
trembling **b** of this matter and the **Ezr 10:9** 5921
granted *them* to me **b** the good hand **Ne 2:8**
and **b** of them we set up a guard **Ne 4:9** 5921
might get grain **b** of the famine." **Ne 5:3**
and we are helpless **b** our fields **Ne 5:5**
walk in the fear of our God **b** of **Ne 5:9** 4480
not do so **b** of the fear of God. **Ne 5:15**
4480, 6440
b the servitude was heavy on this **Ne 5:18** 3588
b Tobiah and Sanballat had hired him. **Ne 6:12**
bound by oath to him **b** he was **Ne 6:18** 3588
b they understood the words which **Ne 8:12** 3588
have set over us **b** of our sins; **Ne 9:37**
"Now **b** of all this We are making **Ne 9:38**
b God had given them great joy, **Ne 12:43** 3588
b they did not meet the sons of **Ne 13:2** 3588
b they have defiled the priesthood **Ne 13:29** 5921
b she did not obey the command of **Es 1:15**
5921, 834
hanged on the gallows **b** he had **Es 8:7** 5921, 834
b the dread of Mordecai had fallen **Es 9:3** 3588
b on those days the Jews rid **Es 9:22**
And **b** of the instructions in this **Es 9:26** 5921
B it did not shut the opening of **Jb 3:10** 3588
Which are turbid **b** of ice **Jb 6:16** 4480
B our days on earth are as a **Jb 8:9** 3588
you would trust, **b** there is hope; **Jb 11:18** 3588
B he has stretched out his hand **Jb 15:25** 3588
eye has also grown dim **b** of grief, **Jb 17:7** 4480
Even **b** of my inward agitation. **Jb 20:2** 5668
"**B** he knew no quiet within him, **Jb 20:20** 3588
"Is it **b** of your reverence that **Jb 22:4** 4480
will be buried **b** of the plague, **Jb 27:15**
B I delivered the poor who cried **Jb 29:12** 3588
"**B** He has loosed His bowstring **Jb 30:11** 3588
B I saw I had support in the gate, **Jb 31:21** 3588
And **b** of His majesty I can do **Jb 31:23** 4480
gloated **b** my wealth was great, **Jb 31:25** 3588
And **b** my hand had secured *so* much; **Jb 31:25** 3588
B I feared the great multitude, **Jb 31:34** 3588
b he was righteous in his own eyes. **Jb 32:1** 3588
b he justified himself before God. **Jb 32:2** 5921
b they had found no answer, **Jb 32:3**
5921, 834
b they were years older than he. **Jb 32:4** 3588
Shall I wait, **b** they do not speak, **Jb 32:16** 3588
B they stop *and* no longer answer? **Jb 32:16** 3588
B they turned aside from following **Jb 34:27**
834, 5921, 3651
terms, **b** you have rejected *it?* **Jb 34:33** 3588
B he answers like wicked men. **Jb 34:36** 5921

"**B** of the multitude of **Jb 35:9** 4480
help **b** of the arm of the mighty. **Jb 35:9** 4480
answer **B** of the pride of evil men. **Jb 35:12**
4480, 6440
b He has not visited *in* His anger, **Jb 35:15** 3588
land is still **b** of the south wind? **Jb 37:17** 4480
arrange *our case* **b** of darkness. **Jb 37:19**
4480, 6440
"Will you trust him **b** his **Jb 39:11** 3588
B God has made her forget wisdom, **Jb 39:17** 3588
B of the crashing they are **Jb 41:25** 4480
b you have not spoken of Me what **Jb 42:7** 3588
b you have not spoken of Me what **Jb 42:8** 3588
in Your righteousness **b** of my foes; **Ps 5:8** 4616
Save me **b** of Your lovingkindness. **Ps 6:4** 4616
old **b** of all my adversaries. **Ps 6:7**
strength **B** of Your adversaries, **Ps 8:2** 4616
"**B** of the devastation of the **Ps 12:5** 4480
b of the groaning of the needy, **Ps 12:5** 4480
B He has dealt bountifully with me. **Ps 13:6** 3588
B He is at my right hand, I will **Ps 16:8** 3588
And were shaken, **b** He was angry. **Ps 18:7** 3588
rescued me, **b** He delighted in me. **Ps 18:19** 3588
him, **b** He delights in him." **Ps 22:8** 3588
me in a level path **B** of my foes. **Ps 27:11** 4616
B they do not regard the works of **Ps 28:5** 3588
B He has heard the voice of my **Ps 28:6** 3588
B You have seen my affliction; **Ps 31:7** 834
has failed **b** of my iniquity, **Ps 31:10**
B of all my adversaries, I have **Ps 31:11** 4480
Him, **B** we trust in His holy name. **Ps 33:21** 3588
Do not fret **b** of evildoers, Be not **Ps 37:1**
Do not fret **b** of him who prospers **Ps 37:7**
B of the man who carries out **Ps 37:7**
B the LORD is the One who holds **Ps 37:24** 3588
them, **B** they take refuge in Him. **Ps 37:40** 3588
my flesh **b** of Your indignation; **Ps 38:3**
4480, 6440
no health in my bones **b** of my sin. **Ps 38:3**
4480, 6440
grow foul *and* fester **B** of my folly **Ps 38:5**
4480, 6440
b of the agitation of my heart. **Ps 38:8** 4480
I am full of anxiety **b** of my sin. **Ps 38:18** 4480
me, **b** I follow what is good. **Ps 38:20** 8478
B it is You who have done *it.* **Ps 39:9** 3588
B of the opposition of Your hand I **Ps 39:10** 4480
b of their shame Who say to me, **Ps 40:15**
5921, 6118
B my enemy does not shout in **Ps 41:11** 3588
Why do I go mourning **b** of the **Ps 42:9**
Why do I go mourning **b** of the **Ps 43:2**
B of the voice of him who **Ps 44:16** 4480
B of the presence of the enemy and **Ps 44:16** 4480
B He is your Lord, bow down to Him. **Ps 45:11** 3588
Judah rejoice **B** of Your judgments. **Ps 48:11** 4616
forever, **b** You have done *it,* **Ps 52:9** 3588
to shame, **b** God had rejected them. **Ps 53:5** 3588
B of the voice of the enemy, **Ps 55:3** 4480
B of the pressure of the wicked; **Ps 55:3**
4480, 6440
B of wickedness, cast them forth, **Ps 56:7** 5921
B *of* his strength I will watch **Ps 59:9**
may be displayed **b** of the truth. **Ps 60:4**
4480, 6440
loud, O Philistia, **b** of Me!" **Ps 60:8** 5921
B Your lovingkindness is better **Ps 63:3** 3588
B of the greatness of Your power **Ps 66:3**
B of Your temple at Jerusalem Kings **Ps 68:29** 4480
B for Your sake I have borne **Ps 69:7** 3588
Ransom me **b** of my enemies! **Ps 69:18** 4616
back **b** of their shame Who say, **Ps 70:3**
5921, 6118
B they did not believe in God And **Ps 78:22** 3588
see *it* and be ashamed, **B** You, **Ps 86:17** 3588
has wasted away **b** of affliction; **Ps 88:9** 4480
"**B** he has loved Me, therefore I **Ps 91:14** 3588
on high, **b** he has known My name. **Ps 91:14** 3588
have rejoiced **B** of Your judgments, **Ps 97:8** 4616
B of the loudness of my groaning **Ps 102:5** 4480
B of Your indignation and Your **Ps 102:10**
4480, 6440
B they were rebellious against His **Ps 106:33** 3588
B they had rebelled against the **Ps 107:11** 3588
Fools, **b** of their rebellious way, **Ps 107:17** 4480
way, And **b** of their iniquities, **Ps 107:17** 4480
they were glad **b** they were quiet, **Ps 107:30** 3588
B of the wickedness of those who **Ps 107:34** 4480
B he did not remember to show **Ps 109:16** 3282
B Your lovingkindness is good, **Ps 109:21** 3588
glory **B** of Your lovingkindness, **Ps 115:1** 5921
lovingkindness, **b** of Your truth. **Ps 115:1** 5921
b He hears My voice *and* my **Ps 116:1** 3588
B He has inclined His ear to me, **Ps 116:2** 3588
My soul weeps **b** of grief; **Ps 119:28** 4480
has seized me **b** of the wicked, **Ps 119:53** 4480
B of Your righteous ordinances. **Ps 119:62** 5921
be glad, **B** I wait for Your word. **Ps 119:74** 3588
B I have observed Your precepts. **Ps 119:100** 3588
water, **B** they do not keep Your law. **Ps 119:136** 5921
B my adversaries have forgotten **Ps 119:139** 3588
them, **B** they do not keep Your word. **Ps 119:158** 834
B of Your righteous ordinances. **Ps 119:164** 5921
B I called and you refused **Pr 1:24** 3282
B they hated knowledge And did **Pr 1:29**
8478, 3588
B they refuse to act with justice. **Pr 21:7** 3588
Do not rob the poor **b** he is poor, **Pr 22:22** 3588
Do not fret **b** of evildoers Or be **Pr 24:19**

B for a piece of bread a man will **Pr 28:21** 5921
B in much wisdom there is much **Ec 1:18** 3588
for my heart was pleased **b** of all **Ec 2:10** 4480
b everything is futility and **Ec 2:17** 3588
B all his days his task is painful **Ec 2:23** 3588
Two are better than one **b** they **Ec 4:9** 834
b God keeps him occupied with the **Ec 5:20** 3588
B that is the end of every man, **Ec 7:2** 834
the king **b** of the oath before God. **Ec 8:2** 5921, 1697
B the sentence against an evil **Ec 8:11** 834
a shadow, **b** he does not fear God. **Ec 8:13** 834
b composure allays great offenses. **Ec 10:4** 3588
b childhood and the prime of life **Ec 11:10** 3588
ones stand idle **b** they are few, **Ec 12:3** 3588
b this *applies to* every person. **Ec 12:13** 3588
"Do not stare at me **b** I am swarthy, **SS 1:6**
me with apples, **B** I am lovesick. **SS 2:5** 3588
B they are filled *with influences* **Is 2:6** 3588
B their speech and their actions **Is 3:8** 3588
"**B** the daughters of Zion are **Is 3:16** 3282, 3588
B I am a man of unclean lips, And **Is 6:5** 3588
do not be fainthearted **b** of these **Is 7:4** 4480
'**B** Aram, *with* Ephraim and the son **Is 7:5** 3282, 3588
b of the abundance of the milk **Is 7:22** 4480
b all the land will be briars and **Is 7:24** 3588
word, it is **b** they have no dawn. **Is 8:20** 834
yoke will be broken **b** of fatness. **Is 10:27** 4480, 6440
B you have ruined your country, **Is 14:20** 3588
place of slaughter **B** of the iniquity **Is 14:21**
B the rod that struck you is **Is 14:29** 3588
be in dread **b** of the waving of the **Is 19:16** 4480, 6440
b of the purpose of the LORD of **Is 19:17** 4480, 6440
cry to the LORD **b** of oppressors, **Is 19:20** 4480, 6440
dismayed and ashamed **b** of Cush **Is 20:5** 4480
peace, **B** he trusts in You. **Is 26:3** 3588
B you have said, **Is 28:15** 3588
B the wheel of *his* cart and his **Is 28:28**
"**B** this people draw near with **Is 29:13** 3282, 3588
"Everyone will be ashamed **b** of a **Is 30:5** 5921
trust in chariots **b** they are many And **Is 31:1** 3588
horsemen **b** they are very strong, **Is 31:1** 3588
rock will pass away **b** of panic, **Is 31:9** 4480
B the palace has been abandoned, **Is 32:14** 3588
"Do not be afraid **b** of the words **Is 37:6** 4480, 6440
'**B** you have prayed to Me about **Is 37:21** 834
"**B** of your raging against Me And **Is 37:29** 3282
And **b** your arrogance has come up **Is 37:29**
b of the bitterness of my soul. **Is 38:15** 5921
B of the greatness of His might **Is 40:26** 4480
B I have given waters in the **Is 43:20** 3588
"**B** I know that you are obstinate, **Is 48:4** 4480
B I knew that you would deal very **Is 48:8** 3588
B of the LORD who is faithful, the **Is 49:7** 4616
b of the fury of the oppressor, **Is 51:13** 4480, 6440
death, **B** He had done no violence, **Is 53:9** 5921
B He poured out Himself to death, **Is 53:12** 8478, 834
assails you will fall **b** of you. **Is 54:15** 5921
to you, **B** of the LORD your God, **Is 55:5** 4616
"**B** of the iniquity of his unjust **Is 57:17**
"If **b** of the sabbath, you turn **Is 58:13** 4480
B the abundance of the sea will be **Is 60:5** 3588
of Israel **b** He has glorified you. **Is 60:9** 3588
B the LORD has anointed me To **Is 61:1** 3282
will recognize them **B** they are **Is 61:9** 3588
"**B** they have burned incense on **Is 65:7** 834
B I called, but you did not answer; **Is 65:12** 3282
"**B** he who is blessed in the earth **Is 65:16** 834
B the former troubles are **Is 65:16** 3588
b they are hidden from My sight! **Is 65:16** 3588
B I called, but no one answered; **Is 66:4** 3282
how to speak, **B** I am a youth." **Jer 1:6** 3588
a youth,' **B** everywhere I send you, **Jer 1:7** 3588
into judgment with you **B** you say, **Jer 2:35** 5921
"**B** of the lightness of her harlotry, **Jer 3:9** 4480
B they have perverted their way, **Jer 3:21** 3588
it, **B** of the evil of your deeds." **Jer 4:4** 4480, 6440
B she has rebelled against Me,' **Jer 4:17** 3588
be silent, **B** you have heard, **Jer 4:19** 3588
above be dark, **B** I have spoken, **Jer 4:28** 5921, 3588
B their transgressions are many, **Jer 5:6** 3588
"**B** you have spoken this word, **Jer 5:14** 3282
"Were they ashamed **b** of the **Jer 6:15** 3588
B they have not listened to My **Jer 6:19** 3588, 5921
B the LORD has rejected them. **Jer 6:30** 3588
and see what I did to it **b** of the **Jer 7:12** 4480, 6440
b you have done all these things," **Jer 7:13** 3282
Topheth **b** there is no *other* place. **Jer 7:32** 4480
B from the least even to the **Jer 8:10** 3588
"Were they ashamed **b** of the **Jer 8:12** 3588
B the LORD our God has doomed us **Jer 8:14** 3588
B every brother deals craftily, **Jer 9:4** 3588
b of the daughter of My people? **Jer 9:7** 4480, 6440
a dirge, **B** they are laid waste so **Jer 9:10** 3588

"**B** they have forsaken My law **Jer 9:13** 5921
B they have cast down our **Jer 9:19** 3588
B it is wood cut from the forest, **Jer 10:3** 3588
be carried, **B** they cannot walk! **Jer 10:5** 3588
Woe is me, **b** of my injury! **Jer 10:19** 5921
call to Me **b** of their disaster. **Jer 11:14** 1157
pronounced evil against you **b** of **Jer 11:17** 1558
snatched away, **B** *men* have said, **Jer 12:4** 3588
B no man lays it to heart. **Jer 12:11** 3588
But be ashamed of your harvest **B** **Jer 12:13** 4480
B the flock of the LORD has been **Jer 13:17** 3588
B of the magnitude of your **Jer 13:22**
"**B** you have forgotten Me And **Jer 13:25** 834
"**B** the ground is cracked, For **Jer 14:4** 5668
her young, **B** there is no grass. **Jer 14:5** 3588
b of the famine and the sword; **Jer 14:16** 4480, 6440
of the earth **b** of Manasseh, **Jer 15:4** 1558
B of Your hand *upon me* I sat alone, **Jer 15:17** 4480, 6440
'*It is* **b** your forefathers have **Jer 16:11** 5921, 834
sin, **b** they have polluted My land; **Jer 16:18** 5921
B they have forsaken the fountain **Jer 17:13** 3588
"**B** they have forsaken Me and have **Jer 19:4** 3282, 834
and **b** they have filled this place **Jer 19:4**
and hiss **b** of all its disasters. **Jer 19:8** 5921
and they will bury in Topheth **b** **Jer 19:11** 4480
b of all the houses on whose **Jer 19:13**
b they have stiffened their necks **Jer 19:15** 3588
B for me the word of the LORD has **Jer 20:8** 3588
ashamed, **b** they have failed, **Jer 20:11** 3588
B he did not kill me before birth, **Jer 20:17** 834
it, **B** of the evil of their deeds. **Jer 21:12** 4480, 6440
'**B** they forsook the covenant of **Jer 22:9** 5921, 834
king **b** you are competing in cedar? **Jer 22:15** 3588
B of all your wickedness. **Jer 22:22** 4480
B of the LORD And because of His **Jer 23:9** 4480, 6440
the LORD And **b** of His holy words. **Jer 23:9** 4480, 6440
the land mourns **b** of the curse. **Jer 23:10** 4480, 6440
fathers forgot My name **b** of Baal? **Jer 23:27**
b every man's own word will become **Jer 23:36** 3588
'**B** you said this word, **Jer 23:38** 3282
'**B** you have not obeyed My words, **Jer 25:8** 3282, 834
stagger and go mad **b** of the sword **Jer 25:16** 4480, 6440
and rise no more **b** of the sword **Jer 25:27** 4480, 6440
B the LORD has a controversy with **Jer 25:31** 3588
made silent **B** of the fierce anger of **Jer 25:37** 4480, 6440
For their land has become a horror **B** **Jer 25:38** 4480, 6440
And **b** of His fierce anger." **Jer 25:38** 4480, 6440
b of the evil of their deeds.' **Jer 26:3** 4480, 6440
b you have counseled rebellion **Jer 28:16** 3588
"**B** you have said, **Jer 29:15** 3588
b they have not listened to My **Jer 29:19** 8478, 834
'**B** of them a curse will be used by **Jer 29:22** 4480
b they have acted foolishly in **Jer 29:23** 3282, 834
'**B** you have sent letters in your **Jer 29:25** 3282, 834
"**B** Shemaiah has prophesied to **Jer 29:31** 3282, 834
'**b** he has preached rebellion **Jer 29:32** 3588
B your iniquity is great *And* your **Jer 30:14** 5921
B your iniquity is great *And* your **Jer 30:15** 5921
'**B** they have called you an **Jer 30:17** 3588
children, **B** they are no more." **Jer 31:15** 3588
B I bore the reproach of my youth.' **Jer 31:19** 3588
b Zedekiah king of Judah had shut **Jer 32:3** 834
fight against it, **b** of the sword, **Jer 32:24** 4480, 6440
b of all the evil of the sons of **Jer 32:32** 5921
city **b** of all their wickedness: **Jer 33:5** 5921
fear and tremble **b** of all the good **Jer 33:9** 5921
b I spoke to them but they did not **Jer 35:17** 3282
'**B** you have obeyed the command of **Jer 35:18** 3282, 834
from Jerusalem **b** of Pharaoh's army, **Jer 37:11** 4480, 6440
right where he is **b** of the famine, **Jer 38:9** 4480, 6440
booty, **b** you have trusted in Me," **Jer 39:18** 3588
B you *people* sinned against the **Jer 40:3** 3588
he had struck down **b** of Gedaliah, **Jer 41:9** 3027
b of the Chaldeans; **Jer 41:18** 4480, 6440
b we are left *but* a few out of **Jer 42:2** 3588
b of their wickedness which they **Jer 44:3** 4480, 6440
it, **b** of the evil of your deeds, **Jer 44:22** 4480, 6440
b of the abominations which you **Jer 44:22** 4480, 6440
"**B** you have burned sacrifices and **Jer 44:23** 4480, 6440
b the LORD has thrust them down. **Jer 46:15** 3588

"**B** of the noise of the galloping **Jer 47:3** 4480
B of the limpness of *their* hands, **Jer 47:3** 4480
"For **b** of your trust in your own **Jer 48:7** 3282
destroyed from *being* a people **B** he **Jer 48:42** 3588
their pasture desolate **b** of them. **Jer 49:20** 5921
"**B** you are glad, because you are **Jer 50:11** 3588
you are glad, **b** you are jubilant, **Jer 50:11** 3588
B you skip about like a **Jer 50:11** 3588
"**B** of the indignation of the LORD **Jer 50:13** 4480
And will hiss **b** of all her wounds. **Jer 50:13** 5921
seized **B** you have engaged in conflict **Jer 50:24** 3588
their pasture desolate **b** of them. **Jer 50:45** 5921
B His purpose is against Babylon **Jer 51:11** 3588
ashamed **b** we have heard reproach; **Jer 51:51** 3588
b of the calamity that I am going **Jer 51:64** 4480, 6440
are in mourning **B** no one comes to **La 1:4** 4480, 1097
caused her grief **B** of the multitude **La 1:5** 5921
B they have seen her nakedness; **La 1:8** 3588
B far from me is a comforter, One **La 1:16** 3588
B the enemy has prevailed." **La 1:16** 3588
My eyes fail **b** of tears, My spirit **La 2:11**
B of the destruction of the **La 2:11** 5921
little ones Who are faint **b** of hunger **La 2:19**
B of the rod of His wrath. **La 3:1**
streams of water **B** of the destruction **La 3:48** 5921
My eyes bring pain to my soul **B** of **La 3:51** 4480
the roof of its mouth **b** of thirst; **La 4:4**
They became food for them **B** of the **La 4:10**
B of the sins of her prophets *And* **La 4:13** 4480
B of the sword in the wilderness. **La 5:9** 4480, 6440
B of the burning heat of famine. **La 5:10** 4480, 6440
B of this our heart is faint, **La 5:17** 5921
B of these things our eyes are dim; **La 5:17** 5921
B of Mount Zion which lies **La 5:18** 5921
surely live **b** he took warning; **Ezk 3:21** 3588
b bread and water will be scarce; **Ezk 4:17** 4616
"**B** you have more turmoil than the **Ezk 5:7** 3282
'And **b** of all your abominations, I **Ezk 5:9** 3282
b you have defiled My sanctuary **Ezk 5:11** 3282
b of all the evil abominations of **Ezk 6:11** 413
b their land will be stripped of **Ezk 12:19** 4616
"**B** you have spoken falsehood and **Ezk 13:8** 3282
"It is definitely **b** they have **Ezk 13:10** 3282
"**B** you disheartened the righteous **Ezk 13:22** 3282
pass through it **b** of the beasts, **Ezk 14:15** 4480, 6440
make the land desolate, **b** they have **Ezk 15:8** 3282
for it was perfect **b** of My **Ezk 16:14**
played the harlot **b** of your fame, **Ezk 16:15** 5921
b you were not satisfied; **Ezk 16:28** 4480
b you give money and no money is **Ezk 16:34**
"**B** your lewdness was poured out **Ezk 16:36** 3282
and **b** of the blood of your sons **Ezk 16:36**
"**B** you have not remembered the **Ezk 16:43** 3282, 834
B of your sins in which you acted **Ezk 16:52**
but not **b** of your covenant. **Ezk 16:61** 4480
anymore **b** of your humiliation, **Ezk 16:63** 4480, 6440
father, **b** he practiced extortion, **Ezk 18:18** 3588
b of his righteousness which he **Ezk 18:22**
iniquity and dies **b** of it, **Ezk 18:26** 5921
"**B** he considered and turned away **Ezk 18:28**
B of the sound of his roaring. **Ezk 19:7** 4480
of branches **B** of abundant waters. **Ezk 19:10** 4480
b they rejected My ordinances, and **Ezk 20:16** 3282
b they had not observed My **Ezk 20:24** 3282
them unclean **b** of their gifts, **Ezk 20:26**
"**B** I will cut off from you the **Ezk 21:4** 3282
'**B** of the news that is coming; **Ezk 21:7** 413
'**B** you have made your iniquity to **Ezk 21:24** 3282
b you have come to remembrance, **Ezk 21:24** 3282
'**B** all of you have become dross, **Ezk 22:19** 3282
b of the breasts of your youth. **Ezk 23:21** 4616
to you **b** you have played the harlot **Ezk 23:30**
b you have defiled yourself with **Ezk 23:30** 5921, 834
'**B** you have forgotten Me and cast **Ezk 23:35** 3282
b they are adulteresses and blood **Ezk 23:45** 3588
B I *would* have cleansed you, Yet **Ezk 24:13** 3282
says the Lord GOD, "**B** you said, **Ezk 25:3** 3282
"**B** you have clapped your hands **Ezk 25:6** 3282
"**B** Moab and Seir say, **Ezk 25:8** 3282
"**B** Edom has acted against the **Ezk 25:12** 3282
"**B** the Philistines have acted in **Ezk 25:15** 3282
b Tyre has said concerning **Ezk 26:2** 3282, 834
"**B** of the multitude of his **Ezk 26:10** 4480
"Tarshish was your customer **b** of the **Ezk 27:12** 4480
"Aram was your customer **b** of the **Ezk 27:16** 4480
"Damascus was your customer **b** of **Ezk 27:18**
b of the abundance of all *kinds* of **Ezk 27:18** 4480
b of the wine of Helbon and white **Ezk 27:18**
"**B** your heart is lifted up And **Ezk 28:2** 3282
is lifted up **b** of your riches **Ezk 28:5**
'**B** you have made your heart Like **Ezk 28:6** 3282
was lifted up **b** of your beauty; **Ezk 28:17**
B they have been *only* a staff *made* **Ezk 29:6** 3282
B you said, 'The Nile is mine, **Ezk 29:9** 3282
performed, **b** they acted for Me," **Ezk 29:20** 834
its branches long **B** of many waters **Ezk 31:5** 4480
"**B** it is high in stature **Ezk 31:10** 3282, 834
he will not stumble **b** of it in the **Ezk 33:12**
desolation and a waste **b** of all their **Ezk 33:29** 5921

b My flock has become a prey,	Ezk 34:8	3282
"**B** you push with side and with	Ezk 34:21	3282
"**B** you have had everlasting	Ezk 35:5	3282
"**B** you have said,	Ezk 35:10	3282
b of your hatred against them;	Ezk 35:11	4480
house of Israel **b** it was desolate,	Ezk 35:15	5921, 834
"**B** the enemy has spoken against	Ezk 36:2	3282
in My wrath **b** you have endured	Ezk 36:6	3282
'**B** they say to you,	Ezk 36:13	3282
b they had defiled it with their	Ezk 36:18	
holy name, **b** it was said of them,	Ezk 36:20	
went into exile for their iniquity **b**	Ezk 39:23	5921, 834
I am the LORD their God **b** I made	Ezk 39:28	
B the structure surrounding the	Ezk 41:7	3588
the upper chambers *were* smaller **b**	Ezk 42:5	3588
"**B** they ministered to them before	Ezk 44:12	3282, 834
They will bear every month **b** their	Ezk 47:12	3588
B of this the king became	Da 2:12	3606, 6903
b the king's command *was* urgent	Da 3:22	4481, 1768
queen entered the banquet hall **b**	Da 5:10	6903
was **b** an extraordinary spirit,	Da 5:12	3606, 6903, 1768
"**B** of the grandeur which He bestowed	Da 5:19	4481
b he possessed an extraordinary	Da 6:3	3606, 6903, 1768
him, **b** he had trusted in his God.	Da 6:23	1768
"Then I kept looking **b** of the	Da 7:11	4481
b of their unfaithful deeds which	Da 9:7	
b we have sinned against You.	Da 9:8	834
for **b** of our sins and the	Da 9:16	3588
b Your city and Your people are	Da 9:19	3588
b *it is* still *to come* at the	Da 11:35	3588
B they are children of harlotry.	Hos 2:4	3588
B there is no faithfulness or	Hos 4:1	3588
B you have rejected knowledge, I	Hos 4:6	3588
B they have stopped giving heed to	Hos 4:10	3588
B their shade is pleasant.	Hos 4:13	3588
be ashamed **b** of their sacrifices.	Hos 4:19	4480
B he was determined to follow	Hos 5:11	3588
fall by the sword **B** of the insolence	Hos 7:16	4480
B they have transgressed My	Hos 8:1	3282
begin to diminish **B** of the burden	Hos 8:10	4480
they will go **b** of destruction;	Hos 9:6	4480
B of the grossness of your	Hos 9:7	5921
And **b** your hostility is *so*	Hos 9:7	
B of the wickedness of their deeds	Hos 9:15	5921
B they have not listened to Him;	Hos 9:17	3588
B you have trusted in your way, in	Hos 10:13	3588
Bethel **b** of your great wickedness.	Hos 10:15	4480, 6440
B they refused to return *to Me.*	Hos 11:5	3588
consume *them* **b** of their counsels.	Hos 11:6	4480
have stumbled **b** of your iniquity.	Hos 14:1	
B the harvest of the field is	Jl 1:11	3588
B there is no pasture for them;	Jl 1:18	3588
B of the violence done to the sons	Jl 3:19	4480
B they threshed Gilead with	Am 1:3	5921
B they deported an entire	Am 1:6	5921
B they delivered up an entire	Am 1:9	5921
B he pursued his brother with the	Am 1:11	5921
B they ripped open the pregnant	Am 1:13	5921
B he burned the bones of the king	Am 2:1	5921
B they rejected the law of the	Am 2:4	5921
B they sell the righteous for	Am 2:6	5921
B I will do this to you, Prepare	Am 4:12	6118, 3588
b you impose heavy rent on the	Am 5:11	3282
B I will pass through the midst	Am 5:17	3588
"**B** of this will not the land	Am 8:8	5921
"**B** of violence to your brother	Ob 1:10	4480
"**B** just as you drank on My holy	Ob 1:16	3588
of the LORD, **b** he had told them.	Jon 1:10	3588
B of this I must lament and wail,	Mi 1:8	5921
B a calamity has come down from	Mi 1:12	3588
B in you were found The rebellious acts	Mi 1:13	3588
B of the children of your delight;	Mi 1:16	3588
For this is no place of rest **B** of	Mi 2:10	5668
B they have practiced evil deeds.	Mi 3:4	834
B there is no answer from God.	Mi 3:7	3588
B at that time He will be great To	Mi 5:4	3588
B the LORD has a case against His	Mi 6:2	3588
Desolating *you* **b** of your sins.	Mi 6:13	5921
LORD **B** I have sinned against Him,	Mi 7:9	3588
desolate **b** of her inhabitants,	Mi 7:13	5921
B He delights in unchanging love.	Mi 7:18	3588
Mountains quake **b** of Him And the	Na 1:5	4480
All **b** of the many harlotries of	Na 3:4	4480
B *I am* doing something in your	Hab 1:5	3588
B through these things their catch	Hab 1:16	3588
"**B** you have looted many nations,	Hab 2:8	3588
B of human bloodshed and violence	Hab 2:8	4480
B of human bloodshed and violence	Hab 2:17	4480
B I must wait quietly for the day	Hab 3:16	834
B they have sinned against the	Zph 1:17	3588
b they have taunted and become	Zph 2:10	3588
feel no shame **B** of all your deeds	Zph 3:11	4480
"**B** of My house which *lies*	Hg 1:9	3282
b of you the sky has withheld its	Hg 1:10	5921
b of the multitude of men and	Zch 2:4	4480
his staff in his hand **b** of age.	Zch 8:4	4480
was no peace **b** of his enemies,	Zch 8:10	4480
camp around My house **b** of an army,	Zch 9:8	4480
B of him who passes by and returns;	Zch 9:8	4480
b of the blood of *My* covenant with	Zch 9:11	
afflicted, **b** there is no shepherd.	Zch 10:2	3588
B I have had compassion on them;	Zch 10:6	3588
B the glorious *trees* have been	Zch 11:2	834
b you are not taking *it* to heart.	Mal 2:2	3588
b He no longer regards the	Mal 2:13	4480
B the LORD has been a witness	Mal 2:14	5921, 3588
COMFORTED, **B** THEY WERE NO MORE.	Mt 2:18	3754
say all kinds of evil against you **b**	Mt 5:11	1752a
b they were distressed and	Mt 9:36	3754
"You will be hated by all **b** of My	Mt 10:22	1223
were done, **b** they did not repent.	Mt 11:20	3754
and will condemn it **b** they	Mt 12:41	3754
b she came from the ends of the	Mt 12:42	3754
up, **b** they had no depth of soil.	Mt 13:5	1223
and **b** they had no root, they	Mt 13:6	1223
b while seeing they do not see,	Mt 13:13	3754
blessed are your eyes, **b** they see;	Mt 13:16	3754
and your ears, **b** they hear.	Mt 13:16	3754
persecution arises **b** of the word,	Mt 13:21	1223
there **b** of their unbelief.	Mt 13:58	1223
he bound him and put him in prison **b**	Mt 14:3	1223
b they regarded John as a prophet.	Mt 14:5	3754
it to be given **b** of his oaths,	Mt 14:9	1223
oaths, and **b** of his dinner guests.	Mt 14:9	
b she keeps shouting at us."	Mt 15:23	3754
b they have remained with Me now	Mt 15:32	3754
b we did not bring *any* bread."	Mt 16:7	3754
b flesh and blood did not reveal	Mt 16:17	3754
"**B** of the littleness of your	Mt 17:20	1223
world **b** of *its* stumbling blocks!	Mt 18:7	575
all that debt **b** you pleaded with me.	Mt 18:32	1893
"**B** of your hardness of heart Moses	Mt 19:8	4314
'**B** no one hired us.'	Mt 20:7	3754
your eye envious **b** I am generous?'	Mt 20:15	3754
b they considered Him to be a prophet.	Mt 21:46	1893
b you shut off the kingdom of	Mt 23:13	3754
b you devour widows' houses,	Mt 23:14	3754
b you travel around on sea and land	Mt 23:15	3754
you will be hated by all nations **b** of	Mt 24:9	1223
"**B** lawlessness is increased, most	Mt 24:12	1223
all fall away **b** of Me this night,	Mt 26:31	1722
though all may fall away **b** of You,	Mt 26:33	1722
For he knew that **b** of envy they	Mt 27:18	1223
greatly in a dream **b** of Him."	Mt 27:19	1223
to speak, **b** they knew who He was.	Mk 1:34	3754
to get to Him **b** of the crowd,	Mk 2:4	1223
ready for Him **b** of the crowd,	Mk 3:9	1223
b they were saying,	Mk 3:30	3754
up **b** it had no depth of soil.	Mk 4:5	1223
and **b** it had no root, it withered	Mk 4:6	1223
persecution arises **b** of the word,	Mk 4:17	1223
sickle, **b** the harvest has come."	Mk 4:29	3754
b he had often been bound with	Mk 5:4	1223
Philip, **b** he had married her.	Mk 6:17	3754
yet **b** of his oaths and because of	Mk 6:26	1223
oaths and **b** of his dinner guests,	Mk 6:26	
compassion for them **b** they were	Mk 6:34	3754
b it does not go into his heart,	Mk 7:19	3754
"**B** of this answer go;	Mk 7:29	1223
feel compassion for the people **b**	Mk 8:2	3754
him **b** he was not following us."	Mk 9:38	3754
water to drink **b** of your name as	Mk 9:41	3754
"**B** of your hardness of heart he	Mk 10:5	4314
"You will be hated by all **b** of My	Mk 13:13	1223
all fall away, **b** it is written,	Mk 14:27	3754
had handed Him over **b** of envy.	Mk 15:10	1223
b it was the preparation day,	Mk 15:42	1893
b they had not believed those who	Mk 16:14	3754
no child, **b** Elizabeth was barren,	Lk 1:7	2530
b you did not believe my words,	Lk 1:20	473, 3739
B of the tender mercy of our God,	Lk 1:78	1223
b he was of the house and family	Lk 2:4	1223
b there was no room for them in	Lk 2:7	1360
the tetrarch was reprimanded by him **b**	Lk 3:19	4012
and **b** of all the wicked things which	Lk 3:19	4012
B HE ANOINTED ME TO PREACH THE	Lk 4:18	3739, 1752a
b they knew Him to be the Christ.	Lk 4:41	3754
companions **b** of the catch of fish	Lk 5:9	1909
to bring him in **b** of the crowd,	Lk 5:19	1223
it, **b** it had been well built.	Lk 6:48	1223
away, **b** it had no moisture.	Lk 8:6	1223
to get to Him **b** of the crowd.	Lk 8:19	1223
b it was said by some that John	Lk 9:7	1223
and we tried to prevent him **b** he	Lk 9:49	3754
not receive Him, **b** He was traveling	Lk 9:53	3754
him *anything* **b** he is his friend,	Lk 11:8	1223
yet **b** of his persistence he will	Lk 11:8	1223
b she came from the ends of the	Lk 11:31	3754
b they repented at the preaching	Lk 11:32	3754
b it was they who killed them, and	Lk 11:48	3754
b they suffered this *fate?*	Lk 13:2	3754
indignant **b** Jesus had healed on	Lk 13:14	3754
b he has received him back safe	Lk 15:27	3754
manager **b** he had acted shrewdly;	Lk 16:8	3754
"He does not thank the slave **b** he	Lk 17:9	3754
yet **b** this widow bothers me, I	Lk 18:5	1223
and was unable **b** of the crowd,	Lk 19:3	575
has come to this house, **b** he,	Lk 19:9	2530
parable, **b** He was near Jerusalem,	Lk 19:11	1223
b you have been faithful in a very	Lk 19:17	3754
of you, **b** you are an exacting man;	Lk 19:21	3754
b you did not recognize the time	Lk 19:44	473, 3739
for they cannot even die anymore, **b**	Lk 20:36	1063
and you will be hated by all **b** of My	Lk 21:17	1223
b these are days of vengeance, so	Lk 21:22	3754
b your redemption is drawing near."	Lk 21:28	1360
b he had been hearing about Him	Lk 23:8	1223
b the sun was obscured; and the veil	Lk 23:45	
they still could not believe *it* **b**	Lk 24:41	575
"**B** I said to you that I saw you	Jn 1:50	3754
and **b** He did not need anyone to	Jn 2:25	3754
b he has not believed in the name	Jn 3:18	3754
b there was much water there;	Jn 3:23	3754
b of the bridegroom's voice.	Jn 3:29	1223
believed in Him **b** of the word of	Jn 4:39	1223
Many more believed **b** of His word;	Jn 4:41	1223
"It is no longer **b** of what you	Jn 4:42	1223
b He was doing these things on the	Jn 5:16	3754
b He not only was breaking the	Jn 5:18	3754
judgment, **b** He is *the* Son of Man.	Jn 5:27	3754
just, **b** I do not seek My own will,	Jn 5:30	3754
b you think that in them you have	Jn 5:39	3754
b they saw the signs which	Jn 6:2	3754
up **b** a strong wind was blowing.	Jn 6:18	
you seek Me, not **b** you saw signs,	Jn 6:26	3754
but **b** you ate of the loaves and	Jn 6:26	3754
grumbling about Him, **b** He said,	Jn 6:41	3754
Me, and I live **b** of the Father,	Jn 6:57	1223
Me, he also will live **b** of Me.	Jn 6:57	1223
b the Jews were seeking to kill	Jn 7:1	3754
but it hates Me **b** I testify of it,	Jn 7:7	3754
I do not go up to this feast **b** My	Jn 7:8	3754
(not **b** it is from Moses,	Jn 7:22	3754
are you angry with Me **b** I made an	Jn 7:23	3754
b I am from Him, and He sent Me."	Jn 7:29	3754
Him, **b** His hour had not yet come.	Jn 7:30	3754
b Jesus was not yet glorified.	Jn 7:39	3754
in the crowd **b** of Him.	Jn 7:43	1223
Him, **b** His hour had not yet come.	Jn 8:20	3754
Me, **b** My word has no place in you.	Jn 8:37	3754
It is **b** you cannot hear My word.	Jn 8:43	3754
truth **b** there is no truth in him.	Jn 8:44	3754
"But **b** I speak the truth, you do	Jn 8:45	3754
hear *them,* **b** you are not of God."	Jn 8:47	3754
b He does not keep the Sabbath."	Jn 9:16	3754
b they were afraid of the Jews;	Jn 9:22	3754
follow him **b** they know his voice.	Jn 10:4	3754
b they do not know the voice of	Jn 10:5	3754
"*He flees* **b** he is a hired hand	Jn 10:13	3754
b I lay down My life so that I may	Jn 10:17	3754
among the Jews **b** of these words.	Jn 10:19	1223
b you are not of My sheep.	Jn 10:26	3754
and **b** You, being a man, make	Jn 10:33	3754
'You are blaspheming,' **b** I said,	Jn 10:36	3754
b he sees the light of this world.	Jn 11:9	3754
b the light is not in him."	Jn 11:10	3754
but **b** of the people standing	Jn 11:42	1223
not **b** he was concerned about the	Jn 12:6	3754
the poor, but **b** he was a thief,	Jn 12:6	3754
b on account of him many of the	Jn 12:11	3754
b they heard that He had performed	Jn 12:18	3754
Isaiah said **b** he saw His glory,	Jn 12:41	3754
but **b** of the Pharisees they were	Jn 12:42	1223
b Judas had the money box,	Jn 13:29	1893
otherwise believe **b** of the works	Jn 14:11	1223
b I go to the Father.	Jn 14:12	3754
b it does not see Him or know	Jn 14:17	3754
you know Him **b** He abides with you	Jn 14:17	3754
b I live, you will live also.	Jn 14:19	3754
rejoiced **b** I go to the Father	Jn 14:28	3754
"You are already clean **b** of the	Jn 15:3	1223
but **b** you are not of the world,	Jn 15:19	3754
b of this the world hates you.	Jn 15:19	3754
b they do not know the One who	Jn 15:21	3754
b you have been with Me from the	Jn 15:27	3754
b they have not known the Father or	Jn 16:3	3754
the beginning, **b** I was with you.	Jn 16:4	3754
"But **b** I have said these things	Jn 16:6	3754
sin, **b** they do not believe in Me;	Jn 16:9	3754
b I go to the Father and	Jn 16:10	3754
b the ruler of this world has been	Jn 16:11	3754
'**b** I go to the Father'?"	Jn 16:17	3754
has pain, **b** her hour has come;	Jn 16:21	3754
she no longer remembers the anguish **b**	Jn 16:21	3754
loves you, **b** you have loved Me and	Jn 16:27	3754
alone, **b** the Father is with Me.	Jn 16:32	3754
them, **b** they are not of the world,	Jn 17:14	3754
He ought to die **b** He made Himself	Jn 19:7	3754
b it was the day of preparation,	Jn 19:31	1893
Therefore **b** of the Jewish day of	Jn 19:42	1223
"**B** they have taken away my Lord,	Jn 20:13	3754
"**B** you have seen Me, have you	Jn 20:29	3754
in **b** of the great number of fish.	Jn 21:6	575
b He said to him the third time,	Jn 21:17	3754
b each one of them was hearing them	Ac 2:6	3754
B YOU WILL NOT ABANDON MY SOUL	Ac 2:27	3754
"And so, **b** he was a prophet and	Ac 2:30	
being greatly disturbed **b** they	Ac 4:2	1223
b they were all glorifying God for	Ac 4:21	3754
b their widows were being	Ac 6:1	3754
attention **b** he had for a long time	Ac 8:11	1223
b you thought you could obtain the	Ac 8:20	3754
b the gift of the Holy Spirit had	Ac 10:45	3754
were scattered **b** of the persecution	Ac 11:19	575
b of her joy she did not open the	Ac 12:14	575
b their country was fed by the	Ac 12:20	1223
b he did not give God the glory,	Ac 12:23	473, 3739
b he was the chief speaker.	Ac 14:12	1894
rejoiced **b** of its encouragement.	Ac 15:31	1909
circumcised him **b** of the Jews who	Ac 16:3	1223
b he was preaching Jesus and the	Ac 17:18	3754
b He has fixed a day in which He	Ac 17:31	2530
b Claudius had commanded all the	Ac 18:2	1223

and **b** he was of the same trade, he Ac 18:3 *1223*
he could not find out the facts **b** of Ac 21:34 *1223*
b of the violence of the mob; Ac 21:35 *1223*
"But since I could not see **b** of Ac 22:11 *575*
b they will not accept your Ac 22:18 *1360*
and **b** he had put him in chains. Ac 22:29 *3754*
especially **b** you are an expert in Ac 26:3
Cyprus **b** the winds were contrary. Ac 27:4 *1223*
B the harbor was not suitable for Ac 27:12
for **b** of the rain that had set in Ac 28:2 *1223*
that had set in and **b** of the cold, Ac 28:2 *1223*
a viper came out **b** of the heat and Ac 28:3 *575*
willing to release me **b** there was Ac 28:18 *1223*
b your faith is being proclaimed Ro 1:8 *3754*
b that which is known about God is Ro 1:19 *1360*
But **b** of your stubbornness and Ro 2:5 *2596*
AMONG THE GENTILES **B** OF YOU," Ro 2:24 *1223*
b by the works of the Law no flesh Ro 3:20 *1360*
b in the forbearance of God He Ro 3:25 *1223*
over **b** of our transgressions, Ro 4:25 *1223*
was raised **b** of our justification. Ro 4:25 *1223*
b the love of God has been poured Ro 5:5 *3754*
spread to all men, **b** all sinned Ro 5:12
1909, 3739
Shall we sin **b** we are not under Ro 6:15 *3754*
b of the weakness of your flesh. Ro 6:19 *1223*
b the mind set on the flesh is Ro 8:7 *1360*
though the body is dead **b** of sin, Ro 8:10 *1223*
is alive **b** of righteousness. Ro 8:10 *1223*
but **b** of Him who subjected it, Ro 8:20 *1223*
b He intercedes for the saints Ro 8:27 *3754*
nor are they all children **b** Ro 9:7 *3754*
would stand, not **b** of works Ro 9:11 *1537*
of works but **b** of Him who calls, Ro 9:11 *1537*
B *they did* not *pursue it* by faith, Ro 9:32 *3754*
mercy **b** of their disobedience, Ro 11:30
that **b** of the mercy shown Ro 11:31
subjection, not only **b** of wrath, Ro 13:5 *1223*
For **b** of this you also pay taxes, Ro 13:6 *1223*
if **b** of food your brother is hurt, Ro 14:15 *1223*
b *his eating is* not from faith; Ro 14:23 *3754*
b of the grace that was given me Ro 15:15 *1223*
B the foolishness of God is wiser 1Co 1:25 *3754*
b they are spiritually appraised. 1Co 2:14 *3754*
b it is *to be* revealed with fire, 1Co 3:13 *3754*
b we have become a spectacle to 1Co 4:9 *3754*
But **b** of immoralities, each 1Co 7:2 *1223*
you **b** of your lack of self-control. 1Co 7:5 *1223*
b the plowman ought to plow in 1Co 9:10 *3754*
b you remember me in everything and 1Co 11:2 *3754*
on her head, **b** of the angels. 1Co 11:10 *1223*
b you come together not for the 1Co 11:17 *3754*
"**B** I am not a hand, I am not *a* 1Co 12:15 *3754*
"**B** I am not an eye, I am not *a* 1Co 12:16 *3754*
b I persecuted the church of God. 1Co 15:9 *1360*
b we testified against God that He 1Co 15:15 *3754*
b they have supplied what was 1Co 16:17 *3754*
Moses **b** of the glory of his face, 2Co 3:7 *1223*
in this case has no glory **b** of 2Co 3:10 *1752a*
b it is removed in Christ. 2Co 3:14 *3754*
the things hidden **b** of shame, 2Co 4:2
b we do not want to be unclothed but 2Co 5:4
1909, 3739
b his spirit has been refreshed by 2Co 7:13 *3754*
b of *his* great confidence in you. 2Co 8:22
B of the proof given by this 2Co 9:13 *1223*
yearn for you **b** of the surpassing 2Co 9:14 *1223*
b I preached the gospel of God to 2Co 11:7 *3754*
B I do not love you? 2Co 11:11 *3754*
B of the surpassing greatness of 2Co 12:7
He was crucified **b** of weakness, 2Co 13:4 *1537*
He lives **b** of the power of God. 2Co 13:4 *1537*
yet we will live with Him **b** of 2Co 13:4 *1537*
they were glorifying God **b** of me. Ga 1:24 *1722*
It was **b** of a revelation that Ga 2:2 *2596*
But *it was* **b** of the false brethren Ga 2:4 *1223*
to his face, **b** he stood condemned. Ga 2:11 *3754*
It was added **b** of transgressions, Ga 3:19 *5484*
B you are sons, God has sent forth Ga 4:6 *3754*
know that it was **b** of a bodily illness Ga 4:13 *1223*
b of His great love with which He Eph 2:4 *1223*
b of the ignorance that is in Eph 4:18 *1223*
b of the hardness of their heart; Eph 4:18 *1223*
for **b** of these things the wrath of Eph 5:6 *1223*
of your time, **b** the days are evil. Eph 5:16 *3754*
b we are members of His body. Eph 5:30 *3754*
you all, **b** I have you in my heart, Php 1:7 *1223*
in the Lord **b** of my imprisonment, Php 1:14
reason to glory **b** I did not run in vain Php 2:16 *3754*
b he was longing for you all and Php 2:26 *1894*
distressed **b** you had heard that he Php 2:26 *1360*
b he came close to death for the Php 2:30 *3754*
b of the hope laid up for you in Col 1:5 *1223*
For it is **b** of these things that Col 3:6 *1223*
b you had become very dear to us. 1Th 2:8 *1360*
b the Lord is *the* avenger in all these 1Th 4:6 *1360*
highly in love **b** of their work. 1Th 5:13 *1223*
b your faith is greatly enlarged, 2Th 1:3 *3754*
b they did not receive the love of 2Th 2:10
473, 3739
b God has chosen you from the 2Th 2:13 *3754*
b we did not act in an 2Th 3:7 *3754*
not **b** we do not have the right *to* 2Th 3:9 *3754*
me, **b** He considered me faithful, 1Tm 1:12 *3754*
b I acted ignorantly in unbelief; 1Tm 1:13 *3754*
b we have fixed our hope on the 1Tm 4:10 *3754*
b they have set aside their 1Tm 5:12 *3754*
to them **b** they are brethren, 1Tm 6:2 *3754*
b those who partake of the benefit 1Tm 6:2 *3754*
who must be silenced **b** they are Ti 1:11 *3748*
b I hear of your love and of the Phm 1:5
b the hearts of the saints have Phm 1:7 *3754*
b of the suffering of death Heb 2:9 *1223*
not able to enter **b** of unbelief. Heb 3:19 *1223*
b it was not united by faith in Heb 4:2
failed to enter **b** of disobedience, Heb 4:6 *1223*
and **b** of it he is obligated to Heb 5:3 *1223*
and He was heard **b** of His piety. Heb 5:7 *575*
who **b** of practice have their Heb 5:14 *1223*
commandment **b** of its weakness Heb 7:18 *1223*
b they were prevented by death Heb 7:23 *1223*
other hand, **b** He continues forever, Heb 7:24 *1223*
b this He did once for all when He Heb 7:27 *1063*
to be offered, **b** the worshipers, Heb 10:2 *1223*
WAS NOT FOUND **B** GOD TOOK HIM UP; Heb 11:5 *1360*
b they saw he was a beautiful Heb 11:23 *1360*
b God had provided something Heb 11:40
b like flowering grass he will Jas 1:10 *3754*
You do not have **b** you do not ask. Jas 4:2 *1223*
b you ask with wrong motives, Jas 4:3 *1360*
b it is written, 1Pe 1:16 *1360*
for they stumble **b** they are 1Pe 2:8
they may **b** of your good deeds, as 1Pe 2:12 *1537*
b he who has suffered in the flesh 1Pe 4:1 *3754*
b love covers a multitude of sins. 1Pe 4:8 *3754*
b the Spirit of glory and of God 1Pe 4:14 *3754*
on Him, **b** He cares for you. 1Pe 5:7 *3754*
and **b** of them the way of the truth 2Pe 2:2 *1223*
b of which the heavens will be 2Pe 3:12 *1223*
b the darkness is passing away and 1Jn 2:8 *3754*
b the darkness has blinded his eyes. 1Jn 2:11 *3754*
b your sins have been forgiven you for 1Jn 2:12 *3754*
b you know Him who has been 1Jn 2:13 *3754*
b you have overcome the evil one. 1Jn 2:13 *3754*
children, **b** you know the Father. 1Jn 2:13 *3754*
b you know Him who has been 1Jn 2:14 *3754*
you, young men, **b** you are strong, 1Jn 2:14 *3754*
you **b** you do not know the truth, 1Jn 2:21 *3754*
the truth, but **b** you do know it, 1Jn 2:21 *3754*
it, and **b** no lie is of the truth. 1Jn 2:21 *3754*
know us, **b** it did not know Him. 1Jn 3:1 *3754*
b we will see Him just as He is. 1Jn 3:2 *3754*
sin, **b** His seed abides in him; 1Jn 3:9 *3754*
cannot sin, **b** he is born of God. 1Jn 3:9 *3754*
B his deeds were evil, and his 1Jn 3:12 *3754*
into life, **b** we love the brethren. 1Jn 3:14 *3754*
b we keep His commandments and do 1Jn 3:22 *3754*
b many false prophets have gone 1Jn 4:1 *3754*
b greater is He who is in you than 1Jn 4:4 *3754*
b He has given us of His Spirit. 1Jn 4:13 *3754*
b as He is, so also are we in this 1Jn 4:17 *3754*
fear, **b** fear involves punishment, 1Jn 4:18 *3754*
We love, **b** He first loved us. 1Jn 4:19 *3754*
b the Spirit is the truth. 1Jn 5:6 *3754*
b he has not believed in the 1Jn 5:10 *3754*
b of the word of God and the Rv 1:9 *1223*
b you have there some who hold the Rv 2:14 *3754*
shut, **b** you have a little power, Rv 3:8 *3754*
'**B** you have kept the word of My Rv 3:10 *3754*
'So **b** you are lukewarm, and Rv 3:16 *3754*
'**B** you say, "I am rich, and have Rv 3:17 *3754*
and **b** of Your will they existed, Rv 4:11 *1223*
b no one was found worthy to open Rv 5:4 *3754*
been slain **b** of the word of God, Rv 6:9 *1223*
and **b** of the testimony which they Rv 6:9 *1223*
waters, **b** they were made bitter. Rv 8:11 *3754*
b of the remaining blasts of the Rv 8:13 *1537*
b these two prophets tormented Rv 11:10 *3754*
b You have taken Your great power Rv 11:17 *3754*
"And they overcame him **b** of the Rv 12:11 *1223*
and **b** of the word of their testimony Rv 12:11 *1223*
b the devil has come down to you, Rv 12:12 *3754*
b he gave his authority to the Rv 13:4 *3754*
b of the signs which it was given him Rv 13:14 *1223*
b the hour of His judgment has Rv 14:7 *3754*
b the harvest of the earth is ripe." Rv 14:15 *3754*
earth, **b** her grapes are ripe." Rv 14:18 *3754*
b in them the wrath of God is Rv 15:1 *3754*
b You judged these things; Rv 16:5 *3754*
gnawed their tongues **b** of pain, Rv 16:10 *1537*
blasphemed the God of heaven **b** of Rv 16:11 *1537*
God **b** of the plague of the hail, Rv 16:21 *1537*
b its plague was extremely severe. Rv 16:21 *3754*
b He is Lord of lords and King of Rv 17:14 *3754*
b of the fear of her torment, Rv 18:10 *1223*
b no one buys their cargoes any Rv 18:11 *3754*
b of the fear of her torment, Rv 18:15 *1223*
b God has pronounced judgment for Rv 18:20 *3754*
b all the nations were deceived by Rv 18:23 *3754*
B HIS JUDGMENTS ARE TRUE AND Rv 19:2 *3754*
been beheaded **b** of their testimony Rv 20:4 *1223*
of Jesus and **b** of the word of God, Rv 20:4 *1223*
b the Lord God will illumine them; Rv 22:5 *3754*

BECHER
Bela and **B** and Ashbel, Gera and Gn 46:21 1071
of **B**, the family of the Becherites; Nu 26:35 1071
Bela and **B** and Jediael. 1Ch 7:6 1071
The sons of **B** *were* Zemirah, 1Ch 7:8 1071
All these *were* the sons of **B**. 1Ch 7:8 1071

BECHERITES
of Becher, the family of the **B**; Nu 26:35 1076

BECOME
and they shall **b** one flesh. Gn 2:24 1961
the man has **b** like one of Us, Gn 3:22 1961
b a flood to destroy all flesh. Gn 9:15 1961
b the father of twelve princes, Gn 17:20 3205
"After I have **b** old, shall I have Gn 18:12 1086
b a great and mighty nation, Gn 18:18 1961
because their outcry has **b** so Gn 19:13 1431
my master, so that he has **b** rich; Gn 24:35 1431
B thousands of ten thousands, Gn 24:60 1961
come about when you **b** restless, Gn 27:40 7300
you may **b** a company of peoples. Gn 28:3 1961
my husband will **b** attached to me, Gn 29:34 3867a
and now I have **b** two companies. Gn 32:10 1961
if you will **b** like us, in that Gn 34:15 1961
live with you and **b** one people. Gn 34:16 1961
to live with us, to **b** one people: Gn 34:22 1961
For their property had **b** too great Gn 36:7 1961
see what will **b** of his dreams!" Gn 37:20 1961
we will **b** a laughingstock. Gn 38:23 1961
"Let the food **b** as a reserve Gn 41:36 1961
of the priests did not **b** Pharaoh's. Gn 47:26 1961
he also will **b** a people and he Gn 48:19 1961
shall **b** a multitude of nations." Gn 48:19 1961
"Surely the matter has **b** known." Ex 2:14
will **b** blood on the dry ground." Ex 4:9 1961
that it may **b** a serpent.' " Ex 7:9 1961
die, and the Nile will **b** foul, Ex 7:18 887
of water, that they may **b** blood; Ex 7:19 1961
that it may **b** gnats through all Ex 8:16 1961
"It will **b** fine dust over all Ex 9:9 1961
and will **b** boils breaking out with Ex 9:9 1961
For it had not **b** leavened, since Ex 12:39 2556a
song, And He has **b** my salvation; Ex 15:2 1961
ordered, and it did not **b** foul nor Ex 16:24 887
and the dead *animal* shall **b** his. Ex 21:34 1961
and the dead *animal* shall **b** his. Ex 21:36 1961
and your wives shall **b** widows and Ex 22:24 1961
that the land may not **b** desolate and Ex 23:29 1961
beasts of the field **b** too numerous Ex 23:29 7231
until you **b** fruitful and take Ex 23:30 6509
do not know what has **b** of him." Ex 32:1 1961
we do not know what has **b** of him.' Ex 32:23 1961
or it will **b** a snare in your midst. Ex 34:12 1961
not to be done, and they **b** guilty; Lv 4:13 816
then *the rest* shall **b** the priest's, Lv 5:13 1961
them will **b** consecrated.' " Lv 6:18 6942
its flesh will **b** consecrated; Lv 6:27 6942
and that He will not **b** wrathful Lv 10:6 7107
water comes, shall **b** unclean, Lv 11:34 2930
in every vessel shall **b** unclean. Lv 11:34 2930
with them so that you **b** unclean. Lv 11:43 2930
has **b** visible to me in the house.' Lv 14:35 7200
in the house need not **b** unclean; Lv 14:36 2930
running water and will **b** clean. Lv 15:13 2891
then he will **b** clean. Lv 17:15 2891
out before you have **b** defiled. Lv 18:24 2930
'For the land has **b** defiled, Lv 18:25 2930
and the land has **b** defiled); Lv 18:27 2930
and the land **b** full of lewdness. Lv 19:29 4390
they also may **b** your possession. Lv 25:45 1961
desolate and your cities **b** waste. Lv 26:33 1961
and its substitute shall **b** holy. Lv 27:10 1961
and its substitute shall **b** holy. Lv 27:33 1961
will **b** a curse among her people. Nu 5:27 1961
our little ones will **b** plunder; Nu 14:3 1961
whom you said would **b** a prey Nu 14:31 1961
that he will not **b** like Korah and Nu 16:40 1961
whom you let remain of them *will* **b** Nu 33:55
This shall **b** theirs as pasture Nu 35:5 1961
ones who you said would **b** a prey, Dt 1:39 1961
"When you **b** the father of Dt 4:25 3205
then your heart will **b** proud and you Dt 8:14 7311
found in it shall **b** your forced labor Dt 20:11 1961
of the vineyard will **b** defiled. Dt 22:9 6942
and she shall **b** his wife because Dt 22:29 1961
to the LORD and it **b** sin in you. Dt 24:15 1961
This day you have **b** a people for Dt 27:9 1961
"You shall **b** a horror, a Dt 28:37 1961
"They shall **b** a sign and a Dt 28:46 1961
are satisfied and **b** prosperous, Dt 31:20 1878
So these stones shall **b** a memorial Jos 4:7 1961
enemies, for they have **b** accursed. Jos 7:12 1961
was dry *and* had **b** crumbled. Jos 9:5 1961
it is dry and has **b** crumbled. Jos 9:12 1961
and they shall **b** your refuge from Jos 20:3 1961
will **b** *as thorns* in your sides Jg 2:3 1961
hands, for Israel would **b** boastful, Jg 7:2 6286
He shall **b** head over all the Jg 10:18 1961
sons of Ammon and **b** head over all Jg 11:8 1961
up to me, will I **b** your head?" Jg 11:9 1961
then I will **b** weak and be like Jg 16:7 2470a
then I will **b** weak and be like Jg 16:11 2470a
then I will **b** weak and be like Jg 16:13
b weak and be like any *other* man." Jg 16:17 2470a
sons, that he might **b** his priest. Jg 17:5 1961
me and I have **b** his priest." Jg 18:4 1961
and **b** famous in Bethlehem. Ru 4:11 7121
may his name **b** famous in Israel. Ru 4:14 7121
or you will **b** slaves to the Hebrews, 1Sa 4:9 5647
yourselves will **b** his servants. 1Sa 8:17 1961
donkeys and will **b** anxious for us." 1Sa 9:5 1672
had **b** odious to the Philistines. 1Sa 13:4 887
me, then we will **b** your servants; 1Sa 17:9 1961
b our servants and serve us." 1Sa 17:9 1961
him that she may **b** a snare to him, 1Sa 18:21 1961
b the king's son-in-law.' " 1Sa 18:22 2859
sight to **b** the king's son-in-law, 1Sa 18:23 2859
David to **b** the king's son-in-law. 1Sa 18:26 2859
he might **b** the king's son-in-law. 1Sa 18:27 2859
he will **b** my servant forever." 1Sa 27:12 1961
from you and has **b** your adversary? 1Sa 28:16 1961
battle he may **b** an adversary to us. 1Sa 29:4 1961
You, O LORD, have **b** their God. 2Sa 7:24 1961
that they had **b** odious to David, 2Sa 10:6 887

attend the king and **b** his nurse;	**1Ki 1:2**	1961
the son of Haggith has **b** king,	**1Ki 1:11**	4427a
Why then has Adonijah **b** king?"	**1Ki 1:13**	4427a
turned about and **b** my brother's,	**1Ki 2:15**	1961
So Israel will **b** a proverb and a	**1Ki 9:7**	1961
this house will **b** a heap of ruins;	**1Ki 9:8**	1961
nor did the jar of oil **b** empty,	**1Ki 17:16**	2637
Edom, and your heart has **b** proud.	**2Ki 14:10**	5375
and they will **b** officials in the	**2Ki 20:18**	1961
and they will **b** as plunder and	**2Ki 21:14**	1961
should **b** a desolation and a curse,	**2Ki 22:19**	1961
"But they will **b** his slaves so	**2Ch 12:8**	1961
b a priest of *what are* no gods.	**2Ch 13:9**	1961
heart has **b** proud in boasting.	**2Ch 25:19**	5375
"They will **b** discouraged with the	**Ne 6:9**	3027, 7503
that I might **b** frightened and act	**Ne 6:13**	3372a
"For the queen's conduct will **b**	**Es 1:17**	3318
with you, will you **b** impatient?	**Jb 4:2**	3811
"When they **b** waterless, they are	**Jb 6:17**	2215
"Indeed, you have now **b** such,	**Jb 6:21**	1961
"An idiot will **b** intelligent	**Jb 11:12**	3823a
And that it would **b** your wisdom!	**Jb 13:5**	1961
Or they **b** insignificant, but he	**Jb 14:21**	6819
Which are destined to **b** ruins.	**Jb 15:28**	
"He will not **b** rich, nor will his	**Jb 15:29**	6238
me up, It has **b** a witness;	**Jb 16:8**	1961
Continue on, also **b** very powerful?	**Jb 21:7**	1396
"And now I have **b** their taunt, I	**Jb 30:9**	1961
I have even **b** a byword to them.	**Jb 30:9**	1961
And I have **b** like dust and ashes.	**Jb 30:19**	4911a
"You have **b** cruel to me;	**Jb 30:21**	2015
"I have **b** a brother to jackals And	**Jb 30:29**	1961
his flesh **b** fresher than in youth,	**Jb 33:25**	7375
"Their offspring **b** strong, they	**Jb 39:4**	2492a
to the Son, that He not **b** angry,	**Ps 2:12**	599
long will my honor **b** a reproach?	**Ps 4:2**	
It has **b** old because of all my	**Ps 6:7**	6275
together they have **b** corrupt;	**Ps 14:3**	444
I will **b** like those who go down to the	**Ps 28:1**	4911a
adversaries, I have **b** a reproach,	**Ps 31:11**	1961
"I have **b** mute, I do not open my	**Ps 39:9**	481
have you **b** disturbed within me?	**Ps 42:5**	1993
have you **b** disturbed within me?	**Ps 42:11**	1993
together they have **b** corrupt;	**Ps 53:3**	444
have **b** estranged from my brothers And	**Ps 69:8**	1961
their table before them **b** a snare;	**Ps 69:22**	1961
may it **b** a trap.	**Ps 69:22**	
I have **b** a marvel to many,	**Ps 71:7**	1961
b a reproach to our neighbors,	**Ps 79:4**	1961
b a help to the children of Lot.Selah.	**Ps 83:8**	1961
b like a man without strength,	**Ps 88:4**	1961
has **b** a reproach to his neighbors.	**Ps 89:41**	1961
I have **b** like an owl of the waste	**Ps 102:6**	1961
I have **b** like a lonely bird on a	**Ps 102:7**	1961
And let his prayer **b** sin.	**Ps 109:7**	1961
I also have **b** a reproach to them;	**Ps 109:25**	1961
who make them will **b** like them,	**Ps 115:8**	1961
song, And He has **b** my salvation.	**Ps 118:14**	1961
And You have **b** my salvation.	**Ps 118:21**	1961
Has **b** the chief corner *stone.*	**Ps 118:22**	1961
This has **b** mine, That I observe	**Ps 119:56**	1961
b like a wineskin in the smoke,	**Ps 119:83**	1961
They have **b** my enemies.	**Ps 139:22**	1961
Or I will **b** like those who go down	**Ps 143:7**	4911a
have **b** surety for your neighbor,	**Pr 6:1**	6148
and the naive may **b** shrewd,	**Pr 19:25**	6191
not love sleep, or you will **b** poor;	**Pr 20:13**	3423
He who loves pleasure *will* **b**	**Pr 21:17**	
wine and oil will not **b** rich.	**Pr 21:17**	6238
those who **b** guarantors for debts.	**Pr 22:26**	6148
struck me, *but* I did not **b** ill;	**Pr 23:35**	2470a
he will **b** weary of you and hate you.	**Pr 25:17**	7646
All his ministers **b** wicked.	**Pr 29:12**	
has come out of prison to **b** king,	**Ec 4:14**	4427a
They have **b** a burden to Me;	**Is 1:14**	1961
the faithful city has **b** a harlot,	**Is 1:21**	1961
Your silver has **b** dross, Your	**Is 1:22**	1961
The strong man will **b** tinder,	**Is 1:31**	1961
and it will **b** trampled ground.	**Is 5:5**	1961
many houses shall **b** desolate,	**Is 5:9**	1961
So their root will **b** like rot and	**Is 5:24**	1961
silver, will **b** briars and thorns.	**Is 7:23**	1961
but they will **b** a place for	**Is 7:25**	1961
"Then He shall **b** a sanctuary;	**Is 8:14**	1961
And the light of Israel will **b** a	**Is 10:17**	1961
song, And He has **b** my salvation."	**Is 12:2**	1961
weak as we, You have **b** like us.	**Is 14:10**	4911a
city And will **b** a fallen ruin.	**Is 17:1**	1961
fatness of his flesh will **b** lean.	**Is 17:4**	7329
fields by the Nile Will **b** dry,	**Is 19:7**	3001
wisest advisers has **b** stupid.	**Is 19:11**	1197b
the Egyptians will **b** like women,	**Is 19:16**	1961
of Judah will **b** a terror to Egypt;	**Is 19:17**	1961
It will **b** a sign and a witness	**Is 19:20**	1961
And he will **b** a father to the	**Is 22:21**	1961
And he will **b** a throne of glory to	**Is 22:23**	1961
but her gain will **b** sufficient	**Is 23:18**	1961
LORD of hosts will **b** a beautiful crown	**Is 28:5**	1961
Then you **b** its trampling *place.*	**Is 28:18**	1961
enemies will **b** like fine dust,	**Is 29:5**	1961
They **b** drunk, but not with wine,	**Is 29:9**	7937
young men will **b** forced laborers.	**Is 31:8**	1961
watch-tower have **b** caves forever,	**Is 32:14**	1961
And their dust **b** greasy with fat.	**Is 34:7**	1878
its land will **b** burning pitch.	**Is 34:9**	1961
The scorched land will **b** a pool	**Is 35:7**	1961
and they will **b** officials in the	**Is 39:7**	1961
let the rough ground **b** a plain,	**Is 40:4**	1961
earth Does not **b** weary or tired.	**Is 40:28**	3286
They will walk and not **b** weary.	**Is 40:31**	3286
They have **b** a prey with none to	**Is 42:22**	1961
But you have **b** weary of Me, O	**Is 43:22**	3021
"Behold, they have **b** like stubble,	**Is 47:14**	1961
"So have those **b** to you with whom	**Is 47:15**	1961
And they will **b** drunk with their	**Is 49:26**	7937
in darkness And your gloom *will* **b**	**Is 58:10**	
Their webs will not **b** clothing,	**Is 59:6**	1961
"The smallest one will **b** a clan,	**Is 60:22**	1961
turned Himself to **b** their enemy,	**Is 63:10**	
We have **b** *like* those over whom	**Is 63:19**	1961
us have **b** like one who is unclean,	**Is 64:6**	1961
holy cities have **b** a wilderness,	**Is 64:10**	1961
Zion has **b** a wilderness,	**Is 64:10**	1961
our precious things have **b** a ruin.	**Is 64:11**	1961
Why has he **b** a prey?	**Jer 2:14**	1961
All who seek her will not **b** weary;	**Jer 2:24**	3286
they have **b** great and rich.	**Jer 5:27**	1431
the LORD has **b** a reproach to them;	**Jer 6:10**	1961
b a den of robbers in your sight?	**Jer 7:11**	1961
for the land will **b** a ruin.	**Jer 7:34**	1961
For the shepherds have **b** stupid	**Jer 10:21**	1197b
"My inheritance has **b** to Me Like	**Jer 12:8**	1961
You will **b** My spokesman.	**Jer 15:19**	1961
and their carcasses will **b** food	**Jer 16:4**	1961
wives **b** childless and widowed.	**Jer 18:21**	1961
b a laughingstock all day long;	**Jer 20:7**	1961
house will **b** a desolation.	**Jer 22:5**	1961
"Do you **b** a king because you are	**Jer 22:15**	4427a
I have **b** like a drunken man, Even	**Jer 23:9**	1961
of them have **b** to Me like Sodom,	**Jer 23:14**	1961
man's own word will **b** the oracle,	**Jer 23:36**	1961
For their land has **b** a horror	**Jer 25:38**	1961
field, And Jerusalem will **b** ruins,	**Jer 26:18**	1961
Why should this city **b** a ruin?	**Jer 27:17**	1961
'Take wives and **b** the fathers of	**Jer 29:6**	3205
And you will **b** a curse, an object	**Jer 42:18**	1961
so they have **b** a ruin and a	**Jer 44:6**	1961
cut off and **b** a curse and a reproach	**Jer 44:8**	1961
not **b** contrite even to this day,	**Jer 44:10**	1792
and they will **b** a curse, an object	**Jer 44:12**	1961
thus your land has **b** a ruin,	**Jer 44:22**	1961
have your mighty ones **b** prostrate?	**Jer 46:15**	5502
For Memphis will **b** a desolation;	**Jer 46:19**	1961
And **b** an overflowing torrent,	**Jer 47:2**	1961
her cities will **b** a desolation,	**Jer 48:9**	1961
he has **b** arrogant toward the LORD;	**Jer 48:26**	1431
he also will **b** a laughingstock.	**Jer 48:26**	1961
waters of Nimrim will **b** desolate.	**Jer 48:34**	1961
So Moab will **b** a laughingstock and	**Jer 48:39**	1961
he has **b** arrogant toward the LORD.	**Jer 48:42**	1431
And it will **b** a desolate heap, And	**Jer 49:2**	1961
Bozrah will **b** an object of horror,	**Jer 49:13**	1961
cities will **b** perpetual ruins."	**Jer 49:13**	1961
Edom will **b** an object of horror;	**Jer 49:17**	1961
"Damascus has **b** helpless;	**Jer 49:24**	7503
"Their camels will **b** plunder,	**Jer 49:32**	1961
Hazor will **b** a haunt of jackals,	**Jer 49:33**	1961
"My people have **b** lost sheep;	**Jer 50:6**	1961
"Chaldea will **b** plunder;	**Jer 50:10**	1961
How Babylon has **b** An object of	**Jer 50:23**	1961
has **b** arrogant against the LORD,	**Jer 50:29**	2102
priests, and they will **b** fools!	**Jer 50:36**	2973
of her, And they will **b** women!	**Jer 50:37**	1961
Babylon will **b** a heap *of ruins,*	**Jer 51:37**	1961
"When they **b** heated up, I will	**Jer 51:39**	2552
that they may **b** jubilant And may	**Jer 51:39**	5937
How Babylon has **b** an object of	**Jer 51:41**	1961
cities have **b** an object of horror,	**Jer 51:43**	1961
b exhausted *only* for fire."	**Jer 51:58**	3286
and they will **b** exhausted.' "	**Jer 51:64**	3286
She has **b** like a widow Who was	**La 1:1**	1961
provinces Has **b** a forced laborer!	**La 1:1**	1961
They have **b** her enemies.	**La 1:2**	1961
adversaries have **b** her masters,	**La 1:5**	1961
Her princes have **b** like deer That	**La 1:6**	1961
she has **b** an unclean thing.	**La 1:8**	1961
has **b** an unclean thing among them.	**La 1:17**	1961
That they may **b** like me.	**La 1:21**	1961
The Lord has **b** like an enemy.	**La 2:5**	1961
I have **b** a laughingstock to all my	**La 3:14**	1961
How dark the gold has **b**,	**La 4:1**	6004
daughter of my people has **b** cruel	**La 4:3**	
is withered, it has **b** like wood.	**La 4:8**	1961
b drunk and make yourself naked.	**La 4:21**	7937
have **b** orphans without a father,	**La 5:3**	1961
Our skin has **b** as hot as an oven,	**La 5:10**	3648
"So your altars will **b** desolate and	**Ezk 6:4**	8074
cities will **b** waste and the high	**Ezk 6:6**	2717b
altars may **b** waste and desolate,	**Ezk 6:6**	2717b
and all knees will **b** *like* water.	**Ezk 7:17**	1980
gold will **b** an abhorrent thing;	**Ezk 7:19**	1961
has **b** an occasion of stumbling.	**Ezk 7:19**	1961
when you **b** a consolation to them.	**Ezk 16:54**	5162
so now you have **b** the reproach of	**Ezk 16:57**	
fruit *and* **b** a splendid vine." '	**Ezk 17:8**	1961
bear fruit and **b** a stately cedar.	**Ezk 17:23**	1961
not **b** a stumbling block to you.	**Ezk 18:30**	1961
and has **b** a lamentation.	**Ezk 19:14**	1961
"You have **b** guilty by the blood	**Ezk 22:4**	816
house of Israel has **b** dross to Me;	**Ezk 22:18**	1961
'Because all of you have **b** dross,	**Ezk 22:19**	1961
I had **b** disgusted with her sister.	**Ezk 23:18**	5361
she will **b** spoil for the nations.	**Ezk 26:5**	1961
You have **b** terrified And you will	**Ezk 27:36**	1961
You have **b** terrified And you will	**Ezk 28:19**	1961
will **b** a desolation and waste.	**Ezk 29:9**	1961
because My flock has **b** a prey,	**Ezk 34:8**	1961
My flock has even **b** food for all	**Ezk 34:8**	1961
And you will **b** a desolation.	**Ezk 35:4**	1961
heights have **b** our possession,'	**Ezk 36:2**	1961
that you would **b** a possession of	**Ezk 36:3**	1961
which have **b** a prey and a derision	**Ezk 36:4**	1961
that you will **b** their inheritance	**Ezk 36:12**	1961
has **b** like the garden of Eden;	**Ezk 36:35**	1961
that they may **b** one in your hand.	**Ezk 37:17**	1961
and the waters *of the sea* **b** fresh.	**Ezk 47:8**	7495
go there and *the others* **b** fresh;	**Ezk 47:9**	7495
and marshes will not **b** fresh;	**Ezk 47:11**	7495
you have **b** great and grown strong,	**Da 4:22**	7236
and your majesty has **b** great and	**Da 4:22**	7236
Jerusalem and Your people *have* **b**	**Da 9:16**	
and will return and **b** enraged at	**Da 11:30**	2194
harlot, Do not let Judah **b** guilty;	**Hos 4:15**	816
Ephraim will **b** a desolation in the	**Hos 5:9**	1961
The princes of Judah have **b** like	**Hos 5:10**	1961
Ephraim has **b** a cake not turned.	**Hos 7:8**	1961
Ephraim has **b** like a silly dove,	**Hos 7:11**	1961
have **b** altars of sinning for him.	**Hos 8:11**	1961
"Surely I have **b** rich, I have	**Hos 12:8**	6238
And his fountain will **b** dry And	**Hos 13:15**	954
Their branches have **b** white.	**Jl 1:7**	3835a
Egypt will **b** a waste, And Edom	**Jl 3:19**	1961
Edom will **b** a desolate wilderness,	**Jl 3:19**	1961
wife will **b** a harlot in the city,	**Am 7:17**	2181
b as if they had never existed.	**Ob 1:16**	1961
we do to you that the sea may **b** calm	**Jon 1:11**	8367
Then the sea will **b** calm for you,	**Jon 1:12**	8367
The houses of Achzib *will* **b** a	**Mi 1:14**	
And the day will **b** dark over them.	**Mi 3:6**	6937
Jerusalem will **b** a heap of ruins,	**Mi 3:12**	1961
the mountain of the temple *will* **b**	**Mi 3:12**	
And the earth will **b** desolate	**Mi 7:13**	1961
You too will **b** drunk, You will be	**Na 3:11**	7937
you will **b** plunder for them.	**Hab 2:7**	1961
their wealth will **b** plunder And	**Zph 1:13**	1961
b arrogant against their territory.	**Zph 2:8**	1431
because they have taunted and **b**	**Zph 2:10**	1431
How she has **b** a desolation, A	**Zph 2:15**	1961
there is not *enough* to **b** drunk;	**Hg 1:6**	7937
other food, will it **b** holy?' "	**Hg 2:12**	6942
will *the latter* **b** unclean?"	**Hg 2:13**	2930
"It will **b** unclean."	**Hg 2:13**	2930
in that day and will **b** My people.	**Zch 2:11**	1961
Before Zerubbabel *you will* **b** a	**Zch 4:7**	
"Now the crown will **b** a reminder	**Zch 6:14**	1961
you that you may **b** a blessing.	**Zch 8:13**	1961
of the tenth *months* will **b** joy,	**Zch 8:19**	1961
be the LORD, for I have **b** rich!'	**Zch 11:5**	6238
that these stones **b** bread."	**Mt 4:3**	*1096*
but if the salt has **b** tasteless,	**Mt 5:13**	*3471*
disciple that he **b** like his teacher,	**Mt 10:25**	*1096*
HEART OF THIS PEOPLE HAS **B** DULL,	**Mt 13:15**	*3975*
"Therefore every scribe who has **b**	**Mt 13:52**	*3100*
are converted and **b** like children,	**Mt 18:3**	*1096*
AND THE TWO SHALL **B** ONE FLESH'?	**Mt 19:5**	*1510, 1519*
but whoever wishes to **b** great	**Mt 20:26**	*1096*
outside of it may **b** clean also.	**Mt 23:26**	*1096*
its branch has already **b** tender and	**Mt 24:32**	*1096*
had also **b** a disciple of Jesus.	**Mt 27:57**	*3100*
will make you **b** fishers of men."	**Mk 1:17**	*1096*
it, for His name had **b** well known;	**Mk 6:14**	*1096*
AND THE TWO SHALL **B** ONE FLESH	**Mk 10:8**	*1510, 1519*
but whoever wishes to **b** great	**Mk 10:43**	*1096*
its branch has already **b** tender and	**Mk 13:28**	*1096*
grow and to **b** strong in spirit,	**Lk 1:80**	*2901*
continued to grow and **b** strong,	**Lk 2:40**	*2901*
THE CROOKED WILL **B** STRAIGHT,	**Lk 3:5**	*1510, 1519*
God, tell this stone to **b** bread."	**Lk 4:3**	*1096*
hidden that will not **b** evident,	**Lk 8:17**	*1096*
but if even salt has **b** tasteless,	**Lk 14:34**	*3471*
"I tell you, if these **b** silent,	**Lk 19:40**	*4623*
among you must **b** like the youngest,	**Lk 22:26**	*1096*
the right to **b** children of God,	**Jn 1:12**	*1096*
tasted the water which had **b** wine,	**Jn 2:9**	*1096*
will **b** in him a well of water	**Jn 4:14**	*1096*
"Behold, you have **b** well;	**Jn 5:14**	*1096*
It had already **b** dark,	**Jn 6:17**	*1096*
"How has this man **b** learned,	**Jn 7:15**	*3609a*
'You will **b** free'?"	**Jn 8:33**	*1096*
not want to **b** His disciples too,	**Jn 9:27**	*1096*
that those who see may **b** blind."	**Jn 9:39**	*1096*
b one flock *with* one shepherd.	**Jn 10:16**	*1096*
"Now My soul has **b** troubled;	**Jn 12:27**	
that you may **b** sons of Light."	**Jn 12:36**	*1096*
b a witness with us of His resurrection.	**Ac 1:22**	*1096*
and murderers you have now **b**;	**Ac 7:52**	*1096*
granted that He **b** visible,	**Ac 10:40**	*1096*
as to what could have **b** of Peter.	**Ac 12:18**	*1096*
"The gods have **b** like men and	**Ac 14:11**	*3666*
good to us, having **b** of one mind,	**Ac 15:25**	*1096*
persuade me to **b** a Christian."	**Ac 26:28**	*4160*
me this day, might **b** such as I am,	**Ac 26:29**	*1096*
HEART OF THIS PEOPLE HAS **B** DULL,	**Ac 28:27**	*3975*
circumcision has **b** uncircumcision.	**Ro 2:25**	*1096*
TOGETHER THEY HAVE **B** USELESS;	**Ro 3:12**	*889*
world may **b** accountable to God;	**Ro 3:19**	*1096*
might **b** a father of many nations	**Ro 4:18**	*1096*
For if we have **b** united with *Him*	**Ro 6:5**	*1096*
is good **b** *a cause of* death for me?	**Ro 7:13**	*1096*
sin would **b** utterly sinful.	**Ro 7:13**	*1096*
He also predestined *to* **b**	**Ro 8:29**	
WE WOULD HAVE **B** LIKE SODOM,	**Ro 9:29**	*1096*
THEIR TABLE **B** A SNARE AND A TRAP,	**Ro 11:9**	*1096*

For I say that Christ has **b** a **Ro 15:8** *1096*
the Gentiles may **b** acceptable, **Ro 15:16** *1096*
each man's work will **b** evident; **1Co 3:13** *1096*
he must **b** foolish, so that he may **1Co 3:18** *1096*
so that he may **b** wise. **1Co 3:18** *1096*
no one of you will **b** arrogant in **1Co 4:6**
filled, you have already **b** rich, **1Co 4:8** *4147*
rich, you have **b** kings without us; **1Co 4:8** *936*
indeed, *I* wish that you had **b** kings **1Co 4:8** *936*
have **b** a spectacle to the world, **1Co 4:9** *1096*
have **b** as the scum of the world, **1Co 4:13** *1096*
Now some have **b** arrogant, as **1Co 4:18**
You have **b** arrogant and have **1Co 5:2**
"THE TWO SHALL **B** ONE FLESH." **1Co 6:16**
1510, 1519
He is not to **b** uncircumcised. **1Co 7:18** *1986a*
if you are able also to **b** free, **1Co 7:21** *1096*
do not **b** slaves of men. **1Co 7:23** *1096*
b a stumbling block to the weak. **1Co 8:9** *1096*
I have **b** all things to all men, **1Co 9:22** *1096*
I may **b** a fellow partaker of it. **1Co 9:23** *1096*
want you to **b** sharers in demons. **1Co 10:20** *1096*
may **b** evident among you. **1Co 11:19** *1096*
and our less presentable members **b** **1Co 12:23** *2192*
I have **b** a noisy gong or a **1Co 13:1** *1096*
B sober-minded as you ought, and **1Co 15:34** *1594*
that we might **b** the righteousness **2Co 5:21** *1096*
through His poverty might **b** rich. **2Co 8:9** *4147*
also may **b** *a supply* for your need, **2Co 8:14** *1096*
I have **b** foolish; **2Co 12:11** *1096*
myself did not **b** a burden to you? **2Co 12:13**
to **b** acquainted with Cephas, **Ga 1:18** *2477*
the Law, having **b** a curse for us **Ga 3:13** *1096*
Therefore the Law has **b** our tutor **Ga 3:24** *1096*
I beg of you, brethren, **b** as I *am,* **Ga 4:12** *1096*
for I also *have* **b** as you *are.* **Ga 4:12**
So have I **b** your enemy by **Ga 4:16** *1096*
Let us not **b** boastful, challenging **Ga 5:26** *1096*
and they, having **b** callous, **Eph 4:19** *524*
But all things **b** visible when they **Eph 5:13** *5319*
AND THE TWO SHALL **B** ONE FLESH. **Eph 5:31**
1510, 1519
cause of Christ has **b** well known **Php 1:13** *1096*
it or have already **b** perfect, **Php 3:12**
because you had **b** very dear to us. **1Th 2:8** *1096*
he will not **b** conceited and fall into **1Tm 3:6**
have learned and **b** convinced of, **2Tm 3:14**
your faith may **b** effective through **Phm 1:6** *1096*
having **b** as much better than the **Heb 1:4** *1096*
THEY ALL WILL **B** OLD LIKE A GARMENT, **Heb 1:11** *3822*
that He might **b** a merciful and **Heb 2:17** *1096*
For we have **b** partakers of Christ, **Heb 3:14** *1096*
Himself so as to **b** a high priest, **Heb 5:5** *1096*
since you have **b** dull of hearing. **Heb 5:11** *1096*
having **b** a high priest forever **Heb 6:20** *1096*
who has **b** *such* not on the basis of **Heb 7:16** *1096*
so much the more also Jesus has **b** **Heb 7:22** *1096*
of which all have **b** partakers, **Heb 12:8** *1096*
not having **b** a forgetful hearer **Jas 1:25** *1096*
and **b** judges with evil motives? **Jas 2:4** *1096*
one *point,* he has **b** guilty of all. **Jas 2:10** *1096*
have **b** a transgressor of the law. **Jas 2:11** *1096*
Let not many *of you* **b** teachers, **Jas 3:1** *1096*
your garments have **b** moth-eaten. **Jas 5:2** *1096*
and you have **b** her children if you **1Pe 3:6** *1096*
WHAT WILL **B** OF THE GODLESS MAN **1Pe 4:18** *5316*
by them you may **b** partakers **2Pe 1:4** *1096*
b worse for them than the first. **2Pe 2:20** *1096*
"I am rich, and have **b** wealthy, **Rv 3:17** *4147*
by fire so that you may **b** rich, **Rv 3:18** *4147*
has **b** *the kingdom* of our Lord and **Rv 11:15** *1096*
She has **b** a dwelling place of **Rv 18:2** *1096*
merchants of the earth have **b** rich **Rv 18:3** *4147*

BECOMES
which they have committed **b** known, **Lv 4:14** 3045
not to be done, and he **b** guilty, **Lv 4:22** 816
not to be done, and **b** guilty, **Lv 4:27** 816
may be with which he **b** unclean, **Lv 5:3** 2930
when he **b** guilty in one of these, **Lv 5:5** 816
be, when he sins and **b** guilty, **Lv 6:4** 816
carcasses **b** unclean until evening, **Lv 11:24** 2930
whoever touches them **b** unclean. **Lv 11:26** 2930
carcasses **b** unclean until evening, **Lv 11:27** 2930
are dead **b** unclean until evening. **Lv 11:31** 2930
when they are dead **b** unclean, **Lv 11:32** 2930
until evening, then it **b** clean. **Lv 11:32** 2891
whatever is in it **b** unclean and **Lv 11:33** 2930
their carcass may fall **b** unclean; **Lv 11:35** 2930
carcass **b** unclean until evening. **Lv 11:39** 2930
and it **b** an infection of leprosy **Lv 13:2** 1961
flesh of the burn **b** a bright spot, **Lv 13:24** 1961
b bald at the front and sides, **Lv 13:41** 4803
it, **b** unclean until evening. **Lv 14:46** 2930
with the discharge lies **b** unclean, **Lv 15:4** 2930
on which he sits **b** unclean. **Lv 15:4** 2930
the discharge rides **b** unclean. **Lv 15:9** 2930
b cleansed from his discharge, **Lv 15:13** 2891
she **b** clean from her discharge, **Lv 15:28** 2891
daughter **b** a widow or divorced, **Lv 22:13** 1961
'If a fellow countryman of yours **b** **Lv 25:25** 4134
countryman of yours **b** poor and **Lv 25:35** 4134
If a countryman of yours **b** so poor **Lv 25:39** 4134
a sojourner with you **b** sufficient, **Lv 25:47** 5381
a countryman of yours **b** so poor **Lv 25:47** 4134
as your land **b** desolate and your **Lv 26:33** 1961
uncircumcised heart **b** humbled **Lv 26:41** 3665
gives to the priest, it **b** his.' " **Nu 5:10** 1961
head on the day when he **b** clean; **Nu 6:9** 2893
b unclean because of a *dead* person, **Nu 9:10** 1961
nostrils and **b** loathsome to you; **Nu 11:20** 1961
and goes and **b** another man's *wife,* **Dt 24:2** 1961
a river **b** parched and dried up, **Jb 14:11** 2717a
"Water **b** hard like stone, And the **Jb 38:30** 2244
not be afraid when a man **b** rich, **Ps 49:16** 6238
appoint darkness and it **b** night, **Ps 104:20** 1961
And **b** guarantor in the presence of **Pr 17:18** 6148
when he **b** surety for a stranger; **Pr 20:16** 6148
is punished, the naive **b** wise; **Pr 21:11** 2449
borrower **b** the lender's slave. **Pr 22:7** 1961
when he **b** surety for a stranger; **Pr 27:13** 6148
Under a slave when he **b** king, **Pr 30:22** 4427a
And the flower **b** a ripening grape, **Is 18:5** 1961
And the wilderness **b** a fertile **Is 32:15** 1961
Grass **b** reeds and rushes. **Is 35:7**
he drinks no water and **b** weary. **Is 44:12** 3286
it **b** *something* for a man to burn, **Is 44:15** 1961
Then in my heart it **b** like a **Jer 20:9** 1961
as he **b** strong through his riches, **Da 11:2**
of Maroth **B** weak waiting for good, **Mi 1:12** 2342a
that man **b** worse than the first. **Mt 12:45** *1096*
the word, and it **b** unfruitful. **Mt 13:22** *1096*
the garden plants and **b** a tree, **Mt 13:32** *1096*
and when he **b** one, you make him **Mt 23:15** *1096*
the word, and it **b** unfruitful. **Mk 4:19** *1096*
grows up and **b** larger than all the **Mk 4:32** *1096*
but if the salt **b** unsalty, with **Mk 9:50** *1096*
that man **b** worse than the first." **Lk 11:26** *1096*
for everything that **b** visible is light. **Eph 5:13** *5319*

BECOMING
torn *by beasts,* **b** unclean by it; **Lv 22:8** 2930
Praise is **b** to the upright. **Ps 33:1** 5000
it is pleasant *and* praise is **b**. **Ps 147:1** 5000
exhausted, They are **b** *like* women; **Jer 51:30** 1961
the sea was **b** increasingly stormy. **Jon 1:11** 1980
was **b** *even* stormier against them. **Jon 1:13** 1980
were **b** obedient to the faith. **Ac 6:7** *5219*
b jealous and taking along some **Ac 17:5** *2206*
were **b** hardened and disobedient, **Ac 19:9** *4645*
Without **b** weak in faith he **Ro 4:19** *770*
He humbled Himself by **b** obedient **Php 2:8** *1096*
But whatever is **b** obsolete and **Heb 8:13** *3822*
and partly by **b** sharers with those **Heb 10:33** *1096*

BECORATH
the son of Zeror, the son of **B**, **1Sa 9:1** 1064

BED
in worship at the head of the **b**. **Gn 47:31** 4296
his strength and sat up in the **b**. **Gn 48:2** 4296
you went up to your father's **b**; **Gn 49:4** 4904
into the **b** and breathed his last, **Gn 49:33** 4296
into your bedroom and on your **b**, **Ex 8:3** 4296
he does not die but remains in **b**, **Ex 21:18** 4904
'Every **b** on which the person with **Lv 15:4** 4904
who touches his **b** shall wash his **Lv 15:5** 4904
'Anyone who touches her **b** **Lv 15:21** 4904
'Whether it be on the **b** or on the **Lv 15:23** 4904
and every **b** on which he lies shall **Lv 15:24** 4904
'Any **b** on which she lies all the **Lv 15:26** 4904
to her like her **b** at menstruation; **Lv 15:26** 4904
idol and laid *it* on the **b**, **1Sa 19:13** 4296
"Bring him up to me on his **b**, **1Sa 19:15** 4296
the household idol *was* on the **b** **1Sa 19:16** 4296
from the ground and sat on the **b**. **1Sa 28:23** 4296
was lying on his **b** in his bedroom, **2Sa 4:7** 4296
man in his own house on his **b**, **2Sa 4:11** 4904
David arose from his **b** and walked **2Sa 11:2** 4904
on his **b** with his lord's servants, **2Sa 11:13** 4904
on your **b** and pretend to be ill; **2Sa 13:5** 4904
the king bowed himself on the **b**. **1Ki 1:47** 4904
living, and laid him on his own **b**. **1Ki 17:19** 4296
And he lay down on his **b** and **1Ki 21:4** 4296
from the **b** where you have gone up, **2Ki 1:4** 4296
from the **b** where you have gone up, **2Ki 1:6** 4296
from the **b** where you have gone up, **2Ki 1:16** 4296
and let us set a **b** for him there, **2Ki 4:10** 4296
him on the **b** of the man of God, **2Ki 4:21** 4296
lad was dead and laid on his **b**. **2Ki 4:32** 4296
because he defiled his father's **b**, **1Ch 5:1** 3326
priest, and murdered him on his **b**. **2Ch 24:25** 4296
'My **b** will comfort me, My couch **Jb 7:13** 6210
home, I make my **b** in the darkness; **Jb 17:13** 3326
also chastened with pain on his **b**, **Jb 33:19** 4904
in your heart upon your **b**, **Ps 4:4** 4904
Every night I make my **b** swim, **Ps 6:6** 4296
He plans wickedness upon his **b**; **Ps 36:4** 4904
When I remember You on my **b**, **Ps 63:6** 3326
enter my house, Nor lie on my **b**; **Ps 132:3**
6210, 3326
If I make my **b** in Sheol, behold, **Ps 139:8** 3331
"I have sprinkled my **b** With myrrh, **Pr 7:17** 4904
he take your **b** from under you? **Pr 22:27** 4904
So *does* the sluggard on his **b**. **Pr 26:14** 4296
"On my **b** night after night I **SS 3:1** 4904
"His cheeks are like a **b** of balsam, **SS 5:13** 6170
Maggots are spread out *as your* **b** **Is 14:11**
The **b** is too short on which to **Is 28:20** 4702
mountain You have made your **b**. **Is 57:7** 4904
have gone up and made your **b** wide. **Is 57:8** 4904
with them, You have loved their **b**, **Is 57:8** 4904
out sackcloth and ashes as a **b**? **Is 58:5**
came to her to the **b** of love and **Ezk 23:17** 4904
your **b** with the uncircumcised.' **Ezk 32:19** 7901
'They have made a **b** for her among **Ezk 32:25** 4904
in your mind *while* on your **b**. **Da 2:28** 4903
while on your **b** your thoughts **Da 2:29** 4903
I lay on my **b** and the visions in **Da 4:5** 4903
in my mind *as I lay* on my **b**: **Da 4:10** 4903
in my mind *as I lay* on my **b**, **Da 4:13** 4903
in his mind *as he lay* on his **b**; **Da 7:1** 4903
of a **b** and *the* cover of a couch! **Am 3:12** 4296
lying sick in **b** with a fever. **Mt 8:14**
to Him a paralytic lying on a **b** **Mt 9:2** *2825b*
"Get up, pick up your **b** and go home." **Mt 9:6** *2825b*
basket, is it, or under a **b**? **Mk 4:21** *2825b*
to **b** at night and gets up by day, **Mk 4:27** *2518*
found the child lying on the **b**, **Mk 7:30** *2825b*
on a **b** a man who was paralyzed; **Lk 5:18** *2825b*
a container, or puts it under a **b**; **Lk 8:16** *2825b*
and my children and I are in **b**; **Lk 11:7** *2845*
there will be two in one **b**; **Lk 17:34** *2825b*
get up and make your **b**." **Ac 9:34** *4766*
father of Publius was lying *in* **b** **Ac 28:8**
the *marriage* **b** *is to be* undefiled; **Heb 13:4** *2845*
throw her on a **b** *of sickness,* **Rv 2:22** *2825b*

BEDAD
died, and Hadad the son of **B**, **Gn 36:35** 911
Husham died, Hadad the son of **B**, **1Ch 1:46** 911

BEDAN
and **B** and Jephthah and Samuel, **1Sa 12:11** 917
The son of Ulam *was* **B**. **1Ch 7:17** 917

BEDCHAMBER
in your **b** do not curse a king, **Ec 10:20** 4093

BEDEIAH
Benaiah, **B**, Cheluhi, **Ezr 10:35** 912

BEDRIDDEN
who had been **b** eight years, **Ac 9:33**
2621, 1909, 2895

BEDROOM
and into your **b** and on your bed, **Ex 8:3**
2315, 4904
he was lying on his bed in his **b**, **2Sa 4:7**
2315, 4904
"Bring the food into the **b**, **2Sa 13:10** 2315
into the **b** to her brother Amnon. **2Sa 13:10** 2315
went in to the king in the **b**. **1Ki 1:15** 2315
words that you speak in your **b**." **2Ki 6:12**
2315, 4904
placed him and his nurse in the **b**. **2Ki 11:2**
2315, 4296
placed him and his nurse in the **b**. **2Ch 22:11**
2315, 4296

BEDS
brought **b**, basins, pottery, wheat, **2Sa 17:28** 4904
While they slumber in their **b**, **Jb 33:15** 4904
Let them sing for joy on their **b**. **Ps 149:5** 4904
to his garden, To the **b** of balsam, **SS 6:2** 6170
They rest in their **b**, **Is 57:2** 4904
from the **b** where it was planted, **Ezk 17:7** 6170
on the **b** where it grew? **Ezk 17:10** 6170
heart When they wail on their **b**; **Hos 7:14** 4904
Those who recline on **b** of ivory **Am 6:4** 4296
Who work out evil on their **b**! **Mi 2:1** 4904

BEDSTEAD
his **b** was an iron bedstead; **Dt 3:11** 6210
his bedstead was an iron **b**; **Dt 3:11** 6210

BEE
and for the **b** that is in the land **Is 7:18** 1682

BEELIADA
Elishama, **B** and Eliphelet. **1Ch 14:7** 1182

BEELZEBUL
called the head of the house **B**, **Mt 10:25** *954*
by **B** the ruler of the demons." **Mt 12:24** *954*
"If I by **B** cast out demons, **Mt 12:27** *954*
"He is possessed by **B**," **Mk 3:22** *954*
"He casts out demons by **B**, **Lk 11:15** *954*
say that I cast out demons by **B**. **Lk 11:18** *954*
"And if I by **B** cast out demons, **Lk 11:19** *954*

BEEN
his tent had **b** at the beginning, **Gn 13:3** 1961
his relative had **b** taken captive, **Gn 14:14**
when he had **b** there a long time, **Gn 26:8**
wells of water which had **b** dug **Gn 26:18**
that the LORD has **b** with you; **Gn 26:28** 1961
the name of the city had **b** Luz. **Gn 28:19**
God of my father has **b** with me. **Gn 31:5** 1961
all that Laban has **b** doing to you. **Gn 31:12**
"These twenty years I *have* **b** **Gn 31:38**
years I have **b** in your house; **Gn 31:41**
fear of Isaac, had not **b** for me, **Gn 31:42** 1961
yet my life has **b** preserved." **Gn 32:30**
gift which has **b** brought to you, **Gn 33:11**
b with me wherever I have gone." **Gn 35:3** 1961
has surely **b** torn to pieces!" **Gn 37:33**
had not **b** given to him as a wife. **Gn 38:14**
has **b** no temple prostitute here." **Gn 38:21** 1961
b no temple prostitute here.' " **Gn 38:22** 1961
Joseph had **b** taken down to Egypt; **Gn 39:1**
which had **b** in the land of Egypt **Gn 41:53** 1961
"My money has **b** returned, and **Gn 42:28**
possession the cup has **b** found." **Gn 44:16**
possession the cup has **b** found, **Gn 44:17**
"For the famine *has* **b** in **Gn 45:6**
they have **b** keepers of livestock; **Gn 46:32** 1961
'Your servants have **b** keepers of **Gn 46:34** 1961
have **b** the years of my life, **Gn 47:9** 1961
"But your offspring that have **b** **Gn 48:6**
The God who has **b** my shepherd all **Gn 48:15**
b a sojourner in a foreign land." **Ex 2:22** 1961
what has **b** done to you in Egypt. **Ex 3:16**
Lord, I have never **b** eloquent, **Ex 4:10**
have **b** cut off from the earth. **Ex 9:15**
such as has not **b** *seen* in Egypt **Ex 9:18** 1961
such as had not **b** in all the land **Ex 9:24** 1961
for there has **b** enough of God's **Ex 9:28**
There had never **b** so *many* locusts, **Ex 10:14** 1961

such as there has not **b** *before* and	Ex 11:6	1961
For it would have **b** better for us	Ex 14:12	
who had **b** going before the camp of	Ex 14:19	
b a sojourner in a foreign land."	Ex 18:3	1961
and its owner has **b** warned,	Ex 21:29	
for what has **b** torn to pieces.	Ex 22:13	
you have **b** shown in the mountain.	Ex 26:30	
for every man has **b** against his son	Ex 32:29	
not **b** produced in all the earth nor	Ex 34:10	
of Israel what he had **b** commanded,	Ex 34:34	
to do as has **b** done this day,	Lv 8:34	
die, for so I have **b** commanded."	Lv 8:35	
for thus I have **b** commanded.	Lv 10:13	
for they have **b** given as your due	Lv 10:14	
and behold, it had **b** burned up!	Lv 10:16	
blood had not **b** brought inside,	Lv 10:18	
b good in the sight of the LORD?"	Lv 10:19	
with the mark has **b** washed,	Lv 13:55	
has faded after it has **b** washed,	Lv 13:56	
leprosy has **b** healed in the leper,	Lv 14:3	
and after it has **b** replastered,	Lv 14:43	
after the house has **b** replastered,	Lv 14:48	
with the discharge has **b** sitting,	Lv 15:6	
men of the land who have **b** before	Lv 18:27	
the nation which has **b** before you.	Lv 18:28	
which have **b** practiced before you,	Lv 18:30	
but who has in no way **b** redeemed nor	Lv 19:20	
the anointing oil has **b** poured and	Lv 21:10	
and who has **b** consecrated to wear	Lv 21:10	
right after he has **b** sold.	Lv 25:48	
'No one who may have **b** set apart	Lv 27:29	
men who had **b** designated by name,	Nu 1:17	
LORD, just as he had **b** commanded.	Nu 3:16	
she has not **b** caught in the act,	Nu 5:13	
has **b** unfaithful to her husband,	Nu 5:27	4603
the ram's shoulder *when it has* **b**	Nu 6:19	
You **b** so hard on Your servant?	Nu 11:11	
among those who had **b** registered,	Nu 11:26	
the people who had **b** greedy.	Nu 11:34	183
has **b** removed from them,	Nu 14:9	
because it had not **b** declared	Nu 15:34	
for the plague had **b** checked.	Nu 16:50	
which a yoke has never **b** placed.	Nu 19:2	
touches one who has **b** slain with	Nu 19:16	
has not **b** sprinkled on him,	Nu 19:20	
If there had **b** a sword in my hand,	Nu 22:29	3426
b accustomed to do so to you?"	Nu 22:30	
for they have **b** hostile to you	Nu 25:18	6887c
the LORD your God has **b** with you;	Dt 2:7	
Has *anything* **b** done like this great	Dt 4:32	
or has *anything* **b** heard like it?	Dt 4:32	
b rebellious against the LORD.	Dt 9:7	1961
"You have **b** rebellious against	Dt 9:24	1961
abomination has **b** done among you,	Dt 13:14	
LORD's remission has **b** proclaimed.	Dt 15:2	
thing has **b** done in Israel,	Dt 17:4	
which has not **b** worked and which	Dt 21:3	
which has not **b** plowed or sown,	Dt 21:4	
his wife, since she has **b** defiled;	Dt 24:4	
b rebellious against the LORD;	Dt 31:27	1961
Just as I have **b** with Moses, I	Jos 1:5	1961
that just as I have **b** with Moses,	Jos 3:7	1961
of Egypt had not **b** circumcised.	Jos 5:5	
If only we had **b** willing to dwell	Jos 7:7	
place has **b** called the valley of Achor	Jos 7:26	
for the people who had **b** fleeing	Jos 8:20	
"The five kings have **b** found	Jos 10:17	
is He who has **b** fighting for you.	Jos 23:3	
all have **b** fulfilled for you, not	Jos 23:14	
on the altar which had **b** built.	Jg 6:28	
companion who had **b** his friend.	Jg 14:20	
fresh cords that have not **b** dried,	Jg 16:7	
fresh cords that had not **b** dried,	Jg 16:8	
new ropes which have not **b** used,	Jg 16:11	
for I have **b** a Nazirite to God	Jg 16:17	
inheritance had not **b** allotted to	Jg 18:1	
happened or **b** seen from the day	Jg 19:30	
she has **b** sitting in the house for	Ru 2:7	
has **b** fully reported to me,	Ru 2:11	
"A son has **b** born to Naomi!"	Ru 4:17	
of the LORD yet **b** revealed to him.	1Sa 3:7	
as they have **b** slaves to you;	1Sa 4:9	5647
there has also **b** a great slaughter	1Sa 4:17	1961
and the ark of God has **b** taken."	1Sa 4:17	
Now the ark of the LORD had **b** in	1Sa 6:1	1961
on which there has never **b** a yoke;	1Sa 6:7	5927
on them, for they have **b** found.	1Sa 9:20	
"Here is what has **b** reserved!	1Sa 9:24	
because it has **b** kept for you	1Sa 9:24	
you went to look for have **b** found.	1Sa 10:2	
that the donkeys had **b** found."	1Sa 10:16	
because the LORD has **b** pleased to	1Sa 12:22	
the Philistines has not **b** great."	1Sa 14:30	
has **b** a warrior from his youth."	1Sa 17:33	
should have **b** given to David,	1Sa 18:19	
and since his deeds *have* **b** very	1Sa 19:4	
evil has **b** decided by my father to	1Sa 20:9	
you as He has **b** with my father.	1Sa 20:13	1961
"Surely women have **b** kept from us	1Sa 21:5	
were with him had **b** discovered.	1Sa 22:6	
now your shepherds have **b** with us	1Sa 25:7	1961
surely there would not have **b** left	1Sa 25:34	
'So has David done and so *has* **b**	1Sa 27:11	
who has **b** with me these days,	1Sa 29:3	1961
you *have* **b** upright, and your	1Sa 29:6	
daughters had **b** taken captive.	1Sa 30:3	
two wives had **b** taken captive,	1Sa 30:5	
also **b** left at the brook Besor,	1Sa 30:21	
So it has **b** from that day forward,	1Sa 30:25	1961

You have **b** very pleasant to me.	2Sa 1:26	
had not **b** *the will* of the king to put	2Sa 3:37	1961
b aliens there until this day).	2Sa 4:3	1961
I have **b** moving about in a tent,	2Sa 7:6	1961
"I have **b** with you wherever	2Sa 7:9	1961
Hadadezer had **b** at war with Toi.	2Sa 8:10	1961
they had **b** defeated by Israel,	2Sa 10:15	
and if *that had* **b** too little,	2Sa 12:8	
"Has Amnon your brother **b** with you?	2Sa 13:20	1961
this has **b** determined since the day	2Sa 13:32	1961
like a woman who has **b** mourning	2Sa 14:2	
as I have **b** your father's servant	2Sa 15:34	1961
'There has **b** a slaughter among the	2Sa 17:9	1961
or has anything **b** taken for us?"	2Sa 19:42	
bones of those who had **b** hanged.	2Sa 21:13	
he also had **b** born to the giant.	2Sa 21:20	
thing **b** done by my lord the king,	1Ki 1:27	1961
LORD has **b** with my lord the king,	1Ki 1:37	1961
has **b** no one like you before you,	1Ki 3:12	1961
had always **b** a friend of David.	1Ki 5:1	1961
where they have **b** taken captive,	1Ki 8:47	
nor have they **b** seen to this day.	1Ki 10:12	
the heart of David his father *had* **b**.	1Ki 11:4	
So Israel has **b** in rebellion	1Ki 12:19	
have not **b** like My servant David,	1Ki 14:8	1961
as though it had **b** a trivial thing	1Ki 16:31	
"Has it not **b** told to my master	1Ki 18:13	
of the LORD which had **b** torn down.	1Ki 18:30	
have **b** very zealous for the LORD,	1Ki 19:10	7065
have **b** very zealous for the LORD,	1Ki 19:14	7065
"Naboth has **b** stoned and is dead."	1Ki 21:14	
Naboth had **b** stoned and was dead,	1Ki 21:15	
have **b** purified to this day,	2Ki 2:22	
you have **b** careful for us with all	2Ki 4:13	2729
"Where have you **b**, Gehazi?"	2Ki 5:25	
shields that *had* **b** King David's,	2Ki 11:10	
had **b** carried away into exile.	2Ki 17:33	
he heard that Hezekiah had **b** sick.	2Ki 20:12	2470a
and have **b** provoking Me to anger since	2Ki 21:15	1961
of this book that has **b** found,	2Ki 22:13	
Surely such a Passover had not **b**	2Ki 23:22	
had **b** over the camp of the LORD,	1Ch 9:19	
b anointed king over all Israel,	1Ch 14:8	
"I have **b** with you wherever	1Ch 17:8	1961
Hadadezer had **b** at war with Tou.	1Ch 18:10	1961
they had **b** defeated by Israel,	1Ch 19:16	
had not **b** on any king before him	1Ch 29:25	1961
knowledge have **b** granted to you.	2Ch 1:12	
where they have **b** taken captive,	2Ch 6:38	
there had never **b** spice like that	2Ch 9:9	1961
So Israel has **b** in rebellion	2Ch 10:19	6586
they had **b** unfaithful to the LORD,	2Ch 12:2	4603
with which Baasha had **b** building,	2Ch 16:6	
shields which had **b** King David's,	2Ch 23:9	
for you have **b** unfaithful and	2Ch 26:18	4603
"For our fathers have **b** unfaithful	2Ch 29:6	4603
people **b** gathered to Jerusalem.	2Ch 30:3	
the wall that had **b** broken down and	2Ch 32:5	
money which had **b** brought into	2Ch 34:14	
of the book which has **b** found;	2Ch 34:21	
There had not **b** celebrated a	2Ch 35:18	
temple of the LORD had not **b** laid.	Ezr 3:6	
and we have **b** sacrificing to Him	Ezr 4:2	
b translated and read before me.	Ezr 4:18	
"A decree has **b** issued by me,	Ezr 4:19	
and a search has **b** made and it has	Ezr 4:19	
been made and it has **b** discovered	Ezr 4:19	
revolt have **b** perpetrated in it,	Ezr 4:19	
now it has **b** under construction and	Ezr 5:16	
when these things had **b** completed,	Ezr 9:1	
b foremost in this unfaithfulness."	Ezr 9:2	1961
our fathers to this day we *have* **b**	Ezr 9:7	
our kings *and* our priests have **b**	Ezr 9:7	
has **b** *shown* from the LORD our God,	Ezr 9:8	1961
we have **b** left an escaped remnant,	Ezr 9:15	
"We have **b** unfaithful to our God and	Ezr 10:2	4603
"You have **b** unfaithful and have	Ezr 10:10	4603
those of you who have **b** scattered	Ne 1:9	
I had not **b** sad in his presence.	Ne 2:1	1961
gates have **b** consumed by fire?"	Ne 2:3	
of my God had **b** favorable to me and	Ne 2:18	
as you are saying have not **b** done,	Ne 6:8	1961
this work had **b** accomplished with	Ne 6:16	
which had **b** made known to them.	Ne 8:12	
the Levites had not **b** given *them,*	Ne 13:10	
what had **b** decreed against her.	Es 2:1	
who had **b** taken into exile from	Es 2:6	
captives who had **b** exiled with	Es 2:6	
learned all that had **b** done,	Es 4:1	
text of the edict which had **b** issued	Es 4:8	
And I have not **b** summoned to come	Es 4:11	
"What honor or dignity has **b**	Es 6:3	
"Nothing has **b** done for him."	Es 6:3	
head a royal crown has **b** placed;	Es 6:8	
for we have **b** sold, I and my	Es 7:4	
if we had only **b** sold as slaves,	Es 7:4	
he saw that harm had **b** determined	Es 7:7	
would have lain down and **b** quiet;	Jb 3:13	8252
then, I would have **b** at rest,	Jb 3:13	5117
Therefore my words have **b** rash.	Jb 6:3	3886b
have **b** as though I had not been,	Jb 10:19	1961
have been as though I had not **b**,	Jb 10:19	1961
of the orphans has **b** crushed.	Jb 22:9	
"Others have **b** with those who	Jb 24:13	1961
my heart has **b** enticed by a woman,	Jb 31:9	
And if he has not **b** warmed with	Jb 31:20	
That too would have **b** an iniquity	Jb 31:28	
not **b** satisfied with his meat'?	Jb 31:31	
too have **b** formed out of the clay.	Jb 33:6	

gates of death **b** revealed to you,	Jb 38:17	
hid, their own foot has **b** caught.	Ps 9:15	
have **b** the helper of the orphan.	Ps 10:14	1961
b my God from my mother's womb.	Ps 22:10	
For they have **b** from of old.	Ps 25:6	
You have **b** my help;	Ps 27:9	1961
b thrust down and cannot rise.	Ps 36:12	
I have **b** young and now I am old	Ps 37:25	1961
have **b** my food day and night,	Ps 42:3	1961
in great fear *where* no fear had **b**;	Ps 53:5	1961
For You have **b** my stronghold And	Ps 59:16	1961
You have **b** angry;	Ps 60:1	599
For You have **b** a refuge for me, A	Ps 61:3	1961
For You have **b** my help, And in	Ps 63:7	1961
I have **b** sustained from *my* birth;	Ps 71:6	
I have **b** stricken all day long And	Ps 73:14	
of Your servants which has **b** shed.	Ps 79:10	
You have **b** full of wrath against	Ps 89:38	5674b
You have **b** our dwelling place in	Ps 90:1	1961
we have **b** consumed by Your anger	Ps 90:7	3615
by Your wrath we have **b** dismayed.	Ps 90:7	
I have **b** anointed with fresh oil.	Ps 92:10	
If the LORD had not **b** my help,	Ps 94:17	1961
But the LORD has **b** my stronghold,	Ps 94:22	1961
my days have **b** consumed in smoke,	Ps 102:3	3615
have **b** scorched like a hearth.	Ps 102:3	
My heart has **b** smitten like grass	Ps 102:4	
The LORD has **b** mindful of us;	Ps 115:12	2142
If Your law had not **b** my delight,	Ps 119:92	
b the LORD who was on our side,"	Ps 124:1	1961
b the LORD who was on our side When	Ps 124:2	1961
Our bones have **b** scattered at the	Ps 141:7	
like those who have long **b** dead.	Ps 143:3	
If you have **b** snared with the	Pr 6:2	
Have **b** caught with the words of	Pr 6:2	
If you have **b** foolish in exalting	Pr 30:32	5034a
which has **b** is that which will be,	Ec 1:9	1961
And that which has **b** done is that	Ec 1:9	
b king over Israel in Jerusalem.	Ec 1:12	1961
all that has **b** done under heaven.	Ec 1:13	
which have **b** done under the sun,	Ec 1:14	
except what has already **b** done?	Ec 2:12	
then have I **b** extremely wise?"	Ec 2:15	2449
for the work which had **b** done	Ec 2:17	
That which is has **b** already and	Ec 3:15	1961
that which will be has already **b**,	Ec 3:15	1961
Whatever exists has already **b** named,	Ec 6:10	
What has **b** is remote and	Ec 7:24	1961
deed that has **b** done under the sun	Ec 8:9	
which has **b** done on the earth	Ec 8:16	
which has **b** done under the sun.	Ec 8:17	
conclusion, when all has **b** heard,	Ec 12:13	
has **b** heard in our land.	SS 2:12	
also **b** filled with silver and gold	Is 2:7	
has also **b** filled with horses And	Is 2:7	
land has also **b** filled with idols;	Is 2:8	
So the *common* man has **b** humbled	Is 2:9	7817
man *of importance* has **b** abased,	Is 2:9	8213
The sycamores have **b** cut down,	Is 9:10	
in which you have **b** enslaved,	Is 14:3	
'Even you have **b** made weak as we,	Is 14:10	
Have **b** brought down to Sheol;	Is 14:11	
You have **b** cut down to the earth,	Is 14:12	
"But you have **b** cast out of your	Is 14:19	
A harsh vision has **b** shown to me;	Is 21:2	
b turned for me into trembling.	Is 21:4	
have **b** captured without the bow;	Is 22:3	
have **b** a defense for the helpless,	Is 25:4	1961
of His slain, have they **b** slain?	Is 27:7	
"Rahab who has **b** exterminated."	Is 30:7	
b winnowed with shovel and fork.	Is 30:24	
For Topheth has long **b** ready,	Is 30:33	
it has **b** prepared for the king.	Is 30:33	
the palace has **b** abandoned,	Is 32:14	
he had **b** sick and had recovered.	Is 39:1	2470a
That her iniquity has **b** removed,	Is 40:2	
Has it not **b** declared to you from	Is 40:21	
Scarcely have they **b** planted,	Is 40:24	
Scarcely have they **b** sown,	Is 40:24	
not **b** traversing with his feet.	Is 41:3	
They have **b** quenched *and*	Is 43:17	
Israel has **b** saved by the LORD	Is 45:17	
who have **b** borne by Me from birth	Is 46:3	
And have **b** carried from the womb;	Is 46:3	
things which have not **b** done,	Is 46:10	
long ago your ear has not **b** open,	Is 48:8	
have **b** called a rebel from birth.	Is 48:8	
would have **b** like a river,	Is 48:18	1961
would have **b** like the sand,	Is 48:19	1961
I have **b** bereaved of my children And	Is 49:21	7921
have **b** taken away without cause?"	Is 52:5	
had not **b** told them they will see,	Is 52:15	
the arm of the LORD **b** revealed?	Is 53:1	
"Whereas you have **b** forsaken and	Is 60:15	1961
You, Has **b** burned *by* fire;	Is 64:11	1961
there has **b** such *a thing* as this!	Jer 2:10	1961
His cities have **b** destroyed,	Jer 2:15	
Have I **b** a wilderness to Israel,	Jer 2:31	1961
Where have you not **b** violated?	Jer 3:2	
the showers have **b** withheld,	Jer 3:3	
And there has **b** no spring rain.	Jer 3:3	1961
has **b** cut off from their mouth.	Jer 7:28	
daughter of my people **b** restored?	Jer 8:22	
"A conspiracy has **b** found among	Jer 11:9	
and birds have **b** snatched away,	Jer 12:4	
"It has **b** made a desolation,	Jer 12:11	
whole land has **b** made desolate,	Jer 12:11	
of the LORD has **b** taken captive.	Jer 13:17	
of the Negev have **b** locked up,	Jer 13:19	

Judah has **b** carried into exile, **Jer 13:19**
Your skirts have **b** removed And **Jer 13:22**
And your heels have **b** exposed. **Jer 13:22**
b put to shame and humiliated, **Jer 14:3** 954
there has **b** no rain on the land; **Jer 14:4** 1961
The farmers have **b** put to shame, **Jer 14:4** 954
Truly our apostasies have **b** many, **Jer 14:7** 7231
has **b** crushed with a mighty blow, **Jer 14:17**
She has **b** shamed and humiliated. **Jer 15:9** 954
a fire has **b** kindled in My anger, **Jer 15:14** 6919
For I have **b** called by Your name, O **Jer 15:16**
Why has my pain **b** perpetual And my **Jer 15:18** 1961
"A baby boy has **b** born to you!" **Jer 20:15**
my mother would have **b** my grave, **Jer 20:17** 1961
my days have **b** spent in shame? **Jer 20:18** 3615
deliver the *person* who has **b** robbed **Jer 21:12**
and deliver the one who has **b** **Jer 22:3**
all your lovers have **b** crushed. **Jer 22:20**
b your practice from your youth, **Jer 22:21**
he and his descendants **b** hurled **Jer 22:28**
whom I have **b** sending to you again **Jer 26:5**
have **b** completed for Babylon, **Jer 29:10** 4390
sons of Judah have **b** doing only evil **Jer 32:30**
sons of Israel have **b** only provoking **Jer 32:30**
"Indeed this city has **b** to Me *a* **Jer 32:31** 1961
who has **b** sold to you and has **Jer 34:14**
and when the Chaldeans who had **b** **Jer 37:5**
all of the women who have **b** left **Jer 38:22**
conversation had not **b** overheard. **Jer 38:27**
who had not **b** exiled to Babylon. **Jer 40:7**
places to which they had **b** driven **Jer 40:12**
"As My anger and wrath have **b** **Jer 42:18**
to which they had **b** driven away, **Jer 43:5**
of Egypt has **b** put to shame, **Jer 46:24** 954
Ashkelon has **b** ruined. **Jer 47:5**
to Nebo, for it has **b** destroyed; **Jer 48:1**
Kiriathaim has **b** put to shame, it **Jer 48:1** 954
put to shame, it has **b** captured; **Jer 48:1**
has **b** put to shame and shattered. **Jer 48:1** 954
has **b** at ease since his youth; **Jer 48:11** 7599
b undisturbed, *like wine* on its dregs, **Jer 48:11** 8252
b emptied from vessel to vessel, **Jer 48:11**
"Moab has **b** destroyed and men **Jer 48:15**
has the mighty scepter **b** broken, **Jer 48:17**
"Moab has **b** put to shame, for it **Jer 48:20** 954
to shame, for it has **b** shattered. **Jer 48:20** 2865
Arnon That Moab has **b** destroyed. **Jer 48:20**
"The horn of Moab has **b** cut off and **Jer 48:25**
"Kerioth has **b** captured And the **Jer 48:41**
And the strongholds have **b** seized, **Jer 48:41**
sons have **b** taken away captive And **Jer 48:46**
O Heshbon, for Ai has **b** destroyed! **Jer 49:3**
counsel **b** lost to the prudent? **Jer 49:7** 6
His offspring has **b** destroyed **Jer 49:10**
of it has **b** heard at the Red Sea. **Jer 49:21**
city of praise has not **b** deserted, **Jer 49:25**
'Babylon has **b** captured, Bel has **Jer 50:2**
captured, Bel has **b** put to shame, **Jer 50:2** 954
to shame, Marduk has **b** shattered; **Jer 50:2** 2865
Her images have **b** put to shame, **Jer 50:2** 954
her idols have **b** shattered.' **Jer 50:2** 2865
Her walls have **b** torn down. **Jer 50:15**
earth Has **b** cut off and broken! **Jer 50:23**
You have **b** found and also seized **Jer 50:24**
"Babylon has **b** seized!" **Jer 50:46**
Judah has **b** forsaken By his God, **Jer 51:5**
Babylon has **b** a golden cup in the **Jer 51:7**
Babylon has fallen and **b** broken; **Jer 51:8**
has **b** captured from end *to end;* **Jer 51:31**
The fords also have **b** seized, **Jer 51:32**
"How Sheshak has **b** captured, And **Jer 51:41**
of the whole earth **b** seized! **Jer 51:41**
She has **b** engulfed with its **Jer 51:42**
have **b** written concerning Babylon. **Jer 51:60**
me, For I have **b** very rebellious. **La 1:20**
Like those who have long **b** dead. **La 3:6**
My soul has **b** rejected from peace; **La 3:17** 2186a
of your iniquity has **b** completed, **La 4:22** 8552
has **b** turned over to strangers, **La 5:2**
has **b** turned into mourning. **La 5:15**
that a prophet has **b** among them. **Ezk 2:5** 1961
Behold, I have never **b** defiled; **Ezk 4:14** 2930
how I have **b** hurt by their **Ezk 6:9**
from the cherub on which it had **b**, **Ezk 9:3** 1961
has **b** given us as a possession.' **Ezk 11:15**
among which you have **b** scattered, **Ezk 11:17**
I did so, as I had **b** commanded. **Ezk 12:7**
have **b** like foxes among ruins. **Ezk 13:4** 1961
has **b** put into the fire for fuel, **Ezk 15:4**
and its middle part has **b** charred, **Ezk 15:4** 2787
have **b** in you for the purpose of **Ezk 22:6** 1961
"Slanderous men have **b** in you for **Ezk 22:9** 1961
when she had **b** defiled by them, **Ezk 23:17** 2930
Because they have **b** *only* a staff **Ezk 29:6** 1961
it has not **b** bound up for healing **Ezk 30:21**
and its boughs have **b** broken in **Ezk 31:12**
have all **b** given over to death, **Ezk 31:14**
"The city has **b** taken." **Ezk 33:21**
LORD had **b** upon me in the evening, **Ezk 33:22** 1961
land has **b** given as a possession.' **Ezk 33:24**
a prophet has **b** in their midst." **Ezk 33:33** 1961
who have **b** feeding themselves! **Ezk 34:2** 1961
and you have **b** taken up in the **Ezk 36:3**
has **b** profaned among the nations, **Ezk 36:23**
whose inhabitants have **b** gathered **Ezk 38:8**
which had **b** a continual waste; **Ezk 38:8** 1961
for you have **b** brought here in **Ezk 40:4**
in which they have **b** ministering **Ezk 44:19**
death or has **b** torn to pieces. **Ezk 44:31**
b eating the king's choice food. **Da 1:15**
this mystery has not **b** revealed to **Da 2:30**
b able to reveal this mystery." **Da 2:47** 3202
furnace had **b** made extremely hot, **Da 3:22**
has **b** removed from you, **Da 4:31** 5709
had **b** taken out of the temple, **Da 5:3**
wisdom have **b** found in you. **Da 5:14**
have **b** drinking wine from them; **Da 5:23**
you have **b** weighed on the scales **Da 5:27**
your kingdom has **b** divided and given **Da 5:28** 6537a
God, as he had **b** doing previously. **Da 6:10**
b able to deliver you from the **Da 6:20** 3202
mornings Which has **b** told is true; **Da 8:26**
the curse has **b** poured out on us, **Da 9:11**
there has not **b** done *anything* like **Da 9:12**
have sinned, we have **b** wicked. **Da 9:15** 7561
"Seventy weeks have **b** decreed for **Da 9:24**
had **b** mourning for three entire **Da 10:2** 1961
for I have now **b** sent to you." **Da 10:11**
for I had **b** left there with the **Da 10:13**
nor has any breath **b** left in me." **Da 10:17**
of kingship has not **b** conferred, **Da 11:21**
For you have **b** a snare at Mizpah And **Hos 5:1** 1961
But I *have* **b** the LORD your **Hos 12:9**
Yet I *have* **b** the LORD your **Hos 13:4**
food **b** cut off before our eyes, **Jl 1:16**
has never **b** *anything* like it, **Jl 2:2** 1961
wine of those who have **b** fined. **Am 2:8**
b sent among the nations *saying,* **Ob 1:1**
'I have **b** expelled from Your sight. **Jon 2:4**
b assembled against you Who say, **Mi 4:11**
b indignant these seventy years?" **Zch 1:12** 2194
her expectation has **b** confounded. **Zch 9:5** 954
glorious *trees* have **b** destroyed; **Zch 11:2**
"We have **b** beaten down, but we **Mal 1:4**
and an abomination has **b** committed **Mal 2:11**
Because the LORD has **b** a witness **Mal 2:14**
have **b** arrogant against Me," **Mal 3:13** 2388
of Solomon by Bathsheba who had **b** **Mt 1:6**
Mary had **b** betrothed to Joseph, **Mt 1:18**
for the Child who has **b** conceived in **Mt 1:20**
who has **b** born King of the Jews? **Mt 2:2**
what has **b** written by the prophet **Mt 2:5**
And having **b** warned *by God* in a **Mt 2:12**
This was to fulfill what had **b** **Mt 2:15**
that he had **b** tricked by the magi, **Mt 2:16**
Then what had **b** spoken through **Mt 2:17**
John had **b** taken into custody, **Mt 4:12**
"Blessed are those who have **b** **Mt 5:10**
it had **b** founded on the rock. **Mt 7:25**
a woman who had **b** suffering from a **Mt 9:20**
But when the crowd had **b** sent out, **Mt 9:25**
this has ever **b** seen **Mt 9:33**
"All things have **b** handed over to **Mt 11:27**
"To you it has **b** granted to know **Mt 13:11**
but to them it has not **b** granted. **Mt 13:11**
away what has **b** sown in his heart. **Mt 13:19**
For John had **b** saying to him, **Mt 14:4**
Having **b** prompted by her mother, **Mt 14:8**
help you has **b** given *to God,*" **Mt 15:5**
you bind on earth shall have **b** bound **Mt 16:19**
you loose on earth shall have **b** **Mt 16:19**
you bind on earth shall have **b** bound **Mt 18:18**
you loose on earth shall have **b** **Mt 18:18**
beginning it has not **b** this way. **Mt 19:8** *1096*
only those to whom it has **b** given. **Mt 19:11**
'Why have you **b** standing here idle **Mt 20:6**
it has **b** prepared by My Father." **Mt 20:23**
b invited to the wedding feast, **Mt 22:3**
'Tell those who have **b** invited, **Mt 22:4**
'If we had **b** *living* in the days of **Mt 23:30** *1510*
we would not have **b** partners with **Mt 23:30** *1510*
Unless those days had **b** cut short, **Mt 24:22**
short, no life would have **b** saved; **Mt 24:22**
he would have **b** on the alert and **Mt 24:43**
eternal fire which has **b** prepared **Mt 25:41**
"For this *perfume* might have **b** **Mt 26:9**
It would have **b** good for that man **Mt 26:24** *1510*
that man if he had not **b** born." **Mt 26:24**
"But after I have **b** raised, **Mt 26:32**
Him, saw that He had **b** condemned, **Mt 27:3**
this reason that field has **b** called **Mt 27:8**
HAD **B** SET by the sons of Israel; **Mt 27:9**
The robbers who had **b** crucified **Mt 27:44**
for Jesus who has **b** crucified. **Mt 28:5**
and did as they had **b** instructed; **Mt 28:15**
"All authority has **b** given to Me **Mt 28:18**
John had **b** taken into custody, **Mk 1:14**
"To you has **b** given the mystery **Mk 4:11**
the word which has **b** sown in them. **Mk 4:15**
nor has *anything* **b** secret, **Mk 4:22** *1096*
because he had often **b** bound with **Mk 5:4**
chains had **b** torn apart by him and **Mk 5:4**
For He had **b** saying to him, **Mk 5:8**
had **b** demon-possessed sitting down, **Mk 5:15**
the man who had **b** demon-possessed **Mk 5:18**
For John had **b** saying to Herod, **Mk 6:18**
has this **b** happening to him?" **Mk 9:21** *1510*
and when He has **b** killed, He will **Mk 9:31**
neck, he had **b** cast into the sea. **Mk 9:42**
for whom it has **b** prepared." **Mk 10:40**
John to have **b** a real prophet. **Mk 11:32** *1510*
days, no life would have **b** saved; **Mk 13:20**
"Why has this perfume **b** wasted? **Mk 14:4** *1096*
"For this perfume might have **b** sold **Mk 14:5**
It would have **b** good for that man **Mk 14:21**
that man if he had not **b** born." **Mk 14:21**
"But after I have **b** raised, **Mk 14:28**
The man named Barabbas had **b** **Mk 15:7** *1510*
had **b** accustomed to do for them. **Mk 15:8**
which had **b** hewn out in the rock; **Mk 15:46** *1510*
that the stone had **b** rolled away, **Mk 16:4**
the Nazarene, who has **b** crucified. **Mk 16:6**
to those who had **b** with Him, **Mk 16:10** *1096*
was alive and had **b** seen by her, **Mk 16:11**
and has **b** baptized shall be saved; **Mk 16:16**
the things you have **b** taught. **Lk 1:4**
for your petition has **b** heard, **Lk 1:13**
and I have **b** sent to speak to you and **Lk 1:19**
had **b** spoken to her by the Lord." **Lk 1:45**
there has **b** born for you a Savior, **Lk 2:11**
had **b** told them about this Child. **Lk 2:17**
and seen, just as had **b** told them. **Lk 2:20**
And it had **b** revealed to him by **Lk 2:26** *1510*
b anxiously looking for You." **Lk 2:48**
than what you have **b** ordered to." **Lk 3:13**
for it has **b** handed over to me, **Lk 4:6**
where He had **b** brought up; **Lk 4:16** *1510*
has **b** fulfilled in your hearing." **Lk 4:21**
on which their city had **b** built, **Lk 4:29**
'Your sins have **b** forgiven you,' **Lk 5:23**
picked up what he had **b** lying on, **Lk 5:25**
after he has **b** fully trained, **Lk 6:40**
it, because it had **b** well built. **Lk 6:48**
had **b** sent returned to the house, **Lk 7:10**
having **b** baptized with the baptism **Lk 7:29**
not having **b** baptized by John. **Lk 7:30**
which are many, have **b** forgiven, **Lk 7:47**
"Your sins have **b** forgiven." **Lk 7:48**
also some women who had **b** healed **Lk 8:2** *1510*
"To you it has **b** granted to know **Lk 8:10**
demon-possessed had **b** made well. **Lk 8:36**
they had all **b** waiting for Him. **Lk 8:40** *1510*
how she had **b** immediately healed. **Lk 8:47**
had **b** overcome with sleep; **Lk 9:32** *1510*
For if the miracles had **b** performed **Lk 10:13**
"All things have **b** handed over to **Lk 10:22**
the door has already **b** shut and my **Lk 11:7**
From everyone who has **b** given **Lk 12:48**
had **b** planted in his vineyard; **Lk 13:6**
should she not have **b** released **Lk 13:16**
they had **b** picking out the places **Lk 14:7**
you may have **b** invited by him, **Lk 14:8** *1510*
to say to those who had **b** invited, **Lk 14:17**
what you commanded has **b** done, **Lk 14:22** *1096*
he was lost and has **b** found.' **Lk 15:24**
many years I have **b** serving you and **Lk 15:29**
Son, you have always **b** with me, **Lk 15:31** *1510*
and *was* lost and has **b** found.'" **Lk 15:32**
"Therefore if you have not **b** faithful **Lk 16:11** *1096*
"And if you have not **b** faithful **Lk 16:12** *1096*
gospel of the kingdom of God has **b** **Lk 16:16**
when he saw that he had **b** healed, **Lk 17:15**
Now having **b** questioned by the **Lk 17:20**
because you have **b** faithful in a **Lk 19:17** *1096*
they have **b** hidden from your eyes. **Lk 19:42**
is going as it has **b** determined; **Lk 22:22**
because he had **b** hearing about Him **Lk 23:8**
had **b** enemies with each other. **Lk 23:12**
4391, 1510
deserving death has **b** done by Him. **Lk 23:15** *1510*
(He was one who had **b** thrown into **Lk 23:19**
who had **b** thrown into prison for **Lk 23:25**
had **b** sent from the Pharisees. **Jn 1:24** *1510*
not believe has **b** judged already, **Jn 3:18**
as having **b** wrought in God." **Jn 3:21** *1510*
had not yet **b** thrown into prison. **Jn 3:24** *1510*
it has **b** given him from heaven. **Jn 3:27** *1510*
'I have **b** sent ahead of Him.' **Jn 3:28** *1510*
this joy of mine has **b** made full. **Jn 3:29**
He had **b** speaking with a woman, **Jn 4:27**
who had **b** ill for thirty-eight years. **Jn 5:5** *2192*
b a long time *in that condition,* **Jn 5:6** *2192*
b granted him from the Father." **Jn 6:65** *1510*
having never **b** educated?" **Jn 7:15**
"You have not also **b** led astray, **Jn 7:47**
woman has **b** caught in adultery, **Jn 8:4**
"Even in your law it has **b** written that **Jn 8:17**
"What have I **b** saying to you *from* **Jn 8:25**
He had **b** speaking to them about **Jn 8:27**
never yet **b** enslaved to anyone; **Jn 8:33**
it of him, that he had **b** blind and **Jn 9:18** *1510*
called the man who had **b** blind, **Jn 9:24** *1510*
b heard that anyone opened the eyes **Jn 9:32**
which He had **b** saying to them. **Jn 10:6**
"Has it not **b** written in your **Jn 10:34** *1510*
already **b** in the tomb four days. **Jn 11:17** *2192*
"Lord, if You had **b** here, **Jn 11:21** *1510*
"Lord, if You had **b** here, **Jn 11:32** *1510*
for he has **b** *dead* four days." **Jn 11:39** *1510*
THE ARM OF THE LORD **B** REVEALED?" **Jn 12:38**
"Have I **b** so long with you, and **Jn 14:9** *1510*
have **b** with Me from the beginning. **Jn 15:27** *1510*
ruler of this world has **b** judged. **Jn 16:11**
a child has **b** born into the world. **Jn 16:21**
and I have **b** glorified in them. **Jn 17:10**
For this I have **b** born, and for **Jn 18:37**
it had **b** given you from above; **Jn 19:11** *1510*
things had already **b** accomplished, **Jn 19:28**
in which no one had yet **b** laid. **Jn 19:41** *1510*
which had **b** on His head, **Jn 20:7** *1510*
the body of Jesus had **b** lying. **Jn 20:12**
their sins have **b** forgiven them; **Jn 20:23**
of any, they have **b** retained." **Jn 20:23**
came, the doors having **b** shut, **Jn 20:26**
but these have **b** written so that you **Jn 20:31**
b taken up from you into heaven, **Ac 1:11**
"Therefore having **b** exalted to **Ac 2:33**

And a man who had **b** lame Ac 3:2 5225
to how this man has **b** made well, Ac 4:9
heaven that has **b** given among men by Ac 4:12
them as having **b** with Jesus. Ac 4:13 1510
had **b** healed standing with them, Ac 4:14
of healing had **b** performed. Ac 4:22
When they had **b** released, Ac 4:23
that they had **b** considered worthy Ac 5:41
"And after he had **b** set Ac 7:21
those who had **b** scattered went Ac 8:4
and many who had **b** paralyzed and Ac 8:7
they had simply **b** baptized in the Ac 8:16 5225
who had **b** bedridden eight years, Ac 9:33
men who had **b** sent by Cornelius, Ac 10:17
your prayer has **b** heard and your Ac 10:31
alms have **b** remembered before God. Ac 10:31
you have **b** kind enough to come. Ac 10:33
have **b** commanded by the Lord." Ac 10:33
One who has **b** appointed by God Ac 10:42
Holy Spirit had **b** poured out on Ac 10:45
having **b** sent to me from Caesarea. Ac 11:11
and Manaen who had **b** brought up Ac 13:1
the message of this salvation has **b** Ac 13:26
and as many as had **b** appointed to Ac 13:48 1510
from which they had **b** commended to Ac 14:26 1510
After there had **b** much debate, Ac 15:7 1096
nor we have **b** able to bear? Ac 15:10 2480
which had **b** decided upon by the Ac 16:4
having **b** forbidden by the Holy Ac 16:6
and her household had **b** baptized, Ac 16:15
word of God had **b** proclaimed by Ac 17:13
This man had **b** instructed in the Ac 18:25 1510
"After I have **b** there, I must Ac 19:21 1096
and they have **b** told about you, Ac 21:21
which they have **b** told about you, Ac 21:24
has **b** appointed for you to do.' Ac 22:10
why he had **b** accused by the Jews, Ac 22:30
After *Paul* had **b** summoned, Ac 24:2
you have **b** a judge to this nation, Ac 24:10 1510
in the temple, having **b** purified, Ac 24:18
to have **b** present before you and Ac 24:19 3918b
have **b** sanctified by faith in Me.' Ac 26:18
this has not **b** done in a corner. Ac 26:26 1510
"This man might have **b** set free Ac 26:32 1096
turn out exactly as I have **b** told. Ac 27:25
you have **b** constantly watching Ac 27:33
they had **b** brought safely through, Ac 28:1
he has **b** saved from the sea, Ac 28:4
of God has **b** sent to the Gentiles; Ac 28:28
you (and have **b** prevented so far) Ro 1:13
nature, have **b** clearly seen, Ro 1:20
through what has **b** made, Ro 1:20 4161
of God has **b** manifested, Ro 3:21
LAWLESS DEEDS HAVE **B** FORGIVEN, Ro 4:7
AND WHOSE SINS HAVE **B** COVERED. Ro 4:7
to that which had **b** spoken, Ro 4:18
having **b** justified by faith, Ro 5:1
the love of God has **b** poured out Ro 5:5
now **b** justified by His blood, Ro 5:9
much more, having **b** reconciled, Ro 5:10
all of us who have **b** baptized into Ro 6:3
have **b** baptized into His death? Ro 6:3
Therefore we have **b** buried with Ro 6:4
having **b** raised from the dead, Ro 6:9
and having **b** freed from sin, you Ro 6:18
But now having **b** freed from sin Ro 6:22
we have **b** released from the Law, Ro 7:6
For in hope we have **b** saved, Ro 8:24
but now have **b** shown mercy because Ro 11:30
these also now have **b** disobedient, Ro 11:31
b prevented from coming to you; Ro 15:22
For Macedonia and Achaia have **b** Ro 15:26 2106
has also **b** a helper of many, Ro 16:2 1096
mystery which has **b** kept secret for Ro 16:25
b made known to all the nations, Ro 16:26
have **b** sanctified in Christ Jesus, 1Co 1:2
I have **b** informed concerning you, 1Co 1:11
Has Christ **b** divided? 1Co 1:13
Passover also has **b** sacrificed. 1Co 5:7
you have **b** bought with a price: 1Co 6:20
anyone **b** called in uncircumcision? 1Co 7:18
the time has **b** shortened, 1Co 7:29 1510
just as I also have **b** fully known. 1Co 13:12
He has **b** raised from the dead, 1Co 15:12
not even Christ has **b** raised; 1Co 15:13
and if Christ has not **b** raised, 1Co 15:14
not even Christ has **b** raised; 1Co 15:16
and if Christ has not **b** raised, 1Co 15:17
Christ has **b** raised from the dead, 1Co 15:20
this reason we have **b** comforted. 2Co 7:13
spirit has **b** refreshed by you all. 2Co 7:13
grace of God which has **b** given in 2Co 8:1
but he has also **b** appointed by the 2Co 8:19
has **b** prepared since last year, 2Co 9:2
in what has **b** accomplished 2Co 10:16
that we have **b** weak *by comparison.* 2Co 11:21
I have **b** on frequent journeys, 2Co 11:26
I have **b** in labor and hardship, 2Co 11:27
I should have **b** commended by you, 2Co 12:11
All this time you have **b** thinking 2Co 12:19
that we have **b** speaking in Christ; 2Co 12:19
seeing that I had **b** entrusted with Ga 2:7
just as Peter *had* **b** to Ga 2:7
the grace that had **b** given to me, Ga 2:9
have also **b** found sinners, Ga 2:17
"I have **b** crucified with Christ; Ga 2:20
yet when it has **b** ratified, Ga 3:15
having **b** ordained through angels Ga 3:19
to whom the promise had **b** made. Ga 3:19

For if a law had **b** given which was Ga 3:21
would indeed have **b** based on law. Ga 3:21 1510
You have **b** severed from Christ, Ga 5:4
of the cross has **b** abolished. Ga 5:11
the world has **b** crucified to me, Ga 6:14
having **b** predestined according to Eph 1:11
(by grace you have **b** saved), Eph 2:5 1510
you have **b** saved through faith; Eph 2:8
were far off have **b** brought near by Eph 2:13 1096
having **b** built on the foundation Eph 2:20
as it has now **b** revealed to His Eph 3:5
for ages has **b** hidden in God who Eph 3:9
with which you have **b** called, Eph 4:1
Him and have **b** taught in Him, Eph 4:21
likeness of God has **b** created in Eph 4:24
having **b** filled with the fruit of Php 1:11
it has **b** granted for Christ's sake, Php 1:29
even as *it has* **b** *doing* in you Col 1:6
have **b** created through Him Col 1:16
the mystery which has **b** hidden Col 1:26
now **b** manifested to His saints, Col 1:26
having **b** knit together in love, Col 2:2
having **b** firmly rooted *and now* Col 2:7
in Him you have **b** made complete, Col 2:10 1510
b buried with Him in baptism, Col 2:12
you have **b** raised up with Christ, Col 3:1
as those who have **b** chosen of God, Col 3:12
which I have also **b** imprisoned; Col 4:3
and **b** mistreated in Philippi, 1Th 2:2
but just as we have **b** approved by 1Th 2:4
having **b** taken away from you for 1Th 2:17
that we have **b** destined for this. 1Th 3:3
with which I have **b** entrusted. 1Tm 1:11
which you have **b** following. 1Tm 4:6
and who has **b** left alone, has fixed 1Tm 5:5
having **b** the wife of one man, 1Tm 5:9
guard what has **b** entrusted to you, 1Tm 6:20
but now has **b** revealed by the 2Tm 1:10
which has **b** entrusted to *you.* 2Tm 1:14
having **b** held captive by him to do 2Tm 2:26
have **b** refreshed through you, Phm 1:7
For He has **b** counted worthy of Heb 3:3
a time just as has **b** said before, Heb 4:7
but One who has **b** tempted in all Heb 4:15
And having **b** made perfect, He Heb 5:9
those who have once **b** enlightened Heb 6:4
b made partakers of the Holy Spirit, Heb 6:4 1096
point in what has **b** said *is this:* Heb 8:1
has **b** enacted on better promises. Heb 8:6
first *covenant* had **b** faultless, Heb 8:7 1510
there would have **b** no occasion Heb 8:7
these things have **b** so prepared, Heb 9:6
place has not yet **b** disclosed while Heb 9:8
those who have **b** defiled sanctify Heb 9:13
those who have **b** called may Heb 9:15
every commandment had **b** spoken Heb 9:19
He has **b** manifested to put away sin Heb 9:26
having **b** offered once to bear the Heb 9:28
having once **b** cleansed, Heb 10:2
By this will we have **b** sanctified Heb 10:10 1510
And indeed if they had **b** thinking Heb 11:15
had **b** encircled for seven days. Heb 11:30
to those who have **b** trained by it, Heb 12:11
brother Timothy has **b** released, Heb 13:23
for once he has **b** approved, he Jas 1:12 1096
name by which you have **b** called? Jas 2:7
and has **b** tamed by the human race. Jas 3:7
b made in the likeness of God; Jas 3:9 1096
and which has **b** withheld by you, Jas 5:4
b distressed by various trials, 1Pe 1:6
in these things which now have **b** 1Pe 1:12
for you have **b** born again not of 1Pe 1:23
Him as to a living stone which has **b** 1Pe 2:4
have **b** called for this purpose, 1Pe 2:21
b put to death in the flesh, 1Pe 3:18
and powers had **b** subjected to Him. 1Pe 3:22
has for this purpose **b** preached 1Pe 4:6
and have **b** established in the 2Pe 1:12
the black darkness has **b** reserved 2Pe 2:17
love of God has truly **b** perfected. 1Jn 2:5
because your sins have **b** forgiven you 1Jn 2:12
Him who has **b** from the beginning. 1Jn 2:13
Him who has **b** from the beginning. 1Jn 2:14
for if they had **b** of us, they 1Jn 2:19 1510
darkness has **b** reserved forever. Jude 1:13
has **b** made to glow in a furnace, Rv 1:15
souls of those who had **b** slain Rv 6:9
to be killed even as they had **b**, Rv 6:11
who had **b** prepared for the hour Rv 9:15
for it has **b** given to the nations; Rv 11:2
of our brethren has **b** thrown down, Rv 12:10
of his heads as if it had **b** slain, Rv 13:3
whose name has not **b** written Rv 13:8
life of the Lamb who has **b** slain. Rv 13:8
had **b** purchased from the earth. Rv 14:3
who have not **b** defiled with women, Rv 14:4
These have **b** purchased from among Rv 14:4
and those who had **b** victorious over Rv 15:2
RIGHTEOUS ACTS HAVE **B** REVEALED." Rv 15:4
such as there had not **b** since man Rv 16:18 1096
whose name has not **b** written in Rv 17:8
great wealth has **b** laid waste!' Rv 18:17
in one hour she has **b** laid waste!' Rv 18:19
who have **b** slain on the earth." Rv 18:24
souls of those who had **b** beheaded Rv 20:4

BEER
From there *they continued* to **B**, Nu 21:16 876
and went to **B** and remained there Jg 9:21 876

BEERA
Shamma, Shilshah, Ithran and **B**. 1Ch 7:37 878

BEERAH
B his son, whom Tilgath-pilneser 1Ch 5:6 880

BEER-ELIM
Eglaim and its wailing even to **B**. Is 15:8 879

BEERI
the daughter of **B** the Hittite, Gn 26:34 882
which came to Hosea the son of **B**, Hos 1:1 882

BEER-LAHAI-ROI
Therefore the well was called **B**; Gn 16:14 883
Isaac had come from going to **B**; Gn 24:62 883
and Isaac lived by **B**. Gn 25:11 883

BEEROTH
out from **B** Bene-jaakan to Moserah. Dt 10:6 885
Chephirah and **B** and Kiriath-jearim. Jos 9:17 881
Gibeon and Ramah and **B**, Jos 18:25 881
B is also considered *part* of Benjamin, 2Sa 4:2 881
of Kiriath-arim, Chephirah and **B**, Ezr 2:25 881
Kiriath-jearim, Chephirah and **B**, Ne 7:29 881

BEEROTHITE
Rechab, sons of Rimmon the **B**, 2Sa 4:2 886
So the sons of Rimmon the **B**, 2Sa 4:5 886
his brother, sons of Rimmon the **B**, 2Sa 4:9 886
Zelek the Ammonite, Naharai the **B**, 2Sa 23:37 886

BEEROTHITES
and the **B** fled to Gittaim and 2Sa 4:3 886

BEERSHEBA
about in the wilderness of **B**. Gn 21:14 884
Therefore he called that place **B**, Gn 21:31 884
So they made a covenant at **B**; Gn 21:32 884
planted a tamarisk tree at **B**, Gn 21:33 884
they arose and went together to **B**; Gn 22:19 884
and Abraham lived at **B**. Gn 22:19 884
Then he went up from there to **B**. Gn 26:23 884
name of the city is **B** to this day. Gn 26:33 884
from **B** and went toward Haran. Gn 28:10 884
all that he had, and came to **B**, Gn 46:1 884
Then Jacob arose from **B**; Gn 46:5 884
Hazar-shual and **B** and Biziothiah, Jos 15:28 884
B or Sheba and Moladah, Jos 19:2 884
the sons of Israel from Dan to **B**, Jg 20:1 884
All Israel from Dan even to **B** 1Sa 3:20 884
they were judging in **B**. 1Sa 8:2 884
over Judah, from Dan even to **B**." 2Sa 3:10 884
to you, from Dan even to **B**, 2Sa 17:11 884
tribes of Israel, from Dan to **B**, 2Sa 24:2 884
out to the south of Judah, *to* **B**. 2Sa 24:7 884
of the people from Dan to **B** died. 2Sa 24:15 884
his fig tree, from Dan even to **B**, 1Ki 4:25 884
ran for his life and came to **B**, 1Ki 19:3 884
his mother's name was Zibiah of **B**. 2Ki 12:1 884
burned incense, from Geba to **B**; 2Ki 23:8 884
They lived at **B**, 1Ch 4:28 884
number Israel from **B** even to Dan, 1Ch 21:2 884
people from **B** to the hill country 2Ch 19:4 884
mother's name *was* Zibiah from **B**. 2Ch 24:1 884
all Israel from **B** even to Dan, 2Ch 30:5 884
in Hazar-shual, in **B** and its towns, Ne 11:27 884
So they encamped from **B** as far as Ne 11:30 884
to Gilgal, Nor cross over to **B**; Am 5:5 884
'As the way of **B** lives,' They will Am 8:14 884

BEES
you and chased you as **b** do, Dt 1:44 1682
a swarm of **b** and honey were in the Jg 14:8 1682
They surrounded me like **b**; Ps 118:12 1682

BE-ESHTERAH
and **B** with its pasture lands; Jos 21:27 1203

BEFALL
"I am afraid that harm may **b** him." Gn 42:4 7122
If harm should **b** him on the Gn 42:38 7122
will **b** you in the days to come. Gn 49:1 7122
and no plague will **b** you to Ex 12:13 1961
evil will **b** you in the latter days, Dt 31:29 7122
calamity which will **b** my people, Es 8:6 4672
No evil will **b** you, Nor will any Ps 91:10 579
of the fool, it will also **b** me. Ec 2:15 7136a

BEFALLEN
that had **b** them on the journey, Ex 18:8 4672
all the hardship that has **b** us; Nu 20:14 4672
These two things have **b** you; Is 51:19 7122
therefore this calamity has **b** you, Jer 44:23 7122
Panic and pitfall have **b** us, La 3:47 1961
Remember, O LORD, what has **b** us; La 5:1 1961

BEFALLS
one also from me, and harm **b** him, Gn 44:29 7136a
upon me, And what I dread **b** me. Jb 3:25 935
No harm **b** the righteous, But the Pr 12:21 579
I know that one fate **b** them both. Ec 2:14 7136a

BEFELL
enemy, Or exulted when evil **b** him? Jb 31:29 4672

BEFITS
Holiness **b** Your house, O LORD, Ps 93:5 4998

BEFORE
end of all flesh has come **b** Me; Gn 6:13 6440
to be righteous **b** Me in this time. Gn 7:1 6440
He was a mighty hunter **b** the LORD; Gn 10:9 6440
a mighty hunter **b** the LORD." Gn 10:9 6440
"Is not the whole land **b** you? Gn 13:9 6440
was **b** the LORD destroyed Sodom Gn 13:10 6440
Walk **b** Me, and be blameless. Gn 17:1 6440
that Ishmael might live **b** You!" Gn 17:18 6440
prepared, and placed *it* **b** them; Gn 18:8 6440
was still standing **b** the LORD. Gn 18:22 6440
B they lay down, the men of the Gn 19:4 2962
outcry has become so great **b** the LORD Gn 19:13 6440

where he had stood **b** the LORD;	Gn 19:27	6440
"Behold, my land is **b** you;	Gn 20:15	6440
vindication **b** all who are with you,	Gn 20:16	6440
and **b** all men you are cleared."	Gn 20:16	854
Then Abraham rose from **b** his dead,	Gn 23:3	6440
bowed **b** the people of the land.	Gn 23:12	6440
b all who went in at the gate of	Gn 23:18	
He will send His angel **b** you,	Gn 24:7	6440
B he had finished speaking, behold,	Gn 24:15	2962
when *food* was set **b** him to eat,	Gn 24:33	6440
'The LORD, **b** whom I have walked,	Gn 24:40	6440
"**B** I had finished speaking in my	Gn 24:45	2962
"Here is Rebekah **b** you,	Gn 24:51	6440
himself to the ground **b** the LORD.	Gn 24:52	6440
my soul may bless you **b** I die."	Gn 27:4	2962
presence of the LORD **b** my death.'	Gn 27:7	6440
he may bless you **b** his death."	Gn 27:10	6440
I ate of all *of it* **b** you came,	Gn 27:33	2962
off the younger **b** the firstborn.	Gn 29:26	6440
"For you had little **b** I came and	Gn 30:30	6440
be angry that I cannot rise **b** you,	Gn 31:35	4480, 6440
b my kinsmen and your kinsmen,	Gn 31:37	5048
Then Jacob sent messengers **b** him	Gn 32:3	6440
"Pass on **b** me, and put a space	Gn 32:16	6440
with the present that goes **b** me.	Gn 32:20	6440
So the present passed on **b** him,	Gn 32:21	5921, 6440
and go, and I will go **b** you."	Gn 33:12	5048
let my lord pass on **b** his servant,	Gn 33:14	6440
pace of the cattle that are **b** me	Gn 33:14	6440
Paddan-aram, and camped **b** the city.	Gn 33:18	6440
and the land shall be *open* **b** you;	Gn 34:10	6440
land of Edom **b** any king reigned	Gn 36:31	6440
down **b** you to the ground?"	Gn 37:10	
and **b** he came close to them,	Gn 37:18	2962
for they were just as ugly as **b**.	Gn 41:21	8462
and they proclaimed **b** him,	Gn 41:43	6440
years old when he stood **b** Pharaoh,	Gn 41:46	6440
Now **b** the year of famine came, two	Gn 41:50	2962
them and bound him **b** their eyes.	Gn 42:24	6440
him *back* to you and set him **b** you,	Gn 43:9	6440
me bear the blame **b** you forever.	Gn 43:9	
down to Egypt and stood **b** Joseph.	Gn 43:15	6440
and bowed to the ground **b** him.	Gn 43:26	
Now they were seated **b** him,	Gn 43:33	6440
and they fell to the ground **b** him.	Gn 44:14	6440
the blame **b** my father forever.'	Gn 44:32	
b all those who stood by him,	Gn 45:1	
sent me **b** you to preserve life.	Gn 45:5	6440
"God sent me **b** you to	Gn 45:7	6440
I will go and see him **b** I die."	Gn 45:28	2962
Now he sent Judah **b** him to Joseph,	Gn 46:28	6440
point out *the way* **b** him to Goshen;	Gn 46:28	6440
as soon as he appeared **b** him,	Gn 46:29	413
"Why should we die **b** your eyes,	Gn 47:19	
of Egypt **b** I came to you in Egypt,	Gn 48:5	5704
"The God **b** whom my fathers	Gn 48:15	6440
Thus he put Ephraim **b** Manasseh.	Gn 48:20	6440
of Machpelah, which is **b** Mamre,	Gn 49:30	5921, 6440
of the field of Machpelah **b** Mamre,	Gn 50:13	5921, 6440
"Your father charged **b** he died,	Gn 50:16	6440
came and fell down **b** him and said,	Gn 50:18	6440
b the midwife can get to them."	Ex 1:19	2962
see that you perform **b** Pharaoh	Ex 4:21	6440
But Moses spoke **b** the LORD,	Ex 6:12	6440
But Moses said **b** the LORD,	Ex 6:30	6440
staff and throw *it* down **b** Pharaoh,	Ex 7:9	6440
down **b** Pharaoh and his servants,	Ex 7:10	6440
and present yourself **b** Pharaoh,	Ex 8:20	6440
to the Egyptians **b** their eyes,	Ex 8:26	
from a kiln, and stood **b** Pharaoh;	Ex 9:10	6440
b Moses because of the boils,	Ex 9:11	6440
stand **b** Pharaoh and say to him,	Ex 9:13	6440
refuse to humble yourself **b** Me?	Ex 10:3	4480, 6440
such as there has not been **b**	Ex 11:6	
to me and bow themselves **b** me,	Ex 11:8	
all these wonders **b** Pharaoh;	Ex 11:10	6440
their dough **b** it was leavened,	Ex 12:34	2962
The LORD was going **b** them in a	Ex 13:21	6440
fire by night, from **b** the people.	Ex 13:22	6440
turn back and camp **b** Pi-hahiroth,	Ex 14:2	6440
been going **b** the camp of Israel,	Ex 14:19	6440
from **b** them and stood behind them.	Ex 14:19	4480, 6440
'Come near **b** the LORD, for He has	Ex 16:9	6440
in it, and place it **b** the LORD to	Ex 16:33	6440
Aaron placed it **b** the Testimony,	Ex 16:34	6440
"Pass **b** the people and take with	Ex 17:5	6440
I will stand **b** you there on the	Ex 17:6	6440
meal with Moses' father-in-law **b** God.	Ex 18:12	6440
the people's representative **b** God,	Ex 18:19	4136
and set **b** them all these words	Ex 19:7	6440
"You shall have no other gods **b** Me.	Ex 20:3	5921, 6440
which you are to set **b** them:	Ex 21:1	6440
house shall appear **b** the judges,	Ex 22:8	413
parties shall come **b** the judges;	Ex 22:9	5704
an oath **b** the LORD shall be made	Ex 22:11	
return it to him **b** the sun sets,	Ex 22:26	5704
shall appear **b** Me empty-handed.	Ex 23:15	6440
males shall appear **b** the Lord GOD.	Ex 23:17	6440
I am going to send an angel **b** you	Ex 23:20	6440
guard **b** him and obey his voice;	Ex 23:21	4480, 6440
"For My angel will go **b** you and	Ex 23:23	6440
and the Hittites **b** you.	Ex 23:28	4480, 6440
them out **b** you in a single year,	Ex 23:29	4480
them out **b** you little by little,	Ex 23:30	4480
and you will drive them out **b** you.	Ex 23:31	4480
on the table **b** Me at all times.	Ex 25:30	6440
the veil which is **b** the testimony,	Ex 27:21	5921
evening to morning **b** the LORD;	Ex 27:21	6440
shall bear their names **b** the LORD	Ex 28:12	6440
a memorial **b** the LORD continually.	Ex 28:29	6440
heart when he goes in **b** the LORD;	Ex 28:30	6440
his heart **b** the LORD continually.	Ex 28:30	6440
leaves the holy place **b** the LORD,	Ex 28:35	6440
they may be accepted **b** the LORD.	Ex 28:38	6440
the bull **b** the tent of meeting,	Ex 29:10	6440
shall slaughter the bull **b** the LORD	Ex 29:11	6440
bread which is *set* **b** the LORD;	Ex 29:23	6440
as a wave offering **b** the LORD.	Ex 29:24	6440
for a soothing aroma **b** the LORD;	Ex 29:25	6440
it as a wave offering **b** the LORD;	Ex 29:26	6440
of the tent of meeting **b** the LORD,	Ex 29:42	6440
be perpetual incense **b** the LORD	Ex 30:8	6440
for the sons of Israel **b** the LORD,	Ex 30:16	6440
and put part of it **b** the testimony	Ex 30:36	6440
make us a god who will go **b** us;	Ex 32:1	6440
saw *this,* he built an altar **b** it;	Ex 32:5	6440
a god for us who will go **b** us;	Ex 32:23	6440
Behold, My angel shall go **b** you;	Ex 32:34	6440
"I will send an angel **b** you	Ex 33:2	6440
make all My goodness pass **b** you,	Ex 33:19	5921, 6440
the name of the LORD **b** you;	Ex 33:19	6440
B all your people I will perform	Ex 34:10	5048
to drive out the Amorite **b** you,	Ex 34:11	4480, 6440
shall appear **b** Me empty-handed.	Ex 34:20	6440
are to appear **b** the Lord GOD,	Ex 34:23	6440
b you and enlarge your borders,	Ex 34:24	4480, 6440
to appear **b** the LORD your God.	Ex 34:24	6440
in **b** the LORD to speak with Him,	Ex 34:34	6440
b the ark of the testimony,	Ex 40:5	6440
bread in order on it **b** the LORD,	Ex 40:23	6440
He lighted the lamps **b** the LORD,	Ex 40:25	6440
set the altar of burnt offering **b**	Ex 40:29	6440
he may be accepted **b** the LORD.	Lv 1:3	6440
slay the young bull **b** the LORD;	Lv 1:5	6440
of the altar northward **b** the LORD,	Lv 1:11	6440
it without defect **b** the LORD.	Lv 3:1	6440
then he shall offer it **b** the LORD,	Lv 3:7	6440
and slay it **b** the tent of meeting,	Lv 3:8	6440
then he shall offer it **b** the LORD,	Lv 3:12	6440
and slay it **b** the tent of meeting,	Lv 3:13	6440
of the tent of meeting **b** the LORD,	Lv 4:4	6440
and slay the bull **b** the LORD.	Lv 4:4	6440
the blood seven times **b** the LORD,	Lv 4:6	6440
fragrant incense which is **b** the LORD	Lv 4:7	6440
bring it **b** the tent of meeting.	Lv 4:14	6440
the head of the bull **b** the LORD,	Lv 4:15	6440
bull shall be slain **b** the LORD.	Lv 4:15	6440
it seven times **b** the LORD,	Lv 4:17	6440
horns of the altar which is **b** the LORD	Lv 4:18	6440
the burnt offering **b** the LORD;	Lv 4:24	6440
was certainly guilty **b** the LORD."	Lv 5:19	6440
make atonement for him **b** the LORD,	Lv 6:7	6440
of Aaron shall present it **b** the LORD	Lv 6:14	6440
shall be slain **b** the LORD;	Lv 6:25	6440
as a wave offering **b** the LORD.	Lv 7:30	6440
bread that was **b** the LORD,	Lv 8:26	6440
as a wave offering **b** the LORD.	Lv 8:27	6440
it for a wave offering **b** the LORD;	Lv 8:29	6440
defect, and offer *them* **b** the LORD.	Lv 9:2	6440
to sacrifice **b** the LORD,	Lv 9:4	6440
came near and stood **b** the LORD.	Lv 9:5	6440
as a wave offering **b** the LORD,	Lv 9:21	6440
Then fire came out from **b** the LORD	Lv 9:24	4480, 6440
offered strange fire **b** the LORD,	Lv 10:1	6440
them, and they died **b** the LORD.	Lv 10:2	6440
And **b** all the people I will be	Lv 10:3	5921, 6440
as a wave offering **b** the LORD;	Lv 10:15	6440
atonement for them **b** the LORD.	Lv 10:17	6440
their burnt offering **b** the LORD.	Lv 10:19	6440
'Then he shall offer it **b** the LORD	Lv 12:7	6440
b the LORD at the doorway of	Lv 14:11	6440
as a wave offering **b** the LORD.	Lv 14:12	6440
of the oil seven times **b** the LORD.	Lv 14:16	6440
on his behalf **b** the LORD.	Lv 14:18	6440
the tent of meeting, **b** the LORD.	Lv 14:23	6440
for a wave offering **b** the LORD.	Lv 14:24	6440
left palm seven times **b** the LORD.	Lv 14:27	6440
on his behalf **b** the LORD.	Lv 14:29	6440
make atonement **b** the LORD on	Lv 14:31	6440
empty the house **b** the priest goes	Lv 14:36	2962
and come **b** the LORD to the doorway	Lv 15:14	6440
atonement on his behalf **b** the LORD	Lv 15:15	6440
atonement on her behalf **b** the LORD	Lv 15:30	6440
b the mercy seat which is on the	Lv 16:2	413, 6440
goats and present them **b** the LORD	Lv 16:7	6440
be presented alive **b** the LORD,	Lv 16:10	6440
from upon the altar **b** the LORD and	Lv 16:12	4480, 6440
incense on the fire **b** the LORD,	Lv 16:13	6440
out to the altar that is **b** the LORD	Lv 16:18	6440
from all your sins **b** the LORD.	Lv 16:30	6440
LORD **b** the tabernacle of the LORD,	Lv 17:4	6440
stand **b** an animal to mate with it;	Lv 18:23	6440
out **b** you have become defiled.	Lv 18:24	4480, 6440
men of the land who have been **b** you	Lv 18:27	6440
the nation which has been **b** you.	Lv 18:28	6440
which have been practiced **b** you,	Lv 18:30	6440
a stumbling block **b** the blind,	Lv 19:14	6440
ram of the guilt offering **b** the LORD	Lv 19:22	6440
shall rise up **b** the grayheaded and	Lv 19:32	4480, 6440
which I will drive out **b** you,	Lv 20:23	6440
person shall be cut off from **b** Me;	Lv 22:3	4480, 6440
'He shall wave the sheaf **b** the	Lv 23:11	6440
with two lambs **b** the LORD;	Lv 23:20	6440
your behalf **b** the LORD your God.	Lv 23:28	6440
and you shall rejoice **b** the LORD	Lv 23:40	6440
to morning **b** the LORD continually;	Lv 24:3	6440
lampstand **b** the LORD continually.	Lv 24:4	6440
on the pure *gold* table **b** the LORD.	Lv 24:6	6440
in order **b** the LORD continually;	Lv 24:8	6440
they will fall **b** you by the sword;	Lv 26:7	6440
will fall **b** you by the sword.	Lv 26:8	6440
be struck down **b** your enemies;	Lv 26:17	6440
to stand up **b** your enemies.	Lv 26:37	6440
he shall be placed **b** the priest and	Lv 27:8	6440
place the animal **b** the priest.	Lv 27:11	6440
But Nadab and Abihu died **b** the	Nu 3:4	6440
they offered strange fire **b** the LORD	Nu 3:4	6440
and set them **b** Aaron the priest,	Nu 3:6	6440
b the tent of meeting,	Nu 3:7	6440
to camp **b** the tabernacle eastward,	Nu 3:38	6440
b the tent of meeting toward the	Nu 3:38	6440
and have her stand **b** the LORD,	Nu 5:16	6440
have the woman stand **b** the LORD	Nu 5:18	6440
wave the grain offering **b** the LORD	Nu 5:25	6440
make the woman stand **b** the LORD,	Nu 5:30	6440
priest shall present *them* **b** the LORD	Nu 6:16	6440
for a wave offering **b** the LORD.	Nu 6:20	6440
brought their offering **b** the LORD,	Nu 7:3	6440
presented them **b** the tabernacle.	Nu 7:3	6440
their offering **b** the altar.	Nu 7:10	6440
the Levites **b** the tent of meeting.	Nu 8:9	6440
present the Levites **b** the LORD;	Nu 8:10	6440
present the Levites **b** the LORD as	Nu 8:11	6440
Levites stand **b** Aaron and before	Nu 8:13	6440
stand before Aaron and **b** his sons	Nu 8:13	6440
as a wave offering **b** the LORD.	Nu 8:21	6440
b Aaron and before his sons;	Nu 8:22	6440
before Aaron and **b** his sons;	Nu 8:22	6440
b Moses and Aaron on that day.	Nu 9:6	6440
of Israel, shall assemble **b** you.	Nu 10:4	413
be remembered **b** the LORD your God,	Nu 10:9	6440
as a reminder of you **b** your God.	Nu 10:10	6440
was set up **b** their arrival.	Nu 10:21	5704
those who hate You flee **b** You."	Nu 10:35	4480, 6440
For they weep **b** me, saying,	Nu 11:13	5921
is among you and have wept **b** Him,	Nu 11:20	6440
their teeth, **b** it was chewed,	Nu 11:33	2962
seven years **b** Zoan in Egypt.)	Nu 13:22	6440
Caleb quieted the people **b** Moses and	Nu 13:30	413
and You go **b** them in a	Nu 14:14	6440
land died by a plague **b** the LORD.	Nu 14:37	6440
you will be struck down **b** your enemies,	Nu 14:42	6440
so shall the alien be **b** the LORD.	Nu 15:15	6440
and their sin offering **b** the LORD,	Nu 15:25	6440
shall make atonement **b** the LORD	Nu 15:28	6440
and they rose up **b** Moses,	Nu 16:2	6440
and to stand **b** the congregation to	Nu 16:9	6440
be present **b** the LORD tomorrow,	Nu 16:16	6440
you bring his censer **b** the LORD,	Nu 16:17	6440
them **b** the LORD and they are holy;	Nu 16:38	6440
near to burn incense **b** the LORD;	Nu 16:40	6440
So Moses deposited the rods **b** the	Nu 17:7	6440
"Put back the rod of Aaron **b** the	Nu 17:10	6440
are **b** the tent of the testimony.	Nu 18:2	6440
covenant of salt **b** the LORD to you	Nu 18:19	6440
our brothers perished **b** the LORD!	Nu 20:3	6440
speak to the rock **b** their eyes,	Nu 20:8	
took the rod from **b** the LORD,	Nu 20:9	4480, 6440
gathered the assembly **b** the rock.	Nu 20:10	413, 6440
them in broad daylight **b** the LORD,	Nu 25:4	
offered strange fire **b** the LORD.	Nu 26:61	6440
They stood **b** Moses and before	Nu 27:2	6440
stood before Moses and **b** Eleazar	Nu 27:2	6440
Eleazar the priest and **b** the leaders	Nu 27:2	6440
brought their case **b** the LORD.	Nu 27:5	6440
holy **b** their eyes at the water."	Nu 27:14	6440
will go out and come in **b** them,	Nu 27:17	6440
and have him stand **b** Eleazar the	Nu 27:19	6440
priest and **b** all the congregation,	Nu 27:19	6440
shall stand **b** Eleazar the priest,	Nu 27:21	6440
judgment of the Urim **b** the LORD.	Nu 27:21	6440
and set him **b** Eleazar the priest and	Nu 27:22	6440
and **b** all the congregation.	Nu 27:22	6440
for ourselves **b** the LORD."	Nu 31:50	6440
for the sons of Israel **b** the LORD.	Nu 31:54	6440
b the congregation of Israel,	Nu 32:4	6440
ready *to go* **b** the sons of Israel,	Nu 32:17	6440
yourselves **b** the LORD for the war,	Nu 32:20	6440
cross over the Jordan **b** the LORD	Nu 32:21	6440
driven His enemies out from **b** Him,	Nu 32:21	6440
the land is subdued **b** the LORD,	Nu 32:22	6440
yours for a possession **b** the LORD.	Nu 32:22	6440
the land is subdued **b** you,	Nu 32:29	6440
and they camped **b** Migdol.	Nu 33:7	6440
They journeyed from **b** Hahiroth	Nu 33:8	6440

the mountains of Abarim, **b** Nebo.	**Nu 33:47**	6440
of the land from **b** you,	**Nu 33:52**	6440
of the land from **b** you,	**Nu 33:55**	6440
b the congregation for trial.	**Nu 35:12**	6440
land **b** the death of the priest.	**Nu 35:32**	5704
b Moses and before the leaders,	**Nu 36:1**	6440
before Moses and **b** the leaders,	**Nu 36:1**	6440
'See, I have placed the land **b** you;	**Dt 1:8**	6440
God has placed the land **b** you;	**Dt 1:21**	6440
'Let us send men **b** us, that they	**Dt 1:22**	6440
'The LORD your God who goes **b** you	**Dt 1:30**	6440
did for you in Egypt **b** your eyes,	**Dt 1:30**	
who goes **b** you on *your* way, to	**Dt 1:33**	6440
the son of Nun, who stands **b** you,	**Dt 1:38**	6440
be defeated **b** your enemies."	**Dt 1:42**	6440
you returned and wept **b** the LORD;	**Dt 1:45**	6440
destroyed them from **b** them and	**Dt 2:12**	6440
the LORD destroyed them **b** them.	**Dt 2:21**	6440
destroyed the Horites from **b** them;	**Dt 2:22**	6440
cross over armed **b** your brothers,	**Dt 3:18**	6440
which I am setting **b** you today?	**Dt 4:8**	6440
b the LORD your God at Horeb,	**Dt 4:10**	6440
the former days which were **b** you,	**Dt 4:32**	6440
did for you in Egypt **b** your eyes?	**Dt 4:34**	
driving out from **b** you nations	**Dt 4:38**	6440
Moses set **b** the sons of Israel;	**Dt 4:44**	6440
'You shall have no other gods **b** Me.	**Dt 5:7**	6440
out all your enemies from **b** you,	**Dt 6:19**	6440
wonders **b** our eyes against Egypt,	**Dt 6:22**	6440
commandment **b** the LORD our God,	**Dt 6:25**	6440
clears away many nations **b** you,	**Dt 7:1**	
		4480, 6440
your God delivers them **b** you	**Dt 7:2**	6440
nations **b** you little by little;	**Dt 7:22**	
		4480, 6440
your God will deliver them **b** you,	**Dt 7:23**	6440
no man will be able to stand **b** you	**Dt 7:24**	6440
the LORD makes to perish **b** you,	**Dt 8:20**	
		4480, 6440
'Who can stand **b** the sons of Anak?'	**Dt 9:2**	6440
over **b** you as a consuming fire.	**Dt 9:3**	6440
and He will subdue them **b** you,	**Dt 9:3**	6440
God has driven them out **b** you,	**Dt 9:4**	
		4480, 6440
LORD is dispossessing them **b** you.	**Dt 9:4**	
		4480, 6440
God is driving them out **b** you,	**Dt 9:5**	
		4480, 6440
and smashed them **b** your eyes.	**Dt 9:17**	
"I fell down **b** the LORD, as	**Dt 9:18**	6440
"So I fell down **b** the LORD the	**Dt 9:25**	6440
to stand **b** the LORD to serve Him	**Dt 10:8**	6440
out all these nations from **b** you,	**Dt 11:23**	
		4480, 6440
"No man will be able to stand **b** you;	**Dt 11:25**	6440
I am setting **b** you today a	**Dt 11:26**	6440
which I am setting **b** you today.	**Dt 11:32**	6440
shall eat **b** the LORD your God,	**Dt 12:7**	6440
shall rejoice **b** the LORD your God,	**Dt 12:12**	6440
"But you shall eat them **b** the	**Dt 12:18**	6440
and you shall rejoice **b** the LORD	**Dt 12:18**	6440
your God cuts off **b** you the nations	**Dt 12:29**	
		4480, 6440
after they are destroyed **b** you,	**Dt 12:30**	
		4480, 6440
shall eat it every year **b** the LORD	**Dt 15:20**	6440
shall rejoice **b** the LORD your God,	**Dt 16:11**	6440
your males shall appear **b** the LORD	**Dt 16:16**	6440
not appear **b** the LORD empty-handed.	**Dt 16:16**	6440
who stand there **b** the LORD.	**Dt 18:7**	6440
God will drive them out **b** you.	**Dt 18:12**	
		4480, 6440
be blameless **b** the LORD your God.	**Dt 18:13**	5973
dispute shall stand **b** the LORD,	**Dt 19:17**	6440
b the priests and the judges who	**Dt 19:17**	6440
or panic, or tremble **b** them,	**Dt 20:3**	
		4480, 6440
b the son of the unloved,	**Dt 21:16**	
		5921, 6440
garment **b** the elders of the city.	**Dt 22:17**	6440
and to defeat your enemies **b** you,	**Dt 23:14**	6440
that is an abomination **b** the LORD,	**Dt 24:4**	6440
for you **b** the LORD your God.	**Dt 24:13**	6440
wages on his day **b** the sun sets,	**Dt 24:15**	
set it down **b** the altar of the LORD	**Dt 26:4**	6440
and say **b** the LORD your God,	**Dt 26:5**	6440
set it down **b** the LORD your God,	**Dt 26:10**	6440
and worship **b** the LORD your God;	**Dt 26:10**	6440
You shall say **b** the LORD your God,	**Dt 26:13**	6440
and rejoice **b** the LORD your God.	**Dt 27:7**	6440
against you to be defeated **b** you;	**Dt 28:7**	6440
and will flee **b** you seven ways.	**Dt 28:7**	6440
you to be defeated **b** your enemies;	**Dt 28:25**	6440
you will flee seven ways **b** them,	**Dt 28:25**	6440
shall be slaughtered **b** your eyes,	**Dt 28:31**	
life shall hang in doubt **b** you;	**Dt 28:66**	
seen all that the LORD did **b** your eyes	**Dt 29:2**	
all of you, **b** the LORD your God:	**Dt 29:10**	6440
the curse which I have set **b** you,	**Dt 30:1**	6440
b you today life and prosperity,	**Dt 30:15**	6440
I have set **b** you life and death,	**Dt 30:19**	6440
will destroy these nations **b** you,	**Dt 31:3**	6440
LORD will deliver them up **b** you,	**Dt 31:5**	6440
when all Israel comes to appear **b**	**Dt 31:11**	6440
will testify **b** them as a witness	**Dt 31:21**	6440
b I have brought them into the	**Dt 31:21**	2962
the sons of Israel **b** his death.	**Dt 33:1**	6440
They shall put incense **b** You,	**Dt 33:10**	639

He drove out the enemy from **b** you,	**Dt 33:27**	
		4480, 6440
your enemies will cringe **b** you,	**Dt 33:29**	6440
b you all the days of your life.	**Jos 1:5**	6440
b your brothers in battle array,	**Jos 1:14**	6440
Now **b** they lay down, she came up	**Jos 2:8**	2962
the land have melted away **b** you.	**Jos 2:9**	
		4480, 6440
dried up the water of the Red Sea **b**	**Jos 2:10**	
		4480, 6440
have melted away **b** us."	**Jos 2:24**	
		4480, 6440
they lodged there **b** they crossed.	**Jos 3:1**	2962
you have not passed this way **b**."	**Jos 3:4**	
		4480, 8543, 8032a
from **b** you the Canaanite,	**Jos 3:10**	6440
ark of the covenant **b** the people,	**Jos 3:14**	6440
cut off **b** the ark of the covenant	**Jos 4:7**	
		4480, 6440
the priests crossed **b** the people.	**Jos 4:11**	6440
battle array **b** the sons of Israel,	**Jos 4:12**	6440
crossed for battle **b** the LORD to	**Jos 4:13**	6440
and went over all its banks as **b**.	**Jos 4:18**	
		8543, 8032a
b you until you had crossed,	**Jos 4:23**	
		4480, 6440
the Red Sea, which He dried up **b** us	**Jos 4:23**	
		4480, 6440
dried up the waters of the Jordan **b**	**Jos 5:1**	
		4480, 6440
trumpets of rams' horns **b** the ark;	**Jos 6:4**	6440
horns **b** the ark of the LORD."	**Jos 6:6**	6440
men go on **b** the ark of the LORD."	**Jos 6:7**	6440
trumpets of rams' horns **b** the LORD	**Jos 6:8**	6440
The armed men went **b** the	**Jos 6:9**	6440
rams' horns **b** the ark of the LORD	**Jos 6:13**	6440
and the armed men went **b** them and	**Jos 6:13**	6440
"Cursed **b** the LORD is the man who	**Jos 6:26**	6440
on his face **b** the ark of the LORD	**Jos 7:6**	6440
turned *their* back **b** their enemies?	**Jos 7:8**	6440
cannot stand **b** their enemies;	**Jos 7:12**	6440
turn *their* backs **b** their enemies,	**Jos 7:12**	6440
You cannot stand **b** your enemies	**Jos 7:13**	6440
they poured them out **b** the LORD.	**Jos 7:23**	6440
first, we will flee **b** them.	**Jos 8:5**	6440
are fleeing **b** us as at the first.'	**Jos 8:6**	6440
So we will flee **b** them.	**Jos 8:6**	6440
of Israel **b** the people to Ai.	**Jos 8:10**	6440
place **b** the desert plain.	**Jos 8:14**	6440
pretended to be beaten **b** them,	**Jos 8:15**	6440
standing on both sides of the ark **b**	**Jos 8:33**	5048
Joshua did not read **b** all the assembly	**Jos 8:35**	5048
the inhabitants of the land **b** you;	**Jos 9:24**	
		4480, 6440
not one of them shall stand **b** you."	**Jos 10:8**	6440
the LORD confounded them **b** Israel,	**Jos 10:10**	6440
As they fled from **b** Israel,	**Jos 10:11**	
		4480, 6440
the Amorites **b** the sons of Israel,	**Jos 10:12**	6440
no day like that **b** it or after it,	**Jos 10:14**	6440
all of them slain **b** Israel;	**Jos 11:6**	6440
out from **b** the sons of Israel;	**Jos 13:6**	
		4480, 6440
as far as Aroer which is **b** Rabbah;	**Jos 13:25**	
		5921, 6440
which is **b** the valley of Hinnom	**Jos 15:8**	
		5921, 6440
They came near **b** Eleazar the	**Jos 17:4**	6440
and **b** Joshua the son of Nun	**Jos 17:4**	6440
the son of Nun and **b** the leaders,	**Jos 17:4**	6440
and the land was subdued **b** them.	**Jos 18:1**	6440
for you here **b** the LORD our God.	**Jos 18:6**	6440
you here **b** the LORD in Shiloh."	**Jos 18:8**	6440
for them in Shiloh **b** the LORD,	**Jos 18:10**	6440
which *lies* **b** Beth-horon southward;	**Jos 18:14**	
		5921, 6440
to the brook that is **b** Jokneam.	**Jos 19:11**	
		5921, 6440
by lot in Shiloh **b** the LORD at	**Jos 19:51**	6440
b the congregation for judgment,	**Jos 20:6**	6440
he stands **b** the congregation.	**Jos 20:9**	6440
of all their enemies stood **b** them;	**Jos 21:44**	6440
b Him with our burnt offerings,	**Jos 22:27**	6440
God which is **b** His tabernacle."	**Jos 22:29**	6440
He will thrust them out from **b**	**Jos 23:5**	6440
you and drive them from **b** you;	**Jos 23:5**	6440
and strong nations from **b** you;	**Jos 23:9**	6440
man has stood **b** you to this day.	**Jos 23:9**	6440
these nations out from **b** you;	**Jos 23:13**	6440
they presented themselves **b** God.	**Jos 24:1**	6440
land when I destroyed them **b** you.	**Jos 24:8**	6440
'Then I sent the hornet **b** you and	**Jos 24:12**	6440
kings of the Amorites from **b** you,	**Jos 24:12**	
		4480, 6440
out from **b** us all the peoples,	**Jos 24:18**	6440
'I will not drive them out **b** you;	**Jg 2:3**	
		4480, 6440
no longer stand **b** their enemies.	**Jg 2:14**	6440
I also will no longer drive out **b**	**Jg 2:21**	
		4480, 6440
the LORD has gone out **b** you."	**Jg 4:14**	6440
the edge of the sword **b** Barak;	**Jg 4:15**	6440
of Canaan **b** the sons of Israel.	**Jg 4:23**	6440
b you and gave you their land,	**Jg 6:9**	
		4480, 6440
my offering and lay it **b** You."	**Jg 6:18**	6440
Midian and take the waters **b** them,	**Jg 7:24**	
was subdued **b** the sons of Israel,	**Jg 8:28**	6440
So Gaal went out **b** the leaders of	**Jg 9:39**	6440

chased him, and he fled **b** him;	**Jg 9:40**	
		4480, 6440
his words **b** the LORD at Mizpah.	**Jg 11:11**	6440
Amorites from **b** His people Israel,	**Jg 11:23**	6440
LORD our God has driven out **b** us,	**Jg 11:24**	
		4480, 6440
were subdued **b** the sons of Israel.	**Jg 11:33**	
		4480, 6440
Samson's wife wept **b** him and said,	**Jg 14:16**	5921
However she wept **b** him seven days	**Jg 14:17**	5921
seventh day **b** the sun went down,	**Jg 14:18**	2962
and wept **b** the LORD until evening,	**Jg 20:23**	6440
thus they remained there **b** the	**Jg 20:26**	6440
and peace offerings **b** the LORD.	**Jg 20:26**	6440
b it to *minister* in those days),	**Jg 20:28**	6440
"They are struck down **b** us,	**Jg 20:32**	6440
the LORD struck Benjamin **b** Israel,	**Jg 20:35**	6440
"Surely they are defeated **b** us,	**Jg 20:39**	6440
they turned their backs **b** the men	**Jg 20:42**	6440
and sat there **b** God until evening,	**Jg 21:2**	6440
b one could recognize another;	**Ru 3:14**	2962
it **b** those who are sitting *here*,	**Ru 4:4**	5048
and **b** the elders of my people.	**Ru 4:4**	5048
she continued praying **b** the LORD,	**1Sa 1:12**	6440
poured out my soul **b** the LORD.	**1Sa 1:15**	6440
morning and worshiped **b** the LORD,	**1Sa 1:19**	6440
that he may appear **b** the LORD and	**1Sa 1:22**	6440
to the LORD **b** Eli the priest.	**1Sa 2:11**	6440
Also, **b** they burned the fat, the	**1Sa 2:15**	2962
men was very great **b** the LORD,	**1Sa 2:17**	6440
Samuel was ministering **b** the LORD,	**1Sa 2:18**	6440
the boy Samuel grew **b** the LORD.	**1Sa 2:21**	5973
incense, to carry an ephod **b** Me;	**1Sa 2:28**	6440
father should walk **b** Me forever';	**1Sa 2:30**	6440
he will walk **b** My anointed always.	**1Sa 2:35**	6440
was ministering to the LORD **b** Eli.	**1Sa 3:1**	6440
Israel was defeated **b** the Philistines	**1Sa 4:2**	6440
us today **b** the Philistines?	**1Sa 4:3**	6440
nothing like this has happened **b**.	**1Sa 4:7**	
		8543, 8032a
"Israel has fled **b** the Philistines	**1Sa 4:17**	6440
the ground **b** the ark of the LORD.	**1Sa 5:3**	6440
the ground **b** the ark of the LORD.	**1Sa 5:4**	6440
"Who is able to stand **b** the LORD,	**1Sa 6:20**	6440
and poured it out **b** the LORD,	**1Sa 7:6**	6440
so that they were routed **b** Israel.	**1Sa 7:10**	6440
and they will run **b** his chariots.	**1Sa 8:11**	6440
out **b** us and fight our battles."	**1Sa 8:20**	6440
you will find him **b** he goes up to	**1Sa 9:13**	2962
Now a day **b** Saul's coming, the	**1Sa 9:15**	6440
Go up **b** me to the high place, for	**1Sa 9:19**	6440
what was on it and set *it* **b** Saul.	**1Sa 9:24**	6440
Set *it* **b** you *and* eat, because it	**1Sa 9:24**	6440
flute, and a lyre **b** them,	**1Sa 10:5**	6440
you shall go down **b** me to Gilgal;	**1Sa 10:8**	6440
present yourselves **b** the LORD by	**1Sa 10:19**	6440
the book and placed *it* **b** the LORD.	**1Sa 10:25**	6440
Saul king **b** the LORD in Gilgal.	**1Sa 11:15**	6440
of peace offerings **b** the LORD;	**1Sa 11:15**	6440
here is the king walking **b** you,	**1Sa 12:2**	6440
And I have walked **b** you from my	**1Sa 12:2**	6440
me **b** the LORD and His anointed.	**1Sa 12:3**	5048
that I may plead with you **b** the	**1Sa 12:7**	6440
the LORD will do **b** your eyes.	**1Sa 12:16**	
and they fell **b** Jonathan, and his	**1Sa 14:13**	6440
the man who eats food **b** evening,	**1Sa 14:24**	5704
but please honor me now **b** the	**1Sa 15:30**	5048
elders of my people and **b** Israel,	**1Sa 15:30**	5048
to pieces **b** the LORD at Gilgal.	**1Sa 15:33**	6440
the LORD's anointed is **b** Him."	**1Sa 16:6**	5048
and made him pass **b** Samuel.	**1Sa 16:8**	6440
seven of his sons pass **b** Samuel.	**1Sa 16:10**	6440
your servants who are **b** you.	**1Sa 16:16**	6440
"Let David now stand **b** me,	**1Sa 16:22**	6440
shield-carrier also walked **b** him.	**1Sa 17:7**	6440
answered the same thing as **b**.	**1Sa 17:30**	7223
Abner took him and brought him **b**	**1Sa 17:57**	6440
went out and came in **b** the people.	**1Sa 18:13**	6440
he went out and came in **b** them.	**1Sa 18:16**	6440
B the days had expired	**1Sa 18:26**	
so that they fled **b** him.	**1Sa 19:8**	
		4480, 6440
and he too prophesied **b** Samuel and	**1Sa 19:24**	6440
And what is my sin **b** your father,	**1Sa 20:1**	6440
which was removed from **b** the LORD,	**1Sa 21:6**	6440
that day, detained **b** the LORD;	**1Sa 21:7**	6440
So he disguised his sanity **b** them,	**1Sa 21:13**	5869
them made a covenant **b** the LORD;	**1Sa 23:18**	6440
arose and went to Ziph **b** Saul.	**1Sa 23:24**	6440
"Go on **b** me; behold, I am coming	**1Sa 25:19**	6440
and fell on her face **b** David and	**1Sa 25:23**	639
Hachilah, *which is* **b** Jeshimon?"	**1Sa 26:1**	
		5921, 6440
of Hachilah, which is **b** Jeshimon,	**1Sa 26:3**	
		5921, 6440
men, cursed are they **b** the LORD,	**1Sa 26:19**	6440
let me set a piece of bread **b** you	**1Sa 28:22**	6440
it **b** Saul and his servants,	**1Sa 28:25**	6440
day when I came **b** you to this day,	**1Sa 29:8**	6440
fled from **b** the Philistines and fell	**1Sa 31:1**	6440
arise and hold a contest **b** us."	**2Sa 2:14**	6440
beaten **b** the servants of David.	**2Sa 2:17**	6440
"I and my kingdom are innocent **b**	**2Sa 3:28**	
		4480, 5973
on sackcloth and lament **b** Abner."	**2Sa 3:31**	6440
As one falls **b** the wicked, you	**2Sa 3:34**	6440
else **b** the sun goes down."	**2Sa 3:35**	6440
with them **b** the LORD at Hebron;	**2Sa 5:3**	6440
broken through my enemies **b** me	**2Sa 5:20**	6440

gone out **b** you to strike the army 2Sa 5:24 6440
of Israel were celebrating **b** the LORD 2Sa 6:5 6440
b the LORD with all *his* might, 2Sa 6:14 6440
leaping and dancing **b** the LORD; 2Sa 6:16 6440
and peace offerings **b** the LORD. 2Sa 6:17 6440
"*It was* **b** the LORD, who chose me 2Sa 6:21 6440
I will celebrate **b** the LORD. 2Sa 6:21 6440
off all your enemies from **b** you; 2Sa 7:9 6440
Saul, whom I removed from **b** you. 2Sa 7:15 6440
kingdom shall endure **b** Me forever; 2Sa 7:16 6440
king went in and sat **b** the LORD, 2Sa 7:18 6440
b Your people whom You have 2Sa 7:23
4480, 6440
David be established **b** You. 2Sa 7:26 6440
it may continue forever **b** You. 2Sa 7:29 6440
the Arameans, and they fled **b** him. 2Sa 10:13
4480, 6440
b Abishai and entered the city. 2Sa 10:14
4480, 6440
But the Arameans fled **b** Israel, 2Sa 10:18
4480, 6440
him, and he ate and drank **b** him, 2Sa 11:13 6440
even take your wives **b** your eyes and 2Sa 12:11 6440
I will do this thing **b** all Israel, 2Sa 12:12 5048
they set food **b** him and he ate. 2Sa 12:20 6440
the pan and dished *them* out **b** him, 2Sa 13:9 6440
his face to the ground **b** the king, 2Sa 14:33 6440
and fifty men as runners **b** him. 2Sa 15:1 6440
near to prostrate himself **b** him, 2Sa 15:5 6440
from Gath, passed on **b** the king. 2Sa 15:18 6440
there **b** the servants of David, 2Sa 18:7 6440
And he prostrated himself **b** the 2Sa 18:28 6440
all the people came **b** the king. 2Sa 19:8 6440
not be commander of the army **b** me 2Sa 19:13 6440
rushed to the Jordan **b** the king. 2Sa 19:17 6440
son of Gera fell down **b** the king 2Sa 19:18 6440
but dead men **b** my lord the king; 2Sa 19:28 6440
them **b** the LORD in Gibeah of Saul, 2Sa 21:6 6440
them in the mountain **b** the LORD, 2Sa 21:9 6440
"From the brightness **b** Him Coals 2Sa 22:13 5048
"For all His ordinances *were* **b** me, 2Sa 22:23 5048
to my cleanness **b** His eyes. 2Sa 22:25 5048
Or will you flee three months **b** 2Sa 24:13 6440
his face to the ground **b** the king. 2Sa 24:20 6440
with fifty men to run **b** him. 1Ki 1:5 6440
and prostrated herself **b** the king. 1Ki 1:16 6440
And when he came in **b** the king, 1Ki 1:23 6440
he prostrated himself **b** the king 1Ki 1:23 6440
are eating and drinking **b** him; 1Ki 1:25 6440
presence and stood **b** the king. 1Ki 1:28 6440
herself **b** the king and said, 1Ki 1:31 6440
prostrated himself **b** King Solomon, 1Ki 1:53 6440
to walk **b** Me in truth with all 1Ki 2:4 6440
arose to meet her, bowed **b** her, 1Ki 2:19 6440
of the Lord GOD **b** my father David, 1Ki 2:26 6440
established **b** the LORD forever." 1Ki 2:45 6440
according as he walked **b** You in 1Ki 3:6 6440
has been no one like you **b** you, 1Ki 3:12 6440
stood **b** the ark of the covenant of 1Ki 3:15 6440
came to the king and stood **b** him. 1Ki 3:16 6440
Thus they spoke **b** the king. 1Ki 3:22 6440
they brought a sword **b** the king. 1Ki 3:24 6440
to him, were with him **b** the ark, 1Ki 8:5 6440
holy place **b** the inner sanctuary, 1Ki 8:8
5921, 6440
Then Solomon stood **b** the altar of 1Ki 8:22 6440
walk **b** You with all their heart, 1Ki 8:23 6440
to walk **b** Me as you have walked.' 1Ki 8:25 6440
Your servant prays **b** You today; 1Ki 8:28 6440
oath **b** Your altar in this house, 1Ki 8:31 6440
Israel are defeated **b** an enemy, 1Ki 8:33 6440
objects of compassion **b** those who 1Ki 8:50 6440
from **b** the altar of the LORD, 1Ki 8:54 6440
have made supplication **b** the LORD, 1Ki 8:59 6440
him offered sacrifice **b** the LORD. 1Ki 8:62 6440
that *was* **b** the house of the LORD, 1Ki 8:64 6440
for the bronze altar that *was* **b** 1Ki 8:64 6440
of Egypt, **b** the LORD our God, 1Ki 8:65 6440
which you have made **b** Me; 1Ki 9:3 6440
if you will walk **b** Me as your 1Ki 9:4 6440
My statutes which I have set **b** you 1Ki 9:6 6440
on the altar which *was* **b** the LORD. 1Ki 9:25 6440
these your servants who stand **b** you 1Ki 10:8 6440
Hadad found great favor **b** Pharaoh, 1Ki 11:19 5869
a lamp always **b** Me in Jerusalem, 1Ki 11:36 6440
worship **b** the one as far as Dan. 1Ki 12:30 6440
to him, and it became as it was **b**. 1Ki 13:6 7223
more evil than all who were **b** you, 1Ki 14:9 6440
dispossessed **b** the sons of Israel. 1Ki 14:24
4480, 6440
which he had committed **b** him; 1Ki 15:3 6440
wickedly than all who *were* **b** him. 1Ki 16:25 6440
LORD more than all who were **b** him. 1Ki 16:30 6440
kings of Israel who were **b** him. 1Ki 16:33 6440
of Israel lives, **b** whom I stand, 1Ki 17:1 6440
of hosts lives, **b** whom I stand, 1Ki 18:15 6440
on the mountain **b** the LORD." 1Ki 19:11 6440
in pieces the rocks **b** the LORD; 1Ki 19:11 6440
with twelve pairs *of oxen* **b** him, 1Ki 19:19 6440
and the sons of Israel camped **b** 1Ki 20:27 5048
and seat two worthless men **b** him, 1Ki 21:10 5048
men came in and sat **b** him; 1Ki 21:13 5048
even against Naboth, **b** the people, 1Ki 21:13 5048
cast out **b** the sons of Israel. 1Ki 21:26
4480, 6440
how Ahab has humbled himself **b** Me? 1Ki 21:29
4480, 6440
he has humbled himself **b** Me, 1Ki 21:29
4480, 6440
prophets were prophesying **b** them. 1Ki 22:10 6440
and stood **b** the LORD and said, 1Ki 22:21 6440
bowed down on his knees **b** Elijah, 2Ki 1:13 5048
for you **b** I am taken from you." 2Ki 2:9 2962
themselves to the ground **b** him. 2Ki 2:15 6440
of hosts lives, **b** whom I stand, 2Ki 3:14 6440
so that they fled **b** them; 2Ki 3:24
4480, 6440
had called her, she stood **b** him. 2Ki 4:12 6440
Then Gehazi passed on **b** them and 2Ki 4:31 6440
the prophets were sitting **b** him, 2Ki 4:38 6440
I set this **b** a hundred men?" 2Ki 4:43 6440
So he set *it* **b** them, and they ate 2Ki 4:44 6440
company, and came and stood **b** him, 2Ki 5:15 6440
"As the LORD lives, **b** whom I stand, 2Ki 5:16 6440
and they carried *them* **b** him. 2Ki 5:23 6440
he went in and stood **b** his master. 2Ki 5:25 413
the place **b** you where we are 2Ki 6:1 6440
Set bread and water **b** them, 2Ki 6:22 6440
but **b** the messenger came to him, 2Ki 6:32 2962
he came and stood **b** him and said, 2Ki 8:9 6440
the two kings did not stand **b** him; 2Ki 10:4 6440
the priest of Baal **b** the altars. 2Ki 11:18 6440
him **b** the people and killed him, 2Ki 15:10 6904
out from **b** the sons of Israel. 2Ki 16:3 6440
b the coming of King Ahaz from 2Ki 16:11 5704
altar, which *was* **b** the LORD, 2Ki 16:14 6440
kings of Israel who were **b** him. 2Ki 17:2 6440
driven out **b** the sons of Israel, 2Ki 17:8
4480, 6440
had carried away to exile **b** them; 2Ki 17:11
4480, 6440
nor *among those* who were **b** him. 2Ki 18:5 6440
b this altar in Jerusalem'? 2Ki 18:22 6440
LORD and spread it out **b** the LORD. 2Ki 19:14 6440
prayed **b** the LORD and said, 2Ki 19:15 6440
is scorched **b** it is grown up. 2Ki 19:26 6440
he will not come **b** it with a shield 2Ki 19:32 6923
how I have walked **b** You in truth 2Ki 20:3 6440
B Isaiah had gone out of the middle 2Ki 20:4 3808
dispossessed **b** the sons of Israel. 2Ki 21:2
4480, 6440
destroyed **b** the sons of Israel. 2Ki 21:9
4480, 6440
the Amorites did who *were* **b** him, 2Ki 21:11 6440
you humbled yourself **b** the LORD 2Ki 22:19
4480, 6440
torn your clothes and wept **b** Me, 2Ki 22:19 6440
and made a covenant **b** the LORD, 2Ki 23:3 6440
places which *were* **b** Jerusalem, 2Ki 23:13
5921, 6440
B him there was no king like him who 2Ki 23:25 6440
the sons of Zedekiah **b** his eyes, 2Ki 25:7
reigned in the land of Edom **b** any 1Ch 1:43 6440
whom God had destroyed **b** them. 1Ch 5:25
4480, 6440
ministered with song **b** the tabernacle 1Ch 6:32 6440
of Israel fled **b** the Philistines and 1Ch 10:1
4480, 6440
with them in Hebron **b** the LORD; 1Ch 11:3 6440
the people fled **b** the Philistines. 1Ch 11:13
4480, 6440
me **b** my God that I should do this. 1Ch 11:19 4480
b God with all *their* might, 1Ch 13:8 6440
and he died there **b** God. 1Ch 13:10 6440
for God will have gone out **b** you 1Ch 14:15 6440
the trumpets **b** the ark of God. 1Ch 15:24 6440
and peace offerings **b** God. 1Ch 16:1 6440
ministers **b** the ark of the LORD, 1Ch 16:4 6440
blew trumpets continually **b** the ark 1Ch 16:6 6440
Splendor and majesty are **b** Him, 1Ch 16:27 6440
Bring an offering, and come **b** Him; 1Ch 16:29 6440
Tremble **b** Him, all the earth; 1Ch 16:30
4480, 6440
will sing for joy **b** the LORD; 1Ch 16:33
4480, 6440
his relatives there **b** the ark of 1Ch 16:37 6440
to minister **b** the ark continually, 1Ch 16:37 6440
priests **b** the tabernacle of the LORD 1Ch 16:39 6440
off all your enemies from **b** you; 1Ch 17:8 6440
I took it from him who was **b** you. 1Ch 17:13 6440
in and sat **b** the LORD and said, 1Ch 17:16 6440
out nations from **b** Your people, 1Ch 17:21 6440
servant is established **b** You.' 1Ch 17:24 6440
has found *courage* to pray **b** You. 1Ch 17:25 6440
it may continue forever **b** You; 1Ch 17:27 6440
who came and camped **b** Medeba. 1Ch 19:7 6440
the Arameans, and they fled **b** him. 1Ch 19:14
4480, 6440
also fled **b** Abshai his brother and 1Ch 19:15
4480, 6440
The Arameans fled **b** Israel, 1Ch 19:18
4480, 6440
to be swept away **b** your foes, 1Ch 21:12
4480, 6440
and prostrated himself **b** David 1Ch 21:21 6440
not go **b** it to inquire of God, 1Ch 21:30 6440
ample preparations **b** his death. 1Ch 22:5 6440
so much blood on the earth **b** Me. 1Ch 22:8 6440
and the land is subdued **b** the LORD 1Ch 22:18 6440
before the LORD and **b** His people. 1Ch 22:18 6440
to burn incense **b** the LORD, 1Ch 23:13 6440
them, continually **b** the LORD. 1Ch 23:31 6440
b their father and had no sons. 1Ch 24:2 6440
"For we are sojourners **b** You, 1Ch 29:15 6440
b the LORD with great gladness. 1Ch 29:22 6440
been on any king **b** him in Israel. 1Ch 29:25 6440
b the tabernacle of the LORD, 2Ch 1:5 6440
Solomon went up there **b** the LORD 2Ch 1:6 6440
go out and come in **b** this people, 2Ch 1:10 6440
who were **b** you has possessed nor 2Ch 1:12 6440
to burn fragrant incense **b** Him and 2Ch 2:4 6440
Him, except to burn *incense* **b** Him? 2Ch 2:6 6440
assembled with him **b** the ark, 2Ch 5:6 6440
Then he stood **b** the altar of the 2Ch 6:12 6440
walk **b** You with all their heart; 2Ch 6:14 6440
My law as you have walked **b** Me.' 2Ch 6:16 6440
which Your servant prays **b** You; 2Ch 6:19 6440
oath **b** Your altar in this house, 2Ch 6:22 6440
Israel are defeated **b** an enemy because 2Ch 6:24 6440
supplication **b** You in this house, 2Ch 6:24 6440
offered sacrifice **b** the LORD. 2Ch 7:4 6440
that *was* **b** the house of the LORD, 2Ch 7:7 6440
if you walk **b** Me as your father 2Ch 7:17 6440
My commandments which I have set **b** 2Ch 7:19 6440
which he had built **b** the porch; 2Ch 8:12 6440
ministering **b** the priests according 2Ch 8:14 5048
these your servants who stand **b** you 2Ch 9:7 6440
was seen **b** in the land of Judah. 2Ch 9:11 6440
and all Israel **b** Abijah and Judah. 2Ch 13:15 6440
the sons of Israel fled **b** Judah, 2Ch 13:16
4480, 6440
Ethiopians **b** Asa and before Judah, 2Ch 14:12 6440
Ethiopians before Asa and **b** Judah, 2Ch 14:12 6440
they were shattered **b** the LORD and 2Ch 14:13 6440
before the LORD and **b** His army. 2Ch 14:13 6440
prophets were prophesying **b** them. 2Ch 18:9 6440
and stood **b** the LORD and said, 2Ch 18:20 6440
they may not be guilty **b** the LORD, 2Ch 19:10
Levites shall be officers **b** you. 2Ch 19:11 6440
house of the LORD **b** the new court, 2Ch 20:5 6440
of this land **b** Your people Israel and 2Ch 20:7
4480, 6440
b this house and before You 2Ch 20:9 6440
before this house and **b** You 2Ch 20:9 6440
For we are powerless **b** this great 2Ch 20:12 6440
All Judah was standing **b** the LORD, 2Ch 20:13 6440
of Jerusalem fell down **b** the LORD, 2Ch 20:18 6440
they went out **b** the army and said, 2Ch 20:21 6440
the priest of Baal **b** the altars. 2Ch 23:17 6440
the money **b** the king and Jehoiada; 2Ch 24:14 6440
will bring you down **b** the enemy, 2Ch 25:8 6440
up as his gods, bowed down **b** them and 2Ch 25:14 6440
leprosy broke out on his forehead **b** 2Ch 26:19 6440
his ways **b** the LORD his God. 2Ch 27:6 6440
driven out **b** the sons of Israel. 2Ch 28:3
4480, 6440
left the captives and the spoil **b** the 2Ch 28:14 6440
has chosen you to stand **b** Him, 2Ch 29:11 6440
are **b** the altar of the LORD." 2Ch 29:19 6440
b the king and the assembly, 2Ch 29:23 6440
b those who led them captive and 2Ch 30:9 6440
and true **b** the LORD his God. 2Ch 31:20 6440
"You shall worship **b** one altar, 2Ch 32:12 6440
dispossessed **b** the sons of Israel. 2Ch 33:2
4480, 6440
destroyed **b** the sons of Israel. 2Ch 33:9
4480, 6440
greatly **b** the God of his fathers. 2Ch 33:12
4480, 6440
images, **b** he humbled himself, 2Ch 33:19 6440
he did not humble himself **b** the 2Ch 33:23
4480, 6440
and you humbled yourself **b** God when 2Ch 34:27
4480, 6440
because you humbled yourself **b** Me, 2Ch 34:27 6440
tore your clothes and wept **b** Me, 2Ch 34:27 6440
made a covenant **b** the LORD to walk 2Ch 34:31 6440
he did not humble himself **b** 2Ch 36:12
4480, 6440
this house was laid **b** their eyes, Ezr 3:12 6440
has been translated and read **b** me. Ezr 4:18 6925
document was read **b** Rehum and Ezr 4:23 6925
in full **b** the God of Jerusalem. Ezr 7:19 6925
to me **b** the king and his counselors Ezr 7:28 6440
b all the king's mighty princes. Ezr 7:28
that we might humble ourselves **b** Ezr 8:21 6440
weigh *them* **b** the leading priests, Ezr 8:29 6440
we are **b** You in our guilt, Ezr 9:15 6440
stand **b** You because of this." Ezr 9:15 6440
himself **b** the house of God, Ezr 10:1 6440
Then Ezra rose from **b** the house of Ezr 10:6
4480, 6440
the people sat in the open square **b** Ezr 10:9
and praying **b** the God of heaven. Ne 1:4 6440
which I am praying **b** You now, Ne 1:6 6440
grant him compassion **b** this man." Ne 1:11 6440
Artaxerxes, that wine *was* **b** him, Ne 2:1 6440
servant has found favor **b** you, Ne 2:5 6440
their sin be blotted out **b** You, Ne 4:5
4480, 6440
governors who were **b** me laid burdens Ne 5:15 6440
the law **b** the assembly of men, Ne 8:2 6440
He read from it **b** the square Ne 8:3 6440
heavenly host bows down **b** You. Ne 9:6 6440
found his heart faithful **b** You, Ne 9:8 6440
"You divided the sea **b** them, Ne 9:11 6440
And You subdued **b** them the Ne 9:24 6440
rest, they did evil again **b** You; Ne 9:28 6440
seem insignificant **b** You, Ne 9:32 6440
land which You set **b** them, Ne 9:35 6440
And Ezra the scribe went **b** them. Ne 12:36 6440
gates of Jerusalem **b** the sabbath, Ne 13:19 6440
to bring Queen Vashti **b** the king Es 1:11 6440
b all who knew law and justice Es 1:13 6440
was cast **b** Haman from day to day Es 3:7 6440
did not stand up or tremble **b** him, Es 5:9 4480
and they were read **b** the king. Es 6:1 6440

city square, and proclaim **b** him,	**Es 6:9**	6440
city square, and proclaimed **b** him,	**Es 6:11**	6440
b whom you have begun to fall,	**Es 6:13**	6440
him, but will surely fall **b** him."	**Es 6:13**	6440
terrified **b** the king and queen.	**Es 7:6**	4480, 6440
eunuchs who *were* **b** the king said,	**Es 7:9**	6440
and Mordecai came **b** the king,	**Es 8:1**	6440
Esther arose and stood **b** the king.	**Es 8:4**	6440
king and if I have found favor **b** him	**Es 8:5**	6440
and no one could stand **b** them,	**Es 9:2**	6440
to present themselves **b** the LORD,	**Jb 1:6**	5921
to present themselves **b** the LORD,	**Jb 2:1**	5921
to present himself **b** the LORD.	**Jb 2:1**	5921
A form *was* **b** my eyes;	**Jb 4:16**	5048
'Can mankind be just **b** God?	**Jb 4:17**	4480
Can a man be pure **b** his Maker?	**Jb 4:17**	4480
dust, Who are crushed **b** the moth!	**Jb 4:19**	6440
And I would place my cause **b** God;	**Jb 5:8**	413
Yet it withers **b** any *other* plant.	**Jb 8:12**	6440
"He thrives **b** the sun, And his	**Jb 8:16**	6440
can a man be in the right **b** God?	**Jb 9:2**	5973
Him, *And* choose my words **b** Him?	**Jb 9:14**	5973
B I go—and I shall not return	**Jb 10:21**	2962
silent **b** me so that I may speak;	**Jb 13:13**	4480
I will argue my ways **b** Him.	**Jb 13:15**	413, 6440
man may not come **b** His presence.	**Jb 13:16**	6440
And hinder meditation **b** God.	**Jb 15:4**	6440
you brought forth **b** the hills?	**Jb 15:7**	6440
will be accomplished **b** his time,	**Jb 15:32**	3808
march him **b** the king of terrors.	**Jb 18:14**	
And their offspring **b** their eyes,	**Jb 21:8**	
"Are they as straw **b** the wind,	**Jb 21:18**	6440
While countless ones *go* **b** him.	**Jb 21:33**	6440
were snatched away **b** their time,	**Jb 22:16**	
"I would present *my* case **b** Him	**Jb 23:4**	6440
"Naked is Sheol **b** Him, And Abaddon	**Jb 26:6**	5048
have cast off the bridle **b** me.	**Jb 30:11**	4480, 6440
he justified himself **b** God.	**Jb 32:2**	4480
Array yourselves **b** me,	**Jb 33:5**	6440
he should go **b** God in judgment.	**Jb 34:23**	413
not behold Him, The case is **b** Him,	**Jb 35:14**	6440
then is he that can stand **b** Me?	**Jb 41:10**	6440
strength, And dismay leaps **b** him.	**Jb 41:22**	6440
and all who had known him **b** came	**Jb 42:11**	6440
shall not stand **b** Your eyes;	**Ps 5:5**	5048
Make Your way straight **b** me.	**Ps 5:8**	6440
They stumble and perish **b** You.	**Ps 9:3**	4480, 6440
Let the nations be judged **b** You.	**Ps 9:19**	5921, 6440
set the LORD continually **b** me;	**Ps 16:8**	5048
for help **b** Him came into His ears.	**Ps 18:6**	6440
b Him passed His thick clouds,	**Ps 18:12**	5048
For all His ordinances were **b** me,	**Ps 18:22**	5048
them fine as the dust **b** the wind;	**Ps 18:42**	5921, 6440
pay my vows **b** those who fear Him.	**Ps 22:25**	5048
the nations will worship **b** You.	**Ps 22:27**	6440
down to the dust will bow **b** Him,	**Ps 22:29**	6440
You prepare a table **b** me in	**Ps 23:5**	6440
Your lovingkindness is **b** my eyes,	**Ps 26:3**	6440
refuge in You, **B** the sons of men!	**Ps 31:19**	6440
"I am cut off from **b** Your eyes";	**Ps 31:22**	6440
Let them be like chaff **b** the wind,	**Ps 35:5**	6440
is no fear of God **b** his eyes.	**Ps 36:1**	5048
Lord, all my desire is **b** You;	**Ps 38:9**	5048
And my sorrow is continually **b** me.	**Ps 38:17**	5048
B I depart and am no more."	**Ps 39:13**	2962
shall I come and appear **b** God?	**Ps 42:2**	6440
All day long my dishonor is **b** me And	**Ps 44:15**	5048
Fire devours **b** Him, And it is very	**Ps 50:3**	6440
offerings are continually **b** Me.	**Ps 50:8**	5048
the case in order **b** your eyes.	**Ps 50:21**	
And my sin is ever **b** me.	**Ps 51:3**	5048
They have not set God **b** them.	**Ps 54:3**	5048
So that I may walk **b** God In the	**Ps 56:13**	6440
They dug a pit **b** me;	**Ps 57:6**	6440
B your pots can feel *the fire of*	**Ps 58:9**	2962
He will abide **b** God forever;	**Ps 61:7**	6440
Pour out your heart **b** Him;	**Ps 62:8**	6440
There will be silence **b** You,	**Ps 65:1**	
let those who hate Him flee **b** Him.	**Ps 68:1**	4480, 6440
As wax melts **b** the fire, *So* let	**Ps 68:2**	4480, 6440
So let the wicked perish **b** God.	**Ps 68:2**	4480, 6440
let them exult **b** God;	**Ps 68:3**	6440
name is the LORD, and exult **b** Him.	**Ps 68:4**	6440
You went forth **b** Your people,	**Ps 68:7**	6440
All my adversaries are **b** You.	**Ps 69:19**	5048
their table **b** them become a snare;	**Ps 69:22**	6440
nomads of the desert bow **b** him,	**Ps 72:9**	6440
And let all kings bow down **b** him,	**Ps 72:11**	
I was *like* a beast **b** You.	**Ps 73:22**	5973
wrought wonders **b** their fathers In	**Ps 78:12**	5048
B they had satisfied their desire,	**Ps 78:30**	
also drove out the nations **b** them And	**Ps 78:55**	4480, 6440
of the prisoner come **b** You;	**Ps 79:11**	6440
B Ephraim and Benjamin and	**Ps 80:2**	6440
You cleared *the ground* **b** it,	**Ps 80:9**	6440
Like chaff **b** the wind.	**Ps 83:13**	6440
one of them appears **b** God in Zion.	**Ps 84:7**	413
Righteousness will go **b** Him And	**Ps 85:13**	6440
shall come and worship **b** You,	**Ps 86:9**	6440
And they have not set You **b** them.	**Ps 86:14**	5048
by day and in the night **b** You.	**Ps 88:1**	5048
Let my prayer come **b** You;	**Ps 88:2**	6440
morning my prayer comes **b** You.	**Ps 88:13**	6923
and truth go **b** You.	**Ps 89:14**	6440
shall crush his adversaries **b** him,	**Ps 89:23**	4480, 6440
And his throne as the sun **b** Me.	**Ps 89:36**	5048
B the mountains were born Or You	**Ps 90:2**	2962
have placed our iniquities **b** You,	**Ps 90:8**	5048
Let us come **b** His presence with	**Ps 95:2**	6923
Let us kneel **b** the LORD our Maker.	**Ps 95:6**	6923
Splendor and majesty are **b** Him,	**Ps 96:6**	6923
Tremble **b** Him, all the earth.	**Ps 96:9**	4480, 6440
B the LORD, for He is coming,	**Ps 96:13**	6440
Fire goes **b** Him And burns up His	**Ps 97:3**	6440
horn Shout joyfully **b** the King,	**Ps 98:6**	6440
B the LORD, for He is coming to	**Ps 98:9**	6440
Come **b** Him with joyful singing.	**Ps 100:2**	6440
set no worthless thing **b** my eyes;	**Ps 101:3**	5048
not maintain his position **b** me.	**Ps 101:7**	5048
will be established **b** You."	**Ps 102:28**	6440
He sent a man **b** them, Joseph, *who*	**Ps 105:17**	6440
one stood in the breach **b** Him,	**Ps 106:23**	6440
fathers be remembered **b** the LORD,	**Ps 109:14**	413
them be **b** the LORD continually,	**Ps 109:15**	5048
Tremble, O earth, **b** the Lord,	**Ps 114:7**	4480, 6440
the Lord, **B** the God of Jacob,	**Ps 114:7**	4480, 6440
I shall walk **b** the LORD In the	**Ps 116:9**	6440
I have placed Your ordinances **b** *me*.	**Ps 119:30**	
speak of Your testimonies **b** kings And	**Ps 119:46**	5048
B I was afflicted I went astray,	**Ps 119:67**	2962
I rise **b** dawn and cry for help;	**Ps 119:147**	
For all my ways are **b** You.	**Ps 119:168**	5048
Let my cry come **b** You, O LORD;	**Ps 119:169**	6440
Let my supplication come **b** You;	**Ps 119:170**	6440
Which withers **b** it grows up;	**Ps 129:6**	6927
sing praises to You **b** the gods.	**Ps 138:1**	5048
b there is a word on my tongue,	**Ps 139:4**	
have enclosed me behind and **b**,	**Ps 139:5**	6924a
be counted as incense **b** You;	**Ps 141:2**	6440
I pour out my complaint **b** Him;	**Ps 142:2**	6440
I declare my trouble **b** Him.	**Ps 142:2**	6440
Who can stand **b** His cold?	**Ps 147:17**	6440
a man are **b** the eyes of the LORD,	**Pr 5:21**	5227
of His way, **B** His works of old.	**Pr 8:22**	6924a
"**B** the mountains were settled,	**Pr 8:25**	2962
B the hills I was brought forth;	**Pr 8:25**	6440
delight, Rejoicing always **b** Him,	**Pr 8:30**	6440
The evil will bow down **b** the good,	**Pr 14:19**	6440
and Abaddon *lie open* **b** the LORD,	**Pr 15:11**	5048
And **b** honor *comes* humility.	**Pr 15:33**	6440
Pride *goes* **b** destruction, And a	**Pr 16:18**	6440
And a haughty spirit **b** stumbling.	**Pr 16:18**	6440
the quarrel **b** it breaks out.	**Pr 17:14**	6440
B destruction the heart of man is	**Pr 18:12**	6440
But humility *goes* **b** honor.	**Pr 18:12**	6440
He who gives an answer **b** he hears,	**Pr 18:13**	2962
him And brings him **b** great men.	**Pr 18:16**	6440
He will stand **b** kings;	**Pr 22:29**	6440
He will not stand **b** obscure men.	**Pr 22:29**	6440
Consider carefully what is **b** you,	**Pr 23:1**	6440
away the wicked **b** the king,	**Pr 25:5**	6440
man who gives way **b** the wicked.	**Pr 25:26**	6440
will be revealed **b** the assembly.	**Pr 26:26**	
But who can stand **b** jealousy?	**Pr 27:4**	6440
of You, Do not refuse me **b** I die:	**Pr 30:7**	2962
beasts And does not retreat **b** any,	**Pr 30:30**	4480, 6440
existed for ages Which were **b** us.	**Ec 1:10**	4480, 6440
all who were over Jerusalem **b** me;	**Ec 1:16**	6440
people, to all who were **b** them,	**Ec 4:16**	6440
knowing *how* to walk **b** the living?	**Ec 6:8**	5048
Why should you die **b** your time?	**Ec 7:17**	3808
king because of the oath **b** God.	**Ec 8:2**	
the serpent bites **b** being charmed,	**Ec 10:11**	
b the evil days come and the years	**Ec 12:1**	5704, 834, 3808
b the sun and the light, the moon	**Ec 12:2**	5704, 834, 3808
Remember Him **b** the silver cord is	**Ec 12:6**	5704, 834, 3808
"**B** I was aware, my soul set me	**SS 6:12**	
"When you come to appear **b** Me,	**Is 1:12**	6440
does the widow's plea come **b** them.	**Is 1:23**	413
ground **B** the terror of the LORD And	**Is 2:19**	4480, 6440
B the terror of the LORD and the	**Is 2:21**	4480, 6440
"For **b** the boy will know *enough*	**Is 7:16**	2962
for **b** the boy knows how to cry out	**Is 8:4**	2962
away **b** the king of Assyria.	**Is 8:4**	6440
be dashed to pieces **B** their eyes;	**Is 13:16**	
abandoned **b** the sons of Israel;	**Is 17:9**	4480, 6440
chaff in the mountains **b** the wind,	**Is 17:13**	6440
Or like whirling dust **b** a gale.	**Is 17:13**	6440
B morning they are no more.	**Is 17:14**	2962
For **b** the harvest, as soon as the	**Is 18:5**	6440
His glory will be **b** His elders.	**Is 24:23**	5048
labor pains, Thus were we **b** You,	**Is 26:17**	4480, 6440
little while **B** Lebanon will be turned	**Is 29:17**	
write it on a tablet **b** them And	**Is 30:8**	854
'You shall worship **b** this altar'?	**Is 36:7**	6440
LORD and spread it out **b** the LORD.	**Is 37:14**	6440
is scorched **b** it is grown up.	**Is 37:27**	6440
he will not come **b** it with a shield,	**Is 37:33**	6923
how I have walked **b** You in truth	**Is 38:3**	6440
Him And His recompense **b** Him.	**Is 40:10**	6440
the nations are as nothing **b** Him,	**Is 40:17**	5048
He delivers up nations **b** him And	**Is 41:2**	6440
B they spring forth I proclaim	**Is 42:9**	2962
make darkness into light **b** them	**Is 42:16**	6440
B Me there was no God formed, And	**Is 43:10**	6440
graven image and falls down **b** it.	**Is 44:15**	
He falls down **b** it and worships;	**Is 44:17**	
I fall down **b** a block of wood!"	**Is 44:19**	
hand, To subdue nations **b** him And	**Is 45:1**	6440
To open doors **b** him so that gates	**Is 45:1**	6440
"I will go **b** you and make the	**Is 45:2**	6440
to warm by *Nor* a fire to sit **b**!	**Is 47:14**	5048
B they took place I proclaimed	**Is 48:5**	2962
b today you have not heard them,	**Is 48:7**	6440
Your walls are continually **b** Me.	**Is 49:16**	5048
For the LORD will go **b** you,	**Is 52:12**	6440
grew up **b** Him like a tender shoot,	**Is 53:2**	6440
that is silent **b** its shearers,	**Is 53:7**	6440
forth into shouts of joy **b** you,	**Is 55:12**	6440
the spirit would grow faint **b** Me,	**Is 57:16**	4480, 6440
your righteousness will go **b** you;	**Is 58:8**	6440
are multiplied **b** You,	**Is 59:12**	5048
To spring up **b** all the nations.	**Is 61:11**	5048
Him, and His recompense **b** Him."	**Is 62:11**	6440
Who divided the waters **b** them to	**Is 63:12**	4480, 6440
"Behold, it is written **b** Me,	**Is 65:6**	6440
come to pass that **b** they call,	**Is 65:24**	2962
"**B** she travailed, she brought	**Is 66:7**	2962
B her pain came, she gave birth to	**Is 66:7**	2962
Which I make will endure **b** Me,"	**Is 66:22**	6440
will come to bow down **b** Me,"	**Is 66:23**	6440
"**B** I formed you in the womb I	**Jer 1:5**	2962
And **b** you were born I consecrated	**Jer 1:5**	2962
Do not be dismayed **b** them,	**Jer 1:17**	4480, 6440
them, or I will dismay you **b** them.	**Jer 1:17**	6440
have you turned yourself **b** Me	**Jer 2:21**	
stain of your iniquity is **b** Me,"	**Jer 2:22**	6440
were pulled down **B** the LORD,	**Jer 4:26**	4480, 6440
the LORD, **b** His fierce anger.	**Jer 4:26**	4480, 6440
is me, for I faint **b** murderers."	**Jer 4:31**	
Sickness and wounds are ever **b** Me.	**Jer 6:7**	5921, 6440
stumbling blocks **b** this people.	**Jer 6:21**	413
come and stand **b** Me in this house,	**Jer 7:10**	6440
My law which I set **b** them,	**Jer 9:13**	6440
Desolate, it mourns **b** Me;	**Jer 12:11**	5921
B He brings darkness And before	**Jer 13:16**	2962
Before He brings darkness And **b**	**Jer 13:16**	2962
and Samuel were to stand **b** Me,	**Jer 15:1**	6440
widows will be more numerous **b** Me	**Jer 15:8**	
to the sword **B** their enemies,"	**Jer 15:9**	6440
B Me you will stand;	**Jer 15:19**	6440
b your eyes and in your time,	**Jer 16:9**	
I will scatter them **B** the enemy;	**Jer 18:17**	6440
Remember how I stood **b** You To	**Jer 18:20**	6440
But may they be overthrown **b** You;	**Jer 18:23**	6440
fall by the sword **b** their enemies	**Jer 19:7**	6440
he did not kill me **b** birth,	**Jer 20:17**	4480
I set **b** you the way of life and	**Jer 21:8**	6440
figs set **b** the temple of the LORD!	**Jer 24:1**	6440
in My law which I have set **b** you,	**Jer 26:4**	6440
"The prophets who were **b** me and	**Jer 28:8**	6440
who were before me and **b** you	**Jer 28:8**	6440
he will slay them **b** your eyes.	**Jer 29:21**	
shall be established **b** Me;	**Jer 30:20**	6440
fixed order departs From **b** Me,"	**Jer 31:36**	4480, 6440
being a nation **b** Me forever."	**Jer 31:36**	6440
b all the Jews who were sitting in	**Jer 32:12**	5869
should be removed from **b** My face,	**Jer 32:31**	5921
b all the nations of the earth which	**Jer 33:9**	
man **b** Me to offer burnt offerings,	**Jer 33:18**	4480, 6440
the former kings who were **b** you,	**Jer 34:5**	6440
and you had made a covenant **b** Me	**Jer 34:15**	6440
the covenant which they made **b** Me,	**Jer 34:18**	6440
Then I set **b** the men of the house	**Jer 35:5**	6440
'Come and let us go to Jerusalem **b**	**Jer 35:11**	4480, 6440
and **b** the army of the Arameans.'	**Jer 35:11**	4480, 6440
a man to stand **b** Me always."	**Jer 35:19**	6440
supplication will come **b** the LORD,	**Jer 36:7**	6440
proclaimed a fast **b** the LORD.	**Jer 36:9**	6440
fire burning in the brazier **b** him.	**Jer 36:22**	6440
please let my petition come **b** you and	**Jer 37:20**	6440
from the cistern **b** he dies."	**Jer 38:10**	2962
presenting my petition **b** the king,	**Jer 38:26**	6440
of Zedekiah **b** his eyes at Riblah;	**Jer 39:6**	
will take place **b** you on that day.	**Jer 39:16**	6440
Look, the whole land is **b** you;	**Jer 40:4**	6440
b the Chaldeans who come to us;	**Jer 40:10**	6440
let our petition come **b** you,	**Jer 42:2**	6440
me to present your petition **b** Him:	**Jer 42:9**	6440
b you and before your fathers."	**Jer 44:10**	6440
before you and **b** your fathers."	**Jer 44:10**	6440
b Pharaoh conquered Gaza.	**Jer 47:1**	2962
'So I will shatter Elam **b** their	**Jer 49:37**	6440
And **b** those who seek their lives;	**Jer 49:37**	6440

From **b** the sword of the oppressor	**Jer 50:16**	6440
the shepherd who can stand **b** Me?"	**Jer 50:44**	6440
of guilt **B** the Holy One of Israel.	**Jer 51:5**	4480
have done in Zion **b** your eyes,"	**Jer 51:24**	6440
the sons of Zedekiah **b** his eyes,	**Jer 52:10**	6440
away As captives **b** the adversary.	**La 1:5**	6440
without strength **B** the pursuer.	**La 1:6**	6440
all their wickedness come **b** You;	**La 1:22**	6440
His right hand From **b** the enemy.	**La 2:3**	6440
water **B** the presence of the Lord;	**La 2:19**	5227
When He spread it out **b** me,	**Ezk 2:10**	6440
of them or be dismayed **b** them,	**Ezk 3:9**	
		4480, 6440
and I place an obstacle **b** him,	**Ezk 3:20**	6440
yourself a brick, place it **b** you and	**Ezk 4:1**	6440
the elders of Judah sitting **b** me,	**Ezk 8:1**	6440
the elders who *were* **b** the temple.	**Ezk 9:6**	6440
came to me and sat down **b** me.	**Ezk 14:1**	6440
and have put right **b** their faces	**Ezk 14:3**	5227
puts right **b** his face the	**Ezk 14:4**	5227
puts right **b** his face the	**Ezk 14:7**	5227
My oil and My incense **b** them.	**Ezk 16:18**	6440
offer **b** them for a soothing aroma;	**Ezk 16:19**	6440
and committed abominations **b** Me.	**Ezk 16:50**	6440
b your wickedness was uncovered,	**Ezk 16:57**	2962
inquire of the LORD, and sat **b** me.	**Ezk 20:1**	6440
b whose sight I had brought them	**Ezk 20:14**	6440
in the gap **B** Me for the land,	**Ezk 22:30**	6440
couch with a table arranged **b** it on	**Ezk 23:41**	6440
I put you **b** kings, That they may	**Ezk 28:17**	6440
so that he will groan **b** him with	**Ezk 30:24**	6440
when I brandish My sword **b** them;	**Ezk 32:10**	
		5921, 6440
the evening, **b** the refugees came.	**Ezk 33:22**	6440
come, and sit **b** you *as* My people and	**Ezk 33:31**	6440
their way **B** Me was like the	**Ezk 36:17**	6440
will be in your hand **b** their eyes.	**Ezk 37:20**	6440
sanctified through you **b** their eyes,	**Ezk 38:16**	6440
width, twenty cubits, **b** the nave;	**Ezk 41:4**	
		413, 6440
is the table that is **b** the LORD."	**Ezk 41:22**	6440
B the chambers *was* an inner walk	**Ezk 42:4**	6440
'You shall present them **b** the LORD,	**Ezk 43:24**	6440
as prince to eat bread **b** the LORD;	**Ezk 44:3**	6440
stand **b** them to minister to them.	**Ezk 44:11**	6440
they ministered to them **b** their idols	**Ezk 44:12**	6440
and they shall stand **b** Me to offer	**Ezk 44:15**	6440
doorway of that gate **b** the LORD	**Ezk 46:3**	6440
people of the land come **b** the LORD	**Ezk 46:9**	6440
presented them **b** Nebuchadnezzar.	**Da 1:18**	6440
they came in and stood **b** the king.	**Da 2:2**	6440
to speak lying and corrupt words **b** me	**Da 2:9**	6925
answered **b** the king and said,	**Da 2:27**	6925
its interpretation **b** the king.	**Da 2:36**	6925
and they stood **b** the image that	**Da 3:3**	6903
these men were brought **b** the king.	**Da 3:13**	6925
"But finally Daniel came in **b** me,	**Da 4:8**	6925
Daniel was brought in **b** the king.	**Da 5:13**	6925
the conjurers were brought in **b** me	**Da 5:15**	6925
answered and said **b** the king,	**Da 5:17**	6925
feared and trembled **b** him;	**Da 5:19**	6925
the vessels of His house **b** you,	**Da 5:23**	6925
and giving thanks **b** his God,	**Da 6:10**	6925
and supplication **b** his God.	**Da 6:11**	6925
approached and spoke **b** the king	**Da 6:12**	6925
answered and spoke **b** the king,	**Da 6:13**	6925
entertainment was brought **b** him;	**Da 6:18**	6925
as I was found innocent **b** Him;	**Da 6:22**	6925
the den **b** the lions overpowered them	**Da 6:24**	
		5705, 1768
and tremble **b** the God of Daniel;	**Da 6:26**	
		4481, 6925
all the beasts that were **b** it,	**Da 7:7**	6925
were pulled out by the roots **b** it;	**Da 7:8**	
		4481, 6925
flowing And coming out from **b** Him;	**Da 7:10**	6925
upon myriads were standing **b** Him;	**Da 7:10**	6925
of Days And was presented **b** Him.	**Da 7:13**	6925
and **b** which three *of them* fell,	**Da 7:20**	
		4481, 6925
no *other* beasts could stand **b** him nor	**Da 8:4**	6440
standing **b** me was one who looked	**Da 8:15**	5048
in His teachings which He set **b** us	**Da 9:10**	6440
presenting our supplications **b** You	**Da 9:18**	6440
and presenting my supplication **b**	**Da 9:20**	6440
on humbling yourself **b** your God,	**Da 10:12**	6440
said to him who was standing **b** me,	**Da 10:16**	5048
flooded away **b** him and shattered,	**Da 11:22**	
		4480, 6440
not turn out the way it did **b**.	**Da 11:29**	7223
third day, That we may live **b** Him.	**Hos 6:2**	6440
They are **b** My face.	**Hos 7:2**	5048
not food been cut off **b** our eyes,	**Jl 1:16**	5048
A fire consumes **b** them And behind	**Jl 2:3**	6440
is like the garden of Eden **b** them But	**Jl 2:3**	6440
B them the people are in anguish;	**Jl 2:6**	
		4480, 6440
B them the earth quakes, The	**Jl 2:10**	6440
LORD utters His voice **b** His army;	**Jl 2:11**	6440
The early and latter rain as **b**.	**Jl 2:23**	7223
B the great and awesome day of the	**Jl 2:31**	6440
two years **b** the earthquake.	**Am 1:1**	6440
who destroyed the Amorite **b** them,	**Am 2:9**	
		4480, 6440
walls, Each one straight **b** her,	**Am 4:3**	5048
go into captivity **b** their enemies,	**Am 9:4**	6440
wickedness has come up **b** Me."	**Jon 1:2**	6440
be split, Like wax **b** the fire,	**Mi 1:4**	
		4480, 6440

"The breaker goes up **b** them;	**Mi 2:13**	6440
So their king goes on **b** them,	**Mi 2:13**	6440
plead your case **b** the mountains,	**Mi 6:1**	854
slavery, And I sent **b** you Moses,	**Mi 6:4**	6440
And bow myself **b** the God on high?	**Mi 6:6**	
And they will be afraid **b** You.	**Mi 7:17**	4480
Who can stand **b** His indignation?	**Na 1:6**	6440
destruction and violence are **b** me;	**Hab 1:3**	5048
all the earth be silent **b** Him."	**Hab 2:20**	
		4480, 6440
B Him goes pestilence, And plague	**Hab 3:5**	6440
Be silent **b** the Lord GOD!	**Zph 1:7**	
		4480, 6440
B the decree takes effect	**Zph 2:2**	2962
B the burning anger of the LORD	**Zph 2:2**	
		2962, 3808
B the day of the LORD's anger	**Zph 2:2**	
		2962, 3808
your fortunes **b** your eyes,"	**Zph 3:20**	
And so is this nation **b** Me,'	**Hg 2:14**	6440
b one stone was placed on another	**Hg 2:15**	
		4480, 2962
"Be silent, all flesh, **b** the LORD;	**Zch 2:13**	
		4480, 6440
standing **b** the angel of the LORD,	**Zch 3:1**	6440
garments and standing **b** the angel.	**Zch 3:3**	6440
who were standing **b** him,	**Zch 3:4**	6440
stone that I have set **b** Joshua;	**Zch 3:9**	6440
B Zerubbabel *you will become* a	**Zch 4:7**	6440
b the Lord of all the earth,	**Zch 6:5**	5921
'For **b** those days there was no	**Zch 8:10**	6440
be as numerous as they were **b**.	**Zch 10:8**	
like the angel of the LORD **b** them.	**Zch 12:8**	6440
flee just as you fled **b** the earthquake	**Zch 14:5**	
		4480, 6440
be like the bowls **b** the altar.	**Zch 14:20**	6440
and abased **b** all the people,	**Mal 2:9**	
and he will clear the way **b** Me.	**Mal 3:1**	6440
in mourning **b** the LORD of hosts?	**Mal 3:14**	
		4480, 6440
a book of remembrance was written **b**	**Mal 3:16**	6440
Elijah the prophet **b** the coming	**Mal 4:5**	6440
b they came together she was found	**Mt 1:18**	*4250*
seen in the east, went on **b** them until	**Mt 2:9**	*4254*
the prophets who were **b** you.	**Mt 5:12**	*4253*
"Let your light shine **b** men in	**Mt 5:16**	*1715*
shall be guilty **b** the court;	**Mt 5:22**	
be guilty **b** the supreme court;	**Mt 5:22**	
your offering there **b** the altar and	**Mt 5:24**	*1715*
b men to be noticed by them;	**Mt 6:1**	*1715*
do not sound a trumpet **b** you,	**Mt 6:2**	*1715*
what you need **b** you ask Him.	**Mt 6:8**	*4253*
do not throw your pearls **b** swine,	**Mt 7:6**	*1715*
a leper came to Him and bowed down **b**	**Mt 8:2**	
here to torment us **b** the time?"	**Mt 8:29**	*4253*
official came and bowed down **b** Him,	**Mt 9:18**	*4352*
be brought **b** governors and kings	**Mt 10:18**	*1909*
who confesses Me **b** men,	**Mt 10:32**	*1715*
him **b** My Father who is in heaven.	**Mt 10:32**	*1715*
"But whoever denies Me **b** men,	**Mt 10:33**	*1715*
him **b** My Father who is in heaven.	**Mt 10:33**	*1715*
WILL PREPARE YOUR WAY **B** YOU.'	**Mt 11:10**	*1715*
danced **b** *them* and pleased Herod,	**Mt 14:6**	
		1722, 3319
came and *began* to bow down **b** Him,	**Mt 15:25**	*4352*
And He was transfigured **b** them;	**Mt 17:2**	*1715*
Jesus, falling on his knees **b** Him	**Mt 17:14**	*1120*
to Himself and set him **b** them,	**Mt 18:2**	
		1722, 3319
ground and prostrated himself **b** him,	**Mt 18:26**	*4352*
get into the kingdom of God **b** you.	**Mt 21:31**	*4254*
in those days **b** the flood	**Mt 24:38**	*4253*
nations will be gathered **b** Him;	**Mt 25:32**	*1715*
this *very* night, **b** a rooster crows,	**Mt 26:34**	*4250*
But he denied *it* **b** them all,	**Mt 26:70**	*1715*
"**B** a rooster crows, you will deny Me	**Mt 26:75**	*4250*
Now Jesus stood **b** the governor,	**Mt 27:11**	*1715*
knelt down **b** Him and mocked Him,	**Mt 27:29**	*1715*
and falling on his knees **b** Him,	**Mk 1:40**	*1120*
would fall down **b** Him and shout,	**Mk 3:11**	*4363*
he ran up and bowed down **b** Him;	**Mk 5:6**	*4352*
to her, came and fell down **b** Him and	**Mk 5:33**	*4363*
to the disciples to set **b** them;	**Mk 6:41**	*3908*
And He was transfigured **b** them;	**Mk 9:2**	*1715*
Taking a child, He set him **b** them,	**Mk 9:36**	
		1722, 3319
man ran up to Him and knelt **b** Him,	**Mk 10:17**	*1120*
and you will stand **b** governors and	**Mk 13:9**	*1909*
very night, **b** a rooster crows twice,	**Mk 14:30**	*4250*
"**B** a rooster crows twice, you will	**Mk 14:72**	*4250*
and kneeling and bowing **b** Him.	**Mk 15:19**	*4352*
that is, the day **b** the Sabbath,	**Mk 15:42**	*4315*
up courage and went in **b** Pilate,	**Mk 15:43**	*4314*
service **b** God in the *appointed* order	**Lk 1:8**	*1725*
go *as a forerunner* **b** Him in the spirit	**Lk 1:17**	*1799*
righteousness **b** Him all our days.	**Lk 1:75**	*1799*
B THE LORD TO PREPARE HIS WAYS;	**Lk 1:76**	*1799*
of the Lord suddenly stood **b** them,	**Lk 2:9**	*2186*
had passed, **b** His circumcision,	**Lk 2:21**	
b He was conceived in the womb.	**Lk 2:21**	*4253*
b he had seen the Lord's Christ.	**Lk 2:26**	*4250*
"Therefore if You worship **b** me,	**Lk 4:7**	*1799*
Immediately he got up **b** them,	**Lk 5:25**	*1799*
WHO WILL PREPARE YOUR WAY **B** YOU.'	**Lk 7:27**	*1715*
he cried out and fell **b** Him,	**Lk 8:28**	*4363*
trembling and fell down **b** Him,	**Lk 8:47**	*4363*
disciples to set **b** the people.	**Lk 9:16**	*3908*
you, eat what is set **b** you;	**Lk 10:8**	*3908*
and I have nothing to set **b** him';	**Lk 11:6**	*3908*

ceremonially washed **b** the meal.	**Lk 11:38**	*4253*
one of them is forgotten **b** God.	**Lk 12:6**	*1799*
everyone who confesses Me **b** men,	**Lk 12:8**	*1715*
him also **b** the angels of God;	**Lk 12:8**	*1715*
but he who denies Me **b** men will	**Lk 12:9**	*1715*
be denied **b** the angels of God.	**Lk 12:9**	*1715*
they bring you **b** the synagogues	**Lk 12:11**	*1909*
to appear **b** the magistrate,	**Lk 12:58**	*1909*
he may not drag you **b** the judge,	**Lk 12:58**	*4314*
"But **b** all these things, they	**Lk 21:12**	*4253*
bringing you **b** kings and governors	**Lk 21:12**	*1909*
and to stand **b** the Son of Man."	**Lk 21:36**	*1715*
this Passover with you **b** I suffer;	**Lk 22:15**	*4253*
"**B** a rooster crows today, you will	**Lk 22:61**	*4250*
up and brought Him **b** Pilate.	**Lk 23:1**	*1909*
for **b** they had been enemies with	**Lk 23:12**	*4391*
behold, having examined Him **b** you,	**Lk 23:14**	*1799*
and He took it and ate *it* **b** them.	**Lk 24:43**	*1799*
than I, for He existed **b** me.'"	**Jn 1:15**	*4413*
rank than I, for He existed **b** me.'	**Jn 1:30**	*4413*
"**B** Philip called you, when you	**Jn 1:48**	*4253*
"Sir, come down **b** my child dies."	**Jn 4:49**	*4250*
coming, another steps down **b** me."	**Jn 5:7**	*4253*
I will accuse you **b** the Father;	**Jn 5:45**	*4314*
of Man ascending to where He was **b**?	**Jn 6:62**	*4387*
came to Him **b**, being one of them	**Jn 7:50**	*4387*
I say to you, **b** Abraham was born,	**Jn 8:58**	*4250*
came **b** Me are thieves and robbers,	**Jn 10:8**	*4253*
out of the country **b** the Passover to	**Jn 11:55**	*4253*
six days **b** the Passover,	**Jn 12:1**	*4253*
performed so many signs **b** them,	**Jn 12:37**	*1715*
Now **b** the Feast of the Passover,	**Jn 13:1**	*4253*
am telling you **b** *it* comes to pass,	**Jn 13:19**	*4253*
have told you **b** it happens,	**Jn 14:29**	*4250*
it has hated Me **b** *it hated* you.	**Jn 15:18**	*4413*
I had with You **b** the world was.	**Jn 17:5**	*4253*
Me **b** the foundation of the world.	**Jn 17:24**	*4253*
B THE GREAT AND GLORIOUS DAY OF	**Ac 2:20**	*4250*
stands here **b** you in good health.	**Ac 4:10**	*1799*
they stood them **b** the Council.	**Ac 5:27**	*1722*
these they brought **b** the apostles;	**Ac 6:6**	*1799*
and brought him **b** the Council.	**Ac 6:12**	*1519*
Mesopotamia, **b** he lived in Haran,	**Ac 7:2**	*4250*
'MAKE FOR US GODS WHO WILL GO **B**	**Ac 7:40**	*4313*
whom God drove out **b** our fathers,	**Ac 7:45**	
		575, 4383
for your heart is not right **b** God.	**Ac 8:21**	*1725*
AS A LAMB **B** ITS SHEARER IS SILENT,	**Ac 8:32**	*1727*
to bear My name **b** the Gentiles and	**Ac 9:15**	*1799*
them bound **b** the chief priests?"	**Ac 9:21**	*1909*
have ascended as a memorial **b** God.	**Ac 10:4**	*1715*
stood **b** me in shining garments,	**Ac 10:30**	*1799*
alms have been remembered **b** God.	**Ac 10:31**	*1799*
we are all here present **b** God to	**Ac 10:33**	*1799*
to bring him out **b** the people.	**Ac 12:4**	
after John had proclaimed **b** His	**Ac 13:24**	*4253*
market place **b** the authorities,	**Ac 16:19**	*1909*
he fell down **b** Paul and Silas,	**Ac 16:29**	*4363*
his house and set food **b** them,	**Ac 16:34**	*3908*
brethren **b** the city authorities,	**Ac 17:6**	*1909*
brought him **b** the judgment seat,	**Ac 18:12**	*1909*
evil of the Way **b** the people,	**Ac 19:9**	*1799*
Paul down and set him **b** them.	**Ac 22:30**	*1519*
conscience **b** God up to this day."	**Ac 23:1**	
him **b** he comes near *the place*."	**Ac 23:15**	*4253*
bring charges against him **b** you."	**Ac 23:30**	*1909*
his accusers to come **b** you.	**Ac 24:8**	*1909*
both **b** God and before men.	**Ac 24:16**	*4314*
both before God and **b** men.	**Ac 24:16**	
ought to have been present **b** you and	**Ac 24:19**	*1909*
found when I stood **b** the Council,	**Ac 24:20**	*1909*
I am on trial **b** you today.'"	**Ac 24:21**	*1909*
trial **b** me on these *charges?*"	**Ac 25:9**	*1909*
"I am standing **b** Caesar's	**Ac 25:10**	*1909*
Festus laid Paul's case **b** the king,	**Ac 25:14**	
hand over any man **b** the accused	**Ac 25:16**	*4250*
and ordered the man to be brought **b**	**Ac 25:17**	
Therefore I have brought him **b** you	**Ac 25:26**	*4254*
you *all* and especially **b** you,	**Ac 25:26**	*1909*
to make my defense **b** you today;	**Ac 26:2**	*1909*
But **b** very long there rushed down	**Ac 27:14**	
		3326, 3756
and whom I serve stood **b** me,	**Ac 27:23**	*3936*
you must stand **b** Caesar;	**Ac 27:24**	*3936*
hearers of the Law *who* are just **b** God,	**Ro 2:13**	*3844*
IS NO FEAR OF GOD **B** THEIR EYES."	**Ro 3:18**	*561*
to boast about, but not **b** God.	**Ro 4:2**	*4314*
stand **b** the judgment seat of God.	**Ro 14:10**	*3936*
have as your own conviction **b** God.	**Ro 14:22**	*1799*
who also were in Christ **b** me.	**Ro 16:7**	*4253*
that no man may boast **b** God.	**1Co 1:29**	*1799*
predestined **b** the ages to our glory;	**1Co 2:7**	*4253*
this world is foolishness **b** God.	**1Co 3:19**	*3844*
go on passing judgment **b** the time,	**1Co 4:5**	*4253*
to go to law **b** the unrighteous and	**1Co 6:1**	*1909*
unrighteous and not **b** the saints?	**1Co 6:1**	*1909*
brother, and that **b** unbelievers?	**1Co 6:6**	*1909*
eat anything that is set **b** you without	**1Co 10:27**	*3908*
b the judgment seat of Christ,	**2Co 5:10**	*1715*
for I have said **b** that you are in	**2Co 7:3**	*4275b*
b Titus proved to be *the* truth.	**2Co 7:14**	*1909*
Therefore openly **b** the churches	**2Co 8:24**	
		1519, 4383
my God may humiliate me **b** you,	**2Co 12:21**	*4314*
As we have said **b**, so I say again	**Ga 1:9**	*4275b*
to those who were apostles **b** me;	**Ga 1:17**	*4253*
you **b** God that I am not lying.	**Ga 1:20**	*1799*
b whose eyes Jesus Christ was	**Ga 3:1**	*2596*
by the Law **b** God is evident;	**Ga 3:11**	*3844*

But **b** faith came, we were kept in	Ga 3:23	*4253*
Him **b** the foundation of the world,	Eph 1:4	*4253*
be holy and blameless **b** Him.	Eph 1:4	*2714*
mystery, as I wrote **b** in brief.	Eph 3:3	*4270*
I bow my knees **b** the Father,	Eph 3:14	*4314*
you were concerned **b**, but you	Php 4:10	*4218*
He is **b** all things, and in Him	Col 1:17	*4253*
in order to present you **b** Him holy	Col 1:22	*2714*
rejoice **b** our God on your account,	1Th 3:9	*1715*
blame in holiness **b** our God	1Th 3:13	*1715*
told you **b** and solemnly warned *you.*	1Th 4:6	*4275b*
you, hoping to come to you **b** long;	1Tm 3:14	*5035*
evident, going **b** them to judgment;	1Tm 5:24	*4254*
good confession **b** Pontius Pilate,	1Tm 6:13	*1909*
every effort to come **b** winter.	2Tm 4:21	*4253*
a time just as has been said **b**,	Heb 4:7	*4275b*
take hold of the hope set **b** us.	Heb 6:18	*4295*
the witness that **b** his being taken up	Heb 11:5	*4253*
the race that is set **b** us,	Heb 12:1	*4295*
joy set **b** Him endured the cross,	Heb 12:2	*4295*
b the foundation of the world,	1Pe 1:20	*4253*
judgment against them **b** the Lord.	2Pe 2:11	*3844*
and will assure our heart **b** Him	1Jn 3:19	*1715*
us, we have confidence **b** God;	1Jn 3:21	*4314*
confidence which we have **b** Him,	1Jn 5:14	*4314*
testified to your love **b** the church	3Jn 1:6	*1799*
b all time and now and forever.	Jude 1:25	*4253*
Spirits who are **b** His throne,	Rv 1:4	*1799*
stumbling block **b** the sons of Israel,	Rv 2:14	*1799*
will confess his name **b** My Father and	Rv 3:5	*1799*
My Father and **b** His angels.	Rv 3:5	*1799*
I have put **b** you an open door	Rv 3:8	*1799*
of fire burning **b** the throne,	Rv 4:5	*1799*
b the throne *there was something* like	Rv 4:6	*1799*
down **b** Him who sits on the throne,	Rv 4:10	*1799*
cast their crowns **b** the throne,	Rv 4:10	*1799*
elders fell down **b** the Lamb,	Rv 5:8	*1799*
standing **b** the throne and before	Rv 7:9	*1799*
before the throne and **b** the Lamb,	Rv 7:9	*1799*
b the throne and worshiped God,	Rv 7:11	*1799*
they are **b** the throne of God;	Rv 7:15	*1799*
the seven angels who stand **b** God,	Rv 8:2	*1799*
altar which was **b** the throne.	Rv 8:3	*1799*
up **b** God out of the angel's hand.	Rv 8:4	*1799*
the golden altar which is **b** God,	Rv 9:13	*1799*
stand **b** the Lord of the earth.	Rv 11:4	*1799*
who sit on their thrones **b** God,	Rv 11:16	*1799*
And the dragon stood **b** the woman	Rv 12:4	*1799*
them **b** our God day and night.	Rv 12:10	*1799*
they sang a new song **b** the throne	Rv 14:3	*1799*
throne and **b** the four living creatures	Rv 14:3	*1799*
WILL COME AND WORSHIP **B** YOU,	Rv 15:4	*1799*
the great was remembered **b** God,	Rv 16:19	*1799*
the small, standing **b** the throne,	Rv 20:12	*1799*

BEFOREHAND

and did not hate him **b**.	Jos 20:5	4480, 8543, 8032a
do not worry **b** about what you	Mk 13:11	*4305*
anointed My body **b** for the burial.	Mk 14:8	*4301*
to prepare **b** to defend yourselves;	Lk 21:14	*4304*
things which God announced **b**	Ac 3:18	*4293*
who were chosen **b** by God,	Ac 10:41	*4401*
which He promised **b** through His	Ro 1:2	*4279*
which He prepared **b** for glory,	Ro 9:23	*4282*
arrange **b** your previously promised	2Co 9:5	*4294*
preached the gospel **b** to Abraham,	Ga 3:8	*4283*
good works, which God prepared **b** so	Eph 2:10	*4282*
words spoken **b** by the holy prophets	2Pe 3:2	*4275b*
beloved, knowing this **b**,	2Pe 3:17	*4267*
those who were long **b** marked out	Jude 1:4	*4270*
spoken **b** by the apostles of our Lord	Jude 1:17	*4275b*

BEG

"Please forgive, I **b** you,	Gn 50:17	577
"Oh, my lord, I **b** you, do not	Nu 12:11	994a
'Let nothing, I **b** you, hinder you	Nu 22:16	4994
but Haman stayed to **b** for his life	Es 7:7	1245
his children wander about and **b**;	Ps 109:10	7592
I **b** You, do not torment me."	Lk 8:28	*1189a*
I **b** You to look at my son,	Lk 9:38	*1189a*
I am ashamed to **b**.	Lk 16:3	*1871*
'Then I **b** you, father, that you	Lk 16:27	*2065*
the one who used to sit and **b**?"	Jn 9:8	*4319a*
in order to **b** alms of those who	Ac 3:2	*154*
Beautiful Gate of the temple to **b**	Ac 3:10	
and I **b** you, allow me to speak to	Ac 21:39	*1189a*
any further, I **b** you to grant us,	Ac 24:4	*3870*
I **b** you to listen to me patiently.	Ac 26:3	*1189a*
we **b** you on behalf of Christ, be	2Co 5:20	*1189a*
I **b** of you, brethren, become as I	Ga 4:12	*1189a*

BEGAN

Then *men* **b** to call upon the name	Gn 4:26	2490c
when men **b** to multiply on the face	Gn 6:1	2490c
Then Noah **b** farming and planted a	Gn 9:20	2490c
And this is what they **b** to do,	Gn 11:6	2490c
Rachel **b** to give birth and she	Gn 35:16	
seven years of famine **b** to come,	Gn 41:54	2490c
the people **b** to play the harlot	Nu 25:1	2490c
LORD **b** to stir him in Mahaneh-dan,	Jg 13:25	2490c
Then she **b** to afflict him, and his	Jg 16:19	2490c
the hair of his head **b** to grow	Jg 16:22	2490c
As the day **b** to dawn, the woman	Jg 19:26	
and they **b** to strike and kill some	Jg 20:31	2490c
and Benjamin **b** to strike and kill	Jg 20:39	2490c
But when the cloud **b** to rise from	Jg 20:40	2490c
years old when he **b** to reign,	1Sa 13:1	
that he **b** to build the house of	1Ki 6:1	
Asa **b** to reign as king of Judah.	1Ki 15:9	
Jehoram king of Judah **b** to reign.	2Ki 8:25	
In those days the LORD **b** to cut	2Ki 10:32	2490c
In those days the LORD **b** to send	2Ki 15:37	2490c
he **b** to be a mighty one in the	1Ch 1:10	2490c
Then Solomon **b** to build the house	2Ch 3:1	2490c
He **b** to build on the second	2Ch 3:2	2490c
years old when he **b** to reign,	2Ch 12:13	
Abijah **b** the battle with an	2Ch 13:3	631
When they **b** singing and praising,	2Ch 20:22	2490c
Jehoram king of Judah **b** to reign.	2Ch 22:1	
Now they **b** the consecration on the	2Ch 29:17	2490c
When the burnt offering **b**,	2Ch 29:27	2490c
the LORD also **b** with the trumpets,	2Ch 29:27	2490c
month they **b** to make the heaps,	2Ch 31:7	2490c
"Since the contributions **b** to be	2Ch 31:10	2490c
Every work which he **b** in the	2Ch 31:21	2490c
he **b** to seek the God of his father	2Ch 34:3	2490c
and in the twelfth year he **b** to	2Ch 34:3	2490c
they **b** to offer burnt offerings to	Ezr 3:6	2490c
b *the work* and appointed the	Ezr 3:8	2490c
arose and **b** to rebuild the house of	Ezr 5:2	8271
month he **b** to go up from Babylon;	Ezr 7:9	3246
that the breaches **b** to be closed,	Ne 4:7	2490c
and **b** eating grass like cattle,	Da 4:33	
and my nobles **b** seeking me out;	Da 4:36	
a man's hand emerged and **b** writing	Da 5:5	
and his knees **b** knocking together.	Da 5:6	
Then this Daniel **b** distinguishing	Da 6:3	
satraps **b** trying to find a ground	Da 6:4	
b asking him the exact meaning of all	Da 7:16	
when the spring crop **b** to sprout.	Am 7:1	8462
and **b** to consume the farm land.	Am 7:4	
Then Jonah **b** to go through the	Jon 3:4	2490c
angels came and **b** to minister to	Mt 4:11	
time Jesus **b** to preach and say,	Mt 4:17	*757*
He opened His mouth and **b** to	Mt 5:2	
The demons **b** to entreat Him,	Mt 8:31	
Jesus got up and **b** to follow him,	Mt 9:19	
And they **b** laughing at Him.	Mt 9:24	
Jesus **b** to speak to the crowds	Mt 11:7	*757*
Then He **b** to denounce the cities	Mt 11:20	*757*
became hungry and **b** to pick	Mt 12:1	*757*
He came to His hometown and **b**	Mt 13:54	
from that region came out and **b**	Mt 15:22	
But she came and **b** to bow down	Mt 15:25	
b to discuss *this* among themselves,	Mt 16:7	
Jesus **b** to show His disciples	Mt 16:21	*757*
Him aside and **b** to rebuke Him,	Mt 16:22	*757*
and he seized him and **b** to choke	Mt 18:28	
slave fell *to the ground* and **b**	Mt 18:29	
And they **b** reasoning among	Mt 21:25	
they all got drowsy and **b** to	Mt 25:5	
From then on he **b** looking for a	Mt 26:16	
they each one **b** to say to Him,	Mt 26:22	*757*
b to be grieved and distressed.	Mt 26:37	*757*
Then he **b** to curse and swear,	Mt 26:74	*757*
and took the reed and **b** to beat	Mt 27:30	
And sitting down, they **b** to keep	Mt 27:36	
b saying, "This man is calling	Mt 27:47	
as it **b** to dawn toward the first	Mt 28:1	
He entered the synagogue and **b** to	Mk 1:21	
they **b** bringing to Him all who	Mk 1:32	
But he went out and **b** to proclaim	Mk 1:45	*757*
and His disciples **b** to make their	Mk 2:23	*757*
went out and immediately **b**	Mk 3:6	
b speaking to them in parables,	Mk 3:23	
He **b** to teach again by the sea.	Mk 4:1	*757*
b asking Him *about*	Mk 4:10	
And he **b** to implore Him earnestly	Mk 5:10	
And they **b** to implore Him to	Mk 5:17	*757*
And he went away and **b** to proclaim	Mk 5:20	*757*
They **b** laughing at Him.	Mk 5:40	
Immediately the girl got up and **b**	Mk 5:42	
He **b** to teach in the synagogue;	Mk 6:2	*757*
and **b** to send them out in pairs,	Mk 6:7	*757*
He **b** to teach them many things.	Mk 6:34	*757*
b to carry here and there on their pallets	Mk 6:55	*757*
He **b** saying to them, "Listen to	Mk 7:14	
and he **b** speaking plainly.	Mk 7:35	
came out and **b** to argue with Him,	Mk 8:11	*757*
They **b** to discuss with one	Mk 8:16	
and **b** to see everything clearly.	Mk 8:25	
And He **b** to teach them that the	Mk 8:31	*757*
Him aside and **b** to rebuke Him.	Mk 8:32	*757*
they were amazed and **b** running up	Mk 9:15	
he **b** rolling around and foaming	Mk 9:20	
His disciples **b** questioning Him	Mk 9:28	
From there they went out and **b** to	Mk 9:30	
He **b** to question them, "What	Mk 9:33	
He once more **b** to teach them.	Mk 10:1	
and **b** to question Him whether it	Mk 10:2	
the disciples **b** questioning	Mk 10:10	
And He took them in His arms and **b**	Mk 10:16	
Peter **b** to say to Him,	Mk 10:28	*757*
He took the twelve aside and **b** to tell	Mk 10:32	*757*
the ten **b** to feel indignant with	Mk 10:41	*757*
Nazarene, he **b** to cry out and say,	Mk 10:47	*757*
he regained his sight and **b**	Mk 10:52	
And He entered the temple and **b** to	Mk 11:15	*757*
And He **b** to teach and say to them,	Mk 11:17	
and **b** seeking how to destroy Him;	Mk 11:18	
and **b** saying to Him, "By what	Mk 11:28	
They **b** reasoning among themselves,	Mk 11:31	
He **b** to speak to them in parables:	Mk 12:1	*757*
and **b** questioning Him, saying,	Mk 12:18	
And Jesus **b** to say, as He taught	Mk 12:35	
and **b** observing how the people	Mk 12:41	
And Jesus **b** to say to them,	Mk 13:5	*757*
And he **b** seeking how to betray	Mk 14:11	
They **b** to be grieved and to say to	Mk 14:19	*757*
and **b** to be very distressed and	Mk 14:33	*757*
and fell to the ground and **b** to	Mk 14:35	
Some stood up and **b** to give false	Mk 14:57	
Some **b** to spit at Him, and to	Mk 14:65	*757*
and **b** once more to say to the	Mk 14:69	*757*
But he **b** to curse and swear,	Mk 14:71	*757*
Me three times." And he **b** to weep.	Mk 14:72	
The chief priests **b** to accuse Him	Mk 15:3	
The crowd went up and **b**	Mk 15:8	*757*
and they **b** to acclaim Him,	Mk 15:18	*757*
they **b** saying, "Behold, He is	Mk 15:35	
and he **b** to speak in praise of	Lk 1:64	
the shepherds **b** saying to one	Lk 2:15	
that very moment she came up and **b**	Lk 2:38	
and they **b** looking for Him among	Lk 2:44	
So he **b** saying to the crowds who	Lk 3:7	
When He **b** His ministry, Jesus	Lk 3:23	*757*
And He **b** teaching in their	Lk 4:15	
And He **b** to say to them,	Lk 4:21	*757*
and they **b** talking with one	Lk 4:36	
And He sat down and **b** teaching	Lk 5:3	
and their nets **b** to break;	Lk 5:6	
the boats, so that they **b** to sink.	Lk 5:7	
and the Pharisees **b** to reason,	Lk 5:21	*757*
all struck with astonishment and **b**	Lk 5:26	
and got up and **b** to follow Him.	Lk 5:28	
The Pharisees and their scribes **b**	Lk 5:30	
He **b** to say, "Blessed *are*	Lk 6:20	
dead man sat up and **b** to speak.	Lk 7:15	*757*
Fear gripped them all, and they **b**	Lk 7:16	
He **b** to speak to the crowds	Lk 7:24	*757*
she **b** to wet His feet with her	Lk 7:38	*757*
with Him **b** to say to themselves,	Lk 7:49	*757*
Soon afterwards, He **b** going	Lk 8:1	
His disciples **b** questioning Him	Lk 8:9	
and they **b** to be swamped and to	Lk 8:23	
and **b** to implore Him to come to	Lk 8:41	
And they **b** laughing at Him,	Lk 8:53	
Departing, they **b** going	Lk 9:6	
He **b** speaking to them about	Lk 9:11	
a cloud formed and **b** to	Lk 9:34	
were increasing, He **b** to say,	Lk 11:29	*757*
the Pharisees **b** to be very hostile	Lk 11:53	*757*
He **b** saying to His disciples first	Lk 12:1	*757*
"And he **b** reasoning to himself,	Lk 12:17	
And He **b** telling this parable:	Lk 13:6	
she was made erect again and **b**	Lk 13:13	
b saying to the crowd in response,	Lk 13:14	
And He **b** speaking a parable to	Lk 14:7	
they all alike **b** to make excuses.	Lk 14:18	*757*
'This man **b** to build and was not	Lk 14:30	*757*
the Pharisees and the scribes **b**	Lk 15:2	
country, and he **b** to be impoverished.	Lk 15:14	*757*
And they **b** to celebrate.	Lk 15:24	*757*
summoned one of the servants and **b**	Lk 15:26	
and his father came out and **b**	Lk 15:28	
and he **b** saying to the first,	Lk 16:5	
they **b** rebuking them.	Lk 18:15	
Now hearing a crowd going by, he **b**	Lk 18:36	
he regained his sight and **b**	Lk 18:43	
When they saw it, they all **b** to	Lk 19:7	
disciples **b** to praise God joyfully	Lk 19:37	*757*
entered the temple and **b** to drive out	Lk 19:45	*757*
And He **b** to tell the people this	Lk 20:9	*757*
So he consented, and **b** seeking a	Lk 22:6	
And they **b** to discuss among	Lk 22:23	*757*
and He knelt down and **b** to pray,	Lk 22:41	
another man **b** to insist, saying,	Lk 22:59	
And they **b** to accuse Him, saying,	Lk 23:2	*757*
And their voices **b** to prevail.	Lk 23:23	
he **b** praising God, saying,	Lk 23:47	
b to return, beating their	Lk 23:48	
Jesus Himself approached and **b**	Lk 24:15	
He **b** giving *it* to them.	Lk 24:30	
They **b** to relate their	Lk 24:35	
the hour when he **b** to get better.	Jn 4:52	
and picked up his pallet and **b** to	Jn 5:9	
The sea **b** to be stirred up	Jn 6:18	
Then the Jews **b** to argue with one	Jn 6:52	
the temple, and **b** *to* teach.	Jn 7:14	
and He sat down and **b** to teach	Jn 8:2	
When they heard it, they **b** to go	Jn 8:9	
and **b** to shout, "Hosanna!	Jn 12:13	
and **b** *to* ask him, saying, "Sir,	Jn 12:21	
and **b** to wash the disciples' feet and	Jn 13:5	*757*
The disciples **b** looking at one	Jn 13:22	
and they **b** to come up to Him	Jn 19:3	
all that Jesus **b** to do and teach,	Ac 1:1	*757*
and **b** to speak with other tongues,	Ac 2:4	*757*
and they **b** selling their property	Ac 2:45	
he **b** asking to receive alms.	Ac 3:3	
And he **b** to give them his	Ac 3:5	
With a leap he stood upright and **b**	Ac 3:8	
they **b** *to* inquire, "By what	Ac 4:7	
and **b** to recognize them as having	Ac 4:13	
they **b** to confer with one another,	Ac 4:15	
filled with the Holy Spirit and **b**	Ac 4:31	
the temple about daybreak and **b**	Ac 5:21	
and they **b** gnashing their teeth	Ac 7:54	
they **b** stoning *him;*	Ac 7:58	
And on that day a great persecution **b**	Ac 8:1	*1096*
But Saul **b** ravaging the church,	Ac 8:3	
down to the city of Samaria and **b**	Ac 8:5	
Then they **b** laying their hands on	Ac 8:17	
and immediately he **b** to proclaim	Ac 9:20	
But Peter **b** *speaking* and *proceeded*	Ac 11:4	*757*
"And as I **b** to speak, the Holy	Ac 11:15	*757*
who came to Antioch and **b**	Ac 11:20	
he rejoiced and **b** to encourage	Ac 11:23	

of them named Agabus stood up and **b**	**Ac 11:28**	
took his seat on the rostrum and **b**	**Ac 12:21**	
When they reached Salamis, they **b**	**Ac 13:5**	
were filled with jealousy and **b**	**Ac 13:45**	
they **b** rejoicing and glorifying	**Ac 13:48**	
And he leaped up and **b** to walk.	**Ac 14:10**	
And they **b** calling Barnabas,	**Ac 14:12**	
they **b** to report all things that	**Ac 14:27**	
Some men came down from Judea and **b**	**Ac 15:1**	
and we sat down and **b** speaking to	**Ac 16:13**	
they **b** dragging Jason and some	**Ac 17:6**	
some **b** to sneer, but others said,	**Ac 17:32**	
Paul **b** devoting himself	**Ac 18:5**	
and **b** beating him in front of	**Ac 18:17**	
and he **b** to speak out boldly in	**Ac 18:26**	*757*
and they **b** speaking with tongues	**Ac 19:6**	
brought their books together and **b**	**Ac 19:19**	
they **b** crying out, saying,	**Ac 19:28**	
Paul **b** talking to them,	**Ac 20:7**	
And they **b** to weep aloud	**Ac 20:37**	
we as well as the local residents **b**	**Ac 21:12**	
After he had greeted them, he **b**	**Ac 21:19**	
And when they heard it they **b**	**Ac 21:20**	
b to stir up all the crowd	**Ac 21:27**	
and he **b** asking who he was	**Ac 21:33**	
Paul **b** crying out in the Council,	**Ac 23:6**	
the Pharisaic party stood up and **b**	**Ac 23:9**	
b to inquire of him privately,	**Ac 23:19**	
Tertullus **b** to accuse him,	**Ac 24:2**	*757*
they **b** bringing charges against	**Ac 25:18**	
they **b** talking to one another,	**Ac 26:31**	
Paul **b** to admonish them,	**Ac 27:9**	
they weighed anchor and **b** sailing	**Ac 27:13**	
they **b** to jettison the cargo;	**Ac 27:18**	
about midnight the sailors **b** to	**Ac 27:27**	
and he broke it and **b** to eat.	**Ac 27:35**	*757*
When they had eaten enough, they **b**	**Ac 27:38**	
but the stern **b** to be broken up	**Ac 27:41**	
they **b** saying to one another,	**Ac 28:4**	
they changed their minds and **b** to	**Ac 28:6**	
he **b** saying to them, "Brethren,	**Ac 28:17**	
they **b** leaving after Paul had	**Ac 28:25**	
he **b** to withdraw and hold himself	**Ga 2:12**	
that He who **b** a good work in you	**Php 1:6**	*1728*
Then I **b** to weep greatly because	**Rv 5:4**	
BEGET		
issue from you, whom you will **b**,	**2Ki 20:18**	3205
issue from you, whom you will **b**,	**Is 39:7**	3205
fathers who **b** them in this land:	**Jer 16:3**	3205
BEGETTING		
says to a father, 'What are you **b**?'	**Is 45:10**	3205
BEGGAR		
a blind **b** *named* Bartimaeus,	**Mk 10:46**	*4319b*
who previously saw him as a **b**,	**Jn 9:8**	*4319b*
BEGGED		
Elijah, and **b** him and said to him,	**2Ki 1:13**	2603a
and **b** with *all* his soul to die,	**Jon 4:8**	7592
I **b** Your disciples to cast it out,	**Lk 9:40**	*1189a*
those who heard **b** that no further	**Heb 12:19**	*3868*
BEGGING		
Or his descendants **b** bread.	**Ps 37:25**	1245
b Him that he might accompany Him	**Lk 8:38**	*1189a*
man was sitting by the road **b**.	**Lk 18:35**	*1871*
the people kept **b** that these	**Ac 13:42**	*3870*
kept **b** them to leave the city.	**Ac 16:39**	*2065*
b him not to go up to Jerusalem.	**Ac 21:12**	*3870*
b us with much urging for the	**2Co 8:4**	*1189a*
BEGIN		
b to take possession and contend	**Dt 2:24**	2490c
'This day I will **b** to put the	**Dt 2:25**	2490c
B to occupy, that you may possess	**Dt 2:31**	2490c
you shall **b** to count seven weeks	**Dt 16:9**	2490c
the time you **b** to put the sickle to	**Dt 16:9**	2490c
another man would **b** to use its fruit.	**Dt 20:6**	2490c
"This day I will **b** to exalt you	**Jos 3:7**	2490c
the man who will **b** to fight against	**Jg 10:18**	2490c
and he shall **b** to deliver Israel	**Jg 13:5**	2490c
"Did I *just* **b** to inquire of God	**1Sa 22:15**	2490c
"Who shall **b** the battle?"	**1Ki 20:14**	631
And they will **b** to diminish	**Hos 8:10**	2490c
and do not **b** to say to yourselves,	**Lk 3:8**	*757*
and you **b** to stand outside and	**Lk 13:25**	*757*
"Then you will **b** to say,	**Lk 13:26**	*757*
who observe it **b** to ridicule him,	**Lk 14:29**	*757*
when these things **b** to take place,	**Lk 21:28**	*757*
will **b** TO SAY TO THE MOUNTAINS,	**Lk 23:30**	*757*
and the Sabbath was about to **b**.	**Lk 23:54**	*2020*
who were the first to **b** a year ago	**2Co 8:10**	*4278*
to **b** with the household of God;	**1Pe 4:17**	*757*
BEGINNING		
In the **b** God created the heavens	**Gn 1:1**	7225
The **b** of his kingdom was Babel	**Gn 10:10**	7225
where his tent had been at the **b**,	**Gn 13:3**	8462
b with the oldest and ending with	**Gn 44:12**	2490c
My might and the **b** of my strength,	**Gn 49:3**	7225
shall be the **b** of months for you;	**Ex 12:2**	7218
'Then at the **b** of each of your	**Nu 28:11**	7218
the **b** even to the end of the year.	**Dt 11:12**	7225
for he is the **b** of his strength;	**Dt 21:17**	7225
camp at the **b** of the middle watch,	**Jg 7:19**	7218
at the **b** of barley harvest.	**Ru 1:22**	8462
his house, from **b** to end.	**1Sa 3:12**	2490c
at the **b** of barley harvest.	**2Sa 21:9**	8462
from the **b** of harvest until it	**2Sa 21:10**	8462
At the **b** of their living there,	**2Ki 17:25**	8462
Ahasuerus, in the **b** of his reign,	**Ezr 4:6**	8462
in **b** the thanksgiving at prayer,	**Ne 11:17**	8462
"Though your **b** was insignificant,	**Jb 8:7**	7225
days of Job more than his **b**;	**Jb 42:12**	7225
of the LORD is the **b** of wisdom;	**Ps 111:10**	7225
of the LORD is the **b** of knowledge;	**Pr 1:7**	7225
"The **b** of wisdom *is:*	**Pr 4:7**	7225
possessed me at the **b** of His way,	**Pr 8:22**	7225
I was established, From the **b**,	**Pr 8:23**	7218
fear of the LORD is the **b** of wisdom,	**Pr 9:10**	8462
The **b** of strife is *like* letting	**Pr 17:14**	7225
gained hurriedly at the **b** Will	**Pr 20:21**	7223
done from the **b** even to the end.	**Ec 3:11**	7218
of a matter is better than its **b**;	**Ec 7:8**	7225
the **b** of his talking is folly and	**Ec 10:13**	8462
And your counselors as at the **b**;	**Is 1:26**	8462
been declared to you from the **b**?	**Is 40:21**	7218
forth the generations from the **b**?	**Is 41:4**	7218
Who has declared *this* from the **b**,	**Is 41:26**	7218
Declaring the end from the **b**,	**Is 46:10**	7225
b Is the place of our sanctuary.	**Jer 17:12**	7223
I am **b** to work calamity in *this*	**Jer 25:29**	2490c
In the **b** of the reign of Jehoiakim	**Jer 26:1**	7225
In the **b** of the reign of Zedekiah	**Jer 27:1**	7225
in the **b** of the reign of Zedekiah	**Jer 28:1**	7225
at the **b** of the reign of Zedekiah	**Jer 49:34**	7225
At the **b** of the night watches;	**La 2:19**	7218
your shrine at the **b** of every street	**Ezk 16:31**	7218
our exile, at the **b** of the year,	**Ezk 40:1**	7218
"At the **b** of your supplications	**Da 9:23**	8462
the **b** of sin To the daughter of Zion	**Mi 1:13**	7225
he became frightened, and **b** to sink,	**Mt 14:30**	*757*
the **b** MADE THEM MALE AND FEMALE	**Mt 19:4**	*746*
from the **b** it has not been this way.	**Mt 19:8**	*746*
b with the last *group* to the first.'	**Mt 20:8**	*757*
are *merely* the **b** of birth pangs.	**Mt 24:8**	*746*
the **b** of the world until now,	**Mt 24:21**	*746*
b of the gospel of Jesus Christ,	**Mk 1:1**	*746*
"But from the **b** of creation, *God*	**Mk 10:6**	*746*
are *merely* the **b** of birth pangs.	**Mk 13:8**	*746*
since the **b** of the creation which	**Mk 13:19**	*746*
by those who from the **b** were	**Lk 1:2**	*746*
everything carefully from the **b**,	**Lk 1:3**	*509*
Then **b** with Moses and with all the	**Lk 24:27**	*757*
all the nations, **b** from Jerusalem.	**Lk 24:47**	*757*
In the **b** was the Word, and the	**Jn 1:1**	*746*
He was in the **b** with God.	**Jn 1:2**	*746*
This **b** of *His* signs Jesus did in	**Jn 2:11**	*746*
For Jesus knew from the **b** who they	**Jn 6:64**	*746*
one by one, **b** with the older ones,	**Jn 8:9**	*757*
I been saying to you *from* the **b**?	**Jn 8:25**	*746*
He was a murderer from the **b**,	**Jn 8:44**	*746*
"Since the **b** of time it has never	**Jn 9:32**	*165*
you have been with Me from the **b**.	**Jn 15:27**	*746*
I did not say to you at the **b**,	**Jn 16:4**	*746*
b with the baptism of John until	**Ac 1:22**	*757*
and **b** from this Scripture he	**Ac 8:35**	*757*
just as *He did* upon us at the **b**.	**Ac 11:15**	*746*
which from the **b** was spent among	**Ac 26:4**	*746*
we **b** to commend ourselves again?	**2Co 3:1**	*757*
as he had previously made a **b**,	**2Co 8:6**	*4278*
and He is the **b**, the firstborn	**Col 1:18**	*746*
God has chosen you from the **b** for	**2Th 2:13**	*746*
IN THE **B** LAID THE FOUNDATION	**Heb 1:10**	*746*
if we hold fast the **b** of our	**Heb 3:14**	*746*
neither **b** of days nor end of life,	**Heb 7:3**	*746*
it was from the **b** of creation."	**2Pe 3:4**	*746*
What was from the **b**,	**1Jn 1:1**	*746*
which you have had from the **b**;	**1Jn 2:7**	*746*
know Him who has been from the **b**.	**1Jn 2:13**	*746*
know Him who has been from the **b**.	**1Jn 2:14**	*746*
in you which you heard from the **b**.	**1Jn 2:24**	*746*
heard from the **b** abides in you,	**1Jn 2:24**	*746*
the devil has sinned from the **b**.	**1Jn 3:8**	*746*
which you have heard from the **b**,	**1Jn 3:11**	*746*
one which we have had from the **b**,	**2Jn 1:5**	*746*
just as you have heard from the **b**,	**2Jn 1:6**	*746*
the **B** of the creation of God,	**Rv 3:14**	*746*
and the Omega, the **b** and the end.	**Rv 21:6**	*746*
and the last, the **b** and the end."	**Rv 22:13**	*746*
BEGINS		
and **b** to beat his fellow slaves	**Mt 24:49**	*757*
coming,' and **b** to beat the slaves,	**Lk 12:45**	*757*
and if *it* **b** with us first,	**1Pe 4:17**	
BEGOT		
"You neglected the Rock who **b** you,	**Dt 32:18**	3205
Listen to your father who **b** you,	**Pr 23:22**	3205
BEGOTTEN		
Or who has **b** the drops of dew?	**Jb 38:28**	3205
are My Son, Today I have **b** You.	**Ps 2:7**	3205
'Who has **b** these for me, Since I	**Is 49:21**	3205
as of the only **b** from the Father,	**Jn 1:14**	*3439*
the only **b** God who is in the	**Jn 1:18**	*3439*
that He gave His only **b** Son,	**Jn 3:16**	*3439*
the name of the only **b** Son of God.	**Jn 3:18**	*3439*
TODAY I HAVE **B** YOU.'	**Ac 13:33**	*1080*
whom I have **b** in my imprisonment,	**Phm 1:10**	*1080*
ARE MY SON, TODAY I HAVE **B** YOU"?	**Heb 1:5**	*1080*
ARE MY SON, TODAY I HAVE **B** YOU";	**Heb 5:5**	*1080*
was offering up his only **b** *son;*	**Heb 11:17**	*3439*
that God has sent His only **b** Son	**1Jn 4:9**	*3439*
BEGS		
So he **b** during the harvest and has	**Pr 20:4**	7592
BEGUN		
from the LORD, the plague has **b**!"	**Nu 16:46**	2490c
the plague had **b** among the people.	**Nu 16:47**	2490c
I have **b** to deliver Sihon and his	**Dt 2:31**	2490c
You have **b** to show Your servant	**Dt 3:24**	2490c
and has not **b** to use its fruit?	**Dt 20:6**	2490c
his eyesight had **b** to grow dim	**1Sa 3:2**	2490c
of Zeruiah had **b** to count *them,*	**1Ch 27:24**	2490c
before whom you have **b** to fall,	**Es 6:13**	2490c
"When he had **b** to settle	**Mt 18:24**	*757*
brother of yours was dead and *has* **b**	**Lk 15:32**	
Having **b** by the Spirit, are you	**Ga 3:3**	*1728*
great power and have **b** to reign.	**Rv 11:17**	
BEHALF		
to the LORD on **b** of his wife,	**Gn 25:21**	5227
him to make atonement on his **b**.	**Lv 1:4**	5921
atonement on his **b** for his sin.	**Lv 5:6**	5921
make atonement on his **b** for his sin	**Lv 5:10**	5921
day, to make atonement on your **b**.	**Lv 8:34**	5921
on his **b** before the LORD.	**Lv 14:18**	5921
on his **b** before the LORD.	**Lv 14:29**	5921
on **b** of the one to be cleansed.	**Lv 14:31**	5921
atonement on his **b** before the LORD	**Lv 15:15**	5921
atonement on her **b** before the LORD	**Lv 15:30**	5921
your **b** before the LORD your God.	**Lv 23:28**	5921
on **b** of the sons of Israel,	**Nu 8:19**	5921
you will Himself fight on your **b**,	**Dt 1:30**	
spoke all these words on his **b**	**Jg 9:3**	5921
salvation of the LORD on your **b**,	**2Ch 20:17**	5973
on **b** of the sons of Israel Your	**Ne 1:6**	5921
who spoke good on **b** of the king!"	**Es 7:9**	5921
is yet more to be said in God's **b**.	**Jb 36:2**	
O God, who have acted on our **b**.	**Ps 68:28**	
Remember, O LORD, on David's **b**,	**Ps 132:1**	
the dead on **b** of the living?	**Is 8:19**	1157
in **b** of the one who waits for Him.	**Is 64:4**	
So I will act on **b** of My servants	**Is 65:8**	4616
You To speak good on their **b**,	**Jer 18:20**	5921
inquire of the LORD on our **b**,	**Jer 21:2**	1157
and pray to the LORD on its **b**;	**Jer 29:7**	1157
to the LORD our God on our **b**."	**Jer 37:3**	1157
in **b** of the holy mountain of my God	**Da 9:20**	5921
b of My people and My inheritance,	**Jl 3:2**	5921
gifts On **b** of Moresheth-gath;	**Mi 1:14**	5921
"This is He on **b** of whom I said,	**Jn 1:30**	*5228*
will request of the Father on your **b**;	**Jn 16:26**	*4012*
"I ask on their **b**;	**Jn 17:9**	*4012*
I do not ask on **b** of the world,	**Jn 17:9**	*4012*
"I do not ask on **b** of these alone,	**Jn 17:20**	*4012*
one man to die on **b** of the people.	**Jn 18:14**	*5228*
on **b** of the truth of God to confirm	**Ro 15:8**	*5228*
in **b** of one against the other.	**1Co 4:6**	*5228*
on our **b** for the favor bestowed on	**2Co 1:11**	*5228*
died and rose again on their **b**.	**2Co 5:15**	*5228*
we beg you on **b** of Christ, be	**2Co 5:20**	*5228*
knew no sin *to be* sin on our **b**,	**2Co 5:21**	*5228*
great is my boasting on your **b**.	**2Co 7:4**	*5228*
your earnestness on our **b** might be	**2Co 7:12**	*5228*
on your **b** in the heart of Titus.	**2Co 8:16**	*5228*
they also, by prayer on your **b**,	**2Co 9:14**	*5228*
On **b** of such a man I will boast;	**2Co 12:5**	*5228*
but on my own **b** I will not boast,	**2Co 12:5**	*5228*
at my tribulations on your **b**,	**Eph 3:13**	*5228*
and *pray* on my **b**, that utterance	**Eph 6:19**	*5228*
servant of Christ on our **b**,	**Col 1:7**	*5228*
I do my share on **b** of His body	**Col 1:24**	*5228*
great a struggle I have on your **b** and	**Col 2:1**	*5228*
be made on **b** of all men,	**1Tm 2:1**	*5228*
that on your **b** he might minister	**Phm 1:13**	*5228*
b of men in things pertaining to God,	**Heb 5:1**	*5228*
BEHAVE		
b thus toward the LORD your God,	**Dt 12:31**	6213a
Let us **b** properly as in the day,	**Ro 13:13**	*4043*
so that you will **b** properly toward	**1Th 4:12**	*4043*
BEHAVED		
that David **b** himself more wisely	**1Sa 18:30**	7919a
iniquity, we have **b** wickedly.	**Ps 106:6**	7561
so proud that he **b** arrogantly,	**Da 5:20**	2103
we **b** toward you believers;	**1Th 2:10**	*1096*
BEHAVING		
you see the man **b** as a madman.	**1Sa 21:14**	7696
BEHAVIOR		
To receive instruction in wise **b**,	**Pr 1:3**	7919a
not a cause of fear for good **b**,	**Ro 13:3**	*2041*
are to be reverent in their **b**,	**Ti 2:3**	*2688*
Let him show by his good **b** his	**Jas 3:13**	*391*
yourselves also in all *your* **b**;	**1Pe 1:15**	*391*
b excellent among the Gentiles,	**1Pe 2:12**	*391*
a word by the **b** of their wives,	**1Pe 3:1**	*391*
your chaste and respectful **b**.	**1Pe 3:2**	*391*
who revile your good **b** in Christ	**1Pe 3:16**	*391*
BEHEADED		
him and killed him and **b** him.	**2Sa 4:7**	5493, 7218
sent and had John **b** in the prison.	**Mt 14:10**	*607*
"John, whom I **b**, has risen!"	**Mk 6:16**	*607*
went and had him **b** in the prison,	**Mk 6:27**	*607*
"I myself had John **b**;	**Lk 9:9**	*607*
saw the souls of those who had been **b**	**Rv 20:4**	*3990*
BEHELD		
for You have **b** mischief and	**Ps 10:14**	5027
BEHEMOTH		
"Behold now, **B**, which I made as	**Jb 40:15**	930
BEHIND		
and the LORD closed *it* **b** him.	**Gn 7:16**	1157
at the tent door, which was **b** him.	**Gn 18:10**	310
doorway, and shut the door **b** him,	**Gn 19:6**	310
Do not look **b** you, and do not stay	**Gn 19:17**	310
But his wife, from **b** him,	**Gn 19:26**	310
b *him* a ram caught in the thicket	**Gn 22:13**	310
And behold, he also is **b** us.' "	**Gn 32:18**	310
servant Jacob also is **b** us.' "	**Gn 32:20**	310
it that you have left the man **b**?	**Ex 2:20**	5800a
not a hoof shall be left **b**,	**Ex 10:26**	7604

girl who is **b** the millstones;	**Ex 11:5**	310
of Israel, moved and went **b** them;	**Ex 14:19**	4480, 310
from before them and stood **b** them.	**Ex 14:19**	4480, 310
to camp **b** the tabernacle westward,	**Nu 3:23**	310
Set an ambush for the city **b** it."	**Jos 8:2**	4480, 310
to ambush the city from **b** it.	**Jos 8:4**	310
an ambush against him **b** the city.	**Jos 8:14**	4480, 310
doors of the roof chamber **b** him,	**Jg 3:23**	1157
of smoke, Benjamin looked **b** them;	**Jg 20:40**	310
coming from the field **b** the oxen,	**1Sa 11:5**	310
feet, with his armor bearer **b** him;	**1Sa 14:13**	310
is wrapped in a cloth **b** the ephod;	**1Sa 21:9**	310
And when Saul looked **b** him,	**1Sa 24:8**	310
four hundred men went up **b** David	**1Sa 25:13**	310
where those left **b** remained.	**1Sa 30:9**	3498
to cross the brook Besor remained **b**.	**1Sa 30:10**	
and my master left me **b** when I	**1Sa 30:13**	5800a
"When he looked **b** him,	**2Sa 1:7**	310
Then Abner looked **b** him and said,	**2Sa 2:20**	310
gathered together **b** Abner	**2Sa 2:25**	310
And King David walked **b** the bier.	**2Sa 3:31**	310
circle around **b** them and come at	**2Sa 5:23**	310
and lock the door **b** her."	**2Sa 13:17**	310
her out and locked the door **b** her.	**2Sa 13:18**	310
people were coming from the road **b**	**2Sa 13:34**	310
and have cast Me **b** your back	**1Ki 14:9**	310
When he looked **b** him and saw them,	**2Ki 2:24**	310
shut the door **b** you and your sons,	**2Ki 4:4**	1157
shut the door **b** her and her sons;	**2Ki 4:5**	1157
of God, and shut *the door* **b** him and	**2Ki 4:21**	1157
and shut the door **b** them both and	**2Ki 4:33**	1157
sound of his master's feet **b** him?"	**2Ki 6:32**	310
Turn **b** me." And the watchman	**2Ki 9:18**	413, 310
you to do with peace? Turn **b** me,"	**2Ki 9:19**	413, 310
third at the gate **b** the guards),	**2Ki 11:6**	310
She has shaken *her* head **b** you,	**2Ki 19:21**	310
circle around **b** them and come at	**1Ch 14:14**	4480, 5921
Judah and the ambush was **b** them.	**2Ch 13:13**	4480, 310
parts of the space **b** the wall,	**Ne 4:13**	310
were **b** the whole house of Judah.	**Ne 4:16**	310
And cast Your law **b** their backs And	**Ne 9:26**	310
"**B** him he makes a wake to shine;	**Jb 41:32**	310
And you cast My words **b** you.	**Ps 50:17**	310
have enclosed me **b** and before,	**Ps 139:5**	268
Behold, he is standing **b** our wall,	**SS 2:9**	310
eyes are *like* doves **b** your veil;	**SS 4:1**	4480, 1157
of a pomegranate **B** your veil.	**SS 4:3**	4480, 1157
of a pomegranate **B** your veil.	**SS 6:7**	4480, 1157
rooms And close your doors **b** you;	**Is 26:20**	1157
Your ears will hear a word **b** you,	**Is 30:21**	4480, 310
She has shaken *her* head **b** you,	**Is 37:22**	310
have cast all my sins **b** Your back.	**Is 38:17**	310
They will walk **b** you, they will	**Is 45:14**	310
"**B** the door and the doorpost You	**Is 57:8**	310
left **b** in the land of Judah,	**Jer 39:10**	7604
"Leave your orphans **b**,	**Jer 49:11**	5800a
heard a great rumbling sound **b** me,	**Ezk 3:12**	310
I will unsheathe a sword **b** them.	**Ezk 5:2**	310
I will unsheathe a sword **b** them.	**Ezk 5:12**	310
Me and cast Me **b** your back,	**Ezk 23:35**	310
left **b** will fall by the sword.	**Ezk 24:21**	5800a
front of the separate area **b** it,	**Ezk 41:15**	5921, 310
"**B** you, Benjamin!"	**Hos 5:8**	310
them And **b** them a flame burns.	**Jl 2:3**	310
But a desolate wilderness **b** them,	**Jl 2:3**	310
And leave a blessing **b** Him,	**Jl 2:14**	310
sorrel and white horses **b** him.	**Zch 1:8**	310
Thus the land is desolated **b** them so	**Zch 7:14**	310
came up **b** Him and touched the	**Mt 9:20**	*3693*
"Get **b** Me, Satan!	**Mt 16:23**	*3694*
Jesus, she came up in the crowd **b** *Him*	**Mk 5:27**	*3693*
"Get **b** Me, Satan;	**Mk 8:33**	*3694*
BROTHER DIES and leaves **b** a wife	**Mk 12:19**	*2641*
and died leaving **b** no children;	**Mk 12:21**	*2641*
boy Jesus stayed **b** in Jerusalem.	**Lk 2:43**	*5278*
And he left everything **b**,	**Lk 5:28**	*2641*
and standing **b** *Him* at His feet,	**Lk 7:38**	*3694*
came up **b** Him and touched the	**Lk 8:44**	*3693*
on him the cross to carry **b** Jesus.	**Lk 23:26**	*3693*
not lagging **b** in diligence,	**Ro 12:11**	*3636*
forgetting what *lies* **b** and	**Php 3:13**	*3694*
best to be left **b** at Athens alone,	**1Th 3:1**	*2641*
B the second veil there was a	**Heb 9:3**	*3326*
and I heard **b** me a loud voice like	**Rv 1:10**	*3694*
full of eyes in front and **b**.	**Rv 4:6**	*3693*

BEHOLD

"**B**, I have given you every plant	**Gn 1:29**	2009
He had made, and **b**, it was very good.	**Gn 1:31**	2009
"**B**, the man has become like one	**Gn 3:22**	2005
"**B**, You have driven me this day	**Gn 4:14**	2005
and **b**, it was corrupt; for all flesh	**Gn 6:12**	2009
and **b**, I am about to destroy them	**Gn 6:13**	2009
"**B**, I, even I am bringing	**Gn 6:17**	2009
and **b**, in her beak was a freshly	**Gn 8:11**	2009
b, the surface of the ground was dried	**Gn 8:13**	2009
"Now **b**, I Myself do establish My	**Gn 9:9**	2009
"**B**, they are one people, and they	**Gn 11:6**	2005
Then **b**, the word of the LORD came	**Gn 15:4**	2009
and **b**, terror *and* great darkness	**Gn 15:12**	2009
and **b**, *there appeared* a smoking oven	**Gn 15:17**	2009
"Now **b**, the LORD has prevented me	**Gn 16:2**	2009
"**B**, your maid is in your power;	**Gn 16:6**	2009
"**B**, you are with child, And you	**Gn 16:11**	2009
b, it is between Kadesh and Bered.	**Gn 16:14**	2009
"As for Me, **b**, My covenant is	**Gn 17:4**	2009
b, I will bless him, and will make	**Gn 17:20**	2009
b, three men were standing opposite	**Gn 18:2**	2009
and **b**, Sarah your wife will have	**Gn 18:10**	2009
"Now **b**, I have ventured to speak	**Gn 18:27**	2009
"Now **b**, I have ventured to speak	**Gn 18:31**	2009
"Now **b**, my lords, please turn	**Gn 19:2**	2009
"Now **b**, I have two daughters who	**Gn 19:8**	2009
"Now **b**, your servant has found	**Gn 19:19**	2009
now **b**, this town is near *enough* to	**Gn 19:20**	2009
"**B**, I grant you this request	**Gn 19:21**	2009
b, the smoke of the land ascended	**Gn 19:28**	2009
"**B**, I lay last night with my	**Gn 19:34**	2005
"**B**, you are a dead man because of	**Gn 20:3**	2009
"**B**, my land is before you;	**Gn 20:15**	2009
"**B**, I have given your brother a	**Gn 20:16**	2009
b, it is your vindication before	**Gn 20:16**	2009
"**B**, the fire and the wood, but	**Gn 22:7**	2009
and **b**, behind *him* a ram caught	**Gn 22:13**	2009
"**B**, Milcah also has borne	**Gn 22:20**	2009
"**B**, I am standing by the spring,	**Gn 24:13**	2009
b, Rebekah who was born to Bethuel	**Gn 24:15**	2009
and **b**, he was standing by the	**Gn 24:30**	2009
b, I am standing by the spring,	**Gn 24:43**	2009
b, Rebekah came out with her jar	**Gn 24:45**	2009
looked, and **b**, camels were coming.	**Gn 24:63**	2009
b, there were twins in her womb.	**Gn 25:24**	2009
"**B**, I am about to die;	**Gn 25:32**	2009
and **b**, Isaac was caressing his wife	**Gn 26:8**	2009
"**B**, certainly she is your wife!	**Gn 26:9**	2009
"**B** now, I am old *and* I do not	**Gn 27:2**	2009
"**B**, I heard your father speak to	**Gn 27:6**	2009
"**B**, Esau my brother is a hairy	**Gn 27:11**	2005
b, now he has taken away my blessing	**Gn 27:36**	2009
"**B**, I have made him your master,	**Gn 27:37**	2005
"**B**, away from the fertility of	**Gn 27:39**	2009
"**B** your brother Esau is consoling	**Gn 27:42**	2009
had a dream, and **b**, a ladder was set	**Gn 28:12**	2009
and **b**, the angels of God were	**Gn 28:12**	2009
And **b**, the LORD stood above it and	**Gn 28:13**	2009
"**B**, I am with you and will keep you	**Gn 28:15**	2009
and **b**, three flocks of sheep were lying	**Gn 29:2**	2009
"**B**, it is still high day;	**Gn 29:7**	2005
b, it was Leah! And he said to Laban,	**Gn 29:25**	2009
and **b**, it was not *friendly* toward him	**Gn 31:2**	2009
b, the male goats which were mating	**Gn 31:10**	2009
"**B** this heap and behold the	**Gn 31:51**	2009
b the pillar which I have set between	**Gn 31:51**	2009
And **b**, he also is behind us.'"	**Gn 32:18**	2009
'**B**, your servant Jacob also is	**Gn 32:20**	2009
and **b**, Esau was coming, and four	**Gn 33:1**	2009
b, the land is large enough for them.	**Gn 34:21**	2009
for **b**, we were binding sheaves in	**Gn 37:7**	2009
and **b**, your sheaves gathered	**Gn 37:7**	2009
and **b**, the sun and the moon and	**Gn 37:9**	2009
and **b**, he was wandering in the field;	**Gn 37:15**	2009
b, a caravan of Ishmaelites was	**Gn 37:25**	2009
and **b**, Joseph was not in the pit;	**Gn 37:29**	2009
"**B**, your father-in-law is going	**Gn 38:13**	2009
b, she is also with child by harlotry."	**Gn 38:24**	2009
that **b**, there were twins in her womb.	**Gn 38:27**	2009
that **b**, his brother came out.	**Gn 38:29**	2009
"**B**, with me *here*, my master does	**Gn 39:8**	2005
b, they were dejected.	**Gn 40:6**	2009
"In my dream, **b**, *there was* a vine	**Gn 40:9**	2009
dream, and **b**, *there were* three baskets	**Gn 40:16**	2009
and **b**, he was standing by the Nile.	**Gn 41:1**	2009
Then **b**, seven other cows came up	**Gn 41:3**	2009
and **b**, seven ears of grain came up	**Gn 41:5**	2009
Then **b**, seven ears, thin and	**Gn 41:6**	2009
Pharaoh awoke, and **b**, *it was* a dream.	**Gn 41:7**	2009
"In my dream, **b**, I was standing	**Gn 41:17**	2009
and **b**, seven cows, fat and sleek	**Gn 41:18**	2009
and **b**, seven ears, full and good,	**Gn 41:22**	2009
"**B**, seven years of great	**Gn 41:29**	2009
"**B**, I have heard that there is	**Gn 42:2**	2009
and **b**, the youngest is with our	**Gn 42:13**	2009
and **b**, it was in the mouth of his	**Gn 42:27**	2009
and **b**, it is even in my sack."	**Gn 42:28**	2009
that **b**, every man's bundle of money	**Gn 42:35**	2009
our sacks, and **b**, each man's money	**Gn 43:21**	2009
"**B**, the money which we found in	**Gn 44:8**	2005
b, we are my lord's slaves, both	**Gn 44:16**	2009
"**B**, your eyes see, and the eyes of	**Gn 45:12**	2009
and **b**, they are in the land of	**Gn 47:1**	2009
"**B**, I have today bought you and	**Gn 47:23**	2005
"**B**, your father is sick."	**Gn 48:1**	2009
"**B**, your son Joseph has come to	**Gn 48:2**	2009
"**B**, I will make you fruitful and	**Gn 48:4**	2009
b, God has let me see your children	**Gn 48:11**	2009
"**B**, I am about to die, but God	**Gn 48:21**	2009
"**B**, I am about to die;	**Gn 50:5**	2009
"**B**, we are your servants."	**Gn 50:18**	2009
"**B**, the people of the sons of	**Ex 1:9**	2009
and **b**, *the* boy was crying.	**Ex 2:6**	2009
and **b**, two Hebrews were fighting	**Ex 2:13**	2009
and **b**, the bush was burning with fire,	**Ex 3:2**	2009
"Now, **b**, the cry of the sons	**Ex 3:9**	2009
"**B**, I am going to the sons of	**Ex 3:13**	2009
b, his hand was leprous like snow.	**Ex 4:6**	2009
b, it was restored like *the rest of* his	**Ex 4:7**	2009
And moreover, **b**, he is coming out	**Ex 4:14**	2009
B, I will kill your son, your	**Ex 4:23**	2009
And **b**, your servants are being	**Ex 5:16**	2009
"**B**, the sons of Israel have not	**Ex 6:12**	2005
"**B**, I am unskilled in speech;	**Ex 6:30**	2005
But **b**, you have not listened until	**Ex 7:16**	2009
b, I will strike the water that is	**Ex 7:17**	2009
refuse to let *them* go, **b**, I will smite	**Ex 8:2**	2009
b, I will send swarms of insects	**Ex 8:21**	2009
"**B**, I am going out from you, and	**Ex 8:29**	2009
b, the hand of the LORD will come	**Ex 9:3**	2009
Pharaoh sent, and **b**, there was not	**Ex 9:7**	2009
"**B**, about this time tomorrow, I	**Ex 9:18**	2009
b, tomorrow I will bring locusts	**Ex 10:4**	2009
b, the Egyptians were marching after	**Ex 14:10**	2009
"As for Me, **b**, I will harden	**Ex 14:17**	2009
"**B**, I will rain bread from heaven	**Ex 16:4**	2009
b, the glory of the LORD appeared	**Ex 16:10**	2009
b, on the surface of the wilderness	**Ex 16:14**	2009
"**B**, I will stand before you there	**Ex 17:6**	2009
"**B**, I will come to you in a	**Ex 19:9**	2009
"**B**, I am going to send an angel	**Ex 23:20**	2009
"**B** the blood of the covenant,	**Ex 24:8**	2009
And **b**, Aaron and Hur are with you;	**Ex 24:14**	2009
"And **b**, I Myself have appointed	**Ex 31:6**	2009
and **b**, they are an obstinate people.	**Ex 32:9**	2009
B, My angel shall go before you;	**Ex 32:34**	2009
"**B**, there is a place by Me, and	**Ex 33:21**	2009
"**B**, I am going to make a covenant.	**Ex 34:10**	2009
b, I am going to drive out the	**Ex 34:11**	2009
Moses, **b**, the skin of his face shone,	**Ex 34:30**	2009
b, they had done it; just as the LORD	**Ex 39:43**	2009
and **b**, it had been burned up!	**Lv 10:16**	2009
"**B**, since its blood had not been	**Lv 10:18**	2005
"**B**, this very day they presented	**Lv 10:19**	2005
b, *if* the leprosy has covered all his	**Lv 13:13**	2009
b, *if* the infection has turned to white,	**Lv 13:17**	2009
look, and **b**, *if* it appears to be lower	**Lv 13:20**	2009
and **b**, there are no white hairs in it	**Lv 13:21**	2009
"Now, **b**, I have taken the Levites	**Nu 3:12**	2009
the tent, **b**, Miriam *was* leprous,	**Nu 12:10**	2009
toward Miriam, **b**, she *was* leprous.	**Nu 12:10**	2009
and **b**, the cloud covered it	**Nu 16:42**	2009
for **b**, the plague had begun among	**Nu 16:47**	2009
and **b**, the rod of Aaron for the	**Nu 17:8**	2009
"**B**, we perish, we are dying, we	**Nu 17:12**	2005
"**B**, I Myself have taken your fellow	**Nu 18:6**	2009
"Now **b**, I Myself have given you	**Nu 18:8**	2009
of Levi, **b**, I have given all the tithe	**Nu 18:21**	2009
now **b**, we are at Kadesh, a town on	**Nu 20:16**	2009
"**B**, a people came out of Egypt;	**Nu 22:5**	2009
b, they cover the surface of the	**Nu 22:5**	2009
'**B**, there is a people who came out	**Nu 22:11**	2009
B, I have come out as an	**Nu 22:32**	2009
"**B**, I have come now to you!	**Nu 22:38**	2009
b, he was standing beside his burnt	**Nu 23:6**	2009
B, a people *who* dwells apart, And	**Nu 23:9**	2005
b, you have actually blessed them!"	**Nu 23:11**	2009
b, he was standing beside his burnt	**Nu 23:17**	2009
"**B**, I have received *a command* to	**Nu 23:20**	2009
"**B**, a people rises like a	**Nu 23:24**	2005
b, you have persisted in blessing them	**Nu 24:10**	2009
but **b**, the LORD has held you back	**Nu 24:11**	2009
"And now, **b**, I am going to my	**Nu 24:14**	2009
I **b** him, but not near;	**Nu 24:17**	7789
Then **b**, one of the sons of Israel	**Nu 25:6**	2009
"**B**, I give him My covenant of	**Nu 25:12**	2009
"**B**, these caused the sons of	**Nu 31:16**	2005
"Now **b**, you have risen up in your	**Nu 32:14**	2009
b, you have sinned against the LORD,	**Nu 32:23**	2009
and **b**, you are this day like the stars	**Dt 1:10**	2009
B, his bedstead was an iron	**Dt 3:11**	2009
'**B**, the LORD our God has shown us	**Dt 5:24**	2005
"**B**, to the LORD your God belong	**Dt 10:14**	2005
B, if it is true and the thing	**Dt 17:4**	2009
and **b**, he has charged her with	**Dt 22:17**	2009
'Now **b**, I have brought the	**Dt 26:10**	2009
"**B**, the time for you to die is	**Dt 31:14**	2005
"**B**, you are about to lie down	**Dt 31:16**	2009
b, while I am still alive with you	**Dt 31:27**	2005
"**B**, men from the sons of Israel	**Jos 2:2**	2009
"**B**, the ark of the covenant of	**Jos 3:11**	2009
b, a man was standing opposite him	**Jos 5:13**	2009
and **b**, they are concealed in the	**Jos 7:21**	2009
and **b**, it was concealed in his	**Jos 7:22**	2009
b, the smoke of the city ascended	**Jos 8:20**	2009
but now **b**, it is dry and has	**Jos 9:12**	2009
b, they are torn; and these our clothes	**Jos 9:13**	2009
"Now **b**, we are in your hands;	**Jos 9:25**	2009
"Now **b**, the LORD has let me	**Jos 14:10**	2009
and now **b**, I am eighty-five years	**Jos 14:10**	2009
"**B**, the sons of Reuben and the	**Jos 22:11**	2009
"Now **b**, today I am going the way	**Jos 23:14**	2009
"**B**, this stone shall be for a	**Jos 24:27**	2009
b, I have given the land into his	**Jg 1:2**	2009
and **b**, the doors of the roof chamber	**Jg 3:24**	2009
but **b**, he did not open the doors	**Jg 3:25**	2009
b, their master had fallen to the floor	**Jg 3:25**	2009
"**B**, the LORD, the God of Israel,	**Jg 4:6**	3808
b, the LORD has gone out before	**Jg 4:14**	3808
And **b**, as Barak pursued Sisera,	**Jg 4:22**	2009
and **b** Sisera was lying dead with	**Jg 4:22**	2009
B, my family is the least in	**Jg 6:15**	2009
b, the altar of Baal was torn down,	**Jg 6:28**	2009
b, I will put a fleece of wool on	**Jg 6:37**	2009
b, a man was relating a dream	**Jg 7:13**	2009
"**B**, I had a dream;	**Jg 7:13**	2009
And **b**, when I come to the	**Jg 7:17**	2009
"**B** Zebah and Zalmunna, concerning	**Jg 8:15**	2009
b, Gaal the son of Ebed and his	**Jg 9:31**	2009
and **b**, they are stirring up the	**Jg 9:31**	2009
and **b**, when he and the people who	**Jg 9:33**	2009

"**B**, people are coming down from **Jg 9:37** 2009
b, his daughter was coming out **Jg 11:34** 2009
"**B** now, you are barren and have **Jg 13:3** 2009
"For **b**, you shall conceive and **Jg 13:5** 2009
'**B**, you shall conceive and give **Jg 13:7** 2009
"**B**, the man who came the *other* **Jg 13:10** 2009
and **b**, a young lion *came* roaring **Jg 14:5** 2009
and **b**, a swarm of bees and honey **Jg 14:8** 2009
"**B**, I have not told *it* to my **Jg 14:16** 2009
"**B**, you have deceived me and told **Jg 16:10** 2009
b, the silver is with me; I took it." **Jg 17:2** 2009
b, it is very good. And will you sit **Jg 18:9** 2009
b, it is west of Kiriath-jearim. **Jg 18:12** 2009
"**B** now, the day has drawn to a **Jg 19:9** 2009
Then **b**, an old man was coming out **Jg 19:16** 2009
celebrating, **b**, the men of the city, **Jg 19:22** 2009
then **b**, his concubine was lying **Jg 19:27** 2009
"**B**, all you sons of Israel, give **Jg 20:7** 2009
and **b**, the whole city was going up **Jg 20:40** 2009
And **b**, no one had come to the camp **Jg 21:8** 2009
b, not one of the inhabitants **Jg 21:9** 2009
"**B**, there is a feast of the LORD **Jg 21:19** 2009
and **b**, if the daughters of Shiloh **Jg 21:21** 2009
"**B**, your sister-in-law has gone **Ru 1:15** 2009
Now **b**, Boaz came from Bethlehem **Ru 2:4** 2009
B, he winnows barley at the **Ru 3:2** 2009
and **b**, a woman was lying at his **Ru 3:8** 2009
b, the close relative of whom Boaz **Ru 4:1** 2009
'**B**, the days are coming when I **1Sa 2:31** 2009
"**B**, I am about to do a thing in **1Sa 3:11** 2009
When he came, **b**, Eli was sitting **1Sa 4:13** 2009
b, Dagon had fallen on his face **1Sa 5:3** 2009
b, Dagon had fallen on his face **1Sa 5:4** 2009
"**B**, you have grown old, and your **1Sa 8:5** 2009
"**B** now, there is a man of God in **1Sa 9:6** 2009
"But **b**, if we go, what shall we **1Sa 9:7** 2009
"**B**, I have in my hand a fourth of **1Sa 9:8** 2009
b, Samuel was coming out toward **1Sa 9:14** 2009
"**B**, the man of whom I spoke to **1Sa 9:17** 2009
Now **b**, your father has ceased to **1Sa 10:2** 2009
and **b**, I will come down to you to **1Sa 10:8** 2009
b, a group of prophets met him; **1Sa 10:10** 2009
"**B**, he is hiding himself by the **1Sa 10:22** 2009
Now **b**, Saul was coming from the **1Sa 11:5** 2009
"**B**, I have listened to your voice **1Sa 12:1** 2009
gray, and **b** my sons are with you. **1Sa 12:2** 2009
b, the LORD has set a king over you. **1Sa 12:13** 2009
b, Samuel came; and Saul went out **1Sa 13:10** 2009
"**B**, we will cross over to the men **1Sa 14:8** 2009
"**B**, Hebrews are coming out of the **1Sa 14:11** 2009
and **b**, the multitude melted away; **1Sa 14:16** 2009
b, Jonathan and his armor bearer **1Sa 14:17** 2009
and **b**, every man's sword was **1Sa 14:20** 2009
b, *there was* a flow of honey; **1Sa 14:26** 2009
"**B**, the people are sinning **1Sa 14:33** 2009
b, he set up a monument for himself, **1Sa 15:12** 2009
B, to obey is better than **1Sa 15:22** 2009
and **b**, he is tending the sheep." **1Sa 16:11** 2009
"**B** now, an evil spirit from God **1Sa 16:15** 2009
"**B**, I have seen a son of Jesse **1Sa 16:18** 2009
b, the champion, the Philistine from **1Sa 17:23** 2009
'**B**, the king delights in you, and **1Sa 18:22** 2009
b, the household idol *was* on the bed **1Sa 19:16** 2009
"**B**, David is at Naioth in Ramah." **1Sa 19:19** 2009
"**B**, they are at Naioth in Ramah." **1Sa 19:22** 2009
B, my father does nothing either **1Sa 20:2** 2009
"**B**, tomorrow is the new moon, and **1Sa 20:5** 2009
b, if there is good *feeling* toward **1Sa 20:12** 2009
"And **b**, I will send the lad, **1Sa 20:21** 2009
'**B**, the arrows are on this side of **1Sa 20:21** 2009
'**B**, the arrows are beyond you,' **1Sa 20:22** 2009
b, the LORD is between you and me **1Sa 20:23** 2009
b, it is wrapped in a cloth behind the **1Sa 21:9** 2009
"**B**, you see the man behaving as a **1Sa 21:14** 2009
"**B**, the Philistines are fighting **1Sa 23:1** 2009
"**B**, we are afraid here in Judah. **1Sa 23:3** 2009
"**B**, David is in the wilderness of **1Sa 24:1** 2009
"**B**, *this is* the day of which the **1Sa 24:4** 2009
'**B**; I am about to give your enemy **1Sa 24:4** 2009
'**B**, David seeks to harm you'? **1Sa 24:9** 2009
"**B**, this day your eyes have seen **1Sa 24:10** 2009
"Now, **b**, I know that you **1Sa 24:20** 2009
"**B**, David sent messengers from **1Sa 25:14** 2009
b, I am coming after you." **1Sa 25:19** 2009
b, David and his men were coming **1Sa 25:20** 2009
b, he was holding a feast in his house, **1Sa 25:36** 2009
"**B**, your maidservant is a maid to **1Sa 25:41** 2009
b, Saul lay sleeping inside the circle **1Sa 26:7** 2009
B, I have played the fool and have **1Sa 26:21** 2009
"**B** the spear of the king! **1Sa 26:22** 2009
"Now **b**, as your life was highly **1Sa 26:24** 2009
"**B**, there is a woman who is a **1Sa 28:7** 2009
"**B**, you know what Saul has done, **1Sa 28:9** 2009
"**B**, your maidservant has obeyed **1Sa 28:21** 2009
the city, **b**, it was burned with fire, **1Sa 30:3** 2009
b, they were spread over all the land, **1Sa 30:16** 2009
"**B**, a gift for you from the spoil **1Sa 30:26** 2009
b, a man came out of the camp **2Sa 1:2** 2009
and **b**, Saul was leaning on his spear. **2Sa 1:6** 2009
And **b**, the chariots and the **2Sa 1:6** 2009
b, it is written in the book of **2Sa 1:18** 2009
b, my hand shall be with you to bring **2Sa 3:12** 2009
And **b**, the servants of David and **2Sa 3:22** 2009
B, Abner came to you; **2Sa 3:24** 2009
"**B**, the head of Ish-bosheth the **2Sa 4:8** 2009
'**B**, Saul is dead,' and thought he **2Sa 4:10** 2009
"**B**, we are your bone and your **2Sa 5:1** 2009
"**B**, he is in the house of Machir **2Sa 9:4** 2009
'**B**, I will raise up evil against **2Sa 12:11** 2009
"**B**, while the child was *still* **2Sa 12:18** 2009
"**B** now, your servant has **2Sa 13:24** 2009
b, many people were coming **2Sa 13:34** 2009
"**B**, the king's sons have come; **2Sa 13:35** 2009
b, the king's sons came and lifted **2Sa 13:36** 2009
"Now **b**, the whole family has **2Sa 14:7** 2009
"**B** now, I will surely do this **2Sa 14:21** 2009
"**B**, I sent for you, saying, **2Sa 14:32** 2009
"**B**, your servants *are ready to do* **2Sa 15:15** 2009
Now **b**, Zadok also *came,* and all **2Sa 15:24** 2009
b, here I am, let Him do to me as **2Sa 15:26** 2009
that **b**, Hushai the Archite met him **2Sa 15:32** 2009
"**B** their two sons are with them **2Sa 15:36** 2009
b, Ziba the servant of Mephibosheth **2Sa 16:1** 2009
"**B**, he is staying in Jerusalem, **2Sa 16:3** 2009
"**B**, all that belongs to **2Sa 16:4** 2009
b, there came out from there a man **2Sa 16:5** 2009
And **b**, you are *taken* in your own **2Sa 16:8** 2009
"**B**, my son who came out from me **2Sa 16:11** 2009
"**B**, he has now hidden himself in **2Sa 17:9** 2009
"**B**, I saw Absalom hanging in an **2Sa 18:10** 2009
"Now **b**, you saw *him!* **2Sa 18:11** 2009
and **b**, a man running by himself. **2Sa 18:24** 2009
"**B**, *another* man running by **2Sa 18:26** 2009
B, the Cushite arrived, **2Sa 18:31** 2009
"**B**, the king is weeping and **2Sa 19:1** 2009
"**B**, the king is sitting in the **2Sa 19:8** 2009
therefore **b**, I have come today, **2Sa 19:20** 2009
And **b**, all the men of Israel came **2Sa 19:41** 2009
"**B**, his head will be thrown to **2Sa 20:21** 2009
"**B**, it is I who have sinned, and **2Sa 24:17** 2009
"**B**, while you are still there **1Ki 1:14** 2009
"Now, **b**, Adonijah is king; **1Ki 1:18** 2009
B, while she was still speaking with **1Ki 1:22** 2009
and **b**, they are eating and drinking **1Ki 1:25** 2009
b, Jonathan the son of Abiathar **1Ki 1:42** 2009
"**B**, Adonijah is afraid of King **1Ki 1:51** 2009
for **b**, he has taken hold of the horns **1Ki 1:51** 2009
"**B**, there is with you Shimei **1Ki 2:8** 2009
and **b**, he is beside the altar. **1Ki 2:29** 2009
"**B**, your servants are in Gath." **1Ki 2:39** 2009
b, I have done according to your **1Ki 3:12** 2009
B, I have given you a wise and **1Ki 3:12** 2009
Solomon awoke, and **b**, it was a dream. **1Ki 3:15** 2009
to nurse my son, **b**, he was dead; **1Ki 3:21** 2009
morning, **b**, he was not my son, **1Ki 3:21** 2009
"**B**, I intend to build a house for **1Ki 5:5** 2009
B, heaven and the highest heaven **1Ki 8:27** 2009
And **b**, the half was not told me. **1Ki 10:7** 2009
b, you are seeking to go to your own **1Ki 11:22** 2009
'**B**, I will tear the kingdom out of **1Ki 11:31** 2009
b your gods, O Israel, that **1Ki 12:28** 2009
Now **b**, there came a man of God **1Ki 13:1** 2009
'**B**, a son shall be born to the **1Ki 13:2** 2009
'**B**, the altar shall be split apart **1Ki 13:3** 2009
And **b**, men passed by and saw the **1Ki 13:25** 2009
b, Ahijah the prophet is there, **1Ki 14:2** 2009
"**B**, the wife of Jeroboam is **1Ki 14:5** 2009
therefore **b**, I am bringing **1Ki 14:10** 2009
b, they are written in the Book of the **1Ki 14:19** 2009
B, I have sent you a present of **1Ki 15:19** 2009
b, I will consume Baasha and his **1Ki 16:3** 2009
b, I have commanded a widow there **1Ki 17:9** 2009
b, a widow was there gathering sticks; **1Ki 17:10** 2009
and **b**, I am gathering a few sticks **1Ki 17:12** 2009
b, Elijah met him, and he recognized **1Ki 18:7** 2009
'**B**, Elijah *is here.*' " **1Ki 18:8** 2009
"**B**, Elijah *is here.*" ' **1Ki 18:11** 2009
"**B**, Elijah *is here*" **1Ki 18:14** 2009
"**B**, a cloud as small as a man's **1Ki 18:44** 2009
and **b**, there was an angel touching **1Ki 19:5** 2009
b, there was at his head a bread cake **1Ki 19:6** 2009
and **b**, the word of the LORD *came* **1Ki 19:9** 2009
And **b**, the LORD was passing by! **1Ki 19:11** 2009
And **b**, a voice *came* to him and **1Ki 19:13** 2009
Now **b**, a prophet approached Ahab **1Ki 20:13** 2009
B, I will deliver them into your **1Ki 20:13** 2009
"**B** now, we have heard that the **1Ki 20:31** 2009
b, as soon as you have departed from **1Ki 20:36** 2009
and **b**, a man turned aside and **1Ki 20:39** 2009
b, he is in the vineyard of Naboth **1Ki 21:18** 2009
"**B**, I will bring evil upon you, **1Ki 21:21** 2009
"**B** now, the words of the prophets **1Ki 22:13** 2009
b, the LORD has put a deceiving spirit **1Ki 22:23** 2009
"**B**, you shall see on that day **1Ki 22:25** 2009
b, he was sitting on the top of the hill. **2Ki 1:9** 2009
"**B** fire came down from heaven and **2Ki 1:14** 2009
b, *there appeared* a chariot of fire **2Ki 2:11** 2009
"**B** now, there are with your **2Ki 2:16** 2009
"**B** now, the situation of this **2Ki 2:19** 2009
b, water came by the way of Edom, **2Ki 3:20** 2009
"**B** now, I perceive that this is a **2Ki 4:9** 2009
'**B**, you have been careful for us **2Ki 4:13** 2009
"**B**, there is the Shunammite. **2Ki 4:25** 2009
b the lad was dead and laid on his **2Ki 4:32** 2009
b, I have sent Naaman my servant **2Ki 5:6** 2009
B, I thought, 'He will surely come out **2Ki 5:11** 2009
"**B** now, I know that there is no **2Ki 5:15** 2009
"**B**, my master has spared this **2Ki 5:20** 2009
"**B**, just now two young men of the **2Ki 5:22** 2009
"**B** now, the place before you **2Ki 6:1** 2009
"**B**, he is in Dothan." **2Ki 6:13** 2009
b, an army with horses and chariots **2Ki 6:15** 2009
and **b**, the mountain was full of **2Ki 6:17** 2009
and **b**, they were in the midst of **2Ki 6:20** 2009
and **b**, they besieged it, until a **2Ki 6:25** 2009
b, he had sackcloth beneath on his **2Ki 6:30** 2009
b, the messenger came down to him and **2Ki 6:33** 2009
"**B**, this evil is from the LORD; **2Ki 6:33** 2009
"**B**, if the LORD should make **2Ki 7:2** 2009
"**B**, you will see it with your own **2Ki 7:2** 2009
b, there was no one there. **2Ki 7:5** 2009
"**B**, the king of Israel has hired **2Ki 7:6** 2009
and **b**, there was no one there, **2Ki 7:10** 2009
B, they *will be in any case* like **2Ki 7:13** 2009
b, they *will be in any case* like **2Ki 7:13** 2009
and **b**, all the way was full of clothes **2Ki 7:15** 2009
"Now **b**, if the LORD should make **2Ki 7:19** 2009
"**B**, you will see it with your **2Ki 7:19** 2009
b, the woman whose son he had **2Ki 8:5** 2009
When he came, **b**, the captains of **2Ki 9:5** 2009
"**B**, the two kings did not stand **2Ki 10:4** 2009
b, I conspired against my master **2Ki 10:9** 2009
b, the king was standing by the pillar, **2Ki 11:14** 2009
b, they saw a marauding band; **2Ki 13:21** 2009
b they are written in the Book of **2Ki 15:11** 2009
b they are written in the Book of **2Ki 15:15** 2009
b they are written in the Book of **2Ki 15:26** 2009
b, they are written in the Book of the **2Ki 15:31** 2009
b, they kill them because they do not **2Ki 17:26** 2009
"Now **b**, you rely on the staff of **2Ki 18:21** 2009
"**B**, I will put a spirit in him so **2Ki 19:7** 2009
"**B**, he has come out to fight **2Ki 19:9** 2009
'**B**, you have heard what the kings **2Ki 19:11** 2009
the morning, **b**, all of them were dead. **2Ki 19:35** 2009
b, I will heal you. **2Ki 20:5** 2009
'**B**, the days are coming when all **2Ki 20:17** 2009
'**B**, I am bringing *such* calamity on **2Ki 21:12** 2009
"**B**, I bring evil on this place **2Ki 22:16** 2009
"Therefore, **b**, I will gather you **2Ki 22:20** 2009
and **b**, they are written in the **1Ch 9:1** 2009
"**B**, we are your bone and your **1Ch 11:1** 2009
B, he was honored among the **1Ch 11:25** 2009
"**B**, I am dwelling in a house of **1Ch 17:1** 2009
'**B**, a son will be born to you, **1Ch 22:9** 2009
"Now **b**, with great pains I have **1Ch 22:14** 2009
"Now **b**, *there are* the divisions **1Ch 28:21** 2009
"**B**, I am about to build a house **2Ch 2:4** 2009
"Now **b**, I will give to your **2Ch 2:10** 2009
B, heaven and the highest heaven **2Ch 6:18** 2009
And **b**, the half of the greatness **2Ch 9:6** 2009
"Now **b**, God is with us at *our* **2Ch 13:12** 2009
b, they were attacked both front and **2Ch 13:14** 2009
B, I have sent you silver and gold; **2Ch 16:3** 2009
b, they are written in the Book of the **2Ch 16:11** 2009
"**B**, the words of the prophets are **2Ch 18:12** 2009
b, the LORD has put a deceiving **2Ch 18:22** 2009
"**B**, you will see on that day **2Ch 18:24** 2009
"**B**, Amariah the chief priest will **2Ch 19:11** 2009
and **b**, they are in Hazazon-tamar **2Ch 20:2** 2009
"Now **b**, the sons of Ammon and **2Ch 20:10** 2009
B, they will come up by the ascent **2Ch 20:16** 2009
and **b**, they *were* corpses lying on **2Ch 20:24** 2009
b, they are written in the annals of **2Ch 20:34** 2009
b, the LORD is going to strike **2Ch 21:14** 2009
"**B**, the king's son shall reign, **2Ch 23:3** 2009
b, the king was standing by his pillar **2Ch 23:13** 2009
b, they are written in the treatise of **2Ch 24:27** 2009
'**B**, you have defeated Edom.' **2Ch 25:19** 2009
b, are they not written in the Book of **2Ch 25:26** 2009
b, he *was* leprous on his forehead; **2Ch 26:20** 2009
b, they are written in the Book of the **2Ch 27:7** 2009
"**B**, because the LORD, the God of **2Ch 28:9** 2009
b, they are written in the Book of the **2Ch 28:26** 2009
"For **b**, our fathers have fallen **2Ch 29:9** 2009
and **b**, they are before the altar **2Ch 29:19** 2009
deeds of devotion, **b**, they are written **2Ch 32:32** 2009
b, they are among the records **2Ch 33:18** 2009
humbled himself, **b**, they are written **2Ch 33:19** 2009
"**B**, I am bringing evil on this **2Ch 34:24** 2009
"**B**, I will gather you to your **2Ch 34:28** 2009
b, they are also written in the **2Ch 35:25** 2009
b, they are written in the Book of the **2Ch 35:27** 2009
found against him, **b**, they are written **2Ch 36:8** 2009
b, we are before You in our **Ezr 9:15** 2009
Yet **b**, we are forcing our sons and **Ne 5:5** 2009
"**B**, we are slaves today, And as **Ne 9:36** 2009
and its bounty, **B**, we are slaves in it. **Ne 9:36** 2009
"**B**, Haman is standing in the **Es 6:5** 2009
"**B** indeed, the gallows standing **Es 7:9** 2009
"**B**, I have given the house of **Es 8:7** 2009
"**B**, all that he has is in your **Jb 1:12** 2009
and **b**, a great wind came from **Jb 1:19** 2009
"**B**, he is in your power, only **Jb 2:6** 2009
"**B**, let that night be barren; **Jb 3:7** 2009
"**B** you have admonished many, And **Jb 4:3** 2009
"**B**, how happy is the man whom God **Jb 5:17** 2009
"**B** this; we have investigated it, **Jb 5:27** 2009
him who sees me will **b** me no longer; **Jb 7:8** 7789
"**B**, this is the joy of His way; **Jb 8:19** 2005
b, *He is* the strong one! **Jb 9:19** 2009
"**B**, He tears down, and it cannot **Jb 12:14** 2005
"**B**, He restrains the waters, and **Jb 12:15** 2005
"**B**, my eye has seen all *this,* My **Jb 13:1** 2005
"**B** now, I have prepared my case; **Jb 13:18** 2009
"**B**, He puts no trust in His holy **Jb 15:15** 2005
"Even now, **b**, my witness is in **Jb 16:19** 2009
"**B**, I cry, 'Violence!' but I get no **Jb 19:7** 2005
Whom I myself shall **b**, **Jb 19:27** 2372
"**B**, their prosperity is not in **Jb 21:16** 2005
"**B**, I know your thoughts, And the **Jb 21:27** 2005
"**B**, I go forward but He is not **Jb 23:8** 2005
acts on the left, I cannot **b** *Him;* **Jb 23:9** 2372
"**B**, as wild donkeys in the **Jb 24:5** 2005
"**B**, these are the fringes of His **Jb 26:14** 2005
"**B**, all of you have seen *it;* **Jb 27:12** 2005
'**B**, the fear of the Lord, that is **Jb 28:28** 2005
B, here is my signature; **Jb 31:35** 2005

Context	Reference	Number
“**B**, I waited for your words, I	**Jb 32:11**	2005
“**B**, my belly is like unvented	**Jb 32:19**	2009
“**B** now, I open my mouth, My	**Jb 33:2**	2009
‘**B**, I belong to God like you;	**Jb 33:6**	2005
‘**B**, no fear of me should terrify	**Jb 33:7**	2009
‘**B**, He invents pretexts against me;	**Jb 33:10**	2005
‘**B**, let me tell you, you are not	**Jb 33:12**	2005
“**B**, God does all these oftentimes	**Jb 33:29**	2005
His face, who then can **b** Him,	**Jb 34:29**	7789
heavens and see; And **b** the clouds	**Jb 35:5**	7789
when you say you do not **b** Him,	**Jb 35:14**	7789
“**B**, God is mighty but does not	**Jb 36:5**	2005
“**B**, God is exalted in His power;	**Jb 36:22**	2005
“**B**, God is exalted, and we do not	**Jb 36:26**	2005
“**B**, He spreads His lightning	**Jb 36:30**	2005
“**B**, I am insignificant;	**Jb 40:4**	2005
“**B** now, Behemoth, which I made as	**Jb 40:15**	2009
“**B** now, his strength in his	**Jb 40:16**	2009
“**B**, your expectation is false;	**Jb 41:9**	2005
B, he travails with wickedness,	**Ps 7:14**	2009
For, **b**, the wicked bend the bow,	**Ps 11:2**	2009
His eyes **b**, His eyelids test the	**Ps 11:4**	2372
The upright will **b** His face.	**Ps 11:7**	2372
shall **b** Your face in righteousness;	**Ps 17:15**	2372
life, To **b** the beauty of the LORD And	**Ps 27:4**	2372
B, the eye of the LORD is on those	**Ps 33:18**	2009
blameless man, and **b** the upright;	**Ps 37:37**	7200
“**B**, You have made my days *as*	**Ps 39:5**	2009
Then I said, “**B**, I come; In the scroll	**Ps 40:7**	2009
B, I will not restrain my lips, O	**Ps 40:9**	2009
Come, **b** the works of the LORD, Who	**Ps 46:8**	2372
B, I was brought forth in	**Ps 51:5**	2005
B, You desire truth in the	**Ps 51:6**	2005
“**B**, the man who would not make	**Ps 52:7**	2009
B, God is my helper;	**Ps 54:4**	2009
“**B**, I would wander far away, I	**Ps 55:7**	2009
For **b**, they have set an ambush for	**Ps 59:3**	2009
B, they belch forth with their	**Ps 59:7**	2009
B, He speaks forth with His voice,	**Ps 68:33**	2005
B, these are the wicked;	**Ps 73:12**	2009
B, I would have betrayed	**Ps 73:15**	2009
For, **b**, those who are far from	**Ps 73:27**	2009
“**B**, He struck the rock so that	**Ps 78:20**	2005
For **b**, Your enemies make an	**Ps 83:2**	2009
B our shield, O God, And look upon	**Ps 84:9**	7200
B, Philistia and Tyre with	**Ps 87:4**	2009
For, **b**, Your enemies, O LORD,	**Ps 92:9**	2009
For, **b**, Your enemies will perish;	**Ps 92:9**	2009
to **b** *The things that are* in heaven	**Ps 113:6**	7200
b Wonderful things from Your law.	**Ps 119:18**	5027
B, I long for Your precepts;	**Ps 119:40**	2009
I **b** the treacherous and loathe	**Ps 119:158**	7200
B, He who keeps Israel Will	**Ps 121:4**	2009
B, as the eyes of servants *look* to	**Ps 123:2**	2009
B, children are a gift of the LORD,	**Ps 127:3**	2009
B, for thus shall the man be	**Ps 128:4**	2009
B, we heard of it in Ephrathah,	**Ps 132:6**	2009
B, how good and how pleasant it is	**Ps 133:1**	2009
B, bless the LORD, all servants of	**Ps 134:1**	2009
B, O LORD, You know it all.	**Ps 139:4**	2005
my bed in Sheol, **b**, You are there.	**Ps 139:8**	2009
B, I will pour out my spirit on you;	**Pr 1:23**	2009
And **b**, a woman *comes* to meet him,	**Pr 7:10**	2009
And **b**, it was completely overgrown	**Pr 24:31**	2009
b, all is vanity and striving after wind.	**Ec 1:14**	2009
“**B**, I have magnified and	**Ec 1:16**	2009
And **b**, it too was futility.	**Ec 2:1**	2009
and **b** all was vanity and striving	**Ec 2:11**	2009
And **b** *I saw* the tears of the	**Ec 4:1**	2009
“**B**, I have discovered this,”	**Ec 7:27**	7200
“**B**, I have found only this, that	**Ec 7:29**	7200
B, he is coming, Climbing on the	**SS 2:8**	2009
B, he is standing behind our wall,	**SS 2:9**	2009
‘For **b**, the winter is past, The	**SS 2:11**	2009
“**B**, it is the *traveling* couch of	**SS 3:7**	2009
For **b**, the Lord GOD of hosts is	**Is 3:1**	2009
He looked for justice, but **b**, bloodshed;	**Is 5:7**	2009
righteousness, but **b**, a cry of distress.	**Is 5:7**	2009
And **b**, it will come with speed	**Is 5:26**	2009
b, there is darkness *and* distress;	**Is 5:30**	2009
“**B**, this has touched your lips;	**Is 6:7**	2009
B, a virgin will be with child and	**Is 7:14**	2009
b, the Lord is about to bring on them	**Is 8:7**	2009
B, I and the children whom the	**Is 8:18**	2009
b, distress and darkness, the gloom	**Is 8:22**	2009
B, the Lord, the GOD of hosts,	**Is 10:33**	2009
“**B**, God is my salvation, I will	**Is 12:2**	2009
B, the day of the LORD is coming,	**Is 13:9**	2009
B, I am going to stir up the Medes	**Is 13:17**	2009
“**B**, Damascus is about to be	**Is 17:1**	2009
At evening time, **b**, *there is* terror!	**Is 17:14**	2009
B, the LORD is riding on a swift	**Is 19:1**	2009
‘**B**, such is our hope, where we	**Is 20:6**	2009
“Now **b**, here comes a troop of	**Is 21:9**	2009
‘**B**, the LORD is about to hurl you	**Is 22:17**	2009
B, the land of the Chaldeans	**Is 23:13**	2005
B, the LORD lays the earth waste,	**Is 24:1**	2009
“**B**, this is our God for whom we	**Is 25:9**	2009
For **b**, the LORD is about to come	**Is 26:21**	2009
B, the Lord has a strong and	**Is 28:2**	2009
“**B**, I am laying in Zion a stone,	**Is 28:16**	2009
And **b**, he is eating; But when he	**Is 29:8**	2009
And **b**, he is drinking, But when he	**Is 29:8**	2009
b, he is faint And his thirst is not	**Is 29:8**	2009
Therefore **b**, I will once again	**Is 29:14**	2009
but your eyes will **b** your Teacher.	**Is 30:20**	7200
B, the name of the LORD comes from	**Is 30:27**	2009
B, a king will reign righteously And	**Is 32:1**	2005
B, their brave men cry in the	**Is 33:7**	2005

Context	Reference	Number
They will **b** a far-distant land.	**Is 33:17**	7200
B it shall descend for judgment	**Is 34:5**	2009
B, your God will come *with*	**Is 35:4**	2009
“**B**, you rely on the staff of this	**Is 36:6**	2009
“**B**, I will put a spirit in him so	**Is 37:7**	2009
‘**B**, you have heard what the kings	**Is 37:11**	2009
the morning, **b**, all of these were dead.	**Is 37:36**	2009
b, I will add fifteen years to	**Is 38:5**	2009
“**B**, I will cause the shadow on	**Is 38:8**	2009
‘**B**, the days are coming when all	**Is 39:6**	2009
B, the Lord GOD will come with	**Is 40:10**	2009
B, His reward is with Him And His	**Is 40:10**	2009
B, the nations are like a drop	**Is 40:15**	2005
B, He lifts up the islands like	**Is 40:15**	2005
“**B**, all those who are angered at	**Is 41:11**	2005
“**B**, I have made you a new, sharp	**Is 41:15**	2009
B, you are of no account, And your	**Is 41:24**	2005
‘**B**, here they are.’	**Is 41:27**	2009
“**B**, all of them are false;	**Is 41:29**	2005
“**B**, My Servant, whom I uphold;	**Is 42:1**	2005
“**B**, the former things have come	**Is 42:9**	2009
“**B**, I will do something new, Now	**Is 43:19**	2009
B, all his companions will be put	**Is 44:11**	2005
“**B**, they have become like	**Is 47:14**	2009
‘**B**, I knew them.’	**Is 48:7**	2009
“**B**, I have refined you, but not	**Is 48:10**	2009
“**B**, these will come from afar;	**Is 49:12**	2009
“**B**, I have inscribed you on the	**Is 49:16**	2005
B, I was left alone;	**Is 49:21**	2005
“**B**, I will lift up My hand to the	**Is 49:22**	2009
B, you were sold for your	**Is 50:1**	2005
B, I dry up the sea with My	**Is 50:2**	2005
B, the Lord GOD helps Me;	**Is 50:9**	2005
B, they will all wear out like a	**Is 50:9**	2005
B, all you who kindle a fire, Who	**Is 50:11**	2005
“**B**, I have taken out of your hand	**Is 51:22**	2009
B, My servant will prosper, He	**Is 52:13**	2009
B, I will set your stones in antimony,	**Is 54:11**	2009
“**B**, I Myself have created the	**Is 54:16**	2005
“**B**, I have made him a witness to	**Is 55:4**	2005
“**B**, you will call a nation you do	**Is 55:5**	2005
“**B**, I am a dry tree.”	**Is 56:3**	2005
B, on the day of your fast you find	**Is 58:3**	2005
“**B**, you fast for contention and	**Is 58:4**	2005
B, the LORD’s hand is not so short	**Is 59:1**	2005
We hope for light, but **b**, darkness,	**Is 59:9**	2009
“For **b**, darkness will cover the	**Is 60:2**	2009
B, the LORD has proclaimed to the	**Is 62:11**	2009
B His reward is with Him, and His	**Is 62:11**	2009
B, You were angry, for we sinned,	**Is 64:5**	2005
B, look now, all of us are Your	**Is 64:9**	2005
“**B**, it is written before Me, I	**Is 65:6**	2009
“**B**, My servants will eat, but	**Is 65:13**	2009
B, My servants will drink, but	**Is 65:13**	2009
B, My servants will rejoice, but	**Is 65:13**	2009
“**B**, My servants will shout	**Is 65:14**	2009
“For **b**, I create new heavens and	**Is 65:17**	2009
For **b**, I create Jerusalem *for*	**Is 65:18**	2009
“**B**, I extend peace to her like a	**Is 66:12**	2009
For **b**, the LORD will come in fire	**Is 66:15**	2009
B, I do not know how to speak,	**Jer 1:6**	2009
“**B**, I have put My words in your	**Jer 1:9**	2009
“For, **b**, I am calling all the	**Jer 1:15**	2009
“Now **b**, I have made you today as	**Jer 1:18**	2009
B, I will enter into judgment with you	**Jer 2:35**	2009
B, you have spoken And have done	**Jer 3:5**	2009
“**B**, we come to You;	**Jer 3:22**	2009
“**B**, he goes up like clouds, And	**Jer 4:13**	2009
and **b**, *it was* formless and void;	**Jer 4:23**	2009
mountains, and **b**, they were quaking,	**Jer 4:24**	2009
I looked, and **b**, there was no man,	**Jer 4:25**	2009
I looked, and **b**, the fruitful land	**Jer 4:26**	2009
B, I am making My words in your	**Jer 5:14**	2009
“**B**, I am bringing a nation	**Jer 5:15**	2009
B, their ears are closed And they	**Jer 6:10**	2009
B, the word of the LORD has become	**Jer 6:10**	2009
b, I am bringing disaster on this	**Jer 6:19**	2009
“**B**, I am laying stumbling blocks	**Jer 6:21**	2009
“**B**, a people is coming from the	**Jer 6:22**	2009
“**B**, you are trusting in deceptive	**Jer 7:8**	2009
B, I, even I, have seen *it*,”	**Jer 7:11**	2009
“**B**, My anger and My wrath will be	**Jer 7:20**	2009
“Therefore, **b**, days are coming,”	**Jer 7:32**	2009
But **b**, the lying pen of the	**Jer 8:8**	2009
B, they have rejected the word of	**Jer 8:9**	2009
For a time of healing, but **b**, terror!	**Jer 8:15**	2009
“For **b**, I am sending serpents	**Jer 8:17**	2009
B, listen! The cry of the daughter of	**Jer 8:19**	2009
“**B**, I will refine them and assay	**Jer 9:7**	2009
“**b**, I will feed them, this	**Jer 9:15**	2009
“**B**, the days are coming,”	**Jer 9:25**	2009
“**B**, I am slinging out the	**Jer 10:18**	2009
The sound of a report! **B**, it comes	**Jer 10:22**	2009
“**B** I am bringing disaster on them	**Jer 11:11**	2009
“**B**, I am about to punish them!	**Jer 11:22**	2009
“**B** I am about to uproot them from	**Jer 12:14**	2009
“**B** I am about to fill all the	**Jer 13:13**	2009
B, those slain with the sword!	**Jer 14:18**	2009
I enter the city, **B**, diseases of famine!	**Jer 14:18**	2009
for a time of healing, but **b**, terror!	**Jer 14:19**	2009
“**B**, I am going to eliminate from	**Jer 16:9**	2009
for **b**, you are each one walking	**Jer 16:12**	2009
“Therefore **b**, days are coming,”	**Jer 16:14**	2009
“**B**, I am going to send for many	**Jer 16:16**	2009
“Therefore **b**, I am going to make	**Jer 16:21**	2009
“**B**, like the clay in the potter’s	**Jer 18:6**	2009
“**B**, I am fashioning calamity	**Jer 18:11**	2009
“**B** I am about to bring a calamity	**Jer 19:3**	2009
therefore, **b**, days are coming,”	**Jer 19:6**	2009

Context	Reference	Number
‘**B**, I am about to bring on this	**Jer 19:15**	2009
‘**B**, I am going to make you a	**Jer 20:4**	2009
“**B**, I am about to turn back the	**Jer 21:4**	2009
“**B**, I set before you the way of	**Jer 21:8**	2009
“**B**, I am against you, O valley	**Jer 21:13**	2009
b, I am about to attend to you for	**Jer 23:2**	2009
“**B**, *the* days are coming,”	**Jer 23:5**	2009
“Therefore **b**, *the* days are	**Jer 23:7**	2009
‘**B**, I am going to feed them	**Jer 23:15**	2009
“**B**, the storm of the LORD has	**Jer 23:19**	2009
“Therefore **b**, I am against the	**Jer 23:30**	2009
“**B**, I am against the prophets,”	**Jer 23:31**	2009
“**B**, I am against those who have	**Jer 23:32**	2009
‘Therefore **b**, I will surely	**Jer 23:39**	2009
b, two baskets of figs set before	**Jer 24:1**	2009
b, I will send and take all the	**Jer 25:9**	2009
‘For **b**, I am beginning to work	**Jer 25:29**	2009
‘**B**, evil is going forth From	**Jer 25:32**	2009
“But as for me, **b**, I am in your	**Jer 26:14**	2009
‘**B**, the vessels of the LORD’s	**Jer 27:16**	2009
‘**B**, I am about to remove you from	**Jer 28:16**	2009
‘**B**, I am sending upon them the	**Jer 29:17**	2009
‘**B**, I will deliver them into the	**Jer 29:21**	2009
“**B**, I am about to punish Shemaiah	**Jer 29:32**	2009
‘For **b**, days are coming,’	**Jer 30:3**	2009
For **b**, I will save you from afar And	**Jer 30:10**	2009
‘**B**, I will restore the fortunes of	**Jer 30:18**	2009
B, the tempest of the LORD!	**Jer 30:23**	2009
“**B**, I am bringing them from the	**Jer 31:8**	2009
“**B**, days are coming,”	**Jer 31:27**	2009
“**B**, days are coming,”	**Jer 31:31**	2009
“**B**, days are coming,”	**Jer 31:38**	2009
“**B**, I am about to give this city	**Jer 32:3**	2009
‘**B**, Hanamel the son of Shallum	**Jer 32:7**	2009
B, You have made the heavens and	**Jer 32:17**	2009
‘**B**, the siege ramps have reached	**Jer 32:24**	2009
and **b**, You see *it*.	**Jer 32:24**	2009
“**B**, I am the LORD, the God of all	**Jer 32:27**	2009
“**B**, I am about to give this city	**Jer 32:28**	2009
“**B**, I will gather them out of all	**Jer 32:37**	2009
‘**B**, I will bring to it health and	**Jer 33:6**	2009
‘**B**, days are coming,’ declares the	**Jer 33:14**	2009
‘**B**, I am giving this city into the	**Jer 34:2**	2009
B, I am proclaiming a release to	**Jer 34:17**	2009
‘**B**, I am going to command,’	**Jer 34:22**	2009
‘**B**, I am bringing on Judah and on	**Jer 35:17**	2009
And **b**, all the officials were	**Jer 36:12**	2009
“**B**, Pharaoh’s army which has come	**Jer 37:7**	2009
“**B**, he is in your hands;	**Jer 38:5**	2009
‘Then **b**, all of the women who have	**Jer 38:22**	2009
“**B**, I am about to bring My words	**Jer 39:16**	2009
“But now, **b**, I am freeing you	**Jer 40:4**	2009
“Now as for me, **b**, I am going to	**Jer 40:10**	2009
B, I am going to pray to the LORD	**Jer 42:4**	2009
“**B**, I am going to send and get	**Jer 43:10**	2009
and **b**, this day they are in ruins	**Jer 44:2**	2009
‘**B**, I am going to set My face	**Jer 44:11**	2009
‘**B**, I have sworn by My great	**Jer 44:26**	2009
‘**B**, I am watching over them for	**Jer 44:27**	2009
‘**B**, I am going to give over	**Jer 44:30**	2009
“**B**, what I have built I am about	**Jer 45:4**	2009
for **b**, I am going to bring	**Jer 45:5**	2009
“**B**, I am going to punish Amon of	**Jer 46:25**	2009
“**B**, waters are going to rise from	**Jer 47:2**	2009
“Therefore **b**, the days are	**Jer 48:12**	2009
“**B**, one will fly swiftly like an	**Jer 48:40**	2009
“Therefore **b**, the days are	**Jer 49:2**	2009
“**B**, I am going to bring terror	**Jer 49:5**	2009
“**B**, those who were not sentenced	**Jer 49:12**	2009
“For **b**, I have made you small	**Jer 49:15**	2009
“**B**, one will come up like a lion	**Jer 49:19**	2009
B, He will mount up and swoop like	**Jer 49:22**	2009
‘**B**, I am going to break the bow of	**Jer 49:35**	2009
“For **b**, I am going to arouse and	**Jer 50:9**	2009
B, *she will be* the least of the	**Jer 50:12**	2009
‘**B**, I am going to punish the king	**Jer 50:18**	2009
“**B**, I am against you, O arrogant	**Jer 50:31**	2009
“**B**, a people is coming from the	**Jer 50:41**	2009
“**B**, one will come up like a lion	**Jer 50:44**	2009
“**B**, I am going to arouse against	**Jer 51:1**	2009
“**B**, I am against you, O	**Jer 51:25**	2009
“**B**, I am going to plead your case	**Jer 51:36**	2009
Therefore **b**, days are coming When	**Jer 51:47**	2009
“Therefore **b**, the days are	**Jer 51:52**	2009
now, all peoples, And **b** my pain;	**La 1:18**	7200
I looked, **b**, a storm wind was coming	**Ezk 1:4**	2009
b, there was one wheel on the earth	**Ezk 1:15**	2009
Then I looked, and **b**, a hand was	**Ezk 2:9**	2009
“**B**, I have made your face as hard	**Ezk 3:8**	2009
and **b**, the glory of the LORD was	**Ezk 3:23**	2009
“Now **b**, I will put ropes on you	**Ezk 4:8**	2009
B, I have never been defiled;	**Ezk 4:14**	2009
“Son of man, **b**, I am going to	**Ezk 4:16**	2009
‘**B**, I, even I, am against you, and	**Ezk 5:8**	2009
“**B**, I Myself am going to bring a	**Ezk 6:3**	2009
unique disaster, **b** it is coming!	**Ezk 7:5**	2009
awakened against you; **b**, it has come!	**Ezk 7:6**	2009
‘**B**, the day! Behold, it is coming!	**Ezk 7:10**	2009
B, it is coming! *Your* doom has gone	**Ezk 7:10**	2009
and **b**, a likeness as the appearance	**Ezk 8:2**	2009
And **b**, the glory of the God of	**Ezk 8:4**	2009
b, to the north of the altar gate *was*	**Ezk 8:5**	2009
when I looked, **b**, a hole in the wall.	**Ezk 8:7**	2009
through the wall, and **b**, an entrance.	**Ezk 8:8**	2009
and **b**, every form of creeping things	**Ezk 8:10**	2009
and **b**, women were sitting there	**Ezk 8:14**	2009
And **b**, at the entrance to the	**Ezk 8:16**	2009
For **b**, they are putting the twig	**Ezk 8:17**	2009
B, six men came from the direction	**Ezk 9:2**	2009

Then **b**, the man clothed in linen **Ezk 9:11** 2009
and **b**, in the expanse that was over **Ezk 10:1** 2009
b, four wheels beside the cherubim, **Ezk 10:9** 2009
And **b**, *there were* twenty-five men **Ezk 11:1** 2009
"Son of man, **b**, the house of **Ezk 12:27** 2009
a lie, therefore **b**, I am against you," **Ezk 13:8** 2009
b, they plaster it over with whitewash; **Ezk 13:10** 2009
"**B**, when the wall has fallen, **Ezk 13:12** 2009
"**B**, I am against your *magic* bands **Ezk 13:20** 2009
"Yet, **b**, survivors will be left **Ezk 14:22** 2009
B, they are going to come forth to **Ezk 14:22** 2009
"**B**, while it is intact, it is not **Ezk 15:5** 2009
and **b**, you were at the time for love; **Ezk 16:8** 2009
"**B** now, I have stretched out My **Ezk 16:27** 2009
therefore, **b**, I will gather all **Ezk 16:37** 2009
b, I in turn will bring your conduct **Ezk 16:43** 1887
"**B**, everyone who quotes proverbs **Ezk 16:44** 2009
"**B**, this was the guilt of your **Ezk 16:49** 2009
and **b**, this vine bent its roots **Ezk 17:7** 2009
"**B**, though it is planted, will it **Ezk 17:10** 2009
'**B**, the king of Babylon came to **Ezk 17:12** 2009
and **b**, he pledged his allegiance, **Ezk 17:18** 2009
"**B**, all souls are Mine; **Ezk 18:4** 2005
"Now **b**, he has a son who has **Ezk 18:14** 2009
b, he will die for his iniquity. **Ezk 18:18** 2009
"**B**, I am about to kindle a fire **Ezk 20:47** 2009
"**B**, I am against you; **Ezk 21:3** 2009
B, it comes and it will happen,' **Ezk 21:7** 2009
"**B**, the rulers of Israel, each **Ezk 22:6** 2009
"**B**, then, I smite My hand at your **Ezk 22:13** 2009
therefore, **b**, I am going to gather you **Ezk 22:19** 2009
'**B** I will arouse your lovers **Ezk 23:22** 2009
'**B**, I will give you into the hand **Ezk 23:28** 2009
"Son of man, **b**, I am about to **Ezk 24:16** 2009
'**B**, I am about to profane My **Ezk 24:21** 2009
therefore, **b**, I am going to give **Ezk 25:4** 2009
therefore, **b**, I have stretched out **Ezk 25:7** 2009
'**B**, the house of Judah is like all **Ezk 25:8** 2009
therefore, **b**, I am going to **Ezk 25:9** 2009
"**B**, I will stretch out My hand **Ezk 25:16** 2009
'**B**, I am against you, O Tyre, and **Ezk 26:3** 2009
"**B**, I will bring upon Tyre from **Ezk 26:7** 2009
B, you are wiser than Daniel; **Ezk 28:3** 2009
Therefore, **b**, I will bring **Ezk 28:7** 2009
"**B**, I am against you, O Sidon, **Ezk 28:22** 2009
"**B**, I am against you, Pharaoh king **Ezk 29:3** 2009
"**B**, I will bring upon you a **Ezk 29:8** 2009
therefore, **b**, I am against you and **Ezk 29:10** 2009
"**B**, I will give the land of **Ezk 29:19** 2009
for **b**, it comes!" **Ezk 30:9** 2009
and, **b**, it has not been bound up **Ezk 30:21** 2009
'**B**, I am against Pharaoh king of **Ezk 30:22** 2009
'**B**, Assyria *was* a cedar in Lebanon **Ezk 31:3** 2009
"**B**, you are to them like a sensual **Ezk 33:32** 2009
"**B**, I am against the shepherds, **Ezk 34:10** 2009
"**B**, I Myself will search for My **Ezk 34:11** 2009
B, I will judge between one sheep **Ezk 34:17** 2009
"**B**, I, even I, will judge between **Ezk 34:20** 2009
"**B**, I am against you, Mount Seir, **Ezk 35:3** 2009
'**B**, I have spoken in My jealousy **Ezk 36:6** 2009
'For, **b**, I am for you, and I will **Ezk 36:9** 2009
and **b**, *there were* very many **Ezk 37:2** 2009
'**B**, I will cause breath to enter **Ezk 37:5** 2009
and **b**, a rattling; and the bones came **Ezk 37:7** 2009
and **b**, sinews were on them, and flesh **Ezk 37:8** 2009
b, they say, 'Our bones are dried up and **Ezk 37:11** 2009
"**B**, I will open your graves and **Ezk 37:12** 2009
"**B**, I will take the stick of **Ezk 37:19** 2009
"**B**, I will take the sons of **Ezk 37:21** 2009
"**B**, I am against you, O Gog, **Ezk 38:3** 2009
'**B**, I am against you, O Gog, **Ezk 39:1** 2009
"**B**, it is coming and it shall be **Ezk 39:8** 2009
and **b**, there was a man whose **Ezk 40:3** 2009
And **b**, there was a wall on the **Ezk 40:5** 2009
and **b**, *there were* chambers and **Ezk 40:17** 2009
b, there was a gate toward the south; **Ezk 40:24** 2009
and **b**, *the length of those* facing **Ezk 42:8** 2009
and **b**, the glory of the God of **Ezk 43:2** 2009
and **b**, the glory of the LORD **Ezk 43:5** 2009
B, this is the law of the house. **Ezk 43:12** 2009
and **b**, the glory of the LORD filled **Ezk 44:4** 2009
and **b**, there *was* a place at the **Ezk 46:19** 2009
and **b**, in every corner of the **Ezk 46:21** 2009
and **b**, water was flowing from **Ezk 47:1** 2009
And **b**, water was trickling from **Ezk 47:2** 2009
b, on the bank of the river there *were* **Ezk 47:7** 2009
and **b**, there was a single great statue; **Da 2:31** 431
and **b**, *there was* a tree in the midst **Da 4:10** 431
and **b**, an *angelic* watcher, a holy one, **Da 4:13** 431
and **b**, the four winds of heaven were **Da 7:2** 718
"And **b**, another beast, a second **Da 7:5** 718
and **b**, another one, like a leopard, **Da 7:6** 718
and **b**, a fourth beast, dreadful and **Da 7:7** 718
b, another horn, a little one, came up **Da 7:8** 431
and **b**, this horn possessed eyes **Da 7:8** 431
b, with the clouds of heaven One like **Da 7:13** 718
b, a ram which had two horns was **Da 8:3** 2009
b, a male goat was coming from **Da 8:5** 2009
and **b**, standing before me was one **Da 8:15** 2009
"**B**, I am going to let you know **Da 8:19** 2009
b, there was a certain man dressed **Da 10:5** 2009
Then **b**, a hand touched me and set **Da 10:10** 2009
then **b**, Michael, one of the chief **Da 10:13** 2009
And **b**, one who resembled a human **Da 10:16** 2009
and **b**, the prince of Greece is about **Da 10:20** 2009
B, three more kings are going to **Da 11:2** 2009
Daniel, looked and **b**, two others were **Da 12:5** 2009
"Therefore, **b**, I will hedge up **Hos 2:6** 2009
"Therefore, **b**, I will allure her, **Hos 2:14** 2009

For **b**, they will go because of **Hos 9:6** 2009
"**B**, I am going to send you grain, **Jl 2:19** 2009
"For **b**, in those days and at that **Jl 3:1** 2009
b, I am going to arouse them from **Jl 3:7** 2009
"**B**, I am weighted down beneath **Am 2:13** 2009
"**B**, the days are coming upon you **Am 4:2** 2009
For **b**, He who forms mountains and **Am 4:13** 2009
For **b**, the LORD is going to **Am 6:11** 2009
"For **b**, I am going to raise up a **Am 6:14** 2009
b, He was forming a locust-swarm **Am 7:1** 2009
And **b**, the spring crop *was* after **Am 7:1** 2009
and **b**, the Lord GOD was calling **Am 7:4** 2009
b, the Lord was standing by a vertical **Am 7:7** 2009
"**B** I am about to put a plumb line **Am 7:8** 2009
b, *there was* a basket of summer fruit. **Am 8:1** 2009
"**B**, days are coming," **Am 8:11** 2009
"**B**, the eyes of the Lord GOD are **Am 9:8** 2009
"For **b**, I am commanding, And I **Am 9:9** 2009
"**B**, days are coming," **Am 9:13** 2009
"**B**, I will make you small among **Ob 1:2** 2009
For **b**, the LORD is coming forth **Mi 1:3** 2009
"**B**, I am planning against this **Mi 2:3** 2009
B, on the mountains the feet of **Na 1:15** 2009
"**B**, I am against you," **Na 2:13** 2009
"**B**, I am against you," **Na 3:5** 2009
B, your people are women in your **Na 3:13** 2009
"For **b**, I am raising up the **Hab 1:6** 2009
"**B**, as for the proud one, His **Hab 2:4** 2009
B, it is overlaid with gold and **Hab 2:19** 2009
"**B**, I am going to deal at that **Zph 3:19** 2009
look for much, but **b**, *it comes* to little; **Hg 1:9** 2009
b, a man was riding on a red horse, **Zch 1:8** 2009
b, all the earth is peaceful and quiet." **Zch 1:11** 2009
looked, and **b**, *there were* four horns. **Zch 1:18** 2009
b, *there was* a man with a measuring **Zch 2:1** 2009
And **b**, the angel who was speaking **Zch 2:3** 2009
"For **b**, I will wave My hand over **Zch 2:9** 2009
for **b** I am coming and I will dwell **Zch 2:10** 2009
b, I am going to bring in My servant **Zch 3:8** 2009
'For **b**, the stone that I have set **Zch 3:9** 2009
B, I will engrave an inscription **Zch 3:9** 2009
"I see, and **b**, a lampstand all of **Zch 4:2** 2009
and **b**, *there was* a flying scroll. **Zch 5:1** 2009
(and **b**, a lead cover was lifted up); **Zch 5:7** 2009
b, four chariots were coming forth **Zch 6:1** 2009
"**B**, a man whose name is Branch, **Zch 6:12** 2009
'**B**, I am going to save My people **Zch 8:7** 2009
B, the Lord will dispossess her **Zch 9:4** 2009
B, your king is coming to you; **Zch 9:9** 2009
"but **b**, I will cause the men to **Zch 11:6** 2009
"For **b**, I am going to raise up a **Zch 11:16** 2009
"**B**, I am going to make Jerusalem **Zch 12:2** 2009
B, a day is coming for the LORD **Zch 14:1** 2009
"**B**, I am going to rebuke your **Mal 2:3** 2009
"**B**, I am going to send My **Mal 3:1** 2009
b, He is coming," says the LORD **Mal 3:1** 2009
"For **b**, the day is coming, **Mal 4:1** 2009
"**B**, I am going to send you Elijah **Mal 4:5** 2009
b, an angel of the Lord appeared **Mt 1:20** 2400
"**B**, THE VIRGIN SHALL BE WITH **Mt 1:23** 2400
b, an angel of the Lord appeared to **Mt 2:13** 2400
b, an angel of the Lord appeared in a **Mt 2:19** 2400
and **b**, the heavens were opened, **Mt 3:16** 2400
and **b**, a voice out of the heavens said **Mt 3:17** 2400
and **b**, angels came and *began* to **Mt 4:11** 2400
and **b**, the log is in your own eye? **Mt 7:4** 2400
And **b**, there arose a great storm **Mt 8:24** 2400
And **b**, the whole city came out to **Mt 8:34** 2400
b, many tax collectors and sinners **Mt 9:10** 2400
"**B**, I send you out as sheep in **Mt 10:16** 2400
'**B**, I SEND MY MESSENGER AHEAD **Mt 11:10** 2400
'**B**, a gluttonous man and a **Mt 11:19** 2400
"**B**, MY SERVANT WHOM I HAVE **Mt 12:18** 2400
and **b**, something greater than **Mt 12:41** 2400
and **b**, something greater than **Mt 12:42** 2400
b, His mother and brothers were **Mt 12:46** 2400
"**B**, Your mother and Your brothers **Mt 12:47** 2400
"**B** My mother and My brothers! **Mt 12:49** 2400
"**B**, the sower went out to sow; **Mt 13:3** 2400
And **b**, Moses and Elijah appeared **Mt 17:3** 2400
and **b**, a voice out of the cloud said **Mt 17:5** 2400
"**B**, we have left everything and **Mt 19:27** 2400
"**B**, we are going up to Jerusalem; **Mt 20:18** 2400
'**B** YOUR KING IS COMING TO YOU, **Mt 21:5** 2400
"**B**, I have prepared my dinner; **Mt 22:4** 2400
"Therefore, **b**, I am sending you **Mt 23:34** 2400
'**B**, your house is being left to **Mt 23:38** 2400
'**B**, here is the Christ,' or **Mt 24:23** 2400
'**B**, I have told you in advance. **Mt 24:25** 2400
'**B**, He is in the wilderness,' do **Mt 24:26** 2400
'**B**, He is in the inner rooms,' do **Mt 24:26** 2400
'**B**, the bridegroom! **Mt 25:6** 2400
B, the hour is at hand and the Son **Mt 26:45** 2400
b, the one who betrays Me is at **Mt 26:46** 2400
b, Judas, one of the twelve, came up **Mt 26:47** 2400
And **b**, one of those who were with **Mt 26:51** 2400
b, you have now heard the **Mt 26:65** 2396
And **b**, the veil of the temple was **Mt 27:51** 2400
And **b**, a severe earthquake had **Mt 28:2** 2400
and **b**, He is going ahead of you into **Mt 28:7** 2400
b, I have told you." **Mt 28:7** 2400
And **b**, Jesus met them and greeted **Mt 28:9** 2400
"**B**, I SEND MY MESSENGER AHEAD **Mk 1:2** 2400
"**B**, Your mother and Your brothers **Mk 3:32** 2400
"**B** My mother and My brothers! **Mk 3:34** 2396
B, the sower went out to sow; **Mk 4:3** 2400
"**B**, we have left everything and **Mk 10:28** 2400
"**B**, we are going up to Jerusalem, **Mk 10:33** 2400
b what wonderful stones and what **Mk 13:1** 2396

'**B**, here is the Christ'; **Mk 13:21** 2396
B, *He is* there'; **Mk 13:21** 2396
b, I have told you everything in **Mk 13:23** 2400
b, the Son of Man is being **Mk 14:41** 2400
b, the one who betrays Me is at **Mk 14:42** 2400
"**B**, He is calling for Elijah." **Mk 15:35** 2396
b, *here is* the place where they **Mk 16:6** 2396
"And **b**, you shall be silent and **Lk 1:20** 2400
"And **b**, you will conceive in your **Lk 1:31** 2400
"And **b**, even your relative **Lk 1:36** 2400
"**B**, the bondslave of the Lord; **Lk 1:38** 2400
"For **b**, when the sound of your **Lk 1:44** 2400
For **b**, from this time on all **Lk 1:48** 2400
for **b**, I bring you good news of great **Lk 2:10** 2400
"**B**, this *Child* is appointed for **Lk 2:34** 2400
B, Your father and I have been **Lk 2:48** 2400
b, *there was* a man covered with **Lk 5:12** 2400
for **b**, your reward is great in heaven. **Lk 6:23** 2400
'**B**, I SEND MY MESSENGER AHEAD **Lk 7:27** 2400
'**B**, a gluttonous man and a **Lk 7:34** 2400
And **b**, two men were talking with **Lk 9:30** 2400
b, I send you out as lambs in the **Lk 10:3** 2400
"**B**, I have given you authority to **Lk 10:19** 2400
and **b**, something greater than **Lk 11:31** 2400
and **b**, something greater than **Lk 11:32** 2400
'**B**, for three years I have come **Lk 13:7** 2400
"And **b**, *some* are last who will be **Lk 13:30** 2400
'**B**, I cast out demons and perform **Lk 13:32** 2400
"**B**, your house is left to you **Lk 13:35** 2400
For **b**, the kingdom of God is in **Lk 17:21** 2400
"**B**, we have left our own *homes* **Lk 18:28** 2400
"**B**, we are going up to Jerusalem, **Lk 18:31** 2400
"**B**, Lord, half of my possessions **Lk 19:8** 2400
"**B** the fig tree and all the trees; **Lk 21:29** 3708
"But **b**, the hand of the one **Lk 22:21** 2400
"Simon, Simon, **b**, Satan has **Lk 22:31** 2400
b, a crowd *came*, and the one **Lk 22:47** 2400
b, having examined Him before you, **Lk 23:14** 2400
and **b**, nothing deserving death has **Lk 23:15** 2400
"For **b**, the days are coming when **Lk 23:29** 2400
b, two men suddenly stood near them **Lk 24:4** 2400
And **b**, two of them were going that **Lk 24:13** 2400
"And **b**, I am sending forth the **Lk 24:49** 2400
"**B**, the Lamb of God who takes **Jn 1:29** 2396
"**B**, the Lamb of God!" **Jn 1:36** 2396
"**B**, an Israelite indeed, in whom **Jn 1:47** 2396
b, He is baptizing and all are coming **Jn 3:26** 2396
B, I say to you, lift up your **Jn 4:35** 2400
"**B**, you have become well; **Jn 5:14** 2396
"Lord, **b**, he whom You love is **Jn 11:3** 2396
B, YOUR KING IS COMING, SEATED ON **Jn 12:15** 2400
"**B**, an hour is coming, and has **Jn 16:32** 2400
"**B**, I am bringing Him out to you so **Jn 19:4** 2396
Pilate said to them, "**B**, the Man **Jn 19:5** 2400
"**B**, your King!" **Jn 19:14** 2396
"Woman, **b**, your son!" **Jn 19:26** 2396
"**B**, your mother!" **Jn 19:27** 2396
b, two men in white clothing stood **Ac 1:10** 2400
B, the feet of those who have **Ac 5:9** 2400
"**B**, I see the heavens opened up **Ac 7:56** 2400
b, the men who had been sent **Ac 10:17** 2400
"**B**, three men are looking for you. **Ac 10:19** 2400
"**B**, I am the one you are looking **Ac 10:21** 2400
and **b**, a man stood before me in **Ac 10:30** 2400
"And **b**, at that moment three men **Ac 11:11** 2400
And **b**, an angel of the Lord **Ac 12:7** 2400
"Now, **b**, the hand of the Lord **Ac 13:11** 2400
But **b**, one is coming after me the **Ac 13:25** 2400
'**B**, YOU SCOFFERS, AND MARVEL, AND **Ac 13:41** 3708
b, we are turning to the Gentiles. **Ac 13:46** 2400
"And now, **b**, bound by the spirit, I **Ac 20:22** 2400
"And now, **b**, I know that all of **Ac 20:25** 2400
and **b**, God has granted you all **Ac 27:24** 2400
"**B**, I LAY IN ZION A STONE OF **Ro 9:33** 2400
B then the kindness and severity **Ro 11:22** 3708
B, I tell you a mystery; **1Co 15:51** 2400
b, new things have come. **2Co 5:17** 2400
B, now is "THE ACCEPTABLE TIME," **2Co 6:2** 2400
b, now is "THE DAY OF SALVATION" **2Co 6:2** 2400
yet **b**, we live; as punished yet not put **2Co 6:9** 2400
For **b** what earnestness this very **2Co 7:11** 2400
B I, Paul, say to you that if you **Ga 5:2** 2396
"**B**, I AND THE CHILDREN WHOM GOD **Heb 2:13** 2400
"**B**, DAYS ARE COMING, SAYS THE **Heb 8:8** 2400
"THEN I SAID, '**B**, I HAVE COME **Heb 10:7** 2400
"**B**, I HAVE COME TO DO YOUR WILL." **Heb 10:9** 2400
B, the pay of the laborers who **Jas 5:4** 2400
b, the Judge is standing right at **Jas 5:9** 2400
"**B**, I LAY IN ZION A CHOICE STONE, **1Pe 2:6** 2400
"**B**, the Lord came with many **Jude 1:14** 2400
B, HE IS COMING WITH THE CLOUDS, **Rv 1:7** 2400
and **b**, I am alive forevermore, **Rv 1:18** 2400
B, the devil is about to cast some **Rv 2:10** 2400
'**B**, I will throw her on a bed *of sickness* **Rv 2:22** 2400
B, I have put before you an open **Rv 3:8** 2400
'**B**, I will cause *those* of the **Rv 3:9** 2400
'**B**, I stand at the door and knock; **Rv 3:20** 2400
and **b**, a door *standing* open in heaven, **Rv 4:1** 2400
and **b**, a throne was standing in **Rv 4:2** 2400
b, the Lion that is from the tribe **Rv 5:5** 2400
b, a white horse, and he who sat on it **Rv 6:2** 2400
I looked, and **b**, a black horse; **Rv 6:5** 2400
I looked, and **b**, an ashen horse; **Rv 6:8** 2400
b, a great multitude which no one **Rv 7:9** 2400
b, two woes are still coming after **Rv 9:12** 2400
b, the third woe is coming quickly. **Rv 11:14** 2400
and **b**, a great red dragon having **Rv 12:3** 2400
b, the Lamb *was* standing on Mount **Rv 14:1** 2400
b, a white cloud, and sitting on the **Rv 14:14** 2400

("**B**, I am coming like a thief.	**Rv 16:15**	*2400*
and **b**, a white horse, and He who	**Rv 19:11**	*2400*
"**B**, the tabernacle of God is	**Rv 21:3**	*2400*
"**B**, I am making all things new."	**Rv 21:5**	*2400*
"And **b**, I am coming quickly.	**Rv 22:7**	*2400*
"**B**, I am coming quickly, and My	**Rv 22:12**	*2400*

BEHOLDING

with unveiled face, **b** as in a	**2Co 3:18**	*2734*

BEHOLDS

And he **b** the form of the LORD.	**Nu 12:8**	5027
And his place no longer **b** him.	**Jb 20:9**	7789
men have seen it; Man **b** from afar.	**Jb 36:25**	5027
who **b** the Son and believes in Him will	**Jn 6:40**	*2334*

BEING

and man became a living **b**.	**Gn 2:7**	5315
pleasure, my lord **b** old also?"	**Gn 18:12**	2204
and my men **b** few in number, they	**Gn 34:30**	
It was while she was **b** brought out	**Gn 38:25**	
time that we are **b** brought in,	**Gn 43:18**	
your servants are **b** beaten;	**Ex 5:16**	
their hooks *also* **b** *of* gold, on	**Ex 26:32**	
their hooks *also* **b** *of* gold;	**Ex 26:37**	
its horns **b** *of one piece* with it,	**Ex 38:2**	1961
man takes the life of any human **b**,	**Lv 24:17**	5315
b under *the authority of* your	**Nu 5:19**	
b under *the authority of* your	**Nu 5:20**	
b under *the authority of* her	**Nu 5:29**	
their names **b** changed	**Nu 32:38**	
b cases of dispute in your courts,	**Dt 17:8**	
b careful to do all His	**Dt 28:1**	8104
you shall never cease **b** slaves,	**Jos 9:23**	
Arba **b** the father of Anak	**Jos 15:13**	
Arba **b** the father of Anak	**Jos 21:11**	
b one hundred and ten years old.	**Jos 24:29**	
rejected Me from **b** king over them.	**1Sa 8:7**	4427a
He has also rejected you from **b**	**1Sa 15:23**	
you from **b** king over Israel."	**1Sa 15:26**	1961
him from **b** king over Israel?	**1Sa 16:1**	4427a
b coming up out of the earth."	**1Sa 28:13**	430
was very old, **b** eighty years old;	**2Sa 19:32**	
from **b** priest to the LORD,	**1Ki 2:27**	1961
The house, while it was **b** built,	**1Ki 6:7**	
in the house while it was **b** built.	**1Ki 6:7**	
removed Maacah his mother from **b**	**1Ki 15:13**	
in **b** like the house of Jeroboam,	**1Ki 16:7**	1961
b then the king of Judah,	**2Ki 8:16**	
sons who were **b** put to death,	**2Ki 11:2**	
b *stationed* until now at	**1Ch 9:18**	
All these, **b** men of war who could	**1Ch 12:38**	
Mikloth **b** the chief officer;	**1Ch 27:4**	
this **b** *required* forever in Israel.	**2Ch 2:4**	
b a great multitude and *having*	**2Ch 13:8**	
sons who were **b** put to death,	**2Ch 22:11**	
in a separate house, **b** a leper,	**2Ch 26:21**	6879
"Beware of **b** negligent in	**Ezr 4:22**	
which is **b** built with huge stones,	**Ezr 5:8**	
and beams are **b** laid in the walls;	**Ezr 5:8**	
its height **b** 60 cubits and its	**Ezr 6:3**	
last ones, these **b** their names,	**Ezr 8:13**	
away their wives, and **b** guilty,	**Ezr 10:19**	
of our God, **b** related to Tobiah,	**Ne 13:4**	
his provinces **b** in his presence.	**Es 1:3**	
b written in the name of King	**Es 3:12**	
now, who *ever* perished **b** innocent?	**Jb 4:7**	
B wholly at ease and satisfied;	**Jb 21:23**	
has put wisdom in the innermost **b** Or	**Jb 38:36**	2910
desire truth in the innermost **b**,	**Ps 51:6**	2910
His strength, **B** girded with might;	**Ps 65:6**	
b wrongfully my enemies	**Ps 69:4**	
But He, **b** compassionate, forgave	**Ps 78:38**	
to my God while I have my **b**.	**Ps 104:33**	
to my God while I have my **b**.	**Ps 146:2**	
will you love **b** simple-minded?	**Pr 1:22**	
will keep your foot from **b** caught.	**Pr 3:26**	
But he who hates **b** a guarantor is	**Pr 11:15**	
all the innermost parts of his **b**.	**Pr 20:27**	990
And my inmost **b** will rejoice When	**Pr 23:16**	3629
who are **b** taken away to death,	**Pr 24:11**	
which were **b** done under the sun.	**Ec 4:1**	
riches **b** hoarded by their owner to	**Ec 5:13**	
serpent bites before **b** charmed,	**Ec 10:11**	
In addition to **b** a wise man, the	**Ec 12:9**	1961
about to be removed from **b** a city And	**Is 17:1**	
all these things came into **b**,"	**Is 66:2**	1961
"Keep your feet from **b** unshod And	**Jer 2:25**	
I have not hurried away from **b** a	**Jer 17:16**	
And a great storm is **b** stirred up	**Jer 25:32**	
From **b** a nation before Me forever."	**Jer 31:36**	1961
who were **b** exiled to Babylon.	**Jer 40:1**	
'Come and let us cut her off from **b**	**Jer 48:2**	
"Moab will be destroyed from **b** a	**Jer 48:42**	
b stricken For lack of the fruits	**La 4:9**	
each had two touching another **b**,	**Ezk 1:11**	
their appearance and workmanship **b**	**Ezk 1:16**	
"For you are not **b** sent to a	**Ezk 3:5**	
are **b** committed in its midst."	**Ezk 9:4**	
cultivated instead of **b** a desolation	**Ezk 36:34**	1961
b a cubit and a handbreadth):	**Ezk 43:13**	
sea, **b** made to flow into the sea,	**Ezk 47:8**	
a human **b** was touching my lips;	**Da 10:16**	1121, 120
will reject you from **b** My priest.	**Hos 4:6**	
became satisfied, And **b** satisfied,	**Hos 13:6**	7646
"Is it **b** said, O house of Jacob:	**Mi 2:7**	
her husband, **b** a righteous man and	**Mt 1:19**	*1510*
after **b** warned *by God* in a dream, he	**Mt 2:22**	
and they were **b** baptized by him in	**Mt 3:6**	
After **b** baptized, Jesus came	**Mt 3:16**	
"And who of you by **b** worried	**Mt 6:27**	
"If you then, **b** evil, know how to	**Mt 7:11**	*1510*
so that the boat was **b** covered with	**Mt 8:24**	*2572*
of vipers, how can you, **b** evil,	**Mt 12:34**	*1510*
prophecy of Isaiah is **b** fulfilled,	**Mt 13:14**	
places, and **b** called Rabbi by men	**Mt 23:7**	
house is **b** left to you desolate!	**Mt 23:38**	
B deeply grieved, they each one	**Mt 26:22**	
the Son of Man is **b** betrayed	**Mt 26:45**	
And while He was **b** accused by the	**Mt 27:12**	
and they were **b** baptized by him in	**Mk 1:5**	
forty days **b** tempted by Satan;	**Mk 1:13**	
B unable to get to Him because of	**Mk 2:4**	
overhearing what was **b** spoken,	**Mk 5:36**	
many as touched it were **b** cured.	**Mk 6:56**	
B reminded, Peter said to Him,	**Mk 11:21**	
Passover *lamb* was **b** sacrificed,	**Mk 14:12**	
the Son of Man is **b** betrayed into	**Mk 14:41**	
all these matters were **b** talked about	**Lk 1:65**	
b rescued from the hand of our	**Lk 1:74**	
which were **b** said about Him.	**Lk 2:33**	
b, as was supposed, the son of Joseph,	**Lk 3:23**	*1510*
days, **b** tempted by the devil.	**Lk 4:2**	
with unclean spirits were **b** cured.	**Lk 6:18**	
a dead man was **b** carried out,	**Lk 7:12**	
"If you then, **b** evil, know how to	**Lk 11:13**	*5225*
His opponents were **b** humiliated;	**Lk 13:17**	
the glorious things **b** done by Him.	**Lk 13:17**	*1096*
just a few who are **b** saved?"	**Lk 13:23**	
of God, but yourselves **b** thrown out.	**Lk 13:28**	
lifted up his eyes, **b** in torment,	**Lk 16:23**	*5225*
but now he is **b** comforted here,	**Lk 16:25**	
they were **b** given in marriage,	**Lk 17:27**	
and **b** amazed at His answer, they	**Lk 20:26**	*2296*
God, **b** sons of the resurrection.	**Lk 20:36**	*1510*
And **b** in agony He was praying very	**Lk 22:44**	*1096*
were **b** led away to be put to death	**Lk 23:32**	
All things came into **b** through Him,	**Jn 1:3**	*1096*
into **b** that has come into being.	**Jn 1:3**	*1096*
into being that has come into **b**.	**Jn 1:3**	*1096*
were coming and were **b** baptized	**Jn 3:23**	
b wearied from His journey,	**Jn 4:6**	
"How is it that You, **b** a Jew,	**Jn 4:9**	*1510*
'From his innermost **b** will flow	**Jn 7:38**	*2836*
to Him before, **b** one of them) said	**Jn 7:50**	*1510*
and because You, **b** a man,	**Jn 10:33**	*1510*
again **b** deeply moved within,	**Jn 11:38**	
but **b** high priest that year, he	**Jn 11:51**	*1510*
b a relative of the one whose ear	**Jn 18:26**	*1510*
Arimathea, **b** a disciple of Jesus,	**Jn 19:38**	*1510*
day by day those who were **b** saved.	**Ac 2:47**	
mother's womb was **b** carried along,	**Ac 3:2**	
were taking note of him as **b** the one	**Ac 3:10**	*1510*
b greatly disturbed because they	**Ac 4:2**	
and they were all **b** healed.	**Ac 5:16**	
their widows were **b** overlooked	**Ac 6:1**	
one *of them* **b** treated unjustly,	**Ac 7:24**	
But **b** full of the Holy Spirit, he	**Ac 7:55**	*5225*
Christ, they were **b** baptized,	**Ac 8:12**	
and after **b** baptized, he continued	**Ac 8:13**	
prevents me from **b** baptized?"	**Ac 8:36**	
Samaria enjoyed peace, **b** built up;	**Ac 9:31**	
gaze on him and **b** much alarmed,	**Ac 10:4**	*1096*
but prayer for him was **b** made	**Ac 12:5**	*1096*
was **b** done by the angel was real,	**Ac 12:9**	*1096*
So, **b** sent out by the Holy Spirit,	**Ac 13:4**	
b amazed at the teaching of the	**Ac 13:12**	
the word of the Lord was **b** spread	**Ac 13:49**	
b sent on their way by the church,	**Ac 15:3**	
Silas, also **b** prophets themselves,	**Ac 15:32**	*1510*
b committed by the brethren to the	**Ac 15:40**	
were **b** strengthened in the faith,	**Ac 16:5**	
our city into confusion, **b** Jews,	**Ac 16:20**	*5225*
accept or to observe, **b** Romans."	**Ac 16:21**	*1510*
his spirit was **b** provoked within	**Ac 17:16**	
"**B** then the children of God, we	**Ac 17:29**	*5225*
were believing and **b** baptized.	**Ac 18:8**	
and **b** fervent in spirit, he was	**Ac 18:25**	*2204*
b acquainted only with the baptism	**Ac 18:25**	*1987*
of the Lord Jesus was **b** magnified.	**Ac 19:17**	
indeed we are in danger of **b** accused	**Ac 19:40**	
of our fathers, **b** zealous for God just	**Ac 22:3**	*5225*
of Your witness Stephen was **b** shed,	**Ac 22:20**	
are **b** carried out for this nation,	**Ac 24:2**	*1096*
Paul was **b** kept in custody at Caesarea	**Ac 25:4**	
"**B** at a loss how to investigate such	**Ac 25:20**	*639*
O King, I am **b** accused by Jews.	**Ac 26:7**	
also when they were **b** put to death	**Ac 26:10**	
and **b** furiously enraged at them, I	**Ac 26:11**	
than by what was **b** said by Paul.	**Ac 27:11**	
we were **b** violently storm-tossed,	**Ac 27:18**	
b saved was gradually abandoned.	**Ac 27:20**	
as we were **b** driven about in the	**Ac 27:27**	
Some were **b** persuaded by the	**Ac 28:24**	
because your faith is **b** proclaimed	**Ro 1:8**	
b understood through what has been	**Ro 1:20**	
b filled with all unrighteousness,	**Ro 1:29**	
b instructed out of the Law,	**Ro 2:18**	
I also still **b** judged as a sinner?	**Ro 3:7**	
b witnessed by the Law and the	**Ro 3:21**	
b justified as a gift by His grace	**Ro 3:24**	
who believe without **b** circumcised,	**Ro 4:11**	*203*
calls into **b** that which does not exist.	**Ro 4:17**	*1510*
and **b** fully assured that what God	**Ro 4:21**	
are **b** led by the Spirit of God,	**Ro 8:14**	
ARE **B** PUT TO DEATH ALL DAY LONG;	**Ro 8:36**	
off, and you, **b** a wild olive,	**Ro 11:17**	*1510*
b saved it is the power of God.	**1Co 1:18**	
his heart, **b** under no constraint,	**1Co 7:37**	*2192*
b accustomed to the idol until	**1Co 8:7**	
conscience **b** weak is defiled.	**1Co 8:7**	*1510*
though not **b** myself under the Law,	**1Co 9:20**	*1510*
though not **b** without the law of	**1Co 9:21**	*1510*
to God among those who are **b** saved	**2Co 2:15**	
b manifested that you are a letter	**2Co 3:3**	
are **b** transformed into the same	**2Co 3:18**	
we who live are constantly **b** delivered	**2Co 4:11**	
inner man is **b** renewed day by day.	**2Co 4:16**	
this tent, we groan, **b** burdened,	**2Co 5:4**	
b always of good courage,	**2Co 5:6**	
this present time your abundance **b**	**2Co 8:14**	
but **b** himself very earnest,	**2Co 8:17**	*5225*
which is **b** administered by us for	**2Co 8:19**	
myself from **b** a burden to you,	**2Co 11:9**	*4*
For you, **b** *so* wise, tolerate the	**2Co 11:19**	*1510*
Who is weak without my **b** weak?	**2Co 11:29**	
b more extremely zealous for my	**Ga 1:14**	*5225*
"If you, **b** a Jew, live like the	**Ga 2:14**	*5225*
you now **b** perfected by the flesh?	**Ga 3:3**	
b shut up to the faith which was	**Ga 3:23**	
But God, **b** rich in mercy, because	**Eph 2:4**	*1510*
Jesus Himself **b** the corner *stone*,	**Eph 2:20**	*1510*
b fitted together, is growing into	**Eph 2:21**	
in whom you also are **b** built	**Eph 2:22**	
b rooted and grounded in love,	**Eph 3:17**	
b diligent to preserve the unity	**Eph 4:3**	
b fitted and held together by what	**Eph 4:16**	
b darkened in their understanding,	**Eph 4:18**	*1510*
which is **b** corrupted in accordance	**Eph 4:22**	
He Himself **b** the Savior of	**Eph 5:23**	
complete by **b** of the same mind,	**Php 2:2**	
and **b** made in the likeness of men.	**Php 2:7**	*1096*
B found in appearance as a man, He	**Php 2:8**	
But even if I am **b** poured out as a	**Php 2:17**	
b conformed to His death;	**Php 3:10**	
the secret of **b** filled and going hungry,	**Php 4:12**	
been firmly rooted *and now* **b** built up	**Col 2:7**	
b supplied and held together by	**Col 2:19**	
put on the new self who is **b** renewed	**Col 3:10**	
God, displaying himself as **b** God.	**2Th 2:4**	*1510*
but the woman **b** deceived,	**1Tm 2:14**	
worse, deceiving and **b** deceived.	**2Tm 3:13**	
For I am already **b** poured out as a	**2Tm 4:6**	
Him, **b** detestable and disobedient and	**Ti 1:16**	*1510*
b subject to their own husbands,	**Ti 2:5**	
that **b** justified by His grace we	**Ti 3:7**	
and is sinning, **b** self-condemned.	**Ti 3:11**	*1510*
b designated by God as a high	**Heb 5:10**	
worthless and close to **b** cursed,	**Heb 6:8**	
cursed, and it ends up **b** burned.	**Heb 6:8**	
days, when, after **b** enlightened,	**Heb 10:32**	
by **b** made a public spectacle	**Heb 10:33**	
his **b** taken up he was pleasing to God.	**Heb 11:5**	*3331*
b warned *by God* about things not	**Heb 11:7**	
in goatskins, **b** destitute,	**Heb 11:37**	
b content with what you have;	**Heb 13:5**	
b a double-minded man, unstable	**Jas 1:8**	
"I am **b** tempted by God";	**Jas 1:13**	
is dead, **b** by itself.	**Jas 2:17**	
of the soil, **b** patient about it,	**Jas 5:7**	
so that the proof of your faith, **b**	**1Pe 1:7**	
are **b** built up as a spiritual	**1Pe 2:5**	
and while **b** reviled, He did not	**1Pe 2:23**	
b submissive to their own husbands;	**1Pe 3:5**	
without **b** frightened by any fear.	**1Pe 3:6**	
always **b** ready to make a defense	**1Pe 3:15**	
are **b** accomplished by your brethren	**1Pe 5:9**	
destroyed, **b** flooded with water.	**2Pe 3:6**	
heavens and earth are **b** reserved for fire,	**2Pe 3:7**	
b in labor and in pain to give	**Rv 12:2**	*2192*

BEINGS

and of human **b**, of the women who	**Nu 31:35**	5315
and the human **b** were 16,000, from	**Nu 31:40**	5315
and the human **b** were 16,000	**Nu 31:46**	5315
figures resembling four living **b**.	**Ezk 1:5**	2421b
In the midst of the living **b** there	**Ezk 1:13**	2421b
back and forth among the living **b**.	**Ezk 1:13**	2421b
And the living **b** ran to and fro	**Ezk 1:14**	2421b
Now as I looked at the living **b**,	**Ezk 1:15**	2421b
on the earth beside the living **b**,	**Ezk 1:15**	2421b
Whenever the living **b** moved,	**Ezk 1:19**	2421b
the living **b** rose from the earth,	**Ezk 1:19**	2421b
of the living **b** *was* in the wheels.	**Ezk 1:20**	2421b
of the living **b** *was* in the wheels.	**Ezk 1:21**	2421b
over the heads of the living **b** *there was*	**Ezk 1:22**	2421b
the living **b** touching one another and	**Ezk 3:13**	2421b
They are the living **b** that I saw	**Ezk 10:15**	2421b
of the living **b** *was* in them.	**Ezk 10:17**	2421b
These are the living **b** that I saw	**Ezk 10:20**	2421b

BEKA

a **b** a head (*that is,* half a shekel	**Ex 38:26**	1235

BEL

B has bowed down, Nebo stoops over;	**Is 46:1**	1078
captured, **B** has been put to shame,	**Jer 50:2**	1078
"I will punish **B** in Babylon,	**Jer 51:44**	1078

BELA

of Zeboiim, and the king of **B**	**Gn 14:2**	1106b
king of Zeboiim and the king of **B**	**Gn 14:8**	1106b
B the son of Beor reigned in Edom,	**Gn 36:32**	1106a
Then **B** died, and Jobab the son of	**Gn 36:33**	1106a
B and Becher and Ashbel, Gera and	**Gn 46:21**	1106a
of **B**, the family of the Belaites;	**Nu 26:38**	1106a
The sons of **B** were Ard and Naaman:	**Nu 26:40**	1106a
B was the son of Beor, and the	**1Ch 1:43**	1106a
When **B** died, Jobab the son of	**1Ch 1:44**	1106a
and **B** the son of Azaz, the son of	**1Ch 5:8**	1106a
B and Becher and Jediael.	**1Ch 7:6**	1106a

The sons of **B** were five: 1Ch 7:7 1106a
the father of **B** his firstborn, 1Ch 8:1 1106a
B had sons: Addar, Gera, Abihud, 1Ch 8:3 1106a

BELAITES
of Bela, the family of the **B**; Nu 26:38 1108

BELCH
they **b** forth with their mouth; Ps 59:7 5042

BELIAL
Or what harmony has Christ with **B**, 2Co 6:15 *955*

BELIEVE
stunned, for he did not **b** them. Gn 45:26 539
"What if they will not **b** me or Ex 4:1 539
"that they may **b** that the LORD, Ex 4:5 539
"If they will not **b** you or heed Ex 4:8 539
b the witness of the last sign. Ex 4:8 539
if they will not **b** even these two signs Ex 4:9 539
and may also **b** in you forever." Ex 19:9 539
how long will they not **b** in Me, Nu 14:11 539
I did not **b** the reports, 1Ki 10:7 539
did not **b** in the LORD their God. 2Ki 17:14 539
"Nevertheless I did not **b** their 2Ch 9:6 539
you like this, and do not **b** him, 2Ch 32:15 539
I could not **b** that He was Jb 9:16 539
"He does not **b** that he will Jb 15:22 539
on them when they did not **b**, Jb 29:24 539
Because they did not **b** in God And Ps 78:22 539
did not **b** in His wonderful works. Ps 78:32 539
They did not **b** in His word, Ps 106:24 539
For I **b** in Your commandments. Ps 119:66 539
speaks graciously, do not **b** him, Pr 26:25 539
If you will not **b**, you surely Is 7:9 539
So that you may know and **b** Me Is 43:10 539
Do not **b** them, although they may Jer 12:6 539
the son of Ahikam did not **b** them. Jer 40:14 539
The kings of the earth did not **b**, La 4:12 539
You would not **b** if you were told. Hab 1:5 539
you **b** that I am able to do this?" Mt 9:28 *4100*
ones who **b** in Me to stumble, Mt 18:6 *4100*
'Then why did you not **b** him?' Mt 21:25 *4100*
and you did not **b** him; Mt 21:32 *4100*
and prostitutes did **b** him; Mt 21:32 *4100*
remorse afterward so as to **b** him. Mt 21:32 *4100*
'There *He is*,' do not **b** *him*. Mt 24:23 *4100*
in the inner rooms,' do not **b** *them*. Mt 24:26 *4100*
the cross, and we will **b** in Him. Mt 27:42 *4100*
repent and **b** in the gospel." Mk 1:15 *4100*
be afraid *any longer*, only **b**." Mk 5:36 *4100*
said, "I do **b**; help my unbelief." Mk 9:24 *4100*
little ones who **b** to stumble, Mk 9:42 *4100*
b that you have received them, Mk 11:24 *4100*
'Then why did you not **b** him?' Mk 11:31 *4100*
'Behold, *He is* there'; do not **b** *him*; Mk 13:21 *4100*
cross, so that we may see and **b**!" Mk 15:32 *4100*
seen by her, they refused to **b** it. Mk 16:11 *569*
but they did not **b** them either. Mk 16:13 *4100*
because you did not **b** my words, Lk 1:20 *4100*
that they will not **b** and be saved. Lk 8:12 *4100*
they **b** for a while, and in time of Lk 8:13 *4100*
only **b**, and she will be made well." Lk 8:50 *4100*
'Why did you not **b** him?' Lk 20:5 *4100*
"If I tell you, you will not **b**; Lk 22:67 *4100*
and they would not **b** them. Lk 24:11 *569*
"O foolish men and slow of heart to **b** Lk 24:25 *4100*
they still could not **b** *it* because of Lk 24:41 *569*
that all might **b** through him. Jn 1:7 *4100*
even to those who **b** in His name, Jn 1:12 *4100*
you under the fig tree, do you **b**? Jn 1:50 *4100*
earthly things and you do not **b**, Jn 3:12 *4100*
b if I tell you heavenly things? Jn 3:12 *4100*
not **b** has been judged already, Jn 3:18 *4100*
"Woman, **b** Me, an hour is coming Jn 4:21 *4100*
of what you said that we **b**, Jn 4:42 *4100*
wonders, you *simply* will not **b**." Jn 4:48 *4100*
for you do not **b** Him whom He sent. Jn 5:38 *4100*
"How can you **b**, when you receive Jn 5:44 *4100*
believed Moses, you would **b** Me, Jn 5:46 *4100*
"But if you do not **b** his writings, Jn 5:47 *4100*
how will you **b** My words?" Jn 5:47 *4100*
you **b** in Him whom He has sent." Jn 6:29 *4100*
sign, so that we may see, and **b** You? Jn 6:30 *4100*
have seen Me, and yet do not **b**. Jn 6:36 *4100*
are some of you who do not **b**." Jn 6:64 *4100*
who they were who did not **b**, Jn 6:64 *4100*
for unless you **b** that I am *He*, you Jn 8:24 *4100*
things, many came to **b** in Him. Jn 8:30 *4100*
speak the truth, you do not **b** Me. Jn 8:45 *4100*
speak truth, why do you not **b** Me? Jn 8:46 *4100*
then did not **b** *it* of him, Jn 9:18 *4100*
"Do you **b** in the Son of Man?" Jn 9:35 *4100*
He, Lord, that I may **b** in Him?" Jn 9:36 *4100*
"Lord, I **b**." And he worshiped Him. Jn 9:38 *4100*
"I told you, and you do not **b**; Jn 10:25 *4100*
"But you do not **b** because you Jn 10:26 *4100*
works of My Father, do not **b** Me; Jn 10:37 *4100*
I do them, though you do not **b** Me, Jn 10:38 *4100*
do not believe Me, **b** the works, Jn 10:38 *4100*
was not there, so that you may **b**; Jn 11:15 *4100*
in Me will never die. Do you **b** this? Jn 11:26 *4100*
"Did I not say to you that if you **b**, Jn 11:40 *4100*
may **b** that You sent Me." Jn 11:42 *4100*
like this, all men will **b** in Him, Jn 11:48 *4100*
have the Light, **b** in the Light, Jn 12:36 *4100*
For this reason they could not **b**, Jn 12:39 *4100*
believes in Me, does not **b** in Me Jn 12:44 *4100*
occur, you may **b** that I am *He*. Jn 13:19 *4100*
b in God, believe also in Me. Jn 14:1 *4100*
believe in God, **b** also in Me. Jn 14:1 *4100*
you not **b** that I am in the Father, Jn 14:10 *4100*
"**B** Me that I am in the Father and Jn 14:11 *4100*
otherwise **b** because of the Jn 14:11 *4100*
when it happens, you may **b**. Jn 14:29 *4100*
sin, because they do not **b** in Me; Jn 16:9 *4100*
we **b** that You came from God." Jn 16:30 *4100*
Jesus answered them, "Do you now **b** Jn 16:31 *4100*
who **b** in Me through their word; Jn 17:20 *4100*
may **b** that You sent Me. Jn 17:21 *4100*
the truth, so that you also may **b**. Jn 19:35 *4100*
into His side, I will not **b**." Jn 20:25 *4100*
may **b** that Jesus is the Christ, Jn 20:31 *4100*
"If you **b** with all your heart, Ac 8:37 *4100*
"I **b** that Jesus Christ is the Son Ac 8:37 *4100*
A WORK WHICH YOU WILL NEVER **B**, Ac 13:41 *4100*
hear the word of the gospel and **b**. Ac 15:7 *4100*
"But we **b** that we are saved Ac 15:11 *4100*
"**B** in the Lord Jesus, and you Ac 16:31 *4100*
telling the people to **b** in Him who Ac 19:4 *4100*
Agrippa, do you **b** the Prophets? Ac 26:27 *4100*
up your courage, men, for I **b** God that Ac 27:25 *4100*
spoken, but others would not **b**. Ac 28:24 *569*
If some did not **b**, their unbelief Ro 3:3 *569*
Jesus Christ for all those who **b**; Ro 3:22 *4100*
who **b** without being circumcised, Ro 4:11 *4100*
as those who **b** in Him who raised Ro 4:24 *4100*
we **b** that we shall also live with Ro 6:8 *4100*
and **b** in your heart that God Ro 10:9 *4100*
How will they **b** in Him whom Ro 10:14 *4100*
preached to save those who **b**. 1Co 1:21 *4100*
and in part I **b** it. 1Co 11:18 *4100*
for a sign, not to those who **b** but 1Co 14:22 *4100*
unbelievers but to those who **b**. 1Co 14:22 *4100*
we also **b**, therefore we also speak, 2Co 4:13 *4100*
might be given to those who **b**. Ga 3:22 *4100*
of His power toward us who **b**. Eph 1:19 *4100*
sake, not only to **b** in Him, Php 1:29 *4100*
performs its work in you who **b**. 1Th 2:13 *4100*
For if we **b** that Jesus died and 1Th 4:14 *4100*
that they will **b** what is false, 2Th 2:11 *4100*
be judged who did not **b** the truth, 2Th 2:12 *4100*
would **b** in Him for eternal life. 1Tm 1:16 *4100*
by those who **b** and know the truth. 1Tm 4:3 *4103*
an example of those who **b**. 1Tm 4:12 *4103*
one wife, having children who **b**, Ti 1:6 *4103*
comes to God must **b** that He is and Heb 11:6 *4100*
You **b** that God is one. Jas 2:19 *4100*
the demons also **b**, and shudder. Jas 2:19 *4100*
do not see Him now, but **b** in Him, 1Pe 1:8 *4100*
value, then, is for you who **b**; 1Pe 2:7 *4100*
that we **b** in the name of His Son 1Jn 3:23 *4100*
Beloved, do not **b** every spirit, 1Jn 4:1 *4100*
not **b** God has made Him a liar, 1Jn 5:10 *4100*
b in the name of the Son of God, 1Jn 5:13 *4100*
destroyed those who did not **b**. Jude 1:5 *4100*

BELIEVED
Then he **b** in the LORD; Gn 15:6 539
So the people **b**; and when they heard Ex 4:31 539
and they **b** in the LORD and in His Ex 14:31 539
"Because you have not **b** Me, Nu 20:12 539
b Him nor listened to His voice. Dt 9:23 539
So Achish **b** David, saying, 1Sa 27:12 539
I would have despaired unless I had **b** Ps 27:13 539
Then they **b** His words; Ps 106:12 539
I **b** when I said, Ps 116:10 539
Who has **b** our message? Is 53:1 539
the people of Nineveh **b** in God; Jon 3:5 539
shall be done for you as you have **b**." Mt 8:13 *4100*
because they had not **b** those who Mk 16:14 *4100*
"He who has **b** and has been Mk 16:16 *4100*
will accompany those who have **b**: Mk 16:17 *4100*
"And blessed *is* she who **b** that Lk 1:45 *4100*
glory, and His disciples **b** in Him. Jn 2:11 *4100*
and they **b** the Scripture and the Jn 2:22 *4100*
the feast, many **b** in His name, Jn 2:23 *4100*
because he has not **b** in the name Jn 3:18 *4100*
many of the Samaritans **b** in Him Jn 4:39 *4100*
Many more **b** because of His word; Jn 4:41 *4100*
The man **b** the word that Jesus Jn 4:50 *4100*
and he himself **b** and his whole Jn 4:53 *4100*
"For if you **b** Moses, you would Jn 5:46 *4100*
"We have **b** and have come to Jn 6:69 *4100*
many of the crowd **b** in Him; Jn 7:31 *4100*
who **b** in Him were to receive; Jn 7:39 *4100*
rulers or Pharisees has **b** in Him, Jn 7:48 *4100*
to those Jews who had **b** Him, Jn 8:31 *4100*
Many **b** in Him there. Jn 10:42 *4100*
I have **b** that You are the Christ, Jn 11:27 *4100*
saw what He had done, **b** in Him. Jn 11:45 *4100*
"LORD, WHO HAS **B** OUR REPORT? Jn 12:38 *4100*
many even of the rulers **b** in Him, Jn 12:42 *4100*
and have **b** that I came forth from Jn 16:27 *4100*
they **b** that You sent Me. Jn 17:8 *4100*
then also entered, and he saw and **b**. Jn 20:8 *4100*
you have seen Me, have you **b**? Jn 20:29 *4100*
they who did not see, and *yet* **b**." Jn 20:29 *4100*
all those who had **b** were together and Ac 2:44 *4100*
those who had heard the message **b**; Ac 4:4 *4100*
who **b** were of one heart and soul; Ac 4:32 *4100*
But when they **b** Philip preaching Ac 8:12 *4100*
Even Simon himself **b**; Ac 8:13 *4100*
Joppa, and many **b** in the Lord. Ac 9:42 *4100*
number who **b** turned to the Lord. Ac 11:21 *4100*
b when he saw what had happened, Ac 13:12 *4100*
been appointed to eternal life **b**. Ac 13:48 *4100*
a large number of people **b**, Ac 14:1 *4100*
to the Lord in whom they had **b**. Ac 14:23 *4100*
sect of the Pharisees who had **b** stood Ac 15:5 *4100*
having **b** in God with his whole Ac 16:34 *4100*
Therefore many of them **b**, Ac 17:12 *4100*
But some men joined him and **b**, Ac 17:34 *4100*
b in the Lord with all his Ac 18:8 *4100*
those who had **b** through grace, Ac 18:27 *4100*
the Holy Spirit when you **b**?" Ac 19:2 *4100*
of those who had **b** kept coming, Ac 19:18 *4100*
the Jews of those who have **b**, Ac 21:20 *4100*
the Gentiles who have **b**, Ac 21:25 *4100*
and beat those who **b** in You. Ac 22:19 *4100*
"ABRAHAM **B** GOD, AND IT WAS Ro 4:3 *4100*
in the presence of Him whom he **b**, Ro 4:17 *4100*
In hope against hope he **b**, Ro 4:18 *4100*
on Him in whom they have not **b**? Ro 10:14 *4100*
"LORD, WHO HAS **B** OUR REPORT?" Ro 10:16 *4100*
is nearer to us than when we **b**. Ro 13:11 *4100*
Servants through whom you **b**, 1Co 3:5 *4100*
to you, unless you **b** in vain. 1Co 15:2 *4100*
they, so we preach and so you **b**. 1Co 15:11 *4100*
"I **B**, THEREFORE I SPOKE," 2Co 4:13 *4100*
even we have **b** in Christ Jesus, Ga 2:16 *4100*
Even so Abraham **B** GOD, AND IT Ga 3:6 *4100*
having also **b**, you were sealed in Him Eph 1:13 *4100*
be marveled at among all who have **b** 2Th 1:10 *4100*
our testimony to you was **b**. 2Th 1:10 *4100*
the nations, **B** on in the world, 1Tm 3:16 *4100*
for I know whom I have **b** and I am 2Tm 1:12 *4100*
so that those who have **b** God will Ti 3:8 *4100*
For we who have **b** enter that rest, Heb 4:3 *4100*
"AND ABRAHAM **B** GOD, AND IT WAS Jas 2:23 *4100*
b the love which God has for us. 1Jn 4:16 *4100*
because he has not **b** in the 1Jn 5:10 *4100*

BELIEVER
son of a Jewish woman who was a **b**, Ac 16:1 *4103*
a **b** in common with an unbeliever? 2Co 6:15 *4103*
are blessed with Abraham, the **b**. Ga 3:9 *4103*
who is a **b** has *dependent* widows, 1Tm 5:16 *4103*

BELIEVERS
And all the more **b** in the Lord, Ac 5:14 *4100*
All the circumcised **b** who came Ac 10:45 *4103*
the **b** in Macedonia and in Achaia. 1Th 1:7 *4100*
we behaved toward you **b**; 1Th 2:10 *4100*
of all men, especially of **b**. 1Tm 4:10 *4103*
Those who have **b** as their 1Tm 6:2 *4103*
of the benefit are **b** and beloved. 1Tm 6:2 *4103*
who through Him are **b** in God, 1Pe 1:21 *4103*

BELIEVES
The naive **b** everything, But the Pr 14:15 539
who **b** *in it* will not be disturbed. Is 28:16 539
are possible to him who **b**." Mk 9:23 *4100*
but **b** that what he says is going Mk 11:23 *4100*
b will in Him have eternal life. Jn 3:15 *4100*
b in Him shall not perish, Jn 3:16 *4100*
"He who **b** in Him is not judged; Jn 3:18 *4100*
who **b** in the Son has eternal life; Jn 3:36 *4100*
My word, and **b** Him who sent Me, Jn 5:24 *4100*
he who **b** in Me will never thirst. Jn 6:35 *4100*
who beholds the Son and **b** in Him will Jn 6:40 *4100*
to you, he who **b** has eternal life. Jn 6:47 *4100*
"He who **b** in Me, as the Scripture Jn 7:38 *4100*
he who **b** in Me will live even if Jn 11:25 *4100*
lives and **b** in Me will never die. Jn 11:26 *4100*
b in Me, does not believe in Me Jn 12:44 *4100*
that everyone who **b** in Me will not Jn 12:46 *4100*
I say to you, he who **b** in Me, Jn 14:12 *4100*
who **b** in Him receives forgiveness Ac 10:43 *4100*
who **b** is freed from all things, Ac 13:39 *4100*
for salvation to everyone who **b**, Ro 1:16 *4100*
but **b** in Him who justifies the Ro 4:5 *4100*
AND HE WHO **B** IN HIM WILL NOT BE Ro 9:33 *4100*
righteousness to everyone who **b**. Ro 10:4 *4100*
for with the heart a person **b**, Ro 10:10 *4100*
"WHOEVER **B** IN HIM WILL NOT BE Ro 10:11 *4100*
bears all things, **b** all things, 1Co 13:7 *4100*
AND HE WHO **B** IN HIM WILL NOT 1Pe 2:6 *4100*
Whoever **b** that Jesus is the Christ 1Jn 5:1 *4100*
b that Jesus is the Son of God? 1Jn 5:5 *4100*
The one who **b** in the Son of God 1Jn 5:10 *4100*

BELIEVING
all things you ask in prayer, **b**, Mt 21:22 *4100*
even His brothers were **b** in Him. Jn 7:5 *4100*
going away and were **b** in Jesus. Jn 12:11 *4100*
them, *yet* they were not **b** in Him. Jn 12:37 *4100*
be unbelieving, but **b**." Jn 20:27 *4103*
b you may have life in His name. Jn 20:31 *4100*
him, not **b** that he was a disciple. Ac 9:26 *4100*
after **b** in the Lord Jesus Christ, Ac 11:17 *4100*
heard were **b** and being baptized. Ac 18:8 *4100*
b everything that is in accordance Ac 24:14 *4100*
you with all joy and peace in **b**, Ro 15:13 *4100*
sanctified through her **b** husband; 1Co 7:14 *80*
a right to take along a **b** wife, 1Co 9:5 *79*

BELL
a golden **b** and a pomegranate, a Ex 28:34 6472
a golden **b** and a pomegranate, Ex 28:34 6472
alternating a **b** and a pomegranate Ex 39:26 6472

BELLOWS
The **b** blow fiercely, The lead is Jer 6:29 4647

BELLS
and **b** of gold between them all Ex 28:33 6472
They also made **b** of pure gold, and Ex 39:25 6472
and put the **b** between the Ex 39:25 6472
inscribed on the **b** of the horses, Zch 14:20 4698

BELLY
On your **b** you will go, And dust Gn 3:14 1512
'Whatever crawls on its **b**, Lv 11:42 1512
thigh and thrust it into his **b**. Jg 3:21 990
not draw the sword out of his **b**; Jg 3:22 990
therefore Abner struck him in the **b** 2Sa 2:23 2570

and there he struck him in the **b** 2Sa 3:27 2570
and they struck him in the **b**; 2Sa 4:6 2570
Joab's hand so he struck him in the **b** 2Sa 20:10 2570
God will expel them from his **b**. Jb 20:15 990
"When he fills his **b**, Jb 20:23 990
my **b** is like unvented wine, Jb 32:19 990
his power in the muscles of his **b**. Jb 40:16 990
And whose **b** You fill with Ps 17:14 990
Your **b** is like a heap of wheat SS 7:2 990
its **b** and its thighs of bronze, Da 2:32 4577
IN THE **B** OF THE SEA MONSTER, Mt 12:40 *2836*

BELONG
'To whom do you **b**, and where are Gn 32:17
these *animals* in front of you **b**?' Gn 32:17
'*These* **b** to your servant Jacob; Gn 32:18
the man to whom these things **b**." Gn 38:25
"Do not interpretations **b** to God? Gn 40:8
the males **b** to the LORD. Ex 13:12
children shall **b** to her master, Ex 21:4 1961
b to the priest who presents it. Lv 7:9 1961
shall **b** to all the sons of Aaron, Lv 7:10 1961
it shall **b** to the priest who Lv 7:14 1961
offerings which **b** to the LORD, Lv 7:20
offerings which **b** to the LORD, Lv 7:21
shall **b** to Aaron and his sons. Lv 7:31 1961
of the tribe to which they **b**; Nu 36:3 1961
of the tribe to which they **b**; Nu 36:4 1961
to the LORD your God **b** heaven and Dt 10:14
things **b** to the LORD our God, Dt 29:29
b to us and to our sons forever, Dt 29:29
Let Your Thummim and Your Urim **b** Dt 33:8
sisters, with all who **b** to them, Jos 2:13
as one male of any who **b** to him." 1Sa 25:22
"To whom do you **b**? 1Sa 30:13
and vineyards **b** to others." Ne 5:5
of one in despair **b** to the wind? Jb 6:26
Him **b** counsel and understanding. Jb 12:13
misled and the misleader **b** to Him. Jb 12:16
"Dominion and awe **b** to Him Who Jb 25:2
"Behold, I **b** to God like you; Jb 33:6
the shields of the earth **b** to God; Ps 47:9
GOD the Lord **b** escapes from death. Ps 68:20
The plans of the heart **b** to man, Pr 16:1
balance and scales **b** to the LORD; Pr 16:11
his sons, it shall **b** to his sons; Ezk 46:16 1961
it shall **b** to them. Ezk 46:17 1961
For wisdom and power **b** to Him. Da 2:20
God **b** compassion and forgiveness, Da 9:9
priests who **b** to the house of the Zch 7:3
an angel of the God to whom I **b** Ac 27:23 *1510*
of Christ, he does not **b** to Him. Ro 8:9 *1510*
For all things **b** to you, 1Co 3:21 *1510*
all things **b** to you, 1Co 3:22
and you **b** to Christ; 1Co 3:23
And if you **b** to Christ, then you Ga 3:29
Now those who **b** to Christ Jesus Ga 5:24
and glory and power **b** to our God; Rv 19:1

BELONGED
his wife and all that **b** to him. Gn 12:20
his wife and all that **b** to him, Gn 13:1
and from what **b** to our father he Gn 31:1
and all the men who **b** to Korah with Nu 16:32
So they and all that **b** to them Nu 16:33
his tent and all that **b** to him; Jos 7:24
And the land of Gilead **b** to the Jos 17:6 1961
The land of Tappuah **b** to Manasseh, Jos 17:8 1961
Tappuah on the border of Manasseh **b** Jos 17:8
of the brook (these cities **b** to Jos 17:9
The south side **b** to Ephraim Jos 17:10
which **b** to Joash the Abiezrite as Jg 6:11
and the priest who had **b** to him, Jg 18:27 1961
which **b** to our brother Elimelech. Ru 4:3
hand of Naomi all that **b** to Elimelech Ru 4:9
all that **b** to Chilion and Mahlon. Ru 4:9
was missed of all that **b** to him; 1Sa 25:21
therefore Ziklag has **b** to the 1Sa 27:6
"All that **b** to Saul and to all 2Sa 9:9 1961
and the mighty men who **b** to David, 1Ki 1:8
which **b** to the Philistines, 1Ki 15:27
which **b** to the Philistines. 1Ki 16:15
which had **b** to Judah, are they 2Ki 14:28
taken all that **b** to the king of Egypt 2Ki 24:7 1961
yet the birthright **b** to Joseph), 1Ch 5:2
of thousands who **b** to Manasseh. 1Ch 12:20
property which **b** to King David. 1Ch 27:31
at Beth-shemesh, which **b** to Judah. 2Ch 25:21
of the grave which **b** to the kings, 2Ch 26:23
divisions in Judah **b** to Benjamin. Ne 11:36
palace which **b** to King Ahasuerus. Es 1:9
Now the bronze pillars which **b** to Jer 52:17
cubits which **b** to the inner court, Ezk 42:3
which **b** to the outer court, Ezk 42:3
that He **b** to Herod's jurisdiction, Lk 23:7
1510, 1537
hands on some who **b** to the church in Ac 12:1 *575*

BELONGING
All the persons **b** to Jacob, who Gn 46:26
of persons **b** to the LORD. Lv 27:2
on the side **b** *to* the sons of Jos 22:11
portion of the field **b** to Boaz, Ru 2:3
Philistines **b** to the five lords, 1Sa 6:18
"Anyone **b** to Jeroboam who dies in 1Ki 14:11
"The one **b** to Ahab, who dies in 1Ki 21:24
of the Gershonites **b** to Ladan, 1Ch 26:21
b to Ladan the Gershonite. 1Ch 26:21
b to the king and his sons, 1Ch 28:1
the lands **b** to the sons of Israel, 2Ch 34:33
meddles with strife not **b** to him. Pr 26:17

'**B** to the LORD,' And will name Is 44:5
the wheels **b** to all four of them. Ezk 10:12
columns **b** to the side pillars, Ezk 40:49
the side chambers **b** to the temple Ezk 41:9
seven spouts **b** to each of the lamps Zch 4:2
b to the number of the twelve. Lk 22:3
1510, 1537
anything **b** to him was his own, Ac 4:32 *5225*
that if he found any **b** to the Way, Ac 9:2 *1510*
were lands **b** to the leading man Ac 28:7

BELONGINGS
my **b** and take *it* for yourself." Gn 31:32 5973

BELONGS
father **b** to us and our children; Gn 31:16
b to the sons of Israel. Ex 9:4
both of man and beast; it **b** to Me." Ex 13:2
that **b** to your neighbor." Ex 20:17
offspring from every womb **b** to Me, Ex 34:19
table and arrange what **b** on it; Ex 40:4 6187
offering **b** to Aaron and his sons: Lv 2:3
offering **b** to Aaron and his sons: Lv 2:10
shall give it to the one to whom it **b** Lv 6:5
the sin offering, **b** to the priest; Lv 14:13
b to the Levites may be redeemed Lv 25:33 4480
whom the possession of the land **b**. Lv 27:24
as a firstborn **b** to the LORD, Lv 27:26
and over all that **b** to it. Nu 1:50
and touch nothing that **b** to them, Nu 16:26
anything that **b** to your neighbor.' Dt 5:21
firstborn son **b** to the unloved, Dt 21:15
him **b** the right of the firstborn. Dt 21:17
all that is in it **b** to the LORD; Jos 6:17
fire, he and all that **b** to him, Jos 7:15
Mearah that **b** to the Sidonians, Jos 13:4
of Baal which **b** to your father, Jg 6:25
near Gibeah which **b** to Benjamin. Jg 19:14
at Gibeah which **b** to Benjamin. Jg 20:4
at Socoh which **b** to Judah, 1Sa 17:1
and on that which **b** to Judah, 1Sa 30:14
"Am I a dog's head that **b** to Judah? 2Sa 3:8
of Obed-edom and all that **b** to him, 2Sa 6:12
that **b** to Mephibosheth is yours." 2Sa 16:4
go to Zarephath, which **b** to Sidon, 1Ki 17:9
to Beersheba, which **b** to Judah, 1Ki 19:3
know that Ramoth-gilead **b** to us, 1Ki 22:3
at Beth-shemesh, which **b** to Judah. 2Ki 14:11
Kiriath-jearim, which **b** to Judah, 1Ch 13:6
"But the earth **b** to the mighty Jb 22:8
Salvation **b** to the LORD; Ps 3:8
That power **b** to God; Ps 62:11
For our shield **b** to the LORD, And Ps 89:18
battle, But victory **b** to the LORD. Pr 21:31
from him And **b** to another man, Jer 3:1 1961
day **b** to the Lord GOD of hosts, Jer 46:10
of that which **b** to the prince, Ezk 48:22 1961
"Righteousness **b** to You, O Lord, Da 9:7
"Open shame **b** to us, O Lord, to Da 9:8
of heaven **b** to such as these." Mt 19:14 *1510*
kingdom of God **b** to such as these. Mk 10:14 *1510*
kingdom of God **b** to such as these. Lk 18:16 *1510*
to whom **b** the adoption as sons, Ro 9:4
and Christ **b** to God. 1Co 3:23
which **b** to the fullness of Christ. Eph 4:13
but the substance **b** to Christ. Col 2:17
are spoken **b** to another tribe, Heb 7:13 *3348*
to whom **b** the glory and dominion 1Pe 4:11 *1510*

BELOVED
"May the **b** of the LORD dwell in Dt 33:12 3039
b and pleasant in their life, 2Sa 1:23 157
That Your **b** may be delivered, Save Ps 60:5 3039
That Your **b** may be delivered, Save Ps 108:6 3039
gives to His **b** *even in his* sleep. Ps 127:2 3039
"My **b** is to me a pouch of myrrh SS 1:13 1730
"My **b** is to me a cluster of henna SS 1:14 1730
"How handsome you are, my **b**, SS 1:16 1730
So is my **b** among the young men. SS 2:3 1730
"Listen! My **b**! Behold, he is coming, SS 2:8 1730
"My **b** is like a gazelle or a SS 2:9 1730
"My **b** responded and said to me, SS 2:10 1730
"My **b** is mine, and I am his; SS 2:16 1730
the shadows flee away, Turn, my **b**, SS 2:17 1730
May my **b** come into his garden And SS 4:16 1730
My **b** was knocking: SS 5:2 1730
"My **b** extended his hand through SS 5:4 1730
"I arose to open to my **b**; SS 5:5 1730
"I opened to my **b**, But my beloved SS 5:6 1730
my **b** had turned away *and* had gone! SS 5:6 1730
of Jerusalem, If you find my **b**, SS 5:8 1730
"What kind of **b** is your beloved, SS 5:9 1730
"What kind of beloved is your **b**, SS 5:9 1730
What kind of **b** is your beloved, SS 5:9 1730
What kind of beloved is your **b**, SS 5:9 1730
"My **b** is dazzling and ruddy, SS 5:10 1730
is my **b** and this is my friend, SS 5:16 1730
"Where has your **b** gone, O most SS 6:1 1730
Where has your **b** turned, That we SS 6:1 1730
"My **b** has gone down to his SS 6:2 1730
"I am my beloved's and my **b** is mine, SS 6:3 1730
"It goes *down* smoothly for my **b**, SS 7:9 1730
"Come, my **b**, let us go out into SS 7:11 1730
I have saved up for you, my **b**. SS 7:13 1730
wilderness Leaning on her **b**?" SS 8:5 1730
"Hurry, my **b**, And be like a SS 8:14 1730
of my **b** concerning His vineyard. Is 5:1 1730
"What right has My **b** in My house Jer 11:15 3039
I have given the **b** of My soul Into Jer 12:7 3033
"This is My **b** Son, in whom I am Mt 3:17 *27*
MY **B** IN WHOM MY SOUL is Mt 12:18 *27*

"This is My **b** Son, with whom I am Mt 17:5 *27*
"You are My **b** Son, in You I am Mk 1:11 *27*
"This is My **b** Son, listen to Him!" Mk 9:7 *27*
"He had one more *to send*, a **b** son; Mk 12:6 *27*
"You are My **b** Son, in You I am Lk 3:22 *27*
I will send my **b** son; Lk 20:13 *27*
you with our **b** Barnabas and Paul, Ac 15:25 *27*
to all who are **b** of God in Rome, Ro 1:7 *27*
AND HER WHO WAS NOT **B**, 'BELOVED Ro 9:25 *25*
HER WHO WAS NOT BELOVED, '**B**.' " Ro 9:25 *25*
are **b** for the sake of the fathers; Ro 11:28 *27*
Never take your own revenge, **b**, Ro 12:19 *27*
Greet Epaenetus, my **b**, Ro 16:5 *27*
Greet Ampliatus, my **b** in the Lord. Ro 16:8 *27*
in Christ, and Stachys my **b**. Ro 16:9 *27*
Greet Persis the **b**, Ro 16:12 *27*
to admonish you as my **b** children. 1Co 4:14 *27*
who is my **b** and faithful child in 1Co 4:17 *27*
Therefore, my **b**, flee from 1Co 10:14 *27*
Therefore, my **b** brethren, be 1Co 15:58 *27*
having these promises, **b**, 2Co 7:1 *27*
and all for your upbuilding, **b**. 2Co 12:19 *27*
He freely bestowed on us in the **B**. Eph 1:6 *25*
imitators of God, as **b** children; Eph 5:1 *27*
Tychicus, the **b** brother and faithful Eph 6:21 *27*
So then, my **b**, just as you have Php 2:12 *27*
my **b** brethren whom I long *to see*, Php 4:1 *27*
way stand firm in the Lord, my **b**. Php 4:1 *27*
our **b** fellow bond-servant, Col 1:7 *27*
us to the kingdom of His **b** Son, Col 1:13 *26*
been chosen of God, holy and **b**, Col 3:12 *25*
our **b** brother and faithful servant Col 4:7 *27*
our faithful and **b** brother, Col 4:9 *27*
Luke, the **b** physician, sends you Col 4:14 *27*
knowing, brethren **b** by God, 1Th 1:4 *25*
for you, brethren **b** by the Lord, 2Th 2:13 *25*
the benefit are believers and **b**. 1Tm 6:2 *27*
To Timothy, my **b** son: 2Tm 1:2 *27*
Philemon our **b** *brother* and fellow Phm 1:1 *27*
more than a slave, a **b** brother, Phm 1:16 *27*
But, **b**, we are convinced of better Heb 6:9 *27*
Do not be deceived, my **b** brethren. Jas 1:16 *27*
This you know, my **b** brethren. Jas 1:19 *27*
Listen, my **b** brethren: Jas 2:5 *27*
B, I urge you as aliens and 1Pe 2:11 *27*
B, do not be surprised at the 1Pe 4:12 *27*
"This is My **b** Son with whom I am 2Pe 1:17 *27*
This is now, **b**, the second letter 2Pe 3:1 *27*
one *fact* escape your notice, **b**, 2Pe 3:8 *27*
Therefore, **b**, since you look for 2Pe 3:14 *27*
just as also our **b** brother Paul, 2Pe 3:15 *27*
You therefore, **b**, knowing this 2Pe 3:17 *27*
B, I am not writing a new 1Jn 2:7 *27*
B, now we are children of God, and 1Jn 3:2 *27*
B, if our heart does not condemn 1Jn 3:21 *27*
B, do not believe every spirit, 1Jn 4:1 *27*
B, let us love one another, for 1Jn 4:7 *27*
B, if God so loved us, we also 1Jn 4:11 *27*
The elder to the **b** Gaius, 3Jn 1:1 *27*
B, I pray that in all respects you 3Jn 1:2 *27*
B, you are acting faithfully in 3Jn 1:5 *27*
B, do not imitate what is evil, 3Jn 1:11 *27*
the called, **b** in God the Father, Jude 1:1 *25*
B, while I was making every effort Jude 1:3 *27*
But you, **b**, ought to remember the Jude 1:17 *27*
But you, **b**, building yourselves up Jude 1:20 *27*
camp of the saints and the **b** city, Rv 20:9 *25*

BELOVED'S
"I am my **b** and my beloved is SS 6:3 1730
"I am my **b**, And his desire is for SS 7:10 1730

BELOW
and separated the waters which were **b** Gn 1:7
4480, 8478
"Let the waters **b** the heavens be Gn 1:9
4480, 8478
was buried **b** Bethel under the oak; Gn 35:8
4480, 8478
that is in the water **b** the earth. Dt 4:18
4480, 8478
heaven above and on the earth **b**; Dt 4:39
4480, 8478
from Baal-gad **b** Mount Hermon as Jos 13:5 8478
of Midian was **b** him in the valley. Jg 7:8
4480, 8478
them down as far as **b** Beth-car. 1Sa 7:11
4480, 8478
is beside Zarethan **b** Jezreel, 1Ki 4:12
4480, 8478
"His roots are dried **b**, Jb 18:16
4480, 8478
he may keep away from Sheol **b**. Pr 15:24 4295
of the earth searched out **b**, Jer 31:37 4295
B these chambers *was* the entrance Ezk 42:9 4480
his fruit above and his root **b**. Am 2:9
4480, 8478
gone **b** into the hold of the ship, Jon 1:5 3381
As Peter was **b** in the courtyard, Mk 14:66 *2736*
"You are from **b**, I am from above; Jn 8:23 *2736*
SKY ABOVE AND SIGNS ON THE EARTH **B**, Ac 2:19 *2736*

BELSHAZZAR
B the king held a great feast for Da 5:1 1113
When **B** tasted the wine, he gave Da 5:2 1113
Then King **B** was greatly alarmed, Da 5:9 1113
"Yet you, his son, **B**, Da 5:22 1113
Then **B** gave orders, and they Da 5:29 1113
B the Chaldean king was slain. Da 5:30 1113
In the first year of **B** king of Babylon Da 7:1 1113
third year of the reign of **B** the king Da 8:1 1112

BELT
his sword and his bow and his **b**. 1Sa 18:4 2290a
ten *pieces* of silver and a **b**." 2Sa 18:11 2290b
and over it was a **b** with a sword 2Sa 20:8 2290a
of war on his **b** about his waist, 1Ki 2:5 2290b
And loosens the **b** of the strong. Jb 12:21 4206b
And for a **b** with which he Ps 109:19 4206a
Instead of a **b**, a rope; Is 3:24 2290b
Nor is the **b** at its waist undone, Is 5:27 232
will be the **b** about His loins, Is 11:5 232
the **b** about His waist. Is 11:5 232
whose waist was girded with *a* **b** *of* Da 10:5
and a leather **b** around his waist; Mt 3:4 *2223*
wore a leather **b** around his waist, Mk 1:6 *2223*
no bag, no money in their **b** Mk 6:8 *2223*
"Carry no money **b**, no bag, no Lk 10:4 *905*
"When I sent you out without money **b** Lk 22:35 *905*
whoever has a money **b** is to take it Lk 22:36 *905*
he took Paul's **b** and bound his own Ac 21:11 *2223*
will bind the man who owns this **b** Ac 21:11 *2223*

BELTESHAZZAR
to Daniel he assigned *the name* **B**, Da 1:7 1095
said to Daniel, whose name was **B**, Da 2:26 1096
whose name is **B** according to the Da 4:8 1096
'O **B**, chief of the magicians, Da 4:9 1096
Now you, **B**, tell *me* its Da 4:18 1096
"Then Daniel, whose name is **B**, Da 4:19 1096
'**B**, do not let the dream or its Da 4:19 1096
B replied, Da 4:19 1096
Daniel, whom the king named **B**. Da 5:12 1096
to Daniel, who was named **B**; Da 10:1 1095

BELTS
And supplies **b** to the tradesmen. Pr 31:24 2290a
girded with **b** on their loins, with Ezk 23:15 232
or copper for your money **b**, Mt 10:9 *2223*
make yourselves money **b** which do not Lk 12:33 *905*

BEN
of the second rank, Zechariah, **B**, 1Ch 15:18 1122

BEN-ABINADAB
B, *in* all the height of Dor 1Ki 4:11 1125

BENAIAH
B the son of Jehoiada was over 2Sa 8:18 1141
and **B** the son of Jehoiada was over 2Sa 20:23 1141
Then **B** the son of Jehoiada, the 2Sa 23:20 1141
things **B** the son of Jehoiada did, 2Sa 23:22 1141
B a Pirathonite, Hiddai of the 2Sa 23:30 1141
the priest, **B** the son of Jehoiada, 1Ki 1:8 1141
not invite Nathan the prophet, **B**, 1Ki 1:10 1141
and Zadok the priest and **B** the son 1Ki 1:26 1141
and **B** the son of Jehoiada." 1Ki 1:32 1141
B the son of Jehoiada answered 1Ki 1:36 1141
prophet, **B** the son of Jehoiada, 1Ki 1:38 1141
prophet, **B** the son of Jehoiada, 1Ki 1:44 1141
sent **B** the son of Jehoiada; 1Ki 2:25 1141
sent **B** the son of Jehoiada, 1Ki 2:29 1141
So **B** came to the tent of the LORD and 1Ki 2:30 1141
And **B** brought the king word again, 1Ki 2:30 1141
Then **B** the son of Jehoiada went up 1Ki 2:34 1141
The king appointed **B** the son 1Ki 2:35 1141
commanded **B** the son of Jehoiada, 1Ki 2:46 1141
and **B** the son of Jehoiada *was* over 1Ki 4:4 1141
Asaiah, Adiel, Jesimiel, **B**, 1Ch 4:36 1141
B the son of Jehoiada, the son of 1Ch 11:22 1141
things **B** the son of Jehoiada did, 1Ch 11:24 1141
of Benjamin, **B** the Pirathonite, 1Ch 11:31 1141
Jehiel, Unni, Eliab, **B**, 1Ch 15:18 1141
Unni, Eliab, Maaseiah and **B**, 1Ch 15:20 1141
Nethanel, Amasai, Zechariah, **B** and 1Ch 15:24 1141
Jehiel, Mattithiah, Eliab, **B**, 1Ch 16:5 1141
and **B** and Jahaziel the priests 1Ch 16:6 1141
and **B** the son of Jehoiada *was* over 1Ch 18:17 1141
army for the third month *was* **B**, 1Ch 27:5 1141
This **B** *was* the mighty man of the 1Ch 27:6 1141
eleventh month *was* **B** the Pirathonite 1Ch 27:14 1141
Jehoiada the son of **B**, 1Ch 27:34 1141
son of Zechariah, the son of **B**, 2Ch 20:14 1141
and **B** *were* overseers under the 2Ch 31:13 1141
Eleazar, Malchijah and **B**; Ezr 10:25 1141
Adna, Chelal, **B**, Maaseiah, Ezr 10:30 1141
B, Bedeiah, Cheluhi, Ezr 10:35 1141
Zebina, Jaddai, Joel *and* **B**. Ezr 10:43 1141
of Azzur and Pelatiah son of **B**, Ezk 11:1 1141
that Pelatiah son of **B** died. Ezk 11:13 1141

BEN-AMMI
bore a son, and called his name **B**; Gn 19:38 1151

BEND
my arms can **b** a bow of bronze. 2Sa 22:35 5181
will not **b** down to the ground. Jb 15:29 5186
For, behold, the wicked **b** the bow, Ps 11:2 1869
my arms can **b** a bow of bronze. Ps 18:34 5181
b their tongue *like* their bow; Jer 9:3 1869
that handle *and* **b** the bow. Jer 46:9 1869
every side, All you who **b** the bow; Jer 50:14 1869
Babylon, All those who **b** the bow: Jer 50:29 1869
not him who bends his bow **b** *it*, Jer 51:3 1869
For I will **b** Judah as My bow, I Zch 9:13 1869
AND **B** THEIR BACKS FOREVER." Ro 11:10 *4781*

BEN-DEKER
B in Makaz and Shaalbim and 1Ki 4:9 1128

BENDS
"He **b** his tail like a cedar; Jb 40:17 2654b
"Let not him who **b** his bow bend Jer 51:3 1869

BENEATH
Blessings of the deep that lies **b**, Gn 49:25 8478
is in heaven above or on the earth **b** Ex 20:4 8478
"They shall be double **b**, Ex 26:24 4295
"You shall put it **b**, Ex 27:5 8478
They were double **b**, Ex 36:29 4295
a grating of bronze network **b**, Ex 38:4 8478
earth **b** or in the water under the earth. Dt 5:8 4480, 8478
dew, And from the deep lying **b**, Dt 33:13 8478
in heaven above and on earth **b**. Jos 2:11 4480, 8478
and **b** the lions and oxen *were* 1Ki 7:29 4480, 8478
b the basin *were* cast supports 1Ki 7:30 4480, 8478
in heaven above or on earth **b**, 1Ki 8:23 4480, 8478
hill and **b** every luxuriant tree. 1Ki 14:23 8478
he had sackcloth **b** on his body. 2Ki 6:30 1004
B Him crouch the helpers of Rahab. Jb 9:13 8478
"**B** the apple tree I awakened you; SS 8:5 8478
"Sheol from **b** is excited over you Is 14:9 4480, 8478
are spread out *as your bed* **b** you And Is 14:11 8478
the sky, Then look to the earth **b**; Is 51:6 4480, 8478
palace to *a place* **b** the storeroom Jer 38:11 8478
beings that I saw **b** the God of Israel Ezk 10:20 8478
and **b** their wings *was* the form of Ezk 10:21 8478
over to death, to the earth **b**, Ezk 31:14 8482
were comforted in the earth **b**. Ezk 31:16 8482
the trees of Eden to the earth **b**; Ezk 31:18 8482
I am weighted down **b** you As a Am 2:13 8478
clouds are the dust **b** His feet. Na 1:3
PUT YOUR ENEMIES **B** YOUR FEET"'? Mt 22:44 *5270*
PUT YOUR ENEMIES **B** YOUR FEET."' Mk 12:36 *5270*

BENE-BERAK
and Jehud and **B** and Gath-rimmon, Jos 19:45 1139

BENEFACTORS
over them are called '**B**.' Lk 22:25 *2110*

BENEFICIAL
his deeds *have been* very **b** to you. 1Sa 19:4 2896a

BENEFIT
it will not be reckoned to his **b**. Lv 7:18
no return for the **b** he received, 2Ch 32:25 1576
destroy it, for there is **b** in it,' Is 65:8 1293
this people the slightest **b**," Jer 23:32 3276
today for a **b** done to a sick man, Ac 4:9 *2108*
Or what is the **b** of circumcision? Ro 3:1 *5622*
Therefore what **b** were you then Ro 6:21 *2590*
to God, you derive your **b**, Ro 6:22 *2590*
This I say for your own **b**; 1Co 7:35 *4851b*
Christ will be of no **b** to you. Ga 5:2 *5623*
God bestowed on me for your **b**, Col 1:25 *1519*
who partake of the **b** are believers 1Tm 6:2 *2108*
let me **b** from you in the Lord; Phm 1:20 *3685*

BENEFITED
who were so occupied were not **b**. Heb 13:9 *5623*

BENEFITS
my soul, And forget none of His **b**; Ps 103:2 1576
the LORD For all His **b** toward me? Ps 116:12 8408

BENE-JAAKAN
from Moseroth and camped at **B**. Nu 33:31 1142
They journeyed from **B** and Nu 33:32 1142
set out from Beeroth **B** to Moserah. Dt 10:6 885

BEN-GEBER
B, in Ramoth-gilead 1Ki 4:13 1127

BEN-HADAD
them to **B** the son of Tabrimmon, 1Ki 15:18 1130
So **B** listened to King Asa and sent 1Ki 15:20 1130
Now **B** king of Aram gathered all 1Ki 20:1 1130
and said to him, "Thus says **B**, 1Ki 20:2 1130
"Thus says **B**, 'Surely, I sent to you 1Ki 20:5 1130
So he said to the messengers of **B**, 1Ki 20:9 1130
B sent to him and said, 1Ki 20:10 1130
When **B** heard this message, as he 1Ki 20:12 1130
while **B** was drinking himself drunk 1Ki 20:16 1130
and **B** sent out and they told him, 1Ki 20:17 1130
and **B** king of Aram escaped on a 1Ki 20:20 1130
B mustered the Arameans and 1Ki 20:26 1130
And **B** fled and came into the city 1Ki 20:30 1130
"Your servant **B** says, 1Ki 20:32 1130
"Your brother **B**." 1Ki 20:33 1130
Then **B** came out to him, and he 1Ki 20:33 1130
B said to him, "The cities 1Ki 20:34 1130
that **B** king of Aram gathered all 2Ki 6:24 1130
Now **B** king of Aram was sick, and 2Ki 8:7 1130
"Your son **B** king of Aram has sent 2Ki 8:9 1130
the hand of **B** the son of Hazael. 2Ki 13:3 1130
B his son became king in his place. 2Ki 13:24 1130
from the hand of **B** the son of Hazael 2Ki 13:25 1130
and sent them to **B** king of Aram, 2Ch 16:2 1130
So **B** listened to King Asa and sent 2Ch 16:4 1130
the fortified towers of **B**." Jer 49:27 1130
it will consume the citadels of **B**. Am 1:4 1130

BEN-HAIL
reign he sent his officials, **B**, 2Ch 17:7 1134

BENHANAN
Amnon and Rinnah, **B** and Tilon. 1Ch 4:20 1135

BEN-HESED
B, in Arubboth 1Ki 4:10 1136

BEN-HINNOM
valley of **B** to the slope of the Jebusite Jos 15:8 1121, 2011
hill which is in the valley of **B**, Jos 18:16 1121, 2011
burned incense in the valley of **B** and 2Ch 28:3 1121, 2011
the fire in the valley of **B**; 2Ch 33:6 1121, 2011
"Then go out to the valley of **B**, Jer 19:2 1121, 2011
called Topheth or the valley of **B**, Jer 19:6 1121, 2011
of Baal that are in the valley of **B** Jer 32:35 1121, 2011

BEN-HUR
B, in the hill country of Ephraim; 1Ki 4:8 1133

BENINU
Hodiah, Bani, **B**. Ne 10:13 1148

BENJAMIN
but his father called him **B**. Gn 35:18 1144
the sons of Rachel: Joseph and **B**; Gn 35:24 1144
brother **B** with his brothers, Gn 42:4 1144
is no more, and you would take **B**; Gn 42:36 1144
to you your other brother and **B**. Gn 43:14 1144
the money in their hand, and **B**; Gn 43:15 1144
When Joseph saw **B** with them, he Gn 43:16 1144
his eyes and saw his brother **B**, Gn 43:29 1144
and the eyes of my brother **B** *see*, Gn 45:12 1144
and **B** wept on his neck. Gn 45:14 1144
but to **B** he gave three hundred Gn 45:22 1144
of Jacob's wife Rachel: Joseph and **B**. Gn 46:19 1144
The sons of **B**: Gn 46:21 1144
"**B** is a ravenous wolf; Gn 49:27 1144
Issachar, Zebulun and **B**; Ex 1:3 1144
of **B**, Abidan the son of Gideoni; Nu 1:11 1144
Of the sons of **B**, their Nu 1:36 1144
numbered men of the tribe of **B** Nu 1:37 1144
"Then *comes* the tribe of **B**, Nu 2:22 1144
and the leader of the sons of **B**: Nu 2:22 1144
Gideoni, leader of the sons of **B**; Nu 7:60 1144
the tribal army of the sons of **B**. Nu 10:24 1144
from the tribe of **B**, Nu 13:9 1144
of **B** according to their families: Nu 26:38 1144
of **B** according to their families; Nu 26:41 1144
"Of the tribe of **B**, Elidad the Nu 34:21 1144
Judah, Issachar, Joseph, and **B**. Dt 27:12 1144
Of **B** he said, "May the beloved Dt 33:12 1144
the lot of the tribe of the sons of **B** Jos 18:11 1144
the inheritance of the sons of **B**, Jos 18:20 1144
cities of the tribe of the sons of **B** Jos 18:21 1144
of **B** according to their families. Jos 18:28 1144
and from the tribe of **B**. Jos 21:4 1144
From the tribe of **B**, Jos 21:17 1144
But the sons of **B** did not drive Jg 1:21 1144
of **B** in Jerusalem to this day. Jg 1:21 1144
came down, Following you, **B**, Jg 5:14 1144
to fight also against Judah, **B**, Jg 10:9 1144
near Gibeah which belongs to **B**. Jg 19:14 1144
(Now the sons of **B** heard that the Jg 20:3 1144
at Gibeah which belongs to **B**. Jg 20:4 1144
when they come to Gibeah of **B**, Jg 20:10 1144
men through the entire tribe of **B**, Jg 20:12 1144
But the sons of **B** would not listen Jg 20:13 1144
The sons of **B** gathered from Jg 20:14 1144
day the sons of **B** were numbered, Jg 20:15 1144
of Israel besides **B** were numbered, Jg 20:17 1144
to battle against the sons of **B**?" Jg 20:18 1144
went out to battle against **B**, Jg 20:20 1144
Then the sons of **B** came out of Jg 20:21 1144
the sons of my brother **B**?" Jg 20:23 1144
the sons of **B** the second day. Jg 20:24 1144
B went out against them from Jg 20:25 1144
against the sons of my brother **B**, Jg 20:28 1144
Israel went up against the sons of **B** Jg 20:30 1144
The sons of **B** went out against Jg 20:31 1144
The sons of **B** said, Jg 20:32 1144
but **B** did not know that disaster Jg 20:34 1144
the LORD struck **B** before Israel, Jg 20:35 1144
25,100 men of **B** that day, Jg 20:35 1144
of **B** saw that they were defeated. Jg 20:36 1144
the men of Israel gave ground to **B** Jg 20:36 1144
and **B** began to strike and kill Jg 20:39 1144
of smoke, **B** looked behind them; Jg 20:40 1144
and the men of **B** were terrified; Jg 20:41 1144
They surrounded **B**, pursued them Jg 20:43 1144
Thus 18,000 men of **B** fell; Jg 20:44 1144
So all of **B** who fell that day were Jg 20:46 1144
then turned back against the sons of **B** Jg 20:48 1144
his daughter to **B** in marriage." Jg 21:1 1144
for their brother **B** and said, Jg 21:6 1144
sent *word* and spoke to the sons of **B** Jg 21:13 1144
B returned at that time, and Jg 21:14 1144
And the people were sorry for **B** Jg 21:15 1144
women are destroyed out of **B**?" Jg 21:16 1144
for the survivors of **B**, Jg 21:17 1144
is he who gives a wife to **B**." Jg 21:18 1144
And they commanded the sons of **B**, Jg 21:20 1144
Shiloh, and go to the land of **B**. Jg 21:21 1144
we did not take for each man *of* **B** Jg 21:22
The sons of **B** did so, and took Jg 21:23 1144
Now a man of **B** ran from the battle 1Sa 4:12 1144
Now there was a man of **B** whose 1Sa 9:1 1144
send you a man from the land of **B**, 1Sa 9:16 1144
the families of the tribe of **B**? 1Sa 9:21 1144
in the territory of **B** at Zelzah; 1Sa 10:2 1144
the tribe of **B** was taken by lot. 1Sa 10:20 1144
tribe of **B** near by its families, 1Sa 10:21 1144
were with Jonathan at Gibeah of **B**. 1Sa 13:2 1144
up from Gilgal to Gibeah of **B**. 1Sa 13:15 1144
in Geba of **B** while the Philistines 1Sa 13:16 1144
watchmen in Gibeah of **B** looked, 1Sa 14:16 1144
Jezreel, over Ephraim, and over **B**, 2Sa 2:9 1144
twelve for **B** and Ish-bosheth the 2Sa 2:15 1144
The sons of **B** gathered 2Sa 2:25 1144
down many of **B** and Abner's men, 2Sa 2:31 1144
also spoke in the hearing of **B**; 2Sa 3:19 1144

and to the whole house of **B**. **2Sa 3:19** 1144
the Beerothite, of the sons of **B** **2Sa 4:2** 1144
is also considered *part* of **B**, **2Sa 4:2** 1144
were a thousand men of **B** with him, **2Sa 19:17** 1144
son in the country of **B** in Zela, **2Sa 21:14** 1144
Ribai of Gibeah of the sons of **B**, **2Sa 23:29** 1144
Shimei the son of Ela, in **B**; **1Ki 4:18** 1144
house of Judah and the tribe of **B**, **1Ki 12:21** 1144
B and to the rest of the people, **1Ki 12:23** 1144
with them Geba of **B** and Mizpah. **1Ki 15:22** 1144
Dan, Joseph, **B**, Naphtali, Gad and **1Ch 2:2** 1144
and from the tribe of **B**: **1Ch 6:60** 1144
and the tribe of the sons of **B**, **1Ch 6:65** 1144
The sons of **B** *were* three: **1Ch 7:6** 1144
the sons of Bilhan *were* Jeush, **B**, **1Ch 7:10** 1144
And **B** became the father of Bela **1Ch 8:1** 1144
All these *were* of the sons of **B**. **1Ch 8:40** 1144
sons of Judah, of the sons of **B** and **1Ch 9:3** 1144
From the sons of **B** *were* Sallu **1Ch 9:7** 1144
Ribai of Gibeah of the sons of **B**, **1Ch 11:31** 1144
they were Saul's kinsmen from **B**. **1Ch 12:2** 1144
Then some of the sons of **B** and **1Ch 12:16** 1144
Of the sons of **B**, **1Ch 12:29** 1144
not number Levi and **B** among them, **1Ch 21:6** 1144
for **B**, Jaasiel the son of Abner; **1Ch 27:21** 1144
the house of Judah and **B**, **2Ch 11:1** 1144
and to all Israel in Judah and **B**, **2Ch 11:3** 1144
cities in Judah and in **B**. **2Ch 11:10** 1144
So he held Judah and **B**. **2Ch 11:12** 1144
and **B** to all the fortified cities, **2Ch 11:23** 1144
and spears, and 280,000 from **B**, **2Ch 14:8** 1144
to me, Asa, and all Judah and **B**: **2Ch 15:2** 1144
idols from all the land of Judah and **B** **2Ch 15:8** 1144
and **B** and those from Ephraim, **2Ch 15:9** 1144
and of **B**, Eliada a valiant **2Ch 17:17** 1144
hundreds throughout Judah and **B**; **2Ch 25:5** 1144
altars throughout all Judah and **B**, **2Ch 31:1** 1144
and from all Judah and **B** and the **2Ch 34:9** 1144
Jerusalem and **B** to stand *with him*. **2Ch 34:32** 1144
of fathers' *households* of Judah and **B** **Ezr 1:5** 1144
the enemies of Judah and **B** heard **Ezr 4:1** 1144
So all the men of Judah and **B** **Ezr 10:9** 1144
B, Malluch *and* Shemariah; **Ezr 10:32** 1144
After them **B** and Hasshub carried **Ne 3:23** 1144
the sons of **B** lived in Jerusalem. **Ne 11:4** 1144
Now these are the sons of **B**: **Ne 11:7** 1144
of **B** also *lived* from Geba *onward*, **Ne 11:31** 1144
divisions in Judah belonged to **B**. **Ne 11:36** 1144
Judah, **B**, Shemaiah, Jeremiah, **Ne 12:34** 1144
There is **B**, the youngest, ruling **Ps 68:27** 1144
Before Ephraim and **B** and Manasseh, **Ps 80:2** 1144
were in Anathoth in the land of **B**, **Jer 1:1** 1144
"Flee for safety, O sons of **B**, **Jer 6:1** 1144
of Jerusalem, from the land of **B**, **Jer 17:26** 1144
that were at the upper **B** Gate, **Jer 20:2** 1144
which is in the land of **B**; **Jer 32:8** 1144
in witnesses in the land of **B**, **Jer 32:44** 1144
of the Negev, in the land of **B**, **Jer 33:13** 1144
from Jerusalem to go to the land of **B** **Jer 37:12** 1144
While he was at the Gate of **B**, **Jer 37:13** 1144
king was sitting in the Gate of **B**; **Jer 38:7** 1144
border of **B** shall be for the prince. **Ezk 48:22** 1144
the east side to the west side, **B**, **Ezk 48:23** 1144
"Beside the border of **B**, **Ezk 48:24** 1144
the gate of **B**, one; **Ezk 48:32** 1144
alarm at Beth-aven: "Behind you, **B**!" **Hos 5:8** 1144
And **B** *will possess* Gilead. **Ob 1:19** 1144
of Kish, a man of the tribe of **B**, **Ac 13:21** *958*
of Abraham, of the tribe of **B**. **Ro 11:1** *958*
of Israel, of the tribe of **B**, **Php 3:5** *958*
thousand, from the tribe of **B**, **Rv 7:8** *958*

BENJAMIN'S
but **B** portion was five times as **Gn 43:34** 1144
and the cup was found in **B** sack. **Gn 44:12** 1144
on his brother **B** neck and wept, **Gn 45:14** 1144
remain on its site from **B** Gate **Zch 14:10** 1144

BENJAMITE
them, Ehud the son of Gera, the **B**, **Jg 3:15** 1145
the son of Aphiah, the son of a **B**, **1Sa 9:1** 376, 3228
"Am I not a **B**, of the smallest of **1Sa 9:21** 1145
how much more now this **B**? **2Sa 16:11** 1145
Gera, the **B** who was from Bahurim, **2Sa 19:16** 1145
was Sheba, the son of Bichri, a **B**; **2Sa 20:1**
376, 3228
you Shimei the son of Gera the **B**, **1Ki 2:8** 1145
of Shimei, the son of Kish, a **B**, **Es 2:5** 376, 3228

BENJAMITES
but the men of the place were **B**. **Jg 19:16** 1145
passed through the land of the **B**, **1Sa 9:4** 1145
Hear now, O **B**! Will the son of Jesse **1Sa 22:7** 1145
Abiezer the Anathothite of the **B**; **1Ch 27:12** 1145

BENO
the sons of Jaaziah, **B**. **1Ch 24:26** 1131a
by Jaaziah *were* **B**, Shoham, Zaccur and **1Ch 24:27** 1131a

BEN-ONI
that she named him **B**; **Gn 35:18** 1126

BENT
And he **b** with all his might so **Jg 16:30** 5186
man was startled and **b** forward; **Ru 3:8** 3943
has **b** His bow and made it ready. **Ps 7:12** 1869
drawn the sword and **b** their bow To **Ps 37:14** 1869
am **b** over and greatly bowed down; **Ps 38:6** 5753a
able to straighten what He has **b**? **Ec 7:13** 5791
are sharp and all its bows are **b**; **Is 5:28** 1869
drawn sword, and from the **b** bow And **Is 21:15** 1869
He has **b** His bow like an enemy; He **La 2:4** 1869
He **b** His bow And set me as a **La 3:12** 1869
this vine **b** its roots toward him **Ezk 17:7** 3719
And I **b** down *and* fed them. **Hos 11:4** 5186
people are **b** on turning from Me. **Hos 11:7** 8511
and she was **b** double, and could **Lk 13:11** *4794*

BENUMBED
I am **b** and badly crushed; **Ps 38:8** 6313

BEN-ZOHETH
sons of Ishi *were* Zoheth and **B**. **1Ch 4:20** 1132

BEON
Elealeh, Sebam, Nebo and **B**, **Nu 32:3** 1194

BEOR
Bela the son of **B** reigned in Edom, **Gn 36:32** 1160
messengers to Balaam the son of **B**, **Nu 22:5** 1160
"The oracle of Balaam the son of **B**, **Nu 24:3** 1160
"The oracle of Balaam the son of **B**, **Nu 24:15** 1160
the son of **B** with the sword. **Nu 31:8** 1160
Balaam the son of **B** from Pethor **Dt 23:4** 1160
also killed Balaam the son of **B**, **Jos 13:22** 1160
Balaam the son of **B** to curse you. **Jos 24:9** 1160
Bela was the son of **B**, **1Ch 1:43** 1160
what Balaam son of **B** answered him, **Mi 6:5** 1160
the way of Balaam, the *son* of **B**, **2Pe 2:15** *961b*

BEQUEATH
b them to your sons after you, **Lv 25:46** 5157
possess the good land and **b** *it* to your **1Ch 28:8** 5157

BERA
made war with **B** king of Sodom, **Gn 14:2** 1298

BERACAH
and **B** and Jehu the Anathothite, **1Ch 12:3** 1294
they assembled in the valley of **B**, **2Ch 20:26** 1294
"The Valley of **B**" **2Ch 20:26** 1294

BERAIAH
Adaiah, **B** and Shimrath *were* the **1Ch 8:21** 1256

BEREA
Paul and Silas away by night to **B**, **Ac 17:10** *960*
been proclaimed by Paul in **B** also, **Ac 17:13** *960*
was accompanied by Sopater of **B**, **Ac 20:4** *961a*

BEREAVE
which will **b** you of your children **Lv 26:22** 7921
'Outside the sword will **b**, **Dt 32:25** 7921
I will **b** *them* of children, I will **Jer 15:7** 7921
and they will **b** you of children; **Ezk 5:17** 7921
never again **b** them of children.' **Ezk 36:12** 7921
longer **b** your nation of children,' **Ezk 36:14** 7921
b them until not a man is left. **Hos 9:12** 7921

BEREAVED
I be **b** of you both in one day?" **Gn 27:45** 7921
"You have **b** me of my children: **Gn 42:36** 7921
for me, if I am **b** of my children, **Gn 43:14** 7921
bereaved of my children, I am **b**." **Gn 43:14** 7921
were **b** will yet say in your ears, **Is 49:20** 7923
I have been **b** of my children And **Is 49:21** 7909a
have **b** your nation of children," **Ezk 36:13** 7921

BEREAVEMENT
for good, *To* the **b** of my soul. **Ps 35:12** 7908

BERECHIAH
and Hashubah, Ohel, **B**, **1Ch 3:20** 1296
hand, even Asaph the son of **B**, **1Ch 6:39** 1296
of Jeduthun, and **B** the son of Asa, **1Ch 9:16** 1296
his relatives, Asaph the son of **B**; **1Ch 15:17** 1296
B and Elkanah were gatekeepers **1Ch 15:23** 1296
B the son of Meshillemoth, **2Ch 28:12** 1296
next to him Meshullam the son of **B** **Ne 3:4** 1296
After him Meshullam the son of **B** **Ne 3:30** 1296
of Meshullam the son of **B**. **Ne 6:18** 1296
the prophet, the son of **B**, **Zch 1:1** 1296
the prophet, the son of **B**, **Zch 1:7** 1296
blood of Zechariah, the son of **B**, **Mt 23:35** *914*

BERED
it is between Kadesh and **B**. **Gn 16:14** 1260
were Shuthelah and **B** his son, **1Ch 7:20** 1260

BEREFT
and the woman was **b** of her two **Ru 1:5** 7604
burned down *and* **b** of inhabitants. **Jer 46:19**
4480, 369

BERI
were Suah, Harnepher, Shual, **B** and **1Ch 7:36** 1275

BERIAH
and **B** and their sister Serah. **Gn 46:17** 1283
And the sons of **B**: **Gn 46:17** 1283
of **B**, the family of the Beriites. **Nu 26:44** 1283
Of the sons of **B**: **Nu 26:45** 1283
bore a son, and he named him **B**, **1Ch 7:23** 1283
were Imnah, Ishvah, Ishvi and **B**, **1Ch 7:30** 1283
sons of **B** *were* Heber and Malchiel, **1Ch 7:31** 1283
and **B** and Shema, who were heads of **1Ch 8:13** 1283
and Joha *were* the sons of **B**. **1Ch 8:16** 1283
were Jahath, Zina, Jeush and **B**. **1Ch 23:10** 1283
and **B** did not have many sons, **1Ch 23:11** 1283

BERIITES
of Beriah, the family of the **B**. **Nu 26:44** 1284

BERITES
even Beth-maacah, and all the **B**; **2Sa 20:14** 1276

BERNICE
Agrippa and **B** arrived at Caesarea and **Ac 25:13** *959*
Agrippa came together with **B** **Ac 25:23** *959*
king stood up and the governor and **B**, **Ac 26:30** *959*

BERODACH-BALADAN
At that time **B** a son of Baladan, **2Ki 20:12** 1255

BEROTHAH
Hamath, **B**, Sibraim, which is **Ezk 47:16** 1268

BEROTHAI
From Betah and from **B**, **2Sa 8:8** 1307a

BEROTHITE
Zelek the Ammonite, Naharai the **B**, **1Ch 11:39** 1307b

BERYL
row a **b** and an onyx and a jasper; **Ex 28:20** 8658
and the fourth row, a **b**, **Ex 39:13** 8658
hands are rods of gold Set with **b**; **SS 5:14** 8658
workmanship *was* like sparkling **b**, **Ezk 1:16** 8658
The **b**, the onyx and the jasper; **Ezk 28:13** 8658
His body also *was* like **b**, **Da 10:6** 8658
the seventh, chrysolite; the eighth, **b**; **Rv 21:20** *969*

BESAI
the sons of Paseah, the sons of **B**, **Ezr 2:49** 1153
the sons of **B**, the sons of Meunim, **Ne 7:52** 1153

BESEECH
"Remember now, O LORD, I **b** You, **2Ki 20:3** 577
"I **b** You, O LORD God of heaven, **Ne 1:5** 577
"O Lord, I **b** You, may Your ear **Ne 1:11** 577
hosts, turn again now, we **b** You; **Ps 80:14** 4994
"O LORD, I **b** You, save my life!" **Ps 116:4** 577
O LORD, do save, we **b** You; **Ps 118:25** 577
O LORD, we **b** You, do send **Ps 118:25** 577
"Remember now, O LORD, I **b** You, **Is 38:3** 577
"Therefore **b** the Lord of the **Mt 9:38** *1189a*
therefore **b** the Lord of the **Lk 10:2** *1189a*

BESEECHING
b Him and falling on his knees **Mk 1:40** *3870*

BESET
himself also is **b** with weakness; **Heb 5:2** *4029*

BESIDE
of sheep were lying there **b** it, **Gn 29:2** 5921
not listen to her to lie **b** her **Gn 39:10** 681a
he left his garment **b** me and fled and **Gn 39:15** 681a
So she left his garment **b** her **Gn 39:16** 681a
garment **b** me and fled outside." **Gn 39:18** 681a
camping by the sea, **b** Pi-hahiroth, **Ex 14:9** 5921
they camped there **b** the waters. **Ex 15:27** 5921
and cast it **b** the altar eastward, **Lv 1:16** 681a
altar and place them **b** the altar. **Lv 6:10** 681a
and eat it unleavened **b** the altar, **Lv 10:12** 681a
'But if a man dies very suddenly **b** **Nu 6:9** 5921
sea, and let *them* fall **b** the camp, **Nu 11:31** 5921
"Stand **b** your burnt offering, and **Nu 23:3** 5921
was standing **b** his burnt offering, **Nu 23:6** 5921
"Stand here **b** your burnt offering **Nu 23:15** 5921
was standing **b** his burnt offering, **Nu 23:17** 5921
out, Like gardens **b** the river, **Nu 24:6** 5921
LORD, Like cedars **b** the waters. **Nu 24:6** 5921
Gilgal, **b** the oaks of Moreh? **Dt 11:30** 681a
b the altar of the LORD your God **Dt 16:21** 681a
place it **b** the ark of the covenant **Dt 31:26**
4480, 6654
Adam, the city that is **b** Zarethan; **Jos 3:16**
4480, 6654
the king of Ai, which is **b** Bethel, **Jos 12:9**
4480, 6654
cut down the Asherah that is **b** it; **Jg 6:25** 5921
which was **b** it was cut down, **Jg 6:28** 5921
down the Asherah which was **b** it." **Jg 6:30** 5921
and camped **b** the spring of Harod; **Jg 7:1** 5921
So she sat **b** the reapers; **Ru 2:14**
4480, 6654
am the woman who stood here **b** you, **1Sa 1:26** 5973
camped **b** Ebenezer while the **1Sa 4:1** 5921
off the seat backward **b** the gate, **1Sa 4:18**
5704, 3027
"I will go out and stand **b** my **1Sa 19:3** 3027
is before Jeshimon, **b** the road, **1Sa 26:3** 5921
spear and the jug of water from **b** **1Sa 26:12**
'Please stand **b** me and kill me, **2Sa 1:9** 5921
"So I stood **b** him and killed him, **2Sa 1:10** 5921
hung them up **b** the pool in Hebron. **2Sa 4:12** 5921
elders of his household stood **b** him **2Sa 12:17** 5921
and stand **b** the way to the gate; **2Sa 15:2**
5921, 3027
all his servants passed on **b** him, **2Sa 15:18**
5921, 3027
So the king stood **b** the gate, and **2Sa 18:4**
413, 3027
of Zoheleth, which is **b** En-rogel; **1Ki 1:9** 681a
and behold, he is **b** the altar. **1Ki 2:29** 681a
took my son from **b** me while your **1Ki 3:20** 681a
which is **b** Zarethan below Jezreel, **1Ki 4:12** 681a
which was **b** the network; **1Ki 7:20** 5676
and two lions standing **b** the arms. **1Ki 10:19** 681a
with the donkey standing **b** it; **1Ki 13:24** 681a
lion also was standing **b** the body. **1Ki 13:24** 681a
and the lion standing **b** the body; **1Ki 13:25** 681a
and the lion standing **b** the body; **1Ki 13:28** 681a
lay my bones **b** his bones. **1Ki 13:31** 681a
was in Jezreel **b** the palace of Ahab **1Ki 21:1** 681a
because it is close **b** my house, **1Ki 21:2** 681a
and the trumpeters **b** the king; **2Ki 11:14** 413
its lid and put it **b** the altar, **2Ki 12:9** 681a
the two walls **b** the king's garden, **2Ki 25:4** 5921
and two lions standing **b** the arms. **2Ch 9:18** 681a
the trumpeters *were* **b** the king. **2Ch 23:13** 5921
the LORD, **b** the altar of incense. **2Ch 26:19**
4480, 5921
to me, the queen sitting **b** him, **Ne 2:6** 681a
carried out repairs **b** his house. **Ne 3:23** 681a
And **b** him stood Mattithiah, Shema, **Ne 8:4** 681a
and the donkeys feeding **b** them, **Jb 1:14**
5921, 3027
He leads me **b** quiet waters. **Ps 23:2** 5921
B them the birds of the heavens **Ps 104:12** 5921

While he lives securely **b** you. **Pr 3:29** 854
On top of the heights **b** the way, **Pr 8:2** 5921
B the gates, at the opening to the **Pr 8:3** 3027
Then I was **b** Him, *as* a master **Pr 8:30** 681a
B the flocks of your companions?" **SS 1:7** 5921
like doves **B** streams of water, **SS 5:12** 5921
you be, you who sow **b** all waters, **Is 32:20** 5921
officials who stood **b** the king. **Jer 36:21** 4480, 5921
Chimham, which is **b** Bethlehem, **Jer 41:17** 681a
In the north **b** the river Euphrates **Jer 46:6** 5921, 3027
on the earth **b** the living beings, **Ezk 1:15** 681a
And the wheels rose close **b** them; **Ezk 1:20** 5980
the wheels rose close **b** them; **Ezk 1:21** 5980
the sound of the wheels **b** them, **Ezk 3:13** 5980
b the river Chebar at Tel-abib, **Ezk 3:15** 413
in and stood **b** the bronze altar. **Ezk 9:2** 681a
he entered and stood **b** a wheel. **Ezk 10:6** 681a
four wheels **b** the cherubim, **Ezk 10:9** 681a
cherubim, one wheel **b** each cherub; **Ezk 10:9** 681a
moved, the wheels would go **b** them; **Ezk 10:16** 681a
wheels would not turn from **b** them. **Ezk 10:16** 681a
my sight with the wheels **b** them; **Ezk 10:19** 5980
wings with the wheels **b** them, **Ezk 11:22** 5980
He placed *it* **b** abundant waters; **Ezk 17:5** 5921
in good soil **b** abundant waters, **Ezk 17:8** 413
all its cattle from **b** many waters; **Ezk 32:13** 5921
"Nor do they lie **b** the fallen **Ezk 32:27** 854
while a man was standing **b** me. **Ezk 43:6** 681a
their door post **b** My door post, **Ezk 43:8** 681a
that fishermen will stand **b** it; **Ezk 47:10** 5921
b the way of Hethlon to **Ezk 48:1** 413, 3027
toward the north **b** Hamath, **Ezk 48:1** 413, 3027
"**B** the border of Dan, from the east **Ezk 48:2** 5921
"**B** the border of Asher, from **Ezk 48:3** 5921
"**B** the border of Naphtali, from **Ezk 48:4** 5921
"**B** the border of Manasseh, from **Ezk 48:5** 5921
"**B** the border of Ephraim, from **Ezk 48:6** 5921
"**B** the border of Reuben, from **Ezk 48:7** 5921
"And **b** the border of Judah, from **Ezk 48:8** 5921
"**B** the border of Benjamin, from **Ezk 48:24** 5921
"**B** the border of Simeon, from **Ezk 48:25** 5921
"**B** the border of Issachar, from **Ezk 48:26** 5921
"**B** the border of Zebulun, from **Ezk 48:27** 5921
"And **b** the border of Gad, at the **Ezk 48:28** 5921
and I myself was **b** the Ulai Canal. **Da 8:2** 5921
I saw him come **b** the ram, **Da 8:7** 681a
heaps **B** the furrows of the field. **Hos 12:11** 5921
they stretch out **b** every altar, **Am 2:8** 681a
saw the Lord standing **b** the altar, **Am 9:1** 5921
which are **b** the two golden pipes, **Zch 4:12** 3027
sowed, some *seeds* fell **b** the road, **Mt 13:4** *3844*
on whom seed was sown **b** the road. **Mt 13:19** *3844*
sowing, some *seed* fell **b** the road, **Mk 4:4** *3844*
These are the ones who are **b** the road **Mk 4:15** *3844*
as he sowed, some fell **b** the road, **Lk 8:5** *3844*
"Those **b** the road are those **Lk 8:12** *3844*
in white clothing stood **b** them. **Ac 1:10** *3936*
out and buried her **b** her husband. **Ac 5:10** *4314*
the widows stood **b** him, **Ac 9:39** *3936*
commanded those standing **b** him **Ac 23:2** *3936*
For if we are **b** ourselves, it is **2Co 5:13** *1839*

BESIDES
"**B**, she actually is my sister, **Gn 20:12** 1571
b the previous famine that had **Gn 26:1** 4480, 905
married, **b** the wives that he had, **Gn 28:9** 5921
if you take wives **b** my daughters, **Gn 31:50** 5921
I do not know the LORD, and **b**, **Ex 5:2** 1571
shall not make *other gods* **b** Me; **Ex 20:23** 854
b the burnt offering of the **Lv 9:17** 4480, 905
b *those of* the sabbaths of the **Lv 23:38** 4480, 905
of the LORD, and **b** your gifts and **Lv 23:38** 4480, 905
and **b** all your votive and freewill **Lv 23:38** 4480, 905
priest, **b** the ram of atonement, **Nu 5:8** 4480, 905
b those who died on account of **Nu 16:49** 4480, 905
'You shall present these **b** the **Nu 28:23** 4480, 905
'**B** the continual burnt offering **Nu 28:31** 4480, 905
b the burnt offering of the new **Nu 29:6** 4480, 905
b the sin offering of atonement **Nu 29:11** 4480, 905
b the continual burnt offering, **Nu 29:16** 4480, 905
b the continual burnt offering and **Nu 29:19** 4480, 905
b the continual burnt offering and **Nu 29:22** 4480, 905
b the continual burnt offering, **Nu 29:25** 4480, 905
b the continual burnt offering and **Nu 29:28** 4480, 905
b the continual burnt offering, **Nu 29:31** 4480, 905
b the continual burnt offering, **Nu 29:34** 4480, 905
b the continual burnt offering and **Nu 29:38** 4480, 905
b your votive offerings and your **Nu 29:39** 905, 4480
And **b**, we saw the sons of the **Dt 1:28** 1571
b a great many unwalled towns. **Dt 3:5** 905, 4480
there is no other **b** Him. **Dt 4:35** 4480, 905
for yourself, **b** these three. **Dt 19:9** 5921
b the covenant which He had made **Dt 29:1** 4480, 905
I am He, And there is no god **b** Me; **Dt 32:39** 5973
b the land of Gilead and Bashan, **Jos 17:5** 905, 4480
b the altar of the LORD our God. **Jos 22:19** 4480, 1107
b the altar of the LORD our God **Jos 22:29** 4480, 905
b the crescent ornaments and the **Jg 8:26** 905, 4480
and **b** the neck bands that *were* on **Jg 8:26** 905, 4480
b her he had no son or **Jg 11:34** 4480
gone away, and what do I have **b**? **Jg 18:24** 5750
b the inhabitants of Gibeah who **Jg 20:15** 905, 4480
Israel **b** Benjamin were numbered, **Jg 20:17** 905, 4480
Indeed, there is no one **b** You, **1Sa 2:2** 1115
servants **b** Asahel were missing. **2Sa 2:30**
You, and there is no God **b** You, **2Sa 7:22** 2108
"**B**, whom should I serve? *Should* **2Sa 16:19** 8145
"For who is God, **b** the LORD? **2Sa 22:32** 1107
And who is a rock, **b** our God? **2Sa 22:32** 1107
"**B**, Solomon has even taken his **1Ki 1:46** 1571
oxen, a hundred sheep **b** deer, **1Ki 4:23** 905, 4480
b Solomon's 3,300 chief deputies **1Ki 5:16** 905, 4480
b what he gave her according to **1Ki 10:13** 4480
b *that* from the traders and the **1Ki 10:15** 905, 4480
b all the land of Naphtali. **1Ki 15:20** 5921
b his sin with which he made Judah **2Ki 21:16** 905, 4480
b the sons of the concubines; **1Ch 3:9** 4480, 905
nor is there any God **b** You, **1Ch 17:20** 2108
which she requested **b** *a return for* **2Ch 9:12** 4480, 905
b that which the traders and **2Ch 9:14** 905, 4480
there is no one **b** You to help *in* **2Ch 14:11** 5973
b their male and female servants who **Ezr 2:65** 4480, 905
wine **b** forty shekels of silver; **Ne 5:15** 310
b those who came to us from the **Ne 5:17**
b their male and their female **Ne 7:67** 4480, 905
I have no good **b** You." **Ps 16:2** 5921
And **b** You, I desire nothing on **Ps 73:25** 5973
masters **b** You have ruled us; **Is 26:13** 2108
And there is no savior **b** Me. **Is 43:11** 4480, 1107
last, And there is no God **b** Me. **Is 44:6** 4480, 1107
Is there any God **b** Me, **Is 44:8** 4480, 1107
B Me there is no God. **Is 45:5** 2108
the sun That there is no one **b** Me. **Is 45:6** 1107
And there is no other God **b** Me, **Is 45:21** 4480, 1107
'I am, and there is no one **b** me. **Is 47:8** 5750
'I am, and there is no one **b** me.' **Is 47:10** 5750
has the eye seen a God **b** You, **Is 64:4** 2108
B, if I give you advice, you will **Jer 38:15**
"**B** all your abominations **Ezk 16:22** 854
petition to any god or man **b** you, **Da 6:7** 3861b, 4481
petition to any god or man **b** you, **Da 6:12** 3861b, 4481
and *given* to others **b** them. **Da 11:4** 4480, 905
Me, For there is no savior **b** Me. **Hos 13:4** 1115
"I am, and there is no one **b** me." **Zph 2:15** 5750
b women and children. **Mt 14:21** *5565*
men, **b** women and children. **Mt 15:38** *5565*
and more will be given you **b**. **Mk 4:24** *4369*
AND THERE IS NO ONE ELSE **B** HIM; **Mk 12:32** *4133*
b, even the dogs were coming and **Lk 16:21** *235*
'And **b** all this, between us and **Lk 16:26** *1722*
Indeed, **b** all this, it is the **Lk 24:21** *2532, 4862*
and **b** he has even brought Greeks **Ac 21:28** *2089*
And **b** our comfort, we rejoiced **2Co 7:13** *1909*

BESIEGE
against you, then you shall **b** it. **Dt 20:12** 6696a
"When you **b** a city a long time, **Dt 20:19** 6696a
"It shall **b** you in all your **Dt 28:52** 6887a
and it shall **b** you in all your **Dt 28:52** 6887a
to Keilah to **b** David and his men. **1Sa 23:8** 6696a
if their enemies **b** them in the **2Ch 6:28** 6887a
that it is under siege, and **b** it. **Ezk 4:3** 6696a, 5921

BESIEGED
a man, that it should be **b** by you? **Dt 20:19** 4692
came up and **b** Jabesh-gilead; **1Sa 11:1** 2583, 5921
the sons of Ammon and **b** Rabbah. **2Sa 11:1** 6696a, 5921
came and **b** him in Abel Beth-maacah, **2Sa 20:15** 6696a, 5921
from Gibbethon and **b** Tirzah. **1Ki 16:17** 6696a, 5921
And he went up and **b** Samaria and **1Ki 20:1** 6696a, 5921
army and went up and **b** Samaria. **2Ki 6:24** 6696a, 5921
and behold, they **b** it, **2Ki 6:25** 6696a, 5921
and they **b** Ahaz, but could not **2Ki 16:5** 6696a, 5921
to Samaria and **b** it three years. **2Ki 17:5** 6696a, 5921
came up against Samaria and **b** it. **2Ki 18:9** 6696a, 5921
of Ammon, and came and **b** Rabbah. **1Ch 20:1** 6696a
Judah and **b** the fortified cities, **2Ch 32:1** 2583, 5921
lovingkindness to me in a **b** city. **Ps 31:21** 4692
Who will bring me into the **b** city? **Ps 60:9** 4692
Who will bring me into the **b** city? **Ps 108:10** 4013
a cucumber field, like a **b** city. **Is 1:8** 5341
He has **b** and encompassed me with **La 3:5** 1129, 5921
and is **b** will die by the famine. **Ezk 6:12** 5341
came to Jerusalem and **b** it. **Da 1:1** 6696a, 5921

BESIEGERS
'**B** come from a far country, And **Jer 4:16** 5341

BESIEGES
if their enemy **b** them in the land **1Ki 8:37** 6887a

BESIEGING
while his servants were **b** it. **2Ki 24:11** 6696a, 5921
he *was* **b** Lachish with all his forces **2Ch 32:9** 5921
who are **b** you outside the wall; **Jer 21:4** 6696a, 5921
Chaldeans who are **b** you will live, **Jer 21:9** 6696a, 5921
king of Babylon was **b** Jerusalem, **Jer 32:2** 6696a, 5921
been **b** Jerusalem heard the report **Jer 37:5** 6696a, 5921

BESODEIAH
son of **B** repaired the Old Gate; **Ne 3:6** 1152

BESOR
with him, and came to the brook **B**, **1Sa 30:9** 1308
exhausted to cross the brook **B** remained **1Sa 30:10** 1308
had also been left at the brook **B**, **1Sa 30:21** 1308

BEST
Then Rebekah took the **b** garments **Gn 27:15** 2536b
take some of the **b** products of the **Gn 43:11** 2173
and I will give you the **b** of the **Gn 45:18** 2898
for the **b** of all the land of Egypt **Gn 45:20** 2898
loaded with the **b** things of Egypt, **Gn 45:23** 2898
brothers in the **b** of the land, **Gn 47:6** 4315
of Egypt, in the **b** of the land, **Gn 47:11** 4315
restitution from the **b** of his own **Ex 22:5** 4315
and the **b** of his own vineyard. **Ex 22:5** 4315
"All the **b** of the fresh oil and **Nu 18:12** 2459
b of the fresh wine **Nu 18:12** 2459
the LORD, from all the **b** of them, **Nu 18:29** 2459
have offered from it the **b** of it, **Nu 18:30** 2459
when you have offered the **b** of it. **Nu 18:32** 2459
"And with the **b** things of the **Dt 33:15** 7218
anoint yourself and put on your **b** **Ru 3:3**
"Do what seems **b** to you. **1Sa 1:23** 2896a
"He will take the **b** of your **1Sa 8:14** 2896a
your **b** young men and your donkeys **1Sa 8:16** 2896a
Agag and the **b** of the sheep, **1Sa 15:9** 4315
the **b** of the sheep and oxen, **1Sa 15:15** 4315
seems **b** to you I will do." **2Sa 18:4** 3190
select the **b** and fittest of your **2Ki 10:3** 2896a
maids to the **b** place in the harem. **Es 2:9** 2896a
b is a mere breath. **Ps 39:5** 5324
And your mouth like the **b** wine!" **SS 7:9** 2896a
You will eat the **b** of the land; **Is 1:19** 2898
with the **b** of all *kinds* of spices, **Ezk 27:22** 7218
the choicest and **b** of Lebanon, **Ezk 31:16** 2896a
The **b** of them is like a briar, The **Mi 7:4** 2896a
'Quickly bring out the **b** robe and put **Lk 15:22** *4413*
I also do my **b** to maintain always **Ac 24:16** *778*
we thought it **b** to be left behind **1Th 3:1** *2106*
a short time as seemed **b** to them, **Heb 12:10** *1380*

BESTOW
may **b** a blessing upon you today." **Ex 32:29** 5414
on these we **b** more abundant honor, **1Co 12:23** *4060*

BESTOWED
you the priesthood as a **b** service, **Nu 18:7** 4979
say to You concerning the honor **b** **1Ch 17:18**
and **b** on him royal majesty which **1Ch 29:25** 5414
has been **b** on Mordecai for this?" **Es 6:3** 6213a
of My splendor which I **b** on you," **Ezk 16:14** 7760
"She **b** her harlotries on **Ezk 23:7** 5414
of the grandeur which He **b** on him, **Da 5:19** 3052
Spirit was **b** through the laying on **Ac 8:18** *1325*
b on us through *the prayers* **2Co 1:11** *1519*
He freely **b** on us in the Beloved. **Eph 1:6** *5487*
and **b** on Him the name which is **Php 2:9** *5483*
from God **b** on me for your benefit, **Col 1:25** *1325*
which was **b** on you through **1Tm 4:14** *1325*
a love the Father has **b** on us, **1Jn 3:1** *1325*

BESTOWER
against Tyre, the **b** of crowns, **Is 23:8** 5849b

BESTOWS
And **b** it on whom He wishes And **Da 4:17** 5415

and **b** it on whomever He wishes. **Da 4:25** 5415
and **b** it on whomever He wishes.' **Da 4:32** 5415

BETAH
From **B** and from Berothai, **2Sa 8:8** 984

BETEN
and Hali and **B** and Achshaph, **Jos 19:25** 991

BETH-ANATH
Horem and **B** and Beth-shemesh; **Jos 19:38** 1043
or the inhabitants of **B**, **Jg 1:33** 1043
B became forced labor for them. **Jg 1:33** 1043

BETH-ANOTH
and Maarath and **B** and Eltekon; **Jos 15:59** 1042

BETHANY
them and went out of the city to **B**, **Mt 21:17** *963*
Now when Jesus was in **B**, **Mt 26:6** *963*
Jerusalem, at Bethphage and **B**, **Mk 11:1** *963*
He left for **B** with the twelve, **Mk 11:11** *963*
when they had left **B**, **Mk 11:12** *963*
While He was in **B** at the home **Mk 14:3** *963*
He approached Bethphage and **B**, **Lk 19:29** *963*
And He led them out as far as **B**, **Lk 24:50** *963*
took place in **B** beyond the Jordan, **Jn 1:28** *963*
man was sick, Lazarus of **B**, **Jn 11:1** *963*
Now **B** was near Jerusalem, about **Jn 11:18** *963*
came to **B** where Lazarus was, **Jn 12:1** *963*

BETH-ARABAH
and continued on the north of **B**, **Jos 15:6** 1026
B, Middin and Secacah, **Jos 15:61** 1026
and **B** and Zemaraim and Bethel, **Jos 18:22** 1026

BETH-ARBEL
destroyed **B** on the day of battle, **Hos 10:14** 1009

BETH-ASHBEA
house of the linen workers at **B**; **1Ch 4:21** 1004, 791

BETH-AVEN
Jericho to Ai, which is near **B**, **Jos 7:2** 1007b
it ended at the wilderness of **B**. **Jos 18:12** 1007b
and camped in Michmash, east of **B**. **1Sa 13:5** 1007b
and the battle spread beyond **B**. **1Sa 14:23** 1007b
not go to Gilgal, Or go up to **B** And **Hos 4:15** 1007b
Sound an alarm at **B**: **Hos 5:8** 1007b
will fear For the calf of **B**. **Hos 10:5** 1007b

BETH-AZMAVETH
the men of **B**, 42; **Ne 7:28** 1041

BETH-BAAL-MEON
Dibon and Bamoth-baal and **B**, **Jos 13:17** 1010

BETH-BARAH
as far as **B** and the Jordan." **Jg 7:24** 1012
waters as far as **B** and the Jordan. **Jg 7:24** 1012

BETH-BIRI
Beth-marcaboth, Hazar-susim, **B** and **1Ch 4:31** 1011

BETH-CAR
them down as far as below **B**. **1Sa 7:11** 1033

BETH-DAGON
B and Naamah and Makkedah; **Jos 15:41** 1016
It turned toward the east to **B** **Jos 19:27** 1016

BETH-DIBLATHAIM
against Dibon, Nebo and **B**, **Jer 48:22** 1015

BETH-EDEN
him who holds the scepter, from **B**; **Am 1:5** 1040

BETH-EKED
he was at **B** of the shepherds, **2Ki 10:12** 1044
and killed them at the pit of **B**, **2Ki 10:14** 1044

BETHEL
to the mountain on the east of **B**, **Gn 12:8** 1008
with **B** on the west and Ai on the **Gn 12:8** 1008
from the Negev as far as **B**, **Gn 13:3** 1008
the beginning, between **B** and Ai, **Gn 13:3** 1008
called the name of that place **B**; **Gn 28:19** 1008
'I am the God *of* **B**, where you **Gn 31:13** 1008
"Arise, go up to **B** and live **Gn 35:1** 1008
and let us arise and go up to **B**, **Gn 35:3** 1008
So Jacob came to Luz (that is, **B**), **Gn 35:6** 1008
was buried below **B** under the oak; **Gn 35:8** 1008
where God had spoken with him, **B**. **Gn 35:15** 1008
Then they journeyed from **B**; **Gn 35:16** 1008
which is near Beth-aven, east of **B**, **Jos 7:2** 1008
and remained between **B** and Ai, **Jos 8:9** 1008
them in ambush between **B** and Ai, **Jos 8:12** 1008
So not a man was left in Ai or **B** **Jos 8:17** 1008
the king of Ai, which is beside **B**, **Jos 12:9** 1008
the king of **B**, one; **Jos 12:16** 1008
through the hill country to **B**. **Jos 16:1** 1008
It went from **B** to Luz, **Jos 16:2** 1008
to the side of Luz (that is, **B**) **Jos 18:13** 1008
and Beth-arabah and Zemaraim and **B**, **Jos 18:22** 1008
house of Joseph went up against **B**, **Jg 1:22** 1008
The house of Joseph spied out **B** **Jg 1:23** 1008
B in the hill country of Ephraim; **Jg 4:5** 1008
of Israel arose, went up to **B**, **Jg 20:18** 1008
went up and came to **B** and wept; **Jg 20:26** 1008
up to **B** and the other to Gibeah, **Jg 20:31** 1008
So the people came to **B** and sat **Jg 21:2** 1008
which is on the north side of **B**, **Jg 21:19** 1008
that goes up from **B** to Shechem, **Jg 21:19** 1008
to **B** and Gilgal and Mizpah, **1Sa 7:16** 1008
up to God at **B** will meet you, **1Sa 10:3** 1008
and in the hill country of **B**, **1Sa 13:2** 1008
to those who were in **B**, **1Sa 30:27** 1008
He set one in **B**, **1Ki 12:29** 1008
thus he did in **B**, sacrificing to **1Ki 12:32** 1008
And he stationed in **B** the priests **1Ki 12:32** 1008
had made in **B** on the fifteenth day **1Ki 12:33** 1008
to **B** by the word of the LORD, **1Ki 13:1** 1008
he cried against the altar in **B**, **1Ki 13:4** 1008
by the way which he came to **B**. **1Ki 13:10** 1008
an old prophet was living in **B**; **1Ki 13:11** 1008
man of God had done that day in **B**; **1Ki 13:11** 1008
against the altar in **B** and against all **1Ki 13:32** 1008
LORD has sent me as far as **B**." **2Ki 2:2** 1008
So they went down to **B**. **2Ki 2:2** 1008
sons of the prophets who *were at* **B** **2Ki 2:3** 1008
Then he went up from there to **B**; **2Ki 2:23** 1008
were at **B** and that *were* at Dan. **2Ki 10:29** 1008
from Samaria came and lived at **B**, **2Ki 17:28** 1008
and carried their ashes to **B**. **2Ki 23:4** 1008
the altar that *was* at **B** *and* the **2Ki 23:15** 1008
done against the altar of **B**." **2Ki 23:17** 1008
to them just as he had done in **B**. **2Ki 23:19** 1008
settlements *were* **B** with its towns, **1Ch 7:28** 1008
cities, **B** with its villages, **2Ch 13:19** 1008
the men of **B** and Ai, 223; **Ezr 2:28** 1008
the men of **B** and Ai, 123; **Ne 7:32** 1008
and Aija, at **B** and its towns, **Ne 11:31** 1008
house of Israel was ashamed of **B**, **Jer 48:13** 1008
Thus it will be done to you at **B** **Hos 10:15** 1008
He found Him at **B** and there He **Hos 12:4** 1008
will also punish the altars of **B**; **Am 3:14** 1008
"Enter **B** and transgress; **Am 4:4** 1008
"But do not resort to **B** And **Am 5:5** 1008
And **B** will come to trouble. **Am 5:5** 1008
with none to quench *it* for **B**, **Am 5:6** 1008
Then Amaziah, the priest of **B**, **Am 7:10** 1008
"But no longer prophesy at **B**, **Am 7:13** 1008
Now *the town of* **B** had sent **Zch 7:2** 1008

BETHELITE
his days Hiel the **B** built Jericho; **1Ki 16:34** 1017

BETH-EMEK
Iphtahel northward to **B** and Neiel; **Jos 19:27** 1025

BETHER
stag on the mountains of **B**." **SS 2:17** 1336

BETHESDA
pool, which is called in Hebrew **B**, **Jn 5:2** *964*

BETH-EZEL
The lamentation of **B**: "He will take **Mi 1:11** 1018

BETH-GADER
and Hareph the father of **B**. **1Ch 2:51** 1013

BETH-GAMUL
against Kiriathaim, **B** and **Jer 48:23** 1014

BETH-GILGAL
from **B** and from *their* fields in **Ne 12:29** 1019

BETH-HACCEREM
Tekoa And raise a signal over **B**; **Jer 6:1** 1021

BETH-HACCHEREM
of **B** repaired the Refuse Gate. **Ne 3:14** 1021

BETH-HARAM
B and Beth-nimrah and Succoth and **Jos 13:27** 1027

BETH-HARAN
and **B** as fortified cities, **Nu 32:36** 1027

BETH-HOGLAH
Then the border went up to **B**, **Jos 15:6** 1031
to the side of **B** northward; **Jos 18:19** 1031
were Jericho and **B** and Emek-keziz, **Jos 18:21** 1031

BETH-HORON
by the way of the ascent of **B** and **Jos 10:10** 1032
they were at the descent of **B**, **Jos 10:11** 1032
of lower **B** even to Gezer, **Jos 16:3** 1032
Ataroth-addar, as far as upper **B**. **Jos 16:5** 1032
lies on the south of lower **B**. **Jos 18:13** 1032
which *lies* before **B** southward; **Jos 18:14** 1032
and **B** with its pasture lands; **Jos 21:22** 1032
another company turned toward **B**, **1Sa 13:18** 1032
rebuilt Gezer and the lower **B** **1Ki 9:17** 1032
lands, **B** with its pasture lands, **1Ch 6:68** 1032
who built lower and upper **B**, **1Ch 7:24** 1032
built upper **B** and lower Beth-horon, **2Ch 8:5** 1032
built upper Beth-horon and lower **B**, **2Ch 8:5** 1032
of Judah, from Samaria to **B**, **2Ch 25:13** 1032

BETH-JESHIMOTH
from **B** as far as Abel-shittim in **Nu 33:49** 1020
the Salt Sea, eastward toward **B**, **Jos 12:3** 1020
and the slopes of Pisgah and **B**, **Jos 13:20** 1020
the glory of the land, **B**, **Ezk 25:9** 1020

BETH-LE-APHRAH
At **B** roll yourself in the dust. **Mi 1:10** 1036

BETH-LEBAOTH
and **B** and Sharuhen; thirteen **Jos 19:6** 1034

BETHLEHEM
on the way to Ephrath (that is, **B**). **Gn 35:19** 1035
the way to Ephrath (that is, **B**)." **Gn 48:7** 1035
and Shimron and Idalah and **B**; **Jos 19:15** 1035
of **B** judged Israel after him. **Jg 12:8** 1035
Ibzan died and was buried in **B**. **Jg 12:10** 1035
was a young man from **B** in Judah, **Jg 17:7** 1035
from the city, from **B** in Judah, **Jg 17:8** 1035
"I am a Levite from **B** in Judah, **Jg 17:9** 1035
for himself from **B** in Judah. **Jg 19:1** 1035
her father's house in **B** in Judah, **Jg 19:2** 1035
"We are passing from **B** in Judah **Jg 19:18** 1035
there, and I went to **B** in Judah. **Jg 19:18** 1035
And a certain man of **B** in Judah **Ru 1:1** 1035
Ephrathites of **B** in Judah. **Ru 1:2** 1035
both went until they came to **B**. **Ru 1:19** 1035
And when they had come to **B**, **Ru 1:19** 1035
And they came to **B** at the **Ru 1:22** 1035
from **B** and said to the reapers, **Ru 2:4** 1035
Ephrathah and become famous in **B**. **Ru 4:11** 1035
what the LORD said, and came to **B**. **1Sa 16:4** 1035
of the Ephrathite of **B** in Judah, **1Sa 17:12** 1035
to tend his father's flock at **B**. **1Sa 17:15** 1035
leave of me to run to **B** his city, **1Sa 20:6** 1035
asked leave of me *to go* to **B**, **1Sa 20:28** 1035
his father's tomb which was in **B**. **2Sa 2:32** 1035
of the Philistines was then in **B**. **2Sa 23:14** 1035
well of **B** which is by the gate!" **2Sa 23:15** 1035
well of **B** which was by the gate, **2Sa 23:16** 1035
Elhanan the son of Dodo of **B**, **2Sa 23:24** 1035
Salma the father of **B** *and* Hareph **1Ch 2:51** 1035
were **B** and the Netophathites, **1Ch 2:54** 1035
of Ephrathah, the father of **B**. **1Ch 4:4** 1035
of the Philistines *was* then in **B**. **1Ch 11:16** 1035
water to drink from the well of **B**, **1Ch 11:17** 1035
well of **B** which *was* by the gate, **1Ch 11:18** 1035
Elhanan the son of Dodo of **B**, **1Ch 11:26** 1035
Thus he built **B**, Etam, Tekoa, **2Ch 11:6** 1035
the men of **B**, 123; **Ezr 2:21** 1035
the men of **B** and Netophah, 188; **Ne 7:26** 1035
Geruth Chimham, which is beside **B**, **Jer 41:17** 1035
"But as for you, **B** Ephrathah, *Too* **Mi 5:2** 1035
Now after Jesus was born in **B** of **Mt 2:1** *965*
"In **B** of Judea; for this is what **Mt 2:5** *965*
'AND YOU, **B**, LAND OF JUDAH, ARE **Mt 2:6** *965*
And he sent them to **B** and **Mt 2:8** *965*
were in **B** and all its vicinity, **Mt 2:16** *965*
city of David which is called **B**, **Lk 2:4** *965*
"Let us go straight to **B** then, **Lk 2:15** *965*
descendants of David, and from **B**, **Jn 7:42** *965*

BETHLEHEMITE
I will send you to Jesse the **B**, **1Sa 16:1** 1022
the **B** who is a skillful musician, **1Sa 16:18** 1022
son of your servant Jesse the **B**." **1Sa 17:58** 1022
the **B** killed Goliath the Gittite, **2Sa 21:19** 1022

BETH-MAACAH
even **B**, and all the Berites; **2Sa 20:14** 1038
came and besieged him in Abel **B**, **2Sa 20:15** 1038

BETH-MARCABOTH
and Ziklag and **B** and Hazar-susah, **Jos 19:5** 1024
B, Hazar-susim, Beth-biri and **1Ch 4:31** 1024

BETH-MEON
Kiriathaim, Beth-gamul and **B**, **Jer 48:23** 1010

BETH-MILLO
and all **B** assembled together, **Jg 9:6** 1037
consume the men of Shechem and **B**; **Jg 9:20** 1037
the men of Shechem and from **B**, **Jg 9:20** 1037

BETH-NIMRAH
and **B** and Beth-haran as fortified **Nu 32:36** 1039
and **B** and Succoth and Zaphon, **Jos 13:27** 1039

BETH-PAZZEZ
and En-gannim and En-haddah and **B**. **Jos 19:21** 1048

BETH-PELET
and Hazar-gaddah and Heshmon and **B**, **Jos 15:27** 1046
and in Jeshua, in Moladah and **B**, **Ne 11:26** 1046

BETH-PEOR
remained in the valley opposite **B**. **Dt 3:29** 1047
Jordan, in the valley opposite **B**, **Dt 4:46** 1047
in the land of Moab, opposite **B**; **Dt 34:6** 1047
and **B** and the slopes of Pisgah and **Jos 13:20** 1047

BETHPHAGE
Jerusalem and had come to **B**, **Mt 21:1** *967*
Jerusalem, at **B** and Bethany, **Mk 11:1** *967*
When He approached **B** and Bethany, **Lk 19:29** *967*

BETH-RAPHA
became the father of **B** and Paseah, **1Ch 4:12** 1051

BETH-REHOB
was in the valley which is near **B**. **Jg 18:28** 1050
of **B** and the Arameans of Zobah, **2Sa 10:6** 1050

BETHSAIDA
Woe to you, **B**! For if the miracles **Mt 11:21** *966*
of *Him* to the other side to **B**, **Mk 6:45** *966*
And they came to **B**. **Mk 8:22** *966*
by Himself to a city called **B**. **Lk 9:10** *966*
Woe to you, **B**! For if the miracles **Lk 10:13** *966*
Now Philip was from **B**, **Jn 1:44** *966*
Philip, who was from **B** of Galilee, **Jn 12:21** *966*

BETH-SHAN
his body to the wall of **B**. **1Sa 31:10** 1052
of his sons from the wall of **B**, **1Sa 31:12** 1052
stolen them from the open square of **B**, **2Sa 21:12** 1052

BETH-SHEAN
Manasseh had **B** and its towns and **Jos 17:11** 1052
those who are in **B** and its towns and **Jos 17:16** 1052
possession of **B** and its villages, **Jg 1:27** 1052
and all **B** which is beside Zarethan **1Ki 4:12** 1052
from **B** to Abel-meholah as far as **1Ki 4:12** 1052
of Manasseh, **B** with its towns, **1Ch 7:29** 1052

BETH-SHEMESH
to **B** and continued through Timnah. **Jos 15:10** 1053
to Tabor and Shahazumah and **B**, **Jos 19:22** 1053
Horem and Beth-anath and **B**; **Jos 19:38** 1053
and **B** with its pasture lands; **Jos 21:16** 1053
drive out the inhabitants of **B**, **Jg 1:33** 1053
and the inhabitants of **B** and **Jg 1:33** 1053
the way of its own territory to **B**, **1Sa 6:9** 1053
way in the direction of **B**; **1Sa 6:12** 1053
followed them to the border of **B**. **1Sa 6:12** 1053
Now *the people of* **B** were reaping **1Sa 6:13** 1053
and the men of **B** offered burnt **1Sa 6:15** 1053
struck down some of the men of **B** **1Sa 6:19** 1053
The men of **B** said, **1Sa 6:20** 1053
Shaalbim and **B** and Elonbeth-hanan; **1Ki 4:9** 1053
of Judah faced each other at **B**, **2Ki 14:11** 1053
Jehoash the son of Ahaziah, at **B**, **2Ki 14:13** 1053
and **B** with its pasture lands; **1Ch 6:59** 1053
of Judah faced each other at **B**, **2Ch 25:21** 1053
Joash the son of Jehoahaz, at **B**, **2Ch 25:23** 1053
Negev of Judah, and had taken **B**, **2Ch 28:18** 1053

BETH-SHEMITE
came into the field of Joshua the **B** 1Sa 6:14 1030
day in the field of Joshua the **B**. 1Sa 6:18 1030
BETH-SHITTAH
fled as far as **B** toward Zererah, Jg 7:22 1029
BETH-TAPPUAH
and Janum and **B** and Aphekah, Jos 15:53 1054
BETH-TOGARMAH
"Those from **B** gave horses and war Ezk 27:14 1004, 8425
B *from* the remote parts of the Ezk 38:6 1004, 8425
BETHUEL
and Pildash and Jidlaph and **B**." Gn 22:22 1328a
B became the father of Rebekah; Gn 22:23 1328a
was born to **B** the son of Milcah, Gn 24:15 1328a
"I am the daughter of **B**, Gn 24:24 1328a
'The daughter of **B**, Nahor's son, Gn 24:47 1328a
Laban and **B** replied, Gn 24:50 1328a
of **B** the Aramean of Paddan-aram, Gn 25:20 1328a
house of **B** your mother's father; Gn 28:2 1328a
to Laban, son of **B** the Aramean, Gn 28:5 1328a
B, Hormah, Ziklag, 1Ch 4:30 1328b
BETHUL
and Eltolad and **B** and Hormah, Jos 19:4 1329
BETHZUR
and Maon *was* the father of **B**. 1Ch 2:45 1049
BETH-ZUR
Halhul, **B** and Gedor, Jos 15:58 1049
B, Soco, Adullam, 2Ch 11:7 1049
of half the district of **B**, Ne 3:16 1049
BETONIM
as far as Ramath-mizpeh and **B**, Jos 13:26 993
BETRAY
but if to **b** me to my adversaries, 1Ch 12:17 7411b
outcasts, do not **b** the fugitive. Is 16:3 1540
"Brother will **b** brother to death, Mt 10:21 *3860*
time many will fall away and will **b** Mt 24:10 *3860*
"What are you willing to give me to **b** Mt 26:15 *3860*
for a good opportunity to **b** Jesus. Mt 26:16 *3860*
you that one of you will **b** Me." Mt 26:21 *3860*
the bowl is the one who will **b** Me. Mt 26:23 *3860*
"Brother will **b** brother to death, Mk 13:12 *3860*
in order to **b** Him to them. Mk 14:10 *3860*
how to **b** Him at an opportune time. Mk 14:11 *3860*
say to you that one of you will **b** Me Mk 14:18 *3860*
how he might **b** Him to them. Lk 22:4 *3860*
good opportunity to **b** Him to them Lk 22:6 *3860*
and who it was that would **b** Him. Jn 6:64 *3860*
of the twelve, was going to **b** Him. Jn 6:71 *3860*
who was intending to **b** Him, Jn 12:4 *3860*
the son of Simon, to **b** Him, Jn 13:2 *3860*
you, that one of you will **b** Me." Jn 13:21 *3860*
BETRAYED
I would have **b** the generation of Ps 73:15 898
Judas Iscariot, the one who **b** Him. Mt 10:4 *3860*
man by whom the Son of Man is **b**! Mt 26:24 *3860*
being **b** into the hands of sinners. Mt 26:45 *3860*
Then when Judas, who had **b** Him, Mt 27:3 *3860*
Judas Iscariot, who **b** Him. Mk 3:19 *3860*
man by whom the Son of Man is **b**! Mk 14:21 *3860*
being **b** into the hands of sinners. Mk 14:41 *3860*
"But you will be **b** even by parents Lk 21:16 *3860*
woe to that man by whom He is **b**!" Lk 22:22 *3860*
in which He was **b** took bread; 1Co 11:23 *3860*
BETRAYERS
whose **b** and murderers you have now Ac 7:52 *4273*
BETRAYING
And Judas, who was **b** Him, Mt 26:25 *3860*
he who was **b** Him gave them a sign, Mt 26:48 *3860*
have sinned by **b** innocent blood." Mt 27:4 *3860*
was **b** Him had given them a signal, Mk 14:44 *3860*
one **b** Me is with Mine on the table. Lk 22:21 *3860*
b the Son of Man with a kiss?" Lk 22:48 *3860*
For He knew the one who was **b** Him; Jn 13:11 *3860*
Now Judas also, who was **b** Him, Jn 18:2 *3860*
And Judas also, who was **b** Him, Jn 18:5 *3860*
BETRAYS
wine **b** the haughty man, Hab 2:5 898
the one who **b** Me is at hand!" Mt 26:46 *3860*
the one who **b** Me is at hand!" Mk 14:42 *3860*
"Lord, who is the one who **b** You?" Jn 21:20 *3860*
BETROTH
"You shall **b** a wife, but another Dt 28:30 781
"I will **b** you to Me forever; Hos 2:19 781
I will **b** you to Me in Hos 2:19 781
will **b** you to Me in faithfulness. Hos 2:20 781
BETROTHALS
of your youth, The love of your **b**, Jer 2:2 3623
BETROTHED
to whom I was **b** for a hundred 2Sa 3:14 781
mother Mary had been **b** to Joseph, Mt 1:18 *3423*
for I **b** you to one husband, so 2Co 11:2 *718*
BETTER
"It is **b** that I give her to you Gn 29:19 2896a
For it would have been **b** for us to Ex 14:12 2896a
be **b** for us to return to Egypt?" Nu 14:3 2896a
b than the vintage of Abiezer? Jg 8:2 2896a
'Which is **b** for you, that seventy Jg 9:2 2896a
b than Balak the son of Zippor, Jg 11:25 2896a
Is it **b** for you to be a priest to Jg 18:19 2896a
last kindness to be **b** than the first Ru 3:10 3190
and is **b** to you than seven sons, Ru 4:15 2896a
Am I not **b** to you than ten sons?" 1Sa 1:8 2896a
to obey is **b** than sacrifice, 1Sa 15:22 2896a
your neighbor, who is **b** than you. 1Sa 15:28 2896a
There is nothing **b** for me than to 1Sa 27:1 2896a
be **b** for me still to be there." 2Sa 14:32 2896a
counsel of Hushai the Archite is **b** 2Sa 17:14 2896a
therefore now it is **b** that you *be* 2Sa 18:3 2896a
name of Solomon **b** than your name 1Ki 1:47 3190
two men more righteous and **b** than 1Ki 2:32 2896a
for I am not **b** than my fathers." 1Ki 19:4 2896a
a **b** vineyard than it in its place; 1Ki 21:2 2896a
b than all the waters of Israel? 2Ki 5:12 2896a
own family, who were **b** than you, 2Ch 21:13 2896a
B is the little of the righteous Ps 37:16 2896a
Your lovingkindness is **b** than life, Ps 63:3 2896a
And it will please the LORD **b** than Ps 69:31 3190
is **b** than a thousand *outside*. Ps 84:10 2896a
It is **b** to take refuge in the LORD Ps 118:8 2896a
It is **b** to take refuge in the LORD Ps 118:9 2896a
The law of Your mouth is **b** to me Ps 119:72 2896a
is **b** than the profit of silver And Pr 3:14 2896a
the profit of silver And her gain **b** Pr 3:14
"For wisdom is **b** than jewels; Pr 8:11 2896a
"My fruit is **b** than gold, even Pr 8:19 2896a
And my yield **b** than choicest Pr 8:19
B is he who is lightly esteemed Pr 12:9 2896a
B is a little with the fear of the Pr 15:16 2896a
B is a dish of vegetables where Pr 15:17 2896a
B is a little with righteousness Pr 16:8 2896a
b it is to get wisdom than gold! Pr 16:16 2896a
It is **b** to be humble in spirit Pr 16:19 2896a
to anger is **b** than the mighty, Pr 16:32 2896a
B is a dry morsel and quietness Pr 17:1 2896a
B is a poor man who walks in his Pr 19:1 2896a
is **b** to be a poor man than a liar. Pr 19:22 2896a
b to live in a corner of a roof Than Pr 21:9 2896a
It is **b** to live in a desert land Than Pr 21:19 2896a
Favor is **b** than silver and gold. Pr 22:1 2896a
it is **b** that it be said to you, Pr 25:7 2896a
It is **b** to live in a corner of the Pr 25:24 2896a
B is open rebuke Than love that is Pr 27:5 2896a
B is a neighbor who is near than a Pr 27:10 2896a
B is the poor who walks in his Pr 28:6 2896a
There is nothing **b** for a man *than* Ec 2:24 2896a
I know that there is nothing **b** for Ec 3:12 2896a
I have seen that nothing is **b** Ec 3:22 2896a
But **b** *off* than both of them is the Ec 4:3 2896a
One hand full of rest is **b** than Ec 4:6 2896a
Two are **b** than one because they Ec 4:9 2896a
yet wise lad is **b** than an old and Ec 4:13 2896a
It is **b** that you should not vow Ec 5:5 2896a
"**B** the miscarriage than he, Ec 6:3 2896a
it is **b** off than he. Ec 6:5 5183a
is **b** than what the soul desires. Ec 6:9 2896a
name is **b** than a good ointment, Ec 7:1 2896a
is **b** than the day of one's birth. Ec 7:1
It is **b** to go to a house of Ec 7:2 2896a
Sorrow is **b** than laughter, For Ec 7:3 2896a
It is **b** to listen to the rebuke of Ec 7:5 2896a
a matter is **b** than its beginning; Ec 7:8 2896a
is **b** than haughtiness of spirit. Ec 7:8 2896a
former days were **b** than these?" Ec 7:10 2896a
a live dog is **b** than a dead lion. Ec 9:4 2896a
"Wisdom is **b** than strength." Ec 9:16 2896a
the wise heard in quietness are **b** Ec 9:17
Wisdom is **b** than weapons of war, Ec 9:18 2896a
For your love is **b** than wine. SS 1:2 2896a
How much **b** is your love than wine, SS 4:10 2896a
And a name **b** than that of sons and Is 56:5 2896a
then I will think **b** of the good Jer 18:10 5162
B are those slain with the sword La 4:9 2896a
how is the wood of the vine **b** Ezk 15:2
treat you **b** than at the first. Ezk 36:11 3190
seemed **b** and they were fatter than Da 1:15 2896a
he found them ten times **b** than all Da 1:20 5921
it was **b** for me then than now!' Hos 2:7 2896a
The **b** he made the *sacred* pillars. Hos 10:1 3190
Are they **b** than these kingdoms, Or Am 6:2 2896a
for death is **b** to me than life." Jon 4:3 2896a
"Death is **b** to me than life." Jon 4:8 2896a
Are you **b** than No-amon, Which was Na 3:8 3190
for it is **b** for you to lose one Mt 5:29 *4851a*
for it is **b** for you to lose one Mt 5:30 *4851a*
b for him to have a heavy millstone Mt 18:6 *4851a*
it is **b** for you to enter life Mt 18:8 *2570*
It is **b** for you to enter life with Mt 18:9 *2570*
like this, it is **b** not to marry." Mt 19:10 *4851a*
stumble, it would be **b** for him if, Mk 9:42 *2570, 3123*
it is **b** for you to enter life Mk 9:43 *2570*
is **b** for you to enter life lame, Mk 9:45 *2570*
it is **b** for you to enter the Mk 9:47 *2570*
"It would be **b** for him if a Lk 17:2 *3081*
the hour when he began to get **b**. Jn 4:52 *2866*
Are we **b** than they? Ro 3:9 *4284*
for it is **b** to marry than to burn 1Co 7:9 *2909*
give her in marriage will do **b**. 1Co 7:38 *2909*
not eat, nor the **b** if we do eat. 1Co 8:8 *4052*
for it would be **b** for me to die 1Co 9:15 *2570, 3123*
not for the **b** but for the worse. 1Co 11:17 *2909*
Christ, for *that* is very much **b**; Php 1:23 *2909*
become as much **b** than the angels, Heb 1:4 *2909*
of **b** things concerning you, Heb 6:9 *2909*
is a bringing in of a **b** hope, Heb 7:19 *2909*
the guarantee of a **b** covenant. Heb 7:22 *2909*
also the mediator of a **b** covenant, Heb 8:6 *2909*
has been enacted on **b** promises. Heb 8:6 *2909*
with **b** sacrifices than these. Heb 9:23 *2909*
a **b** possession and a lasting one. Heb 10:34 *2909*
to God a **b** sacrifice than Cain, Heb 11:4 *4183*
as it is, they desire a **b** *country*, Heb 11:16 *2909*
might obtain a **b** resurrection; Heb 11:35 *2909*
had provided something **b** for us, Heb 11:40 *2909*
speaks **b** than *the blood* of Abel. Heb 12:24 *2909*
For it is **b**, if God should will it 1Pe 3:17 *2909*
For it would be **b** for them not to 2Pe 2:21 *2909*
BETWEEN
put enmity **B** you and the woman, Gn 3:15 996
And **b** your seed and her seed; Gn 3:15 996
which I am making **b** Me and you Gn 9:12 996
of a covenant **b** Me and the earth. Gn 9:13 996
which is **b** Me and you and every Gn 9:15 996
covenant **b** God and every living Gn 9:16 996
established **b** Me and all flesh that Gn 9:17 996
and Resen **b** Nineveh and Calah; Gn 10:12 996
at the beginning, **b** Bethel and Ai, Gn 13:3 996
And there was strife **b** the Gn 13:7 996
there be no strife **b** you and me, Gn 13:8 996
b my herdsmen and your herdsmen, Gn 13:8 996
torch which passed **b** these pieces. Gn 15:17 996
May the LORD judge **b** you and me." Gn 16:5 996
behold, it is **b** Kadesh and Bered. Gn 16:14 996
My covenant **b** Me and you, Gn 17:2 996
b Me and you and your descendants Gn 17:7 996
b Me and you and your descendants Gn 17:10 996
sign of the covenant **b** Me and you. Gn 17:11 996
and settled **b** Kadesh and Shur; Gn 20:1 996
silver, what is that **b** me and you? Gn 23:15 996
'Let there now be an oath **b** us, Gn 26:28 996
between us, *even* **b** you and us, Gn 26:28 996
days' journey **b** himself and Jacob, Gn 30:36 996
that they may decide **b** us two. Gn 31:37 996
it be a witness **b** you and me." Gn 31:44 996
a witness **b** you and me this day." Gn 31:48 996
"May the LORD watch **b** you and me Gn 31:49 996
God is witness **b** you and me." Gn 31:50 996
which I have set **b** you and me. Gn 31:51 996
God of their father, judge **b** us." Gn 31:53 996
me, and put a space **b** droves." Gn 32:16 996
there was an interpreter **b** them. Gn 42:23 996
the ruler's staff from **b** his feet, Gn 49:10 996
Lying down **b** the sheepfolds. Gn 49:14 996
b My people and your people. Ex 8:23 996
make a distinction **b** the livestock of Ex 9:4 996
a distinction **b** Egypt and Israel.' Ex 11:7 996
Pi-hahiroth, **b** Migdol and the sea; Ex 14:2 996
So it came **b** the camp of Egypt and Ex 14:20 996
of Sin, which is **b** Elim and Sinai, Ex 16:1 996
I judge **b** a man and his neighbor and Ex 18:16 996
from **b** the two cherubim which are Ex 25:22 996
a partition **b** the holy place and the Ex 26:33 996
bells of gold **b** them all around: Ex 28:33 8432
and you shall put it **b** the tent of Ex 30:18 996
for *this* is a sign **b** Me and you Ex 31:13 996
"It is a sign **b** Me and the sons Ex 31:17 996
and put the bells **b** the Ex 39:25 8432
"You shall set the laver **b** Ex 40:7 996
He placed the laver **b** the tent Ex 40:30 996
b the holy and the profane, Lv 10:10 996
and **b** the unclean and the clean, Lv 10:10 996
b the unclean and the clean, Lv 11:47 996
and **b** the edible creature and the Lv 11:47 996
distinction **b** the clean animal and Lv 20:25 996
and **b** the unclean bird and the Lv 20:25 996
established **b** Himself and the sons Lv 26:46 996
from **b** the two cherubim, Nu 7:89 996
grind *it* **b** two millstones or beat *it* Nu 11:8
the meat was still **b** their teeth, Nu 11:33 996
carried it on a pole **b** two *men*, Nu 13:23
stand **b** the dead and the living, Nu 16:48 996
of Moab, **b** Moab and the Amorites. Nu 21:13 996
divided **b** the larger and the smaller Nu 26:56 996
Moses, *as* **b** a man and his wife, Nu 30:16 996
as **b** a father and his daughter, Nu 30:16 996
and divide the booty **b** the warriors Nu 31:27 996
congregation shall judge **b** the slayer Nu 35:24 996
b Paran and Tophel and Laban and Dt 1:1 996
cases **b** your fellow countrymen, Dt 1:16 996
and judge righteously **b** a man and Dt 1:16 996
b the LORD and you at that time, Dt 5:5 996
b one kind of homicide or another, Dt 17:8 996
b one kind of lawsuit or another, Dt 17:8 996
and **b** one kind of assault or Dt 17:8 996
b men and they go to court, Dt 25:1 996
issues from **b** her legs and toward Dt 28:57 996
And he dwells **b** His shoulders." Dt 33:12 996
there shall be **b** you and it a Jos 3:4 996
and remained **b** Bethel and Ai, Jos 8:9 996
there was a valley **b** him and Ai. Jos 8:11 996
them in ambush **b** Bethel and Ai, Jos 8:12 996
territory of their lot lay **b** the sons Jos 18:11 996
the Jordan a border **b** us and you, Jos 22:25 996
rather it shall be a witness **b** us Jos 22:27 996
and **b** our generations after us, Jos 22:27 996
it is a witness **b** us and you." Jos 22:28 996
b us that the LORD is God." Jos 22:34 996
darkness **b** you and the Egyptians, Jos 24:7 996
b Ramah and Bethel in the hill Jg 4:5 996
for *there was* peace **b** Jabin the Jg 4:17 996
"**B** her feet he bowed, he fell, he Jg 5:27 996
B her feet he bowed, he fell; Jg 5:27 996
Then God sent an evil spirit **b** Jg 9:23 996
"The LORD is witness **b** us; Jg 11:10 996
"What is **b** you and me, that you Jg 11:12
judge today **b** the sons of Israel Jg 11:27 996
Mahaneh-dan, **b** Zorah and Eshtaol. Jg 13:25 996
torch in the middle **b** two tails. Jg 15:4 996
they made him stand **b** the pillars. Jg 16:25 996
and buried him **b** Zorah and Eshtaol Jg 16:31 996
Now the appointed sign **b** the men Jg 20:38

and set it **b** Mizpah and Shen, 1Sa 7:12 996
peace **b** Israel and the Amorites. 1Sa 7:14 996
B the passes by which Jonathan sought 1Sa 14:4 996
lots **b** me and Jonathan my son." 1Sa 14:42 996
they camped **b** Socoh and Azekah, 1Sa 17:1 996
side, with the valley **b** them. 1Sa 17:3 996
javelin *slung* **b** his shoulders. 1Sa 17:6 996
is hardly a step **b** me and death." 1Sa 20:3 996
LORD is **b** you and me forever." 1Sa 20:23 996
'The LORD will be **b** me and you, 1Sa 20:42 996
and **b** my descendants and your 1Sa 20:42 996
"May the LORD judge **b** you and me, 1Sa 24:12 996
be judge and decide **b** you and me; 1Sa 24:15 996
distance *with* a large area **b** them. 1Sa 26:13 996
was a long war **b** the house of Saul 2Sa 3:1 996
there was war **b** the house of Saul 2Sa 3:6 996
left hanging **b** heaven and earth, 2Sa 18:9 996
David was sitting **b** the two gates; 2Sa 18:24 996
Can I distinguish **b** good and bad? 2Sa 19:35 996
oath of the LORD which was **b** them, 2Sa 21:7 996
b David and Saul's son Jonathan. 2Sa 21:7 996
people to discern **b** good and evil. 1Ki 3:9 996
was peace **b** Hiram and Solomon, 1Ki 5:12 996
even borders **b** the frames, 1Ki 7:28 996
were **b** the frames *were* lions, 1Ki 7:29 996
ground **b** Succoth and Zarethan. 1Ki 7:46 996
There was war **b** Rehoboam and 1Ki 14:30 996
There was war **b** Rehoboam and 1Ki 15:6 996
was war **b** Abijam and Jeroboam. 1Ki 15:7 996
Now there was war **b** Asa and Baasha 1Ki 15:16 996
there be a treaty **b** you and me, 1Ki 15:19 996
as **b** my father and your father. 1Ki 15:19 996
There was war **b** Asa and Baasha 1Ki 15:32 996
the land **b** them to survey it; 1Ki 18:6 996
will you hesitate **b** two opinions? 1Ki 18:21 5921
and put his face **b** his knees. 1Ki 18:42 996
without war **b** Aram and Israel. 1Ki 22:1 996
and shot Joram **b** his arms; 2Ki 9:24 996
"Bring her out **b** the ranks, and 2Ki 11:15
413, 4480, 1004
Then Jehoiada made a covenant **b** 2Ki 11:17 996
also **b** the king and the people. 2Ki 11:17 996
from **b** *his* altar and the house of 2Ki 16:14 996
by way of the gate **b** the two walls 2Ki 25:4 996
LORD standing **b** earth and heaven, 1Ch 21:16 996
clay ground **b** Succoth and Zeredah. 2Ch 4:17 996
they may learn *the difference* **b** 2Ch 12:8
And *there were* wars **b** Rehoboam and 2Ch 12:15
was war **b** Abijah and Jeroboam. 2Ch 13:2 996
help *in the battle* **b** the powerful and 2Ch 14:11 996
there be a treaty **b** you and me, 2Ch 16:3 996
as **b** my father and your father. 2Ch 16:3 996
their cities, **b** blood and blood, 2Ch 19:10 996
and blood, **b** law and commandment, 2Ch 19:10 996
"Bring her out **b** the ranks; 2Ch 23:14
413, 4480, 1004
Then Jehoiada made a covenant **b** 2Ch 23:16 996
B the upper room of the corner Ne 3:32 996
'**B** morning and evening they are Jb 4:20 4480
"There is no umpire **b** us, Jb 9:33 996
That no air can come **b** them. Jb 41:16 996
They flow **b** the mountains; Ps 104:10 996
And decides **b** the mighty ones Pr 18:18 996
rivalry **b** a man and his neighbor. Ec 4:4
Which lies all night **b** my breasts. SS 1:13 996
And He will judge **b** the nations, Is 2:4 996
Judah, Judge **b** Me and My vineyard. Is 5:3 996
And you made a reservoir **b** the two Is 22:11 996
a separation **b** you and your God, Is 59:2 996
justice **b** a man and his neighbor, Jer 7:5 996
in two and passed **b** its parts Jer 34:18 996
passed **b** the parts of the calf Jer 34:19 996
through the gate **b** the two walls; Jer 39:4 996
by way of the gate **b** the two walls Jer 52:7 996
an iron wall **b** you and the city, Ezk 4:3 996
and the Spirit lifted me up **b** Ezk 8:3 996
LORD, **b** the porch and the altar, Ezk 8:16 996
"Enter **b** the whirling wheels Ezk 10:2 996
coals of fire from **b** the cherubim and Ezk 10:2 996
fire from **b** the whirling wheels, Ezk 10:6 996
wheels, from **b** the cherubim," Ezk 10:6 996
from **b** the cherubim to the fire Ezk 10:7 996
the fire which was **b** the cherubim, Ezk 10:7 996
true justice **b** man and man, Ezk 18:8 996
to be a sign **b** Me and them, Ezk 20:12 996
they shall be a sign **b** Me and you, Ezk 20:20 996
b the holy and the profane, Ezk 22:26 996
b the unclean and the clean; Ezk 22:26 996
judge **b** one sheep and another, Ezk 34:17 996
b the rams and the male goats. Ezk 34:17 996
will judge **b** the fat sheep and the Ezk 34:20 996
judge **b** one sheep and another. Ezk 34:22 996
were five cubits **b** the guardrooms. Ezk 40:7 996
But the free space **b** the side Ezk 41:9 1007a
palm tree was **b** cherub and cherub, Ezk 41:18 996
divide **b** the holy and the profane. Ezk 42:20 996
with *only* the wall **b** Me and them. Ezk 43:8 996
b the holy and the profane, Ezk 44:23 996
b the unclean and the clean. Ezk 44:23 996
which is **b** the border of Damascus Ezk 47:16 996
"The east side, from **b** Hauran, Ezk 47:18 996
everything **b** the border of Judah Ezk 48:22 996
were in its mouth **b** its teeth; Da 7:5 997
had a conspicuous horn **b** his eyes. Da 8:5 996
of a man **b** *the banks of* Ulai, Da 8:16 996
is **b** his eyes is the first king. Da 8:21 996
tents of his royal pavilion **b** the seas Da 11:45 996
her adultery from **b** her breasts, Hos 2:2 996
Weep **b** the porch and the altar, Jl 2:17 996
b their right and left hand, Jon 4:11 996
And He will judge **b** many peoples Mi 4:3 996
ephah **b** the earth and the heavens. Zch 5:9 996
forth from **b** the two mountains; Zch 6:1 996
will be **b** the two offices." Zch 6:13 996
things from **b** their teeth. Zch 9:7 996
brotherhood **b** Judah and Israel. Zch 11:14 996
are these wounds **b** your arms?' Zch 13:6 996
b you and the wife of your youth, Mal 2:14 996
b the righteous and the wicked, Mal 3:18 996
b one who serves God and one who Mal 3:18 996
b the temple and the altar. Mt 23:35 *3342*
who was killed **b** the altar and the Lk 11:51 *3342*
So he divided his wealth **b** them. Lk 15:12 *1244*
b us and you there is a great Lk 16:26 *3342*
was passing **b** Samaria and Galilee. Lk 17:11
1223, 3319
on either side, and Jesus in **b**. Jn 19:18 *3319*
Peter was sleeping **b** two soldiers, Ac 12:6 *3342*
made no distinction **b** us and them, Ac 15:9 *3342*
b the Pharisees and Sadducees, Ac 23:7
is no distinction **b** Jew and Greek; Ro 10:12
be able to decide **b** his brethren, 1Co 6:5 *303, 3319*
in which there is no *distinction* **b** Col 3:11
one mediator also **b** God and men, 1Tm 2:5
and constant friction **b** men of 1Tm 6:5
And I saw **b** the throne Rv 5:6
1722, 3319

BEWAIL

shall **b** the burning which the LORD Lv 10:6 1058

BEWARE

"**B** that you do not take my son back Gn 24:6 8104
B, do not see my face again, for Ex 10:28 8104
'**B** that you do not go up on the Ex 19:12 8104
"And **b** not to lift up your eyes Dt 4:19 8104
"**B** that you do not forget the LORD Dt 8:11 8104
"**B** that your hearts are not deceived, Dt 11:16 8104
b that you are not ensnared to Dt 12:30 8104
"**B** that there is no base thought Dt 15:9 8104
"**B** that you do not pass this 2Ki 6:9 8104
"**B** of being negligent in carrying Ezr 4:22 1934
"**B** that wrath does not entice Jb 36:18 8104
"**B** that Hezekiah does not Is 36:18
"**B** of practicing your Mt 6:1 *4337*
"**B** of the false prophets, who Mt 7:15 *4337*
b of men, for they will hand you Mt 10:17 *4337*
"Watch out and **b** of the leaven of Mt 16:6 *4337*
But **b** of the leaven of the Mt 16:11 *4337*
say to **b** of the leaven of bread, Mt 16:12 *4337*
B of the leaven of the Pharisees Mk 8:15 *991*
"**B** of the scribes who like to Mk 12:38 *991*
"**B** of the leaven of the Lk 12:1 *4337*
"**B**, and be on your guard against Lk 12:15 *3708*
"**B** of the scribes, who like to Lk 20:46 *4337*
B of the dogs, beware of the evil Php 3:2 *991*
the dogs, **b** of the evil workers, Php 3:2 *991*
b of the false circumcision; Php 3:2 *991*

BEWILDERED

of the crashing they are **b**. Jb 41:25 2398
I am so **b** I cannot hear, so Is 21:3 5753a
came together, and were **b** because Ac 2:6 *4797*

BEWILDERMENT

blindness and with **b** of heart; Dt 28:28 8541
"I will strike every horse with **b** and Zch 12:4 8541

BEWITCHED

foolish Galatians, who has **b** you, Ga 3:1 *940*

BEYOND

his tent **b** the tower of Eder. Gn 35:21
4480, 1973
it, for it was **b** measure. Gn 41:49 369
of Atad, which is **b** the Jordan, Gn 50:10 5676
which is **b** the Jordan. Gn 50:11 5676
she has a discharge **b** that period, Lv 15:25 5921
who are in excess **b** the Levites, Nu 3:46 5921
b those ransomed by the Levites; Nu 3:49 5921
b the Jordan *opposite* Jericho. Nu 22:1
4480, 5676
other side of the Jordan and **b**, Nu 32:19 1973
any time goes **b** the border of his city Nu 35:26 3318
b our brothers the sons of Esau, Dt 2:8
5674a, 4480
Amorites who were **b** the Jordan, Dt 3:8 5676
God will give them **b** the Jordan. Dt 3:20 5676
fair land that is **b** the Jordan, Dt 3:25 5676
"Nor is it **b** the sea, that you Dt 30:13
4480, 5676
which Moses gave you **b** the Jordan, Jos 1:14 5676
b the Jordan toward the sunrise." Jos 1:15 5676
Amorites who were **b** the Jordan, Jos 2:10 5676
who *were* **b** the Jordan to the west, Jos 5:1 5676
willing to dwell **b** the Jordan! Jos 7:7 5676
the kings who were **b** the Jordan, Jos 9:1 5676
Amorites who were **b** the Jordan, Jos 9:10 5676
b the Jordan toward the sunrise, Jos 12:1 5676
b the Jordan toward the west, Jos 12:7 5676
them **b** the Jordan to the east, Jos 13:8 5676
b the Jordan to the east. Jos 13:27 5676
b the Jordan at Jericho to the Jos 13:32
4480, 5676
and the half-tribe **b** the Jordan; Jos 14:3
4480, 5676
to Taanath-shiloh and continued **b** Jos 16:6
and Bashan, which is **b** the Jordan, Jos 17:5
4480, 5676
inheritance eastward **b** the Jordan, Jos 18:7
4480, 5676
the sons of Dan proceeded **b** them; Jos 19:47
3318, 4480
B the Jordan east of Jericho, they Jos 20:8 4480
of the LORD gave you **b** the Jordan. Jos 22:4 5676
brothers westward **b** the Jordan. Jos 22:7 5676
your fathers lived **b** the River, Jos 24:2 5676
father Abraham from **b** the River, Jos 24:3
4480, 5676
Amorites who lived **b** the Jordan, Jos 24:8 5676
served **b** the River and in Egypt, Jos 24:14 5676
served which were **b** the River, Jos 24:15 5676
sons of Israel who were **b** the Jordan Jg 10:8 5676
Moab, and they camped **b** the Arnon; Jg 11:18 5676
and the battle spread **b** Beth-aven. 1Sa 14:23 5674a
'Behold, the arrows are **b** you,' 1Sa 20:22
4480, 1973
"Is not the arrow **b** you?" 1Sa 20:37
4480, 1973
with those who were **b** the Jordan, 1Sa 31:7 5676
the Arameans who were **b** the River, 2Sa 10:16
4480, 5676
had passed a little **b** the summit, 2Sa 16:1 5674a
them **b** the *Euphrates* River, 1Ki 14:15
4480, 5676
of all these vessels was **b** weight. 2Ki 25:16 3808
and **b** the Jordan at Jericho, on 1Ch 6:78
4480, 5676
the Arameans who were **b** the River, 1Ch 19:16
4480, 5676
timbers of cedar logs **b** number, 1Ch 22:4 369
and bronze and iron **b** weight, 1Ch 22:14 369
coming against you from **b** the sea, 2Ch 20:2 5676
rest of the region **b** the River. Ezr 4:10 5675
the men in the region **b** the River, Ezr 4:11 5675
in *the province* **b** the River." Ezr 4:16 5675
rest of *the provinces* **b** the River: Ezr 4:17 5675
all *the provinces* **b** the River, Ezr 4:20 5675
of *the province* **b** the River, Ezr 5:3 5675
of *the province* **b** the River, Ezr 5:6 5675
officials, who were **b** the River, Ezr 5:6 5675
of *the province* **b** the River, Ezr 6:6 5675
of *the provinces* **b** the River, Ezr 6:6 5675
of *the provinces* **b** the River, Ezr 6:8 5675
of *the province* **b** the River, Ezr 6:13 5675
are *in the provinces* **b** the River, Ezr 7:21 5675
are in *the province* **b** the River, Ezr 7:25 5675
in the provinces **b** the River, Ezr 8:36 5676
of the provinces **b** the River, Ne 2:7 5676
b the River and gave them the king's Ne 2:9 5676
of the province **b** the River. Ne 3:7 5676
evils **b** number have surrounded me; Ps 40:12
5704, 369
Will suddenly be broken **b** remedy. Pr 29:1 369
But **b** this, my son, be warned: Ec 12:12 3148
from regions **b** the Euphrates Is 7:20 5676
Which lies **b** the rivers of Cush, Is 18:1
4480, 5676
Do not be angry **b** measure, O LORD, Is 64:9 5704
silent and afflict us **b** measure? Is 64:12 5704
My sorrow is **b** healing, My heart Jer 8:18
us so that we are **b** healing? Jer 14:19 369
out **b** the gates of Jerusalem. Jer 22:19
4480, 1973
coastlands which are **b** the sea; Jer 25:22 5676
nests **B** the mouth of the chasm. Jer 48:28 5676
of all these vessels was **b** weight. Jer 52:20 3808
you go into exile **b** Damascus," Am 5:27
4480, 1973
"From **b** the rivers of Ethiopia My Zph 3:10 5676
b the border of Israel!" Mal 1:5
4480, 5921
THE WAY OF THE SEA, **B** THE JORDAN, Mt 4:15 *4008*
and Judea and *from* **b** the Jordan. Mt 4:25 *4008*
anything **b** these is of evil. Mt 5:37 *4053*
the region of Judea **b** the Jordan; Mt 19:1 *4008*
And He went a little **b** *them,* Mt 26:39 *4281*
and from Idumea, and **b** the Jordan, Mk 3:8 *4008*
region of Judea and **b** the Jordan; Mk 10:1 *4008*
And He went a little **b** *them,* Mk 14:35 *4281*
place in Bethany **b** the Jordan, Jn 1:28 *4008*
He who was with you **b** the Jordan, Jn 3:26 *4008*
And He went away again **b** the Jn 10:40 *4008*
ALSO WILL REMOVE YOU **B** BABYLON.' Ac 7:43 *1900*
"But if you want anything **b** this, Ac 19:39 *4007b*
b that, I do not know whether I 1Co 1:16 *3062*
to be tempted **b** what you are able, 1Co 10:13 *5228*
excessively, **b** our strength, 2Co 1:8 *5228*
of glory far **b** all comparison, 2Co 4:17 *1519*
and **b** their ability, *they gave* of 2Co 8:3 *3844*
we will not boast **b** *our* measure, 2Co 10:13
1519, 280
not boasting **b** *our* measure, *that* 2Co 10:15
1519, 280
gospel even to the regions **b** you, 2Co 10:16 *5238a*
the church of God **b** measure and Ga 1:13
2596, 5236
and I was advancing in Judaism **b** Ga 1:14 *5228*
b all that we ask or think, Eph 3:20 *5228*
holy and blameless and **b** reproach Col 1:22 *410*
B all these things *put on* love, Col 3:14 *1909*
as deacons if they are **b** reproach. 1Tm 3:10 *410*
in speech which is **b** reproach, Ti 2:8 *176*
even **b** the proper time of life, Heb 11:11 *3844*

BEZAI

the sons of **B**, 323; Ezr 2:17 1209
the sons of **B**, 324; Ne 7:23 1209
Hodiah, Hashum, **B**, Ne 10:18 1209

BEZALEL

"See, I have called by name **B**, Ex 31:2 1212
called by name **B** the son of Uri, Ex 35:30 1212

“Now **B** and Oholiab, and every Ex 36:1 1212
Then Moses called **B** and Oholiab Ex 36:2 1212
a skillful workman, **B** made them. Ex 36:8
Now **B** made the ark of acacia wood; Ex 37:1 1212
Now **B** the son of Uri, the son of Ex 38:22 1212
and Uri became the father of **B**. 1Ch 2:20 1212
altar, which **B** the son of Uri, 2Ch 1:5 1212
Benaiah, Maaseiah, Mattaniah, **B**, Ezr 10:30 1212

BEZEK
defeated ten thousand men at **B**. Jg 1:4 966
They found Adoni-bezek in **B** Jg 1:5 966
He numbered them in **B**; 1Sa 11:8 966

BEZER
B in the wilderness on the plateau Dt 4:43 1221
they designated **B** in the Jos 20:8 1221
they gave **B** with its pasture lands Jos 21:36 1221
B in the wilderness with its 1Ch 6:78 1221
B, Hod, Shamma, Shilshah, Ithran and 1Ch 7:37 1221

BIAS
these *principles* without **b**, 1Tm 5:21 *4299*

BICHRI
name was Sheba, the son of **B**, 2Sa 20:1 1075
and followed Sheba the son of **B**; 2Sa 20:2 1075
“Now Sheba the son of **B** will do 2Sa 20:6 1075
to pursue Sheba the son of **B**. 2Sa 20:7 1075
pursued Sheba the son of **B**. 2Sa 20:10 1075
Joab to pursue Sheba the son of **B**. 2Sa 20:13 1075
Sheba the son of **B** by name, 2Sa 20:21 1075
the son of **B** and threw it to Joab. 2Sa 20:22 1075

BID
and go in and **b** him arise from 2Ki 9:2

BIDDING
After **b** them farewell, He Mk 6:46 *657*

BIDKAR
Then *Jehu* said to **B** his officer, 2Ki 9:25 920

BIER
King David walked behind the **b**. 2Sa 3:31 4296

BIG
on the **b** toes of their right feet, Ex 29:20 931
on the **b** toe of his right foot, Lv 8:23 931
on the **b** toe of their right foot. Lv 8:24 931
on the **b** toe of his right foot. Lv 14:14 931
on the **b** toe of his right foot, Lv 14:17 931
on the **b** toe of his right foot. Lv 14:25 931
on the **b** toe of his right foot, Lv 14:28 931
and cut off his thumbs and **b** toes. Jg 1:6 931
their thumbs and their **b** toes cut off Jg 1:7 931
king of Egypt *is but* a **b** noise; Jer 46:17 7588
And Levi gave a **b** reception for Lk 5:29 *3173*
A man was giving a **b** dinner, Lk 14:16 *3173*

BIGGER
people are **b** and taller than we; Dt 1:28 1419
bushel smaller and the shekel **b**, Am 8:5 1431

BIGTHA
Mehuman, Biztha, Harbona, **B**, Es 1:10 903

BIGTHAN
at the king’s gate, **B** and Teresh, Es 2:21 904

BIGTHANA
reported concerning **B** and Teresh, Es 6:2 904

BIGVAI
Mordecai, Bilshan, Mispar, **B**, Ezr 2:2 902
the sons of **B**, 2,056; Ezr 2:14 902
and of the sons of **B**, Ezr 8:14 902
Mordecai, Bilshan, Mispereth, **B**, Ne 7:7 902
the sons of **B**, 2,067; Ne 7:19 902
Adonijah, **B**, Adin, Ne 10:16 902

BILDAD
the Temanite, **B** the Shuhite and Jb 2:11 1085
Then **B** the Shuhite answered, Jb 8:1 1085
Then **B** the Shuhite responded, Jb 18:1 1085
Then **B** the Shuhite answered, Jb 25:1 1085
So Eliphaz the Temanite and **B** the Jb 42:9 1085

BILEAM
and **B** with its pasture lands, 1Ch 6:70 1109b

BILGAH
the fifteenth for **B**, 1Ch 24:14 1083
Mijamin, Maadiah, **B**, Ne 12:5 1083
of **B**, Shammua; of Shemaiah, Ne 12:18 1083

BILGAI
Maaziah, **B**, Shemaiah. Ne 10:8 1084

BILHAH
Laban also gave his maid **B** to his Gn 29:29 1090a
“Here is my maid **B**, go in to her that Gn 30:3 1090a
she gave him her maid **B** as a wife, Gn 30:4 1090a
B conceived and bore Jacob a Gn 30:5 1090a
Rachel’s maid **B** conceived Gn 30:7 1090a
lay with **B** his father’s concubine, Gn 35:22 1090a
and the sons of **B**, Rachel’s maid: Gn 35:25 1090a
sons of **B** and the sons of Zilpah, Gn 37:2 1090a
These are the sons of **B**, Gn 46:25 1090a
at **B**, Ezem, Tolad, 1Ch 4:29 1090b
Jezer, and Shallum, the sons of **B**. 1Ch 7:13 1090a

BILHAN
B and Zaavan and Akan. Gn 36:27 1092
The sons of Ezer *were* **B**, 1Ch 1:42 1092
The son of Jediael *was* **B**. 1Ch 7:10 1092
And the sons of **B** *were* Jeush, 1Ch 7:10 1092

BILL
‘Take your **b**, and sit down quickly Lk 16:6 *1121*
‘Take your **b**, and write eighty.’ Lk 16:7 *1121*

BILLOWS
Your breakers and **b** passed over me. Jon 2:3 1530

BILSHAN
Seraiah, Reelaiah, Mordecai, **B**, Ezr 2:2 1114
Raamiah, Nahamani, Mordecai, **B**, Ne 7:7 1114

BIMHAL
sons of Japhlet *were* Pasach, **B** and 1Ch 7:33 1118

BIND
“They shall **b** the breastpiece Ex 28:28 7405
and his sons, and **b** caps on them, Ex 29:9 2280
or takes an oath to **b** himself with Nu 30:2 631
“You shall **b** them as a sign Dt 6:8 7194
b them as a sign on your hand, Dt 11:18 7194
and **b** the money in your hand and Dt 14:25 6696a
“We have come up to **b** Samson in Jg 15:10 631
“We have come down to **b** you so Jg 15:12 631
but we will **b** you fast and give Jg 15:13 631
that we may **b** him to afflict him. Jg 16:5 631
“If they **b** me with seven fresh Jg 16:7 631
“If they **b** me tightly with new Jg 16:11 631
would **b** it to myself like a crown. Jb 31:36 6029
you **b** the chains of the Pleiades, Jb 38:31 7194
“Can you **b** the wild ox in a Jb 39:10 7194
B them in the hidden *place*. Jb 40:13 2280
will you **b** him for your maidens? Jb 41:5 7194
B the festival sacrifice with Ps 118:27 631
To **b** their kings with chains And Ps 149:8 631
B them around your neck, Write Pr 3:3 7194
B them continually on your heart; Pr 6:21 7194
B them on your fingers; Pr 7:3 7194
B up the testimony, seal the law Is 8:16 6887a
jewels and **b** them on as a bride. Is 49:18 7194
sent me to **b** up the brokenhearted, Is 61:1 2280
ropes on you and **b** you with them so Ezk 3:25 631
b them in the edges of your *robes*. Ezk 5:3 6696a
B on your turban and put your Ezk 24:17 2280
the scattered, **b** up the broken and Ezk 34:16 2280
“First gather up the tares and **b** Mt 13:30 *1210*
and whatever you **b** on earth Mt 16:19 *1210*
whatever you **b** on earth Mt 18:18 *1210*
‘**B** him hand and foot, and throw him Mt 22:13 *1210*
no one was able to **b** him anymore, Mk 5:3 *1210*
to **b** all who call on Your name.” Ac 9:14 *1210*
will **b** the man who owns this belt Ac 21:11 *1210*

BINDER
Or the **b** of sheaves his bosom; Ps 129:7 6014a

BINDING
we were **b** sheaves in the field, Gn 37:7 481
there shall be a **b** of woven work, Ex 28:32 8193
with a **b** all around its opening, Ex 39:23 8193
bind himself with a **b** obligation, Nu 30:2 632
every **b** oath to humble herself, Nu 30:13 632
Your vows are **b** upon me, O God; Ps 56:12
and **b** Jesus, they led Him away and Mk 15:1 *1210*
b and putting both men and women Ac 22:4 *1195*

BINDS
and **b** herself by an obligation in Nu 30:3 631
And **b** their loins with a girdle. Jb 12:18 631
It **b** me about as the collar of my Jb 30:18 247
not cry for help when He **b** them. Jb 36:13 631
And **b** up their wounds. Ps 147:3 2280
Like one who **b** a stone in a sling, Pr 26:8 6887a
on the day the LORD **b** up the Is 30:26 2280
unless he first **b** the strong *man?* Mt 12:29 *1210*
unless he first **b** the strong man, Mk 3:27 *1210*

BINEA
Moza became the father of **B**; 1Ch 8:37 1150
father of **B** and Rephaiah his son, 1Ch 9:43 1150

BINNUI
Jeshua and Noadiah the son of **B**. Ezr 8:33 1131b
Maaseiah, Mattaniah, Bezalel, **B** and Ezr 10:30 1131b
Bani, **B**, Shimei, Ezr 10:38 1131b
After him **B** the son of Henadad Ne 3:24 1131b
the sons of **B**, 648; Ne 7:15 1131b
Azaniah, **B** of the sons of Henadad, Ne 10:9 1131b
The Levites *were* Jeshua, **B**, Ne 12:8 1131b

BIRD
and every winged **b** after its kind; Gn 1:21 5775
every **b** of the sky and to every thing Gn 1:30 5775
the field and every **b** of the sky, Gn 2:19 5775
kind, and every **b** after its kind, Gn 7:14 5775
every creeping thing, and every **b**, Gn 8:19 5775
clean animal and of every clean **b** Gn 8:20 5775
earth and on every **b** of the sky; Gn 9:2 5775
any blood, either of **b** or animal, Lv 7:26 5775
regarding the animal and the **b**, Lv 11:46 5775
shall also give orders to slay the one **b** Lv 14:5 6833
“*As for* the live **b**, he shall take Lv 14:6 6833
dip them and the live **b** in the blood Lv 14:6 6833
in the blood of the **b** that was slain Lv 14:6 6833
b go free over the open field. Lv 14:7 6833
and he shall slaughter the one **b** Lv 14:50 6833
scarlet string, with the live **b**, Lv 14:51 6833
them in the blood of the slain **b** as Lv 14:51 6833
the **b** and with the running water, Lv 14:52 6833
along with the live **b** and with the Lv 14:52 6833
he shall let the live **b** go free Lv 14:53 6833
a beast or a **b** which may be eaten, Lv 17:13 5775
the unclean **b** and the clean; Lv 20:25 5775
by animal or by **b** or by anything Lv 20:25 5775
winged **b** that flies in the sky, Dt 4:17 6833
“You may eat any clean **b**. Dt 14:11 6833
“You may eat any clean **b**. Dt 14:20 5775
“The path no **b** of prey knows, Nor Jb 28:7 5861
you play with him as with a **b**, Jb 41:5 6833
“Flee *as* a **b** to your mountain; Ps 11:1 6833
“I know every **b** of the mountains, Ps 50:11 5775
The **b** also has found a house, And Ps 84:3 6833
like a lonely **b** on a housetop. Ps 102:7 6833
Our soul has escaped as a **b** out of Ps 124:7 6833
baited net In the sight of any **b**; Pr 1:17 1167, 3671
a **b** from the hand of the fowler. Pr 6:5 6833
As a **b** hastens to the snare, So he Pr 7:23 6833
a **b** that wanders from her nest, Pr 27:8 6833
for a **b** of the heavens will carry Ec 10:20 5775
will arise at the sound of the **b**, Ec 12:4 6833
Calling a **b** of prey from the east, Is 46:11 5861
like a speckled **b** of prey to Me? Jer 12:9 5861
cause Hunted me down like a **b**; La 3:52 6833
b and beast of the field. Ezk 39:4 6833
‘Speak to every kind of **b** and to Ezk 39:17 6833
“The priests shall not eat any **b** Ezk 44:31 5775
had on its back four wings of a **b**; Da 7:6 5776
the snare of a **b** catcher is in all his Hos 9:8 3352
their glory will fly away like a **b** Hos 9:11 5775
Does a **b** fall into a trap on the Am 3:5 6833
of every unclean and hateful **b**. Rv 18:2 *3732*

BIRD'S
come upon a **b** nest along the way, Dt 22:6 6833

BIRDS
and let **b** fly above the earth in Gn 1:20 5775
and let **b** multiply on the earth.” Gn 1:22 5775
fish of the sea and over the **b** of the Gn 1:26 5775
the sea and over the **b** of the sky and Gn 1:28 5775
cattle, and to the **b** of the sky, Gn 2:20 5775
things and to **b** of the sky; Gn 6:7 5775
“Of the **b** after their kind, and Gn 6:20 5775
also of the **b** of the sky, by Gn 7:3 5775
and **b** and everything that creeps Gn 7:8 5775
after its kind, all sorts of **b**. Gn 7:14 6833
b and cattle and beasts and every Gn 7:21 5775
things and to **b** of the sky, Gn 7:23 5775
b and animals and every creeping Gn 8:17 5775
creature that is with you, the **b**, Gn 9:10 5775
but he did not cut the **b**. Gn 15:10 6833
The **b** of prey came down upon Gn 15:11 5861
and the **b** were eating them out of Gn 40:17 5775
b will eat your flesh off you.” Gn 40:19 5775
the LORD is a burnt offering of **b**, Lv 1:14 5775
you shall detest among the **b**; Lv 11:13 5775
give orders to take two live clean **b** Lv 14:4 6833
he shall take two **b** and cedar wood Lv 14:49 6833
“Your carcasses will be food to all **b** Dt 28:26 5775
give your flesh to the **b** of the sky 1Sa 17:44 5775
b of the sky and the wild beasts 1Sa 17:46 5775
and she allowed neither the **b** of 2Sa 21:10 5775
b and creeping things and fish. 1Ki 4:33 5775
the **b** of the heavens will eat; 1Ki 14:11 5775
the **b** of the heavens will eat.” 1Ki 16:4 5775
field the **b** of heaven will eat.” 1Ki 21:24 5775
also **b** were prepared for me; Ne 5:18 6833
And the **b** of the heavens, and let Jb 12:7 5775
concealed from the **b** of the sky. Jb 28:21 5775
wiser than the **b** of the heavens?’ Jb 35:11 5775
The **b** of the heavens and the fish Ps 8:8 6833
for food to the **b** of the heavens, Ps 79:2 5775
them the **b** of the heavens dwell; Ps 104:12 5775
Where the **b** build their nests, *And* Ps 104:17 6833
net and **b** trapped in a snare, Ec 9:12 6833
fleeing **b** *or* scattered nestlings, Is 16:2 5775
together for mountain **b** of prey, Is 18:6 5861
And the **b** of prey will spend the Is 18:6 5861
Like flying **b** so the LORD of hosts Is 31:5 6833
all the **b** of the heavens had fled. Jer 4:25 5775
‘Like a cage full of **b**, Jer 5:27 5775
will be food for the **b** of the sky and Jer 7:33 5775
Both the **b** of the sky and the Jer 9:10 5775
and **b** have been snatched away, Jer 12:4 5775
Are the **b** of prey against her on Jer 12:9 5861
and the **b** of the sky and the Jer 15:3 5775
carcasses will become food for the **b** Jer 16:4 5775
carcasses as food for the **b** of the Jer 19:7 5775
dead bodies will be food for the **b** Jer 34:20 5775
which you hunt lives there as **b** and Ezk 13:20 6524c
those lives whom you hunt as **b**. Ezk 13:20 6524c
And **b** of every kind will nest Ezk 17:23 6833
the earth and to the **b** of the sky. Ezk 29:5 5775
‘All the **b** of the heavens nested Ezk 31:6 5775
the **b** of the heavens will dwell, Ezk 31:13 5775
And I will cause all the **b** of the Ezk 32:4 5775
of the sea, the **b** of the heavens, Ezk 38:20 5775
of the field, or the **b** of the sky, Da 2:38 5776
And the **b** of the sky dwelt in its Da 4:12 6853
it And the **b** from its branches. Da 4:14 6853
branches the **b** of the sky lodged Da 4:21 6853
of the field, The **b** of the sky And Hos 2:18 5775
of the field and the **b** of the sky, Hos 4:3 5775
them down like the **b** of the sky. Hos 7:12 5775
come trembling like **b** from Egypt And Hos 11:11 6833
I will remove the **b** of the sky And Zph 1:3 5775
B will sing in the window, Zph 2:14 6963
“Look at the **b** of the air, that Mt 6:26 *4071*
and the **b** of the air *have* nests, Mt 8:20 *4071*
and the **b** came and ate them up. Mt 13:4 *4071*
so that THE **B** OF THE AIR come and Mt 13:32 *4071*
and the **b** came and ate it up. Mk 4:4 *4071*
so that THE **B** OF THE AIR can NEST Mk 4:32 *4071*
and the **b** of the air ate it up. Lk 8:5 *4071*
and the **b** of the air *have* nests, Lk 9:58 *4071*
more valuable you are than the **b**! Lk 12:24 *4071*
and THE **B** OF THE AIR NESTED IN ITS Lk 13:19 *4071*
of the earth and **b** of the air. Ac 10:12 *4071*
creatures and the **b** of the air. Ac 11:6 *4071*
form of corruptible man and of **b** Ro 1:23 *4071*
of beasts, and another flesh of **b**, 1Co 15:39 *4421*
For every species of beasts and **b**, Jas 3:7 *4071*
all the **b** which fly in midheaven, Rv 19:17 *3732*
b were filled with their flesh. Rv 19:21 *3732*

BIRDS'
and his nails like **b** *claws.* Da 4:33 6853
BIRSHA
and with **B** king of Gomorrah, Gn 14:2 1306
BIRTH
she conceived and gave **b** to Cain, Gn 4:1 3205
she gave **b** to his brother Abel. Gn 4:2 3205
conceived, and gave **b** to Enoch; Gn 4:17 3205
Adah gave **b** to Jabal; Gn 4:20 3205
she also gave **b** to Tubal-cain, Gn 4:22 3205
and she gave **b** to a son, and named Gn 4:25 3205
father Terah in the land of his **b**, Gn 11:28 4138
house and from the land of my **b**, Gn 24:7 4138
names, in the order of their **b**: Gn 25:13 8435
years old when she gave **b** to them. Gn 25:26 3205
return to the land of your **b**.'" Gn 31:13 4138
b and she suffered severe labor. Gn 35:16 3205
at the time she was giving **b**, Gn 38:27 3205
took place while she was giving **b**, Gn 38:28 3205
helping the Hebrew women to give **b** Ex 1:16 3205
and give **b** before the midwife Ex 1:19 3205
Then she gave **b** to a son, and he Ex 2:22 3205
so that she gives **b** prematurely, Ex 21:22 3205
other stone, according to their **b**. Ex 28:10 8435
gives **b** and bears a male *child*, Lv 12:2 2232
"No one of illegitimate **b** shall Dt 23:2 4464
And forgot the God who gave you **b**. Dt 32:18 2342a
conceive and give **b** to a son. Jg 13:3 3205
conceive and give **b** to a son, Jg 13:5 3205
conceive and give **b** to a son, Jg 13:7 3205
b to a son and named him Samson; Jg 13:24 3205
mother and the land of your **b**, Ru 2:11 4138
brothers or from the court of his **b** Ru 4:10
conceive, and she gave **b** to a son. Ru 4:13 3205
seven sons, has given **b** to him." Ru 4:15 3205
that she gave **b** to a son; 1Sa 1:20 3205
Even the barren gives **b** to seven, 1Sa 2:5 3205
and she conceived and gave **b** to 1Sa 2:21 3205
was pregnant and about to give **b**; 1Sa 4:19 3205
died, she kneeled down and gave **b**, 1Sa 4:19 3205
for you have given **b** to a son." 1Sa 4:20 3205
and she gave **b** to a son, and he 2Sa 12:24 3205
and I gave **b** to a child while she 1Ki 3:17 3205
on the third day after I gave **b**, 1Ki 3:18 3205
this woman also gave **b** to a child, 1Ki 3:18 3205
for children have come to **b** and 2Ki 19:3 4866
mouth and cursed the day of his **b**. Jb 3:1
"Why did I not die at **b**, Jb 3:11 7358
of heaven, who has given it **b**? Jb 38:29 3205
time the mountain goats give **b**? Jb 39:1 3205
do you know the time they give **b**? Jb 39:2 3205
Upon You I was cast from **b**; Ps 22:10 7358
who speak lies go astray from **b**. Ps 58:3 990
I have been sustained from *my* **b**; Ps 71:6 990
gave **b** to the earth and the world, Ps 90:2 2342a
let her rejoice who gave **b** to you. Pr 23:25 3205
A time to give **b** and a time to Ec 3:2 3205
is better than the day of one's **b**. Ec 7:1 3205
she was in labor *and* gave you **b**. SS 8:5 3205
she conceived and gave **b** to a son. Is 8:3 3205
neither travailed nor given **b**, Is 23:4 3205
approaches *the time* to give **b**, Is 26:17 3205
we writhed *in labor,* We gave **b**, Is 26:18 3205
give **b** to the departed spirits. Is 26:19 5307
chaff, you will give **b** to stubble; Is 33:11 3205
for children have come to **b**, Is 37:3 4866
'To what are you giving **b**?'" Is 45:10 2342a
who have been borne by Me from **b** Is 46:3 990
have been called a rebel from **b**. Is 48:8 990
Sarah who gave **b** to you in pain; Is 51:2 2342a
pain came, she gave **b** to a boy. Is 66:7 4422
"Shall I bring to the point of **b** and Is 66:9 7665
And to a stone, 'You gave me **b**.' Jer 2:27 3205
one giving **b** to her first child, Jer 4:31 1069
given **b** only to abandon *her young*, Jer 14:5 3205
he did not kill me before **b**, Jer 20:17 7358
and see If a male can give **b**. Jer 30:6 3205
who gave you **b** will be humiliated. Jer 50:12 3205
"Your origin and your **b** are from Ezk 16:3 4138
"As for your **b**, on the day you Ezk 16:4 4138
in Chaldea, the land of their **b**. Ezk 23:15 4138
the beasts of the field gave **b**, Ezk 31:6 3205
again and gave **b** to a daughter. Hos 1:6 3205
she conceived and gave **b** to a son. Hos 1:8 3205
No **b**, no pregnancy and no Hos 9:11 3205
"Writhe and labor to give **b**, Mi 4:10 1518
his father and mother who gave **b** Zch 13:3 3205
his father and mother who gave **b** Zch 13:3 3205
Now the **b** of Jesus Christ was as Mt 1:18 *1078*
virgin until she gave **b** to a Son; Mt 1:25 *5088*
merely the beginning of **b** pangs. Mt 24:8 *5604*
merely the beginning of **b** pangs. Mk 13:8 *5604*
and many will rejoice at his **b**. Lk 1:14 *1078*
had come for Elizabeth to give **b**, Lk 1:57 *5088*
and she gave **b** to a son. Lk 1:57 *5088*
were completed for her to give **b**. Lk 2:6 *5088*
she gave **b** to her firstborn son; Lk 2:7 *5088*
by, He saw a man blind from **b**. Jn 9:1 *1079a*
but when she gives **b** to the child, Jn 16:21 *1080*
Now Joseph, a Levite of Cyprian **b**, Ac 4:36 *1085*
Apollos, an Alexandrian by **b**, Ac 18:24 *1085*
so also the man *has his* **b** through 1Co 11:12
has conceived, it gives **b** to sin; Jas 1:15 *5088*
in labor and in pain to give **b**. Rv 12:2 *5088*
the woman who was about to give **b**, Rv 12:4 *5088*
gave **b** he might devour her child. Rv 12:4 *5088*
And she gave **b** to a son, a male Rv 12:5 *5088*
who gave **b** to the male *child*. Rv 12:13 *5088*

BIRTHDAY
third day, *which was* Pharaoh's **b**, Gn 40:20
3205, 3117
But when Herod's **b** came, the Mt 14:6 *1077*
Herod on his **b** gave a banquet for Mk 6:21 *1077*
BIRTHRIGHT
"First sell me your **b**." Gn 25:31 1062
of what *use* then is the **b** to me?" Gn 25:32 1062
to him, and sold his **b** to Jacob. Gn 25:33 1062
Thus Esau despised his **b**. Gn 25:34 1062
He took away my **b**, and behold, now Gn 27:36 1062
the firstborn according to his **b** Gn 43:33 1062
his **b** was given to the sons of 1Ch 5:1 1062
the genealogy according to the **b**. 1Ch 5:1 1062
yet the **b** belonged to Joseph), 1Ch 5:2 1062
sold his own **b** for a *single* meal. Heb 12:16 *4415*
BIRTHSTOOL
birth and see *them* upon the **b**, Ex 1:16 70
BIRZAITH
Malchiel, who was the father of **B**. 1Ch 7:31 1269
BISHLAM
And in the days of Artaxerxes, **B**, Ezr 4:7 1312
BIT
the people and they **b** the people, Nu 21:6 5391a
that if a serpent **b** any man, Nu 21:9 5391a
Whose trappings include **b** and Ps 32:9 4964
BITE
b him who breaks through a wall. Ec 10:8 5391a
no charm, And they will **b** you," Jer 8:17 5391a
the serpent and it will **b** them. Am 9:3 5391a
something to **b** with their teeth, Mi 3:5 5391a
if you **b** and devour one another, Ga 5:15 *1143*
BITES
the path, That **b** the horse's heels, Gn 49:17 5391a
At the last it **b** like a serpent And Pr 23:32 5391a
serpent **b** before being charmed, Ec 10:11 5391a
the wall And a snake **b** him. Am 5:19 5391a
BITHIA
sons of **B** the daughter of Pharaoh, 1Ch 4:17 1332
BITHYNIA
they were trying to go into **B**, Ac 16:7 *978*
Galatia, Cappadocia, Asia, and **B**, 1Pe 1:1 *978*
BITS
you shall break it into **b** and Lv 2:6 6595
Now if we put the **b** into the Jas 3:3 *5469*
BITTEN
about, that everyone who is **b**, Nu 21:8 5391a
BITTER
an exceedingly great and **b** cry, Gn 27:34 4751
and they made their lives **b** with Ex 1:14 4843
with unleavened bread and **b** herbs. Ex 12:8 4844
waters of Marah, for they were **b**; Ex 15:23 4751
with unleavened bread and **b** herbs. Nu 9:11 4844
by plague And **b** destruction; Dt 32:24 4815
of poison, Their clusters, **b**. Dt 32:32 4846
know that it will be **b** in the end? 2Sa 2:26 4751
of Israel, *which was* very **b**; 2Ki 14:26 4784
And life to the **b** of soul, Jb 3:20 4751
You write **b** things against me Jb 13:26 4846
While another dies with a **b** soul, Jb 21:25 4751
aimed **b** speech *as* their arrow, Ps 64:3 4751
in the end she is **b** as wormwood, Pr 5:4 4751
famished man any **b** thing is sweet. Pr 27:7 4751
And wine to him whose life is **b**. Pr 31:6 4751
And I discovered more **b** than death Ec 7:26 4751
Who substitute **b** for sweet and Is 5:20 4751
bitter for sweet and sweet for **b**! Is 5:20 4751
drink is **b** to those who drink it. Is 24:9 4843
it is evil and **b** For you to forsake Jer 2:19 4751
This is your evil. How **b**! Jer 4:18 4751
an only son, A lamentation most **b**. Jer 6:26 8563
Ramah, Lamentation *and* **b** weeping. Jer 31:15 8563
afflicted, And she herself is **b**. La 1:4 4843
with breaking heart and **b** grief, Ezk 21:6 4814
of soul With **b** mourning. Ezk 27:31 4751
Ephraim has provoked to **b** anger; Hos 12:14 8563
end of it will be like a **b** day. Am 8:10 4751
And utter a **b** lamentation *and* say, Mi 2:4 5093
the **b** weeping over a firstborn. Zch 12:10 4843
opening *both* fresh and **b** *water?* Jas 3:11 *4089*
But if you have **b** jealousy and Jas 3:14 *4089*
waters, because they were made **b**. Rv 8:11 *4087*
it will make your stomach **b**, Rv 10:9 *4087*
eaten it, my stomach was made **b**. Rv 10:10 *4087*
BITTERLY
"The archers **b** attacked him, And Gn 49:23 4843
lifted up their voices and wept **b**. Jg 21:2
1419, 1065
Almighty has dealt very **b** with me. Ru 1:20 4843
provoke her **b** to irritate her, 1Sa 1:6
1571, 3708a
prayed to the LORD and wept **b**. 1Sa 1:10 1058
and all his servants wept very **b**. 2Sa 13:36
1419, 1065
And Hezekiah wept **b**. 2Ki 20:3
1419, 1065
for the people wept **b**. Ezr 10:1
7235a, 1059
the city and wailed loudly and **b**. Es 4:1 4751
Therefore I will weep **b** for Jazer, Is 16:9 1065
eyes away from me, Let me weep **b**, Is 22:4 4843
The ambassadors of peace weep **b**. Is 33:7 4751
And Hezekiah wept **b**. Is 38:3 1419
And my eyes will **b** weep And flow Jer 13:17 1830
She weeps **b** in the night And her La 1:2 1058
heard over you And will cry **b**. Ezk 27:30 4751

In it the warrior cries out **b**. Zph 1:14 4751
and they will weep **b** over Him like Zch 12:10 4843
And he went out and wept **b**. Mt 26:75 *4090*
And he went out and wept **b**. Lk 22:62 *4090*
BITTERNESS
water of **b** that brings a curse. Nu 5:18 4751
water of **b** that brings a curse; Nu 5:19 4751
wash them off into the water of **b**. Nu 5:23 4751
water of **b** that brings a curse, Nu 5:24 4751
will go into her and *cause* **b**. Nu 5:24 4751
will go into her and *cause* **b**, Nu 5:27 4751
"Surely the **b** of death is past." 1Sa 15:32 4751
will complain in the **b** of my soul. Jb 7:11 4751
breath, But saturates me with **b**. Jb 9:18 4472
I will speak in the **b** of my soul. Jb 10:1 4751
The heart knows its own **b**, Pr 14:10 4787a
father And **b** to her who bore him. Pr 17:25 4470
years because of the **b** of my soul. Is 38:15 4751
for *my own* welfare I had great **b**; Is 38:17 4751
me with **b** and hardship. La 3:5 7219
He has filled me with **b**, La 3:15 4844
my wandering, the wormwood and **b**. La 3:19 7219
in **b** of soul With bitter mourning. Ezk 27:31 4751
in the gall of **b** and in the bondage Ac 8:23 *4088*
MOUTH IS FULL OF CURSING AND **B**"; Ro 3:14 *4088*
Let all **b** and wrath and anger and Eph 4:31 *4088*
of **b** springing up causes trouble, Heb 12:15 *4088*
BIZIOTHIAH
Hazar-shual and Beersheba and **B**, Jos 15:28 964
BIZTHA
wine, he commanded Mehuman, **B**, Es 1:10 968
BLACK
and every **b** one among the lambs and Gn 30:32 2345
the goats and **b** among the lambs, Gn 30:33 2345
all the **b** ones among the sheep, Gn 30:35 2345
all the **b** in the flock of Laban; Gn 30:40 2345
and there is no **b** hair in it, Lv 13:31 7838
and **b** hair has grown in it, Lv 13:37 7838
sky grew **b** with clouds and wind, 1Ki 18:45 6937
"Let darkness and **b** gloom claim it; Jb 3:5 6757
"My skin turns **b** on me, And my Jb 30:30 7835
"I am **b** but lovely, O daughters SS 1:5 7838
of dates *And* **b** as a raven. SS 5:11 7838
with the second chariot **b** horses, Zch 6:2 7838
with one of which the **b** horses are Zch 6:6 7838
cannot make one hair white or **b**. Mt 5:36 *3189*
the **b** darkness has been reserved. 2Pe 2:17 *2217*
for whom the **b** darkness has been Jude 1:13 *2217*
I looked, and behold, a **b** horse; Rv 6:5 *3189*
b as sackcloth *made* of hair, Rv 6:12 *3189*
BLACKER
Their appearance is **b** than soot, La 4:8 2821
BLACKNESS
Let the **b** of the day terrify it. Jb 3:5 3650
"I clothe the heavens with **b** And Is 50:3 6940
BLACKSMITH
Now no **b** could be found in all the 1Sa 13:19 2796
BLADE
handle also went in after the **b**, Jg 3:22 3851
and the fat closed over the **b**, Jg 3:22 3851
first the **b**, then the head, then Mk 4:28 *5528*
BLAME
me bear the **b** before you forever. Gn 43:9 2398
the **b** before my father forever.' Gn 44:32 2398
"On me alone, my lord, be the **b**. 1Sa 25:24 5771
Job did not sin nor did he **b** God. Jb 1:22
5414, 8604
may establish your hearts without **b** 1Th 3:13 *273*
without **b** at the coming of our 1Th 5:23 *274*
BLAMELESS
a righteous man, **b** in his time; Gn 6:9 8549
Walk before Me, and be **b**. Gn 17:1 8549
You slay a nation, even *though* **b**? Gn 20:4 6662
be **b** before the LORD your God. Dt 18:13 8549
"This time I shall be **b** in regard Jg 15:3 5352
"I was also **b** toward Him, And I 2Sa 22:24 8549
With the **b** You show Yourself 2Sa 22:26 8549
You show Yourself **b**; 2Sa 22:26 8552
"As for God, His way is **b**; 2Sa 22:31 8549
And He sets the **b** in His way. 2Sa 22:33 8549
Asa's heart was **b** all his days. 2Ch 15:17 8003
name was Job; and that man was **b**, Jb 1:1 8535
on the earth, a **b** and upright man, Jb 1:8 8535
a **b** and upright man fearing God Jb 2:3 8535
The just *and* **b** *man* is a joke. Jb 12:4 8549
I was also **b** with Him, And I kept Ps 18:23 8549
With the **b** You show Yourself Ps 18:25 8549
You show Yourself **b**; Ps 18:25 8552
As for God, His way is **b**; Ps 18:30 8549
with strength And makes my way **b**? Ps 18:32 8549
Then I will be **b**, And I shall be Ps 19:13 8552
The LORD knows the days of the **b**, Ps 37:18 8549
Mark the **b** man, and behold the Ps 37:37 8535
speak And **b** when You judge. Ps 51:4 2135
shoot from concealment at the **b**; Ps 64:4 8535
I will give heed to the **b** way. Ps 101:2 8549
He who walks in a **b** way is the one Ps 101:6 8549
blessed are those whose way is **b**, Ps 119:1 8549
May my heart be **b** in Your statutes, Ps 119:80 8549
land And the **b** will remain in it; Pr 2:21 8549
of the **b** will smooth his way, Pr 11:5 8549
b in *their* walk are His delight. Pr 11:20 8549
guards the one whose way is **b**, Pr 13:6 8537
pit, But the **b** will inherit good. Pr 28:10 8549
Men of bloodshed hate the **b**, Pr 29:10 8535
"You were **b** in your ways From the Ezk 28:15 8549
to maintain always a **b** conscience Ac 24:16 *677*

b in the day of our Lord Jesus	**1Co 1:8**	*410*
would be holy and **b** before Him.	**Eph 1:4**	*299b*
but that she would be holy and **b**.	**Eph 5:27**	*299b*
and **b** until the day of Christ;	**Php 1:10**	*677*
yourselves to be **b** and innocent,	**Php 2:15**	*273*
which is in the Law, found **b**.	**Php 3:6**	*273*
holy and **b** and beyond reproach	**Col 1:22**	*299b*
by Him in peace, spotless and **b**,	**2Pe 3:14**	*298*
of His glory **b** with great joy,	**Jude 1:24**	*299b*
found in their mouth; they are **b**.	**Rv 14:5**	*299b*
BLAMELESSLY		
He who walks **b** will be delivered,	**Pr 28:18**	8549
walking **b** in all the commandments	**Lk 1:6**	*273*
how devoutly and uprightly and **b**	**1Th 2:10**	*274*
BLANKET		
And the **b** is too small to wrap	**Is 28:20**	4541b
BLASPHEME		
to the enemies of the LORD to **b**,	**2Sa 12:14**	5006
I tried to force them to **b**;	**Ac 26:11**	*987*
that they will be taught not to **b**.	**1Tm 1:20**	*987*
Do they not **b** the fair name by	**Jas 2:7**	*987*
to **b** His name and His tabernacle,	**Rv 13:6**	*987*
BLASPHEMED		
woman **b** the Name and cursed.	**Lv 24:11**	6895
of the king of Assyria have **b** Me.	**2Ki 19:6**	1442
'Whom have you reproached and **b**?	**2Ki 19:22**	1442
of the king of Assyria have **b** Me.	**Is 37:6**	1442
"Whom have you reproached and **b**?	**Is 37:23**	1442
is continually **b** all day long.	**Is 52:5**	5006
"Yet in this your fathers have **b**	**Ezk 20:27**	1442
tore his robes and said, "He has **b**!	**Mt 26:65**	*987*
But when they resisted and **b**,	**Ac 18:6**	*987*
"THE NAME OF GOD IS **B** AMONG THE	**Ro 2:24**	*987*
and they **b** the name of God who has	**Rv 16:9**	*987*
and they **b** the God of heaven	**Rv 16:11**	*987*
and men **b** God because of the	**Rv 16:21**	*987*
BLASPHEMER		
even though I was formerly a **b** and	**1Tm 1:13**	*989*
BLASPHEMERS		
of temples nor **b** of our goddess.	**Ac 19:37**	*987*
BLASPHEMES		
the one who **b** the name of the LORD	**Lv 24:16**	5344b
as the native, when he **b** the Name,	**Lv 24:16**	5344b
said to themselves, "This *fellow* **b**."	**Mt 9:3**	*987*
but whoever **b** against the Holy	**Mk 3:29**	*987*
he who **b** against the Holy Spirit,	**Lk 12:10**	*987*
BLASPHEMIES		
from Egypt,' And committed great **b**,	**Ne 9:18**	5007b
You, And they committed great **b**.	**Ne 9:26**	5007b
of men, and whatever **b** they utter;	**Mk 3:28**	*988*
"Who is this *man* who speaks **b**?	**Lk 5:21**	*988*
speaking arrogant words and **b**,	**Rv 13:5**	*988*
opened his mouth in **b** against God,	**Rv 13:6**	*988*
BLASPHEMING		
an alien, that one is **b** the LORD;	**Nu 15:30**	1442
this man speak that way? He is **b**;	**Mk 2:7**	*987*
many other things against Him, **b**.	**Lk 22:65**	*987*
'You are **b**,' because I said,	**Jn 10:36**	*987*
things spoken by Paul, and were **b**.	**Ac 13:45**	*987*
BLASPHEMOUS		
"We have heard him speak **b** words	**Ac 6:11**	*989*
and on his heads *were* **b** names.	**Rv 13:1**	*988*
a scarlet beast, full of **b** names,	**Rv 17:3**	*988*
BLASPHEMY		
sin and **b** shall be forgiven people,	**Mt 12:31**	*988*
but **b** against the Spirit shall not	**Mt 12:31**	*988*
Behold, you have now heard the **b**;	**Mt 26:65**	*988*
"You have heard the **b**;	**Mk 14:64**	*988*
we do not stone You, but for **b**;	**Jn 10:33**	*988*
and the **b** by those who say they	**Rv 2:9**	*988*
BLAST		
"At the **b** of Your nostrils the	**Ex 15:8**	7307
the ram's horn sounds a long **b**,	**Ex 19:13**	4900
make a long **b** with the ram's horn,	**Jos 6:5**	4900
b of the breath of His nostrils.	**2Sa 22:16**	5397
And by the **b** of His anger they	**Jb 4:9**	7307
b of the breath of Your nostrils.	**Ps 18:15**	5397
"That I will cause a trumpet **b**	**Jer 49:2**	8643
and to the **b** of a trumpet and the	**Heb 12:19**	*2279*
BLASTING		
work of your hands with **b** wind,	**Hg 2:17**	7711b
BLASTS		
because of the remaining **b** of the	**Rv 8:13**	*5456*
BLASTUS		
won over **B** the king's chamberlain,	**Ac 12:20**	*986*
BLAZE		
censers out of the midst of the **b**,	**Nu 16:37**	8316
a firebrand snatched from a **b**;	**Am 4:11**	8316
BLAZED		
And a fire **b** up in their company;	**Ps 106:18**	1197a
BLAZING		
a **b** fire from the midst of a bush;	**Ex 3:2**	3852
the **b** flame will not be quenched and	**Ezk 20:47**	3852
"In My zeal and in My **b** wrath	**Ezk 38:19**	784
midst of a furnace of **b** fire."	**Da 3:6**	3345
the midst of a furnace of **b** fire.	**Da 3:11**	3345
the midst of a furnace of **b** fire;	**Da 3:15**	3345
us from the furnace of **b** fire;	**Da 3:17**	3345
them into the furnace of **b** fire.	**Da 3:20**	3345
midst of the furnace of **b** fire.	**Da 3:21**	3345
furnace of **b** fire *still* tied up.	**Da 3:23**	3345
the door of the furnace of **b** fire;	**Da 3:26**	3345
can be touched and to a **b** fire,	**Heb 12:18**	*2545*
BLEATING		
is this **b** of the sheep in my ears,	**1Sa 15:14**	6963

BLEMISH		
young bull and two rams without **b**,	**Ex 29:1**	8549
sheep which has a **b** *or* any defect,	**Dt 17:1**	4140b
darling, And there is no **b** in you.	**SS 4:7**	4140b
goat without **b** for a sin offering,	**Ezk 43:22**	8549
present a young bull without **b**	**Ezk 43:23**	8549
a ram without **b** from the flock.	**Ezk 43:23**	8549
a ram from the flock, without **b**,	**Ezk 43:25**	8549
b and cleanse the sanctuary.	**Ezk 45:18**	8549
seven rams without **b** on every day	**Ezk 45:23**	8549
b and a ram without blemish;	**Ezk 46:4**	8549
blemish and a ram without **b**;	**Ezk 46:4**	8549
offer a young bull without **b**,	**Ezk 46:6**	8549
a ram, *which* shall be without **b**.	**Ezk 46:6**	8549
provide a lamb a year old without **b**	**Ezk 46:13**	8549
offered Himself without **b** to God,	**Heb 9:14**	*299b*
BLEMISHED		
sacrifices a **b** animal to the Lord,	**Mal 1:14**	7843
BLEMISHES		
They are stains and **b**,	**2Pe 2:13**	*3470*
BLENDED		
kinds **b** by the perfumers' art;	**2Ch 16:14**	7543
BLESS		
a great nation, And I will **b** you,	**Gn 12:2**	1288
And I will **b** those who bless you,	**Gn 12:3**	1288
And I will bless those who **b** you,	**Gn 12:3**	1288
"I will **b** her, and indeed I	**Gn 17:16**	1288
Then I will **b** her, and she shall	**Gn 17:16**	1288
behold, I will **b** him, and will	**Gn 17:20**	1288
indeed I will greatly **b** you,	**Gn 22:17**	1288
and I will be with you and **b** you,	**Gn 26:3**	1288
I will **b** you, and multiply your	**Gn 26:24**	1288
my soul may **b** you before I die."	**Gn 27:4**	1288
and **b** you in the presence of the	**Gn 27:7**	1288
he may **b** you before his death."	**Gn 27:10**	1288
of my game, that you may **b** me."	**Gn 27:19**	1288
my son's game, that I may **b** you."	**Gn 27:25**	1288
And blessed be those who **b** you."	**Gn 27:29**	1288
son's game, that you may **b** me."	**Gn 27:31**	1288
"**B** me, *even* me also, O my father!"	**Gn 27:34**	1288
B me, *even* me also, O my father."	**Gn 27:38**	1288
"May God Almighty **b** you and	**Gn 28:3**	1288
not let you go unless you **b** me."	**Gn 32:26**	1288
me, please, that I may **b** them."	**Gn 48:9**	1288
me from all evil, **B** the lads;	**Gn 48:16**	1288
said, and go, and **b** me also."	**Ex 12:32**	1288
I will come to you and **b** you.	**Ex 20:24**	1288
will **b** your bread and your water;	**Ex 23:25**	1288
you shall **b** the sons of Israel.	**Nu 6:23**	1288
The LORD **b** you, and keep you;	**Nu 6:24**	1288
Israel, and I *then* will **b** them."	**Nu 6:27**	1288
that he whom you **b** is blessed,	**Nu 22:6**	1288
I have received *a command* to **b**;	**Nu 23:20**	1288
them at all nor **b** them at all!"	**Nu 23:25**	1288
it pleased the LORD to **b** Israel,	**Nu 24:1**	1288
more than you are and **b** you,	**Dt 1:11**	1288
you and **b** you and multiply you;	**Dt 7:13**	1288
He will also **b** the fruit of your	**Dt 7:13**	1288
you shall **b** the LORD your God for	**Dt 8:10**	1288
to **b** in His name until this day.	**Dt 10:8**	1288
LORD your God may **b** you in all	**Dt 14:29**	1288
since the LORD will surely **b** you	**Dt 15:4**	1288
b you as He has promised you,	**Dt 15:6**	1288
LORD your God will **b** you in all	**Dt 15:10**	1288
God will **b** you in whatever you do.	**Dt 15:18**	1288
because the LORD your God will **b**	**Dt 16:15**	1288
and to **b** in the name of the LORD;	**Dt 21:5**	1288
so that the LORD your God may **b**	**Dt 23:20**	1288
may sleep in his cloak and **b** you;	**Dt 24:13**	1288
LORD your God may **b** you in all	**Dt 24:19**	1288
heaven, and **b** Your people Israel,	**Dt 26:15**	1288
on Mount Gerizim to **b** the people:	**Dt 27:12**	1288
and He will **b** you in the land	**Dt 28:8**	1288
to **b** all the work of your hand;	**Dt 28:12**	1288
and that the LORD your God may **b**	**Dt 30:16**	1288
"O LORD, **b** his substance, And	**Dt 33:11**	1288
first to **b** the people of Israel.	**Jos 8:33**	1288
So he had to **b** you, and I	**Jos 24:10**	1288
people volunteered, **B** the LORD!	**Jg 5:2**	1288
among the people; **B** the LORD!	**Jg 5:9**	1288
"May the LORD **b** you."	**Ru 2:4**	1288
b Elkanah and his wife and say,	**1Sa 2:20**	1288
because he must **b** the sacrifice;	**1Sa 9:13**	1288
David returned to **b** his household,	**2Sa 6:20**	1288
to **b** the house of Your servant,	**2Sa 7:29**	1288
King David to greet him and **b** him,	**2Sa 8:10**	1288
b the inheritance of the LORD?"	**2Sa 21:3**	1288
came to **b** our lord King David,	**1Ki 1:47**	1288
"Oh that You would **b** me indeed and	**1Ch 4:10**	1288
David returned to **b** his household.	**1Ch 16:43**	1288
to **b** the house of Your servant,	**1Ch 17:27**	1288
David to greet him and to **b** him,	**1Ch 18:10**	1288
Him and to **b** in His name forever.	**1Ch 23:13**	1288
"Now **b** the LORD your God."	**1Ch 29:20**	1288
b the LORD your God forever and	**Ne 9:5**	1288
b the LORD who has counseled me;	**Ps 16:7**	1288
congregations I shall **b** the LORD.	**Ps 26:12**	1288
people and **b** Your inheritance;	**Ps 28:9**	1288
LORD will **b** His people with peace.	**Ps 29:11**	1288
I will **b** the LORD at all times;	**Ps 34:1**	1288
They **b** with their mouth, But	**Ps 62:4**	1288
I will **b** You as long as I live;	**Ps 63:4**	1288
You **b** its growth.	**Ps 65:10**	1288
B our God, O peoples, And sound	**Ps 66:8**	1288
God be gracious to us and **b** us,	**Ps 67:1**	1288
B God in the congregations, *Even*	**Ps 68:26**	1288
Let them **b** him all day long.	**Ps 72:15**	1288
And let *men* **b** themselves by him;	**Ps 72:17**	1288

Sing to the LORD, **b** His name;	**Ps 96:2**	1288
Give thanks to Him, **b** His name.	**Ps 100:4**	1288
B the LORD, O my soul,	**Ps 103:1**	1288
within me, **b** His holy name.	**Ps 103:1**	
B the LORD, O my soul, And forget	**Ps 103:2**	1288
B the LORD, you His angels, Mighty	**Ps 103:20**	1288
B the LORD, all you His hosts, You	**Ps 103:21**	1288
B the LORD, all you works of His,	**Ps 103:22**	1288
B the LORD, O my soul!	**Ps 103:22**	1288
B the LORD, O my soul!	**Ps 104:1**	1288
B the LORD, O my soul.	**Ps 104:35**	1288
Let them curse, but You **b**;	**Ps 109:28**	1288
He will **b** *us;* He will bless the house	**Ps 115:12**	1288
He will **b** the house of Israel;	**Ps 115:12**	1288
He will **b** the house of Aaron.	**Ps 115:12**	1288
He will **b** those who fear the LORD,	**Ps 115:13**	1288
we will **b** the LORD From this time	**Ps 115:18**	1288
The LORD **b** you from Zion, And may	**Ps 128:5**	1288
b you in the name of the LORD."	**Ps 129:8**	1288
"I will abundantly **b** her provision;	**Ps 132:15**	1288
Behold, **b** the LORD, all servants	**Ps 134:1**	1288
to the sanctuary And **b** the LORD.	**Ps 134:2**	1288
May the LORD **b** you from Zion, He	**Ps 134:3**	1288
O house of Israel, **b** the LORD;	**Ps 135:19**	1288
O house of Aaron, **b** the LORD;	**Ps 135:19**	1288
O house of Levi, **b** the LORD;	**Ps 135:20**	1288
who revere the LORD, **b** the LORD.	**Ps 135:20**	1288
will **b** Your name forever and ever.	**Ps 145:1**	1288
Every day I will **b** You,	**Ps 145:2**	1288
And Your godly ones shall **b** You.	**Ps 145:10**	1288
And all flesh will **b** His holy name	**Ps 145:21**	1288
father And does not **b** his mother.	**Pr 30:11**	1288
Her children rise up and **b** her;	**Pr 31:28**	833
nations will **b** themselves in Him,	**Jer 4:2**	1288
with which I had promised to **b** it.	**Jer 18:10**	3190
'The LORD **b** you, O abode of	**Jer 31:23**	1288
from this day on I will **b** *you.*' "	**Hg 2:19**	1288
b those who curse you, pray for	**Lk 6:28**	*2127*
and sent Him to **b** you by turning	**Ac 3:26**	*2127*
B those who persecute you;	**Ro 12:14**	*2127*
who persecute you; **b** and do not curse.	**Ro 12:14**	*2127*
when we are reviled, we **b**;	**1Co 4:12**	*2127*
b a sharing in the blood of Christ?	**1Co 10:16**	*2127*
if you **b** in the spirit *only,*	**1Co 14:16**	*2127*
"I WILL SURELY **B** YOU AND I WILL	**Heb 6:14**	*2127*
With it we **b** *our* Lord and Father,	**Jas 3:9**	*2127*
BLESSED		
God **b** them, saying,	**Gn 1:22**	1288
God **b** them; and God said to them,	**Gn 1:28**	1288
Then God **b** the seventh day and	**Gn 2:3**	1288
and He **b** them and named them Man	**Gn 5:2**	1288
And God **b** Noah and his sons and	**Gn 9:1**	1288
"**B** be the LORD, The God of Shem;	**Gn 9:26**	1288
of the earth will be **b**."	**Gn 12:3**	1288
He **b** him and said,	**Gn 14:19**	1288
"**B** be Abram of God Most High,	**Gn 14:19**	1288
And **b** be God Most High, Who has	**Gn 14:20**	1288
nations of the earth will be **b**?	**Gn 18:18**	1288
nations of the earth shall be **b**,	**Gn 22:18**	1288
LORD had **b** Abraham in every way.	**Gn 24:1**	1288
"**B** be the LORD, the God of my	**Gn 24:27**	1288
"Come in, **b** of the LORD!	**Gn 24:31**	1288
The LORD has greatly **b** my master,	**Gn 24:35**	1288
the LORD, and **b** the LORD,	**Gn 24:48**	1288
They **b** Rebekah and said to her,	**Gn 24:60**	1288
Abraham, that God **b** his son Isaac;	**Gn 25:11**	1288
nations of the earth shall be **b**;	**Gn 26:4**	1288
And the LORD **b** him,	**Gn 26:12**	1288
You are now the **b** of the LORD.' "	**Gn 26:29**	1288
brother Esau's hands; so he **b** him.	**Gn 27:23**	1288
his garments, he **b** him and said,	**Gn 27:27**	1288
of a field which the LORD has **b**;	**Gn 27:27**	1288
And **b** be those who bless you."	**Gn 27:29**	1288
of it before you came, and **b** him?	**Gn 27:33**	1288
Yes, and he shall be **b**."	**Gn 27:33**	1288
with which his father had **b** him;	**Gn 27:41**	1288
Jacob and **b** him and charged him,	**Gn 28:1**	1288
Now Esau saw that Isaac had **b**	**Gn 28:6**	1288
that when he **b** him he charged him,	**Gn 28:6**	1288
the families of the earth be **b**.	**Gn 28:14**	1288
LORD has **b** me on your account."	**Gn 30:27**	1288
LORD has **b** you wherever I turned.	**Gn 30:30**	1288
sons and his daughters and **b** them.	**Gn 31:55**	1288
And he **b** him there.	**Gn 32:29**	1288
from Paddan-aram, and He **b** him.	**Gn 35:9**	1288
the LORD **b** the Egyptian's house on	**Gn 39:5**	1288
and Jacob **b** Pharaoh.	**Gn 47:7**	1288
And Jacob **b** Pharaoh, and went out	**Gn 47:10**	1288
in the land of Canaan and **b** me,	**Gn 48:3**	1288
He **b** Joseph, and said,	**Gn 48:15**	1288
He **b** them that day, saying,	**Gn 48:20**	1288
said to them when he **b** them.	**Gn 49:28**	1288
He **b** them, every one with the	**Gn 49:28**	1288
"**B** be the LORD who delivered you	**Ex 18:10**	1288
therefore the LORD **b** the sabbath	**Ex 20:11**	1288
they had done. So Moses **b** them.	**Ex 39:43**	1288
toward the people and **b** them,	**Lv 9:22**	1288
they came out and **b** the people,	**Lv 9:23**	1288
know that he whom you bless is **b**,	**Nu 22:6**	1288
for they are **b**."	**Nu 22:12**	1288
you have actually **b** them!"	**Nu 23:11**	1288
When He has **b**, then I cannot	**Nu 23:20**	1288
B is everyone who blesses you, And	**Nu 24:9**	1288
b you in all that you have done;	**Dt 2:7**	1288
"You shall be **b** above all peoples;	**Dt 7:14**	1288
which the LORD your God has **b** you.	**Dt 12:7**	1288
as the LORD your God has **b** you.	**Dt 15:14**	1288
"**B** *shall* you *be* in the city, and	**Dt 28:3**	1288
and **b** *shall* you *be* in the country.	**Dt 28:3**	1288

“**B** *shall be* the offspring of your Dt 28:4 1288
“**B** *shall be* your basket and your Dt 28:5 1288
“**B** *shall* you *be* when you come in, Dt 28:6 1288
b *shall* you *be* when you go out. Dt 28:6 1288
Moses the man of God **b** the sons Dt 33:1 1288
“**B** of the LORD *be* his land, With Dt 33:13 1288
“**B** is the one who enlarges Gad; Dt 33:20 1288
“More **b** than sons is Asher; Dt 33:24 1288
“**B** are you, O Israel; Dt 33:29 835
So Joshua **b** him and gave Hebron Jos 14:13 1288
whom the LORD has thus far **b**?” Jos 17:14 1288
Joshua **b** them and sent them away, Jos 22:6 1288
away to their tents, he **b** them, Jos 22:7 1288
and the sons of Israel **b** God; Jos 22:33 1288
“Most **b** of women is Jael, The Jg 5:24 1288
Most **b** is she of women in the Jg 5:24 1288
child grew up and the LORD **b** him. Jg 13:24 1288
“**B** be my son by the LORD.” Jg 17:2 1288
he who took notice of you be **b**.” Ru 2:19 1288
“May he be **b** of the LORD who has Ru 2:20 1288
“May you be **b** of the LORD, my Ru 3:10 1288
“**B** is the LORD who has not left Ru 4:14 1288
“**B** are you of the LORD! 1Sa 15:13 1288
“May you be **b** of the LORD, 1Sa 23:21 1288
“**B** be the LORD God of Israel, who 1Sa 25:32 1288
and **b** be your discernment, and 1Sa 25:33 1288
be your discernment, and **b** be you, 1Sa 25:33 1288
“**B** be the LORD, who has pleaded 1Sa 25:39 1288
“**B** are you, my son David; 1Sa 26:25 1288
“May you be **b** of the LORD because 2Sa 2:5 1288
and the LORD **b** Obed-edom and all 2Sa 6:11 1288
“The LORD has **b** the house of 2Sa 6:12 1288
he **b** the people in the name of the 2Sa 6:18 1288
of Your servant be **b** forever.” 2Sa 7:29 1288
him, he would not go, but **b** him. 2Sa 13:25 1288
prostrated himself and **b** the king; 2Sa 14:22 1288
“**B** is the LORD your God, who has 2Sa 18:28 1288
then kissed Barzillai and **b** him, 2Sa 19:39 1288
“The LORD lives, and **b** be my rock; 2Sa 22:47 1288
‘**B** be the LORD, the God of Israel, 1Ki 1:48 1288
“But King Solomon shall be **b**, 1Ki 2:45 1288
“**B** be the LORD today, who has 1Ki 5:7 1288
and **b** all the assembly of Israel, 1Ki 8:14 1288
“**B** be the LORD, the God of 1Ki 8:15 1288
And he stood and **b** all the 1Ki 8:55 1288
“**B** be the LORD, who has given 1Ki 8:56 1288
people away and they **b** the king. 1Ki 8:66 1288
“How **b** are your men, how blessed 1Ki 10:8 835
how **b** are these your servants who 1Ki 10:8 835
“**B** be the LORD your God who 1Ki 10:9 1288
and the LORD **b** the family of 1Ch 13:14 1288
he **b** the people in the name of the 1Ch 16:2 1288
B be the LORD, the God of Israel, 1Ch 16:36 1288
for You, O LORD, have **b**, 1Ch 17:27 1288
blessed, and it is **b** forever.” 1Ch 17:27 1288
God had indeed **b** him. 1Ch 26:5 1288
So David **b** the LORD in the sight 1Ch 29:10 1288
“**B** are You, O LORD God of Israel 1Ch 29:10 1288
And all the assembly **b** the LORD, 1Ch 29:20 1288
“**B** be the LORD, the God of 2Ch 2:12 1288
and **b** all the assembly of Israel, 2Ch 6:3 1288
“**B** be the LORD, the God of 2Ch 6:4 1288
“How **b** are your men, how blessed 2Ch 9:7 835
how **b** are these your servants who 2Ch 9:7 835
“**B** be the LORD your God who 2Ch 9:8 1288
for there they **b** the LORD. 2Ch 20:26 1288
priests arose and **b** the people; 2Ch 30:27 1288
they **b** the LORD and His people 2Ch 31:8 1288
for the LORD has **b** His people, 2Ch 31:10 1288
B be the LORD, the God of our Ezr 7:27 1288
Ezra **b** the LORD the great God. Ne 8:6 1288
O may Your glorious name be **b** And Ne 9:5 1288
And the people **b** all the men who Ne 11:2 1288
You have **b** the work of his hands, Jb 1:10 1288
B be the name of the LORD.” Jb 1:21 1288
the ear heard, it called me **b**, Jb 29:11 833
The LORD **b** the latter *days* of Jb 42:12 1288
How **b** is the man who does not walk Ps 1:1 835
How **b** are all who take refuge in Ps 2:12 835
The LORD lives, and **b** be my rock; Ps 18:46 1288
You make him most **b** forever; Ps 21:6 1293
B be the LORD, Because He has Ps 28:6 1288
B be the LORD, For He has made Ps 31:21 1288
How **b** is he whose transgression is Ps 32:1 835
How **b** is the man to whom the LORD Ps 32:2 835
B is the nation whose God is the Ps 33:12 835
How **b** is the man who takes refuge Ps 34:8 835
b by Him will inherit the land, Ps 37:22 1288
How **b** is the man who has made the Ps 40:4 835
How **b** is he who considers the Ps 41:1 835
shall be called **b** upon the earth; Ps 41:2 833
B be the LORD, the God of Israel, Ps 41:13 1288
Therefore God has **b** You forever. Ps 45:2 1288
How **b** is the one whom You choose Ps 65:4 835
B be God, Who has not turned away Ps 66:20 1288
B be the Lord, who daily bears our Ps 68:19 1288
power to the people. **B** be God! Ps 68:35 1288
Let all nations call him **b**. Ps 72:17 833
B be the LORD God, the God of Ps 72:18 1288
b be His glorious name forever; Ps 72:19 1288
How **b** are those who dwell in Your Ps 84:4 835
How **b** is the man whose strength is Ps 84:5 835
b is the man who trusts in You! Ps 84:12 835
How **b** are the people who know the Ps 89:15 835
B be the LORD forever! Ps 89:52 1288
B is the man whom You chasten Ps 94:12 835
How **b** are those who keep justice, Ps 106:3 835
B be the LORD, the God of Israel, Ps 106:48 1288
b is the man who fears the LORD, Ps 112:1 835

of the upright will be **b**. Ps 112:2 1288
B be the name of the LORD From Ps 113:2 1288
May you be **b** of the LORD, Maker of Ps 115:15 1288
B is the one who comes in the name Ps 118:26 1288
We have **b** you from the house of Ps 118:26 1288
How **b** are those whose way is Ps 119:1 835
How **b** are those who observe His Ps 119:2 835
B are You, O LORD; Ps 119:12 1288
B be the LORD, Who has not given Ps 124:6 1288
How **b** is the man whose quiver is Ps 127:5 835
How **b** is everyone who fears the Ps 128:1 835
the man be **b** Who fears the LORD. Ps 128:4 1288
B be the LORD from Zion, Who Ps 135:21 1288
How **b** will be the one who repays Ps 137:8 835
How **b** will be the one who seizes Ps 137:9 835
B be the LORD, my rock, Who trains Ps 144:1 1288
How **b** are the people who are so Ps 144:15 835
How **b** are the people whose God is Ps 144:15 835
How **b** is he whose help is the God Ps 146:5 835
He has **b** your sons within you. Ps 147:13 1288
How **b** is the man who finds wisdom Pr 3:13 835
Let your fountain be **b**, Pr 5:18 1288
For **b** are they who keep my ways. Pr 8:32 835
“**B** is the man who listens to me, Pr 8:34 835
The memory of the righteous is **b**, Pr 10:7 1293
b is he who trusts in the LORD. Pr 16:20 835
How **b** are his sons after him. Pr 20:7 835
Will not be **b** in the end. Pr 20:21 1288
He who is generous will be **b**, Pr 22:9 1288
How **b** is the man who fears always, Pr 28:14 835
B are you, O land, whose king is Ec 10:17 835
maidens saw her and called her **b**, SS 6:9 833
whom the LORD of hosts has **b**, Is 19:25 1288
“**B** is Egypt My people, and Is 19:25 1288
How **b** are all those who long for Is 30:18 835
How **b** will you be, you who sow Is 32:20 835
Then I **b** him and multiplied him.” Is 51:2 1288
“How **b** is the man who does this, Is 56:2 835
the offspring *whom* the LORD has **b**. Is 61:9 1288
“Because he who is **b** in the earth Is 65:16 1288
Will be **b** by the God of truth; Is 65:16 1288
offspring of those **b** by the LORD, Is 65:23 1288
“**B** is the man who trusts in the Jer 17:7 1288
not be **b** when my mother bore me! Jer 20:14 1288
“**B** be the glory of the LORD in Ezk 3:12 1288
Then Daniel **b** the God of heaven; Da 2:19 1289
name of God be **b** forever and ever, Da 2:20 1289
“**B** be the God of Shadrach, Da 3:28 1289
and I **b** the Most High and praised Da 4:34 1289
“How **b** is he who keeps waiting Da 12:12 835
‘**B** be the LORD, for I have become Zch 11:5 1288
All the nations will call you **b**, Mal 3:12 833
‘So now we call the arrogant **b**; Mal 3:15 833
“**B** are the poor in spirit, for Mt 5:3 *3107*
“**B** are those who mourn, for they Mt 5:4 *3107*
“**B** are the gentle, for they shall Mt 5:5 *3107*
“**B** are those who hunger and Mt 5:6 *3107*
“**B** are the merciful, for they Mt 5:7 *3107*
“**B** are the pure in heart, for Mt 5:8 *3107*
“**B** are the peacemakers, for they Mt 5:9 *3107*
“**B** are those who have been Mt 5:10 *3107*
“**B** are you when *people* insult Mt 5:11 *3107*
“And **b** is he who does not Mt 11:6 *3107*
“But **b** are your eyes, because Mt 13:16 *3107*
up toward heaven, He **b** *the food,* Mt 14:19 *2127*
“**B** are you, Simon Barjona, Mt 16:17 *3107*
B IS HE WHO COMES IN THE NAME OF Mt 21:9 *2127*
‘**B** IS HE WHO COMES IN THE NAME OF Mt 23:39 *2127*
“**B** is that slave whom his master Mt 24:46 *3107*
‘Come, you who are **b** of My Father, Mt 25:34 *2127*
He **b** *the food* and broke the loaves Mk 6:41 *2127*
and after He had **b** them, Mk 8:7 *2127*
B IS HE WHO COMES IN THE NAME OF Mk 11:9 *2127*
B *is* the coming kingdom of our Mk 11:10 *2127*
Christ, the Son of the **B** *One?*” Mk 14:61 *2128*
“**B** *are* you among women, and Lk 1:42 *2127*
and **b** *is* the fruit of your womb! Lk 1:42 *2127*
“And **b** *is* she who believed that Lk 1:45 *3107*
all generations will count me **b**. Lk 1:48 *3106*
“**B** *be* the Lord God of Israel, For Lk 1:68 *2128*
took Him into his arms, and **b** God, Lk 2:28 *2127*
And Simeon **b** them and said to Lk 2:34 *2127*
“**B** *are* you *who are* poor, for Lk 6:20 *3107*
“**B** *are* you who hunger now, for Lk 6:21 *3107*
B *are* you who weep now, for you Lk 6:21 *3107*
“**B** are you when men hate you, and Lk 6:22 *3107*
“**B** is he who does not take offense Lk 7:23 *3107*
looking up to heaven, He **b** them, Lk 9:16 *2127*
“**B** *are* the eyes which see the Lk 10:23 *3107*
“**B** is the womb that bore You and Lk 11:27 *3107*
b are those who hear the word of Lk 11:28 *3107*
“**B** are those slaves whom the Lk 12:37 *3107*
finds *them* so, **b** are those *slaves.* Lk 12:38 *3107*
“**B** is that slave whom his master Lk 12:43 *3107*
‘**B** IS HE WHO COMES IN THE NAME OF Lk 13:35 *2127*
and you will be **b**, since they do Lk 14:14 *3107*
“**B** is everyone who will eat Lk 14:15 *3107*
“**B** IS THE KING WHO COMES IN THE Lk 19:38 *2127*
‘**B** are the barren, and the wombs Lk 23:29 *3107*
them, He took the bread and **b** *it,* Lk 24:30 *2127*
He lifted up His hands and **b** them. Lk 24:50 *2127*
B IS HE WHO COMES IN THE NAME OF Jn 12:13 *2127*
things, you are **b** if you do them. Jn 13:17 *3107*
B *are* they who did not see, and Jn 20:29 *3107*
FAMILIES OF THE EARTH SHALL BE **B**.’ Ac 3:25 *1757*
‘It is more **b** to give than to receive.’ ” Ac 20:35 *3107*
the Creator, who is **b** forever. Ro 1:25 *2128*
B ARE THOSE WHOSE LAWLESS DEEDS Ro 4:7 *3107*
“**B** IS THE MAN WHOSE SIN THE LORD Ro 4:8 *3107*

who is over all, God **b** forever. Ro 9:5 *2128*
B *be* the God and Father of our 2Co 1:3 *2128*
Lord Jesus, He who is **b** forever, 2Co 11:31 *2128*
THE NATIONS WILL BE **B** IN YOU.” Ga 3:8 *1757*
are of faith are **b** with Abraham, Ga 3:9 *2127*
B *be* the God and Father of our Eph 1:3 *2128*
who has **b** us with every spiritual Eph 1:3 *2127*
the glorious gospel of the **b** God, 1Tm 1:11 *3107*
who is the **b** and only Sovereign, 1Tm 6:15 *3107*
looking for the **b** hope and the Ti 2:13 *3107*
slaughter of the kings and **b** him, Heb 7:1 *2127*
b the one who had the promises. Heb 7:6 *2127*
the lesser is **b** by the greater. Heb 7:7 *2127*
By faith Isaac **b** Jacob and Esau, Heb 11:20 *2127*
b each of the sons of Joseph, Heb 11:21 *2127*
B is a man who perseveres under Jas 1:12 *3107*
man will be **b** in what he does. Jas 1:25 *3107*
We count those **b** who endured. Jas 5:11 *3106*
B be the God and Father of our 1Pe 1:3 *2128*
sake of righteousness, *you are* **b**. 1Pe 3:14 *3107*
for the name of Christ, you are **b**, 1Pe 4:14 *3107*
B is he who reads and those who Rv 1:3 *3107*
‘**B** are the dead who die in the Rv 14:13 *3107*
B is the one who stays awake and Rv 16:15 *3107*
‘**B** are those who are invited to Rv 19:9 *3107*
B and holy is the one who has a Rv 20:6 *3107*
B is he who heeds the words of the Rv 22:7 *3107*
B are those who wash their robes, Rv 22:14 *3107*

BLESSES

And by the Almighty who **b** you *With* Gn 49:25 1288
Blessed is everyone who **b** you, Nu 24:9 1288
you when the LORD your God **b** you, Dt 14:24 1288
just as the LORD your God **b** you; Dt 16:10 1288
For it is You who **b** the righteous man, Ps 5:12 1288
God, our God, **b** us. Ps 67:6 1288
God **b** us, That all the ends of the Ps 67:7 1288
Also He **b** them and they multiply Ps 107:38 1288
b the dwelling of the righteous. Pr 3:33 1288
He who **b** his friend with a loud Pr 27:14 1288
is *like* the one who **b** an idol. Is 66:3 1288

BLESSING

And so you shall be a **b**; Gn 12:2 1293
upon myself a curse and not a **b**.” Gn 27:12 1293
as Isaac had finished **b** Jacob, Gn 27:30 1288
and has taken away your **b**.” Gn 27:35 1293
now he has taken away my **b**.” Gn 27:36 1293
you not reserved a **b** for me?” Gn 27:36 1293
“Do you have only one **b**, Gn 27:38 1293
against Jacob because of the **b** with Gn 27:41 1293
He also give you the **b** of Abraham, Gn 28:4 1293
b was upon all that he owned, Gn 39:5 1293
“By you Israel will pronounce **b**, Gn 48:20 1288
one with the **b** appropriate to him. Gn 49:28 1293
may bestow a **b** upon you today.” Ex 32:29 1293
then I will so order My **b** for you Lv 25:21 1293
in **b** them these three times! Nu 24:10 1288
before you today a **b** and a curse: Dt 11:26 1293
the **b**, if you listen to the Dt 11:27 1293
that you shall place the **b** on Dt 11:29 1293
according to the **b** of the LORD Dt 12:15 1293
according to the **b** of the LORD Dt 16:17 1293
God turned the curse into a **b** for you Dt 23:5 1293
“The LORD will command the **b** upon Dt 28:8 1293
the **b** and the curse which I have Dt 30:1 1293
and death, the **b** and the curse. Dt 30:19 1293
Now this is the **b** with which Moses Dt 33:1 1293
And full of the **b** of the LORD, Dt 33:23 1293
of the law, the **b** and the curse, Jos 8:34 1293
Then she said, “Give me a **b**; Jos 15:19 1293
“Give me a **b**, since you have Jg 1:15 1293
and with Your **b** may the house of 2Sa 7:29 1293
exalted above all **b** and praise! Ne 9:5 1293
our God turned the curse into a **b**. Ne 13:2 1293
“The **b** of the one ready to perish Jb 29:13 1293
Your **b** *be* upon Your people! Ps 3:8 1293
He shall receive a **b** from the LORD Ps 24:5 1293
And his descendants are a **b**. Ps 37:26 1293
And he did not delight in **b**, Ps 109:17 1293
“The **b** of the LORD be upon you; Ps 129:8 1293
there the LORD commanded the **b** Ps 133:3 1293
the **b** of the LORD that makes rich, Pr 10:22 1293
By the **b** of the upright a city is Pr 11:11 1293
But **b** will be on the head of him Pr 11:26 1293
And a good **b** will come upon them. Pr 24:25 1293
a **b** in the midst of the earth, Is 19:24 1293
And My **b** on your descendants; Is 44:3 1293
and the places around My hill a **b**. Ezk 34:26 1293
they will be showers of **b**. Ezk 34:26 1293
cause a **b** to rest on your house. Ezk 44:30 1293
relent And leave a **b** behind Him, Jl 2:14 1293
save you that you may become a **b**. Zch 8:13 1293
pour out for you a **b** until it Mal 3:10 1293
give it your **b** *of* peace. But if Mt 10:13
take back your **b** *of* peace. Mt 10:13
took *some* bread, and after a **b**, Mt 26:26 *2127*
them in His arms and *began* **b** them, Mk 10:16 *2721a*
bread, and after a **b** He broke *it* Mk 14:22 *2127*
While He was **b** them, Lk 24:51 *2127*
just as David also speaks of the **b** Ro 4:6 *3108*
this **b** then on the circumcised, Ro 4:9 *3108*
in the fullness of the **b** of Christ. Ro 15:29 *2129*
Is not the cup of **b** which we bless 1Co 10:16 *2129*
that you might twice receive a **b**; 2Co 1:15 *5485*
in Christ Jesus the **b** of Abraham Ga 3:14 *2129*
then is that sense of **b** you had? Ga 4:15 *3108*
spiritual **b** in the heavenly *places* Eph 1:3 *2129*
tilled, receives a **b** from God; Heb 6:7 *2129*
when he desired to inherit the **b**, Heb 12:17 *2129*

mouth come *both* **b** and cursing. **Jas 3:10** *2129*
insult, but giving a **b** instead; **1Pe 3:9** *2127*
that you might inherit a **b**. **1Pe 3:9** *2129*
might and honor and glory and **b**." **Rv 5:12** *2129*
be **b** and honor and glory and **Rv 5:13** *2129*
b and glory and wisdom and **Rv 7:12** *2129*

BLESSINGS
you *With* **b** of heaven above, **Gn 49:25** 1293
B of the deep that lies beneath, **Gn 49:25** 1293
B of the breasts and of the womb. **Gn 49:25** 1293
"The **b** of your father Have **Gn 49:26** 1293
surpassed the **b** of my ancestors **Gn 49:26** 1293
"All these **b** will come upon **Dt 28:2** 1293
him with the **b** of good things; **Ps 21:3** 1293
early rain also covers it with **b**. **Ps 84:6** 1293
B are on the head of the **Pr 10:6** 1293
A faithful man will abound with **b**, **Pr 28:20** 1293
upon you and I will curse your **b**; **Mal 2:2** 1293
YOU THE HOLY *and* SURE **B** **Ac 13:34**

BLEW
"You **b** with Your wind, the sea **Ex 15:10** 5398
went forward and **b** the trumpets; **Jos 6:8** 8628
the priests who **b** the trumpets, **Jos 6:9** 8628
continually, and **b** the trumpets; **Jos 6:13** 8628
when the priests **b** the trumpets, **Jos 6:16** 8628
and *priests* **b** the trumpets; **Jos 6:20** 8628
that he **b** the trumpet in the hill **Jg 3:27** 8628
and he **b** a trumpet, and the **Jg 6:34** 8628
and they **b** the trumpets and **Jg 7:19** 8628
When the three companies **b** the **Jg 7:20** 8628
When they **b** 300 trumpets, the **Jg 7:22** 8628
Then Saul **b** the trumpet throughout **1Sa 13:3** 8628
So Joab **b** the trumpet; **2Sa 2:28** 8628
Then Joab **b** the trumpet, and the **2Sa 18:16** 8628
and he **b** the trumpet and said, **2Sa 20:1** 8628
So he **b** the trumpet, and they were **2Sa 20:22** 8628
Then they **b** the trumpet, and all **1Ki 1:39** 8628
the bare steps, and **b** the trumpet, **2Ki 9:13** 8628
the land rejoiced and **b** trumpets. **2Ki 11:14** 8628
b the trumpets before the ark of **1Ch 15:24** 2690
Benaiah and Jahaziel the priests **b** **1Ch 16:6** 2690
on the other side **b** trumpets; **2Ch 7:6** 2690
and the priests **b** the trumpets. **2Ch 13:14** 2690
the land rejoiced and **b** trumpets, **2Ch 23:13** 8628
the floods came, and the winds **b** and **Mt 7:25** *4154*
the floods came, and the winds **b** and **Mt 7:27** *4154*

BLIGHT
sword and with **b** and with mildew, **Dt 28:22** 7711b
if there is **b** *or* mildew, **1Ki 8:37** 7711b
if there is **b** or mildew, **2Ch 6:28** 7711b

BLIND
him mute or deaf, or seeing or **b**? **Ex 4:11** 5787
a stumbling block before the **b**, **Lv 19:14** 5787
a **b** man, or a lame man, or he who **Lv 21:18** 5787
'Those *that are* **b** or fractured or **Lv 22:22** 5788b
misleads a **b** *person* on the road.' **Dt 27:18** 5787
as the **b** man gropes in darkness, **Dt 28:29** 5787
a bribe to **b** my eyes with it? **1Sa 12:3** 5956
b and lame will turn you away"; **2Sa 5:6** 5787
let him reach the lame and the **b**, **2Sa 5:8** 5787
"The **b** or the lame shall not come **2Sa 5:8** 5787
"I was eyes to the **b** And **Jb 29:15** 5787
The LORD opens *the eyes of* the **b**; **Ps 146:8** 5787
B yourselves and be blind; **Is 29:9** 8173a
Blind yourselves and be **b**; **Is 29:9** 8173a
the eyes of the **b** will see. **Is 29:18** 5787
the eyes of the **b** will be opened And **Is 35:5** 5787
To open **b** eyes, To bring out **Is 42:7** 5787
the **b** by a way they do not know, **Is 42:16** 5787
And look, you **b**, that you may see. **Is 42:18** 5787
Who is **b** but My servant, Or so **Is 42:19** 5787
Who is so **b** as he that is at peace **Is 42:19** 5787
so **b** as the servant of the LORD? **Is 42:19** 5787
Bring out the people who are **b**, **Is 43:8** 5787
His watchmen are **b**, **Is 56:10** 5787
grope along the wall like **b** men, **Is 59:10** 5787
Among them the **b** and the lame, **Jer 31:8** 5787
They wandered, **b**, in the streets; **La 4:14** 5787
So that they will walk like the **b**, **Zph 1:17** 5787
And his right eye will be **b**." **Zch 11:17** 3543a
you present the **b** for sacrifice, **Mal 1:8** 5787
there, two **b** men followed Him, **Mt 9:27** *5185*
house, the **b** men came up to Him, **Mt 9:28** *5185*
the **B** RECEIVE SIGHT and *the* lame **Mt 11:5** *5185*
man *who was* **b** and mute was **Mt 12:22** *5185*
they are **b** guides of the blind. **Mt 15:14** *5185*
they are blind guides of the **b**. **Mt 15:14** *5185*
And if a **b** man guides a blind man, **Mt 15:14** *5185*
And if a blind man guides a **b** man, **Mt 15:14** *5185*
those who were lame, crippled, **b**, **Mt 15:30** *5185*
lame walking, and the **b** seeing; **Mt 15:31** *5185*
two **b** men sitting by the road, **Mt 20:30** *5185*
And *the* **b** and *the* lame came to Him **Mt 21:14** *5185*
"Woe to you, **b** guides, who say, **Mt 23:16** *5185*
"You fools and **b** men! **Mt 23:17** *5185*
"You **b** men, which is more **Mt 23:19** *5185*
"You **b** guides, who strain out a **Mt 23:24** *5185*
"You **b** Pharisee, first clean the **Mt 23:26** *5185*
And they brought a **b** man to Jesus **Mk 8:22** *5185*
Taking the **b** man by the hand, **Mk 8:23** *5185*
a **b** beggar *named* Bartimaeus, **Mk 10:46** *5185*
So they called the **b** man, **Mk 10:49** *5185*
And the **b** man said to Him, **Mk 10:51** *5185*
AND RECOVERY OF SIGHT TO THE **B**, **Lk 4:18** *5185*
"A **b** man cannot guide a blind **Lk 6:39** *5185*
"A blind man cannot guide a **b** man, **Lk 6:39** *5185*
gave sight to many *who were* **b**. **Lk 7:21** *5185*
the **B** RECEIVE SIGHT, *the* lame **Lk 7:22** *5185*
the crippled, *the* lame, *the* **b**, **Lk 14:13** *5185*
poor and crippled and **b** and lame.' **Lk 14:21** *5185*
b man was sitting by the road begging **Lk 18:35** *5185*
of those who were sick, **b**, **Jn 5:3** *5185*
by, He saw a man **b** from birth. **Jn 9:1** *5185*
that he would be born **b**?" **Jn 9:2** *5185*
Pharisees the man who was formerly **b**. **Jn 9:13** *5185*
said to the **b** man again, **Jn 9:17** *5185*
it of him, that he had been **b** and **Jn 9:18** *5185*
your son, who you say was born **b**? **Jn 9:19** *5185*
our son, and that he was born **b**; **Jn 9:20** *5185*
called the man who had been **b**, **Jn 9:24** *5185*
I do know, that though I was **b**, **Jn 9:25** *5185*
the eyes of a person born **b**. **Jn 9:32** *5185*
that those who see may become **b**." **Jn 9:39** *5185*
"We are not **b** too, are we?" **Jn 9:40** *5185*
"If you were **b**, you would have no **Jn 9:41** *5185*
cannot open the eyes of the **b**, **Jn 10:21** *5185*
opened the eyes of the **b** man, **Jn 11:37** *5185*
and you will be **b** and not see the **Ac 13:11** *5185*
you yourself are a guide to the **b**, **Ro 2:19** *5185*
qualities is **b** *or* short-sighted, **2Pe 1:9** *5185*
and poor and **b** and naked, **Rv 3:17** *5185*

BLINDED
of those who see will not be **b**, **Is 32:3** 8173a
He then **b** Zedekiah's eyes and **Jer 39:7** 5786
Then he **b** the eyes of Zedekiah; **Jer 52:11** 5786
"HE HAS **B** THEIR EYES AND HE **Jn 12:40** *5186*
b the minds of the unbelieving so **2Co 4:4** *5186*
the darkness has **b** his eyes. **1Jn 2:11** *5186*

BLINDFOLD
to spit at Him, and to **b** Him, **Mk 14:65** *4028*

BLINDFOLDED
they **b** Him and were asking Him, **Lk 22:64** *4028*

BLINDNESS
the doorway of the house with **b**, **Gn 19:11** 5575
any defect, *such as* lameness or **b**, **Dt 15:21** 5787
smite you with madness and with **b** **Dt 28:28** 5788a
"Strike this people with **b**, **2Ki 6:18** 5575
So He struck them with **b** according **2Ki 6:18** 5575
every horse of the peoples with **b**. **Zch 12:4** 5788a

BLINDS
for a bribe **b** the clear-sighted **Ex 23:8** 5786
for a bribe **b** the eyes of the wise **Dt 16:19** 5786

BLOCK
a stumbling **b** before the blind, **Lv 19:14** 4383
I fall down before a **b** of wood!" **Is 44:19** 944
the stumbling **b** of their iniquity. **Ezk 14:3** 4383
the stumbling **b** of his iniquity, **Ezk 14:4** 4383
the stumbling **b** of his iniquity, **Ezk 14:7** 4383
not become a stumbling **b** to you. **Ezk 18:30** 4383
it will **b** off those who would pass by. **Ezk 39:11** 2629
became a stumbling **b** of iniquity to **Ezk 44:12** 4383
You are a stumbling **b** to Me; **Mt 16:23** *4625*
whom the stumbling **b** comes! **Mt 18:7** *4625*
A STUMBLING **B** AND A RETRIBUTION **Ro 11:9** *4625*
a stumbling **b** in a brother's way. **Ro 14:13** *4625*
crucified, to Jews a stumbling **b** and **1Co 1:23** *4625*
become a stumbling **b** to the weak. **1Co 8:9** *4348*
Then the stumbling **b** of the cross **Ga 5:11** *4625*
stumbling **b** before the sons of Israel, **Rv 2:14** *4625*

BLOCKED
He has **b** my ways with hewn stone; **La 3:9** 1443

BLOCKS
stumbling **b** before this people. **Jer 6:21** 4383
of His kingdom all stumbling **b**, **Mt 13:41** *4625*
world because of *its* stumbling **b**! **Mt 18:7** *4625*
inevitable that stumbling **b** come; **Mt 18:7** *4625*
that stumbling **b** come, **Lk 17:1** *4625*

BLOOD
The voice of your brother's **b** is **Gn 4:10** 1818
your brother's **b** from your hand. **Gn 4:11** 1818
with its life, *that is,* its **b**. **Gn 9:4** 1818
"Whoever sheds man's **b**, **Gn 9:6** 1818
blood, By man his **b** shall be shed, **Gn 9:6** 1818
"Shed no **b**. Throw him into this pit **Gn 37:22** 1818
our brother and cover up his **b**? **Gn 37:26** 1818
and dipped the tunic in the **b**; **Gn 37:31** 1818
comes the reckoning for his **b**." **Gn 42:22** 1818
And his robes in the **b** of grapes. **Gn 49:11** 1818
will become **b** on the dry ground." **Ex 4:9** 1818
indeed a bridegroom of **b** to me." **Ex 4:25** 1818
"*You are* a bridegroom of **b**" **Ex 4:26** 1818
hand, and it will be turned to **b**. **Ex 7:17** 1818
of water, that they may become **b**; **Ex 7:19** 1818
and there will be **b** throughout **Ex 7:19** 1818
was in the Nile was turned to **b**. **Ex 7:20** 1818
And the **b** was through all the land **Ex 7:21** 1818
they shall take some of the **b** and **Ex 12:7** 1818
'The **b** shall be a sign for you **Ex 12:13** 1818
I see the **b** I will pass over you, **Ex 12:13** 1818
it in the **b** which is in the basin, **Ex 12:22** 1818
and apply some of the **b** that is in **Ex 12:22** 1818
and when He sees the **b** on the **Ex 12:23** 1818
"You shall not offer the **b** of My **Ex 23:18** 1818
of the **b** and put *it* in basins, **Ex 24:6** 1818
the **b** he sprinkled on the altar. **Ex 24:6** 1818
So Moses took the **b** and sprinkled **Ex 24:8** 1818
"Behold the **b** of the covenant, **Ex 24:8** 1818
"You shall take some of the **b** **Ex 29:12** 1818
the **b** at the base of the altar. **Ex 29:12** 1818
take its **b** and sprinkle it around **Ex 29:16** 1818
and take some of its **b** and put *it* **Ex 29:20** 1818
rest of the **b** around on the altar. **Ex 29:20** 1818
some of the **b** that is on the altar **Ex 29:21** 1818
b of the sin offering of atonement **Ex 30:10** 1818
"You shall not offer the **b** of My **Ex 34:25** 1818
shall offer up the **b** and sprinkle **Lv 1:5** 1818
sprinkle the **b** around on the altar **Lv 1:5** 1818
its **b** around on the altar. **Lv 1:11** 1818
and its **b** is to be drained out on **Lv 1:15** 1818
the **b** around on the altar. **Lv 3:2** 1818
its **b** around on the altar. **Lv 3:8** 1818
its **b** around on the altar. **Lv 3:13** 1818
not eat any fat or any **b**.'" **Lv 3:17** 1818
take some of the **b** of the bull and **Lv 4:5** 1818
shall dip his finger in the **b** and **Lv 4:6** 1818
the **b** seven times before the LORD, **Lv 4:6** 1818
put some of the **b** on the horns of **Lv 4:7** 1818
and all the **b** of the bull he shall **Lv 4:7** 1818
bring some of the **b** of the bull to **Lv 4:16** 1818
shall dip his finger in the **b** and **Lv 4:17** 1818
'He shall put some of the **b** on **Lv 4:18** 1818
and all the **b** he shall pour out at **Lv 4:18** 1818
take some of the **b** of the sin offering **Lv 4:25** 1818
and *the rest of* its **b** he shall **Lv 4:25** 1818
priest shall take some of its **b** with **Lv 4:30** 1818
and all *the rest of* its **b** he shall **Lv 4:30** 1818
priest is to take some of the **b** of the **Lv 4:34** 1818
and all *the rest of* its **b** he shall **Lv 4:34** 1818
'He shall also sprinkle some of the **b** **Lv 5:9** 1818
while the rest of the **b** shall be **Lv 5:9** 1818
of its **b** splashes on a garment, **Lv 6:27** 1818
any of the **b** is brought into the tent **Lv 6:30** 1818
its **b** around on the altar. **Lv 7:2** 1818
the **b** of the peace offerings. **Lv 7:14** 1818
'You are not to eat any **b**, **Lv 7:26** 1818
'Any person who eats any **b**, **Lv 7:27** 1818
sons of Aaron who offers the **b** of **Lv 7:33** 1818
Moses slaughtered *it* and took the **b** **Lv 8:15** 1818
rest of the **b** at the base of the altar **Lv 8:15** 1818
the **b** around on the altar. **Lv 8:19** 1818
some of its **b** and put it on the lobe **Lv 8:23** 1818
and Moses put some of the **b** on the **Lv 8:24** 1818
rest of the **b** around on the altar. **Lv 8:24** 1818
of the **b** which was on the altar and **Lv 8:30** 1818
sons presented the **b** to him; **Lv 9:9** 1818
and he dipped his finger in the **b** and **Lv 9:9** 1818
rest of the **b** at the base of the altar. **Lv 9:9** 1818
and Aaron's sons handed the **b** to **Lv 9:12** 1818
and Aaron's sons handed the **b** to **Lv 9:18** 1818
its **b** had not been brought inside, **Lv 10:18** 1818
'Then she shall remain in the **b** of **Lv 12:4** 1818
and she shall remain in the **b** of **Lv 12:5** 1818
cleansed from the flow of her **b**. **Lv 12:7** 1818
dip them and the live bird in the **b** **Lv 14:6** 1818
of the **b** of the guilt offering, **Lv 14:14** 1818
on the **b** of the guilt offering; **Lv 14:17** 1818
some of the **b** of the guilt offering **Lv 14:25** 1818
of the **b** of the guilt offering. **Lv 14:28** 1818
them in the **b** of the slain bird as **Lv 14:51** 1818
cleanse the house with the **b** **Lv 14:52** 1818
if her discharge in her body is **b**, **Lv 15:19** 1818
a discharge of her **b** many days, **Lv 15:25** 1818
he shall take some of the **b** of the **Lv 16:14** 1818
the **b** with his finger seven times. **Lv 16:14** 1818
and bring its **b** inside the veil and **Lv 16:15** 1818
and do with its **b** as he did with **Lv 16:15** 1818
as he did with the **b** of the bull, **Lv 16:15** 1818
and shall take some of the **b** of **Lv 16:18** 1818
the bull and of the **b** of the goat and **Lv 16:18** 1818
some of the **b** on it seven times and **Lv 16:19** 1818
whose **b** was brought in to make **Lv 16:27** 1818
He has shed **b** and that man shall **Lv 17:4** 1818
priest shall sprinkle the **b** on the altar **Lv 17:6** 1818
among them, who eats any **b**, **Lv 17:10** 1818
against that person who eats **b** and **Lv 17:10** 1818
the life of the flesh is in the **b**, **Lv 17:11** 1818
for it is the **b** by reason of the **Lv 17:11** 1818
'No person among you may eat **b**, **Lv 17:12** 1818
who sojourns among you eat **b**.' **Lv 17:12** 1818
out its **b** and cover it with earth. **Lv 17:13** 1818
its **b** is *identified* with its life. **Lv 17:14** 1818
are not to eat the **b** of any flesh, **Lv 17:14** 1818
the life of all flesh is its **b**; **Lv 17:14** 1818
'None of you shall approach any **b** **Lv 18:6** 7607
she is your father's **b** relative. **Lv 18:12** 7607
she is your mother's **b** relative. **Lv 18:13** 7607
they are **b** relatives. **Lv 18:17** 7607
shall not eat *anything* with the **b**, **Lv 19:26** 1818
she has exposed the flow of her **b**; **Lv 20:18** 1818
one has made naked his **b** relative; **Lv 20:19** 7607
or one of his **b** relatives from his **Lv 25:49** 7607
You shall sprinkle their **b** on the **Nu 18:17** 1818
some of its **b** with his finger and **Nu 19:4** 1818
and sprinkle some of its **b** toward **Nu 19:4** 1818
its hide and its flesh and its **b**, **Nu 19:5** 1818
And drinks the **b** of the slain." **Nu 23:24** 1818
'The **b** avenger himself shall put **Nu 35:19** 1818
the **b** avenger shall put the **Nu 35:21** 1818
between the slayer and the **b** avenger **Nu 35:24** 1818
from the hand of the **b** avenger, **Nu 35:25** 1818
and the **b** avenger finds him **Nu 35:27** 1818
the **b** avenger kills the manslayer, **Nu 35:27** 1818
he will not be guilty of **b** **Nu 35:27** 1818
for **b** pollutes the land and no **Nu 35:33** 1818
land for the **b** that is shed on it, **Nu 35:33** 1818
by the **b** of him who shed it. **Nu 35:33** 1818
"Only you shall not eat the **b**; **Dt 12:16** 1818
"Only be sure not to eat the **b**, **Dt 12:23** 1818
the blood, for the **b** is the life, **Dt 12:23** 1818
offerings, the flesh and the **b**, **Dt 12:27** 1818
and the **b** of your sacrifices shall **Dt 12:27** 1818
"Only you shall not eat its **b**; **Dt 15:23** 1818
otherwise the avenger of **b** might pursue **Dt 19:6** 1818
"So innocent **b** will not be shed **Dt 19:10** 1818

into the hand of the avenger of **b**, **Dt 19:12** 1818
the **b** of the innocent from Israel, **Dt 19:13** 1818
'Our hands did not shed this **b**, **Dt 21:7** 1818
do not place the guilt of innocent **b** **Dt 21:8** 1818
of innocent **b** from your midst, **Dt 21:9** 1818
of the **b** of grapes you drank wine. **Dt 32:14** 1818
will make My arrows drunk with **b**, **Dt 32:42** 1818
b of the slain and the captives, **Dt 32:42** 1818
will avenge the **b** of His servants, **Dt 32:43** 1818
his **b** *shall be* on his own head, **Jos 2:19** 1818
house, his **b** *shall be* on our head if **Jos 2:19** 1818
your refuge from the avenger of **b**. **Jos 20:3** 1818
if the avenger of **b** pursues him, **Jos 20:5** 1818
die by the hand of the avenger of **b** **Jos 20:9** 1818
and their **b** might be laid on **Jg 9:24** 1818
the people ate *them* with the **b**. **1Sa 14:32** 1818
the LORD by eating with the **b**." **1Sa 14:33** 1818
the LORD by eating with the **b**.' " **1Sa 14:34** 1818
will you sin against innocent **b** by **1Sa 19:5** 1818
restrained you from shedding **b**, **1Sa 25:26** 1818
both by having shed **b** without **1Sa 25:31** 1818
do not let my **b** fall to the ground **1Sa 26:20** 1818
"Your **b** is on your head, for your **2Sa 1:16** 1818
"From the **b** of the slain, from **2Sa 1:22** 1818
of the **b** of Asahel his brother. **2Sa 3:27** 1818
of the **b** of Abner the son of Ner. **2Sa 3:28** 1818
now require his **b** from your hand and **2Sa 4:11** 1818
of **b** will not continue to destroy, **2Sa 14:11** 1818
b in the middle of the highway. **2Sa 20:12** 1818
Shall I drink the **b** of the men who **2Sa 23:17** 1818
also shed the **b** of war in peace. **1Ki 2:5** 1818
And he put the **b** of war on his **1Ki 2:5** 1818
gray hair down to Sheol with **b**." **1Ki 2:9** 1818
b which Joab shed without cause. **1Ki 2:31** 1818
will return his **b** on his own head, **1Ki 2:32** 1818
"So shall their **b** return on the **1Ki 2:33** 1818
b shall be on your own head." **1Ki 2:37** 1818
until the **b** gushed out on them. **1Ki 18:28** 1818
the dogs licked up the **b** of Naboth **1Ki 21:19** 1818
the dogs will lick up your **b**, **1Ki 21:19** 1818
and the **b** from the wound ran into **1Ki 22:35** 1818
and the dogs licked up his **b** **1Ki 22:38** 1818
water opposite *them* as red as **b**. **2Ki 3:22** 1818
Then they said, "This is **b**; **2Ki 3:23** 1818
the **b** of My servants the prophets, **2Ki 9:7** 1818
and the **b** of all the servants of **2Ki 9:7** 1818
I have seen yesterday the **b** of Naboth **2Ki 9:26** 1818
of Naboth and the **b** of his sons,' **2Ki 9:26** 1818
and some of her **b** was sprinkled on **2Ki 9:33** 1818
sprinkled the **b** of his peace offerings on **2Ki 16:13** 1818
and sprinkle on it all the **b** of **2Ki 16:15** 1818
and all the **b** of the sacrifice. **2Ki 16:15** 1818
Manasseh shed very much innocent **b** **2Ki 21:16** 1818
for the innocent **b** which he shed, **2Ki 24:4** 1818
filled Jerusalem with innocent **b**; **2Ki 24:4** 1818
Shall I drink the **b** of these men **1Ch 11:19** 1818
'You have shed much **b** and **1Ch 22:8** 1818
so much **b** on the earth before Me. **1Ch 22:8** 1818
are a man of war and have shed **b**.' **1Ch 28:3** 1818
their cities, between **b** and blood, **2Ch 19:10** 1818
their cities, between blood and **b**, **2Ch 19:10** 1818
the **b** of the son of Jehoiada the priest, **2Ch 24:25** 1818
b and sprinkled it on the altar. **2Ch 29:22** 1818
and sprinkled the **b** on the altar; **2Ch 29:22** 1818
and sprinkled the **b** on the altar. **2Ch 29:22** 1818
their **b** to atone for all Israel, **2Ch 29:24** 1818
the priests sprinkled the **b** *which* **2Ch 30:16** 1818
the **b** *received* from their hand, **2Ch 35:11** 1818
"O earth, do not cover my **b**, **Jb 16:18** 1818
"His young ones also suck up **b**; **Jb 39:30** 1818
He who requires **b** remembers them; **Ps 9:12** 1818
not pour out their drink offerings of **b**, **Ps 16:4** 1818
"What profit is there in my **b**, **Ps 30:9** 1818
Or drink the **b** of male goats? **Ps 50:13** 1818
his feet in the **b** of the wicked. **Ps 58:10** 1818
your foot may shatter *them* in **b**, **Ps 68:23** 1818
b will be precious in his sight; **Ps 72:14** 1818
And turned their rivers to **b**, **Ps 78:44** 1818
They have poured out their **b** like **Ps 79:3** 1818
for the **b** of Your servants which **Ps 79:10** 1818
He turned their waters into **b** And **Ps 105:29** 1818
And shed innocent **b**, **Ps 106:38** 1818
The **b** of their sons and their **Ps 106:38** 1818
the land was polluted with the **b**. **Ps 106:38** 1818
with us, Let us lie in wait for **b**, **Pr 1:11** 1818
evil And they hasten to shed **b**. **Pr 1:16** 1818
they lie in wait for their own **b**; **Pr 1:18** 1818
And hands that shed innocent **b**, **Pr 6:17** 1818
of the wicked lie in wait for **b**, **Pr 12:6** 1818
laden with the guilt of human **b** **Pr 28:17** 1818
pressing the nose brings forth **b**; **Pr 30:33** 1818
no pleasure in the **b** of bulls, **Is 1:11** 1818
Your hands are covered with **b**. **Is 1:15** 1818
tumult, And cloak rolled in **b**, **Is 9:5** 1818
the waters of Dimon are full of **b**; **Is 15:9** 1818
will be drenched with their **b**. **Is 34:3** 1818
of the LORD is filled with **b**, **Is 34:6** 1818
with the **b** of lambs and goats, **Is 34:6** 1818
their land will be soaked with **b**, **Is 34:7** 1818
their own **b** as with sweet wine; **Is 49:26** 1818
For your hands are defiled with **b** And **Is 59:3** 1818
they hasten to shed innocent **b**; **Is 59:7** 1818
is like one who offers swine's **b**; **Is 66:3** 1818
not shed innocent **b** in this place, **Jer 7:6** 1818
place with the **b** of the innocent **Jer 19:4** 1818
not shed innocent **b** in this place. **Jer 22:3** 1818
And on shedding innocent **b** And on **Jer 22:17** 1818
bring innocent **b** on yourselves, **Jer 26:15** 1818
And drink its fill of their **b**; **Jer 46:10** 1818
who restrains his sword from **b**. **Jer 48:10** 1818
"May my **b** be upon the inhabitants **Jer 51:35** 1818
her midst The **b** of the righteous; **La 4:13** 1818
They were defiled with **b** So that **La 4:14** 1818
his **b** I will require at your hand. **Ezk 3:18** 1818
his **b** I will require at your hand. **Ezk 3:20** 1818
and the land is filled with **b** and **Ezk 9:9** 1818
and pour out My wrath in **b** on it to **Ezk 14:19** 1818
and saw you squirming in your **b**, **Ezk 16:6** 1818
to you *while you were* in your **b**, **Ezk 16:6** 1818
to you *while you were* in your **b**, **Ezk 16:6** 1818
water, washed off your **b** from you and **Ezk 16:9** 1818
and bare and squirming in your **b**. **Ezk 16:22** 1818
and because of the **b** of your sons **Ezk 16:36** 1818
adultery or shed **b** are judged; **Ezk 16:38** 1818
you the **b** of wrath and jealousy. **Ezk 16:38** 1818
have a violent son who sheds **b** and **Ezk 18:10** 1818
his **b** will be on his own head. **Ezk 18:13** 1818
your **b** will be in the midst of the **Ezk 21:32** 1818
"A city shedding **b** in her midst, **Ezk 22:3** 1818
by the **b** which you have shed, **Ezk 22:4** 1818
you for the purpose of shedding **b**. **Ezk 22:6** 1818
you for the purpose of shedding **b**, **Ezk 22:9** 1818
they have taken bribes to shed **b**; **Ezk 22:12** 1818
by shedding **b** *and* destroying lives **Ezk 22:27** 1818
adultery, and **b** is on their hands. **Ezk 23:37** 1818
the judgment of women who shed **b**, **Ezk 23:45** 1818
and **b** is on their hands. **Ezk 23:45** 1818
"For her **b** is in her midst; **Ezk 24:7** 1818
I have put her **b** on the bare rock, **Ezk 24:8** 1818
to her And **b** to her streets, **Ezk 28:23** 1818
drink the discharge of your **b** As **Ezk 32:6** 1818
his **b** will be on his *own* head. **Ezk 33:4** 1818
his **b** will be on himself. **Ezk 33:5** 1818
but his **b** I will require from the **Ezk 33:6** 1818
b I will require from your hand. **Ezk 33:8** 1818
"You eat *meat* with the **b** *in it,* **Ezk 33:25** 1818
eyes to your idols as you shed **b**. **Ezk 33:25** 1818
the **b** which they had shed on the land, **Ezk 36:18** 1818
"With pestilence and with **b** I **Ezk 38:22** 1818
you may eat flesh and drink **b**. **Ezk 39:17** 1818
the **b** of the princes of the earth, **Ezk 39:18** 1818
and drink **b** until you are drunk, **Ezk 39:19** 1818
on it and to sprinkle **b** on it. **Ezk 43:18** 1818
'You shall take some of its **b** and **Ezk 43:20** 1818
My food, the fat and the **b**; **Ezk 44:7** 1818
to offer Me the fat and the **b**," **Ezk 44:15** 1818
The priest shall take some of the **b** **Ezk 45:19** 1818
in the sky and on the earth, **B**, **Jl 2:30** 1818
darkness And the moon into **b** **Jl 2:31** 1818
land they have shed innocent **b**. **Jl 3:19** 1818
their **b** which I have not avenged, **Jl 3:21** 1818
and do not put innocent **b** on us; **Jon 1:14** 1818
b will be poured out like dust And **Zph 1:17** 1818
remove their **b** from their mouth And **Zch 9:7** 1818
of the **b** of *My* covenant with you, **Zch 9:11** 1818
and **b** did not reveal *this* to you, **Mt 16:17** *129*
shedding the **b** of the prophets.' **Mt 23:30** *129*
all the righteous **b** shed on earth, **Mt 23:35** *129*
from the **b** of righteous Abel to **Mt 23:35** *129*
Abel to the **b** of Zechariah, **Mt 23:35** *129*
for this is My **b** of the covenant, **Mt 26:28** *129*
sinned by betraying innocent **b**." **Mt 27:4** *129*
since it is the price of **b**." **Mt 27:6** *129*
called the Field of **B** to this day. **Mt 27:8** *129*
"I am innocent of this Man's **b**; **Mt 27:24** *129*
b shall be on us and on our children!" **Mt 27:25** *129*
the flow of her **b** was dried up; **Mk 5:29** *129*
"This is My **b** of the covenant, **Mk 14:24** *129*
that the **b** of all the prophets, **Lk 11:50** *129*
from the **b** of Abel to the blood of **Lk 11:51** *129*
of Abel to the **b** of Zechariah, **Lk 11:51** *129*
whose **b** Pilate had mixed with **Lk 13:1** *129*
you is the new covenant in My **b**. **Lk 22:20** *129*
His sweat became like drops of **b**, **Lk 22:44** *129*
who were born, not of **b** **Jn 1:13** *129*
of the Son of Man and drink His **b**, **Jn 6:53** *129*
and drinks My **b** has eternal life, **Jn 6:54** *129*
true food, and My **b** is true drink. **Jn 6:55** *129*
and drinks My **b** abides in Me, **Jn 6:56** *129*
b and water came out. **Jn 19:34** *129*
Hakeldama, that is, Field of **B**.) **Ac 1:19** *129*
SIGNS ON THE EARTH BELOW, **B**, **Ac 2:19** *129*
DARKNESS AND THE MOON INTO **B**, **Ac 2:20** *129*
to bring this man's **b** upon us." **Ac 5:28** *129*
from what is strangled and from **b**. **Ac 15:20** *129*
from **b** and from things strangled **Ac 15:29** *129*
"Your **b** *be* on your own heads! **Ac 18:6** *129*
I am innocent of the **b** of all men. **Ac 20:26** *129*
which He purchased with His own **b**. **Ac 20:28** *129*
from **b** and from what is strangled **Ac 21:25** *129*
'And when the **b** of Your witness **Ac 22:20** *129*
"THEIR FEET ARE SWIFT TO SHED **B**, **Ro 3:15** *129*
propitiation in His **b** through faith. **Ro 3:25** *129*
now been justified by His **b**, **Ro 5:9** *129*
a sharing in the **b** of Christ? **1Co 10:16** *129*
cup is the new covenant in My **b**; **1Co 11:25** *129*
of the body and the **b** of the Lord. **1Co 11:27** *129*
that flesh and **b** cannot inherit **1Co 15:50** *129*
consult with flesh and **b**, **Ga 1:16** *129*
we have redemption through His **b**, **Eph 1:7** *129*
brought near by the **b** of Christ. **Eph 2:13** *129*
is not against flesh and **b**, **Eph 6:12** *129*
peace through the **b** of His cross; **Col 1:20** *129*
the children share in flesh and **b**, **Heb 2:14** *129*
once a year, not without *taking* **b**, **Heb 9:7** *129*
through the **b** of goats and calves, **Heb 9:12** *129*
and calves, but through His own **b**, **Heb 9:12** *129*
For if the **b** of goats and bulls **Heb 9:13** *129*
much more will the **b** of Christ, **Heb 9:14** *129*
was not inaugurated without **b**. **Heb 9:18** *129*
the **b** of the calves and the goats, **Heb 9:19** *129*
"THIS IS THE **B** OF THE COVENANT **Heb 9:20** *129*
of the ministry with the **b**. **Heb 9:21** *129*
all things are cleansed with **b**, **Heb 9:22** *129*
without shedding of **b** there is no **Heb 9:22** *130*
year by year with **b** that is not his **Heb 9:25** *129*
For it is impossible for the **b** of **Heb 10:4** *129*
the holy place by the **b** of Jesus, **Heb 10:19** *129*
has regarded as unclean the **b** **Heb 10:29** *129*
and the sprinkling of the **b**, **Heb 11:28** *129*
b in your striving against sin; **Heb 12:4** *129*
covenant, and to the sprinkled **b**, **Heb 12:24** *129*
which speaks better than *the* **b** of **Heb 12:24**
of those animals whose **b** is brought **Heb 13:11** *129*
the people through His own **b**, **Heb 13:12** *129*
the **b** of the eternal covenant, **Heb 13:20** *129*
and be sprinkled with His **b**: **1Pe 1:2** *129*
but with precious **b**, as of a lamb **1Pe 1:19** *129*
and spotless, *the* **b** of Christ. **1Pe 1:19**
and the **b** of Jesus His Son **1Jn 1:7** *129*
the One who came by water and **b**, **1Jn 5:6** *129*
but with the water and with the **b**. **1Jn 5:6** *129*
Spirit and the water and the **b**; **1Jn 5:8** *129*
us from our sins by His **b** **Rv 1:5** *129*
purchased for God with Your **b** *men* **Rv 5:9** *129*
avenging our **b** on those who dwell **Rv 6:10** *129*
and the whole moon became like **b**; **Rv 6:12** *129*
them white in the **b** of the Lamb. **Rv 7:14** *129*
came hail and fire, mixed with **b**, **Rv 8:7** *129*
and a third of the sea became **b**, **Rv 8:8** *129*
the waters to turn them into **b**, **Rv 11:6** *129*
they overcame him because of the **b** **Rv 12:11** *129*
b came out from the wine press, **Rv 14:20** *129*
became **b** like *that* of a dead man; **Rv 16:3** *129*
and they became **b**. **Rv 16:4** *129*
out the **b** of saints and prophets, **Rv 16:6** *129*
You have given them **b** to drink. **Rv 16:6** *129*
drunk with the **b** of the saints, **Rv 17:6** *129*
the **b** of the witnesses of Jesus. **Rv 17:6** *129*
in her was found the **b** of prophets **Rv 18:24** *129*
B OF HIS BOND-SERVANTS ON HER." **Rv 19:2** *129*
clothed with a robe dipped in **b**, **Rv 19:13** *129*

BLOODGUILT

that you will not bring **b** on your **Dt 22:8** 1818
his Lord will leave his **b** on him And **Hos 12:14** 1818

BLOODGUILTINESS

there will be no **b** on his account. **Ex 22:2** 1818
there will be **b** on his account. **Ex 22:3** 1818
b is to be reckoned to that man. **Lv 17:4** 1818
or his mother, his **b** is upon him. **Lv 20:9** 1818
to death, their **b** is upon them. **Lv 20:11** 1818
incest, their **b** is upon them. **Lv 20:12** 1818
Their **b** is upon them. **Lv 20:13** 1818
Their **b** is upon them. **Lv 20:16** 1818
stones, their **b** is upon them.' " **Lv 20:27** 1818
an inheritance, and **b** be on you. **Dt 19:10** 1818
And the **b** shall be forgiven them. **Dt 21:8** 1818
Deliver me from **b**, O God, the God **Ps 51:14** 1818

BLOODSHED

who have kept me this day from **b** and **1Sa 25:33** 1818
"Get out, get out, you man of **b**, **2Sa 16:7** 1818
all the **b** of the house of Saul, **2Sa 16:8** 1818
evil, for you are a man of **b**!" **2Sa 16:8** 1818
abhors the man of **b** and deceit. **Ps 5:6** 1818
Nor my life with men of **b**, **Ps 26:9** 1818
Men of **b** and deceit will not live **Ps 55:23** 1818
And save me from men of **b**. **Ps 59:2** 1818
from me, therefore, men of **b**. **Ps 139:19** 1818
Men of **b** hate the blameless, But **Pr 29:10** 1818
the **b** of Jerusalem from her midst, **Is 4:4** 1818
looked for justice, but behold, **b**; **Is 5:7** 4939
And the earth will reveal her **b** And **Is 26:21** 1818
his ears from hearing about **b** And **Is 33:15** 1818
and **b** also will pass through you, **Ezk 5:17** 1818
and at the **b** which is among you. **Ezk 22:13** 1818
"I will give you over to **b**, **Ezk 35:6** 1818
bloodshed, and **b** will pursue you; **Ezk 35:6** 1818
since you have not hated **b**, **Ezk 35:6** 1818
therefore **b** will pursue you. **Ezk 35:6** 1818
of Jehu for the **b** of Jezreel, **Hos 1:4** 1818
so that **b** follows bloodshed. **Hos 4:2** 1818
so that bloodshed follows **b**. **Hos 4:2** 1818
Who build Zion with **b** And **Mi 3:10** 1818
All of them lie in wait for **b**; **Mi 7:2** 1818
b and violence done to the land, **Hab 2:8** 1818
"Woe to him who builds a city with **b** **Hab 2:12** 1818
b and violence done to the land, **Hab 2:17** 1818

BLOODY

"It is for Saul and his **b** house, **2Sa 21:1** 1818
for the land is full of **b** crimes and **Ezk 7:23** 1818
will you judge the **b** city? **Ezk 22:2** 1818
"Woe to the **b** city, To the pot in **Ezk 24:6** 1818
"Woe to the **b** city! **Ezk 24:9** 1818
Tracked with **b** *footprints.* **Hos 6:8** 1818
Woe to the **b** city, completely full **Na 3:1** 1818

BLOOMED

budded *Or* the pomegranates had **b**. **SS 6:11** 5340b
whether the pomegranates have **b**. **SS 7:12** 5340b

BLOSSOM

the brim of a cup, *as* a lily **b**; **1Ki 7:26** 6525
the brim of a cup, *like* a lily **b**; **2Ch 4:5** 6525
And the vines in **b** have given **SS 2:13** 5563
While our vineyards are in **b**." **SS 2:15** 5563
rot and their **b** blow away as dust; **Is 5:24** 6525
morning you bring your seed to **b**; **Is 17:11** 6524a
root, Israel will **b** and sprout, **Is 27:6** 6692a

Context	Reference	Number
And the Arabah will rejoice and **b**;	Is 35:1	6524a
It will **b** profusely And rejoice	Is 35:2	6524a
He will **b** like the lily, And he	Hos 14:5	6524a
And they will **b** like the vine.	Hos 14:7	6524a
Though the fig tree should not **b** And	Hab 3:17	6524a

BLOSSOMED

Context	Reference	Number
rod has budded, arrogance has **b**.	Ezk 7:10	6524a

BLOSSOMS

Context	Reference	Number
as it was budding, its **b** came out,	Gn 40:10	5322a
shall be shaped like almond **b**	Ex 25:33	
and three cups shaped like almond **b**	Ex 25:33	
four cups shaped like almond **b**,	Ex 25:34	
three cups shaped like almond **b**,	Ex 37:19	
and three cups shaped like almond **b**,	Ex 37:19	
four cups shaped like almond **b**,	Ex 37:20	
and put forth buds and produced **b**,	Nu 17:8	6692a
the almond tree **b**, the	Ec 12:5	5340b
b In the vineyards of Engedi."	SS 1:14	
trees To see the **b** of the valley,	SS 6:11	3
has budded *And its* **b** have opened,	SS 7:12	5563
as soon as the bud **b** And the	Is 18:5	8552
The **b** of Lebanon wither.	Na 1:4	6525

BLOT

Context	Reference	Number
"I will **b** out man whom I have	Gn 6:7	4229a
and I will **b** out from the face of	Gn 7:4	4229a
that I will utterly **b** out the	Ex 17:14	4229a
please **b** me out from Your book	Ex 32:32	4229a
Me, I will **b** him out of My book.	Ex 32:33	4229a
that I may destroy them and **b** out	Dt 9:14	4229a
you shall **b** out the memory of	Dt 25:19	4229a
and the LORD will **b** out his name	Dt 29:20	4229a
even to **b** *it* out and destroy *it*	1Ki 13:34	3582
He would **b** out the name of Israel	2Ki 14:27	4229a
and do not **b** out my loyal deeds	Ne 13:14	4229a
b out my transgressions.	Ps 51:1	4229a
sins And **b** out all my iniquities.	Ps 51:9	4229a
Or **b** out their sin from Your sight.	Jer 18:23	4229a

BLOTTED

Context	Reference	Number
Thus He **b** out every living thing	Gn 7:23	4229a
they were **b** out from the earth;	Gn 7:23	4229a
name will not be **b** out from Israel.	Dt 25:6	4229a
will not be **b** out from Israel.	Jg 21:17	4229a
their sin be **b** out before You,	Ne 4:5	4229a
You have **b** out their name forever	Ps 9:5	4229a
they be **b** out of the book of life And	Ps 69:28	4229a
let their name be **b** out.	Ps 109:13	4229a
the sin of his mother be **b** out.	Ps 109:14	4229a
his reproach will not be **b** out.	Pr 6:33	4229a
down, and your works may be **b** out.	Ezk 6:6	4229a

BLOW

Context	Reference	Number
"But when you **b** an alarm, the	Nu 10:5	8628
you **b** an alarm the second time,	Nu 10:6	8628
shall **b** without sounding an alarm.	Nu 10:7	8628
moreover, shall **b** the trumpets;	Nu 10:8	8628
you shall **b** the trumpets over your	Nu 10:10	8628
the priests shall **b** the trumpets.	Jos 6:4	8628
they continued to **b** the trumpets.	Jos 6:9	8628
they continued to **b** the trumpets.	Jos 6:13	8628
all who are with me **b** the trumpet,	Jg 7:18	8628
then you also **b** the trumpets all	Jg 7:18	8628
Israel, and **b** the trumpet and say,	1Ki 1:34	8628
the east wind to **b** in the heavens And	Ps 78:26	5265
B the trumpet at the new moon, At	Ps 81:3	8628
wind to **b** and the waters to flow.	Ps 147:18	5380
and their blossom **b** away as dust;	Is 5:24	5927
every **b** of the rod of punishment,	Is 30:32	4569a
"**B** the trumpet in the land;	Jer 4:5	8628
Now **b** a trumpet in Tekoa And	Jer 6:1	8628
The bellows **b** fiercely, The lead	Jer 6:29	2787
has been crushed with a mighty **b**,	Jer 14:17	4347
B a trumpet among the nations!	Jer 51:27	8628
I will **b** on you with the fire of	Ezk 21:31	6315
to **b** fire on it in order to melt *it*,	Ezk 22:20	5301
'I will gather you and **b** on	Ezk 22:21	5301
the desire of your eyes with a **b**;	Ezk 24:16	4046
"The **b** of his battering rams	Ezk 26:9	4239
coming and does not **b** the trumpet and	Ezk 33:6	8628
B the horn in Gibeah, The trumpet	Hos 5:8	8628
B a trumpet in Zion, And sound an	Jl 2:1	8628
B a trumpet in Zion, Consecrate a	Jl 2:15	8628
you bring *it* home, I **b** it *away*.	Hg 1:9	5301
the Lord GOD will **b** the trumpet,	Zch 9:14	8628
so that no wind would **b** on the	Rv 7:1	*4154*

BLOWING

Context	Reference	Number
rest, a reminder by **b** *of trumpets*,	Lv 23:24	8643
be to you a day for **b** trumpets.	Nu 29:1	8643
in their right hands for **b**,	Jg 7:20	8628
the fire a sound of a gentle **b**.	1Ki 19:12	1851
and twenty priests **b** trumpets	2Ch 5:12	2690
B toward the south, Then turning	Ec 1:6	1980
"And when *you see* a south wind **b**,	Lk 12:55	*4154*
up because a strong wind was **b**.	Jn 6:18	*4154*

BLOWN

Context	Reference	Number
"When both are **b**,	Nu 10:3	8628
"Yet if *only* one is **b**,	Nu 10:4	8628
is to be **b** for them to set out.	Nu 10:6	8628
And as soon as the trumpet is **b**,	Is 18:3	8628
that a great trumpet will be **b**,	Is 27:13	8628
'They have **b** the trumpet and made	Ezk 7:14	8628
b away from the threshing floor And	Hos 13:3	5590
If a trumpet is **b** in a city will	Am 3:6	8628

BLOWS

Context	Reference	Number
Than a hundred **b** into a fool.	Pr 17:10	5221
strife, And his mouth calls for **b**.	Pr 18:6	4112
And **b** for the back of fools.	Pr 19:29	4112
ones like the chaff which **b** away;	Is 29:5	5674a
the breath of the LORD **b** upon it;	Is 40:7	5380
earth, But He merely **b** on them,	Is 40:24	5398
the smith who **b** the fire of coals And	Is 54:16	5301
and **b** on the trumpet and warns	Ezk 33:3	8628
"The wind **b** where it wishes and	Jn 3:8	*4154*
had struck them with many **b**,	Ac 16:23	*4127*

BLUE

Context	Reference	Number
b, purple and scarlet *material*,	Ex 25:4	8504
curtains of fine twisted linen and **b**	Ex 26:1	8504
"You shall make loops of **b** on	Ex 26:4	8504
"You shall make a veil of **b**	Ex 26:31	8504
screen for the doorway of the tent of **b**	Ex 26:36	8504
of **b** and purple and scarlet	Ex 27:16	8504
They shall take the gold and the **b**	Ex 28:5	8504
of **b** and purple *and* scarlet	Ex 28:6	8504
of **b** and purple and scarlet	Ex 28:8	8504
of **b** and purple and scarlet	Ex 28:15	8504
rings of the ephod with a **b** cord,	Ex 28:28	8504
the robe of the ephod all of **b**.	Ex 28:31	8504
make on its hem pomegranates of **b**	Ex 28:33	8504
"You shall fasten it on a **b** cord,	Ex 28:37	8504
and **b**, purple and scarlet	Ex 35:6	8504
who had in his possession **b** and	Ex 35:23	8504
in **b** and purple *and* scarlet	Ex 35:25	8504
in **b** and in purple *and* in scarlet	Ex 35:35	8504
of fine twisted linen and **b** and	Ex 36:8	8504
He made loops of **b** on the edge	Ex 36:11	8504
he made the veil of **b** and purple	Ex 36:35	8504
of **b** and purple and scarlet	Ex 36:37	8504
of **b** and purple and scarlet	Ex 38:18	8504
a skillful workman and a weaver in **b**	Ex 38:23	8504
from the **b** and purple and scarlet	Ex 39:1	8504
and of **b** and purple and scarlet	Ex 39:2	8504
into threads to be woven in *with* the **b**	Ex 39:3	8504
of gold *and* of **b** and purple and	Ex 39:5	8504
of gold *and* of **b** and purple and	Ex 39:8	8504
rings of the ephod with a **b** cord,	Ex 39:21	8504
the ephod of woven work, all of **b**;	Ex 39:22	8504
They made pomegranates of **b**	Ex 39:24	8504
and **b** and purple and scarlet	Ex 39:29	8504
They fastened a **b** cord to it,	Ex 39:31	8504
spread over *it* a cloth of pure **b**,	Nu 4:6	8504
they shall also spread a cloth of **b**	Nu 4:7	8504
"Then they shall take a **b** cloth	Nu 4:9	8504
golden altar they shall spread a **b** cloth	Nu 4:11	8504
and put them in a **b** cloth and	Nu 4:12	8504
tassel of each corner a cord of **b**.	Nu 15:38	8504
in royal robes of **b** and white,	Es 8:15	8504
Your awning was **b** and purple from	Ezk 27:7	8504
clothes of **b** and embroidered work,	Ezk 27:24	8504

BLUSH

Context	Reference	Number
They did not even know how to **b**.	Jer 6:15	3637
And they did not know how to **b**;	Jer 8:12	3637

BOANERGES

Context	Reference	Number
James (to them He gave the name **B**,	Mk 3:17	*993*

BOAR

Context	Reference	Number
A **b** from the forest eats it away And	Ps 80:13	2386

BOARD

Context	Reference	Number
shall be the length of each **b** and	Ex 26:16	7175b
a half cubits the width of each **b**.	Ex 26:16	7175b
shall be two tenons for each **b**,	Ex 26:17	7175b
two sockets under one **b** for its	Ex 26:19	7175b
another **b** for its two tenons;	Ex 26:19	7175b
two sockets under one **b** and two	Ex 26:21	7175b
and two sockets under another **b**.	Ex 26:21	7175b
two sockets under one **b** and two	Ex 26:25	7175b
and two sockets under another **b**.	Ex 26:25	7175b
cubits *was* the length of each **b**	Ex 36:21	7175b
a half cubits the width of each **b**.	Ex 36:21	7175b
There were two tenons for each **b**,	Ex 36:22	7175b
two sockets under one **b** for its	Ex 36:24	7175b
another **b** for its two tenons.	Ex 36:24	7175b
two sockets under one **b** and two	Ex 36:26	7175b
and two sockets under another **b**.	Ex 36:26	7175b
sockets, two under every **b**.	Ex 36:30	7175b
from there to take Paul on **b**;	Ac 20:13	*353*
him on **b** and came to Mitylene.	Ac 20:14	*353*
Then we went on **b** the ship, and	Ac 21:6	*1684*

BOARDS

Context	Reference	Number
shall make the **b** for the tabernacle	Ex 26:15	7175b
for all the **b** of the tabernacle.	Ex 26:17	7175b
make the **b** for the tabernacle:	Ex 26:18	7175b
twenty **b** for the south side.	Ex 26:18	7175b
of silver under the twenty **b**,	Ex 26:19	7175b
on the north side, twenty **b**,	Ex 26:20	7175b
to the west, you shall make six **b**.	Ex 26:22	7175b
You shall make two **b** for the corners	Ex 26:23	7175b
b with their sockets of silver,	Ex 26:25	7175b
b of one side of the tabernacle,	Ex 26:26	7175b
and five bars for the **b** of the	Ex 26:27	7175b
and five bars for the **b** of the	Ex 26:27	7175b
The middle bar in the center of the **b**	Ex 26:28	7175b
"You shall overlay the **b** with	Ex 26:29	7175b
its covering, its hooks and its **b**,	Ex 35:11	7175b
he made the **b** for the tabernacle	Ex 36:20	7175b
for all the **b** of the tabernacle.	Ex 36:22	7175b
He made the **b** for the tabernacle:	Ex 36:23	7175b
twenty **b** for the south side;	Ex 36:23	7175b
of silver under the twenty **b**;	Ex 36:24	7175b
the north side, he made twenty **b**,	Ex 36:25	7175b
to the west, he made six **b**.	Ex 36:27	7175b
He made two **b** for the corners	Ex 36:28	7175b
b with their sockets of silver,	Ex 36:30	7175b
b of one side of the tabernacle,	Ex 36:31	7175b
and five bars for the **b** of the	Ex 36:32	7175b
and five bars for the **b** of the	Ex 36:32	7175b
center of the **b** from end to end.	Ex 36:33	7175b
He overlaid the **b** with gold	Ex 36:34	7175b
its clasps, its **b**, its bars, and	Ex 39:33	7175b
its sockets, and set up its **b**,	Ex 40:18	7175b
the **b** of the tabernacle and its	Nu 4:31	7175b
on the inside with **b** of cedar;	1Ki 6:15	6763
of the house with **b** of cypress.	1Ki 6:15	6763
rear part of the house with **b** of cedar	1Ki 6:16	6763

BOAST

Context	Reference	Number
of this curse, that he will **b**,	Dt 29:19	1288
"**B** no more so very proudly, Do	1Sa 2:3	1696, 7235a
b like him who takes *it* off.'"	1Ki 20:11	1984b
Some **b** in chariots and some in	Ps 20:7	
we will **b** in the name of the LORD,	Ps 20:7	2142
soul will make its **b** in the LORD;	Ps 34:2	1984b
And **b** in the abundance of their	Ps 49:6	1984b
Why do you **b** in evil, O mighty man?	Ps 52:1	1984b
'Do not **b**,' And to the wicked,	Ps 75:4	1984b
images, Who **b** themselves of idols;	Ps 97:7	1984b
Do not **b** about tomorrow, For you	Pr 27:1	1984b
Is the axe to **b** itself over the	Is 10:15	6286
Cush their hope and Egypt their **b**.	Is 20:5	8597
And in their riches you will **b**.	Is 61:6	3235
not a wise man **b** of his wisdom,	Jer 9:23	1984b
not the mighty man **b** of his might,	Jer 9:23	1984b
not a rich man **b** of his riches;	Jer 9:23	1984b
but let him who boasts **b** of this,	Jer 9:24	1984b
do not **b** In the day of *their* distress.	Ob 1:12	1431, 6310
rely upon the Law and **b** in God,	Ro 2:17	*2744*
You who **b** in the Law, through your	Ro 2:23	*2744*
he has something to **b** about,	Ro 4:2	*2745*
that no man may **b** before God.	1Co 1:29	*2744*
HIM WHO BOASTS, **B** IN THE LORD."	1Co 1:31	*2744*
So then let no one **b** in men.	1Co 3:21	*2744*
b as if you had not received it?	1Co 4:7	*2744*
any man make my **b** an empty one.	1Co 9:15	*2745*
gospel, I have nothing to **b** of,	1Co 9:16	*2745*
I **b** about you to the Macedonians,	2Co 9:2	*2744*
For even if I **b** somewhat	2Co 10:8	*2744*
we will not **b** beyond *our* measure,	2Co 10:13	*2744*
and not to **b** in what has been	2Co 10:16	*2744*
But HE WHO BOASTS IS TO **B** IN	2Co 10:17	*2744*
that I also may **b** a little.	2Co 11:16	*2744*
many **b** according to the flesh,	2Co 11:18	*2744*
to the flesh, I will **b** also.	2Co 11:18	*2744*
If I have to **b**, I will boast of	2Co 11:30	*2744*
I will **b** of what pertains to my	2Co 11:30	*2744*
On behalf of such a man I will **b**;	2Co 12:5	*2744*
but on my own behalf I will not **b**,	2Co 12:5	*2744*
wish to **b** I will not be foolish,	2Co 12:6	*2744*
will rather **b** about my weaknesses,	2Co 12:9	*2744*
that they may **b** in your flesh.	Ga 6:13	*2744*
may it never be that I would **b**,	Ga 6:14	*2744*
of works, so that no one may **b**.	Eph 2:9	*2744*
our confidence and the **b** of our hope	Heb 3:6	*2745*
as it is, you **b** in your arrogance;	Jas 4:16	*2744*

BOASTED

Context	Reference	Number
In God we have **b** all day long, And	Ps 44:8	1984b
I have **b** to him about you,	2Co 7:14	*2744*

BOASTERS

Context	Reference	Number
Causing the omens of **b** to fail,	Is 44:25	907

BOASTFUL

Context	Reference	Number
their hands, for Israel would become **b**,	Jg 7:2	6286
The **b** shall not stand before Your	Ps 5:5	1984b
"I said to the **b**,	Ps 75:4	1984b
"How **b** you are about the valleys!	Jer 49:4	1984b
b words which the horn was speaking	Da 7:11	7229
of God, insolent, arrogant, **b**,	Ro 1:30	*213*
Let us not become **b**,	Ga 5:26	*2755*
lovers of money, **b**, arrogant,	2Tm 3:2	*213*
the eyes and the **b** pride of life,	1Jn 2:16	*212*

BOASTING

Context	Reference	Number
"Where is your **b** now with which you	Jg 9:38	6310
your heart has become proud in **b**.	2Ch 25:19	3513
their falsehoods and reckless **b**;	Jer 23:32	6350
Where then is **b**? It is excluded.	Ro 3:27	*2746a*
for **b** in things pertaining to God.	Ro 15:17	*2746a*
Your **b** is not good.	1Co 5:6	*2745*
brethren, by the **b** in you which	1Co 15:31	*2746a*
you; great is my **b** on your behalf	2Co 7:4	*2746a*
so also our **b** before Titus proved	2Co 7:14	*2746a*
and of our reason for **b** about you.	2Co 8:24	*2746a*
that our **b** about you may not be	2Co 9:3	*2745*
not **b** beyond *our* measure, *that is,*	2Co 10:15	*2744*
this **b** of mine will not be stopped	2Co 11:10	*2746a*
the matter about which they are **b**.	2Co 11:12	*2744*
in this confidence of **b**.	2Co 11:17	*2746a*
B is necessary, though it is not	2Co 12:1	*2744*
for **b** in regard to himself alone,	Ga 6:4	*2745*
all such **b** is evil.	Jas 4:16	*2746a*

BOASTS

Context	Reference	Number
"Shall your **b** silence men?	Jb 11:3	907
the wicked **b** of his heart's desire,	Ps 10:3	1984b
when he goes his way, then he **b**.	Pr 20:14	1984b
a man who **b** of his gifts falsely.	Pr 25:14	1984b
His idle **b** are false.	Is 16:6	907
but let him who **b** boast of this,	Jer 9:24	1984b
idle **b** have accomplished nothing.	Jer 48:30	907
a man and a mouth uttering great **b**	Da 7:8	
eyes and a mouth uttering great **b**	Da 7:20	
HIM WHO **B**, BOAST IN THE LORD."	1Co 1:31	*2744*
But HE WHO **B** IS TO BOAST IN THE	2Co 10:17	*2744*
and *yet* it **b** of great things.	Jas 3:5	*850a*

BOAT

Context	Reference	Number
On which no **b** with oars will go,	Is 33:21	590
the **b** with Zebedee their father,	Mt 4:21	*4143*
left the **b** and their father,	Mt 4:22	*4143*
When He got into the **b**,	Mt 8:23	*4143*

the **b** was being covered with the waves; **Mt 8:24** *4143*
Getting into a **b**, **Mt 9:1** *4143*
so He got into a **b** and sat down, **Mt 13:2** *4143*
He withdrew from there in a **b** **Mt 14:13** *4143*
made the disciples get into the **b** and **Mt 14:22** *4143*
But the **b** was already a long distance **Mt 14:24** *4143*
And Peter got out of the **b**, **Mt 14:29** *4143*
When they got into the **b**, **Mt 14:32** *4143*
who were in the **b** worshiped Him, **Mt 14:33** *4143*
the crowds, Jesus got into the **b** **Mt 15:39** *4143*
also in the **b** mending the nets. **Mk 1:19** *4143*
in the **b** with the hired servants, **Mk 1:20** *4143*
that a **b** should stand ready for Him **Mk 3:9** *4142*
into a **b** in the sea and sat down; **Mk 4:1** *4143*
them in the **b**, just as He was; **Mk 4:36** *4143*
the waves were breaking over the **b** **Mk 4:37** *4143*
that the **b** was already filling up. **Mk 4:37** *4143*
When He got out of the **b**, **Mk 5:2** *4143*
As He was getting into the **b**, **Mk 5:18** *4143*
again in the **b** to the other side, **Mk 5:21** *4143*
They went away in the **b** to a **Mk 6:32** *4143*
Jesus made His disciples get into the **b** **Mk 6:45** *4143*
the **b** was in the middle of the sea, **Mk 6:47** *4143*
Then He got into the **b** with them, **Mk 6:51** *4143*
When they got out of the **b**, **Mk 6:54** *4143*
entered the **b** with His disciples and **Mk 8:10** *4143*
than one loaf in the **b** with them. **Mk 8:14** *4143*
the people from the **b**. **Lk 5:3** *4143*
to their partners in the other **b** for **Lk 5:7** *4143*
Jesus and His disciples got into a **b**, **Lk 8:22** *4143*
and He got into a **b** and **Lk 8:37** *4143*
and after getting into a **b**, **Jn 6:17** *4143*
the sea and drawing near to the **b**; **Jn 6:19** *4143*
to receive Him into the **b**, **Jn 6:21** *4143*
and immediately the **b** was at the **Jn 6:21** *4143*
there was no other small **b** there, **Jn 6:22** *4142*
with His disciples into the **b**, **Jn 6:22** *4143*
They went out and got into the **b**; **Jn 21:3** *4143*
on the right-hand side of the **b** and **Jn 21:6** *4143*
disciples came in the little **b**, **Jn 21:8** *4142*
to get the *ship's* **b** under control. **Ac 27:16** *4627*
let down the *ship's* **b** into the sea, **Ac 27:30** *4627*
cut away the ropes of the *ship's* **b** and **Ac 27:32** *4627*

BOATS
"They slip by like reed **b**, **Jb 9:26** 591
and other **b** were with Him. **Mk 4:36** *4143*
b lying at the edge of the lake; **Lk 5:2** *4142*
And He got into one of the **b**, **Lk 5:3** *4143*
came and filled both of the **b**, **Lk 5:7** *4143*
they had brought their **b** to land, **Lk 5:11** *4143*
There came other small **b** from **Jn 6:23** *4142*
themselves got into the small **b**, **Jn 6:24** *4142*

BOAZ
of Elimelech, whose name was **B**. **Ru 2:1** 1162
of the field belonging to **B**, **Ru 2:3** 1162
B came from Bethlehem and said to **Ru 2:4** 1162
Then **B** said to his servant who was **Ru 2:5** 1162
Then **B** said to Ruth, **Ru 2:8** 1162
B replied to her, **Ru 2:11** 1162
At mealtime **B** said to her, **Ru 2:14** 1162
glean, **B** commanded his servants, **Ru 2:15** 1162
with whom I worked today is **B**." **Ru 2:19** 1162
So she stayed close by the maids of **B** **Ru 2:23** 1162
"Now is not **B** our kinsman, **Ru 3:2** 1162
When **B** had eaten and drunk and his **Ru 3:7** 1162
Now **B** went up to the gate and sat **Ru 4:1** 1162
of whom **B** spoke was passing by, **Ru 4:1** 1162
B said, "On the day you buy the field **Ru 4:5** 1162
So the closest relative said to **B**, **Ru 4:8** 1162
Then **B** said to the elders and all **Ru 4:9** 1162
So **B** took Ruth, and she became his **Ru 4:13** 1162
and to Salmon was born **B**, **Ru 4:21** 1162
to Salmon was born Boaz, and to **B**, **Ru 4:21** 1162
up the left pillar and named it **B**. **1Ki 7:21** 1162
Salma became the father of **B**, **1Ch 2:11** 1162
B became the father of Obed, and **1Ch 2:12** 1162
Jachin and the one on the left **B**. **2Ch 3:17** 1162
Salmon was the father of **B** by Rahab, **Mt 1:5** *1003*
B was the father of Obed by Ruth, **Mt 1:5** *1003*
the son of Obed, the son of **B**, **Lk 3:32** *1003*

BOCHERU
Azrikam, **B**, Ishmael, Sheariah, **1Ch 8:38** 1074
B and Ishmael and Sheariah and **1Ch 9:44** 1074

BOCHIM
the LORD came up from Gilgal to **B**. **Jg 2:1** 1066
So they named that place **B**; **Jg 2:5** 1066

BODIES
lord except our **b** and our lands. **Gn 47:18** 1472a
skin of their **b** are a faint white, **Lv 13:39** 1320
then I will thrash your **b** with the **Jg 8:7** 1320
I will give the dead **b** of the army **1Sa 17:46** 6297
the body of Saul and the **b** of his sons **1Sa 31:12** 1472a
of Saul and the **b** of his sons and **1Ch 10:12** 1480
They also rule over our **b** And over **Ne 9:37** 1472a
the dead **b** of Your servants for food **Ps 79:2** 5038
"The dead **b** of this people **Jer 7:33** 5038
of the dead **b** and of the ashes, **Jer 31:40** 6297
And their dead **b** will be food for **Jer 34:20** 5038
clothes torn and their **b** gashed, **Jer 41:5**
being, and two covering their **b**. **Ezk 1:11** 1472a
"I will also lay the dead **b** of **Ezk 6:5** 6297
the fire had no effect on the **b** of **Da 3:27** 1655
and yielded up their **b** so as not **Da 3:28** 1655
And countless dead **b** **Na 3:3** 1472a
They stumble over the dead **b**! **Na 3:3** 1472a
and many **b** of the saints who had **Mt 27:52** *4983*
so that the **b** would not remain on **Jn 19:31** *4983*
that their **b** would be dishonored **Ro 1:24** *4983*
will also give life to your mortal **b** **Ro 8:11** *4983*
b a living and holy sacrifice, **Ro 12:1** *4983*
that your **b** are members of Christ? **1Co 6:15** *4983*
heavenly **b** and earthly bodies, **1Co 15:40** *4983*
heavenly bodies and earthly **b**, **1Co 15:40** *4983*
their own wives as their own **b**. **Eph 5:28** *4983*
whose **b** fell in the wilderness? **Heb 3:17** *2966*
and our **b** washed with pure water. **Heb 10:22** *4983*
For the **b** of those animals whose **Heb 13:11** *4983*
And their dead **b** *will lie* in the **Rv 11:8** *4430*
dead **b** for three and a half days, **Rv 11:9** *4430*
their dead **b** to be laid in a tomb. **Rv 11:9** *4430*

BODILY
upon Him in **b** form like a dove, **Lk 3:22** *4984*
because of a **b** illness that I preached **Ga 4:13** *4561*
was a trial to you in my **b** condition **Ga 4:14** *4561*
fullness of Deity dwells in **b** form, **Col 2:9** *4985*
for **b** discipline is only of little **1Tm 4:8** *4984*

BODY
will come forth from your own **b**, **Gn 15:4** 4578
it will be separated from your **b**; **Gn 25:23** 4578
it is his cloak for his **b**. **Ex 22:27** 5785
shall not be poured on anyone's **b**, **Ex 30:32** 1320
"When a man has on the skin of his **b** **Lv 13:2** 1320
of leprosy on the skin of his **b**, **Lv 13:2** 1320
at the mark on the skin of the **b**, **Lv 13:3** 1320
be deeper than the skin of his **b**, **Lv 13:3** 1320
is white on the skin of his **b**, **Lv 13:4** 1320
leprosy on the skin of his **b**, **Lv 13:11** 1320
the leprosy has covered all his **b**, **Lv 13:13** 1320
When the **b** has a boil on its skin **Lv 13:18** 1320
"Or if the **b** sustains in its skin **Lv 13:24** 1320
bright spots on the skin of the **b**, **Lv 13:38** 1320
of leprosy in the skin of the **b**, **Lv 13:43** 1320
bathe his **b** in water and be clean. **Lv 14:9** 1320
man has a discharge from his **b**, **Lv 15:2** 1320
whether his **b** allows its discharge to **Lv 15:3** 1320
his **b** obstructs its discharge. **Lv 15:3** 1320
then wash his clothes and bathe his **b** **Lv 15:13** 1320
he shall bathe all his **b** in water **Lv 15:16** 1320
her discharge in her **b** is blood, **Lv 15:19** 1320
shall be next to his **b**, **Lv 16:4** 1320
Then he shall bathe his **b** in water **Lv 16:4** 1320
"He shall bathe his **b** with **Lv 16:24** 1320
and bathe his **b** with water; **Lv 16:26** 1320
and bathe his **b** with water, **Lv 16:28** 1320
does not wash *them* or bathe his **b**, **Lv 17:16** 1320
any cuts in your **b** for the dead nor **Lv 19:28** 1320
he has bathed his **b** in water. **Lv 22:6** 1320
use a razor over their whole **b** and **Nu 8:7** 1320
clothes and bathe his **b** in water, **Nu 19:7** 1320
in water and bathe his **b** in water, **Nu 19:8** 1320
the **b** of a man who has died, **Nu 19:13** 5315
and the woman, through the **b**. **Nu 25:8** 6896
Blessed *shall be* the offspring of your **b** **Dt 28:4** 990
in the offspring of your **b** and in **Dt 28:11** 990
Cursed *shall be* the offspring of your **b** **Dt 28:18** 990
eat the offspring of your own **b**, **Dt 28:53** 990
in the offspring of your **b** and in **Dt 30:9** 990
took his **b** down from the tree and **Jos 8:29** 5038
honey were in the **b** of the lion. **Jg 14:8** 1472a
honey out of the **b** of the lion. **Jg 14:9** 1472a
his **b** to the wall of Beth-shan. **1Sa 31:10** 1472a
and took the **b** of Saul and the **1Sa 31:12** 1472a
your **b** shall not come to the grave **1Ki 13:22** 5038
and his **b** was thrown on the road, **1Ki 13:24** 5038
also was standing beside the **b**. **1Ki 13:24** 5038
and saw the **b** thrown on the road, **1Ki 13:25** 5038
the lion standing beside the **b**; **1Ki 13:25** 5038
He went and found his **b** thrown **1Ki 13:28** 5038
the lion standing beside the **b**; **1Ki 13:28** 5038
eaten the **b** nor torn the donkey. **1Ki 13:28** 5038
So the prophet took up the **b** of **1Ki 13:29** 5038
He laid his **b** in his own grave, **1Ki 13:30** 5038
he had sackcloth beneath on his **b**. **2Ki 6:30** 1320
his **b** in a chariot from Megiddo, **2Ki 23:30** 4191
arose and took away the **b** of Saul **1Ch 10:12** 1480
shields, spears, helmets, **b** armor, **2Ch 26:14** 8302
"But his **b** pains him, And he **Jb 14:22** 1320
from grief, my soul and my **b** *also.* **Ps 31:9** 990
And my **b** has wasted away. **Ps 31:10** 6106
my **b** wasted away Through my **Ps 32:3** 6106
Our **b** cleaves to the earth. **Ps 44:25** 990
And their **b** is fat. **Ps 73:4** 193a
it entered into his **b** like water And **Ps 109:18** 7130
b I will set upon your throne. **Ps 132:11** 990
It will be healing to your **b** And **Pr 3:8** 8270
And health to all their **b**. **Pr 4:22** 1320
flesh and your **b** are consumed; **Pr 5:11** 7607
A tranquil heart is life to the **b**, **Pr 14:30** 1320
into the innermost parts of the **b**. **Pr 18:8** 990
into the innermost parts of the **b**. **Pr 26:22** 990
how to stimulate my **b** with wine **Ec 2:3** 1320
and put away pain from your **b**, **Ec 11:10** 1320
to books is wearying to the **b**. **Ec 12:12** 1320
fruitful garden, both soul and **b**, **Is 10:18** 1320
the **b** of My mother He named Me. **Is 49:1** 4578
and cast his dead **b** into the **Jer 26:23** 5038
and his dead **b** shall be cast out **Jer 36:30** 5038
were more ruddy *in* **b** than corals, **La 4:7** 6106
one also had two wings covering its **b** **Ezk 1:23** 1472a
and fill your **b** with this scroll **Ezk 3:3** 4578
Their whole **b**, their backs, **Ezk 10:12** 1320
and his **b** was drenched with the **Da 4:33** 1655
and his **b** was drenched with the **Da 5:21** 1655
and its **b** was destroyed and given **Da 7:11** 1655
His **b** also *was* like beryl, his **Da 10:6** 1472a
of my **b** for the sin of my soul? **Mi 6:7** 990
Also anguish is in the whole **b** And **Na 2:10** 4975
one of the parts of your **b**, **Mt 5:29**
whole **b** to be thrown into hell. **Mt 5:29** *4983*
one of the parts of your **b**, **Mt 5:30**
for your whole **b** to go into hell. **Mt 5:30** *4983*
"The eye is the lamp of the **b**; **Mt 6:22** *4983*
whole **b** will be full of light. **Mt 6:22** *4983*
whole **b** will be full of darkness. **Mt 6:23** *4983*
nor for your **b**, *as to* what you **Mt 6:25** *4983*
food, and the **b** more than clothing? **Mt 6:25** *4983*
Do not fear those who kill the **b** **Mt 10:28** *4983*
destroy both soul and **b** in hell. **Mt 10:28** *4983*
and took away the **b** and buried it; **Mt 14:12** *4430*
she poured this perfume on My **b**, **Mt 26:12** *4983*
"Take, eat; this is My **b**." **Mt 26:26** *4983*
and asked for the **b** of Jesus. **Mt 27:58** *4983*
And Joseph took the **b** and wrapped **Mt 27:59** *4983*
and she felt in her **b** that she was **Mk 5:29** *4983*
away his **b** and laid it in a tomb. **Mk 6:29** *4430*
My **b** beforehand for the burial. **Mk 14:8** *4983*
"Take *it;* this is My **b**." **Mk 14:22** *4983*
linen sheet over *his* naked **b**; **Mk 14:51**
and asked for the **b** of Jesus. **Mk 15:43** *4983*
he granted the **b** to Joseph. **Mk 15:45** *4430*
"The eye is the lamp of your **b**; **Lk 11:34** *4983*
whole **b** also is full of light; **Lk 11:34** *4983*
your **b** also is full of darkness. **Lk 11:34** *4983*
your whole **b** is full of light, **Lk 11:36** *4983*
be afraid of those who kill the **b** and **Lk 12:4** *4983*
nor for your **b**, *as to* what you **Lk 12:22** *4983*
food, and the **b** more than clothing. **Lk 12:23** *4983*
"Where the **b** *is,* there also the **Lk 17:37** *4983*
is My **b** which is given for you; **Lk 22:19** *4983*
Then the whole **b** of them got up and **Lk 23:1** *4128*
and asked for the **b** of Jesus. **Lk 23:52** *4983*
the tomb and how His **b** was laid. **Lk 23:55** *4983*
not find the **b** of the Lord Jesus. **Lk 24:3** *4983*
and did not find His **b**, **Lk 24:23** *4983*
speaking of the temple of His **b**. **Jn 2:21** *4983*
he might take away the **b** of Jesus; **Jn 19:38** *4983*
So he came and took away His **b**. **Jn 19:38** *4983*
So they took the **b** of Jesus and **Jn 19:40** *4983*
the **b** of Jesus had been lying. **Jn 20:12** *4983*
and when they had washed her **b**, **Ac 9:37**
and prayed, and turning to the **b**, **Ac 9:40** *4983*
carried from his **b** to the sick, **Ac 19:12** *5559*
faith he contemplated his own **b**, **Ro 4:19** *4983*
that our **b** of sin might be done **Ro 6:6** *4983*
do not let sin reign in your mortal **b** **Ro 6:12** *4983*
presenting the members of your **b** **Ro 6:13**
the Law through the **b** of Christ, **Ro 7:4** *4983*
of our **b** to bear fruit for death. **Ro 7:5**
law in the members of my **b**, **Ro 7:23**
me free from the **b** of this death? **Ro 7:24** *4983*
the **b** is dead because of sin, **Ro 8:10** *4983*
to death the deeds of the **b**, **Ro 8:13** *4983*
as sons, the redemption of our **b**. **Ro 8:23** *4983*
we have many members in one **b** **Ro 12:4** *4983*
who are many, are one **b** in Christ, **Ro 12:5** *4983*
absent in **b** but present in spirit, **1Co 5:3** *4983*
Yet the **b** is not for immorality, **1Co 6:13** *4983*
and the Lord is for the **b**. **1Co 6:13** *4983*
to a prostitute is one **b** *with her?* **1Co 6:16** *4983*
a man commits is outside the **b**, **1Co 6:18** *4983*
man sins against his own **b**. **1Co 6:18** *4983*
Or do you not know that your **b** is **1Co 6:19** *4983*
therefore glorify God in your **b**. **1Co 6:20** *4983*
not have authority over her own **b**, **1Co 7:4** *4983*
not have authority over his own **b**, **1Co 7:4** *4983*
may be holy both in **b** and spirit; **1Co 7:34** *4983*
discipline my **b** and make it my slave, **1Co 9:27** *4983*
a sharing in the **b** of Christ? **1Co 10:16** *4983*
bread, we who are many are one **b**; **1Co 10:17** *4983*
"This is My **b**, which is for you; **1Co 11:24** *4983*
the **b** and the blood of the Lord. **1Co 11:27** *4983*
he does not judge the **b** rightly. **1Co 11:29** *4983*
For even as the **b** is one and *yet* **1Co 12:12** *4983*
and all the members of the **b**, **1Co 12:12** *4983*
though they are many, are one **b**, **1Co 12:12** *4983*
we were all baptized into one **b**, **1Co 12:13** *4983*
For the **b** is not one member, but **1Co 12:14** *4983*
hand, I am not *a part* of the **b**," **1Co 12:15** *4983*
any the less *a part* of the **b**. **1Co 12:15** *4983*
eye, I am not *a part* of the **b**," **1Co 12:16** *4983*
any the less *a part* of the **b**. **1Co 12:16** *4983*
If the whole **b** were an eye, where **1Co 12:17** *4983*
each one of them, in the **b**, **1Co 12:18** *4983*
one member, where would the **b** be? **1Co 12:19** *4983*
there are many members, but one **b**. **1Co 12:20** *4983*
much truer that the members of the **b** **1Co 12:22** *4983*
and those *members* of the **b** which **1Co 12:23** *4983*
But God has *so* composed the **b**, **1Co 12:24** *4983*
may be no division in the **b**, **1Co 12:25** *4983*
Now you are Christ's **b**, **1Co 12:27** *4983*
if I surrender my **b** to be burned, **1Co 13:3** *4983*
what kind of **b** do they come?" **1Co 15:35** *4983*
do not sow the **b** which is to be, **1Co 15:37** *4983*
gives it a **b** just as He wished, **1Co 15:38** *4983*
each of the seeds a **b** of its own. **1Co 15:38** *4983*
It is sown a perishable **b**, it is **1Co 15:42**
it is raised an imperishable **b**; **1Co 15:42**
it is sown a natural **b**, **1Co 15:44** *4983*
body, it is raised a spiritual **b**. **1Co 15:44** *4983*
If there is a natural **b**, **1Co 15:44** *4983*
there is also a spiritual **b**. **1Co 15:44**
about in the **b** the dying of Jesus, **2Co 4:10** *4983*
also may be manifested in our **b**. **2Co 4:10** *4983*
the **b** we are absent from the Lord **2Co 5:6** *4983*
prefer rather to be absent from the **b** **2Co 5:8** *4983*

for his deeds in the **b**, 2Co 5:10 *4983*
whether in the **b** I do not know, 2Co 12:2 *4983*
or out of the **b** I do not know, 2Co 12:2 *4983*
in the **b** or apart from the body 2Co 12:3 *4983*
or apart from the **b** I do not know, 2Co 12:3 *4983*
on my **b** the brand-marks of Jesus. Ga 6:17 *4983*
which is His **b**, the fullness of Him Eph 1:23 *4983*
in one **b** to God through the cross, Eph 2:16 *4983*
heirs and fellow members of the **b**, Eph 3:6 *4954*
There is one **b** and one Spirit, Eph 4:4 *4983*
building up of the **b** of Christ; Eph 4:12 *4983*
from whom the whole **b**, being fitted Eph 4:16 *4983*
causes the growth of the **b** for the Eph 4:16 *4983*
Himself *being* the Savior of the **b**. Eph 5:23 *4983*
because we are members of His **b**. Eph 5:30 *4983*
as always, be exalted in my **b**, Php 1:20 *4983*
who will transform the **b** of our Php 3:21 *4983*
with the **b** of His glory, Php 3:21 *4983*
He is also head of the **b**, Col 1:18 *4983*
in His fleshly **b** through death, Col 1:22 *4983*
I do my share on behalf of His **b** Col 1:24 *4983*
For even though I am absent in **b**, Col 2:5 *4561*
in the removal of the **b** of the flesh Col 2:11 *4983*
the head, from whom the entire **b**, Col 2:19 *4983*
and severe treatment of the **b**, Col 2:23 *4983*
earthly **b** as dead to immorality, Col 3:5
indeed you were called in one **b**; Col 3:15 *4983*
soul and **b** be preserved complete, 1Th 5:23 *4983*
regulations for the **b** imposed Heb 9:10 *4561*
A **B** YOU HAVE PREPARED FOR ME; Heb 10:5 *4983*
b of Jesus Christ once for all. Heb 10:10 *4983*
you yourselves also are in the **b**. Heb 13:3 *4983*
what is necessary for *their* **b**, Jas 2:16 *4983*
the **b** without *the* spirit is dead, Jas 2:26 *4983*
to bridle the whole **b** as well. Jas 3:2 *4983*
we direct their entire **b** as well. Jas 3:3 *4983*
tongue is a small part of the **b**, Jas 3:5
that which defiles the entire **b**, Jas 3:6 *4983*
our sins in His **b** on the cross, 1Pe 2:24 *4983*
and argued about the **b** of Moses, Jude 1:9 *4983*
BODYGUARD
officer, the captain of the **b**. Gn 37:36 2876
of Pharaoh, the captain of the **b**, Gn 39:1 2876
the house of the captain of the **b**, Gn 40:3 2876
b put Joseph in charge of them, Gn 40:4 2876
the house of the captain of the **b**, Gn 41:10 2876
a servant of the captain of the **b**, Gn 41:12 2876
I will make you my **b** for life." 1Sa 28:2
8104, 7218
Nebuzaradan the captain of the **b** Jer 39:9 2876
Nebuzaradan the captain of the **b** Jer 39:10 2876
Nebuzaradan the captain of the **b**, Jer 39:11 2876
the captain of the **b** sent *word*, Jer 39:13 2876
the **b** had released him from Ramah, Jer 40:1 2876
Now the captain of the **b** had taken Jer 40:2 2876
So the captain of the **b** gave him a Jer 40:5 2876
Nebuzaradan the captain of the **b** Jer 41:10 2876
Nebuzaradan the captain of the **b** Jer 43:6 2876
Nebuzaradan the captain of the **b**, Jer 52:12 2876
the captain of the king's **b**, Da 2:14 2877
BOHAN
the stone of **B** the son of Reuben. Jos 15:6 932
the stone of **B** the son of Reuben. Jos 18:17 932
BOIL
bake and **b** what you will boil, Ex 16:23 1310
bake and boil what you will **b**, Ex 16:23 1310
not to **b** a young goat in the milk Ex 23:19 1310
and **b** its flesh in a holy place. Ex 29:31 1310
not **b** a young goat in its mother's milk." Ex 34:26 1310
"**B** the flesh at the doorway of Lv 8:31 1310
When the body has a **b** on its skin Lv 13:18 7822
and in the place of the **b** there is Lv 13:19 7822
it has broken out in the **b**. Lv 13:20 7822
it is *only* the scar of the **b**; Lv 13:23 7822
and **b** *it* in the pot and make cakes Nu 11:8 1310
not **b** a young goat in its mother's milk. Dt 14:21 1310
"Put on the large pot and **b** stew 2Ki 4:38 1310
they took and laid *it* on the **b**, 2Ki 20:7 7822
"He makes the depths **b** like a pot; Jb 41:31 7570
of figs and apply it to the **b**, Is 38:21 7822
as fire causes water to **b** Is 64:2 1158
Make it **b** vigorously. Ezk 24:5 7570
kindle the fire, **B** the flesh well And Ezk 24:10 8552
the priests shall **b** the guilt offering Ezk 46:20 1310
b the sacrifices of the people." Ezk 46:24 1310
and take of them and **b** in them. Zch 14:21 1310
BOILED
of it raw or **b** at all with water, Ex 12:9 1310
in which it was **b** shall be broken; Lv 6:28 1310
if it was **b** in a bronze vessel, Lv 6:28 1310
ram's shoulder *when it has been* **b**, Nu 6:19 1311
he will not take **b** meat from you, 1Sa 2:15 1310
sacrificed them and **b** their flesh 1Ki 19:21 1310
"So we **b** my son and ate him; 2Ki 6:29 1310
they **b** the holy things in pots, 2Ch 35:13 1310
women **B** their own children; La 4:10 1310
BOILING
would come while the meat was **b**, 1Sa 2:13 1310
from a **b** pot and *burning* rushes. Jb 41:20 5301
"I see a **b** pot, facing away from Jer 1:13 5301
and **b** places were made under the Ezk 46:23 4018a
"These are the **b** places where the Ezk 46:24 1310
BOILS
and will become **b** breaking out Ex 9:9 7822
and became **b** breaking out with Ex 9:10 7822
before Moses because of the **b**, Ex 9:11 7822
for the **b** were on the magicians as Ex 9:11 7822
"The LORD will smite you with the **b** Dt 28:27 7822
on the knees and legs with sore **b**, Dt 28:35 7822
and smote Job with sore **b** from the Jb 2:7 7822
BOISTEROUS
She is **b** and rebellious, Pr 7:11 1993
The woman of folly is **b**, Pr 9:13 1993
were full of noise, You **b** town, Is 22:2 1993
will drink *and* be **b** as with wine; Zch 9:15 1993
BOLD
me **b** with strength in my soul. Ps 138:3 7292
A wicked man displays a **b** face, Pr 21:29 5810
But the righteous are **b** as a lion. Pr 28:1 982
And Isaiah is very **b** and says, Ro 10:20 *662*
you, but **b** toward you when absent! 2Co 10:1 *2292*
when I am present I *need* not be **b** 2Co 10:2 *2292*
For we are not **b** to class or 2Co 10:12 *5111*
whatever respect anyone *else* is **b** 2Co 11:21 *5111*
I am just as **b** myself. 2Co 11:21 *5111*
BOLD-FACED
things, the actions of a **b** harlot. Ezk 16:30 7989
BOLDLY
sons of Israel were going out **b**. Ex 14:8
7311, 3027
Israel started out **b** in the sight of all Nu 33:3
7311, 3027
mouth speaks **b** against my enemies, 1Sa 2:1 7337
spoken out **b** in the name of Jesus. Ac 9:27 *3955*
out **b** in the name of the Lord. Ac 9:28 *3955*
and Barnabas spoke out **b** and said, Ac 13:46 *3955*
b *with reliance* upon the Lord, Ac 14:3 *3955*
to speak out **b** in the synagogue. Ac 18:26 *3955*
speaking out **b** for three months, Ac 19:8 *3955*
very **b** to you on some points so Ro 15:15 *5112*
in *proclaiming* it I may speak **b**, Eph 6:20 *3955*
BOLDNESS
to speak the word of God with **b**. Ac 4:31 *3954*
we use great **b** in *our* speech, 2Co 3:12 *3954*
in whom we have **b** and confident Eph 3:12 *3954*
with **b** the mystery of the gospel, Eph 6:19 *3954*
in anything, but *that* with all **b**, Php 1:20 *3954*
we had the **b** in our God to speak 1Th 2:2 *3955*
BOLT
let them shut and **b** the doors. Ne 7:3 270
on it And set a **b** and doors, Jb 38:10 1280
myrrh, On the handles of the **b**. SS 5:5 4514
BOLTS
its doors with its **b** and bars. Ne 3:3 4514
doors with its **b** and its bars. Ne 3:6 4514
its doors with its **b** and its bars, Ne 3:13 4514
its doors with its **b** and its bars. Ne 3:14 4514
its doors with its **b** and its bars, Ne 3:15 4514
And their herds to **b** of lightning. Ps 78:48 7565
to and fro like **b** of lightning. Ezk 1:14 965
BOND
is none *remaining*, **b** or free. Dt 32:36 6113
person, both **b** and free in Israel. 1Ki 14:10 6113
male, both **b** and free in Israel; 1Ki 21:21 6113
person both **b** and free in Israel. 2Ki 9:8 6113
for there was neither **b** nor free, 2Ki 14:26 6113
"He loosens the **b** of kings And Jb 12:18 4147
rich and the poor have a common **b**, Pr 22:2 6298
you into the **b** of the covenant; Ezk 20:37 4562
from this **b** on the Sabbath day?" Lk 13:16 *1199*
of the Spirit in the **b** of peace. Eph 4:3 *4886*
which is the perfect **b** of unity. Col 3:14 *4886*
BONDAGE
of Israel sighed because of the **b**, Ex 2:23 5656
because of *their* **b** rose up to God. Ex 2:23 5656
Egyptians are holding them in **b**, Ex 6:5 5647
I will deliver you from their **b**. Ex 6:6 5656
of *their* despondency and cruel **b**. Ex 6:9 5656
of Egypt, from the house of **b**, Jos 24:17 5650
father when they were in Egypt *in* **b** 1Sa 2:27
us a little reviving in our **b**. Ezr 9:8 5659
yet in our **b** our God has not Ezr 9:9 5659
are forced into **b** *already*, Ne 5:5 3533
them, a Jew his brother, in **b**. Jer 34:9 5647
should keep them any longer in **b**; Jer 34:10 5647
of Egypt, from the house of **b**, Jer 34:13 5650
WILL BE IN **B** I MYSELF WILL JUDGE,' Ac 7:7 *1398*
and in the **b** of iniquity." Ac 8:23 *4886*
I am of flesh, sold into **b** to sin. Ro 7:14
is not under **b** in such *cases*, 1Co 7:15 *1402*
in order to bring us into **b**. Ga 2:4 *2615*
were held in **b** under the elemental Ga 4:3 *1402*
BONDS
and his **b** dropped from his hands. Jg 15:14 612
loosed the **b** of the swift donkey, Jb 39:5 4147
handmaid, You have loosed my **b**. Ps 116:16 4147
To loosen the **b** of wickedness, Is 58:6 2784
your yoke *And* tore off your **b**; Jer 2:20 4147
broken the yoke *And* burst the **b**. Jer 5:5 4147
"Make for yourself **b** and yokes Jer 27:2 4147
neck and will tear off their **b**; Jer 30:8 4147
cords of a man, with **b** of love, Hos 11:4 5688
and *yet* he would break his **b** Lk 8:29 *1199*
that **b** and afflictions await me. Ac 20:23 *1199*
He has kept in eternal **b** under Jude 1:6 *1199*
BOND-SERVANT
releasing Your **b** to depart in peace, Lk 2:29 *1401*
Paul, a **b** of Christ Jesus, called Ro 1:1 *1401*
men, I would not be a **b** of Christ. Ga 1:10 *1401*
Himself, taking the form of a **b**, Php 2:7 *1401*
Epaphras, our beloved fellow **b**, Col 1:7 *4889*
servant and fellow **b** in the Lord, Col 4:7 *4889*
Lord's **b** must not be quarrelsome, 2Tm 2:24 *1401*
Paul, a **b** of God and an apostle Ti 1:1 *1401*
a **b** of God and of the Lord Jesus Jas 1:1 *1401*
a **b** and apostle of Jesus Christ, 2Pe 1:1 *1401*
Jude, a **b** of Jesus Christ, and Jude 1:1 *1401*
it by His angel to His **b** John, Rv 1:1 *1401*
sang the song of Moses, the **b** of God Rv 15:3 *1401*
BOND-SERVANTS
and grant that Your **b** may speak Your Ac 4:29 *1401*
men are **b** of the Most High God, Ac 16:17 *1401*
ourselves as your **b** for Jesus' sake. 2Co 4:5 *1401*
and Timothy, **b** of Christ Jesus, Php 1:1 *1401*
God gave Him to show to His **b**, Rv 1:1 *1401*
she teaches and leads My **b** astray so Rv 2:20 *1401*
b of our God on their foreheads." Rv 7:3 *1401*
reward Your **b** the prophets Rv 11:18 *1401*
THE BLOOD OF HIS **B** ON HER." Rv 19:2 *1401*
praise to our God, all you His **b**, Rv 19:5 *1401*
in it, and His **b** will serve Him; Rv 22:3 *1401*
sent His angel to show to His **b** Rv 22:6 *1401*
BONDSLAVE
"Behold, the **b** of the Lord; Lk 1:38 *1401*
for the humble state of His **b**; Lk 1:48 *1401*
your number, a **b** of Jesus Christ, Col 4:12 *1401*
BONDSLAVES
EVEN ON MY **B**, BOTH MEN AND Ac 2:18 *1401*
Urge **b** to be subject to their own Ti 2:9 *1401*
for evil, but *use it* as **b** of God. 1Pe 2:16 *1401*
BONDWOMAN
the **b** and one by the free woman. Ga 4:22 *3814*
But the son by the **b** was born Ga 4:23 *3814*
"CAST OUT THE **B** AND HER SON, FOR Ga 4:30 *3814*
FOR THE SON OF THE **B** SHALL NOT BE Ga 4:30 *3814*
we are not children of a **b**, Ga 4:31 *3814*
BONE
"This is now **b** of my bones, And Gn 2:23 6106
you are my **b** and my flesh." Gn 29:14 6106
nor are you to break any **b** of it. Ex 12:46 6106
morning, nor break a **b** of it; Nu 9:12 6106
or a human **b** or a grave, Nu 19:16 6106
and on the one who touched the **b** Nu 19:18 6106
that I am your **b** and your flesh." Jg 9:2 6106
we are your **b** and your flesh. 2Sa 5:1 6106
you are my **b** and my flesh. 2Sa 19:12 6106
'Are you not my **b** and my flesh? 2Sa 19:13 6106
we are your **b** and your flesh. 1Ch 11:1 6106
and touch his **b** and his flesh; Jb 2:5 6106
"My **b** clings to my skin and my Jb 19:20 6106
And a soft tongue breaks the **b**. Pr 25:15 1634
came together, **b** to its bone. Ezk 37:7 6106
came together, bone to its **b**. Ezk 37:7 6106
through and anyone sees a man's **b**, Ezk 39:15 6106
"NOT A **B** OF HIM SHALL BE BROKEN." Jn 19:36 *3747*
BONES
"This is now bone of my **b**, Gn 2:23 6106
shall carry my **b** up from here." Gn 50:25 6106
took the **b** of Joseph with him, Ex 13:19 6106
carry my **b** from here with you." Ex 13:19 6106
And will crush their **b** in pieces, Nu 24:8 6106
Now they buried the **b** of Joseph, Jos 24:32 6106
They took their **b** and buried 1Sa 31:13 6106
then David went and took the **b** of 2Sa 21:12 6106
bones of Saul and the **b** of Jonathan 2Sa 21:12 6106
He brought up the **b** of Saul 2Sa 21:13 6106
Saul and the **b** of Jonathan his son 2Sa 21:13 6106
b of those who had been hanged. 2Sa 21:13 6106
They buried the **b** of Saul and 2Sa 21:14 6106
b shall be burned on you.'" 1Ki 13:2 6106
lay my **b** beside his bones. 1Ki 13:31 6106
lay my bones beside his **b**. 1Ki 13:31 6106
And when the man touched the **b** of 2Ki 13:21 6106
filled their places with human **b**. 2Ki 23:14 6106
and he sent and took the **b** from 2Ki 23:16 6106
let no one disturb his **b**." 2Ki 23:18 6106
So they left his **b** undisturbed 2Ki 23:18 6106
undisturbed with the **b** of the prophet 2Ki 23:18 6106
altars and burned human **b** on them; 2Ki 23:20 6106
their **b** under the oak in Jabesh, 1Ch 10:12 6106
Then he burned the **b** of the priests 2Ch 34:5 6106
And made all my **b** shake. Jb 4:14 6106
me together with **b** and sinews? Jb 10:11 6106
"His **b** are full of his youthful Jb 20:11 6106
And the marrow of his **b** is moist, Jb 21:24 6106
night it pierces my **b** within me, Jb 30:17 6106
on me, And my **b** burn with fever. Jb 30:30 6106
with unceasing complaint in his **b**; Jb 33:19 6106
b which were not seen stick out. Jb 33:21 6106
"His **b** are tubes of bronze; Jb 40:18 6106
me, O LORD, for my **b** are dismayed. Ps 6:2 6106
And all my **b** are out of joint; Ps 22:14 6106
I can count all my **b**. Ps 22:17 6106
He keeps all his **b**, Ps 34:20 6106
All my **b** will say, Ps 35:10 6106
health in my **b** because of my sin. Ps 38:3 6106
As a shattering of my **b**, Ps 42:10 6106
Let the **b** which You have broken Ps 51:8 6106
For God scattered the **b** of him who Ps 53:5 6106
And my **b** have been scorched like a Ps 102:3 6106
groaning My **b** cling to my flesh. Ps 102:5 6106
water And like oil into his **b**. Ps 109:18 6106
Our **b** have been scattered at the Ps 141:7 6106
body And refreshment to your **b**. Pr 3:8 6106
him is like rottenness in his **b**. Pr 12:4 6106
passion is rottenness to the **b**. Pr 14:30 6106
Good news puts fat on the **b**. Pr 15:30 6106
to the soul and healing to the **b**. Pr 16:24 6106
a broken spirit dries up the **b**. Pr 17:22 1634
how **b** *are formed* in the womb Ec 11:5 6106
Like a lion—so He breaks all my **b**, Is 38:13 6106
And give strength to your **b**; Is 58:11 6106
And your **b** will flourish like the Is 66:14 6106

out the **b** of the kings of Judah and **Jer 8:1** 6106
Judah and the **b** of its princes, **Jer 8:1** 6106
princes, and the **b** of the priests and **Jer 8:1** 6106
and the **b** of the prophets, **Jer 8:1** 6106
and the **b** of the inhabitants of **Jer 8:1** 6106
a burning fire Shut up in my **b**; **Jer 20:9** 6106
within me, All my **b** tremble; **Jer 23:9** 6106
has broken his **b** is Nebuchadnezzar **Jer 50:17** 6105c
on high He sent fire into my **b**, **La 1:13** 6106
to waste away, He has broken my **b**. **La 3:4** 6106
skin is shriveled on their **b**, **La 4:8** 6106
scatter your **b** around your altars. **Ezk 6:5** 6106
Fill *it* with choice **b**. **Ezk 24:4** 6106
Also seethe its **b** in it." **Ezk 24:5** 6106
spices, And let the **b** be burned. **Ezk 24:10** 6106
their iniquity rested on their **b**, **Ezk 32:27** 6106
and it was full of **b**. **Ezk 37:1** 6106
"Son of man, can these **b** live?" **Ezk 37:3** 6106
"Prophesy over these **b** and **Ezk 37:4** 6106
'O dry **b**, hear the word of the **Ezk 37:4** 6106
"Thus says the Lord GOD to these **b**, **Ezk 37:5** 6106
and the **b** came together, bone to **Ezk 37:7** 6106
b are the whole house of Israel; **Ezk 37:11** 6106
'Our **b** are dried up and our hope **Ezk 37:11** 6106
them and crushed all their **b**. **Da 6:24** 1635
the **b** of the king of Edom to lime. **Am 2:1** 6106
to carry out *his* **b** from the house, **Am 6:10** 6106
them And their flesh from their **b**, **Mi 3:2** 6106
skin from them, Break their **b** And **Mi 3:3** 6106
Decay enters my **b**, And in my place **Hab 3:16** 6106
dead men's **b** and all uncleanness. **Mt 23:27** *3747*
and **b** as you see that I have." **Lk 24:39** *3747*
and gave orders concerning his **b**. **Heb 11:22** *3747*

BOOK

the **b** of the generations of Adam. **Gn 5:1** 5612
"Write this in a **b** as a memorial and **Ex 17:14** 5612
Then he took the **b** of the covenant **Ex 24:7** 5612
Your **b** which You have written!" **Ex 32:32** 5612
Me, I will blot him out of My **b**. **Ex 32:33** 5612
in the **B** of the Wars of the LORD, **Nu 21:14** 5612
law which are written in this **b**, **Dt 28:58** 5612
not written in the **b** of this law, **Dt 28:61** 5612
every curse which is written in this **b** **Dt 29:20** 5612
are written in this **b** of the law. **Dt 29:21** 5612
curse which is written in this **b**; **Dt 29:27** 5612
are written in this **b** of the law, **Dt 30:10** 5612
writing the words of this law in a **b** **Dt 31:24** 5612
"Take this **b** of the law and place **Dt 31:26** 5612
"This **b** of the law shall not **Jos 1:8** 5612
in the **b** of the law of Moses, **Jos 8:31** 5612
is written in the **b** of the law. **Jos 8:34** 5612
it not written in the **b** of Jashar? **Jos 10:13** 5612
cities in seven divisions in a **b**; **Jos 18:9** 5612
in the **b** of the law of Moses, **Jos 23:6** 5612
words in the **b** of the law of God; **Jos 24:26** 5612
b and placed *it* before the LORD. **1Sa 10:25** 5612
it is written in the **b** of Jashar. **2Sa 1:18** 5612
in the **b** of the acts of Solomon? **1Ki 11:41** 5612
written in the **B** of the Chronicles **1Ki 14:19** 5612
written in the **B** of the Chronicles **1Ki 14:29** 5612
written in the **B** of the Chronicles **1Ki 15:7** 5612
written in the **B** of the Chronicles **1Ki 15:23** 5612
written in the **B** of the Chronicles **1Ki 15:31** 5612
written in the **B** of the Chronicles **1Ki 16:5** 5612
written in the **B** of the Chronicles **1Ki 16:14** 5612
written in the **B** of the Chronicles **1Ki 16:20** 5612
written in the **B** of the Chronicles **1Ki 16:27** 5612
written in the **B** of the Chronicles **1Ki 22:39** 5612
written in the **B** of the Chronicles **1Ki 22:45** 5612
written in the **B** of the Chronicles **2Ki 1:18** 5612
written in the **B** of the Chronicles **2Ki 8:23** 5612
written in the **B** of the Chronicles **2Ki 10:34** 5612
written in the **B** of the Chronicles **2Ki 12:19** 5612
written in the **B** of the Chronicles **2Ki 13:8** 5612
written in the **B** of the Chronicles **2Ki 13:12** 5612
in the **b** of the Law of Moses, **2Ki 14:6** 5612
written in the **B** of the Chronicles **2Ki 14:15** 5612
written in the **B** of the Chronicles **2Ki 14:18** 5612
written in the **B** of the Chronicles **2Ki 14:28** 5612
written in the **B** of the Chronicles **2Ki 15:6** 5612
written in the **B** of the Chronicles **2Ki 15:11** 5612
written in the **B** of the Chronicles **2Ki 15:15** 5612
written in the **B** of the Chronicles **2Ki 15:21** 5612
written in the **B** of the Chronicles **2Ki 15:26** 5612
written in the **B** of the Chronicles **2Ki 15:31** 5612
written in the **B** of the Chronicles **2Ki 15:36** 5612
written in the **B** of the Chronicles **2Ki 16:19** 5612
written in the **B** of the Chronicles **2Ki 20:20** 5612
written in the **B** of the Chronicles **2Ki 21:17** 5612
written in the **B** of the Chronicles **2Ki 21:25** 5612
"I have found the **b** of the law in **2Ki 22:8** 5612
gave the **b** to Shaphan who read it. **2Ki 22:8** 5612
the priest has given me a **b**." **2Ki 22:10** 5612
the words of the **b** of the law, **2Ki 22:11** 5612
of this **b** that has been found, **2Ki 22:13** 5612
listened to the words of this **b**, **2Ki 22:13** 5612
even all the words of the **b** which **2Ki 22:16** 5612
words of the **b** of the covenant which **2Ki 23:2** 5612
that were written in this **b**. **2Ki 23:3** 5612
in this **b** of the covenant." **2Ki 23:21** 5612
the **b** that Hilkiah the priest found **2Ki 23:24** 5612
written in the **B** of the Chronicles **2Ki 23:28** 5612
written in the **B** of the Chronicles **2Ki 24:5** 5612
in the **B** of the Kings of Israel. **1Ch 9:1** 5612
written in the **B** of the Kings **2Ch 16:11** 5612
having the **b** of the law of the **2Ch 17:9** 5612
in the **B** of the Kings of Israel. **2Ch 20:34** 5612
treatise of the **B** of the Kings. **2Ch 24:27** 5612
in the law in the **b** of Moses, **2Ch 25:4** 5612
written in the **B** of the Kings **2Ch 25:26** 5612
written in the **B** of the Kings **2Ch 27:7** 5612
they are written in the **B** of the **2Ch 28:26** 5612
in the **B** of the Kings of Judah and **2Ch 32:32** 5612
Hilkiah the priest found the **b** of **2Ch 34:14** 5612
"I have found the **b** of the law in **2Ch 34:15** 5612
And Hilkiah gave the **b** to Shaphan. **2Ch 34:15** 5612
Then Shaphan brought the **b** to the **2Ch 34:16** 5612
"Hilkiah the priest gave me a **b**." **2Ch 34:18** 5612
of the **b** which has been found; **2Ch 34:21** 5612
all that is written in this **b**." **2Ch 34:21** 5612
even all the curses written in the **b** **2Ch 34:24** 5612
their hearing all the words of the **b** **2Ch 34:30** 5612
of the covenant written in this **b**. **2Ch 34:31** 5612
it is written in the **b** of Moses. **2Ch 35:12** 5612
written in the **B** of the Kings **2Ch 35:27** 5612
written in the **B** of the Kings **2Ch 36:8** 5612
it is written in the **b** of Moses. **Ezr 6:18** 5609
Then I found the **b** of the genealogy **Ne 7:5** 5612
asked Ezra the scribe to bring the **b** **Ne 8:1** 5612
attentive to the **b** of the law. **Ne 8:3** 5612
Ezra opened the **b** in the sight **Ne 8:5** 5612
They read from the **b**, **Ne 8:8** 5612
the **b** of the law of God daily, **Ne 8:18** 5612
they read from the **b** of the law of **Ne 9:3** 5612
registered in the **B** of the Chronicles **Ne 12:23** 5612
they read aloud from the **b** of Moses **Ne 13:1** 5612
written in the **B** of the Chronicles **Es 2:23** 5612
order to bring the **b** of records, **Es 6:1** 5612
and it was written in the **b**. **Es 9:32** 5612
written in the **B** of the Chronicles **Es 10:2** 5612
that they were inscribed in a **b**! **Jb 19:23** 5612
of the **b** it is written of me. **Ps 40:7** 5612
Are *they* not in Your **b**? **Ps 56:8** 5613c
be blotted out of the **b** of life And **Ps 69:28** 5612
in Your **b** were all written **Ps 139:16** 5612
you like the words of a sealed **b**, **Is 29:11** 5612
Then the **b** will be given to the **Is 29:12** 5612
the deaf will hear words of a **b**, **Is 29:18** 5612
Seek from the **b** of the LORD, and **Is 34:16** 5612
it, all that is written in this **b** which **Jer 25:13** 5612
which I have spoken to you in a **b**. **Jer 30:2** 5612
reading from the **b** the words of **Jer 36:8** 5612
Then Baruch read from the **b** the **Jer 36:10** 5612
the words of the LORD from the **b**, **Jer 36:11** 5612
read from the **b** to the people. **Jer 36:13** 5612
I wrote them with ink on the **b**." **Jer 36:18** 5612
the **b** which Jehoiakim king of Judah **Jer 36:32** 5612
in a **b** at Jeremiah's dictation, **Jer 45:1** 5612
who is found written in the **b**, **Da 12:1** 5612
seal up the **b** until the end of time; **Da 12:4** 5612
The **b** of the vision of Nahum the **Na 1:1** 5612
and a **b** of remembrance was written **Mal 3:16** 5612
you not read in the **b** of Moses,. **Mk 12:26** *976*
in the **b** of the words of Isaiah **Lk 3:4** *976*
And the **b** of the prophet Isaiah **Lk 4:17** *975*
And He opened the **b** and **Lk 4:17** *975*
And He closed the **b**, **Lk 4:20** *975*
himself says in the **b** of Psalms, **Lk 20:42** *976*
which are not written in this **b**; **Jn 20:30** *975*
it is written in the **b** of Psalms, **Ac 1:20** *976*
written in the **b** of the prophets, **Ac 7:42** *976*
WRITTEN IN THE **B** OF THE LAW, **Ga 3:10** *975*
whose names are in the **b** of life. **Php 4:3** *976*
sprinkled both the **b** itself and all **Heb 9:19** *975*
SCROLL OF THE **B** IT IS WRITTEN OF ME) **Heb 10:7** *975*
"Write in a **b** what you see, and **Rv 1:11** *975*
erase his name from the **b** of life, **Rv 3:5** *976*
a **b** written inside and on the back, **Rv 5:1** *975*
the **b** and to break its seals?" **Rv 5:2** *975*
the earth was able to open the **b** **Rv 5:3** *975*
was found worthy to open the **b** or **Rv 5:4** *975*
open the **b** and its seven seals." **Rv 5:5** *975*
And He came and took the **b** out of **Rv 5:7**
When He had taken the **b**, **Rv 5:8** *975*
"Worthy are You to take the **b** and **Rv 5:9** *975*
hand a little **b** which was open. **Rv 10:2** *974*
take the **b** which is open in the **Rv 10:8** *975*
him to give me the little **b**. **Rv 10:9** *974*
I took the little **b** out of the **Rv 10:10** *974*
world in the **b** of life of the Lamb **Rv 13:8** *975*
name has not been written in the **b** **Rv 17:8** *975*
and another **b** was opened, which is **Rv 20:12** *975*
which is *the* **b** of life; **Rv 20:12**
found written in the **b** of life, **Rv 20:15** *976*
written in the Lamb's **b** of life. **Rv 21:27** *975*
words of the prophecy of this **b**." **Rv 22:7** *975*
who heed the words of this **b**. **Rv 22:9** *975*
words of the prophecy of this **b**, **Rv 22:10** *975*
words of the prophecy of this **b**: **Rv 22:18** *975*
which are written in this **b**; **Rv 22:18** *975*
words of the **b** of this prophecy, **Rv 22:19** *975*
city, which are written in this **b**. **Rv 22:19** *975*

BOOKS

in the record **b** of your fathers. **Ezr 4:15** 5609
you will discover in the record **b** and **Ezr 4:15** 5609
the writing of many **b** is endless, **Ec 12:12** 5612
and excessive devotion *to* **b** is **Ec 12:12**
court sat, And the **b** were opened. **Da 7:10** 5609
observed in the **b** the number of **Da 9:2** 5612
contain the **b** that would be written. **Jn 21:25** *975*
who practiced magic brought their **b** **Ac 19:19** *976*
at Troas with Carpus, and the **b**, **2Tm 4:13** *975*
the throne, and **b** were opened; **Rv 20:12** *975*
which were written in the **b**, **Rv 20:12** *975*

BOOT

For every **b** of the booted warrior **Is 9:5** 5430

BOOTED

b warrior in the *battle* tumult, **Is 9:5** 5431

BOOTH

His tabernacle like a garden **b**; **La 2:6**
raise up the fallen **b** of David, **Am 9:11** 5521
sitting in the tax collector's **b**; **Mt 9:9** *5058*
of Alphaeus sitting in the tax **b**, **Mk 2:14** *5058*
named Levi sitting in the tax **b**, **Lk 5:27** *5058*

BOOTHS

and made **b** for his livestock; **Gn 33:17** 5521
of **B** for seven days to the LORD. **Lv 23:34** 5521
shall live in **b** for seven days; **Lv 23:42** 5521
in Israel shall live in **b**, **Lv 23:42** 5521
I had the sons of Israel live in **b** **Lv 23:43** 5521
"You shall celebrate the Feast of **B** **Dt 16:13** 5521
of Weeks and at the Feast of **B**, **Dt 16:16** 5521
of debts, at the Feast of **B**, **Dt 31:10** 5521
of Weeks and the Feast of **B**. **2Ch 8:13** 5521
They celebrated the Feast of **B**, **Ezr 3:4** 5521
the sons of Israel should live in **b** **Ne 8:14** 5521
of *other* leafy trees, to make **b**, **Ne 8:15** 5521
them and made **b** for themselves, **Ne 8:16** 5521
made **b** and lived in them. **Ne 8:17** 5521
and to celebrate the Feast of **B**. **Zch 14:16** 5521
go up to celebrate the Feast of **B**. **Zch 14:18** 5521
go up to celebrate the Feast of **B**. **Zch 14:19** 5521
feast of the Jews, the Feast of **B**, **Jn 7:2** *4634*

BOOTY

count of the **b** that was captured, **Nu 31:26** 4455a
and divide the **b** between the **Nu 31:27** 4455a
Now the **b** that remained from the **Nu 31:32** 4455a
The men of war had taken **b**, **Nu 31:53** 962
"We took only the animals as our **b** **Dt 2:35** 962
of the cities we took as our **b**. **Dt 3:7** 962
"Then you shall gather all its **b** **Dt 13:16** 7998
burn the city and all its **b** with fire **Dt 13:16** 7998
you shall take as **b** for yourself; **Dt 20:14** 962
wicked man desires the **b** of evil men, **Pr 12:12** 4685b
Swift is the **b**, speedy is the prey. **Is 8:1** 7998
To capture **b** and to seize plunder, **Is 10:6** 7998
will divide the **b** with the strong; **Is 53:12** 7998
I will give for **b** without cost, **Jer 15:13** 957
and all your treasures for **b**, **Jer 17:3** 957
he will have his own life as **b**. **Jer 21:9** 7998
his *own* life as **b** and stay alive.' **Jer 38:2** 7998
you will have your *own* life as **b**, **Jer 39:18** 7998
'but I will give your life to you as **b** **Jer 45:5** 7998
their many cattle for **b**, **Jer 49:32** 7998
he will distribute plunder, **b** and **Da 11:24** 7998

BOR-ASHAN

and to those who were in **B**, **1Sa 30:30** 953b

BORDER

within all the confines of its **b**, **Gn 23:17** 1366
one end of Egypt's **b** to the other. **Gn 47:21** 1366
to the **b** of the land of Canaan. **Ex 16:35** 7097a
the mountain or touch the **b** of it; **Ex 19:12** 7097a
gold and make a gold **b** around it. **Ex 25:24** 2213
a gold **b** for the rim around it. **Ex 25:25** 2213
Hor by the **b** of the land of Edom, **Nu 20:23** 1366
out of the **b** of the Amorites, **Nu 21:13** 1366
for the Arnon is the **b** of Moab, **Nu 21:13** 1366
Ar, And leans to the **b** of Moab." **Nu 21:15** 1366
we have passed through your **b**." **Nu 21:22** 1366
Israel to pass through his **b**. **Nu 21:23** 1366
for the **b** of the sons of Ammon *was* **Nu 21:24** 1366
of Moab, which is on the Arnon **b**, **Nu 22:36** 1366
at the extreme end of the **b**. **Nu 22:36** 1366
at Iye-abarim, at the **b** of Moab. **Nu 33:44** 1366
and your southern **b** shall extend **Nu 34:3** 1366
'Then your **b** shall turn *direction* **Nu 34:4** 1366
'The **b** shall turn *direction* **Nu 34:5** 1366
'As for the western **b**, **Nu 34:6** 1366
this shall be your west **b**. **Nu 34:6** 1366
'And this shall be your north **b**: **Nu 34:7** 1366
you shall draw your **b** line from **Nu 34:7**
of the **b** shall be at Zedad; **Nu 34:8** 1366
the **b** shall proceed to Ziphron, **Nu 34:9** 1366
This shall be your north **b**. **Nu 34:9** 1366
'For your eastern **b** you shall also **Nu 34:10** 1366
and the **b** shall go down from **Nu 34:11** 1366
and the **b** shall go down and reach **Nu 34:11** 1366
'And the **b** shall go down to the **Nu 34:12** 1366
goes beyond the **b** of his city of refuge **Nu 35:26** 1366
the **b** of his city of refuge, **Nu 35:27** 1366
cross over Ar, the **b** of Moab. **Dt 2:18** 1366
as far as the **b** of the Geshurites and **Dt 3:14** 1366
the middle of the valley as a **b** **Dt 3:16** 1366
the **b** of the sons of Ammon; **Dt 3:16** 1366
also, with the Jordan as *a* **b**, **Dt 3:17** 1366
your **b** will be from the **Dt 11:24** 1366
your **b** as He has promised you, **Dt 12:20** 1366
the **b** of the sons of Ammon; **Jos 12:2** 1366
as far as the **b** of the Geshurites **Jos 12:5** 1366
as the **b** of Sihon king of Heshbon. **Jos 12:5** 1366
as the **b** of Ekron to the north **Jos 13:3** 1366
as Aphek, to the **b** of the Amorite; **Jos 13:4** 1366
far as the **b** of the sons of Ammon; **Jos 13:10** 1366
The **b** of the sons of Reuben **Jos 13:23** 1366
Mahanaim as far as the **b** of Debir; **Jos 13:26** 1366
Heshbon, with the Jordan as a **b**, **Jos 13:27** 1366
families reached the **b** of Edom, **Jos 15:1** 1366
Their south **b** was from the **Jos 15:2** 1366
and the **b** ended at the sea. **Jos 15:4** 1366
This shall be your south **b**. **Jos 15:4** 1366
The east **b** *was* the Salt Sea, **Jos 15:5** 1366
And the **b** of the north side was **Jos 15:5** 1366
Then the **b** went up to Beth-hoglah, **Jos 15:6** 1366
and the **b** went up to the stone of **Jos 15:6** 1366

The **b** went up to Debir from	**Jos 15:7**	1366
and the **b** continued to the waters	**Jos 15:7**	1366
Then the **b** went up the valley of	**Jos 15:8**	1366
and the **b** went up to the top of	**Jos 15:8**	1366
the top of the mountain the **b** curved	**Jos 15:9**	1366
then the **b** curved to Baalah	**Jos 15:9**	1366
The **b** turned about from Baalah	**Jos 15:10**	1366
The **b** proceeded to the side of	**Jos 15:11**	1366
Then the **b** curved to Shikkeron and	**Jos 15:11**	1366
and the **b** ended at the sea.	**Jos 15:11**	1366
The west **b** *was* at the Great Sea,	**Jos 15:12**	1366
This is the **b** around the sons of	**Jos 15:12**	1366
toward the **b** of Edom in the south	**Jos 15:21**	1366
the **b** of the Archites at Ataroth.	**Jos 16:2**	1366
the **b** of their inheritance	**Jos 16:5**	1366
Then the **b** went westward at	**Jos 16:6**	1366
and the **b** turned about eastward to	**Jos 16:6**	1366
From Tappuah the **b** continued	**Jos 16:8**	1366
The **b** of Manasseh ran from	**Jos 17:7**	1366
then the **b** went southward to the	**Jos 17:7**	1366
but Tappuah on the **b** of Manasseh	**Jos 17:8**	1366
The **b** went down to the brook	**Jos 17:9**	1366
and the **b** of Manasseh *was* on the	**Jos 17:9**	1366
Manasseh, and the sea was their **b**;	**Jos 17:10**	1366
Their **b** on the north side was	**Jos 18:12**	1366
then the **b** went up to the side of	**Jos 18:12**	1366
From there the **b** continued to Luz,	**Jos 18:13**	1366
the **b** went down to Ataroth-addar,	**Jos 18:13**	1366
The **b** extended *from there* and	**Jos 18:14**	1366
and the **b** went westward and went	**Jos 18:15**	1366
The **b** went down to the edge of	**Jos 18:16**	1366
The **b** continued to the side of	**Jos 18:19**	1366
and the **b** ended at the north bay	**Jos 18:19**	1366
This *was* the south **b**.	**Jos 18:19**	1366
Jordan was its **b** on the east side.	**Jos 18:20**	1379
Then their **b** went up to the west	**Jos 19:11**	1366
as far as the **b** of Chisloth-tabor,	**Jos 19:12**	1366
The **b** circled around it on the	**Jos 19:14**	1366
The **b** reached to Tabor and	**Jos 19:22**	1366
and their **b** ended at the Jordan;	**Jos 19:22**	1366
The **b** turned to Ramah and to	**Jos 19:29**	1366
then the **b** turned to Hosah, and it	**Jos 19:29**	1366
Their **b** was from Heleph, from	**Jos 19:33**	1366
Then the **b** turned westward to	**Jos 19:34**	1366
the Jordan a **b** between us and you,	**Jos 22:25**	1366
The **b** of the Amorites ran from	**Jg 1:36**	1366
for the Arnon *was* the **b** of Moab.	**Jg 11:18**	1366
them to the **b** of Beth-shemesh.	**1Sa 6:12**	1366
anymore within the **b** of Israel.	**1Sa 7:13**	1366
another company turned toward the **b**	**1Sa 13:18**	1366
remaining within any **b** of Israel,	**2Sa 21:5**	1366
Philistines and to the **b** of Egypt;	**1Ki 4:21**	1366
were summoned and stood on the **b**.	**2Ki 3:21**	1366
He restored the **b** of Israel from	**2Ki 14:25**	1366
bless me indeed and enlarge my **b**,	**1Ch 4:10**	1366
and as far as the **b** of Egypt.	**2Ch 9:26**	1366
fame extended to the **b** of Egypt,	**2Ch 26:8**	935
a pillar to the LORD near its **b**.	**Is 19:19**	1366
Come to her from the farthest **b**;	**Jer 50:26**	7093
judge you to the **b** of Israel;	**Ezk 11:10**	1366
judge you to the **b** of Israel.	**Ezk 11:11**	1366
and even to the **b** of Ethiopia.	**Ezk 29:10**	1366
and its **b** on its edge round about	**Ezk 43:13**	1366
the **b** around it *shall be* half a	**Ezk 43:17**	1366
ledge and on the **b** round about;	**Ezk 43:20**	1366
the west **b** to the east border.	**Ezk 45:7**	1366
the west border to the east **b**.	**Ezk 45:7**	1366
which is between the **b** of Damascus	**Ezk 47:16**	1366
of Damascus and the **b** of Hamath;	**Ezk 47:16**	1366
which is by the **b** of Hauran.	**Ezk 47:16**	1366
to Hazar-enan *at* the **b** of Damascus,	**Ezk 47:17**	1366
the north is the **b** of Hamath.	**Ezk 47:17**	1366
from the *north* **b** to the eastern	**Ezk 47:18**	1366
from the *south* **b** to a point	**Ezk 47:20**	1366
as Hazar-enan *at* the **b** of Damascus,	**Ezk 48:1**	1366
"Beside the **b** of Dan, from	**Ezk 48:2**	1366
"Beside the **b** of Asher, from	**Ezk 48:3**	1366
"Beside the **b** of Naphtali,	**Ezk 48:4**	1366
"Beside the **b** of Manasseh,	**Ezk 48:5**	1366
"Beside the **b** of Ephraim,	**Ezk 48:6**	1366
"Beside the **b** of Reuben, from	**Ezk 48:7**	1366
"And beside the **b** of Judah, from	**Ezk 48:8**	1366
place, by the **b** of the Levites.	**Ezk 48:12**	1366
"Alongside the **b** of the priests	**Ezk 48:13**	1366
the allotment toward the east **b**,	**Ezk 48:21**	1366
of the 25,000 toward the west **b**,	**Ezk 48:21**	1366
everything between the **b** of Judah	**Ezk 48:22**	1366
and the **b** of Benjamin shall be	**Ezk 48:22**	1366
"Beside the **b** of Benjamin,	**Ezk 48:24**	1366
"Beside the **b** of Simeon, from	**Ezk 48:25**	1366
"Beside the **b** of Issachar,	**Ezk 48:26**	1366
"Beside the **b** of Zebulun,	**Ezk 48:27**	1366
"And beside the **b** of Gad, at the	**Ezk 48:28**	1366
the **b** shall be from Tamar to the	**Ezk 48:28**	1366
you Will send you forth to the **b**,	**Ob 1:7**	1366
beyond the **b** of Israel!"	**Mal 1:5**	1366

BORDERED

the Arabs who **b** the Ethiopians;	**2Ch 21:16**	5921, 3027

BORDERS

be seen among you in all your **b**.	**Ex 13:7**	1366
before you and enlarge your **b**,	**Ex 34:24**	1366
land of Canaan according to its **b**.	**Nu 34:2**	1367
according to its **b** all around.' "	**Nu 34:12**	1367
its farthest **b** it shall be yours;	**Jos 17:18**	8444
and according to its **b** all around.	**Jos 18:20**	1367
the land for inheritance by its **b**,	**Jos 19:49**	1367
they had **b**, even borders between	**1Ki 7:28**	4526
even **b** between the frames,	**1Ki 7:28**	4526
and on the **b** which were between	**1Ki 7:29**	4526
and their **b** were square,	**1Ki 7:31**	4526
four wheels *were* underneath the **b**,	**1Ki 7:32**	4526
stays and its **b** *were* part of it.	**1Ki 7:35**	4526
plates of its stays and on its **b**,	**1Ki 7:36**	4526
were in it and its **b** from Tirzah,	**2Ki 15:16**	1366
Ahaz cut off the **b** of the stands,	**2Ki 16:17**	4526
of Sharon, as far as their **b**.	**1Ch 5:16**	8444
to their camps within their **b**.	**1Ch 6:54**	1366
the **b** of the sons of Manasseh,	**1Ch 7:29**	3027
He makes peace in your **b**;	**Ps 147:14**	1366
extended all the **b** of the land.	**Is 26:15**	7099
or destruction within your **b**;	**Is 60:18**	1366
your sins And within all your **b**.	**Jer 15:13**	1366
places for sin throughout your **b**.	**Jer 17:3**	1366
b are in the heart of the seas;	**Ezk 27:4**	1366
In order to enlarge their **b**.	**Am 1:13**	1366
And Hamath also, which **b** on it;	**Zch 9:2**	1379

BORE

men, and they **b** *children* to them.	**Gn 6:4**	3205
So Hagar **b** Abram a son;	**Gn 16:15**	3205
the name of his son, whom Hagar **b**,	**Gn 16:15**	3205
old when Hagar **b** Ishmael to him.	**Gn 16:16**	3205
The firstborn **b** a son,	**Gn 19:37**	3205
for the younger, she also **b** a son,	**Gn 19:38**	3205
maids, so that they **b** *children*.	**Gn 20:17**	3205
So Sarah conceived and **b** a son to	**Gn 21:2**	3205
born to him, whom Sarah **b** to him,	**Gn 21:3**	3205
these eight Milcah **b** to Nahor,	**Gn 22:23**	3205
also **b** Tebah and Gaham and Tahash	**Gn 22:24**	3205
of Milcah, whom she **b** to Nahor."	**Gn 24:24**	3205
"Now Sarah my master's wife **b** a	**Gn 24:36**	3205
Nahor's son, whom Milcah **b** to him';	**Gn 24:47**	3205
She **b** to him Zimran and	**Gn 25:2**	3205
Sarah's maid, **b** to Abraham;	**Gn 25:12**	3205
So Esau **b** a grudge against Jacob	**Gn 27:41**	7852
and **b** a son and named him Reuben,	**Gn 29:32**	3205
again and **b** a son and said,	**Gn 29:33**	3205
again and **b** a son and said,	**Gn 29:34**	3205
again and **b** a son and said,	**Gn 29:35**	3205
saw that she **b** Jacob no children,	**Gn 30:1**	3205
conceived and **b** Jacob a son.	**Gn 30:5**	3205
again and **b** Jacob a second son.	**Gn 30:7**	3205
Leah's maid Zilpah **b** Jacob a son.	**Gn 30:10**	3205
maid Zilpah **b** Jacob a second son.	**Gn 30:12**	3205
conceived and **b** Jacob a fifth son.	**Gn 30:17**	3205
again and **b** a sixth son to Jacob.	**Gn 30:19**	3205
Afterward she **b** a daughter and	**Gn 30:21**	3205
conceived and **b** a son and said,	**Gn 30:23**	3205
I **b** the loss of it myself.	**Gn 31:39**	2398
Adah **b** Eliphaz to Esau, and	**Gn 36:4**	3205
to Esau, and Basemath **b** Reuel,	**Gn 36:4**	3205
b Jeush and Jalam and Korah.	**Gn 36:5**	3205
and she **b** Amalek to Eliphaz.	**Gn 36:12**	3205
she **b** to Esau, Jeush and Jalam and	**Gn 36:14**	3205
and **b** a son and he named him Er.	**Gn 38:3**	3205
and **b** a son and named him Onan.	**Gn 38:4**	3205
She **b** still another son and	**Gn 38:5**	3205
it was at Chezib that she **b** him.	**Gn 38:5**	3205
Potiphera priest of On, **b** to him.	**Gn 41:50**	3205
know that my wife **b** me two sons;	**Gn 44:27**	3205
whom she **b** to Jacob in Paddan-aram,	**Gn 46:15**	3205
and she **b** to Jacob these sixteen	**Gn 46:18**	3205
Potiphera, priest of On, **b** to him.	**Gn 46:20**	3205
Rachel, and she **b** these to Jacob;	**Gn 46:25**	3205
The woman conceived and **b** a son;	**Ex 2:2**	3205
and she **b** him Aaron and Moses;	**Ex 6:20**	3205
and she **b** him Nadab and Abihu,	**Ex 6:23**	3205
of Putiel, and she **b** him Phinehas.	**Ex 6:25**	3205
and *how* I **b** you on eagles' wings,	**Ex 19:4**	5375
blossoms, and it **b** ripe almonds.	**Nu 17:8**	1580
she **b** to Amram: Aaron and Moses	**Nu 26:59**	3205
was in Shechem also **b** him a son,	**Jg 8:31**	3205
Gilead's wife **b** him sons;	**Jg 11:2**	3205
of Perez whom Tamar **b** to Judah,	**Ru 4:12**	3205
then she **b** him a son.	**2Sa 11:27**	3205
that Uriah's widow **b** to David,	**2Sa 12:15**	3205
of Tahpenes **b** his son Genubath,	**1Ki 11:20**	3205
The woman conceived and **b** a	**2Ki 4:17**	3205
Abraham's concubine, *whom* she **b**,	**1Ch 1:32**	3205
b him Perez and Zerah.	**1Ch 2:4**	3205
Abigail **b** Amasa, and the	**1Ch 2:17**	3205
married Ephrath, who **b** him Hur.	**1Ch 2:19**	3205
and she **b** him Segub.	**1Ch 2:21**	3205
b him Ashhur the father of Tekoa.	**1Ch 2:24**	3205
and she **b** him Ahban and Molid.	**1Ch 2:29**	3205
in marriage, and she **b** him Attai.	**1Ch 2:35**	3205
Ephah, Caleb's concubine, **b** Haran,	**1Ch 2:46**	3205
concubine, **b** Sheber and Tirhanah.	**1Ch 2:48**	3205
She also **b** Shaaph the father of	**1Ch 2:49**	3205
Naarah **b** him Ahuzzam, Hepher,	**1Ch 4:6**	3205
"Because I **b** *him* with pain."	**1Ch 4:9**	3205
and she conceived *and* **b**	**1Ch 4:17**	
wife **b** Jered the father of Gedor,	**1Ch 4:18**	3205
men who **b** shield and sword and	**1Ch 5:18**	5375
whom his Aramean concubine **b**;	**1Ch 7:14**	3205
she **b** Machir the father of Gilead.	**1Ch 7:14**	3205
Maacah the wife of Machir **b** a son,	**1Ch 7:16**	3205
b Ishhod and Abiezer and Mahlah.	**1Ch 7:18**	3205
and she conceived and **b** a son,	**1Ch 7:23**	3205
who **b** shield and spear *were* 6,800,	**1Ch 12:24**	5375
and she **b** him sons:	**2Ch 11:19**	3205
of Absalom, and she **b** him Abijah,	**2Ch 11:20**	3205
"However, You **b** with them for many	**Ne 9:30**	4900
And bitterness to her who **b** him.	**Pr 17:25**	3205
pure *child* of the one who **b** her.	**SS 6:9**	3205
Surely our griefs He Himself **b**,	**Is 53:4**	5375
Yet He Himself **b** the sin of many,	**Is 53:12**	5375
"She who **b** seven *sons* pines away;	**Jer 15:9**	3205
be blessed when my mother **b** me!	**Jer 20:14**	3205
hurl you and your mother who **b** you	**Jer 22:26**	3205
I **b** the reproach of my youth.'	**Jer 31:19**	5375
Those whom I **b** and reared, My	**La 2:22**	2946
and they **b** sons and daughters.	**Ezk 23:4**	3205
their sons, whom they **b** to Me,	**Ezk 23:37**	3205
and **b** their disgrace with those	**Ezk 32:24**	5375
and they **b** their disgrace with	**Ezk 32:25**	5375
and **b** their disgrace with those	**Ezk 32:30**	5375
and she conceived and **b** him a son.	**Hos 1:3**	3205
the wheat sprouted and **b** grain,	**Mt 13:26**	*4160*
"Blessed is the womb that **b** You and	**Lk 11:27**	*941*
and the wombs that never **b**,	**Lk 23:29**	*1080*
and He Himself **b** our sins in His	**1Pe 2:24**	*399*

BORED

a chest and **b** a hole in its lid and	**2Ki 12:9**	5344a

BORN

Now to Enoch was **b** Irad,	**Gn 4:18**	3205
To Seth, to him also a son was **b**;	**Gn 4:26**	3205
and daughters were **b** to them,	**Gn 6:1**	3205
were **b** to them after the flood.	**Gn 10:1**	3205
of Japheth, children were **b**.	**Gn 10:21**	3205
Two sons were **b** to Eber;	**Gn 10:25**	3205
his trained men, **b** in his house,	**Gn 14:14**	3211
one **b** in my house is my heir."	**Gn 15:3**	1121
a *servant* who is **b** in the house or	**Gn 17:12**	3211
"A *servant* who is **b** in your house	**Gn 17:13**	3211
"Will a child be **b** to a man one	**Gn 17:17**	3205
and all *the servants* who were **b** in	**Gn 17:23**	3211
who were **b** in the house or bought	**Gn 17:27**	3211
name of his son who was **b** to him,	**Gn 21:3**	3205
when his son Isaac was **b** to him.	**Gn 21:5**	3205
b to Bethuel the son of Milcah,	**Gn 24:15**	3205
who were **b** to him in Paddan-aram.	**Gn 35:26**	3205
b to him in the land of Canaan.	**Gn 36:5**	3205
came, two sons were **b** to Joseph,	**Gn 41:50**	3205
Egypt were **b** Manasseh and Ephraim,	**Gn 46:20**	3205
of Rachel, who were **b** to Jacob;	**Gn 46:22**	3205
were **b** to him in Egypt were two;	**Gn 46:27**	3205
who were **b** to you in the land of	**Gn 48:5**	3205
been **b** after them shall be yours;	**Gn 48:6**	3205
Manasseh, were **b** on Joseph's knees.	**Gn 50:23**	3205
b you are to cast into the Nile,	**Ex 1:22**	3209
whether **b** at home or born outside,	**Lv 18:9**	4138
whether born at home or **b** outside,	**Lv 18:9**	4138
wife's daughter, **b** to your father,	**Lv 18:11**	4138
and those who are **b** in his house	**Lv 22:11**	3211
an ox or a sheep or a goat is **b**,	**Lv 22:27**	3205
Levi, who was **b** to Levi in Egypt;	**Nu 26:59**	3205
To Aaron were **b** Nadab and Abihu,	**Nu 26:60**	3205
all the firstborn males that are **b**	**Dt 15:19**	3205
sons of the third generation who are **b**	**Dt 23:8**	3205
but all the people who were **b** in	**Jos 5:5**	3209
do for the boy who is to be **b**."	**Jg 13:8**	3205
their father who was **b** in Israel;	**Jg 18:29**	3205
"A son has been **b** to Naomi!"	**Ru 4:17**	3205
to Perez was **b** Hezron,	**Ru 4:18**	3205
and to Hezron was **b** Ram,	**Ru 4:19**	3205
and to Amminadab was **b** Nahshon,	**Ru 4:20**	3205
and to Salmon was **b** Boaz,	**Ru 4:21**	3205
and to Obed was **b** Jesse, and to	**Ru 4:22**	3205
Sons were **b** to David at Hebron:	**2Sa 3:2**	3205
These were **b** to David at Hebron.	**2Sa 3:5**	3205
and daughters were **b** to David.	**2Sa 5:13**	3205
who were **b** to him in Jerusalem:	**2Sa 5:14**	3209
is **b** to you shall surely die."	**2Sa 12:14**	3209
Absalom there were **b** three sons,	**2Sa 14:27**	3205
he also had been **b** to the giant.	**2Sa 21:20**	3205
four were **b** to the giant in Gath,	**2Sa 21:22**	3205
and he was **b** after Absalom.	**1Ki 1:6**	3205
your son who will be **b** to you,	**1Ki 8:19**	3318, 2504
shall be **b** to the house of David,	**1Ki 13:2**	3205
Two sons were **b** to Eber,	**1Ch 1:19**	3205
these three were **b** to him by	**1Ch 2:3**	3205
who were **b** to him *were* Jerahmeel,	**1Ch 2:9**	3205
David who were **b** to him in Hebron:	**1Ch 3:1**	3205
Six were **b** to him in Hebron, and	**1Ch 3:4**	3205
These were **b** to him in Jerusalem:	**1Ch 3:5**	3205
who were **b** in the land killed,	**1Ch 7:21**	3205
children **b** *to him* in Jerusalem:	**1Ch 14:4**	3205
'Behold, a son will be **b** to you,	**1Ch 22:9**	3205
Also to his son Shemaiah sons were **b**	**1Ch 26:6**	3205
your son who will be **b** to you,	**2Ch 6:9**	3318, 2504
and three daughters were **b** to him.	**Jb 1:2**	3205
day perish on which I was to be **b**,	**Jb 3:3**	3205
For man is **b** for trouble, As	**Jb 5:7**	3205
foal of a wild donkey is **b** a man.	**Jb 11:12**	3205
"Man, who is **b** of woman, Is	**Jb 14:1**	3205
"Were you the first man to be **b**,	**Jb 15:7**	3205
pure, Or he who is **b** of a woman,	**Jb 15:14**	3205
can he be clean who is **b** of woman?	**Jb 25:4**	3205
"You know, for you were **b** then,	**Jb 38:21**	3205
To a people who will be **b**,	**Ps 22:31**	3205
even the children *yet* to be **b**,	**Ps 78:6**	3205
'This one was **b** there.' "	**Ps 87:4**	3205
one and that one were **b** in her';	**Ps 87:5**	3205
"This one was **b** there."	**Ps 87:6**	3205
Before the mountains were **b** Or	**Ps 90:2**	3205
And a brother is **b** for adversity.	**Pr 17:17**	3205
he was **b** poor in his kingdom.	**Ec 4:14**	3205
exactly as a man is **b**, thus will he die.	**Ec 5:16**	935
For a child will be **b** to us,	**Is 9:6**	3205
were inhabitants of the world **b**.	**Is 26:18**	5307
Can a land be **b** in one day?	**Is 66:8**	2342a

you were **b** I consecrated you; Jer 1:5 3318, 7358
and daughters **b** in this place, Jer 16:3 3209
Cursed be the day when I was **b**; Jer 20:14 3205
"A baby boy has been **b** to you!" Jer 20:15 3205
country where you were not **b**, Jer 22:26 3205
little ones who were **b** healthy? La 2:20 2949
b your navel cord was not cut, Ezk 16:4 3205
abhorred on the day you were **b**. Ezk 16:5 3205
her as on the day when she was **b**. Hos 2:3 3205
of Mary, by whom Jesus was **b**, Mt 1:16 *1080*
Now after Jesus was **b** in Bethlehem Mt 2:1 *1080*
who has been **b** King of the Jews? Mt 2:2 *5088*
them where the Messiah was to be **b**. Mt 2:4 *1080*
among those **b** of women there has Mt 11:11 *1084*
"For there are eunuchs who were **b** Mt 19:12 *1080*
that man if he had not been **b**." Mt 26:24 *1080*
that man if he had not been **b**." Mk 14:21 *1080*
there has been **b** for you a Savior, Lk 2:11 *5088*
to you, among those **b** of women there Lk 7:28 *1084*
who were **b**, not of blood nor of Jn 1:13 *1080*
say to you, unless one is **b** again he Jn 3:3 *1080*
"How can a man be **b** when he is old? Jn 3:4 *1080*
into his mother's womb and be **b**, Jn 3:4 *1080*
one is **b** of water and the Spirit he Jn 3:5 *1080*
which is **b** of the flesh is flesh, Jn 3:6 *1080*
is **b** of the Spirit is spirit. Jn 3:6 *1080*
'You must be **b** again.' Jn 3:7 *1080*
everyone who is **b** of the Spirit." Jn 3:8 *1080*
"We were not **b** of fornication; Jn 8:41 *1080*
say to you, before Abraham was **b**, Jn 8:58 *1096*
that he would be **b** blind?" Jn 9:2 *1080*
your son, who you say was **b** blind? Jn 9:19 *1080*
our son, and that he was **b** blind; Jn 9:20 *1080*
the eyes of a person **b** blind. Jn 9:32 *1080*
"You were **b** entirely in sins, and Jn 9:34 *1080*
a child has been **b** into the world. Jn 16:21 *1080*
For this I have been **b**, Jn 18:37 *1080*
own language to which we were **b**? Ac 2:8 *1080*
was at this time that Moses was **b**; Ac 7:20 *1080*
am a Jew, **b** in Tarsus of Cilicia, Ac 22:3 *1080*
"But I was actually **b** *a citizen*." Ac 22:28 *1080*
who was **b** of a descendant of David Ro 1:3 *1096*
though *the twins* were not yet **b** and Ro 9:11 *1080*
all, as to one untimely **b**, 1Co 15:8 *1626*
sent forth His Son, **b** of a woman, Ga 4:4 *1096*
born of a woman, **b** under the Law, Ga 4:4 *1096*
was **b** according to the flesh, Ga 4:23 *1080*
he who was **b** according to the flesh Ga 4:29 *1080*
the flesh persecuted him *who was* **b** Ga 4:29
there was **b** even of one man, Heb 11:12 *1096*
By faith Moses, when he was **b**, Heb 11:23 *1080*
mercy has caused us to be **b** again 1Pe 1:3 *313*
for you have been **b** again not of 1Pe 1:23 *313*
b as creatures of instinct to be 2Pe 2:12 *1080*
righteousness is **b** of Him. 1Jn 2:29 *1080*
No one who is **b** of God practices sin, 1Jn 3:9 *1080*
sin, because he is **b** of God. 1Jn 3:9 *1080*
loves is **b** of God and knows God. 1Jn 4:7 *1080*
Jesus is the Christ is **b** of God, 1Jn 5:1 *1080*
Father loves the *child* **b** of Him. 1Jn 5:1 *1080*
is **b** of God overcomes the world; 1Jn 5:4 *1080*
that no one who is **b** of God sins; 1Jn 5:18 *1080*
but He who was **b** of God keeps him 1Jn 5:18 *1080*

BORNE
Abram's wife had **b** him no *children*, Gn 16:1 3205
have **b** him a son in his old age." Gn 21:7 3205
whom she had **b** to Abraham, Gn 21:9 3205
Milcah also has **b** children to your Gn 22:20 3205
because I have **b** him three sons." Gn 29:34 3205
because I have **b** him six sons." Gn 30:20 3205
about when Rachel had **b** Joseph, Gn 30:25 3205
their children whom they have **b**? Gn 31:43 3205
of Leah, whom she had **b** to Jacob, Gn 34:1 3205
and the unloved have **b** him sons, Dt 21:15 3205
was barren and had **b** no *children*. Jg 13:2 3205
are barren and have **b** no *children*, Jg 13:3 3205
whom she had **b** to Saul, 2Sa 21:8 3205
whom she had **b** to Adriel the son 2Sa 21:8 3205
he was not my son, whom I had **b**." 1Ki 3:21 3205
'I have **b** *chastisement;* Jb 34:31 5375
for Your sake I have **b** reproach; Ps 69:7 5375
who have been **b** by Me from birth Is 46:3 6006
her among all the sons she has **b**, Is 51:18 3205
one, you who have **b** no *child;* Is 54:1 3205
that you have **b** me *As* a man of Jer 15:10 3205
is we who have **b** their iniquities. La 5:7 5445
daughters whom you had **b** to Me and Ezk 16:20 3205
"You have **b** *the penalty of* your Ezk 16:58 5375
they have **b** illegitimate children. Hos 5:7 3205
For the tree has **b** its fruit, Jl 2:22 5375
she who is in labor has **b** a child. Mi 5:3 3205
olive tree, it has not **b** *fruit*. Hg 2:19 5375
equal to us who have **b** the burden Mt 20:12 *941*
we have **b** the image of the earthy, 1Co 15:49 *5409*

BORROW
many nations, but you will not **b**; Dt 15:6 5670
many nations, but you shall not **b**. Dt 28:12 3867b
b vessels at large for yourself 2Ki 4:3 7592
from him who wants to **b** from you. Mt 5:42 *1155*

BORROWED
"Alas, my master! For it was **b**." 2Ki 6:5 7592
"We have **b** money for the king's Ne 5:4 3867b

BORROWER
the **b** *becomes* the lender's slave. Pr 22:7 3867b
the seller, the lender like the **b**, Is 24:2 3867b

BORROWS
man **b** *anything* from his neighbor, Ex 22:14 7592

wicked **b** and does not pay back, Ps 37:21 3867b

BOSOM
"Now put your hand into your **b**." Ex 4:6 2436
So he put his hand into his **b**, Ex 4:6 2436
"Put your hand into your **b** again." Ex 4:7 2436
he put his hand into his **b** again, Ex 4:7 2436
and when he took it out of his **b**, Ex 4:7 2436
'Carry them in your **b** as a nurse Nu 11:12 2436
drink of his cup and lie in his **b**, 2Sa 12:3 2436
and let her lie in your **b**, 1Ki 1:2 2436
slept, and laid him in her **b**, 1Ki 3:20 2436
and laid her dead son in my **b**. 1Ki 3:20 2436
Then he took him from her **b** and 1Ki 17:19 2436
By hiding my iniquity in my **b**, Jb 31:33 2243
my prayer kept returning to my **b**. Ps 35:13 2436
From within Your **b**, destroy *them!* Ps 74:11 2436
our neighbors sevenfold into their **b** Ps 79:12 2436
How I bear in my **b** *the reproach* Ps 89:50 2436
Or the binder of sheaves his **b**; Ps 129:7 2683
And embrace the **b** of a foreigner? Pr 5:20 2436
Can a man take fire in his **b** And Pr 6:27 2436
man receives a bribe from the **b** Pr 17:23 2436
anger, And a bribe in the **b**, Pr 21:14 2436
anger resides in the **b** of fools. Ec 7:9 2436
lambs And carry *them* in His **b**; Is 40:11 2436
will bring your sons in *their* **b**, Is 49:22 2684
I will even repay into their **b**, Is 65:6 2436
their former work into their **b**." Is 65:7 2436
delighted with her bountiful **b**." Is 66:11 3519b
b of their children after them, Jer 32:18 2436
is poured out On their mothers' **b**. La 2:12 2436
there their virgin **b** was handled. Ezk 23:3 1717
and they handled her virgin **b** and Ezk 23:8 1717
when the Egyptians handled your **b** Ezk 23:21 1717
From her who lies in your **b** Guard Mi 7:5 2436
away by the angels to Abraham's **b**; Lk 16:22 *2859*
far away and Lazarus in his **b**. Lk 16:23 *2859*
who is in the **b** of the Father, Jn 1:18 *2859*
There was reclining on Jesus' **b** one Jn 13:23 *2859*
He, leaning back thus on Jesus' **b**, Jn 13:25 *4738*
one who also had leaned back on His **b** Jn 21:20 *4738*

BOTH
were **b** naked and were not ashamed. Gn 2:25 8147
the eyes of **b** of them were opened, Gn 3:7 8147
"**B** thorns and thistles it shall Gn 3:18
laid it upon **b** their shoulders Gn 9:23 8147
the house, **b** young and old, Gn 19:4 4480
with blindness, **b** small and great, Gn 19:11 4480
Thus **b** the daughters of Lot were Gn 19:36 8147
have plenty of **b** straw and feed, Gn 24:25 1571
be bereaved of you **b** in one day?" Gn 27:45 8147
b had a dream the same night, Gn 40:5 8147
b me and the chief baker. Gn 41:10
b we and the one in whose Gn 44:16 1571
until now, **b** we and our fathers,' Gn 46:34 1571
shepherds, **b** we and our fathers." Gn 47:3 1571
your eyes, **b** we and our land? Gn 47:19 1571
Joseph took them **b**, Gn 48:13 8147
with him **b** chariots and horsemen; Gn 50:9 1571
b in *vessels of* wood and in Ex 7:19
land of Egypt, **b** man and beast; Ex 9:25 4480
b in the sight of Pharaoh's Ex 11:3
b its head and its legs along Ex 12:9
land of Egypt, **b** man and beast; Ex 12:12 4480
b you and the sons of Israel; Ex 12:31 1571
"Take **b** your flocks and your Ex 12:32 1571
of Israel, **b** of man and beast; Ex 13:2
b the firstborn of man and the Ex 13:15 4480
b yourself and these people who Ex 18:18 1571
the case of **b** parties shall come Ex 22:9 8147
thus it shall be with **b** of them: Ex 26:24 8147
which were written on **b** sides; Ex 32:15 8147
moved them, **b** men and women, Ex 35:22
heart to teach, **b** he and Oholiab, Ex 35:34
b of them for the two corners. Ex 36:29 8147
On **b** sides of the gate of the Ex 38:15
4480, 2088
b without defect, and offer Lv 9:2
a calf and a lamb, **b** one year old, Lv 9:3
they shall **b** bathe in water and be Lv 15:18
"Then Aaron shall lay **b** of his Lv 16:21 8147
cut off from among their people **b** him Lv 20:5
b of them shall surely be put to Lv 20:11 8147
b of them shall surely be put to Lv 20:12 8147
b of them have committed a Lv 20:13 8147
b he and they shall be burned with Lv 20:14
thus **b** of them shall be cut off Lv 20:18 8147
b of the most holy and of Lv 21:22
you shall not kill **b** it and its Lv 22:28
then **b** it and its substitute shall Lv 27:10
then **b** it and its substitute shall Lv 27:33
shall send away **b** male and female; Nu 5:3 4480
b of them full of fine flour mixed Nu 7:13 8147
b of them full of fine flour mixed Nu 7:19 8147
b of them full of fine flour mixed Nu 7:25 8147
b of them full of fine flour mixed Nu 7:31 8147
b of them full of fine flour mixed Nu 7:37 8147
b of them full of fine flour mixed Nu 7:43 8147
b of them full of fine flour mixed Nu 7:49 8147
b of them full of fine flour mixed Nu 7:55 8147
b of them full of fine flour mixed Nu 7:61 8147
b of them full of fine flour mixed Nu 7:67 8147
b of them full of fine flour mixed Nu 7:73 8147
b of them full of fine flour mixed Nu 7:79 8147
b for the alien and for the native Nu 9:14
"When **b** are blown, all the Nu 10:3 1992a
Then Moses returned to the camp, **b** Nu 11:30
When they had **b** come forward, Nu 12:5 8147

b you and they along with Aaron. Nu 16:16
altar, or **b** they and you will die. Nu 18:3 1571
and pierced **b** of them through, Nu 25:8 8147
b he and the sons of Israel with Nu 27:21
the prey, **b** of man and of beast. Nu 31:11
captured, **b** of man and of animal; Nu 31:26
fifty, **b** of man and of animals, Nu 31:47 4480
then **b** the men who have the Dt 19:17 8147
and **b** the loved and the unloved Dt 21:15 8147
woman, then **b** of them shall die, Dt 22:22
1571, 8147
then you shall bring them **b** out to Dt 22:24 8147
for **b** of these are an abomination Dt 23:18
1571, 8147
but **b** with those who stand here Dt 29:15
B young man and virgin, Dt 32:25 1571
in the city, **b** man and woman, Jos 6:21
4480, 5704
b he and the elders of Israel; Jos 7:6
and have **b** stolen and deceived. Jos 7:11 1571
fell that day, **b** men and women, Jos 8:25 4480
their judges were standing on **b** sides Jos 8:33
4480, 2088
b hewers of wood and drawers of Jos 9:23
b the middle of the valley and Jos 12:2
b those who are in Beth-shean and Jos 17:16
b they and their camels were Jg 6:5
"Rule over us, **b** you and your Jg 8:22 1571
thus burning up **b** the shocks and Jg 15:5 4480
So **b** of them sat down and ate and Jg 19:6 8147
so **b** of them ate. Jg 19:8 8147
"Yet there is **b** straw and fodder Jg 19:19 1571
b the entire city with the cattle Jg 20:48 4480
b Mahlon and Chilion also died, Ru 1:5
8147, 1992a
So they **b** went until they came to Ru 1:19 8147
b of whom built the house of Ru 4:11 8147
b with the LORD and with men. 1Sa 2:26 1571
the same day **b** of them will die. 1Sa 2:34 8147
b ears of everyone who hears it will 1Sa 3:11 8147
b the palms of his hands *were* cut off 1Sa 5:4 8147
b Ashdod and its territories. 1Sa 5:6
men of the city, **b** young and old, 1Sa 5:9 4480
b of fortified cities and of 1Sa 6:18 4480
and **b** he and Samuel went out into 1Sa 9:26 8147
then **b** you and also the king who 1Sa 12:14 1571
b you and your king will be swept 1Sa 12:25 1571
When **b** of them revealed 1Sa 14:11 8147
but put to death **b** man and woman, 1Sa 15:3 4480
killed **b** the lion and the bear; 1Sa 17:36 1571
b of them went out to the field. 1Sa 20:11 8147
of the sword, **b** men and women, 1Sa 22:19 4480
wall to us **b** by night and by day, 1Sa 25:16 1571
b by having shed blood without 1Sa 25:31
and they **b** became his wives. 1Sa 25:43
1571, 8147
you will **b** accomplish much and 1Sa 26:25 1571
who were in it, **b** small and great, 1Sa 30:2 4480
of Israel, **b** to men and women, 2Sa 6:19 4480
who is crippled in **b** feet." 2Sa 9:3
Now he was lame in **b** feet. 2Sa 9:13 8147
who would destroy **b** me and my son 2Sa 14:16 3162
show me **b** it and His habitation. 2Sa 15:25
regarded by **b** David and Absalom. 2Sa 16:23 1571
not asked, **b** riches and honor, 1Ki 3:13 1571
b the nave and the inner sanctuary; 1Ki 6:5
b the cherubim were of the same 1Ki 6:25 8147
measured the circumference of **b**. 1Ki 7:15 8147
hundred in rows around **b** capitals. 1Ki 7:20 8145
and the hinges **b** for the doors of 1Ki 7:50
and **b** of them were alone in the 1Ki 11:29 8147
person, **b** bond and free in Israel, 1Ki 14:10
b because of all the evil which he 1Ki 16:7
male, **b** bond and free in Israel; 1Ki 21:21
b you and your cattle and your 2Ki 3:17
and shut the door behind them **b** and 2Ki 4:33 8147
person **b** bond and free in Israel. 2Ki 9:8
b the money of each man's 2Ki 12:4
of it, **b** his ears will tingle. 2Ki 21:12 8147
all the people, **b** small and great; 2Ki 23:2 4480
all the people, **b** small and great, 2Ki 25:26 4480
using **b** the right hand and the 1Ch 12:2
b to the east and to the west. 1Ch 12:15
b you and your relatives, 1Ch 15:12
of Israel, **b** man and woman, 1Ch 16:3 4480
b from the descendants of Eleazar 1Ch 24:5
"**B** riches and honor *come* from 1Ch 29:12
were attacked **b** front and rear; 2Ch 13:14
b in the lowland and in the plain. 2Ch 26:10
b the sojourners who came from the 2Ch 30:25
b the priests and the Levites, 2Ch 31:2
b he and the inhabitants of 2Ch 32:26
Whatever is needed, **b** young bulls, Ezr 6:9
b for their brothers the priests Ezr 6:20
they were **b** hanged on a gallows; Es 2:23 8147
all the Jews, **b** young and old, Es 3:13 4480
of King Ahasuerus, **b** near and far, Es 9:20
b what they had seen in this Es 9:26
Who may lay his hand upon us **b**. Jb 9:33 8147
"**B** the gray-haired and the aged Jb 15:10 1571
in regard to **b** nation and man? Jb 34:29 3162
peace I will **b** lie down and sleep, Ps 4:8 3162
B low and high, Rich and poor Ps 49:2 1571
B rider and horse were cast into a Ps 76:6
number, Animals **b** small and great. Ps 104:25
of Egypt, **B** of man and beast. Ps 135:8 4480
B young men and virgins; Ps 148:12
B of them alike are an abomination Pr 17:15
1571, 8147

B of them are abominable to the Pr 20:10 1571, 8147
eye, The LORD has made **b** of them. Pr 20:12 1571, 8147
ruin *that comes* from **b** of them? Pr 24:22 8147
a fool is heavier than **b** of them. Pr 27:3 8147
LORD gives light to the eyes of **b**. Pr 29:13 8147
know that one fate befalls them **b**. Ec 2:14 3605
"God will judge **b** the righteous Ec 3:17
But better *off* than **b** of them is Ec 4:3 8147
God comes forth with **b** of them. Ec 7:18 3605
b of them alike will be good. Ec 11:6 8147
all choice *fruits,* **B** new and old, SS 7:13
Thus they shall **b** burn together And Is 1:31 8147
and Judah **B** supply and support, Is 3:1
But to **b** the houses of Israel, a Is 8:14 8147
B palm branch and bulrush in a Is 9:14
fruitful garden, **b** soul and body, Is 10:18 4480
groan, I will **b** gasp and pant. Is 42:14 3162
B their own iniquities and the Is 65:7
B the autumn rain and the spring Jer 5:24
For **b** husband and wife shall be Jer 6:11 1571
B the birds of the sky and the Jer 9:10 4480
b the fathers and the sons Jer 13:14
For **b** prophet and priest Have gone Jer 14:18 1571
"**B** great men and small will die Jer 16:6
of this city, **b** man and beast; Jer 21:6
"For **b** prophet and priest are Jer 23:11 1571
b the sealed *copy containing* the Jer 32:11
day **b** in Israel and among mankind; Jer 32:20
b they and their men. Jer 40:8
b small and great approached Jer 42:1 4480
all the people **b** small and great, Jer 42:8 4480
B small and great will die by the Jer 44:12 4480
And **b** of them have fallen down Jer 46:12 8147
B man and beast have wandered off, Jer 50:3 4480
b they and the sons of Judah as Jer 50:4
For the LORD has **b** purposed and Jer 51:12 1571
High That **b** good and ill go forth? La 3:38
what he sold as long as they **b** Ezk 7:13
cut off from it **b** man and beast, Ezk 14:13
b sons and daughters. Behold, Ezk 14:22
fire has consumed **b** of its ends and Ezk 15:4 8147
b your older and your younger; Ezk 16:61
b of them will go out of one land. Ezk 21:19 8147
they **b** took the same way. Ezk 23:13 8147
b your lewdness and your Ezk 23:29
arms, **b** the strong and the broken; Ezk 30:22
burn *them,* **b** shields and bucklers, Ezk 39:9
b according to their arrangements and Ezk 42:11
so as to allow **b** the holy place Da 8:13
"As for **b** kings, their hearts Da 11:27 8147
"But **b** man and beast must be Jon 3:8
evil, **b** hands do it well. Mi 7:3
B the pelican and the hedgehog Zph 2:14 1571
wineskins, and **b** are preserved." Mt 9:17 *297*
destroy **b** soul and body in hell. Mt 10:28 *2532*
'Allow **b** to grow together until Mt 13:30 *297*
man, **b** will fall into a pit." Mt 15:14 *297*
all they found, **b** evil and good; Mt 22:10 *5037*
swears **b** by the altar and by Mt 23:20
swears **b** by the temple and by Him Mt 23:21
swears **b** by the throne of God Mt 23:22
b into the fire and into the water Mk 9:22 *2532*
b righteous in the sight of God, Lk 1:6 *297*
and they were **b** advanced in years. Lk 1:7 *297*
the teachers, **b** listening to them and Lk 2:46 *2532*
came and filled **b** of the boats, Lk 5:7 *297*
otherwise he will **b** tear the new, Lk 5:36 *2532*
Will they not **b** fall into a pit? Lk 6:39 *297*
he graciously forgave them **b**. Lk 7:42 *297*
b men and women, and to eat Lk 12:45
you **b** will come and say to you, Lk 14:9 *2532, 846*
B the Pharisees and the scribes Lk 15:2 *5037*
to go **b** to prison and to death!" Lk 22:33 *2532*
b chief priests and scribes, Lk 22:66 *5037*
and **b** Jesus and His disciples were Jn 2:2 *2532*
"You **b** know Me and know where I Jn 7:28 *2532*
"You have **b** seen Him, and He is Jn 9:37 *2532*
away **b** our place and our nation." Jn 11:48 *2532*
"I have **b** glorified it, and will Jn 12:28 *2532*
but now they have **b** seen and hated Jn 15:24 *2532*
them **b** His hands and His side. Jn 20:20 *2532*
be My witnesses **b** in Jerusalem, Ac 1:8 *5037*
from Rome, **b** Jews and proselytes, Ac 2:10 *5037*
MY BONDSLAVES, B MEN AND WOMEN, Ac 2:18
that he **b** died and was buried, Ac 2:29 *2532*
this which you **b** see and hear. Ac 2:33 *2532*
God has made Him **b** Lord and Christ Ac 2:36 *2532*
b Herod and Pontius Pilate, Ac 4:27 *5037*
b Cyrenians and Alexandrians, Ac 6:9 *5037*
sent *to be* **b** a ruler and a deliverer Ac 7:35 *2532*
they **b** went down into the water, Ac 8:38 *297*
to the Way, **b** men and women, Ac 9:2 *5037*
He did **b** in the land of the Jews Ac 10:39 *5037*
believed, **b** of Jews and of Greeks. Ac 14:1 *5037*
And when an attempt was made by **b** Ac 14:5 *5037*
through **b** Phoenicia and Samaria, Ac 15:3 *5037*
of the Lord, **b** Jews and Greeks. Ac 19:10 *5037*
known to all, **b** Jews and Greeks, Ac 19:17 *5037*
solemnly testifying to **b** Jews and Ac 20:21 *5037*
b men and women into prisons, Ac 22:4 *5037*
of **b** the righteous and the wicked. Ac 24:15 *5037*
always a blameless conscience **b** Ac 24:16
to me, **b** at Jerusalem and here, Ac 25:24 *5037*
b to those of Damascus first, Ac 26:20 *5037*
testifying **b** to small and great, Ac 26:22 *5037*
proclaim light **b** to the *Jewish* people Ac 26:23 *5037*
from **b** the Law of Moses and from Ac 28:23 *5037*
other's faith, **b** yours and mine. Ro 1:12 *5037*
b to Greeks and to barbarians, Ro 1:14 *5037*
b to the wise and to the foolish. Ro 1:14 *5037*
b Jews and Greeks are all under sin; Ro 3:9 *5037*
depth of the riches **b** of the wisdom Ro 11:33 *2532*
b of the dead and of the living. Ro 14:9 *2532*
are the called, **b** Jews and Greeks, 1Co 1:24 *5037*
will **b** bring to light the things hidden 1Co 4:5 *2532*
the world, **b** to angels and to men. 1Co 4:9 *2532*
hour we are **b** hungry and thirsty, 1Co 4:11 *2532*
God will do away with **b** of them. 1Co 6:13 *2532*
may be holy **b** in body and spirit; 1Co 7:34 *2532*
So then **b** he who gives his own 1Co 7:38 *2532*
peace, who made **b** *groups into* one and Eph 2:14 *297*
and might reconcile them **b** in one Eph 2:16 *297*
for through Him we **b** have our Eph 2:18 *297*
knowing that **b** their Master and Eph 6:9 *2532*
since **b** in my imprisonment and in Php 1:7 *5037*
am hard-pressed from **b** *directions,* Php 1:23 *1417*
b to will and to work for *His* good Php 2:13 *2532*
b of having abundance and Php 4:12 *2532*
b in the heavens and on earth, Col 1:16
who **b** killed the Lord Jesus and 1Th 2:15 *2532*
b for yourself and for those who hear 1Tm 4:16 *2532*
that he will be able **b** to exhort in Ti 1:9 *2532*
but **b** their mind and their Ti 1:15 *2532*
now is useful **b** to you and to me. Phm 1:11 *2532*
b in the flesh and in the Lord. Phm 1:16 *2532*
b by signs and wonders and by Heb 2:4 *5037*
For **b** He who sanctifies and those Heb 2:11 *5037*
spirit, of **b** joints and marrow, Heb 4:12 *5037*
b gifts and sacrifices for sins; Heb 5:1 *5037*
He offered up **b** prayers and Heb 5:7 *5037*
a *hope* **b** sure and steadfast and Heb 6:19 *5037*
to offer **b** gifts and sacrifices; Heb 8:3 *5037*
Accordingly **b** gifts and sacrifices Heb 9:9 *5037*
and sprinkled **b** the book itself Heb 9:19 *5037*
he sprinkled **b** the tabernacle and all Heb 9:21 *2532*
from the same mouth come **b** Jas 3:10
send out from the same opening **b** Jas 3:11
b now and to the day of eternity. 2Pe 3:18 *2532*
he has **b** the Father and the Son. 2Jn 1:9 *2532*
of all men, **b** free men and slaves, Rv 19:18 *5037*

BOTHER

"Why do you **b** the woman? Mt 26:10 *2873, 3930*
why do you **b** her? Mk 14:6 *2873, 3930*
'Do not **b** me; Lk 11:7 *2873, 3930*

BOTHERED

that David's conscience **b** him because 1Sa 24:5 5221
and **b** about so many things; Lk 10:41 *2350a*

BOTHERS

yet because this widow **b** me, Lk 18:5 *3930, 2873*

BOTTLE

a **b** of milk and gave him a drink; Jg 4:19 4997
Put my tears in Your **b**. Ps 56:8 4997

BOTTOM

rings of gold and put them on the **b** Ex 28:27 4295
gold rings and placed them on the **b** Ex 39:20 4295
ran into the **b** of the chariot. 1Ki 22:35 2436
and they had not reached the **b** of Da 6:24 773
was torn in two from top to **b**; Mt 27:51 *2736*
was torn in two from top to **b**. Mk 15:38 *2736*

BOTTOMLESS

key of the **b** pit was given to him. Rv 9:1 *12*
He opened the **b** pit, Rv 9:2 *12*

BOUGH

"Joseph is a fruitful **b**, Gn 49:22 1121
bough, A fruitful **b** by a spring; Gn 49:22 1121
or three olives on the topmost **b**, Is 17:6 534

BOUGHS

palm branches and **b** of leafy trees Lv 23:40 6057
you shall not go over the **b** again; Dt 24:20 6287a
And the cedars of God with its **b**. Ps 80:10 6057
off the **b** with a terrible crash; Is 10:33 6333a
may bring forth **b** and bear fruit and Ezk 17:23 6057
b became many and its branches long Ezk 31:5 5634
of the heavens nested in its **b**, Ezk 31:6 5589a
could not compare with its **b**, Ezk 31:8 5589a
and its **b** have been broken in all Ezk 31:12 6288

BOUGHT

b with money from any foreigner, Gn 17:12 4736
who is born in your house or who is **b** Gn 17:13 4736
and all who were **b** with his money, Gn 17:23 4736
or **b** with money from a foreigner, Gn 17:27 4736
He **b** the piece of land where Gn 33:19 7069
b him from the Ishmaelites, Gn 39:1 7069
Canaan for the grain which they **b**, Gn 47:14 7666
So Joseph **b** all the land of Egypt Gn 47:20 7069
b you and your land for Pharaoh; Gn 47:23 7069
which Abraham **b** along with the Gn 49:30 7069
which Abraham had **b** along with the Gn 50:13 7069
'But if it is not **b** back for him Lv 25:30 1350
the LORD a field which he has **b**, Lv 27:22 4736
to the one from whom he **b** it, Lv 27:24 7069
not He your Father who has **b** you? Dt 32:6 7069
piece of ground which Jacob had **b** Jos 24:32 7069
I have **b** from the hand of Naomi all Ru 4:9 7069
ewe lamb Which he **b** and nourished; 2Sa 12:3 7069
So David **b** the threshing floor and 2Sa 24:24 7069
He **b** the hill Samaria from 1Ki 16:24 7069
I **b** male and female slaves and I Ec 2:7 7069
b Me not sweet cane with money, Is 43:24 7069
So I **b** the waistband in accordance Jer 13:2 7069
the waistband that you have **b**, Jer 13:4 7069
"I **b** the field which was at Jer 32:9 7069
will again be **b** in this land."' Jer 32:15 7069
'Fields will be **b** in this land Jer 32:43 7069
So I **b** her for myself for fifteen Hos 3:2 3739
sold all that he had and **b** it. Mt 13:46 *59*
with the money **b** the Potter's Field Mt 27:7 *59*
Joseph **b** a linen cloth, took Mk 15:46 *59*
of James, and Salome, **b** spices, Mk 16:1 *59*
'I have **b** a piece of land and I Lk 14:18 *59*
'I have **b** five yoke of oxen, and I Lk 14:19 *59*
For you have been **b** with a price: 1Co 6:20 *59*
You were **b** with a price; 1Co 7:23 *59*
denying the Master who **b** them, 2Pe 2:1 *59*

BOUND

the wood, and **b** his son Isaac and Gn 22:9 6123
them and **b** him before their eyes. Gn 42:24 631
his life is **b** up in the lad's life, Gn 44:30 7194
utmost **b** of the everlasting hills; Gn 49:26 8379
with their kneading bowls **b** up in Ex 12:34 6887a
They **b** the breastpiece by its Ex 39:21 7405
with sashes and **b** caps on them, Lv 8:13 2280
by which she has **b** herself, Nu 30:4 631
she has **b** herself shall stand. Nu 30:4 631
she has **b** herself shall stand; Nu 30:5 631
lips by which she has **b** herself, Nu 30:6 631
she has **b** herself shall stand. Nu 30:7 631
lips by which she has **b** herself; Nu 30:8 631
by which she has **b** herself, Nu 30:9 631
or **b** herself by an obligation with Nu 30:10 631
which she **b** herself shall stand. Nu 30:11 631
and he **b** it on his right thigh Jg 3:16 2296
Then they **b** him with two new ropes Jg 15:13 631
how you may be **b** to afflict you." Jg 16:6 631
dried, and she **b** him with them. Jg 16:8 631
tell me how you may be **b**." Jg 16:10 631
b him with them and said to him, Jg 16:12 631
tell me how you may be **b**." Jg 16:13 631
Gaza and **b** him with bronze chains, Jg 16:21 631
then the life of my lord shall be **b** 1Sa 25:29 6887a
"Your hands were not **b**, 2Sa 3:34 631
girdle **b** about his loins." 2Ki 1:8 247
and **b** two talents of silver in two 2Ki 5:23 6696a
shut him up and **b** him in prison. 2Ki 17:4 631
and **b** him with bronze fetters 2Ki 25:7 631
hooks, **b** him with bronze *chains* 2Ch 33:11 631
b him with bronze *chains* to take him 2Ch 36:6 631
For many in Judah were **b** by oath Ne 6:18 1167
"And if they are **b** in fetters, Jb 36:8 631
is **b** up in the heart of a child; Pr 22:15 7194
Saying to those who are **b**, Is 49:9 631
blinded Zedekiah's eyes and **b** him Jer 39:7 631
when he had taken him **b** in chains Jer 40:1 631
and the king of Babylon **b** him with Jer 52:11 631
yoke of my transgressions is **b**; La 1:14 8244
it has not been **b** up for healing Ezk 30:21 2280
the broken you have not **b** up, Ezk 34:4 2280
b into the midst of the fire?" Da 3:24 3729
they are **b** for their double guilt. Hos 10:10 631
The iniquity of Ephraim is **b** up; Hos 13:12 6887a
her great men were **b** with fetters. Na 3:10 7576
Herod had John arrested, he **b** him and Mt 14:3 *1210*
on earth shall have been **b** in heaven, Mt 16:19 *1210*
on earth shall have been **b** in heaven; Mt 18:18 *1210*
and they **b** Him, and led Him away and Mt 27:2 *1210*
been **b** with shackles and chains, Mk 5:4 *1210*
had John arrested and **b** in prison Mk 6:17 *1210*
and he was **b** with chains and Lk 8:29 *1195*
has **b** for eighteen long years, Lk 13:16 *1210*
b hand and foot with wrappings, Jn 11:44 *1210*
Jews, arrested Jesus and **b** Him, Jn 18:12 *1210*
Him **b** to Caiaphas the high priest. Jn 18:24 *1210*
and **b** it in linen wrappings with Jn 19:40 *1210*
might bring them **b** to Jerusalem. Ac 9:2 *1210*
them **b** before the chief priests?" Ac 9:21 *1210*
two soldiers, **b** with two chains, Ac 12:6 *1210*
"And now, behold, **b** by the spirit, Ac 20:22 *1210*
belt and **b** his own feet and hands, Ac 21:11 *1210*
For I am ready not only to be **b**, Ac 21:13 *1210*
him to be **b** with two chains; Ac 21:33 *1210*
and **b** themselves under an oath, Ac 23:12 *332*
"We have **b** ourselves under a Ac 23:14 *332*
b themselves under a curse not to eat Ac 23:21 *332*
For the married woman is **b** by law Ro 7:2 *1210*
died to that by which we were **b**, Ro 7:6 *2722*
Are you **b** to a wife? 1Co 7:27 *1210*
is **b** as long as her husband lives; 1Co 7:39 *1210*
be **b** together with unbelievers; 2Co 6:14 *2086*
b at the great river Euphrates." Rv 9:14 *1210*
and **b** him for a thousand years; Rv 20:2 *1210*

BOUNDARIES

He set the **b** of the peoples Dt 32:8 1367
And I placed **b** on it And set a Jb 38:10 2706
all the **b** of the earth; Ps 74:17 1367
I removed the **b** of the peoples And Is 10:13 1367
and the **b** of their habitation, Ac 17:26 *3734*

BOUNDARY

"I will fix your **b** from the Ex 23:31 1366
not move your neighbor's **b** mark, Dt 19:14 1366
who moves his neighbor's **b** mark.' Dt 27:17 1366
allotted *them* to them as a **b**. Ne 9:22 6285
At the **b** of light and darkness. Jb 26:10 8503
a **b** that they may not pass over, Ps 104:9 1366
When He set for the sea its **b** So Pr 8:29 2706
will establish the **b** of the widow. Pr 15:25 1366
b Which your fathers have set. Pr 22:28 1366
Do not move the ancient **b** Or Pr 23:10 1366

the sand as a **b** for the sea,	**Jer 5:22**	1366
holy within all its **b** round about.	**Ezk 45:1**	1366
"This *shall be* the **b** by which you	**Ezk 47:13**	1366
This *shall be* the **b** of the land:	**Ezk 47:15**	1366
"The **b** shall extend from the	**Ezk 47:17**	1366
become like those who move a **b**;	**Hos 5:10**	1366
that day will your **b** be extended.	**Mi 7:11**	2706

BOUNDING

Galloping horses And **b** chariots!	**Na 3:2**	7540

BOUNDS

set **b** for the people all around,	**Ex 19:12**	1379
'Set **b** about the mountain and	**Ex 19:23**	1379

BOUNTIFUL

be delighted with her **b** bosom."	**Is 66:11**	2123b
your previously promised **b** gift,	**2Co 9:5**	*2129*
same would be ready as a **b** gift	**2Co 9:5**	*2129*

BOUNTIFULLY

Because He has dealt **b** with me.	**Ps 13:6**	1580
For the LORD has dealt **b** with you.	**Ps 116:7**	1580
Deal **b** with Your servant, That I	**Ps 119:17**	1580
For You will deal **b** with me."	**Ps 142:7**	1580
he who sows **b** will also reap	**2Co 9:6**	*2129*
bountifully will also reap **b**.	**2Co 9:6**	*2129*

BOUNTY

gave her according to his royal **b**.	**1Ki 10:13**	3027
to eat of its fruit and its **b**,	**Ne 9:36**	2898
according to the king's **b**.	**Es 1:7**	3027
gifts according to the king's **b**.	**Es 2:18**	3027
have crowned the year with Your **b**,	**Ps 65:11**	2899b
be radiant over the **b** of the LORD	**Jer 31:12**	2898

BOW

I set My **b** in the cloud, and it	**Gn 9:13**	7198
the **b** will be seen in the cloud,	**Gn 9:14**	7198
"When the **b** is in the cloud, then	**Gn 9:16**	7198
your gear, your quiver and your **b**,	**Gn 27:3**	7198
you, And nations **b** down to you;	**Gn 27:29**	7812
your mother's sons **b** down to you.	**Gn 27:29**	7812
come to **b** ourselves down before you	**Gn 37:10**	7812
proclaimed before him, "**B** the knee!"	**Gn 41:43**	86
Amorite with my sword and my **b**."	**Gn 48:22**	7198
father's sons shall **b** down to you.	**Gn 49:8**	7812
But his **b** remained firm, And his	**Gn 49:24**	7198
to me and **b** themselves before me,	**Ex 11:8**	7812
Moses made haste to **b** low	**Ex 34:8**	6915
in your land to **b** down to it;	**Lv 26:1**	7812
or serve them, or **b** down to them.	**Jos 23:7**	7812
other gods and **b** down to them,	**Jos 23:16**	7812
but not by your sword or your **b**.	**Jos 24:12**	7198
to serve them and **b** down to them;	**Jg 2:19**	7812
b down to him for a piece of silver	**1Sa 2:36**	7812
his sword and his **b** and his belt.	**1Sa 18:4**	7198
sons of Judah *the song of* the **b**;	**2Sa 1:18**	7198
b of Jonathan did not turn back,	**2Sa 1:22**	7198
my arms can bend a **b** of bronze.	**2Sa 22:35**	7198
Now a certain man drew his **b** at	**1Ki 22:34**	7198
I **b** myself in the house of Rimmon,	**2Ki 5:18**	7812
I **b** myself in the house of Rimmon,	**2Ki 5:18**	7812
with your sword and with your **b**?	**2Ki 6:22**	7198
And Jehu drew his **b** with his full	**2Ki 9:24**	7198
"Take a **b** and arrows."	**2Ki 13:15**	7198
So he took a **b** and arrows.	**2Ki 13:15**	7198
"Put your hand on the **b**."	**2Ki 13:16**	7198
nor **b** down yourselves to them nor	**2Ki 17:35**	7812
Him you shall **b** yourselves down,	**2Ki 17:36**	7812
shield and sword and shot with **b** and	**1Ch 5:18**	7198
and *to shoot* arrows from the **b**;	**1Ch 12:2**	7198
200,000 armed with **b** and shield;	**2Ch 17:17**	7198
A certain man drew his **b** at	**2Ch 18:33**	7198
But the bronze **b** will pierce him.	**Jb 20:24**	7198
And my **b** is renewed in my hand.'	**Jb 29:20**	7198
I will **b** in reverence for You.	**Ps 5:7**	7812
has bent His **b** and made it ready.	**Ps 7:12**	7198
behold, the wicked bend the **b**,	**Ps 11:2**	7198
my arms can bend a **b** of bronze.	**Ps 18:34**	7198
to the dust will **b** before Him,	**Ps 22:29**	3766
drawn the sword and bent their **b** To	**Ps 37:14**	7198
For I will not trust in my **b**,	**Ps 44:6**	7198
He is your Lord, **b** down to Him.	**Ps 45:11**	7812
the **b** and cuts the spear in two;	**Ps 46:9**	7198
nomads of the desert **b** before him,	**Ps 72:9**	3766
let all kings **b** down before him,	**Ps 72:11**	7812
turned aside like a treacherous **b**.	**Ps 78:57**	7198
Come, let us worship and **b** down,	**Ps 95:6**	3766
b down toward Your holy temple And	**Ps 138:2**	7812
B Your heavens, O LORD, and come	**Ps 144:5**	5186
evil will **b** down before the good,	**Pr 14:19**	7817
drawn sword, and from the bent **b** And	**Is 21:15**	7198
have been captured without the **b**;	**Is 22:3**	7198
the wind-driven chaff with his **b**.	**Is 41:2**	7198
in chains And will **b** down to you;	**Is 45:14**	7812
That to Me every knee will **b**,	**Is 45:23**	3766
They **b** down, indeed they worship	**Is 46:6**	5456
arise, Princes will also **b** down	**Is 49:7**	7812
They will **b** down to you with their	**Is 49:23**	7812
And all those who despised you will **b**	**Is 60:14**	7812
you will **b** down to the slaughter.	**Is 65:12**	3766
will come to **b** down before Me,"	**Is 66:23**	7812
"They seize **b** and spear;	**Jer 6:23**	7198
bend their tongue *like* their **b**;	**Jer 9:3**	7198
serve them and to **b** down to them,	**Jer 13:10**	7812
that handle *and* bend the **b**.	**Jer 46:9**	7198
I am going to break the **b** of Elam,	**Jer 49:35**	7198
side, All you who bend the **b**;	**Jer 50:14**	7198
Babylon, All those who bend the **b**:	**Jer 50:29**	7198
"They seize *their* **b** and javelin;	**Jer 50:42**	7198
not him who bends his **b** bend *it*,	**Jer 51:3**	7198
He has bent His **b** like an enemy;	**La 2:4**	7198
He bent His **b** And set me as a	**La 3:12**	7198
strike your **b** from your left hand and	**Ezk 39:3**	7198
that day I will break the **b** of Israel	**Hos 1:5**	7198
and will not deliver them by **b**,	**Hos 1:7**	7198
And I will abolish the **b**,	**Hos 2:18**	7198
They are like a deceitful **b**;	**Hos 7:16**	7198
the **b** will not stand *his ground*,	**Am 2:15**	7198
So that you will no longer **b** down	**Mi 5:13**	7812
b myself before the God on high?	**Mi 6:6**	3721
Your **b** was made bare, The rods of	**Hab 3:9**	7198
"And those who **b** down on the	**Zph 1:5**	7812
And those who **b** down *and* swear to	**Zph 1:5**	7812
of the nations will **b** down to Him,	**Zph 2:11**	7812
And the **b** of war will be cut off.	**Zch 9:10**	7198
For I will bend Judah as My **b**,	**Zch 9:13**	7198
I will fill the **b** with Ephraim.	**Zch 9:13**	7198
peg, From them the **b** of battle,	**Zch 10:4**	7198
and *began* to **b** down before Him,	**Mt 15:25**	*4352*
to lay out anchors from the **b**,	**Ac 27:30**	*4408*
LORD, EVERY KNEE SHALL **B** TO ME,	**Ro 14:11**	*2578*
I **b** my knees before the Father,	**Eph 3:14**	*2578*
name of Jesus EVERY KNEE WILL **B**,	**Php 2:10**	*2578*
them come and **b** down at your feet,	**Rv 3:9**	*4352*
and he who sat on it had a **b**;	**Rv 6:2**	*5115*

BOWED

them and **b** himself to the earth,	**Gn 18:2**	7812
he rose to meet them and **b** down	**Gn 19:1**	7812
and **b** to the people of the land,	**Gn 23:7**	7812
b before the people of the land.	**Gn 23:12**	7812
man **b** low and worshiped the LORD.	**Gn 24:26**	6915
I **b** low and worshiped the LORD,	**Gn 24:48**	6915
he **b** himself to the ground	**Gn 24:52**	7812
b down to the ground seven times,	**Gn 33:3**	7812
their children, and they **b** down.	**Gn 33:6**	7812
her children, and they **b** down;	**Gn 33:7**	7812
near with Rachel, and they **b** down.	**Gn 33:7**	7812
around and **b** down to my sheaf."	**Gn 37:7**	7812
And Joseph's brothers came and **b**	**Gn 42:6**	7812
and **b** to the ground before him.	**Gn 43:26**	7812
They **b** down in homage.	**Gn 43:28**	6915
Then Israel **b** *in worship* at the	**Gn 47:31**	7812
and **b** with his face to the ground.	**Gn 48:12**	7812
He **b** his shoulder to bear *burdens*,	**Gn 49:15**	5186
then they **b** low and worshiped.	**Ex 4:31**	6915
the people **b** low and worshiped.	**Ex 12:27**	6915
and he **b** down and kissed him;	**Ex 18:7**	7812
he **b** all the way to the ground.	**Nu 22:31**	6915
ate and **b** down to their gods.	**Nu 25:2**	7812
his face to the earth, and **b** down,	**Jos 5:14**	7812
and **b** themselves down to them;	**Jg 2:12**	7812
and **b** themselves down to them.	**Jg 2:17**	7812
"Between her feet he **b**,	**Jg 5:27**	3766
Between her feet he **b**,	**Jg 5:27**	3766
Where he **b**, there he fell dead.	**Jg 5:27**	3766
he **b** in worship.	**Jg 7:15**	7812
to the ground, and **b** three times.	**1Sa 20:41**	7812
David **b** with his face to the	**1Sa 24:8**	6915
and **b** herself to the ground.	**1Sa 25:23**	7812
She arose and **b** with her face	**1Sa 25:41**	7812
and he **b** with his face to the	**1Sa 28:14**	6915
So the Cushite **b** to Joab and ran.	**2Sa 18:21**	7812
"He **b** the heavens also, and came	**2Sa 22:10**	5186
and Araunah went out and **b** his	**2Sa 24:20**	7812
Then Bathsheba **b** and prostrated	**1Ki 1:16**	6915
b with her face to the ground,	**1Ki 1:31**	6915
And the king **b** himself on the bed.	**1Ki 1:47**	7812
arose to meet her, **b** before her,	**1Ki 2:19**	7812
all the knees that have not **b** to	**1Ki 19:18**	3766
he came and **b** down on his knees	**2Ki 1:13**	3766
And they came to meet him and **b**	**2Ki 2:15**	7812
feet and **b** herself to the ground,	**2Ki 4:37**	7812
and **b** low and did homage to the	**1Ch 29:20**	6915
b down on the pavement with their	**2Ch 7:3**	3766
Jehoshaphat **b** his head with	**2Ch 20:18**	6915
Judah came and **b** down to the king,	**2Ch 24:17**	7812
as his gods, **b** down before them and	**2Ch 25:14**	7812
with him **b** down and worshiped.	**2Ch 29:29**	3766
joy, and **b** down and worshiped.	**2Ch 29:30**	6915
then they **b** low and worshiped the	**Ne 8:6**	6915
b down and paid homage to Haman;	**Es 3:2**	3766
neither **b** down nor paid homage.	**Es 3:2**	3766
b down nor paid homage to him,	**Es 3:5**	3766
He **b** the heavens also, and came	**Ps 18:9**	5186
They have **b** down and fallen,	**Ps 20:8**	3766
I **b** down mourning, as one who	**Ps 35:14**	7817
I am bent over and greatly **b** down;	**Ps 38:6**	7817
My soul is **b** down;	**Ps 57:6**	3721
and **b** down Through oppression,	**Ps 107:39**	7817
And raises up all who are **b** down.	**Ps 145:14**	3721
raises up those who are **b** down;	**Ps 146:8**	3721
Bel has **b** down, Nebo stoops over;	**Is 46:1**	3766
over, they have **b** down together;	**Is 46:2**	3766
served them and **b** down to them;	**Jer 16:11**	7812
b down to other gods and served them.	**Jer 22:9**	7812
Have **b** their heads to the ground.	**La 2:10**	3381
remembers And is **b** down within me.	**La 3:20**	7743
came to Him and **b** down before Him,	**Mt 8:2**	*4352*
official came and **b** down before Him,	**Mt 9:18**	*4352*
he ran up and **b** down before Him;	**Mk 5:6**	*4352*
and **b** their faces to the ground,	**Lk 24:5**	*2827*
And He **b** His head and gave up His	**Jn 19:30**	*2827*
WHO HAVE NOT **B** THE KNEE TO BAAL."	**Ro 11:4**	*2578*

BOWELS

sickness, a disease of your **b**,	**2Ch 21:15**	4578
until your **b** come out because of	**2Ch 21:15**	4578
his **b** with an incurable sickness.	**2Ch 21:18**	4578
that his **b** came out because of his	**2Ch 21:19**	4578

BOWING

eleven stars were **b** down to me."	**Gn 37:9**	7812
b to the ground and said to him,	**Ru 2:10**	7812
Is it for **b** one's head like a reed And	**Is 58:5**	3721
afflicted you will come **b** to you,	**Is 60:14**	7817
came to Jesus with her sons, **b** down	**Mt 20:20**	*4352*
and kneeling and **b** before Him.	**Mk 15:19**	*4352*

BOWL

one silver **b** of seventy shekels,	**Nu 7:13**	4219
one silver **b** of seventy shekels,	**Nu 7:19**	4219
one silver **b** of seventy shekels,	**Nu 7:25**	4219
one silver **b** of seventy shekels,	**Nu 7:31**	4219
one silver **b** of seventy shekels,	**Nu 7:37**	4219
one silver **b** of seventy shekels,	**Nu 7:43**	4219
one silver **b** of seventy shekels,	**Nu 7:49**	4219
one silver **b** of seventy shekels,	**Nu 7:55**	4219
one silver **b** of seventy shekels,	**Nu 7:61**	4219
one silver **b** of seventy shekels,	**Nu 7:67**	4219
one silver **b** of seventy shekels,	**Nu 7:73**	4219
one silver **b** of seventy shekels,	**Nu 7:79**	4219
thirty *shekels* and each **b** seventy;	**Nu 7:85**	4219
your basket and your kneading **b**.	**Dt 28:5**	4863
your basket and your kneading **b**.	**Dt 28:17**	4863
b she brought him curds.	**Jg 5:25**	5602
the fleece, a **b** full of water.	**Jg 6:38**	5602
the **b** and a little oil in the jar;	**1Ki 17:12**	3537
'The **b** of flour shall not be	**1Ki 17:14**	3537
The **b** of flour was not exhausted	**1Ki 17:16**	3537
bowls with the weight for each **b**;	**1Ch 28:17**	3713a
bowls with the weight for each **b**;	**1Ch 28:17**	3713a
and the golden **b** is crushed,	**Ec 12:6**	1543
gold with its **b** on the top of it,	**Zch 4:2**	1543
one on the right side of the **b** and	**Zch 4:3**	1543
b is the one who will betray Me.	**Mt 26:23**	*5165*
one who dips with Me in the **b**.	**Mk 14:20**	*5165*
poured out his **b** on the earth;	**Rv 16:2**	*5357*
poured out his **b** into the sea,	**Rv 16:3**	*5357*
poured out his **b** into the rivers	**Rv 16:4**	*5357*
poured out his **b** upon the sun,	**Rv 16:8**	*5357*
b on the throne of the beast	**Rv 16:10**	*5357*
out his **b** on the great river,	**Rv 16:12**	*5357*
poured out his **b** upon the air,	**Rv 16:17**	*5357*

BOWLS

ovens and into your kneading **b**.	**Ex 8:3**	4863
with their kneading **b** bound up in	**Ex 12:34**	4863
its pans and its jars and its **b** with	**Ex 25:29**	4518
its pans and its **b** and its jars,	**Ex 37:16**	4518
b and the jars for the drink offering,	**Nu 4:7**	4518
silver dishes, twelve silver **b**,	**Nu 7:84**	4219
basins and the shovels and the **b**.	**1Ki 7:40**	4219
the two pillars and the *two* **b** of	**1Ki 7:41**	1543
to cover the two **b** of the capitals	**1Ki 7:41**	1543
for each network to cover the two **b**	**1Ki 7:42**	1543
pails and the shovels and the **b**;	**1Ki 7:45**	4219
the **b** and the spoons and the firepans,	**1Ki 7:50**	4219
the LORD silver cups, snuffers, **b**,	**2Ki 12:13**	4219
b with the weight for each bowl;	**1Ch 28:17**	3713a
b with the weight for each bowl;	**1Ch 28:17**	3713a
And he made one hundred golden **b**.	**2Ch 4:8**	4219
the pails, the shovels and the **b**.	**2Ch 4:11**	4219
the **b** and the two capitals on top	**2Ch 4:12**	1543
the two networks to cover the two **b**	**2Ch 4:12**	1543
to cover the two **b** of the capitals	**2Ch 4:13**	1543
and the snuffers, the **b**,	**2Ch 4:22**	4219
30 gold **b**, 410 silver bowls of a	**Ezr 1:10**	3713a
410 silver **b** of a second *kind and*	**Ezr 1:10**	3713a
and 20 gold **b** *worth* 1,000 darics	**Ezr 8:27**	3713a
vessels, from **b** to all the jars.	**Is 22:24**	3627, 101
of the guard also took away the **b**,	**Jer 52:19**	5592a
the pans and the drink offering **b**,	**Jer 52:19**	4518
Who drink wine from sacrificial **b**	**Am 6:6**	4219
be like the **b** before the altar.	**Zch 14:20**	4219
and golden **b** full of incense,	**Rv 5:8**	*5357*
golden **b** full of the wrath of God,	**Rv 15:7**	*5357*
pour out on the earth the seven **b** of	**Rv 16:1**	*5357*
seven **b** came and spoke with me,	**Rv 17:1**	*5357*
seven **b** full of the seven last plagues	**Rv 21:9**	*5357*

BOWMAN

horseman and **b** every city flees;	**Jer 4:29**	7411a, 7198

BOWMEN

the remainder of the number of **b**,	**Is 21:17**	7198

BOWS

"The **b** of the mighty are	**1Sa 2:4**	7198
They were equipped with **b**,	**1Ch 12:2**	7198
bearing shields and wielding **b**;	**2Ch 14:8**	7198
body armor, **b** and sling stones.	**2Ch 26:14**	7198
with their swords, spears and **b**.	**Ne 4:13**	7198
the spears, the shields, the **b** and	**Ne 4:16**	7198
heavenly host **b** down before You.	**Ne 9:6**	7812
He crouches, he **b** down, And the	**Ps 10:10**	7817
heart, And their **b** will be broken.	**Ps 37:15**	7198
were archers equipped with **b**,	**Ps 78:9**	7198
are sharp and all its **b** are bent;	**Is 5:28**	7198
People will come there with **b** and	**Is 7:24**	7198
b will mow down the young men,	**Is 13:18**	7198
captured, Their **b** are shattered;	**Jer 51:56**	7198
and bucklers, **b** and arrows,	**Ezk 39:9**	7198

BOWSHOT

down opposite him, about a **b** away,	**Gn 21:16**	2909, 7198

BOWSTRING

has loosed His **b** and afflicted me,	**Jb 30:11**	3499b

BOWSTRINGS

aim with Your **b** at their faces.	**Ps 21:12**	4340

BOX

guilt offering in a **b** by its side.	**1Sa 6:8**	712
and the **b** with the golden mice and	**1Sa 6:11**	712

LORD and the **b** that was with it, — **1Sa 6:15** — 712
with the **b** tree and the cypress, — **Is 41:19** — 8410
to you, The juniper, the **b** tree and — **Is 60:13** — 8410
thief, and as he had the money **b**, — **Jn 12:6** — *1101*
because Judas had the money **b**, — **Jn 13:29** — *1101*
I **b** in such a way, as not beating — **1Co 9:26** — *4438*

BOXES
ankle chains, sashes, perfume **b**, — **Is 3:20** — 1004

BOXWOOD
b from the coastlands of Cyprus. — **Ezk 27:6** — 839

BOY
And a **b** for striking me; — **Gn 4:23** — 3206
her shoulder, and *gave her* the **b**, — **Gn 21:14** — 3206
she left the **b** under one of the bushes. — **Gn 21:15** — 3206
"Do not let me see the **b** die." — **Gn 21:16** — 3206
"The **b** is not *there;* — **Gn 37:30** — 3206
'Do not sin against the **b**' — **Gn 42:22** — 3206
and behold, *the* **b** was crying. — **Ex 2:6** — 5288
for the **b** shall be a Nazirite to — **Jg 13:5** — 5288
for the **b** shall be a Nazirite to — **Jg 13:7** — 5288
do for the **b** who is to be born." — **Jg 13:8** — 5288
to the **b** who was holding his hand, — **Jg 16:26** — 5288
bull, and brought the **b** to Eli. — **1Sa 1:25** — 5288
"For this **b** I prayed, and the — **1Sa 1:27** — 5288
But the **b** ministered to the LORD — **1Sa 2:11** — 5288
as a **b** wearing a linen ephod. — **1Sa 2:18** — 5288
the **b** Samuel grew before the LORD. — **1Sa 2:21** — 5288
Now the **b** Samuel was growing in — **1Sa 2:26** — 5288
Now the **b** Samuel was ministering — **1Sa 3:1** — 5288
that the LORD was calling the **b**. — **1Sa 3:8** — 5288
And she called the **b** Ichabod, — **1Sa 4:21** — 5288
him, while Hadad *was* a young **b**. — **1Ki 11:17** — 5288
you what will happen to the **b**." — **1Ki 14:3** — 5288
'A **b** is conceived.' — **Jb 3:3** — 1397
"For before the **b** will know — **Is 7:16** — 5288
before the **b** knows how to cry out — **Is 8:4** — 5288
And a little **b** will lead them. — **Is 11:6** — 5288
pain came, she gave birth to a **b**. — **Is 66:7** — 2145
"A baby **b** has been born to you!" — **Jer 20:15** — 2145
people, Traded a **b** for a harlot And — **Jl 3:3** — 3206
him, and the **b** was cured at once. — **Mt 17:18** — *3816*
They brought the **b** to Him. — **Mk 9:20**
and *the* **b** became so much like a — **Mk 9:26**
the **b** Jesus stayed behind in — **Lk 2:43** — *3816*
for he is my only **b**, — **Lk 9:38**
unclean spirit, and healed the **b** and — **Lk 9:42** — *3816*
They took away the **b** alive, — **Ac 20:12** — *3816*

BOY'S
b mode of life and his vocation?" — **Jg 13:12** — 5288
Immediately the **b** father cried out — **Mk 9:24** — *3813*

BOYS
When the **b** grew up, Esau became a — **Gn 25:27** — 5288
them, but let the **b** live. — **Ex 1:17** — 3206
this thing, and let the **b** live?" — **Ex 1:18** — 3206
b and girls playing in its streets.' — **Zch 8:5** — 3206

BOZEZ
and the name of the one was **B**, — **1Sa 14:4** — 949

BOZKATH
Lachish and **B** and Eglon, — **Jos 15:39** — 1218
the daughter of Adaiah of **B**. — **2Ki 22:1** — 1218

BOZRAH
Jobab the son of Zerah of **B** became — **Gn 36:33** — 1224a
Jobab the son of Zerah of **B** became — **1Ch 1:44** — 1224a
For the LORD has a sacrifice in **B** And — **Is 34:6** — 1224a
garments of glowing colors from **B**, — **Is 63:1** — 1224a
against Kerioth, **B** and — **Jer 48:24** — 1224a
"that **B** will become an object of — **Jer 49:13** — 1224a
spread out His wings against **B**; — **Jer 49:22** — 1224a
will consume the citadels of **B**." — **Am 1:12** — 1224a

BRACED
and **b** himself against them, — **Jg 16:29** — 5564

BRACELET
and the **b** which *was* on his arm, — **2Sa 1:10** — 685

BRACELETS
two **b** for her wrists weighing ten — **Gn 24:22** — 6781a
and the **b** on his sister's wrists, — **Gn 24:30** — 6781a
her nose, and the **b** on her wrists. — **Gn 24:47** — 6781a
earrings and signet rings and **b**, — **Ex 35:22** — 3558
articles of gold, armlets and **b**, — **Nu 31:50** — 6781a
dangling earrings, **b**, — **Is 3:19** — 8285
ornaments, put **b** on your hands and — **Ezk 16:11** — 6781a
And they put **b** on the hands of the — **Ezk 23:42** — 6781a

BRAG
does not **b** *and* is not arrogant, — **1Co 13:4** — *4068*

BRAIDED
not with **b** hair and gold or pearls — **1Tm 2:9** — *4117*

BRAIDING
b the hair, and wearing gold jewelry, — **1Pe 3:3** — *1708*

BRAMBLE
all the trees said to the **b**, — **Jg 9:14** — 329
"The **b** said to the trees, — **Jg 9:15** — 329
may fire come out from the **b** and — **Jg 9:15** — 329

BRANCH
like almond *blossoms* in the one **b**, — **Ex 25:33** — 7070
almond *blossoms* in the other **b**, — **Ex 25:33** — 7070
a bulb and a flower in one **b**, — **Ex 37:19** — 7070
bulb and a flower in the other **b** — **Ex 37:19** — 7070
cut down a **b** with a single cluster — **Nu 13:23** — 2156
and cut down a **b** from the trees, — **Jg 9:48** — 7754b
one his **b** and followed Abimelech, — **Jg 9:49** — 7754a
And his palm **b** will not be green. — **Jb 15:32** — 3712
below, And his **b** is cut off above. — **Jb 18:16** — 7105b
And dew lies all night on my **b**. — **Jb 29:19** — 7105b
In that day the **B** of the LORD will — **Is 4:2** — 6780
b and bulrush in a single day. — **Is 9:14** — 3712
And a **b** from his roots will bear — **Is 11:1** — 5342
of your tomb Like a rejected **b**, — **Is 14:19** — 5342
or tail, *its* palm **b** or bulrush, — **Is 19:15** — 3712
forever, The **b** of My planting, — **Is 60:21** — 5342
raise up for David a righteous **B**; — **Jer 23:5** — 6780
B of David to spring forth; — **Jer 33:15** — 6780
vine *better* than any wood of a **b** — **Ezk 15:2** — 2156
Its strong **b** was torn off So that — **Ezk 19:12** — 4294
'And fire has gone out from *its* **b**; — **Ezk 19:14** — 4294
there is not in it a strong **b**, — **Ezk 19:14** — 4294
showing intelligence in every **b** *of* — **Da 1:4**
and intelligence in every **b** *of* — **Da 1:17**
to bring in My servant the **B**. — **Zch 3:8** — 6780
"Behold, a man whose name is **B**, — **Zch 6:12** — 6780
He will **b** out from where He is; — **Zch 6:12** — 6779
leave them neither root nor **b**." — **Mal 4:1** — 6057
its **b** has already become tender and — **Mt 24:32** — *2798*
its **b** has already become tender and — **Mk 13:28** — *2798*
"Every **b** in Me that does not bear — **Jn 15:2** — *2814*
and every **b** that bears fruit, He — **Jn 15:2**
the **b** cannot bear fruit of itself unless — **Jn 15:4** — *2814*
in Me, he is thrown away as a **b** and — **Jn 15:6** — *2814*
full of the sour wine upon *a* **b** — **Jn 19:29**

BRANCHES
and on the vine *were* three **b**. — **Gn 40:10** — 8299
the three **b** are three days; — **Gn 40:12** — 8299
Its **b** run over a wall. — **Gn 49:22** — 1323
Six **b** shall go out from its sides; — **Ex 25:32** — 7070
three **b** of the lampstand from its — **Ex 25:32** — 7070
and three **b** of the lampstand from — **Ex 25:32** — 7070
b going out from the lampstand; — **Ex 25:33** — 7070
first pair of **b** *coming* out of it, — **Ex 25:35** — 7070
second pair of **b** *coming* out of it, — **Ex 25:35** — 7070
third pair of **b** *coming* out of it, — **Ex 25:35** — 7070
six **b** coming out of the lampstand. — **Ex 25:35** — 7070
b *shall be of one piece* with it; — **Ex 25:36** — 7070
were six **b** going out of its sides; — **Ex 37:18** — 7070
three **b** of the lampstand from the — **Ex 37:18** — 7070
and three **b** of the lampstand from — **Ex 37:18** — 7070
six **b** going out of the lampstand. — **Ex 37:19** — 7070
first pair of **b** *coming* out of it, — **Ex 37:21** — 7070
second pair of **b** *coming* out of it, — **Ex 37:21** — 7070
third pair of **b** *coming* out of it, — **Ex 37:21** — 7070
six **b** coming out of the lampstand. — **Ex 37:21** — 7070
their **b** were *of one piece* with it; — **Ex 37:22** — 7070
palm **b** and boughs of leafy trees — **Lv 23:40** — 3709
under the thick **b** of a great oak. — **2Sa 18:9** — 7730
to the hills, and bring olive **b** and — **Ne 8:15** — 5929
olive branches and wild olive **b**, — **Ne 8:15** — 5929
and wild olive branches, myrtle **b**, — **Ne 8:15** — 5929
branches, myrtle branches, palm **b** and — **Ne 8:15** — 5929
and **b** of *other* leafy trees, — **Ne 8:15** — 5929
was sending out its **b** to the sea And — **Ps 80:11** — 7105b
lift up *their* voices among the **b**. — **Ps 104:12** — 6074b
five on the **b** of a fruitful tree, — **Is 17:6** — 5585
Or like **b** which they abandoned — **Is 17:9** — 534
and cut away the spreading **b**. — **Is 18:5** — 5189
will lie down and feed on its **b**. — **Is 27:10** — 5585
Strip away her **b**, For they are not — **Jer 5:10** — 5189
a grape gatherer Over the **b**." — **Jer 6:9** — 5552
on it, And its **b** are worthless. — **Jer 11:16** — 1808
vine with its **b** turned toward him, — **Ezk 17:6** — 1808
and yielded shoots and sent out **b**. — **Ezk 17:6** — 6288
sent out its **b** toward him from — **Ezk 17:7** — 1808
it might yield **b** and bear fruit — **Ezk 17:8** — 6057
will nest in the shade of its **b**. — **Ezk 17:23** — 1808
of **b** Because of abundant waters. — **Ezk 19:10** — 6058
b *fit* for scepters of rulers, — **Ezk 19:11** — 4294
its height with the mass of its **b**. — **Ezk 19:11** — 1808
With beautiful **b** and forest shade, — **Ezk 31:3** — 6057
boughs became many and its **b** long — **Ezk 31:5** — 6288
And under its **b** all the beasts of — **Ezk 31:6** — 6288
greatness, in the length of its **b**; — **Ezk 31:7** — 1808
plane trees could not match its **b**. — **Ezk 31:8** — 6288
with the multitude of its **b**, — **Ezk 31:9** — 1808
all the valleys its **b** have fallen and — **Ezk 31:12** — 1808
field will be on its *fallen* **b** — **Ezk 31:13** — 6288
you will put forth your **b** and bear — **Ezk 36:8** — 6057
birds of the sky dwelt in its **b**, — **Da 4:12** — 6056
down the tree and cut off its **b**, — **Da 4:14** — 6056
it And the birds from its **b**. — **Da 4:14** — 6056
b the birds of the sky lodged — **Da 4:21** — 6056
Their **b** have become white. — **Jl 1:7** — 8299
them And destroyed their vine **b**. — **Na 2:2** — 2156
"What are the two olive **b** which — **Zch 4:12** — 7641
THE AIR come and NEST IN ITS **B**." — **Mt 13:32** — *2798*
were cutting **b** from the trees and — **Mt 21:8** — *2798*
garden plants and forms large **b**; — **Mk 4:32** — *2798*
and others *spread* leafy **b** which — **Mk 11:8** — *4742a*
OF THE AIR NESTED IN ITS **B**." — **Lk 13:19** — *2798*
took the **b** of the palm trees and — **Jn 12:13** — *902*
"I am the vine, you are the **b**; — **Jn 15:5** — *2814*
the root is holy, the **b** are too. — **Ro 11:16** — *2798*
if some of the **b** were broken off, — **Ro 11:17** — *2798*
do not be arrogant toward the **b**; — **Ro 11:18** — *2798*
"**B** were broken off so that I — **Ro 11:19** — *2798*
God did not spare the natural **b**, — **Ro 11:21** — *2798*
will these who are the natural **b** — **Ro 11:24**
and palm **b** *were* in their hands; — **Rv 7:9** — *5404*

BRAND
not a **b** plucked from the fire?" — **Zch 3:2** — 181

BRANDING
And **b** instead of beauty. — **Is 3:24** — 3587
own conscience as with a **b** iron, — **1Tm 4:2** — *2741b*

BRANDISH
you when I **b** My sword before them; — **Ezk 32:10** — 5774a

BRANDISHED
And the cypress *spears* are **b**. — **Na 2:3** — 7477

BRANDISHING
And in battles, **b** weapons, He will — **Is 30:32** — 8573

BRAND-MARKS
I bear on my body the **b** of Jesus. — **Ga 6:17** — *4742b*

BRANDS
among the **b** you have set ablaze. — **Is 50:11** — 2131

BRASS
silver, and 18,000 talents of **b**, — **1Ch 29:7** — 5178
work in gold, silver, **b** and iron, — **2Ch 2:7** — 5178
and of **b** and of stone and of wood, — **Rv 9:20** — *5470*

BRAVE
their **b** men cry in the streets, — **Is 33:7** — 691

BRAVEST
"Even the **b** among the warriors — **Am 2:16** — 533, 3820

BRAWLER
is a mocker, strong drink a **b**, — **Pr 20:1** — 1993

BRAY
the wild donkey **b** over *his* grass, — **Jb 6:5** — 5101

BRAZEN
And with a **b** face she says to him: — **Pr 7:13** — 5810

BRAZIER
fire burning in the **b** before him. — **Jer 36:22** — 254
into the fire that was in the **b**, — **Jer 36:23** — 254
in the fire that was in the **b**. — **Jer 36:23** — 254

BREACH
a **b** you have made for yourself!" — **Gn 38:29** — 6556
"For every **b** of trust, *whether it* — **Ex 22:9** — 6588
made a **b** in the tribes of Israel. — **Jg 21:15** — 6556
and closed up the **b** of the city of — **1Ki 11:27** — 6556
and *that* no **b** remained in it, — **Ne 6:1** — 6556
through me with **b** after breach; — **Jb 16:14** — 6556
through me with breach after **b**; — **Jb 16:14** — 6556
"As *through* a wide **b** they come, — **Jb 30:14** — 6556
one stood in the **b** before Him, — **Ps 106:23** — 6556
for ourselves a **b** in its walls and — **Is 7:6** — 1234
be to you Like a **b** about to fall, — **Is 30:13** — 6556
be called the repairer of the **b**, — **Is 58:12** — 6556

BREACHED
of the month, the city *wall* was **b**. — **Jer 39:2** — 1234
as men enter a city that is **b**. — **Ezk 26:10** — 1234
in anguish, Thebes will be **b** And — **Ezk 30:16** — 1234

BREACHES
and that the **b** began to be closed, — **Ne 4:7** — 6555
Heal its **b**, for it totters. — **Ps 60:2** — 7667
And you saw that the **b** In the *wall* — **Is 22:9** — 1233
"You have not gone up into the **b**, — **Ezk 13:5** — 6556
go out *through* **b** *in the walls,* — **Am 4:3** — 6556
booth of David, And wall up its **b**; — **Am 9:11** — 6556

BREAD
of your face You will eat **b**, — **Gn 3:19** — 3899
of Salem brought out **b** and wine; — **Gn 14:18** — 3899
and I will bring a piece of **b**, — **Gn 18:5** — 3899
knead *it* and make **b** cakes." — **Gn 18:6** — 5692
for them, and baked unleavened **b**, — **Gn 19:3** — 4682
and took **b** and a skin of water and — **Gn 21:14** — 3899
Jacob gave Esau **b** and lentil stew; — **Gn 25:34** — 3899
gave the savory food and the **b**, — **Gn 27:17** — 3899
baskets of white **b** on my head; — **Gn 40:16** — 2751
all the land of Egypt there was **b**. — **Gn 41:54** — 3899
people cried out to Pharaoh for **b**; — **Gn 41:55** — 3899
could not eat **b** with the Hebrews, — **Gn 43:32** — 3899
donkeys loaded with grain and **b** — **Gn 45:23** — 3899
unleavened **b** and bitter herbs. — **Ex 12:8** — 4682
days you shall eat unleavened **b**, — **Ex 12:15** — 4682
observe the *Feast of* Unleavened **B**, — **Ex 12:17** — 4682
you shall eat unleavened **b**, — **Ex 12:18** — 4682
you shall eat unleavened **b**.' " — **Ex 12:20** — 4682
Egypt into cakes of unleavened **b**. — **Ex 12:39** — 4682
days you shall eat unleavened **b**, — **Ex 13:6** — 4682
"Unleavened **b** shall be eaten — **Ex 13:7** — 4682
meat, when we ate **b** to the full; — **Ex 16:3** — 3899
I will rain **b** from heaven for you; — **Ex 16:4** — 3899
and **b** to the full in the morning; — **Ex 16:8** — 3899
you shall be filled with **b**; — **Ex 16:12** — 3899
"It is the **b** which the LORD has — **Ex 16:15** — 3899
day they gathered twice as much **b**, — **Ex 16:22** — 3899
b for two days on the sixth day. — **Ex 16:29** — 3899
that they may see the **b** that I fed — **Ex 16:32** — 3899
observe the Feast of Unleavened **B**; — **Ex 23:15** — 4682
days you are to eat unleavened **b**, — **Ex 23:15** — 4682
of My sacrifice with leavened **b**; — **Ex 23:18** — 2557
will bless your **b** and your water; — **Ex 23:25** — 3899
You shall set the **b** of the Presence — **Ex 25:30** — 3899
and unleavened **b** and unleavened — **Ex 29:2** — 4682
and one cake of **b** and one cake of — **Ex 29:23** — 3899
one cake of **b** *mixed with* oil — **Ex 29:23** — 3899
b which is *set* before the LORD; — **Ex 29:23** — 4682
and the **b** that is in the basket, — **Ex 29:32** — 3899
of the **b** remains until morning, — **Ex 29:34** — 3899
observe the Feast of Unleavened **B**. — **Ex 34:18** — 4682
days you are to eat unleavened **b**, — **Ex 34:18** — 4682
of My sacrifice with leavened **b**, — **Ex 34:25** — 2557
he did not eat **b** or drink water. — **Ex 34:28** — 3899
and the **b** of the Presence; — **Ex 35:13** — 3899
and the **b** of the Presence; — **Ex 39:36** — 3899
He set the arrangement of **b** in — **Ex 40:23** — 3899
offering with cakes of leavened **b**. — **Lv 7:13** — 3899
and the basket of unleavened **b**, — **Lv 8:2** — 4682
b that was before the LORD, — **Lv 8:26** — 4682
of **b** *mixed with* oil and one wafer, — **Lv 8:26** — 3899
eat it there together with the **b** — **Lv 8:31** — 3899
the **b** you shall burn in the fire. — **Lv 8:32** — 3899
Feast of Unleavened **B** to the LORD; — **Lv 23:6** — 4682
days you shall eat unleavened **b**. — **Lv 23:6** — 4682
you shall eat neither **b** nor — **Lv 23:14** — 3899

loaves of **b** for a wave offering,	**Lv 23:17**	3899
'Along with the **b** you shall	**Lv 23:18**	3899
wave them with the **b** of the first fruits	**Lv 23:20**	3899
be a memorial portion for the **b**,	**Lv 24:7**	3899
'When I break your staff of **b**,	**Lv 26:26**	3899
will bake your **b** in one oven,	**Lv 26:26**	3899
back your **b** in rationed amounts,	**Lv 26:26**	3899
table of the **b** of the Presence	**Nu 4:7**	
the continual **b** shall be on it.	**Nu 4:7**	3899
unleavened **b** and bitter herbs.	**Nu 9:11**	4682
b *shall be* eaten for seven days.	**Nu 28:17**	4682
that man does not live by **b** alone,	**Dt 8:3**	3899
I neither ate **b** nor drank water.	**Dt 9:9**	3899
I neither ate **b** nor drank water,	**Dt 9:18**	3899
shall not eat leavened **b** with it;	**Dt 16:3**	2557
shall eat with it unleavened **b**,	**Dt 16:3**	4682
bread, the **b** of affliction	**Dt 16:3**	3899
days you shall eat unleavened **b**,	**Dt 16:8**	4682
at the Feast of Unleavened **B** and	**Dt 16:16**	4682
"You have not eaten **b**,	**Dt 29:6**	3899
and all the **b** of their provision	**Jos 9:5**	3899
"This our **b** *was* warm *when* we took	**Jos 9:12**	3899
b from an ephah of flour;	**Jg 6:19**	4682
b and lay them on this rock,	**Jg 6:20**	4682
the meat and the unleavened **b**;	**Jg 6:21**	4682
the meat and the unleavened **b**.	**Jg 6:21**	4682
a loaf of barley **b** was tumbling	**Jg 7:13**	3899
"Please give loaves of **b** to the	**Jg 8:5**	3899
we should give **b** to your army?"	**Jg 8:6**	3899
b to your men who are weary?' "	**Jg 8:15**	3899
yourself with a piece of **b**,	**Jg 19:5**	3899
and also **b** and wine for me,	**Jg 19:19**	3899
that you may eat of the **b** and dip	**Ru 2:14**	3899
your piece of **b** in the vinegar."	**Ru 2:14**	6595
full hire themselves out for **b**,	**1Sa 2:5**	3899
a piece of silver or a loaf of **b** and	**1Sa 2:36**	3899
I may eat a piece of **b**.	**1Sa 2:36**	3899
For the **b** is gone from our sack	**1Sa 9:7**	3899
carrying three loaves of **b**,	**1Sa 10:3**	3899
you and give you two *loaves* of **b**,	**1Sa 10:4**	3899
donkey *loaded with* **b** and a jug	**1Sa 16:20**	3899
Give me five loaves of **b**,	**1Sa 21:3**	3899
"There is no ordinary **b** on hand,	**1Sa 21:4**	3899
hand, but there is consecrated **b**;	**1Sa 21:4**	3899
the priest gave him consecrated **b**;	**1Sa 21:6**	
for there was no **b** there but the	**1Sa 21:6**	3899
was no bread there but the **b** of	**1Sa 21:6**	3899
in order to put hot **b** *in its place*	**1Sa 21:6**	3899
in that you have given him **b** and a	**1Sa 22:13**	3899
"Shall I then take my **b** and my	**1Sa 25:11**	3899
took two hundred *loaves* of **b** and	**1Sa 25:18**	3899
and let me set a piece of **b** before	**1Sa 28:22**	3899
and baked unleavened **b** from it.	**1Sa 28:24**	4682
David, and gave him **b** and he ate,	**1Sa 30:11**	3899
For he had not eaten **b** or drunk	**1Sa 30:12**	3899
by the sword, or who lacks **b**."	**2Sa 3:29**	3899
to eat **b** while it was still day;	**2Sa 3:35**	3899
if I taste **b** or anything else	**2Sa 3:35**	3899
a cake of **b** and one of dates and	**2Sa 6:19**	3899
It would eat of his **b** and drink of	**2Sa 12:3**	6595
them *were* two hundred loaves of **b**,	**2Sa 16:1**	3899
and the **b** and summer fruit for the	**2Sa 16:2**	3899
which *was* the **b** of the Presence;	**1Ki 7:48**	3899
b or drink water in this place.	**1Ki 13:8**	3899
'You shall eat no **b**,	**1Ki 13:9**	3899
"Come home with me and eat **b**."	**1Ki 13:15**	3899
nor will I eat **b** or drink water	**1Ki 13:16**	3899
'You shall eat no **b**,	**1Ki 13:17**	3899
he may eat **b** and drink water.' "	**1Ki 13:18**	3899
b in his house and drank water.	**1Ki 13:19**	3899
but have returned and eaten **b** and	**1Ki 13:22**	3899
"Eat no **b** and drink no water";	**1Ki 13:22**	3899
eaten **b** and after he had drunk,	**1Ki 13:23**	3899
The ravens brought him **b** and	**1Ki 17:6**	3899
and **b** and meat in the evening,	**1Ki 17:6**	3899
me a piece of **b** in your hand."	**1Ki 17:11**	3899
LORD your God lives, I have no **b**,	**1Ki 17:12**	4580
me a little **b** cake from it first and	**1Ki 17:13**	5692
provided them with **b** and water.)	**1Ki 18:4**	3899
provided them with **b** and water?	**1Ki 18:13**	3899
head a **b** cake *baked on* hot stones,	**1Ki 19:6**	5692
Arise, eat **b**, and let your heart	**1Ki 21:7**	3899
and feed him sparingly with **b** and	**1Ki 22:27**	3899
man of God **b** of the first fruits,	**2Ki 4:42**	3899
Set **b** and water before them, that	**2Ki 6:22**	3899
wine, a land of **b** and vineyards,	**2Ki 18:32**	3899
unleavened **b** among their brothers.	**2Ki 23:9**	4682
to everyone a loaf of **b** and a	**1Ch 16:3**	3899
the **b** of the Presence on them,	**2Ch 4:19**	3899
the Feast of Unleavened **B**,	**2Ch 8:13**	4682
and feed him sparingly with **b** and	**2Ch 18:26**	3899
Unleavened **B** in the second month,	**2Ch 30:13**	4682
B *for* seven days with great joy,	**2Ch 30:21**	4682
Feast of Unleavened **B** seven days.	**2Ch 35:17**	4682
Unleavened **B** seven days with joy,	**Ezr 6:22**	4682
he went there, he did not eat **b** nor	**Ezr 10:6**	3899
took from them **b** and wine besides	**Ne 5:15**	3899
"You provided **b** from heaven	**Ne 9:15**	3899
sons of Israel with **b** and water,	**Ne 13:2**	3899
the hungry you have withheld **b**.	**Jb 22:7**	3899
As **b** for *their* children in the	**Jb 24:5**	3899
will not be satisfied with **b**.	**Jb 27:14**	3899
So that his life loathes **b**,	**Jb 33:20**	3899
they ate **b** with him in his house;	**Jb 42:11**	3899
eat up my people *as* they eat **b**,	**Ps 14:4**	3899
Or his descendants begging **b**.	**Ps 37:25**	3899
in whom I trusted, Who ate my **b**,	**Ps 41:9**	3899
up My people *as though* they ate **b** And	**Ps 53:4**	3899
Can He give **b** also?	**Ps 78:20**	3899
Man did eat the **b** of angels;	**Ps 78:25**	3899
have fed them with the **b** of tears,	**Ps 80:5**	3899
Indeed, I forget to eat my **b**.	**Ps 102:4**	3899
For I have eaten ashes like **b** And	**Ps 102:9**	3899
He broke the whole staff of **b**.	**Ps 105:16**	3899
them with the **b** of heaven.	**Ps 105:40**	3899
To eat the **b** of painful labors;	**Ps 127:2**	3899
I will satisfy her needy with **b**.	**Ps 132:15**	3899
For they eat the **b** of wickedness And	**Pr 4:17**	3899
one is reduced to a loaf of **b**,	**Pr 6:26**	3899
b *eaten* in secret is pleasant."	**Pr 9:17**	3899
he who honors himself and lacks **b**.	**Pr 12:9**	3899
his land will have plenty of **b**,	**Pr 12:11**	3899
B obtained by falsehood is sweet	**Pr 20:17**	3899
Do not eat the **b** of a selfish man,	**Pr 23:6**	3899
piece of **b** a man will transgress.	**Pr 28:21**	3899
does not eat the **b** of idleness.	**Pr 31:27**	3899
Go *then,* eat your **b** in happiness and	**Ec 9:7**	3899
and neither is **b** to the wise nor	**Ec 9:11**	3899
b on the surface of the waters,	**Ec 11:1**	3899
support, the whole supply of **b** And	**Is 3:1**	3899
there is neither **b** nor cloak;	**Is 3:7**	3899
"We will eat our own **b** and wear our	**Is 4:1**	3899
of Tema, Meet the fugitive with **b**.	**Is 21:14**	3899
Grain for **b** is crushed, Indeed, he	**Is 28:28**	3899
Although the Lord has given you **b**	**Is 30:20**	3899
b *from* the yield of the ground,	**Is 30:23**	3899
His **b** will be given *him,*	**Is 33:16**	3899
wine, a land of **b** and vineyards.	**Is 36:17**	3899
he also makes a fire to bake **b**.	**Is 44:15**	3899
also have baked **b** over its coals.	**Is 44:19**	3899
nor will his **b** be lacking.	**Is 51:14**	3899
you spend money for what is not **b**,	**Is 55:2**	3899
to the sower and **b** to the eater;	**Is 55:10**	3899
to divide your **b** with the hungry And	**Is 58:7**	3899
"Men will not break **b** in	**Jer 16:7**	
of **b** daily from the bakers' street,	**Jer 37:21**	3899
all the **b** in the city was gone.	**Jer 37:21**	3899
there is no more **b** in the city."	**Jer 38:9**	3899
eating **b** together there in Mizpah,	**Jer 41:1**	3899
of a trumpet or hunger for **b**,	**Jer 42:14**	3899
All her people groan seeking **b**;	**La 1:11**	3899
The little ones ask for **b**,	**La 4:4**	3899
Egypt *and* Assyria to get enough **b**.	**La 5:6**	3899
We get our **b** at the risk of our	**La 5:9**	3899
and make them into **b** for yourself;	**Ezk 4:9**	3899
sons of Israel eat their **b** unclean	**Ezk 4:13**	3899
which you will prepare your **b**."	**Ezk 4:15**	3899
break the staff of **b** in Jerusalem,	**Ezk 4:16**	3899
eat **b** by weight and with anxiety,	**Ezk 4:16**	3899
b and water will be scarce;	**Ezk 4:17**	3899
you and break the staff of **b**.	**Ezk 5:16**	3899
of man, eat your **b** with trembling and	**Ezk 12:18**	3899
"They will eat their **b** with anxiety	**Ezk 12:19**	3899
of barley and fragments of **b**,	**Ezk 13:19**	3899
it, destroy its supply of **b**,	**Ezk 14:13**	3899
"Also My **b** which I gave you, fine	**Ezk 16:19**	3899
but gives his **b** to the hungry and	**Ezk 18:7**	3899
but he gives his **b** to the hungry and	**Ezk 18:16**	3899
and do not eat the **b** of men."	**Ezk 24:17**	3899
and you will not eat the **b** of men.	**Ezk 24:22**	3899
prince to eat **b** before the LORD;	**Ezk 44:3**	3899
unleavened **b** shall be eaten.	**Ezk 45:21**	4682
Who give *me* my **b** and my water,	**Hos 2:5**	3899
b *will be* like mourners' bread;	**Hos 9:4**	
bread will be like mourners' **b**;	**Hos 9:4**	3899
b will be for themselves *alone;*	**Hos 9:4**	3899
And lack of **b** in all your places,	**Am 4:6**	3899
there eat **b** and there do your	**Am 7:12**	3899
for **b** or a thirst for water,	**Am 8:11**	3899
your **b** Will set an ambush for you.	**Ob 1:7**	3899
and touches **b** with this fold,	**Hg 2:12**	3899
that these stones become **b**."	**Mt 4:3**	*740*
'MAN SHALL NOT LIVE ON **B** ALONE,	**Mt 4:4**	*740*
'Give us this day our daily **b**.	**Mt 6:11**	*740*
and they ate the consecrated **b**,	**Mt 12:4**	*740*
their hands when they eat **b**."	**Mt 15:2**	*740*
not good to take the children's **b** and	**Mt 15:26**	*740*
they had forgotten to bring *any* **b**.	**Mt 16:5**	*740*
because we did not bring *any* **b**."	**Mt 16:7**	*740*
yourselves that you have no **b**?	**Mt 16:8**	*740*
did not speak to you concerning **b**?	**Mt 16:11**	*740*
say to beware of the leaven of **b**,	**Mt 16:12**	*740*
on the first *day* of Unleavened **B**	**Mt 26:17**	
were eating, Jesus took *some* **b**,	**Mt 26:26**	*740*
priest, and ate the consecrated **b**,	**Mk 2:26**	*740*
no **b**, no bag, no money in their	**Mk 6:8**	*740*
spend two hundred denarii on **b**	**Mk 6:37**	*740*
eating their **b** with impure hands,	**Mk 7:2**	*740*
eat their **b** with impure hands?"	**Mk 7:5**	*740*
not good to take the children's **b** and	**Mk 7:27**	*740*
b here in *this* desolate place	**Mk 8:4**	*740*
And they had forgotten to take **b**,	**Mk 8:14**	*740*
the fact that they had no **b**.	**Mk 8:16**	*740*
the fact that you have no **b**?	**Mk 8:17**	*740*
and Unleavened **B** were two days away;	**Mk 14:1**	
On the first day of Unleavened **B**,	**Mk 14:12**	
they were eating, He took *some* **b**,	**Mk 14:22**	*740*
tell this stone to become **b**."	**Lk 4:3**	*740*
'MAN SHALL NOT LIVE ON **B** ALONE.' "	**Lk 4:4**	*740*
and took and ate the consecrated **b**	**Lk 6:4**	*740*
eating no **b** and drinking no wine,	**Lk 7:33**	*740*
neither a staff, nor a bag, nor **b**,	**Lk 9:3**	*740*
'Give us each day our daily **b**.	**Lk 11:3**	*740*
Pharisees on the Sabbath to eat **b**,	**Lk 14:1**	*740*
eat **b** in the kingdom of God!"	**Lk 14:15**	*740*
hired men have more than enough **b**,	**Lk 15:17**	*740*
Now the Feast of Unleavened **B**,	**Lk 22:1**	
came the *first* day of Unleavened **B**	**Lk 22:7**	
had taken *some* **b** *and* given thanks,	**Lk 22:19**	*740*
He took the **b** and blessed *it,*	**Lk 24:30**	*740*
by them in the breaking of the **b**.	**Lk 24:35**	*740*
"Where are we to buy **b**,	**Jn 6:5**	*740*
of **b** is not sufficient for them,	**Jn 6:7**	*740*
ate the **b** after the Lord had given	**Jn 6:23**	*740*
THEM **B** OUT OF HEAVEN TO EAT.' "	**Jn 6:31**	*740*
has given you the **b** out of heaven,	**Jn 6:32**	*740*
you the true **b** out of heaven.	**Jn 6:32**	*740*
"For the **b** of God is that which	**Jn 6:33**	*740*
"Lord, always give us this **b**."	**Jn 6:34**	*740*
"I am the **b** of life;	**Jn 6:35**	*740*
b that came down out of heaven."	**Jn 6:41**	*740*
"I am the **b** of life.	**Jn 6:48**	*740*
"This is the **b** which comes down	**Jn 6:50**	*740*
b that came down out of heaven;	**Jn 6:51**	*740*
if anyone eats of this **b**,	**Jn 6:51**	*740*
and the **b** also which I will give	**Jn 6:51**	*740*
b which came down out of heaven;	**Jn 6:58**	*740*
eats this **b** will live forever."	**Jn 6:58**	*740*
'HE WHO EATS MY **B** HAS LIFTED UP	**Jn 13:18**	*740*
and fish placed on it, and **b**.	**Jn 21:9**	*740*
Jesus came and took the **b** and	**Jn 21:13**	*740*
the breaking of **b** and to prayer.	**Ac 2:42**	*740*
breaking **b** from house to house,	**Ac 2:46**	*740*
during the days of Unleavened **B**.	**Ac 12:3**	
after the days of Unleavened **B**,	**Ac 20:6**	
were gathered together to break **b**,	**Ac 20:7**	*740*
and had broken the **b** and eaten,	**Ac 20:11**	*740*
he took **b** and gave thanks to God	**Ac 27:35**	*740*
b of sincerity and truth.	**1Co 5:8**	
Is not the **b** which we break a	**1Co 10:16**	*740*
Since there is one **b**,	**1Co 10:17**	*740*
for we all partake of the one **b**.	**1Co 10:17**	*740*
in which He was betrayed took **b**;	**1Co 11:23**	*740*
you eat this **b** and drink the cup,	**1Co 11:26**	*740*
Therefore whoever eats the **b** or	**1Co 11:27**	*740*
eat of the **b** and drink of the cup.	**1Co 11:28**	*740*
seed to the sower and **b** for food will	**2Co 9:10**	*740*
anyone's **b** without paying for it,	**2Th 3:8**	*740*
quiet fashion and eat their own **b**.	**2Th 3:12**	*740*
and the table and the sacred **b**;	**Heb 9:2**	*740*

BREADTH

cubits, its **b** fifty cubits,	**Gn 6:15**	7341
the land through its length and **b**;	**Gn 13:17**	7341
great discernment and **b** of mind,	**1Ki 4:29**	7341
will fill the **b** of your land,	**Is 8:8**	7341
what is the **b** and length and height	**Eph 3:18**	*4114*

BREAK

Lot and came near to **b** the door.	**Gn 19:9**	7665
will **b** his yoke from your neck."	**Gn 27:40**	6561
nor are you to **b** any bone of it.	**Ex 12:46**	7665
it, then you shall **b** its neck;	**Ex 13:13**	6202
b through to the LORD to gaze,	**Ex 19:21**	2040
the LORD will **b** out against them."	**Ex 19:22**	6555
b through to come up to the LORD,	**Ex 19:24**	2040
LORD, or He will **b** forth upon them."	**Ex 19:24**	6555
and **b** their *sacred* pillars in	**Ex 23:24**	7665
it, then you shall **b** its neck.	**Ex 34:20**	6202
you shall **b** it into bits and pour	**Lv 2:6**	6626
and you shall **b** the vessel.	**Lv 11:33**	7665
and so **b** My covenant,	**Lv 26:15**	6565a
also **b** down your pride of power;	**Lv 26:19**	7665
'When I **b** your staff of bread, ten	**Lv 26:26**	7665
until morning, nor **b** a bone of it;	**Nu 9:12**	7665
and shall **b** the heifer's neck	**Dt 21:4**	6202
and will forsake Me and **b** My	**Dt 31:16**	6565a
and spurn Me and **b** My covenant.	**Dt 31:20**	6565a
will never **b** My covenant with you,	**Jg 2:1**	6565a
days are coming when I will **b** your	**1Sa 2:31**	1438
b your treaty with Baasha king of	**1Ki 15:19**	6565a
to **b** through to the king of Edom;	**2Ki 3:26**	1234
b your treaty with Baasha king of	**2Ch 16:3**	6565a
to **b** into them for himself.	**2Ch 32:1**	1234
shall we again **b** Your commandments	**Ezr 9:14**	6565a
would **b** their stone wall down!"	**Ne 4:3**	6555
"They **b** up my path, They profit	**Jb 30:13**	5420
shall **b** them with a rod of iron,	**Ps 2:9**	7489b
B the arm of the wicked and the	**Ps 10:15**	7665
You **b** the ships of Tarshish.	**Ps 48:7**	7665
But God will **b** you down forever;	**Ps 52:5**	5422
B out the fangs of the young	**Ps 58:6**	5422
"But I will not **b** off My	**Ps 89:33**	6565a
B forth and sing for joy and sing	**Ps 98:4**	6476
I will **b** down its wall and it will	**Is 5:5**	6555
For You shall **b** the yoke of their	**Is 9:4**	2865
They **b** forth into shouts of joy.	**Is 14:7**	6476
to **b** Assyria in My land, and I	**Is 14:25**	7665
it will even **b** off and fall, and	**Is 22:25**	1438
For waters will **b** forth in the	**Is 35:6**	1234
"A bruised reed He will not **b** And	**Is 42:3**	7665
B forth into a shout of joy, you	**Is 44:23**	6476
B forth into joyful shouting, O	**Is 49:13**	6476
B forth, shout joyfully together,	**Is 52:9**	6476
B forth into joyful shouting and	**Is 54:1**	6476
mountains and the hills will **b** forth	**Is 55:12**	6476
go free And **b** every yoke?	**Is 58:6**	5423
light will **b** out like the dawn,	**Is 58:8**	1234
To pluck up and to **b** down,	**Jer 1:10**	5422
"Out of the north the evil will **b**	**Jer 1:14**	6605a
"**B** up your fallow ground, And do	**Jer 4:3**	5214
not **b** *bread* in mourning for them,	**Jer 16:7**	6536
"Then you are to **b** the jar in the	**Jer 19:10**	7665
I **b** this people and this city,	**Jer 19:11**	7665
'for I will **b** the yoke of the king	**Jer 28:4**	7665
so will I **b** within two full years the	**Jer 28:11**	7665
b his yoke from off their neck and	**Jer 30:8**	7665
over them to pluck up, to **b** down,	**Jer 31:28**	5422

you can **b** My covenant for the day and **Jer 33:20** 6565a
I am going to **b** the bow of Elam, **Jer 49:35** 7665
I am going to **b** the staff of bread **Ezk 4:16** 7665
you and **b** the staff of bread. **Ezk 5:16** 7665
and a violent wind will **b** out. **Ezk 13:11** 1234
a violent wind **b** out in My wrath. **Ezk 13:13** 1234
indeed **b** the covenant and escape? **Ezk 17:15** 6565a
of Tyre and **b** down her towers; **Ezk 26:4** 2040
axes he will **b** down your towers. **Ezk 26:9** 5422
b down your walls and destroy your **Ezk 26:12** 2040
I **b** there the yoke bars of Egypt. **Ezk 30:18** 7665
king of Egypt and will **b** his arms, **Ezk 30:22** 7665
and I will **b** the arms of Pharaoh, **Ezk 30:24** 7665
crush and **b** all these in pieces. **Da 2:40** 7490
b away now from your sins by *doing* **Da 4:27** 6562
at dawn, at the **b** of day, **Da 6:19** 5053
that day I will **b** the bow of Israel in **Hos 1:5** 7665
The LORD will **b** down their altars **Hos 10:2** 6202
B up your fallow ground, For it is **Hos 10:12** 5214
the defenses, They do not **b** ranks. **Jl 2:8** 1214
also **b** the *gate* bar of Damascus, **Am 1:5** 7665
live, Or He will **b** forth like a fire, **Am 5:6** 6743a
b them on the heads of them all! **Am 9:1** 1214
that the ship was about to **b** up **Jon 1:4** 7665
They **b** out, pass through the gate and **Mi 2:13** 6555
skin from them, **B** their bones And **Mi 3:3** 6476
will **b** his yoke bar from upon you, **Na 1:13** 7665
to **b** my covenant which I had made **Zch 11:10** 6565a
to **b** the brotherhood between Judah **Zch 11:14** 6565a
and where thieves **b** in and steal. **Mt 6:19** *1358*
thieves do not **b** in or steal; **Mt 6:20** *1358*
in the temple **b** the Sabbath and **Mt 12:5** *953*
"A BATTERED REED HE WILL NOT **B** **Mt 12:20** *2608a*
"Why do Your disciples **b** **Mt 15:2** *3862*
and their nets *began* to **b**; **Lk 5:6** *1284*
and *yet* he would **b** his bonds **Lk 8:29** *1284*
dead, they did not **b** His legs. **Jn 19:33** *2608a*
were gathered together to **b** bread, **Ac 20:7** *2806*
Is not the bread which we **b** a **1Co 10:16** *2806*
B FORTH AND SHOUT, YOU WHO ARE **Ga 4:27** *4486*
the book and to **b** its seals?" **Rv 5:2** *3089*
take the book and to **b** its seals; **Rv 5:9** *455*

BREAKDOWN
There is no relief for your **b**, **Na 3:19** 7667

BREAKER
"The **b** goes up before them; **Mi 2:13** 6555

BREAKERS
All Your **b** and Your waves have **Ps 42:7** 4867
Than the mighty **b** of the sea, **Ps 93:4** 4867
Your **b** and billows passed over me. **Jon 2:3** 4867

BREAKFAST
"Come *and* have **b**." **Jn 21:12** *709*
So when they had finished **b**, **Jn 21:15** *709*

BREAKING
"Let me go, for the dawn is **b**." **Gn 32:26** 5927
and will become boils **b** out with **Ex 9:9** 6524b
and it became boils **b** out with **Ex 9:10** 6524b
"If the thief is caught while **b** in and **Ex 22:2** 4290
it is leprosy **b** out on his bald **Lv 13:42** 6524b
them, **b** My covenant with them; **Lv 26:44** 6565a
are each **b** away from his master. **1Sa 25:10** 6555
mountains and **b** in pieces the rocks **1Ki 19:11** 7665
And let it not see the **b** dawn; **Jb 3:9** 6079
A **b** down of walls And a crying to **Is 22:5** 7175a
You did not find them **b** in. **Jer 2:34** 4290
the oath by **b** the covenant. **Ezk 16:59** 6565a
the oath by **b** the covenant, **Ezk 17:18** 6565a
with **b** heart and bitter grief, **Ezk 21:6** 7670
and **b** the loaves He gave them to **Mt 14:19** *2806*
and the waves were **b** over the boat **Mk 4:37** *1911*
bread and blessed *it,* and **b** *it,* **Lk 24:30** *2806*
by them in the **b** of the bread. **Lk 24:35** *2800*
He not only was **b** the Sabbath, **Jn 5:18** *3089*
But when the day was now **b**, **Jn 21:4**
1096, 4407b
to the **b** of bread and to prayer. **Ac 2:42** *2800*
and **b** bread from house to house, **Ac 2:46** *2806*
you doing, weeping and **b** my heart? **Ac 21:13** *4919*
the Law, through your **b** the Law, **Ro 2:23** *3847*

BREAKS
"If a fire **b** out and spreads to **Ex 22:6** 3318
leprosy **b** out farther on the skin, **Lv 13:12** 6524b
the mark **b** out again in the house after **Lv 14:43** 6524b
"He **b** through me with breach **Jb 16:14** 6555
"He **b** me down on every side, and **Jb 19:10** 5422
"He **b** in pieces mighty men **Jb 34:24** 7489b
voice of the LORD **b** the cedars; **Ps 29:5** 7665
the LORD **b** in pieces the cedars of **Ps 29:5** 7665
He **b** the bow and cuts the spear in **Ps 46:9** 7665
one plows and **b** open the earth, **Ps 141:7** 1234
the quarrel before it **b** out. **Pr 17:14** 1566
And a soft tongue **b** the bone. **Pr 25:15** 7665
may bite him who **b** through a wall. **Ec 10:8** 6555
so He **b** all my bones, **Is 38:13** 7665
which is crushed a snake **b** forth. **Is 59:5** 1234
is *like* the one who **b** a dog's neck; **Is 66:3** 6202
even as one **b** a potter's vessel, **Jer 19:11** 7665
bread, *But* no one **b** *it* for them. **La 4:4** 6536
so, like iron that **b** in pieces, **Da 2:40** 7490

BREAKTHROUGH
before me like the **b** of waters." **2Sa 5:20** 6556
my hand, like the **b** of waters." **1Ch 14:11** 6556

BREAST
the **b** of Aaron's ram of ordination, **Ex 29:26** 2373
"You shall consecrate the **b** **Ex 29:27** 2373
He shall bring the fat with the **b**, **Lv 7:30** 2373
that the **b** may be presented as a **Lv 7:30** 2373
but the **b** shall belong to Aaron **Lv 7:31** 2373
'For I have taken the **b** of the **Lv 7:34** 2373
Moses also took the **b** and **Lv 8:29** 2373
"The **b** of the wave offering, **Lv 10:14** 2373
up and the **b** offered by waving they **Lv 10:15** 2373
together with the **b** offered by **Nu 6:20** 2373
it shall be yours like the **b** of a **Nu 18:18** 2373
snatch the orphan from the **b**, **Jb 24:9** 7699b
Those *just* taken from the **b**? **Is 28:9** 7699a
And suck the **b** of kings; **Is 60:16** 7699b
Even jackals offer the **b**, **La 4:3** 7699a
its **b** and its arms of silver, **Da 2:32** 2306
to heaven, but was beating his **b**, **Lk 18:13** *4738*

BREASTPIECE
for the ephod and for the **b**. **Ex 25:7** 2833
a **b** and an ephod and a robe and a **Ex 28:4** 2833
You shall make a **b** of judgment, **Ex 28:15** 2833
"You shall make on the **b** **Ex 28:22** 2833
make on the **b** two rings of gold, **Ex 28:23** 2833
rings on the two ends of the **b**. **Ex 28:23** 2833
two rings at the ends of the **b**. **Ex 28:24** 2833
them on the two ends of the **b**, **Ex 28:26** 2833
"They shall bind the **b** by its **Ex 28:28** 2833
and that the **b** will not come loose **Ex 28:28** 2833
in the **b** of judgment over his heart **Ex 28:29** 2833
"You shall put in the **b** of **Ex 28:30** 2833
the ephod and the ephod and the **b**, **Ex 29:5** 2833
for the ephod and for the **b**. **Ex 35:9** 2833
for the ephod and for the **b**; **Ex 35:27** 2833
He made the **b**, the work of a **Ex 39:8** 2833
they made the **b** folded double, a **Ex 39:9** 2833
made on the **b** chains like cords, **Ex 39:15** 2833
rings on the two ends of the **b**. **Ex 39:16** 2833
two rings at the ends of the **b**. **Ex 39:17** 2833
them on the two ends of the **b**, **Ex 39:19** 2833
They bound the **b** by its rings **Ex 39:21** 2833
and that the **b** would not come **Ex 39:21** 2833
He then placed the **b** on him, **Lv 8:8** 2833
and in the **b** he put the Urim and **Lv 8:8** 2833

BREASTPLATE
He put on righteousness like a **b**, **Is 59:17** 8302
PUT ON THE **B** OF RIGHTEOUSNESS, **Eph 6:14** *2382*
put on the **b** of faith and love, **1Th 5:8** *2382*

BREASTPLATES
the shields, the bows and the **b**; **Ne 4:16** 8302
had **b** like breastplates of iron; **Rv 9:9** *2382*
had breastplates like **b** of iron; **Rv 9:9** *2382*
the riders had **b** *the color* of fire **Rv 9:17** *2382*

BREASTS
of the **b** and of the womb. **Gn 49:25** 7699a
the portions of fat on the **b**; **Lv 9:20** 2373
But the **b** and the right thigh **Lv 9:21** 2373
knees receive me, And why the **b**, **Jb 3:12** 7699a
me trust *when* upon my mother's **b**. **Ps 22:9** 7699a
her **b** satisfy you at all times; **Pr 5:19** 1717
Which lies all night between my **b**. **SS 1:13** 7699a
"Your two **b** are like two fawns, **SS 4:5** 7699a
"Your two **b** are like two fawns, **SS 7:3** 7699a
And your **b** are *like its* clusters. **SS 7:7** 7699a
b be like clusters of the vine, **SS 7:8** 7699a
to me Who nursed at my mother's **b**. **SS 8:1** 7699a
a little sister, And she has no **b**; **SS 8:8** 7699a
a wall, and my **b** were like towers; **SS 8:10** 7699a
your **b** for the pleasant fields, **Is 32:12** 7699a
satisfied with her comforting **b**, **Is 66:11** 7699b
your **b** were formed and your hair **Ezk 16:7** 7699a
there their **b** were pressed and **Ezk 23:3** 7699a
because of the **b** of your youth. **Ezk 23:21** 7699a
its fragments And tear your **b**; **Ezk 23:34** 7699a
her adultery from between her **b**, **Hos 2:2** 7699a
them a miscarrying womb and dry **b**. **Hos 9:14** 7699a
of doves, Beating on their **b**. **Na 2:7** 3824
and the **b** at which You nursed." **Lk 11:27** *3149*
and the **b** that never nursed.' **Lk 23:29** *3149*
began to return, beating their **b**. **Lk 23:48** *4738*

BREATH
into his nostrils the **b** of life; **Gn 2:7** 5397
flesh in which is the **b** of life, **Gn 6:17** 7307
flesh in which was the **b** of life. **Gn 7:15** 7307
was the **b** of the spirit of life, **Gn 7:22** 5397
blast of the **b** of His nostrils. **2Sa 22:16** 7307
that there was no **b** left in him. **1Ki 17:17** 5397
"By the **b** of God they perish, And **Jb 4:9** 5397
"Remember that my life is *but* **b**; **Jb 7:7** 7307
me alone, for my days are *but* a **b**. **Jb 7:16** 1892
"He will not allow me to get my **b**, **Jb 9:18** 7307
thing, And the **b** of all mankind? **Jb 12:10** 7307
b of His mouth he will go away. **Jb 15:30** 7307
"My **b** is offensive to my wife, **Jb 19:17** 7307
"By His **b** the heavens are cleared; **Jb 26:13** 7307
the **b** of God is in my nostrils, **Jb 27:3** 5397
And the **b** of the Almighty gives **Jb 32:8** 5397
b of the Almighty gives me life. **Jb 33:4** 5397
to Himself His spirit and His **b**, **Jb 34:14** 5397
"From the **b** of God ice is made, **Jb 37:10** 5397
"His **b** kindles coals, And a flame **Jb 41:21** 5315
blast of the **b** of Your nostrils. **Ps 18:15** 7307
the **b** of His mouth all their host. **Ps 33:6** 7307
every man at his best is a mere **b**. **Ps 39:5** 1892
Surely every man is a mere **b** **Ps 39:11** 1892
They are together lighter than **b**. **Ps 62:9** 1892
of man, That they are a *mere* **b**. **Ps 94:11** 1892
any **b** at all in their mouths. **Ps 135:17** 7307
Man is like a mere **b**; **Ps 144:4** 1892
that has **b** praise the LORD. **Ps 150:6** 5397
they all have the same **b** and there **Ec 3:19** 7307
Who knows that the **b** of man **Ec 3:21** 7307
b of the beast descends downward **Ec 3:21** 7307
fragrance of your **b** like apples, **SS 7:8** 639
b *of life* is in his nostrils; **Is 2:22** 5397
And with the **b** of His lips He will **Is 11:4** 7307
For the **b** of the ruthless Is like **Is 25:4** 7307
His **b** is like an overflowing **Is 30:28** 7307
The **b** of the LORD, like a torrent **Is 30:33** 5397
My **b** will consume you like a fire. **Is 33:11** 7307
the **b** of the LORD blows upon it; **Is 40:7** 7307
Who gives **b** to the people on it And **Is 42:5** 5397
up, *And* a **b** will take *them away.* **Is 57:13** 1892
the **b** *of those whom* I have made. **Is 57:16** 5397
daughter of Zion gasping for **b**, **Jer 4:31** 3306
And there is no **b** in them. **Jer 10:14** 7307
And there is no **b** in them. **Jer 51:17** 7307
The **b** of our nostrils, the LORD's **La 4:20** 7307
I will cause **b** to enter you that **Ezk 37:5** 7307
and put **b** in you that you may come **Ezk 37:6** 7307
but there was no **b** in them. **Ezk 37:8** 7307
"Prophesy to the **b**, prophesy, son **Ezk 37:9** 7307
son of man, and say to the **b**, **Ezk 37:9** 7307
"Come from the four winds, O **b**, **Ezk 37:9** 7307
me, and the **b** came into them, **Ezk 37:10** 7307
nor has any **b** been left in me." **Da 10:17** 5397
there is no **b** at all inside it. **Hab 2:19** 7307
to all *people* life and **b** and all things; **Ac 17:25** *4157*
will slay with the **b** of His mouth **2Th 2:8** *4151*
b of life from God came into them, **Rv 11:11** *4151*
give **b** to the image of the beast, **Rv 13:15** *4151*

BREATHE
their hope is to **b** their last." **Jb 11:20** 4646
me, And such as **b** out violence. **Ps 27:12** 3307
lie among those who **b** forth fire, **Ps 57:4** 3857
Make my garden **b** out *fragrance,* **SS 4:16** 6315
O breath, and **b** on these slain, **Ezk 37:9** 5301

BREATHED
and **b** into his nostrils the breath **Gn 2:7** 5301
Abraham **b** his last and died in **Gn 25:8** 1478
and he **b** his last and died, and **Gn 25:17** 1478
Isaac **b** his last and died and **Gn 35:29** 1478
feet into the bed and **b** his last, **Gn 49:33** 1478
he utterly destroyed all who **b**, **Jos 10:40** 5397
there was no one left who **b**. **Jos 11:11** 5397
They left no one who **b**. **Jos 11:14** 5397
a loud cry, and **b** His last. **Mk 15:37** *1606*
of Him, saw the way He **b** His last, **Mk 15:39** *1606*
Having said this, He **b** His last. **Lk 23:46** *1606*
He had said this, He **b** on them and **Jn 20:22** *1720*
Ananias fell down and **b** his last; **Ac 5:5** *1634*
at his feet and **b** her last **Ac 5:10** *1634*

BREATHES
not leave alive anything that **b**. **Dt 20:16** 5397

BREATHING
Her **b** is labored. **Jer 15:9** 5301
still **b** threats and murder against **Ac 9:1** *1709*

BREATHLESS
the house of the LORD, she was **b**. **2Ch 9:4**
3808, 7307

BRED
and it **b** worms and became foul; **Ex 16:20** 7426b

BREECHES
linen **b** to cover *their* bare flesh; **Ex 28:42** 4370
the linen **b** of fine twisted linen, **Ex 39:28** 4370

BREED
may **b** abundantly on the earth, **Gn 8:17** 8317
You shall not **b** together two kinds **Lv 19:19** 7250
lambs, And rams, the **b** of Bashan, **Dt 32:14** 1121

BREEDER
Mesha king of Moab was a sheep **b**, **2Ki 3:4** 5349

BRETHREN
that he went out to his **b** and **Ex 2:11** 251
beating a Hebrew, one of his **b**. **Ex 2:11** 251
return to my **b** who are in Egypt, **Ex 4:18** 251
Our **b** have made our hearts melt, **Dt 1:28** 251
"Nevertheless my **b** who went up **Jos 14:8** 251
"Listen to me, my **b** and my people; **1Ch 28:2** 251
your **b** who live in their cities, **2Ch 19:10** 251
may *not* come on you and your **b**. **2Ch 19:10** 251
captive of their **b** 200,000 women, **2Ch 28:8** 251
of your **b** the lay people, **2Ch 35:5** 251
and prepare for your **b** to do **2Ch 35:6** 251
Levites their **b** prepared for them. **2Ch 35:15** 251
Bakbukiah, the second among his **b**; **Ne 11:17** 251
Akkub, Talmon and their **b** **Ne 11:19** 251
I will tell of Your name to my **b**; **Ps 22:22** 251
"Then they shall bring all your **b** **Is 66:20** 251
Then the remainder of His **b** Will **Mi 5:3** 251
word to My **b** to leave for Galilee, **Mt 28:10** *80*
but go to My **b** and say to them, **Jn 20:17** *80*
saying went out among the **b** **Jn 21:23** *80*
stood up in the midst of the **b** **Ac 1:15** *80*
"**B**, the Scripture had to be **Ac 1:16** *435, 80*
"**B**, I may confidently say to you **Ac 2:29** *435, 80*
"**B**, what shall we do?" **Ac 2:37** *435, 80*
"And now, **b**, I know that you **Ac 3:17** *80*
A PROPHET LIKE ME FROM YOUR **B**; **Ac 3:22** *80*
"Therefore, **b**, select from among you **Ac 6:3** *80*
"Hear me, **b** and fathers! **Ac 7:2** *435, 80*
entered his mind to visit his **b**, **Ac 7:23** *80*
"And he supposed that his **b** **Ac 7:25** *80*
'Men, you are **b**, why do you injure **Ac 7:26** *80*
A PROPHET LIKE ME FROM YOUR **B**.' **Ac 7:37** *80*
But when the **b** learned *of it,* they **Ac 9:30** *80*
the **b** from Joppa accompanied him. **Ac 10:23** *80*
Now the apostles and the **b** who **Ac 11:1** *80*
These six **b** also went with me **Ac 11:12** *80*
relief of the **b** living in Judea. **Ac 11:29** *80*
these things to James and the **b**." **Ac 12:17** *80*

"**B**, if you have any word of	**Ac 13:15**	*435, 80*
"**B**, sons of Abraham's family, and	**Ac 13:26**	*435, 80*
let it be known to you, **b**,	**Ac 13:38**	*435, 80*
and embittered them against the **b**.	**Ac 14:2**	*80*
Judea and *began* teaching the **b**,	**Ac 15:1**	*80*
the **b** determined that Paul	**Ac 15:2**	*80*
bringing great joy to all the **b**.	**Ac 15:3**	*80*
"**B**, you know that in the early	**Ac 15:7**	*435, 80*
"**B**, listen to me.	**Ac 15:13**	*435, 80*
Silas, leading men among the **b**,	**Ac 15:22**	*80*
apostles and the **b** who are elders,	**Ac 15:23**	*80*
to the **b** in Antioch and Syria and	**Ac 15:23**	*80*
the **b** with a lengthy message.	**Ac 15:32**	*80*
they were sent away from the **b** in	**Ac 15:33**	*80*
"Let us return and visit the **b** in	**Ac 15:36**	*80*
by the **b** to the grace of the Lord.	**Ac 15:40**	*80*
by the **b** who were in Lystra	**Ac 16:2**	*80*
of Lydia, and when they saw the **b**,	**Ac 16:40**	*80*
b before the city authorities,	**Ac 17:6**	*80*
The **b** immediately sent Paul	**Ac 17:10**	*80*
Then immediately the **b** sent	**Ac 17:14**	*80*
b and put out to sea for Syria,	**Ac 18:18**	*80*
the **b** encouraged him and wrote to	**Ac 18:27**	*80*
and after greeting the **b**,	**Ac 21:7**	*80*
the **b** received us gladly.	**Ac 21:17**	*80*
"**B** and fathers, hear my defense	**Ac 22:1**	*435, 80*
I also received letters to the **b**,	**Ac 22:5**	*80*
"**B**, I have lived my life with a	**Ac 23:1**	*435, 80*
"I was not aware, **b**,	**Ac 23:5**	*80*
"**B**, I am a Pharisee, a son of	**Ac 23:6**	*435, 80*
There we found *some* **b**,	**Ac 28:14**	*80*
And the **b**, when they heard about	**Ac 28:15**	*80*
"**B**, though I had done nothing	**Ac 28:17**	*435, 80*
nor have any of the **b** come here	**Ac 28:21**	*80*
do not want you to be unaware, **b**,	**Ro 1:13**	*80*
Or do you not know, **b**	**Ro 7:1**	*80*
Therefore, my **b**, you also were	**Ro 7:4**	*80*
So then, **b**, we are under	**Ro 8:12**	*80*
be the firstborn among many **b**;	**Ro 8:29**	*80*
from Christ for the sake of my **b**,	**Ro 9:3**	*80*
B, my heart's desire and my prayer	**Ro 10:1**	*80*
For I do not want you, **b**,	**Ro 11:25**	*80*
I urge you, **b**,	**Ro 12:1**	*80*
And concerning you, my **b**,	**Ro 15:14**	*80*
Now I urge you, **b**, by our Lord	**Ro 15:30**	*80*
Hermas and the **b** with them.	**Ro 16:14**	*80*
Now I urge you, **b**, keep your eye	**Ro 16:17**	*80*
Now I exhort you, **b**,	**1Co 1:10**	*80*
informed concerning you, my **b**,	**1Co 1:11**	*80*
For consider your calling, **b**,	**1Co 1:26**	*80*
And when I came to you, **b**,	**1Co 2:1**	*80*
And I, **b**, could not speak to you	**1Co 3:1**	*80*
Now these things, **b**,	**1Co 4:6**	*80*
be able to decide between his **b**,	**1Co 6:5**	*80*
defraud. *You do* this even to *your* **b**.	**1Co 6:8**	*80*
B, each one is to remain with God in	**1Co 7:24**	*80*
But this I say, **b**, the time has	**1Co 7:29**	*80*
by sinning against the **b** and	**1Co 8:12**	*80*
do not want you to be unaware, **b**,	**1Co 10:1**	*80*
So then, my **b**, when you come	**1Co 11:33**	*80*
Now concerning spiritual *gifts*, **b**,	**1Co 12:1**	*80*
But now, **b**, if I come to you	**1Co 14:6**	*80*
B, do not be children in your	**1Co 14:20**	*80*
What is *the outcome* then, **b**?	**1Co 14:26**	*80*
Therefore, my **b**, desire earnestly	**1Co 14:39**	*80*
Now I make known to you, **b**,	**1Co 15:1**	*80*
than five hundred **b** at one time,	**1Co 15:6**	*80*
I affirm, **b**, by the boasting in	**1Co 15:31**	*80*
Now I say this, **b**, that flesh and	**1Co 15:50**	*80*
Therefore, my beloved **b**,	**1Co 15:58**	*80*
for I expect him with the **b**.	**1Co 16:11**	*80*
greatly to come to you with the **b**;	**1Co 16:12**	*80*
Now I urge you, **b**	**1Co 16:15**	*80*
All the **b** greet you.	**1Co 16:20**	*80*
do not want you to be unaware, **b**,	**2Co 1:8**	*80*
Now, **b**, we *wish to* make known to	**2Co 8:1**	*80*
as for our **b**, *they are* messengers	**2Co 8:23**	*80*
But I have sent the **b**,	**2Co 9:3**	*80*
I thought it necessary to urge the **b**	**2Co 9:5**	*80*
when the **b** came from Macedonia they	**2Co 11:9**	*80*
on the sea, dangers among false **b**;	**2Co 11:26**	*5569*
Finally, **b**, rejoice, be made	**2Co 13:11**	*80*
and all the **b** who are with me, To	**Ga 1:2**	*80*
For I would have you know, **b**,	**Ga 1:11**	*80*
But *it was* because of the false **b**	**Ga 2:4**	*5569*
B, I speak in terms of human	**Ga 3:15**	*80*
I beg of you, **b**, become as I *am*,	**Ga 4:12**	*80*
And you **b**, like Isaac, are	**Ga 4:28**	*80*
So then, **b**, we are not children of	**Ga 4:31**	*80*
But I, **b**, if I still preach	**Ga 5:11**	*80*
For you were called to freedom, **b**;	**Ga 5:13**	*80*
B, even if anyone is caught in any	**Ga 6:1**	*80*
Christ be with your spirit, **b**.	**Ga 6:18**	*80*
Peace be to the **b**, and love with	**Eph 6:23**	*80*
Now I want you to know, **b**,	**Php 1:12**	*80*
and that most of the **b**,	**Php 1:14**	*80*
Finally, my **b**, rejoice in the Lord.	**Php 3:1**	*80*
B, I do not regard myself as	**Php 3:13**	*80*
B, join in following my example,	**Php 3:17**	*80*
my beloved **b** whom I long *to see*,	**Php 4:1**	*80*
Finally, **b**, whatever is true,	**Php 4:8**	*80*
The **b** who are with me greet you.	**Php 4:21**	*80*
b in Christ *who are* at Colossae:	**Col 1:2**	*80*
Greet the **b** who are in Laodicea	**Col 4:15**	*80*
knowing, **b** beloved by God, *His*	**1Th 1:4**	*80*
For you yourselves know, **b**,	**1Th 2:1**	*80*
For you recall, **b**, our labor and	**1Th 2:9**	*80*
For you, **b**, became imitators of	**1Th 2:14**	*80*
But we, **b**, having been taken away from	**1Th 2:17**	*80*
for this reason, **b**,	**1Th 3:7**	*80*
Finally then, **b**, we request and	**1Th 4:1**	*80*
Now as to the love of the **b**,	**1Th 4:9**	*5360*
the **b** who are in all Macedonia.	**1Th 4:10**	*80*
But we urge you, **b**,	**1Th 4:10**	*80*
not want you to be uninformed, **b**,	**1Th 4:13**	*80*
as to the times and the epochs, **b**,	**1Th 5:1**	*80*
But you, **b**, are not in darkness,	**1Th 5:4**	*80*
But we request of you, **b**,	**1Th 5:12**	*80*
We urge you, **b**,	**1Th 5:14**	*80*
B, pray for us.	**1Th 5:25**	*80*
Greet all the **b** with a holy kiss.	**1Th 5:26**	*80*
this letter read to all the **b**.	**1Th 5:27**	*80*
to give thanks to God for you, **b**,	**2Th 1:3**	*80*
Now we request you, **b**,	**2Th 2:1**	*80*
for you, **b** beloved by the Lord,	**2Th 2:13**	*80*
So then, **b**, stand firm and hold to	**2Th 2:15**	*80*
Finally, **b**, pray for us that the	**2Th 3:1**	*80*
Now we command you, **b**,	**2Th 3:6**	*80*
But as for you, **b**, do not grow weary	**2Th 3:13**	*80*
out these things to the **b**,	**1Tm 4:6**	*80*
to them because they are **b**,	**1Tm 6:2**	*80*
Linus and Claudia and all the **b**.	**2Tm 4:21**	*80*
He is not ashamed to call them **b**,	**Heb 2:11**	*80*
WILL PROCLAIM YOUR NAME TO MY **B**,	**Heb 2:12**	*80*
be made like His **b** in all things,	**Heb 2:17**	*80*
Therefore, holy **b**, partakers of a	**Heb 3:1**	*80*
Take care, **b**, that there not be	**Heb 3:12**	*80*
the people, that is, from their **b**,	**Heb 7:5**	*80*
Therefore, **b**, since	**Heb 10:19**	*80*
Let love of the **b** continue.	**Heb 13:1**	*5360*
But I urge you, **b**, bear with this	**Heb 13:22**	*80*
Consider it all joy, my **b**,	**Jas 1:2**	*80*
Do not be deceived, my beloved **b**.	**Jas 1:16**	*80*
This you know, my beloved **b**.	**Jas 1:19**	*80*
My **b**, do not hold your faith in	**Jas 2:1**	*80*
Listen, my beloved **b**:	**Jas 2:5**	*80*
What use is it, my **b**,	**Jas 2:14**	*80*
many *of you* become teachers, my **b**,	**Jas 3:1**	*80*
My **b**, these things ought not to be	**Jas 3:10**	*80*
Can a fig tree, my **b**,	**Jas 3:12**	*80*
not speak against one another, **b**.	**Jas 4:11**	*80*
Therefore be patient, **b**,	**Jas 5:7**	*80*
Do not complain, **b**,	**Jas 5:9**	*80*
As an example, **b**, of suffering and	**Jas 5:10**	*80*
But above all, my **b**,	**Jas 5:12**	*80*
My **b**, if any among you strays from	**Jas 5:19**	*80*
souls for a sincere love of the **b**,	**1Pe 1:22**	*5360*
by your **b** who are in the world.	**1Pe 5:9**	*81*
Therefore, **b**, be all the more	**2Pe 1:10**	*80*
Do not be surprised, **b**, if the world	**1Jn 3:13**	*80*
into life, because we love the **b**.	**1Jn 3:14**	*80*
to lay down our lives for the **b**.	**1Jn 3:16**	*80*
For I was very glad when **b** came	**3Jn 1:3**	*80*
whatever you accomplish for the **b**,	**3Jn 1:5**	*80*
himself does not receive the **b**, either,	**3Jn 1:10**	*80*
fellow servants and their **b** who	**Rv 6:11**	*80*
accuser of our **b** has been thrown	**Rv 12:10**	*80*
b who hold the testimony of Jesus;	**Rv 19:10**	*80*
yours and of your **b** the prophets	**Rv 22:9**	*80*

BRIAR

The best of them is like a **b**,	**Mi 7:4**	2312
do they pick grapes from a **b** bush.	**Lk 6:44**	*942*

BRIARS

Let **b** grow instead of wheat, And	**Jb 31:40**	2336
But **b** and thorns will come up.	**Is 5:6**	8068
silver, will become **b** and thorns.	**Is 7:23**	8068
all the land will be **b** and thorns.	**Is 7:24**	8068
go there for fear of **b** and thorns;	**Is 7:25**	8068
It consumes **b** and thorns;	**Is 9:18**	8068
thorns and his **b** in a single day.	**Is 10:17**	8068
give Me **b** *and* thorns in battle,	**Is 27:4**	8068
which thorns *and* **b** shall come up;	**Is 32:13**	8068

BRIBE

"You shall not take a **b**,	**Ex 23:8**	7810
for a **b** blinds the clear-sighted	**Ex 23:8**	7810
not show partiality nor take a **b**.	**Dt 10:17**	7810
and you shall not take a **b**,	**Dt 16:19**	7810
for a **b** blinds the eyes of the	**Dt 16:19**	7810
'Cursed is he who accepts a **b** to	**Dt 27:25**	7810
a **b** to blind my eyes with it?	**1Sa 12:3**	3724a
or the taking of a **b**."	**2Ch 19:7**	7810
'Offer a **b** for me from your	**Jb 6:22**	7809
he take a **b** against the innocent.	**Ps 15:5**	7810
A **b** is a charm in the sight of its	**Pr 17:8**	7810
A wicked man receives a **b** from the	**Pr 17:23**	7810
anger, And a **b** in the bosom,	**Pr 21:14**	7810
mad, And a **b** corrupts the heart.	**Ec 7:7**	4979
Everyone loves a **b** And	**Is 1:23**	7810
Who justify the wicked for a **b**,	**Is 5:23**	7810
his hands so that they hold no **b**;	**Is 33:15**	7810
gifts to all your lovers to **b** them	**Ezk 16:33**	7809
pronounce judgment for a **b**,	**Mi 3:11**	7810
asks, also the judge, for a **b**,	**Mi 7:3**	7966

BRIBES

and took **b** and perverted justice.	**1Sa 8:3**	7810
And whose right hand is full of **b**.	**Ps 26:10**	7810
But he who hates **b** will live.	**Pr 15:27**	4979
a man who takes **b** overthrows it.	**Pr 29:4**	8641
they have taken **b** to shed blood;	**Ezk 22:12**	7810
the righteous *and* accept **b** And	**Am 5:12**	3724a

BRICK

And they used **b** for stone, and	**Gn 11:3**	3843
straw to make **b** as previously;	**Ex 5:7**	3835b
today in making **b** as previously?"	**Ex 5:14**	3835b
b *terrace* which is at the entrance	**Jer 43:9**	4404
you son of man, get yourself a **b**,	**Ezk 4:1**	3843
Take hold of the **b** mold!	**Na 3:14**	4404

BRICKKILN

and made them pass through the **b**.	**2Sa 12:31**	4404

BRICKS

make **b** and burn *them* thoroughly."	**Gn 11:3**	3835b
bitter with hard labor in mortar and **b**	**Ex 1:14**	3843
"But the quota of **b** which they	**Ex 5:8**	3843
they keep saying to us, 'Make **b**!'	**Ex 5:16**	3843
you must deliver the quota of **b**."	**Ex 5:18**	3843
reduce *your* daily amount of **b**."	**Ex 5:19**	3843
"The **b** have fallen down, But we	**Is 9:10**	3843
gardens and burning incense on **b**;	**Is 65:3**	3843

BRIDAL

ever so much **b** payment and gift,	**Gn 34:12**	4119
And the bride out of her **b** chamber.	**Jl 2:16**	

BRIDE

"*Come* with me from Lebanon, *my* **b**,	**SS 4:8**	3618
beat faster, my sister, *my* **b**;	**SS 4:9**	3618
is your love, my sister, *my* **b**!	**SS 4:10**	3618
"Your lips, *my* **b**, drip honey;	**SS 4:11**	3618
garden locked is my sister, *my* **b**,	**SS 4:12**	3618
into my garden, my sister, *my* **b**;	**SS 5:1**	3618
jewels and bind them on as a **b**.	**Is 49:18**	3618
And as a **b** adorns herself with her	**Is 61:10**	3618
bridegroom rejoices over the **b**,	**Is 62:5**	3618
her ornaments, Or a **b** her attire?	**Jer 2:32**	3618
bridegroom and the voice of the **b**;	**Jer 7:34**	3618
the groom and the voice of the **b**,	**Jer 16:9**	3618
bridegroom and the voice of the **b**,	**Jer 25:10**	3618
bridegroom and the voice of the **b**,	**Jer 33:11**	3618
the **b** out of her *bridal* chamber.	**Jl 2:16**	3618
who has the **b** is the bridegroom;	**Jn 3:29**	*3565*
voice of the bridegroom and **b** will	**Rv 18:23**	*3565*
His **b** has made herself ready."	**Rv 19:7**	*1135*
as a **b** adorned for her husband.	**Rv 21:2**	*3565*
"Come here, I will show you the **b**,	**Rv 21:9**	*3565*
The Spirit and the **b** say,	**Rv 22:17**	*3565*

BRIDEGROOM

are indeed a **b** of blood to me."	**Ex 4:25**	2860a
she said, "*You are* a **b** of blood"	**Ex 4:26**	2860a
as a **b** coming out of his chamber;	**Ps 19:5**	2860a
a **b** decks himself with a garland,	**Is 61:10**	2860a
as the **b** rejoices over the bride,	**Is 62:5**	2860a
the **b** and the voice of the bride;	**Jer 7:34**	2860a
the **b** and the voice of the bride,	**Jer 25:10**	2860a
the **b** and the voice of the bride,	**Jer 33:11**	2860a
sackcloth For the **b** of her youth.	**Jl 1:8**	1167
Let the **b** come out of his room And	**Jl 2:16**	2860a
"The attendants of the **b** cannot	**Mt 9:15**	*3567*
as long as the **b** is with them,	**Mt 9:15**	*3566*
the **b** is taken away from them,	**Mt 9:15**	*3566*
lamps and went out to meet the **b**.	**Mt 25:1**	*3566*
"Now while the **b** was delaying,	**Mt 25:5**	*3566*
there was a shout, 'Behold, the **b**!	**Mt 25:6**	*3566*
to make the purchase, the **b** came,	**Mt 25:10**	*3566*
"While the **b** is with them, the	**Mk 2:19**	*3566*
attendants of the **b** cannot fast,	**Mk 2:19**	*3567*
long as they have the **b** with them,	**Mk 2:19**	*3566*
the **b** is taken away from them,	**Mk 2:20**	*3566*
make the attendants of the **b** fast	**Lk 5:34**	*3567*
fast while the **b** is with them,	**Lk 5:34**	*3566*
the **b** is taken away from them,	**Lk 5:35**	*3566*
the headwaiter called the **b**,	**Jn 2:9**	*3566*
"He who has the bride is the **b**;	**Jn 3:29**	*3566*
but the friend of the **b**,	**Jn 3:29**	*3566*
and the voice of the **b** and bride	**Rv 18:23**	*3566*

BRIDEGROOM'S

greatly because of the **b** voice.	**Jn 3:29**	*3566*

BRIDES

And your **b** commit adultery.	**Hos 4:13**	3618
your **b** when they commit adultery,	**Hos 4:14**	3618

BRIDLE

your nose, And My **b** in your lips,	**2Ki 19:28**	4964
have cast off the **b** before me.	**Jb 30:11**	7448
bit and **b** to hold them in check,	**Ps 32:9**	7448
for the horse, a **b** for the donkey,	**Pr 26:3**	4964
peoples the **b** which leads to ruin.	**Is 30:28**	7448
your nose And My **b** in your lips,	**Is 37:29**	4964
and yet does not **b** his tongue but	**Jas 1:26**	*5468*
able to **b** the whole body as well.	**Jas 3:2**	*5468*

BRIDLES

wine press, up to the horses' **b**,	**Rv 14:20**	*5469*

BRIEF

"But now for a **b** moment grace has	**Ezr 9:8**	4592
"For a **b** moment I forsook you,	**Is 54:7**	6996b
us, by your kindness, a **b** hearing.	**Ac 24:4**	*4935*
mystery, as I wrote before in **b**.	**Eph 3:3**	*3641*

BRIEFLY

for I have written to you **b**.	**Heb 13:22**	*1223, 1024*
I have written to you **b**,	**1Pe 5:12**	*3641*

BRIER

a prickling **b** or a painful thorn	**Ezk 28:24**	5544

BRIERS

of the wilderness and with **b**."	**Jg 8:7**	1303
thorns of the wilderness and **b**,	**Jg 8:16**	1303

BRIGHT

a swelling or a scab or a **b** spot,	**Lv 13:2**	934
"But if the **b** spot is white on	**Lv 13:4**	934
or a reddish-white, **b** spot,	**Lv 13:19**	934
the **b** spot remains in its place and	**Lv 13:23**	934
of the burn becomes a **b** spot,	**Lv 13:24**	934
in the **b** spot has turned white and	**Lv 13:25**	934
is no white hair in the **b** spot and	**Lv 13:26**	934
the **b** spot remains in its place and	**Lv 13:28**	934
b spots on the skin of the body,	**Lv 13:38**	934
of the body, *even* white **b** spots,	**Lv 13:38**	934

and if the **b** spots on the skin of	**Lv 13:39**	934
and for a scab, and for a **b** spot	**Lv 14:56**	934
the light which is **b** in the skies;	**Jb 37:21**	925
And the night is as **b** as the day.	**Ps 139:12**	215
B eyes gladden the heart;	**Pr 15:30**	3974
with cedar and painting *it* **b** red.'	**Jer 22:14**	8350
and a **b** light around it,	**Ezk 1:4**	5051
The fire was **b**, and lightning was	**Ezk 1:13**	5051
a **b** cloud overshadowed them,	**Mt 17:5**	*5460*
a very **b** light suddenly flashed	**Ac 22:6**	*2425*
clothed in linen, clean *and* **b**,	**Rv 15:6**	*2986*
in fine linen, **b** *and* clean;	**Rv 19:8**	*2986*
of David, the **b** morning star."	**Rv 22:16**	*2986*

BRIGHTENED

hand to his mouth, and his eyes **b**.	**1Sa 14:27**	215
how my eyes have **b** because I	**1Sa 14:29**	215

BRIGHTER

Your life would be **b** than noonday;	**Jb 11:17**	6965
That shines **b** and brighter until	**Pr 4:18**	1980
brighter and **b** until the full day.	**Pr 4:18**	1980
of the sun will be seven times **b**,	**Is 30:26**	
light from heaven, **b** than the sun,	**Ac 26:13**	*2987*

BRIGHTLY

Those who have insight will shine **b**	**Da 12:3**	2094a

BRIGHTNESS

"From the **b** before Him Coals of	**2Sa 22:13**	5051
"If even the moon has no **b** And	**Jb 25:5**	166
From the **b** before Him passed His	**Ps 18:12**	5051
the **b** of a flaming fire by night;	**Is 4:5**	5051
For **b**, but we walk in gloom.	**Is 59:9**	5054
And kings to the **b** of your rising.	**Is 60:3**	5051
b will the moon give you light;	**Is 60:19**	5051
righteousness goes forth like **b**,	**Is 62:1**	5051
and upward the appearance of **b**,	**Ezk 8:2**	2096
the **b** of the glory of the LORD.	**Ezk 10:4**	5051
the **b** of the expanse of heaven,	**Da 12:3**	2096
dark And the stars lose their **b**.	**Jl 2:10**	5051
dark And the stars lose their **b**.	**Jl 3:15**	5051
light, Even gloom with no **b** in it?	**Am 5:20**	5051
because of the **b** of that light,	**Ac 22:11**	*1391*

BRILLIANCE

b was like a very costly stone,	**Rv 21:11**	*5458*

BRIM

metal ten cubits from **b** to brim,	**1Ki 7:23**	8193
metal ten cubits from brim to **b**,	**1Ki 7:23**	8193
Under its **b** gourds went around	**1Ki 7:24**	8193
and its **b** was made like the brim	**1Ki 7:26**	8193
brim was made like the **b** of a cup,	**1Ki 7:26**	8193
sea, ten cubits from **b** to brim,	**2Ch 4:2**	8193
sea, ten cubits from brim to **b**,	**2Ch 4:2**	8193
and its **b** was made like the brim	**2Ch 4:5**	8193
brim was made like the **b** of a cup,	**2Ch 4:5**	8193
So they filled them up to the **b**.	**Jn 2:7**	*507*

BRIMSTONE

rained on Sodom and Gomorrah **b**	**Gn 19:24**	1614
'All its land is **b** and salt, a	**Dt 29:23**	1614
B is scattered on his habitation.	**Jb 18:15**	1614
Fire and **b** and burning wind will	**Ps 11:6**	1614
of the LORD, like a torrent of **b**,	**Is 30:33**	1614
pitch, And its loose earth into **b**,	**Is 34:9**	1614
with hailstones, fire and **b**.	**Ezk 38:22**	1614
it rained fire and **b** from heaven	**Lk 17:29**	*2303*
of fire and of hyacinth and of **b**;	**Rv 9:17**	*2306*
proceed fire and smoke and **b**.	**Rv 9:17**	*2303*
the fire and the smoke and the **b** which	**Rv 9:18**	*2303*
will be tormented with fire and **b**	**Rv 14:10**	*2303*
lake of fire which burns with **b**.	**Rv 19:20**	*2303*
into the lake of fire and **b**,	**Rv 20:10**	*2303*
lake that burns with fire and **b**,	**Rv 21:8**	*2303*

BRING

"Let the earth **b** forth living	**Gn 1:24**	3318
pain you will **b** forth children;	**Gn 3:16**	3205
you shall **b** two of every *kind* into	**Gn 6:19**	935
"**B** out with you every living	**Gn 8:17**	3318
when I **b** a cloud over the earth,	**Gn 9:14**	6049b
"**B** Me a three year old heifer,	**Gn 15:9**	3947
and I will **b** a piece of bread,	**Gn 18:5**	3947
so that the LORD may **b** upon	**Gn 18:19**	935
B them out to us that we may have	**Gn 19:5**	3318
please let me **b** them out to you,	**Gn 19:8**	3318
the city, **b** *them* out of the place;	**Gn 19:12**	3318
and **b** it to me that I may eat,	**Gn 27:4**	935
field to hunt for game to **b** *home,*	**Gn 27:5**	935
'**B** me *some* game and prepare a	**Gn 27:7**	935
b me two choice young goats from there,	**Gn 27:9**	3947
you shall **b** *it* to your father,	**Gn 27:10**	935
and I will **b** upon myself a curse	**Gn 27:12**	935
"**B** *it* to me, and I will eat of my	**Gn 27:25**	5066
and will **b** you back to this land;	**Gn 28:15**	7725
torn *of beasts* I did not **b** to you;	**Gn 31:39**	935
and **b** word back to me."	**Gn 37:14**	7725
their way to **b** *them* down to Egypt.	**Gn 37:25**	3381
"**B** her out and let her be burned!"	**Gn 38:24**	3318
and God will quickly **b** it about.	**Gn 41:32**	6213a
and **b** your youngest brother to me,	**Gn 42:20**	935
'But **b** your youngest brother to me	**Gn 42:34**	935
if I do not **b** him *back* to you;	**Gn 42:37**	935
then you will **b** my gray hair down	**Gn 42:38**	3381
'**B** your brother down'?"	**Gn 43:7**	3381
If I do not **b** him *back* to you and	**Gn 43:9**	935
"**B** the men into the house, and	**Gn 43:16**	935
'**B** him down to me that I may set	**Gn 44:21**	3381
you will **b** my gray hair down to	**Gn 44:29**	3381
Thus your servants will **b** the gray	**Gn 44:31**	3381
'If I do not **b** him *back* to you,	**Gn 44:32**	935
hurry and **b** my father down here."	**Gn 45:13**	3381
wives, and **b** your father and come.	**Gn 45:19**	5375
I will also surely **b** you up again;	**Gn 46:4**	5927
"**B** them to me, please, that I may	**Gn 48:9**	3947
and **b** you back to the land of your	**Gn 48:21**	7725
to **b** about this present result,	**Gn 50:20**	6213a
and **b** you up from this land to the	**Gn 50:24**	5927
and to **b** them up from that land to	**Ex 3:8**	5927
so that you may **b** My people,	**Ex 3:10**	3318
and that I should **b** the sons of	**Ex 3:11**	3318
I will **b** you up out of the	**Ex 3:17**	5927
and I will **b** you out from under	**Ex 6:6**	3318
'I will **b** you to the land	**Ex 6:8**	935
to **b** the sons of Israel out of the	**Ex 6:13**	3318
"**B** out the sons of Israel from	**Ex 6:26**	3318
hand on Egypt and **b** out My hosts,	**Ex 7:4**	3318
on Egypt and **b** out the sons of Israel	**Ex 7:5**	3318
secret arts to **b** forth gnats,	**Ex 8:18**	3318
b your livestock and whatever you	**Ex 9:19**	5756
b locusts into your territory.	**Ex 10:4**	935
I will **b** on Pharaoh and on Egypt;	**Ex 11:1**	935
you are not to **b** forth any of the	**Ex 12:46**	3318
"You will **b** them and plant them	**Ex 15:17**	935
when they prepare what they **b** in,	**Ex 16:5**	935
and you **b** the disputes to God,	**Ex 18:19**	935
major dispute they will **b** to you,	**Ex 18:22**	935
dispute they would **b** to Moses,	**Ex 18:26**	935
his master shall **b** him to God,	**Ex 21:6**	5066
then he shall **b** him to the door or	**Ex 21:6**	5066
pieces, let him **b** it as evidence;	**Ex 22:13**	935
"You shall **b** the choice first	**Ex 23:19**	935
and to **b** you into the place which	**Ex 23:20**	935
b you in to *the land of* the Amorites,	**Ex 23:23**	935
and shall **b** in the ark of the	**Ex 26:33**	935
that they **b** you clear oil of	**Ex 27:20**	3947
"Then **b** near to yourself Aaron	**Ex 28:1**	7126
"Then you shall **b** Aaron and his	**Ex 29:4**	7126
"You shall **b** his sons and put	**Ex 29:8**	7126
"Then you shall **b** the bull before	**Ex 29:10**	7126
daughters, and **b** *them* to me."	**Ex 32:2**	935
'**B** up this people!'	**Ex 33:12**	5927
"You shall **b** the very first of	**Ex 34:26**	935
b it as the LORD's contribution:	**Ex 35:5**	935
to **b** *material* for all the work,	**Ex 35:29**	935
"You shall **b** in the table and	**Ex 40:4**	935
and you shall **b** in the lampstand	**Ex 40:4**	935
"Then you shall **b** Aaron and his	**Ex 40:12**	7126
"You shall **b** his sons and put	**Ex 40:14**	7126
you shall **b** your offering of	**Lv 1:2**	7126
then he shall **b** his offering from	**Lv 1:14**	7126
'The priest shall **b** it to the	**Lv 1:15**	7126
'He shall then **b** it to Aaron's	**Lv 2:2**	935
'Now when you **b** an offering of a	**Lv 2:4**	7126
'When you **b** in the grain offering	**Lv 2:8**	935
and he shall **b** it to the altar.	**Lv 2:8**	5066
offering, which you **b** to the LORD,	**Lv 2:11**	7126
you shall **b** them to the LORD,	**Lv 2:12**	7126
'Also if you **b** a grain offering of	**Lv 2:14**	7126
you shall **b** fresh heads of grain	**Lv 2:14**	7126
he shall **b** as an offering by fire to	**Lv 3:9**	7126
so as to **b** guilt on the people,	**Lv 4:3**	819
'He shall **b** the bull to the	**Lv 4:4**	935
and **b** it to the tent of meeting,	**Lv 4:5**	935
he is to **b** out to a clean place	**Lv 4:12**	3318
b it before the tent of meeting.	**Lv 4:14**	935
'Then the anointed priest is to **b**	**Lv 4:16**	935
'Then he is to **b** out the bull to *a*	**Lv 4:21**	3318
shall **b** for his offering a goat,	**Lv 4:23**	935
shall **b** for his offering a goat,	**Lv 4:28**	935
for a sin offering, he shall **b** it,	**Lv 4:32**	935
'He shall also **b** his guilt	**Lv 5:6**	935
then he shall **b** to the LORD his	**Lv 5:7**	935
'He shall **b** them to the	**Lv 5:8**	935
he shall **b** the tenth of an ephah	**Lv 5:11**	935
'He shall **b** it to the priest,	**Lv 5:12**	935
then he shall **b** his guilt offering	**Lv 5:15**	935
"He is then to **b** to the priest a	**Lv 5:18**	935
"Then he shall **b** to the priest	**Lv 6:6**	935
is *well* stirred, you shall **b** it.	**Lv 6:21**	935
shall **b** his offering to the LORD	**Lv 7:29**	935
b offerings by fire to the LORD.	**Lv 7:30**	935
shall **b** the fat with the breast,	**Lv 7:30**	935
they shall **b** along with the	**Lv 10:15**	935
she shall **b** to the priest at the	**Lv 12:6**	935
and **b** it for a guilt offering,	**Lv 14:12**	7126
"Then the eighth day he shall **b**	**Lv 14:23**	935
and **b** them in to the priest,	**Lv 15:29**	935
incense, and **b** *it* inside the veil.	**Lv 16:12**	935
and **b** its blood inside the veil and	**Lv 16:15**	935
sons of Israel may **b** their sacrifices	**Lv 17:5**	935
they may **b** them in to the LORD,	**Lv 17:5**	935
and does not **b** it to the doorway	**Lv 17:9**	935
'He shall **b** his guilt offering	**Lv 19:21**	935
then you shall **b** in the sheaf of	**Lv 23:10**	935
'You shall **b** in from your dwelling	**Lv 23:17**	935
b to you clear oil from beaten olives	**Lv 24:2**	3947
"**B** the one who has cursed outside	**Lv 24:14**	3318
will **b** forth the crop for three years.	**Lv 25:21**	6213a
'I will also **b** upon you a sword	**Lv 26:25**	935
and they will **b** back your bread in	**Lv 26:26**	7725
I will also **b** weakness into their	**Lv 26:36**	935
to **b** them into the land of their	**Lv 26:41**	935
"**B** the tribe of Levi near and set	**Nu 3:6**	7126
then **b** his wife to the priest,	**Nu 5:15**	935
and shall **b** *as* an offering for her	**Nu 5:15**	935
'Then the priest shall **b** her near	**Nu 5:16**	7126
the LORD and **b** it to the altar;	**Nu 5:25**	7126
'Then on the eighth day he shall **b**	**Nu 6:10**	935
and shall **b** a male lamb a year old	**Nu 6:12**	935
he shall **b** the offering to the	**Nu 6:13**	935
and **b** them to the tent of meeting,	**Nu 11:16**	3947
then He will **b** us into this land and	**Nu 14:8**	935
'Because the LORD could not **b** this	**Nu 14:16**	935
I will **b** into the land which he	**Nu 14:24**	935
I will **b** them in, and they will know	**Nu 14:31**	935
you enter the land where I **b** you,	**Nu 15:18**	935
and will **b** *him* near to Himself;	**Nu 16:5**	7126
choose, He will **b** near to Himself.	**Nu 16:5**	7126
Israel, to **b** you near to Himself,	**Nu 16:9**	7126
you **b** his censer before the LORD,	**Nu 16:17**	7126
also you and Aaron *shall* each **b**	**Nu 16:17**	
then **b** it quickly to the	**Nu 16:46**	1980
"But **b** with you also your	**Nu 18:2**	7126
land, which they **b** to the LORD,	**Nu 18:13**	935
they **b** you an unblemished red heifer	**Nu 19:2**	3947
to **b** us in to this wretched place?	**Nu 20:5**	935
You shall thus **b** forth water for	**Nu 20:8**	3318
shall we **b** forth water for you out	**Nu 20:10**	3318
therefore you shall not **b** this	**Nu 20:12**	935
and **b** them up to Mount Hor;	**Nu 20:25**	5927
and I will **b** word back to you as	**Nu 22:8**	7725
will lead them out and **b** them in,	**Nu 27:17**	935
hard for you, you shall **b** to me,	**Dt 1:17**	7126
and **b** back to us word of the way	**Dt 1:22**	7725
to **b** you in *and* to give you their	**Dt 4:38**	935
from there in order to **b** us in,	**Dt 6:23**	935
"You shall not **b** an	**Dt 7:26**	935
LORD was not able to **b** them into	**Dt 9:28**	935
you shall **b** your burnt offerings,	**Dt 12:6**	935
shall **b** all that I command you:	**Dt 12:11**	935
you are not able to **b** *the tithe,*	**Dt 14:24**	5375
third year you shall **b** out all the tithe	**Dt 14:28**	3318
then you shall **b** out that man or	**Dt 17:5**	3318
elders of that city shall **b** the heifer	**Dt 21:4**	3381
shall **b** her home to your house,	**Dt 21:12**	935
and **b** him out to the elders of his	**Dt 21:19**	3318
b them back to your countryman.	**Dt 22:1**	7725
you shall **b** it home to your house,	**Dt 22:2**	622
that you will not **b** bloodguilt on	**Dt 22:8**	7760
shall take and **b** out the *evidence*	**Dt 22:15**	3318
then they shall **b** out the girl to	**Dt 22:21**	3318
then you shall **b** them both out to	**Dt 22:24**	3318
"You shall not **b** the hire of a	**Dt 23:18**	935
and you shall not **b** sin on the	**Dt 24:4**	2398
shall **b** the pledge out to you.	**Dt 24:11**	3318
which you **b** in from your land	**Dt 26:2**	935
"The LORD will **b** you and your	**Dt 28:36**	1980
"You shall **b** out much seed to the	**Dt 28:38**	3318
"The LORD will **b** a nation against	**Dt 28:49**	5375
then the LORD will **b** extraordinary	**Dt 28:59**	6381
"He will **b** back on you all	**Dt 28:60**	7725
the LORD will **b** on you until you	**Dt 28:61**	5927
will **b** you back to Egypt in ships,	**Dt 28:68**	7725
to **b** upon it every curse which is	**Dt 29:27**	935
and from there He will **b** you back.	**Dt 30:4**	3947
"The LORD your God will **b** you	**Dt 30:5**	935
"For when I **b** them into the land	**Dt 31:20**	935
for you shall **b** the sons of Israel	**Dt 31:23**	935
of Judah, And **b** him to his people.	**Dt 33:7**	935
"**B** out the men who have come to	**Jos 2:3**	3318
accursed and **b** trouble on it.	**Jos 6:18**	5916
"Go into the harlot's house and **b**	**Jos 6:22**	3318
b this people over the Jordan,	**Jos 7:7**	5674a
"Open the mouth of the cave and **b**	**Jos 10:22**	3318
and **b** *the description* here to me.	**Jos 18:6**	935
will **b** upon you all the threats,	**Jos 23:15**	935
not the LORD **b** us up from Egypt?'	**Jg 6:13**	5927
and **b** out my offering and lay it	**Jg 6:18**	3318
"**B** out your son, that he may die,	**Jg 6:30**	3318
b them down to the water and I	**Jg 7:4**	3381
to her in order to **b** her back,	**Jg 19:3**	7725
"**B** out the man who came into your	**Jg 19:22**	3318
Please let me **b** them out that you	**Jg 19:24**	3318
then I will **b** him, that he may	**1Sa 1:22**	935
a little robe and **b** it to him from year	**1Sa 2:19**	5927
if we go, what shall we **b** the man?	**1Sa 9:7**	935
no present to **b** to the man of God.	**1Sa 9:7**	935
"**B** the portion that I gave you,	**1Sa 9:23**	5414
him and did not **b** him any present.	**1Sa 10:27**	935
B the men, that we may put them	**1Sa 11:12**	5414
"**B** to me the burnt offering and	**1Sa 13:9**	5066
"**B** the ark of God here."	**1Sa 14:18**	5066
of you **b** me his ox or his sheep,	**1Sa 14:34**	5066
"**B** me Agag, the king of the	**1Sa 15:32**	5066
said to Jesse, "Send and **b** him;	**1Sa 16:11**	3947
can play well and **b** *him* to me."	**1Sa 16:17**	935
"**B** also these ten cuts of cheese	**1Sa 17:18**	935
brothers, and **b** back news of them.	**1Sa 17:18**	3947
"**B** him up to me on his bed, that	**1Sa 19:15**	5927
should you **b** me to your father?"	**1Sa 20:8**	935
now, send and **b** him to me,	**1Sa 20:31**	3947
"Go, **b** *them* to the city."	**1Sa 20:40**	935
Why do you **b** him to me?	**1Sa 21:14**	935
"**B** the ephod here."	**1Sa 23:9**	5066
or a woman alive to **b** to Gath,	**1Sa 27:11**	935
and **b** up for me whom I shall name	**1Sa 28:8**	5927
for my life to **b** about my death?"	**1Sa 28:9**	4191
"Whom shall I **b** up for you?"	**1Sa 28:11**	5927
"**B** up Samuel for me."	**1Sa 28:11**	5927
"Please **b** me the ephod."	**1Sa 30:7**	5066
"Will you **b** me down to this band?"	**1Sa 30:15**	3381
I will **b** you down to this band."	**1Sa 30:15**	3381
you to **b** all Israel over to you."	**2Sa 3:12**	5437
my face unless you first **b** Michal,	**2Sa 3:13**	935
to **b** up from there the ark of God	**2Sa 6:2**	5927
that they might **b** it from the house	**2Sa 6:3**	5375
and you shall **b** in *the produce* so	**2Sa 9:10**	935
Can I **b** him back again?	**2Sa 12:23**	7725
"**B** the food into the bedroom,	**2Sa 13:10**	935
speaks to you, **b** him to me,	**2Sa 14:10**	935

Context	Reference	Number
does not **b** back his banished one.	**2Sa 14:13**	7725
b back the young man Absalom."	**2Sa 14:21**	7725
indeed **b** me back to Jerusalem,	**2Sa 15:8**	7725
b down calamity on us and strike	**2Sa 15:14**	5080
then He will **b** me back again and	**2Sa 15:25**	7725
will **b** back all the people to you.	**2Sa 17:3**	7725
Israel shall **b** ropes to that city,	**2Sa 17:13**	5375
LORD might **b** calamity on Absalom.	**2Sa 17:14**	935
"Please let me run and **b** the king	**2Sa 18:19**	1319
to **b** the king back to his house,	**2Sa 19:11**	7725
be the last to **b** back the king?'	**2Sa 19:12**	7725
to **b** the king across the Jordan.	**2Sa 19:15**	5674a
to **b** over the king's household,	**2Sa 19:18**	5674a
advice first to **b** back our king?"	**2Sa 19:43**	7725
own mule, and **b** him down to Gihon.	**1Ki 1:33**	3381
a valiant man and **b** good news."	**1Ki 1:42**	1319
and you will **b** his gray hair down	**1Ki 2:9**	3381
"My servants will **b** *them* down	**1Ki 5:9**	3381
to **b** up the ark of the covenant of	**1Ki 8:1**	5927
and **b** them back to the land which	**1Ki 8:34**	7725
'**B** him back with you to your	**1Ki 13:18**	7725
carry them and would **b** them back	**1Ki 14:28**	7725
"Please **b** me a piece of bread in	**1Ki 17:11**	3947
from it first and **b** *it* out to me,	**1Ki 17:13**	3318
to **b** my iniquity to remembrance and	**1Ki 17:18**	2142
Then he said, "Go, **b** him."	**1Ki 20:33**	3947
"Behold, I will **b** evil upon you,	**1Ki 21:21**	935
I will not **b** the evil in his days,	**1Ki 21:29**	935
but I will **b** the evil upon his	**1Ki 21:29**	935
"**B** quickly Micaiah son of Imlah."	**1Ki 22:9**	4116
"**B** me a new jar, and put salt in	**2Ki 2:20**	3947
"But now **b** me a minstrel."	**2Ki 3:15**	3947
"**B** me another vessel."	**2Ki 4:6**	5066
But he said, "Now **b** meal." He	**2Ki 4:41**	3947
b you to the man whom you seek."	**2Ki 6:19**	1980
and **b** him to an inner room.	**2Ki 9:2**	935
"**B** out garments for all the	**2Ki 10:22**	3318
I **b** into your hands to escape shall	**2Ki 10:24**	935
"**B** her out between the ranks, and	**2Ki 11:15**	3318
to **b** into the house of the LORD,	**2Ki 12:4**	935
I **b** evil on this place and on its	**2Ki 22:16**	935
I will **b** on this place.	**2Ki 22:20**	935
to **b** out of the temple of the LORD	**2Ki 23:4**	3318
b back the ark of our God to us,	**1Ch 13:3**	5437
to **b** the ark of God from	**1Ch 13:5**	935
to **b** up from there the ark of God,	**1Ch 13:6**	5927
I **b** the ark of God *home* to me?"	**1Ch 13:12**	935
to **b** up the ark of the LORD to its	**1Ch 15:3**	5927
that you may **b** up the ark of the	**1Ch 15:12**	5927
to **b** up the ark of the LORD God	**1Ch 15:14**	5927
who went to **b** up the ark of the	**1Ch 15:25**	5927
B an offering, and come before Him;	**1Ch 16:29**	5375
and **b** me *word* that I may know	**1Ch 21:2**	935
so that you may **b** the ark of the	**1Ch 22:19**	935
and **b** it to you on rafts by sea to	**2Ch 2:16**	935
to **b** up the ark of the covenant of	**2Ch 5:2**	5927
and **b** them back to the land which	**2Ch 6:25**	7725
"**B** quickly Micaiah, Imla's son."	**2Ch 18:8**	4116
who hate the LORD and so **b**	**2Ch 19:2**	
"**B** her out between the ranks;	**2Ch 23:14**	3318
not required the Levites to **b** in from	**2Ch 24:6**	935
b to the LORD the levy *fixed by* Moses	**2Ch 24:9**	935
them to **b** them back to the LORD;	**2Ch 24:19**	7725
will **b** you down before the enemy,	**2Ch 25:8**	3782
has power to help and to **b** down."	**2Ch 25:8**	3782
must not **b** the captives in here,	**2Ch 28:13**	935
for you are proposing *to* **b** upon	**2Ch 28:13**	
for they did not **b** him into the	**2Ch 28:27**	935
come near and **b** sacrifices and	**2Ch 29:31**	935
evil which I will **b** on this place	**2Ch 34:28**	935
to **b** cedar wood from Lebanon to	**Ezr 3:7**	935
and to **b** the silver and gold,	**Ezr 7:15**	2987
to **b** ministers to us for the house	**Ezr 8:17**	935
to **b** *them* to Jerusalem to the	**Ezr 8:30**	935
b them to the place where I have	**Ne 1:9**	935
b the book of the law of Moses	**Ne 8:1**	935
the hills, and **b** olive branches and	**Ne 8:15**	935
peoples of the land who **b** wares	**Ne 10:31**	935
b it to the house of our God,	**Ne 10:34**	935
and that they might **b** the	**Ne 10:35**	935
and **b** to the house of our God the	**Ne 10:36**	935
also **b** the first of our dough,	**Ne 10:37**	935
and the Levites shall **b** up the	**Ne 10:38**	5927
b the contribution of the grain,	**Ne 10:39**	935
people cast lots to **b** one out of ten	**Ne 11:1**	935
to **b** them to Jerusalem so that	**Ne 12:27**	935
to **b** Queen Vashti before the king	**Es 1:11**	935
"**B** Haman quickly that we may do	**Es 5:5**	4116
an order to **b** the book of records,	**Es 6:1**	935
let them **b** a royal robe which the	**Es 6:8**	935
b forth words from their minds?	**Jb 8:10**	3318
And **b** him into judgment with	**Jb 14:3**	935
mischief and **b** forth iniquity,	**Jb 15:35**	3205
"For I know that You will **b** me	**Jb 30:23**	7725
And his life to those who **b** death.	**Jb 33:22**	4191
To **b** back his soul from the pit,	**Jb 33:30**	7725
b rain on a land without people,	**Jb 38:26**	4305
down, they **b** forth their young,	**Jb 39:3**	6398
Let his maker **b** near his sword.	**Jb 40:19**	5066
"Surely the mountains **b** him food,	**Jb 40:20**	5375
O LORD, confront him, **b** him low;	**Ps 17:13**	3766
B me out of my distresses.	**Ps 25:17**	3318
He will **b** forth your	**Ps 37:6**	3318
Let them **b** me to Your holy hill And	**Ps 43:3**	935
For they **b** down trouble upon me And	**Ps 55:3**	4131
will **b** them down to the pit of	**Ps 55:23**	3381
by Your power, and **b** them down,	**Ps 59:11**	3381
will **b** me into the besieged city?	**Ps 60:9**	2986
choose and **b** near *to You*	**Ps 65:4**	7126

Context	Reference	Number
"I will **b** *them* back from Bashan.	**Ps 68:22**	7725
I will **b** *them* back from the depths	**Ps 68:22**	7725
Kings will **b** gifts to You.	**Ps 68:29**	2986
And will **b** me up again from the	**Ps 71:20**	5927
mountains **b** peace to the people,	**Ps 72:3**	5375
and of the islands **b** presents;	**Ps 72:10**	7725
Let all who are around Him **b** gifts	**Ps 76:11**	2986
B an offering and come into His	**Ps 96:8**	5375
may **b** forth food from the earth,	**Ps 104:14**	3318
will **b** me into the besieged city?	**Ps 108:10**	2986
"**B** my soul out of prison, So that	**Ps 142:7**	3318
b my soul out of trouble.	**Ps 143:11**	3318
And our flocks **b** forth thousands	**Ps 144:13**	503
b forth what is acceptable,	**Pr 10:32**	3045
And he who pursues evil *will* **b**	**Pr 11:19**	
A fool's lips **b** strife, And his	**Pr 18:6**	935
not even **b** it back to his mouth.	**Pr 19:24**	7725
not know what a day may **b** forth.	**Pr 27:1**	3205
And the goats *will* **b** the price of	**Pr 27:26**	
A man's pride will **b** him low,	**Pr 29:23**	8213
For who will **b** him to see what	**Ec 3:22**	935
b up a matter in the presence of God.	**Ec 5:2**	3318
Yet know that God will **b** you to	**Ec 11:9**	935
God will **b** every act to judgment,	**Ec 12:14**	935
"I would lead you *and* **b** you Into	**SS 8:2**	935
Each one was to **b** a thousand	**SS 8:11**	935
"**B** your worthless offerings no	**Is 1:13**	935
"The LORD will **b** on you, on your	**Is 7:17**	935
the Lord is about to **b** on them the	**Is 8:7**	5927
along and **b** them to their place,	**Is 14:2**	935
I will **b** added *woes* upon Dimon,	**Is 15:9**	7896
you **b** your seed to blossom;	**Is 17:11**	6524a
B water for the thirsty, O	**Is 21:14**	857
of your walls He will **b** down,	**Is 25:12**	7817
I will **b** distress to Ariel,	**Is 29:2**	6693
also is wise and will **b** disaster And	**Is 31:2**	935
"**B** forward your strong *arguments*,"	**Is 41:21**	5066
Let them **b** forth and declare to us	**Is 41:22**	5066
b forth justice to the nations.	**Is 42:1**	3318
will faithfully **b** forth justice.	**Is 42:3**	3318
To **b** out prisoners from the	**Is 42:7**	3318
b your offspring from the east,	**Is 43:5**	935
B My sons from afar And	**Is 43:6**	935
B out the people who are blind,	**Is 43:8**	3318
will **b** them all down as fugitives,	**Is 43:14**	3381
truly I will **b** it to pass.	**Is 46:11**	935
"I **b** near My righteousness, it is	**Is 46:13**	7126
Servant, To **b** Jacob back to Him,	**Is 49:5**	7725
will **b** your sons in *their* bosom,	**Is 49:22**	935
I will **b** to My holy mountain And	**Is 56:7**	935
And **b** the homeless poor into the	**Is 58:7**	935
mischief and **b** forth iniquity.	**Is 59:4**	3205
They will **b** gold and frankincense,	**Is 60:6**	5375
first, To **b** your sons from afar,	**Is 60:9**	935
So that *men* may **b** to you the	**Is 60:11**	935
"Instead of bronze I will **b** gold,	**Is 60:17**	935
instead of iron I will **b** silver,	**Is 60:17**	935
To **b** good news to the afflicted;	**Is 61:1**	1319
will **b** forth offspring from Jacob,	**Is 65:9**	3318
And will **b** on them what they dread.	**Is 66:4**	935
"Shall I **b** to the point of birth and	**Is 66:9**	7665
"Then they shall **b** all your	**Is 66:20**	935
"just as the sons of Israel **b**	**Is 66:20**	935
family, And I will **b** you to Zion.'	**Jer 3:14**	935
"they will **b** out the bones of the	**Jer 8:1**	3318
anger, or You will **b** me to nothing.	**Jer 10:24**	4591
for I will **b** disaster on the men	**Jer 11:23**	935
of the field, **B** them to devour!	**Jer 12:9**	857
and I will **b** them back, each one	**Jer 12:15**	7725
I will **b** against them, against the	**Jer 15:8**	935
I will suddenly **b** down on her	**Jer 15:8**	5307
will cause your enemies to **b** *it*	**Jer 15:14**	5674a
B on them a day of disaster, And	**Jer 17:18**	935
b anything in through the gates of	**Jer 17:21**	935
"You shall not **b** a load out	**Jer 17:22**	3318
"to **b** no load in through the	**Jer 17:24**	935
the calamity I planned to **b** on it.	**Jer 18:8**	6213a
You suddenly **b** raiders upon them;	**Jer 18:22**	935
to **b** a calamity upon this place,	**Jer 19:3**	935
I am about to **b** on this city and	**Jer 19:15**	935
them away and **b** them to Babylon.	**Jer 20:5**	935
b them back to their pasture,	**Jer 23:3**	7725
For I will **b** calamity upon them,	**Jer 23:12**	935
I will **b** punishment upon that man	**Jer 23:34**	6485
I will **b** them again to this land;	**Jer 24:6**	7725
and will **b** them against this land and	**Jer 25:9**	935
'I will **b** upon that land all	**Jer 25:13**	935
b innocent blood on yourselves,	**Jer 26:15**	5414
"But the nation which will **b** its	**Jer 27:11**	935
"**B** your necks under the yoke of	**Jer 27:12**	935
'Then I will **b** them back and	**Jer 27:22**	5927
'Within two years I am going to **b**	**Jer 28:3**	7725
'I am also going to **b** back to this	**Jer 28:4**	7725
b back the vessels of the LORD's	**Jer 28:6**	7725
you, to **b** you back to this place.	**Jer 29:10**	7725
'and I will **b** you back to the	**Jer 29:14**	7725
'I will also **b** them back to the	**Jer 30:3**	7725
And I will **b** him near and he	**Jer 30:21**	7126
B me back that I may be restored,	**Jer 31:18**	7725
to destroy and to **b** disaster,	**Jer 31:28**	7489a
b them out of the land of Egypt,	**Jer 31:32**	3318
and I will **b** them back to this	**Jer 32:37**	7725
so I am going to **b** on them all the	**Jer 32:42**	935
I will **b** to it health and healing,	**Jer 33:6**	5927
and of those who **b** a thank	**Jer 33:11**	935
I will **b** them back to this city;	**Jer 34:22**	7725
and **b** them into the house of the	**Jer 35:2**	935
which I plan to **b** on them,	**Jer 36:3**	6213a
and I will **b** on them and the	**Jer 36:31**	935

Context	Reference	Number
and **b** up Jeremiah the prophet from	**Jer 38:10**	5927
'They will also **b** out all your	**Jer 38:23**	3318
of bronze to **b** him to Babylon.	**Jer 39:7**	935
I am about to **b** My words on this	**Jer 39:16**	935
to **b** to the house of the LORD.	**Jer 41:5**	935
I am going to **b** on them.	**Jer 42:17**	935
going to **b** disaster on all flesh,'	**Jer 45:5**	935
For I shall **b** upon her, *even* upon	**Jer 48:44**	935
I am going to **b** terror upon you,"	**Jer 49:5**	935
For I will **b** the disaster of Esau	**Jer 49:8**	935
I will **b** you down from there,"	**Jer 49:16**	3381
And I will **b** their disaster from	**Jer 49:32**	935
'I will **b** upon Elam the four	**Jer 49:36**	935
And I will **b** calamity upon them,	**Jer 49:37**	935
I am going to arouse and **b** up	**Jer 50:9**	5927
b Israel back to his pasture and	**Jer 50:19**	7725
that He may **b** rest to the earth,	**Jer 50:34**	7280b
B balm for her pain;	**Jer 51:8**	3947
B up the horses like bristly	**Jer 51:27**	5927
"I will **b** them down like lambs	**Jer 51:40**	3381
that I am going to **b** upon her;	**Jer 51:64**	935
that You would **b** the day which	**La 1:21**	935
My eyes **b** pain to my soul Because	**La 3:51**	5953a
and I will **b** the sword on you.	**Ezk 5:17**	935
am going to **b** a sword on you,	**Ezk 6:3**	935
and **b** all your abominations	**Ezk 7:3**	5414
but I will **b** your ways upon you,	**Ezk 7:4**	5414
b on you all your abominations.	**Ezk 7:8**	5414
will **b** the worst of the nations,	**Ezk 7:24**	935
but I will **b** their conduct upon	**Ezk 9:10**	5414
but I will **b** you out of it.	**Ezk 11:7**	3318
so I will **b** a sword upon you,"	**Ezk 11:8**	935
"And I will **b** you out of the	**Ezk 11:9**	3318
Will You **b** the remnant of Israel	**Ezk 11:13**	6213a
I will **b** their conduct down on	**Ezk 11:21**	5414
"**B** your baggage out by day in their	**Ezk 12:4**	3318
hole through the wall to **b** *it* out.	**Ezk 12:12**	3318
And I will **b** him to Babylon in	**Ezk 12:13**	935
and **b** it down to the ground,	**Ezk 13:14**	5060
"Or *if* I should **b** a sword on that	**Ezk 14:17**	935
and I will **b** on you the blood of	**Ezk 16:38**	5414
I in turn will **b** your conduct down	**Ezk 16:43**	5414
Then I will **b** him to Babylon and	**Ezk 17:20**	935
may **b** forth boughs and bear fruit and	**Ezk 17:23**	5375
I **b** down the high tree, exalt the	**Ezk 17:24**	8213
to **b** them out from the land of	**Ezk 20:6**	3318
I would not **b** them into the land	**Ezk 20:15**	935
"I will **b** you out from the	**Ezk 20:34**	3318
and I will **b** you into the	**Ezk 20:35**	935
and I will **b** you into the bond of	**Ezk 20:37**	935
I will **b** them out of the land	**Ezk 20:38**	3318
when I **b** you out from the peoples	**Ezk 20:41**	3318
I **b** you into the land of Israel,	**Ezk 20:42**	935
and I will **b** them against you from	**Ezk 23:22**	935
'**B** up a company against them and	**Ezk 23:46**	5927
b up many nations against you,	**Ezk 26:3**	5927
I will **b** upon Tyre from the north	**Ezk 26:7**	935
I **b** up the deep over you	**Ezk 26:19**	5927
then I will **b** you down with those	**Ezk 26:20**	3381
"I will **b** terrors on you and	**Ezk 26:21**	5414
I will **b** strangers upon you,	**Ezk 28:7**	935
'They will **b** you down to the pit,	**Ezk 28:8**	3381
And I will **b** you up out of the	**Ezk 29:4**	5927
I will **b** upon you a sword	**Ezk 29:8**	935
when I **b** your destruction among	**Ezk 32:9**	935
hordes of Egypt and **b** it down,	**Ezk 32:18**	3381
'If I **b** a sword upon a land, and	**Ezk 33:2**	935
"I will **b** them out from the	**Ezk 34:13**	3318
and **b** them to their own land;	**Ezk 34:13**	935
the lost, **b** back the scattered,	**Ezk 34:16**	7725
and **b** you into your own land.	**Ezk 36:24**	935
and I will not **b** a famine on you.	**Ezk 36:29**	5414
b you into the land of Israel.	**Ezk 37:12**	935
and **b** them into their own land;	**Ezk 37:21**	935
your jaws, and I will **b** you out,	**Ezk 38:4**	3318
I will **b** you against My land,	**Ezk 38:16**	935
that I would **b** you against them?	**Ezk 38:17**	935
and **b** you against the mountains of	**Ezk 39:2**	935
"When I **b** them back from the	**Ezk 39:27**	7725
in order that they may not **b** *them*	**Ezk 46:20**	3318
who **b** forth sons in your midst.	**Ezk 47:22**	3205
b in some of the sons of Israel,	**Da 1:3**	935
anger gave orders to **b** Shadrach,	**Da 3:13**	858
"So I gave orders to **b** into my	**Da 4:6**	5954
he gave orders to **b** the gold and	**Da 5:2**	858
aloud to **b** in the conjurers,	**Da 5:7**	5954
us, to **b** on us great calamity;	**Da 9:12**	935
to **b** in everlasting righteousness,	**Da 9:24**	935
her, **B** her into the wilderness And	**Hos 2:14**	1980
I will **b** them down like the birds	**Hos 7:12**	3381
Though they **b** up their children,	**Hos 9:12**	1431
But Ephraim will **b** out his	**Hos 9:13**	3318
And **b** back his reproach to him.	**Hos 12:14**	7725
And **b** them down to the valley of	**Jl 3:2**	3381
B down, O LORD, Your mighty ones.	**Jl 3:11**	5181
"**B** now, that we may drink!"	**Am 4:1**	935
B your sacrifices every morning,	**Am 4:4**	935
you **b** near the seat of violence?	**Am 6:3**	5066
And I will **b** sackcloth on	**Am 8:10**	5927
From there will I **b** them down.	**Am 9:2**	3381
'Who will **b** me down to earth?'	**Ob 1:3**	3381
From there I will **b** you down,"	**Ob 1:4**	3381
had declared He would **b** upon them.	**Jon 3:10**	6213a
I will **b** on you The one who takes	**Mi 1:15**	935
He will **b** me out to the light, *And*	**Mi 7:9**	3318
b all of them up with a hook,	**Hab 1:15**	5927
I will **b** distress on men So	**Zph 1:17**	6887a
ones, Will **b** My offerings.	**Zph 3:10**	2986
"At that time I will **b** you in,	**Zph 3:20**	935

b wood and rebuild the temple,	**Hg 1:8**	935
when you **b** *it* home, I blow it *away.*	**Hg 1:9**	935
to **b** in My servant the Branch.	**Zch 3:8**	935
and he will **b** forth the top stone	**Zch 4:7**	3318
and I will **b** them *back* and they	**Zch 8:8**	935
Joseph, And I will **b** them back,	**Zch 10:6**	7725
"I will **b** them back from the land	**Zch 10:10**	7725
And I will **b** them into the land of	**Zch 10:10**	935
"And I will **b** the third part	**Zch 13:9**	935
you **b** what was taken by robbery and	**Mal 1:13**	935
so you **b** the offering!	**Mal 1:13**	935
"**B** the whole tithe into the	**Mal 3:10**	935
I came to **b** peace on the earth;	**Mt 10:34**	*906*
I did not come to **b** peace,	**Mt 10:34**	*906*
"**B** them here to Me."	**Mt 14:18**	*5342*
but they had forgotten to **b** *any*	**Mt 16:5**	*2983*
"*He said that* because we did not **b**	**Mt 16:7**	*2983*
B him here to Me."	**Mt 17:17**	*5342*
untie them and **b** them to Me.	**Mt 21:2**	*71*
"He will **b** those wretches to a	**Mt 21:41**	*622*
commanded *him* to **b** *back* his head.	**Mk 6:27**	*5342*
I put up with you? **B** him to Me!"	**Mk 9:19**	*5342*
untie it and **b** it *here.*	**Mk 11:2**	*5342*
B Me a denarius to look at."	**Mk 12:15**	*5342*
many charges they **b** against You!"	**Mk 15:4**	*2723*
you and to **b** you this good news.	**Lk 1:19**	*2097*
I **b** you good news of great joy	**Lk 2:10**	*2097*
and they were trying to **b** him in and	**Lk 5:18**	*1533*
to **b** him in because of the crowd,	**Lk 5:19**	*1533*
life, and **b** no fruit to maturity.	**Lk 8:14**	*5052*
B your son here."	**Lk 9:41**	*4317*
"When they **b** you before the	**Lk 12:11**	*1533*
b in here the poor and crippled	**Lk 14:21**	*1521*
'Quickly **b** out the best robe and	**Lk 15:22**	*1627*
and **b** the fattened calf, kill it,	**Lk 15:23**	*5342*
God **b** about justice for His elect who	**Lk 18:7**	*4160*
"I tell you that He will **b** about	**Lk 18:8**	*4160*
b them here and slay them in my	**Lk 19:27**	*71*
untie it and **b** it *here.*	**Lk 19:30**	*71*
"Why did you not **b** Him?"	**Jn 7:45**	*71*
I must **b** them also, and they will	**Jn 10:16**	*71*
and **b** to your remembrance all that	**Jn 14:26**	*5279*
do you **b** against this Man?"	**Jn 18:29**	*5342*
"**B** some of the fish which you	**Jn 21:10**	*5342*
and **b** you where you do not wish to	**Jn 21:18**	*5342*
and **b** the proceeds of the sales	**Ac 4:34**	*5342*
to **b** them *back* without violence	**Ac 5:26**	*71*
to **b** this man's blood upon us."	**Ac 5:28**	*1863*
might **b** them bound to Jerusalem.	**Ac 9:2**	*71*
to **b** him out before the people.	**Ac 12:4**	*321*
Herod was about to **b** him forward,	**Ac 12:6**	*4254*
THAT YOU MAY **B** SALVATION TO	**Ac 13:47**	
		1510, 1519
come themselves and **b** us out."	**Ac 16:37**	*1806*
to **b** them out to the people.	**Ac 17:5**	*4254*
b charges against one another.	**Ac 19:38**	*1458*
for Damascus in order to **b** even those	**Ac 22:5**	*71*
and **b** him into the barracks.	**Ac 23:10**	*71*
commander to **b** him down to you,	**Ac 23:15**	*2609*
ask you to **b** Paul down tomorrow	**Ac 23:20**	*2609*
b him safely to Felix the governor.	**Ac 23:24**	*1295*
instructing his accusers to **b** charges	**Ac 23:30**	*3004*
after several years I came to **b** alms	**Ac 24:17**	*4160*
wanting to **b** Paul safely through,	**Ac 27:43**	*1295*
to **b** about *the* obedience of faith	**Ro 1:5**	*1519*
b a charge against God's elect?	**Ro 8:33**	*1458*
(that is, to **b** Christ down),	**Ro 10:6**	*2609*
to **b** Christ up from the dead)."	**Ro 10:7**	*321*
B GOOD NEWS OF GOOD THINGS!"	**Ro 10:15**	*2097*
Lord comes who will both **b** to light	**1Co 4:5**	*5461*
in order to **b** us into bondage.	**Ga 2:4**	*2615*
and to **b** to light what is the	**Eph 3:9**	*5461*
but **b** them up in the discipline	**Eph 6:4**	*1625*
the Lord, will **b** you information.	**Col 4:7**	*1107*
even so God will **b** with Him those	**1Th 4:14**	*71*
and He also will **b** it to pass.	**1Th 5:24**	*4160*
b to an end by the appearance of	**2Th 2:8**	*2673*
which He will **b** about at the	**1Tm 6:15**	*1166*
Pick up Mark and **b** him with you,	**2Tm 4:11**	*71*
When you come **b** the cloak which I	**2Tm 4:13**	*5342*
and will **b** me safely to His	**2Tm 4:18**	*4982*
so that He might **b** us to God,	**1Pe 3:18**	*4317*
do not **b** a reviling judgment against	**2Pe 2:11**	*5342*
you and does not **b** this teaching,	**2Jn 1:10**	*5342*
earth will **b** their glory into it.	**Rv 21:24**	*5342*
and they will **b** the glory and the	**Rv 21:26**	*5342*

BRINGING

even I am **b** the flood of water	**Gn 6:17**	935
b out the sons of Israel from Egypt;	**Ex 6:27**	3318
us in this way, **b** us out of Egypt?	**Ex 14:11**	3318
And they still *continued* **b** to him	**Ex 36:3**	935
"The people are **b** much more than	**Ex 36:5**	935
were restrained from **b** *any more.*	**Ex 36:6**	935
land of Canaan where I am **b** you;	**Lv 18:3**	935
so that the land to which I am **b**	**Lv 20:22**	935
is the LORD **b** us into this land,	**Nu 14:3**	935
by **b** out a bad report concerning	**Nu 14:36**	3318
God is **b** you into a good land,	**Dt 8:7**	935
you disturbed me by **b** me up?"	**1Sa 28:15**	5927
and thought he was **b** good news,	**2Sa 4:10**	1319
house of Israel were **b** up the ark	**2Sa 6:15**	5927
servants to David, **b** tribute.	**2Sa 8:2**	5375
servants to David, **b** tribute.	**2Sa 8:6**	5375
"This one also is **b** good news."	**2Sa 18:26**	1319
silent about **b** the king back?"	**2Sa 19:10**	7725
condemning the wicked by **b** his way	**1Ki 8:32**	5414
Tarshish came **b** gold and silver,	**1Ki 10:22**	5375
I am **b** calamity on the house of	**1Ki 14:10**	935
they were **b** *the vessels* to her and	**2Ki 4:5**	5066
I am **b** *such* calamity on Jerusalem	**2Ki 21:12**	935
servants to David, **b** tribute.	**1Ch 18:2**	5375
servants to David, **b** tribute.	**1Ch 18:6**	5375
punishing the wicked by **b** his way	**2Ch 6:23**	5414
Tarshish came **b** gold and silver,	**2Ch 9:21**	5375
And they were **b** horses for Solomon	**2Ch 9:28**	3318
And many were **b** gifts to the LORD	**2Ch 32:23**	935
When they were **b** out the money	**2Ch 34:14**	3318
I am **b** evil on this place and on	**2Ch 34:24**	935
and **b** in sacks of grain and	**Ne 13:15**	935
He was **b** up Hadassah, that is	**Es 2:7**	539
of joy, **b** his sheaves *with him.*	**Ps 126:6**	5375
weary of **b** it to his mouth again.	**Pr 26:15**	7725
For I am **b** evil from the north,	**Jer 4:6**	935
I am **b** a nation against you from	**Jer 5:15**	935
I am **b** disaster on this people,	**Jer 6:19**	935
"Behold I am **b** disaster on them	**Jer 11:11**	935
from the Negev, **b** burnt offerings,	**Jer 17:26**	935
and **b** sacrifices of thanksgiving	**Jer 17:26**	935
am **b** them from the north country,	**Jer 31:8**	935
I am **b** on Judah and on all the	**Jer 35:17**	935
b them out of the land of Egypt.	**Ezk 20:9**	3318
b to mind the iniquity of their	**Ezk 29:16**	2142
b with him a proposal of peace	**Da 11:17**	
b with them *those who were* lame,	**Mt 15:30**	*2192*
they *began* **b** to Him all who were	**Mk 1:32**	*5342*
they came, **b** to Him a paralytic,	**Mk 2:3**	*5342*
And they were **b** children to Him so	**Mk 10:13**	*4374*
And they were **b** even their babies	**Lk 18:15**	*4374*
b you before kings and governors	**Lk 21:12**	*520*
b the spices which they had	**Lk 24:1**	*5342*
"Behold, I am **b** Him out to you so	**Jn 19:4**	*71*
b a mixture of myrrh and aloes,	**Jn 19:39**	*5342*
knowledge, and **b** a portion of it,	**Ac 5:2**	*5342*
b people who were sick or	**Ac 5:16**	*5342*
come here for the purpose of **b** them	**Ac 9:21**	*71*
b great joy to all the brethren.	**Ac 15:3**	*4160*
who was **b** her masters much profit	**Ac 16:16**	*3930*
"For you are **b** some strange	**Ac 17:20**	*1533*
was **b** no little business to the	**Ac 19:24**	*3930*
b many and serious charges against	**Ac 25:7**	*2702*
they *began* **b** charges against him	**Ac 25:18**	*5342*
appeared, **b** salvation to all men,	**Ti 2:11**	*4992*
things, in **b** many sons to glory,	**Heb 2:10**	*71*
there is a **b** in of a better hope,	**Heb 7:19**	*1898a*
b swift destruction upon	**2Pe 2:1**	*1863*

BRINGS

"It shall be when the LORD **b**	**Ex 13:5**	935
when the LORD **b** you to the land	**Ex 13:11**	935
of you **b** an offering to the LORD,	**Lv 1:2**	7126
'But if he **b** a lamb as his	**Lv 4:32**	935
of bitterness that **b** a curse.	**Nu 5:18**	779
of bitterness that **b** a curse;	**Nu 5:19**	779
and this water that **b** a curse	**Nu 5:22**	779
of bitterness that **b** a curse,	**Nu 5:24**	779
so that the water which **b** a curse	**Nu 5:24**	779
that the water which **b** a curse	**Nu 5:27**	779
"But if the LORD **b** about an	**Nu 16:30**	1254a
"God **b** them out of Egypt, He is	**Nu 23:22**	3318
"God **b** him out of Egypt, He is	**Nu 24:8**	3318
LORD your God **b** you into the land	**Dt 6:10**	935
"When the LORD your God **b** you	**Dt 7:1**	935
when the LORD your God **b** you into	**Dt 11:29**	935
He **b** down to Sheol and raises up.	**1Sa 2:6**	3381
He **b** low, He also exalts.	**1Sa 2:7**	8213
me, And **b** down peoples under me,	**2Sa 22:48**	3381
Who also **b** me out from my enemies;	**2Sa 22:49**	3381
Whom God **b** into their power.	**Jb 12:6**	935
b the deep darkness into light.	**Jb 12:22**	3318
And his own scheme **b** him down.	**Jb 18:7**	7993
For wrath **b** the punishment of	**Jb 19:29**	
is hidden he **b** out to the light.	**Jb 28:11**	3318
mischief and **b** forth falsehood.	**Ps 7:14**	3205
Who **b** forth the wind from His	**Ps 135:7**	3318
b down the wicked to the ground.	**Ps 147:6**	8213
the tongue of the wise **b** healing.	**Pr 12:18**	4832
But a faithful envoy **b** healing.	**Pr 13:17**	
his lips **b** evil to pass.	**Pr 16:30**	3615
him And **b** him before great men.	**Pr 18:16**	5148
And **b** down the stronghold in which	**Pr 21:22**	3381
when he **b** it with evil intent!	**Pr 21:27**	935
The north wind **b** forth rain, And a	**Pr 25:23**	2342a
his own way **b** shame to his mother.	**Pr 29:15**	954
The fear of man **b** a snare, But he	**Pr 29:25**	5414
pressing the nose **b** forth blood;	**Pr 30:33**	3318
She **b** her food from afar.	**Pr 31:14**	935
Who **b** forth the chariot and the	**Is 43:17**	3318
the feet of him who **b** good news,	**Is 52:7**	1319
And **b** good news of happiness,	**Is 52:7**	1319
And **b** out a weapon for its work;	**Is 54:16**	3318
as the earth **b** forth its sprouts,	**Is 61:11**	3318
And **b** out the wind from His	**Jer 10:13**	3318
Before He **b** darkness And before	**Jer 13:16**	2821
And **b** forth the wind from His	**Jer 51:16**	3318
But he **b** iniquity to remembrance,	**Ezk 21:23**	2142
you, as the sea **b** up its waves.	**Ezk 26:3**	5927
uncleanness that **b** on destruction,	**Mi 2:10**	2254b
the feet of him who **b** good news,	**Na 1:15**	1319
morning He **b** His justice to light;	**Zph 3:5**	5414
good man **b** out of *his* good treasure	**Mt 12:35**	*1544b*
evil man **b** out of *his* evil treasure	**Mt 12:35**	*1544b*
indeed bears fruit and **b** forth,	**Mt 13:23**	*4160*
who **b** out of his treasure	**Mt 13:52**	*1544b*
of his heart **b** forth what is good;	**Lk 6:45**	*4393*
treasure **b** forth what is evil;	**Lk 6:45**	*4393*
for the Law **b** about wrath, but	**Ro 4:15**	*2716*
tribulation **b** about perseverance;	**Ro 5:3**	*2716*
an avenger who **b** wrath on the	**Ro 13:4**	
b the firstborn into the world,	**Heb 1:6**	*1521*
b forth vegetation useful to those	**Heb 6:7**	*5088*
is accomplished, it **b** forth death.	**Jas 1:15**	*616*

BRISTLED

The hair of my flesh **b** up.	**Jb 4:15**	5568

BRISTLY

up the horses like **b** locusts.	**Jer 51:27**	5569

BRITTLE

strong and part of it will be **b**.	**Da 2:42**	8406

BROAD

in **b** daylight before the LORD,	**Nu 25:4**	5048
lie with your wives in **b** daylight.	**2Sa 12:11**	5869
brought me forth into a **b** place;	**2Sa 22:20**	4800
land was **b** and quiet and peaceful;	**1Ch 4:40**	7342
Jerusalem as far as the **B** Wall.	**Ne 3:8**	7342
With the **b** and rich land which	**Ne 9:35**	7342
Tower of Furnaces, to the **B** Wall,	**Ne 12:38**	7342
it, a **b** place with no constraint;	**Jb 36:16**	7338
me forth also into a **b** place;	**Ps 18:19**	4800
There is the sea, great and **b**,	**Ps 104:25**	7342
the chief men over a **b** country.	**Ps 110:6**	7227a
Your commandment is exceedingly **b**.	**Ps 119:96**	7342
And the rugged terrain a **b** valley;	**Is 40:4**	1237
"The **b** wall of Babylon will be	**Jer 51:58**	7342
make the earth dark in **b** daylight.	**Am 8:9**	216
is **b** that leads to destruction,	**Mt 7:13**	*2149*
And they came up on the **b** plain of	**Rv 20:9**	*4114*

BROADEN

for they **b** their phylacteries and	**Mt 23:5**	*4115*

BROADER

the earth And **b** than the sea.	**Jb 11:9**	7342

BROILED

They gave Him a piece of a **b** fish;	**Lk 24:42**	*3702*

BROKE

and I **b** the bars of your yoke and	**Lv 26:13**	7665
because you **b** faith with Me in the	**Dt 32:51**	4603
the trumpets and **b** the pitchers,	**Jg 7:20**	7665
in ambush **b** out of their place,	**Jg 20:33**	1518
old, so that tumors **b** out on them.	**1Sa 5:9**	8368
So the three mighty men **b** through	**2Sa 23:16**	1234
They also **b** down the *sacred* pillar	**2Ki 10:27**	5422
Baal and **b** down the house of Baal,	**2Ki 10:27**	5422
they **b** in pieces thoroughly,	**2Ki 11:18**	7665
and **b** down the *sacred* pillars and cut	**2Ki 18:4**	7665
He also **b** in pieces the bronze	**2Ki 18:4**	3807
He also **b** down the houses of the	**2Ki 23:7**	5422
and he **b** down the high places of	**2Ki 23:8**	5422
of the LORD, the king **b** down;	**2Ki 23:12**	5422
He **b** in pieces the *sacred*	**2Ki 23:14**	7665
and the high place he **b** down.	**2Ki 23:15**	5422
b down the walls around Jerusalem.	**2Ki 25:10**	5422
the Chaldeans **b** in pieces and	**2Ki 25:13**	7665
So the three **b** through the camp of	**1Ch 11:18**	1234
that war **b** out at Gezer with the	**1Ch 20:4**	5975
and they **b** in pieces his altars	**2Ch 23:17**	7665
and **b** down the wall of Gath and	**2Ch 26:6**	6555
the leprosy **b** out on his forehead	**2Ch 26:19**	2224
of Judah, **b** the pillars in pieces,	**2Ch 31:1**	7665
and the molten images he **b** in	**2Ch 34:4**	7665
and **b** down the wall of Jerusalem	**2Ch 36:19**	5422
"I **b** the jaws of the wicked And	**Jb 29:17**	7665
You **b** the heads of the sea monsters	**Ps 74:13**	7665
You **b** open springs and torrents; You	**Ps 74:15**	1234
There He **b** the flaming arrows, The	**Ps 76:3**	7665
He **b** the whole staff of bread.	**Ps 105:16**	7665
And the plague **b** out among them.	**Ps 106:29**	6555
of death And **b** their bands apart.	**Ps 107:14**	5423
b the everlasting covenant.	**Is 24:5**	6565a
"For long ago I **b** your yoke *And*	**Jer 2:20**	7665
of Jeremiah the prophet and **b** it.	**Jer 28:10**	7665
Egypt, My covenant which they **b**,	**Jer 31:32**	6565a
b down the walls of Jerusalem.	**Jer 39:8**	5422
b down all the walls around	**Jer 52:14**	5422
the Chaldeans **b** in pieces and	**Jer 52:17**	7665
despised and whose covenant he **b**,	**Ezk 17:16**	6565a
and My covenant which he **b**,	**Ezk 17:19**	6565a
You **b** and tore all their hands;	**Ezk 29:7**	7533
You **b** and made all their loins	**Ezk 29:7**	7665
He **b** them and started giving them	**Mt 15:36**	*2806*
He **b** *it* and gave *it* to the	**Mt 26:26**	*2806*
He blessed *the food* and **b** the	**Mk 6:41**	*2622*
loaves, He gave thanks and **b** them,	**Mk 8:6**	*2806*
when I **b** the five loaves for the	**Mk 8:19**	*2806*
"When *I* **b** the seven for the four	**Mk 8:20**	
and she **b** the vial and poured it	**Mk 14:3**	*4937*
and after a blessing He **b** *it*	**Mk 14:22**	*2806*
He blessed them, and **b** *them,*	**Lk 9:16**	*2622*
bread *and* given thanks, He **b** it	**Lk 22:19**	*2806*
and **b** the legs of the first man and	**Jn 19:32**	*2608a*
and he **b** it and began to eat.	**Ac 27:35**	*2806*
when He had given thanks, He **b** it and	**1Co 11:24**	*2806*
and **b** down the barrier of the	**Eph 2:14**	*3089*
the Lamb **b** one of the seven seals,	**Rv 6:1**	*455*
When He **b** the second seal, I	**Rv 6:3**	*455*
When He **b** the third seal, I	**Rv 6:5**	*455*
When the Lamb **b** the fourth seal, I	**Rv 6:7**	*455*
When the Lamb **b** the fifth seal, I	**Rv 6:9**	*455*
I looked when He **b** the sixth seal,	**Rv 6:12**	*455*
When the Lamb **b** the seventh seal,	**Rv 8:1**	*455*

BROKEN

he has **b** My covenant."	**Gn 17:14**	6565a
in which it was boiled shall be **b**;	**Lv 6:28**	7665
leprosy, it has **b** out in the boil.	**Lv 13:20**	6524b
it has **b** out in the burn.	**Lv 13:25**	6524b
eczema that has **b** out on the skin;	**Lv 13:39**	6524b
the discharge touches shall be **b**,	**Lv 15:12**	7665
who has a **b** foot or broken hand,	**Lv 21:19**	7667
who has a broken foot or **b** hand,	**Lv 21:19**	7667

LORD and has **b** His commandment,	**Nu 15:31**	6565a
whose neck was **b** in the valley;	**Dt 21:6**	6202
and his neck was **b** and he died,	**1Sa 4:18**	7665
"The LORD has **b** through my	**2Sa 5:20**	6555
and I will have them **b** up there,	**1Ki 5:9**	5310a
the ships were **b** at Ezion-geber.	**1Ki 22:48**	7665
Then the city was **b** into,	**2Ki 25:4**	1234
b through my enemies by my hand,	**1Ch 14:11**	6555
So the ships were **b** and could not go	**2Ch 20:37**	7665
sons of the wicked Athaliah had **b**	**2Ch 24:7**	6555
all the wall that had been **b** down and	**2Ch 32:5**	6555
Hezekiah his father had **b** down;	**2Ch 33:3**	5422
and the wall of Jerusalem is **b**	**Ne 1:3**	6555
walls of Jerusalem which were **b**	**Ne 2:13**	6555
teeth of the young lions are **b**.	**Jb 4:10**	5421
and evening they are **b** in pieces;	**Jb 4:20**	3807
"My spirit is **b**, my days are	**Jb 17:1**	2254b
wickedness will be **b** like a tree.	**Jb 24:20**	7665
And my arm be **b** off at the elbow.	**Jb 31:22**	7665
And the uplifted arm is **b**.	**Jb 38:15**	7665
out of mind; I am like a **b** vessel.	**Ps 31:12**	6
Not one of them is **b**.	**Ps 34:20**	7665
heart, And their bows will be **b**.	**Ps 37:15**	7665
the arms of the wicked will be **b**,	**Ps 37:17**	7665
bones which You have **b** rejoice.	**Ps 51:8**	1794
sacrifices of God are a **b** spirit;	**Ps 51:17**	7665
A **b** and a contrite heart, O God,	**Ps 51:17**	7665
have rejected us. You have **b** us;	**Ps 60:1**	6555
Reproach has **b** my heart and I am	**Ps 69:20**	7665
Why have You **b** down its hedges,	**Ps 80:12**	6555
You have **b** down all his walls;	**Ps 89:40**	6555
to act, *For* they have **b** Your law.	**Ps 119:126**	6565a
snare is **b** and we have escaped.	**Ps 124:7**	7665
His knowledge the deeps were **b** up And	**Pr 3:20**	1234
Instantly he will be **b** and	**Pr 6:15**	7665
the heart is sad, the spirit is **b**.	**Pr 15:13**	5218b
But a **b** spirit dries up the bones.	**Pr 17:22**	5218b
as for a **b** spirit who can bear it?	**Pr 18:14**	5218b
And its stone wall was **b** down.	**Pr 24:31**	2040
Like a city that is **b** into *and*	**Pr 25:28**	6555
Will suddenly be **b** beyond remedy.	**Pr 29:1**	7665
silver cord is **b** and the golden bowl	**Ec 12:6**	7576
undone, Nor its sandal strap **b**.	**Is 5:27**	5423
"Be **b**, O peoples, and be	**Is 8:9**	7489b
Then they will fall and be **b**;	**Is 8:15**	7665
yoke will be **b** because of fatness.	**Is 10:27**	2254b
has **b** the staff of the wicked,	**Is 14:5**	7665
the rod that struck you is **b**;	**Is 14:29**	7665
The city of chaos is **b** down;	**Is 24:10**	7665
The earth is **b** asunder, The earth	**Is 24:19**	7489b
its limbs are dry, they are **b** off;	**Is 27:11**	7665
may go and stumble backward, be **b**,	**Is 28:13**	7665
has ceased, He has **b** the covenant,	**Is 33:8**	6565a
you will wail with a **b** spirit.	**Is 65:14**	7665
themselves cisterns, **B** cisterns That	**Jer 2:13**	7665
b the yoke *And* burst the bonds.	**Jer 5:5**	7665
the daughter of my people I am **b**;	**Jer 8:21**	7665
destroyed, And all my ropes are **b**;	**Jer 10:20**	5423
house of Judah have **b** My covenant	**Jer 11:10**	6565a
My heart is **b** within me, All my	**Jer 23:9**	7665
'I have **b** the yoke of the king of	**Jer 28:2**	7665
after Hananiah the prophet had **b**	**Jer 28:12**	7665
"You have **b** the yokes of wood,	**Jer 28:13**	7665
which are **b** down *to make a defense*	**Jer 33:4**	5422
then My covenant may also be **b**	**Jer 33:21**	6565a
"Moab is **b**, Her little ones have	**Jer 48:4**	7665
'How has the mighty scepter been **b**,	**Jer 48:17**	7665
has been cut off and his arm **b**,"	**Jer 48:25**	7665
for I have **b** Moab like an	**Jer 48:38**	7665
and this last one *who* has **b** his	**Jer 50:17**	6105c
earth Has been cut off and **b**!	**Jer 50:23**	7665
Babylon has fallen and been **b**;	**Jer 51:8**	7665
fire, The bars of her *gates* are **b**.	**Jer 51:30**	7665
Then the city was **b** into,	**Jer 52:7**	1234
He has destroyed and **b** her bars.	**La 2:9**	7665
to waste away, He has **b** my bones.	**La 3:4**	7665
He has **b** my teeth with gravel;	**La 3:16**	1638
may be **b** and brought to an end,	**Ezk 6:6**	7665
the gateway of the peoples is **b**;	**Ezk 26:2**	7665
b you In the heart of the seas.	**Ezk 27:26**	7665
'Now that you are **b** by the seas In	**Ezk 27:34**	7665
Egypt And all her helpers are **b**.	**Ezk 30:8**	7665
I have **b** the arm of Pharaoh king	**Ezk 30:21**	7665
arms, both the strong and the **b**;	**Ezk 30:22**	7665
and its boughs have been **b** in all	**Ezk 31:12**	7665
you will be **b** and lie with those slain	**Ezk 32:28**	7665
the **b** you have not bound up,	**Ezk 34:4**	7665
back the scattered, bind up the **b** and	**Ezk 34:16**	7665
when I have **b** the bars of their	**Ezk 34:27**	7665
was mighty, the large horn was **b**;	**Da 8:8**	7665
"The **b** *horn* and the four	**Da 8:22**	7665
he will be **b** without human agency.	**Da 8:25**	7665
his kingdom will be **b** up and	**Da 11:4**	7665
of Samaria will be **b** to pieces.	**Hos 8:6**	7616
And the rocks are **b** up by Him.	**Na 1:6**	5422
So it was **b** on that day, and thus	**Zch 11:11**	6565a
seek the scattered, heal the **b**,	**Zch 11:16**	7665
was left over of the **b** pieces,	**Mt 14:20**	*2801*
was left over of the **b** pieces,	**Mt 15:37**	*2801*
on this stone will be **b** to pieces;	**Mt 21:44**	*4917*
allowed his house to be **b** into.	**Mt 24:43**	*1358*
him and the shackles **b** in pieces,	**Mk 5:4**	*4937*
full baskets of the **b** pieces,	**Mk 6:43**	*2801*
was left over of the **b** pieces.	**Mk 8:8**	*2801*
full of **b** pieces you picked up?"	**Mk 8:19**	*2801*
large baskets full of **b** pieces did you	**Mk 8:20**	*2801*
and the **b** pieces which they had	**Lk 9:17**	*2801*
allowed his house to be **b** into.	**Lk 12:39**	*1358*
on that stone will be **b** to pieces;	**Lk 20:18**	*4917*
the Law of Moses will not be **b**,	**Jn 7:23**	*3089*
(and the Scripture cannot be **b**),	**Jn 10:35**	*3089*
Pilate that their legs might be **b**,	**Jn 19:31**	*2608a*
"NOT A BONE OF HIM SHALL BE **B**."	**Jn 19:36**	*4937*
meeting of the synagogue had **b** up,	**Ac 13:43**	*3089*
up and had **b** the bread and eaten,	**Ac 20:11**	*2806*
be **b** up by the force *of the waves*.	**Ac 27:41**	*3089*
some of the branches were **b** off,	**Ro 11:17**	*1575*
"Branches were **b** off so that I	**Ro 11:19**	*1575*
were **b** off for their unbelief,	**Ro 11:20**	*1575*
OF THE POTTER ARE **B** TO PIECES,	**Rv 2:27**	*4937*

BROKENHEARTED

The LORD is near to the **b** And	**Ps 34:18**	7665, 3820
He heals the **b** And binds up their	**Ps 147:3**	7665, 3820
He has sent me to bind up the **b**,	**Is 61:1**	7665, 3820

BROKENNESS

the **b** of My people superficially,	**Jer 6:14**	7667
They heal the **b** of the daughter	**Jer 8:11**	7667
For the **b** of the daughter of my	**Jer 8:21**	7667

BRONZE

of all implements of **b** and iron;	**Gn 4:22**	5178
gold, silver and **b**,	**Ex 25:3**	5178
You shall make fifty clasps of **b**,	**Ex 26:11**	5178
cast five sockets of **b** for them.	**Ex 26:37**	5178
and you shall overlay it with **b**.	**Ex 27:2**	5178
shall make all its utensils of **b**.	**Ex 27:3**	5178
for it a grating of network of **b**,	**Ex 27:4**	5178
four **b** rings at its four corners.	**Ex 27:4**	5178
wood, and overlay them with **b**.	**Ex 27:6**	5178
with their twenty sockets of **b**;	**Ex 27:10**	5178
with their twenty sockets of **b**;	**Ex 27:11**	5178
of silver and their sockets of **b**.	**Ex 27:17**	5178
linen, and their sockets of **b**.	**Ex 27:18**	5178
pegs of the court, *shall be* of **b**.	**Ex 27:19**	5178
"You shall also make a laver of **b**,	**Ex 30:18**	5178
of bronze, with its base of **b**,	**Ex 30:18**	5178
work in gold, in silver, and in **b**,	**Ex 31:4**	5178
gold, silver, and **b**,	**Ex 35:5**	5178
burnt offering with its **b** grating,	**Ex 35:16**	5178
make a contribution of silver and **b**	**Ex 35:24**	5178
in gold and in silver and in **b**,	**Ex 35:32**	5178
of **b** to join the tent together so	**Ex 36:18**	5178
but their five sockets were of **b**.	**Ex 36:38**	5178
it, and he overlaid it with **b**.	**Ex 38:2**	5178
he made all its utensils of **b**.	**Ex 38:3**	5178
a grating of **b** network beneath,	**Ex 38:4**	5178
four ends of the **b** grating *as* holders	**Ex 38:5**	5178
wood and overlaid them with **b**.	**Ex 38:6**	5178
he made the laver of **b** with its base	**Ex 38:8**	5178
of bronze with its base of **b**,	**Ex 38:8**	5178
their twenty sockets, *made* of **b**;	**Ex 38:10**	5178
their twenty sockets *were* of **b**,	**Ex 38:11**	5178
sockets for the pillars *were* of **b**,	**Ex 38:17**	5178
and their four sockets *were* of **b**;	**Ex 38:19**	5178
of the court all around *were* of **b**.	**Ex 38:20**	5178
The **b** of the wave offering was	**Ex 38:29**	5178
b altar and its bronze grating,	**Ex 38:30**	5178
bronze altar and its **b** grating,	**Ex 38:30**	5178
b altar and its bronze grating,	**Ex 39:39**	5178
bronze altar and its **b** grating,	**Ex 39:39**	5178
if it was boiled in a **b** vessel,	**Lv 6:28**	5178
like iron and your earth like **b**.	**Lv 26:19**	5154
So Eleazar the priest took the **b**	**Nu 16:39**	5178
And Moses made a **b** serpent and set	**Nu 21:9**	5178
when he looked to the **b** serpent,	**Nu 21:9**	5178
the gold and the silver, the **b**,	**Nu 31:22**	5178
is over your head shall be **b**,	**Dt 28:23**	5178
"Your locks will be iron and **b**,	**Dt 33:25**	5178
b and iron are holy to the LORD;	**Jos 6:19**	5178
gold, and articles of **b** and iron,	**Jos 6:24**	5178
livestock, with silver, gold, **b**,	**Jos 22:8**	5178
Gaza and bound him with **b** chains,	**Jg 16:21**	5178
He had a **b** helmet on his head,	**1Sa 17:5**	5178
five thousand shekels of **b**.	**1Sa 17:5**	5178
He also *had* **b** greaves on his legs	**1Sa 17:6**	5178
b javelin *slung* between his shoulders.	**1Sa 17:6**	5178
and put a **b** helmet on his head,	**1Sa 17:38**	5178
took a very large amount of **b**.	**2Sa 8:8**	5178
of silver, of gold and of **b**.	**2Sa 8:10**	5178
hundred *shekels* of **b** in weight,	**2Sa 21:16**	5178
that my arms can bend a bow of **b**.	**2Sa 22:35**	5154
with walls and **b** bars *were* his);	**1Ki 4:13**	5178
was a man of Tyre, a worker in **b**;	**1Ki 7:14**	5178
and skill for doing any work in **b**.	**1Ki 7:14**	5178
He fashioned the two pillars of **b**;	**1Ki 7:15**	5178
also made two capitals of molten **b**	**1Ki 7:16**	5178
Then he made the ten stands of **b**;	**1Ki 7:27**	5178
four **b** wheels with bronze axles,	**1Ki 7:30**	5178
four bronze wheels with **b** axles,	**1Ki 7:30**	5178
He made ten basins of **b**,	**1Ki 7:38**	5178
of the LORD *were* of polished **b**.	**1Ki 7:45**	5178
of the **b** could not be ascertained.	**1Ki 7:47**	5178
for the **b** altar that *was* before	**1Ki 8:64**	5178
made shields of **b** in their place,	**1Ki 14:27**	5178
The **b** altar, which *was* before	**2Ki 16:14**	5178
But the **b** altar shall be for me to	**2Ki 16:15**	5178
the **b** oxen which were under it and	**2Ki 16:17**	5178
the **b** serpent that Moses had made,	**2Ki 18:4**	5178
bound him with **b** fetters and	**2Ki 25:7**	5178
Now the **b** pillars which were in	**2Ki 25:13**	5178
and the stands and the **b** sea which	**2Ki 25:13**	5178
and carried the **b** to Babylon.	**2Ki 25:13**	5178
and all the **b** vessels which were	**2Ki 25:14**	5178
b of all these vessels was beyond	**2Ki 25:16**	5178
cubits, and a **b** capital was on it;	**2Ki 25:17**	5178
the capital all around, all of **b**.	**2Ki 25:17**	5178
to sound aloud cymbals of **b**;	**1Ch 15:19**	5178
took a very large amount of **b**,	**1Ch 18:8**	5178
with which Solomon made the **b** sea	**1Ch 18:8**	5178
the pillars and the **b** utensils.	**1Ch 18:8**	5178
articles of gold and silver and **b**.	**1Ch 18:10**	5178
and more **b** than could be weighed;	**1Ch 22:3**	5178
and **b** and iron beyond weight,	**1Ch 22:14**	5178
the silver and the **b** and the iron there	**1Ch 22:16**	5178
the **b** for the *things of* bronze,	**1Ch 29:2**	5178
the bronze for the *things of* **b**,	**1Ch 29:2**	5178
Now the **b** altar, which Bezalel the	**2Ch 1:5**	5178
before the LORD to the **b** altar	**2Ch 1:6**	5178
how to work in gold, silver, **b**,	**2Ch 2:14**	5178
Then he made a **b** altar, twenty	**2Ch 4:1**	5178
and overlaid their doors with **b**.	**2Ch 4:9**	5178
Huram-abi made of polished **b** for	**2Ch 4:16**	5178
of the **b** could not be found out.	**2Ch 4:18**	5178
Now Solomon had made a **b** platform,	**2Ch 6:13**	5178
because the **b** altar which Solomon	**2Ch 7:7**	5178
made shields of **b** in their place and	**2Ch 12:10**	5178
and also workers in iron and **b** to	**2Ch 24:12**	5178
hooks, bound him with **b** *chains*	**2Ch 33:11**	5178
b *chains* to take him to Babylon.	**2Ch 36:6**	5178
and two utensils of fine shiny **b**,	**Ezr 8:27**	5178
of stones, Or is my flesh **b**?	**Jb 6:12**	5153
But the **b** bow will pierce him.	**Jb 20:24**	5154
"His bones are tubes of **b**;	**Jb 40:18**	5154
iron as straw, **B** as rotten wood.	**Jb 41:27**	5154
that my arms can bend a bow of **b**.	**Ps 18:34**	5154
For He has shattered gates of **b** And	**Ps 107:16**	5178
I will shatter the doors of **b** and	**Is 45:2**	5154
iron sinew And your forehead **b**,	**Is 48:4**	5154
"Instead of **b** I will bring gold,	**Is 60:17**	5178
silver, And instead of wood, **b**,	**Is 60:17**	5178
walls of **b** against the whole land,	**Jer 1:18**	5178
They are **b** and iron;	**Jer 6:28**	5178
iron, Iron from the north, or **b**?	**Jer 15:12**	5178
this people A fortified wall of **b**;	**Jer 15:20**	5178
bound him in fetters of **b**	**Jer 39:7**	5178
bound him with **b** fetters and	**Jer 52:11**	5178
Now the **b** pillars which belonged	**Jer 52:17**	5178
LORD and the stands and the **b** sea,	**Jer 52:17**	5178
carried all their **b** to Babylon.	**Jer 52:17**	5178
and all the **b** vessels which were	**Jer 52:18**	5178
b bulls that were under the sea,	**Jer 52:20**	5178
the **b** of all these vessels was beyond	**Jer 52:20**	5178
Now a capital of **b** was on it;	**Jer 52:22**	5178
the capital all around, all of **b**.	**Jer 52:22**	5178
and they gleamed like burnished **b**.	**Ezk 1:7**	5178
in and stood beside the **b** altar.	**Ezk 9:2**	5178
all of them are **b** and tin and iron	**Ezk 22:18**	5178
'As they gather silver and **b** and	**Ezk 22:20**	5178
it may be hot And its **b** may glow	**Ezk 24:11**	5178
the lives of men and vessels of **b**	**Ezk 27:13**	5178
was like the appearance of **b**,	**Ezk 40:3**	5178
its belly and its thighs of **b**,	**Da 2:32**	5174
"Then the iron, the clay, the **b**,	**Da 2:35**	5174
then another third kingdom of **b**,	**Da 2:39**	5174
that it crushed the iron, the **b**,	**Da 2:45**	5174
But with a band of iron and **b**	**Da 4:15**	5174
but with a band of iron and **b**	**Da 4:23**	5174
the gods of gold and silver, of **b**,	**Da 5:4**	5174
the gods of silver and gold, of **b**,	**Da 5:23**	5174
teeth of iron and its claws of **b**,	**Da 7:19**	5174
feet like the gleam of polished **b**,	**Da 10:6**	5178
iron And your hoofs I will make **b**,	**Mi 4:13**	5154
the mountains *were* **b** mountains.	**Zch 6:1**	5178
His feet *were* like burnished **b**,	**Rv 1:15**	*5474*
and His feet are like burnished **b**,	**Rv 2:18**	*5474*
wood and **b** and iron and marble,	**Rv 18:12**	*5475*

BROOCHES

came *and* brought **b** and earrings	**Ex 35:22**	2397

BROOD

fathers' place, a **b** of sinful men,	**Nu 32:14**	8635
"On the right hand their **b** arises;	**Jb 30:12**	6526
"You **b** of vipers, who warned you	**Mt 3:7**	*1081*
"You **b** of vipers, how can you,	**Mt 12:34**	*1081*
"You serpents, you **b** of vipers,	**Mt 23:33**	*1081*
"You **b** of vipers, who warned you	**Lk 3:7**	*1081*
hen *gathers* her **b** under her wings,	**Lk 13:34**	*3555*

BROOK

leafy trees and willows of the **b**,	**Lv 23:40**	5158a
from Azmon to the **b** of Egypt,	**Nu 34:5**	5158a
over the **b** Zered yourselves.'	**Dt 2:13**	5158a
So we crossed over the **b** Zered.	**Dt 2:13**	5158a
until we crossed over the **b** Zered was	**Dt 2:14**	5158a
and I threw its dust into the **b**	**Dt 9:21**	5158a
even as far as the **b** Jabbok,	**Jos 12:2**	5158a
and proceeded to the **b** of Egypt,	**Jos 15:4**	5158a
the **b** of Egypt and the Great Sea,	**Jos 15:47**	5158a
westward to the **b** of Kanah,	**Jos 16:8**	5158a
went down to the **b** of Kanah,	**Jos 17:9**	5158a
of Kanah, southward of the **b**	**Jos 17:9**	5158a
was on the north side of the **b** and	**Jos 17:9**	5158a
to the **b** that is before Jokneam.	**Jos 19:11**	5158a
five smooth stones from the **b**,	**1Sa 17:40**	5158a
with him, and came to the **b** Besor,	**1Sa 30:9**	5158a
exhausted to cross the **b** Besor remained	**1Sa 30:10**	5158a
had also been left at the **b** Besor,	**1Sa 30:21**	5158a
also passed over the **b** Kidron,	**2Sa 15:23**	5158a
have crossed the **b** of water."	**2Sa 17:20**	4323
out and cross over the **b** Kidron,	**1Ki 2:37**	5158a
of Hamath to the **b** of Egypt,	**1Ki 8:65**	5158a
and burned *it* at the **b** Kidron.	**1Ki 15:13**	5158a
hide yourself by the **b** Cherith,	**1Ki 17:3**	5158a
be that you will drink of the **b**,	**1Ki 17:4**	5158a
went and lived by the **b** Cherith,	**1Ki 17:5**	5158a

and he would drink from the **b**.	**1Ki 17:6**	5158a
a while that the **b** dried up,	**1Ki 17:7**	5158a
brought them down to the **b** Kishon,	**1Ki 18:40**	5158a
outside Jerusalem to the **b** Kidron,	**2Ki 23:6**	5158a
and burned it at the **b** Kidron,	**2Ki 23:6**	5158a
their dust into the **b** Kidron.	**2Ki 23:12**	5158a
from the **b** of Egypt to the river	**2Ki 24:7**	5158a
of Hamath to the **b** of Egypt.	**2Ch 7:8**	5158a
it and burned *it* at the **b** Kidron.	**2Ch 15:16**	5158a
and cast *them* into the **b** Kidron.	**2Ch 30:14**	5158a
The willows of the **b** surround him.	**Jb 40:22**	5158a
drink from the **b** by the wayside;	**Ps 110:7**	5158a
of wisdom is a bubbling **b**.	**Pr 18:4**	5158a
carry off over the **b** of Arabim.	**Is 15:7**	5158a
the Euphrates to the **b** of Egypt,	**Is 27:12**	5158a
the fields as far as the **b** Kidron,	**Jer 31:40**	5158a
Meribath-kadesh, to the **b** *of Egypt and*	**Ezk 47:19**	5158a
Meribath-kadesh, to the **b** *of Egypt,*	**Ezk 48:28**	5158a
of Hamath To the **b** of the Arabah.	**Am 6:14**	5158a

BROOKS

a good land, a land of **b** of water,	**Dt 8:7**	5158a
Jotbathah, a land of **b** of water.	**Dt 10:7**	5158a
Hiddai of the **b** of Gaash,	**2Sa 23:30**	5158a
Hurai of the **b** of Gaash, Abiel the	**1Ch 11:32**	5158a
Ophir among the stones of the **b**,	**Jb 22:24**	5158a
As the deer pants for the water **b**,	**Ps 42:1**	650
For the water **b** are dried up And	**Jl 1:20**	650
b of Judah will flow with water;	**Jl 3:18**	650

BROOM

food is the root of the **b** shrub.	**Jb 30:4**	7574
the *burning* coals of the **b** tree.	**Ps 120:4**	7574
it with the **b** of destruction,"	**Is 14:23**	4292

BROTH

in a basket and the **b** in a pot,	**Jg 6:19**	4839
this rock, and pour out the **b**."	**Jg 6:20**	4839
And the **b** of unclean meat is *in*	**Is 65:4**	4839

BROTHER

she gave birth to his **b** Abel.	**Gn 4:2**	251
Cain told Abel his **b**.	**Gn 4:8**	251
against Abel his **b** and killed him.	**Gn 4:8**	251
"Where is Abel your **b**?"	**Gn 4:9**	251
from every man's **b** I will require	**Gn 9:5**	251
Eber, *and* the older **b** of Japheth,	**Gn 10:21**	251
b of Eshcol and brother of Aner,	**Gn 14:13**	251
brother of Eshcol and **b** of Aner,	**Gn 14:13**	251
And she herself said, 'He is my **b**.'	**Gn 20:5**	251
"He is my **b**."	**Gn 20:13**	251
b a thousand pieces of silver;	**Gn 20:16**	251
borne children to your **b** Nahor:	**Gn 22:20**	251
Uz his firstborn and Buz his **b**	**Gn 22:21**	251
Milcah bore to Nahor, Abraham's **b**.	**Gn 22:23**	251
the wife of Abraham's **b** Nahor,	**Gn 24:15**	251
had a **b** whose name was Laban;	**Gn 24:29**	251
things to her **b** and to her mother.	**Gn 24:53**	251
But her **b** and her mother said,	**Gn 24:55**	251
Afterward his **b** came forth	**Gn 25:26**	251
your father speak to your **b** Esau,	**Gn 27:6**	251
Esau my **b** is a hairy man and I am	**Gn 27:11**	251
were hairy like his **b** Esau's hands;	**Gn 27:23**	251
his **b** came in from his hunting.	**Gn 27:30**	251
"Your **b** came deceitfully and has	**Gn 27:35**	251
live, And your **b** you shall serve;	**Gn 27:40**	251
then I will kill my **b** Jacob."	**Gn 27:41**	251
"Behold your **b** Esau is consoling	**Gn 27:42**	251
flee to Haran, to my **b** Laban!	**Gn 27:43**	251
daughters of Laban your mother's **b**.	**Gn 28:2**	251
the Aramean, the **b** of Rebekah,	**Gn 28:5**	251
daughter of Laban his mother's **b**,	**Gn 29:10**	251
the sheep of Laban his mother's **b**,	**Gn 29:10**	251
the flock of Laban his mother's **b**.	**Gn 29:10**	251
to his **b** Esau in the land of Seir,	**Gn 32:3**	251
"We came to your **b** Esau, and	**Gn 32:6**	251
me, I pray, from the hand of my **b**,	**Gn 32:11**	251
with him a present for his **b** Esau:	**Gn 32:13**	251
my **b** Esau meets you and asks you,	**Gn 32:17**	251
until he came near to his **b**.	**Gn 33:3**	251
"I have plenty, my **b**;	**Gn 33:9**	251
when you fled from your **b** Esau."	**Gn 35:1**	251
to him when he fled from his **b**.	**Gn 35:7**	251
land away from his **b** Jacob.	**Gn 36:6**	251
kill our **b** and cover up his blood?	**Gn 37:26**	251
for he is our **b**, our *own* flesh."	**Gn 37:27**	251
raise up offspring for your **b**."	**Gn 38:8**	251
not to give offspring to his **b**.	**Gn 38:9**	251
hand, that behold, his **b** came out.	**Gn 38:29**	251
Afterward his **b** came out who	**Gn 38:30**	251
b Benjamin with his brothers,	**Gn 42:4**	251
unless your youngest **b** comes here!	**Gn 42:15**	251
one of you that he may get your **b**,	**Gn 42:16**	251
and bring your youngest **b** to me,	**Gn 42:20**	251
we are guilty concerning our **b**,	**Gn 42:21**	251
'But bring your youngest **b** to me	**Gn 42:34**	251
I will give your **b** to you,	**Gn 42:34**	251
for his **b** is dead, and he alone is	**Gn 42:38**	251
face unless your **b** is with you.'	**Gn 43:3**	251
"If you send our **b** with us, we	**Gn 43:4**	251
unless your **b** is with you.' "	**Gn 43:5**	251
whether you still had *another* **b**?"	**Gn 43:6**	251
Have you *another* **b**?'	**Gn 43:7**	251
'Bring your **b** down'?"	**Gn 43:7**	251
"Take your **b** also, and arise,	**Gn 43:13**	251
to you your other **b** and Benjamin.	**Gn 43:14**	251
his eyes and saw his **b** Benjamin,	**Gn 43:29**	251
"Is this your youngest **b**,	**Gn 43:29**	251
he was deeply stirred over his **b**,	**Gn 43:30**	251
'Have you a father or a **b**?'	**Gn 44:19**	251
Now his **b** is dead, so he alone is	**Gn 44:20**	251
youngest **b** comes down with you,	**Gn 44:23**	251
If our youngest **b** is with us, then	**Gn 44:26**	251
unless our youngest **b** is with us.'	**Gn 44:26**	251
"I am your **b** Joseph, whom you	**Gn 45:4**	251
and the eyes of my **b** Benjamin *see,*	**Gn 45:12**	251
on his **b** Benjamin's neck and wept,	**Gn 45:14**	251
b shall be greater than he,	**Gn 48:19**	251
there not your **b** Aaron the Levite?	**Ex 4:14**	251
b Aaron shall be your prophet.	**Ex 7:1**	251
and your **b** Aaron shall speak to	**Ex 7:2**	251
the justice *due* to your needy **b**	**Ex 23:6**	251
near to yourself Aaron your **b**,	**Ex 28:1**	251
holy garments for Aaron your **b**,	**Ex 28:2**	251
for Aaron your **b** and his sons,	**Ex 28:4**	251
your **b** and on his sons with him;	**Ex 28:41**	251
camp, and kill every man his **b**,	**Ex 32:27**	251
against his son and against his **b**	**Ex 32:29**	251
"Tell your **b** Aaron that he shall	**Lv 16:2**	251
the nakedness of your father's **b**;	**Lv 18:14**	251
son and his daughter and his **b**,	**Lv 21:2**	251
for his **b** or for his sister,	**Nu 6:7**	251
and you and your **b** Aaron assemble	**Nu 20:8**	251
'Thus your **b** Israel has said,	**Nu 20:14**	251
your people, as Aaron your **b** was;	**Nu 27:13**	251
Zelophehad our **b** to his daughters.	**Nu 36:2**	251
"If your **b**, your mother's son, or	**Dt 13:6**	251
it of his neighbor and his **b**,	**Dt 15:2**	251
whatever of yours is with your **b**.	**Dt 15:3**	251
close your hand from your poor **b**;	**Dt 15:7**	251
eye is hostile toward your poor **b**,	**Dt 15:9**	251
freely open your hand to your **b**,	**Dt 15:11**	251
and he has accused his **b** falsely,	**Dt 19:18**	251
as he had intended to do to his **b**.	**Dt 19:19**	251
an Edomite, for he is your **b**;	**Dt 23:7**	251
your **b** is not degraded in your eyes.	**Dt 25:3**	251
Her husband's **b** shall go in to her	**Dt 25:5**	2993
the duty of a husband's **b** to her.	**Dt 25:5**	2992
assume the name of his dead **b**,	**Dt 25:6**	251
'My husband's **b** refuses to	**Dt 25:7**	2993
a name for his **b** in Israel;	**Dt 25:7**	251
the duty of a husband's **b** to me.'	**Dt 25:7**	2992
shall be hostile toward his **b** and	**Dt 28:54**	251
as Aaron your **b** died on Mount Hor	**Dt 32:50**	251
the son of Kenaz, the **b** of Caleb,	**Jos 15:17**	251
Then Judah said to Simeon his **b**,	**Jg 1:3**	251
son of Kenaz, Caleb's younger **b**,	**Jg 1:13**	251
Then Judah went with Simeon his **b**,	**Jg 1:17**	251
son of Kenaz, Caleb's younger **b**.	**Jg 3:9**	251
there because of Abimelech his **b**.	**Jg 9:21**	251
be laid on Abimelech their **b**,	**Jg 9:24**	251
the sons of my **b** Benjamin?"	**Jg 20:23**	251
against the sons of my **b** Benjamin,	**Jg 20:28**	251
for their **b** Benjamin and said,	**Jg 21:6**	251
which belonged to our **b** Elimelech.	**Ru 4:3**	251
the son of Ahitub, Ichabod's **b**,	**1Sa 14:3**	251
Now Eliab his oldest **b** heard when	**1Sa 17:28**	251
my **b** has commanded me to attend.	**1Sa 20:29**	251
the son of Zeruiah, Joab's **b**,	**1Sa 26:6**	251
distressed for you, my **b** Jonathan;	**2Sa 1:26**	251
lift up my face to your **b** Joab?"	**2Sa 2:22**	251
each from following his **b**."	**2Sa 2:27**	251
of the blood of Asahel his **b**.	**2Sa 3:27**	251
So Joab and Abishai his **b** killed	**2Sa 3:30**	251
he had put their **b** Asahel to death	**2Sa 3:30**	251
Rechab and Baanah his **b** escaped.	**2Sa 4:6**	251
answered Rechab and Baanah his **b**,	**2Sa 4:9**	251
in the hand of Abishai his **b**,	**2Sa 10:10**	251
the son of Shimeah, David's **b**;	**2Sa 13:3**	251
the sister of my **b** Absalom."	**2Sa 13:4**	251
"Go now to your **b** Amnon's house,	**2Sa 13:7**	251
Tamar went to her **b** Amnon's house,	**2Sa 13:8**	251
into the bedroom to her **b** Amnon.	**2Sa 13:10**	251
"No, my **b**, do not violate me, for	**2Sa 13:12**	251
Then Absalom her **b** said to her,	**2Sa 13:20**	251
"Has Amnon your **b** been with you?	**2Sa 13:20**	251
silent, my sister, he is your **b**;	**2Sa 13:20**	251
desolate in her **b** Absalom's house.	**2Sa 13:20**	251
let my **b** Amnon go with us."	**2Sa 13:26**	251
the son of Shimeah, David's **b**,	**2Sa 13:32**	251
over the one who struck his **b**,	**2Sa 14:7**	251
the life of his **b** whom he killed,	**2Sa 14:7**	251
the son of Zeruiah, Joab's **b**,	**2Sa 18:2**	251
"Is it well with you, my **b**?"	**2Sa 20:9**	251
Then Joab and Abishai his **b**	**2Sa 20:10**	251
the son of Shimei, David's **b**,	**2Sa 21:21**	251
Abishai, the **b** of Joab,	**2Sa 23:18**	251
b of Joab was among the thirty;	**2Sa 23:24**	251
the mighty men, and Solomon his **b**.	**1Ki 1:10**	251
when I fled from Absalom your **b**.	**1Ki 2:7**	251
to Adonijah your **b** as a wife."	**1Ki 2:21**	251
for he is my older **b**	**1Ki 2:22**	251
which you have given me, my **b**?"	**1Ki 9:13**	251
over him, *saying,* "Alas, my **b**!"	**1Ki 13:30**	251
"Is he still alive? He is my **b**."	**1Ki 20:32**	251
"Your **b** Ben-hadad."	**1Ki 20:33**	251
The sons of Jada the **b** of	**1Ch 2:32**	251
sons of Caleb, the **b** of Jerahmeel,	**1Ch 2:42**	251
Chelub the **b** of Shuhah became	**1Ch 4:11**	251
b Asaph stood at his right hand,	**1Ch 6:39**	251
and the name of his **b** *was* Sheresh,	**1Ch 7:16**	251
sons of his **b** Helem *were* Zophah,	**1Ch 7:35**	251
his **b** *were* Ulam his firstborn,	**1Ch 8:39**	251
As for Abshai the **b** of Joab,	**1Ch 11:20**	251
armies *were* Asahel the **b** of Joab,	**1Ch 11:26**	251
Joel the **b** of Nathan, Mibhar the	**1Ch 11:38**	251
the son of Shimri and Joha his **b**,	**1Ch 11:45**	251
in the hand of Abshai his **b**;	**1Ch 19:11**	251
also fled before Abshai his **b** and	**1Ch 19:15**	251
the **b** of Goliath the Gittite,	**1Ch 20:5**	251
the son of Shimea, David's **b**,	**1Ch 20:7**	251
The **b** of Micah, Isshiah;	**1Ch 24:25**	251
as well as those of his younger **b**.	**1Ch 24:31**	251
of Jehieli, Zetham and Joel his **b**,	**1Ch 26:22**	251
month *was* Asahel the **b** of Joab,	**1Ch 27:7**	251
them and his **b** Shimei *was* second.	**2Ch 31:12**	251
Conaniah and Shimei his **b** by the	**2Ch 31:13**	251
his **b** king over Judah and	**2Ch 36:4**	251
his **b** and brought him to Egypt.	**2Ch 36:4**	251
exacting usury, each from his **b**!"	**Ne 5:7**	251
then I put Hanani my **b**,	**Ne 7:2**	251
"I have become a **b** to jackals And	**Jb 30:29**	251
as though it were my friend or **b**;	**Ps 35:14**	251
man can by any means redeem *his* **b** Or	**Ps 49:7**	251
"You sit and speak against your **b**;	**Ps 50:20**	251
And a **b** is born for adversity.	**Pr 17:17**	251
his work Is **b** to him who destroys.	**Pr 18:9**	251
A **b** offended *is harder to be won*	**Pr 18:19**	251
friend who sticks closer than a **b**.	**Pr 18:24**	251
who is near than a **b** far away.	**Pr 27:10**	251
having neither a son nor a **b**,	**Ec 4:8**	251
"Oh that you were like a **b** to me	**SS 8:1**	251
of his **b** in his father's house,	**Is 3:6**	251
No man spares his **b**.	**Is 9:19**	251
will each fight against his **b** and	**Is 19:2**	251
his neighbor And says to his **b**,	**Is 41:6**	251
neighbor, And do not trust any **b**;	**Jer 9:4**	251
Because every **b** deals craftily,	**Jer 9:4**	251
not lament for him: 'Alas, my **b**!'	**Jer 22:18**	251
say to his neighbor and to his **b**,	**Jer 23:35**	251
to his neighbor and each man his **b**,	**Jer 31:34**	251
one should keep them, a Jew his **b**,	**Jer 34:9**	251
you shall set free his Hebrew **b** who	**Jer 34:14**	251
release each man to his **b** and	**Jer 34:17**	251
does any of these things to a **b**	**Ezk 18:10**	251
practiced extortion, robbed *his* **b** and	**Ezk 18:18**	251
to one another, each to his **b**,	**Ezk 33:30**	251
man's sword will be against his **b**.	**Ezk 38:21**	251
for son, for daughter, for **b**,	**Ezk 44:25**	251
womb he took his **b** by the heel,	**Hos 12:3**	251
he pursued his **b** with the sword,	**Am 1:11**	251
of violence to your **b** Jacob,	**Ob 1:10**	251
and compassion each to his **b**;	**Zch 7:9**	251
"*Was* not Esau Jacob's **b**?"	**Mal 1:2**	251
deal treacherously each against his **b**	**Mal 2:10**	251
called Peter, and Andrew his **b**,	**Mt 4:18**	80
son of Zebedee, and John his **b**,	**Mt 4:21**	80
everyone who is angry with his **b**	**Mt 5:22**	80
and whoever says to his **b**,	**Mt 5:22**	80
your **b** has something against you,	**Mt 5:23**	80
first be reconciled to your **b**,	**Mt 5:24**	80
"Or how can you say to your **b**,	**Mt 7:4**	80
is called Peter, and Andrew his **b**;	**Mt 10:2**	80
son of Zebedee, and John his **b**;	**Mt 10:2**	80
"**B** will betray brother to death,	**Mt 10:21**	80
will betray **b** to death,	**Mt 10:21**	80
is My **b** and sister and mother."	**Mt 12:50**	80
the wife of his **b** Philip.	**Mt 14:3**	80
Peter and James and John his **b**,	**Mt 17:1**	80
"If your **b** sins, go and	**Mt 18:15**	80
to you, you have won your **b**.	**Mt 18:15**	80
how often shall my **b** sin against	**Mt 18:21**	80
forgive his **b** from your heart."	**Mt 18:35**	80
HIS **B** AS NEXT OF KIN SHALL MARRY	**Mt 22:24**	80
RAISE UP CHILDREN FOR HIS **B**.'	**Mt 22:24**	80
children left his wife to his **b**;	**Mt 22:25**	80
Simon and Andrew, the **b** of Simon,	**Mk 1:16**	80
son of Zebedee, and John his **b**,	**Mk 1:19**	80
Zebedee, and John the **b** of James	**Mk 3:17**	80
he is My **b** and sister and mother."	**Mk 3:35**	80
and James and John the **b** of James.	**Mk 5:37**	80
the son of Mary, and **b** of James and	**Mk 6:3**	80
the wife of his **b** Philip,	**Mk 6:17**	80
for us that IF A MAN'S **B** DIES and	**Mk 12:19**	80
CHILD, HIS **B** SHOULD MARRY THE WIFE	**Mk 12:19**	80
AND RAISE UP CHILDREN TO HIS **B**.	**Mk 12:19**	80
"**B** will betray brother to death,	**Mk 13:12**	80
"Brother will betray **b** to death,	**Mk 13:12**	80
and his **b** Philip was tetrarch of	**Lk 3:1**	80
named Peter, and Andrew his **b**;	**Lk 6:14**	80
"Or how can you say to your **b**,	**Lk 6:42**	80
'**B**, let me take out the speck that	**Lk 6:42**	80
tell my **b** to divide the *family*	**Lk 12:13**	80
'Your **b** has come, and your father	**Lk 15:27**	80
for this **b** of yours was dead and	**Lk 15:32**	80
If your **b** sins, rebuke him;	**Lk 17:3**	80
for us that IF A MAN'S **B** DIES,	**Lk 20:28**	80
HIS **B** SHOULD MARRY THE WIFE AND	**Lk 20:28**	80
AND RAISE UP CHILDREN TO HIS **B**.	**Lk 20:28**	80
Him, was Andrew, Simon Peter's **b**.	**Jn 1:40**	80
He found first his own **b** Simon and	**Jn 1:41**	80
disciples, Andrew, Simon Peter's **b**,	**Jn 6:8**	80
hair, whose **b** Lazarus was sick.	**Jn 11:2**	80
console them concerning *their* **b**.	**Jn 11:19**	80
here, my **b** would not have died.	**Jn 11:21**	80
"Your **b** will rise again."	**Jn 11:23**	80
here, my **b** would not have died."	**Jn 11:32**	80
"**B** Saul, the Lord Jesus, who	**Ac 9:17**	80
And he had James the **b** of John put	**Ac 12:2**	80
"You see, **b**, how many thousands	**Ac 21:20**	80
'**B** Saul, receive your sight!'	**Ac 22:13**	80
But you, why do you judge your **b**?	**Ro 14:10**	80
you regard your **b** with contempt?	**Ro 14:10**	80
if because of food your **b** is hurt,	**Ro 14:15**	80
anything by which your **b** stumbles.	**Ro 14:21**	80
greets you, and Quartus, the **b**.	**Ro 16:23**	80
will of God, and Sosthenes our **b**,	**1Co 1:1**	80
not to associate with any so-called **b**	**1Co 5:11**	80
but **b** goes to law with brother,	**1Co 6:6**	80
but brother goes to law with **b**,	**1Co 6:6**	80

that if any **b** has a wife who is an **1Co 7:12** *80*
the **b** or the sister is not under **1Co 7:15** *80*
the **b** for whose sake Christ died. **1Co 8:11** *80*
if food causes my **b** to stumble, **1Co 8:13** *80*
I will not cause my **b** to stumble. **1Co 8:13** *80*
But concerning Apollos our **b**, **1Co 16:12** *80*
will of God, and Timothy *our* **b**, **2Co 1:1** *80*
my spirit, not finding Titus my **b**; **2Co 2:13** *80*
sent along with him the **b** whose fame **2Co 8:18** *80*
We have sent with them our **b**, **2Co 8:22** *80*
to go, and I sent the **b** with him. **2Co 12:18** *80*
except James, the Lord's **b**. **Ga 1:19** *80*
the beloved **b** and faithful **Eph 6:21** *80*
my **b** and fellow worker and fellow **Php 2:25** *80*
will of God, and Timothy our **b**, **Col 1:1** *80*
our beloved **b** and faithful servant **Col 4:7** *80*
our faithful and beloved **b**, **Col 4:9** *80*
our **b** and God's fellow worker in **1Th 3:2** *80*
no man transgress and defraud his **b** **1Th 4:6** *80*
that you keep away from every **b** **2Th 3:6** *80*
an enemy, but admonish him as a **b**. **2Th 3:15** *80*
Christ Jesus, and Timothy our **b**, **Phm 1:1** *80*
To Philemon our beloved **b** **Phm 1:1**
been refreshed through you, **b**. **Phm 1:7** *80*
more than a slave, a beloved **b**, **Phm 1:16** *80*
Yes, **b**, let me benefit from you in **Phm 1:20** *80*
AND EVERYONE HIS **B**, SAYING, **Heb 8:11** *80*
our **b** Timothy has been released, **Heb 13:23** *80*
But the **b** of humble **Jas 1:9** *80*
If a **b** or sister is without **Jas 2:15** *80*
He who speaks against a **b** or **Jas 4:11** *80*
a brother or judges his **b**, **Jas 4:11** *80*
Through Silvanus, our faithful **b** **1Pe 5:12** *80*
just as also our beloved **b** Paul, **2Pe 3:15** *80*
b is in the darkness until now. **1Jn 2:9** *80*
The one who loves his **b** abides in **1Jn 2:10** *80*
But the one who hates his **b** is in **1Jn 2:11** *80*
the one who does not love his **b**. **1Jn 3:10** *80*
of the evil one and slew his **b**. **1Jn 3:12** *80*
who hates his **b** is a murderer; **1Jn 3:15** *80*
and sees his **b** in need and **1Jn 3:17** *80*
"I love God," and hates his **b**, **1Jn 4:20** *80*
not love his **b** whom he has seen, **1Jn 4:20** *80*
loves God should love his **b** also. **1Jn 4:21** *80*
If anyone sees his **b** committing a **1Jn 5:16** *80*
of Jesus Christ, and **b** of James, **Jude 1:1** *80*
your **b** and fellow partaker in the **Rv 1:9** *80*

BROTHERHOOD
not remember *the* covenant of **b**. **Am 1:9** 251
the **b** between Judah and Israel. **Zch 11:14** 264
love the **b**, fear God, honor the **1Pe 2:17** *81*

BROTHER-IN-LAW
perform your duty as a **b** to her, **Gn 38:8** 2992

BROTHERLY
devoted to one another in **b** love; **Ro 12:10** *5360*
you be harmonious, sympathetic, **b** **1Pe 3:8** *5361*
and in *your* godliness, **b** kindness, **2Pe 1:7** *5360*
kindness, and in *your* **b** kindness, **2Pe 1:7** *5360*

BROTHER'S
Am I my **b** keeper?" **Gn 4:9** 251
The voice of your **b** blood is **Gn 4:10** 251
your **b** blood from your hand. **Gn 4:11** 251
His **b** name was Jubal; **Gn 4:21** 251
and his **b** name *was* Joktan. **Gn 10:25** 251
days, until your **b** fury subsides, **Gn 27:44** 251
your **b** anger against you subsides and **Gn 27:45** 251
"Go in to your **b** wife, and **Gn 38:8** 251
when he went in to his **b** wife, **Gn 38:9** 251
the nakedness of your **b** wife; **Lv 18:16** 251
it is your **b** nakedness. **Lv 18:16** 251
is a man who takes his **b** wife, **Lv 20:21** 251
he has uncovered his **b** nakedness. **Lv 20:21** 251
not desire to take his **b** wife, **Dt 25:7** 2994
then his **b** wife shall go up to the **Dt 25:7** 2994
then his **b** wife shall come to him **Dt 25:9** 251
does not build up his **b** house.' **Dt 25:9** 251
has turned about and become my **b**, **1Ki 2:15** 251
and his **b** name was Joktan. **1Ch 1:19** 251
wine in their oldest **b** house, **Jb 1:13** 251
wine in their oldest **b** house, **Jb 1:18** 251
And do not go to your **b** house in **Pr 27:10** 251
"Do not gloat over your **b** day, **Ob 1:12** 251
the speck that is in your **b** eye, **Mt 7:3** *80*
take the speck out of your **b** eye. **Mt 7:5** *80*
for you to have your **b** wife." **Mk 6:18** *80*
because of Herodias, his **b** wife, **Lk 3:19** *80*
the speck that is in your **b** eye, **Lk 6:41** *80*
the speck that is in your **b** eye. **Lk 6:42** *80*
or a stumbling block in a **b** way. **Ro 14:13** *80*
evil, and his **b** were righteous. **1Jn 3:12** *80*

BROTHERS
and told his two **b** outside. **Gn 9:22** 251
servants He shall be to his **b**." **Gn 9:25** 251
and your herdsmen, for we are **b**. **Gn 13:8** 251
live to the east of all his **b**." **Gn 16:12** 251
"Please, my **b**, do not act **Gn 19:7** 251
to the house of my master's **b**." **Gn 24:27** 251
Be master of your **b**, **Gn 27:29** 251
"My **b**, where are you from?" **Gn 29:4** 251
said to her father and to her **b**, **Gn 34:11** 251
sons, Simeon and Levi, Dinah's **b**, **Gn 34:25** 251
his **b** while he was *still* a youth, **Gn 37:2** 251
His **b** saw that their father **Gn 37:4** 251
loved him more than all his **b**; **Gn 37:4** 251
and when he told it to his **b**, **Gn 37:5** 251
Then his **b** said to him, **Gn 37:8** 251
dream, and related it to his **b**, **Gn 37:9** 251
it to his father and to his **b**; **Gn 37:10** 251
your mother and your **b** actually come **Gn 37:10** 251
His **b** were jealous of him, but **Gn 37:11** 251
Then his **b** went to pasture their **Gn 37:12** 251
"Are not your **b** pasturing *the* **Gn 37:13** 251
b and the welfare of the flock, **Gn 37:14** 251
"I am looking for my **b**; **Gn 37:16** 251
his **b** and found them at Dothan. **Gn 37:17** 251
about, when Joseph reached his **b**, **Gn 37:23** 251
Judah said to his **b**, **Gn 37:26** 251
And his **b** listened *to him*. **Gn 37:27** 251
He returned to his **b** and said, **Gn 37:30** 251
that Judah departed from his **b** and **Gn 38:1** 251
that he too may die like his **b**." **Gn 38:11** 251
Then ten **b** of Joseph went down to **Gn 42:3** 251
brother Benjamin with his **b**, **Gn 42:4** 251
And Joseph's **b** came and bowed down **Gn 42:6** 251
saw his **b** he recognized them, **Gn 42:7** 251
But Joseph had recognized his **b**, **Gn 42:8** 251
"Your servants are twelve **b** *in all*, **Gn 42:13** 251
your **b** be confined in your prison; **Gn 42:19** 251
Then he said to his **b**, **Gn 42:28** 251
'We are twelve **b**, sons of our **Gn 42:32** 251
leave one of your **b** with me and **Gn 42:33** 251
and his **b** came to Joseph's house, **Gn 44:14** 251
and let the lad go up with his **b**. **Gn 44:33** 251
made himself known to his **b**. **Gn 45:1** 251
Then Joseph said to his **b**, **Gn 45:3** 251
But his **b** could not answer him, **Gn 45:3** 251
Then Joseph said to his **b**, **Gn 45:4** 251
kissed all his **b** and wept on them, **Gn 45:15** 251
afterward his **b** talked with him. **Gn 45:15** 251
house that Joseph's **b** had come, **Gn 45:16** 251
"Say to your **b**, **Gn 45:17** 251
So he sent his **b** away, and as they **Gn 45:24** 251
b and to his father's household, **Gn 46:31** 251
'My **b** and my father's household, **Gn 46:31** 251
"My father and my **b** and their **Gn 47:1** 251
He took five men from among his **b** **Gn 47:2** 251
Then Pharaoh said to his **b**, **Gn 47:3** 251
and your **b** have come to you. **Gn 47:5** 251
your **b** in the best of the land, **Gn 47:6** 251
settled his father and his **b** and **Gn 47:11** 251
Joseph provided his father and his **b** **Gn 47:12** 251
of their **b** in their inheritance. **Gn 48:6** 251
you one portion more than your **b**, **Gn 48:22** 251
"Simeon and Levi are **b**; **Gn 49:5** 251
"Judah, your **b** shall praise you; **Gn 49:8** 251
the one distinguished among his **b**. **Gn 49:26** 251
his **b** and his father's household; **Gn 50:8** 251
returned to Egypt, he and his **b**, **Gn 50:14** 251
When Joseph's **b** saw that their **Gn 50:15** 251
of your **b** and their sin, **Gn 50:17** 251
Then his **b** also came and fell down **Gn 50:18** 251
Joseph said to his **b**, **Gn 50:24** 251
all his **b** and all that generation. **Ex 1:6** 251
who is the highest among his **b**, **Lv 21:10** 251
One of his **b** may redeem him, **Lv 25:48** 251
their **b** in the tent of meeting, **Nu 8:26** 251
you near, *Korah*, and all your **b**, **Nu 16:10** 251
"But bring with you also your **b**, **Nu 18:2** 251
our **b** perished before the LORD! **Nu 20:3** 251
possession among our father's **b**." **Nu 27:4** 251
possession among their father's **b**, **Nu 27:7** 251
give his inheritance to his **b**. **Nu 27:9** 251
'If he has no **b**, **Nu 27:10** 251
his inheritance to his father's **b**. **Nu 27:10** 251
'If his father has no **b**, **Nu 27:11** 251
"Shall your **b** go to war while you **Nu 32:6** 251
territory of your **b** the sons of Esau **Dt 2:4** 251
beyond our **b** the sons of Esau, **Dt 2:8** 251
cross over armed before your **b**, **Dt 3:18** 251
portion or inheritance with his **b**; **Dt 10:9** 251
poor man with you, one of your **b**, **Dt 15:7** 251
"When **b** live together and one of **Dt 25:5** 251
And he did not acknowledge his **b**, **Dt 33:9** 251
the one distinguished among his **b**. **Dt 33:16** 251
May he be favored by his **b**, **Dt 33:24** 251
before your **b** in battle array, **Jos 1:14** 251
until the LORD gives your **b** rest, **Jos 1:15** 251
my mother and my **b** and my sisters, **Jos 2:13** 251
father and your mother and your **b** **Jos 2:18** 251
mother and her **b** and all she had; **Jos 6:23** 251
us an inheritance among our **b**." **Jos 17:4** 251
inheritance among their father's **b**. **Jos 17:4** 251
"You have not forsaken your **b** **Jos 22:3** 251
your God has given rest to your **b**, **Jos 22:4** 251
b westward beyond the Jordan. **Jos 22:7** 251
of your enemies with your **b**." **Jos 22:8** 251
"They *were* my **b**, the sons of my **Jg 8:19** 251
his **b** the sons of Jerubbaal, **Jg 9:5** 251
his hands to kill his **b**. **Jg 9:24** 251
father in killing his seventy **b**. **Jg 9:56** 251
b and lived in the land of Tob; **Jg 11:3** 251
Then his **b** and all his father's **Jg 16:31** 251
to their **b** at Zorah and Eshtaol, **Jg 18:8** 251
and Eshtaol, their **b** said to them, **Jg 18:8** 251
listen to the voice of their **b**, **Jg 20:13** 251
or their **b** come to complain to us, **Jg 21:22** 251
will not be cut off from his **b** or from **Ru 4:10** 251
him in the midst of his **b**; **1Sa 16:13** 251
"Take now for your **b** an ephah of **1Sa 17:17** 251
and run to the camp to your **b**. **1Sa 17:17** 251
look into the welfare of your **b**, **1Sa 17:18** 251
entered in order to greet his **b**. **1Sa 17:22** 251
me get away that I may see my **b**.' **1Sa 20:29** 251
and when his **b** and all his **1Sa 22:1** 251
"You must not do so, my **b**, **1Sa 30:23** 251
back from following their **b**?" **2Sa 2:26** 251
to his **b** and to his friends, **2Sa 3:8** 251
Return and take back your **b**; **2Sa 15:20** 251
b; you are my bone and my flesh. **2Sa 19:12** 251
"Why had our **b** the men of Judah **2Sa 19:41** 251
and he invited all his **b**, **1Ki 1:9** 251
bid him arise from among his **b**, **2Ki 9:2** 251
unleavened bread among their **b**. **2Ki 23:9** 251
was more honorable than his **b**, **1Ch 4:9** 251
but his **b** did not have many sons, **1Ch 4:27** 251
Though Judah prevailed over his **b**, **1Ch 5:2** 251
but daughters only, so their **b**, **1Ch 23:22** 251
Obed and Elzabad, whose **b**, **1Ch 26:7** 251
for Judah, Elihu, *one* of David's **b**; **1Ch 27:18** 251
as head and leader among his **b**, **2Ch 11:22** 251
He had **b**, the sons of **2Ch 21:2** 251
killed all his **b** with the sword, **2Ch 21:4** 251
and you have also killed your **b**, **2Ch 21:13** 251
Judah and the sons of Ahaziah's **b** **2Ch 22:8** 251
whom you captured from your **b**, **2Ch 28:11** 251
city of palm trees, to their **b**; **2Ch 28:15** 251
They assembled their **b**, **2Ch 29:15** 251
therefore their **b** the Levites **2Ch 29:34** 251
be like your fathers and your **b**, **2Ch 30:7** 251
your **b** and your sons *will find* **2Ch 30:9** 251
portions to their **b** by divisions, **2Ch 31:15** 251
and Shemaiah and Nethanel, his **b**, **2Ch 35:9** 251
of Jozadak and his **b** the priests, **Ezr 3:2** 251
and his **b** arose and built the **Ezr 3:2** 251
b the priests and the Levites, **Ezr 3:8** 251
Then Jeshua *with* his sons and **b** **Ezr 3:9** 251
with their sons and **b** the Levites, **Ezr 3:9** 251
both for their **b** the priests and **Ezr 6:20** 251
seems good to you and to your **b** **Ezr 7:18** 252
what to say to Iddo *and* his **b**, **Ezr 8:17** 251
Sherebiah, and his sons and **b**, **Ezr 8:18** 251
Merari, with his **b** and their sons, **Ezr 8:19** 251
and with them ten of their **b**; **Ezr 8:24** 251
the son of Jozadak, and his **b**: **Ezr 10:18** 251
that Hanani, one of my **b**, **Ne 1:2** 251
arose with his **b** the priests and built **Ne 3:1** 251
After him their **b** carried out **Ne 3:18** 251
He spoke in the presence of his **b** **Ne 4:2** 251
and awesome, and fight for your **b**, **Ne 4:14** 251
So neither I, my **b**, **Ne 4:23** 251
wives against their Jewish **b**. **Ne 5:1** 251
flesh is like the flesh of our **b**, **Ne 5:5** 251
b who were sold to the nations; **Ne 5:8** 251
b that they may be sold to us?" **Ne 5:8** 251
likewise I, my **b** and my servants are **Ne 5:10** 251
also their **b** Shebaniah, Hodiah, **Ne 10:10** 251
and their **b**, valiant warriors, 128. **Ne 11:14** 251
of thanksgiving, he and his **b**. **Ne 12:8** 251
Also Bakbukiah and Unni, their **b**, **Ne 12:9** 251
with their **b** opposite them, **Ne 12:24** 251
"My **b** have acted deceitfully like **Jb 6:15** 251
"He has removed my **b** far from me, **Jb 19:13** 251
And I am loathsome to my own **b**. **Jb 19:17** 1121, 990
pledges of your **b** without cause, **Jb 22:6** 251
Then all his **b** and all his **Jb 42:11** 251
them inheritance among their **b**. **Jb 42:15** 251
I have become estranged from my **b** **Ps 69:8** 251
the sake of my **b** and my friends, **Ps 122:8** 251
For **b** to dwell together in unity! **Ps 133:1** 251
one who spreads strife among **b**. **Pr 6:19** 251
share in the inheritance among **b**. **Pr 17:2** 251
All the **b** of a poor man hate him; **Pr 19:7** 251
"Your **b** who hate you, who exclude **Is 66:5** 251
as I have cast out all your **b**, **Jer 7:15** 251
"For even your **b** and the **Jer 12:6** 251
your **b** who did not go with you **Jer 29:16** 251
son of Habazziniah, and his **b** and **Jer 35:3** 251
"Son of man, your **b**, **Ezk 11:15** 251
Say to your **b**, "Ammi," **Hos 2:1** 251
Jacob the father of Judah and his **b**. **Mt 1:2** *80*
became the father of Jeconiah and his **b**, **Mt 1:11** *80*
the Sea of Galilee, He saw two **b**, **Mt 4:18** *80*
on from there He saw two other **b**, **Mt 4:21** *80*
"If you greet only your **b**, **Mt 5:47** *80*
and **b** were standing outside, **Mt 12:46** *80*
Your mother and Your **b** are **Mt 12:47** *80*
is My mother and who are My **b**?" **Mt 12:48** *80*
"Behold My mother and My **b**! **Mt 12:49** *80*
His mother called Mary, and His **b**, **Mt 13:55** *80*
who has left houses or **b** or sisters **Mt 19:29** *80*
became indignant with the two **b**. **Mt 20:24** *80*
"Now there were seven **b** with us; **Mt 22:25** *80*
your Teacher, and you are all **b**. **Mt 23:8** *80*
did it to one of these **b** of Mine, **Mt 25:40** *80*
Then His mother and His **b** arrived, **Mk 3:31** *80*
b are outside looking for You." **Mk 3:32** *80*
"Who are My mother and My **b**?" **Mk 3:33** *80*
"Behold My mother and My **b**! **Mk 3:34** *80*
is no one who has left house or **b** or **Mk 10:29** *80*
houses and **b** and sisters and **Mk 10:30** *80*
"There were seven **b**; **Mk 12:20** *80*
And His mother and **b** came to Him, **Lk 8:19** *80*
and Your **b** are standing outside, **Lk 8:20** *80*
"My mother and My **b** are these who **Lk 8:21** *80*
do not invite your friends or your **b** **Lk 14:12** *80*
and children and **b** and sisters, **Lk 14:26** *80*
for I have five **b** **Lk 16:28** *80*
wife or **b** or parents or children, **Lk 18:29** *80*
"Now there were seven **b**; **Lk 20:29** *80*
and **b** and relatives and friends, **Lk 21:16** *80*
turned again, strengthen your **b**." **Lk 22:32** *80*
He and His mother and *His* **b** **Jn 2:12** *80*
His **b** said to Him, **Jn 7:3** *80*
even His **b** were believing in Him. **Jn 7:5** *80*
His **b** had gone up to the feast, **Jn 7:10** *80*

mother of Jesus, and with His **b**.	**Ac 1:14**	*80*
made himself known to his **b**,	**Ac 7:13**	*80*
had the Twin **B** for its figurehead.	**Ac 28:11**	*1359*
apostles and the **b** of the Lord	**1Co 9:5**	*80*
a father, *to* the younger men as **b**,	**1Tm 5:1**	*80*

BROTHERS'

he might not make his **b** hearts	**Dt 20:8**	251

BROUGHT

The earth **b** forth vegetation,	**Gn 1:12**	3318
and **b** *them* to the man to see what	**Gn 2:19**	935
the man, and **b** her to the man.	**Gn 2:22**	935
Cain **b** an offering to the LORD	**Gn 4:3**	935
on his part also **b** of the	**Gn 4:4**	935
and **b** her into the ark to himself.	**Gn 8:9**	935
He **b** back all the goods, and	**Gn 14:16**	7725
and also **b** back his relative Lot	**Gn 14:16**	7725
of Salem **b** out bread and wine;	**Gn 14:18**	3318
"I am the LORD who **b** you out of	**Gn 15:7**	3318
Then he **b** all these to Him and cut	**Gn 15:10**	3947
water be **b** and wash your feet,	**Gn 18:4**	3947
b Lot into the house with them,	**Gn 19:10**	935
and they **b** him out, and put him	**Gn 19:16**	3318
When they had **b** them outside,	**Gn 19:17**	3318
that you have **b** on me and on my	**Gn 20:9**	935
The servant **b** out articles of	**Gn 24:53**	3318
Then Isaac **b** her into his mother	**Gn 24:67**	935
you would have **b** guilt upon us."	**Gn 26:10**	935
they **b** grief to Isaac and Rebekah.	**Gn 26:35**	1961
them, and **b** *them* to his mother;	**Gn 27:14**	935
And he **b** *it* to him, and he ate;	**Gn 27:25**	5066
he also **b** him wine and he drank.	**Gn 27:25**	935
food, and **b** it to his father;	**Gn 27:31**	935
that hunted game and **b** *it* to me,	**Gn 27:33**	935
him and **b** him to his house.	**Gn 29:13**	935
daughter Leah, and **b** her to him;	**Gn 29:23**	935
and **b** them to his mother Leah.	**Gn 30:14**	935
and the flocks **b** forth striped,	**Gn 30:39**	3205
all the flock **b** forth speckled;	**Gn 31:8**	3205
all the flock **b** forth striped.	**Gn 31:8**	3205
my gift which has been **b** to you,	**Gn 33:11**	935
"You have **b** trouble on me by	**Gn 34:30**	5916
And Joseph **b** back a bad report	**Gn 37:2**	935
Thus they **b** Joseph into Egypt.	**Gn 37:28**	935
and **b** it to their father and said,	**Gn 37:32**	935
It was while she was being **b** out	**Gn 38:25**	3318
he has **b** in a Hebrew to us to make	**Gn 39:14**	935
Hebrew slave, whom you **b** to us,	**Gn 39:17**	935
b him out of the dungeon;	**Gn 41:14**	7323
the land **b** forth abundantly.	**Gn 41:47**	6213a
grain which they had **b** from Egypt,	**Gn 43:2**	935
and **b** the men to Joseph's house.	**Gn 43:17**	935
they were **b** to Joseph's house;	**Gn 43:18**	935
first time that we are being **b** in,	**Gn 43:18**	935
So we have **b** it back in our hand.	**Gn 43:21**	7725
"We have also **b** down other money	**Gn 43:22**	3381
Then he **b** Simeon out to them.	**Gn 43:23**	3318
Then the man **b** the men into	**Gn 43:24**	935
they **b** into the house to him the	**Gn 43:26**	935
mouth of our sacks we have **b** back	**Gn 44:8**	7725
he **b** with him to Egypt.	**Gn 46:7**	935
and they have **b** their flocks and	**Gn 46:32**	935
Then Joseph **b** his father Jacob and	**Gn 47:7**	935
and Joseph **b** the money into	**Gn 47:14**	935
they **b** their livestock to Joseph,	**Gn 47:17**	935
Then Joseph **b** them close to him,	**Gn 48:10**	5066
right, and **b** them close to him.	**Gn 48:13**	5066
her maid, and she **b** it *to her.*	**Ex 2:5**	3947
she **b** him to Pharaoh's daughter and	**Ex 2:10**	935
have **b** the people out of Egypt,	**Ex 3:12**	3318
have You **b** harm to this people?	**Ex 5:22**	7489a
who **b** you out from under the	**Ex 6:7**	3318
in the field and is not **b** home,	**Ex 9:19**	622
and Aaron were **b** back to Pharaoh,	**Ex 10:8**	7725
the east wind **b** the locusts.	**Ex 10:13**	5375
for on this very day I **b** your	**Ex 12:17**	3318
dough which they had **b** out of Egypt	**Ex 12:39**	3318
b them out from the land of Egypt;	**Ex 12:42**	3318
day the LORD **b** the sons of Israel out	**Ex 12:51**	3318
LORD **b** you out from this place.	**Ex 13:3**	3318
hand the LORD **b** you out of Egypt.	**Ex 13:9**	3318
hand the LORD **b** us out of Egypt,	**Ex 13:14**	3318
hand the LORD **b** us out of Egypt."	**Ex 13:16**	3318
pillar of fire and cloud and **b** the army	**Ex 14:24**	2000
and the LORD **b** back the waters of	**Ex 15:19**	7725
for you have **b** us out into this	**Ex 16:3**	3318
b you out of the land of Egypt;	**Ex 16:6**	3318
I **b** you out of the land of Egypt.' "	**Ex 16:32**	3318
now, have you **b** us up from Egypt,	**Ex 17:3**	5927
LORD had **b** Israel out of Egypt.	**Ex 18:1**	3318
eagles' wings, and **b** you to Myself.	**Ex 19:4**	935
And Moses **b** back the words of the	**Ex 19:8**	7725
And Moses **b** the people out of the	**Ex 19:17**	3318
b you out of the land of Egypt,	**Ex 20:2**	3318
b them out of the land of Egypt,	**Ex 29:46**	3318
b us up from the land of Egypt,	**Ex 32:1**	5927
their ears and **b** *them* to Aaron.	**Ex 32:3**	935
b you up from the land of Egypt."	**Ex 32:4**	5927
offerings, and **b** peace offerings;	**Ex 32:6**	5066
you **b** up from the land of Egypt,	**Ex 32:7**	5927
b you up from the land of Egypt!' "	**Ex 32:8**	5927
have **b** out from the land of Egypt	**Ex 32:11**	3318
'With evil *intent* He **b** them out to	**Ex 32:12**	3318
have **b** *such* great sin upon them?"	**Ex 32:21**	935
b us up from the land of Egypt,	**Ex 32:23**	5927
have **b** up from the land of Egypt,	**Ex 33:1**	5927
came *and* **b** the LORD's contribution	**Ex 35:21**	935
came *and* **b** brooches and earrings	**Ex 35:22**	935
red and porpoise skins, **b** them.	**Ex 35:23**	935
bronze **b** the LORD's contribution;	**Ex 35:24**	935
for any work of the service **b** it.	**Ex 35:24**	935
hands, and **b** what they had spun,	**Ex 35:25**	935
The rulers **b** the onyx stones	**Ex 35:27**	935
b a freewill offering to the LORD.	**Ex 35:29**	935
which the sons of Israel had **b**	**Ex 36:3**	935
They **b** the tabernacle to Moses,	**Ex 39:33**	935
He **b** the ark into the tabernacle,	**Ex 40:21**	935
the blood is **b** into the tent of meeting	**Lv 6:30**	935
he **b** the bull of the sin offering,	**Lv 8:14**	5066
which the LORD has **b** about.	**Lv 10:6**	8313
its blood had not been **b** inside,	**Lv 10:18**	935
b you up from the land of Egypt to	**Lv 11:45**	5927
he shall be **b** to Aaron the priest or	**Lv 13:2**	935
then he shall be **b** to the priest.	**Lv 13:9**	935
Now he shall be **b** to the priest,	**Lv 14:2**	935
whose blood was **b** in to make	**Lv 16:27**	935
and has not **b** it to the doorway of	**Lv 17:4**	935
therefore I have **b** its punishment	**Lv 18:25**	6485
who **b** you out from the land of	**Lv 19:36**	3318
who **b** you out from the land of	**Lv 22:33**	3318
b in the offering of your God,	**Lv 23:14**	935
from the day when you **b** in the	**Lv 23:15**	935
live in booths when I **b** them out from	**Lv 23:43**	3318
So they **b** him to Moses.	**Lv 24:11**	935
and they **b** the one who had cursed	**Lv 24:23**	3318
who **b** you out of the land of Egypt	**Lv 25:38**	3318
I **b** out from the land of Egypt;	**Lv 25:42**	3318
I **b** out from the land of Egypt.	**Lv 25:55**	3318
who **b** you out of the land of Egypt	**Lv 26:13**	3318
whom I **b** out of the land of Egypt	**Lv 26:45**	3318
When they **b** their offering before	**Nu 7:3**	935
Was it I who **b** them forth, that	**Nu 11:12**	3205
LORD and it **b** quail from the sea,	**Nu 11:31**	1468
and they **b** back word to them and	**Nu 13:26**	7725
for by Your strength You **b** up this	**Nu 14:13**	5927
even those men who **b** out the very	**Nu 14:37**	3318
and they have **b** their offering,	**Nu 15:25**	935
wood **b** him to Moses and Aaron and	**Nu 15:33**	7126
b him outside the camp and	**Nu 15:36**	3318
"I am the LORD your God who **b** you	**Nu 15:41**	3318
and that He has **b** you near, *Korah,*	**Nu 16:10**	7126
"Is it not enough that you have **b**	**Nu 16:13**	5927
you have not **b** us into a land	**Nu 16:14**	935
Moses then **b** out all the rods from	**Nu 17:9**	3318
and it shall be **b** outside the camp	**Nu 19:3**	3318
"Why then have you **b** the LORD's	**Nu 20:4**	935
an angel and **b** us out from Egypt;	**Nu 20:16**	3318
"Why have you **b** us up out of	**Nu 21:5**	5927
and **b** him up to the high places of	**Nu 22:41**	5927
"From Aram Balak has **b** me,	**Nu 23:7**	5148
b to his relatives a Midianite woman,	**Nu 25:6**	7126
b their case before the LORD.	**Nu 27:5**	7126
They **b** the captives and the	**Nu 31:12**	935
"So we have **b** as an offering to	**Nu 31:50**	7126
and **b** it to the tent of meeting as	**Nu 31:54**	935
we have **b** them to their place,	**Nu 32:17**	935
their hands and **b** it down to us;	**Dt 1:25**	3381
they **b** us back a report and said,	**Dt 1:25**	7725
He has **b** us out of the land of	**Dt 1:27**	3318
and **b** you out of the iron furnace,	**Dt 4:20**	3318
And He personally **b** you from Egypt	**Dt 4:37**	3318
b you out of the land of Egypt,	**Dt 5:6**	3318
and the LORD your God **b** you out of	**Dt 5:15**	3318
who **b** you from the land of Egypt,	**Dt 6:12**	3318
and the LORD **b** us from Egypt with	**Dt 6:21**	3318
He **b** us out from there in	**Dt 6:23**	3318
LORD **b** you out by a mighty hand and	**Dt 7:8**	3318
which the LORD your God **b** you out.	**Dt 7:19**	3318
forget the LORD your God who **b** you	**Dt 8:14**	3318
He **b** water for you out of the rock	**Dt 8:15**	3318
has **b** me in to possess this land,'	**Dt 9:4**	935
for your people whom you **b** out of	**Dt 9:12**	3318
whom You have **b** out of Egypt with	**Dt 9:26**	3318
'Otherwise the land from which You **b**	**Dt 9:28**	3318
hated them He has **b** them out to slay	**Dt 9:28**	3318
whom You have **b** out by Your great	**Dt 9:29**	3318
against the LORD your God who **b** you	**Dt 13:5**	3318
God who **b** you out from the land	**Dt 13:10**	3318
God **b** you out of Egypt by night.	**Dt 16:1**	3318
b you up from the land of Egypt,	**Dt 20:1**	5927
and the LORD **b** us out of Egypt	**Dt 26:8**	3318
and He has **b** us to this place and	**Dt 26:9**	935
I have **b** the first of the produce	**Dt 26:10**	935
b them out of the land of Egypt.	**Dt 29:25**	3318
before I have **b** them into the land	**Dt 31:21**	935
But she had **b** them up to the roof	**Jos 2:6**	5927
spies went in and **b** out Rahab	**Jos 6:23**	3318
they also **b** out all her relatives and	**Jos 6:23**	3318
and **b** Israel near by tribes,	**Jos 7:16**	7126
He **b** the family of Judah near,	**Jos 7:17**	7126
and he **b** the family of the	**Jos 7:17**	7126
b his household near man by man;	**Jos 7:18**	7126
inside the tent and **b** them to Joshua	**Jos 7:23**	935
and they **b** them up to the valley	**Jos 7:24**	5927
king of Ai and **b** him to Joshua.	**Jos 8:23**	7126
and **b** these five kings out to him	**Jos 10:23**	3318
they **b** these kings out to Joshua,	**Jos 10:24**	3318
and I **b** word back to him as *it was*	**Jos 14:7**	7725
Israel, and **b** back word to them.	**Jos 22:32**	7725
and afterward I **b** you out.	**Jos 24:5**	3318
'I **b** your fathers out of	**Jos 24:6**	3318
and **b** the sea upon them and	**Jos 24:7**	935
'Then I **b** you into the land of the	**Jos 24:8**	935
for the LORD our God is He who **b**	**Jos 24:17**	5927
sons of Israel **b** up from Egypt,	**Jos 24:32**	5927
So they **b** him to Jerusalem and he	**Jg 1:7**	935
"I **b** you up out of Egypt and led	**Jg 2:1**	5927
b them out of the land of Egypt,	**Jg 2:12**	3318
magnificent bowl she **b** him curds.	**Jg 5:25**	7126
was **b** very low because of Midian,	**Jg 6:6**	1809
'It was I who **b** you up from Egypt and	**Jg 6:8**	5927
and **b** you out from the house of	**Jg 6:8**	3318
b *them* out to him under the oak and	**Jg 6:19**	3318
he **b** the people down to the water.	**Jg 7:5**	3381
and they **b** the heads of Oreb and	**Jg 7:25**	935
You have **b** me very low, and you	**Jg 11:35**	3766
and he **b** in thirty daughters from	**Jg 12:9**	935
b thirty companions to be with him.	**Jg 14:11**	3947
ropes and **b** him up from the rock.	**Jg 15:13**	5927
the Philistines **b** up to her seven fresh	**Jg 16:8**	5927
and **b** the money in their hands.	**Jg 16:18**	5927
and they **b** him down to Gaza and	**Jg 16:21**	3381
came down, took him, **b** him up and	**Jg 16:31**	5927
"Who **b** you here? And what are you	**Jg 18:3**	935
she **b** him into her father's house,	**Jg 19:3**	935
concubine and **b** *her* out to them;	**Jg 19:25**	3318
they **b** them to the camp at Shiloh,	**Jg 21:12**	935
but the LORD has **b** me back empty.	**Ru 1:21**	7725
and **b** him to the house of the LORD	**1Sa 1:24**	935
the bull, and **b** the boy to Eli.	**1Sa 1:25**	935
all that the fork **b** up the priest	**1Sa 2:14**	5927
because his sons **b** a curse on	**1Sa 3:13**	7043
who **b** the news replied,	**1Sa 4:17**	1319
and **b** it from Ebenezer to Ashdod.	**1Sa 5:1**	935
and **b** it to the house of Dagon and	**1Sa 5:2**	935
of Israel be **b** around to Gath."	**1Sa 5:8**	5437
And they **b** the ark of the God of	**1Sa 5:8**	5437
After they had **b** it around,	**1Sa 5:9**	5437
"They have **b** the ark of the God	**1Sa 5:10**	5437
have **b** back the ark of the LORD;	**1Sa 6:21**	7725
ark of the LORD and **b** it into the house	**1Sa 7:1**	935
the day that I **b** them up from Egypt	**1Sa 8:8**	5927
servant and **b** them into the hall and	**1Sa 9:22**	935
'I **b** Israel up from Egypt, and I	**1Sa 10:18**	5927
b all the tribes of Israel near,	**1Sa 10:20**	7126
Then he **b** the tribe of Benjamin	**1Sa 10:21**	7126
and Aaron and who **b** your fathers up	**1Sa 12:6**	5927
Moses and Aaron who **b** your fathers	**1Sa 12:8**	3318
night **b** each one his ox with him and	**1Sa 14:34**	5066
who has **b** about this great	**1Sa 14:45**	6213a
have **b** them from the Amalekites,	**1Sa 15:15**	935
b back Agag the king of Amalek,	**1Sa 15:20**	935
So he sent and **b** him in.	**1Sa 16:12**	935
head and **b** it to Jerusalem,	**1Sa 17:54**	935
Abner took him and **b** him before	**1Sa 17:57**	935
Then David **b** their foreskins, and	**1Sa 18:27**	935
and the LORD **b** about a great	**1Sa 19:5**	6213a
And Jonathan **b** David to Saul, and	**1Sa 19:7**	935
for you have **b** your servant into a	**1Sa 20:8**	935
For I **b** neither my sword nor my	**1Sa 21:8**	3947
that you have **b** this one to act	**1Sa 21:15**	935
I have **b** about *the death* of every	**1Sa 22:22**	5437
this gift which your maidservant has **b**	**1Sa 25:27**	935
from her hand what she had **b** him and	**1Sa 25:35**	935
She **b** *it* before Saul and his	**1Sa 28:25**	5066
So Abiathar **b** the ephod to David.	**1Sa 30:7**	5066
in the field and **b** him to David,	**1Sa 30:11**	3947
When he had **b** him down,	**1Sa 30:16**	3381
David **b** *it* all back.	**1Sa 30:19**	7725
I have **b** them here to my lord."	**2Sa 1:10**	935
b up his men who *were* with him,	**2Sa 2:3**	5927
Saul and **b** him over to Mahanaim.	**2Sa 2:8**	5674a
a raid and **b** much spoil with them;	**2Sa 3:22**	935
and they **b** him back from the well	**2Sa 3:26**	7725
Then they **b** the head of	**2Sa 4:8**	935
So they **b** it with the ark of God	**2Sa 6:4**	5375
David went and **b** up the ark of	**2Sa 6:12**	5927
So they **b** in the ark of the LORD	**2Sa 6:17**	935
I **b** up the sons of Israel from Egypt,	**2Sa 7:6**	5927
that You have **b** me this far?	**2Sa 7:18**	935
and **b** them to Jerusalem.	**2Sa 8:7**	935
b with him articles of silver,	**2Sa 8:10**	
Then King David sent and **b** him	**2Sa 9:5**	3947
And Hadadezer sent and **b** out the	**2Sa 10:16**	3318
David sent and **b** her to his house	**2Sa 11:27**	622
And he **b** out the spoil of the city	**2Sa 12:30**	3318
b out the people who were in it,	**2Sa 12:31**	3318
cakes which she had made and **b** them	**2Sa 13:10**	935
When she **b** *them* to him to eat, he	**2Sa 13:11**	5066
So Joab sent to Tekoa and **b** a wise	**2Sa 14:2**	3947
and **b** Absalom to Jerusalem.	**2Sa 14:23**	935
b beds, basins, pottery, wheat,	**2Sa 17:28**	5066
and **b** the king and his household	**2Sa 19:41**	5674a
He **b** up the bones of Saul and	**2Sa 21:13**	5927
b me forth into a broad place;	**2Sa 22:20**	3318
and the LORD **b** about a great	**2Sa 23:10**	6213a
the LORD **b** about a great victory.	**2Sa 23:12**	6213a
and took *it* and **b** *it* to David.	**2Sa 23:16**	935
Shunammite, and **b** her to the king.	**1Ki 1:3**	935
David's mule, and **b** him to Gihon.	**1Ki 1:38**	1980
they **b** him down from the altar.	**1Ki 1:53**	3381
And Benaiah **b** the king word again,	**1Ki 2:30**	7725
went and **b** his servants from Gath.	**1Ki 2:40**	935
and **b** her to the city of David until	**1Ki 3:1**	935
So they **b** a sword before the king.	**1Ki 3:24**	935
they **b** tribute and served Solomon	**1Ki 4:21**	5066
They also **b** barley and straw for	**1Ki 4:28**	935
sent and **b** Hiram from Tyre.	**1Ki 7:13**	3947
And Solomon **b** in the things	**1Ki 7:51**	935
They **b** up the ark of the LORD	**1Ki 8:4**	5927
priests and the Levites **b** them up.	**1Ki 8:4**	5927
Then the priests **b** the ark of the	**1Ki 8:6**	935
I **b** My people Israel from Egypt,	**1Ki 8:16**	3318
b them from the land of Egypt."	**1Ki 8:21**	3318
You have **b** forth from Egypt,	**1Ki 8:51**	3318
when You **b** our fathers forth from	**1Ki 8:53**	3318
who **b** their fathers out of the	**1Ki 9:9**	3318

b all this adversity on them.' " **1Ki 9:9** 935
there, and **b** *it* to King Solomon. **1Ki 9:28** 935
of Hiram, which **b** gold from Ophir, **1Ki 10:11** 5375
b in from Ophir a very great **1Ki 10:11** 935
They **b** every man his gift, **1Ki 10:25** 935
b you up from the land of Egypt." **1Ki 12:28** 5927
to the prophet who had **b** him back; **1Ki 13:20** 7725
the prophet whom he had **b** back. **1Ki 13:23** 7725
Now when the prophet who **b** him **1Ki 13:26** 7725
and **b** it back, and he came to the **1Ki 13:29** 7725
He **b** into the house of the **1Ki 15:15** 935
The ravens **b** him bread and **1Ki 17:6** 935
have You also **b** calamity to the **1Ki 17:20** 7489a
and **b** him down from the upper room **1Ki 17:23** 3381
and **b** the prophets together at **1Ki 18:20** 6908
b them down to the brook Kishon, **1Ki 18:40** 3381
departed and **b** him word again. **1Ki 20:9** 7725
aside and **b** a man to me and said, **1Ki 20:39** 935
king died and was **b** to Samaria, **1Ki 22:37** 935
So they **b** *it* to him. **2Ki 2:20** 3947
taken him and **b** him to his mother, **2Ki 4:20** 935
and **b** the man of God bread of the **2Ki 4:42** 935
He **b** the letter to the king of **2Ki 5:6** 935
from his hands what he **b**. **2Ki 5:20** 935
And he **b** them to Samaria. **2Ki 6:19** 1980
b the heads of the king's sons," **2Ki 10:8** 935
So he **b** out garments for them. **2Ki 10:22** 3318
They **b** out the *sacred* pillars **2Ki 10:26** 3318
Jehoiada sent and **b** the captains **2Ki 11:4** 3947
and **b** them to him in the house of **2Ki 11:4** 935
Then he **b** the king's son out and **2Ki 11:12** 3318
and they **b** the king down from the **2Ki 11:19** 3381
is **b** into the house of the LORD, **2Ki 12:4** 935
was **b** into the house of the LORD. **2Ki 12:9** 935
was **b** into the house of the LORD; **2Ki 12:13** 935
not **b** into the house of the LORD; **2Ki 12:16** 935
Then they **b** him on horses and he **2Ki 14:20** 5375
he **b** from the front of the house, **2Ki 16:14** 7126
who had **b** them up from the land of **2Ki 17:7** 5927
The king of Assyria **b** *men* from **2Ki 17:24** 935
who **b** you up from the land of **2Ki 17:36** 5927
Now I have **b** it to pass, That you **2Ki 19:25** 935
And He **b** the shadow on the **2Ki 20:11** 7725
and **b** water into the city, **2Ki 20:20** 935
count the money **b** in to the house **2Ki 22:4** 935
scribe came to the king and **b** back **2Ki 22:9** 7725
So they **b** back word to the king. **2Ki 22:20** 7725
He **b** out the Asherah from the **2Ki 23:6** 3318
Then he **b** all the priests from the **2Ki 23:8** 935
and **b** him to Jerusalem and buried **2Ki 23:30** 935
Jehoahaz away and **b** *him* to Egypt, **2Ki 23:34** 935
Babylon **b** into exile to Babylon. **2Ki 24:16** 935
Then they captured the king and **b** **2Ki 25:6** 5927
fetters and **b** him to Babylon. **2Ki 25:7** 935
and **b** them to the king of Babylon **2Ki 25:20** 1980
of Manasseh, and **b** them to Halah, **1Ch 5:26** 935
counted them when they **b** them in **1Ch 9:28** 935
and **b** them to Jabesh, and they buried **1Ch 10:12** 935
one who led out and **b** in Israel; **1Ch 11:2** 935
and took *it* and **b** *it* to David; **1Ch 11:18** 935
risk of their lives they **b** it." **1Ch 11:19** 935
and Naphtali, **b** food on donkeys, **1Ch 12:40** 935
and the LORD **b** the fear of him on **1Ch 14:17** 5414
Thus all Israel **b** up the ark of **1Ch 15:28** 5927
And they **b** in the ark of God and **1Ch 16:1** 935
that I **b** up Israel to this day, **1Ch 17:5** 5927
that You have **b** me this far? **1Ch 17:16** 935
and **b** them to Jerusalem. **1Ch 18:7** 935
And *Hadoram* **b** all kinds of **1Ch 18:10**
and **b** out the Arameans who were **1Ch 19:16** 3318
he **b** out the spoil of the city, **1Ch 20:2** 3318
b out the people who *were* in it, **1Ch 20:3** 3318
for the Sidonians and Tyrians **b** **1Ch 22:4** 935
David had **b** up the ark of God from **2Ch 1:4** 5927
And Solomon **b** in the things that **2Ch 5:1** 935
They **b** up the ark and the tent **2Ch 5:5** 5927
the Levitical priests **b** them up. **2Ch 5:5** 5927
Then the priests **b** the ark of the **2Ch 5:7** 935
'Since the day that I **b** My people **2Ch 6:5** 3318
who **b** them from the land of Egypt, **2Ch 7:22** 3318
b all this adversity on them.' " **2Ch 7:22** 935
Then Solomon **b** Pharaoh's daughter **2Ch 8:11** 5927
gold and **b** them to King Solomon. **2Ch 8:18** 935
of Solomon who **b** gold from Ophir, **2Ch 9:10** 935
also **b** algum trees and precious **2Ch 9:10** 935
for what she had **b** to the king. **2Ch 9:12** 935
which the traders and merchants **b**; **2Ch 9:14** 935
b gold and silver to Solomon. **2Ch 9:14** 935
They **b** every man his gift, **2Ch 9:24** 935
b them back into the guards' room. **2Ch 12:11** 7725
sheep from the spoil they had **b**. **2Ch 15:11** 935
He **b** into the house of God the **2Ch 15:18** 935
Then Asa **b** out silver and gold **2Ch 16:2** 3318
Then King Asa **b** all Judah, and **2Ch 16:6** 3947
Judah **b** tribute to Jehoshaphat, **2Ch 17:5** 5414
Some of the Philistines **b** **2Ch 17:11** 935
the Arabians also **b** him flocks, **2Ch 17:11** 935
and **b** them back to the LORD, **2Ch 19:4** 7725
they **b** him to Jehu, put him to **2Ch 22:9** 935
Then they **b** out the king's son and **2Ch 23:11** 3318
Jehoiada the priest **b** out the **2Ch 23:14** 3318
and **b** the king down from the house **2Ch 23:20** 3381
people rejoiced and **b** in their levies **2Ch 24:10** 935
the chest was **b** in to the king's officer **2Ch 24:11** 935
they **b** the rest of the money **2Ch 24:14** 935
b them to the top of the cliff and **2Ch 25:12** 935
he **b** the gods of the sons of Seir, **2Ch 25:14** 935
and **b** him to Jerusalem and **2Ch 25:23** 935
Then they **b** him on horses and **2Ch 25:28** 5375
captives and **b** *them* to Damascus. **2Ch 28:5** 935
and **b** the spoil to Samaria. **2Ch 28:8** 935
on donkeys, and **b** them to Jericho, **2Ch 28:15** 935
for he had **b** about a lack of **2Ch 28:19** 6544a
He **b** in the priests and the **2Ch 29:4** 935
they **b** out to the court of the house **2Ch 29:16** 3318
They **b** seven bulls, seven **2Ch 29:21** 935
Then they **b** the male goats of the **2Ch 29:23** 5066
And the assembly **b** sacrifices and **2Ch 29:31** 935
and all those who were willing **b** **2Ch 29:31**
which the assembly **b** was 70 bulls, **2Ch 29:32** 935
and **b** burnt offerings to the house **2Ch 30:15** 935
and they **b** in abundantly the tithe **2Ch 31:5** 935
also **b** in the tithe of oxen and **2Ch 31:6** 935
be **b** into the house of the LORD, **2Ch 31:10** 935
They faithfully **b** in the **2Ch 31:12** 935
Therefore the LORD **b** the **2Ch 33:11** 935
and **b** him again to Jerusalem to **2Ch 33:13** 7725
that was **b** into the house of God, **2Ch 34:9** 935
been **b** into the house of the LORD, **2Ch 34:14** 935
Then Shaphan **b** the book to the **2Ch 34:16** 935
And they **b** back word to the king. **2Ch 34:28** 7725
and **b** him to Jerusalem where he **2Ch 35:24** 1980
his brother and **b** him to Egypt. **2Ch 36:4** 935
Nebuchadnezzar also **b** *some* of the **2Ch 36:7** 935
King Nebuchadnezzar sent and **b** him **2Ch 36:10** 935
Therefore He **b** up against them the **2Ch 36:17** 5927
he **b** *them* all to Babylon. **2Ch 36:18** 935
Also King Cyrus **b** out the articles **Ezr 1:7** 3318
had them **b** out by the hand of **Ezr 1:8** 3318
Sheshbazzar **b** them all up with the **Ezr 1:11** 5927
of Assyria, who **b** us up here." **Ezr 4:2** 5927
b them to the temple of Babylon, **Ezr 5:14** 2987
in Jerusalem and **b** to Babylon, **Ezr 6:5** 2987
be returned and **b** to their places **Ezr 6:5** 1981
they **b** us a man of insight of the sons **Ezr 8:18** 935
Then Ezra the priest **b** the law **Ne 8:2** 935
So the people went out and **b** *them* **Ne 8:16** 935
Who chose Abram And **b** him out from **Ne 9:7** 3318
You **b** forth water from a rock for **Ne 9:15** 3318
your God Who **b** you up from Egypt,' **Ne 9:18** 5927
And You **b** them into the land Which **Ne 9:23** 935
then **b** the tithe of the grain, **Ne 13:12** 935
and they **b** *them* into Jerusalem on **Ne 13:15** 935
the same, so that our God **b** on us **Ne 13:18** 935
Vashti to be **b** in to his presence, **Es 1:17** 935
b Haman to the banquet **Es 6:14** 935
"Now a word was **b** to me **Jb 4:12** 1589
have You **b** me out of the womb? **Jb 10:18** 3318
were you **b** forth before the hills? **Jb 15:7** 2342a
they are **b** low and like everything **Jb 24:24** 4355
adversities that the LORD had **b** on him. **Jb 42:11** 935
He **b** me forth also into a broad **Ps 18:19** 3318
Yet You are He who **b** me forth from **Ps 22:9** 1518
You have **b** up my soul from Sheol; **Ps 30:3** 5927
He **b** me up out of the pit of **Ps 40:2** 5927
rejected us and **b** us to dishonor, **Ps 44:9** 3637
who follow her, Will be **b** to You. **Ps 45:14** 935
Behold, I was **b** forth in iniquity, **Ps 51:5** 2342a
You **b** us into the net; You laid an **Ps 66:11** 935
Yet You **b** us out into *a place of* **Ps 66:12** 3318
He **b** forth streams also from the **Ps 78:16** 3318
So He **b** their days to an end in **Ps 78:33** 3615
So He **b** them to His holy land, To **Ps 78:54** 935
ewes with suckling lambs He **b** him To **Ps 78:71** 935
For we are **b** very low. **Ps 79:8** 1809
b you up from the land of Egypt; **Ps 81:10** 5927
have **b** his strongholds to ruin. **Ps 89:40** 7760
He has **b** back their wickedness **Ps 94:23** 7725
b them out with silver and gold, **Ps 105:37** 3318
They asked, and He **b** quail, **Ps 105:40** 935
He **b** forth His people with joy, **Ps 105:43** 3318
He **b** them out of darkness and the **Ps 107:14** 3318
He **b** them out of their distresses. **Ps 107:28** 3318
I was **b** low, and He saved me. **Ps 116:6** 1809
b back the captive ones of Zion, **Ps 126:1** 7725
And **b** Israel out from their midst, **Ps 136:11** 3318
to my cry, For I am **b** very low; **Ps 142:6** 1809
were no depths I was **b** forth, **Pr 8:24** 2342a
Before the hills I was **b** forth; **Pr 8:25** 2342a
king has **b** me into his chambers." **SS 1:4** 935
"He has **b** me to *his* banquet hall, **SS 2:4** 935
I had **b** him to my mother's house, **SS 3:4** 935
"Sons I have reared and **b** up, **Is 1:2** 7311
they have **b** evil on themselves. **Is 3:9** 1580
guided by them are **b** to confusion. **Is 9:16** 1104
man I **b** down *their* inhabitants, **Is 10:13** 3381
harps Have been **b** down to Sheol; **Is 14:11** 3381
homage will be **b** to the LORD of hosts **Is 18:7** 2986
I have neither **b** up young *men nor* **Is 23:4** 1431
has **b** low those who dwell on high, **Is 26:5** 7817
Then you will be **b** low; **Is 29:4** 8213
Now I have **b** it to pass, That you **Is 37:26** 935
"You have not **b** to Me the sheep **Is 43:23** 935
I have called him, I have **b** him, **Is 48:15** 935
His own arm **b** salvation to Him, **Is 59:16** 3467
So My own arm **b** salvation to Me, **Is 63:5** 3467
Where is He who **b** them up out of **Is 63:11** 5927
"Before she travailed, she **b** forth; **Is 66:7** 3205
a nation be **b** forth all at once? **Is 66:8** 3205
she also **b** forth her sons. **Is 66:8** 3205
'Where is the LORD Who **b** us up out **Jer 2:6** 5927
I **b** you into the fruitful land To **Jer 2:7** 935
deeds Have **b** these things to you. **Jer 4:18** 6213a
I **b** them out of the land of Egypt, **Jer 7:22** 3318
punishment they shall be **b** down," **Jer 8:12** 3782
Beaten silver is **b** from Tarshish, **Jer 10:9** 935
I **b** them out of the land of Egypt, **Jer 11:4** 3318
I **b** them up from the land of Egypt, **Jer 11:7** 5927
therefore I **b** on them all the **Jer 11:8** 935
who **b** up the sons of Israel out of **Jer 16:14** 5927
who **b** up the sons of Israel from **Jer 16:15** 5927
man who **b** the news To my father, **Jer 20:15** 1319
who **b** up the sons of Israel from **Jer 23:7** 5927
who **b** up and led back the **Jer 23:8** 5927
and had **b** them to Babylon, **Jer 24:1** 935
And they **b** Uriah from Egypt and **Jer 26:23** 3318
shortly be **b** again from Babylon'; **Jer 27:16** 7725
'You **b** Your people Israel out of **Jer 32:21** 3318
'Just as I **b** all this great **Jer 32:42** 935
and **b** them into subjection for **Jer 34:11** 3533
I **b** them out of the land of Egypt, **Jer 34:13** 3318
and you **b** them into subjection to **Jer 34:16** 3533
and I **b** them into the house of the **Jer 35:4** 935
and **b** him to the officials. **Jer 37:14** 935
had Jeremiah the prophet **b** to him **Jer 38:14** 3947
king of Judah are going to be **b** out **Jer 38:22** 3318
and they seized him and **b** him up **Jer 39:5** 5927
and the LORD has **b** it on and done **Jer 40:3** 935
whom he had **b** back from Gibeon. **Jer 41:16** 7725
calamity that I have **b** on Jerusalem **Jer 44:2** 935
opened His armory And has **b** forth **Jer 50:25** 3318
LORD has **b** about our vindication; **Jer 51:10** 3318
Then they captured the king and **b** **Jer 52:9** 5927
fetters and **b** him to Babylon and **Jer 52:11** 935
and **b** them to the king of Babylon **Jer 52:26** 1980
of Judah and **b** him out of prison. **Jer 52:31** 3318
He has **b** *them* down to the ground; **La 2:2** 5060
may be broken and **b** to an end, **Ezk 6:6** 7673a
and **b** me in the visions of God **Ezk 8:3** 935
Then He **b** me to the entrance of **Ezk 8:7** 935
Then He **b** me to the entrance of **Ezk 8:14** 935
Then He **b** me into the inner court **Ezk 8:16** 935
the Spirit lifted me up and **b** me **Ezk 11:1** 935
And the Spirit lifted me up and **b** **Ezk 11:24** 935
By day I **b** out my baggage like the **Ezk 12:7** 3318
I the LORD will be **b** to give him **Ezk 14:4** 6030a
I the LORD will be **b** to answer him **Ezk 14:7** 6030a
be left in it who will be **b** out, **Ezk 14:22** 3318
which I have **b** against Jerusalem **Ezk 14:22** 935
everything which I have **b** upon it. **Ezk 14:22** 935
and **b** it to a land of merchants; **Ezk 17:4** 935
and **b** them to him in Babylon. **Ezk 17:12** 935
'When she **b** up one of her cubs, He **Ezk 19:3** 5927
And they **b** him with hooks To the **Ezk 19:4** 935
And **b** him to the king of Babylon; **Ezk 19:9** 935
They **b** him in hunting nets So that **Ezk 19:9** 935
and **b** them into the wilderness. **Ezk 20:10** 935
whose sight I had **b** them out. **Ezk 20:14** 3318
in whose sight I had **b** them out. **Ezk 20:22** 3318
"When I had **b** them into the land **Ezk 20:28** 935
Thus you have **b** your day near and **Ezk 22:4** 7126
way I have **b** upon their heads," **Ezk 22:31** 5414
your lewdness and your harlotry **b** **Ezk 23:27**
and drunkards were **b** from the **Ezk 23:42** 935
and ebony they **b** as your payment. **Ezk 27:15** 7725
have **b** you Into great waters; **Ezk 27:26** 935
have **b** fire from the midst of you; **Ezk 28:18** 3318
not be **b** together or gathered. **Ezk 29:5** 622
Will be **b** in to destroy the land; **Ezk 30:11** 935
Yet you will be **b** down with the **Ezk 31:18** 3381
the scattered you have not **b** back, **Ezk 34:4** 7725
and He **b** me out by the Spirit of **Ezk 37:1** 3318
were **b** out from the nations, **Ezk 38:8** 3318
was upon me and He **b** me there. **Ezk 40:1** 935
He **b** me into the land of Israel and **Ezk 40:2** 935
So He **b** me there; **Ezk 40:3** 935
for you have been **b** here in order **Ezk 40:4** 935
Then he **b** me into the outer court, **Ezk 40:17** 935
Then he **b** me to the inner court by **Ezk 40:28** 935
He **b** me into the inner court **Ezk 40:32** 935
Then he **b** me to the north gate; **Ezk 40:35** 935
Then he **b** me to the porch of the **Ezk 40:48** 935
Then he **b** me to the nave and **Ezk 41:1** 935
he **b** me out into the outer court, **Ezk 42:1** 3318
and he **b** me to the chamber which **Ezk 42:1** 935
he **b** me out by the way of the gate **Ezk 42:15** 3318
up and **b** me into the inner court; **Ezk 43:5** 935
Then He **b** me back by the way of **Ezk 44:1** 7725
Then He **b** me by way of the north **Ezk 44:4** 935
when you **b** in foreigners, **Ezk 44:7** 935
Then he **b** me through the entrance, **Ezk 46:19** 935
Then he **b** me out into the outer **Ezk 46:21** 3318
Then he **b** me back to the door of **Ezk 47:1** 7725
He **b** me out by way of the **Ezk 47:2** 3318
Then he **b** me back to the bank of **Ezk 47:6** 7725
he **b** them to the land of Shinar, **Da 1:2** 935
and he **b** the vessels into the **Da 1:2** 935
Then Arioch hurriedly **b** Daniel **Da 2:25** 5954
and **b** charges against the Jews. **Da 3:8** 399
these men were **b** before the king. **Da 3:13** 858
Then they **b** the gold vessels that **Da 5:3** 858
Daniel was **b** in before the king. **Da 5:13** 5954
my father the king **b** from Judah? **Da 5:13** 858
the conjurers were **b** in before me **Da 5:15** 5954
and they have **b** the vessels of His **Da 5:23** 858
and Daniel was **b** in and cast into **Da 6:16** 858
A stone was **b** and laid over **Da 6:17** 858
no entertainment was **b** before him; **Da 6:18** 5954
and they **b** those men who had **Da 6:24** 858
calamity in store and **b** it on us; **Da 9:14** 935
who have **b** Your people out of the **Da 9:15** 3318
up, along with those who **b** her in and **Da 11:6** 935
the LORD **b** Israel from Egypt, **Hos 12:13** 5927
b My precious treasures to your **Jl 3:5** 935
b you up from the land of Egypt, **Am 2:10** 5927
He **b** up from the land of Egypt: **Am 3:1** 5927
"Have I not **b** up Israel from the **Am 9:7** 5927

have **b** up my life from the pit, Jon 2:6 5927
I **b** you up from the land of Egypt Mi 6:4 5927
pride of Assyria will be **b** down And Zch 10:11 3381
they **b** to Him all who were ill, Mt 4:24 *4374*
they **b** to Him many who were Mt 8:16 *4374*
And they **b** to Him a paralytic lying Mt 9:2 *4374*
demon-possessed man was **b** to Him. Mt 9:32 *4374*
and you will even be **b** before Mt 10:18 *71*
blind and mute was **b** to Jesus, Mt 12:22 *4374*
And his head was **b** on a platter Mt 14:11 *5342*
and she **b** it to her mother. Mt 14:11 *5342*
and **b** to Him all who were sick; Mt 14:35 *4374*
"I **b** him to Your disciples, Mt 17:16 *4374*
ten thousand talents was **b** to him. Mt 18:24 *4317*
Then *some* children were **b** to Him Mt 19:13 *4374*
and **b** the donkey and the colt, and Mt 21:7 *71*
And they **b** Him a denarius. Mt 22:19 *4374*
came up and **b** five more talents, Mt 25:20 *4374*
"A lamp is not **b** to be put under Mk 4:21 *2064*
Is it not **b** to be put on Mk 4:21
and **b** his head on a platter, and Mk 6:28 *5342*
They **b** to Him one who was deaf Mk 7:32 *5342*
And they **b** a blind man to Jesus and Mk 8:22 *5342*
hand, He **b** him out of the village; Mk 8:23 *1627*
and **b** them up on a high mountain Mk 9:2 *399*
"Teacher, I **b** You my son, Mk 9:17 *5342*
They **b** the boy to Him. Mk 9:20 *5342*
They **b** the colt to Jesus and Mk 11:7 *5342*
They **b** *one.* And He said to them, Mk 12:16 *5342*
they **b** Him to the place Golgotha, Mk 15:22 *5342*
"He has **b** down rulers from *their* Lk 1:52 *2507*
they **b** Him up to Jerusalem to Lk 2:22 *321*
the parents **b** in the child Jesus, Lk 2:27 *1521*
MOUNTAIN AND HILL WILL BE **B** LOW; Lk 3:5 *5013*
Nazareth, where He had been **b** up; Lk 4:16 *5142*
various diseases **b** them to Him; Lk 4:40 *71*
they had **b** their boats to land, Lk 5:11 *2609*
b an alabaster vial of perfume, Lk 7:37 *2865*
You will be **b** down to Hades! Lk 10:15 *2597*
own beast, and **b** him to an inn and Lk 10:34 *71*
and commanded that he be **b** to Him; Lk 18:40 *71*
They **b** it to Jesus, and they Lk 19:35 *71*
and **b** Him to the house of the high Lk 22:54 *1521*
up and **b** Him before Pilate. Lk 23:1 *71*
"You **b** this man to me as one who Lk 23:14 *4374*
He **b** him to Jesus. Jn 1:42 *71*
"No one **b** Him *anything* to eat, Jn 4:33 *5342*
b a woman caught in adultery, Jn 8:3 *71*
They **b** to the Pharisees the man who Jn 9:13 *71*
to the doorkeeper, and **b** Peter in. Jn 18:16 *1521*
heard these words, he **b** Jesus out, Jn 19:13 *71*
hyssop and **b** it up to His mouth. Jn 19:29 *4374*
sold it and **b** the money and laid Ac 4:37 *5342*
the prison house for them to be **b**. Ac 5:21 *71*
When they had **b** them, Ac 5:27 *71*
these they **b** before the apostles; Ac 6:6 *2476*
and **b** him before the Council. Ac 6:12 *71*
and **b** a sacrifice to the idol, Ac 7:41 *321*
our fathers **b** it in with Joshua Ac 7:45 *1521*
hand, they **b** him into Damascus. Ac 9:8 *1521*
Barnabas took hold of him and **b** him Ac 9:27 *71*
they **b** him down to Caesarea and Ac 9:30 *2609*
they **b** him into the upper room; Ac 9:39 *321*
who is also called Peter, **b** here; Ac 11:13 *3343*
numbers were **b** to the Lord. Ac 11:24 *4369*
found him, he **b** him to Antioch. Ac 11:26 *71*
been **b** up with Herod the tetrarch, Ac 13:1 *4939*
God has **b** to Israel a Savior, Ac 13:23 *71*
b oxen and garlands to the gates, Ac 14:13 *5342*
b them to the chief magistrates, Ac 16:20 *4317*
and after he **b** them out, he said, Ac 16:30 *4254*
And he **b** them into his house and Ac 16:34 *321*
and when they had **b** them out, Ac 16:39 *1806*
Paul **b** him as far as Athens; Ac 17:15 *71*
him and **b** him to the Areopagus, Ac 17:19 *71*
b him before the judgment seat, Ac 18:12 *71*
practiced magic **b** their books together Ac 19:19 *4851a*
"For you have **b** these men *here* Ac 19:37 *71*
and besides he has even **b** Greeks Ac 21:28 *1521*
Paul had **b** him into the temple. Ac 21:29 *1521*
him to be **b** into the barracks. Ac 21:34 *71*
about to be **b** into the barracks, Ac 21:37 *1521*
of Cilicia, but **b** up in this city, Ac 22:3 *397*
him to be **b** into the barracks, Ac 22:24 *1521*
and **b** Paul down and set him before Ac 22:30 *2609*
I **b** him down to their Council; Ac 23:28 *2609*
and **b** him by night to Antipatris. Ac 23:31 *71*
and they **b** charges to the governor Ac 24:1 *1718*
the Jews **b** charges against Paul, Ac 25:2 *1718*
he might have him **b** to Jerusalem Ac 25:3 *3343*
tribunal and ordered Paul to be **b**. Ac 25:6 *71*
of the Jews **b** charges against him, Ac 25:15 *1718*
and ordered the man to be **b** before Ac 25:17 *71*
command of Festus, Paul was **b** in. Ac 25:23 *71*
Therefore I have **b** him before you Ac 25:26 *4254*
they all were **b** safely to land. Ac 27:44 *1295*
they had been **b** safely through, Ac 28:1 *1295*
of the false brethren secretly **b** in, Ga 2:4 *3920*
which He **b** about in Christ, when Eph 1:20 *1754*
b near by the blood of Christ. Eph 2:13 *1096*
and has **b** us good news of your 1Th 3:6 *2097*
and if she has **b** up children, if 1Tm 5:10 *5044*
we have **b** nothing into the world, 1Tm 6:7 *1533*
and **b** life and immortality to 2Tm 1:10 *5461*
animals whose blood is **b** into the holy Heb 13:11 *1533*
who **b** up from the dead the great Heb 13:20 *321*
b us forth by the word of truth, Jas 1:18 *616*
grace to be **b** to you at the revelation 1Pe 1:13 *5342*
were **b** safely through *the* water. 1Pe 3:20 *1295*
when He **b** a flood upon the world 2Pe 2:5 *1863*

BROW
and led Him to the **b** of the hill Lk 4:29 *3790*

BRUISE
He shall **b** you on the head, And Gn 3:15 7779
And you shall **b** him on the heel." Gn 3:15 7779
wound for wound, **b** for bruise. Ex 21:25 2250
wound for wound, bruise for **b**. Ex 21:25 2250
and heals the **b** He has inflicted. Is 30:26 4273

BRUISED
b or crushed or torn or cut, Lv 22:24 4600
"A **b** reed He will not break And Is 42:3 7533

BRUISES
"For He **b** me with a tempest And Jb 9:17 7779
is nothing sound in it, *Only* **b**, Is 1:6 6482

BRUSHWOOD
As fire kindles the **b**, Is 64:2 2003

BRUTAL
give you into the hand of **b** men, Ezk 21:31 1197b
gossips, without self-control, **b**, 2Tm 3:3 *434*

BUBBLING
fountain of wisdom is a **b** brook. Pr 18:4 5042

BUCKET
nations are like a drop from a **b**, Is 40:15 1805

BUCKETS
"Water will flow from his **b**, Nu 24:7 1805

BUCKLER
Take hold of **b** and shield And Ps 35:2 4043
"Line up the shield and **b**, Jer 46:3 6793c
side with **b** and shield and helmet; Ezk 23:24 6793c
a great company *with* **b** and shield, Ezk 38:4 6793c

BUCKLERS
and burn *them,* both shields and **b**, Ezk 39:9 6793c

BUD
in the ear and the flax was in **b**. Ex 9:31 1392
as soon as the **b** blossoms And the Is 18:5 6525

BUDDED
To see whether the vine had **b** *Or* SS 6:11 6524a
b *And its* blossoms have opened, SS 7:12 6524a
the rod has **b**, arrogance has Ezk 7:10 6692a
the manna, and Aaron's rod which **b**, Heb 9:4 *985*

BUDDING
And as it was **b**, its blossoms came Gn 40:10 6524a

BUDS
put forth **b** and produced blossoms, Nu 17:8 6525

BUGLE
b produces an indistinct sound, 1Co 14:8 *4536*

BUILD
let us **b** for ourselves a city, Gn 11:4 1129
you shall not **b** it of cut stones, Ex 20:25 1129
"**B** seven altars for me here, and Nu 23:1 1129
"**B** seven altars for me here and Nu 23:29 1129
"We will **b** here sheepfolds for Nu 32:16 1129
"**B** yourselves cities for your Nu 32:24 1129
cities which you did not **b**, Dt 6:10 1129
"When you **b** a new house, you Dt 22:8 1129
does not **b** up his brother's house.' Dt 25:9 1129
you shall **b** there an altar to the Dt 27:5 1129
"You shall **b** the altar of the Dt 27:6 1129
you shall **b** a house, but you will Dt 28:30 1129
'Let us **b** an altar, not for burnt Jos 22:26 6213a, 1129
and **b** an altar to the LORD your Jg 6:26 1129
I will **b** him an enduring house, 1Sa 2:35 1129
should **b** Me a house to dwell in? 2Sa 7:5 1129
"He shall **b** a house for My name, 2Sa 7:13 1129
'I will **b** you a house'; 2Sa 7:27 1129
order to **b** an altar to the LORD, 2Sa 24:21 1129
"**B** for yourself a house in 1Ki 2:36 1129
that David my father was unable to **b** 1Ki 5:3 1129
I intend to **b** a house for the name 1Ki 5:5 1129
he will **b** the house for My name.' 1Ki 5:5 1129
and the stones to **b** the house. 1Ki 5:18 1129
began to **b** the house of the LORD. 1Ki 6:1 1129
to **b** a house that My name might be 1Ki 8:16 1129
heart of my father David to **b** a house 1Ki 8:17 1129
heart to **b** a house for My name, 1Ki 8:18 1129
you shall not **b** the house, 1Ki 8:19 1129
he will **b** the house for My name.' 1Ki 8:19 1129
levied to **b** the house of the LORD, 1Ki 9:15 1129
pleased Solomon to **b** in Jerusalem, 1Ki 9:19 1129
then I will be with you and **b** you 1Ki 11:38 1129
carpenters, to **b** a house for him. 1Ch 14:1 1129
not **b** a house for Me to dwell in; 1Ch 17:4 1129
the LORD will **b** a house for you. 1Ch 17:10 1129
"He shall **b** for Me a house, and I 1Ch 17:12 1129
that You will **b** for him a house; 1Ch 17:25 1129
that David should go up and **b** an 1Ch 21:18 6965
may **b** on it an altar to the LORD; 1Ch 21:22 1129
out stones to **b** the house of God. 1Ch 22:2 1129
and charged him to **b** a house for 1Ch 22:6 1129
I had intended to **b** a house to the 1Ch 22:7 1129
shall not **b** a house to My name, 1Ch 22:8 1129
'He shall **b** a house for My name, 1Ch 22:10 1129
and **b** the house of the LORD your 1Ch 22:11 1129
b the sanctuary of the LORD God, 1Ch 22:19 1129
I *had* intended to **b** a permanent 1Ch 28:2 1129
I had made preparations to **b** *it.* 1Ch 28:2 1129
'You shall not **b** a house for My 1Ch 28:3 1129
shall **b** My house and My courts; 1Ch 28:6 1129
to **b** a house for the sanctuary; 1Ch 28:10 1129
to **b** You a house for Your holy name, 1Ch 29:16 1129
do *them* all, and to **b** the temple, 1Ch 29:19 1129
Now Solomon decided to **b** a house 2Ch 2:1 1129
to **b** him a house to dwell in, 2Ch 2:3 1129
I am about to **b** a house for the 2Ch 2:4 1129
I am about to **b** *will be* great, 2Ch 2:5 1129
who is able to **b** a house for Him, 2Ch 2:6 1129
that I should **b** a house for Him, 2Ch 2:6 1129
to **b** *will be* great and wonderful. 2Ch 2:9 1129
who will **b** a house for the LORD 2Ch 2:12 1129
Then Solomon began to **b** the house 2Ch 3:1 1129
He began to **b** on the second 2Ch 3:2 1129
tribes of Israel *in which* to **b** a house 2Ch 6:5 1129
heart of my father David to **b** a house 2Ch 6:7 1129
heart to **b** a house for My name, 2Ch 6:8 1129
you shall not **b** the house, 2Ch 6:9 1129
he shall **b** the house for My name.' 2Ch 6:9 1129
pleased Solomon to **b** in Jerusalem, 2Ch 8:6 1129
"Let us **b** these cities and 2Ch 14:7 1129
me to **b** Him a house in Jerusalem, 2Ch 36:23 1129
me to **b** Him a house in Jerusalem, Ezr 1:2 1129
"Let us **b** with you, for we, like Ezr 4:2 1129
b to the LORD God of Israel, Ezr 4:3 1129
"Let us arise and **b**." Ne 2:18 1129
we His servants will arise and **b**, Ne 2:20 1129
And **b** up their way against me And Jb 19:12 5549
They thrust aside my feet and **b** up Jb 30:12 5549
tear them down and not **b** them up. Ps 28:5 1129
B the walls of Jerusalem. Ps 51:18 1129
Zion and **b** the cities of Judah, Ps 69:35 1129
And **b** up your throne to all Ps 89:4 1129
Where the birds **b** their nests, *And* Ps 104:17 7077
They labor in vain who **b** it; Ps 127:1 1129
Afterwards, then, **b** your house. Pr 24:27 1129
to tear down and a time to **b** up. Ec 3:3 1129
b on her a battlement of silver; SS 8:9 1129
He will **b** My city and will let My Is 45:13 1129
"**B** up, build up, prepare the way, Is 57:14 5549
"Build up, **b** up, prepare the way, Is 57:14 5549
Foreigners will **b** up your walls, Is 60:10 1129
B up, build up the highway, Is 62:10 5549
Build up, **b** up the highway, Is 62:10 5549
will **b** houses and inhabit *them;* Is 65:21 1129
"They will not **b** and another Is 65:22 1129
is a house you could **b** for Me? Is 66:1 1129
to overthrow, To **b** and to plant." Jer 1:10 1129
a kingdom to **b** up or to plant *it;* Jer 18:9 1129
'I will **b** myself a roomy house Jer 22:14 1129
and I will **b** them up and not Jer 24:6 1129
'**B** houses and live *in them;* Jer 29:5 1129
b houses and live *in them* and Jer 29:28 1129
"Again I will **b** you and you Jer 31:4 1129
over them to **b** and to plant," Jer 31:28 1129
'You shall not **b** a house, Jer 35:7 1129
to **b** ourselves houses to dwell in; Jer 35:9 1129
I will **b** you up and not tear you down, Jer 42:10 1129
siege against it, **b** a siege wall, Ezk 4:2 1129
'*The time* is not near to **b** houses. Ezk 11:3 1129
nor did you **b** the wall around the Ezk 13:5 1443
when they cast up ramps and **b** Ezk 17:17 1129
cast up ramps, to **b** a siege wall. Ezk 21:22 1129
who would **b** up the wall and stand in Ezk 22:30 1443
and they will **b** houses, plant Ezk 28:26 1129
And I will **b** a wall against her so Hos 2:6 1443
"Though you **b** high like the Ob 1:4 1361b
Who **b** Zion with bloodshed And Mi 3:10 1129
b houses but not inhabit *them,* Zph 1:13 1129
"To **b** a temple for her in the Zch 5:11 1129
He will **b** the temple of the LORD. Zch 6:12 1129
who will **b** the temple of the LORD, Zch 6:13 1129
and **b** the temple of the LORD." Zch 6:15 1129
will return and **b** up the ruins"; Mal 1:4 1129
"They may **b**, but I will tear down; Mal 1:4 1129
upon this rock I will **b** My church; Mt 16:18 *3618*
For you **b** the tombs of the Mt 23:29 *3618*
b another made without hands.' " Mk 14:58 *3618*
you **b** the tombs of the prophets, Lk 11:47 *3618*
them, and you **b** *their tombs.* Lk 11:48 *3618*
down my barns and **b** larger ones, Lk 12:18 *3618*
you, when he wants to **b** a tower, Lk 14:28 *3618*
to **b** and was not able to finish.' Lk 14:30 *3618*
forty-six years to **b** this temple, Jn 2:20 *3618*
KIND OF HOUSE WILL YOU **B** FOR ME? Ac 7:49 *3618*
which is able to **b** *you* up and to Ac 20:32 *3618*
b on another man's foundation; Ro 15:20 *3618*
one another and **b** up one another, 1Th 5:11 *3618*

BUILDER
wise master **b** I laid a foundation, 1Co 3:10 *753*
by just so much as the **b** of the Heb 3:3 *2680*
but the **b** of all things is God. Heb 3:4 *2680*
whose architect and **b** is God. Heb 11:10 *1217*

BUILDERS
So Solomon's **b** and Hiram's 1Ki 5:18 1129
b and the Gebalites cut them, 1Ki 5:18 1129
out to the carpenters and the **b** who 2Ki 12:11 1129
to the carpenters and the **b** and 2Ki 22:6 1129
gave *it* to the carpenters and to the **b** 2Ch 34:11 1129
Now when the **b** had laid the Ezr 3:10 1129
for they have demoralized the **b**. Ne 4:5 1129
As for the **b**, each *wore* his sword Ne 4:18 1129
The stone which the **b** rejected Has Ps 118:22 1129
"Your **b** hurry; Is 49:17 1121
Your **b** have perfected your beauty. Ezk 27:4 1129
'THE STONE WHICH THE **B** REJECTED, Mt 21:42 *3618*
'THE STONE WHICH THE **B** REJECTED, Mk 12:10 *3618*
'THE STONE WHICH THE **B** REJECTED, Lk 20:17 *3618*
WHICH WAS REJECTED by you, THE **B**, Ac 4:11 *3620b*
"THE STONE WHICH THE **B** REJECTED, 1Pe 2:7 *3618*

BUILDING
and they stopped **b** the city. Gn 11:8 1129
day, by **b** yourselves an altar, Jos 22:16 1129
us by **b** an altar for yourselves, Jos 22:19 1129
by **b** an altar for burnt offering, Jos 22:29 1129

until he had finished **b** his own 1Ki 3:1 1129
this house which you are **b**, 1Ki 6:12 1129
So he was seven years in **b** it. 1Ki 6:38 1129
b his own house thirteen years, 1Ki 7:1 1129
finished **b** the house of the LORD, 1Ki 9:1 1129
laid for **b** the house of God. 2Ch 3:3 1129
with which Baasha had been **b**, 2Ch 16:6 1129
the people of the exile were **b** a temple Ezr 4:1 1129
with us in **b** a house to our God; Ezr 4:3 1129
Judah, and frightened them from **b**, Ezr 4:4 1129
who were reconstructing this **b**. Ezr 5:4 1147
b through the prophesying of Haggai Ezr 6:14 1124
And they finished **b** according to Ezr 6:14 1124
and he said, "Even what they are **b** Ne 4:3 1129
The **b** that *was* in front of the Ezk 41:12 1146
and the wall of the **b** *was* five Ezk 41:12 1146
the separate area with the **b** and Ezk 41:13 1140
He measured the length of the **b** along Ezk 41:15 1146
opposite the **b** toward the north. Ezk 42:1 1146
lower and middle ones in the **b**. Ezk 42:5 1146
separate area and facing the **b**, Ezk 42:10 1146
It will be a day for **b** your walls. Mi 7:11 1129
he is like a man **b** a house, Lk 6:48 *3618*
they were planting, they were **b**; Lk 17:28 *3618*
peace and the **b** up of one another. Ro 14:19 *3619*
you are God's field, God's **b**. 1Co 3:9 *3619*
and another is **b** on it. 1Co 3:10 *2026*
torn down, we have a **b** from God, 2Co 5:1 *3619*
which the Lord gave for **b** you up 2Co 10:8 *3619*
for **b** up and not for tearing down. 2Co 13:10 *3619*
in whom the whole **b**, Eph 2:21 *3619*
to the **b** up of the body of Christ; Eph 4:12 *3619*
for the **b** up of itself in love. Eph 4:16 *3619*
b yourselves up on your most holy Jude 1:20 *2026*

BUILDINGS

of the porch *of the temple,* its **b**, 1Ch 28:11 1004
to overlay the walls of the **b**; 1Ch 29:4 1004
all its fortified **b** with fire and 2Ch 36:19 759
to point out the temple **b** to Him. Mt 24:1 *3619*
stones and what wonderful **b**!" Mk 13:1 *3619*
"Do you see these great **b**? Mk 13:2 *3619*

BUILDS

rises up and **b** this city Jericho; Jos 6:26 1129
Unless the LORD **b** the house, They Ps 127:1 1129
The LORD **b** up Jerusalem; Ps 147:2 1129
The wise woman **b** her house, But Pr 14:1 1129
"Woe to him who **b** his house Jer 22:13 1129
And when anyone **b** a wall, behold, Ezk 13:10 1129
The One who **b** His upper chambers Am 9:6 1129
"Woe to him who **b** a city with Hab 2:12 1129
man must be careful how he **b** on it. 1Co 3:10 *2026*
b on the foundation with gold, 1Co 3:12 *2026*

BUILT

and he **b** a city, and called the Gn 4:17 1129
Then Noah **b** an altar to the LORD, Gn 8:20 1129
and **b** Nineveh and Rehoboth-Ir and Gn 10:11 1129
tower which the sons of men had **b**. Gn 11:5 1129
So he **b** an altar there to the LORD Gn 12:7 1129
and there he **b** an altar to the Gn 12:8 1129
there he **b** an altar to the LORD. Gn 13:18 1129
and Abraham **b** the altar there and Gn 22:9 1129
So he **b** an altar there and called Gn 26:25 1129
and **b** for himself a house and Gn 33:17 1129
He **b** an altar there, and Gn 35:7 1129
they **b** for Pharaoh storage cities, Ex 1:11 1129
Moses **b** an altar and named it Ex 17:15 1129
and **b** an altar at the foot of the Ex 24:4 1129
saw *this,* he **b** an altar before it; Ex 32:5 1129
(Now Hebron was **b** seven years Nu 13:22 1129
"Come to Heshbon! Let it be **b**! Nu 21:27 1129
and **b** seven altars and offered a Nu 23:14 1129
Gad **b** Dibon and Ataroth and Aroer, Nu 32:34 1129
The sons of Reuben **b** Heshbon Nu 32:37 1129
names to the cities which they **b**. Nu 32:38 1129
b good houses and lived *in them,* Dt 8:12 1129
'Who is the man that has **b** a new Dt 20:5 1129
Joshua **b** an altar to the LORD, Jos 8:30 1129
he **b** the city and settled in it. Jos 19:50 1129
b an altar there by the Jordan, Jos 22:10 1129
half-tribe of Manasseh have **b** an altar Jos 22:11 1129
"If we have **b** us an altar to turn Jos 22:23 1129
and cities which you had not **b**, Jos 24:13 1129
Hittites and **b** a city and named it Luz Jg 1:26 1129
Then Gideon **b** an altar there to Jg 6:24 1129
on the altar which had been **b**. Jg 6:28 1129
arose early and **b** an altar there and Jg 21:4 1129
of whom **b** the house of Israel; Ru 4:11 1129
he **b** there an altar to the LORD. 1Sa 7:17 1129
And Saul **b** an altar to the LORD; 1Sa 14:35 1129
first altar that he **b** to the LORD. 1Sa 14:35 1129
And David **b** all around from the 2Sa 5:9 1129
and they **b** a house for David. 2Sa 5:11 1129
not **b** Me a house of cedar? 2Sa 7:7 1129
b there an altar to the LORD and 2Sa 24:25 1129
because there was no house **b** for 1Ki 3:2 1129
which King Solomon **b** for the LORD, 1Ki 6:2 1129
Against the wall of the house he **b** 1Ki 6:5 1129
The house, while it was being **b**, 1Ki 6:7 1129
was **b** of stone prepared at the 1Ki 6:7 1129
in the house while it was being **b**. 1Ki 6:7 1129
So he **b** the house and finished it; 1Ki 6:9 1129
He also **b** the stories against the 1Ki 6:10 1129
b the house and finished it. 1Ki 6:14 1129
Then he **b** the walls of the house 1Ki 6:15 1129
He **b** twenty cubits on the rear 1Ki 6:16 1129
he **b** *them* for it on the inside as 1Ki 6:16 1129
He **b** the inner court with 1Ki 6:36 1129
He **b** the house of the forest 1Ki 7:2 1129
have surely **b** You a lofty house, 1Ki 8:13 1129
and have **b** the house for the name 1Ki 8:20 1129
less this house which I have **b**! 1Ki 8:27 1129
I have **b** is called by Your name. 1Ki 8:43 1129
house which I have **b** for Your name, 1Ki 8:44 1129
house which I have **b** for Your name; 1Ki 8:48 1129
house which you have **b** by putting 1Ki 9:3 1129
Solomon had **b** the two houses, 1Ki 9:10 1129
house which *Solomon* had **b** for her, 1Ki 9:24 1129
for her, then he **b** the Millo. 1Ki 9:24 1129
the altar which he **b** to the LORD, 1Ki 9:25 1129
King Solomon also **b** a fleet of 1Ki 9:26 6213a
Solomon, the house that he had **b**, 1Ki 10:4 1129
Then Solomon **b** a high place for 1Ki 11:7 1129
Solomon **b** the Millo, *and* closed up 1Ki 11:27 1129
enduring house as I **b** for David, 1Ki 11:38 1129
Then Jeroboam **b** Shechem in the 1Ki 12:25 1129
went out from there and **b** Penuel. 1Ki 12:25 1129
For they also **b** for themselves 1Ki 14:23 1129
timber with which Baasha had **b**. 1Ki 15:22 1129
And King Asa **b** with them Geba of 1Ki 15:22 1129
he did and the cities which he **b**, 1Ki 15:23 1129
and he **b** on the hill, and named 1Ki 16:24 1129
named the city which he **b** Samaria, 1Ki 16:24 1129
of Baal which he **b** in Samaria. 1Ki 16:32 1129
days Hiel the Bethelite **b** Jericho; 1Ki 16:34 1129
So with the stones he **b** an altar 1Ki 18:32 1129
house which he **b** and all the cities 1Ki 22:39 1129
and all the cities which he **b**, 1Ki 22:39 1129
He **b** Elath and restored it to 2Ki 14:22 1129
He **b** the upper gate of the house 2Ki 15:35 1129
So Urijah the priest **b** an altar; 2Ki 16:11 1129
which they had **b** in the house, 2Ki 16:18 1129
they **b** for themselves high places 2Ki 17:9 1129
He **b** altars in the house of 2Ki 21:4 1129
For he **b** altars for all the host 2Ki 21:5 1129
Solomon the king of Israel had **b** for 2Ki 23:13 1129
and **b** a siege wall all around it. 2Ki 25:1 1129
which Solomon **b** in Jerusalem), 1Ch 6:10 1129
until Solomon had **b** the house of 1Ch 6:32 1129
who **b** lower and upper Beth-horon, 1Ch 7:24 1129
and Shemed, who **b** Ono and Lod, 1Ch 8:12 1129
He **b** the city all around, from 1Ch 11:8 1129
Now *David* **b** houses for himself in 1Ch 15:1 6213a
b for Me a house of cedar? 1Ch 17:6 1129
b an altar to the LORD there and 1Ch 21:26 1129
and the house that is to be **b** for 1Ch 22:5 1129
be **b** for the name of the LORD." 1Ch 22:19 1129
"I have **b** You a lofty house, And 2Ch 6:2 1129
and have **b** the house for the name 2Ch 6:10 1129
less this house which I have **b**. 2Ch 6:18 1129
I have **b** is called by Your name. 2Ch 6:33 1129
house which I have **b** for Your name, 2Ch 6:34 1129
house which I have **b** for Your name, 2Ch 6:38 1129
Solomon had **b** the house of the LORD 2Ch 8:1 1129
that he **b** the cities which Huram 2Ch 8:2 1129
He **b** Tadmor in the wilderness 2Ch 8:4 1129
cities which he had **b** in Hamath. 2Ch 8:4 1129
He also **b** upper Beth-horon and 2Ch 8:5 1129
the house which he had **b** for her, 2Ch 8:11 1129
which he had **b** before the porch; 2Ch 8:12 1129
Solomon, the house which he had **b**, 2Ch 9:3 1129
and **b** cities for defense in Judah. 2Ch 11:5 1129
Thus he **b** Bethlehem, Etam, Tekoa, 2Ch 11:6 1129
He **b** fortified cities in Judah, 2Ch 14:6 1129
So they **b** and prospered. 2Ch 14:7 1129
and he **b** fortresses and store 2Ch 17:12 1129
and have **b** You a sanctuary there 2Ch 20:8 1129
He **b** Eloth and restored it to 2Ch 26:2 1129
and he **b** cities in *the area of* 2Ch 26:6 1129
Uzziah **b** towers in Jerusalem at 2Ch 26:9 1129
He **b** towers in the wilderness 2Ch 26:10 1129
He **b** the upper gate of the house 2Ch 27:3 1129
b extensively the wall of Ophel. 2Ch 27:3 1129
he **b** cities in the hill country of 2Ch 27:4 1129
and he **b** fortresses and towers on 2Ch 27:4 1129
and **b** another outside wall 2Ch 32:5
He **b** altars in the house of 2Ch 33:4 1129
For he **b** altars for all the host 2Ch 33:5 1129
Now after this he **b** the outer wall 2Ch 33:14 1129
altars which he had **b** on the mountain 2Ch 33:15 1129
and the sites on which he **b** high 2Ch 33:19 1129
the son of David king of Israel **b**; 2Ch 35:3 1129
and his brothers arose and **b** the Ezr 3:2 1129
which is being **b** with huge stones, Ezr 5:8 1124
temple that was **b** many years ago, Ezr 5:11 1124
king of Israel **b** and finished. Ezr 5:11 1124
the priests and **b** the Sheep Gate; Ne 3:1 1129
Next to him the men of Jericho **b**, Ne 3:2 1129
to them Zaccur the son of Imri **b**. Ne 3:2 1129
sons of Hassenaah **b** the Fish Gate; Ne 3:3 1129
They **b** it and hung its doors with Ne 3:13 1129
He **b** it and hung its doors with Ne 3:14 1129
He **b** it, covered it and hung its Ne 3:15 1129
So we **b** the wall and the whole Ne 4:6 1129
sword girded at his side as he **b**, Ne 4:18 1129
few and the houses were not **b**. Ne 7:4 1129
for the singers had **b** themselves Ne 12:29 1129
seized a house which he has not **b**. Jb 20:19 1129
"He has **b** his house like the Jb 27:18 1129
And He **b** His sanctuary like the Ps 78:69 1129
will be **b** up forever; Ps 89:2 1129
For the LORD has **b** up Zion; Ps 102:16 1129
that is **b** As a city that is Ps 122:3 1129
Wisdom has **b** her house, She has Pr 9:1 1129
By wisdom a house is **b**, Pr 24:3 1129
I **b** houses for myself, I planted Ec 2:4 1129
of David, **B** with rows of stones SS 4:4 1129
He **b** a tower in the middle of it And Is 5:2 1129
'They shall be **b**.' Is 44:26 1129
'She will be **b**,' And of the Is 44:28 1129
have **b** the high places of Topheth, Jer 7:31 1129
be **b** up in the midst of My people. Jer 12:16 1129
and have **b** the high places of Baal Jer 19:5 1129
wrath from the day that they **b** it, Jer 32:31 1129
"They **b** the high places of Jer 32:35 1129
I have **b** I am about to tear down, Jer 45:4 1129
and **b** a siege wall all around it. Jer 52:4 1129
that you **b** yourself a shrine and Ezk 16:24 1129
"You **b** yourself a high place at Ezk 16:25 1129
"When you **b** your shrine at the Ezk 16:31 1129
You will be **b** no more, for I the Ezk 26:14 1129
for the altar on the day it is **b**, Ezk 43:18 6213a
which I myself have **b** as a royal Da 4:30 1124
it will be **b** again, with plaza and Da 9:25 1129
forgotten his Maker and **b** palaces; Hos 8:14 1129
have **b** houses of well-hewn stone, Am 5:11 1129
My house will be **b** in it," Zch 1:16 1129
end that the temple might be **b**. Zch 8:9 1129
For Tyre **b** herself a fortress And Zch 9:3 1129
are the doers of wickedness **b** up but Mal 3:15 1129
who **b** his house on the rock. Mt 7:24 *3618*
who **b** his house on the sand. Mt 7:26 *3618*
A WINE PRESS IN IT, AND **B** A TOWER, Mt 21:33 *3618*
THE WINE PRESS AND **B** A TOWER, Mk 12:1 *3618*
on which their city had been **b**, Lk 4:29 *3618*
it, because it had been well **b**. Lk 6:48 *3618*
is like a man who **b** a house on Lk 6:49 *3618*
was he who **b** us our synagogue." Lk 7:5 *3618*
was Solomon who **b** a house for Him. Ac 7:47 *3618*
Samaria enjoyed peace, being **b** up; Ac 9:31 *3618*
which he has **b** on it remains, 1Co 3:14 *2026*
having been **b** on the foundation Eph 2:20 *2026*
in whom you also are being **b** Eph 2:22 *4925*
rooted *and now* being **b** up in Him Col 2:7 *2026*
For every house is **b** by someone, Heb 3:4 *2680*
are being **b** up as a spiritual 1Pe 2:5 *2026*

BUKKI

Dan a leader, **B** the son of Jogli. Nu 34:22 1231
Abishua became the father of **B**, 1Ch 6:5 1231
and **B** became the father of Uzzi, 1Ch 6:5 1231
B his son, Uzzi his son, Zerahiah 1Ch 6:51 1231
Zerahiah, son of Uzzi, son of **B**, Ezr 7:4 1231

BUKKIAH

B, Mattaniah, Uzziel, Shebuel and 1Ch 25:4 1232
the sixth to **B**, his sons and his 1Ch 25:13 1232

BUL

eleventh year, in the month of **B**, 1Ki 6:38 945

BULB

the one branch, a **b** and a flower, Ex 25:33 3730
in the other branch, a **b** and a flower Ex 25:33 3730
"A **b** shall be under the *first* Ex 25:35 3730
and a **b** under the *second* pair of Ex 25:35 3730
and a **b** under the *third* pair of Ex 25:35 3730
a **b** and a flower in one branch, Ex 37:19 3730
a **b** and a flower in the other Ex 37:19 3730
and a **b** was under the *first* pair Ex 37:21 3730
and a **b** under the *second* pair of Ex 37:21 3730
and a **b** under the *third* pair of Ex 37:21 3730

BULBS

its **b** and its flowers shall be *of one* Ex 25:31 3730
blossoms, its **b** and its flowers. Ex 25:34 3730
"Their **b** and their branches *shall* Ex 25:36 3730
its **b** and its flowers were *of one* Ex 37:17 3730
blossoms, its **b** and its flowers; Ex 37:20 3730
Their **b** and their branches were *of* Ex 37:22 3730

BULGE

about to fall, A **b** in a high wall, Is 30:13 1158

BULGES

Their eye **b** from fatness; Ps 73:7 3318

BULL

b and two rams without blemish, Ex 29:1 6499
along with the **b** and the two rams. Ex 29:3 6499
the **b** before the tent of meeting, Ex 29:10 6499
their hands on the head of the **b**. Ex 29:10 6499
"You shall slaughter the **b** Ex 29:11 6499
blood of the **b** and put *it* on the horns Ex 29:12 6499
the **b** and its hide and its refuse, Ex 29:14 6499
"Each day you shall offer a **b** Ex 29:36 6499
slay the young **b** before the LORD; Lv 1:5 1241
offer to the LORD a **b** without defect Lv 4:3
6499, 1121, 1241
'He shall bring the **b** to the Lv 4:4 6499
lay his hand on the head of the **b** and Lv 4:4 6499
and slay the **b** before the LORD. Lv 4:4 6499
blood of the **b** and bring it to the tent Lv 4:5 6499
and all the blood of the **b** he Lv 4:7 6499
fat of the **b** of the sin offering: Lv 4:8 6499
'But the hide of the **b** and all its Lv 4:11 6499
that is, all *the rest of* the **b**, Lv 4:12 6499
assembly shall offer a **b** of the herd Lv 4:14 6499
the head of the **b** before the LORD, Lv 4:15 6499
and the **b** shall be slain before Lv 4:15 6499
to bring some of the blood of the **b** Lv 4:16 6499
'He shall also do with the **b** just Lv 4:20 6499
with the **b** of the sin offering; Lv 4:20 6499
the **b** to *a place* outside the camp and Lv 4:21 6499
burn it as he burned the first **b**; Lv 4:21 6499
oil and the **b** of the sin offering, Lv 8:2 6499
brought the **b** of the sin offering, Lv 8:14 6499
head of the **b** of the sin offering. Lv 8:14 6499
But the **b** and its hide and its Lv 8:17 6499
"Take for yourself a calf, a **b**, Lv 9:2
1121, 1241
with a **b** for a sin offering and a Lv 16:3
6499, 1121, 1241

“Then Aaron shall offer the **b** for	**Lv 16:6**	6499
“Then Aaron shall offer the **b** of	**Lv 16:11**	6499
and he shall slaughter the **b** of	**Lv 16:11**	6499
blood of the **b** and sprinkle *it* with his	**Lv 16:14**	6499
as he did with the blood of the **b**,	**Lv 16:15**	6499
b and of the blood of the goat and	**Lv 16:18**	6499
“But the **b** of the sin offering	**Lv 16:27**	6499
defect, and a **b** of the herd and	**Lv 23:18**	
		6499, 1121, 1241
one **b**, one ram, one male lamb one	**Nu 7:15**	
		6499, 1121, 1241
one **b**, one ram, one male lamb one	**Nu 7:21**	
		6499, 1121, 1241
one young **b**, one ram, one male	**Nu 7:27**	6499
one **b**, one ram, one male lamb one	**Nu 7:33**	
		6499, 1121, 1241
one **b**, one ram, one male lamb one	**Nu 7:39**	
		6499, 1121, 1241
one **b**, one ram, one male lamb one	**Nu 7:45**	
		6499, 1121, 1241
one **b**, one ram, one male lamb one	**Nu 7:51**	
		6499, 1121, 1241
one **b**, one ram, one male lamb one	**Nu 7:57**	
		6499, 1121, 1241
one **b**, one ram, one male lamb one	**Nu 7:63**	
		6499, 1121, 1241
one **b**, one ram, one male lamb one	**Nu 7:69**	
		6499, 1121, 1241
one **b**, one ram, one male lamb one	**Nu 7:75**	
		6499, 1121, 1241
one **b**, one ram, one male lamb one	**Nu 7:81**	
		6499, 1121, 1241
take a **b** with its grain offering,	**Nu 8:8**	
		6499, 1121, 1241
and a second **b** you shall take for	**Nu 8:8**	6499
“When you prepare a **b** as a	**Nu 15:8**	
		1121, 1241
then you shall offer with the **b** a	**Nu 15:9**	
		1121, 1241
offer one **b** for a burnt offering,	**Nu 15:24**	
		6499, 1121, 1241
up a **b** and a ram on each altar.	**Nu 23:2**	6499
up a **b** and a ram on each altar.”	**Nu 23:4**	6499
a **b** and a ram on *each* altar.	**Nu 23:14**	6499
up a **b** and a ram on *each* altar.	**Nu 23:30**	6499
for a grain offering, for each **b**;	**Nu 28:12**	6499
half a hin of wine for a **b** and a third	**Nu 28:14**	6499
for a **b** and two-tenths for the ram.	**Nu 28:20**	6499
of an ephah for each **b**,	**Nu 28:28**	6499
one **b**, one ram, *and* seven male	**Nu 29:2**	
		6499, 1121, 1241
three-tenths *of an ephah* for the **b**,	**Nu 29:3**	6499
one **b**, one ram, seven male lambs	**Nu 29:8**	
		6499, 1121, 1241
three-tenths *of an ephah* for the **b**,	**Nu 29:9**	6499
one **b**, one ram, seven male lambs	**Nu 29:36**	6499
and their drink offerings for the **b**,	**Nu 29:37**	6499
“Take your father's **b** and a	**Jg 6:25**	6499
and a second **b** seven years old,	**Jg 6:25**	6499
and take a second **b** and offer a	**Jg 6:26**	6499
and the second **b** was offered on	**Jg 6:28**	6499
with a three-year-old **b** and one	**1Sa 1:24**	6499
Then they slaughtered the **b**,	**1Sa 1:25**	6499
with a young **b** and seven rams,	**2Ch 13:9**	6499
take no young **b** out of your house Nor	**Ps 50:9**	6499
Or a young **b** with horns and hoofs.	**Ps 69:31**	6499
and the face of a **b** on the left,	**Ezk 1:10**	7794
‘a young **b** for a sin offering.	**Ezk 43:19**	6499
take the **b** for the sin offering,	**Ezk 43:21**	6499
as they cleansed *it* with the **b**.	**Ezk 43:22**	6499
you shall present a young **b**	**Ezk 43:23**	6499
young **b** and a ram from the flock,	**Ezk 43:25**	6499
you shall take a young **b** without	**Ezk 45:18**	6499
the land a **b** for a sin offering.	**Ezk 45:22**	6499
grain offering an ephah with a **b**,	**Ezk 45:24**	6499
offer a young **b** without blemish,	**Ezk 46:6**	6499
offering, an ephah with the **b** and	**Ezk 46:7**	6499
with a **b** and an ephah with a ram,	**Ezk 46:11**	6499

BULLS

their colts, forty cows and ten **b**,	**Gn 32:15**	6499
sacrificed young **b** as peace offerings	**Ex 24:5**	6499
for the burnt offering twelve **b**,	**Nu 7:87**	6499
sacrifice of peace offerings 24 **b**,	**Nu 7:88**	6499
their hands on the heads of the **b**;	**Nu 8:12**	6499
b and seven rams for me here.”	**Nu 23:1**	6499
b and seven rams for me here.”	**Nu 23:29**	6499
two **b** and one ram, seven male	**Nu 28:11**	
		6499, 1121, 1241
two **b** and one ram and seven male	**Nu 28:19**	
		6499, 1121, 1241
aroma to the LORD: two young **b**,	**Nu 28:27**	
		6499, 1121, 1241
thirteen **b**, two rams, fourteen	**Nu 29:13**	
		6499, 1121, 1241
ephah for each of the thirteen **b**,	**Nu 29:14**	6499
twelve **b**, two rams, fourteen male	**Nu 29:17**	
		6499, 1121, 1241
and their drink offerings for the **b**,	**Nu 29:18**	6499
eleven **b**, two rams, fourteen male	**Nu 29:20**	6499
and their drink offerings for the **b**,	**Nu 29:21**	6499
ten **b**, two rams, fourteen male	**Nu 29:23**	6499
and their drink offerings for the **b**,	**Nu 29:24**	6499
nine **b**, two rams, fourteen male	**Nu 29:26**	6499
and their drink offerings for the **b**,	**Nu 29:27**	6499
eight **b**, two rams, fourteen male	**Nu 29:29**	6499
and their drink offerings for the **b**,	**Nu 29:30**	6499
seven **b**, two rams, fourteen male	**Nu 29:32**	6499
and their drink offerings for the **b**,	**Nu 29:33**	6499
sacrificed seven **b** and seven rams.	**1Ch 15:26**	6499
offerings to the LORD, 1,000 **b**,	**1Ch 29:21**	6499
They brought seven **b**,	**2Ch 29:21**	6499
So they slaughtered the **b**,	**2Ch 29:22**	1241
the assembly brought was 70 **b**,	**2Ch 29:32**	1241
things were 600 **b** and 3,000 sheep.	**2Ch 29:33**	1241
assembly 1,000 **b** and 7,000 sheep,	**2Ch 30:24**	6499
assembly 1,000 **b** and 10,000 sheep;	**2Ch 30:24**	6499
numbering 30,000 plus 3,000 **b**;	**2Ch 35:7**	1241
2,600 *from the flocks* and 300 **b**.	**2Ch 35:8**	1241
5,000 *from the flocks* and 500 **b**.	**2Ch 35:9**	1241
They did this also with the **b**.	**2Ch 35:12**	1241
Whatever is needed, both young **b**,	**Ezr 6:9**	8450
of this temple of God 100 **b**,	**Ezr 6:17**	8450
you shall diligently buy **b**,	**Ezr 7:17**	8450
12 **b** for all Israel, 96 rams, 77	**Ezr 8:35**	6499
yourselves seven **b** and seven rams,	**Jb 42:8**	6499
Many **b** have surrounded me;	**Ps 22:12**	6499
Strong **b** of Bashan have encircled	**Ps 22:12**	
“Shall I eat the flesh of **b** Or	**Ps 50:13**	47
Then young **b** will be offered on	**Ps 51:19**	6499
an offering of **b** with male goats.	**Ps 66:15**	1241
The herd of **b** with the calves of	**Ps 68:30**	47
no pleasure in the blood of **b**,	**Is 1:11**	6499
And young **b** with strong ones;	**Is 34:7**	6499
Put all her young **b** to the sword;	**Jer 50:27**	6499
bronze **b** that were under the sea,	**Jer 52:20**	1241
were rams, lambs, goats and **b**,	**Ezk 39:18**	6499
a burnt offering to the LORD seven **b**	**Ezk 45:23**	6499
In Gilgal they sacrifice **b**,	**Hos 12:11**	7794
For if the blood of goats and **b**	**Heb 9:13**	*5022*
of **b** and goats to take away sins.	**Heb 10:4**	*5022*

BULRUSH

palm branch and **b** in a single day.	**Is 9:14**	100
or tail, *its* palm branch or **b**,	**Is 19:15**	100

BULRUSHES

The **b** by the Nile, by the edge of	**Is 19:7**	6169

BULWARK

faithfulness is a shield and **b**.	**Ps 91:4**	5507

BUNAH

were Ram the firstborn, then **B**,	**1Ch 2:25**	946

BUNCH

“You shall take a **b** of hyssop	**Ex 12:22**	92

BUNCHES

cakes, fig cakes and **b** of raisins,	**1Ch 12:40**	6778

BUNDLE

man's **b** of money *was* in his sack;	**Gn 42:35**	6872a
shall be bound in the **b** of the living	**1Sa 25:29**	6872a
Pick up your **b** from the ground,	**Jer 10:17**	3666
But when Paul had gathered a **b** of	**Ac 28:3**	*4128*

BUNDLES

their father saw their **b** of money,	**Gn 42:35**	6872a
pull out for her *some grain* from the **b**	**Ru 2:16**	6653
bind them in **b** to burn them up;	**Mt 13:30**	*1197*

BUNNI

Bani, Kadmiel, Shebaniah, **B**,	**Ne 9:4**	1138
B, Azgad, Bebai,	**Ne 10:15**	1138
son of Hashabiah, the son of **B**;	**Ne 11:15**	1138

BURDEN

and they will bear *the* **b** with you.	**Ex 18:22**	
the **b** of all this people on me?	**Nu 11:11**	4853a
bear the **b** of the people with you,	**Nu 11:17**	4853a
‘I am not able to bear *the* **b** of	**Dt 1:9**	
load and **b** of you and your strife?	**Dt 1:12**	4853a
me, then you will be a **b** to me.	**2Sa 15:33**	4853a
be an added **b** to my lord the king?	**2Sa 19:35**	4853a
They were also over the **b** bearers,	**2Ch 34:13**	5449
a **b** on *your* shoulders no longer.	**2Ch 35:3**	4853a
of the **b** bearers is failing,	**Ne 4:10**	5449
So that I am a **b** to myself?	**Jb 7:20**	4853a
b they weigh too much for me.	**Ps 38:4**	4853a
Cast your **b** upon the LORD and He	**Ps 55:22**	3053
an oppressive **b** upon our loins.	**Ps 66:11**	4157
the Lord, who daily bears our **b**,	**Ps 68:19**	6006
“I relieved his shoulder of the **b**,	**Ps 81:6**	5447
They have become a **b** to Me;	**Is 1:14**	2960
You shall break the yoke of their **b**	**Is 9:4**	5448
that his **b** will be removed from	**Is 10:27**	5448
his **b** removed from their shoulder.	**Is 14:25**	5448
They could not rescue the **b**,	**Is 46:2**	4853a
“This **b** *concerns* the prince in	**Ezk 12:10**	4853b
of the **b** of the king of princes.	**Hos 8:10**	4853a
reproach *of exile* is a **b** on them.	**Zph 3:18**	4864
The **b** of the word of the LORD is	**Zch 9:1**	4853b
The **b** of the word of the LORD	**Zch 12:1**	4853b
“For My yoke is easy and My **b** is	**Mt 11:30**	*5413*
equal to us who have borne the **b**	**Mt 20:12**	*922*
THE FOAL OF A BEAST OF **B**.’”	**Mt 21:5**	*5268*
greater **b** than these essentials:	**Ac 15:28**	*922*
in need, I was not a **b** to anyone;	**2Co 11:9**	*2655*
kept myself from being a **b** to you,	**2Co 11:9**	*4*
myself did not become a **b** to you?	**2Co 12:13**	*2655*
you, and I will not be a **b** to you;	**2Co 12:14**	*2655*
as it may, I did not **b** you myself;	**2Co 12:16**	*2599a*
so as not to be a **b** to any of you,	**1Th 2:9**	*1912*
we would not be a **b** to any of you;	**2Th 3:8**	*1912*
I place no other **b** on you.	**Rv 2:24**	*922*

BURDENED

I have not **b** you with offerings,	**Is 43:23**	5647
you have **b** Me with your sins,	**Is 43:24**	5647
Asia, that we were **b** excessively,	**2Co 1:8**	*916*
in this tent, we groan, being **b**,	**2Co 5:4**	*916*
them and the church must not be **b**,	**1Tm 5:16**	*916*

BURDENS

He bowed his shoulder to bear **b**,	**Gn 49:15**	
from under the **b** of the Egyptians,	**Ex 6:6**	5450
from under the **b** of the Egyptians.	**Ex 6:7**	5450
those who carried **b** took *their* load	**Ne 4:17**	5447
governors who were before me laid **b**	**Ne 5:15**	3513
“They tie up heavy **b** and lay them on	**Mt 23:4**	*5413*
men down with **b** hard to bear,	**Lk 11:46**	*5413*
the **b** with one of your fingers.	**Lk 11:46**	*5413*
Bear one another's **b**,	**Ga 6:2**	*922*

BURDENSOME

because it is too **b** for me.	**Nu 11:14**	3515
not all go, for we will be **b**	**2Sa 13:25**	3513
The things that you carry are **b**,	**Is 46:1**	6006
and His commandments are not **b**.	**1Jn 5:3**	*926*

BURIAL

give me a **b** site among you that I	**Gn 23:4**	6913
in your presence for a **b** site.”	**Gn 23:9**	6913
for a **b** site by the sons of Heth.	**Gn 23:20**	6913
and bury me in their **b** place.”	**Gn 47:30**	6900
Ephron the Hittite for a **b** site.	**Gn 49:30**	6913
a **b** site from Ephron the Hittite.	**Gn 50:13**	6913
man knows his **b** place to this day.	**Dt 34:6**	6900
he does not even have a *proper* **b**,	**Ec 6:3**	6900
will not be united with them in **b**,	**Is 14:20**	6900
there is no *other* place for **b**.	**Jer 19:11**	6912
will be buried with a donkey's **b**,	**Jer 22:19**	6900
the **b** place of the common people.	**Jer 26:23**	6913
Gog a **b** ground there in Israel,	**Ezk 39:11**	6913
she did it to prepare Me for **b**.	**Mt 26:12**	*1779*
Field as a **b** place for strangers.	**Mt 27:7**	*5027*
My body beforehand for the **b**.	**Mk 14:8**	*1780*
may keep it for the day of My **b**.	**Jn 12:7**	*1780*
as is the **b** custom of the Jews.	**Jn 19:40**	*1779*

BURIED

you will be **b** at a good old age.	**Gn 15:15**	6912
Abraham **b** Sarah his wife in the	**Gn 23:19**	6912
b him in the cave of Machpelah,	**Gn 25:9**	6912
Abraham was **b** with Sarah his wife.	**Gn 25:10**	6912
was **b** below Bethel under the oak;	**Gn 35:8**	6912
and was **b** on the way to Ephrath	**Gn 35:19**	6912
and his sons Esau and Jacob **b** him.	**Gn 35:29**	6912
and I **b** her there on the way to	**Gn 48:7**	6912
they **b** Abraham and his wife Sarah,	**Gn 49:31**	6912
they **b** Isaac and his wife Rebekah,	**Gn 49:31**	6912
wife Rebekah, and there I **b** Leah	**Gn 49:31**	6912
and **b** him in the cave of the field	**Gn 50:13**	6912
After he had **b** his father,	**Gn 50:14**	6912
because there they **b** the people	**Nu 11:34**	6912
Miriam died there and was **b** there.	**Nu 20:1**	6912
There Aaron died and there he was **b**	**Dt 10:6**	6912
And He **b** him in the valley in the	**Dt 34:6**	6912
And they **b** him in the territory of	**Jos 24:30**	6912
Now they **b** the bones of Joseph,	**Jos 24:32**	6912
and they **b** him at Gibeah of	**Jos 24:33**	6912
And they **b** him in the territory of	**Jg 2:9**	6912
Joash died at a ripe old age and was **b**	**Jg 8:32**	6912
Then he died and was **b** in Shamir.	**Jg 10:2**	6912
And Jair died and was **b** in Kamon.	**Jg 10:5**	6912
Jephthah the Gileadite died and was **b**	**Jg 12:7**	6912
Ibzan died and was **b** in Bethlehem.	**Jg 12:10**	6912
Elon the Zebulunite died and was **b**	**Jg 12:12**	6912
Hillel the Pirathonite died and was **b**	**Jg 12:15**	6912
and **b** him between Zorah and	**Jg 16:31**	6912
I will die, and there I will be **b**.	**Ru 1:17**	6912
and **b** him at his house in Ramah.	**1Sa 25:1**	6912
and **b** him in Ramah, his own city.	**1Sa 28:3**	6912
They took their bones and **b**	**1Sa 31:13**	6912
men of Jabesh-gilead who **b** Saul.”	**2Sa 2:4**	6912
to Saul your lord, and have **b** him.	**2Sa 2:5**	6912
And they took up Asahel and **b** him	**2Sa 2:32**	6912
Thus they **b** Abner in Hebron;	**2Sa 3:32**	6912
took the head of Ish-bosheth and **b** it	**2Sa 4:12**	6912
was **b** in the grave of his father.	**2Sa 17:23**	6912
They **b** the bones of Saul and	**2Sa 21:14**	6912
and was **b** in the city of David.	**1Ki 2:10**	6912
and he was **b** at his own house in	**1Ki 2:34**	6912
was **b** in the city of his father David,	**1Ki 11:43**	6912
After he had **b** him,	**1Ki 13:31**	6912
in which the man of God is **b**;	**1Ki 13:31**	6912
Israel **b** him and mourned for him,	**1Ki 14:18**	6912
and was **b** with his fathers in the	**1Ki 14:31**	6912
they **b** him in the city of David;	**1Ki 15:8**	6912
Asa slept with his fathers and was **b**	**1Ki 15:24**	6912
his fathers and was **b** in Tirzah,	**1Ki 16:6**	6912
his fathers and was **b** in Samaria;	**1Ki 16:28**	6912
and they **b** the king in Samaria.	**1Ki 22:37**	6912
slept with his fathers and was **b** with	**1Ki 22:50**	6912
and was **b** with his fathers in the	**2Ki 8:24**	6912
and **b** him in his grave with his	**2Ki 9:28**	6912
and they **b** him in Samaria.	**2Ki 10:35**	6912
and they **b** him with his fathers in	**2Ki 12:21**	6912
and they **b** him in Samaria;	**2Ki 13:9**	6912
and Joash was **b** in Samaria with	**2Ki 13:13**	6912
Elisha died, and they **b** him.	**2Ki 13:20**	6912
b in Samaria with the kings of Israel;	**2Ki 14:16**	6912
he was **b** at Jerusalem with his fathers	**2Ki 14:20**	6912
and they **b** him with his fathers in	**2Ki 15:7**	6912
and he was **b** with his fathers in	**2Ki 15:38**	6912
and was **b** with his fathers in the	**2Ki 16:20**	6912
was **b** in the garden of his own house,	**2Ki 21:18**	6912
He was **b** in his grave in the	**2Ki 21:26**	6912
and **b** him in his own tomb.	**2Ki 23:30**	6912
b their bones under the oak in Jabesh,	**1Ch 10:12**	6912
was **b** in the city of his father David;	**2Ch 9:31**	6912
and was **b** in the city of David;	**2Ch 12:16**	6912
they **b** him in the city of David,	**2Ch 14:1**	6912
They **b** him in his own tomb	**2Ch 16:14**	6912
slept with his fathers and was **b**	**2Ch 21:1**	6912
they **b** him in the city of David,	**2Ch 21:20**	6912
Jehu, put him to death and **b** him.	**2Ch 22:9**	6912
They **b** him in the city of	**2Ch 24:16**	6912
they **b** him in the city of David,	**2Ch 24:25**	6912

they brought him on horses and **b** him **2Ch 25:28** 6912
and they **b** him with his fathers in **2Ch 26:23** 6912
they **b** him in the city of David; **2Ch 27:9** 6912
and they **b** him in the city, **2Ch 28:27** 6912
and they **b** him in the upper **2Ch 32:33** 6912
and they **b** him in his own house. **2Ch 33:20** 6912
was **b** in the tombs of his fathers. **2Ch 35:24** 6912
will be **b** because of the plague, **Jb 27:15** 6912
So then, I have seen the wicked **b**, **Ec 8:10** 6912
They will not be gathered or **b**; **Jer 8:2** 6912
they will not be lamented or **b**; **Jer 16:4** 6912
they will not be **b**, **Jer 16:6** 6912
will die and there you will be **b**, **Jer 20:6** 6912
will be **b** with a donkey's burial, **Jer 22:19** 6912
not be lamented, gathered or **b**; **Jer 25:33** 6912
b it in the valley of Hamon-gog. **Ezk 39:15** 6912
and took away the body and **b** it; **Mt 14:12** *2290*
the rich man also died and was **b**. **Lk 16:22** *2290*
David that he both died and was **b**, **Ac 2:29** *2290*
carrying him out, they **b** him. **Ac 5:6** *2290*
those who have **b** your husband **Ac 5:9** *2290*
out and **b** her beside her husband. **Ac 5:10** *2290*
Some devout men **b** Stephen, **Ac 8:2** *4792*
Therefore we have been **b** with Him **Ro 6:4** *4916*
and that He was **b**, and that He was **1Co 15:4** *2290*
having been **b** with Him in baptism, **Col 2:12** *4916*

BURIERS

marker by it until the **b** have buried it **Ezk 39:15** 6912

BURIES

sluggard **b** his hand in the dish, **Pr 19:24** 2934
sluggard **b** his hand in the dish; **Pr 26:15** 2934

BURN

bricks and **b** *them* thoroughly." **Gn 11:3** 8313
morning, you shall **b** with fire. **Ex 12:10** 8313
b for burn, wound for wound, **Ex 21:25** 3555
burn for **b**, wound for wound, **Ex 21:25** 3555
to make a lamp **b** continually. **Ex 27:20** 5927
b with fire outside the camp; **Ex 29:14** 8313
shall **b** the remainder with fire; **Ex 29:34** 8313
shall **b** fragrant incense on it; **Ex 30:7** 6999
he shall **b** it every morning when **Ex 30:7** 6999
at twilight, he shall **b** incense. **Ex 30:8** 6999
that My anger may **b** against them and **Ex 32:10** 2734
why does Your anger **b** against Your **Ex 32:11** 2734
"Do not let the anger of my lord **b**; **Ex 32:22** 2734
out, and **b** it on wood with fire; **Lv 4:12** 8313
and **b** it as he burned the first **Lv 4:21** 8313
shall **b** wood on it every morning; **Lv 6:12** 1197a
the bread you shall **b** in the fire. **Lv 8:32** 8313
sustains in its skin a **b** by fire, **Lv 13:24** 4348
of the **b** becomes a bright spot, **Lv 13:24** 4348
it has broken out in the **b**. **Lv 13:25** 4348
it is the swelling from the **b**; **Lv 13:28** 4348
for it is *only* the scar of the **b**. **Lv 13:28** 4348
"So he shall **b** the garment, **Lv 13:52** 8313
you shall **b** it in the fire, **Lv 13:55** 8313
and they shall **b** their hides, **Lv 16:27** 8313
to make a lamp **b** continually. **Lv 24:2** 5927
near to **b** incense before the LORD; **Nu 16:40** 6999
b their graven images with fire. **Dt 7:5** 8313
their gods you are to **b** with fire; **Dt 7:25** 8313
and **b** their Asherim with fire, **Dt 12:3** 8313
for they even **b** their sons and **Dt 12:31** 8313
b the city and all its booty with fire **Dt 13:16** 8313
jealousy will **b** against that man, **Dt 29:20** 6225
and **b** their chariots with fire." **Jos 11:6** 8313
Israel did not **b** any cities that **Jos 11:13** 8313
of the LORD will **b** against you, **Jos 23:16** 2734
"Do not let Your anger **b** against **Jg 6:39** 2734
of the tower to **b** it with fire. **Jg 9:52** 8313
will **b** your house down on you." **Jg 12:1** 8313
or we will **b** you and your father's **Jg 14:15** 8313
"They must surely **b** the fat first, **1Sa 2:16** 6999
go up to My altar, to **b** incense, **1Sa 2:28** 6999
went up to the altar to **b** incense. **1Ki 12:33** 6999
by the altar to **b** incense. **1Ki 13:1** 6999
high places who **b** incense on you, **1Ki 13:2** 6999
"Upon the great altar **b** the **2Ki 16:15** 6999
of Judah had appointed to **b** incense **2Ki 23:5** 6999
to **b** incense before the LORD, **1Ch 23:13** 6999
to **b** fragrant incense before Him and **2Ch 2:4** 6999
except to **b** *incense* before Him? **2Ch 2:6** 6999
to **b** in front of the inner **2Ch 4:20** 1197a
and evening they **b** to the LORD burnt **2Ch 13:11** 6999
the temple of the LORD to **b** incense **2Ch 26:16** 6999
Uzziah, to **b** incense to the LORD, **2Ch 26:18** 6999
who are consecrated to **b** incense. **2Ch 26:18** 6999
places to **b** incense to other gods, **2Ch 28:25** 6999
be His ministers and **b** incense." **2Ch 29:11** 6999
and on it you shall **b** incense"? **2Ch 32:12** 6999
to **b** on the altar of the LORD our **Ne 10:34** 1197a
on me, And my bones **b** with fever. **Jb 30:30** 2787
Will Your jealousy **b** like fire? **Ps 79:5** 1197a
Will Your wrath **b** like fire? **Ps 89:46** 1197a
Thus they shall both **b** together And **Is 1:31** 1197a
And it will **b** and devour his **Is 10:17** 1197a
them, I would **b** them completely. **Is 27:4** 3341
Even Lebanon is not enough to **b**, **Is 40:16** 1197a
Nor will the flame **b** you. **Is 43:2** 1197a
becomes *something* for a man to **b**, **Is 44:15** 1197a
fire And **b** with none to quench it, **Jer 4:4** 1197a
it will **b** and not be quenched." **Jer 7:20** 1197a
to **b** their sons and their **Jer 7:31** 8313
the gods to whom they **b** incense, **Jer 11:12** 6999
altars to **b** incense to Baal. **Jer 11:13** 6999
in My anger, It will **b** upon you." **Jer 15:14** 3344
in My anger Which will **b** forever. **Jer 17:4** 3344
They **b** incense to worthless gods **Jer 18:15** 6999
the high places of Baal to **b** their sons **Jer 19:5** 8313
and he will **b** it with fire." **Jer 21:10** 8313
And **b** with none to extinguish *it*, **Jer 21:12** 1197a
set this city on fire and **b** it, **Jer 32:29** 8313
offerings, to **b** grain offerings and **Jer 33:18** 6999
and he will **b** it with fire. **Jer 34:2** 8313
so they will **b** *spices* for you; **Jer 34:5** 8313
it and take it and **b** it with fire; **Jer 34:22** 8313
the king not to **b** the scroll, **Jer 36:25** 8313
capture it and **b** it with fire." **Jer 37:8** 8313
up and **b** this city with fire.' " **Jer 37:10** 8313
and they will **b** it with fire, and **Jer 38:18** 8313
will **b** them and take them captive. **Jer 43:12** 8313
Egypt he will **b** with fire. **Jer 43:13** 8313
to anger by continuing to **b** sacrifices **Jer 44:3** 6999
not to **b** sacrifices to other gods. **Jer 44:5** 6999
to **b** sacrifices to the queen of **Jer 44:25** 6999
"One third you shall **b** in the **Ezk 5:2** 1197a
the fire and **b** them in the fire; **Ezk 5:4** 8313
"They will **b** your houses with **Ezk 16:41** 8313
and **b** their houses with fire. **Ezk 23:47** 8313
fires with the weapons and **b** *them*, **Ezk 39:9** 8026b
And **b** incense on the hills, **Hos 4:13** 6999
"I will **b** up her chariots in **Na 2:13** 1197a
b incense to their fishing net; **Hab 1:16** 6999
but He will **b** up the chaff with **Mt 3:12** *2618*
bind them in bundles to **b** them up; **Mt 13:30** *2618*
temple of the Lord and **b** incense. **Lk 1:9** *2370*
but He will **b** up the chaff with **Lk 3:17** *2618*
it is better to marry than to **b** **1Co 7:9** *4448*
flesh and will **b** her up with fire. **Rv 17:16** *2618*

BURNED

Jacob's anger **b** against Rachel, **Gn 30:2** 2734
"Bring her out and let her be **b**!" **Gn 38:24** 8313
slave did to me," his anger **b**. **Gn 39:19** 2734
sight, why the bush is not **b** up." **Ex 3:3** 1197a
anger of the LORD **b** against Moses, **Ex 4:14** 2734
and Moses' anger **b**, and he threw **Ex 32:19** 2734
they had made and **b** *it* with fire, **Ex 32:20** 8313
and he **b** fragrant incense on it, **Ex 40:27** 6999
are poured out it shall be **b**. **Lv 4:12** 8313
burn it as he **b** the first bull; **Lv 4:21** 8313
of the priest shall be **b** entirely. **Lv 6:23** 3632
it shall be **b** with fire. **Lv 6:30** 8313
third day shall be **b** with fire. **Lv 7:17** 8313
it shall be **b** with fire. **Lv 7:19** 8313
he **b** in the fire outside the camp, **Lv 8:17** 8313
he **b** with fire outside the camp. **Lv 9:11** 8313
and behold, it had been **b** up! **Lv 10:16** 8313
it shall be **b** in the fire. **Lv 13:52** 8313
the mark shall be **b** in the fire. **Lv 13:57** 8313
third day shall be **b** with fire. **Lv 19:6** 8313
he and they shall be **b** with fire, **Lv 20:14** 8313
she shall be **b** with fire. **Lv 21:9** 8313
and the fire of the LORD **b** among **Nu 11:1** 1197a
the fire of the LORD **b** among them. **Nu 11:3** 1197a
b against them and He departed. **Nu 12:9** 2734
the men who were **b** had offered, **Nu 16:39** 8313
heifer shall be **b** in his sight; **Nu 19:5** 8313
with its refuse, shall be **b**. **Nu 19:5** 8313
Balak's anger **b** against Balaam, **Nu 24:10** 2734
Then they **b** all their cities where **Nu 31:10** 8313
"So the LORD's anger **b** in that day, **Nu 32:10** 2734
the LORD's anger **b** against Israel, **Nu 32:13** 2734
and the mountain **b** with fire to **Dt 4:11** 1197a
and **b** it with fire and crushed it, **Dt 9:21** 8313
of the LORD **b** against that land, **Dt 29:27** 2734
They **b** the city with fire, and **Jos 6:24** 8313
LORD **b** against the sons of Israel. **Jos 7:1** 2734
the ban shall be **b** with fire, **Jos 7:15** 8313
and they **b** them with fire after **Jos 7:25** 8313
b Ai and made it a heap forever, **Jos 8:28** 8313
and **b** their chariots with fire. **Jos 11:9** 8313
And he **b** Hazor with fire. **Jos 11:11** 8313
Hazor alone, *which* Joshua **b**. **Jos 11:13** 8313
of the LORD **b** against Israel, **Jg 2:14** 2734
of the LORD **b** against Israel, **Jg 2:20** 2734
Gaal the son of Ebed, his anger **b**. **Jg 9:30** 2734
of the LORD **b** against Israel, **Jg 10:7** 2734
And his anger **b**, and he went up to **Jg 14:19** 2734
b her and her father with fire. **Jg 15:6** 8313
were as flax that is **b** with fire, **Jg 15:14** 1197a
and they **b** the city with fire. **Jg 18:27** 8313
Also, before they **b** the fat, **1Sa 2:15** 6999
anger **b** against David and he said, **1Sa 17:28** 2734
Then Saul's anger **b** against **1Sa 20:30** 2734
Ziklag and **b** it with fire; **1Sa 30:1** 8313
city, behold, it was **b** with fire, **1Sa 30:3** 8313
and we **b** Ziklag with fire." **1Sa 30:14** 8313
came to Jabesh and **b** them there. **1Sa 31:12** 8313
anger of the LORD **b** against Uzzah, **2Sa 6:7** 2734
anger **b** greatly against the man, **2Sa 12:5** 2734
b with fire in *their* place." **2Sa 23:7** 8313
of the LORD **b** against Israel, **2Sa 24:1** 2734
and **b** incense on the high places. **1Ki 3:3** 6999
Gezer and **b** it with fire, **1Ki 9:16** 8313
who **b** incense and sacrificed to **1Ki 11:8** 6999
human bones shall be **b** on you.' " **1Ki 13:2** 8313
and **b** *it* at the brook Kidron. **1Ki 15:13** 8313
b the king's house over him with fire, **1Ki 16:18** 8313
of the house of Baal and **b** them. **2Ki 10:26** 8313
and **b** incense on the high places. **2Ki 12:3** 6999
and **b** incense on the high places. **2Ki 14:4** 6999
and **b** incense on the high places. **2Ki 15:4** 6999
and **b** incense on the high places. **2Ki 15:35** 6999
He sacrificed and **b** incense on **2Ki 16:4** 6999
and **b** his burnt offering and his **2Ki 16:13** 6999
and there they **b** incense on all **2Ki 17:11** 6999
and the Sepharvites **b** their **2Ki 17:31** 8313
sons of Israel **b** incense to it; **2Ki 18:4** 6999
have forsaken Me and have **b** incense **2Ki 22:17** 6999
and he **b** them outside Jerusalem in **2Ki 23:4** 8313
also those who **b** incense to Baal, **2Ki 23:5** 6999
and **b** it at the brook Kidron, **2Ki 23:6** 8313
where the priests had **b** incense, **2Ki 23:8** 6999
and he **b** the chariots of the sun **2Ki 23:11** 8313
them to dust, and **b** the Asherah. **2Ki 23:15** 8313
the bones from the graves and **b** *them* **2Ki 23:16** 8313
altars and **b** human bones on them; **2Ki 23:20** 8313
which His anger **b** against Judah, **2Ki 23:26** 2734
He **b** the house of the LORD, **2Ki 25:9** 8313
every great house he **b** with fire. **2Ki 25:9** 8313
anger of the LORD **b** against Uzza, **1Ch 13:10** 2734
order and they were **b** with fire. **1Ch 14:12** 8313
it and **b** *it* at the brook Kidron. **2Ch 15:16** 8313
so their anger **b** against Judah and **2Ch 25:10** 2734
them and **b** incense to them. **2Ch 25:14** 6999
of the LORD **b** against Amaziah, **2Ch 25:15** 2734
he **b** incense in the valley of **2Ch 28:3** 6999
Ben-hinnom and **b** his sons in fire, **2Ch 28:3** 1197a
and **b** incense on the high places, **2Ch 28:4** 6999
and have not **b** incense or offered **2Ch 29:7** 6999
Then he **b** the bones of the priests **2Ch 34:5** 8313
and have **b** incense to other gods, **2Ch 34:25** 6999
Then they **b** the house of God and **2Ch 36:19** 8313
wall of Jerusalem, and **b** all its fortified **2Ch 36:19** 8313
and its gates are **b** with fire." **Ne 1:3** 3341
desolate and its gates **b** by fire. **Ne 2:17** 3341
dusty rubble even the **b** ones?" **Ne 4:2** 8313
angry and his wrath **b** within him. **Es 1:12** 1197a
fire of God fell from heaven and **b** up **Jb 1:16** 1197a
Buzite, of the family of Ram **b**; **Jb 32:2** 2734
against Job his anger **b** because **Jb 32:2** 2734
And his anger **b** against his three **Jb 32:3** 2734
of the three men his anger **b**. **Jb 32:5** 2734
While I was musing the fire **b**; **Ps 39:3** 1197a
b Your sanctuary to the ground; **Ps 74:7**
7971, 784
They have **b** all the meeting places **Ps 74:8** 8313
It is **b** with fire, it is cut down; **Ps 80:16** 8313
bosom And his clothes not be **b**? **Pr 6:27** 8313
am swarthy, For the sun has **b** me. **SS 1:6** 7805
Your cities are **b** with fire, **Is 1:7** 8313
the LORD has **b** against His people, **Is 5:25** 2734
LORD of hosts the land is **b** up, **Is 9:19** 6272
inhabitants of the earth are **b**, **Is 24:6** 2787
"The peoples will be **b** to lime, **Is 33:12** 4955
thorns which are **b** in the fire. **Is 33:12** 3341
And it **b** him, but he paid no **Is 42:25** 1197a
"I have **b** half of it in the fire and **Is 44:19** 8313
praised You, Has been **b** *by* fire; **Is 64:11** 8316
have **b** incense on the mountains And **Is 65:7** 6999
have **b** sacrifices in it to other gods **Jer 19:4** 6999
on whose rooftops they **b** sacrifices **Jer 19:13** 6999
as *spices* were **b** for your fathers, **Jer 34:5** 4955
came to Jeremiah after the king had **b** **Jer 36:27** 8313
Jehoiakim the king of Judah **b**. **Jer 36:28** 8313
"You have **b** this scroll, saying, **Jer 36:29** 8313
king of Judah had **b** in the fire; **Jer 36:32** 8313
this city will not be **b** with fire, **Jer 38:17** 8313
this city will be **b** with fire.' " **Jer 38:23** 8313
The Chaldeans also **b** with fire the **Jer 39:8** 8313
poured out and **b** in the cities of Judah **Jer 44:6** 1197a
sacrifices that you **b** in the cities **Jer 44:21** 6999
"Because you have **b** sacrifices **Jer 44:23** 6999
It will even be **b** down *and* bereft **Jer 46:19** 3341
they have **b** the marshes with fire, **Jer 51:32** 8313
He **b** the house of the LORD, **Jer 52:13** 8313
every large house he **b** with fire. **Jer 52:13** 8313
And He has **b** in Jacob like a **La 2:3** 1197a
south to north will be **b** by it. **Ezk 20:47** 6866a
spices, And let the bones be **b**. **Ezk 24:10** 2787
and it *shall be* **b** in the appointed **Ezk 43:21** 8313
b up all the trees of the field. **Jl 1:19** 3857
Because he **b** the bones of the king **Am 2:1** 8313
her earnings will be **b** with fire And **Mi 1:7** 8313
are gathered up and **b** with fire, **Mt 13:40** *2618*
into the fire and they are **b**. **Jn 15:6** *2545*
b in their desire toward one another, **Ro 1:27** *1572*
If any man's work is **b** up, **1Co 3:15** *2618*
and if I surrender my body to be **b**, **1Co 13:3** *2545*
cursed, and it ends up being **b**. **Heb 6:8** *2740*
for sin, are **b** outside the camp. **Heb 13:11** *2618*
earth and its works will be **b** up. **2Pe 3:10** *2618*
and a third of the earth was **b** up, **Rv 8:7** *2618*
a third of the trees were **b** up, **Rv 8:7** *2618*
and all the green grass was **b** up. **Rv 8:7** *2618*
and she will be **b** up with fire; **Rv 18:8** *2618*

BURNING

behold, the bush was **b** with fire, **Ex 3:2** 1197a
You send forth Your **b** anger, **Ex 15:7** 2740
an altar as a place for **b** incense; **Ex 30:1** 4729a
Turn from Your **b** anger and change **Ex 32:12** 2740
the altar is to be kept **b** on it. **Lv 6:9** 3344
the altar shall be kept **b** on it. **Lv 6:12** 3344
kept **b** continually on the altar; **Lv 6:13** 3344
shall bewail the **b** which the LORD **Lv 10:6** 8316
you scatter the **b** coals abroad. **Nu 16:37** 784
it into the midst of the **b** heifer. **Nu 19:6** 8316
to add still more to the **b** anger **Nu 32:14** 2740
the mountain was **b** with fire, **Dt 5:23** 1197a
the mountain was **b** with fire, **Dt 9:15** 1197a
His **b** anger and show mercy to you, **Dt 13:17** 2740
is brimstone and salt, a **b** waste, **Dt 29:23** 8316
thus **b** up both the shocks and the **Jg 15:5** 1197a
b incense with them *on the altar* **1Ki 9:25** 6999
censer in his hand for **b** incense, **2Ch 26:19** 6999
for the **b** anger of the LORD is **2Ch 28:11** 2740

His **b** anger is against Israel."	**2Ch 28:13**	2740
His **b** anger may turn away from us.	**2Ch 29:10**	2740
b anger may turn away from you.	**2Ch 30:8**	2740
"Out of his mouth go **b** torches;	**Jb 41:19**	3940
As *from* a boiling pot and **b**	**Jb 41:20**	
Fire and brimstone and **b** wind will	**Ps 11:6**	2152
And chasten me not in Your **b** anger.	**Ps 38:1**	2534
For my loins are filled with **b**,	**Ps 38:7**	7033
the green and the **b** alike.	**Ps 58:9**	2740
And may Your **b** anger overtake them.	**Ps 69:24**	2740
He sent upon them His **b** anger,	**Ps 78:49**	2740
turned away from Your **b** anger.	**Ps 85:3**	2740
Your **b** anger has passed over me;	**Ps 88:16**	2740
B indignation has seized me	**Ps 119:53**	2152
With the **b** coals of the broom	**Ps 120:4**	
"May **b** coals fall upon them;	**Ps 140:10**	784
you will heap **b** coals on his head,	**Pr 25:22**	
Are **b** lips and a wicked heart.	**Pr 26:23**	1814
of judgment and the spirit of **b**,	**Is 4:4**	1197a
with a **b** coal in his hand, which he	**Is 6:6**	7531a
And it will again be *subject* to **b**,	**Is 6:13**	1197a
rolled in blood, will be for **b**,	**Is 9:5**	8316
will be kindled like a **b** flame.	**Is 10:16**	3350
Cruel, with fury and **b** anger,	**Is 13:9**	2740
hosts In the day of His **b** anger.	**Is 13:13**	2740
B is His anger and dense is *His*	**Is 30:27**	1197a
us can live with continual **b**?"	**Is 33:14**	4168
And its land will become **b** pitch.	**Is 34:9**	1197a
b wick He will not extinguish;	**Is 42:3**	
salvation like a torch that is **b**.	**Is 62:1**	1197a
gardens and **b** incense on bricks;	**Is 65:3**	6999
like a **b** fire Shut up in my bones;	**Jer 20:9**	1197a
fire **b** in the brazier before him.	**Jer 36:22**	1197a
b sacrifices to other gods in the	**Jer 44:8**	6999
were **b** sacrifices to other gods,	**Jer 44:15**	6999
by **b** sacrifices to the queen of	**Jer 44:17**	6999
"But since we stopped **b** sacrifices	**Jer 44:18**	6999
"when we were **b** sacrifices to the	**Jer 44:19**	6999
Because of the **b** heat of famine.	**La 5:10**	2152
that looked like **b** coals of fire,	**Ezk 1:13**	1197a
flames, Its wheels *were* a **b** fire.	**Da 7:9**	1815
destroyed and given to the **b** fire.	**Da 7:11**	3346
the Baals And **b** incense to idols.	**Hos 11:2**	6999
and withdraw His **b** anger so that	**Jon 3:9**	2740
Who can endure the **b** of His anger?	**Na 1:6**	2740
Before the **b** anger of the LORD comes	**Zph 2:2**	2740
My indignation, All My **b** anger;	**Zph 3:8**	2740
day is coming, **b** like a furnace;	**Mal 4:1**	1197a
passage about *the* **b** bush,	**Mk 12:26**	
in the *passage about the* **b** bush,	**Lk 20:37**	
"Were not our hearts **b** within us	**Lk 24:32**	*2545*
"He was the lamp that was **b** and	**Jn 5:35**	*2545*
IN THE FLAME OF A **B** THORN BUSH	**Ac 7:30**	*4442*
began **b** them in the sight of everyone;	**Ac 19:19**	*2618*
WILL HEAP **B** COALS ON HIS HEAD."	**Ro 12:20**	*4442*
heavens will be destroyed by **b**,	**2Pe 3:12**	*4448*
lamps of fire **b** before the throne,	**Rv 4:5**	*2545*
great mountain **b** with fire was thrown	**Rv 8:8**	*2545*
fell from heaven, **b** like a torch,	**Rv 8:10**	*2545*
when they see the smoke of her **b**,	**Rv 18:9**	*4451*
as they saw the smoke of her **b**,	**Rv 18:18**	*4451*

BURNISHED

and they gleamed like **b** bronze.	**Ezk 1:7**	7044
His feet *were* like **b** bronze,	**Rv 1:15**	*5474*
and His feet are like **b** bronze,	**Rv 2:18**	*5474*

BURNS

"Then the one who **b** them shall	**Lv 16:28**	8313
'The one who **b** it shall also wash	**Nu 19:8**	8313
And **b** to the lowest part of Sheol,	**Dt 32:22**	3344
of the LORD that **b** against us,	**2Ki 22:13**	3341
My wrath **b** against this place,	**2Ki 22:17**	3341
He **b** the chariots with fire.	**Ps 46:9**	8313
Like fire that **b** the forest And	**Ps 83:14**	1197a
And **b** up His adversaries round	**Ps 97:3**	3857
For wickedness **b** like a fire;	**Is 9:18**	1197a
Half of it he **b** in the fire;	**Is 44:16**	8313
become like stubble, Fire **b** them;	**Is 47:14**	8313
A fire that **b** all the day.	**Is 65:5**	3344
He who **b** incense is *like* the one	**Is 66:3**	2142
the one who **b** incense to his gods.	**Jer 48:35**	6999
morning it **b** like a flaming fire.	**Hos 7:6**	1197a
"My anger **b** against them!"	**Hos 8:5**	2734
them And behind them a flame **b**.	**Jl 2:3**	3857
of fire which **b** with brimstone.	**Rv 19:20**	*2545*
that **b** with fire and brimstone,	**Rv 21:8**	*2545*

BURNT

offered **b** offerings on the altar.	**Gn 8:20**	5930a
and offer him there as a **b**	**Gn 22:2**	5930a
he split wood for the **b** offering,	**Gn 22:3**	5930a
Abraham took the wood of the **b**	**Gn 22:6**	5930a
is the lamb for the **b** offering?"	**Gn 22:7**	5930a
the lamb for the **b** offering,	**Gn 22:8**	5930a
and offered him up for a **b**	**Gn 22:13**	5930a
have sacrifices and **b** offerings,	**Ex 10:25**	5930a
took a **b** offering and sacrifices	**Ex 18:12**	5930a
shall sacrifice on it your **b** offerings	**Ex 20:24**	5930a
and they offered **b** offerings and	**Ex 24:5**	5930a
it is a **b** offering to the LORD:	**Ex 29:18**	5930a
b offering for a soothing aroma before	**Ex 29:25**	5930a
"It shall be a continual **b** offering	**Ex 29:42**	5930a
or **b** offering or meal offering;	**Ex 30:9**	5930a
b offering and all its utensils,	**Ex 30:28**	5930a
the altar of **b** offering also with	**Ex 31:9**	5930a
early and offered **b** offerings,	**Ex 32:6**	5930a
the altar of **b** offering with its	**Ex 35:16**	5930a
of **b** offering of acacia wood,	**Ex 38:1**	5930a
You shall set the altar of **b** offering	**Ex 40:6**	5930a
b offering and all its utensils,	**Ex 40:10**	5930a
He set the altar of **b** offering	**Ex 40:29**	5930a
and offered on it the **b** offering	**Ex 40:29**	5930a
is a **b** offering from the herd,	**Lv 1:3**	5930a
on the head of the **b** offering,	**Lv 1:4**	5930a
'He shall then skin the **b** offering	**Lv 1:6**	5930a
it on the altar for a **b** offering,	**Lv 1:9**	5930a
or of the goats, for a **b** offering,	**Lv 1:10**	5930a
it is a **b** offering, an offering by	**Lv 1:13**	5930a
the LORD is a **b** offering of birds,	**Lv 1:14**	5930a
it is a **b** offering, an offering by	**Lv 1:17**	5930a
on the altar on the **b** offering,	**Lv 3:5**	5930a
b offering which is at the doorway	**Lv 4:7**	5930a
smoke on the altar of **b** offering.	**Lv 4:10**	5930a
at the base of the altar of **b** offering	**Lv 4:18**	5930a
the **b** offering before the LORD;	**Lv 4:24**	5930a
horns of the altar of **b** offering;	**Lv 4:25**	5930a
base of the altar of **b** offering.	**Lv 4:25**	5930a
at the place of the **b** offering.	**Lv 4:29**	5930a
horns of the altar of **b** offering;	**Lv 4:30**	5930a
where they slay the **b** offering.	**Lv 4:33**	5930a
horns of the altar of **b** offering,	**Lv 4:34**	5930a
and the other for a **b** offering.	**Lv 5:7**	5930a
he shall then prepare as a **b** offering	**Lv 5:10**	5930a
is the law for the **b** offering:	**Lv 6:9**	5930a
the **b** offering itself *shall remain*	**Lv 6:9**	5930a
the **b** offering on the altar and	**Lv 6:10**	5930a
lay out the **b** offering on it,	**Lv 6:12**	5930a
in the place where the **b** offering	**Lv 6:25**	5930a
place where they slay the **b** offering	**Lv 7:2**	5930a
who presents any man's **b** offering,	**Lv 7:8**	5930a
for himself the skin of the **b** offering	**Lv 7:8**	5930a
This is the law of the **b** offering,	**Lv 7:37**	5930a
the ram of the **b** offering,	**Lv 8:18**	5930a
a **b** offering for a soothing aroma;	**Lv 8:21**	5930a
on the altar with the **b** offering.	**Lv 8:28**	5930a
and a ram for a **b** offering,	**Lv 9:2**	5930a
without defect, for a **b** offering,	**Lv 9:3**	5930a
sin offering and your **b** offering,	**Lv 9:7**	5930a
he slaughtered the **b** offering;	**Lv 9:12**	5930a
They handed the **b** offering to	**Lv 9:13**	5930a
with the **b** offering on the altar.	**Lv 9:14**	5930a
He also presented the **b** offering,	**Lv 9:16**	5930a
the **b** offering of the morning.	**Lv 9:17**	5930a
sin offering and the **b** offering	**Lv 9:22**	5930a
and consumed the **b** offering and the	**Lv 9:24**	5930a
their **b** offering before the LORD.	**Lv 10:19**	5930a
year old lamb for a **b** offering and	**Lv 12:6**	5930a
the one for a **b** offering and the	**Lv 12:8**	5930a
sin offering and the **b** offering,	**Lv 14:13**	5930a
he shall slaughter the **b** offering.	**Lv 14:19**	5930a
The priest shall offer up the **b** offering	**Lv 14:20**	5930a
and the other a **b** offering.	**Lv 14:22**	5930a
and the other for a **b** offering,	**Lv 14:31**	5930a
and the other for a **b** offering.	**Lv 15:15**	5930a
and the other for a **b** offering.	**Lv 15:30**	5930a
and a ram for a **b** offering.	**Lv 16:3**	5930a
and one ram for a **b** offering.	**Lv 16:5**	5930a
come forth and offer his **b** offering	**Lv 16:24**	5930a
and the **b** offering of the people and	**Lv 16:24**	5930a
offers a **b** offering or sacrifice,	**Lv 17:8**	5930a
to the LORD for a **b** offering	**Lv 22:18**	5930a
for a **b** offering to the LORD.	**Lv 23:12**	5930a
to be a **b** offering to the LORD,	**Lv 23:18**	5930a
b offerings and grain offerings,	**Lv 23:37**	5930a
and *the* other for a **b** offering,	**Nu 6:11**	5930a
lamb a year old without defect for a **b**	**Nu 6:14**	5930a
sin offering and his **b** offering.	**Nu 6:16**	5930a
one year old, for a **b** offering;	**Nu 7:15**	5930a
one year old, for a **b** offering;	**Nu 7:21**	5930a
one year old, for a **b** offering;	**Nu 7:27**	5930a
one year old, for a **b** offering;	**Nu 7:33**	5930a
one year old, for a **b** offering;	**Nu 7:39**	5930a
one year old, for a **b** offering;	**Nu 7:45**	5930a
one year old, for a **b** offering;	**Nu 7:51**	5930a
one year old, for a **b** offering;	**Nu 7:57**	5930a
one year old, for a **b** offering;	**Nu 7:63**	5930a
one year old, for a **b** offering;	**Nu 7:69**	5930a
one year old, for a **b** offering;	**Nu 7:75**	5930a
one year old, for a **b** offering;	**Nu 7:81**	5930a
for the **b** offering twelve bulls,	**Nu 7:87**	5930a
for a **b** offering to the LORD,	**Nu 8:12**	5930a
trumpets over your **b** offerings,	**Nu 10:10**	5930a
a **b** offering or a sacrifice to	**Nu 15:3**	5930a
b offering or for the sacrifice,	**Nu 15:5**	5930a
as a **b** offering or a sacrifice,	**Nu 15:8**	5930a
offer one bull for a **b** offering,	**Nu 15:24**	5930a
some of the ashes of the **b** purification	**Nu 19:17**	8316
"Stand beside your **b** offering,	**Nu 23:3**	5930a
standing beside his **b** offering,	**Nu 23:6**	5930a
"Stand here beside your **b** offering	**Nu 23:15**	5930a
standing beside his **b** offering,	**Nu 23:17**	5930a
a continual **b** offering every day.	**Nu 28:3**	5930a
'It is a continual **b** offering	**Nu 28:6**	5930a
This is the **b** offering of every	**Nu 28:10**	5930a
b offering and its drink offering.	**Nu 28:10**	5930a
present a **b** offering to the LORD:	**Nu 28:11**	5930a
a **b** offering of a soothing aroma,	**Nu 28:13**	5930a
this is the **b** offering of each	**Nu 28:14**	5930a
to the continual **b** offering.	**Nu 28:15**	5930a
by fire, a **b** offering to the LORD:	**Nu 28:19**	5930a
the **b** offering of the morning,	**Nu 28:23**	5930a
is for a continual **b** offering.	**Nu 28:23**	5930a
to the continual **b** offering.	**Nu 28:24**	5930a
'You shall offer a **b** offering	**Nu 28:27**	5930a
'Besides the continual **b** offering	**Nu 28:31**	5930a
'You shall offer a **b** offering	**Nu 29:2**	5930a
the **b** offering of the new moon and	**Nu 29:6**	5930a
and the continual **b** offering and	**Nu 29:6**	5930a
'You shall present a **b** offering	**Nu 29:8**	5930a
the continual **b** offering and its grain	**Nu 29:11**	5930a
You shall present a **b** offering,	**Nu 29:13**	5930a
besides the continual **b** offering,	**Nu 29:16**	5930a
besides the continual **b** offering	**Nu 29:19**	5930a
besides the continual **b** offering	**Nu 29:22**	5930a
besides the continual **b** offering,	**Nu 29:25**	5930a
besides the continual **b** offering	**Nu 29:28**	5930a
besides the continual **b** offering,	**Nu 29:31**	5930a
besides the continual **b** offering,	**Nu 29:34**	5930a
you shall present a **b** offering,	**Nu 29:36**	5930a
besides the continual **b** offering	**Nu 29:38**	5930a
for your **b** offerings and for your	**Nu 29:39**	5930a
you shall bring your **b** offerings,	**Dt 12:6**	5930a
b offerings and your sacrifices,	**Dt 12:11**	5930a
do not offer your **b** offerings in every	**Dt 12:13**	5930a
you shall offer your **b** offerings,	**Dt 12:14**	5930a
you shall offer your **b** offerings,	**Dt 12:27**	5930a
b offering to the LORD your God;	**Dt 13:16**	3632
and you shall offer on it **b**	**Dt 27:6**	5930a
whole **b** offering on Your altar.	**Dt 33:10**	3632
b offerings on it to the LORD,	**Jos 8:31**	5930a
or if to offer a **b** offering or	**Jos 22:23**	5930a
for **b** offering or for sacrifice;	**Jos 22:26**	5930a
before Him with our **b** offerings,	**Jos 22:27**	5930a
for **b** offering or for sacrifice;	**Jos 22:28**	5930a
building an altar for **b** offering,	**Jos 22:29**	5930a
a second bull and offer a **b** offering	**Jg 6:26**	5930a
offer it up as a **b** offering."	**Jg 11:31**	5930a
but if you prepare a **b** offering,	**Jg 13:16**	5930a
He would not have accepted a **b**	**Jg 13:23**	5930a
And they offered **b** offerings and	**Jg 20:26**	5930a
b offerings and peace offerings.	**Jg 21:4**	5930a
cows as a **b** offering to the LORD.	**1Sa 6:14**	5930a
the men of Beth-shemesh offered **b**	**1Sa 6:15**	5930a
a whole **b** offering to the LORD;	**1Sa 7:9**	5930a
was offering up the **b** offering,	**1Sa 7:10**	5930a
come down to you to offer **b** offerings	**1Sa 10:8**	5930a
"Bring to me the **b** offering and	**1Sa 13:9**	5930a
And he offered the **b** offering.	**1Sa 13:9**	5930a
finished offering the **b** offering,	**1Sa 13:10**	5930a
and offered the **b** offering."	**1Sa 13:12**	5930a
LORD as much delight in **b** offerings	**1Sa 15:22**	5930a
and David offered **b** offerings and	**2Sa 6:17**	5930a
David had finished offering the **b**	**2Sa 6:18**	5930a
Look, the oxen for the **b** offering,	**2Sa 24:22**	5930a
for I will not offer **b** offerings	**2Sa 24:24**	5930a
b offerings and peace offerings.	**2Sa 24:25**	5930a
b offerings on that altar.	**1Ki 3:4**	5930a
and offered **b** offerings and made	**1Ki 3:15**	5930a
because there he offered the **b**	**1Ki 8:64**	5930a
was too small to hold the **b** offering	**1Ki 8:64**	5930a
Solomon offered **b** offerings and peace	**1Ki 9:25**	5930a
the **b** offering and on the wood."	**1Ki 18:34**	5930a
and consumed the **b** offering and	**1Ki 18:38**	5930a
and **b** incense on the high places.	**1Ki 22:43**	6999
him as a **b** offering on the wall.	**2Ki 3:27**	5930a
servant will no longer offer **b** offering	**2Ki 5:17**	5930a
offer sacrifices and **b** offerings.	**2Ki 10:24**	5930a
finished offering the **b** offering,	**2Ki 10:25**	5930a
and burned his **b** offering and his	**2Ki 16:13**	5930a
altar burn the morning **b** offering and	**2Ki 16:15**	5930a
king's **b** offering and his meal offering,	**2Ki 16:15**	5930a
with the **b** offering of all the	**2Ki 16:15**	5930a
sprinkle on it all the blood of the **b**	**2Ki 16:15**	5930a
sons offered on the altar of **b** offering	**1Ch 6:49**	5930a
and they offered **b** offerings and	**1Ch 16:1**	5930a
David had finished offering the **b**	**1Ch 16:2**	5930a
to offer **b** offerings to the LORD	**1Ch 16:40**	5930a
to the LORD on the altar of **b** offering	**1Ch 16:40**	5930a
I will give the oxen for **b** offerings	**1Ch 21:23**	5930a
or offer a **b** offering which costs	**1Ch 21:24**	5930a
b offerings and peace offerings.	**1Ch 21:26**	5930a
heaven on the altar of **b** offering.	**1Ch 21:26**	5930a
and the altar of **b** offering *were*	**1Ch 21:29**	5930a
altar of **b** offering for Israel."	**1Ch 22:1**	5930a
offer all **b** offerings to the LORD,	**1Ch 23:31**	5930a
offered **b** offerings to the LORD,	**1Ch 29:21**	5930a
a thousand **b** offerings on it.	**2Ch 1:6**	5930a
b offerings morning and evening,	**2Ch 2:4**	5930a
rinse things for the **b** offering;	**2Ch 4:6**	5930a
the **b** offering and the sacrifices,	**2Ch 7:1**	5930a
for there he offered the **b**	**2Ch 7:7**	5930a
able to contain the **b** offering,	**2Ch 7:7**	5930a
Then Solomon offered **b** offerings	**2Ch 8:12**	5930a
they burn to the LORD **b** offerings	**2Ch 13:11**	5930a
offer the **b** offerings of the LORD,	**2Ch 23:18**	5930a
the service and the **b** offering,	**2Ch 24:14**	5930a
And they offered **b** offerings in	**2Ch 24:14**	5930a
burned incense or offered **b** offerings	**2Ch 29:7**	5930a
the altar of **b** offering with all	**2Ch 29:18**	5930a
for the king ordered the **b**	**2Ch 29:24**	5930a
offer the **b** offering on the altar.	**2Ch 29:27**	5930a
When the **b** offering began, the	**2Ch 29:27**	5930a
until the **b** offering was finished.	**2Ch 29:28**	5930a
the completion of the **b** offerings,	**2Ch 29:29**	5927
were willing *brought* **b** offerings.	**2Ch 29:31**	5930a
The number of the **b** offerings	**2Ch 29:32**	5930a
were for a **b** offering to the LORD.	**2Ch 29:32**	5930a
to skin all the **b** offerings;	**2Ch 29:34**	5930a
There *were* also many **b**	**2Ch 29:35**	5930a
the libations for the **b** offerings.	**2Ch 29:35**	5930a
and brought **b** offerings to the	**2Ch 30:15**	5930a
for **b** offerings and for peace	**2Ch 31:2**	5930a
of his goods for the **b** offerings,	**2Ch 31:3**	5930a
morning and evening **b** offerings,	**2Ch 31:3**	5930a
and the **b** offerings for the	**2Ch 31:3**	5930a
Then they removed the **b** offerings	**2Ch 35:12**	5930a
were offering the **b** offerings and	**2Ch 35:14**	5930a
and to offer **b** offerings on the	**2Ch 35:16**	5930a

to offer **b** offerings on it, **Ezr 3:2** 5930a
b offerings on it to the LORD, **Ezr 3:3** 5930a
b offerings morning and evening. **Ezr 3:3** 5930a
fixed number of **b** offerings daily, **Ezr 3:4** 5930a
there was a continual **b** offering, **Ezr 3:5** 5930a
to offer **b** offerings to the LORD, **Ezr 3:6** 5930a
a **b** offering to the God of heaven, **Ezr 6:9** 5928
captivity offered **b** offerings to the God **Ezr 8:35** 5930a
all as a **b** offering to the LORD. **Ezr 8:35** 5930a
for the continual **b** offering, **Ne 10:33** 5930a
the morning and offering **b** offerings **Jb 1:5** 5930a
up a **b** offering for yourselves, **Jb 42:8** 5930a
find your **b** offering acceptable! **Ps 20:3** 5930a
B offering and sin offering You **Ps 40:6** 5930a
And your **b** offerings are **Ps 50:8** 5930a
are not pleased with **b** offering. **Ps 51:16** 5930a
In **b** offering and whole burnt **Ps 51:19** 5930a
offering and whole **b** offering; **Ps 51:19** 3632
into Your house with **b** offerings; **Ps 66:13** 5930a
to You **b** offerings of fat beasts, **Ps 66:15** 5930a
had enough of **b** offerings of rams And **Is 1:11** 5930a
beasts enough for a **b** offering. **Is 40:16** 5930a
Me the sheep of your **b** offerings, **Is 43:23** 5930a
Their **b** offerings and their **Is 56:7** 5930a
I hate robbery in the **b** offering; **Is 61:8** 5930a
b offerings are not acceptable And **Jer 6:20** 5930a
"Add your **b** offerings to your **Jer 7:21** 5930a
b offerings and sacrifices. **Jer 7:22** 5930a
b offering and grain offering, **Jer 14:12** 5930a
the Negev, bringing **b** offerings, **Jer 17:26** 5930a
the fire as **b** offerings to Baal, **Jer 19:5** 5930a
before Me to offer **b** offerings, **Jer 33:18** 5930a
I will make you a **b** out mountain. **Jer 51:25** 8316
there they rinse the **b** offering. **Ezk 40:38** 5930a
which to slaughter the **b** offering, **Ezk 40:39** 5930a
For the **b** offering *there were* **Ezk 40:42** 5930a
the **b** offering and the sacrifice. **Ezk 40:42** 5930a
to offer **b** offerings on it and to **Ezk 43:18** 5930a
up as a **b** offering to the LORD. **Ezk 43:24** 5930a
your **b** offerings on the altar, **Ezk 43:27** 5930a
they shall slaughter the **b** **Ezk 44:11** 5930a
grain offering, for a **b** offering and **Ezk 45:15** 5930a
part *to provide* the **b** offerings, **Ezk 45:17** 5930a
grain offering, the **b** offering and **Ezk 45:17** 5930a
as a **b** offering to the LORD seven bulls **Ezk 45:23** 5930a
the sin offering, the **b** offering, **Ezk 45:25** 5930a
priests shall provide his **b** offering and **Ezk 46:2** 5930a
"The **b** offering which the **Ezk 46:4** 5930a
a freewill offering, a **b** offering, **Ezk 46:12** 5930a
And he shall provide his **b** offering **Ezk 46:12** 5930a
a **b** offering to the LORD daily; **Ezk 46:13** 5930a
for a continual **b** offering." **Ezk 46:15** 5930a
of God rather than **b** offerings. **Hos 6:6** 5930a
"Even though you offer up to Me **b** **Am 5:22** 5930a
I come to Him with **b** offerings, **Mi 6:6** 5930a
all **b** offerings and sacrifices." **Mk 12:33** *3646*
IN WHOLE **B** OFFERINGS AND **Heb 10:6** *3646*
B OFFERINGS AND *sacrifices* FOR SIN **Heb 10:8** *3646*

BURST
of the great deep **b** open, **Gn 7:11** 1234
the cloud does not **b** under them. **Jb 26:8** 1234
new wineskins it is about to **b**. **Jb 32:19** 1234
broken the yoke *And* **b** the bonds. **Jer 5:5** 5423
will **b** on the head of the wicked. **Jer 30:23** 2342a
And you **b** forth in your rivers And **Ezk 32:2** 1518
When they **b** through the defenses, **Jl 2:8** 5307
otherwise the wineskins **b**, **Mt 9:17** *4486*
the wine will **b** the skins, **Mk 2:22** *4486*
the new wine will **b** the skins and **Lk 5:37** *4486*
the torrent **b** against that house **Lk 6:48** *4366*
and the torrent **b** against it and **Lk 6:49** *4366*
he **b** open in the middle and all **Ac 1:18** *2997*

BURSTING
the sea with doors When, **b** forth, **Jb 38:8** 1518

BURY
I may **b** my dead out of my sight." **Gn 23:4** 6912
b your dead in the choicest of our **Gn 23:6** 6912
me to **b** my dead out of my sight, **Gn 23:8** 6912
I give it to you; **b** your dead." **Gn 23:11** 6912
me that I may **b** my dead there." **Gn 23:13** 6912
So **b** your dead." **Gn 23:15** 6912
Please do not **b** me in Egypt, **Gn 47:29** 6912
and **b** me in their burial place." **Gn 47:30** 6912
b me with my fathers in the cave **Gn 49:29** 6912
of Canaan, there you shall **b** me." **Gn 50:5** 6912
let me go up and **b** my father; **Gn 50:5** 6912
"Go up and **b** your father, as he **Gn 50:6** 6912
So Joseph went up to **b** his father, **Gn 50:7** 6912
gone up with him to **b** his father. **Gn 50:14** 6912
surely **b** him on the same day **Dt 21:23** 6912
and fall upon him and **b** him, **1Ki 2:31** 6912
army had gone up to **b** the slain, **1Ki 11:15** 6912
old prophet to mourn and to **b** him. **1Ki 13:29** 6912
b me in the grave in which the man **1Ki 13:31** 6912
shall mourn for him and **b** him, **1Ki 14:13** 6912
Jezreel, and none shall **b** *her.*'" **2Ki 9:10** 6912
to this cursed woman and **b** her, **2Ki 9:34** 6912
They went to **b** her, **2Ki 9:35** 6912
b him in the tombs of the kings. **2Ch 24:25** 6912
And there was no one to **b** them. **Ps 79:3** 6912
for they will **b** in Topheth because **Jer 7:32** 6912
and there will be no one to **b** them **Jer 14:16** 6912
and they will **b** in Topheth because **Jer 19:11** 6912
So they will **b** Gog there with all **Ezk 39:11** 6912
people of the land will **b** *them;* **Ezk 39:13** 6912
them up, Memphis will **b** them. **Hos 9:6** 6912
me first to go and **b** my father." **Mt 8:21** *2290*
the dead to **b** their own dead." **Mt 8:22** *2290*
me first to go and **b** my father." **Lk 9:59** *2290*
the dead to **b** their own dead; **Lk 9:60** *2290*

BURYING
you his grave for **b** your dead." **Gn 23:6** 6912
while the Egyptians were **b** all **Nu 33:4** 6912
As they were **b** a man, **2Ki 13:21** 6912
be **b** them in order to cleanse the land **Ezk 39:12** 6912
b those who were passing through, **Ezk 39:14** 6912

BUSH
fire from the midst of a **b**; **Ex 3:2** 5572
the **b** was burning with fire, **Ex 3:2** 5572
fire, yet the **b** was not consumed. **Ex 3:2** 5572
why the **b** is not burned up." **Ex 3:3** 5572
to him from the midst of the **b** and **Ex 3:4** 5572
favor of Him who dwelt in the **b**. **Dt 33:16** 5572
"The thorn **b** which was in Lebanon **2Ki 14:9** 2336
Lebanon, and trampled the thorn **b**. **2Ki 14:9** 2336
"The thorn **b** which was in Lebanon **2Ch 25:18** 2336
Lebanon and trampled the thorn **b**. **2Ch 25:18** 2336
thorn **b** the cypress will come up, **Is 55:13** 5285
"For he will be like a **b** in the **Jer 17:6** 6176
the *passage* about *the burning* **b**, **Mk 12:26** *942*
they pick grapes from a briar **b**. **Lk 6:44** *942*
the *passage about the burning* **b**, **Lk 20:37** *942*
THE FLAME OF A BURNING THORN **B**. **Ac 7:30** *942*
appeared to him in the thorn **b**. **Ac 7:35** *942*

BUSHEL
b smaller and the shekel bigger, **Am 8:5** 374

BUSHES
left the boy under one of the **b**. **Gn 21:15** 7880
breaks out and spreads to thorn **b**, **Ex 22:6** 6975
Who pluck mallow by the **b**, **Jb 30:4** 7880
"Among the **b** they cry out; **Jb 30:7** 7880
crackling of thorn **b** under a pot, **Ec 7:6** 5518b
of the cliffs, on all the thorn **b** and **Is 7:19** 5285
are not gathered from thorn **b** nor **Mt 7:16**

BUSINESS
not eat until I have told my **b**." **Gn 24:33** 1697
if you do not tell this **b** of ours, **Jos 2:14** 1697
"But if you tell this **b** of ours, **Jos 2:20** 1697
man in Maon whose **b** was in Carmel; **1Sa 25:2** 4639
of those who carry on the *king's* **b**, **Es 3:9** 4399
the king's **b** assisted the Jews, **Es 9:3** 4399
ships, Who do **b** on great waters; **Ps 107:23** 4399
again and carried on the king's **b**; **Da 8:27** 4399
"What **b** do we have with each other, **Mt 8:29**
to his own farm, another to his **b**, **Mt 22:5** *1171*
saying, "What **b** do we have with **Mk 1:24**
"What **b** do we have with each other, **Mk 5:7**
"Let us alone! What **b** do we have **Lk 4:34**
"What **b** do we have with each other, **Lk 8:28**
'Do **b** *with this* until I come *back.*' **Lk 19:13** *4231*
might know what **b** they had done. **Lk 19:15** *1281*
My Father's house a place of **b**." **Jn 2:16** *1712*
no little **b** to the craftsmen; **Ac 19:24** *2039*
prosperity depends upon this **b**. **Ac 19:25** *2039*
own **b** and work with your hands, **1Th 4:11**
engage in **b** and make a profit." **Jas 4:13** *1710*

BUSY
your servant was **b** here and there, **1Ki 20:40** 6213a

BUSYBODIES
no work at all, but acting like **b**. **2Th 3:11** *4020*
idle, but also gossips and **b**, **1Tm 5:13** *4021*

BUTCHERED
are *all* **b** and everything is ready; **Mt 22:4** *2380*

BUTT
belly with the **b** end of the spear, **2Sa 2:23** 310

BUTTER
When my steps were bathed in **b**, **Jb 29:6** 2529
His speech was smoother than **b**, **Ps 55:21** 4260
the churning of milk produces **b**, **Pr 30:33** 2529

BUTTING
I saw the ram **b** westward, **Da 8:4** 5055

BUTTOCKS
and barefoot with **b** uncovered, **Is 20:4** 8351

BUTTRESS
the corner **b** and fortified them. **2Ch 26:9** 4740

BUY
to Egypt to **b** grain from Joseph, **Gn 41:57** 7666
and **b** *some* for us from that place, **Gn 42:2** 7666
went down to **b** grain from Egypt. **Gn 42:3** 7666
So the sons of Israel came to **b** **Gn 42:5** 7666
the land of Canaan, to **b** food." **Gn 42:7** 7666
your servants have come to **b** food. **Gn 42:10** 7666
"Go back, **b** us a little food." **Gn 43:2** 7666
we will go down and **b** you food. **Gn 43:4** 7666
down the first time to **b** food, **Gn 43:20** 7666
other money in our hand to **b** food; **Gn 43:22** 7666
'Go back, **b** us a little food.' **Gn 44:25** 7666
B us and our land for food, and we **Gn 47:19** 7069
land of the priests he did not **b**, **Gn 47:22** 7069
"If you **b** a Hebrew slave, he **Ex 21:2** 7069
or **b** from your friend's hand, **Lv 25:14** 7069
you shall **b** from your friend; **Lv 25:15** 7069
kinsman is to come and **b** back what **Lv 25:25** 1350
"You shall **b** food from them with **Dt 2:6** 7666
'**B** *it* before those who are sitting **Ru 4:4** 7069
"On the day you **b** the field from **Ru 4:5** 7069
"**B** *it* for yourself." **Ru 4:8** 7069
"To **b** the threshing floor from **2Sa 24:21** 7069
surely **b** *it* from you for a price, **2Sa 24:24** 7069
surely **b** *it* for the full price; **1Ch 21:24** 7069
and to the builders to **b** quarried stone **2Ch 34:11** 7069
you shall diligently **b** bulls, **Ezr 7:17** 7066
we did not **b** any land, and all my **Ne 5:16** 7069
we will not **b** from them on the **Ne 10:31** 3947
in the hand of a fool to **b** wisdom, **Pr 17:16** 7069
B truth, and do not sell *it, Get* **Pr 23:23** 7069
who have no money come, **b** and eat. **Is 55:1** 7666
b wine and milk Without money **Is 55:1** 7666
and **b** yourself a linen waistband and **Jer 13:1** 7069
and **b** a potter's earthenware jar, **Jer 19:1** 7069
"**B** for yourself my field which is **Jer 32:7** 7069
right of redemption to **b** *it.*" **Jer 32:7** 7069
'**B** my field, please, that is at **Jer 32:8** 7069
b *it* for yourself.' **Jer 32:8** 7069
"**B** for yourself the field with **Jer 32:25** 7069
'Men will **b** fields for money, **Jer 32:44** 7069
So as to **b** the helpless for money **Am 8:6** 7069
"Those who **b** them slay them and **Zch 11:5** 7069
and **b** food for themselves." **Mt 14:15** *59*
and **b** *some* for yourselves.' **Mt 25:9** *59*
b themselves something to eat." **Mk 6:36** *59*
and **b** food for all these people." **Lk 9:13** *59*
no sword is to sell his coat and **b** one. **Lk 22:36** *59*
gone away into the city to **b** food. **Jn 4:8** *59*
"Where are we to **b** bread, so **Jn 6:5** *59*
"**B** the things we have need of for **Jn 13:29** *59*
and those who **b**, as though they **1Co 7:30** *59*
to **b** from Me gold refined by fire so **Rv 3:18** *59*
will be able to **b** or to sell, **Rv 13:17** *59*

BUYER
slaves, but there will be no **b**." **Dt 28:68** 7069
"Bad, bad," says the **b**, **Pr 20:14** 7069
mistress, the **b** like the seller, **Is 24:2** 7069
b rejoice nor the seller mourn; **Ezk 7:12** 7069

BUYING
and for **b** timber and hewn stone to **2Ki 12:12** 7069
for **b** timber and hewn stone to repair **2Ki 22:6** 7069
were **b** and selling in the temple, **Mt 21:12** *59*
were **b** and selling in the temple, **Mk 11:15** *59*
they were drinking, they were **b**, **Lk 17:28** *59*

BUYS
'But if a priest **b** a slave as *his* **Lv 22:11** 7069
She considers a field and **b** it; **Pr 31:16** 3947
all that he has and **b** that field. **Mt 13:44** *59*
no one **b** their cargoes any more **Rv 18:11** *59*

BUZ
Uz his firstborn and **B** his **Gn 22:21** 938
the son of Jahdo, the son of **B**; **1Ch 5:14** 938
and Dedan, Tema, **B** and **Jer 25:23** 938

BUZI
to Ezekiel the priest, son of **B**, **Ezk 1:3** 941

BUZITE
Elihu the son of Barachel the **B**, **Jb 32:2** 940
Barachel the **B** spoke out and said, **Jb 32:6** 940

BUZZARD
eagle and the vulture and the **b**, **Lv 11:13** 5822
eagle and the vulture and the **b**, **Dt 14:12** 5822

BYPATHS
the ancient paths, To walk in **b**, **Jer 18:15** 5410b

BYSTANDERS
the **b** came up and said to Peter, **Mt 26:73** *2476*
Some of the **b** were saying to them, **Mk 11:5** *1563, 2476*
began once more to say to the **b**, **Mk 14:69** *3936*
the **b** were again saying to Peter, **Mk 14:70** *3936*
When some of the **b** heard it, **Mk 15:35** *3936*
"Then he said to the **b**, **Lk 19:24** *3936*
the **b** said, "Do you revile God's high **Ac 23:4** *3936*

BYWORD
proverb and a **b** among all peoples. **1Ki 9:7** 8148
proverb and a **b** among all peoples. **2Ch 7:20** 8148
He has made me a **b** of the people, **Jb 17:6** 4914
I have even become a **b** to them. **Jb 30:9** 4405
make us a **b** among the nations, **Ps 44:14** 4912
my clothing, I became a **b** to them. **Ps 69:11** 4912
Thus she became a **b** among women, **Ezk 23:10** 8034
a reproach, A **b** among the nations. **Jl 2:17** 4912

C

CABBON
and **C** and Lahmas and Chitlish, **Jos 15:40** 3522

CABLES
c in undergirding the ship; **Ac 27:17** *996*

CABUL
then it proceeded on north to **C**, **Jos 19:27** 3521
called the land of **C** to this day. **1Ki 9:13** 3521

CAESAR
it lawful to give a poll-tax to **C**, **Mt 22:17** *2541*
to **C** the things that are Caesar's; **Mt 22:21** *2541*
Is it lawful to pay a poll-tax to **C**, **Mk 12:14** *2541*
to **C** the things that are Caesar's, **Mk 12:17** *2541*
a decree went out from **C** Augustus, **Lk 2:1** *2541*
year of the reign of Tiberius **C**, **Lk 3:1** *2541*
lawful for us to pay taxes to **C**, **Lk 20:22** *2541*
to **C** the things that are Caesar's, **Lk 20:25** *2541*
and forbidding to pay taxes to **C**, **Lk 23:2** *2541*
this Man, you are no friend of **C**; **Jn 19:12** *2541*
out *to be* a king opposes **C**." **Jn 19:12** *2541*
"We have no king but **C**." **Jn 19:15** *2541*
act contrary to the decrees of **C**, **Ac 17:7** *2541*
against the temple or against **C**." **Ac 25:8** *2541*
hand me over to them. I appeal to **C**." **Ac 25:11** *2541*
"You have appealed to **C**, **Ac 25:12** *2541*
to Caesar, to **C** you shall go." **Ac 25:12** *2541*
custody until I send him to **C**." **Ac 25:21** *2541*
if he had not appealed to **C**." **Ac 26:32** *2541*

Context	Reference	Number
you must stand before **C**;	**Ac 27:24**	*2541*
I was forced to appeal to **C**,	**Ac 28:19**	*2541*
CAESAREA		
into the district of **C** Philippi,	**Mt 16:13**	*2542*
to the villages of **C** Philippi;	**Mk 8:27**	*2542*
the cities until he came to **C**.	**Ac 8:40**	*2542*
to **C** and sent him away to Tarsus.	**Ac 9:30**	*2542*
a man at **C** named Cornelius,	**Ac 10:1**	*2542*
On the following day he entered **C**.	**Ac 10:24**	*2542*
having been sent to me from **C**.	**Ac 11:11**	*2542*
to **C** and was spending time there.	**Ac 12:19**	*2542*
When he had landed at **C**,	**Ac 18:22**	*2542*
day we left and came to **C**	**Ac 21:8**	*2542*
from **C** also came with us,	**Ac 21:16**	*2542*
hour of the night to proceed to **C**,	**Ac 23:23**	*2542*
When these had come to **C** and	**Ac 23:33**	*2542*
later went up to Jerusalem from **C**.	**Ac 25:1**	*2542*
Paul was being kept in custody at **C**	**Ac 25:4**	*2542*
among them, he went down to **C**,	**Ac 25:6**	*2542*
Agrippa and Bernice arrived at **C** and	**Ac 25:13**	*2542*
CAESAR'S		
They said to Him, "**C**."	**Mt 22:21**	*2541*
to Caesar the things that are **C**;	**Mt 22:21**	*2541*
And they said to Him, "**C**."	**Mk 12:16**	*2541*
to Caesar the things that are **C**,	**Mk 12:17**	*2541*
They said, "**C**."	**Lk 20:24**	*2541*
to Caesar the things that are **C**,	**Lk 20:25**	*2541*
"I am standing before **C** tribunal,	**Ac 25:10**	*2541*
especially those of **C** household.	**Php 4:22**	*2541*
CAGE		
'Like a **c** full of birds, So their	**Jer 5:27**	3619
'They put him in a **c** with	**Ezk 19:9**	5474
CAIAPHAS		
court of the high priest, named **C**;	**Mt 26:3**	*2533*
seized Jesus led Him away to **C**,	**Mt 26:57**	*2533*
high priesthood of Annas and **C**,	**Lk 3:2**	*2533*
But one of them, **C**,	**Jn 11:49**	*2533*
for he was father-in-law of **C**,	**Jn 18:13**	*2533*
Now **C** was the one who had advised	**Jn 18:14**	*2533*
Him bound to **C** the high priest.	**Jn 18:24**	*2533*
from **C** into the Praetorium,	**Jn 18:28**	*2533*
and **C** and John and Alexander,	**Ac 4:6**	*2533*
CAIN		
she conceived and gave birth to **C**,	**Gn 4:1**	7014b
but **C** was a tiller of the ground.	**Gn 4:2**	7014b
C brought an offering to the LORD	**Gn 4:3**	7014b
but for **C** and for his offering He	**Gn 4:5**	7014b
So **C** became very angry and his	**Gn 4:5**	7014b
Then the LORD said to **C**,	**Gn 4:6**	7014b
C told Abel his brother.	**Gn 4:8**	7014b
that **C** rose up against Abel his	**Gn 4:8**	7014b
Then the LORD said to **C**,	**Gn 4:9**	7014b
C said to the LORD,	**Gn 4:13**	7014b
"Therefore whoever kills **C**,	**Gn 4:15**	7014b
the LORD appointed a sign for **C**,	**Gn 4:15**	7014b
Then **C** went out from the presence	**Gn 4:16**	7014b
C had relations with his wife	**Gn 4:17**	7014b
If **C** is avenged sevenfold, Then	**Gn 4:24**	7014b
for **C** killed him."	**Gn 4:25**	7014b
to God a better sacrifice than **C**,	**Heb 11:4**	*2535*
not as **C**, *who* was of the evil one and	**1Jn 3:12**	*2535*
For they have gone the way of **C**,	**Jude 1:11**	*2535*
CAINAN		
the son of **C**, the son of Arphaxad,	**Lk 3:36**	*2536*
son of Mahalaleel, the son of **C**,	**Lk 3:37**	*2536*
CAKE		
and one **c** of bread and one cake of	**Ex 29:23**	3603
and one cake of bread and one **c** of	**Ex 29:23**	2471
he took one unleavened **c** and one	**Lv 8:26**	2471
one **c** of bread *mixed with* oil	**Lv 8:26**	2471
of an ephah shall be *in* each **c**.	**Lv 24:5**	2471
unleavened **c** out of the basket and	**Nu 6:19**	2471
shall lift up a **c** as an offering;	**Nu 15:20**	2471
fig **c** and two clusters of raisins,	**1Sa 30:12**	1690
a **c** of bread and one of dates and	**2Sa 6:19**	2471
me a little bread **c** from it first and	**1Ki 17:13**	5692
a bread **c** *baked on* hot stones,	**1Ki 19:6**	5692
"Take a **c** of figs."	**2Ki 20:7**	1690
a portion *of meat* and a raisin **c**.	**1Ch 16:3**	809
"Let them take a **c** of figs and	**Is 38:21**	1690
You shall eat it as a barley **c**,	**Ezk 4:12**	5692
Ephraim has become a **c** not turned.	**Hos 7:8**	5692
CAKES		
knead *it* and make bread **c**."	**Gn 18:6**	5692
Egypt into **c** of unleavened bread.	**Ex 12:39**	5692
and unleavened **c** mixed with oil,	**Ex 29:2**	2471
c of fine flour mixed with oil,	**Lv 2:4**	2471
as unleavened **c** in a holy place;	**Lv 6:16**	4682
offer unleavened **c** mixed with oil,	**Lv 7:12**	2471
and **c** *of well* stirred fine flour	**Lv 7:12**	2471
offering with **c** of leavened bread.	**Lv 7:13**	2471
flour and bake twelve **c** with it;	**Lv 24:5**	2471
and a basket of unleavened **c** of	**Nu 6:15**	2471
with the basket of unleavened **c**;	**Nu 6:17**	4682
it in the pot and make **c** with it;	**Nu 11:8**	5692
as the taste of **c** baked with oil.	**Nu 11:8**	3955
unleavened **c** and parched *grain*.	**Jos 5:11**	4682
raisins and two hundred **c** of figs,	**1Sa 25:18**	1690
make me a couple of **c** in my sight,	**2Sa 13:6**	3834
kneaded *it*, made **c** in his sight,	**2Sa 13:8**	3823b
in his sight, and baked the **c**.	**2Sa 13:8**	3834
So Tamar took the **c** which she had	**2Sa 13:10**	3834
you, *some* **c** and a jar of honey,	**1Ki 14:3**	5350
oxen, great quantities of flour **c**,	**1Ch 12:40**	7058
fig **c** and bunches of raisins,	**1Ch 12:40**	1690
"Sustain me with raisin **c**,	**SS 2:5**	809
You will moan for the raisin **c** of	**Is 16:7**	809
to make **c** for the queen of heaven;	**Jer 7:18**	3561
made for her *sacrificial* **c** in her image	**Jer 44:19**	3561
with the wheat of Minnith, **c**,	**Ezk 27:17**	6436
to other gods and love raisin **c**."	**Hos 3:1**	809
CALAH		
Nineveh and Rehoboth-Ir and **C**,	**Gn 10:11**	3625
and Resen between Nineveh and **C**;	**Gn 10:12**	3625
CALAMITIES		
all your **c** and your distresses;	**1Sa 10:19**	7463a
Cannot my palate discern **c**?	**Jb 6:30**	1942
CALAMITY		
For the day of their **c** is near,	**Dt 32:35**	343
bring down **c** on us and strike the city	**2Sa 15:14**	7463a
the LORD might bring **c** on Absalom.	**2Sa 17:14**	7463a
confronted me in the day of my **c**,	**2Sa 22:19**	343
it, the LORD relented from the **c** and	**2Sa 24:16**	7463a
c on the house of Jeroboam,	**1Ki 14:10**	7463a
have You also brought **c** to the	**1Ki 17:20**	7489a
such **c** on Jerusalem and Judah,	**2Ki 21:12**	7463a
LORD saw and was sorry over the **c**,	**1Ch 21:15**	7463a
your possessions with a great **c**;	**2Ch 21:14**	4046
c which will befall my people,	**Es 8:6**	7463a
in the balances together with my **c**!	**Jb 6:2**	1942
is at ease holds **c** in contempt,	**Jb 12:5**	6365
And **c** is ready at his side.	**Jb 18:12**	343
out, Or does their **c** fall on them?	**Jb 21:17**	343
is reserved for the day of **c**;	**Jb 21:30**	343
"Is it not **c** to the unjust And	**Jb 31:3**	343
"For **c** from God is a terror to	**Jb 31:23**	343
confronted me in the day of my **c**,	**Ps 18:18**	343
I will also laugh at your **c**;	**Pr 1:26**	343
your **c** comes like a whirlwind,	**Pr 1:27**	343
his **c** will come suddenly;	**Pr 6:15**	343
at **c** will not go unpunished.	**Pr 17:5**	343
the wicked stumble in *time of* **c**.	**Pr 24:16**	7463a
For their **c** will rise suddenly,	**Pr 24:22**	343
house in the day of your **c**;	**Pr 27:10**	343
his heart will fall into **c**.	**Pr 28:14**	7463a
Causing well-being and creating **c**;	**Is 45:7**	7451b
in vain, Or bear *children* for **c**;	**Is 65:23**	928
all this great **c** against us?	**Jer 16:10**	7463a
the **c** I planned to bring on it.	**Jer 18:8**	7463a
I am fashioning **c** against you and	**Jer 18:11**	7463a
My face In the day of their **c**.' "	**Jer 18:17**	343
to bring a **c** upon this place,	**Jer 19:3**	7463a
entire **c** that I have declared against it,	**Jer 19:15**	7463a
For I will bring **c** upon them,	**Jer 23:12**	7463a
'**C** will not come upon you.'	**Jer 23:17**	7463a
I am beginning to work **c** in *this*	**Jer 25:29**	7489a
that I may repent of the **c** which I	**Jer 26:3**	7463a
of war and of **c** and of pestilence.	**Jer 28:8**	7463a
'plans for welfare and not for **c**	**Jer 29:11**	7463a
made all this **c** come upon them.	**Jer 32:23**	7463a
c which I plan to bring on them,	**Jer 36:3**	7463a
all the **c** that I have declared to them	**Jer 36:31**	7463a
this **c** against this place;	**Jer 40:2**	7463a
c that I have inflicted on you.	**Jer 42:10**	7463a
no survivors or refugees from the **c**	**Jer 42:17**	7463a
c that I have brought on Jerusalem	**Jer 44:2**	7463a
therefore this **c** has befallen you,	**Jer 44:23**	7463a
day of their **c** has come upon them,	**Jer 46:21**	343
they have devised **c** against her:	**Jer 48:2**	7463a
And his **c** has swiftly hastened.	**Jer 48:16**	7463a
And I will bring **c** upon them,	**Jer 49:37**	7463a
to her In the day of *her* **c**.	**Jer 51:2**	7463a
c which would come upon Babylon,	**Jer 51:60**	7463a
because of the **c** that I am going	**Jer 51:64**	7463a
All my enemies have heard of my **c**;	**La 1:21**	7463a
then you will be comforted for the **c**	**Ezk 14:22**	7463a
the sword at the time of their **c**,	**Ezk 35:5**	343
ruled us, to bring on us great **c**;	**Da 9:12**	7463a
Moses, all this **c** has come on us;	**Da 9:13**	7463a
c in store and brought it on us;	**Da 9:14**	7463a
If a **c** occurs in a city has not	**Am 3:6**	7451b
Do you put off the day of **c**,	**Am 6:3**	7451b
'The **c** will not overtake or	**Am 9:10**	7463a
c In the day of their disaster.	**Ob 1:13**	7463a
account this **c** *has struck* us."	**Jon 1:7**	7463a
account *has* this **c** *struck* us?	**Jon 1:8**	7463a
then God relented concerning the **c**	**Jon 3:10**	7463a
and one who relents concerning **c**.	**Jon 4:2**	7463a
Because a **c** has come down from the	**Mi 1:12**	7451b
I am planning against this family a **c**	**Mi 2:3**	7463a
C will not come upon us."	**Mi 3:11**	7463a
be delivered from the hand of **c**!	**Hab 2:9**	7451b
CALAMUS		
Nard and saffron, **c** and cinnamon,	**SS 4:14**	7070
CALCOL		
the Ezrahite, Heman, **C** and Darda,	**1Ki 4:31**	3633
Zerah *were* Zimri, Ethan, Heman, **C** and	**1Ch 2:6**	3633
CALCULATE		
then he shall **c** the years since	**Lv 25:27**	2803
c from the year when he sold himself	**Lv 25:50**	2803
jubilee, he shall so **c** with him.	**Lv 25:52**	2803
then the priest shall **c** the price	**Lv 27:18**	2803
then the priest shall **c** for him	**Lv 27:23**	2803
not first sit down and **c** the cost to	**Lk 14:28**	*5585*
c the number of the beast,	**Rv 13:18**	*5585*
CALCULATED		
And **c** the dust of the earth by the	**Is 40:12**	3557
CALDRON		
it into the pan, or kettle, or **c**,	**1Sa 2:14**	7037
CALEB		
of Judah, **C** the son of Jephunneh;	**Nu 13:6**	3612
Then **C** quieted the people before	**Nu 13:30**	3612
of Nun and **C** the son of Jephunneh,	**Nu 14:6**	3612
"But My servant **C**, because he has	**Nu 14:24**	3612
except **C** the son of Jephunneh and	**Nu 14:30**	3612
But Joshua the son of Nun and **C**	**Nu 14:38**	3612
except **C** the son of Jephunneh and	**Nu 26:65**	3612
except **C** the son of Jephunneh the	**Nu 32:12**	3612
of Judah, **C** the son of Jephunneh.	**Nu 34:19**	3612
except **C** the son of Jephunneh;	**Dt 1:36**	3612
and **C** the son of Jephunneh the	**Jos 14:6**	3612
and gave Hebron to **C** the son of	**Jos 14:13**	3612
Hebron became the inheritance of **C**	**Jos 14:14**	3612
Now he gave to **C** the son of	**Jos 15:13**	3612
C drove out from there the	**Jos 15:14**	3612
And **C** said, "The one who attacks	**Jos 15:16**	3612
son of Kenaz, the brother of **C**,	**Jos 15:17**	3612
the donkey, and **C** said to her,	**Jos 15:18**	3612
they gave to **C** the son of	**Jos 21:12**	3612
And **C** said, "The one who attacks	**Jg 1:12**	3612
her donkey, and **C** said to her,	**Jg 1:14**	3612
So **C** gave her the upper springs	**Jg 1:15**	3612
Then they gave Hebron to **C**,	**Jg 1:20**	3612
to Judah, and on the Negev of **C**,	**1Sa 30:14**	3612
Now **C** the son of Hezron had sons	**1Ch 2:18**	3612
Azubah died, **C** married Ephrath,	**1Ch 2:19**	3612
Now the sons of **C**, the brother of	**1Ch 2:42**	3612
and the daughter of **C** *was* Achsah.	**1Ch 2:49**	3612
These were the sons of **C**.	**1Ch 2:50**	3612
C the son of Jephunneh *were* Iru,	**1Ch 4:15**	3612
gave to **C** the son of Jephunneh.	**1Ch 6:56**	3612
CALEB-EPHRATHAH		
After the death of Hezron in **C**,	**1Ch 2:24**	3613
CALEBITE		
in *his* dealings, and he was a **C**),	**1Sa 25:3**	3614
CALEB'S		
son of Kenaz, **C** younger brother,	**Jg 1:13**	3612
son of Kenaz, **C** younger brother.	**Jg 3:9**	3612
Ephah, **C** concubine, bore	**1Ch 2:46**	3612
Maacah, **C** concubine, bore Sheber	**1Ch 2:48**	3612
CALF		
and took a tender and choice **c** and	**Gn 18:7**	1121, 1241
and the **c** which he had prepared,	**Gn 18:8**	1121, 1241
tool and made it into a molten **c**;	**Ex 32:4**	5695
made for themselves a molten **c**,	**Ex 32:8**	5695
that he saw the **c** and *the* dancing;	**Ex 32:19**	5695
He took the **c** which they had	**Ex 32:20**	5695
the fire, and out came this **c**."	**Ex 32:24**	5695
with the **c** which Aaron had made.	**Ex 32:35**	5695
"Take for yourself a **c**,	**Lv 9:2**	5695
sin offering, and a **c** and a lamb,	**Lv 9:3**	5695
slaughtered the **c** of the sin offering	**Lv 9:8**	5695
made for yourselves a molten **c**;	**Dt 9:16**	5695
thing, the **c** which you had made,	**Dt 9:21**	5695
had a fattened **c** in the house,	**1Sa 28:24**	5695
A **c** of molten metal And said,	**Ne 9:18**	5695
He makes Lebanon skip like a **c**,	**Ps 29:6**	5695
They made a **c** in Horeb And	**Ps 106:19**	5695
And the **c** and the young lion and	**Is 11:6**	5695
There the **c** will graze, And there	**Is 27:10**	5695
chastised, Like an untrained **c**;	**Jer 31:18**	5695
when they cut the **c** in two and	**Jer 34:18**	5695
passed between the parts of the **c**	**Jer 34:19**	5695
He has rejected your **c**,	**Hos 8:5**	5695
Surely the **c** of Samaria will be	**Hos 8:6**	5695
will fear For the **c** of Beth-aven.	**Hos 10:5**	5697
and bring the fattened **c**,	**Lk 15:23**	*3448*
father has killed the fattened **c** because	**Lk 15:27**	*3448*
killed the fattened **c** for him.'	**Lk 15:30**	*3448*
"At that time they made a **c**	**Ac 7:41**	*3447*
and the second creature like a **c**,	**Rv 4:7**	*3448*
CALF'S		
their feet were like a **c** hoof,	**Ezk 1:7**	5695
CALL		
man to see what he would **c** them;	**Gn 2:19**	7121
to **c** upon the name of the LORD.	**Gn 4:26**	7121
And you shall **c** his name Ishmael,	**Gn 16:11**	7121
you shall not **c** her name Sarai,	**Gn 17:15**	7121
and you shall **c** his name Isaac;	**Gn 17:19**	7121
"We will **c** the girl and consult	**Gn 24:57**	7121
For women will **c** me happy."	**Gn 30:13**	7121
"Shall I go and **c** a nurse for you	**Ex 2:7**	7121
the sons of his people, to **c** him,	**Nu 22:5**	7121
"If the men have come to **c** you,	**Nu 22:20**	7121
not urgently send to you to **c** you?	**Nu 22:37**	7121
but the Moabites **c** them Emim.	**Dt 2:11**	7121
the Ammonites **c** them Zamzummin,	**Dt 2:20**	7121
(Sidonians **c** Hermon Sirion, and	**Dt 3:9**	7121
and the Amorites **c** it Senir):	**Dt 3:9**	7121
LORD our God whenever we **c** on Him?	**Dt 4:7**	7121
I **c** heaven and earth to witness	**Dt 4:26**	5749b
and you **c** *them* to mind in all	**Dt 30:1**	7725
"I **c** heaven and earth to witness	**Dt 30:19**	5749b
c Joshua, and present yourselves	**Dt 31:14**	7121
c the heavens and the earth to witness	**Dt 31:28**	5749b
will **c** peoples *to* the mountain;	**Dt 33:19**	7121
"**C** for Samson, that he may amuse	**Jg 16:25**	7121
"Do not **c** me Naomi;	**Ru 1:20**	7121
c me Mara, for the Almighty has	**Ru 1:20**	7121
Why do you **c** me Naomi, since the	**Ru 1:21**	7121
"I did not **c**, lie down again."	**1Sa 3:5**	7121
"I did not **c**, my son, lie down	**1Sa 3:6**	7121
I will **c** to the LORD, that He may	**1Sa 12:17**	7121
Absalom would **c** to him and say,	**2Sa 15:2**	7121
"Now **c** Hushai the Archite also,	**2Sa 17:5**	7121
"**C** out the men of Judah for me	**2Sa 20:4**	2199
went to **c** out *the men of* Judah,	**2Sa 20:5**	2199
"I **c** upon the LORD, who is worthy	**2Sa 22:4**	7121
"**C** Bathsheba to me."	**1Ki 1:28**	7121
"**C** to me Zadok the priest, Nathan	**1Ki 1:32**	7121

to them whenever they **c** to You.	**1Ki 8:52**	7121
you **c** on the name of your god,	**1Ki 18:24**	7121
I will **c** on the name of the LORD,	**1Ki 18:24**	7121
and **c** on the name of your god,	**1Ki 18:25**	7121
"**C** out with a loud voice, for he	**1Ki 18:27**	7121
"**C** this Shunammite."	**2Ki 4:12**	7121
He said, "**C** her."	**2Ki 4:15**	7121
"**C** this Shunammite."	**2Ki 4:36**	7121
and stand and **c** on the name of the	**2Ki 5:11**	7121
to the LORD, **c** upon His name;	**1Ch 16:8**	7121
"**C** now, is there anyone who will	**Jb 5:1**	7121
"Then **c**, and I will answer;	**Jb 13:22**	7121
"You will **c**, and I will answer	**Jb 14:15**	7121
If I **c** to the pit,	**Jb 17:14**	7121
"I **c** to my servant, but he does	**Jb 19:16**	7121
Will he **c** on God at all times?	**Jb 27:10**	7121
Answer me when I **c**,	**Ps 4:1**	7121
The LORD hears when I **c** to Him.	**Ps 4:3**	7121
bread, *And* do not **c** upon the Lord?	**Ps 14:4**	7121
I **c** upon the LORD, who is worthy	**Ps 18:3**	7121
King answer us in the day we **c**.	**Ps 20:9**	7121
To You, O LORD, I **c**;	**Ps 28:1**	7121
shame, O LORD, for I **c** upon You;	**Ps 31:17**	7121
C upon Me in the day of trouble;	**Ps 50:15**	7121
As for me, I shall **c** upon God,	**Ps 55:16**	7121
turn back in the day when I **c**;	**Ps 56:9**	7121
the end of the earth I **c** to You when	**Ps 61:2**	7121
Let all nations **c** him blessed.	**Ps 72:17**	833
which do not **c** upon Your name.	**Ps 79:6**	7121
us, and we will **c** upon Your name.	**Ps 80:18**	7121
to all who **c** upon You.	**Ps 86:5**	7121
of my trouble I shall **c** upon You,	**Ps 86:7**	7121
"He will **c** upon Me, and I will	**Ps 91:15**	7121
day when I **c** answer me quickly.	**Ps 102:2**	7121
to the LORD, **c** upon His name;	**Ps 105:1**	7121
c *upon Him* as long as I live.	**Ps 116:2**	7121
And **c** upon the name of the LORD.	**Ps 116:13**	7121
And **c** upon the name of the LORD.	**Ps 116:17**	7121
O Lord, I **c** upon You;	**Ps 141:1**	7121
ear to my voice when I **c** to You!	**Ps 141:1**	7121
is near to all who **c** upon Him,	**Ps 145:18**	7121
To all who **c** upon Him in truth.	**Ps 145:18**	7121
"Then they will **c** on me, but I	**Pr 1:28**	7121
And **c** understanding *your* intimate	**Pr 7:4**	7121
Does not wisdom **c**, And	**Pr 8:1**	7121
"To you, O men, I **c**,	**Pr 8:4**	7121
do evil, Men will **c** a schemer.	**Pr 24:8**	7121
Woe to those who **c** evil good,	**Is 5:20**	559
and she will **c** His name Immanuel.	**Is 7:14**	7121
that this people **c** a conspiracy,	**Is 8:12**	559
thanks to the LORD, **c** on His name.	**Is 12:4**	7121
And **c** out to her, that her warfare	**Is 40:2**	7121
A voice says, "**C** out."	**Is 40:6**	7121
"What shall I **c** out?"	**Is 40:6**	7121
of the sun he will **c** on My name;	**Is 41:25**	7121
not **c** to mind the former things,	**Is 43:18**	2142
one will **c** on the name of Jacob;	**Is 44:5**	7121
"For they **c** themselves after the	**Is 48:2**	7121
When I **c** to them, they stand	**Is 48:13**	7121
will **c** a nation you do not know,	**Is 55:5**	7121
C upon Him while He is near.	**Is 55:6**	7121
Will you **c** this a fast, even an	**Is 58:5**	7121
"Then you will **c**, and the LORD	**Is 58:9**	7121
day, And **c** the sabbath a delight,	**Is 58:13**	7121
will **c** you the city of the LORD,	**Is 60:14**	7121
you will **c** your walls salvation,	**Is 60:18**	7121
And they will **c** them,	**Is 62:12**	7121
nation which did not **c** on My name.	**Is 65:1**	7121
come to pass that before they **c**,	**Is 65:24**	7121
that time they will **c** Jerusalem	**Jer 3:17**	7121
'You shall **c** Me, My Father, And	**Jer 3:19**	7121
They **c** them rejected silver,	**Jer 6:30**	7121
and you shall **c** to them, but they	**Jer 7:27**	7121
and **c** for the mourning women,	**Jer 9:17**	7121
families that do not **c** Your name;	**Jer 10:25**	7121
for I will not listen when they **c** to Me	**Jer 11:14**	7121
and **c** their sins to account."	**Jer 14:10**	6485
'Then you will **c** upon Me and come	**Jer 29:12**	7121
the hills of Ephraim **c** out,	**Jer 31:6**	7121
field with money and **c** in witnesses	**Jer 32:25**	5749b
and **c** in witnesses in the land of	**Jer 32:44**	5749b
'**C** to Me and I will answer you,	**Jer 33:3**	7121
they will **c** out to one another,	**Jer 49:29**	7121
when I cry out and **c** for help,	**La 3:8**	7768
c for the grain and multiply it,	**Ezk 36:29**	7121
"I will **c** for a sword	**Ezk 38:21**	7121
will **c** *it* the valley of Hamon-gog.	**Ezk 39:11**	7121
gave orders to **c** in the magicians,	**Da 2:2**	7121
"That you will **c** Me Ishi And will	**Hos 2:16**	7121
And will no longer **c** Me Baali.	**Hos 2:16**	7121
They **c** to Egypt, they go to	**Hos 7:11**	7121
they **c** them to *the One* on high,	**Hos 11:7**	7121
They also **c** the farmer to mourning	**Am 5:16**	7121
Get up, **c** on your god.	**Jon 1:6**	7121
and let men **c** on God earnestly	**Jon 3:8**	7121
The voice of the LORD will **c** to	**Mi 6:9**	7121
long, O LORD, will I **c** for help,	**Hab 1:2**	7768
may **c** on the name of the LORD,	**Zph 3:9**	7121
They will **c** on My name, And I will	**Zch 13:9**	7121
will **c** them the wicked territory,	**Mal 1:4**	7121
the nations will **c** you blessed,	**Mal 3:12**	833
'So now we **c** the arrogant blessed;	**Mal 3:15**	833
and you shall **c** His name Jesus,	**Mt 1:21**	*2564*
THEY SHALL **C** HIS NAME IMMANUEL,"	**Mt 1:23**	*2564*
I did not come to **c** the righteous,	**Mt 9:13**	*2564*
who **c** out to the other *children*,	**Mt 11:16**	*4377*
'**C** the laborers and pay them their	**Mt 20:8**	*2564*
"And he sent out his slaves to **c**	**Mt 22:3**	*2564*
how does David in the Spirit **c** Him	**Mt 22:43**	*2564*
not **c** *anyone* on earth your father;	**Mt 23:9**	*2564*
I did not come to **c** the righteous,	**Mk 2:17**	*2564*
"Why do you **c** Me good?	**Mk 10:18**	*3004*
Jesus stopped and said, "**C** him *here*."	**Mk 10:49**	*5455*
whom you **c** the King of the Jews?"	**Mk 15:12**	*3004*
were going to **c** him Zacharias,	**Lk 1:59**	*2564*
"I have not come to **c** the	**Lk 5:32**	*2564*
"Why do you **c** Me,	**Lk 6:46**	*2564*
market place and **c** to one another,	**Lk 7:32**	*4377*
said these things, He would **c** out,	**Lk 8:8**	*5455*
"Why do you **c** Me good?	**Lk 18:19**	*3004*
"Go, **c** your husband and come	**Jn 4:16**	*5455*
"You **c** Me Teacher and Lord;	**Jn 13:13**	*5455*
"No longer do I **c** you slaves, for	**Jn 15:15**	*3004*
Lord our God will **c** to Himself."	**Ac 2:39**	*4341*
to bind all who **c** on Your name."	**Ac 9:14**	*1941*
not **c** any man unholy or unclean.	**Ac 10:28**	*3004*
the Way which they **c** a sect I do serve	**Ac 24:14**	*3004*
C THOSE WHO WERE NOT MY PEOPLE,	**Ro 9:25**	*2564*
in riches for all who **c** on Him;	**Ro 10:12**	*1941*
WHOEVER WILL **C** ON THE NAME OF	**Ro 10:13**	*1941*
How then will they **c** on Him in	**Ro 10:14**	*1941*
with all who in every place **c** on	**1Co 1:2**	*1941*
But I **c** God as witness to my soul,	**2Co 1:23**	*1941*
upward **c** of God in Christ Jesus.	**Php 3:14**	*2821*
c on the Lord from a pure heart.	**2Tm 2:22**	*1941*
is not ashamed to **c** them brethren,	**Heb 2:11**	*2564*
c for the elders of the church and	**Jas 5:14**	*4341*
be able to **c** these things to mind.	**2Pe 1:15**	*4160*
I will **c** attention to his deeds	**3Jn 1:10**	*5279*
those who **c** themselves apostles,	**Rv 2:2**	*3004*
deep things of Satan, as they **c** them	**Rv 2:24**	*3004*

CALLED

God **c** the light day, and the	**Gn 1:5**	7121
day, and the darkness He **c** night.	**Gn 1:5**	7121
God **c** the expanse heaven.	**Gn 1:8**	7121
God **c** the dry land earth, and	**Gn 1:10**	7121
gathering of the waters He **c** seas;	**Gn 1:10**	7121
the man **c** a living creature,	**Gn 2:19**	7121
She shall be **c** Woman, Because she	**Gn 2:23**	7121
Then the LORD God **c** to the man,	**Gn 3:9**	7121
Now the man **c** his wife's name Eve,	**Gn 3:20**	7121
and **c** the name of the city Enoch,	**Gn 4:17**	7121
and he **c** his name Enosh.	**Gn 4:26**	7121
Now he **c** his name Noah, saying,	**Gn 5:29**	7121
Therefore its name was **c** Babel,	**Gn 11:9**	7121
and **c** upon the name of the LORD.	**Gn 12:8**	7121
Then Pharaoh **c** Abram and said,	**Gn 12:18**	7121
Abram **c** on the name of the LORD.	**Gn 13:4**	7121
Then she **c** the name of the LORD	**Gn 16:13**	7121
the well was **c** Beer-lahai-roi;	**Gn 16:14**	7121
and Abram **c** the name of his son,	**Gn 16:15**	7121
longer shall your name be **c** Abram,	**Gn 17:5**	7121
and they **c** to Lot and said to him,	**Gn 19:5**	7121
the name of the town was **c** Zoar.	**Gn 19:22**	7121
bore a son, and **c** his name Moab;	**Gn 19:37**	7121
a son, and **c** his name Ben-ammi;	**Gn 19:38**	7121
in the morning and **c** all his servants	**Gn 20:8**	7121
c Abraham and said to him,	**Gn 20:9**	7121
Abraham **c** the name of his son	**Gn 21:3**	7121
of God **c** to Hagar from heaven and	**Gn 21:17**	7121
he **c** that place Beersheba,	**Gn 21:31**	7121
he **c** on the name of the LORD,	**Gn 21:33**	7121
of the LORD **c** to him from heaven and	**Gn 22:11**	7121
Abraham **c** the name of that	**Gn 22:14**	7121
Then the angel of the LORD **c** to	**Gn 22:15**	7121
they **c** Rebekah and said to her,	**Gn 24:58**	7121
heel, so his name was **c** Jacob;	**Gn 25:26**	7121
Therefore his name was **c** Edom.	**Gn 25:30**	7121
Then Abimelech **c** Isaac and said,	**Gn 26:9**	7121
and **c** upon the name of the LORD,	**Gn 26:25**	7121
So he **c** it Shibah;	**Gn 26:33**	7121
that he **c** his older son Esau and	**Gn 27:1**	7121
sent and **c** her younger son Jacob,	**Gn 27:42**	7121
So Isaac **c** Jacob and blessed him	**Gn 28:1**	7121
c the name of that place Bethel;	**Gn 28:19**	7121
So Jacob sent and **c** Rachel and	**Gn 31:4**	7121
Now Laban **c** it Jegar-sahadutha,	**Gn 31:47**	7121
but Jacob **c** it Galeed.	**Gn 31:47**	7121
and **c** his kinsmen to the meal;	**Gn 31:54**	7121
an altar and **c** it El-Elohe-Israel.	**Gn 33:20**	7121
there, and **c** the place El-bethel,	**Gn 35:7**	7121
You shall no longer be **c** Jacob,	**Gn 35:10**	7121
Thus He **c** him Israel.	**Gn 35:10**	7121
but his father **c** him Benjamin.	**Gn 35:18**	7121
she **c** to the men of her household and	**Gn 39:14**	7121
so he sent and **c** for all the	**Gn 41:8**	7121
Pharaoh sent and **c** for Joseph,	**Gn 41:14**	7121
he **c** his son Joseph and said to	**Gn 47:29**	7121
they shall be **c** by the names of	**Gn 48:6**	7121
king of Egypt **c** for the midwives and	**Ex 1:18**	7121
girl went and **c** the child's mother.	**Ex 2:8**	7121
God **c** to him from the midst of the	**Ex 3:4**	7121
Then Pharaoh also **c** for *the* wise	**Ex 7:11**	7121
c for Moses and Aaron and said,	**Ex 8:8**	7121
c for Moses and Aaron and said,	**Ex 8:25**	7121
hurriedly **c** for Moses and Aaron,	**Ex 10:16**	7121
Then Pharaoh **c** to Moses, and said,	**Ex 10:24**	7121
c for all the elders of Israel and	**Ex 12:21**	7121
Then he **c** for Moses and Aaron at	**Ex 12:31**	7121
LORD **c** to him from the mountain,	**Ex 19:3**	7121
and **c** the elders of the people,	**Ex 19:7**	7121
and the LORD **c** Moses to the top of	**Ex 19:20**	7121
and on the seventh day He **c** to	**Ex 24:16**	7121
"See, I have **c** by name Bezalel,	**Ex 31:2**	7121
and he **c** it the tent of meeting.	**Ex 33:7**	7121
as he **c** upon the name of the LORD.	**Ex 34:5**	7121
Then Moses **c** to them, and Aaron	**Ex 34:31**	7121
the LORD has **c** by name Bezalel the	**Ex 35:30**	7121
Then Moses **c** Bezalel and Oholiab	**Ex 36:2**	7121
Then the LORD **c** to Moses and spoke	**Lv 1:1**	7121
Moses **c** Aaron and his sons	**Lv 9:1**	7121
c also to Mishael and Elzaphan,	**Lv 10:4**	7121
who were **c** of the congregation,	**Nu 1:16**	7148
name of that place was **c** Taberah,	**Nu 11:3**	7121
that place was **c** Kibroth-hattaavah,	**Nu 11:34**	7121
tent, and He **c** Aaron and Miriam.	**Nu 12:5**	7121
but Moses **c** Hoshea the son of Nun,	**Nu 13:16**	7121
place was **c** the valley of Eshcol,	**Nu 13:24**	7121
name of the place was **c** Hormah.	**Nu 21:3**	7121
"I **c** you to curse my enemies, but	**Nu 24:10**	7121
who were **c** by the congregation,	**Nu 26:9**	7148
its towns, and **c** them Havvoth-jair.	**Nu 32:41**	7121
and **c** it Nobah after his own name.	**Nu 32:42**	7121
it is **c** the land of Rephaim.	**Dt 3:13**	7121
and **c** it, *that is,* Bashan, after his own	**Dt 3:14**	7121
"In Israel his name shall be **c**,	**Dt 25:10**	7121
you are **c** by the name of the LORD,	**Dt 28:10**	7121
Then Moses **c** to Joshua and said to	**Dt 31:7**	7121
So Joshua **c** the twelve men whom he	**Jos 4:4**	7121
place is **c** Gilgal to this day.	**Jos 5:9**	7121
c the priests and said to them,	**Jos 6:6**	7121
place has been **c** the valley of Achor	**Jos 7:26**	7121
were **c** together to pursue them,	**Jos 8:16**	2199
c for them and spoke to them,	**Jos 9:22**	7121
c for all the men of Israel,	**Jos 10:24**	7121
and they **c** Leshem Dan after the	**Jos 19:47**	7121
sons of Gad **c** the altar *Witness;*	**Jos 22:34**	7121
that Joshua **c** for all Israel, for	**Jos 23:2**	7121
and **c** for the elders of Israel and	**Jos 24:1**	7121
the name of the city was **c** Hormah.	**Jg 1:17**	7121
Barak **c** Zebulun and Naphtali	**Jg 4:10**	2199
c together all his chariots,	**Jg 4:13**	2199
were **c** together to follow him.	**Jg 6:34**	2199
were **c** together to follow him;	**Jg 6:35**	2199
and lifted his voice and **c** out.	**Jg 9:7**	7121
he **c** quickly to the young man,	**Jg 9:54**	7121
are **c** Havvoth-jair to this day.	**Jg 10:4**	7121
when I **c** you, you did not deliver	**Jg 12:2**	2199
and he **c** to the LORD and said,	**Jg 15:18**	7121
c the lords of the Philistines,	**Jg 16:18**	7121
and **c** for a man and had him shave	**Jg 16:19**	7121
they **c** for Samson from the prison,	**Jg 16:25**	7121
Samson **c** to the LORD and said,	**Jg 16:28**	7121
Therefore they **c** that place	**Jg 18:12**	7121
They **c** the name of the city Dan,	**Jg 18:29**	7121
that the LORD **c** Samuel;	**1Sa 3:4**	7121
"Here I am, for you **c** me."	**1Sa 3:5**	7121
The LORD **c** yet again,	**1Sa 3:6**	7121
"Here I am, for you **c** me."	**1Sa 3:6**	7121
So the LORD **c** Samuel again for the	**1Sa 3:8**	7121
"Here I am, for you **c** me."	**1Sa 3:8**	7121
and stood and **c** as at other times,	**1Sa 3:10**	7121
Then Eli **c** Samuel and said,	**1Sa 3:16**	7121
And she **c** the boy Ichabod, saying,	**1Sa 4:21**	7121
And the Philistines **c** for the	**1Sa 6:2**	7121
for *he who is* **c** a prophet now was	**1Sa 9:9**	
now was formerly **c** a seer.)	**1Sa 9:9**	7121
daybreak Samuel **c** to Saul on the roof,	**1Sa 9:26**	7121
Thereafter Samuel **c** the people	**1Sa 10:17**	6817
So Samuel **c** to the LORD, and the	**1Sa 12:18**	7121
Then Jesse **c** Abinadab and made	**1Sa 16:8**	7121
Then Jonathan **c** David, and	**1Sa 19:7**	7121
shot, Jonathan **c** after the lad and	**1Sa 20:37**	7121
And Jonathan **c** after the lad,	**1Sa 20:38**	7121
c that place the Rock of Escape.	**1Sa 23:28**	7121
out of the cave and **c** after Saul,	**1Sa 24:8**	7121
David **c** to the people and to	**1Sa 26:14**	7121
therefore I have **c** you,	**1Sa 28:15**	7121
Achish **c** David and said to him,	**1Sa 29:6**	7121
behind him, he saw me and **c** to me.	**2Sa 1:7**	7121
c one of the young men and said,	**2Sa 1:15**	7121
that place was **c** Helkath-hazzurim,	**2Sa 2:16**	7121
Then Abner **c** to Joab and said,	**2Sa 2:26**	7121
and **c** it the city of David.	**2Sa 5:9**	7121
ark of God which is **c** by the Name,	**2Sa 6:2**	7121
place is **c** Perez-uzzah to this day.	**2Sa 6:8**	7121
was Ziba, and they **c** him to David;	**2Sa 9:2**	7121
the king **c** Saul's servant Ziba and	**2Sa 9:9**	7121
Now David **c** him, and he ate and	**2Sa 11:13**	7121
Then he **c** his young man who	**2Sa 13:17**	7121
and told him, he **c** for Absalom.	**2Sa 14:33**	7121
and it is **c** Absalom's Monument to	**2Sa 18:18**	7121
The watchman **c** and told the king.	**2Sa 18:25**	7121
c to the gatekeeper and said,	**2Sa 18:26**	7121
Ahimaaz **c** and said to the king,	**2Sa 18:28**	7121
Then a wise woman **c** from the city,	**2Sa 20:16**	7121
So the king **c** the Gibeonites and	**2Sa 21:2**	7121
"In my distress I **c** upon the LORD,	**2Sa 22:7**	7121
he was **c** Adino the Eznite,	**2Sa 23:8**	
and **c** for Shimei and said to him,	**1Ki 2:36**	7121
and **c** for Shimei and said to him,	**1Ki 2:42**	7121
I have built is **c** by Your name.	**1Ki 8:43**	7121
c the land of Cabul to this day.	**1Ki 9:13**	7121
Then they sent and **c** him,	**1Ki 12:3**	7121
that they sent and **c** him to the	**1Ki 12:20**	7121
and he **c** to her and said,	**1Ki 17:10**	7121
to get *it,* he **c** to her and said,	**1Ki 17:11**	7121
He **c** to the LORD and said,	**1Ki 17:20**	7121
three times, and **c** to the LORD and	**1Ki 17:21**	7121
Ahab **c** Obadiah who *was* over	**1Ki 18:3**	7121
prepared it and **c** on the name of Baal	**1Ki 18:26**	7121
Then the king of Israel **c** all the	**1Ki 20:7**	7121
of Israel **c** an officer and said,	**1Ki 22:9**	7121
For the LORD has **c** these three	**2Ki 3:10**	7121
for the LORD has **c** these three	**2Ki 3:13**	7121
And when he had **c** her, she stood	**2Ki 4:12**	7121
When he had **c** her, she stood in	**2Ki 4:15**	7121

she c to her husband and said,	2Ki 4:22	7121
He c Gehazi and said,	2Ki 4:36	7121
"Call this Shunammite." So he c her.	2Ki 4:36	7121
c his servants and said to them,	2Ki 6:11	7121
So they came and c to the	2Ki 7:10	7121
The gatekeepers c and	2Ki 7:11	7121
for the LORD has c for a famine,	2Ki 8:1	7121
Now Elisha the prophet c one of	2Ki 9:1	7121
Jehoash c for Jehoiada the priest,	2Ki 12:7	7121
and it was c Nehushtan.	2Ki 18:4	7121
When they c to the king, Eliakim	2Ki 18:18	7121
Now Jabez c on the God of Israel,	1Ch 4:10	7121
it was c the city of David.	1Ch 11:7	7121
the cherubim, where His name is c.	1Ch 13:6	7121
and he c that place Perez-uzza to	1Ch 13:11	7121
Then David c for Zadok and	1Ch 15:11	7121
And he c to the LORD and He	1Ch 21:26	7121
Then he c for his son Solomon, and	1Ch 22:6	7121
I have built is c by Your name.	2Ch 6:33	7121
and My people who are c by My name	2Ch 7:14	7121
Then Asa c to the LORD his God and	2Ch 14:11	7121
of Israel c an officer and said,	2Ch 18:8	7121
They c this out with a loud	2Ch 32:18	7121
and he was c by their name.	Ezr 2:61	7121
So I c the priests and took an	Ne 5:12	7121
So the king's scribes were c at	Es 8:9	7121
Therefore they c these days Purim	Es 9:26	7121
"If I c and He answered me, I	Jb 9:16	7121
The one who c on God and He	Jb 12:4	7121
the ear heard, it c me blessed,	Jb 29:11	833
in gold, And c fine gold my trust,	Jb 31:24	559
I have c upon You, for You will	Ps 17:6	7121
In my distress I c upon the LORD,	Ps 18:6	7121
To You, O LORD, I c,	Ps 30:8	7121
shall be c blessed upon the earth;	Ps 41:2	833
They have c their lands after	Ps 49:11	7121
bread And have not c upon God?	Ps 53:4	7121
"You c in trouble and I rescued	Ps 81:7	7121
I have c upon You every day, O	Ps 88:9	7121
was among those who c on His name;	Ps 99:6	7121
They c upon the LORD and He	Ps 99:6	7121
He c for a famine upon the land;	Ps 105:16	7121
I c upon the name of the LORD:	Ps 116:4	7121
my distress I c upon the LORD;	Ps 118:5	7121
the day I c, You answered me;	Ps 138:3	7121
Because I c and you refused	Pr 1:24	7121
in heart will be c understanding,	Pr 16:21	7121
I c him but he did not answer me.	SS 5:6	7121
maidens saw her and c her blessed,	SS 6:9	833
be c the city of righteousness,	Is 1:26	7121
only let us be c by your name;	Is 4:1	7121
remains in Jerusalem will be c holy	Is 4:3	559
And one c out to another and said,	Is 6:3	7121
at the voice of him who c out,	Is 6:4	7121
will be c Wonderful Counselor,	Is 9:6	7121
I have even c My mighty warriors,	Is 13:3	7121
will be c the City of Destruction.	Is 19:18	559
Then the lookout c,	Is 21:8	7121
GOD of hosts c *you* to weeping,	Is 22:12	7121
Therefore, I have c her	Is 30:7	7121
a band of shepherds is c out,	Is 31:4	7121
longer will the fool be c noble,	Is 32:5	7121
will be c the Highway of Holiness.	Is 35:8	7121
And c from its remotest parts And	Is 41:9	7121
I have c you in righteousness,	Is 42:6	7121
I have c you by name;	Is 43:1	7121
Everyone who is c by My name, And	Is 43:7	7121
"Yet you have not c on Me,	Is 43:22	7121
I have also c you by your name;	Is 45:4	7121
longer be c tender and delicate.	Is 47:1	7121
no longer be c The queen of kingdoms.	Is 47:5	7121
have been c a rebel from birth.	Is 48:8	7121
Me, O Jacob, even Israel whom I c;	Is 48:12	7121
indeed I have c him, I have	Is 48:15	7121
The LORD c Me from the womb;	Is 49:1	7121
When I c, *why* was there none to	Is 50:2	7121
When *he was but* one I c him,	Is 51:2	7121
Who is c the God of all the earth.	Is 54:5	7121
"For the LORD has c you,	Is 54:6	7121
For My house will be c a house of	Is 56:7	7121
be c the repairer of the breach,	Is 58:12	7121
will be c oaks of righteousness,	Is 61:3	7121
will be c the priests of the LORD;	Is 61:6	7121
And you will be c by a new name Which	Is 62:2	7121
But you will be c,	Is 62:4	7121
And you will be c,	Is 62:12	7121
those who were not c by Your name.	Is 63:19	7121
Because I c, but you did not	Is 65:12	7121
will be c by another name.	Is 65:15	7121
Because I c, but no one answered;	Is 66:4	7121
'Have you not just now c to Me,	Jer 3:4	7121
this house, which is c by My name,	Jer 7:10	7121
this house, which is c by My name,	Jer 7:11	7121
I c you but you did not answer,	Jer 7:13	7121
the house which is c by My name,	Jer 7:14	7121
the house which is c by My name,	Jer 7:30	7121
"when it will no longer be c Topheth,	Jer 7:32	559
The LORD c your name,	Jer 11:16	7121
O LORD, And we are c by Your name;	Jer 14:9	7121
For I have been c by Your name, O	Jer 15:16	7121
this place will no longer be c Topheth	Jer 19:6	7121
not the name the LORD has c you,	Jer 20:3	7121
is His name by which He will be c,	Jer 23:6	7121
this city which is c by My name,	Jer 25:29	7121
they have c you an outcast,	Jer 30:17	7121
the deed, and c in witnesses,	Jer 32:10	5749b
the house which is c by My name,	Jer 32:34	7121
the name by which she will be c:	Jer 33:16	7121
the house which is c by My name.	Jer 34:15	7121
I have c them but they did not answer.	Jer 35:17	7121
c Baruch the son of Neriah,	Jer 36:4	7121
c for Johanan the son of Kareah and	Jer 42:8	7121
He has c an appointed time against	La 1:15	7121
"I c to my lovers, *but* they	La 1:19	7121
You c as in the day of an appointed	La 2:22	7121
I c on Your name, O LORD, Out of	La 3:55	7121
drew near when I c on You;	La 3:57	7121
And He c to the man clothed in	Ezk 9:3	7121
The wheels were c in my hearing,	Ezk 10:13	7121
name is c Bamah to this day."	Ezk 20:29	7121
The king c aloud to bring in the	Da 5:7	7123
of Ulai, and he c out and said,	Da 8:16	7121
the city which is c by Your name;	Da 9:18	7121
Your people are c by Your name."	Da 9:19	7121
him, And out of Egypt I c My son.	Hos 11:1	7121
The more they c them, The more	Hos 11:2	7121
nations who are c by My name,"	Am 9:12	7121
Then they c on the LORD and said,	Jon 1:14	7121
"I c out of my distress to the	Jon 2:2	7121
and they c a fast and put on	Jon 3:5	7121
"I c for a drought on the	Hg 1:11	7121
as He c and they would not listen,	Zch 7:13	7121
they c and I would not listen,"	Zch 7:13	7121
will be c the City of Truth,	Zch 8:3	7121
of the LORD of hosts *will be* c	Zch 8:3	
the one I c Favor and the other I	Zch 11:7	7121
Favor and the other I c Union;	Zch 11:7	7121
Jesus was born, who is c the Messiah.	Mt 1:16	*3004*
and he c His name Jesus.	Mt 1:25	*2564*
Then Herod secretly c the magi and	Mt 2:7	*2564*
"OUT OF EGYPT I C MY SON."	Mt 2:15	*2564*
and lived in a city c Nazareth	Mt 2:23	*3004*
"He shall be c a Nazarene."	Mt 2:23	*2564*
brothers, Simon who was c Peter,	Mt 4:18	*3004*
mending their nets; and He c them.	Mt 4:21	*2564*
for they shall be c sons of God.	Mt 5:9	*2564*
shall be c least in the kingdom of	Mt 5:19	*2564*
he shall be c great in the kingdom	Mt 5:19	*2564*
there, He saw a man c Matthew,	Mt 9:9	*3004*
The first, Simon, who is c Peter,	Mt 10:2	*3004*
If they have c the head of the	Mt 10:25	*1941*
Is not His mother c Mary,	Mt 13:55	*3004*
After Jesus c the crowd to Him,	Mt 15:10	*4341*
And Jesus c His disciples to Him,	Mt 15:32	*4341*
And He c a child to Himself and	Mt 18:2	*4341*
But Jesus c them to Himself and	Mt 20:25	*4341*
And Jesus stopped and c them,	Mt 20:32	*5455*
SHALL BE C A HOUSE OF PRAYER';	Mt 21:13	*2564*
"For many are c, but few *are*	Mt 22:14	*2822*
places, and being c Rabbi by men	Mt 23:7	*2564*
"But do not be c Rabbi;	Mt 23:8	*2564*
"Do not be c leaders;	Mt 23:10	*2564*
a journey, who c his own slaves and	Mt 25:14	*2564*
with them to a place c Gethsemane,	Mt 26:36	*3004*
field has been c the Field of Blood	Mt 27:8	*2564*
a notorious prisoner, c Barabbas.	Mt 27:16	*3004*
or Jesus who is c Christ?"	Mt 27:17	*3004*
I do with Jesus who is c Christ?"	Mt 27:22	*3004*
came to a place c Golgotha,	Mt 27:33	*3004*
Immediately He c them;	Mk 1:20	*2564*
And He c them to Himself and began	Mk 3:23	*4341*
they sent *word* to Him and c Him.	Mk 3:31	*2564*
He c the crowd to Him again,	Mk 7:14	*4341*
Jesus c His disciples and said to	Mk 8:1	*4341*
He c the twelve and said to them,	Mk 9:35	*5455*
So they c the blind man, saying	Mk 10:49	*5455*
'MY HOUSE SHALL BE C A HOUSE OF	Mk 11:17	*2564*
and they c together the whole	Mk 15:16	*4779*
to a city in Galilee c Nazareth,	Lk 1:26	*3686*
be c the Son of the Most High;	Lk 1:32	*2564*
shall be c the Son of God.	Lk 1:35	*2564*
and she who was c barren is now in	Lk 1:36	*2564*
but he shall be c John."	Lk 1:60	*2564*
relatives who is c by that name."	Lk 1:61	*2564*
as to what he wanted him c.	Lk 1:62	*2564*
be c the prophet of the Most High;	Lk 1:76	*2564*
of David which is c Bethlehem,	Lk 2:4	*2564*
His name was *then* c Jesus,	Lk 2:21	*2564*
SHALL BE C HOLY TO THE LORD"),	Lk 2:23	*2564*
came, He c His disciples to Him and	Lk 6:13	*4377*
and Simon who was c the Zealot;	Lk 6:15	*2564*
afterwards He went to a city c Nain;	Lk 7:11	*2564*
Mary who was c Magdalene, from	Lk 8:2	*2564*
took her by the hand and c,	Lk 8:54	*5455*
And He c the twelve together, and	Lk 9:1	*4779*
by Himself to a city c Bethsaida.	Lk 9:10	*2564*
She had a sister c Mary,	Lk 10:39	*2564*
He c her over and said to her,	Lk 13:12	*4377*
no longer worthy to be c your son;	Lk 15:19	*2564*
longer worthy to be c your son.'	Lk 15:21	*2564*
"And he c him and said to him,	Lk 16:2	*5455*
But Jesus c for them, saying,	Lk 18:16	*4341*
And he c out, saying,	Lk 18:38	*994*
a man c by the name of Zaccheus;	Lk 19:2	*2564*
"And he c ten of his slaves, and	Lk 19:13	*2564*
be c to him so that he might	Lk 19:15	*5455*
near the mount that is c Olivet,	Lk 19:29	*2564*
on the mount that is c Olivet.	Lk 21:37	*2564*
Bread, which is c the Passover,	Lk 22:1	*3004*
into Judas who was c Iscariot,	Lk 22:3	*2564*
who have authority over them are c	Lk 22:25	*2564*
came, and the one c Judas,	Lk 22:47	*3004*
came to the place c The Skull,	Lk 23:33	*2564*
you shall be c Cephas"	Jn 1:42	*2564*
"Before Philip c you, when you	Jn 1:48	*5455*
the headwaiter c the bridegroom,	Jn 2:9	*5455*
to a city of Samaria c Sychar,	Jn 4:5	*3004*
(He who is c Christ);	Jn 4:25	*3004*
which is c in Hebrew Bethesda,	Jn 5:2	*1951*
"The man who is c Jesus made	Jn 9:11	*3004*
until they c the parents of the	Jn 9:18	*5455*
they c the man who had been blind,	Jn 9:24	*5455*
"If he c them gods, to whom the	Jn 10:35	*3004*
Thomas, who is c Didymus,	Jn 11:16	*3004*
went away and c Mary her sister,	Jn 11:28	*5455*
wilderness, into a city c Ephraim;	Jn 11:54	*3004*
when He c Lazarus out of the tomb and	Jn 12:17	*5455*
but I have c you friends, for all	Jn 15:15	*3004*
seat at a place c The Pavement,	Jn 19:13	*3004*
the place c the Place of a Skull,	Jn 19:17	*3004*
of a Skull, which is c in Hebrew,	Jn 19:17	*3004*
one of the twelve, c Didymus,	Jn 20:24	*3004*
Simon Peter, and Thomas c Didymus,	Jn 21:2	*3004*
Jerusalem from the mount c Olivet,	Ac 1:12	*2564*
that field was c Hakeldama,	Ac 1:19	*2564*
two men, Joseph c Barsabbas	Ac 1:23	*2564*
Barsabbas (who was also c Justus),	Ac 1:23	*1941*
the temple which is c Beautiful,	Ac 3:2	*3004*
also c Barnabas by the apostles	Ac 4:36	*1941*
came, they c the Council together,	Ac 5:21	*4779*
c the Synagogue of the Freedmen,	Ac 6:9	*3004*
as he c on *the Lord* and said,	Ac 7:59	*1941*
is c the Great Power of God."	Ac 8:10	*2564*
and go to the street c Straight,	Ac 9:11	*2564*
those who c on this name,	Ac 9:21	*1941*
translated *in Greek* is c Dorcas);	Ac 9:36	*3004*
of what was c the Italian cohort,	Ac 10:1	*2564*
named Simon, who is also c Peter;	Ac 10:5	*1941*
Simon, who was also c Peter,	Ac 10:18	*1941*
and had c together his relatives	Ac 10:24	*4779*
invite Simon, who is also c Peter,	Ac 10:32	*1941*
have Simon, who is also c Peter,	Ac 11:13	*1941*
first c Christians in Antioch.	Ac 11:26	*5537*
of John who was also c Mark,	Ac 12:12	*1941*
them John, who was also c Mark.	Ac 12:25	*1941*
and Simeon who was c Niger,	Ac 13:1	*2564*
the work to which I have c them."	Ac 13:2	*4341*
GENTILES WHO ARE C BY MY NAME,'	Ac 15:17	*1941*
Judas c Barsabbas, and Silas, leading	Ac 15:22	*2564*
wanted to take John, c Mark,	Ac 15:37	*2564*
concluding that God had c us to	Ac 16:10	*4341*
he c for lights and rushed in,	Ac 16:29	*154*
and c to him the elders of the church.	Ac 20:17	*3333*
Paul c one of the centurions	Ac 23:17	*4341*
"Paul the prisoner c me to him	Ac 23:18	*4341*
he c to him two of the centurions and	Ac 23:23	*4341*
to a place c Fair Havens,	Ac 27:8	*2564*
land a violent wind, c Euraquilo;	Ac 27:14	*2564*
of a small island c Clauda,	Ac 27:16	*2564*
out that the island was c Malta.	Ac 28:1	*2564*
After three days Paul c together those	Ac 28:17	*4779*
of Christ Jesus, c *as* an apostle,	Ro 1:1	*2822*
also are the c of Jesus Christ;	Ro 1:6	*2822*
of God in Rome, c *as* saints:	Ro 1:7	*2822*
man, she shall be c an adulteress;	Ro 7:3	*5537*
are c according to *His* purpose.	Ro 8:28	*2822*
He predestined, He also c;	Ro 8:30	*2564*
and these whom He c, He also	Ro 8:30	*2564*
even us, whom He also c,	Ro 9:24	*2564*
BE C SONS OF THE LIVING GOD."	Ro 9:26	*2564*
c *as* an apostle of Jesus Christ by	1Co 1:1	*2822*
c into fellowship with His Son,	1Co 1:9	*2564*
but to those who are the c,	1Co 1:24	*2822*
cases, but God has c us to peace.	1Co 7:15	*2564*
to each one, as God has c each,	1Co 7:17	*2564*
any man c *when he was already*	1Co 7:18	*2564*
anyone been c in uncircumcision?	1Co 7:18	*2564*
that condition in which he was c.	1Co 7:20	*2564*
Were you c while a slave?	1Co 7:21	*2564*
was c in the Lord while a slave,	1Co 7:22	*2564*
likewise he who was c while free,	1Co 7:22	*2564*
that *condition* in which he was c.	1Co 7:24	*2564*
by all, he is c to account by all;	1Co 14:24	*350*
and not fit to be c an apostle,	1Co 15:9	*2564*
who c you by the grace of Christ,	Ga 1:6	*2564*
womb and c me through His grace,	Ga 1:15	*2564*
For you were c to freedom,	Ga 5:13	*2564*
Gentiles in the flesh, who are c	Eph 2:11	*3004*
with which you have been c,	Eph 4:1	*2564*
c in one hope of your calling;	Eph 4:4	*2564*
indeed you were c in one body;	Col 3:15	*2564*
and *also* Jesus who is c Justus;	Col 4:11	*3004*
For God has not c us for the	1Th 4:7	*2564*
this He c you through our gospel,	2Th 2:14	*2564*
eternal life to which you were c,	1Tm 6:12	*2564*
arguments of what is falsely c	1Tm 6:20	*5581*
us and c us with a holy calling,	2Tm 1:9	*2564*
day, as long as it is *still* c "Today,"	Heb 3:13	*2564*
receives it when he is c by God,	Heb 5:4	*2564*
this is c the holy place.	Heb 9:2	*3004*
which is c the Holy of Holies,	Heb 9:3	*3004*
those who have been c may receive	Heb 9:15	*2564*
By faith Abraham, when he was c,	Heb 11:8	*2564*
is not ashamed to be c their God;	Heb 11:16	*1941*
YOUR DESCENDANTS SHALL BE C."	Heb 11:18	*2564*
be c the son of Pharaoh's daughter,	Heb 11:24	*3004*
name by which you have been c?	Jas 2:7	*1941*
and he was c the friend of God.	Jas 2:23	*2564*
but like the Holy One who c you,	1Pe 1:15	*2564*
Him who has c you out of darkness	1Pe 2:9	*2564*
you have been c for this purpose,	1Pe 2:21	*2564*
for you were c for the very	1Pe 3:9	*2564*
who c you to His eternal glory in	1Pe 5:10	*2564*
Him who c us by His own glory	2Pe 1:3	*2564*
we would be c children of God;	1Jn 3:1	*2564*
of James, To those who are the c,	Jude 1:1	*2822*
Jesus, was on the island c Patmos	Rv 1:9	*2564*

name of the star is **c** Wormwood; **Rv 8:11** *3004*
mystically is **c** Sodom and Egypt, **Rv 11:8** *2564*
old who is **c** the devil and Satan, **Rv 12:9** *2564*
and he **c** with a loud voice to him **Rv 14:18** *5455*
which in Hebrew is **c** Har-Magedon. **Rv 16:16** *2564*
the **c** and chosen and faithful." **Rv 17:14** *2822*
on it *is* **c** Faithful and True **Rv 19:11** *2564*
and His name is **c** The Word of God. **Rv 19:13** *2564*

CALLING
not **c** us when you went to fight **Jg 8:1** 7121
Ammon without **c** us to go with you? **Jg 12:1** 7121
that the LORD was **c** the boy. **1Sa 3:8** 7121
too would have been an iniquity **c** **Jb 31:28**
C to those who pass by, Who are **Pr 9:15** 7121
and sabbath, the **c** of assemblies **Is 1:13** 7121
One keeps **c** to me from Seir, **Is 21:11** 7121
is **c**, "Clear the way for the LORD **Is 40:3** 7121
C forth the generations from the **Is 41:4** 7121
C a bird of prey from the east, **Is 46:11** 7121
I am **c** all the families of the **Jer 1:15** 7121
c to contend *with them* by fire, **Am 7:4** 7121
"This man is **c** for Elijah." **Mt 27:47** *5455*
C them to Himself, Jesus said to **Mk 10:42** *4341*
He is **c** for you." **Mk 10:49** *5455*
C His disciples to Him, He said to **Mk 12:43** *4341*
"Behold, He is **c** for Elijah." **Mk 15:35** *5455*
but they kept on **c** out, **Lk 23:21** *2019*
but also was **c** God His own Father, **Jn 5:18** *3004*
is here and is **c** for you." **Jn 11:28** *5455*
and after **c** the apostles in, they **Ac 5:40** *4341*
and **c** the saints and widows, he **Ac 9:41** *5455*
and **c** out, they were asking **Ac 10:18** *5455*
And they *began* **c** Barnabas, Zeus, **Ac 14:12** *2564*
away your sins, **c** on His name.' **Ac 22:16** *1941*
and the **c** of God are irrevocable. **Ro 11:29** *2821*
in Christ Jesus, saints by **c**, **1Co 1:2** *2822*
For consider your **c**, **1Co 1:26** *2821*
know what is the hope of His **c**, **Eph 1:18** *2821*
walk in a manner worthy of the **c** **Eph 4:1** *2821*
were called in one hope of your **c**; **Eph 4:4** *2821*
will count you worthy of your **c**, **2Th 1:11** *2821*
us and called us with a holy **c**, **2Tm 1:9** *2821*
partakers of a heavenly **c**, **Heb 3:1** *2821*
Sarah obeyed Abraham, **c** him lord, **1Pe 3:6** *2564*
about His **c** and choosing you; **2Pe 1:10** *2821*

CALLOUS
and they, having become **c**, **Eph 4:19** *524*

CALLS
"When Pharaoh **c** you and says, **Gn 46:33** 7121
or one who **c** up the dead. **Dt 18:11** 1875
down, and it shall be if He **c** you, **1Sa 3:9** 7121
"Who are you who **c** to the king?" **1Sa 26:14** 7121
for which the foreigner **c** to You, **1Ki 8:43** 7121
for which the foreigner **c** to You, **2Ch 6:33** 7121
by or shuts up, Or **c** an assembly, **Jb 11:10** 6950
And when He **c** me to account, **Jb 31:14** 6485
Deep **c** to deep at the sound of Your **Ps 42:7** 7121
she **c** From the tops of the heights **Pr 9:3** 7121
strife, And his mouth **c** for blows. **Pr 18:6** 7121
by number, He **c** them all by name; **Is 40:26** 7121
He **c** in righteousness to His feet? **Is 41:2** 7121
of Israel, who **c** you by your name. **Is 45:3** 7121
There is no one who **c** on Your name, **Is 64:7** 7121
None of them **c** on Me. **Hos 7:7** 7121
whoever **c** on the name of the LORD **Jl 2:32** 7121
the survivors whom the LORD **c**. **Jl 2:32** 7121
Who **c** for the waters of the sea **Am 5:8** 7121
He who **c** for the waters of the sea **Am 9:6** 7121
"If David then **c** Him 'Lord,' **Mt 22:45** *2564*
"David himself **c** Him 'Lord'; **Mk 12:37** *3004*
he **c** together his friends and his **Lk 15:6** *4779*
she **c** together her friends and **Lk 15:9** *4779*
he **c** the Lord THE GOD OF ABRAHAM **Lk 20:37** *3004*
"Therefore David **c** Him 'Lord,' **Lk 20:44** *2564*
and he **c** his own sheep by name and **Jn 10:3** *5455*
EVERYONE WHO **C** ON THE NAME OF **Ac 2:21** *1941*
who gives life to the dead and **c** **Ro 4:17** *2564*
works but because of Him who **c**, **Ro 9:11** *2564*
did not *come* from Him who **c** you. **Ga 5:8** *2564*
manner worthy of the God who **c** you **1Th 2:12** *2564*
Faithful is He who **c** you, **1Th 5:24** *2564*
who **c** herself a prophetess, **Rv 2:20** *3004*

CALM
'Take care and be **c**, **Is 7:4** 8252
"So I will **c** My fury against **Ezk 16:42** 5117
that the sea may become **c** for us?" **Jon 1:11** 8367
the sea will become **c** for you, **Jon 1:12** 8367
and it became perfectly **c**. **Mt 8:26** *1055*
down and it became perfectly **c**. **Mk 4:39** *1055*
and they stopped, and it became **c**. **Lk 8:24** *1055*
to keep **c** and to do nothing rash. **Ac 19:36** *2687*

CALMED
So the Levites **c** all the people, **Ne 8:11** 2814
by the sea, It cannot be **c**. **Jer 49:23** 8252

CALMS
But the slow to anger **c** a dispute. **Pr 15:18** 8252

CALNEH
Babel and Erech and Accad and **C**, **Gn 10:10** 3641a
Go over to **C** and look, And go from **Am 6:2** 3641b

CALNO
"Is not **C** like Carchemish, Or **Is 10:9** 3641b

CALVE
of the LORD makes the deer to **c** And **Ps 29:9** 2342a

CALVES
to the cart and take their **c** home, **1Sa 6:7** 1121
cart, and shut up their **c** at home. **1Sa 6:10** 1121
and took sheep and oxen and **c**, **1Sa 14:32** 1121, 1241
consulted, and made two golden **c**, **1Ki 12:28** 5695
to the **c** which he had made. **1Ki 12:32** 5695
even the golden **c** that *were* at **2Ki 10:29** 5695
molten images, *even* two **c**, **2Ki 17:16** 5695
and for the **c** which he had made. **2Ch 11:15** 5695
the golden **c** which Jeroboam made **2Ch 13:8** 5695
His cow **c** and does not abort. **Jb 21:10** 6403
bulls with the **c** of the peoples, **Ps 68:30** 5695
in her midst Are like fattened **c**, **Jer 46:21** 5695
men who sacrifice kiss the **c**!" **Hos 13:2** 5695
And **c** from the midst of the stall, **Am 6:4** 5695
burnt offerings, With yearling **c**? **Mi 6:6** 5695
skip about like **c** from the stall. **Mal 4:2** 5695
through the blood of goats and **c**, **Heb 9:12** *3448*
the blood of the **c** and the goats, **Heb 9:19** *3448*

CALVING
Do you observe the **c** of the deer? **Jb 39:1** 2342a

CAME
So it **c** about in the course of **Gn 4:3** 1961
And it **c** about when they were in **Gn 4:8** 1961
Now it **c** about, when men began to **Gn 6:1** 1961
God **c** in to the daughters of men, **Gn 6:4** 935
flood of water **c** upon the earth. **Gn 7:6** 1961
It **c** about after the seven days, **Gn 7:10** 1961
of the flood **c** upon the earth. **Gn 7:10** 1961
c upon the earth for forty days, **Gn 7:17** 1961
Then it **c** about at the end of **Gn 8:6** 1961
The dove **c** to him toward evening **Gn 8:11** 935
Now it **c** about in the six hundred **Gn 8:13** 1961
Now the sons of Noah who **c** out of **Gn 9:18** 3318
(from which **c** the Philistines) **Gn 10:14** 3318
It **c** about as they journeyed east, **Gn 11:2** 1961
The LORD **c** down to see the **Gn 11:5** 3381
thus they **c** to the land of Canaan. **Gn 12:5** 935
It **c** about when he came near **Gn 12:11** 1961
about when he **c** near to Egypt, **Gn 12:11** 7126, 935
It **c** about when Abram came **Gn 12:14** 1961
about when Abram **c** into Egypt, **Gn 12:14** 935
Then Abram moved his tent and **c** **Gn 13:18** 935
And it **c** about in the days of **Gn 14:1** 1961
All these **c** as allies to the **Gn 14:3** 2266
c and defeated the Rephaim in **Gn 14:5** 935
turned back and **c** to En-mishpat **Gn 14:7** 935
the king of Bela (that is, Zoar) **c** out; **Gn 14:8** 3318
c and told Abram the Hebrew. **Gn 14:13** 935
the LORD **c** to Abram in a vision, **Gn 15:1** 1961
the word of the LORD **c** to him, **Gn 15:4**
of prey **c** down upon the carcasses, **Gn 15:11** 3381
It **c** about when the sun had set, **Gn 15:17** 1961
Abraham **c** near and said, **Gn 18:23** 5066
Now the two angels **c** to Sodom in **Gn 19:1** 935
are the men who **c** to you tonight? **Gn 19:5** 935
"This one **c** in as an alien, and **Gn 19:9** 935
Lot and **c** near to break the door. **Gn 19:9** 5066
over the earth when Lot **c** to Zoar. **Gn 19:23** 935
Thus it **c** about, when God **Gn 19:29** 1961
But God **c** to Abimelech in a dream **Gn 20:3** 935
and it **c** about, when God caused me **Gn 20:13** 1961
Now it **c** about at that time that **Gn 21:22** 1961
Now it **c** about after these things, **Gn 22:1** 1961
Then they **c** to the place of which **Gn 22:9** 935
Now it **c** about after these things, **Gn 22:20** 1961
to the land from where you **c**?" **Gn 24:5** 3318
c out with her jar on her shoulder. **Gn 24:15** 3318
and filled her jar and **c** up. **Gn 24:16** 5927
"So I **c** today to the spring, and **Gn 24:42** 935
Rebekah **c** out with her jar on her **Gn 24:45** 3318
It **c** about after the death of **Gn 25:11** 1961
Now the first **c** forth red, all **Gn 25:25** 3318
Afterward his brother **c** forth **Gn 25:26** 3318
Esau **c** in from the field and he **Gn 25:29** 935
It **c** about, when he had been **Gn 26:8** 1961
Then Abimelech **c** to him from Gerar **Gn 26:26** 1980
Now it **c** about on the same day, **Gn 26:32** 1961
that Isaac's servants **c** in and **Gn 26:32** 935
Now it **c** about, when Isaac was **Gn 27:1** 1961
Then he **c** to his father and said, **Gn 27:18** 935
Jacob **c** close to Isaac his father, **Gn 27:22** 5066
So he **c** close and kissed him; **Gn 27:27** 5066
Now it **c** about, as soon as Isaac **Gn 27:30** 1961
his brother **c** in from his hunting. **Gn 27:30** 935
I ate of all *of it* before you **c**, **Gn 27:33** 935
"Your brother **c** deceitfully and **Gn 27:35** 935
He **c** to a certain place and **Gn 28:11** 6293
and **c** to the land of the sons of **Gn 29:1** 1980
Rachel **c** with her father's sheep, **Gn 29:9** 935
So it **c** about in the morning that, **Gn 29:25** 1961
When Jacob **c** in from the field in **Gn 30:16** 935
Now it **c** about when Rachel had **Gn 30:25** 1961
"For you had little before I **c** and **Gn 30:30**
where the flocks **c** to drink; **Gn 30:38** 935
they mated when they **c** to drink. **Gn 30:38** 935
"And it **c** about at the time when **Gn 31:10** 1961
God **c** to Laban the Aramean in **Gn 31:24** 935
"We **c** to your brother Esau, and **Gn 32:6** 935
until he **c** near to his brother. **Gn 33:3** 5066
maids **c** near with their children, **Gn 33:6** 5066
likewise **c** near with her children, **Gn 33:7** 5066
Joseph **c** near with Rachel, **Gn 33:7** 5066
c safely to the city of Shechem, **Gn 33:18** 935
Canaan, when he **c** from Paddan-aram, **Gn 33:18** 935
Jacob kept silent until they **c** in. **Gn 34:5** 935
Now the sons of Jacob **c** in from **Gn 34:7** 935
c to the gate of their city and **Gn 34:20** 935
Now it **c** about on the third day, **Gn 34:25** 1961
and **c** upon the city unawares, **Gn 34:25** 935
Jacob's sons **c** upon the slain and **Gn 34:27** 935
So Jacob **c** to Luz **Gn 35:6** 935
again when he **c** from Paddan-aram, **Gn 35:9** 935
It **c** about as her soul was **Gn 35:18** 1961
It **c** about while Israel was **Gn 35:22** 1961
Jacob **c** to his father Isaac at **Gn 35:27** 935
of Hebron, and he **c** to Shechem. **Gn 37:14** 935
and before he **c** close to them, **Gn 37:18** 7126
So it **c** about, when Joseph reached **Gn 37:23** 1961
And it **c** about at that time, that **Gn 38:1** 1961
It **c** about at the time she was **Gn 38:27** 1961
"This one **c** out first." **Gn 38:28** 3318
But it **c** about as he drew back his **Gn 38:29** 1961
that behold, his brother **c** out. **Gn 38:29** 3318
Afterward his brother **c** out **Gn 38:30** 3318
It **c** about that from the time **Gn 39:5** 1961
It **c** about after these events **Gn 39:7** 1961
he **c** in to me to lie with me, and **Gn 39:14** 935
her until his master **c** home. **Gn 39:16** 935
c in to me to make sport of me; **Gn 39:17** 935
Then it **c** about after these things **Gn 40:1** 1961
When Joseph **c** to them in the **Gn 40:6** 935
was budding, its blossoms **c** out, **Gn 40:10** 5927
Thus it **c** about on the third day, **Gn 40:20** 1961
the Nile there **c** up seven cows, **Gn 41:2** 5927
c up after them from the Nile, **Gn 41:3** 5927
of grain **c** up on a single stalk, **Gn 41:5** 5927
his clothes, he **c** to Pharaoh. **Gn 41:14** 935
and sleek **c** up out of the Nile, **Gn 41:18** 5927
seven other cows **c** up after them, **Gn 41:19** 5927
and good, **c** up on a single stalk; **Gn 41:22** 5927
cows that **c** up after them are seven **Gn 41:27** 5927
Now before the year of famine **c**, **Gn 41:50** 935
in the land of Egypt **c** to an end, **Gn 41:53** 3615
The people of all the earth **c** **Gn 41:57** 935
So the sons of Israel **c** to buy **Gn 42:5** 935
And Joseph's brothers **c** and bowed **Gn 42:6** 935
When they **c** to their father Jacob **Gn 42:29** 935
Now it **c** about as they were **Gn 42:35** 1961
So it **c** about when they had **Gn 43:2** 1961
So they **c** near to Joseph's house **Gn 43:19** 5066
we indeed **c** down the first time to **Gn 43:20** 3381
and it **c** about when we came to the **Gn 43:21** 1961
when we **c** to the lodging place, **Gn 43:21** 935
When Joseph **c** home, they brought **Gn 43:26** 935
he washed his face and **c** out; **Gn 43:31** 3318
his brothers **c** to Joseph's house, **Gn 44:14** 935
"Thus it **c** about when we went up **Gn 44:24** 1961
And they **c** closer. **Gn 45:4** 5066
and **c** to the land of Canaan to **Gn 45:25** 935
that he had, and **c** to Beersheba, **Gn 46:1** 935
land of Canaan, and **c** to Egypt, **Gn 46:6** 935
to Jacob, who **c** to Egypt, **Gn 46:26** 935
house of Jacob, who **c** to Egypt, **Gn 46:27** 935
they **c** into the land of Goshen. **Gn 46:28** 935
Egyptians **c** to Joseph and said, **Gn 47:15** 935
they **c** to him the next year and **Gn 47:18** 935
Now it **c** about after these things **Gn 48:1** 1961
Egypt before I **c** to you in Egypt, **Gn 48:5** 935
as for me, when I **c** from Paddan, **Gn 48:7** 935
When they **c** to the threshing floor **Gn 50:10** 935
Then his brothers also **c** and fell **Gn 50:18** 1980
Israel who **c** to Egypt with Jacob; **Ex 1:1** 935
c each one with his household: **Ex 1:1** 935
All the persons who **c** from the **Ex 1:5** 3318
c down to bathe at the Nile, **Ex 2:5** 3381
Now it **c** about in those days, when **Ex 2:11** 1961
and they **c** to draw water and **Ex 2:16** 935
shepherds **c** and drove them away, **Ex 2:17** 935
When they **c** to Reuel their father, **Ex 2:18** 935
Now it **c** about in *the course of* **Ex 2:23** 1961
of the wilderness and **c** to Horeb, **Ex 3:1** 935
Now it **c** about at the lodging **Ex 4:24** 1961
and Aaron **c** and said to Pharaoh, **Ex 5:1** 935
Israel **c** and cried out to Pharaoh, **Ex 5:15** 935
"Ever since I **c** to Pharaoh to **Ex 5:23** 935
Now it **c** about on the day when the **Ex 6:28** 1961
So Moses and Aaron **c** to Pharaoh, **Ex 7:10** 935
and the frogs **c** up and covered the **Ex 8:6** 5927
And there **c** great swarms of **Ex 8:24** 935
c upon the earth until this day.'" **Ex 10:6** 1961
The locusts **c** up over all the **Ex 10:14** 5927
Now it **c** about at midnight that **Ex 12:29** 1961
did for me when I **c** out of Egypt.' **Ex 13:8** 3318
'It **c** about, when Pharaoh was **Ex 13:15** 1961
So it **c** between the camp of Egypt **Ex 14:20** 935
When they **c** to Marah, they **Ex 15:23** 935
Then they **c** to Elim where there **Ex 15:27** 935
Israel **c** to the wilderness of Sin, **Ex 16:1** 935
It **c** about as Aaron spoke to **Ex 16:10** 1961
So it **c** about at evening that the **Ex 16:13** 1961
quails **c** up and covered the camp, **Ex 16:13** 5927
the congregation **c** and told Moses, **Ex 16:22** 935
It **c** about on the seventh day **Ex 16:27** 1961
until they **c** to an inhabited land; **Ex 16:35** 935
they ate the manna until they **c** to **Ex 16:35** 935
Then Amalek **c** and fought against **Ex 17:8** 935
So it **c** about when Moses held his **Ex 17:11** 1961
c with his sons and his wife to **Ex 18:5** 935
and Aaron **c** with all the elders of **Ex 18:12** 935
It **c** about the next day that **Ex 18:13** 1961
c into the wilderness of Sinai. **Ex 19:1** 935
they **c** to the wilderness of Sinai and **Ex 19:2** 935
So Moses **c** and called the elders **Ex 19:7** 935
So it **c** about on the third day, **Ex 19:16** 1961
The LORD **c** down on Mount Sinai, **Ex 19:20** 3381
if it is hired, it **c** for its hire. **Ex 22:15** 935
for in it you **c** out of Egypt. **Ex 23:15** 3318

Then Moses **c** and recounted to the	Ex 24:3	935
It **c** about, as soon as Moses	Ex 32:19	1961
as soon as Moses **c** near the camp,	Ex 32:19	7126
the fire, and out **c** this calf."	Ex 32:24	3318
And it **c** about, whenever Moses	Ex 33:8	1961
month of Abib you **c** out of Egypt.	Ex 34:18	3318
It **c** about when Moses was	Ex 34:29	1961
all the sons of Israel **c** near,	Ex 34:32	5066
take off the veil until he **c** out;	Ex 34:34	3318
and whenever he **c** out and spoke to	Ex 34:34	3318
everyone whose spirit moved him **c**	Ex 35:21	935
c *and* brought brooches and	Ex 35:22	935
all the work of the sanctuary **c**,	Ex 36:4	935
Now it **c** about on the eighth day	Lv 9:1	1961
and the whole congregation **c** near	Lv 9:5	7126
So Aaron **c** near to the altar and	Lv 9:8	7126
they **c** out and blessed the people,	Lv 9:23	3318
Then fire **c** out from before the	Lv 9:24	3318
And fire **c** out from the presence	Lv 10:2	3318
So they **c** forward and carried them	Lv 10:5	7126
so they **c** before Moses and Aaron	Nu 9:6	7126
Then it **c** about when the ark set	Nu 10:35	1961
When it **c** to rest, he said,	Nu 10:36	5117
Then the LORD **c** down in the cloud	Nu 11:25	3381
So the three of them **c** out.	Nu 12:4	3318
Then the LORD **c** down in a pillar	Nu 12:5	3381
they **c** to Hebron where Ahiman,	Nu 13:22	935
Then they **c** to the valley of	Nu 13:23	935
lived in that hill country **c** down,	Nu 14:45	3381
and Dathan and Abiram **c** out *and*	Nu 16:27	3318
Fire also **c** forth from the LORD	Nu 16:35	3318
It **c** about, however, when the	Nu 16:42	1961
Then Moses and Aaron **c** to the	Nu 16:43	935
c to the wilderness of Zin in the	Nu 20:1	935
Then Moses and Aaron **c** in from the	Nu 20:6	935
and water **c** forth abundantly, and	Nu 20:11	3318
And Edom **c** out against him with a	Nu 20:20	3318
congregation, **c** to Mount Hor.	Nu 20:22	935
Eleazar **c** down from the mountain.	Nu 20:28	3381
So the people **c** to Moses and said,	Nu 21:7	935
and it **c** about, that if a serpent	Nu 21:9	1961
and **c** to Jahaz and fought against	Nu 21:23	935
"Behold, a people **c** out of Egypt;	Nu 22:5	3318
and they **c** to Balaam and repeated	Nu 22:7	935
Then God **c** to Balaam and said,	Nu 22:9	935
there is a people who **c** out of	Nu 22:11	3318
They **c** to Balaam and said to him,	Nu 22:16	935
God **c** to Balaam at night and	Nu 22:20	935
and they **c** to Kiriath-huzoth.	Nu 22:39	935
Then it **c** about in the morning	Nu 22:41	1961
He **c** to him, and behold, he	Nu 23:17	935
and the Spirit of God **c** upon him.	Nu 24:2	1961
one of the sons of Israel **c** and	Nu 25:6	935
Then it **c** about after the plague,	Nu 26:1	1961
c out of the land of Egypt *were:*	Nu 26:4	3318
the son of Joseph, **c** near;	Nu 27:1	7126
sons of Reuben **c** and spoke to Moses	Nu 32:2	935
of the men who **c** up from Egypt,	Nu 32:11	5927
Then they **c** near to him and said,	Nu 32:16	5066
by which they **c** out from the land	Nu 33:1	3318
from Marah and **c** to Elim;	Nu 33:9	935
c near and spoke before Moses and	Nu 36:1	7126
and we **c** to Kadesh-barnea.	Dt 1:19	935
and **c** to the valley of Eshcol and	Dt 1:24	935
until you **c** to this place.'	Dt 1:31	935
hill country **c** out against you and	Dt 1:44	3318
"So it **c** about when all the men	Dt 2:16	1961
the Caphtorim who **c** from Caphtor,	Dt 2:23	3318
"Then Sihon with all his people **c**	Dt 2:32	3318
with all his people **c** out to meet	Dt 3:1	3318
"You **c** near and stood at the	Dt 4:11	7126
when they **c** out from Egypt,	Dt 4:45	3318
when they **c** out from Egypt.	Dt 4:46	3318
with fire, you **c** near to me,	Dt 5:23	7126
"It **c** about at the end of	Dt 9:11	1961
"So I turned and **c** down from the	Dt 9:15	3381
that **c** down from the mountain.	Dt 9:21	3381
and **c** down from the mountain and	Dt 10:5	3381
until you **c** to this place;	Dt 11:5	935
land of Egypt from which you **c**,	Dt 11:10	3318
you **c** out of the land of Egypt	Dt 16:3	3318
you **c** out of the land of Egypt.	Dt 16:3	3318
the time that you **c** out of Egypt.	Dt 16:6	3318
this woman, *but* when I **c** near her,	Dt 22:14	7126
the way when you **c** out of Egypt,	Dt 23:4	3318
on the way as you **c** out of Egypt.	Dt 24:9	3318
the way when you **c** out from Egypt,	Dt 25:17	3318
c out to meet us for battle,	Dt 29:7	3318
and how we **c** through the midst of	Dt 29:16	5674a
It **c** about, when Moses	Dt 31:24	1961
not known, New *gods* who **c** lately,	Dt 32:17	935
Then Moses **c** and spoke all the	Dt 32:44	935
"The LORD **c** from Sinai, And	Dt 33:2	935
And He **c** from the midst of ten	Dt 33:2	857
And he **c** *with* the leaders of the	Dt 33:21	857
mourning for Moses **c** to an end.	Dt 34:8	8552
Now it **c** about after the death of	Jos 1:1	1961
So they went and **c** into the house	Jos 2:1	935
"Yes, the men **c** to me, but I did	Jos 2:4	935
"It **c** about when *it was time*	Jos 2:5	1961
she **c** up to them on the roof,	Jos 2:8	5927
you when you **c** out of Egypt,	Jos 2:10	3318
and **c** to the hill country,	Jos 2:22	935
Then the two men returned and **c**	Jos 2:23	3381
and **c** to Joshua the son of Nun,	Jos 2:23	935
from Shittim and **c** to the Jordan,	Jos 3:1	935
carried the ark **c** into the Jordan,	Jos 3:15	935
It **c** about when the priests	Jos 4:18	1961
Now the people **c** up from the	Jos 4:19	5927
Now it **c** about when all the kings	Jos 5:1	1961
who **c** out of Egypt who were males,	Jos 5:4	3318
way after they **c** out of Egypt.	Jos 5:4	3318
people who **c** out were circumcised,	Jos 5:5	3318
along the way as they **c** out of Egypt	Jos 5:5	3318
the men of war who **c** out of Egypt,	Jos 5:6	3318
Now it **c** about when Joshua was by	Jos 5:13	1961
no one went out and no one **c** in.	Jos 6:1	935
the rear guard **c** after the ark,	Jos 6:9	1980
then they **c** into the camp and	Jos 6:11	935
guard **c** after the ark of the LORD,	Jos 6:13	1980
It **c** about when the king of Ai	Jos 8:14	1961
The others **c** out from the city	Jos 8:22	3318
Now it **c** about when all the kings	Jos 9:1	1961
It **c** about at the end of three	Jos 9:16	1961
and **c** to their cities on the third day.	Jos 9:17	935
Now it **c** about when Adoni-zedek	Jos 10:1	1961
So Joshua **c** upon them suddenly by	Jos 10:9	935
It **c** about when Joshua and the	Jos 10:20	1961
So they **c** near and put their feet	Jos 10:24	7126
It **c** about at sunset that	Jos 10:27	1961
of Gezer **c** up to help Lachish,	Jos 10:33	5927
Then it **c** about, when Jabin king	Jos 11:1	1961
They **c** out, they and all their	Jos 11:4	3318
c and encamped together at the	Jos 11:5	935
people of war with him **c** upon them	Jos 11:7	935
Then Joshua **c** at that time and cut	Jos 11:21	935
It **c** about that when she came	Jos 15:18	1961
came about that when she **c** *to him,*	Jos 15:18	935
Jericho and **c** out at the Jordan.	Jos 16:7	3318
They **c** near before Eleazar the	Jos 17:4	7126
It **c** about when the sons of	Jos 17:13	1961
and they **c** to Joshua to the camp	Jos 18:9	935
tribe of the sons of Benjamin **c** up	Jos 18:11	5927
Now the third lot **c** up for the	Jos 19:10	5927
Then the lot **c** out for the	Jos 21:4	3318
house of Israel failed; all **c** to pass.	Jos 21:45	935
When they **c** to the region of	Jos 22:10	935
They **c** to the sons of Reuben	Jos 22:15	935
although a plague **c** on the	Jos 22:17	1961
Now it **c** about after many days,	Jos 23:1	1961
of Egypt, and you **c** to the sea;	Jos 24:6	935
the Jordan and **c** to Jericho;	Jos 24:11	935
It **c** about after these things	Jos 24:29	1961
Now it **c** about after the death of	Jg 1:1	1961
it **c** about when she came *to him,*	Jg 1:14	1961
it came about when she **c** *to him,*	Jg 1:14	935
It **c** about when Israel became	Jg 1:28	1961
LORD **c** up from Gilgal to Bochim.	Jg 2:1	5927
it **c** about when the judge died,	Jg 2:19	1961
The Spirit of the LORD **c** upon him,	Jg 3:10	1961
It **c** about when he had	Jg 3:18	1961
Ehud **c** to him while he was	Jg 3:20	935
and the refuse **c** out.	Jg 3:22	3318
out, his servants **c** and looked,	Jg 3:24	935
It **c** about when he had arrived,	Jg 3:27	1961
him **c** Shamgar the son of Anath,	Jg 3:31	1961
Israel **c** up to her for judgment.	Jg 4:5	5927
Jael **c** out to meet him and said to	Jg 4:22	3318
survivors **c** down to the nobles;	Jg 5:13	3381
the LORD **c** down to me as warriors.	Jg 5:13	3381
those whose root is in Amalek **c**	Jg 5:14	
From Machir commanders **c** down,	Jg 5:14	3381
"The kings **c** *and* fought;	Jg 5:19	935
c into the land to devastate it.	Jg 6:5	935
Now it **c** about when the sons of	Jg 6:7	1961
Then the angel of the LORD **c** and	Jg 6:11	935
Spirit of the LORD **c** upon Gideon;	Jg 6:34	3847
and they **c** up to meet them.	Jg 6:35	5927
Now the same night it **c** about that	Jg 7:9	1961
When Gideon **c**, behold, a man was	Jg 7:13	935
and it **c** to the tent and struck it	Jg 7:13	935
c to the outskirts of the camp	Jg 7:19	935
c to the Jordan *and* crossed over,	Jg 8:4	935
He **c** to the men of Succoth and	Jg 8:15	935
Then it **c** about, as soon as Gideon	Jg 8:33	1961
son of Ebed **c** with his relatives,	Jg 9:26	935
Now it **c** about the next day, that	Jg 9:42	1961
So Abimelech **c** to the tower and	Jg 9:52	935
the son of Jerubbaal **c** upon them.	Jg 9:57	935
It **c** about after a while that	Jg 11:4	1961
my land when they **c** up from Egypt,	Jg 11:13	5927
'For when they **c** up from Egypt,	Jg 11:16	5927
to the Red Sea and **c** to Kadesh,	Jg 11:16	935
and **c** to the east side of the land	Jg 11:18	935
of the LORD **c** upon Jephthah,	Jg 11:29	1961
Jephthah **c** to his house at Mizpah,	Jg 11:34	935
the woman **c** and told her husband,	Jg 13:6	935
"A man of God **c** to me and his	Jg 13:6	935
And I did not ask him where he **c**	Jg 13:6	
and the angel of God **c** again to	Jg 13:9	935
the man who **c** the *other* day has	Jg 13:10	935
he **c** to the man he said to him,	Jg 13:11	935
For it **c** about when the flame went	Jg 13:20	1961
So he **c** back and told his father	Jg 14:2	5927
and **c** as far as the vineyards of	Jg 14:5	935
a young lion **c** roaring toward him.	Jg 14:5	
Spirit of the LORD **c** upon him	Jg 14:6	6743a
he **c** to his father and mother,	Jg 14:9	1980
of the eater **c** something to eat,	Jg 14:14	3318
of the strong **c** something sweet."	Jg 14:14	3318
Then it **c** about on the fourth day	Jg 14:15	1961
of the LORD **c** upon him mightily,	Jg 14:19	6743a
So the Philistines **c** up and burned	Jg 15:6	5927
When he **c** to Lehi, the Philistines	Jg 15:14	935
And the Spirit of the LORD **c** upon	Jg 15:14	6743a
in Lehi so that water **c** out of it.	Jg 15:19	3318
After this it **c** about that he	Jg 16:4	1961
of the Philistines **c** up to her and	Jg 16:5	5927
It **c** about when she pressed	Jg 16:16	1961
of the Philistines **c** up to her and	Jg 16:18	5927
all his father's household **c** down,	Jg 16:31	3381
he **c** to the hill country of	Jg 17:8	935
And they **c** to the hill country of	Jg 18:2	935
Then the five men departed and **c**	Jg 18:7	935
When they **c** back to their brothers	Jg 18:8	935
and **c** to the house of Micah.	Jg 18:13	935
c to the house of the young man,	Jg 18:15	935
belonged to him, and **c** to Laish,	Jg 18:27	935
Now it **c** about in those days, when	Jg 19:1	1961
and **c** to *a place* opposite Jebus	Jg 19:10	935
"Bring out the man who **c** into	Jg 19:22	935
the woman **c** and fell down at the	Jg 19:26	935
Israel **c** up from the land of Egypt	Jg 19:30	5927
the land of Gilead, **c** out,	Jg 20:1	3318
"I **c** with my concubine to spend	Jg 20:4	935
Then the sons of Benjamin **c** out of	Jg 20:21	3318
Then the sons of Israel **c** against	Jg 20:24	7126
went up and **c** to Bethel and wept;	Jg 20:26	935
from all Israel **c** against Gibeah,	Jg 20:34	935
those who **c** out of the cities destroyed	Jg 20:42	
So the people **c** to Bethel and sat	Jg 21:2	935
It **c** about the next day that	Jg 21:4	1961
Now it **c** about in the days when	Ru 1:1	1961
went until they **c** to Bethlehem.	Ru 1:19	935
And they **c** to Bethlehem at the	Ru 1:22	935
Boaz **c** from Bethlehem and said to	Ru 2:4	935
Thus she **c** and has remained from	Ru 2:7	935
and **c** to a people that you did not	Ru 2:11	1980
and she **c** secretly, and uncovered	Ru 3:7	935
woman **c** to the threshing floor."	Ru 3:14	935
When she **c** to her	Ru 3:16	935
the day **c** that Elkanah sacrificed,	1Sa 1:4	1961
Now it **c** about, as she continued	1Sa 1:12	1961
It **c** about in due time, after	1Sa 1:20	1961
to all the Israelites who **c** there.	1Sa 2:14	935
of God **c** to Eli and said to him,	1Sa 2:27	935
Then the LORD **c** and stood and	1Sa 3:10	935
word of Samuel **c** to all Israel.	1Sa 4:1	1961
When the people **c** into the camp,	1Sa 4:3	935
of the LORD **c** into the camp,	1Sa 4:5	935
and **c** to Shiloh the same day	1Sa 4:12	935
When he **c**, behold, Eli was sitting	1Sa 4:13	935
the man **c** to tell *it* in the city,	1Sa 4:13	935
the man **c** hurriedly and told Eli.	1Sa 4:14	935
one who **c** from the battle line.	1Sa 4:16	935
birth, for her pains **c** upon her.	1Sa 4:19	2015
as the ark of God **c** to Ekron	1Sa 5:10	935
The cart **c** into the field of	1Sa 6:14	935
And the men of Kiriath-jearim **c**	1Sa 7:1	935
And it **c** about when Samuel was old	1Sa 8:1	1961
together and **c** to Samuel at Ramah;	1Sa 8:4	935
When they **c** to the land of Zuph,	1Sa 9:5	935
As they **c** into the city, behold,	1Sa 9:14	935
When they **c** down from the high	1Sa 9:25	3381
those signs **c** about on that day.	1Sa 10:9	935
When they **c** to the hill there,	1Sa 10:10	935
Spirit of God **c** upon him mightily,	1Sa 10:10	6743a
It **c** about, when all who knew	1Sa 10:11	1961
he **c** to the high place.	1Sa 10:13	935
c up and besieged Jabesh-gilead;	1Sa 11:1	5927
Then the messengers **c** to Gibeah of	1Sa 11:4	935
Then the Spirit of God **c** upon Saul	1Sa 11:6	6743a
people, and they **c** out as one man.	1Sa 11:7	3318
and they **c** into the midst of the	1Sa 11:11	935
the sons of Ammon **c** against you,	1Sa 12:12	935
they **c** up and camped in Michmash,	1Sa 13:5	5927
offering, behold, Samuel **c**;	1Sa 13:10	935
And the raiders **c** from the camp of	1Sa 13:17	3318
So it **c** about on the day of battle	1Sa 13:22	1961
Now the day **c** that Jonathan, the	1Sa 14:1	1961
him rallied and **c** to the battle;	1Sa 14:20	935
Saul **c** to the city of Amalek and	1Sa 15:5	935
when they **c** up from Egypt."	1Sa 15:6	5927
the word of the LORD **c** to Samuel,	1Sa 15:10	1961
"Saul **c** to Carmel, and behold, he	1Sa 15:12	935
Samuel **c** to Saul, and Saul	1Sa 15:13	935
And Agag **c** to him cheerfully.	1Sa 15:32	1980
the LORD said, and **c** to Bethlehem.	1Sa 16:4	935
And the elders of the city **c**	1Sa 16:4	2729
and the Spirit of the LORD **c**	1Sa 16:13	6743a
David **c** to Saul and attended him;	1Sa 16:21	935
So it **c** about whenever the *evil*	1Sa 16:23	1961
evil spirit from God **c** to Saul,	1Sa 16:23	1961
Then a champion **c** out from the	1Sa 17:4	3318
The Philistine **c** forward	1Sa 17:16	5066
And he **c** to the circle of the camp	1Sa 17:20	935
When a lion or a bear **c** and took a	1Sa 17:34	935
c on and approached David,	1Sa 17:41	1980
and **c** and drew near to meet David,	1Sa 17:48	1980
Now it **c** about when he had	1Sa 18:1	1961
that the women **c** out of all the	1Sa 18:6	3318
Now it **c** about on the next day	1Sa 18:10	1961
from God **c** mightily upon Saul,	1Sa 18:10	6743a
out and **c** in before the people.	1Sa 18:13	935
he went out and **c** in before them.	1Sa 18:16	935
it **c** about at the time when Merab,	1Sa 18:19	1961
escaped and **c** to Samuel at Ramah,	1Sa 19:18	935
God **c** upon the messengers of Saul;	1Sa 19:20	1961
and **c** as far as the large well	1Sa 19:22	935
the Spirit of God **c** upon him also,	1Sa 19:23	1961
until he **c** to Naioth in Ramah.	1Sa 19:23	935
Ramah, and **c** and said to Jonathan,	1Sa 20:1	935
and when the new moon **c**,	1Sa 20:24	1961
It **c** about the next day, the	1Sa 20:27	1961
Now it **c** about in the morning that	1Sa 20:35	1961
up the arrow and **c** to his master.	1Sa 20:38	935
Then David **c** to Nob to Ahimelech	1Sa 21:1	935

c trembling to meet David and	1Sa 21:1	2729
and all of them **c** to the king.	1Sa 22:11	935
Now it **c** about, when Abiathar the	1Sa 23:6	1961
that he **c** down *with* an ephod in	1Sa 23:6	3381
Ziphites **c** up to Saul at Gibeah,	1Sa 23:19	5927
and he **c** down to the rock and	1Sa 23:25	3381
But a messenger **c** to Saul, saying,	1Sa 23:27	935
He **c** to the sheepfolds on the way,	1Sa 24:3	935
It **c** about afterward that	1Sa 24:5	1961
And it **c** about while he was	1Sa 25:2	1961
When David's young men **c**,	1Sa 25:9	935
and they **c** and told him according	1Sa 25:12	935
It **c** about as she was riding	1Sa 25:20	1961
Then Abigail **c** to Nabal, and	1Sa 25:36	935
of David **c** to Abigail at Carmel,	1Sa 25:40	935
the Ziphites **c** to Saul at Gibeah,	1Sa 26:1	935
c after him into the wilderness,	1Sa 26:3	935
David then arose and **c** to the	1Sa 26:5	935
Abishai **c** to the people by night,	1Sa 26:7	935
c to destroy the king your lord.	1Sa 26:15	935
Then he returned and **c** to Achish.	1Sa 27:9	935
Now it **c** about in those days that	1Sa 28:1	1961
and **c** and camped in Shunem;	1Sa 28:4	935
and they **c** to the woman by night;	1Sa 28:8	935
The woman **c** to Saul and saw	1Sa 28:21	935
when I **c** before you to this day,	1Sa 29:8	1961
men **c** to Ziklag on the third day,	1Sa 30:1	935
David and his men **c** to the city,	1Sa 30:3	935
him, and **c** to the brook Besor,	1Sa 30:9	935
When David **c** to the two hundred	1Sa 30:21	935
hand the band that **c** against us.	1Sa 30:23	935
Now when David **c** to Ziklag, he	1Sa 30:26	935
Philistines **c** and lived in them.	1Sa 31:7	935
It **c** about on the next day	1Sa 31:8	1961
Philistines **c** to strip the slain,	1Sa 31:8	935
of Beth-shan, and they **c** to Jabesh and	1Sa 31:12	935
c about after the death of Saul,	2Sa 1:1	1961
a man **c** out of the camp from Saul,	2Sa 1:2	935
And it **c** about when he came to	2Sa 1:2	1961
And it came about when he **c** to	2Sa 1:2	935
Then it **c** about afterwards that	2Sa 2:1	1961
Then the men of Judah **c** and there	2Sa 2:4	935
that the spear **c** out at his back.	2Sa 2:23	3318
And it **c** about that all who came	2Sa 2:23	1961
And it came about that all who **c**	2Sa 2:23	935
down, they **c** to the hill of Ammah,	2Sa 2:24	935
all morning, and **c** to Mahanaim.	2Sa 2:29	935
It **c** about while there was war	2Sa 3:6	1961
men with him **c** to David at Hebron.	2Sa 3:20	935
the servants of David and Joab **c**	2Sa 3:22	935
the son of Ner **c** to the king,	2Sa 3:23	935
Then Joab **c** to the king and said,	2Sa 3:24	935
Behold, Abner **c** to you;	2Sa 3:24	935
that he **c** to deceive you and to	2Sa 3:25	935
When Joab **c** out from David, he	2Sa 3:26	3318
Then all the people **c** to persuade	2Sa 3:35	935
Saul and Jonathan **c** from Jezreel,	2Sa 4:4	935
departed and **c** to the house of	2Sa 4:5	935
They **c** to the middle of the	2Sa 4:6	935
Now when they **c** into the house, as	2Sa 4:7	935
c to David at Hebron and said,	2Sa 5:1	935
of Israel **c** to the king at Hebron,	2Sa 5:3	935
Jerusalem, after he **c** from Hebron;	2Sa 5:13	935
Now the Philistines **c** and spread	2Sa 5:18	935
So David **c** to Baal-perazim and	2Sa 5:20	935
Now the Philistines **c** up once	2Sa 5:22	5927
But when they **c** to the threshing	2Sa 6:6	935
as the ark of the LORD **c** into the city	2Sa 6:16	935
Saul **c** out to meet David and said,	2Sa 6:20	3318
Now it **c** about when the king lived	2Sa 7:1	1961
the word of the LORD **c** to Nathan,	2Sa 7:4	1961
Now after this it **c** about that	2Sa 8:1	1961
of Damascus **c** to help Hadadezer,	2Sa 8:5	935
c to David and fell on his face	2Sa 9:6	935
c to the land of the Ammonites,	2Sa 10:2	935
The sons of Ammon **c** out and	2Sa 10:8	3318
sons of Ammon and **c** to Jerusalem.	2Sa 10:14	935
the River, and they **c** to Helam;	2Sa 10:16	935
the Jordan, and **c** to Helam.	2Sa 10:17	935
Now when evening **c** David arose	2Sa 11:2	1961
took her, and when she **c** to him,	2Sa 11:4	935
When Uriah **c** to him, David asked	2Sa 11:7	935
So the messenger departed and **c**	2Sa 11:22	935
and **c** out against us in the field,	2Sa 11:23	3318
And he **c** to him and said,	2Sa 12:1	935
"Now a traveler **c** to the rich	2Sa 12:4	935
and he **c** into the house of the	2Sa 12:20	935
Then he **c** to his own house, and	2Sa 12:20	935
when the king **c** to see him, Amnon	2Sa 13:6	935
Now it **c** about after two full	2Sa 13:23	1961
Absalom **c** to the king and said,	2Sa 13:24	935
way that the report **c** to David,	2Sa 13:30	935
the king's sons **c** and lifted their	2Sa 13:36	935
c to Absalom at his house and said	2Sa 14:31	935
Joab **c** to the king and told him,	2Sa 14:33	935
Thus he **c** to the king and	2Sa 14:33	935
Now it **c** about after this that	2Sa 15:1	1961
And when a man **c** near	2Sa 15:5	7126
who **c** to the king for judgment;	2Sa 15:6	935
Now it **c** about at the end of forty	2Sa 15:7	1961
Then a messenger **c** to David,	2Sa 15:13	935
"You **c** *only* yesterday, and shall	2Sa 15:20	935
Now behold, Zadok also **c**,	2Sa 15:24	
and Abiathar **c** up until all the	2Sa 15:24	5927
David's friend, **c** into the city,	2Sa 15:37	935
and Absalom **c** into Jerusalem.	2Sa 15:37	935
When King David **c** to Bahurim,	2Sa 16:5	935
there **c** out from there a man of	2Sa 16:5	3318
he **c** out cursing continually as he	2Sa 16:5	3318

out cursing continually as he **c**.	2Sa 16:5	3318
who **c** out from me seeks my life;	2Sa 16:11	3318
c about when Hushai the Archite,	2Sa 16:16	1961
David's friend, **c** to Absalom,	2Sa 16:16	935
c to the house of a man in Bahurim,	2Sa 17:18	935
Then Absalom's servants **c** to the	2Sa 17:20	935
It **c** about after they had	2Sa 17:21	1961
c up out of the well and went and told	2Sa 17:21	5927
Then David **c** to Mahanaim.	2Sa 17:24	935
And he **c** nearer and nearer.	2Sa 18:25	1980
Then Joab **c** into the house to the	2Sa 19:5	935
all the people **c** before the king.	2Sa 19:8	935
and **c** as far as the Jordan.	2Sa 19:15	935
And Judah **c** to Gilgal in order to	2Sa 19:15	935
hurried and **c** down with the men of	2Sa 19:16	3381
the king **c** out from Jerusalem,	2Sa 19:19	3318
of Saul **c** down to meet the king;	2Sa 19:24	3381
until the day he **c** *home* in peace.	2Sa 19:24	935
It was when he **c** from	2Sa 19:25	935
all the men of Israel **c** to the	2Sa 19:41	935
David **c** to his house at Jerusalem,	2Sa 20:3	935
in Gibeon, Amasa **c** to meet them.	2Sa 20:8	935
everyone who **c** by him stood still.	2Sa 20:12	935
They **c** and besieged him in	2Sa 20:15	935
woman wisely **c** to all the people.	2Sa 20:22	935
Now it **c** about after this that	2Sa 21:18	1961
And my cry for help **c** into His	2Sa 22:7	
and **c** down With thick darkness	2Sa 22:10	3381
chief men went down and **c** to David	2Sa 23:13	935
Then they **c** to Gilead and to the	2Sa 24:6	935
and they **c** to Dan-jaan and around	2Sa 24:6	935
and **c** to the fortress of Tyre and	2Sa 24:7	935
they **c** to Jerusalem at the end of	2Sa 24:8	935
of the LORD **c** to the prophet Gad,	2Sa 24:11	1961
So Gad **c** to David and told him,	2Sa 24:13	935
So Gad **c** to David that day and	2Sa 24:18	935
the king, Nathan the prophet **c** in.	1Ki 1:22	935
And when he **c** in before the king,	1Ki 1:23	935
And she **c** into the king's presence	1Ki 1:28	935
they **c** into the king's presence.	1Ki 1:32	935
the son of Abiathar the priest **c**.	1Ki 1:42	935
c to bless our lord King David,	1Ki 1:47	935
And he **c** and prostrated himself	1Ki 1:53	935
he **c** down to me at the Jordan,	1Ki 2:8	3381
Now Adonijah the son of Haggith **c**	1Ki 2:13	935
Now the news **c** to Joab, for Joab	1Ki 2:28	935
Benaiah **c** to the tent of the LORD and	1Ki 2:30	935
But it **c** about at the end of three	1Ki 2:39	1961
And he **c** to Jerusalem and stood	1Ki 3:15	935
Then two women who were harlots **c**	1Ki 3:16	935
all who **c** to King Solomon's table,	1Ki 4:27	7131
Men **c** from all peoples to hear	1Ki 4:34	935
Now it **c** about in the four hundred	1Ki 6:1	1961
Israel **c** out of the land of Egypt,	1Ki 6:1	3318
of the LORD **c** to Solomon saying,	1Ki 6:11	1961
So he **c** to King Solomon and	1Ki 7:14	935
Then all the elders of Israel **c**,	1Ki 8:3	935
they **c** out of the land of Egypt.	1Ki 8:9	3318
the priests **c** from the holy place,	1Ki 8:10	3318
Now it **c** about when Solomon had	1Ki 9:1	1961
It **c** about at the end of	1Ki 9:10	1961
So Hiram **c** out from Tyre to see	1Ki 9:12	3318
As soon as Pharaoh's daughter **c** up	1Ki 9:24	5927
she **c** to test him with difficult	1Ki 10:1	935
So she **c** to Jerusalem with a very	1Ki 10:2	935
When she **c** to Solomon, she spoke	1Ki 10:2	935
until I **c** and my eyes had seen it.	1Ki 10:7	935
Now the weight of gold which **c** in	1Ki 10:14	935
c bringing gold and silver,	1Ki 10:22	935
For it **c** about, when David was in	1Ki 11:15	1961
arose from Midian and **c** to Paran;	1Ki 11:18	935
them from Paran and **c** to Egypt,	1Ki 11:18	935
It **c** about at that time, when	1Ki 11:29	1961
of Israel **c** and spoke to Rehoboam,	1Ki 12:3	935
the people **c** to Rehoboam	1Ki 12:12	935
It **c** about when all Israel	1Ki 12:20	1961
God **c** to Shemaiah the man of God,	1Ki 12:22	1961
there **c** a man of God from Judah to	1Ki 13:1	935
return by the way which you **c**.' "	1Ki 13:9	1980
by the way which he **c** to Bethel.	1Ki 13:10	935
and his sons **c** and told him all	1Ki 13:11	935
of God who **c** from Judah had gone.	1Ki 13:12	935
the man of God who **c** from Judah?"	1Ki 13:14	935
"For a command **c** to me by	1Ki 13:17	
by going the way which you **c**.' "	1Ki 13:17	1980
Now it **c** about, as they were	1Ki 13:20	1961
that the word of the LORD **c** to the	1Ki 13:20	1961
the man of God who **c** from Judah,	1Ki 13:21	935
It **c** about after he had eaten	1Ki 13:23	1961
so they **c** and told *it* in the city	1Ki 13:25	935
and brought it back, and he **c** to	1Ki 13:29	935
and **c** to the house of Ahijah.	1Ki 14:4	935
and departed and **c** to Tirzah.	1Ki 14:17	935
king of Egypt **c** up against Jerusalem.	1Ki 14:25	5927
It **c** about as soon as he was	1Ki 15:29	1961
Now the word of the LORD **c** to Jehu	1Ki 16:1	1961
son of Hanani also **c** against Baasha	1Ki 16:7	1961
It **c** about when he became	1Ki 16:11	1961
It **c** about, as though it had	1Ki 16:31	1961
The word of the LORD **c** to him,	1Ki 17:2	1961
the word of the LORD **c** to him,	1Ki 17:8	1961
when he **c** to the gate of the city,	1Ki 17:10	935
Now it **c** about after these things that	1Ki 17:17	1961
c to Elijah in the third year,	1Ki 18:1	1961
Elijah **c** near to all the	1Ki 18:21	5066
It **c** about at noon, that	1Ki 18:27	1961
So all the people **c** near to him.	1Ki 18:30	5066
the prophet **c** near and said,	1Ki 18:36	5066
It **c** about at the seventh *time*,	1Ki 18:44	1961

for his life and **c** to Beersheba,	1Ki 19:3	935
and **c** and sat down under a juniper	1Ki 19:4	935
The angel of the LORD **c** again	1Ki 19:7	7725
Then he **c** there to a cave and	1Ki 19:9	935
the word of the LORD **c** to him,	1Ki 19:9	
a voice **c** to him and said,	1Ki 19:13	
c near to the king of Israel and	1Ki 20:22	5066
Then a man of God **c** near and spoke	1Ki 20:28	5066
And Ben-hadad fled and **c** into the	1Ki 20:30	935
and **c** to the king of Israel and	1Ki 20:32	935
Then Ben-hadad **c** out to him, and	1Ki 20:33	3318
and vexed, and **c** to Samaria.	1Ki 20:43	935
Now it **c** about after these things that	1Ki 21:1	1961
So Ahab **c** into his house sullen	1Ki 21:4	935
his wife **c** to him and said to him,	1Ki 21:5	935
men **c** in and sat before him;	1Ki 21:13	935
the LORD **c** to Elijah the Tishbite,	1Ki 21:17	1961
It **c** about when Ahab heard	1Ki 21:27	1961
the LORD **c** to Elijah the Tishbite,	1Ki 21:28	1961
c down to the king of Israel.	1Ki 22:2	3381
When he **c** to the king, the king	1Ki 22:15	935
"Then a spirit **c** forward and	1Ki 22:21	3318
Zedekiah the son of Chenaanah **c** near	1Ki 22:24	5066
c up to meet us and said to us,	2Ki 1:6	5927
"What kind of man was he who **c** up	2Ki 1:7	5927
Then fire **c** down from heaven and	2Ki 1:10	3381
Then the fire of God **c** down from	2Ki 1:12	3381
he **c** and bowed down on his knees	2Ki 1:13	935
"Behold fire **c** down from heaven and	2Ki 1:14	3381
And it **c** about when the LORD was	2Ki 2:1	1961
c out to Elisha and said to him,	2Ki 2:3	3318
So they **c** to Jericho.	2Ki 2:4	935
And they **c** to meet him and bowed	2Ki 2:15	935
young lads **c** out from the city and	2Ki 2:23	3318
Then two female bears **c** out of the	2Ki 2:24	3318
And it **c** about, when the minstrel	2Ki 3:15	1961
the hand of the LORD **c** upon him.	2Ki 3:15	1961
water **c** by the way of Edom,	2Ki 3:20	935
when they **c** to the camp of Israel,	2Ki 3:24	935
c great wrath against Israel,	2Ki 3:27	1961
she **c** and told the man of God.	2Ki 4:7	935
Now there **c** a day when Elisha	2Ki 4:8	1961
One day he **c** there and turned in	2Ki 4:11	935
the day **c** that he went out to his	2Ki 4:18	1961
So she went and **c** to the man of	2Ki 4:25	935
c to the man of God to the hill,	2Ki 4:27	935
Gehazi **c** near to push her away;	2Ki 4:27	5066
When Elisha **c** into the house,	2Ki 4:32	935
And when she **c** in to him, he said,	2Ki 4:36	935
and **c** and sliced them into the pot	2Ki 4:39	935
Now a man **c** from Baal-shalishah,	2Ki 4:42	935
So Naaman **c** with his horses and	2Ki 5:9	935
Then his servants **c** near and spoke	2Ki 5:13	5066
and **c** and stood before him,	2Ki 5:15	935
he **c** down from the chariot to meet	2Ki 5:21	5307
When he **c** to the hill, he took	2Ki 5:24	935
and when they **c** to the Jordan,	2Ki 6:4	935
and they **c** by night and surrounded	2Ki 6:14	935
When they **c** down to him,	2Ki 6:18	3381
Now it **c** about after this, that	2Ki 6:24	1961
but before the messenger **c** to him,	2Ki 6:32	935
the messenger **c** down to him and	2Ki 6:33	3381
when they **c** to the outskirts of	2Ki 7:5	935
c to the outskirts of the camp,	2Ki 7:8	935
So they **c** and called to the	2Ki 7:10	935
"We **c** to the camp of the	2Ki 7:10	935
spoke when the king **c** down to him.	2Ki 7:17	3381
Then Elisha **c** to Damascus.	2Ki 8:7	935
c and stood before him and said,	2Ki 8:9	935
When he **c**, behold, the captains of	2Ki 9:5	935
Now Jehu **c** out to the servants of	2Ki 9:11	3318
saw the company of Jehu as he **c**,	2Ki 9:17	935
"The messenger **c** to them, but he	2Ki 9:18	935
horseman, who **c** to them and said,	2Ki 9:19	935
"He **c** even to them, and he did	2Ki 9:20	935
When Jehu **c** to Jezreel, Jezebel	2Ki 9:30	935
When he **c** in, he ate and drank;	2Ki 9:34	935
When the letter **c** to them,	2Ki 10:7	935
When the messenger **c** and told him,	2Ki 10:8	935
When he **c** to Samaria, he	2Ki 10:17	935
and all the worshipers of Baal **c**,	2Ki 10:21	935
Then it **c** about, as soon as he had	2Ki 10:25	1961
and **c** to Jehoiada the priest.	2Ki 11:9	935
she **c** to the people in the house	2Ki 11:13	935
and **c** by the way of the gate of	2Ki 11:19	935
But it **c** about that in the	2Ki 12:6	1961
the high priest **c** up and tied *it* in bags	2Ki 12:10	5927
Joash the king of Israel **c** down to	2Ki 13:14	3381
Now it **c** about, as soon as the	2Ki 14:5	1961
and **c** to Jerusalem and tore down	2Ki 14:13	935
up from Tirzah and **c** to Samaria,	2Ki 15:14	935
of Assyria, **c** against the land,	2Ki 15:19	935
Tiglath-pileser king of Assyria **c**	2Ki 15:29	935
c up to Jerusalem to *wage* war;	2Ki 16:5	5927
and the Arameans **c** to Elath and	2Ki 16:6	935
When the king **c** from Damascus,	2Ki 16:12	935
king of Assyria **c** up against him,	2Ki 17:3	5927
Now *this* **c** about because the sons	2Ki 17:7	1961
Samaria **c** and lived at Bethel,	2Ki 17:28	935
Now it **c** about in the third year	2Ki 18:1	1961
king of Assyria **c** up against Samaria	2Ki 18:9	5927
Sennacherib king of Assyria **c** up	2Ki 18:13	5927
they went up and **c** to Jerusalem.	2Ki 18:17	935
they **c** and stood by the conduit of	2Ki 18:17	935
Asaph the recorder, **c** out to them.	2Ki 18:18	3318
c to Hezekiah with their clothes	2Ki 18:37	935
of King Hezekiah **c** to Isaiah.	2Ki 19:5	935
"With my many chariots I **c** up to	2Ki 19:23	5927
you back by the way which you **c**.	2Ki 19:28	935

“By the way that he **c**, **2Ki 19:33** 935
It **c** about as he was **2Ki 19:37** 1961
of Amoz **c** to him and said to him, **2Ki 20:1** 935
the word of the LORD **c** to him, **2Ki 20:4** 1961
Then Isaiah the prophet **c** to King **2Ki 20:14** 935
day their fathers **c** from Egypt, **2Ki 21:15** 3318
Shaphan the scribe **c** to the **2Ki 22:9** 935
who **c** from Judah and proclaimed **2Ki 23:17** 935
of the prophet who **c** from Samaria. **2Ki 23:18** 935
king of Babylon **c** up, **2Ki 24:1** 5927
of the LORD it **c** upon Judah, **2Ki 24:3** 1961
and the city **c** under siege. **2Ki 24:10** 935
the king of Babylon **c** to the city, **2Ki 24:11** 935
this **c** about in Jerusalem and Judah **2Ki 24:20** 1961
Nebuchadnezzar king of Babylon **c**, **2Ki 25:1** 935
king of Babylon, **c** to Jerusalem. **2Ki 25:8** 935
they **c** to Gedaliah to Mizpah, **2Ki 25:23** 935
it **c** about in the seventh month, **2Ki 25:25** 1961
c with ten men and struck Gedaliah **2Ki 25:25** 935
Now it **c** about in the **2Ki 25:27** 1961
from which the Philistines **c**, **1Ch 1:12** 3318
from these **c** the Zorathites and **1Ch 2:53** 3318
the Kenites who **c** from Hammath, **1Ch 2:55** 935
c in the days of Hezekiah king of **1Ch 4:41** 935
and from him **c** the leader, yet **1Ch 5:2**
c down to take their livestock. **1Ch 7:21** 3381
his relatives **c** to comfort him. **1Ch 7:22** 935
Philistines **c** and lived in them. **1Ch 10:7** 935
It **c** about the next day, when **1Ch 10:8** 1961
Philistines **c** to strip the slain, **1Ch 10:8** 935
of Israel **c** to the king at Hebron, **1Ch 11:3** 935
the ones who **c** to David at Ziklag, **1Ch 12:1** 935
From the Gadites there **c** over **1Ch 12:8** 914
c to the stronghold to David. **1Ch 12:16** 935
Then the Spirit **c** upon Amasai, who **1Ch 12:18** 3847
by day *men* **c** to David to help him, **1Ch 12:22** 935
for war, who **c** to David at Hebron, **1Ch 12:23** 935
c to Hebron with a perfect heart to **1Ch 12:38** 935
When they **c** to the threshing floor **1Ch 13:9** 935
So they **c** up to Baal-perazim, and **1Ch 14:11** 5927
the LORD **c** to the city of David, **1Ch 15:29** 935
And it **c** about, when David dwelt **1Ch 17:1** 1961
It **c** about the same night that **1Ch 17:3** 1961
that the word of God **c** to Nathan, **1Ch 17:3** 1961
Now after this it **c** about that **1Ch 18:1** 1961
When the Arameans of Damascus **c** to **1Ch 18:5** 935
Now it **c** about after this, that **1Ch 19:1** 1961
And David's servants **c** into the **1Ch 19:2** 935
who **c** and camped before Medeba. **1Ch 19:7** 935
from their cities and **c** to battle. **1Ch 19:7** 935
The sons of Ammon **c** out and **1Ch 19:9** 3318
Then Joab **c** to Jerusalem. **1Ch 19:15** 935
and **c** upon them and drew up in **1Ch 19:17** 935
Ammon, and **c** and besieged Rabbah. **1Ch 20:1** 935
Now it **c** about after this, that **1Ch 20:4** 1961
all Israel, and **c** to Jerusalem. **1Ch 21:4** 935
So Gad **c** to David and said to him, **1Ch 21:11** 935
As David **c** to Ornan, Ornan **1Ch 21:21** 935
“But the word of the LORD **c** to me, **1Ch 22:8** 1961
the first lot **c** out for Jehoiarib, **1Ch 24:7** 3318
when *they* **c** in to the house of the **1Ch 24:19** 935
lot **c** out for Asaph to Joseph, **1Ch 25:9** 3318
and his lot **c** out to the north. **1Ch 26:14** 3318
divisions which **c** in and went out **1Ch 27:1** 935
of this, wrath **c** upon Israel, **1Ch 27:24** 1961
the circumstances which **c** on him, **1Ch 29:30** 5674a
Then all the elders of Israel **c**, **2Ch 5:4** 935
Israel, when they **c** out of Egypt. **2Ch 5:10** 3318
c forth from the holy place **2Ch 5:11** 3318
fire **c** down from heaven and **2Ch 7:1** 3381
a very great assembly *who* **c** from **2Ch 7:8** 935
Now it **c** about at the end of the **2Ch 8:1** 1961
she **c** to Jerusalem to test Solomon **2Ch 9:1** 935
and when she **c** to Solomon, she **2Ch 9:1** 935
until I **c** and my eyes had seen it. **2Ch 9:6** 935
Now the weight of gold which **c** to **2Ch 9:13** 935
c bringing gold and silver, **2Ch 9:21** 935
When Jeroboam and all Israel **c**, **2Ch 10:3** 935
So Jeroboam and all the people **c** **2Ch 10:12** 935
LORD **c** to Shemaiah the man of God, **2Ch 11:2** 1961
and **c** to Judah and Jerusalem, **2Ch 11:14** 1980
And it **c** about in King Rehoboam's **2Ch 12:2** 1961
of Egypt **c** up against Jerusalem **2Ch 12:2** 5927
And the people who **c** with him from **2Ch 12:3** 935
Judah and **c** as far as Jerusalem. **2Ch 12:4** 935
Then Shemaiah the prophet **c** to **2Ch 12:5** 935
word of the LORD **c** to Shemaiah, **2Ch 12:7** 1961
of Egypt **c** up against Jerusalem, **2Ch 12:9** 5927
the guards **c** and carried them and **2Ch 12:11** 935
Now Zerah the Ethiopian **c** out **2Ch 14:9** 3318
chariots, and he **c** to Mareshah. **2Ch 14:9** 935
the Spirit of God **c** on Azariah **2Ch 15:1** 1961
who went out or to him who **c** in, **2Ch 15:5** 935
Baasha king of Israel **c** up against **2Ch 16:1** 5927
At that time Hanani the seer **c** to **2Ch 16:7** 935
When he **c** to the king, the **2Ch 18:14** 935
“Then a spirit **c** forward and **2Ch 18:20** 3318
son of Chenaanah **c** near and struck **2Ch 18:23** 5066
Now it **c** about after this that the **2Ch 20:1** 1961
c to make war against Jehoshaphat. **2Ch 20:1** 935
c and reported to Jehoshaphat, **2Ch 20:2** 935
they even **c** from all the cities of **2Ch 20:4** 935
they **c** out of the land of Egypt **2Ch 20:10** 935
Spirit of the LORD **c** upon Jahaziel **2Ch 20:14** 1961
When Judah **c** to the lookout of the **2Ch 20:24** 935
his people **c** to take their spoil, **2Ch 20:25** 935
They **c** to Jerusalem with harps, **2Ch 20:28** 935
Then a letter **c** to him from Elijah **2Ch 21:12** 935
c against Judah and invaded it, **2Ch 21:17** 5927
it **c** about in the course of time, **2Ch 21:19** 1961
that his bowels **c** out because of **2Ch 21:19** 3318
for the band of men who **c** with the **2Ch 22:1** 935
For when he **c**, he went out with **2Ch 22:7** 935
It **c** about when Jehu was **2Ch 22:8** 1961
Israel, and they **c** to Jerusalem. **2Ch 23:2** 935
she **c** into the house of the LORD **2Ch 23:12** 935
and **c** through the upper gate to **2Ch 23:20** 935
Now it **c** about after this that **2Ch 24:4** 1961
It **c** about whenever the chest **2Ch 24:11** 1961
c and bowed down to the king, **2Ch 24:17** 935
so wrath **c** upon Judah and **2Ch 24:18** 1961
Then the Spirit of God **c** on **2Ch 24:20** 3847
of the Arameans **c** up against him; **2Ch 24:23** 5927
and they **c** to Judah and Jerusalem, **2Ch 24:23** 935
c with a small number of men; **2Ch 24:24** 935
Now it **c** about as soon as the **2Ch 25:3** 1961
But a man of God **c** to him saying, **2Ch 25:7** 935
which **c** to him from Ephraim, **2Ch 25:10** 935
Now after Amaziah **c** from slaughtering **2Ch 25:14** 1961
c to Samaria and said to them, **2Ch 28:9** 935
So Tilgath-pilneser king of Assyria **c** **2Ch 28:20** 935
the thing **c** about suddenly. **2Ch 29:36** 1961
themselves and **c** to Jerusalem. **2Ch 30:11** 935
the assembly that **c** from Israel, **2Ch 30:25** 935
both the sojourners who **c** from the **2Ch 30:25** 935
c to His holy dwelling place, **2Ch 30:27** 935
the rulers **c** and saw the heaps, **2Ch 31:8** 935
Sennacherib king of Assyria **c** **2Ch 32:1** 935
therefore wrath **c** on him and on **2Ch 32:25** 1961
They **c** to Hilkiah the high **2Ch 34:9** 935
Neco king of Egypt **c** up to make **2Ch 35:20** 5927
but **c** to make war on the plain of **2Ch 35:22** 935
Nebuchadnezzar king of Babylon **c** **2Ch 36:6** 5927
c up out of the captivity of the exiles **Ezr 2:1** 5927
These **c** with Zerubbabel, Jeshua, **Ezr 2:2** 935
are those who **c** up from Tel-melah, **Ezr 2:59** 5927
Now when the seventh month **c**, **Ezr 3:1** 5060
and all who **c** from the captivity **Ezr 3:8** 935
that the Jews who **c** up from you **Ezr 4:12** 5559b
their colleagues **c** to them and spoke **Ezr 5:3** 858
'Then that Sheshbazzar **c** *and* laid **Ezr 5:16** 858
He **c** to Jerusalem in the fifth **Ezr 7:8** 935
the fifth month he **c** to Jerusalem, **Ezr 7:9** 935
Thus we **c** to Jerusalem and **Ezr 8:32** 935
and some men from Judah **c**; **Ne 1:2** 935
And it **c** about in the month Nisan, **Ne 2:1** 1961
Then I **c** to the governors *of the* **Ne 2:9** 935
So I **c** to Jerusalem and was there **Ne 2:11** 935
Now it **c** about that when Sanballat **Ne 4:1** 1961
near them **c** and told us ten times, **Ne 4:12** 935
besides those who **c** to us from the **Ne 5:17** 935
and Tobiah's *letters* **c** to them. **Ne 6:17** 935
the genealogy of those who **c** up first **Ne 7:5** 5927
c up from the captivity of the exiles **Ne 7:6** 5927
who **c** with Zerubbabel, Jeshua, **Ne 7:7** 935
were they who **c** up from Tel-melah, **Ne 7:61** 5927
And when the seventh month **c**, **Ne 7:73** 5060
“Then You **c** down on Mount Sinai, **Ne 9:13** 3381
the Levites who **c** up with Zerubbabel **Ne 12:1** 5927
and I **c** to Jerusalem and learned **Ne 13:7** 935
It **c** about that just as it **Ne 13:19** 1961
So it **c** about when the command and **Es 2:8** 1961
lady **c** to go in to King Ahasuerus, **Es 2:12** 5060
daughter, **c** to go in to the king, **Es 2:15** 5060
command and decree of the king **c**, **Es 4:3** 5060
and her eunuchs **c** and told her, **Es 4:4** 935
Hathach **c** back and related **Es 4:9** 935
Now it **c** about on the third day **Es 5:1** 1961
So Esther **c** near and touched the **Es 5:2** 7126
So the king and Haman **c** to the **Es 5:5** 935
c in and the king said to him, **Es 6:6** 935
Now the king and Haman **c** to drink **Es 7:1** 935
and Mordecai **c** before the king, **Es 8:1** 935
when it **c** to the king's attention, **Es 9:25** 935
sons of God **c** to present themselves **Jb 1:6** 935
LORD, and Satan also **c** among them. **Jb 1:6** 935
a messenger **c** to Job and said, **Jb 1:14** 935
speaking, another also **c** and said, **Jb 1:16** 935
speaking, another also **c** and said, **Jb 1:17** 935
speaking, another also **c** and said, **Jb 1:18** 935
a great wind **c** from across the **Jb 1:19** 935
“Naked I **c** from my mother's womb, **Jb 1:21** 3318
sons of God **c** to present themselves **Jb 2:1** 935
and Satan also **c** among them to **Jb 2:1** 935
c each one from his own place, **Jb 2:11** 935
Dread **c** upon me, and trembling, **Jb 4:14** 7122
They **c** there and were confounded. **Jb 6:20** 935
the one ready to perish **c** upon me, **Jb 29:13** 935
“When I expected good, then evil **c**; **Jb 30:26** 935
waited for light, then darkness **c**. **Jb 30:26** 935
It **c** about after the LORD had **Jb 42:7** 1961
had known him before **c** to him, **Jb 42:11** 935
help before Him **c** into His ears. **Ps 18:6** 935
and **c** down With thick darkness **Ps 18:9** 3381
c upon me to devour my flesh, **Ps 27:2** 7126
me, my feet **c** close to stumbling, **Ps 73:2** 5186
I **c** into the sanctuary of God; **Ps 73:17** 935
the time that his word **c** to pass, **Ps 105:19** 935
Israel also **c** into Egypt; **Ps 105:23** 935
and there **c** a swarm of flies *And* **Ps 105:31** 935
He spoke, and locusts **c**, **Ps 105:34** 935
loved cursing, so it **c** to him; **Ps 109:17** 935
the terrors of Sheol **c** upon me; **Ps 116:3** 4672
All **c** from the dust and all return **Ec 3:20** 1961
womb, so will he return as he **c**. **Ec 5:15** 935
Also this I **c** to see as wisdom **Ec 9:13**
in it and a great king **c** to it, **Ec 9:14** 935
it **c** about in the days of Ahaz, **Is 7:1** 1961
c up out of the land of Egypt. **Is 11:16** 5927
that King Ahaz died this oracle **c**: **Is 14:28** 1961
that the commander **c** to Ashdod, **Is 20:1** 935
Sennacherib king of Assyria **c** up **Is 36:1** 5927
Asaph, the recorder, **c** out to him. **Is 36:3** 3318
c to Hezekiah with their clothes **Is 36:22** 935
of King Hezekiah **c** to Isaiah. **Is 37:5** 935
'With my many chariots I **c** up to **Is 37:24** 5927
you back by the way which you **c**. **Is 37:29** 935
'By the way that he **c**, **Is 37:34** 935
It **c** about as he was **Is 37:38** 1961
of Amoz **c** to him and said to him, **Is 38:1** 935
the word of the LORD **c** to Isaiah, **Is 38:4** 1961
Then Isaiah the prophet **c** to King **Is 39:3** 935
c forth from the loins of Judah, **Is 48:1** 3318
I acted, and they **c** to pass. **Is 48:3** 935
“Why was there no man when I **c**? **Is 50:2** 935
You **c** down, the mountains quaked at **Is 64:3** 3381
all these things **c** into being,” **Is 66:2** 1961
Before her pain **c**, she gave birth **Is 66:7** 935
the LORD **c** in the days of Josiah the **Jer 1:2** 1961
c also in the days of Jehoiakim the **Jer 1:3** 1961
word of the LORD **c** to me saying, **Jer 1:4** 1961
word of the LORD **c** to me saying, **Jer 1:11** 1961
LORD **c** to me a second time saying, **Jer 1:13** 1961
word of the LORD **c** to me saying, **Jer 2:1** 1961
Evil **c** upon them,” **Jer 2:3** 935
But you **c** and defiled My land, And **Jer 2:7** 935
that **c** to Jeremiah from the LORD, **Jer 7:1** 1961
Since the day that your fathers **c** out **Jer 7:25** 3318
but no good **c**; For a time of **Jer 8:15**
which **c** to Jeremiah from the LORD, **Jer 11:1** 1961
of the LORD **c** to me a second time, **Jer 13:3** 1961
Then the word of the LORD **c** to me, **Jer 13:8** 1961
That which **c** as the word of the **Jer 14:1** 1961
but nothing good **c**; And for a **Jer 14:19**
of the LORD also **c** to me saying, **Jer 16:1** 1961
The word which **c** to Jeremiah from **Jer 18:1** 1961
word of the LORD **c** to me saying, **Jer 18:5** 1961
Then Jeremiah **c** from Topheth, **Jer 19:14** 935
The word which **c** to Jeremiah from **Jer 21:1** 1961
Then the word of the LORD **c** to me, **Jer 24:4** 1961
The word that **c** to Jeremiah **Jer 25:1** 1961
Judah, this word **c** from the LORD, **Jer 26:1** 1961
they **c** up from the king's house to **Jer 26:10** 5927
word **c** to Jeremiah from the LORD, **Jer 27:1** 1961
word of the LORD **c** to Jeremiah after **Jer 28:12** 1961
Then **c** the word of the LORD to **Jer 29:30** 1961
which **c** to Jeremiah from the LORD, **Jer 30:1** 1961
The word that **c** to Jeremiah from **Jer 32:1** 1961
“The word of the LORD **c** to me, **Jer 32:6** 1961
“Then Hanamel my uncle's son **c** to **Jer 32:8** 935
c in and took possession of it, **Jer 32:23** 935
word of the LORD **c** to Jeremiah, **Jer 32:26** 1961
c to Jeremiah the second time, **Jer 33:1** 1961
word of the LORD **c** to Jeremiah, **Jer 33:19** 1961
word of the LORD **c** to Jeremiah, **Jer 33:23** 1961
which **c** to Jeremiah from the LORD, **Jer 34:1** 1961
which **c** to Jeremiah from the LORD **Jer 34:8** 1961
LORD **c** to Jeremiah from the LORD, **Jer 34:12** 1961
The word which **c** to Jeremiah from **Jer 35:1** 1961
king of Babylon **c** up against the land **Jer 35:11** 5927
word of the LORD **c** to Jeremiah, **Jer 35:12** 1961
word **c** to Jeremiah from the LORD, **Jer 36:1** 1961
people who **c** from the cities of Judah **Jer 36:9** 935
Then the word of the LORD **c** to **Jer 36:27** 1961
LORD **c** to Jeremiah the prophet, **Jer 37:6** 1961
Then all the officials **c** to **Jer 38:27** 935
king of Babylon and all his army **c** **Jer 39:1** 935
officials of the king of Babylon **c** in **Jer 39:3** 935
The word which **c** to Jeremiah from **Jer 40:1** 1961
So they **c** to Gedaliah at Mizpah, **Jer 40:8** 935
away and **c** to the land of Judah, **Jer 40:12** 935
the forces that were in the field **c** to **Jer 40:13** 935
c to Mizpah to Gedaliah the son of **Jer 41:1** 935
that eighty men **c** from Shechem, **Jer 41:5** 935
as soon as they **c** inside the city, **Jer 41:7** 935
Mizpah turned around and **c** back, **Jer 41:14** 7725
word of the LORD **c** to Jeremiah. **Jer 42:7** 1961
LORD **c** to Jeremiah in Tahpanhes, **Jer 43:8** 1961
The word that **c** to Jeremiah for **Jer 44:1** 1961
That which **c** as the word of the **Jer 46:1** 1961
That which **c** as the word of the **Jer 47:1** 1961
“If grape gatherers **c** to you, **Jer 49:9** 935
If thieves **c** by night, They **Jer 49:9** 935
That which **c** as the word of the **Jer 49:34** 1961
c upon them have devoured them; **Jer 50:7** 4672
through the anger of the LORD *this* **c** **Jer 52:3** 1961
Now it **c** about in the ninth year **Jer 52:4** 1961
Nebuchadnezzar king of Babylon **c**, **Jer 52:4** 935
king of Babylon, **c** to Jerusalem. **Jer 52:12** 935
Now it **c** about in the **Jer 52:31** 1961
it **c** about in the thirtieth year, **Ezk 1:1** 1961
the word of the LORD **c** expressly **Ezk 1:3** 1961
the hand of the LORD **c** upon him.) **Ezk 1:3** 1961
And there **c** a voice from above the **Ezk 1:25** 1961
Then I **c** to the exiles who lived **Ezk 3:15** 935
days the word of the LORD **c** to me, **Ezk 3:16** 1961
word of the LORD **c** to me saying, **Ezk 6:1** 1961
word of the LORD **c** to me saying, **Ezk 7:1** 1961
It **c** about in the sixth year, **Ezk 8:1** 1961
six men **c** from the direction of **Ezk 9:2** 935
It **c** about when He commanded **Ezk 10:6** 1961
Now it **c** about as I prophesied, **Ezk 11:13** 1961
Then the word of the LORD **c** to me, **Ezk 11:14** 1961
word of the LORD **c** to me, **Ezk 12:1** 1961
the word of the LORD **c** to me, **Ezk 12:8** 1961
word of the LORD **c** to me saying, **Ezk 12:17** 1961
word of the LORD **c** to me, **Ezk 12:21** 1961

word of the LORD **c** to me,	**Ezk 12:26**	1961
word of the LORD **c** to me saying,	**Ezk 13:1**	1961
c to me and sat down before me.	**Ezk 14:1**	935
word of the LORD **c** to me,	**Ezk 14:2**	1961
word of the LORD **c** to me saying,	**Ezk 14:12**	1961
word of the LORD **c** to me,	**Ezk 15:1**	1961
word of the LORD **c** to me,	**Ezk 16:1**	1961
"Then it **c** about after all your	**Ezk 16:23**	1961
word of the LORD **c** to me saying,	**Ezk 17:1**	1961
c to Lebanon and took away the top	**Ezk 17:3**	935
word of the LORD **c** to me,	**Ezk 17:11**	1961
king of Babylon **c** to Jerusalem,	**Ezk 17:12**	935
word of the LORD **c** to me,	**Ezk 18:1**	1961
Israel **c** to inquire of the LORD,	**Ezk 20:1**	935
word of the LORD **c** to me saying,	**Ezk 20:2**	1961
word of the LORD **c** to me,	**Ezk 20:45**	1961
word of the LORD **c** to me saying,	**Ezk 21:1**	1961
word of the LORD **c** to me,	**Ezk 21:8**	1961
word of the LORD **c** to me saying,	**Ezk 21:18**	1961
his right hand **c** the divination,	**Ezk 21:22**	1961
word of the LORD **c** to me,	**Ezk 22:1**	1961
word of the LORD **c** to me,	**Ezk 22:17**	1961
word of the LORD **c** to me,	**Ezk 22:23**	1961
of the LORD **c** to me again,	**Ezk 23:1**	1961
c to her to the bed of love and	**Ezk 23:17**	935
a messenger was sent; and lo, they **c**	**Ezk 23:40**	935
LORD **c** to me in the ninth year,	**Ezk 24:1**	1961
word of the LORD **c** to me saying,	**Ezk 24:15**	1961
word of the LORD **c** to me saying,	**Ezk 24:20**	1961
word of the LORD **c** to me saying,	**Ezk 25:1**	1961
word of the LORD **c** to me saying,	**Ezk 26:1**	1961
word of the LORD **c** to me saying,	**Ezk 27:1**	1961
of the LORD **c** again to me,	**Ezk 28:1**	1961
word of the LORD **c** to me saying,	**Ezk 28:11**	1961
word of the LORD **c** to me saying,	**Ezk 28:20**	1961
word of the LORD **c** to me saying,	**Ezk 29:1**	1961
word of the LORD **c** to me saying,	**Ezk 29:17**	1961
of the LORD **c** again to me saying,	**Ezk 30:1**	1961
word of the LORD **c** to me saying,	**Ezk 30:20**	1961
word of the LORD **c** to me saying,	**Ezk 31:1**	1961
word of the LORD **c** to me saying,	**Ezk 32:1**	1961
word of the LORD **c** to me saying,	**Ezk 32:17**	1961
word of the LORD **c** to me,	**Ezk 33:1**	1961
refugees from Jerusalem **c** to me,	**Ezk 33:21**	935
evening, before the refugees **c**.	**Ezk 33:22**	935
time *they* **c** to me in the morning;	**Ezk 33:22**	935
word of the LORD **c** to me saying,	**Ezk 33:23**	1961
word of the LORD **c** to me saying,	**Ezk 34:1**	1961
word of the LORD **c** to me saying,	**Ezk 35:1**	1961
word of the LORD **c** to me saying,	**Ezk 36:16**	1961
"When they **c** to the nations where	**Ezk 36:20**	935
and the bones **c** together, bone to	**Ezk 37:7**	7126
me, and the breath **c** into them,	**Ezk 37:10**	935
into them, and they **c** to life and	**Ezk 37:10**	2421a
of the LORD **c** again to me saying,	**Ezk 37:15**	1961
word of the LORD **c** to me saying,	**Ezk 38:1**	1961
saw when He **c** to destroy the city.	**Ezk 43:3**	935
And the glory of the LORD **c** into	**Ezk 43:4**	935
c to Jerusalem and besieged it.	**Da 1:1**	935
c in and stood before the king.	**Da 2:2**	935
time certain Chaldeans **c** forward	**Da 3:8**	7127
Then Nebuchadnezzar **c** near to the	**Da 3:26**	7127
c out of the midst of the fire.	**Da 3:26**	5312
Chaldeans and the diviners **c** in	**Da 4:7**	5954
"But finally Daniel **c** in before me,	**Da 4:8**	5954
mouth, a voice **c** from heaven,	**Da 4:31**	5308
Then all the king's wise men **c** in,	**Da 5:8**	5954
satraps **c** by agreement to the king	**Da 6:6**	7284
Then these men **c** by agreement and	**Da 6:11**	7284
Then these men **c** by agreement to	**Da 6:15**	7284
a little one, **c** up among them,	**Da 7:8**	5559b
And He **c** up to the Ancient of Days	**Da 7:13**	4291
and the other *horn* which **c** up	**Da 7:20**	5559b
until the Ancient of Days **c** and	**Da 7:22**	858
He **c** up to the ram that had	**Da 8:6**	935
and in its place there **c** up four	**Da 8:8**	5927
Out of one of them **c** forth a	**Da 8:9**	3318
he **c** near to where I was standing,	**Da 8:17**	935
and when he **c** I was frightened and	**Da 8:17**	935
c to me in *my* extreme weariness	**Da 9:21**	5060
the chief princes, **c** to help me,	**Da 10:13**	935
"Do you understand why I **c** to you?	**Da 10:20**	935
which **c** to Hosea the son of Beeri,	**Hos 1:1**	1961
she **c** up from the land of Egypt.	**Hos 2:15**	5927
But they **c** to Baal-peor and	**Hos 9:10**	935
Indeed, I **c** to hate them there!	**Hos 9:15**	
word of the LORD that **c** to Joel,	**Jl 1:1**	1961
And it **c** about, when it had	**Am 7:2**	1961
"If thieves **c** to you, If robbers	**Ob 1:5**	935
If grape gatherers **c** to you,	**Ob 1:5**	935
The word of the LORD **c** to Jonah	**Jon 1:1**	1961
And my prayer **c** to You, Into Your	**Jon 2:7**	935
LORD **c** to Jonah the second time,	**Jon 3:1**	1961
a worm when dawn **c** the next day and	**Jon 4:7**	5927
When the sun **c** up	**Jon 4:8**	2224
which **c** up overnight and perished	**Jon 4:10**	1961
The word of the LORD which **c** *to*	**Mi 1:1**	1961
you **c** out from the land of Egypt,	**Mi 7:15**	3318
which **c** to Zephaniah son of Cushi,	**Zph 1:1**	1961
They **c** from you, *O Zion;*	**Zph 3:18**	1961
the word of the LORD **c** by the	**Hg 1:1**	1961
c by Haggai the prophet,	**Hg 1:3**	1961
and they **c** and worked on the house	**Hg 1:14**	935
c by Haggai the prophet saying,	**Hg 2:1**	1961
made you when you **c** out of Egypt,	**Hg 2:5**	3318
c to Haggai the prophet,	**Hg 2:10**	1961
from that time *when* one **c** to a	**Hg 2:16**	935
and *when* one **c** to the wine vat to	**Hg 2:16**	935
Then the word of the LORD **c** a	**Hg 2:20**	1961
LORD **c** to Zechariah the prophet,	**Zch 1:1**	1961
LORD **c** to Zechariah the prophet,	**Zch 1:7**	1961
word of the LORD **c** to me,	**Zch 4:8**	1961
of the LORD also **c** to me,	**Zch 6:9**	1961
the word of the LORD **c** to	**Zch 7:1**	1961
the LORD of hosts **c** to me,	**Zch 7:4**	1961
of the LORD **c** to Zechariah saying,	**Zch 7:8**	1961
wrath **c** from the LORD of hosts.	**Zch 7:12**	1961
of the LORD of hosts **c**,	**Zch 8:1**	1961
and for him who went out or **c** in	**Zch 8:10**	935
the LORD of hosts **c** to me,	**Zch 8:18**	1961
before they **c** together she was	**Mt 1:18**	*4905*
until it **c** and stood over	**Mt 2:9**	*2064*
and **c** into the land of Israel.	**Mt 2:21**	*1525*
and **c** and lived in a city called	**Mt 2:23**	*2064*
in those days John the Baptist **c**,	**Mt 3:1**	*3854*
After being baptized, Jesus **c** up	**Mt 3:16**	*305*
And the tempter **c** and said to Him,	**Mt 4:3**	*4334*
c and *began* to minister to Him.	**Mt 4:11**	*4334*
He **c** and settled in Capernaum,	**Mt 4:13**	*2064*
sat down, His disciples **c** to Him.	**Mt 5:1**	*4334*
"Do not think that I **c** to abolish	**Mt 5:17**	*2064*
rain fell, and the floods **c**,	**Mt 7:25**	*2064*
rain fell, and the floods **c**,	**Mt 7:27**	*2064*
When Jesus **c** down from the mountain,	**Mt 8:1**	*2597*
And a leper **c** to Him	**Mt 8:2**	*4334*
Capernaum, a centurion **c** to Him,	**Mt 8:5**	*4334*
When Jesus **c** into Peter's home, He	**Mt 8:14**	*2064*
When evening **c**, they brought to Him	**Mt 8:16**	*1096*
a scribe **c** and said to Him,	**Mt 8:19**	*4334*
And they **c** to *Him* and woke Him,	**Mt 8:25**	*4334*
When He **c** to the other side into	**Mt 8:28**	*2064*
And they **c** out and went into the	**Mt 8:32**	*1831*
whole city **c** out to meet Jesus;	**Mt 8:34**	*1831*
over *the sea* and **c** to His own city.	**Mt 9:1**	*2064*
sinners **c** and were dining with Jesus	**Mt 9:10**	*2064*
the disciples of John **c** to Him,	**Mt 9:14**	*4334*
a *synagogue* official **c**	**Mt 9:18**	*4334*
c up behind Him and touched the	**Mt 9:20**	*4334*
Jesus **c** into the official's house,	**Mt 9:23**	*2064*
house, the blind men **c** up to Him,	**Mt 9:28**	*4334*
I **c** to bring peace on the earth;	**Mt 10:34**	*2064*
"For I **c** to SET A MAN AGAINST HIS	**Mt 10:35**	*2064*
c neither eating nor drinking,	**Mt 11:18**	*2064*
Son of Man **c** eating and drinking,	**Mt 11:19**	*2064*
because she **c** from the ends of the	**Mt 12:42**	*2064*
return to my house from which I **c**'	**Mt 12:44**	*1831*
and the birds **c** and ate them up.	**Mt 13:4**	*2064*
thorns **c** up and choked them out.	**Mt 13:7**	*305*
the disciples **c** and said to Him,	**Mt 13:10**	*4334*
his enemy **c** and sowed tares among	**Mt 13:25**	*2064*
the landowner **c** and said to him,	**Mt 13:27**	*4334*
And His disciples **c** to Him and	**Mt 13:36**	*4334*
He **c** to His hometown and *began*	**Mt 13:54**	*2064*
But when Herod's birthday **c**,	**Mt 14:6**	*1096*
His disciples **c** and took away	**Mt 14:12**	*4334*
evening, the disciples **c** to Him and	**Mt 14:15**	*4334*
watch of the night He **c** to them,	**Mt 14:25**	*2064*
on the water and **c** toward Jesus.	**Mt 14:29**	*2064*
they **c** to land at Gennesaret.	**Mt 14:34**	*2064*
scribes **c** to Jesus from Jerusalem and	**Mt 15:1**	*4334*
the disciples **c** and said to Him,	**Mt 15:12**	*4334*
woman from that region **c** out	**Mt 15:22**	*1831*
c and implored Him,	**Mt 15:23**	*4334*
But she **c** and *began* to bow down	**Mt 15:25**	*2064*
And large crowds **c** to Him,	**Mt 15:30**	*4334*
and **c** to the region of Magadan.	**Mt 15:39**	*2064*
The Pharisees and Sadducees **c** up,	**Mt 16:1**	*4334*
And the disciples **c** to the other	**Mt 16:5**	*2064*
Now when Jesus **c** into the district	**Mt 16:13**	*2064*
And Jesus **c** to *them* and touched	**Mt 17:7**	*4334*
say to you that Elijah already **c**,	**Mt 17:12**	*2064*
When they **c** to the crowd,	**Mt 17:14**	*2064*
the crowd, a man **c** up to Jesus,	**Mt 17:14**	*4334*
him, and the demon **c** out of him,	**Mt 17:18**	*1831*
c to Jesus privately and said,	**Mt 17:19**	*4334*
When they **c** to Capernaum, those who	**Mt 17:24**	*4334*
the two-drachma *tax* **c** to Peter and	**Mt 17:24**	*4334*
And when he **c** into the house,	**Mt 17:25**	*2064*
time the disciples **c** to Jesus and	**Mt 18:1**	*4334*
Then Peter **c** and said to Him,	**Mt 18:21**	*4334*
they were deeply grieved and **c** and	**Mt 18:31**	*2064*
and **c** into the region of Judea	**Mt 19:1**	*2064*
Some Pharisees **c** to Jesus,	**Mt 19:3**	*4334*
And someone **c** to Him and said,	**Mt 19:16**	*4334*
"When evening **c**, the owner of	**Mt 20:8**	*1096*
hired about the eleventh hour **c**,	**Mt 20:9**	*2064*
"When those *hired* first **c**,	**Mt 20:10**	*2064*
of Zebedee **c** to Jesus with her sons,	**Mt 20:20**	*4334*
the lame **c** to Him in the temple,	**Mt 21:14**	*4334*
fig tree by the road, He **c** to it	**Mt 21:19**	*2064*
c to Him while He was teaching,	**Mt 21:23**	*4334*
and he **c** to the first and said,	**Mt 21:28**	*4334*
"The man **c** to the second and said	**Mt 21:30**	*4334*
"For John **c** to you in the way of	**Mt 21:32**	*2064*
THIS **C** ABOUT FROM THE LORD, AND	**Mt 21:42**	*1096*
"But when the king **c** in to look	**Mt 22:11**	*1525*
c to Jesus and questioned Him,	**Mt 22:23**	*4334*
Jesus **c** out from the temple	**Mt 24:1**	*1831*
was going away when His disciples **c**	**Mt 24:1**	*4334*
the disciples **c** to Him privately,	**Mt 24:3**	*4334*
flood **c** and took them all away;	**Mt 24:39**	*2064*
the purchase, the bridegroom **c**,	**Mt 25:10**	*2064*
Later the other virgins also **c**,	**Mt 25:11**	*2064*
master of those slaves **c** and settled	**Mt 25:19**	*2064*
who had received the five talents **c** up	**Mt 25:20**	*4334*
who *had received* the two talents **c**	**Mt 25:22**	*4334*
who had received the one talent **c** up	**Mt 25:24**	*4334*
I was in prison, and you **c** to Me.'	**Mt 25:36**	*2064*
a woman **c** to Him with an alabaster	**Mt 26:7**	*4334*
Bread the disciples **c** to Jesus and	**Mt 26:17**	*4334*
Now when evening **c**, Jesus was	**Mt 26:20**	*1096*
Then Jesus **c** with them to a place	**Mt 26:36**	*2064*
And He **c** to the disciples and	**Mt 26:40**	*2064*
He **c** and found them sleeping,	**Mt 26:43**	*2064*
Then He **c** to the disciples and	**Mt 26:45**	*2064*
Judas, one of the twelve, **c** up	**Mt 26:47**	*2064*
who **c** from the chief priests	**Mt 26:47**	
Then they **c** and laid hands on	**Mt 26:50**	*4334*
many false witnesses **c** forward.	**Mt 26:60**	*4334*
But later on two **c** forward,	**Mt 26:60**	*4334*
servant-girl **c** to him and said,	**Mt 26:69**	*4334*
bystanders **c** up and said to Peter,	**Mt 26:73**	*4334*
Now when morning **c**, all the chief	**Mt 27:1**	*1096*
And when they **c** to a place called	**Mt 27:33**	*2064*
there **c** a rich man from Arimathea,	**Mt 27:57**	*2064*
other Mary **c** to look at the grave.	**Mt 28:1**	*2064*
c and rolled away the stone and sat	**Mt 28:2**	*4334*
And they **c** up and took hold of His	**Mt 28:9**	*4334*
some of the guard **c** into the city	**Mt 28:11**	*2064*
'His disciples **c** by night and	**Mt 28:13**	*2064*
And Jesus **c** up and spoke to them,	**Mt 28:18**	*4334*
Jesus **c** from Nazareth in Galilee and	**Mk 1:9**	*2064*
and a voice **c** out of the heavens:	**Mk 1:11**	*1096*
custody, Jesus **c** into Galilee,	**Mk 1:14**	*2064*
a loud voice and **c** out of him.	**Mk 1:26**	*1831*
And immediately after they **c** out of	**Mk 1:29**	*2064*
they **c** into the house of Simon and	**Mk 1:29**	*2064*
And He **c** to her and raised her up,	**Mk 1:31**	*4334*
When evening **c**, after the sun had	**Mk 1:32**	*1096*
for that is what I **c** for."	**Mk 1:38**	*1831*
And a leper **c** to Jesus, beseeching	**Mk 1:40**	*2064*
And they **c**, bringing to Him a	**Mk 2:3**	*2064*
and they **c** and said to Him,	**Mk 2:18**	*2064*
that He was doing and **c** to Him.	**Mk 3:8**	*2064*
Himself wanted, and they **c** to Him.	**Mk 3:13**	*565*
And He **c** home, and the crowd	**Mk 3:20**	*2064*
The scribes who **c** down from	**Mk 3:22**	*2597*
and the birds **c** and ate it up.	**Mk 4:4**	*2064*
and the thorns **c** up and choked it,	**Mk 4:7**	*305*
On that day, when evening **c**, He	**Mk 4:35**	*1096*
c to the other side of the sea,	**Mk 5:1**	*2064*
And *the people* **c** to see what it	**Mk 5:14**	*2064*
They **c** to Jesus and observed	**Mk 5:15**	*2064*
officials named Jairus **c** up,	**Mk 5:22**	*2064*
c up in the crowd behind *Him*	**Mk 5:27**	*2064*
her, **c** and fell down before Him and	**Mk 5:33**	*2064*
they **c** from the *house of* the	**Mk 5:35**	*2064*
They **c** to the house of the	**Mk 5:38**	*2064*
and **c** into His hometown;	**Mk 6:1**	*2064*
When the Sabbath **c**, He began to	**Mk 6:2**	*1096*
A strategic day **c** when Herod	**Mk 6:21**	*1096*
the daughter of Herodias herself **c** in	**Mk 6:22**	*1525*
Immediately she **c** in a	**Mk 6:25**	*1525*
they **c** and took away his body and	**Mk 6:29**	*2064*
c to Him and said,	**Mk 6:35**	*4334*
watch of the night He **c** to them,	**Mk 6:48**	*2064*
over they **c** to land at Gennesaret,	**Mk 6:53**	*2064*
c and fell at His feet.	**Mk 7:25**	*2064*
and **c** through Sidon to the Sea of	**Mk 7:31**	*2064*
c to the district of Dalmanutha.	**Mk 8:10**	*2064*
The Pharisees **c** out and began	**Mk 8:11**	*1831*
And they **c** to Bethsaida.	**Mk 8:22**	*2064*
and a voice **c** out of the cloud,	**Mk 9:7**	*1096*
When they **c** *back* to the disciples,	**Mk 9:14**	*2064*
terrible convulsions, it **c** out;	**Mk 9:26**	*1831*
When He **c** into *the* house, His	**Mk 9:28**	*1525*
They **c** to Capernaum;	**Mk 9:33**	*2064*
Some Pharisees **c** up to Jesus,	**Mk 10:2**	*4334*
two sons of Zebedee, **c** up to Jesus,	**Mk 10:35**	*4365*
Then they **c** to Jericho.	**Mk 10:46**	*2064*
he jumped up and **c** to Jesus.	**Mk 10:50**	*2064*
Jesus entered Jerusalem *and* **c**	**Mk 11:11**	
and when He **c** to it, He found	**Mk 11:13**	*2064*
Then they **c** to Jerusalem.	**Mk 11:15**	*2064*
When evening **c**,	**Mk 11:19**	*1096*
They **c** again to Jerusalem.	**Mk 11:27**	*2064*
the scribes and the elders **c** to Him,	**Mk 11:27**	*2064*
THIS **C** ABOUT FROM THE LORD, AND	**Mk 12:11**	*1096*
They **c** and said to Him,	**Mk 12:14**	*2064*
c to Jesus, and *began* questioning	**Mk 12:18**	*2064*
scribes **c** and heard them arguing,	**Mk 12:28**	*4334*
A poor widow **c** and put in two	**Mk 12:42**	*2064*
there **c** a woman with an alabaster	**Mk 14:3**	*2064*
went out and **c** to the city,	**Mk 14:16**	*2064*
was evening He **c** with the twelve.	**Mk 14:17**	*2064*
c to a place named Gethsemane;	**Mk 14:32**	*2064*
And He **c** and found them sleeping,	**Mk 14:37**	*2064*
He **c** and found them sleeping,	**Mk 14:40**	*2064*
And He **c** the third time, and said	**Mk 14:41**	*2064*
Judas, one of the twelve, **c** up	**Mk 14:43**	*3854*
The high priest stood up *and* **c**	**Mk 14:60**	
servant-girls of the high priest **c**,	**Mk 14:66**	*2064*
When the sixth hour **c**, darkness fell	**Mk 15:33**	*1096*
there were many other women who **c**	**Mk 15:41**	*4872*
Joseph of Arimathea **c**,	**Mk 15:43**	*2064*
they **c** to the tomb when the sun	**Mk 16:2**	*2064*
But when he **c** out, he was unable	**Lk 1:22**	*1831*
they **c** to circumcise the child,	**Lk 1:59**	*2064*
Fear **c** on all those living	**Lk 1:65**	*1096*
So they **c** in a hurry and found	**Lk 2:16**	*2064*
c in the Spirit into the temple;	**Lk 2:27**	*2064*
At that very moment she **c** up	**Lk 2:38**	*2186*
down with them and **c** to Nazareth	**Lk 2:51**	*2064*
the word of God **c** to John,	**Lk 3:2**	*1096*
And he **c** into all the district	**Lk 3:3**	*2064*
also **c** to be baptized,	**Lk 3:12**	*2064*
dove, and a voice **c** out of heaven,	**Lk 3:22**	*1096*

And He **c** to Nazareth, where He had	**Lk 4:16**	*2064*
great famine **c** over all the land;	**Lk 4:25**	*1096*
And He **c** down to Capernaum, a city	**Lk 4:31**	*2718*
he **c** out of him without doing him	**Lk 4:35**	*1831*
And amazement **c** upon them all, and	**Lk 4:36**	*1096*
When day **c**, Jesus left and	**Lk 4:42**	*1096*
searching for Him, and **c** to Him and	**Lk 4:42**	*2064*
And they **c** and filled both of the	**Lk 5:7**	*2064*
And he got up and **c** forward.	**Lk 6:8**	*2476*
And when day **c**, He called His	**Lk 6:13**	*1096*
Jesus **c** down with them and stood on a	**Lk 6:17**	*2597*
When they **c** to Jesus, they earnestly	**Lk 7:4**	*3854*
He **c** up and touched the coffin;	**Lk 7:14**	*4334*
and the bearers **c** to a halt.	**Lk 7:14**	*2476*
When the men **c** to Him, they said,	**Lk 7:20**	*3854*
but she, since the time I **c** in,	**Lk 7:45**	*1525*
His mother and brothers **c** to Him,	**Lk 8:19**	*3854*
They **c** to Jesus and woke Him up,	**Lk 8:24**	*4334*
And when He **c** out onto the land, He	**Lk 8:27**	*1831*
And the demons **c** out of the man	**Lk 8:33**	*1831*
and they **c** to Jesus, and found the	**Lk 8:35**	*2064*
there **c** a man named Jairus,	**Lk 8:41**	*2064*
c up behind Him and touched the	**Lk 8:44**	*4334*
she **c** trembling and fell down	**Lk 8:47**	*2064*
someone **c** from *the house of* the	**Lk 8:49**	*2064*
When He **c** to the house, He did not	**Lk 8:51**	*2064*
and the twelve **c** and said to Him,	**Lk 9:12**	*4334*
Then a voice **c** out of the cloud,	**Lk 9:35**	*1096*
On the next day, when they **c** down	**Lk 9:37**	*1096*
he **c** to the place and saw him,	**Lk 10:32**	*2064*
who was on a journey, **c** upon him;	**Lk 10:33**	*2064*
and **c** to him and bandaged up his	**Lk 10:34**	*4334*
and she **c** up *to Him* and said,	**Lk 10:40**	*2186*
to my house from which I **c**.'	**Lk 11:24**	*1831*
because she **c** from the ends of the	**Lk 11:31**	*2064*
that I **c** to grant peace on earth?	**Lk 12:51**	*3854*
and he **c** looking for fruit on it and	**Lk 13:6**	*2064*
"And the slave **c** *back* and	**Lk 14:21**	*3854*
"But when he **c** to his senses, he	**Lk 15:17**	*2064*
"So he got up and **c** to his father.	**Lk 15:20**	*2064*
he **c** and approached the house,	**Lk 15:25**	*2064*
c out and *began* pleading with him.	**Lk 15:28**	*1831*
but when this son of yours **c**,	**Lk 15:30**	*2064*
flood **c** and destroyed them all.	**Lk 17:27**	*2064*
and when he **c** near, He questioned	**Lk 18:40**	*1448*
When Jesus **c** to the place, He	**Lk 19:5**	*2064*
And he hurried and **c** down and	**Lk 19:6**	*2597*
"The second **c**, saying,	**Lk 19:18**	*2064*
"Another **c**, saying,	**Lk 19:20**	*2064*
that they did not know where *it* **c**	**Lk 20:7**	
c to Him some of the Sadducees	**Lk 20:27**	*4334*
Then **c** the *first* day of Unleavened	**Lk 22:7**	*2064*
And He **c** out and proceeded as was	**Lk 22:39**	*1831*
He **c** to the disciples and found	**Lk 22:45**	*2064*
a crowd **c**, and the one called	**Lk 22:47**	
c to the place called The Skull,	**Lk 23:33**	*2064*
who **c** together for this spectacle,	**Lk 23:48**	*4836*
dawn, they **c** to the tomb bringing	**Lk 24:1**	*2064*
and did not find His body, they **c**,	**Lk 24:23**	*2064*
All things **c** into being through Him,	**Jn 1:3**	*1096*
and apart from Him nothing **c** into	**Jn 1:3**	*1096*
There **c** a man sent from God,	**Jn 1:6**	*1096*
He **c** as a witness,	**Jn 1:7**	*2064*
He was not the Light, but *he* **c**	**Jn 1:8**	
He **c** to His own, and those who	**Jn 1:11**	*2064*
Israel, I **c** baptizing in water."	**Jn 1:31**	*2064*
So they **c** and saw where He	**Jn 1:39**	*2064*
and did not know where it **c** from	**Jn 2:9**	*1510*
this man **c** to Jesus by night and	**Jn 3:2**	*2064*
c into the land of Judea,	**Jn 3:22**	*2064*
they **c** to John and said to him,	**Jn 3:26**	*2064*
So He **c** to a city of Samaria called	**Jn 4:5**	*2064*
There **c** a woman of Samaria to draw	**Jn 4:7**	*2064*
At this point His disciples **c**,	**Jn 4:27**	*2064*
So when the Samaritans **c** to Jesus,	**Jn 4:40**	*2064*
So when He **c** to Galilee, the	**Jn 4:45**	*2064*
He **c** again to Cana of	**Jn 4:46**	*2064*
Now when evening **c**,	**Jn 6:16**	*1096*
There **c** other small boats from	**Jn 6:23**	*2064*
small boats, and **c** to Capernaum	**Jn 6:24**	*2064*
bread that **c** down out of heaven."	**Jn 6:41**	*2597*
bread that **c** down out of heaven;	**Jn 6:51**	*2597*
bread which **c** down out of heaven;	**Jn 6:58**	*2597*
The officers then **c** to the	**Jn 7:45**	*2064*
(he who **c** to Him before, being one	**Jn 7:50**	*2064*
He **c** again into the temple,	**Jn 8:2**	*3854*
for I know where I **c** from and	**Jn 8:14**	*2064*
things, many **c** to believe in Him.	**Jn 8:30**	
and washed, and **c** *back* seeing.	**Jn 9:7**	*2064*
"For judgment I **c** into this	**Jn 9:39**	*2064*
"All who **c** before Me are thieves	**Jn 10:8**	*2064*
I **c** that they may have life, and	**Jn 10:10**	*2064*
gods, to whom the word of God **c**	**Jn 10:35**	*1096*
Many **c** to Him and were saying,	**Jn 10:41**	*2064*
So when Jesus **c**, He found that he	**Jn 11:17**	*2064*
when Mary **c** where Jesus was,	**Jn 11:32**	*2064*
and the Jews who **c** with her	**Jn 11:33**	*4905*
moved within, **c** to the tomb.	**Jn 11:38**	*2064*
man who had died **c** forth, bound	**Jn 11:44**	*1831*
Therefore many of the Jews who **c** to	**Jn 11:45**	*2064*
c to Bethany where Lazarus was,	**Jn 12:1**	*2064*
and they **c**, not for Jesus' sake	**Jn 12:9**	*2064*
these then **c** to Philip, who	**Jn 12:21**	*4334*
Philip **c** and told Andrew;	**Jn 12:22**	*2064*
Andrew and Philip **c** and	**Jn 12:22**	*2064*
for this purpose I **c** to this hour.	**Jn 12:27**	*2064*
Then a voice **c** out of heaven:	**Jn 12:28**	*2064*
So He **c** to Simon Peter.	**Jn 13:6**	*2064*
that I **c** forth from the Father.	**Jn 16:27**	*1831*
"I **c** forth from the Father and	**Jn 16:28**	*1831*
we believe that You **c** from God."	**Jn 16:30**	*1831*
that I **c** forth from You,	**Jn 17:8**	*1831*
c there with lanterns and torches	**Jn 18:3**	*2064*
Pilate **c** out again and said	**Jn 19:4**	*1831*
Jesus then **c** out, wearing the	**Jn 19:5**	*1831*
So the soldiers **c**,	**Jn 19:32**	*2064*
blood and water **c** out.	**Jn 19:34**	*1831*
For these things **c** to pass to	**Jn 19:36**	*1096*
So he **c** and took away His	**Jn 19:38**	*2064*
first come to Him by night, also **c**,	**Jn 19:39**	*2064*
Magdalene **c** early to the tomb,	**Jn 20:1**	*2064*
So she ran and **c** to Simon Peter	**Jn 20:2**	*2064*
Peter and **c** to the tomb first;	**Jn 20:4**	*2064*
Simon Peter also **c**,	**Jn 20:6**	*2064*
Mary Magdalene **c**, announcing to	**Jn 20:18**	*2064*
Jesus **c** and stood in their midst and	**Jn 20:19**	*2064*
was not with them when Jesus **c**.	**Jn 20:24**	*2064*
Jesus **c**, the doors having been	**Jn 20:26**	*2064*
disciples **c** in the little boat,	**Jn 21:8**	*2064*
Jesus **c** and took the bread and	**Jn 21:13**	*2064*
And suddenly there **c** from heaven a	**Ac 2:2**	*1096*
the crowd **c** together,	**Ac 2:6**	*4905*
and the Sadducees **c** up to them,	**Ac 4:1**	*2186*
men **c** to be about five thousand.	**Ac 4:4**	*1096*
fear **c** over all who heard of it.	**Ac 5:5**	*1096*
three hours, and his wife **c** in,	**Ac 5:7**	*1525*
young men **c** in and found her dead,	**Ac 5:10**	*1525*
fear **c** over the whole church,	**Ac 5:11**	*1096*
pallets, so that when Peter **c** by at	**Ac 5:15**	*2064*
the high priest and his associates **c**,	**Ac 5:21**	*1525*
But the officers who **c** did not	**Ac 5:22**	*3854*
someone **c** and reported to them,	**Ac 5:25**	*3854*
were dispersed and **c** to nothing.	**Ac 5:36**	*1096*
c up to him and dragged him away	**Ac 6:12**	*2186*
c over all Egypt and Canaan,	**Ac 7:11**	*2064*
there **c** the voice of the Lord:	**Ac 7:31**	*1096*
who **c** down and prayed for them that	**Ac 8:15**	*2597*
the road they **c** to some water;	**Ac 8:36**	*2064*
When they **c** up out of the water,	**Ac 8:39**	*305*
cities until he **c** to Caesarea.	**Ac 8:40**	*2064*
When he **c** to Jerusalem, he was	**Ac 9:26**	*3854*
he **c** down also to the saints who	**Ac 9:32**	*2718*
A voice **c** to him,	**Ac 10:13**	*1096*
Again a voice **c** to him a second	**Ac 10:15**	
"That is why I **c** without even	**Ac 10:29**	*2064*
All the circumcised believers who **c**	**Ac 10:45**	*4905*
And when Peter **c** up to Jerusalem,	**Ac 11:2**	*305*
and it **c** right down to me,	**Ac 11:5**	*2064*
who **c** to Antioch and *began*	**Ac 11:20**	*2064*
Now at this time some prophets **c**	**Ac 11:27**	*2718*
they **c** to the iron gate that leads	**Ac 12:10**	*2064*
When Peter **c** to himself, he	**Ac 12:11**	*1096*
named Rhoda **c** to answer.	**Ac 12:13**	*4334*
Now when day **c**, there was no small	**Ac 12:18**	*1096*
and with one accord they **c** to him,	**Ac 12:20**	*3918b*
and **c** to Perga in Pamphylia;	**Ac 13:13**	*2064*
appeared to those who **c** up with Him	**Ac 13:31**	*4872*
Jews **c** from Antioch and Iconium,	**Ac 14:19**	*1904*
Pisidia and **c** into Pamphylia.	**Ac 14:24**	*2064*
Some men **c** down from Judea and	**Ac 15:1**	*2718*
The apostles and the elders **c**	**Ac 15:6**	*4863*
Paul **c** also to Derbe and to Lystra.	**Ac 16:1**	*2658*
and after they **c** to Mysia, they were	**Ac 16:7**	*2064*
by Mysia, they **c** down to Troas.	**Ac 16:8**	*2597*
And it **c** out at that very moment.	**Ac 16:18**	*1831*
there **c** a great earthquake,	**Ac 16:26**	*1096*
Now when day **c**, the chief	**Ac 16:35**	*1096*
and they **c** and appealed to them,	**Ac 16:39**	*2064*
Apollonia, they **c** to Thessalonica,	**Ac 17:1**	*2064*
Berea also, they **c** there as	**Ac 17:13**	*2064*
Jews to leave Rome. He **c** to them,	**Ac 18:2**	*4334*
and Timothy **c** down from Macedonia,	**Ac 18:5**	*2718*
They **c** to Ephesus, and he left	**Ac 18:19**	*2658*
an eloquent man, **c** to Ephesus;	**Ac 18:24**	*2658*
the upper country and **c** to Ephesus,	**Ac 19:1**	*2064*
them, the Holy Spirit **c** on them,	**Ac 19:6**	*2064*
much exhortation, he **c** to Greece.	**Ac 20:2**	*2064*
and **c** to them at Troas within five	**Ac 20:6**	*2064*
him on board and **c** to Mitylene.	**Ac 20:14**	*2064*
the day following we **c** to Miletus.	**Ac 20:15**	*2064*
tears and with trials which **c** upon me	**Ac 20:19**	*4819*
When we **c** in sight of Cyprus,	**Ac 21:3**	*398*
day we left and **c** to Caesarea	**Ac 21:8**	*2064*
named Agabus **c** down from Judea.	**Ac 21:10**	*2718*
from Caesarea also **c** with us,	**Ac 21:16**	*4905*
a report **c** up to the commander of	**Ac 21:31**	*305*
commander **c** up and took hold	**Ac 21:33**	*1448*
were with me and **c** into Damascus.	**Ac 22:11**	*2064*
c to me, and standing near said to	**Ac 22:13**	*2064*
The commander **c** and said to him,	**Ac 22:27**	*4334*
They **c** to the chief priests	**Ac 23:14**	*4334*
and he **c** and entered the barracks	**Ac 23:16**	*3854*
I **c** up to them with the troops and	**Ac 23:27**	*2186*
Ananias **c** down with some elders,	**Ac 24:1**	*2597*
"But Lysias the commander **c** along,	**Ac 24:7**	*3928*
"Now after several years I **c** to	**Ac 24:17**	*3854*
So, on the next day when Agrippa **c**	**Ac 25:23**	*2064*
we **c** to a place called Fair	**Ac 27:8**	*2064*
When a moderate south wind **c** up,	**Ac 27:13**	*5285*
But when the fourteenth night **c**, as	**Ac 27:27**	*1096*
When day **c**, they could not	**Ac 27:39**	*1096*
a viper **c** out because of the heat and	**Ac 28:3**	*1831*
on the second day we **c** to Puteoli.	**Ac 28:13**	*2064*
and thus we **c** to Rome.	**Ac 28:14**	*2064*
c from there as far as the Market	**Ac 28:15**	*2064*
and when they **c** together, he *began*	**Ac 28:17**	*4905*
they **c** to him at his lodging in	**Ac 28:23**	*2064*
was welcoming all who **c** to him,	**Ac 28:30**	*1531*
The gift is not like *that which* **c**	**Ro 5:16**	
The Law **c** in so that the	**Ro 5:20**	*3922*
but when the commandment **c**,	**Ro 7:9**	*2064*
And when I **c** to you, brethren, I	**1Co 2:1**	*2064*
For since by a man **c** death, by a	**1Co 15:21**	
by a man also **c** the resurrection	**1Co 15:21**	
affliction which **c** *to us* in Asia,	**2Co 1:8**	*1096*
thing I wrote you, so that when I **c**,	**2Co 2:3**	*2064*
Now when I **c** to Troas for the	**2Co 2:12**	*2064*
engraved on stones, **c** with glory,	**2Co 3:7**	*1096*
For even when we **c** into Macedonia	**2Co 7:5**	*2064*
the brethren **c** from Macedonia they	**2Co 11:9**	*2064*
But when Cephas **c** to Antioch, I	**Ga 2:11**	*2064*
but when they **c**, he *began* to	**Ga 2:12**	*2064*
which **c** four hundred and thirty	**Ga 3:17**	*1096*
But before faith **c**,	**Ga 3:23**	*2064*
when the fullness of the time **c**,	**Ga 4:4**	*2064*
HE **C** AND PREACHED PEACE TO YOU	**Eph 2:17**	*2064*
because he **c** close to death for	**Php 2:30**	*1448*
we never **c** with flattering speech,	**1Th 2:5**	*1096*
and so it **c** to pass, as you know.	**1Th 3:4**	*1096*
that Christ Jesus **c** into the world	**1Tm 1:15**	*2064*
who **c** out of Egypt *led* by Moses?	**Heb 3:16**	*1831*
the oath, which **c** after the Law,	**Heb 7:28**	
the One who **c** by water and blood,	**1Jn 5:6**	*2064*
glad when brethren **c** and testified	**3Jn 1:3**	*2064*
the Lord **c** with many thousands of	**Jude 1:14**	*2064*
mouth **c** a sharp two-edged sword;	**Rv 1:16**	*1607*
And He **c** and took the book out of	**Rv 5:7**	*2064*
angel **c** and stood at the altar,	**Rv 8:3**	*2064*
and there **c** hail and fire,	**Rv 8:7**	*1096*
c locusts upon the earth	**Rv 9:3**	*1831*
breath of life from God **c** into them,	**Rv 11:11**	*1525*
were enraged, and Your wrath **c**,	**Rv 11:18**	*2064*
and the time **c** for the dead to be	**Rv 11:18**	
another angel **c** out of the temple,	**Rv 14:15**	*1831*
And another angel **c** out of the	**Rv 14:17**	*1831*
over fire, **c** out from the altar;	**Rv 14:18**	*1831*
blood **c** out from the wine press,	**Rv 14:20**	*1831*
seven plagues **c** out of the temple,	**Rv 15:6**	*1831*
and a loud voice **c** out of the	**Rv 16:17**	*1831*
since man **c** to be upon the earth,	**Rv 16:18**	*1096*
each, **c** down from heaven upon men;	**Rv 16:21**	*2597*
angels who had the seven bowls **c**	**Rv 17:1**	*2064*
And a voice **c** from the throne,	**Rv 19:5**	*1831*
sword which **c** from the mouth of Him	**Rv 19:21**	*1831*
and they **c** to life and reigned	**Rv 20:4**	
And they **c** up on the broad plain	**Rv 20:9**	*305*
and fire **c** down from heaven and	**Rv 20:9**	*2597*
last plagues **c** and spoke with me,	**Rv 21:9**	*2064*

CAMEL

Isaac she dismounted from the **c**.	**Gn 24:64**	1581
the **c**, for though it chews cud, it	**Lv 11:4**	1581
the **c** and the rabbit and the	**Dt 14:7**	1581
ox and sheep, **c** and donkey.'"	**1Sa 15:3**	1581
swift young **c** entangling her ways,	**Jer 2:23**	1072
on the horse, the mule, the **c**,	**Zch 14:15**	1581
it is easier for a **c** to go through	**Mt 19:24**	*2574*
strain out a gnat and swallow a **c**!	**Mt 23:24**	*2574*
"It is easier for a **c** to go	**Mk 10:25**	*2574*
"For it is easier for a **c** to go	**Lk 18:25**	*2574*

CAMEL'S

and put them in the **c** saddle,	**Gn 31:34**	1581
himself had a garment of **c** hair and	**Mt 3:4**	*2574*
John was clothed with **c** hair	**Mk 1:6**	*2574*

CAMELS

servants and female donkeys and **c**.	**Gn 12:16**	1581
c from the camels of his master,	**Gn 24:10**	1581
camels from the **c** of his master,	**Gn 24:10**	1581
He made the **c** kneel down	**Gn 24:11**	1581
'Drink, and I will water your **c** also'	**Gn 24:14**	1581
"I will draw also for your **c**	**Gn 24:19**	1581
draw, and she drew for all his **c**.	**Gn 24:20**	1581
When the **c** had finished drinking,	**Gn 24:22**	1581
standing by the **c** at the spring.	**Gn 24:30**	1581
house, and a place for the **c**?"	**Gn 24:31**	1581
Then Laban unloaded the **c**,	**Gn 24:32**	1581
he gave straw and feed to the **c**,	**Gn 24:32**	1581
and maids, and **c** and donkeys.	**Gn 24:35**	1581
and I will draw for your **c** also";	**Gn 24:44**	1581
and I will water your **c** also';	**Gn 24:46**	1581
drank, and she watered the **c** also.	**Gn 24:46**	1581
the **c** and followed the man.	**Gn 24:61**	1581
looked, and behold, **c** were coming.	**Gn 24:63**	1581
male servants and **c** and donkeys.	**Gn 30:43**	1581
his children and his wives upon **c**;	**Gn 31:17**	1581
flocks and the herds and the **c**,	**Gn 32:7**	1581
thirty milking **c** and their colts,	**Gn 32:15**	1581
with their **c** bearing aromatic gum	**Gn 37:25**	1581
horses, on the donkeys, on the **c**,	**Ex 9:3**	1581
they and their **c** were innumerable;	**Jg 6:5**	1581
and their **c** were without number,	**Jg 7:12**	1581
the cattle, the donkeys, the **c**,	**1Sa 27:9**	1581
young men who rode on **c** and fled.	**1Sa 30:17**	1581
with **c** carrying spices and very	**1Ki 10:2**	1581
their 50,000 **c**, 250,000 sheep,	**1Ch 5:21**	1581
brought food on donkeys, **c**,	**1Ch 12:40**	1581
Ishmaelite had charge of the **c**;	**1Ch 27:30**	1581
retinue, with **c** carrying spices and	**2Ch 9:1**	1581
away large numbers of sheep and **c**.	**2Ch 14:15**	1581
their **c**, 435; *their* donkeys, 6,720.	**Ezr 2:67**	1581
their **c**, 435; *their* donkeys, 6,720.	**Ne 7:69**	1581
also were 7,000 sheep, 3,000 **c**,	**Jb 1:3**	1581
made a raid on the **c** and took them	**Jb 1:17**	1581
he had 14,000 sheep and 6,000 **c**	**Jb 42:12**	1581
A train of donkeys, a train of **c**,	**Is 21:7**	1581
"A multitude of **c** will cover you,	**Is 60:6**	1581
The young **c** of Midian and Ephah;	**Is 60:6**	1072

in litters, on mules and on **c**, Is 66:20 3753
all their goods and their **c**, Jer 49:29 1581
"Their **c** will become plunder, Jer 49:32 1581
I will make Rabbah a pasture for **c** Ezk 25:5 1581

CAMELS'

which were on their **c** necks. Jg 8:21 1581
bands that *were* on their **c** necks. Jg 8:26 1581
forty **c** loads; and he came 2Ki 8:9 1581
And their treasures on **c** humps, Is 30:6 1581

CAMP

"This is God's **c**." Gn 32:2 4264
himself spent that night in the **c**. Gn 32:21 4264
turn back and **c** before Pi-hahiroth, Ex 14:2 2583
shall **c** in front of Baal-zephon, Ex 14:2 2583
been going before the **c** of Israel, Ex 14:19 4264
So it came between the **c** of Egypt Ex 14:20 4264
camp of Egypt and the **c** of Israel; Ex 14:20 4264
quails came up and covered the **c**, Ex 16:13 4264
was a layer of dew around the **c**. Ex 16:13 4264
people who *were* in the **c** trembled. Ex 19:16 4264
people out of the **c** to meet God, Ex 19:17 4264
burn with fire outside the **c**; Ex 29:14 4264
is a sound of war in the **c**." Ex 32:17 4264
as soon as Moses came near the **c**, Ex 32:19 4264
Moses stood in the gate of the **c**, Ex 32:26 4264
forth from gate to gate in the **c**, Ex 32:27 4264
tent and pitch it outside the **c**, Ex 33:7 4264
camp, a good distance from the **c**, Ex 33:7 4264
meeting which was outside the **c**. Ex 33:7 4264
When Moses returned to the **c**, Ex 33:11 4264
was circulated throughout the **c**, Ex 36:6 4264
out to a clean place outside the **c** Lv 4:12 4264
the bull to *a place* outside the **c** and Lv 4:21 4264
outside the **c** to a clean place. Lv 6:11 4264
burned in the fire outside the **c**, Lv 8:17 4264
he burned with fire outside the **c**. Lv 9:11 4264
to the outside of the **c**." Lv 10:4 4264
tunics to the outside of the **c**, Lv 10:5 4264
dwelling shall be outside the **c**. Lv 13:46 4264
go out to the outside of the **c**. Lv 14:3 4264
Now afterward, he may enter the **c**, Lv 14:8 4264
he shall come into the **c**. Lv 16:26 4264
shall be taken outside the **c**, Lv 16:27 4264
he shall come into the **c**. Lv 16:28 4264
ox or a lamb or a goat in the **c**, Lv 17:3 4264
who slaughters it outside the **c**, Lv 17:3 4264
with each other in the **c**. Lv 24:10 4264
one who has cursed outside the **c**, Lv 24:14 4264
the **c** and stoned him with stones. Lv 24:23 4264
also **c** around the tabernacle. Nu 1:50 2583
"The sons of Israel shall **c**, Nu 1:52 2583
shall camp, each man by his own **c**, Nu 1:52 4264
"But the Levites shall **c** around Nu 1:53 2583
"The sons of Israel shall **c**, Nu 2:2 2583
they shall **c** around the tent of Nu 2:2 2583
"Now those who **c** on the east side Nu 2:3 2583
of the standard of the **c** of Judah, Nu 2:3 4264
"Those who **c** next to him Nu 2:5 2583
numbered men of the **c** of Judah: Nu 2:9 4264
the **c** of Reuben by their armies, Nu 2:10 4264
"Those who **c** next to him Nu 2:12 2583
numbered men of the **c** of Reuben: Nu 2:16 4264
with the **c** of the Levites in the midst Nu 2:17 4264
just as they **c**, so they shall set Nu 2:17 2583
the **c** of Ephraim by their armies, Nu 2:18 4264
numbered men of the **c** of Ephraim: Nu 2:24 4264
of the **c** of Dan by their armies, Nu 2:25 4264
"Those who **c** next to him Nu 2:27 2583
the numbered men of the **c** of Dan Nu 2:31 4264
the Gershonites were to **c** behind Nu 3:23 2583
Kohath were to **c** on the southward Nu 3:29 2583
They *were* to **c** on the northward Nu 3:35 2583
Now those who were to **c** before the Nu 3:38 2583
"When the **c** sets out, Aaron and Nu 4:5 4264
when the **c** is to set out, Nu 4:15 4264
they send away from the **c** every leper Nu 5:2 4264
you shall send them outside the **c** Nu 5:3 4264
c where I dwell in their midst." Nu 5:3 4264
so and sent them outside the **c**; Nu 5:4 4264
there the sons of Israel would **c**. Nu 9:17 2583
command of the LORD they would **c**; Nu 9:18 2583
of the **c** of the sons of Judah, Nu 10:14 4264
the standard of the **c** of Reuben, Nu 10:18 4264
of the **c** of the sons of Ephraim, Nu 10:22 4264
of the **c** of the sons of Dan, Nu 10:25 4264
we should **c** in the wilderness, Nu 10:31 2583
day when they set out from the **c**. Nu 10:34 4264
some of the outskirts of the **c**. Nu 11:1 4264
the dew fell on the **c** at night, Nu 11:9 4264
But two men had remained in the **c**; Nu 11:26 4264
and they prophesied in the **c**. Nu 11:26 4264
Medad are prophesying in the **c**." Nu 11:27 4264
Then Moses returned to the **c**, Nu 11:30 4264
and let *them* fall beside the **c**, Nu 11:31 4264
the other side, all around the **c** and Nu 11:31 4264
for themselves all around the **c**. Nu 11:32 4264
up for seven days outside the **c**, Nu 12:14 4264
up outside the **c** for seven days, Nu 12:15 4264
of the LORD nor Moses left the **c**. Nu 14:44 4264
him with stones outside the **c**." Nu 15:35 4264
brought him outside the **c** and Nu 15:36 4264
outside the **c** and be slaughtered Nu 19:3 4264
and afterward come into the **c**, Nu 19:7 4264
outside the **c** in a clean place, Nu 19:9 4264
to the **c** at the plains of Moab, Nu 31:12 4264
out to meet them outside the **c**. Nu 31:13 4264
c outside the camp seven days; Nu 31:19 2583
camp outside the **c** seven days; Nu 31:19 4264
afterward you may enter the **c**." Nu 31:24 4264
of war perished from within the **c**, Dt 2:14 4264
to destroy them from within the **c** until Dt 2:15 4264
then he must go outside the **c**; Dt 23:10 4264
he may not reenter the **c**. Dt 23:10 4264
at sundown he may reenter the **c**. Dt 23:11 4264
outside the **c** and go out there, Dt 23:12 4264
your God walks in the midst of your **c** Dt 23:14 4264
therefore your **c** must be holy; Dt 23:14 4264
of the **c** and command the people, Jos 1:11 4264
went through the midst of the **c**; Jos 3:2 4264
in the **c** until they were healed. Jos 5:8 4264
then they came into the **c** and Jos 6:11 4264
camp and spent the night in the **c**. Jos 6:11 4264
city once and returned to the **c**; Jos 6:14 4264
and make the **c** of Israel Jos 6:18 4264
them outside the **c** of Israel. Jos 6:23 4264
went to Joshua to the **c** at Gilgal and Jos 9:6 4264
word to Joshua to the **c** at Gilgal, Jos 10:6 4264
him returned to the **c** to Gilgal. Jos 10:15 4264
the people returned to the **c** to Joshua Jos 10:21 4264
him returned to the **c** at Gilgal. Jos 10:43 4264
came to Joshua to the **c** at Shiloh. Jos 18:9 4264
So they would **c** against them and Jg 6:4 2583
and the **c** of Midian was on the Jg 7:1 4264
and the **c** of Midian was below him Jg 7:8 4264
"Arise, go down against the **c**, Jg 7:9 4264
Purah your servant down to the **c**, Jg 7:10 4264
you may go down against the **c**." Jg 7:11 4264
of the army that was in the **c**. Jg 7:11 4264
was tumbling into the **c** of Midian, Jg 7:13 4264
and all the **c** into his hand." Jg 7:14 4264
He returned to the **c** of Israel Jg 7:15 4264
the **c** of Midian into your hands." Jg 7:15 4264
I come to the outskirts of the **c**, Jg 7:17 4264
the trumpets all around the **c** and Jg 7:18 4264
came to the outskirts of the **c** Jg 7:19 4264
stood in his place around the **c**; Jg 7:21 4264
and Jogbehah, and attacked the **c** when Jg 8:11 4264
camp when the **c** was unsuspecting. Jg 8:11 4264
no one had come to the **c** from Jg 21:8 4264
brought them to the **c** at Shiloh, Jg 21:12 4264
When the people came into the **c**, 1Sa 4:3 4264
of the LORD came into the **c**, 1Sa 4:5 4264
in the **c** of the Hebrews *mean?*" 1Sa 4:6 4264
of the LORD had come into the **c**. 1Sa 4:6 4264
"God has come into the **c**." 1Sa 4:7 4264
of the **c** at the morning watch and 1Sa 11:11 4264
And the raiders came from the **c** of 1Sa 13:17 4264
there was a trembling in the **c**, 1Sa 14:15 4264
the commotion in the **c** of the 1Sa 14:19 4264
up with them all around in the **c**, 1Sa 14:21 4264
and run to the **c** to your brothers. 1Sa 17:17 4264
And he came to the circle of the **c** 1Sa 17:20 4570
was lying in the circle of the **c**, 1Sa 26:5 4570
down with me to Saul in the **c**?" 1Sa 26:6 4264
inside the circle of the **c** with 1Sa 26:7 4570
you will go out with me in the **c**, 1Sa 28:1 4264
Saul saw the **c** of the Philistines, 1Sa 28:5 4264
a man came out of the **c** from Saul, 2Sa 1:2 4264
escaped from the **c** of Israel." 2Sa 1:3 4264
and **c** against the city and capture it, 2Sa 12:28 2583
through the **c** of the Philistines, 2Sa 23:16 4264
over Israel that day in the **c**. 1Ki 16:16 4264
when they came to the **c** of Israel, 2Ki 3:24 4264
and such a place shall be my **c**." 2Ki 6:8 8466
go over to the **c** of the Arameans. 2Ki 7:4 4264
to go to the **c** of the Arameans; 2Ki 7:5 4264
outskirts of the **c** of the Arameans, 2Ki 7:5 4264
even the **c** just as it was, 2Ki 7:7 4264
came to the outskirts of the **c**, 2Ki 7:8 4264
"We came to the **c** of the 2Ki 7:10 4264
gone from the **c** to hide themselves 2Ki 7:12 4264
through the **c** of the Arameans. 2Ki 7:16 4264
185,000 in the **c** of the Assyrians; 2Ki 19:35 4264
for the **c** of the sons of Levi. 1Ch 9:18 4264
had been over the **c** of the LORD, 1Ch 9:19 4264
through the **c** of the Philistines and 1Ch 11:18 4264
c had slain all the older *sons*. 2Ch 22:1 4264
in the gates of the **c** of the LORD. 2Ch 31:2 4264
of the **c** of the king of Assyria. 2Ch 32:21 4264
against me And **c** around my tent. Jb 19:12 2583
May their **c** be desolate; Ps 69:25 2918
them fall in the midst of their **c**, Ps 78:28 4264
became envious of Moses in the **c**, Ps 106:16 4264
will **c** against you encircling *you*, Is 29:3 2583
185,000 in the **c** of the Assyrians; Is 37:36 4264
like the sound of an army **c**; Ezk 1:24 4264
Surely His **c** is very great, For Jl 2:11 4264
stench of your **c** rise up in your Am 4:10 4264
But I will **c** around My house Zch 9:8 2583
for sin, are burned outside the **c**. Heb 13:11 *3925b*
us go out to Him outside the **c**, Heb 13:13 *3925b*
and surrounded the **c** of the saints Rv 20:9 *3925b*

CAMPED

and **c** in the valley of Gerar, Gn 26:17 2583
c in the hill country of Gilead. Gn 31:25 8628
Paddan-aram, and **c** before the city. Gn 33:18 2583
set out from Succoth and **c** in Etham Ex 13:20 2583
they **c** there beside the waters. Ex 15:27 2583
of the LORD, and **c** at Rephidim, Ex 17:1 2583
in the wilderness where he was **c**, Ex 18:5 2583
of Sinai and **c** in the wilderness; Ex 19:2 2583
Israel **c** in front of the mountain. Ex 19:2 2583
so they **c** by their standards, Nu 2:34 2583
the tabernacle, they remained **c**. Nu 9:18 2583
of the LORD they remained **c**. Nu 9:20 2583
remained **c** and did not set out; Nu 9:22 2583
At the command of the LORD they **c**, Nu 9:23 2583
and **c** in the wilderness of Paran. Nu 12:16 2583
Israel moved out and **c** in Oboth. Nu 21:10 2583
from Oboth and **c** at Iyeabarim, Nu 21:11 2583
they set out and **c** in Wadi Zered. Nu 21:12 2583
From there they journeyed and **c** on Nu 21:13 2583
and **c** in the plains of Moab beyond Nu 22:1 2583
from Rameses and **c** in Succoth. Nu 33:5 2583
from Succoth and **c** in Etham, Nu 33:6 2583
and they **c** before Migdol. Nu 33:7 2583
of Etham and **c** at Marah. Nu 33:8 2583
and they **c** there. Nu 33:9 2583
from Elim and **c** by the Red Sea. Nu 33:10 2583
and **c** in the wilderness of Sin. Nu 33:11 2583
of Sin and **c** at Dophkah. Nu 33:12 2583
from Dophkah and **c** at Alush. Nu 33:13 2583
from Alush and **c** at Rephidim; Nu 33:14 2583
and **c** in the wilderness of Sinai. Nu 33:15 2583
Sinai and **c** at Kibroth-hattaavah. Nu 33:16 2583
and **c** at Hazeroth. Nu 33:17 2583
from Hazeroth and **c** at Rithmah. Nu 33:18 2583
Rithmah and **c** at Rimmon-perez. Nu 33:19 2583
from Rimmon-perez and **c** at Libnah. Nu 33:20 2583
from Libnah and **c** at Rissah. Nu 33:21 2583
from Rissah and **c** in Kehelathah. Nu 33:22 2583
and **c** at Mount Shepher. Nu 33:23 2583
Mount Shepher and **c** at Haradah. Nu 33:24 2583
from Haradah and **c** at Makheloth. Nu 33:25 2583
from Makheloth and **c** at Tahath. Nu 33:26 2583
from Tahath and **c** at Terah. Nu 33:27 2583
from Terah and **c** at Mithkah. Nu 33:28 2583
from Mithkah and **c** at Hashmonah. Nu 33:29 2583
from Hashmonah and **c** at Moseroth. Nu 33:30 2583
Moseroth and **c** at Bene-jaakan. Nu 33:31 2583
Bene-jaakan and **c** at Hor-haggidgad. Nu 33:32 2583
Hor-haggidgad and **c** at Jotbathah. Nu 33:33 2583
from Jotbathah and **c** at Abronah. Nu 33:34 2583
from Abronah and **c** at Ezion-geber. Nu 33:35 2583
and **c** in the wilderness of Zin, Nu 33:36 2583
from Kadesh and **c** at Mount Hor, Nu 33:37 2583
from Mount Hor and **c** at Zalmonah. Nu 33:41 2583
from Zalmonah and **c** at Punon. Nu 33:42 2583
from Punon and **c** at Oboth. Nu 33:43 2583
from Oboth and **c** at Iye-abarim, Nu 33:44 2583
from Iyim and **c** at Dibon-gad. Nu 33:45 2583
and **c** at Almon-diblathaim. Nu 33:46 2583
and **c** in the mountains of Abarim, Nu 33:47 2583
and **c** in the plains of Moab by the Nu 33:48 2583
They **c** by the Jordan, from Nu 33:49 2583
and **c** at Gilgal on the eastern edge Jos 4:19 2583
the sons of Israel **c** at Gilgal they Jos 5:10 2583
and **c** on the north side of Ai. Jos 8:11 2583
and **c** by Gibeon and fought against Jos 10:5 2583
c by it and fought against it. Jos 10:31 2583
c by it and fought against it. Jos 10:34 2583
and **c** in the valley of Jezreel. Jg 6:33 2583
and **c** beside the spring of Harod; Jg 7:1 2583
and he **c** against Thebez and Jg 9:50 2583
summoned and they **c** in Gilead. Jg 10:17 2583
together and **c** in Mizpah. Jg 10:17 2583
Moab, and they **c** beyond the Arnon; Jg 11:18 2583
all his people and **c** in Jahaz and Jg 11:20 2583
went up and **c** in Judah, Jg 15:9 2583
and **c** at Kiriath-jearim in Judah. Jg 18:12 2583
the morning and **c** against Gibeah. Jg 20:19 2583
c beside Ebenezer while the Philistines 1Sa 4:1 2583
while the Philistines **c** in Aphek. 1Sa 4:1 2583
they came up and **c** in Michmash, 1Sa 13:5 2583
the Philistines **c** at Michmash. 1Sa 13:16 2583
they **c** between Socoh and Azekah, 1Sa 17:1 2583
and **c** in the valley of Elah, 1Sa 17:2 2583
Saul **c** in the hill of Hachilah, 1Sa 26:3 2583
to the place where Saul had **c**. 1Sa 26:5 2583
and the people were **c** around him. 1Sa 26:5 2583
together and came and **c** in Shunem; 1Sa 28:4 2583
together and they **c** in Gilboa. 1Sa 28:4 2583
Absalom **c** in the land of Gilead. 2Sa 17:26 2583
crossed the Jordan and **c** in Aroer, 2Sa 24:5 2583
people were **c** against Gibbethon, 1Ki 16:15 2583
people who were **c** heard it said, 1Ki 16:16 2583
and the sons of Israel **c** before 1Ki 20:27 2583
So they **c** one over against the 1Ki 20:29 2583
against Jerusalem, **c** against it and 2Ki 25:1 2583
who came and **c** before Medeba. 1Ch 19:7 2583
Ahava, where we **c** for three days; Ezr 8:15 2583
"The Arameans have **c** in Ephraim," Is 7:2 5117
Ariel the city *where* David *once* **c**! Is 29:1 2583
against Jerusalem, **c** against it and Jer 52:4 2583

CAMPING

they overtook them **c** by the sea, Ex 14:9 2583
and saw Israel **c** tribe by tribe; Nu 24:2 7931
while the Israelites were **c** by the 1Sa 29:1 2583
my lord are **c** in the open field. 2Sa 11:11 2583
was **c** in the valley of Rephaim. 2Sa 23:13 2583
was **c** in the valley of Rephaim. 1Ch 11:15 2583

CAMPS

by their villages, and by their **c**; Gn 25:16 2918
the Levites in the midst of the **c**; Nu 2:17 4264
men of the **c** by their armies, Nu 2:32 4264
and for having the **c** set out. Nu 10:2 4264
the **c** that are pitched on the east Nu 10:5 4264
the **c** that are pitched on the Nu 10:6 4264
the rear guard for all the **c**, Nu 10:25 4264
open **c** or with fortifications? Nu 13:19 4264
lived and all their **c** with fire. Nu 31:10 2918
the alien who is within your **c**, Dt 29:11 4264
Philistines and plundered their **c**. 1Sa 17:53 4264
gathered their armed **c** for war, 1Sa 28:1 4264
to their **c** within their borders. 1Ch 6:54 2918

wall, raise up a ramp, pitch c and	Ezk 4:2	4264
cattle that will be in those c.	Zch 14:15	4264

CAN

c number the dust of the earth,	Gn 13:16	3201
descendants c also be numbered.	Gn 13:16	
Now as for you then, what c I do,	Gn 27:37	
But what c I do this day to these	Gn 31:43	
dream, but no one c interpret it;	Gn 41:15	
hear a dream you c interpret it."	Gn 41:15	
"C we find a man like this, in	Gn 41:38	
food, as much as they c carry,	Gn 44:1	3201
I c indeed practice divination?"	Gn 44:15	
"What c we say to my lord?	Gn 44:16	
we say to my lord? What c we speak?	Gn 44:16	
And how c we justify ourselves?	Gn 44:16	
the midwife c get to them."	Ex 1:19	935
yourselves wherever you c find *it*,	Ex 5:11	
I c make atonement for your sin."	Ex 32:30	
"For how then c it be known that	Ex 33:16	
for no man c see Me and live!"	Ex 33:20	
feet, as far as the priest c see,	Lv 13:12	
"*He shall offer* what he c afford,	Lv 14:31	
so that you c eat your fill and	Lv 25:19	
you c still eat old things from	Lv 25:22	
c use them as permanent slaves.	Lv 25:46	
which men c present as an offering	Lv 27:9	
addition to what *else* he c afford;	Nu 6:21	
And how c I denounce whom the	Nu 23:8	
"Who c count the dust of Jacob,	Nu 23:10	
who c live except God has ordained	Nu 24:23	
everything that c stand the fire,	Nu 31:23	
no expiation c be made for the land	Nu 35:33	
'How c I alone bear the load and	Dt 1:12	
'Where c we go up?	Dt 1:28	
who c do such works and mighty acts	Dt 3:24	
how c I dispossess them?'	Dt 7:17	3201
of whose hills you c dig copper.	Dt 8:9	
c stand before the sons of Anak?'	Dt 9:2	
there will be nothing you c do.	Dt 28:32	
no one who c deliver from My hand.	Dt 32:39	
what c I say since Israel has	Jos 7:8	
shall do to them whatever you c."	Jg 9:33	
"How c you say,	Jg 16:15	
So how c you say to me,	Jg 18:24	
LORD, who c intercede for him?"	1Sa 2:25	
perhaps he c tell us about our	1Sa 9:6	
"How c this one deliver us?"	1Sa 10:27	
which c not profit or deliver,	1Sa 12:21	
But Samuel said, "How c I go?	1Sa 16:2	
for me now a man who c play well and	1Sa 16:17	
more c he have but the kingdom?"	1Sa 18:8	
bread, or whatever c be found."	1Sa 21:3	
man that no one c speak to him."	1Sa 25:17	
for who c stretch out his hand	1Sa 26:9	
know what your servant c do."	1Sa 28:2	
"How c the ark of the LORD come	2Sa 6:9	
what more c David say to You?	2Sa 7:20	
How then c we tell him that the	2Sa 12:18	
C I bring him back again?	2Sa 12:23	3201
no one c turn to the right or to	2Sa 14:19	
then you c thwart the counsel of	2Sa 15:34	
of the places where he c be found,	2Sa 17:12	
C I distinguish between good and	2Sa 19:35	
Or c your servant taste what I eat	2Sa 19:35	
Or c I hear anymore the voice of	2Sa 19:35	
And how c I make atonement that	2Sa 21:3	
"For by You I c run upon a troop;	2Sa 22:30	
By my God I c leap over a wall.	2Sa 22:30	
my arms c bend a bow of bronze.	2Sa 22:35	
your sons c live on the rest."	2Ki 4:7	
to us, *that* he c turn in there."	2Ki 4:10	
what c I do for you?	2Ki 4:13	
sojourn wherever you c sojourn;	2Ki 8:1	
how then c we stand?"	2Ki 10:4	
"How then c you repulse one	2Ki 18:24	
"How c I bring the ark of God	1Ch 13:12	
"What more c David still *say* to	1Ch 17:18	
for who c rule this great people	2Ch 1:10	
that no one c stand against You.	2Ch 20:6	
for no one c stand before You	Ezr 9:15	
Nor c the task *be done* in one	Ezr 10:13	
C they offer sacrifices?	Ne 4:2	
C they finish in a day?	Ne 4:2	
C they revive the stones from the	Ne 4:2	
that you in the king's palace c escape	Es 4:13	
"For how c I endure to see the	Es 8:6	3201
"and how c I endure to see the	Es 8:6	3201
But who c refrain from speaking?	Jb 4:2	3201
'C mankind be just before God?	Jb 4:17	
C a man be pure before his Maker?	Jb 4:17	
"C something tasteless be eaten	Jb 6:6	
"C the papyrus grow up without	Jb 8:11	
C the rushes grow without water?	Jb 8:11	
But how c a man be in the right	Jb 9:2	
"How then c I answer Him, *And*	Jb 9:14	
of justice, who c summon Him?	Jb 9:19	
"C you discover the depths of God?	Jb 11:7	
C you discover the limits of the	Jb 11:7	
as the heavens, what c you do?	Jb 11:8	
than Sheol, what c you know?	Jb 11:8	
an assembly, who c restrain Him?	Jb 11:10	
a man, and there c be no release.	Jb 12:14	
"Who c make the clean out of the	Jb 14:4	
understanding and then we c talk.	Jb 18:2	
for a case against him c we find?'	Jb 19:28	
"C anyone teach God knowledge, In	Jb 21:22	
"C a vigorous man be of use to	Jb 22:2	
C He judge through the thick	Jb 22:13	
'What c the Almighty do to them?'	Jb 22:17	
He is unique and who c turn Him?	Jb 23:13	
is not so, who c prove me a liar,	Jb 24:25	
"How then c a man be just with God?	Jb 25:4	
Or how c he be clean who is born	Jb 25:4	
thunder, who c understand?"	Jb 26:14	
"But where c wisdom be found?	Jb 28:12	
Nor c silver be weighed as its	Jb 28:15	
Nor c it be exchanged for articles	Jb 28:17	
Nor c it be valued in pure gold.	Jb 28:19	
of His majesty I c do nothing.	Jb 31:23	3201
'Who c find one who has not been	Jb 31:31	
"Refute me if you c;	Jb 33:5	3201
keeps quiet, who then c condemn?	Jb 34:29	
His face, who then c behold Him,	Jb 34:29	
"C anyone understand the	Jb 36:29	
"C you, with Him, spread out the	Jb 37:18	
"C you bind the chains of the	Jb 38:31	
"C you lead forth a constellation	Jb 38:32	
"C you lift up your voice to the	Jb 38:34	
"C you send forth lightnings that	Jb 38:35	
"Who c count the clouds by	Jb 38:37	
"C you hunt the prey for the	Jb 38:39	
"C you count the months they	Jb 39:2	
"C you bind the wild ox in a	Jb 39:10	
what c I reply to You?	Jb 40:4	
And c you thunder with a voice	Jb 40:9	
your own right hand c save you.	Jb 40:14	
"C anyone capture him when he is	Jb 40:24	
barbs c anyone pierce *his* nose?	Jb 40:24	
"C you draw out Leviathan with a	Jb 41:1	
"C you put a rope in his nose Or	Jb 41:2	
"C you fill his skin with	Jb 41:7	
then is he that c stand before Me?	Jb 41:10	
"Who c strip off his outer armor?	Jb 41:13	
Who c come within his double mail?	Jb 41:13	
"Who c open the doors of his face?	Jb 41:14	
That no air c come between them.	Jb 41:16	
"I know that You c do all things,	Jb 42:2	3201
no purpose of Yours c be thwarted.	Jb 42:2	
How c you say to my soul,	Ps 11:1	
What c the righteous do?"	Ps 11:3	
For by You I c run upon a troop;	Ps 18:29	
by my God I c leap over a wall.	Ps 18:29	
my arms c bend a bow of bronze.	Ps 18:34	
Who c discern *his* errors?	Ps 19:12	
I c count all my bones.	Ps 22:17	
No man c by any means redeem *his*	Ps 49:7	
What c *mere* man do to me?	Ps 56:4	
What c man do to me?	Ps 56:11	
pots c feel *the fire of* thorns He	Ps 58:9	
"Who c see them?"	Ps 64:5	
"C God prepare a table in the	Ps 78:19	3201
C He give bread also?	Ps 78:20	3201
What man c live and not see death?	Ps 89:48	
C he deliver his soul from the	Ps 89:48	
C a throne of destruction be	Ps 94:20	
Who c speak of the mighty deeds of	Ps 106:2	
Or c show forth all His praise?	Ps 106:2	
What c man do to me?	Ps 118:6	
c a young man keep his way pure?	Ps 119:9	
How c we sing the LORD's song In a	Ps 137:4	
Where c I go from Your Spirit?	Ps 139:7	
where c I flee from Your presence?	Ps 139:7	
Who c stand before His cold?	Ps 147:17	
C a man take fire in his bosom And	Pr 6:27	
Or c a man walk on hot coals And	Pr 6:28	
of a man c endure his sickness,	Pr 18:14	
a broken spirit who c bear it?	Pr 18:14	
But who c find a trustworthy man?	Pr 20:6	
Who c say, "I have cleansed my heart	Pr 20:9	
How then c man understand his way?	Pr 20:24	
men who c give a discreet answer.	Pr 26:16	
But who c stand before jealousy?	Pr 27:4	
An excellent wife, who c find?	Pr 31:10	
For who c eat and who can have	Ec 2:25	
who c have enjoyment without Him?	Ec 2:25	
warm, but how c one be warm *alone?*	Ec 4:11	
one c overpower him who is alone,	Ec 4:12	
who is alone, two c resist him.	Ec 4:12	
labor that he c carry in his hand.	Ec 5:15	
For who c tell a man what will be	Ec 6:12	
Who c discover it?	Ec 7:24	
c tell him when it will happen?	Ec 8:7	
and who c tell him what will come	Ec 10:14	
my dress, How c I put it on *again?*	SS 5:3	
my feet, How c I dirty them *again?*	SS 5:3	
planned, and who c frustrate *it?*	Is 14:27	
hand, who c turn it back?"	Is 14:27	
How c you *men* say to Pharaoh,	Is 19:11	
us c live with the consuming fire?	Is 33:14	
Who among us c live with continual	Is 33:14	
"How then c you repulse one	Is 36:9	
Who, if I ask, c give an answer.	Is 41:28	
Who among them c declare this And	Is 43:9	
none who c deliver out of My hand;	Is 43:13	
I act and who c reverse it?"	Is 43:13	
For how c *My name* be profaned?	Is 48:11	
"C a woman forget her nursing	Is 49:15	
"C the prey be taken from the	Is 49:24	
C a land be born in one day?	Is 66:8	
C a nation be brought forth all at	Is 66:8	
cisterns That c hold no water.	Jer 2:13	3201
"How c you say,	Jer 2:23	
of her heat who c turn her away?	Jer 2:24	
if they c save you In the time of	Jer 2:28	
"C a virgin forget her ornaments,	Jer 2:32	
open squares, If you c find a man,	Jer 5:1	
c you understand what they say.	Jer 5:15	
"How c you say,	Jer 8:8	
For what *else* c I do, because of	Jer 9:7	
fear them, For they c do no harm,	Jer 10:5	
no harm, Nor c they do any good."	Jer 10:5	
C the sacrificial flesh take away	Jer 11:15	
disaster, So *that* you c rejoice?"	Jer 11:15	
how c you compete with horses?	Jer 12:5	
"C the Ethiopian change his skin	Jer 13:23	
Then you also c do good Who are	Jer 13:23	3201
Or c the heavens grant showers?	Jer 14:22	
"C anyone smash iron, Iron from	Jer 15:12	
C man make gods for himself?	Jer 16:20	
Who c understand it?	Jer 17:9	
"C I not, O house of Israel, deal	Jer 18:6	3201
"C a man hide himself in hiding	Jer 23:24	
and see If a male c give birth.	Jer 30:6	
the heavens above c be measured And	Jer 31:37	
c break My covenant for the day and	Jer 33:20	
king c *do* nothing against you."	Jer 38:5	3201
"How c it be quiet, When the LORD	Jer 47:7	
"How c you say,	Jer 48:14	
shepherd who c stand against Me?"	Jer 49:19	
shepherd who c stand before Me?"	Jer 50:44	
Who c heal you?	La 2:13	
So that no prayer c pass through.	La 3:44	
nor c they fill their stomachs,	Ezk 7:19	
will cover his face so that he c not see	Ezk 12:12	
"C wood be taken from it to make	Ezk 15:3	
or c *men* take a peg from it on	Ezk 15:3	
c it still be made into anything!	Ezk 15:5	
nor by many people c it be raised	Ezk 17:9	
C he indeed break the covenant and	Ezk 17:15	
"C your heart endure, or can your	Ezk 22:14	
endure, or c your hands be strong in	Ezk 22:14	
how then c we survive?"	Ezk 33:10	
"Son of man, c these bones live?"	Ezk 37:3	
that I may know that you c declare	Da 2:9	
who c make the interpretation known	Da 2:25	
c deliver you out of my hands?"	Da 3:15	
And no one c ward off His hand Or	Da 4:35	
"Any man who c read this	Da 5:7	
"For how c such a servant of my	Da 10:17	3201
C the LORD now pasture them Like a	Hos 4:16	
the king, what c he do for us?"	Hos 10:3	
How c I give you up, O Ephraim?	Hos 11:8	
How c I surrender you, O Israel?	Hos 11:8	
How c I make you like Admah?	Hos 11:8	
How c I treat you like Zeboiim?	Hos 11:8	
very awesome, And who c endure it?	Jl 2:11	
Who c but prophesy?	Am 3:8	
How c Jacob stand, For he is small?"	Am 7:2	
How c Jacob stand, for he is small?"	Am 7:5	
"C I justify wicked scales And a	Mi 6:11	
Who c stand before His indignation?	Na 1:6	
Who c endure the burning of His	Na 1:6	
And You c not look on wickedness	Hab 1:13	3201
Until no *room* c be found for them.	Zch 10:10	
"But who c endure the day of His	Mal 3:2	
And who c stand when He appears?	Mal 3:2	
that you c say to yourselves,	Mt 3:9	
how c it be made salty *again?* It	Mt 5:13	
"No one c serve two masters;	Mt 6:24	*1410*
by being worried c add a *single* hour	Mt 6:27	*1410*
"Or how c you say to your	Mt 7:4	
c a bad tree produce good fruit.	Mt 7:18	
willing, You c make me clean."	Mt 8:2	*1410*
bridegroom is with them, c they?	Mt 9:15	
be the Son of David, c he?"	Mt 12:23	
"Or how c anyone enter the strong	Mt 12:29	*1410*
"You brood of vipers, how c you,	Mt 12:34	*1410*
"Not all men c accept this	Mt 19:11	
"Then who c be saved?"	Mt 19:25	*1410*
willing, You c make me clean."	Mk 1:40	*1410*
c forgive sins but God alone?"	Mk 2:7	*1410*
c they? So long as they have	Mk 2:19	
"How c Satan cast out Satan?	Mk 3:23	*1410*
"But no one c enter the strong	Mk 3:27	*1410*
THE AIR C NEST UNDER ITS SHADE."	Mk 4:32	*1410*
which c defile him if it goes into him;	Mk 7:15	*1410*
launderer on earth c whiten them.	Mk 9:3	*1410*
But if You c do anything, take	Mk 9:22	*1410*
And Jesus said to him, "'If You c?'	Mk 9:23	*1410*
"Then who c be saved?"	Mk 10:26	*1410*
you wish you c do good to them;	Mk 14:7	*1410*
"How c this be, since I am a virgin?"	Lk 1:34	
willing, You c make me clean."	Lk 5:12	*1410*
Who c forgive sins, but God alone?"	Lk 5:21	*1410*
bridegroom is with them, c you?	Lk 5:34	
cannot guide a blind man, c he?	Lk 6:39	
"Or how c you say to your	Lk 6:42	*1410*
that have no more that they c do.	Lk 12:4	
by worrying c add a *single* hour	Lk 12:25	*1410*
none of you c be My disciple who	Lk 14:33	*1410*
for you c no longer be manager.'	Lk 16:2	*1410*
"No servant c serve two masters;	Lk 16:13	*1410*
"Then who c be saved?"	Lk 18:26	*1410*
"C any good thing come out of	Jn 1:46	*1410*
for no one c do these signs that	Jn 3:2	*1410*
c a man be born when he is old?	Jn 3:4	*1410*
mother's womb and be born, c he?"	Jn 3:4	
"How c these things be?"	Jn 3:9	*1410*
"A man c receive nothing unless	Jn 3:27	*1410*
the Son c do nothing of Himself,	Jn 5:19	*1410*
"I c do nothing on My own	Jn 5:30	*1410*
"How c you believe, when you	Jn 5:44	*1410*
"No one c come to Me unless the	Jn 6:44	*1410*
"How c this man give us *His* flesh	Jn 6:52	*1410*
who c listen to it?"	Jn 6:60	*1410*
to you, that no one c come to Me unless	Jn 6:65	*1410*
is coming when no one c work.	Jn 9:4	*1410*

“How **c** a man who is a sinner **Jn 9:16** *1410*
the eyes of the blind, **c** he?” **Jn 10:21**
and how **c** You say, **Jn 12:34**
why **c** I not follow You right now? **Jn 13:37** *1410*
how **c** you say, ‘Show us **Jn 14:9**
so neither **c** you *unless* you abide **Jn 15:4**
apart from Me you **c** do nothing. **Jn 15:5** *1410*
“Surely no one **c** refuse the water **Ac 10:47** *1410*
Spirit just as we *did*, **c** he?” **Ac 10:47**
Council of the elders **c** testify. **Ac 22:5**
since you **c** take note of the fact **Ac 24:11** *1410*
“Nor **c** they prove to you **Ac 24:13** *1410*
me, no one **c** hand me over to them. **Ac 25:11** *1410*
For no man **c** lay a foundation **1Co 3:11** *1410*
and no one **c** say, **1Co 12:3** *1410*
For you **c** all prophesy one by one, **1Co 14:31** *1410*
we **c** do nothing against the truth, **2Co 13:8** *1410*
when you read you **c** understand my **Eph 3:4** *1410*
I **c** do all things through Him who **Php 4:13** *2480*
For what thanks **c** we render to God **1Th 3:9** *1410*
whom no man has seen or **c** see. **1Tm 6:16** *1410*
he **c** deal gently with the ignorant **Heb 5:2** *1410*
c never, by the same sacrifices **Heb 10:1** *1410*
which **c** never take away sins; **Heb 10:11** *1410*
not come to *a mountain* that **c** be **Heb 12:18**
of those things which **c** be shaken, **Heb 12:27**
C that faith save him? **Jas 2:14** *1410*
But no one **c** tame the tongue; **Jas 3:8** *1410*
C a fig tree, my brethren, produce **Jas 3:12** *1410*
Nor **c** salt water produce fresh. **Jas 3:12**
a righteous man **c** accomplish much. **Jas 5:16** *2480*
an open door which no one **c** shut, **Rv 3:8** *1410*
c neither see nor hear nor walk; **Rv 9:20** *1410*

CANA
was a wedding in **C** of Galilee, **Jn 2:1** *2580*
signs Jesus did in **C** of Galilee, **Jn 2:11** *2580*
He came again to **C** of **Jn 4:46** *2580*
and Nathanael of **C** in Galilee, **Jn 21:2** *2580*

CANAAN
and Ham was the father of **C**. **Gn 9:18** 3667a
Ham, the father of **C**, **Gn 9:22** 3667a
“Cursed be **C**; A servant of servants **Gn 9:25** 3667a
And let **C** be his servant. **Gn 9:26** 3667a
And let **C** be his servant.” **Gn 9:27** 3667a
Cush and Mizraim and Put and **C**. **Gn 10:6** 3667a
C became the father of Sidon, **Gn 10:15** 3667a
in order to enter the land of **C**; **Gn 11:31** 3667a
they set out for the land of **C**; **Gn 12:5** 3667a
thus they came to the land of **C**. **Gn 12:5** 3667a
Abram settled in the land of **C**, **Gn 13:12** 3667a
lived ten years in the land of **C**, **Gn 16:3** 3667a
sojournings, all the land of **C**, **Gn 17:8** 3667a
in the land of **C**; **Gn 23:2** 3667a
in the land of **C**. **Gn 23:19** 3667a
a wife from the daughters of **C**. **Gn 28:1** 3667a
a wife from the daughters of **C**,” **Gn 28:6** 3667a
of **C** displeased his father Isaac; **Gn 28:8** 3667a
the land of **C** to his father Isaac. **Gn 31:18** 3667a
which is in the land of **C**, **Gn 33:18** 3667a
which is in the land of **C**, **Gn 35:6** 3667a
his wives from the daughters of **C**: **Gn 36:2** 3667a
were born to him in the land of **C**. **Gn 36:5** 3667a
he had acquired in the land of **C**, **Gn 36:6** 3667a
had sojourned, in the land of **C**. **Gn 37:1** 3667a
famine was in the land of **C** *also*. **Gn 42:5** 3667a
“From the land of **C**, **Gn 42:7** 3667a
sons of one man in the land of **C**; **Gn 42:13** 3667a
father Jacob in the land of **C**, **Gn 42:29** 3667a
father today in the land of **C**.’ **Gn 42:32** 3667a
back to you from the land of **C**. **Gn 44:8** 3667a
beasts and go to the land of **C**, **Gn 45:17** 3667a
land of **C** to their father Jacob. **Gn 45:25** 3667a
had acquired in the land of **C**, **Gn 46:6** 3667a
and Onan died in the land of **C**). **Gn 46:12** 3667a
who *were* in the land of **C**, **Gn 46:31** 3667a
have come out of the land of **C**; **Gn 47:1** 3667a
famine is severe in the land of **C**. **Gn 47:4** 3667a
C languished because of the famine. **Gn 47:13** 3667a
C for the grain which they bought, **Gn 47:14** 3667a
of Egypt and in the land of **C**, **Gn 47:15** 3667a
in the land of **C** and blessed me, **Gn 48:3** 3667a
in the land of **C** on the journey, **Gn 48:7** 3667a
is before Mamre, in the land of **C**, **Gn 49:30** 3667a
I dug for myself in the land of **C**, **Gn 50:5** 3667a
sons carried him to the land of **C** and **Gn 50:13** 3667a
them, to give them the land of **C**, **Ex 6:4** 3667a
inhabitants of **C** have melted away. **Ex 15:15** 3667a
to the border of the land of **C**. **Ex 16:35** 3667a
“When you enter the land of **C**, **Lv 14:34** 3667a
land of **C** where I am bringing you; **Lv 18:3** 3667a
the land of **C** *and* to be your God. **Lv 25:38** 3667a
they may spy out the land of **C**, **Nu 13:2** 3667a
them to spy out the land of **C**, **Nu 13:17** 3667a
Er and Onan died in the land of **C**. **Nu 26:19** 3667a
among you in the land of **C**.” **Nu 32:30** 3667a
of the LORD into the land of **C**, **Nu 32:32** 3667a
in the Negev in the land of **C**, **Nu 33:40** 3667a
the Jordan into the land of **C**, **Nu 33:51** 3667a
‘When you enter the land of **C**, **Nu 34:2** 3667a
of **C** according to its borders. **Nu 34:2** 3667a
sons of Israel in the land of **C**. **Nu 34:29** 3667a
the Jordan into the land of **C**, **Nu 35:10** 3667a
and three cities in the land of **C**; **Nu 35:14** 3667a
and look at the land of **C**, **Dt 32:49** 3667a
of the land of **C** during that year. **Jos 5:12** 3667a
Israel inherited in the land of **C**, **Jos 14:1** 3667a
them at Shiloh in the land of **C**, **Jos 21:2** 3667a
Shiloh which is in the land of **C**, **Jos 22:9** 3667a
Jordan which is in the land of **C**, **Jos 22:10** 3667a
at the frontier of the land of **C**, **Jos 22:11** 3667a
land of Gilead to the land of **C**, **Jos 22:32** 3667a
led him through all the land of **C**, **Jos 24:3** 3667a
experienced any of the wars of **C**; **Jg 3:1** 3667a
into the hand of Jabin king of **C**, **Jg 4:2** 3667a
of **C** before the sons of Israel. **Jg 4:23** 3667a
heavier upon Jabin the king of **C**, **Jg 4:24** 3667a
had destroyed Jabin the king of **C**. **Jg 4:24** 3667a
Then fought the kings of **C** At **Jg 5:19** 3667a
Shiloh, which is in the land of **C**. **Jg 21:12** 3667a
were Cush, Mizraim, Put, and **C**. **1Ch 1:8** 3667a
C became the father of Sidon, **1Ch 1:13** 3667a
“To you I will give the land of **C**, **1Ch 16:18** 3667a
“To you I will give the land of **C** **Ps 105:11** 3667a
they sacrificed to the idols of **C**; **Ps 106:38** 3667a
Bashan, And all the kingdoms of **C**; **Ps 135:11** 3667a
will be speaking the language of **C** **Is 19:18** 3667a
C to demolish its strongholds. **Is 23:11** 3667a
the people of **C** will be silenced; **Zph 1:11** 3667a
of the LORD is against you, O **C**, **Zph 2:5** 3667a
famine came over all Egypt and **C**, **Ac 7:11** *5477*
seven nations in the land of **C**, **Ac 13:19** *5477*

CANAANITE
of the **C** were spread abroad. **Gn 10:18** 3669a
The territory of the **C** **Gn 10:19** 3669a
Now the **C** *was* then in the land. **Gn 12:6** 3669a
Now the **C** and the Perizzite were **Gn 13:7** 3669a
and the Amorite and the **C** and the **Gn 15:21** 3669a
a certain **C** whose name was Shua; **Gn 38:2** 3669a
and Shaul the son of a **C** woman. **Gn 46:10** 3669a
to the place of the **C** and the **Ex 3:8** 3669a
to the land of the **C** and the Hittite **Ex 3:17** 3669a
and Shaul the son of a **C** woman; **Ex 6:15** 3669a
brings you to the land of the **C**, **Ex 13:5** 3669a
brings you to the land of the **C**, **Ex 13:11** 3669a
you and I will drive out the **C**, **Ex 33:2** 3669a
the Amorite before you, and the **C**, **Ex 34:11** 3669a
When the **C**, the king of Arad, who **Nu 21:1** 3669a
Now the **C**, the king of Arad who **Nu 33:40** 3669a
Amorite, the **C** and the Perizzite, **Dt 20:17** 3669a
dispossess from before you the **C**, **Jos 3:10** 3669a
Hittite and the Amorite, the **C**, **Jos 9:1** 3669a
the **C** on the east and on the west, **Jos 11:3** 3669a
Hittite, the Amorite and the **C**, **Jos 12:8** 3669a
(it is counted as **C**); **Jos 13:3** 3669a
the south, all the land of the **C**, **Jos 13:4** 3669a
the Perizzite and the **C** and the Hittite **Jos 24:11** 3669a
him To give *him* the land of the **C**, **Ne 9:8** 3669a
birth are from the land of the **C**, **Ezk 16:3** 3669a
And there will no longer be a **C** in **Zch 14:21** 3669a
a **C** woman from that region came out **Mt 15:22** *5478*

CANAANITES
son from the daughters of the **C**, **Gn 24:3** 3669a
son from the daughters of the **C**, **Gn 24:37** 3669a
among the **C** and the Perizzites; **Gn 34:30** 3669a
inhabitants of the land, the **C**, **Gn 50:11** 3669a
Hittites, the Perizzites, the **C**, **Ex 23:23** 3669a
will drive out the Hivites, the **C**, **Ex 23:28** 3669a
and the **C** are living by the sea **Nu 13:29** 3669a
and the **C** live in the valleys; **Nu 14:25** 3669a
C will be there in front of you, **Nu 14:43** 3669a
Then the Amalekites and the **C** who **Nu 14:45** 3669a
of Israel and delivered up the **C**; **Nu 21:3** 3669a
the seacoast, the land of the **C**, **Dt 1:7** 3669a
Amorites and the **C** and the Perizzites **Dt 7:1** 3669a
of the **C** who live in the Arabah, **Dt 11:30** 3669a
of the **C** who *were* by the sea, **Jos 5:1** 3669a
“For the **C** and all the **Jos 7:9** 3669a
out the **C** who lived in Gezer, **Jos 16:10** 3669a
so the **C** live in the midst of **Jos 16:10** 3669a
because the **C** persisted in living **Jos 17:12** 3669a
they put the **C** to forced labor, **Jos 17:13** 3669a
and all the **C** who live in the **Jos 17:16** 3669a
for you shall drive out the **C**, **Jos 17:18** 3669a
go up first for us against the **C**, **Jg 1:1** 3669a
that we may fight against the **C**; **Jg 1:3** 3669a
and the LORD gave the **C** and the **Jg 1:4** 3669a
defeated the **C** and the Perizzites. **Jg 1:5** 3669a
to fight against the **C** living in the hill **Jg 1:9** 3669a
against the **C** who lived in Hebron **Jg 1:10** 3669a
struck the **C** living in Zephath, **Jg 1:17** 3669a
so the **C** persisted in living in **Jg 1:27** 3669a
they put the **C** to forced labor, **Jg 1:28** 3669a
the **C** who were living in Gezer; **Jg 1:29** 3669a
the **C** lived in Gezer among them. **Jg 1:29** 3669a
so the **C** lived among them and **Jg 1:30** 3669a
the Asherites lived among the **C**, **Jg 1:32** 3669a
Beth-anath, but lived among the **C**, **Jg 1:33** 3669a
C and the Sidonians and the Hivites **Jg 3:3** 3669a
sons of Israel lived among the **C**, **Jg 3:5** 3669a
of the Hivites and of the **C**, **2Sa 24:7** 3669a
the **C** who lived in the city, **1Ki 9:16** 3669a
abominations, *those* of the **C**, **Ezr 9:1** 3669a
inhabitants of the land, the **C**, **Ne 9:24** 3669a
among the **C** as far as Zarephath, **Ob 1:20** 3669a

CANAANITESS
born to him by Bath-shua the **C**. **1Ch 2:3** 3669a

CANAL
I myself was beside the Ulai **C**. **Da 8:2** 180
was standing in front of the **c**. **Da 8:3** 180
seen standing in front of the **c**, **Da 8:6** 180

CANALS
The **c** will emit a stench, The **Is 19:6** 5104
us A place of rivers *and* wide **c** **Is 33:21** 2975
I will make the Nile **c** dry And **Ezk 30:12** 2975

CANCELED
covenant with death will be **c**, **Is 28:18** 3722a
having **c** out the certificate of **Col 2:14** *1813*

CANDACE
eunuch, a court official of **C**, **Ac 8:27** *2582*

CANE
fragrant **c** two hundred and fifty, **Ex 30:23** 7070
bought Me not sweet **c** with money, **Is 43:24** 7070
the sweet **c** from a distant land? **Jer 6:20** 7070
c were among your merchandise. **Ezk 27:19** 7070

CANNEH
“Haran, **C**, Eden, the traders of **Ezk 27:23** 3656

CANNOT
but I **c** escape to the mountains, **Gn 19:19**
3201, 3808
for I **c** do anything until you **Gn 19:22**
3201, 3808
so we **c** speak to you bad or good. **Gn 24:50**
3201, 3808
“We **c**, until all the flocks are **Gn 29:8**
3201, 3808
be angry that I **c** rise before you, **Gn 31:35**
3201, 3808
“We **c** do this thing, to give our **Gn 34:14**
3201, 3808
‘The lad **c** leave his father, for **Gn 44:22**
3201, 3808
“But we said, ‘We **c** go down. **Gn 44:26**
3201, 3808
for we **c** see the man’s face unless **Gn 44:26**
3201, 3808
you **c** do it alone. **Ex 18:18**
3201, 3808
people **c** come up to Mount Sinai, **Ex 19:23**
3201, 3808
“You **c** see My face, for no man **Ex 33:20**
3201, 3808
‘But if he **c** afford a lamb, then **Lv 5:7** 3808
‘But if she **c** afford a lamb, then **Lv 12:8** 3808
has blessed, then I **c** revoke it. **Nu 23:20** 3808
But whatever **c** stand the fire you **Nu 31:23** 3808
he **c** make the son of the loved the **Dt 21:16**
3201, 3808
he **c** divorce her all his days. **Dt 22:19**
3201, 3808
he **c** divorce her all his days. **Dt 22:29**
3201, 3808
itch, from which you **c** be healed. **Dt 28:27**
3201, 3808
boils, from which you **c** be healed, **Dt 28:35**
3201, 3808
sons of Israel **c** stand before their **Jos 7:12**
3201, 3808
You **c** stand before your enemies **Jos 7:13**
3201, 3808
Israel, and now we **c** touch them. **Jos 9:19**
3201, 3808
the LORD, and I **c** take *it* back.” **Jg 11:35**
3201, 3808
“But we **c** give them wives of our **Jg 21:18**
3201, 3808
“I **c** redeem *it* for myself, because I **Ru 4:6**
3201, 3808
redemption, for I **c** redeem *it*.” **Ru 4:6**
3201, 3808
“I **c** go with these, for I have **1Sa 17:39**
3201, 3808
“David **c** enter here.” **2Sa 5:6** 3808
which **c** be gathered up again. **2Sa 14:14** 3808
Because they **c** be taken in hand; **2Sa 23:6** 3808
the highest heaven **c** contain You, **1Ki 8:27** 3808
“I **c** return with you, nor go with **1Ki 13:16**
3201, 3808
and tell Ahab and he **c** find you, **1Ki 18:12** 3808
do, but this thing I **c** do.’ ” **1Ki 20:9**
3201, 3808
of Jezreel, so they **c** say, **2Ki 9:37** 3808
the highest heavens **c** contain Him? **2Ch 2:6** 3808
the highest heaven **c** contain You; **2Ch 6:18** 3808
a great work and I **c** come down. **Ne 6:3**
3201, 3808
Media so that it **c** be repealed, **Es 1:19** 3808
that their hands **c** attain success. **Jb 5:12** 3808
C my palate discern calamities? **Jb 6:30** 3808
tears down, and it **c** be rebuilt; **Jb 12:14** 3808
You have set so that he **c** pass. **Jb 14:5** 3808
walled up my way so that I **c** pass, **Jb 19:8** 3808
like a dream, and they **c** find him; **Jb 20:8** 3808
he has attained And **c** swallow *it*; **Jb 20:18** 3808
his trading, He **c** even enjoy *them*. **Jb 20:18** 3808
Or darkness, so that you **c** see, **Jb 22:11** 3808
place for Him, so that He **c** see; **Jb 22:14** 3808
backward, but I **c** perceive *Him*; **Jb 23:8** 3808
acts on the left, I **c** behold *Him*; **Jb 23:9** 3808
turns on the right, I **c** see Him. **Jb 23:9** 3808
c be given in exchange for it, **Jb 28:15** 3808
“It **c** be valued in the gold of **Jb 28:16** 3808
“Gold or glass **c** equal it, Nor **Jb 28:17** 3808
“The topaz of Ethiopia **c** equal it, **Jb 28:19** 3808
“I am seething within and **c** relax; **Jb 30:27** 3808
things which we **c** comprehend. **Jb 37:5** 3808
We **c** arrange *our case* because of **Jb 37:19** 3808
we **c** find Him; He is exalted **Jb 37:23** 3808
each other and **c** be separated. **Jb 41:17** 3808
sword that reaches him **c** avail, **Jb 41:26** 1097
“The arrow **c** make him flee; **Jb 41:28** 3808
Even he who **c** keep his soul alive. **Ps 22:29** 3808
have been thrust down and **c** rise. **Ps 36:12**
3201, 3808
eyes grow dim so that they **c** see, **Ps 69:23** 4480

I am so troubled that I **c** speak. Ps 77:4 3808
I am shut up and **c** go out. Ps 88:8 3808
have mouths, but they **c** speak; Ps 115:5 3808
They have eyes, but they **c** see; Ps 115:5 3808
They have ears, but they **c** hear; Ps 115:6 3808
They have noses, but they **c** smell; Ps 115:6 3808
They have hands, but they **c** feel; Ps 115:7 3808
They have feet, but they **c** walk; Ps 115:7 3808
They **c** make a sound with their Ps 115:7 3808
as Mount Zion, which **c** be moved but Ps 125:1 3808
It is *too* high, I **c** attain to it. Ps 139:6 3201, 3808
deep pits from which they **c** rise. Ps 140:10 1077
they **c** sleep unless they do evil; Pr 4:16 3808
And all desirable things **c** compare Pr 8:11 3808
And under four, it **c** bear up: Pr 30:21 3201, 3808
What is crooked **c** be straightened and Ec 1:15 3201, 3808
and what is lacking **c** be counted. Ec 1:15 3201, 3808
for he **c** dispute with him who is Ec 6:10 3201, 3808
I concluded that man **c** discover Ec 8:17 3201, 3808
"I know," he **c** discover. Ec 8:17 3201, 3808
"Many waters **c** quench love, Nor SS 8:7 3201, 3808
I **c** endure iniquity and the solemn Is 1:13 3201, 3808
I am so bewildered I **c** hear, Is 21:3 4480
cannot hear, so terrified I **c** see. Is 21:3 4480
"I **c**, for it is sealed." Is 29:11 3201, 3808
read this." And he will say, "I **c** read. Is 29:12 3808
of a people who **c** profit them, Is 30:5 3808
To a people who **c** profit *them;* Is 30:6 3808
It **c** hold the base of its mast Is 33:23 1077
"For Sheol **c** thank You, Death Is 38:18 3808
thank You, Death **c** praise You; Is 38:18 3808
pit **c** hope for Your faithfulness. Is 38:18 3808
over their eyes so that they **c** see Is 44:18 4480
hearts so that they **c** comprehend. Is 44:18 4480
And he **c** deliver himself, nor say, Is 44:20 3808
And pray to a god who **c** save. Is 45:20 3808
one may cry to it, it **c** answer; Is 46:7 3808
c deliver him from his distress. Is 46:7 3808
fall on you For which you **c** atone; Is 47:11 3201, 3808
They **c** deliver themselves from the Is 47:14 3808
My hand so short that it **c** ransom? Is 50:2 4480
tossing sea, For it **c** be quiet, Is 57:20 3201, 3808
is not so short That it **c** save; Is 59:1 4480
is His ear so dull That it **c** hear. Is 59:1 4480
street, And uprightness **c** enter. Is 59:14 3201, 3808
I **c** be silent, Because you have Jer 4:19 3808
decree, so it **c** cross over it. Jer 5:22 3808
waves toss, yet they **c** prevail; Jer 5:22 3808
roar, yet they **c** cross over it. Jer 5:22 3808
are closed And they **c** listen. Jer 6:10 3201, 3808
field are they, And they **c** speak; Jer 10:5 3808
be carried, Because they **c** walk! Jer 10:5 3808
nations **c** endure His indignation. Jer 10:10 3808
Like a mighty man who **c** save? Jer 14:9 3201, 3808
vessel, which **c** again be repaired; Jer 19:11 3201, 3808
holding *it* in, And I **c** endure *it.* Jer 20:9 3808
c be eaten due to rottenness." Jer 24:3 3808
like the bad figs which **c** be eaten Jer 24:8 3808
that **c** be eaten due to rottenness. Jer 29:17 3808
the host of heaven **c** be counted and Jer 33:22 3808
the sand of the sea **c** be measured, Jer 33:22 3808
I **c** go into the house of the LORD. Jer 36:5 3201, 3808
by the sea, It **c** be calmed. Jer 49:23 3201, 3808
walled me in so that I **c** go out; La 3:7 3808
whose words you **c** understand. Ezk 3:6 3808
so that you **c** go out among them. Ezk 3:25 3808
and **c** be a man who rebukes them, Ezk 3:26 3808
put ropes on you so that you **c** turn Ezk 4:8 3808
They **c** satisfy their appetite nor Ezk 7:19 3808
shall cover your face so that you **c** Ezk 12:6 3808
Which **c** be measured or numbered; Hos 1:10 3808
her so that she **c** find her paths. Hos 2:6 3808
which you **c** remove your necks; Mi 2:3 3808
A city set on a hill **c** be hidden; Mt 5:14 *1410, 3756*
c make one hair white or black. Mt 5:36 *1410, 3756*
You **c** serve God and wealth. Mt 6:24 *1410, 3756*
"A good tree **c** produce bad fruit, Mt 7:18 *1410, 3756*
attendants of the bridegroom **c** mourn Mt 9:15 *1410, 3361*
"This man **c** be the Son of David, Mt 12:23 *3385*
but **c** *discern* the signs of the Mt 16:3 *1410, 3756*
c pass away unless I drink it, Mt 26:42 *1410, 3756*
that I **c** appeal to My Father, Mt 26:53 *1410, 3756*
He **c** save Himself. Mt 27:42 *1410, 3756*
the attendants of the bridegroom **c** Mk 2:19 *1410*
bridegroom with them, they **c** fast. Mk 2:19 *1410, 3756*
itself, that kingdom **c** stand. Mk 3:24 *1410, 3756*
and is divided, he **c** stand, Mk 3:26 *1410, 3756*
the man from outside **c** defile him, Mk 7:18 *1410, 3756*
"This kind **c** come out by anything Mk 9:29 *1410, 3762*
He **c** save Himself. Mk 15:31 *1410, 3756*
"You **c** make the attendants of the Lk 5:34 *1410, 3361*
"A blind man **c** guide a blind man, Lk 6:39 *1410, 3385*
I **c** get up and give you *anything.'* Lk 11:7 *1410, 3756*
you **c** do even a very little thing, Lk 12:26 *1410, 3761*
for it **c** be that a prophet would Lk 13:33 *1735, 3756*
and for that reason I **c** come.' Lk 14:20 *1410, 3756*
his own life, he **c** be My disciple. Lk 14:26 *1410, 3756*
come after Me **c** be My disciple. Lk 14:27 *1410, 3756*
You **c** serve God and wealth." Lk 16:13 *1410, 3756*
for they **c** even die anymore, because Lk 20:36 *1410, 3761*
he **c** see the kingdom of God." Jn 3:3 *1410, 3756*
He **c** enter a second time into his Jn 3:4 *1410, 3361*
c enter into the kingdom of God. Jn 3:5 *1410, 3756*
"The world **c** hate you, Jn 7:7 *1410, 3756*
and where I am, you **c** come." Jn 7:34 *1410, 3756*
and where I am, you **c** come'?" Jn 7:36 *1410, 3756*
where I am going, you **c** come." Jn 8:21 *1410, 3756*
'Where I am going, you **c** come'?" Jn 8:22 *1410, 3756*
It is because you **c** hear My word. Jn 8:43 *1410, 3756*
c open the eyes of the blind, Jn 10:21 *1410, 3361*
(and the Scripture **c** be broken), Jn 10:35 *1410, 3756*
'Where I am going, you **c** come.' Jn 13:33 *1410, 3756*
"Where I go, you **c** follow Me now; Jn 13:36 *1410, 3756*
truth, whom the world **c** receive, Jn 14:17 *1410, 3756*
the branch **c** bear fruit of itself unless Jn 15:4 *1410, 3756*
to you, but you **c** bear *them* now. Jn 16:12 *1410, 3756*
in Jerusalem, and we **c** deny it. Ac 4:16 *1410, 3756*
for we **c** stop speaking about what we Ac 4:20 *1410, 3756*
custom of Moses, you **c** be saved." Ac 15:1 *1410, 3756*
ship, you yourselves **c** be saved." Ac 27:31 *1410, 3756*
who are in the flesh **c** please God. Ro 8:8 *1410, 3756*
to him; and he **c** understand them, 1Co 2:14 *1410, 3756*
You **c** drink the cup of the Lord 1Co 10:21 *1410, 3756*
you **c** partake of the table of the 1Co 10:21 *1410, 3756*
And the eye **c** say to the hand, 1Co 12:21 *1410, 3756*
c inherit the kingdom of God; 1Co 15:50 *1410, 3756*
are otherwise **c** be concealed. 1Tm 5:25 *1410, 3756*
so we **c** take anything out of it 1Tm 6:7 *1410, 3761*
for He **c** deny Himself. 2Tm 2:13 *1410, 3756*
life, which God, who **c** lie, Ti 1:2 *893*
high priest who **c** sympathize with our Heb 4:15 *1410, 3361*
things we **c** now speak in detail. Heb 9:5 *3756*
which **c** make the worshiper perfect Heb 9:9 *1410, 3361*
which **c** be shaken may remain. Heb 12:27 *3361*
a kingdom which **c** be shaken, Heb 12:28 *761*
for God **c** be tempted by evil, and Jas 1:13 *551*
You are envious and **c** obtain; Jas 4:2 *1410, 3756*
and he **c** sin, because he is born 1Jn 3:9 *1410, 3756*
c love God whom he has not seen. 1Jn 4:20 *1410, 3756*
and that you **c** tolerate evil men, Rv 2:2 *1410, 3756*

CANOPIES
"And He made darkness **c** around Him, 2Sa 22:12 5521

CANOPY
hiding place, His **c** around Him, Ps 18:11 5521
over all the glory will be a **c**. Is 4:5 2646
he will spread his **c** over them. Jer 43:10 8237

CAPABILITY
and men of outstanding **c** were 1Ch 26:31 2428

CAPABLE
if you know any **c** men among *them,* Gn 47:6 2428
and his relatives, 1,700 **c** men, 1Ch 26:30 2428
and his relatives, **c** men, 1Ch 26:32 2428

CAPACITY
in measurement of weight, or **c**. Lv 19:35 4884

CAPERBERRY
along, and the **c** is ineffective. Ec 12:5 35

CAPERNAUM
He came and settled in **C**, Mt 4:13 *2746b*
And when Jesus entered **C**, Mt 8:5 *2746b*
"And you, **C**, will not be exalted Mt 11:23 *2746b*
When they came to **C**, Mt 17:24 *2746b*
They went into **C**; Mk 1:21 *2746b*
back to **C** several days afterward, Mk 2:1 *2746b*
They came to **C**; Mk 9:33 *2746b*
Whatever we heard was done at **C**, Lk 4:23 *2746b*
And He came down to **C**, Lk 4:31 *2746b*
of the people, He went to **C**. Lk 7:1 *2746b*
"And you, **C**, will not be exalted Lk 10:15 *2746b*
After this He went down to **C**, Jn 2:12 *2746b*
official whose son was sick at **C**. Jn 4:46 *2746b*
started to cross the sea to **C**. Jn 6:17 *2746b*
the small boats, and came to **C** seeking Jn 6:24 *2746b*
the synagogue as He taught in **C**. Jn 6:59 *2746b*

CAPHTOR
the Caphtorim who came from **C**, Dt 2:23 3731
which the Philistines came, and **C**. 1Ch 1:12 3732
The remnant of the coastland of **C**. Jer 47:4 3731
from **C** and the Arameans from Kir? Am 9:7 3731

CAPHTORIM
which came the Philistines) and **C**. Gn 10:14 3732
Gaza, the **C** who came from Caphtor, Dt 2:23 3732

CAPITAL
the height of the one **c** was five 1Ki 7:16 3805
of the other **c** was five cubits. 1Ki 7:16 3805
seven for the one **c** and seven for 1Ki 7:17 3805
capital and seven for the other **c**. 1Ki 7:17 3805
and so he did for the other **c**. 1Ki 7:18 3805
cubits, and a bronze **c** was on it; 2Ki 25:17 3805
height of the **c** was three cubits, 2Ki 25:17 3805
pomegranates on the **c** all around, 2Ki 25:17 3805
and the **c** on the top of each *was* 2Ch 3:15 6858
Now a **c** of bronze was on it; Jer 52:22 3805
height of each **c** was five cubits, Jer 52:22 3805
upon the **c** all around, Jer 52:22 3805

CAPITALS
He also made two **c** of molten 1Ki 7:16 3805
c which were on the top of the pillars; 1Ki 7:17 3805
on the one network to cover the **c** 1Ki 7:18 3805
The **c** which *were* on the top of 1Ki 7:19 3805
There were **c** on the two pillars, 1Ki 7:20 3805
two hundred in rows around both **c**. 1Ki 7:20 3805
two pillars and the *two* bowls of the **c** 1Ki 7:41 3805
the two bowls of the **c** which 1Ki 7:41 3805
c which *were* on the tops of the pillars 1Ki 7:42 3805
the two **c** on top of the pillars, 2Ch 4:12 3805
the **c** which were on top of the pillars, 2Ch 4:12 3805
the **c** which were on the pillars. 2Ch 4:13 3805
"Smite the **c** so that the Am 9:1 3730

CAPITOL
year, while I was in Susa the **c**, Ne 1:1 1002

CAPPADOCIA
of Mesopotamia, Judea and **C**, Ac 2:9 *2587*
throughout Pontus, Galatia, **C**, 1Pe 1:1 *2587*

CAPRICIOUS
c children will rule over them, Is 3:4 8586

CAPS
and you shall make **c** for them, Ex 28:40 4021
and his sons, and bind **c** on them, Ex 29:9 4021
and the decorated **c** of fine linen, Ex 39:28 4021
with sashes and bound **c** on them, Lv 8:13 4021
their **c** and their *other* clothes, Da 3:21 3737

CAPTAIN
officer, the **c** of the bodyguard. Gn 37:36 8269
Pharaoh, the **c** of the bodyguard, Gn 39:1 8269
house of the **c** of the bodyguard, Gn 40:3 8269
The **c** of the bodyguard put Gn 40:4 8269
house of the **c** of the bodyguard, Gn 41:10 8269
servant of the **c** of the bodyguard, Gn 41:12 8269
as **c** of the host of the LORD." Jos 5:14 8269
The **c** of the LORD's host said Jos 5:15 8269
of Sisera, **c** of the army of Hazor, 1Sa 12:9 8269
And the name of the **c** of his army 1Sa 14:50 8269
and he became **c** over them. 1Sa 22:2 8269
who is **c** over your guard, 1Sa 22:14
him a **c** of fifty with his fifty. 2Ki 1:9 8269
replied to the **c** of fifty, 2Ki 1:10 8269
another **c** of fifty with his fifty. 2Ki 1:11 8269
So he again sent the **c** of a third 2Ki 1:13 8269
When the third **c** of fifty went up, 2Ki 1:13 8269
king or to the **c** of the army?' " 2Ki 4:13 8269
c of the army of the king of Aram, 2Ki 5:1 8269
"I have a word for you, O **c**." 2Ki 9:5 8269
And he said, "For you, O **c**." 2Ki 9:5 8269
Nebuzaradan the **c** of the guard, 2Ki 25:8 7227b

who *were with* the **c** of the guard 2Ki 25:10 7227b
Nebuzaradan the **c** of the guard 2Ki 25:11 7227b
But the **c** of the guard left some 2Ki 25:12 7227b
The **c** of the guard also took away 2Ki 25:15 7227b
Then the **c** of the guard took 2Ki 25:18 7227b
the scribe of the **c** of the army who 2Ki 25:19 8269
Nebuzaradan the **c** of the guard 2Ki 25:20 7227b
The **c** of fifty and the honorable Is 3:3 8269
a **c** of the guard whose name was Jer 37:13 1167
Nebuzaradan the **c** of the bodyguard Jer 39:9 7227b
Nebuzaradan the **c** of the bodyguard Jer 39:10 7227b
the **c** of the bodyguard, Jer 39:11 7227b
the **c** of the bodyguard sent *word,* Jer 39:13 7227b
after Nebuzaradan **c** of the bodyguard Jer 40:1 7227b
Now the **c** of the bodyguard had Jer 40:2 7227b
So the **c** of the bodyguard gave him Jer 40:5 7227b
whom Nebuzaradan the **c** of the Jer 41:10 7227b
Nebuzaradan the **c** of the bodyguard Jer 43:6 7227b
the **c** of the bodyguard, Jer 52:12 7227b
with the **c** of the guard broke down Jer 52:14 7227b
Then Nebuzaradan the **c** of the Jer 52:15 7227b
But Nebuzaradan the **c** of the guard Jer 52:16 7227b
The **c** of the guard also took away Jer 52:19 7227b
Then the **c** of the guard took Jer 52:24 7227b
Nebuzaradan the **c** of the guard Jer 52:26 7227b
Nebuzaradan the **c** of the guard Jer 52:30 7227b
the **c** of the king's bodyguard, Da 2:14 7229
So the **c** approached him and said, Jon 1:6 7227b, 2259
and the **c** of the temple *guard* Ac 4:1 *4755*
Now when the **c** of the temple *guard* Ac 5:24 *4755*
Then the **c** went along with the Ac 5:26 *4755*
the pilot and the **c** of the ship than Ac 27:11 *3490*

CAPTAINS

the **c** of thousands and the Nu 31:14 8269
thousands and the **c** of hundreds, Nu 31:14 8269
the **c** of thousands and the Nu 31:48 8269
thousands and the **c** of hundreds, Nu 31:48 8269
from the **c** of thousands and the Nu 31:52 8269
thousands and the **c** of hundreds, Nu 31:52 8269
c of thousands and of hundreds, Nu 31:54 8269
a Tahchemonite, chief of the **c**, 2Sa 23:8 7991c
his servants, his princes, his **c**, 1Ki 9:22 7991c
place, and put **c** in their place, 1Ki 20:24 6346
the thirty-two **c** of his chariots, 1Ki 22:31 8269
when the **c** of the chariots saw 1Ki 22:32 8269
When the **c** of the chariots saw 1Ki 22:33 8269
two **c** of fifty with their fifties; 2Ki 1:14 8269
him and the **c** of the chariots; 2Ki 8:21 8269
the **c** of the army were sitting, 2Ki 9:5 8269
the **c** of hundreds of the Carites 2Ki 11:4 8269
So the **c** of hundreds did according 2Ki 11:9 8269
The priest gave to the **c** of 2Ki 11:10 8269
with the **c** and the trumpeters 2Ki 11:14 8269
Jehoiada the priest commanded the **c** 2Ki 11:15 8269
He took the **c** of hundreds and 2Ki 11:19 8269
and his **c** and his officials. 2Ki 24:12 8269
the **c** and all the mighty men of valor, 2Ki 24:14 8269
When all the **c** of the forces, they 2Ki 25:23 8269
and the **c** of the forces arose and 2Ki 25:26 8269
sons of Gad were **c** of the army; 1Ch 12:14 7218
them and made them **c** of the band. 1Ch 12:18 7218
c of thousands who belonged to 1Ch 12:20 7218
of valor, and were **c** in the army. 1Ch 12:21 8269
of his father's house twenty-two **c**. 1Ch 12:28 8269
Of Naphtali *there were* 1,000 **c**, 1Ch 12:34 8269
Then David consulted with the **c** of 1Ch 13:1 8269
Israel and the **c** over thousands, 1Ch 15:25 8269
they were men of war, his chief **c** and 2Ch 8:9 7991c
commanded the **c** of his chariots, 2Ch 18:30 8269
when the **c** of the chariots saw 2Ch 18:31 8269
When the **c** of the chariots saw that it 2Ch 18:32 8269
himself, and took **c** of hundreds: 2Ch 23:1 8269
gave to the **c** of hundreds the spears 2Ch 23:9 8269
and the **c** and the trumpeters *were* 2Ch 23:13 8269
priest brought out the **c** of hundreds 2Ch 23:14 8269
He took the **c** of hundreds, the 2Ch 23:20 8269
and the **c** *were* behind the whole Ne 4:16 8269
from afar, And the thunder of the **c** Jb 39:25 8269
"Rise up, **c**, oil the shields," Is 21:5 8269

CAPTIVATE

and **c** weak women weighed down 2Tm 3:6 *163*

CAPTIVATED

The king is **c** by *your* tresses. SS 7:5 631

CAPTIVE

his relative had been taken **c**, Gn 14:14 7617
of the **c** who was in the dungeon, Ex 12:29 7628b
Israel and took some of them **c**. Nu 21:1 7628b
long will Asshur keep you **c**?" Nu 24:22 7628b
hands and you take them away **c**, Dt 21:10 7628b
and they took **c** the women *and all* 1Sa 30:2 7628b
their daughters had been taken **c**. 1Sa 30:3 7628b
David's two wives had been taken **c**, 1Sa 30:5 7628b
away **c** to the land of the enemy, 1Ki 8:46 7628b
land where they have been taken **c**, 1Ki 8:47 7628b
of those who have taken them **c**, 1Ki 8:47 7628b
enemies who have taken them **c**, 1Ki 8:48 7628b
those who have taken them **c**, 1Ki 8:50 7628b
and had taken **c** a little girl from 2Ki 5:2 7628b
you have taken **c** with your sword 2Ki 6:22 7628b
and he carried them **c** to Assyria. 2Ki 15:29 1540
So the king of Babylon took him **c** 2Ki 24:12
away **c** to a land far off or near, 2Ch 6:36 7617
the land where they are taken **c**, 2Ch 6:37 7617
where they have been taken **c**, 2Ch 6:38 7617
Israel carried away **c** of their brethren 2Ch 28:8 7617
before those who led them **c** and 2Ch 30:9 7617
the LORD restores His **c** people, Ps 14:7 7622
When God restores His **c** people, Ps 53:6 7622
You have led **c** *Your* captives; Ps 68:18 7617
brought back the **c** ones of Zion, Ps 126:1 7622
they will take their captors **c** and Is 14:2 7617
were found were taken **c** together, Is 22:3 631
be broken, snared and taken **c**. Is 28:13 3920
the dust, rise up, O **c** Jerusalem; Is 52:2 7628b
your neck, O **c** daughter of Zion. Is 52:2 7628a
of the LORD has been taken **c**. Jer 13:17 7617
in the place where they led him **c**, Jer 22:12 1540
c Jeconiah the son of Jehoiakim, Jer 24:1 1540
Then Ishmael took **c** all the Jer 41:10 7617
the son of Nethaniah took them **c** Jer 41:10 7617
Ishmael had taken **c** from Mizpah Jer 41:14 7617
he will burn them and take them **c**. Jer 43:12 7617
your sons have been taken away **c** And Jer 48:46 7628b
From there she will be taken **c**. Jer 50:9 3920
took them **c** have held them fast, Jer 50:33 7617
to which they will be carried **c**, Ezk 6:9 7617
be led **c** into all the nations; Lk 21:24 *163*
every thought **c** to the obedience 2Co 10:5 *163*
HIGH, HE LED C A HOST OF CAPTIVES, Eph 4:8 *162*
See to it that no one takes you **c** Col 2:8 *4812*
been held **c** by him to do his will. 2Tm 2:26 *2221*

CAPTIVES

my daughters like **c** of the sword? Gn 31:26 7617
They brought the **c** and the Nu 31:12 7628b
purify yourselves, you and your **c**, Nu 31:19 7628b
see among the **c** a beautiful woman, Dt 21:11 7633
the blood of the slain and the **c**, Dt 32:42 7633
Barak, and take away your **c**, Jg 5:12 7628b
men of valor, ten thousand **c**, 2Ki 24:14 1540
away from him a great number of **c** and 2Ch 28:5 7633
listen to me and return the **c** whom 2Ch 28:11 7633
"You must not bring the **c** in here, 2Ch 28:13 7633
So the armed men left the **c** and 2Ch 28:14 7633
by name arose, took the **c**, 2Ch 28:15 7633
Judah and carried away **c**. 2Ch 28:17 7628b
c who had been exiled with Jeconiah Es 2:6 1473
high, You have led captive *Your* **c**; Ps 68:18 7628b
the **c** Or fall among the slain. Is 10:4 616
Assyria will lead away the **c** of Egypt Is 20:4 7628b
Or the **c** of a tyrant be rescued?" Is 49:24 7628b
"Even the **c** of the mighty man Is 49:25 7628b
To proclaim liberty to **c** And Is 61:1 7617
regard as good the **c** of Judah, Jer 24:5 1546
away As **c** before the adversary. La 1:5 7628b
They collect **c** like sand. Hab 1:9 7628b
ME TO PROCLAIM RELEASE TO THE C, Lk 4:18 *164*
HIGH, HE LED CAPTIVE A HOST OF C, Eph 4:8 *161*

CAPTIVITY

And his daughters into **c**, Nu 21:29 7622
shall also remove the clothes of her **c** Dt 21:13 7628b
yours, for they will go into **c**. Dt 28:41 7628b
your God will restore you from **c**, Dt 30:3 7622
the day of the **c** of the land. Jg 18:30 1540
to You in the land of their **c**, 2Ch 6:37 7628b
their soul in the land of their **c**, 2Ch 6:38 7628b
and our wives are in **c** for this. 2Ch 29:9 7628b
c of the exiles whom Nebuchadnezzar Ezr 2:1 7628b
who came from the **c** to Jerusalem, Ezr 3:8 7628b
c offered burnt offerings to the God Ezr 8:35 7628b
of the lands, to the sword, to **c** and Ezr 9:7 7628b
escaped *and* had survived the **c**, Ne 1:2 7628b
who survived the **c** are in great distress Ne 1:3 7628b
up for plunder in a land of **c**. Ne 4:4 7633
c of the exiles whom Nebuchadnezzar Ne 7:6 7628b
c made booths and lived in them. Ne 8:17 7628b
And gave up His strength to **c** And Ps 78:61 7628b
You restored the **c** of Jacob. Ps 85:1 7622
Restore our **c**, O LORD, As the Ps 126:4 7622
But have themselves gone into **c**. Is 46:2 7628b
And those *destined* for **c**, Jer 15:2 7628b
destined for captivity, to **c**." Jer 15:2 7628b
live in your house will go into **c**; Jer 20:6 7628b
And your lovers will go into **c**; Jer 22:22 7628b
from the land of their **c**. Jer 30:10 7628b
one of them, will go into **c**; Jer 30:16 7628b
and those for **c** to captivity, Jer 43:11 7628b
and those for captivity to **c**, Jer 43:11 7628b
from the land of their **c**. Jer 46:27 7628b
And your daughters into **c**. Jer 48:46 7633
and my young men Have gone into **c**. La 1:18 7628b
So as to restore you from **c**, La 2:14 7622
they will go into exile, into **c**.' Ezk 12:11 7628b
I will restore their **c**, Ezk 16:53 7622
the **c** of Sodom and her daughters, Ezk 16:53 7622
the **c** of Samaria and her Ezk 16:53 7622
and along with them your own **c**, Ezk 16:53 7622
And the women will go into **c**. Ezk 30:17 7628b
And her daughters will go into **c**. Ezk 30:18 7628b
gold he will take into **c** to Egypt, Da 11:8 7628b
and by flame, by **c** and by plunder for Da 11:33 7628b
Gilgal will certainly go into **c** And Am 5:5 1540
go into **c** before their enemies, Am 9:4 7628b
restore the **c** of My people Israel, Am 9:14 7622
became an exile, She went into **c**; Na 3:10 7628b
If anyone *is destined* for **c**, Rv 13:10 *161*
for captivity, to **c** he goes; Rv 13:10 *161*

CAPTORS

In the presence of all their **c**. Ps 106:46 7617
there our **c** demanded of us songs, Ps 137:3 7617
they will take their **c** captive and Is 14:2 7617

CAPTURE

war against it in order to **c** it, Dt 20:19 8610
camp against the city and **c** it, 2Sa 12:28 3920
or I will **c** the city myself and it 2Sa 12:28 3920
we will **c** them alive and get into 2Ki 7:12 8610
anyone **c** him when he is on watch, Jb 40:24 3947
own iniquities will **c** the wicked, Pr 5:22 3920
Nor let her **c** you with her eyelids. Pr 6:25 3947
To **c** booty and to seize plunder, Is 10:6 7997b
For they have dug a pit to **c** me Jer 18:22 3920
c it and burn it with fire." Jer 37:8 3920
of Babylon and he will **c** it.' " Jer 38:3 3920
and **c** her spoil and seize her Ezk 29:19 7997b
to **c** spoil and to seize plunder, Ezk 38:12 7997b
'Have you come to **c** spoil? Ezk 38:13 7997b
and goods, to **c** great spoil? Ezk 38:13 7997b
ramp and **c** a well-fortified city; Da 11:15 3920
face to the coastlands and **c** many. Da 11:18 3920
And heap up rubble to **c** it. Hab 1:10 3920

CAPTURED

and they **c** and looted all their Gn 34:29 7617
and they **c** its villages and Nu 21:32 3920
The sons of Israel **c** the women Nu 31:9 7617
a count of the booty that was **c**, Nu 31:26 7628b
we **c** all his cities at that time and Dt 2:34 3920
of the cities which we had **c**. Dt 2:35 3920
We **c** all his cities at that time; Dt 3:4 3920
ran and entered the city and **c** it, Jos 8:19 3920
the *men in* ambush had **c** the city Jos 8:21 3920
heard that Joshua had **c** Ai, Jos 10:1 3920
Now Joshua **c** Makkedah on that day, Jos 10:28 3920
and he **c** it on the second day, and Jos 10:32 3920
They **c** it on that day and Jos 10:35 3920
They **c** it and struck it and Jos 10:37 3920
He **c** it and its king and all Jos 10:39 3920
Joshua **c** all these kings and Jos 10:42 3920
and **c** Hazor and struck its king Jos 11:10 3920
c all the cities of these kings, Jos 11:12 3920
And he **c** all their kings and Jos 11:17 3920
Kenaz, the brother of Caleb, **c** it; Jos 15:17 3920
and fought with Leshem and **c** it. Jos 19:47 3920
Judah fought against Jerusalem and **c** Jg 1:8 3920
Caleb's younger brother, **c** it; Jg 1:13 3920
They **c** the two leaders of Midian, Jg 7:25 3920
and **c** the two kings of Midian, Jg 8:12 3920
And he **c** a youth from Succoth and Jg 8:14 3920
and he **c** the city and killed the Jg 9:45 3920
he camped against Thebez and **c** it. Jg 9:50 3920
The Gileadites **c** the fords of Jg 12:5 3920
He **c** Agag the king of the 1Sa 15:8 8610
So David had **c** all the sheep and 1Sa 30:20 3947
David **c** the stronghold of Zion, 2Sa 5:7 3920
David **c** from him 1,700 2Sa 8:4 3920
of Ammon and **c** the royal city. 2Sa 12:26 3920
I have even **c** the city of waters. 2Sa 12:27 3920
fought against it and **c** it. 2Sa 12:29 3920
of Egypt had gone up and **c** Gezer and 1Ki 9:16 3920
and fought against Gath and **c** it, 2Ki 12:17 3920
of Israel **c** Amaziah king of Judah, 2Ki 14:13 8610
king of Assyria came and **c** Ijon and 2Ki 15:29 3947
went up against Damascus and **c** it, 2Ki 16:9 8610
the king of Assyria **c** Samaria and 2Ki 17:6 3920
the end of three years they **c** it; 2Ki 18:10 3920
king of Israel, Samaria was **c**. 2Ki 18:10 3920
Then they **c** the king and brought 2Ki 25:6 8610
David **c** the stronghold of Zion 1Ch 11:5 3920
went to Hamath-zobah and **c** it. 2Ch 8:3 2388
He **c** the fortified cities of 2Ch 12:4 3920
and **c** from him *several* cities, 2Ch 13:19 3920
had **c** in the hill country of Ephraim. 2Ch 15:8 3920
which Asa his father had **c**. 2Ch 17:2 3920
The sons of Judah also **c** 10,000 2Ch 25:12 7617
of Israel **c** Amaziah king of Judah, 2Ch 25:23 8610
whom you **c** from your brothers, 2Ch 28:11 7617
and they **c** Manasseh with hooks, 2Ch 33:11 3920
"They **c** fortified cities and Ne 9:25 3920
but the sinner will be **c** by her. Ec 7:26 3920
who is **c** will fall by the sword. Is 13:15 5595
he fought against Ashdod and **c** it, Is 20:1 3920
And have been **c** without the bow; Is 22:3 631
be **c** and delivered into his hand; Jer 34:3 8610
the day that Jerusalem was **c**. Jer 38:28 3920
Jerusalem was **c** in the ninth year of Jer 39:1 3920
been put to shame, it has been **c**; Jer 48:1 3920
Even you yourself will be **c**; Jer 48:7 3920
"Kerioth has been **c** And the Jer 48:41 3920
'Babylon has been **c**, Jer 50:2 3920
city has been **c** from end *to end;* Jer 51:31 3920
"How Sheshak has been **c**, Jer 51:41 3920
And her mighty men will be **c**, Jer 51:56 3920
Then they **c** the king and brought Jer 52:9 8610
anointed, Was **c** in their pits, La 4:20 3920
He was **c** in their pit, And they Ezk 19:4 8610
He was **c** in their pit. Ezk 19:8 8610
his den unless he has **c** *something?* Am 3:4 3920
sword along with your **c** horses, Am 4:10 7628b
to battle, and the city will be **c**, Zch 14:2 3920
of instinct to be **c** and killed, 2Pe 2:12 *259*

CAPTURES

attacks Kiriath-sepher and **c** it, Jos 15:16 3920
attacks Kiriath-sepher and **c** it, Jg 1:12 3920
"He **c** the wise by their own Jb 5:13 3920
his spirit, than he who **c** a city. Pr 16:32 3920
earth when it **c** nothing at all? Am 3:5 3920

CARAVAN

a **c** of Ishmaelites was coming from Gn 37:25 736
but supposed Him to be in the **c**, Lk 2:44 *4923*

CARAVANS

"The **c** of Tema looked, The Jb 6:19 734
spend the night, O **c** of Dedanites. Is 21:13 736

CARCASS

whether a **c** of an unclean beast or Lv 5:2 5038
beast or the **c** of unclean cattle Lv 5:2 5038

or a c of unclean swarming things, Lv 5:2 5038
their c may fall becomes unclean; Lv 11:35 5038
touches their c shall be unclean. Lv 11:36 5038
'If a part of their c falls on Lv 11:37 5038
and a part of their c falls on it, Lv 11:38 5038
c becomes unclean until evening. Lv 11:39 5038
who eats some of its c shall wash Lv 11:40 5038
and the one who picks up its c Lv 11:40 5038
to look at the c of the lion; Jg 14:8 4658

CARCASSES

of prey came down upon the c, Gn 15:11 6297
of their flesh nor touch their c; Lv 11:8 5038
and their c you shall detest. Lv 11:11 5038
c becomes unclean until evening. Lv 11:24 5038
whoever picks up any of their c shall Lv 11:25 5038
whoever touches their c becomes Lv 11:27 5038
and the one who picks up their c Lv 11:28 5038
of their flesh nor touch their c. Dt 14:8 5038
"Your c will be food to all Dt 28:26 5038
and their c will become food for Jer 16:4 5038
with the c of their detestable idols Jer 16:18 5038
and I will give over their c as Jer 19:7 5038

CARCHEMISH

to make war at C on the Euphrates, 2Ch 35:20 3751
"Is not Calno like C, Is 10:9 3751
was by the Euphrates River at C, Jer 46:2 3751

CARE

gave them into the c of his sons. Gn 30:35 3027
which are nursing are a c to me. Gn 33:13 5921
of them, and he took c of them; Gn 40:4 8334
put him in my c, and I will return Gn 42:37 3027
but God will surely take c of you and Gn 50:24 6485
"God will surely take c of you, Gn 50:25 6485
"God will surely take c of you Ex 13:19 6485
and shall take c of him until he Ex 21:19 7495
and they shall take c of it; Nu 1:50 8334
Only let me *take* c *of* all your Jg 19:20
in the c of the baggage keeper, 1Sa 17:22 3027
your master's wives into your c, 2Sa 12:8 2436
flee, they will not c about us; 2Sa 18:3 7760, 3820
us die, they will not c about us. 2Sa 18:3 7760, 3820
and committed them to the c of the 1Ki 14:27 3027
careful for us with all this c; 2Ki 4:13 2731
all of this was in the c of 1Ch 26:28 3027
in c of Jehiel the Gershonite. 1Ch 29:8 3027
and committed them to the c of the 2Ch 12:10 3027
this work is going on with great c Ezr 5:8 629
as she had done when under his c. Es 2:20 545
Let not God above c for it, Jb 3:4 1875
And Your c has preserved my spirit. Jb 10:12 6486
he c for his household after him, Jb 21:21 2656
of man that You c for him? Ps 8:4 6485
From the c of the ewes with Ps 78:71 310
and see, and take c of this vine, Ps 80:14 6485
not taken c of my own vineyard. SS 1:6 5201
those who take c of its fruit." SS 8:12 5201
'Take c and be calm, have no fear Is 7:4 8104
so I will c for My sheep and will Ezk 34:12 1239
For the LORD their God will c for Zph 2:7 6485
who will not c for the perishing, Zch 11:16 6485
for tomorrow will c for itself. Mt 6:34 *3309*
and did not take c of You?' Mt 25:44 *1247*
"Take c what you listen to. Mk 4:24 *991*
You not c that we are perishing?" Mk 4:38 *3199*
"So take c how you listen; Lk 8:18 *991*
him to an inn and took c of him. Lk 10:34 *1959*
innkeeper and said, 'Take c of him; Lk 10:35 *1959*
do You not c that my sister has Lk 10:40 *3199*
take c what you propose to do with Ac 5:35 *4337*
go to his friends and receive c. Ac 27:3 *1958*
But take c that this liberty of 1Co 8:9 *991*
have the same c for one another. 1Co 12:25 *3309*
take c that you are not consumed by Ga 5:15 *991*
he take c of the church of God?), 1Tm 3:5 *1959*
Take c, brethren, that there Heb 3:12 *991*
AND I DID NOT C FOR THEM, Heb 8:9 *272*

CARED

He encircled him, He c for him, Dt 32:10 995
and he had neither c for his feet, 2Sa 19:24 6213a
I c for you in the wilderness, In Hos 13:5 3045
a letter of Christ, c for by us, 2Co 3:3 *1247*

CAREFREE

of a c multitude was with her; Ezk 23:42 7961

CAREFUL

"Be c that you do not speak to Gn 31:24 8104
'Be c not to speak either good or Gn 31:29 8104
"Tell Aaron and his sons to be c Lv 22:2 5144a
"Must I not be c to speak what Nu 23:12 8104
shall be c to present My offering, Nu 28:2 8104
will be afraid of you. So be very c; Dt 2:4 8104
should listen and be c to do *it,* Dt 6:3 8104
c to observe all this commandment Dt 6:25 8104
you today you shall be c to do, Dt 8:1 8104
"For if you are c to keep all Dt 11:22 8104
and you shall be c to do all the Dt 11:32 8104
"Be c that you do not offer your Dt 12:13 8104
"Be c that you do not forsake the Dt 12:19 8104
"Be c to listen to all these Dt 12:28 8104
command you, you shall be c to do; Dt 12:32 8104
be c to observe these statutes. Dt 16:12 8104
and you shall be c to observe Dt 17:10 8104
"You shall be c to perform what Dt 23:23 8104
"Be c against an infection of Dt 24:8 8104
them, so you shall be c to do. Dt 24:8 8104
You shall therefore be c to do Dt 26:16 8104
being c to do all His commandments Dt 28:1 8104
"If you are not c to observe all Dt 28:58 8104
and be c to observe all the words Dt 31:12 8104
be c to do according to all the Jos 1:7 8104
so that you may be c to do Jos 1:8 8104
"Only be very c to observe the Jos 22:5 8104
be c not to drink wine or strong Jg 13:4 8104
'If your sons are c of their way, 1Ki 2:4 8104
been c for us with all this care; 2Ki 4:13 2729
But Jehu was not c to walk in the 2Ki 10:31 8104
if you are c to observe the 1Ch 22:13 8104
be very c what you do, for the 2Ch 19:7 8104
"Be c, do not turn to evil, Jb 36:21 8104
they c to observe My ordinances, Ezk 20:21 8104
be c to observe My ordinances. Ezk 36:27 8104
must be c how he builds on it. 1Co 3:10 *991*
Therefore be c how you walk, not Eph 5:15 *991, 199*
will be c to engage in good deeds. Ti 3:8 *5431*
to you made c searches and inquiries, 1Pe 1:10 *1567a, 1830*

CAREFULLY

But Moses searched c for the goat Lv 10:16 1875
"So watch yourselves c, Dt 4:15 3966
may learn them and observe them c. Dt 5:1 6213a
judgments which you shall c observe Dt 12:1 6213a
to observe c all this commandment Dt 15:5 6213a
by c observing all the words of Dt 17:19 6213a
c observe all this commandment which Dt 19:9 6213a
you today, to observe *them* c, Dt 28:13 6213a
command your sons to observe c, Dt 32:46 6213a
"Listen c, my daughter. Ru 2:8 3808
I looked at him c in the morning, 1Ki 3:21 995
"Listen c to my speech, And let Jb 13:17 8085
"Listen c to my speech, And let Jb 21:2 8085
And you will look c for his place and Ps 37:10 995
Consider c what is before you, Pr 23:1 995
you plant *it* you c fence *it* in, Is 17:11 5473
Listen c to Me, and eat what is Is 55:2 8085
"Go and search c for the Child; Mt 2:8 *199*
unless they c wash their hands, Mk 7:3 *4435*
everything c from the beginning, Lk 1:3 *199*
and search c until she finds it? Lk 15:8 *1960*
But examine everything *c;* 1Th 5:21

CARELESS

But a fool is arrogant and c. Pr 14:16 982
he who is c of conduct will die. Pr 19:16 959
abundant food and c ease, Ezk 16:49 8252
every c word that people speak, Mt 12:36 *692*

CARES

for which the LORD your God c; Dt 11:12 1875
No one c for my soul. Ps 142:4 1875
And he who c for his master will Pr 27:18 8104
no one c for her." Jer 30:17 1875
"As a shepherd c for his herd in Ezk 34:12 1243
tenderly c for her own children. 1Th 2:7 *2282*
on Him, because He c for you. 1Pe 5:7 *3199*

CARESSES

Let us delight ourselves with c. Pr 7:18 159

CARESSING

Isaac was c his wife Rebekah. Gn 26:8 6711

CARETAKER

They made me c of the vineyards, SS 1:6 5201

CARETAKERS

He entrusted the vineyard to c. SS 8:11 5201

CARGO

and they threw the c which was in Jon 1:5 3627
the ship was to unload its c. Ac 21:3 *1117*
not only of the c and the ship, Ac 27:10 *5413*
they began to jettison the c; Ac 27:18 *1546*

CARGOES

no one buys their c any more Rv 18:11 *1117*
c of gold and silver and precious Rv 18:12 *1117*
and c of horses and chariots Rv 18:13

CARING

without fear, c for themselves; Jude 1:12 *4165*

CARITES

of the C and of the guard, 2Ki 11:4 3746
C and the guards and all the people 2Ki 11:19 3746

CARKAS

Bigtha, Abagtha, Zethar and C, Es 1:10 3752

CARMEL

the king of Jokneam in C, Jos 12:22 3760
Maon, C and Ziph and Juttah, Jos 15:55 3760
and it reached to C on the west Jos 19:26 3760
"Saul came to C, and behold, he 1Sa 15:12 3760
in Maon whose business was in C; 1Sa 25:2 3760
he was shearing his sheep in C 1Sa 25:2 3760
"Go up to C, visit Nabal and 1Sa 25:5 3760
all the days they were in C. 1Sa 25:7 3760
of David came to Abigail at C, 1Sa 25:40 3760
to me all Israel at Mount C, 1Ki 18:19 3760
the prophets together at Mount C. 1Ki 18:20 3760
Elijah went up to the top of C; 1Ki 18:42 3760
He went from there to Mount C, 2Ki 2:25 3760
came to the man of God to Mount C. 2Ki 4:25 3760
"Your head crowns you like C, SS 7:5 3760
Bashan and C lose *their foliage.* Is 33:9 3760
it, The majesty of C and Sharon. Is 35:2 3760
mountains, Or like C by the sea. Jer 46:18 3760
and he will graze on C and Bashan, Jer 50:19 3760
And the summit of C dries up." Am 1:2 3760
they hide on the summit of C, Am 9:3 3760
Bashan and C wither; Na 1:4 3760

CARMELITE

Abigail the widow of Nabal the C. 1Sa 30:5 3761
Abigail the widow of Nabal the C. 2Sa 2:2 3761
Abigail the widow of Nabal the C; 2Sa 3:3 3761
Hezro the C, Paarai the Arbite, 2Sa 23:35
Hezro the C, Naarai the son of 1Ch 11:37

CARMELITESS

Jezreelitess, and Abigail the C, 1Sa 27:3 3761
was Daniel, by Abigail the C; 1Ch 3:1 3762

CARMI

Hanoch and Pallu and Hezron and C. Gn 46:9 3756
Hanoch and Pallu, Hezron and C; Ex 6:14 3756
of C, the family of the Carmites. Nu 26:6 3756
the ban, for Achan, the son of C, Jos 7:1 3756
and Achan, son of C, Jos 7:18 3756
The son of C *was* Achar, the *1Ch 2:7* 3756
of Judah *were* Perez, Hezron, C, 1Ch 4:1 3756
Hanoch and Pallu, Hezron and C. 1Ch 5:3 3756

CARMITES

of Carmi, the family of the C. Nu 26:6 3757

CARNAGE

And set them apart for a day of c! Jer 12:3 2028

CARNALLY

'Now if a man lies c with a woman Lv 19:20 7902, 2233

CAROUSE

deceptions, as they c with you, 2Pe 2:13 *4910*

CAROUSING

the day, not in c and drunkenness, Ro 13:13 *2970*
envying, drunkenness, c, Ga 5:21 *2970*
c, drinking parties and abominable 1Pe 4:3 *2970*

CARPENTER

"Is not this the c, the son of Mk 6:3 *5045*

CARPENTER'S

"Is not this the c son? Mt 13:55 *5045*

CARPENTERS

cedar trees and c and stonemasons; 2Sa 5:11 2796, 6086
it out to the c and the builders who 2Ki 12:11 2796, 6086
to the c and the builders and the 2Ki 22:6 2796
with cedar trees, masons and c, 1Ch 14:1 2796, 6086
and masons of stone and c, 1Ch 22:15 2796, 6086
and they hired masons and c to 2Ch 24:12 2796
They in turn gave *it* to the c and 2Ch 34:11 2796
gave money to the masons and c, Ezr 3:7 2796

CARPETS

donkeys, You who sit on *rich* c, Jg 5:10 4055
work, and in c of many colors Ezk 27:24 1595

CARPUS

which I left at Troas with C, 2Tm 4:13 *2591*

CARRIED

and the sons of Israel c their Gn 46:5 5375
sons c him to the land of Canaan and Gn 50:13 5375
that with them the table may be c. Ex 25:28 5375
sides of the altar when it is c. Ex 27:7 5375
So they came forward and c them Lv 10:5 5375
which they c on the shoulder. Nu 7:9 5375
c it on a pole between two *men,* Nu 13:23 5375
saw how the LORD your God c you, Dt 1:31 5375
the sons of Levi who c the ark of Dt 31:9 5375
Levites who c the ark of the covenant Dt 31:25 5375
them, He c them on His pinions. Dt 32:11 5375
c the ark came into the Jordan, Jos 3:15 5375
And the priests who c the ark of Jos 3:17 5375
and they c them over with them to Jos 4:8 5674a
priests who c the ark of the covenant Jos 4:9 5375
For the priests who c the ark were Jos 4:10 5375
priests who c the ark of the covenant Jos 4:18 5375
the Levitical priests who c the ark Jos 8:33 5375
the people who had c the tribute. Jg 3:18 5375
c them up to the top of the mountain Jg 16:3 5927
who danced, whom they c away. Jg 21:23 1497
and from there they c the ark of 1Sa 4:4 5375
and has not c out My commands." 1Sa 15:11 6965
c out the command of the LORD." 1Sa 15:13 6965
and c *them* off and went their way. 1Sa 30:2 5090a
so David and his men c them away. 2Sa 5:21 5375
c by the servants of Hadadezer and 2Sa 8:7 413
And ten young men who c Joab's 2Sa 18:15 5375
because you c the ark of the Lord 1Ki 2:26 5375
and they c away the stones of Ramah 1Ki 15:22 5375
and his conspiracy which he c out, 1Ki 16:20 7194
and c him up to the upper room 1Ki 17:19 5927
and they c *them* before him. 2Ki 5:23 5375
and c from there silver and gold 2Ki 7:8 5375
tent and c from there *also,* 2Ki 7:8 5375
c him in a chariot to Jerusalem and 2Ki 9:28 7392
and he c them captive to Assyria. 2Ki 15:29 1540
and c *the people of* it away into 2Ki 16:9 1540
c Israel away into exile to Assyria, 2Ki 17:6 1540
had c away to exile before them; 2Ki 17:11 1540
So Israel was c away into exile 2Ki 17:23 1540
"The nations whom you have c away 2Ki 17:26 1540
whom you c away into exile and 2Ki 17:27 1540
the priests whom they had c away 2Ki 17:28 1540
they had been c away into exile. 2Ki 17:33 1540
Then the king of Assyria c Israel 2Ki 18:11 1540
to this day will be c to Babylon; 2Ki 20:17 5375
and c their ashes to Bethel. 2Ki 23:4 5375
He c out from there all the 2Ki 24:13 3318
of the guard c away into exile. 2Ki 25:11 1540
and c the bronze to Babylon. 2Ki 25:13 5375
king of Assyria c away into exile; 1Ch 5:6 1540
and he c them away into exile, 1Ch 5:26 1540
LORD c Judah and Jerusalem away 1Ch 6:15 1540
c them into exile to Manahath, 1Ch 8:6 1540
he c them into exile; 1Ch 8:7 1540

And Judah was **c** away into exile to	**1Ch 9:1**	1540
They **c** the ark of God on a new	**1Ch 13:7**	7392
The sons of the Levites **c** the	**1Ch 15:15**	5375
c by the servants of Hadadezer and	**1Ch 18:7**	5921
had **c** away from all the nations:	**1Ch 18:11**	5375
all the work of Solomon was **c** out	**2Ch 8:16**	3559
the guards came and **c** them and	**2Ch 12:11**	5375
And they **c** away very much plunder.	**2Ch 14:13**	5375
and they **c** away large numbers of	**2Ch 14:15**	7617
and they **c** away the stones of	**2Ch 16:6**	5375
and **c** away all the possessions	**2Ch 21:17**	7617
and they defeated him and **c** away	**2Ch 28:5**	7617
The sons of Israel **c** away	**2Ch 28:8**	7617
Judah and **c** away captives.	**2Ch 28:17**	7617
and **c** *them* speedily to all the lay	**2Ch 35:13**	7323
and **c** him in the second chariot	**2Ch 35:24**	7392
the sword he **c** away to Babylon;	**2Ch 36:20**	1540
which Nebuchadnezzar had **c** away	**Ezr 1:7**	3318
of Babylon had **c** away to Babylon,	**Ezr 2:1**	1540
it be **c** out with all diligence!"	**Ezr 6:12**	5648
and their colleagues **c** out *the*	**Ezr 6:13**	5648
After him the Levites **c** out	**Ne 3:17**	2388
c out repairs for his district.	**Ne 3:17**	2388
After him their brothers **c** out	**Ne 3:18**	2388
men of the valley, **c** out repairs.	**Ne 3:22**	2388
After them Benjamin and Hasshub **c**	**Ne 3:23**	2388
c out repairs beside his house.	**Ne 3:23**	2388
Gate the priests **c** out repairs,	**Ne 3:28**	2388
Zadok the son of Immer **c** out repairs	**Ne 3:29**	2388
of the East Gate, **c** out repairs.	**Ne 3:29**	2388
son of Berechiah **c** out repairs in front	**Ne 3:30**	2388
c out repairs as far as the house	**Ne 3:31**	2388
and the merchants **c** out repairs.	**Ne 3:32**	2388
half of my servants **c** on the	**Ne 4:16**	6213a
those who **c** burdens took *their* load	**Ne 4:17**	5375
So we **c** on the work with half of	**Ne 4:21**	6213a
the king of Babylon had **c** away,	**Ne 7:6**	1540
not been, **C** from womb to tomb.'	**Jb 10:19**	2986
"While he is **c** to the grave, *Men*	**Jb 21:32**	2986
the spoil of Samaria will be **c** away	**Is 8:4**	5375
to this day will be **c** to Babylon;	**Is 39:6**	5375
And have been **c** from the womb;	**Is 46:3**	5375
will be **c** on *their* shoulders.	**Is 49:22**	5375
bore, And our sorrows He **c**;	**Is 53:4**	5445
daughters will be **c** in the arms.	**Is 60:4**	539
and **c** them all the days of old.	**Is 63:9**	5375
you will be **c** on the hip and	**Is 66:12**	5375
They must be **c**, Because they	**Jer 10:5**	5375
All Judah has been **c** into exile,	**Jer 13:19**	1540
into exile, Wholly **c** into exile.	**Jer 13:19**	1540
c out the purposes of His heart;	**Jer 23:20**	6965
Babylon had **c** away captive Jeconiah	**Jer 24:1**	1540
when he **c** into exile Jeconiah the son	**Jer 27:20**	1540
'They will be **c** to Babylon and	**Jer 27:22**	935
from this place and **c** to Babylon.	**Jer 28:3**	935
c *them* into exile in Babylon.	**Jer 39:9**	1540
c away into exile some of the poorest	**Jer 52:15**	1540
and **c** all their bronze to Babylon.	**Jer 52:17**	5375
Nebuchadnezzar **c** away into exile:	**Jer 52:28**	1540
c into exile 745 Jewish people;	**Jer 52:30**	1540
to which they will be **c** captive,	**Ezk 6:9**	7617
I went out in the dark *and* **c** *the*	**Ezk 12:7**	5375
and the wind **c** them away so that	**Da 2:35**	5376
slew those men who **c** up Shadrach,	**Da 3:22**	5559a
again and **c** on the king's business;	**Da 8:27**	6213a
"When the multitude is **c** away,	**Da 11:12**	5375
The thing itself will be **c** to	**Hos 10:6**	2986
Assyria, And oil is **c** to Egypt.	**Hos 12:1**	2986
"You also **c** along Sikkuth your	**Am 5:26**	5375
that strangers **c** off his wealth,	**Ob 1:11**	7617
She is stripped, she is **c** away,	**Na 2:7**	5927
Who have **c** out His ordinances;	**Zph 2:3**	6466
AND **C** AWAY OUR DISEASES."	**Mt 8:17**	*941*
to Him a paralytic, **c** by four men.	**Mk 2:3**	*142*
a dead man was being **c** out,	**Lk 7:12**	*1580*
died and was **c** away by the angels	**Lk 16:22**	*667*
He parted from them and was **c** up into	**Lk 24:51**	*1339*
"Sir, if you have **c** Him away,	**Jn 20:15**	*941*
mother's womb was being **c** along,	**Ac 3:2**	*941*
and they **c** her out and buried her	**Ac 5:10**	*1627*
c the sick out into the streets and	**Ac 5:15**	*1627*
"When they had **c** out all that	**Ac 13:29**	*5055*
even **c** from his body to the sick,	**Ac 19:12**	*667*
he was **c** by the soldiers	**Ac 21:35**	*941*
are being **c** out for this nation,	**Ac 24:2**	*1096*
was **c** away by their hypocrisy.	**Ga 2:13**	*4879*
He **c** out in Christ Jesus our Lord,	**Eph 3:11**	*4160*
and **c** about by every wind of	**Eph 4:14**	*4064*
Do not be **c** away by varied and	**Heb 13:9**	*3911*
c away and enticed by his own lust.	**Jas 1:14**	*1828*
have **c** out the desire of the Gentiles,	**1Pe 4:3**	*2716*
not **c** away by the error of	**2Pe 3:17**	*4879*
without water, **c** along by winds;	**Jude 1:12**	*3911*
And he **c** me away in the Spirit	**Rv 17:3**	*667*
And he **c** me away in the Spirit to	**Rv 21:10**	*667*

CARRIERS

were the **c** for your merchandise.	**Ezk 27:25**	7788

CARRIES

and he who **c** them shall wash his	**Lv 15:10**	5375
as a nurse **c** a nursing infant,	**Nu 11:12**	5375
you, just as a man **c** his son,	**Dt 1:31**	5375
like chaff which the storm **c** away?	**Jb 21:18**	1589
"The east wind **c** him away, and he	**Jb 27:21**	5375
the man who **c** out wicked schemes.	**Ps 37:7**	6213a
And **c** *it* off with no one to	**Is 5:29**	6403
storm **c** them away like stubble.	**Is 40:24**	5375
strong is he who **c** out His word.	**Jl 2:11**	6213a
'If a man **c** holy meat in the fold	**Hg 2:12**	5375
and *yet* none of you **c** out the Law?	**Jn 7:19**	*4160*
woman and of the beast that **c** her,	**Rv 17:7**	*941*

CARRION

and the pelican and the **c** vulture,	**Lv 11:18**	7360
the pelican, the **c** vulture,	**Dt 14:17**	7360

CARRY

c grain for the famine of your	**Gn 42:19**	935
c down to the man as a present,	**Gn 43:11**	3381
with food, as much as they can **c**,	**Gn 44:1**	5375
that Joseph had sent to **c** him,	**Gn 45:27**	5375
which Pharaoh had sent to **c** him.	**Gn 46:5**	5375
you shall **c** me out of Egypt and	**Gn 47:30**	5375
shall **c** my bones up from here."	**Gn 50:25**	5927
c my bones from here with you."	**Ex 13:19**	5927
the ark, to **c** the ark with them.	**Ex 25:14**	5375
for the poles to **c** the table.	**Ex 25:27**	5375
"Aaron shall **c** the names of	**Ex 28:29**	5375
and Aaron shall **c** the judgment of	**Ex 28:30**	5375
for poles with which to **c** it.	**Ex 30:4**	5375
which to **c** on their priesthood;	**Ex 31:10**	3547
on the sides of the ark, to **c** it.	**Ex 37:5**	5375
for the poles to **c** the table.	**Ex 37:14**	5375
them with gold, to **c** the table.	**Ex 37:15**	5375
for poles with which to **c** it.	**Ex 37:27**	5375
of the altar, with which to **c** it.	**Ex 38:7**	5375
and **c** the ashes outside the camp	**Lv 6:11**	3318
c your relatives away from the	**Lv 10:4**	5375
My judgments, so as to **c** them out,	**Lv 25:18**	6213a
commandments so as to **c** them out,	**Lv 26:3**	6213a
not **c** out all these commandments,	**Lv 26:14**	6213a
not to **c** out all My commandments,	**Lv 26:15**	6213a
They shall **c** the tabernacle and	**Nu 1:50**	5375
of Kohath shall come to **c** *them*,	**Nu 4:15**	5375
which the sons of Kohath are to **c**.	**Nu 4:15**	4853a
they shall **c** the curtains of the	**Nu 4:25**	5375
man by name the items he is to **c**.	**Nu 4:32**	4853a
'**C** them in your bosom as a nurse	**Nu 11:12**	5375
am not able to **c** all this people,	**Nu 11:14**	5375
set apart the tribe of Levi to **c** the ark	**Dt 10:8**	5375
priests who **c** the ark of the LORD,	**Jos 3:13**	5375
firm, and **c** them over with you and	**Jos 4:3**	5674a
"Command the priests who **c** the	**Jos 4:16**	5375
"Also seven priests shall **c** seven	**Jos 6:4**	5375
and let seven priests **c** seven	**Jos 6:6**	5375
incense, to **c** an ephod before Me;	**1Sa 2:28**	5375
"In that day I will **c** out against	**1Sa 3:12**	6965
to **c** the good news to the house of	**1Sa 31:9**	1319
Shall we **c** out his plan?	**2Sa 17:6**	6213a
not the man to **c** news this day,	**2Sa 18:20**	1309
but you shall **c** news another day;	**2Sa 18:20**	1319
you shall **c** no news today because	**2Sa 18:20**	1319
so that the LORD may **c** out His	**1Ki 2:4**	6965
there, and you shall **c** *them* away.	**1Ki 5:9**	5375
then I will **c** out My word with you	**1Ki 6:12**	6965
that the guards would **c** them and	**1Ki 14:28**	5375
will **c** you where I do not know;	**1Ki 18:12**	5375
take in their hand and **c** away.' "	**1Ki 20:6**	3947
"**C** him to his mother."	**2Ki 4:19**	5375
to **c** out the words of this	**2Ki 23:3**	6965
to **c** the good news to their idols	**1Ch 10:9**	1319
"No one is to **c** the ark of God	**1Ch 15:2**	5375
chose them to **c** the ark of God and	**1Ch 15:2**	5375
"Because you did not **c** *it* at	**1Ch 15:13**	
will no longer need to **c** the tabernacle	**1Ch 23:26**	5375
assigned 70,000 men to **c** loads and	**2Ch 2:2**	5449
you may **c** it up to Jerusalem."	**2Ch 2:16**	5927
70,000 of them to **c** loads and	**2Ch 2:18**	5449
more than they could **c**.	**2Ch 20:25**	4853a
and **c** the uncleanness out from the	**2Ch 29:5**	3318
it to **c** out to the Kidron valley.	**2Ch 29:16**	3318
those who **c** on the *king's* business,	**Es 3:9**	6213a
"Why does your heart **c** you away?	**Jb 15:12**	3947
I would **c** it on my shoulder,	**Jb 31:36**	5375
shepherd also, and **c** them forever.	**Ps 28:9**	5375
he dies he will **c** nothing away;	**Ps 49:17**	3947
labor that he can **c** in his hand.	**Ec 5:15**	1980
of the heavens will **c** the sound and	**Ec 10:20**	1980
c off over the brook of Arabim.	**Is 15:7**	5375
Whose feet used to **c** her to	**Is 23:7**	2986
And now do not **c** on as scoffers,	**Is 28:22**	3917b
They **c** their riches on the backs	**Is 30:6**	5375
lambs And **c** *them* in His bosom;	**Is 40:11**	5375
and the wind will **c** them away,	**Is 41:16**	5375
Who **c** about their wooden idol And	**Is 45:20**	5375
things that you **c** are burdensome,	**Is 46:1**	5385
I have done *it*, and I will **c** *you;*	**Is 46:4**	5375
it upon the shoulder *and* **c** it;	**Is 46:7**	5445
he will **c** out His good pleasure	**Is 48:14**	6213a
You who **c** the vessels of the LORD.	**Is 52:11**	5375
the wind will **c** all of them up,	**Is 57:13**	5375
and do not **c** any load on the	**Jer 17:21**	5375
and he will **c** them away as exiles	**Jer 20:4**	1540
we will certainly **c** out every word	**Jer 44:17**	6213a
They will **c** off for themselves	**Jer 49:29**	5375
sight *and* **c** *it* out in the dark.	**Ezk 12:6**	3318
And he will **c** off her wealth and	**Ezk 29:19**	5375
to **c** away silver and gold,	**Ezk 38:13**	5375
to **c** out a peaceful arrangement.	**Da 11:6**	6213a
pieces and go away, I will **c** away,	**Hos 5:14**	5375
to **c** out *his* bones from the house,	**Am 6:10**	3318
man's house and **c** off his property,	**Mt 12:29**	*726*
c here and there on their pallets those	**Mk 6:55**	*4064*
to **c** merchandise through the temple.	**Mk 11:16**	*1308*
to **c** out for Him the custom of the	**Lk 2:27**	*4160*
"**C** no money belt, no bag, no shoes;	**Lk 10:4**	*941*
"Whoever does not **c** his own cross	**Lk 14:27**	*941*
him the cross to **c** behind Jesus.	**Lk 23:26**	*5342*
for you to **c** your pallet."	**Jn 5:10**	*142*
they will **c** you out *as well*."	**Ac 5:9**	*1627*
to **c** your gift to Jerusalem;	**1Co 16:3**	*667*
not **c** out the desire of the flesh.	**Ga 5:16**	*5055*
that I might fully **c** out the	**Col 1:25**	*4137*

CARRYING

and **c** away my daughters like captives	**Gn 31:26**	5090a
and shall put it on the **c** bars.	**Nu 4:10**	4132
skin, and put them on the **c** bars.	**Nu 4:12**	4132
Gershonites, in serving and in **c**:	**Nu 4:24**	4853a
work of **c** in the tent of meeting.	**Nu 4:47**	4853a
everyone by his serving or **c**;	**Nu 4:49**	4853a
Merari, who were **c** the tabernacle,	**Nu 10:17**	5375
set out, **c** the holy *objects;*	**Nu 10:21**	5375
with the Levitical priests **c** it,	**Jos 3:3**	5375
who are **c** the ark of the covenant,	**Jos 3:8**	5375
the priests **c** the ark of the covenant	**Jos 3:14**	5375
the feet of the priests **c** the ark	**Jos 3:15**	5375
the seven priests **c** the seven	**Jos 6:8**	5375
The seven priests **c** the seven	**Jos 6:13**	5375
will meet you, one **c** three young goats,	**1Sa 10:3**	5375
another **c** three loaves of bread,	**1Sa 10:3**	5375
and another **c** a jug of wine;	**1Sa 10:3**	5375
the young man who was **c** his armor,	**1Sa 14:1**	5375
the young man who was **c** his armor,	**1Sa 14:6**	5375
and all the Levites with him **c** the	**2Sa 15:24**	5375
with camels **c** spices and very much	**1Ki 10:2**	5375
helping the Levites who were **c** the ark	**1Ch 15:26**	5375
the Levites who were **c** the ark,	**1Ch 15:27**	5375
retinue, with camels **c** spices and	**2Ch 9:1**	5375
negligent in **c** out this *matter;*	**Ezr 4:22**	5648
fro weeping, **c** *his* bag of seed,	**Ps 126:6**	5375
the sabbath day holy by not **c** a load	**Jer 17:27**	5375
meet you **c** a pitcher of water;	**Mk 14:13**	*941*
some men *were* **c** on a bed a man who	**Lk 5:18**	*5342*
meet you **c** a pitcher of water;	**Lk 22:10**	*941*
after **c** him out, they buried him.	**Ac 5:6**	*1627*
find me **c** on a discussion with anyone	**Ac 24:12**	*1256*
always **c** about in the body the	**2Co 4:10**	*4064*

CARSHENA

C, Shethar, Admatha, Tarshish,	**Es 1:14**	3771

CART

a **c** for *every* two of the leaders	**Nu 7:3**	5699
prepare a new **c** and two milch cows	**1Sa 6:7**	5699
the **c** and take their calves home,	**1Sa 6:7**	5699
of the LORD and place it on the **c**;	**1Sa 6:8**	5699
cows and hitched them to the **c**,	**1Sa 6:10**	5699
put the ark of the LORD on the **c**,	**1Sa 6:11**	5699
The **c** came into the field of	**1Sa 6:14**	5699
and they split the wood of the **c**	**1Sa 6:14**	5699
placed the ark of God on a new **c**	**2Sa 6:3**	5699
Abinadab, were leading the new **c**.	**2Sa 6:3**	5699
new **c** from the house of Abinadab,	**1Ch 13:7**	5699
and Uzza and Ahio drove the **c**.	**1Ch 13:7**	5699
And sin as if with **c** ropes;	**Is 5:18**	5699
Because the wheel of *his* **c** and his	**Is 28:28**	5699

CARTS

six covered **c** and twelve oxen,	**Nu 7:3**	5699
So Moses took the **c** and the oxen and	**Nu 7:6**	5699
Two **c** and four oxen he gave to the	**Nu 7:7**	5699
and four **c** and eight oxen he gave	**Nu 7:8**	5699

CARTWHEEL

Nor is the **c** driven over cummin;	**Is 28:27**	5699

CARVE

You who **c** a resting place for	**Is 22:16**	2710

CARVED

c *in the shape* of gourds and open	**1Ki 6:18**	4734
Then he **c** all the walls of the	**1Ki 6:29**	7049b
with **c** engravings of cherubim,	**1Ki 6:29**	6603
he **c** on them carvings of cherubim,	**1Ki 6:32**	7049b
He **c** *on it* cherubim, palm	**1Ki 6:35**	7049b
Then he set the **c** image of Asherah	**2Ki 21:7**	6459
and he **c** cherubim on the walls.	**2Ch 3:7**	6605b
Then he put the **c** image of the	**2Ch 33:7**	6459
the Asherim and the **c** images,	**2Ch 33:19**	6456
and Amon sacrificed to all the **c**	**2Ch 33:22**	6456
places, the Asherim, the **c** images and	**2Ch 34:3**	6456
also the Asherim, the **c** images and	**2Ch 34:4**	6456
and the **c** images into powder,	**2Ch 34:7**	6456
And now all its **c** work They smash	**Ps 74:6**	6603
is **c** ivory Inlaid with sapphires.	**SS 5:14**	6247
were **c** on the wall all around.	**Ezk 8:10**	2707
man in the room of his **c** images?	**Ezk 8:12**	4906
c with cherubim and palm trees;	**Ezk 41:18**	6213a
c on all the house all around.	**Ezk 41:19**	6213a
cherubim and palm trees were **c**,	**Ezk 41:20**	6213a
Also there were **c** on them, on the	**Ezk 41:25**	6213a
trees like those **c** on the walls;	**Ezk 41:25**	6213a
"I will cut off your **c** images And	**Mi 5:13**	6456
the idol when its maker has **c** it,	**Hab 2:18**	6458

CARVING

settings, and in the **c** of wood,	**Ex 31:5**	2799
settings and in the **c** of wood,	**Ex 35:33**	2799

CARVINGS

he carved on them **c** of cherubim,	**1Ki 6:32**	4734

CASE

the **c** of both parties shall come	**Ex 22:9**	1697
in smoke on the altar as *in the* **c**	**Lv 4:26**	
'Or in **c** a man has no kinsman, but	**Lv 25:26**	3588
'Now in **c** a countryman of yours	**Lv 25:35**	3588
brought their **c** before the LORD.	**Nu 27:5**	4941
The **c** that is too hard for you,	**Dt 1:17**	1697
has done in the **c** of Baal-peor,	**Dt 4:3**	
"If any **c** is too difficult for	**Dt 17:8**	1697
to you the verdict in the **c**.	**Dt 17:9**	4941
this is the **c** of the manslayer	**Dt 19:4**	1697
and murders him, so is this **c**.	**Dt 22:26**	1697
and the judges decide their **c**,	**Dt 25:1**	

state his **c** in the hearing of the elders Jos 20:4 1697
"Such is not the **c**. 2Sa 20:21 1697
in the **c** of Uriah the Hittite. 1Ki 15:5 1697
they *will be in any* **c** like all 2Ki 7:13
they *will be in any* **c** like all 2Ki 7:13
"Behold now, I have prepared my **c**; Jb 13:18 4941
for a **c** against him can we find?" Jb 19:28 1697
"I would present *my* **c** before Him Jb 23:4 4941
the **c** which I did not know. Jb 29:16 7379
behold Him, The **c** is before Him, Jb 35:14 1779
We cannot arrange *our* **c** because Jb 37:19
my **c** against an ungodly nation; Ps 43:1 7379
I will reprove you and state *the* **c** Ps 50:21
first to plead his **c** *seems* right, Pr 18:17 7379
For the LORD will plead their **c** And Pr 22:23 7379
He will plead their **c** against you. Pr 23:11 7379
not go out hastily to argue *your* **c**; Pr 25:8
Argue your **c** with your neighbor, Pr 25:9 7379
"Present your **c**," Is 41:21 7379
let us argue our **c** together; Is 43:26 8199
"Declare and set forth *your* **c**; Is 45:21
Who has a **c** against Me? Is 50:8
1167, 4941
that I would plead *my* **c** with You; Jer 12:1 7378
then in that **c** listen to the word Jer 42:15 3651
He will vigorously plead their **c** So Jer 50:34 7379
I am going to plead your **c** And Jer 51:36 7379
have seen my oppression; Judge my **c**. La 3:59 4941
with a writing **c** at his loins. Ezk 9:2 7083
at whose loins was the writing **c**. Ezk 9:3 7083
loins was the writing **c** reported, Ezk 9:11 7083
in **c** there may be a prolonging of Da 4:27 2006
For the LORD has a **c** against the Hos 4:1 7379
plead your **c** before the mountains, Mi 6:1 7378
LORD has a **c** against His people; Mi 6:2 7379
my **c** and executes justice for me. Mi 7:9 7379
"In their **c** the prophecy of Mt 13:14
in **c** he should come suddenly and find Mk 13:36 *3361*
"For in this **c** the saying is Jn 4:37
"So in the present **c**, Ac 5:38 *3568*
For *in the* **c** *of* many who had Ac 8:7
determine his **c** by a more thorough Ac 23:15
3588, 4012
down, I will decide your **c**." Ac 24:22
3588, 2596
laid Paul's **c** before the king, Ac 25:14
3588, 2596
In this **c**, moreover, it is 1Co 4:2 *5602*
he has a **c** against his neighbor, 1Co 6:1 *4229*
that it will be done so in my **c**; 1Co 9:15 *1722*
in this **c** has no glory because 2Co 3:10 *3313*
in whose **c** the god of this world 2Co 4:4 *1722*
may not be made empty in this **c**, 2Co 9:3 *3313*
but in **c** I am delayed, *I write* so 1Tm 3:15 *1437*
For in the **c** of those who have Heb 6:4
this **c** mortal men receive tithes, Heb 7:8 *5602*
but in that **c** one *receives them,* Heb 7:8 *1563*

CASES
'Hear *the* **c** between your fellow Dt 1:16
being **c** of dispute in your courts, Dt 17:8 1697
is not under bondage in such **c**, 1Co 7:15

CASIPHIA
the leading man at the place **C**; Ezr 8:17 3703
temple servants at the place **C**, Ezr 8:17 3703

CASLUH
Pathrus, **C**, from which the 1Ch 1:12 3695

CASLUHIM
and Pathrusim and **C** Gn 10:14 3695

CASSIA
and of **c** five hundred, according Ex 30:24 6916
with myrrh and aloes *and* **c**; Ps 45:8 7102
wrought iron, **c** and sweet cane Ezk 27:19 6916

CAST
born you are to **c** into the Nile, Ex 1:22 7993
his army He has **c** into the sea; Ex 15:4 3384
shall **c** four gold rings for it and Ex 25:12 3332
and you shall **c** five sockets of Ex 26:37 3332
and he **c** four sockets of silver Ex 36:36 3332
He **c** four rings of gold for it Ex 37:3 3332
He **c** four gold rings for it Ex 37:13 3332
He **c** four rings on the four Ex 38:5 3332
c it beside the altar eastward, Lv 1:16 7993
shall **c** lots for the two goats, Lv 16:8 5414
and **c** it into the midst of the Nu 19:6 7993
"But we have **c** them down, Heshbon Nu 21:30 3384
and **c** them into another land, Dt 29:28 7993
I will **c** lots for you here Jos 18:6 3384
then I will **c** lots for you here Jos 18:8 7993
And Joshua **c** lots for them in Jos 18:10 7993
"**C** *lots* between me and Jonathan 1Sa 14:42 5307
one will not be **c** out from him. 2Sa 14:14 5080
c stones and threw dust at him. 2Sa 16:13 5619
They took Absalom and **c** him 2Sa 18:17 7993
c up a siege ramp against the city, 2Sa 20:15 8210
Now he made the sea of **c** *metal* ten 1Ki 7:23 3332
were in two rows, **c** with the rest. 1Ki 7:24 3332
beneath the basin *were* **c** supports 1Ki 7:30 3332
spokes, and their hubs were all **c**. 1Ki 7:33 3332
and he set the sea *of* **c** *metal* on 1Ki 7:39
of the Jordan the king **c** them, 1Ki 7:46 3332
My name, I will **c** out of My sight. 1Ki 9:7 7971
and have **c** Me behind your back 1Ki 14:9 7993
c out before the sons of Israel. 1Ki 21:26 3423
LORD has taken him up and **c** him on 2Ki 2:16 7993
"Take *him* up and **c** him into the 2Ki 9:25 7993
take and **c** him into the property, 2Ki 9:26 7993
and they **c** the man into the grave 2Ki 13:21 7993
and would not destroy them or **c** 2Ki 13:23 7993
He had **c** them out of His sight. 2Ki 17:20 7993
have **c** their gods into the fire, 2Ki 19:18 5414
And I will **c** off Jerusalem, this 2Ki 23:27 3988a
He **c** them out from His presence. 2Ki 24:20 7993
These also **c** lots just as their 1Ch 24:31 5307
They **c** lots for their duties, 1Ch 25:8 5307
They **c** lots, the small and the 1Ch 26:13 5307
they **c** lots *for* his son Zechariah, 1Ch 26:14 5307
Also he made the **c** *metal* sea, 2Ch 4:2 3332
were in two rows, **c** in one piece. 2Ch 4:3 3332
of the Jordan the king **c** them in 2Ch 4:17 3332
My name I will **c** out of My sight and 2Ch 7:20 7993
and **c** *them* into the brook Kidron. 2Ch 30:14 7993
And **c** Your law behind their backs Ne 9:26 7993
Likewise we **c** lots for the supply Ne 10:34 5307
but the rest of the people **c** lots Ne 11:1 5307
was **c** before Haman from day to day Es 3:7 5307
to destroy them and had **c** Pur, Es 9:24 5307
would even **c** *lots* for the orphans And Jb 6:27 5307
And will **c** off his flower like the Jb 15:33 7993
"When you are **c** down, you will Jb 22:29 8213
of my face they did not **c** down. Jb 29:24 5307
have **c** off the bridle before me. Jb 30:11 7971
"He has **c** me into the mire, And I Jb 30:19 3384
And **c** away their cords from us!" Ps 2:3 7993
eyes to **c** *us* down to the ground. Ps 17:11 5186
Upon You I was **c** from birth; Ps 22:10 7993
And for my clothing they **c** lots. Ps 22:18 5307
To **c** down the afflicted and the Ps 37:14 5307
And you **c** My words behind you. Ps 50:17 7993
not **c** me away from Your presence And Ps 51:11 7993
C your burden upon the LORD and Ps 55:22 7993
of wickedness, **c** them forth, Ps 56:7 6405
c me off in the time of old age; Ps 71:9 7993
You **c** them down to destruction. Ps 73:18 5307
horse were **c** into a dead sleep. Ps 76:6 7290a
But You have **c** off and rejected, Ps 89:38 2186a
And **c** his throne to the ground. Ps 89:44 4048
have lifted me up and **c** me away. Ps 102:10 7993
c them down in the wilderness, Ps 106:26 5307
c their seed among the nations And Ps 106:27 5307
May they be **c** into the fire, Into Ps 140:10 5307
are the victims she has **c** down, Pr 7:26 5307
The lot is **c** into the lap, But its Pr 16:33 2904
The **c** lot puts an end to strife Pr 18:18
C your bread on the surface of the Ec 11:1 7971
In that day men will **c** away to the Is 2:20 7993
"But you have been **c** out of your Is 14:19 7993
C your shadow like night at high Is 16:3 7896
And all those who **c** a line into Is 19:8 7993
To be **c** into a vast country; Is 22:18
Lay low *and* **c** to the ground, Is 25:12 5060
He has **c** *it* down to the earth with Is 28:2 5117
every man will **c** away his silver idols Is 31:7 3988a
He has **c** the lot for them, And Is 34:17 5307
have **c** their gods into the fire, Is 37:19 5414
C all my sins behind Your back. Is 38:17 7993
a god or **c** an idol to no profit? Is 44:10 5258a
c up a siege against Jerusalem. Jer 6:6 8210
them, They shall be **c** down," Jer 6:15 3782
"I will **c** you out of My Jer 7:15 7993
as I have **c** out all your brothers, Jer 7:15 7993
'Cut off your hair and **c** *it* away, Jer 7:29 7993
have **c** down our dwellings.'" Jer 9:19 7993
c into a land that they had not known Jer 22:28 7993
and **c** you away from My presence, Jer 23:39 5203
and **c** his dead body into the Jer 26:23 7993
Then I will also **c** off all the Jer 31:37 3988a
and his dead body shall be **c** out Jer 36:30 7993
Then they took Jeremiah and **c** him Jer 38:6 7993
whom they have **c** into the cistern; Jer 38:9 7993
with him slaughtered them *and* **c** Jer 41:7
where Ishmael had **c** all the corpses Jer 41:9 7993
He **c** them out from His presence. Jer 52:3 7993
He has **c** from heaven to earth The La 2:1 7993
when they **c** up ramps and build Ezk 17:17 8210
"**C** away from you all your Ezk 18:31 7993
It was **c** down to the ground; Ezk 19:12 7993
'**C** away, each of you, the Ezk 20:7 7993
they did not **c** away the detestable Ezk 20:8 7993
against the gates, to **c** up ramps, Ezk 21:22 8210
Me and **c** Me behind your back, Ezk 23:35 7993
you, **c** up a ramp against you Ezk 26:8 8210
They will **c** dust on their heads, Ezk 27:30 5927
Therefore I have **c** you as profane Ezk 28:16 2490c
I **c** you to the ground; Ezk 28:17 7993
I will **c** you on the open field. Ezk 32:4 2904
be **c** into the midst of a furnace Da 3:6 7412
shall be **c** into the midst of a furnace Da 3:11 7412
you will immediately be **c** into the Da 3:15 7412
in order to **c** *them* into the Da 3:20 7412
and were **c** into the midst of the Da 3:21 7412
"Was it not three men we **c** bound Da 3:24 7412
shall be **c** into the lions' den. Da 6:7 7412
is to be **c** into the lions' den?" Da 6:12 7412
in and **c** into the lions' den. Da 6:16 7412
accused Daniel, and they **c** them, Da 6:24 7412
will come, **c** up a siege ramp Da 11:15 8210
My God will **c** them away Because Hos 9:17 3988a
them bare and **c** *them* away; Jl 1:7 7993
have also **c** lots for My people, Jl 3:3 3032
And you will be **c** to Harmon," Am 4:3 7993
And **c** righteousness down to the earth Am 5:7 5117
will **c** them forth in silence." Am 8:3 7993
And **c** lots for Jerusalem Ob 1:11 3032
let us **c** lots so we may learn on Jon 1:7 5307
So they **c** lots and the lot fell on Jon 1:7 5307
"For You had **c** me into the Jon 2:3 7993
You will **c** all their sins Into Mi 7:19 7993
They **c** lots for her honorable men, Na 3:10 3032
and **c** the lead weight on its opening. Zch 5:8 7993
her And **c** her wealth into the sea; Zch 9:4 5221
vine in the field **c** *its grapes,*" Mal 3:11 7921
and in Your name **c** out demons, Mt 7:22 *1544b*
be **c** out into the outer darkness; Mt 8:12 *1544b*
He **c** out the spirits with a word, Mt 8:16 *1544b*
"If You *are going to* **c** us out, Mt 8:31 *1544b*
After the demon was **c** out, Mt 9:33 *1544b*
unclean spirits, to **c** them out, Mt 10:1 *1544b*
cleanse *the* lepers, **c** out demons. Mt 10:8 *1544b*
If I by Beelzebul **c** out demons, Mt 12:27 *1544b*
by whom do your sons **c** *them* out? Mt 12:27 *1544b*
"But if I **c** out demons by the Mt 12:28 *1544b*
is like a dragnet **c** into the sea, Mt 13:47 *906*
and be **c** into the eternal fire. Mt 18:8 *906*
eyes and be **c** into the fiery hell. Mt 18:9 *906*
'Be taken up and **c** into the sea,' Mt 21:21 *906*
diseases, and **c** out many demons; Mk 1:34 *1544b*
authority to **c** out the demons. Mk 3:15 *1544b*
"How can Satan **c** out Satan? Mk 3:23 *1544b*
c the demon out of her daughter. Mk 7:26 *1544b*
I told Your disciples to **c** it out, Mk 9:18 *1544b*
neck, he had been **c** into the sea. Mk 9:42 *906*
your two feet, to be **c** into hell, Mk 9:45 *906*
two eyes, to be **c** into hell, Mk 9:47 *1544b*
'Be taken up and **c** into the sea,' Mk 11:23 *906*
whom He had **c** out seven demons. Mk 16:9 *1544b*
in My name they will **c** out demons, Mk 16:17 *1544b*
begged Your disciples to **c** it out, Lk 9:40 *1544b*
that I **c** out demons by Beelzebul. Lk 11:18 *1544b*
if I by Beelzebul **c** out demons, Lk 11:19 *1544b*
by whom do your sons **c** them out? Lk 11:19 *1544b*
"But if I **c** out demons by the Lk 11:20 *1544b*
has authority to **c** into hell; Lk 12:5 *1685*
come to **c** fire upon the earth; Lk 12:49 *906*
I **c** out demons and perform cures Lk 13:32 *1544b*
one also they wounded and **c** out. Lk 20:12 *1544b*
And they **c** lots, dividing up His Lk 23:34 *906*
to Me I will certainly not **c** out. Jn 6:37 *1544b*
of this world will be **c** out. Jn 12:31 *1544b*
them, and **c** them into the fire and Jn 15:6 *906*
us not tear it, but **c** lots for it, Jn 19:24 *2975*
AND FOR MY CLOTHING THEY **C** LOTS." Jn 19:24 *906*
"**C** the net on the right-hand side Jn 21:6 *906*
So they **c**, and then they Jn 21:6 *906*
to death I **c** my vote against them. Ac 26:10 *2702*
they **c** four anchors from the stern Ac 27:29 *4496*
"**C** OUT THE BONDWOMAN AND HER Ga 4:30 *1544b*
but **c** them into hell and committed 2Pe 2:4 *5020*
to **c** some of you into prison, Rv 2:10 *906*
and will **c** their crowns before the Rv 4:10 *906*

CASTANETS
harps, tambourines, **c** and cymbals. 2Sa 6:5 4517

CASTER
Or a skillful **c** of spells. Ps 58:5 2266

CASTING
talents of silver were for **c** the sockets Ex 38:27 3332
nations which I am **c** out before you Lv 18:24 7971
all of them had one **c**, 1Ki 7:37 4165
his brother, **c** a net into the sea; Mt 4:18 *906*
garments among themselves by **c** lots Mt 27:35 *906*
of Simon, **c** a net in the sea; Mk 1:16 *293a*
preaching and **c** out the demons. Mk 1:39 *1544b*
And they were **c** out many demons Mk 6:13 *1544b*
someone **c** out demons in Your name, Mk 9:38 *1544b*
among themselves, **c** lots for them Mk 15:24 *906*
someone **c** out demons in Your name; Lk 9:49 *1544b*
And He was **c** out a demon Lk 11:14 *1544b*
And **c** off the anchors, they left Ac 27:40 *4014*
c all your anxiety on Him, 1Pe 5:7 *1977*
c up their own shame like foam; Jude 1:13 *1890*

CASTLE
in the **c** of the king's house with 2Ki 15:25 759

CASTS
or one who **c** a spell, or a medium, Dt 18:11 2266
He **c** forth His ice as fragments; Ps 147:17 7993
Laziness **c** into a deep sleep, And Pr 19:15 5307
the ground, He **c** it to the dust. Is 26:5 5060
As for the idol, a craftsman **c** it, Is 40:19 5258a
"He **c** out the demons by the ruler Mt 9:34 *1544b*
"This man **c** out demons only by Mt 12:24 *1544b*
"If Satan **c** out Satan, he is Mt 12:26 *1544b*
"He **c** out the demons by the ruler Mk 3:22 *1544b*
a man who **c** seed upon the soil; Mk 4:26 *906*
"He **c** out demons by Beelzebul, Lk 11:15 *1544b*
but perfect love **c** out fear, 1Jn 4:18 *906*
as a fig tree **c** its unripe figs Rv 6:13 *906*

CASUALTIES
who inflicted him with heavy **c**. 2Ch 28:5 4347

CATCH
c his wife from the daughters of Shiloh Jg 21:21 2414
He lurks to **c** the afflicted; Ps 10:9 2414
let the net which he hid **c** himself; Ps 35:8 3920
"**C** the foxes for us, The little SS 2:15 270
They set a trap, They **c** men. Jer 5:26 3920
these things their **c** is large, Hab 1:16 2506
and let down your nets for a **c**." Lk 5:4 *61*
c of fish which they had taken; Lk 5:9 *61*
c *Him* in something He might say. Lk 11:54 *2340*
might **c** Him in some statement, Lk 20:20 *1949*
And they were unable to **c** Him in a Lk 20:26 *1949*
of the boat and you will find *a* **c**." Jn 21:6

CATCHER
snare of a bird **c** is in all his ways, Hos 9:8 3352

CATCHES
in hunting **c** a beast or a bird Lv 17:13 6679

He c the afflicted when he draws Ps 10:9 2414
C THE WISE IN THEIR CRAFTINESS"; 1Co 3:19 *1405*

CATCHING

omen, and quickly c his word said, 1Ki 20:33 2480
from now on you will be c men." Lk 5:10 *2221*

CATERPILLAR

is gathered *as* the c gathers; Is 33:4 2625
And the c was devouring Your many Am 4:9 1501

CATTLE

c and creeping things and beasts Gn 1:24 929
kind, and the c after their kind, Gn 1:25 929
over the c and over all the earth, Gn 1:26 929
The man gave names to all the c, Gn 2:20 929
Cursed are you more than all c, Gn 3:14 929
and all the c after their kind, Gn 7:14 929
birds and c and beasts and every Gn 7:21 929
c that were with him in the ark; Gn 8:1 929
is with you, the birds, the c, Gn 9:10 929
and how your c have fared with me. Gn 30:29 4735
according to the pace of the c Gn 33:14 4399
and his livestock and all his c Gn 36:6 929
all spent, and the c are my lord's. Gn 47:18
4735, 929
the firstborn of the c as well. Ex 11:5 929
and all the firstborn of c. Ex 12:29 929
servant or your c or your sojourner Ex 20:10 929
first offspring from c and sheep. Ex 34:19 7794
or the carcass of unclean c or Lv 5:2 929
together two kinds of your c; Lv 19:19 929
a male without defect from the c, Lv 22:19 1241
'Even your c and the animals that Lv 25:7 929
destroy your c and reduce your number Lv 26:22 929
and the c of the Levites instead Nu 3:41 929
the c of the sons of Israel." Nu 3:41 929
Israel and the c of the Levites. Nu 3:45 929
and all their c and all their Nu 31:9 929
c and of the donkeys and of the sheep Nu 31:28 1241
fifty of the persons, of the c, Nu 31:30 1241
and 72,000 c, Nu 31:33 1241
and the c were 36,000, from which Nu 31:38 1241
and 36,000 c, Nu 31:44 1241
our livestock and all our c shall Nu 32:26 929
shall be for their c and for their herds Nu 35:3 929
ox or your donkey or any of your c Dt 5:14 929
barren among you or among your c. Dt 7:14 929
grass in your fields for your c, Dt 11:15 929
its c with the edge of the sword. Dt 13:15 929
offspring of your c and in the produce Dt 30:9 929
and your c shall remain in the Jos 1:14 4735
its c as plunder for yourselves. Jos 8:2 929
Israel took only the c and the Jos 8:27 929
spoil of these cities and the c, Jos 11:14 929
their pasture lands for our c." Jos 21:2 929
the c and all that they found; Jg 20:48 929
and he took away the sheep, the c, 1Sa 27:9 1241
had captured all the sheep and the c 1Sa 30:20 1241
not have to kill some of the c." 1Ki 18:5 929
or for the c that followed them. 2Ki 3:9 929
you and your c and your beasts. 2Ki 3:17 4735
because their c had increased in 1Ch 5:9 4735
They took away their c: 1Ch 5:21 4735
charge of the c which were 1Ch 27:29 1241
charge of the c in the valleys. 1Ch 27:29 1241
c and sheepfolds for the flocks. 2Ch 32:28 929
silver and gold, with goods and c, Ezr 1:4 929
with gold, with goods, with c and Ezr 1:6 929
And over our c as they please, Ne 9:37 929
firstborn of our sons and of our c, Ne 10:36 929
The c also, concerning what is Jb 36:33 4735
Mine, The c on a thousand hills. Ps 50:10 929
their c also to the hailstones And Ps 78:48 1165
the grass to grow for the c, Ps 104:14 929
He does not let their c decrease. Ps 107:38 929
Let our c bear Without mishap and Ps 144:14 441a
Beasts and all c; Ps 148:10 929
of rams And the fat of fed c; Is 1:11 4806
Killing of c and slaughtering of sheep, Is 22:13 1241
consigned to the beasts and the c. Is 46:1 929
c which go down into the valley, Is 63:14 929
the lowing of the c is not heard; Jer 9:10 4735
their many c for booty, Jer 49:32 4735
all its c from beside many waters; Ezk 32:13 929
who have acquired c and goods, Ezk 38:12 4735
gold, to take away c and goods, Ezk 38:13 4735
and you be given grass to eat like c Da 4:25 8450
will be given grass to eat like c, Da 4:32 8450
and began eating grass like c, Da 4:33 8450
He was given grass to eat like c, Da 5:21 8450
The herds of c wander aimlessly Jl 1:18 1241
And there be no c in the stalls, Hab 3:17 1241
the ground produces, on men, on c, Hg 1:11 929
multitude of men and c within it. Zch 2:4 929
the c that will be in those camps. Zch 14:15 929
and his sons and his c?" Jn 4:12 *2353*
flour and wheat and c and sheep, Rv 18:13 *2934*

CAUGHT

ram c in the thicket by his horns; Gn 22:13 270
Laban c up with Jacob. Gn 31:25 5381
She c him by his garment, Gn 39:12 8610
stretched out his hand and c it, Ex 4:4 2388
the thief is c while breaking in and Ex 22:2 4672
the man's house, if the thief is c, Ex 22:7 4672
"If the thief is not c, Ex 22:8 4672
and she has not been c in the act, Nu 5:13 8610
"If a man is c kidnapping any of Dt 24:7 4672
He spread His wings and c them, Dt 32:11 3947
and they pursued him and c him and Jg 1:6 270
went and c three hundred foxes, Jg 15:4 3920
but they c 5,000 of them on the Jg 20:45 5953b
And his head c fast in the oak, so 2Sa 18:9 2388
the hill, she c hold of his feet. 2Ki 4:27 2388
and they c him while he was hiding 2Ch 22:9 3920
has the falcon's eye c sight of it. Jb 28:7 7805
are c in the cords of affliction, Jb 36:8 3920
hid, their own foot has been c. Ps 9:15 3920
Let them be c in the plots which Ps 10:2 8610
Let them even be c in their pride, Ps 59:12 3920
will keep your foot from being c. Pr 3:26 3921
c with the words of your mouth, Pr 6:2 3920
will be c by *their own* greed. Pr 11:6 3920
like fish c in a treacherous net and Ec 9:12 270
They will even be snared and c." Is 8:15 3920
of the pit will be c in the snare; Is 24:18 3920
to shame, They are dismayed and c; Jer 8:9 3920
Or was he c among thieves? Jer 48:27 4672
of the pit Will be c in the snare; Jer 48:44 3920
for you and you were also c, Jer 50:24 3920
and c me by a lock of my head; Ezk 8:3 3947
him, and he will be c in My snare. Ezk 12:13 8610
him, and he will be c in My snare. Ezk 17:20 8610
hard all night and c nothing, Lk 5:5 *2983*
brought a woman c in adultery, Jn 8:3 *2638*
this woman has been c in adultery, Jn 8:4 *2638*
and that night they c nothing. Jn 21:3 *4084*
the fish which you have now c." Jn 21:10 *4084*
and when the ship was c *in it* Ac 27:15 *4884*
man was c up to the third heaven. 2Co 12:2 *726*
was c up into Paradise and heard 2Co 12:4 *726*
if anyone is c in any trespass, Ga 6:1 *4301*
c up together with them in the clouds 1Th 4:17 *726*
was c up to God and to His throne. Rv 12:5 *726*

CAUSE

I c My name to be remembered, Ex 20:24
and subverts the c of the just. Ex 23:8 1697
and c your sons *also* to play the Ex 34:16
and *so* c them to bear punishment Lv 22:16
eyes and c the soul to pine away; Lv 26:16
a curse will go into her and c Nu 5:24
a curse will go into her and c Nu 5:27
he will c Israel to inherit it. Dt 1:38
nor shall he c the people to Dt 17:16
"The LORD shall c your enemies who Dt 28:7 5414
"The LORD shall c you to be Dt 28:25 5414
David to death without a c?" 1Sa 19:5 2600
and may He see and plead my c and 1Sa 24:15 7379
this will not c grief or a 1Sa 25:31 1961
both by having shed blood without c 1Sa 25:31 2600
who has pleaded the c of my 1Sa 25:39 7379
any suit or c could come to me and 2Sa 15:4 4941
blood which Joab shed without c. 1Ki 2:31 2600
and maintain their c. 1Ki 8:45 4941
place, and maintain their c, 1Ki 8:49 4941
that He may maintain the c of His 1Ki 8:59 4941
and the c of His people Israel, 1Ki 8:59 4941
he be a c of guilt to Israel?" 1Ch 21:3 819
and maintain their c. 2Ch 6:35 4941
and maintain their c and 2Ch 6:39 4941
chosen to c My name to dwell.' Ne 1:9
and to c a disturbance in it. Ne 4:8 6213a
him to ruin him without c." Jb 2:3 2600
And I would place my c before God; Jb 5:8 1700
multiplies my wounds without c. Jb 9:17 2600
You c a driven leaf to tremble? Jb 13:25 6206
of your brothers without c, Jb 22:6 2600
"They c *the poor* to go about Jb 24:10
up to the wind *and* c me to ride; Jb 30:22
who without c was my adversary, Ps 7:4 7387
You have maintained my just c; Ps 9:4 1779
of the earth will no longer c terror. Ps 10:18 6206
Hear a just c, O LORD, give heed Ps 17:1 6664
without c will be ashamed. Ps 25:3 7387
without c they hid their net for me; Ps 35:7 2600
Without c they dug a pit for my soul. Ps 35:7 2600
me without c wink maliciously. Ps 35:19 2600
awake to my right And to my c, Ps 35:23 7379
You c us to turn back from Ps 44:10
For the c of truth and meekness Ps 45:4 1697
I will c Your name to be remembered Ps 45:17
the earth and c it to overflow; Ps 65:9
And c His face to shine upon Ps 67:1
Those who hate me without a c are Ps 69:4 2600
O God, *and* plead Your own c; Ps 74:22 7379
And c Your face to shine *upon us,* Ps 80:3
And c Your face to shine *upon us,* Ps 80:7
C Your face to shine *upon us,* and Ps 80:19
And c Your indignation toward us Ps 85:4
And fought against me without c. Ps 109:3 2600
will maintain his c in judgment. Ps 112:5 1697
Plead my c and redeem me; Ps 119:154 7379
Princes persecute me without c, Ps 119:161 2600
"There I will c the horn of David Ps 132:17
maintain the c of the afflicted And Ps 140:12 1779
us ambush the innocent without c; Pr 1:11 2600
not contend with a man without c, Pr 3:30 2600
Who has wounds without c? Pr 23:29 2600
against your neighbor without c, Pr 24:28 2600
a curse without c does not alight. Pr 26:2 2600
Do not let your speech c you to Ec 5:6
Who c a person to be indicted by a Is 29:21
And the LORD will c His voice of Is 30:30
of recompense for the c of Zion. Is 34:8 7379
will c the shadow on the stairway, Is 38:8 7725
State your c, that you may be Is 43:26
Perhaps you may c trembling. Is 47:12 6206
Assyrian oppressed them without c. Is 52:4 657
have been taken away without c?" Is 52:5 2600
So the Lord GOD will c Is 61:11
You c us to stray from Your ways And Is 63:17
They do not plead the c, Jer 5:28 1779
the cause, The c of the orphan, Jer 5:28 1779
time, And will c them distress, Jer 10:18 6887a
For to You have I committed my c. Jer 11:20 7379
Surely I will c the enemy to make Jer 15:11
"Then I will c your enemies to Jer 15:14
and I will c them to fall by the Jer 19:7
For to You I have set forth my c. Jer 20:12 7379
the c of the afflicted and needy; Jer 22:16 1779
My hand and c all the nations Jer 25:15
'There is no one to plead your c; Jer 30:13 1779
valley of Ben-hinnom to c their sons Jer 32:35
abomination, to c Judah to sin. Jer 32:35
I will c a righteous Branch of David Jer 33:15
"That I will c a trumpet blast Jer 49:2
My enemies without c Hunted me La 3:52 2600
Lord, You have pleaded my soul's c; La 3:58 7379
when I did not c him grief, Ezk 13:22 3510
"If I were to c wild beasts to Ezk 14:15
and I did not c their annihilation Ezk 20:17 6213a
when you c your sons to pass Ezk 20:31
the slaughter, to c it to consume, Ezk 21:28
Then c her to know all her Ezk 22:2
"That it may c wrath to come up Ezk 24:8
And I will c all the birds of the Ezk 32:4
I will c your hordes to fall; Ezk 32:12
c their rivers to run like oil," Ezk 32:14
And I will c showers to come down Ezk 34:26
and I will c you to be inhabited Ezk 36:11
'Yes, I will c men Ezk 36:12
nor will you c your nation to Ezk 36:15
and c you to walk in My statutes, Ezk 36:27 6213a
will c the cities to be inhabited, Ezk 36:33
I will c breath to enter you that Ezk 37:5
I will open your graves and c you Ezk 37:12
and c them to discern between the Ezk 44:23
to c a blessing to rest on your house. Ezk 44:30
He will c deceit to succeed Da 8:25
will c tens of thousands to fall; Da 11:12
will c them to rule over the many, Da 11:39
and *which* you did not c to grow, Jon 4:10
And c *me* to look on wickedness? Hab 1:3
and I will c the remnant of this Zch 8:12
behold, I will c the men to fall, Zch 11:6
and c them to be put to death. Mt 10:21 *2289*
than that he would c one of these Lk 17:2 *4624*
"Does this c you to stumble? Jn 6:61 *4624*
'THEY HATED ME WITHOUT A C.' Jn 15:25 *1431*
since there is no *real* c *for it,* Ac 19:40 *159a*
witnessed to My c at Jerusalem, Ac 23:11
3588, 4012
did that which is good become *a* c Ro 7:13
not a c of fear for good behavior, Ro 13:3 *5401*
keep your eye on those who c Ro 16:17 *4160*
will not c my brother to stumble. 1Co 8:13 *4624*
that we will c no hindrance to the 1Co 9:12 *1325*
with you without c to be afraid, 1Co 16:10 *870*
For if I c you sorrow, who then 2Co 2:2 *3076*
may c the giving of thanks to abound 2Co 4:15 *4052*
no c for offense in anything, 2Co 6:3 *4349*
on let no one c trouble for me, Ga 6:17 *3930*
so that my imprisonment in *the* c *of* Php 1:13
thinking to c me distress in my Php 1:17 *1453*
have shared my struggle in *the* c *of* Php 4:3
without c by his fleshly mind, Col 2:18 *1500*
and may the Lord c you to increase 1Th 3:12
4121, 4052
is no c for stumbling in him. 1Jn 2:10 *4625*
are the ones who c divisions, Jude 1:19 *592*
I will c *those* of the synagogue of Rv 3:9 *1325*
so that he might c her to be swept Rv 12:15 *4160*
and c as many as do not worship Rv 13:15 *4160*

CAUSED

the LORD God c to grow every tree Gn 2:9
So the LORD God c a deep sleep to Gn 2:21
c a wind to pass over the earth, Gn 8:1
when God c me to wander from my Gn 20:13
your God c *it* to happen to me." Gn 27:20
the LORD c all that he did to prosper Gn 39:3
He c their chariot wheels to Ex 14:25
"You are the ones who have c the Nu 16:41 4191
these c the sons of Israel, Nu 31:16 1961
until they have c you to perish. Dt 28:51
son of Nebat, who c Israel to sin. 1Ki 22:52
For the Lord had c the army of the 2Ki 7:6
and c the inhabitants of Jerusalem 2Ch 21:11
and have c Judah and the 2Ch 21:13
"May the God who has c His Ezr 6:12
the LORD had c them to rejoice, Ezr 6:22
foreign women c even him to sin. Ne 13:26
c the eyes of the widow to fail, Jb 31:16
Or have c its owners to lose their Jb 31:39
So that they c the cry of the poor Jb 34:28
And c the dawn to know its place, Jb 38:12
You c judgment to be heard from Ps 76:8
sea and c them to pass through Ps 78:13
And c waters to run down like Ps 78:16
He c the east wind to blow in the Ps 78:26
And He c His people to be very Ps 105:24
blood And c their fish to die. Ps 105:29
He c the storm to be still, So Ps 107:29 6965
end of all the groaning she has c. Is 21:2
But the LORD has c the iniquity of Is 53:6
Who c His glorious arm to go at Is 63:12
For the LORD has c her grief La 1:5 3013
The LORD has c to be forgotten The La 2:6
has c rampart and wall to lament; La 2:8
c the enemy to rejoice over you; La 2:17

He has **c** my flesh and my skin to — **La 3:4**
in that they **c** all their — **Ezk 20:26**
their idols and even **c** their sons, — **Ezk 23:37**
down to Sheol I **c** lamentations; — **Ezk 31:15** 56
He **c** me to pass among them — **Ezk 37:2**
c you to come up out of your graves, — **Ezk 37:13**
has **c** you to rule over them all. — **Da 2:38**
Then the king **c** Shadrach, Meshach — **Da 3:30**
host of heaven and **c** some of the host — **Da 8:10**
you have **c** many to stumble by the — **Mal 2:8**
had had a sickness **c** by a spirit; — **Lk 13:11**
But if any has **c** sorrow, he has — **2Co 2:5** *3076*
sorrow, he has **c** sorrow not to me, — **2Co 2:5** *3076*
I **c** you sorrow by my letter, — **2Co 7:8** *3076*
see that that letter **c** you sorrow, — **2Co 7:8** *3076*
c us to be born again to a living hope — **1Pe 1:3**

CAUSES
lovingkindness, He **c** it to happen. — **Jb 37:13**
He **c** the grass to grow for the — **Ps 104:14**
And nothing **c** them to stumble. — **Ps 119:165**
He **c** the vapors to ascend from the — **Ps 135:7**
He **c** His wind to blow and the — **Ps 147:18**
He who winks the eye **c** trouble, — **Pr 10:10** 5414
him and **c** his stern face to beam. — **Ec 8:1**
And as a garden **c** the things sown — **Is 61:11**
as fire **c** water to boil — **Is 64:2**
And He **c** the clouds to ascend from — **Jer 10:13**
And He **c** the clouds to ascend from — **Jer 51:16**
For if He **c** grief, Then He will — **La 3:32** 3013
while the transgression **c** horror, — **Da 8:13** 8074
make Jerusalem a cup that **c** reeling — **Zch 12:2**
for He **c** His sun to rise on *the* — **Mt 5:45** *393*
but whoever **c** one of these little — **Mt 18:6** *4624*
or your foot **c** you to stumble, — **Mt 18:8** *4624*
"If your eye **c** you to — **Mt 18:9** *4624*
"Whoever **c** one of these — **Mk 9:42** *4624*
"If your hand **c** you to stumble, — **Mk 9:43** *4624*
"If your foot **c** you to stumble, — **Mk 9:45** *4624*
"If your eye **c** you to — **Mk 9:47** *4624*
And we know that God **c** all things — **Ro 8:28** *4903*
but God who **c** the growth. — **1Co 3:7** *837*
if food **c** my brother to stumble, — **1Co 8:13** *4624*
c the growth of the body for the — **Eph 4:16** *4160*
bitterness springing up **c** trouble, — **Heb 12:15** *1776*
And he **c** all, the small and the — **Rv 13:16** *4160*

CAUSING
am staying, by **c** her son to die?" — **1Ki 17:20**
women **c** them to look with contempt — **Es 1:17**
C the omens of boasters to fail, — **Is 44:25**
diviners, **C** wise men to draw back And — **Is 44:25**
C well-being and creating calamity; — **Is 45:7** 6213a
c consternation among them. — **Ezk 3:15** 8074
c them to pass through *the fire.* — **Ezk 16:21**
with anyone or **c** a riot. — **Ac 24:12** *4160*
watered, but God was **c** the growth. — **1Co 3:6** *837*

CAUTIOUS
man is **c** and turns away from evil, — **Pr 14:16** 3372a

CAVALRY
kings, with horses, chariots, **c** and — **Ezk 26:7** 6571b
of **c** and wagons and chariots when — **Ezk 26:10** 6571b

CAVE
and he stayed in a **c**, — **Gn 19:30** 4631
the **c** of Machpelah which he owns, — **Gn 23:9** 4631
I give you the **c** that is in it. — **Gn 23:11** 4631
the field and **c** which was in it, — **Gn 23:17** 4631
buried Sarah his wife in the **c** — **Gn 23:19** 4631
field and the **c** that is in it, — **Gn 23:20** 4631
buried him in the **c** of Machpelah, — **Gn 25:9** 4631
bury me with my fathers in the **c** — **Gn 49:29** 4631
in the **c** that is in the field of — **Gn 49:30** 4631
the field and the **c** that is in it, — **Gn 49:32** 4631
and buried him in the **c** of the — **Gn 50:13** 4631
themselves in the **c** at Makkedah. — **Jos 10:16** 4631
hidden in the **c** at Makkedah." — **Jos 10:17** 4631
stones against the mouth of the **c**, — **Jos 10:18** 4631
"Open the mouth of the **c** and — **Jos 10:22** 4631
five kings out to me from the **c**." — **Jos 10:22** 4631
five kings out to him from the **c**: — **Jos 10:23** 4631
c where they had hidden themselves, — **Jos 10:27** 4631
stones over the mouth of the **c**, — **Jos 10:27** 4631
and escaped to the **c** of Adullam; — **1Sa 22:1** 4631
on the way, where there *was* a **c**; — **1Sa 24:3** 4631
in the inner recesses of the **c**. — **1Sa 24:3** 4631
And Saul arose, left the **c**, — **1Sa 24:7** 4631
of the **c** and called after Saul, — **1Sa 24:8** 4631
you today into my hand in the **c**, — **1Sa 24:10** 4631
harvest time to the **c** of Adullam, — **2Sa 23:13** 4631
and hid them by fifties in a **c**, — **1Ki 18:4** 4631
of the LORD by fifties in a **c**, — **1Ki 18:13** 4631
Then he came there to a **c** and — **1Ki 19:9** 4631
stood in the entrance of the **c**. — **1Ki 19:13** 4631
to David, into the **c** of Adullam, — **1Ch 11:15** 4631
Now it was a **c**, and a stone was — **Jn 11:38** *4693*

CAVERNS
In order to go into the **c** of the — **Is 2:21** 5366

CAVES
and the **c** and the strongholds. — **Jg 6:2** 4631
the people hid themselves in **c**, — **1Sa 13:6** 4631
one of the **c** or in another place; — **2Sa 17:9** 6354
Men will go into **c** of the rocks — **Is 2:19** 4631
watch-tower have become **c** forever, — **Is 32:14** 4631
All of them are trapped in **c**, — **Is 42:22** 2352b
in the **c** will die of pestilence. — **Ezk 33:27** 4631
With **c** for shepherds and folds for — **Zph 2:6** 3741
and **c** and holes in the ground. — **Heb 11:38** *4693*
hid themselves in the **c** and among — **Rv 6:15** *4693*

CEASE
And day and night Shall not **c**." — **Gn 8:22** 7673a
have them **c** from their labors!" — **Ex 5:5** 7673a
the thunder will **c** and — **Ex 9:29** 2308
the seventh day you shall **c** *from labor* — **Ex 23:12** 7673a
will never **c** *to be* in the land; — **Dt 15:11** 2308
you shall never **c** being slaves, — **Jos 9:23** 3772
brother Benjamin, or shall I **c**?" — **Jg 20:28** 2308
those who were hungry **c** *to hunger.* — **1Sa 2:5** 2308
"Do not **c** to cry to the LORD our — **1Sa 7:8** 2790b
my father will **c** *to be concerned* — **1Sa 9:5** 2308
"There the wicked **c** from raging, — **Jb 3:17** 2308
the enemy and the revengeful **c**. — **Ps 8:2** 7673a
C from anger and forsake wrath; — **Ps 37:8** 7503
wars to **c** to the end of the earth; — **Ps 46:9** 7673a
"**C** *striving* and know that I am — **Ps 46:10** 7503
And he should **c** *trying* forever — **Ps 49:8** 2308
Your indignation toward us to **c**. — **Ps 85:4** 6565a
You have made his splendor to **c** And — **Ps 89:44** 7673a
C listening, my son, to — **Pr 19:27** 2308
Even strife and dishonor will **c**. — **Pr 22:10** 7673a
C from your consideration *of it.* — **Pr 23:4** 2308
deeds from My sight. **C** to do evil, — **Is 1:16** 2308
For I have made the shouting to **c**. — **Is 16:10** 7673a
you **c** to deal treacherously, — **Is 33:1** 5239
"Then I will make to **c** from the — **Jer 7:34** 7673a
night and day, And let them not **c**; — **Jer 14:17** 1820
of drought Nor **c** to yield fruit. — **Jer 17:8** 4185
will **c** From being a nation before Me — **Jer 31:36** 7673a
man and beast to **c** from it?'" — **Jer 36:29** 7673a
wine to **c** from the wine presses; — **Jer 48:33** 7673a
lovingkindnesses indeed never **c**, — **La 3:22** 8552
the pride of the strong ones **c**, — **Ezk 7:24** 7673a
"I will make this proverb **c** so — **Ezk 12:23** 7673a
the land of Egypt to **c** from you, — **Ezk 23:27** 7673a
make lewdness **c** from the land, — **Ezk 23:48** 7673a
have become terrified And you will **c** — **Ezk 27:36** 369
have become terrified And you will **c** — **Ezk 28:19** 369
also make the hordes of Egypt **c** — **Ezk 30:10** 7673a
make the images **c** from Memphis. — **Ezk 30:13** 7673a
pride of her power will **c** in her; — **Ezk 30:18** 7673a
and the pride of her power will **c**; — **Ezk 33:28** 7673a
make them **c** from feeding sheep. — **Ezk 34:10** 7673a
will you not **c** to make crooked the — **Ac 13:10** *3973*
not **c** to admonish each one with tears — **Ac 20:31** *3973*
if *there are* tongues, they will **c**; — **1Co 13:8** *3973*
do not **c** giving thanks for you, — **Eph 1:16** *3973*
adultery that never **c** from sin, — **2Pe 2:14** *180*
and night they do not **c** to say, — **Rv 4:8** *372*

CEASED
and the thunder and the hail **c**, — **Ex 9:33** 2308
the hail and the thunder had **c**, — **Ex 9:34** 2308
the seventh day He **c** *from labor,* — **Ex 31:17** 7673a
The manna **c** on the day after — **Jos 5:12** 7673a
"The peasantry **c**, they ceased in — **Jg 5:7** 2308
ceased, they **c** in Israel, — **Jg 5:7** 2308
your father has **c** to be concerned — **1Sa 10:2** 5203
of it, he **c** fortifying Ramah — **1Ki 15:21** 2308
When Baasha heard *of it,* he **c** fortifying — **2Ch 16:5** 2308
the house of God in Jerusalem **c**, — **Ezr 4:24** 989
these three men **c** answering Job, — **Jb 32:1** 7673a
has **c** to be wise *and* to do good. — **Ps 36:3** 2308
Has His lovingkindness **c** forever? — **Ps 77:8** 656
"How the oppressor has **c**, — **Is 14:4** 7673a
has ceased, *And how* fury has **c**! — **Is 14:4** 7673a
come to an end, destruction has **c**, — **Is 16:4** 3615
are desolate, the traveler has **c**, — **Is 33:8** 7673a
and they **c** speaking with him, — **Jer 38:27** 2790b
men of Babylon have **c** fighting, — **Jer 51:30** 2308
The joy of our hearts has **c**; — **La 5:15** 7673a
in, has not **c** to kiss My feet. — **Lk 7:45** *1257*
After the uproar had **c**, — **Ac 20:1** *3973*
we have not **c** to pray for you and — **Col 1:9** *3973*
they not have **c** to be offered, — **Heb 10:2** *3973*
in the flesh has **c** from sin, — **1Pe 4:1** *3973*

CEASES
LORD, for the godly man **c** to be, — **Ps 12:1** 1584
The gaiety of tambourines **c**, — **Is 24:8** 7673a
stops, The gaiety of the harp **c**. — **Is 24:8** 7673a
Who **c** to stir up *the fire* From the — **Hos 7:4** 7673a

CEASING
the LORD by **c** to pray for you; — **1Sa 12:23** 2308
me, They slandered me without **c**. — **Ps 35:15** 1826a
pray without **c**; — **1Th 5:17** *89*

CEDAR
take two live clean birds and **c** wood — **Lv 14:4** 730
together with the **c** wood and the — **Lv 14:6** 730
he shall take two birds and **c** wood — **Lv 14:49** 730
"Then he shall take the **c** wood — **Lv 14:51** 730
with the live bird and with the **c** wood — **Lv 14:52** 730
"The priest shall take **c** wood — **Nu 19:6** 730
sent messengers to David with **c** trees — **2Sa 5:11** 730
"See now, I dwell in a house of **c**, — **2Sa 7:2** 730
not built Me a house of **c**?' — **2Sa 7:7** 730
from the **c** that is in Lebanon even — **1Ki 4:33** 730
the **c** and cypress timber. — **1Ki 5:8** 730
of the **c** and cypress timber. — **1Ki 5:10** 730
house with beams and planks of **c**. — **1Ki 6:9** 730
to the house with timbers of **c**. — **1Ki 6:10** 730
on the inside with boards of **c**; — **1Ki 6:15** 730
c from the floor to the ceiling; — **1Ki 6:16** 730
There was **c** on the house within, — **1Ki 6:18** 730
all was **c**, there was no stone seen. — **1Ki 6:18** 730
He also overlaid the altar with **c**. — **1Ki 6:20** 730
cut stone and a row of **c** beams. — **1Ki 6:36** 730
on four rows of **c** pillars with — **1Ki 7:2** 730
with **c** beams on the pillars. — **1Ki 7:2** 730
It was paneled with **c** above — **1Ki 7:3** 730
with **c** from floor to floor. — **1Ki 7:7** 730
cut according to measure, and **c**. — **1Ki 7:11** 730
cut stone and a row of **c** beams — **1Ki 7:12** 730
Tyre had supplied Solomon with **c** — **1Ki 9:11** 730
to the **c** which was in Lebanon, — **2Ki 14:9** 730
messengers to David with **c** trees, — **1Ch 14:1** 730
I am dwelling in a house of **c**, — **1Ch 17:1** 730
built for Me a house of **c**? — **1Ch 17:6** 730
timbers of **c** logs beyond number, — **1Ch 22:4** 730
quantities of **c** timber to David. — **1Ch 22:4** 730
"Send me also **c**, cypress and — **2Ch 2:8** 730
to the **c** which was in Lebanon, — **2Ch 25:18** 730
to bring **c** wood from Lebanon to — **Ezr 3:7** 730
"He bends his tail like a **c**; — **Jb 40:17** 730
He will grow like a **c** in Lebanon. — **Ps 92:12** 730
barricade her with planks of **c**." — **SS 8:9** 730
will put the **c** in the wilderness, — **Is 41:19** 730
c and painting *it* bright red.' — **Jer 22:14** 730
because you are competing in **c**? — **Jer 22:15** 730
and took away the top of the **c**. — **Ezk 17:3** 730
lofty top of the **c** and set *it* out; — **Ezk 17:22** 730
fruit and become a stately **c**. — **Ezk 17:23** 730
They have taken a **c** from Lebanon — **Ezk 27:5** 730
Assyria *was* a **c** in Lebanon With — **Ezk 31:3** 730
For He has laid bare the **c** work. — **Zph 2:14** 731
O cypress, for the **c** has fallen, — **Zch 11:2** 730

CEDARS
LORD, Like **c** beside the waters. — **Nu 24:6** 730
and consume the **c** of Lebanon.' — **Jg 9:15** 730
they cut for me **c** from Lebanon, — **1Ki 5:6** 730
and he made **c** as plentiful as — **1Ki 10:27** 730
tall **c** *and* its choice cypresses. — **2Ki 19:23** 730
and he made **c** as plentiful as — **2Ch 1:15** 730
and sent him **c** to build him a — **2Ch 2:3** 730
and he made **c** as plentiful as — **2Ch 9:27** 730
voice of the LORD breaks the **c**; — **Ps 29:5** 730
breaks in pieces the **c** of Lebanon. — **Ps 29:5** 730
Its fruit will wave like *the* **c** *of* — **Ps 72:16**
And the **c** of God with its boughs. — **Ps 80:10** 730
The **c** of Lebanon which He planted, — **Ps 104:16** 730
Fruit trees and all **c**; — **Ps 148:9** 730
"The beams of our houses are **c**, — **SS 1:17** 730
is like Lebanon Choice as the **c**. — **SS 5:15** 730
And *it will be* against all the **c** — **Is 2:13** 730
But we will replace *them* with **c**." — **Is 9:10** 730
over you, *and* the **c** of Lebanon, — **Is 14:8** 730
tall **c** *and* its choice cypresses. — **Is 37:24** 730
Surely he cuts **c** for himself, and — **Is 44:14** 730
they will cut down your choicest **c** — **Jer 22:7** 730
dwell in Lebanon, Nested in the **c**, — **Jer 22:23** 730
'The **c** in God's garden could not — **Ezk 31:8** 730
And he will take root like *the* **c** *of* — **Hos 14:5**
tree And his fragrance like *the* **c** — **Hos 14:6**
his height *was* like the height of **c** — **Am 2:9** 730
That a fire may feed on your **c**. — **Zch 11:1** 730

CEILING
from the floor of the house to the **c** — **1Ki 6:15** 7023, 5604
of cedar from the floor to the **c**; — **1Ki 6:16** 7023

CELEBRATE
that they may **c** a feast to Me in the — **Ex 5:1** 2287
shall **c** it *as* a feast to the LORD; — **Ex 12:14** 2287
to **c** it *as* a permanent ordinance. — **Ex 12:14** 2287
of Israel are to **c** this. — **Ex 12:47** 6213a
then let him come near to **c** it; — **Ex 12:48** 6213a
a year you shall **c** a feast to Me. — **Ex 23:14** 2287
to **c** the sabbath throughout their — **Ex 31:16** 6213a
You shall **c** the Feast of Weeks, — **Ex 34:22** 6213a
you shall **c** the feast of the LORD — **Lv 23:39** 2287
'You shall thus **c** it *as* a feast to — **Lv 23:41** 2287
shall **c** it in the seventh month. — **Lv 23:41** 2287
"Observe the month of Abib and **c** — **Dt 16:1** 6213a
"Then you shall **c** the Feast of — **Dt 16:10** 6213a
"You shall **c** the Feast of Booths — **Dt 16:13** 6213a
"Seven days you shall **c** a feast — **Dt 16:15** 2287
I will **c** before the LORD. — **2Sa 6:21** 7832
"**C** the Passover to the LORD your — **2Ki 23:21** 6213a
even to **c** and to thank and praise — **1Ch 16:4** 2142
to **c** the Passover to the LORD God — **2Ch 30:1** 6213a
to **c** the Passover in the second month, — **2Ch 30:2** 6213a
they could not **c** it at that time, — **2Ch 30:3** 6213a
that they should come to **c** the — **2Ch 30:5** 6213a
to **c** the Feast of Unleavened Bread — **2Ch 30:13** 6213a
to **c** *the feast* another seven days, — **2Ch 30:23** 6213a
on that day to **c** the Passover, — **2Ch 35:16** 6213a
and to **c** a great festival, — **Ne 8:12** 6213a
c the dedication with gladness, — **Ne 12:27** 6213a
obliging them to **c** the fourteenth — **Es 9:21** 6213a
would not fail to **c** these two days — **Es 9:27** 6213a
And the voice of those who **c**; — **Jer 30:19** 7832
C your feasts, O Judah; — **Na 1:15** 2287
and to **c** the Feast of Booths. — **Zch 14:16** 2287
go up to **c** the Feast of Booths. — **Zch 14:18** 2287
go up to **c** the Feast of Booths. — **Zch 14:19** 2287
and let us eat and **c**; — **Lk 15:23** *2165*
And they began to **c**. — **Lk 15:24** *2165*
so that I might **c** with my friends; — **Lk 15:29** *2165*
'But we had to **c** and rejoice, for — **Lk 15:32** *2165*
Therefore let us **c** the feast, — **1Co 5:8** *1858b*
will rejoice over them and **c**; — **Rv 11:10** *2165*

CELEBRATED
Passover had not been **c** from the days — **2Ki 23:22** 6213a
For they had not **c** *it* in great — **2Ch 30:5** 6213a
c the Feast of Unleavened Bread — **2Ch 30:21** 6213a
so they **c** the seven days with joy. — **2Ch 30:23** 6213a
Then Josiah **c** the Passover to the — **2Ch 35:1** 6213a
c the Passover at that time, — **2Ch 35:17** 6213a
had not been **c** a Passover like it — **2Ch 35:18** 6213a

Israel c such a Passover as Josiah did 2Ch 35:18 6213a
Josiah's reign this Passover was c. 2Ch 35:19 6213a
They c the Feast of Booths, as Ezr 3:4 6213a
c the dedication of this house of Ezr 6:16 5648
And they c the feast seven days, Ne 8:18 6213a
and c throughout every generation, Es 9:28 6213a

CELEBRATES
and c the Passover to the LORD, Ex 12:48 6213a

CELEBRATING
While they were c, behold, the men Jg 19:22 3190, 3820
were c before the LORD with all kinds 2Sa 6:5 7832
David and all Israel were c 1Ch 13:8 7832
and saw King David leaping and c; 1Ch 15:29 7832

CELL
dungeon, that is, the vaulted c; Jer 37:16 2588
and a light shone in the c; Ac 12:7 *3612*

CELLAR
a lamp, puts it away in a c nor Lk 11:33 *2926*

CELLARS
in thickets, in cliffs, in c, 1Sa 13:6 6877
vineyards *stored* in the wine c. 1Ch 27:27 214

CENCHREA
In C he had his hair cut, for he Ac 18:18 *2747*
of the church which is at C; Ro 16:1 *2747*

CENSER
you bring his c before the LORD, Nu 16:17 4289
took his *own* c and put fire on it, Nu 16:18 4289
"Take your c and put in it fire Nu 16:46 4289
with a c in his hand for burning 2Ch 26:19 4730
each man with his c in his hand and Ezk 8:11 4730
at the altar, holding a golden c; Rv 8:3 *3031*
Then the angel took the c Rv 8:5 *3031*

CENSERS
take c for yourselves, Korah and Nu 16:6 4289
c out of the midst of the blaze, Nu 16:37 4289
"As for the c of these men who Nu 16:38 4289
Eleazar the priest took the bronze c Nu 16:39 4289

CENSUS
"When you take a c of the sons of Ex 30:12 7218
"Take a c of all the congregation Nu 1:2 7218
their c among the sons of Israel. Nu 1:49 7218
"Take a c of the descendants of Nu 4:2 7218
a c of the sons of Gershon also, Nu 4:22 7218
"Take a c of all the congregation Nu 26:2 7218
"*Take a c of the people* from Nu 26:4
"Your servants have taken a c of Nu 31:49 7218
the c of *all* the people to David. 1Ch 21:5 4662
number by c of men was 38,000. 1Ch 23:3 1538
in the number of names by their c, 1Ch 23:24 1538
following the c which his father 2Ch 2:17 5610
and he took a c of those from 2Ch 25:5 6485
that a c be taken of all the Lk 2:1 *583*
This was the first c taken while Lk 2:2 *582*
way to register for the c, Lk 2:3 *583*
rose up in the days of the c and Ac 5:37 *582*

CENT
until you have paid up the last c. Mt 5:26 *2835*
"Are not two sparrows sold for a c? Mt 10:29 *787*
copper coins, which amount to a c. Mk 12:42 *2835*
you have paid the very last c." Lk 12:59 *3016*

CENTER
"The middle bar in the c of Ex 26:28 8432
c of the boards from end to end. Ex 36:33 8432
the robe was *at the top* in the c, Ex 39:23 8432
cubits, with the city in the c. Nu 35:5 8432
strong tower in the c of the city, Jg 9:51 8432
each other in the c of the house. 1Ki 6:27 8432
gardens, Following one in the c, Is 66:17 8432
them into the c of this city. Jer 21:4 8432
in the fire at the c of the city, Ezk 5:2 8432
set her at the c of the nations, Ezk 5:5 8432
who live at the c of the world.' Ezk 38:12 2872
and having set her in the c *of* Jn 8:3 *3319*
in the c *of the court.* Jn 8:9 *3319*
they had placed them in the c, Ac 4:7 *3319*
in the c and around the throne, Rv 4:6 *3319*
I heard *something* like a voice in the c Rv 6:6 *3319*
the Lamb in the c of the throne Rv 7:17 *3319*

CENTS
not five sparrows sold for two c? Lk 12:6 *787*

CENTURION
Capernaum, a c came to Him, Mt 8:5 *1543*
But the c said, Mt 8:8 *1543*
And Jesus said to the c, Mt 8:13 *1543*
Now the c, and those who were with Mt 27:54 *1543*
When the c, who was standing Mk 15:39 *2760*
by this time, and summoning the c, Mk 15:44 *2760*
And ascertaining this from the c, Mk 15:45 *2760*
the house, the c sent friends, Lk 7:6 *1543*
when the c saw what had happened, Lk 23:47 *1543*
a c of what was called the Italian Ac 10:1 *1543*
"Cornelius, a c, a righteous and Ac 10:22 *1543*
said to the c who was standing by, Ac 22:25 *1543*
When the c heard *this,* he went Ac 22:26 *1543*
Then he gave orders to the c for Ac 24:23 *1543*
a c of the Augustan cohort named Ac 27:1 *1543*
There the c found an Ac 27:6 *1543*
But the c was more persuaded by Ac 27:11 *1543*
said to the c and to the soldiers, Ac 27:31 *1543*
but the c, wanting to bring Paul Ac 27:43 *1543*

CENTURION'S
And a c slave, who was Lk 7:2 *1543*

CENTURIONS
he took along *some* soldiers and c and Ac 21:32 *1543*
one of the c to him and said, Ac 23:17 *1543*
And he called to him two of the c and Ac 23:23 *1543*

CEPHAS
you shall be called C" Jn 1:42 *2786*
and "I of C," and "I of Christ." 1Co 1:12 *2786*
whether Paul or Apollos or C or 1Co 3:22 *2786*
the brothers of the Lord and C? 1Co 9:5 *2786*
and that He appeared to C, 1Co 15:5 *2786*
to become acquainted with C, Ga 1:18 *2786*
given to me, James and C and John, Ga 2:9 *2786*
But when C came to Antioch, I Ga 2:11 *2786*
said to C in the presence of all, Ga 2:14 *2786*

CEREMONIALLY
first c washed before the meal. Lk 11:38 *907*

CERTAIN
"Know for c that your descendants Gn 15:13 3045
He came to a c place and spent Gn 28:11
and visited a c Adullamite, Gn 38:1 376
a c Canaanite whose name was Shua; Gn 38:2 376
if it is true and the thing c that Dt 17:4 3559
But a c woman threw an upper Jg 9:53 259
There was a c man of Zorah, of Jg 13:2 259
that there was a c Levite staying Jg 19:1 376
of the city, c worthless fellows, Jg 19:22 376
And a c man of Bethlehem in Judah Ru 1:1
Now there was a c man from 1Sa 1:1 259
But c worthless men said, 1Sa 10:27
the young men to a c place.' 1Sa 21:2 492, 6423
Your servant has heard for c that 1Sa 23:10 8085
they stood on the top of a c hill. 2Sa 2:25 259
When a c man saw *it,* he told Joab 2Sa 18:10 259
for c that you shall surely die; 1Ki 2:37 3045
'You will know for c that on the 1Ki 2:42 3045
he and c Edomites of his father's 1Ki 11:17 376
Now a c man of the sons of the 1Ki 20:35 259
Now a c man drew his bow at random 1Ki 22:34
Now a c woman of the wives of the 2Ki 4:1 259
appointed for her a c officer, 2Ki 8:6 259
Then c *persons* went and told 1Ch 19:5
A c man drew his bow at random 2Ch 18:33
"There is a c people scattered Es 3:8 259
was a c man without a dependent, Ec 4:8 259
for c that if you put me to death, Jer 26:15 3045
Elnathan the son of Achbor and c Jer 26:22
and among them was a c man clothed Ezk 9:2 259
c of the elders of Israel Ezk 20:1 376
"I know for c that you are Da 2:8 3330a
For this reason at that time c Da 3:8 1400
"There are c Jews whom you have Da 3:12 1400
He commanded c valiant Da 3:20 1400
was a c man dressed in linen, Da 10:5 259
going forth is as c as the dawn; Hos 6:3 3559
"Go into the city to a c man, Mt 26:18 *1170*
"How will I know this *for c?* Lk 1:18
while Jesus was praying in a c place, Lk 11:1 *5100*
"In a c city there was a judge Lk 18:2 *5100*
down at c seasons into the pool and Jn 5:4 *2596*
Now a c man was sick, Lazarus of Jn 11:1 *5100*
know for c that God has made Him Ac 2:36 *806*
"A c Ananias, a man who was Ac 22:12 *5100*
wishing to know for c why he had Ac 22:30 *804*
must run aground on a c island." Ac 27:26 *5100*
to the coming of c men from James, Ga 2:12 *5100*
that you may instruct c men not to 1Tm 1:3 *5100*
He again fixes a c day, Heb 4:7 *5100*
diligent to make c about His calling 2Pe 1:10 *949*
For c persons have crept in Jude 1:4 *5100*

CERTAINLY
"Behold, c she is your wife! Gn 26:9 389
"C I will be with you, and this Ex 3:12 3588
he was c guilty before the LORD." Lv 5:19 816
use, but you must c not eat it. Lv 7:24 398
you should c have eaten it in the Lv 10:18 398
congregation shall c stone him. Lv 24:16 7275
c does flow with milk and honey, Nu 13:27 1571
shall c not sell her for money, Dt 21:14 4376
you shall c bring them back to Dt 22:1 7725
shall c help him to raise *them* up. Dt 22:4 6965
you shall c let the mother go, but Dt 22:7 7971
"Because it was c told your Jos 9:24 5046
for the LORD will c make for my 1Sa 25:28 6213a
for I will c give the Philistines 2Sa 5:19 5414
has shown me that he will c die." 2Ki 8:10 4191
My lips c will not speak unjustly, Jb 27:4 518
But c God has heard; Ps 66:19 403
For *wealth* c makes itself wings Like Pr 23:5 6213a
They c were not ashamed, And they Jer 8:12 1571
him, I c *still* remember him; Jer 31:20 2142
c come and destroy this land, Jer 36:29 935
'This city will c be given into Jer 38:3 5414
will you not c put me to death? Jer 38:15 4191
"For I will c rescue you, and you Jer 39:18 4422
"But rather we will c accomplish every word Jer 44:17 6213a
"We will c perform our vows that Jer 44:25 6213a
vows, and c perform your vows!' Jer 44:25 6213a
to drink the cup will c drink *it,* Jer 49:12 8354
but you will c drink *it.* Jer 49:12 8354
replied to the king, "C, O king." Da 3:24 3330a
Gilgal will c go into captivity And Am 5:5 1540
c go from its land into exile.' " Am 7:11 1540
c go from its land into exile.' " Am 7:17 1540
For it will c come, it will not Hab 2:3 935
"You are c God's Son!" Mt 14:33 *230*
hand of the Lord was c with him. Lk 1:66 *2532*
"C this man also was with Him, Lk 22:59 *1909, 225*
"C this man was innocent." Lk 23:47 *3689*
comes to Me I will c not cast out. Jn 6:37 *3756, 3361*
"This c is the Prophet." Jn 7:40 *230*
'I HAVE C SEEN THE OPPRESSION OF Ac 7:34 *3708*
"I most c understand *now* that God Ac 10:34 *1909, 225*
c be a great famine all over the world. Ac 11:28 *3195*
will c hear that you have come. Ac 21:22 *3843*
that there shall c be a resurrection Ac 24:15 *3195*
voyage will c be with damage Ac 27:10 *3195*
c we shall also be *in the likeness* Ro 6:5 *235*
declaring that God is c among you. 1Co 14:25 *3689*
C I have not taken advantage of 2Co 12:17

CERTAINTY
know with c that the LORD your God Jos 23:13 3045
himself and return to me with c, 1Sa 23:23 3559
To make you know the c of the Pr 22:21 7189b
For this you know with c, Eph 5:5 *1097*

CERTIFICATE
and he writes her a c of divorce Dt 24:1 5612
writes her a c of divorce and puts *it* in Dt 24:3 5612
"Where is the c of divorce By Is 50:1 5612
HIM GIVE HER A C OF DIVORCE'; Mt 5:31 *647*
GIVE HER A C OF DIVORCE Mt 19:7 *975*
C OF DIVORCE AND SEND *her* AWAY." Mk 10:4 *975*
having canceled out the c of debt Col 2:14 *5498*

CHAFF
anger, *and* it consumes them as c. Ex 15:7 7179
Or will You pursue the dry c? Jb 13:25 7179
c which the storm carries away? Jb 21:18 4671b
like c which the wind drives away. Ps 1:4 4671b
them be like c before the wind, Ps 35:5 4671b
Like c before the wind. Ps 83:13 7179
And be chased like c in the Is 17:13 4671b
ones like the c which blows away; Is 29:5 4671b
"You have conceived c, Is 33:11 2842
As the wind-driven c with his bow. Is 41:2 7179
And will make the hills like c. Is 41:15 4671b
and became like c from the summer Da 2:35 5784
Like c which is blown away from Hos 13:3 4671b
The day passes like the c Zph 2:2 4671b
and every evildoer will be c; Mal 4:1 7179
up the c with unquenchable fire." Mt 3:12 *892*
up the c with unquenchable fire." Lk 3:17 *892*

CHAIN
He has made my c heavy. La 3:7 5178
'Make the c, for the land is full Ezk 7:23 7569
bind him anymore, even with a c; Mk 5:3 *254*
for I am wearing this c for the Ac 28:20 *254*
abyss and a great c in his hand. Rv 20:1 *254*

CHAINS
and two c of pure gold; Ex 28:14 8333
corded c on the filigree *settings.* Ex 28:14 8333
c of twisted cordage work in pure gold Ex 28:22 8333
on the breastpiece c like cords, Ex 39:15 8333
Gaza and bound him with bronze c, Jg 16:21 5178
And he drew c of gold across the 1Ki 6:21 7569
it with palm trees and c. 2Ch 3:5 8333
He made c in the inner sanctuary 2Ch 3:16 8333
and placed *them* on the c. 2Ch 3:16 8333
bound him with bronze c and took 2Ch 33:11
him and bound him with bronze c 2Ch 36:6
you bind the c of the Pleiades, Jb 38:31 4575a
death, Prisoners in misery and c, Ps 107:10 1270
To bind their kings with c And Ps 149:8 2203b
and nets, whose hands are c. Ec 7:26 612
headdresses, ankle c, Is 3:20 6807b
silversmith *fashions* c of silver. Is 40:19 7577
in c And will bow down to you; Is 45:14 2203b
from the c around your neck, Is 52:2 4147
when he had taken him bound in c Jer 40:1 246
the c which are on your hands. Jer 40:4 246
been bound with shackles and c, Mk 5:4 *254*
the c had been torn apart by him and Mk 5:4 *254*
and he was bound with c and Lk 8:29 *254*
two soldiers, bound with two c, Ac 12:6 *254*
And his c fell off his hands. Ac 12:7 *254*
and everyone's c were unfastened. Ac 16:26 *1199*
him to be bound with two c; Ac 21:33 *254*
and because he had put him in c. Ac 22:29 *1210*
as I am, except for these c." Ac 26:29 *1199*
for which I am an ambassador in c; Eph 6:20 *254*
me and was not ashamed of my c; 2Tm 1:16 *254*
yes, also c and imprisonment. Heb 11:36 *1199*

CHAINWORK
twisted threads of c for the capitals 1Ki 7:17 4639, 8333

CHAIR
a table and a c and a lampstand; 2Ki 4:10 3678
c From the timber of Lebanon. SS 3:9 668
themselves in the c of Moses; Mt 23:2 *2515*

CHALCEDONY
the second, sapphire; the third, c; Rv 21:19 *5472*

CHALDEA
"C will become plunder; Jer 50:10 3778
Babylon and all the inhabitants of C Jer 51:24 3778
be upon the inhabitants of C," Jer 51:35 3778
Spirit of God to the exiles in C. Ezk 11:24 3778
with the land of merchants, C, Ezk 16:29 3778
like the Babylonians *in* C, Ezk 23:15 3778
and sent messengers to them in C. Ezk 23:16 3778

CHALDEAN
king of Babylon, the C, Ezr 5:12 3779
of any magician, conjurer or C. Da 2:10 3779
Belshazzar the C king was slain. Da 5:30 3779

CHALDEANS
land of his birth, in Ur of the C. Gn 11:28 3778

went out together from Ur of the **C** **Gn 11:31** 3778
brought you out of Ur of the **C**, **Gn 15:7** 3778
LORD sent against him bands of **C**, **2Ki 24:2** 3778
the **C** were all around the city. **2Ki 25:4** 3778
But the army of the **C** pursued the **2Ki 25:5** 3778
So all the army of the **C** who *were* **2Ki 25:10** 3778
the **C** broke in pieces and carried **2Ki 25:13** 3778
afraid of the servants of the **C**; **2Ki 25:24** 3778
the **C** who were with him at Mizpah. **2Ki 25:25** 3778
for they were afraid of the **C**. **2Ki 25:26** 3778
king of the **C** who slew their young **2Ch 36:17** 3778
"The **C** formed three bands and **Jb 1:17** 3778
Behold, the land of the **C** **Is 23:13** 3778
all down as fugitives, Even the **C**, **Is 43:14** 3778
a throne, O daughter of the **C**! **Is 47:1** 3778
darkness, O daughter of the **C**, **Is 47:5** 3778
His arm *will be against* the **C**. **Is 48:14** 3778
forth from Babylon! Flee from the **C**! **Is 48:20** 3778
the **C** who are besieging you outside **Jer 21:4** 3778
who goes out and falls away to the **C** **Jer 21:9** 3778
and into the hand of the **C**. **Jer 22:25** 3778
this place *into* the land of the **C**. **Jer 24:5** 3778
iniquity, and the land of the **C**; **Jer 25:12** 3778
escape out of the hand of the **C**; **Jer 32:4** 3778
"If you fight against the **C**, **Jer 32:5** 3778
of the **C** who fight against it, **Jer 32:24** 3778
given into the hand of the **C**.' " **Jer 32:25** 3778
give this city into the hand of the **C** **Jer 32:28** 3778
"The **C** who are fighting **Jer 32:29** 3778
is given into the hand of the **C**." **Jer 32:43** 3778
are coming to fight with the **C** and **Jer 33:5** 3778
to Jerusalem before the army of the **C** **Jer 35:11** 3778
and when the **C** who had been **Jer 37:5** 3778
"The **C** will also return and fight **Jer 37:8** 3778
C will surely go away from us," **Jer 37:9** 3778
C who were fighting against you, **Jer 37:10** 3778
when the army of the **C** had lifted **Jer 37:11** 3778
"You are going over to the **C**!" **Jer 37:13** 3778
I am not going over to the **C**"; **Jer 37:14** 3778
but he who goes out to the **C** will **Jer 38:2** 3778
given over to the hand of the **C**, **Jer 38:18** 3778
Jews who have gone over to the **C**, **Jer 38:19** 3778
your wives and your sons to the **C**, **Jer 38:23** 3778
But the army of the **C** pursued them **Jer 39:5** 3778
The **C** also burned with fire the **Jer 39:8** 3778
"Do not be afraid of serving the **C**; **Jer 40:9** 3778
you before the **C** who come to us; **Jer 40:10** 3778
and the **C** who were found there, **Jer 41:3** 3778
because of the **C**; **Jer 41:18** 3778
us over into the hand of the **C**, **Jer 43:3** 3778
Babylon, the land of the **C**, **Jer 50:1** 3778
go forth from the land of the **C**; **Jer 50:8** 3778
God of hosts In the land of the **C**. **Jer 50:25** 3778
"A sword against the **C**," **Jer 50:35** 3778
against the land of the **C**: **Jer 50:45** 3778
down slain in the land of the **C**, **Jer 51:4** 3778
from the land of the **C**! **Jer 51:54** 3778
the **C** were all around the city. **Jer 52:7** 3778
But the army of the **C** pursued the **Jer 52:8** 3778
So all the army of the **C** who *were* **Jer 52:14** 3778
the **C** broke in pieces and carried **Jer 52:17** 3778
land of the **C** by the river Chebar; **Ezk 1:3** 3778
to Babylon in the land of the **C**; **Ezk 12:13** 3778
of the **C** portrayed with vermilion, **Ezk 23:14** 3778
the Babylonians and all the **C**, **Ezk 23:23** 3778
literature and language of the **C**. **Da 1:4** 3778
the sorcerers and the **C** to **Da 2:2** 3778
C spoke to the king in Aramaic: **Da 2:4** 3778
king replied to the **C**, **Da 2:5** 3779
The **C** answered the king and said, **Da 2:10** 3779
C came forward and brought charges **Da 3:8** 3779
magicians, the conjurers, the **C** and **Da 4:7** 3779
conjurers, the **C** and the diviners. **Da 5:7** 3779
of the magicians, conjurers, **C** **Da 5:11** 3779
king over the kingdom of the **C** **Da 9:1** 3778
"For behold, I am raising up the **C**, **Hab 1:6** 3778
The **C** bring all of them up with a **Hab 1:15**
left the land of the **C** **Ac 7:4** *5466*

CHALDEANS'
the glory of the **C** pride, Will be **Is 13:19** 3778

CHALDEES
brought him out from Ur of the **C**, **Ne 9:7** 3778

CHALICE
The **c** of reeling you have drained **Is 51:17** 3563a, 6907
The **c** of My anger; You will never **Is 51:22** 3563a, 6907

CHALK
stones like pulverized **c** stones; **Is 27:9** 1615
he outlines it with red **c**. **Is 44:13** 8279

CHALLENGING
become boastful, **c** one another, **Ga 5:26** *4292*

CHAMBER
he entered his **c** and wept there. **Gn 43:30** 2315
sitting alone in his cool roof **c**. **Jg 3:20** 5944
doors of the roof **c** behind him, **Jg 3:23** 5944
doors of the roof **c** were locked; **Jg 3:24** 5944
not open the doors of the roof **c**. **Jg 3:25** 5944
inner **c** of the temple of El-berith. **Jg 9:46** 6877
and put *them* on the inner **c** and **Jg 9:49** 6877
inner **c** on fire over those *inside*, **Jg 9:49** 6877
to the **c** over the gate and wept. **2Sa 18:33** 5944
The doorway for the lowest side **c** **1Ki 6:8** 6763
into the city into an inner **c**. **1Ki 20:30** 2315
his upper **c** which *was* in Samaria, **2Ki 1:2** 5944
let us make a little walled upper **c** **2Ki 4:10** 5944
in to the upper **c** and rested. **2Ki 4:11** 5944
c of Nathan-melech the official, **2Ki 23:11** 3957
on the roof, the upper **c** of Ahaz, **2Ki 23:12** 5944
and went into the **c** of Jehohanan **Ezr 10:6** 3957
a bridegroom coming out of his **c**; **Ps 19:5** 2646
into the **c** of the sons of Hanan **Jer 35:4** 3957
was near the **c** of the officials, **Jer 35:4** 3957
which was above the **c** of Maaseiah **Jer 35:4** 3957
the **c** of Gemariah the son of Shaphan **Jer 36:10** 3957
king's house, into the scribe's **c**. **Jer 36:12** 3957
in the **c** of Elishama the scribe, **Jer 36:20** 3957
of the **c** of Elishama the scribe. **Jer 36:21** 3957
A **c** with its doorway was by **Ezk 40:38** 3957
c which faces toward the south, **Ezk 40:45** 3957
but the **c** which faces toward the **Ezk 40:46** 3957
and he brought me to the **c** which **Ezk 42:1** 3957
in his roof **c** he had windows open **Da 6:10** 5952
And the bride out of her *bridal* **c**. **Jl 2:16** 2646
led Him away to their council **c**, **Lk 22:66**

CHAMBERLAIN
won over Blastus the king's **c**, **Ac 12:20** *1909, 2846*

CHAMBERS
thus he made side **c** all around. **1Ki 6:5** 6763
c which were on the 45 pillars, **1Ki 7:3** 6763
and were over the **c** and over the **1Ch 9:26** 3957
who lived in the **c** *of the temple* **1Ch 9:33** 3957
in the courts and in the **c** and in **1Ch 23:28** 3957
the **c** of the house of the LORD." **Ezr 8:29** 3957
at the **c** of the house of our God, **Ne 10:37** 3957
God, to the **c** of the storehouse. **Ne 10:38** 3957
new wine and the oil to the **c**; **Ne 10:39** 3957
over the **c** for the stores, **Ne 12:44** 5393
the **c** of the house of our God, **Ne 13:4** 3957
Pleiades, And the **c** of the south; **Jb 9:9** 2315
of His upper **c** in the waters; **Ps 104:3** 5944
the mountains from His upper **c**; **Ps 104:13** 5944
Even in the **c** of their kings. **Ps 105:30** 2315
Descending to the **c** of death. **Pr 7:27** 2315
king has brought me into his **c**." **SS 1:4** 2315
of the LORD, into one of the **c**, **Jer 35:2** 3957
there were **c** and a pavement made **Ezk 40:17** 3957
thirty **c** faced the pavement. **Ezk 40:17** 3957
c for the singers in the inner court, **Ezk 40:44** 3957
and the width of the side **c**, **Ezk 41:5** 6763
The side **c** were in three stories, **Ezk 41:6** 6763
and the side **c** extended to the **Ezk 41:6** 6763
The side **c** surrounding the **Ezk 41:7** 6763
the foundations of the side **c** were **Ezk 41:8** 6763
of the side **c** *was* five cubits. **Ezk 41:9** 6763
side **c** belonging to the temple **Ezk 41:9** 6763
and the *outer* **c** *was* twenty cubits **Ezk 41:10** 3957
The doorways of the side **c** **Ezk 41:11** 6763
thus *were* the side **c** of the house **Ezk 41:26** 6763
Before the **c** *was* an inner walk **Ezk 42:4** 3957
Now the upper **c** *were* smaller **Ezk 42:5** 3957
therefore *the upper* **c** were set **Ezk 42:6**
outer wall by the side of the **c**, **Ezk 42:7** 3957
the outer court facing the **c**, **Ezk 42:7** 3957
For the length of the **c** which *were* **Ezk 42:8** 3957
Below these **c** *was* the entrance **Ezk 42:9** 3957
facing the building, *there were* **c**. **Ezk 42:10** 3957
of the **c** which *were* on the north, **Ezk 42:11** 3957
Corresponding to the openings of the **c** **Ezk 42:12** 3957
north **c** *and* the south chambers, **Ezk 42:13** 3957
north chambers *and* the south **c**, **Ezk 42:13** 3957
they are the holy **c** where the **Ezk 42:13** 3957
and lay them in the holy **c**; **Ezk 44:19** 3957
into the holy **c** for the priests, **Ezk 46:19** 3957
builds His upper **c** in the heavens And **Am 9:6** 4609b

CHAMELEON
and the sand reptile, and the **c**. **Lv 11:30** 8580

CHAMPION
Then a **c** came out from the armies **1Sa 17:4** 376, 996
talking with them, behold, the **c**, **1Sa 17:23** 376, 996
saw that their **c** was dead, **1Sa 17:51** 1368
will send them a Savior and a **C**, **Is 19:20** 7227b
LORD is with me like a dread **c**; **Jer 20:11** 1368

CHANCE
it happened to us by **c**." **1Sa 6:9** 4745
"By **c** I happened to be on Mount **2Sa 1:6** 7122
for time and **c** overtake them all. **Ec 9:11** 6294
"And by **c** a priest was **Lk 10:31** *4795*

CHANGE
yourselves and **c** your garments; **Gn 35:2** 2498
c their minds when they see war, **Ex 13:17** 5162
a **c** of heart toward the people, **Ex 14:5** 2015
C Your mind about *doing* harm to Your **Ex 32:12** 5162
Israel will not lie or **c** His mind; **1Sa 15:29** 5162
a man that He should **c** His mind." **1Sa 15:29** 5162
in order to **c** the appearance of **2Sa 14:20** 5437
or people who attempts to **c** *it*, **Ezr 6:12** 8133
I will wait Until my **c** comes. **Jb 14:14** 2487
You **c** his appearance and **Jb 14:20** 8132
to his own hurt and does not **c**; **Ps 15:4** 4171
fear, though the earth should **c** And **Ps 46:2** 4171
With whom there is no **c**, **Ps 55:19** 2487
Like clothing You will **c** them and **Ps 102:26** 2498
has sworn and will not **c** His mind, **Ps 110:4** 5162
with those who are given to **c**, **Pr 24:21** 8132
And I will not **c** My mind, **Jer 4:28** 5162
"Can the Ethiopian **c** his skin Or **Jer 13:23** 2015
and the LORD will **c** His mind about **Jer 26:13** 5162
I will **c** their glory into shame. **Hos 4:7** 4171
"For I, the LORD, do not **c**; **Mal 3:6** 8132
with you now and to **c** my tone, **Ga 4:20** *236*
there takes place a **c** of law also. **Heb 7:12** *3331*
SWORN AND WILL NOT **C** HIS MIND, **Heb 7:21** *3338*

CHANGED
me and **c** my wages ten times; **Gn 31:7** 2498
and you **c** my wages ten times. **Gn 31:41** 2498
shaved himself and **c** his clothes, **Gn 41:14** 2498
So the LORD **c** His mind about the **Ex 32:14** 5162
his eyes the infection has not **c** **Lv 13:5** 5975
turns again and is **c** to white, **Lv 13:16** 2015
the mark has not **c** its appearance, **Lv 13:55** 2015
their names being **c** **Nu 32:38** 5437
them and be **c** into another man. **1Sa 10:6** 2015
to leave Samuel, God **c** his heart; **1Sa 10:9** 2015
himself, and **c** his clothes; **2Sa 12:20** 2498
and **c** his name to Jehoiakim. **2Ki 23:34** 5437
place, and **c** his name to Zedekiah. **2Ki 24:17** 5437
Jehoiachin **c** his prison clothes and **2Ki 25:29** 8132
and **c** his name to Jehoiakim. **2Ch 36:4** 5437
Yet his food in his stomach is **c** **Jb 20:14** 2015
"It is **c** like clay *under* the seal; **Jb 38:14** 2015
hand of the Most High has **c**." **Ps 77:10** 8132
change them and they will be **c**. **Ps 102:26** 2498
"Has a nation **c** gods When they **Jer 2:11** 4171
But My people have **c** their glory **Jer 2:11** 4171
and the LORD **c** His mind about the **Jer 26:19** 5162
flavor, And his aroma has not **c**. **Jer 48:11** 4171
Jehoiachin **c** his prison clothes, **Jer 52:33** 8132
become, *How* the pure gold has **c**! **La 4:1** 8132
me until the situation is **c**; **Da 2:9** 8133
his mind be **c** from *that of* a man And **Da 4:16** 8133
document so that it may not be **c**, **Da 6:8** 8133
the king establishes may be **c**." **Da 6:15** 8133
would be **c** in regard to Daniel. **Da 6:17** 8133
The LORD **c** His mind about this. **Am 7:3** 5162
The LORD **c** His mind about this. **Am 7:6** 5162
All the land will be **c** into a **Zch 14:10** 5437
they **c** their minds and *began* to **Ac 28:6** *3328*
all sleep, but we will all be **c**, **1Co 15:51** *236*
imperishable, and we will be **c**. **1Co 15:52** *236*
LIKE A GARMENT THEY WILL ALSO BE **C**. **Heb 1:12** *236*
For when the priesthood is **c**, **Heb 7:12** *3346a*

CHANGERS
overturned the tables of the money **c** **Mt 21:12** *2855a*
overturned the tables of the money **c** **Mk 11:15** *2855a*
and the money **c** seated *at their* **Jn 2:14** *2773*
poured out the coins of the money **c** **Jn 2:15** *2855a*

CHANGES
of them he gave **c** of garments, **Gn 45:22** 2487
of silver and five **c** of garments. **Gn 45:22** 2487
wraps and thirty **c** of clothes. **Jg 14:12** 2487
wraps and thirty **c** of clothes." **Jg 14:13** 2487
and gave the **c** *of clothes* to those **Jg 14:19** 2487
of gold and ten **c** of clothes. **2Ki 5:5** 2487
silver and two **c** of clothes.' " **2Ki 5:22** 2487
in two bags with two **c** of clothes and **2Ki 5:23** 2487
"It **c** direction, turning **Jb 37:12** 4524
He **c** rivers into a wilderness And **Ps 107:33** 7760
He **c** a wilderness into a pool of **Ps 107:35** 7760
He who **c** the times and the epochs; **Da 2:21** 8133
And **c** deep darkness into morning, **Am 5:8** 2015

CHANGING
you go around so much **C** your way? **Jer 2:36** 8132

CHANNEL
"Who has cleft a **c** for the flood, **Jb 38:25** 8585a

CHANNELS
"Then the **c** of the sea appeared, **2Sa 22:16** 650
"He hews out **c** through the rocks, **Jb 28:10** 2975
Then the **c** of water appeared, And **Ps 18:15** 650
The king's heart is *like* **c** of **Pr 21:1** 6388
its **c** and go over all its banks. **Is 8:7** 650
c to all the trees of the field. **Ezk 31:4** 8585a

CHANT
a lamentation and they shall **c** it. **Ezk 32:16** 6969
of the nations shall **c** it. **Ezk 32:16** 6969
her hordes they shall **c** it," **Ezk 32:16** 6969

CHANTED
Then David **c** with this lament over **2Sa 1:17** 6969
c a *lament* for Abner and said, **2Sa 3:33** 6969
Jeremiah **c** a lament for Josiah. **2Ch 35:25** 6969

CHAOS
The city of **c** is broken down; **Is 24:10** 8414

CHARACTER
and perseverance, proven **c**; **Ro 5:4** *1382*
and proven **c**, hope; **Ro 5:4** *1382*
Make sure that your **c** is free from **Heb 13:5** *5158*

CHARCOAL
Like **c** to hot embers and wood to **Pr 26:21** 6352
there, having made a **c** fire, **Jn 18:18** *439*
they saw a **c** fire *already* laid and **Jn 21:9** *439*

CHARGE
who had **c** of all that he owned, **Gn 24:2** 4910
Abraham obeyed Me and kept My **c**, **Gn 26:5** 4931
all that he owned he put in his **c**. **Gn 39:4** 3027
everything he owned in Joseph's **c**; **Gn 39:6** 3027
has put all that he owns in my **c**. **Gn 39:8** 3027
chief jailer committed to Joseph's **c** all **Gn 39:22** 3027
c because the LORD was with him; **Gn 39:23** 3027
bodyguard put Joseph in **c** of them, **Gn 40:4** 6485
overseers in **c** of the land, **Gn 41:34** 5921
put them in **c** of my livestock." **Gn 47:6** 8269
and gave them a **c** to the sons of **Ex 6:13** 6680
you shall not **c** him interest. **Ex 22:25** 7760, 5921
"Keep far from a false **c**, **Ex 23:7** 1697
You shall **c** the sons of Israel, **Ex 27:20** 6680
days and keep the **c** of the LORD, **Lv 8:35** 4931
'Thus you are to keep My **c**, **Lv 18:30** 4931
'They shall therefore keep My **c**, **Lv 22:9** 4931
So the Levites shall keep **c** of the **Nu 1:53** 4931
keep the LORD's **c** and not set out. **Nu 9:19** 4931
they kept the LORD's **c**, **Nu 9:23** 4931

have given you **c** of My offerings, **Nu 18:8** 4931
c of the tabernacle of the LORD." **Nu 31:30** 4931
c of the tabernacle of the LORD, **Nu 31:47** 4931
of men of war who are in our **c**, **Nu 31:49** 3027
'But **c** Joshua and encourage him **Dt 3:28** 6680
your God, and always keep His **c**, **Dt 11:1** 4931
"But if this **c** is true, that the **Dt 22:20** 1697
not **c** interest to your countrymen: **Dt 23:19** 5391b
"You may **c** interest to a **Dt 23:20** 5391b
you shall not **c** interest, **Dt 23:20** 5391b
your God, which I **c** you today, **Dt 28:13** 6680
statutes with which I **c** you today, **Dt 28:15** 6680
but have kept the **c** of the **Jos 22:3** 4931
who was in **c** of the reapers, **Ru 2:5** 5324
The servant in **c** of the **Ru 2:6** 5324
The **c** was two-thirds of a **1Sa 13:21** 6477
and yet today you **c** me with a **2Sa 3:8** 6485
Keep the **c** of the LORD your God, **1Ki 2:3** 4931
be, each according to his **c**. **1Ki 4:28** 4941
he leaned to have **c** of the gate; **2Ki 7:17** 5921
one who *was* in **c** of the wardrobe, **2Ki 10:22** 5921
So they and their sons had **c** of **1Ch 9:23** 5921
and they *were* in **c** of opening *it* **1Ch 9:27** 5921
had **c** of the utensils of service, **1Ch 9:28** 5921
was *in* **c** *of* the singing; **1Ch 15:22**
and give you **c** over Israel, **1Ch 22:12** 6680
to keep **c** of the tent of meeting, **1Ch 23:32** 4931
meeting, and **c** of the holy place, **1Ch 23:32** 4931
and **c** of the sons of Aaron their **1Ch 23:32** 4931
had **c** of the treasures of the **1Ch 26:20** 5921
had **c** of the treasures of the **1Ch 26:22** 5921
Shelomoth and his relatives had **c** **1Ch 26:26** 5921
had **c** of the affairs of Israel **1Ch 26:30**
the son of Zabdiel had **c** of the first **1Ch 27:2** 5921
the Ahohite and his division had **c** **1Ch 27:4** 5921
the thirty, and had **c** of thirty; **1Ch 27:6** 5921
Now in **c** of the tribes of Israel: **1Ch 27:16** 5921
had **c** of the king's storehouses. **1Ch 27:25** 5921
Jonathan the son of Uzziah had **c** **1Ch 27:25** 5921
Ezri the son of Chelub had **c** **1Ch 27:26** 5921
Ramathite had **c** of the vineyards; **1Ch 27:27** 5921
and Zabdi the Shiphmite had **c** of **1Ch 27:27** 5921
Baal-hanan the Gederite had **c** **1Ch 27:28** 5921
Joash had **c** of the stores of oil. **1Ch 27:28** 5921
Shitrai the Sharonite had **c** of **1Ch 27:29** 5921
had **c** of the cattle in the **1Ch 27:29** 5921
Ishmaelite had **c** of the camels; **1Ch 27:30** 5921
Meronothite had **c** of the donkeys. **1Ch 27:30** 5921
the Hagrite had **c** of the flocks. **1Ch 27:31** 5921
we keep the **c** of the LORD our God, **2Ch 13:11** 4931
the people keep the **c** of the LORD. **2Ch 23:6** 4931
the Levite *was* the officer in **c** of them **2Ch 31:12** 5921
the fortress, in **c** of Jerusalem, **Ne 7:2** 5921
who were in **c** of the outside work **Ne 11:16** 5921
were in **c** of the temple servants. **Ne 11:21** 5921
in **c** of the songs of thanksgiving, **Ne 12:8** 5921
In **c** of the storehouses I **Ne 13:13** 5921
eunuch, who is in **c** of the women; **Es 2:3** 8104
Hegai, who was in **c** of the women. **Es 2:8** 8104
who was in **c** of the concubines. **Es 2:14** 8104
eunuch who was in **c** of the women, **Es 2:15** 8104
give His angels **c** concerning you, **Ps 91:11** 6680
ruins will be under your **c**," **Is 3:6** 3027
I will also **c** the clouds to rain **Is 5:6** 6680
is in **c** of the *royal* household, **Is 22:15** 5921
he had put him in **c** of the men, **Jer 40:7** 6485
had put under the **c** of Gedaliah **Jer 41:10** 6485
priests who keep **c** of the temple; **Ezk 40:45** 4931
priests who keep **c** of the altar. **Ezk 40:46** 4931
c of My holy things yourselves, **Ezk 44:8** 4931
to keep **c** of My sanctuary." **Ezk 44:8** 4931
them to keep **c** of the house, **Ezk 44:14** 4931
who kept **c** of My sanctuary when **Ezk 44:15** 4931
to minister to Me and keep My **c**. **Ezk 44:16** 4931
sons of Zadok, who have kept My **c**, **Ezk 48:11** 4931
be in **c** of the whole kingdom, **Da 6:1**
and also have **c** of My courts, **Zch 3:7** 8104
is it that we have kept His **c**, **Mal 3:14** 4931
slave whom his master put in **c** of his **Mt 24:45** *2525*
him in **c** of all his possessions. **Mt 24:47** *2525*
will put you in **c** of many things; **Mt 25:21** *2525*
will put you in **c** of many things; **Mt 25:23** *2525*
with regard to even a *single* **c**, **Mt 27:14** *4487*
up the **c** against Him which read, **Mt 27:37** *156*
house and putting his slaves in **c**, **Mk 13:34** *1849*
of the **c** against Him read, **Mk 15:26** *156*
will put in **c** of his servants, **Lk 12:42** *2525*
him in **c** of all his possessions. **Lk 12:44** *2525*
whom we may put in **c** of this task. **Ac 6:3** *2525*
who was in **c** of all her treasure; **Ac 8:27** *1909*
sending it in **c** of Barnabas and **Ac 11:30** *1223, 5495*
"And wanting to ascertain the **c** **Ac 23:28** *156*
will bring a **c** against God's elect? **Ro 8:33** *1458*
I may offer the gospel without **c**, **1Co 9:18** *77*
gospel of God to you without **c**? **2Co 11:7** *1431*
and have **c** over you in the Lord **1Th 5:12** *4291b*
I solemnly **c** you in the presence **1Tm 5:21** *1263*
I **c** you in the presence of God, **1Tm 6:13** *3853*
and solemnly **c** *them* in the **2Tm 2:14** *1263*
I solemnly **c** *you* in the presence **2Tm 4:1** *1263*
anything, **c** that to my account; **Phm 1:18** *1677*
it over those allotted to your **c**, **1Pe 5:3** *2819*

CHARGED

So Abimelech **c** all the people, **Gn 26:11** 6680
Jacob and blessed him and **c** him, **Gn 28:1** 6680
that when he blessed him he **c** him, **Gn 28:6** 6680
Then he **c** them and said to them, **Gn 49:29** 6680
sons did for him as he had **c** them; **Gn 50:12** 6680
"Your father **c** before he died, **Gn 50:16** 6680
"Then I **c** your judges at that **Dt 1:16** 6680
he has **c** her with shameful deeds, **Dt 22:17** 7760
the army nor be **c** with any duty; **Dt 24:5** 5674a
the elders of Israel **c** the people, **Dt 27:1** 6680
also **c** the people on that day, **Dt 27:11** 6680
"Moses **c** us with a law, A **Dt 33:4** 6680
He **c** the messenger, saying, **2Sa 11:19** 6680
king **c** Joab and Abishai and Ittai, **2Sa 18:5** 6680
when the king **c** all the commanders **2Sa 18:5** 6680
king **c** you and Abishai and Ittai, **2Sa 18:12** 6680
drew near, he **c** Solomon his son, **1Ki 2:1** 6680
and **c** him to build a house for the **1Ch 22:6** 6680
Then he **c** them saying, **2Ch 19:9** 6680
may be **c** against this generation, **Lk 11:50** *1567a*
be **c** against this generation.' **Lk 11:51** *1567a*
for we have already **c** that both **Ro 3:9** *4256*

CHARGES

and **c** her with shameful deeds and **Dt 22:14** 7760
And against His angels He **c** error. **Jb 4:18** 7760
and brought **c** against the Jews. **Da 3:8** 7170
many **c** they bring against You!" **Mk 15:4** *2723*
the **c** which you make against Him. **Lk 23:14** *2723*
them bring **c** against one another. **Ac 19:38** *1458*
bring **c** against him before you." **Ac 23:30** *3004*
c to the governor against Paul. **Ac 24:1** *1718*
"Nor can they prove to you *the* **c** **Ac 24:13**
the Jews brought **c** against Paul, **Ac 25:2** *1718*
bringing many and serious **c** **Ac 25:7** *159b*
stand trial before me on these **c**?" **Ac 25:9**
of the Jews brought **c** against him, **Ac 25:15** *1718*
to make his defense against the **c**. **Ac 25:16** *1462*
they *began* bringing **c** against him **Ac 25:18** *156*
indicate also the **c** against him." **Ac 25:27** *156*

CHARGING

When Jacob finished **c** his sons, **Gn 49:33** 6680
Like a horse **c** into the battle. **Jer 8:6** 7857
Horsemen **c**, Swords flashing, **Na 3:3** 5927

CHARIOT

He had him ride in his second **c**; **Gn 41:43** 4818
Joseph prepared his **c** and went **Gn 46:29** 4818
So he made his **c** ready and took **Ex 14:6** 7393
caused their **c** wheels to swerve, **Ex 14:25** 4818
from *his* **c** and fled away on foot. **Jg 4:15** 4818
'Why does his **c** delay in coming? **Jg 5:28** 7393
and David hamstrung the **c** horses, **2Sa 8:4** 7393
for himself a **c** and horses and **2Sa 15:1** 4818
like the workmanship of a **c** wheel. **1Ki 7:33** 4818
his captains, his **c** commanders, **1Ki 9:22** 7393
and he stationed them in the **c** **1Ki 10:26** 7393
A **c** was imported from Egypt **1Ki 10:29** 4818
mount his **c** to flee to Jerusalem. **1Ki 12:18** 4818
'Prepare *your* **c** and go down, **1Ki 18:44**
for horse, and **c** for chariot. **1Ki 20:25** 7393
for horse, and chariot for **c**. **1Ki 20:25** 7393
and he took him up into the **c**. **1Ki 20:33** 4818
So he said to the driver of his **c**, **1Ki 22:34** 7395
in his **c** in front of the Arameans, **1Ki 22:35** 4818
ran into the bottom of the **c**. **1Ki 22:35** 7393
the **c** by the pool of Samaria, **1Ki 22:38** 7393
there appeared a **c** of fire and **2Ki 2:11** 7393
from the **c** to meet him and said, **2Ki 5:21** 4818
man turned from his **c** to meet you? **2Ki 5:26** 4818
rode in a **c** and went to Jezreel, **2Ki 9:16** 7392
And they made his **c** ready. **2Ki 9:21** 7393
of Judah went out, each in his **c**, **2Ki 9:21** 7393
his heart and he sank in his **c**. **2Ki 9:24** 7393
"Shoot him too, in the **c**." **2Ki 9:27** 4818
carried him in a **c** to Jerusalem and **2Ki 9:28** 7392
he took him up to him into the **c**. **2Ki 10:15** 4818
So he made him ride in his **c**. **2Ki 10:16** 7393
his body in a **c** from Megiddo, **2Ki 23:30** 7392
David hamstrung all the **c** horses, **1Ch 18:4** 7393
and gold for the model of the **c**, **1Ch 28:18** 4818
and he stationed them in the **c** **2Ch 1:14** 7393
and he stationed them in the **c** **2Ch 9:25** 7393
mount his **c** to flee to Jerusalem. **2Ch 10:18** 4818
So he said to the driver of the **c**, **2Ch 18:33** 7395
of Israel propped himself up in his **c** **2Ch 18:34** 4818
So his servants took him out of the **c** **2Ch 35:24** 4818
him in the second **c** which he had, **2Ch 35:24** 7393
He makes the clouds His **c**; **Ps 104:3** 7398
horses seem like flint and its **c** **Is 5:28**
brings forth the **c** and the horse, **Is 43:17** 7393
you I shatter the **c** and its rider, **Jer 51:21** 7393
the **c** to the team of horses, **Mi 1:13** 4818
With the first **c** *were* red horses, **Zch 6:2** 4818
with the second **c** black horses, **Zch 6:2** 4818
with the third **c** white horses, and **Zch 6:3** 4818
fourth **c** strong dappled horses. **Zch 6:3** 4818
I will cut off the **c** from Ephraim And **Zch 9:10** 7393
returning and sitting in his **c**, **Ac 8:28** *716*
"Go up and join this **c**." **Ac 8:29** *716*
And he ordered the **c** to stop; **Ac 8:38** *716*

CHARIOTEERS

and David killed 700 **c** of the **2Sa 10:18** 7393
7,000 **c** and 40,000 foot soldiers, **1Ch 19:18** 7393
at My table with horses and **c**, **Ezk 39:20** 7393

CHARIOTS

up with him both **c** and horsemen; **Gn 50:9** 7393
and he took six hundred select **c**, **Ex 14:7** 7393
and all the *other* **c** of Egypt with **Ex 14:7** 7393
all the horses *and* **c** of Pharaoh, **Ex 14:9** 7393
through his **c** and his horsemen. **Ex 14:17** 7393
through his **c** and his horsemen." **Ex 14:18** 7393
his **c** and his horsemen went in **Ex 14:23** 7393
over their **c** and their horsemen." **Ex 14:26** 7393
covered the **c** and the horsemen, **Ex 14:28** 7393
"Pharaoh's **c** and his army He has **Ex 15:4** 4818
For the horses of Pharaoh with his **c** **Ex 15:19** 7393
army, to its horses and its **c**, **Dt 11:4** 7393
c *and* people more numerous than you **Dt 20:1** 7393
with very many horses and **c**. **Jos 11:4** 7393
and burn their **c** with fire." **Jos 11:6** 4818
and burned their **c** with fire. **Jos 11:9** 4818
in the valley land have **c** of iron, **Jos 17:16** 7393
even though they have **c** of iron **Jos 17:18** 7393
c and horsemen to the Red Sea. **Jos 24:6** 7393
valley because they had iron **c**. **Jg 1:19** 7393
for he had nine hundred iron **c**, **Jg 4:3** 7393
with his **c** and his many *troops* to **Jg 4:7** 7393
Sisera called together all his **c**, **Jg 4:13** 7393
his chariots, nine hundred iron **c**, **Jg 4:13** 7393
and all *his* **c** and all *his* army with **Jg 4:15** 7393
But Barak pursued the **c** and the **Jg 4:16** 7393
do the hoofbeats of his **c** tarry?' **Jg 5:28** 4818
and place *them* for himself in his **c** **1Sa 8:11** 4818
and they will run before his **c**. **1Sa 8:11** 4818
of war and equipment for his **c**. **1Sa 8:12** 7393
30,000 **c** and 6,000 horsemen, **1Sa 13:5** 7393
the **c** and the horsemen pursued him **2Sa 1:6** 7393
reserved *enough* of them for 100 **c**. **2Sa 8:4** 7393
So he prepared for himself **c** and **1Ki 1:5** 7393
40,000 stalls of horses for his **c**, **1Ki 4:26** 4817
even the cities for his **c** and the **1Ki 9:19** 7393
Solomon gathered **c** and horsemen; **1Ki 10:26** 7393
had 1,400 **c** and 12,000 horsemen, **1Ki 10:26** 7393
Zimri, commander of half his **c**, **1Ki 16:9** 7393
kings with him, and horses and **c**. **1Ki 20:1** 7393
out and struck the horses and **c**, **1Ki 20:21** 7393
the thirty-two captains of his **c**, **1Ki 22:31** 7393
captains of the **c** saw Jehoshaphat, **1Ki 22:32** 7393
When the captains of the **c** saw **1Ki 22:33** 7393
c of Israel and its horsemen!" **2Ki 2:12** 7393
came with his horses and his **c** and **2Ki 5:9** 7393
and **c** and a great army there, **2Ki 6:14** 7393
and **c** was circling the city. **2Ki 6:15** 7393
and **c** of fire all around Elisha. **2Ki 6:17** 7393
sound of **c** and a sound of horses, **2Ki 7:6** 7393
took therefore two **c** with horses, **2Ki 7:14** 7393
to Zair, and all his **c** with him. **2Ki 8:21** 7393
him and the captains of the **c**; **2Ki 8:21** 7393
as well as the **c** and horses and a **2Ki 10:2** 7393
and ten **c** and 10,000 footmen, **2Ki 13:7** 7393
c of Israel and its horsemen!" **2Ki 13:14** 7393
on Egypt for **c** and for horsemen? **2Ki 18:24** 7393
"With my many **c** I came up to the **2Ki 19:23** 7393
burned the **c** of the sun with fire. **2Ki 23:11** 4818
David took from him 1,000 **c** **1Ch 18:4** 7393
reserved *enough* of them for 100 **c**. **1Ch 18:4** 7393
c and horsemen from Mesopotamia, **1Ch 19:6** 7393
hired for themselves 32,000 **c**, **1Ch 19:7** 7393
Solomon amassed **c** and horsemen. **2Ch 1:14** 7393
He had 1,400 **c** and 12,000 **2Ch 1:14** 7393
They imported **c** from Egypt for **2Ch 1:17** 4818
his **c** and cities for his horsemen, **2Ch 8:6** 7393
of his **c** and his horsemen. **2Ch 8:9** 7393
horses and **c** and 12,000 horsemen, **2Ch 9:25** 4818
with 1,200 **c** and 60,000 horsemen. **2Ch 12:3** 7393
army of a million men and 300 **c**, **2Ch 14:9** 4818
with very many **c** and horsemen? **2Ch 16:8** 7393
commanded the captains of his **c**, **2Ch 18:30** 7393
captains of the **c** saw Jehoshaphat, **2Ch 18:31** 7393
captains of the **c** saw that it was not **2Ch 18:32** 7393
commanders and all his **c** with him. **2Ch 21:9** 7393
him and the commanders of the **c**. **2Ch 21:9** 7393
Some *boast* in **c** and some in **Ps 20:7** 7393
He burns the **c** with fire. **Ps 46:9** 5699
The **c** of God are myriads, **Ps 68:17** 7393
My mare among the **c** of Pharaoh. **SS 1:9** 7393
Over the **c** of my noble people." **SS 6:12** 4818
And there is no end to their **c**. **Is 2:7** 4818
took up the quiver With the **c**, **Is 22:6** 7393
choicest valleys were full of **c**, **Is 22:7** 7393
And there your splendid **c** will be, **Is 22:18** 4818
trust in **c** because they are many And **Is 31:1** 7393
on Egypt for **c** and for horsemen? **Is 36:9** 7393
'With my many **c** I came up to the **Is 37:24** 7393
fire And His **c** like the whirlwind, **Is 66:15** 4818
to the LORD, on horses, in **c**, **Is 66:20** 7393
And his **c** like the whirlwind; **Jer 4:13** 4818
David, riding in **c** and on horses, **Jer 17:25** 7393
throne, riding in **c** and on horses, **Jer 22:4** 7393
horses, and drive madly, you **c**, **Jer 46:9** 7393
stallions, The tumult of his **c**, **Jer 47:3** 7393
their horses and against their **c** And **Jer 50:37** 7393
come against you with weapons, **c** and **Ezk 23:24** 7393
king of kings, with horses, **c**, **Ezk 26:7** 7393
noise of cavalry and wagons and **c** when **Ezk 26:10** 7393
will storm against him with **c**, **Da 11:40** 7393
With a noise as of **c** They leap on **Jl 2:5** 4818
from among you And destroy your **c**. **Mi 5:10** 4818
The **c** are *enveloped* in flashing **Na 2:3** 7393
The **c** race madly in the streets, **Na 2:4** 7393
"I will burn up her **c** in smoke, **Na 2:13** 7393
Galloping horses And bounding **c**! **Na 3:2** 4818
Your horses, On Your **c** of salvation? **Hab 3:8** 4818
overthrow the **c** and their riders, **Hg 2:22** 4818
four **c** were coming forth from **Zch 6:1** 4818
wings was like the sound of **c**, **Rv 9:9** *716*
and **c** and slaves and human lives. **Rv 18:13** *4480*

CHARITY

give that which is within as **c**, **Lk 11:41** *1654*
your possessions and give to **c**; **Lk 12:33** *1654*
with deeds of kindness and **c** which **Ac 9:36** *1654*

Context	Reference	Number
CHARM		
is a **c** in the sight of its owner;	Pr 17:8	68, 2580
C is deceitful and beauty is vain,	Pr 31:30	2580
you will not know how to **c** away;	Is 47:11	7837
Adders, for which there is no **c**,	Jer 8:17	3908
CHARMED		
the serpent bites before being **c**,	Ec 10:11	3908
CHARMER		
there is no profit for the **c**.	Ec 10:11	1167, 3956
CHARMERS		
it does not hear the voice of **c**,	Ps 58:5	3907
CHARMING		
of the harlot, The **c** one,	Na 3:4	2580, 2896a
CHARMS		
you are, *My* love, with *all* your **c**!	SS 7:6	8588
CHARRED		
and its middle part has been **c**,	Ezk 15:4	2787
fire has consumed it and it is **c**,	Ezk 15:5	2787
CHASE		
heart, and he will **c** after them;	Ex 14:4	7291
'But you will **c** your enemies and	Lv 26:7	7291
five of you will **c** a hundred,	Lv 26:8	7291
of you will **c** ten thousand,	Lv 26:8	7291
the sound of a driven leaf will **c** them	Lv 26:36	7291
"How could one **c** a thousand, And	Dt 32:30	7291
CHASED		
and he **c** after the sons of Israel	Ex 14:8	7291
Then the Egyptians **c** after them	Ex 14:9	7291
against you and **c** you as bees do,	Dt 1:44	7291
Abimelech **c** him, and he fled	Jg 9:40	7291
And **c** from the inhabited world.	Jb 18:18	5074
vision of the night he is **c** away.	Jb 20:8	5074
And be **c** like chaff in the	Is 17:13	7291
They **c** us on the mountains,	La 4:19	1814
CHASES		
a bribe And **c** after rewards.	Is 1:23	7291
CHASING		
Israel returned from **c** the Philistines	1Sa 17:53	1814
CHASM		
nests Beyond the mouth of the **c**.	Jer 48:28	6354
and you there is a great **c** fixed,	Lk 16:26	*5490*
CHASTE		
your **c** and respectful behavior.	1Pe 3:2	*53*
for they have kept themselves **c**.	Rv 14:4	*3933*
CHASTEN		
anger, Nor **c** me in Your wrath.	Ps 6:1	3256
And **c** me not in Your burning anger.	Ps 38:1	3256
You **c** a man for iniquity;	Ps 39:11	3256
is the man whom You **c**,	Ps 94:12	3256
But I will **c** you justly And will	Jer 30:11	3256
CHASTENED		
is also **c** with pain on his bed,	Jb 33:19	3198
all day long And **c** every morning.	Ps 73:14	8433b
CHASTENING		
a prayer, Your **c** was upon them.	Is 26:16	4148
The **c** for our well-being *fell* upon	Is 53:5	4148
They accepted no **c**.	Jer 2:30	4148
CHASTENS		
He who **c** the nations, will He not	Ps 94:10	3256
CHASTISE		
his mother, and when they **c** him,	Dt 21:18	3256
city shall take the man and **c** him,	Dt 22:18	3256
But I will **c** all of them.	Hos 5:2	4148
I will **c** them in accordance with	Hos 7:12	3256
it is My desire, I will **c** them;	Hos 10:10	3256
CHASTISED		
'You have **c** me, and I was	Jer 31:18	3256
have chastised me, and I was **c**,	Jer 31:18	3256
CHASTISEMENT		
'I have borne **c**; I will not	Jb 34:31	
The rods of **c** were sworn.	Hab 3:9	561
CHATTER		
avoiding worldly *and* empty **c** *and*	1Tm 6:20	*2757*
But avoid worldly *and* empty **c**,	2Tm 2:16	*2757*
CHEAPLY		
You sell Your people **c**,	Ps 44:12	3808, 1952
CHEAT		
And to **c** with dishonest scales,	Am 8:5	5791
CHEATED		
"Yet your father has **c** me and	Gn 31:7	8524
CHEBAR		
by the river **C** among the exiles,	Ezk 1:1	3529
of the Chaldeans by the river **C**;	Ezk 1:3	3529
beside the river **C** at Tel-abib,	Ezk 3:15	3529
glory which I saw by the river **C**,	Ezk 3:23	3529
beings that I saw by the river **C**,	Ezk 10:15	3529
the God of Israel by the river **C**;	Ezk 10:20	3529
I had seen by the river **C**.	Ezk 10:22	3529
vision which I saw by the river **C**;	Ezk 43:3	3529
CHECK		
bit and bridle to hold them in **c**,	Ps 32:9	1102
have not kept their feet in **c**.	Jer 14:10	2820
CHECKED		
living, so that the plague was **c**.	Nu 16:48	6113
for the plague had been **c**.	Nu 16:50	6113
on the sons of Israel was **c**.	Nu 25:8	6113
CHECKERED		
and a robe and a tunic of **c** work,	Ex 28:4	8665
the tunic of **c** work of fine linen,	Ex 28:39	7660
CHEDORLAOMER		
king of Ellasar, **C** king of Elam,	Gn 14:1	3540
Twelve years they had served **C**,	Gn 14:4	3540
In the fourteenth year **C** and	Gn 14:5	3540
against **C** king of Elam and Tidal	Gn 14:9	3540
after his return from the defeat of **C**	Gn 14:17	3540
CHEEK		
struck Micaiah on the **c** and said,	1Ki 22:24	3895
struck Micaiah on the **c** and said,	2Ch 18:23	3895
slapped me on the **c** with contempt;	Jb 16:10	3895
smitten all my enemies on the **c**;	Ps 3:7	3895
Let him give his **c** to the smiter,	La 3:30	3895
the judge of Israel on the **c**.	Mi 5:1	3895
whoever slaps you on your right **c**,	Mt 5:39	*4600*
"Whoever hits you on the **c**,	Lk 6:29	*4600*
CHEEKS		
and the two **c** and the stomach.	Dt 18:3	3895
"Your **c** are lovely with	SS 1:10	3895
"His **c** are like a bed of balsam,	SS 5:13	3895
And My **c** to those who pluck out	Is 50:6	3895
night And her tears are on her **c**;	La 1:2	3895
CHEER		
me that I may have a little **c**	Jb 10:20	1082
CHEERFUL		
off my *sad* countenance and be **c**,'	Jb 9:27	1082
A joyful heart makes a **c** face,	Pr 15:13	3190
a **c** heart *has* a continual feast.	Pr 15:15	2896a
drink your wine with a **c** heart;	Ec 9:7	2896a
c feasts for the house of Judah;	Zch 8:19	2896a
for God loves a **c** giver.	2Co 9:7	*2431*
Is anyone **c**? He is to sing praises.	Jas 5:13	*2114*
CHEERFULLY		
And Agag came to him **c**.	1Sa 15:32	4575b
this nation, I **c** make my defense,	Ac 24:10	*2115b*
CHEERFULNESS		
he who shows mercy, with **c**.	Ro 12:8	*2432*
CHEERS		
my new wine, which **c** God and men,	Jg 9:13	8055
CHEESE		
"Bring also these ten cuts of **c**	1Sa 17:18	2461
curds, sheep, and **c** of the herd,	2Sa 17:29	8194
like milk And curdle me like **c**;	Jb 10:10	1385
CHELAL		
Adna, **C**, Benaiah, Maaseiah,	Ezr 10:30	3636
CHELUB		
C the brother of Shuhah became	1Ch 4:11	3620
Ezri the son of **C** had charge	1Ch 27:26	3620
CHELUBAI		
to him *were* Jerahmeel, Ram and **C**.	1Ch 2:9	3621
CHELUHI		
Benaiah, Bedeiah, **C**,	Ezr 10:35	3622
CHEMOSH		
You are ruined, O people of **C**!	Nu 21:29	3645
C your god gives you to possess?	Jg 11:24	3645
for **C** the detestable idol of Moab,	1Ki 11:7	3645
the Sidonians, **C** the god of Moab,	1Ki 11:33	3645
and for **C** the abomination of Moab,	2Ki 23:13	3645
And **C** will go off into exile	Jer 48:7	3645
"And Moab will be ashamed of **C**,	Jer 48:13	3645
The people of **C** have perished;	Jer 48:46	3645
CHENAANAH		
Then Zedekiah the son of **C** made	1Ki 22:11	3668
Then Zedekiah the son of **C** came	1Ki 22:24	3668
were Jeush, Benjamin, Ehud, **C**,	1Ch 7:10	3668
Zedekiah the son of **C** made	2Ch 18:10	3668
Then Zedekiah the son of **C** came	2Ch 18:23	3668
CHENANI		
Bunni, Sherebiah, Bani *and* **C**,	Ne 9:4	3662
CHENANIAH		
C, chief of the Levites, was	1Ch 15:22	3663
and the singers and **C** the leader	1Ch 15:27	3663
C and his sons were *assigned* to	1Ch 26:29	3663
CHEPHAR-AMMONI		
and **C** and Ophni and Geba;	Jos 18:24	3726
CHEPHIRAH		
Now their cities *were* Gibeon and **C**	Jos 9:17	3716a
and Mizpeh and **C** and Mozah,	Jos 18:26	3716a
the sons of Kiriath-arim, **C** and	Ezr 2:25	3716a
the men of Kiriath-jearim, **C** and	Ne 7:29	3716a
CHEPHIRIM		
at **C** in the plain of Ono."	Ne 6:2	3716b
CHERAN		
and Eshban and Ithran and **C**.	Gn 36:26	3763
Hamran, Eshban, Ithran and **C**.	1Ch 1:41	3763
CHERETHITES		
made a raid on the Negev of the **C**,	1Sa 30:14	3774
was over the **C** and the Pelethites;	2Sa 8:18	3774
passed on beside him, all the **C**,	2Sa 15:18	3774
along with the **C** and the	2Sa 20:7	3774
was over the **C** and the Pelethites;	2Sa 20:23	3774
the son of Jehoiada, the **C**,	1Ki 1:38	3774
the son of Jehoiada, the **C**,	1Ki 1:44	3774
was over the **C** and the Pelethites,	1Ch 18:17	3774
even cut off the **C** and destroy the	Ezk 25:16	3774
the seacoast, The nation of the **C**!	Zph 2:5	3774
CHERISH		
or daughter, or the wife you **c**,	Dt 13:6	2436
God, which these men **c** themselves,	Ac 24:15	*4327*
CHERISHES		
his brother and toward the wife he **c**	Dt 28:54	2436
be hostile toward the husband she **c**	Dt 28:56	2436
own flesh, but nourishes and **c** it,	Eph 5:29	*2282*
CHERITH		
and hide yourself by the brook **C**,	1Ki 17:3	3747
he went and lived by the brook **C**,	1Ki 17:5	3747
CHERUB		
"Make one **c** at one end and	Ex 25:19	3742
end and one **c** at the other end;	Ex 25:19	3742
one **c** at the one end and one	Ex 37:8	3742
end and one **c** at the other end;	Ex 37:8	3742
"And He rode on a **c** and flew;	2Sa 22:11	3742
Five cubits *was* the one wing of the **c**	1Ki 6:24	3742
cubits the other wing of the **c**;	1Ki 6:24	3742
The other **c** *was* ten cubits;	1Ki 6:25	3742
of the one **c** *was* ten cubits,	1Ki 6:26	3742
cubits, and so *was* the other **c**.	1Ki 6:26	3742
c was touching the other wall.	1Ki 6:27	3742
touched the wing of the other **c**.	2Ch 3:11	3742
The wing of the other **c**,	2Ch 3:12	3742
to the wing of the first **c**.	2Ch 3:12	3742
up from Tel-melah, Tel-harsha, **C**,	Ezr 2:59	3743
up from Tel-melah, Tel-harsha, **C**,	Ne 7:61	3743
He rode upon a **c** and flew;	Ps 18:10	3742
from the **c** on which it had been,	Ezk 9:3	3742
glory of the LORD went up from the **c**	Ezk 10:4	3742
Then the **c** stretched out his hand	Ezk 10:7	3742
cherubim, one wheel beside each **c**;	Ezk 10:9	3742
first face *was* the face of a **c**,	Ezk 10:14	3742
were the anointed **c** who covers,	Ezk 28:14	3742
have destroyed you, O covering **c**,	Ezk 28:16	3742
tree was between **c** and cherub,	Ezk 41:18	3742
tree was between cherub and **c**,	Ezk 41:18	3742
cherub, and every **c** had two faces,	Ezk 41:18	3742
CHERUBIM		
garden of Eden He stationed the **c** and	Gn 3:24	3742
"You shall make two **c** of gold,	Ex 25:18	3742
you shall make the **c** *of one piece*	Ex 25:19	3742
"The **c** shall have *their* wings	Ex 25:20	3742
the faces of the **c** are to be	Ex 25:20	3742
from between the two **c** which are	Ex 25:22	3742
you shall make them with **c**,	Ex 26:1	3742
it shall be made with **c**,	Ex 26:31	3742
and scarlet *material,* with **c**,	Ex 36:8	3742
he made it with **c**, the work of a	Ex 36:35	3742
He made two **c** of gold;	Ex 37:7	3742
he made the **c** *of one piece* with	Ex 37:8	3742
c had *their* wings spread upward,	Ex 37:9	3742
the **c** were toward the mercy seat.	Ex 37:9	3742
testimony, from between the two **c**,	Nu 7:89	3742
of hosts who sits *above* the **c**;	1Sa 4:4	3742
who is enthroned *above* the **c**.	2Sa 6:2	3742
he made two **c** of olive wood,	1Ki 6:23	3742
both the **c** were of the same	1Ki 6:25	3742
He placed the **c** in the midst	1Ki 6:27	3742
wings of the **c** were spread out,	1Ki 6:27	3742
He also overlaid the **c** with gold.	1Ki 6:28	3742
about with carved engravings of **c**,	1Ki 6:29	3742
he carved on them carvings of **c**,	1Ki 6:32	3742
on the **c** and on the palm trees.	1Ki 6:32	3742
He carved *on it* **c**,	1Ki 6:35	3742
the frames *were* lions, oxen and **c**;	1Ki 7:29	3742
its stays and on its borders, **c**,	1Ki 7:36	3742
place, under the wings of the **c**.	1Ki 8:6	3742
For the **c** spread *their* wings over	1Ki 8:7	3742
and the **c** made a covering over the	1Ki 8:7	3742
who are enthroned *above* the **c**,	2Ki 19:15	3742
LORD who is enthroned *above* the **c**,	1Ch 13:6	3742
model of the chariot, *even* the **c** that	1Ch 28:18	3742
and he carved **c** on the walls.	2Ch 3:7	3742
Then he made two sculptured **c** in	2Ch 3:10	3742
of the **c** *was* twenty cubits;	2Ch 3:11	3742
of these **c** extended twenty cubits,	2Ch 3:13	3742
fine linen, and he worked **c** on it.	2Ch 3:14	3742
holies, under the wings of the **c**.	2Ch 5:7	3742
For the **c** spread their wings over	2Ch 5:8	3742
so that the **c** made a covering over	2Ch 5:8	3742
who are enthroned *above* the **c**,	Ps 80:1	3742
He is enthroned *above* the **c**,	Ps 99:1	3742
who is enthroned *above* the **c**,	Is 37:16	3742
that was over the heads of the **c**	Ezk 10:1	3742
the whirling wheels under the **c** and	Ezk 10:2	3742
coals of fire from between the **c** and	Ezk 10:2	3742
Now the **c** were standing on the	Ezk 10:3	3742
the sound of the wings of the **c**	Ezk 10:5	3742
wheels, from between the **c**,"	Ezk 10:6	3742
hand from between the **c** to the fire	Ezk 10:7	3742
the fire which was between the **c**,	Ezk 10:7	3742
The **c** appeared to have the	Ezk 10:8	3742
behold, four wheels beside the **c**,	Ezk 10:9	3742
Then the **c** rose up.	Ezk 10:15	3742
Now when the **c** moved, the wheels	Ezk 10:16	3742
also when the **c** lifted up their	Ezk 10:16	3742
When the **c** stood still, the wheels	Ezk 10:17	
the temple and stood over the **c**.	Ezk 10:18	3742
When the **c** departed, they lifted	Ezk 10:19	3742
so I knew that they *were* **c**.	Ezk 10:20	3742
Then the **c** lifted up their wings	Ezk 11:22	3742
was carved with **c** and palm trees;	Ezk 41:18	3742
c and palm trees were carved,	Ezk 41:20	3742
c and palm trees like those carved	Ezk 41:25	3742
and above it *were* the **c** of glory	Heb 9:5	*5502*
CHESALON		
Jearim on the north (that is, **C**),	Jos 15:10	3693
CHESED		
and **C** and Hazo and Pildash and	Gn 22:22	3777
CHESIL		
and Eltolad and **C** and Hormah,	Jos 15:30	3686
CHEST		
a **c** and bored a hole in its lid and	2Ki 12:9	727
there was much money in the **c**,	2Ki 12:10	727
and they made a **c** and set it	2Ch 24:8	727
the **c** until they had finished.	2Ch 24:10	727
It came about whenever the **c**	2Ch 24:11	727

officer would come, empty the c, 2Ch 24:11 727
and girded across His c with a golden Rv 1:13 3149

CHESTS
And I will tear open their c; Hos 13:8 5458, 3820
and girded around their c with golden Rv 15:6 4738

CHESULLOTH
Jezreel and *included* C and Shunem, Jos 19:18 3694

CHEW
among those which c the cud, Lv 11:4 5927
a split hoof, it does not c cud, Lv 11:7 1641
split *hoof,* or which do not c cud, Lv 11:26 5927
these among those which c the cud, Dt 14:7 5927
for though they c the cud, Dt 14:7 5927
divides the hoof but *does* not c Dt 14:8

CHEWED
their teeth, before it was c, Nu 11:33 3772

CHEWS
making split hoofs, *and* c the cud, Lv 11:3 5927
the camel, for though it c cud, Lv 11:4 5927
shaphan, for though it c cud, Lv 11:5 5927
rabbit also, for though it c cud, Lv 11:6 5927
hoof split in two *and* c the cud, Dt 14:6 5927

CHEZIB
and it was at C that she bore him. Gn 38:5 3580

CHICKS
hen gathers her c under her wings, Mt 23:37 3556a

CHIDON
came to the threshing floor of C, 1Ch 13:9 3592

CHIEF
firstborn of Esau, are c Teman, Gn 36:15 441b
of Esau, are chief Teman, c Omar, Gn 36:15 441b
chief Teman, chief Omar, c Zepho, Gn 36:15 441b
chief Omar, chief Zepho, c Kenaz, Gn 36:15 441b
c Korah, chief Gatam, chief Amalek. Gn 36:16 441b
chief Korah, c Gatam, chief Amalek. Gn 36:16 441b
Korah, chief Gatam, c Amalek. Gn 36:16 441b
c Nahath, chief Zerah, chief Gn 36:17 441b
chief Nahath, c Zerah, chief Gn 36:17 441b
Nahath, chief Zerah, c Shammah, Gn 36:17 441b
Zerah, chief Shammah, c Mizzah. Gn 36:17 441b
c Jeush, chief Jalam, chief Korah. Gn 36:18 441b
chief Jeush, c Jalam, chief Korah. Gn 36:18 441b
chief Jeush, chief Jalam, c Korah. Gn 36:18 441b
c Lotan, chief Shobal, chief Gn 36:29 441b
chief Lotan, c Shobal, chief Gn 36:29 441b
Lotan, chief Shobal, c Zibeon, Gn 36:29 441b
Shobal, chief Zibeon, c Anah, Gn 36:29 441b
c Dishon, chief Ezer, chief Dishan. Gn 36:30 441b
chief Dishon, c Ezer, chief Dishan. Gn 36:30 441b
Dishon, chief Ezer, c Dishan. Gn 36:30 441b
c Timna, chief Alvah, chief Gn 36:40 441b
chief Timna, c Alvah, chief Gn 36:40 441b
Timna, chief Alvah, c Jetheth, Gn 36:40 441b
c Oholibamah, chief Elah, chief Gn 36:41 441b
chief Oholibamah, c Elah, Gn 36:41 441b
Oholibamah, chief Elah, c Pinon, Gn 36:41 441b
c Kenaz, chief Teman, chief Gn 36:42 441b
chief Kenaz, c Teman, chief Gn 36:42 441b
Kenaz, chief Teman, c Mibzar, Gn 36:42 441b
c Magdiel, chief Iram. Gn 36:43 441b
chief Magdiel, c Iram. Gn 36:43 441b
in the sight of the c jailer. Gn 39:21 8269
The c jailer committed to Gn 39:22 8269
The c jailer did not supervise Gn 39:23 8269
c cupbearer and the chief baker. Gn 40:2 8269
chief cupbearer and the c baker. Gn 40:2 8269
So the c cupbearer told his dream Gn 40:9 8269
When the c baker saw that he had Gn 40:16 8269
lifted up the head of the c cupbearer Gn 40:20 8269
of the c baker among his servants. Gn 40:20 8269
the c cupbearer to his office, Gn 40:21 8269
but he hanged the c baker, Gn 40:22 8269
Yet the c cupbearer did not Gn 40:23 8269
the c cupbearer spoke to Pharaoh, Gn 41:9 8269
both me and the c baker. Gn 41:10 8269
was the c of the leaders of Levi, Nu 3:32 5387a
one c for each father's household Jos 22:14 5387a
"Come and be our c that we may Jg 11:6 7101
made him head and c over them; Jg 11:11 7101
Edomite, the c of Saul's shepherds. 1Sa 21:7 47
and David took control of the c 2Sa 8:1 522b
and David's sons were c ministers. 2Sa 8:18 3548
a Tahchemonite, c of the captains, 2Sa 23:8 7218
Then three of the thirty c men 2Sa 23:13 7218
of Zeruiah, was c of the thirty. 2Sa 23:18 7218
besides Solomon's 3,300 c deputies 1Ki 5:16 8269
These *were* the c officers who 1Ki 9:23 8269
the guard took Seraiah the c priest 2Ki 25:18 7218
c Timna, chief Aliah, chief 1Ch 1:51 441b
chief Timna, c Aliah, chief 1Ch 1:51 441b
Timna, chief Aliah, c Jetheth, 1Ch 1:51 441b
c Oholibamah, chief Elah, chief 1Ch 1:52 441b
chief Oholibamah, c Elah, 1Ch 1:52 441b
Oholibamah, chief Elah, c Pinon, 1Ch 1:52 441b
c Kenaz, chief Teman, chief 1Ch 1:53 441b
chief Kenaz, c Teman, chief 1Ch 1:53 441b
Kenaz, chief Teman, c Mibzar, 1Ch 1:53 441b
c Magdiel, chief Iram. 1Ch 1:54 441b
chief Magdiel, c Iram. 1Ch 1:54 441b
generations, *were* Jeiel the c, 1Ch 5:7 7218
Joel *was* the c and Shapham the 1Ch 5:12 7218
all five of them *were* c men. 1Ch 7:3 7218
to their generations, c men who 1Ch 8:28 7218
the c officer of the house of God; 1Ch 9:11 5057
their relatives (Shallum the c 1Ch 9:17 7218
c gatekeepers who *were* Levites, 1Ch 9:26 5057
to their generations, c men, 1Ch 9:34 7218
first shall be c and commander." 1Ch 11:6 7218
went up first, so he became c. 1Ch 11:6 7218
a Hachmonite, the c of the thirty; 1Ch 11:11 7218
Now three of the thirty c men went 1Ch 11:15 7218
of Joab, he was c of the thirty, 1Ch 11:20 7218
Reubenite, a c of the Reubenites, 1Ch 11:42 7218
The c was Ahiezer, then Joash, the 1Ch 12:3 7218
who was the c of the thirty, 1Ch 12:18 7218
the sons of Kohath, Uriel the c, 1Ch 15:5 8269
the sons of Merari, Asaiah the c, 1Ch 15:6 8269
the sons of Gershom, Joel the c, 1Ch 15:7 8269
sons of Elizaphan, Shemaiah the c, 1Ch 15:8 8269
the sons of Hebron, Eliel the c, 1Ch 15:9 8269
sons of Uzziel, Amminadab the c, 1Ch 15:10 8269
Chenaniah, c of the Levites, 1Ch 15:22 8269
Asaph the c, and second to him 1Ch 16:5 7218
son of Gershom *was* Shebuel the c. 1Ch 23:16 7218
son of Eliezer was Rehabiah the c; 1Ch 23:17 7218
son of Izhar was Shelomith the c. 1Ch 23:18 7218
Since more c men were found from 1Ch 24:4 7218
of the gatekeepers, the c men, 1Ch 26:12 7218
for the Hebronites, Jerijah the c 1Ch 26:31 7218
and was c of all the commanders of 1Ch 27:3 7218
Mikloth *being* the c officer; 1Ch 27:4 5057
son of Jehoiada the priest, *as* c; 1Ch 27:5 7218
c officer for the Reubenites was 1Ch 27:16 5057
were men of war, his c captains and 2Ch 8:9 8269
the c officers of King Solomon, 2Ch 8:10 8269
Amariah the c priest will be over 2Ch 19:11 7218
the c *priest* and said to him, 2Ch 24:6 7218
the c priest's officer would come, 2Ch 24:11 7218
Azariah the c priest and all 2Ch 26:20 7218
Azariah the c priest of the 2Ch 31:10 7218
and Azariah *was* the c officer 2Ch 31:13
son of Aaron the c priest. Ezr 7:5 7218
chose a way for them and sat as c, Jb 29:25 7218
the c men over a broad country. Ps 110:6 7218
Has become the c corner *stone.* Ps 118:22 7218
exalt Jerusalem Above my c joy. Ps 137:6 7218
Which, having no c, Pr 6:7 7101
as the c of the mountains, Is 2:2 7218
who was c officer in the house of Jer 20:1 5057
And shout among the c of the nations; Jer 31:7 7218
one of the c officers of the king, Jer 41:1 7227b
the guard took Seraiah the c priest Jer 52:24 7218
Ashpenaz, the c of his officials, Da 1:3 7227b
and c prefect over all the wise men Da 2:48 7229
Belteshazzar, c of the magicians, Da 4:9 7229
appointed him c of the magicians, Da 5:11 7229
Michael, one of the c princes, Da 10:13 7223
as the c of the mountains. Mi 4:1 7218
Gathering together all the c Mt 2:4 749
elders and c priests and scribes, Mt 16:21 749
to the c priests and scribes, Mt 20:18 749
But when the c priests and the Mt 21:15 749
the c priests and the elders of Mt 21:23 749
THIS BECAME THE C CORNER *stone;* Mt 21:42 2776
When the c priests and the Mt 21:45 749
and the c seats in the synagogues, Mt 23:6 4410
Then the c priests and the elders Mt 26:3 749
Iscariot, went to the c priests Mt 26:14 749
from the c priests and elders of Mt 26:47 749
Now the c priests and the whole Mt 26:59 749
all the c priests and the elders Mt 27:1 749
to the c priests and elders, Mt 27:3 749
The c priests took the pieces Mt 27:6 749
by the c priests and elders, Mt 27:12 749
But the c priests and the elders Mt 27:20 749
the same way the c priests also, Mt 27:41 749
the c priests and the Pharisees Mt 27:62 749
c priests all that had happened. Mt 28:11 749
and the c priests and the scribes, Mk 8:31 749
to the c priests and the scribes; Mk 10:33 749
The c priests and the scribes Mk 11:18 749
in the temple, the c priests and Mk 11:27 749
THIS BECAME THE C CORNER *stone* Mk 12:10 2776
and c seats in the synagogues and Mk 12:39 4410
and the c priests and the scribes Mk 14:1 749
twelve, went off to the c priests in Mk 14:10 749
from the c priests and the scribes Mk 14:43 749
and all the c priests and the Mk 14:53 749
Now the c priests and the whole Mk 14:55 749
c priests with the elders and scribes and Mk 15:1 749
The c priests *began* to accuse Mk 15:3 749
For he was aware that the c Mk 15:10 749
But the c priests stirred up the Mk 15:11 749
the same way the c priests also, Mk 15:31 749
elders and c priests and scribes, Lk 9:22 749
For you love the c seats in Lk 11:43 4410
he was a c tax collector and Lk 19:2 754
but the c priests and the scribes Lk 19:47 749
the c priests and the scribes Lk 20:1 749
THIS BECAME THE C CORNER *stone'?* Lk 20:17 2776
The scribes and the c priests Lk 20:19 749
and c seats in the synagogues and Lk 20:46 4410
The c priests and the scribes Lk 22:2 749
away and discussed with the c priests Lk 22:4 749
Then Jesus said to the c priests Lk 22:52 749
both c priests and scribes, Lk 22:66 749
the c priests and the crowds, Lk 23:4 749
And the c priests and the scribes Lk 23:10 749
Pilate summoned the c priests Lk 23:13 749
and how the c priests and our Lk 24:20 749
and the c priests and the Jn 7:32 749
to the c priests and Pharisees, Jn 7:45 749
Therefore the c priests and the Jn 11:47 749
Now the c priests and the Jn 11:57 749
But the c priests planned Jn 12:10 749
the c priests and the Pharisees, Jn 18:3 749
Your own nation and the c priests Jn 18:35 749
So when the c priests and Jn 19:6 749
The c priests answered, Jn 19:15 749
So the c priests of the Jews Jn 19:21 749
but WHICH BECAME THE C CORNER Ac 4:11 2776
and reported all that the c Ac 4:23 749
the c priests heard these words, Ac 5:24 749
authority from the c priests to bind all Ac 9:14 749
them bound before the c priests?" Ac 9:21 749
because he was the c speaker. Ac 14:12 2233
brought them to the c magistrates, Ac 16:20 4755
and the c magistrates tore their Ac 16:22 4755
the c magistrates sent their Ac 16:35 4755
"The c magistrates have sent to Ac 16:36 4755
these words to the c magistrates. Ac 16:38 4755
of one Sceva, a Jewish c priest, Ac 19:14 749
released him and ordered the c priests Ac 22:30 749
to the c priests and the elders and Ac 23:14 749
And the c priests and the leading Ac 25:2 749
the c priests and the elders of Ac 25:15 749
authority from the c priests, Ac 26:10 749
and commission of the c priests, Ac 26:12 749
And when the C Shepherd appears, 1Pe 5:4 750

CHIEFS
are the c of the sons of Esau. Gn 36:15 441b
These are the c descended from Gn 36:16 441b
These are the c descended from Gn 36:17 441b
These are the c descended from Gn 36:18 441b
and these are their c. Gn 36:19 441b
the c descended from the Horites, Gn 36:21 441b
the c descended from the Horites: Gn 36:29 441b
the c descended from the Horites, Gn 36:30 441b
various c in the land of Seir. Gn 36:30 441b
of the c descended from Esau, Gn 36:40 441b
These are the c of Edom Gn 36:43 441b
"Then the c of Edom were dismayed; Ex 15:15 441b
your c, your tribes, your elders Dt 29:10 7218
and said to the c of the men of Jos 10:24 7101
Moses struck with the c of Midian, Jos 13:21 5387a
and with him ten c, Jos 22:14 5387a
The c of all the people, *even* Jg 20:2 6438
here, all you c of the people, 1Sa 14:38 6438
Now the c of Edom were: 1Ch 1:51 441b
These *were* the c of Edom. 1Ch 1:54 441b
do, their c *were* two hundred; 1Ch 12:32 7218
Then David spoke to the c of the 1Ch 15:16 8269
of David *were* c at the king's side. 1Ch 18:17 7223
the c of the earth's people And Jb 12:24 7218
"There also are the c of the north, Ezk 32:30 5257b

CHILD
Sarai was barren; she had no c. Gn 11:30 2056
"Behold, you are with c, Gn 16:11 2030
"Will a c be born to a man one Gn 17:17
ninety years old, bear *a* c?" Gn 17:17
'Shall I indeed bear *a* c, when Gn 18:13
Lot were with c by their father. Gn 19:36 2029
The c grew and was weaned, and Gn 21:8 3206
she is also with c by harlotry." Gn 38:24 2030
"I am with c by the man to whom Gn 38:25 2030
and a little c of *his* old age. Gn 44:20 3206
Then she put the c into it and Ex 2:3 3206
When she opened *it,* she saw the c, Ex 2:6 3206
she may nurse the c for you?" Ex 2:7 3206
"Take this c away and nurse him Ex 2:9 3206
woman took the c and nursed him. Ex 2:9 3206
The c grew, and she brought Ex 2:10 3206
c so that she gives birth prematurely, Ex 21:22 2030
gives birth and bears a male c, Lv 12:2
'But if she bears a female c, Lv 12:5
is the law for her who bears *a* c, Lv 12:7
and has no c and returns to her Lv 22:13 2233
Now she was his one *and* only c; Jg 11:34 3173
and the c grew up and the LORD Jg 13:24 5288
the c and laid him in her lap, Ru 4:16 3206
not go up until the c is weaned; 1Sa 1:22 5288
Shiloh, although the c was young. 1Sa 1:24 5288
both man and woman, c and infant, 1Sa 15:3 5768
had no c to the day of her death. 2Sa 6:23 3206
the c also that is born to you 2Sa 12:14 1121
Then the LORD struck the c that 2Sa 12:15 3206
inquired of God for the c; 2Sa 12:16 5288
the seventh day that the c died. 2Sa 12:18 3206
to tell him that the c was dead, 2Sa 12:18 3206
while the c was *still* alive, 2Sa 12:18 3206
we tell him that the c is dead, 2Sa 12:18 3206
perceived that the c was dead; 2Sa 12:19 3206
said to his servants, "Is the c dead?" 2Sa 12:19 3206
While the c was alive, you fasted 2Sa 12:21 3206
but when the c died, you arose and 2Sa 12:21 3206
"While the c was *still* alive, I 2Sa 12:22 3206
to me, that the c may live.' 2Sa 12:22 3206
David, yet I am but a little c; 1Ki 3:7 5288
to a c while she *was* in the house. 1Ki 3:17 3205
this woman also gave birth to a c, 1Ki 3:18 3205
"Divide the living c in two, 1Ki 3:25 3206
woman whose c *was* the living one 1Ki 3:26 1121
my lord, give her the living c, 1Ki 3:26 3205
"Give the first woman the living c, 1Ki 3:27 3205
enter the city the c will die. 1Ki 14:12 3206
of the house, the c died. 1Ki 14:17 5288
himself upon the c three times, 1Ki 17:21 3206
and the life of the c returned to 1Ki 17:22 3206
Elijah took the c and 1Ki 17:23 3206
When the c was grown, the day came 2Ki 4:18 3206
Is it well with the c?' " 2Ki 4:26 3206
And he went up and lay on the c, 2Ki 4:34 3206
the flesh of the c became warm. 2Ki 4:34 3206

like the flesh of a little **c** and **2Ki 5:14** 5288
women with **c** you will rip up." **2Ki 8:12** 2030
up all its women who were with **c**. **2Ki 15:16** 2030
weaned **c** *rests* against his mother, **Ps 131:2**
soul is like a weaned **c** within me. **Ps 131:2**
up a **c** in the way he should go, **Pr 22:6** 5288
is bound up in the heart of a **c**; **Pr 22:15** 5288
hold back discipline from the **c**, **Pr 23:13** 5288
But a **c** who gets his own way **Pr 29:15** 5288
She is the pure **c** of the one **SS 6:9**
will be with **c** and bear a son, **Is 7:14** 2030
For a **c** will be born to us, a son **Is 9:6** 3206
That a **c** could write them down. **Is 10:19** 5288
The nursing **c** will play by the **Is 11:8**
And the weaned **c** will put his hand **Is 11:8**
"Can a woman forget her nursing **c** And **Is 49:15** 5764
you who have borne no **c**; Break **Is 54:1**
one giving birth to her first **c**, **Jer 4:31** 1069
The woman with **c** and she who is in **Jer 31:8** 2030
and she who is in labor with **c**, **Jer 31:8**
Is he a delightful **c**? **Jer 31:20** 3206
you man and woman, **c** and infant, **Jer 44:7** 5768
she who is in labor has borne a **c**. **Mi 5:3**
to be with **c** by the Holy Spirit. **Mt 1:18** *1722, 1064*
for the **C** who has been conceived in **Mt 1:20**
THE VIRGIN SHALL BE WITH **C** **Mt 1:23** *1722, 1064*
and search carefully for the **C**; **Mt 2:8** *3813*
stood over *the place* where the **C** was. **Mt 2:9** *3813*
saw the **C** with Mary His mother; **Mt 2:11** *3813*
Take the **C** and His mother **Mt 2:13** *3813*
search for the **C** to destroy Him." **Mt 2:13** *3813*
the **C** and His mother while it **Mt 2:14** *3813*
take the **C** and His mother, **Mt 2:20** *3813*
took the **C** and His mother, **Mt 2:21** *3813*
to death, and a father *his* **c**; **Mt 10:21** *5043*
And He called a **c** to Himself and **Mt 18:2** *3813*
then humbles himself as this **c**, **Mt 18:4** *3813*
one such **c** in My name receives Me; **Mt 18:5** *3813*
The **c** has not died, but is asleep." **Mk 5:39** *3813*
entered *the room* where the **c** was. **Mk 5:40** *3813*
Taking the **c** by the hand, He **Mk 5:41** *3813*
she found the **c** lying on the bed, **Mk 7:30** *3813*
Taking a **c**, He set him before **Mk 9:36** *3813*
"Whoever receives one **c** like this **Mk 9:37** *3813*
a **c** will not enter it *at all*." **Mk 10:15** *3813*
behind a wife AND LEAVES NO **C**, **Mk 12:19** *5043*
to death, and a father *his* **c**; **Mk 13:12** *5043*
But they had no **c**, because **Lk 1:7** *5043*
and for that reason the holy **C** shall **Lk 1:35** *1080*
day they came to circumcise the **c**, **Lk 1:59** *3813*
then will this **c** *turn out to* be?" **Lk 1:66** *3813*
"And you, **c**, will be called the **Lk 1:76** *3813*
And the **c** continued to grow and **Lk 1:80** *3813*
engaged to him, and was with **c**. **Lk 2:5** *1471*
had been told them about this **C**. **Lk 2:17** *3813*
parents brought in the **c** Jesus, **Lk 2:27** *3813*
this **C** is appointed for the fall **Lk 2:34**
The **C** continued to grow and **Lk 2:40** *3813*
hand and called, saying, "**C**, arise!" **Lk 8:54** *3816*
a **c** and stood him by His side, **Lk 9:47** *3813*
this **c** in My name receives Me, **Lk 9:48** *3813*
'**C**, remember that during your life **Lk 16:25** *5043*
a **c** will not enter it *at all*." **Lk 18:17** *3813*
"Sir, come down before my **c** dies." **Jn 4:49** *3813*
but when she gives birth to the **c**, **Jn 16:21** *3813*
a **c** has been born into the world. **Jn 16:21** *444*
and *yet,* even when he had no **c**, **Ac 7:5** *5043*
and faithful **c** in the Lord, **1Co 4:17** *5043*
When I was a **c**, I used to speak like **1Co 13:11** *3516*
a child, I used to speak like a **c**, **1Co 13:11** *3516*
think like a **c**, reason like a child; **1Co 13:11** *3516*
reason like a **c**; when I became a man, **1Co 13:11** *3516*
I say, as long as the heir is a **c**, **Ga 4:1** *3516*
like a **c** *serving* his father. **Php 2:22** *5043*
labor pains upon a woman with **c**, **1Th 5:3** *1722, 1064*
Timothy, *my* true **c** in the faith: **1Tm 1:2** *5043*
my true **c** in a common faith: **Ti 1:4** *5043*
I appeal to you for my **c** Onesimus **Phm 1:10** *5043*
they saw he was a beautiful **c**; **Heb 11:23** *3813*
loves the Father loves the **c** born **1Jn 5:1**
and she was with **c**; **Rv 12:2** *1722, 1064*
gave birth he might devour her **c**. **Rv 12:4** *5043*
a male **c**, who is to rule all **Rv 12:5**
and her **c** was caught up to God and **Rv 12:5** *5043*
woman who gave birth to the male **c**. **Rv 12:13**

CHILDBEARING
Sarah was past **c**. **Gn 18:11** 734, 802

CHILDBIRTH
greatly multiply Your pain in **c**, **Gn 3:16** 2032
Anguish, as of a woman in **c**. **Ps 48:6** 3205
us, Pain as of a woman in **c**. **Jer 6:24** 3205
hold of you Like a woman in **c**? **Jer 13:21** 3205
upon you, Pain like a woman in **c**! **Jer 22:23** 3205
on his loins, as a woman in **c**? **Jer 30:6** 3205
hold of her Like a woman in **c**. **Jer 49:24** 3205
him, Agony like a woman in **c**. **Jer 50:43** 3205
The pains of **c** come upon him; **Hos 13:13** 3205
has gripped you like a woman in **c**? **Mi 4:9** 3205
of Zion, Like a woman in **c**; **Mi 4:10** 3205
the pains of **c** together until now. **Ro 8:22** *4944*

CHILDHOOD
He who pampers his slave from **c** **Pr 29:21** 5290
Rejoice, young man, during your **c**, **Ec 11:9** 3208
because **c** and the prime of life **Ec 11:10** 3208
to him?" And he said, "From **c**. **Mk 9:21** *3812*
and that from **c** you have known the **2Tm 3:15** *1025*

CHILDISH
a man, I did away with **c** things. **1Co 13:11** *3516*

CHILDLESS
will You give me, since I am **c**, **Gn 15:2** 6185
They will die **c**. **Lv 20:20** 6185
brother's nakedness. They will be **c**. **Lv 20:21** 6185
"As your sword has made women **c**, **1Sa 15:33** 7921
your mother be **c** among women." **1Sa 15:33** 7921
their wives become **c** and widowed. **Jer 18:21** 7909b
'Write this man down **c**, **Jer 22:30** 6185
DIES, having a wife, AND HE IS **C**, **Lk 20:28** *815*
the first took a wife and died **c**; **Lk 20:29** *815*

CHILDREN
In pain you will bring forth **c**; **Gn 3:16** 1121
and they bore **c** to them. **Gn 6:4**
the father of all the **c** of Eber, **Gn 10:21** 1121
brother of Japheth, **c** were born. **Gn 10:21**
Abram's wife had borne him no **c**, **Gn 16:1**
has prevented me from bearing **c**. **Gn 16:2**
I will obtain **c** through her." **Gn 16:2** 1129
may command his **c** and his household **Gn 18:19** 1121
so that they bore **c**. **Gn 20:17**
Abraham that Sarah would nurse **c**? **Gn 21:7** 1121
has borne **c** to your brother Nahor: **Gn 22:20** 1121
c struggled together within her; **Gn 25:22** 1121
saw that she bore Jacob no **c**, **Gn 30:1**
"Give me **c**, or else I die." **Gn 30:1** 1121
through her I too may have **c**." **Gn 30:3** 1129
my **c** for whom I have served you, **Gn 30:26** 3206
father belongs to us and our **c**; **Gn 31:16** 1121
his **c** and his wives upon camels; **Gn 31:17** 1121
and the **c** are my children, **Gn 31:43** 1121
and the children are my **c**, **Gn 31:43** 1121
to their **c** whom they have borne? **Gn 31:43** 1121
attack me *and* the mothers with the **c**. **Gn 32:11** 1121
his two maids and his eleven **c**, **Gn 32:22** 3206
So he divided the **c** among Leah and **Gn 33:1** 3206
the maids and their **c** in front, **Gn 33:2** 3206
in front, and Leah and her **c** next, **Gn 33:2** 3206
eyes and saw the women and the **c**, **Gn 33:5** 3206
"The **c** whom God has graciously **Gn 33:5** 3206
the maids came near with their **c**, **Gn 33:6** 3206
likewise came near with her **c**, **Gn 33:7** 3206
"My lord knows that the **c** are **Gn 33:13** 3206
according to the pace of the **c**, **Gn 33:14** 3206
These are the **c** of Anah: **Gn 36:25** 1121
"You have bereaved me of my **c**: **Gn 42:36** 7921
for me, if I am bereaved of my **c**, **Gn 43:14** 7921
you and your **c** and your children's **Gn 45:10** 1121
and your children's **c** and your flocks **Gn 45:10** 1121
has let me see your **c** as well." **Gn 48:11** 2233
"This is one of the Hebrews' **c**." **Ex 2:6** 3206
for you and your **c** forever. **Ex 12:24** 1121
when your **c** say to you, **Ex 12:26** 1121
men on foot, aside from **c**. **Ex 12:37** 2945
c and our livestock with thirst?" **Ex 17:3** 1121
iniquity of the fathers on the **c**, **Ex 20:5** 1121
her **c** shall belong to her master, **Ex 21:4** 3206
love my master, my wife and my **c**; **Ex 21:5** 1121
widows and your **c** fatherless. **Ex 22:24** 1121
visiting the iniquity of fathers on the **c** **Ex 34:7** 1121
which will bereave you of your **c** **Lv 26:22** 7921
and they had no **c**. **Nu 3:4** 1121
will then be free and conceive **c**. **Nu 5:28** 2233
leader of the **c** of Simeon; **Nu 7:36** 1121
the iniquity of the fathers on the **c** **Nu 14:18** 1121
'Your **c**, however, whom you said **Nu 14:31** 2945
Moses spoke to the **c** of Israel, **Dt 1:3** 1121
men, women and **c** of every city. **Dt 2:34** 2945
men, women and **c** of every city. **Dt 3:6** 2945
and that they may teach their **c**.' **Dt 4:10** 1121
"When you become the father of **c** **Dt 4:25** 1121
the father of children and children's **c** **Dt 4:25** 1121
you and with your **c** after you, **Dt 4:40** 1121
iniquity of the fathers on the **c**, **Dt 5:9** 1121
"Only the women and the **c** and the **Dt 20:14** 2945
the rest of his **c** who remain, **Dt 28:54** 1121
flesh of his **c** which he will eat, **Dt 28:55** 1121
and toward her **c** whom she bears; **Dt 28:57** 1121
the men and the women and **c** and **Dt 31:12** 2945
"Their **c**, who have not known, **Dt 31:13** 1121
toward Him, *They are* not His **c**, **Dt 32:5** 1121
so that when your **c** ask later, **Jos 4:6** 1121
"When your **c** ask their fathers in **Jos 4:21** 1121
then you shall inform your **c**, **Jos 4:22** 1121
Their **c** whom He raised up in **Jos 5:7** 1121
to you and to your **c** forever, **Jos 14:9** 1121
Ahiman and Talmai, the **c** of Anak. **Jos 15:14** 3211
wife was barren and had borne no **c**. **Jg 13:2**
you are barren and have borne no **c**, **Jg 13:3**
of her two **c** and her husband. **Ru 1:5** 3206
and Peninnah had **c**, **1Sa 1:2** 3206
had children, but Hannah had no **c**. **1Sa 1:2** 3206
But she who has many **c** languishes. **1Sa 2:5** 1121
"May the LORD give you **c** from **1Sa 2:20** 2233
"Are these all the **c**?" **1Sa 16:11** 5288
both men and women, **c** and infants; **1Sa 22:19** 5768
to every man his wife and his **c**, **1Sa 30:22** 1121
up together with him and his **c**. **2Sa 12:3** 1121
wives and **c** are also mine.'" **1Ki 20:3** 1121
gold and your wives and your **c**," **1Ki 20:5** 1121
my **c** and my silver and my gold, **1Ki 20:7** 1121
take my two **c** to be his slaves." **2Ki 4:1** 3206
and to the guardians of *the* **c** *of* **2Ki 10:1**
and the guardians of *the* **c**, sent **2Ki 10:5**
Sepharvites burned their **c** in the fire **2Ki 17:31** 1121
their **c** likewise and their **2Ki 17:41** 1121
for **c** have come to birth and **2Ki 19:3** 1121
The **c** of Amram *were* Aaron, **1Ch 6:3** 1121
of **c** in the country of Moab after **1Ch 8:8** 1121
of the **c** born *to him* in Jerusalem: **1Ch 14:4** 3205
infants, their wives and their **c**. **2Ch 20:13** 1121
he did not put their **c** to death, **2Ch 25:4** 1121
included all their little **c**, **2Ch 31:18** 2945
some of his own **c** killed him there **2Ch 32:21** 3329, 4578
large assembly, men, women and **c**, **Ezr 10:1** 3206
away all the wives and their **c**, **Ezr 10:3** 3205
them had wives *by whom* they had **c**. **Ezr 10:44** 1121
our **c** like their children. **Ne 5:5** 1121
our children like their **c**. **Ne 5:5** 1121
even the women and **c** rejoiced, **Ne 12:43** 3206
As for their **c**, half spoke in the **Ne 13:24** 1121
both young and old, women and **c**, **Es 3:13** 2945
them, including **c** and women, **Es 8:11** 2945
eyes of his **c** also will languish. **Jb 17:5** 1121
"Even young **c** despise me; **Jb 19:18** 5759
the flock, And their **c** skip about. **Jb 21:11** 3206
bread for *their* **c** in the desert. **Jb 24:5** 5288
with me, *And* my **c** were around me; **Jb 29:5** 5288
They are satisfied with **c**, **Ps 17:14** 1121
Come, you **c**, listen to me; **Ps 34:11** 1121
And the **c** of men take refuge in **Ps 36:7** 1121
people, Save the **c** of the needy And **Ps 72:4** 1121
betrayed the generation of Your **c**. **Ps 73:15** 1121
not conceal them from their **c**, **Ps 78:4** 1121
they should teach them to their **c**, **Ps 78:5** 1121
know, *even* the **c** *yet* to be born, **Ps 78:6** 1121
arise and tell *them* to their **c**, **Ps 78:6** 1121
have become a help to the **c** of Lot. **Ps 83:8** 1121
"Return, O **c** of men." **Ps 90:3** 1121
And Your majesty to their **c**. **Ps 90:16** 1121
c of Your servants will continue, **Ps 102:28** 1121
a father has compassion on *his* **c**, **Ps 103:13** 1121
His righteousness to children's **c**, **Ps 103:17** 1121
Let his **c** be fatherless And his **Ps 109:9** 1121
Let his **c** wander about and beg; **Ps 109:10** 1121
be gracious to his fatherless **c**. **Ps 109:12** 3490
the house *As* a joyful mother of **c**. **Ps 113:9** 1121
give you increase, You and your **c**. **Ps 115:14** 1121
Behold, **c** are a gift of the LORD, **Ps 127:3** 1121
So are the **c** of one's youth. **Ps 127:4** 1121
Your **c** like olive plants Around **Ps 128:3** 1121
may you see your children's **c**. **Ps 128:6** 1121
men and virgins; Old men and **c**. **Ps 148:12** 5288
an inheritance to his children's **c**, **Pr 13:22** 1121
And his **c** will have refuge. **Pr 14:26** 1121
Her **c** rise up and bless her; **Pr 31:28** 1121
If a man fathers a hundred **c** **Ec 6:3**
bargains with the **c** of foreigners. **Is 2:6** 3206
capricious **c** will rule over them, **Is 3:4** 8586
Their oppressors are **c**, **Is 3:12** 5953c
I and the **c** whom the LORD has **Is 8:18** 3206
womb, *Nor* will their eye pity **c**. **Is 13:18** 1121
But when he sees his **c**, **Is 29:23** 3206
"Woe to the rebellious **c**," **Is 30:1** 1121
for **c** have come to birth, and **Is 37:3** 1121
Nor know loss of **c**.' **Is 47:8** 7908
Loss of **c** and widowhood. **Is 47:9** 7908
"The **c** of whom you were bereaved **Is 49:20** 1121
I have been bereaved of my **c** And **Is 49:21** 7909a
Are you not **c** of rebellion, **Is 57:4** 3206
slaughter the **c** in the ravines, **Is 57:5** 3206
Or bear **c** for calamity; For they **Is 65:23**
They are stupid **c** And have **Jer 4:22** 1121
it out on the **c** in the street And **Jer 6:11** 5768
"The **c** gather wood, and the **Jer 7:18** 1121
To cut off the **c** from the streets, **Jer 9:21** 5768
I will bereave *them* of **c**, **Jer 15:7** 7921
As they remember their **c**, **Jer 17:2** 1121
give their **c** over to famine And **Jer 18:21** 1121
'Their **c** also will be as **Jer 30:20** 1121
Rachel is weeping for her **c**; **Jer 31:15** 1121
refuses to be comforted for her **c**, **Jer 31:15** 1121
"And *your* **c** will return to their **Jer 31:17** 1121
the bosom of their **c** after them, **Jer 32:18** 1121
the good of their **c** after them. **Jer 32:39** 1121
in charge of the men, women and **c**, **Jer 40:7** 2945
were soldiers, *the* women, *the* **c**, **Jer 41:16** 2945
the men, the women, the **c**, **Jer 43:6** 2945
have not turned back for *their* **c**, **Jer 47:3** 1121
My **c** are desolate Because the **La 1:16** 1121
women Boiled their own **c**; **La 4:10** 3206
who are stubborn and obstinate **c**, **Ezk 2:4** 1121
and they will bereave you of **c**; **Ezk 5:17** 7921
men, young men, maidens, little **c**, **Ezk 9:6** 2945
"You slaughtered My **c** and **Ezk 16:21** 1121
who loathed her husband and **c**. **Ezk 16:45** 1121
who loathed their husbands and **c**. **Ezk 16:45** 1121
said to their **c** in the wilderness, **Ezk 20:18** 1121
"But the **c** rebelled against Me; **Ezk 20:21** 1121
their **c** for their idols, **Ezk 23:39** 1121
never again bereave them of **c**.' **Ezk 36:12** 7921
have bereaved your nation of **c**," **Ezk 36:13** 7921
longer bereave your nation of **c**,' **Ezk 36:14** 7921
and they cast them, their **c** and **Da 6:24** 1123
harlotry and *have* **c** of harlotry; **Hos 1:2** 3206
will have no compassion on her **c**, **Hos 2:4** 1121
Because they are **c** of harlotry. **Hos 2:4** 1121
God, I also will forget your **c**. **Hos 4:6** 1121
they have borne illegitimate **c**. **Hos 5:7** 1121
Though they bring up their **c**, **Hos 9:12** 1121
bring out his **c** for slaughter. **Hos 9:13** 1121
Even though they bear **c**, **Hos 9:16**

dashed in pieces with *their* **c**. **Hos 10:14** 1121
the **c** and the nursing infants. **Jl 2:16** 5768
Because of the **c** of your delight; **Mi 1:16** 1121
c you take My splendor forever. **Mi 2:9** 5768
Also her small **c** were dashed to **Na 3:10** 5768
their **c** will see *it* and be glad, **Zch 10:7** 1121
their **c** will live and come back. **Zch 10:9** 1121
hearts of the fathers to *their* **c** and **Mal 4:6** 1121
hearts of the **c** to their fathers, **Mal 4:6** 1121
and sent and slew all the male **c** **Mt 2:16** *3816*
RACHEL WEEPING FOR HER **C**; **Mt 2:18** *5043*
able to raise up **c** to Abraham. **Mt 3:9** *5043*
how to give good gifts to your **c**, **Mt 7:11** *5043*
c will rise up against parents and **Mt 10:21** *5043*
c sitting in the market places, **Mt 11:16** *3813*
who call out to the other **c**, **Mt 11:16** *3813*
who ate, besides women and **c**. **Mt 14:21** *3813*
thousand men, besides women and **c**. **Mt 15:38** *3813*
are converted and become like **c**, **Mt 18:3** *3813*
wife and **c** and all that he had, **Mt 18:25** *5043*
Then *some* **c** were brought to Him so **Mt 19:13** *3813*
"Let the **c** alone, and do not **Mt 19:14** *3813*
or **c** or farms for My name's sake, **Mt 19:29** *5043*
and the **c** who were shouting in **Mt 21:15** *3816*
"Do You hear what these **c** are **Mt 21:16** *5043*
'IF A MAN DIES HAVING NO **C**, **Mt 22:24** *5043*
AND RAISE UP **C** FOR HIS BROTHER.' **Mt 22:24** *5043*
and having no **c** left his wife to his **Mt 22:25** *4690*
wanted to gather your **c** together, **Mt 23:37** *5043*
blood shall be on us and on our **c**!" **Mt 27:25** *5043*
"Let the **c** be satisfied first, **Mk 7:27** *5043*
And they were bringing **c** to Him so **Mk 10:13** *3813*
"Permit the **c** to come to Me; **Mk 10:14** *3813*
"**C**, how hard it is to enter the **Mk 10:24** *5043*
or mother or father or **c** or farms, **Mk 10:29** *5043*
and mothers and **c** and farms, **Mk 10:30** *5043*
SHOULD MARRY THE WIFE AND RAISE UP **C** **Mk 12:19** *4690*
and died leaving no **c**. **Mk 12:20** *4690*
and died leaving behind no **c**; **Mk 12:21** *4690*
and *so* all seven left no **c**. **Mk 12:22** *4690*
and **c** will rise up against parents **Mk 13:12** *5043*
OF THE FATHERS BACK TO THE **C**, **Lk 1:17** *5043*
able to raise up **c** to Abraham. **Lk 3:8** *5043*
"They are like **c** who sit in the **Lk 7:32** *3813*
is vindicated by all her **c**." **Lk 7:35** *5043*
shut and my **c** and I are in bed; **Lk 11:7** *3813*
how to give good gifts to your **c**, **Lk 11:13** *5043*
wanted to gather your **c** together, **Lk 13:34** *5043*
and **c** and brothers and sisters, **Lk 14:26** *5043*
"Permit the **c** to come to Me, and **Lk 18:16** *3813*
wife or brothers or parents or **c**, **Lk 18:29** *5043*
the ground and your **c** within you, **Lk 19:44** *5043*
SHOULD MARRY THE WIFE AND RAISE UP **C** **Lk 20:28** *4690*
way all seven died, leaving no **c**. **Lk 20:31** *5043*
for yourselves and for your **c**. **Lk 23:28** *5043*
gave the right to become **c** of God, **Jn 1:12** *5043*
"If you are Abraham's **c**, **Jn 8:39** *5043*
c of God who are scattered abroad. **Jn 11:52** *5043*
"Little **c**, I am with you a little **Jn 13:33** *5040*
"**C**, you do not have any fish, do **Jn 21:5** *3813*
the promise is for you and your **c** and **Ac 2:39** *5043*
our **c** in that He raised up Jesus, **Ac 13:33** *5043*
'For we also are His **c**.' **Ac 17:28** *2085*
"Being then the **c** of God, we ought **Ac 17:29** *2085*
while they all, with wives and **c**, **Ac 21:5** *5043*
telling them not to circumcise their **c** **Ac 21:21** *5043*
our spirit that we are **c** of God, **Ro 8:16** *5043*
and if **c**, heirs also, heirs of God **Ro 8:17** *5043*
of the glory of the **c** of God. **Ro 8:21** *5043*
nor are they all **c** because **Ro 9:7** *5043*
it is not the **c** of the flesh who **Ro 9:8** *5043*
of the flesh who are **c** of God, **Ro 9:8** *5043*
but the **c** of the promise are **Ro 9:8** *5043*
to admonish you as my beloved **c**. **1Co 4:14** *5043*
for otherwise your **c** are unclean, **1Co 7:14** *5043*
do not be **c** in your thinking; **1Co 14:20** *3813*
I speak as to **c** **2Co 6:13** *5043*
for **c** are not responsible to save **2Co 12:14** *5043*
parents, but parents for *their* **c**. **2Co 12:14** *5043*
So also we, while we were **c**, **Ga 4:3** *3516*
My **c**, with whom I am again in **Ga 4:19** *5043*
bearing **c** who are to be slaves; **Ga 4:24** *1080*
for she is in slavery with her **c**. **Ga 4:25** *5043*
NUMEROUS ARE THE **C** OF THE DESOLATE **Ga 4:27** *5043*
like Isaac, are **c** of promise. **Ga 4:28** *5043*
we are not **c** of a bondwoman, **Ga 4:31** *5043*
and were by nature **c** of wrath, **Eph 2:3** *5043*
result, we are no longer to be **c**, **Eph 4:14** *3516*
be imitators of God, as beloved **c**; **Eph 5:1** *5043*
walk as **c** of Light **Eph 5:8** *5043*
C, obey your parents in the Lord, **Eph 6:1** *5043*
do not provoke your **c** to anger, **Eph 6:4** *5043*
c of God above reproach in the **Php 2:15** *5043*
C, be obedient to your parents in **Col 3:20** *5043*
Fathers, do not exasperate your **c**, **Col 3:21** *5043*
tenderly cares for her own **c**. **1Th 2:7** *5043*
you as a father *would* his own **c**, **1Th 2:11** *5043*
be preserved through the bearing of **c** **1Tm 2:15** *5042*
keeping his **c** under control with **1Tm 3:4** *5043*
their **c** and their own households. **1Tm 3:12** *5043*
any widow has **c** or grandchildren, **1Tm 5:4** *5043*
and if she has brought up **c**, **1Tm 5:10** *5044*
widows to get married, bear **c**, **1Tm 5:14** *5041*
of one wife, having **c** who believe, **Ti 1:6** *5043*
their husbands, to love their **c**, **Ti 2:4** *5388*
THE **C** WHOM GOD HAS GIVEN ME." **Heb 2:13** *3813*
the **c** share in flesh and blood, **Heb 2:14** *3813*
are illegitimate **c** and not sons. **Heb 12:8** *3541*
As obedient **c**, do not be conformed **1Pe 1:14** *5043*
and you have become her **c** if you **1Pe 3:6** *5043*
trained in greed, accursed **c**; **2Pe 2:14** *5043*
My little **c**, I am writing these **1Jn 2:1** *5040*
I am writing to you, little **c**, **1Jn 2:12** *5040*
I have written to you, **c**, **1Jn 2:13** *3813*
C, it is the last hour; **1Jn 2:18** *3813*
Now, little **c**, abide in Him, **1Jn 2:28** *5040*
that we would be called **c** of God; **1Jn 3:1** *5043*
Beloved, now we are **c** of God, **1Jn 3:2** *5043*
Little **c**, make sure no one deceives you; **1Jn 3:7** *5040*
By this the **c** of God and the **1Jn 3:10** *5043*
the **c** of the devil are obvious: **1Jn 3:10** *5043*
Little **c**, let us not love with **1Jn 3:18** *5040*
You are from God, little **c**, **1Jn 4:4** *5040*
we know that we love the **c** of God, **1Jn 5:2** *5043*
Little **c**, guard yourselves from **1Jn 5:21** *5040*
to the chosen lady and her **c**, **2Jn 1:1** *5043*
some of your **c** walking in truth, **2Jn 1:4** *5043*
The **c** of your chosen sister greet **2Jn 1:13** *5043*
hear of my **c** walking in the truth. **3Jn 1:4** *5043*
I will kill her **c** with pestilence, **Rv 2:23** *5043*
to make war with the rest of her **c**, **Rv 12:17** *4690*

CHILDREN'S
you and your children and your **c** **Gn 45:10** 1121
the father of children and **c** children **Dt 4:25** 1121
His righteousness to **c** children, **Ps 103:17** 1121
may you see your **c** children. **Ps 128:6** 1121
an inheritance to his **c** children, **Pr 13:22** 1121
And the **c** teeth are set on edge.' **Jer 31:29** 1121
But the **c** teeth are set on edge'? **Ezk 18:2** 1121
"It is not good to take the **c** **Mt 15:26** *5043*
for it is not good to take the **c** **Mk 7:27** *5043*
the table feed on the **c** crumbs." **Mk 7:28** *3813*

CHILD'S
girl went and called the **c** mother. **Ex 2:8** 3206
let this **c** life return to him." **1Ki 17:21** 3206
who sought the **C** life are dead." **Mt 2:20** *3813*
He took along the **c** father and **Mk 5:40** *3813*

CHILEAB
and his second, **C**, by Abigail the **2Sa 3:3** 3609

CHILION
of his two sons *were* Mahlon and **C**, **Ru 1:2** 3630
Then both Mahlon and **C** also died, **Ru 1:5** 3630
all that belonged to **C** and Mahlon. **Ru 4:9** 3630

CHILMAD
Asshur *and* **C** traded with you. **Ezk 27:23** 3638

CHIMHAM
However, here is your servant **C**, **2Sa 19:37** 3643
"**C** shall cross over with me, and **2Sa 19:38** 3643
to Gilgal, and **C** went on with him; **2Sa 19:40** 3643
they went and stayed in Geruth **C**, **Jer 41:17** 3643

CHIMNEY
floor And like smoke from a **c**. **Hos 13:3** 699

CHINNERETH
on the east side of the Sea of **C**. **Nu 34:11** 3672
from **C** even as far as the sea of **Dt 3:17** 3672
C beyond the Jordan to the east. **Jos 13:27** 3672
Zer and Hammath, Rakkath and **C**, **Jos 19:35** 3672

CHINNEROTH
south of **C** and in the lowland **Jos 11:2** 3672
as the Sea of **C** toward the east, **Jos 12:3** 3672
Dan, Abel-beth-maacah and all **C**, **1Ki 15:20** 3672

CHIOS
the following day opposite **C**; **Ac 20:15** *5508*

CHIRPED
wing or opened *its* beak or **c**." **Is 10:14** 6850

CHISLEV
Now it happened in the month **C**, **Ne 1:1** 3691
of the ninth month, *which is* **C**. **Zch 7:1** 3691

CHISLON
of Benjamin, Elidad the son of **C**. **Nu 34:21** 3692

CHISLOTH-TABOR
sunrise as far as the border of **C**, **Jos 19:12** 3696

CHITLISH
and Cabbon and Lahmas and **C**, **Jos 15:40** 3798

CHLOE'S
you, my brethren, by **C** *people*, **1Co 1:11** *5514*

CHOICE
and took a tender and **c** calf and **Gn 18:7** 2896a
bring me two **c** young goats from there, **Gn 27:9** 2896a
his donkey's colt to the **c** vine; **Gn 49:11** 8321b
"You shall bring the **c** first **Ex 23:19** 7225
and all your **c** votive offerings **Dt 12:11** 977
land, With the **c** things of heaven, **Dt 33:13** 4022
And with the **c** yield of the sun, **Dt 33:14** 4022
with the **c** produce of the months. **Dt 33:14** 4022
And with the **c** things of the **Dt 33:15** 4022
And with the **c** things of the earth **Dt 33:16** 4022
who were numbered, 700 **c** men. **Jg 20:15** 977
people 700 **c** men were left-handed; **Jg 20:16** 977
When ten thousand **c** men from all **Jg 20:34** 977
was Saul, a **c** and handsome *man*, **1Sa 9:2** 970
from all the **c** men of Israel, **2Sa 10:9** 977
fortified city and every **c** city, **2Ki 3:19** 4004
tall cedars *and* its **c** cypresses. **2Ki 19:23** 4004
houses, **c** and mighty men of valor, **1Ch 7:40** 1305
he selected from all the **c** men of **1Ch 19:10** 970
found them to be 300,000 **c** men, **2Ch 25:5** 970
c presents to Hezekiah king of Judah, **2Ch 32:23** 4030
day was one ox *and* six **c** sheep, **Ne 5:18** 1305
c maids from the king's palace and **Es 2:9** 7200
be your gold And **c** silver to you. **Jb 22:25** 8443
And subdued the **c** men of Israel. **Ps 78:31** 970
of the righteous is *as* **c** silver, **Pr 10:20** 977
of pomegranates With **c** fruits, **SS 4:13** 4022
his garden And eat its **c** fruits!" **SS 4:16** 4022
is like Lebanon **C** as the cedars. **SS 5:15** 977
over our doors are all **c** *fruits*, **SS 7:13** 4022
have trampled down its **c** clusters **Is 16:8** 8291
food and **c** attire for those who dwell **Is 23:18** 6266
aged wine, **c** pieces with marrow, **Is 25:6** 8081
tall cedars *and* its **c** cypresses. **Is 37:24** 4004
"Yet I planted you a **c** vine, **Jer 2:21** 8321a
you will fall like a **c** vessel. **Jer 25:34** 2532
"All the **c** men in all his **Ezk 17:21** 4005
Fill *it* with **c** bones. **Ezk 24:4** 4005
after piece, Without making a **c**. **Ezk 24:6** 1486
traded with you in **c** garments, **Ezk 27:24** 4360
alienate this **c** *portion* of land; **Ezk 48:14** 7225
a daily ration from the king's **c** food **Da 1:5** 6598
defile himself with the king's **c** food **Da 1:8** 6598
who are eating the king's **c** food; **Da 1:13** 6598
had been eating the king's **c** food. **Da 1:15** 6598
continued to withhold their **c** food **Da 1:16** 6598
eat his **c** food will destroy him, **Da 11:26** 6598
early days God made a **c** among you, **Ac 15:7** *1586*
according to *His* **c** would stand, **Ro 9:11** *1589*
according to *God's* gracious **c**. **Ro 11:5** *1589*
standpoint of *God's* **c** they are beloved **Ro 11:28** *1589*
Greet Rufus, a **c** man in the Lord, **Ro 16:13** *1588*
beloved by God, *His* **c** of you; **1Th 1:4** *1589*
but is **c** and precious in the sight of **1Pe 2:4** *1588*
"BEHOLD, I LAY IN ZION A **C** STONE, **1Pe 2:6** *1588*

CHOICEST
your dead in the **c** of our graves; **Gn 23:6** 4005
And the **c** of his officers are **Ex 15:4** 4005
fat with the **c** of every offering of My **1Sa 2:29** 7225
the **c** of the things devoted to **1Sa 15:21** 7225
And knowledge rather than **c** gold. **Pr 8:10** 977
gold, And my yield *better* than **c** silver. **Pr 8:19** 977
And planted it with the **c** vine. **Is 5:2** 8321a
c valleys were full of chariots, **Is 22:7** 4005
And they will cut down your **c** **Jer 22:7** 4005
His **c** young men have also gone **Jer 48:15** 4005
and the **c** of your gifts, **Ezk 20:40** 7225
of whom *were* the **c** men of Assyria; **Ezk 23:7** 4005
"Take the **c** of the flock, And **Ezk 24:5** 4005
Eden, the **c** and best of Lebanon, **Ezk 31:16** 4005
ground, not even their **c** troops, **Da 11:15** 4005
gave a tenth of the **c** spoils. **Heb 7:4** *205*

CHOIR
second **c** proceeded to the left, **Ne 12:38** 8426
For the **c** director, on my stringed **Hab 3:19** 5329

CHOIRS
wall, and I appointed two great **c**, **Ne 12:31** 8426
Then the two **c** took their stand in **Ne 12:40** 8426

CHOKE
of wealth **c** the word, **Mt 13:22** *4846*
he seized him and *began* to **c** *him*, **Mt 18:28** *4155*
things enter in and **c** the word, **Mk 4:19** *4846*

CHOKED
the thorns came up and **c** them out. **Mt 13:7** *638*
and the thorns came up and **c** it, **Mk 4:7** *4846*
grew up with it and **c** it out. **Lk 8:7** *638*
they are **c** with worries and riches **Lk 8:14** *4846*

CHOOSE
"**C** men for us and go out, fight **Ex 17:9** 977
even the one whom He will **c**, **Nu 16:5** 977
of the man whom I **c** will sprout. **Nu 17:5** 977
'**C** wise and discerning and **Dt 1:13** 3051
did not set His love on you nor **c** you **Dt 7:7** 977
God will **c** from all your tribes, **Dt 12:5** 977
God will **c** for His name to dwell, **Dt 12:11** 977
which the LORD your God will **c**, **Dt 12:18** 977
in the place which he shall **c** in **Dt 23:16** 977
So **c** life in order that you may **Dt 30:19** 977
God at the place which He will **c**, **Dt 31:11** 977
in the place which He would **c**. **Jos 9:27** 977
c for yourselves today whom you **Jos 24:15** 977
'Did I *not* **c** them from all the **1Sa 2:28** 977
C a man for yourselves and let him **1Sa 17:8** 1262
"Please let me **c** 12,000 men that **2Sa 17:1** 977
c for yourself one of them, which **2Sa 24:12** 977
I did not **c** a city out of all the **1Ki 8:16** 977
and let them **c** one ox for **1Ki 18:23** 977
"**C** one ox for yourselves and **1Ki 18:25** 977
c for yourself one of them, which I **1Ch 21:10** 977
I did not **c** a city out of all the **2Ch 6:5** 977
nor did I **c** any man for a leader **2Ch 6:5** 977
that my soul would **c** suffocation, **Jb 7:15** 977
Him, *And* **c** my words before Him? **Jb 9:14** 977
you **c** the language of the crafty. **Jb 15:5** 977
us **c** for ourselves what is right; **Jb 34:4** 977
For you must **c**, and not I; **Jb 34:33** 977
him in the way he should **c**. **Ps 25:12** 977
is the one whom You **c** **Ps 65:4** 977
did not **c** the tribe of Ephraim, **Ps 78:67** 977
did not **c** the fear of the LORD. **Pr 1:29** 977
And do not **c** any of his ways. **Pr 3:31** 977
enough to refuse evil and **c** good. **Is 7:15** 977
enough to refuse evil and **c** good, **Is 7:16** 977
on Jacob and again **c** Israel, **Is 14:1** 977
sabbaths, And **c** what pleases Me, **Is 56:4** 977
"Is it a fast like this which I **c**, **Is 58:5** 977
"Is this not the fast which I **c**, **Is 58:6** 977
So I will **c** their punishments And **Is 66:4** 977
Zion and again **c** Jerusalem. **Zch 1:17** 977
land, and will again **c** Jerusalem. **Zch 2:12** 977
"Did I Myself not **c** you, **Jn 6:70** *1586*
"You did not **c** Me but I chose **Jn 15:16** *1586*
to **c** men from among them to send **Ac 15:22** *1586*
and I do not know which to **c**. **Php 1:22** *138*
did not God **c** the poor of this **Jas 2:5** *1586*

CHOOSES
the man whom the LORD **c** *shall be* Nu 16:7 977
the LORD **c** in one of your tribes, Dt 12:14 977
the place which the LORD your God **c** Dt 12:21 977
go to the place which the LORD **c**. Dt 12:26 977
where He **c** to establish His name, Dt 14:23 977
the LORD your God **c** to set His name Dt 14:24 977
place which the LORD your God **c**. Dt 14:25 977
God in the place which the LORD **c**. Dt 15:20 977
the LORD **c** to establish His name. Dt 16:2 977
your God **c** to establish His name, Dt 16:6 977
place which the LORD your God **c**. Dt 16:7 977
your God **c** to establish His name. Dt 16:11 977
God in the place which the LORD **c**, Dt 16:15 977
your God in the place which He **c**, Dt 16:16 977
place which the LORD your God **c**. Dt 17:8 977
from that place which the LORD **c**; Dt 17:10 977
over you whom the LORD your God **c**, Dt 17:15 977
to the place which the LORD **c**, Dt 18:6 977
your God **c** to establish His name. Dt 26:2 977
do whatever my lord the king **c**." 2Sa 15:15 977
He **c** our inheritance for us, The Ps 47:4 977
He who **c** you is an abomination. Is 41:24 977

CHOOSING
Do I not know that you are **c** the 1Sa 20:30 977
c rather to endure ill-treatment Heb 11:25 *138*
about His calling and **c** you; 2Pe 1:10 *1589*

CHOP
"**C** down the tree and cut off its Da 4:14 1414
"**C** down the tree and destroy it; Da 4:23 1414
And **c** *them* up as for the pot And Mi 3:3 6566

CHOPPED
were high above them he **c** down; 2Ch 34:4 1438
and **c** down all the incense altars 2Ch 34:7 1438

CHOPS
from the one who **c** your wood to Dt 29:11 2404
itself over the one who **c** with it? Is 10:15 2672

CHORAZIN
"Woe to you, **C**! Woe to you, Mt 11:21 *5523*
"Woe to you, **C**! Woe to you, Lk 10:13 *5523*

CHOSE
for themselves, whomever they **c**. Gn 6:2 977
So Lot **c** for himself all the Gn 13:11 977
c able men out of all Israel and Ex 18:25 977
He **c** their descendants after them. Dt 4:37 977
He **c** their descendants after them, Dt 10:15 977
and Joshua **c** 30,000 men, valiant Jos 8:3 977
Now Saul **c** for himself 3,000 men 1Sa 13:2 977
and **c** for himself five smooth stones 1Sa 17:40 977
who **c** me above your father and 2Sa 6:21 977
but I **c** David to be over My people 1Ki 8:16 977
sake of My servant David whom I **c**, 1Ki 11:34 977
c them to carry the ark of God and 1Ch 15:2 977
c me from all the house of my 1Ch 28:4 977
Who **c** Abram And brought him out Ne 9:7 977
"I **c** a way for them and sat as Jb 29:25 977
But **c** the tribe of Judah, Mount Ps 78:68 977
He also **c** David His servant And Ps 78:70 977
And **c** that in which I did not Is 65:12 977
And **c** that in which I did not delight. Is 66:4 977
'The two families which the LORD **c**, Jer 33:24 977
"On the day when I **c** Israel and Ezk 20:5 977
the sake of the elect, whom He **c**, Mk 13:20 *1586*
and **c** twelve of them, whom He also Lk 6:13 *1586*
did not choose Me but I **c** you, Jn 15:16 *1586*
but I **c** you out of the world, Jn 15:19 *1586*
and they **c** Stephen, a man full of Ac 6:5 *1586*
this people Israel **c** our fathers and Ac 13:17 *1586*
But Paul **c** Silas and left, Ac 15:40 *1951*
just as He **c** us in Him before the Eph 1:4 *1586*

CHOSEN
"For I have **c** him, so that Gn 18:19 3045
congregation, **c** in the assembly, Nu 16:2 7148
the LORD your God has **c** you to be Dt 7:6 977
and the LORD has **c** you to be a Dt 14:2 977
"For the LORD your God has **c** him Dt 18:5 977
for the LORD your God has **c** them Dt 21:5 977
have **c** for yourselves the LORD, Jos 24:22 977
"New gods were **c**; Then war *was* Jg 5:8 977
out to the gods which you have **c**; Jg 10:14 977
whom you have **c** for yourselves; 1Sa 8:18 977
you see him whom the LORD has **c**? 1Sa 10:24 977
here is the king whom you have **c**, 1Sa 12:13 977
"The LORD has not **c** this one either." 1Sa 16:8 977
"The LORD has not **c** this one either." 1Sa 16:9 977
"The LORD has not **c** these." 1Sa 16:10 977
thousand **c** men from all Israel and 1Sa 24:2 977
three thousand **c** men of Israel, 1Sa 26:2 977
gathered all the **c** men of Israel, 2Sa 6:1 977
and all the men of Israel have **c**, 2Sa 16:18 977
of Saul, the **c** of the LORD." 2Sa 21:6 972
of Your people which You have **c**, 1Ki 3:8 977
toward the city which You have **c** 1Ki 8:44 977
the city which You have **c**, 1Ki 8:48 977
of Jerusalem which I have **c**." 1Ki 11:13 977
c from all the tribes of Israel), 1Ki 11:32 977
have **c** for Myself to put My name. 1Ki 11:36 977
180,000 **c** men who were warriors, 1Ki 12:21 977
the city which the LORD had **c** from 1Ki 14:21 977
c from all the tribes of Israel, 2Ki 21:7 977
this city which I have **c**, 2Ki 23:27 977
these who were **c** to be gatekeepers 1Ch 9:22 1305
Sons of Jacob, His **c** ones! 1Ch 16:13 972
Jeduthun, and the rest who were **c**, 1Ch 16:41 1305
For He has **c** Judah to be a leader; 1Ch 28:4 977
He has **c** my son Solomon to sit on 1Ch 28:5 977
I have **c** him to be a son to Me, 1Ch 28:6 977
for the LORD has **c** you to build a 1Ch 28:10 977
son Solomon, whom alone God has **c**, 1Ch 29:1 977
but I have **c** Jerusalem that My 2Ch 6:6 977
and I have **c** David to be over My 2Ch 6:6 977
this city which You have **c** and 2Ch 6:34 977
and the city which You have **c**, 2Ch 6:38 977
and have **c** this place for Myself 2Ch 7:12 977
"For now I have **c** and consecrated 2Ch 7:16 977
180,000 **c** men who were warriors, 2Ch 11:1 977
c from all the tribes of Israel, 2Ch 12:13 977
valiant warriors, 400,000 **c** men, 2Ch 13:3 977
800,000 **c** men *who were* valiant 2Ch 13:3 977
500,000 **c** men of Israel fell slain. 2Ch 13:17 977
has **c** you to stand before Him, 2Ch 29:11 977
c from all the tribes of Israel, 2Ch 33:7 977
have **c** to cause My name to dwell.' Ne 1:9 977
He has **c** for His own inheritance. Ps 33:12 977
"I have made a covenant with My **c**; Ps 89:3 972
exalted one **c** from the people. Ps 89:19 977
O sons of Jacob, His **c** ones! Ps 105:6 972
servant, *And* Aaron, whom He had **c**. Ps 105:26 977
His **c** ones with a joyful shout. Ps 105:43 972
see the prosperity of Your **c** ones, Ps 106:5 972
Had not Moses His **c** one stood in Ps 106:23 972
I have **c** the faithful way; Ps 119:30 977
me, For I have **c** Your precepts. Ps 119:173 977
For the LORD has **c** Zion; Ps 132:13 977
the LORD has **c** Jacob for Himself, Ps 135:4 977
is to be **c** above silver. Pr 16:16 977
at the gardens which you have **c**. Is 1:29 977
My servant, Jacob whom I have **c**, Is 41:8 977
I have **c** you and not rejected you. Is 41:9 977
My **c** one *in whom* My soul delights. Is 42:1 972
"And My servant whom I have **c**, Is 43:10 977
To give drink to My **c** people. Is 43:20 972
And Israel, whom I have **c**: Is 44:1 977
And you Jeshurun whom I have **c**. Is 44:2 977
My servant, And Israel My **c** *one*, Is 45:4 972
Holy One of Israel who has **c** You." Is 49:7 977
Even My **c** ones shall inherit it, Is 65:9 972
name for a curse to My **c** ones, Is 65:15 972
And My **c** ones will wear out the Is 65:22 972
As they have **c** their *own* ways, And Is 66:3 977
"And death will be **c** rather than Jer 8:3 977
whoever is **c** I shall appoint over it. Jer 49:19 977
whoever is **c** I will appoint over it. Jer 50:44 977
"You only have I **c** among all the Am 3:2 3045
signet *ring*, for I have **c** you,'" Hg 2:23 977
who has **c** Jerusalem rebuke you! Zch 3:2 977
MY SERVANT WHOM I HAVE **C**; Mt 12:18 *140*
many are called, but few *are* **c**." Mt 22:14 *1588*
he was **c** by lot to enter the Lk 1:9 *2975*
"This is My Son, *My* **C** One; Lk 9:35 *1586*
necessary, for Mary has **c** the good part, Lk 10:42 *1586*
for your Father has **c** gladly to Lk 12:32 *2106*
is the Christ of God, His **C** One." Lk 23:35 *1588*
I know the ones I have **c**; Jn 13:18 *1586*
to the apostles whom He had **c**. Ac 1:2 *1586*
one of these two You have **c** Ac 1:24 *1586*
for he is a **c** instrument of Mine, Ac 9:15 *1589*
who were **c** beforehand by God, Ac 10:41 *4401*
but those who were **c** obtained it, Ro 11:7 *1589*
but God has **c** the foolish things 1Co 1:27 *1586*
and God has **c** the weak things of 1Co 1:27 *1586*
world and the despised God has **c**, 1Co 1:28 *1586*
as those who have been **c** of God, Col 3:12 *1588*
because God has **c** you from the 2Th 2:13 *138*
Christ Jesus and of *His* **c** angels, 1Tm 5:21 *1588*
for the sake of those who are **c**, 2Tm 2:10 *1588*
for the faith of those **c** of God Ti 1:1 *1588*
Asia, and Bithynia, who are **c** 1Pe 1:1 *1588*
But you are A **C** RACE, A royal 1Pe 2:9 *1588*
in Babylon, **c** together with you, 1Pe 5:13 *4899*
to the **c** lady and her children, 2Jn 1:1 *1588*
of your **c** sister greet you. 2Jn 1:13 *1588*
the called and **c** and faithful." Rv 17:14 *1588*

CHRIST
birth of Jesus **C** was as follows: Mt 1:18 *5547*
imprisoned, heard of the works of **C**, Mt 11:2 *5547*
"You are the **C**, the Son of the Mt 16:16 *5547*
tell no one that He was the **C**. Mt 16:20 *5547*
"What do you think about the **C**, Mt 22:42 *5547*
One is your Leader, *that is*, **C**. Mt 23:10 *5547*
'I am the **C**,' and will mislead Mt 24:5 *5547*
'Behold, here is the **C**,' Mt 24:23 *5547*
You tell us whether You are the **C**, Mt 26:63 *5547*
"Prophesy to us, You **C**; Mt 26:68 *5547*
or Jesus who is called **C**?" Mt 27:17 *5547*
I do with Jesus who is called **C**?" Mt 27:22 *5547*
of the gospel of Jesus **C**, Mk 1:1 *5547*
"You are the **C**." Mk 8:29 *5547*
of your name as *followers* of **C**, Mk 9:41 *5547*
that the **C** is the son of David? Mk 12:35 *5547*
'Behold, here is the **C**' Mk 13:21 *5547*
"Are You the **C**, the Son of the Mk 14:61 *5547*
"Let *this* **C**, the King of Israel, Mk 15:32 *5547*
you a Savior, who is **C** the Lord. Lk 2:11 *5547*
before he had seen the Lord's **C**. Lk 2:26 *5547*
as to whether he was the **C**, Lk 3:15 *5547*
because they knew Him to be the **C**. Lk 4:41 *5547*
Peter answered and said, "The **C** Lk 9:20 *5547*
that they say the **C** is David's son? Lk 20:41 *5547*
"If You are the **C**, tell us." Lk 22:67 *5547*
and saying that He Himself is **C**, Lk 23:2 *5547*
Himself if this is the **C** of God, Lk 23:35 *5547*
"Are You not the **C**? Lk 23:39 *5547*
"Was it not necessary for the **C** Lk 24:26 *5547*
that the **C** would suffer and rise Lk 24:46 *5547*
were realized through Jesus **C**. Jn 1:17 *5547*
"I am not the **C**." Jn 1:20 *5547*
baptizing, if you are not the **C**, Jn 1:25 *5547*
Messiah" (which translated means **C**). Jn 1:41 *5547*
'I am not the **C**,' but, Jn 3:28 *5547*
(He who is called **C**); Jn 4:25 *5547*
this is not the **C**, is it?" Jn 4:29 *5547*
really know that this is the **C**, Jn 7:26 *5547*
but whenever the **C** may come, Jn 7:27 *5547*
"When the **C** comes, He will Jn 7:31 *5547*
Others were saying, "This is the **C**." Jn 7:41 *5547*
"Surely the **C** is not going to Jn 7:41 *5547*
C comes from the descendants of David, Jn 7:42 *5547*
anyone confessed Him to be **C**, Jn 9:22 *5547*
If You are the **C**, tell us plainly." Jn 10:24 *5547*
have believed that You are the **C**, Jn 11:27 *5547*
that the **C** is to remain forever; Jn 12:34 *5547*
and Jesus **C** whom You have sent. Jn 17:3 *5547*
may believe that Jesus is the **C**, Jn 20:31 *5547*
of the resurrection of the **C**, Ac 2:31 *5547*
God has made Him both Lord and **C** Ac 2:36 *5547*
be baptized in the name of Jesus **C** Ac 2:38 *5547*
In the name of Jesus **C** the Nazarene Ac 3:6 *5547*
that His **C** would suffer, Ac 3:18 *5547*
Jesus, the **C** appointed for you, Ac 3:20 *5547*
the name of Jesus **C** the Nazarene, Ac 4:10 *5547*
THE LORD AND AGAINST HIS **C**,' Ac 4:26 *5547*
and preaching Jesus *as* the **C**. Ac 5:42 *5547*
and *began* proclaiming **C** to them. Ac 8:5 *5547*
of God and the name of Jesus **C**, Ac 8:12 *5547*
that Jesus **C** is the Son of God." Ac 8:37 *5547*
proving that this *Jesus* is the **C**. Ac 9:22 *5547*
"Aeneas, Jesus **C** heals you; Ac 9:34 *5547*
preaching peace through Jesus **C** Ac 10:36 *5547*
baptized in the name of Jesus **C**. Ac 10:48 *5547*
believing in the Lord Jesus **C**, Ac 11:17 *5547*
for the name of our Lord Jesus **C**. Ac 15:26 *5547*
of Jesus **C** to come out of her!" Ac 16:18 *5547*
evidence that the **C** had to suffer Ac 17:3 *5547*
am proclaiming to you is the **C**." Ac 17:3 *5547*
to the Jews that Jesus was the **C**. Ac 18:5 *5547*
Scriptures that Jesus was the **C**. Ac 18:28 *5547*
God and faith in our Lord Jesus **C**. Ac 20:21 *5547*
him *speak* about faith in **C** Jesus. Ac 24:24 *5547*
that the **C** was to suffer, *and* that Ac 26:23 *5547*
Lord Jesus **C** with all openness, Ac 28:31 *5547*
Paul, a bond-servant of **C** Jesus, Ro 1:1 *5547*
of holiness, Jesus **C** our Lord, Ro 1:4 *5547*
also are the called of Jesus **C**; Ro 1:6 *5547*
our Father and the Lord Jesus **C**. Ro 1:7 *5547*
God through Jesus **C** for you all, Ro 1:8 *5547*
secrets of men through **C** Jesus. Ro 2:16 *5547*
Jesus **C** for all those who believe; Ro 3:22 *5547*
redemption which is in **C** Jesus; Ro 3:24 *5547*
with God through our Lord Jesus **C**, Ro 5:1 *5547*
right time **C** died for the ungodly. Ro 5:6 *5547*
were yet sinners, **C** died for us. Ro 5:8 *5547*
in God through our Lord Jesus **C**, Ro 5:11 *5547*
the grace of the one Man, Jesus **C**, Ro 5:15 *5547*
in life through the One, Jesus **C**. Ro 5:17 *5547*
life through Jesus **C** our Lord. Ro 5:21 *5547*
have been baptized into **C** Jesus Ro 6:3 *5547*
so that as **C** was raised from Ro 6:4 *5547*
Now if we have died with **C**, Ro 6:8 *5547*
knowing that **C**, having been raised Ro 6:9 *5547*
sin, but alive to God in **C** Jesus. Ro 6:11 *5547*
eternal life in **C** Jesus our Lord. Ro 6:23 *5547*
to the Law through the body of **C**, Ro 7:4 *5547*
to God through Jesus **C** our Lord! Ro 7:25 *5547*
for those who are in **C** Jesus. Ro 8:1 *5547*
law of the Spirit of life in **C** Jesus Ro 8:2 *5547*
does not have the Spirit of **C**, Ro 8:9 *5547*
If **C** is in you, though the Ro 8:10 *5547*
He who raised **C** Jesus from the Ro 8:11 *5547*
of God and fellow heirs with **C**, Ro 8:17 *5547*
C Jesus is He who died, yes, Ro 8:34 *5547*
separate us from the love of **C**? Ro 8:35 *5547*
God, which is in **C** Jesus our Lord. Ro 8:39 *5547*
I am telling the truth in **C**, Ro 9:1 *5547*
C for the sake of my brethren, Ro 9:3 *5547*
is the **C** according to the flesh, Ro 9:5 *5547*
For **C** is the end of the law for Ro 10:4 *5547*
(that is, to bring **C** down), Ro 10:6 *5547*
to bring **C** up from the dead)." Ro 10:7 *5547*
and hearing by the word of **C**. Ro 10:17 *5547*
who are many, are one body in **C**, Ro 12:5 *5547*
But put on the Lord Jesus **C**, Ro 13:14 *5547*
this end **C** died and lived again, Ro 14:9 *5547*
your food him for whom **C** died. Ro 14:15 *5547*
For he who in this *way* serves **C** is Ro 14:18 *5547*
For even **C** did not please Himself; Ro 15:3 *5547*
one another according to **C** Jesus, Ro 15:5 *5547*
and Father of our Lord Jesus **C**. Ro 15:6 *5547*
just as **C** also accepted us to the Ro 15:7 *5547*
For I say that **C** has become a Ro 15:8 *5547*
of **C** Jesus to the Gentiles, Ro 15:16 *5547*
Therefore in **C** Jesus I have found Ro 15:17 *5547*
C has accomplished through me, Ro 15:18 *5547*
fully preached the gospel of **C**. Ro 15:19 *5547*
not where **C** was *already* named, Ro 15:20 *5547*
the fullness of the blessing of **C**. Ro 15:29 *5547*
C and by the love of the Spirit, Ro 15:30 *5547*
my fellow workers in **C** Jesus, Ro 16:3 *5547*
the first convert to **C** from Asia. Ro 16:5 *5547*
who also were in **C** before me. Ro 16:7 *5547*
Urbanus, our fellow worker in **C**, Ro 16:9 *5547*
Greet Apelles, the approved in **C**. Ro 16:10 *5547*
All the churches of **C** greet you. Ro 16:16 *5547*
Lord **C** but of their own appetites; Ro 16:18 *5547*
our Lord Jesus **C** be with you all. Ro 16:24 *5547*

and the preaching of Jesus **C**, **Ro 16:25** *5547*
only wise God, through Jesus **C**, **Ro 16:27** *5547*
of Jesus **C** by the will of God, **1Co 1:1** *5547*
have been sanctified in **C** Jesus, **1Co 1:2** *5547*
on the name of our Lord Jesus **C**, **1Co 1:2** *5547*
our Father and the Lord Jesus **C**. **1Co 1:3** *5547*
which was given you in **C** Jesus, **1Co 1:4** *5547*
concerning **C** was confirmed in you, **1Co 1:6** *5547*
revelation of our Lord Jesus **C**, **1Co 1:7** *5547*
in the day of our Lord Jesus **C**. **1Co 1:8** *5547*
with His Son, Jesus **C** our Lord. **1Co 1:9** *5547*
by the name of our Lord Jesus **C**, **1Co 1:10** *5547*
and "I of Cephas," and "I of **C**." **1Co 1:12** *5547*
Has **C** been divided? **1Co 1:13** *5547*
For **C** did not send me to baptize, **1Co 1:17** *5547*
cross of **C** would not be made void. **1Co 1:17** *5547*
but we preach **C** crucified, to Jews **1Co 1:23** *5547*
C the power of God and the wisdom **1Co 1:24** *5547*
by His doing you are in **C** Jesus, **1Co 1:30** *5547*
nothing among you except Jesus **C**, **1Co 2:2** *5547*
But we have the mind of **C**. **1Co 2:16** *5547*
to men of flesh, as to infants in **C**. **1Co 3:1** *5547*
which is laid, which is Jesus **C**. **1Co 3:11** *5547*
and you belong to **C**; **1Co 3:23** *5547*
and **C** belongs to God. **1Co 3:23** *5547*
in this manner, as servants of **C** and **1Co 4:1** *5547*
sake, but you are prudent in **C**; **1Co 4:10** *5547*
to have countless tutors in **C**, **1Co 4:15** *5547*
for in **C** Jesus I became your **1Co 4:15** *5547*
you of my ways which are in **C**, **1Co 4:17** *5547*
For **C** our Passover also has been **1Co 5:7** *5547*
in the name of the Lord Jesus **C** and **1Co 6:11** *5547*
that your bodies are members of **C**? **1Co 6:15** *5547*
take away the members of **C** and **1Co 6:15** *5547*
and one Lord, Jesus **C**, **1Co 8:6** *5547*
the brother for whose sake **C** died. **1Co 8:11** *5547*
it is weak, you sin against **C**. **1Co 8:12** *5547*
no hindrance to the gospel of **C**. **1Co 9:12** *5547*
law of God but under the law of **C**, **1Co 9:21** *5547*
and the rock was **C**. **1Co 10:4** *5547*
bless a sharing in the blood of **C**? **1Co 10:16** *5547*
break a sharing in the body of **C**? **1Co 10:16** *5547*
of me, just as I also am of **C**. **1Co 11:1** *5547*
that **C** is the head of every man, **1Co 11:3** *5547*
a woman, and God is the head of **C**. **1Co 11:3** *5547*
many, are one body, so also is **C**. **1Co 12:12** *5547*
that **C** died for our sins according **1Co 15:3** *5547*
Now if **C** is preached, that He has **1Co 15:12** *5547*
dead, not even **C** has been raised; **1Co 15:13** *5547*
and if **C** has not been raised, then **1Co 15:14** *5547*
against God that He raised **C**, **1Co 15:15** *5547*
not even **C** has been raised; **1Co 15:16** *5547*
and if **C** has not been raised, your **1Co 15:17** *5547*
fallen asleep in **C** have perished. **1Co 15:18** *5547*
have hoped in **C** in this life only, **1Co 15:19** *5547*
C has been raised from the dead, **1Co 15:20** *5547*
also in **C** all will be made alive. **1Co 15:22** *5547*
C the first fruits, after that **1Co 15:23** *5547*
which I have in **C** Jesus our Lord, **1Co 15:31** *5547*
victory through our Lord Jesus **C**. **1Co 15:57** *5547*
love be with you all in **C** Jesus. **1Co 16:24** *5547*
of **C** Jesus by the will of God, **2Co 1:1** *5547*
our Father and the Lord Jesus **C**. **2Co 1:2** *5547*
and Father of our Lord Jesus **C**, **2Co 1:3** *5547*
just as the sufferings of **C** are ours **2Co 1:5** *5547*
our comfort is abundant through **C**. **2Co 1:5** *5547*
For the Son of God, **C** Jesus, **2Co 1:19** *5547*
you in **C** and anointed us is God, **2Co 1:21** *5547*
your sakes in the presence of **C**, **2Co 2:10** *5547*
I came to Troas for the gospel of **C** **2Co 2:12** *5547*
leads us in triumph in **C**, **2Co 2:14** *5547*
For we are a fragrance of **C** to God **2Co 2:15** *5547*
we speak in **C** in the sight of God. **2Co 2:17** *5547*
that you are a letter of **C**, **2Co 3:3** *5547*
we have through **C** toward God. **2Co 3:4** *5547*
because it is removed in **C**. **2Co 3:14** *5547*
of the gospel of the glory of **C**, **2Co 4:4** *5547*
ourselves but **C** Jesus as Lord, **2Co 4:5** *5547*
the glory of God in the face of **C**. **2Co 4:6** *5547*
before the judgment seat of **C**, **2Co 5:10** *5547*
For the love of **C** controls us, **2Co 5:14** *5547*
known **C** according to the flesh, **2Co 5:16** *5547*
Therefore if anyone is in **C**, **2Co 5:17** *5547*
us to Himself through **C** and **2Co 5:18** *5547*
that God was in **C** reconciling the **2Co 5:19** *5547*
we are ambassadors for **C**, **2Co 5:20** *5547*
we beg you on behalf of **C**, **2Co 5:20** *5547*
Or what harmony has **C** with Belial, **2Co 6:15** *5547*
the grace of our Lord Jesus **C**, **2Co 8:9** *5547*
of the churches, a glory to **C**. **2Co 8:23** *5547*
confession of the gospel of **C** and **2Co 9:13** *5547*
by the meekness and gentleness of **C** **2Co 10:1** *5547*
captive to the obedience of **C**, **2Co 10:5** *5547*
as far as you in the gospel of **C**; **2Co 10:14** *5547*
that to **C** I might present you *as* a **2Co 11:2** *5547*
and purity *of devotion* to **C**. **2Co 11:3** *5547*
As the truth of **C** is in me, this **2Co 11:10** *5547*
themselves as apostles of **C**. **2Co 11:13** *5547*
Are they servants of **C**? **2Co 11:23** *5547*
I know a man in **C** who fourteen **2Co 12:2** *5547*
the power of **C** may dwell in me. **2Co 12:9** *5547*
that we have been speaking in **C**; **2Co 12:19** *5547*
proof of the **C** who speaks in me, **2Co 13:3** *5547*
yourselves, that Jesus **C** is in you **2Co 13:5** *5547*
The grace of the Lord Jesus **C**, **2Co 13:14** *5547*
of man, but through Jesus **C** and **Ga 1:1** *5547*
our Father and the Lord Jesus **C**, **Ga 1:3** *5547*
who called you by the grace of **C**, **Ga 1:6** *5547*
want to distort the gospel of **C**. **Ga 1:7** *5547*
I would not be a bond-servant of **C**. **Ga 1:10** *5547*
through a revelation of Jesus **C**. **Ga 1:12** *5547*
churches of Judea which were in **C**; **Ga 1:22** *5547*
liberty which we have in **C** Jesus, **Ga 2:4** *5547*
Law but through faith in **C** Jesus, **Ga 2:16** *5547*
even we have believed in **C** Jesus, **Ga 2:16** *5547*
we may be justified by faith in **C** and **Ga 2:16** *5547*
seeking to be justified in **C**, **Ga 2:17** *5547*
is **C** then a minister of sin? **Ga 2:17** *5547*
"I have been crucified with **C**; **Ga 2:20** *5547*
I who live, but **C** lives in me; **Ga 2:20** *5547*
the Law, then **C** died needlessly." **Ga 2:21** *5547*
before whose eyes Jesus **C** was **Ga 3:1** *5547*
C redeemed us from the curse of **Ga 3:13** *5547*
in **C** Jesus the blessing of Abraham **Ga 3:14** *5547*
"And to your seed," that is, **C**. **Ga 3:16** *5547*
that the promise by faith in Jesus **C** **Ga 3:22** *5547*
become our tutor *to lead us* to **C**, **Ga 3:24** *5547*
of God through faith in **C** Jesus. **Ga 3:26** *5547*
all of you who were baptized into **C** **Ga 3:27** *5547*
have clothed yourselves with **C**. **Ga 3:27** *5547*
for you are all one in **C** Jesus. **Ga 3:28** *5547*
And if you belong to **C**, **Ga 3:29** *5547*
angel of God, as **C** Jesus *Himself.* **Ga 4:14** *5547*
in labor until **C** is formed in you **Ga 4:19** *5547*
for freedom that **C** set us free; **Ga 5:1** *5547*
C will be of no benefit to you. **Ga 5:2** *5547*
You have been severed from **C**, **Ga 5:4** *5547*
For in **C** Jesus neither **Ga 5:6** *5547*
Now those who belong to **C** Jesus **Ga 5:24** *5547*
and thereby fulfill the law of **C**. **Ga 6:2** *5547*
be persecuted for the cross of **C**. **Ga 6:12** *5547*
in the cross of our Lord Jesus **C**, **Ga 6:14** *5547*
Lord Jesus **C** be with your spirit, **Ga 6:18** *5547*
of **C** Jesus by the will of God, **Eph 1:1** *5547*
and *who are* faithful in **C** Jesus: **Eph 1:1** *5547*
our Father and the Lord Jesus **C**. **Eph 1:2** *5547*
and Father of our Lord Jesus **C**, **Eph 1:3** *5547*
in the heavenly *places* in **C**, **Eph 1:3** *5547*
sons through Jesus **C** to Himself, **Eph 1:5** *5547*
the summing up of all things in **C**, **Eph 1:10** *5547*
we who were the first to hope in **C** **Eph 1:12** *5547*
that the God of our Lord Jesus **C**, **Eph 1:17** *5547*
which He brought about in **C**, **Eph 1:20** *5547*
made us alive together with **C** **Eph 2:5** *5547*
the heavenly *places* in **C** Jesus, **Eph 2:6** *5547*
in kindness toward us in **C** Jesus. **Eph 2:7** *5547*
created in **C** Jesus for good works, **Eph 2:10** *5547*
were at that time separate from **C**, **Eph 2:12** *5547*
in **C** Jesus you who formerly were far **Eph 2:13** *5547*
brought near by the blood of **C**. **Eph 2:13** *5547*
C Jesus Himself being the corner **Eph 2:20** *5547*
the prisoner of **C** Jesus for the **Eph 3:1** *5547*
my insight into the mystery of **C**, **Eph 3:4** *5547*
in **C** Jesus through the gospel, **Eph 3:6** *5547*
the unfathomable riches of **C**, **Eph 3:8** *5547*
carried out in **C** Jesus our Lord, **Eph 3:11** *5547*
so that **C** may dwell in your hearts **Eph 3:17** *5547*
of **C** which surpasses knowledge, **Eph 3:19** *5547*
glory in the church and in **C** Jesus **Eph 3:21** *5547*
the building up of the body of **C**; **Eph 4:12** *5547*
which belongs to the fullness of **C**. **Eph 4:13** *5547*
into Him who is the head, *even* **C**, **Eph 4:15** *5547*
you did not learn **C** in this way, **Eph 4:20** *5547*
as God in **C** also has forgiven you. **Eph 4:32** *5547*
in love, just as **C** also loved you and **Eph 5:2** *5547*
in the kingdom of **C** and God. **Eph 5:5** *5547*
And **C** will shine on you." **Eph 5:14** *5547*
name of our Lord Jesus **C** to God, **Eph 5:20** *5547*
to one another in the fear of **C**. **Eph 5:21** *5547*
as **C** also is the head of the **Eph 5:23** *5547*
But as the church is subject to **C**, **Eph 5:24** *5547*
just as **C** also loved the church **Eph 5:25** *5547*
just as **C** also *does* the church, **Eph 5:29** *5547*
reference to **C** and the church. **Eph 5:32** *5547*
sincerity of your heart, as to **C**; **Eph 6:5** *5547*
men-pleasers, but as slaves of **C**, **Eph 6:6** *5547*
the Father and the Lord Jesus **C**. **Eph 6:23** *5547*
Jesus **C** with incorruptible *love.* **Eph 6:24** *5547*
Timothy, bond-servants of **C** Jesus, **Php 1:1** *5547*
in **C** Jesus who are in Philippi, **Php 1:1** *5547*
our Father and the Lord Jesus **C**. **Php 1:2** *5547*
perfect it until the day of **C** Jesus. **Php 1:6** *5547*
all with the affection of **C** Jesus. **Php 1:8** *5547*
and blameless until the day of **C**; **Php 1:10** *5547*
which *comes* through Jesus **C**, **Php 1:11** *5547*
my imprisonment in *the cause of* **C** **Php 1:13** *5547*
C even from envy and strife, **Php 1:15** *5547*
C out of selfish ambition rather **Php 1:17** *5547*
or in truth, **C** is proclaimed; **Php 1:18** *5547*
the provision of the Spirit of Jesus **C**, **Php 1:19** *5547*
all boldness, **C** will even now, **Php 1:20** *5547*
For to me, to live is **C** and **Php 1:21** *5547*
desire to depart and be with **C**, **Php 1:23** *5547*
may abound in **C** Jesus through my **Php 1:26** *5547*
manner worthy of the gospel of **C**, **Php 1:27** *5547*
there is any encouragement in **C**, **Php 2:1** *5547*
which was also in **C** Jesus, **Php 2:5** *5547*
confess that Jesus **C** is Lord, **Php 2:11** *5547*
so that in the day of **C** I will have **Php 2:16** *5547*
interests, not those of **C** Jesus. **Php 2:21** *5547*
close to death for the work of **C**, **Php 2:30** *5547*
Spirit of God and glory in **C** Jesus **Php 3:3** *5547*
counted as loss for the sake of **C**. **Php 3:7** *5547*
value of knowing **C** Jesus my Lord, **Php 3:8** *5547*
so that I may gain **C**, **Php 3:8** *5547*
that which is through faith in **C**, **Php 3:9** *5547*
I was laid hold of by **C** Jesus. **Php 3:12** *5547*
the upward call of God in **C** Jesus. **Php 3:14** *5547*
are enemies of the cross of **C**, **Php 3:18** *5547*
for a Savior, the Lord Jesus **C**; **Php 3:20** *5547*
hearts and your minds in **C** Jesus. **Php 4:7** *5547*
to His riches in glory in **C** Jesus. **Php 4:19** *5547*
Greet every saint in **C** Jesus. **Php 4:21** *5547*
Lord Jesus **C** be with your spirit. **Php 4:23** *5547*
of Jesus **C** by the will of God, **Col 1:1** *5547*
brethren in **C** *who are* at Colossae: **Col 1:2** *5547*
the Father of our Lord Jesus **C**, **Col 1:3** *5547*
since we heard of your faith in **C** **Col 1:4** *5547*
servant of **C** on our behalf, **Col 1:7** *5547*
the Gentiles, which is **C** in you, **Col 1:27** *5547*
present every man complete in **C**. **Col 1:28** *5547*
God's mystery, *that is,* **C** *Himself,* **Col 2:2** *5547*
the stability of your faith in **C**. **Col 2:5** *5547*
have received **C** Jesus the Lord, **Col 2:6** *5547*
world, rather than according to **C**. **Col 2:8** *5547*
flesh by the circumcision of **C**; **Col 2:11** *5547*
but the substance belongs to **C**. **Col 2:17** *5547*
If you have died with **C** to the **Col 2:20** *5547*
you have been raised up with **C**, **Col 3:1** *5547*
the things above, where **C** is, **Col 3:1** *5547*
your life is hidden with **C** in God. **Col 3:3** *5547*
When **C**, who is our life, is **Col 3:4** *5547*
slave and freeman, but **C** is all, **Col 3:11** *5547*
peace of **C** rule in your hearts, **Col 3:15** *5547*
word of **C** richly dwell within you, **Col 3:16** *5547*
It is the Lord **C** whom you serve. **Col 3:24** *5547*
may speak forth the mystery of **C**, **Col 4:3** *5547*
number, a bondslave of Jesus **C**, **Col 4:12** *5547*
the Father and the Lord Jesus **C**: **1Th 1:1** *5547*
hope in our Lord Jesus **C** **1Th 1:3** *5547*
even though as apostles of **C** we **1Th 2:6** *5547*
God in **C** Jesus that are in Judea, **1Th 2:14** *5547*
fellow worker in the gospel of **C**, **1Th 3:2** *5547*
the dead in **C** will rise first. **1Th 4:16** *5547*
through our Lord Jesus **C**, **1Th 5:9** *5547*
is God's will for you in **C** Jesus. **1Th 5:18** *5547*
at the coming of our Lord Jesus **C**. **1Th 5:23** *5547*
of our Lord Jesus **C** be with you. **1Th 5:28** *5547*
our Father and the Lord Jesus **C**: **2Th 1:1** *5547*
the Father and the Lord Jesus **C**. **2Th 1:2** *5547*
of our God and *the* Lord Jesus **C**. **2Th 1:12** *5547*
to the coming of our Lord Jesus **C** and **2Th 2:1** *5547*
the glory of our Lord Jesus **C**. **2Th 2:14** *5547*
C Himself and God our Father, **2Th 2:16** *5547*
and into the steadfastness of **C**. **2Th 3:5** *5547*
in the name of our Lord Jesus **C**, **2Th 3:6** *5547*
exhort in the Lord Jesus **C** to work **2Th 3:12** *5547*
our Lord Jesus **C** be with you all. **2Th 3:18** *5547*
an apostle of **C** Jesus according to **1Tm 1:1** *5547*
of God our Savior, and of **C** Jesus, **1Tm 1:1** *5547*
the Father and **C** Jesus our Lord. **1Tm 1:2** *5547*
I thank **C** Jesus our Lord, who has **1Tm 1:12** *5547*
love which are *found* in **C** Jesus. **1Tm 1:14** *5547*
that **C** Jesus came into the world **1Tm 1:15** *5547*
Jesus **C** might demonstrate His **1Tm 1:16** *5547*
God and men, *the* man **C** Jesus, **1Tm 2:5** *5547*
in the faith that is in **C** Jesus. **1Tm 3:13** *5547*
will be a good servant of **C** Jesus, **1Tm 4:6** *5547*
sensual desires in disregard of **C**, **1Tm 5:11** *5547*
presence of God and of **C** Jesus **1Tm 5:21** *5547*
words, those of our Lord Jesus **C**, **1Tm 6:3** *5547*
to all things, and of **C** Jesus, **1Tm 6:13** *5547*
the appearing of our Lord Jesus **C**, **1Tm 6:14** *5547*
of **C** Jesus by the will of God, **2Tm 1:1** *5547*
to the promise of life in **C** Jesus, **2Tm 1:1** *5547*
the Father and **C** Jesus our Lord. **2Tm 1:2** *5547*
us in **C** Jesus from all eternity, **2Tm 1:9** *5547*
appearing of our Savior **C** Jesus, **2Tm 1:10** *5547*
and love which are in **C** Jesus. **2Tm 1:13** *5547*
in the grace that is in **C** Jesus. **2Tm 2:1** *5547*
me, as a good soldier of **C** Jesus. **2Tm 2:3** *5547*
Remember Jesus **C**, risen from the **2Tm 2:8** *5547*
the salvation which is in **C** Jesus **2Tm 2:10** *5547*
who desire to live godly in **C** Jesus **2Tm 3:12** *5547*
through faith which is in **C** Jesus. **2Tm 3:15** *5547*
presence of God and of **C** Jesus, **2Tm 4:1** *5547*
of God and an apostle of Jesus **C**, **Ti 1:1** *5547*
the Father and **C** Jesus our Savior. **Ti 1:4** *5547*
our great God and Savior, **C** Jesus, **Ti 2:13** *5547*
richly through Jesus **C** our Savior, **Ti 3:6** *5547*
Paul, a prisoner of **C** Jesus, **Phm 1:1** *5547*
our Father and the Lord Jesus **C**. **Phm 1:3** *5547*
I have enough confidence in **C** to **Phm 1:8** *5547*
now also a prisoner of **C** Jesus **Phm 1:9** *5547*
refresh my heart in **C**. **Phm 1:20** *5547*
my fellow prisoner in **C** Jesus, **Phm 1:23** *5547*
Lord Jesus **C** be with your spirit. **Phm 1:25** *5547*
but **C** *was faithful* as a Son over **Heb 3:6** *5547*
For we have become partakers of **C**, **Heb 3:14** *5547*
So also **C** did not glorify Himself **Heb 5:5** *5547*
elementary teaching about the **C**, **Heb 6:1** *5547*
when **C** appeared *as* a high priest **Heb 9:11** *5547*
how much more will the blood of **C**, **Heb 9:14** *5547*
For **C** did not enter a holy place **Heb 9:24** *5547*
so **C** also, having been offered **Heb 9:28** *5547*
the body of Jesus **C** once for all. **Heb 10:10** *5547*
considering the reproach of **C** **Heb 11:26** *5547*
Jesus **C** *is* the same yesterday and **Heb 13:8** *5547*
in His sight, through Jesus **C**, **Heb 13:21** *5547*
of God and of the Lord Jesus **C**, **Jas 1:1** *5547*
faith in our glorious Lord Jesus **C** **Jas 2:1** *5547*
Peter, an apostle of Jesus **C**, **1Pe 1:1** *5547*
to obey Jesus **C** and be **1Pe 1:2** *5547*
and Father of our Lord Jesus **C**, **1Pe 1:3** *5547*
resurrection of Jesus **C** from the dead **1Pe 1:3** *5547*
at the revelation of Jesus **C**; **1Pe 1:7** *5547*
Spirit of **C** within them was indicating **1Pe 1:11** *5547*

of **C** and the glories to follow. **1Pe 1:11** *5547*
you at the revelation of Jesus **C**. **1Pe 1:13** *5547*
and spotless, *the blood* of **C**. **1Pe 1:19** *5547*
acceptable to God through Jesus **C**. **1Pe 2:5** *5547*
since **C** also suffered for you, **1Pe 2:21** *5547*
sanctify **C** as Lord in your hearts, **1Pe 3:15** *5547*
who revile your good behavior in **C** **1Pe 3:16** *5547*
For **C** also died for sins once for **1Pe 3:18** *5547*
the resurrection of Jesus **C**, **1Pe 3:21** *5547*
since **C** has suffered in the flesh, **1Pe 4:1** *5547*
may be glorified through Jesus **C**, **1Pe 4:11** *5547*
you share the sufferings of **C**, **1Pe 4:13** *5547*
you are reviled for the name of **C**, **1Pe 4:14** *5547*
witness of the sufferings of **C**, **1Pe 5:1** *5547*
you to His eternal glory in **C**, **1Pe 5:10** *5547*
Peace be to you all who are in **C**. **1Pe 5:14** *5547*
and apostle of Jesus **C**, **2Pe 1:1** *5547*
of our God and Savior, Jesus **C**: **2Pe 1:1** *5547*
knowledge of our Lord Jesus **C**. **2Pe 1:8** *5547*
Savior Jesus **C** will be abundantly **2Pe 1:11** *5547*
Lord Jesus **C** has made clear to me. **2Pe 1:14** *5547*
and coming of our Lord Jesus **C**, **2Pe 1:16** *5547*
of the Lord and Savior Jesus **C**, **2Pe 2:20** *5547*
of our Lord and Savior Jesus **C**. **2Pe 3:18** *5547*
Father, and with His Son Jesus **C**. **1Jn 1:3** *5547*
the Father, Jesus **C** the righteous, **1Jn 2:1** *5547*
who denies that Jesus is the **C**? **1Jn 2:22** *5547*
in the name of His Son Jesus **C**, **1Jn 3:23** *5547*
that Jesus **C** has come in the flesh **1Jn 4:2** *5547*
Jesus is the **C** is born of God, **1Jn 5:1** *5547*
came by water and blood, Jesus **C**; **1Jn 5:6** *5547*
who is true, in His Son Jesus **C**. **1Jn 5:20** *5547*
God the Father and from Jesus **C**, **2Jn 1:3** *5547*
Jesus **C** *as* coming in the flesh. **2Jn 1:7** *5547*
not abide in the teaching of **C**, **2Jn 1:9** *5547*
Jude, a bond-servant of Jesus **C**, **Jude 1:1** *5547*
the Father, and kept for Jesus **C**: **Jude 1:1** *5547*
our only Master and Lord, Jesus **C**. **Jude 1:4** *5547*
the apostles of our Lord Jesus **C**, **Jude 1:17** *5547*
our Lord Jesus **C** to eternal life. **Jude 1:21** *5547*
Savior, through Jesus **C** our Lord, **Jude 1:25** *5547*
The Revelation of Jesus **C**, **Rv 1:1** *5547*
and to the testimony of Jesus **C**, **Rv 1:2** *5547*
from Jesus **C**, the faithful witness, **Rv 1:5** *5547*
kingdom of our Lord and of His **C**; **Rv 11:15** *5547*
the authority of His **C** have come, **Rv 12:10** *5547*
with **C** for a thousand years. **Rv 20:4** *5547*
priests of God and of **C** and will reign **Rv 20:6** *5547*

CHRISTIAN
will persuade me to become a **C**." **Ac 26:28** *5546*
but if *anyone suffers* as a **C**, **1Pe 4:16** *5546*

CHRISTIANS
were first called **C** in Antioch. **Ac 11:26** *5546*

CHRIST'S
We are fools for **C** sake, **1Co 4:10** *5547*
was called while free, is **C** slave. **1Co 7:22** *5547*
Now you are **C** body, and **1Co 12:27** *5547*
those who are **C** at His coming, **1Co 15:23** *5547*
confident in himself that he is **C**, **2Co 10:7** *5547*
himself, that just as he is **C**, **2Co 10:7** *5547*
with difficulties, for **C** sake; **2Co 12:10** *5547*
to the measure of **C** gift. **Eph 4:7** *5547*
it has been granted for **C** sake, **Php 1:29** *5547*
what is lacking in **C** afflictions. **Col 1:24** *5547*
thing which is in you for **C** sake. **Phm 1:6** *5547*

CHRISTS
"For false **C** and false prophets **Mt 24:24** *5580*
C and false prophets will arise, **Mk 13:22** *5580*

CHRONIC
it is a **c** leprosy on the skin of **Lv 13:11** 3462
and miserable and **c** sicknesses. **Dt 28:59** 539

CHRONICLES
Book of the **C** of the Kings of Israel. **1Ki 14:19** 1697, 3117
Book of the **C** of the Kings of Judah? **1Ki 14:29** 1697, 3117
Book of the **C** of the Kings of Judah? **1Ki 15:7** 1697, 3117
Book of the **C** of the Kings of Judah? **1Ki 15:23** 1697, 3117
Book of the **C** of the Kings of Israel? **1Ki 15:31** 1697, 3117
Book of the **C** of the Kings of Israel? **1Ki 16:5** 1697, 3117
Book of the **C** of the Kings of Israel? **1Ki 16:14** 1697, 3117
Book of the **C** of the Kings of Israel? **1Ki 16:20** 1697, 3117
Book of the **C** of the Kings of Israel? **1Ki 16:27** 1697, 3117
Book of the **C** of the Kings of Israel? **1Ki 22:39** 1697, 3117
Book of the **C** of the Kings of Judah? **1Ki 22:45** 1697, 3117
Book of the **C** of the Kings of Israel? **2Ki 1:18** 1697, 3117
Book of the **C** of the Kings of Judah? **2Ki 8:23** 1697, 3117
Book of the **C** of the Kings of Israel? **2Ki 10:34** 1697, 3117
Book of the **C** of the Kings of Judah? **2Ki 12:19** 1697, 3117
Book of the **C** of the Kings of Israel? **2Ki 13:8** 1697, 3117
Book of the **C** of the Kings of Israel? **2Ki 13:12** 1697, 3117
Book of the **C** of the Kings of Israel? **2Ki 14:15** 1697, 3117
Book of the **C** of the Kings of Judah? **2Ki 14:18** 1697, 3117
Book of the **C** of the Kings of Israel? **2Ki 14:28** 1697, 3117
Book of the **C** of the Kings of Judah? **2Ki 15:6** 1697, 3117
Book of the **C** of the Kings of Israel. **2Ki 15:11** 1697, 3117
Book of the **C** of the Kings of Israel. **2Ki 15:15** 1697, 3117
Book of the **C** of the Kings of Israel? **2Ki 15:21** 1697, 3117
Book of the **C** of the Kings of Israel. **2Ki 15:26** 1697, 3117
Book of the **C** of the Kings of Israel. **2Ki 15:31** 1697, 3117
Book of the **C** of the Kings of Judah? **2Ki 15:36** 1697, 3117
Book of the **C** of the Kings of Judah? **2Ki 16:19** 1697, 3117
Book of the **C** of the Kings of Judah? **2Ki 20:20** 1697, 3117
Book of the **C** of the Kings of Judah? **2Ki 21:17** 1697, 3117
Book of the **C** of the Kings of Judah? **2Ki 21:25** 1697, 3117
Book of the **C** of the Kings of Judah? **2Ki 23:28** 1697, 3117
Book of the **C** of the Kings of Judah? **2Ki 24:5** 1697, 3117
account of the **c** of King David. **1Ch 27:24** 1697, 3117
in the **c** of Samuel the seer, **1Ch 29:29** 1697
in the **c** of Nathan the prophet and **1Ch 29:29** 1697
and in the **c** of Gad the seer, **1Ch 29:29** 1697
were registered in the Book of the **C** **Ne 12:23** 1697, 3117
Book of the **C** in the king's presence. **Es 2:23** 1697, 3117
bring the book of records, the **c**, **Es 6:1** 1697, 3117
C of the Kings of Media and Persia? **Es 10:2** 1697, 3117

CHRYSOLITE
the seventh, **c**; the eighth, beryl; **Rv 21:20** *5555*

CHRYSOPRASE
the tenth, **c**; the eleventh, jacinth; **Rv 21:20** *5556*

CHURCH
upon this rock I will build My **c**; **Mt 16:18** *1577*
listen to them, tell it to the **c**; **Mt 18:17** *1577*
refuses to listen even to the **c**, **Mt 18:17** *1577*
great fear came over the whole **c**, **Ac 5:11** *1577*
began against the **c** in Jerusalem **Ac 8:1** *1577*
But Saul *began* ravaging the **c**, **Ac 8:3** *1577*
So the **c** throughout all Judea and **Ac 9:31** *1577*
the ears of the **c** at Jerusalem, **Ac 11:22** *1577*
entire year they met with the **c** and **Ac 11:26** *1577*
on some who belonged to the **c** in **Ac 12:1** *1577*
made fervently by the **c** to God. **Ac 12:5** *1577*
Antioch, in the **c** that was *there*, **Ac 13:1** *1577*
elders for them in every **c**, **Ac 14:23** *1577*
and gathered the **c** together, **Ac 14:27** *1577*
being sent on their way by the **c**, **Ac 15:3** *1577*
they were received by the **c** and **Ac 15:4** *1577*
and the elders, with the whole **c**, **Ac 15:22** *1577*
he went up and greeted the **c**, **Ac 18:22** *1577*
called to him the elders of the **c**. **Ac 20:17** *1577*
to shepherd the **c** of God which He **Ac 20:28** *1577*
of the **c** which is at Cenchrea; **Ro 16:1** *1577*
the **c** that is in their house. **Ro 16:5** *1577*
host to me and to the whole **c**, **Ro 16:23** *1577*
the **c** of God which is at Corinth, **1Co 1:2** *1577*
as I teach everywhere in every **c**. **1Co 4:17** *1577*
judge those who are within *the c*? **1Co 5:12** *1577*
who are of no account in the **c**? **1Co 6:4** *1577*
or to Greeks or to the **c** of God; **1Co 10:32** *1577*
when you come together as a **c**, **1Co 11:18** *1577*
Or do you despise the **c** of God and **1Co 11:22** *1577*
And God has appointed in the **c**, **1Co 12:28** *1577*
one who prophesies edifies the **c**. **1Co 14:4** *1577*
that the **c** may receive edifying. **1Co 14:5** *1577*
for the edification of the **c**. **1Co 14:12** *1577*
in the **c** I desire to speak five **1Co 14:19** *1577*
Therefore if the whole **c** assembles **1Co 14:23** *1577*
he must keep silent in the **c**; **1Co 14:28** *1577*
for a woman to speak in **c**. **1Co 14:35** *1577*
because I persecuted the **c** of God. **1Co 15:9** *1577*
with the **c** that is in their house. **1Co 16:19** *1577*
To the **c** of God which is at **2Co 1:1** *1577*
the **c** of God beyond measure and **Ga 1:13** *1577*
as head over all things to the **c**, **Eph 1:22** *1577*
now be made known through the **c** **Eph 3:10** *1577*
to Him *be* the glory in the **c** and **Eph 3:21** *1577*
Christ also is the head of the **c**, **Eph 5:23** *1577*
But as the **c** is subject to Christ, **Eph 5:24** *1577*
Christ also loved the **c** and gave **Eph 5:25** *1577*
to Himself the **c** in all her glory, **Eph 5:27** *1577*
just as Christ also *does* the **c**, **Eph 5:29** *1577*
reference to Christ and the **c**. **Eph 5:32** *1577*
as to zeal, a persecutor of the **c**; **Php 3:6** *1577*
no **c** shared with me in the matter **Php 4:15** *1577*
is also head of the body, the **c**; **Col 1:18** *1577*
behalf of His body, which is the **c**, **Col 1:24** *1577*
Of *this* **c** I was made a minister **Col 1:25** *1577*
and the **c** that is in her house. **Col 4:15** *1577*
read in the **c** of the Laodiceans; **Col 4:16** *1577*
To the **c** of the Thessalonians in God **1Th 1:1** *1577*
To the **c** of the Thessalonians in God **2Th 1:1** *1577*
he take care of the **c** of God?), **1Tm 3:5** *1577*
reputation with those outside *the c*, **1Tm 3:7** *1577*
which is the **c** of the living God, **1Tm 3:15** *1577*
and the **c** must not be burdened, **1Tm 5:16** *1577*
and to the **c** in your house: **Phm 1:2** *1577*
to the general assembly and **c** of **Heb 12:23** *1577*
must call for the elders of the **c** **Jas 5:14** *1577*
testified to your love before the **c** **3Jn 1:6** *1577*
I wrote something to the **c**; **3Jn 1:9** *1577*
do so and puts *them* out of the **c**. **3Jn 1:10** *1577*
angel of the **c** in Ephesus write: **Rv 2:1** *1577*
angel of the **c** in Smyrna write: **Rv 2:8** *1577*
angel of the **c** in Pergamum write: **Rv 2:12** *1577*
angel of the **c** in Thyatira write: **Rv 2:18** *1577*
angel of the **c** in Sardis write: **Rv 3:1** *1577*
to the angel of the **c** in Philadelphia **Rv 3:7** *1577*
angel of the **c** in Laodicea write: **Rv 3:14** *1577*

CHURCHES
and Cilicia, strengthening the **c**. **Ac 15:41** *1577*
So the **c** were being strengthened **Ac 16:5** *1577*
also all the **c** of the Gentiles; **Ro 16:4** *1577*
All the **c** of Christ greet you. **Ro 16:16** *1577*
And so I direct in all the **c**. **1Co 7:17** *1577*
practice, nor have the **c** of God. **1Co 11:16** *1577*
as in all the **c** of the saints. **1Co 14:33** *1577*
The women are to keep silent in the **c**; **1Co 14:34** *1577*
as I directed the **c** of Galatia, **1Co 16:1** *1577*
The **c** of Asia greet you. **1Co 16:19** *1577*
been given in the **c** of Macedonia, **2Co 8:1** *1577*
has spread through all the **c**; **2Co 8:18** *1577*
also been appointed by the **c** to travel **2Co 8:19** *1577*
they are messengers of the **c**, **2Co 8:23** *1577*
Therefore openly before the **c**, **2Co 8:24** *1577*
I robbed other **c** by taking wages **2Co 11:8** *1577*
on me *of* concern for all the **c**. **2Co 11:28** *1577*
as inferior to the rest of the **c**, **2Co 12:13** *1577*
are with me, To the **c** of Galatia: **Ga 1:2** *1577*
c of Judea which were in Christ; **Ga 1:22** *1577*
became imitators of the **c** of God **1Th 2:14** *1577*
speak proudly of you among the **c** of **2Th 1:4** *1577*
to the seven **c** that are in Asia: **Rv 1:4** *1577*
see, and send *it* to the seven **c**: **Rv 1:11** *1577*
are the angels of the seven **c**, **Rv 1:20** *1577*
seven lampstands are the seven **c**. **Rv 1:20** *1577*
what the Spirit says to the **c**. **Rv 2:7** *1577*
what the Spirit says to the **c**. **Rv 2:11** *1577*
what the Spirit says to the **c**. **Rv 2:17** *1577*
and all the **c** will know that I am **Rv 2:23** *1577*
what the Spirit says to the **c**.' **Rv 2:29** *1577*
what the Spirit says to the **c**.' **Rv 3:6** *1577*
what the Spirit says to the **c**.' **Rv 3:13** *1577*
what the Spirit says to the **c**.' " **Rv 3:22** *1577*
to you these things for the **c**. **Rv 22:16** *1577*

CHURNING
For the **c** of milk produces butter, **Pr 30:33** 4330
So the **c** of anger produces strife. **Pr 30:33** 4330

CHUZA
and Joanna the wife of **C**, **Lk 8:3** *5529a*

CILICIA
and some from **C** and Asia, **Ac 6:9** *2791*
and **C** who are from the Gentiles, **Ac 15:23** *2791*
was traveling through Syria and **C**, **Ac 15:41** *2791*
"I am a Jew of Tarsus in **C**, **Ac 21:39** *2791*
"I am a Jew, born in Tarsus of **C**, **Ac 22:3** *2791*
he learned that he was from **C**, **Ac 23:34** *2791*
the coast of **C** and Pamphylia, **Ac 27:5** *2791*
into the regions of Syria and **C**. **Ga 1:21** *2791*

CINNAMON
and of fragrant **c** half as much, **Ex 30:23** 7076
my bed With myrrh, aloes and **c**. **Pr 7:17** 7076
Nard and saffron, calamus and **c**, **SS 4:14** 7076
and **c** and spice and incense and **Rv 18:13** *2796b*

CIRCLE
And he came to the **c** of the camp **1Sa 17:20** 4570
was lying in the **c** of the camp, **1Sa 26:5** 4570
sleeping inside the **c** of the camp with **1Sa 26:7** 4570
c around behind them and come at **2Sa 5:23** 5437
c around behind them and come at **1Ch 14:14** 5437
a **c** on the surface of the waters At **Jb 26:10** 2328
a **c** on the face of the deep, **Pr 8:27** 2329
It is He who sits above the **c** of **Is 40:22** 2329
not sit in the **c** of merrymakers, **Jer 15:17** 5475

CIRCLED
and **c** Mount Seir for many days. **Dt 2:1** 5437
have **c** this mountain long enough. **Dt 2:3** 5437
The border **c** around it on the **Jos 19:14** 5437

CIRCLING
the men of war **c** the city once. **Jos 6:3** 5362b
taken around the city, **c** *it* once; **Jos 6:11** 5362b
and chariots was **c** the city. **2Ki 6:15** 5437

CIRCUIT
He used to go annually on **c** to **1Sa 7:16** 5437
made a **c** of seven days' journey, **2Ki 3:9** 5437
its **c** to the other end of them; **Ps 19:6** 8622

CIRCULAR
from brim to brim, **c** in form, **1Ki 7:23** 5696
was a **c** form half a cubit high, **1Ki 7:35** 5696
from brim to brim, **c** in form, **2Ch 4:2** 5696
on its **c** courses the wind returns. **Ec 1:6** 5439

CIRCULATE
So they established a decree to **c** **2Ch 30:5** 5674a

CIRCULATED
was **c** throughout the camp, **Ex 36:6** 5674a
c a proclamation in all their cities **Ne 8:15** 5674a

CIRCULATING
which I hear the LORD's people **c**. **1Sa 2:24** 5674a

CIRCUMCISE
"So **c** your heart, and stiffen your **Dt 10:16** 4135
the LORD your God will **c** your heart **Dt 30:6** 4135
knives and **c** again the sons of Israel **Jos 5:2** 4135
"**C** yourselves to the LORD And **Jer 4:4** 4135
day they came to **c** the child, **Lk 1:59** *4059*
and on *the* Sabbath you **c** a man. **Jn 7:22** *4059*
"It is necessary to **c** them and **Ac 15:5** *4059*
telling them not to **c** their children **Ac 21:21** *4059*

CIRCUMCISED
every male among you shall be **c**. **Gn 17:10** 4135
c in the flesh of your foreskin, **Gn 17:11** 4135
be **c** throughout your generations, **Gn 17:12** 4135
with your money shall surely be **c**; **Gn 17:13** 4135
c in the flesh of his foreskin, **Gn 17:14** 4135
and **c** the flesh of their foreskin **Gn 17:23** 4135
c in the flesh of his foreskin. **Gn 17:24** 4135
c in the flesh of his foreskin. **Gn 17:25** 4135
the very same day Abraham was **c**, **Gn 17:26** 4135
from a foreigner, were **c** with him. **Gn 17:27** 4135
Then Abraham **c** his son Isaac when **Gn 21:4** 4135
in that every male of you be **c**, **Gn 34:15** 4135
you will not listen to us to be **c**, **Gn 34:17** 4135
every male among us be **c** as they are **Gn 34:22** 4135
us be circumcised as they are **c**. **Gn 34:22** 4135
son Shechem, and every male was **c**, **Gn 34:24** 4135
with money, after you have **c** him, **Ex 12:44** 4135
the LORD, let all his males be **c**, **Ex 12:48** 4135
flesh of his foreskin shall be **c**. **Lv 12:3** 4135
flint knives and **c** the sons of Israel **Jos 5:3** 4135
is the reason why Joshua **c** them: **Jos 5:4** 4135
the people who came out were **c**, **Jos 5:5** 4135
came out of Egypt had not been **c**. **Jos 5:5** 4135
up in their place, Joshua **c**; **Jos 5:7** 4135
they had not **c** them along the way. **Jos 5:7** 4135
who are **c** and yet uncircumcised **Jer 9:25** 4135
and **c** him on the eighth day; **Ac 7:8** *4059*
All the **c** believers who came **Ac 10:45** *4061*
who were **c** took issue with him, **Ac 11:2** *4061*
"Unless you are **c** according to **Ac 15:1** *4059*
and he took him and **c** him because **Ac 16:3** *4059*
God who will justify the **c** by faith **Ro 3:30** *4061*
Is this blessing then on the **c**, **Ro 4:9** *4061*
While he was **c**, or uncircumcised? **Ro 4:10** *4061*
Not while **c**, but while **Ro 4:10** *4061*
all who believe without being **c**, **Ro 4:11** *203*
any man called *when he was already* **c**? **1Co 7:18** *4059*
He is not to be **c**. **1Co 7:18** *4059*
a Greek, was compelled to be **c**. **Ga 2:3** *4059*
just as Peter *had been* to the **c** **Ga 2:7** *4061*
for Peter in *his* apostleship to the **c** **Ga 2:8** *4061*
the Gentiles and they to the **c**. **Ga 2:9** *4061*
flesh try to compel you to be **c**, **Ga 6:12** *4059*
For those who are **c** do not even **Ga 6:13** *4059*
but they desire to have you **c** so **Ga 6:13** *4059*
c the eighth day, of the nation of **Php 3:5** *4061*
and in Him you were also **c** with a **Col 2:11** *4059*
and Jew, **c** and uncircumcised, **Col 3:11** *4061*

CIRCUMCISING
had finished **c** all the nation, **Jos 5:8** 4135

CIRCUMCISION
because of the **c**. **Ex 4:26** 4139
days had passed, before His **c**, **Lk 2:21** *4059*
reason Moses has given you **c** **Jn 7:22** *4061*
"If a man receives **c** on *the* **Jn 7:23** *4061*
"And He gave him the covenant of **c**; **Ac 7:8** *4061*
For indeed **c** is of value if you **Ro 2:25** *4061*
your **c** has become uncircumcision. **Ro 2:25** *4061*
uncircumcision be regarded as **c**? **Ro 2:26** *4061*
c are a transgressor of the Law? **Ro 2:27** *4061*
nor is **c** that which is outward **Ro 2:28** *4061*
c is that which is of the heart, **Ro 2:29** *4061*
Or what is the benefit of **c**? **Ro 3:1** *4061*
and he received the sign of **c**, **Ro 4:11** *4061*
and the father of **c** to those who **Ro 4:12** *4061*
those who not only are of the **c**, **Ro 4:12** *4061*
Christ has become a servant to the **c** **Ro 15:8** *4061*
C is nothing, and uncircumcision **1Co 7:19** *4061*
aloof, fearing the party of the **c**. **Ga 2:12** *4061*
say to you that if you receive **c**, **Ga 5:2** *4059*
again to every man who receives **c**, **Ga 5:3** *4059*
For in Christ Jesus neither **c** nor **Ga 5:6** *4061*
I, brethren, if I still preach **c**, **Ga 5:11** *4061*
For neither is **c** anything, nor **Ga 6:15** *4061*
by the so-called "**C**," **Eph 2:11** *4061*
workers, beware of the false **c**; **Php 3:2** *2699*
for we are the *true* **c**, **Php 3:3** *4061*
with a **c** made without hands, **Col 2:11** *4061*
of the flesh by the **c** of Christ; **Col 2:11** *4061*
kingdom of God who are from the **c**, **Col 4:11** *4061*
especially those of the **c**, **Ti 1:10** *4061*

CIRCUMFERENCE
cubits measured the **c** of both. **1Ki 7:15** 5437
cubits, and thirty cubits in **c**. **1Ki 7:23** 6961a, 5437, 5439
cubits and its **c** thirty cubits. **2Ch 4:2** 6957b, 5437, 5439
and it *was* twelve cubits in **c** **Jer 52:21** 5437, 2339

CIRCUMSTANCE
in any and every **c** I have learned **Php 4:12** *1722*
grant you peace in every **c**. **2Th 3:16** *5158*

CIRCUMSTANCES
and the **c** which came on him, **1Ch 29:30** 6256
Is a word spoken in right **c**. **Pr 25:11** 655
Under these **c**, after so many **Lk 12:1** *1722*
that you also may know about my **c**, **Eph 6:21** *3588, 2596*
that my **c** have turned out for the **Php 1:12** *3588, 2596*
to be content in whatever **c** I am. **Php 4:11** *1722*
that you may know about our **c** and **Col 4:8** *3588, 4012*
brother of humble **c** is to glory **Jas 1:9**

CISTERN
a spring or a **c** collecting water **Lv 11:36** 953a
each of the waters of his own **c**, **2Ki 18:31** 953a
Drink water from your own **c** And **Pr 5:15** 953a
and the wheel at the **c** is crushed; **Ec 12:6** 953a
Or to scoop water from a **c**." **Is 30:14** 1360
each of the waters of his own **c**, **Is 36:16** 953a
the **c** *of* Malchijah the king's son, **Jer 38:6** 953a
Now in the **c** there was no water **Jer 38:6** 953a
they had put Jeremiah into the **c**. **Jer 38:7** 953a
whom they have cast into the **c**; **Jer 38:9** 953a
from the **c** before he dies." **Jer 38:10** 953a
by ropes into the **c** to Jeremiah. **Jer 38:11** 953a
ropes and lifted him out of the **c**, **Jer 38:13** 953a
them *and cast them* into the **c**. **Jer 41:7** 953a
Now as for the **c** where Ishmael had **Jer 41:9** 953a

CISTERNS
and hewn **c** which you did not dig, **Dt 6:11** 953a
the wilderness and hewed many **c**, **2Ch 26:10** 953a
full of every good thing, Hewn **c**, **Ne 9:25** 953a
waters, To hew for themselves **c**, **Jer 2:13** 877
for themselves cisterns, Broken **c** That **Jer 2:13** 877
come to the **c** and found no water. **Jer 14:3** 1356a

CITADEL
went into the **c** of the king's house **1Ki 16:18** 759
royal throne which *was* at the **c** **Es 1:2** 1002
the people who were present at the **c** **Es 1:5** 1002
every beautiful young virgin to the **c** **Es 2:3** 1002
Now there was at the **c** in Susa **Es 2:5** 1002
young ladies were gathered to the **c** **Es 2:8** 1002
while the decree was issued at the **c** **Es 3:15** 1002
and the decree was given out at the **c** **Es 8:14** 1002
At the **c** in Susa the Jews killed **Es 9:6** 1002
of those who were killed at the **c** in **Es 9:11** 1002
and the ten sons of Haman at the **c** in **Es 9:12** 1002
contentions are like the bars of a **c**. **Pr 18:19** 759
looking I was in the **c** of Susa, **Da 8:2** 1002

CITADELS
it will consume the **c** of Ben-hadad. **Am 1:4** 759
Gaza And it will consume her **c**. **Am 1:7** 759
Tyre And it will consume her **c**." **Am 1:10** 759
it will consume the **c** of Bozrah." **Am 1:12** 759
And it will consume her **c** Amid war **Am 1:14** 759
it will consume the **c** of Kerioth; **Am 2:2** 759
will consume the **c** of Jerusalem." **Am 2:5** 759
Proclaim on the **c** in Ashdod and on **Am 3:9** 759
on the **c** in the land of Egypt **Am 3:9** 759
and devastation in their **c**." **Am 3:10** 759
you And your **c** will be looted." **Am 3:11** 759
of Jacob, And detest his **c**; **Am 6:8** 759
land, When he tramples on our **c**, **Mi 5:5** 759

CITIES
settled in the **c** of the valley, **Gn 13:12** 5892b
and He overthrew those **c**, **Gn 19:25** 5892b
and all the inhabitants of the **c**, **Gn 19:25** 5892b
God destroyed the **c** of the valley, **Gn 19:29** 5892b
the **c** in which Lot lived. **Gn 19:29** 5892b
there was a great terror upon the **c** **Gn 35:5** 5892b
in the **c** under Pharaoh's authority, **Gn 41:35** 5892b
and placed the food in the **c**; **Gn 41:48** 5892b
he removed them to the **c** from one **Gn 47:21** 5892b
they built for Pharaoh storage **c**, **Ex 1:11** 5892b
'As for **c** of the Levites, the **Lv 25:32** 5892b
the **c** which are their possession. **Lv 25:32** 5892b
for the houses of the **c** of the Levites **Lv 25:33** 5892b
of their **c** shall not be sold, **Lv 25:34** 5892b
you gather together into your **c**, **Lv 26:25** 5892b
'I will lay waste your **c** as well and **Lv 26:31** 5892b
desolate and your **c** become waste. **Lv 26:33** 5892b
how are the **c** in which they live, **Nu 13:19** 5892b
c are fortified *and* very large; **Nu 13:28** 5892b
I will utterly destroy their **c**." **Nu 21:2** 5892b
destroyed them and their **c**. **Nu 21:3** 5892b
Israel took all these **c** and **Nu 21:25** 5892b
in all the **c** of the Amorites, **Nu 21:25** 5892b
Then they burned all their **c** where **Nu 31:10** 5892b
and **c** for our little ones; **Nu 32:16** 5892b
our little ones live in the fortified **c** **Nu 32:17** 5892b
yourselves **c** for your little ones, **Nu 32:24** 5892b
remain there in the **c** of Gilead; **Nu 32:26** 5892b
land with its **c** with *their* territories, **Nu 32:33** 5892b
the **c** of the surrounding land. **Nu 32:33** 5892b
and Beth-haran as fortified **c**, **Nu 32:36** 5892b
names to the **c** which they built. **Nu 32:38** 5892b
of their possession **c** to live in; **Nu 35:2** 5892b
pasture lands around the **c**. **Nu 35:2** 5892b
The **c** shall be theirs to live in; **Nu 35:3** 5892b
"The pasture lands of the **c** **Nu 35:4** 5892b
theirs as pasture lands for the **c**. **Nu 35:5** 5892b
"The **c** which you shall give **Nu 35:6** 5892b
shall be the six **c** of refuge, **Nu 35:6** 5892b
to them you shall give forty-two **c**. **Nu 35:6** 5892b
"All the **c** which you shall give **Nu 35:7** 5892b
the Levites *shall be* forty-eight **c**, **Nu 35:7** 5892b
"As for the **c** which you shall **Nu 35:8** 5892b
each shall give some of his **c** to **Nu 35:8** 5892b
c to be your cities of refuge, **Nu 35:11** 5892b
cities to be your **c** of refuge, **Nu 35:11** 5892b
'The **c** shall be to you as a refuge **Nu 35:12** 5892b
'The **c** which you are to give **Nu 35:13** 5892b
shall be your six **c** of refuge. **Nu 35:13** 5892b
'You shall give three **c** across the **Nu 35:14** 5892b
and three **c** in the land of Canaan; **Nu 35:14** 5892b
they are to be **c** of refuge. **Nu 35:14** 5892b
'These six **c** shall be for refuge **Nu 35:15** 5892b
and the **c** which we shall enter.' **Dt 1:22** 5892b
the **c** are large and fortified to **Dt 1:28** 5892b
captured all his **c** at that time and **Dt 2:34** 5892b
of the **c** which we had captured. **Dt 2:35** 5892b
and the **c** of the hill country, **Dt 2:37** 5892b
captured all his **c** at that time; **Dt 3:4** 5892b
sixty **c**, all the region of Argob, **Dt 3:4** 5892b
were **c** fortified with high walls, **Dt 3:5** 5892b
of the **c** we took as our booty. **Dt 3:7** 5892b
all the **c** of the plateau and all **Dt 3:10** 5892b
c of the kingdom of Og in Bashan. **Dt 3:10** 5892b
hill country of Gilead and its **c** I **Dt 3:12** 5892b
in your **c** which I have given you, **Dt 3:19** 5892b
c across the Jordan to the east, **Dt 4:41** 5892b
to one of these **c** he might live: **Dt 4:42** 5892b
c which you did not build, **Dt 6:10** 5892b
you, great **c** fortified to heaven, **Dt 9:1** 5892b
"If you hear in one of your **c**, **Dt 13:12** 5892b
in their **c** and in their houses, **Dt 19:1** 5892b
you shall set aside three **c** for **Dt 19:2** 5892b
flee to one of these **c** and live; **Dt 19:5** 5892b
set aside three **c** for yourself.' **Dt 19:7** 5892b
add three more **c** for yourself, **Dt 19:9** 5892b
and he flees to one of these **c**, **Dt 19:11** 5892b
the **c** that are very far from you, **Dt 20:15** 5892b
of the **c** of these nations nearby. **Dt 20:15** 5892b
"Only in the **c** of these peoples **Dt 20:16** 5892b
measure *the distance* to the **c** which **Dt 21:2** 5892b
came to their **c** on the third day. **Jos 9:17** 5892b
Now their **c** *were* Gibeon and **Jos 9:17** 5892b
city, like one of the royal **c**, **Jos 10:2** 5892b
not allow them to enter their **c**, **Jos 10:19** 5892b
them had entered the fortified **c**, **Jos 10:20** 5892b
struck it and its king and all its **c** and **Jos 10:37** 5892b
it and its king and all its **c**, **Jos 10:39** 5892b
captured all the **c** of these kings, **Jos 11:12** 5892b
any **c** that stood on their mounds, **Jos 11:13** 5892b
spoil of these **c** and the cattle, **Jos 11:14** 5892b
destroyed them with their **c**. **Jos 11:21** 5892b
c of Sihon king of the Amorites, **Jos 13:10** 5892b
all its **c** which are on the plain: **Jos 13:17** 5892b
even all the **c** of the plain and **Jos 13:21** 5892b
the **c** and their villages. **Jos 13:23** 5892b
Jazer, and all the **c** of Gilead, **Jos 13:25** 5892b
the **c** and their villages. **Jos 13:28** 5892b
which are in Bashan, sixty **c**; **Jos 13:30** 5892b
the **c** of the kingdom of Og in **Jos 13:31** 5892b
in the land, except **c** to live in, **Jos 14:4** 5892b
there, with great fortified **c**; **Jos 14:12** 5892b
to the **c** of Mount Ephron, **Jos 15:9** 5892b
Now the **c** at the extremity of the **Jos 15:21** 5892b
twenty-nine **c** with their villages. **Jos 15:32** 5892b
fourteen **c** with their villages. **Jos 15:36** 5892b
sixteen **c** with their villages. **Jos 15:41** 5892b
nine **c** with their villages. **Jos 15:44** 5892b
eleven **c** with their villages. **Jos 15:51** 5892b
nine **c** with their villages. **Jos 15:54** 5892b
ten **c** with their villages. **Jos 15:57** 5892b
six **c** with their villages. **Jos 15:59** 5892b
two **c** with their villages. **Jos 15:60** 5892b
six **c** with their villages. **Jos 15:62** 5892b
together with the **c** which were set **Jos 16:9** 5892b
all the **c** with their villages. **Jos 16:9** 5892b
these **c** *belonged* to Ephraim **Jos 17:9** 5892b
Ephraim among the **c** of Manasseh), **Jos 17:9** 5892b
not take possession of these **c**, **Jos 17:12** 5892b
by **c** in seven divisions in a book; **Jos 18:9** 5892b
Now the **c** of the tribe of the sons **Jos 18:21** 5892b
twelve **c** with their villages. **Jos 18:24** 5892b
fourteen **c** with their villages. **Jos 18:28** 5892b
thirteen **c** with their villages; **Jos 19:6** 5892b
Ashan; four **c** with their villages; **Jos 19:7** 5892b
these **c** as far as Baalath-beer, **Jos 19:8** 5892b
twelve **c** with their villages. **Jos 19:15** 5892b
these **c** with their villages. **Jos 19:16** 5892b
sixteen **c** with their villages. **Jos 19:22** 5892b
the **c** with their villages. **Jos 19:23** 5892b
twenty-two **c** with their villages. **Jos 19:30** 5892b
these **c** with their villages. **Jos 19:31** 5892b
The fortified **c** *were* Ziddim, **Jos 19:35** 5892b
nineteen **c** with their villages. **Jos 19:38** 5892b
the **c** with their villages. **Jos 19:39** 5892b
these **c** with their villages. **Jos 19:48** 5892b
'Designate the **c** of refuge, of **Jos 20:2** 5892b
He shall flee to one of these **c**, **Jos 20:4** 5892b
These were the appointed **c** for all **Jos 20:9** 5892b
Moses to give us **c** to live in, **Jos 21:2** 5892b
these **c** with their pasture lands, **Jos 21:3** 5892b
received thirteen **c** by lot from **Jos 21:4** 5892b
sons of Kohath received ten **c** by lot **Jos 21:5** 5892b
sons of Gershon received thirteen **c** **Jos 21:6** 5892b
their families received twelve **c** from **Jos 21:7** 5892b
these **c** with their pasture lands, **Jos 21:8** 5892b
They gave these **c** which are **Jos 21:9** 5892b
nine **c** from these two tribes. **Jos 21:16** 5892b
Almon with its pasture lands; four **c**. **Jos 21:18** 5892b
All the **c** of the sons of Aaron, **Jos 21:19** 5892b
c with their pasture lands. **Jos 21:19** 5892b
Then the **c** from the tribe of Ephraim **Jos 21:20** 5892b
with its pasture lands; four **c**. **Jos 21:22** 5892b
with its pasture lands; four **c**. **Jos 21:24** 5892b

with its pasture lands; two **c**. Jos 21:25 5892b
All the **c** with their pasture lands Jos 21:26 5892b
with its pasture lands; two **c**. Jos 21:27 5892b
with its pasture lands; four **c**. Jos 21:29 5892b
Rehob with its pasture lands; four **c**. Jos 21:31 5892b
Kartan with its pasture lands; three **c**. Jos 21:32 5892b
All the **c** of the Gershonites Jos 21:33 5892b
c with their pasture lands. Jos 21:33 5892b
with its pasture lands; four **c**. Jos 21:35 5892b
with its pasture lands; four **c**. Jos 21:37 5892b
Jazer with its pasture lands; four **c** Jos 21:39 5892b
All *these were* the **c** of the sons Jos 21:40 5892b
and their lot was twelve **c**. Jos 21:40 5892b
All the **c** of the Levites in the Jos 21:41 5892b
forty-eight **c** with their pasture lands. Jos 21:41 5892b
These **c** each had its surrounding Jos 21:42 5892b
thus *it was* with all these **c**. Jos 21:42 5892b
and **c** which you had not built, Jos 24:13 5892b
and they had thirty **c** in the land Jg 10:4 5892b
and in all the **c** that are on the Jg 11:26 5892b
the entrance of Minnith, twenty **c**, Jg 11:33 5892b
buried in *one of* the **c** of Gilead. Jg 12:7 5892b
gathered from the **c** to Gibeah, Jg 20:14 5892b
From the **c** on that day the Jg 20:15 5892b
who came out of the **c** destroyed them Jg 20:42 5892b
fire all the **c** which they found. Jg 20:48 5892b
rebuilt the **c** and lived in them. Jg 21:23 5892b
number of all the **c** of the Philistines 1Sa 6:18 5892b
c and of country villages. 1Sa 6:18 5892b
The **c** which the Philistines 1Sa 7:14 5892b
came out of all the **c** of Israel, 1Sa 18:6 5892b
in one of the **c** in the country, 1Sa 27:5 5892b
in the **c** of the Jerahmeelites, 1Sa 30:29 5892b
who were in the **c** of the Kenites, 1Sa 30:29 5892b
they abandoned the **c** and fled; 1Sa 31:7 5892b
go up to one of the **c** of Judah?" 2Sa 2:1 5892b
and they lived in the **c** of Hebron. 2Sa 2:3 5892b
and from Berothai, **c** of Hadadezer, 2Sa 8:8 5892b
people and for the **c** of our God; 2Sa 10:12 5892b
to all the **c** of the sons of Ammon. 2Sa 12:31 5892b
c and escape from our sight." 2Sa 20:6 5892b
c of the Hivites and of the Canaanites, 2Sa 24:7 5892b
sixty great **c** with walls and 1Ki 4:13 5892b
them in the land of their **c**, 1Ki 8:37 8179
twenty **c** in the land of Galilee. 1Ki 9:11 5892b
the **c** which Solomon had given him, 1Ki 9:12 5892b
these **c** which you have given me, 1Ki 9:13 5892b
the storage **c** which Solomon had, 1Ki 9:19 5892b
even the **c** for his chariots and 1Ki 9:19 5892b
and the **c** for his horsemen, 1Ki 9:19 5892b
he stationed them in the chariot **c** 1Ki 10:26 5892b
who lived in the **c** of Judah, 1Ki 12:17 5892b
which are in the **c** of Samaria." 1Ki 13:32 5892b
armies against the **c** of Israel, 1Ki 15:20 5892b
he did and the **c** which he built, 1Ki 15:23 5892b
"The **c** which my father took from 1Ki 20:34 5892b
and all the **c** which he built, 1Ki 22:39 5892b
Thus they destroyed the **c**; 2Ki 3:25 5892b
Hazael the **c** which he had taken 2Ki 13:25 5892b
him and recovered the **c** of Israel. 2Ki 13:25 5892b
Gozan, and in the **c** of the Medes. 2Ki 17:6 5892b
and settled *them* in the **c** of Samaria 2Ki 17:24 5892b
Samaria and lived in its **c**. 2Ki 17:24 5892b
away into exile in the **c** of Samaria 2Ki 17:26 5892b
in their **c** in which they lived. 2Ki 17:29 5892b
Gozan, and in the **c** of the Medes, 2Ki 18:11 5892b
c of Judah and seized them. 2Ki 18:13 5892b
fortified **c** into ruinous heaps. 2Ki 19:25 5892b
in the high places in the **c** of Judah 2Ki 23:5 5892b
the priests from the **c** of Judah, 2Ki 23:8 5892b
which *were* in the **c** of Samaria, 2Ki 23:19 5892b
c in the land of Gilead. 1Ch 2:22 5892b
and its villages, *even* sixty **c**. 1Ch 2:23 5892b
their **c** until the reign of David. 1Ch 4:31 5892b
Rimmon, Tochen and Ashan, five **c**; 1Ch 4:32 5892b
around the same **c** as far as Baal. 1Ch 4:33 5892b
gave the *following* **c** of refuge: 1Ch 6:57 5892b
All their **c** throughout their 1Ch 6:60 5892b
their families were thirteen **c**. 1Ch 6:60 5892b
the half of Manasseh, ten **c**. 1Ch 6:61 5892b
of Manasseh, thirteen **c** in Bashan. 1Ch 6:62 5892b
the tribe of Zebulun, twelve **c**. 1Ch 6:63 5892b
the **c** with their pasture lands. 1Ch 6:64 5892b
c which are mentioned by name. 1Ch 6:65 5892b
families of the sons of Kohath had **c** 1Ch 6:66 5892b
to them the *following* **c** of refuge: 1Ch 6:67 5892b
in their **c** *were* Israel, 1Ch 9:2 5892b
they forsook their **c** and fled; 1Ch 10:7 5892b
in their **c** with pasture lands, 1Ch 13:2 5892b
and from Cun, **c** of Hadadezer, 1Ch 18:8 5892b
from their **c** and came to battle. 1Ch 19:7 5892b
people and for the **c** of our God; 1Ch 19:13 5892b
to all the **c** of the sons of Ammon. 1Ch 20:3 5892b
in the country, in the **c**, 1Ch 27:25 5892b
he stationed them in the chariot **c** 2Ch 1:14 5892b
them in the land of their **c**, 2Ch 6:28 8179
c which Huram had given to him, 2Ch 8:2 5892b
c which he had built in Hamath. 2Ch 8:4 5892b
Beth-horon, fortified **c** *with* walls, 2Ch 8:5 5892b
the storage **c** that Solomon had, 2Ch 8:6 5892b
and all the **c** for his chariots and 2Ch 8:6 5892b
chariots and **c** for his horsemen, 2Ch 8:6 5892b
in the chariot **c** and with the king 2Ch 9:25 5892b
who lived in the **c** of Judah, 2Ch 10:17 5892b
and built **c** for defense in Judah. 2Ch 11:5 5892b
c in Judah and in Benjamin. 2Ch 11:10 5892b
Benjamin to all the fortified **c**, 2Ch 11:23 5892b
He captured the fortified **c** of Judah 2Ch 12:4 5892b
and captured from him *several* **c**, 2Ch 13:19 5892b
altars from all the **c** of Judah. 2Ch 14:5 5892b
He built fortified **c** in Judah, 2Ch 14:6 5892b
"Let us build these **c** and 2Ch 14:7 5892b
destroyed all the **c** around Gerar, 2Ch 14:14 5892b
and they despoiled all the **c**, 2Ch 14:14 5892b
from the **c** which he had captured 2Ch 15:8 5892b
armies against the **c** of Israel, 2Ch 16:4 5892b
and all the store **c** of Naphtali. 2Ch 16:4 5892b
in all the fortified **c** of Judah, 2Ch 17:2 5892b
and in the **c** of Ephraim which Asa 2Ch 17:2 5892b
to teach in the **c** of Judah; 2Ch 17:7 5892b
went throughout all the **c** of Judah 2Ch 17:9 5892b
fortresses and store **c** in Judah. 2Ch 17:12 5892b
large supplies in the **c** of Judah, 2Ch 17:13 5892b
the fortified **c** through all Judah. 2Ch 17:19 5892b
in all the fortified **c** of Judah, 2Ch 19:5 5892b
your brethren who live in their **c**, 2Ch 19:10 5892b
the **c** of Judah to seek the LORD. 2Ch 20:4 5892b
things, with fortified **c** in Judah, 2Ch 21:3 5892b
Levites from all the **c** of Judah, 2Ch 23:2 5892b
"Go out to the **c** of Judah and 2Ch 24:5 5892b
to battle, raided the **c** of Judah, 2Ch 25:13 5892b
and he built **c** in *the area of* 2Ch 26:6 5892b
c in the hill country of Judah, 2Ch 27:4 5892b
had invaded the **c** of the lowland 2Ch 28:18 5892b
went out to the **c** of Judah, 2Ch 31:1 5892b
of Israel returned to their **c**, 2Ch 31:1 5892b
Judah who lived in the **c** of Judah also 2Ch 31:6 5892b
Shecaniah in the **c** of the priests, 2Ch 31:15 5892b
in the pasture lands of their **c**, 2Ch 31:19 5892b
and besieged the fortified **c**, 2Ch 32:1 5892b
He made **c** for himself and 2Ch 32:29 5892b
in all the fortified **c** of Judah. 2Ch 33:14 5892b
In the **c** of Manasseh, Ephraim, 2Ch 34:6 5892b
temple servants lived in their **c**, Ezr 2:70 5892b
cities, and all Israel in their **c**. Ezr 2:70 5892b
the sons of Israel *were* in the **c**, Ezr 3:1 5892b
all those in our **c** who have married Ezr 10:14 5892b
and all Israel, lived in their **c**. Ne 7:73 5892b
sons of Israel *were* in their **c**. Ne 7:73 5892b
in all their **c** and in Jerusalem, Ne 8:15 5892b
fortified **c** and a fertile land. Ne 9:25 5892b
remained in the *other* **c**. Ne 11:1 5892b
but in the **c** of Judah each lived Ne 11:3 5892b
lived on his own property in their **c** Ne 11:3 5892b
were in all the **c** of Judah, Ne 11:20 5892b
fields of the **c** the portions required Ne 12:44 5892b
The Jews assembled in their **c** Es 9:2 5892b
"He has lived in desolate **c**, Jb 15:28 5892b
And You have uprooted the **c**; Ps 9:6 5892b
Zion and build the **c** of Judah, Ps 69:35 5892b
Your **c** are burned with fire, Is 1:7 5892b
"Until **c** are devastated *and* Is 6:11 5892b
a wilderness And overthrew its **c**, Is 14:17 5892b
the face of the world with **c**." Is 14:21 5892b
"The **c** of Aroer are forsaken; Is 17:2 5892b
In that day their strong **c** will be Is 17:9 5892b
five **c** in the land of Egypt will be Is 19:18 5892b
C of ruthless nations will revere Is 25:3 7151
covenant, he has despised the **c**, Is 33:8 5892b
and thistles in its fortified **c**; Is 34:13 4013
up against all the fortified **c** of Judah Is 36:1 5892b
fortified **c** into ruinous heaps. Is 37:26 5892b
Say to the **c** of Judah, Is 40:9 5892b
and its **c** lift up *their voices*, Is 42:11 5892b
And of the **c** of Judah, Is 44:26 5892b
And will resettle the desolate **c**. Is 54:3 5892b
And they will repair the ruined **c**, Is 61:4 5892b
holy **c** have become a wilderness, Is 64:10 5892b
and against all the **c** of Judah. Jer 1:15 5892b
His **c** have been destroyed, without Jer 2:15 5892b
number of your **c** Are your gods, Jer 2:28 5892b
let us go Into the fortified **c**.' Jer 4:5 5892b
Your **c** will be ruins Without Jer 4:7 5892b
voices against the **c** of Judah. Jer 4:16 5892b
And all its **c** were pulled down Jer 4:26 5892b
A leopard is watching their **c**. Jer 5:6 5892b
fortified **c** in which you trust. Jer 5:17 5892b
what they are doing in the **c** of Judah Jer 7:17 5892b
make to cease from the **c** of Judah Jer 7:34 5892b
let us go into the fortified **c** And Jer 8:14 5892b
make the **c** of Judah a desolation, Jer 9:11 5892b
make the **c** of Judah A desolation, Jer 10:22 5892b
"Proclaim all these words in the **c** Jer 11:6 5892b
"Then the **c** of Judah and the Jer 11:12 5892b
your gods are as many as your **c**, Jer 11:13 5892b
The **c** of the Negev have been Jer 13:19 5892b
"They will come in from the **c** of Jer 17:26 5892b
But let that man be like the **c** Jer 20:16 5892b
Like **c** which are not inhabited. Jer 22:6 5892b
Jerusalem and the **c** of Judah and Jer 25:18 5892b
and speak to all the **c** of Judah who Jer 26:2 5892b
of Israel, Return to these your **c**. Jer 31:21 5892b
in the land of Judah and in its **c** when Jer 31:23 5892b
its **c** will dwell together in it, Jer 31:24 5892b
of Jerusalem, in the **c** of Judah, Jer 32:44 5892b
in the **c** of the hill country, Jer 32:44 5892b
country, in the **c** of the lowland and Jer 32:44 5892b
and in the **c** of the Negev; Jer 32:44 5892b
in the **c** of Judah and in the Jer 33:10 5892b
man or beast, and in all its **c**, Jer 33:12 5892b
'In the **c** of the hill country, in Jer 33:13 5892b
country, in the **c** of the lowland, Jer 33:13 5892b
lowland, in the **c** of the Negev, Jer 33:13 5892b
Jerusalem and in the **c** of Judah, Jer 33:13 5892b
Jerusalem and against all its **c**, Jer 34:1 5892b
all the remaining **c** of Judah, Jer 34:7 5892b
c among the cities of Judah. Jer 34:7 5892b
cities among the **c** of Judah. Jer 34:7 5892b
and I will make the **c** of Judah a Jer 34:22 5892b
of Judah who come from their **c**. Jer 36:6 5892b
from the **c** of Judah to Jerusalem Jer 36:9 5892b
has appointed over the **c** of Judah, Jer 40:5 5892b
your **c** that you have taken over." Jer 40:10 5892b
Jerusalem and all the **c** of Judah; Jer 44:2 5892b
were poured out and burned in the **c** Jer 44:6 5892b
in the **c** of Judah and in the streets Jer 44:17 5892b
sacrifices that you burned in the **c** of Jer 44:21 5892b
her **c** will become a desolation, Jer 48:9 5892b
and men have gone up to his **c**; Jer 48:15 5892b
and all the **c** of the land of Moab, Jer 48:24 5892b
the **c** and dwell among the crags, Jer 48:28 5892b
And his people settled in its **c**? Jer 49:1 5892b
c will become perpetual ruins." Jer 49:13 5892b
And I will set fire to his **c** Jer 50:32 5892b
"Her **c** have become an object of Jer 51:43 5892b
The virgins in the **c** of Judah. La 5:11 5892b
c will become waste and the high Ezk 6:6 5892b
inhabited **c** will be laid waste and Ezk 12:20 5892b
towers And laid waste their **c**; Ezk 19:7 5892b
the flank of Moab of *its* **c**, Ezk 25:9 5892b
its **c** which are on its frontiers, Ezk 25:9 5892b
the **c** which are not inhabited, Ezk 26:19 5892b
And her **c**, in the midst of cities Ezk 29:12 5892b
midst of **c** that are laid waste, Ezk 29:12 5892b
And her **c** will be In the midst of Ezk 30:7 5892b
In the midst of the devastated **c**. Ezk 30:7 5892b
"I will lay waste your **c** And Ezk 35:4 5892b
and your **c** will not be inhabited. Ezk 35:9 5892b
wastes and to the forsaken **c** which Ezk 36:4 5892b
and the **c** will be inhabited and Ezk 36:10 5892b
will cause the **c** to be inhabited, Ezk 36:33 5892b
c are fortified *and* inhabited.' Ezk 36:35 5892b
c be filled with flocks of men. Ezk 36:38 5892b
the **c** of Israel will go out and Ezk 39:9 5892b
their possession **c** to dwell in. Ezk 45:5
Judah has multiplied fortified **c**, Hos 8:14 5892b
But I will send a fire on its **c** Hos 8:14 5892b
sword will whirl against their **c**, Hos 11:6 5892b
he may save you in all your **c**, Hos 13:10 5892b
also cleanness of teeth in all your **c** Am 4:6 5892b
"So two or three **c** would stagger Am 4:8 5892b
they will rebuild the ruined **c** and live Am 9:14 5892b
Will possess the **c** of the Negev. Ob 1:20 5892b
"I will also cut off the **c** of Mi 5:11 5892b
from among you And destroy your **c**. Mi 5:14 5892b
From Assyria and the **c** of Egypt, Mi 7:12 5892b
c And the high corner towers. Zph 1:16 5892b
Their **c** are laid waste, Without a Zph 3:6 5892b
for Jerusalem and the **c** of Judah, Zch 1:12 5892b
"My **c** will again overflow with Zch 1:17 5892b
prosperous along with its **c** around it, Zch 7:7 5892b
even the inhabitants of many **c**. Zch 8:20 5892b
through all the **c** and villages, Mt 9:35 *4172*
going through the **c** of Israel until Mt 10:23 *4172*
to teach and preach in their **c**. Mt 11:1 *4172*
Then He began to denounce the **c** in Mt 11:20 *4172*
followed Him on foot from the **c**. Mt 14:13 *4172*
together on foot from all the **c**, Mk 6:33 *4172*
He entered villages, or **c**, Mk 6:56 *4172*
of God to the other **c** also, Lk 4:43 *4172*
While He was in one of the **c**, Lk 5:12 *4172*
various **c** were journeying to Him, Lk 8:4 *4172*
be in authority over ten **c**.' Lk 19:17 *4172*
'And you are to be over five **c**.' Lk 19:19 *4172*
Also the people from the **c** in Ac 5:16 *4172*
preaching the gospel to all the **c** until Ac 8:40 *4172*
it and fled to the **c** of Lycaonia, Ac 14:6 *4172*
they were passing through the **c**, Ac 16:4 *4172*
pursuing them even to foreign **c**. Ac 26:11 *4172*
and *if* He condemned the **c** of Sodom 2Pe 2:6 *4172*
Gomorrah and the **c** around them, Jude 1:7 *4172*
and the **c** of the nations fell. Rv 16:19 *4172*

CITIZEN

a **c** of no insignificant city; Ac 21:39 *4177*
"But I was actually born *a* **c**." Ac 22:28
NOT TEACH EVERYONE HIS FELLOW **C**, Heb 8:11 *4177*

CITIZENS

c of Jericho fought against you, Jos 24:11 1167
son of man, say to your fellow **c**, Ezk 33:12 5971a
"Yet your fellow **c** say, Ezk 33:17 5971a
your fellow **c** who talk about you Ezk 33:30 5971a
to one of the **c** of that country, Lk 15:15 *4177*
"But his **c** hated him and sent a Lk 19:14 *4177*
you are fellow **c** with the saints, Eph 2:19 *4847*

CITIZENSHIP

c with a large sum of money." Ac 22:28 *4174*
For our **c** is in heaven, from which Php 3:20 *4175*

CITRON

and every *kind of* **c** wood and every Rv 18:12 *2367*

CITY

and he built a **c**, and called the Gn 4:17 5892b
called the name of the **c** Enoch, Gn 4:17 5892b
that is the great **c**. Gn 10:12 5892b
let us build for ourselves a **c**, Gn 11:4 5892b
The LORD came down to see the **c** Gn 11:5 5892b
and they stopped building the **c**. Gn 11:8 5892b
are fifty righteous within the **c**; Gn 18:24 5892b
fifty righteous within the **c**, Gn 18:26 5892b
the whole **c** because of five?" Gn 18:28 5892b
they lay down, the men of the **c**, Gn 19:4 5892b
and whomever you have in the **c**, Gn 19:12 5892b
for the LORD will destroy the **c**." Gn 19:14 5892b
away in the punishment of the **c**." Gn 19:15 5892b
out, and put him outside the **c**. Gn 19:16 5892b
who went in at the gate of his **c**, Gn 23:10 5892b
who went in at the gate of his **c**. Gn 23:18 5892b

to Mesopotamia, to the **c** of Nahor.	**Gn 24:10**	5892b
camels kneel down outside the **c**	**Gn 24:11**	5892b
c are coming out to draw water;	**Gn 24:13**	5892b
of the **c** is Beersheba to this day.	**Gn 26:33**	5892b
the name of the **c** had been Luz.	**Gn 28:19**	5892b
came safely to the **c** of Shechem,	**Gn 33:18**	5892b
and camped before the **c**.	**Gn 33:18**	5892b
came to the gate of their **c** and	**Gn 34:20**	5892b
and spoke to the men of their **c**,	**Gn 34:20**	5892b
went out of the gate of his **c** listened	**Gn 34:24**	5892b
who went out of the gate of his **c**.	**Gn 34:24**	5892b
and came upon the **c** unawares,	**Gn 34:25**	5892b
upon the slain and looted the **c**,	**Gn 34:27**	5892b
and that which was in the **c** and	**Gn 34:28**	5892b
the name of his **c** was Dinhabah.	**Gn 36:32**	5892b
and the name of his **c** was Avith.	**Gn 36:35**	5892b
and the name of his **c** was Pau;	**Gn 36:39**	5892b
he placed in every **c** the food from	**Gn 41:48**	5892b
They had *just* gone out of the **c**,	**Gn 44:4**	5892b
donkey, they returned to the **c**.	**Gn 44:13**	5892b
"As soon as I go out of the **c**,	**Ex 9:29**	5892b
went out of the **c** from Pharaoh,	**Ex 9:33**	5892b
at an unclean place outside the **c**.	**Lv 14:40**	5892b
at an unclean place outside the **c**.	**Lv 14:41**	5892b
outside the **c** to an unclean place.	**Lv 14:45**	5892b
outside the **c** into the open field.	**Lv 14:53**	5892b
a dwelling house in a walled **c**,	**Lv 25:29**	5892b
house that is in the walled **c** passes	**Lv 25:30**	5892b
house sale in the **c** of this possession	**Lv 25:33**	5892b
For Heshbon was the **c** of Sihon,	**Nu 21:26**	5892b
let the **c** of Sihon be established.	**Nu 21:27**	5892b
out to meet him at the **c** of Moab,	**Nu 22:36**	5892b
destroy the remnant from the **c**."	**Nu 24:19**	5892b
shall extend from the wall of the **c**	**Nu 35:4**	5892b
measure outside the **c** on the east side	**Nu 35:5**	5892b
cubits, with the **c** in the center.	**Nu 35:5**	5892b
his **c** of refuge to which he fled;	**Nu 35:25**	5892b
beyond the border of his **c** of refuge	**Nu 35:26**	5892b
the border of his **c** of refuge,	**Nu 35:27**	5892b
he should have remained in his **c**	**Nu 35:28**	5892b
who has fled to his **c** of refuge,	**Nu 35:32**	5892b
women and children of every **c**.	**Dt 2:34**	5892b
from the **c** which is in the valley,	**Dt 2:36**	5892b
was no **c** that was too high for us;	**Dt 2:36**	7151
there was not a **c** which we did not	**Dt 3:4**	7151
women and children of every **c**.	**Dt 3:6**	5892b
the inhabitants of their **c**,	**Dt 13:13**	5892b
that **c** with the edge of the sword,	**Dt 13:15**	5892b
burn the **c** and all its booty with fire	**Dt 13:16**	5892b
then the elders of his **c** shall	**Dt 19:12**	5892b
approach a **c** to fight against it,	**Dt 20:10**	5892b
animals and all that is in the **c**,	**Dt 20:14**	5892b
"When you besiege a **c** a long time,	**Dt 20:19**	5892b
construct siegeworks against the **c**	**Dt 20:20**	5892b
"It shall be that the **c** which	**Dt 21:3**	5892b
that is, the elders of that **c**,	**Dt 21:3**	5892b
and the elders of that **c** shall	**Dt 21:4**	5892b
"All the elders of that **c**	**Dt 21:6**	5892b
bring him out to the elders of his **c**	**Dt 21:19**	5892b
shall say to the elders of his **c**,	**Dt 21:20**	5892b
of his **c** shall stone him to death;	**Dt 21:21**	5892b
the elders of the **c** at the gate.	**Dt 22:15**	5892b
before the elders of the **c**.	**Dt 22:17**	5892b
"So the elders of that **c** shall	**Dt 22:18**	5892b
and the men of her **c** shall stone	**Dt 22:21**	5892b
finds her in the **c** and lies with her,	**Dt 22:23**	5892b
the gate of that **c** and you shall stone	**Dt 22:24**	5892b
she did not cry out in the **c**,	**Dt 22:24**	5892b
"Then the elders of his **c** shall	**Dt 25:8**	5892b
"Blessed *shall* you *be* in the **c**,	**Dt 28:3**	5892b
"Cursed *shall* you *be* in the **c**,	**Dt 28:16**	5892b
of Jericho, the **c** of palm trees,	**Dt 34:3**	5892b
for her house was on the **c** wall,	**Jos 2:15**	7023
the **c** that is beside Zarethan;	**Jos 3:16**	5892b
"You shall march around the **c**,	**Jos 6:3**	5892b
men of war circling the **c** once.	**Jos 6:3**	5892b
march around the **c** seven times,	**Jos 6:4**	5892b
wall of the **c** will fall down flat,	**Jos 6:5**	5892b
forward, and march around the **c**,	**Jos 6:7**	5892b
of the LORD taken around the **c**,	**Jos 6:11**	5892b
c once and returned to the camp;	**Jos 6:14**	5892b
marched around the **c** in the same	**Jos 6:15**	5892b
marched around the **c** seven times.	**Jos 6:15**	5892b
For the LORD has given you the **c**.	**Jos 6:16**	5892b
"The **c** shall be under the	**Jos 6:17**	5892b
the people went up into the **c**,	**Jos 6:20**	5892b
ahead, and they took the **c**.	**Jos 6:20**	5892b
destroyed everything in the **c**,	**Jos 6:21**	5892b
They burned the **c** with fire,	**Jos 6:24**	5892b
up and builds this **c** Jericho;	**Jos 6:26**	5892b
the king of Ai, his people, his **c**,	**Jos 8:1**	5892b
an ambush for the **c** behind it."	**Jos 8:2**	5892b
to ambush the **c** from behind it.	**Jos 8:4**	5892b
Do not go very far from the **c**,	**Jos 8:4**	5892b
are with me will approach the **c**.	**Jos 8:5**	5892b
have drawn them away from the **c**,	**Jos 8:6**	5892b
and take possession of the **c**,	**Jos 8:7**	5892b
be when you have seized the **c**,	**Jos 8:8**	5892b
that you shall set the **c** on fire.	**Jos 8:8**	5892b
and arrived in front of the **c**,	**Jos 8:11**	5892b
and Ai, on the west side of the **c**.	**Jos 8:12**	5892b
was on the north side of the **c**,	**Jos 8:13**	5892b
guard on the west side of the **c**,	**Jos 8:13**	5892b
that the men of the **c** hurried and	**Jos 8:14**	5892b
ambush against him behind the **c**.	**Jos 8:14**	5892b
people who were in the **c** were called	**Jos 8:16**	5892b
and were drawn away from the **c**.	**Jos 8:16**	5892b
c unguarded and pursued Israel.	**Jos 8:17**	5892b
that was in his hand toward the **c**.	**Jos 8:18**	5892b

and entered the **c** and captured it,	**Jos 8:19**	5892b
they quickly set the **c** on fire.	**Jos 8:19**	5892b
smoke of the **c** ascended to the sky,	**Jos 8:20**	5892b
men in ambush had captured the **c**	**Jos 8:21**	5892b
that the smoke of the **c** ascended,	**Jos 8:21**	5892b
out from the **c** to encounter them,	**Jos 8:22**	5892b
the spoil of that **c** as plunder for	**Jos 8:27**	5892b
it at the entrance of the **c** gate,	**Jos 8:29**	5892b
because Gibeon *was* a great **c**,	**Jos 10:2**	5892b
There was not a **c** which made peace	**Jos 11:19**	5892b
with the **c** which is in the middle	**Jos 13:9**	5892b
with the **c** which is in the middle	**Jos 13:16**	5892b
and the **C** of Salt and Engedi;	**Jos 15:62**	5898
a **c** of the sons of Judah.	**Jos 18:14**	5892b
and to the fortified **c** of Tyre;	**Jos 19:29**	5892b
gave him the **c** for which he asked,	**Jos 19:50**	5892b
he built the **c** and settled in it.	**Jos 19:50**	5892b
of the gate of the **c** and state his case	**Jos 20:4**	5892b
hearing of the elders of that **c**;	**Jos 20:4**	5892b
c to them and give him a place,	**Jos 20:4**	5892b
'He shall dwell in that **c**	**Jos 20:6**	5892b
to his own **c** and to his own house,	**Jos 20:6**	5892b
to the **c** from which he fled.' "	**Jos 20:6**	5892b
fields of the **c** and its villages they	**Jos 21:12**	5892b
the **c** of refuge for the manslayer,	**Jos 21:13**	5892b
the **c** of refuge for the manslayer,	**Jos 21:21**	5892b
the **c** of refuge for the manslayer,	**Jos 21:27**	5892b
the **c** of refuge for the manslayer,	**Jos 21:32**	5892b
the **c** of refuge for the manslayer,	**Jos 21:38**	5892b
the sword and set the **c** on fire.	**Jg 1:8**	5892b
went up from the **c** of palms with	**Jg 1:16**	5892b
name of the **c** was called Hormah.	**Jg 1:17**	5892b
name of the **c** was formerly Luz).	**Jg 1:23**	5892b
saw a man coming out of the **c** and	**Jg 1:24**	5892b
"Please show us the entrance to the **c**	**Jg 1:24**	5892b
showed them the entrance to the **c**,	**Jg 1:25**	5892b
the **c** with the edge of the sword,	**Jg 1:25**	5892b
Hittites and built a **c** and named it Luz	**Jg 1:26**	5892b
possessed the **c** of the palm trees.	**Jg 3:13**	5892b
the men of the **c** to do it by day,	**Jg 6:27**	5892b
the **c** arose early in the morning,	**Jg 6:28**	5892b
the men of the **c** said to Joash,	**Jg 6:30**	5892b
He took the elders of the **c**,	**Jg 8:16**	5892b
and killed the men of the **c**.	**Jg 8:17**	5892b
an ephod, and placed it in his **c**,	**Jg 8:27**	5892b
When Zebul the ruler of the **c**	**Jg 9:30**	5892b
are stirring up the **c** against you.	**Jg 9:31**	5892b
rise early and rush upon the **c**;	**Jg 9:33**	5892b
in the entrance of the **c** gate;	**Jg 9:35**	5892b
the people coming out from the **c**,	**Jg 9:43**	5892b
in the entrance of the **c** gate;	**Jg 9:44**	5892b
fought against the **c** all that day,	**Jg 9:45**	5892b
and he captured the **c** and killed	**Jg 9:45**	5892b
he razed the **c** and sowed it with salt.	**Jg 9:45**	5892b
tower in the center of the **c**,	**Jg 9:51**	5892b
women with all the leaders of the **c**	**Jg 9:51**	5892b
So the men of the **c** said to him on	**Jg 14:18**	5892b
all night at the gate of the **c**.	**Jg 16:2**	5892b
took hold of the doors of the **c** gate	**Jg 16:3**	5892b
Then the man departed from the **c**,	**Jg 17:8**	5892b
and they burned the **c** with fire.	**Jg 18:27**	5892b
rebuilt the **c** and lived in it.	**Jg 18:28**	5892b
They called the name of the **c** Dan,	**Jg 18:29**	5892b
name of the **c** formerly was Laish.	**Jg 18:29**	5892b
turn aside into this **c** of the Jebusites	**Jg 19:11**	5892b
not turn aside into the **c** of foreigners	**Jg 19:12**	5892b
down in the open square of the **c**,	**Jg 19:15**	5892b
in the open square of the **c**;	**Jg 19:17**	5892b
celebrating, behold, the men of the **c**,	**Jg 19:22**	5892b
were gathered against the **c**,	**Jg 20:11**	5892b
and were drawn away from the **c**,	**Jg 20:31**	5892b
away from the **c** to the highways."	**Jg 20:32**	5892b
the **c** with the edge of the sword.	**Jg 20:37**	5892b
cloud of smoke rise from the **c**.	**Jg 20:38**	5892b
from the **c** in a column of smoke,	**Jg 20:40**	5892b
the whole **c** was going up *in smoke*	**Jg 20:40**	5892b
both the entire **c** with the cattle	**Jg 20:48**	5892b
the **c** was stirred because of them,	**Ru 1:19**	5892b
took *it* up and went into the **c**,	**Ru 2:18**	5892b
for all my people in the **c** know	**Ru 3:11**	8179
Then she went into the **c**.	**Ru 3:15**	5892b
of the elders of the **c** and said,	**Ru 4:2**	5892b
go up from his **c** yearly to worship	**1Sa 1:3**	5892b
the man came to tell *it* in the **c**,	**1Sa 4:13**	5892b
the city, and all the **c** cried out.	**1Sa 4:13**	5892b
the **c** with very great confusion;	**1Sa 5:9**	5892b
and He smote the men of the **c**,	**1Sa 5:9**	5892b
deadly confusion throughout the **c**;	**1Sa 5:11**	5892b
cry of the **c** went up to heaven.	**1Sa 5:12**	5892b
"Go every man to his **c**."	**1Sa 8:22**	5892b
there is a man of God in this **c**,	**1Sa 9:6**	5892b
to the **c** where the man of God was.	**1Sa 9:10**	5892b
they went up the slope to the **c**,	**1Sa 9:11**	5892b
for he has come into the **c** today,	**1Sa 9:12**	5892b
"As soon as you enter the **c** you	**1Sa 9:13**	5892b
So they went up to the **c**.	**1Sa 9:14**	5892b
As they came into the **c**,	**1Sa 9:14**	5892b
from the high place into the **c**,	**1Sa 9:25**	5892b
going down to the edge of the **c**,	**1Sa 9:27**	5892b
as you have come there to the **c**,	**1Sa 10:5**	5892b
Saul came to the **c** of Amalek and	**1Sa 15:5**	5892b
And the elders of the **c** came	**1Sa 16:4**	5892b
of me to run to Bethlehem his **c**,	**1Sa 20:6**	5892b
family has a sacrifice in the **c**,	**1Sa 20:29**	5892b
"Go, bring *them* to the **c**."	**1Sa 20:40**	5892b
while Jonathan went into the **c**.	**1Sa 20:42**	5892b
And he struck Nob the **c** of the	**1Sa 22:19**	5892b
a **c** with double gates and bars."	**1Sa 23:7**	5892b
to destroy the **c** on my account.	**1Sa 23:10**	5892b

live in the royal **c** with you?"	**1Sa 27:5**	5892b
and buried him in Ramah, his own **c**.	**1Sa 28:3**	5892b
David and his men came to the **c**,	**1Sa 30:3**	5892b
of Zion, that is the **c** of David.	**2Sa 5:7**	5892b
and called it the **c** of David.	**2Sa 5:9**	5892b
LORD into the **c** of David with him;	**2Sa 6:10**	5892b
into the **c** of David with gladness.	**2Sa 6:12**	5892b
ark of the LORD came into the **c** of	**2Sa 6:16**	5892b
David took control of the chief **c**	**2Sa 8:1**	522b
to you in order to search the **c**,	**2Sa 10:3**	5892b
array at the entrance of the **c**,	**2Sa 10:8**	8179
before Abishai and entered the **c**.	**2Sa 10:14**	5892b
was as Joab kept watch on the **c**,	**2Sa 11:16**	5892b
The men of the **c** went out and	**2Sa 11:17**	5892b
you go so near to the **c** to fight?	**2Sa 11:20**	5892b
the **c** stronger and overthrow it'	**2Sa 11:25**	5892b
"There were two men in one **c**,	**2Sa 12:1**	5892b
Ammon and captured the royal **c**.	**2Sa 12:26**	5892b
even captured the **c** of waters.	**2Sa 12:27**	5892b
camp against the **c** and capture it,	**2Sa 12:28**	5892b
or I will capture the **c** myself	**2Sa 12:28**	5892b
spoil of the **c** in great amounts.	**2Sa 12:30**	5892b
"From what **c** are you?"	**2Sa 15:2**	5892b
counselor, from his **c** Giloh,	**2Sa 15:12**	5892b
c with the edge of the sword."	**2Sa 15:14**	5892b
had finished passing from the **c**.	**2Sa 15:24**	5892b
"Return the ark of God to the **c**.	**2Sa 15:25**	5892b
Return to the **c** in peace and your	**2Sa 15:27**	5892b
"But if you return to the **c**,	**2Sa 15:34**	5892b
David's friend, came into the **c**,	**2Sa 15:37**	5892b
"If he withdraws into a **c**,	**2Sa 17:13**	5892b
shall bring ropes to that **c**,	**2Sa 17:13**	5892b
could not be seen entering the **c**.	**2Sa 17:17**	5892b
and went to his home, to his **c**,	**2Sa 17:23**	5892b
be ready to help us from the **c**."	**2Sa 18:3**	5892b
by stealth into the **c** that day,	**2Sa 19:3**	5892b
that I may die in my own **c** near	**2Sa 19:37**	5892b
cast up a siege ramp against the **c**,	**2Sa 20:15**	5892b
a wise woman called from the **c**,	**2Sa 20:16**	5892b
a **c**, even a mother in Israel.	**2Sa 20:19**	5892b
and I will depart from the **c**."	**2Sa 20:21**	5892b
they were dispersed from the **c**,	**2Sa 20:22**	5892b
on the right side of the **c** that is	**2Sa 24:5**	5892b
is the **c** making such an uproar?"	**1Ki 1:41**	7151
so that the **c** is in an uproar.	**1Ki 1:45**	7151
and was buried in the **c** of David.	**1Ki 2:10**	5892b
and brought her to the **c** of David until	**1Ki 3:1**	5892b
of the LORD from the **c** of David,	**1Ki 8:1**	5892b
I did not choose a **c** out of all	**1Ki 8:16**	5892b
pray to the LORD toward the **c**	**1Ki 8:44**	5892b
the **c** which You have chosen,	**1Ki 8:48**	5892b
the Canaanites who lived in the **c**,	**1Ki 9:16**	5892b
daughter came up from the **c** of David	**1Ki 9:24**	5892b
of the **c** of his father David.	**1Ki 11:27**	5892b
the **c** which I have chosen from all	**1Ki 11:32**	5892b
the **c** where I have chosen for	**1Ki 11:36**	5892b
in the **c** of his father David,	**1Ki 11:43**	5892b
the **c** where the old prophet lived.	**1Ki 13:25**	5892b
he came to the **c** of the old prophet	**1Ki 13:29**	5892b
dies in the **c** the dogs will eat.	**1Ki 14:11**	5892b
enter the **c** the child will die.	**1Ki 14:12**	5892b
the **c** which the LORD had chosen	**1Ki 14:21**	5892b
his fathers in the **c** of David;	**1Ki 14:31**	5892b
they buried him in the **c** of David;	**1Ki 15:8**	5892b
in the **c** of David his father;	**1Ki 15:24**	5892b
dies in the **c** the dogs will eat,	**1Ki 16:4**	5892b
Zimri saw that the **c** was taken,	**1Ki 16:18**	5892b
the **c** which he built Samaria,	**1Ki 16:24**	5892b
when he came to the gate of the **c**,	**1Ki 17:10**	5892b
to the **c** to Ahab king of Israel and	**1Ki 20:2**	5892b
themselves against the **c**.	**1Ki 20:12**	5892b
So these went out from the **c**,	**1Ki 20:19**	5892b
the rest fled to Aphek into the **c**,	**1Ki 20:30**	5892b
into the **c** into an inner chamber.	**1Ki 20:30**	5892b
were living with Naboth in his **c**.	**1Ki 21:8**	5892b
So the men of his **c**,	**1Ki 21:11**	5892b
and the nobles who lived in his **c**,	**1Ki 21:11**	5892b
So they took him outside the **c** and	**1Ki 21:13**	5892b
to Ahab, who dies in the **c**,	**1Ki 21:24**	5892b
to Amon the governor of the **c**	**1Ki 22:26**	5892b
c and every man to his country."	**1Ki 22:36**	5892b
in the **c** of his father David,	**1Ki 22:50**	5892b
the men of the **c** said to Elisha,	**2Ki 2:19**	5892b
situation of this **c** is pleasant,	**2Ki 2:19**	5892b
young lads came out from the **c** and	**2Ki 2:23**	5892b
fortified **c** and every choice city,	**2Ki 3:19**	5892b
fortified city and every choice **c**,	**2Ki 3:19**	5892b
by night and surrounded the **c**.	**2Ki 6:14**	5892b
and chariots was circling the **c**.	**2Ki 6:15**	5892b
is not the way, nor is this the **c**;	**2Ki 6:19**	5892b
'We will enter the **c**,'	**2Ki 7:4**	5892b
in the **c** and we will die there;	**2Ki 7:4**	5892b
to the gatekeepers of the **c**,	**2Ki 7:10**	5892b
'When they come out of the **c**,	**2Ki 7:12**	5892b
them alive and get into the **c**.' "	**2Ki 7:12**	5892b
remain, which are left in the **c**.	**2Ki 7:13**	5892b
his fathers in the **c** of David;	**2Ki 8:24**	5892b
the **c** to go tell *it* in Jezreel."	**2Ki 9:15**	5892b
his fathers in the **c** of David.	**2Ki 9:28**	5892b
and a fortified **c** and the weapons,	**2Ki 10:2**	5892b
and he who *was* over the **c**,	**2Ki 10:5**	5892b
were with the great men of the **c**,	**2Ki 10:6**	5892b
land rejoiced and the **c** was quiet.	**2Ki 11:20**	5892b
his fathers in the **c** of David,	**2Ki 12:21**	5892b
his fathers in the **c** of David.	**2Ki 14:20**	5892b
his fathers in the **c** of David,	**2Ki 15:7**	5892b
in the **c** of David his father;	**2Ki 15:38**	5892b
his fathers in the **c** of David;	**2Ki 16:20**	5892b
from watchtower to fortified **c**.	**2Ki 17:9**	5892b

from watchtower to fortified c. 2Ki 18:8 5892b
and this c will not be given into 2Ki 18:30 5892b
the king of the c of Sepharvaim, 2Ki 19:13 5892b
to this c or shoot an arrow there; 2Ki 19:32 5892b
he shall not come to this c," 2Ki 19:33 5892b
'For I will defend this c to save 2Ki 19:34 5892b
I will deliver you and this c from 2Ki 20:6 5892b
and I will defend this c for My 2Ki 20:6 5892b
and brought water into the c, 2Ki 20:20 5892b
of Joshua the governor of the c, 2Ki 23:8 5892b
were on one's left at the c gate. 2Ki 23:8 5892b
And the men of the c told him, 2Ki 23:17 5892b
this c which I have chosen, 2Ki 23:27 5892b
and the c came under siege. 2Ki 24:10 5892b
the king of Babylon came to the c, 2Ki 24:11 5892b
So the c was under siege until the 2Ki 25:2 5892b
the famine was so severe in the c 2Ki 25:3 5892b
Then the c was broken into, and 2Ki 25:4 5892b
Chaldeans were all around the c. 2Ki 25:4 5892b
of the people who were left in the c 2Ki 25:11 5892b
From the c he took one 2Ki 25:19 5892b
advisers who were found in the c; 2Ki 25:19 5892b
the land who were found in the c. 2Ki 25:19 5892b
the name of his c was Dinhabah. 1Ch 1:43 5892b
and the name of his c *was* Avith. 1Ch 1:46 5892b
and the name of his c was Pai, 1Ch 1:50 5892b
fields of the c and its villages, 1Ch 6:56 5892b
of Zion (that is, the c of David). 1Ch 11:5 5892b
it was called the c of David. 1Ch 11:7 5892b
He built the c all around, 1Ch 11:8 5892b
Joab repaired the rest of the c. 1Ch 11:8 5892b
ark with him to the c of David, 1Ch 13:13 5892b
for himself in the c of David; 1Ch 15:1 5892b
the LORD came to the c of David, 1Ch 15:29 5892b
array at the entrance of the c, 1Ch 19:9 5892b
his brother and entered the c. 1Ch 19:15 5892b
he brought out the spoil of the c, 1Ch 20:2 5892b
of the LORD out of the c of David, 2Ch 5:2 5892b
I did not choose a c out of all 2Ch 6:5 5892b
this c which You have chosen and 2Ch 6:34 5892b
and the c which You have chosen, 2Ch 6:38 5892b
up from the c of David to the house 2Ch 8:11 5892b
in the c of his father David; 2Ch 9:31 5892b
c and strengthened them greatly. 2Ch 11:12 5892b
the c which the LORD had chosen 2Ch 12:13 5892b
and was buried in the c of David; 2Ch 12:16 5892b
they buried him in the c of David, 2Ch 14:1 5892b
crushed by nation, and c by city, 2Ch 15:6 5892b
crushed by nation, and city by c, 2Ch 15:6 5892b
out for himself in the c of David, 2Ch 16:14 5892b
him to Amon the governor of the c and 2Ch 18:25 5892b
cities of Judah, c by city. 2Ch 19:5 5892b
cities of Judah, city by c. 2Ch 19:5 5892b
his fathers in the c of David, 2Ch 21:1 5892b
they buried him in the c of David, 2Ch 21:20 5892b
land rejoiced and the c was quiet. 2Ch 23:21 5892b
in the c of David among the kings, 2Ch 24:16 5892b
they buried him in the c of David, 2Ch 24:25 5892b
his fathers in the c of Judah. 2Ch 25:28 5892b
they buried him in the c of David; 2Ch 27:9 5892b
to Jericho, the c of palm trees, 2Ch 28:15 5892b
In every c of Judah he made 2Ch 28:25 5892b
and they buried him in the c, 2Ch 28:27 5892b
assembled the princes of the c and 2Ch 29:20 5892b
So the couriers passed from c to city 2Ch 30:10 5892b
from city to c through the country 2Ch 30:10 5892b
cities, or in each and every c, 2Ch 31:19 5892b
springs which *were* outside the c, 2Ch 32:3 5892b
the Millo *in* the c of David, 2Ch 32:5 5892b
him in the square at the c gate, 2Ch 32:6 5892b
so that they might take the c. 2Ch 32:18 5892b
the west side of the c of David. 2Ch 32:30 5892b
built the outer wall of the c of David 2Ch 33:14 5892b
and he threw *them* outside the c. 2Ch 33:15 5892b
and Maaseiah an official of the c, 2Ch 34:8 5892b
and Judah, each to his c. Ezr 2:1 5892b
and settled in the c of Samaria, Ezr 4:10 7149
the rebellious and evil c and Ezr 4:12 7149
that if that c is rebuilt and the Ezr 4:13 7149
learn that that c is a rebellious city Ezr 4:15 7149
rebellious c and damaging to kings Ezr 4:15 7149
therefore that c was laid waste. Ezr 4:15 7149
if that c is rebuilt and the walls Ezr 4:16 7149
that c has risen up against the kings Ezr 4:19 7149
that this c may not be rebuilt Ezr 4:21 7149
the elders and judges of each c, Ezr 10:14 5892b
my face not be sad when the c, Ne 2:3 5892b
to the c of my fathers' tombs, Ne 2:5 5892b
the temple, for the wall of the c and Ne 2:8 5892b
that descend from the c of David. Ne 3:15 5892b
Now the c was large and spacious, Ne 7:4 5892b
and Judah, each to his c, Ne 7:6 5892b
to live in Jerusalem, the holy c, Ne 11:1 5892b
was second in command of the c. Ne 11:9 5892b
Levites in the holy c *were* 284. Ne 11:18 5892b
directly up the steps of the c of David Ne 12:37 5892b
God brought on us and on this c Ne 13:18 5892b
the c of Susa was in confusion. Es 3:15 5892b
out into the midst of the c and wailed Es 4:1 5892b
went out to Mordecai to the c square Es 4:6 5892b
on horseback through the c square, Es 6:9 5892b
on horseback through the c square, Es 6:11 5892b
Jews who were in each and every c Es 8:11 5892b
c of Susa shouted and rejoiced. Es 8:15 5892b
province and in each and every c, Es 8:17 5892b
every province and every c; Es 9:28 5892b
"From the c men groan, And the Jb 24:12 5892b
I went out to the gate of the c, Jb 29:7 7176
"He scorns the tumult of the c, Jb 39:7 7151

to me in a besieged c. Ps 31:21 5892b
streams make glad the c of God, Ps 46:4 5892b
be praised, In the c of our God, Ps 48:1 5892b
north, The c of the great King. Ps 48:2 7151
In the c of the LORD of hosts, Ps 48:8 5892b
of hosts, in the c of our God; Ps 48:8 5892b
seen violence and strife in the c. Ps 55:9 5892b
like a dog, And go around the c. Ps 59:6 5892b
like a dog, And go around the c. Ps 59:14 5892b
will bring me into the besieged c? Ps 60:9 5892b
And may those from the c flourish Ps 72:16 5892b
are spoken of you, O c of God. Ps 87:3 5892b
to cut off from the c of the LORD Ps 101:8 5892b
not find a way to an inhabited c. Ps 107:4 5892b
way, To go to an inhabited c. Ps 107:7 5892b
they may establish an inhabited c, Ps 107:36 5892b
will bring me into the besieged c? Ps 108:10 5892b
As a c that is compact together; Ps 122:3 5892b
Unless the LORD guards the c, Ps 127:1 5892b
entrance of the gates in the c she Pr 1:21 5892b
gates, at the opening to the c, Pr 8:3 7176
the tops of the heights of the c: Pr 9:3 7176
seat by the high places of the c, Pr 9:14 7176
the righteous, the c rejoices, Pr 11:10 7151
of the upright a c is exalted, Pr 11:11 7176
spirit, than he who captures a c. Pr 16:32 5892b
rich man's wealth is his strong c, Pr 18:11 7151
harder to be won than a strong c, Pr 18:19 7151
man scales the c of the mighty And Pr 21:22 5892b
Like a c that is broken into *and* Pr 25:28 5892b
Scorners set a c aflame, But wise Pr 29:8 7151
than ten rulers who are in a c. Ec 7:19 5892b
in the c where they did thus. Ec 8:10 5892b
There was a small c with few men Ec 9:14 5892b
he delivered the c by his wisdom. Ec 9:15 5892b
not *even* know how to go to a c. Ec 10:15 5892b
must arise now and go about the c; SS 3:2 5892b
make the rounds in the c found me, SS 3:3 5892b
make the rounds in the c found me, SS 5:7 5892b
cucumber field, like a besieged c. Is 1:8 5892b
faithful c has become a harlot, Is 1:21 7151
be called the c of righteousness, Is 1:26 5892b
of righteousness, A faithful c." Is 1:26 7151
"Wail, O gate; cry, O c; Is 14:31 5892b
to be removed from being a c And Is 17:1 5892b
c will disappear from Ephraim, Is 17:3 4013
his neighbor, C against city Is 19:2 5892b
his neighbor, City against c Is 19:2 5892b
be called the C of Destruction. Is 19:18 5892b
boisterous town, you exultant c; Is 22:2 7151
wall of the c of David were many; Is 22:9 5892b
Is this your jubilant c, Whose Is 23:7
Take *your* harp, walk about the c, Is 23:16 5892b
The c of chaos is broken down; Is 24:10 7151
Desolation is left in the c And Is 24:12 5892b
You have made a c into a heap, Is 25:2 5892b
a heap, A fortified c into a ruin; Is 25:2 7151
A palace of strangers is a c no more, Is 25:2 5892b
"We have a strong c; Is 26:1 5892b
dwell on high, the unassailable c; Is 26:5 7151
For the fortified c is isolated, Is 27:10 5892b
the c *where* David *once* camped! Is 29:1 7151
And she will be *a c of* lamenting Is 29:2
houses *and for* the jubilant c. Is 32:13 7151
the populated c forsaken. Is 32:14 5892b
the c will be utterly laid low. Is 32:19 5892b
the c of our appointed feasts; Is 33:20 7151
this c will not be given into the Is 36:15 5892b
the king of the c of Sepharvaim, Is 37:13 5892b
'He will not come to this c Is 37:33 5892b
and he will not come to this c,' Is 37:34 5892b
'For I will defend this c to save Is 37:35 5892b
deliver you and this c from the hand Is 38:6 5892b
and I will defend this c." Is 38:6 5892b
He will build My c and Is 45:13 5892b
call themselves after the holy c And Is 48:2 5892b
garments, O Jerusalem, the holy c; Is 52:1 5892b
will call you the c of the LORD, Is 60:14 5892b
"Sought out, a c not forsaken." Is 62:12 5892b
"A voice of uproar from the c, Is 66:6 5892b
made you today as a fortified c and Jer 1:18 5892b
from a c and two from a family, Jer 3:14 5892b
horseman and bowman every c flees; Jer 4:29 5892b
Every c is forsaken, And no man Jer 4:29 5892b
This is the c to be punished, In Jer 6:6 5892b
The c and its inhabitants. Jer 8:16 5892b
Or if I enter the c, Jer 14:18 5892b
of this c on the sabbath day, Jer 17:24 5892b
through the gates of this c kings Jer 17:25 5892b
this c will be inhabited forever. Jer 17:25 5892b
"I will also make this c a desolation Jer 19:8 5892b
I break this people and this c, Jer 19:11 5892b
"so as to make this c like Topheth. Jer 19:12 5892b
I am about to bring on this c and Jer 19:15 5892b
over all the wealth of this c, Jer 20:5 5892b
them into the center of this c. Jer 21:4 5892b
down the inhabitants of this c, Jer 21:6 5892b
survive in this c from the pestilence, Jer 21:7 5892b
"He who dwells in this c will die Jer 21:9 5892b
set My face against this c for harm Jer 21:10 5892b
Many nations will pass by this c; Jer 22:8 5892b
LORD done thus to this great c?' Jer 22:8 5892b
along with the c which I gave you Jer 23:39 5892b
this c which is called by My name, Jer 25:29 5892b
and this c I will make a curse to Jer 26:6 5892b
and this c will be desolate, Jer 26:9 5892b
For he has prophesied against this c Jer 26:11 5892b
against this house and against this c Jer 26:12 5892b
on yourselves, and on this c and Jer 26:15 5892b

and he prophesied against this c Jer 26:20 5892b
Why should this c become a ruin? Jer 27:17 5892b
vessels that are left in this c, Jer 27:19 5892b
'Seek the welfare of the c Jer 29:7 5892b
the people who dwell in this c, Jer 29:16 5892b
c will be rebuilt on its ruin, Jer 30:18 5892b
"when the c will be rebuilt for Jer 31:38 5892b
I am about to give this c into the Jer 32:3 5892b
have reached the c to take it; Jer 32:24 5892b
and the c is given into the hand Jer 32:24 5892b
although the c is given into the hand Jer 32:25 5892b
I am about to give this c into the Jer 32:28 5892b
who are fighting against this c will Jer 32:29 5892b
set this c on fire and burn it, Jer 32:29 5892b
"Indeed this c has been to Me *a* Jer 32:31 5892b
this c of which you say, Jer 32:36 5892b
concerning the houses of this c, Jer 33:4 5892b
hidden My face from this c because Jer 33:5 5892b
I am giving this c into the hand Jer 34:2 5892b
I will bring them back to this c; Jer 34:22 5892b
return and fight against this c, Jer 37:8 5892b
up and burn this c with fire.' " Jer 37:10 5892b
all the bread in the c was gone. Jer 37:21 5892b
'He who stays in this c will die Jer 38:2 5892b
'This c will certainly be given Jer 38:3 5892b
left in this c and all the people, Jer 38:4 5892b
there is no more bread in the c." Jer 38:9 5892b
c will not be burned with fire, Jer 38:17 5892b
then this c will be given over to Jer 38:18 5892b
c will be burned with fire.' " Jer 38:23 5892b
month, the c *wall* was breached. Jer 39:2 5892b
fled and went out of the c at night Jer 39:4 5892b
the people who were left in the c, Jer 39:9 5892b
bring My words on this c for disaster Jer 39:16 5892b
as soon as they came inside the c, Jer 41:7 5892b
the c and its inhabitants." Jer 46:8 5892b
The c and those who live in it; Jer 47:2 5892b
A destroyer will come to every c, Jer 48:8 5892b
city, So that no c will escape; Jer 48:8 5892b
"How the c of praise has not been Jer 49:25 5892b
Babylon That his c has been captured Jer 51:31 5892b
So the c was under siege until the Jer 52:5 5892b
famine was so severe in the c that Jer 52:6 5892b
Then the c was broken into, and Jer 52:7 5892b
went forth from the c at night by Jer 52:7 5892b
Chaldeans were all around the c. Jer 52:7 5892b
the people who were left in the c, Jer 52:15 5892b
He also took from the c one Jer 52:25 5892b
advisers who were found in the c, Jer 52:25 5892b
were found in the midst of the c. Jer 52:25 5892b
the c That was full of people! La 1:1 5892b
and my elders perished in the c While La 1:19 5892b
faint In the streets of the c. La 2:11 7151
man In the streets of the c, La 2:12 5892b
"Is this the c of which they La 2:15 5892b
of all the daughters of my c. La 3:51 5892b
you and inscribe a c on it, Ezk 4:1 5892b
iron wall between you and the c, Ezk 4:3 5892b
the fire at the center of the c, Ezk 5:2 5892b
with the sword all around the c, Ezk 5:2
will also consume those in the c. Ezk 7:15 5892b
and the c is full of violence. Ezk 7:23 5892b
near, O executioners of the c, Ezk 9:1 5892b
"Go through the midst of the c, Ezk 9:4 5892b
Go through the c after him and strike Ezk 9:5 5892b
struck down *the people* in the c. Ezk 9:7 5892b
and the c is full of perversion; Ezk 9:9 5892b
and scatter *them* over the c." Ezk 10:2 5892b
and give evil advice in this c, Ezk 11:2 5892b
This c is the pot and we are Ezk 11:3
multiplied your slain in this c, Ezk 11:6 5892b
the midst of the c are the flesh and Ezk 11:7
the city are the flesh and this c Ezk 11:7
you out of the midst of the c and Ezk 11:9
"This c will not be a pot for Ezk 11:11
went up from the midst of the c and Ezk 11:23 5892b
mountain which is east of the c. Ezk 11:23 5892b
he set it in a c of traders. Ezk 17:4 5892b
at the head of the way to the c. Ezk 21:19 5892b
will you judge the bloody c? Ezk 22:2 5892b
"A c shedding blood in her midst, Ezk 22:3 5892b
"Woe to the bloody c, Ezk 24:6 5892b
"Woe to the bloody c! Ezk 24:9 5892b
as men enter a c that is breached. Ezk 26:10 5892b
one, From the seas, O renowned c, Ezk 26:17 5892b
I make you a desolate c, Ezk 26:19 5892b
"The c has been taken." Ezk 33:21 5892b
the name of *the* c will be Hamonah. Ezk 39:16 5892b
year after the c was taken, Ezk 40:1 5892b
there was a structure like a c. Ezk 40:2 5892b
saw when He came to destroy the c. Ezk 43:3 5892b
"You shall give the c Ezk 45:6 5892b
and the property of the c, Ezk 45:7 5892b
and the property of the c, Ezk 45:7 5892b
shall be for common use for the c, Ezk 48:15 5892b
and the c shall be in its midst. Ezk 48:15 5892b
"The c shall have open spaces: Ezk 48:17 5892b
be food for the workers of the c. Ezk 48:18 5892b
"The workers of the c, Ezk 48:19 5892b
with the property of the c. Ezk 48:20 5892b
and of the property of the c; Ezk 48:21 5892b
Levites and the property of the c, Ezk 48:22 5892b
"These are the exits of the c: Ezk 48:30 5892b
shall be the gates of the c, Ezk 48:31 5892b
"*The* c *shall be* 18,000 Ezk 48:35
name of the c from *that* day *shall be*, Ezk 48:35 5892b
turn away from Your c Jerusalem, Da 9:16 5892b
the c which is called by Your name; Da 9:18 5892b
because Your c and Your people are Da 9:19 5892b

for your people and your holy c, Da 9:24 5892b
destroy the c and the sanctuary. Da 9:26 5892b
and capture a well-fortified c; Da 11:15 5892b
Gilead is a c of wrongdoers, Hos 6:8 7151
They rush on the c, Jl 2:9 5892b
a c will not the people tremble? Am 3:6 5892b
in a c has not the LORD done it? Am 3:6 5892b
Then I would send rain on one c Am 4:7 5892b
another c I would not send rain; Am 4:7 5892b
to another c to drink water, Am 4:8 5892b
"The c which goes forth a Am 5:3 5892b
I will deliver up *the* c and all it Am 6:8 5892b
will become a harlot in the c, Am 7:17 5892b
"Arise, go to Nineveh the great c and Jon 1:2 5892b
go to Nineveh the great c and Jon 3:2 5892b
was an exceedingly great c, Jon 3:3 5892b
to go through the c one day's walk; Jon 3:4 5892b
out from the c and sat east of it. Jon 4:5 5892b
see what would happen in the c. Jon 4:5 5892b
Nineveh, the great c in which there Jon 4:11 5892b
For now you will go out of the c, Mi 4:10 7151
voice of the LORD will call to the c Mi 6:9 5892b
men of *the* c are full of violence, Mi 6:12
Woe to the bloody c, Na 3:1 5892b
"Woe to him who builds a c with Hab 2:12 5892b
exultant c Which dwells securely, Zph 2:15 5892b
and defiled, The tyrannical c! Zph 3:1 5892b
will be called the C of Truth, Zch 8:3 5892b
'And the streets of the c will be Zch 8:5 5892b
and the c will be captured, Zch 14:2 5892b
and half of the c exiled, Zch 14:2 5892b
will not be cut off from the c. Zch 14:2 5892b
lived in a c called Nazareth Mt 2:23 4172
devil took Him into the holy c and Mt 4:5 4172
A c set on a hill cannot be hidden; Mt 5:14 4172
for it is THE C OF THE GREAT KING. Mt 5:35 4172
ran away, and went to the c and Mt 8:33 4172
whole c came out to meet Jesus; Mt 8:34 4172
over *the sea* and came to His own c. Mt 9:1 4172
not enter *any* c of the Samaritans; Mt 10:5 4172
whatever c or village you enter, Mt 10:11 4172
at his house until you leave *that* c Mt 10:11
go out of that house or that c, Mt 10:14 4172
day of judgment than for that c. Mt 10:15 4172
they persecute you in one c, Mt 10:23 4172
and any c or house divided against Mt 12:25 4172
Jerusalem, all the c was stirred, Mt 21:10 4172
and went out of the c to Bethany, Mt 21:17 4172
when He was returning to the c, Mt 21:18 4172
and set their c on fire. Mt 22:7 4172
and persecute from c to city, Mt 23:34 4172
and persecute from city to c, Mt 23:34 4172
"Go into the c to a certain man, Mt 26:18 4172
the holy c and appeared to many. Mt 27:53 4172
some of the guard came into the c Mt 28:11 4172
whole c had gathered at the door. Mk 1:33 4172
no longer publicly enter a c, Mk 1:45 4172
ran away and reported it in the c Mk 5:14 4172
came, they would go out of the c. Mk 11:19 4172
"Go into the c, and a man will Mk 14:13 4172
went out and came to the c, Mk 14:16 4172
sent from God to a c in Galilee called Lk 1:26 4172
the hill country, to a c of Judah, Lk 1:39 4172
the census, each to his own c. Lk 2:3 4172
Galilee, from the c of Nazareth, Lk 2:4 4172
to Judea, to the c of David which Lk 2:4 4172
for today in the c of David there Lk 2:11 4172
to their own c of Nazareth. Lk 2:39 4172
got up and drove Him out of the c, Lk 4:29 4172
on which their c had been built, Lk 4:29 4172
down to Capernaum, a c of Galilee, Lk 4:31 4172
afterwards He went to a c called Nain; Lk 7:11 4172
He approached the gate of the c, Lk 7:12 4172
crowd from the c was with her. Lk 7:12 4172
a woman in the c who was a sinner; Lk 7:37 4172
from one c and village to another, Lk 8:1 4172
was met by a man from the c Lk 8:27 4172
ran away and reported it in the c Lk 8:34 4172
proclaiming throughout the whole c Lk 8:39 4172
stay there until you leave that c. Lk 9:4 *1563*
you, as you go out from that c, Lk 9:5 4172
Himself to a c called Bethsaida. Lk 9:10 4172
in pairs ahead of Him to every c Lk 10:1 4172
"Whatever c you enter and Lk 10:8 4172
"But whatever c you enter and Lk 10:10 4172
the dust of your c which clings to our Lk 10:11 4172
day for Sodom than for that c. Lk 10:12 4172
from one c and village to another, Lk 13:22 4172
"O Jerusalem, Jerusalem, *the* c Lk 13:34 4172
into the streets and lanes of the c Lk 14:21 4172
saying, "In a certain c there was a Lk 18:2 4172
"There was a widow in that c, Lk 18:3 4172
He saw the c and wept over it, Lk 19:41 4172
are in the midst of the c must Lk 21:21 *846*
are in the country must not enter the c; Lk 21:21 *846*
When you have entered the c, Lk 22:10 4172
insurrection made in the c, Lk 23:19 4172
from Arimathea, a c of the Jews, Lk 23:51 4172
but you are to stay in the c until Lk 24:49 4172
of the c of Andrew and Peter. Jn 1:44 4172
So He came to a c of Samaria called Jn 4:5 4172
gone away into the c to buy food. Jn 4:8 4172
her waterpot, and went into the c and Jn 4:28 4172
They went out of the c, Jn 4:30 4172
From that c many of the Jn 4:39 4172
into a c called Ephraim; Jn 11:54 4172
was crucified was near the c; Jn 19:20 4172
When they had entered *the* c, Ac 1:13 4172
"For truly in this c there were Ac 4:27 4172
they had driven him out of the c, Ac 7:58 4172
Philip went down to the c of Samaria Ac 8:5 4172
was much rejoicing in that c. Ac 8:8 4172
was practicing magic in the c and Ac 8:9 4172
but get up and enter the c, Ac 9:6 4172
their way and approaching the c, Ac 10:9 4172
"I was in the c of Joppa praying; Ac 11:5 4172
iron gate that leads into the c, Ac 12:10 4172
Sabbath nearly the whole c assembled Ac 13:44 4172
and the leading men of the c, Ac 13:50 4172
people of the c were divided; Ac 14:4 4172
temple was just outside the c, Ac 14:13 4172
Paul and dragged him out of the c, Ac 14:19 4172
him, he got up and entered the c. Ac 14:20 4172
c and had made many disciples, Ac 14:21 4172
in every c those who preach him, Ac 15:21 4172
in every c in which we proclaimed Ac 15:36 4172
c of the district of Macedonia, Ac 16:12 4172
staying in this c for some days. Ac 16:12 4172
Lydia, from the c of Thyatira, Ac 16:14 4172
are throwing our c into confusion, Ac 16:20 4172
kept begging them to leave the c. Ac 16:39 4172
a mob and set the c in an uproar; Ac 17:5 4172
brethren before the c authorities, Ac 17:6 4173
the crowd and the c authorities who Ac 17:8 4173
was observing the c full of idols. Ac 17:16 4172
I have many people in this c." Ac 18:10 4172
c was filled with the confusion, Ac 19:29 4172
the c of the Ephesians is guardian Ac 19:35 4172
testifies to me in every c, Ac 20:23 4172
us until *we were* out of the c. Ac 21:5 4172
the Ephesian in the c with him, Ac 21:29 4172
Then all the c was provoked, and the Ac 21:30 4172
a citizen of no insignificant c; Ac 21:39 4172
Cilicia, but brought up in this c, Ac 22:3 4172
nor in the c *itself* did they find Ac 24:12 4172
and the prominent men of the c, Ac 25:23 4172
near which was the c of Lasea. Ac 27:8 4172
the c treasurer greets you, Ro 16:23 4172
the Gentiles, dangers in the c, 2Co 11:26 4172
guarding the c of the Damascenes 2Co 11:32 4172
in every c as I directed you, Ti 1:5 4172
for the c which has foundations, Heb 11:10 4172
for He has prepared a c for them. Heb 11:16 4172
and to the c of the living God, Heb 12:22 4172
here we do not have a lasting c, Heb 13:14 4172
but we are seeking *the* c which is Heb 13:14
we will go to such and such a c, Jas 4:13 4172
and the name of the c of My God, Rv 3:12 4172
the holy c for forty-two months. Rv 11:2 4172
lie in the street of the great c which Rv 11:8 4172
and a tenth of the c fell; Rv 11:13 4172
press was trodden outside the c, Rv 14:20 4172
c was split into three parts, Rv 16:19 4172
woman whom you saw is the great c, Rv 17:18 4172
'Woe, woe, the great c, Rv 18:10 4172
great city, Babylon, the strong c! Rv 18:10 4172
'Woe, woe, the great c, Rv 18:16 4172
'What c is like the great city?' Rv 18:18 4172
'What *city* is like the great c?' Rv 18:18 4172
'Woe, woe, the great c, Rv 18:19 4172
"So will Babylon, the great c, Rv 18:21 4172
of the saints and the beloved c, Rv 20:9 4172
And I saw the holy c, Rv 21:2 4172
and showed me the holy c, Rv 21:10 4172
c had twelve foundation stones, Rv 21:14 4172
measuring rod to measure the c, Rv 21:15 4172
The c is laid out as a square, Rv 21:16 4172
he measured the c with the rod, Rv 21:16 4172
and the c was pure gold, like Rv 21:18 4172
The foundation stones of the c Rv 21:19 4172
the street of the c was pure gold, Rv 21:21 4172
And the c has no need of the sun Rv 21:23 4172
may enter by the gates into the c. Rv 22:14 4172
tree of life and from the holy c, Rv 22:19 4172

CLAIM
therefore we also have more c on 2Sa 19:43
"Let darkness and black gloom c it; Jb 3:5 1350
"If I have despised the c of my Jb 31:13 4941
Do not c honor in the presence of Pr 25:6 1921
slanderously reported and as some c Ro 3:8 *5346*
women making a c to godliness. 1Tm 2:10 *1861*

CLAIMED
and not one of *them* c that Ac 4:32 *3004*

CLAIMING
Theudas rose up, c to be somebody, Ac 5:36 *3004*
of Samaria, c to be someone great; Ac 8:9 *3004*

CLAIMS
"See, your c are good and right, 2Sa 15:3 1697

CLAMOR
'A c has come to the end of the Jer 25:31 7588
wrath and anger and c and slander Eph 4:31 *2906*

CLAMPS
doors of the gates and for the c, 1Ch 22:3 4226

CLAN
spoke to them and to the whole c of Jg 9:1 4940
"The smallest one will become a c, Is 60:22 505
our God, And be like a c in Judah, Zch 9:7 441b

CLANGING
become a noisy gong or a c cymbal. 1Co 13:1 *214*

CLANS
by your tribes and by your c." 1Sa 10:19 505
little to be among the c of Judah, Mi 5:2 505
"Then the c of Judah will say in Zch 12:5 441b
I will make the c of Judah like a Zch 12:6 441b

CLAP
"*Men* will c their hands at him And Jb 27:23 5606
O c your hands, all peoples; Ps 47:1 8628
Let the rivers c their hands, Ps 98:8 4222
of the field will c *their* hands. Is 55:12 4222
All who pass along the way C their La 2:15 5606
'C your hand, stamp your foot and Ezk 6:11 5221
and c *your* hands together; Ezk 21:14 5221
"I will also c My hands Ezk 21:17 5221
you Will c *their* hands over you, Na 3:19 8628

CLAPPED
and they c their hands and said, 2Ki 11:12 5221
"Because you have c your hands Ezk 25:6 4222

CLAPS
He c his hands among us, And Jb 34:37 5606

CLASP
They c each other and cannot be Jb 41:17 3920

CLASPS
You shall make fifty c of gold, Ex 26:6 7165
to one another with the c so Ex 26:6 7165
You shall make fifty c of bronze, Ex 26:11 7165
and you shall put the c into the Ex 26:11 7165
hang up the veil under the c, Ex 26:33 7165
He made fifty c of gold and Ex 36:13 7165
to one another with the c, Ex 36:13 7165
He made fifty c of bronze to Ex 36:18 7165
its c, its boards, its bars, and Ex 39:33 7165

CLASS
became a father's household, one c. 1Ch 23:11 6486
For we are not bold to c or compare 2Co 10:12 *1469*

CLAUDA
of a small island called C, Ac 27:16 *2802*

CLAUDIA
Linus and C and all the brethren. 2Tm 4:21 *2803*

CLAUDIUS
this took place in the *reign* of C. Ac 11:28 *2804*
because C had commanded all the Ac 18:2 *2804*
"C Lysias, to the most excellent Ac 23:26 *2804*

CLAWS
and his nails like birds' c. Da 4:33
teeth of iron and its c of bronze, Da 7:19 2953

CLAY
in the c ground between Succoth 1Ki 7:46 4568
in the c ground between Succoth 2Ch 4:17 4568
those who dwell in houses of c, Jb 4:19 2563a
now, that You have made me as c; Jb 10:9 2563a
Your defenses are defenses of c. Jb 13:12 2563a
garments as *plentiful as* the c, Jb 27:16 2563a
too have been formed out of the c. Jb 33:6 2563a
is changed like c *under* the seal; Jb 38:14 2563a
of destruction, out of the miry c, Ps 40:2 2916
be considered as equal with the c, Is 29:16 2563a
Even as the potter treads c." Is 41:25 2563a
Will the c say to the potter, Is 45:9 2563a
You are our Father, We are the c, Is 64:8 2563a
vessel that he was making of c was Jer 18:4 2563a
like the c in the potter's hand, Jer 18:6 2563a
partly of iron and partly of c. Da 2:33 2635
statue on its feet of iron and c and Da 2:34 2635
"Then the iron, the c, Da 2:35 2635
of potter's c and partly of iron, Da 2:41 2635
saw the iron mixed with common c. Da 2:41 2635
saw the iron mixed with common c, Da 2:43 2635
the iron, the bronze, the c, Da 2:45 2635
into the c and tread the mortar! Na 3:14 2916
ground, and made c of the spittle, Jn 9:6 *4081*
and applied the c to his eyes, Jn 9:6 *4081*
man who is called Jesus made c, Jn 9:11 *4081*
on the day when Jesus made the c and Jn 9:14 *4081*
"He applied c to my eyes, and I Jn 9:15 *4081*
potter have a right over the c, Ro 9:21 *4081*

CLEAN
you of every c animal by sevens, Gn 7:2 2889
of the animals that are not c two, Gn 7:2 2889
Of c animals and animals that are Gn 7:8 2889
animals that are not c and birds Gn 7:8 2889
and took of every c animal and of Gn 8:20 2889
clean animal and of every c bird Gn 8:20 2889
he is to bring out to a c place Lv 4:12 2889
outside the camp to a c place. Lv 6:11 2889
who is c may eat *such* flesh. Lv 7:19 2889
and between the unclean and the c, Lv 10:10 2889
offering you may eat in a c place, Lv 10:14 2889
until evening, then it becomes c. Lv 11:32 2891
collecting water shall be c, Lv 11:36 2889
which is to be sown, it is c. Lv 11:37 2889
between the unclean and the c, Lv 11:47 2889
for her, and she will be c.'" Lv 12:8 2891
the priest shall pronounce him c; Lv 13:6 2891
shall wash his clothes and be c. Lv 13:6 2891
c *him who has* the infection; Lv 13:13 2891
has all turned white *and* he is c. Lv 13:13 2889
priest shall pronounce c *him who has* Lv 13:17 2891
him who has the infection; he is c. Lv 13:17 2889
the priest shall pronounce him c. Lv 13:23 2891
the priest shall pronounce him c, Lv 13:28 2891
the priest shall pronounce him c; Lv 13:34 2891
shall wash his clothes and be c. Lv 13:34 2891
it, the scale has healed, he is c; Lv 13:37 2889
the priest shall pronounce him c. Lv 13:37 2891
has broken out on the skin; he is c. Lv 13:39 2889
hair of his head, he is bald; he is c. Lv 13:40 2889
he is bald on the forehead; he is c. Lv 13:41 2889
a second time and will be c." Lv 13:58 2891
for pronouncing it c or unclean. Lv 13:59 2891
give orders to take two live c birds Lv 14:4 2889
and shall pronounce him c, Lv 14:7 2891
hair and bathe in water and be c. Lv 14:8 2891
bathe his body in water and be c. Lv 14:9 2891

priest who pronounces him **c** shall	**Lv 14:11**	2891
for him, and he will be **c**.	**Lv 14:20**	2891
priest shall pronounce the house **c**	**Lv 14:48**	2891
the house, and it will be **c**."	**Lv 14:53**	2891
are unclean and when they are **c**.	**Lv 14:57**	2889
discharge spits on one who is **c**,	**Lv 15:8**	2889
running water and will become **c**.	**Lv 15:13**	2891
she becomes **c** from her discharge,	**Lv 15:28**	2891
and afterward she will be **c**.	**Lv 15:28**	2891
you will be **c** from all your sins	**Lv 16:30**	2891
then he will become **c**.	**Lv 17:15**	2891
the **c** animal and the unclean,	**Lv 20:25**	2889
the unclean bird and the **c**;	**Lv 20:25**	2889
of the holy *gifts* until he is **c**.	**Lv 22:4**	2891
when the sun sets, he will be **c**,	**Lv 22:7**	2891
has not defiled herself and is **c**,	**Nu 5:28**	2889
head on the day when he becomes **c**;	**Nu 6:9**	2893
clothes, and they will be **c**.	**Nu 8:7**	2891
who is **c** and is not on a journey,	**Nu 9:13**	2889
household who is **c** may eat it.	**Nu 18:11**	2889
household who is **c** may eat it.	**Nu 18:13**	2889
'Now a man who is **c** shall gather	**Nu 19:9**	2889
outside the camp in a **c** place,	**Nu 19:9**	2889
day, *and then* he will be **c**;	**Nu 19:12**	2891
seventh day, he will not be **c**.	**Nu 19:12**	2891
'A **c** person shall take hyssop	**Nu 19:18**	2889
"Then the **c** *person* shall sprinkle	**Nu 19:19**	2889
water and shall be **c** by evening.	**Nu 19:19**	2891
the fire, and it shall be **c**,	**Nu 31:23**	2891
on the seventh day and be **c**,	**Nu 31:24**	2891
unclean and the **c** may eat of it,	**Dt 12:15**	2889
and the **c** alike may eat of it.	**Dt 12:22**	2889
"You may eat any **c** bird.	**Dt 14:11**	2889
"You may eat any **c** bird.	**Dt 14:20**	2889
and the **c** alike *may eat it,*	**Dt 15:22**	2889
"It is an accident, he is not **c**,	**1Sa 20:26**	2889
not clean, surely *he is* not **c**."	**1Sa 20:26**	2889
and I will make a **c** sweep of the	**1Ki 14:10**	1197a
to you and *you will* be **c**."	**2Ki 5:10**	2891
I not wash in them and be **c**?"	**2Ki 5:12**	2891
'Wash, and be **c**'?"	**2Ki 5:13**	2891
of a little child and he was **c**.	**2Ki 5:14**	2891
showbread is *set* on the **c** table,	**2Ch 13:11**	2889
can make the **c** out of the unclean?	**Jb 14:4**	2889
And he who has **c** hands will grow	**Jb 17:9**	2889
can he be **c** who is born of woman?	**Jb 25:4**	2135
The fear of the LORD is **c**,	**Ps 19:9**	2889
who has **c** hands and a pure heart,	**Ps 24:4**	5355a
me with hyssop, and I shall be **c**;	**Ps 51:7**	2891
Create in me a **c** heart, O God, And	**Ps 51:10**	2889
no oxen are, the manger is **c**,	**Pr 14:4**	1249
of a man are **c** in his own sight,	**Pr 16:2**	2134
for the good, for the **c** and	**Ec 9:2**	2889
yourselves, make yourselves **c**;	**Is 1:16**	2135
without a *single* **c** place.	**Is 28:8**	
bring their grain offering in a **c** vessel	**Is 66:20**	2889
between the unclean and the **c**;	**Ezk 22:26**	2889
cleansed you, Yet you are not **c**,	**Ezk 24:13**	2891
I will sprinkle **c** water on you,	**Ezk 36:25**	2889
water on you, and you will be **c**;	**Ezk 36:25**	2891
between the unclean and the **c**.	**Ezk 44:23**	2889
them put a **c** turban on his head."	**Zch 3:5**	2889
So they put a **c** turban on his head	**Zch 3:5**	2889
are willing, You can make me **c**."	**Mt 8:2**	*2511*
For you **c** the outside of the cup	**Mt 23:25**	*2511*
first **c** the inside of the cup and	**Mt 23:26**	*2511*
outside of it may become **c** also.	**Mt 23:26**	*2513*
and wrapped it in a **c** linen cloth,	**Mt 27:59**	*2513*
are willing, You can make me **c**."	**Mk 1:40**	*2511*
(*Thus He* declared all foods **c**.)	**Mk 7:19**	*2511*
are willing, You can make me **c**."	**Lk 5:12**	*2511*
"Now you Pharisees **c** the outside	**Lk 11:39**	*2511*
and then all things are **c** for you.	**Lk 11:41**	*2513*
his feet, but is completely **c**;	**Jn 13:10**	*2513*
and you are **c**, but not all *of you.*"	**Jn 13:10**	*2513*
"Not all of you are **c**."	**Jn 13:11**	*2513*
"You are already **c** because of the	**Jn 15:3**	*2513*
I am **c**. From now on I will go to	**Ac 18:6**	*2513*
All things indeed are **c**,	**Ro 14:20**	*2513*
C out the old leaven so that you may	**1Co 5:7**	*1571*
having our hearts sprinkled **c**	**Heb 10:22**	
clothed in linen, **c** *and* bright,	**Rv 15:6**	*2513*
in fine linen, bright *and* **c**;	**Rv 19:8**	*2513*
in fine linen, white *and* **c**,	**Rv 19:14**	*2513*

CLEANNESS

According to the **c** of my hands He	**2Sa 22:21**	1252
According to my **c** before His eyes.	**2Sa 22:25**	1252
through the **c** of your hands."	**Jb 22:30**	1252
According to the **c** of my hands He	**Ps 18:20**	1252
to the **c** of my hands in His eyes.	**Ps 18:24**	1252
"But I gave you also **c** of teeth	**Am 4:6**	5356

CLEANSE

"To **c** the house then, he shall	**Lv 14:49**	2398
"He shall thus **c** the house with	**Lv 14:52**	2398
blood on it seven times and **c** it,	**Lv 16:19**	2891
shall be made for you to **c** you;	**Lv 16:30**	2891
the sons of Israel and **c** them.	**Nu 8:6**	2891
But you shall **c** them and present	**Nu 8:15**	2891
made atonement for them to **c** them.	**Nu 8:21**	2891
in to **c** the house of the LORD,	**2Ch 29:15**	2891
of the house of the LORD to **c** *it,*	**2Ch 29:16**	2891
with snow And **c** my hands with lye,	**Jb 9:30**	2141
my iniquity And **c** me from my sin.	**Ps 51:2**	2891
not to winnow and not to **c**,	**Jer 4:11**	1305
'I will **c** them from all their	**Jer 33:8**	2891
I will **c** you from all your	**Ezk 36:25**	2891
I **c** you from all your iniquities,	**Ezk 36:33**	2891
they have sinned, and will **c** them.	**Ezk 37:23**	2891
them in order to **c** the land.	**Ezk 39:12**	2891
of the ground, in order to **c** it.	**Ezk 39:14**	2891
So they will **c** the land."	**Ezk 39:16**	2891
c it and make atonement for it.	**Ezk 43:20**	2398
and they shall **c** the altar as	**Ezk 43:22**	2398
blemish and **c** the sanctuary.	**Ezk 45:18**	2398
raise *the* dead, **c** *the* lepers,	**Mt 10:8**	*2511*
not eat unless they **c** themselves;	**Mk 7:4**	*4472*
let us **c** ourselves from all	**2Co 7:1**	*2511*
c your conscience from dead works	**Heb 9:14**	*2511*
C your hands, you sinners;	**Jas 4:8**	*2511*
to **c** us from all unrighteousness.	**1Jn 1:9**	*2511*

CLEANSED

be **c** from the flow of her blood.	**Lv 12:7**	2891
hyssop for the one who is to be **c**.	**Lv 14:4**	2891
who is to be **c** from the leprosy and	**Lv 14:7**	2891
"The one to be **c** shall then wash	**Lv 14:8**	2891
shall present the man to be **c** and the	**Lv 14:11**	2891
the right ear of the one to be **c**,	**Lv 14:14**	2891
right ear lobe of the one to be **c**,	**Lv 14:17**	2891
on the head of the one to be **c**.	**Lv 14:18**	2891
one to be **c** from his uncleanness.	**Lv 14:19**	2891
right ear of the one to be **c** and on	**Lv 14:25**	2891
the right ear of the one to be **c**,	**Lv 14:28**	2891
on the head of the one to be **c**,	**Lv 14:29**	2891
LORD on behalf of the one to be **c**.	**Lv 14:31**	2891
becomes **c** from his discharge,	**Lv 15:13**	2891
have not **c** ourselves to this day,	**Jos 22:17**	2891
c the whole house of the LORD,	**2Ch 29:18**	2891
an order and they **c** the rooms;	**Ne 13:9**	2891
"I have **c** my heart, I am pure	**Pr 20:9**	2135
'You are a land that is not **c** or	**Ezk 22:24**	2891
Because I *would* have **c** you,	**Ezk 24:13**	2891
be **c** from your filthiness again Until	**Ezk 24:13**	2891
altar as they **c** *it* with the bull.	**Ezk 43:22**	2398
"After he is **c**, seven days	**Ezk 44:26**	2893
saying, "I am willing; be **c**."	**Mt 8:3**	*2511*
And immediately his leprosy was **c**.	**Mt 8:3**	*2511*
lepers are **c** and *the* deaf hear,	**Mt 11:5**	*2511*
said to him, "I am willing; be **c**."	**Mk 1:41**	*2511*
the leprosy left him and he was **c**.	**Mk 1:42**	*2511*
and none of them was **c**,	**Lk 4:27**	*2511*
saying, "I am willing; be **c**."	**Lk 5:13**	*2511*
the lame walk, *the* lepers are **c**,	**Lk 7:22**	*2511*
as they were going, they were **c**.	**Lk 17:14**	*2511*
"Were there not ten **c**?	**Lk 17:17**	*2511*
"What God has **c**, no *longer*	**Ac 10:15**	*2511*
'What God has **c**, no longer	**Ac 11:9**	*2511*
having **c** her by the washing of	**Eph 5:26**	*2511*
say, all things are **c** with blood,	**Heb 9:22**	*2511*
in the heavens to be **c** with these,	**Heb 9:23**	*2511*
worshipers, having once been **c**,	**Heb 10:2**	*2511*

CLEANSES

anyone **c** himself from these *things,*	**2Tm 2:21**	*1571*
Jesus His Son **c** us from all sin.	**1Jn 1:7**	*2511*

CLEANSING

himself to the priest for his **c**,	**Lv 13:7**	2893
farther in the skin after his **c**,	**Lv 13:35**	2893
of the leper in the day of his **c**.	**Lv 14:2**	2893
them for his **c** to the priest,	**Lv 14:23**	2893
means are limited for his **c**."	**Lv 14:32**	2893
for himself seven days for his **c**;	**Lv 15:13**	2893
you shall do to them, for their **c**:	**Nu 8:7**	2891
were you washed with water for **c**;	**Ezk 16:4**	4935
'When you have finished **c** *it,*	**Ezk 43:23**	2398
for your **c** what Moses commanded,	**Mk 1:44**	*2512*
and make an offering for your **c**,	**Lk 5:14**	*2512*
and them, **c** their hearts by faith.	**Ac 15:9**	*2511*
sanctify for the **c** of the flesh,	**Heb 9:13**	*2514*

CLEAR

sapphire, as **c** as the sky itself.	**Ex 24:10**	2892a
they bring you **c** oil of beaten olives	**Ex 27:20**	2134
bring to you **c** oil from beaten olives	**Lv 24:2**	2134
the LORD might be made **c** to them.	**Lv 24:12**	6567a
and **c** out the old because of the new.	**Lv 26:10**	3318
He will by no means **c** *the guilty,*	**Nu 14:18**	5352
"The LORD your God will **c**	**Dt 7:22**	5394
go up to the forest and **c** a place	**Jos 17:15**	1254a
it is a forest, you shall **c** it,	**Jos 17:18**	1254a
according to the **c** space on each,	**1Ki 7:36**	4626
"**C** the way for the LORD in the	**Is 40:3**	6437
C the way for the people;	**Is 62:10**	6437
you should drink of the **c** waters,	**Ezk 34:18**	4950
and he will **c** the way before Me.	**Mal 3:1**	6437
thoroughly **c** His threshing floor;	**Mt 3:12**	*1245b*
if your eye is **c**,	**Mt 6:22**	*573*
thoroughly **c** His threshing floor,	**Lk 3:17**	*1245a*
when your eye is **c**,	**Lk 11:34**	*573*
by the tongue speech that is **c**,	**1Co 14:9**	*2154*
it **c** in the way I ought to speak.	**Col 4:4**	*5319*
of the faith with a **c** conscience.	**1Tm 3:9**	*2513*
whom I serve with a **c** conscience	**2Tm 1:3**	*2513*
those who say such things make it **c**	**Heb 11:14**	*1718*
Jesus Christ has made **c** to me.	**2Pe 1:14**	*1213*
city was pure gold, like **c** glass.	**Rv 21:18**	*2513*
the water of life, **c** as crystal,	**Rv 22:1**	*2986*

CLEARED

and before all men you are **c**."	**Gn 20:16**	3198
and **c** the Judeans out of Elath	**2Ki 16:6**	5394
"By His breath the heavens are **c**;	**Jb 26:13**	8235
the wind has passed and **c** them.	**Jb 37:21**	2891
You **c** *the ground* before it,	**Ps 80:9**	6437
you, He has **c** away your enemies.	**Zph 3:15**	6437

CLEARER

And this is **c** still, if another	**Heb 7:15**	*2612*

CLEARLY

stammerers will hasten to speak **c**.	**Is 32:4**	6703
days you will **c** understand it.	**Jer 23:20**	998
You should **c** understand that today	**Jer 42:19**	3045
you should now **c** understand that	**Jer 42:22**	3045
and then you will see **c** to take	**Mt 7:5**	*1227*
and *began* to see everything **c**.	**Mk 8:25**	*5081*
and then you will see **c** to take	**Lk 6:42**	*1227*
he **c** saw in a vision an angel of God	**Ac 10:3**	*5320*
divine nature, have been **c** seen,	**Ro 1:20**	*2529*

CLEARS

and **c** away many nations before you,	**Dt 7:1**	5394

CLEAR-SIGHTED

for a bribe blinds the **c** and	**Ex 23:8**	6493

CLEAVED

You **c** the earth with rivers.	**Hab 3:9**	1234

CLEAVES

And my tongue **c** to my jaws;	**Ps 22:15**	1692
Our body **c** to the earth.	**Ps 44:25**	1692
My soul **c** to the dust;	**Ps 119:25**	1692
The tongue of the infant **c** To the	**La 4:4**	1692

CLEFT

I will put you in the **c** of the rock	**Ex 33:22**	5366
in the **c** of the rock of Etam.	**Jg 15:8**	5585
Judah went down to the **c** of the rock	**Jg 15:11**	5585
"Who has **c** a channel for the flood,	**Jb 38:25**	6385

CLEFTS

"O my dove, in the **c** of the rock,	**SS 2:14**	2288
the rocks and the **c** of the cliffs Before	**Is 2:21**	5585
ravines, Under the **c** of the crags?	**Is 57:5**	5585
hill and from the **c** of the rocks.	**Jer 16:16**	5357
you who live in the **c** of the rock,	**Jer 49:16**	2288
You who live in the **c** of the rock,	**Ob 1:3**	2288

CLEMENT

the gospel, together with **C** also and	**Php 4:3**	*2815*

CLEOPAS

One *of them,* named **C**,	**Lk 24:18**	*2810*

CLERK

the crowd, the town **c** said,	**Ac 19:35**	*1122*

CLEVER

eyes And **c** in their own sight!	**Is 5:21**	995
OF THE C I WILL SET ASIDE."	**1Co 1:19**	*4908*

CLEVERLY

For we did not follow **c** devised	**2Pe 1:16**	*4679*

CLEVERNESS

the gospel, not in **c** of speech,	**1Co 1:17**	*4678*
AND THE C OF THE CLEVER I WILL SET	**1Co 1:19**	*4907*

CLIFF

And your nest is set in the **c**.	**Nu 24:21**	5553
brought them to the top of the **c** and	**2Ch 25:12**	5553
from the top of the **c**, so that they	**2Ch 25:12**	5553
"On the **c** he dwells and lodges,	**Jb 39:28**	5553
in order to throw Him down the **c**.	**Lk 4:29**	*2630*

CLIFFS

in caves, in thickets, in **c**,	**1Sa 13:6**	5553
The **c** are a refuge for the shephanim	**Ps 104:18**	5553
the rocks and the clefts of the **c** Before	**Is 2:21**	5553
ravines, on the ledges of the **c**,	**Is 7:19**	5553

CLIMB

'I will **c** the palm tree, I will	**SS 7:8**	5927
thickets and **c** among the rocks;	**Jer 4:29**	5927
They **c** the wall like soldiers;	**Jl 2:7**	5927
They **c** into the houses, They enter	**Jl 2:9**	5927

CLIMBED

c up on his hands and feet,	**1Sa 14:13**	5927
and **c** up into a sycamore tree	**Lk 19:4**	*305*

CLIMBING

he is coming, **C** on the mountains,	**SS 2:8**	1801

CLIMBS

And he who **c** out of the pit will	**Is 24:18**	5927
And the one who **c** up out of the pit	**Jer 48:44**	5927
sheep, but **c** up some other way,	**Jn 10:1**	*305*

CLING

you shall serve Him and **c** to Him,	**Dt 10:20**	1692
voice, serve Him, and **c** to Him.	**Dt 13:4**	1692
the ban shall **c** to your hand,	**Dt 13:17**	1692
LORD will make the pestilence **c** to	**Dt 28:21**	1692
afraid, and they will **c** to you.	**Dt 28:60**	1692
you are to **c** to the LORD your God,	**Jos 23:8**	1692
c to the rest of these nations,	**Jos 23:12**	1692
the leprosy of Naaman shall **c** to you	**2Ki 5:27**	1692
groaning My bones **c** to my flesh.	**Ps 102:5**	1692
I **c** to Your testimonies; O LORD,	**Ps 119:31**	1692
May my tongue **c** to the roof of my	**Ps 137:6**	1692
whole household of Judah **c** to Me,'	**Jer 13:11**	1692
of your rivers **c** to your scales.	**Ezk 29:4**	1692
your rivers will **c** to your scales.	**Ezk 29:4**	1692
c to what is good.	**Ro 12:9**	*2853*

CLINGING

"Stop **c** to Me, for I have not yet	**Jn 20:17**	*681*
While he was **c** to Peter and John,	**Ac 3:11**	*2902*

CLINGS

"My bone **c** to my skin and my	**Jb 19:20**	1692
My soul **c** to You;	**Ps 63:8**	1692
waistband **c** to the waist of a man,	**Jer 13:11**	1692
of your city which **c** to our feet we	**Lk 10:11**	*2853*

CLIP

who **c** the hair on their temples;	**Jer 9:26**	7112

CLOAK

take your neighbor's **c** as a pledge,	**Ex 22:26**	8008
it is his **c** for his body.	**Ex 22:27**	8071
may sleep in his **c** and bless you;	**Dt 24:13**	8008
it on his right thigh under his **c**.	**Jg 3:16**	4055
"Give me the **c** that is on you and	**Ru 3:15**	4304
had clothed himself with a new **c**;	**1Ki 11:29**	8008
of the new **c** which was on him and	**1Ki 11:30**	8008
Yourself with light as with a **c**,	**Ps 104:2**	8008

“You have a c, you shall be our Is 3:6 8071
there is neither bread nor c; Is 3:7 8071
tumult, And c rolled in blood, Is 9:5 8071
and touched the fringe of His c; Mt 9:20 2440
just touch the fringe of His c; Mt 14:36 2440
field must not turn back to get his c. Mt 24:18 2440
behind *Him* and touched His c. Mk 5:27 2440
just touch the fringe of His c; Mk 6:56 2440
Throwing aside his c, Mk 10:50 2440
and touched the fringe of His c, Lk 8:44 2440
your c around you and follow me.” Ac 12:8 2440
When you come bring the c which I 2Tm 4:13 5315b

CLOAKS
festal robes, outer tunics, c, Is 3:22 4304
throwing off their c and tossing dust Ac 22:23 2440

CLODS
“The c of the valley will gently Jb 21:33 7263
a mass And the c stick together? Jb 38:38 7263
The seeds shrivel under their c; Jl 1:17 4053

CLOPAS
sister, Mary the *wife* of C, Jn 19:25 2832

CLOSE
“Please come c, that I may feel Gn 27:21 5066
Jacob came c to Isaac his father, Gn 27:22 5066
“Please come c and kiss me, my Gn 27:26 5066
So he came c and kissed him; Gn 27:27 5066
and before he came c to them, Gn 37:18 7126
and Joseph will c your eyes.” Gn 46:4 7896, 3027
Then Joseph brought them c to him, Gn 48:10 5066
right, and brought them c to him. Gn 48:13 5066
“The rings shall be c to the rim Ex 25:27 5980
on the front of it c to the place Ex 28:27 5980
C by the rim were the rings, the Ex 37:14 5980
c to the place where it joined, Ex 39:20 5980
he shall remove c to the backbone, Lv 3:9 5980
nor c your hand from your poor Dt 15:7 7092
now, the day has drawn to a c; Jg 19:9 6150
know that disaster was c to them. Jg 20:34 5060
saw that disaster was c to them. Jg 20:41 5060
‘You should stay c to my servants Ru 2:21 1692
So she stayed c by the maids of Ru 2:23 1692
maid, for you are a c relative.” Ru 3:9 1350
Now it is true I am a c relative; Ru 3:12 1350
the c relative of whom Boaz spoke Ru 4:1 1350
will find two men c to Rachel’s tomb 1Sa 10:2 5973
the king is a c relative to us. 2Sa 19:42 7138
and c to the rounded projection 1Ki 7:20 4480, 5980
because it is c beside my house, 1Ki 21:2 7138
throughout the army c to sunset, 1Ki 22:36
let us c the doors of the temple, Ne 6:10 5462
and were c to him: Es 1:14 7138
“I even paid c attention to you; Jb 32:12 995
Even my c friend in whom I Ps 41:9 7965
me, my feet came c to stumbling, Ps 73:2 4592
camels, Let him pay c attention, Is 21:7 7182
attention, very c attention.” Is 21:7 7182
And c your doors behind you; Is 26:20 5462
“Your c friends Have misled and Jer 38:22 7965
And the wheels rose c beside them; Ezk 1:20 5980
the wheels rose c beside them; Ezk 1:21 5980
c your door and pray to your Father Mt 6:6 2808
his relatives and c friends. Ac 10:24 316
sailing along Crete, c *inshore.* Ac 27:13 788
because he came c to death for the Php 2:30 1448
Pay c attention to yourself and to 1Tm 4:16 1907
worthless and c to being cursed, Heb 6:8 1451

CLOSED
and c up the flesh at that place. Gn 2:21 5462
and the LORD c *it* behind him. Gn 7:16 5462
the floodgates of the sky were c, Gn 8:2 5534a
the LORD had c fast all the wombs Gn 20:18 6113
and the earth c over them, and Nu 16:33 3680
and the fat c over the blade, Jg 3:22 5462
but the LORD had c her womb. 1Sa 1:5 5462
because the LORD had c her womb. 1Sa 1:6 5462
and c up the breach of the city of 1Ki 11:27 5462
and he c the doors of the house of 2Ch 28:24 5462
that the breaches began to be c, Ne 4:7 5640
me And has c His net around me. Jb 19:6 5362b
They have c their unfeeling *heart,* Ps 17:10 5462
They will not be c day or night, Is 60:11 5462
Behold, their ears are c And Jer 6:10 6189
I c the deep over it and held back Ezk 31:15 3680
AND THEY HAVE C THEIR EYES, OTHERWISE Mt 13:15 2576
And He c the book, gave it Lk 4:20 4428
HEAR, AND THEY HAVE C THEIR EYES; Ac 28:27 2576
Law, so that every mouth may be c Ro 3:19 5420
its gates will never be c; Rv 21:25 2808

CLOSELY
also pursued them c in the battle. 1Sa 14:22 1692
and the horsemen pursued him c. 2Sa 1:6 1692
c pursued Saul and his sons, 1Ch 10:2 1692
c to the thunder of His voice, Jb 37:2 8085
And send to Kedar and observe c And Jer 2:10 3966
follow c after you there *in* Egypt, Jer 42:16 1692
will speak to you and listen c. Ezk 3:10 241
the Pharisees were watching Him c Lk 6:7 3906
question Him c on many subjects, Lk 11:53 653
they were watching Him c. Lk 14:1 3906
as he approached to look *more* c, Ac 7:31 2657

CLOSER
“Please come c to me.” Gn 45:4 5066
And they came c. And he said, Gn 45:4 5066
there is a relative c than I. Ru 3:12 7138
who sticks c than a brother. Pr 18:24 1692

c attention to what we have heard, Heb 2:1 4057

CLOSES
When he c his lips, he is *considered* Pr 17:28 331
need and c his heart against him, 1Jn 3:17 2808

CLOSEST
he is one of our c relatives.” Ru 2:20 1350
Then he said to the c relative, Ru 4:3 1350
The c relative said, Ru 4:6 1350
So the c relative said to Boaz, Ru 4:8 1350

CLOTH
spread over *it* a c of pure blue, Nu 4:6 899b
they shall also spread a c of blue Nu 4:7 899b
over them a c of scarlet *material,* Nu 4:8 899b
“Then they shall take a blue c Nu 4:9 899b
shall spread a blue c and cover it Nu 4:11 899b
and put them in a blue c and cover Nu 4:12 899b
and spread a purple c over it. Nu 4:13 899b
wrapped in a c behind the ephod; 1Sa 21:9 8071
the weavers of white c will be utterly Is 19:9 2360a
the table, they spread out the c, Is 21:5 6844
clothed you with embroidered c and Ezk 16:10 7553
linen, silk and embroidered c. Ezk 16:13 7553
embroidered c and covered them, Ezk 16:18 899b
of unshrunk c on an old garment; Mt 9:16 4470
and wrapped it in a clean linen c, Mt 27:59 4616
of unshrunk c on an old garment; Mk 2:21 4470
Joseph bought a linen c, Mk 15:46 4616
down, wrapped Him in the linen c and Mk 15:46 4616
“No one tears a piece of c from a Lk 5:36 1915
down and wrapped it in a linen c, Lk 23:53 4616
face was wrapped around with a c. Jn 11:44 4676

CLOTHE
And she sent garments to c Es 4:4 3847
C me with skin and flesh, And knit Jb 10:11 3847
Do you c his neck with a mane? Jb 39:19 3847
And c yourself with honor and Jb 40:10 3847
also I will c with salvation, Ps 132:16 3847
“His enemies I will c with shame, Ps 132:18 3847
drowsiness will c *one* with rags. Pr 23:21 3847
And I will c him with your tunic And Is 22:21 3847
“I c the heavens with blackness And Is 50:3 3847
C yourself in your strength, Is 52:1 3847
C yourself in your beautiful Is 52:1 3847
will c themselves with trembling; Ezk 26:16 3847
and c yourselves with the wool, Ezk 34:3 3847
And all who c themselves with Zph 1:8 3847
will c you with festal robes.” Zch 3:4 3847
will He not much more c you? Mt 6:30
You in, or naked, and c You? Mt 25:38 4016
naked, and you did not c Me; Mt 25:43 4016
how much more *will He* c you? Lk 12:28
and *properly* c yourself and serve Lk 17:8 4024
c yourselves with humility toward 1Pe 5:5 1463
garments so that you may c yourself, Rv 3:18 4016
to her to c herself in fine linen, Rv 19:8 4016

CLOTHED
for Adam and his wife, and c them. Gn 3:21 3847
c him in garments of fine linen and Gn 41:42 3847
the sash, and c him with the robe and Lv 8:7 3847
come near and c them with tunics, Lv 8:13 3847
and he was c with scale-armor 1Sa 17:5 3847
Then Saul c David with his 1Sa 17:38 3847
his head, and he c him with armor. 1Sa 17:38 3847
Who c you luxuriously in scarlet, 2Sa 1:24 3847
had c himself with a new cloak; 1Ki 11:29 3680
Now David was c with a robe of 1Ch 15:27 3736
sons and kinsmen, c in fine linen, 2Ch 5:12 3847
O LORD God, be c with salvation and 2Ch 6:41 3847
and they c all their naked ones 2Ch 28:15 3847
the king’s gate c in sackcloth. Es 4:2 3830
“My flesh is c with worms and a Jb 7:5 3847
who hate you will be c with shame, Jb 8:22 3847
put on righteousness, and it c me; Jb 29:14 3847
Let those be c with shame and Ps 35:26 3847
The meadows are c with flocks And Ps 65:13 3847
LORD reigns, He is c with majesty; Ps 93:1 3847
The LORD has c and girded Himself Ps 93:1 3847
are c with splendor and majesty, Ps 104:1 3847
But he c himself with cursing as Ps 109:18 3847
my accusers be c with dishonor, Ps 109:29 3847
priests be c with righteousness, Ps 132:9 3847
her household are c with scarlet. Pr 31:21 3847
C with the slain who are pierced Is 14:19 3830
c me with garments of salvation, Is 61:10 3847
the prince will be c with horror, Ezk 7:27 3847
man c in linen with a writing case Ezk 9:2 3847
And He called to the man c in linen Ezk 9:3 3847
the man c in linen at whose loins Ezk 9:11 3847
to the man c in linen and said, Ezk 10:2 3847
He commanded the man c in linen, Ezk 10:6 3847
the hands of the one c in linen, Ezk 10:7 3847
also c you with embroidered cloth and Ezk 16:10 3847
who were c in purple, governors Ezk 23:6 3847
shall be c with linen garments; Ezk 44:17 3847
to me shall be c with purple Da 5:7 3848
you will be c with purple and *wear* Da 5:16 3848
and they c Daniel with purple and Da 5:29 3848
Joshua was c with filthy garments Zch 3:3 3847
his head and c him with garments, Zch 3:5 3847
not even Solomon in all his glory c Mt 6:29 4016
naked, and you c Me; Mt 25:36 4016
John was c with camel’s hair Mk 1:6 1746a
down, c and in his right mind, Mk 5:15 2439
Those who are splendidly c and Lk 7:25 2441
of Jesus, c and in his right mind; Lk 8:35 2439
not even Solomon in all his glory c Lk 12:27 4016
are c with power from on high.” Lk 24:49 1746a
and thirsty, and are poorly c, 1Co 4:11 1130

c with our dwelling from heaven, 2Co 5:2 1902
want to be unclothed but to be c, 2Co 5:4 1902
have c yourselves with Christ. Ga 3:27 1746a
c in a robe reaching to the feet, Rv 1:13 1746a
will thus be c in white garments; Rv 3:5 4016
sitting, c in white garments, Rv 4:4 4016
before the Lamb, c in white robes, Rv 7:9 4016
who are c in the white robes, Rv 7:13 4016
out of heaven, c with a cloud; Rv 10:1 4016
and sixty days, c in sackcloth.” Rv 11:3 4016
a woman c with the sun, and the Rv 12:1 4016
out of the temple, c in linen, Rv 15:6 1746a
woman was c in purple and scarlet, Rv 17:4 4016
she who was c in fine linen and Rv 18:16 4016
is c with a robe dipped in blood Rv 19:13 4016
are in heaven, c in fine linen, Rv 19:14 1746a

CLOTHES
So Jacob tore his c, Gn 37:34 8071
shaved himself and changed his c, Gn 41:14 8071
Then they tore their c, Gn 44:13 8071
up in the c on their shoulders. Ex 12:34 8071
your heads nor tear your c, Lv 10:6 899b
c and be unclean until evening. Lv 11:25 899b
c and be unclean until evening; Lv 11:28 899b
c and be unclean until evening, Lv 11:40 899b
c and be unclean until evening. Lv 11:40 899b
he shall wash his c and be clean. Lv 13:6 899b
he shall wash his c and be clean. Lv 13:34 899b
infection, his c shall be torn, Lv 13:45 899b
his c and shave off all his hair and Lv 14:8 899b
He shall then wash his c and bathe Lv 14:9 899b
in the house shall wash his c, Lv 14:47 899b
in the house shall wash his c, Lv 14:47 899b
shall wash his c and bathe in water Lv 15:5 899b
shall wash his c and bathe in Lv 15:6 899b
shall wash his c and bathe in water Lv 15:7 899b
he too shall wash his c and bathe Lv 15:8 899b
he who carries them shall wash his c Lv 15:10 899b
shall wash his c and bathe in water Lv 15:11 899b
he shall then wash his c and bathe Lv 15:13 899b
touches her bed shall wash his c Lv 15:21 899b
shall wash his c and bathe in water Lv 15:22 899b
shall wash his c and bathe in water Lv 15:27 899b
in a holy place and put on his c, Lv 16:24 899b
c and bathe his body with water; Lv 16:26 899b
c and bathe his body with water, Lv 16:28 899b
wash his c and bathe in water, Lv 17:15 899b
uncover his head nor tear his c; Lv 21:10 899b
whole body and wash their c, Nu 8:7 899b
from sin and washed their c; Nu 8:21 899b
spied out the land, tore their c; Nu 14:6 899b
his c and bathe his body in water, Nu 19:7 899b
also wash his c in water and bathe Nu 19:8 899b
c and be unclean until evening; Nu 19:10 899b
and he shall wash his c and bathe Nu 19:19 899b
for impurity shall wash his c, Nu 19:21 899b
“And you shall wash your c on the Nu 31:24 899b
“She shall also remove the c of Dt 21:13 8071
your c have not worn out on you, Dt 29:5 8008
Then Joshua tore his c and fell to Jos 7:6 8071
feet, and worn-out c on themselves; Jos 9:5 8008
and these our c and our sandals Jos 9:13 8008
iron, and with very many c; Jos 22:8 8008
her, he tore his c and said, Jg 11:35 899b
wraps and thirty changes of c. Jg 14:12 899b
wraps and thirty changes of c.” Jg 14:13 899b
spoil and gave the changes *of* c Jg 14:19
of silver a year, a suit of c, Jg 17:10 899b
yourself and put on your *best* c, Ru 3:3 8071
his c torn and dust on his head. 1Sa 4:12 4055
its head, and covered *it* with c. 1Sa 19:13 899b
He also stripped off his c, 1Sa 19:24 899b
himself by putting on other c, 1Sa 28:8 899b
his c torn and dust on his head. 2Sa 1:2 899b
took hold of his c and tore them, 2Sa 1:11 899b
“Tear your c and gird on 2Sa 3:31 899b
himself, and changed his c; 2Sa 12:20 8071
tore his c and lay on the ground; 2Sa 13:31 899b
were standing by with c torn. 2Sa 13:31 899b
his mustache, nor washed his c, 2Sa 19:24 899b
and they covered him with c, 1Ki 1:1 899b
that he tore his c and put on 1Ki 21:27 899b
own c and tore them in two pieces. 2Ki 2:12 899b
of gold and ten changes of c. 2Ki 5:5 899b
he tore his c and said, 2Ki 5:7 899b
the king of Israel had torn his c, 2Ki 5:8 899b
“Why have you torn your c? 2Ki 5:8 899b
silver and two changes of c.’ ” 2Ki 5:22 899b
in two bags with two changes of c and 2Ki 5:23 899b
receive money and to receive c and 2Ki 5:26 899b
of the woman, he tore his c 2Ki 6:30 899b
from there silver and gold and c, 2Ki 7:8 899b
way was full of c and equipment which 2Ki 7:15 899b
Athaliah tore her c and cried, 2Ki 11:14 899b
came to Hezekiah with their c torn 2Ki 18:37 899b
Hezekiah heard *it,* he tore his c, 2Ki 19:1 899b
of the law, he tore his c. 2Ki 22:11 899b
torn your c and wept before Me, 2Ki 22:19 899b
Jehoiachin changed his prison c and 2Ki 25:29 899b
Then Athaliah tore her c and said, 2Ch 23:13 899b
and they gave them c and sandals, 2Ch 28:15 3847
of the law, he tore his c. 2Ch 34:19 899b
yourself before Me, tore your c and 2Ch 34:27 899b
me, none of us removed our c, Ne 4:23 899b
Their c did not wear out, nor did Ne 9:21 8008
that had been done, he tore his c, Es 4:1 899b
pit, And my own c would abhor me. Jb 9:31 8008
bosom And his c not be burned? Pr 6:27 899b
Let your c be white all the time, Ec 9:8 899b

Instead of fine **c**, a donning of Is 3:24 6614
our own bread and wear our own **c**, Is 4:1 8071
came to Hezekiah with their **c** torn Is 36:22 899b
Hezekiah heard *it,* he tore his **c**, Is 37:1 899b
took from there worn-out **c** and Jer 38:11 5499
"Now put these worn-out **c** and Jer 38:12 5499
c torn and their bodies gashed, Jer 41:5 899b
Jehoiachin changed his prison **c**, Jer 52:33 899b
"You took some of your **c**, Ezk 16:16 899b
strip you of your **c** and take away Ezk 23:26 899b
in **c** of blue and embroidered work, Ezk 27:24 1545
their caps and their *other* **c**, Da 3:21 3831
"But if God so **c** the grass of Mt 6:30 *294*
who was not dressed in wedding **c**, Mt 22:11 *1742*
come in here without wedding **c**?' Mt 22:12 *1742*
Tearing his **c**, the high priest Mk 14:63 *5509*
"But if God so **c** the grass in Lk 12:28 *292b*
no one's silver or gold or **c**. Ac 20:33 *2441*
a gold ring and dressed in fine **c**, Jas 2:2 *2066*
comes in a poor man in dirty **c**, Jas 2:2 *2066*
the one who is wearing the fine **c**, Jas 2:3 *2066*
one who stays awake and keeps his **c**, Rv 16:15 *2440*

CLOTHING
and articles of gold, and **c**; Ex 3:22 8071
and articles of gold, and **c**; Ex 12:35 8071
he may not reduce her food, her **c**, Ex 21:10 3682
ox, for donkey, for sheep, for **c**, Ex 22:9 8008
any wooden article, or **c**, Lv 11:32 899b
"Your **c** did not wear out on you, Dt 8:4 8071
alien by giving him food and **c**. Dt 10:18 8071
"A woman shall not wear man's **c**, Dt 22:5 3627
nor shall a man put on a woman's **c**; Dt 22:5 8071
donkeys, the camels, and the **c**. 1Sa 27:9 899b
spend the night naked, without **c**, Jb 24:7 3830
poor to go about naked without **c**, Jb 24:10 3830
seen anyone perish for lack of **c**, Jb 31:19 3830
them, And for my **c** they cast lots. Ps 22:18 3830
were sick, my **c** was sackcloth; Ps 35:13 3830
Her **c** is interwoven with gold. Ps 45:13 3830
When I made sackcloth my **c**, Ps 69:11 3830
Like **c** You will change them and Ps 102:26 3830
The lambs *will be* for your **c**, Pr 27:26 3830
Her **c** is fine linen and purple. Pr 31:22 3830
Strength and dignity are her **c**, Pr 31:25 3830
Their webs will not become **c**, Is 59:6 899b
on garments of vengeance for **c** And Is 59:17 8516
Violet and purple are their **c**; Jer 10:9 3830
high places, strip you of your **c**, Ezk 16:39 899b
and covers the naked with **c**, Ezk 18:7 899b
and covers the naked with **c**, Ezk 18:16 899b
you put on **c**, but no one is warm Hg 1:6 3847
than food, and the body more than **c**? Mt 6:25 *1742*
"And why are you worried about **c**? Mt 6:28 *1742*
or 'What will we wear for **c**?' Mt 6:31 *4016*
who come to you in sheep's **c**, Mt 7:15 *1742*
A man dressed in soft **c**? Mt 11:8
Those who wear soft **c** are in Mt 11:8
and his **c** as white as snow. Mt 28:3 *1742*
A man dressed in soft **c**? Lk 7:25 *2440*
not put on any **c** for a long time, Lk 8:27 *2440*
His **c** *became* white *and* gleaming. Lk 9:29 *2441*
than food, and the body more than **c**. Lk 12:23 *1742*
stood near them in dazzling **c**; Lk 24:4 *2066*
AND FOR MY **C** THEY CAST LOTS." Jn 19:24 *2441*
men in white **c** stood beside them. Ac 1:10 *2067*
to adorn themselves with proper **c**, 1Tm 2:9 *2689*
c and in need of daily food, Jas 2:15 *1131*

CLOTHS
with salt or even wrapped in **c**. Ezk 16:4 2853
and she wrapped Him in **c**, Lk 2:7 *4683*
you will find a baby wrapped in **c** and Lk 2:12 *4683*

CLOUD
I set My bow in the **c**, Gn 9:13 6051
when I bring a **c** over the earth, Gn 9:14 6051
the bow will be seen in the **c**, Gn 9:14 6051
"When the bow is in the **c**, Gn 9:16 6051
before them in a pillar of **c** by day Ex 13:21 6051
take away the pillar of **c** by day, Ex 13:22 6051
and the pillar of **c** moved from Ex 14:19 6051
was the **c** along with the darkness, Ex 14:20 6051
through the pillar of fire and **c** Ex 14:24 6051
of the LORD appeared in the **c**. Ex 16:10 6051
I will come to you in a thick **c**, Ex 19:9 6051
and a thick **c** upon the mountain Ex 19:16 6051
the thick **c** where God *was.* Ex 20:21 6205
and the **c** covered the mountain. Ex 24:15 6051
and the **c** covered it for six days; Ex 24:16 6051
to Moses from the midst of the **c**. Ex 24:16 6051
c as he went up to the mountain; Ex 24:18 6051
the pillar of **c** would descend and Ex 33:9 6051
people saw the pillar of **c** standing Ex 33:10 6051
The LORD descended in the **c** Ex 34:5 6051
the **c** covered the tent of meeting, Ex 40:34 6051
because the **c** had settled on it, Ex 40:35 6051
whenever the **c** was taken up from Ex 40:36 6051
but if the **c** was not taken up, Ex 40:37 6051
the **c** of the LORD was on the Ex 40:38 6051
in the **c** over the mercy seat. Lv 16:2 6051
that the **c** of incense may cover Lv 16:13 6051
the **c** covered the tabernacle, Nu 9:15 6051
the **c** would cover it *by day,* and Nu 9:16 6051
Whenever the **c** was lifted from over Nu 9:17 6051
place where the **c** settled down, Nu 9:17 6051
the **c** settled over the tabernacle, Nu 9:18 6051
Even when the **c** lingered over the Nu 9:19 6051
If sometimes the **c** remained a few Nu 9:20 6051
If sometimes the **c** remained from Nu 9:21 6051
the **c** was lifted in the morning, Nu 9:21 6051
night, whenever the **c** was lifted, Nu 9:21 6051
c lingered over the tabernacle, Nu 9:22 6051
the **c** was lifted from over Nu 10:11 6051
Then the **c** settled down in the Nu 10:12 6051
The **c** of the LORD was over Nu 10:34 6051
LORD came down in the **c** and spoke Nu 11:25 6051
LORD came down in a pillar of **c** Nu 12:5 6051
But when the **c** had withdrawn from Nu 12:10 6051
eye, while Your **c** stands over them; Nu 14:14 6051
before them in a pillar of **c** by day Nu 14:14 6051
the **c** covered it and the glory of Nu 16:42 6051
in fire by night and **c** by day, Dt 1:33 6051
darkness, **c** and thick gloom. Dt 4:11 6051
of the **c** and *of* the thick gloom, Dt 5:22 6051
in the tent in a pillar of **c**, Dt 31:15 6051
and the pillar of **c** stood at the Dt 31:15 6051
c of smoke rise from the city. Jg 20:38 4864
But when the **c** began to rise from Jg 20:40 4864
c filled the house of the LORD, 1Ki 8:10 6051
to minister because of the **c**, 1Ki 8:11 6051
He would dwell in the thick **c**. 1Ki 8:12 6205
a **c** as small as a man's hand is 1Ki 18:44 5645
of the LORD, was filled with a **c**, 2Ch 5:13 6051
to minister because of the **c**, 2Ch 5:14 6051
He would dwell in the thick **c**. 2Ch 6:1 6205
of **c** You led them by day, Ne 9:12 6051
of **c** did not leave them by day, Ne 9:19 6051
Let a **c** settle on it; Jb 3:5 6053
"When a **c** vanishes, it is gone, Jb 7:9 6051
the **c** does not burst under them. Jb 26:8 6051
moon And spreads His **c** over it. Jb 26:9 6051
has passed away like a **c**. Jb 30:15 5645
moisture He loads the thick **c**; Jb 37:11 5645
disperses the **c** of His lightning. Jb 37:11 6051
the lightning of His **c** to shine? Jb 37:15 6051
When I made a **c** its garment And Jb 38:9 6051
He led them with the **c** by day And Ps 78:14 6051
spoke to them in the pillar of **c**; Ps 99:7 6051
He spread a **c** for a covering, And Ps 105:39 6051
is like a **c** with the spring rain. Pr 16:15 5645
over her assemblies a **c** by day, Is 4:5 6051
c of dew in the heat of harvest." Is 18:4 5645
the LORD is riding on a swift **c** and Is 19:1 5645
Like heat by the shadow of a **c**, Is 25:5 5645
transgressions like a thick **c** And Is 44:22 5645
"Who are these who fly like a **c** And Is 60:8 5645
of Zion With a **c** in His anger! La 2:1 5743
You have covered Yourself with a **c** La 3:44 6051
a great **c** with fire flashing forth Ezk 1:4 6051
of the **c** of incense rising. Ezk 8:11 6051
and the **c** filled the inner court. Ezk 10:3 6051
the temple was filled with the **c** and Ezk 10:4 6051
A **c** will cover her, And her Ezk 30:18 6051
I will cover the sun with a **c** And Ezk 32:7 6051
be like a **c** covering the land, Ezk 38:9 6051
Israel like a **c** to cover the land. Ezk 38:16 6051
your loyalty is like a morning **c** And Hos 6:4 6051
they will be like the morning **c** And Hos 13:3 6051
a bright **c** overshadowed them, Mt 17:5 *3507*
and behold, a voice out of the **c** said Mt 17:5 *3507*
Then a **c** formed, overshadowing Mk 9:7 *3507*
and a voice came out of the **c**, Mk 9:7 *3507*
a **c** formed and *began* to overshadow Lk 9:34 *3507*
were afraid as they entered the **c**. Lk 9:34 *3507*
Then a voice came out of the **c**, Lk 9:35 *3507*
you see a **c** rising in the west, Lk 12:54 *3507*
IN A **C** with power and great glory. Lk 21:27 *3507*
and a **c** received Him out of their Ac 1:9 *3507*
our fathers were all under the **c** and 1Co 10:1 *3507*
Moses in the **c** and in the sea; 1Co 10:2 *3507*
a **c** of witnesses surrounding us, Heb 12:1 *3509*
out of heaven, clothed with a **c**; Rv 10:1 *3507*
they went up into heaven in the **c**, Rv 11:12 *3507*
I looked, and behold, a white **c**, Rv 14:14 *3507*
the **c** *was* one like a son of man, Rv 14:14 *3507*
voice to Him who sat on the **c**, Rv 14:15 *3507*
Then He who sat on the **c** swung His Rv 14:16 *3507*

CLOUDBURST
flame of a consuming fire In **c**, Is 30:30 5311

CLOUDS
dripped, Even the **c** dripped water. Jg 5:4 5645
of waters, thick **c** of the sky. 2Sa 22:12 5645
sun rises, A morning without **c**, 2Sa 23:4 5645
sky grew black with **c** and wind, 1Ki 18:45 5645
And his head touches the **c**, Jb 20:6 5645
'**C** are a hiding place for Him, so Jb 22:14 5645
"He wraps up the waters in His **c**, Jb 26:8 5645
And behold the **c** Jb 35:5 7834
Which the **c** pour down, They drip Jb 36:28 7834
understand the spreading of the **c**, Jb 36:29 5645
about the layers of the thick **c**, Jb 37:16 5645
you lift up your voice to the **c**, Jb 38:34 5645
"Who can count the **c** by wisdom, Jb 38:37 7834
of waters, thick **c** of the skies. Ps 18:11 5645
before Him passed His thick **c**, Ps 18:12 5645
heavens And Your truth to the **c**. Ps 57:10 7834
The **c** poured out water; Ps 77:17 5645
Yet He commanded the **c** above And Ps 78:23 7834
C and thick darkness surround Him; Ps 97:2 6051
He makes the **c** His chariot; Ps 104:3 5645
Who covers the heavens with **c**, Ps 147:8 5645
Fire and hail, snow and **c**; Ps 148:8 7008
Like **c** and wind without rain Is a Pr 25:14 5387b
If the **c** are full, they pour out Ec 11:3 5645
who looks at the **c** will not reap. Ec 11:4 5645
and **c** return after the rain; Ec 12:2 5645
charge the **c** to rain no rain on it." Is 5:6 5645
the light is darkened by its **c**. Is 5:30 6183
ascend above the heights of the **c**; Is 14:14 5645
let the **c** pour down righteousness; Is 45:8 7834
"Behold, he goes up like **c**, Jer 4:13 6051
And He causes the **c** to ascend from Jer 10:13 5387b
And He causes the **c** to ascend from Jer 51:16 5387b
rainbow in the **c** on a rainy day, Ezk 1:28 6051
its height was raised above the **c** Ezk 19:11 5688
It will be a day of **c**, Ezk 30:3 6051
And its top was among the **c**. Ezk 31:3 5645
and has set its top among the **c**, Ezk 31:10 5645
nor set their top among the **c**, Ezk 31:14 5645
with the **c** of heaven One like a Da 7:13 6050
A day of **c** and thick darkness. Jl 2:2 6051
c are the dust beneath His feet. Na 1:3 6051
A day of **c** and thick darkness, Zph 1:15 6051
The LORD who makes the storm **c**; Zch 10:1 2385
the SON OF MAN COMING ON THE **C** Mt 24:30 *3507*
and COMING ON THE **C** OF HEAVEN." Mt 26:64 *3507*
IN **C** with great power and glory. Mk 13:26 *3507*
and COMING WITH THE **C** OF HEAVEN." Mk 14:62 *3507*
the **c** to meet the Lord in the air, 1Th 4:17 *3507*
c without water, carried along by Jude 1:12 *3507*
BEHOLD, HE IS COMING WITH THE **C**, Rv 1:7 *3507*

CLOUDY
scattered on a **c** and gloomy day. Ezk 34:12 6051

CLUB
but he went down to him with a **c** 2Sa 23:21 7626
but he went down to him with a **c** 1Ch 11:23 7626
Like a **c** and a sword and a sharp Pr 25:18 4650
a **c** wielding those who lift it, Is 10:15 7626
with a rod, and cummin with a **c**. Is 28:27 7626

CLUBS
"**C** are regarded as stubble; Jb 41:29 8455
war **c** and spears, and for seven Ezk 39:9 4731
large crowd with swords and **c**, Mt 26:47 *3586*
come out with swords and **c** to arrest Mt 26:55 *3586*
by a crowd with swords and **c**, Mk 14:43 *3586*
with swords and **c** to arrest Me, Mk 14:48 *3586*
c as you would against a robber? Lk 22:52 *3586*

CLUNG
mother-in-law, but Ruth **c** to her. Ru 1:14 1692
hand was weary and **c** to the sword, 2Sa 23:10 1692
he **c** to the sins of Jeroboam the 2Ki 3:3 1692
For he **c** to the LORD; 2Ki 18:6 1692

CLUSTER
branch with a single **c** of grapes; Nu 13:23 811
because of the **c** which the sons of Nu 13:24 811
"My beloved is to me a **c** of henna SS 1:14 811
"As the new wine is found in the **c**, Is 65:8 811
There is not a **c** of grapes to eat, Mi 7:1 811

CLUSTERS
and its **c** produced ripe grapes. Gn 40:10 811
are grapes of poison, Their **c**, bitter. Dt 32:32 811
grain and a hundred **c** of raisins 1Sa 25:18 6778
of fig cake and two **c** of raisins, 1Sa 30:12 6778
of bread, a hundred **c** of raisins, 2Sa 16:1 6778
His locks are *like* **c** of dates SS 5:11 8534
And your breasts are *like its* **c**. SS 7:7 811
breasts be like **c** of the vine, SS 7:8 811
have trampled down its choice **c** Is 16:8 8291
the **c** from the vine of the earth, Rv 14:18 *1009*
to the earth and gathered *the* **c** Rv 14:19

CNIDUS
with difficulty had arrived off **C**, Ac 27:7 *2834*

COAL
extinguish my **c** which is left, 2Sa 14:7 1513
with a burning **c** in his hand, Is 6:6 7531a
There will be no **c** to warm by Is 47:14 1513

COALS
shall take a firepan full of **c** of fire Lv 16:12 1513
you scatter the burning **c** abroad. Nu 16:37 784
C were kindled by it. 2Sa 22:9 1513
before Him **C** of fire were kindled. 2Sa 22:13 1513
"His breath kindles **c**, Jb 41:21 1513
C were kindled by it. Ps 18:8 1513
clouds, Hailstones and **c** of fire. Ps 18:12 1513
voice, Hailstones and **c** of fire. Ps 18:13 1513
the *burning* **c** of the broom tree. Ps 120:4 1513
"May burning **c** fall upon them; Ps 140:10 1513
Or can a man walk on hot **c** And Pr 6:28 1513
will heap burning **c** on his head, Pr 25:22 1513
and does his work over the **c**, Is 44:12 6352
also have baked bread over its **c**. Is 44:19 1513
the smith who blows the fire of **c** And Is 54:16 6352
looked like burning **c** of fire, Ezk 1:13 1513
and fill your hands with **c** of fire Ezk 10:2 1513
"Then set it empty on its **c** So Ezk 24:11 1513
HEAP BURNING **C** ON HIS HEAD." Ro 12:20 *440*

COARSE
and silly talk, or **c** jesting, Eph 5:4 *2160*

COAST
shall come from the **c** of Kittim, Nu 24:24 3027
c of the Great Sea toward Lebanon, Jos 9:1 2348
And the **c** will be For the remnant Zph 2:7 2256a
the regions along the **c** of Asia, Ac 27:2 *2596*
the **c** of Cilicia and Pamphylia, Ac 27:5 *2596*

COASTAL
the **c** region of Tyre and Sidon, Lk 6:17 *3882*

COASTLAND
of this **c** will say in that day, Is 20:6 339
silent, you inhabitants of the **c**, Is 23:2 339
Wail, O inhabitants of the **c**. Is 23:6 339
The remnant of the **c** of Caphtor. Jer 47:4 339

COASTLANDS
From these the **c** of the nations Gn 10:5 339
the land and on the **c** of the sea. Es 10:1 339

Context	Reference	Number
God of Israel, In the **c** of the sea.	Is 24:15	339
"**C**, listen to Me in silence, And	Is 41:1	339
The **c** have seen and are afraid;	Is 41:5	339
And the **c** will wait expectantly	Is 42:4	339
And declare His praise in the **c**.	Is 42:12	339
I will make the rivers into **c** And	Is 42:15	339
The **c** will wait for Me, And for My	Is 51:5	339
To the **c** He will make recompense.	Is 59:18	339
"Surely the **c** will wait for Me;	Is 60:9	339
to the distant **c** that have neither	Is 66:19	339
cross to the **c** of Kittim and see,	Jer 2:10	339
of the **c** which are beyond the sea;	Jer 25:22	339
And declare in the **c** afar off,	Jer 31:10	339
"Shall not the **c** shake at the	Ezk 26:15	339
'Now the **c** will tremble On the day	Ezk 26:18	339
the **c** which are by the sea Will be	Ezk 26:18	339
merchant of the peoples to many **c**,	Ezk 27:3	339
of boxwood from the **c** of Cyprus.	Ezk 27:6	339
and purple from the **c** of Elishah.	Ezk 27:7	339
Many **c** were your market;	Ezk 27:15	339
of the **c** Are appalled at you,	Ezk 27:35	339
those who inhabit the **c** in safety;	Ezk 39:6	339
face to the **c** and capture many.	Da 11:18	339
and all the **c** of the nations will	Zph 2:11	339
COASTLINE		
the Great Sea, that is, *its* **c**;	Nu 34:6	1366
was at the Great Sea, even *its* **c**.	Jos 15:12	1366
and the Great Sea, even *its* **c**.	Jos 15:47	1366
COAT		
like the opening of a **c** of mail,	Ex 28:32	8473
as the opening of a **c** of mail,	Ex 39:23	8473
stones and **c** them with lime	Dt 27:2	7874
and you shall **c** them with lime.	Dt 27:4	7874
Archite met him with his **c** torn and	2Sa 15:32	3801
me about as the collar of my **c**.	Jb 30:18	3801
shirt, let him have your **c** also.	Mt 5:40	*2440*
field must not turn back to get his **c**.	Mk 13:16	*2440*
and whoever takes away your **c**,	Lk 6:29	*2440*
whoever has no sword is to sell his **c**	Lk 22:36	*2440*
COATS		
up in their trousers, their **c**,	Da 3:21	6361
or even two **c**, or sandals, or a	Mt 10:10	*5509*
and laid their **c** on them; and He sat	Mt 21:7	*2440*
and He sat on the **c**.	Mt 21:7	*2440*
Most of the crowd spread their **c** in	Mt 21:8	*2440*
the colt to Jesus and put their **c** on	Mk 11:7	*2440*
And many spread their **c** in the road,	Mk 11:8	*2440*
and they threw their **c** on the colt	Lk 19:35	*2440*
they were spreading their **c** on	Lk 19:36	*2440*
and watching out for the **c** of those	Ac 22:20	*2440*
COBRA		
a deaf **c** that stops up its ear,	Ps 58:4	6620
will tread upon the lion and **c**,	Ps 91:13	6620
will play by the hole of the **c**,	Is 11:8	6620
COBRAS		
And the deadly poison of **c**.	Dt 32:33	6620
To the venom of **c** within him.	Jb 20:14	6620
"He sucks the poison of **c**;	Jb 20:16	6620
COFFIN		
and placed in a **c** in Egypt.	Gn 50:26	727
And He came up and touched the **c**;	Lk 7:14	*4673*
COHABIT		
but the king did not **c** with her.	1Ki 1:4	3045
COHORT		
the whole *Roman* **c** around Him.	Mt 27:27	*4686*
called together the whole *Roman* **c**.	Mk 15:16	*4686*
then, having received the *Roman* **c** and	Jn 18:3	*4686*
So the *Roman* **c** and the commander and	Jn 18:12	*4686*
of what was called the Italian **c**,	Ac 10:1	*4686*
Roman **c** that all Jerusalem was in	Ac 21:31	*4686*
of the Augustan **c** named Julius.	Ac 27:1	*4686*
COIN		
Me the **c** *used* for the poll-tax."	Mt 22:19	*3546*
ten silver coins and loses one **c**,	Lk 15:8	*1406*
found the **c** which I had lost!'	Lk 15:9	*1406*
COINS		
and put in two small copper **c**,	Mk 12:42	*3016*
ten silver **c** and loses one coin,	Lk 15:8	*1406*
putting in two small copper **c**.	Lk 21:2	*3016*
out the **c** of the money	Jn 2:15	*4405*
COLD		
and harvest, And **c** and heat,	Gn 8:22	7120
have no covering against the **c**.	Jb 24:7	7135
storm, And out of the north the **c**.	Jb 37:9	7135
Who can stand before His **c**?	Ps 147:17	7135
Like the **c** of snow in the time of	Pr 25:13	6793b
takes off a garment on a **c** day,	Pr 25:20	7135
Like **c** water to a weary soul, So	Pr 25:25	7119
Or is the **c** flowing water *from* a	Jer 18:14	7119
in the stone walls on a **c** day.	Na 3:17	7135
even a cup of **c** water to drink,	Mt 10:42	*5593*
most people's love will grow **c**.	Mt 24:12	*5594*
for it was **c** and they were warming	Jn 18:18	*5592*
had set in and because of the **c**,	Ac 28:2	*5592*
without food, in **c** and exposure.	2Co 11:27	*5592*
that you are neither **c** nor hot;	Rv 3:15	*5593*
I wish that you were **c** or hot.	Rv 3:15	*5593*
lukewarm, and neither hot nor **c**,	Rv 3:16	*5593*
COL-HOZEH		
Shallum the son of **C**,	Ne 3:15	3626
the son of Baruch, the son of **C**,	Ne 11:5	3626
COLLAPSE		
c comes suddenly in an instant,	Is 30:13	7667
Whose **c** is like the smashing	Is 30:14	7665
down, the steep pathways will **c** and	Ezk 38:20	5307
COLLAPSED		
shattered, The ancient hills **c**.	Hab 3:6	7817
against it and immediately it **c**,	Lk 6:49	*4844b*
COLLAPSES		
And dry grass **c** into the flame,	Is 5:24	7503
COLLAR		
me about as the **c** of my coat.	Jb 30:18	6310
in the stocks and in the iron **c**,	Jer 29:26	6729
COLLEAGUES		
Tabeel and the rest of his **c**	Ezr 4:7	3674
scribe and the rest of their **c**,	Ezr 4:9	3675
and to the rest of their **c** who	Ezr 4:17	3675
Shimshai the scribe and their **c**,	Ezr 4:23	3675
and Shethar-bozenai and their **c**	Ezr 5:3	3675
and his **c** the officials,	Ezr 5:6	3675
River, Shethar-bozenai and your **c**,	Ezr 6:6	3675
and their **c** carried out *the decree*	Ezr 6:13	3675
COLLECT		
and **c** money from all Israel to	2Ch 24:5	6908
They **c** captives like sand.	Hab 1:9	622
And those who **c** from you awaken?	Hab 2:7	2111
of the earth **c** customs or poll-tax,	Mt 17:25	*2983*
"**C** no more than what you have	Lk 3:13	*4238*
Law to **c** a tenth from the people,	Heb 7:5	*586b*
COLLECTED		
Israel **c** his strength and sat up	Gn 48:2	2388
they did daily and **c** much money.	2Ch 24:11	622
had **c** from Manasseh and Ephraim,	2Ch 34:9	622
I **c** for myself silver and gold and	Ec 2:8	3664
c the waters of the lower pool.	Is 22:9	6908
c *them* from a harlot's earnings,	Mi 1:7	6908
those who **c** the two-drachma *tax*	Mt 17:24	*2983*
I would have **c** it with interest?'	Lk 19:23	*4238*
from them **c** a tenth from Abraham and	Heb 7:6	*1183*
COLLECTING		
a cistern **c** water shall be clean,	Lv 11:36	4723b
given the task of gathering and **c**	Ec 2:26	3664
COLLECTION		
let your **c** *of idols* deliver you.	Is 57:13	6899
concerning the **c** for the saints,	1Co 16:1	*3048*
COLLECTIONS		
these **c** are like well-driven nails;	Ec 12:11	627
that no **c** be made when I come.	1Co 16:2	*3048*
COLLECTOR		
Thomas and Matthew the tax **c**; James	Mt 10:3	*5057*
be to you as a Gentile and a tax **c**.	Mt 18:17	*5057*
that He went out and noticed a tax **c**	Lk 5:27	*5057*
and the other a tax **c**.	Lk 18:10	*5057*
or even like this tax **c**.	Lk 18:11	*5057*
"But the tax **c**, standing some	Lk 18:13	*5057*
he was a chief tax **c** and he was rich.	Lk 19:2	*754*
COLLECTOR'S		
sitting in the tax **c** booth; and He	Mt 9:9	*5058*
COLLECTORS		
Do not even the tax **c** do the same?	Mt 5:46	*5057*
many tax **c** and sinners came and were	Mt 9:10	*5057*
is your Teacher eating with the tax **c**	Mt 9:11	*5057*
a friend of tax **c** and sinners!' Yet	Mt 11:19	*5057*
"Truly I say to you that the tax **c**	Mt 21:31	*5057*
but the tax **c** and prostitutes did	Mt 21:32	*5057*
and many tax **c** and sinners were	Mk 2:15	*5057*
was eating with the sinners and tax **c**,	Mk 2:16	*5057*
is He eating and drinking with tax **c**	Mk 2:16	*5057*
And *some* tax **c** also came to be	Lk 3:12	*5057*
and there was a great crowd of tax **c**	Lk 5:29	*5057*
do you eat and drink with the tax **c**	Lk 5:30	*5057*
When all the people and the tax **c**	Lk 7:29	*5057*
a friend of tax **c** and sinners!'	Lk 7:34	*5057*
Now all the tax **c** and the sinners	Lk 15:1	*5057*
COLLECTS		
And **c** to himself all peoples.	Hab 2:5	622
COLLIDE		
king of the South will **c** with him,	Da 11:40	5055
COLONIZE		
to carry her to **c** distant places?	Is 23:7	1481a
COLONY		
district of Macedonia, a *Roman* **c**;	Ac 16:12	*2862*
COLOR		
c turned to a deathly pallor,	Da 10:8	1935
the riders had breastplates *the* **c**	Rv 9:17	
COLORED		
coverings, With **c** linens of Egypt.	Pr 7:16	2405
The shields of his mighty men are **c**	Na 2:3	
COLORS		
antimony and stones of various **c**,	1Ch 29:2	7553
garments of glowing **c** from Bozrah,	Is 63:1	2556b
yourself high places of various **c** and	Ezk 16:16	2921
and a full plumage of many **c** came	Ezk 17:3	7553
work, and in carpets of many **c**	Ezk 27:24	1264
COLOSSAE		
brethren in Christ *who are* at **C**:	Col 1:2	*2857*
COLT		
his donkey's **c** to the choice vine;	Gn 49:11	1121
mounted on a donkey, Even on a **c**,	Zch 9:9	5895
tied *there* and a **c** with her;	Mt 21:2	*4454*
MOUNTED ON A DONKEY, EVEN ON A C	Mt 21:5	*4454*
and brought the donkey and the **c**,	Mt 21:7	*4454*
it, you will find a **c** tied *there*,	Mk 11:2	*4454*
They went away and found a **c**	Mk 11:4	*4454*
are you doing, untying the **c**?"	Mk 11:5	*4454*
They brought the **c** to Jesus	Mk 11:7	*4454*
you enter, you will find a **c** tied	Lk 19:30	*4454*
As they were untying the **c**,	Lk 19:33	*4454*
"Why are you untying the **c**?"	Lk 19:33	*4454*
threw their coats on the **c**	Lk 19:35	*4454*
COMING, SEATED ON A DONKEY'S C."	Jn 12:15	*4454*
COLTS		
thirty milking camels and their **c**,	Gn 32:15	1121
COLUMN		
from the city in a **c** of smoke,	Jg 20:40	5982
they roll upward in a **c** of smoke.	Is 9:18	1348
COLUMNS		
on silver rings and marble **c**,	Es 1:6	5982
the wilderness Like **c** of smoke,	SS 3:6	8490
Jehudi had read three or four **c**,	Jer 36:23	1817
c belonging to the side pillars,	Ezk 40:49	5982
Blood, fire and **c** of smoke.	Jl 2:30	8490
COMB		
from the **c** is sweet to your taste;	Pr 24:13	5317
COMBAT		
which entered **c** by divisions according	2Ch 26:11	6635
COMBED		
linen made from **c** flax	Is 19:9	8305
COMBINE		
they will **c** with one another in	Da 2:43	6151
as iron does not **c** with pottery.	Da 2:43	6151
COMBINING		
c spiritual *thoughts* with	1Co 2:13	*4793*
COME		
end of all flesh has **c** before Me;	Gn 6:13	935
will **c** to you to keep *them* alive.	Gn 6:20	935
"It shall **c** about, when I	Gn 9:14	1961
"**C**, let us make bricks and burn	Gn 11:3	3051
"**C**, let us build for ourselves a	Gn 11:4	3051
"**C**, let Us go down and there	Gn 11:7	3051
will **c** forth from your own body,	Gn 15:4	3318
will **c** out with many possessions.	Gn 15:14	3318
c from and where are you going?"	Gn 16:8	935
and kings will **c** forth from you.	Gn 17:6	3318
of peoples will **c** from her."	Gn 17:16	1961
to its outcry, which has **c** to Me;	Gn 18:21	935
c under the shelter of my roof."	Gn 19:8	935
not a man on earth to **c** in to us	Gn 19:31	935
"**C**, let us make our father drink	Gn 19:32	1980
Now Abimelech had not **c** near her;	Gn 20:4	7126
"**C** in, blessed of the LORD!	Gn 24:31	935
oath, when you **c** to my relatives;	Gn 24:41	935
had **c** from going to Beer-lahai-roi;	Gn 24:62	935
"Why have you **c** to me, since you	Gn 26:27	935
"Please **c** close, that I may feel	Gn 27:21	5066
"Please **c** close and kiss me, my	Gn 27:26	5066
But it shall **c** about when you	Gn 27:40	1961
"You must **c** in to me, for I have	Gn 30:16	935
when you **c** concerning my wages.	Gn 30:33	935
"So now **c**, let us make a	Gn 31:44	1980
fear him, that he will **c** and attack me	Gn 32:11	935
until I **c** to my lord at Seir."	Gn 33:14	935
of nations shall **c** from you,	Gn 35:11	1961
And kings shall **c** forth from you.	Gn 35:11	3318
c to bow ourselves down before you	Gn 37:10	935
C, and I will send you to them."	Gn 37:13	1980
c and let us kill him and throw	Gn 37:20	1980
"**C** and let us sell him to the	Gn 37:27	1980
"Here now, let me **c** in to you";	Gn 38:16	935
me, that you may **c** in to me?"	Gn 38:16	935
them seven years of famine will **c**,	Gn 41:30	6965
seven years of famine began to **c**,	Gn 41:54	935
"Where have you **c** from?"	Gn 42:7	935
you have **c** to look at the	Gn 42:9	935
your servants have **c** to buy food.	Gn 42:10	935
but you have **c** to look at the	Gn 42:12	935
this distress has **c** upon us."	Gn 42:21	935
I **c** to your servant my father,	Gn 44:30	935
"Please **c** closer to me."	Gn 45:4	5066
c down to me, do not delay.	Gn 45:9	3381
are still five years of famine *to* **c**,	Gn 45:11	
house that Joseph's brothers had **c**,	Gn 45:16	935
and your households and **c** to me,	Gn 45:18	935
and bring your father and **c**.	Gn 45:19	935
the land of Canaan, have **c** to me;	Gn 46:31	935
have **c** out of the land of Canaan;	Gn 47:1	935
"We have **c** to sojourn in the	Gn 47:4	935
and your brothers have **c** to you.	Gn 47:5	935
your son Joseph has **c** to you,"	Gn 48:2	935
will befall you in the days to **c**.	Gn 49:1	319
"**C**, let us deal wisely with them,	Ex 1:10	3051
have you **c** *back* so soon today?"	Ex 2:18	935
"Do not **c** near here;	Ex 3:5	7126
"So I have **c** down to deliver them	Ex 3:8	3381
of the sons of Israel has **c** to Me;	Ex 3:9	935
"Therefore, **c** now, and I will	Ex 3:10	1980
will **c** to the king of Egypt and	Ex 3:18	935
which will **c** up and go into your	Ex 8:3	5927
"So the frogs will **c** up on you	Ex 8:4	5927
c up on the land of Egypt.'"	Ex 8:5	5927
frogs **c** up on the land of Egypt.	Ex 8:7	5927
the hand of the LORD will **c** *with* a	Ex 9:3	1961
may **c** up on the land of Egypt and	Ex 10:12	5927
All these your servants will **c** down	Ex 11:8	3381
will not allow the destroyer to **c** in	Ex 12:23	935
let him **c** near to celebrate it;	Ex 12:48	7126
your son asks you in time to **c**,	Ex 13:14	4279
not **c** near the other all night.	Ex 14:20	7126
may **c** back over the Egyptians,	Ex 14:26	7725
'**C** near before the LORD, for He	Ex 16:9	7126
rock, and water will **c** out of it,	Ex 17:6	3318
people **c** to me to inquire of God.	Ex 18:15	935
I will **c** to you in a thick cloud,	Ex 19:9	935
third day the LORD will **c** down on	Ex 19:11	3381
they shall **c** up to the mountain."	Ex 19:13	5927
"Also let the priests who **c**	Ex 19:22	5066
people cannot **c** up to Mount Sinai,	Ex 19:23	5927

"Go down and **c** up *again,* you and Ex 19:24 5927
break through to **c** up to the LORD, Ex 19:24 5927
God has **c** in order to test you, Ex 20:20 935
I will **c** to you and bless you. Ex 20:24 935
parties shall **c** before the judges; Ex 22:9 935
And it shall **c** about that when he Ex 22:27 1961
all the people among whom you **c**, Ex 23:27 935
"**C** up to the LORD, you and Aaron, Ex 24:1 5927
however, shall **c** near to the LORD, Ex 24:2 5066
LORD, but they shall not **c** near, Ex 24:2 5066
shall the people **c** up with him." Ex 24:2 5927
"**C** up to Me on the mountain and Ex 24:12 5927
will not **c** loose from the ephod. Ex 28:28 2118
to **c** down from the mountain, Ex 32:1 3381
"**C**, make us a god who will go Ex 32:1 6965
c to me!" And all the sons of Ex 32:26
and it will **c** about, while My Ex 33:22 1961
and **c** up in the morning to Mount Ex 34:2 5927
"No man is to **c** up with you, Ex 34:3 5927
they were afraid to **c** near him. Ex 34:30 5066
every skillful man among you **c**, Ex 35:10 935
to **c** to the work to perform it. Ex 36:2 7126
would not **c** loose from the ephod, Ex 39:21 2118
had Aaron and his sons **c** near Lv 8:6 7126
Next Moses had Aaron's sons **c** near Lv 8:13 7126
He also had Aaron's sons **c** near; Lv 8:24 7126
"**C** near to the altar and offer Lv 9:7 7126
'By those who **c** near Me I will be Lv 10:3 7126
"**C** forward, carry your relatives Lv 10:4 7126
you **c** into the tent of meeting, Lv 10:9 935
then he shall **c** to the priest, Lv 13:16 935
house shall **c** and tell the priest, Lv 14:35 935
priest shall **c** out of the house, Lv 14:38 3318
shall **c** in and make an inspection. Lv 14:44 935
and **c** before the LORD to the Lv 15:14 935
shall **c** into the tent of meeting and Lv 16:23 935
and **c** forth and offer his burnt Lv 16:24 3318
he shall **c** into the camp. Lv 16:26 935
he shall **c** into the camp. Lv 16:28 935
is to **c** near to offer the LORD's Lv 21:21 5066
he shall not **c** near to offer the Lv 21:21 5066
shall not go in to the veil or **c** near Lv 21:23 5066
'When you **c** into the land which I Lv 25:2 935
then his nearest kinsman is to **c** Lv 25:25 935
had **c** out of the land of Egypt, Nu 1:1 3318
of Kohath shall **c** to carry *them,* Nu 4:15 935
the water, then it shall **c** about, Nu 5:27 1961
had **c** out of the land of Egypt, Nu 9:1 3318
c with us and we will do you good, Nu 10:29 1980
"I will not **c**, but rather will go Nu 10:30 1980
c down and speak with you there, Nu 11:17 3381
word will **c** true for you or not." Nu 11:23 7136a
c out to the tent of meeting." Nu 12:4 3318
When they had both **c** forward, Nu 12:5 3318
they proceeded to **c** to Moses and Nu 13:26 935
'Surely you shall not **c** into the Nu 14:30 935
"We will not **c** up. Nu 16:12 5927
We will not **c** up!" Nu 16:14 5927
descendants of Aaron should **c** near Nu 16:40 7126
"It will **c** about that the rod Nu 17:5 1961
but they shall not **c** near to the Nu 18:3 7126
an outsider may not **c** near you. Nu 18:4 7126
The sons of Israel shall not **c** near Nu 18:22 7126
and afterward **c** into the camp, Nu 19:7 935
have you made us **c** up from Egypt, Nu 20:5 5927
or I will **c** out with the sword Nu 20:18 3318
and it shall **c** about, that Nu 21:8 1961
"**C** to Heshbon! Let it be built! Nu 21:27 935
"Now, therefore, please **c**, Nu 22:6 1980
now **c**, curse them for me; Nu 22:11 1980
"Balaam refused to **c** with us." Nu 22:14 1980
Please **c** then, curse this people Nu 22:17 1980
"If the men have **c** to call you, Nu 22:20 935
I have **c** out as an adversary, Nu 22:32 3318
Why did you not **c** to me? Nu 22:37 1980
"Behold, I have **c** now to you! Nu 22:38 935
perhaps the LORD will **c** to meet me Nu 23:3 7136a
'**C** curse Jacob for me, And come, Nu 23:7 1980
'Come curse Jacob for me, And **c**, Nu 23:7 1980
"Please **c** with me to another Nu 23:13 1980
"Please **c**, I will take you to Nu 23:27 1980
c, *and* I will advise you what this Nu 24:14 1980
to your people in the days to **c**." Nu 24:14 319
A star shall **c** forth from Jacob, Nu 24:17 1869
'But ships *shall* **c** from Nu 24:24
So they also *will* **c** to Nu 24:24
will go out and **c** in before them, Nu 27:17 935
at his command they shall **c** in, Nu 27:21 935
who had **c** from service in the war. Nu 31:14 935
year after the sons of Israel had **c** Nu 33:38 3318
then it shall **c** about that those Nu 33:55 1961
'You have **c** to the hill country of Dt 1:20 935
for us to **c** from Kadesh-barnea until Dt 2:14 1980
you **c** opposite the sons of Ammon, Dt 2:19 7126
all these things have **c** upon you, Dt 4:30 4672
"Then it shall **c** about when the Dt 6:10 1961
your son asks you in time to **c**, Dt 6:20 4279
"Then it shall **c** about, because Dt 7:12 1961
and like it **c** under the ban; Dt 7:26 1961
"It shall **c** about if you ever Dt 8:19 1961
and **c** up to Me on the mountain, Dt 10:1 5927
"It shall **c** about, if you Dt 11:13 1961
"It shall **c** about, when the Dt 11:29 1961
dwelling, and there you shall **c**. Dt 12:5 935
for you have not as yet **c** to the Dt 12:9 935
then it shall **c** about that the Dt 12:11 1961
shall **c** and eat and be satisfied, Dt 14:29 935
shall **c** about if he says to you, Dt 15:16 1961
"So you shall **c** to the Levitical Dt 17:9 935

"Now it shall **c** about when he Dt 17:18 1961
'It shall **c** about that whoever Dt 18:19 1961
does not **c** about or come true, Dt 18:22 1961
does not come about or **c** true, Dt 18:22 935
c near and speak to the people. Dt 20:2 5066
the sons of Levi, shall **c** near, Dt 21:5 5066
"If you happen to **c** upon a bird's Dt 22:6 7122
then his brother's wife shall **c** to Dt 25:9 5066
"Therefore it shall **c** about when Dt 25:19 1961
will **c** upon you and overtake you Dt 28:2 935
shall you *be* when you **c** in, Dt 28:6 935
they will **c** out against you one Dt 28:7 3318
"But it shall **c** about, if you Dt 28:15 1961
will **c** upon you and overtake you: Dt 28:15 935
"Cursed *shall* you *be* when you **c** in, Dt 28:19 935
from heaven it shall **c** down on you Dt 28:24 3381
"So all these curses shall **c** on Dt 28:45 935
c down throughout your land, Dt 28:52 3381
"It shall **c** about that as the Dt 28:63 1961
"Now the generation to **c**, Dt 29:22 314
of these things have **c** upon you, Dt 30:1 935
I am no longer able to **c** and go, Dt 31:2 3318
and troubles will **c** upon them; Dt 31:17 4672
that these evils have **c** upon us?' Dt 31:17 4672
"Then it shall **c** about, when many Dt 31:21 1961
and troubles have **c** upon them, Dt 31:21 4672
Let it **c** to the head of Joseph, Dt 33:16 935
men from the sons of Israel have **c** Jos 2:2 935
out the men who have **c** to you, Jos 2:3 935
for they have **c** to search out Jos 2:3 935
and it shall **c** about when the LORD Jos 2:14 1961
unless, when we **c** into the land, Jos 2:18 935
"It shall **c** about that anyone Jos 2:19 1961
Do not **c** near it, that you may Jos 3:4 7126
'When you **c** to the edge of the Jos 3:8 935
"**C** here, and hear the words of Jos 3:9 5066
"It shall **c** about when the Jos 3:13 1961
that they **c** up from the Jordan." Jos 4:16 5927
"**C** up from the Jordan." Jos 4:17 5927
covenant of the LORD had **c** up Jos 4:18 5927
ask their fathers in time to **c**, Jos 4:21 4279
rather I indeed **c** now *as* captain Jos 5:14 935
you shall **c** near by your tribes. Jos 7:14 7126
by lot shall **c** near by families, Jos 7:14 7126
takes shall **c** near by households, Jos 7:14 7126
takes shall **c** near man by man. Jos 7:14 7126
when they **c** out to meet us as at Jos 8:5 3318
"They will **c** out after us Jos 8:6 3318
"We have **c** from a far country; Jos 9:6 935
you and where do you **c** from?" Jos 9:8 935
"Your servants have **c** from a very Jos 9:9 935
the day that we left to **c** to you; Jos 9:12 1980
"**C** up to me and help me, and let Jos 10:4 5927
c up to us quickly and save us and Jos 10:6 5927
"**C** near, put your feet on the Jos 10:24 7126
'In time to **c** your sons may say to Jos 22:24 4279
not say to our sons in time to **c**, Jos 22:27 4279
'It shall also **c** about if they say Jos 22:28 1961
to our generations in time to **c**, Jos 22:28 4279
"It shall **c** about that just Jos 23:15 1961
God spoke to you have **c** upon you, Jos 23:15 935
"**C** up with me into the territory Jg 1:3 5927
them to **c** down to the valley; Jg 1:34 3381
"**C**, and I will show you the man Jg 4:22 1980
did not **c** to the help of the LORD, Jg 5:23 935
that the Midianites would **c** up Jg 6:3 5927
For they would **c** up with their Jg 6:5 5927
they would **c** in like locusts for Jg 6:5 5927
from here, until I **c** *back* to You, Jg 6:18 935
"Now therefore **c**, proclaim in the Jg 7:3 4994
I **c** to the outskirts of the camp, Jg 7:17 935
"**C** down against Midian and take Jg 7:24 3381
'You **c**, reign over us!' Jg 9:10 1980
'You **c**, reign over us!' Jg 9:12 1980
'You **c**, reign over us!' Jg 9:14 1980
c and take refuge in my shade; Jg 9:15 935
may fire **c** out from the bramble Jg 9:15 3318
let fire **c** out from Abimelech and Jg 9:20 3318
and let fire **c** out from the men of Jg 9:20 3318
seventy sons of Jerubbaal might **c**, Jg 9:24 935
"Increase your army and **c** out." Jg 9:29 3318
his relatives have **c** to Shechem; Jg 9:31 935
are with him **c** out against you, Jg 9:33 3318
"**C** and be our chief that we may Jg 11:6 1980
So why have you **c** to me now when Jg 11:7 935
that you have **c** to me to fight Jg 11:12 935
then have you **c** up to me this day to Jg 12:3 5927
no razor shall **c** upon his head, Jg 13:5 5927
whom You have sent **c** to us again Jg 13:8 935
"Now when your words **c** *to pass,* Jg 13:12 935
so that when your words **c** *to pass,* Jg 13:17 935
"Why have you **c** up against us?" Jg 15:10 5927
"We have **c** up to bind Samson in Jg 15:10 5927
"We have **c** down to bind you so Jg 15:12 3381
"Samson has **c** here," Jg 16:2 935
"A razor has never **c** on my head, Jg 16:17 5927
"**C** up once more, for he has told Jg 16:18 5927
"Where do you **c** from?" Jg 17:9 935
you will **c** to a secure people Jg 18:10 935
over your mouth and **c** with us, Jg 18:19 1980
"Please **c**, and let us turn aside Jg 19:11 1980
"**C** and let us approach one of Jg 19:13 1980
going, and where do you **c** from?" Jg 19:17 935
this man has **c** into my house, Jg 19:23 935
when they **c** to Gibeah of Benjamin, Jg 20:10 935
has this **c** about in Israel, Jg 21:3 1961
not **c** up in the assembly to the LORD? Jg 21:5 5927
not **c** up to the LORD at Mizpah, Jg 21:5 5927
not **c** up to the LORD at Mizpah?" Jg 21:8 5927

no one had **c** to the camp from Jg 21:8 935
if the daughters of Shiloh **c** out Jg 21:21 3318
then you shall **c** out of the Jg 21:21 3318
"It shall **c** about, when their Jg 21:22 1961
brothers **c** to complain to us, Jg 21:22 935
when they had **c** to Bethlehem, Ru 1:19 935
and she happened to **c** to the Ru 2:3 7136a
wings you have **c** to seek refuge." Ru 2:12 935
"**C** here, that you may eat of the Ru 2:14 5066
has **c** back from the land of Moab, Ru 4:3 7725
razor shall never **c** on his head." 1Sa 1:11 5927
let arrogance **c** out of your mouth; 1Sa 2:3 3318
c while the meat was boiling, 1Sa 2:13 935
the priest's servant would **c** and 1Sa 2:15 935
she would **c** up with her husband 1Sa 2:19 5927
will **c** concerning your two sons, 1Sa 2:34 935
will **c** and bow down to him 1Sa 2:36 935
that it may **c** among us and deliver 1Sa 4:3 935
of the LORD had **c** into the camp. 1Sa 4:6 935
"God has **c** into the camp." 1Sa 4:7 935
c down and take it up to you." 1Sa 6:21 3381
did not **c** anymore within the border 1Sa 7:13 935
"**C**, and let us return, or else my 1Sa 9:5 1980
"**C**, and let us go to the seer"; 1Sa 9:9 1980
Well said; **c**, let us go." So they went 1Sa 9:10 1980
for he has **c** into the city today, 1Sa 9:12 935
because their cry has **c** to Me." 1Sa 9:16 935
will **c** as far as the oak of Tabor, 1Sa 10:3 935
"Afterward you will **c** to the hill 1Sa 10:5 935
as you have **c** there to the city, 1Sa 10:5 935
the LORD will **c** upon you mightily, 1Sa 10:6 6743a
be when these signs **c** to you, 1Sa 10:7 935
I will **c** down to you to offer 1Sa 10:8 3381
wait seven days until I **c** to you 1Sa 10:8 935
"Has the man **c** here yet?" 1Sa 10:22 935
us, we will **c** out to you." 1Sa 11:3 3318
"Whoever does not **c** out after 1Sa 11:7 3318
said to the messengers who had **c**, 1Sa 11:9 935
"Tomorrow we will **c** out to you, 1Sa 11:10 3318
"**C** and let us go to Gilgal and 1Sa 11:14 1980
but Samuel did not **c** to Gilgal; 1Sa 13:8 935
not **c** within the appointed days, 1Sa 13:11 935
will **c** down against me at Gilgal, 1Sa 13:12 3381
"**C** and let us cross over to the 1Sa 14:1 1980
"**C** and let us cross over to the 1Sa 14:6 1980
'Wait until we **c** to you'; 1Sa 14:9 5060
'**C** up to us,' then we will go up, 1Sa 14:10 5927
"**C** up to us and we will tell you 1Sa 14:12 5927
"**C** up after me, for the LORD has 1Sa 14:12 5927
have **c** to sacrifice to the LORD.' 1Sa 16:2 935
"Do you **c** in peace?" 1Sa 16:4 935
I have **c** to sacrifice to the LORD. 1Sa 16:5 935
and **c** with me to the sacrifice." 1Sa 16:5 935
and it shall **c** about when the evil 1Sa 16:16 1961
"Why do you **c** out to draw up in 1Sa 17:8 3318
and let him **c** down to me. 1Sa 17:8 3381
"Why have you **c** down? 1Sa 17:28 3381
for you have **c** down in order to 1Sa 17:28 3381
that you **c** to me with sticks?" 1Sa 17:43 935
"**C** to me, and I will give your 1Sa 17:44 1980
"You **c** to me with a sword, a 1Sa 17:45 935
but I **c** to you in the name of the 1Sa 17:45 935
by my father to **c** upon you, 1Sa 20:9 935
"**C**, and let us go out into the 1Sa 20:11 1980
you shall go down quickly and **c** to 1Sa 20:19 935
side of you, get them,' then **c**; 1Sa 20:21 935
son of Jesse not **c** to the meal, 1Sa 20:27 935
he has not **c** to the king's table." 1Sa 20:29 935
Shall this one **c** into my house?" 1Sa 21:15 935
my father and my mother **c** *and stay* 1Sa 22:3 3318
Saul that David had **c** to Keilah, 1Sa 23:7 935
Saul is seeking to **c** to Keilah to 1Sa 23:10 935
Will Saul **c** down just as Your 1Sa 23:11 3381
"He will **c** down." 1Sa 23:11 3381
that Saul had **c** out to seek his life 1Sa 23:15 3318
c down according to all the desire 1Sa 23:20 3381
"Hurry and **c**, for the Philistines 1Sa 23:27 1980
whom has the king of Israel **c** out? 1Sa 24:14 3318
for we have **c** on a festive day. 1Sa 25:8 935
you had **c** quickly to meet me, 1Sa 25:34 935
or his day will **c** that he dies, 1Sa 26:10 935
for the king of Israel has **c** out 1Sa 26:20 3318
the young men **c** over and take it. 1Sa 26:22 5674a
as you **c** to Shur even as far as 1Sa 27:8 935
c upon you for this thing." 1Sa 28:10 7136a
of your lord who have **c** with you, 1Sa 29:10 935
otherwise these uncircumcised will **c** 1Sa 31:4 935
"From where do you **c**?" 2Sa 1:3 935
daughter, when you **c** to see me." 2Sa 3:13 935
"You shall not **c** in here, but the 2Sa 5:6 935
lame shall not **c** into the house." 2Sa 5:8 935
circle around behind them and **c** at 2Sa 5:23 935
can the ark of the LORD **c** to me?" 2Sa 6:9 935
you, who will **c** forth from you, 2Sa 7:12 3318
you, then I will **c** to help you. 2Sa 10:11 1980
"Have you not **c** from a journey? 2Sa 11:10 935
for the wayfarer who had **c** to him; 2Sa 12:4 935
it for the man who had **c** to him." 2Sa 12:4 935
c and give me *some* food to eat, 2Sa 13:5 935
"Please let my sister Tamar **c** and 2Sa 13:6 935
"**C**, lie with me, my sister." 2Sa 13:11 935
"Behold, the king's sons have **c**; 2Sa 13:35 935
"Now the reason I have **c** to speak 2Sa 14:15 935
king, but he would not **c** to him. 2Sa 14:29 935
a second time, but he would not **c**. 2Sa 14:29 935
'**C** here, that I may send you to 2Sa 14:32 935
"Why have I **c** from Geshur? 2Sa 14:32 935
to **c** to the king for judgment, 2Sa 15:2 935
any suit or cause could **c** to me and 2Sa 15:4 935

men who had **c** with him from Gath,	**2Sa 15:18**	935
“I will **c** upon him while he	**2Sa 17:2**	935
When Hushai had **c** to Absalom,	**2Sa 17:6**	935
“So we shall **c** to him in one of	**2Sa 17:12**	935
Now when David had **c** to Mahanaim,	**2Sa 17:27**	935
evil that has **c** upon you from your	**2Sa 19:7**	935
of all Israel has **c** to the king,	**2Sa 19:11**	935
therefore behold, I have **c** today,	**2Sa 19:20**	935
has **c** safely to his own house.”	**2Sa 19:30**	935
Gileadite had **c** down from Rogelim;	**2Sa 19:31**	3381
‘**C** here that I may speak with you.’ ”	**2Sa 20:16**	7126
And **c** trembling out of their	**2Sa 22:46**	2296
of famine **c** to you in your land?	**2Sa 24:13**	935
lord the king **c** to his servant?”	**2Sa 24:21**	935
“So now **c**, please let me give you	**1Ki 1:12**	1980
I will **c** in after you and confirm	**1Ki 1:14**	935
“Otherwise it will **c** about,	**1Ki 1:21**	1961
“Then you shall **c** up after him,	**1Ki 1:35**	5927
and he shall **c** and sit on my	**1Ki 1:35**	935
“**C** in, for you are a valiant man	**1Ki 1:42**	935
have **c** up from there rejoicing,	**1Ki 1:45**	5927
“Do you **c** peacefully?”	**1Ki 2:13**	935
“Thus the king has said, ‘**C** out.’ ”	**1Ki 2:30**	3318
do not know how to go out or **c** in.	**1Ki 3:7**	935
did such abundance of spices **c** in	**1Ki 10:10**	935
almug trees have not **c** in *again*	**1Ki 10:12**	935
had **c** to Shechem to make him king.	**1Ki 12:1**	935
when Rehoboam had **c** to Jerusalem,	**1Ki 12:21**	935
this thing has **c** from Me.	**1Ki 12:24**	1961
“**C** home with me and refresh	**1Ki 13:7**	935
“**C** home with me and eat bread.”	**1Ki 13:15**	1980
your body shall not **c** to the grave	**1Ki 13:22**	935
“For the thing shall surely **c** to	**1Ki 13:32**	1961
“**C** in, wife of Jeroboam, why do	**1Ki 14:6**	935
family will **c** to the grave,	**1Ki 14:13**	935
You have **c** to me to bring my	**1Ki 17:18**	935
“It will **c** about when I leave	**1Ki 18:12**	1961
so when I **c** and tell Ahab and he	**1Ki 18:12**	935
to all the people, “**C** near to me.”	**1Ki 18:30**	5066
whom the word of the LORD had **c**,	**1Ki 18:31**	1961
“It shall **c** about, the one	**1Ki 19:17**	1961
“Men have **c** out from Samaria.”	**1Ki 20:17**	3318
“If they have **c** out for peace,	**1Ki 20:18**	3318
or if they have **c** out for war,	**1Ki 20:18**	3318
of Aram will **c** up against you.”	**1Ki 20:22**	5927
‘You shall not **c** down from the bed	**2Ki 1:4**	3381
Therefore you shall not **c** down	**2Ki 1:6**	3381
God, the king says, ‘**C** down.’ ”	**2Ki 1:9**	3381
let fire **c** down from heaven and	**2Ki 1:10**	3381
‘**C** down quickly.’ ”	**2Ki 1:11**	3381
let fire **c** down from heaven and	**2Ki 1:12**	3381
you shall not **c** down from the bed	**2Ki 1:16**	3381
had **c** up to fight against them.	**2Ki 3:21**	5927
and the creditor has **c** to take my	**2Ki 4:1**	935
Now let him **c** to me, and he shall	**2Ki 5:8**	935
‘He will surely **c** out to me and	**2Ki 5:11**	3318
sons of the prophets have **c** to me	**2Ki 5:22**	935
When they had **c** into Samaria,	**2Ki 6:20**	935
c again into the land of Israel.	**2Ki 6:23**	935
Now therefore **c**, and let us go	**2Ki 7:4**	1980
of the Egyptians, to **c** upon us.”	**2Ki 7:6**	935
Now therefore **c**, let us go and	**2Ki 7:9**	1980
‘When they **c** out of the city, we	**2Ki 7:12**	3318
c on the land for seven years.”	**2Ki 8:1**	935
“The man of God has **c** here.”	**2Ki 8:7**	935
did this mad fellow **c** to you?”	**2Ki 9:11**	935
of Judah had **c** down to see Joram.	**2Ki 9:16**	3381
and **c** to me at Jezreel tomorrow	**2Ki 10:6**	935
and we have **c** down to greet the	**2Ki 10:13**	3381
“**C** with me and see my zeal for	**2Ki 10:16**	1980
was not a man left who did not **c**.	**2Ki 10:21**	935
let none **c** out.”	**2Ki 10:25**	3318
who **c** in on the sabbath and keep	**2Ki 11:5**	935
who were to **c** in on the sabbath,	**2Ki 11:9**	935
“**C**, let us face each other.”	**2Ki 14:8**	1980
c up and deliver me from the hand	**2Ki 16:7**	5927
“Now therefore, **c**, make a bargain	**2Ki 18:23**	4994
“Have I now **c** up without the	**2Ki 18:25**	5927
peace with me and **c** out to me,	**2Ki 18:31**	3318
until I **c** and take you away to a	**2Ki 18:32**	935
for children have **c** to birth and	**2Ki 19:3**	935
has **c** out to fight against you,”	**2Ki 19:9**	3318
arrogance has **c** up to My ears,	**2Ki 19:28**	5927
“He will not **c** to this city or	**2Ki 19:32**	935
not **c** before it with a shield	**2Ki 19:32**	6923
he shall not **c** to this city,”	**2Ki 19:33**	935
from where have they **c** to you?”	**2Ki 20:14**	935
“They have **c** from a far country,	**2Ki 20:14**	935
did not **c** out of his land again,	**2Ki 24:7**	3318
misfortune had **c** upon his house.	**1Ch 7:23**	1961
were to **c** in every seven days from	**1Ch 9:25**	935
uncircumcised will **c** and abuse me.”	**1Ch 10:4**	935
you **c** peacefully to me to help me,	**1Ch 12:17**	935
by name to **c** and make David king.	**1Ch 12:31**	935
Now the Philistines had **c** and made	**1Ch 14:9**	935
and **c** at them in front of the	**1Ch 14:14**	935
an offering, and **c** before Him;	**1Ch 16:29**	935
house for a great while to **c**,	**1Ch 17:17**	7350
Have not his servants **c** to you to	**1Ch 19:3**	935
and the kings who had **c** were by	**1Ch 19:9**	935
“Both riches and honor **c** from	**1Ch 29:12**	
For all things **c** from You, and	**1Ch 29:14**	
out and **c** in before this people,	**2Ch 1:10**	935
nor those who will **c** after you.”	**2Ch 1:12**	
they **c** and pray toward this house,	**2Ch 6:32**	935
seeing the fire **c** down and the	**2Ch 7:3**	3381
had **c** to Shechem to make him king.	**2Ch 10:1**	935
when Rehoboam had **c** to Jerusalem,	**2Ch 11:1**	935
set an ambush to **c** from the rear,	**2Ch 13:13**	935
have **c** against this multitude.	**2Ch 14:11**	935
not **c** on you and your brethren.	**2Ch 19:10**	1961
‘Should evil **c** upon us, the sword,	**2Ch 20:9**	935
will **c** up by the ascent of Ziz,	**2Ch 20:16**	5927
Seir, who had **c** against Judah;	**2Ch 20:22**	935
c out because of the sickness,	**2Ch 21:15**	3318
Levites who **c** in on the sabbath,	**2Ch 23:4**	935
who were to **c** in on the sabbath,	**2Ch 23:8**	935
the chief priest’s officer would **c**,	**2Ch 24:11**	935
“**C**, let us face each other.”	**2Ch 25:17**	1980
Edomites had **c** and attacked Judah and	**2Ch 28:17**	935
c near and bring sacrifices and	**2Ch 29:31**	5066
that they should **c** to the house of	**2Ch 30:1**	935
that they should **c** to celebrate	**2Ch 30:5**	935
saw that Sennacherib had **c** and	**2Ch 32:2**	935
c and find abundant water?”	**2Ch 32:4**	935
wrath of the LORD did not **c** on them	**2Ch 32:26**	935
you have **c** to us at Jerusalem;	**Ezr 4:12**	858
until a report could **c** to Darius,	**Ezr 5:5**	1981
The exiles who had **c** from the	**Ezr 8:35**	935
“After all that has **c** upon us	**Ezr 9:13**	935
would not **c** within three days,	**Ezr 10:8**	935
wives **c** at appointed times,	**Ezr 10:14**	935
pass through until I **c** to Judah,	**Ne 2:7**	935
someone had **c** to seek the welfare	**Ne 2:10**	935
C, let us rebuild the wall of	**Ne 2:17**	1980
conspired together to **c** *and* fight	**Ne 4:8**	935
know or see until we **c** among them,	**Ne 4:11**	935
“They will **c** up against us from	**Ne 4:12**	
“**C**, let us meet together at	**Ne 6:2**	1980
a great work and I cannot **c** down.	**Ne 6:3**	3381
I leave it and **c** down to you?”	**Ne 6:3**	3381
So **c** now, let us take counsel	**Ne 6:7**	1980
before You, Which has **c** upon us,	**Ne 9:32**	4672
just in all that has **c** upon us;	**Ne 9:33**	935
of Judah **c** up on top of the wall,	**Ne 12:31**	5927
on they did not **c** on the sabbath.	**Ne 13:21**	935
c as gatekeepers to sanctify the	**Ne 13:22**	935
But Queen Vashti refused to **c** at	**Es 1:12**	935
his presence, but she did not **c**.’	**Es 1:17**	935
that Vashti may no longer **c** into	**Es 1:19**	935
I have not been summoned to **c** to	**Es 4:11**	935
may the king and Haman **c** this day	**Es 5:4**	935
may the king and Haman **c** to the	**Es 5:8**	935
let no one but me **c** with the king	**Es 5:12**	935
And the king said, “Let him **c** in.”	**Es 6:5**	935
“From where do you **c**?”	**Jb 1:7**	935
“Where have you **c** from?”	**Jb 2:2**	935
adversity that had **c** upon him,	**Jb 2:11**	935
to **c** to sympathize with him and	**Jb 2:11**	935
c into the number of the months.	**Jb 3:6**	935
C forth from the womb and expire?	**Jb 3:11**	3318
“But now it has **c** to you, and you	**Jb 4:5**	935
of His anger they **c** to an end.	**Jb 4:9**	3615
does not **c** from the dust,	**Jb 5:6**	3318
will **c** to the grave in full vigor,	**Jb 5:26**	935
that my request might **c** to pass,	**Jb 6:8**	935
And **c** to an end without hope.	**Jb 7:6**	3615
goes down to Sheol does not **c** up.	**Jb 7:9**	5927
Then let **c** on me what may.	**Jb 13:13**	5674a
man may not **c** before His presence.	**Jb 13:16**	935
“But **c** again all of you now, For	**Jb 17:10**	935
“His troops **c** together, And build	**Jb 19:12**	935
who suffers will **c** *against* him.	**Jb 20:22**	935
Terrors **c** upon him,	**Jb 20:25**	1980
Thereby good will **c** to you.	**Jb 22:21**	935
Him, That I might **c** to His seat!	**Jb 23:3**	935
tried me, I shall **c** forth as gold.	**Jb 23:10**	3318
“Where then does wisdom **c** from?	**Jb 28:20**	935
“As *through* a wide breach they **c**,	**Jb 30:14**	857
the cry of the poor to **c** to Him,	**Jb 34:28**	935
‘Thus far you shall **c**,	**Jb 38:11**	935
“From whose womb has **c** the ice?	**Jb 38:29**	3318
Who can **c** within his double mail?	**Jb 41:13**	935
That no air can **c** between them.	**Jb 41:16**	935
evil of the wicked **c** to an end,	**Ps 7:9**	1584
c to an end in perpetual ruins,	**Ps 9:6**	8552
of Israel would **c** out of Zion!	**Ps 14:7**	
c forth from Your presence;	**Ps 17:2**	3318
And **c** trembling out of their	**Ps 18:45**	2727
They will **c** and will declare His	**Ps 22:31**	935
That the King of glory may **c** in!	**Ps 24:7**	935
That the King of glory may **c** in!	**Ps 24:9**	935
they will not **c** near to you.	**Ps 32:9**	7126
C, you children, listen to me;	**Ps 34:11**	1980
destruction **c** upon him unawares,	**Ps 35:8**	935
not the foot of pride **c** upon me,	**Ps 36:11**	935
Then I said, “Behold, I **c**;	**Ps 40:7**	935
shall I **c** and appear before God?	**Ps 42:2**	935
All this has **c** upon us, but we	**Ps 44:17**	935
The daughter of Tyre *will* **c** with	**Ps 45:12**	
C, behold the works of the LORD,	**Ps 46:8**	1980
our God **c** and not keep silence;	**Ps 50:3**	935
of Israel would **c** out of Zion!	**Ps 53:6**	
Fear and trembling **c** upon me,	**Ps 55:5**	935
Let death **c** deceitfully upon them;	**Ps 55:15**	5378
hear prayer, To You all men **c**.	**Ps 65:2**	935
C and see the works of God, *Who is*	**Ps 66:5**	1980
I shall **c** into Your house with	**Ps 66:13**	935
C *and* hear, all who fear God, And	**Ps 66:16**	1980
Envoys will **c** out of Egypt;	**Ps 68:31**	857
I have **c** into deep waters, and a	**Ps 69:2**	935
they not **c** into Your righteousness.	**Ps 69:27**	935
to which I may continually **c**;	**Ps 71:3**	935
I will **c** with the mighty deeds of	**Ps 71:16**	935
Your power to all who are to **c**.	**Ps 71:18**	935
May he **c** down like rain upon the	**Ps 72:6**	3381
His promise **c** to an end forever?	**Ps 77:8**	1584
to **c** the praises of the LORD,	**Ps 78:4**	314
the generation to **c** might know,	**Ps 78:6**	314
compassion **c** quickly to meet us,	**Ps 79:8**	6923
of the prisoner **c** before You;	**Ps 79:11**	935
up Your power And **c** to save us!	**Ps 80:2**	1980
“**C**, and let us wipe them out as a	**Ps 83:4**	1980
shall **c** and worship before You,	**Ps 86:9**	935
Let my prayer **c** before You;	**Ps 88:2**	935
will any plague **c** near your tent.	**Ps 91:10**	7126
O **c**, let us sing for joy to the	**Ps 95:1**	1980
Let us **c** before His presence with	**Ps 95:2**	6923
C, let us worship and bow down,	**Ps 95:6**	935
offering and **c** into His courts.	**Ps 96:8**	935
C before Him with joyful singing.	**Ps 100:2**	935
When will You **c** to me?	**Ps 101:2**	935
And let my cry for help **c** to You.	**Ps 102:1**	935
her, For the appointed time has **c**.	**Ps 102:13**	935
written for the generation to **c**,	**Ps 102:18**	314
Your years will not **c** to an end.	**Ps 102:27**	8552
is judged, let him **c** forth guilty,	**Ps 109:7**	3318
Your lovingkindnesses also **c** to me,	**Ps 119:41**	935
c to me that I may live,	**Ps 119:77**	935
and anguish have **c** upon me,	**Ps 119:143**	4672
Let my cry **c** before You, O LORD;	**Ps 119:169**	7126
Let my supplication **c** before You;	**Ps 119:170**	935
From where shall my help **c**?	**Ps 121:1**	935
c again with a shout of joy,	**Ps 126:6**	935
Your heavens, O LORD, and **c** down;	**Ps 144:5**	3381
“**C** with us, Let us lie in wait	**Pr 1:11**	1980
distress and anguish **c** upon you.	**Pr 1:27**	935
From His mouth **c** knowledge	**Pr 2:6**	
“Go, and **c** back, And tomorrow I	**Pr 3:28**	7725
Since you have **c** into the hand of	**Pr 6:3**	935
poverty will **c** in like a vagabond And	**Pr 6:11**	935
his calamity will **c** suddenly;	**Pr 6:15**	935
I have **c** out to meet you,	**Pr 7:15**	3318
“**C**, let us drink our fill of love	**Pr 7:18**	1980
At the full moon he will **c** home.”	**Pr 7:20**	935
“**C**, eat of my food And drink of	**Pr 9:5**	1980
the wicked fears will **c** upon him,	**Pr 10:24**	935
evil, evil will **c** to him.	**Pr 11:27**	935
Poverty and shame *will* **c** to him	**Pr 13:18**	
will only **c** *to* poverty.	**Pr 22:16**	
and the glutton will **c** to poverty,	**Pr 23:21**	3423
a good blessing will **c** upon them.	**Pr 24:25**	935
your poverty will **c** *as* a robber And	**Pr 24:34**	935
that it be said to you, “**C** up here,”	**Pr 25:7**	5927
a stone, it will **c** back on him.	**Pr 26:27**	7725
know that want will **c** upon him.	**Pr 28:22**	935
those who will **c** later *still*.	**Ec 1:11**	1961
“**C** now, I will test you with	**Ec 2:1**	1980
the man *do* who will **c** after the king	**Ec 2:12**	935
it to the man who will **c** after me.	**Ec 2:18**	1961
c out of prison to become king,	**Ec 4:14**	3318
and even the ones who will **c** later	**Ec 4:16**	314
had **c** naked from his mother’s womb,	**Ec 5:15**	3318
tell him what will **c** after him?	**Ec 10:14**	1961
that is to **c** *will be* futility.	**Ec 11:8**	935
before the evil days **c** and the	**Ec 12:1**	935
my beautiful one, And **c** along.	**SS 2:10**	1980
my beautiful one, And **c** along!” ”	**SS 2:13**	1980
have **c** up from *their* washing,	**SS 4:2**	5927
“**C** with me from Lebanon, *my*	**SS 4:8**	
May you **c** with me from Lebanon.	**SS 4:8**	935
“Awake, O north *wind*, And **c**,	**SS 4:16**	935
May my beloved **c** into his garden	**SS 4:16**	935
“I have **c** into my garden, my	**SS 5:1**	935
have **c** up from *their* washing,	**SS 6:6**	5927
C back, come back, O Shulammite;	**SS 6:13**	7725
“Come back, **c** back, O Shulammite;	**SS 6:13**	7725
C back, come back, that we may	**SS 6:13**	7725
Come back, **c** back, that we may	**SS 6:13**	7725
“**C**, my beloved, let us go out	**SS 7:11**	1980
“When you **c** to appear before Me,	**Is 1:12**	935
“**C** now, and let us reason	**Is 1:18**	1980
the widow’s plea **c** before them.	**Is 1:23**	935
the LORD will **c** to an end.	**Is 1:28**	3615
c about that In the last days The	**Is 2:2**	1961
And many peoples will **c** and say,	**Is 2:3**	1980
“**C**, let us go up to the mountain	**Is 2:3**	1980
C, house of Jacob, and let us walk	**Is 2:5**	1980
Now it will **c** about that instead	**Is 3:24**	1961
It will **c** about that he who is	**Is 4:3**	1961
But briars and thorns will **c** up.	**Is 5:6**	5927
of Israel draw near And **c** to pass,	**Is 5:19**	935
it will **c** with speed swiftly.	**Is 5:26**	935
not stand nor shall it **c** to pass.	**Is 7:7**	1961
never **c** since the day that Ephraim	**Is 7:17**	935
They will all **c** and settle on	**Is 7:19**	935
And it will **c** about in that day,	**Is 7:23**	1961
People will **c** there with bows and	**Is 7:24**	935
which will **c** from afar?	**Is 10:3**	935
He has **c** against Aiath, He has	**Is 10:28**	935
It will **c** as destruction from the	**Is 13:6**	935
Her *fateful* time also will soon **c**	**Is 13:22**	935
over you to meet you when you **c**;	**Is 14:9**	935
serpent’s root a viper will **c** out,	**Is 14:29**	3318
the extortioner has **c** to an end,	**Is 16:4**	656
So it will **c** about when Moab	**Is 16:12**	1961
cloud and is about to **c** to Egypt;	**Is 19:1**	935
and the Assyrians will **c** into	**Is 19:23**	935
inquire, inquire; **C** back again.”	**Is 21:12**	857
“**C**, go to this steward, To	**Is 22:15**	1980
“Then it will **c** about in that	**Is 22:20**	1961
It will **c** about at the end of	**Is 23:17**	1961
C, my people, enter into your	**Is 26:20**	1980
the LORD is about to **c** out from	**Is 26:21**	3318
days to **c** Jacob will take root,	**Is 27:6**	935
Women **c** *and* make a fire with them,	**Is 27:11**	935
It will **c** about also in that day	**Is 27:13**	1961

c and worship the LORD in the	Is 27:13	1961
you are prostrate Your words *will* **c**.	Is 29:4	
For the ruthless will **c** to an end and	Is 29:20	656
From where **c** lioness and lion,	Is 30:6	
time to **c** As a witness forever.	Is 30:8	314
of them will **c** to an end together.	Is 31:3	3615
So will the LORD of hosts **c** down	Is 31:4	3381
the *fruit* gathering will not **c**.	Is 32:10	935
thorns *and* briars shall **c** up;	Is 32:13	5927
c up in its fortified towers,	Is 34:13	5927
your God will **c** *with* vengeance;	Is 35:4	935
The recompense of God will **c**,	Is 35:4	935
c with joyful shouting to Zion,	Is 35:10	935
c make a bargain with my master	Is 36:8	4994
"Have I now **c** up without the	Is 36:10	5927
peace with me and **c** out to me,	Is 36:16	3318
until I **c** and take you away to a	Is 36:17	935
for children have **c** to birth,	Is 37:3	935
has **c** out to fight against you,"	Is 37:9	3318
arrogance has **c** up to My ears,	Is 37:29	5927
'He will not **c** to this city or	Is 37:33	935
not **c** before it with a shield,	Is 37:33	6923
and he will not **c** to this city,'	Is 37:34	935
from where have they **c** to you?"	Is 39:3	935
have **c** to me from a far country,	Is 39:3	935
the Lord GOD will **c** with might,	Is 40:10	935
Let them **c** forward, then let them	Is 41:1	5066
Let us **c** together for judgment.	Is 41:1	7126
They have drawn near and have **c**.	Is 41:5	857
that are going to **c** afterward,	Is 41:23	857
one from the north, and he has **c**;	Is 41:25	857
will **c** upon rulers as *upon* mortar,	Is 41:25	935
the former things have **c** to pass,	Is 42:9	935
things to **c** concerning My sons,	Is 45:11	857
c over to you and will be yours;	Is 45:14	5674a
they will **c** over in chains And	Is 45:14	5674a
"Gather yourselves and **c**;	Is 45:20	935
Men will **c** to Him, And all who	Is 45:24	935
"**C** down and sit in the dust, O	Is 47:1	3381
these two things will **c** on you	Is 47:9	935
They will **c** on you in full	Is 47:9	935
"But evil will **c** on you Which you	Is 47:11	935
not know Will **c** on you suddenly.	Is 47:11	935
you from what will **c** upon you.	Is 47:13	935
"**C** near to Me, listen to this:	Is 48:16	7126
"Behold, these will **c** from afar;	Is 49:12	935
these *will* **c** from the north	Is 49:12	
gather together, they **c** to you.	Is 49:18	935
From where did these **c**?'"	Is 49:21	
c with joyful shouting to Zion,	Is 51:11	935
unclean Will no longer **c** into you.	Is 52:1	935
for it will not **c** near you.	Is 54:14	7126
one who thirsts, **c** to the waters;	Is 55:1	1980
And you who have no money **c**,	Is 55:1	1980
C, buy wine and milk Without money	Is 55:1	1980
"Incline your ear and **c** to Me.	Is 55:3	1980
and the snow **c** down from heaven,	Is 55:10	3381
thorn bush the cypress will **c** up,	Is 55:13	5927
the nettle the myrtle will **c** up,	Is 55:13	5927
For My salvation is about to **c** And	Is 56:1	935
beasts in the forest, **C** to eat.	Is 56:9	857
"**C**," *they say,* "let us get wine, and	Is 56:12	857
"But **c** here, you sons of a	Is 57:3	7126
He will **c** like a rushing stream Which	Is 59:19	
"A Redeemer will **c** to Zion,	Is 59:20	935
for your light has **c**,	Is 60:1	935
"Nations will **c** to your light,	Is 60:3	1980
gather together, they **c** to you.	Is 60:4	935
Your sons will **c** from afar, And	Is 60:4	935
of the nations will **c** to you.	Is 60:5	935
All those from Sheba will **c**;	Is 60:6	935
And the ships of Tarshish *will* **c**	Is 60:9	
glory of Lebanon will **c** to you,	Is 60:13	935
you will **c** bowing to you,	Is 60:14	1980
And My year of redemption has **c**.	Is 63:4	935
rend the heavens *and* **c** down,	Is 64:1	3381
to yourself, do not **c** near me,	Is 65:5	5066
not be remembered or **c** to mind.	Is 65:17	5927
c to pass that before they call,	Is 65:24	1961
the LORD will **c** in fire And His	Is 66:15	935
will **c** to an end altogether,"	Is 66:17	5486
And they shall **c** and see My glory.	Is 66:18	935
will **c** to bow down before Me,"	Is 66:23	935
"and they will **c** and they will	Jer 1:15	935
We will no longer **c** to You'?	Jer 2:31	935
And it will not **c** to mind, nor	Jer 3:16	5927
and they will **c** together from the	Jer 3:18	935
"Behold, we **c** to You;	Jer 3:22	857
It shall **c** about in that day,"	Jer 4:9	1961
will **c** at My command;	Jer 4:12	935
'Besiegers **c** from a far country,	Jer 4:16	935
Misfortune will not **c** on us,	Jer 5:12	935
It shall **c** about when they say,	Jer 5:19	1961
and their flocks will **c** to her,	Jer 6:3	935
frankincense **c** to Me from Sheba And	Jer 6:20	935
the destroyer Will **c** upon us.	Jer 6:26	935
then **c** and stand before Me in this	Jer 7:10	935
and it did not **c** into My mind.	Jer 7:31	5927
For they **c** and devour the land and	Jer 8:16	935
mourning women, that they may **c**;	Jer 9:17	935
wailing women, that they may **c**!	Jer 9:17	935
death has **c** up through our windows;	Jer 9:21	5927
Therefore I have **c** to hate her.	Jer 12:8	
the wilderness Destroyers have **c**,	Jer 12:12	935
"And it will **c** about that after I	Jer 12:15	1961
crown Has **c** down from your head."	Jer 13:18	3381
They have **c** to the cisterns and	Jer 14:3	935
c to an end by sword and famine,	Jer 16:4	3615
To You the nations will **c** From	Jer 16:19	935

word of the LORD? Let it **c** now!"	Jer 17:15	935
kings of Judah **c** in and go out,	Jer 17:19	935
who **c** in through these gates:	Jer 17:20	935
"But it will **c** about, if you	Jer 17:24	1961
then there will **c** in through the	Jer 17:25	935
"They will **c** in from the cities	Jer 17:26	935
"**C** and let us devise plans	Jer 18:18	1980
C on and let us strike at him with	Jer 18:18	1980
Why did I ever **c** forth from the	Jer 20:18	3318
'Who will **c** down against us?	Jer 21:13	5181
will groan when pangs **c** upon you,	Jer 22:23	935
'Calamity will not **c** upon you.'	Jer 23:17	935
the word of the LORD has **c** to me,	Jer 25:3	1961
has **c** to the end of the earth,	Jer 25:31	935
and your dispersions have **c**,	Jer 25:34	4390
who have **c** to worship *in* the	Jer 26:2	935
the messengers who **c** to Jerusalem	Jer 27:3	935
call upon Me and **c** and pray to Me,	Jer 29:12	1980
'It shall **c** about on that	Jer 30:8	1961
shall **c** forth from their midst;	Jer 30:21	3318
"With weeping they will **c**,	Jer 31:9	935
"They will **c** and shout for	Jer 31:12	935
all this calamity **c** upon them.	Jer 32:23	7122
You have spoken has **c** to pass;	Jer 32:24	1961
'**C** and let us go to Jerusalem	Jer 35:11	935
of Judah who **c** from their cities.	Jer 36:6	935
will **c** before the LORD,	Jer 36:7	5307
have read to the people and **c**."	Jer 36:14	1980
certainly **c** and destroy this land,	Jer 36:29	935
Pharaoh's army which has **c** out for	Jer 37:7	3318
Jeremiah had **c** into the dungeon,	Jer 37:16	935
'The king of Babylon will not **c**	Jer 37:19	935
let my petition **c** before you and	Jer 37:20	5307
you and **c** to you and say to you,	Jer 38:25	935
Now the word of the LORD had **c** to	Jer 39:15	1961
prefer to **c** with me to Babylon,	Jer 40:4	935
come with me to Babylon, **c** *along,*	Jer 40:4	935
not to **c** with me to Babylon,	Jer 40:4	935
before the Chaldeans who **c** to us;	Jer 40:10	935
"**C** to Gedaliah the son of Ahikam!"	Jer 41:6	935
let our petition **c** before you,	Jer 42:2	5307
c and strike the land of Egypt;	Jer 43:11	935
did not *all this* **c** into His mind?	Jer 44:21	5927
"Surely one shall **c** *who looms up*	Jer 46:18	935
of their calamity has **c** upon them,	Jer 46:21	935
c to her as woodcutters with axes.	Jer 46:22	935
"Baldness has **c** upon Gaza;	Jer 47:5	935
'**C** and let us cut her off from	Jer 48:2	1980
A destroyer will **c** to every city,	Jer 48:8	935
"The disaster of Moab will soon **c**,	Jer 48:16	935
"**C** down from your glory And sit	Jer 48:18	3381
destroyer of Moab has **c** up against	Jer 48:18	5927
has also **c** upon the plain,	Jer 48:21	935
'Who will **c** against me?'	Jer 49:4	935
together and **c** against her,	Jer 49:14	935
one will **c** up like a lion from the	Jer 49:19	5927
'But it will **c** about in the last	Jer 49:39	1961
"For a nation has **c** up against	Jer 50:3	5927
"the sons of Israel will **c**,	Jer 50:4	935
they will **c** that they may join	Jer 50:5	935
"**C** to her from the farthest border;	Jer 50:26	935
be upon them, for their day has **c**,	Jer 50:27	935
"For your day has **c**,	Jer 50:31	935
one will **c** up like a lion from the	Jer 50:44	5927
C and let us recount in Zion The	Jer 51:10	935
in treasures, Your end has **c**,	Jer 51:13	935
time of harvest will **c** for her."	Jer 51:33	935
"The sea has **c** up over Babylon;	Jer 51:42	5927
make what he has swallowed **c** out	Jer 51:44	3318
"**C** forth from her midst, My	Jer 51:45	3318
For the report will **c** one year,	Jer 51:46	935
will **c** to her from the north,"	Jer 51:48	935
And let Jerusalem **c** to your mind.	Jer 51:50	5927
Me destroyers will **c** to her,"	Jer 51:53	935
which would **c** upon Babylon,	Jer 51:60	935
"As soon as you **c** to Babylon,	Jer 51:61	935
They have **c** upon my neck;	La 1:14	5927
their wickedness **c** before You;	La 1:22	935
were finished For our end had **c**.	La 4:18	935
cup will **c** around to you as well,	La 4:21	5674a
'An end is coming; the end has **c**!	Ezk 7:6	935
behold, it has **c**!	Ezk 7:6	935
'Your doom has **c** to you, O	Ezk 7:7	935
The time has **c**, the day is	Ezk 7:7	935
'The time has **c**, the day has	Ezk 7:12	935
'Disaster will **c** upon disaster and	Ezk 7:26	935
"When they **c** there, they will	Ezk 11:18	935
A flooding rain will **c**,	Ezk 13:11	1961
they are going to **c** forth to you	Ezk 14:22	3318
they have **c** out of the fire,	Ezk 15:7	3318
should never **c** about nor happen.	Ezk 16:16	935
c to you from every direction for	Ezk 16:33	935
"Do you **c** to inquire of Me?	Ezk 20:3	935
into your mind will not **c** about,	Ezk 20:32	1961
sword of the king of Babylon to **c**;	Ezk 21:19	935
c to Rabbah of the sons of Ammon,	Ezk 21:20	935
you have **c** to remembrance,	Ezk 21:24	2142
prince of Israel, whose day has **c**,	Ezk 21:25	935
who are slain, whose day has **c**,	Ezk 21:29	935
midst, so that her time will **c**,	Ezk 22:3	935
day near and have **c** to your years;	Ezk 22:4	935
will **c** against you with weapons,	Ezk 23:24	935
even sent for men who **c** from afar,	Ezk 23:40	935
wrath to **c** up to take vengeance,	Ezk 24:8	5927
weep, and your tears shall not **c**.	Ezk 24:16	935
he who escapes will **c** to you with	Ezk 24:26	935
pillars will **c** down to the ground.	Ezk 26:11	3381
sea Will **c** down from their ships;	Ezk 27:29	3381
"A sword will **c** upon Egypt,	Ezk 30:4	935

pride of her power will **c** down;	Ezk 30:6	3381
king of Babylon will **c** upon you.	Ezk 32:11	935
'**C** now and hear what the message	Ezk 33:30	935
"They **c** to you as people	Ezk 33:31	935
"They come to you as people **c**,	Ezk 33:31	3996
showers to **c** down in their season;	Ezk 34:26	3381
for they will soon **c**.	Ezk 36:8	935
yet they have **c** out of His land.'	Ezk 36:20	3381
enter you that you may **c** to life.	Ezk 37:5	2421a
in you that you may **c** alive;	Ezk 37:6	2421a
"**C** from the four winds, O breath,	Ezk 37:9	935
slain, that they **c** to life.	Ezk 37:9	2421a
you to **c** up out of your graves,	Ezk 37:12	5927
you to **c** up out of your graves,	Ezk 37:13	5927
you and you will **c** to life,	Ezk 37:14	2421a
in the latter years you will **c**	Ezk 38:8	935
go up, you will **c** like a storm;	Ezk 38:9	935
"It will **c** about on that day,	Ezk 38:10	1961
thoughts will **c** into your mind and	Ezk 38:10	5927
'Have you **c** to capture spoil?	Ezk 38:13	935
"You will **c** from your place	Ezk 38:15	935
and you will **c** up against My	Ezk 38:16	5927
It shall **c** about in the last days	Ezk 38:16	1961
"It will **c** about on that day,	Ezk 38:18	1961
"Assemble and **c**, gather from	Ezk 39:17	935
who from the sons of Levi **c** near	Ezk 40:46	7131
"And they shall not **c** near to Me	Ezk 44:13	5066
c near to any of My holy things,	Ezk 44:13	5066
c near to Me to minister to Me;	Ezk 44:15	7126
they shall **c** near to My table to	Ezk 44:16	7126
c near to minister to the LORD,	Ezk 45:4	7131
people of the land **c** before the LORD	Ezk 46:9	935
"It will **c** about that every	Ezk 47:9	1961
"And it will **c** about that	Ezk 47:10	1961
all the rulers of the provinces to **c**	Da 3:2	858
Meshach and Abed-nego, **c** out,	Da 3:26	5312
the Most High God, and **c** here!"	Da 3:26	858
smell of fire *even* **c** upon them.	Da 3:27	5907
which has **c** upon my lord the king:	Da 4:24	4291
he had **c** near the den to Daniel,	Da 6:20	7127
forever, for all ages to **c**.'	Da 7:18	5957
I saw him **c** beside the ram,	Da 8:7	5060
all this calamity has **c** on us;	Da 9:13	935
I have now **c** forth to give you	Da 9:22	3318
issued, and I have **c** to tell *you,*	Da 9:23	935
the prince who is to **c** will destroy	Da 9:26	935
And its end *will* **c** with a flood;	Da 9:26	
on the wing of abominations *will* **c**	Da 9:27	
have **c** in response to your words.	Da 10:12	935
"Now I have **c** to give you an	Da 10:14	935
the vision anguish has **c** upon me,	Da 10:16	2015
prince of Greece is about to **c**.	Da 10:20	935
king of the South will **c** to the king	Da 11:6	935
and he will **c** against *their* army	Da 11:7	935
"Then the king of the North will **c**,	Da 11:15	935
"He will set his face to **c**	Da 11:17	935
but he will **c** in a time of	Da 11:21	935
for the end is still *to* **c** at	Da 11:27	
will return and **c** into the South,	Da 11:29	935
ships of Kittim will **c** against him;	Da 11:30	935
so he will **c** back and show regard	Da 11:30	7725
because *it is* still *to* **c** at	Da 11:35	
yet he will **c** to his end, and no	Da 11:45	935
"It will **c** about in that day,"	Hos 2:16	1961
"It will **c** about in that day	Hos 2:21	1961
and they will **c** trembling to the	Hos 3:5	6342
"**C**, let us return to the LORD.	Hos 6:1	1980
And He will **c** to us like the rain,	Hos 6:3	935
The days of punishment have **c**,	Hos 9:7	935
The days of retribution have **c**;	Hos 9:7	935
But I will **c** over her fair neck	Hos 10:11	5674a
midst, And I will not **c** in wrath.	Hos 11:9	935
will **c** trembling from the west.	Hos 11:10	2729
They will **c** trembling like birds	Hos 11:11	2729
pains of childbirth **c** upon him;	Hos 13:13	935
the reeds, An east wind will **c**,	Hos 13:15	935
C, spend the night in sackcloth O	Jl 1:13	935
And it will **c** as destruction from	Jl 1:15	935
Let the bridegroom **c** out of his	Jl 2:16	3318
and its foul smell will **c** up,	Jl 2:20	5927
"It will **c** about after this	Jl 2:28	1961
"And it will **c** about that whoever	Jl 2:32	1961
soldiers draw near, let them **c** up!	Jl 3:9	5927
Hasten and **c**, all you surrounding	Jl 3:11	935
Let the nations be aroused And **c**	Jl 3:12	5927
C, tread, for the wine press is	Jl 3:13	935
great houses will **c** to an end,"	Am 3:15	5486
to Bethel And do not **c** to Gilgal,	Am 5:5	935
And Bethel will **c** to trouble.	Am 5:5	1961
end has **c** for My people Israel.	Am 8:2	935
"It will **c** about in that day,"	Am 8:9	1961
wickedness has **c** up before Me."	Jon 1:2	5927
"**C**, let us cast lots so we may	Jon 1:7	1980
And where do you **c** from?	Jon 1:8	935
of me this great storm *has* **c** upon	Jon 1:12	
He will **c** down and tread on the	Mi 1:3	3381
incurable, For it has **c** to Judah;	Mi 1:9	935
Because a calamity has **c** down from	Mi 1:12	3381
Calamity will not **c** upon us."	Mi 3:11	935
And it will **c** about in the last	Mi 4:1	1961
Many nations will **c** and say,	Mi 4:2	1980
"**C** and let us go up to the	Mi 4:2	1980
daughter of Zion, To you it will **c**	Mi 4:8	857
Even the former dominion will **c**,	Mi 4:8	935
With what shall I **c** to the LORD	Mi 6:6	6923
I **c** to Him with burnt offerings,	Mi 6:6	6923
watchmen, Your punishment will **c**.	Mi 7:4	935
It *will be* a day when they will **c**	Mi 7:12	935
They will **c** trembling out of their	Mi 7:17	7264

LORD our God they will **c** in dread And	Mi 7:17	6342
who scatters has **c** up against you.	Na 2:1	5927
"And it will **c** about that all who	Na 3:7	1961
Their horsemen **c** galloping, Their	Hab 1:8	935
Their horsemen **c** from afar;	Hab 1:8	935
"All of them **c** for violence.	Hab 1:9	935
For it will certainly **c**,	Hab 2:3	935
cup in the LORD's right hand will **c**	Hab 2:16	5437
And utter disgrace *will* **c** upon	Hab 2:16	
"Then it will **c** about on the day	Zph 1:8	1961
"It will **c** about at that time	Zph 1:12	1961
"The time has not **c**,	Hg 1:2	935
and they will **c** with the wealth of	Hg 2:7	935
yet you *did* not **c** *back* to	Hg 2:17	
craftsmen have **c** to terrify them,	Zch 1:21	935
"Those who are far off will **c**	Zch 6:15	935
'It will **c** about that just as	Zch 8:13	1961
will yet *be* that peoples will **c**,	Zch 8:20	935
nations will **c** to seek the LORD of	Zch 8:22	935
"From them will **c** the cornerstone,	Zch 10:4	3318
children will live and **c** back.	Zch 10:9	7725
impenetrable forest has **c** down.	Zch 11:2	3381
"It will **c** about in that day	Zch 12:3	1961
nations that **c** against Jerusalem.	Zch 12:9	935
"It will **c** about in that day,"	Zch 13:2	1961
"Also it will **c** about in that day	Zch 13:4	1961
It will **c** about in all the land,"	Zch 13:8	1961
Then the LORD, my God, will **c**,	Zch 14:5	935
but it will **c** about that at	Zch 14:7	1961
It will **c** about in that day	Zch 14:13	1961
Then it will **c** about that any who	Zch 14:16	1961
and all who sacrifice will **c** and	Zch 14:21	935
will suddenly **c** to His temple;	Mal 3:1	935
so that I will not **c** and smite	Mal 4:6	935
east and have **c** to worship Him."	Mt 2:2	*2064*
OUT OF YOU SHALL C FORTH A RULER	Mt 2:6	*1831*
I too may **c** and worship Him."	Mt 2:8	*2064*
you to flee from the wrath to **c**?	Mt 3:7	*3195*
by You, and do You **c** to me?"	Mt 3:14	*2064*
I did not **c** to abolish but to	Mt 5:17	*2064*
then **c** and present your offering.	Mt 5:24	*2064*
you, you will not **c** out of there	Mt 5:26	*1831*
'Your kingdom **c**. Your will be done,	Mt 6:10	*2064*
who **c** to you in sheep's clothing,	Mt 7:15	*2064*
"I will **c** and heal him."	Mt 8:7	*2064*
worthy for You to **c** under my roof,	Mt 8:8	*1525*
and to another, '**C**!' and he comes,	Mt 8:9	*2064*
many will **c** from east and west,	Mt 8:11	*2240*
Have You **c** here to torment us	Mt 8:29	*2064*
I did not **c** to call the righteous,	Mt 9:13	*2064*
But the days will **c** when the	Mt 9:15	*2064*
but **c** and lay Your hand on her,	Mt 9:18	*2064*
I did not **c** to bring peace, but a	Mt 10:34	*2064*
himself is Elijah who was to **c**.	Mt 11:14	*2064*
"**C** to Me, all who are weary and	Mt 11:28	*1205*
the kingdom of God has **c** upon you.	Mt 12:28	*5348*
in this age or in the *age* to **c**.	Mt 12:32	*3195*
BIRDS OF THE AIR **C** AND NEST IN ITS	Mt 13:32	*2064*
the angels will **c** forth	Mt 13:49	*1831*
me to **c** to You on the water."	Mt 14:28	*2064*
And He said, "**C**!"	Mt 14:29	*2064*
out of the mouth **c** from the heart,	Mt 15:18	*1831*
out of the heart **c** evil thoughts,	Mt 15:19	*1831*
"If anyone wishes to **c** after Me,	Mt 16:24	*2064*
"For the Son of Man is going to **c**	Mt 16:27	*2064*
say that Elijah must **c** first?"	Mt 17:10	*2064*
that stumbling blocks **c**;	Mt 18:7	*2064*
c to save that which was lost.	Mt 18:11	*2064*
and **c**, follow Me."	Mt 19:21	*1204*
Son of Man did not **c** to be served,	Mt 20:28	*2064*
Jerusalem and had **c** to Bethphage,	Mt 21:1	*2064*
c, let us kill him and seize his	Mt 21:38	*1205*
and they were unwilling to **c**.	Mt 22:3	*2064*
c to the wedding feast."	Mt 22:4	*1205*
how did you **c** in here without	Mt 22:12	*1525*
will **c** upon this generation.	Mt 23:36	*2240*
"For many will **c** in My name,	Mt 24:5	*2064*
nations, and then the end will **c**.	Mt 24:14	*2240*
the master of that slave will **c** on	Mt 24:50	*2240*
C out to meet *him.*'	Mt 25:6	*1831*
'**C**, you who are blessed of My	Mt 25:34	*1205*
sick, or in prison, and **c** to You?'	Mt 25:39	*2064*
"Friend, *do* what you have **c** for."	Mt 26:50	*3918b*
"Have you **c** out with swords and	Mt 26:55	*1831*
of God, **c** down from the cross."	Mt 27:40	*2597*
let Him now **c** down from the cross,	Mt 27:42	*2597*
Elijah will **c** to save Him."	Mt 27:49	*2064*
His disciples may **c** and steal Him	Mt 27:64	*2064*
C, see the place where He was	Mt 28:6	*1205*
should **c** to the governor's ears,	Mt 28:14	*191*
Have You **c** to destroy us?	Mk 1:24	*2064*
"Be quiet, and **c** out of him!"	Mk 1:25	*1831*
When He had **c** back to	Mk 2:1	*1525*
I did not **c** to call the righteous,	Mk 2:17	*2064*
"But the days will **c** when the	Mk 2:20	*2064*
"Get up and **c** forward!"	Mk 3:3	
but that it would **c** to light.	Mk 4:22	*2064*
because the harvest has **c**."	Mk 4:29	*3936*
"**C** out of the man, you unclean	Mk 5:8	*1831*
c and lay Your hands on her,	Mk 5:23	*2064*
"**C** away by yourselves to a secluded	Mk 6:31	*1205*
when they had **c** from Jerusalem,	Mk 7:1	*2064*
and *when they* **c** from the market	Mk 7:4	
of them have **c** from a great distance."	Mk 8:3	*1510*
"If anyone wishes to **c** after Me,	Mk 8:34	*2064*
God after it has **c** with power."	Mk 9:1	*2064*
say that Elijah must **c** first?"	Mk 9:11	*2064*
first **c** and restore all things.	Mk 9:12	*2064*
to you that Elijah has indeed **c**,	Mk 9:13	*2064*
c out of him and do not enter him	Mk 9:25	*1831*
c out by anything but prayer."	Mk 9:29	*1831*
"Permit the children to **c** to Me;	Mk 10:14	*2064*
and **c**, follow Me."	Mk 10:21	*1204*
and in the age to **c**,	Mk 10:30	*2064*
Son of Man did not **c** to be served,	Mk 10:45	*2064*
c, let us kill him, and the	Mk 12:7	*1205*
c and destroy the vine-growers,	Mk 12:9	*2064*
"Many will **c** in My name, saying,	Mk 13:6	*2064*
when the *appointed* time will **c**.	Mk 13:33	*1510*
he should **c** suddenly and find you	Mk 13:36	*2064*
you may not **c** into temptation;	Mk 14:38	*2064*
hour has **c**; behold, the Son of Man	Mk 14:41	*2064*
"Have you **c** out with swords and	Mk 14:48	*1831*
and **c** down from the cross!"	Mk 15:30	*2597*
Israel, now **c** down from the cross,	Mk 15:32	*2597*
Elijah will **c** to take Him down."	Mk 15:36	*2064*
When evening had already **c**,	Mk 15:42	*1096*
that they might **c** and anoint Him.	Mk 16:1	*2064*
"The Holy Spirit will **c** upon you,	Lk 1:35	*1904*
mother of my Lord would **c** to me?	Lk 1:43	*2064*
had **c** for Elizabeth to give birth,	Lk 1:57	*4092a*
you to flee from the wrath to **c**?	Lk 3:7	*3195*
Have You **c** to destroy us?	Lk 4:34	*2064*
"Be quiet and **c** out of him!"	Lk 4:35	*1831*
unclean spirits and they **c** out."	Lk 4:36	*1831*
boat for them to **c** and help them.	Lk 5:7	*2064*
who had **c** from every village of	Lk 5:17	*2064*
"I have not **c** to call the	Lk 5:32	*2064*
"But *the* days will **c**;	Lk 5:35	*2064*
"Get up and **c** forward!"	Lk 6:8	*2476*
who had **c** to hear Him and to be	Lk 6:18	*2064*
asking Him to **c** and save the life of	Lk 7:3	*2064*
worthy for You to **c** under my roof;	Lk 7:6	*1525*
myself worthy to **c** to You,	Lk 7:7	*2064*
and to another, '**C**!' and he comes,	Lk 7:8	*2064*
"For John the Baptist has **c**	Lk 7:33	*2064*
of Man has **c** eating and drinking,	Lk 7:34	*2064*
those who **c** in may see the light.	Lk 8:16	*1531*
will not be known and **c** to light.	Lk 8:17	*2064*
spirit to **c** out of the man.	Lk 8:29	*1831*
to implore Him to **c** to his house;	Lk 8:41	*1525*
"If anyone wishes to **c** after Me,	Lk 9:23	*2064*
command fire to **c** down from heaven	Lk 9:54	*2597*
did not **c** to destroy men's lives,	Lk 9:56	*2064*
where He Himself was going to **c**.	Lk 10:1	*2064*
kingdom of God has **c** near to you.'	Lk 10:9	*1448*
the kingdom of God has **c** near.'	Lk 10:11	*1448*
be Your name. Your kingdom **c**.	Lk 11:2	*2064*
mine has **c** to me from a journey,	Lk 11:6	*3854*
the kingdom of God has **c** upon you.	Lk 11:20	*5348*
goods laid up for many years *to* **c**;	Lk 12:19	
and will **c** up and wait on them.	Lk 12:37	*3928*
the master of that slave will **c** on	Lk 12:46	*2240*
c to cast fire upon the earth;	Lk 12:49	*2064*
for three years I have **c** looking	Lk 13:7	*2064*
c during them and get healed,	Lk 13:14	*2064*
they will **c** from east and west and	Lk 13:29	*2240*
you both will **c** and say to you,	Lk 14:9	*2064*
to those who had been invited, '**C**;	Lk 14:17	*2064*
and for that reason I cannot **c**.'	Lk 14:20	*2064*
hedges, and compel *them* to **c** in,	Lk 14:23	*1525*
carry his own cross and **c** after Me	Lk 14:27	*2064*
was dead and has **c** to life again;	Lk 15:24	*326*
'Your brother has **c**,	Lk 15:27	*2240*
who wish to **c** over from here to you	Lk 16:26	*1224*
also **c** to this place of torment.'	Lk 16:28	*2064*
that stumbling blocks **c**,	Lk 17:1	*2064*
woe to him through whom they **c**!	Lk 17:1	*2064*
when he has **c** in from the field,	Lk 17:7	*1525*
'**C** immediately and sit down to	Lk 17:7	*3928*
"The days will **c** when you will	Lk 17:22	*2064*
"Permit the children to **c** to Me,	Lk 18:16	*2064*
and **c**, follow Me."	Lk 18:22	*1204*
at this time and in the age to **c**,	Lk 18:30	*2064*
"Zaccheus, hurry and **c** down,	Lk 19:5	*2597*
salvation has **c** to this house,	Lk 19:9	*1096*
"For the Son of Man has **c** to seek	Lk 19:10	*2064*
with this until I **c** *back*.'	Lk 19:13	*2064*
money in the bank, and having **c**,	Lk 19:23	*2064*
"For the days will **c** upon you	Lk 19:43	*2240*
"He will **c** and destroy these	Lk 20:16	*2064*
the days will **c** in which there	Lk 21:6	*2064*
for many will **c** in My name,	Lk 21:8	*2064*
not **c** on you suddenly like a trap;	Lk 21:34	*2186*
for it will **c** upon all those who	Lk 21:35	*1898b*
get up early in the morning *to* **c**	Lk 21:38	
had **c**, He reclined *at the table,*	Lk 22:14	*1096*
and elders who had **c** against Him,	Lk 22:52	*3854*
"Have you **c** out with swords and	Lk 22:52	*1831*
me when You **c** in Your kingdom!"	Lk 23:42	*2064*
Now the women who had **c** with Him	Lk 23:55	*4905*
into being that has **c** into being.	Jn 1:3	*1096*
"**C**, and you will see."	Jn 1:39	*2064*
good thing **c** out of Nazareth?"	Jn 1:46	*1510*
Philip said to him, "**C** and see."	Jn 1:46	*2064*
My hour has not yet **c**."	Jn 2:4	*2240*
You have **c** from God *as* a teacher;	Jn 3:2	*2064*
the Light has **c** into the world,	Jn 3:19	*2064*
and does not **c** to the Light	Jn 3:20	*2064*
nor **c** all the way here to draw."	Jn 4:15	*1330*
call your husband and **c** here."	Jn 4:16	*2064*
"**C**, see a man who told me all the	Jn 4:29	*1205*
Jesus had **c** out of Judea into Galilee,	Jn 4:47	*2240*
Him to **c** down and heal his son;	Jn 4:47	*2597*
c down before my child dies."	Jn 4:49	*2597*
had **c** out of Judea into Galilee.	Jn 4:54	*2064*
and does not **c** into judgment,	Jn 5:24	*2064*
and will **c** forth;	Jn 5:29	*1607*
and you are unwilling to **c** to Me so	Jn 5:40	*2064*
"I have **c** in My Father's name,	Jn 5:43	*2064*
who is to **c** into the world."	Jn 6:14	*2064*
to **c** and take Him by force to	Jn 6:15	*2064*
and Jesus had not yet **c** to them.	Jn 6:17	*2064*
the Father gives Me will **c** to Me,	Jn 6:37	*2240*
"For I have **c** down from heaven,	Jn 6:38	*2597*
'I have **c** down out of heaven'?"	Jn 6:42	*2597*
"No one can **c** to Me unless the	Jn 6:44	*2064*
to you, that no one can **c** to Me unless	Jn 6:65	*2064*
"We have believed and have **c**	Jn 6:69	
My time has not yet fully **c**."	Jn 7:8	*4137*
but whenever the Christ may **c**,	Jn 7:27	*2064*
and I have not **c** of Myself, but He	Jn 7:28	*2064*
because His hour had not yet **c**.	Jn 7:30	*2064*
and where I am, you cannot **c**."	Jn 7:34	*2064*
and where I am, you cannot **c**'?"	Jn 7:36	*2064*
let him **c** to Me and drink.	Jn 7:37	*2064*
is not going to **c** from Galilee,	Jn 7:41	*2064*
you do not know where I **c** from or	Jn 8:14	*2064*
because His hour had not yet **c**.	Jn 8:20	*2064*
where I am going, you cannot **c**."	Jn 8:21	*2064*
'Where I am going, you cannot **c**'?"	Jn 8:22	*2064*
forth and have **c** from God,	Jn 8:42	*2240*
not even **c** on My own initiative,	Jn 8:42	*2064*
and you have not **c** to know Him,	Jn 8:55	
the Jews had **c** to Martha and Mary,	Jn 11:19	*2064*
had not yet **c** into the village,	Jn 11:30	*2064*
"Lord, **c** and see."	Jn 11:34	*2064*
"Lazarus, **c** forth."	Jn 11:43	*1204*
and the Romans will **c** and take	Jn 11:48	*2064*
will not **c** to the feast at all?"	Jn 11:56	*2064*
crowd who had **c** to the feast,	Jn 12:12	*2064*
"The hour has **c** for the Son of	Jn 12:23	*2064*
"This voice has not **c** for My sake,	Jn 12:30	*1096*
"I have **c** *as* Light into the	Jn 12:46	*2064*
I did not **c** to judge the world,	Jn 12:47	*2064*
Jesus knowing that His hour had **c**	Jn 13:1	*2064*
and that He had **c** forth from God and	Jn 13:3	*1831*
'Where I am going, you cannot **c**.'	Jn 13:33	*1831*
a place for you, I will **c** again and	Jn 14:3	*2064*
and *yet* you have not **c** to know Me,	Jn 14:9	
leave you as orphans; I will **c** to you.	Jn 14:18	*2064*
love him, and We will **c** to him and	Jn 14:23	*2064*
'I go away, and I will **c** to you.'	Jn 14:28	*2064*
"If I had not **c** and spoken to	Jn 15:22	*2064*
the Helper will not **c** to you;	Jn 16:7	*2064*
will disclose to you what is to **c**.	Jn 16:13	*2064*
pain, because her hour has **c**;	Jn 16:21	*2064*
Father and have **c** into the world;	Jn 16:28	*2064*
hour is coming, and has *already* **c**,	Jn 16:32	*2064*
"Father, the hour has **c**;	Jn 17:1	*2064*
"Now they have **c** to know that	Jn 17:7	
are in the world, and I **c** to You.	Jn 17:11	*2064*
"But now I **c** to You;	Jn 17:13	*2064*
where all the Jews **c** together;	Jn 18:20	*4905*
for this I have **c** into the world,	Jn 18:37	*2064*
and they *began* to **c** up to Him and	Jn 19:3	*2064*
who had first **c** to Him by night,	Jn 19:39	*2064*
disciple who had first **c** to the tomb	Jn 20:8	*2064*
"We will also **c** with you."	Jn 21:3	*2064*
"**C** *and* have breakfast."	Jn 21:12	*1205*
"If I want him to remain until I **c**,	Jn 21:22	*2064*
"If I want him to remain until I **c**,	Jn 21:23	*2064*
So when they had **c** together,	Ac 1:6	*4905*
the Holy Spirit has **c** upon you;	Ac 1:8	*1904*
will **c** in just the same way as you	Ac 1:11	*2064*
When the day of Pentecost had **c**,	Ac 2:1	*4845*
GLORIOUS DAY OF THE LORD SHALL **C**.	Ac 2:20	*2064*
c from the presence of the Lord;	Ac 3:19	*2064*
them as to what would **c** of this.	Ac 5:24	*1096*
AND **C** INTO THE LAND THAT I WILL	Ac 7:3	*1204*
'AND AFTER THAT THEY WILL **C** OUT	Ac 7:7	*1831*
and all his relatives to **c** to him,	Ac 7:14	
I HAVE **C** DOWN TO RESCUE THEM;	Ac 7:34	*2597*
C NOW, AND I WILL SEND YOU TO	Ac 7:34	*1204*
you have said may **c** upon me."	Ac 8:24	*1904*
he had **c** to Jerusalem to worship,	Ac 8:27	*2064*
Philip to **c** up and sit with him.	Ac 8:31	*305*
c in and lay his hands on him,	Ac 9:12	*1525*
and *who* had **c** here for the purpose	Ac 9:21	*2064*
of God who had *just* **c** in	Ac 10:3	*1525*
the reason for which you have **c**?"	Ac 10:21	*3918b*
a holy angel to send for you *to* **c**	Ac 10:22	
is also called Peter, to **c** to you;	Ac 10:32	
you have been kind enough to **c**.	Ac 10:33	*3854*
the Prophets may not **c** upon *you:*	Ac 13:40	*1904*
like men and have **c** down to us."	Ac 14:11	*2597*
"**C** over to Macedonia and help us."	Ac 16:9	*1224*
Lord, **c** into my house and stay."	Ac 16:15	*1525*
of Jesus Christ to **c** out of her!"	Ac 16:18	*1831*
c out now and go in peace."	Ac 16:36	*1831*
c themselves and bring us out."	Ac 16:37	*2064*
upset the world have **c** here also;	Ac 17:6	*3918b*
to **c** to him as soon as possible,	Ac 17:15	*2064*
having recently **c** from Italy with	Ac 18:2	*2064*
what reason they had **c** together.	Ac 19:32	*4905*
And when they had **c** to him,	Ac 20:18	*3854*
savage wolves will **c** in among you,	Ac 20:29	*1525*
certainly hear that you have **c**.	Ac 21:22	*2064*
"Men of Israel, **c** to our aid!	Ac 21:28	*997*
When these had **c** to Caesarea	Ac 23:33	*1525*
his accusers to **c** before you.	Ac 24:8	*2064*
self-control and the judgment to **c**,	Ac 24:25	*3195*
the Jews who had **c** down from	Ac 25:7	*2597*
nor have any of the brethren **c**	Ac 28:21	*3854*
often I have planned to **c** to you	Ro 1:13	*2064*
"Let us do evil that good may **c**"?	Ro 3:8	*2064*
who is a type of Him who was to **c**.	Ro 5:14	*3195*

I would not have **c** to know sin **Ro 7:7**
things present, nor things to **c**, **Ro 8:38** *3195*
"AT THIS TIME I WILL **C**, **Ro 9:9** *2064*
there has also **c** to be at the **Ro 11:5** *1096*
their transgression salvation *has* **c** **Ro 11:11**
fullness of the Gentiles has **c** in; **Ro 11:25** *1525*
"THE DELIVERER WILL **C** FROM ZION, **Ro 11:26** *2240*
"THERE SHALL **C** THE ROOT OF JESSE, **Ro 15:12** *1510*
many years a longing to **c** to you **Ro 15:23** *2064*
I know that when I **c** to you, **Ro 15:29** *2064*
I will **c** in the fullness of the **Ro 15:29** *2064*
so that I may **c** to you in joy by **Ro 15:32** *2064*
world through its wisdom did not **c** **1Co 1:21**
I did not **c** with superiority of **1Co 2:1** *2064*
or things present or things to **c**; **1Co 3:22** *3195*
praise will **c** to him from God. **1Co 4:5** *1096*
But I will **c** to you soon, if the **1Co 4:19** *2064*
Shall I **c** to you with a rod, **1Co 4:21** *2064*
and **c** together again so that Satan **1Co 7:5** *1510*
whom the ends of the ages have **c**. **1Co 10:11** *2658*
because you **c** together not for the **1Co 11:17** *4905*
when you **c** together as a church, **1Co 11:18** *4905*
when you **c** together to eat, **1Co 11:33** *4905*
will not **c** together for judgment. **1Co 11:34** *4905*
matters I will arrange when I **c**. **1Co 11:34** *2064*
if I **c** to you speaking in tongues, **1Co 14:6** *2064*
Or has it **c** to you only? **1Co 14:36** *2658*
what kind of body do they **c**?" **1Co 15:35** *2064*
does not **c** to life unless it dies; **1Co 15:36** *2227*
then will **c** about the saying that **1Co 15:54** *1096*
no collections be made when I **c**. **1Co 16:2** *2064*
But I will **c** to you after I go **1Co 16:5** *2064*
in peace, so that he may **c** to me; **1Co 16:11** *2064*
to **c** to you with the brethren; **1Co 16:12** *2064*
not at all *his* desire to **c** now, **1Co 16:12** *2064*
he will **c** when he has opportunity. **1Co 16:12** *2064*
I intended at first to **c** to you, **2Co 1:15** *2064*
again from Macedonia to **c** to you, **2Co 1:16** *2064*
that to spare you I did not **c** again **2Co 1:23** *2064*
not **c** to you in sorrow again. **2Co 2:1** *2064*
behold, new things have **c**. **2Co 5:17** *1096*
C OUT FROM THEIR MIDST AND BE **2Co 6:17** *1831*
otherwise if any Macedonians **c** with me **2Co 9:4** *2064*
for we were the first to **c** even as **2Co 10:14** *5348*
third time I am ready to **c** to you, **2Co 12:14** *2064*
I am afraid that perhaps when I **c** I **2Co 12:20** *2064*
I am afraid that when I **c** again my **2Co 12:21** *2064*
rest *as well,* that if I **c** again **2Co 13:2** *2064*
Abraham might **c** to the Gentiles, **Ga 3:14** *1096*
until the seed would **c** to whom **Ga 3:19** *2064*
But now that faith has **c**, **Ga 3:25** *2064*
now that you have **c** to know God, **Ga 4:9**
This persuasion *did* not **c** **Ga 5:8**
age but also in the one to **c**. **Eph 1:21** *3195*
so that in the ages to **c** He **Eph 2:7** *1904*
I **c** and see you or remain absent, **Php 1:27** *2064*
which has **c** to you, just as in all **Col 1:6** *3918b*
so that He Himself will **c** to have **Col 1:18** *1096*
are a *mere* shadow of what is to **c**; **Col 2:17** *3195*
that the wrath of God will **c** upon **Col 3:6** *2064*
did not **c** to you in word only, **1Th 1:5** *1096*
rescues us from the wrath to **c**. **1Th 1:10** *2064*
For our exhortation does not **c** **1Th 2:3**
has **c** upon them to the utmost. **1Th 2:16** *5348*
For we wanted to **c** to you **1Th 2:18** *2064*
that Timothy has **c** to us from you, **1Th 3:6** *2064*
day of the Lord will **c** just like a thief **1Th 5:2** *2064*
then destruction will **c** upon them **1Th 5:3** *2186*
that the day of the Lord has **c**. **2Th 2:2** *1764*
for *it will not* **c** unless **2Th 2:3**
c to the knowledge of the truth. **1Tm 2:4** *2064*
hoping to **c** to you before long; **1Tm 3:14** *2064*
life and *also* for the *life* to **c**. **1Tm 4:8** *3195*
Until I **c**, give attention to the **1Tm 4:13** *2064*
and they may **c** to their senses *and* **2Tm 2:26** *366*
last days difficult times will **c**. **2Tm 3:1** *1764*
c to the knowledge of the truth. **2Tm 3:7** *2064*
For the time will **c** when they will **2Tm 4:3** *1510*
the time of my departure has **c**. **2Tm 4:6** *2186*
Make every effort to **c** to me soon; **2Tm 4:9** *2064*
When you **c** bring the cloak which I **2Tm 4:13** *2064*
every effort to **c** before winter. **2Tm 4:21** *2064*
effort to **c** to me at Nicopolis, **Ti 3:12** *2064*
For I have **c** to have much joy and **Phm 1:7**
YOUR YEARS WILL NOT **C** TO AN END." **Heb 1:12** *1587*
subject to angels the world to **c**, **Heb 2:5** *3195*
He is able to **c** to the aid of **Heb 2:18** *997*
may seem to have **c** short of it. **Heb 4:1** *5302*
and you have **c** to need milk and **Heb 5:12** *1096*
and the powers of the age to **c**, **Heb 6:5** *3195*
priest of the good things to **c**, **Heb 9:11** *1096*
a shadow of the good things to **c** **Heb 10:1** *3195*
'BEHOLD, I HAVE **C** **Heb 10:7** *2240*
"BEHOLD, I HAVE **C** TO DO YOUR WILL. **Heb 10:9** *2240*
WHILE, HE WHO IS COMING WILL **C**, **Heb 10:37** *2240*
Esau, even regarding things to **c**. **Heb 11:20** *3195*
For you have not **c** to *a mountain* **Heb 12:18** *4334*
But you have **c** to Mount Zion and **Heb 12:22** *4334*
seeking *the city* which is to **c**. **Heb 13:14** *3195*
mouth **c** *both* blessing and cursing. **Jas 3:10** *1831*
C now, you who say, **Jas 4:13** *33*
C now, you rich, weep and howl for **Jas 5:1** *33*
of the grace that *would* **c** to you **1Pe 1:10**
mockers will **c** with *their* mocking, **2Pe 3:3** *2064*
but for all to **c** to repentance. **2Pe 3:9** *5562*
of the Lord will **c** like a thief, **2Pe 3:10** *2240*
know that we have **c** to know Him, **1Jn 2:3**
"I have **c** to know Him," **1Jn 2:4**
has **c** in the flesh is from God; **1Jn 4:2** *2064*
We have **c** to know and have **1Jn 4:16** *1097*
we know that the Son of God has **c**, **1Jn 5:20** *2240*
c to you and speak face to face, **2Jn 1:12** *1096*
if I **c**, I will call attention to his deeds **3Jn 1:10** *2064*
is and who was and who is to **c**, **Rv 1:4** *2064*
is and who was and who is to **c**, **Rv 1:8** *2064*
who was dead, and has **c** to life, **Rv 2:8**
you have, hold fast until I **c**. **Rv 2:25** *2240*
wake up, I will **c** like a thief, **Rv 3:3** *2240*
at what hour I will **c** to you. **Rv 3:3** *2240*
them **c** and bow down at your feet, **Rv 3:9** *2240*
about to **c** upon the whole world, **Rv 3:10** *2064*
the door, I will **c** in to him and **Rv 3:20** *1525*
"**C** up here, and I will show you **Rv 4:1** *305*
Out from the throne **c** flashes of **Rv 4:5** *1607*
WAS AND WHO IS AND WHO IS TO **C**." **Rv 4:8** *2064*
as with a voice of thunder, "**C**." **Rv 6:1** *2064*
living creature saying, "**C**." **Rv 6:3** *2064*
living creature saying, "**C**." **Rv 6:5** *2064*
living creature saying, "**C**." **Rv 6:7** *2064*
great day of their wrath has **c**, **Rv 6:17** *2064*
and where have they **c** from?" **Rv 7:13** *2064*
c out of the great tribulation, **Rv 7:14** *2064*
"**C** up here." Then they went up into **Rv 11:12** *305*
authority of His Christ have **c**, **Rv 12:10** *1096*
the devil has **c** down to you, **Rv 12:12** *2597*
so that he even makes fire **c** down **Rv 13:13** *2597*
of the sword and has **c** to life. **Rv 13:14**
the hour of His judgment has **c**; **Rv 14:7** *2064*
for the hour to reap has **c**, **Rv 14:15** *2064*
WILL **C** AND WORSHIP BEFORE YOU, **Rv 15:4** *2240*
"**C** here, I will show you the **Rv 17:1** *1204*
and is about to **c** up out of the **Rv 17:8** *305*
that he was and is not and will **c**. **Rv 17:8** *3918b*
one is, the other has not yet **c**; **Rv 17:10** *2064*
"**C** out of her, my people, so **Rv 18:4** *1831*
in one day her plagues will **c**, **Rv 18:8** *2240*
in one hour your judgment has **c**.' **Rv 18:10** *2064*
marriage of the Lamb has **c** and His **Rv 19:7** *2064*
"**C**, assemble for the great supper **Rv 19:17** *1205*
The rest of the dead did not **c** to life **Rv 20:5**
and will **c** out to deceive the **Rv 20:8** *1831*
"**C** here, I will show you the **Rv 21:9** *1204*
and lying, shall ever **c** into it, **Rv 21:27** *1525*
Spirit and the bride say, "**C**." **Rv 22:17** *2064*
let the one who hears say, "**C**." **Rv 22:17** *2064*
And let the one who is thirsty **c**; **Rv 22:17** *2064*
Amen. **C**, Lord Jesus. **Rv 22:20** *2064*

COMELINESS

what **c** and beauty *will be* theirs! **Zch 9:17** 2898

COMELY

"The **c** and dainty one, the **Jer 6:2** 5000

COMES

of all that **c** out of the ark, even **Gn 9:10** 3318
that the maiden who **c** out to draw, **Gn 24:43** 3318
"The matter **c** from the LORD; **Gn 24:50** 3318
"If Esau **c** to the one company and **Gn 32:8** 935
"Here **c** this dreamer! **Gn 37:19** 935
your youngest brother **c** here! **Gn 42:15** 935
c the reckoning for his blood." **Gn 42:22** 1875
youngest brother **c** down with you, **Gn 44:23** 3381
between his feet, Until Shiloh **c**, **Gn 49:10** 935
Pharaoh, as he **c** out to the water, **Ex 8:20** 3318
when the hail **c** down on them, **Ex 9:19** 3381
they have a dispute, it **c** to me, **Ex 18:16** 935
"If he **c** alone, he shall go out **Ex 21:3** 935
him, and then he **c** to know *it*, **Lv 5:3**
him, and then he **c** to know *it*, **Lv 5:4**
may be eaten, on which water **c**, **Lv 11:34** 935
c in and makes an inspection and **Lv 14:48** 935
tent of meeting until he **c** out, **Lv 16:17** 3318
the ninth year when its crop **c** in. **Lv 25:22** 935
who **c** near shall be put to death. **Nu 1:51** 7131
"*Then* **c** the tribe of Zebulun, **Nu 2:7**
"Then **c** the tribe of Gad, **Nu 2:14**
"Then **c** the tribe of Benjamin, **Nu 2:22**
"Then **c** the tribe of Naphtali, **Nu 2:29**
c near shall be put to death." **Nu 3:10** 7131
if a spirit of jealousy **c** over him **Nu 5:14** 5674a
or if a spirit of jealousy **c** over **Nu 5:14** 5674a
or when a spirit of jealousy **c** **Nu 5:30** 5674a
until it **c** out of your nostrils **Nu 11:20** 3318
when he **c** from his mother's womb!" **Nu 12:12** 3318
"Everyone who **c** near, who comes **Nu 17:13** 7131
who **c** near to the tabernacle of **Nu 17:13** 7131
c near shall be put to death." **Nu 18:7** 7131
everyone who **c** into the tent and **Nu 19:14** 935
c out of the border of the Amorites, **Nu 21:13** 3318
jubilee of the sons of Israel **c**, **Nu 36:4** 1961
"Every daughter who **c** into **Nu 36:8** 3423
and the sign or the wonder **c** true, **Dt 13:2** 935
c out of the field every year. **Dt 14:22** 3318
"Now if a Levite **c** from any of **Dt 18:6** 935
and **c** whenever he desires to the **Dt 18:6** 935
and the wife of one **c** near to **Dt 25:11** 7126
who **c** from a distant land, **Dt 29:22** 935
when all Israel **c** to appear before **Dt 31:11** 935
if anyone **c** and inquires of you, **Jg 4:20** 935
and one company **c** by the way of **Jg 9:37** 935
then it shall be that whatever **c** **Jg 11:31** 3318
not eat anything that **c** from the vine **Jg 13:14** 3318
this night, and when morning **c**, **Ru 3:13** 1961
all that he says surely **c** true. **1Sa 9:6** 935
people will not eat until he **c**, **1Sa 9:13** 935
not sit down until he **c** here." **1Sa 16:11** 935
of the wicked **c** forth wickedness'; **1Sa 24:13** 3318
when your father **c** to see you, **2Sa 13:5** 935
word **c** from you to inform me." **2Sa 15:28** 935
a good man and **c** with good news." **2Sa 18:27** 935
and he **c** *and* takes an oath before **1Ki 8:31** 935
when he **c** from a far country for **1Ki 8:41** 935
he **c** and prays toward this house, **1Ki 8:42** 935
and it shall be, when he **c** to us, **2Ki 4:10** 935
"And now as this letter **c** to you, **2Ki 5:6** 935
Look, when the messenger **c**, **2Ki 6:32** 935
Now, when this letter **c** to you, **2Ki 10:2** 935
and whoever **c** within the ranks **2Ki 11:8** 935
he goes out and when he **c** in." **2Ki 11:8** 935
one **c** into the house of the LORD; **2Ki 12:9** 935
and he **c** *and* takes an oath before **2Ch 6:22** 935
when he **c** from a far country for **2Ch 6:32** 935
Whoever **c** to consecrate himself **2Ch 13:9** 935
"Whenever any dispute **c** to **2Ch 19:10** 935
he **c** in and when he goes out." **2Ch 23:7** 935
man or woman who **c** to the king **Es 4:11** 935
c at the sight of my food, **Jb 3:24** 935
"For what I fear **c** upon me, And **Jb 3:25** 857
I am not at rest, but turmoil **c**." **Jb 3:26** 935
be afraid of violence when it **c**. **Jb 5:21** 935
a flower he **c** forth and withers. **Jb 14:2** 3318
I will wait Until my change **c**. **Jb 14:14** 935
at peace the destroyer **c** upon him. **Jb 15:21** 935
drawn forth and **c** out of his back, **Jb 20:25** 3318
his cry When distress **c** upon him? **Jb 27:9** 935
"The earth, from it **c** food, **Jb 28:5** 3318
"Out of the south **c** the storm, **Jb 37:9** 935
of the north **c** golden *splendor;* **Jb 37:22** 857
From You **c** my praise in the great **Ps 22:25**
But a shout of joy **c** in **Ps 30:5**
And when he **c** to see *me,* he speaks **Ps 41:6** 935
Nor from the desert **c** exaltation; **Ps 75:6**
morning my prayer **c** before You. **Ps 88:13** 6923
one who **c** in the name of the LORD; **Ps 118:26** 935
My help **c** from the LORD, Who **Ps 121:2**
I will mock when your dread **c**, **Pr 1:26** 935
When your dread **c** like a storm And **Pr 1:27** 935
calamity **c** like a whirlwind, **Pr 1:27** 857
onslaught of the wicked when it **c**; **Pr 3:25** 935
And behold, a woman **c** to meet **Pr 7:10**
When pride **c**, then comes dishonor, **Pr 11:2** 935
When pride comes, then **c** dishonor, **Pr 11:2** 935
who opens wide his lips **c** to ruin. **Pr 13:3**
insolence **c** nothing but strife, **Pr 13:10** 5414
But much revenue **c** by **Pr 14:4**
And before honor **c** humility. **Pr 15:33**
When a wicked man **c**, **Pr 18:3** 935
wicked man comes, contempt also **c**, **Pr 18:3** 935
And with dishonor **c** scorn. **Pr 18:3**
Until another **c** and examines him. **Pr 18:17** 935
A man of *too many* friends **c** **Pr 18:24**
But everyone who is hasty **c** **Pr 21:5**
And who knows the ruin *that* **c** **Pr 24:22**
c out a vessel for the smith; **Pr 25:4** 3318
But justice for man **c** from the **Pr 29:26**
goes and a generation **c**, **Ec 1:4** 935
the dream **c** through much effort and **Ec 5:3** 935
for it **c** in futility and goes into **Ec 6:4** 935
God **c** forth with both of them. **Ec 7:18** 3318
no *tree* cutter **c** up against us.' **Is 14:8** 5927
For smoke **c** from the north, And **Is 14:31** 935
And **c** to his sanctuary to pray, **Is 16:12** 935
on, It **c** from the wilderness, **Is 21:1** 935
behold, here **c** a troop of riders, **Is 21:9** 935
"Morning **c** but also night. **Is 21:12** 857
also **c** from the LORD of hosts, **Is 28:29** 3318
collapse **c** suddenly in an instant, **Is 30:13** 935
of the LORD **c** from a remote place; **Is 30:27** 935
will hail when the forest **c** down, **Is 32:19** 3381
"Lo, your salvation **c**; **Is 62:11** 935
Who is this who **c** from Edom, With **Is 63:1** 935
The sound of a report! Behold, it **c** **Jer 10:22** 935
will not see when prosperity **c**, **Jer 17:6** 935
And will not fear when the heat **c**; **Jer 17:8** 935
until the time of his own land **c**; **Jer 27:7** 935
when the word of the prophet **c** to **Jer 28:9** 935
no one **c** to the appointed feasts. **La 1:4** 935
there who speaks and it **c** to pass, **La 3:37** 1961
Our wood **c** *to us* at a price. **La 5:4** 935
'When anguish **c**, they will seek **Ezk 7:25** 935
and *then* **c** to the prophet, **Ezk 14:4** 935
and *then* **c** to the prophet to **Ezk 14:7** 935
"What **c** into your mind will **Ezk 20:32** 5927
Behold, it **c** and it will happen,' **Ezk 21:7** 935
until He **c** whose right it is, **Ezk 21:27** 935
when it **c**, then you will know that **Ezk 24:24** 935
for behold, it **c**!" **Ezk 30:9** 935
and a sword **c** and takes him away, **Ezk 33:4** 935
c and takes a person from them, **Ezk 33:6** 935
is which **c** forth from the LORD.' **Ezk 33:30** 3318
"So when it **c** to pass **Ezk 33:33** 935
c against the land of Israel," **Ezk 38:18** 935
"But he who **c** against him will do **Da 11:16** 935
Like an eagle *the enemy* **c** against **Hos 8:1**
He **c** to rain righteousness on you. **Hos 10:12** 935
From Me **c** your fruit. **Hos 14:8** 4672
and awesome day of the LORD **c**. **Jl 2:31** 935
destruction **c** upon the fortress. **Am 5:9** 935
To whom the house of Israel **c**. **Am 6:1** 935
When morning **c**, they do it, For it **Mi 2:1**
justice **c** out perverted. **Hab 1:4** 3318
God **c** from Teman, And the Holy One **Hab 3:3** 935
And plague **c** after Him. **Hab 3:5** 3318
anger of the LORD **c** upon you, **Zph 2:2** 935
day of the LORD's anger **c** upon you. **Zph 2:2** 935
it **c** to little; when you bring **Hg 1:9**
and he **c**, and to my slave, **Mt 8:9** *2064*
of Israel until the Son of Man **c**. **Mt 10:23** *2064*

and when it **c**, it finds	**Mt 12:44**	*2064*
the evil *one* **c** and snatches away	**Mt 13:19**	*2064*
and take the first fish that **c** up;	**Mt 17:27**	*305*
whom the stumbling block **c**!	**Mt 18:7**	*2064*
HE WHO **C** IN THE NAME OF THE LORD	**Mt 21:9**	*2064*
when the owner of the vineyard **c**,	**Mt 21:40**	*2064*
'BLESSED IS HE WHO **C** IN THE NAME	**Mt 23:39**	*2064*
as the lightning **c** from the east and	**Mt 24:27**	*1831*
master finds so doing when he **c**.	**Mt 24:46**	*2064*
the Son of Man **c** in His glory,	**Mt 25:31**	*2064*
immediately Satan **c** and takes away	**Mk 4:15**	*2064*
when He **c** in the glory of His Father	**Mk 8:38**	*2064*
HE WHO **C** IN THE NAME OF THE LORD	**Mk 11:9**	*2064*
"Everyone who **c** to Me and hears	**Lk 6:47**	*2064*
and he **c**, and to my slave,	**Lk 7:8**	*2064*
then the devil **c** and takes away	**Lk 8:12**	*2064*
ashamed of him when He **c** in His glory,	**Lk 9:26**	*2064*
"And when it **c**, it finds it swept	**Lk 11:25**	*2064*
in heaven, where no thief **c** near nor	**Lk 12:33**	*1448*
door to him when he **c** and knocks.	**Lk 12:36**	*2064*
will find on the alert when he **c**;	**Lk 12:37**	*2064*
"Whether he **c** in the second	**Lk 12:38**	*2064*
master finds so doing when he **c**.	**Lk 12:43**	*2064*
Me until *the time* **c** when you say,	**Lk 13:35**	*2240*
WHO **C** IN THE NAME OF THE LORD!'	**Lk 13:35**	*2064*
the one who has invited you **c**,	**Lk 14:10**	*2064*
"If anyone **c** to Me, and does not	**Lk 14:26**	*2064*
"And when he **c** home, he calls	**Lk 15:6**	*2064*
However, when the Son of Man **c**,	**Lk 18:8**	*2064*
WHO **C** IN THE NAME OF THE LORD;	**Lk 19:38**	*2064*
on until the kingdom of God **c**."	**Lk 22:18**	*2064*
'He who **c** after me has a higher	**Jn 1:15**	*2064*
"*It is* He who **c** after me, the	**Jn 1:27**	*2064*
'After me **c** a Man who has a higher	**Jn 1:30**	*2064*
but do not know where it **c** from and	**Jn 3:8**	*2064*
the truth **c** to the Light,	**Jn 3:21**	*2064*
"He who **c** from above is above	**Jn 3:31**	*2064*
He who **c** from heaven is above all.	**Jn 3:31**	*2064*
when that One **c**, He will declare	**Jn 4:25**	*2064*
months, and *then* **c** the harvest'?	**Jn 4:35**	*2064*
if another **c** in his own name, you	**Jn 5:43**	*2064*
that which **c** down out of heaven,	**Jn 6:33**	*2597*
he who **c** to Me will not hunger,	**Jn 6:35**	*2064*
and the one who **c** to Me I will	**Jn 6:37**	*2064*
learned from the Father, **c** to Me.	**Jn 6:45**	*2064*
bread which **c** down out of heaven,	**Jn 6:50**	*2597*
"When the Christ **c**, He will not	**Jn 7:31**	*2064*
c from the descendants of David,	**Jn 7:42**	*2064*
"The thief **c** only to steal and	**Jn 10:10**	*2064*
even He who **c** into the world."	**Jn 11:27**	*2064*
HE WHO **C** IN THE NAME OF THE LORD	**Jn 12:13**	*2064*
telling you before *it* **c** to pass,	**Jn 13:19**	*1096*
no one **c** to the Father but	**Jn 14:6**	*2064*
"When the Helper **c**, whom I will	**Jn 15:26**	*2064*
to you, so that when their hour **c**,	**Jn 16:4**	*2064*
"And He, when He **c**, will convict	**Jn 16:8**	*2064*
when He, the Spirit of truth, **c**,	**Jn 16:13**	*2064*
and the faith which **c** through Him	**Ac 3:16**	
him before he **c** near *the place*."	**Ac 23:15**	*1448*
"When Lysias the commander **c** down,	**Ac 24:22**	*2597*
for through the Law **c**	**Ro 3:20**	
So faith **c** from hearing,	**Ro 10:17**	
but wait until the Lord **c** who will	**1Co 4:5**	*2064*
the Lord's death until He **c**.	**1Co 11:26**	*2064*
but when the perfect **c**,	**1Co 13:10**	*2064*
then **c** the end, when He hands	**1Co 15:24**	
Now if Timothy **c**, see that he is	**1Co 16:10**	*2064*
For if one **c** and preaches another	**2Co 11:4**	*2064*
for if righteousness **c** through	**Ga 2:21**	
c upon the sons of disobedience.	**Eph 5:6**	*2064*
the fruit of righteousness which **c**	**Php 1:11**	
the righteousness which **c** from	**Php 3:9**	
wealth that **c** from the full assurance	**Col 2:2**	
if he **c** to you, welcome him);	**Col 4:10**	*2064*
when He **c** to be glorified in His	**2Th 1:10**	*2064*
come unless the apostasy **c** first,	**2Th 2:3**	*2064*
men to die once and after this **c**	**Heb 9:27**	
when He **c** into the world,	**Heb 10:5**	*1525*
for he who **c** to God must believe	**Heb 11:6**	*4334*
one **c** short of the grace of God;	**Heb 12:15**	*5302*
released, with whom, if he **c** soon,	**Heb 13:23**	*2064*
For if a man **c** into your assembly	**Jas 2:2**	*1525*
and there also **c** in a poor man in	**Jas 2:2**	*1525*
not that which **c** down from above,	**Jas 3:15**	*2718*
which **c** upon you for your testing,	**1Pe 4:12**	*1096*
If anyone **c** to you and does not	**2Jn 1:10**	*2064*
which **c** down out of heaven from My	**Rv 3:12**	*2597*
the beast that **c** up out of the	**Rv 11:7**	*305*
and when he **c**, he must remain a	**Rv 17:10**	*2064*
From His mouth **c** a sharp sword,	**Rv 19:15**	*1607*

COMFORT

all his daughters arose to **c** him,	**Gn 37:35**	5162
and his relatives came to **c** him.	**1Ch 7:22**	5162
to sympathize with him and **c** him.	**Jb 2:11**	5162
'My bed will **c** me, My couch will	**Jb 7:13**	5162
"How then will you vainly **c** me,	**Jb 21:34**	5162
"I go about mourning without **c**;	**Jb 30:28**	
Your rod and Your staff, they **c** me.	**Ps 23:4**	5162
my greatness And turn *to* **c** me.	**Ps 71:21**	5162
This is my **c** in my affliction,	**Ps 119:50**	5165
from of old, O LORD, And **c** myself.	**Ps 119:52**	5162
O may Your lovingkindness **c** me,	**Ps 119:76**	5162
"When will You **c** me?"	**Ps 119:82**	5162
your son, and he will give you **c**;	**Pr 29:17**	5117
that they had no one to **c** *them;*	**Ec 4:1**	5162
but they had no one to **c** *them.*	**Ec 4:1**	5162
turned away, And You **c** me.	**Is 12:1**	5162
Do not try to **c** me concerning the	**Is 22:4**	5162
"**C**, O comfort My people,"	**Is 40:1**	5162
"Comfort, O **c** My people,"	**Is 40:1**	5162
Indeed, the LORD will **c** Zion;	**Is 51:3**	5162
He will **c** all her waste places.	**Is 51:3**	5162
How shall I **c** you?	**Is 51:19**	5162
c to him and to his mourners,	**Is 57:18**	5150
To **c** all who mourn,	**Is 61:2**	5162
mother comforts, so I will **c** you;	**Is 66:13**	5162
them, to **c** anyone for the dead,	**Jer 16:7**	5162
into joy And will **c** them	**Jer 31:13**	5162
to **c** her Among all her lovers.	**La 1:2**	5162
There is no one to **c** her;	**La 1:17**	5162
There is no one to **c** me;	**La 1:21**	5162
what shall I liken you as I **c** you,	**La 2:13**	5162
"Then they will **c** you when you	**Ezk 14:23**	5162
and the LORD will again **c** Zion and	**Zch 1:17**	5162
tell false dreams; They **c** in vain.	**Zch 10:2**	5162
you are receiving your **c** in full.	**Lk 6:24**	*3874*
and in the **c** of the Holy Spirit,	**Ac 9:31**	*3874*
of mercies and God of all **c**,	**2Co 1:3**	*3874*
to **c** those who are in any affliction	**2Co 1:4**	*3870*
with the **c** with which we ourselves	**2Co 1:4**	*3874*
our **c** is abundant through Christ.	**2Co 1:5**	*3874*
it is for your **c** and salvation;	**2Co 1:6**	*3874*
are comforted, it is for your **c**,	**2Co 1:6**	*3874*
so also you are *sharers* of our **c**.	**2Co 1:7**	*3874*
should rather forgive and **c** *him,*	**2Co 2:7**	*3870*
I am filled with **c**;	**2Co 7:4**	*3874*
but also by the **c** with which he	**2Co 7:7**	*3874*
And besides our **c**, we rejoiced	**2Co 7:13**	*3874*
us, and that he may **c** your hearts.	**Eph 6:22**	*3870*
c one another with these words.	**1Th 4:18**	*3870*
eternal **c** and good hope by grace,	**2Th 2:16**	*3874*
c and strengthen your hearts in	**2Th 2:17**	*3870*
have much joy and **c** in your love,	**Phm 1:7**	*3874*

COMFORTED

was **c** after his mother's death.	**Gn 24:67**	5162
him, but he refused to be **c**.	**Gn 37:35**	5162
c them and spoke kindly to them.	**Gn 50:21**	5162
for you have **c** me and indeed have	**Ru 2:13**	5162
Then David **c** his wife Bathsheba,	**2Sa 12:24**	5162
for he was **c** concerning Amnon,	**2Sa 13:39**	5162
troops, As one who **c** the mourners.	**Jb 29:25**	5162
and they consoled him and **c** him	**Jb 42:11**	5162
My soul refused to be **c**.	**Ps 77:2**	5162
O LORD, have helped me and **c** me.	**Ps 86:17**	5162
For the LORD has **c** His people And	**Is 49:13**	5162
For the LORD has **c** His people,	**Is 52:9**	5162
one, storm-tossed, *and* not **c**,	**Is 54:11**	5162
And you will be **c** in Jerusalem."	**Is 66:13**	5162
refuses to be **c** for her children,	**Jer 31:15**	5162
then you will be **c** for the	**Ezk 14:22**	5162
were **c** in the earth beneath.	**Ezk 31:16**	5162
and he will be **c** for all his	**Ezk 32:31**	5162
AND SHE REFUSED TO BE **C**,	**Mt 2:18**	*3870*
who mourn, for they shall be **c**.	**Mt 5:4**	*3870*
but now he is being **c** here,	**Lk 16:25**	*3870*
the boy alive, and were greatly **c**.	**Ac 20:12**	*3870*
which we ourselves are **c** by God.	**2Co 1:4**	*3870*
or if we are **c**, it is for your	**2Co 1:6**	*3870*
c us by the coming of Titus;	**2Co 7:6**	*3870*
with which he was **c** in you,	**2Co 7:7**	*3870*
For this reason we have been **c**.	**2Co 7:13**	*3870*
rejoice, be made complete, be **c**,	**2Co 13:11**	*3870*
c about you through your faith;	**1Th 3:7**	*3870*

COMFORTER

She has no **c**. "See, O LORD, my	**La 1:9**	5162
Because far from me is a **c**,	**La 1:16**	5162

COMFORTERS

in that he has sent **c** to you?	**1Ch 19:3**	5162
Sorry **c** are you all.	**Jb 16:2**	5162
but there was none, And for **c**,	**Ps 69:20**	5162
Where will I seek **c** for you?"	**Na 3:7**	5162

COMFORTING

the word of my lord the king be **c**,	**2Sa 14:17**	4496
be satisfied with her **c** breasts,	**Is 66:11**	8575
me with gracious words, **c** words.	**Zch 1:13**	5150

COMFORTS

"I, even I, am He who **c** you.	**Is 51:12**	5162
"As one whom his mother **c**,	**Is 66:13**	5162
who **c** us in all our affliction so	**2Co 1:4**	*3870*
But God, who **c** the depressed,	**2Co 7:6**	*3870*

COMING

the city are **c** out to draw water;	**Gn 24:13**	3318
looked, and behold, camels were **c**.	**Gn 24:63**	935
daughter **c** with the sheep."	**Gn 29:6**	935
furthermore he is **c** to meet you,	**Gn 32:6**	1980
looked, and behold, Esau was **c**,	**Gn 33:1**	935
of Ishmaelites was **c** from Gilead,	**Gn 37:25**	935
are **c** in all the land of Egypt;	**Gn 41:29**	935
of these good years that are **c**,	**Gn 41:35**	935
buy grain among those who were **c**,	**Gn 42:5**	935
the present for Joseph's **c** at noon;	**Gn 43:25**	935
behold, he is **c** out to meet you;	**Ex 4:14**	3318
am **c** to you with your wife and her	**Ex 18:6**	935
first pair of branches **c** out	**Ex 25:35**	
second pair of branches **c** out	**Ex 25:35**	
third pair of branches **c** out	**Ex 25:35**	
branches **c** out of the lampstand.	**Ex 25:35**	3318
Moses was **c** down from Mount Sinai	**Ex 34:29**	3381
he was **c** down from the mountain),	**Ex 34:29**	3381
first pair of branches **c** out	**Ex 37:21**	
second pair of branches **c** out	**Ex 37:21**	
third pair of branches **c** out	**Ex 37:21**	
branches **c** out of the lampstand.	**Ex 37:21**	3318
c near was to be put to death.	**Nu 3:38**	7131
their **c** near to the sanctuary."	**Nu 8:19**	5066
was **c** by the way of Atharim,	**Nu 21:1**	935
beg you, hinder you from **c** to me;	**Nu 22:16**	1980
Balak heard that Balaam was **c**,	**Nu 22:36**	935
of the **c** of the sons of Israel.	**Nu 33:40**	935
war and for going out and **c** in.	**Jos 14:11**	935
spies saw a man **c** out of the city and	**Jg 1:24**	3318
'Why does his chariot delay in **c**?	**Jg 5:28**	935
people are **c** down from the tops of	**Jg 9:36**	3381
people are **c** down from the highest	**Jg 9:37**	3381
the people **c** out from the city,	**Jg 9:43**	3318
his daughter was **c** out to meet him	**Jg 11:34**	3318
Lo, the day is **c** to an end;	**Jg 19:9**	2583
an old man was **c** out of the field	**Jg 19:16**	935
the woman who is **c** into your home	**Ru 4:11**	935
the days are **c** when I will break	**1Sa 2:31**	935
Samuel was **c** out toward them to go	**1Sa 9:14**	3318
Now a day before Saul's **c**,	**1Sa 9:15**	935
meet a group of prophets **c** down	**1Sa 10:5**	3381
Saul was **c** from the field behind	**1Sa 11:5**	935
Hebrews are **c** out of the holes	**1Sa 14:11**	3318
way while he was **c** up from Egypt.	**1Sa 15:2**	5927
was **c** up from the army of the	**1Sa 17:23**	5927
you seen this man who is **c** up?	**1Sa 17:25**	5927
Surely he is **c** up to defy Israel.	**1Sa 17:25**	5927
It happened as they were **c**,	**1Sa 18:6**	935
"I saw the son of Jesse **c** to Nob,	**1Sa 22:9**	935
behold, I am **c** after you."	**1Sa 25:19**	935
riding on her donkey and **c** down by	**1Sa 25:20**	3381
his men were **c** down toward her;	**1Sa 25:20**	3381
knew that Saul was definitely **c**.	**1Sa 26:4**	935
"I see a divine being **c** up out of the	**1Sa 28:13**	5927
"An old man is **c** up, and he is	**1Sa 28:14**	5927
and your going out and your **c** in	**1Sa 29:6**	935
day of your **c** to me to this day.	**1Sa 29:6**	935
learn of your going out and **c** in and	**2Sa 3:25**	4126
many people were **c** from the road	**2Sa 13:34**	1980
as David was **c** to the summit,	**2Sa 15:32**	935
the wife of Jeroboam is **c** to	**1Ki 14:5**	935
of her feet **c** in the doorway,	**1Ki 14:6**	935
out or **c** in to Asa king of Judah.	**1Ki 15:17**	935
man's hand is **c** up from the sea."	**1Ki 18:44**	5927
the Arameans are **c** down there."	**2Ki 6:9**	5185
met Jehonadab the son of Rechab **c**	**2Ki 10:15**	
the **c** of King Ahaz from Damascus.	**2Ki 16:11**	935
And your going out and your **c** in,	**2Ki 19:27**	935
the days are **c** when all that is in	**2Ki 20:17**	935
For He is **c** to judge the earth.	**1Ch 16:33**	935
out or **c** in to Asa king of Judah.	**2Ch 16:1**	935
"A great multitude is **c** against	**2Ch 20:2**	935
by **c** to drive us out from Your	**2Ch 20:11**	935
multitude who are **c** against us;	**2Ch 20:12**	935
those who were **c** from the battle,	**2Ch 28:12**	935
I am not **c** against you today	**2Ch 35:21**	
Now in the second year of their **c**	**Ezr 3:8**	935
for they are **c** to kill you,	**Ne 6:10**	935
they are **c** to kill you at night."	**Ne 6:10**	935
also, concerning what is **c** up.	**Jb 36:33**	5927
a bridegroom **c** out of his chamber;	**Ps 19:5**	3318
will be told of the Lord to the **c**	**Ps 22:30**	
For He sees his day is **c**.	**Ps 37:13**	935
Before the LORD, for He is **c**,	**Ps 96:13**	935
For He is **c** to judge the earth.	**Ps 96:13**	935
for He is **c** to judge the earth;	**Ps 98:9**	935
guard your going out and your **c** in	**Ps 121:8**	935
the head, **C** down upon the beard,	**Ps 133:2**	3381
C down upon the edge of his	**Ps 133:2**	3381
C down upon the mountains of Zion;	**Ps 133:3**	3381
the **c** days all will be forgotten.	**Ec 2:16**	935
Behold, he is **c**, Climbing on the	**SS 2:8**	935
"What is this **c** up from the	**SS 3:6**	5927
is this **c** up from the wilderness	**SS 8:5**	5927
They are **c** from a far country,	**Is 13:5**	935
Behold, the day of the LORD is **c**,	**Is 13:9**	935
And your going out and your **c** in And	**Is 37:28**	935
the days are **c** when all that is in	**Is 39:6**	935
Or announce to us what is **c**;	**Is 41:22**	935
declare to them the things that are **c**	**Is 44:7**	857
the time is **c** to gather all	**Is 66:18**	935
a people is **c** from the north land,	**Jer 6:22**	935
"Therefore, behold, days are **c**,"	**Jer 7:32**	935
"Behold, the days are **c**,"	**Jer 9:25**	935
and see Those **c** from the north.	**Jer 13:20**	935
"Therefore behold, days are **c**,"	**Jer 16:14**	935
carrying a load and **c** in through	**Jer 17:27**	935
therefore, behold, days are **c**,"	**Jer 19:6**	935
"Behold, *the* days are **c**,"	**Jer 23:5**	935
behold, *the* days are **c**,"	**Jer 23:7**	935
'For behold, days are **c**,'	**Jer 30:3**	935
"Behold, days are **c**,"	**Jer 31:27**	935
"Behold, days are **c**,"	**Jer 31:31**	935
"Behold, days are **c**,"	**Jer 31:38**	935
of Shallum your uncle is **c** to you,	**Jer 32:7**	935
are **c** to fight with the Chaldeans and	**Jer 33:5**	935
'Behold, days are **c**,'	**Jer 33:14**	935
Now Jeremiah was *still* **c** in and	**Jer 37:4**	935
about the **c** of Nebuchadnezzar king	**Jer 46:13**	935
But a horsefly is **c** from the north	**Jer 46:20**	935
is coming from the north—it is **c**!	**Jer 46:20**	935
On account of the day that is **c** To	**Jer 47:4**	935
behold, the days are **c**,"	**Jer 48:12**	935
"Terror, pit and snare are **c**	**Jer 48:43**	
behold, the days are **c**,"	**Jer 49:2**	935
a people is **c** from the north,	**Jer 50:41**	935
days are **c** When I will punish the	**Jer 51:47**	935
behold, the days are **c**,"	**Jer 51:52**	935
the destroyer is **c** against her,	**Jer 51:56**	935
a storm wind was **c** from the north,	**Ezk 1:4**	935
The end is **c** on the four corners	**Ezk 7:2**	935
unique disaster, behold it is **c**!	**Ezk 7:5**	935
'An end is **c**; the end has come!	**Ezk 7:6**	935
'Behold, the day! Behold, it is **c**!	**Ezk 7:10**	935

'Because of the news that is c;	Ezk 21:7	935
it is c and I will act.	Ezk 24:14	935
he sees the sword c upon the land and	Ezk 33:3	935
c and does not blow the trumpet and	Ezk 33:6	935
it is c and it shall be done,"	Ezk 39:8	935
was c from the way of the east.	Ezk 43:2	935
beasts were c up from the sea,	Da 7:3	5559b
flowing And c out from before Him;	Da 7:10	5312
One like a Son of Man was c,	Da 7:13	858
with the longer one c up last.	Da 8:3	5927
a male goat was c from the west	Da 8:5	935
and one of them will keep on c and	Da 11:10	935
the LORD c up from the wilderness;	Hos 13:15	5927
For the day of the LORD is c;	Jl 2:1	935
the days are c upon you When they	Am 4:2	935
"Behold, days are c,"	Am 8:11	935
"Behold, days are c,"	Am 9:13	935
LORD is c forth from His place.	Mi 1:3	3318
the LORD, Near and c very quickly;	Zph 1:14	4118a
"What are these c to do?"	Zch 1:21	935
angel was c out to meet him,	Zch 2:3	3318
for behold I am c and I will dwell	Zch 2:10	935
and there two women were c out	Zch 5:9	3318
four chariots were c forth from	Zch 6:1	3318
Behold, your king is c to you;	Zch 9:9	935
a day is c for the LORD when the	Zch 14:1	935
you delight, behold, He is c,"	Mal 3:1	935
who can endure the day of His c?	Mal 3:2	935
"For behold, the day is c,	Mal 4:1	935
that is c will set them ablaze,"	Mal 4:1	935
the c of the great and terrible day	Mal 4:5	935
After c into the house they saw	Mt 2:11	2064
and Sadducees c for baptism,	Mt 3:7	2064
but He who is c after me is mightier	Mt 3:11	2064
from Galilee at the Jordan c to	Mt 3:13	2064
as they were c out of the tombs.	Mt 8:28	1831
the Son of Man c in His kingdom."	Mt 16:28	2064
were c down from the mountain,	Mt 17:9	2597
Elijah is c and will restore all things;	Mt 17:11	2064
do not hinder them from c to Me;	Mt 19:14	2064
'BEHOLD YOUR KING IS C TO YOU,	Mt 21:5	2064
what *will be* the sign of Your c,	Mt 24:3	3952
will the c of the Son of Man be.	Mt 24:27	3952
the SON OF MAN C ON THE CLOUDS	Mt 24:30	2064
"For the c of the Son of Man will	Mt 24:37	3952
will the c of the Son of Man be.	Mt 24:39	3952
not know which day your Lord is c.	Mt 24:42	2064
time of the night the thief was c,	Mt 24:43	2064
for the Son of Man is c at an hour	Mt 24:44	2064
master is not c for a long time,'	Mt 24:48	5549
after two days the Passover is c,	Mt 26:2	1096
and C ON THE CLOUDS OF HEAVEN."	Mt 26:64	2064
As they were c out,	Mt 27:32	1831
and c out of the tombs after His	Mt 27:53	1831
One is c who is mightier than I,	Mk 1:7	2064
Immediately c up out of the water,	Mk 1:10	305
were c to Him from everywhere.	Mk 1:45	2064
all the people were c to Him,	Mk 2:13	2064
And c out, the unclean spirits	Mk 5:13	1831
were many *people* c and going,	Mk 6:31	2064
were c down from the mountain,	Mk 9:9	2597
the c kingdom of our father David;	Mk 11:10	2064
see THE SON OF MAN C IN CLOUDS	Mk 13:26	2064
when the master of the house is c,	Mk 13:35	2064
After c, Judas immediately went	Mk 14:45	2064
and C WITH THE CLOUDS OF HEAVEN."	Mk 14:62	2064
a passer-by c from the country,	Mk 15:21	2064
And c in, he said to her,	Lk 1:28	1525
One is c who is mightier than I,	Lk 3:16	2064
Demons also were c out of many,	Lk 4:41	1831
c from Him and healing *them* all.	Lk 6:19	1831
a large crowd was c together,	Lk 8:4	4896
at what hour the thief was c,	Lk 12:39	2064
for the Son of Man is c at an hour	Lk 12:40	2064
master will be a long time in c,'	Lk 12:45	2064
'A shower is c,' and so it turns	Lk 12:54	2064
to encounter the one c against him	Lk 14:31	2064
were c near Him to listen to Him.	Lk 15:1	1448
dogs were c and licking his sores.	Lk 16:21	2064
to when the kingdom of God was c,	Lk 17:20	2064
not c with signs to be observed;	Lk 17:20	2064
that city, and she kept c to him,	Lk 18:3	2064
continually c she will wear me out.'"	Lk 18:5	2064
things which are c upon the world;	Lk 21:26	1904
THE SON OF MAN C IN A CLOUD	Lk 21:27	2064
of Cyrene, c in from the country,	Lk 23:26	2064
the days are c when they will say,	Lk 23:29	2064
also mocked Him, c up to Him,	Lk 23:36	4334
Light which, c into the world,	Jn 1:9	2064
next day he saw Jesus c to him and	Jn 1:29	2064
Jesus saw Nathanael c to Him,	Jn 1:47	2064
were c and were being baptized	Jn 3:23	3854
baptizing and all are c to Him."	Jn 3:26	2064
an hour is c when neither in this	Jn 4:21	2064
"But an hour is c, and now is,	Jn 4:23	2064
"I know that Messiah is c	Jn 4:25	2064
of the city, and were c to Him.	Jn 4:30	2064
is stirred up, but while I am c,	Jn 5:7	2064
to you, an hour is c and now is,	Jn 5:25	2064
for an hour is c, in which all who	Jn 5:28	2064
a large crowd was c to Him,	Jn 6:5	2064
and all the people were c to Him;	Jn 8:2	2064
night is c when no one can work.	Jn 9:4	2064
of the sheep, sees the wolf c,	Jn 10:12	2064
when she heard that Jesus was c,	Jn 11:20	2064
got up quickly and was c to Him.	Jn 11:29	2064
that Jesus was c to Jerusalem,	Jn 12:12	2064
BEHOLD, YOUR KING IS C,	Jn 12:15	2064
for the ruler of the world is c,	Jn 14:30	2064

but an hour is c for everyone who	Jn 16:2	2064
an hour is c when I will no	Jn 16:25	2064
"Behold, an hour is c,	Jn 16:32	2064
the things that were c upon Him,	Jn 18:4	2064
but c to Jesus, when they saw that	Jn 19:33	2064
of Jerusalem were c together,	Ac 5:16	4905
the c of the Righteous One,	Ac 7:52	1660
they were c out *of them* shouting	Ac 8:7	1831
on the road by which you were c,	Ac 9:17	2064
"Do not delay in c to us."	Ac 9:38	1330
object like a great sheet c down,	Ac 10:11	2597
an object c down like a	Ac 11:5	2597
proclaimed before His c a baptism	Ac 13:24	4383, 1529
one is c after me the sandals of	Ac 13:25	2064
in Him who was c after him,	Ac 19:4	2064
of those who had believed kept c,	Ac 19:18	2064
And c to us, he took Paul's belt	Ac 21:11	2064
were c to him and getting cured.	Ac 28:9	4334
of God I may succeed in c to you.	Ro 1:10	2064
often been prevented from c to you;	Ro 15:22	2064
as though I were not c to you.	1Co 4:18	2064
those who are Christ's at His c,	1Co 15:23	3952
I rejoice over the c of	1Co 16:17	3952
ourselves to consider anything as c	2Co 3:5	
comforted us by the c of Titus;	2Co 7:6	3952
and not only by his c,	2Co 7:7	3952
is the third time I am c to you.	2Co 13:1	2064
the c of certain men from James,	Ga 2:12	2064
Jesus through my c to you again.	Php 1:26	3952
I myself also will be c shortly.	Php 2:24	2064
your part read my letter *that is* c	Col 4:16	
that our c to you was not in vain,	1Th 2:1	1529
of our Lord Jesus at His c?	1Th 2:19	3952
the c of our Lord Jesus with all His	1Th 3:13	3952
remain until the c of the Lord,	1Th 4:15	3952
at the c of our Lord Jesus Christ.	1Th 5:23	3952
to the c of our Lord Jesus Christ and	2Th 2:1	3952
an end by the appearance of His c;	2Th 2:8	3952
the one whose c is in accord with	2Th 2:9	3952
"BEHOLD, DAYS ARE C,	Heb 8:8	2064
WHILE, HE WHO IS C WILL COME,	Heb 10:37	2064
c down from the Father of lights,	Jas 1:17	2597
miseries which are c upon you.	Jas 5:1	1904
brethren, until the c of the Lord.	Jas 5:7	3952
for the c of the Lord is near.	Jas 5:8	3952
And c to Him as to a living stone which	1Pe 2:4	4334
and c of our Lord Jesus Christ,	2Pe 1:16	3952
"Where is the promise of His c?	2Pe 3:4	3952
hastening the c of the day of God,	2Pe 3:12	3952
as you heard that antichrist is c,	1Jn 2:18	2064
away from Him in shame at His c.	1Jn 2:28	3952
which you have heard that it is c,	1Jn 4:3	2064
Jesus Christ *as* c in the flesh.	2Jn 1:7	2064
BEHOLD, HE IS C WITH THE CLOUDS,	Rv 1:7	2064
or else I am c to you and will	Rv 2:5	2064
or else I am c to you quickly, and	Rv 2:16	2064
'I am c quickly; hold fast what you	Rv 3:11	2064
are still c after these things.	Rv 9:12	2064
strong angel c down out of heaven,	Rv 10:1	2597
the third woe is c quickly.	Rv 11:14	2064
I saw a beast c up out of the sea,	Rv 13:1	305
beast c up out of the earth;	Rv 13:11	305
And I saw c out of the mouth of	Rv 16:13	
("Behold, I am c like a thief.	Rv 16:15	2064
another angel c down from heaven,	Rv 18:1	2597
I saw an angel c down from heaven,	Rv 20:1	2597
c down out of heaven from God,	Rv 21:2	2597
c down out of heaven from God,	Rv 21:10	2597
c from the throne of God and of	Rv 22:1	1607
"And behold, I am c quickly.	Rv 22:7	2064
"Behold, I am c quickly, and My	Rv 22:12	2064
"Yes, I am c quickly."	Rv 22:20	2064

COMMAND

so that he may c his	Gn 18:19	6680
my son, listen to me as I c you.	Gn 27:8	6680
c all my people shall do homage;	Gn 41:40	6310
according to the c of Pharaoh,	Gn 45:21	6310
"You shall speak all that I c you,	Ex 7:2	6680
according to the c of the LORD,	Ex 17:1	6310
So Moses issued a c,	Ex 36:6	6680
according to the c of Moses,	Ex 38:21	6310
"C Aaron and his sons, saying,	Lv 6:9	6680
"The priest shall then c that they	Lv 14:36	6680
"C the sons of Israel that they	Lv 24:2	6680
c of the LORD might be made clear	Lv 24:12	6310
c of the LORD by their families,	Nu 3:39	6310
to his sons, at the c of the LORD,	Nu 3:51	6310
at the c of Aaron and his sons;	Nu 4:27	6310
"C the sons of Israel that they	Nu 5:2	6680
the LORD will c concerning you."	Nu 9:8	6680
At the c of the LORD the sons of	Nu 9:18	6310
the c of the LORD they would camp;	Nu 9:18	6310
according to the c of the LORD	Nu 9:20	6310
to the c of the LORD they set out.	Nu 9:20	6310
At the c of the LORD they camped,	Nu 9:23	6310
at the c of the LORD they set out;	Nu 9:23	6310
the c of the LORD through Moses.	Nu 9:23	6310
of Paran at the c of the LORD,	Nu 13:3	6310
My c at the waters of Meribah.	Nu 20:24	6310
to the c of the LORD my God.	Nu 22:18	6310
"Behold, I have received *a* c to	Nu 23:20	
contrary to the c of the LORD,	Nu 24:13	6310
you rebelled against My c to treat	Nu 27:14	6310
At his c they shall go out and at	Nu 27:21	6310
and at his c they shall come in,	Nu 27:21	6310
"C the sons of Israel and say to	Nu 28:2	6680
So Moses gave c concerning them to	Nu 32:28	6680
journeys by the c of the LORD,	Nu 33:2	6310

to Mount Hor at the c of the LORD,	Nu 33:38	6310
"C the sons of Israel and say to	Nu 34:2	6680
"C the sons of Israel that they	Nu 35:2	6680
the c of the LORD your God;	Dt 1:26	6310
against the c of the LORD,	Dt 1:43	6310
and c the people, saying,	Dt 2:4	6680
the LORD your God which I c you.	Dt 4:2	6680
His commandments which I c you,	Dt 6:2	6680
the c of the LORD your God;	Dt 9:23	6310
you shall bring all that I c you:	Dt 12:11	6680
you shall do all that I c you.	Dt 12:14	6680
to all these words which I c you,	Dt 12:28	6680
"Whatever I c you, you shall be	Dt 12:32	6680
therefore I c you, saying,	Dt 15:11	6680
therefore I c you this today.	Dt 15:15	6680
speak to them all that I c him.	Dt 18:18	6680
"Therefore, I c you, saying,	Dt 19:7	6680
commandment which I c you today,	Dt 19:9	6680
commandments which I c you today.	Dt 27:1	6680
statutes which I c you today."	Dt 27:10	6680
commandments which I c you today,	Dt 28:1	6680
"The LORD will c the blessing	Dt 28:8	6680
of the words which I c you today,	Dt 28:14	6680
to all that I c you today,	Dt 30:2	6680
commandments which I c you today.	Dt 30:8	6680
"For this commandment which I c	Dt 30:11	6680
in that I c you today to love the	Dt 30:16	6680
which you shall c your sons to	Dt 32:46	6680
of the camp and c the people,	Jos 1:11	6680
"Anyone who rebels against your c	Jos 1:18	6310
your words in all that you c him,	Jos 1:18	6680
c the priests who are carrying the	Jos 3:8	6680
and c them, saying,	Jos 4:3	6680
"C the priests who carry the ark	Jos 4:16	6680
and at sunset Joshua gave c and	Jos 8:29	6680
had given c at first to bless the people	Jos 8:33	6680
about at sunset that Joshua gave a c,	Jos 10:27	6680
to the c of the LORD to Joshua,	Jos 15:13	6310
So according to the c of the LORD	Jos 17:4	6310
In accordance with the c of the	Jos 19:50	6310
according to the c of the LORD.	Jos 21:3	6310
the c of the LORD through Moses.	Jos 22:9	6310
rebel against the c of the LORD,	1Sa 12:14	6310
rebel against the c of the LORD,	1Sa 12:15	6310
carried out the c of the LORD."	1Sa 15:13	1697
the c of the LORD and your words,	1Sa 15:24	6310
"Let our lord now c your servants	1Sa 16:16	559
one third under the c of Joab,	2Sa 18:2	3027
c of Abishai the son of Zeruiah,	2Sa 18:2	3027
under the c of Ittai the Gittite.	2Sa 18:2	3027
the c which I have laid on you?"	1Ki 2:43	4687
c that they cut for me cedars from	1Ki 5:6	6680
that I c you and walk in My ways,	1Ki 11:38	6680
"For a c *came* to me by the word	1Ki 13:17	1697
have disobeyed the c of the LORD,	1Ki 13:21	6310
who disobeyed the c of the LORD;	1Ki 13:26	6310
the money at the c of Pharaoh.	2Ki 23:35	6310
Surely at the c of the LORD it	2Ki 24:3	6310
all their kinsmen *were* at their c.	1Ch 12:32	6310
the king's c was abhorrent to Joab.	1Ch 21:6	1697
will be entirely at your c."	1Ch 28:21	1697
I c the locust to devour the land,	2Ch 7:13	6680
at the c of the king they stoned him	2Ch 24:21	4687
according to the c of David and of	2Ch 29:25	4687
for the c was from the LORD	2Ch 29:25	4687
according to the c of the king,	2Ch 30:6	4687
according to the king's c.	2Ch 35:10	4687
according to the c of David,	2Ch 35:15	4687
according to the c of King Josiah.	2Ch 35:16	4687
building according to the c of the God	Ezr 6:14	2942
was second in c of the city.	Ne 11:9	5921
in accordance with the c of David	Ne 12:45	4687
king's c delivered by the eunuchs.	Es 1:12	1697
because she did not obey the c of	Es 1:15	3982
So it came about when the c and	Es 2:8	1697
you transgressing the king's c?"	Es 3:3	4687
went out impelled by the king's c	Es 3:15	1697
the c and decree of the king came,	Es 4:3	1697
and impelled by the king's c,	Es 8:14	1697
the thirteenth day when the king's c	Es 9:1	1697
The c of Esther established	Es 9:32	3982
departed from the c of His lips;	Jb 23:12	4687
your c that the eagle mounts up And	Jb 39:27	6310
The LORD will c His lovingkindness	Ps 42:8	6680
C victories for Jacob.	Ps 44:4	6680
The Lord gives the c;	Ps 68:11	561
He sends forth His c to the earth;	Ps 147:15	565a
water would not transgress His c,	Pr 8:29	6310
"Keep the c of the king because	Ec 8:2	6310
a *royal* c experiences no trouble,	Ec 8:5	4687
The LORD has given a c concerning	Is 23:11	6680
And all that I c you, you shall speak.	Jer 1:7	6680
speak to them all which I c you.	Jer 1:17	6680
will come at My c; now I will also	Jer 4:12	
or c them in the day that I	Jer 7:22	6680
walk in all the way which I c you,	Jer 7:23	6680
in the fire, which I did not c,	Jer 7:31	6680
do according to all which I c you;	Jer 11:4	6680
yet I did not send them or c them,	Jer 23:32	6680
"C them *to go* to their masters,	Jer 27:4	6680
falsely, which I did not c them;	Jer 29:23	6680
'Behold, I am going to c,'	Jer 34:22	6680
they have obeyed their father's c.	Jer 35:14	4687
the son of Rechab have observed the c	Jer 35:16	4687
the c of Jonadab your father,	Jer 35:18	4687
For I have rebelled against His c;	La 1:18	6310
"The c from me is firm:	Da 2:5	4406
seen that the c from me is firm,	Da 2:8	4406
"To you the c is given, O	Da 3:4	560

because the king's **c** *was* urgent Da 3:22 4406
in Him, violating the king's **c**, Da 3:28 4406
decision is a **c** of the holy ones, Da 4:17 3983
supplications the **c** was issued, Da 9:23 1697
was determined to follow *man's* **c**. Hos 5:11 6673
the LORD is going to **c** that the Am 6:11 6680
From there I will **c** the serpent Am 9:3 6680
c the sword that it slay them, Am 9:4 6680
has issued a **c** concerning you: Na 1:14 6680
c that these stones become bread." Mt 4:3 3004
'HE WILL **C** HIS ANGELS CONCERNING Mt 4:6 1781
c me to come to You on the water." Mt 14:28 2753
"Why then did Moses **c** to GIVE HER Mt 19:7 1781
"**C** that in Your kingdom these two Mt 20:21 3004
"You deaf and mute spirit, I **c** you, Mk 9:25 2004
"What did Moses **c** you?" Mk 10:3 1781
for it is written, 'HE WILL **C** HIS Lk 4:10 1781
c them to go away into the abyss. Lk 8:31 2004
do You want us to **c** fire to come Lk 9:54 3004
have never neglected a **c** of yours; Lk 15:29 1785
friends if you do what I **c** you. Jn 15:14 1781
"This I **c** you, that you love one Jn 15:17 1781
"I **c** you in the name of Jesus Ac 16:18 3853
and he, having received such a **c**, Ac 16:24 3852
and receiving a **c** for Silas and Ac 17:15 1785
of the city, at the **c** of Festus, Ac 25:23 2753
by way of concession, not of **c**. 1Co 7:6 2003
virgins I have no **c** of the Lord, 1Co 7:25 2003
I am not speaking *this* as a **c**, 2Co 8:8 2003
and will *continue to* do what we **c**. 2Th 3:4 3853
Now we **c** you, brethren, in the 2Th 3:6 3853
Now such persons we **c** and exhort 2Th 3:12 3853
This **c** I entrust to you, Timothy, 1Tm 1:18 3852
For they could not bear the **c**, Heb 12:20 1291

COMMANDED

The LORD God **c** the man, Gn 2:16 6680
of which I **c** you not to eat?" Gn 3:11 6680
from the tree about which I **c** you, Gn 3:17 6680
to all that God had **c** him, Gn 6:22 6680
to all that the LORD had **c** him. Gn 7:5 6680
and female, as God had **c** Noah. Gn 7:9 6680
flesh, entered as God had **c** him; Gn 7:16 6680
Pharaoh **c** *his* men concerning him; Gn 12:20 6680
eight days old, as God had **c** him. Gn 21:4 6680
He also **c** them saying, Gn 32:4 6680
He **c** the one in front, saying, Gn 32:17 6680
c also the second and the third, Gn 32:19 6680
Then he **c** his house steward, Gn 44:1 6680
Joseph **c** his servants the Gn 50:2 6680
as the king of Egypt had **c** them, Ex 1:17 1696
Then Pharaoh **c** all his people, Ex 1:22 6680
the signs that He had **c** him *to do*. Ex 4:28 6680
So the same day Pharaoh **c** the Ex 5:6 6680
as the LORD **c** them, thus they did. Ex 7:6 6680
they did just as the LORD had **c**; Ex 7:10 6680
Aaron did even as the LORD had **c**. Ex 7:20 6680
as the LORD had **c** Moses and Aaron, Ex 12:28 6680
as the LORD had **c** Moses and Aaron. Ex 12:50 6680
"This is what the LORD has **c**, Ex 16:16 6680
"This is what the LORD has **c**, Ex 16:32 6680
As the LORD **c** Moses, so Aaron Ex 16:34 6680
words which the LORD had **c** him. Ex 19:7 6680
eat unleavened bread, as I **c** you, Ex 23:15 6680
to all that I have **c** you; Ex 29:35 6680
may make all that I have **c** you: Ex 31:6 6680
to all that I have **c** you." Ex 31:11 6680
aside from the way which I **c** them. Ex 32:8 6680
Sinai, as the LORD had **c** him, Ex 34:4 6680
eat unleavened bread, as I **c** you, Ex 34:18 6680
and he **c** them *to do* everything Ex 34:32 6680
sons of Israel what he had been **c**, Ex 34:34 6680
that the LORD has **c** *you* to do: Ex 35:1 6680
the thing which the LORD has **c**, Ex 35:4 6680
and make all that the LORD has **c**: Ex 35:10 6680
had **c** through Moses to be done, Ex 35:29 6680
with all that the LORD has **c**." Ex 36:1 6680
which the LORD **c** *us* to perform." Ex 36:5 6680
all that the LORD had **c** Moses. Ex 38:22 6680
just as the LORD had **c** Moses. Ex 39:1 6680
just as the LORD had **c** Moses. Ex 39:5 6680
just as the LORD had **c** Moses. Ex 39:7 6680
just as the LORD had **c** Moses. Ex 39:21 6680
just as the LORD had **c** Moses. Ex 39:26 6680
just as the LORD had **c** Moses. Ex 39:29 6680
just as the LORD had **c** Moses. Ex 39:31 6680
to all that the LORD had **c** Moses; Ex 39:32 6680
to all that the LORD had **c** Moses. Ex 39:42 6680
just as the LORD had **c**, Ex 39:43 6680
to all that the LORD had **c** him, Ex 40:16 6680
it, just as the LORD had **c** Moses. Ex 40:19 6680
just as the LORD had **c** Moses. Ex 40:21 6680
just as the LORD had **c** Moses. Ex 40:23 6680
just as the LORD had **c** Moses. Ex 40:25 6680
it, just as the LORD had **c** Moses. Ex 40:27 6680
just as the LORD had **c** Moses. Ex 40:29 6680
just as the LORD had **c** Moses. Ex 40:32 6680
the LORD has **c** not to be done, Lv 4:2 4687
the LORD has **c** not to be done, Lv 4:13 4687
the LORD his God has **c** not to be done, Lv 4:22 4687
the LORD has **c** not to be done, Lv 4:27 4687
the LORD has **c** not to be done, Lv 5:17 4687
'These the LORD had **c** to be given Lv 7:36 6680
which the LORD **c** Moses at Mount Lv 7:38 6680
at Mount Sinai in the day that He **c** Lv 7:38 6680
Moses did just as the LORD **c** him. Lv 8:4 6680
which the LORD has **c** to do." Lv 8:5 6680
just as the LORD had **c** Moses. Lv 8:9 6680
just as the LORD had **c** Moses. Lv 8:13 6680
just as the LORD had **c** Moses. Lv 8:17 6680
just as the LORD had **c** Moses. Lv 8:21 6680
just as the LORD had **c** Moses. Lv 8:29 6680
ordination offering, just as I **c**, Lv 8:31 6680
"The LORD has **c** to do as has been Lv 8:34 6680
not die, for so I have been **c**." Lv 8:35 6680
the LORD had **c** through Moses. Lv 8:36 6680
So they took what Moses had **c** to Lv 9:5 6680
which the LORD has **c** you to do, Lv 9:6 6680
them, just as the LORD has **c**." Lv 9:7 6680
just as the LORD had **c** Moses. Lv 9:10 6680
the LORD, just as Moses had **c**. Lv 9:21 6680
the LORD, which He had not **c** them. Lv 10:1 6680
for thus I have been **c**. Lv 10:13 6680
you, just as the LORD has **c**." Lv 10:15 6680
in the sanctuary, just as I **c**." Lv 10:18 6680
And just as the LORD had **c** Moses, Lv 16:34 6680
'This is what the LORD has **c**, Lv 17:2 6680
did, just as the LORD had **c** Moses. Lv 24:23 6680
commandments which the LORD **c** Lv 27:34 6680
just as the LORD had **c** Moses. Nu 1:19 6680
to all which the LORD had **c** Moses, Nu 1:54 6680
just as the LORD had **c** Moses. Nu 2:33 6680
to all that the LORD **c** Moses, Nu 2:34 6680
the LORD, just as he had been **c**. Nu 3:16 6680
just as the LORD had **c** him; Nu 3:42 6680
just as the LORD had **c** Moses. Nu 3:51 6680
men, just as the LORD had **c** Moses. Nu 4:49 6680
just as the LORD had **c** Moses. Nu 8:3 6680
c Moses concerning the Levites, Nu 8:20 6680
c Moses concerning the Levites, Nu 8:22 6680
to all that the LORD had **c** Moses, Nu 9:5 6680
the LORD has **c** you through Moses, Nu 15:23 6680
just as the LORD had **c** Moses. Nu 15:36 6680
just as the LORD had **c** him, Nu 17:11 6680
of the law which the LORD has **c**, Nu 19:2 6680
the LORD, just as He had **c** him; Nu 20:9 6680
Moses did just as the LORD had **c**, Nu 20:27 6680
upward, as the LORD has **c** Moses." Nu 26:4 6680
just as the LORD **c** Moses.' " Nu 27:11 6680
Moses did just as the LORD **c** him; Nu 27:22 6680
all that the LORD had **c** Moses. Nu 29:40 6680
is the word which the LORD has **c**. Nu 30:1 6680
statutes which the LORD **c** Moses, Nu 30:16 6680
just as the LORD had **c** Moses, Nu 31:7 6680
law which the LORD has **c** Moses: Nu 31:21 6680
did just as the LORD had **c** Moses. Nu 31:31 6680
just as the LORD had **c** Moses. Nu 31:41 6680
just as the LORD had **c** Moses. Nu 31:47 6680
So Moses **c** the sons of Israel, Nu 34:13 6680
which the LORD has **c** to give to Nu 34:13 6680
These are those whom the LORD **c** to Nu 34:29 6680
"The LORD **c** my lord to give the Nu 36:2 6680
and my lord was **c** by the LORD to Nu 36:2 6680
Then Moses **c** the sons of Israel Nu 36:5 6680
"This is what the LORD has **c** Nu 36:6 6680
Just as the LORD had **c** Moses, Nu 36:10 6680
c to the sons of Israel through Moses Nu 36:13 6680
LORD had **c** him *to give* to them, Dt 1:3 6680
"I **c** you at that time all the Dt 1:18 6680
just as the LORD our God had **c** us; Dt 1:19 6680
just as the LORD our God **c** us.' Dt 1:41 6680
the LORD our God had **c** us. Dt 2:37 6680
"Then I **c** you at that time, Dt 3:18 6680
"I **c** Joshua at that time, Dt 3:21 6680
just as the LORD my God **c** me, Dt 4:5 6680
which He **c** you to perform, Dt 4:13 6680
"The LORD **c** me at that time Dt 4:14 6680
which the LORD your God has **c** you. Dt 4:23 6680
holy, as the LORD your God **c** you. Dt 5:12 6680
therefore the LORD your God **c** you Dt 5:15 6680
as the LORD your God has **c** you, Dt 5:16 6680
as the LORD your God has **c** you; Dt 5:32 6680
which the LORD your God has **c** you, Dt 5:33 6680
your God has **c** *me* to teach you, Dt 6:1 6680
His statutes which He has **c** you. Dt 6:17 6680
which the LORD our God **c** you?' Dt 6:20 6680
"So the LORD **c** us to observe all Dt 6:24 6680
the LORD our God, just as He **c** us. Dt 6:25 6680
aside from the way which I **c** them; Dt 9:12 6680
the way which the LORD had **c** you. Dt 9:16 6680
they are, as the LORD **c** me." Dt 10:5 6680
has given you, as I have **c** you; Dt 12:21 6680
the LORD your God **c** you to walk. Dt 13:5 6680
heavenly host, which I have not **c**, Dt 17:3 6680
which I have not **c** him to speak, Dt 18:20 6680
as the LORD your God has **c** you, Dt 20:17 6680
as I have **c** them, so you shall be Dt 24:8 6680
commandments which You have **c** me; Dt 26:13 6680
to all that You have **c** me. Dt 26:14 6680
and His statutes which He **c** you. Dt 28:45 6680
covenant which the LORD **c** Moses Dt 29:1 6680
commandments which I have **c** you. Dt 31:5 6680
Then Moses **c** them, saying, Dt 31:10 6680
that Moses **c** the Levites who Dt 31:25 6680
from the way which I have **c** you; Dt 31:29 6680
and did as the LORD had **c** Moses. Dt 34:9 6680
law which Moses My servant **c** you; Jos 1:7 6680
"Have I not **c** you? Jos 1:9 6680
c the officers of the people, Jos 1:10 6680
the servant of the LORD **c** you, Jos 1:13 6680
"All that you have **c** us we will do, Jos 1:16 6680
and they **c** the people, saying, Jos 3:3 6680
sons of Israel did as Joshua **c**, Jos 4:8 6680
LORD had **c** Joshua to speak Jos 4:10 6680
to all that Moses had **c** Joshua. Jos 4:10 6680
So Joshua **c** the priests, saying, Jos 4:17 6680
But Joshua **c** the people, saying, Jos 6:10 6680
My covenant which I **c** them. Jos 7:11 6680
He **c** them, saying, Jos 8:4 6680
See, I have **c** you." Jos 8:8 6680
of the LORD which He had **c** Joshua. Jos 8:27 6680
the LORD had **c** the sons of Israel, Jos 8:31 6680
of all that Moses had **c** which Joshua Jos 8:35 6680
God had **c** His servant Moses to give Jos 9:24 6680
LORD, the God of Israel, had **c**. Jos 10:40 6680
the servant of the LORD had **c**. Jos 11:12 6680
the LORD had **c** Moses his servant, Jos 11:15 6680
his servant, so Moses **c** Joshua, Jos 11:15 6680
of all that the LORD had **c** Moses. Jos 11:15 6680
just as the LORD had **c** Moses. Jos 11:20 6680
an inheritance as I have **c** you. Jos 13:6 6680
as the LORD had **c** through Moses, Jos 14:2 6680
did just as the LORD had **c** Moses, Jos 14:5 6680
"The LORD **c** Moses to give us an Jos 17:4 6680
and Joshua **c** those who went to Jos 18:8 6680
"The LORD **c** through Moses to give Jos 21:2 6680
as the LORD had **c** through Moses. Jos 21:8 6680
the servant of the LORD **c** you, Jos 22:2 6680
to my voice in all that I **c** you. Jos 22:2 6680
the servant of the LORD **c** you, Jos 22:5 6680
the LORD your God, which He **c** you, Jos 23:16 6680
covenant which I **c** their fathers and Jg 2:20 6680
had **c** their fathers through Moses. Jg 3:4 6680
LORD, the God of Israel, has **c**, Jg 4:6 6680
let her observe all that I **c**." Jg 13:14 6680
warriors there, and **c** them, Jg 21:10 6680
And they **c** the sons of Benjamin, Jg 21:20 6680
c the servants not to touch you. Ru 2:9 6680
to glean, Boaz **c** his servants, Ru 2:15 6680
that her mother-in-law had **c** her. Ru 3:6 6680
which I have **c** *in My* dwelling, 1Sa 2:29 6680
the LORD your God, which He **c** you, 1Sa 13:13 6680
not kept what the LORD **c** you." 1Sa 13:14 6680
and went as Jesse had **c** him. 1Sa 17:20 6680
Then Saul **c** his servants, 1Sa 18:22 6680
and my brother has **c** me to attend. 1Sa 20:29 6680
Then David **c** the young men, and 2Sa 4:12 6680
so, just as the LORD had **c** him, 2Sa 5:25 6680
I **c** to shepherd My people Israel, 2Sa 7:7 6680
even from the day that I **c** judges 2Sa 7:11 6680
Absalom **c** his servants, 2Sa 13:28 6680
have not I myself **c** you? 2Sa 13:28 6680
to Amnon just as Absalom had **c**. 2Sa 13:29 6680
it was your servant Joab who **c** me, 2Sa 14:19 6680
thus they did all that the king **c**, 2Sa 21:14 6680
of Gad, just as the LORD had **c**. 2Sa 24:19 6680
c Benaiah the son of Jehoiada, 1Ki 2:46 6680
Then the king **c**, and they quarried 1Ki 5:17 6680
which He **c** our fathers. 1Ki 8:58 6680
doing according to all that I have **c** 1Ki 9:4 6680
had **c** him concerning this thing, 1Ki 11:10 6680
not observe what the LORD had **c**. 1Ki 11:10 6680
My statutes, which I have **c** you, 1Ki 11:11 6680
was **c** me by the word of the LORD, 1Ki 13:9 6680
which the LORD your God **c** you, 1Ki 13:21 6680
He **c** him all the days of his life, 1Ki 15:5 6680
and I have **c** the ravens to provide 1Ki 17:4 6680
I have **c** a widow there to provide 1Ki 17:9 6680
Now the king of Aram had **c** the 1Ki 22:31 6680
He **c** them, saying, 2Ki 11:5 6680
to all that Jehoiada the priest **c**. 2Ki 11:9 6680
And Jehoiada the priest **c** the 2Ki 11:15 6680
the Law of Moses, as the LORD **c**, 2Ki 14:6 6680
King Ahaz **c** Urijah the priest, 2Ki 16:15 6680
according to all that King Ahaz **c**. 2Ki 16:16 6680
the law which I **c** your fathers, 2Ki 17:13 6680
had **c** them not to do like them. 2Ki 17:15 6680
Then the king of Assyria **c**, 2Ki 17:27 6680
the LORD **c** the sons of Jacob, 2Ki 17:34 6680
LORD made a covenant and **c** them, 2Ki 17:35 6680
which the LORD had **c** Moses. 2Ki 18:6 6680
Moses the servant of the LORD **c**; 2Ki 18:12 6680
to all that I have **c** them, 2Ki 21:8 6680
that My servant Moses **c** them." 2Ki 21:8 6680
the king **c** Hilkiah the priest, 2Ki 22:12 6680
Then the king **c** Hilkiah the high 2Ki 23:4 6680
the king **c** all the people saying, 2Ki 23:21 6680
Moses the servant of God had **c**. 1Ch 6:49 6680
David did just as God had **c** him, 1Ch 14:16 6680
as Moses had **c** according to the word 1Ch 15:15 6680
He **c** to a thousand generations, 1Ch 16:15 6680
of the LORD, which He **c** Israel. 1Ch 16:40 6680
whom I **c** to shepherd My people, 1Ch 17:6 6680
even from the day that I **c** judges 1Ch 17:10 6680
not I who **c** to count the people? 1Ch 21:17 559
of the LORD **c** Gad to say to David, 1Ch 21:18 559
The LORD **c** the angel, and he 1Ch 21:27 559
LORD **c** Moses concerning Israel. 1Ch 22:13 6680
David also **c** all the leaders of 1Ch 22:17 6680
the LORD God of Israel had **c** him. 1Ch 24:19 6680
to do according to all that I have **c** you 2Ch 7:17 6680
for David the man of God had so **c**. 2Ch 8:14 4687
and **c** Judah to seek the LORD God 2Ch 14:4 559
c the captains of his chariots, 2Ch 18:30 6680
to all that Jehoiada the priest **c**. 2Ch 23:8 6680
So the king **c**, and they made a 2Ch 24:8 559
book of Moses, which the LORD **c**, 2Ch 25:4 6680
princes **c** by the word of the LORD. 2Ch 30:12 4687
Also he **c** the people who lived in 2Ch 31:4 559
Then Hezekiah **c** *them* to prepare 2Ch 31:11 559
c them according to all the law, 2Ch 33:8 6680
Then the king **c** Hilkiah, Ahikam 2Ch 34:20 6680
the king of Persia has **c** us." Ezr 4:3 6680
is **c** by the God of heaven, Ezr 7:23 4481, 2942
c by Your servants the prophets, Ezr 9:11 6680
nor the ordinances which You **c** Your Ne 1:7 6680
"Remember the word which You **c** Ne 1:8 6680

how the LORD had **c** through Moses	**Ne 8:14**	6680
I **c** that the doors should be shut	**Ne 13:19**	559
And I **c** the Levites that they	**Ne 13:22**	559
was merry with wine, he **c** Mehuman,	**Es 1:10**	559
'King Ahasuerus **c** Queen Vashti to	**Es 1:17**	559
even as Mordecai had **c** her;	**Es 2:20**	6680
so the king had **c** concerning him.	**Es 3:2**	6680
as Haman **c** to the king's satraps,	**Es 3:12**	6680
and did just as Esther had **c** him.	**Es 4:17**	6680
all that Mordecai **c** to the Jews,	**Es 8:9**	6680
king **c** that it should be done so;	**Es 9:14**	559
he **c** by letter that his wicked	**Es 9:25**	559
ever in your life **c** the morning,	**Jb 38:12**	6680
He **c**, and it stood fast.	**Ps 33:9**	6680
Your God has **c** your strength;	**Ps 68:28**	6680
in Israel, Which He **c** our fathers That	**Ps 78:5**	6680
Yet He **c** the clouds above And	**Ps 78:23**	6680
He **c** to a thousand generations,	**Ps 105:8**	6680
the peoples, As the LORD **c** them,	**Ps 106:34**	559
You have **c** Your testimonies in	**Ps 119:138**	6680
For there the LORD **c** the blessing	**Ps 133:3**	6680
For He **c** and they were created.	**Ps 148:5**	6680
I have **c** My consecrated ones, I	**Is 13:3**	6680
For His mouth has **c**,	**Is 34:16**	6680
and my molten image have **c** them.'	**Is 48:5**	6680
"But this is what I **c** them,	**Jer 7:23**	6680
which I **c** your forefathers in the	**Jer 11:4**	6680
covenant, which I **c** *them* to do,	**Jer 11:8**	6680
Euphrates, as the LORD had **c** me.	**Jer 13:5**	6680
which I **c** you to hide there."	**Jer 13:6**	6680
nor **c** them nor spoken to them;	**Jer 14:14**	6680
day holy, as I **c** your forefathers.	**Jer 17:22**	6680
thing which I never **c** or spoke of,	**Jer 19:5**	6680
I have **c** you to speak to them.	**Jer 26:2**	6680
speaking all that the LORD had **c** *him*	**Jer 26:8**	6680
"And I **c** Baruch in their	**Jer 32:13**	6680
have done nothing of all that You **c**	**Jer 32:23**	6680
which I had not **c** them nor had it	**Jer 32:35**	6680
son of Rechab, our father, **c** us,	**Jer 35:6**	6680
our father, in all that he **c** us,	**Jer 35:8**	6680
all that Jonadab our father **c** us.	**Jer 35:10**	6680
he **c** his sons not to drink wine,	**Jer 35:14**	6680
of their father which he **c** them,	**Jer 35:16**	6680
according to all that he **c** you;	**Jer 35:18**	6680
Jeremiah **c** Baruch, saying,	**Jer 36:5**	6680
that Jeremiah the prophet **c** him,	**Jer 36:8**	6680
king **c** Jerahmeel the king's son,	**Jer 36:26**	6680
king **c** Ebed-melech the Ethiopian,	**Jer 38:10**	6680
these words which the king had **c**;	**Jer 38:27**	6680
to all that I have **c** you.	**Jer 50:21**	6680
c Seraiah the son of Neriah,	**Jer 51:59**	6680
The ones whom You **c** That they should	**La 1:10**	6680
The LORD has **c** concerning Jacob	**La 1:17**	6680
word Which He **c** from days of old.	**La 2:17**	6680
to pass, Unless the Lord has **c** *it?*	**La 3:37**	6680
done just as You have **c** me."	**Ezk 9:11**	6680
He **c** the man clothed in linen,	**Ezk 10:6**	6680
I did so, as I had been **c**.	**Ezk 12:7**	6680
in the morning I did as I was **c**.	**Ezk 24:18**	6680
So I prophesied as I was **c**;	**Ezk 37:7**	6680
So I prophesied as He **c** me,	**Ezk 37:10**	6680
He **c** certain valiant warriors	**Da 3:20**	560
'And in that it was **c** to leave the	**Da 4:26**	560
And you **c** the prophets saying,	**Am 2:12**	6680
Then the LORD **c** the fish, and it	**Jon 2:10**	559
I **c** My servants the prophets,	**Zch 1:6**	6680
I **c** him in Horeb for all Israel.	**Mal 4:4**	6680
as the angel of the Lord **c** him,	**Mt 1:24**	*4367*
present the offering that Moses **c**,	**Mt 8:4**	*4367*
the king **c** *it* to be given because	**Mt 14:9**	*2753*
from the mountain, Jesus **c** them,	**Mt 17:9**	*1781*
repay, his lord **c** him to be sold,	**Mt 18:25**	*2753*
them to observe all that I **c** you;	**Mt 28:20**	*1781*
for your cleansing what Moses **c**,	**Mk 1:44**	*4367*
and **c** *him* to bring *back* his head.	**Mk 6:27**	*2004*
He **c** them all to sit down by	**Mk 6:39**	*2004*
also **c** the doorkeeper to stay on	**Mk 13:34**	*1781*
your cleansing, just as Moses **c**,	**Lk 5:14**	*4367*
For He had **c** the unclean spirit to	**Lk 8:29**	*3853*
'Master, what you **c** has been done,	**Lk 14:22**	*2004*
he did the things which were **c**,	**Lk 17:9**	*1299*
do all the things which are **c** you,	**Lk 17:10**	*1299*
and **c** that he be brought to Him;	**Lk 18:40**	*2753*
Moses **c** us to stone such women;	**Jn 8:5**	*1781*
I do exactly as the Father **c** Me. Get	**Jn 14:31**	*1781*
He **c** them not to leave Jerusalem,	**Ac 1:4**	*3853*
they **c** them not to speak or teach	**Ac 4:18**	*3853*
you have been **c** by the Lord."	**Ac 10:33**	*4367*
"For so the Lord has **c** us,	**Ac 13:47**	*1781*
had **c** all the Jews to leave Rome.	**Ac 18:2**	*1299*
The high priest Ananias **c**	**Ac 23:2**	*2004*
and **c** that those who could swim	**Ac 27:43**	*2753*
with your hands, just as we **c** you,	**1Th 4:11**	*3853*
OF THE COVENANT WHICH GOD C YOU."	**Heb 9:20**	*1781*
love one another, just as He **c** us.	**1Jn 3:23**	*1325, 1785*

COMMANDER

and Phicol, the **c** of his army,	**Gn 21:22**	8269
and Phicol, the **c** of his army,	**Gn 21:32**	8269
and Phicol the **c** of his army.	**Gn 26:26**	8269
and the **c** of his army was Sisera,	**Jg 4:2**	8269
you Sisera, the **c** of Jabin's army,	**Jg 4:7**	8269
cheese to the **c** of *their* thousand,	**1Sa 17:18**	8269
said to Abner the **c** of the army,	**1Sa 17:55**	8269
him as his **c** of a thousand;	**1Sa 18:13**	8269
the son of Ner, the **c** of his army;	**1Sa 26:5**	8269
the son of Ner, **c** of Saul's army,	**2Sa 2:8**	8269
and Shobach the **c** of the army of	**2Sa 10:16**	8269
down Shobach the **c** of their army,	**2Sa 10:18**	8269
if you will not be **c** of the army	**2Sa 19:13**	8269
therefore he became their **c**;	**2Sa 23:19**	8269
c of the army who was with him,	**2Sa 24:2**	8269
priest and Joab the **c** of the army,	**1Ki 1:19**	8269
of Ner, **c** of the army of Israel,	**1Ki 2:32**	8269
of Jether, **c** of the army of Judah.	**1Ki 2:32**	8269
and Joab the **c** of the army had	**1Ki 11:15**	8269
Joab the **c** of the army was dead,	**1Ki 11:21**	8269
Zimri, **c** of half his chariots,	**1Ki 16:9**	8269
made Omri, the **c** of the army,	**1Ki 16:16**	8269
first shall be chief and **c**."	**1Ch 11:6**	8269
most honored and became their **c**;	**1Ch 11:21**	8269
with Shophach the **c** of the army of	**1Ch 19:16**	8269
death Shophach the **c** of the army.	**1Ch 19:18**	8269
The third **c** of the army for the	**1Ch 27:5**	8269
was the **c** Shamhuth the Izrahite;	**1Ch 27:8**	8269
Joab was the **c** of the king's army.	**1Ch 27:34**	8269
of thousands, Adnah *was* the **c**,	**2Ch 17:14**	8269
and next to him *was* Johanan the **c**,	**2Ch 17:15**	8269
c and officer in the camp of the	**2Ch 32:21**	5057
Rehum the **c** and Shimshai the	**Ezr 4:8**	1169, 2942
then *wrote* Rehum the **c** and	**Ezr 4:9**	1169, 2942
sent an answer to Rehum the **c**,	**Ezr 4:17**	1169, 2942
Hananiah the **c** of the fortress,	**Ne 7:2**	8269
year that the **c** came to Ashdod,	**Is 20:1**	8661
A leader and **c** for the peoples.	**Is 55:4**	6680
and the scribe of the **c** of the	**Jer 52:25**	8269
Then the **c** of the officials	**Da 1:7**	8269
permission from the **c** of the officials	**Da 1:8**	8269
sight of the **c** of the officials,	**Da 1:9**	8269
and the **c** of the officials said to	**Da 1:10**	8269
overseer whom the **c** of the officials	**Da 1:11**	8269
the **c** of the officials presented	**Da 1:18**	8269
he said to Arioch, the king's **c**,	**Da 2:15**	7990
be equal with the **C** of the host;	**Da 8:11**	8269
But a **c** will put a stop to his	**Da 11:18**	7101
So the *Roman* cohort and the **c** and	**Jn 18:12**	*5506*
a report came up to the **c** of the	**Ac 21:31**	*5506*
they saw the **c** and the soldiers,	**Ac 21:32**	*5506*
c came up and took hold of him,	**Ac 21:33**	*5506*
the barracks, he said to the **c**,	**Ac 21:37**	*5506*
the **c** ordered him to be brought	**Ac 22:24**	*5506*
he went to the **c** and told him,	**Ac 22:26**	*5506*
The **c** came and said to him,	**Ac 22:27**	*5506*
The **c** answered,	**Ac 22:28**	*5506*
and the **c** also was afraid when he	**Ac 22:29**	*5506*
the **c** was afraid Paul would be	**Ac 23:10**	*5506*
the **c** to bring him down to you,	**Ac 23:15**	*5506*
"Lead this young man to the **c**,	**Ac 23:17**	*5506*
him and led him to the **c** and said,	**Ac 23:18**	*5506*
The **c** took him by the hand and	**Ac 23:19**	*5506*
the **c** let the young man go,	**Ac 23:22**	*5506*
"But Lysias the **c** came along, and	**Ac 24:7**	*5506*
"When Lysias the **c** comes down, I	**Ac 24:22**	*5506*

COMMANDERS

they shall appoint **c** of armies at	**Dt 20:9**	8269
heart *goes out* to the **c** of Israel,	**Jg 5:9**	2710
From Machir **c** came down, And from	**Jg 5:14**	2710
c of thousands and of fifties,	**1Sa 8:12**	8269
Then the **c** of the Philistines went	**1Sa 18:30**	8269
Will he make you all **c** of	**1Sa 22:7**	8269
of thousands and **c** of hundreds?	**1Sa 22:7**	8269
the **c** of the Philistines said,	**1Sa 29:3**	8269
said to the **c** of the Philistines,	**1Sa 29:3**	8269
But the **c** of the Philistines were	**1Sa 29:4**	8269
and the **c** of the Philistines said	**1Sa 29:4**	8269
c of the Philistines have said,	**1Sa 29:9**	8269
had two men who were **c** of bands:	**2Sa 4:2**	8269
and set over them **c** of thousands	**2Sa 18:1**	8269
of thousands and **c** of hundreds.	**2Sa 18:1**	8269
all the **c** concerning Absalom.	**2Sa 18:5**	8269
and against the **c** of the army.	**2Sa 24:4**	8269
So Joab and the **c** of the army went	**2Sa 24:4**	8269
c of the army and Abiathar the priest,	**1Ki 1:25**	8269
the two **c** of the armies of Israel,	**1Ki 2:5**	8269
his captains, his chariot **c**,	**1Ki 9:22**	8269
committed them to the care of the **c**	**1Ki 14:27**	8269
King Asa and sent the **c** of his armies	**1Ki 15:20**	8269
David and the **c** of the army set	**1Ch 25:1**	8269
the **c** of thousands and hundreds,	**1Ch 26:26**	8269
and hundreds, and the **c** of the army,	**1Ch 26:26**	8269
c of thousands and of hundreds,	**1Ch 27:1**	8269
and was chief of all the **c** of the	**1Ch 27:3**	8269
and the **c** of the divisions that	**1Ch 28:1**	8269
the king, and the **c** of thousands,	**1Ch 28:1**	8269
thousands, and the **c** of hundreds,	**1Ch 28:1**	8269
c of thousands and of hundreds,	**1Ch 29:6**	8269
to the **c** of thousands and of	**2Ch 1:2**	8269
and **c** of his chariots and his	**2Ch 8:9**	8269
committed them to the care of the **c**	**2Ch 12:10**	8269
King Asa and sent the **c** of his armies	**2Ch 16:4**	8269
of Judah, **c** of thousands, Adnah	**2Ch 17:14**	8269
c and all his chariots with him.	**2Ch 21:9**	8269
him and the **c** of the chariots.	**2Ch 21:9**	8269
to *their* fathers' households under **c** of	**2Ch 25:5**	8269
and **c** of hundreds throughout Judah	**2Ch 25:5**	8269
Therefore the LORD brought the **c**	**2Ch 33:11**	8269
Then he put army **c** in all the	**2Ch 33:14**	8269
Now all the **c** of the forces that	**Jer 40:7**	8269
c of the forces that were in the field	**Jer 40:13**	8269
son of Kareah and all the **c** of the	**Jer 41:11**	8269
the **c** of the forces that were with him,	**Jer 41:13**	8269
the **c** of the forces that were with him	**Jer 41:16**	8269
Then all the **c** of the forces,	**Jer 42:1**	8269
and all the **c** of the forces that	**Jer 42:8**	8269
and all the **c** of the forces,	**Jer 43:4**	8269
c of the forces took the entire remnant	**Jer 43:5**	8269
banquet for his lords and military **c**	**Mk 6:21**	*5506*
by the **c** and the prominent men of	**Ac 25:23**	*5506*
the earth and the great men and the **c**	**Rv 6:15**	*5506*
the flesh of kings and the flesh of **c**	**Rv 19:18**	*5506*

COMMANDING

observe what I am **c** you this day:	**Ex 34:11**	6680
add to the word which I am **c** you,	**Dt 4:2**	6680
words, which I am **c** you today,	**Dt 6:6**	6680
judgments which I am **c** you today,	**Dt 7:11**	6680
"All the commandments that I am **c**	**Dt 8:1**	6680
statutes which I am **c** you today;	**Dt 8:11**	6680
I am **c** you today for your good?	**Dt 10:13**	6680
which I am **c** you today,	**Dt 11:8**	6680
which I am **c** you today,	**Dt 11:13**	6680
this commandment which I am **c** you to	**Dt 11:22**	6680
your God, which I am **c** you today;	**Dt 11:27**	6680
the way which I am **c** you today,	**Dt 11:28**	6680
which I am **c** you today,	**Dt 13:18**	6680
which I am **c** you today.	**Dt 15:5**	6680
I am **c** you to do this thing.	**Dt 24:18**	6680
I am **c** you to do this thing.	**Dt 24:22**	6680
these stones, as I am **c** you today,	**Dt 27:4**	6680
"For behold, I am **c**,	**Am 9:9**	6680
c the jailer to guard them	**Ac 16:23**	*3853*

COMMANDMENT

stone tablets with the law and the **c**	**Ex 24:12**	4687
you in **c** for the sons of Israel.	**Ex 25:22**	6680
the **c** of the LORD through Moses.	**Nu 4:37**	6310
according to the **c** of the LORD.	**Nu 4:41**	6310
the **c** of the LORD through Moses.	**Nu 4:45**	6310
the **c** of the LORD through Moses,	**Nu 4:49**	6310
the **c** of the LORD through Moses.	**Nu 10:13**	6310
transgressing the **c** of the LORD,	**Nu 14:41**	6310
from the day when the LORD gave **c**	**Nu 15:23**	6680
of the LORD and has broken His **c**,	**Nu 15:31**	4687
"Now this is the **c**, the statutes	**Dt 6:1**	4687
this **c** before the LORD our God,	**Dt 6:25**	4687
you shall keep the **c** and the	**Dt 7:11**	4687
"You shall therefore keep every **c**	**Dt 11:8**	4687
this **c** which I am commanding you to	**Dt 11:22**	4687
to observe carefully all this **c**	**Dt 15:5**	4687
he may not turn aside from the **c**,	**Dt 17:20**	4687
you carefully observe all this **c** which	**Dt 19:9**	4687
"For this **c** which I command you	**Dt 30:11**	4687
of the **c** of the LORD your God.	**Jos 22:3**	4687
"Only be very careful to observe the **c**	**Jos 22:5**	4687
kept the **c** of the LORD your God,	**1Sa 13:13**	4687
and have not observed the **c** which	**1Ki 13:21**	4687
ordinances and the law and the **c** which	**2Ki 17:37**	4687
not a word, for the king's **c** was,	**2Ki 18:36**	4687
up according to the **c** of Moses,	**2Ch 8:13**	4687
did not depart from the **c** of the king	**2Ch 8:15**	4687
and to observe the law and the **c**.	**2Ch 14:4**	4687
and blood, between law and **c**,	**2Ch 19:10**	4687
according to the **c** of the king by	**2Ch 29:15**	4687
the house of God in law and in **c**,	**2Ch 31:21**	4687
who tremble at the **c** of our God;	**Ezr 10:3**	4687
For *there was* a **c** from the king	**Ne 11:23**	4687
king's **c** and his decree arrived,	**Es 8:17**	1697
The **c** of the LORD is pure,	**Ps 19:8**	4687
You have given **c** to save me, For	**Ps 71:3**	6680
Your **c** is exceedingly broad.	**Ps 119:96**	4687
son, observe the **c** of your father And	**Pr 6:20**	4687
For the **c** is a lamp and the	**Pr 6:23**	4687
who fears the **c** will be rewarded.	**Pr 13:13**	4687
He who keeps the **c** keeps his soul,	**Pr 19:16**	4687
for the king's **c** was,	**Is 36:21**	4687
Then King Zedekiah gave **c**,	**Jer 37:21**	6680
"And now this **c** is for you, O	**Mal 2:1**	4687
that I have sent this **c** to you,	**Mal 2:4**	4687
transgress the **c** of God for the sake	**Mt 15:3**	*1785*
which is the great **c** in the Law?"	**Mt 22:36**	*1785*
"This is the great and foremost **c**.	**Mt 22:38**	*1785*
"Neglecting the **c** of God, you	**Mk 7:8**	*1785*
experts at setting aside the **c** of	**Mk 7:9**	*1785*
of heart he wrote you this **c**.	**Mk 10:5**	*1785*
"What **c** is the foremost of all?"	**Mk 12:28**	*1785*
no other **c** greater than these."	**Mk 12:31**	*1785*
they rested according to the **c**.	**Lk 23:56**	*1785*
c I received from My Father."	**Jn 10:18**	*1785*
Himself who sent Me has given Me a **c**	**Jn 12:49**	*1785*
I know that His **c** is eternal life;	**Jn 12:50**	*1785*
"A new **c** I give to you, that you	**Jn 13:34**	*1785*
"This is My **c**, that you love one	**Jn 15:12**	*1785*
taking opportunity through the **c**,	**Ro 7:8**	*1785*
but when the **c** came, sin became	**Ro 7:9**	*1785*
and this **c**, which was to result in	**Ro 7:10**	*1785*
taking an opportunity through the **c**,	**Ro 7:11**	*1785*
and the **c** is holy and righteous	**Ro 7:12**	*1785*
that through the **c** sin would	**Ro 7:13**	*1785*
and if there is any other **c**,	**Ro 13:9**	*1785*
to the **c** of the eternal God,	**Ro 16:26**	*2003*
I write to you are the Lord's **c**.	**1Co 14:37**	*1785*
is the first **c** with a promise),	**Eph 6:2**	*1785*
to the **c** of God our Savior,	**1Tm 1:1**	*2003*
that you keep the **c** without stain	**1Tm 6:14**	*1785*
to the **c** of God our Savior,	**Ti 1:3**	*2003*
have **c** in the Law to collect a tenth	**Heb 7:5**	*1785*
there is a setting aside of a former **c**	**Heb 7:18**	*1785*
For when every **c** had been spoken	**Heb 9:19**	*1785*
from the holy **c** handed on to them.	**2Pe 2:21**	*1785*
c of the Lord and Savior *spoken* by	**2Pe 3:2**	*1785*
I am not writing a new **c** to you,	**1Jn 2:7**	*1785*
but an old **c** which you have had	**1Jn 2:7**	*1785*
the old **c** is the word which you	**1Jn 2:7**	*1785*
hand, I am writing a new **c** to you,	**1Jn 2:8**	*1785*
This is His **c**, that we believe	**1Jn 3:23**	*1785*

And this **c** we have from Him, that 1Jn 4:21 *1785*
received **c** *to do* from the Father. 2Jn 1:4 *1785*
were writing to you a new **c**, 2Jn 1:5 *1785*
This is the **c**, just as you have 2Jn 1:6 *1785*

COMMANDMENTS
Me and kept My charge, My **c**, Gn 26:5 4687
His sight, and give ear to His **c**, Ex 15:26 4687
to keep My **c** and My instructions? Ex 16:28 4687
those who love Me and keep My **c**. Ex 20:6 4687
words of the covenant, the Ten **C**. Ex 34:28 1697
"So you shall keep My **c**, Lv 22:31 4687
keep My **c** so as to carry them out, Lv 26:3 4687
and do not carry out all these **c**, Lv 26:14 4687
so as not to carry out all My **c**, Lv 26:15 4687
These are the **c** which the LORD Lv 27:34 4687
and do not observe all these **c**, Nu 15:22 4687
remember all the **c** of the LORD, Nu 15:39 4687
you may remember to do all My **c** and Nu 15:40 4687
These are the **c** and the ordinances Nu 36:13 4687
that you may keep the **c** of the Dt 4:2 4687
the Ten **C**; and He wrote them on Dt 4:13 1697
His **c** which I am giving you today, Dt 4:40 4687
those who love Me and keep My **c**. Dt 5:10 4687
fear Me and keep all My **c** always, Dt 5:29 4687
that I may speak to you all the **c** and Dt 5:31 4687
keep all His statutes and His **c** which Dt 6:2 4687
keep the **c** of the LORD your God, Dt 6:17 4687
those who love Him and keep His **c**; Dt 7:9 4687
"All the **c** that I am commanding Dt 8:1 4687
you would keep His **c** or not. Dt 8:2 4687
keep the **c** of the LORD your God, Dt 8:6 4687
LORD your God by not keeping His **c** Dt 8:11 4687
the Ten **C** which the LORD had Dt 10:4 1697
and to keep the LORD's **c** and His Dt 10:13 4687
His ordinances, and His **c**. Dt 11:1 4687
if you listen obediently to my **c** Dt 11:13 4687
to the **c** of the LORD your God, Dt 11:27 4687
to the **c** of the LORD your God, Dt 11:28 4687
and you shall keep His **c**, Dt 13:4 4687
keeping all His **c** which I am Dt 13:18 4687
c which You have commanded me; Dt 26:13 4687
or forgotten any of Your **c**. Dt 26:13 4687
His **c** and His ordinances, Dt 26:17 4687
that you should keep all His **c**; Dt 26:18 4687
the **c** which I command you today. Dt 27:1 4687
and do His **c** and His statutes Dt 27:10 4687
His **c** which I command you today, Dt 28:1 4687
keep the **c** of the LORD your God and Dt 28:9 4687
to the **c** of the LORD your God, Dt 28:13 4687
to observe to do all His **c** and His Dt 28:15 4687
by keeping His **c** and His statutes Dt 28:45 4687
His **c** which I command you today. Dt 30:8 4687
to keep His **c** and His statutes which Dt 30:10 4687
walk in His ways and to keep His **c** Dt 30:16 4687
the **c** which I have commanded you. Dt 31:5 4687
walk in all His ways and keep His **c** Jos 22:5 4687
in obeying the **c** of the LORD; Jg 2:17 4687
they would obey the **c** of the LORD, Jg 3:4 4687
ways, to keep His statutes, His **c**, 1Ki 2:3 4687
ways, keeping My statutes and **c**, 1Ki 3:14 4687
keep all My **c** by walking in them, 1Ki 6:12 4687
keep His **c** and His statutes and His 1Ki 8:58 4687
in His statutes and to keep His **c**, 1Ki 8:61 4687
and do not keep My **c** and My 1Ki 9:6 4687
who observed My **c** and My statutes; 1Ki 11:34 4687
by observing My statutes and My **c**, 1Ki 11:38 4687
who kept My **c** and who followed Me 1Ki 14:8 4687
have forsaken the **c** of the LORD and 1Ki 18:18 4687
from your evil ways and keep My **c**, 2Ki 17:13 4687
They forsook all the **c** of the 2Ki 17:16 4687
keep the **c** of the LORD their God, 2Ki 17:19 4687
or the **c** which the LORD commanded 2Ki 17:34 4687
following Him, but kept His **c**, 2Ki 18:6 4687
and to keep His **c** and His 2Ki 23:3 4687
performs My **c** and My ordinances, 1Ch 28:7 4687
observe and seek after all the **c** 1Ch 28:8 4687
a perfect heart to keep Your **c**, 1Ch 29:19 4687
and My **c** which I have set before you 2Ch 7:19 4687
God of his father, followed His **c**, 2Ch 17:4 4687
'Why do you transgress the **c** of 2Ch 24:20 4687
and to keep His **c** and His 2Ch 34:31 4687
learned in the words of the **c** of Ezr 7:11 4687
For we have forsaken Your **c**, Ezr 9:10 4687
shall we again break Your **c** and Ezr 9:14 4687
those who love Him and keep His **c**, Ne 1:5 4687
You and have not kept the **c**, Ne 1:7 4687
to Me and keep My **c** and do them, Ne 1:9 4687
true laws, Good statutes and **c**. Ne 9:13 4687
And laid down for them **c**, Ne 9:14 4687
and would not listen to Your **c**. Ne 9:16 4687
and did not listen to Your **c** but sinned Ne 9:29 4687
Or paid attention to Your **c** and Your Ne 9:34 4687
observe all the **c** of GOD our Lord, Ne 10:29 4687
the works of God, But keep His **c**, Ps 78:7 4687
My statutes And do not keep My **c**, Ps 89:31 4687
have all those who do *His c;* Ps 111:10
Who greatly delights in His **c**. Ps 112:1 4687
When I look upon all Your **c**. Ps 119:6 4687
Do not let me wander from Your **c**. Ps 119:10 4687
Do not hide Your **c** from me. Ps 119:19 4687
the cursed, Who wander from Your **c**. Ps 119:21 4687
I shall run the way of Your **c**, Ps 119:32 4687
Make me walk in the path of Your **c**, Ps 119:35 4687
I shall delight in Your **c**, Ps 119:47 4687
I shall lift up my hands to Your **c**, Ps 119:48 4687
and did not delay To keep Your **c**. Ps 119:60 4687
knowledge, For I believe in Your **c**. Ps 119:66 4687
that I may learn Your **c**. Ps 119:73 4687
All Your **c** are faithful; Ps 119:86 4687
c make me wiser than my enemies, Ps 119:98 4687
I may observe the **c** of my God. Ps 119:115 4687
Therefore I love Your **c** Above gold, Ps 119:127 4687
panted, For I longed for Your **c**. Ps 119:131 4687
Yet Your **c** are my delight. Ps 119:143 4687
O LORD, And all Your **c** are truth. Ps 119:151 4687
salvation, O LORD, And do Your **c**. Ps 119:166 4687
For all Your **c** are righteousness. Ps 119:172 4687
For I do not forget Your **c**. Ps 119:176 4687
And treasure my **c** within you, Pr 2:1 4687
But let your heart keep my **c**; Pr 3:1 4687
Keep my **c** and live; Pr 4:4 4687
And treasure my **c** within you. Pr 7:1 4687
Keep my **c** and live, And my Pr 7:2 4687
fear God and keep His **c**, Ec 12:13 4687
you had paid attention to My **c**! Is 48:18 4687
those who love Him and keep His **c**, Da 9:4 4687
aside from Your **c** and ordinances. Da 9:5 4687
one of the least of these **c**, Mt 5:19 *1785*
to enter into life, keep the **c**." Mt 19:17 *1785*
"On these two **c** depend the whole Mt 22:40 *1785*
"You know the **c**, Mk 10:19 *1785*
c and requirements of the Lord. Lk 1:6 *1785*
"You know the **c**, Lk 18:20 *1785*
you love Me, you will keep My **c**. Jn 14:15 *1785*
"He who has My **c** and keeps them is Jn 14:21 *1785*
"If you keep My **c**, you will abide Jn 15:10 *1785*
just as I have kept My Father's **c** Jn 15:10 *1785*
is the keeping of the **c** of God. 1Co 7:19 *1785*
Law of **c** *contained* in ordinances, Eph 2:15 *1785*
with the **c** and teachings of men? Col 2:22 *1778*
For you know what **c** we gave you by 1Th 4:2 *3852*
c of men who turn away from the truth. Ti 1:14 *1785*
to know Him, if we keep His **c**. 1Jn 2:3 *1785*
know Him," and does not keep His **c**, 1Jn 2:4 *1785*
because we keep His **c** and do the 1Jn 3:22 *1785*
one who keeps His **c** abides in Him, 1Jn 3:24 *1785*
we love God and observe His **c**. 1Jn 5:2 *1785*
love of God, that we keep His **c**; 1Jn 5:3 *1785*
and His **c** are not burdensome. 1Jn 5:3 *1785*
that we walk according to His **c**. 2Jn 1:6 *1785*
who keep the **c** of God and hold to Rv 12:17 *1785*
of the saints who keep the **c** of God Rv 14:12 *1785*

COMMANDS
to the LORD our God as He **c** us." Ex 8:27 559
do this thing and God *so* **c** you, Ex 18:23 6680
will do just as my lord **c**. Nu 32:25 6680
"This day the LORD your God **c** you Dt 26:16 6680
and has not carried out My **c**." 1Sa 15:11 1697
all that my lord the king **c** his servant 2Sa 9:11 6680
Who **c** the sun not to shine, And Jb 9:7 559
And **c** that they return from evil. Jb 36:10 559
And **c** it to strike the mark. Jb 36:32 6680
That it may do whatever He **c** it On Jb 37:12 6680
The wise of heart will receive **c**, Pr 10:8 4687
your father, kept all his **c** and Jer 35:18 4687
He **c** even the unclean spirits, and Mk 1:27 *2004*
power He **c** the unclean spirits and Lk 4:36 *2004*
He **c** even the winds and the water, Lk 8:25 *2004*

COMMEMORATE
yearly to **c** the daughter of Jephthah Jg 11:40 8567

COMMEND
"And now I **c** you to God and to Ac 20:32 *3908*
I **c** to you our sister Phoebe, who Ro 16:1 *4921*
But food will not **c** us to God; 1Co 8:8 *3936*
we beginning to **c** ourselves again? 2Co 3:1 *4921*
some of those who **c** themselves; 2Co 10:12 *4921*

COMMENDABLE
be eagerly sought in a **c** manner, Ga 4:18 *2570*

COMMENDABLY
They eagerly seek you, not **c**, Ga 4:17 *2573*

COMMENDATION
letters of **c** to you or from you? 2Co 3:1 *4956*

COMMENDED
So I **c** pleasure, for there is Ec 8:15 7623b
they **c** them to the Lord in whom Ac 14:23 *3908*
they had been **c** to the grace of God Ac 14:26 *3860*
I should have been **c** by you, 2Co 12:11 *4921*

COMMENDING
c ourselves to every man's conscience 2Co 4:2 *4921*
We are not again **c** ourselves to 2Co 5:12 *4921*
c ourselves as servants of God, 2Co 6:4 *4921*

COMMENDS
he who **c** himself that is approved, 2Co 10:18 *4921*
is approved, but he whom the Lord **c**. 2Co 10:18 *4921*

COMMENSURATE
for the trouble would not be **c** Es 7:4 7737a

COMMERCIAL
shekels of silver, **c** standard. Gn 23:16 5503

COMMISSION
and **c** him in their sight. Nu 27:19 6680
of meeting, that I may **c** him." Dt 31:14 6680
And **c** it against the people of My fury Is 10:6 6680
spoke by the **c** of the LORD to the Hg 1:13 4400
and **c** of the chief priests, Ac 26:12 *2011*

COMMISSIONED
laid his hands on him and **c** him, Nu 27:23 6680
Then He **c** Joshua the son of Nun, Dt 31:23 6680
"The king has **c** me with a matter and 1Sa 21:2 6680
you and with which I have **c** you; 1Sa 21:2 6680

COMMISSIONERS
and over them three **c** Da 6:2 5632
distinguishing himself among the **c** Da 6:3 5632
Then the **c** and satraps began Da 6:4 5632
Then these **c** and satraps came by Da 6:6 5632
"All the **c** of the kingdom, the Da 6:7 5632

COMMIT
"You shall not **c** adultery. Ex 20:14 5003
and they **c** any of the things which Lv 4:13 6213a
'You shall not **c** adultery. Dt 5:18 5003
house, do not **c** this act of folly. Jg 19:23 6213a
But do not **c** such an act of folly Jg 19:24 6213a
LORD and made them **c** a great sin. 2Ki 17:21 2398
peoples who **c** these abominations? Ezr 9:14
"**C** *yourself* to the LORD; Ps 22:8 1556
Into Your hand I **c** my spirit; Ps 31:5 6485
C your way to the LORD, Trust also Ps 37:5 1556
C your works to the LORD And your Pr 16:3 1556
for kings to **c** wicked Pr 16:12 6213a
c to Me the work of My hands. Is 45:11 6680
you steal, murder, and **c** adultery and Jer 7:9 5003
house of Judah to **c** the abominations Ezk 8:17 6213a
like women who **c** adultery or shed Ezk 16:38 5003
"so that you will not **c** this Ezk 16:43 6213a
did not **c** half of your sins, Ezk 16:51 2398
his pledge, does not **c** robbery, Ezk 18:7 1497
or retain a pledge, or **c** robbery, Ezk 18:16 1497
I will **c** the judgment to them, Ezk 23:24 5414
'Will they now **c** adultery with her Ezk 23:43 2181
not **c** lewdness as you have done. Ezk 23:48 6213a
on your sword, you **c** abominations and Ezk 33:26 6213a
And your brides **c** adultery. Hos 4:13 5003
your brides when they **c** adultery, Hos 4:14 5003
'YOU SHALL NOT **C** MURDER' and Mt 5:21 *5407*
'YOU SHALL NOT **C** ADULTERY'; Mt 5:27 *3431*
unchastity, makes her **c** adultery; Mt 5:32 *3431*
and those who **c** lawlessness, Mt 13:41 *4160*
"YOU SHALL NOT **C** MURDER; Mt 19:18 *5407*
YOU SHALL NOT **C** ADULTERY; Mt 19:18 *3431*
NOT MURDER, DO NOT **C** ADULTERY, Mk 10:19 *3431*
NOT **C** ADULTERY, DO NOT MURDER, Lk 18:20 *3431*
INTO YOUR HANDS I **C** MY SPIRIT." Lk 23:46 *3908*
that one should not **c** adultery, Ro 2:22 *3431*
adultery, do you **c** adultery? Ro 2:22 *3431*
"YOU SHALL NOT **C** ADULTERY, YOU Ro 13:9 *3431*
Or did I **c** a sin in humbling 2Co 11:7 *4160*
"DO NOT **C** ADULTERY," Jas 2:11 *3431*
"DO NOT **C** MURDER." Jas 2:11 *5407*
Now if you do not **c** adultery, but Jas 2:11 *3431*
commit adultery, but do **c** murder, Jas 2:11 *5407*
you **c** murder. You are envious Jas 4:2 *5407*
who **c** sin not *leading* to death. 1Jn 5:16 *264*
and to **c** *acts of* immorality. Rv 2:14 *4203*
so that they **c** *acts of* immorality Rv 2:20 *4203*
and those who **c** adultery with her Rv 2:22 *3431*

COMMITS
not to be done, and **c** any of them, Lv 4:2 6213a
congregation of Israel **c** error and Lv 4:13 7686
'If *there is* a man who **c** adultery Lv 20:10 5003
one who **c** adultery with his Lv 20:10 5003
c any of the sins of mankind, Nu 5:6 6213a
when he **c** iniquity, I will correct 2Sa 7:14 5753b
The unfortunate **c** *himself* to You; Ps 10:14 5800a
The one who **c** adultery with a Pr 6:32 5003
his righteousness and **c** iniquity, Ezk 3:20 6213a
the poor and needy, **c** robbery, Ezk 18:12 1497
to the idols *and* **c** abomination, Ezk 18:12 6213a
his righteousness, **c** iniquity and Ezk 18:24 6213a
his righteousness, **c** iniquity and Ezk 18:26 6213a
on the day when he **c** sin.' Ezk 33:12 2398
righteousness that he **c** iniquity, Ezk 33:13 6213a
his righteousness and **c** iniquity, Ezk 33:18 6213a
for the land **c** flagrant harlotry, Hos 1:2 2181
'Whoever **c** murder shall be liable Mt 5:21 *5407*
a divorced woman **c** adultery. Mt 5:32 *3429*
another woman **c** adultery." Mt 19:9 *3429*
woman **c** adultery against her; Mk 10:11 *3429*
and marries another **c** adultery, Lk 16:18 *3431*
from a husband **c** adultery. Lk 16:18 *3431*
who **c** sin is the slave of sin. Jn 8:34 *4160*
that a man **c** is outside the body, 1Co 6:18 *4160*

COMMITTED
The chief jailer **c** to Joseph's Gn 39:22 5414
"You yourselves have **c** a great sin; Ex 32:30 2398
this people has **c** a great sin, Ex 32:31 2398
sin offering for the sin he has **c**. Lv 4:3 2398
which they have **c** becomes known, Lv 4:14 2398
he has **c** is made known to him, Lv 4:23 2398
he has **c** is made known to him, Lv 4:28 2398
for his sin which he has **c**. Lv 4:28 2398
regard to his sin which he has **c**, Lv 4:35 2398
LORD for his sin which he has **c**, Lv 5:6 2398
behalf for his sin which he has **c**, Lv 5:10 2398
which he has **c** from one of these, Lv 5:13 2398
LORD for his sin which he has **c**, Lv 19:22 2398
he has **c** will be forgiven him. Lv 19:22 2398
they have **c** incest, their Lv 20:12 6213a
of them have **c** a detestable act; Lv 20:13 6213a
which they **c** against Me, Lv 26:40 4603
confess his sins which he has **c**, Nu 5:7 6213a
your sin which you had **c** in doing Dt 9:18 2398
or any sin which he has **c**; Dt 19:15 2398
a man has **c** a sin worthy of death and Dt 21:22 1961
has **c** an act of folly in Israel by Dt 22:21 6213a
c a disgraceful thing in Israel.' " Jos 7:15 6213a
have **c** against the God of Israel, Jos 22:16 4603
because you have not **c** this Jos 22:31 4603
for they have **c** a lewd and Jg 20:6 6213a
acts that they have **c** in Israel." Jg 20:10 6213a
You have **c** all this evil, yet do 1Sa 12:20 6213a
fool and have **c** a serious error." 1Sa 26:21 7686
have sinned and have **c** iniquity, 1Ki 8:47 5753b
which he **c** and with which he made 1Ki 14:16 2398
done, with the sins which they **c**. 1Ki 14:22 2398

and **c** them to the care of the **1Ki 14:27** 6485
father which he had **c** before him; **1Ki 15:3** 6213a
"What sin have I **c**, that you are **1Ki 18:9** 2398
he did and his sin which he **c**, **2Ki 21:17** 2398
because the watch was **c** to them; **1Ch 9:27** 5921
which he **c** against the LORD, **1Ch 10:13** 4603
have sinned, we have **c** iniquity and **2Ch 6:37** 5753b
and **c** them to the care of the **2Ch 12:10** 6485
Egypt,' And **c** great blasphemies, **Ne 9:18** 6213a
And they **c** great blasphemies. **Ne 9:26** 6213a
you have **c** all this great evil by acting **Ne 13:27** 6213a
they have **c** abominable deeds; **Ps 14:1** 8581
and have **c** abominable injustice; **Ps 53:1** 8581
our fathers, We have **c** iniquity, **Ps 106:6** 5753b
"For My people have **c** two evils: **Jer 2:13** 6213a
she polluted the land and **c** **Jer 3:9** 5003
They **c** adultery And trooped to the **Jer 5:7** 5003
For to You have I **c** my cause. **Jer 11:20** 1540
have **c** against the LORD our God?' **Jer 16:10** 2398
and have **c** adultery with their **Jer 29:23** 5003
and they **c** Jeremiah to the court **Jer 37:21** 6485
their wickedness which they **c** so as to **Jer 44:3** 6213a
which they **c** in the land of Judah **Jer 44:9** 6213a
the abominations which you have **c**; **Jer 44:22** 6213a
for the evils which they have **c**, **Ezk 6:9** 6213a
which they have **c** here, **Ezk 8:17** 6213a
which are being **c** in its midst." **Ezk 9:4** 6213a
and **c** abominations before Me. **Ezk 16:50** 6213a
abominations which you have **c**. **Ezk 16:51** 6213a
act which he has **c** against Me. **Ezk 17:20** 4603
He has **c** all these abominations, **Ezk 18:13** 6213a
all his father's sins which he **c**, **Ezk 18:14** 6213a
turns from all his sins which he has **c** **Ezk 18:21** 6213a
"All his transgressions which he has **c** **Ezk 18:22** 6213a
for his treachery which he has **c** **Ezk 18:24** 4603
and his sin which he has **c**; **Ezk 18:24** 2398
for his iniquity which he has **c** **Ezk 18:26** 6213a
from his wickedness which he has **c** **Ezk 18:27** 6213a
his transgressions which he had **c**, **Ezk 18:28** 6213a
transgressions which you have **c** and **Ezk 18:31** 6586
they have **c** acts of lewdness. **Ezk 22:9** 6213a
"One has **c** abomination with **Ezk 22:11** 6213a
oppression and **c** robbery, **Ezk 22:29** 1497
"For they have **c** adultery, and **Ezk 23:37** 5003
Thus they have **c** adultery with **Ezk 23:37** 5003
of his which he has **c** he will die. **Ezk 33:13** 6213a
"None of his sins that he has **c** **Ezk 33:16** 2398
abominations which they have **c**. **Ezk 33:29** 6213a
abominations which they have **c**. **Ezk 43:8** 6213a
abominations which they have **c**. **Ezk 44:13** 6213a
you, O king, I have **c** no crime." **Da 6:22** 5648
we have sinned, **c** iniquity, acted **Da 9:5** 5753b
which they have **c** against You. **Da 9:7** 4603
Surely they have **c** crime. **Hos 6:9** 6213a
been **c** in Israel and in Jerusalem; **Mal 2:11** 6213a
has already **c** adultery with her in his **Mt 5:28** *3431*
had **c** murder in the insurrection. **Mk 15:7** *4160*
and **c** deeds worthy of a flogging, **Lk 12:48** *4160*
those who **c** the evil *deeds* to a **Jn 5:29** *4238*
being **c** by the brethren to the **Ac 15:40** *3860*
"I have **c** no offense either **Ac 25:8** *264*
have **c** anything worthy of death, **Ac 25:11** *4238*
he had **c** nothing worthy of death; **Ac 25:25** *4238*
passed over the sins previously **c**; **Ro 3:25** *4266*
of teaching to which you were **c**, **Ro 6:17** *3860*
judged him who has so **c** this, **1Co 5:3** *2716*
and He has **c** to us the word of **2Co 5:19** *5087*
sins of the people **c** in ignorance. **Heb 9:7**
of the transgressions that were **c** **Heb 9:15**
him up, and if he has **c** sins, **Jas 5:15** *4160*
WHO **C** NO SIN, NOR WAS ANY DECEIT **1Pe 2:22** *4160*
and **c** them to pits of darkness, **2Pe 2:4** *3860*
of the earth **c** *acts of* immorality, **Rv 17:2** *4203*
c *acts of* immorality with her, **Rv 18:3** *4203*
who **c** *acts of* immorality and lived **Rv 18:9** *4203*

COMMITTING

They weary themselves **c** iniquity. **Jer 9:5** 5753b
The **c** of adultery and walking in **Jer 23:14** 5003
But we are **c** a great evil against **Jer 26:19** 6213a
the house of Israel are **c** here, **Ezk 8:6** 6213a
abominations that they are **c** here." **Ezk 8:9** 6213a
house of Israel are **c** in the dark, **Ezk 8:12** 6213a
abominations which they are **c**." **Ezk 8:13** 6213a
against Me by **c** unfaithfulness, **Ezk 14:13** 4603
ensure life without **c** iniquity, **Ezk 33:15** 6213a
another man, she is **c** adultery." **Mk 10:12** *3431*
men with men **c** indecent acts and **Ro 1:27** *2716*
you are **c** sin *and* are convicted by **Jas 2:9** *2038b*
c a sin not *leading* to death, **1Jn 5:16** *264*

COMMON

'Now if anyone of the **c** people **Lv 4:27** 776
The king made silver *as* **c** as **1Ki 10:27**
on the graves of the **c** people. **2Ki 23:6** 1121
The king made silver *as* **c** as **2Ch 9:27**
"You have nothing in **c** with us in **Ezr 4:3**
rich and the poor have a **c** bond, **Pr 22:2** 6298
and the oppressor have this in **c**: **Pr 29:13** 6298
So the **c** man has been humbled **Is 2:9**
So the **c** man will be humbled **Is 5:15**
What does straw have *in* **c** with **Jer 23:28**
the burial place of the **c** people. **Jer 26:23** 1121
wilderness with men of the **c** sort. **Ezk 23:42**
7230, 120
shall be for **c** use for the city, **Ezk 48:15** 2455
saw the iron mixed with **c** clay. **Da 2:41** 2917
saw the iron mixed with **c** clay, **Da 2:43** 2917
together and had all things in **c**; **Ac 2:44** *2839*
things were **c** property to them. **Ac 4:32** *2839*
use and another for **c** use? **Ro 9:21** *819*
you but such as is **c** to man; **1Co 10:13** *442*
of the Spirit for the **c** good. **1Co 12:7** *4851a*
believer in **c** with an unbeliever? **2Co 6:15** *3310*
By **c** confession, great is the **1Tm 3:16** *3672*
Titus, my true child in a **c** faith: **Ti 1:4** *2839*
write you about our **c** salvation, **Jude 1:3** *2839*
His purpose by having a **c** purpose, **Rv 17:17** *1520*

COMMONWEALTH

excluded from the **c** of Israel, **Eph 2:12** *4174*

COMMOTION

does the noise of this **c** *mean?*" **1Sa 4:14** 1995
the **c** in the camp of the Philistines **1Sa 14:19** 1995
A great **c** out of the land of the north **Jer 10:22** 7494
and He saw a **c**, and *people* **Mk 5:38** *2351*
"Why make a **c** and weep? **Mk 5:39** *2350b*

COMMUNICATED

and He sent and **c** *it* by His angel **Rv 1:1** *4591*

COMMUNITY

"They are driven from the **c**; **Jb 30:5** 1460b

COMPACT

As a city that is **c** together; **Ps 122:3** 2266

COMPANIES

herds and the camels, into two **c**; **Gn 32:7** 4264
and now I have become two **c**. **Gn 32:10** 4264
divided the 300 men into three **c**, **Jg 7:16** 7218
When the three **c** blew the trumpets **Jg 7:20** 7218
in wait against Shechem in four **c**. **Jg 9:34** 7218
and divided them into three **c**, **Jg 9:43** 7218
the other two **c** then dashed **Jg 9:44** 7218
Saul put the people in three **c**; **1Sa 11:11** 7218
of the Philistines in three **c**: **1Sa 13:17** 7218
As at the dance of the two **c**? **SS 6:13** 4264
c that are assembled about you, **Ezk 38:7** 6951

COMPANION

"Why are you striking your **c**?" **Ex 2:13** 7453
and deceives his **c** in regard to a **Lv 6:2** 5997
or *if* he has extorted from his **c**, **Lv 6:2** 5997
to his **c** who had been his friend. **Jg 14:20** 4828
so I gave her to your **c**. **Jg 15:2** 4828
his wife and gave her to his **c**." **Jg 15:6** 4828
eyes and give *them* to your **c**, **2Sa 12:11** 7453
to jackals And a **c** of ostriches. **Jb 30:29** 7453
My **c** and my familiar friend; **Ps 55:13** 441a
am a **c** of all those who fear You, **Ps 119:63** 2270
That leaves the **c** of her youth And **Pr 2:17** 441a
the **c** of fools will suffer harm. **Pr 13:20** 7462b
But he who is a **c** of gluttons **Pr 28:7** 7462b
Is the **c** of a man who destroys. **Pr 28:24** 2270
falls, the one will lift up his **c**. **Ec 4:10** 2270
your **c** and your wife by covenant. **Mal 2:14** 2278
Indeed, true **c**, I ask you also to **Php 4:3** *4805*

COMPANIONS

of my virginity, I and my **c**." **Jg 11:37** 7464
and she left with her **c**, **Jg 11:38** 7464
brought thirty **c** to be with him. **Jg 14:11** 4828
The virgins, her **c** who follow her, **Ps 45:14** 7464
Beside the flocks of your **c**?" **SS 1:7** 2270
My **c** are listening for your voice **SS 8:13** 2270
are rebels And **c** of thieves; **Is 1:23** 2270
all his **c** will be put to shame, **Is 44:11** 2270
Former **c** to be head over you? **Jer 13:21** 441a
them to death along with their **c**. **Jer 41:8** 251
and for the sons of Israel, his **c**'; **Ezk 37:16** 2270
all the house of Israel, his **c**.' **Ezk 37:16** 2270
and the tribes of Israel, his **c**; **Ezk 37:19** 2270
he became hungry, he and his **c**, **Mt 12:3**
3588, 3326
Simon and his **c** searched for Him; **Mk 1:36**
3588, 3326
and he and his **c** became hungry; **Mk 2:25**
3588, 3326
father and mother and His own **c**, **Mk 5:40**
3588, 3326
these instructions to Peter and his **c**. **Mk 16:20**
amazement had seized him and all his **c** **Lk 5:9**
3588, 4862
alone, and gave it to his **c**?" **Lk 6:4**
3588, 3326
c had been overcome with sleep; **Lk 9:32**
3588, 4862
they went to their own **c** **Ac 4:23**
Now Paul and his **c** put out to sea **Ac 13:13**
3588, 4012
Paul's traveling **c** from Macedonia. **Ac 19:29** *4898*
THE OIL OF GLADNESS ABOVE YOUR **C**." **Heb 1:9** *3353*

COMPANY

you may become a **c** of peoples. **Gn 28:3** 6951
comes to the one **c** and attacks it, **Gn 32:8** 4264
the **c** which is left will escape." **Gn 32:8** 4264
by all this **c** which I have met?" **Gn 33:8** 4264
A nation and a **c** of nations shall **Gn 35:11** 6951
I will make you a **c** of peoples, **Gn 48:4** 6951
and it was a very great **c**. **Gn 50:9** 4264
he spoke to Korah and all his **c**, **Nu 16:5** 5712
yourselves, Korah and all your **c**, **Nu 16:6** 5712
"Therefore you and all your **c** are **Nu 16:11** 5712
"You and all your **c** be present **Nu 16:16** 5712
not become like Korah and his **c** **Nu 16:40** 5712
against Aaron in the **c** of Korah, **Nu 26:9** 5712
with Korah, when that **c** died, **Nu 26:10** 5712
yet he was not among the **c** of **Nu 27:3** 5712
the LORD in the **c** of Korah; **Nu 27:3** 5712
and one **c** comes by the way of the **Jg 9:37** 7218
Then Abimelech and the **c** who was **Jg 9:44** 7218
one **c** turned toward Ophrah, to the **1Sa 13:17** 7218
another **c** turned toward Beth-horon, **1Sa 13:18** 7218
and another **c** turned toward the **1Sa 13:18** 7218
the **c** of the prophets prophesying, **1Sa 19:20** 3862
to the man of God with all his **c**, **2Ki 5:15** 4264
he saw the **c** of Jehu as he came, **2Ki 9:17** 8229
Jehu as he came, and said, "I see a **c**." **2Ki 9:17** 8229
the **c** of the godless is barren, **Jb 15:34** 5712
You have laid waste all my **c**. **Jb 16:7** 5712
in **c** with the workers of iniquity, **Jb 34:8** 2274
And engulfed the **c** of Abiram. **Ps 106:17** 5712
And a fire blazed up in their **c**; **Ps 106:18** 5712
In the **c** of the upright and in the **Ps 111:1** 5475
But he who keeps **c** with harlots **Pr 29:3** 7462b
A great **c**, they will return here. **Jer 31:8** 6951
c will not help him in the war, **Ezk 17:17** 6951
wagons, and with a **c** of peoples. **Ezk 23:24** 6951
'Bring up a **c** against them and **Ezk 23:46** 6951
'The **c** will stone them with **Ezk 23:47** 6951
all your **c** that is in your midst, **Ezk 27:27** 6951
Your merchandise and all your **c** **Ezk 27:34** 6951
over you With a **c** of many peoples, **Ezk 32:3** 6951
"Assyria is there and all her **c**; **Ezk 32:22** 6951
her **c** is round about her grave. **Ezk 32:23** 6951
a great **c** *with* buckler and shield, **Ezk 38:4** 6951
assembled your **c** to seize plunder, **Ezk 38:13** 6951
first enjoyed your **c** for a while **Ro 15:24**
find *refreshing* rest in your **c**. **Ro 15:32**
"Bad **c** corrupts good morals." **1Co 15:33** *3657*

COMPARABLE

who in the skies is **c** to the LORD? **Ps 89:6** 6186a
length **c** to one of the portions, **Ezk 45:7** 5980
heaven will be **c** to ten virgins, **Mt 25:1** *3666*

COMPARE

There is none to **c** with You. **Ps 40:5** 6186a
things cannot **c** with her. **Pr 8:11** 7737a
what likeness will you **c** with Him? **Is 40:18** 6186a
Me And make Me equal and **c** Me, **Is 46:5** 4911a
To what shall I **c** you, O daughter **La 2:13** 1819
could not **c** with its boughs, **Ezk 31:8** 1819
could **c** with it in its beauty. **Ezk 31:8** 1819
to what shall I **c** this generation? **Mt 11:16** *3666*
I **c** the men of this generation, **Lk 7:31** *3666*
like, and to what shall I **c** it? **Lk 13:18** *3666*
what shall I **c** the kingdom of God? **Lk 13:20** *3666*
For we are not bold to class or **c** **2Co 10:12** *4793*
and **c** themselves with themselves, **2Co 10:12** *4793*

COMPARED

'You **c** yourself to a young lion of **Ezk 32:2** 1819
on them, may be **c** to a wise man **Mt 7:24** *3666*
"The kingdom of heaven may be **c** **Mt 13:24** *3666*
heaven may be **c** to a king **Mt 18:23** *3666*
of heaven may be **c** to a king who **Mt 22:2** *3666*
c with the glory that is to be revealed **Ro 8:18**

COMPARES

And nothing you desire **c** with her. **Pr 3:15** 7737a

COMPARISON

have I done now in **c** with you? **Jg 8:2**
was I able to do in **c** with you?" **Jg 8:3**
not seem to you like nothing in **c**? **Hg 2:3** 3644
weight of glory far beyond all **c**, **2Co 4:17** *5236*
say that we have been weak *by* **c**. **2Co 11:21**

COMPASS

planes and outlines it with a **c**, **Is 44:13** 4230
toward the four points of the **c**, **Da 11:4** 8064

COMPASSION

the **c** of the LORD *was* upon him; **Gn 19:16** 2551
and may God Almighty grant you **c** **Gn 43:14** 7356
and will show **c** on whom I will **Ex 33:19** 7355
on whom I will show **c**." **Ex 33:19** 7355
c on you and make you increase, **Dt 13:17** 7355
from captivity, and have **c** on you, **Dt 30:3** 7355
And will have **c** on His servants, **Dt 32:36** 5162
for you have had **c** on me. **1Sa 23:21** 2550
he did this thing and had no **c**." **2Sa 12:6** 2550
and make them *objects of* **c** before **1Ki 8:50** 7356
that they may have **c** on them **1Ki 8:50** 7355
LORD was gracious to them and had **c** **2Ki 13:23** 7355
your brothers and your sons *will find* **c** **2Ch 30:9** 7356
because He had **c** on His people and **2Ch 36:15** 2550
had no **c** on young man or virgin, **2Ch 36:17** 2550
and grant him **c** before this man." **Ne 1:11** 7356
You, in Your great **c**, **Ne 9:19** 7356
and according to Your great **c** You **Ne 9:27** 7356
rescued them according to Your **c**, **Ne 9:28** 7356
in Your great **c** You did not make **Ne 9:31** 7356
and have **c** on me according to the **Ne 13:22** 2347
And implore the **c** of the Almighty, **Jb 8:5** 2603a
Your **c** and Your lovingkindnesses, **Ps 25:6** 7356
will not withhold Your **c** from me; **Ps 40:11** 7356
Your **c** blot out my transgressions. **Ps 51:1** 7356
to the greatness of Your **c**, **Ps 69:16** 7356
will have **c** on the poor and needy, **Ps 72:13** 2347
Or has He in anger withdrawn His **c**? **Ps 77:9** 7356
Let Your **c** come quickly to meet us, **Ps 79:8** 7356
will arise *and* have **c** on Zion; **Ps 102:13** 7355
you with lovingkindness and **c**; **Ps 103:4** 7356
as a father has **c** on *his* children, **Ps 103:13** 7355
LORD has **c** on those who fear Him. **Ps 103:13** 7355
He also made them *objects of* **c** In **Ps 106:46** 7356
Your **c** come to me that I may live, **Ps 119:77** 7356
And will have **c** on His servants. **Ps 135:14** 5162
the **c** of the wicked is cruel. **Pr 12:10** 7356
and forsakes *them* will find **c**. **Pr 28:13** 7355
have **c** on the fruit of the womb, **Is 13:18** 7355
the LORD will have **c** on Jacob and **Is 14:1** 7355
Maker will not have **c** on them. **Is 27:11** 7355
He waits on high to have **c** on you. **Is 30:18** 7355
who has **c** on them will lead them And **Is 49:10** 7355

Context	Reference	No.
And will have c on His afflicted.	Is 49:13	7355
have no c on the son of her womb?	Is 49:15	7355
with great c I will gather you.	Is 54:7	7356
I will have c on you,"	Is 54:8	7355
Says the LORD who has c on you.	Is 54:10	7355
LORD, And He will have c on him,	Is 55:7	7355
in My favor I have had c on you.	Is 60:10	7355
granted them according to His c And	Is 63:7	7356
Your c are restrained toward me.	Is 63:15	7356
them, I will again have c on them;	Jer 12:15	7355
not show pity nor be sorry nor have c	Jer 13:14	7355
"*My* lovingkindness and c.	Jer 16:5	7356
them nor have pity nor c."	Jer 21:7	7355
And have c on his dwelling places;	Jer 30:18	7355
'I will also show you c,	Jer 42:12	7356
so that he will have c on you and	Jer 42:12	7355
Then He will have c According to	La 3:32	7355
things for you, to have c on you.	Ezk 16:5	2550
Now God granted Daniel favor and c	Da 1:9	7356
they might request c from the God of	Da 2:18	7359
our God *belong* c and forgiveness,	Da 9:9	7356
but on account of Your great c.	Da 9:18	7356
have c on the house of Israel,	Hos 1:6	7355
"But I will have c on the house	Hos 1:7	7355
I will have no c on her children,	Hos 2:4	7355
In lovingkindness and in c,	Hos 2:19	7356
I will also have c on her who had	Hos 2:23	7355
on her who had not obtained c,	Hos 2:23	7355
C will be hidden from My sight.	Hos 13:14	5164
the sword, While he stifled his c;	Am 1:11	7356
"You had c on the plant for which	Jon 4:10	2347
Should I not have c on Nineveh,	Jon 4:11	2347
He will again have c on us;	Mi 7:19	7355
how long will You have no c for	Zch 1:12	7355
"I will return to Jerusalem with c;	Zch 1:16	7356
and c each to his brother;	Zch 7:9	7356
Because I have had c on them;	Zch 10:6	7355
'I DESIRE C, AND NOT SACRIFICE,'	Mt 9:13	*1656*
people, He felt c for them,	Mt 9:36	*4697*
'I DESIRE C, AND NOT A SACRIFICE,'	Mt 12:7	*1656*
crowd, and felt c for them	Mt 14:14	*4697*
"I feel c for the people,	Mt 15:32	*4697*
"And the lord of that slave felt c and	Mt 18:27	*4697*
Moved with c, Jesus touched	Mt 20:34	*4697*
Moved with c, Jesus stretched out	Mk 1:41	*4697*
And He felt c for them because	Mk 6:34	*4697*
"I feel c for the people	Mk 8:2	*4697*
Lord saw her, He felt c for her,	Lk 7:13	*4697*
and when he saw him, he felt c,	Lk 10:33	*4697*
saw him and felt c *for him,*	Lk 15:20	*4697*
C ON WHOM I HAVE COMPASSION."	Ro 9:15	*3627*
COMPASSION ON WHOM I HAVE C."	Ro 9:15	*3627*
Spirit, if any affection and c,	Php 2:1	*3628*
and beloved, put on a heart of c,	Col 3:12	*3628*
Lord is full of c and *is* merciful.	Jas 5:11	*4184*
COMPASSIONATE		
the LORD God, c and gracious,	Ex 34:6	7349
"For the LORD your God is a c God;	Dt 4:31	7349
LORD your God is gracious and c,	2Ch 30:9	7349
of forgiveness, Gracious and c,	Ne 9:17	7349
For You are a gracious and c God.	Ne 9:31	7349
But He, being c, forgave *their*	Ps 78:38	7349
The LORD is c and gracious, Slow	Ps 103:8	7349
The LORD is gracious and c.	Ps 111:4	7349
is gracious and c and righteous.	Ps 112:4	7349
Yes, our God is c.	Ps 116:5	7355
The hands of c women Boiled their	La 4:10	7362
God, For He is gracious and c,	Jl 2:13	7349
You are a gracious and c God,	Jon 4:2	7349
COMPASSIONS		
never cease, For His c never fail.	La 3:22	7356
within Me, All My c are kindled.	Hos 11:8	5150
COMPEL		
the hedges, and c *them* to come in,	Lk 14:23	*315*
how *is it that* you c the Gentiles	Ga 2:14	*315*
try to c you to be circumcised,	Ga 6:12	*315*
COMPELLED		
The Egyptians c the sons of	Ex 1:13	
you yourselves c me.	2Co 12:11	*315*
a Greek, was c to be circumcised.	Ga 2:3	*315*
COMPENSATE		
the king c me *with* this reward?	2Sa 19:36	1580
COMPENSATION		
for it is your c in return for	Nu 18:31	7939
COMPETE		
Then how can you c with horses?	Jer 12:5	2734
COMPETENT		
are you not c *to constitute* the	1Co 6:2	*370*
COMPETES		
Everyone who c in the games	1Co 9:25	*75*
Also if anyone c as an athlete,	2Tm 2:5	*118*
he c according to the rules.	2Tm 2:5	*118*
COMPETING		
a king because you are c in cedar?	Jer 22:15	2734
COMPILE		
have undertaken to c an account of	Lk 1:1	*392*
COMPLACENCY		
the c of fools will destroy them.	Pr 1:32	7962
COMPLACENT		
ear to my word, You c daughters.	Is 32:9	982
will be troubled, O c *daughters;*	Is 32:10	982
Be troubled, you c *daughters;*	Is 32:11	982
COMPLAIN		
became like those who c of adversity	Nu 11:1	596
or their brothers come to c to us,	Jg 21:22	7378
I should c anymore to the king?"	2Sa 19:28	2199
c in the bitterness of my soul.	Jb 7:11	7878
"Why do you c against Him That	Jb 33:13	7378
and at noon, I will c and murmur,	Ps 55:17	7878
Do not c, brethren, against one	Jas 5:9	*4727*
COMPLAINED		
But Abraham c to Abimelech because	Gn 21:25	3198
COMPLAINING		
Who has contentions? Who has c?	Pr 23:29	7879
COMPLAINT		
me, My couch will ease my c,'	Jb 7:13	7879
'I will forget my c,	Jb 9:27	7879
I will give full vent to my c;	Jb 10:1	7879
"As for me, is my c to man?	Jb 21:4	7879
"Even today my c is rebellion;	Jb 23:2	7879
When they filed a c against me,	Jb 31:13	7379
And with unceasing c in his bones;	Jb 33:19	7379
in my c and am surely distracted,	Ps 55:2	7879
Hear my voice, O God, in my c;	Ps 64:1	7879
I pour out my c before Him;	Ps 142:2	7879
man, Offer c in view of his sins?	La 3:39	596
a c arose on the part of the	Ac 6:1	*1112*
with him have a c against any man,	Ac 19:38	*3056*
whoever has a c against anyone;	Col 3:13	*3437*
to one another without c.	1Pe 4:9	*1112*
COMPLAINTS		
heard the c of the sons of Israel,	Nu 14:27	8519b
COMPLETE		
of the Amorite is not yet c."	Gn 15:16	8003
"C the week of this one, and we	Gn 29:27	4390
"C your work quota, *your* daily	Ex 5:13	3615
be c to its top to the first ring;	Ex 26:24	8535
day there is a sabbath of c rest,	Ex 31:15	7677
a sabbath of c rest to the LORD;	Ex 35:2	7677
c to its top to the first ring;	Ex 36:29	8535
day there is a sabbath of c rest,	Lv 23:3	7677
there shall be seven c sabbaths.	Lv 23:15	8549
to be a sabbath of c rest to you,	Lv 23:32	7677
according to your c number from	Nu 14:29	3605
law in a book until they were c,	Dt 31:24	8552
of this song, until they were c:	Dt 31:30	8552
"When your days are c and you lie	2Sa 7:12	4390
until seventy years were c.	2Ch 36:21	4390
C darkness is held in reserve for	Jb 20:26	3605
For a c destruction, one that is	Is 10:23	3617
will not execute a c destruction.	Jer 4:27	3617
do not execute a c destruction;	Jer 5:10	3617
will not make you a c destruction.	Jer 5:18	3617
remnant of Israel to a c end?"	Ezk 11:13	3617
even until a c destruction,	Da 9:27	3617
He will make a c end of its site,	Na 1:8	3617
LORD, He will make a c end of it.	Na 1:9	3617
For He will make a c end,	Zph 1:18	3617
"If you wish to be c,	Mt 19:21	*5046*
to see if he has enough to c it?	Lk 14:28	*535*
you be made c in the same mind	1Co 1:10	*2675*
so he would also c in you this	2Co 8:6	*2005*
whenever your obedience is c.	2Co 10:6	*4137*
also pray for, that you be made c.	2Co 13:9	*2676*
brethren, rejoice, be made c,	2Co 13:11	*2675*
joy c by being of the same mind,	Php 2:2	*4137*
risking his life to c what was	Php 2:30	*378*
may present every man c in Christ.	Col 1:28	*5046*
and in Him you have been made c,	Col 2:10	*4137*
c what is lacking in your faith?	1Th 3:10	*2675*
and soul and body be preserved c,	1Th 5:23	*3648*
that you may be perfect and c,	Jas 1:4	*3648*
so that our joy may be made c.	1Jn 1:4	*4137*
COMPLETED		
the heavens and the earth were c,	Gn 2:1	3615
God c His work which He had done,	Gn 2:2	3615
"Give *me* my wife, for my time is c,	Gn 29:21	4390
Jacob did so and c her week,	Gn 29:28	4390
"Why have you not c your required	Ex 5:14	3615
of the tent of meeting was c;	Ex 39:32	3615
days of her purification are c.	Lv 12:4	4390
days of her purification are c,	Lv 12:6	4390
until everything was c that the LORD	Jos 4:10	8552
and successfully c all that he had	2Ch 7:11	6743b
So the house of the LORD was c.	2Ch 8:16	8003
helped them until the work was c and	2Ch 29:34	3615
and it is not *yet* c.'	Ezr 5:16	8000
This temple was c on the third	Ezr 6:15	3319
Now when these things had been c,	Ezr 9:1	3615
So the wall was c on the	Ne 6:15	7999a
When these days were c,	Es 1:5	4390
beautification were c as follows:	Es 2:12	4390
of feasting had c their cycle,	Jb 1:5	5362b
has c all His work on Mount Zion	Is 10:12	1214
when seventy years are c I will punish	Jer 25:12	4390
years have been c for Babylon,	Jer 29:10	4390
of your iniquity has been c,	La 4:22	8552
"When you have c these, you shall	Ezk 4:6	3615
you have c the days of your siege.	Ezk 4:8	3615
when the days of the siege are c.	Ezk 5:2	4390
'When they have c the days,	Ezk 43:27	3615
the entire three weeks were c.	Da 10:3	4390
all these *events* will be c.	Da 12:7	3615
days were c for her to give birth.	Lk 2:6	*4092a*
to the law of Moses were c,	Lk 2:22	*4092a*
When He had c all His discourse in	Lk 7:1	*4137*
deeds c in the sight of My God.	Rv 3:2	*4137*
they had been, would be c also.	Rv 6:11	*4137*
until the thousand years were c;	Rv 20:3	*5055*
until the thousand years were c.	Rv 20:5	*5055*
When the thousand years are c,	Rv 20:7	*5055*
COMPLETELY		
surely drive you out from here c.	Ex 11:1	3617
care of him until he is c healed.	Ex 21:19	7495
and I will c destroy them.	Ex 23:23	3582
that person shall be c cut off;	Nu 15:31	3772
Are we to perish c?"	Nu 17:13	8552
and the LORD c destroyed them;	Dt 11:4	5704, 3117, 2088
the Salt Sea, were c cut off.	Jos 3:16	8552
but they did not drive them out c.	Jos 17:13	3423
but they did not drive them out c.	Jg 1:28	3423
of a lion, will c lose heart;	2Sa 17:10	4549
And they will be c burned with	2Sa 23:7	8313
to a cubit, c surrounding the sea;	1Ki 7:24	5439
all the lands, destroying them c.	2Ki 19:11	2763a
him, so as not to destroy *him* c;	2Ch 12:12	3617
those whose heart is c His.	2Ch 16:9	8003
of Mount Seir destroying *them* c;	2Ch 20:23	8045
"O that you would be c silent,	Jb 13:5	2790b
are c estranged from me.	Jb 19:13	389
"Let us c subdue them."	Ps 74:8	3162
it was c overgrown with thistles;	Pr 24:31	3605
Therefore I c despaired of all the	Ec 2:20	5437, 3820
But the idols will c vanish.	Is 2:18	3632
have c *disappeared* from the land.	Is 16:4	8552
The earth will be c laid waste and	Is 24:3	1238b
laid waste and c despoiled,	Is 24:3	962
step on them, I would burn them c.	Is 27:4	3162
all the lands, destroying them c.	Is 37:11	2763a
a choice vine, A c faithful seed.	Jer 2:21	3605
Will not that land be c polluted?	Jer 3:1	2610
Have You c rejected Judah?	Jer 14:19	3988a
you be c free from punishment?	Jer 25:29	5352
For I will destroy c all the	Jer 30:11	3617
Only I will not destroy you c.	Jer 30:11	3617
by famine until they are c gone.	Jer 44:27	3615
the one who will be c acquitted?	Jer 49:12	5352
But she will be c desolate;	Jer 50:13	3605
wall of Babylon will be c razed And	Jer 51:58	6209
Will it not c wither as soon as	Ezk 17:10	3001
We are c cut off.'	Ezk 37:11	
king of Israel will be c cut off.	Hos 10:15	1820
'We are c destroyed!	Mi 2:4	7703
consumed As stubble c withered.	Na 1:10	4392
pass through you; He is cut off c.	Na 1:15	3605
city, c full of lies *and* pillage;	Na 3:1	3605
"I will c remove all *things* From	Zph 1:2	5486
if you c obey the LORD your God.	Zch 6:15	8085
immediately they were c astounded.	Mk 5:42	*1611, 3173*
to wash his feet, but is c clean;	Jn 13:10	*3650*
devoting himself c to the word,	Ac 18:5	*4912*
fix your hope c on the grace to be	1Pe 1:13	*5049*
COMPLETING		
"And while John was c his course,	Ac 13:25	*4137*
COMPLETION		
at the c of the burnt offerings,	2Ch 29:29	3615
the c of the desolations of Jerusalem,	Da 9:2	4390
the c of the days of purification,	Ac 21:26	*1604*
also the c of it by your ability.	2Co 8:11	*2005*
COMPLIMENTS		
you have eaten, And waste your c.	Pr 23:8	1697, 5273a
COMPOSE		
I could c words against you And	Jb 16:4	2266
COMPOSED		
I have c and quieted my soul;	Ps 131:2	7737a
"I c *my soul* until morning.	Is 38:13	7737a
David have c songs for themselves,	Am 6:5	2803
The first account I c,	Ac 1:1	*4160*
But God has *so* c the body, giving	1Co 12:24	*4786*
COMPOSURE		
because c allays great offenses.	Ec 10:4	4832
not be quickly shaken from your c or	2Th 2:2	*3563*
COMPREHEND		
great things which we cannot c.	Jb 37:5	3045
hearts so that they cannot c.	Is 44:18	7919a
not c the things that were said.	Lk 18:34	*1097*
and the darkness did not c it.	Jn 1:5	*2638*
may be able to c with all the	Eph 3:18	*2638*
COMPREHENDS		
speech which no one c,	Is 33:19	8085
COMPREHENSION		
of God, which surpasses all c,	Php 4:7	*3563*
COMPRESSES		
c his lips brings evil to pass.	Pr 16:30	7169
COMPULSION		
permit you to go, except under c.	Ex 3:19	2389, 3027
for under c he will let them go,	Ex 6:1	2389, 3027
and under c he will drive them	Ex 6:1	2389, 3027
to the law, there was no c,	Es 1:8	597
to boast of, for I am under c;	1Co 9:16	*318*
not grudgingly or under c,	2Co 9:7	*318*
would not be, in effect, by c	Phm 1:14	*318*
exercising oversight not under c,	1Pe 5:2	*317*
CONANIAH		
and C the Levite *was* the officer	2Ch 31:12	3562
overseers under the authority of C and	2Ch 31:13	3562
C also, and Shemaiah and Nethanel,	2Ch 35:9	3562
CONCEAL		
him, nor shall you spare or c him.	Dt 13:8	3680
That You would c me until Your	Jb 14:13	5641
is with the Almighty I will not c.	Jb 27:11	3582
He will c me in His tabernacle;	Ps 27:5	6845

not c them from their children, Ps 78:4 3582
is the glory of God to c a matter, Pr 25:2 5641
They do not *even* c *it.* Is 3:9 3582
he will not be able to c himself; Jer 49:10 2247
Do not c *it but* say, Jer 50:2 3582
c these words and seal up the book Da 12:4 5640
And though they c themselves from Am 9:3 5641

CONCEALED
they are c in the earth inside my Jos 7:21 2934
it was c in his tent with the Jos 7:22 2934
things You have c in Your heart; Jb 10:13 6845
And have not c from their fathers, Jb 15:18 3582
And c from the birds of the sky. Jb 28:21 5641
I have not c Your lovingkindness Ps 40:10 3582
open rebuke Than love that is c. Pr 27:5 5641
have c ourselves with deception." Is 28:15 5641
their discerning men will be c. Is 29:14 5641
shadow of His hand He has c Me; Is 49:2 2244
is their iniquity c from My eyes. Jer 16:17 6845
for *these* words are c and sealed Da 12:9 5640
for there is nothing c that will not Mt 10:26 2572
and it was c from them so that Lk 9:45 3871
For you are like c tombs, Lk 11:44 82
which are otherwise cannot be c. 1Tm 5:25 2928

CONCEALMENT
To shoot from c at the blameless, Ps 64:4 4565

CONCEALS
mouth of the wicked c violence. Pr 10:6 3680
mouth of the wicked c violence. Pr 10:11 3680
He who c hatred *has* lying lips, Pr 10:18 3680
he who is trustworthy c a matter. Pr 11:13 3680
But a prudent man c dishonor. Pr 12:16 3680
A prudent man c knowledge, But the Pr 12:23 3680
He who c a transgression seeks love, Pr 17:9 3680
He who c his transgressions will Pr 28:13 3680

CONCEIT
from selfishness or empty c, Php 2:3 2754

CONCEITED
Do not be c, but fear; Ro 11:20
5426, 5308
so that he will not become c 1Tm 3:6 5187
he is c *and* understands nothing; 1Tm 6:4 5187
rich in this present world not to be c 1Tm 6:17 5309
treacherous, reckless, c, 2Tm 3:4 5187

CONCEIVE
will then be free and c children. Nu 5:28 2232
shall c and give birth to a son. Jg 13:3 2029
shall c and give birth to a son, Jg 13:5 2030
shall c and give birth to a son, Jg 13:7 2030
And the LORD enabled her to c, Ru 4:13 2032
"They c mischief and bring forth Jb 15:35 2029
They c mischief and bring forth Is 59:4 2029
behold, you will c in your womb and Lk 1:31 4815
herself received ability to c, Heb 11:11
2602, 4690

CONCEIVED
and she c and gave birth to Cain, Gn 4:1 2029
relations with his wife and she c, Gn 4:17 2029
He went in to Hagar, and she c; Gn 16:4 2029
and when she saw that she had c, Gn 16:4 2029
but when she saw that she had c, Gn 16:5 2029
So Sarah c and bore a son to Gn 21:2 2029
him and Rebekah his wife c. Gn 25:21 2029
Leah c and bore a son and Gn 29:32 2029
c again and bore a son and said, Gn 29:33 2029
c again and bore a son and said, Gn 29:34 2029
c again and bore a son and said, Gn 29:35 2029
Bilhah c and bore Jacob a son. Gn 30:5 2029
Rachel's maid Bilhah c again Gn 30:7 2029
she c and bore Jacob a fifth son. Gn 30:17 2029
Leah c again and bore a sixth Gn 30:19 2029
So she c and bore a son and said, Gn 30:23 2029
So she c and bore a son and he Gn 38:3 2029
Then she c again and bore a son Gn 38:4 2029
went in to her, and she c by him. Gn 38:18 2029
The woman c and bore a son; Ex 2:2 2029
"Was it I who c all this people? Nu 11:12 2029
in due time, after Hannah had c, 1Sa 1:20 2029
and she c and gave birth to three 1Sa 2:21 2029
The woman c; and she sent and told 2Sa 11:5 2029
The woman c and bore a son at 2Ki 4:17 2029
and she c *and bore* Miriam, 1Ch 4:17 2029
wife, and she c and bore a son, 1Ch 7:23 2029
the night *which* said, 'A boy is c.' Jb 3:3 2029
And in sin my mother c me. Ps 51:5 3179
into the room of her who c me." SS 3:4 2029
and she c and gave birth to a son. Is 8:3 2029
"You have c chaff, you will give Is 33:11 2029
and she c and bore him a son. Hos 1:3 2029
Then she c again and gave birth to Hos 1:6 2029
she c and gave birth to a son. Hos 1:8 2029
who c them has acted shamefully. Hos 2:5 2029
c in her is of the Holy Spirit. Mt 1:20 1080
has also c a son in her old age; Lk 1:36 4815
angel before He was c in the womb. Lk 2:21 4815
have c this deed in your heart? Ac 5:4 5087
when she had c *twins* by one man, Ro 9:10
2845, 2192
when lust has c, it gives birth to sin; Jas 1:15 4815

CONCEIVES
wickedness, And he c mischief and Ps 7:14 2029

CONCEIVING
C *in* and uttering from the heart Is 59:13 2029

CONCEPTION
No birth, no pregnancy and no c! Hos 9:11 2032

CONCERN
with him *there* he did not c himself Gn 39:6 3045
my master does not c himself with Gn 39:8 3045
not c yourselves with your goods, Gn 45:20
2347, 5869
his house with no c even for this. Ex 7:23
7896, 3820
truly we have done this out of c, Jos 22:24 1674
of my great c and provocation." 1Sa 1:16 7879
"We have no c of silver or gold 2Sa 21:4
the weights of the bag are His c. Pr 16:11 4639
wicked does not understand *such* c. Pr 29:7 1847
"But I had c for My holy name, Ezk 36:21 2550
But I want you to be free from c. 1Co 7:32 275
on me *of* c for all the churches. 2Co 11:28 3308
led into sin without my intense c? 2Co 11:29 4448
you have revived your c for me; Php 4:10 5426
he has a deep c for you and for those Col 4:13 4192

CONCERNED
"I am indeed c about you and what Ex 3:16 6485
when they heard that the LORD was c Ex 4:31 6485
to be c whether *it is* good or bad, Lv 27:33 1239
else my father will cease *to be* c 1Sa 9:5
your father has ceased to be c 1Sa 10:2 1697
And that You are c about him, Jb 7:17
7896, 3820
is c for the rights of the poor, Pr 29:7 3045
the upright are c for his life. Pr 29:10 1245
Perhaps *your* god will be c about Jon 1:6 6245b
and is not c about the sheep. Jn 10:13 3199
because he was c about the poor, Jn 12:6 3199
related how God first c Himself about Ac 15:14 1980a
not c about any of these things. Ac 18:17 3199
is c about the things of the Lord, 1Co 7:32 3309
c about the things of the world, 1Co 7:33 3309
is c about the things of the Lord, 1Co 7:34 3309
c about the things of the world, 1Co 7:34 3309
God is not c about oxen, is He? 1Co 9:9 3199
genuinely be c for your welfare. Php 2:20 3309
and I may be less c *about you.* Php 2:28 253
indeed, you were c *before,* Php 4:10 5426
OF MAN, THAT YOU ARE C ABOUT HIM? Heb 2:6 1980a

CONCERNING
Pharaoh commanded *his* men c him; Gn 12:20 5921
and swore to him c this matter. Gn 24:9 5921
Esau is consoling himself c you Gn 27:42
later, when you come c my wages. Gn 30:33 5921
"Truly we are guilty c our brother, Gn 42:21 5921
Joseph made it a statute c the Gn 47:26 5921
and Moses cried to the LORD c the Ex 8:12
5921, 1697
"Now c everything which I have Ex 23:13
atonement for him c his sin which he Lv 5:13 5921
make atonement for him c his error Lv 5:18 5921
'C all the animals which divide Lv 11:26
to all the service c them. Nu 3:26
and all the service c them; Nu 3:31
equipment, and the service c them, Nu 3:36
c the most holy things. Nu 4:4
and make atonement for him c his Nu 6:11
4480, 834
had commanded Moses c the Levites, Nu 8:20
had commanded Moses c the Levites, Nu 8:22 5921
the Levites c their obligations." Nu 8:26
the LORD will command c you." Nu 9:8
LORD has promised good c Israel." Nu 10:29 5921
out a bad report c the land, Nu 14:36 5921
c the altar and inside the veil, Nu 18:7 1697
therefore I have said c them, Nu 18:24
proceeds out of her lips c her vows Nu 30:12
or c the obligation of herself shall Nu 30:12
c them to Eleazar the priest, Nu 32:28
c the daughters of Zelophehad, Nu 36:6
(c all Bashan, it is called the land of Dt 3:13
ask now c the former days which Dt 4:32
true, c which he spoke to you, Dt 13:2
God c you and me in Kadesh-barnea. Jos 14:6
5921, 182
your God spoke c you has failed; Jos 23:14 5921
Zalmunna, c whom you taunted me, Jg 8:15
they had taken a great oath c him Jg 21:5
times in Israel c the redemption and Ru 4:7 5921
which will come c your two sons, 1Sa 2:34 413
that I have spoken c his house, 1Sa 3:12 413
I gave you, c which I said to you, 1Sa 9:23
c all the righteous acts of the LORD 1Sa 12:7 854
the good that He has spoken c you, 1Sa 25:30 5921
me with a guilt c the woman. 2Sa 3:8
Your servant c the distant future. 2Sa 7:19
c Your servant and his house, 2Sa 7:25 5921
to console him c his father. 2Sa 10:2 413
David asked c the welfare of Joab 2Sa 11:7
for he was comforted c Amnon, 2Sa 13:39 5921
and I will give orders c you." 2Sa 14:8 5921
all the commanders c Absalom. 2Sa 18:5
5921, 1697
His promise which He spoke c me, 1Ki 2:4 5921
c the house of Eli in Shiloh. 1Ki 2:27 5921
c the cedar and cypress timber. 1Ki 5:8
"C this house which you are 1Ki 6:12
"Also c the foreigner who is not 1Ki 8:41 413
of Solomon c the name of the LORD, 1Ki 10:1
from the nations c which the LORD 1Ki 11:2
had commanded him c this thing, 1Ki 11:10 5921
who spoke c me *that I would be* 1Ki 14:2 5921
to inquire of you c her son, 1Ki 14:5 413
he does not prophesy good c me, 1Ki 22:8 5921
he would not prophesy good c me, 1Ki 22:18 5921
LORD spoke c the house of Ahab, 2Ki 10:10 5921
c which the LORD had said to them, 2Ki 17:12
c which the LORD had commanded 2Ki 17:15
them say c Tirhakah king of Cush, 2Ki 19:9 413
the LORD c the king of Assyria, 2Ki 19:32 413
all Judah c the words of this book 2Ki 22:13 5921
to all that is written c us." 2Ki 22:13 5921
to the word of the LORD c Israel. 1Ch 11:10 5921
David still *say* to You c the honor 1Ch 17:18
that You have spoken c Your servant 1Ch 17:23
Your servant and c his house be 1Ch 17:23 5921
to console him c his father. 1Ch 19:2 5921
God just as He has spoken c you. 1Ch 22:11 5921
the LORD commanded Moses c Israel. 1Ch 22:13 5921
set by the ordinance c them, 1Ch 23:31 5921
the Manassites c all the affairs of God 1Ch 26:32
"Also c the foreigner who is not 2Ch 6:32 413
any manner or c the storehouses. 2Ch 8:15
seer c Jeroboam the son of Nebat? 2Ch 9:29 5921
All Judah rejoiced c the oath, 2Ch 15:15 5921
good c me but always evil. 2Ch 18:7 5921
he would not prophesy good c me, 2Ch 18:17 5921
has spoken c the sons of David. 2Ch 23:3 5921
and the Levites c the heaps. 2Ch 31:9 5921
c the words of the book which has 2Ch 34:21 5921
a written reply be returned c it. Ezr 5:5 5922
us his decision c this *matter.*" Ezr 5:17 5922
'C the house of God at Jerusalem, Ezr 6:3
I issue a decree c what you are to Ezr 6:8
to inquire c Judah and Jerusalem Ezr 7:14 5922
and sought our God c this *matter,* Ezr 8:23 5921
and I asked them c the Jews who Ne 1:2 5921
to proclaim in Jerusalem c you, Ne 6:7 5921
commandment from the king c them Ne 11:23 5921
in all matters c the people. Ne 11:24
so the king had commanded c him. Es 3:2
reported c Bigthana and Teresh, Es 6:2 5921
Should I lie c my right? Jb 34:6 5921
cattle also, c what is coming up. Jb 36:33 5921
will not keep silence c his limbs, Jb 41:12
C the discovery of his iniquity Ps 36:2
will give His angels charge c you, Ps 91:11
all *Your* precepts c everything, Ps 119:128
seek and explore by wisdom c all that Ec 1:13 5921
said to myself c the sons of men, Ec 3:18
5921, 1700
c Judah and Jerusalem, which he saw Is 1:1 5921
of Amoz saw c Judah and Jerusalem. Is 2:1 5921
That He may teach us c His ways And Is 2:3 4480
song of my beloved c His vineyard. Is 5:1
The oracle c Babylon which Isaiah Is 13:1
The oracle c Moab. Is 15:1
the LORD spoke earlier c Moab. Is 16:13 413
The oracle c Damascus. Is 17:1
The oracle c Egypt. Is 19:1
c the wilderness of the sea. Is 21:1
The oracle c Edom. Is 21:11
The oracle c the valley of vision. Is 22:1
Do not try to comfort me c the Is 22:4 5921
The oracle c Tyre. Is 23:1
The LORD has given a command c Is 23:11 413
outcry in the streets c the wine; Is 24:11 5921
west c the majesty of the LORD. Is 24:14
Abraham, c the house of Jacob: Is 29:22 413
oracle c the beasts of the Negev. Is 30:6
them say c Tirhakah king of Cush, Is 37:9 5921
the LORD c the king of Assyria, Is 37:33 413
the things to come c My sons, Is 45:11 5921
Shall I relent c these things? Is 57:6 5921
on them c all their wickedness, Jer 1:16 5921
"I remember c you the devotion of Jer 2:2
c burnt offerings and sacrifices. Jer 7:22
5921, 1697
the LORD c the men of Anathoth, Jer 11:21 5921
Thus says the LORD c all My wicked Jer 12:14 5921
"Therefore thus says the LORD c Jer 14:15 5921
For thus says the LORD c the sons Jer 16:3 5921
and c their mothers who bear them, Jer 16:3 5921
"At one moment I might speak c a Jer 18:7 5921
a nation or c a kingdom to uproot, Jer 18:7 5921
I will relent c the calamity I Jer 18:8 5921
moment I might speak c a nation Jer 18:9 5921
c a kingdom to build up or to plant Jer 18:9 5921
For thus says the LORD c the house Jer 22:6 5921
thus says the LORD God of Israel c Jer 23:2 5921
the LORD of hosts c the prophets, Jer 23:15 5921
c all the people of Judah, Jer 25:1 5921
the LORD of hosts c the pillars, Jer 27:19 413
concerning the pillars, c the sea, Jer 27:19 5921
concerning the sea, c the stands and Jer 27:19 5921
and c the rest of the vessels that Jer 27:19 5921
c the vessels that are left in the Jer 27:21 5921
for thus says the LORD c the king Jer 29:16 413
and c all the people who dwell in Jer 29:16 413
c Ahab the son of Kolaiah and Jer 29:21 413
c Zedekiah the son of Maaseiah, Jer 29:21 413
LORD c Shemaiah the Nehelamite, Jer 29:31 413
c Israel and concerning Judah: Jer 30:4 413
concerning Israel and c Judah: Jer 30:4 413
c this city of which you say, Jer 32:36 413
Israel c the houses of this city, Jer 33:4 5921
and c the houses of the kings of Jer 33:4 5921
I have spoken c the house of Israel Jer 33:14 413
Thus says the LORD c you, Jer 34:4 5921
I have spoken to you c Israel and Jer 36:2 5921
concerning Israel and c Judah, Jer 36:2 5921
Judah, and c all the nations, Jer 36:2 5921
"And c Jehoiakim king of Judah Jer 36:29 5921
LORD c Jehoiakim king of Judah, Jer 36:30 5921
for I will relent c the calamity Jer 42:10 413
the prophet c the nations. Jer 46:1 5921

c the army of Pharaoh Neco king of — Jer 46:2 — 5921
the prophet c the Philistines, — Jer 47:1 — 413
C Moab. Thus says the LORD — Jer 48:1
C the sons of Ammon. — Jer 49:1
C Edom. Thus says the LORD — Jer 49:7
C Damascus. "Hamath and Arpad — Jer 49:23
C Kedar and the kingdoms of Hazor, — Jer 49:28
to Jeremiah the prophet c Elam, — Jer 49:34 — 413
which the LORD spoke c Babylon, — Jer 50:1 — 413
c the inhabitants of Babylon. — Jer 51:12 — 413
which have been written c Babylon. — Jer 51:60 — 413
c this place to cut it off, — Jer 51:62 — 413
The LORD has commanded c Jacob — La 1:17
'Thus says the Lord GOD c the — Ezk 12:19
people have c the land of Israel, — Ezk 12:22 — 5921
will quote *this* proverb c you, — Ezk 16:44 — 5921
c the land of Israel, — Ezk 18:2 — 5921
'Thus says the Lord GOD c the sons — Ezk 21:28 — 413
of Ammon and c their reproach,' — Ezk 21:28 — 413
"Then I said c her who was worn — Ezk 23:43
because Tyre has said c Jerusalem, — Ezk 26:2 — 5921
prophesy c the land of Israel and — Ezk 36:6 — 5921
all that I say to you c all the statutes — Ezk 44:5
of the LORD and c all its laws; — Ezk 44:5
the God of heaven c this mystery, — Da 2:18 — 5922
give you an answer c this matter. — Da 3:16 — 5922
c Nebuchadnezzar was fulfilled; — Da 4:33 — 5922
and issued a proclamation c him — Da 5:29 — 5922
which he envisioned in visions c — Am 1:1 — 5921
Thus says the Lord GOD c Edom — Ob 1:1
then God relented c the calamity — Jon 3:10 — 5921
and one who relents c calamity. — Jon 4:2 — 5921
he saw c Samaria and Jerusalem. — Mi 1:1 — 5921
do not speak out c these things, — Mi 2:6
out to you c wine and liquor,' — Mi 2:11
Thus says the LORD c the prophets — Mi 3:5 — 5921
C evil, both hands do it well. — Mi 7:3 — 5921
LORD has issued a command c you: — Na 1:14 — 5921
all that I have appointed c her. — Zph 3:7 — 5921
of the word of the LORD c Israel. — Zch 12:1 — 5921
COMMAND HIS ANGELS C YOU'; — Mt 4:6 — *4012*
I did not speak to you c bread? — Mt 16:11 — *4012*
ANGELS C YOU TO GUARD — Lk 4:10 — *4012*
c Him went out all over Judea and — Lk 7:17 — *4012*
c Himself in all the Scriptures. — Lk 24:27 — *4012*
testify c man, for He Himself knew — Jn 2:25 — *4012*
among the crowds c Him; — Jn 7:12 — *4012*
to speak and to judge c you, — Jn 8:26 — *4012*
to console them c *their* brother. — Jn 11:19 — *4012*
will convict the world c sin and — Jn 16:8 — *4012*
c sin, because they do not believe — Jn 16:9 — *4012*
and c righteousness, because I go — Jn 16:10 — *4012*
and c judgment, because the ruler — Jn 16:11 — *4012*
the things c the kingdom of God. — Ac 1:3 — *4012*
by the mouth of David c Judas, — Ac 1:16 — *4012*
c whom He also testified and said, — Ac 13:22
out all that was written c Him, — Ac 13:29 — *4012*
apostles and elders c this issue. — Ac 15:2 — *4012*
"We shall hear you again c this." — Ac 17:32 — *4012*
accurately the things c Jesus, — Ac 18:25 — *4012*
no small disturbance c the Way. — Ac 19:23 — *4012*
"But c the Gentiles who have — Ac 21:25 — *4012*
him yourself c all these matters you — Ac 24:8 — *4012*
received letters from Judea c you, — Ac 28:21 — *4012*
for c this sect, it is known to us — Ac 28:22 — *4012*
trying to persuade them c Jesus, — Ac 28:23 — *4012*
and teaching c the Lord Jesus — Ac 28:31 — *4012*
c His Son, who was born of a — Ro 1:3 — *4012*
from the law c the husband. — Ro 7:2
Isaiah cries out c Israel, — Ro 9:27 — *5228*
And c you, my brethren, I myself — Ro 15:14 — *4012*
I thank my God always c you for — 1Co 1:4 — *4012*
c Christ was confirmed in you, — 1Co 1:6
For I have been informed c you, — 1Co 1:11 — *4012*
Now c the things about which you — 1Co 7:1 — *4012*
Now c virgins I have no command of — 1Co 7:25 — *4012*
Now c things sacrificed to idols, — 1Co 8:1 — *4012*
Therefore c the eating of things — 1Co 8:4 — *4012*
c that for which I give thanks? — 1Co 10:30 — *5228*
Now c spiritual *gifts,* brethren, I — 1Co 12:1 — *4012*
c the collection for the saints, — 1Co 16:1 — *4012*
But c Apollos our brother, I — 1Co 16:12 — *4012*
C this I implored the Lord three — 2Co 12:8 — *5228*
have confidence in the Lord c you, — 2Th 3:4 — *1909*
prophecies previously made c you, — 1Tm 1:18 — *1909*
and c these things I want you to — Ti 3:8 — *4012*
to come, c which we are speaking. — Heb 2:5 — *4012*
said somewhere c the seventh *day:* — Heb 4:4 — *4012*
C him we have much to say, and *it* — Heb 5:11 — *4012*
convinced of better things c you, — Heb 6:9 — *4012*
For the one c whom these things — Heb 7:13 — *1909*
Moses spoke nothing c priests. — Heb 7:14 — *4012*
and gave orders c his bones. — Heb 11:22 — *4012*
hands, c the Word of Life — 1Jn 1:1 — *4012*
c those who are trying to deceive you. — 1Jn 2:26 — *4012*
He has testified c His Son. — 1Jn 5:9 — *4012*
that God has given c His Son. — 1Jn 5:10 — *4012*
"You must prophesy again c many — Rv 10:11 — *1909*

CONCERNS
LORD will accomplish what c me; — Ps 138:8 — 1157
"This burden c the prince in — Ezk 12:10

CONCESSION
requesting a c against Paul, that — Ac 25:3 — *5485*
But this I say by way of c, — 1Co 7:6 — *4774*

CONCILIATE
we are slandered, we try to c; — 1Co 4:13 — *3870*

CONCLUDED
and I saw every work of God, *I* c — Ec 8:17
of the crowd c *it was* Alexander, — Ac 19:33 — *4822*
Christ controls us, having c this, — 2Co 5:14 — *2919*

CONCLUDING
c that God had called us to preach — Ac 16:10 — *4822*

CONCLUSION
The c, when all has been heard, *is:* — Ec 12:13 — 5490, 1697

CONCUBINE
His c, whose name was Reumah, — Gn 22:24 — 6370
and lay with Bilhah his father's c, — Gn 35:22 — 6370
Timna was a c of Esau's son — Gn 36:12 — 6370
His c who was in Shechem also — Jg 8:31 — 6370
who took a c for himself from — Jg 19:1 — 6370
c played the harlot against him, — Jg 19:2 — 6370
go along with his c and servant, — Jg 19:9 — 6370
his c also was with him. — Jg 19:10 — 6370
is my virgin daughter and his c. — Jg 19:24 — 6370
his c and brought *her* out to them; — Jg 19:25 — 6370
his c was lying at the doorway of — Jg 19:27 — 6370
c and cut her in twelve pieces, — Jg 19:29 — 6370
"I came with my c to spend the — Jg 20:4 — 6370
ravished my c so that she died. — Jg 20:5 — 6370
"And I took hold of my c and cut — Jg 20:6 — 6370
had a c whose name was Rizpah, — 2Sa 3:7 — 6370
you gone in to my father's c?" — 2Sa 3:7 — 6370
daughter of Aiah, the c of Saul, — 2Sa 21:11 — 6370
The sons of Keturah, Abraham's c, — 1Ch 1:32 — 6370
Ephah, Caleb's c, — 1Ch 2:46 — 6370
Maacah, Caleb's c, bore Sheber and — 1Ch 2:48 — 6370
Asriel, whom his Aramean c bore; — 1Ch 7:14 — 6370

CONCUBINES
but to the sons of his c, — Gn 25:6 — 6370
more c and wives from Jerusalem, — 2Sa 5:13 — 6370
king left ten c to keep the house. — 2Sa 15:16 — 6370
"Go in to your father's c, — 2Sa 16:21 — 6370
c in the sight of all Israel. — 2Sa 16:22 — 6370
wives, and the lives of your c, — 2Sa 19:5 — 6370
the c whom he had left to keep the — 2Sa 20:3 — 6370
princesses, and three hundred c, — 1Ki 11:3 — 6370
David, besides the sons of the c; — 1Ch 3:9 — 6370
than all his *other* wives and c. — 2Ch 11:21 — 6370
had taken eighteen wives and sixty c — 2Ch 11:21 — 6370
eunuch who was in charge of the c. — Es 2:14 — 6370
and the pleasures of men—many c. — Ec 2:8 — 7705
are sixty queens and eighty c, — SS 6:8 — 6370
The queens and the c *also,* — SS 6:9 — 6370
and his c might drink from them. — Da 5:2 — 3904
wives and his c drank from them. — Da 5:3 — 3904
your wives and your c have been — Da 5:23 — 3904

CONCUR
For I joyfully c with the law of — Ro 7:22 — *4913*

CONDEMN
he whom the judges c shall pay — Ex 22:9 — 7561
the righteous and c the wicked, — Dt 25:1 — 7561
am righteous, my mouth will c me; — Jb 9:20 — 7561
"I will say to God, 'Do not c me; — Jb 10:2 — 7561
will you c the righteous mighty One, — Jb 34:17 — 7561
He keeps quiet, who then can c? — Jb 34:29 — 7561
c Me that you may be justified? — Jb 40:8 — 7561
And c the innocent to death. — Ps 94:21 — 7561
He will c a man who devises evil. — Pr 12:2 — 7561
you in judgment you will c. — Is 54:17 — 7561
and will c it because they — Mt 12:41 — *2632*
at the judgment and will c it, — Mt 12:42 — *2632*
and they will c Him to death, — Mt 20:18 — *2632*
and they will c Him to death and — Mk 10:33 — *2632*
and do not c, and you will not be — Lk 6:37 — *2613a*
at the judgment and c them, — Lk 11:31 — *2632*
at the judgment and c it, — Lk 11:32 — *2632*
Did no one c you?" — Jn 8:10 — *2632*
"I do not c you, either. — Jn 8:11 — *2632*
you judge another, you c yourself; — Ro 2:1 — *2632*
not c himself in what he approves. — Ro 14:22 — *2919*
I do not speak to c you, — 2Co 7:3 — *2633*
if our heart does not c us, — 1Jn 3:21 — *2607*

CONDEMNATION
you will receive greater c. — Mt 23:14 — *2917*
these will receive greater c." — Mk 12:40 — *2917*
These will receive greater c." — Lk 20:47 — *2917*
are under the same sentence of c? — Lk 23:40 — *2917*
for a sentence of c against him. — Ac 25:15 — *2613b*
good may come"? Their c is just. — Ro 3:8 — *2917*
one *transgression* resulting in c, — Ro 5:16 — *2631*
there resulted c to all men, — Ro 5:18 — *2631*
Therefore there is now no c for — Ro 8:1 — *2631*
will receive c upon themselves. — Ro 13:2 — *2917*
if the ministry of c has glory, — 2Co 3:9 — *2633*
into the c incurred by the devil. — 1Tm 3:6 — *2917*
thus incurring c, because they — 1Tm 5:12 — *2917*
beforehand marked out for this c, — Jude 1:4 — *2917*

CONDEMNED
no answer, and yet had c Job. — Jb 32:3 — 7561
who hate the righteous will be c. — Ps 34:21 — 816
who take refuge in Him will be c. — Ps 34:22 — 816
Or let him be c when he is judged. — Ps 37:33 — 7561
you would not have c the innocent. — Mt 12:7 — *2613a*
by your words you will be c." — Mt 12:37 — *2613a*
Him, saw that He had been c, — Mt 27:3 — *2632*
c Him to be deserving of death. — Mk 14:64 — *2632*
he who has disbelieved shall be c. — Mk 16:16 — *2632*
condemn, and you will not be c; — Lk 6:37 — *2613a*
for sin, He c sin in the flesh, — Ro 8:3 — *2632*
But he who doubts is c if he eats, — Ro 14:23 — *2632*
last of all, as men c to death; — 1Co 4:9 — *1935*
will not be c along with the world. — 1Co 11:32 — *2632*
to his face, because he stood c. — Ga 2:11 — *2607*
by which he c the world, — Heb 11:7 — *2632*
You have c and put to death the — Jas 5:6 — *2613a*
and *if* He c the cities of Sodom — 2Pe 2:6 — *2632*

CONDEMNING
c the wicked by bringing his way — 1Ki 8:32 — 7561
Sabbath, fulfilled *these* by c *Him.* — Ac 13:27 — *2919*

CONDEMNS
"Your own mouth c you, and not I; — Jb 15:6 — 7561
and he who c the righteous, — Pr 17:15 — 7561
Who is he who c Me? — Is 50:9 — 7561
who is the one who c? — Ro 8:34 — *2632*
in whatever our heart c us; — 1Jn 3:20 — *2607*

CONDITION
"Only on this c will we consent — Gn 34:15
"Only on this c will the men — Gn 34:22
"I will make *it* with you on this c, — 1Sa 11:2
Know well the c of your flocks, — Pr 27:23 — 6440
already been a long time *in that* c, — Jn 5:6
in that c in which he was called. — 1Co 7:20 — *2821*
one is to remain with God in that c — 1Co 7:24
c you did not despise or loathe, — Ga 4:14 — *4561*
encouraged when I learn of your c. — Php 2:19 — *3588, 4012*

CONDITIONS
and also c were good in Judah. — 2Ch 12:12 — 1697
copy containing the terms and c and — Jer 32:11 — 2706
one sets it aside or adds c to it. — Ga 3:15 — *1928*

CONDUCT
"For the queen's c will become — Es 1:17 — 1697
who have heard of the queen's c will — Es 1:18 — 1697
He may turn man aside *from his* c, — Jb 33:17 — 4639
slay those who are upright in c. — Ps 37:14 — 1870
But he who is careless of c will — Pr 19:16 — 1870
If his c is pure and right. — Pr 20:11 — 6467
as for the pure, his c is upright. — Pr 21:8 — 6467
to their c I will deal with them, — Ezk 7:27 — 1870
bring their c upon their heads." — Ezk 9:10 — 1870
their c down on their heads," — Ezk 11:21 — 1870
you will see their c and actions; — Ezk 14:22 — 1870
when you see their c and actions, — Ezk 14:23 — 1870
who are ashamed of your lewd c. — Ezk 16:27 — 1870
your c down on your own head," — Ezk 16:43 — 1870
corruptly in all your c than they. — Ezk 16:47 — 1870
Israel, each according to his c," — Ezk 18:30 — 1870
Did we not c ourselves in the same — 2Co 12:18 — *4043*
Only c yourselves in a manner — Php 1:27 — *4176*
C yourselves with wisdom toward — Col 4:5 — *4043*
to c himself in the household of God, — 1Tm 3:15 — *390*
in speech, c, love, faith *and* purity, — 1Tm 4:12 — *391*
Now you followed my teaching, c, — 2Tm 3:10 — *72*
considering the result of their c, — Heb 13:7 — *391*
desiring to c ourselves honorably — Heb 13:18 — *390*
c yourselves in fear during the — 1Pe 1:17 — *390*
the sensual c of unprincipled men — 2Pe 2:7 — *391*
you to be in holy c and godliness, — 2Pe 3:11 — *391*

CONDUCTED
be c in the king's treasure house, — Ezr 5:17 — 1240
we have c ourselves in the world, — 2Co 1:12 — *390*

CONDUCTS
And c himself arrogantly against — Jb 15:25 — 1396

CONDUIT
stood by the c of the upper pool, — 2Ki 18:17 — 8585a
how he made the pool and the c and — 2Ki 20:20 — 8585a
end of the c of the upper pool, — Is 7:3 — 8585a
And he stood by the c of the upper — Is 36:2 — 8585a

CONFER
they *began* to c with one another, — Ac 4:15 — *4820*

CONFERRED
He had c with Joab the son of — 1Ki 1:7 — 1697
honor of kingship has not been c, — Da 11:21 — 5414
and the elders of the people c — Mt 27:1 — *4824, 2983*
And they c together and with — Mt 27:7 — *4824, 2983*
Festus had c with his council, — Ac 25:12 — *4814*

CONFESS
c that in which he has sinned. — Lv 5:5 — 3034
and c over it all the iniquities — Lv 16:21 — 3034
'If they c their iniquity and the — Lv 26:40 — 3034
then he shall c his sins which he — Nu 5:7 — 3034
if they turn to You again and c — 1Ki 8:33 — 3034
pray toward this place and c Your — 1Ki 8:35 — 3034
return *to You* and c Your name, — 2Ch 6:24 — 3034
toward this place and c Your name, — 2Ch 6:26 — 3034
"Then I will also c to you, — Jb 40:14 — 3034
c my transgressions to the LORD"; — Ps 32:5 — 3034
For I c my iniquity; — Ps 38:18 — 5046
through You alone we c Your name. — Is 26:13 — 2142
I will also c him before My Father — Mt 10:32 — *3670*
the Son of Man will c him also — Lk 12:8 — *3670*
c with your mouth Jesus *as* Lord, — Ro 10:9 — *3670*
c that Jesus Christ is Lord, — Php 2:11 — *1843*
c your sins to one another, — Jas 5:16 — *1843*
If we c our sins, He is faithful — 1Jn 1:9 — *3670*
does not c Jesus is not from God; — 1Jn 4:3 — *3670*
will c his name before My Father and — Rv 3:5 — *3670*

CONFESSED
and stood and c their sins and the — Ne 9:2 — 3034
they c and worshiped the LORD — Ne 9:3 — 3034
to the LORD my God and c and said, — Da 9:4 — 3034
River, as they c their sins. — Mt 3:6 — *1843*
And he c and did not deny, but — Jn 1:20 — *3670*
and did not deny, but c, — Jn 1:20 — *3670*
had already agreed that if anyone c — Jn 9:22 — *3670*
and having c that they were strangers — Heb 11:13 — *3670*

CONFESSES
But he who c and forsakes *them* — Pr 28:13 — 3034

“Therefore everyone who **c** Me before **Mt 10:32** *3670*
you, everyone who **c** Me before men, **Lk 12:8** *3670*
and with the mouth he **c**, **Ro 10:10** *3670*
who **c** the Son has the Father also. **1Jn 2:23** *3670*
every spirit that **c** that Jesus **1Jn 4:2** *3670*
c that Jesus is the Son of God, **1Jn 4:15** *3670*

CONFESSING
c the sins of the sons of Israel **Ne 1:6** 3034
and **c** my sin and the sin of my **Da 9:20** 3034
in the Jordan River, **c** their sins. **Mk 1:5** *1843*
the Pharisees they were not **c** *Him,* **Jn 12:42** *3670*
c and disclosing their practices. **Ac 19:18** *1843*
c that the Law is good. **Ro 7:16** *3670*

CONFESSION
Ezra was praying and making **c**, **Ezr 10:1** 3034
make **c** to the LORD God of your **Ezr 10:11** 8426
to your **c** of the gospel of Christ and **2Co 9:13** *3671*
By common **c**, great is the **1Tm 3:16** *3672*
and you made the good **c** in the **1Tm 6:12** *3671*
the good **c** before Pontius Pilate, **1Tm 6:13** *3671*
Apostle and High Priest of our **c**; **Heb 3:1** *3671*
of God, let us hold fast our **c**. **Heb 4:14** *3671*
c of our hope without wavering, **Heb 10:23** *3671*

CONFIDENCE
“What is this **c** that you have? **2Ki 18:19** 986
us saw *it,* they lost their **c**; **Ne 6:16** 5869
“Is not your fear *of God* your **c**, **Jb 4:6** 3690
Whose **c** is fragile, And whose **Jb 8:14** 3689
you will speak with **c**, And the **Jb 22:29** 1466
“If I have put my **c** *in* gold, **Jb 31:24** 3689
GOD, *You are* my **c** from my youth. **Ps 71:5** 4009
they should put their **c** in God And **Ps 78:7** 3689
For the LORD will be your **c** And **Pr 3:26** 3689
of the LORD there is strong **c**, **Pr 14:26** 4009
c in a faithless man in time of trouble. **Pr 25:19** 4009
quietness and **c** forever. **Is 32:17** 983
“What is this **c** that you have? **Is 36:4** 986
was ashamed of Bethel, their **c**. **Jer 48:13** 4009
be the **c** of the house of Israel, **Ezk 29:16** 4009
Do not have **c** in a friend. **Mi 7:5** 982
observed the **c** of Peter and John and **Ac 4:13** *3954*
may speak Your word with all **c**, **Ac 4:29** *3954*
and I speak to him also with **c**, **Ac 26:26** *3955*
For our proud **c** is this: the **2Co 1:12** *2746a*
In this **c** I intended at first **2Co 1:15** *4006*
having **c** in you all that my joy **2Co 2:3** *3982*
Such **c** we have through Christ **2Co 3:4** *4006*
Great is my **c** in you; great is my **2Co 7:4** *3954*
in everything I have **c** in you. **2Co 7:16** *2292*
because of *his* great **c** in you. **2Co 8:22** *4006*
will be put to shame by this **c**. **2Co 9:4** *5287*
with the **c** with which I propose to be **2Co 10:2** *4006*
in this **c** of boasting. **2Co 11:17** *5287*
I have **c** in you in the Lord that **Ga 5:10** *3982*
so that your proud **c** in me may **Php 1:26** *2745*
Jesus and put no **c** in the flesh, **Php 3:3** *3982*
might have **c** even in the flesh. **Php 3:4** *4006*
has a mind to put **c** in the flesh, **Php 3:4** *3982*
have **c** in the Lord concerning you, **2Th 3:4** *3982*
great **c** in the faith that is in Christ **1Tm 3:13** *3954*
though I have enough **c** in Christ **Phm 1:8** *3954*
Having **c** in your obedience, I **Phm 1:21** *3982*
if we hold fast our **c** and the **Heb 3:6** *3954*
with **c** to the throne of grace, **Heb 4:16** *3954*
we have **c** to enter the holy place **Heb 10:19** *3954*
do not throw away your **c**, **Heb 10:35** *3954*
we may have **c** and not shrink away **1Jn 2:28** *3954*
condemn us, we have **c** before God; **1Jn 3:21** *3954*
may have **c** in the day of judgment; **1Jn 4:17** *3954*
is the **c** which we have before Him, **1Jn 5:14** *3954*

CONFIDENT
He is **c**, though the Jordan rushes **Jb 40:23** 982
me, In *spite of* this I shall be **c**. **Ps 27:3** 982
and are **c** that you yourself are a **Ro 2:19** *3982*
If anyone is **c** in himself that he **2Co 10:7** *3982*
and **c** access through faith in Him. **Eph 3:12** *4006*
For I am **c** of this very thing, **Php 1:6** *3982*
which they make **c** assertions. **1Tm 1:7** *1226*

CONFIDENTLY
I may **c** say to you regarding the **Ac 2:29** *3954*
things I want you to speak **c**, **Ti 3:8** *1226*
so that we **c** say, **Heb 13:6** *2292*

CONFINE
been warned, yet he does not **c** it and **Ex 21:29** 8104

CONFINED
where the king's prisoners were **c**; **Gn 39:20** 631
king of Egypt, who were **c** in jail, **Gn 40:5** 631
your brother, while you remain **c**, **Gn 42:16** 631
your brothers be **c** in your prison; **Gn 42:19** 631
yet its owner has not **c** it, **Ex 21:36** 8104
of Mehetabel, who was **c** at home, **Ne 6:10** 6113
dungeon, And will be **c** in prison; **Is 24:22** 5462
still **c** in the court of the guard, **Jer 33:1** 6113
Jeremiah while he was **c** in the court **Jer 39:15** 6113

CONFINEMENT
So he put them in **c** in the house **Gn 40:3** 4929
and they were in **c** for some time. **Gn 40:4** 4929
him in **c** in his master's house, **Gn 40:7** 4929
and he put me in **c** in the house of **Gn 41:10** 4929

CONFINES
within all the **c** of its border, **Gn 23:17** 5439

CONFIRM
and I will **c** My covenant with you. **Lv 26:9** 6965
her husband may **c** it or her **Nu 30:13** 6965
that He may **c** His covenant which **Dt 8:18** 6965
in order to **c** the oath which the **Dt 9:5** 6965
'Cursed is he who does not **c** the **Dt 27:26** 6965
exchange *of land* to **c** any matter: **Ru 4:7** 6965
only may the LORD **c** His word.” **1Sa 1:23** 6965
and his house, **c** *it* forever, **2Sa 7:25** 6965
in after you and **c** your words.” **1Ki 1:14** 4390
that he might **c** the words of the **2Ki 23:24** 6965
wrote with full authority to **c** **Es 9:29** 6965
And **c** for us the work of our hands; **Ps 90:17** 3559
Yes, **c** the work of our hands. **Ps 90:17** 3559
I have sworn and I will **c** it, **Ps 119:106** 6965
in order to **c** the oath which I **Jer 11:5** 6965
may the LORD **c** your words which **Jer 28:6** 6965
Go ahead and **c** your vows, and **Jer 44:25** 6965
to **c** the promises *given* to the fathers, **Ro 15:8** *950*
who will also **c** you to the end, **1Co 1:8** *950*
Christ, will Himself perfect, **c**, **1Pe 5:10** *4741*

CONFIRMATION
the defense and **c** of the gospel, **Php 1:7** *951*
as **c** is an end of every dispute. **Heb 6:16** *951*

CONFIRMED
he has **c** them, because he said **Nu 30:14** 6965
witnesses a matter shall be **c**. **Dt 19:15** 6965
was **c** as a prophet of the LORD. **1Sa 3:20** 539
be **c** which You have spoken to Your **1Ki 8:26** 539
also **c** it to Jacob for a statute, **1Ch 16:17** 5975
let Your word be **c** which You have **2Ch 6:17** 539
You **c** Your inheritance when it was **Ps 68:9** 3559
And My covenant shall be **c** to him. **Ps 89:28** 539
Your testimonies are fully **c**; **Ps 93:5** 539
He **c** it to Jacob for a statute, **Ps 105:10** 5975
“Thus He has **c** His words which He **Da 9:12** 6965
WITNESSES EVERY FACT MAY BE **C**. **Mt 18:16** *2476*
and **c** the word by the signs that **Mk 16:20** *950*
concerning Christ was **c** in you, **1Co 1:6** *950*
EVERY FACT IS TO BE **C** BY THE **2Co 13:1** *2476*
it was **c** to us by those who heard, **Heb 2:3** *950*

CONFIRMING
C the word of His servant And **Is 44:26** 6965

CONFIRMS
then he **c** all her vows or all her **Nu 30:14** 6965

CONFISCATION
c of goods or for imprisonment.” **Ezr 7:26** 6065

CONFLICT
have engaged in **c** with the LORD.” **Jer 50:24** 1624
was true and *one of* great **c**, **Da 10:1** 6635
the same **c** which you saw in me, **Php 1:30** *73*
endured a great **c** of sufferings, **Heb 10:32** *119*

CONFLICTS
c without, fears within. **2Co 7:5** *3163*
of quarrels and **c** among you? **Jas 4:1** *3163*

CONFORMED
become **c** to the image of His Son, **Ro 8:29** *4832b*
And do not be **c** to this world, but **Ro 12:2** *4964*
sufferings, being **c** to His death; **Php 3:10** *4832a*
do not be **c** to the former lusts **1Pe 1:14** *4964*

CONFORMING
with the doctrine **c** to godliness, **1Tm 6:3** *2596*

CONFORMITY
into **c** with the body of His glory, **Php 3:21** *4832b*

CONFOUND
And I will **c** their strategy, So **Is 19:3** 1104

CONFOUNDED
And the LORD **c** them before Israel, **Jos 10:10** 2000
They came there and were **c**. **Jb 6:20** 2659
Be ashamed and **c** for your ways, O **Ezk 36:32** 3637
for her expectation has been **c**. **Zch 9:5** 954

CONFOUNDING
increasing in strength and **c** the Jews **Ac 9:22** *4797*

CONFRONT
“Who will **c** him with his actions, **Jb 21:31** 5046, 5921, 6440
Days of affliction **c** me. **Jb 30:27** 6923
Arise, O LORD, **c** him, bring him **Ps 17:13** 6923
Terror and pit and snare **C** you, **Is 24:17** 5921
will not overtake or **c** us.' **Am 9:10** 6923

CONFRONTED
The snares of death **c** me. **2Sa 22:6** 6923
c me in the day of my calamity, **2Sa 22:19** 6923
The snares of death **c** me. **Ps 18:5** 6923
c me in the day of my calamity, **Ps 18:18** 6923
the scribes with the elders **c** *Him,* **Lk 20:1** *2186*

CONFUSE
down and there **c** their language, **Gn 11:7** 1101a
C, O Lord, divide their tongues, **Ps 55:9** 1104
Send out Your arrows and **c** them. **Ps 144:6** 2000
And **c** the direction of your paths. **Is 3:12** 1104

CONFUSED
because there the LORD **c** the **Gn 11:9** 1101a
the Philistines and **c** them, **1Sa 7:10** 2000
away from me, For they have **c** me; **SS 6:5** 7292
strong drink, They are **c** by wine, **Is 28:7** 1104

CONFUSION
the army of the Egyptians into **c**. **Ex 14:24** 2000
and throw into **c** all the people **Ex 23:27** 2000
great **c** until they are destroyed. **Dt 7:23** 4103
LORD will send upon you curses, **c**, **Dt 28:20** 4103
the city with very great **c**; **1Sa 5:9** 4103
a deadly **c** throughout the city; **1Sa 5:11** 4103
and there was very great **c**. **1Sa 14:20** 4103
drink, the city of Susa was in **c**. **Es 3:15** 943
guided by them are brought to **c**. **Is 9:16** 1104
and **c** In the valley of vision, **Is 22:5** 3998
They trust in **c** and speak lies; **Is 59:4** 8414
Then their **c** will occur. **Mi 7:4** 3998
men are throwing our city into **c**, **Ac 16:20** *1613*
The city was filled with the **c**, **Ac 19:29** *4799*
for the assembly was in **c** and **Ac 19:32** *4797*
that all Jerusalem was in **c**. **Ac 21:31** *4797*
is not *a God* of **c** but of peace, **1Co 14:33** *181*

CONGEALED
were **c** in the heart of the sea. **Ex 15:8** 7087a

CONGRATULATED
So I **c** the dead who are already **Ec 4:2** 7623b

CONGRATULATES
Though while he lives he **c** himself **Ps 49:18** 1288

CONGREGATION
“Speak to all the **c** of Israel, **Ex 12:3** 5712
then the whole assembly of the **c** **Ex 12:6** 5712
be cut off from the **c** of Israel, **Ex 12:19** 5712
“All the **c** of Israel are to **Ex 12:47** 5712
and all the **c** of the sons of **Ex 16:1** 5712
The whole **c** of the sons of **Ex 16:2** 5712
all the **c** of the sons of Israel, **Ex 16:9** 5712
the whole **c** of the sons of Israel, **Ex 16:10** 5712
of the **c** came and told Moses, **Ex 16:22** 5712
Then all the **c** of the sons of **Ex 17:1** 5712
rulers in the **c** returned to him; **Ex 34:31** 5712
all the **c** of the sons of Israel, **Ex 35:1** 5712
all the **c** of the sons of Israel, **Ex 35:4** 5712
Then all the **c** of the sons of **Ex 35:20** 5712
The silver of those of the **c** **Ex 38:25** 5712
whole **c** of Israel commits error and **Lv 4:13** 5712
'Then the elders of the **c** shall **Lv 4:15** 5712
and assemble all the **c** at the **Lv 8:3** 5712
When the **c** was assembled at the **Lv 8:4** 5712
Moses said to the **c**, **Lv 8:5** 5712
and the whole **c** came near and **Lv 9:5** 5712
become wrathful against all the **c**. **Lv 10:6** 5712
to bear away the guilt of the **c**, **Lv 10:17** 5712
“He shall take from the **c** of **Lv 16:5** 5712
“Speak to all the **c** of the sons **Lv 19:2** 5712
then let all the **c** stone him. **Lv 24:14** 5712
the **c** shall certainly stone him. **Lv 24:16** 5712
all the **c** of the sons of Israel, **Nu 1:2** 5712
are they who were called of the **c**, **Nu 1:16** 5712
and they assembled all the **c** **Nu 1:18** 5712
on the **c** of the sons of Israel. **Nu 1:53** 5712
c before the tent of meeting, **Nu 3:7** 5712
and Aaron and the leaders of the **c** **Nu 4:34** 5712
the whole **c** of the sons of Israel, **Nu 8:9** 5712
Moses and Aaron and all the **c** of the **Nu 8:20** 5712
shall use them for summoning the **c** **Nu 10:2** 5712
all the **c** shall gather themselves **Nu 10:3** 5712
and to all the **c** of the sons of Israel **Nu 13:26** 5712
to all the **c** and showed them the fruit **Nu 13:26** 5712
Then all the **c** lifted up their **Nu 14:1** 5712
and the whole **c** said to them, **Nu 14:2** 5712
of the **c** of the sons of Israel. **Nu 14:5** 5712
all the **c** of the sons of Israel, **Nu 14:7** 5712
But all the **c** said to stone them **Nu 14:10** 5712
c who are grumbling against Me? **Nu 14:27** 5712
surely this I will do to all this evil **c** **Nu 14:35** 5712
made all the **c** grumble against him **Nu 14:36** 5712
without the knowledge of the **c**, **Nu 15:24** 5712
that all the **c** shall offer one **Nu 15:24** 5712
all the **c** of the sons of Israel, **Nu 15:25** 5712
'So all the **c** of the sons of **Nu 15:26** 5712
Moses and Aaron and to all the **c**; **Nu 15:33** 5712
all the **c** shall stone him with **Nu 15:35** 5712
c brought him outside the camp and **Nu 15:36** 5712
and fifty leaders of the **c**, **Nu 16:2** 5712
enough, for all the **c** are holy, **Nu 16:3** 5712
from the *rest of* the **c** of Israel, **Nu 16:9** 5712
before the **c** to minister to them; **Nu 16:9** 5712
Thus Korah assembled all the **c** **Nu 16:19** 5712
of the LORD appeared to all the **c**. **Nu 16:19** 5712
yourselves from among this **c**, **Nu 16:21** 5712
You be angry with the entire **c**?” **Nu 16:22** 5712
“Speak to the **c**, saying, **Nu 16:24** 5712
and he spoke to the **c**, **Nu 16:26** 5712
But on the next day all the **c** of **Nu 16:41** 5712
when the **c** had assembled against **Nu 16:42** 5712
'Get away from among this **c**, **Nu 16:45** 5712
the **c** and make atonement for them, **Nu 16:46** 5712
and the **c** of the sons of Israel **Nu 19:9** 5712
the sons of Israel, the whole **c**, **Nu 20:1** 5712
There was no water for the **c**, **Nu 20:2** 5712
assemble the **c** and speak to the rock **Nu 20:8** 5712
the **c** and their beasts drink.” **Nu 20:8** 5712
and the **c** and their beasts drank. **Nu 20:11** 5712
the sons of Israel, the whole **c**, **Nu 20:22** 5712
Hor in the sight of all the **c**. **Nu 20:27** 5712
all the **c** saw that Aaron had died, **Nu 20:29** 5712
all the **c** of the sons of Israel, **Nu 25:6** 5712
he arose from the midst of the **c** and **Nu 25:7** 5712
“Take a census of all the **c** of **Nu 26:2** 5712
Abiram who were called by the **c**, **Nu 26:9** 5712
before the leaders and all the **c**, **Nu 27:2** 5712
Zin, during the strife of the **c**, **Nu 27:14** 5712
flesh, appoint a man over the **c**, **Nu 27:16** 5712
that the **c** of the LORD will not be **Nu 27:17** 5712
the priest and before all the **c**, **Nu 27:19** 5712
in order that all the **c** of the **Nu 27:20** 5712
Israel with him, even all the **c**.” **Nu 27:21** 5712
the priest and before all the **c**. **Nu 27:22** 5712
to the **c** of the sons of Israel, **Nu 31:12** 5712
leaders of the **c** went out to meet them **Nu 31:13** 5712
was among the **c** of the LORD. **Nu 31:16** 5712
the fathers' *households* of the **c** take **Nu 31:26** 5712
went out to battle and all the **c**. **Nu 31:27** 5712
and to the leaders of the **c**, **Nu 32:2** 5712
conquered before the **c** of Israel, **Nu 32:4** 5712
he stands before the **c** for trial. **Nu 35:12** 5712
then the **c** shall judge between the **Nu 35:24** 5712

'The c shall deliver the Nu 35:25 5712
and the c shall restore him to his Nu 35:25 5712
of the c swore *an oath* to them. Jos 9:15 5712
leaders of the c had sworn to them by Jos 9:18 5712
c grumbled against the leaders. Jos 9:18 5712
the leaders said to the whole c, Jos 9:19 5712
drawers of water for the whole c, Jos 9:21 5712
c and for the altar of the LORD, Jos 9:27 5712
Then the whole c of the sons of Jos 18:1 5712
stands before the c for judgment, Jos 20:6 5712
until he stands before the c. Jos 20:9 5712
the whole c of the sons of Israel Jos 22:12 5712
"Thus says the whole c of the LORD, Jos 22:16 5712
plague came on the c of the LORD, Jos 22:17 5712
the whole c of Israel tomorrow. Jos 22:18 5712
wrath fall on all the c of Israel? Jos 22:20 5712
priest and the leaders of the c, Jos 22:30 5712
and the c assembled as one man to Jg 20:1 5712
And the c sent 12,000 of the Jg 21:10 5712
Then the whole c sent *word* and Jg 21:13 5712
Then the elders of the c said, Jg 21:16 5712
Solomon and all the c of Israel, 1Ki 8:5 5712
And King Solomon and all the c of 2Ch 5:6 5712
servant of the LORD on the c of Israel 2Ch 24:6 6951
give You thanks in the great c; Ps 35:18 6951
of righteousness in the great c; Ps 40:9 6951
and Your truth from the great c. Ps 40:10 6951
Remember Your c, which You have Ps 74:2 5712
God takes His stand in His own c; Ps 82:1 5712
Him also in the c of the people, Ps 107:32 6951
praise in the c of the godly ones. Ps 149:1 6951
the midst of the assembly and c." Pr 5:14 5712
hear, O nations, And know, O c, Jer 6:18 5712
And their c shall be established Jer 30:20 5712
they should not enter into Your c. La 1:10 6951
Gather the people, sanctify the c, Jl 2:16 6951
And the c of those who believed Ac 4:32 *4128*
the c of the disciples and said, Ac 6:2 *4128*
found approval with the whole c; Ac 6:5 *4128*
"This is the one who was in the c Ac 7:38 *1577*
having gathered the c together, Ac 15:30 *4128*
OF THE C I WILL SING YOUR PRAISE." Heb 2:12 *1577*

CONGREGATION'S
now the c half was 337,500 sheep, Nu 31:43 5712

CONGREGATIONS
In the c I shall bless the LORD. Ps 26:12 4721
Bless God in the c, Ps 68:26 4721

CONIAH
"even though C the son of Jer 22:24 3078
"Is this man C a despised, Jer 22:28 3078
place of C the son of Jehoiakim. Jer 37:1 3078

CONJUGAL
her clothing, or her c rights. Ex 21:10 5772b

CONJURE
"C up for me, please, and bring 1Sa 28:8 7080

CONJURER
of any magician, c or Chaldean. Da 2:10 826

CONJURERS
and c who *were* in all his realm. Da 1:20 825
to call in the magicians, the c, Da 2:2 825
has inquired, neither wise men, c, Da 2:27 826
"Then the magicians, the c, Da 4:7 826
called aloud to bring in the c, Da 5:7 826
him chief of the magicians, c, Da 5:11 826
"Just now the wise men *and* the c Da 5:15 826

CONNECTION
by which they serve in c with it: Nu 4:14 5921
the guilt in c with the sanctuary, Nu 18:1
guilt in c with your priesthood. Nu 18:1
the persecution that occurred in c with Ac 11:19 *1909*
of a riot in c with today's events, Ac 19:40 *4012*
and in this c we will be unable Ac 19:40 *4012*

CONQUER
against it, but could not c it. Is 7:1
3898a, 5921
c through Him who loved us. Ro 8:37 *5245*
he went out conquering and to c. Rv 6:2 *3528*

CONQUERED
and c all the country of the Gn 14:7 5221
the land which the LORD c before Nu 32:4 5221
the cities of Israel, and c Ijon, 1Ki 15:20 5221
and the sons of Judah c because 2Ch 13:18 553
cities of Israel, and they c Ijon, 2Ch 16:4 5221
before Pharaoh c Gaza. Jer 47:1 5221
who by faith c kingdoms, performed Heb 11:33 *2610*

CONQUERING
and he went out c and to conquer. Rv 6:2 *3528*

CONSCIENCE
David's c bothered him because he had 1Sa 24:5 3820
c before God up to this day." Ac 23:1 *4893*
best to maintain always a blameless c Ac 24:16 *4893*
hearts, their c bearing witness and Ro 2:15 *4893*
my c testifies with me in the Ro 9:1 *4893*
and their c being weak is defiled. 1Co 8:7 *4893*
will not his c, if he is weak, be 1Co 8:10 *4893*
wounding their c when it is weak, 1Co 8:12 *4893*
I mean not your own c, 1Co 10:29 *4893*
my freedom judged by another's c? 1Co 10:29 *4893*
is this: the testimony of our c, 2Co 1:12 *4893*
every man's c in the sight of God. 2Co 4:2 *4893*
and a good c and a sincere faith. 1Tm 1:5 *4893*
keeping faith and a good c, 1Tm 1:19 *4893*
of the faith with a clear c. 1Tm 3:9 *4893*
own c as with a branding iron, 1Tm 4:2 *4893*
c the way my forefathers did, 2Tm 1:3 *4893*
mind and their c are defiled. Ti 1:15 *4893*
make the worshiper perfect in c, Heb 9:9 *4893*
cleanse your c from dead works to Heb 9:14 *4893*
hearts sprinkled *clean* from an evil c Heb 10:22 *4893*
we are sure that we have a good c, Heb 13:18 *4893*
if for the sake of c toward God a 1Pe 2:19 *4893*
and keep a good c so that in the 1Pe 3:16 *4893*
but an appeal to God for a good c 1Pe 3:21 *4893*

CONSCIENCE'
but also for c sake. Ro 13:5 *4893*
without asking questions for c sake; 1Co 10:25 *4893*
asking questions for c sake. 1Co 10:27 *4893*
and for c sake; 1Co 10:28 *4893*

CONSCIENCES
are made manifest also in your c. 2Co 5:11 *4893*

CONSCIENTIOUS
For the Levites were more c to 2Ch 29:34
3477, 3824

CONSCIOUS
with disgrace and c of my misery. Jb 10:15 7202
c that His disciples grumbled at Jn 6:61
3609a, 1722, 1438
I am c of nothing against myself, 1Co 4:4 *4924a*

CONSCIOUSNESS
no longer have had c of sins? Heb 10:2 *4893*

CONSECRATE
and c them today and tomorrow, Ex 19:10 6942
near to the LORD c themselves, Ex 19:22 6942
about the mountain and c it.' " Ex 19:23 6942
make Aaron's garments to c him, Ex 28:3 6942
things which the sons of Israel c, Ex 28:38 6942
them and ordain them and c them, Ex 28:41 6942
to c them to minister as priests to Me: Ex 29:1 6942
"You shall c the breast of Ex 29:27 6942
and you shall anoint it to c it. Ex 29:36 6942
atonement for the altar and c it; Ex 29:37 6942
"I will c the tent of meeting Ex 29:44 6942
I will also c Aaron and his sons Ex 29:44 6942
"You shall also c them, that they Ex 30:29 6942
Aaron and his sons, and c them, Ex 30:30 6942
c it and all its furnishings; Ex 40:9 6942
all its utensils, and c the altar, Ex 40:10 6942
the laver and its stand, and c it. Ex 40:11 6942
on Aaron and anoint him and c him, Ex 40:13 6942
basin and its stand, to c them. Lv 8:11 6942
head and anointed him, to c him. Lv 8:12 6942
C yourselves therefore, and be Lv 11:44 6942
of the sons of Israel c it. Lv 16:19 6942
'You shall c yourselves therefore Lv 20:7 6942
'You shall c him, therefore, for Lv 21:8 6942
'You shall thus c the fiftieth Lv 25:10 6942
to the LORD, no man may c it; Lv 27:26 6942
that same day he shall c his head, Nu 6:11 6942
'C yourselves for tomorrow, and Nu 11:18 6942
"You shall c to the LORD your God Dt 15:19 6942
"C yourselves, for tomorrow the Jos 3:5 6942
C the people and say, Jos 7:13 6942
'C yourselves for tomorrow, for Jos 7:13 6942
C yourselves and come with me to 1Sa 16:5 6942
c yourselves both you and your 1Ch 15:12 6942
c himself this day to the LORD?" 1Ch 29:5
4390, 3027
Whoever comes to c himself with a 2Ch 13:9
4390, 3027
C yourselves now, and consecrate 2Ch 29:5 6942
now, and c the house of the LORD, 2Ch 29:5 6942
to c themselves than the priests. 2Ch 29:34 6942
in order to c *them* to the LORD. 2Ch 30:17 6942
Job would send and c them, Jb 1:5 6942
C the nations against her, Summon Jer 51:27 6942
C the nations against her, The Jer 51:28 6942
so shall they c it. Ezk 43:26
4390, 3027
C a fast, Proclaim a solemn Jl 1:14 6942
Blow a trumpet in Zion, C a fast, Jl 2:15 6942

CONSECRATED
to the people and c the people, Ex 19:14 6942
so he and his garments shall be c, Ex 29:21 6942
and it shall be c by My glory. Ex 29:43 6942
touches them will become c.' " Lv 6:18 6942
touches its flesh will become c; Lv 6:27 6942
'This is that which is c to Aaron Lv 7:35 4888b
Aaron and that which is c to his sons Lv 7:35 4888b
all that was in it, and c them. Lv 8:10 6942
at the base of the altar and c it, Lv 8:15 6942
and he c Aaron, his garments, and Lv 8:30 6942
she shall not touch any c thing, Lv 12:4 6944
has been c to wear the garments, Lv 21:10
4390, 3027
he anointed it and c it with all Nu 7:1 6942
he anointed them and c them also. Nu 7:1 6942
a c people to the LORD your God, Dt 26:19 6918
idols and c one of his sons, Jg 17:5
4390, 3027
So Micah c the Levite, and the Jg 17:12
4390, 3027
and c Eleazar his son to keep the 1Sa 7:1 6942
He also c Jesse and his sons and 1Sa 16:5 6942
on hand, but there is c bread; 1Sa 21:4 6944
So the priest gave him c *bread;* 1Sa 21:6 6944
On the same day the king c the 1Ki 8:64 6942
I have c this house which you have 1Ki 9:3 6942
house which I have c for My name, 1Ki 9:7 6942
So the priests and the Levites c 1Ch 15:14 6942
Then Solomon c the middle of the 2Ch 7:7 6942
"For now I have chosen and c this 2Ch 7:16 6942
and this house which I have c for 2Ch 7:20 6942
Aaron who are c to burn incense. 2Ch 26:18 6942
their brothers, c themselves, 2Ch 29:15 6942
Then they c the house of the LORD 2Ch 29:17 6942
we have prepared and c; 2Ch 29:19 6942
you have c yourselves to the LORD, 2Ch 29:31
4390, 3027
The c things were 600 bulls 2Ch 29:33 6944
other priests had c themselves. 2Ch 29:34 6942
because the priests had not c 2Ch 30:3 6942
sanctuary which He has c forever, 2Ch 30:8 6942
of themselves, and c themselves 2Ch 30:15 6942
assembly who had not c themselves; 2Ch 30:17 6942
number of priests c themselves. 2Ch 30:24 6942
were c to the LORD their God, 2Ch 31:6 6942
and the tithes and the c things; 2Ch 31:12 6944
for they c themselves faithfully 2Ch 31:18 6942
festivals of the LORD that were c, Ezr 3:5 6942
they c it and hung its doors. Ne 3:1 6942
They c the wall to the Tower of Ne 3:1 6942
the c *portion* for the Levites, Ne 12:47 6942
Levites set apart the c *portion* Ne 12:47 6942
I have commanded My c ones, Is 13:3 6942
And before you were born I c you; Jer 1:5 6942
Her c ones were purer than snow, La 4:7 5139
a sacrifice, He has c His guests. Zph 1:7 6942
of God, and they ate the c bread, Mt 12:4 *4286*
high priest, and ate the c bread, Mk 2:26 *4286*
and took and ate the c bread which Lk 6:4 *4286*

CONSECRATES
c his house as holy to the LORD, Lv 27:14 6942
'Yet if the one who c it should Lv 27:15 6942
if a man c to the LORD part of the Lv 27:16 6942
'If he c his field as of the year Lv 27:17 6942
he c his field after the jubilee, Lv 27:18 6942
'If the one who c it should Lv 27:19 6942
'Or if he c to the LORD a field Lv 27:22 6942

CONSECRATION
made at their ordination *and* c; Ex 29:33 6942
for the c of the anointing oil of Lv 21:12 5145
Now they began the c on the first 2Ch 29:17 6942

CONSECUTIVE
write *it* out for you in c order, Lk 1:3 *2517*

CONSENT
this *condition* will we c to you: Gn 34:15 225
the men c to us to live with us, Gn 34:22 225
Only let us c to them, and they Gn 34:23 225
king of Moab, but he would not c. Jg 11:17 14
"Do not listen or c." 1Ki 20:8 14
"Will the wild ox c to serve you, Jb 39:9 14
if sinners entice you, Do not c. Pr 1:10 14
"If you c and obey, You will eat Is 1:19 14
for a longer time, he did not c, Ac 18:20 *1962*
without your c I did not want to do Phm 1:14 *1106*

CONSENTED
So he c, and *began* seeking a good Lk 22:6 *1843*
not c to their plan and action), Lk 23:51 *4784*

CONSENTS
and she c to live with him, 1Co 7:12 *4909*
and he c to live with her, 1Co 7:13 *4909*

CONSEQUENCES
he who does wrong will receive the c Col 3:25

CONSIDER
C too, that this nation is Your Ex 33:13 7200
C the years of all generations. Dt 32:7 995
'I did not c them'; Dt 33:9 7200
therefore, c what you should do." Jg 18:14 3045
C it, take counsel and speak up!" Jg 19:30 7760
"Do not c your maidservant as a 1Sa 1:16 5414
for c what great things He has 1Sa 12:24 7200
know and c what you should do, 1Sa 25:17 7200
"Let not my lord c me guilty, nor 2Sa 19:19 2803
Now c and see what answer I shall 2Sa 24:13 3045
But c now, and see how he is 2Ki 5:7 3045
c what answer I shall return to 1Ch 21:12 7200
"C now, for the LORD has chosen 1Ch 28:10 7200
"C what you are doing, for you do 2Ch 19:6 7200
And c the things searched out by Jb 8:8 3559
Your face And c me Your enemy? Jb 13:24 2803
and my maids c me a stranger. Jb 19:15 2803
When I c, I am terrified of Him. Jb 23:15 995
does not *need to* c a man further, Jb 34:23 7760
Stand and c the wonders of God. Jb 37:14 995
my words, O LORD, C my groaning. Ps 5:1 995
When I c Your heavens, the work of Ps 8:3 7200
C *and* answer me, O LORD my God; Ps 13:3 5027
C her ramparts; Go through her Ps 48:13
7896, 3820
"Now c this, you who forget God, Ps 50:22 995
God, And will c what He has done. Ps 64:9 7919a
C the covenant; For the dark places Ps 74:20 5027
c the lovingkindnesses of the LORD. Ps 107:43 995
diligently c Your testimonies. Ps 119:95 995
C how I love Your precepts; Ps 119:159 7200
C carefully what is before you, Pr 23:1 995
He not c *it* who weighs the hearts? Pr 24:12 995
So I turned to c wisdom, madness Ec 2:12 7200
not often c the years of his life, Ec 5:20 2142
C the work of God, For who is able Ec 7:13 7200
But in the day of adversity c Ec 7:14 7200
do they c the work of His hands. Is 5:12 7200
And c and gain insight as well, Is 41:20 7760
they *were,* That we may c them and Is 41:22 7760
These things you did not c Nor Is 47:7
7760, 5921, 3820
"C and call for the mourning Jer 9:17 995
She did not c her future. La 1:9 2142
And they do not c in their hearts Hos 7:2 559
says the LORD of hosts, "C your ways Hg 1:5
7760, 3824, 5921

says the LORD of hosts, "**C** your ways **Hg 1:7** 7760, 3824, 5921
now, do **c** from this day onward: **Hg 2:15** 7760, 3824
'Do **c** from this day onward, from **Hg 2:18** 7760, 3824
temple of the LORD was founded, **c**: **Hg 2:18** 7760, 3824
c myself worthy to come to You, **Lk 7:7** *515*
"**C** the ravens, for they neither **Lk 12:24** *2657*
"**C** the lilies, how they grow: **Lk 12:27** *2657*
please **c** me excused.' **Lk 14:18** *2192*
please **c** me excused.' **Lk 14:19** *2192*
will not first sit down and **c** whether **Lk 14:31** *1011*
cleansed, no *longer* **c** unholy." **Ac 10:15** *2840*
has cleansed, no longer **c** unholy.' **Ac 11:9** *2840*
"But I do not **c** my life of any **Ac 20:24** *4160*
by the Jews, I **c** myself fortunate, **Ac 26:2** *2233*
so **c** yourselves to be dead to sin, **Ro 6:11** *3049*
For I **c** that the sufferings of **Ro 8:18** *3049*
For **c** your calling, brethren, that **1Co 1:26** *991*
to **c** anything as *coming* from ourselves **2Co 3:5** *3049*
him **c** this again within himself, **2Co 10:7** *3049*
Let such a person **c** this, **2Co 10:11** *3049*
For I **c** myself not in the least **2Co 11:5** *3049*
Therefore **c** the members of your **Col 3:5** *3499*
C what I say, for the Lord will **2Tm 2:7** *3539*
of a heavenly calling, **c** Jesus, **Heb 3:1** *2657*
and let us **c** how to stimulate one **Heb 10:24** *2657*
For **c** Him who has endured such **Heb 12:3** *357*
C it all joy, my brethren, when **Jas 1:2** *2233*
I **c** it right, as long as I am **2Pe 1:13** *2233*

CONSIDERABLE
Now after a **c** time Shua's **Gn 38:12** 7235a
And **c** numbers were brought to the **Ac 11:24** *2425*
the church and taught **c** numbers; **Ac 11:26** *2425*
turned away a **c** number of people, **Ac 19:26** *2425*
When **c** time had passed and the **Ac 27:9** *2425*

CONSIDERATION
wealth, Cease from your **c** *of it.* **Pr 23:4** 998
Nor did you take into **c** Him who **Is 22:11** 7200
and Julius treated Paul with **c** and **Ac 27:3** *5364*
showing every **c** for all men. **Ti 3:2** *4240*

CONSIDERED
found with me, will be **c** stolen." **Gn 30:33**
wall shall be **c** as open fields; **Lv 25:31** 2803
Beeroth is also **c** *part* of Benjamin, **2Sa 4:2** 2803
son Solomon will be **c** offenders." **1Ki 1:21**
it was not **c** valuable in the days **1Ki 10:21** 2803
silver was not **c** valuable in the **2Ch 9:20** 2803
therefore they were **c** unclean *and* **Ezr 2:62**
therefore they were **c** unclean *and* **Ne 7:64**
for they were **c** reliable, and it **Ne 13:13** 2803
"Have you **c** My servant Job? **Jb 1:8** 7760, 3820, 5921
"Have you **c** My servant Job? **Jb 2:3** 7760, 3820, 5921
against me And **c** me as His enemy. **Jb 19:11** 2803
are **c** as sheep to be slaughtered. **Ps 44:22** 2803
I have **c** the days of old, The **Ps 77:5** 2803
I **c** my ways And turned my feet to **Ps 119:59** 2803
when he keeps silent, is **c** wise; **Pr 17:28** 2803
he is **c** prudent. **Pr 17:28**
Thus I **c** all my activities which **Ec 2:11** 6437
be **c** as equal with the clay, **Is 29:16** 2803
field will be **c** as a forest? **Is 29:17** 2803
fertile field is **c** as a forest. **Is 32:15** 2803
who **c** That He was cut off out of **Is 53:8** 7878
"Because he **c** and turned away **Ezk 18:28** 7200
But when he had **c** this, behold, an **Mt 1:20** *1760*
because they **c** Him to be a prophet. **Mt 21:46** *2192*
for everyone **c** John to have been a **Mk 11:32** *2192*
but those who are **c** worthy to **Lk 20:35** *2661*
rejoicing that they had been **c** **Ac 5:41** *2661*
"Why is it **c** incredible among you **Ac 26:8** *2919*
C AS SHEEP TO BE SLAUGHTERED." **Ro 8:36** *3049*
be **c** worthy of the kingdom of God, **2Th 1:5** *2661*
me, because He **c** me faithful, **1Tm 1:12** *2233*
to be **c** worthy of double honor, **1Tm 5:17** *515*
c Him faithful who had promised. **Heb 11:11** *2233*
He **c** that God is able to raise *people* **Heb 11:19** *3049*

CONSIDERING
c the reproach of Christ greater **Heb 11:26** *2233*
and **c** the result of their conduct, **Heb 13:7** *333*

CONSIDERS
blessed is he who **c** the helpless; **Ps 41:1** 7919a
But the sensible man **c** his steps. **Pr 14:15** 995
one **c** the house of the wicked, **Pr 21:12** 7919a
She **c** a field and buys it; **Pr 31:16** 2161

CONSIGN
And I will **c** Jacob to the ban and **Is 43:28** 5414

CONSIGNED
Their images are **c** to the beasts **Is 46:1**

CONSIST
his life **c** of his possessions." **Lk 12:15** *1510*
of God does not **c** in words but **1Co 4:20**

CONSISTED
chambers toward the free space **c** *of* **Ezk 41:11**
Whose wall **c** of the sea? **Na 3:8**

CONSISTENT
but their testimony was not **c**. **Mk 14:56** *2470*
respect was their testimony **c**. **Mk 14:59** *2470*

CONSISTING
c of valiant men, men who bore **1Ch 5:18**
certificate of debt **c** of decrees against **Col 2:14**

CONSISTS
Me **c** of tradition learned *by rote,* **Is 29:13** 1961

(for the fruit of the Light **c** in **Eph 5:9**

CONSOLATION
"But it is still my **c**, **Jb 6:10** 5165
And let this be your *way of* **c**. **Jb 21:2** 8575
nor give them a cup of **c** to drink **Jer 16:7** 8575
done when you become a **c** to them. **Ezk 16:54** 5162
looking for the **c** of Israel; **Lk 2:25** *3874*
edification and exhortation and **c**. **1Co 14:3** *3889*
Christ, if there is any **c** of love, **Php 2:1** *3890*

CONSOLATIONS
the **c** of God too small for you, **Jb 15:11** 8575
within me, Your **c** delight my soul. **Ps 94:19** 8575

CONSOLE
to **c** him concerning his father. **2Sa 10:2** 5162
to **c** him concerning his father. **1Ch 19:2** 5162
sons of Ammon to Hanun to **c** him. **1Ch 19:2** 5162
or go to lament or to **c** them; **Jer 16:5** 5110
c them concerning *their* brother. **Jn 11:19** *3888*

CONSOLED
and they **c** him and comforted him **Jb 42:11** 5110

CONSOLERS
because he has sent **c** to you? **2Sa 10:3** 5162

CONSOLING
Esau is **c** himself concerning you **Gn 27:42** 5162
with her in the house, and **c** her, **Jn 11:31** *3888*

CONSPICUOUS
had a **c** horn between his eyes. **Da 8:5** 2380
in its place there came up four **c** *horns* **Da 8:8** 2380

CONSPIRACIES
of Your presence from the **c** of man; **Ps 31:20** 7407

CONSPIRACY
And the **c** was strong, for the **2Sa 15:12** 7195
Zimri and his **c** which he carried out, **1Ki 16:20** 7195
His servants arose and made a **c** **2Ki 12:20** 7195
Shallum and his **c** which he made, **2Ki 15:15** 7195
son of Elah made a **c** against Pekah **2Ki 15:30** 7195
king of Assyria found **c** in Hoshea, **2Ki 17:4** 7195
"You are not to say, '*It is* a **c**!' **Is 8:12** 7195
to all that this people call a **c**, **Is 8:12** 7195
"A **c** has been found among the men **Jer 11:9** 7195
a **c** of her prophets in her midst like **Ezk 22:25** 7195
the Jews formed a **c** and bound **Ac 23:12** *4160*

CONSPIRATORS
is among the **c** with Absalom." **2Sa 15:31** 7194
all the **c** against King Amon, **2Ch 33:25** 7194

CONSPIRE
And **c** together against Your **Ps 83:3** 3289

CONSPIRED
"For all of you have **c** against me **1Sa 22:8** 7194
and the son of Jesse **c** against me, **1Sa 22:13** 7194
house of Issachar **c** against him, **1Ki 15:27** 7194
half his chariots, **c** against him. **1Ki 16:9** 7194
"Zimri has **c** and has also struck **1Ki 16:16** 7194
the son of Nimshi **c** against Joram. **2Ki 9:14** 7194
I **c** against my master and killed **2Ki 10:9** 7194
They **c** against him in Jerusalem, **2Ki 14:19** 7194
Then Shallum the son of Jabesh **c** **2Ki 15:10** 7194
c against him and struck him in **2Ki 15:25** 7194
The servants of Amon **c** against **2Ki 21:23** 7194
those who had **c** against King Amon, **2Ki 21:24** 7194
So they **c** against him and at the **2Ch 24:21** 7194
his own servants **c** against him **2Ch 24:25** 7194
these are those who **c** against him: **2Ch 24:26** 7194
they **c** against him in Jerusalem, **2Ch 25:27** 7194
Finally his servants **c** against him **2Ch 33:24** 7194
All of them **c** together to come **Ne 4:8** 7194
have **c** together with one mind; **Ps 83:5** 3289
"Amos has **c** against you in the **Am 7:10** 7194
But the Pharisees went out and **c** **Mt 12:14** *4824, 2983*

CONSPIRING
went out and immediately *began* **c** **Mk 3:6** *4824*

CONSTANT
of a wife are a **c** dripping. **Pr 19:13** 2956
A **c** dripping on a day of steady **Pr 27:15** 2956
and **c** friction between men of **1Tm 6:5** *1275*

CONSTANTLY
with which he **c** girds himself. **Ps 109:19** 8548
who **c** record unjust decisions, **Is 10:1**
who will **c** pass through the land, **Ezk 39:14** 8548
"Your God whom you **c** serve will **Da 6:16** 8411
has your God, whom you **c** serve, **Da 6:20** 8411
C, night and day, he was screaming **Mk 5:5** *1223*
were **c** added to *their number,* **Ac 5:14**
taking place, he was **c** amazed. **Ac 8:13**
c watching and going without eating, **Ac 27:33** *1300*
For we who live are **c** being delivered **2Co 4:11** *104*
is **c** bearing fruit and increasing, **Col 1:6**
c bearing in mind your work of **1Th 1:3** *89*
For this reason we also **c** thank God **1Th 2:13** *89*
c nourished on the words of **1Tm 4:6**
as I **c** remember you in my prayers **2Tm 1:3** *88*

CONSTELLATION
you lead forth a **c** in its season, **Jb 38:32** 4216

CONSTELLATIONS
c and to all the host of heaven. **2Ki 23:5** 4208
stars of heaven and their **c** Will not **Is 13:10** 3685

CONSTERNATION
were living, causing **c** among them. **Ezk 3:15** 8074

CONSTITUTE
These **c** the list of the mighty **1Ch 11:11**
are you not competent *to* **c** **1Co 6:2**

CONSTRAINS
The spirit within me **c** me. **Jb 32:18** 6693

CONSTRAINT
of it, a broad place with no **c**; **Jb 36:16** 4164
in his heart, being under no **c**, **1Co 7:37** *318*

CONSTRUCT
"Let them **c** a sanctuary for **Ex 25:8** 6213a
furniture, just so you shall **c** *it.* **Ex 25:9** 6213a
"They shall **c** an ark of **Ex 25:10** 6213a
that you may **c** siegeworks against **Dt 20:20** 1129

CONSTRUCTED
and **c** large siegeworks against it. **Ec 9:14** 1129

CONSTRUCTION
work in the **c** of the sanctuary, **Ex 36:1** 5656
work in the **c** of the sanctuary. **Ex 36:3** 5656
c work which the LORD commanded **Ex 36:5** 5656
until now it has been under **c** and **Ezr 5:16** 1124
of Noah, during the **c** of the ark, **1Pe 3:20** *2680*

CONSULT
call the girl and **c** her wishes." **Gn 24:57** 7592
"**C** the mediums and the spiritists **Is 8:19** 1875
should not a people **c** their God? **Is 8:19** 1875
Should they **c** the dead on **Is 8:19**
With whom did He **c** and *who* gave **Is 40:14** 3289
Indeed, let them **c** together. **Is 45:21** 3289
My people **c** their wooden idol, and **Hos 4:12** 7592
c with flesh and blood, **Ga 1:16** *4323*

CONSULTATION
had **c** with the elders of Israel, **2Sa 3:17** 1697
Philistines after **c** sent him away, **1Ch 12:19** 6098
Without **c**, plans are frustrated, **Pr 15:22** 5475
Prepare plans by **c**, **Pr 20:18** 6098
Council, immediately held a **c**; **Mk 15:1** *4824*

CONSULTED
King Rehoboam **c** with the elders **1Ki 12:6** 3289
and **c** with the young men who grew **1Ki 12:8** 3289
So the king **c**, and made two golden **1Ki 12:28** 3289
Then David **c** with the captains of **1Ch 13:1** 3289
King Rehoboam **c** with the elders **2Ch 10:6** 3289
and **c** with the young men who grew **2Ch 10:8** 3289
When he had **c** with the people, **2Ch 20:21** 3289
I **c** with myself and contended **Ne 5:7** 4427b
watch for my life have **c** together, **Ps 71:10** 3289
Should I be **c** by them at all? **Ezk 14:3** 1875
about which the king **c** them, **Da 1:20** 1245
high officials and the governors have **c** **Da 6:7** 3272b
had assembled with the elders and **c** **Mt 28:12** *4824, 2983*

CONSULTING
down to Egypt Without **c** Me, **Is 30:2** 7592

CONSULTS
arrows, he **c** the household idols, **Ezk 21:21** 7592

CONSUME
and your enemies' land will **c** you. **Lv 26:38** 398
that I may **c** them instantly." **Nu 16:21** 3615
that I may **c** them instantly." **Nu 16:45** 3615
For this great fire will **c** us; **Dt 5:25** 398
"You shall **c** all the peoples **Dt 7:16** 398
little, for the locust will **c** it. **Dt 28:38** 2628
He will turn and do you harm and **c** **Jos 24:20** 3615
and **c** the cedars of Lebanon.' **Jg 9:15** 398
fire come out from Abimelech and **c** **Jg 9:20** 398
from Beth-millo, and **c** Abimelech." **Jg 9:20** 398
I will **c** Baasha and his house, **1Ki 16:3** 1197a
heaven and **c** you and your fifty." **2Ki 1:10** 398
heaven and **c** you and your fifty." **2Ki 1:12** 398
will **c** the survivor in his tent. **Jb 20:26** 7462a
and heat **c** the snow waters, **Jb 24:19** 1497
You **c** as a moth what is **Ps 39:11** 4529
form shall be for Sheol to **c** So **Ps 49:14** 1086
those who **c** them increase. **Ec 5:11** 398
while the lips of a fool **c** him; **Ec 10:12** 1104
My breath will **c** you like a fire. **Is 33:11** 398
people wood, and it will **c** them. **Jer 5:14** 398
will also **c** those in the city. **Ezk 7:15** 398
and hailstones to **c** *it* in wrath. **Ezk 13:13** 3615
fire, yet the fire will **c** them. **Ezk 15:7** 398
will **c** every green tree in you, **Ezk 20:47** 398
the slaughter, to cause it to **c**, **Ezk 21:28** 398
will **c** your uncleanness from you. **Ezk 22:15** 8552
an oven, And they **c** their rulers; **Hos 7:7** 398
it may **c** its palatial dwellings. **Hos 8:14** 398
And **c** *them* because of their counsels. **Hos 11:6** 3615
will **c** the citadels of Ben-hadad. **Am 1:4** 398
Gaza And it will **c** her citadels. **Am 1:7** 398
And it will **c** her citadels." **Am 1:10** 398
will **c** the citadels of Bozrah." **Am 1:12** 398
And it will **c** her citadels Amid **Am 1:14** 398
it will **c** the citadels of Kerioth; **Am 2:2** 398
c the citadels of Jerusalem." **Am 2:5** 398
And it will **c** with none to quench *it* **Am 5:6** 398
deep and began to **c** the farm land. **Am 7:4** 398
will set them on fire and **c** them, **Ob 1:18** 398
There fire will **c** you, The sword **Na 3:15** 398
It will **c** you as the locust *does.* **Na 3:15** 398
c it with its timber and stones." **Zch 5:4** 3615
so they will **c** on the right hand **Zch 12:6** 398
down from heaven and **c** them?" **Lk 9:54** *355*
"ZEAL FOR YOUR HOUSE WILL **C** ME." **Jn 2:17** *2719*
FIRE WHICH WILL **C** THE ADVERSARIES. **Heb 10:27** *2068*
and will **c** your flesh like fire. **Jas 5:3** *2068*

CONSUMED
entirely **c** our purchase price. **Gn 31:15** 398
by day the heat **c** me and the **Gn 31:40** 398
with fire, yet the bush was not **c**. **Ex 3:2** 398
grain or the field *itself* is **c**, **Ex 22:6** 398
from before the LORD and **c** the burnt **Lv 9:24** 398
presence of the LORD and **c** them, **Lv 10:2** 398
c *some* of the outskirts of the camp. **Nu 11:1** 398

and **c** the two hundred and fifty men **Nu 16:35** 398
"Nevertheless Kain will be **c**; **Nu 24:22** 1197a
until He has **c** you from the land where **Dt 28:21** 3615
from them, and they will be **c**, **Dt 31:17** 398
wasted by famine, and **c** by plague **Dt 32:24** 3898b
fire sprang up from the rock and **c** **Jg 6:21** 398
"The man who **c** us and who **2Sa 21:5** 3615
not turn back until they were **c**. **2Sa 22:38** 3615
and **c** the burnt offering and the **1Ki 18:38** 398
the Arameans until they are **c**.' " **1Ki 22:11** 3615
heaven and **c** him and his fifty. **2Ki 1:10** 398
heaven and **c** him and his fifty. **2Ki 1:12** 398
and **c** the first two captains of **2Ki 1:14** 398
fire came down from heaven and **c** **2Ch 7:1** 398
Arameans until they are **c**.' " **2Ch 18:10** 3615
its gates have been **c** by *fire*?" **Ne 2:3** 398
its gates which were **c** by fire. **Ne 2:13** 398
sheep and the servants and **c** them, **Jb 1:16** 398
their abundance the fire has **c**.' **Jb 22:20** 398
not turn back until they were **c**. **Ps 18:37** 3615
For zeal for Your house has **c** me, **Ps 69:9** 398
of my soul be ashamed *and* **c**; **Ps 71:13** 3615
For we have been **c** by Your anger **Ps 90:7** 3615
For my days have been **c** in smoke, **Ps 102:3** 3615
Let sinners be **c** from the earth And **Ps 104:35** 8552
The flame **c** the wicked. **Ps 106:18** 3857
My zeal has **c** me, Because my **Ps 119:139** 6789
your flesh and your body are **c**; **Pr 5:11** 3615
remove its hedge and it will be **c**; **Is 5:5** 1197a
"But the shameful thing has **c** the **Jer 3:24** 398
You have **c** them, But they refused **Jer 5:3** 3615
The lead is **c** by the fire; **Jer 6:29** 8552
They have devoured him and **c** him And **Jer 10:25** 3615
until all the scroll was **c** in the **Jer 36:23** 8552
after them Until I have **c** them. **Jer 49:37** 3615
Zion Which has **c** its foundations. **La 4:11** 398
or be **c** by famine among you, **Ezk 5:12** 3615
falls, you will be **c** in its midst. **Ezk 13:14** 3615
the fire has **c** both of its ends and **Ezk 15:4** 398
fire has **c** it and it is charred, **Ezk 15:5** 398
So that it withered; The fire **c** it. **Ezk 19:12** 398
It has **c** its shoots *and* fruit, So **Ezk 19:14** 398
I have **c** them with the fire of My **Ezk 22:31** 3615
survivors will be **c** by the fire. **Ezk 23:25** 398
may be melted in it, Its rust **c**. **Ezk 24:11** 8552
It has **c** you, And I have turned **Ezk 28:18** 398
So I have **c** them in My anger. **Ezk 43:8** 3615
and it **c** the great deep and began **Am 7:4** 398
They are **c** As stubble completely **Na 1:10** 398
And she will be **c** with fire. **Zch 9:4** 398
you, O sons of Jacob, are not **c**. **Mal 3:6** 3615
care that you are not **c** by one another. **Ga 5:15** *355*

CONSUMES
anger, *and* it **c** them as chaff. **Ex 15:7** 398
And **c** the earth with its yield, **Dt 32:22** 398
fire **c** the tents of the corrupt. **Jb 15:34** 398
would be fire that **c** to Abaddon, **Jb 31:12** 398
his hands and **c** his own flesh. **Ec 4:5** 398
as a tongue of fire **c** stubble And **Is 5:24** 398
It **c** briars and thorns; **Is 9:18** 398
A fire **c** before them And behind **Jl 2:3** 398
Fire **c** your gate bars. **Na 3:13** 398

CONSUMING
like a **c** fire on the mountain top. **Ex 24:17** 398
"For the LORD your God is a **c** fire, **Dt 4:24** 398
over before you as a **c** fire. **Dt 9:3** 398
tempest and the flame of a **c** fire. **Is 29:6** 398
And His tongue is like a **c** fire; **Is 30:27** 398
And *in* the flame of a **c** fire In **Is 30:30** 398
among us can live with the **c** fire? **Is 33:14** 398
like a flaming fire **C** round about. **La 2:3** 398
of a flame of fire **c** the stubble, **Jl 2:5** 398
for our God is a **c** fire. **Heb 12:29** *2654*

CONSUMMATION
but now once at the **c** of the ages **Heb 9:26** *4930*

CONSUMPTION
c and fever that will waste away **Lv 26:16** 7829
"The LORD will smite you with **c** **Dt 28:22** 7829

CONTAIN
the highest heaven cannot **c** You, **1Ki 8:27** 3557
the highest heavens cannot **c** Him? **2Ch 2:6** 3557
the highest heaven cannot **c** You; **2Ch 6:18** 3557
not able to **c** the burnt offering, **2Ch 7:7** 3557
of our life, they **c** seventy years, **Ps 90:10**
the bath will **c** a tenth of a homer **Ezk 45:11** 5375
c the books that would be written. **Jn 21:25** *5562*

CONTAINED
is the Law of commandments **c** in **Eph 2:15**
For *this* is **c** in Scripture: **1Pe 2:6** *4023*

CONTAINER
a lamp covers it over with a **c**, **Lk 8:16** *4632*

CONTAINERS
and gathered the good *fish* into **c**, **Mt 13:48** *32b*

CONTAINING
both the sealed *copy* **c** the terms **Jer 32:11**
c twenty or thirty gallons each. **Jn 2:6** *5562*

CONTAINS
Let the sea roar, and all it **c**; **1Ch 16:32** 4393
And its dust **c** gold. **Jb 28:6**
earth is the LORD's, and all it **c**, **Ps 24:1** 4393
the world is Mine, and all it **c**. **Ps 50:12** 4393
The world and all it **c**, **Ps 89:11** 4393
Let the sea roar, and all it **c**; **Ps 96:11** 4393
Let the sea roar and all it **c**, **Ps 98:7** 4393
Let the earth and all it **c** hear, **Is 34:1** 4393
and held in derision; It **c** much. **Ezk 23:32** 3557
will deliver up *the* city and all it **c**." **Am 6:8** 4393
Listen, O earth and all it **c**, **Mi 1:2** 4393
EARTH IS THE LORD'S, AND ALL IT C. **1Co 10:26** *4138*

CONTAMINATED
they abstain from things **c** by idols **Ac 15:20** *234*

CONTEMPLATED
weak in faith he **c** his own body, **Ro 4:19** *2657*

CONTEMPLATING
"While I was **c** the horns, behold, **Da 7:8** 7920

CONTEMPORARIES
many of my **c** among my countrymen, **Ga 1:14** *4915*

CONTEMPT
Why then did you treat us with **c**? **2Sa 19:43** 7043
to look with **c** on their husbands **Es 1:17** 959
will be plenty of **c** and anger. **Es 1:18** 963
is at ease holds calamity in **c**, **Jb 12:5** 937
"He pours **c** on nobles And **Jb 12:21** 937
slapped me on the cheek with **c**; **Jb 16:10** 2781
the **c** of families terrified me, **Jb 31:34** 937
the righteous With pride and **c**. **Ps 31:18** 937
He pours **c** upon princes And makes **Ps 107:40** 937
Take away reproach and **c** from me, **Ps 119:22** 937
For we are greatly filled with **c**. **Ps 123:3** 937
ease, *And* with the **c** of the proud. **Ps 123:4** 937
a wicked man comes, **c** also comes, **Pr 18:3** 937
and the land of Naphtali with **c**, **Is 9:1** 7043
to disgrace *and* everlasting **c**. **Da 12:2** 1860
hiss *And* wave his hand *in* **c**. **Zph 2:15**
many things and be treated with **c**? **Mk 9:12** *1847*
and viewed others with **c**: **Lk 18:9** *1848*
Him with **c** and mocking Him, **Lk 23:11** *1848*
eats is not to regard with **c** **Ro 14:3** *1848*
do you regard your brother with **c**? **Ro 14:10** *1848*

CONTEMPTIBLE
your grave, For you are **c**." **Na 1:14** 7043
unimpressive and his speech **c**." **2Co 10:10** *1848*

CONTEMPTUOUSLY
For son treats father **c**, **Mi 7:6** 5034a

CONTEND
and **c** with him in battle. **Dt 2:24** 1624
"Will you **c** for Baal, or will you **Jg 6:31** 7378
is a god, let him **c** for himself, **Jg 6:31** 7378
"Let Baal **c** against him," **Jg 6:32** 7378
"Those who **c** with the LORD will **1Sa 2:10** 7378
me know why You **c** with me. **Jb 10:2** 7378
Will you **c** for God? **Jb 13:8** 7378
"Who will **c** with me? **Jb 13:19** 7378
"Would He **c** with me by the **Jb 23:6** 7378
faultfinder **c** with the Almighty? **Jb 40:2** 7378
C, O LORD, with those who contend **Ps 35:1** 7378
O LORD, with those who **c** with me; **Ps 35:1** 3401
Do not **c** with a man without cause, **Pr 3:30** 7378
The LORD arises to **c**, **Is 3:13** 7378
who **c** with you will be as nothing and **Is 41:11** 7379
I will **c** with the one who contends **Is 49:25** 7378
Who will **c** with Me? **Is 50:8** 7378
"For I will not **c** forever, **Is 57:16** 7378
"Therefore I will yet **c** with you," **Jer 2:9** 7378
"And with your sons' sons I will **c**. **Jer 2:9** 7378
"Why do you **c** with Me? **Jer 2:29** 7378
"**C** with your mother, contend, For **Hos 2:2** 7378
"Contend with your mother, **c**, **Hos 2:2** 7378
like those who **c** with the priest. **Hos 4:4** 7378
calling to **c** *with them* by fire, **Am 7:4** 7378
that you **c** earnestly for the faith **Jude 1:3** *1864*

CONTENDED
Esek, because they **c** with him. **Gn 26:20** 6229
became angry and **c** with Laban; **Gn 31:36** 7378
thus **c** with Moses and spoke, **Nu 20:3** 7378
sons of Israel **c** with the LORD, **Nu 20:13** 7378
who **c** against Moses and against **Nu 26:9** 5327b
when they **c** against the LORD, **Nu 26:9** 5327b
With his hands he **c** for them, **Dt 33:7** 7378
With whom You **c** at the waters of **Dt 33:8** 7378
And they **c** with him vigorously. **Jg 8:1** 7378
and **c** with the nobles and the **Ne 5:7** 7378
So I **c** with them and cursed them **Ne 13:25** 7378
You **c** with them by banishing them, **Is 27:8** 7378
And in his maturity he **c** with God. **Hos 12:3** 8280

CONTENDS
I will contend with the one who **c** **Is 49:25** 3401
your God Who **c** for His people, **Is 51:22** 7378

CONTENT
and be **c** with your wages." **Lk 3:14** *714*
I am well **c** with weaknesses, **2Co 12:10** *2106*
for I have learned to be **c** in **Php 4:11** *842*
with these we shall be **c**. **1Tm 6:8** *714*
money, being **c** with what you have; **Heb 13:5** *714*

CONTENTION
an object of **c** to our neighbors, **Ps 80:6** 4066
the scoffer, and **c** will go out, **Pr 22:10** 4066
is no whisperer, **c** quiets down. **Pr 26:20** 4066
you fast for **c** and strife and to **Is 58:4** 7379
and a man of **c** to all the land! **Jer 15:10** 4066
Strife exists and **c** arises. **Hab 1:3** 4066

CONTENTIONS
me from the **c** of my people; **2Sa 22:44** 7379
And listen to the **c** of my lips. **Jb 13:6** 7379
me from the **c** of the people; **Ps 18:43** 7379
c are like the bars of a citadel. **Pr 18:19** 4066
And the **c** of a wife are a constant **Pr 19:13** 4066
Who has **c**? Who has complaining? **Pr 23:29** 4066

CONTENTIOUS
in a house shared with a **c** woman. **Pr 21:9** 4066
Than with a **c** and vexing woman. **Pr 21:19** 4066
in a house shared with a **c** woman. **Pr 25:24** 4066
So is a **c** man to kindle strife. **Pr 26:21** 4066
rain And a **c** woman are alike; **Pr 27:15** 4066
But if one is inclined to be **c**, **1Co 11:16** *5380*

CONTENTMENT
great gain when accompanied by **c**. **1Tm 6:6** *841*

CONTEST
arise and hold a **c** before us." **2Sa 2:14** 7832

CONTINUAL
"It shall be a **c** burnt offering **Ex 29:42** 8548
and the **c** bread shall be on it. **Nu 4:7** 8548
c grain offering and the anointing oil **Nu 4:16** 8548
as a **c** burnt offering every day. **Nu 28:3** 8548
'It is a **c** burnt offering which **Nu 28:6** 8548
in addition to the **c** burnt offering **Nu 28:10** 8548
addition to the **c** burnt offering. **Nu 28:15** 8548
which is for a **c** burnt offering. **Nu 28:23** 8548
addition to the **c** burnt offering. **Nu 28:24** 8548
'Besides the **c** burnt offering and **Nu 28:31** 8548
and the **c** burnt offering and its **Nu 29:6** 8548
c burnt offering and its grain offering, **Nu 29:11** 8548
besides the **c** burnt offering, **Nu 29:16** 8548
besides the **c** burnt offering and **Nu 29:19** 8548
besides the **c** burnt offering and **Nu 29:22** 8548
besides the **c** burnt offering, **Nu 29:25** 8548
besides the **c** burnt offering and **Nu 29:28** 8548
besides the **c** burnt offering, **Nu 29:31** 8548
besides the **c** burnt offering, **Nu 29:34** 8548
besides the **c** burnt offering and **Nu 29:38** 8548
there was a **c** burnt offering, **Ezr 3:5** 8548
for the **c** grain offering, **Ne 10:33** 8548
for the **c** burnt offering, **Ne 10:33** 8548
a cheerful heart *has* a **c** feast. **Pr 15:15** 8548
us can live with **c** burning?" **Is 33:14** 5769
Turned away in **c** apostasy? **Jer 8:5** 5329
They will ascend with **c** weeping; **Jer 48:5** 1065
Israel which had been a **c** waste; **Ezk 38:8** 8548
morning, for a **c** burnt offering." **Ezk 46:15** 8548

CONTINUALLY
of his heart was only evil **c**. **Gn 6:5** 3605, 3117
c in the midst of the hail, **Ex 9:24**
the light, to make a lamp burn **c**. **Ex 27:20** 8548
for a memorial before the LORD **c**. **Ex 28:29** 8548
over his heart before the LORD **c**. **Ex 28:30** 8548
be kept burning **c** on the altar; **Lv 6:13** 8548
the light, to make a lamp burn **c**. **Lv 24:2** 8548
to morning before the LORD **c**; **Lv 24:3** 8548
gold lampstand before the LORD **c**. **Lv 24:4** 8548
set it in order before the LORD **c**; **Lv 24:8** 8548
only be oppressed and robbed **c**, **Dt 28:29** 3605, 3117
look on and yearn for them **c**; **Dt 28:32** 3605, 3117
but oppressed and crushed **c**. **Dt 28:33** 3605, 3117
the ark of the LORD went on **c**, **Jos 6:13** 1980
Thus Saul was David's enemy **c**. **1Sa 18:29** 3605, 3117
prophesying **c** until he came to Naioth **1Sa 19:23** 1980
the house of Saul grew weaker **c**. **2Sa 3:1** 1980
people increased **c** with Absalom. **2Sa 15:12** 1980
he came out cursing **c** as he came. **2Sa 16:5**
before me **c** in place of Joab.' " **2Sa 19:13** 3605, 3117
your servants who stand before you **c** **1Ki 10:8** 8548
between Rehoboam and Jeroboam **c**. **1Ki 14:30** 3605, 3117
a holy man of God passing by us **c**. **2Ki 4:9** 8548
and He gave them **c** into the hand **2Ki 13:3** 3605, 3117
priests *blew* trumpets **c** before the ark **1Ch 16:6** 8548
Seek His face **c**. **1Ch 16:11** 8548
to minister before the ark **c**, **1Ch 16:37** 8548
offering **c** morning and evening, **1Ch 16:40** 8548
them, **c** before the LORD. **1Ch 23:31** 8548
and *to set out* the showbread **c**, **2Ch 2:4** 8548
your servants who stand before you **c** **2Ch 9:7** 8548
between Rehoboam and Jeroboam **c**. **2Ch 12:15** 3605, 3117
LORD **c** all the days of Jehoiada. **2Ch 24:14** 8548
but they **c** mocked the messengers **2Ch 36:16**
God in their hearts." Thus Job did **c**. **Jb 1:5** 3605, 3117
And I am **c** tossing until dawn. **Jb 7:4** 7646
I have set the LORD **c** before me; **Ps 16:8** 8548
My eyes are **c** toward the LORD, For **Ps 25:15** 8548
His praise shall **c** be in my mouth. **Ps 34:1** 8548
And let them say **c**, **Ps 35:27** 8548
And my sorrow is **c** before me. **Ps 38:17** 8548
and Your truth will **c** preserve me. **Ps 40:11** 8548
who love Your salvation say **c**, **Ps 40:16** 8548
burnt offerings are **c** before Me. **Ps 50:8** 8548
see, And make their loins shake **c**. **Ps 69:23** 8548
who love Your salvation say **c**, **Ps 70:4** 8548
habitation to which I may **c** come; **Ps 71:3** 8548
My praise is **c** of You. **Ps 71:6** 8548
But as for me, I will hope **c**, **Ps 71:14** 8548
And let them pray for him **c**; **Ps 72:15** 8548
Nevertheless I am **c** with You; **Ps 73:23** 8548
rise against You which ascends **c**. **Ps 74:23** 8548
Seek His face **c**. **Ps 105:4** 8548
Let them be before the LORD **c**, **Ps 109:15** 8548
So I will keep Your law **c**, **Ps 119:44** 8548
My life is **c** in my hand, Yet I do **Ps 119:109** 8548
have regard for Your statutes **c**. **Ps 119:117** 8548
They **c** stir up wars. **Ps 140:2** 3605, 3117
in his heart **c** devises evil, **Pr 6:14** 3605, 6256

Bind them **c** on your heart; Pr 6:21 8548
not a righteous man on earth who **c** Ec 7:20
stand **c** by day on the watchtower, Is 21:8 8548
the farmer plow **c** to plant seed? Is 28:24 3605, 3117
Does he **c** turn and harrow Is 28:24
Your walls are **c** before Me. Is 49:16 8548
That you fear **c** all day long Is 51:13 8548
name is **c** blasphemed all day long. Is 52:5 8548
"And the LORD will **c** guide you, Is 58:11 8548
"Your gates will be open **c**; Is 60:11 8548
who **c** provoke Me to My face, Is 65:3 8548
weep **c** for the one who goes away; Jer 22:10 1058
and to prepare sacrifices **c**.'" Jer 33:18 3605, 3117
great cloud with fire flashing forth **c** Ezk 1:4
heart **c** went after their idols. Ezk 20:16
With its rivers it **c** extended all Ezk 31:4
LORD **c** by a perpetual ordinance. Ezk 46:14 8548
gone, They play the harlot **c**; Hos 4:18 2181
wind, And pursues the east wind **c**; Hos 12:1 3605, 3117
justice, And wait for your God **c**. Hos 12:6 8548
His anger also tore **c**, Am 1:11 5703
All the nations will drink **c**. Ob 1:16 8548
whom has not your evil passed **c**? Na 3:19 8548
c slay nations without sparing? Hab 1:17 8548
angels in heaven **c** see the face Mt 18:10 *1223, 3956*
by **c** coming she will wear me out.'" Lk 18:5 *1519, 5056*
and were **c** in the temple praising Lk 24:53 *1223, 3956*
c devoting themselves to prayer, Ac 1:14 *4342*
They were **c** devoting themselves Ac 2:42 *4342*
and charity which she **c** did. Ac 9:36
people and prayed to God **c**. Ac 10:2 *1223, 3956*
And the disciples were **c** filled Ac 13:52
the Lord of peace Himself **c** grant you 2Th 3:16 *1223, 3956*
c entering the outer tabernacle Heb 9:6 *1223, 3956*
which they offer **c** year by year, Heb 10:1 *1336*
let us **c** offer up a sacrifice of Heb 13:15 *1223, 3956*
you were **c** straying like sheep, 1Pe 2:25

CONTINUE
let *them* go and **c** to hold them, Ex 9:2 5750
and shall **c** as unclean to you. Lv 11:35 1961
she shall **c** in her menstrual Lv 15:19 1961
she shall **c** as though in her menstrual Lv 15:25 1961
ascent of Akrabbim and **c** to Zin, Nu 34:4 5674a
reach Hazaraddar and **c** to Azmon. Nu 34:4 5674a
his sons may **c** long in his kingdom Dt 17:20 748
God will not **c** to drive these nations Jos 23:13 3254
nor did they **c** to fight anymore. 2Sa 2:28 3254
that it may **c** forever before You. 2Sa 7:29 1961
of blood will not **c** to destroy, 2Sa 14:11 7235a
that it may **c** forever before You; 1Ch 17:27 1961
do the wicked *still* live, **C** on, Jb 21:7 6275
O **c** Your lovingkindness to those Ps 36:10 4900
children of Your servants will **c**, Ps 102:28 7931
again, *As* you **c** in *your* rebellion? Is 1:5 3254
does not **c** to thresh it forever. Is 28:28 1758
shall not **c** to dwell *with us*." La 4:15 3254
He will not **c** to regard them; La 4:16 3254
his covenant that it might **c**. Ezk 17:14 5975
My covenant may **c** with Levi," Mal 2:4 1961
"If you **c** in My word, *then* you Jn 8:31 *3306*
not to **c** teaching in this name, Ac 5:28
them to **c** in the grace of God. Ac 13:43 *4357*
encouraging them to **c** in the faith, Ac 14:22 *1696*
Are we to **c** in sin so that grace Ro 6:1 *1961*
if you **c** in His kindness; Ro 11:22 *1961*
they do not **c** in their unbelief, Ro 11:23 *1961*
to you, and will **c** to do so. 2Co 11:9 *5083*
what I am doing I will **c** to do, 2Co 11:12 *2532*
I know that I will remain and **c** Php 1:25 *3887*
if indeed you **c** in the faith Col 1:23 *1961*
that you are doing and will **c** *to* 2Th 3:4
bearing of children if they **c** in faith 1Tm 2:15 *3306*
Those who **c** in sin, rebuke in the 1Tm 5:20
c in the things you have learned 2Tm 3:14 *3306*
THEY DID NOT **C** IN MY COVENANT, Heb 8:9 *1696*
Let love of the brethren **c**. Heb 13:1 *3306*

CONTINUED
and **c** to grow richer until he Gn 26:13 1980
He **c**, "Name me your wages, Gn 30:28 559
And they still **c** bringing to him Ex 36:3
From there *they* **c** to Beer, that Nu 21:16
And from the wilderness *they* **c** to Nu 21:18
while they **c** to blow the trumpets. Jos 6:9 1980
while they **c** to blow the trumpets. Jos 6:13 1980
ascent of Akrabbim and **c** to Zin, Jos 15:3 5674a
of Kadesh-barnea and **c** to Hezron, Jos 15:3 5674a
It **c** to Azmon and proceeded to Jos 15:4 5674a
and **c** on the north of Beth-arabah, Jos 15:6 5674a
c to the waters of En-shemesh and Jos 15:7 5674a
and **c** to the slope of Mount Jearim Jos 15:10 5674a
Beth-shemesh and **c** through Timnah. Jos 15:10 5674a
to Shikkeron and **c** to Mount Baalah Jos 15:11 5674a
and **c** to the border of the Jos 16:2 5674a
and **c** *beyond* it to the east of Jos 16:6 5674a
From Tappuah the border **c** westward Jos 16:8 1980
From there the border **c** to Luz, Jos 18:13 5674a
It **c** to the side in front of Jos 18:18 5674a
The border **c** to the side of Jos 18:19 5674a
From there it **c** eastward Jos 19:13 5674a
as she **c** praying before the LORD, 1Sa 1:12 7235a
the Philistines **c** and increased; 1Sa 14:19 1980
Then Huram **c**, "Blessed be the LORD, 2Ch 2:12 559
He **c** to seek God in the days 2Ch 26:5 1961
But the people **c** acting corruptly. 2Ch 27:2 5750
all this **c** until the burnt 2Ch 29:28
Then Job **c** his discourse and said, Jb 27:1 3254, 5375
Then Elihu **c** and said, Jb 34:1 6030a
Then Elihu **c** and said, Jb 35:1 6030a
Then Elihu **c** and said, Jb 36:1 3254
they still **c** to sin against Him, Ps 78:17 3254
We **c** in them a long time; Is 64:5
So the overseer **c** to withhold Da 1:16 1961
And Daniel **c** until the first year Da 1:21 1961
"You **c** looking until a stone was Da 2:34 1934
and he **c** kneeling on his knees Da 6:10
more widely they **c** to proclaim it. Mk 7:36
And He **c** by questioning them, Mk 8:29
And the child **c** to grow and to Lk 1:80
and **c** to speak of Him to all those Lk 2:38
Child **c** to grow and become strong, Lk 2:40
and He **c** in subjection to them; Lk 2:51
Then He **c** by saying to them, Lk 21:10
Jesus no longer **c** to walk Jn 11:54
c to testify *about Him.* Jn 12:17 *3140*
they all **c** in amazement and great Ac 2:12
number of the disciples **c** to increase Ac 6:7
baptized, he **c** on with Philip, Ac 8:13 *4342*
those hearing him **c** to be amazed, Ac 9:21
the Holy Spirit, it **c** to increase. Ac 9:31
And he went out and **c** to follow, Ac 12:9
But Peter **c** knocking; Ac 12:16 *1961*
c to grow and to be multiplied. Ac 12:24
there they **c** to preach the gospel. Ac 14:7
She **c** doing this for many days. Ac 16:18
entered the synagogue and **c** speaking Ac 19:8

CONTINUES
But the night **c**, And I am Jb 7:4 4058
Your faithfulness **c** throughout Ps 119:90
north, The wind **c** swirling along; Ec 1:6 1980
and **c** in entreaties and prayers 1Tm 5:5 *4357*
because He **c** forever, holds His Heb 7:24 *3306*
all **c** just as it was from the 2Pe 3:4 *1265*

CONTINUING
journeyed on, **c** toward the Negev. Gn 12:9 1980, 5265
to provoke Me to anger by **c** to burn Jer 44:3 1980
day **c** with one mind in the temple, Ac 2:46 *4342*
were prevented by death from **c**, Heb 7:23 *3887*

CONTINUOUSLY
one year old lambs each day, **c**. Ex 29:38 8548
So it was **c**; the cloud would cover it Nu 9:16 8548

CONTRADICT
and to refute those who **c**. Ti 1:9 *483*

CONTRADICTING
began **c** the things spoken by Paul, Ac 13:45 *483*

CONTRARY
c to the command of the LORD my Nu 22:18 5674a
because your way was **c** to me. Nu 22:32 3399
c to the command of the LORD, Nu 24:13 5674a
it was turned to the **c** so that the Es 9:1
makes idols, **c** to her *interest,* Ezk 22:3 5921
for the wind was **c**. Mt 14:24 *1727*
"On the **c**, blessed are those who Lk 11:28 *3303a, 3767*
"No, on the **c**, He leads the Jn 7:12 *235*
act **c** to the decrees of Caesar, Ac 17:7 *561*
men to worship God **c** to the law." Ac 18:13 *3844*
Cyprus because the winds were **c**. Ac 27:4 *1727*
On the **c**, we establish the Law. Ro 3:31 *235*
On the **c**, I would not have come to Ro 7:7 *235*
On the **c**, who are you, O man, who Ro 9:20 *3304*
and were grafted **c** to nature into Ro 11:24 *3844*
hindrances **c** to the teaching which Ro 16:17 *3844*
On the **c**, you yourselves wrong and 1Co 6:8 *235*
On the **c**, it is much truer that 1Co 12:22 *235*
on the **c** you should rather forgive 2Co 2:7 *5121*
should preach to you a gospel **c** to Ga 1:8 *3844*
c to what you received, Ga 1:9 *3844*
But on the **c**, seeing that I had Ga 2:7 *5121*
the Law is not of faith; on the **c**, Ga 3:12 *235*
Law then **c** to the promises of God? Ga 3:21 *2596*
else is **c** to sound teaching, 1Tm 1:10 *480*

CONTRIBUTE
ourselves under obligation to **c** yearly Ne 10:32 5414

CONTRIBUTED
For Hezekiah king of Judah had **c** 2Ch 30:24 7311
and the princes had **c** to the 2Ch 30:24 7311
Josiah **c** to the lay people, to 2Ch 35:7 7311
His officers also **c** a freewill 2Ch 35:8 7311
c to the Levites for the Passover 2Ch 35:9 7311
of reputation **c** nothing to me. Ga 2:6 *4323*

CONTRIBUTING
and many others who were **c** to Lk 8:3 *1247*
c to the needs of the saints, Ro 12:13 *2841*

CONTRIBUTION
of Israel to raise a **c** for Me; Ex 25:2 8641
moves him you shall raise My **c**. Ex 25:2 8641
This is the **c** which you are to raise Ex 25:3 8641
half a shekel as a **c** to the LORD. Ex 30:13 8641
shall give the **c** to the LORD. Ex 30:14 8641
when you give the **c** to the LORD to Ex 30:15 8641
from among you a **c** to the LORD; Ex 35:5 8641
let him bring it as the LORD's **c**: Ex 35:5 8641
brought the LORD's **c** for the work Ex 35:21 8641
Everyone who could make a **c** of Ex 35:24 8641
and bronze brought the LORD's **c**; Ex 35:24 8641
every offering as a **c** to the LORD; Lv 7:14 8641
to the priest as a **c** from the sacrifices Lv 7:32 8641
thigh of the **c** from the sons of Israel Lv 7:34 8641
'Also every **c** pertaining to all Nu 5:9 8641
your tithes, the **c** of your hand, Dt 12:6 8641
tithes and the **c** of your hand, Dt 12:11 8641
offerings, or the **c** of your hand. Dt 12:17 8641
shall bring the **c** of the grain, Ne 10:39 8641
kind and every **c** of every kind, Ezk 44:30 8641
each of them determined to send *a* **c** Ac 11:29
Achaia have been pleased to make a **c** Ro 15:26 *2842*
for the liberality of your **c** to them 2Co 9:13 *2842*

CONTRIBUTIONS
They received from Moses all the **c** Ex 36:3 8641
work for the **c** of the sanctuary." Ex 36:6 8641
"Since the **c** began to be brought 2Ch 31:10 8641
They faithfully brought in the **c** 2Ch 31:12 8641
to apportion the **c** for the LORD 2Ch 31:14 8641
the first of our dough, our **c**, Ne 10:37 8641
chambers for the stores, the **c**, Ne 12:44 8641
and the **c** for the priests. Ne 13:5 8641
and there I will seek your **c** and Ezk 20:40 8641
of every kind, from all your **c**, Ezk 44:30 8641

CONTRIBUTORS
than all the **c** to the treasury; Mk 12:43 *906*

CONTRITE
A broken and a **c** heart, O God, Ps 51:17 1794
And *also* with the **c** and lowly of Is 57:15 1793a
And to revive the heart of the **c**. Is 57:15 1792
him who is humble and **c** of spirit, Is 66:2 5223
not become **c** even to this day, Jer 44:10 1792

CONTROL
Then Joseph could not **c** himself Gn 45:1 662
saw that the people were out of **c** Ex 32:25 6544a
for Aaron had let them get out of **c** Ex 32:25 6544a
and David took **c** of the chief city 2Sa 8:1 4964
established the kingdom in his **c**, 2Ch 17:5 3027
man who has no **c** over his spirit. Pr 25:28 4623
Yet he will have **c** over all the Ec 2:19 7980
"But he will gain **c** over the Da 11:43 4910
was sold, was it not under your **c**? Ac 5:4 *1849*
to get the *ship's* boat under **c**. Ac 27:16 *4031*
children under **c** with all dignity 1Tm 3:4 *5292*

CONTROLLED
and he **c** himself and said, Gn 43:31 662
Haman **c** himself, however, went to Es 5:10 662

CONTROLS
For the love of Christ **c** us, 2Co 5:14 *4912*

CONTROVERSIAL
he has a morbid interest in **c** questions 1Tm 6:4 *2214*

CONTROVERSIES
But avoid foolish **c** and genealogies Ti 3:9 *2214*

CONTROVERSY
man has a **c** with a foolish man, Pr 29:9 8199
the LORD has a **c** with the nations. Jer 25:31 7379

CONVENED
So they **c** on the first day of the Ezr 10:16 3427
and the Pharisees **c** a council, Jn 11:47 *4863*

CONVENING
"When **c** the assembly, however, Nu 10:7 6950

CONVERSATION
the **c** had not been overheard. Jer 38:27 1697

CONVERSE
him quite often and **c** with him. Ac 24:26 *3656*

CONVERSING
philosophers were **c** with him. Ac 17:18 *4820*

CONVERSION
in detail the **c** of the Gentiles, Ac 15:3 *1995*

CONVERT
the first **c** to Christ from Asia. Ro 16:5 *536*
and not a new **c**, so that he 1Tm 3:6 *3504*

CONVERTED
And sinners will be **c** to You. Ps 51:13 7725
are **c** and become like children, Mt 18:3 *4762*
WITH THEIR HEART, AND BE **C** Jn 12:40 *4762*

CONVICT
will **c** the world concerning sin and Jn 16:8 *1651*
and to **c** all the ungodly of all Jude 1:15 *1651*

CONVICTED
man enters, he is **c** by all, 1Co 14:24 *1651*
are **c** by the law as transgressors. Jas 2:9 *1651*

CONVICTION
have as your own **c** before God. Ro 14:22 *4572*
the Holy Spirit and with full **c**; 1Th 1:5 *4136*
for, the **c** of things not seen. Heb 11:1 *1650*

CONVICTS
"Which one of you **c** Me of sin? Jn 8:46 *1651*

CONVINCED
are **c** that John was a prophet." Lk 20:6 *3982*
For I am **c** that neither death, nor Ro 8:38 *3982*
must be fully **c** in his own mind. Ro 14:5 *4135*
I know and am **c** in the Lord Jesus Ro 14:14 *3982*
I myself also am **c** that you Ro 15:14 *3982*
C of this, I know that I will remain Php 1:25 *3982*
and I am **c** that He is able to guard 2Tm 1:12 *3982*
you have learned and become **c** of, 2Tm 3:14 *4104*
we are **c** of better things Heb 6:9 *3982*

CONVINCING
His suffering, by many **c** proofs, Ac 1:3 *5039*

CONVOCATION
of complete rest, a holy **c**. Lv 23:3 4744
first day you shall have a holy **c**; Lv 23:7 4744

On the seventh day is a holy c; Lv 23:8 4744
you are to have a holy c. Lv 23:21 4744
by blowing *of trumpets,* a holy c. Lv 23:24 4744
it shall be a holy c for you, Lv 23:27 4744
'On the first day is a holy c; Lv 23:35 4744
the eighth day you shall have a holy c Lv 23:36 4744
the first day *shall be* a holy c; Nu 28:18 4744
day you shall have a holy c; Nu 28:25 4744
of Weeks, you shall have a holy c; Nu 28:26 4744
you shall also have a holy c; Nu 29:1 4744
month you shall have a holy c, Nu 29:7 4744
month you shall have a holy c; Nu 29:12 4744

CONVOCATIONS
which you shall proclaim as holy c Lv 23:2 4744
holy c which you shall proclaim at Lv 23:4 4744
you shall proclaim as holy c, Lv 23:37 4744

CONVULSION
the spirit threw him into a c, Mk 9:20 *4952*
a c with foaming *at the mouth* Lk 9:39 *4682*
ground and threw him into a c. Lk 9:42 *4952*

CONVULSIONS
Throwing him into c, Mk 1:26 *4682*
and throwing him into terrible c, Mk 9:26 *4682*

COOK
"You shall c and eat *it* in Dt 16:7 1310
Samuel said to the c, 1Sa 9:23 2876
Then the c took up the leg with 1Sa 9:24 2876

COOKED
When Jacob had c stew, Gn 25:29 2102
bread with this fold, or c food, Hg 2:12 5138

COOKING
And the c pots in the LORD's house Zch 14:20 5518a
Every c pot in Jerusalem and Zch 14:21 5518a

COOKS
for perfumers and c and bakers. 1Sa 8:13 2879

COOL
in the garden in the c of the day, Gn 3:8 7307
alone in his c roof chamber. Jg 3:20 4747
relieving himself in the c room." Jg 3:24 4747
And he who has a c spirit is a man Pr 17:27 7119
"Until the c of the day when the SS 2:17 6315
"Until the c of the day When the SS 4:6 6315
in water and c off my tongue, Lk 16:24 *2711*

COPE
But they were unable to c with Ac 6:10 *436*

COPIES
it was necessary for the c of the things Heb 9:23 *5262*

COPING
even from the foundation to the c, 1Ki 7:9 2947

COPPER
out of whose hills you can dig c. Dt 8:9 5178
dust, And c is smelted from rock. Jb 28:2 5154
silver, or c for your money belts, Mt 10:9 *5475*
of cups and pitchers and c pots.) Mk 7:4 *5473*
came and put in two small c coins, Mk 12:42 *3016*
putting in two small c coins. Lk 21:2 *3016*

COPPERSMITH
Alexander the c did me much harm; 2Tm 4:14 *5471*

COPY
he shall write for himself a c of Dt 17:18 4932
stones a c of the law of Moses, Jos 8:32 4932
"See the c of the altar of the LORD Jos 22:28 8403
this is the c of the letter which Ezr 4:11 6573
Then as soon as the c of King Ezr 4:23 6573
c of the letter which Tattenai, Ezr 5:6 6573
Now this is the c of the decree Ezr 7:11 6572
A c of the edict to be issued as Es 3:14 6572
He also gave him a c of the text Es 4:8 6572
A c of the edict to be issued as Es 8:13 6572
both the sealed c *containing* Jer 32:11 5612
terms and conditions and the open c; Jer 32:11 5612
who serve a c and shadow of the Heb 8:5 *5262*
hands, a *mere* c of the true one, Heb 9:24 *499*

CORAL
"C and crystal are not to be Jb 28:18 7215
embroidered work, fine linen, c and Ezk 27:16 7215

CORALS
were more ruddy *in* body than c, La 4:7 6443

CORBAN
would help you is C Mk 7:11 *2878a*

CORD
"Your seal and your c, Gn 38:18 6616
rings of the ephod with a blue c, Ex 28:28 6616
"You shall fasten it on a blue c, Ex 28:37 6616
rings of the ephod with a blue c, Ex 39:21 6616
They fastened a blue c to it, Ex 39:31 6616
tassel of each corner a c of blue. Nu 15:38 6616
you tie this c of scarlet thread Jos 2:18 8615a
tied the scarlet c in the window. Jos 2:21 8615a
Or press down his tongue with a c? Jb 41:1 2256a
A c of three *strands* is not Ec 4:12 2339
Remember Him before the silver c Ec 12:6 2256a
born your navel c was not cut, Ezk 16:4 8270

CORDAGE
shall make them of twisted c work, Ex 28:14 5688
of twisted c work in pure gold. Ex 28:22 5688
of twisted c work in pure gold. Ex 39:15 5688

CORDED
shall put the c chains on the filigree Ex 28:14 5688

CORDS
ring and c and staff are these?" Gn 38:25 6616
"You shall put the two c of gold Ex 28:24 5688
c on the two filigree *settings,* Ex 28:25 5688
the pegs of the court and their c; Ex 35:18 4340
on the breastpiece chains like c, Ex 39:15 5688
Then they put the two gold c in Ex 39:17 5688
c on the two filigree *settings,* Ex 39:18 5688
its c and its pegs and all the Ex 39:40 4340
and the altar, and its c, Nu 3:26 4340
and their pegs and their c. Nu 3:37 4340
and their c and all the equipment Nu 4:26 4340
and their pegs and their c, Nu 4:32 4340
fresh c that have not been dried, Jg 16:7 3499b
fresh c that had not been dried, Jg 16:8 3499b
But he snapped the c as a string Jg 16:9 3499b
The c of Sheol surrounded me; 2Sa 22:6 2256a
linen held by c of fine purple linen Es 1:6 2256a
are caught in the c of affliction, Jb 36:8 2256a
Pleiades, Or loose the c of Orion? Jb 38:31 4189
And cast away their c from us!" Ps 2:3 5688
The c of death encompassed me, And Ps 18:4 2256a
The c of Sheol surrounded me; Ps 18:5 2256a
The c of death encompassed me And Ps 116:3 2256a
with c to the horns of the altar. Ps 118:27 5688
The c of the wicked have encircled Ps 119:61 2256a
cut in two the c of the wicked. Ps 129:4 5688
have hidden a trap for me, and c; Ps 140:5 2256a
be held with the c of his sin. Pr 5:22 2256a
iniquity with the c of falsehood, Is 5:18 2256a
up, Nor any of its c be torn apart. Is 33:20 2256a
Lengthen your c And strengthen Is 54:2 4340
many colors *and* tightly wound c, Ezk 27:24 2256a
I led them with c of a man, with Hos 11:4 2256a
And He made a scourge of c, Jn 2:15 *4979*

CORIANDER
it manna, and it was like c seed, Ex 16:31 1407
Now the manna was like c seed, Nu 11:7 1407

CORINTH
he left Athens and went to C. Ac 18:1 *2882*
happened that while Apollos was at C, Ac 19:1 *2882*
the church of God which is at C, 1Co 1:2 *2882*
To the church of God which is at C 2Co 1:1 *2882*
I did not come again to C. 2Co 1:23 *2882*
Erastus remained at C, 2Tm 4:20 *2882*

CORINTHIANS
and many of the C when they heard Ac 18:8 *2881*
has spoken freely to you, O C, 2Co 6:11 *2881*

CORMORANT
owl and the c and the great owl, Lv 11:17 7994
the carrion vulture, the c, Dt 14:17 7994

CORNELIUS
a man at Caesarea named C, Ac 10:1 *2883*
in and said to him, "C!" Ac 10:3 *2883*
the men who had been sent by C, Ac 10:17 *2883*
"C, a centurion, a righteous and Ac 10:22 *2883*
Now C was waiting for them and Ac 10:24 *2883*
When Peter entered, C met him, Ac 10:25 *2883*
C said, "Four days ago to this hour, Ac 10:30 *2883*
'C, your prayer has been heard and Ac 10:31 *2883*

CORNER
tassel of each c a cord of blue. Nu 15:38 3671
the Gate of Ephraim to the C Gate, 2Ki 14:13 6438
the Gate of Ephraim to the C Gate, 2Ch 25:23 6438
towers in Jerusalem at the C Gate 2Ch 26:9 6438
the c buttress and fortified them. 2Ch 26:9 4740
himself in every c of Jerusalem. 2Ch 28:24 6438
as the Angle and as far as the c. Ne 3:24 6438
as far as the upper room of the c. Ne 3:31 6438
Between the upper room of the c Ne 3:32 6438
Has become the chief c *stone.* Ps 118:22 6438
And our daughters as c pillars Ps 144:12 2106
through the street near her c; Pr 7:8 6438
the squares, And lurks by every c. Pr 7:12 6438
better to live in a c of a roof Than Pr 21:9 6438
It is better to live in a c of the Pr 25:24 6438
Tower of Hananel to the C Gate. Jer 31:38 6438
to the c of the Horse Gate toward Jer 31:40 6438
a c Nor a stone for foundations, Jer 51:26 6438
out At the c of every street. La 4:1 7218
in every c of the court *there was* Ezk 46:21 4740
c of a bed and *the* cover of a couch! Am 3:12 6285
cities And the high c towers. Zph 1:16 6438
Their c towers are in ruins. Zph 3:6 6438
of the First Gate to the C Gate, Zch 14:10 6438
THIS BECAME THE CHIEF C *stone;* Mt 21:42 *1137*
THIS BECAME THE CHIEF C *stone* Mk 12:10 *1137*
THIS BECAME THE CHIEF C *stone*'? Lk 20:17 *1137*
but WHICH BECAME THE CHIEF C *stone.* Ac 4:11 *1137*
for this has not been done in a c. Ac 26:26 *1137*
Jesus Himself being the c *stone,* Eph 2:20 *204*
CHOICE STONE, A PRECIOUS C *stone,* 1Pe 2:6 *204*
THIS BECAME THE VERY C *stone,*" 1Pe 2:7 *1137*

CORNERS
four c which are on its four feet. Ex 25:26 6285
c of the tabernacle at the rear. Ex 26:23 4740
they shall form the two c. Ex 26:24 4740
make its horns on its four c; Ex 27:2 6438
four bronze rings at its four c. Ex 27:4 7098
c of the tabernacle at the rear. Ex 36:28 4740
with both of them for the two c. Ex 36:29 4740
four c that were on its four feet. Ex 37:13 6285
He made its horns on its four c, Ex 38:2 6438
reap to the very c of your field, Lv 19:9 6285
reap to the very c of your field nor Lv 23:22 6285
tassels on the c of their garments Nu 15:38 3671
tassels on the four c of your garment Dt 22:12 3671
at the four c of each stand; 1Ki 7:34 6438
to be on the towers and on the c for 2Ch 26:15 6438
struck the four c of the house, Jb 1:19 6438
From the four c of the earth. Is 11:12 3671
all who cut the c *of their hair;* Jer 25:23 6285
those who cut the c *of their hair;* Jer 49:32 6285
coming on the four c of the land. Ezk 7:2 3671
its c, its base and its sides Ezk 41:22 4740
and on the four c of the ledge and Ezk 43:20 6438
four c of the ledge of the altar and Ezk 45:19 6438
across to the four c of the court; Ezk 46:21 4740
In the four c of the court *there* Ezk 46:22 4740
four in the c *were* the same size. Ezk 46:22 7106b
Drenched like the c of the altar. Zch 9:15 2106
synagogues and on the street c so Mt 6:5 *1137*
lowered by four c to the ground, Ac 10:11 *746*
lowered by four c from the sky; Ac 11:5 *746*
at the four c of the earth, Rv 7:1 *1137*
are in the four c of the earth, Rv 20:8 *1137*

CORNERSTONE
Or who laid its c, Jb 38:6 68, 6438
Those who are the c of her tribes Is 19:13 6438
A costly c *for* the foundation, Is 28:16 6438
"From them will come the c, Zch 10:4 6438

CORPSE
touches anything made unclean by a c Lv 22:4 5315
'The one who touches the c of any Nu 19:11 4191
'Anyone who touches a c, Nu 19:13 4191
his c shall not hang all night on Dt 21:23 5038
and the c of Jezebel will be as 2Ki 9:37 5038
of the pit Like a trampled c. Is 14:19 6297
from a c touches any of these, Hg 2:13 5315
"Wherever the c is, there the Mt 24:28 *4430*
like a c that most *of them* said, Mk 9:26 *3498*

CORPSES
c will fall in this wilderness, Nu 14:29 6297
c will fall in this wilderness. Nu 14:32 6297
your c lie in the wilderness. Nu 14:33 6297
they *were* c lying on the ground, 2Ch 20:24 6297
nations, He will fill *them* with c, Ps 110:6 1472a
and their c lay like refuse in the Is 5:25 5038
Their c will rise. Is 26:19 5038
c will give off their stench, Is 34:3 6297
go forth and look On the c of the men Is 66:24 6297
'The c of men will fall like dung Jer 9:22 5038
and to fill them with the c of men Jer 33:5 6297
Ishmael had cast all the c of the men Jer 41:9 6297
c of their kings when they die, Ezk 43:7 6297
the c of their kings far from Me; Ezk 43:9 6297
"Many *will be* the c; Am 8:3 6297
gleaming, Many slain, a mass of c, Na 3:3 6297

CORRECT
I will c him with the rod of men 2Sa 7:14 3198
C your son, and he will give you Pr 29:17 3256
Your own wickedness will c you, Jer 2:19 3256
C me, O LORD, but with justice; Jer 10:24 3256
But I will c you properly And by Jer 46:28 3256
Rock, have established them to c. Hab 1:12 3198

CORRECTING
c those who are in opposition, 2Tm 2:25 *3811*

CORRECTION
"Whether for c, or for His world, Jb 37:13 7626
them, But they refused to take c. Jer 5:3 4148
of the LORD their God or accept c; Jer 7:28 4148
in order not to listen or take c. Jer 17:23 4148
for teaching, for reproof, for c, 2Tm 3:16 *1882*

CORRECTLY
for he could not pronounce it c. Jg 12:6 3651
may c answer him who sent you? Pr 22:21 571
and to write words of truth c. Ec 12:10 3476
"You have judged c." Lk 7:43 *3723*
"You have answered c; Lk 10:28 *3723*
know that You speak and teach c, Lk 20:21 *3723*
"You have c said, 'I have no Jn 4:17 *2573*
"You say c that I am a king. Jn 18:37

CORRECTOR
a c of the foolish, a teacher of Ro 2:20 *3810*

CORRECTS
Even as a father c the son in Pr 3:12
He who c a scoffer gets dishonor Pr 9:7 3256

CORRESPOND
shall c to the number of years. Lv 25:50 1961

CORRESPONDED
Guard c to guard. 1Ch 26:16 5980

CORRESPONDING
c to the hangings of the court. Ex 38:18 5980
The stones were c to the names Ex 39:14 5921
were twelve, c to their names, Ex 39:14 5921
'C to the number of years after Lv 25:15
c to the width of the house, 1Ki 6:3
5921, 6440
c to the number of the tribes of Ezr 6:17
of God, division c to division. Ne 12:24 5980
days c to the years of their iniquity, Ezk 4:5
c to the length of the gates. Ezk 40:18 5980
c to gallery in three stories. Ezk 42:3
413, 6440
C to the openings of the chambers Ezk 42:12
C to that, baptism now saves 1Pe 3:21 *499*

CORRESPONDS
and c to the present Jerusalem, Ga 4:25 *4960*

CORRUPT
earth was c in the sight of God, Gn 6:11 7843
the earth, and behold, it was c; Gn 6:12 7843
less one who is detestable and c, Jb 15:16 444
fire consumes the tents of the c. Jb 15:34 7810
They are c, they have committed Ps 14:1 7843
together they have become c; Ps 14:3 444
"There is no God," They are c, Ps 53:1 7843
together they have become c; Ps 53:3 444
They, all of them, are c. Jer 6:28 7843
ways or according to your c deeds, Ezk 20:44 7843

Context	Reference	Number
was more c in her lust than she,	Ezk 23:11	7843
to speak lying and c words before me	Da 2:9	7844
were eager to c all their deeds.	Zph 3:7	7843
c desires and despise authority.	2Pe 2:10	*3394*

CORRUPTED

Context	Reference	Number
had c their way upon the earth.	Gn 6:12	7843
land of Egypt, have c *themselves.*	Ex 32:7	7843
You c your wisdom by reason of	Ezk 28:17	7843
you have c the covenant of Levi,"	Mal 2:8	7843
we wronged no one, we c no one,	2Co 7:2	*5351*
which is being c in accordance	Eph 4:22	*5351*

CORRUPTIBLE

Context	Reference	Number
for an image in the form of c man	Ro 1:23	*5349*

CORRUPTING

Context	Reference	Number
c the earth with her immorality,	Rv 19:2	*5351*

CORRUPTION

Context	Reference	Number
for their c is in them, they have	Lv 22:25	4893a
of accusation or *evidence of* c,	Da 6:4	7844
or c was *to be* found in him.	Da 6:4	7844
will be set free from its slavery to c	Ro 8:21	*5356*
flesh will from the flesh reap c,	Ga 6:8	*5356*
c that is in the world by lust.	2Pe 1:4	*5356*
they themselves are slaves of c;	2Pe 2:19	*5356*

CORRUPTLY

Context	Reference	Number
do not act c and make a graven	Dt 4:16	7843
long in the land, and act c,	Dt 4:25	7843
brought out of Egypt have acted c.	Dt 9:12	7843
after my death you will act c and turn	Dt 31:29	7843
"They have acted c toward Him,	Dt 32:5	7843
and act more c than their fathers,	Jg 2:19	7843
was so proud that he acted c,	2Ch 26:16	7843
But the people continued acting c.	2Ch 27:2	7843
"We have acted very c against	Ne 1:7	2254b
of evildoers, Sons who act c!	Is 1:4	7843
you acted more c in all your conduct	Ezk 16:47	7843

CORRUPTS

Context	Reference	Number
man mad, And a bribe c the heart.	Ec 7:7	6
"Bad company c good morals."	1Co 15:33	*5351*

COS

Context	Reference	Number
we ran a straight course to C and	Ac 21:1	*2972*

COSAM

Context	Reference	Number
the son of Addi, the son of C,	Lk 3:28	*2973*

COSMETICS

Context	Reference	Number
and let their c be given *them.*	Es 2:3	8562
provided her with her c and food,	Es 2:9	8562
with spices and the c for women	Es 2:12	8562

COST

Context	Reference	Number
sinned at the c of their lives,	Nu 16:38	
LORD my God which c me nothing."	2Sa 24:24	2600
"At *the* c *of* our heads he may	1Ch 12:19	
And let the c be paid from the	Ezr 6:4	5313
the full c is to be paid to these	Ezr 6:8	5313
So he does not know that it *will* c	Pr 7:23	
milk Without money and without c.	Is 55:1	4242
I will give for booty without c,	Jer 15:13	4242
sit down and calculate the c to	Lk 14:28	*1160a*
of the water of life without c.	Rv 21:6	*1431*
take the water of life without c.	Rv 22:17	*1431*

COSTLY

Context	Reference	Number
quarried great stones, c stones,	1Ki 5:17	3368
All these were of c stones,	1Ki 7:9	3368
The foundation was of c stones,	1Ki 7:10	3368
And above were c stones, stone cut	1Ki 7:11	3368
the redemption of his soul is c,	Ps 49:8	3365
A c cornerstone *for* the foundation,	Is 28:16	3368
its produce and all its c things;	Jer 20:5	3366
him with gold, silver, c stones and	Da 11:38	3368
alabaster vial of very c perfume,	Mt 26:7	*927*
of very c perfume of pure nard;	Mk 14:3	*4185*
of very c perfume of pure nard,	Jn 12:3	*4186*
and gold or pearls or c garments,	1Tm 2:9	*4185*
every article *made* from very c wood	Rv 18:12	*5093*
Her brilliance was like a very c stone,	Rv 21:11	*5093*

COSTS

Context	Reference	Number
offering which c me nothing."	1Ch 21:24	2600

COTS

Context	Reference	Number
and laid them on c and pallets,	Ac 5:15	*2825a*

COUCH

Context	Reference	Number
he went up to my c.	Gn 49:4	3326
falling on the c where Esther was.	Es 7:8	4296
me, My c will ease my complaint,'	Jb 7:13	4904
I dissolve my c with my tears.	Ps 6:6	6210
"I have spread my c with coverings,	Pr 7:16	6210
Indeed, our c is luxuriant!	SS 1:16	6210
it is the *traveling* c of Solomon;	SS 3:7	4296
and you sat on a splendid c with a	Ezk 23:41	4296
of a bed and *the* cover of a c!	Am 3:12	6210

COUCHES

Context	Reference	Number
He c, he lies down as a lion, And	Gn 49:9	3766
"He c, he lies down as a lion,	Nu 24:9	3766
and c of gold and silver on a	Es 1:6	4296
of ivory And sprawl on their c,	Am 6:4	6210

COULD

Context	Reference	Number
And the land c not sustain them	Gn 13:6	
where they sojourned c not sustain	Gn 36:7	3201
and *so* they hated him and c not	Gn 37:4	3201
How then c I do this great evil and	Gn 39:9	
who c interpret them to Pharaoh.	Gn 41:8	
it c not be detected that they had	Gn 41:21	
no one who c explain it to me."	Gn 41:24	
C we possibly know that he would	Gn 43:7	
by now we c have returned twice."	Gn 43:10	
because the Egyptians c not eat	Gn 43:32	3201
How then c we steal silver or gold	Gn 44:8	
Then Joseph c not control himself	Gn 45:1	3201
But his brothers c not answer him,	Gn 45:3	3201
so dim from age *that* he c not see.	Gn 48:10	3201
But when she c hide him no longer,	Ex 2:3	3201
c not drink water from the Nile.	Ex 7:21	3201
for they c not drink of the water	Ex 7:24	3201
bring forth gnats, but they c not;	Ex 8:18	3201
The magicians c not stand	Ex 9:11	3201
out of Egypt and c not delay,	Ex 12:39	3201
c not drink the waters of Marah,	Ex 15:23	3201
Everyone who c make a contribution	Ex 35:24	
everyone who c enter to do the	Nu 4:47	
so that they c not observe	Nu 9:6	3201
'Because the LORD c not bring this	Nu 14:16	3201
and gold, I c not do anything,	Nu 22:18	3201
I c not do anything contrary to	Nu 24:13	3201
"How c one chase a thousand, And	Dt 32:30	
of Judah c not drive them out;	Jos 15:63	3201
But the sons of Manasseh c not	Jos 17:12	3201
but they c not drive out the	Jg 1:19	
so that they c no longer stand	Jg 2:14	3201
that they c not remain in Shechem	Jg 9:41	
and He c bear the misery of Israel	Jg 10:16	7114a
he c not pronounce it correctly.	Jg 12:6	3559
But they c not tell the riddle in	Jg 14:14	3201
each one c sling a stone at a hair	Jg 20:16	
before one c recognize another;	Ru 3:14	
grow dim *and* he c not see *well*),	1Sa 3:2	3201
were set so that he c not see.	1Sa 4:15	3201
we saw that they c not be found,	1Sa 10:14	
looked for him, he c not be found.	1Sa 10:21	
Now no blacksmith c be found in	1Sa 13:19	
and they went wherever they c go.	1Sa 23:13	
For with what c this *man* make	1Sa 29:4	
he c not live after he had fallen.	2Sa 1:10	
How then c I lift up my face to	2Sa 2:22	
c no longer answer Abner a word,	2Sa 3:11	3201
where c I get rid of my reproach?	2Sa 13:13	
any suit or cause c come to me and	2Sa 15:4	
c not be seen entering the city.	2Sa 17:17	3201
they searched and c not find *them,*	2Sa 17:20	
clothes, but he c not keep warm.	1Ki 1:1	
it c hold two thousand baths.	1Ki 7:26	
the bronze c not be ascertained.	1Ki 7:47	
they c not be counted or numbered.	1Ki 8:5	
poles c be seen from the holy place	1Ki 8:8	
but they c not be seen outside;	1Ki 8:8	
so that the priests c not stand to	1Ki 8:11	3201
he c not draw it back to himself.	1Ki 13:4	3201
Now Ahijah c not see, for his eyes	1Ki 14:4	3201
swear that they c not find you.	1Ki 18:10	
to the king of Edom; but they c not.	2Ki 3:26	3201
C I not wash in them and be clean?"	2Ki 5:12	
in heaven, c this thing be?"	2Ki 7:2	
in heaven, c such a thing be?"	2Ki 7:19	
Ahaz, but c not overcome him.	2Ki 16:5	3201
who c handle shield and spear,	1Ch 12:8	
who c draw up in battle formation	1Ch 12:33	
who c draw up in battle formation,	1Ch 12:35	
who c draw up in battle formation,	1Ch 12:38	
But David c not go before it to	1Ch 21:30	3201
and more bronze than c be weighed;	1Ch 22:3	
it c hold 3,000 baths.	2Ch 4:5	
of the bronze c not be found out.	2Ch 4:18	
they c not be counted or numbered.	2Ch 5:6	
ends of the poles of the ark c be seen	2Ch 5:9	
but they c not be seen outside;	2Ch 5:9	
so that the priests c not stand to	2Ch 5:14	3201
The priests c not enter into	2Ch 7:2	3201
c not hold his own against them.	2Ch 13:7	
fell that they c not recover,	2Ch 14:13	
more than they c carry.	2Ch 20:25	
broken and c not go to Tarshish.	2Ch 20:37	6113
who c wage war with great power,	2Ch 26:13	
c not celebrate it at that time,	2Ch 30:3	3201
c deliver his people out of my hand,	2Ch 32:14	3201
but they c not be located;	Ezr 2:62	
so that the people c not distinguish	Ezr 3:13	
did not stop them until a report c	Ezr 5:5	
and c not find a word *to say.*	Ne 5:8	
And c one such as I go into the	Ne 6:11	
in order that they c reproach me.	Ne 6:13	
but they c not show their fathers'	Ne 7:61	3201
but it c not be located;	Ne 7:64	
women and all who c listen with	Ne 8:2	
and women, those who c understand;	Ne 8:3	
During that night the king c not	Es 6:1	5074
and no one c stand before them,	Es 9:2	
I c not discern its appearance;	Jb 4:16	
He c not answer Him once in a	Jb 9:3	
snatch away, who c restrain Him?	Jb 9:12	
Who c say to Him,	Jb 9:12	
I were right, I c not answer;	Jb 9:15	
I c not believe that He was	Jb 9:16	
you c lift up your face without	Jb 11:15	
"I too c speak like you, If I	Jb 16:4	
I c compose words against you And	Jb 16:4	
"I c strengthen you with my	Jb 16:5	
of my lips c lessen *your pain.*	Jb 16:5	
How then c I gaze at a virgin?	Jb 31:1	
What then c I do when God arises?	Jb 31:14	
for him, but he c not be found.	Ps 37:36	
reproaches me, Then I c bear *it;*	Ps 55:12	
me, Then I c hide myself from him.	Ps 55:12	
of the warriors c use his hands.	Ps 76:5	
their streams, they c not drink.	Ps 78:44	
And His widows c not weep.	Ps 78:64	
iniquities, O Lord, who c stand?	Ps 130:3	
until I c see what good there is	Ec 2:3	
against it, but c not conquer it.	Is 7:1	3201
That a child c write them down.	Is 10:19	
They c only whisper a prayer, Your	Is 26:16	
We c not accomplish deliverance	Is 26:18	
They c not rescue the burden, But	Is 46:2	3201
is a house you c build for Me?	Is 66:1	
which c not be eaten due to	Jer 24:2	
C enter the gates of Jerusalem.	La 4:12	
no one c touch their garments.	La 4:14	3201
For a nation that c not save.	La 4:17	
that we c not walk in our streets;	La 4:18	
they c *only* deliver themselves,"	Ezk 14:14	
"they c not deliver either *their*	Ezk 14:16	
"they c not deliver either *their*	Ezk 14:18	
"they c not deliver either *their*	Ezk 14:20	
by which they c not live;	Ezk 20:25	
in God's garden c not match it;	Ezk 31:8	
c not compare with its boughs,	Ezk 31:8	
trees c not match its branches.	Ezk 31:8	
c compare with it in its beauty.	Ezk 31:8	
it was a river that I c not ford,	Ezk 47:5	3201
in, a river that c not be forded.	Ezk 47:5	
who c declare the matter for the king,	Da 2:10	3202
and there is no one else who c	Da 2:11	
but they c not make its	Da 4:7	
but they c not read the	Da 5:8	3546
but they c not declare the	Da 5:15	3546
but they c find no ground of	Da 6:4	3202
other beasts c stand before him nor	Da 8:4	
me, I heard but c not understand;	Da 12:8	
"How c you do this?"	Jon 1:10	
to return to land but they c not,	Jon 1:13	3201
sat under it in the shade until he c see	Jon 4:5	
hearts *like* flint so that they c not hear	Zch 7:12	
that no one c pass by that way.	Mt 8:28	*2480*
and they c not cure him."	Mt 17:16	*1410*
"Why c we not drive it out?"	Mt 17:19	*1410*
you *men* c not keep watch with Me	Mt 26:40	*2480*
to such an extent that Jesus c no	Mk 1:45	*1410*
would be with Him and that He c	Mk 3:14	
that they c not even eat a meal.	Mk 3:20	*1410*
And He c do no miracle there	Mk 6:5	*1410*
put him to death and c not *do so;*	Mk 6:19	*1410*
yet He c not escape notice.	Mk 7:24	*1410*
it out, and they c not *do it.*"	Mk 9:18	*2480*
"Why c we not drive it out?"	Mk 9:28	*1410*
"She has done what she c;	Mk 14:8	*2192*
C you not keep watch for one hour?	Mk 14:37	*2480*
that house and c not shake it,	Lk 6:48	*2480*
and c not be healed by anyone,	Lk 8:43	*2480*
to cast it out, and they c not."	Lk 9:40	*1410*
and c not straighten up at all.	Lk 13:11	*1410*
And they c make no reply to this.	Lk 14:6	*2480*
began inquiring what these things c	Lk 15:26	
and they c not find anything that	Lk 19:48	
so that they c deliver Him to	Lk 20:20	
While they still c not believe	Lk 24:41	
not from God, He c do nothing."	Jn 9:33	*1410*
"C not this man, who opened the	Jn 11:37	*1410*
For this reason they c not believe,	Jn 12:39	*1410*
and our fathers c find no food.	Ac 7:11	
because you thought you c obtain	Ac 8:20	
"Well, how c I, unless someone	Ac 8:31	*1410*
eyes were open, he c see nothing;	Ac 9:8	
I that I c stand in God's way?"	Ac 11:17	*1415*
as to what c have become of Peter.	Ac 12:18	
from which you c not be freed	Ac 13:39	*1410*
and when he c not find out the	Ac 21:34	*1410*
"But since I c not see because of	Ac 22:11	
him which they c not prove,	Ac 25:7	*2480*
if somehow they c reach Phoenix,	Ac 27:12	*1410*
in it and c not face the wind,	Ac 27:15	*1410*
they c not recognize the land;	Ac 27:39	
drive the ship onto it if they c.	Ac 27:39	*1410*
commanded that those who c swim	Ac 27:43	*1410*
For what the Law c not do,	Ro 8:3	*102*
For I c wish that I myself were	Ro 9:3	
c not speak to you as to spiritual	1Co 3:1	*1410*
so that the sons of Israel c not	2Co 3:7	*1410*
but I c wish to be present with	Ga 4:20	
when we c endure *it* no longer,	1Th 3:1	
when I c endure *it* no longer,	1Th 3:5	
He c swear by no one greater,	Heb 6:13	*2192*
For they c not bear the command,	Heb 12:20	
multitude which no one c count,	Rv 7:9	*1410*
so that she c fly into the wilderness	Rv 12:14	
and no one c learn the song except	Rv 14:3	*1410*

COUNCIL

Context	Reference	Number
my soul not enter into their c;	Gn 49:6	5475
feared in the c of the holy ones,	Ps 89:7	5475
has stood in the c of the LORD,	Jer 23:18	5475
"But if they had stood in My c,	Jer 23:22	5475
no place in the c of My people,	Ezk 13:9	5475
C kept trying to obtain false testimony	Mt 26:59	*4892*
C kept trying to obtain testimony	Mk 14:55	*4892*
and scribes and the whole C,	Mk 15:1	*4892*
came, a prominent member of the C,	Mk 15:43	*1010*
the C of elders of the people	Lk 22:66	*4244*
led Him away to their c *chamber,*	Lk 22:66	*4892*
Joseph, who was a member of the C,	Lk 23:50	*1010*
and the Pharisees convened a c,	Jn 11:47	*4892*
them to leave the C,	Ac 4:15	*4892*
came, they called the C together,	Ac 5:21	*4892*
they stood them before the C.	Ac 5:27	*4892*
stood up in the C and gave orders	Ac 5:34	*4892*
way from the presence of the C,	Ac 5:41	*4892*
and brought him before the C.	Ac 6:12	*4892*
all who were sitting in the C saw	Ac 6:15	*4892*
the C of the elders can testify.	Ac 22:5	*4244*
priests and all the C to assemble,	Ac 22:30	*4892*
Paul, looking intently at the C,	Ac 23:1	*4892*

Paul *began* crying out in the **C**, Ac 23:6 4892
you and the **C** notify the commander Ac 23:15 4892
bring Paul down tomorrow to the **C**, Ac 23:20 4892
I brought him down to their **C**; Ac 23:28 4892
found when I stood before the **C**, Ac 24:20 4892
Festus had conferred with his **c**, Ac 25:12 4824

COUNSEL
I will give you **c**, Ex 18:19 3289
Israel, through the **c** of Balaam, Nu 31:16 1697
they are a nation lacking in **c**, Dt 32:28 6098
did not ask for the **c** of the LORD. Jos 9:14 6310
it, take **c** and speak up!" Jg 19:30 5779
give your advice and **c** here." Jg 20:7 6098
the **c** of Ahithophel foolishness." 2Sa 15:31 6098
thwart the **c** of Ahithophel for me. 2Sa 15:34 6098
"But I **c** that all Israel be 2Sa 17:11 3289
"The **c** of Hushai the Archite is 2Sa 17:14 6098
better than the **c** of Ahithophel." 2Sa 17:14 6098
thwart the good **c** of Ahithophel, 2Sa 17:14 6098
saw that his **c** was not followed, 2Sa 17:23 6098
please let me give you **c** and save 1Ki 1:12 6098
you **c** *me* to answer this people?" 1Ki 12:6 3289
But he forsook the **c** of the elders 1Ki 12:8 6098
"What **c** do you give that we may 1Ki 12:9 3289
have **c** and strength for the war.' 2Ki 18:20 6098
because he asked **c** of a medium, 1Ch 10:13 6098
you **c** *me* to answer this people?" 2Ch 10:6 3289
But he forsook the **c** of the elders 2Ch 10:8 6098
"What **c** do you give that we may 2Ch 10:9 3289
forsook the **c** of the elders. 2Ch 10:13 6098
also walked according to their **c**, 2Ch 22:5 6098
and have not listened to my **c**." 2Ch 25:16 6098
Then Amaziah king of Judah took **c** 2Ch 25:17 3289
frustrate their **c** all the days of Cyrus Ezr 4:5 6098
according to the **c** of my lord and Ezr 10:3 6098
c of the leaders and the elders, Ezr 10:8 6098
now, let us take **c** together." Ne 6:7 3289
To Him belong **c** and understanding. Jb 12:13 6098
"Do you hear the secret **c** of God, Jb 15:8 5475
c of the wicked is far from me. Jb 21:16 6098
c of the wicked is far from me. Jb 22:18 6098
"What **c** you have given to *one* Jb 26:3 3289
waited, And kept silent for my **c**. Jb 29:21 6098
c By words without knowledge? Jb 38:2 6098
'Who is this that hides **c** Jb 42:3 6098
not walk in the **c** of the wicked, Ps 1:1 6098
And the rulers take **c** together Ps 2:2 3245
long shall I take **c** in my soul, Ps 13:2 6098
to shame the **c** of the afflicted, Ps 14:6 6098
desire And fulfill all your **c**! Ps 20:4 6098
they took **c** together against me, Ps 31:13 3245
I will **c** you with My eye upon you. Ps 32:8 3289
nullifies the **c** of the nations; Ps 33:10 6098
The **c** of the LORD stands forever, Ps 33:11 6098
me from the secret **c** of evildoers, Ps 64:2 5475
With Your **c** You will guide me, And Ps 73:24 6098
They did not wait for His **c**, Ps 106:13 6098
were rebellious in their **c**, Ps 106:43 6098
spurned the **c** of the Most High. Ps 107:11 6098
understanding will acquire wise **c**, Pr 1:5 8458
And you neglected all my **c** And Pr 1:25 6098
"They would not accept my **c**, Pr 1:30 6098
"**C** is mine and sound wisdom; Pr 8:14 6098
a wise man is he who listens to **c**. Pr 12:15 6098
wisdom is with those who receive **c**. Pr 13:10 3289
Listen to **c** and accept discipline, Pr 19:20 6098
man's heart, But the **c** of the LORD will Pr 19:21 6098
And no **c** against the LORD. Pr 21:30 6098
a man's **c** is sweet to his friend. Pr 27:9 6098
The spirit of **c** and strength, Is 11:2 6098
Who has made *His* **c** wonderful and Is 28:29 6098
'Your **c** and strength for the war Is 36:5 6098
to the priest, nor **c** to the sage, Jer 18:18 6098
I will make void the **c** of Judah Jer 19:7 6098
great in **c** and mighty in deed, Jer 32:19 6098
good **c** been lost to the prudent? Jer 49:7 6098
the priest and **c** from the elders. Ezk 7:26 6098
will be ashamed of its own **c**. Hos 10:6 6098
Unless He reveals His secret **c** Am 3:7 5475
and the **c** of peace will be between Zch 6:13 6098
things after the **c** of His will, Eph 1:11 *1012*

COUNSELED
because he has **c** rebellion against Dt 13:5 1696
"This is what Ahithophel **c** 2Sa 17:15 3289
Israel, and this is what I have **c**. 2Sa 17:15 3289
Ahithophel has **c** against you." 2Sa 17:21 3289
and he **c** with his servants saying, 2Ki 6:8 3289
will bless the LORD who has **c** me; Ps 16:7 3289
They have **c** only to thrust him Ps 62:4 3289
c rebellion against the LORD.'" Jer 28:16 1696
What Balak king of Moab **c** Mi 6:5 3289

COUNSELOR
Ahithophel the Gilonite, David's **c**, 2Sa 15:12 3289
son Zechariah, a **c** with insight, 1Ch 26:14 3289
Jonathan, David's uncle, *was* a **c**, 1Ch 27:32 3289
Ahithophel *was* **c** to the king; 1Ch 27:33 3289
mother was his **c** to do wickedly. 2Ch 22:3 3289
"Have we appointed you a royal **c**? 2Ch 25:16 3289
man, The **c** and the expert artisan, Is 3:3 3289
name will be called Wonderful **C**, Is 9:6 3289
Or as His **c** has informed Him? Is 40:13 376, 6098
And there is no **c** among them Who, Is 41:28 3289
among you, Or has your **c** perished, Mi 4:9 3289
evil against the LORD, A wicked **c**. Na 1:11 3289
OF THE LORD, OR WHO BECAME HIS **C**? Ro 11:34 *4825*

COUNSELORS
c after the death of his father, 2Ch 22:4 3289
and hired **c** against them to Ezr 4:5 3289
are sent by the king and his seven **c** Ezr 7:14 3272a
which the king and his **c** have Ezr 7:15 3272a
before the king and his **c** and before Ezr 7:28 3289
king and his **c** and his princes and Ezr 8:25 3289
kings and *with* **c** of the earth, Jb 3:14 3289
"He makes **c** walk barefoot And Jb 12:17 3289
also are my delight; *They are* my **c**. Ps 119:24 376, 6098
abundance of **c** there is victory. Pr 11:14 3289
evil, But **c** of peace have joy. Pr 12:20 3289
But with many **c** they succeed. Pr 15:22 3289
abundance of **c** there is victory. Pr 24:6 3289
And your **c** as at the beginning; Is 1:26 3289
prefects and the governors, the **c**, Da 3:2 148
prefects and the governors, the **c**, Da 3:3 148
and my **c** and my nobles began Da 4:36 1907

COUNSELS
the **c** of the wicked are deceitful. Pr 12:5 8458
things Of **c** and knowledge, Pr 22:20 4156
"You are wearied with your many **c**; Is 47:13 6098
but walked in *their own* **c** *and* in Jer 7:24 4156
consume *them* because of their **c**. Hos 11:6 4156

COUNT
the heavens, and **c** the stars, Gn 15:5 5608
if you are able to **c** them." Gn 15:5 5608
they will be too many to **c**." Gn 16:10 5608
then he shall **c** off for himself Lv 15:13 5608
c off for herself seven days; Lv 15:28 5608
shall **c** their fruit as forbidden. Lv 19:23 6188
'You shall also **c** for yourselves Lv 23:15 5608
'You shall **c** fifty days to the day Lv 23:16 5608
'You are also to **c** off seven Lv 25:8 5608
"Who can **c** the dust of Jacob, Or Nu 23:10 4487
take a **c** of the booty that was Nu 31:26 7218
shall **c** seven weeks for yourself; Dt 16:9 5608
you shall begin to **c** seven weeks Dt 16:9 5608
So they arose and went over by **c**, 2Sa 2:15 4557
high priest that he may **c** the money 2Ki 22:4 8552
I who commanded to **c** the people? 1Ch 21:17 4487
But David did not **c** those twenty 1Ch 27:23 5375, 4557
of Zeruiah had begun to **c** *them*, 1Ch 27:24 4487
"Who can **c** the clouds by wisdom, Jb 38:37 5608
"Can you **c** the months they Jb 39:2 5608
I can **c** all my bones. Ps 22:17 5608
They would be too numerous to **c**. Ps 40:5 5608
and go around her; **C** her towers; Ps 48:12 5608
c when He registers the peoples, Ps 87:6 5608
If I should **c** them, they would Ps 139:18 5608
as a hired man would **c** them, Is 16:14 8141
a year, as a hired man would **c** it, Is 21:16 8141
all generations will **c** me blessed. Lk 1:48 *3106*
I **c** all things to be loss in view Php 3:8 *2233*
and **c** them but rubbish so that Php 3:8 *2233*
will **c** you worthy of your calling, 2Th 1:11 *515*
We **c** those blessed who endured. Jas 5:11 *3106*
They **c** it a pleasure to revel in 2Pe 2:13 *2233*
His promise, as some **c** slowness, 2Pe 3:9 *2233*
multitude which no one could **c**, Rv 7:9 *705*

COUNTED
the north (it is **c** as Canaanite); Jos 13:3 2803
too many to be numbered or **c**. 1Ki 3:8 5608
they could not be **c** or numbered. 1Ki 8:5 5608
and tied *it* in bags and **c** the money 2Ki 12:10 4487
for they **c** them when they brought 1Ch 9:28 4557
of those of them who were **c**, 1Ch 23:24 6485
they could not be **c** or numbered. 2Ch 5:6 5608
and he **c** them out to Sheshbazzar, Ezr 1:8 5608
be **c** as incense before You; Ps 141:2 3559
and what is lacking cannot be **c**. Ec 1:15 4487
you **c** the houses of Jerusalem And Is 22:10 5608
'As the host of heaven cannot be **c** and Jer 33:22 5608
"For he was **c** among us and Ac 1:17 *2674*
and they **c** up the price of them Ac 19:19 *4860*
those things I have **c** as loss for Php 3:7 *2233*
may it not be **c** against them. 2Tm 4:16 *3049*
For He has been **c** worthy of more Heb 3:3 *515*

COUNTENANCE
became very angry and his **c** fell. Gn 4:5 6440
And why has your **c** fallen? Gn 4:6 6440
"If you do well, will not *your* **c** Gn 4:7
The LORD lift up His **c** on you, Nu 6:26 6440
a nation of fierce **c** who will Dt 28:50 6440
off my *sad* **c** and be cheerful,' Jb 9:27 6440
up the light of Your **c** upon us, Ps 4:6 6440
in the haughtiness of his **c**, Ps 10:4 639
yet praise Him, The help of my **c** and Ps 42:11 6440
praise Him, The help of my **c** and Ps 43:5 6440
perish at the rebuke of Your **c**. Ps 80:16 6440
they walk in the light of Your **c**. Ps 89:15 6440
a backbiting tongue, an angry **c**. Pr 25:23 6440
They are troubled in **c**. Ezk 27:35 6440

COUNTING
c their trespasses against them, 2Co 5:19 *3049*

COUNTLESS
him, While **c** ones *go* before him. Jb 21:33 369, 4557
a mass of corpses, And **c** dead bodies Na 3:3 369, 7097b
were to have **c** tutors in Christ, 1Co 4:15 *3463*

COUNTRIES
Solomon from Egypt and from all **c**. 2Ch 9:28 776
of the kingdoms of the **c**." 2Ch 12:8 776
all the **c** and their lands, Is 37:18 776
the **c** where He had banished them.' Jer 16:15 776
remnant of My flock out of all the **c** Jer 23:3 776
the **c** where I had driven them.' Jer 23:8 776
and who were in all the *other* **c**, Jer 40:11 776
you are scattered among the **c**. Ezk 6:8 776
I had scattered them among the **c**, Ezk 11:16 776
in the **c** where they had gone." Ezk 11:16 776
and assemble you out of the **c** Ezk 11:17 776
and spread them among the **c**. Ezk 12:15 776
gather them from the **c** and bring Ezk 34:13 776
the **c** to which You have driven them, Da 9:7 776
and he will enter **c**, Da 11:40 776
and many **c** will fall; but these Da 11:41
out his hand against *other* **c**, Da 11:42 776
They will remember Me in far **c**, Zch 10:9 4801

COUNTRY
Sephar, the hill **c** of the east. Gn 10:30 2022
"Go forth from your **c**, Gn 12:1 776
all the **c** of the Amalekites, Gn 14:7 7704
who survived fled to the hill **c**. Gn 14:10 2022
go to my **c** and to my relatives, Gn 24:4 776
to my own place and to my own **c**. Gn 30:25 776
face toward the hill **c** of Gilead. Gn 31:21 2022
him in the hill **c** of Gilead. Gn 31:23 2022
pitched his tent in the hill **c**, Gn 31:25 2022
camped in the hill **c** of Gilead. Gn 31:25 2022
the land of Seir, the **c** of Edom. Gn 32:3 7704
to your **c** and to your relatives, Gn 32:9 776
Esau lived in the hill **c** of Seir; Gn 36:8 2022
Edomites in the hill **c** of Seir. Gn 36:9 2022
and took us for spies of the **c**. Gn 42:30 776
then go up into the hill **c**. Nu 13:17 2022
Amorites are living in the hill **c**, Nu 13:29 2022
up to the ridge of the hill **c**, Nu 14:40 2022
to the ridge of the hill **c**; Nu 14:44 2022
Canaanites who lived in that hill **c** Nu 14:45 2022
go to the hill **c** of the Amorites, Dt 1:7 2022
in the hill **c** and in the lowland Dt 1:7 2022
way to the hill **c** of the Amorites, Dt 1:19 2022
'You have come to the hill **c** of Dt 1:20 2022
and went up into the hill **c**, Dt 1:24 2022
as easy to go up into the hill **c**. Dt 1:41 2022
and went up into the hill **c**. Dt 1:43 2022
The Amorites who lived in that hill **c** Dt 1:44 2022
and the cities of the hill **c**, Dt 2:37 2022
hill **c** of Gilead and its cities I Dt 3:12 2022
that good hill **c** and Lebanon.' Dt 3:25 2022
person is found lying in the open **c** Dt 21:1 7704
and blessed *shall* you *be* in the **c**. Dt 28:3 7704
and cursed *shall* you *be* in the **c**. Dt 28:16 7704
"Go to the hill **c**, so that the Jos 2:16 2022
departed and came to the hill **c**, Jos 2:22 2022
came down from the hill **c** and crossed Jos 2:23 2022
in the hill **c** and in the lowland Jos 9:1 2022
"We have come from a far **c**; Jos 9:6 776
servants have come from a very far **c** Jos 9:9 776
inhabitants of our **c** spoke to us, Jos 9:11 776
c have assembled against us." Jos 10:6 2022
the hill **c** and the Negev and the Jos 10:40 2022
and all the **c** of Goshen even as Jos 10:41 776
were of the north in the hill **c**, Jos 11:2 2022
and the Jebusite in the hill **c**, Jos 11:3 2022
the hill **c** and all the Negev, all Jos 11:16 2022
hill **c** of Israel and its lowland Jos 11:16 2022
off the Anakim from the hill **c**, Jos 11:21 2022
Anab and from all the hill **c** of Judah Jos 11:21 2022
and from all the hill **c** of Israel. Jos 11:21 2022
in the hill **c**, in the lowland, in Jos 12:8 2022
inhabitants of the hill **c** from Lebanon Jos 13:6 2022
give me this hill **c** about which Jos 14:12 2022
In the hill **c**: Jos 15:48 2022
through the hill **c** to Bethel. Jos 16:1 2022
since the hill **c** of Ephraim is too Jos 17:15 2022
"The hill **c** is not enough for us, Jos 17:16 2022
but the hill **c** shall be yours. Jos 17:18 2022
up through the hill **c** westward, Jos 18:12 2022
in the hill **c** of Ephraim. Jos 19:50 2022
in the hill **c** of Naphtali and Shechem Jos 20:7 2022
Shechem in the hill **c** of Ephraim, Jos 20:7 2022
in the hill **c** of Judah. Jos 20:7 2022
in the hill **c** of Judah, with its Jos 21:11 2022
lands, in the hill **c** of Ephraim, Jos 21:21 2022
which is in the hill **c** of Ephraim, Jos 24:30 2022
him in the hill **c** of Ephraim. Jos 24:33 2022
the Canaanites living in the hill **c** Jg 1:9 2022
took possession of the hill **c**; Jg 1:19 2022
the sons of Dan into the hill **c**, Jg 1:34 2022
in the hill **c** of Ephraim, Jg 2:9 2022
trumpet in the hill **c** of Ephraim; Jg 3:27 2022
down with him from the hill **c**, Jg 3:27 2022
Bethel in the hill **c** of Ephraim; Jg 4:5 2022
all the hill **c** of Ephraim, Jg 7:24 2022
Shamir in the hill **c** of Ephraim. Jg 10:1 2022
the inhabitants of that **c**. Jg 11:21 776
in the hill **c** of the Amalekites. Jg 12:15 2022
Even the destroyer of our **c**, Jg 16:24 776
Now there was a man of the hill **c** Jg 17:1 2022
he came to the hill **c** of Ephraim Jg 17:8 2022
came to the hill **c** of Ephraim, Jg 18:2 2022
from there to the hill **c** of Ephraim Jg 18:13 2022
who went to spy out the **c** of Laish Jg 18:14 776
part of the hill **c** of Ephraim, Jg 19:1 2022
was from the hill **c** of Ephraim, Jg 19:16 2022
part of the hill **c** of Ephraim, Jg 19:18 2022
from the hill **c** of Ephraim, 1Sa 1:1 2022
the ark of the LORD had been in the **c** 1Sa 6:1 7704
cities and of **c** villages. 1Sa 6:18 6521
passed through the hill **c** of Ephraim 1Sa 9:4 2022
and in the hill **c** of Bethel, 1Sa 13:2 2022
themselves in the hill **c** of Ephraim 1Sa 14:22 2022
hill **c** in the wilderness of Ziph. 1Sa 23:14 2022

in one of the cities in the **c**, **1Sa 27:5** 7704
David lived in the **c** of the Philistines **1Sa 27:7** 7704
in the **c** of the Philistines.' " **1Sa 27:11** 7704
c was weeping with a loud voice, **2Sa 15:23** 776
a man from the hill **c** of Ephraim, **2Sa 20:21** 2022
son in the **c** of Benjamin in Zela, **2Sa 21:14** 776
Ben-hur, in the hill **c** of Ephraim; **1Ki 4:8** 2022
the **c** of Sihon king of the **1Ki 4:19** 776
from a far **c** for Your name's sake **1Ki 8:41** 776
Arabs and the governors of the **c**. **1Ki 10:15** 776
away, that I may go to my own **c**." **1Ki 11:21** 776
are seeking to go to your own **c**?" **1Ki 11:22** 776
Shechem in the hill **c** of Ephraim, **1Ki 12:25** 2022
but the Arameans filled the **c**. **1Ki 20:27** 776
his city and every man to his **c**." **1Ki 22:36** 776
and the **c** was filled with water. **2Ki 3:20** 776
to me from the hill **c** of Ephraim. **2Ki 5:22** 2022
"They have come from a far **c**, **2Ki 20:14** 776
Shechem in the hill **c** of Ephraim **1Ch 6:67** 2022
of children in the **c** of Moab after **1Ch 8:8** 7704
of the storehouses in the **c**, **1Ch 27:25** 7704
when he comes from a far **c** for Your **2Ch 6:32** 776
the governors of the **c** brought gold **2Ch 9:14** 776
which is in the hill **c** of Ephraim, **2Ch 13:4** 2022
captured in the hill **c** of Ephraim. **2Ch 15:8** 2022
Beersheba to the hill **c** of Ephraim **2Ch 19:4** 2022
the hill **c** and the fertile fields, **2Ch 26:10** 2022
cities in the hill **c** of Judah, **2Ch 27:4** 2022
the **c** of Ephraim and Manasseh, **2Ch 30:10** 776
To this hill **c** which His right **Ps 78:54** 2022
the chief men over a broad **c**. **Ps 110:6** 776
beloved, let us go out into the **c**, **SS 7:11** 7704
far **c**, From the farthest horizons, **Is 13:5** 776
Because you have ruined your **c**, **Is 14:20** 776
a ball, *To be cast* into a vast **c**; **Is 22:18** 776
Like streams of water in a dry **c**, **Is 32:2** 6724
"They have come to me from a far **c**, **Is 39:3** 776
man of My purpose from a far **c**. **Is 46:11** 776
'Besiegers come from a far **c**, **Jer 4:16** 776
'If I go out to the **c**, **Jer 14:18** 7704
from the lowland, from the hill **c** and **Jer 17:26** 2022
forsake the rock of the open **c**? **Jer 18:14** 7706a
another **c** where you were not born, **Jer 22:26** 776
am bringing them from the north **c**, **Jer 31:8** 776
in the cities of the hill **c**, **Jer 32:44** 2022
'In the cities of the hill **c**, **Jer 33:13** 2022
the hill **c** of Ephraim and Gilead. **Jer 50:19** 2022
and let us each go to his own **c**, **Jer 51:9** 776
if a **c** sins against Me by **Ezk 14:13** 776
but the **c** would be desolate. **Ezk 14:16** 776
bring a sword on that **c** and say, **Ezk 14:17** 776
'Let the sword pass through the **c** **Ezk 14:17** 776
I should send a plague against that **c** **Ezk 14:19** 776
'Surely in the **c** of the king who **Ezk 17:16** 4725
do you come from? What is your **c**? **Jon 1:8** 776
while I was still in my *own* **c**? **Jon 4:2** 127
a heap of ruins in the open **c**, **Mi 1:6** 7704
are going forth to the north **c**; **Zch 6:6** 776
ones go forth to the south **c**. **Zch 6:6** 776
for their own **c** by another way. **Mt 2:12** *5561*
side into the **c** of the Gadarenes, **Mt 8:28** *5561*
c of Judea was going out to him, **Mk 1:5** *5561*
sea, into the **c** of the Gerasenes. **Mk 5:1** *5561*
not to send them out of the **c**. **Mk 5:10** *5561*
it in the city and in the **c**. **Mk 5:14** *68*
and ran about that whole **c** and **Mk 6:55** *5561*
a passer-by coming from the **c**, **Mk 15:21** *68*
along on their way to the **c**. **Mk 16:12** *68*
and went in a hurry to the hill **c**, **Lk 1:39** *3714*
about in all the hill **c** of Judea. **Lk 1:65** *3714*
sailed to the **c** of the Gerasenes, **Lk 8:26** *5561*
it in the city and *out* in the **c**. **Lk 8:34** *68*
the people of the **c** of the Gerasenes **Lk 8:37** *4066*
on a journey into a distant **c**, **Lk 15:13** *5561*
severe famine occurred in that **c**, **Lk 15:14** *5561*
to one of the citizens of that **c**, **Lk 15:15** *5561*
A nobleman went to a distant **c** **Lk 19:12** *5561*
in the **c** must not enter the city; **Lk 21:21** *5561*
of Cyrene, coming in from the **c**, **Lk 23:26** *68*
prophet has no honor in his own **c**. **Jn 4:44** *3968*
to the **c** near the wilderness, **Jn 11:54** *5561*
out of the **c** before the Passover to **Jn 11:55** *5561*
LEAVE YOUR C AND YOUR RELATIVES, **Ac 7:3** *1093*
c in which you are now living. **Ac 7:4** *1093*
c was fed by the king's country. **Ac 12:20** *5561*
country was fed by the king's **c**. **Ac 12:20**
the upper **c** and came to Ephesus, **Ac 19:1** *3313*
they are seeking a **c** of their own. **Heb 11:14** *3968*
if they had been thinking of that **c** **Heb 11:15**
they desire a better **c**, that is, **Heb 11:16**

COUNTRYMAN

hate your fellow **c** in your heart; **Lv 19:17** 251
'If a fellow **c** of yours becomes so **Lv 25:25** 251
'Now in case a **c** of yours becomes **Lv 25:35** 251
that your **c** may live with you. **Lv 25:36** 251
'If a **c** of yours becomes so **Lv 25:39** 251
and a **c** of yours becomes so poor **Lv 25:47** 251
between a man and his fellow **c**, **Dt 1:16** 251
over yourselves who is not your **c**. **Dt 17:15** 251
bring them back to your **c**. **Dt 22:1** 251
"If your **c** is not near you, **Dt 22:2** 251
you until your **c** looks for it; **Dt 22:2** 251
with anything lost by your **c**, **Dt 22:3** 251
"If *two* men, a man and his **c**, **Dt 25:11** 251

COUNTRYMAN'S

c ox or his sheep straying away, **Dt 22:1** 251
"You shall not see your **c** donkey **Dt 22:4** 251

COUNTRYMEN

But in respect to your **c**, **Lv 25:46** 251
the cases between your fellow **c**, **Dt 1:16** 251
rest to your fellow **c** as to you, **Dt 3:20** 251
one from among your **c** you shall **Dt 17:15** 251
heart may not be lifted up above his **c** **Dt 17:20** 251
have no inheritance among their **c**; **Dt 18:2** 251
me from among you, from your **c**, **Dt 18:15** 251
from among their **c** like you, **Dt 18:18** 251
not charge interest to your **c**: **Dt 23:19** 251
but to your **c** you shall not charge **Dt 23:20** 251
of his **c** of the sons of Israel, **Dt 24:7** 251
whether *he is* one of your **c** or one **Dt 24:14** 251
my fellow **c** and save some of them. **Ro 11:14** *4561*
from robbers, dangers from *my* **c**, **2Co 11:26** *1085*
of my contemporaries among my **c**, **Ga 1:14** *1085*
at the hands of your own **c**, **1Th 2:14** *4853*

COUNTRYSIDE

there was spread over the whole **c**, **2Sa 18:8** 776
the vegetation of the **c** to wither? **Jer 12:4** 3605, 7704
O mountain of Mine in the **c**, **Jer 17:3** 7704
go into the surrounding **c** and villages **Mk 6:36** *68*
entered villages, or cities, or **c**, **Mk 6:56** *68*
go into the surrounding villages and **c** **Lk 9:12** *68*

COUNTS

He **c** me as His enemy. **Jb 33:10** 2803
He **c** the number of the stars; **Ps 147:4** 4487
"Where is he who **c**? **Is 33:18** 5608
Where is he who **c** the towers?" **Is 33:18** 5608

COUPLE

make me a **c** of cakes in my sight, **2Sa 13:6** 8147
him with a **c** of saddled donkeys, **2Sa 16:1** 6776
a **c** of legs or a piece of an ear, **Am 3:12** 8147

COUPLINGS

buy quarried stone and timber for **c** **2Ch 34:11** 4226

COURAGE

our hearts melted and no **c** **Jos 2:11** 7307
"Take **c** and be men, O **1Sa 4:9** 2388
had died in Hebron, he lost **c**, **2Sa 4:1** 3027, 7503
c to pray this prayer to You. **2Sa 7:27** 3820
therefore Your servant has found **c** **1Ch 17:25**
you, be strong and do not lose **c**, **2Ch 15:7** 3027, 7503
he took **c** and removed the **2Ch 15:8** 2388
And he took **c** and rebuilt all the **2Ch 32:5** 2388
strong and let your heart take **c**; **Ps 27:14** 553
strong and let your heart take **c**, **Ps 31:24** 553
"Take **c**, fear not. **Is 35:4** 2388
take **c** and be courageous!" **Da 10:19** 2388
and **c** against the king of the South **Da 11:25** 3824
with justice and **c** To make known **Mi 3:8** 1369
'But now take **c**, Zerubbabel,' **Hg 2:4** 2388
'take **c** also, Joshua son of **Hg 2:4** 2388
all you people of the land take **c**,' **Hg 2:4** 2388
"Take **c**, son; your sins are **Mt 9:2** *2293*
"Daughter, take **c**; **Mt 9:22** *2293*
"Take **c**, it is I; **Mt 14:27** *2293*
and said to them, "Take **c**; it is I, **Mk 6:50** *2293*
blind man, saying to him, "Take **c**, **Mk 10:49** *2293*
up **c** and went in before Pilate, **Mk 15:43** *5111*
they did not have **c** to question Him **Lk 20:40** *5111*
you have tribulation, but take **c**; **Jn 16:33** *2293*
stood at his side and said, "Take **c**; **Ac 23:11** *2293*
now I urge you to keep up your **c**, **Ac 27:22** *2114*
"Therefore, keep up your **c**, **Ac 27:25** *2114*
them, he thanked God and took **c**. **Ac 28:15** *2294*
Therefore, being always of good **c**, **2Co 5:6** *2292*
we are of good **c**, I say, and **2Co 5:8** *2292*
have far more **c** to speak the word **Php 1:14** *5111*

COURAGEOUS

"Be strong and **c**, do not be **Dt 31:6** 553
"Be strong and **c**, for you shall **Dt 31:7** 553
"Be strong and **c**, for you shall **Dt 31:23** 553
"Be strong and **c**, for you shall **Jos 1:6** 553
"Only be strong and very **c**; **Jos 1:7** 553
Be strong and **c**! Do not tremble **Jos 1:9** 553
only be strong and **c**." **Jos 1:18** 553
Be strong and **c**, for thus the LORD **Jos 10:25** 553
and let us show ourselves **c** for **2Sa 10:12** 2388
Be **c** and be valiant." **2Sa 13:28** 2388
and let us show ourselves **c** for **1Ch 19:13** 2388
Be strong and **c**, do not fear nor **1Ch 22:13** 553
house for the sanctuary; be **c** and act. **1Ch 28:10** 2388
"Be strong and **c**, and act; **1Ch 28:20** 553
"Be strong and **c**, do not fear or **2Ch 32:7** 553
but we will be with you; be **c** and act. **Ezr 10:4** 2388
take courage and be **c**!" **Da 10:19** 2388
I propose to be **c** against some, **2Co 10:2** *5111*

COURIER

One **c** runs to meet another, And **Jer 51:31** 7323

COURIERS

The **c** went throughout all **2Ch 30:6** 7323
So the **c** passed from city to city **2Ch 30:10** 7323
Letters were sent by **c** to all **Es 3:13** 7323
The **c** went out impelled by the **Es 3:15** 7323
and sent letters by **c** on horses, **Es 8:10** 7323
The **c**, hastened and impelled by **Es 8:14** 7323

COURSE

So it came about in the **c** of time **Gn 4:3** 4480, 7093
Now it came about in *the* **c** *of* **Ex 2:23**
it came about in the **c** of time, **2Ch 21:19** 4480, 3117
"The paths of their **c** wind along, **Jb 6:18** 1870
rain And a **c** for the thunderbolt, **Jb 28:26** 1870
as a strong man to run his **c**. **Ps 19:5** 734
And equity *and* every good **c**. **Pr 2:9** 4570
Until indignation runs *its* **c**. **Is 26:20** 5674a
Everyone turned to his **c**, **Jer 8:6** 4794
Their **c** also is evil And their **Jer 23:10** 4794
the transgressors have run *their* **c**, **Da 8:23**
while John was completing his **c**, **Ac 13:25** *1408*
we ran a straight **c** to Samothrace, **Ac 16:11** *2113*
so that I may finish my **c** **Ac 20:24** *1408*
we ran a straight **c** to Cos and the **Ac 21:1** *2113*
according to the **c** of this world, **Eph 2:2** *165*
good fight, I have finished the **c**, **2Tm 4:7** *1408*
sets on fire the **c** of *our* life, **Jas 3:6** *5164*
having pursued a **c** of sensuality, **1Pe 4:3** *4198*

COURSES

c they fought against Sisera. **Jg 5:20** 4546
its circular **c** the wind returns. **Ec 1:6** 5439

COURT

make the **c** of the tabernacle. **Ex 27:9** 2691a
hangings for the **c** of fine twisted linen **Ex 27:9** 2691a
"*For* the width of the **c** on **Ex 27:12** 2691a
"The width of the **c** on the **Ex 27:13** 2691a
"For the gate of the **c** **Ex 27:16** 2691a
"All the pillars around the **c** **Ex 27:17** 2691a
the **c** *shall be* one hundred cubits, **Ex 27:18** 2691a
pegs, and all the pegs of the **c**, **Ex 27:19** 2691a
the hangings of the **c**, **Ex 35:17** 2691a
the screen for the gate of the **c**; **Ex 35:17** 2691a
the pegs of the **c** and their cords; **Ex 35:18** 2691a
Then he made the **c**: **Ex 38:9** 2691a
hangings of the **c** were of fine twisted **Ex 38:9** 2691a
On both sides of the gate of the **c** **Ex 38:15** 2691a
All the hangings of the **c** all **Ex 38:16** 2691a
and all the pillars of the **c** were **Ex 38:17** 2691a
the **c** was the work of the weaver, **Ex 38:18** 2691a
to the hangings of the **c**. **Ex 38:18** 2691a
pegs of the tabernacle and of the **c** **Ex 38:20** 2691a
and the sockets of the **c** all **Ex 38:31** 2691a
the sockets of the gate of the **c**, **Ex 38:31** 2691a
all the pegs of the **c** all around. **Ex 38:31** 2691a
the hangings for the **c**, **Ex 39:40** 2691a
the screen for the gate of the **c**, **Ex 39:40** 2691a
"You shall set up the **c** all **Ex 40:8** 2691a
the veil for the gateway of the **c**. **Ex 40:8** 2691a
He erected the **c** all around **Ex 40:33** 2691a
the veil for the gateway of the **c**. **Ex 40:33** 2691a
in the **c** of the tent of meeting. **Lv 6:16** 2691a
in the **c** of the tent of meeting. **Lv 6:26** 2691a
and the hangings of the **c**, **Nu 3:26** 2691a
screen for the doorway of the **c** which **Nu 3:26** 2691a
and the pillars around the **c** with **Nu 3:37** 2691a
and the hangings of the **c**, **Nu 4:26** 2691a
for the doorway of the gate of the **c** **Nu 4:26** 2691a
and the pillars around the **c** and **Nu 4:32** 2691a
between men and they go to **c**, **Dt 25:1** 4941
or from the **c** of his *birth* place; **Ru 4:10** 8179
All the people who were in the **c**, **Ru 4:11** 8179
He built the inner **c** with **1Ki 6:36** 2691a
the other **c** inward from the hall, **1Ki 7:8** 2691a
so on the outside to the great **c**. **1Ki 7:9** 2691a
So the great **c** all around **1Ki 7:12** 2691a
inner **c** of the house of the LORD, **1Ki 7:12** 2691a
king consecrated the middle of the **c** **1Ki 8:64** 2691a
had gone out of the middle **c**, **2Ki 20:4** 2691a
Then he made the **c** of the priests **2Ch 4:9** 2691a, 5835
great **c** and doors for the court, **2Ch 4:9** 5835
great court and doors for the **c**, **2Ch 4:9** 5835
had set it in the midst of the **c**; **2Ch 6:13** 5835
consecrated the middle of the **c** that **2Ch 7:7** 2691a
of the LORD before the new **c**, **2Ch 20:5** 2691a
in the **c** of the house of the LORD. **2Ch 24:21** 2691a
to the **c** of the house of the LORD. **2Ch 29:16** 2691a
which is by the **c** of the guard. **Ne 3:25** 2691a
in the **c** of the garden of the **Es 1:5** 2691a
forth in front of the **c** of the harem **Es 2:11** 2691a
the inner **c** who is not summoned, **Es 4:11** 2691a
in the inner **c** of the king's palace in **Es 5:1** 2691a
the queen standing in the **c**, **Es 5:2** 2691a
"Who is in the **c**?" **Es 6:4** 2691a
Haman had just entered the outer **c** **Es 6:4** 2691a
Haman is standing in the **c**." **Es 6:5** 2691a
Him, That we may go to **c** together. **Jb 9:32** 4941
he stood in the **c** of the LORD's house **Jer 19:14** 2691a
'Stand in the **c** of the LORD's **Jer 26:2** 2691a
the queen mother, the **c** officials, **Jer 29:2** 5631
was shut up in the **c** of the guard, **Jer 32:2** 2691a
my uncle's son came to me in the **c** **Jer 32:8** 2691a
sitting in the **c** of the guard. **Jer 32:12** 2691a
confined in the **c** of the guard, **Jer 33:1** 2691a
of Jerusalem, the **c** officers and **Jer 34:19** 5631
the scribe, in the upper **c**, **Jer 36:10** 2691a
So they went to the king in the **c**, **Jer 36:20** 2691a
Jeremiah to the **c** of the guardhouse **Jer 37:21** 2691a
in the **c** of the guardhouse. **Jer 37:21** 2691a
was in the **c** of the guardhouse; **Jer 38:6** 2691a
stayed in the **c** of the guardhouse. **Jer 38:13** 2691a
So Jeremiah stayed in the **c** of the **Jer 38:28** 2691a
sent and took Jeremiah out of the **c** **Jer 39:14** 2691a
in the **c** of the guardhouse, **Jer 39:15** 2691a
and who will summon Me *into* **c**? **Jer 49:19**
and who will summon Me *into* **c**? **Jer 50:44**
of the north gate of the inner **c**, **Ezk 8:3**
me to the entrance of the **c**, **Ezk 8:7** 2691a
the inner **c** of the LORD's house. **Ezk 8:16** 2691a
and the cloud filled the inner **c**. **Ezk 10:3** 2691a
and the **c** was filled with the **Ezk 10:4** 2691a
was heard as far as the outer **c**, **Ezk 10:5** 2691a

he brought me into the outer **c**, Ezk 40:17 2691a
made for the **c** all around; Ezk 40:17 2691a
of the exterior of the inner **c**, Ezk 40:19 2691a
the outer **c** which faced the north, Ezk 40:20 2691a
The inner **c** had a gate Ezk 40:23 2691a
c had a gate toward the south; Ezk 40:27 2691a
to the inner **c** by the south gate; Ezk 40:28 2691a
porches *were* toward the outer **c**; Ezk 40:31 2691a
into the inner **c** toward the east. Ezk 40:32 2691a
porches *were* toward the outer **c**; Ezk 40:34 2691a
pillars *were* toward the outer **c**; Ezk 40:37 2691a
for the singers in the inner **c**, Ezk 40:44 2691a
He measured the **c**, Ezk 40:47 2691a
nave and the porches of the **c**. Ezk 41:15 2691a
brought me out into the outer **c**, Ezk 42:1 2691a
which belonged to the inner **c**, Ezk 42:3 2691a
which belonged to the outer **c**, Ezk 42:3 2691a
the outer **c** facing the chambers, Ezk 42:7 2691a
in the outer **c** *was* fifty cubits; Ezk 42:8 2691a
one enters them from the outer **c**. Ezk 42:9 2691a
the wall of the **c** toward the east, Ezk 42:10 2691a
they shall not go out into the outer **c** Ezk 42:14 2691a
and brought me into the inner **c**; Ezk 43:5 2691a
enter at the gates of the inner **c**, Ezk 44:17 2691a
of the inner **c** and in the house. Ezk 44:17 2691a
When they go out into the outer **c**, Ezk 44:19 2691a
into the outer **c** to the people, Ezk 44:19 2691a
wine when they enter the inner **c**. Ezk 44:21 2691a
c to minister in the sanctuary, Ezk 44:27 2691a
posts of the gate of the inner **c**. Ezk 45:19 2691a
"The gate of the inner **c** facing Ezk 46:1 2691a
not bring *them* out into the outer **c** Ezk 46:20 2691a
he brought me out into the outer **c** Ezk 46:21 2691a
to the four corners of the **c**; Ezk 46:21 2691a
in every corner of the **c** *there was* a Ezk 46:21 2691a
of the court *there was a small* **c**. Ezk 46:21 2691a
the **c** *there were* enclosed courts, Ezk 46:22 2691a
for serving in the king's **c**; Da 1:4 1964
while Daniel *was* at the king's **c**. Da 2:49 8651
The **c** sat, And the books were Da 7:10 1780
'But the **c** will sit *for judgment*, Da 7:26 1780
murder shall be liable to the **c**.' Mt 5:21 *2920*
shall be guilty before the **c**; Mt 5:22 *2920*
be guilty before the supreme **c**; Mt 5:22 *4892*
in the **c** of the high priest, Mt 26:3 *833*
set her in the center *of the* **c**, Jn 8:3
in the center *of the* **c**. Jn 8:9
into the **c** of the high priest, Jn 18:15 *833*
eunuch, a **c** official of Candace, Ac 8:27 *1413*
by you, or by *any* human **c**; 1Co 4:3 *2250*
and personally drag you into **c**? Jas 2:6 *2922*
the **c** which is outside the temple and Rv 11:2 *833*

COURTEOUSLY
and entertained us **c** three days. Ac 28:7 *5390*

COURTS
of the houses, the **c**, and the fields. Ex 8:13 2691a
being cases of dispute in your **c**, Dt 17:8 8179
two **c** of the house of the LORD. 2Ki 21:5 2691a
two **c** of the house of the LORD, 2Ki 23:12 2691a
in the **c** and in the chambers and 1Ch 23:28 2691a
who shall build My house and My **c**; 1Ch 28:6 2691a
the **c** of the house of the LORD, 1Ch 28:12 2691a
in the **c** of the house of the LORD. 2Ch 23:5 2691a
two **c** of the house of the LORD. 2Ch 33:5 2691a
each on his roof, and in their **c** and Ne 8:16 2691a
and in the **c** of the house of God, Ne 8:16 2691a
him in the **c** of the house of God. Ne 13:7 2691a
near *to You* To dwell in Your **c**. Ps 65:4 2691a
yearned for the **c** of the LORD; Ps 84:2 2691a
For a day in Your **c** is better than Ps 84:10 2691a
will flourish in the **c** of our God. Ps 92:13 2691a
an offering and come into His **c**. Ps 96:8 2691a
And His **c** with praise. Ps 100:4 2691a
In the **c** of the LORD's house, In Ps 116:19 2691a
In the **c** of the house of our God! Ps 135:2 2691a
of you this trampling of My **c**? Is 1:12 2691a
drink it in the **c** of My sanctuary. Is 62:9 2691a
and fill the **c** with the slain. Ezk 9:7 2691a
pillars like the pillars of the **c**; Ezk 42:6 2691a
the court *there were* enclosed **c**, Ezk 46:22 2691a
and also have charge of My **c**, Zch 3:7 2691a
they will hand you over to *the* **c** Mt 10:17 *4892*
they will deliver you to *the* **c**, Mk 13:9 *4892*
the **c** are in session and Ac 19:38 *60*
to constitute the smallest law **c**? 1Co 6:2 *2922*
So if you have law **c** dealing 1Co 6:4 *2922*

COURTYARD
Bahurim, who had a well in his **c**, 2Sa 17:18 2691a
about to the side pillar of the **c**. Ezk 40:14 2691a
far as the **c** of the high priest, Mt 26:58 *833*
was sitting outside in the **c**, Mt 26:69 *833*
into the **c** of the high priest; Mk 14:54 *833*
As Peter was below in the **c**, Mk 14:66 *833*
the **c** and had sat down together, Lk 22:55 *833*

COUSIN
and *also* Barnabas's **c** Mark Col 4:10 *431*

COVENANT
I will establish My **c** with you; Gn 6:18 1285
Myself do establish My **c** with you, Gn 9:9 1285
"I establish My **c** with you; Gn 9:11 1285
"This is the sign of the **c** which Gn 9:12 1285
of a **c** between Me and the earth. Gn 9:13 1285
and I will remember My **c**, Gn 9:15 1285
to remember the everlasting **c** Gn 9:16 1285
"This is the sign of the **c** which Gn 9:17 1285
day the LORD made a **c** with Abram, Gn 15:18 1285
establish My **c** between Me and you, Gn 17:2 1285
for Me, behold, My **c** is with you, Gn 17:4 1285
"I will establish My **c** Gn 17:7 1285
generations for an everlasting **c**, Gn 17:7 1285
as for you, you shall keep My **c**, Gn 17:9 1285
"This is My **c**, which you shall Gn 17:10 1285
sign of the **c** between Me and you. Gn 17:11 1285
thus shall My **c** be in your flesh Gn 17:13 1285
your flesh for an everlasting **c**. Gn 17:13 1285
he has broken My **c**." Gn 17:14 1285
and I will establish My **c** with him Gn 17:19 1285
c for his descendants after him. Gn 17:19 1285
My **c** I will establish with Isaac, Gn 17:21 1285
and the two of them made a **c**. Gn 21:27 1285
So they made a **c** at Beersheba; Gn 21:32 1285
us, and let us make a **c** with you, Gn 26:28 1285
"So now come, let us make a **c**, Gn 31:44 1285
God remembered His **c** with Abraham, Ex 2:24 1285
I also established My **c** with them, Ex 6:4 1285
and I have remembered My **c**. Ex 6:5 1285
obey My voice and keep My **c**, Ex 19:5 1285
no **c** with them or with their gods. Ex 23:32 1285
Then he took the book of the **c** and Ex 24:7 1285
"Behold the blood of the **c**, Ex 24:8 1285
generations as a perpetual **c**.' Ex 31:16 1285
"Behold, I am going to make a **c**. Ex 34:10 1285
you make no **c** with the inhabitants Ex 34:12 1285
otherwise you might make a **c** with the Ex 34:15 1285
a **c** with you and with Israel." Ex 34:27 1285
on the tablets the words of the **c**, Ex 34:28 1285
so that the salt of the **c** of your God Lv 2:13 1285
c for the sons of Israel. Lv 24:8 1285
and I will confirm My **c** with you. Lv 26:9 1285
commandments, *and* so break My **c**, Lv 26:15 1285
will execute vengeance for the **c**; Lv 26:25 1285
I will remember My **c** with Jacob, Lv 26:42 1285
remember also My **c** with Isaac, Lv 26:42 1285
and My **c** with Abraham as well, Lv 26:42 1285
them, breaking My **c** with them; Lv 26:44 1285
them the **c** with their ancestors, Lv 26:45 1285
with the ark of the **c** of the LORD Nu 10:33 1285
neither the ark of the **c** of the LORD Nu 14:44 1285
It is an everlasting **c** of salt Nu 18:19 1285
'Behold, I give him My **c** of peace; Nu 25:12 1285
a **c** of a perpetual priesthood, Nu 25:13 1285
"So He declared to you His **c** Dt 4:13 1285
forget the **c** of the LORD your God Dt 4:23 1285
nor forget the **c** with your fathers Dt 4:31 1285
our God made a **c** with us at Horeb. Dt 5:2 1285
not make this **c** with our fathers, Dt 5:3 1285
You shall make no **c** with them and Dt 7:2 1285
who keeps His **c** and His Dt 7:9 1285
your God will keep with you His **c** Dt 7:12 1285
that He may confirm His **c** which He Dt 8:18 1285
the tablets of the **c** which the Dt 9:9 1285
of stone, the tablets of the **c**. Dt 9:11 1285
of the **c** were in my two hands. Dt 9:15 1285
the ark of the **c** of the LORD, Dt 10:8 1285
your God, by transgressing His **c**, Dt 17:2 1285
These are the words of the **c** which Dt 29:1 1285
besides the **c** which He had made Dt 29:1 1285
the words of this **c** to do them, Dt 29:9 1285
into the **c** with the LORD your God, Dt 29:12 1285
am I making this **c** and this oath, Dt 29:14 1285
the curses of the **c** which are written Dt 29:21 1285
they forsook the **c** of the LORD, Dt 29:25 1285
the ark of the **c** of the LORD, Dt 31:9 1285
My **c** which I have made with them. Dt 31:16 1285
them, and spurn Me and break My **c**. Dt 31:20 1285
the ark of the **c** of the LORD, Dt 31:25 1285
ark of the **c** of the LORD your God, Dt 31:26 1285
observed Your word, And kept Your **c**. Dt 33:9 1285
"When you see the ark of the **c** of Jos 3:3 1285
"Take up the ark of the **c** and Jos 3:6 1285
So they took up the ark of the **c** Jos 3:6 1285
who are carrying the ark of the **c**, Jos 3:8 1285
the ark of the **c** of the Lord of Jos 3:11 1285
ark of the **c** before the people, Jos 3:14 1285
priests who carried the ark of the **c** Jos 3:17 1285
the ark of the **c** of the LORD; Jos 4:7 1285
the ark of the **c** were standing, Jos 4:9 1285
priests who carried the ark of the **c** Jos 4:18 1285
"Take up the ark of the **c**, Jos 6:6 1285
the **c** of the LORD followed them. Jos 6:8 1285
My **c** which I commanded them. Jos 7:11 1285
transgressed the **c** of the LORD, Jos 7:15 1285
the ark of the **c** of the LORD, Jos 8:33 1285
now therefore, make a **c** with us." Jos 9:6 1285
then shall we make a **c** with you?" Jos 9:7 1285
now then, make a **c** with us." Jos 9:11 1285
with them and made a **c** with them, Jos 9:15 1285
after they had made a **c** with them, Jos 9:16 1285
the **c** of the LORD your God, Jos 23:16 1285
made a **c** with the people that day, Jos 24:25 1285
'I will never break My **c** with you, Jg 2:1 1285
you shall make no **c** with the Jg 2:2 1285
this nation has transgressed My **c** Jg 2:20 1285
the ark of the **c** of God *was* there Jg 20:27 1285
the ark of the **c** of the LORD, 1Sa 4:3 1285
carried the ark of the **c** of the LORD 1Sa 4:4 1285
with the ark of the **c** of God. 1Sa 4:4 1285
As the ark of the **c** of the LORD 1Sa 4:5 1285
"Make a **c** with us and we will serve 1Sa 11:1 1285
Then Jonathan made a **c** with David 1Sa 18:3 1285
into a **c** of the LORD with you. 1Sa 20:8 1285
So Jonathan made a **c** with 1Sa 20:16
to me when my son makes *a* **c** with 1Sa 22:8
of them made a **c** before the LORD; 1Sa 23:18 1285
Make your **c** with me, and behold, 2Sa 3:12 1285
I will make a **c** with you, but I 2Sa 3:13 1285
that they may make a **c** with you, 2Sa 3:21 1285
and King David made a **c** with them 2Sa 5:3 1285
carrying the ark of the **c** of God. 2Sa 15:24 1285
sons of Israel made a **c** with them, 2Sa 21:2 7650
has made an everlasting **c** with me, 2Sa 23:5 1285
the ark of the **c** of the Lord, 1Ki 3:15 1285
and the two of them made a **c**. 1Ki 5:12 1285
the ark of the **c** of the LORD. 1Ki 6:19 1285
to bring up the ark of the **c** of 1Ki 8:1 1285
of the **c** of the LORD to its place, 1Ki 8:6 1285
made a **c** with the sons of Israel, 1Ki 8:9
ark, in which is the **c** of the LORD, 1Ki 8:21 1285
keeping **c** and *showing* 1Ki 8:23 1285
not kept My **c** and My statutes, 1Ki 11:11 1285
of Israel have forsaken Your **c**, 1Ki 19:10 1285
of Israel have forsaken Your **c**, 1Ki 19:14 1285
I will let you go with this **c**." 1Ki 20:34 1285
made a **c** with him and let him go. 1Ki 20:34 1285
Then he made a **c** with them and put 2Ki 11:4 1285
Then Jehoiada made a **c** between the 2Ki 11:17 1285
because of His **c** with Abraham, 2Ki 13:23 1285
They rejected His statutes and His **c** 2Ki 17:15 1285
LORD made a **c** and commanded them, 2Ki 17:35 1285
The **c** that I have made with you, 2Ki 17:38 1285
their God, but transgressed His **c**, 2Ki 18:12 1285
the words of the book of the **c** which 2Ki 23:2 1285
and made a **c** before the LORD, 2Ki 23:3 1285
to carry out the words of this **c** 2Ki 23:3 1285
all the people entered into the **c**. 2Ki 23:3 1285
written in this book of the **c**." 2Ki 23:21 1285
and David made a **c** with them in 1Ch 11:3 1285
who went to bring up the ark of the **c** 1Ch 15:25 1285
the ark of the **c** of the LORD, 1Ch 15:26 1285
the **c** of the LORD with shouting, 1Ch 15:28 1285
It happened when the ark of the **c** 1Ch 15:29 1285
before the ark of the **c** of God. 1Ch 16:6 1285
Remember His **c** forever, The word 1Ch 16:15 1285
The **c** which He made with Abraham, 1Ch 16:16
To Israel as an everlasting **c**, 1Ch 16:17 1285
the ark of the **c** of the LORD to 1Ch 16:37 1285
c of the LORD is under curtains." 1Ch 17:1 1285
the ark of the **c** of the LORD and 1Ch 22:19 1285
permanent home for the ark of the **c** 1Ch 28:2 1285
the ark of the **c** of the LORD. 1Ch 28:18 1285
to bring up the ark of the **c** of 2Ch 5:2 1285
of the **c** of the LORD to its place, 2Ch 5:7 1285
made a **c** with the sons of Israel, 2Ch 5:10
in which is the **c** of the LORD, 2Ch 6:11
keeping **c** and *showing* 2Ch 6:14 1285
David and his sons by a **c** of salt? 2Ch 13:5 1285
They entered into the **c** to 2Ch 15:12 1285
c which He had made with David, 2Ch 21:7 1285
they entered into a **c** with him. 2Ch 23:1 1285
Then all the assembly made a **c** 2Ch 23:3 1285
Then Jehoiada made a **c** between 2Ch 23:16 1285
a **c** with the LORD God of Israel, 2Ch 29:10 1285
all the words of the book of the **c** 2Ch 34:30 1285
king stood in his place and made a **c** 2Ch 34:31 1285
of the **c** written in this book. 2Ch 34:31 1285
did according to the **c** of God, 2Ch 34:32 1285
now let us make a **c** with our God Ezr 10:3 1285
who preserves the **c** and Ne 1:5 1285
And made a **c** with him To Ne 9:8 1285
keeps **c** and lovingkindness, Ne 9:32 1285
have defiled the priesthood and the **c** Ne 13:29 1285
"I have made a **c** with my eyes; Jb 31:1 1285
"Will he make a **c** with you? Jb 41:4 1285
keep His **c** and His testimonies. Ps 25:10 1285
And He will make them know His **c**. Ps 25:14 1285
have not dealt falsely with Your **c**. Ps 44:17 1285
made a **c** with Me by sacrifice." Ps 50:5 1285
And to take My **c** in your mouth? Ps 50:16 1285
He has violated his **c**. Ps 55:20 1285
Consider the **c**; For the dark places Ps 74:20 1285
They did not keep the **c** of God And Ps 78:10 1285
Nor were they faithful in His **c**. Ps 78:37 1285
Against You they make a **c**: Ps 83:5 1285
"I have made a **c** with My chosen; Ps 89:3 1285
My **c** shall be confirmed to him. Ps 89:28 1285
"My **c** I will not violate, Nor Ps 89:34 1285
have spurned the **c** of Your servant; Ps 89:39 1285
To those who keep His **c** And Ps 103:18 1285
He has remembered His **c** forever, Ps 105:8 1285
The **c** which He made with Ps 105:9
To Israel as an everlasting **c**, Ps 105:10 1285
remembered His **c** for their sake, Ps 106:45 1285
He will remember His **c** forever. Ps 111:5 1285
He has ordained His **c** forever; Ps 111:9 1285
"If your sons will keep My **c** And Ps 132:12 1285
And forgets the **c** of her God; Pr 2:17 1285
statutes, broke the everlasting **c**. Is 24:5 1285
"We have made a **c** with death, And Is 28:15 1285
c with death will be canceled, Is 28:18 1285
has ceased, He has broken the **c**, Is 33:8 1285
appoint you as a **c** to the people, Is 42:6 1285
give You for a **c** of the people, Is 49:8 1285
c of peace will not be shaken," Is 54:10 1285
make an everlasting **c** with you, Is 55:3 1285
pleases Me, And hold fast My **c**; Is 56:4 1285
the sabbath And holds fast My **c**; Is 56:6 1285
for Me, this is My **c** with them," Is 59:21 1285
make an everlasting **c** with them. Is 61:8 1285
'The ark of the **c** of the LORD.' Jer 3:16 1285
"Hear the words of this **c**, Jer 11:2 1285
not heed the words of this **c** Jer 11:3 1285
the words of this **c** and do them. Jer 11:6 1285
on them all the words of this **c**, Jer 11:8 1285
the house of Judah have broken My **c** Jer 11:10 1285
and do not annul Your **c** with us. Jer 14:21 1285
'Because they forsook the **c** of the Jer 22:9 1285

“when I will make a new **c** with **Jer 31:31** 1285
not like the **c** which I made **Jer 31:32** 1285
of Egypt, My **c** which they broke, **Jer 31:32** 1285
“But this is the **c** which I will **Jer 31:33** 1285
“I will make an everlasting **c** **Jer 32:40** 1285
‘If you can break My **c** for the day and **Jer 33:20** 1285
the day and My **c** for the night, **Jer 33:20** 1285
then My **c** may also be broken with **Jer 33:21** 1285
My **c** *for* day and night *stand* not, **Jer 33:25** 1285
after King Zedekiah had made a **c** **Jer 34:8** 1285
who had entered into the **c** that **Jer 34:10** 1285
‘I made a **c** with your forefathers **Jer 34:13** 1285
and you had made a **c** before Me in **Jer 34:15** 1285
men who have transgressed My **c**, **Jer 34:18** 1285
the **c** which they made before Me, **Jer 34:18** 1285
c that will not be forgotten. **Jer 50:5** 1285
c with you so that you became Mine,” **Ezk 16:8** 1285
the oath by breaking the **c**. **Ezk 16:59** 1285
I will remember My **c** with you in **Ezk 16:60** 1285
an everlasting **c** with you. **Ezk 16:60** 1285
but not because of your **c**. **Ezk 16:61** 1285
I will establish My **c** with you, **Ezk 16:62** 1285
family and made a **c** with him, **Ezk 17:13** 1285
itself, *but* keeping his **c** that **Ezk 17:14** 1285
he indeed break the **c** and escape? **Ezk 17:15** 1285
he despised and whose **c** he broke, **Ezk 17:16** 1285
the oath by breaking the **c**, **Ezk 17:18** 1285
despised and My **c** which he broke, **Ezk 17:19** 1285
bring you into the bond of the **c**; **Ezk 20:37** 1285
“I will make a **c** of peace **Ezk 34:25** 1285
will make a **c** of peace with them; **Ezk 37:26** 1285
be an everlasting **c** with them. **Ezk 37:26** 1285
for they made My **c** void **Ezk 44:7** 1285
who keeps His **c** and lovingkindness **Da 9:4** 1285
firm **c** with the many for one week, **Da 9:27** 1285
and also the prince of the **c**. **Da 11:22** 1285
will be *set* against the holy **c**, **Da 11:28** 1285
and become enraged at the holy **c** **Da 11:30** 1285
for those who forsake the holy **c**. **Da 11:30** 1285
who act wickedly toward the **c**, **Da 11:32** 1285
“In that day I will also make a **c** **Hos 2:18** 1285
Adam they have transgressed the **c**; **Hos 6:7** 1285
they have transgressed My **c** And **Hos 8:1** 1285
he makes a **c** with Assyria, **Hos 12:1** 1285
not remember *the* **c** of brotherhood. **Am 1:9** 1285
of the blood of *My* **c** with you, **Zch 9:11** 1285
to break my **c** which I had made **Zch 11:10** 1285
My **c** may continue with Levi,” **Mal 2:4** 1285
“My **c** with him was *one of* life **Mal 2:5** 1285
have corrupted the **c** of Levi,” **Mal 2:8** 1285
to profane the **c** of our fathers? **Mal 2:10** 1285
your companion and your wife by **c**. **Mal 2:14** 1285
and the messenger of the **c**, **Mal 3:1** 1285
for this is My blood of the **c**, **Mt 26:28** *1242*
“This is My blood of the **c**, **Mk 14:24** *1242*
And to remember His holy **c**, **Lk 1:72** *1242*
for you is the new **c** in My blood. **Lk 22:20** *1242*
and of the **c** which God made with **Ac 3:25** *1242*
He gave him the **c** of circumcision; **Ac 7:8** *1242*
“THIS IS MY **C** WITH THEM, **Ro 11:27** *1242*
“This cup is the new **c** in My blood; **1Co 11:25** *1242*
adequate *as* servants of a new **c**, **2Co 3:6** *1242*
the reading of the old **c** the same veil **2Co 3:14** *1242*
even though it is *only* a man’s **c**, **Ga 3:15** *1242*
a **c** previously ratified by God, **Ga 3:17** *1242*
the guarantee of a better **c**. **Heb 7:22** *1242*
also the mediator of a better **c**, **Heb 8:6** *1242*
For if that first **c** had been **Heb 8:7**
WHEN I WILL EFFECT A NEW **C** WITH **Heb 8:8** *1242*
NOT LIKE THE **C** WHICH I MADE WITH **Heb 8:9** *1242*
THEY DID NOT CONTINUE IN MY **C**, **Heb 8:9** *1242*
“FOR THIS IS THE **C** THAT I WILL **Heb 8:10** *1242*
When He said, “A new **c**,” He **Heb 8:13**
Now even the first **c** had **Heb 9:1**
ark of the **c** covered on all sides with **Heb 9:4** *1242*
budded, and the tables of the **c**; **Heb 9:4** *1242*
He is the mediator of a new **c**, **Heb 9:15** *1242*
were *committed* under the first **c**, **Heb 9:15** *1242*
For where a **c** is, there must of **Heb 9:16** *1242*
For a **c** is valid *only* when men are **Heb 9:17** *1242*
Therefore even the first **c** was **Heb 9:18**
THE **C** WHICH GOD COMMANDED YOU.” **Heb 9:20** *1242*
“THIS IS THE **C** THAT I WILL MAKE **Heb 10:16** *1242*
the **c** by which he was sanctified, **Heb 10:29** *1242*
to Jesus, the mediator of a new **c**, **Heb 12:24** *1242*
the blood of the eternal **c**, **Heb 13:20** *1242*
of His **c** appeared in His temple, **Rv 11:19** *1242*

COVENANTED

as I **c** with your father David, **2Ch 7:18** 3772

COVENANTS

With worthless oaths they make **c**; **Hos 10:4** 1285
and the **c** and the giving of the Law **Ro 9:4** *1242*
for these *women* are two **c**: **Ga 4:24** *1242*
and strangers to the **c** of promise, **Eph 2:12** *1242*

COVER

c it inside and out with pitch. **Gn 6:14** 3722b
our brother and **c** up his blood? **Gn 37:26** 3680
shall **c** the surface of the land, **Ex 10:5** 3680
“The deeps **c** them; **Ex 15:5** 3680
digs a pit and does not **c** it over, **Ex 21:33** 3680
side and on the other, to **c** it. **Ex 26:13** 3680
breeches to **c** *their* bare flesh; **Ex 28:42** 3680
of the rock and **c** you with My hand **Ex 33:22** 7917b
he shall **c** his mustache and cry, **Lv 13:45** 5844a
cloud of incense may **c** the mercy seat **Lv 16:13** 3680
out its blood and **c** it with earth. **Lv 17:13** 3680
c the ark of the testimony with it; **Nu 4:5** 3680
and **c** the same with a covering of **Nu 4:8** 3680
and **c** the lampstand for the light, **Nu 4:9** 3680
c it with a covering of porpoise skin, **Nu 4:11** 3680
put them in a blue cloth and **c** them **Nu 4:12** 3680
and they shall spread a **c** of **Nu 4:14** 3681
the cloud would **c** it *by day*, and **Nu 9:16** 3680
they **c** the surface of the land, **Nu 22:5** 3680
they **c** the surface of the land; **Nu 22:11** 3680
garment with which you **c** yourself. **Dt 22:12** 3680
shall turn to **c** up your excrement. **Dt 23:13** 3680
on the one network to **c** the capitals **1Ki 7:18** 3680
and the two networks to **c** the two **1Ki 7:41** 3680
to **c** the two bowls of the capitals **1Ki 7:42** 3680
he took the **c** and dipped it **2Ki 8:15** 4345
and the two networks to **c** the two **2Ch 4:12** 3680
to **c** the two bowls of the capitals **2Ch 4:13** 3680
“O earth, do not **c** my blood, And **Jb 16:18** 3680
in the dust, And worms **c** them. **Jb 21:26** 3680
of the valley will gently **c** him; **Jb 21:33** 4985
an abundance of water will **c** you? **Jb 38:34** 3680
“The lotus plants **c** him with shade; **Jb 40:22** 5526a
He will **c** you with His pinions, **Ps 91:4** 5526a
will not return to **c** the earth. **Ps 104:9** 3680
And let them **c** themselves with **Ps 109:29** 5844a
the mischief of their lips **c** them. **Ps 140:9** 3680
the LORD As the waters **c** the sea. **Is 11:9** 3680
And will no longer **c** her slain. **Is 26:21** 3680
I did not **c** My face from **Is 50:6** 5641
When you see the naked, to **c** him; **Is 58:7** 3680
c themselves with their works; **Is 59:6** 3680
behold, darkness will **c** the earth And **Is 60:2** 3680
“A multitude of camels will **c** you, **Is 60:6** 3680
and let our humiliation **c** us; **Jer 3:25** 3680
And they **c** their heads. **Jer 14:3** 2645
“I will rise and **c** *that* land; **Jer 46:8** 3680
You shall **c** your face so that you **Ezk 12:6** 3680
He will **c** his face so that he can **Ezk 12:12** 3680
on the ground To **c** it with dust. **Ezk 24:7** 3680
feet, and do not **c** *your* mustache and **Ezk 24:17** 5844a
you will not **c** *your* mustache and **Ezk 24:22** 5844a
dust *raised by* them will **c** you; **Ezk 26:10** 3680
and the great waters **c** you, **Ezk 26:19** 3680
A cloud will **c** her, And her **Ezk 30:18** 3680
you, I will **c** the heavens and **Ezk 32:7** 3680
I will **c** the sun with a cloud And **Ezk 32:7** 3680
grow back on you, **c** you with skin and **Ezk 37:6** 7159
Israel like a cloud to **c** the land. **Ezk 38:16** 3680
My flax *Given* to **c** her nakedness. **Hos 2:9** 3680
will say to the mountains, “**C** us! **Hos 10:8** 3680
of a bed and *the* **c** of a couch! **Am 3:12** 1833
they will all **c** *their* mouths **Mi 3:7** 5844a
shame will **c** her who said to me, **Mi 7:10** 3680
the LORD, As the waters **c** the sea. **Hab 2:14** 3680
behold, a lead **c** was lifted up); **Zch 5:7** 3603
you **c** the altar of the LORD with **Mal 2:13** 3680
AND TO THE HILLS, ‘**C** US.’ **Lk 23:30** *2572*
if a woman does not **c** her head, **1Co 11:6** *2619*
head shaved, let her **c** her head. **1Co 11:6** *2619*
and will **c** a multitude of sins. **Jas 5:20** *2572*

COVERED

under the heavens were **c**. **Gn 7:19** 3680
higher, and the mountains were **c**. **Gn 7:20** 3680
c the nakedness of their father; **Gn 9:23** 3680
she took her veil and **c** herself. **Gn 24:65** 3680
and **c** *herself* with a veil, **Gn 38:14** 3680
a harlot, for she had **c** her face. **Gn 38:15** 3680
and **c** it over with tar and pitch. **Ex 2:3** 2560b
came up and **c** the land of Egypt. **Ex 8:6** 3680
c the surface of the whole land, **Ex 10:15** 3680
c the chariots and the horsemen, **Ex 14:28** 3680
with Your wind, the sea **c** them; **Ex 15:10** 3680
the quails came up and **c** the camp, **Ex 16:13** 3680
and the cloud **c** the mountain. **Ex 24:15** 3680
and the cloud **c** it for six days; **Ex 24:16** 3680
the cloud **c** the tent of meeting, **Ex 40:34** 3680
if the leprosy has **c** all his body, **Lv 13:13** 3680
LORD, six **c** carts and twelve oxen, **Nu 7:3** 6632a
the cloud **c** the tabernacle, **Nu 9:15** 3680
the cloud **c** it and the glory of **Nu 16:42** 3680
the sea upon them and **c** them; **Jos 24:7** 3680
tent, and she **c** him with a rug. **Jg 4:18** 3680
gave him a drink; then she **c** him. **Jg 4:19** 3680
its head, and **c** *it* with clothes. **1Sa 19:13** 3680
head was **c** and he walked barefoot. **2Sa 15:30** 2645
each **c** his head and went up weeping **2Sa 15:30** 2645
The king **c** his face and cried **2Sa 19:4** 3813
“Today you have **c** with shame the **2Sa 19:5** 954
and they **c** him with clothes, but **1Ki 1:1** 3680
and he **c** the house with beams and **1Ki 6:9** 5603
The **c** way for the sabbath **2Ki 16:18** 4146b
c himself with sackcloth and **2Ki 19:1** 3680
of the priests, **c** with sackcloth, **2Ki 19:2** 3680
and the elders, **c** with sackcloth, **1Ch 21:16** 3680
and **c** the ark of the covenant of **1Ch 28:18** 5526a
He built it, **c** it and hung its **Ne 3:15** 2926
home, mourning, with *his* head **c**. **Es 6:12** 2645
king’s mouth, they **c** Haman’s face. **Es 7:8** 2645
he has **c** his face with his fat And **Jb 15:27** 3680
I **c** my transgressions like Adam, **Jb 31:33** 3680
is forgiven, Whose sin is **c**! **Ps 32:1** 3680
And **c** us with the shadow of death. **Ps 44:19** 3680
And the valleys are **c** with grain; **Ps 65:13** 5848b
the wings of a dove **c** with silver, **Ps 68:13** 2645
Dishonor has **c** my face. **Ps 69:7** 3680
be **c** with reproach and dishonor, **Ps 71:13** 5844a
mountains were **c** with its shadow, **Ps 80:10** 3680
You **c** all their sin. Selah. **Ps 85:2** 3680
You have **c** him with shame. **Ps 89:45** 5844a
You **c** it with the deep as with a **Ps 104:6** 3680
The waters **c** their adversaries; **Ps 106:11** 3680
Their heart is **c** with fat, *But* I **Ps 119:70** 2954
c my head in the day of battle. **Ps 140:7** 5526a
Its surface was **c** with nettles, **Pr 24:31** 3680
and its name is **c** in obscurity. **Ec 6:4** 3680
Your hands are **c** with blood. **Is 1:15** 4390
with two he **c** his face, and with **Is 6:2** 3680
face, and with two he **c** his feet, **Is 6:2** 3680
And He has **c** your heads, the seers. **Is 29:10** 3680
c himself with sackcloth and **Is 37:1** 3680
of the priests, **c** with sackcloth, **Is 37:2** 3680
and have **c** you with the shadow of **Is 51:16** 3680
to shame, They have **c** their heads. **Jer 14:4** 2645
Disgrace has **c** our faces, For **Jer 51:51** 3680
How the Lord has **c** the daughter of **La 2:1** 5743
You have **c** *Yourself* with anger And **La 3:43** 5526a
You have **c** Yourself with a cloud **La 3:44** 5526a
over you and **c** your nakedness. **Ezk 16:8** 3680
fine linen and **c** you with silk. **Ezk 16:10** 3680
your embroidered cloth and **c** them, **Ezk 16:18** 3680
bare rock, That it may not be **c**.” **Ezk 24:8** 3680
and flesh grew and skin **c** them; **Ezk 37:8** 7159, 4605
windows (but the windows were **c**), **Ezk 41:16** 3680
Jacob, You will be **c** *with* shame, **Ob 1:10** 3680
him, **c** *himself* with sackcloth and **Jon 3:6** 3680
beast must be **c** with sackcloth; **Jon 3:8** 3680
the boat was being **c** with the waves; **Mt 8:24** *2572*
there was a man **c** with leprosy; **Lk 5:12** *4134*
c up that will not be revealed, **Lk 12:2** *4780*
laid at his gate, **c** with sores, **Lk 16:20** *1669*
The young men got up and **c** him up, **Ac 5:6** *4958*
a loud voice, and **c** their ears and **Ac 7:57** *4912*
AND WHOSE SINS HAVE BEEN **C**. **Ro 4:7** *1943*
man ought not to have his head **c**, **1Co 11:7** *2619*
covenant **c** on all sides with gold, **Heb 9:4** *4028*

COVERING

Noah removed the **c** of the ark, **Gn 8:13** 4372
for that is his only **c**; **Ex 22:27** 3682
c the mercy seat with their wings **Ex 25:20** 5526a
“You shall make a **c** for the **Ex 26:14** 4372
and a **c** of porpoise skins above. **Ex 26:14** 4372
tabernacle, its tent and its **c**, **Ex 35:11** 4372
He made a **c** for the tent of **Ex 36:19** 4372
and a **c** of porpoise skins above. **Ex 36:19** 4372
c the mercy seat with their wings, **Ex 37:9** 5526a
and the **c** of rams’ skins dyed red, **Ex 39:34** 4372
red, and the **c** of porpoise skins, **Ex 39:34** 4372
the **c** of the tent on top of it, **Ex 40:19** 4372
ram, the fat tail, and the *fat* **c**, **Lv 9:19** 4374
tabernacle and the tent, its **c**, **Nu 3:25** 4372
lay a **c** of porpoise skin on it, **Nu 4:6** 3681
same with a **c** of porpoise skin, **Nu 4:8** 4372
utensils in a **c** of porpoise skin, **Nu 4:10** 4372
it with a **c** of porpoise skin, **Nu 4:11** 4372
them with a **c** of porpoise skin, **Nu 4:12** 4372
sons have finished **c** the holy *objects* **Nu 4:15** 3680
and the tent of meeting *with* its **c** **Nu 4:25** 4372
its covering and the **c** of porpoise skin **Nu 4:25** 4372
which has no **c** tied down on it, **Nu 19:15** 6781b
So spread your **c** over your maid, **Ru 3:9** 3671
And the woman took a **c** and spread **2Sa 17:19** 4539
and the cherubim made a **c** over the **1Ki 8:7** 5526a
a **c** over the ark and its poles. **2Ch 5:8** 3680
And have no **c** against the cold. **Jb 24:7** 3682
before Him, And Abaddon has no **c**. **Jb 26:6** 3682
Or that the needy had no **c**, **Jb 31:19** 3682
C Yourself with light as with a **Ps 104:2** 5844a
He spread a cloud for a **c**, **Ps 105:39** 4539
you And worms are your **c**.’ **Is 14:11** 4374
the **c** which is over all peoples, **Is 25:7** 6440, 3875
And make sackcloth their **c**.” **Is 50:3** 3682
being, and two **c** their bodies. **Ezk 1:11** 3680
each one also had two wings **c** **Ezk 1:23** 3680
Every precious stone was your **c**: **Ezk 28:13** 4540
I have destroyed you, O **c** cherub, **Ezk 28:16** 5526a
will be like a cloud **c** the land, **Ezk 38:9** 3680
her hair is given to her for a **c**. **1Co 11:15** *4018*
If we have food and **c**, **1Tm 6:8** *4629*
use your freedom as a **c** for evil, **1Pe 2:16** *1942*

COVERINGS

and made themselves loin **c**. **Gn 3:7** 2290b
“I have spread my couch with **c**, **Pr 7:16** 4765
She makes **c** for herself; **Pr 31:22** 4765

COVERS

shall take all the fat that **c** the entrails **Ex 29:13** 3680
and the fat that **c** the entrails **Ex 29:22** 3680
the fat that **c** the entrails and **Lv 3:3** 3680
and the fat that **c** the entrails **Lv 3:9** 3680
the fat that **c** the entrails and **Lv 3:14** 3680
the fat that **c** the entrails, and **Lv 4:8** 3680
and the fat that **c** the entrails, **Lv 7:3** 3680
and the leprosy **c** all the skin of **Lv 13:12** 3680
He **c** the faces of its judges. **Jb 9:24** 3680
And an abundance of water **c** you. **Jb 22:11** 3680
Nor deep gloom *which* **c** me. **Jb 23:17** 3680
And He **c** the depths of the sea. **Jb 36:30** 3680
“He **c** *His* hands with the lightning, **Jb 36:32** 3680
The garment of violence **c** them. **Ps 73:6** 5848b
rain also **c** it with blessings. **Ps 84:6** 5844a
a garment with which he **c** himself, **Ps 109:19** 5844a
Who **c** the heavens with clouds, Who **Ps 147:8** 3680
But love **c** all transgressions. **Pr 10:12** 3680
his hatred **c** itself with guile, **Pr 26:26** 3680
and **c** the naked with clothing, **Ezk 18:7** 3680
and **c** the naked with clothing, **Ezk 18:16** 3680
were the anointed cherub who **c**, **Ezk 28:14** 5526a
His splendor **c** the heavens, And **Hab 3:3** 3680

who c his garment with wrong," Mal 2:16 3680
a lamp c it over with a container, Lk 8:16 2572
love c a multitude of sins. 1Pe 4:8 2572

COVERT
the c of the reeds and the marsh. Jb 40:21 5643a

COVET
shall not c your neighbor's house; Ex 20:17 2530
you shall not c your neighbor's Ex 20:17 2530
and no man shall c your land when Ex 34:24 2530
shall not c your neighbor's wife, Dt 5:21 2530
you shall not c the silver or the Dt 7:25 2530
so that you do not c *them* and take Jos 6:18 2763a
They c fields and then seize *them,* Mi 2:2 2530
"YOU SHALL NOT C." Ro 7:7 1937
NOT STEAL, YOU SHALL NOT C," Ro 13:9 1937

COVETED
then I c them and took them; Jos 7:21 2530
"I have c no one's silver or gold Ac 20:33 1937

COVETING
deeds of c *and* wickedness, *as well* Mk 7:22 4124
about c if the Law had not said, Ro 7:7 1939
produced in me c of every kind; Ro 7:8 1939

COVETOUS
or with the c and swindlers, 1Co 5:10 4123
is an immoral person, or c, 1Co 5:11 4123
nor thieves, nor *the* c, 1Co 6:10 4123
immoral or impure person or c man, Eph 5:5 4123

COVETOUSNESS
gift and not affected by c. 2Co 9:5 4124

COW
His c calves and does not abort. Jb 21:10 6510
the c and the bear will graze, Is 11:7 6510

COWARDLY
"But for the c and unbelieving Rv 21:8 1169

COWER
He has made me c in the dust. La 3:16 3728

COW'S
I will give you c dung in place Ezk 4:15 1241

COWS
colts, forty c and ten bulls, Gn 32:15 6510
the Nile there came up seven c, Gn 41:2 6510
seven other c came up after them Gn 41:3 6510
other c on the bank of the Nile. Gn 41:3 6510
The ugly and gaunt c ate up Gn 41:4 6510
ate up the seven sleek and fat c. Gn 41:4 6510
and behold, seven c, fat and sleek Gn 41:18 6510
seven other c came up after them, Gn 41:19 6510
and the lean and ugly c ate up the Gn 41:20 6510
cows ate up the first seven fat c. Gn 41:20 6510
"The seven good c are seven years; Gn 41:26 6510
"The seven lean and ugly c Gn 41:27 6510
Curds of c, and milk of the flock, Dt 32:14 1241
prepare a new cart and two milch c 1Sa 6:7 6510
and hitch the c to the cart and 1Sa 6:7 6510
c and hitched them to the cart, 1Sa 6:10 6510
And the c took the straight way in 1Sa 6:12 6510
and offered the c as a burnt offering 1Sa 6:14 6510
you c of Bashan who are on the Am 4:1 6510

COZBI
slain was C the daughter of Zur, Nu 25:15 3579
of Peor and in the affair of C, Nu 25:18 3579

COZEBA
and Jokim, the men of C, 1Ch 4:22 3578

CRACKED
"Because the ground is c, Jer 14:4 2865

CRACKLING
the c of thorn bushes under a pot, Ec 7:6 6963
Like the c of a flame of fire Jl 2:5 6963

CRAFT
And against all the beautiful c. Is 2:16 7914b
and no craftsman of any c will be Rv 18:22 5078

CRAFTILY
his neighbor, so as to kill him c, Ex 21:14 6195
acted c and set out as envoys, Jos 9:4 6195
To deal c with His servants. Ps 105:25 5230
Because every brother deals c, Jer 9:4 6117

CRAFTINESS
WHO CATCHES THE WISE IN THEIR C"; 1Co 3:19 3834
not walking in c or adulterating 2Co 4:2 3834
the serpent deceived Eve by his c, 2Co 11:3 3834
men, by c in deceitful scheming; Eph 4:14 3834

CRAFTSMAN
the work of the hands of the c, Dt 27:15 2796
As for the idol, a c casts it, Is 40:19 2796
He seeks out for himself a skillful c Is 40:20 2796
So the c encourages the smelter, Is 41:7 2796
hands of a c with a cutting tool. Jer 10:3 2796
The work of a c and of the hands Jer 10:9 2796
A c made it, so it is not God; Hos 8:6 2796
and no c of any craft will be Rv 18:22 5079

CRAFTSMANSHIP
knowledge, and in all *kinds of* c, Ex 31:3 4399
he may work in all *kinds of* c. Ex 31:5 4399
and in knowledge and in all c; Ex 35:31 4399

CRAFTSMEN
and all the c and the smiths. 2Ki 24:14 2796
and the c and the smiths, 2Ki 24:16 2796
of Ge-harashim, for they were c. 1Ch 4:14 2796
for all the work done by the c. 1Ch 29:5 2796
Lod and Ono, the valley of c. Ne 11:35 2796
for the c themselves are mere men. Is 44:11 2796
with the c and smiths from Jerusalem Jer 24:1 2796
the c and the smiths had departed Jer 29:2 2796
silver, All of them the work of c. Hos 13:2 2796
Then the LORD showed me four c. Zch 1:20 2796
but these c have come to terrify Zch 1:21
no little business to the c; Ac 19:24 5079
if Demetrius and the c who are Ac 19:38 5079

CRAFTY
Now the serpent was more c than Gn 3:1 6175
you choose the language of the c. Jb 15:5 6175
nevertheless, c fellow that I am, 2Co 12:16 3835

CRAG
was a sharp c on the one side and 1Sa 14:4 5553
and a sharp c on the other side, 1Sa 14:4 5553
The one c rose on the north 1Sa 14:5 8127
and lodges, Upon the rocky c, Jb 39:28 8127

CRAGS
Under the clefts of the c? Is 57:5 5553
the cities and dwell among the c, Jer 48:28 5553
And roll you down from the c, And I Jer 51:25 5553

CRAMPED
of his plenty he will be c; Jb 20:22 6887a
will be too c for the inhabitants, Is 49:19 6887a
'The place is too c for me; Is 49:20 6862a

CRANE
"Like a swallow, *like* a c, Is 38:14 5693

CRASH
off the boughs with a terrible c; Is 10:33 4637
And a loud c from the hills. Zph 1:10 7667

CRASHING
of the c they are bewildered. Jb 41:25 7667

CRAVE
eat, *Or* a first-ripe fig *which* I c. Mi 7:1 183
that we would not c evil things 1Co 10:6 1510, 1938

CRAVED
But c intensely in the wilderness, Ps 106:14 183
crave evil things as they also c. 1Co 10:6 1937

CRAVES
the sluggard c and *gets* nothing, Pr 13:4 183
generation c for a sign; Mt 12:39 1934

CRAVING
David had a c and said, 2Sa 23:15 183
David had a c and said, 1Ch 11:17 183
reject the c of the wicked. Pr 10:3 1942
All day long he is c, Pr 21:26 183

CRAWLING
the venom of c things of the dust. Dt 32:24 2119a
animals and c creatures of the earth Ac 10:12 2062
the wild beasts and the c creatures Ac 11:6 2062
animals and c creatures. Ro 1:23 2062

CRAWLS
'Whatever c on its belly, and Lv 11:42 1980

CREATE
C in me a clean heart, O God, And Ps 51:10 1254a
then the LORD will c over the Is 4:5 1254a
it *and* did not c it a waste place, Is 45:18 1254a
I c new heavens and a new earth; Is 65:17 1254a
and rejoice forever in what I c; Is 65:18 1254a
I c Jerusalem *for* rejoicing And Is 65:18 1254a

CREATED
God c the heavens and the earth. Gn 1:1 1254a
God c the great sea monsters and Gn 1:21 1254a
God c man in His own image, in Gn 1:27 1254a
in the image of God He c him; Gn 1:27 1254a
male and female He c them. Gn 1:27 1254a
His work which God had c and made. Gn 2:3 1254a
and the earth when they were c, Gn 2:4 1254a
In the day when God c man, Gn 5:1 1254a
He c them male and female, and He Gn 5:2 1254a
Man in the day when they were c. Gn 5:2 1254a
have c from the face of the land, Gn 6:7 1254a
day that God c man on the earth, Dt 4:32 1254a
and the south, You have c them; Ps 89:12 1254a
You have c all the sons of men! Ps 89:47 1254a
yet to be c may praise the LORD. Ps 102:18 1254a
send forth Your Spirit, they are c; Ps 104:30 1254a
For He commanded and they were c. Ps 148:5 1254a
And see who has c these *stars,* Is 40:26 1254a
the Holy One of Israel has c it. Is 41:20 1254a
Who c the heavens and stretched Is 42:5 1254a
And whom I have c for My glory, Is 43:7 1254a
I, the LORD, have c it. Is 45:8 1254a
made the earth, and c man upon it. Is 45:12 1254a
says the LORD, who c the heavens Is 45:18 1254a
"They are c now and not long ago; Is 48:7 1254a
I Myself have c the smith who Is 54:16 1254a
I have c the destroyer to ruin. Is 54:16 1254a
For the LORD has c a new thing in Jer 31:22 1254a
In the place where you were c, Ezk 21:30 1254a
you were c They were prepared. Ezk 28:13 1254a
your ways From the day you were c Ezk 28:15 1254a
Has not one God c us? Mal 2:10 1254a
that He who c *them* from the Mt 19:4 2936
of the creation which God c until Mk 13:19 2936
nor depth, nor any other c thing, Ro 8:39 2937
man was not c for the woman's sake, 1Co 11:9 2936
c in Christ Jesus for good works, Eph 2:10 2936
hidden in God who c all things; Eph 3:9 2936
been c in righteousness and holiness Eph 4:24 2936
For by Him all things were c, Col 1:16 2936
have been c through Him and for Him. Col 1:16 2936
to the image of the One who c him Col 3:10 2936
For it was Adam who was first c, 1Tm 2:13 4111
which God has c to be gratefully 1Tm 4:3 2936
For everything c by God is good, 1Tm 4:4 2938
can be shaken, as of c things, Heb 12:27 4160
for You c all things, and because of Rv 4:11 2936
will they existed, and were c." Rv 4:11 2936
And every c thing which is in Rv 5:13 2938
WHO C HEAVEN AND THE THINGS IN IT Rv 10:6 2936

CREATES
He who forms mountains and c the Am 4:13 1254a

CREATING
One forming light and c darkness, Is 45:7 1254a
Causing well-being and c calamity; Is 45:7 1254a
C the praise of the lips. Is 57:19 1254a

CREATION
"But from the beginning of c, Mk 10:6 2937
of the c which God created until Mk 13:19 2937
and preach the gospel to all c. Mk 16:15 2937
For since the c of the world His Ro 1:20 2937
For the anxious longing of the c Ro 8:19 2937
the c was subjected to futility, Ro 8:20 2937
that the c itself also will be set Ro 8:21 2937
For we know that the whole c Ro 8:22 2937
nor uncircumcision, but a new c. Ga 6:15 2937
God, the firstborn of all c. Col 1:15 2937
proclaimed in all c under heaven, Col 1:23 2937
that is to say, not of this c; Heb 9:11 2937
it was from the beginning of c." 2Pe 3:4 2937
the Beginning of the c of God, Rv 3:14 2937

CREATOR
your C in the days of your youth, Ec 12:1 1254a
C will not be gracious to them. Is 27:11 3335
the C of the ends of the earth Is 40:28 1254a
now, thus says the LORD, your C, Is 43:1 1254a
your Holy One, The C of Israel, Is 43:15 1254a
the creature rather than the C, Ro 1:25 2936
faithful C in doing what is right. 1Pe 4:19 2939

CREATURE
and every living c that moves, Gn 1:21 5315
the man called a living c, Gn 2:19 5315
every living c that is with you, Gn 9:10 5315
every living c that is with you, Gn 9:12 5315
and every living c of all flesh; Gn 9:15 5315
between God and every living c Gn 9:16 5315
and between the edible c and the Lv 11:47 2421b
the c which is not to be eaten. Lv 11:47 2421b
c will make the matter known. Ec 10:20
It will come about that every living c Ezk 47:9 5315
saw the c hanging from his hand, Ac 28:4 2342
However he shook the c off into Ac 28:5 2342
the c rather than the Creator, Ro 1:25 2937
anyone is in Christ, *he is* a new c; 2Co 5:17 2937
is no c hidden from His sight, Heb 4:13 2937
The first c *was* like a lion, Rv 4:7 2226
and the second c like a calf, Rv 4:7 2226
c had a face like that of a man, Rv 4:7 2226
fourth c *was* like a flying eagle. Rv 4:7 2226
heard the second living c saying, Rv 6:3 2226
I heard the third living c saying, Rv 6:5 2226
of the fourth living c saying, Rv 6:7 2226

CREATURES
teem with swarms of living c, Gn 1:20 5315
forth living c after their kind: Gn 1:24 5315
'These are the c which you may eat Lv 11:2 2421b
living c that are in the water, Lv 11:10 5315
all the c that walk on *all* fours, Lv 11:27 2421b
Your c settled in it; Ps 68:10 2421b
food for the c of the wilderness. Ps 74:14 5971a
But desert c will lie down there, Is 13:21 6716b
Assyria appointed it for desert c Is 23:13 6716b
c will meet with the wolves, Is 34:14 6716b
"Therefore the desert c will live Jer 50:39 6716b
living c fed themselves from it. Da 4:12 1321
and crawling c of the earth and birds Ac 10:12 2062
c and the birds of the air. Ac 11:6 2062
four-footed animals and crawling c. Ro 1:23 2062
of first fruits among His c. Jas 1:18 2938
of reptiles and c of the sea, Jas 3:7 1724
born as c of instinct to be 2Pe 2:12 5446
of those c also be destroyed, 2Pe 2:12
four living c full of eyes in Rv 4:6 2226
And the four living c, Rv 4:8 2226
And when the living c give glory Rv 4:9 2226
the throne (with the four living c) Rv 5:6 2226
the four living c and the Rv 5:8 2226
and the living c and the elders; Rv 5:11 2226
And the four living c kept saying, Rv 5:14 2226
I heard one of the four living c saying Rv 6:1 2226
of the four living c saying, Rv 6:6 2226
the elders and the four living c; Rv 7:11 2226
and a third of the c which Rv 8:9 2938
the four living c and the elders; Rv 14:3 2226
Then one of the four living c gave Rv 15:7 2226
living c fell down and worshiped God Rv 19:4 2226

CREDIT
love you, what c is *that* to you? Lk 6:32 5485
to you, what c is *that* to you? Lk 6:33 5485
to receive, what c is *that* to you? Lk 6:34 5485
so that no one will c me with more 2Co 12:6 3049
For what c is there if, when you 1Pe 2:20 2811

CREDITED
AND IT WAS C TO HIM AS RIGHTEOUSNESS." Ro 4:3 3049
his wage is not c as a favor, but as Ro 4:4 3049
his faith is c as righteousness, Ro 4:5 3049
"FAITH WAS C TO ABRAHAM AS Ro 4:9 3049
How then was it c? While he was Ro 4:10 3049
that righteousness might be c to them, Ro 4:11 3049
Therefore IT WAS ALSO C TO HIM AS Ro 4:22 3049
only was it written that it was c to Ro 4:23 3049
to whom it will be c, as those who Ro 4:24 3049

CREDITOR
you are not to act as a c to him; Ex 22:25 5383
every c shall release what he has Dt 15:2 1167, 4874, 3027

and the **c** has come to take my two	**2Ki 4:1**	5383
Let the **c** seize all that he has,	**Ps 109:11**	5383
borrower, the **c** like the debtor.	**Is 24:2**	5383
CREDITORS		
Or to whom of My **c** did I sell you?	**Is 50:1**	5383
"Will not your **c** rise up	**Hab 2:7**	5391a
CREDITS		
the blessing on the man to whom God **c**	**Ro 4:6**	*3049*
CREEP		
things that **c** on the earth,	**Ezk 38:20**	7430
CREEPING		
cattle and **c** things and beasts of	**Gn 1:24**	7431
and over every **c** thing that creeps	**Gn 1:26**	7431
from man to animals to **c** things	**Gn 6:7**	7431
of every **c** thing of the ground	**Gn 6:20**	7431
and every **c** thing that creeps on	**Gn 7:14**	7431
from man to animals to **c** things	**Gn 7:23**	7431
birds and animals and every **c**	**Gn 8:17**	7431
Every beast, every **c** thing,	**Gn 8:19**	7431
and birds and **c** things and fish.	**1Ki 4:33**	7431
C things and winged fowl;	**Ps 148:10**	7431
every form of **c** things and beasts	**Ezk 8:10**	7431
all the **c** things that creep on the	**Ezk 38:20**	7431
And the **c** things of the ground.	**Hos 2:18**	7431
has left, the **c** locust has eaten;	**Jl 1:4**	3218
And what the **c** locust has left,	**Jl 1:4**	3218
locust has eaten, The **c** locust,	**Jl 2:25**	3218
yourself like the **c** locust,	**Na 3:15**	3218
c locust strips and flies away.	**Na 3:16**	3218
Like **c** things without a ruler over	**Hab 1:14**	7431
CREEPS		
c on the ground after its kind;	**Gn 1:25**	7431
thing that **c** on the earth."	**Gn 1:26**	7430
everything that **c** on the ground,	**Gn 7:8**	7430
c on the earth after its kind,	**Gn 7:14**	7430
thing that **c** on the earth,	**Gn 8:17**	7430
everything that **c** on the ground,	**Gn 9:2**	7430
by anything that **c** on the ground,	**Lv 20:25**	7430
of anything that **c** on the ground,	**Dt 4:18**	7430
CREPT		
persons have **c** in unnoticed,	**Jude 1:4**	*3921*
CRESCENS		
C *has gone* to Galatia, Titus to	**2Tm 4:10**	*2913*
CRESCENT		
and took the **c** ornaments which	**Jg 8:21**	7720
besides the **c** ornaments and the	**Jg 8:26**	7720
anklets, headbands, **c** ornaments,	**Is 3:18**	7720
CRETANS		
C and Arabs—we hear them in our	**Ac 2:11**	*2912*
"**C** are always liars, evil beasts,	**Ti 1:12**	*2912*
CRETE		
we sailed under the shelter of **C**,	**Ac 27:7**	*2914*
reach Phoenix, a harbor of **C**,	**Ac 27:12**	*2914*
anchor and *began* sailing along **C**,	**Ac 27:13**	*2914*
and not to have set sail from **C** and	**Ac 27:21**	*2914*
For this reason I left you in **C**,	**Ti 1:5**	*2914*
CREVICE		
it there in a **c** of the rock."	**Jer 13:4**	5357
CRICKET		
its kinds, and the **c** in its kinds,	**Lv 11:22**	2728
"The **c** shall possess all your	**Dt 28:42**	6767c
CRIED		
he **c** out with an exceedingly great	**Gn 27:34**	6817
people **c** out to Pharaoh for bread;	**Gn 41:55**	6817
those who stood by him, and he **c**,	**Gn 45:1**	7121
of the bondage, and they **c** out;	**Ex 2:23**	2199
Israel came and **c** out to Pharaoh,	**Ex 5:15**	6817
and Moses **c** to the LORD concerning	**Ex 8:12**	6817
sons of Israel **c** out to the LORD.	**Ex 14:10**	6817
Then he **c** out to the LORD, and the	**Ex 15:25**	6817
So Moses **c** out to the LORD,	**Ex 17:4**	6817
people therefore **c** out to Moses,	**Nu 11:2**	6817
Moses **c** out to the LORD,	**Nu 12:13**	6817
lifted up their voices and **c**,	**Nu 14:1**	5414
'But when we **c** out to the LORD, He	**Nu 20:16**	6817
the field, the engaged girl **c** out,	**Dt 22:27**	6817
'Then we **c** to the LORD, the God of	**Dt 26:7**	6817
'But when they **c** out to the LORD,	**Jos 24:7**	6817
the sons of Israel **c** to the LORD,	**Jg 3:9**	2199
the sons of Israel **c** to the LORD,	**Jg 3:15**	2199
The sons of Israel **c** to the LORD;	**Jg 4:3**	6817
the sons of Israel **c** to the LORD.	**Jg 6:6**	2199
c to the LORD on account of Midian,	**Jg 6:7**	2199
right hands for blowing, and **c**,	**Jg 7:20**	7121
sons of Israel **c** out to the LORD,	**Jg 10:10**	2199
oppressed you, you **c** out to Me,	**Jg 10:12**	6817
They **c** to the sons of Dan, who	**Jg 18:23**	7121
the city, and all the city **c** out.	**1Sa 4:13**	2199
to Ekron the Ekronites **c** out,	**1Sa 5:10**	2199
and Samuel **c** to the LORD for	**1Sa 7:9**	2199
your fathers **c** out to the LORD,	**1Sa 12:8**	2199
They **c** out to the LORD and said,	**1Sa 12:10**	2199
and **c** out to the LORD all night.	**1Sa 15:11**	2199
she **c** out with a loud voice;	**1Sa 28:12**	2199
face and **c** out with a loud voice,	**2Sa 19:4**	2199
upon the LORD, Yes, I **c** to my God;	**2Sa 22:7**	7121
He **c** against the altar by the	**1Ki 13:2**	7121
he **c** against the altar in Bethel,	**1Ki 13:4**	7121
and he **c** to the man of God who	**1Ki 13:21**	7121
which he **c** by the word of the LORD	**1Ki 13:32**	7121
So they **c** with a loud voice and	**1Ki 18:28**	7121
by, he **c** to the king and said,	**1Ki 20:39**	6817
him, and Jehoshaphat **c** out.	**1Ki 22:32**	2199
Elisha saw *it* and **c** out,	**2Ki 2:12**	6817
of the prophets **c** out to Elisha,	**2Ki 4:1**	6817
stew, they **c** out and said,	**2Ki 4:40**	6817
and he **c** out and said,	**2Ki 6:5**	6817
on the wall a woman **c** out to him,	**2Ki 6:26**	6817
Athaliah tore her clothes and **c**,	**2Ki 11:14**	7121
and **c** with a loud voice in Judean,	**2Ki 18:28**	7121
Isaiah the prophet **c** to the LORD,	**2Ki 20:11**	7121
they **c** out to God in the battle,	**1Ch 5:20**	2199
so they **c** to the LORD, and the	**2Ch 13:14**	6817
But Jehoshaphat **c** out, and the	**2Ch 18:31**	2199
about this and **c** out to heaven.	**2Ch 32:20**	2199
and they **c** with a loud voice to	**Ne 9:4**	2199
But when they **c** to You in the	**Ne 9:27**	6817
When they **c** again to You, You	**Ne 9:28**	2199
delivered the poor who **c** for help,	**Jb 29:12**	7768
LORD, And **c** to my God for help;	**Ps 18:6**	7768
They **c** for help, but there was	**Ps 18:41**	7768
To You they **c** out and were	**Ps 22:5**	2199
But when he **c** to Him for help, He	**Ps 22:24**	7768
LORD my God, I **c** to You for help,	**Ps 30:2**	7768
my supplications When I **c** to You.	**Ps 31:22**	7768
poor man **c**, and the LORD heard him	**Ps 34:6**	7121
I **c** to Him with my mouth, And He	**Ps 66:17**	7121
I have **c** out by day and in the	**Ps 88:1**	6817
LORD, have **c** out to You for help,	**Ps 88:13**	7768
Then they **c** out to the LORD in	**Ps 107:6**	6817
Then they **c** out to the LORD in	**Ps 107:13**	2199
Then they **c** out to the LORD in	**Ps 107:19**	2199
c to the LORD in their trouble,	**Ps 107:28**	6817
I **c** with all my heart;	**Ps 119:145**	7121
c to You; save me And I shall keep	**Ps 119:146**	7121
In my trouble I **c** to the LORD, And	**Ps 120:1**	7121
of the depths I have **c** to You,	**Ps 130:1**	7121
I **c** out to You, O LORD;	**Ps 142:5**	2199
and **c** with a loud voice in Judean and	**Is 36:13**	7121
Even they have **c** aloud after you.	**Jer 12:6**	7121
They **c** there, 'Pharaoh king of Egypt	**Jer 46:17**	7121
Their heart **c** out to the Lord,	**La 2:18**	6817
Unclean!" they **c** of themselves.	**La 4:15**	7121
Then He **c** out in my hearing with a	**Ezk 9:1**	7121
fell on my face and **c** out saying,	**Ezk 9:8**	2199
Then I fell on my face and **c** out	**Ezk 11:13**	2199
he **c** out with a troubled voice.	**Da 6:20**	2200
and every man **c** to his god,	**Jon 1:5**	2199
I **c** for help from the depth of	**Jon 2:2**	7768
and he **c** out and said,	**Jon 3:4**	7121
Then He **c** out to me and spoke to	**Zch 6:8**	2199
And they **c** out,	**Mt 8:29**	*2896*
And they **c** out in fear.	**Mt 14:26**	*2896*
and beginning to sink, he **c** out,	**Mt 14:30**	*2896*
that Jesus was passing by, **c** out,	**Mt 20:30**	*2896*
but they **c** out all the more,	**Mt 20:31**	*2896*
Jesus **c** out with a loud voice,	**Mt 27:46**	*310*
c out again with a loud voice,	**Mt 27:50**	*2896*
with an unclean spirit; and he **c** out,	**Mk 1:23**	*349*
spirit **c** out with a loud voice and	**Mk 1:26**	*5455*
that it was a ghost, and **c** out;	**Mk 6:49**	*349*
father **c** out and said,	**Mk 9:24**	*2896*
Jesus **c** out with a loud voice,	**Mk 15:34**	*994*
And she **c** out with a loud voice and	**Lk 1:42**	*400*
and he **c** out with a loud voice,	**Lk 4:33**	*349*
he **c** out and fell before Him,	**Lk 8:28**	*349*
"And he **c** out and said,	**Lk 16:24**	*5455*
But they **c** out all together,	**Lk 23:18**	*349*
testified about Him and **c** out,	**Jn 1:15**	*2896*
Jesus **c** out in the temple,	**Jn 7:28**	*2896*
the feast, Jesus stood and **c** out,	**Jn 7:37**	*2896*
He **c** out with a loud voice,	**Jn 11:43**	*2905*
And Jesus **c** out and said,	**Jn 12:44**	*2896*
So they **c** out again,	**Jn 18:40**	*2905*
the officers saw Him, they **c** out saying	**Jn 19:6**	*2905*
release Him, but the Jews **c** out saying	**Jn 19:12**	*2905*
So they **c** out,	**Jn 19:15**	*2905*
But they **c** out with a loud voice,	**Ac 7:57**	*2896*
knees, he **c** out with a loud voice,	**Ac 7:60**	*2896*
But Paul **c** out with a loud voice,	**Ac 16:28**	*5455*
and they **c** out with a loud voice,	**Rv 6:10**	*2896*
and he **c** out with a loud voice to	**Rv 7:2**	*2896*
and he **c** out with a loud voice, as	**Rv 10:3**	*2896*
and when he had **c** out, the seven	**Rv 10:3**	*2896*
and she **c** out, being in labor and	**Rv 12:2**	*2896*
And he **c** out with a mighty voice,	**Rv 18:2**	*2896*
and he **c** out with a loud voice,	**Rv 19:17**	*2896*
CRIES		
about that when he **c** out to Me,	**Ex 22:27**	6817
And my **c** pour out like water.	**Jb 3:24**	7581
"If my land **c** out against me, And	**Jb 31:38**	2199
the needy when he **c** for help,	**Ps 72:12**	7768
of the noisy *streets* she **c** out;	**Pr 1:21**	7121
entrance of the doors, she **c** out:	**Pr 8:3**	7442
My heart **c** out for Moab;	**Is 15:5**	2199
no **c** of joy or jubilant shouting,	**Is 16:10**	7442
and **c** out in her labor pains,	**Is 26:17**	2199
Amid war **c** on the day of battle	**Am 1:14**	8643
war **c** and the sound of a trumpet.	**Am 2:2**	8643
In it the warrior **c** out bitterly.	**Zph 1:14**	6873
Isaiah **c** out concerning Israel,	**Ro 9:27**	*2896*
by you, **c** out *against you;*	**Jas 5:4**	*2896*
CRIME		
"For that would be a lustful **c**;	**Jb 31:11**	2154
O king, I have committed no **c**."	**Da 6:22**	2248
Surely they have committed **c**.	**Hos 6:9**	2154
a matter of wrong or of vicious **c**,	**Ac 18:14**	*4467*
CRIMES		
for the land is full of bloody **c** and	**Ezk 7:23**	4941
not of such **c** as I was expecting,	**Ac 25:18**	*4190*
CRIMINAL		
even to imprisonment as a **c**;	**2Tm 2:9**	*2557*
CRIMINALS		
Two others also, who were **c**,	**Lk 23:32**	*2557*
they crucified Him and the **c**,	**Lk 23:33**	*2557*
One of the **c** who were hanged	**Lk 23:39**	*2557*
CRIMSON		
in purple, **c** and violet *fabrics,*	**2Ch 2:7**	3758
violet, linen and **c** fabrics,	**2Ch 2:14**	3758
violet, purple, **c** and fine linen,	**2Ch 3:14**	3758
Though they are red like **c**,	**Is 1:18**	8438
CRINGE		
your enemies will **c** before you,	**Dt 33:29**	3584
CRIPPLED		
son, had a son **c** in his feet.	**2Sa 4:4**	5223
Jonathan who is **c** in both feet."	**2Sa 9:3**	5223
with them *those who were* lame, **c**,	**Mt 15:30**	*2948*
the mute speaking, the **c** restored,	**Mt 15:31**	*2948*
for you to enter life **c** or lame,	**Mt 18:8**	*2948*
is better for you to enter life **c**,	**Mk 9:43**	*2948*
reception, invite *the* poor, *the* **c**,	**Lk 14:13**	*376b*
poor and **c** and blind and lame.'	**Lk 14:21**	*376b*
CRISPUS		
C, the leader of the synagogue,	**Ac 18:8**	*2921*
none of you except **C** and Gaius,	**1Co 1:14**	*2921*
CRITICIZE		
who **c** will accept instruction.	**Is 29:24**	7279
CROCODILE		
and the gecko, and the **c**,	**Lv 11:30**	3581a
CROCUS		
will rejoice and blossom; Like the **c**	**Is 35:1**	2261
CROOKED		
are a perverse and **c** generation.	**Dt 32:5**	6618
c You show Yourself astute.	**Ps 18:26**	6141
who turn aside to their **c** ways,	**Ps 125:5**	6128
Whose paths are **c**, And who are	**Pr 2:15**	6141
is nothing **c** or perverted in them.	**Pr 8:8**	6617
He who has a **c** mind finds no good,	**Pr 17:20**	6141
The way of a guilty man is **c**,	**Pr 21:8**	2019
he who is **c** though he be rich.	**Pr 28:6**	6141, 1870
he who is **c** will fall all at once.	**Pr 28:18**	6140, 1870
What is **c** cannot be straightened and	**Ec 1:15**	5791
They have made their paths **c**,	**Is 59:8**	6140
He has made my paths **c**.	**La 3:9**	5753a
THE C WILL BECOME STRAIGHT,	**Lk 3:5**	*4646*
c the straight ways of the Lord?	**Ac 13:10**	*1294*
of a **c** and perverse generation,	**Php 2:15**	*4646*
CROOKEDNESS		
But the **c** of the treacherous will	**Pr 11:3**	5558
CROP		
take away its **c** with its feathers and	**Lv 1:16**	4760
your vineyard and gather in its **c**,	**Lv 25:3**	8393
bring forth the **c** for three years.	**Lv 25:21**	8393
still eat old things from the **c**,	**Lv 25:22**	8393
ninth year when its **c** comes in.	**Lv 25:22**	8393
when the spring **c** began to sprout.	**Am 7:1**	3954
the spring **c** *was* after the king's	**Am 7:1**	3954
on the good soil and yielded a **c**,	**Mt 13:8**	*2590*
choked it, and it yielded no **c**.	**Mk 4:7**	*2590*
yielded a **c** and produced thirty,	**Mk 4:8**	*2590*
"But when the **c** permits, he	**Mk 4:29**	*2590*
a **c** a hundred times as great."	**Lk 8:8**	*2590*
CROPS		
gathered in the **c** of the land,	**Lv 23:39**	8393
land shall have all its **c** to eat.	**Lv 25:7**	8393
shall eat its **c** out of the field.	**Lv 25:12**	8393
to the number of years of **c**.	**Lv 25:15**	8393
number of **c** he is selling to you.	**Lv 25:16**	8393
do not sow or gather in our **c**?"	**Lv 25:20**	8393
and we will forego *the* **c**	**Ne 10:31**	
eat, And let my **c** be uprooted.	**Jb 31:8**	6631
also their **c** to the grasshopper And	**Ps 78:46**	2981
"The soil produces **c** by itself;	**Mk 4:28**	*2592*
I have no place to store my **c**?'	**Lk 12:17**	*2590*
thresh in hope of sharing *the* **c**.	**1Co 9:10**	
to receive his share of the **c**.	**2Tm 2:6**	*2590*
CROSS		
and all of you armed men **c** over	**Nu 32:21**	5674a
will **c** over in the presence of the	**Nu 32:27**	5674a
will **c** with you over the Jordan in	**Nu 32:29**	5674a
will not **c** over with you armed,	**Nu 32:30**	5674a
"We ourselves will **c** over armed	**Nu 32:32**	5674a
'When you **c** over the Jordan into	**Nu 33:51**	5674a
'When you **c** the Jordan into the	**Nu 35:10**	5674a
'Now arise and **c** over the brook	**Dt 2:13**	5674a
you shall **c** over Ar, the border	**Dt 2:18**	5674a
until I **c** over the Jordan into the	**Dt 2:29**	5674a
all you valiant men shall **c** over	**Dt 3:18**	5674a
into which you are about to **c**.	**Dt 3:21**	5674a
c over and see the fair land that	**Dt 3:25**	5674a
you shall not **c** over this Jordan.	**Dt 3:27**	5674a
that I would not **c** the Jordan,	**Dt 4:21**	5674a
land, I shall not **c** the Jordan,	**Dt 4:22**	5674a
but you shall **c** and take	**Dt 4:22**	5674a
you are about to **c** to possess it;	**Dt 11:8**	5674a
you are about to **c** to possess it,	**Dt 11:11**	5674a
"For you are about to **c** the	**Dt 11:31**	5674a
"When you **c** the Jordan and live	**Dt 12:10**	5674a
the day when you **c** the Jordan	**Dt 27:2**	5674a
of this law, when you **c** over,	**Dt 27:3**	5674a
it shall be when you **c** the Jordan,	**Dt 27:4**	5674a
"When you **c** the Jordan, these	**Dt 27:12**	5674a
'Who will **c** the sea for us to get	**Dt 30:13**	5674a
'You shall not **c** this Jordan.'	**Dt 31:2**	5674a
your God who will **c** ahead of you;	**Dt 31:3**	5674a
the one who will **c** ahead of you,	**Dt 31:3**	5674a
to **c** the Jordan to possess."	**Dt 31:13**	5674a
to **c** the Jordan to possess."	**Dt 32:47**	5674a
therefore arise, **c** this Jordan,	**Jos 1:2**	5674a

days you are to **c** this Jordan, **Jos 1:11** 5674a
but you shall **c** before your **Jos 1:14** 5674a
and **c** over ahead of the people." **Jos 3:6** 5674a
set out from their tents to **c** the Jordan **Jos 3:14** 5674a
"**C** again to the ark of the LORD **Jos 4:5** 5674a
then **c** into the land of the **Jos 22:19** 5674a
and did not allow anyone to **c**. **Jg 3:28** 5674a
"Why did you **c** over to fight **Jg 12:1** 5674a
of Ephraim said, "Let me **c** over," **Jg 12:5** 5674a
"Come and let us **c** over to the **1Sa 14:1** 5674a
by which Jonathan sought to **c** over **1Sa 14:4** 5674a
"Come and let us **c** over to the **1Sa 14:6** 5674a
we will **c** over to the men and **1Sa 14:8** 5674a
exhausted to **c** the brook Besor remained **1Sa 30:10** 5674a
but by all means **c** over, **2Sa 17:16** 5674a
"Arise and **c** over the water **2Sa 17:21** 5674a
as he was about to **c** the Jordan. **2Sa 19:18** 5674a
"You **c** over with me and I will **2Sa 19:33** 5674a
c over the Jordan with the king. **2Sa 19:36** 5674a
him **c** over with my lord the king, **2Sa 19:37** 5674a
"Chimham shall **c** over with me, **2Sa 19:38** 5674a
out and **c** over the brook Kidron, **1Ki 2:37** 5674a
Uncover the leg, **c** the rivers. **Is 47:2** 5674a
For the redeemed to **c** over? **Is 51:10** 5674a
"For **c** to the coastlands of **Jer 2:10** 5674a
decree, so it cannot **c** over it. **Jer 5:22** 5674a
roar, yet they cannot **c** over it. **Jer 5:22** 5674a
to **c** over to the sons of Ammon. **Jer 41:10** 5674a
Gilgal, Nor **c** over to Beersheba; **Am 5:5** 5674a
"And he who does not take his **c** **Mt 10:38** *4716*
deny himself, and take up his **c** and **Mt 16:24** *4716*
into service to bear His **c**. **Mt 27:32** *4716*
of God, come down from the **c**." **Mt 27:40** *4716*
let Him now come down from the **c**, **Mt 27:42** *4716*
deny himself, and take up his **c** and **Mk 8:34** *4716*
to bear His **c**. **Mk 15:21** *4716*
and come down from the **c**!" **Mk 15:30** *4716*
Israel, now come down from the **c**, **Mk 15:32** *4716*
himself, and take up his **c** daily and **Lk 9:23** *4716*
"Whoever does not carry his own **c** **Lk 14:27** *4716*
none may **c** over from there to us.' **Lk 16:26** *1276*
him the **c** to carry behind Jesus. **Lk 23:26** *4716*
started to **c** the sea to Capernaum. **Jn 6:17** *4008*
He went out, bearing His own **c**, **Jn 19:17** *4716*
and put it on the **c**. **Jn 19:19** *4716*
by the **c** of Jesus were His mother, **Jn 19:25** *4716*
remain on the **c** on the Sabbath **Jn 19:31** *4716*
you nailed to a **c** by the hands of **Ac 2:23** *4362*
to death by hanging Him on a **c**. **Ac 5:30** *3586*
to death by hanging Him on a **c**. **Ac 10:39** *3586*
from the **c** and laid Him in a tomb. **Ac 13:29** *3586*
that the **c** of Christ would not be **1Co 1:17** *4716*
word of the **c** is foolishness **1Co 1:18** *4716*
block of the **c** has been abolished. **Ga 5:11** *4716*
be persecuted for the **c** of Christ. **Ga 6:12** *4716*
in the **c** of our Lord Jesus Christ, **Ga 6:14** *4716*
in one body to God through the **c**, **Eph 2:16** *4716*
point of death, even death on a **c**. **Php 2:8** *4716*
are enemies of the **c** of Christ, **Php 3:18** *4716*
peace through the blood of His **c**; **Col 1:20** *4716*
way, having nailed it to the **c**. **Col 2:14** *4716*
joy set before Him endured the **c**, **Heb 12:2** *4716*
our sins in His body on the **c**, **1Pe 2:24** *3586*

CROSSED

arose and **c** the *Euphrates* River, **Gn 31:21** 5674a
my staff *only* I **c** this Jordan, **Gn 32:10** 5674a
and **c** the ford of the Jabbok. **Gn 32:22** 5674a
upon him just as he **c** over Penuel, **Gn 32:31** 5674a
So we **c** over the brook Zered. **Dt 2:13** 5674a
until we **c** over the brook Zered was **Dt 2:14** 5674a
and **c** over and came to Joshua **Jos 2:23** 5674a
they lodged there before they **c**. **Jos 3:1** 5674a
So the people **c** opposite Jericho. **Jos 3:16** 5674a
while all Israel **c** on dry ground, **Jos 3:17** 5674a
when it **c** the Jordan, the waters **Jos 4:7** 5674a
And the people hurried and **c**; **Jos 4:10** 5674a
the priests **c** before the people. **Jos 4:11** 5674a
Manasseh **c** over in battle array **Jos 4:12** 5674a
c for battle before the LORD to **Jos 4:13** 5674a
c this Jordan on dry ground.' **Jos 4:22** 5674a
Jordan before you until you had **c**, **Jos 4:23** 5674a
dried up before us until we had **c**; **Jos 4:23** 5674a
sons of Israel until they had **c**, **Jos 5:1** 5674a
'You **c** the Jordan and came to **Jos 24:11** 5674a
and they **c** over and camped in the **Jg 6:33** 5674a
him came to the Jordan *and* **c** over, **Jg 8:4** 5674a
and **c** over into Shechem; **Jg 9:26** 5674a
The sons of Ammon **c** the Jordan **Jg 10:9** 5674a
So Jephthah **c** over to the sons of **Jg 11:32** 5674a
and they **c** to Zaphon and said to **Jg 12:1** 5674a
I took my life in my hands and **c** **Jg 12:3** 5674a
Also *some of* the Hebrews **c** the **1Sa 13:7** 5674a
David **c** over to the other side and **1Sa 26:13** 5674a
So David arose and **c** over, **1Sa 27:2** 5674a
so they **c** the Jordan, walked all **2Sa 2:29** 5674a
Israel together and **c** the Jordan, **2Sa 10:17** 5674a
"They have **c** the brook of water." **2Sa 17:20** 5674a
with him arose and **c** the Jordan; **2Sa 17:22** 5674a
remained who had not **c** the Jordan. **2Sa 17:22** 5674a
And Absalom **c** the Jordan, he and **2Sa 17:24** 5674a
All the people **c** over the Jordan **2Sa 19:39** 5674a
the Jordan and the king **c** too. **2Sa 19:39** 5674a
They **c** the Jordan and camped **2Sa 24:5** 5674a
never **c** him at any time by asking, **1Ki 1:6** 6087a
two of them **c** over on dry ground. **2Ki 2:8** 5674a
When they had **c** over, **2Ki 2:9** 5674a
and Elisha **c** over. **2Ki 2:14** 5674a
Then Joram **c** over to Zair, and all **2Ki 8:21** 5674a
These are the ones who **c** the **1Ch 12:15** 5674a
Israel together and **c** the Jordan, **1Ch 19:17** 5674a
Then Jehoram **c** over with his **2Ch 21:9** 5674a
Your messengers **c** the sea **Is 23:2** 5674a
no one **c** And where no man dwelt?' **Jer 2:6** 5674a
Getting into a boat, Jesus **c** over **Mt 9:1** *1276*
When they had **c** over, **Mt 14:34** *1276*
When Jesus had **c** over again in **Mk 5:21** *1276*
When they had **c** over they came **Mk 6:53** *1276*
the next day we **c** over to Samos; **Ac 20:15** *3846*

CROSSING

on Manasseh's head, **c** his hands, **Gn 48:14** 7919b
discouraging the sons of Israel from **c** **Nu 32:7** 5674a
You are **c** over the Jordan today to **Dt 9:1** 5674a
your God who is **c** over before you **Dt 9:3** 5674a
c the Jordan to enter and possess it. **Dt 30:18** 5674a
is **c** over ahead of you into the Jordan. **Jos 3:11** 5674a
nation had finished **c** the Jordan. **Jos 3:17** 5674a
nation had finished **c** the Jordan, **Jos 4:1** 5674a
all the people had finished **c**, **Jos 4:11** 5674a
Then they kept **c** the ford to bring **2Sa 19:18** 5674a
his servants **c** over toward him; **2Sa 24:20** 5674a
found a ship **c** over to Phoenicia, **Ac 21:2** *1276*

CROUCH

Him **c** the helpers of Rahab. **Jb 9:13** 7817
When they **c** in *their* dens *And* lie **Jb 38:40** 7817
Nothing *remains* but to **c** among the **Is 10:4** 3766

CROUCHED

and he **c** down on the earth and **1Ki 18:42** 1457

CROUCHES

He **c**, he bows down, And the **Ps 10:10** 1794

CROUCHING

not do well, sin is **c** at the door; **Gn 4:7** 7257

CROW

the rooster will not **c** today until **Lk 22:34** *5455*
I say to you, a rooster will not **c** **Jn 13:38** *5455*

CROWD

"They will incite a **c** against you and **Ezk 16:40** 6951
They do not **c** each other, **Jl 2:8** 1766
Now when Jesus saw a **c** around Him, **Mt 8:18** *3793*
and the **c** in noisy disorder, **Mt 9:23** *3793*
But when the **c** had been sent out, **Mt 9:25** *3793*
and the whole **c** was standing on **Mt 13:2** *3793*
he feared the **c**, because they **Mt 14:5** *3793*
He saw a large **c**, and felt **Mt 14:14** *3793*
After Jesus called the **c** to Him, He **Mt 15:10** *3793*
So the **c** marveled as they saw **Mt 15:31** *3793*
place to satisfy such a large **c**?" **Mt 15:33** *3793*
When they came to the **c**, a man came **Mt 17:14** *3793*
a large **c** followed Him. **Mt 20:29** *3793*
The **c** sternly told them to be quiet, **Mt 20:31** *3793*
Most of the **c** spread their coats in **Mt 21:8** *3793*
came up accompanied by a large **c** with **Mt 26:47** *3793*
washed his hands in front of the **c**, **Mt 27:24** *3793*
to get to Him because of the **c**, **Mk 2:4** *3793*
stand ready for Him because of the **c**, **Mk 3:9** *3793*
so that they would not **c** Him; **Mk 3:9** *2346*
And He came home, and the **c** gathered **Mk 3:20** *3793*
A **c** was sitting around Him, and they **Mk 3:32** *3793*
And such a very large **c** gathered to **Mk 4:1** *3793*
and the whole **c** was by the sea on **Mk 4:1** *3793*
Leaving the **c**, they took Him along **Mk 4:36** *3793*
a large **c** gathered around Him; **Mk 5:21** *3793*
and a large **c** was following Him **Mk 5:24** *3793*
came up in the **c** behind *Him* **Mk 5:27** *3793*
turned around in the **c** and said, **Mk 5:30** *3793*
"You see the **c** pressing in on You, **Mk 5:31** *3793*
He saw a large **c**, and He felt **Mk 6:34** *3793*
while He Himself was sending the **c** **Mk 6:45** *3793*
After He called the **c** to Him again, **Mk 7:14** *3793*
When he had left the **c** *and* **Mk 7:17** *3793*
Jesus took him aside from the **c**, **Mk 7:33** *3793*
when there was again a large **c** **Mk 8:1** *3793*
And He summoned the **c** with His **Mk 8:34** *3793*
they saw a large **c** around them, **Mk 9:14** *3793*
when the entire **c** saw Him, **Mk 9:15** *3793*
And one of the **c** answered Him, **Mk 9:17** *3793*
that a **c** was rapidly gathering, **Mk 9:25** *3793*
with His disciples and a large **c**, **Mk 10:46** *3793*
for the whole **c** was astonished at His **Mk 11:18** *3793*
large **c** enjoyed listening to Him. **Mk 12:37** *3793*
came up accompanied by a **c** with **Mk 14:43** *3793*
The **c** went up and began asking him **Mk 15:8** *3793*
the chief priests stirred up the **c** **Mk 15:11** *3793*
Wishing to satisfy the **c**, Pilate **Mk 15:15** *3793*
Now it happened that while the **c** was **Lk 5:1** *3793*
to bring him in because of the **c**, **Lk 5:19** *3793*
into the middle *of the* **c**, in **Lk 5:19**
and there was a great **c** of **Lk 5:29** *3793*
and *there was* a large **c** of His **Lk 6:17** *3793*
and turned and said to the **c** that was **Lk 7:9** *3793*
accompanied by a large **c**. **Lk 7:11** *3793*
c from the city was with her. **Lk 7:12** *3793*
When a large **c** was coming together, **Lk 8:4** *3793*
to get to Him because of the **c**. **Lk 8:19** *3793*
"Send the **c** away, that they may go **Lk 9:12** *3793*
a large **c** met Him. **Lk 9:37** *3793*
And a man from the **c** shouted, saying, **Lk 9:38** *3793*
women in the **c** raised her voice and **Lk 11:27** *3793*
Someone in the **c** said to Him, **Lk 12:13** *3793*
began saying to the **c** in response, **Lk 13:14** *3793*
and the entire **c** was rejoicing over **Lk 13:17** *3793*
Now hearing a **c** going by, he *began* **Lk 18:36** *3793*
and was unable because of the **c**, **Lk 19:3** *3793*
the whole **c** of the disciples began to **Lk 19:37** *4128*
Some of the Pharisees in the **c** said **Lk 19:39** *3793*
betray Him to them apart from the **c**. **Lk 22:6** *3793*
a **c** *came*, and the one called **Lk 22:47** *3793*
And following Him was a large **c** of **Lk 23:27** *4128*
while there was a **c** in *that* place. **Jn 5:13** *3793*
A large **c** followed Him, because they **Jn 6:2** *3793*
up His eyes and seeing that a large **c** **Jn 6:5** *3793*
The next day the **c** that stood on **Jn 6:22** *3793*
So when the **c** saw that Jesus was not **Jn 6:24** *3793*
The **c** answered, "You have a demon! **Jn 7:20** *3793*
But many of the **c** believed in Him; **Jn 7:31** *3793*
The Pharisees heard the **c** muttering **Jn 7:32** *3793*
So a division occurred in the **c** **Jn 7:43** *3793*
"But this **c** which does not know **Jn 7:49** *3793*
The large **c** of the Jews then learned **Jn 12:9** *3793*
On the next day the large **c** who had **Jn 12:12** *3793*
So the **c** *of people* who stood by **Jn 12:29** *3793*
The **c** then answered Him, "We have **Jn 12:34** *3793*
And when this sound occurred, the **c** **Ac 2:6** *4128*
robes and rushed out into the **c**, **Ac 14:14** *3793*
c rose up together against them, **Ac 16:22** *3793*
They stirred up the **c** and the **Ac 17:8** *3793*
the **c** concluded *it was* Alexander, **Ac 19:33** *3793*
After quieting the **c**, the town clerk **Ac 19:35** *3793*
began to stir up all the **c** **Ac 21:27** *3793*
But among the **c** some were shouting **Ac 21:34** *3793*
purified, without *any* **c** or uproar. **Ac 24:18** *3793*

CROWDING

are **c** and pressing in on You." **Lk 8:45** *4912*

CROWDS

Large **c** followed Him from Galilee **Mt 4:25** *3793*
When Jesus saw the **c**, He went up on **Mt 5:1** *3793*
the **c** were amazed at His teaching; **Mt 7:28** *3793*
large **c** followed Him. **Mt 8:1** *3793*
But when the **c** saw *this*, they **Mt 9:8** *3793*
and the **c** were amazed, *and were* **Mt 9:33** *3793*
Jesus began to speak to the **c** about **Mt 11:7** *3793*
All the **c** were amazed, and were **Mt 12:23** *3793*
While He was still speaking to the **c**, **Mt 12:46** *3793*
And large **c** gathered to Him, so He **Mt 13:2** *3793*
All these things Jesus spoke to the **c** **Mt 13:34** *3793*
Then He left the **c** and went into **Mt 13:36** *3793*
so send the **c** away, that they may go **Mt 14:15** *3793*
the disciples *gave them* to the **c**, **Mt 14:19** *3793*
while He sent the **c** away. **Mt 14:22** *3793*
After He had sent the **c** away, He **Mt 14:23** *3793*
And large **c** came to Him, bringing **Mt 15:30** *3793*
And sending away the **c**, Jesus got **Mt 15:39** *3793*
and large **c** followed Him, and He **Mt 19:2** *3793*
The **c** going ahead of Him, and those **Mt 21:9** *3793*
And the **c** were saying, "This is **Mt 21:11** *3793*
When the **c** heard *this*, they were **Mt 22:33** *3793*
Then Jesus spoke to the **c** and to His **Mt 23:1** *3793*
At that time Jesus said to the **c**, **Mt 26:55** *3793*
and the elders persuaded the **c** to ask **Mt 27:20** *3793*
c gathered around Him again, **Mk 10:1** *3793*
So he *began* saying to the **c** who **Lk 3:7** *3793*
And the **c** were questioning him, **Lk 3:10** *3793*
and the **c** were searching for Him, **Lk 4:42** *3793*
and large **c** were gathering to hear **Lk 5:15** *3793*
He began to speak to the **c** about John, **Lk 7:24** *3793*
the **c** were pressing against Him. **Lk 8:42** *3793*
But the **c** were aware of this **Lk 9:11** *3793*
and the **c** were amazed. **Lk 11:14** *3793*
As the **c** were increasing, He **Lk 11:29** *3793*
And He was also saying to the **c**, **Lk 12:54** *3793*
Now large **c** were going along with Him; **Lk 14:25** *3793*
said to the chief priests and the **c**, **Lk 23:4** *3793*
And all the **c** who came together for **Lk 23:48** *3793*
There was much grumbling among the **c** **Jn 7:12** *3793*
The **c** with one accord were giving **Ac 8:6** *3793*
But when the Jews saw the **c**, **Ac 13:45** *3793*
When the **c** saw what Paul had done, **Ac 14:11** *3793*
to offer sacrifice with the **c**. **Ac 14:13** *3793*
restrained the **c** from offering sacrifice **Ac 14:18** *3793*
and having won over the **c**, they **Ac 14:19** *3793*
agitating and stirring up the **c**. **Ac 17:13** *3793*

CROWED

And immediately a rooster **c**. **Mt 26:74** *5455*
a rooster **c** a second time. **Mk 14:72** *5455*
he was still speaking, a rooster **c**. **Lk 22:60** *5455*
and immediately a rooster **c**. **Jn 18:27** *5455*

CROWN

And on the **c** of the head of the **Gn 49:26** 6936
and put the holy **c** on the turban. **Ex 29:6** 5145
plate of the holy **c** of pure gold, **Ex 39:30** 5145
the golden plate, the holy **c**, **Lv 8:9** 5145
your foot to the **c** of your head. **Dt 28:35** 6936
And to the **c** of the head of the **Dt 33:16** 6936
the arm, also the **c** of the head. **Dt 33:20** 6936
And I took the **c** which *was* on his **2Sa 1:10** 5145
the **c** of their king from his head; **2Sa 12:30** 5850
the sole of his foot to the **c** of his head **2Sa 14:25** 6936
the **c** at the top *was* a cubit, **1Ki 7:31** 3805
son out and put the **c** on him and **2Ki 11:12** 5145
the **c** of their king from his head, **1Ch 20:2** 5850
king's son and put the **c** on him, **2Ch 23:11** 5145
Vashti before the king with *her* royal **c** **Es 1:11** 3804
so that he set the royal **c** on her **Es 2:17** 3804
head a royal **c** has been placed; **Es 6:8** 3804
with a large **c** of gold and a **Es 8:15** 5850
of his foot to the **c** of his head. **Jb 2:7** 6936
And removed the **c** from my head. **Jb 19:9** 5850
would bind it to myself like a **c**. **Jb 31:36** 5850
You **c** him with glory and majesty! **Ps 8:5** 5849b
set a **c** of fine gold on his head. **Ps 21:3** 5850
The hairy **c** of him who goes on in **Ps 68:21** 6936
have profaned his **c** in the dust. **Ps 89:39** 5145
upon himself his **c** shall shine." **Ps 132:18** 5145
present you with a **c** of beauty." **Pr 4:9** 5850

wife is the **c** of her husband, **Pr 12:4** 5850
The **c** of the wise is their riches, **Pr 14:24** 5850
A gray head is a **c** of glory; **Pr 16:31** 5850
are the **c** of old men, **Pr 17:6** 5850
a **c** *endure* to all generations. **Pr 27:24** 5145
gaze on King Solomon with the **c** **SS 3:11** 5850
c of the drunkards of Ephraim, **Is 28:1** 5850
The proud **c** of the drunkards of **Is 28:3** 5850
of hosts will become a beautiful **c** **Is 28:5** 5850
You will also be a **c** of beauty in **Is 62:3** 5850
Have shaved the **c** of your head. **Jer 2:16** 6936
c Has come down from your head." **Jer 13:18** 5850
The **c** has fallen from our head; **La 5:16** 5850
and a beautiful **c** on your head. **Ezk 16:12** 5850
the turban and take off the **c**; **Ezk 21:26** 5850
silver and gold, make an *ornate* **c** and **Zch 6:11** 5850
"Now the **c** will become a reminder **Zch 6:14** 5850
For *they are as* the stones of a **c**, **Zch 9:16** 5145
And after twisting together a **c** of thorns, **Mt 27:29** *4735*
and after twisting a **c** of thorns, **Mk 15:17** *4735*
And the soldiers twisted together a **c** of **Jn 19:2** *4735*
c of thorns and the purple robe. **Jn 19:5** *4735*
whom I long *to see,* my joy and **c**, **Php 4:1** *4735*
hope or joy or **c** of exultation? **1Th 2:19** *4735*
up for me the **c** of righteousness, **2Tm 4:8** *4735*
he will receive the **c** of life which **Jas 1:12** *4735*
receive the unfading **c** of glory. **1Pe 5:4** *4735*
and I will give you the **c** of life. **Rv 2:10** *4735*
so that no one will take your **c**. **Rv 3:11** *4735*
and a **c** was given to him, **Rv 6:2** *4735*
on her head a **c** of twelve stars; **Rv 12:1** *4735*
having a golden **c** on His head and **Rv 14:14** *4735*

CROWNED
have **c** the year with Your bounty, **Ps 65:11** 5849b
the sensible are **c** with knowledge. **Pr 14:18** 3803
c him On the day of his wedding, **SS 3:11** 5849b
HAVE **C** HIM WITH GLORY AND HONOR, **Heb 2:7** *4737*
of death **c** with glory and honor, **Heb 2:9** *4737*

CROWNS
Who **c** you with lovingkindness and **Ps 103:4** 5849b
"Your head **c** you like Carmel, And **SS 7:5** 5921
against Tyre, the bestower of **c**, **Is 23:8** 5849b
and beautiful **c** on their heads. **Ezk 23:42** 5850
and golden **c** on their heads. **Rv 4:4** *4735*
cast their **c** before the throne, **Rv 4:10** *4735*
heads appeared to be **c** like gold, **Rv 9:7** *4735*

CROWS
this *very* night, before a rooster **c**, **Mt 26:34** *5455*
"Before a rooster **c**, you will deny **Mt 26:75** *5455*
the rooster **c**, or in the morning **Mk 13:35** *219*
very night, before a rooster **c** twice, **Mk 14:30** *5455*
"Before a rooster **c** twice, you will **Mk 14:72** *5455*
"Before a rooster **c** today, you will **Lk 22:61** *5455*

CRUCIBLE
The **c** is for silver and the **Pr 27:21** 4715

CRUCIFIED
he handed Him over to be **c**. **Mt 27:26** *4717*
And when they had **c** Him, **Mt 27:35** *4717*
time two robbers were **c** with Him, **Mt 27:38** *4717*
robbers who had been **c** with Him **Mt 27:44** *4957*
looking for Jesus who has been **c**. **Mt 28:5** *4717*
he handed Him over to be **c**. **Mk 15:15** *4717*
And they **c** Him, and divided up His **Mk 15:24** *4717*
the third hour when they **c** Him. **Mk 15:25** *4717*
They **c** two robbers with Him, **Mk 15:27** *4717*
Those who were **c** with Him were **Mk 15:32** *4957*
the Nazarene, who has been **c**. **Mk 16:6** *4717*
loud voices asking that He be **c**. **Lk 23:23** *4717*
they **c** Him and the criminals, **Lk 23:33** *4717*
the hands of sinful men, and be **c**, **Lk 24:7** *4717*
the sentence of death, and **c** Him. **Lk 24:20** *4717*
handed Him over to them to be **c**. **Jn 19:16** *4717*
There they **c** Him, and with Him two **Jn 19:18** *4717*
Jesus was **c** was near the city; **Jn 19:20** *4717*
soldiers, when they had **c** Jesus, **Jn 19:23** *4717*
the other who was **c** with Him; **Jn 19:32** *4957*
where He was **c** there was a garden, **Jn 19:41** *4717*
this Jesus whom you **c**." **Ac 2:36** *4717*
Christ the Nazarene, whom you **c**, **Ac 4:10** *4717*
that our old self was **c** with *Him,* **Ro 6:6** *4957*
Paul was not **c** for you, was he? **1Co 1:13** *4717*
but we preach Christ **c**, **1Co 1:23** *4717*
except Jesus Christ, and Him **c**. **1Co 2:2** *4717*
not have **c** the Lord of glory; **1Co 2:8** *4717*
He was **c** because of weakness, **2Co 13:4** *4717*
"I have been **c** with Christ; **Ga 2:20** *4957*
was publicly portrayed *as* **c**? **Ga 3:1** *4717*
belong to Christ Jesus have **c** the flesh **Ga 5:24** *4717*
which the world has been **c** to me, **Ga 6:14** *4717*
where also their Lord was **c**. **Rv 11:8** *4717*

CRUCIFIXION
Man is *to be* handed over for **c**." **Mt 26:2** *4717*

CRUCIFY
to mock and scourge and **c** *Him,* **Mt 20:19** *4717*
some of them you will kill and **c**, **Mt 23:34** *4717*
They all said, "**C** Him!" **Mt 27:22** *4717*
more, saying, "**C** Him!" **Mt 27:23** *4717*
on Him, and led Him away to **c** Him. **Mt 27:31** *4717*
They shouted back, "**C** Him!" **Mk 15:13** *4717*
they shouted all the more, "**C** Him!" **Mk 15:14** *4717*
And they led Him out to **c** Him. **Mk 15:20** *4717*
"**C**, crucify Him!" **Lk 23:21** *4717*
"Crucify, **c** Him!" **Lk 23:21** *4717*
they cried out saying, "**C**, crucify!" **Jn 19:6** *4717*
they cried out saying, "Crucify, **c**!" **Jn 19:6** *4717*
"Take Him yourselves and **c** Him, **Jn 19:6** *4717*
and I have authority to **c** You?" **Jn 19:10** *4717*

with *Him,* away with *Him,* **c** Him!" **Jn 19:15** *4717*
"Shall I **c** your King?" **Jn 19:15** *4717*
c to themselves the Son of God and **Heb 6:6** *388*

CRUEL
And their wrath, for it is **c**. **Gn 49:7** 7185
their despondency and **c** bondage. **Ex 6:9** 7186
"You have become **c** to me; **Jb 30:21** 393
And your years to the **c** one; **Pr 5:9** 394
But the **c** man does himself harm. **Pr 11:17** 394
the compassion of the wicked is **c**. **Pr 12:10** 394
So a **c** messenger will be sent **Pr 17:11** 394
the day of the LORD is coming, **C**, **Is 13:9** 394
into the hand of a **c** master, **Is 19:4** 7186
They are **c** and have no mercy; **Jer 6:23** 394
With the punishment of a **c** one, **Jer 30:14** 394
They are **c** and have no mercy. **Jer 50:42** 394
daughter of my people has become **c** **La 4:3** 393

CRUELLY
"She treats her young **c**, **Jb 39:16** 7188
my daughter is **c** demon-possessed." **Mt 15:22** *2560*

CRUMBLED
was dry *and* had become **c**. **Jos 9:5** 5350
it is dry and has become **c**. **Jos 9:12** 5350

CRUMBLES
"But the falling mountain **c** away, **Jb 14:18** 5034b

CRUMBS
but even the dogs feed on the **c** **Mt 15:27** *5589*
table feed on the children's **c**." **Mk 7:28** *5589*
and longing to be fed with the **c** **Lk 16:21**

CRUSH
And will **c** their bones in pieces, **Nu 24:8** 1633b
c through the forehead of Moab, **Nu 24:17** 4272
that God were willing to **c** me, **Jb 6:9** 1792
torment me And **c** me with words? **Jb 19:2** 1792
forgets that a foot may **c** them, **Jb 39:15** 2115
of the needy And **c** the oppressor. **Ps 72:4** 1792
c his adversaries before him, **Ps 89:23** 3807
They **c** Your people, O LORD, And **Ps 94:5** 1792
Or **c** the afflicted at the gate; **Pr 22:22** 1792
But the LORD was pleased To **c** Him, **Is 53:10** 1792
c them with twofold destruction! **Jer 17:18** 7665
time against me To **c** my young men; **La 1:15** 7665
To **c** under His feet All the **La 3:34** 1792
c and break all these in pieces. **Da 2:40** 1855
it will **c** and put an end to all **Da 2:44** 1855
earth and tread it down and **c** it. **Da 7:23** 1855
oppress the poor, who **c** the needy, **Am 4:1** 7533
will soon **c** Satan under your feet. **Ro 16:20** *4937*

CRUSHED
or eczema or scabs or **c** testicles. **Lv 21:20** 4790
bruised or **c** or torn or cut, **Lv 22:24** 3807
do, and **c** you from Seir to Hormah. **Dt 1:44** 3807
and burned it with fire and **c** it, **Dt 9:21** 3807
but oppressed and **c** continually. **Dt 28:33** 7533
c the sons of Israel that year; **Jg 10:8** 7533
I **c** *and* stamped them as the mire **2Sa 22:43** 1854
rely on the staff of this **c** reed, **2Ki 18:21** 7533
timber, 20,000 kors of **c** wheat and **2Ch 2:10** 4347
"Nation was **c** by nation, and **2Ch 15:6** 3807
c *it* and burned *it* at the brook **2Ch 15:16** 1854
dust, Who are **c** before the moth! **Jb 4:19** 1792
of the orphans has been **c**. **Jb 22:9** 1792
them in the night, And they are **c**. **Jb 34:25** 1792
saves those who are **c** in spirit. **Ps 34:18** 1793a
I am benumbed and badly **c**; **Ps 38:8** 1794
have **c** us in a place of jackals And **Ps 44:19** 1794
You **c** the heads of Leviathan; You **Ps 74:14** 7533
You Yourself **c** Rahab like one who is **Ps 89:10** 1792
My soul is **c** with longing After **Ps 119:20** 1638
He has **c** my life to the ground; **Ps 143:3** 1792
with a pestle along with **c** grain, **Pr 27:22** 7383
broken and the golden bowl is **c**, **Ec 12:6** 7533
and the wheel at the cistern is **c**; **Ec 12:6** 7533
and sinners will be **c** together, **Is 1:28** 7667
the pillars *of Egypt* will be **c**; **Is 19:10** 1792
O **c** virgin daughter of Sidon. **Is 23:12** 6231
Grain for bread is **c**, **Is 28:28** 1854
rely on the staff of this **c** reed, **Is 36:6** 7533
"He will not be disheartened or **c** Until **Is 42:4** 7533
He was **c** for our iniquities; **Is 53:5** 1792
which is **c** a snake breaks forth. **Is 59:5** 2115
has been **c** with a mighty blow, **Jer 14:17** 7665
For all your lovers have been **c**. **Jer 22:20** 7665
Babylon has devoured me *and* **c** me, **Jer 51:34** 2000
and **c** you from every side, **Ezk 36:3** 7602b
feet of iron and clay and **c** them. **Da 2:34** 1855
gold were **c** all at the same time and **Da 2:35** 1855
hands and that it **c** the iron, **Da 2:45** 1855
them and **c** all their bones. **Da 6:24** 1855
It devoured and **c** and trampled **Da 7:7** 1855
of bronze, *and which* devoured, **c** and **Da 7:19** 1855
is oppressed, **c** in judgment, **Hos 5:11** 7533
afflicted in every way, but not **c**; **2Co 4:8** *4729*

CRUSHES
But perversion in it **c** the spirit. **Pr 15:4** 7667
A lying tongue hates those it **c**, **Pr 26:28** 1790
as iron **c** and shatters all things, **Da 2:40** 1855

CRUSHING
on Abimelech's head, **c** his skull. **Jg 9:53** 7533
"What do you mean by **c** My people **Is 3:15** 1792

CRUST
with worms and a **c** of dirt, **Jb 7:5** 1487

CRY
an exceedingly great and bitter **c**, **Gn 27:34** 6818
and their **c** for help because of **Ex 2:23** 7775
c because of their taskmasters, **Ex 3:7** 6818
the **c** of the sons of Israel has **Ex 3:9** 6818
are lazy, therefore they **c** out, **Ex 5:8** 6817
great **c** in all the land of Egypt, **Ex 11:6** 6818
and there was a great **c** in Egypt, **Ex 12:30** 6818
all, *and* if he does **c** out to Me, **Ex 22:23** 6817
to Me, I will surely hear his **c**; **Ex 22:23** 6818
not the sound of the **c** of triumph, **Ex 32:18** 6031b
it the sound of the **c** of defeat; **Ex 32:18** 6031b
he shall cover his mustache and **c**, **Lv 13:45** 7121
he may **c** to the LORD against you, **Dt 15:9** 7121
she did not **c** out in the city, **Dt 22:24** 6817
so that he will not **c** against you **Dt 24:15** 7121
"Go and **c** out to the gods which **Jg 10:14** 2199
c of the city went up to heaven. **1Sa 5:12** 7775
to **c** to the LORD our God for us, **1Sa 7:8** 2199
"Then you will **c** out in that day **1Sa 8:18** 2199
because their **c** has come to Me." **1Sa 9:16** 6818
battle array shouting the war **c**. **1Sa 17:20** 7321
my **c** for help *came* into His ears. **2Sa 22:7** 7775
to listen to the **c** and to the **1Ki 8:28** 7440
Then a **c** passed throughout the **1Ki 22:36** 7440
to listen to the **c** and to the **2Ch 6:19** 7440
the men of Judah raised a war **c**, **2Ch 13:15** 7321
the men of Judah raised the war **c**, **2Ch 13:15** 7321
and **c** to You in our distress, and **2Ch 20:9** 2199
heard their **c** by the Red Sea. **Ne 9:9** 2201
be no *resting* place for my **c**. **Jb 16:18** 2201
"Behold, I **c**, 'Violence!' but I get no **Jb 19:7** 6817
the souls of the wounded **c** out; **Jb 24:12** 7768
"Will God hear his **c** When **Jb 27:9** 6818
"Among the bushes they **c** out; **Jb 30:7** 5101
"I **c** out to You for help, but **Jb 30:20** 7768
disaster therefore **c** out for help? **Jb 30:24** 7769
the assembly *and* **c** out for help. **Jb 30:28** 7768
the **c** of the poor to come to Him, **Jb 34:28** 6818
might hear the **c** of the afflicted **Jb 34:28** 6818
of oppressions they **c** out; **Jb 35:9** 2199
They **c** for help because of the arm **Jb 35:9** 7768
"There they **c** out, but He does **Jb 35:12** 6817
God will not listen to an empty **c**, **Jb 35:13**
not **c** for help when He binds them. **Jb 36:13** 7768
When its young **c** to God And **Jb 38:41** 7768
of the captains and the war **c**. **Jb 39:25** 8643
Heed the sound of my **c** for help, **Ps 5:2** 7768
not forget the **c** of the afflicted. **Ps 9:12** 6818
cause, O LORD, give heed to my **c**; **Ps 17:1** 7440
And my **c** for help before Him came **Ps 18:6** 7775
O my God, I **c** by day, but You **Ps 22:2** 7121
O LORD, when I **c** with my voice, **Ps 27:7** 7121
when I **c** to You for help, **Ps 28:2** 7768
And His ears are *open* to their **c**. **Ps 34:15** 7775
righteous **c**, and the LORD hears **Ps 34:17** 6817
O LORD, and give ear to my **c**; **Ps 39:12** 7775
He inclined to me and heard my **c**. **Ps 40:1** 7775
I will **c** to God Most High, To God **Ps 57:2** 7121
Hear my **c**, O God; **Ps 61:1** 7440
rises to God, and I will **c** aloud; **Ps 77:1** 6817
For to You I **c** all day long. **Ps 86:3** 7121
Incline Your ear to my **c**! **Ps 88:2** 7440
"He will **c** to Me, **Ps 89:26** 7121
let my **c** for help come to You. **Ps 102:1** 7775
distress When He heard their **c**; **Ps 106:44** 7440
I rise before dawn and **c** for help; **Ps 119:147** 7768
Let my **c** come before You, O LORD; **Ps 119:169** 7440
I **c** aloud with my voice to the **Ps 142:1** 2199
"Give heed to my **c**, For I am **Ps 142:6** 7440
hear their **c** and will save them. **Ps 145:19** 7775
And to the young ravens which **c**. **Ps 147:9** 7121
For if you **c** for discernment, Lift **Pr 2:3** 7121
He who shuts his ear to the **c** of **Pr 21:13** 2201
c himself and not be answered. **Pr 21:13** 7121
but behold, a **c** of distress. **Is 5:7** 6818
before the boy knows how to **c** out **Is 8:4** 7121
C aloud with your voice, O **Is 10:30** 6670a
C aloud and shout for joy, O **Is 12:6** 6670a
"Wail, O gate; **c**, O city; Melt away, **Is 14:31** 2199
Heshbon and Elealeh also **c** out, **Is 15:4** 2199
the armed men of Moab **c** aloud; **Is 15:4** 7321
a **c** of distress over *their* ruin. **Is 15:5** 2201
For the **c** of distress has gone **Is 15:8** 2201
for they will **c** to the LORD **Is 19:20** 6817
They **c** out from the west **Is 24:14** 6670a
to you at the sound of your **c**; **Is 30:19** 2199
their brave men **c** in the streets, **Is 33:7** 6817
goat also will **c** to its kind; **Is 34:14** 7121
will not **c** out or raise *His voice,* **Is 42:2** 6817
shout, yes, He will raise a war **c**. **Is 42:13** 6873
Though one may **c** to it, it cannot **Is 46:7** 6817
into joyful shouting and **c** aloud, **Is 54:1** 6670a
"When you **c** out, let your **Is 57:13** 2199
"**C** loudly, do not hold back; **Is 58:1** 7121
You will **c**, and He will say, **Is 58:9** 7768
will **c** out with a heavy heart, **Is 65:14** 6817
C aloud and say, **Jer 4:5** 7121
heard a **c** as of a woman in labor, **Jer 4:31** 6963
The **c** of the daughter of Zion **Jer 4:31** 6963
not lift up **c** or prayer for them, **Jer 7:16** 7440
The **c** of the daughter of my people **Jer 8:19** 7775
though they will **c** to Me, **Jer 11:11** 2199
of Jerusalem will go and **c** to the gods **Jer 11:12** 2199
lift up a **c** or prayer for them; **Jer 11:14** 7440
the **c** of Jerusalem has ascended. **Jer 14:2** 6682
am not going to listen to their **c**; **Jer 14:12** 7440
For each time I speak, I **c** aloud; **Jer 20:8** 2199
"Go up to Lebanon and **c** out, **Jer 22:20** 6817
C out also from Abarim, For all **Jer 22:20** 6817
"Wail, you shepherds, and **c**; **Jer 25:34** 2199
sound of the **c** of the shepherds; **Jer 25:36** 6818
'Why do you **c** out over your injury? **Jer 30:15** 2199
is full of your **c** *of distress;* **Jer 46:12** 6682

And the men will **c** out, **Jer 47:2** 2199
have sounded out a **c** *of distress.* **Jer 48:4** 2201
the anguished **c** of destruction. **Jer 48:5** 6818
Wail and **c** out; Declare by the Arnon **Jer 48:20** 2199
Even for all Moab will I **c** out; **Jer 48:31** 2199
C out, O daughters of Rabbah, Gird **Jer 49:3** 6817
c against her on every side! **Jer 50:15** 7321
And they will **c** out with shouts of **Jer 51:14** 6031b
c aloud in the night At the **La 2:19** 7442
when I **c** out and call for help, **La 3:8** 2199
for relief, From my **c** for help." **La 3:56** 7775
c in My ears with a loud voice, **Ezk 8:18** 7121
"**C** out and wail, son of man; **Ezk 21:12** 2199
lift up the voice with a battle **c**, **Ezk 21:22** 8643
"At the sound of the **c** of your **Ezk 27:28** 2201
over you And will **c** bitterly. **Ezk 27:30** 2199
And they do not **c** to Me from their **Hos 7:14** 2199
They **c** out to Me, **Hos 8:2** 2199
priests will **c** out over it, **Hos 10:5** 1523
your God, And **c** out to the LORD. **Jl 1:14** 2199
To You, O LORD, I **c**; **Jl 1:19** 7121
the great city and **c** against it, **Jon 1:2** 7121
Then they will **c** out to the LORD, **Mi 3:4** 2199
They **c**, "Peace," But against him **Mi 3:5** 7121
"Now, why do you **c** out loudly? **Mi 4:9** 7321
I **c** out to You, "Violence!" **Hab 1:2** 2199
stone will **c** out from the wall, **Hab 2:11** 2199
sound of a **c** from the Fish Gate, **Zph 1:10** 6818
A day of trumpet and battle **c** Against **Zph 1:16** 8643
"HE WILL NOT QUARREL, NOR **C** OUT; **Mt 12:19** *2905*
and *began* to **c** out, **Mt 15:22** *2896*
he began to **c** out and say, **Mk 10:47** *2896*
And Jesus uttered a loud **c**, **Mk 15:37** *5456*
elect who **c** to Him day and night, **Lk 18:7** *994*
silent, the stones will **c** out!" **Lk 19:40** *2896*
as sons by which we **c** out, **Ro 8:15** *2896*
and they **c** out with a loud voice, **Rv 7:10** *2896*

CRYING
blood is **c** to Me from the ground. **Gn 4:10** 6817
God heard the lad **c**; **Gn 21:17** 6963
child, and behold, *the* boy was **c**. **Ex 2:6** 1058
"Why are you **c** out to Me? **Ex 14:15** 6817
the army ran, **c** out as they fled. **Jg 7:21** 7321
went away, **c** aloud as she went. **2Sa 13:19** 2199
I was **c** to the LORD with my voice, **Ps 3:4** 7121
I am weary with my **c**; **Ps 69:3** 7121
of walls And a **c** to the mountain. **Is 22:5** 7771b
of weeping and the sound of **c**. **Is 65:19** 2201
VOICE OF ONE **C** IN THE WILDERNESS, **Mt 3:3** *994*
two blind men followed Him, **c** out, **Mt 9:27** *2896*
VOICE OF ONE **C** IN THE WILDERNESS, **Mk 1:3** *994*
After **c** out and throwing him **Mk 9:26** *2896*
but he kept **c** out all the more, **Mk 10:48** *2896*
VOICE OF ONE **C** IN THE WILDERNESS, **Lk 3:4** *994*
but he kept **c** out all the more, **Lk 18:39** *2905*
Jesus, **c** out with a loud voice, **Lk 23:46** *5455*
VOICE OF ONE **C** IN THE WILDERNESS, **Jn 1:23** *994*
The people kept **c** out, **Ac 12:22** *2019*
rushed out into the crowd, **c** out **Ac 14:14** *2896*
after Paul and us, she kept **c** out, **Ac 16:17** *2896*
with rage, they *began* **c** out, **Ac 19:28** *2896*
c out, "Men of Israel, come **Ac 21:28** *2896*
And as they were **c** out and **Ac 22:23** *2905*
Paul *began* **c** out in the Council, **Ac 23:6** *2896*
into our hearts, **c**, "Abba! Father!" **Ga 4:6** *2896*
supplications with loud **c** and tears **Heb 5:7** *2906*
c out with a loud voice to Him who **Rv 14:15** *2896*
and were **c** out as they saw the **Rv 18:18** *2896*
on their heads and were **c** out, **Rv 18:19** *2896*
no longer be *any* mourning, or **c**, **Rv 21:4** *2906*

CRYSTAL
and **c** are not to be mentioned; **Jb 28:18** 1378
of rubies, And your gates of **c**, **Is 54:12** 688
like the awesome gleam of **c**, **Ezk 1:22** 7140
something like a sea of glass, like **c**; **Rv 4:6** *2930*
of the water of life, clear as **c**, **Rv 22:1** *2930*

CRYSTAL-CLEAR
stone, as a stone of **c** jasper. **Rv 21:11** *2929*

CUB
lioness and lion's **c** prowled, **Na 2:11** 1482

CUBIT
and finish it to a **c** from the top; **Gn 6:16** 520
two cubits long and one **c** wide and **Ex 25:23** 520
"The **c** on one side and the **Ex 26:13** 520
one side and the **c** on the other, **Ex 26:13** 520
"Its length *shall be* a **c**, **Ex 30:2** 520
be a cubit, and its width a **c**, **Ex 30:2** 520
two cubits long and a **c** wide and **Ex 37:10** 520
a **c** long and a cubit wide, square, **Ex 37:25** 520
a cubit long and a **c** wide, **Ex 37:25** 520
width four cubits by ordinary **c**.) **Dt 3:11** 520
had two edges, a **c** in length, **Jg 3:16** 1574
around encircling it ten to a **c**, **1Ki 7:24** 520
the crown at the top *was* a **c**, **1Ki 7:31** 520
of a pedestal, a **c** and a half; **1Ki 7:31** 520
of a wheel *was* a **c** and a half. **1Ki 7:32** 520
was a circular form half a **c** high, **1Ki 7:35** 520
which was a **c** and a handbreadth. **Ezk 40:5** 520
There was a barrier *wall* one **c** *wide* **Ezk 40:12** 520
hewn stone, a **c** and a half long, **Ezk 40:42** 520
a half long, a **c** and a half wide and **Ezk 40:42** 520
and a half wide and one **c** high, **Ezk 40:42** 520
the **c** being a cubit and a handbreadth **Ezk 43:13** 520
being a **c** and a handbreadth): **Ezk 43:13** 520
the base *shall be* a **c** and **Ezk 43:13** 520
shall be a cubit and the width a **c**, **Ezk 43:13** 520
two cubits and the width one **c**; **Ezk 43:14** 520
four cubits and the width one **c**. **Ezk 43:14** 520

around it *shall be* half a **c** and **Ezk 43:17** 520
its base *shall be* a **c** round about; **Ezk 43:17** 520

CUBITS
length of the ark three hundred **c**, **Gn 6:15** 520
cubits, its breadth fifty **c**, **Gn 6:15** 520
cubits, and its height thirty **c**. **Gn 6:15** 520
water prevailed fifteen **c** higher, **Gn 7:20** 520
acacia wood two and a half **c** long, **Ex 25:10** 520
long, and one and a half **c** wide, **Ex 25:10** 520
wide, and one and a half **c** high. **Ex 25:10** 520
two and a half **c** long and one and **Ex 25:17** 520
long and one and a half **c** wide. **Ex 25:17** 520
two **c** long and one cubit wide and **Ex 25:23** 520
wide and one and a half **c** high. **Ex 25:23** 520
curtain shall be twenty-eight **c**, **Ex 26:2** 520
the width of each curtain four **c**; **Ex 26:2** 520
of each curtain *shall be* thirty **c**, **Ex 26:8** 520
the width of each curtain four **c**; **Ex 26:8** 520
"Ten **c** *shall be* the length of **Ex 26:16** 520
a half **c** the width of each board. **Ex 26:16** 520
five **c** long and five cubits wide; **Ex 27:1** 520
five cubits long and five **c** wide; **Ex 27:1** 520
and its height shall be three **c**. **Ex 27:1** 520
one hundred **c** long for one side; **Ex 27:9** 520
shall be hangings one hundred **c** **Ex 27:11**
hangings of fifty **c** *with* their ten pillars **Ex 27:12** 520
on the east side *shall be* fifty **c**. **Ex 27:13** 520
one side *of the gate shall be* fifteen **c** **Ex 27:14** 520
side *shall be* hangings of fifteen **c** **Ex 27:15**
shall be a screen of twenty **c**, **Ex 27:16** 520
the court *shall be* one hundred **c**, **Ex 27:18** 520
five **c** of fine twisted linen, **Ex 27:18** 520
and its height *shall be* two **c**; **Ex 30:2** 520
of each curtain was twenty-eight **c** and **Ex 36:9** 520
the width of each curtain four **c**; **Ex 36:9** 520
of each curtain *was* thirty **c** **Ex 36:15** 520
four **c** the width of each curtain; **Ex 36:15** 520
c *was* the length of each board **Ex 36:21** 520
a half **c** the width of each board. **Ex 36:21** 520
its length was two and a half **c**, **Ex 37:1** 520
and its width one and a half **c**, **Ex 37:1** 520
and its height one and a half **c**; **Ex 37:1** 520
pure gold, two and a half **c** long and **Ex 37:6** 520
long and one and a half **c** wide. **Ex 37:6** 520
two **c** long and a cubit wide and **Ex 37:10** 520
wide and one and a half **c** high. **Ex 37:10** 520
wide, square, and two **c** high; **Ex 37:25** 520
of acacia wood, five **c** long, **Ex 38:1** 520
five cubits long, and five **c** wide, **Ex 38:1** 520
wide, square, and three **c** high. **Ex 38:1** 520
fine twisted linen, one hundred **c**; **Ex 38:9** 520
side *there were* one hundred **c**; **Ex 38:11** 520
west side *there were* hangings of fifty **c** **Ex 38:12** 520
For the east side fifty **c**. **Ex 38:13** 520
side *of the gate were* fifteen **c**, **Ex 38:14** 520
court *were* hangings of fifteen **c**, **Ex 38:15** 520
And the length *was* twenty **c** and **Ex 38:18** 520
cubits and the height *was* five **c**, **Ex 38:18** 520
and about two **c** *deep* on the **Nu 11:31** 520
city outward a thousand **c** around. **Nu 35:4** 520
on the east side two thousand **c**, **Nu 35:5** 520
on the south side two thousand **c**, **Nu 35:5** 520
on the west side two thousand **c**, **Nu 35:5** 520
on the north side two thousand **c**, **Nu 35:5** 520
Its length was nine **c** and its **Dt 3:11** 520
width four **c** by ordinary cubit.) **Dt 3:11** 520
of about 2,000 **c** by measure. **Jos 3:4** 520
whose height was six **c** and a span. **1Sa 17:4** 520
its length *was* sixty **c** and its **1Ki 6:2** 520
sixty cubits and its width twenty **c** **1Ki 6:2**
cubits and its height thirty **c**. **1Ki 6:2** 520
the house *was* twenty **c** in length, **1Ki 6:3** 520
the front of the house *was* ten **c**. **1Ki 6:3** 520
The lowest story *was* five **c** wide, **1Ki 6:6** 520
and the middle *was* six **c** wide, **1Ki 6:6** 520
and the third *was* seven **c** wide; **1Ki 6:6** 520
the whole house, each five **c** high; **1Ki 6:10** 520
He built twenty **c** on the rear **1Ki 6:16** 520
inner sanctuary, was forty **c** *long.* **1Ki 6:17** 520
sanctuary *was* twenty **c** in length, **1Ki 6:20** 520
in length, twenty **c** in width, **1Ki 6:20** 520
in width, and twenty **c** in height, **1Ki 6:20** 520
of olive wood, each ten **c** high. **1Ki 6:23** 520
Five **c** *was* the one wing of the **1Ki 6:24** 520
c the other wing of the cherub; **1Ki 6:24** 520
end of the other wing *were* ten **c**. **1Ki 6:24** 520
The other cherub *was* ten **c**; **1Ki 6:25** 520
of the one cherub *was* ten **c**, **1Ki 6:26** 520
its length was 100 **c** and its width **1Ki 7:2** 520
50 **c** and its height 30 cubits, **1Ki 7:2** 520
50 cubits and its height 30 **c**, **1Ki 7:2** 520
was 50 **c** and its width 30 cubits, **1Ki 7:6** 520
was 50 cubits and its width 30 **c**, **1Ki 7:6** 520
ten **c** and stones of eight cubits. **1Ki 7:10** 520
ten cubits and stones of eight **c**. **1Ki 7:10** 520
c was the height of one pillar, **1Ki 7:15** 520
and a line of twelve **c** measured **1Ki 7:15** 520
height of the one capital was five **c** **1Ki 7:16** 520
of the other capital was five **c**. **1Ki 7:16** 520
porch were of lily design, four **c**. **1Ki 7:19** 520
metal ten **c** from brim to brim, **1Ki 7:23** 520
form, and its height was five **c**, **1Ki 7:23** 520
and thirty **c** in circumference. **1Ki 7:23** 520
the length of each stand was four **c** **1Ki 7:27** 520
its width four **c** and its height **1Ki 7:27** 520
cubits and its height three **c**. **1Ki 7:27** 520
each basin *was* four **c**, **1Ki 7:38** 520
Ephraim to the Corner Gate, 400 **c**. **2Ki 14:13** 520
of the one pillar was eighteen **c**, **2Ki 25:17** 520

height of the capital was three **c**, **2Ki 25:17** 520
man of *great* stature five **c** tall. **1Ch 11:23** 520
The length in **c**, according to the **2Ch 3:3** 520
to the old standard *was* sixty **c**, **2Ch 3:3** 520
cubits, and the width twenty **c**. **2Ch 3:3** 520
the width of the house, twenty **c**, **2Ch 3:4** 520
width of the house *was* twenty **c**, **2Ch 3:8** 520
and its width *was* twenty **c**; **2Ch 3:8** 520
of the cherubim *was* twenty **c**; **2Ch 3:11** 520
the wing of one, of five **c**, **2Ch 3:11** 520
and *its* other wing, of five **c**, **2Ch 3:11** 520
of the other cherub, of five **c**, **2Ch 3:12** 520
and its other wing of five **c** was **2Ch 3:12** 520
these cherubim extended twenty **c**, **2Ch 3:13** 520
of the house, thirty-five **c** high, **2Ch 3:15** 520
on the top of each *was* five **c**. **2Ch 3:15** 520
twenty **c** in length and twenty **2Ch 4:1** 520
cubits in length and twenty **c** in width **2Ch 4:1** 520
in width and ten **c** in height. **2Ch 4:1** 520
sea, ten **c** from brim to brim, **2Ch 4:2** 520
and its height *was* five **c** and its **2Ch 4:2** 520
and its circumference thirty **c**. **2Ch 4:2** 520
under it *and* all around it, ten **c**, **2Ch 4:3** 520
a bronze platform, five **c** long, **2Ch 6:13** 520
five cubits long, five **c** wide and **2Ch 6:13** 520
cubits wide and three **c** high, **2Ch 6:13** 520
Ephraim to the Corner Gate, 400 **c**. **2Ch 25:23** 520
60 **c** and its width 60 cubits; **Ezr 6:3** 521
60 cubits and its width 60 **c**; **Ezr 6:3** 521
and a thousand **c** of the wall to **Ne 3:13** 520
"Have a gallows fifty **c** high made **Es 5:14** 520
at Haman's house fifty **c** high, **Es 7:9** 520
of each pillar *was* eighteen **c**, **Jer 52:21** 520
and it *was* twelve **c** in **Jer 52:21** 520
height of each capital was five **c**, **Jer 52:22** 520
hand was a measuring rod of six **c**, **Ezk 40:5** 520
five **c** between the guardrooms. **Ezk 40:7** 520
the porch of the gate, eight **c**; **Ezk 40:9** 520
and its side pillars, two **c**. **Ezk 40:9** 520
the width of the gateway, ten **c**, **Ezk 40:11** 520
length of the gate, thirteen **c**. **Ezk 40:11** 520
were six **c** *square* on each side. **Ezk 40:12** 520
a width of twenty-five **c** from *one* **Ezk 40:13** 520
the side pillars sixty **c** *high;* **Ezk 40:14** 520
porch of the gate *was* fifty **c**. **Ezk 40:15** 520
c on the east and on the north. **Ezk 40:19** 520
Its length *was* fifty **c** and **Ezk 40:21** 520
and the width twenty-five **c**. **Ezk 40:21** 520
a hundred **c** from gate to gate. **Ezk 40:23** 520
the length *was* fifty **c** and the **Ezk 40:25** 520
cubits and the width twenty-five **c**. **Ezk 40:25** 520
toward the south, a hundred **c**. **Ezk 40:27** 520
it *was* fifty **c** long and **Ezk 40:29** 520
cubits long and twenty-five **c** wide. **Ezk 40:29** 520
c long and five cubits wide. **Ezk 40:30** 520
cubits long and five **c** wide. **Ezk 40:30** 520
it *was* fifty **c** long and **Ezk 40:33** 520
cubits long and twenty-five **c** wide. **Ezk 40:33** 520
the length *was* fifty **c** and the **Ezk 40:36** 520
cubits and the width twenty-five **c**. **Ezk 40:36** 520
a hundred **c** long and a hundred **Ezk 40:47** 520
cubits long and a hundred **c** wide; **Ezk 40:47** 520
of the porch, five **c** on each side; **Ezk 40:48** 520
the gate was three **c** on each side. **Ezk 40:48** 520
length of the porch *was* twenty **c** **Ezk 40:49** 520
cubits and the width eleven **c**; **Ezk 40:49** 520
six **c** wide on each side *was* the **Ezk 41:1** 520
width of the entrance *was* ten **c** and **Ezk 41:2** 520
entrance *were* five **c** on each side. **Ezk 41:2** 520
the length of the nave, forty **c**, **Ezk 41:2** 520
cubits, and the width, twenty **c**. **Ezk 41:2** 520
side pillar of the doorway, two **c**, **Ezk 41:3** 520
and the doorway, six **c** *high;* **Ezk 41:3** 520
the width of the doorway, seven **c**. **Ezk 41:3** 520
He measured its length, twenty **c**, **Ezk 41:4** 520
cubits, and the width, twenty **c**, **Ezk 41:4** 520
the wall of the temple, six **c**; **Ezk 41:5** 520
of the side chambers, four **c**, **Ezk 41:5** 520
full rod of six long **c** *in height.* **Ezk 41:8** 520
of the side chambers *was* five **c**. **Ezk 41:9** 520
outer chambers *was* twenty **c** in width **Ezk 41:10** 520
free space *was* five **c** all around. **Ezk 41:11** 520
the west *was* seventy **c** wide; **Ezk 41:12** 520
was five **c** thick all around, **Ezk 41:12** 520
and its length *was* ninety **c**. **Ezk 41:12** 520
the temple, a hundred **c** long; **Ezk 41:13** 520
walls *were* also a hundred **c** long. **Ezk 41:13** 520
the east *side totaled* a hundred **c**. **Ezk 41:14** 520
gallery on each side, a hundred **c**; **Ezk 41:15** 520
altar *was* of wood, three **c** high and **Ezk 41:22** 520
cubits high and its length two **c**; **Ezk 41:22** 520
the length, *which was* a hundred **c**, **Ezk 42:2** 520
the width *was* fifty **c**. **Ezk 42:2** 520
Opposite the twenty **c** which **Ezk 42:3**
was an inner walk ten **c** wide, **Ezk 42:4** 520
wide, a way of one *hundred* **c**; **Ezk 42:4** 520
chambers, its length *was* fifty **c**, **Ezk 42:7** 520
in the outer court *was* fifty **c**; **Ezk 42:8** 520
facing the temple *was* a hundred **c**. **Ezk 42:8** 520
measurements of the altar by **c** **Ezk 43:13** 520
to the lower ledge *shall be* two **c** and **Ezk 43:14** 520
the larger ledge *shall be* four **c** and **Ezk 43:14** 520
The altar hearth *shall be* four **c**; **Ezk 43:15** 520
altar hearth *shall be* twelve **c** **Ezk 43:16**
"The ledge *shall be* fourteen **c** **Ezk 43:17**
25,000 **c**, and the width shall be **Ezk 45:1**
five hundred by five hundred **c**, **Ezk 45:2**
and fifty **c** for its open space **Ezk 45:2** 520
25,000 **c** and a width of 10,000 **Ezk 45:3**

10,000 **c**; and in it shall be **Ezk 45:3**
"An area 25,000 **c** in **Ezk 45:5**
5,000 **c** wide and 25,000 *cubits* **Ezk 45:6**
25,000 **c** long, alongside **Ezk 45:6**
forty **c** long and thirty wide; **Ezk 46:22**
hand, he measured a thousand **c**, **Ezk 47:3** 520
25,000 **c** in width, **Ezk 48:8**
25,000 **c** in length and 10,000 **Ezk 48:9**
25,000 **c** *in length,* toward the west **Ezk 48:10**
25,000 **c** in length and 10,000 in **Ezk 48:13**
25,000 **c** and the width 10,000. **Ezk 48:13**
"The remainder, 5,000 **c** in **Ezk 48:15**
4,500 **c**, the south side **Ezk 48:16**
4,500 **c**, the east side 4,500 **Ezk 48:16**
4,500 **c**, and the west side **Ezk 48:16**
west side 4,500 **c**. **Ezk 48:16**
on the north 250 **c**, on the south **Ezk 48:17**
on the south 250 **c**, on **Ezk 48:17**
on the east 250 **c**, and on **Ezk 48:17**
and on the west 250 **c**. **Ezk 48:17**
10,000 **c** toward the east **Ezk 48:18**
25,000 **c**; you shall set apart **Ezk 48:20**
25,000 **c** of the allotment toward **Ezk 48:21**
4,500 **c** by measurement, **Ezk 48:30**
"On the east side, 4,500 **c**, **Ezk 48:32**
"On the south side, 4,500 **c** **Ezk 48:33**
"On the west side, 4,500 **c**, **Ezk 48:34**
"The city shall be 18,000 **c** **Ezk 48:35**
sixty **c** *and* its width six cubits; **Da 3:1** 521
sixty cubits *and* its width six **c**; **Da 3:1** 521
c and its width ten cubits." **Zch 5:2** 520
cubits and its width ten **c**." **Zch 5:2** 520

CUBS
bear robbed of her **c** in the field. **2Sa 17:8** 7909b
a man meet a bear robbed of her **c**, **Pr 17:12** 7909b
They will growl like lions' **c**. **Jer 51:38** 1484
young lions, She reared her **c**. **Ezk 19:2** 1482
'When she brought up one of her **c**, **Ezk 19:3** 1482
her **c** And made him a young lion. **Ezk 19:5** 1482
them like a bear robbed of her **c**, **Hos 13:8** 7909b
The lion tore enough for his **c**, **Na 2:12** 1484

CUCUMBER
Like a watchman's hut in a **c** field, **Is 1:8** 4750
a scarecrow in a **c** field are they, **Jer 10:5** 4750

CUCUMBERS
the **c** and the melons and the leeks **Nu 11:5** 7180

CUD
split hoofs, *and* chews the **c**, **Lv 11:3** 1625
among those which chew the **c**, **Lv 11:4** 1625
the camel, for though it chews **c**, **Lv 11:4** 1625
shaphan, for though it chews **c**, **Lv 11:5** 1625
also, for though it chews **c**, **Lv 11:6** 1625
a split hoof, it does not chew **c**, **Lv 11:7** 1625
hoof, or which do not chew **c**, **Lv 11:26** 1625
hoof split in two *and* chews the **c**, **Dt 14:6** 1625
among those which chew the **c**, **Dt 14:7** 1625
for though they chew the **c**, **Dt 14:7** 1625
the hoof but *does* not *chew* the **c**, **Dt 14:8** 1625

CULPRITS
were *worse* **c** than all the men who **Lk 13:4** *3781*

CULT
of Israel shall be a **c** prostitute, **Dt 23:17** 6945
sons of Israel be a **c** prostitute. **Dt 23:17** 6945
male **c** prostitutes in the land. **1Ki 14:24** 6945
male **c** prostitutes from the land and **1Ki 15:12** 6945
the houses of the *male* **c** prostitutes **2Ki 23:7** 6945
perishes among the **c** prostitutes. **Jb 36:14** 6945

CULTIC
your burnt offerings in every **c** **Dt 12:13**

CULTIVATE
there was no man to **c** the ground. **Gn 2:5** 5647
of Eden to **c** it and keep it. **Gn 2:15** 5647
to **c** the ground from which he was **Gn 3:23** 5647
"When you **c** the ground, it will **Gn 4:12** 5647
"You shall plant and **c** vineyards, **Dt 28:39** 5647
servants shall **c** the land for him, **2Sa 9:10** 5647
in the land and **c** faithfulness. **Ps 37:3** 7462b
the tribes of Israel, shall **c** it. **Ezk 48:19** 5647

CULTIVATED
which used to be **c** with the hoe, **Is 7:25** 5737b
you, and you will be **c** and sown. **Ezk 36:9** 5647
"The desolate land will be **c** **Ezk 36:34** 5647
to nature into a **c** olive tree, **Ro 11:24** *2565*

CULTIVATES
a king who **c** the field is an **Ec 5:9** 5647

CUMMIN
And sow dill and scatter **c** And **Is 28:25** 3646
is the cartwheel driven over **c**; **Is 28:27** 3646
out with a rod, and **c** with a club. **Is 28:27** 3646
For you tithe the mint and dill and **c**, **Mt 23:23** *2951*

CUN
Also from Tibhath and from **C**, **1Ch 18:8** 3560

CUNNING
for I am told that he is very **c**. **1Sa 23:22** 6191
But Jehu did it in **c**, **2Ki 10:19** 6122
of the **c** is quickly thwarted. **Jb 5:13** 6617
as a harlot and **c** of heart. **Pr 7:10** 5341

CUP
"Now Pharaoh's **c** was in my hand; **Gn 40:11** 3563a
and squeezed them into Pharaoh's **c**, **Gn 40:11** 3563a
I put the **c** into Pharaoh's hand." **Gn 40:11** 3563a
and you will put Pharaoh's **c** into **Gn 40:13** 3563a
he put the **c** into Pharaoh's hand; **Gn 40:21** 3563a
"Put my **c**, the silver cup, in **Gn 44:2** 1375
"Put my cup, the silver **c**, **Gn 44:2** 1375
the **c** was found in Benjamin's sack. **Gn 44:12** 1375
possession the **c** has been found." **Gn 44:16** 1375
possession the **c** has been found, **Gn 44:17** 1375
of his **c** and lie in his bosom, **2Sa 12:3** 3563a
was made like the brim of a **c**, **1Ki 7:26** 3563a
was made like the brim of a **c**, **2Ch 4:5** 3563a
will be the portion of their **c**. **Ps 11:6** 3563a
of my inheritance and my **c**; **Ps 16:5** 3563a
my head with oil; My **c** overflows. **Ps 23:5** 3563a
a **c** is in the hand of the LORD, **Ps 75:8** 3563a
shall lift up the **c** of salvation And **Ps 116:13** 3563a
is red, When it sparkles in the **c**, **Pr 23:31** 3563a
the LORD's hand the **c** of His anger; **Is 51:17** 3563a
out of your hand the **c** of reeling, **Is 51:22** 3563a
nor give them a **c** of consolation **Jer 16:7** 3563a
"Take this **c** of the wine of wrath **Jer 25:15** 3563a
I took the **c** from the LORD's hand and **Jer 25:17** 3563a
the **c** from your hand to drink, **Jer 25:28** 3563a
the **c** will certainly drink *it,* **Jer 49:12** 3563a
golden **c** in the hand of the LORD, **Jer 51:7** 3563a
But the **c** will come around to you **La 4:21** 3563a
I will give her **c** into your hand.' **Ezk 23:31** 3563a
'You will drink your sister's **c**, **Ezk 23:32** 3563a
The **c** of horror and desolation, **Ezk 23:33** 3563a
The **c** of your sister Samaria. **Ezk 23:33** 3563a
The **c** in the LORD's right hand **Hab 2:16** 3563a
I am going to make Jerusalem a **c** **Zch 12:2** 5592a
even a **c** of cold water to drink, **Mt 10:42** *4221*
the **c** that I am about to drink?" **Mt 20:22** *4221*
"My **c** you shall drink; **Mt 20:23** *4221*
outside of the **c** and of the dish, **Mt 23:25** *4221*
inside of the **c** and of the dish, **Mt 23:26** *4221*
He had taken a **c** and given thanks, **Mt 26:27** *4221*
possible, let this **c** pass from Me; **Mt 26:39** *4221*
"For whoever gives you a **c** of **Mk 9:41** *4221*
able to drink the **c** that I drink, **Mk 10:38** *4221*
c that I drink you shall drink; **Mk 10:39** *4221*
And when He had taken a **c** **Mk 14:23** *4221*
remove this **c** from Me; **Mk 14:36** *4221*
of the **c** and of the platter; **Lk 11:39** *4221*
He had taken a **c** *and* given thanks, **Lk 22:17** *4221*
took the **c** after they had eaten, **Lk 22:20** *4221*
"This **c** which is poured out for **Lk 22:20** *4221*
willing, remove this **c** from Me; **Lk 22:42** *4221*
c which the Father has given Me, **Jn 18:11** *4221*
Is not the **c** of blessing which we **1Co 10:16** *4221*
You cannot drink the **c** of the Lord **1Co 10:21** *4221*
of the Lord and the **c** of demons; **1Co 10:21** *4221*
the same way *He took* the **c** also after **1Co 11:25** *4221*
"This **c** is the new covenant in My **1Co 11:25** *4221*
eat this bread and drink the **c**, **1Co 11:26** *4221*
whoever eats the bread or drinks the **c** **1Co 11:27** *4221*
of the bread and drink of the **c**. **1Co 11:28** *4221*
strength in the **c** of His anger; **Rv 14:10** *4221*
to give her the **c** of the wine of **Rv 16:19** *4221*
having in her hand a gold **c** full **Rv 17:4** *4221*
in the **c** which she has mixed, mix **Rv 18:6** *4221*

CUPBEARER
c and the baker for the king of Egypt **Gn 40:1** 4945a
the chief **c** and the chief baker. **Gn 40:2** 4945a
Then the **c** and the baker for the **Gn 40:5** 4945a
chief **c** told his dream to Joseph, **Gn 40:9** 4945a
former custom when you were his **c**. **Gn 40:13** 4945a
he lifted up the head of the chief **c** **Gn 40:20** 4945a
the chief **c** to his office, **Gn 40:21** 4945a
chief **c** did not remember Joseph, **Gn 40:23** 4945a
Then the chief **c** spoke to Pharaoh, **Gn 41:9** 4945a
Now I was the **c** to the king. **Ne 1:11** 4945a

CUPBEARERS
waiters and their attire, his **c**, **1Ki 10:5** 4945a
attire, his **c** and their attire, **2Ch 9:4** 4945a

CUPS
its **c**, its bulbs and its flowers **Ex 25:31** 1375
"Three **c** *shall be* shaped like **Ex 25:33** 1375
and three **c** shaped like almond **Ex 25:33** 1375
c shaped like almond *blossoms,* **Ex 25:34** 1375
its **c**, its bulbs and its flowers **Ex 37:17** 1375
c shaped like almond *blossoms,* **Ex 37:19** 1375
c shaped like almond *blossoms,* **Ex 37:19** 1375
c shaped like almond *blossoms,* **Ex 37:20** 1375
and the **c** and the snuffers and the **1Ki 7:50** 5592a
the house of the LORD silver **c**, **2Ki 12:13** 5592a
And who fill **c** with mixed wine **Is 65:11**
pitchers full of wine and **c**; **Jer 35:5** 3563a
c and pitchers and copper pots.) **Mk 7:4** *4221*

CURDLE
like milk And **c** me like cheese; **Jb 10:10** 7087a

CURDS
He took **c** and milk and the **Gn 18:8** 2529
C of cows, and milk of the flock, **Dt 32:14** 2529
bowl she brought him **c**. **Jg 5:25** 2529
honey, **c**, sheep, and cheese of the **2Sa 17:29** 2529
rivers flowing with honey and **c**. **Jb 20:17** 2529
"He will eat **c** and honey at the **Is 7:15** 2529
the milk produced he will eat **c**, **Is 7:22** 2529
the land will eat **c** and honey. **Is 7:22** 2529

CURE
he would **c** him of his leprosy." **2Ki 5:3** 622
you may **c** him of his leprosy." **2Ki 5:6** 622
to me to **c** a man of his leprosy? **2Ki 5:7** 622
over the place and **c** the leper.' **2Ki 5:11** 622
you, Or to **c** you of your wound. **Hos 5:13** 1455
and they could not **c** him." **Mt 17:16** *2323*

CURED
and as many as touched *it* were **c**. **Mt 14:36** *1295*
of him, and the boy was **c** at once. **Mt 17:18** *2323*
many as touched it were being **c**. **Mk 6:56** *4982*
with unclean spirits were being **c**. **Lk 6:18** *2323*
At that very time He **c** many *people* **Lk 7:21** *2323*
Jews were saying to the man who was **c**, **Jn 5:10** *2323*
were coming to him and getting **c**. **Ac 28:9** *2323*

CURES
and perform **c** today and tomorrow, **Lk 13:32** *2392*

CURING
c those who had need of healing. **Lk 9:11** *2390*

CURRENT
the house of the LORD, in **c** money, **2Ki 12:4** 5674a
the seas, And the **c** engulfed me. **Jon 2:3** 5104

CURSE
c the ground on account of man, **Gn 8:21** 7043
the one who curses you I will **c**. **Gn 12:3** 779
myself a **c** and not a blessing." **Gn 27:12** 7045
"Your **c** be on me, my son; **Gn 27:13** 7045
Cursed be those who **c** you, **Gn 27:29** 779
"You shall not **c** God, nor curse a **Ex 22:28** 7043
God, nor **c** a ruler of your people. **Ex 22:28** 779
'You shall not **c** a deaf man, nor **Lv 19:14** 7043
of bitterness that brings a **c**. **Nu 5:18** 779
of bitterness that brings a **c**; **Nu 5:19** 779
swear with the oath of the **c**, **Nu 5:21** 423
"the LORD make you a **c** and an **Nu 5:21** 423
a **c** shall go into your stomach, **Nu 5:22** 779
of bitterness that brings a **c**, **Nu 5:24** 779
water which brings a **c** will go into her **Nu 5:24** 779
that the water which brings a **c** **Nu 5:27** 779
will become a **c** among her people. **Nu 5:27** 423
c this people for me since they **Nu 22:6** 779
and he whom you **c** is cursed." **Nu 22:6** 779
now come, **c** them for me; **Nu 22:11** 6895
you shall not **c** the people, **Nu 22:12** 779
then, **c** this people for me.' " **Nu 22:17** 6895
'Come **c** Jacob for me, And come, **Nu 23:7** 779
"How shall I **c** whom God has not **Nu 23:8** 6895
I took you to **c** my enemies, but **Nu 23:11** 6895
and **c** them for me from there." **Nu 23:13** 6895
"Do not **c** them at all nor bless **Nu 23:25** 6895
you **c** them for me from there." **Nu 23:27** 6895
"I called you to **c** my enemies, **Nu 24:10** 6895
you today a blessing and a **c**: **Dt 11:26** 7045
and the **c**, if you do not listen to **Dt 11:28** 7045
Gerizim and the **c** on Mount Ebal. **Dt 11:29** 7045
Pethor of Mesopotamia, to **c** you. **Dt 23:4** 7043
your God turned the **c** into a blessing **Dt 23:5** 7045
"For the **c**, these shall stand **Dt 27:13** 7045
when he hears the words of this **c**, **Dt 29:19** 423
and every **c** which is written in **Dt 29:20** 423
c which is written in this book; **Dt 29:27** 7045
the **c** which I have set before you, **Dt 30:1** 7045
and death, the blessing and the **c**. **Dt 30:19** 7045
the law, the blessing and the **c**, **Jos 8:34** 7045
Balaam the son of Beor to **c** you. **Jos 24:9** 7043
'**C** Meroz,' said the angel of the **Jg 5:23** 779
'Utterly **c** its inhabitants; **Jg 5:23** 779
and the **c** of Jotham the son of **Jg 9:57** 7045
you uttered a **c** in my hearing, **Jg 17:2** 422
because his sons brought a **c** on **1Sa 3:13** 7043
this dead dog **c** my lord the king? **2Sa 16:9** 7043
'**C** David,' then who shall say, **2Sa 16:10** 7043
Let him alone and let him **c**, **2Sa 16:11** 7043
c on the day I went to Mahanaim. **1Ki 2:8** 7045
become a desolation and a **c**, **2Ki 22:19** 7045
and are taking on themselves a **c** **Ne 10:29** 423
Balaam against them to **c** them. **Ne 13:2** 7043
God turned the **c** into a blessing. **Ne 13:2** 7045
will surely **c** You to Your face." **Jb 1:11** 1288
he will **c** You to Your face." **Jb 2:5** 1288
fast your integrity? **C** God and die!" **Jb 2:9** 1288
"Let those **c** it who curse the **Jb 3:8** 6895
"Let those curse it who **c** the day, **Jb 3:8** 779
sin By asking for his life in a **c**. **Jb 31:30** 423
their mouth, But inwardly they **c**. **Ps 62:4** 7043
me have used my *name* as a **c**. **Ps 102:8** 7650
Let them **c**, but You bless; **Ps 109:28** 7043
The **c** of the LORD is on the house **Pr 3:33** 3994
grain, the people will **c** him, **Pr 11:26** 6895
are righteous," Peoples will **c** him, **Pr 24:24** 6895
a **c** without cause does not alight. **Pr 26:2** 7045
It will be reckoned a **c** to him. **Pr 27:14** 7045
c you and you will be found guilty. **Pr 30:10** 7043
your bedchamber do not **c** a king, **Ec 10:20** 7043
rooms do not **c** a rich man, **Ec 10:20** 7043
they will be enraged and **c** their **Is 8:21** 7043
Therefore, a **c** devours the earth, **Is 24:6** 423
name for a **c** to My chosen ones, **Is 65:15** 7621
the land mourns because of the **c**. **Jer 23:10** 423
a taunt and a **c** in all places **Jer 24:9** 7045
a horror, a hissing and a **c**, **Jer 25:18** 7045
and this city I will make a **c** to **Jer 26:6** 7045
kingdoms of the earth, to be a **c** and **Jer 29:18** 423
'Because of them a **c** will be **Jer 29:22** 7045
And you will become a **c**, **Jer 42:18** 7045
cut off and become a **c** and a reproach **Jer 44:8** 7045
and they will become a **c**, **Jer 44:12** 7045
ruin, an object of horror and a **c**, **Jer 44:22** 7045
a reproach, a ruin and a **c**; **Jer 49:13** 7045
of heart, Your **c** will be on them. **La 3:65** 8381
the **c** has been poured out on us, **Da 9:11** 423
"This is the **c** that is going **Zch 5:3** 423
as you were a **c** among the nations, **Zch 8:13** 7045
it, and there will no longer be a **c**, **Zch 14:11** 2764a
"then I will send the **c** upon you and **Mal 2:2** 3994
you and I will **c** your blessings; **Mal 2:2** 779
"You are cursed with a **c**, **Mal 3:9** 3994
and smite the land with a **c**." **Mal 4:6** 2764a
Then he began to **c** and swear, **Mt 26:74** *2617a*
But he began to **c** and swear, **Mk 14:71** *332*

bless those who **c** you, pray for **Lk 6:28** *2672*
who have bound themselves under a **c** **Ac 23:21** *332*
who persecute you; bless and do not **c**. **Ro 12:14** *2672*
works of the Law are under a **c**; **Ga 3:10** *2671*
redeemed us from the **c** of the Law, **Ga 3:13** *2671*
the Law, having become a **c** for us **Ga 3:13** *2671*
and with it we **c** men, who have **Jas 3:9** *2672*
There will no longer be any **c**; **Rv 22:3** *2616b*

CURSED
C are you more than all cattle, **Gn 3:14** 779
C is the ground because of you; **Gn 3:17** 779
"Now you are **c** from the **Gn 4:11** 779
the ground which the LORD has **c**." **Gn 5:29** 779
"**C** be Canaan; A servant of servants **Gn 9:25** 779
C be those who curse you, And **Gn 27:29** 779
"**C** be their anger, for it is **Gn 49:7** 779
he has **c** his father or his mother, **Lv 20:9** 7043
woman blasphemed the Name and **c**. **Lv 24:11** 7043
one who has **c** outside the camp, **Lv 24:14** 7043
brought the one who had **c** outside **Lv 24:23** 7043
and he whom you curse is **c**." **Nu 22:6** 779
shall I curse whom God has not **c**? **Nu 23:8** 6895
c is everyone who curses you." **Nu 24:9** 779
'**C** is the man who makes an idol or **Dt 27:15** 779
'**C** is he who dishonors his father **Dt 27:16** 779
'**C** is he who moves his neighbor's **Dt 27:17** 779
'**C** is he who misleads a blind **Dt 27:18** 779
'**C** is he who distorts the justice **Dt 27:19** 779
'**C** is he who lies with his **Dt 27:20** 779
'**C** is he who lies with any animal.' **Dt 27:21** 779
'**C** is he who lies with his sister, **Dt 27:22** 779
'**C** is he who lies with his **Dt 27:23** 779
'**C** is he who strikes his neighbor **Dt 27:24** 779
'**C** is he who accepts a bribe to **Dt 27:25** 779
'**C** is he who does not confirm the **Dt 27:26** 779
"**C** *shall* you *be* in the city, and **Dt 28:16** 779
and **c** *shall* you *be* in the country. **Dt 28:16** 779
"**C** *shall be* your basket and your **Dt 28:17** 779
"**C** *shall be* the offspring of your **Dt 28:18** 779
"**C** *shall* you *be* when you come in, **Dt 28:19** 779
c *shall* you *be* when you go out. **Dt 28:19** 779
"**C** before the LORD is the man who **Jos 6:26** 779
"Now therefore, you are **c**, **Jos 9:23** 779
and ate and drank and **c** Abimelech. **Jg 9:27** 7043
"**C** is he who gives a wife to **Jg 21:18** 779
"**C** be the man who eats food **1Sa 14:24** 779
'**C** be the man who eats food today.' " **1Sa 14:28** 779
Philistine **c** David by his gods. **1Sa 17:43** 7043
men, **c** are they before the LORD, **1Sa 26:19** 779
Thus Shimei said when he **c**, **2Sa 16:7** 7043
with him and as he went he **c** and **2Sa 16:13** 7043
because he **c** the LORD's anointed?" **2Sa 19:21** 7043
now it was he who **c** me with a **1Ki 2:8** 7043
'You **c** God and the king.' **1Ki 21:10** 1288
"Naboth **c** God and the king." **1Ki 21:13** 1288
he **c** them in the name of the LORD. **2Ki 2:24** 7043
now to this **c** woman and bury her, **2Ki 9:34** 779
So I contended with them and **c** **Ne 13:25** 7043
and **c** God in their hearts." **Jb 1:5** 1288
mouth and **c** the day of his *birth*. **Jb 3:1** 7043
And I **c** his abode immediately. **Jb 5:3** 6895
Their portion is **c** on the earth. **Jb 24:18** 7043
those **c** by Him will be cut off. **Ps 37:22** 7043
You rebuke the arrogant, the **c**, **Ps 119:21** 779
c of the LORD will fall into it. **Pr 22:14** 2194
likewise have many times **c** others. **Ec 7:22** 7043
"**C** is the man who does not heed **Jer 11:3** 779
"**C** is the man who trusts in **Jer 17:5** 779
C be the day when I was born; **Jer 20:14** 779
C be the man who brought the news **Jer 20:15** 779
"**C** be the one who does the LORD's **Jer 48:10** 779
And **c** be the one who restrains his **Jer 48:10** 779
And a short measure *that is* **c**? **Mi 6:10** 2194
"But **c** be the swindler who has a **Mal 1:14** 779
and indeed, I have **c** them *already*, **Mal 2:2** 779
"You are **c** with a curse, for you **Mal 3:9** 779
tree which You **c** has withered." **Mk 11:21** *2672*
C IS EVERYONE WHO DOES NOT ABIDE **Ga 3:10** *1944*
"**C** IS EVERYONE WHO HANGS ON A **Ga 3:13** *1944*
is worthless and close to being **c**, **Heb 6:8** *2671*

CURSES
the one who **c** you I will curse. **Gn 12:3** 7043
"He who **c** his father or his **Ex 21:17** 7043
who **c** his father or his mother, **Lv 20:9** 7043
'If anyone **c** his God, then he **Lv 24:15** 7043
then write these **c** on a scroll, **Nu 5:23** 423
cursed is everyone who **c** you." **Nu 24:9** 779
that all these **c** will come upon **Dt 28:15** 7045
"The LORD will send upon you **c**, **Dt 28:20** 3994
"So all these **c** shall come on you **Dt 28:45** 7045
according to all the **c** of the **Dt 29:21** 423
will inflict all these **c** on your enemies **Dt 30:7** 423
If he **c**, and if the LORD has told **2Sa 16:10** 7043
even all the **c** written in the book **2Ch 34:24** 423
greedy man **c** *and* spurns the LORD. **Ps 10:3** 1288
of **c** and deceit and oppression; **Ps 10:7** 423
of **c** and lies which they utter. **Ps 59:12** 423
He who **c** his father or his mother, **Pr 20:20** 7043
shuts his eyes will have many **c**. **Pr 28:27** 3994
is a kind of *man* who **c** his father And **Pr 30:11** 7043
money to me, *Yet* everyone **c** me. **Jer 15:10** 7043

CURSING
came out **c** continually as he came. **2Sa 16:5** 7043
to me instead of his **c** this day." **2Sa 16:12** 7045
He also loved **c**, so it came to him; **Ps 109:17** 7045
with **c** as with his garment, **Ps 109:18** 7045
you will not hear your servant **c** you. **Ec 7:21** 7043
IS FULL OF **C** AND BITTERNESS"; **Ro 3:14** *685*

mouth come *both* blessing and **c**. **Jas 3:10** *2671*

CURTAIN
"The length of each **c** shall be **Ex 26:2** 3407
the width of each **c** four cubits; **Ex 26:2** 3407
the outermost **c** in the *first* set, **Ex 26:4** 3407
shall make *them* on the edge of the **c** **Ex 26:4** 3407
make fifty loops in the one **c**, **Ex 26:5** 3407
the **c** that is in the second set; **Ex 26:5** 3407
of each **c** *shall be* thirty cubits, **Ex 26:8** 3407
the width of each **c** four cubits; **Ex 26:8** 3407
sixth **c** at the front of the tent. **Ex 26:9** 3407
make fifty loops on the edge of the **c** **Ex 26:10** 3407
and fifty loops on the edge of the **c** **Ex 26:10** 3407
the half **c** that is left over, **Ex 26:12** 3407
seat, and the **c** of the screen; **Ex 35:12** 6532
of each **c** was twenty-eight cubits and **Ex 36:9** 3407
the width of each **c** four cubits; **Ex 36:9** 3407
the outermost **c** in the first set; **Ex 36:11** 3407
he did likewise on the edge of the **c** **Ex 36:11** 3407
He made fifty loops in the one **c** **Ex 36:12** 3407
the **c** that was in the second set; **Ex 36:12** 3407
of each **c** *was* thirty cubits **Ex 36:15** 3407
four cubits the width of each **c**; **Ex 36:15** 3407
made fifty loops on the edge of the **c** **Ex 36:17** 3407
the **c** *that was outermost in* the second **Ex 36:17** 3407
out heaven like a *tent* **c**. **Ps 104:2** 3407
Who stretches out the heavens like a **c** **Is 40:22** 1852

CURTAINS
shall make the tabernacle with ten **c** **Ex 26:1** 3407
all the **c** shall have the same **Ex 26:2** 3407
"Five **c** shall be joined to one **Ex 26:3** 3407
and *the other* five **c** *shall be* **Ex 26:3** 3407
and join the **c** to one another with **Ex 26:6** 3407
"Then you shall make **c** of goats' **Ex 26:7** 3407
you shall make eleven **c** in all. **Ex 26:7** 3407
the eleven **c** shall have the same **Ex 26:8** 3407
shall join five **c** by themselves and **Ex 26:9** 3407
and the *other* six **c** by themselves, **Ex 26:9** 3407
is left over in the **c** of the tent, **Ex 26:12** 3407
the length of the **c** of the tent, **Ex 26:13** 3407
made the tabernacle with ten **c**; **Ex 36:8** 3407
the **c** had the same measurements. **Ex 36:9** 3407
He joined five **c** to one another **Ex 36:10** 3407
five **c** he joined to one another. **Ex 36:10** 3407
and joined the **c** to one another **Ex 36:13** 3407
Then he made **c** of goats' *hair* for **Ex 36:14** 3407
he made eleven **c** in all. **Ex 36:14** 3407
c had the same measurements. **Ex 36:15** 3407
He joined five **c** by themselves and **Ex 36:16** 3407
and *the other* six **c** by themselves. **Ex 36:16** 3407
they shall carry the **c** of the **Nu 4:25** 3407
ark of God dwells within tent **c**." **2Sa 7:2** 3407
covenant of the LORD is under **c**." **1Ch 17:1** 3407
of Kedar, Like the **c** of Solomon. **SS 1:5** 3407
out the **c** of your dwellings, **Is 54:2** 3407
devastated, My **c** in an instant. **Jer 4:20** 3407
my tent again Or to set up my **c**. **Jer 10:20** 3407
off for themselves Their tent **c**, **Jer 49:29** 3407
The tent **c** of the land of Midian **Hab 3:7** 3407

CURVED
the top of the mountain the border **c** **Jos 15:9** 8388a
then the border **c** to Baalah **Jos 15:9** 8388a
Then the border **c** to Shikkeron and **Jos 15:11** 8388a

CURVES
c of your hips are like jewels, **SS 7:1** 2542

CUSH
flows around the whole land of **C**. **Gn 2:13** 3568a
The sons of Ham *were* **C** and **Gn 10:6** 3568a
The sons of **C** *were* Seba and **Gn 10:7** 3568a
Now **C** became the father of Nimrod; **Gn 10:8** 3568a
say concerning Tirhakah king of **C**, **2Ki 19:9** 3568a
The sons of Ham *were* **C**, **1Ch 1:8** 3568a
The sons of **C** *were* Seba, **1Ch 1:9** 3568a
C became the father of Nimrod; **1Ch 1:10** 3568a
From Assyria, Egypt, Pathros, **C**, **Is 11:11** 3568a
Which lies beyond the rivers of **C**, **Is 18:1** 3568a
and token against Egypt and **C**, **Is 20:3** 3568a
of Egypt and the exiles of **C**, **Is 20:4** 3568a
ashamed because of **C** their hope **Is 20:5** 3568a
say concerning Tirhakah king of **C**, **Is 37:9** 3568a
ransom, **C** and Seba in your place. **Is 43:3** 3568a
merchandise of **C** And the Sabeans, **Is 45:14** 3568a

CUSHAN
saw the tents of **C** under distress, **Hab 3:7** 3572

CUSHAN-RISHATHAIM
hands of **C** king of Mesopotamia; **Jg 3:8** 3573
of Israel served **C** eight years. **Jg 3:8** 3573
the LORD gave **C** king of **Jg 3:10** 3573
hand, so that he prevailed over **C**. **Jg 3:10** 3573

CUSHI
son of Shelemiah, the son of **C**, **Jer 36:14** 3570
which came to Zephaniah son of **C**, **Zph 1:1** 3570

CUSHION
was in the stern, asleep on the **c**; **Mk 4:38** *4344*

CUSHITE
the **C** woman whom he had married **Nu 12:1** 3571
(for he had married a **C** woman); **Nu 12:1** 3571
Then Joab said to the **C**, **2Sa 18:21** 3569
So the **C** bowed to Joab and ran. **2Sa 18:21** 3569
let me also run after the **C**." **2Sa 18:22** 3569
of the plain and passed up the **C**. **2Sa 18:23** 3569
Behold, the **C** arrived, and the **2Sa 18:31** 3569
Cushite arrived, and the **C** said, **2Sa 18:31** 3569
Then the king said to the **C**, **2Sa 18:32** 3569
And the **C** answered, **2Sa 18:32** 3569

CUSTODY
They put him in **c** so that the **Lv 24:12** 4929
and they put him in **c** because it **Nu 15:34** 4929
to the harem, into the **c** of Hegai, **Es 2:3** 3027
into the **c** of Hegai, **Es 2:8** 3027
king's palace into the **c** of Hegai, **Es 2:8** 3027
harem, to the **c** of Shaashgaz, **Es 2:14** 3027
that John had been taken into **c**, **Mt 4:12** *3860*
after John had been taken into **c**, **Mk 1:14** *3860*
they went out to take **c** of Him; **Mk 3:21** *2902*
Jesus in **c** were mocking Him and **Lk 22:63** *4912*
in **c** and *yet* have *some* freedom, **Ac 24:23** *5083*
Paul was being kept in **c** at Caesarea **Ac 25:4** *5083*
in **c** for the Emperor's decision, **Ac 25:21** *5083*
in **c** until I send him to Caesar." **Ac 25:21** *5083*
we were kept in **c** under the law, **Ga 3:23** *5432*

CUSTOM
c when you were his cupbearer. **Gn 40:13** 4941
according to the **c** of daughters. **Ex 21:9** 4941
Thus it became a **c** in Israel, **Jg 11:39** 2706
Now this was *the* **c** in former **Ru 4:7**
and the **c** of the priests with the **1Sa 2:13** 4941
And this is the **c** of man, O Lord **2Sa 7:19** 8451
cut themselves according to their **c** **1Ki 18:28** 4941
by the pillar, according to the **c**, **2Ki 11:14** 4941
know the **c** of the god of the land; **2Ki 17:26** 4941
the **c** of the god of the land." **2Ki 17:26** 4941
the **c** of the god of the land." **2Ki 17:27** 4941
according to the **c** of the nations **2Ki 17:33** 4941
did according to their earlier **c**. **2Ki 17:40** 4941
at their stations after their **c**, **2Ch 30:16** 4941
they will not pay tribute, **c** or **Ezr 4:13** 1093
the River, and that tribute, **c** and **Ezr 4:20** 1093
for it was the **c** of the king so *to speak* **Es 1:13** 1697
and made a **c** for themselves and **Es 9:27** 6901
again, and, according to His **c**, **Mk 10:1** *1486*
to the **c** of the priestly office, **Lk 1:9** *1485*
out for Him the **c** of the Law, **Lk 2:27** *1480*
according to the **c** of the Feast; **Lk 2:42** *1485*
and as was His **c**, He entered the **Lk 4:16** *1486*
was His **c** to the Mount of Olives; **Lk 22:39** *1485*
for the Jewish **c** of purification, **Jn 2:6**
"But you have a **c** that I **Jn 18:39** *4914*
as is the burial **c** of the Jews. **Jn 19:40** *1485*
according to the **c** of Moses, **Ac 15:1** *1485*
And according to Paul's **c**, **Ac 17:2** *1486*
not the **c** of the Romans to hand over **Ac 25:16** *1485*
c to whom custom; **Ro 13:7** *5056*
custom to whom **c**; **Ro 13:7** *5056*

CUSTOMARILY
for the young men **c** did this. **Jg 14:10**

CUSTOMER
"Tarshish was your **c** because of **Ezk 27:12** 5503
"Aram was your **c** because of the **Ezk 27:16** 5503
"Damascus was your **c** because of **Ezk 27:18** 5503

CUSTOMERS
Kedar, they were your **c** for lambs, **Ezk 27:21** 5503
for these they were your **c**. **Ezk 27:21** 5503

CUSTOMS
not practice any of the abominable **c** **Lv 18:30** 2708
you shall not follow the **c** of the **Lv 20:23** 2708
and walked in the **c** of the nations **2Ki 17:8** 2708
and *in the* **c** of the kings of **2Ki 17:8**
the **c** which Israel had introduced. **2Ki 17:19** 2708
do according to the earlier **c**: **2Ki 17:34** 4941
established these **c** for Purim, **Es 9:32** 1697
the **c** of the peoples are delusion; **Jer 10:3** 2708
judge you according to their **c**. **Ezk 23:24** 4941
of the earth collect **c** or poll-tax, **Mt 17:25** *5056*
c which Moses handed down to us." **Ac 6:14** *1485*
and are proclaiming **c** which it is **Ac 16:21** *1485*
nor to walk according to the **c**. **Ac 21:21** *1485*
c and questions among *the* Jews; **Ac 26:3** *1485*
people or the **c** of our fathers, **Ac 28:17** *1485*

CUT
c off by the water of the flood, **Gn 9:11** 3772
these to Him and **c** them in two, **Gn 15:10** 1334
but he did not **c** the birds. **Gn 15:10** 1334
shall be **c** off from his people; **Gn 17:14** 3772
Then Zipporah took a flint and **c** **Ex 4:25** 3772
have been **c** off from the earth. **Ex 9:15** 3582
person shall be **c** off from Israel. **Ex 12:15** 3772
that person shall be **c** off from **Ex 12:19** 3772
shall not build it of **c** stones, **Ex 20:25** 1496
shall **c** the ram into its pieces, **Ex 29:17** 5408
be **c** off from his people.' " **Ex 30:33** 3772
shall be **c** off from his people." **Ex 30:38** 3772
be **c** off from among his people. **Ex 31:14** 3772
"**C** out for yourself two stone **Ex 34:1** 6458
So he **c** out two stone tablets like **Ex 34:4** 6458
pillars and **c** down their Asherim **Ex 34:13** 3772
hammered out gold sheets and **c** *them* **Ex 39:3** 7112
offering and **c** it into its pieces. **Lv 1:6** 5408
'He shall then **c** it into its **Lv 1:12** 5408
shall be **c** off from his people. **Lv 7:20** 3772
be **c** off from his people.' " **Lv 7:21** 3772
shall be **c** off from his people. **Lv 7:25** 3772
be **c** off from his people.' " **Lv 7:27** 3772
he had **c** the ram into its pieces, **Lv 8:20** 5408
be **c** off from among his people. **Lv 17:4** 3772
shall be **c** off from his people. **Lv 17:9** 3772
c him off from among his people. **Lv 17:10** 3772
whoever eats it shall be **c** off.' **Lv 17:14** 3772
be **c** off from among their people. **Lv 18:29** 3772
shall be **c** off from his people. **Lv 19:8** 3772
c him off from among his people, **Lv 20:3** 3772
and I will **c** off from among their **Lv 20:5** 3772
c him off from among his people. **Lv 20:6** 3772
and they shall be **c** off in the **Lv 20:17** 3772
be **c** off from among their people. **Lv 20:18** 3772

shall be c off from before Me; Lv 22:3 3772
bruised or crushed or torn or c, Lv 22:24 3772
he shall be c off from his people. Lv 23:29 3772
and c down your incense altars, Lv 26:30 3772
be c off from among the Levites. Nu 4:18 3772
then be c off from his people, Nu 9:13 3772
c down a branch with a single cluster Nu 13:23 3772
sons of Israel c down from there. Nu 13:24 3772
be c off from among his people. Nu 15:30 3772
person shall be completely c off; Nu 15:31 3772
person shall be c off from Israel. Nu 19:13 3772
that person shall be c off from Nu 19:20 3772
'C out for yourself two tablets of Dt 10:1 6458
and c out two tablets of stone Dt 10:3 6458
and you shall c down the engraved Dt 12:3 1438
you shall not c yourselves nor Dt 14:1 1413
forest with his friend to c wood, Dt 19:5 2404
swings the axe to c down the tree, Dt 19:5 3772
and you shall not c them down. Dt 20:19 3772
you shall destroy and c down, Dt 20:20 3772
or has his male organ c off shall Dt 23:1 3772
then you shall c off her hand; Dt 25:12 7112
'I will c them to pieces, I will Dt 32:26 6284
of the Jordan will be c off, Jos 3:13 3772
Salt Sea, were completely c off. Jos 3:16 3772
the waters of the Jordan were c off Jos 4:7 3772
waters of the Jordan were c off.' Jos 4:7 3772
and c off our name from the earth. Jos 7:9 3772
c off the Anakim from the hill country Jos 11:21 3772
the nations which I have c off, Jos 23:4 3772
and c off his thumbs and big toes. Jg 1:6 7112
their thumbs and their big toes c off Jg 1:7 7112
and c down the Asherah that is Jg 6:25 3772
Asherah which you shall c down." Jg 6:26 3772
which was beside it was c down, Jg 6:28 3772
he has c down the Asherah which Jg 6:30 3772
c down a branch from the trees, Jg 9:48 3772
All the people also c down Jg 9:49 3772
and c her in twelve pieces, Jg 19:29 5408
my concubine and c her in pieces Jg 20:6 5408
tribe is c off from Israel today. Jg 21:6 1438
name of the deceased will not be c off Ru 4:10 3772
'Yet I will not c off every man of 1Sa 2:33 3772
hands were c off on the threshold; 1Sa 5:4 3772
yoke of oxen and c them in pieces, 1Sa 11:7 5408
him, and c off his head with it. 1Sa 17:51 3772
"You shall not c off your 1Sa 20:15 3772
Then David arose and c off the 1Sa 24:4 3772
had c off the edge of Saul's robe. 1Sa 24:5 3772
For in that I c off the edge of 1Sa 24:11 3772
not c off my descendants after me and 1Sa 24:21 3772
how he has c off those who are 1Sa 28:9 3772
They c off his head and 1Sa 31:9 3772
"Go, c him down." 2Sa 1:15 6293
and c off their hands and feet and 2Sa 4:12 7112
c off all your enemies from before you 2Sa 7:9 3772
and c off their garments in the 2Sa 10:4 3772
When he c the hair of his head 2Sa 14:26 1548
end of every year that he c it, 2Sa 14:26 1548
it was heavy on him so he c it), 2Sa 14:26 1548
go over now and c off his head." 2Sa 16:9 5493
And they c off the head of Sheba 2Sa 20:22 3772
they c for me cedars from Lebanon, 1Ki 5:6 3772
to c timber like the Sidonians." 1Ki 5:6 3772
of the house with c stones. 1Ki 5:17 1496
builders and the Gebalites c them, 1Ki 5:18 6458
inner court with three rows of c stone 1Ki 6:36 1496
of stone c according to measure, 1Ki 7:9 1496
stone c according to measure, 1Ki 7:11 1496
had three rows of c stone and a row 1Ki 7:12 1496
then I will c off Israel from the 1Ki 9:7 3772
he had c off every male in Edom), 1Ki 11:16 3772
and will c off from Jeroboam every 1Ki 14:10 3772
who will c off the house of Jeroboam 1Ki 14:14 3772
and Asa c down her horrid image 1Ki 15:13 3772
one ox for themselves and c it up, 1Ki 18:23 5408
c themselves according to their custom 1Ki 18:28 1413
Then he arranged the wood and c 1Ki 18:33 5408
will c off from Ahab every male, 1Ki 21:21 3772
to the Jordan, they c down trees. 2Ki 6:4 1504
him the place, he c off a stick and 2Ki 6:6 7094
and I will c off from Ahab every 2Ki 9:8 3772
to c off portions from Israel; 2Ki 10:32 7096
c off the borders of the stands, 2Ki 16:17 7112
pillars and c down the Asherah. 2Ki 18:4 3772
At that time Hezekiah c off the 2Ki 18:16 7112
And I c down its tall cedars and 2Ki 19:23 3772
sacred pillars and c down the Asherim 2Ki 23:14 3772
and c in pieces all the vessels of 2Ki 24:13 7112
and have c off all your enemies 1Ch 17:8 3772
and c off their garments in the 1Ch 19:4 3772
and c them with saws and with 1Ch 20:3 7787
know how to c timber of Lebanon; 2Ch 2:8 3772
the woodsmen who c the timber, 2Ch 2:10 3772
"We will c whatever timber 2Ch 2:16 3772
pillars, c down the Asherim, 2Ch 14:3 1438
and Asa c down her horrid image, 2Ch 15:16 3772
tomb which he had c out for himself 2Ch 16:14 3738a
to c off the house of Ahab. 2Ch 22:7 3772
for he was c off from the house of 2Ch 26:21 1504
he c the utensils of the house of 2Ch 28:24 7112
in pieces, c down the Asherim and 2Ch 31:1 1438
warriors to c off the supply of water 2Ch 32:3 5640
would loose His hand and c me off! Jb 6:9 1214
it is still green and not c down, Jb 8:12 6998
for a tree, When it is c down, Jb 14:7 3772
And his branch is c off above. Jb 18:16 4448c
number of his months is c off? Jb 21:21 2686a
'Truly our adversaries are c off, Jb 22:20 3582
the heads of grain they are c off. Jb 24:24 4448c
of the godless when he is c off, Jb 27:8 1214
LORD c off all flattering lips, Ps 12:3 3772
am c off from before Your eyes"; Ps 31:22 1629a
To c off the memory of them from Ps 34:16 3772
For evildoers will be c off, Ps 37:9 3772
those cursed by Him will be c off. Ps 37:22 3772
of the wicked will be c off. Ps 37:28 3772
When the wicked are c off, Ps 37:34 3772
of the wicked will be c off. Ps 37:38 3772
horns of the wicked He will c off, Ps 75:10 1438
will c off the spirit of princes; Ps 76:12 1219
is burned with fire, it is c down; Ps 80:16 3683
And they are c off from Your hand. Ps 88:5 1504
So as to c off from the city of Ps 101:8 3772
And c bars of iron asunder. Ps 107:16 1438
Let his posterity be c off; Ps 109:13 3772
That He may c off their memory Ps 109:15 3772
the LORD I will surely c them off. Ps 118:10 4135
the LORD I will surely c them off. Ps 118:11 4135
the LORD I will surely c them off. Ps 118:12 4135
He has c in two the cords of the Ps 129:4 7112
lovingkindness, c off my enemies Ps 143:12 6789
will be c off from the land And Pr 2:22 3772
perverted tongue will be c out. Pr 10:31 3772
And your hope will not be c off. Pr 23:18 3772
And your hope will not be c off. Pr 24:14 3772
The sycamores have been c down, Is 9:10 1438
And to c off many nations. Is 10:7 3772
tall in stature will be c down And Is 10:33 1438
He will c down the thickets of Is 10:34 5362a
who harass Judah will be c off; Is 11:13 3772
You have been c down to the earth, Is 14:12 1438
"and will c off from Babylon name Is 14:22 3772
is bald and every beard is c off. Is 15:2 1639
Then He will c off the sprigs with Is 18:5 3772
and c away the spreading branches. Is 18:5 8456
load hanging on it will be c off, Is 22:25 3772
on doing evil will be c off; Is 29:20 3772
Like c thorns which are burned in Is 33:12 3683
And I c down its tall cedars and Is 37:24 3772
and c through their iron bars. Is 45:2 1438
you, In order not to c you off. Is 48:9 3772
Their name would never be c off or Is 48:19 3772
it not You who c Rahab in pieces, Is 51:9 2672
who considered That He was c off Is 53:8 1504
sign which will not be c off." Is 55:13 3772
name which will not be c off. Is 56:5 3772
daughter of Zion, I will c off. Jer 6:2 1820
"C down her trees And cast up a Jer 6:6 3772
has been c off from their mouth. Jer 7:28 3772
'C off your hair and cast it away, Jer 7:29 1494
To c off the children from the streets, Jer 9:21 3772
it is wood c from the forest, Jer 10:3 3772
And let us c him off from the land Jer 11:19 3772
And they will c down your choicest Jer 22:7 3772
rooms, And c out its windows, Jer 22:14 7167
who c the corners of their hair; Jer 25:23 7112
when they c the calf in two and Jer 34:18 3772
the king c it with a scribe's Jer 36:23 7167
to c off from you man and woman, Jer 44:7 3772
so that you might be c off and Jer 44:8 3772
for woe, even to c off all Judah. Jer 44:11 3772
"They have c down her forest," Jer 46:23 3772
To c off from Tyre and Sidon Every Jer 47:4 3772
us c her off from being a nation!' Jer 48:2 3772
"The horn of Moab has been c off and Jer 48:25 1438
is bald and every beard c short; Jer 48:37 1639
who c the corners of their hair; Jer 49:32 7112
"C off the sower from Babylon And Jer 50:16 3772
earth Has been c off and broken! Jer 50:23 1438
concerning this place to c it off, Jer 51:62 3772
In fierce anger He has c off All La 2:3 1438
over my head; I said, "I am c off!" La 3:54 1504
your incense altars may be c down, Ezk 6:6 1438
c him off from among My people. Ezk 14:8 3772
and c off from it both man and Ezk 14:13 3772
and c off man and beast from it,' Ezk 14:17 3772
to c off man and beast from it, Ezk 14:19 3772
to c off man and beast from it! Ezk 14:21 3772
born your navel cord was not c, Ezk 16:4 3772
and they will stone you and c you Ezk 16:40 1333
up its roots and c off its fruit, Ezk 17:9 7082
siege walls to c off many lives. Ezk 17:17 3772
and c off from you the righteous Ezk 21:3 3772
"Because I will c off from you Ezk 21:4 3772
and c them down with their swords; Ezk 23:47 1254a
And I will c you off from the Ezk 25:7 3772
and c off man and beast from it. Ezk 25:13 3772
even c off the Cherethites and Ezk 25:16 3772
c off from you man and beast. Ezk 29:8 3772
c off the hordes of Thebes. Ezk 30:15 3772
have c it down and left it; Ezk 31:12 3772
and I will c off from it the one Ezk 35:7 3772
We are completely c off.' Ezk 37:11 1504
a stone was c out without hands, Da 2:34 1505
a stone was c out of the mountain Da 2:45 1505
the tree and c off its branches, Da 4:14 7113
will be c off and have nothing, Da 9:26 3772
That they might be c off. Hos 8:4 3772
will be c off with her king Like Hos 10:7 1820
Israel will be completely c off. Hos 10:15 1820
That is c off from your mouth. Jl 1:5 3772
offering and the drink offering are c off Jl 1:9 3772
food been c off before our eyes, Jl 1:16 3772
And c off the inhabitant from the Am 1:5 3772
"I will also c off the inhabitant Am 1:8 3772
c off the judge from her midst And Am 2:3 3772
horns of the altar will be c off And Am 3:14 1438
So that everyone may be c Ob 1:9 3772
And you will be c off forever. Ob 1:10 3772
road To c down their fugitives; Ob 1:14 3772
yourself bald and c off your hair, Mi 1:16 1494
all your enemies will be c off. Mi 5:9 3772
"That I will c off your horses Mi 5:10 3772
"I will also c off the cities of Mi 5:11 3772
c off sorceries from your hand, Mi 5:12 3772
"I will c off your carved images Mi 5:13 3772
they will be c off and pass away. Na 1:12 1494
I will c off idol and image From Na 1:14 3772
He is c off completely. Na 1:15 3772
c off your prey from the land, Na 2:13 3772
you, The sword will c you down; Na 3:15 3772
should be c off from the fold And Hab 3:17 1504
And I will c off man from the face Zph 1:3 3772
And I will c off the remnant of Zph 1:4 3772
weigh out silver will be c off. Zph 1:11 3772
"I have c off nations; Zph 3:6 3772
So her dwelling will not be c off Zph 3:7 3772
And I will c off the pride of the Zch 9:6 3772
c off the chariot from Ephraim And Zch 9:10 3772
And the bow of war will be c off. Zch 9:10 3772
staff Favor and c it in pieces, Zch 11:10 1438
I c in pieces my second staff Union, Zch 11:14 1438
"that I will c off the names of Zch 13:2 3772
in it will be c off and perish; Zch 13:8 3772
will not be c off from the city. Zch 14:2 3772
may the LORD c off from the tents Mal 2:12 3772
c down and thrown into the fire. Mt 3:10 1581
hand makes you stumble, c it off and Mt 5:30 1581
c down and thrown into the fire. Mt 7:19 1581
c it off and throw it from you; Mt 18:8 1581
those days had been c short, Mt 24:22 2856
elect those days will be c short. Mt 24:22 2856
and will c him in pieces and Mt 24:51 1371
high priest and c off his ear. Mt 26:51 851
causes you to stumble, c it off; Mk 9:43 609
causes you to stumble, c it off; Mk 9:45 609
which they had c from the fields. Mk 11:8 2875
high priest and c off his ear. Mk 14:47 851
c down and thrown into the fire." Lk 3:9 1581
know, and will c him in pieces, Lk 12:46 1371
tree without finding any. C it down! Lk 13:7 1581
but if not, c it down.' " Lk 13:9 1581
priest and c off his right ear. Lk 22:50 851
Him in a tomb c into the rock, Lk 23:53 2991
slave, and c off his right ear; Jn 18:10 609
of the one whose ear Peter c off, Jn 18:26 609
they were c to the quick and intended Ac 5:33 1282
this, they were c to the quick, Ac 7:54 1282
In Cenchrea he had his hair c, Ac 18:18 2751
Then the soldiers c away the ropes Ac 27:32 609
otherwise you also will be c off. Ro 11:22 1581
For if you were c off from what is Ro 11:24 1581
let her also have her hair c off; 1Co 11:6 2751
her hair c off or her head shaved, 1Co 11:6 2751
that I may c off opportunity from 2Co 11:12 1581

CUTH
the men of C made Nergal, 2Ki 17:30 3575

CUTHAH
men from Babylon and from C 2Ki 17:24 3575

CUTS
any c in your body for the dead nor Lv 19:28 8296a
nor make any c in their flesh. Lv 21:5 8295
"When the LORD your God c off Dt 12:29 3772
LORD your God c off the nations, Dt 19:1 3772
"Bring also these ten c of cheese 1Sa 17:18 2757
not even when the LORD c off every 1Sa 20:15 3772
the bow and c the spear in two; Ps 46:9 7112
He c off his own feet and drinks Pr 26:6 7096
c off head and tail from Israel, Is 9:14 3772
He c me off from the loom; Is 38:12 1214
Surely he c cedars for himself, Is 44:14 3772

CUTTER
no tree c comes up against us.' Is 14:8 3772

CUTTING
in the c of stones for settings, Ex 31:5 2799
in the c of stones for settings and Ex 35:33 2799
The man shapes iron into a c tool and Is 44:12 4621
of a craftsman with a c tool. Jer 10:3 4621
your house By c off many peoples; Hab 2:10 7096
were c branches from the trees and Mt 21:8 2875

CYCLE
of feasting had completed their c, Jb 1:5 5362b

CYMBAL
a noisy gong or a clanging c. 1Co 13:1 2950

CYMBALS
tambourines, castanets and c. 2Sa 6:5 6767d
with lyres, harps, tambourines, c and 1Ch 13:8 4700
harps, lyres, loud-sounding c, 1Ch 15:16 4700
to sound aloud c of bronze; 1Ch 15:19 4700
trumpets, with loud-sounding c, 1Ch 15:28 4700
also Asaph played loud-sounding c, 1Ch 16:5 4700
and Jeduthun with trumpets and c 1Ch 16:42 4700
prophesy with lyres, harps and c; 1Ch 25:1 4700
in the house of the LORD, with c, 1Ch 25:6 4700
clothed in fine linen, with c, 2Ch 5:12 4700
and c and instruments of music, 2Ch 5:13 4700
in the house of the LORD with c, 2Ch 29:25 4700
the sons of Asaph, with c, Ezr 3:10 4700
songs to the accompaniment of c, Ne 12:27 4700
Praise Him with loud c; Ps 150:5 6767d
Praise Him with resounding c. Ps 150:5 6767d

CYPRESS
concerning the cedar and c timber. 1Ki 5:8 1265
desired of the cedar and c timber. 1Ki 5:10 1265

of the house with boards of **c**. 1Ki 6:15 1265
and two doors of **c** wood; 1Ki 6:34 1265
supplied Solomon with cedar and **c** 1Ki 9:11 1265
c and algum timber from Lebanon, 2Ch 2:8 1265
overlaid the main room with **c** wood 2Ch 3:5 1265
"Even the **c** trees rejoice over Is 14:8 1265
with the box tree and the **c**, Is 41:19 8391
himself, and takes a **c** or an oak and Is 44:14 8645
the thorn bush the **c** will come up, Is 55:13 1265
the box tree and the **c** together, Is 60:13 8391
I am like a luxuriant **c**; Hos 14:8 1265
And the **c** *spears* are brandished. Na 2:3 1265
Wail, O **c**, for the cedar has Zch 11:2 1265

CYPRESSES
its tall cedars *and* its choice **c**. 2Ki 19:23 1265
houses are cedars, Our rafters, **c**. SS 1:17 1266
its tall cedars *and* its choice **c**. Is 37:24 1265
The **c** could not compare with its Ezk 31:8 1265

CYPRIAN
Now Joseph, a Levite of **C** birth, Ac 4:36 *2953*

CYPRUS
to them from the land of **C**. Is 23:1 3794
Arise, pass over to **C**; Is 23:12 3794
boxwood from the coastlands of **C**. Ezk 27:6 3794
to Phoenicia and **C** and Antioch, Ac 11:19 *2954*
some of them, men of **C** and Cyrene, Ac 11:20 *2953*
and from there they sailed to **C**. Ac 13:4 *2954*
with him and sailed away to **C**. Ac 15:39 *2954*
When we came in sight of **C**, Ac 21:3 *2954*
with us, taking us to Mnason of **C**, Ac 21:16 *2953*
and sailed under the shelter of **C** Ac 27:4 *2954*

CYRENE
they found a man of **C** named Simon, Mt 27:32 *2956*
from the country, Simon of **C** Mk 15:21 *2956*
they seized a man, Simon of **C** Lk 23:26 *2956*
the districts of Libya around **C**, Ac 2:10 *2957*
some of them, men of Cyprus and **C**, Ac 11:20 *2956*
was called Niger, and Lucius of **C**, Ac 13:1 *2956*

CYRENIANS
including both **C** and Alexandrians, Ac 6:9 *2956*

CYRUS
Now in the first year of **C** king of 2Ch 36:22 3566
up the spirit of **C** king of Persia, 2Ch 36:22 3566
"Thus says **C** king of Persia, 2Ch 36:23 3566
first year of **C** king of Persia, Ezr 1:1 3566
up the spirit of **C** king of Persia, Ezr 1:1 3566
"Thus says **C** king of Persia, Ezr 1:2 3566
Also King **C** brought out the Ezr 1:7 3566
and **C**, king of Persia, had them Ezr 1:8 3566
they had from **C** king of Persia. Ezr 3:7 3566
the LORD God of Israel, as King **C**, Ezr 4:3 3566
all the days of **C** king of Persia, Ezr 4:5 3566
first year of **C** king of Babylon, Ezr 5:13 3567
King **C** issued a decree to rebuild Ezr 5:13 3567
these King **C** took from the temple Ezr 5:14 3567
issued by King **C** to rebuild this house Ezr 5:17 3567
"In the first year of King **C**, Ezr 6:3 3567
Cyrus, **C** the king issued a decree: Ezr 6:3 3567
God of Israel and the decree of **C**, Ezr 6:14 3567
"*It is I* who says of **C**, Is 44:28 3566
says the LORD to **C** His anointed, Is 45:1 3566
the first year of **C** the king. Da 1:21 3566
and in the reign of **C** the Persian. Da 6:28 3567
In the third year of **C** king of Da 10:1 3566

D

DABBESHETH
and to Maralah, it then touched **D** and Jos 19:11 1708

DABERATH
proceeded to **D** and up to Japhia. Jos 19:12 1705
lands, **D** with its pasture lands, Jos 21:28 1705
lands, **D** with its pasture lands 1Ch 6:72 1705

DAGON
a great sacrifice to **D** their god, Jg 16:23 1712
and brought it to the house of **D** and 1Sa 5:2 1712
house of Dagon and set it by **D**. 1Sa 5:2 1712
D had fallen on his face to the 1Sa 5:3 1712
So they took **D** and set him in his 1Sa 5:3 1712
D had fallen on his face to the 1Sa 5:4 1712
And the head of **D** and both the 1Sa 5:4 1712
the trunk of **D** was left to him. 1Sa 5:4 1712
neither the priests of **D** nor all who 1Sa 5:5 1712
of **D** in Ashdod to this day. 1Sa 5:5 1712
severe on us and on **D** our god." 1Sa 5:7 1712
his head in the house of **D**. 1Ch 10:10 1712

DAGON'S
of Dagon nor all who enter **D** house 1Sa 5:5 1712

DAILY
your work quota, *your* **d** amount, Ex 5:13 3117
reduce *your* **d** amount of bricks." Ex 5:19 3117
twice as much as they gather **d**." Ex 16:5 3117
this manner you shall present **d**, Nu 28:24 3117
d with her words and urged him, Jg 16:16 3117
six Levites, on the north four **d**, 1Ch 26:17 3117
four daily, on the south four **d**, 1Ch 26:17 3117
did so according to the **d** rule, 2Ch 8:13 3117
priests according to the **d** rule, 2Ch 8:14 3117
did **d** and collected much money. 2Ch 24:11 3117
of the LORD for his **d** obligations 2Ch 31:16 3117
fixed number of burnt offerings **d**, Ezr 3:4 3117
be given to them **d** without fail, Ezr 6:9 3118
from the book of the law of God **d**, Ne 8:18 3117
Now it was when they had spoken **d** Es 3:4 3117
the Lord, who **d** bears our burden, Ps 68:19 3117
And I was **d** *His* delight, Rejoicing Pr 8:30 3117
to me, Watching **d** at my gates, Pr 8:34 3117
d rising early and sending *them.* Jer 7:25 3117
of bread **d** from the bakers' street, Jer 37:21 3117
a **d** portion all the days of his Jer 52:34 3117
Memphis *will have* distresses **d**. Ezk 30:16 3119
d a goat for a sin offering; Ezk 43:25 3117
a male goat **d** for a sin offering. Ezk 45:23 3117
a burnt offering to the LORD **d**; Ezk 46:13 3117
a **d** ration from the king's choice food Da 1:5 3117
'Give us this day our **d** bread. Mt 6:11 *1967*
himself, and take up his cross **d** and Lk 9:23 *2596, 2250*
'Give us each day our **d** bread. Lk 11:3 *1967*
He was teaching **d** in the temple; Lk 19:47 *2596, 2250*
I was with you **d** in the temple, Lk 22:53 *2596, 2250*
in the **d** serving *of food.* Ac 6:1 *2522*
and were increasing in number **d**. Ac 16:5 *2596, 2250*
examining the Scriptures **d** Ac 17:11 *2596, 2250*
d in the school of Tyrannus. Ac 19:9 *2596, 2250*
in Christ Jesus our Lord, I die **d**. 1Co 15:31 *2596, 2250*
there is the **d** pressure on me *of* 2Co 11:28 *2596, 2250*
who does not need **d**, Heb 7:27 *2596, 2250*
Every priest stands **d** ministering Heb 10:11 *2596, 2250*
clothing and in need of **d** food, Jas 2:15 *2184*

DAINTIES
rich, And he will yield royal **d**. Gn 49:20 4574

DAINTY
of a whisperer are like **d** morsels, Pr 18:8 3859
of a whisperer are like **d** morsels, Pr 26:22 3859
"The comely and **d** one, the Jer 6:2 6026

DALMANUTHA
and came to the district of **D**. Mk 8:10 *1148*

DALMATIA
has gone to Galatia, Titus to **D**. 2Tm 4:10 *1149*

DALPHON
and Parshandatha, **D**, Es 9:7 1813

DAMAGE
house wherever any **d** may be found. 2Ki 12:5 919
will **d** the revenue of the kings. Ezr 4:13 5142
why should **d** increase to the Ezr 4:22 2257
So that no one will **d** it, I guard Is 27:3 6485
and his horses *eventually* **d** *it,* Is 28:28 2000
be with **d** and great loss, Ac 27:10 *5196*
and incurred this **d** and loss. Ac 27:21 *5196*
and do not **d** the oil and the wine." Rv 6:6 *91*

DAMAGED
The enemy has **d** everything within Ps 74:3 7489a
singed, nor were their trousers **d**, Da 3:27 8133

DAMAGES
and they shall repair the **d** of the 2Ki 12:5 919
not repaired the **d** of the house. 2Ki 12:6 919
you not repair the **d** of the house? 2Ki 12:7 919
pay it for the **d** of the house." 2Ki 12:7 919
nor repair the **d** of the house. 2Ki 12:8 919
the **d** to the house of the LORD, 2Ki 12:12 919
LORD to repair the **d** of the house, 2Ki 22:5 919

DAMAGING
city and **d** to kings and provinces, Ezr 4:15 5142

DAMARIS
a woman named **D** and others Ac 17:34 *1152*

DAMASCENES
king was guarding the city of the **D** 2Co 11:32 *1153*

DAMASCUS
far as Hobah, which is north of **D**. Gn 14:15 1834
of my house is Eliezer of **D**?" Gn 15:2 1834
of **D** came to help Hadadezer, 2Sa 8:5 1834
garrisons among the Arameans of **D**, 2Sa 8:6 1834
they went to **D** and stayed there, 1Ki 11:24 1834
stayed there, and reigned in **D**. 1Ki 11:24 1834
king of Aram, who lived in **D**, 1Ki 15:18 1834
your way to the wilderness of **D**, 1Ki 19:15 1834
make streets for yourself in **D**, 1Ki 20:34 1834
and Pharpar, the rivers of **D**, 2Ki 5:12 1834
Then Elisha came to **D**. 2Ki 8:7 1834
every kind of good thing of **D**, 2Ki 8:9 1834
for Israel, **D** and Hamath, 2Ki 14:28 1834
went up against **D** and captured it, 2Ki 16:9 1834
Now King Ahaz went to **D** to meet 2Ki 16:10 1834
and saw the altar which *was* at **D**; 2Ki 16:10 1834
that King Ahaz had sent from **D**, 2Ki 16:11 1834
the coming of King Ahaz from **D**. 2Ki 16:11 1834
When the king came from **D**, 2Ki 16:12 1834
When the Arameans of **D** came to 1Ch 18:5 1834
garrisons among the Arameans of **D**; 1Ch 18:6 1834
king of Aram, who lived in **D**, 2Ch 16:2 1834
all their spoil to the king of **D**. 2Ch 24:23 1834
captives and brought *them* to **D**. 2Ch 28:5 1834
gods of **D** which had defeated him, 2Ch 28:23 1834
of Lebanon, Which faces toward **D**. SS 7:4 1834
"For the head of Aram is **D** and Is 7:8 1834
and the head of **D** is Rezin Is 7:8 1834
the wealth of **D** and the spoil of Is 8:4 1834
like Arpad, Or Samaria like **D**? Is 10:9 1834
The oracle concerning **D**. Is 17:1 1834
D is about to be removed from Is 17:1 1834
from **D** And the remnant of Aram; Is 17:3 1834
Concerning **D**. "Hamath and Arpad Jer 49:23 1834
"**D** has become helpless; Jer 49:24 1834
I will set fire to the wall of **D**, Jer 49:27 1834
"**D** was your customer because of Ezk 27:18 1834
of **D** and the border of Hamath; Ezk 47:16 1834
to Hazar-enan *at* the border of **D**, Ezk 47:17 1834
east side, from between Hauran, **D**, Ezk 47:18 1834
as Hazar-enan *at* the border of **D**, Ezk 48:1 1834
"For three transgressions of **D** Am 1:3 1834
will also break the *gate* bar of **D**, Am 1:5 1834
make you go into exile beyond **D**," Am 5:27 1834
with **D** as its resting place Zch 9:1 1834
from him to the synagogues at **D**, Ac 9:2 *1154*
it happened that he was approaching **D**, Ac 9:3 *1154*
the hand, they brought him into **D**. Ac 9:8 *1154*
there was a disciple at **D** Ac 9:10 *1154*
with the disciples who were at **D**, Ac 9:19 *1154*
confounding the Jews who lived at **D** Ac 9:22 *1154*
and how at **D** he had spoken out Ac 9:27 *1154*
and started off for **D** in order to Ac 22:5 *1154*
way, approaching **D** about noontime, Ac 22:6 *1154*
'Get up and go on into **D**, Ac 22:10 *1154*
who were with me and came into **D**. Ac 22:11 *1154*
journeying to **D** with the authority Ac 26:12 *1154*
both to those of **D** first, Ac 26:20 *1154*
In **D** the ethnarch under Aretas the 2Co 11:32 *1154*
and returned once more to **D**. Ga 1:17 *1154*

DAMP
My locks with the **d** of the night.' SS 5:2 7447a

DAMS
"He **d** up the streams from flowing, Jb 28:11 2280

DAN
and went in pursuit as far as **D**. Gn 14:14 1835
Therefore she named him **D**. Gn 30:6 1835
sons of Bilhah, Rachel's maid: **D** and Gn 35:25 1835
The sons of **D**: Gn 46:23 1835
"**D** shall judge his people, As one Gn 49:16 1835
"**D** shall be a serpent in the way, Gn 49:17 1835
D and Naphtali, Gad and Asher. Ex 1:4 1835
of Ahisamach, of the tribe of **D**; Ex 31:6 1835
of Ahisamach, of the tribe of **D**. Ex 35:34 1835
of Ahisamach, of the tribe of **D**, Ex 38:23 1835
of Dibri, of the tribe of **D**.) Lv 24:11 1835
of **D**, Ahiezer the son of Nu 1:12 1835
Of the sons of **D**, their Nu 1:38 1835
numbered men of the tribe of **D** Nu 1:39 1835
of the camp of **D** by their armies, Nu 2:25 1835
and the leader of the sons of **D**: Nu 2:25 1835
the numbered men of the camp of **D** Nu 2:31 1835
leader of the sons of **D**; Nu 7:66 1835
of the camp of the sons of **D**, Nu 10:25 1835
from the tribe of **D**, Nu 13:12 1835
of **D** according to their families: Nu 26:42 1835
of **D** according to their families. Nu 26:42 1835
tribe of the sons of **D** a leader, Nu 34:22 1835
Reuben, Gad, Asher, Zebulun, **D**, Dt 27:13 1835
Of **D** he said, Dt 33:22 1835
"**D** is a lion's whelp, That leaps Dt 33:22 1835
all the land, Gilead as far as **D**, Dt 34:1 1835
of **D** according to their families. Jos 19:40 1835
sons of **D** proceeded beyond them; Jos 19:47 1835
for the sons of **D** went up and Jos 19:47 1835
and they called Leshem **D** after the Jos 19:47 1835
after the name of **D** their father. Jos 19:47 1835
of **D** according to their families, Jos 19:48 1835
of Ephraim and from the tribe of **D** Jos 21:5 1835
From the tribe of **D**, Jos 21:23 1835
sons of **D** into the hill country, Jg 1:34 1835
And why did **D** stay in ships? Jg 5:17 1835
So the sons of **D** sent from their Jg 18:2 1835
of war, who were of the sons of **D**, Jg 18:16 1835
and overtook the sons of **D**. Jg 18:22 1835
They cried to the sons of **D**, Jg 18:23 1835
The sons of **D** said to him, Jg 18:25 1835
the sons of **D** went on their way; Jg 18:26 1835
called the name of the city **D**, Jg 18:29 1835
after the name of **D** their father Jg 18:29 1835
The sons of **D** set up for Jg 18:30 1835
of Israel from **D** to Beersheba, Jg 20:1 1835
All Israel from **D** even to 1Sa 3:20 1835
Judah, from **D** even to Beersheba." 2Sa 3:10 1835
to you, from **D** even to Beersheba, 2Sa 17:11 1835
of Israel, from **D** to Beersheba, 2Sa 24:2 1835
people from **D** to Beersheba died. 2Sa 24:15 1835
tree, from **D** even to Beersheba, 1Ki 4:25 1835
Bethel, and the other he put in **D**. 1Ki 12:29 1835
before the one as far as **D**. 1Ki 12:30 1835
of Israel, and conquered Ijon, **D**, 1Ki 15:20 1835
were at Bethel and that *were* at **D**. 2Ki 10:29 1835
D, Joseph, Benjamin, Naphtali, 1Ch 2:2 1835
Israel from Beersheba even to **D**, 1Ch 21:2 1835
for **D**, Azarel the son of Jeroham. 1Ch 27:22 1835
and they conquered Ijon, **D**, 2Ch 16:4 1835
Israel from Beersheba even to **D**, 2Ch 30:5 1835
For a voice declares from **D**, Jer 4:15 1835
From **D** is heard the snorting of Jer 8:16 1835
running from east to west, **D**, Ezk 48:1 1835
'Beside the border of **D**, Ezk 48:2 1835
the gate of **D**, one. Ezk 48:32 1835
'As your god lives, O **D**,' Am 8:14 1835

DANCE
A time to mourn and a time to **d**. Ec 3:4 7540
As at the **d** of the two companies? SS 6:13 4246
the virgin will rejoice in the **d**, Jer 31:13 4234
flute for you, and you did not **d**; Mt 11:17 *3738*
flute for you, and you did not **d**; Lk 7:32 *3738*

DANCED
to their number from those who **d**, Jg 21:23 2342a

not sing of this one as they **d**, 1Sa 21:11 4246
d before *them* and pleased Herod, Mt 14:6 *3738*
of Herodias herself came in and **d**, Mk 6:22 *3738*

DANCES
come out to take part in the **d**, Jg 21:21 4246
David, of whom they sing in the **d**, 1Sa 29:5 4246
forth to the **d** of the merrymakers. Jer 31:4 4234

DANCING
her with timbrels and with **d**. Ex 15:20 4246
that he saw the calf and *the* **d**; Ex 32:19 4246
him with tambourines and with **d**. Jg 11:34 4246
cities of Israel, singing and **d**, 1Sa 18:6 4246
eating and drinking and **d** because 1Sa 30:16 2287
And David was **d** before the LORD 2Sa 6:14 3769
leaping and **d** before the LORD; 2Sa 6:16 3769
turned for me my mourning into **d**; Ps 30:11 4234
Let them praise His name with **d**; Ps 149:3 4234
Praise Him with timbrel and **d**; Ps 150:4 4234
d has been turned into mourning. La 5:15 4234
the house, he heard music and **d**. Lk 15:25 *5525*

DANGER
to be swamped and to be in **d**. Lk 8:23 *2793*
"Not only is there **d** that Ac 19:27 *2793*
"For indeed we are in **d** of being Ac 19:40 *2793*
Why are we also in **d** every hour? 1Co 15:30 *2793*
number, often in **d** of death. 2Co 11:23 *2288*

DANGEROUS
passed and the voyage was now **d**, Ac 27:9 *2000*

DANGERS
journeys, in **d** from rivers, 2Co 11:26 *2794*
from rivers, **d** from robbers, 2Co 11:26 *2794*
robbers, **d** from *my* countrymen, 2Co 11:26 *2794*
countrymen, **d** from the Gentiles, 2Co 11:26 *2794*
from the Gentiles, **d** in the city, 2Co 11:26 *2794*
in the city, **d** in the wilderness, 2Co 11:26 *2794*
in the wilderness, **d** on the sea, 2Co 11:26 *2794*
the sea, **d** among false brethren; 2Co 11:26 *2794*

DANGLING
d earrings, bracelets, veils, Is 3:19 5188

DANIEL
the second *was* **D**, by Abigail the 1Ch 3:1 1840
of the sons of Ithamar, **D**; Ezr 8:2 1840
D, Ginnethon, Baruch, Ne 10:6 1840
though these three men, Noah, **D** and Ezk 14:14 1840
even *though* Noah, **D** and Ezk 14:20 1840
Behold, you are wiser than **D**; Ezk 28:3 1840
from the sons of Judah were **D**, Da 1:6 1840
and to **D** he assigned the *name* Da 1:7 1840
But **D** made up his mind that he Da 1:8 1840
Now God granted **D** favor and Da 1:9 1840
of the officials said to **D**, Da 1:10 1840
But **D** said to the overseer whom Da 1:11 1840
officials had appointed over **D**, Da 1:11 1840
D even understood all *kinds of* Da 1:17 1840
them all not one was found like **D**, Da 1:19 1840
And **D** continued until the first Da 1:21 1840
D and his friends to kill *them.* Da 2:13 1841
Then **D** replied with discretion and Da 2:14 1841
informed **D** about the matter. Da 2:15 1841
So **D** went in and requested of the Da 2:16 1841
Then **D** went to his house and Da 2:17 1841
so that **D** and his friends would Da 2:18 1841
revealed to **D** in a night vision. Da 2:19 1841
Then **D** blessed the God of heaven; Da 2:19 1841
D said, "Let the name of God Da 2:20 1841
Therefore, **D** went in to Arioch, Da 2:24 1841
Then Arioch hurriedly brought **D** Da 2:25 1841
The king said to **D**, Da 2:26 1841
D answered before the king and Da 2:27 1841
on his face and did homage to **D**, Da 2:46 1841
The king answered **D** and said, Da 2:47 1841
the king promoted **D** and gave him Da 2:48 1841
And **D** made request of the king, Da 2:49 1841
while **D** *was* at the king's court. Da 2:49 1841
"But finally **D** came in before me, Da 4:8 1841
D, whose name is Belteshazzar, Da 4:19 1841
problems were found in this **D**, Da 5:12 1841
Let **D** now be summoned and he will Da 5:12 1841
Then **D** was brought in before the Da 5:13 1841
The king spoke and said to **D**, Da 5:13 1841
"Are you that **D** who is one of the Da 5:13 1841
Then **D** answered and said before Da 5:17 1841
they clothed **D** with purple and Da 5:29 1841
commissioners (of whom **D** was one), Da 6:2 1841
Then this **D** began distinguishing Da 6:3 1841
find a ground of accusation against **D** Da 6:4 1841
ground of accusation against this **D** Da 6:5 1841
Now when **D** knew that the document Da 6:10 1841
D making petition and supplication Da 6:11 1841
"**D**, who is one of the exiles from Da 6:13 1841
and set *his* mind on delivering **D**; Da 6:14 1841
and **D** was brought in and cast into Da 6:16 1841
The king spoke and said to **D**, Da 6:16 1841
would be changed in regard to **D**. Da 6:17 1841
he had come near the den to **D**, Da 6:20 1841
The king spoke and said to **D**, Da 6:20 1841
"**D**, servant of the living God, Da 6:20 1841
Then **D** spoke to the king, Da 6:21 1841
D to be taken up out of the den. Da 6:23 1841
So **D** was taken up out of the den and Da 6:23 1841
men who had maliciously accused **D**, Da 6:24 1841
and tremble before the God of **D**; Da 6:26 1841
D from the power of the lions." Da 6:27 1841
So this **D** enjoyed success in the Da 6:28 1841
D saw a dream and visions Da 7:1 1841
D said, "I was looking in my vision Da 7:2 1841
"As for me, **D**, my spirit was Da 7:15 1841
As for me, **D**, my thoughts were Da 7:28 1841
king a vision appeared to me, **D**, Da 8:1 1840
When I, **D**, had seen the vision, Da 8:15 1840
Then I, **D**, was exhausted and sick Da 8:27 1840
the first year of his reign, I, **D**, Da 9:2 1840
"O **D**, I have now come forth to Da 9:22 1840
a message was revealed to **D**, Da 10:1 1840
In those days, I, **D**, Da 10:2 1840
Now I, **D**, alone saw the vision, Da 10:7 1840
"O **D**, man of high esteem, Da 10:11 1840
"Do not be afraid, **D**, Da 10:12 1840
"But as for you, **D**, conceal these Da 12:4 1840
Then I, **D**, looked and behold, two Da 12:5 1840
"Go *your way*, **D**, for *these* words Da 12:9 1840
spoken of through **D** the prophet, Mt 24:15 *1158*

DANITE
of a **D** woman and a Tyrian father, 2Ch 2:14 1323, 1835

DANITES
of Zorah, of the family of the **D**, Jg 13:2 1839
the tribe of the **D** was seeking an Jg 18:1 1839
Then from the family of the **D**, Jg 18:11 1839
sons were priests to the tribe of the **D** Jg 18:30 1839
Of the **D** who could draw up in 1Ch 12:35 1839

DAN-JAAN
came to **D** and around to Sidon, 2Sa 24:6 1842

DANNAH
and **D** and Kiriath-sannah Jos 15:49 1837

DAPPLED
fourth chariot strong **d** horses. Zch 6:3 1261
while the **d** ones go forth to the Zch 6:6 1261

DARA
Ethan, Heman, Calcol and **D**; 1Ch 2:6 1873

DARDA
the Ezrahite, Heman, Calcol and **D**, 1Ki 4:31 1862

DARE
I **d** not lift up my head. Jb 10:15
For who would **d** to risk his life Jer 30:21 6148
nor did anyone **d** from that day on Mt 22:46 *5111*
man someone would **d** even to die. Ro 5:7 *5111*
d to go to law before the 1Co 6:1 *5111*
did not **d** pronounce against him a Jude 1:9 *5111*

DARED
none of the rest **d** to associate with Ac 5:13 *5111*

DARES
And as a lion, who **d** rouse him up? Gn 49:9
And as a lion, who **d** rouse him? Nu 24:9
so fierce that he **d** to arouse him; Jb 41:10

DARICS
talents and 10,000 **d** of gold, 1Ch 29:7 150
and 20 gold bowls *worth* 1,000 **d** Ezr 8:27 150

DARING
D, self-willed, they do not 2Pe 2:10 *5113*

DARIUS
the reign of **D** king of Persia. Ezr 4:5 1867
of the reign of **D** king of Persia. Ezr 4:24 1868
until a report could come to **D**, Ezr 5:5 1868
the River, sent to **D** the king. Ezr 5:6 1868
"To **D** the king, all peace. Ezr 5:7 1868
Then King **D** issued a decree, and Ezr 6:1 1868
I, **D**, have issued *this* decree, let Ezr 6:12 1868
just as King **D** had sent. Ezr 6:13 1868
Israel and the decree of Cyrus, **D**, Ezr 6:14 1868
sixth year of the reign of King **D**. Ezr 6:15 1868
in the reign of **D** the Persian. Ne 12:22 1867
So **D** the Mede received the kingdom Da 5:31 1868
It seemed good to **D** to appoint 120 Da 6:1 1868
"King **D**, live forever! Da 6:6 1868
King **D** signed the document, Da 6:9 1868
Then **D** the king wrote to all the Da 6:25 1868
enjoyed success in the reign of **D** Da 6:28 1868
year of **D** the son of Ahasuerus, Da 9:1 1867
In the first year of **D** the Mede, Da 11:1 1867
In the second year of **D** the king, Hg 1:1 1867
in the second year of **D** the king. Hg 1:15 1867
month, in the second year of **D**, Hg 2:10 1867
month of the second year of **D**, Zch 1:1 1867
Shebat, in the second year of **D**, Zch 1:7 1867
In the fourth year of King **D**, Zch 7:1 1867

DARK
sun had set, that it was very **d**, Gn 15:17 5939
Even openly, and not in **d** sayings, Nu 12:8 2420
was time to shut the gate at **d**, Jos 2:5 2822
as it grew **d** at the gates of Jerusalem Ne 13:19 6751
"In the **d** they dig into houses, Jb 24:16 2822
Let their way be **d** and slippery, Ps 35:6 2822
For the **d** places of the land are Ps 74:20 4285
I will utter **d** sayings of old, Ps 78:2 2420
me in the lowest pit, In **d** places, Ps 88:6 4285
He sent darkness and made *it* **d**; Ps 105:28 2821
the darkness is not **d** to You, Ps 139:12 2821
He has made me dwell in **d** places, Ps 143:3 4285
Those who live in a **d** land, Is 9:2 6757
The sun will be **d** when it rises And Is 13:10 2821
whose deeds are *done* in a **d** place, Is 29:15 4285
spoken in secret, In some **d** land; Is 45:19 2822
mourn And the heavens above be **d**. Jer 4:28 6937
In **d** places He has made me dwell, La 3:6 4285
How **d** the gold has become, *How* the La 4:1 6004
of Israel are committing in the **d**, Ezk 8:12 2822
sight *and carry it* out in the **d**. Ezk 12:6 5939
I went out in the **d** *and* carried Ezk 12:7 5939
his shoulder in the **d** and go out. Ezk 12:12 5939
"In Tehaphnehes the day will be **d** Ezk 30:18 2821
The sun and the moon grow **d** And Jl 2:10 6937
The sun and moon grow **d** And Jl 3:15 6937
the earth **d** in broad daylight. Am 8:9 2821
the day will become **d** over them. Mi 3:6 6937
morning, while it was still **d**, Mk 1:35 *1773*
of light, with no **d** part in it, Lk 11:36 *4652*
the **d** will be heard in the light, Lk 12:3 *4653*
It had already become **d**, Jn 6:17 *4653*
to the tomb, while it was still **d**, Jn 20:1 *4653*
as to a lamp shining in a **d** place, 2Pe 1:19 *850b*

DARKEN
the heavens and **d** their stars; Ezk 32:7 6937
lights in the heavens I will **d** over you Ezk 32:8 6937

DARKENED
land, so that the land was **d**; Ex 10:15 2821
the stars of its twilight be **d**; Jb 3:9 2821
"The light in his tent is **d**, Jb 18:6 2821
the moon and the stars are **d**, Ec 12:2 2821
Even the light is **d** by its clouds. Is 5:30 2821
of those days THE SUN WILL BE **D**, Mt 24:29 *4654*
tribulation, THE SUN WILL BE **D** AND Mk 13:24 *4654*
and their foolish heart was **d**. Ro 1:21 *4654*
"LET THEIR EYES BE **D** TO SEE NOT, Ro 11:10 *4654*
being **d** in their understanding, Eph 4:18 *4656*
so that a third of them would be **d** Rv 8:12 *4654*
were **d** by the smoke of the pit. Rv 9:2 *4656*
and his kingdom became **d**; Rv 16:10 *4656*

DARKENS
"Who is this that **d** counsel By Jb 38:2 2821
Who also **d** day *into* night, Am 5:8 2821

DARKNESS
and **d** was over the surface of the Gn 1:2 2822
separated the light from the **d**. Gn 1:4 2822
day, and the **d** He called night. Gn 1:5 2822
to separate the light from the **d**; Gn 1:18 2822
terror *and* great **d** fell upon him. Gn 15:12 2825
may be **d** over the land of Egypt, Ex 10:21 2822
even a **d** which may be felt." Ex 10:21 2822
was thick **d** in all the land of Egypt Ex 10:22 2822
was the cloud along with the **d**, Ex 14:20 2822
d, cloud and thick gloom. Dt 4:11 2822
the voice from the midst of the **d**, Dt 5:23 2822
as the blind man gropes in **d**, Dt 28:29 653
d between you and the Egyptians, Jos 24:7 3990
the wicked ones are silenced in **d**; 1Sa 2:9 2822
down With thick **d** under His feet. 2Sa 22:10 6205
"And He made **d** canopies around 2Sa 22:12 2822
And the LORD illumines my **d**. 2Sa 22:29 2822
"May that day be **d**; Jb 3:4 2822
"Let **d** and black gloom claim it; Jb 3:5 2822
"*As for* that night, let **d** seize it; Jb 3:6 652
"By day they meet with **d**, Jb 5:14 2822
To the land of **d** and deep shadow, Jb 10:21 2822
land of utter gloom as **d** *itself,* Jb 10:22 652
And which shines as the **d**." Jb 10:22 652
D would be like the morning. Jb 11:17 8591b
"He reveals mysteries from the **d** And Jb 12:22 2822
And brings the deep **d** into light. Jb 12:22 6757
"They grope in **d** with no light, Jb 12:25 2822
that he will return from **d**, Jb 15:22 2822
knows that a day of **d** is at hand. Jb 15:23 2822
"He will not escape from **d**; Jb 15:30 2822
And deep **d** is on my eyelids, Jb 16:16 6757
in the presence of **d**. Jb 17:12 2822
my home, I make my bed in the **d**; Jb 17:13 2822
"He is driven from light into **d**, Jb 18:18 2822
And He has put **d** on my paths. Jb 19:8 2822
Complete **d** is held in reserve for Jb 20:26 2822
Or **d**, so that you cannot see, And Jb 22:11 2822
Can He judge through the thick **d**? Jb 22:13 6205
But I am not silenced by the **d**, Jb 23:17 2822
is the same to him as thick **d**, Jb 24:17 6757
with the terrors of thick **d**. Jb 24:17 6757
At the boundary of light and **d**. Jb 26:10 2822
"*Man* puts an end to **d**, Jb 28:3 2822
by His light I walked through **d**; Jb 29:3 2822
I waited for light, then **d** came. Jb 30:26 652
"There is no **d** or deep shadow Jb 34:22 2822
arrange *our case* because of **d**. Jb 37:19 2822
And thick **d** its swaddling band, Jb 38:9 6205
have you seen the gates of deep **d**? Jb 38:17 6757
And **d**, where is its place, Jb 38:19 2822
To shoot in **d** at the upright in heart. Ps 11:2 652
down With thick **d** under His feet. Ps 18:9 6205
He made **d** His hiding place, His Ps 18:11 2822
canopy around Him, **D** of waters, Ps 18:11 2825
The LORD my God illumines my **d**. Ps 18:28 2822
They walk about in **d**; Ps 82:5 2825
wonders be made known in the **d**? Ps 88:12 2822
My acquaintances are *in* **d**. Ps 88:18 4285
the pestilence that stalks in **d**, Ps 91:6 652
Clouds and thick **d** surround Him; Ps 97:2 6205
appoint **d** and it becomes night, Ps 104:20 2822
He sent **d** and made *it* dark; Ps 105:28 2822
in **d** and in the shadow of death, Ps 107:10 2822
out of **d** and the shadow of death And Ps 107:14 2822
arises in the **d** for the upright; Ps 112:4 2822
"Surely the **d** will overwhelm me, Ps 139:11 2822
Even the **d** is not dark to You, Ps 139:12 2822
D and light are alike *to You.* Ps 139:12 2825
To walk in the ways of **d**; Pr 2:13 2822
The way of the wicked is like **d**; Pr 4:19 653
middle of the night and *in the* **d**. Pr 7:9 653
His lamp will go out in time of **d**. Pr 20:20 2822
excels folly as light excels **d**. Ec 2:13 2822
his head, but the fool walks in **d**. Ec 2:14 2822
eats in **d** with great vexation, Ec 5:17 2822
let him remember the days of **d**, Ec 11:8 2822
Who substitute **d** for light and Is 5:20 2822
for light and light for **d**; Is 5:20 2822

behold, there is **d** *and* distress; Is 5:30 2822
earth, and behold, distress and **d**, Is 8:22 2825
they will be driven away into **d**. Is 8:22 653
walk in **d** Will see a great light; Is 9:2 2822
And out of *their* gloom and **d** the Is 29:18 2822
who dwell in **d** from the prison. Is 42:7 2822
I will make **d** into light before Is 42:16 4285
will give you the treasures of **d** And Is 45:3 2822
One forming light and creating **d**, Is 45:7 2822
"Sit silently, and go into **d**, Is 47:5 2822
'Go forth,' To those who are in **d**, Is 49:9 2822
That walks in **d** and has no light? Is 50:10 2825
Then your light will rise in **d** And Is 58:10 2822
We hope for light, but behold, **d**, Is 59:9 2822
behold, **d** will cover the earth And Is 60:2 2822
the earth And deep **d** the peoples; Is 60:2 6205
a land of drought and of deep **d**, Jer 2:6 6757
to Israel, Or a land of thick **d**? Jer 2:31 3991
Before He brings **d** And before your Jer 13:16 2821
for light He makes it into deep **d**, Jer 13:16 6757
me walk In **d** and not in light. La 3:2 2822
you And will set **d** on your land," Ezk 32:8 2822
He knows what is in the **d**, Da 2:22 2816
A day of **d** and gloom, A day of Jl 2:2 2822
A day of clouds and thick **d**. Jl 2:2 6205
"The sun will be turned into **d** And Jl 2:31 2822
He who makes dawn into **d** And Am 4:13 5890
And changes deep **d** into morning, Am 5:8 6757
It *will be* **d** and not light; Am 5:18 2822
of the LORD *be* **d** instead of light, Am 5:20 2822
without vision, And **d** for you Mi 3:6 2825
Though I dwell in **d**, Mi 7:8 2822
will pursue His enemies into **d**. Na 1:8 2822
desolation, A day of **d** and gloom, Zph 1:15 2822
A day of clouds and thick **d**, Zph 1:15 6205
SITTING IN **D** SAW A GREAT LIGHT, Mt 4:16 *4653*
your whole body will be full of **d**. Mt 6:23 *4652*
the light that is in you is **d**, Mt 6:23 *4655*
is darkness, how great is the **d**! Mt 6:23 *4655*
be cast out into the outer **d**; Mt 8:12 *4655*
"What I tell you in the **d**, Mt 10:27 *4653*
and throw him into the outer **d**; Mt 22:13 *4655*
worthless slave into the outer **d**; Mt 25:30 *4655*
Now from the sixth hour **d** fell Mt 27:45 *4655*
d fell over the whole land until Mk 15:33 *4655*
SIT IN **D** AND THE SHADOW OF DEATH, Lk 1:79 *4655*
bad, your body also is full of **d**. Lk 11:34 *4652*
the light in you is not **d**. Lk 11:35 *4655*
and the power of **d** are yours." Lk 22:53 *4655*
and **d** fell over the whole land Lk 23:44 *4655*
The Light shines in the **d**, Jn 1:5 *4653*
and the **d** did not comprehend it. Jn 1:5 *4653*
loved the **d** rather than the Light Jn 3:19 *4655*
follows Me will not walk in the **d**, Jn 8:12 *4653*
that **d** will not overtake you; Jn 12:35 *4653*
the **d** does not know where he goes. Jn 12:35 *4653*
believes in Me will not remain in **d**. Jn 12:46 *4653*
THE SUN WILL BE TURNED INTO **D** Ac 2:20 *4655*
a mist and a **d** fell upon him, Ac 13:11 *4655*
so that they may turn from **d** to light Ac 26:18 *4655*
a light to those who are in **d**, Ro 2:19 *4655*
d and put on the armor of light. Ro 13:12 *4655*
to light the things hidden in the **d** 1Co 4:5 *4655*
"Light shall shine out of **d**," 2Co 4:6 *4655*
what fellowship has light with **d**? 2Co 6:14 *4655*
for you were formerly **d**, Eph 5:8 *4655*
in the unfruitful deeds of **d**, Eph 5:11 *4655*
against the world forces of this **d**, Eph 6:12 *4655*
rescued us from the domain of **d**, Col 1:13 *4655*
But you, brethren, are not in **d**, 1Th 5:4 *4655*
We are not of night nor of **d**; 1Th 5:5 *4655*
and to **d** and gloom and whirlwind, Heb 12:18 *1105*
out of **d** into His marvelous light; 1Pe 2:9 *4655*
and committed them to pits of **d**, 2Pe 2:4 *2217*
the black **d** has been reserved. 2Pe 2:17 *4655*
and in Him there is no **d** at all. 1Jn 1:5 *4653*
with Him and *yet* walk in the **d**, 1Jn 1:6 *4655*
because the **d** is passing away and 1Jn 2:8 *4653*
his brother is in the **d** until now. 1Jn 2:9 *4653*
the **d** and walks in the darkness, 1Jn 2:11 *4653*
the darkness and walks in the **d**, 1Jn 2:11 *4653*
the **d** has blinded his eyes. 1Jn 2:11 *4653*
He has kept in eternal bonds under **d** Jude 1:6 *2217*
black **d** has been reserved forever. Jude 1:13 *4655*

DARKON

the sons of Jaalah, the sons of **D**, Ezr 2:56 1874
the sons of Jaala, the sons of **D**, Ne 7:58 1874

DARLING

"To me, my **d**, you are like My SS 1:9 7474
"How beautiful you are, my **d**, SS 1:15 7474
So is my **d** among the maidens." SS 2:2 7474
'Arise, my **d**, my beautiful one, SS 2:10 7474
Arise, my **d**, my beautiful one, And SS 2:13 7474
"How beautiful you are, my **d**, SS 4:1 7474
are altogether beautiful, my **d**, SS 4:7 7474
'Open to me, my sister, my **d**, SS 5:2 7474
are as beautiful as Tirzah, my **d**, SS 6:4 7474

DART

Nor the spear, the **d** or Jb 41:26 4551b

DARTING

like torches **d** back and forth Ezk 1:13 1980

DASH

little ones you will **d** in pieces, 2Ki 8:12 7376
I will **d** them against each other, Jer 13:14 5310a
and **d** down your arrows from your Ezk 39:3 5307
They **d** to and fro like lightning Na 2:4 7323

DASHED

d forward and stood in the entrance Jg 9:44 6584
the other two companies then **d** Jg 9:44 6584
so that they were all **d** to pieces. 2Ch 25:12 1234
be **d** to pieces Before their eyes; Is 13:16 7376
d in pieces with *their* children. Hos 10:14 7376
little ones will be **d** in pieces, Hos 13:16 7376
her small children were **d** to pieces Na 3:10 7376

DASHES

d your little ones Against the rock. Ps 137:9 5310a

DASHING

the horses' hoofs beat From the **d**, Jg 5:22 1726
the **d** of his valiant steeds. Jg 5:22 1726

DATE

of water and seventy **d** palms, Ex 15:27 8558
until the **d** set by the father. Ga 4:2 *4287*

DATES

a cake of bread and one of **d** and 2Sa 6:19 829
His locks are *like* clusters of **d** SS 5:11 8534

DATHAN

son of Levi, with **D** and Abiram, Nu 16:1 1885
sent a summons to **D** and Abiram, Nu 16:12 1885
of Korah, **D** and Abiram.' " Nu 16:24 1885
arose and went to **D** and Abiram, Nu 16:25 1885
dwellings of Korah, **D** and Abiram; Nu 16:27 1885
and **D** and Abiram came out *and* Nu 16:27 1885
Nemuel and **D** and Abiram. Nu 26:9 1885
These are the **D** and Abiram who Nu 26:9 1885
and what He did to **D** and Abiram, Dt 11:6 1885
earth opened and swallowed up **D**, Ps 106:17 1885

DAUGHTER

wife was Milcah, the **d** of Haran, Gn 11:29 1323
is my sister, the **d** of my father, Gn 20:12 1323
but not the **d** of my mother, Gn 20:12 1323
"Whose **d** are you? Please tell me, Gn 24:23 1323
"I am the **d** of Bethuel, the son Gn 24:24 1323
'Whose **d** are you?' Gn 24:47 1323
'The **d** of Bethuel, Nahor's son, Gn 24:47 1323
to take the **d** of my master's kinsman Gn 24:48 1323
the **d** of Bethuel the Aramean of Gn 25:20 1323
Judith the **d** of Beeri the Hittite, Gn 26:34 1323
Basemath the **d** of Elon the Hittite; Gn 26:34 1323
he had, Mahalath the **d** of Ishmael, Gn 28:9 1323
his **d** coming with the sheep." Gn 29:6 1323
d of Laban his mother's brother, Gn 29:10 1323
years for your younger **d** Rachel." Gn 29:18 1323
evening he took his **d** Leah, Gn 29:23 1323
Zilpah to his **d** Leah as a maid. Gn 29:24 1323
gave him his **d** Rachel as his wife. Gn 29:28 1323
gave his maid Bilhah to his **d** Rachel Gn 29:29 1323
she bore a **d** and named her Dinah. Gn 30:21 1323
Now Dinah the **d** of Leah, whom she Gn 34:1 1323
attracted to Dinah the **d** of Jacob, Gn 34:3 1323
that he had defiled Dinah his **d**; Gn 34:5 1323
in Israel by lying with Jacob's **d**, Gn 34:7 1323
my son Shechem longs for your **d**; Gn 34:8 1323
then we will take our **d** and go." Gn 34:17 1323
he was delighted with Jacob's **d**. Gn 34:19 1323
Adah the **d** of Elon the Hittite, Gn 36:2 1323
and Oholibamah the **d** of Anah and Gn 36:2 1323
also Basemath, Ishmael's **d**, Gn 36:3 1323
the **d** of Anah and the Gn 36:14 1323
wife Oholibamah, the **d** of Anah. Gn 36:18 1323
and Oholibamah, the **d** of Anah. Gn 36:25 1323
was Mehetabel, the **d** of Matred, Gn 36:39 1323
daughter of Matred, **d** of Mezahab. Gn 36:39 1323
Judah saw there a **d** of a Gn 38:2 1323
after a considerable time Shua's **d**, Gn 38:12 1323
the **d** of Potiphera priest of On, Gn 41:45 1323
the **d** of Potiphera priest of On, Gn 41:50 1323
in Paddan-aram, with his **d** Dinah; Gn 46:15 1323
whom Laban gave to his **d** Leah; Gn 46:18 1323
whom Asenath, the **d** of Potiphera, Gn 46:20 1323
whom Laban gave to his **d** Rachel, Gn 46:25 1323
but if it is a **d**, then she shall live." Ex 1:16 1323
every **d** you are to keep alive." Ex 1:22 1323
Levi went and married a **d** of Levi. Ex 2:1 1323
The **d** of Pharaoh came down to Ex 2:5 1323
his sister said to Pharaoh's **d**, Ex 2:7 1323
Pharaoh's **d** said to her, Ex 2:8 1323
Then Pharaoh's **d** said to her, Ex 2:9 1323
and she brought him to Pharaoh's **d** and Ex 2:10 1323
he gave his **d** Zipporah to Moses. Ex 2:21 1323
Elisheba, the **d** of Amminadab, Ex 6:23 1323
work, you or your son or your **d**, Ex 20:10 1323
man sells his **d** as a female slave, Ex 21:7 1323
"Whether it gores a son or a **d**, Ex 21:31 1323
completed, for a son or for a **d**, Lv 12:6 1323
d or your mother's daughter, Lv 18:9 1323
daughter or your mother's **d**, Lv 18:9 1323
son's **d** or your daughter's daughter, Lv 18:10 1323
son's daughter or your daughter's **d**, Lv 18:10 1323
nakedness of your father's wife's **d**, Lv 18:11 1323
nakedness of a woman and of her **d**, Lv 18:17 1323
son's **d** or her daughter's daughter, Lv 18:17 1323
son's daughter or her daughter's **d**, Lv 18:17 1323
your **d** by making her a harlot, Lv 19:29 1323
father's **d** or his mother's daughter, Lv 20:17 1323
father's daughter or his mother's **d**, Lv 20:17 1323
his son and his **d** and his brother, Lv 21:2 1323
'Also the **d** of any priest, if she Lv 21:9 1323
priest's **d** is married to a layman, Lv 22:12 1323
d becomes a widow or divorced, Lv 22:13 1323
was Shelomith, the **d** of Dibri, Lv 24:11 1323
was slain was Cozbi the **d** of Zur, Nu 25:15 1323
the **d** of the leader of Midian, Nu 25:18 1323
name of the **d** of Asher *was* Serah. Nu 26:46 1323
wife was Jochebed, the **d** of Levi, Nu 26:59 1323
transfer his inheritance to his **d**. Nu 27:8 1323
'If he has no **d**, Nu 27:9 1323
and as between a father and his **d**, Nu 30:16 1323
Every **d** who comes into possession Nu 36:8 1323
you or your son or your **d** or your Dt 5:14 1323
choose, you and your son and **d**, Dt 12:18 1323
mother's son, or your son or **d**, Dt 13:6 1323
you and your son and your **d** and Dt 16:11 1323
you and your son and your **d** and Dt 16:14 1323
or his **d** pass through the fire, Dt 18:10 1323
gave my **d** to this man for a wife, Dt 22:16 1323
"I did not find your **d** a virgin." Dt 22:17 1323
the **d** of his father or of his mother.' Dt 27:22 1323
and toward her son and **d**, Dt 28:56 1323
give him Achsah my **d** as a wife." Jos 15:16 1323
gave him Achsah his **d** as a wife. Jos 15:17 1323
give him my **d** Achsah for a wife." Jg 1:12 1323
gave him his **d** Achsah for a wife. Jg 1:13 1323
his **d** was coming out to meet him Jg 11:34 1323
her he had no son or **d**. Jg 11:34 1323
tore his clothes and said, "Alas, my **d** Jg 11:35 1323
to commemorate the **d** of Jephthah Jg 11:40 1323
is my virgin **d** and his concubine. Jg 19:24 1323
his **d** to Benjamin in marriage." Jg 21:1 1323
And she said to her, "Go, my **d**." Ru 2:2 1323
"Listen carefully, my **d**. Ru 2:8 1323
"It is good, my **d**, that you go Ru 2:22 1323
"My **d**, shall I not seek security Ru 3:1 1323
you be blessed of the LORD, my **d**. Ru 3:10 1323
"Now, my **d**, do not fear. Ru 3:11 1323
"How did it go, my **d**?" Ru 3:16 1323
"Wait, my **d**, until you know how Ru 3:18 1323
wife was Ahinoam the **d** of Ahimaaz. 1Sa 14:50 1323
great riches and will give him his **d** 1Sa 17:25 1323
"Here is my older **d** Merab; 1Sa 18:17 1323
at the time when Merab, Saul's **d**, 1Sa 18:19 1323
Michal, Saul's **d**, loved David. 1Sa 18:20 1323
gave him Michal his **d** for a wife. 1Sa 18:27 1323
David, and *that* Michal, Saul's **d**, 1Sa 18:28 1323
Now Saul had given Michal his **d**, 1Sa 25:44 1323
son of Maacah, the **d** of Talmai, 2Sa 3:3 1323
name was Rizpah, the **d** of Aiah; 2Sa 3:7 1323
you first bring Michal, Saul's **d**, 2Sa 3:13 1323
Michal the **d** of Saul looked out 2Sa 6:16 1323
Michal the **d** of Saul came out to 2Sa 6:20 1323
Michal the **d** of Saul had no child 2Sa 6:23 1323
not Bathsheba, the **d** of Eliam, 2Sa 11:3 1323
bosom, And was like a **d** to him. 2Sa 12:3 1323
and one **d** whose name was Tamar; 2Sa 14:27 1323
in to Abigail the **d** of Nahash, 2Sa 17:25 1323
two sons of Rizpah the **d** of Aiah, 2Sa 21:8 1323
five sons of Merab the **d** of Saul, 2Sa 21:8 1323
And Rizpah the **d** of Aiah took 2Sa 21:10 1323
David what Rizpah the **d** of Aiah, 2Sa 21:11 1323
and took Pharaoh's **d** and brought 1Ki 3:1 1323
the **d** of Solomon was his wife); 1Ki 4:11 1323
Basemath the **d** of Solomon); 1Ki 4:15 1323
like this hall for Pharaoh's **d**, 1Ki 7:8 1323
had given it *as* a dowry to his **d**, 1Ki 9:16 1323
As soon as Pharaoh's **d** came up 1Ki 9:24 1323
women along with the **d** of Pharaoh: 1Ki 11:1 1323
was Maacah the **d** of Abishalom. 1Ki 15:2 1323
was Maacah the **d** of Abishalom. 1Ki 15:10 1323
that he married Jezebel the **d** of 1Ki 16:31 1323
name was Azubah the **d** of Shilhi. 1Ki 22:42 1323
for the **d** of Ahab became his wife; 2Ki 8:18 1323
bury her, for she is a king's **d**." 2Ki 9:34 1323
Jehosheba, the **d** of King Joram, 2Ki 11:2 1323
your **d** to my son in marriage.' 2Ki 14:9 1323
name *was* Jerusha the **d** of Zadok. 2Ki 15:33 1323
name was Abi the **d** of Zechariah. 2Ki 18:2 1323
mocked you, The virgin **d** of Zion; 2Ki 19:21 1323
behind you, The **d** of Jerusalem! 2Ki 19:21 1323
the **d** of Haruz of Jotbah. 2Ki 21:19 1323
the **d** of Adaiah of Bozkath. 2Ki 22:1 1323
man might make his son or his **d** pass 2Ki 23:10 1323
the **d** of Jeremiah of Libnah. 2Ki 23:31 1323
Zebidah the **d** of Pedaiah of Rumah. 2Ki 23:36 1323
the **d** of Elnathan of Jerusalem. 2Ki 24:8 1323
the **d** of Jeremiah of Libnah. 2Ki 24:18 1323
was Mehetabel, the **d** of Matred, 1Ch 1:50 1323
of Matred, the **d** of Mezahab. 1Ch 1:50 1323
Afterward Hezron went in to the **d** 1Ch 2:21 1323
Sheshan gave his **d** to Jarha 1Ch 2:35 1323
and the **d** of Caleb *was* Achsah. 1Ch 2:49 1323
the **d** of Talmai king of Geshur; 1Ch 3:2 1323
four, by Bath-shua the **d** of Ammiel; 1Ch 3:5 1323
sons of Bithia the **d** of Pharaoh, 1Ch 4:17 1323
His **d** was Sheerah, who built 1Ch 7:24 1323
that Michal the **d** of Saul looked 1Ch 15:29 1323
Then Solomon brought Pharaoh's **d** 2Ch 8:11 1323
as a wife Mahalath the **d** of Jerimoth 2Ch 11:18 1323
the **d** of Eliab the son of Jesse, 2Ch 11:18 1323
he took Maacah the **d** of Absalom, 2Ch 11:20 1323
Rehoboam loved Maacah the **d** of 2Ch 11:21 1323
Micaiah the **d** of Uriel of Gibeah. 2Ch 13:2 1323
name *was* Azubah the **d** of Shilhi. 2Ch 20:31 1323
did (for Ahab's **d** was his wife), 2Ch 21:6 1323
d took Joash the son of Ahaziah, 2Ch 22:11 1323
the **d** of King Jehoram, 2Ch 22:11 1323
your **d** to my son in marriage.' 2Ch 25:18 1323
name was Jerushah the **d** of Zadok. 2Ch 27:1 1323
was Abijah, the **d** of Zechariah. 2Ch 29:1 1323
son Jehohanan had married the **d** of Ne 6:18 1323
that is Esther, his uncle's **d**, Es 2:7 1323
Mordecai took her as his own **d**. Es 2:7 1323
the **d** of Abihail the uncle of Es 2:15 1323
who had taken her as his **d**, Es 2:15 1323
Then Queen Esther, **d** of Abihail, Es 9:29 1323
That in the gates of the **d** of Zion Ps 9:14 1323
Listen, O **d**, give attention and Ps 45:10 1323

d of Tyre *will come* with a gift;	Ps 45:12	1323
King's **d** is all glorious within;	Ps 45:13	1323
O **d** of Babylon, you devastated	Ps 137:8	1323
She is her mother's only **d**;	SS 6:9	1323
your feet in sandals, O prince's **d**!	SS 7:1	1323
The **d** of Zion is left like a	Is 1:8	1323
with your voice, O **d** of Gallim!	Is 10:30	1323
at the mountain of the **d** of Zion,	Is 10:32	1004
to the mountain of the **d** of Zion.	Is 16:1	1323
destruction of the **d** of my people."	Is 22:4	1323
like the Nile, O **d** of Tarshish,	Is 23:10	1323
more, O crushed virgin **d** of Sidon.	Is 23:12	1323
mocked you, The virgin **d** of Zion;	Is 37:22	1323
behind you, The **d** of Jerusalem!	Is 37:22	1323
the dust, O virgin **d** of Babylon;	Is 47:1	1323
a throne, O **d** of the Chaldeans!	Is 47:1	1323
darkness, O **d** of the Chaldeans,	Is 47:5	1323
your neck, O captive **d** of Zion.	Is 52:2	1323
the earth, Say to the **d** of Zion,	Is 62:11	1323
direction of the **d** of My people	Jer 4:11	1323
the **d** of Zion gasping for breath,	Jer 4:31	1323
and dainty one, the **d** of Zion,	Jer 6:2	1323
battle Against you, O **d** of Zion!"	Jer 6:23	1323
O **d** of my people, put on sackcloth	Jer 6:26	1323
the **d** of My people superficially,	Jer 8:11	1323
The cry of the **d** of my people from	Jer 8:19	1323
of the **d** of my people I am broken;	Jer 8:21	1323
the **d** of my people been restored?	Jer 8:22	1323
the slain of the **d** of my people!	Jer 9:1	1323
do, because of the **d** of My people?	Jer 9:7	1323
For the virgin **d** of my people has	Jer 14:17	1323
go here and there, O faithless **d**?	Jer 31:22	1323
obtain balm, O virgin **d** of Egypt!	Jer 46:11	1323
for exile, O **d** dwelling in Egypt,	Jer 46:19	1323
"The **d** of Egypt has been put to	Jer 46:24	1323
ground, O **d** dwelling in Dibon,	Jer 48:18	1323
d Who trusts in her treasures,	Jer 49:4	1323
Against you, O **d** of Babylon.	Jer 50:42	1323
"The **d** of Babylon is like a	Jer 51:33	1323
the **d** of Jeremiah of Libnah.	Jer 52:1	1323
Has departed from the **d** of Zion;	La 1:6	1323
wine press The virgin **d** of Judah.	La 1:15	1323
How the Lord has covered the **d** of	La 2:1	1323
The strongholds of the **d** of Judah;	La 2:2	1323
In the tent of the **d** of Zion He	La 2:4	1323
d of Judah Mourning and moaning.	La 2:5	1323
destroy The wall of the **d** of Zion.	La 2:8	1323
the **d** of Zion Sit on the ground,	La 2:10	1323
destruction of the **d** of my people,	La 2:11	1323
I compare you, O **d** of Jerusalem?	La 2:13	1323
I comfort you, O virgin **d** of Zion?	La 2:13	1323
their heads At the **d** of Jerusalem,	La 2:15	1323
"O wall of the **d** of Zion, Let	La 2:18	1323
destruction of the **d** of my people.	La 3:48	1323
But the **d** of my people has become	La 4:3	1323
For the iniquity of the **d** of my	La 4:6	1323
destruction of the **d** of my people.	La 4:10	1323
Rejoice and be glad, O **d** of Edom,	La 4:21	1323
has been completed, O **d** of Zion;	La 4:22	1323
punish your iniquity, O **d** of Edom;	La 4:22	1323
either *their* son or *their* **d**.	Ezk 14:20	1323
'Like mother, like **d**.'	Ezk 16:44	1323
"You are the **d** of your mother,	Ezk 16:45	1323
humbled his sister, his father's **d**.	Ezk 22:11	1323
for mother, for son, for **d**,	Ezk 44:25	1323
and the **d** of the king of the South	Da 11:6	1323
him the **d** of women to ruin it.	Da 11:17	1323
and took Gomer the **d** of Diblaim,	Hos 1:3	1323
again and gave birth to a **d**.	Hos 1:6	1323
the beginning of sin To the **d** of Zion	Mi 1:13	1323
the flock, Hill of the **d** of Zion,	Mi 4:8	1323
The kingdom of the **d** of Jerusalem.	Mi 4:8	1323
labor to give birth, **D** of Zion,	Mi 4:10	1323
"Arise and thresh, **d** of Zion,	Mi 4:13	1323
yourselves in troops, **d** of troops;	Mi 5:1	1323
D rises up against her mother,	Mi 7:6	1323
Shout for joy, O **d** of Zion!	Zph 3:14	1323
all *your* heart, O **d** of Jerusalem!	Zph 3:14	1323
living with the **d** of Babylon."	Zch 2:7	1323
for joy and be glad, O **d** of Zion;	Zch 2:10	1323
Rejoice greatly, O **d** of Zion!	Zch 9:9	1323
Shout *in triumph*, O **d** of Jerusalem!	Zch 9:9	1323
married the **d** of a foreign god.	Mal 2:11	1323
"My **d** has just died;	Mt 9:18	*2364*
"**D**, take courage; your faith has	Mt 9:22	*2364*
AND A **D** AGAINST HER MOTHER,	Mt 10:35	*2364*
and he who loves son or **d** more	Mt 10:37	*2364*
the **d** of Herodias danced before	Mt 14:6	*2364*
my **d** is cruelly demon-possessed."	Mt 15:22	*2364*
And her **d** was healed at once.	Mt 15:28	*2364*
"SAY TO THE **D** OF ZION	Mt 21:5	*2364*
little **d** is at the point of death;	Mk 5:23	*2365*
"**D**, your faith has made you well;	Mk 5:34	*2364*
"Your **d** has died; why trouble the	Mk 5:35	*2364*
and when the **d** of Herodias herself	Mk 6:22	*2364*
little **d** had an unclean spirit	Mk 7:25	*2365*
to cast the demon out of her **d**.	Mk 7:26	*2364*
demon has gone out of your **d**."	Mk 7:29	*2364*
prophetess, Anna the **d** of Phanuel,	Lk 2:36	*2364*
for he had an only **d**,	Lk 8:42	*2364*
"**D**, your faith has made you well;	Lk 8:48	*2364*
"Your **d** has died; do not trouble the	Lk 8:49	*2364*
mother against **d** and daughter	Lk 12:53	*2364*
daughter and **d** against mother	Lk 12:53	*2364*
woman, a **d** of Abraham as she is,	Lk 13:16	*2364*
"FEAR NOT, **D** OF ZION;	Jn 12:15	*2364*
outside, Pharaoh's **d** took him away	Ac 7:21	*2364*
unbecomingly toward his virgin **d**,	1Co 7:36	
to keep his own virgin **d**, he	1Co 7:37	
both he who gives his own virgin **d**	1Co 7:38	
be called the son of Pharaoh's **d**,	Heb 11:24	*2364*

DAUGHTER-IN-LAW

his grandson, and Sarai his **d**,	Gn 11:31	3618
Then Judah said to his **d** Tamar,	Gn 38:11	3618
did not know that she was his **d**.	Gn 38:16	3618
d Tamar has played the harlot,	Gn 38:24	3618
uncover the nakedness of your **d**;	Lv 18:15	3618
is a man who lies with his **d**,	Lv 20:12	3618
her Ruth the Moabitess, her **d**,	Ru 1:22	3618
Naomi said to her **d**,	Ru 2:20	3618
Naomi said to Ruth her **d**,	Ru 2:22	3618
for your **d**, who loves you and is	Ru 4:15	3618
Now his **d**, Phinehas's wife, was	1Sa 4:19	3618
his **d** bore him Perez and Zerah.	1Ch 2:4	3618
another has lewdly defiled his **d**.	Ezk 22:11	3618
mother, **D** against her mother-in-law;	Mi 7:6	3618
A **D** AGAINST HER MOTHER-IN-LAW;	Mt 10:35	*3565*
mother-in-law against **d** and	Lk 12:53	*3565*
and **d** against mother-in-law."	Lk 12:53	*3565*

DAUGHTER'S

son's daughter or your **d** daughter,	Lv 18:10	1323
son's daughter or her **d** daughter,	Lv 18:17	1323
the evidence of my **d** virginity.'	Dt 22:17	1323

DAUGHTERS

and he had *other* sons and **d**.	Gn 5:4	1323
and he had *other* sons and **d**.	Gn 5:7	1323
and he had *other* sons and **d**.	Gn 5:10	1323
and he had *other* sons and **d**.	Gn 5:13	1323
and he had *other* sons and **d**.	Gn 5:16	1323
and he had *other* sons and **d**.	Gn 5:19	1323
and he had *other* sons and **d**.	Gn 5:22	1323
and he had *other* sons and **d**.	Gn 5:26	1323
Noah, and he had *other* sons and **d**.	Gn 5:30	1323
the land, and **d** were born to them,	Gn 6:1	1323
that the **d** of men were beautiful;	Gn 6:2	1323
of God came in to the **d** of men,	Gn 6:4	1323
and he had *other* sons and **d**.	Gn 11:11	1323
and he had *other* sons and **d**.	Gn 11:13	1323
Eber, and he had *other* sons and **d**.	Gn 11:15	1323
and he had *other* sons and **d**.	Gn 11:17	1323
Reu, and he had *other* sons and **d**.	Gn 11:19	1323
and he had *other* sons and **d**.	Gn 11:21	1323
and he had *other* sons and **d**.	Gn 11:23	1323
and he had *other* sons and **d**.	Gn 11:25	1323
I have two **d** who have not had	Gn 19:8	1323
and your sons, and your **d**,	Gn 19:12	1323
who were to marry his **d**,	Gn 19:14	1323
"Up, take your wife and your two **d** who	Gn 19:15	1323
his wife and the hands of his two **d**,	Gn 19:16	1323
mountains, and his two **d** with him;	Gn 19:30	1323
in a cave, he and his two **d**.	Gn 19:30	1323
Thus both the **d** of Lot were with	Gn 19:36	1323
son from the **d** of the Canaanites,	Gn 24:3	1323
and the **d** of the men of the city	Gn 24:13	1323
son from the **d** of the Canaanites,	Gn 24:37	1323
living because of the **d** of Heth;	Gn 27:46	1323
takes a wife from the **d** of Heth,	Gn 27:46	1323
these, from the **d** of the land,	Gn 27:46	1323
take a wife from the **d** of Canaan.	Gn 28:1	1323
to yourself a wife from the **d** of Laban	Gn 28:2	1323
a wife from the **d** of Canaan,"	Gn 28:6	1323
So Esau saw that the **d** of Canaan	Gn 28:8	1323
Now Laban had two **d**;	Gn 29:16	1323
my **d** like captives of the sword?	Gn 31:26	1323
allow me to kiss my sons and my **d**?	Gn 31:28	1323
take your **d** from me by force.	Gn 31:31	1323
you fourteen years for your two **d** and	Gn 31:41	1323
"The **d** are my daughters, and the	Gn 31:43	1323
"The daughters are my **d**,	Gn 31:43	1323
what can I do this day to these my **d**	Gn 31:43	1323
"If you mistreat my **d**,	Gn 31:50	1323
or if you take wives besides my **d**,	Gn 31:50	1323
sons and his **d** and blessed them.	Gn 31:55	1323
out to visit the **d** of the land.	Gn 34:1	1323
give your **d** to us and take our	Gn 34:9	1323
us and take our **d** for yourselves.	Gn 34:9	1323
then we will give our **d** to you,	Gn 34:16	1323
we will take your **d** for ourselves,	Gn 34:16	1323
Let us take their **d** in marriage,	Gn 34:21	1323
marriage, and give our **d** to them.	Gn 34:21	1323
his wives from the **d** of Canaan:	Gn 36:2	1323
and his **d** and all his household,	Gn 36:6	1323
all his **d** arose to comfort him,	Gn 37:35	1323
him, his **d** and his granddaughters,	Gn 46:7	1323
and his **d** *numbered* thirty-three.	Gn 46:15	1323
the priest of Midian had seven **d**;	Ex 2:16	1323
He said to his **d**,	Ex 2:20	1323
will put them on your sons and **d**.	Ex 3:22	1323
married one of the **d** of Putiel,	Ex 6:25	1323
with our sons and our **d**,	Ex 10:9	1323
wife, and she bears him sons or **d**,	Ex 21:4	1323
her according to the custom of **d**.	Ex 21:9	1323
your wives, your sons, and your **d**,	Ex 32:2	1323
take some of his **d** for your sons,	Ex 34:16	1323
and his **d** might play the harlot with	Ex 34:16	1323
and your sons and your **d** with you;	Lv 10:14	1323
the flesh of your **d** you will eat.	Lv 26:29	1323
and to your sons and **d** with you as	Nu 18:11	1323
and your sons and your **d** with you,	Nu 18:19	1323
And his **d** into captivity,	Nu 21:29	1323
the harlot with the **d** of Moab.	Nu 25:1	1323
of Hepher had no sons, but only **d**;	Nu 26:33	1323
the **d** of Zelophehad were Mahlah,	Nu 26:33	1323
Then the **d** of Zelophehad, the son	Nu 27:1	1323
and these are the names of his **d**:	Nu 27:1	1323
"The **d** of Zelophehad are right in	Nu 27:7	1323
Zelophehad our brother to his **d**.	Nu 36:2	1323
concerning the **d** of Zelophehad,	Nu 36:6	1323
Moses, so the **d** of Zelophehad did:	Nu 36:10	1323
the **d** of Zelophehad married their	Nu 36:11	1323
not give your **d** to their sons,	Dt 7:3	1323
you take their **d** for your sons.	Dt 7:3	1323
your God, you and your sons and **d**,	Dt 12:12	1323
and **d** in the fire to their gods.	Dt 12:31	1323
"None of the **d** of Israel shall be	Dt 23:17	1323
"Your sons and your **d** shall be	Dt 28:32	1323
and **d** but they will not be yours,	Dt 28:41	1323
the flesh of your sons and of your **d**	Dt 28:53	1323
the provocation of His sons and **d**.	Dt 32:19	1323
the bar of gold, his sons, his **d**,	Jos 7:24	1323
of Manasseh, had no sons, only **d**;	Jos 17:3	1323
and these are the names of his **d**:	Jos 17:3	1323
because the **d** of Manasseh received	Jos 17:6	1323
their **d** for themselves as wives,	Jg 3:6	1323
gave their own **d** to their sons,	Jg 3:6	1323
that the **d** of Israel went yearly	Jg 11:40	1323
and thirty **d** *whom* he gave in	Jg 12:9	1323
and he brought in thirty **d** from	Jg 12:9	1323
one of the **d** of the Philistines.	Jg 14:1	1323
one of the **d** of the Philistines;	Jg 14:2	1323
among the **d** of your relatives,	Jg 14:3	1323
give them any of our **d** in marriage?"	Jg 21:7	1323
cannot give them wives of our **d**."	Jg 21:18	1323
if the **d** of Shiloh come out to	Jg 21:21	1323
his wife from the **d** of Shiloh,	Jg 21:21	1323
But Naomi said, "Return, my **d**.	Ru 1:11	1323
"Return, my **d**! Go, for I am too old	Ru 1:12	1323
refrain from marrying? No, my **d**;	Ru 1:13	1323
and to all her sons and her **d**;	1Sa 1:4	1323
birth to three sons and two **d**.	1Sa 2:21	1323
"He will also take your **d** for	1Sa 8:13	1323
the names of his two **d** *were these:*	1Sa 14:49	1323
their **d** had been taken captive.	1Sa 30:3	1323
one because of his sons and his **d**.	1Sa 30:6	1323
whether small or great, sons or **d**,	1Sa 30:19	1323
the **d** of the Philistines will rejoice,	2Sa 1:20	1323
The **d** of the uncircumcised will exult.	2Sa 1:20	1323
"O **d** of Israel, weep over Saul,	2Sa 1:24	1323
sons and **d** were born to David.	2Sa 5:13	1323
for in this manner the virgin **d** of	2Sa 13:18	1323
and the lives of your sons and **d**,	2Sa 19:5	1323
and their **d** pass through the fire,	2Ki 17:17	1323
Now Sheshan had no sons, only **d**.	1Ch 2:34	1323
Shimei had sixteen sons and six **d**;	1Ch 4:27	1323
Zelophehad, and Zelophehad had **d**.	1Ch 7:15	1323
the father of more sons and **d**.	1Ch 14:3	1323
died and had no sons, but **d** only,	1Ch 23:22	1323
sons and three **d** to Heman.	1Ch 25:5	1323
twenty-eight sons and sixty **d**.	2Ch 11:21	1323
of twenty-two sons and sixteen **d**.	2Ch 13:21	1323
became the father of sons and **d**.	2Ch 24:3	1323
200,000 women, sons and **d**;	2Ch 28:8	1323
and our sons and our **d** and our	2Ch 29:9	1323
wives, their sons and their **d**,	2Ch 31:18	1323
the **d** of Barzillai the Gileadite,	Ezr 2:61	1323
have taken some of their **d** *as wives*	Ezr 9:2	1323
'So now do not give your **d** to	Ezr 9:12	1323
nor take their **d** to your sons,	Ezr 9:12	1323
made repairs, he and his **d**.	Ne 3:12	1323
your brothers, your sons, your **d**,	Ne 4:14	1323
"We, our sons and our **d** are many;	Ne 5:2	1323
our sons and our **d** to be slaves,	Ne 5:5	1323
and some of our **d** are forced into	Ne 5:5	1323
took a wife of the **d** of Barzillai,	Ne 7:63	1323
wives, their sons and their **d**,	Ne 10:28	1323
and that we will not give our **d** to	Ne 10:30	1323
land or take their **d** for our sons.	Ne 10:30	1323
not give your **d** to their sons,	Ne 13:25	1323
nor take of their **d** for your sons	Ne 13:25	1323
sons and three **d** were born to him.	Jb 1:2	1323
when his sons and his **d** were eating	Jb 1:13	1323
"Your sons and your **d** were eating	Jb 1:18	1323
He had seven sons and three **d**.	Jb 42:13	1323
were found so fair as Job's **d**;	Jb 42:15	1323
d are among Your noble ladies;	Ps 45:9	1323
glad, Let the **d** of Judah rejoice Because	Ps 48:11	1323
And the **d** of Judah have rejoiced	Ps 97:8	1323
sons and their **d** to the demons,	Ps 106:37	1323
blood of their sons and their **d**,	Ps 106:38	1323
And our **d** as corner pillars	Ps 144:12	1323
The leech has two **d**,	Pr 30:15	1323
"Many **d** have done nobly, But you	Pr 31:29	1323
the **d** of song will sing softly.	Ec 12:4	1323
but lovely, O **d** of Jerusalem,	SS 1:5	1323
"I adjure you, O **d** of Jerusalem,	SS 2:7	1323
"I adjure you, O **d** of Jerusalem,	SS 3:5	1323
fitted out By the **d** of Jerusalem.	SS 3:10	1323
"Go forth, O **d** of Zion, And gaze	SS 3:11	1323
"I adjure you, O **d** of Jerusalem,	SS 5:8	1323
is my friend, O **d** of Jerusalem."	SS 5:16	1323
you to swear, O **d** of Jerusalem,	SS 8:4	1323
"Because the **d** of Zion are proud And	Is 3:16	1323
will afflict the scalp of the **d** of Zion	Is 3:17	1323
away the filth of the **d** of Zion and	Is 4:4	1323
The **d** of Moab will be at the fords	Is 16:2	1323
ear to my word, You complacent **d**.	Is 32:9	1323
O complacent **d**; For the vintage	Is 32:10	1323
you complacent **d**; Strip,	Is 32:11	1323
My **d** from the ends of the earth,	Is 43:6	1323
And your **d** will be carried on	Is 49:22	1323
better than that of sons and **d**;	Is 56:5	1323
d will be carried in the arms.	Is 60:4	1323
herds, their sons and their **d**.	Jer 3:24	1323
will devour your sons and your **d**;	Jer 5:17	1323
sons and their **d** in the fire,	Jer 7:31	1323
Teach your **d** wailing, And everyone	Jer 9:20	1323

sons and **d** will die by famine;	**Jer 11:22**	1323
their wives, nor their sons, nor their **d**	**Jer 14:16**	1323
have sons or **d** in this place."	**Jer 16:2**	1323
the sons and **d** born in this place,	**Jer 16:3**	1323
sons and the flesh of their **d**,	**Jer 19:9**	1323
become the fathers of sons and **d**,	**Jer 29:6**	1323
sons and give your **d** to husbands,	**Jer 29:6**	1323
that they may bear sons and **d**;	**Jer 29:6**	1323
d to pass through *the fire* to Molech,	**Jer 32:35**	1323
we, our wives, our sons or our **d**,	**Jer 35:8**	1323
the king's **d** and all the people	**Jer 41:10**	1323
the king's **d** and every person that	**Jer 43:6**	1323
And your **d** into captivity.	**Jer 48:46**	1323
Cry out, O **d** of Rabbah, Gird	**Jer 49:3**	1323
Because of all the **d** of my city.	**La 3:51**	1323
set your face against the **d** of	**Ezk 13:17**	1323
either *their* sons or *their* **d**.	**Ezk 14:16**	1323
either *their* sons or *their* **d**,	**Ezk 14:18**	1323
be brought out, *both* sons and **d**.	**Ezk 14:22**	1323
and **d** whom you had borne to Me and	**Ezk 16:20**	1323
you, the **d** of the Philistines,	**Ezk 16:27**	1323
who lives north of you with her **d**;	**Ezk 16:46**	1323
south of you, is Sodom with her **d**.	**Ezk 16:46**	1323
"Sodom, your sister and her **d**	**Ezk 16:48**	1323
done as you and your **d** have done.	**Ezk 16:48**	1323
she and her **d** had arrogance,	**Ezk 16:49**	1323
the captivity of Sodom and her **d**,	**Ezk 16:53**	1323
captivity of Samaria and her **d**,	**Ezk 16:53**	1323
Sodom with her **d** and Samaria with	**Ezk 16:55**	1323
daughters and Samaria with her **d**,	**Ezk 16:55**	1323
and you with your **d** will *also*	**Ezk 16:55**	1323
the reproach of the **d** of Edom and	**Ezk 16:57**	1323
around her, of the **d** of the Philistines	**Ezk 16:57**	1323
and I will give them to you as **d**,	**Ezk 16:61**	1323
two women, the **d** of one mother;	**Ezk 23:2**	1323
Mine, and they bore sons and **d**.	**Ezk 23:4**	1323
they took her sons and her **d**,	**Ezk 23:10**	1323
will take your sons and your **d**;	**Ezk 23:25**	1323
slay their sons and their **d** and burn	**Ezk 23:47**	1323
and your sons and your **d** whom you	**Ezk 24:21**	1323
delight, their sons and their **d**,	**Ezk 24:25**	1323
'Also her **d** who are on the	**Ezk 26:6**	1323
"He will slay your **d** on the	**Ezk 26:8**	1323
And her **d** will go into captivity.	**Ezk 30:18**	1323
d of the nations shall chant it.	**Ezk 32:16**	1323
and the **d** of the powerful nations,	**Ezk 32:18**	1323
Therefore your **d** play the harlot And	**Hos 4:13**	1323
I will not punish your **d** when they	**Hos 4:14**	1323
And your sons and **d** will prophesy,	**Jl 2:28**	1323
"Also I will sell your sons and your **d**	**Jl 3:8**	1323
and your **d** will fall by the sword,	**Am 7:17**	1323
he had a wife from the **d** of Aaron,	**Lk 1:5**	*2364*
"**D** of Jerusalem, stop weeping for	**Lk 23:28**	*2364*
SONS AND YOUR **D** SHALL PROPHESY,	**Ac 2:17**	*2364*
virgin **d** who were prophetesses.	**Ac 21:9**	*2364*
you shall be sons and **d** to Me,"	**2Co 6:18**	*2364*

DAUGHTERS-IN-LAW

Then she arose with her **d** that she	**Ru 1:6**	3618
she was, and her two **d** with her;	**Ru 1:7**	3618
And Naomi said to her two **d**,	**Ru 1:8**	3618

DAVID

father of Jesse, the father of **D**.	**Ru 4:17**	1732
was born Jesse, and to Jesse, **D**.	**Ru 4:22**	1732
upon **D** from that day forward.	**1Sa 16:13**	1732
son **D** who is with the flock."	**1Sa 16:19**	1732
sent *them* to Saul by **D** his son.	**1Sa 16:20**	1732
D came to Saul and attended him;	**1Sa 16:21**	1732
"Let **D** now stand before me,	**1Sa 16:22**	1732
D would take the harp and play *it*	**1Sa 16:23**	1732
Now **D** was the son of the	**1Sa 17:12**	1732
D was the youngest.	**1Sa 17:14**	1732
but **D** went back and forth from	**1Sa 17:15**	1732
Then Jesse said to **D** his son,	**1Sa 17:17**	1732
So **D** arose early in the morning	**1Sa 17:20**	1732
Then **D** left his baggage in the	**1Sa 17:22**	1732
and **D** heard *them*.	**1Sa 17:23**	1732
Then **D** spoke to the men who were	**1Sa 17:26**	1732
burned against **D** and he said,	**1Sa 17:28**	1732
But **D** said, "What have I done now?	**1Sa 17:29**	1732
words which **D** spoke were heard,	**1Sa 17:31**	1732
D said to Saul,	**1Sa 17:32**	1732
Then Saul said to **D**,	**1Sa 17:33**	1732
But **D** said to Saul,	**1Sa 17:34**	1732
D said, "The LORD who delivered me	**1Sa 17:37**	1732
And Saul said to **D**,	**1Sa 17:37**	1732
Then Saul clothed **D** with his	**1Sa 17:38**	1732
D girded his sword over his	**1Sa 17:39**	1732
So **D** said to Saul,	**1Sa 17:39**	1732
And **D** took them off.	**1Sa 17:39**	1732
came on and approached **D**,	**1Sa 17:41**	1732
the Philistine looked and saw **D**,	**1Sa 17:42**	1732
The Philistine said to **D**,	**1Sa 17:43**	1732
Philistine cursed **D** by his gods.	**1Sa 17:43**	1732
The Philistine also said to **D**,	**1Sa 17:44**	1732
Then **D** said to the Philistine,	**1Sa 17:45**	1732
and came and drew near to meet **D**,	**1Sa 17:48**	1732
that **D** ran quickly toward the	**1Sa 17:48**	1732
And **D** put his hand into his bag	**1Sa 17:49**	1732
Thus **D** prevailed over the Philistine	**1Sa 17:50**	1732
D ran and stood over the Philistine	**1Sa 17:51**	1732
Then **D** took the Philistine's head	**1Sa 17:54**	1732
Now when Saul saw **D** going out	**1Sa 17:55**	1732
So when **D** returned from killing	**1Sa 17:57**	1732
D answered, "*I am* the son of your	**1Sa 17:58**	1732
was knit to the soul of **D**,	**1Sa 18:1**	1732
Jonathan made a covenant with **D**	**1Sa 18:3**	1732
that was on him and gave it to **D**,	**1Sa 18:4**	1732
So **D** went out wherever Saul sent	**1Sa 18:5**	1732
when **D** returned from killing the	**1Sa 18:6**	1732
And **D** his ten thousands."	**1Sa 18:7**	1732
have ascribed to **D** ten thousands,	**1Sa 18:8**	1732
Saul looked at **D** with	**1Sa 18:9**	1732
while **D** was playing *the harp* with	**1Sa 18:10**	1732
"I will pin **D** to the wall."	**1Sa 18:11**	1732
But **D** escaped from his presence	**1Sa 18:11**	1732
Now Saul was afraid of **D**,	**1Sa 18:12**	1732
D was prospering in all his	**1Sa 18:14**	1732
But all Israel and Judah loved **D**,	**1Sa 18:16**	1732
Then Saul said to **D**,	**1Sa 18:17**	1732
But **D** said to Saul,	**1Sa 18:18**	1732
should have been given to **D**,	**1Sa 18:19**	1732
Michal, Saul's daughter, loved **D**.	**1Sa 18:20**	1732
Therefore Saul said to **D**,	**1Sa 18:21**	1732
"Speak to **D** secretly, saying,	**1Sa 18:22**	1732
servants spoke these words to **D**.	**1Sa 18:23**	1732
But **D** said, "Is it trivial in your sight	**1Sa 18:23**	1732
to these words *which* **D** spoke.	**1Sa 18:24**	1732
"Thus you shall say to **D**,	**1Sa 18:25**	1732
Now Saul planned to make **D** fall by	**1Sa 18:25**	1732
his servants told **D** these words,	**1Sa 18:26**	1732
it pleased **D** to become the king's	**1Sa 18:26**	1732
D rose up and went, he and his	**1Sa 18:27**	1732
Then **D** brought their foreskins,	**1Sa 18:27**	1732
and knew that the LORD was with **D**,	**1Sa 18:28**	1732
Saul was even more afraid of **D**.	**1Sa 18:29**	1732
that **D** behaved himself more wisely	**1Sa 18:30**	1732
his servants to put **D** to death.	**1Sa 19:1**	1732
Saul's son, greatly delighted in **D**.	**1Sa 19:1**	1732
So Jonathan told **D** saying,	**1Sa 19:2**	1732
Jonathan spoke well of **D** to Saul	**1Sa 19:4**	1732
king sin against his servant **D**,	**1Sa 19:4**	1732
putting **D** to death without a cause?"	**1Sa 19:5**	1732
Then Jonathan called **D**,	**1Sa 19:7**	1732
And Jonathan brought **D** to Saul,	**1Sa 19:7**	1732
D went out and fought with the	**1Sa 19:8**	1732
and **D** was playing *the harp* with	**1Sa 19:9**	1732
pin **D** to the wall with the spear,	**1Sa 19:10**	1732
And **D** fled and escaped that night.	**1Sa 19:10**	1732
let **D** down through a window,	**1Sa 19:12**	1732
Saul sent messengers to take **D**,	**1Sa 19:14**	1732
Saul sent messengers to see **D**,	**1Sa 19:15**	1732
Now **D** fled and escaped and came to	**1Sa 19:18**	1732
"Behold, **D** is at Naioth in Ramah."	**1Sa 19:19**	1732
Saul sent messengers to take **D**,	**1Sa 19:20**	1732
"Where are Samuel and **D**?"	**1Sa 19:22**	1732
Then **D** fled from Naioth in Ramah,	**1Sa 20:1**	1732
Yet **D** vowed again, saying,	**1Sa 20:3**	1732
Then Jonathan said to **D**,	**1Sa 20:4**	1732
So **D** said to Jonathan,	**1Sa 20:5**	1732
'**D** earnestly asked *leave* of me to	**1Sa 20:6**	1732
Then **D** said to Jonathan,	**1Sa 20:10**	1732
Jonathan said to **D**,	**1Sa 20:11**	1732
Then Jonathan said to **D**,	**1Sa 20:12**	1732
if there is good *feeling* toward **D**,	**1Sa 20:12**	1732
of **D** from the face of the earth."	**1Sa 20:15**	1732
a *covenant* with the house of **D**,	**1Sa 20:16**	1732
Jonathan made **D** vow again	**1Sa 20:17**	1732
So **D** hid in the field;	**1Sa 20:24**	1732
'**D** earnestly asked leave of me *to*	**1Sa 20:28**	1732
had decided to put **D** to death.	**1Sa 20:33**	1732
for he was grieved over **D** because	**1Sa 20:34**	1732
field for the appointment with **D**,	**1Sa 20:35**	1732
and **D** knew about the matter.	**1Sa 20:39**	1732
D rose from the south side and	**1Sa 20:41**	1732
and wept together, but **D** *wept* the more.	**1Sa 20:41**	1732
Jonathan said to **D**,	**1Sa 20:42**	1732
Then **D** came to Nob to Ahimelech	**1Sa 21:1**	1732
came trembling to meet **D** and	**1Sa 21:1**	1732
D said to Ahimelech the priest,	**1Sa 21:2**	1732
The priest answered **D** and said,	**1Sa 21:4**	1732
D answered the priest and said	**1Sa 21:5**	1732
D said to Ahimelech,	**1Sa 21:8**	1732
And **D** said, "There is none like it;	**1Sa 21:9**	1732
Then **D** arose and fled that day	**1Sa 21:10**	1732
"Is this not **D** the king of the land?	**1Sa 21:11**	1732
And **D** his ten thousands'?"	**1Sa 21:11**	1732
D took these words to heart and	**1Sa 21:12**	1732
So **D** departed from there and	**1Sa 22:1**	1732
And **D** went from there to Mizpah of	**1Sa 22:3**	1732
time that **D** was in the stronghold.	**1Sa 22:4**	1732
The prophet Gad said to **D**,	**1Sa 22:5**	1732
So **D** departed and went into the	**1Sa 22:5**	1732
Then Saul heard that **D** and the men	**1Sa 22:6**	1732
your servants is as faithful as **D**,	**1Sa 22:14**	1732
because their hand also is with **D**	**1Sa 22:17**	1732
Abiathar, escaped and fled after **D**.	**1Sa 22:20**	1732
Abiathar told **D** that Saul had	**1Sa 22:21**	1732
Then **D** said to Abiathar,	**1Sa 22:22**	1732
Then they told **D**, saying,	**1Sa 23:1**	1732
So **D** inquired of the LORD, saying,	**1Sa 23:2**	1732
And the LORD said to **D**,	**1Sa 23:2**	1732
Then **D** inquired of the LORD once	**1Sa 23:4**	1732
So **D** and his men went to Keilah	**1Sa 23:5**	1732
Thus **D** delivered the inhabitants	**1Sa 23:5**	1732
of Ahimelech fled to **D** at Keilah,	**1Sa 23:6**	1732
Saul that **D** had come to Keilah,	**1Sa 23:7**	1732
Keilah to besiege **D** and his men.	**1Sa 23:8**	1732
Now **D** knew that Saul was plotting	**1Sa 23:9**	1732
Then **D** said, "O LORD God of Israel,	**1Sa 23:10**	1732
D said, "Will the men of Keilah	**1Sa 23:12**	1732
Then **D** and his men, about six	**1Sa 23:13**	1732
that **D** had escaped from Keilah,	**1Sa 23:13**	1732
D stayed in the wilderness in	**1Sa 23:14**	1732
Now **D** became aware that Saul had	**1Sa 23:15**	1732
while **D** was in the wilderness of Ziph	**1Sa 23:15**	1732
arose and went to **D** at Horesh,	**1Sa 23:16**	1732
and **D** stayed at Horesh while	**1Sa 23:18**	1732
"Is **D** not hiding with us in the	**1Sa 23:19**	1732
Now **D** and his men were in the	**1Sa 23:24**	1732
men went to seek *him*, they told **D**,	**1Sa 23:25**	1732
D in the wilderness of Maon.	**1Sa 23:25**	1732
and **D** and his men on the other	**1Sa 23:26**	1732
and **D** was hurrying to get away	**1Sa 23:26**	1732
D and his men to seize them.	**1Sa 23:26**	1732
So Saul returned from pursuing **D** and	**1Sa 23:28**	1732
D went up from there and	**1Sa 23:29**	1732
D is in the wilderness of Engedi."	**1Sa 24:1**	1732
and went to seek **D** and his men in	**1Sa 24:2**	1732
Now **D** and his men were sitting in	**1Sa 24:3**	1732
The men of **D** said to him,	**1Sa 24:4**	1732
Then **D** arose and cut off the edge	**1Sa 24:4**	1732
D persuaded his men with *these*	**1Sa 24:7**	1732
Now afterward **D** arose and went out	**1Sa 24:8**	1732
D bowed with his face to the	**1Sa 24:8**	1732
D said to Saul,	**1Sa 24:9**	1732
'Behold, **D** seeks to harm you'?	**1Sa 24:9**	1732
When **D** had finished speaking	**1Sa 24:16**	1732
"Is this your voice, my son **D**?"	**1Sa 24:16**	1732
He said to **D**,	**1Sa 24:17**	1732
D swore to Saul.	**1Sa 24:22**	1732
but **D** and his men went up to the	**1Sa 24:22**	1732
And **D** arose and went down to the	**1Sa 25:1**	1732
that **D** heard in the wilderness	**1Sa 25:4**	1732
So **D** sent ten young men; and David	**1Sa 25:5**	1732
men; and **D** said to the young men,	**1Sa 25:5**	1732
servants and to your son **D**.'"	**1Sa 25:8**	1732
"Who is **D**? And who is the son	**1Sa 25:10**	1732
D said to his men,	**1Sa 25:13**	1732
And **D** also girded on his sword,	**1Sa 25:13**	1732
four hundred men went up behind **D**	**1Sa 25:13**	1732
D sent messengers from the	**1Sa 25:14**	1732
D and his men were coming down	**1Sa 25:20**	1732
Now **D** had said, "Surely in vain I	**1Sa 25:21**	1732
"May God do so to the enemies of **D**,	**1Sa 25:22**	1732
When Abigail saw **D**,	**1Sa 25:23**	1732
and fell on her face before **D** and	**1Sa 25:23**	1732
Then **D** said to Abigail,	**1Sa 25:32**	1732
So **D** received from her hand what	**1Sa 25:35**	1732
When **D** heard that Nabal was dead,	**1Sa 25:39**	1732
Then **D** sent a proposal to Abigail,	**1Sa 25:39**	1732
the servants of **D** came to Abigail	**1Sa 25:40**	1732
"**D** has sent us to you to take	**1Sa 25:40**	1732
she followed the messengers of **D** and	**1Sa 25:42**	1732
D had also taken Ahinoam of	**1Sa 25:43**	1732
"Is not **D** hiding on the hill of	**1Sa 26:1**	1732
for **D** in the wilderness of Ziph.	**1Sa 26:2**	1732
D was staying in the wilderness.	**1Sa 26:3**	1732
D sent out spies, and he knew that	**1Sa 26:4**	1732
D then arose and came to the place	**1Sa 26:5**	1732
D saw the place where Saul lay,	**1Sa 26:5**	1732
Then **D** said to Ahimelech the Hittite	**1Sa 26:6**	1732
So **D** and Abishai came to the	**1Sa 26:7**	1732
Then Abishai said to **D**,	**1Sa 26:8**	1732
But **D** said to Abishai,	**1Sa 26:9**	1732
D also said, "As the LORD lives,	**1Sa 26:10**	1732
So **D** took the spear and the jug of	**1Sa 26:12**	1732
Then **D** crossed over to the other	**1Sa 26:13**	1732
D called to the people and to	**1Sa 26:14**	1732
So **D** said to Abner,	**1Sa 26:15**	1732
"Is this your voice, my son **D**?"	**1Sa 26:17**	1732
And **D** said, "It is my voice, my lord	**1Sa 26:17**	1732
Return, my son **D**, for I will not	**1Sa 26:21**	1732
D replied, "Behold the spear	**1Sa 26:22**	1732
Then Saul said to **D**,	**1Sa 26:25**	1732
"Blessed are you, my son **D**;	**1Sa 26:25**	1732
So **D** went on his way, and Saul	**1Sa 26:25**	1732
Then **D** said to himself,	**1Sa 27:1**	1732
So **D** arose and crossed over, he	**1Sa 27:2**	1732
And **D** lived with Achish at Gath,	**1Sa 27:3**	1732
even **D** with his two wives,	**1Sa 27:3**	1732
told Saul that **D** had fled to Gath,	**1Sa 27:4**	1732
Then **D** said to Achish,	**1Sa 27:5**	1732
The number of days that **D**	**1Sa 27:7**	1732
Now **D** and his men went up and	**1Sa 27:8**	1732
D attacked the land and did	**1Sa 27:9**	1732
D said, "Against the Negev of Judah	**1Sa 27:10**	1732
D did not leave a man or a	**1Sa 27:11**	1732
'So has **D** done and so *has been* his	**1Sa 27:11**	1732
So Achish believed **D**,	**1Sa 27:12**	1732
And Achish said to **D**,	**1Sa 28:1**	1732
D said to Achish,	**1Sa 28:2**	1732
So Achish said to **D**,	**1Sa 28:2**	1732
given it to your neighbor, to **D**.	**1Sa 28:17**	1732
and **D** and his men were proceeding	**1Sa 29:2**	1732
"Is this not **D**, the servant of	**1Sa 29:3**	1732
"Is this not **D**, of whom they sing	**1Sa 29:5**	1732
And **D** his ten thousands'?"	**1Sa 29:5**	1732
Achish called **D** and said to him,	**1Sa 29:6**	1732
D said to Achish,	**1Sa 29:8**	1732
But Achish replied to **D**,	**1Sa 29:9**	1732
So **D** arose early, he and his men,	**1Sa 29:11**	1732
Then it happened when **D** and his	**1Sa 30:1**	1732
D and his men came to the city,	**1Sa 30:3**	1732
Then **D** and the people who were	**1Sa 30:4**	1732
Moreover **D** was greatly distressed	**1Sa 30:6**	1732
But **D** strengthened himself in the	**1Sa 30:6**	1732
D said to Abiathar the priest,	**1Sa 30:7**	1732
Abiathar brought the ephod to **D**.	**1Sa 30:7**	1732
D inquired of the LORD,	**1Sa 30:8**	1732
So **D** went, he and the six hundred	**1Sa 30:9**	1732
But **D** pursued, he and four hundred	**1Sa 30:10**	1732
in the field and brought him to **D**,	**1Sa 30:11**	1732
D said to him,	**1Sa 30:13**	1732
Then **D** said to him,	**1Sa 30:15**	1732
D slaughtered them from the	**1Sa 30:17**	1732
So **D** recovered all that the	**1Sa 30:18**	1732

D brought *it* all back.	1Sa 30:19	1732
So **D** had captured all the sheep	1Sa 30:20	1732
When **D** came to the two hundred men	1Sa 30:21	1732
were too exhausted to follow **D**,	1Sa 30:21	1732
and they went out to meet **D** and to	1Sa 30:21	1732
then **D** approached the people and	1Sa 30:21	1732
who went with **D** said,	1Sa 30:22	1732
Then **D** said, "You must not do so,	1Sa 30:23	1732
Now when **D** came to Ziklag, he sent	1Sa 30:26	1732
and to all the places where **D**	1Sa 30:31	1732
when **D** had returned from the	2Sa 1:1	1732
D remained two days in Ziklag.	2Sa 1:1	1732
when he came to **D** that he fell to the	2Sa 1:2	1732
Then **D** said to him,	2Sa 1:3	1732
D said to him,	2Sa 1:4	1732
So **D** said to the young man who	2Sa 1:5	1732
Then **D** took hold of his clothes	2Sa 1:11	1732
D said to the young man who	2Sa 1:13	1732
Then **D** said to him,	2Sa 1:14	1732
And **D** called one of the young men	2Sa 1:15	1732
D said to him,	2Sa 1:16	1732
Then **D** chanted with this lament	2Sa 1:17	1732
that **D** inquired of the LORD,	2Sa 2:1	1732
So **D** said, "Where shall I go up?"	2Sa 2:1	1732
So **D** went up there, and his two	2Sa 2:2	1732
And **D** brought up his men who *were*	2Sa 2:3	1732
D king over the house of Judah.	2Sa 2:4	1732
And they told **D**, saying,	2Sa 2:4	1732
D sent messengers to the men	2Sa 2:5	1732
of Judah, however, followed **D**.	2Sa 2:10	1732
The time that **D** was king in	2Sa 2:11	1732
servants of **D** went out and met them	2Sa 2:13	1732
and twelve of the servants of **D**.	2Sa 2:15	1732
beaten before the servants of **D**.	2Sa 2:17	1732
But the servants of **D** had struck	2Sa 2:31	1732
house of Saul and the house of **D**;	2Sa 3:1	1732
and **D** grew steadily stronger, but	2Sa 3:1	1732
Sons were born to **D** at Hebron:	2Sa 3:2	1732
These were born to **D** at Hebron.	2Sa 3:5	1732
the house of Saul and the house of **D**	2Sa 3:6	1732
delivered you into the hands of **D**;	2Sa 3:8	1732
if as the LORD has sworn to **D**,	2Sa 3:9	1732
of **D** over Israel and over Judah,	2Sa 3:10	1732
sent messengers to **D** in his place,	2Sa 3:12	1732
So **D** sent messengers to	2Sa 3:14	1732
seeking for **D** to be king over you.	2Sa 3:17	1732
For the LORD has spoken of **D**,	2Sa 3:18	1732
'By the hand of My servant **D** I	2Sa 3:18	1732
speak in the hearing of **D** in Hebron	2Sa 3:19	1732
men with him came to **D** at Hebron.	2Sa 3:20	1732
And **D** made a feast for Abner and	2Sa 3:20	1732
Abner said to **D**,	2Sa 3:21	1732
So **D** sent Abner away, and he went	2Sa 3:21	1732
the servants of **D** and Joab came	2Sa 3:22	1732
Abner was not with **D** in Hebron,	2Sa 3:22	1732
When Joab came out from **D**,	2Sa 3:26	1732
but **D** did not know *it.*	2Sa 3:26	1732
Afterward when **D** heard it,	2Sa 3:28	1732
Then **D** said to Joab and to all the	2Sa 3:31	1732
And King **D** walked behind the bier.	2Sa 3:31	1732
the people came to persuade **D** to eat	2Sa 3:35	1732
but **D** vowed, saying,	2Sa 3:35	1732
head of Ish-bosheth to **D** at Hebron and	2Sa 4:8	1732
D answered Rechab and Baanah	2Sa 4:9	1732
Then **D** commanded the young men,	2Sa 4:12	1732
came to **D** at Hebron and said,	2Sa 5:1	1732
and King **D** made a covenant with	2Sa 5:3	1732
they anointed **D** king over Israel.	2Sa 5:3	1732
D was thirty years old when he	2Sa 5:4	1732
of the land, and they said to **D**,	2Sa 5:6	1732
"**D** cannot enter here."	2Sa 5:6	1732
D captured the stronghold of Zion,	2Sa 5:7	1732
of Zion, that is the city of **D**.	2Sa 5:7	1732
D said on that day,	2Sa 5:8	1732
So **D** lived in the stronghold and	2Sa 5:9	1732
and called it the city of **D**.	2Sa 5:9	1732
And **D** built all around from the	2Sa 5:9	1732
D became greater and greater,	2Sa 5:10	1732
king of Tyre sent messengers to **D**	2Sa 5:11	1732
and they built a house for **D**.	2Sa 5:11	1732
And **D** realized that the LORD had	2Sa 5:12	1732
Meanwhile **D** took more concubines	2Sa 5:13	1732
sons and daughters were born to **D**.	2Sa 5:13	1732
had anointed **D** king over Israel,	2Sa 5:17	1732
Philistines went up to seek out **D**;	2Sa 5:17	1732
and when **D** heard *of it,* he went	2Sa 5:17	1732
Then **D** inquired of the LORD,	2Sa 5:19	1732
And the LORD said to **D**,	2Sa 5:19	1732
So **D** came to Baal-perazim and	2Sa 5:20	1732
D and his men carried them away.	2Sa 5:21	1732
When **D** inquired of the LORD,	2Sa 5:23	1732
Then **D** did so, just as the LORD	2Sa 5:25	1732
Now **D** again gathered all the	2Sa 6:1	1732
And **D** arose and went with all the	2Sa 6:2	1732
D and all the house of Israel were	2Sa 6:5	1732
D became angry because of the	2Sa 6:8	1732
So **D** was afraid of the LORD that	2Sa 6:9	1732
And **D** was unwilling to move the	2Sa 6:10	1732
LORD into the city of **D** with him;	2Sa 6:10	1732
but **D** took it aside to the house	2Sa 6:10	1732
Now it was told King **D**,	2Sa 6:12	1732
D went and brought up the ark	2Sa 6:12	1732
into the city of **D** with gladness.	2Sa 6:12	1732
And **D** was dancing before the LORD	2Sa 6:14	1732
and **D** was wearing a linen ephod.	2Sa 6:14	1732
So **D** and all the house of Israel	2Sa 6:15	1732
of the LORD came into the city of **D**	2Sa 6:16	1732
and saw King **D** leaping and dancing	2Sa 6:16	1732
tent which **D** had pitched for it;	2Sa 6:17	1732
and **D** offered burnt offerings and	2Sa 6:17	1732
When **D** had finished offering	2Sa 6:18	1732
But when **D** returned to bless his	2Sa 6:20	1732
Saul came out to meet **D** and said,	2Sa 6:20	1732
So **D** said to Michal,	2Sa 6:21	1732
"Go and say to My servant **D**,	2Sa 7:5	1732
you shall say to My servant **D**,	2Sa 7:8	1732
this vision, so Nathan spoke to **D**.	2Sa 7:17	1732
Then **D** the king went in and sat	2Sa 7:18	1732
Again what more can **D** say to You?	2Sa 7:20	1732
D be established before You.	2Sa 7:26	1732
D defeated the Philistines and subdued	2Sa 8:1	1732
and **D** took control of the chief city	2Sa 8:1	1732
the Moabites became servants to **D**,	2Sa 8:2	1732
Then **D** defeated Hadadezer, the son	2Sa 8:3	1732
D captured from him 1,700	2Sa 8:4	1732
D hamstrung the chariot horses,	2Sa 8:4	1732
Zobah, **D** killed 22,000 Arameans.	2Sa 8:5	1732
Then **D** put garrisons among the	2Sa 8:6	1732
the Arameans became servants to **D**,	2Sa 8:6	1732
LORD helped **D** wherever he went.	2Sa 8:6	1732
D took the shields of gold	2Sa 8:7	1732
King **D** took a very large amount of	2Sa 8:8	1732
Toi king of Hamath heard that **D** had	2Sa 8:9	1732
King **D** to greet him and bless him,	2Sa 8:10	1732
King **D** also dedicated these to the	2Sa 8:11	1732
So **D** made a name *for himself* when	2Sa 8:13	1732
the Edomites became servants to **D**.	2Sa 8:14	1732
LORD helped **D** wherever he went.	2Sa 8:14	1732
So **D** reigned over all Israel;	2Sa 8:15	1732
and **D** administered justice and	2Sa 8:15	1732
Then **D** said, "Is there yet anyone left	2Sa 9:1	1732
Ziba, and they called him to **D**;	2Sa 9:2	1732
Then King **D** sent and brought him	2Sa 9:5	1732
came to **D** and fell on his face and	2Sa 9:6	1732
And **D** said, "Mephibosheth."	2Sa 9:6	1732
D said to him,	2Sa 9:7	1732
Then **D** said, "I will show kindness	2Sa 10:2	1732
So **D** sent some of his servants to	2Sa 10:2	1732
"Do you think that **D** is honoring	2Sa 10:3	1732
Has **D** not sent his servants to you	2Sa 10:3	1732
When they told *it* to **D**,	2Sa 10:5	1732
that they had become odious to **D**,	2Sa 10:6	1732
When **D** heard *of it,* he sent Joab	2Sa 10:7	1732
Now when it was told **D**,	2Sa 10:17	1732
to meet **D** and fought against him.	2Sa 10:17	1732
and **D** killed 700 charioteers of	2Sa 10:18	1732
that **D** sent Joab and his servants	2Sa 11:1	1732
But **D** stayed at Jerusalem.	2Sa 11:1	1732
Now when evening came **D** arose from	2Sa 11:2	1732
So **D** sent and inquired about the	2Sa 11:3	1732
D sent messengers and took her,	2Sa 11:4	1732
and she sent and told **D**,	2Sa 11:5	1732
Then **D** sent to Joab, *saying,*	2Sa 11:6	1732
So Joab sent Uriah to **D**.	2Sa 11:6	1732
D asked concerning the welfare of	2Sa 11:7	1732
Then **D** said to Uriah,	2Sa 11:8	1732
Now when they told **D**,	2Sa 11:10	1732
to his house," **D** said to Uriah,	2Sa 11:10	1732
Uriah said to **D**,	2Sa 11:11	1732
Then **D** said to Uriah,	2Sa 11:12	1732
Now **D** called him, and he ate and	2Sa 11:13	1732
morning **D** wrote a letter to Joab	2Sa 11:14	1732
to **D** all the events of the war.	2Sa 11:18	1732
reported to **D** all that Joab had sent	2Sa 11:22	1732
The messenger said to **D**,	2Sa 11:23	1732
Then **D** said to the messenger,	2Sa 11:25	1732
D sent and brought her to his	2Sa 11:27	1732
But the thing that **D** had done was	2Sa 11:27	1732
Then the LORD sent Nathan to **D**.	2Sa 12:1	1732
Nathan then said to **D**,	2Sa 12:7	1732
Then **D** said to Nathan,	2Sa 12:13	1732
And Nathan said to **D**,	2Sa 12:13	1732
child that Uriah's widow bore to **D**,	2Sa 12:15	1732
D therefore inquired of God for	2Sa 12:16	1732
and **D** fasted and went and lay all	2Sa 12:16	1732
And the servants of **D** were afraid	2Sa 12:18	1732
But when **D** saw that his servants	2Sa 12:19	1732
D perceived that the child was	2Sa 12:19	1732
so **D** said to his servants,	2Sa 12:19	1732
So **D** arose from the ground,	2Sa 12:20	1732
D comforted his wife Bathsheba,	2Sa 12:24	1732
sent messengers to **D** and said,	2Sa 12:27	1732
So **D** gathered all the people and	2Sa 12:29	1732
Then **D** and all the people returned	2Sa 12:31	1732
the son of **D** had a beautiful sister	2Sa 13:1	1732
and Amnon the son of **D** loved her.	2Sa 13:1	1732
D sent to the house for Tamar,	2Sa 13:7	1732
King **D** heard of all these matters,	2Sa 13:21	1732
the way that the report came to **D**,	2Sa 13:30	1732
And **D** mourned for his son every	2Sa 13:37	1732
D longed to go out to Absalom;	2Sa 13:39	1732
Then a messenger came to **D**,	2Sa 15:13	1732
D said to all his servants who	2Sa 15:14	1732
Therefore **D** said to Ittai,	2Sa 15:22	1732
And **D** went up the ascent of the	2Sa 15:30	1732
Now someone told **D**,	2Sa 15:31	1732
And **D** said, "O LORD, I pray, make	2Sa 15:31	1732
as **D** was coming to the summit,	2Sa 15:32	1732
D said to him,	2Sa 15:33	1732
when **D** had passed a little beyond	2Sa 16:1	1732
When King **D** came to Bahurim,	2Sa 16:5	1732
He threw stones at **D** and at	2Sa 16:6	1732
and at all the servants of King **D**;	2Sa 16:6	1732
'Curse **D**,' then who shall say,	2Sa 16:10	1732
Then **D** said to Abishai and to all	2Sa 16:11	1732
So **D** and his men went on the way;	2Sa 16:13	1732
regarded by both **D** and Absalom.	2Sa 16:23	1732
I may arise and pursue **D** tonight.	2Sa 17:1	1732
send quickly and tell **D**,	2Sa 17:16	1732
and they would go and tell King **D**,	2Sa 17:17	1732
the well and went and told King **D**;	2Sa 17:21	1732
and they said to **D**,	2Sa 17:21	1732
Then **D** and all the people who *were*	2Sa 17:22	1732
Then **D** came to Mahanaim.	2Sa 17:24	1732
Now when **D** had come to Mahanaim,	2Sa 17:27	1732
for **D** and for the people who *were*	2Sa 17:29	1732
Then **D** numbered the people who	2Sa 18:1	1732
D sent the people out, one	2Sa 18:2	1732
there before the servants of **D**,	2Sa 18:7	1732
to meet the servants of **D**.	2Sa 18:9	1732
Now **D** was sitting between the two	2Sa 18:24	1732
Then King **D** sent to Zadok and	2Sa 19:11	1732
the men of Judah to meet King **D**.	2Sa 19:16	1732
D then said, "What have I to do with	2Sa 19:22	1732
have more *claim* on **D** than you.	2Sa 19:43	1732
"We have no portion in **D**,	2Sa 20:1	1732
Israel withdrew from following **D**	2Sa 20:2	1732
Then **D** came to his house at	2Sa 20:3	1732
And **D** said to Abishai,	2Sa 20:6	1732
favors Joab and whoever is for **D**,	2Sa 20:11	1732
lifted up his hand against King **D**.	2Sa 20:21	1732
Jairite was also a priest to **D**.	2Sa 20:26	1732
in the days of **D** for three years,	2Sa 21:1	1732
D sought the presence of the LORD.	2Sa 21:1	1732
Thus **D** said to the Gibeonites,	2Sa 21:3	1732
between **D** and Saul's son Jonathan.	2Sa 21:7	1732
When it was told **D** what Rizpah the	2Sa 21:11	1732
then **D** went and took the bones of	2Sa 21:12	1732
D went down and his servants	2Sa 21:15	1732
the Philistines, **D** became weary.	2Sa 21:15	1732
sword, and he intended to kill **D**.	2Sa 21:16	1732
Then the men of **D** swore to him,	2Sa 21:17	1732
and they fell by the hand of **D** and	2Sa 21:22	1732
And **D** spoke the words of this song	2Sa 22:1	1732
D and his descendants forever."	2Sa 22:51	1732
Now these are the last words of **D**.	2Sa 23:1	1732
D the son of Jesse declares, The	2Sa 23:1	1732
of the mighty men whom **D** had:	2Sa 23:8	1732
one of the three mighty men with **D**	2Sa 23:9	1732
chief men went down and came to **D**	2Sa 23:13	1732
D was then in the stronghold,	2Sa 23:14	1732
D had a craving and said,	2Sa 23:15	1732
and took *it* and brought *it* to **D**.	2Sa 23:16	1732
D appointed him over his guard.	2Sa 23:23	1732
it incited **D** against them to say,	2Sa 24:1	1732
So **D** said to the LORD,	2Sa 24:10	1732
When **D** arose in the morning, the	2Sa 24:11	1732
"Go and speak to **D**,	2Sa 24:12	1732
So Gad came to **D** and told him, and	2Sa 24:13	1732
Then **D** said to Gad,	2Sa 24:14	1732
Then **D** spoke to the LORD when he	2Sa 24:17	1732
So Gad came to **D** that day and said	2Sa 24:18	1732
D went up according to the	2Sa 24:19	1732
D said, "To buy the threshing floor	2Sa 24:21	1732
Araunah said to **D**,	2Sa 24:22	1732
So **D** bought the threshing floor	2Sa 24:24	1732
D built there an altar to the LORD and	2Sa 24:25	1732
King **D** was old, advanced in age;	1Ki 1:1	1732
the mighty men who belonged to **D**,	1Ki 1:8	1732
and **D** our lord does not know *it?*	1Ki 1:11	1732
at once to King **D** and say to him,	1Ki 1:13	1732
Then King **D** said,	1Ki 1:28	1732
"May my lord King **D** live forever."	1Ki 1:31	1732
Then King **D** said,	1Ki 1:32	1732
the throne of my lord King **D**!"	1Ki 1:37	1732
lord King **D** has made Solomon king.	1Ki 1:43	1732
came to bless our lord King **D**,	1Ki 1:47	1732
Then **D** slept with his fathers and	1Ki 2:10	1732
and was buried in the city of **D**.	1Ki 2:10	1732
The days that **D** reigned over	1Ki 2:11	1732
sat on the throne of **D** his father,	1Ki 2:12	1732
me on the throne of **D** my father and	1Ki 2:24	1732
the Lord GOD before my father **D**,	1Ki 2:26	1732
while my father **D** did not know *it:*	1Ki 2:32	1732
but to **D** and his descendants and	1Ki 2:33	1732
which you did to my father **D**;	1Ki 2:44	1732
and the throne of **D** shall be	1Ki 2:45	1732
and brought her to the city of **D** until	1Ki 3:1	1732
in the statutes of his father **D**,	1Ki 3:3	1732
to Your servant **D** my father,	1Ki 3:6	1732
king in place of my father **D**,	1Ki 3:7	1732
as your father **D** walked,	1Ki 3:14	1732
had always been a friend of **D**.	1Ki 5:1	1732
"You know that **D** my father was	1Ki 5:3	1732
as the LORD spoke to **D** my father,	1Ki 5:5	1732
who has given to **D** a wise son over	1Ki 5:7	1732
which I spoke to **D** your father.	1Ki 6:12	1732
things dedicated by his father **D**,	1Ki 7:51	1732
of the LORD from the city of **D**,	1Ki 8:1	1732
spoke with His mouth to my father **D**	1Ki 8:15	1732
D to be over My people Israel.'	1Ki 8:16	1732
it was in the heart of my father **D**	1Ki 8:17	1732
"But the LORD said to my father **D**,	1Ki 8:18	1732
I have risen in place of my father **D**	1Ki 8:20	1732
with Your servant, my father **D**,	1Ki 8:24	1732
keep with Your servant **D** my father	1Ki 8:25	1732
to Your servant, my father **D**.	1Ki 8:26	1732
the LORD had shown to **D** His servant	1Ki 8:66	1732
before Me as your father **D** walked,	1Ki 9:4	1732
as I promised to your father **D**,	1Ki 9:5	1732
daughter came up from the city of **D**	1Ki 9:24	1732
heart of **D** his father *had been.*	1Ki 11:4	1732
fully, as **D** his father *had done.*	1Ki 11:6	1732
for the sake of your father **D**,	1Ki 11:12	1732
your son for the sake of My servant **D**	1Ki 11:13	1732
it came about, when **D** was in Edom,	1Ki 11:15	1732
that **D** slept with his fathers and	1Ki 11:21	1732

Context	Reference	Strong's
band, after **D** slew them of *Zobah;*	**1Ki 11:24**	1732
of the city of his father **D**.	**1Ki 11:27**	1732
D and for the sake of Jerusalem,	**1Ki 11:32**	1732
ordinances, as his father **D** *did.*	**1Ki 11:33**	1732
sake of My servant **D** whom I chose,	**1Ki 11:34**	1732
that My servant **D** may have a lamp	**1Ki 11:36**	1732
commandments, as My servant **D** did,	**1Ki 11:38**	1732
enduring house as I built for **D**,	**1Ki 11:38**	1732
the descendants of **D** for this,	**1Ki 11:39**	1732
in the city of his father **D**.	**1Ki 11:43**	1732
"What portion do we have in **D**?	**1Ki 12:16**	1732
look after your own house, **D**!"	**1Ki 12:16**	1732
the house of **D** to this day.	**1Ki 12:19**	1732
of Judah followed the house of **D**.	**1Ki 12:20**	1732
will return to the house of **D**.	**1Ki 12:26**	1732
shall be born to the house of **D**,	**1Ki 13:2**	1732
kingdom away from the house of **D**	**1Ki 14:8**	1732
have not been like My servant **D**,	**1Ki 14:8**	1732
with his fathers in the city of **D**;	**1Ki 14:31**	1732
like the heart of his father **D**.	**1Ki 15:3**	1732
because **D** did what was right in	**1Ki 15:5**	1732
they buried him in the city of **D**;	**1Ki 15:8**	1732
of the LORD, like **D** his father.	**1Ki 15:11**	1732
in the city of **D** his father;	**1Ki 15:24**	1732
in the city of his father **D**,	**1Ki 22:50**	1732
for the sake of **D** His servant,	**2Ki 8:19**	1732
with his fathers in the city of **D**;	**2Ki 8:24**	1732
with his fathers in the city of **D**.	**2Ki 9:28**	1732
with his fathers in the city of **D**,	**2Ki 12:21**	1732
LORD, yet not like **D** his father;	**2Ki 14:3**	1732
with his fathers in the city of **D**.	**2Ki 14:20**	1732
with his fathers in the city of **D**,	**2Ki 15:7**	1732
in the city of **D** his father;	**2Ki 15:38**	1732
his God, as his father **D** *had done.*	**2Ki 16:2**	1732
with his fathers in the city of **D**;	**2Ki 16:20**	1732
torn Israel from the house of **D**,	**2Ki 17:21**	1732
to all that his father **D** had done.	**2Ki 18:3**	1732
LORD, the God of your father **D**,	**2Ki 20:5**	1732
said to **D** and to his son Solomon,	**2Ki 21:7**	1732
in all the way of his father **D**,	**2Ki 22:2**	1732
Ozem the sixth, **D** the seventh;	**1Ch 2:15**	1732
Now these were the sons of **D** who	**1Ch 3:1**	1732
All *these were* the sons of **D**,	**1Ch 3:9**	1732
their cities until the reign of **D**.	**1Ch 4:31**	1732
Now these are those whom **D**	**1Ch 6:31**	1732
in the days of **D** was 22,600.	**1Ch 7:2**	1732
whom **D** and Samuel the seer	**1Ch 9:22**	1732
the kingdom to **D** the son of Jesse.	**1Ch 10:14**	1732
gathered to **D** at Hebron and said,	**1Ch 11:1**	1732
and **D** made a covenant with them in	**1Ch 11:3**	1732
they anointed **D** king over Israel,	**1Ch 11:3**	1732
Then **D** and all Israel went to	**1Ch 11:4**	1732
inhabitants of Jebus said to **D**,	**1Ch 11:5**	1732
Nevertheless **D** captured the	**1Ch 11:5**	1732
of Zion (that is, the city of **D**).	**1Ch 11:5**	1732
D had said, "Whoever strikes down a	**1Ch 11:6**	1732
Then **D** dwelt in the stronghold;	**1Ch 11:7**	1732
it was called the city of **D**.	**1Ch 11:7**	1732
D became greater and greater,	**1Ch 11:9**	1732
of the mighty men whom **D** had,	**1Ch 11:10**	1732
list of the mighty men whom **D** had:	**1Ch 11:11**	1732
He was with **D** at Pasdammim when	**1Ch 11:13**	1732
men went down to the rock to **D**,	**1Ch 11:15**	1732
D was then in the stronghold,	**1Ch 11:16**	1732
D had a craving and said,	**1Ch 11:17**	1732
and took *it* and brought *it* to **D**;	**1Ch 11:18**	1732
nevertheless **D** would not drink it,	**1Ch 11:18**	1732
D appointed him over his guard.	**1Ch 11:25**	1732
the ones who came to **D** at Ziklag,	**1Ch 12:1**	1732
came over to **D** in the stronghold	**1Ch 12:8**	1732
Judah came to the stronghold to **D**.	**1Ch 12:16**	1732
D went out to meet them, and	**1Ch 12:17**	1732
"*We* are yours, O **D**, And with you,	**1Ch 12:18**	1732
Then **D** received them and made them	**1Ch 12:18**	1732
Manasseh also some defected to **D** when	**1Ch 12:19**	1732
D against the band of raiders,	**1Ch 12:21**	1732
by day *men* came to **D** to help him,	**1Ch 12:22**	1732
for war, who came to **D** at Hebron,	**1Ch 12:23**	1732
by name to come and make **D** king.	**1Ch 12:31**	1732
of weapons of war and helped **D**	**1Ch 12:33**	1732
to make **D** king over all Israel;	**1Ch 12:38**	1732
were of one mind to make **D** king.	**1Ch 12:38**	1732
They were there with **D** three days,	**1Ch 12:39**	1732
Then **D** consulted with the captains	**1Ch 13:1**	1732
D said to all the assembly of	**1Ch 13:2**	1732
D assembled all Israel together,	**1Ch 13:5**	1732
D and all Israel went up to	**1Ch 13:6**	1732
D and all Israel were	**1Ch 13:8**	1732
Then **D** became angry because of the	**1Ch 13:11**	1732
D was afraid of God that day,	**1Ch 13:12**	1732
So **D** did not take the ark with him	**1Ch 13:13**	1732
the ark with him to the city of **D**,	**1Ch 13:13**	1732
messengers to **D** with cedar trees,	**1Ch 14:1**	1732
And **D** realized that the LORD had	**1Ch 14:2**	1732
D took more wives at Jerusalem,	**1Ch 14:3**	1732
and **D** became the father of more	**1Ch 14:3**	1732
When the Philistines heard that **D**	**1Ch 14:8**	1732
went up in search of **D**;	**1Ch 14:8**	1732
and **D** heard of it and went out	**1Ch 14:8**	1732
D inquired of God, saying,	**1Ch 14:10**	1732
and **D** defeated them there;	**1Ch 14:11**	1732
D said, "God has broken through	**1Ch 14:11**	1732
so **D** gave the order and they were	**1Ch 14:12**	1732
D inquired again of God, and	**1Ch 14:14**	1732
D did just as God had	**1Ch 14:16**	1732
of **D** went out into all the lands;	**1Ch 14:17**	1732
Now **D** built houses for himself in	**1Ch 15:1**	1732
for himself in the city of **D**;	**1Ch 15:1**	1732
D said, "No one is to carry the ark	**1Ch 15:2**	1732
And **D** assembled all Israel at	**1Ch 15:3**	1732
D gathered together the sons	**1Ch 15:4**	1732
Then **D** called for Zadok and	**1Ch 15:11**	1732
Then **D** spoke to the chiefs of the	**1Ch 15:16**	1732
So *it was* **D**, with the elders of	**1Ch 15:25**	1732
Now **D** was clothed with a robe of	**1Ch 15:27**	1732
D also wore an ephod of linen.	**1Ch 15:27**	1732
of the LORD came to the city of **D**,	**1Ch 15:29**	1732
King **D** leaping and celebrating;	**1Ch 15:29**	1732
tent which **D** had pitched for it,	**1Ch 16:1**	1732
When **D** had finished offering the	**1Ch 16:2**	1732
Then on that day **D** first assigned	**1Ch 16:7**	1732
and **D** returned to bless his	**1Ch 16:43**	1732
about, when **D** dwelt in his house,	**1Ch 17:1**	1732
that **D** said to Nathan the prophet,	**1Ch 17:1**	1732
Then Nathan said to **D**,	**1Ch 17:2**	1732
"Go and tell **D** My servant,	**1Ch 17:4**	1732
shall you say to My servant **D**,	**1Ch 17:7**	1732
this vision, so Nathan spoke to **D**.	**1Ch 17:15**	1732
Then **D** the king went in and sat	**1Ch 17:16**	1732
"What more can **D** still *say* to	**1Ch 17:18**	1732
and the house of **D** Your servant is	**1Ch 17:24**	1732
about that **D** defeated the Philistines	**1Ch 18:1**	1732
the Moabites became servants to **D**,	**1Ch 18:2**	1732
D also defeated Hadadezer king of	**1Ch 18:3**	1732
D took from him 1,000 chariots	**1Ch 18:4**	1732
and **D** hamstrung all the chariot	**1Ch 18:4**	1732
D killed 22,000 men of the	**1Ch 18:5**	1732
Then **D** put *garrisons* among the	**1Ch 18:6**	1732
the Arameans became servants to **D**,	**1Ch 18:6**	1732
LORD helped **D** wherever he went.	**1Ch 18:6**	1732
D took the shields of gold	**1Ch 18:7**	1732
D took a very large amount of	**1Ch 18:8**	1732
king of Hamath heard that **D** had	**1Ch 18:9**	1732
he sent Hadoram his son to King **D** to	**1Ch 18:10**	1732
King **D** also dedicated these to the	**1Ch 18:11**	1732
the Edomites became servants to **D**.	**1Ch 18:13**	1732
LORD helped **D** wherever he went.	**1Ch 18:13**	1732
So **D** reigned over all Israel;	**1Ch 18:14**	1732
and the sons of **D** *were* chiefs at	**1Ch 18:17**	1732
Then **D** said, "I will show kindness	**1Ch 19:2**	1732
So **D** sent messengers to console	**1Ch 19:2**	1732
that **D** is honoring your father,	**1Ch 19:3**	1732
went and told **D** about the men.	**1Ch 19:5**	1732
had made themselves odious to **D**,	**1Ch 19:6**	1732
When **D** heard *of it,* he sent Joab	**1Ch 19:8**	1732
When it was told **D**,	**1Ch 19:17**	1732
And when **D** drew up in battle array	**1Ch 19:17**	1732
and **D** killed of the Arameans 7,000	**1Ch 19:18**	1732
made peace with **D** and served him.	**1Ch 19:19**	1732
But **D** stayed at Jerusalem.	**1Ch 20:1**	1732
D took the crown of their king	**1Ch 20:2**	1732
And thus **D** did to all the cities	**1Ch 20:3**	1732
Then **D** and all the people returned	**1Ch 20:3**	1732
and they fell by the hand of **D** and	**1Ch 20:8**	1732
and moved **D** to number Israel.	**1Ch 21:1**	1732
So **D** said to Joab and to the	**1Ch 21:2**	1732
the census of *all* the people to **D**.	**1Ch 21:5**	1732
D said to God,	**1Ch 21:8**	1732
"Go and speak to **D**, saying,	**1Ch 21:10**	1732
So Gad came to **D** and said to him,	**1Ch 21:11**	1732
D said to Gad,	**1Ch 21:13**	1732
Then **D** lifted up his eyes and saw	**1Ch 21:16**	1732
Then **D** and the elders, covered	**1Ch 21:16**	1732
D said to God,	**1Ch 21:17**	1732
LORD commanded Gad to say to **D**,	**1Ch 21:18**	1732
that **D** should go up and build an	**1Ch 21:18**	1732
So **D** went up at the word of Gad,	**1Ch 21:19**	1732
As **D** came to Ornan, Ornan	**1Ch 21:21**	1732
to Ornan, Ornan looked and saw **D**,	**1Ch 21:21**	1732
prostrated himself before **D** with his	**1Ch 21:21**	1732
Then **D** said to Ornan,	**1Ch 21:22**	1732
Ornan said to **D**,	**1Ch 21:23**	1732
But King **D** said to Ornan,	**1Ch 21:24**	1732
So **D** gave Ornan 600 shekels of	**1Ch 21:25**	1732
Then **D** built an altar to the LORD	**1Ch 21:26**	1732
when **D** saw that the LORD had	**1Ch 21:28**	1732
But **D** could not go before it to	**1Ch 21:30**	1732
D said, "This is the house of the	**1Ch 22:1**	1732
So **D** gave orders to gather the	**1Ch 22:2**	1732
D prepared large quantities of	**1Ch 22:3**	1732
quantities of cedar timber to **D**.	**1Ch 22:4**	1732
D said, "My son Solomon is young	**1Ch 22:5**	1732
So **D** made ample preparations	**1Ch 22:5**	1732
D said to Solomon,	**1Ch 22:7**	1732
D also commanded all the leaders	**1Ch 22:17**	1732
Now when **D** reached old age, he	**1Ch 23:1**	1732
which **D** made for giving praise.	**1Ch 23:5**	1732
D divided them into divisions	**1Ch 23:6**	1732
For **D** said, "The LORD God of Israel	**1Ch 23:25**	1732
For by the last words of **D** the	**1Ch 23:27**	1732
D, with Zadok of the sons of	**1Ch 24:3**	1732
in the presence of **D** the king,	**1Ch 24:31**	1732
D and the commanders of the army	**1Ch 25:1**	1732
which King **D** and the heads of the	**1Ch 26:26**	1732
And King **D** made them overseers of	**1Ch 26:32**	1732
But **D** did not count those twenty	**1Ch 27:23**	1732
of the chronicles of King **D**.	**1Ch 27:24**	1732
property which belonged to King **D**.	**1Ch 27:31**	1732
Now **D** assembled at Jerusalem all	**1Ch 28:1**	1732
King **D** rose to his feet and said,	**1Ch 28:2**	1732
Then **D** gave to his son Solomon the	**1Ch 28:11**	1732
"All *this,*" *said* **D**,	**1Ch 28:19**	1732
Then **D** said to his son Solomon,	**1Ch 28:20**	1732
D said to the entire assembly,	**1Ch 29:1**	1732
and King **D** also rejoiced greatly.	**1Ch 29:9**	1732
So **D** blessed the LORD in the sight	**1Ch 29:10**	1732
D said, "Blessed are You, O LORD	**1Ch 29:10**	1732
Then **D** said to all the assembly,	**1Ch 29:20**	1732
the son of **D** king a second time,	**1Ch 29:22**	1732
as king instead of **D** his father;	**1Ch 29:23**	1732
and also all the sons of King **D**	**1Ch 29:24**	1732
Now **D** the son of Jesse reigned	**1Ch 29:26**	1732
Now the acts of King **D**,	**1Ch 29:29**	1732
Now Solomon the son of **D**	**2Ch 1:1**	1732
D had brought up the ark of God	**2Ch 1:4**	1732
D with great lovingkindness,	**2Ch 1:8**	1732
to my father **D** is fulfilled,	**2Ch 1:9**	1732
"As you dealt with **D** my father and	**2Ch 2:3**	1732
whom **D** my father provided.	**2Ch 2:7**	1732
who has given King **D** a wise son,	**2Ch 2:12**	1732
those of my lord **D** your father.	**2Ch 2:14**	1732
which his father **D** had taken;	**2Ch 2:17**	1732
LORD had appeared to his father **D**,	**2Ch 3:1**	1732
at the place that **D** had prepared on	**2Ch 3:1**	1732
that **D** his father had dedicated,	**2Ch 5:1**	1732
of the LORD out of the city of **D**,	**2Ch 5:2**	1732
spoke with His mouth to my father **D**	**2Ch 6:4**	1732
D to be over My people Israel.'	**2Ch 6:6**	1732
in the heart of my father **D** to build a	**2Ch 6:7**	1732
"But the LORD said to my father **D**,	**2Ch 6:8**	1732
have risen in the place of my father **D**	**2Ch 6:10**	1732
who has kept with Your servant **D**,	**2Ch 6:15**	1732
Israel, keep with Your servant **D**,	**2Ch 6:16**	1732
You have spoken to Your servant **D**.	**2Ch 6:17**	1732
lovingkindness to Your servant **D**."	**2Ch 6:42**	1732
which King **D** had made for giving	**2Ch 7:6**	1732
that the LORD had shown to **D** and to	**2Ch 7:10**	1732
before Me as your father **D** walked	**2Ch 7:17**	1732
I covenanted with your father **D**,	**2Ch 7:18**	1732
from the city of **D** to the house which	**2Ch 8:11**	1732
in the house of **D** king of Israel,	**2Ch 8:11**	1732
to the ordinance of his father **D**,	**2Ch 8:14**	1732
for **D** the man of God had so	**2Ch 8:14**	1732
in the city of his father **D**;	**2Ch 9:31**	1732
"What portion do we have in **D**?	**2Ch 10:16**	1732
look after your own house, **D**."	**2Ch 10:16**	1732
the house of **D** to this day.	**2Ch 10:19**	1732
of **D** and Solomon for three years.	**2Ch 11:17**	1732
the daughter of Jerimoth the son of **D**	**2Ch 11:18**	1732
and was buried in the city of **D**;	**2Ch 12:16**	1732
gave the rule over Israel forever to **D**	**2Ch 13:5**	1732
servant of Solomon the son of **D**,	**2Ch 13:6**	1732
of the LORD through the sons of **D**,	**2Ch 13:8**	1732
they buried him in the city of **D**,	**2Ch 14:1**	1732
out for himself in the city of **D**,	**2Ch 16:14**	1732
with his fathers in the city of **D**,	**2Ch 21:1**	1732
not willing to destroy the house of **D**	**2Ch 21:7**	1732
covenant which He had made with **D**,	**2Ch 21:7**	1732
the LORD God of your father **D**,	**2Ch 21:12**	1732
they buried him in the city of **D**,	**2Ch 21:20**	1732
spoken concerning the sons of **D**.	**2Ch 23:3**	1732
whom **D** had assigned over the house	**2Ch 23:18**	1732
according to the order of **D**.	**2Ch 23:18**	1732
in the city of **D** among the kings,	**2Ch 24:16**	1732
they buried him in the city of **D**,	**2Ch 24:25**	1732
they buried him in the city of **D**;	**2Ch 27:9**	1732
the LORD as **D** his father *had done.*	**2Ch 28:1**	1732
to all that his father **D** had done.	**2Ch 29:2**	1732
of **D** and of Gad the king's seer,	**2Ch 29:25**	1732
with the *musical* instruments of **D**,	**2Ch 29:26**	1732
by the instruments of **D**,	**2Ch 29:27**	1732
the words of **D** and Asaph the seer.	**2Ch 29:30**	1732
the days of Solomon the son of **D**,	**2Ch 30:26**	1732
the Millo *in* the city of **D**,	**2Ch 32:5**	1732
to the west side of the city of **D**.	**2Ch 32:30**	1732
of the tombs of the sons of **D**;	**2Ch 32:33**	1732
said to **D** and to Solomon his son,	**2Ch 33:7**	1732
of **D** on the west side of Gihon,	**2Ch 33:14**	1732
walked in the ways of his father **D**	**2Ch 34:2**	1732
to seek the God of his father **D**;	**2Ch 34:3**	1732
the son of **D** king of Israel built;	**2Ch 35:3**	1732
according to the writing of **D** king	**2Ch 35:4**	1732
according to the command of **D**,	**2Ch 35:15**	1732
directions of King **D** of Israel.	**Ezr 3:10**	1732
of the sons of **D**, Hattush;	**Ezr 8:2**	1732
whom **D** and the princes had given	**Ezr 8:20**	1732
that descend from the city of **D**.	**Ne 3:15**	1732
a point opposite the tombs of **D**,	**Ne 3:16**	1732
as prescribed by **D** the man of God,	**Ne 12:24**	1732
instruments of **D** the man of God.	**Ne 12:36**	1732
directly up the steps of the city of **D**	**Ne 12:37**	1732
the wall above the house of **D** to the	**Ne 12:37**	1732
of **D** *and* of his son Solomon.	**Ne 12:45**	1732
For in the days of **D** and Asaph,	**Ne 12:46**	1732
To **D** and his descendants forever.	**Ps 18:50**	1732
prayers of **D** the son of Jesse are	**Ps 72:20**	1732
He also chose **D** His servant And	**Ps 78:70**	1732
I have sworn to **D** My servant,	**Ps 89:3**	1732
"I have found **D** My servant;	**Ps 89:20**	1732
I will not lie to **D**.	**Ps 89:35**	1732
swore to **D** in Your faithfulness?	**Ps 89:49**	1732
The thrones of the house of **D**.	**Ps 122:5**	1732
For the sake of **D** Your servant, Do	**Ps 132:10**	1732
The LORD has sworn to **D** A	**Ps 132:11**	1732
the horn of **D** to spring forth;	**Ps 132:17**	1732
Who rescues **D** His servant from	**Ps 144:10**	1732
proverbs of Solomon the son of **D**,	**Pr 1:1**	1732
of the Preacher, the son of **D**,	**Ec 1:1**	1732
"Your neck is like the tower of **D**	**SS 4:4**	1732
it was reported to the house of **D**,	**Is 7:2**	1732
"Listen now, O house of **D**!	**Is 7:13**	1732
throne of **D** and over his kingdom,	**Is 9:7**	1732
in faithfulness in the tent of **D**;	**Is 16:5**	1732
wall of the city of **D** were many;	**Is 22:9**	1732
of the house of **D** on his shoulder,	**Is 22:22**	1732
the city *where* **D** *once* camped!	**Is 29:1**	1732
LORD, the God of your father **D**,	**Is 38:5**	1732

the faithful mercies shown to **D**. **Is 55:3** 1732
that sit for **D** on his throne, **Jer 13:13** 1732
sitting on the throne of **D**, **Jer 17:25** 1732
O house of **D**, thus says the LORD: **Jer 21:12** 1732
of **D** Or ruling again in Judah.' " **Jer 22:30** 1732
raise up for **D** a righteous Branch; **Jer 23:5** 1732
king who sits on the throne of **D**, **Jer 29:16** 1732
LORD their God and **D** their king, **Jer 30:9** 1732
Branch of **D** to spring forth; **Jer 33:15** 1732
'**D** shall never lack a man to sit **Jer 33:17** 1732
covenant may also be broken with **D** **Jer 33:21** 1732
I will multiply the descendants of **D** **Jer 33:22** 1732
of Jacob and **D** My servant, **Jer 33:26** 1732
no one to sit on the throne of **D**, **Jer 36:30** 1732
them one shepherd, My servant **D**, **Ezk 34:23** 1732
D will be prince among them; **Ezk 34:24** 1732
servant **D** will be king over them, **Ezk 37:24** 1732
and **D** My servant will be their **Ezk 37:25** 1732
LORD their God and **D** their king; **Hos 3:5** 1732
And like **D** have composed songs for **Am 6:5** 1732
raise up the fallen booth of **D**, **Am 9:11** 1732
so that the glory of the house of **D** **Zch 12:7** 1732
them in that day will be like **D**, **Zch 12:8** 1732
the house of **D** *will be* like God, **Zch 12:8** 1732
"I will pour out on the house of **D** **Zch 12:10** 1732
of the house of **D** by itself and **Zch 12:12** 1732
will be opened for the house of **D** **Zch 13:1** 1732
of Jesus the Messiah, the son of **D**, **Mt 1:1** *1160b*
Jesse was the father of **D** the king. **Mt 1:6** *1160b*
D was the father of Solomon **Mt 1:6** *1160b*
to **D** are fourteen generations; **Mt 1:17** *1160b*
from **D** to the deportation to **Mt 1:17** *1160b*
"Joseph, son of **D**, do not be **Mt 1:20** *1160b*
"Have mercy on us, Son of **D**!" **Mt 9:27** *1160b*
"Have you not read what **D** did when **Mt 12:3** *1160b*
"This man cannot be the Son of **D**, **Mt 12:23** *1160b*
mercy on me, Lord, Son of **D**; **Mt 15:22** *1160b*
have mercy on us, Son of **D**!" **Mt 20:30** *1160b*
Son of **D**, have mercy on us!" **Mt 20:31** *1160b*
"Hosanna to the Son of **D**; **Mt 21:9** *1160b*
"Hosanna to the Son of **D**," **Mt 21:15** *1160b*
They said to Him, "*The son* of **D**." **Mt 22:42** *1160b*
how does **D** in the Spirit call Him **Mt 22:43** *1160b*
"If **D** then calls Him **Mt 22:45** *1160b*
"Have you never read what **D** did **Mk 2:25** *1160b*
"Jesus, Son of **D**, have mercy on **Mk 10:47** *1160b*
"Son of **D**, have mercy on me!" **Mk 10:48** *1160b*
coming kingdom of our father **D**; **Mk 11:10** *1160b*
that the Christ is the son of **D**? **Mk 12:35** *1160b*
"**D** himself said in the Holy Spirit, **Mk 12:36** *1160b*
"**D** himself calls Him 'Lord'; **Mk 12:37** *1160b*
Joseph, of the descendants of **D**; **Lk 1:27** *1160b*
Him the throne of His father **D**; **Lk 1:32** *1160b*
us In the house of **D** His servant **Lk 1:69** *1160b*
to Judea, to the city of **D** which **Lk 2:4** *1160b*
was of the house and family of **D**, **Lk 2:4** *1160b*
for today in the city of **D** there **Lk 2:11** *1160b*
the son of Nathan, the son of **D**, **Lk 3:31** *1160b*
what **D** did when he was hungry, **Lk 6:3** *1160b*
"Jesus, Son of **D**, have mercy on **Lk 18:38** *1160b*
"Son of **D**, have mercy on me!" **Lk 18:39** *1160b*
"For **D** himself says in the book **Lk 20:42** *1160b*
"Therefore **D** calls Him 'Lord,' **Lk 20:44** *1160b*
comes from the descendants of **D**, **Jn 7:42** *1160b*
the village where **D** was?" **Jn 7:42** *1160b*
the mouth of **D** concerning Judas, **Ac 1:16** *1160b*
"For **D** says of Him, **Ac 2:25** *1160b*
say to you regarding the patriarch **D** **Ac 2:29** *1160b*
not **D** who ascended into heaven, **Ac 2:34** *1160b*
mouth of our father **D** Your servant, **Ac 4:25** *1160b*
our fathers, until the time of **D**. **Ac 7:45** *1160b*
"**D** found favor in God's sight, **Ac 7:46** *1160b*
He raised up **D** to be their king, **Ac 13:22** *1160b*
'I HAVE FOUND **D** the son of Jesse, **Ac 13:22** *1160b*
THE HOLY *and* SURE *blessings* OF **D**.' **Ac 13:34** *1160b*
"For **D**, after he had served the **Ac 13:36** *1160b*
REBUILD THE TABERNACLE OF **D** **Ac 15:16** *1160b*
of **D** according to the flesh, **Ro 1:3** *1160b*
just as **D** also speaks of the **Ro 4:6** *1160b*
D says, "LET THEIR TABLE BECOME **Ro 11:9** *1160b*
from the dead, descendant of **D**, **2Tm 2:8** *1160b*
saying through **D** after so long a **Heb 4:7** *1160b*
of **D** and Samuel and the prophets, **Heb 11:32** *1160b*
who is true, who has the key of **D**, **Rv 3:7** *1160b*
the tribe of Judah, the Root of **D**, **Rv 5:5** *1160b*
the root and the descendant of **D**, **Rv 22:16** *1160b*

DAVID'S

but there was no sword in **D** hand. **1Sa 17:50** 1732
Thus Saul was **D** enemy continually. **1Sa 18:29** 1732
to **D** house to watch him, **1Sa 19:11** 1732
But Michal, **D** wife, told him, **1Sa 19:11** 1732
it at the hands of **D** enemies." **1Sa 20:16** 1732
Saul's side, but **D** place was empty. **1Sa 20:25** 1732
new moon, that **D** place was empty; **1Sa 20:27** 1732
But **D** men said to him, **1Sa 23:3** 1732
afterward that **D** conscience bothered **1Sa 24:5** 1732
When **D** young men came, they spoke **1Sa 25:9** 1732
to all these words in **D** name; **1Sa 25:9** 1732
But Nabal answered **D** servants and **1Sa 25:10** 1732
So **D** young men retraced their way **1Sa 25:12** 1732
given Michal his daughter, **D** wife, **1Sa 25:44** 1732
Saul recognized **D** voice and said, **1Sa 26:17** 1732
Now **D** two wives had been taken **1Sa 30:5** 1732
"This is **D** spoil." **1Sa 30:20** 1732
nineteen of **D** servants besides **2Sa 2:30** 1732
sixth, Ithream, by **D** wife Eglah. **2Sa 3:5** 1732
blind, who are hated by **D** soul, **2Sa 5:8** 1732
and **D** sons were chief ministers. **2Sa 8:18** 1732
So Mephibosheth ate at **D** table as **2Sa 9:11** 1732
But when **D** servants came to the **2Sa 10:2** 1732
So Hanun took **D** servants and **2Sa 10:4** 1732
the people among **D** servants fell; **2Sa 11:17** 1732
Then **D** anger burned greatly **2Sa 12:5** 1732
and it was *placed* on **D** head. **2Sa 12:30** 1732
the son of Shimeah, **D** brother; **2Sa 13:3** 1732
the son of Shimeah, **D** brother, **2Sa 13:32** 1732
the Gilonite, **D** counselor, **2Sa 15:12** 1732
So Hushai, **D** friend, came into the **2Sa 15:37** 1732
when Hushai the Archite, **D** friend, **2Sa 16:16** 1732
D men with him over the Jordan?" **2Sa 19:41** 1732
the son of Shimei, **D** brother, **2Sa 21:21** 1732
Now **D** heart troubled him after he **2Sa 24:10** 1732
came to the prophet Gad, **D** seer, **2Sa 24:11** 1732
had Solomon ride on King **D** mule, **1Ki 1:38** 1732
As **D** time to die drew near, he **1Ki 2:1** 1732
But for **D** sake the LORD his God **1Ki 15:4** 1732
and shields that *had been* King **D**, **2Ki 11:10** 1732
and for My servant **D** sake.' " **2Ki 19:34** 1732
and for My servant **D** sake. **2Ki 20:6** 1732
And **D** servants came into the land **1Ch 19:2** 1732
took **D** servants and shaved them and **1Ch 19:4** 1732
and it was placed on **D** head. **1Ch 20:2** 1732
the son of Shimea, **D** brother, **1Ch 20:7** 1732
The LORD spoke to Gad, **D** seer, **1Ch 21:9** 1732
In the fortieth year of **D** reign, **1Ch 26:31** 1732
Judah, Elihu, *one* of **D** brothers; **1Ch 27:18** 1732
Also Jonathan, **D** uncle, *was* a **1Ch 27:32** 1732
example of his father **D** earlier days **2Ch 17:3** 1732
shields which had been King **D**, **2Ch 23:9** 1732
Remember, O LORD, on **D** behalf, **Ps 132:1** 1732
and for My servant **D** sake.' " **Is 37:35** 1732
of Judah, who sits on **D** throne, **Jer 22:2** 1732
sitting in **D** place on his throne, **Jer 22:4** 1732
that they say the Christ is **D** son? **Lk 20:41** *1160b*

DAWN

"Let me go, for the **d** is breaking." **Gn 32:26** 7837
let her go at the approach of **d**. **Jg 19:25** 7837
As the day began to **d**, **Jg 19:26**
6437, 1242
and by **d** not even one remained who **2Sa 17:22**
216, 1242
from **d** until the stars appeared. **Ne 4:21**
5927, 7837
And let it not see the breaking **d**; **Jb 3:9** 7837
I am continually tossing until **d**. **Jb 7:4** 5399
"The murderer arises at **d**; **Jb 24:14** 216
caused the **d** to know its place, **Jb 38:12** 7837
and lyre! I will awaken the **d**. **Ps 57:8** 7837
d and the sunset shout for joy. **Ps 65:8** 1242
I will awaken the **d**! **Ps 108:2** 7837
array, from the womb of the **d**, **Ps 110:3** 4891
I rise before **d** and cry for help; **Ps 119:147** 5399
If I take the wings of the **d**, **Ps 139:9** 7837
righteous is like the light of **d**, **Pr 4:18** 5051
'Who is this that grows like the **d**, **SS 6:10** 7837
it is because they have no **d**. **Is 8:20** 7837
star of the morning, son of the **d**! **Is 14:12** 7837
your dew *is as* the dew of the **d**, **Is 26:19** 219a
light will break out like the **d**, **Is 58:8** 7837
Then the king arose at **d**, **Da 6:19** 8238
forth is as certain as the **d**; **Hos 6:3** 7837
At **d** the king of Israel will be **Hos 10:15** 7837
d is spread over the mountains, **Jl 2:2** 7837
He who makes **d** into darkness And **Am 4:13** 7837
a worm when **d** came the next day and **Jon 4:7** 7837
as it began to **d** toward the first **Mt 28:1** *2020*
first day of the week, at early **d**, **Lk 24:1** *3722*
Until the day was about to **d**, **Ac 27:33** *1096*

DAWNED

When morning **d**, **Gn 19:15** 5927
Sinai, And **d** on them from Seir; **Dt 33:2** 2224
night until the day **d** at Hebron. **2Sa 2:32** 215
OF DEATH, UPON THEM A LIGHT **D**." **Mt 4:16** *393*

DAWNING

they rose early at the **d** of the day **Jos 6:15** 7837

DAWNS

God will help her when morning **d**. **Ps 46:5** 6437
until the day **d** and the morning **2Pe 1:19** *1306a*

DAY

God called the light **d**, **Gn 1:5** 3117
and there was morning, one **d**. **Gn 1:5** 3117
and there was morning, a second **d**. **Gn 1:8** 3117
and there was morning, a third **d**. **Gn 1:13** 3117
to separate the **d** from the night, **Gn 1:14** 3117
the greater light to govern the **d**, **Gn 1:16** 3117
and to govern the **d** and the night, **Gn 1:18** 3117
and there was morning, a fourth **d**. **Gn 1:19** 3117
and there was morning, a fifth **d**. **Gn 1:23** 3117
there was morning, the sixth **d**. **Gn 1:31** 3117
By the seventh **d** God completed **Gn 2:2** 3117
and He rested on the seventh **d** **Gn 2:2** 3117
the seventh **d** and sanctified it, **Gn 2:3** 3117
in the **d** that the LORD God made **Gn 2:4** 3117
for in the **d** that you eat from it **Gn 2:17** 3117
"For God knows that in the **d** you **Gn 3:5** 3117
the garden in the cool of the **d**, **Gn 3:8** 3117
You have driven me this **d** from the **Gn 4:14** 3117
In the **d** when God created man, He **Gn 5:1** 3117
in the **d** when they were created. **Gn 5:2** 3117
on the seventeenth **d** of the month, **Gn 7:11** 3117
on the same **d** all the fountains of **Gn 7:11** 3117
On the very same **d** Noah and Shem **Gn 7:13** 3117
on the seventeenth **d** of the month, **Gn 8:4** 3117
on the first **d** of the month, **Gn 8:5**
the twenty-seventh **d** of the month, **Gn 8:14** 3117
And **d** and night Shall not cease." **Gn 8:22** 3117
On that **d** the LORD made a covenant **Gn 15:18** 3117
their foreskin in the very same **d**, **Gn 17:23** 3117
same **d** Abraham was circumcised, **Gn 17:26** 3117
tent door in the heat of the **d**. **Gn 18:1** 3117
On the following **d**, the firstborn **Gn 19:34** 4283
father of the Moabites to this **d**. **Gn 19:37** 3117
of the sons of Ammon to this **d**. **Gn 19:38** 3117
on the **d** that Isaac was weaned. **Gn 21:8** 3117
On the third **d** Abraham raised his **Gn 22:4** 3117
Provide, as it is said to this **d**, **Gn 22:14** 3117
Now it came about on the same **d**, **Gn 26:32** 3117
the city is Beersheba to this **d**. **Gn 26:33** 3117
I do not know the **d** of my death. **Gn 27:2** 3117
bereaved of you both in one **d**?" **Gn 27:45** 3117
"Behold, it is still high **d**; **Gn 29:7** 3117
So he removed on that **d** the **Gn 30:35** 3117
the third **d** that Jacob had fled, **Gn 31:22** 3117
stolen by **d** or stolen by night. **Gn 31:39** 3117
by **d** the heat consumed me and the **Gn 31:40** 3117
But what can I do this **d** to these **Gn 31:43** 3117
between you and me this **d**." **Gn 31:48** 3117
to this **d** the sons of Israel do **Gn 32:32** 3117
And if they are driven hard one **d**, **Gn 33:13** 3117
that **d** on his way to Seir. **Gn 33:16** 3117
Now it came about on the third **d**, **Gn 34:25** 3117
me in the **d** of my distress and **Gn 35:3** 3117
pillar of Rachel's grave to this **d**. **Gn 35:20** 3117
she spoke to Joseph **d** after day, **Gn 39:10** 3117
she spoke to Joseph day after **d**, **Gn 39:10** 3117
Now it happened one **d** that he went **Gn 39:11** 3117
Thus it came about on the third **d**, **Gn 40:20** 3117
said to them on the third **d**, **Gn 42:18** 3117
the land of Egypt *valid* to this **d**, **Gn 47:26** 3117
my shepherd all my life to this **d**, **Gn 48:15** 3117
He blessed them that **d**, **Gn 48:20** 3117
He went out the next **d**, **Ex 2:13** 3117
So the same **d** Pharaoh commanded **Ex 5:6** 3117
Now it came about on the **d** when **Ex 6:28** 3117
"But on that **d** I will set apart **Ex 8:22** 3117
LORD did this thing on the next **d**, **Ex 9:6** 4283
the **d** it was founded until now. **Ex 9:18** 3117
from the **d** that they came upon the **Ex 10:6** 3117
upon the earth until this **d**.' " **Ex 10:6** 3117
all that **d** and all that night; **Ex 10:13** 3117
d you see my face you shall die!" **Ex 10:28** 3117
fourteenth **d** of the same month, **Ex 12:6** 3117
this **d** will be a memorial to you, **Ex 12:14** 3117
but on the first **d** you shall **Ex 12:15** 3117
the first **d** until the seventh day, **Ex 12:15** 3117
the first day until the seventh **d**, **Ex 12:15** 3117
'On the first **d** you shall have **Ex 12:16** 3117
holy assembly on the seventh **d**; **Ex 12:16** 3117
for on this very **d** I brought your **Ex 12:17** 3117
you shall observe this **d** throughout **Ex 12:17** 3117
d of the month at evening, **Ex 12:18** 3117
d of the month at evening. **Ex 12:18** 3117
and thirty years, to the very **d**, **Ex 12:41** 3117
And on that same **d** **Ex 12:51** 3117
"Remember this **d** in which you **Ex 13:3** 3117
"On this **d** in the month of Abib, **Ex 13:4** 3117
and on the seventh **d** there shall **Ex 13:6** 3117
You shall tell your son on that **d**, **Ex 13:8** 3117
by **d** to lead them on the way, **Ex 13:21** 3119
might travel by **d** and by night. **Ex 13:21** 3119
away the pillar of cloud by **d**, **Ex 13:22** 3119
Thus the LORD saved Israel that **d** **Ex 14:30** 3117
on the fifteenth **d** of the second **Ex 16:1** 3117
and gather a day's portion every **d**, **Ex 16:4** 3117
"On the sixth **d**, when they prepare **Ex 16:5** 3117
Now on the sixth **d** they gathered **Ex 16:22** 3117
gather it, but on the seventh **d**, **Ex 16:26** 3117
It came about on the seventh **d** that **Ex 16:27** 3117
bread for two days on the sixth **d**. **Ex 16:29** 3117
of his place on the seventh **d**." **Ex 16:29** 3117
people rested on the seventh **d**. **Ex 16:30** 3117
It came about the next **d** that **Ex 18:13** 4283
on that very **d** they came into the **Ex 19:1** 3117
let them be ready for the third **d**, **Ex 19:11** 3117
for on the third **d** the LORD will **Ex 19:11** 3117
"Be ready for the third **d**; **Ex 19:15** 3117
So it came about on the third **d**, **Ex 19:16** 3117
"Remember the sabbath **d**, **Ex 20:8** 3117
but the seventh **d** is a sabbath of **Ex 20:10** 3117
them, and rested on the seventh **d**; **Ex 20:11** 3117
the sabbath **d** and made it holy. **Ex 20:11** 3117
however, he survives a **d** or two, **Ex 21:21** 3117
eighth **d** you shall give it to Me. **Ex 22:30** 3117
but on the seventh **d** you shall cease **Ex 23:12** 3117
and on the seventh **d** He called to **Ex 24:16** 3117
"Each **d** you shall offer a **Ex 29:36** 3117
two one year old lambs each **d**, **Ex 29:38** 3117
but on the seventh **d** there is a **Ex 31:15** 3117
does any work on the sabbath **d** **Ex 31:15** 3117
seventh **d** He ceased *from labor*, **Ex 31:17** 3117
So the next **d** they rose early and **Ex 32:6** 4283
men of the people fell that **d**. **Ex 32:28** 3117
d Moses said to the people, **Ex 32:30** 4283
in the **d** when I punish, **Ex 32:34** 3117
what I am commanding you this **d**: **Ex 34:11** 3117
on the seventh **d** you shall rest; **Ex 34:21** 3117
on the seventh **d** you shall have a **Ex 35:2** 3117
seventh day you shall have a holy **d**, **Ex 35:2**
your dwellings on the sabbath **d**." **Ex 35:3** 3117
"On the first **d** of the first **Ex 40:2** 3117
year, on the first **d** of the month, **Ex 40:17**
until the **d** when it was taken up. **Ex 40:37** 3117
LORD was on the tabernacle by **d**, **Ex 40:38** 3119
on the **d** *he presents* his guilt offering. **Lv 6:5** 3117
LORD on the **d** when he is anointed; **Lv 6:20** 3117
be eaten on the **d** of his offering; **Lv 7:15** 3117

Context	Reference	Number
d that he offers his sacrifice,	Lv 7:16	3117
and on the next **d** what is left of	Lv 7:16	4283
third **d** shall be burned with fire.	Lv 7:17	3117
ever be eaten on the third **d**,	Lv 7:18	3117
in that **d** when he presented them	Lv 7:35	3117
in the **d** that He anointed them.	Lv 7:36	3117
in the **d** that He commanded the sons	Lv 7:38	3117
until the **d** that the period of	Lv 8:33	3117
to do as has been done this **d**,	Lv 8:34	3117
remain **d** and night for seven days and	Lv 8:35	3119
Now it came about on the eighth **d**	Lv 9:1	3117
this very **d** they presented their	Lv 10:19	3117
'On the eighth **d** the flesh of	Lv 12:3	3117
look at him on the seventh **d**,	Lv 13:5	3117
at him again on the seventh **d**,	Lv 13:6	3117
look at him on the seventh **d**.	Lv 13:27	3117
"On the seventh **d** the priest	Lv 13:32	3117
"Then on the seventh **d** the priest	Lv 13:34	3117
look at the mark on the seventh **d**;	Lv 13:51	3117
leper in the **d** of his cleansing.	Lv 14:2	3117
"It will be on the seventh **d**	Lv 14:9	3117
"Now on the eighth **d** he is to	Lv 14:10	3117
"Then the eighth **d** he shall bring	Lv 14:23	3117
seventh **d** and make an inspection.	Lv 14:39	3117
'Then on the eighth **d** he shall	Lv 15:14	3117
'Then on the eighth **d** she shall	Lv 15:29	3117
on the tenth **d** of the month,	Lv 16:29	
for it is on this **d** that atonement	Lv 16:30	3117
be eaten the same **d** you offer *it*,	Lv 19:6	3117
day you offer *it*, and the next **d**;	Lv 19:6	4283
third **d** shall be burned with fire.	Lv 19:6	3117
it is eaten at all on the third **d**,	Lv 19:7	3117
and from the eighth **d** on it shall	Lv 22:27	3117
both it and its young in one **d**.	Lv 22:28	3117
"It shall be eaten on the same **d**,	Lv 22:30	3117
but on the seventh **d** there is a	Lv 23:3	3117
on the fourteenth **d** of the month	Lv 23:5	
'Then on the fifteenth **d** of the	Lv 23:6	3117
'On the first **d** you shall have a	Lv 23:7	3117
seventh **d** is a holy convocation;	Lv 23:8	3117
on the **d** after the sabbath the	Lv 23:11	4283
on the **d** when you wave the sheaf,	Lv 23:12	3117
'Until this same **d**, until you have	Lv 23:14	3117
from the **d** after the sabbath,	Lv 23:15	4283
from the **d** when you brought in the	Lv 23:15	3117
the **d** after the seventh sabbath;	Lv 23:16	4283
'On this same **d** you shall make a	Lv 23:21	3117
"On exactly the tenth **d** of this	Lv 23:27	
month is the **d** of atonement;	Lv 23:27	3117
not do any work on this same **d**,	Lv 23:28	3117
day, for it is a **d** of atonement,	Lv 23:28	3117
not humble himself on this same **d**,	Lv 23:29	3117
who does any work on this same **d**,	Lv 23:30	3117
the first **d** is a holy convocation;	Lv 23:35	3117
On the eighth **d** you shall have a	Lv 23:36	3117
each day's matter on its own **d**	Lv 23:37	3117
fifteenth **d** of the seventh month,	Lv 23:39	3117
d and a rest on the eighth day.	Lv 23:39	3117
day and a rest on the eighth **d**.	Lv 23:39	3117
'Now on the first **d** you shall take	Lv 23:40	3117
"Every sabbath **d** he shall set it	Lv 24:8	3117
the tenth **d** of the seventh month;	Lv 25:9	
on the **d** of atonement you shall	Lv 25:9	3117
and he shall on that **d** give your	Lv 27:23	3117
on the **d** that I struck down all	Nu 3:13	3117
on the **d** when he becomes clean;	Nu 6:9	3117
shall shave it on the seventh **d**.	Nu 6:9	3117
'Then on the eighth **d** he shall	Nu 6:10	3117
d he shall consecrate his head,	Nu 6:11	3117
Now on the **d** that Moses	Nu 7:1	3117
their offering, one leader each **d**,	Nu 7:11	3117
offering on the first **d** was Nahshon	Nu 7:12	3117
second **d** Nethanel the son of Zuar,	Nu 7:18	3117
d *it was* Eliab the son of Helon,	Nu 7:24	3117
On the fourth **d** *it was* Elizur the	Nu 7:30	3117
On the fifth **d** *it was* Shelumiel	Nu 7:36	3117
On the sixth **d** *it was* Eliasaph the	Nu 7:42	3117
On the seventh **d** *it was* Elishama	Nu 7:48	3117
On the eighth **d** *it was* Gamaliel	Nu 7:54	3117
On the ninth **d** *it was* Abidan the	Nu 7:60	3117
On the tenth **d** *it was* Ahiezer the	Nu 7:66	3117
On the eleventh **d** *it was* Pagiel	Nu 7:72	3117
d *it was* Ahira the son of Enan,	Nu 7:78	3117
on the **d** that I struck down all	Nu 8:17	3117
"On the fourteenth **d** of this month,	Nu 9:3	3117
on the fourteenth **d** of the month,	Nu 9:5	3117
not observe Passover on that **d**;	Nu 9:6	3117
before Moses and Aaron on that **d**.	Nu 9:6	3117
on the fourteenth **d** at twilight,	Nu 9:11	3117
Now on the **d** that the tabernacle	Nu 9:15	3117
the cloud would cover it *by* **d**,	Nu 9:16	
"Also in the **d** of your gladness	Nu 10:10	3117
of the LORD was over them by **d** when	Nu 10:34	3119
'You shall eat, not one **d**,	Nu 11:19	3117
The people spent all **d** and all	Nu 11:32	3117
and all night and all the next **d**,	Nu 11:32	3117
before them in a pillar of cloud by **d**	Nu 14:14	3119
for every **d** you shall bear your	Nu 14:34	3117
from the **d** when the LORD gave	Nu 15:23	3117
gathering wood on the sabbath **d**.	Nu 15:32	3117
But on the next **d** all the	Nu 16:41	4283
Now on the next **d** Moses went	Nu 17:8	4283
third **d** and on the seventh day,	Nu 19:12	3117
third day and on the seventh **d**,	Nu 19:12	3117
third **d** and on the seventh day,	Nu 19:12	3117
third day and on the seventh **d**,	Nu 19:12	3117
third **d** and on the seventh day;	Nu 19:19	3117
third day and on the seventh **d**;	Nu 19:19	3117
and on the seventh **d** he shall	Nu 19:19	3117
ridden all your life to this **d**?	Nu 22:30	3117
d of the plague because of Peor."	Nu 25:18	
continual burnt offering every **d**.	Nu 28:3	
'Then on the sabbath **d** two male	Nu 28:9	
'Then on the fourteenth **d** of the	Nu 28:16	3117
'On the fifteenth **d** of this	Nu 28:17	3117
d *shall be* a holy convocation;	Nu 28:18	3117
'On the seventh **d** you shall	Nu 28:25	3117
'Also on the **d** of the first	Nu 28:26	3117
on the first **d** of the month,	Nu 29:1	
to you a **d** for blowing trumpets.	Nu 29:1	3117
'Then on the tenth **d** of this	Nu 29:7	
'Then on the fifteenth **d** of the	Nu 29:12	3117
'Then on the second **d**:	Nu 29:17	3117
'Then on the third **d**:	Nu 29:20	3117
'Then on the fourth **d**:	Nu 29:23	3117
'Then on the fifth **d**:	Nu 29:26	3117
'Then on the sixth **d**:	Nu 29:29	3117
'Then on the seventh **d**:	Nu 29:32	3117
'On the eighth **d** you shall have a	Nu 29:35	3117
her on the **d** he hears *of it*,	Nu 30:5	3117
to her on the **d** he hears *it*,	Nu 30:7	3117
on the **d** her husband hears *of it*,	Nu 30:8	3117
them on the **d** he hears *them*,	Nu 30:12	3117
says nothing to her from **d** to day,	Nu 30:14	3117
says nothing to her from day to **d**,	Nu 30:14	3117
to her on the **d** he heard them.	Nu 30:14	3117
third **d** and on the seventh day.	Nu 31:19	3117
third day and on the seventh **d**.	Nu 31:19	3117
on the seventh **d** and be clean,	Nu 31:24	3117
the LORD's anger burned in that **d**,	Nu 32:10	3117
fifteenth **d** of the first month;	Nu 33:3	3117
on the next **d** after the Passover	Nu 33:3	4283
on the first **d** in the fifth month.	Nu 33:38	
the first **d** of the eleventh month,	Dt 1:3	
you are this **d** like the stars of	Dt 1:10	3117
in fire by night and cloud by **d**,	Dt 1:33	3119
who this **d** have no knowledge of	Dt 1:39	3117
in their place even to this **d**.	Dt 2:22	3117
'This **d** I will begin to put the	Dt 2:25	3117
Havvoth-jair, *as it is* to this **d**.)	Dt 3:14	3117
"*Remember* the **d** you stood before	Dt 4:10	3117
the **d** the LORD spoke to you at Horeb	Dt 4:15	3117
since the **d** that God created man	Dt 4:32	3117
the sabbath **d** to keep it holy,	Dt 5:12	3117
but the seventh **d** is a sabbath of	Dt 5:14	3117
you to observe the sabbath **d**.	Dt 5:15	3117
to your fathers, as *it is* this **d**.	Dt 8:18	3117
from the **d** that you left the land	Dt 9:7	3117
the fire on the **d** of the assembly.	Dt 9:10	3117
the LORD from the **d** I knew you.	Dt 9:24	3117
the fire on the **d** of the assembly;	Dt 10:4	3117
to bless in His name until this **d**.	Dt 10:8	3117
all peoples, as *it is* this **d**.	Dt 10:15	3117
"Know this **d** that I *am* not	Dt 11:2	3117
the **d** when you came out of the land	Dt 16:3	3117
sacrifice on the evening of the first **d**	Dt 16:4	3117
and on the seventh **d** there shall	Dt 16:8	3117
in Horeb on the **d** of the assembly,	Dt 18:16	3117
then it shall be in the **d** he wills	Dt 21:16	3117
surely bury him on the same **d**	Dt 21:23	3117
on his **d** before the sun sets,	Dt 24:15	3117
'I declare this **d** to the LORD my	Dt 26:3	3117
"This **d** the LORD your God	Dt 26:16	3117
"So it shall be on the **d** when you	Dt 27:2	3117
This **d** you have become a people	Dt 27:9	3117
also charged the people on that **d**,	Dt 27:11	3117
you will be in dread night and **d**,	Dt 28:66	3119
"Yet to this **d** the LORD has not	Dt 29:4	3117
another land, as *it is* this **d**.'	Dt 29:28	3117
be kindled against them in that **d**,	Dt 31:17	3117
so that they will say in that **d**,	Dt 31:17	3117
I will surely hide My face in that **d**	Dt 31:18	3117
Moses wrote this song the same **d**,	Dt 31:22	3117
the **d** of their calamity is near,	Dt 32:35	3117
spoke to Moses that very same **d**,	Dt 32:48	3117
by Him, Who shields him all the **d**,	Dt 33:12	3117
knows his burial place to this **d**.	Dt 34:6	3117
shall meditate on it **d** and night,	Jos 1:8	3119
"This **d** I will begin to exalt you	Jos 3:7	3117
and they are there to this **d**.	Jos 4:9	3117
On that **d** the LORD exalted Joshua	Jos 4:14	3117
place is called Gilgal to this **d**.	Jos 5:9	3117
on the evening of the fourteenth **d**	Jos 5:10	3117
On the **d** after the Passover,	Jos 5:11	4283
the Passover, on that very **d**,	Jos 5:11	3117
The manna ceased on the **d**	Jos 5:12	4283
then on the seventh **d** you shall	Jos 6:4	3117
mouth, until the **d** I tell you,	Jos 6:10	3117
Thus the second **d** they marched	Jos 6:14	3117
on the seventh **d** they rose early	Jos 6:15	3117
rose early at the dawning of the **d**	Jos 6:15	7837
only on that **d** they marched around	Jos 6:15	3117
in the midst of Israel to this **d**,	Jos 6:25	3117
LORD will trouble you this **d**."	Jos 7:25	3117
of stones that stands to this **d**,	Jos 7:26	3117
the valley of Achor to this **d**.	Jos 7:26	3117
All who fell that **d**,	Jos 8:25	3117
a desolation until this **d**.	Jos 8:28	3117
of stones *that stands* to this **d**.	Jos 8:29	3117
the **d** that we left to come to you;	Jos 9:12	3117
to their cities on the third **d**.	Jos 9:17	3117
But Joshua made them that **d** hewers	Jos 9:27	3117
the altar of the LORD, to this **d**,	Jos 9:27	3117
Joshua spoke to the LORD in the **d**	Jos 10:12	3117
to go *down* for about a whole **d**.	Jos 10:13	3117
There was no **d** like that	Jos 10:14	3117
mouth of the cave, to this very **d**.	Jos 10:27	3117
captured Makkedah on that **d**,	Jos 10:28	3117
he captured it on the second **d**,	Jos 10:32	3117
They captured it on that **d** and	Jos 10:35	3117
that **d** every person who *was* in it,	Jos 10:35	3117
live among Israel until this **d**.	Jos 13:13	3117
"So Moses swore on that **d**,	Jos 14:9	3117
as I was in the **d** Moses sent me;	Jos 14:11	3117
which the LORD spoke on that **d**,	Jos 14:12	3117
on that **d** that Anakim *were* there,	Jos 14:12	3117
the Kenizzite until this **d**.	Jos 14:14	3117
Judah at Jerusalem until this **d**.	Jos 15:63	3117
in the midst of Ephraim to this **d**,	Jos 16:10	3117
these many days to this **d**,	Jos 22:3	3117
from following the LORD this **d**,	Jos 22:16	3117
to rebel against the LORD this **d**?	Jos 22:16	3117
not cleansed ourselves to this **d**,	Jos 22:17	3117
this **d** from following the LORD?	Jos 22:18	3117
LORD do not save us this **d**!	Jos 22:22	3117
from following the LORD this **d**,	Jos 22:29	3117
God, as you have done to this **d**.	Jos 23:8	3117
has stood before you to this **d**.	Jos 23:9	3117
a covenant with the people that **d**,	Jos 24:25	3117
Benjamin in Jerusalem to this **d**.	Jg 1:21	3117
Luz which is its name to this **d**.	Jg 1:26	3117
that **d** under the hand of Israel.	Jg 3:30	3117
For this is the **d** in which the	Jg 4:14	3117
So God subdued on that **d** Jabin the	Jg 4:23	3117
the son of Abinoam sang on that **d**,	Jg 5:1	3117
To this **d** it is still in Ophrah of	Jg 6:24	3117
the men of the city to do it by **d**,	Jg 6:27	3119
on that **d** he named him Jerubbaal,	Jg 6:32	3117
Jerubbaal and his house this **d**,	Jg 9:19	3117
Now it came about the next **d**,	Jg 9:42	4283
against the city all that **d**,	Jg 9:45	3117
are called Havvoth-jair to this **d**.	Jg 10:4	3117
only please deliver us this **d**."	Jg 10:15	3117
have you come up to me this **d** to	Jg 12:3	3117
womb to the **d** of his death.' "	Jg 13:7	3117
the man who came the *other* **d** has	Jg 13:10	3117
fourth **d** that they said to Samson's	Jg 14:15	3117
on the seventh **d** he told her	Jg 14:17	3117
d before the sun went down,	Jg 14:18	3117
which is in Lehi to this **d**.	Jg 15:19	3117
for until that **d** an inheritance	Jg 18:1	3117
that place Mahaneh-dan to this **d**;	Jg 18:12	3117
d of the captivity of the land.	Jg 18:30	3117
Now on the fourth **d** they got up	Jg 19:5	3117
On the fifth **d** he arose to go	Jg 19:8	3117
now, the **d** has drawn to a close;	Jg 19:9	3117
Lo, the **d** is coming to an end;	Jg 19:9	3117
near Jebus, the **d** was almost gone;	Jg 19:11	3117
As the **d** began to dawn, the woman	Jg 19:26	1242
from the **d** when the sons of Israel	Jg 19:30	3117
from the land of Egypt to this **d**.	Jg 19:30	3117
From the cities on that **d** the	Jg 20:15	3117
on that **d** 22,000 men of Israel.	Jg 20:21	3117
arrayed themselves the first **d**.	Jg 20:22	3117
the sons of Benjamin the second **d**.	Jg 20:24	3117
from Gibeah the second **d** and felled	Jg 20:25	3117
and fasted that **d** until evening.	Jg 20:26	3117
the sons of Benjamin on the third **d**	Jg 20:30	3117
25,100 men of Benjamin that **d**,	Jg 20:35	3117
all of Benjamin who fell that **d** were	Jg 20:46	3117
It came about the next **d** that	Jg 21:4	4283
"On the **d** you buy the field from	Ru 4:5	3117
d came that Elkanah sacrificed,	1Sa 1:4	3117
the same **d** both of them will die.	1Sa 2:34	3117
"In that **d** I will carry out	1Sa 3:12	3117
and came to Shiloh the same **d**	1Sa 4:12	3117
of Dagon in Ashdod to this **d**.	1Sa 5:5	3117
sacrifices that **d** to the LORD.	1Sa 6:15	3117
it, they returned to Ekron that **d**.	1Sa 6:16	3117
witness to this **d** in the field of Joshua	1Sa 6:18	3117
From the **d** that the ark remained	1Sa 7:2	3117
the LORD, and fasted on that **d** and	1Sa 7:6	3117
a great thunder on that **d** against the	1Sa 7:10	3117
since the **d** that I brought them up	1Sa 8:8	3117
them up from Egypt even to this **d**	1Sa 8:8	3117
"Then you will cry out in that **d**	1Sa 8:18	3117
will not answer you in that **d**."	1Sa 8:18	3117
Now a **d** before Saul's coming, the	1Sa 9:15	3117
So Saul ate with Samuel that **d**.	1Sa 9:24	3117
those signs came about on that **d**.	1Sa 10:9	3117
Ammonites until the heat of the **d**.	1Sa 11:11	3117
man shall be put to death this **d**,	1Sa 11:13	3117
you from my youth even to this **d**.	1Sa 12:2	3117
and His anointed is witness this **d**	1Sa 12:5	3117
LORD sent thunder and rain that **d**;	1Sa 12:18	3117
So it came about on the **d** of	1Sa 13:22	3117
Now the **d** came that Jonathan, the	1Sa 14:1	3117
the LORD delivered Israel that **d**,	1Sa 14:23	3117
Israel were hard-pressed on that **d**,	1Sa 14:24	3117
that **d** from Michmash to Aijalon.	1Sa 14:31	3117
He did not answer him on that **d**.	1Sa 14:37	3117
he has worked with God this **d**."	1Sa 14:45	3117
again until the **d** of his death;	1Sa 15:35	3117
upon David from that **d** forward.	1Sa 16:13	3117
"I defy the ranks of Israel this **d**;	1Sa 17:10	3117
"This **d** the LORD will deliver you	1Sa 17:46	3117
of the army of the Philistines this **d**	1Sa 17:46	3117
Saul took him that **d** and did	1Sa 18:2	3117
with suspicion from that **d** on.	1Sa 18:9	3117
Now it came about on the next **d**	1Sa 18:10	4283
all that **d** and all that night.	1Sa 19:24	3117
time tomorrow, *or* the third **d**,	1Sa 20:12	
hid yourself on that eventful **d**,	1Sa 20:19	3117
did not speak anything that **d**,	1Sa 20:26	3117
It came about the next **d**,	1Sa 20:27	4283
the second **d** of the new moon,	1Sa 20:27	
on the second **d** of the new moon,	1Sa 20:34	3117

servants of Saul was there that **d**,	**1Sa 21:7**	3117
arose and fled that **d** from Saul,	**1Sa 21:10**	3117
lie in ambush, as *it is* this **d**."	**1Sa 22:8**	3117
lying in ambush as *it is* this **d**?"	**1Sa 22:13**	3117
and he killed that **d** eighty-five	**1Sa 22:18**	3117
"I knew on that **d**, when Doeg the	**1Sa 22:22**	3117
And Saul sought him every **d**,	**1Sa 23:14**	3117
d of which the LORD said to you,	**1Sa 24:4**	3117
this **d** your eyes have seen that	**1Sa 24:10**	3117
what you have done to me this **d**.	**1Sa 24:19**	3117
for we have come on a festive **d**.	**1Sa 25:8**	3117
wall to us both by night and by **d**,	**1Sa 25:16**	3119
who sent you this **d** to meet me,	**1Sa 25:32**	3117
kept me this **d** from bloodshed and	**1Sa 25:33**	3117
or his **d** will come that he dies,	**1Sa 26:10**	3117
was precious in your sight this **d**.	**1Sa 26:21**	3117
highly valued in my sight this **d**,	**1Sa 26:24**	3117
perish one **d** by the hand of Saul.	**1Sa 27:1**	3117
So Achish gave him Ziklag that **d**;	**1Sa 27:6**	3117
to the kings of Judah to this **d**.	**1Sa 27:6**	3117
has done this thing to you this **d**.	**1Sa 28:18**	3117
eaten no food all **d** and all night.	**1Sa 28:20**	3117
d he deserted *to me* to this day?"	**1Sa 29:3**	3117
day he deserted *to me* to this **d**?"	**1Sa 29:3**	3117
from the **d** of your coming to me	**1Sa 29:6**	3117
of your coming to me to this **d**.	**1Sa 29:6**	3117
d when I came before you to this day,	**1Sa 29:8**	3117
when I came before you to this **d**,	**1Sa 29:8**	3117
men came to Ziklag on the third **d**,	**1Sa 30:1**	3117
until the evening of the next **d**;	**1Sa 30:17**	4283
it has been from that **d** forward,	**1Sa 30:25**	3117
an ordinance for Israel to this **d**.	**1Sa 30:25**	3117
all his men on that **d** together.	**1Sa 31:6**	3117
It came about on the next **d**	**1Sa 31:8**	4283
On the third **d**, behold, a man	**2Sa 1:2**	3117
That **d** the battle was very severe,	**2Sa 2:17**	3117
until the **d** dawned at Hebron.	**2Sa 2:32**	3117
to eat bread while it was still **d**;	**2Sa 3:35**	3117
all Israel understood that **d** that it had	**2Sa 3:37**	3117
man has fallen this **d** in Israel?	**2Sa 3:38**	3117
have been aliens there until this **d**).	**2Sa 4:3**	3117
Ish-bosheth in the heat of the **d** while	**2Sa 4:5**	3117
d on Saul and his descendants."	**2Sa 4:8**	3117
David said on that **d**,	**2Sa 5:8**	3117
is called Perez-uzzah to this **d**.	**2Sa 6:8**	3117
was afraid of the LORD that **d**;	**2Sa 6:9**	3117
no child to the **d** of her death.	**2Sa 6:23**	3117
the **d** I brought up the sons of Israel	**2Sa 7:6**	3117
Israel from Egypt, even to this **d**;	**2Sa 7:6**	3117
even from the **d** that I commanded	**2Sa 7:11**	3117
in Jerusalem that **d** and the next.	**2Sa 11:12**	3117
the seventh **d** that the child died.	**2Sa 12:18**	3117
the **d** that he violated his sister Tamar.	**2Sa 13:32**	3117
David mourned for his son every **d**.	**2Sa 13:37**	3117
instead of his cursing this **d**."	**2Sa 16:12**	3117
slaughter there that **d** was great,	**2Sa 18:7**	3117
that **d** than the sword devoured.	**2Sa 18:8**	3117
Absalom's Monument to this **d**.	**2Sa 18:18**	3117
not the man to carry news this **d**,	**2Sa 18:20**	3117
you shall carry news another **d**;	**2Sa 18:20**	3117
for the LORD has freed you this **d**	**2Sa 18:31**	3117
The victory that **d** was turned	**2Sa 19:2**	3117
the people heard *it* said that **d**,	**2Sa 19:2**	3117
by stealth into the city that **d**,	**2Sa 19:3**	3117
for I know this **d** that if Absalom	**2Sa 19:6**	3117
the **d** when my lord the king came out	**2Sa 19:19**	3117
this **d** be an adversary to me?	**2Sa 19:22**	3117
from the **d** the king departed until	**2Sa 19:24**	3117
until the **d** he came *home* in peace.	**2Sa 19:24**	3117
up until the **d** of their death,	**2Sa 20:3**	3117
birds of the sky to rest on them by **d**	**2Sa 21:10**	3119
the **d** the Philistines struck down Saul	**2Sa 21:12**	3117
in the **d** that the LORD delivered him	**2Sa 22:1**	3117
me in the **d** of my calamity,	**2Sa 22:19**	3117
about a great victory that **d**;	**2Sa 23:10**	3117
the middle of a pit on a snowy **d**.	**2Sa 23:20**	3117
to David that **d** and said to him,	**2Sa 24:18**	3117
I will indeed do so this **d**."	**1Ki 1:30**	3117
curse on the **d** I went to Mahanaim.	**1Ki 2:8**	3117
"For on the **d** you go out and	**1Ki 2:37**	3117
the **d** you depart and go anywhere,	**1Ki 2:42**	3117
on his throne, as *it is* this **d**.	**1Ki 3:6**	3117
on the third **d** after I gave birth,	**1Ki 3:18**	3117
Solomon's provision for one **d**	**1Ki 4:22**	3117
they are there to this **d**.	**1Ki 8:8**	3117
'Since the **d** that I brought My	**1Ki 8:16**	3117
it with Your hand as it is this **d**.	**1Ki 8:24**	3117
toward this house night and **d**,	**1Ki 8:29**	3117
to the LORD our God **d** and night,	**1Ki 8:59**	3119
people Israel, as each **d** requires,	**1Ki 8:59**	3117
His commandments, as at this **d**."	**1Ki 8:61**	3117
On the same **d** the king consecrated	**1Ki 8:64**	3117
On the eighth **d** he sent the people	**1Ki 8:66**	3117
the land of Cabul to this **d**.	**1Ki 9:13**	3117
forced laborers, even to this **d**.	**1Ki 9:21**	3117
nor have they been seen to this **d**.	**1Ki 10:12**	3117
third **d** as the king had directed,	**1Ki 12:12**	3117
"Return to me on the third **d**."	**1Ki 12:12**	3117
the house of David to this **d**.	**1Ki 12:19**	3117
on the fifteenth **d** of the month,	**1Ki 12:32**	3117
fifteenth **d** in the eighth month,	**1Ki 12:33**	3117
Then he gave a sign the same **d**,	**1Ki 13:3**	3117
of God had done that **d** in Bethel;	**1Ki 13:11**	3117
Jeroboam this **d** and from now on.	**1Ki 14:14**	3117
over Israel that **d** in the camp.	**1Ki 16:16**	3117
until the **d** that the LORD sends	**1Ki 17:14**	3117
on the seventh **d** the battle was joined,	**1Ki 20:29**	3117
100,000 foot soldiers in one **d**.	**1Ki 20:29**	3117
you shall see on that **d** when you	**1Ki 22:25**	3117

The battle raged that **d**,	**1Ki 22:35**	3117
have been purified to this **d**,	**2Ki 2:22**	3117
Now there came a **d** when Elisha	**2Ki 4:8**	3117
One **d** he came there and turned in	**2Ki 4:11**	3117
the **d** came that he went out to his	**2Ki 4:18**	3117
and I said to her on the next **d**,	**2Ki 6:29**	3117
This **d** is a day of good news, but	**2Ki 7:9**	3117
This day is a **d** of good news, but	**2Ki 7:9**	3117
from the **d** that she left the land even	**2Ki 8:6**	3117
On the following **d**, he took	**2Ki 8:15**	4283
revolted against Judah to this **d**.	**2Ki 8:22**	3117
and made it a latrine to this **d**.	**2Ki 10:27**	3117
and named it Joktheel to this **d**.	**2Ki 14:7**	3117
was a leper to the **d** of his death.	**2Ki 15:5**	3117
and have lived there to this **d**.	**2Ki 16:6**	3117
own land to Assyria until this **d**.	**2Ki 17:23**	3117
To this **d** they do according to the	**2Ki 17:34**	3117
fathers did, so they do to this **d**.	**2Ki 17:41**	3117
'This **d** is a day of distress,	**2Ki 19:3**	3117
'This day is a **d** of distress,	**2Ki 19:3**	3117
On the third **d** you shall go up to	**2Ki 20:5**	3117
house of the LORD the third **d**?"	**2Ki 20:8**	3117
d will be carried to Babylon;	**2Ki 20:17**	3117
d their fathers came from Egypt,	**2Ki 21:15**	3117
from Egypt, even to this **d**.'"	**2Ki 21:15**	3117
on the tenth **d** of the tenth month,	**2Ki 25:1**	3117
On the ninth **d** of the *fourth* month	**2Ki 25:3**	3117
the seventh **d** of the fifth month,	**2Ki 25:8**	3117
on the twenty-seventh **d** of	**2Ki 25:27**	3117
by the king, a portion for each **d**,	**2Ki 25:30**	3117
destroyed them utterly to this **d**,	**1Ch 4:41**	3117
and have lived there to this **d**.	**1Ch 4:43**	3117
to the river of Gozan, to this **d**.	**1Ch 5:26**	3117
engaged in their work **d** and night.	**1Ch 9:33**	3119
It came about the next **d**,	**1Ch 10:8**	4283
a lion inside a pit on a snowy **d**.	**1Ch 11:22**	3117
For **d** by day *men* came to David to	**1Ch 12:22**	3117
d *men* came to David to help him,	**1Ch 12:22**	3117
that place Perez-uzza to this **d**.	**1Ch 13:11**	3117
David was afraid of God that **d**,	**1Ch 13:12**	3117
Then on that **d** David first	**1Ch 16:7**	3117
of His salvation from **d** to day.	**1Ch 16:23**	3117
of His salvation from day to **d**.	**1Ch 16:23**	3117
since the **d** that I brought up Israel	**1Ch 17:5**	3117
I brought up Israel to this **d**,	**1Ch 17:5**	3117
even from the **d** that I commanded	**1Ch 17:10**	3117
himself this **d** to the LORD?"	**1Ch 29:5**	3117
On the next **d** they made	**1Ch 29:21**	3117
So they ate and drank that **d**	**1Ch 29:22**	3117
He began to build on the second **d**	**2Ch 3:2**	3117
and they are there to this **d**.	**2Ch 5:9**	3117
'Since the **d** that I brought My	**2Ch 6:5**	3117
it with Your hand, as it is this **d**.	**2Ch 6:15**	3117
toward this house **d** and night,	**2Ch 6:20**	3119
d they held a solemn assembly,	**2Ch 7:9**	3117
Then on the twenty-third **d** of the	**2Ch 7:10**	3117
as forced laborers to this **d**.	**2Ch 8:8**	3117
the **d** of the foundation of the house	**2Ch 8:16**	3117
third **d** as the king had directed,	**2Ch 10:12**	3117
"Return to me on the third **d**."	**2Ch 10:12**	3117
the house of David to this **d**.	**2Ch 10:19**	3117
sacrificed to the LORD that **d** 700 oxen	**2Ch 15:11**	3117
"Behold, you will see on that **d**	**2Ch 18:24**	3117
The battle raged that **d**,	**2Ch 18:34**	3117
Then on the fourth **d** they	**2Ch 20:26**	3117
revolted against Judah to this **d**.	**2Ch 21:10**	3117
of the sickness, **d** by day.'"	**2Ch 21:15**	3117
of the sickness, day by **d**.'"	**2Ch 21:15**	3117
was a leper to the **d** of his death;	**2Ch 26:21**	3117
slew in Judah 120,000 in one **d**,	**2Ch 28:6**	3117
the consecration on the first **d**	**2Ch 29:17**	3117
and on the eighth **d** of the month	**2Ch 29:17**	3117
sixteenth **d** of the first month.	**2Ch 29:17**	3117
priests praised the LORD **d** after day	**2Ch 30:21**	3117
day after **d** with loud instruments	**2Ch 30:21**	3117
animals on the fourteenth **d**	**2Ch 35:1**	3117
that **d** to celebrate the Passover,	**2Ch 35:16**	3117
in their lamentations to this **d**.	**2Ch 35:25**	3117
the ordinance, as each **d** required;	**Ezr 3:4**	3117
From the first **d** of the seventh	**Ezr 3:6**	3117
on the third **d** of the month Adar;	**Ezr 6:15**	3118
On the fourth **d** the silver and	**Ezr 8:33**	3117
"Since the days of our fathers to this **d**	**Ezr 9:7**	3117
to open shame, as *it is* this **d**.	**Ezr 9:7**	3117
escaped remnant, as *it is* this **d**;	**Ezr 9:15**	3117
So they convened on the first **d** of	**Ezr 10:16**	3117
married foreign wives by the first **d**	**Ezr 10:17**	3117
before You now, **d** and night,	**Ne 1:6**	3119
Can they finish in a **d**?	**Ne 4:2**	3117
a guard against them **d** and night.	**Ne 4:9**	3119
From that **d** on,	**Ne 4:16**	3117
us by night and a laborer by **d**."	**Ne 4:22**	3117
to them this very **d** their fields,	**Ne 5:11**	3117
from the **d** that I was appointed to	**Ne 5:14**	3117
prepared for each **d** was one ox *and*	**Ne 5:18**	3117
the first **d** of the seventh month.	**Ne 8:2**	3117
d is holy to the LORD your God;	**Ne 8:9**	3117
for this **d** is holy to our Lord.	**Ne 8:10**	3117
"Be still, for the **d** is holy;	**Ne 8:11**	3117
Then on the second **d** the heads of	**Ne 8:13**	3117
Joshua the son of Nun to that **d**.	**Ne 8:17**	3117
from the first **d** to the last day.	**Ne 8:18**	3117
from the first day to the last **d**.	**Ne 8:18**	3117
and on the eighth **d** *there was a*	**Ne 8:18**	3117
Now on the twenty-fourth **d** of this	**Ne 9:1**	3117
their God for a fourth of the **d**;	**Ne 9:3**	3117
name for Yourself as *it is* this **d**.	**Ne 9:10**	3117
cloud You led them by **d**,	**Ne 9:12**	3119
of cloud did not leave them by **d**,	**Ne 9:19**	3119

of the kings of Assyria to this **d**.	**Ne 9:32**	3117
grain on the sabbath **d** to sell,	**Ne 10:31**	3117
them on the sabbath or a holy **d**;	**Ne 10:31**	3117
for the song leaders **d** by day.	**Ne 11:23**	3117
for the song leaders day by **d**.	**Ne 11:23**	3117
and on that **d** they offered great	**Ne 12:43**	3117
On that **d** men were also appointed	**Ne 12:44**	3117
gatekeepers as each **d** required,	**Ne 12:47**	3117
On that **d** they read aloud from the	**Ne 13:1**	3117
into Jerusalem on the sabbath **d**.	**Ne 13:15**	3117
them on the **d** they sold food.	**Ne 13:15**	3117
doing, by profaning the sabbath **d**?	**Ne 13:17**	3117
would enter on the sabbath **d**.	**Ne 13:19**	3117
to sanctify the sabbath **d**.	**Ne 13:22**	3117
On the seventh **d**, when the heart	**Es 1:10**	3117
"This **d** the ladies of Persia	**Es 1:18**	3117
Every **d** Mordecai walked back	**Es 2:11**	3117
was cast before Haman from **d** to	**Es 3:7**	3117
day to **d** and from month *to month,*	**Es 3:7**	3117
thirteenth **d** of the first month,	**Es 3:12**	3117
old, women and children, in one **d**,	**Es 3:13**	3117
the thirteenth **d** of the twelfth	**Es 3:13**	3117
they should be ready for this **d**.	**Es 3:14**	3117
drink for three days, night or **d**.	**Es 4:16**	3117
Now it came about on the third **d**	**Es 5:1**	3117
may the king and Haman come this **d**	**Es 5:4**	3117
that **d** glad and pleased of heart;	**Es 5:9**	3117
king said to Esther on the second **d**	**Es 7:2**	3117
On that **d** King Ahasuerus gave the	**Es 8:1**	3117
on the twenty-third **d**;	**Es 8:9**	3117
on one **d** in all the provinces of	**Es 8:12**	3117
the thirteenth **d** of the twelfth	**Es 8:12**	3117
the Jews would be ready for this **d**	**Es 8:13**	3117
on the thirteenth **d** when the	**Es 9:1**	3117
on the **d** when the enemies of the	**Es 9:1**	3117
On that **d** the number of those who	**Es 9:11**	3117
the fourteenth **d** of the month Adar	**Es 9:15**	3117
thirteenth **d** of the month Adar,	**Es 9:17**	3117
and on the fourteenth **d** they	**Es 9:17**	3117
it a **d** of feasting and rejoicing.	**Es 9:17**	3117
and they rested on the fifteenth **d**	**Es 9:18**	3117
it a **d** of feasting and rejoicing.	**Es 9:18**	3117
make the fourteenth **d** of the month	**Es 9:19**	3117
fourteenth **d** of the month Adar,	**Es 9:21**	3117
the fifteenth **d** of the same month,	**Es 9:21**	3117
in the house of each one on his **d**,	**Jb 1:4**	3117
Now there was a **d** when the sons of	**Jb 1:6**	3117
Now on the **d** when his	**Jb 1:13**	3117
Again there was a **d** when the sons	**Jb 2:1**	3117
and cursed the **d** of his *birth.*	**Jb 3:1**	3117
"Let the **d** perish on which I was	**Jb 3:3**	3117
"May that **d** be darkness;	**Jb 3:4**	3117
the blackness of the **d** terrify it.	**Jb 3:5**	3117
those curse it who curse the **d**,	**Jb 3:8**	3117
"By **d** they meet with darkness,	**Jb 5:14**	3119
fulfills his **d** like a hired man.	**Jb 14:6**	3117
that a **d** of darkness is at hand.	**Jb 15:23**	3117
"They make night into **d**,	**Jb 17:12**	3117
flow away in the **d** of His anger.	**Jb 20:28**	3117
is reserved for the **d** of calamity;	**Jb 21:30**	3117
be led forth at the **d** of fury.	**Jb 21:30**	3117
They shut themselves up by **d**;	**Jb 24:16**	3119
For the **d** of war and battle?	**Jb 38:23**	3117
His law he meditates **d** and night.	**Ps 1:2**	3119
a God who has indignation every **d**.	**Ps 7:11**	3117
sorrow in my heart all the **d**?	**Ps 13:2**	3119
me in the **d** of my calamity,	**Ps 18:18**	3117
D to day pours forth speech, And	**Ps 19:2**	3117
Day to **d** pours forth speech, And	**Ps 19:2**	3117
answer you in the **d** of trouble!	**Ps 20:1**	3117
King answer us in the **d** we call.	**Ps 20:9**	3117
O my God, I cry by **d**,	**Ps 22:2**	3119
For You I wait all the **d**.	**Ps 25:5**	3117
For in the **d** of trouble He will	**Ps 27:5**	3117
Through my groaning all **d** long.	**Ps 32:3**	3117
For **d** and night Your hand was heavy	**Ps 32:4**	3119
And Your praise all **d** long.	**Ps 35:28**	3117
For He sees his **d** is coming.	**Ps 37:13**	3117
d long he is gracious and lends,	**Ps 37:26**	3117
I go mourning all **d** long.	**Ps 38:6**	3117
they devise treachery all **d** long.	**Ps 38:12**	3117
deliver him in a **d** of trouble.	**Ps 41:1**	3117
have been my food **d** and night,	**Ps 42:3**	3119
While *they* say to me all **d** long,	**Ps 42:3**	3117
While they say to me all **d** long,	**Ps 42:10**	3117
In God we have boasted all **d** long,	**Ps 44:8**	3117
d long my dishonor is before me And	**Ps 44:15**	3117
Your sake we are killed all **d** long;	**Ps 44:22**	3117
Call upon Me in the **d** of trouble;	**Ps 50:15**	3117
of God *endures* all **d** long.	**Ps 52:1**	3117
D and night they go around her	**Ps 55:10**	3119
all **d** long he oppresses me.	**Ps 56:1**	3117
have trampled upon me all **d** long,	**Ps 56:2**	3117
All **d** long they distort my words;	**Ps 56:5**	3117
turn back in the **d** when I call;	**Ps 56:9**	3117
a refuge in the **d** of my distress.	**Ps 59:16**	3117
That I may pay my vows **d** by day.	**Ps 61:8**	3117
That I may pay my vows day by **d**.	**Ps 61:8**	3117
And with Your glory all **d** long.	**Ps 71:8**	3117
And of Your salvation all **d** long;	**Ps 71:15**	3117
Your righteousness all **d** long;	**Ps 71:24**	3117
Let them bless him all **d** long.	**Ps 72:15**	3117
I have been stricken all **d** long And	**Ps 73:14**	3117
Yours is the **d**, Yours also is the night;	**Ps 74:16**	3117
man reproaches You all **d** long.	**Ps 74:22**	3117
In the **d** of my trouble I sought	**Ps 77:2**	3117
turned back in the **d** of battle.	**Ps 78:9**	3117
He led them with the cloud by **d** And	**Ps 78:14**	3119
The **d** when He redeemed them from	**Ps 78:42**	3117

At the full moon, on our feast **d**.	**Ps 81:3**	3117
For a **d** in Your courts is better	**Ps 84:10**	3117
For to You I cry all **d** long.	**Ps 86:3**	3117
In the **d** of my trouble I shall	**Ps 86:7**	3117
by **d** and in the night before You.	**Ps 88:1**	3117
I have called upon You every **d**,	**Ps 88:9**	3117
me like water all **d** long;	**Ps 88:17**	3117
Your name they rejoice all the **d**,	**Ps 89:16**	3117
Or of the arrow that flies by **d**;	**Ps 91:5**	3119
the **d** of Massah in the wilderness,	**Ps 95:8**	3117
of His salvation from **d** to day.	**Ps 96:2**	3117
of His salvation from day to **d**.	**Ps 96:2**	3117
from me in the **d** of my distress;	**Ps 102:2**	3117
In the **d** when I call answer me	**Ps 102:2**	3117
have reproached me all **d** long;	**Ps 102:8**	3117
freely in the **d** of Your power;	**Ps 110:3**	3117
kings in the **d** of His wrath.	**Ps 110:5**	3117
is the **d** which the LORD has made;	**Ps 118:24**	3117
d according to Your ordinances,	**Ps 119:91**	3117
It is my meditation all the **d**.	**Ps 119:97**	3117
Seven times a **d** I praise You,	**Ps 119:164**	3117
The sun will not smite you by **d**,	**Ps 121:6**	3119
The sun to rule by **d**,	**Ps 136:8**	3119
sons of Edom The **d** of Jerusalem,	**Ps 137:7**	3117
d I called, You answered me;	**Ps 138:3**	3117
the night is as bright as the **d**.	**Ps 139:12**	3117
my head in the **d** of battle.	**Ps 140:7**	3117
Every **d** I will bless You, And I	**Ps 145:2**	3117
that very **d** his thoughts perish.	**Ps 146:4**	3117
and brighter until the full **d**.	**Pr 4:18**	3117
not spare in the **d** of vengeance.	**Pr 6:34**	3117
do not profit in the **d** of wrath,	**Pr 11:4**	3117
Even the wicked for the **d** of evil.	**Pr 16:4**	3117
All **d** long he is craving, While	**Pr 21:26**	3117
is prepared for the **d** of battle,	**Pr 21:31**	3117
are slack in the **d** of distress,	**Pr 24:10**	3117
takes off a garment on a cold **d**,	**Pr 25:20**	3117
not know what a **d** may bring forth.	**Pr 27:1**	3117
house in the **d** of your calamity;	**Pr 27:10**	3117
A constant dripping on a **d** of	**Pr 27:15**	3117
And the **d** of *one's* death is better	**Ec 7:1**	3117
better than the **d** of one's birth.	**Ec 7:1**	3117
In the **d** of prosperity be happy,	**Ec 7:14**	3117
But in the **d** of adversity	**Ec 7:14**	3117
or authority over the **d** of death;	**Ec 8:8**	3117
should never sleep **d** or night),	**Ec 8:16**	3117
in the **d** that the watchmen of the	**Ec 12:3**	3117
the **d** when the shadows flee away,	**SS 2:17**	3117
him On the **d** of his wedding,	**SS 3:11**	3117
the **d** of his gladness of heart."	**SS 3:11**	3117
the **d** When the shadows flee away,	**SS 4:6**	3117
On the **d** when she is spoken for?	**SS 8:8**	3117
alone will be exalted in that **d**.	**Is 2:11**	3117
of hosts will have a **d** *of reckoning*	**Is 2:12**	3117
alone will be exalted in that **d**,	**Is 2:17**	3117
In that **d** men will cast away to	**Is 2:20**	3117
He will protest on that **d**, saying,	**Is 3:7**	3117
In that **d** the Lord will take away	**Is 3:18**	3117
take hold of one man in that **d**,	**Is 4:1**	3117
In that **d** the Branch of the LORD	**Is 4:2**	3117
over her assemblies a cloud by **d**,	**Is 4:5**	3119
to *give* shade from the heat by **d**,	**Is 4:6**	3119
d like the roaring of the sea.	**Is 5:30**	3117
d that Ephraim separated from Judah,	**Is 7:17**	3117
In that **d** the LORD will whistle for	**Is 7:18**	3117
In that **d** the Lord will shave with	**Is 7:20**	3117
Now in that **d** a man may	**Is 7:21**	3117
And it will come about in that **d**,	**Is 7:23**	3117
branch and bulrush in a single **d**.	**Is 9:14**	3117
you do in the **d** of punishment,	**Is 10:3**	3117
and his briars in a single **d**.	**Is 10:17**	3117
that **d** the remnant of Israel,	**Is 10:20**	3117
So it will be in that **d**,	**Is 10:27**	3117
Then in that **d** The nations	**Is 11:10**	3117
Then it will happen on that **d** that	**Is 11:11**	3117
d that they came up out of the land	**Is 11:16**	3117
Then you will say on that **d**,	**Is 12:1**	3117
And in that **d** you will say,	**Is 12:4**	3117
for the **d** of the LORD is near!	**Is 13:6**	3117
the **d** of the LORD is coming,	**Is 13:9**	3117
In the **d** of His burning anger.	**Is 13:13**	3117
And it will be in the **d** when the	**Is 14:3**	3117
Now in that **d** the glory of Jacob	**Is 17:4**	3117
In that **d** man will have regard for	**Is 17:7**	3117
In that **d** their strong cities will	**Is 17:9**	3117
In the **d** that you plant it you	**Is 17:11**	3117
In a **d** of sickliness and incurable pain	**Is 17:11**	3117
In that **d** the Egyptians will	**Is 19:16**	3117
In that **d** five cities in the land	**Is 19:18**	3117
In that **d** there will be an altar	**Is 19:19**	3117
will know the LORD in that **d**.	**Is 19:21**	3117
In that **d** there will be a highway	**Is 19:23**	3117
In that **d** Israel will be the third	**Is 19:24**	3117
this coastland will say in that **d**,	**Is 20:6**	3117
by **d** on the watchtower,	**Is 21:8**	3119
GOD of hosts has a **d** of panic,	**Is 22:5**	3117
In that **d** you depended on the	**Is 22:8**	3117
in that **d** the Lord GOD of hosts called	**Is 22:12**	3117
"Then it will come about in that **d**,	**Is 22:20**	3117
"In that **d**," declares the LORD	**Is 22:25**	3117
Now in that **d** Tyre	**Is 23:15**	3117
So it will happen in that **d**,	**Is 24:21**	3117
And it will be said in that **d**,	**Is 25:9**	3117
In that **d** this song will be sung	**Is 26:1**	3117
In that **d** the LORD will punish	**Is 27:1**	3117
In that **d**, "A vineyard of wine,	**Is 27:2**	3117
damage it, I guard it night and **d**.	**Is 27:3**	3117
them on the **d** of the east wind.	**Is 27:8**	3117
In that **d** the LORD	**Is 27:12**	3117
It will come about also in that **d**	**Is 27:13**	3117
In that **d** the LORD of hosts will	**Is 28:5**	3117
anytime during the **d** or night,	**Is 28:19**	3117
On that **d** the deaf will hear	**Is 29:18**	3117
on that **d** your livestock will	**Is 30:23**	3117
on the **d** of the great slaughter,	**Is 30:25**	3117
on the **d** the LORD binds up the	**Is 30:26**	3117
For in that **d** every man will cast	**Is 31:7**	3117
For the LORD has a **d** of vengeance,	**Is 34:8**	3117
will not be quenched night or **d**;	**Is 34:10**	3119
'This **d** is a day of distress,	**Is 37:3**	3117
'This day is a **d** of distress,	**Is 37:3**	3117
From **d** until night You make	**Is 38:12**	3117
From **d** until night You make	**Is 38:13**	3117
d will be carried to Babylon;	**Is 39:6**	3117
come on you suddenly in one **d**:	**Is 47:9**	3117
And in a **d** of salvation I have	**Is 49:8**	3117
That you fear continually all **d**	**Is 51:13**	3117
continually blasphemed all **d** long.	**Is 52:5**	3117
in that **d** I am the one who is	**Is 52:6**	3117
"Yet they seek Me **d** by day and	**Is 58:2**	3117
"Yet they seek Me day by **d** and	**Is 58:2**	3117
on the **d** of your fast you find	**Is 58:3**	3117
a **d** for a man to humble himself?	**Is 58:5**	3117
even an acceptable **d** to the LORD?	**Is 58:5**	3117
your *own* pleasure on My holy **d**,	**Is 58:13**	3117
the holy **d** of the LORD	**Is 58:13**	
will not be closed **d** or night,	**Is 60:11**	3119
you have the sun for light by **d**,	**Is 60:19**	3119
And the **d** of vengeance of our God;	**Is 61:2**	3117
All **d** and all night they will	**Is 62:6**	3117
d of vengeance was in My heart,	**Is 63:4**	3117
all **d** long to a rebellious people,	**Is 65:2**	3117
A fire that burns all the **d**.	**Is 65:5**	3117
Can a land be born in one **d**?	**Is 66:8**	3117
I have appointed you this **d** over	**Jer 1:10**	3117
from our youth even to this **d**.	**Jer 3:25**	3117
It shall come about in that **d**,"	**Jer 4:9**	3117
Woe to us, for the **d** declines,	**Jer 6:4**	3117
or command them in the **d** that I	**Jer 7:22**	3117
"Since the **d** that your fathers	**Jer 7:25**	3117
of the land of Egypt until this **d**,	**Jer 7:25**	3117
That I might weep **d** and night For	**Jer 9:1**	3119
in the **d** that I brought them out of	**Jer 11:4**	3117
with milk and honey, as *it is* this **d**	**Jer 11:5**	3117
warned your fathers in the **d** that I	**Jer 11:7**	3117
the land of Egypt, even to this **d**,	**Jer 11:7**	3117
set them apart for a **d** of carnage!	**Jer 12:3**	3117
flow down with tears night and **d**,	**Jer 14:17**	3119
sun has set while it was yet **d**;	**Jer 15:9**	3119
will serve other gods **d** and night,	**Jer 16:13**	3119
my refuge in the **d** of distress,	**Jer 16:19**	3117
have I longed for the woeful **d**;	**Jer 17:16**	3117
my refuge in the **d** of disaster.	**Jer 17:17**	3117
Bring on them a **d** of disaster, And	**Jer 17:18**	3117
not carry any load on the sabbath **d**	**Jer 17:21**	3117
on the sabbath **d** nor do any work,	**Jer 17:22**	3117
work, but keep the sabbath **d** holy,	**Jer 17:22**	3117
of this city on the sabbath **d**,	**Jer 17:24**	3117
but to keep the sabbath **d** holy	**Jer 17:24**	3117
not listen to Me to keep the sabbath **d**	**Jer 17:27**	3117
of Jerusalem on the sabbath **d**,	**Jer 17:27**	3117
In the **d** of their calamity.'"	**Jer 18:17**	3117
On the next **d**, when Pashhur released	**Jer 20:3**	4283
become a laughingstock all **d** long;	**Jer 20:7**	3117
reproach and derision all **d** long.	**Jer 20:8**	3117
Cursed be the **d** when I was born;	**Jer 20:14**	3117
Let the **d** not be blessed when my	**Jer 20:14**	3117
king of Judah, even to this **d**,	**Jer 25:3**	3117
and a curse, as it is this **d**;	**Jer 25:18**	3117
Those slain by the LORD on that **d**	**Jer 25:33**	3117
be there until the **d** I visit them,'	**Jer 27:22**	3117
for that **d** is great, There is none	**Jer 30:7**	3117
'It shall come about on that **d**,'	**Jer 30:8**	3117
"For there will be a **d** when	**Jer 31:6**	3117
in the **d** I took them by the hand	**Jer 31:32**	3117
Who gives the sun for light by **d** And	**Jer 31:35**	3119
and even to this **d** both in Israel	**Jer 32:20**	3117
a name for Yourself, as at this **d**.	**Jer 32:20**	3117
from the **d** that they built it,	**Jer 32:31**	3117
they built it, even to this **d**,	**Jer 32:31**	3117
can break My covenant for the **d** and	**Jer 33:20**	3117
so that **d** and night will not be at	**Jer 33:20**	3119
'If My covenant *for* **d** and night	**Jer 33:25**	3119
in the **d** that I brought them out	**Jer 34:13**	3117
they do not drink *wine* to this **d**,	**Jer 35:14**	3117
from the **d** I *first* spoke to you,	**Jer 36:2**	3117
days of Josiah, even to this **d**.	**Jer 36:2**	3117
in the LORD's house on a fast **d**.	**Jer 36:6**	3117
the **d** and the frost of the night.	**Jer 36:30**	3117
the **d** that Jerusalem was captured.	**Jer 38:28**	3117
in the ninth **d** of the month,	**Jer 39:2**	
take place before you on that **d**.	**Jer 39:16**	3117
I will deliver you on that **d**,"	**Jer 39:17**	3117
d after the killing of Gedaliah,	**Jer 41:4**	3117
this **d** they are in ruins and no	**Jer 44:2**	3117
and a desolation as it is this **d**.	**Jer 44:6**	3117
become contrite even to this **d**,	**Jer 44:10**	3117
an inhabitant, as *it is* this **d**.	**Jer 44:22**	3117
befallen you, as *it has* this **d**."	**Jer 44:23**	3117
For that **d** belongs to the Lord GOD	**Jer 46:10**	3117
GOD of hosts, A **d** of vengeance,	**Jer 46:10**	3117
For the **d** of their calamity has	**Jer 46:21**	3117
On account of the **d** that is coming	**Jer 47:4**	3117
the mighty men of Moab in that **d**	**Jer 48:41**	3117
the mighty men of Edom in that **d**	**Jer 49:22**	3117
war will be silenced in that **d**,"	**Jer 49:26**	3117
upon them, for their **d** has come,	**Jer 50:27**	3117
war will be silenced in that **d**,"	**Jer 50:30**	3117
"For your **d** has come, The time	**Jer 50:31**	3117
to her In the **d** of *her* calamity.	**Jer 51:2**	3117
on the tenth **d** of the tenth month,	**Jer 52:4**	
On the ninth **d** of the fourth month	**Jer 52:6**	
prison until the **d** of his death.	**Jer 52:11**	3117
on the tenth **d** of the fifth month,	**Jer 52:12**	
his life until the **d** of his death.	**Jer 52:34**	3117
on the **d** of His fierce anger.	**La 1:12**	3117
me desolate, Faint all **d** long.	**La 1:13**	3117
the **d** which You have proclaimed,	**La 1:21**	3117
footstool In the **d** of His anger.	**La 2:1**	3117
As in the **d** of an appointed feast.	**La 2:7**	3117
this is the **d** for which we waited;	**La 2:16**	3117
run down like a river **d** and night;	**La 2:18**	3119
them in the **d** of Your anger,	**La 2:21**	3117
You called as in the **d** of an	**La 2:22**	3117
In the **d** of the LORD's anger.	**La 2:22**	3117
His hand Repeatedly all the **d**.	**La 3:3**	3117
Their *mocking* song all the **d**.	**La 3:14**	3117
Are against me all **d** long.	**La 3:62**	3117
on the fifth **d** of the fourth	**Ezk 1:1**	
in the clouds on a rainy **d**,	**Ezk 1:28**	3117
against Me to this very **d**.	**Ezk 2:3**	3117
for forty days, a **d** for each year.	**Ezk 4:6**	3117
be twenty shekels a **d** by weight;	**Ezk 4:10**	3117
The time has come, the **d** is near	**Ezk 7:7**	3117
'Behold, the **d**! Behold, it is coming!	**Ezk 7:10**	3117
time has come, the **d** has arrived.	**Ezk 7:12**	3117
in the **d** of the wrath of the LORD.	**Ezk 7:19**	3117
on the fifth **d** of the sixth month,	**Ezk 8:1**	
go into exile by **d** in their sight;	**Ezk 12:3**	3119
Bring your baggage out by **d** in their	**Ezk 12:4**	3119
By **d** I brought out my baggage like	**Ezk 12:7**	3119
the battle on the **d** of the LORD.	**Ezk 13:5**	3117
on the **d** you were born your navel	**Ezk 16:4**	3117
abhorred on the **d** you were born.	**Ezk 16:5**	3117
from your lips in your **d** of pride,	**Ezk 16:56**	3117
"On the **d** when I chose Israel and	**Ezk 20:5**	3117
on that **d** I swore to them, to	**Ezk 20:6**	3117
is called Bamah to this **d**."	**Ezk 20:29**	3117
with all your idols to this **d**.	**Ezk 20:31**	3117
of Israel, whose **d** has come,	**Ezk 21:25**	3117
who are slain, whose **d** has come,	**Ezk 21:29**	3117
Thus you have brought your **d** near	**Ezk 22:4**	3117
on in the **d** of indignation.'	**Ezk 22:24**	3117
defiled My sanctuary on the same **d**	**Ezk 23:38**	3117
on the same **d** to profane it;	**Ezk 23:39**	3117
of man, write the name of the **d**,	**Ezk 24:2**	3117
the name of the day, this very **d**.	**Ezk 24:2**	3117
siege to Jerusalem this very **d**.	**Ezk 24:2**	3117
will *it* not be on the **d** when I	**Ezk 24:25**	3117
that on that **d** he who escapes will	**Ezk 24:26**	3117
'On that **d** your mouth will be	**Ezk 24:27**	3117
tremble On the **d** of your fall;	**Ezk 26:18**	3117
seas On the **d** of your overthrow.	**Ezk 27:27**	3117
On the **d** that you were created	**Ezk 28:13**	3117
ways From the **d** you were created Until	**Ezk 28:15**	3117
"On that **d** I will make a horn	**Ezk 29:21**	3117
Lord GOD, "Wail, 'Alas for the **d**!'	**Ezk 30:2**	3117
"For the **d** is near, Even the day	**Ezk 30:3**	3117
Even the **d** of the LORD is near;	**Ezk 30:3**	3117
It will be a **d** of clouds, A time	**Ezk 30:3**	3117
"On that **d** messengers will go	**Ezk 30:9**	3117
be on them as on the **d** of Egypt;	**Ezk 30:9**	3117
"In Tehaphnehes the **d** will be	**Ezk 30:18**	3117
"On the **d** when it went down to	**Ezk 31:15**	3117
own life, on the **d** of your fall."	**Ezk 32:10**	3117
him in the **d** of his transgression,	**Ezk 33:12**	3117
d when he turns from his wickedness;	**Ezk 33:12**	3117
on the **d** when he commits sin.'	**Ezk 33:12**	3117
shepherd cares for his herd in the **d**	**Ezk 34:12**	3117
on a cloudy and gloomy **d**.	**Ezk 34:12**	3117
"On the **d** that I cleanse you from	**Ezk 36:33**	3117
"It will come about on that **d**,	**Ezk 38:10**	3117
"On that **d** when My people Israel	**Ezk 38:14**	3117
"It will come about on that **d**,	**Ezk 38:18**	3117
I declare *that* on that **d** there will	**Ezk 38:19**	3117
is the **d** of which I have spoken.	**Ezk 39:8**	3117
"On that **d** I will give Gog a burial	**Ezk 39:11**	3117
on the **d** that I glorify Myself,"	**Ezk 39:13**	3117
LORD their God from that **d** onward.	**Ezk 39:22**	3117
on that same **d** the hand of the	**Ezk 40:1**	3117
the altar on the **d** it is built,	**Ezk 43:18**	3117
'On the second **d** you shall	**Ezk 43:22**	3117
that on the eighth **d** and onward,	**Ezk 43:27**	3117
"On the **d** that he goes into	**Ezk 44:27**	3117
"Thus you shall do on the seventh **d**	**Ezk 45:20**	
on the fourteenth **d** of the month,	**Ezk 45:21**	3117
"On that **d** the prince shall	**Ezk 45:22**	3117
on every **d** of the seven days,	**Ezk 45:23**	3117
on the fifteenth **d** of the month,	**Ezk 45:25**	3117
shall be opened on the sabbath **d** and	**Ezk 46:1**	3117
opened on the **d** of the new moon.	**Ezk 46:1**	3117
offer to the LORD on the sabbath **d**	**Ezk 46:4**	3117
"On the **d** of the new moon *he*	**Ezk 46:6**	3117
as he does on the sabbath **d**.	**Ezk 46:12**	3117
of the city from *that* **d** *shall be*,	**Ezk 48:35**	3117
on his knees three times a **d**,	**Da 6:10**	3118
his petition three times a **d**."	**Da 6:13**	3118
at dawn, at the break of **d**,	**Da 6:19**	5053
but to us open shame, as it is this **d**	**Da 9:7**	3117
a name for Yourself, as it is this **d**	**Da 9:15**	3117
twenty-fourth **d** of the first month,	**Da 10:4**	3117
for from the first **d** that you set	**Da 10:12**	3117
"On that **d** I will break the bow	**Hos 1:5**	3117
great will be the **d** of Jezreel.	**Hos 1:11**	3117
her as on the **d** when she was born.	**Hos 2:3**	3117
As in the **d** when she came up from	**Hos 2:15**	3117
It will come about in that **d**,"	**Hos 2:16**	3117

"In that **d** I will also make a	**Hos 2:18**	3117
in that **d** that I will respond,"	**Hos 2:21**	3117
So you will stumble by **d**,	**Hos 4:5**	3117
a desolation in the **d** of rebuke;	**Hos 5:9**	3117
d, That we may live before Him.	**Hos 6:2**	3117
On the **d** of our king, the princes	**Hos 7:5**	3117
What will you do on the **d** of the	**Hos 9:5**	3117
on the **d** of the feast of the LORD?	**Hos 9:5**	3117
Beth-arbel on the **d** of battle,	**Hos 10:14**	3117
Alas for the **d**!	**Jl 1:15**	3117
For the **d** of the LORD is near, And	**Jl 1:15**	3117
For the **d** of the LORD is coming;	**Jl 2:1**	3117
A **d** of darkness and gloom, A day	**Jl 2:2**	3117
A **d** of clouds and thick darkness.	**Jl 2:2**	3117
The **d** of the LORD is indeed great	**Jl 2:11**	3117
and awesome **d** of the LORD comes.	**Jl 2:31**	3117
For the **d** of the LORD is near in	**Jl 3:14**	3117
And in that **d** The mountains	**Jl 3:18**	3117
Amid war cries on the **d** of battle	**Am 1:14**	3117
And a storm on the **d** of tempest.	**Am 1:14**	3117
will flee naked in that **d**,"	**Am 2:16**	3117
"For on the **d** that I punish	**Am 3:14**	3117
Who also darkens **d** *into* night,	**Am 5:8**	3117
are longing for the **d** of the LORD,	**Am 5:18**	3117
will the **d** of the LORD *be* to you?	**Am 5:18**	3117
Will not the **d** of the LORD *be*	**Am 5:20**	3117
Do you put off the **d** of calamity,	**Am 6:3**	3117
will turn to wailing in that **d**,"	**Am 8:3**	3117
It will come about in that **d**,"	**Am 8:9**	3117
end of it will be like a bitter **d**.	**Am 8:10**	3117
"In that **d** the beautiful virgins	**Am 8:13**	3117
"In that **d** I will raise up the	**Am 9:11**	3117
"Will I not on that **d**,"	**Ob 1:8**	3117
"On the **d** that you stood aloof,	**Ob 1:11**	3117
On the **d** that strangers carried	**Ob 1:11**	3117
"Do not gloat over your brother's **d**,	**Ob 1:12**	3117
day, The **d** of his misfortune.	**Ob 1:12**	3117
In the **d** of their destruction;	**Ob 1:12**	3117
boast In the **d** of *their* distress.	**Ob 1:12**	3117
people In the **d** of their disaster.	**Ob 1:13**	3117
In the **d** of their disaster.	**Ob 1:13**	3117
wealth In the **d** of their disaster.	**Ob 1:13**	3117
In the **d** of their distress.	**Ob 1:14**	3117
"For the **d** of the LORD draws near	**Ob 1:15**	3117
a worm when dawn came the next **d** and	**Jon 4:7**	4283
"On that **d** they will take up	**Mi 2:4**	3117
the **d** will become dark over them.	**Mi 3:6**	3117
"In that **d**," declares the LORD,	**Mi 4:6**	3117
"It will be in that **d**,"	**Mi 5:10**	3117
The **d** when you post your watchmen,	**Mi 7:4**	3117
be a **d** for building your walls.	**Mi 7:11**	3117
On that **d** will your boundary be	**Mi 7:11**	3117
It *will be* a **d** when they will come	**Mi 7:12**	3117
A stronghold in the **d** of trouble,	**Na 1:7**	3117
in the stone walls on a cold **d**.	**Na 3:17**	3117
quietly for the **d** of distress,	**Hab 3:16**	3117
For the **d** of the LORD is near, For	**Zph 1:7**	3117
on the **d** of the LORD's sacrifice That	**Zph 1:8**	3117
"And I will punish on that **d** all	**Zph 1:9**	3117
"On that **d**," declares the LORD,	**Zph 1:10**	3117
Near is the great **d** of the LORD,	**Zph 1:14**	3117
Listen, the **d** of the LORD!	**Zph 1:14**	3117
A **d** of wrath is that day, A day of	**Zph 1:15**	3117
A day of wrath is that **d**,	**Zph 1:15**	3117
day, A **d** of trouble and distress,	**Zph 1:15**	3117
A **d** of destruction and desolation,	**Zph 1:15**	3117
A **d** of darkness and gloom,	**Zph 1:15**	3117
A **d** of clouds and thick darkness,	**Zph 1:15**	3117
A **d** of trumpet and battle cry Against	**Zph 1:16**	3117
them On the **d** of the LORD's wrath;	**Zph 1:18**	3117
The **d** passes like the chaff	**Zph 2:2**	3117
Before the **d** of the LORD's anger	**Zph 2:2**	3117
In the **d** of the LORD's anger.	**Zph 2:3**	3117
the **d** when I rise up as a witness.	**Zph 3:8**	3117
"In that **d** you will feel no shame	**Zph 3:11**	3117
d it will be said to Jerusalem:	**Zph 3:16**	3117
on the first **d** of the sixth month,	**Hg 1:1**	3117
on the twenty-fourth **d** of the	**Hg 1:15**	3117
do consider from this **d** onward:	**Hg 2:15**	3117
'Do consider from this **d** onward,	**Hg 2:18**	3117
twenty-fourth **d** of the ninth *month;*	**Hg 2:18**	3117
from the **d** when the temple of the	**Hg 2:18**	3117
this **d** on I will bless *you.*' "	**Hg 2:19**	3117
to Haggai on the twenty-fourth **d**	**Hg 2:20**	3117
'On that **d**,' declares the LORD of	**Hg 2:23**	3117
d of the eleventh month,	**Zch 1:7**	3117
that **d** and will become My people.	**Zch 2:11**	3117
iniquity of that land in one **d**.	**Zch 3:9**	3117
'In that **d**,' declares the LORD of	**Zch 3:10**	3117
despised the **d** of small things?	**Zch 4:10**	3117
and you go the same **d** and enter	**Zch 6:10**	3117
came to Zechariah on the fourth **d**	**Zch 7:1**	
those who *spoke* in the **d** that the	**Zch 8:9**	3117
This very **d** I am declaring that I	**Zch 9:12**	3117
that **d** As the flock of His people;	**Zch 9:16**	3117
So it was broken on that **d**,	**Zch 11:11**	3117
"It will come about in that **d**	**Zch 12:3**	3117
"In that **d**," declares the LORD,	**Zch 12:4**	3117
"In that **d** I will make the clans	**Zch 12:6**	3117
"In that **d** the LORD will defend	**Zch 12:8**	3117
them in that **d** will be like David,	**Zch 12:8**	3117
"And in that **d** I will set about	**Zch 12:9**	3117
"In that **d** there will be great	**Zch 12:11**	3117
"In that **d** a fountain will be	**Zch 13:1**	3117
It will come about in that **d**,"	**Zch 13:2**	3117
in that **d** that the prophets will each	**Zch 13:4**	3117
a **d** is coming for the LORD when	**Zch 14:1**	3117
when He fights on a **d** of battle.	**Zch 14:3**	3117
In that **d** His feet will stand	**Zch 14:4**	3117

d there will be no light;	**Zch 14:6**	3117
d which is known to the LORD,	**Zch 14:7**	3117
to the LORD, neither **d** nor night,	**Zch 14:7**	3117
And in that **d** living waters will flow	**Zch 14:8**	3117
d the LORD will be *the only* one,	**Zch 14:9**	3117
It will come about in that **d**	**Zch 14:13**	3117
In that **d** there will *be inscribed*	**Zch 14:20**	3117
of the LORD of hosts in that **d**.	**Zch 14:21**	3117
can endure the **d** of His coming?	**Mal 3:2**	3117
"on the **d** that I prepare *My* own	**Mal 3:17**	3117
"For behold, the **d** is coming,	**Mal 4:1**	3117
and the **d** that is coming will set	**Mal 4:1**	3117
on the **d** which I am preparing,"	**Mal 4:3**	3117
great and terrible **d** of the LORD.	**Mal 4:5**	3117
'Give us this **d** our daily bread.	**Mt 6:11**	*4594*
d has enough trouble of its own.	**Mt 6:34**	*2250*
"Many will say to Me on that **d**,	**Mt 7:22**	*2250*
and Gomorrah in the **d** of judgment than	**Mt 10:15**	*2250*
and Sidon in *the* **d** of judgment than	**Mt 11:22**	*2250*
it would have remained to this **d**.	**Mt 11:23**	*4594*
of Sodom in *the* **d** of judgment,	**Mt 11:24**	*2250*
for it in the **d** of judgment.	**Mt 12:36**	*2250*
d Jesus went out of the house and	**Mt 13:1**	*2250*
and be raised up on the third **d**.	**Mt 16:21**	*2250*
will be raised on the third **d**."	**Mt 17:23**	*2250*
laborers for a denarius for the **d**,	**Mt 20:2**	*2250*
standing here idle all **d** long?'	**Mt 20:6**	*2250*
and the scorching heat of the **d**.'	**Mt 20:12**	*2250*
third **d** He will be raised up."	**Mt 20:19**	*2250*
On that **d** *some* Sadducees	**Mt 22:23**	*2250*
nor did anyone dare from that **d** on	**Mt 22:46**	*2250*
of that **d** and hour no one knows,	**Mt 24:36**	*2250*
the **d** that Noah entered the ark,	**Mt 24:38**	*2250*
know which **d** your Lord is coming.	**Mt 24:42**	*2250*
come on a **d** when he does not expect	**Mt 24:50**	*2250*
do not know the **d** nor the hour.	**Mt 25:13**	*2250*
Now on the first **d** of Unleavened	**Mt 26:17**	
that **d** when I drink it new with you	**Mt 26:29**	*2250*
Every **d** I used to sit in the	**Mt 26:55**	*2250*
the Field of Blood to this **d**.	**Mt 27:8**	*4594*
Now on the next **d**, the day after	**Mt 27:62**	*1887*
Now on the next day, the **d** after	**Mt 27:62**	*1887*
be made secure until the third **d**,	**Mt 27:64**	*2250*
it began to dawn toward the first **d**	**Mt 28:1**	
among the Jews, *and is* to this **d**.	**Mt 28:15**	*4594*
and then they will fast in that **d**.	**Mk 2:20**	*2250*
to bed at night and gets up by **d**,	**Mk 4:27**	*2250*
On that **d**, when evening came	**Mk 4:35**	*2250*
Constantly, night and **d**,	**Mk 5:5**	*2250*
A strategic **d** came when Herod	**Mk 6:21**	*2250*
On the next **d**, when they had	**Mk 11:12**	*1887*
of that **d** or hour no one knows,	**Mk 13:32**	*2250*
the first **d** of Unleavened Bread,	**Mk 14:12**	*2250*
d when I drink it new in the kingdom	**Mk 14:25**	*2250*
"Every **d** I was with you in the	**Mk 14:49**	*2250*
because it was the preparation **d**,	**Mk 15:42**	*3904*
that is, the **d** before the Sabbath,	**Mk 15:42**	*4315*
early on the first **d** of the week,	**Mk 16:2**	
early on the first **d** of the week,	**Mk 16:9**	
d when these things take place,	**Lk 1:20**	*2250*
the eighth **d** they came to circumcise	**Lk 1:59**	*2250*
lived in the deserts until the **d** of his	**Lk 1:80**	*2250*
and **d** with fastings and prayers.	**Lk 2:37**	*2250*
When **d** came, Jesus left and	**Lk 4:42**	*2250*
One **d** He was teaching;	**Lk 5:17**	*2250*
And when **d** came, He called His	**Lk 6:13**	*2250*
"Be glad in that **d** and leap *for*	**Lk 6:23**	*2250*
Now the **d** was ending, and	**Lk 9:12**	*2250*
and be raised up on the third **d**."	**Lk 9:22**	*2250*
On the next **d**, when they came down	**Lk 9:37**	*2250*
tolerable in that **d** for Sodom than	**Lk 10:12**	*2250*
"On the next **d** he took out	**Lk 10:35**	*839*
'Give us each **d** our daily bread.	**Lk 11:3**	*2250*
a **d** when he does not expect *him*	**Lk 12:46**	*2250*
'It will be a hot **d**,'	**Lk 12:55**	
and not on the Sabbath **d**."	**Lk 13:14**	*2250*
from this bond on the Sabbath **d**?"	**Lk 13:16**	*2250*
and the third **d** I reach My goal.'	**Lk 13:32**	
today and tomorrow and the next **d**;	**Lk 13:33**	
pull him out on a Sabbath **d**?"	**Lk 14:5**	*2250*
joyously living in splendor every **d**.	**Lk 16:19**	*2250*
sins against you seven times a **d**,	**Lk 17:4**	*2250*
will the Son of Man be in His **d**.	**Lk 17:24**	*2250*
the **d** that Noah entered the ark,	**Lk 17:27**	*2250*
but on the **d** that Lot went out	**Lk 17:29**	*2250*
the **d** that the Son of Man is revealed.	**Lk 17:30**	*2250*
"On that **d**, the one who	**Lk 17:31**	*2250*
elect who cry to Him **d** and night,	**Lk 18:7**	*2250*
the third **d** He will rise again."	**Lk 18:33**	*2250*
"If you had known in this **d**,	**Lk 19:42**	*2250*
that **d** will not come on you suddenly	**Lk 21:34**	*2250*
d He was teaching in the temple,	**Lk 21:37**	*2250*
Then came the *first* **d** of	**Lk 22:7**	*2250*
When it was **d**, the Council of	**Lk 22:66**	*2250*
with one another that very **d**;	**Lk 23:12**	*2250*
It was the preparation **d**,	**Lk 23:54**	*2250*
But on the first **d** of the week,	**Lk 24:1**	
and the third **d** rise again."	**Lk 24:7**	*2250*
very **d** to a village named Emmaus,	**Lk 24:13**	*2250*
d since these things happened.	**Lk 24:21**	*2250*
and the **d** is now nearly over."	**Lk 24:29**	*2250*
again from the dead the third **d**,	**Lk 24:46**	*2250*
next **d** he saw Jesus coming to him and	**Jn 1:29**	*1887*
Again the next **d** John was standing	**Jn 1:35**	*1887*
and they stayed with Him that **d**,	**Jn 1:39**	*2250*
The next **d** He purposed to go into	**Jn 1:43**	*1887*
On the third **d** there was a	**Jn 2:1**	*2250*
Now it was the Sabbath on that **d**.	**Jn 5:9**	*2250*
The next **d** the crowd that	**Jn 6:22**	*1887*

but raise it up on the last **d**.	**Jn 6:39**	*2250*
will raise him up on the last **d**."	**Jn 6:40**	*2250*
I will raise him up on the last **d**.	**Jn 6:44**	*2250*
I will raise him up on the last **d**.	**Jn 6:54**	*2250*
Now on the last **d**, the great *day*	**Jn 7:37**	*2250*
Now on the last day, the great **d**	**Jn 7:37**	
Abraham rejoiced to see My **d**,	**Jn 8:56**	*2250*
who sent Me as long as it is **d**;	**Jn 9:4**	*2250*
on the **d** when Jesus made the clay and	**Jn 9:14**	*2250*
"Are there not twelve hours in the **d**?	**Jn 11:9**	*2250*
If anyone walks in the **d**,	**Jn 11:9**	*2250*
the resurrection on the last **d**."	**Jn 11:24**	*2250*
So from that **d** on they planned	**Jn 11:53**	*2250*
keep it for the **d** of My burial.	**Jn 12:7**	*2250*
On the next **d** the large crowd	**Jn 12:12**	*1887*
what will judge him at the last **d**.	**Jn 12:48**	*2250*
"In that **d** you will know that I	**Jn 14:20**	*2250*
d you will not question Me	**Jn 16:23**	*2250*
"In that **d** you will ask in My name,	**Jn 16:26**	*2250*
Now it was the **d** of preparation	**Jn 19:14**	*3904*
it was the **d** of preparation,	**Jn 19:31**	*3904*
(for that Sabbath was a high **d**),	**Jn 19:31**	*3904*
of the Jewish **d** of preparation,	**Jn 19:42**	*3904*
Now on the first **d** of the week	**Jn 20:1**	
it was evening on that **d**,	**Jn 20:19**	*2250*
the first **d** of the week,	**Jn 20:19**	
But when the **d** was now breaking,	**Jn 21:4**	*4407b*
until the **d** when He was taken up	**Ac 1:2**	*2250*
until the **d** that He was taken up	**Ac 1:22**	*2250*
When the **d** of Pentecost had come,	**Ac 2:1**	*2250*
is *only* the third hour of the **d**;	**Ac 2:15**	*2250*
GLORIOUS **D** OF THE LORD SHALL COME.	**Ac 2:20**	*2250*
and his tomb is with us to this **d**.	**Ac 2:29**	*2250*
and that **d** there were added about	**Ac 2:41**	*2250*
D by day continuing with one mind in	**Ac 2:46**	*2250*
Day by **d** continuing with one	**Ac 2:46**	*2250*
Lord was adding to their number **d** by	**Ac 2:47**	*2250*
by **d** those who were being saved.	**Ac 2:47**	*2250*
used to set down every **d** at the gate	**Ac 3:2**	*2250*
put them in jail until the next **d**,	**Ac 4:3**	*839*
On the next **d**, their rulers and	**Ac 4:5**	*839*
And every **d**, in the temple and	**Ac 5:42**	*2250*
circumcised him on the eighth **d**;	**Ac 7:8**	*2250*
"On the following **d** he	**Ac 7:26**	*2250*
And on that **d** a great persecution	**Ac 8:1**	*2250*
also watching the gates **d** and night	**Ac 9:24**	*2250*
About the ninth hour of the **d** he	**Ac 10:3**	*2250*
On the next **d**, as they were on	**Ac 10:9**	*1887*
And on the next **d** he got up	**Ac 10:23**	*1887*
following **d** he entered Caesarea.	**Ac 10:24**	*1887*
"God raised Him up on the third **d** and	**Ac 10:40**	*2250*
Now when **d** came, there was no	**Ac 12:18**	*2250*
On an appointed **d** Herod,	**Ac 12:21**	*2250*
and on the Sabbath **d** they went	**Ac 13:14**	*2250*
The next **d** he went away with	**Ac 14:20**	*1887*
on the **d** following to Neapolis;	**Ac 16:11**	
And on the Sabbath **d** we went	**Ac 16:13**	*2250*
Now when **d** came, the chief	**Ac 16:35**	*2250*
and in the market place every **d**	**Ac 17:17**	*2250*
because He has fixed a **d** in which	**Ac 17:31**	*2250*
On the first **d** of the week,	**Ac 20:7**	
intending to leave the next **d**,	**Ac 20:7**	*1887*
the following **d** opposite Chios;	**Ac 20:15**	
next **d** we crossed over to Samos;	**Ac 20:15**	
d following we came to Miletus.	**Ac 20:15**	
possible, on the **d** of Pentecost.	**Ac 20:16**	*2250*
first **d** that I set foot in Asia,	**Ac 20:18**	*2250*
"Therefore, I testify to you this **d**	**Ac 20:26**	*2250*
remembering that night and **d** for a	**Ac 20:31**	*2250*
the next **d** to Rhodes and from there	**Ac 21:1**	
we stayed with them for a **d**.	**Ac 21:7**	*2250*
On the next **d** we left and	**Ac 21:8**	*1887*
the following **d** Paul went in with us	**Ac 21:18**	
Paul took the men, and the next **d**,	**Ac 21:26**	*2250*
But on the next **d**, wishing to know	**Ac 22:30**	*1887*
before God up to this **d**."	**Ac 23:1**	*2250*
When it was **d**, the Jews formed	**Ac 23:12**	*2250*
But the next **d**, leaving the	**Ac 23:32**	*1887*
and on the next **d** he took his seat	**Ac 25:6**	*1887*
d took my seat on the tribunal and	**Ac 25:17**	
on the next **d** when Agrippa came	**Ac 25:23**	*1887*
earnestly serve *God* night and **d**.	**Ac 26:7**	*2250*
I stand to this **d** testifying both	**Ac 26:22**	*2250*
but also all who hear me this **d**,	**Ac 26:29**	*4594*
The next **d** we put in at Sidon;	**Ac 27:3**	
The next **d** as we were being	**Ac 27:18**	
and on the third **d** they threw the	**Ac 27:19**	
Until the **d** was about to dawn,	**Ac 27:33**	*2250*
"Today is the fourteenth **d** that	**Ac 27:33**	*2250*
When **d** came, they could not	**Ac 27:39**	*2250*
a **d** later a south wind sprang up,	**Ac 28:13**	*2250*
the second **d** we came to Puteoli.	**Ac 28:13**	*1206*
When they had set a **d** for Paul,	**Ac 28:23**	*2250*
storing up wrath for yourself in the **d**	**Ro 2:5**	*2250*
on the **d** when, according to my	**Ro 2:16**	*2250*
BEING PUT TO DEATH ALL **D** LONG;	**Ro 8:36**	*2250*
"ALL THE **D** LONG I HAVE STRETCHED	**Ro 10:21**	*2250*
HEAR NOT, DOWN TO THIS VERY **D**."	**Ro 11:8**	*2250*
almost gone, and the **d** is near.	**Ro 13:12**	*2250*
Let us behave properly as in the **d**,	**Ro 13:13**	*2250*
person regards one **d** above another,	**Ro 14:5**	*2250*
another regards every **d** *alike.*	**Ro 14:5**	*2250*
He who observes the **d**,	**Ro 14:6**	*2250*
in the **d** of our Lord Jesus Christ.	**1Co 1:8**	*2250*
for the **d** will show it because it	**1Co 3:13**	*2250*
saved in the **d** of the Lord Jesus.	**1Co 5:5**	*2250*
thousand fell in one **d**.	**1Co 10:8**	*2250*
d according to the Scriptures,	**1Co 15:4**	*2250*
On the first **d** of every week each	**1Co 16:2**	

ours, in the **d** of our Lord Jesus. **2Co 1:14** *2250*
for until this very **d** at the **2Co 3:14** *2250*
to this **d** whenever Moses is read, **2Co 3:15** *4594*
man is being renewed **d** by day. **2Co 4:16** *2250*
man is being renewed day by **d**. **2Co 4:16** *2250*
THE **D** OF SALVATION I HELPED YOU." **2Co 6:2** *2250*
behold, now is "THE **D** OF SALVATION" **2Co 6:2** *2250*
and a **d** I have spent in the deep. **2Co 11:25** *3574*
sealed for the **d** of redemption. **Eph 4:30** *2250*
be able to resist in the evil **d**, **Eph 6:13** *2250*
gospel from the first **d** until now. **Php 1:5** *2250*
it until the **d** of Christ Jesus. **Php 1:6** *2250*
blameless until the **d** of Christ; **Php 1:10** *2250*
so that in the **d** of Christ I will **Php 2:16** *2250*
circumcised the eighth **d**, **Php 3:5** *3637*
in you also since the **d** you heard *of it* **Col 1:6** *2250*
also, since the **d** we heard *of it*, **Col 1:9** *2250*
or a new moon or a Sabbath **d** **Col 2:16**
how working night and **d** so as not **1Th 2:9** *2250*
as we night and **d** keep praying **1Th 3:10** *2250*
the **d** of the Lord will come just like a **1Th 5:2** *2250*
that the **d** would overtake you **1Th 5:4** *2250*
all sons of light and sons of **d**. **1Th 5:5** *2250*
But since we are of *the* **d**, **1Th 5:8** *2250*
glorified in His saints on that **d**, **2Th 1:10** *2250*
that the **d** of the Lord has come. **2Th 2:2** *2250*
we *kept* working night and **d** so that **2Th 3:8** *2250*
and prayers night and **d**. **1Tm 5:5** *2250*
you in my prayers night and **d**, **2Tm 1:3** *2250*
entrusted to Him until that **d**. **2Tm 1:12** *2250*
to find mercy from the Lord on that **d** **2Tm 1:18** *2250*
Judge, will award to me on that **d**; **2Tm 4:8** *2250*
THE **D** OF TRIAL IN THE WILDERNESS, **Heb 3:8** *2250*
encourage one another **d** after day, **Heb 3:13** *2250*
encourage one another day after **d**, **Heb 3:13** *2250*
somewhere concerning the seventh **d**: **Heb 4:4**
SEVENTH **D** FROM ALL HIS WORKS"; **Heb 4:4** *2250*
He again fixes a certain **d**, **Heb 4:7** *2250*
spoken of another **d** after that. **Heb 4:8** *2250*
ON THE **D** WHEN I TOOK THEM BY THE **Heb 8:9** *2250*
as you see the **d** drawing near. **Heb 10:25** *2250*
your hearts in a **d** of slaughter. **Jas 5:5** *2250*
God in the **d** of visitation. **1Pe 2:12** *2250*
until the **d** dawns and the morning **2Pe 1:19** *2250*
righteous soul tormented **d** after day **2Pe 2:8** *2250*
after **d** by *their* lawless deeds), **2Pe 2:8** *2250*
punishment for the **d** of judgment, **2Pe 2:9** *2250*
kept for the **d** of judgment and **2Pe 3:7** *2250*
Lord one **d** is like a thousand years, **2Pe 3:8** *2250*
and a thousand years like one **d**. **2Pe 3:8** *2250*
But the **d** of the Lord will come **2Pe 3:10** *2250*
the coming of the **d** of God, **2Pe 3:12** *2250*
both now and to the **d** of eternity. **2Pe 3:18** *2250*
confidence in the **d** of judgment; **1Jn 4:17** *2250*
for the judgment of the great **d**, **Jude 1:6** *2250*
was in the Spirit on the Lord's **d**, **Rv 1:10** *2250*
and **d** and night they do not cease **Rv 4:8** *2250*
great **d** of their wrath has come, **Rv 6:17** *2250*
they serve Him **d** and night in His **Rv 7:15** *2250*
the **d** would not shine for a third **Rv 8:12** *2250*
the hour and **d** and month and year, **Rv 9:15** *2250*
them before our God **d** and night. **Rv 12:10** *2250*
they have no rest **d** and night, **Rv 14:11** *2250*
for the war of the great **d** of God, **Rv 16:14** *2250*
in one **d** her plagues will come, **Rv 18:8** *2250*
d and night forever and ever. **Rv 20:10** *2250*

DAYBREAK
a man wrestled with him until **d**. **Gn 32:24** *7837*
returned to its normal state at **d**, **Ex 14:27** *1242*
and at **d** Samuel **1Sa 9:26** *7837*
entered into the temple about **d** and **Ac 5:21** *3722*
with them a long while until **d**, **Ac 20:11** *827*
from the stern and wished for **d**. **Ac 27:29** *2250*

DAYLIGHT
them in broad **d** before the LORD, **Nu 25:4** 8121
her master was, until *full* **d**. **Jg 19:26** 216
lie with your wives in broad **d**. **2Sa 12:11** 8121, 2088
make the earth dark in broad **d**. **Am 8:9** 3117, 216

DAY'S
and gather a **d** portion every day, **Ex 16:4** 3117
each **d** matter on its own day **Lv 23:37** 3117
about a **d** journey on this side and **Nu 11:31** 3117
and a **d** journey on the other side, **Nu 11:31** 3117
a **d** journey into the wilderness, **1Ki 19:4** 3117
as every **d** work required; **1Ch 16:37** 3117
to go through the city one **d** walk; **Jon 3:4** 3117
the caravan, and went a **d** journey; **Lk 2:44** *2250*
a Sabbath **d** journey away. **Ac 1:12**

DAYS
for seasons and for **d** and years; **Gn 1:14** 3117
you will eat All the **d** of your life; **Gn 3:14** 3117
eat of it All the **d** of your life. **Gn 3:17** 3117
Then the **d** of Adam after he became **Gn 5:4** 3117
So all the **d** that Adam lived were **Gn 5:5** 3117
So all the **d** of Seth were nine **Gn 5:8** 3117
So all the **d** of Enosh were nine **Gn 5:11** 3117
So all the **d** of Kenan were nine **Gn 5:14** 3117
So all the **d** of Mahalalel were **Gn 5:17** 3117
So all the **d** of Jared were nine **Gn 5:20** 3117
So all the **d** of Enoch were three **Gn 5:23** 3117
So all the **d** of Methuselah were **Gn 5:27** 3117
So all the **d** of Lamech were seven **Gn 5:31** 3117
nevertheless his **d** shall be one **Gn 6:3** 3117
were on the earth in those **d**, **Gn 6:4** 3117
"For after seven more **d**, **Gn 7:4** 3117
earth forty **d** and forty nights; **Gn 7:4** 3117
It came about after the seven **d**, **Gn 7:10** 3117
for forty **d** and forty nights. **Gn 7:12** 3117
came upon the earth for forty **d**, **Gn 7:17** 3117
the earth one hundred and fifty **d**. **Gn 7:24** 3117
and fifty **d** the water decreased. **Gn 8:3** 3117
came about at the end of forty **d**, **Gn 8:6** 3117
So he waited yet another seven **d**; **Gn 8:10** 3117
he waited yet another seven **d**, **Gn 8:12** 3117
So all the **d** of Noah were nine **Gn 9:29** 3117
in his **d** the earth was divided; **Gn 10:25** 3117
The **d** of Terah were two **Gn 11:32** 3117
the **d** of Amraphel king of Shinar, **Gn 14:1** 3117
male among you who is eight **d** old **Gn 17:12** 3117
son Isaac when he was eight **d** old, **Gn 21:4** 3117
of the Philistines for many **d**. **Gn 21:34** 3117
"Let the girl stay with us *a few* **d**, **Gn 24:55** 3117
When her **d** to be delivered were **Gn 25:24** 3117
had occurred in the **d** of Abraham. **Gn 26:1** 3117
in the **d** of Abraham his father, **Gn 26:15** 3117
in the **d** of his father Abraham, **Gn 26:18** 3117
"The **d** of mourning for my father **Gn 27:41** 3117
"Stay with him a few **d**, **Gn 27:44** 3117
few **d** because of his love for her. **Gn 29:20** 3117
Now in the **d** of wheat harvest **Gn 30:14** 3117
Now the **d** of Isaac were one **Gn 35:28** 3117
and mourned for his son many **d**. **Gn 37:34** 3117
the three branches are three **d**; **Gn 40:12** 3117
within three more **d** Pharaoh will **Gn 40:13** 3117
the three baskets are three **d**; **Gn 40:18** 3117
within three more **d** Pharaoh will **Gn 40:19** 3117
together in prison for three **d**. **Gn 42:17** 3117
the **d** of their sojourning." **Gn 47:9** 3117
will befall you in the **d** to come. **Gn 49:1** 3117
Now forty **d** were required for it, **Gn 50:3** 3117
Egyptians wept for him seventy **d**. **Gn 50:3** 3117
d of mourning for him were past, **Gn 50:4** 3117
seven **d** mourning for his father. **Gn 50:10** 3117
Now it came about in those **d**, **Ex 2:11** 3117
d that the king of Egypt died. **Ex 2:23** 3117
Seven **d** passed after the LORD **Ex 7:25** 3117
all the land of Egypt for three **d**. **Ex 10:22** 3117
rise from his place for three **d**, **Ex 10:23** 3117
'Seven **d** you shall eat unleavened **Ex 12:15** 3117
'Seven **d** there shall be no leaven **Ex 12:19** 3117
"For seven **d** you shall eat **Ex 13:6** 3117
be eaten throughout the seven **d**; **Ex 13:7** 3117
and they went three **d** in the **Ex 15:22** 3117
"Six **d** you shall gather it, but **Ex 16:26** 3117
He gives you bread for two **d** **Ex 16:29** 3117
"Six **d** you shall labor and do all **Ex 20:9** 3117
"For in six **d** the LORD made the **Ex 20:11** 3117
that your **d** may be prolonged in **Ex 20:12** 3117
shall be with its mother seven **d**; **Ex 22:30** 3117
"Six **d** you are to do your work, **Ex 23:12** 3117
for seven **d** you are to eat **Ex 23:15** 3117
will fulfill the number of your **d**. **Ex 23:26** 3117
the cloud covered it for six **d**; **Ex 24:16** 3117
mountain forty **d** and forty nights. **Ex 24:18** 3117
"For seven **d** the one of his sons **Ex 29:30** 3117
shall ordain them through seven **d**. **Ex 29:35** 3117
"For seven **d** you shall make **Ex 29:37** 3117
'For six **d** work may be done, but **Ex 31:15** 3117
for in six **d** the LORD made heaven **Ex 31:17** 3117
For seven **d** you are to eat **Ex 34:18** 3117
"You shall work six **d**, **Ex 34:21** 3117
the LORD forty **d** and forty nights; **Ex 34:28** 3117
"For six **d** work may be done, but **Ex 35:2** 3117
the tent of meeting for seven **d**, **Lv 8:33** 3117
will ordain you through seven **d**. **Lv 8:33** 3117
remain day and night for seven **d** and **Lv 8:35** 3117
she shall be unclean for seven **d**, **Lv 12:2** 3117
as in the **d** of her menstruation **Lv 12:2** 3117
purification for thirty-three **d**; **Lv 12:4** 3117
until the **d** of her purification **Lv 12:4** 3117
her purification for sixty-six **d**. **Lv 12:5** 3117
When the **d** of her purification **Lv 12:6** 3117
who has the infection for seven **d**. **Lv 13:4** 3117
isolate him for seven more **d**. **Lv 13:5** 3117
shall isolate him for seven **d**; **Lv 13:21** 3117
shall isolate him for seven **d**; **Lv 13:26** 3117
the scaly infection for seven **d**. **Lv 13:31** 3117
with the scale seven more **d**. **Lv 13:33** 3117
remain unclean all the **d** during which **Lv 13:46** 3117
article with the mark for seven **d**. **Lv 13:50** 3117
quarantine it for seven more **d**. **Lv 13:54** 3117
stay outside his tent for seven **d**. **Lv 14:8** 3117
quarantine the house for seven **d**. **Lv 14:38** 3117
himself seven **d** for his cleansing; **Lv 15:13** 3117
menstrual impurity for seven **d**; **Lv 15:19** 3117
him, he shall be unclean seven **d**, **Lv 15:24** 3117
a discharge of her blood many **d**, **Lv 15:25** 3117
all the **d** of her impure discharge **Lv 15:25** 3117
bed on which she lies all the **d** of her **Lv 15:26** 3117
count off for herself seven **d**; **Lv 15:28** 3117
remain seven **d** with its mother, **Lv 22:27** 3117
'For six **d** work may be done, **Lv 23:3** 3117
for seven **d** you shall eat **Lv 23:6** 3117
'But for seven **d** you shall present **Lv 23:8** 3117
'You shall count fifty **d** to the **Lv 23:16** 3117
of Booths for seven **d** to the LORD. **Lv 23:34** 3117
'For seven **d** you shall present an **Lv 23:36** 3117
the feast of the LORD for seven **d**, **Lv 23:39** 3117
the LORD your God for seven **d**. **Lv 23:40** 3117
the LORD for seven **d** in the year. **Lv 23:41** 3117
shall live in booths for seven **d**; **Lv 23:42** 3117
It is like the **d** of a hired man **Lv 25:50** 3117
all the **d** of the desolation, **Lv 26:34** 3117
'All the **d** of *its* desolation it **Lv 26:35** 3117
'All the **d** of his separation he **Nu 6:4** 3117
'All the **d** of his vow of **Nu 6:5** 3117
He shall be holy until the **d** are **Nu 6:5** 3117
'All the **d** of his separation to **Nu 6:6** 3117
'All the **d** of his separation he is **Nu 6:8** 3117
to the LORD his **d** as a Nazirite, **Nu 6:12** 3117
but the former **d** will be void **Nu 6:12** 3117
Nazirite when the **d** of his separation **Nu 6:13** 3117
over the tabernacle for many **d**, **Nu 9:19** 3117
a few **d** over the tabernacle, **Nu 9:20** 3117
Whether it was two **d** or a month or **Nu 9:22** 3117
and on the first **d** of your months, **Nu 10:10** 3117
in front of them for the three **d**, **Nu 10:33** 3117
shall eat, not one day, nor two **d**, **Nu 11:19** 3117
one day, nor two days, nor five **d**, **Nu 11:19** 3117
days, nor five days, nor ten **d**, **Nu 11:19** 3117
days, nor ten days, nor twenty **d**, **Nu 11:19** 3117
not bear her shame for seven **d**? **Nu 12:14** 3117
up for seven **d** outside the camp, **Nu 12:14** 3117
up outside the camp for seven **d**, **Nu 12:15** 3117
the land, at the end of forty **d**, **Nu 13:25** 3117
of **d** which you spied out the land, **Nu 14:34** 3117
you spied out the land, forty **d**, **Nu 14:34** 3117
shall be unclean for seven **d**. **Nu 19:11** 3117
tent shall be unclean for seven **d**. **Nu 19:14** 3117
shall be unclean for seven **d**. **Nu 19:16** 3117
of Israel wept for Aaron thirty **d**. **Nu 20:29** 3117
to your people in the **d** to come." **Nu 24:14** 3117
bread *shall be* eaten for seven **d**. **Nu 28:17** 3117
shall present daily, for seven **d**, **Nu 28:24** 3117
a feast to the LORD for seven **d**. **Nu 29:12** 3117
camp outside the camp seven **d**; **Nu 31:19** 3117
"So you remained in Kadesh many **d**, **Dt 1:46** 3117
days, the **d** that you spent *there*. **Dt 1:46** 3117
and circled Mount Seir for many **d**. **Dt 2:1** 3117
your heart all the **d** of your life; **Dt 4:9** 3117
all the **d** they live on the earth, **Dt 4:10** 3117
come upon you, in the latter **d** you **Dt 4:30** 3117
former **d** which were before you, **Dt 4:32** 3117
'Six **d** you shall labor and do all **Dt 5:13** 3117
you, that your **d** may be prolonged and **Dt 5:16** 3117
and that you may prolong *your* **d** in **Dt 5:33** 3117
you, all the **d** of your life, **Dt 6:2** 3117
and that your **d** may be prolonged. **Dt 6:2** 3117
the mountain forty **d** and nights; **Dt 9:9** 3117
at the end of forty **d** and nights **Dt 9:11** 3117
at the first, forty **d** and nights; **Dt 9:18** 3117
the LORD the forty **d** and nights, **Dt 9:25** 3117
stayed on the mountain forty **d** and **Dt 10:10** 3117
so that you may prolong *your* **d** on **Dt 11:9** 3117
so that your **d** and the **d** of your **Dt 11:21** 3117
so that your days and the **d** of **Dt 11:21** 3117
seven **d** you shall eat with it **Dt 16:3** 3117
may remember all the **d** of your life **Dt 16:3** 3117
"For seven **d** no leaven shall be **Dt 16:4** 3117
"Six **d** you shall eat unleavened **Dt 16:8** 3117
celebrate the Feast of Booths seven **d** **Dt 16:13** 3117
"Seven **d** you shall celebrate a **Dt 16:15** 3117
judge who is *in office* in those **d**, **Dt 17:9** 3117
read it all the **d** of his life, **Dt 17:19** 3117
who will be *in office* in those **d**. **Dt 19:17** 3117
and that you may prolong your **d**. **Dt 22:7** 3117
he cannot divorce her all his **d**. **Dt 22:19** 3117
he cannot divorce her all his **d**. **Dt 22:29** 3117
or their prosperity all your **d**. **Dt 23:6** 3117
that your **d** may be prolonged in **Dt 25:15** 3117
You will not prolong *your* **d** in **Dt 30:18** 3117
life and the length of your **d**, **Dt 30:20** 3117
will befall you in the latter **d**, **Dt 31:29** 3117
"Remember the **d** of old, Consider **Dt 32:7** 3117
will prolong your **d** in the land, **Dt 32:47** 3117
bronze, And according to your **d**, **Dt 33:25** 3117
in the plains of Moab thirty **d**; **Dt 34:8** 3117
then the **d** of weeping *and* mourning **Dt 34:8** 3117
before you all the **d** of your life. **Jos 1:5** 3117
d you are to cross this Jordan, **Jos 1:11** 3117
hide yourselves there for three **d** until **Jos 2:16** 3117
d until the pursuers returned. **Jos 2:22** 3117
At the end of three **d** **Jos 3:2** 3117
its banks all the **d** of harvest), **Jos 3:15** 3117
Moses all the **d** of his life. **Jos 4:14** 3117
You shall do so for six **d**. **Jos 6:3** 3117
they did so for six **d**. **Jos 6:14** 3117
It came about at the end of three **d** **Jos 9:16** 3117
one who is high priest in those **d**. **Jos 20:6** 3117
brothers these many **d** to this day, **Jos 22:3** 3117
Now it came about after many **d**, **Jos 23:1** 3117
served the LORD all the **d** of Joshua **Jos 24:31** 3117
of Joshua and all the **d** of the elders **Jos 24:31** 3117
the LORD all the **d** of Joshua, **Jg 2:7** 3117
and all the **d** of the elders who **Jg 2:7** 3117
enemies all the **d** of the judge; **Jg 2:18** 3117
the **d** of Shamgar the son of Anath, **Jg 5:6** 3117
son of Anath, In the **d** of Jael, **Jg 5:6** 3117
forty years in the **d** of Gideon. **Jg 8:28** 3117
the Gileadite four **d** in the year. **Jg 11:40** 3117
within the seven **d** of the feast, **Jg 14:12** 3117
not tell the riddle in three **d**. **Jg 14:14** 3117
seven **d** while their feast lasted. **Jg 14:17** 3117
years in the **d** of the Philistines. **Jg 15:20** 3117
d there was no king in Israel; **Jg 17:6** 3117
In those **d** there was no king of **Jg 18:1** 3117
and in those **d** the tribe of the **Jg 18:1** 3117
Now it came about in those **d**, **Jg 19:1** 3117
and he remained with him three **d**. **Jg 19:4** 3117
of God *was* there in those **d**, **Jg 20:27** 3117
before it to *minister* in those **d**), **Jg 20:28** 3117
d there was no king in Israel; **Jg 21:25** 3117
in the **d** when the judges governed, **Ru 1:1** 3117
to the LORD all the **d** of his life, **1Sa 1:11** 3117
the **d** are coming when I will break **1Sa 2:31** 3117

from the LORD was rare in those **d**,	1Sa 3:1	3117
Philistines all the **d** of Samuel.	1Sa 7:13	3117
Israel all the **d** of his life.	1Sa 7:15	3117
which were lost three **d** ago,	1Sa 9:20	3117
You shall wait seven **d** until I	1Sa 10:8	3117
"Let us alone for seven **d**,	1Sa 11:3	3117
Now he waited seven **d**,	1Sa 13:8	3117
not come within the appointed **d**,	1Sa 13:11	3117
was severe all the **d** of Saul;	1Sa 14:52	3117
Jesse was old in the **d** of Saul,	1Sa 17:12	3117
morning and evening for forty **d** and	1Sa 17:16	3117
Before the **d** had expired	1Sa 18:26	3117
"When you have stayed for three **d**,	1Sa 20:19	8027
all the **d** they were in Carmel.	1Sa 25:7	3117
not be found in you all your **d**.	1Sa 25:28	3117
About ten **d** later, the LORD struck	1Sa 25:38	3117
The number of **d** that David	1Sa 27:7	3117
Now it came about in those **d** that	1Sa 28:1	3117
who has been with me these **d**,	1Sa 29:3	3117
for three **d** and three nights.	1Sa 30:12	3117
when I fell sick three **d** ago.	1Sa 30:13	3117
at Jabesh, and fasted seven **d**.	1Sa 31:13	3117
David remained two **d** in Ziklag.	2Sa 1:1	3117
"When your **d** are complete and you	2Sa 7:12	3117
been mourning for the dead many **d**;	2Sa 14:2	3117
which he gave in those **d**,	2Sa 16:23	3117
of Judah for me within three **d**,	2Sa 20:4	3117
in the **d** of David for three years,	2Sa 21:1	3117
put to death in the first **d** of harvest	2Sa 21:9	3117
end of nine months and twenty **d**.	2Sa 24:8	3117
The **d** that David reigned over	1Ki 2:11	3117
Shimei lived in Jerusalem many **d**.	1Ki 2:38	3117
name of the LORD until those **d**.	1Ki 3:2	3117
the kings like you all your **d**.	1Ki 3:13	3117
then I will prolong your **d**."	1Ki 3:14	3117
Solomon all the **d** of his life.	1Ki 4:21	3117
Beersheba, all the **d** of Solomon.	1Ki 4:25	3117
that they may fear You all the **d**	1Ki 8:40	3117
for seven **d** and seven *more* days,	1Ki 8:65	3117
for seven days and seven *more* **d**,	1Ki 8:65	3117
seven *more* days, *even* fourteen **d**.	1Ki 8:65	3117
valuable in the **d** of Solomon.	1Ki 10:21	3117
I will not do it in your **d** for the sake	1Ki 11:12	3117
to Israel all the **d** of Solomon,	1Ki 11:25	3117
him ruler all the **d** of his life,	1Ki 11:34	3117
"Depart for three **d**,	1Ki 12:5	3117
him all the **d** of his life,	1Ki 15:5	3117
Jeroboam all the **d** of his life.	1Ki 15:6	3117
devoted to the LORD all his **d**.	1Ki 15:14	3117
Baasha king of Israel all their **d**.	1Ki 15:16	3117
Baasha king of Israel all their **d**.	1Ki 15:32	3117
Zimri reigned seven **d** at Tirzah.	1Ki 16:15	3117
In his **d** Hiel the Bethelite built	1Ki 16:34	3117
and her household ate for *many* **d**.	1Ki 17:15	3117
Now it happened *after* many **d**	1Ki 18:1	3117
forty **d** and forty nights to Horeb,	1Ki 19:8	3117
over against the other seven **d**.	1Ki 20:29	3117
will not bring the evil in his **d**,	1Ki 21:29	3117
upon his house in his son's **d**."	1Ki 21:29	3117
in the **d** of his father Asa,	1Ki 22:46	3117
and they searched three **d** but	2Ki 2:17	3117
In his **d** Edom revolted from under	2Ki 8:20	3117
In those **d** the LORD began to cut	2Ki 10:32	3117
all his **d** in which Jehoiada the priest	2Ki 12:2	3117
Israel all the **d** of Jehoahaz.	2Ki 13:22	3117
he did not depart all his **d** from	2Ki 15:18	3117
In the **d** of Pekah king of Israel,	2Ki 15:29	3117
In those **d** the LORD began to send	2Ki 15:37	3117
for until those **d** the sons of	2Ki 18:4	3117
In those **d** Hezekiah became mortally	2Ki 20:1	3117
the **d** are coming when all that is	2Ki 20:17	3117
be peace and truth in my **d**?"	2Ki 20:19	3117
the **d** of the judges who judged Israel,	2Ki 23:22	3117
nor in all the **d** of the kings of	2Ki 23:22	3117
In his **d** Pharaoh Neco king of	2Ki 23:29	3117
In his **d** Nebuchadnezzar king of	2Ki 24:1	3117
regularly all the **d** of his life;	2Ki 25:29	3117
each day, all the **d** of his life.	2Ki 25:30	3117
in his **d** the earth was divided,	1Ch 1:19	3117
the **d** of Hezekiah king of Judah,	1Ch 4:41	3117
In the **d** of Saul they made war	1Ch 5:10	3117
in the **d** of Jotham king of Judah	1Ch 5:17	3117
the **d** of Jeroboam king of Israel.	1Ch 5:17	3117
in the **d** of David was 22,600.	1Ch 7:2	3117
father Ephraim mourned many **d**,	1Ch 7:22	3117
villages *were* to come in every seven **d**	1Ch 9:25	3117
oak in Jabesh, and fasted seven **d**.	1Ch 10:12	3117
were there with David three **d**,	1Ch 12:39	3117
not seek it in the **d** of Saul."	1Ch 13:3	3117
"When your **d** are fulfilled	1Ch 17:11	3117
three **d** of the sword of the LORD,	1Ch 21:12	3117
and quiet to Israel in his **d**.	1Ch 22:9	3117
our **d** on the earth are like a	1Ch 29:15	3117
died in a ripe old age, full of **d**,	1Ch 29:28	3117
feast at that time for seven **d**,	2Ch 7:8	3117
the altar they observed seven **d** and	2Ch 7:9	3117
seven days and the feast seven **d**.	2Ch 7:9	3117
valuable in the **d** of Solomon.	2Ch 9:20	3117
"Return to me again in three **d**."	2Ch 10:5	3117
strength in the **d** of Abijah;	2Ch 13:20	3117
for ten years during his **d**.	2Ch 14:1	3117
"For many **d** Israel was	2Ch 15:3	3117
heart was blameless all his **d**.	2Ch 15:17	3117
d and did not seek the Baals,	2Ch 17:3	3117
And they were three **d** taking the	2Ch 20:25	3117
In his **d** Edom revolted against the	2Ch 21:8	3117
all the **d** of Jehoiada the priest.	2Ch 24:2	3117
continually all the **d** of Jehoiada.	2Ch 24:14	3117
to seek God in the **d** of Zechariah,	2Ch 26:5	3117

the house of the LORD in eight **d**,	2Ch 29:17	3117
Bread *for* seven **d** with great joy,	2Ch 30:21	3117
ate for the appointed seven **d**,	2Ch 30:22	3117
the feast another seven **d**,	2Ch 30:23	3117
celebrated the seven **d** with joy.	2Ch 30:23	3117
the **d** of Solomon the son of David,	2Ch 30:26	3117
d Hezekiah became mortally ill;	2Ch 32:24	3117
come on them in the **d** of Hezekiah.	2Ch 32:26	3117
Feast of Unleavened Bread seven **d**.	2Ch 35:17	3117
since the **d** of Samuel the prophet;	2Ch 35:18	3117
months and ten **d** in Jerusalem,	2Ch 36:9	3117
All the **d** of its desolation it	2Ch 36:21	3117
d of Esarhaddon king of Assyria,	Ezr 4:2	3117
all the **d** of Cyrus king of Persia,	Ezr 4:5	3117
And in the **d** of Artaxerxes,	Ezr 4:7	3117
revolt within it in past **d**;	Ezr 4:15	3118
up against the kings in past **d**,	Ezr 4:19	3118
Unleavened Bread seven **d** with joy,	Ezr 6:22	3117
where we camped for three **d**;	Ezr 8:15	3117
and remained there three **d**.	Ezr 8:32	3117
"Since the **d** of our fathers to	Ezr 9:7	3117
would not come within three **d**,	Ezr 10:8	3117
at Jerusalem within the three **d**.	Ezr 10:9	3117
the task *be done* in one or two **d**,	Ezr 10:13	3117
down and wept and mourned for **d**;	Ne 1:4	3117
Jerusalem and was there three **d**.	Ne 2:11	3117
and once in ten **d** all sorts of	Ne 5:18	3117
of *the month* Elul, in fifty-two **d**.	Ne 6:15	3117
Also in those **d** many letters went	Ne 6:17	3117
from the **d** of Joshua the son of Nun	Ne 8:17	3117
they celebrated the feast seven **d**,	Ne 8:18	3117
From the **d** of the kings of Assyria	Ne 9:32	3117
their kinsmen in the **d** of Jeshua.	Ne 12:7	3117
in the **d** of Joiakim, the priests,	Ne 12:12	3117
registered in the **d** of Eliashib,	Ne 12:22	3117
the **d** of Johanan the son of Eliashib.	Ne 12:23	3117
These *served* in the **d** of Joiakim	Ne 12:26	3117
and in the **d** of Nehemiah the	Ne 12:26	3117
For in the **d** of David and Asaph,	Ne 12:46	3117
So all Israel in the **d** of Zerubbabel	Ne 12:47	3117
In those **d** I saw in Judah some who	Ne 13:15	3117
In those **d** I also saw that the	Ne 13:23	3117
took place in the **d** of Ahasuerus,	Es 1:1	3117
in those **d** as King Ahasuerus sat	Es 1:2	3117
of his great majesty for many **d**,	Es 1:4	3117
majesty for many days, 180 **d**.	Es 1:4	3117
When these **d** were completed,	Es 1:5	3117
king gave a banquet lasting seven **d**	Es 1:5	3117
for the **d** of their beautification were	Es 2:12	3117
In those **d**, while Mordecai was	Es 2:21	3117
to the king for these thirty **d**."	Es 4:11	3117
do not eat or drink for three **d**,	Es 4:16	3117
because on those **d** the Jews rid	Es 9:22	3117
that they should make them **d** of	Es 9:22	3117
d Purim after the name of Pur.	Es 9:26	3117
d according to their regulation and	Es 9:27	3117
So these **d** were to be remembered	Es 9:28	3117
and these **d** of Purim were not to	Es 9:28	3117
to establish these **d** of Purim at	Es 9:31	3117
When the **d** of feasting had	Jb 1:5	3117
on the ground with him for seven **d**	Jb 2:13	3117
rejoice among the **d** of the year;	Jb 3:6	3117
d like the days of a hired man?	Jb 7:1	3117
days like the **d** of a hired man?	Jb 7:1	3117
"My **d** are swifter than a weaver's	Jb 7:6	3117
alone, for my **d** are *but* a breath.	Jb 7:16	3117
our **d** on earth are as a shadow.	Jb 8:9	3117
my **d** are swifter than a runner;	Jb 9:25	3117
'Are Your **d** as the days of a	Jb 10:5	3117
'Are Your days as the **d** of a mortal,	Jb 10:5	3117
"Would He not let my few **d** alone?	Jb 10:20	3117
"Since his **d** are determined, The	Jb 14:5	3117
the **d** of my struggle I will wait Until	Jb 14:14	3117
man writhes in pain all *his* **d**,	Jb 15:20	3117
is broken, my **d** are extinguished,	Jb 17:1	3117
"My **d** are past, my plans are torn	Jb 17:11	3117
"They spend their **d** in prosperity,	Jb 21:13	3117
those who know Him not see His **d**?	Jb 24:1	3117
does not reproach any of my **d**.	Jb 27:6	3117
in the **d** when God watched over me;	Jb 29:2	3117
As I was in the prime of my **d**,	Jb 29:4	3117
I shall multiply *my* **d** as the sand.	Jb 29:18	3117
D of affliction have seized me.	Jb 30:16	3117
D of affliction confront me.	Jb 30:27	3117
to the **d** of his youthful vigor;	Jb 33:25	3117
will end their **d** in prosperity	Jb 36:11	3117
And the number of your **d** is great!	Jb 38:21	3117
The LORD blessed the latter **d**	Jb 42:12	3117
died, an old man and full of **d**.	Jb 42:17	3117
him, Length of **d** forever and ever.	Ps 21:4	3117
follow me all the **d** of my life,	Ps 23:6	3117
of the LORD all the **d** of my life,	Ps 27:4	3117
length of **d** that he may see good?	Ps 34:12	3117
LORD knows the **d** of the blameless,	Ps 37:18	3117
And in the **d** of famine they will	Ps 37:19	3117
And what is the extent of my **d**;	Ps 39:4	3117
have made my **d** *as* handbreadths,	Ps 39:5	3117
work that You did in their **d**,	Ps 44:1	3117
in their days, In the **d** of old.	Ps 44:1	3117
should I fear in **d** of adversity,	Ps 49:5	3117
will not live out half their **d**.	Ps 55:23	3117
his **d** may the righteous flourish,	Ps 72:7	3117
I have considered the **d** of old,	Ps 77:5	3117
their **d** to an end in futility And	Ps 78:33	3117
And his throne as the **d** of heaven.	Ps 89:29	3117
have shortened the **d** of his youth;	Ps 89:45	3117
our **d** have declined in Your fury;	Ps 90:9	3117
As for the **d** of our life, they	Ps 90:10	3117
So teach us to number our **d**,	Ps 90:12	3117

for joy and be glad all our **d**.	Ps 90:14	3117
to the **d** You have afflicted us,	Ps 90:15	3117
relief from the **d** of adversity,	Ps 94:13	3117
my **d** have been consumed in smoke,	Ps 102:3	3117
My **d** are like a lengthened shadow,	Ps 102:11	3117
He has shortened my **d**.	Ps 102:23	3117
take me away in the midst of my **d**,	Ps 102:24	3117
As for man, his **d** are like grass;	Ps 103:15	3117
Let his **d** be few;	Ps 109:8	3117
How many are the **d** of Your servant?	Ps 119:84	3117
Jerusalem all the **d** of your life.	Ps 128:5	3117
The **d** that were ordained *for me,*	Ps 139:16	3117
I remember the **d** of old;	Ps 143:5	3117
His **d** are like a passing shadow.	Ps 144:4	3117
For length of **d** and years of life And	Pr 3:2	3117
by me your **d** will be multiplied,	Pr 9:11	3117
the **d** of the afflicted are bad,	Pr 15:15	3117
may be wise the rest of your **d**.	Pr 19:20	
unjust gain will prolong *his* **d**.	Pr 28:16	3117
not evil All the **d** of her life.	Pr 31:12	3117
coming **d** all will be forgotten.	Ec 2:16	3117
Because all his **d** his task is	Ec 2:23	3117
former **d** were better than these?"	Ec 7:10	3117
not lengthen his **d** like a shadow,	Ec 8:13	3117
d of his life which God has given him	Ec 8:15	3117
all the **d** of your fleeting life which He	Ec 9:9	3117
for you will find it after many **d**.	Ec 11:1	3117
him remember the **d** of darkness,	Ec 11:8	3117
during the **d** of young manhood.	Ec 11:9	3117
Creator in the **d** of your youth,	Ec 12:1	3117
before the evil **d** come and the	Ec 12:1	3117
come about that In the last **d** The	Is 2:2	3117
it came about in the **d** of Ahaz,	Is 7:1	3117
and on your father's house such **d**	Is 7:17	3117
And her **d** will not be prolonged.	Is 13:22	3117
years like the **d** of one king.	Is 23:15	3117
many **d** they *will be* punished.	Is 24:22	3117
d to come Jacob will take root,	Is 27:6	
like the light of seven **d**,	Is 30:26	3117
Within a year and *a few* **d** You	Is 32:10	3117
d Hezekiah became mortally ill.	Is 38:1	3117
d of our life at the house of the LORD.	Is 38:20	3117
the **d** are coming when all that is	Is 39:6	3117
will be peace and truth in my **d**."	Is 39:8	3117
Awake as in the **d** of old, the	Is 51:9	3117
offspring, He will prolong *His* **d**,	Is 53:10	3117
this is like the **d** of Noah to Me,	Is 54:9	3117
And the **d** of your mourning will be	Is 60:20	3117
and carried them all the **d** of old.	Is 63:9	3117
people remembered the **d** of old,	Is 63:11	3117
For from **d** of old they have not heard	Is 64:4	5769
an infant *who lives but a few* **d**,	Is 65:20	3117
man who does not live out his **d**;	Is 65:20	3117
so will be the **d** of My people,	Is 65:22	3117
the LORD came in the **d** of Josiah the	Jer 1:2	3117
came also in the **d** of Jehoiakim the	Jer 1:3	3117
forgotten Me **D** without number.	Jer 2:32	3117
to me in the **d** of Josiah the king,	Jer 3:6	3117
"It shall be in those **d** when	Jer 3:16	3117
"In those **d** the house of Judah	Jer 3:18	3117
"Yet even in those **d**,"	Jer 5:18	3117
"Therefore, behold, **d** are coming,"	Jer 7:32	3117
"Behold, the **d** are coming,"	Jer 9:25	3117
many **d** the LORD said to me,	Jer 13:6	3117
"Therefore behold, **d** are coming,"	Jer 16:14	3117
of his **d** it will forsake him,	Jer 17:11	3117
therefore, behold, **d** are coming,"	Jer 19:6	3117
my **d** have been spent in shame?	Jer 20:18	3117
man who will not prosper in his **d**;	Jer 22:30	3117
"Behold, *the* **d** are coming,"	Jer 23:5	3117
"In His **d** Judah will be saved,	Jer 23:6	3117
behold, *the* **d** are coming,"	Jer 23:7	3117
In the last **d** you will clearly	Jer 23:20	3117
For the **d** of your slaughter and	Jer 25:34	3117
the **d** of Hezekiah king of Judah;	Jer 26:18	3117
'For behold, **d** are coming,'	Jer 30:3	3117
latter **d** you will understand this.	Jer 30:24	3117
"Behold, **d** are coming,"	Jer 31:27	3117
those **d** they will not say again,	Jer 31:29	3117
"Behold, **d** are coming,"	Jer 31:31	3117
house of Israel after those **d**,"	Jer 31:33	3117
"Behold, **d** are coming,"	Jer 31:38	3117
"Behold, **d** are coming,' declares	Jer 33:14	3117
'In those **d** and at that time I	Jer 33:15	3117
'In those **d** Judah will be saved	Jer 33:16	3117
from the LORD in the **d** of Jehoiakim	Jer 35:1	3117
tents you shall dwell all your **d**,	Jer 35:7	3117
d in the land where you sojourn.'	Jer 35:7	3117
us, not to drink wine all our **d**,	Jer 35:8	3117
to you, from the **d** of Josiah,	Jer 36:2	3117
and Jeremiah stayed there many **d**.	Jer 37:16	3117
Now at the end of ten **d**	Jer 42:7	3117
be inhabited as in the **d** of old,"	Jer 46:26	3117
behold, the **d** are coming,"	Jer 48:12	3117
of Moab In the latter **d**,"	Jer 48:47	3117
behold, the **d** are coming,"	Jer 49:2	3117
about in the last **d** That I will restore	Jer 49:39	3117
"In those **d** and at that time,"	Jer 50:4	3117
'In those **d** and at that time,'	Jer 50:20	3117
d are coming When I will punish	Jer 51:47	3117
behold, the **d** are coming,"	Jer 51:52	3117
regularly all the **d** of his life.	Jer 52:33	3117
a daily portion all the **d** of his	Jer 52:34	3117
In the **d** of her affliction and	La 1:7	3117
things That were from the **d** of old	La 1:7	3117
Which He commanded from **d** of old.	La 2:17	3117
Our **d** were finished For our end	La 4:18	3117
Renew our **d** as of old,	La 5:21	3117
seven **d** where they were living,	Ezk 3:15	3117

At the end of seven **d**	**Ezk 3:16**	3117
number of **d** that you lie on it.	**Ezk 4:4**	3117
I have assigned you a number of **d**	**Ezk 4:5**	3117
three hundred and ninety **d**;	**Ezk 4:5**	3117
assigned it to you for forty **d**,	**Ezk 4:6**	3117
completed the **d** of your siege.	**Ezk 4:8**	3117
the **d** that you lie on your side,	**Ezk 4:9**	3117
side, three hundred and ninety **d**.	**Ezk 4:9**	3117
the **d** of the siege are completed.	**Ezk 5:2**	3117
'The **d** are long and every vision	**Ezk 12:22**	3117
"The **d** draw near as well as the	**Ezk 12:23**	3117
longer be delayed, for in your **d**,	**Ezk 12:25**	3117
not remember the **d** of your youth,	**Ezk 16:22**	3117
not remembered the **d** of your youth	**Ezk 16:43**	3117
with you in the **d** of your youth,	**Ezk 16:60**	3117
the **d** that I will deal with you?	**Ezk 22:14**	3117
remembering the **d** of her youth,	**Ezk 23:19**	3117
"After many **d** you will be summoned;	**Ezk 38:8**	3117
It shall come about in the last **d**	**Ezk 38:16**	3117
the one of whom I spoke in former **d**	**Ezk 38:17**	3117
who prophesied in those **d** for *many*	**Ezk 38:17**	3117
'For seven **d** you shall prepare	**Ezk 43:25**	3117
'For seven **d** they shall make	**Ezk 43:26**	3117
When they have completed the **d**,	**Ezk 43:27**	3117
seven **d** shall elapse for him.	**Ezk 44:26**	3117
the Passover, a feast of seven **d**;	**Ezk 45:21**	3117
"*During* the seven **d** of the	**Ezk 45:23**	3117
on every day of the seven **d**,	**Ezk 45:23**	3117
seven **d** for the sin offering,	**Ezk 45:25**	3117
shall be shut the six working **d**;	**Ezk 46:1**	3117
test your servants for ten **d**,	**Da 1:12**	3117
matter and tested them for ten **d**.	**Da 1:14**	3117
At the end of ten **d** their	**Da 1:15**	3117
Then at the end of the **d** which the	**Da 1:18**	3117
will take place in the latter **d**.	**Da 2:28**	3118
"In the **d** of those kings the	**Da 2:44**	3118
and in the **d** of your father,	**Da 5:11**	3118
besides you, O king, for thirty **d**,	**Da 6:7**	3118
besides you, O king, for thirty **d**,	**Da 6:12**	3118
the Ancient of **D** took *His* seat;	**Da 7:9**	3118
He came up to the Ancient of **D**	**Da 7:13**	3118
until the Ancient of **D** came and	**Da 7:22**	3118
to many **d** *in the future*."	**Da 8:26**	3117
was exhausted and sick for **d**.	**Da 8:27**	3117
In those **d**, I, Daniel, had been	**Da 10:2**	3117
withstanding me for twenty-one **d**;	**Da 10:13**	3117
to your people in the latter **d**,	**Da 10:14**	3117
pertains to the **d** yet *future*."	**Da 10:14**	3117
within a few **d** he will be shattered,	**Da 11:20**	3117
and by plunder for *many* **d**.	**Da 11:33**	3117
is set up, *there will be* 1,290 **d**.	**Da 12:11**	3117
and attains to the 1,335 **d**!	**Da 12:12**	3117
of Beeri, during the **d** of Uzziah,	**Hos 1:1**	3117
and during the **d** of Jeroboam the son	**Hos 1:1**	3117
will punish her for the **d** of the Baals	**Hos 2:13**	3117
there as in the **d** of her youth,	**Hos 2:15**	3117
"You shall stay with me for many **d**.	**Hos 3:3**	3117
for many **d** without king or prince,	**Hos 3:4**	3117
and to His goodness in the last **d**.	**Hos 3:5**	3117
"He will revive us after two **d**;	**Hos 6:2**	3117
The **d** of punishment have come, The	**Hos 9:7**	3117
The **d** of retribution have come;	**Hos 9:7**	3117
depravity As in the **d** of Gibeah;	**Hos 9:9**	3117
the **d** of Gibeah you have sinned,	**Hos 10:9**	3117
the **d** of the appointed festival.	**Hos 12:9**	3117
in your **d** Or in your fathers' days?	**Jl 1:2**	3117
your days Or in your fathers' **d**?	**Jl 1:2**	3117
pour out My Spirit in those **d**.	**Jl 2:29**	3117
in those **d** and at that time,	**Jl 3:1**	3117
in the **d** of Uzziah king of Judah,	**Am 1:1**	3117
in the **d** of Jeroboam son of Joash,	**Am 1:1**	3117
the **d** are coming upon you When	**Am 4:2**	3117
Your tithes every three **d**.	**Am 4:4**	3117
"Behold, **d** are coming,"	**Am 8:11**	3117
And rebuild it as in the **d** of old;	**Am 9:11**	3117
"Behold, **d** are coming,"	**Am 9:13**	3117
the fish three **d** and three nights.	**Jon 1:17**	3117
"Yet forty **d** and Nineveh will be	**Jon 3:4**	3117
of Moresheth in the **d** of Jotham,	**Mi 1:1**	3117
And it will come about in the last **d**	**Mi 4:1**	3117
ago, From the **d** of eternity."	**Mi 5:2**	3117
and Gilead As in the **d** of old.	**Mi 7:14**	3117
"As in the **d** when you came out	**Mi 7:15**	3117
our forefathers From the **d** of old.	**Mi 7:20**	3117
a pool of water throughout her **d**,	**Na 2:8**	3117
I am doing something in your **d**	**Hab 1:5**	3117
in the **d** of Josiah son of Amon,	**Zph 1:1**	3117
remnant of this people in those **d**,	**Zch 8:6**	3117
you who are listening in these **d**	**Zch 8:9**	3117
'For before those **d** there was no	**Zch 8:10**	3117
of this people as in the former **d**,'	**Zch 8:11**	3117
again purposed in these **d** to do good	**Zch 8:15**	3117
'In those **d** ten men from all the	**Zch 8:23**	3117
in the **d** of Uzziah king of Judah.	**Zch 14:5**	3117
d of old and as in former years.	**Mal 3:4**	3117
"From the **d** of your fathers you	**Mal 3:7**	3117
Judea in the **d** of Herod the king,	**Mt 2:1**	*2250*
in those **d** John the Baptist came,	**Mt 3:1**	*2250*
fasted forty **d** and forty nights,	**Mt 4:2**	*2250*
But the **d** will come when the	**Mt 9:15**	*2250*
"From the **d** of John the	**Mt 11:12**	*2250*
for just as JONAH WAS THREE **D** AND	**Mt 12:40**	*2250*
so will the Son of Man be three **d**	**Mt 12:40**	*2250*
three **d** and have nothing to eat;	**Mt 15:32**	*2250*
Six **d** later Jesus took with	**Mt 17:1**	*2250*
living in the **d** of our fathers,	**Mt 23:30**	*2250*
who are nursing babies in those **d**!	**Mt 24:19**	*2250*
Unless those **d** had been cut short,	**Mt 24:22**	*2250*
elect those **d** will be cut short.	**Mt 24:22**	*2250*
those **d** THE SUN WILL BE DARKENED,	**Mt 24:29**	*2250*
will be just like the **d** of Noah.	**Mt 24:37**	*2250*
"For as in those **d** before the flood	**Mt 24:38**	*2250*
after two **d** the Passover is coming,	**Mt 26:2**	*2250*
and to rebuild it in three **d**.' "	**Mt 26:61**	*2250*
temple and rebuild it in three **d**,	**Mt 27:40**	*2250*
'After three **d** I *am to* rise again.'	**Mt 27:63**	*2250*
In those **d** Jesus came	**Mk 1:9**	*2250*
forty **d** being tempted by Satan;	**Mk 1:13**	*2250*
to Capernaum several **d** afterward,	**Mk 2:1**	*2250*
"But the **d** will come when the	**Mk 2:20**	*2250*
In those **d**, when there was again a	**Mk 8:1**	*2250*
have remained with Me now three **d** and	**Mk 8:2**	*2250*
and after three **d** rise again.	**Mk 8:31**	*2250*
Six **d** later, Jesus took with	**Mk 9:2**	*2250*
He will rise three **d** later."	**Mk 9:31**	*2250*
and three **d** later He will rise again."	**Mk 10:34**	*2250*
those who are nursing babies in those **d**!	**Mk 13:17**	*2250*
"For those **d** will be a *time of*	**Mk 13:19**	*2250*
the Lord had shortened *those* **d**,	**Mk 13:20**	*2250*
whom He chose, He shortened the **d**.	**Mk 13:20**	*2250*
"But in those **d**, after that	**Mk 13:24**	*2250*
Unleavened Bread were two **d** away;	**Mk 14:1**	*2250*
and in three **d** I will build	**Mk 14:58**	*2250*
temple and rebuild it in three **d**,	**Mk 15:29**	*2250*
In the **d** of Herod, king of Judea,	**Lk 1:5**	*2250*
When the **d** of his priestly service	**Lk 1:23**	*2250*
After these **d** Elizabeth his	**Lk 1:24**	*2250*
d when He looked *with favor* upon *me*,	**Lk 1:25**	*2250*
before Him all our **d**.	**Lk 1:75**	*2250*
Now in those **d** a decree went out	**Lk 2:1**	*2250*
the **d** were completed for her to	**Lk 2:6**	*2250*
And when eight **d** had passed,	**Lk 2:21**	*2250*
And when the **d** for their	**Lk 2:22**	*2250*
spending the full number of **d**,	**Lk 2:43**	*2250*
after three **d** they found Him in the	**Lk 2:46**	*2250*
for forty **d**, being tempted by the	**Lk 4:2**	*2250*
And He ate nothing during those **d**,	**Lk 4:2**	*2250*
in Israel in the **d** of Elijah,	**Lk 4:25**	*2250*
"But *the* **d** will come;	**Lk 5:35**	*2250*
then they will fast in those **d**."	**Lk 5:35**	*2250*
Now on one of *those* **d**	**Lk 8:22**	*2250*
Some eight **d** after these sayings,	**Lk 9:28**	*2250*
and reported to no one in those **d** any	**Lk 9:36**	*2250*
When the **d** were approaching for	**Lk 9:51**	*2250*
six **d** in which work should be done;	**Lk 13:14**	*2250*
"And not many **d** later, the	**Lk 15:13**	*2250*
"The **d** will come when you will	**Lk 17:22**	*2250*
one of the **d** of the Son of Man,	**Lk 17:22**	*2250*
as it happened in the **d** of Noah,	**Lk 17:26**	*2250*
also in the **d** of the Son of Man:	**Lk 17:26**	*2250*
same as happened in the **d** of Lot:	**Lk 17:28**	*2250*
"For the **d** will come upon you	**Lk 19:43**	*2250*
On one of the **d**	**Lk 20:1**	*2250*
the **d** will come in which there	**Lk 21:6**	*2250*
because these are **d** of vengeance,	**Lk 21:22**	*2250*
those who are nursing babies in those **d**;	**Lk 21:23**	*2250*
d are coming when they will say,	**Lk 23:29**	*2250*
have happened here in these **d**?"	**Lk 24:18**	*2250*
and they stayed there a few **d**.	**Jn 2:12**	*2250*
in three **d** I will raise it up."	**Jn 2:19**	*2250*
will You raise it up in three **d**?"	**Jn 2:20**	*2250*
and He stayed there two **d**.	**Jn 4:40**	*2250*
After the two **d** He went forth	**Jn 4:43**	*2250*
He then stayed two **d** *longer* in the	**Jn 11:6**	*2250*
already been in the tomb four **d**.	**Jn 11:17**	*2250*
for he has been *dead* four **d**."	**Jn 11:39**	*5066b*
six **d** before the Passover,	**Jn 12:1**	*2250*
After eight **d** His	**Jn 20:26**	*2250*
to them over *a period of* forty **d** and	**Ac 1:3**	*2250*
Holy Spirit not many **d** from now."	**Ac 1:5**	*2250*
'AND IT SHALL BE IN THE LAST **D**,'	**Ac 2:17**	*2250*
I WILL IN THOSE **D** POUR FORTH	**Ac 2:18**	*2250*
onward, also announced these **d**.	**Ac 3:24**	*2250*
rose up in the **d** of the census and	**Ac 5:37**	*2250*
And he was three **d** without sight,	**Ac 9:9**	*2250*
Now for several **d** he was with the	**Ac 9:19**	*2250*
When many **d** had elapsed, the	**Ac 9:23**	*2250*
stayed many **d** in Joppa with a tanner	**Ac 9:43**	*2250*
"Four **d** ago to this hour, I was	**Ac 10:30**	*2250*
asked him to stay on for a few **d**.	**Ac 10:48**	*2250*
during the **d** of Unleavened Bread.	**Ac 12:3**	*2250*
and for many **d** He appeared to	**Ac 13:31**	*2250*
ACCOMPLISHING A WORK IN YOUR **D**,	**Ac 13:41**	*2250*
in the early **d** God made a choice	**Ac 15:7**	*2250*
some **d** Paul said to Barnabas,	**Ac 15:36**	*2250*
staying in this city for some **d**.	**Ac 16:12**	*2250*
continued doing this for many **d**.	**Ac 16:18**	*2250*
having remained many **d** longer,	**Ac 18:18**	*2250*
after the **d** of Unleavened Bread,	**Ac 20:6**	*2250*
to them at Troas within five **d**;	**Ac 20:6**	*2250*
and there we stayed seven **d**.	**Ac 20:6**	*2250*
we stayed there seven **d**;	**Ac 21:4**	*2250*
When our **d** there were ended,	**Ac 21:5**	*2250*
we were staying there for some **d**,	**Ac 21:10**	*2250*
After these **d** we got ready and	**Ac 21:15**	*2250*
of the **d** of purification,	**Ac 21:26**	*2250*
When the seven **d** were almost over,	**Ac 21:27**	*2250*
After five **d** the high priest	**Ac 24:1**	*2250*
twelve **d** ago I went up to Jerusalem	**Ac 24:11**	*2250*
But some **d** later Felix arrived	**Ac 24:24**	*2250*
three **d** later went up to Jerusalem	**Ac 25:1**	*2250*
spent not more than eight or ten **d**	**Ac 25:6**	*2250*
Now when several **d** had elapsed,	**Ac 25:13**	*2250*
they were spending many **d** there,	**Ac 25:14**	*2250*
sailed slowly for a good many **d**,	**Ac 27:7**	*2250*
sun nor stars appeared for many **d**,	**Ac 27:20**	*2250*
entertained us courteously three **d**.	**Ac 28:7**	*2250*
we stayed there for three **d**.	**Ac 28:12**	*2250*
to stay with them for seven **d**;	**Ac 28:14**	*2250*
After three **d** Paul called together those	**Ac 28:17**	*2250*
and stayed with him fifteen **d**.	**Ga 1:18**	*2250*
You observe **d** and months and	**Ga 4:10**	*2250*
your time, because the **d** are evil.	**Eph 5:16**	*2250*
last **d** difficult times will come.	**2Tm 3:1**	*2250*
d has spoken to us in His Son,	**Heb 1:2**	*2250*
In the **d** of His flesh, He offered	**Heb 5:7**	*2250*
beginning of **d** nor end of life,	**Heb 7:3**	*2250*
"BEHOLD, **D** ARE COMING, SAYS THE	**Heb 8:8**	*2250*
HOUSE OF ISRAEL AFTER THOSE **D**,	**Heb 8:10**	*2250*
MAKE WITH THEM AFTER THOSE **D**,	**Heb 10:16**	*2250*
But remember the former **d**,	**Heb 10:32**	*2250*
had been encircled for seven **d**.	**Heb 11:30**	*2250*
It is in the last **d** that you have	**Jas 5:3**	*2250*
DESIRES LIFE, TO LOVE AND SEE GOOD **D**,	**1Pe 3:10**	*2250*
God kept waiting in the **d** of Noah,	**1Pe 3:20**	*2250*
that in the last **d** mockers will	**2Pe 3:3**	*2250*
you will have tribulation for ten **d**.	**Rv 2:10**	*2250*
faith even in the **d** of Antipas,	**Rv 2:13**	*2250*
And in those **d** men will seek death	**Rv 9:6**	*2250*
but in the **d** of the voice of the	**Rv 10:7**	*2250*
for twelve hundred and sixty **d**,	**Rv 11:3**	*2250*
during the **d** of their prophesying;	**Rv 11:6**	*2250*
bodies for three and a half **d**,	**Rv 11:9**	*2250*
But after the three and a half **d**	**Rv 11:11**	*2250*
thousand two hundred and sixty **d**.	**Rv 12:6**	*2250*

DAYS'

a distance of three **d** journey	**Gn 30:36**	3117
a distance of seven **d** journey,	**Gn 31:23**	3117
let us go a three **d** journey into	**Ex 3:18**	3117
let us go a three **d** journey into	**Ex 5:3**	3117
"We must go a three **d** journey into	**Ex 8:27**	3117
of the LORD three **d** journey,	**Nu 10:33**	3117
and they went three **d** journey in	**Nu 33:8**	3117
It is eleven **d** *journey* from	**Dt 1:2**	3117
there be three **d** pestilence	**2Sa 24:13**	3117
made a circuit of seven **d** journey,	**2Ki 3:9**	3117
great city, a three **d** walk.	**Jon 3:3**	3117

DAYTIME

it remained in the **d** and at night,	**Nu 9:21**	3119
His lovingkindness in the **d**;	**Ps 42:8**	3119
it a pleasure to revel in the **d**.	**2Pe 2:13**	*2250*
In the **d**	**Rv 21:25**	*2250*

DAZZLING

"My beloved is **d** and ruddy,	**SS 5:10**	6703
Like **d** heat in the sunshine,	**Is 18:4**	6703
stood near them in **d** clothing;	**Lk 24:4**	*797*

DEACONS

including the overseers and **d**:	**Php 1:1**	*1249*
D likewise *must be* men of dignity,	**1Tm 3:8**	*1249*
as **d** if they are beyond reproach.	**1Tm 3:10**	*1247*
D must be husbands of *only* one	**1Tm 3:12**	*1249*
For those who have served well as **d**	**1Tm 3:13**	*1247*

DEAD

you are a **d** man because of the	**Gn 20:3**	4191
Abraham rose from before his **d**,	**Gn 23:3**	4191
I may bury my **d** out of my sight."	**Gn 23:4**	4191
bury your **d** in the choicest of our	**Gn 23:6**	4191
his grave for burying your **d**."	**Gn 23:6**	4191
me to bury my **d** out of my sight,	**Gn 23:8**	4191
people I give it to you; bury your **d**."	**Gn 23:11**	4191
me that I may bury my **d** there."	**Gn 23:13**	4191
So bury your **d**."	**Gn 23:15**	4191
for his brother is **d**,	**Gn 42:38**	4191
Now his brother is **d**,	**Gn 44:20**	4191
saw that their father was **d**,	**Gn 50:15**	4191
were seeking your life are **d**."	**Ex 4:19**	4191
one of the livestock of Israel **d**.	**Ex 9:7**	4191
where there was not someone **d**.	**Ex 12:30**	4191
"We will all be **d**."	**Ex 12:33**	4191
the Egyptians **d** on the seashore.	**Ex 14:30**	4191
and the **d** *animal* shall become his.	**Ex 21:34**	4191
also they shall divide the **d** *ox*.	**Ex 21:35**	4191
and the **d** *animal* shall become his.	**Ex 21:36**	4191
touches them when they are **d**	**Lv 11:31**	4194
may fall when they are **d** becomes	**Lv 11:32**	4194
any cuts in your body for the **d** nor	**Lv 19:28**	5315
'No one shall defile himself for a **d**	**Lv 21:1**	
shall he approach any **d** person,	**Lv 21:11**	4191
who is unclean because of a **d**	**Nu 5:2**	
shall not go near to a **d** person.	**Nu 6:6**	4191
concerning his sin because of the **d**	**Nu 6:11**	
unclean because of *the* **d** person,	**Nu 9:6**	5315
unclean because of *the* **d** person,	**Nu 9:7**	5315
becomes unclean because of a **d**	**Nu 9:10**	
"Oh, do not let her be like one **d**,	**Nu 12:12**	4191
between the **d** and the living,	**Nu 16:48**	4191
forehead for the sake of the **d**.	**Dt 14:1**	4191
or one who calls up the **d**.	**Dt 18:11**	4191
assume the name of his **d** brother,	**Dt 25:6**	4191
nor offered any of it to the **d**.	**Dt 26:14**	4191
"Moses My servant is **d**;	**Jos 1:2**	4191
master had fallen to the floor **d**.	**Jg 3:25**	4191
and behold Sisera was lying **d** with	**Jg 4:22**	4191
Where he bowed, there he fell **d**.	**Jg 5:27**	7703
about, as soon as Gideon was **d**,	**Jg 8:33**	4191
Israel saw that Abimelech was **d**,	**Jg 9:55**	4191
So the **d** whom he killed at his	**Jg 16:30**	4191
have dealt with the **d** and with me.	**Ru 1:8**	4191
to the living and to the **d**."	**Ru 2:20**	4191
also, Hophni and Phinehas, are **d**,	**1Sa 4:17**	4191
And I will give the **d** bodies of	**1Sa 17:46**	6297
saw that their champion was **d**,	**1Sa 17:51**	4191
A **d** dog, a single flea?	**1Sa 24:14**	4191
When David heard that Nabal was **d**,	**1Sa 25:39**	4191
Now Samuel was **d**, and all Israel	**1Sa 28:3**	4191
armor bearer saw that Saul was **d**,	**1Sa 31:5**	4191

Context	Reference	Number
and that Saul and his sons were **d**,	**1Sa 31:7**	4191
the people have fallen and are **d**;	**2Sa 1:4**	4191
and Jonathan his son are **d** also."	**2Sa 1:4**	4191
Saul and his son Jonathan are **d**?"	**2Sa 1:5**	4191
for Saul your lord is **d**,	**2Sa 2:7**	4191
'Behold, Saul is **d**,' and thought	**2Sa 4:10**	4191
should regard a **d** dog like me?"	**2Sa 9:8**	4191
Uriah the Hittite is **d** also.' "	**2Sa 11:21**	4191
some of the king's servants are **d**,	**2Sa 11:24**	4191
Uriah the Hittite is also **d**."	**2Sa 11:24**	4191
that Uriah her husband was **d**,	**2Sa 11:26**	4191
to tell him that the child was **d**,	**2Sa 12:18**	4191
we tell him that the child is **d**,	**2Sa 12:18**	4191
perceived that the child was **d**;	**2Sa 12:19**	4191
"Is the child **d**?"	**2Sa 12:19**	4191
child dead?" And they said, "He is **d**	**2Sa 12:19**	4191
king's sons, for Amnon alone is **d**;	**2Sa 13:32**	4191
'all the king's sons are **d**,'	**2Sa 13:33**	4191
are dead,' for only Amnon is **d**."	**2Sa 13:33**	4191
concerning Amnon, since he was **d**.	**2Sa 13:39**	4191
been mourning for the **d** many days;	**2Sa 14:2**	4191
I am a widow, for my husband is **d**.	**2Sa 14:5**	4191
this **d** dog curse my lord the king?	**2Sa 16:9**	4191
because the king's son is **d**."	**2Sa 18:20**	4191
alive and all of us were **d** today,	**2Sa 19:6**	4191
but **d** men before my lord the king;	**2Sa 19:28**	4194
and laid her **d** son in my bosom	**1Ki 3:20**	4191
to nurse my son, behold, he was **d**;	**1Ki 3:21**	4191
son, and the **d** one is your son."	**1Ki 3:22**	4191
For the **d** one is your son, and the	**1Ki 3:22**	4191
and your son is the **d** one';	**1Ki 3:23**	4191
For your son is the **d** one,	**1Ki 3:23**	4191
the commander of the army was **d**,	**1Ki 11:21**	4191
has been stoned and is **d**."	**1Ki 21:14**	4191
Naboth had been stoned and was **d**,	**1Ki 21:15**	4191
for Naboth is not alive, but **d**."	**1Ki 21:15**	4191
When Ahab heard that Naboth was **d**,	**1Ki 21:16**	4191
"Your servant my husband is **d**,	**2Ki 4:1**	4191
the lad was **d** and laid on his bed.	**2Ki 4:32**	4191
restored to life the one who was **d**,	**2Ki 8:5**	4191
of Ahaziah saw that her son was **d**,	**2Ki 11:1**	4191
behold, all of them were **d**.	**2Ki 19:35**	4191, 6297
armor bearer saw that Saul was **d**,	**1Ch 10:5**	4191
and that Saul and his sons were **d**,	**1Ch 10:7**	4191
of Ahaziah saw that her son was **d**,	**2Ch 22:10**	4191
I am forgotten as a **d** man,	**Ps 31:12**	4191
horse were cast into a **d** sleep.	**Ps 76:6**	7290a
They have given the **d** bodies of	**Ps 79:2**	5038
Forsaken among the **d**,	**Ps 88:5**	4191
You perform wonders for the **d**?	**Ps 88:10**	4191
ate sacrifices offered to the **d**.	**Ps 106:28**	4191
The **d** do not praise the LORD, Nor	**Ps 115:17**	4191
like those who have long been **d**.	**Ps 143:3**	4191
And her tracks *lead* to the **d**;	**Pr 2:18**	7496
not know that the **d** are there,	**Pr 9:18**	7496
rest in the assembly of the **d**.	**Pr 21:16**	7496
So I congratulated the **d** who are	**Ec 4:2**	4191
are already **d** more than the living	**Ec 4:2**	4191
Afterwards they *go* to the **d**.	**Ec 9:3**	4191
live dog is better than a **d** lion.	**Ec 9:4**	4191
but the **d** do not know anything,	**Ec 9:5**	4191
D flies make a perfumer's oil stink	**Ec 10:1**	4194
the **d** on behalf of the living?	**Is 8:19**	4191
for you the spirits of the **d**,	**Is 14:9**	7496
to idols and ghosts of the **d** And	**Is 19:3**	330b
The **d** will not live, the departed	**Is 26:14**	4191
Your **d** will live;	**Is 26:19**	4191
behold, all of these were **d**.	**Is 37:36**	4191, 6297
are vigorous *we are* like **d** men.	**Is 59:10**	4191
"The **d** bodies of this people	**Jer 7:33**	5038
them, to comfort anyone for the **d**,	**Jer 16:7**	4191
Do not weep for the **d** or mourn	**Jer 22:10**	4191
and cast his **d** body into the	**Jer 26:23**	5038
of the **d** bodies and of the ashes,	**Jer 31:40**	6297
And their **d** bodies will be food	**Jer 34:20**	5038
and his **d** body shall be cast out	**Jer 36:30**	5038
Like those who have long been **d**.	**La 3:6**	4191
"I will also lay the **d** bodies of	**Ezk 6:5**	6297
make no mourning for the **d**.	**Ezk 24:17**	4191
a **d** person to defile *themselves;*	**Ezk 44:25**	4191
And countless **d** bodies	**Na 3:3**	1472a
They stumble over the **d** bodies!	**Na 3:3**	1472a
sought the Child's life are **d**."	**Mt 2:20**	2348
the **d** to bury their own dead."	**Mt 8:22**	3498
the dead to bury their own **d**."	**Mt 8:22**	3498
"Heal *the* sick, raise *the* **d**,	**Mt 10:8**	3498
hear, *the* **d** are raised up,	**Mt 11:5**	3498
he has risen from the **d**,	**Mt 14:2**	3498
Son of Man has risen from the **d**."	**Mt 17:9**	3498
the resurrection of the **d**,	**Mt 22:31**	3498
He is not the God of the **d** but of the	**Mt 22:32**	3498
but inside they are full of **d**	**Mt 23:27**	3498
'He has risen from the **d**,'	**Mt 27:64**	3498
of him and became like **d** men.	**Mt 28:4**	3498
that He has risen from the **d**;	**Mt 28:7**	3498
the Baptist has risen from the **d**,	**Mk 6:14**	3498
Son of Man rose from the **d**.	**Mk 9:9**	3498
what rising from the **d** meant.	**Mk 9:10**	3498
most *of them* said, "He is **d**!"	**Mk 9:26**	599
"For when they rise from the **d**,	**Mk 12:25**	3498
the fact that the **d** rise again,	**Mk 12:26**	3498
"He is not the God of the **d**,	**Mk 12:27**	3498
wondered if He was **d** by this time,	**Mk 15:44**	2348
as to whether He was already **d**.	**Mk 15:44**	599
a **d** man was being carried out,	**Lk 7:12**	2348
The **d** man sat up and began to	**Lk 7:15**	3498
deaf hear, *the* **d** are raised up,	**Lk 7:22**	3498
that John had risen from the **d**,	**Lk 9:7**	3498
the **d** to bury their own dead;	**Lk 9:60**	3498
the dead to bury their own **d**;	**Lk 9:60**	3498
and went away leaving him half **d**.	**Lk 10:30**	2253
for this son of mine was **d** and	**Lk 15:24**	3498
this brother of yours was **d** and *has*	**Lk 15:32**	3498
someone goes to them from the **d**,	**Lk 16:30**	3498
if someone rises from the **d**.' "	**Lk 16:31**	3498
and the resurrection from the **d**,	**Lk 20:35**	3498
"But that the **d** are raised, even	**Lk 20:37**	3498
"Now He is not the God of the **d** but	**Lk 20:38**	3498
seek the living One among the **d**?	**Lk 24:5**	3498
again from the **d** the third day,	**Lk 24:46**	3498
He was raised from the **d**,	**Jn 2:22**	3498
raises the **d** and gives them life,	**Jn 5:21**	3498
when the **d** will hear the voice of	**Jn 5:25**	3498
said to them plainly, "Lazarus is **d**,	**Jn 11:14**	599
for he has been **d** four days."	**Jn 11:39**	
whom Jesus had raised from the **d**.	**Jn 12:1**	3498
whom He raised from the **d**.	**Jn 12:9**	3498
tomb and raised him from the **d**,	**Jn 12:17**	3498
they saw that He was already **d**,	**Jn 19:33**	2348
He must rise again from the **d**.	**Jn 20:9**	3498
after He was raised from the **d**.	**Jn 21:14**	3498
one whom God raised from the **d**,	**Ac 3:15**	3498
Jesus the resurrection from the **d**.	**Ac 4:2**	3498
whom God raised from the **d**—	**Ac 4:10**	3498
young men came in and found her **d**,	**Ac 5:10**	3498
Him after He arose from the **d**.	**Ac 10:41**	3498
as Judge of the living and the **d**.	**Ac 10:42**	3498
"But God raised Him from the **d**;	**Ac 13:30**	3498
that He raised Him up from the **d**,	**Ac 13:34**	3498
the city, supposing him to be **d**.	**Ac 14:19**	2348
suffer and rise again from the **d**,	**Ac 17:3**	3498
men by raising Him from the **d**."	**Ac 17:31**	3498
of the resurrection of the **d**,	**Ac 17:32**	3498
third floor and was picked up **d**.	**Ac 20:9**	3498
hope and resurrection of the **d**!"	**Ac 23:6**	3498
'For the resurrection of the **d** I	**Ac 24:21**	3498
and about a **d** man,	**Ac 25:19**	2348
people if God does raise the **d**?	**Ac 26:8**	3498
reason of *His* resurrection from the **d**	**Ac 26:23**	3498
swell up or suddenly fall down **d**.	**Ac 28:6**	3498
by the resurrection from the **d**,	**Ro 1:4**	3498
who gives life to the **d** and calls	**Ro 4:17**	3498
now as good as **d** since he was	**Ro 4:19**	3499
raised Jesus our Lord from the **d**,	**Ro 4:24**	3498
Christ was raised from the **d** through	**Ro 6:4**	3498
having been raised from the **d**,	**Ro 6:9**	3498
consider yourselves to be **d** to sin,	**Ro 6:11**	3498
to God as those alive from the **d**,	**Ro 6:13**	3498
to Him who was raised from the **d**,	**Ro 7:4**	3498
for apart from the Law sin *is* **d**.	**Ro 7:8**	3498
the body is **d** because of sin,	**Ro 8:10**	3498
Jesus from the **d** dwells in you,	**Ro 8:11**	3498
He who raised Christ Jesus from the **d**	**Ro 8:11**	3498
to bring Christ up from the **d**)."	**Ro 10:7**	3498
that God raised Him from the **d**,	**Ro 10:9**	3498
acceptance be but life from the **d**?	**Ro 11:15**	3498
both of the **d** and of the living.	**Ro 14:9**	3498
but if her husband is **d**,	**1Co 7:39**	2837
He has been raised from the **d**,	**1Co 15:12**	3498
there is no resurrection of the **d**?	**1Co 15:12**	3498
there is no resurrection of the **d**,	**1Co 15:13**	3498
if in fact the **d** are not raised.	**1Co 15:15**	3498
For if the **d** are not raised, not	**1Co 15:16**	3498
Christ has been raised from the **d**,	**1Co 15:20**	3498
came the resurrection of the **d**.	**1Co 15:21**	3498
do who are baptized for the **d**?	**1Co 15:29**	3498
If the **d** are not raised at all,	**1Co 15:29**	3498
If the **d** are not raised, LET US	**1Co 15:32**	3498
"How are the **d** raised?	**1Co 15:35**	3498
also is the resurrection of the **d**.	**1Co 15:42**	3498
the **d** will be raised imperishable,	**1Co 15:52**	3498
but in God who raises the **d**;	**2Co 1:9**	3498
Father, who raised Him from the **d**),	**Ga 1:1**	3498
when He raised Him from the **d** and	**Eph 1:20**	3498
d in your trespasses and sins,	**Eph 2:1**	3498
we were **d** in our transgressions,	**Eph 2:5**	3498
sleeper, And arise from the **d**,	**Eph 5:14**	3498
to the resurrection from the **d**.	**Php 3:11**	3498
the firstborn from the **d**,	**Col 1:18**	3498
of God, who raised Him from the **d**.	**Col 2:12**	3498
When you were **d** in your	**Col 2:13**	3498
earthly body as **d** to immorality,	**Col 3:5**	3499
heaven, whom He raised from the **d**,	**1Th 1:10**	3498
the **d** in Christ will rise first.	**1Th 4:16**	3498
is **d** even while she lives.	**1Tm 5:6**	2348
Jesus Christ, risen from the **d**,	**2Tm 2:8**	3498
is to judge the living and the **d**,	**2Tm 4:1**	3498
d works and of faith toward God,	**Heb 6:1**	3498
and the resurrection of the **d** and	**Heb 6:2**	3498
cleanse your conscience from **d** works	**Heb 9:14**	3498
is valid *only* when men are **d**,	**Heb 9:17**	3498
and through faith, though he is **d**,	**Heb 11:4**	599
man, and him as good as **d** at that,	**Heb 11:12**	3499
able to raise *people* even from the **d**	**Heb 11:19**	3498
Women received *back* their **d** by	**Heb 11:35**	3498
who brought up from the **d** the	**Heb 13:20**	3498
faith, if it has no works, is **d**,	**Jas 2:17**	3498
the body without *the* spirit is **d**,	**Jas 2:26**	3498
so also faith without works is **d**.	**Jas 2:26**	3498
of Jesus Christ from the **d**,	**1Pe 1:3**	3498
God, who raised Him from the **d** and	**1Pe 1:21**	3498
to judge the living and the **d**.	**1Pe 4:5**	3498
preached even to those who are **d**,	**1Pe 4:6**	3498
trees without fruit, doubly **d**,	**Jude 1:12**	599
witness, the firstborn of the **d**,	**Rv 1:5**	3498
I fell at His feet like a **d** man.	**Rv 1:17**	3498
I was **d**, and behold, I am alive	**Rv 1:18**	3498
The first and the last, who was **d**,	**Rv 2:8**	3498
that you are alive, but you are **d**.	**Rv 3:1**	3498
And their **d** bodies *will lie* in the	**Rv 11:8**	4430
nations *will* look at their **d** bodies	**Rv 11:9**	4430
their **d** bodies to be laid in a tomb.	**Rv 11:9**	4430
time *came* for the **d** to be judged,	**Rv 11:18**	3498
'Blessed are the **d** who die in the	**Rv 14:13**	3498
became blood like *that* of a **d** man;	**Rv 16:3**	3498
The rest of the **d** did not come to	**Rv 20:5**	3498
And I saw the **d**, the great and the	**Rv 20:12**	3498
and the **d** were judged from the	**Rv 20:12**	3498
gave up the **d** which were in it,	**Rv 20:13**	3498
gave up the **d** which were in them;	**Rv 20:13**	3498

DEADLY

Context	Reference	Number
or with any **d** object of stone, and	**Nu 35:23**	834, 4191
And the **d** poison of cobras.	**Dt 32:33**	393
a **d** confusion throughout the city;	**1Sa 5:11**	4194
prepared for Himself **d** weapons;	**Ps 7:13**	4194
who despoil me, My **d** enemies who	**Ps 17:9**	5315
And from the **d** pestilence.	**Ps 91:3**	1942
"Their tongue is a **d** arrow;	**Jer 9:8**	7819
"They will die of **d** diseases,	**Jer 16:4**	4463
All their **d** designs against me;	**Jer 18:23**	4194
"When I send against them the **d**	**Ezk 5:16**	7451a
and if they drink any **d** *poison,*	**Mk 16:18**	2286
evil *and* full of **d** poison.	**Jas 3:8**	2287

DEADNESS

Context	Reference	Number
old, and the **d** of Sarah's womb;	**Ro 4:19**	3500

DEAF

Context	Reference	Number
Or who makes *him* mute or **d**,	**Ex 4:11**	2795
'You shall not curse a **d** man,	**Lv 19:14**	2795
My rock, do not be **d** to me,	**Ps 28:1**	2790b
But I, like a **d** man, do not hear;	**Ps 38:13**	2795
a **d** cobra that stops up its ear,	**Ps 58:4**	2795
the **d** will hear words of a book,	**Is 29:18**	2795
ears of the **d** will be unstopped.	**Is 35:5**	2795
Hear, you **d**! And look, you blind,	**Is 42:18**	2795
so **d** as My messenger whom I send?	**Is 42:19**	2795
the **d**, even though they have ears.	**Is 43:8**	2795
their mouth, Their ears will be **d**.	**Mi 7:16**	2790b
are cleansed and *the* **d** hear,	**Mt 11:5**	2974
was **d** and spoke with difficulty,	**Mk 7:32**	2974
He makes even the **d** to hear and	**Mk 7:37**	2974
"You **d** and mute spirit, I command	**Mk 9:25**	2974
are cleansed, and *the* **d** hear,	**Lk 7:22**	2974

DEAL

Context	Reference	Number
Judge of all the earth **d** justly?"	**Gn 18:25**	6213a
you will not **d** falsely with me or	**Gn 21:23**	8266
if you are going to **d** kindly and truly	**Gn 24:49**	6213a
d with me in kindness and faithfulness	**Gn 47:29**	6213a
"Come, let us **d** wisely with them,	**Ex 1:10**	2449
you **d** this way with your servants?	**Ex 5:15**	6213a
only do not let Pharaoh **d**	**Ex 8:29**	8524
he shall **d** with her according to	**Ex 21:9**	6213a
shall not steal, nor **d** falsely,	**Lv 19:11**	8266
Thus you shall **d** with the Levites	**Nu 8:26**	6213a
You are going to **d** thus with me,	**Nu 11:15**	6213a
that you also will **d** kindly with	**Jos 2:12**	6213a
will **d** kindly and faithfully with you."	**Jos 2:14**	6213a
May the LORD **d** kindly with you as	**Ru 1:8**	6213a
d kindly with your servant,	**1Sa 20:8**	6213a
"**D** gently for my sake with	**2Sa 18:5**	
hands, for they **d** faithfully."	**2Ki 22:7**	6213a
also a great **d** of spoil from them,	**2Ch 28:8**	7227a
Those who **d** treacherously without	**Ps 25:3**	898
D with them as with Midian, As	**Ps 83:9**	6213a
Nor **d** falsely in My faithfulness.	**Ps 89:33**	8266
To **d** craftily with His servants.	**Ps 105:25**	5230
d *kindly* with me for Your name's	**Ps 109:21**	6213a
D bountifully with Your servant,	**Ps 119:17**	1580
D with Your servant according to	**Ps 119:124**	6213a
You will **d** bountifully with me."	**Ps 142:7**	1580
who **d** faithfully are His delight.	**Pr 12:22**	6213a
The treacherous **d** treacherously,	**Is 24:16**	898
And the treacherous **d** very	**Is 24:16**	898
d marvelously with this people,	**Is 29:14**	6381
did not **d** treacherously with him.	**Is 33:1**	898
you cease to **d** treacherously,	**Is 33:1**	898
will **d** treacherously with you.	**Is 33:1**	898
you would **d** very treacherously;	**Is 48:8**	898
Sons who will not **d** falsely."	**Is 63:8**	8266
those who **d** in treachery at ease?	**Jer 12:1**	898
d with you as this potter *does?*"	**Jer 18:6**	6213a
D with them in the time of Your	**Jer 18:23**	6213a
perhaps the LORD will **d** with us	**Jer 21:2**	6213a
d with him just as he tells you."	**Jer 39:12**	6213a
And **d** with them as You have dealt	**La 1:22**	5953a
their conduct I will **d** with them,	**Ezk 7:27**	6213a
I indeed will **d** in wrath.	**Ezk 8:18**	6213a
My ordinances so as to **d** faithfully	**Ezk 18:9**	6213a
the days that I will **d** with you?	**Ezk 22:14**	6213a
that they may **d** with you in wrath.	**Ezk 23:25**	6213a
They will **d** with you in hatred,	**Ezk 23:29**	6213a
in order to **d** in your merchandise.	**Ezk 27:9**	6148
he will thoroughly **d** with it.	**Ezk 31:11**	6213a
"I will **d** *with you* according to	**Ezk 35:11**	6213a
and **d** with your servants according	**Da 1:13**	6213a
and he will **d** with them and	**Da 11:7**	6213a
of Samaria, For they **d** falsely;	**Hos 7:1**	6466
On those who **d** treacherously?	**Hab 1:13**	898
I am going to **d** at that time With	**Zph 3:19**	6213a
Why do we **d** treacherously each	**Mal 2:10**	898
and let no one **d** treacherously	**Mal 2:15**	898
that you do not **d** treacherously."	**Mal 2:16**	898
he can **d** gently with the ignorant	**Heb 5:2**	3356

Context	Reference	Number
DEALERS		
of seams, your **d** in merchandise And	**Ezk 27:27**	6148
go instead to the **d** and buy *some*	**Mt 25:9**	*4453*
DEALING		
you have law courts **d** with matters	**1Co 6:4**	
d out retribution to those who do	**2Th 1:8**	*1325*
DEALINGS		
and had no **d** with anyone.	**Jg 18:7**	1697
and they had no **d** with anyone,	**Jg 18:28**	1697
man was harsh and evil in *his* **d**,	**1Sa 25:3**	4611
d will return on your own head.	**Ob 1:15**	1576
Jews have no **d** with Samaritans.)	**Jn 4:9**	*4798*
seen the outcome of the Lord's **d**,	**Jas 5:11**	
DEALS		
and he **d** with him violently or	**Dt 24:7**	6014b
When the LORD **d** well with my lord,	**1Sa 25:31**	3190
one *still* **d** treacherously,	**Is 21:2**	898
He **d** unjustly in the land of	**Is 26:10**	5765
to the priest Everyone **d** falsely.	**Jer 6:13**	6213a
Because every brother **d** craftily,	**Jer 9:4**	6117
God **d** with you as with sons;	**Heb 12:7**	*4374*
DEALT		
God has **d** graciously with me and	**Gn 33:11**	2603a
have you **d** with us in this way,	**Ex 14:11**	6213a
d proudly against the people."	**Ex 18:11**	2102
since I have **d** kindly with you,	**Jos 2:12**	6213a
if you have **d** in truth and	**Jg 9:16**	6213a
if you have **d** well with Jerubbaal	**Jg 9:16**	6213a
have **d** with him as he deserved	**Jg 9:16**	6213a
if then you have **d** in truth and	**Jg 9:19**	6213a
d treacherously with Abimelech,	**Jg 9:23**	898
have **d** with the dead and with me.	**Ru 1:8**	6213a
has **d** very bitterly with me.	**Ru 1:20**	4843
When He had severely **d** with them,	**1Sa 6:6**	5953a
for you have **d** well with me, while	**1Sa 24:17**	1580
while I have **d** wickedly with you.	**1Sa 24:17**	1580
In this manner Absalom **d** with	**2Sa 15:6**	6213a
if I had **d** treacherously against	**2Sa 18:13**	6213a
the work, for they **d** faithfully.	**2Ki 12:15**	6213a
and **d** with mediums and spiritists.	**2Ki 21:6**	6213a
"You have **d** with my father David	**2Ch 1:8**	6213a
"As you **d** with David my father and	**2Ch 2:3**	6213a
and **d** with mediums and spiritists.	**2Ch 33:6**	6213a
For You have **d** faithfully, but we	**Ne 9:33**	6213a
He has **d** bountifully with me.	**Ps 13:6**	1580
not **d** falsely with Your covenant.	**Ps 44:17**	8266
d with us according to our sins,	**Ps 103:10**	6213a
LORD has **d** bountifully with you.	**Ps 116:7**	1580
You have **d** well with Your servant,	**Ps 119:65**	6213a
He has not **d** thus with any nation;	**Ps 147:20**	6213a
you have **d** treacherously with Me,	**Jer 3:20**	898
d very treacherously with Me,"	**Jer 5:11**	898
have **d** treacherously with you,	**Jer 12:6**	898
have **d** treacherously with her;	**La 1:2**	898
Which was severely **d** out to me,	**La 1:12**	5953a
with them as You have **d** with me	**La 1:22**	5953a
With whom have You **d** thus?	**La 2:20**	5953a
have **d** with you for My name's sake,	**Ezk 20:44**	6213a
transgressions I **d** with them,	**Ezk 39:24**	6213a
They have **d** treacherously against	**Hos 5:7**	898
have **d** treacherously against Me.	**Hos 6:7**	898
Who has **d** wondrously with you;	**Jl 2:26**	6213a
so He has **d** with us.	**Zch 1:6**	6213a
"Judah has **d** treacherously, and	**Mal 2:11**	898
whom you have **d** treacherously,	**Mal 2:14**	898
"This is the way the Lord has **d**	**Lk 1:25**	*4160*
DEAR		
"Is Ephraim My **d** son?	**Jer 31:20**	3357
of any account as **d** to myself,	**Ac 20:24**	*5093*
you had become very **d** to us.	**1Th 2:8**	*27*
DEARLY		
Their rulers **d** love shame.	**Hos 4:18**	157
DEARTH		
the **d** of people is a prince's ruin.	**Pr 14:28**	657
DEATH		
was comforted after his mother's **d**.	**Gn 24:67**	
came about after the **d** of Abraham,	**Gn 25:11**	4194
wife shall surely be put to **d**."	**Gn 26:11**	4191
them up after the **d** of Abraham;	**Gn 26:18**	4194
and I do not know the day of my **d**.	**Gn 27:2**	4194
presence of the LORD before my **d**.'	**Gn 27:7**	4194
he may bless you before his **d**."	**Gn 27:10**	4194
against him to put him to **d**.	**Gn 37:18**	4191
"You may put my two sons to **d** if	**Gn 42:37**	4191
son, then you shall put him to **d**;	**Ex 1:16**	4191
him and sought to put him to **d**.	**Ex 4:24**	4191
only remove this **d** from me."	**Ex 10:17**	4194
mountain shall surely be put to **d**.	**Ex 19:12**	4191
he dies shall surely be put to **d**.	**Ex 21:12**	4191
mother shall surely be put to **d**.	**Ex 21:15**	4191
shall surely be put to **d**.	**Ex 21:16**	4191
mother shall surely be put to **d**.	**Ex 21:17**	4191
an ox gores a man or a woman to **d**,	**Ex 21:28**	4191
its owner also shall be put to **d**.	**Ex 21:29**	4191
animal shall surely be put to **d**.	**Ex 22:19**	4191
it shall surely be put to **d**;	**Ex 31:14**	4191
day shall surely be put to **d**.	**Ex 31:15**	4191
any work on it shall be put to **d**.	**Ex 35:2**	4191
the **d** of the two sons of Aaron,	**Lv 16:1**	4194
shall not, *however,* be put to **d**,	**Lv 19:20**	4191
Molech, shall surely be put to **d**;	**Lv 20:2**	4191
Molech, so as not to put him to **d**,	**Lv 20:4**	4191
he shall surely be put to **d**;	**Lv 20:9**	4191
the adulteress shall surely be put to **d**.	**Lv 20:10**	4191
of them shall surely be put to **d**,	**Lv 20:11**	4191
of them shall surely be put to **d**;	**Lv 20:12**	4191
they shall surely be put to **d**.	**Lv 20:13**	4191
he shall surely be put to **d**;	**Lv 20:15**	4191
they shall surely be put to **d**.	**Lv 20:16**	4191
a spiritist shall surely be put to **d**.	**Lv 20:27**	4191
shall surely be put to **d**;	**Lv 24:16**	4191
the Name, shall be put to **d**.	**Lv 24:16**	4191
he shall surely be put to **d**.	**Lv 24:17**	4191
who kills a man shall be put to **d**.	**Lv 24:21**	4191
he shall surely be put to **d**.	**Lv 27:29**	4191
who comes near shall be put to **d**.	**Nu 1:51**	4191
comes near shall be put to **d**."	**Nu 3:10**	4191
coming near was to be put to **d**.	**Nu 3:38**	4191
"The man shall surely be put to **d**;	**Nu 15:35**	4191
and stoned him to **d** with stones,	**Nu 15:36**	4191
"If these men die the **d** of all men or	**Nu 16:29**	4194
the **d** of the LORD's people."	**Nu 16:41**	4191
comes near shall be put to **d**."	**Nu 18:7**	4191
Let me die the **d** of the upright,	**Nu 23:10**	4194
murderer shall surely be put to **d**.	**Nu 35:16**	4191
murderer shall surely be put to **d**.	**Nu 35:17**	4191
murderer shall surely be put to **d**.	**Nu 35:18**	4191
shall put the murderer to **d**;	**Nu 35:19**	4191
put him to **d** when he meets him.	**Nu 35:19**	4191
him shall surely be put to **d**,	**Nu 35:21**	4191
shall put the murderer to **d** when	**Nu 35:21**	4191
live in it until the **d** of the high priest	**Nu 35:25**	4194
until the **d** of the high priest.	**Nu 35:28**	4194
But after the **d** of the high priest	**Nu 35:28**	4194
the murderer shall be put to **d** at the	**Nu 35:30**	7523
but no person shall be put to **d** on	**Nu 35:30**	4191
of a murderer who is guilty of **d**,	**Nu 35:31**	4191
but he shall surely be put to **d**.	**Nu 35:31**	4191
land before the **d** of the priest.	**Nu 35:32**	4194
of dreams shall be put to **d**,	**Dt 13:5**	4191
first against him to put him to **d**,	**Dt 13:9**	4191
"So you shall stone him to **d**	**Dt 13:10**	4191
and you shall stone them to **d**.	**Dt 17:5**	4191
who is to die shall be put to **d**;	**Dt 17:6**	4191
he shall not be put to **d** on the	**Dt 17:6**	4191
first against him to put him to **d**,	**Dt 17:7**	4191
though he was not deserving of **d**,	**Dt 19:6**	4194
of his city shall stone him to **d**;	**Dt 21:21**	4191
has committed a sin worthy of **d** and	**Dt 21:22**	4194
of death and he is put to **d**,	**Dt 21:22**	4191
men of her city shall stone her to **d**	**Dt 22:21**	4191
and you shall stone them to **d**;	**Dt 22:24**	4191
is no sin in the girl worthy of **d**,	**Dt 22:26**	4194
not be put to **d** for *their* sons,	**Dt 24:16**	4191
be put to **d** for *their* fathers;	**Dt 24:16**	4191
shall be put to **d** for his own sin.	**Dt 24:16**	4191
prosperity, and **d** and adversity;	**Dt 30:15**	4194
I have set before you life and **d**,	**Dt 30:19**	4194
how much more, then, after my **d**?	**Dt 31:27**	4194
"For I know that after my **d** you	**Dt 31:29**	4194
is I who put to **d** and give life.	**Dt 32:39**	4191
the sons of Israel before his **d**.	**Dt 33:1**	4194
after the **d** of Moses the servant of	**Jos 1:1**	4194
command him, shall be put to **d**;	**Jos 1:18**	4191
and deliver our lives from **d**."	**Jos 2:13**	4194
struck them and put them to **d**,	**Jos 10:26**	4191
them down and put them to **d**.	**Jos 11:17**	4191
until the **d** of the one who is high	**Jos 20:6**	4194
it came about after the **d** of Joshua	**Jg 1:1**	4194
despised their lives *even* to **d**,	**Jg 5:18**	4191
him shall be put to **d** by morning.	**Jg 6:31**	4191
from the womb to the day of his **d**.' "	**Jg 13:7**	4194
that his soul was annoyed to **d**.	**Jg 16:16**	4191
the dead whom he killed at his **d** were	**Jg 16:30**	4194
that we may put them to **d** and	**Jg 20:13**	4191
"He shall surely be put to **d**."	**Jg 21:5**	4191
anything but **d** parts you and me."	**Ru 1:17**	4194
your mother-in-law after the **d** of your	**Ru 2:11**	4194
the LORD desired to put them to **d**.	**1Sa 2:25**	4191
And about the time of her **d** the	**1Sa 4:20**	4191
men, that we may put them to **d**."	**1Sa 11:12**	4191
a man shall be put to **d** this day,	**1Sa 11:13**	4191
bearer put some to **d** after him.	**1Sa 14:13**	4191
but put to **d** both man and woman,	**1Sa 15:3**	4191
the bitterness of **d** is past."	**1Sa 15:32**	4194
Saul again until the day of his **d**;	**1Sa 15:35**	4194
his servants to put David to **d**.	**1Sa 19:1**	4191
father is seeking to put you to **d**.	**1Sa 19:2**	4191
David to **d** without a cause?"	**1Sa 19:5**	4191
lives, he shall not be put to **d**."	**1Sa 19:6**	4191
to put him to **d** in the morning.	**1Sa 19:11**	4191
tomorrow you will be put to **d**."	**1Sa 19:11**	4191
bed, that I may put him to **d**."	**1Sa 19:15**	4191
Why should I put you to **d**?' "	**1Sa 19:17**	4191
hardly a step between me and **d**."	**1Sa 20:3**	4194
in me, put me to **d** yourself;	**1Sa 20:8**	4191
"Why should he be put to **d**?	**1Sa 20:32**	4191
had decided to put David to **d**.	**1Sa 20:33**	4191
put the priests of the LORD to **d**,	**1Sa 22:17**	4191
I have brought about *the* **d** of	**1Sa 22:22**	
for my life to bring about my **d**?"	**1Sa 28:9**	4191
it came about after the **d** of Saul,	**2Sa 1:1**	4194
in their **d** they were not parted;	**2Sa 1:23**	4194
he had put their brother Asahel to **d**	**2Sa 3:30**	4191
to put Abner the son of Ner to **d**.	**2Sa 3:37**	4191
had no child to the day of her **d**.	**2Sa 6:23**	4194
and he measured two lines to put to **d**	**2Sa 8:2**	4191
'Strike Amnon,' then put him to **d**.	**2Sa 13:28**	4191
have put to **d** all the young men,	**2Sa 13:32**	4191
that we may put him to **d** for the	**2Sa 14:7**	4191
in me, let him put me to **d**."	**2Sa 14:32**	4191
may be, whether for **d** or for life,	**2Sa 15:21**	4194
not Shimei be put to **d** for this,	**2Sa 19:21**	4191
man be put to **d** in Israel today?	**2Sa 19:22**	4191
shut up until the day of their **d**,	**2Sa 20:3**	4191
he put the Gibeonites to **d**."	**2Sa 21:1**	4191
to put any man to **d** in Israel."	**2Sa 21:4**	4191
and they were put to **d** in the	**2Sa 21:9**	4191
"For the waves of **d** encompassed me;	**2Sa 22:5**	4194
The snares of **d** confronted me.	**2Sa 22:6**	4194
he will not put his servant to **d**	**1Ki 1:51**	4191
not put you to **d** with the sword.'	**1Ki 2:8**	4191
Adonijah shall be put to **d** today."	**1Ki 2:24**	4191
not put you to **d** at this time,	**1Ki 2:26**	4191
fell upon him and put him to **d**,	**1Ki 2:34**	4191
therefore to put Jeroboam to **d**;	**1Ki 11:40**	4191
in Egypt until the **d** of Solomon.	**1Ki 11:40**	4194
and all Israel stoned him to **d**.	**1Ki 12:18**	4191
and struck him and put him to **d** in	**1Ki 16:10**	4191
and to put my son to **d**!"	**1Ki 17:18**	4191
the hand of Ahab to put me to **d**?	**1Ki 18:9**	4191
of Hazael, Jehu shall put to **d**,	**1Ki 19:17**	4191
of Jehu, Elisha shall put to **d**.	**1Ki 19:17**	4191
take him out and stone him to **d**."	**1Ki 21:10**	4191
and stoned him to **d** with stones.	**1Ki 21:13**	4191
Israel after the **d** of Ahab.	**2Ki 1:1**	4194
not be from there **d** or unfruitfulness	**2Ki 2:21**	4194
of God, there is **d** in the pot."	**2Ki 4:40**	4194
sons who were being put to **d**,	**2Ki 11:2**	4191
Athaliah, and he was not put to **d**.	**2Ki 11:2**	4191
the ranks shall be put to **d**."	**2Ki 11:8**	4191
her put to **d** with the sword,"	**2Ki 11:15**	4191
to **d** in the house of the LORD."	**2Ki 11:15**	4191
house, she was put to **d** there.	**2Ki 11:16**	4191
For they had put Athaliah to **d**	**2Ki 11:20**	4191
the slayers he did not put to **d**,	**2Ki 14:6**	4191
not be put to **d** for the sons,	**2Ki 14:6**	4191
sons be put to **d** for the fathers;	**2Ki 14:6**	4191
be put to **d** for his own sin."	**2Ki 14:6**	4191
after the **d** of Jehoash son of Jehoahaz	**2Ki 14:17**	4194
was a leper to the day of his **d**.	**2Ki 15:5**	4194
put him to **d** and became king in his	**2Ki 15:30**	4191
exile to Kir, and put Rezin to **d**.	**2Ki 16:9**	4191
put them to **d** at Riblah in the land	**2Ki 25:21**	4191
of the LORD, so He put him to **d**.	**1Ch 2:3**	4191
the **d** of Hezron in Caleb-ephrathah,	**1Ch 2:24**	4194
and put to **d** Shophach the	**1Ch 19:18**	4191
ample preparations before his **d**.	**1Ch 22:5**	4194
sons of Israel stoned him to **d**.	**2Ch 10:18**	4191
of Israel should be put to **d**	**2Ch 15:13**	4191
after the **d** of his father,	**2Ch 22:4**	4194
brought him to Jehu, put him to **d** and	**2Ch 22:9**	4191
sons who were being put to **d**,	**2Ch 22:11**	4191
that she would not put him to **d**.	**2Ch 22:11**	4191
her, put to **d** with the sword."	**2Ch 23:14**	4191
to **d** in the house of the LORD."	**2Ch 23:14**	4191
house, they put her to **d** there.	**2Ch 23:15**	4191
put Athaliah to **d** with the sword.	**2Ch 23:21**	4191
and thirty years old at his **d**.	**2Ch 24:15**	4194
But after the **d** of Jehoiada the	**2Ch 24:17**	4194
they stoned him to **d** in the court	**2Ch 24:21**	68
did not put their children to **d**,	**2Ch 25:4**	4191
shall not be put to **d** for sons,	**2Ch 25:4**	4191
nor sons be put to **d** for fathers,	**2Ch 25:4**	4191
be put to **d** for his own sin."	**2Ch 25:4**	4191
years after the **d** of Joash,	**2Ch 25:25**	4194
was a leper to the day of his **d**;	**2Ch 26:21**	4194
of Jerusalem honored him at his **d**.	**2Ch 32:33**	4194
and put him to **d** in his own house.	**2Ch 33:24**	4191
whether for **d** or for banishment or	**Ezr 7:26**	4193
but one law, that he be put to **d**,	**Es 4:11**	4191
Who long for **d**, but there is none,	**Jb 3:21**	4194
famine He will redeem you from **d**,	**Jb 5:20**	4194
D rather than my pains.	**Jb 7:15**	4194
firstborn of **d** devours his limbs.	**Jb 18:13**	4194
"Abaddon and **D** say,	**Jb 28:22**	4194
I know that You will bring me to **d**	**Jb 30:23**	4194
And his life to those who bring **d**.	**Jb 33:22**	4191
gates of **d** been revealed to you,	**Jb 38:17**	4194
there is no mention of You in **d**;	**Ps 6:5**	4194
lift me up from the gates of **d**,	**Ps 9:13**	4194
eyes, or I will sleep the *sleep of* **d**,	**Ps 13:3**	4194
The cords of **d** encompassed me, And	**Ps 18:4**	4194
The snares of **d** confronted me.	**Ps 18:5**	4194
You lay me in the dust of **d**.	**Ps 22:15**	4194
the valley of the shadow of **d**,	**Ps 23:4**	6757
To deliver their soul from **d** And	**Ps 33:19**	4194
covered us with the shadow of **d**.	**Ps 44:19**	6757
He will guide us until **d**.	**Ps 48:14**	4192
D shall be their shepherd;	**Ps 49:14**	4194
terrors of **d** have fallen upon me.	**Ps 55:4**	4194
Let **d** come deceitfully upon them;	**Ps 55:15**	4194
have delivered my soul from **d**,	**Ps 56:13**	4194
the Lord belong escapes from **d**.	**Ps 68:20**	4194
For there are no pains in their **d**,	**Ps 73:4**	4194
did not spare their soul from **d**,	**Ps 78:50**	4194
What man can live and not see **d**?	**Ps 89:48**	4194
And condemn the innocent to **d**.	**Ps 94:21**	1818
free those who were doomed to **d**,	**Ps 102:20**	8546
darkness and in the shadow of **d**,	**Ps 107:10**	6757
of darkness and the shadow of **d** And	**Ps 107:14**	6757
they drew near to the gates of **d**.	**Ps 107:18**	4194
in heart, to put *them* to **d**.	**Ps 109:16**	4191
The cords of **d** encompassed me And	**Ps 116:3**	4194
You have rescued my soul from **d**,	**Ps 116:8**	4194
LORD Is the **d** of His godly ones.	**Ps 116:15**	4194
But He has not given me over to **d**.	**Ps 118:18**	4194
For her house sinks down to **d** And	**Pr 2:18**	4194
Her feet go down to **d**,	**Pr 5:5**	4194
Descending to the chambers of **d**.	**Pr 7:27**	4194
All those who hate me love **d**."	**Pr 8:36**	4194
But righteousness delivers from **d**.	**Pr 10:2**	4194
But righteousness delivers from **d**.	**Pr 11:4**	4194
evil *will bring about* his own **d**.	**Pr 11:19**	4194
And in *its* pathway there is no **d**.	**Pr 12:28**	4194

turn aside from the snares of **d**. Pr 13:14 4194
man, But its end is the way of **d**. Pr 14:12 4194
one may avoid the snares of **d**. Pr 14:27 4194
of a king is *like* messengers of **d**, Pr 16:14 4194
man, But its end is the way of **d**. Pr 16:25 4194
D and life are in the power of the Pr 18:21 4194
is hope, And do not desire his **d**. Pr 19:18 4191
fleeting vapor, the pursuit of **d**. Pr 21:6 4194
of the sluggard puts him to **d**, Pr 21:25 4191
who are being taken away to **d**, Pr 24:11 4194
throws Firebrands, arrows and **d**, Pr 26:18 4194
blood Will be a fugitive until **d**; Pr 28:17 953a
And the day of *one's* **d** is better Ec 7:1 4194
more bitter than **d** the woman whose Ec 7:26 4194
or authority over the day of **d**; Ec 8:8 4194
For love is as strong as **d**, SS 8:6 4194
In the year of King Uzziah's **d** I Is 6:1 4194
He will swallow up **d** for all time, Is 25:8 4194
"We have made a covenant with **d**, Is 28:15 4194
covenant with **d** will be canceled, Is 28:18 4194
thank You, **D** cannot praise You; Is 38:18 4194
He was with a rich man in His **d**, Is 53:9 4194
He poured out Himself to **d**, Is 53:12 4194
"And **d** will be chosen rather than Jer 8:3 4194
For **d** has come up through our Jer 9:21 4194
"Those *destined* for **d**, Jer 15:2 4194
"Those *destined* for death, to **d**; Jer 15:2 4194
their men also be smitten to **d**, Jer 18:21 4194
the way of life and the way of **d**. Jer 21:8 4194
"A **d** sentence for this man! Jer 26:11 4194
certain that if you put me to **d**, Jer 26:15 4191
"No **d** sentence for this man! Jer 26:16 4194
Judah and all Judah put him to **d**? Jer 26:19 4191
the king sought to put him to **d**; Jer 26:21 4191
of the people to put him to **d**. Jer 26:24 4191
"Now let this man be put to **d**, Jer 38:4 4191
you not certainly put me to **d**? Jer 38:15 4191
surely I will not put you to **d** nor Jer 38:16 4191
us and we will not put you to **d**,' Jer 38:25 4191
with the sword and put to **d** the Jer 41:2 4191
"Do not put us to **d**; Jer 41:8 4191
to **d** along with their companions. Jer 41:8 4191
they will put us to **d** or exile us Jer 43:3 4191
for **d** *will be given over* to death, Jer 43:11 4194
for death *will be given over* to **d**, Jer 43:11 4194
in prison until the day of his **d**. Jer 52:11 4194
struck them down and put them to **d** Jer 52:27 4191
his life until the day of his **d**. Jer 52:34 4194
In the house it is like **d**. La 1:20 4194
to put to **d** some who should not die Ezk 13:19 4191
he will surely be put to **d**; Ezk 18:13 4191
pleasure in the **d** of the wicked," Ezk 18:23 4194
in the **d** of anyone who dies," Ezk 18:32 4194
And you will die the **d** of those Ezk 28:8 4463
'You will die the **d** of the Ezk 28:10 4194
have all been given over to **d**, Ezk 31:14 4194
pleasure in the **d** of the wicked, Ezk 33:11 4194
or beast that has died a natural **d** Ezk 44:31 5038
Shall I redeem them from **d**? Hos 13:14 4194
O **D**, where are your thorns? Hos 13:14 4194
encompassed me to the point of **d**. Jon 2:5 5315
for **d** is better to me than life." Jon 4:3 4194
"**D** is better to me than life." Jon 4:8 4194
reason to be angry, even to **d**." Jon 4:9 4194
like Sheol, And he is like **d**, Hab 2:5 4194
remained there until the **d** of Herod Mt 2:15 *5054*
IN THE LAND AND SHADOW OF **D**, Mt 4:16 *2288*
will betray brother to **d**, Mt 10:21 *2288*
and cause them to be put to **d**. Mt 10:21 *2289*
Herod wanted to put him to **d**, Mt 14:5 *615*
OR MOTHER IS TO BE PUT TO **D**.' Mt 15:4 *2288*
will not taste **d** until they see the Son Mt 16:28 *2288*
and they will condemn Him to **d**, Mt 20:18 *2288*
deeply grieved, to the point of **d**; Mt 26:38 *2288*
that they might put Him to **d**. Mt 26:59 *2289*
"He deserves **d**!" Mt 26:66 *2288*
against Jesus to put Him to **d**; Mt 27:1 *2289*
Barabbas and to put Jesus to **d**. Mt 27:20 *622*
daughter is at the point of **d**; Mk 5:23 *2079*
put him to **d** and could not *do so;* Mk 6:19 *615*
IS TO BE PUT TO **D**'; Mk 7:10 *2288*
not taste **d** until they see the kingdom Mk 9:1 *2288*
and they will condemn Him to **d** and Mk 10:33 *2288*
"Brother will betray brother to **d**, Mk 13:12 *2288*
parents and have them put to **d**. Mk 13:12 *2289*
deeply grieved to the point of **d**; Mk 14:34 *2288*
against Jesus to put Him to **d**, Mk 14:55 *2289*
Him to be deserving of **d**. Mk 14:64 *2288*
IN DARKNESS AND THE SHADOW OF **D**, Lk 1:79 *2288*
that he would not see **d** before he had Lk 2:26 *2288*
not taste **d** until they see the kingdom Lk 9:27 *2288*
all the people will stone us to **d**, Lk 20:6 *2642*
they will put *some* of you to **d**, Lk 21:16 *2289*
how they might put Him to **d**; Lk 22:2 *337*
to go both to prison and to **d**!" Lk 22:33 *2288*
nothing deserving **d** has been done Lk 23:15 *2288*
found in Him no guilt *demanding* **d**; Lk 23:22 *2288*
led away to be put to **d** with Him. Lk 23:32 *337*
Him to the sentence of **d**, Lk 24:20 *2288*
for he was at the point of **d**. Jn 4:47 *599*
but has passed out of **d** into life. Jn 5:24 *2288*
My word he will never see **d**." Jn 8:51 *2288*
word, he will never taste of **d**.' Jn 8:52 *2288*
"This sickness is not to end in **d**, Jn 11:4 *2288*
Now Jesus had spoken of his **d**, Jn 11:13 *2288*
put Lazarus to **d** also; Jn 12:10 *615*
kind of **d** by which He was to die. Jn 12:33 *2288*
permitted to put anyone to **d**," Jn 18:31 *615*
kind of **d** He was about to die. Jn 18:32 *2288*
signifying by what kind of **d** he Jn 21:19 *2288*
of godless men and put *Him* to **d**. Ac 2:23 *337*
putting an end to the agony of **d**, Ac 2:24 *2288*
but put to **d** the Prince of life, Ac 3:15 *615*
to **d** by hanging Him on a cross. Ac 5:30 *1315a*
agreement with putting him to **d**. Ac 8:1 *336*
so that they might put him to **d**; Ac 9:24 *337*
were attempting to put him to **d**. Ac 9:29 *337*
put Him to **d** by hanging Him on a Ac 10:39 *337*
of John put to **d** with a sword. Ac 12:2 *337*
no ground for *putting Him to* **d**, Ac 13:28
I persecuted this Way to the **d**, Ac 22:4 *2288*
deserving **d** or imprisonment. Ac 23:29 *2288*
committed anything worthy of **d**, Ac 25:11 *2288*
had committed nothing worthy of **d**; Ac 25:25 *2288*
when they were being put to **d** Ac 26:10 *337*
temple and tried to put me to **d**. Ac 26:21 *1315a*
worthy of **d** or imprisonment." Ac 26:31 *2288*
was no ground for putting me to **d**. Ac 28:18 *2288*
such things are worthy of **d**, Ro 1:32 *2288*
to God through the **d** of His Son, Ro 5:10 *2288*
into the world, and **d** through sin, Ro 5:12 *2288*
sin, and so **d** spread to all men, Ro 5:12 *2288*
d reigned from Adam until Moses, Ro 5:14 *2288*
one, **d** reigned through the one, Ro 5:17 *2288*
that, as sin reigned in **d**, Ro 5:21 *2288*
have been baptized into His **d**? Ro 6:3 *2288*
with Him through baptism into **d**, Ro 6:4 *2288*
with *Him* in the likeness of His **d**, Ro 6:5 *2288*
d no longer is master over Him. Ro 6:9 *2288*
For the **d** that He died, He died to Ro 6:10
either of sin resulting in **d**, Ro 6:16 *2288*
the outcome of those things is **d**. Ro 6:21 *2288*
For the wages of sin is **d**, Ro 6:23 *2288*
of our body to bear fruit for **d**. Ro 7:5 *2288*
proved to result in **d** for me; Ro 7:10 *2288*
good become *a cause of* **d** for me? Ro 7:13 *2288*
my **d** through that which is good, Ro 7:13 *2288*
me free from the body of this **d**? Ro 7:24 *2288*
free from the law of sin and of **d**. Ro 8:2 *2288*
the mind set on the flesh is **d**, Ro 8:6 *2288*
you are putting to **d** the deeds of the Ro 8:13 *2289*
ARE BEING PUT TO **D** ALL DAY LONG; Ro 8:36 *2289*
neither **d**, nor life, nor angels, nor Ro 8:38 *2288*
or life or **d** or things present or things 1Co 3:22 *2288*
of all, as men condemned to **d**; 1Co 4:9 *1935*
the Lord's **d** until He comes. 1Co 11:26 *2288*
For since by a man *came* **d**, 1Co 15:21 *2288*
enemy that will be abolished is **d**. 1Co 15:26 *2288*
"**D** IS SWALLOWED UP in victory. 1Co 15:54 *2288*
"O **D**, WHERE IS YOUR VICTORY? 1Co 15:55 *2288*
O **D**, WHERE IS YOUR STING?" 1Co 15:55 *2288*
The sting of **d** is sin, and the 1Co 15:56 *2288*
we had the sentence of **d** within 2Co 1:9 *2288*
us from so great a *peril of* **d**, 2Co 1:10 *2288*
the one an aroma from **d** to death, 2Co 2:16 *2288*
the one an aroma from death to **d**, 2Co 2:16 *2288*
But if the ministry of **d**, 2Co 3:7 *2288*
delivered over to **d** for Jesus' sake, 2Co 4:11 *2288*
So **d** works in us, but life in you. 2Co 4:12 *2288*
as punished yet not put to **d**, 2Co 6:9 *2289*
sorrow of the world produces **d**. 2Co 7:10 *2288*
number, often in danger of **d**. 2Co 11:23 *2288*
by it having put to **d** the enmity. Eph 2:16 *615*
my body, whether by life or by **d**. Php 1:20 *2288*
obedient to the point of **d**, Php 2:8 *2288*
point of death, even **d** on a cross. Php 2:8 *2288*
he was sick to the point of **d**, Php 2:27 *2288*
close to **d** for the work of Christ, Php 2:30 *2288*
being conformed to His **d**; Php 3:10 *2288*
you in His fleshly body through **d**, Col 1:22 *2288*
Christ Jesus, who abolished **d** and 2Tm 1:10 *2288*
of **d** crowned with glory and honor, Heb 2:9 *2288*
God He might taste **d** for everyone. Heb 2:9 *2288*
that through **d** He might render Heb 2:14 *2288*
him who had the power of **d**, Heb 2:14 *2288*
who through fear of **d** were subject Heb 2:15 *2288*
the One able to save Him from **d**, Heb 5:7 *2288*
prevented by **d** from continuing, Heb 7:23 *2288*
so that, since a **d** has taken Heb 9:15 *2288*
be the **d** of the one who made it. Heb 9:16 *2288*
up so that he would not see **d**; Heb 11:5 *2288*
they were put to **d** with the sword; Heb 11:37 *599, 1722, 5408*
accomplished, it brings forth **d**. Jas 1:15 *2288*
and put to **d** the righteous *man* Jas 5:6 *5407*
his way will save his soul from **d** and Jas 5:20 *2288*
having been put to **d** in the flesh, 1Pe 3:18 *2289*
we have passed out of **d** into life, 1Jn 3:14 *2288*
He who does not love abides in **d**. 1Jn 3:14 *2288*
committing a sin not *leading* to **d**, 1Jn 5:16 *2288*
who commit sin not *leading* to **d**. 1Jn 5:16 *2288*
There is a sin *leading* to **d**; 1Jn 5:16 *2288*
there is a sin not *leading* to **d**. 1Jn 5:17 *2288*
I have the keys of **d** and of Hades. Rv 1:18 *2288*
Be faithful until **d**, Rv 2:10 *2288*
not be hurt by the second **d**.' Rv 2:11 *2288*
he who sat on it had the name **D**; Rv 6:8 *2288*
will seek **d** and will not find it; Rv 9:6 *2288*
long to die, and **d** flees from them. Rv 9:6 *2288*
even when faced with **d**. Rv 12:11 *2288*
these the second **d** has no power, Rv 20:6 *2288*
and **d** and Hades gave up the dead Rv 20:13 *2288*
Then **d** and Hades were thrown into Rv 20:14 *2288*
This is the second **d**, Rv 20:14 *2288*
there will no longer be *any* **d**; Rv 21:4 *2288*
which is the second **d**." Rv 21:8 *2288*

DEATHLY

color turned to a **d** pallor, Da 10:8 4889

DEBATE

great dissension and **d** with them, Ac 15:2 *2214*
After there had been much **d**, Ac 15:7 *2214*

DEBATED

so that they **d** among themselves, Mk 1:27 *4802*

DEBATER

Where is the **d** of this age? 1Co 1:20 *4804*

DEBIR

of Lachish and to **D** king of Eglon, Jos 10:3 1688
all Israel with him returned to **D**, Jos 10:38 1688
so he did to **D** and its king, Jos 10:39 1688
hill country, from Hebron, from **D**, Jos 11:21 1688
the king of **D**, one; Jos 12:13 1688
as far as the border of **D**; Jos 13:26 1688
up to **D** from the valley of Achor, Jos 15:7 1688
against the inhabitants of **D**; Jos 15:15 1688
of **D** formerly was Kiriath-sepher. Jos 15:15 1688
and Kiriath-sannah (that is, **D**), Jos 15:49 1688
and **D** with its pasture lands, Jos 21:15 1688
went against the inhabitants of **D** Jg 1:11 1688
of **D** formerly *was* Kiriath-sepher). Jg 1:11 1688
lands, **D** with its pasture lands, 1Ch 6:58 1688

DEBORAH

Now **D**, Rebekah's nurse, died, and Gn 35:8 1683
Now **D**, a prophetess, the wife of Jg 4:4 1683
tree of **D** between Ramah and Bethel Jg 4:5 1683
Then **D** arose and went with Barak Jg 4:9 1683
D also went up with him. Jg 4:10 1683
D said to Barak, Jg 4:14 1683
Then **D** and Barak the son of Jg 5:1 1683
ceased in Israel, Until I, **D**, arose, Jg 5:7 1683
"Awake, awake, **D**; Awake, awake, Jg 5:12 1683
princes of Issachar *were* with **D**; Jg 5:15 1683

DEBRIS

and I will scrape her **d** from her Ezk 26:4 6083
timbers and your **d** into the water. Ezk 26:12 6083

DEBT

and everyone who was in **d**, 1Sa 22:2 5377
"Go, sell the oil and pay your **d**, 2Ki 4:7 5386
year and the exaction of every **d**. Ne 10:31 3027
the word will be in **d** to it, Pr 13:13 2254a
him and forgave him the **d**. Mt 18:27 *1156*
I forgave you all that **d** because you Mt 18:32 *3782*
canceled out the certificate of **d** Col 2:14 *5498*

DEBTOR

borrower, the creditor like the **d**. Is 24:2 5377
but restores to the **d** his pledge, Ezk 18:7 2326

DEBTORS

as we also have forgiven our **d**. Mt 6:12 *3781*
"A moneylender had two **d**: Lk 7:41 *5533*
each one of his master's **d**, Lk 16:5 *5533*

DEBTS

you shall grant a remission *of* **d**. Dt 15:1
of the year of remission of **d**, Dt 31:10
those who become guarantors for **d**. Pr 22:26 4859
'And forgive us our **d**, Mt 6:12 *3783*

DECAPOLIS

Him from Galilee and *the* **D** Mt 4:25 *1179*
proclaim in **D** what great things Jesus Mk 5:20 *1179*
Galilee, within the region of **D**. Mk 7:31 *1179*

DECAY

"Let his own eyes see his **d**, Jb 21:20 3589
allow Your Holy One to undergo **d**. Ps 16:10 7845
That he should not undergo **d**. Ps 49:9 7845
D enters my bones, And in my place Hab 3:16 7538
YOUR HOLY ONE TO UNDERGO **D**. Ac 2:27 *1312*
HADES, NOR DID His flesh SUFFER **D**. Ac 2:31 *1312*
the dead, no longer to return to **d**, Ac 13:34 *1312*
YOUR HOLY ONE TO UNDERGO **D**.' Ac 13:35 *1312*
his fathers and underwent **d**; Ac 13:36 *1312*
whom God raised did not undergo **d**. Ac 13:37 *1312*

DECAYED

Has their wisdom **d**? Jer 49:7 5628

DECAYING

While I am **d** like a rotten thing, Jb 13:28 1086
but though our outer man is **d**, 2Co 4:16 *1311*

DECAYS

The new wine mourns, The vine **d**, Is 24:7 535

DECEASED

the wife of the **d** shall not be Dt 25:5 4191
the Moabitess, the widow of the **d**, Ru 4:5 4191
of the **d** on his inheritance." Ru 4:5 4191
name of the **d** on his inheritance, Ru 4:10 4191
so that the name of the **d** will not Ru 4:10 4191
Martha, the sister of the **d**, Jn 11:39 *5053*

DECEIT

and his father Hamor with **d**, Gn 34:13 4820
Nor will my tongue mutter **d**. Jb 27:4 7423a
And my foot has hastened after **d**, Jb 31:5 4820
abhors the man of bloodshed and **d**. Ps 5:6 4820
of curses and **d** and oppression; Ps 10:7 4820
And in whose spirit there is no **d**! Ps 32:2 7423a
And your lips from speaking **d**. Ps 34:13 4820
of his mouth are wickedness and **d**; Ps 36:3 4820
in evil And your tongue frames **d**. Ps 50:19 4820
Like a sharp razor, O worker of **d**. Ps 52:2 7423a
Oppression and **d** do not depart Ps 55:11 4820
Men of bloodshed and **d** will not Ps 55:23 4820
He who practices **d** shall not dwell Ps 101:7 7423a
Whose mouths speak **d**, Ps 144:8 7723
of aliens, Whose mouth speaks **d** And Ps 144:11 7723
is right, But a false witness, **d**. Pr 12:17 4820
D is in the heart of those who Pr 12:20 4820
way, But the foolishness of fools is **d**. Pr 14:8 4820
But he lays up **d** in his heart. Pr 26:24 4820
Nor was there any **d** in His mouth. Is 53:9 4820

of rebellion, Offspring of **d**, **Is 57:4** 8267
So their houses are full of **d**; **Jer 5:27** 4820
They hold fast to **d**, **Jer 8:5** 8649b
the priest Everyone practices **d**. **Jer 8:10** 8267
dwelling is in the midst of **d**; **Jer 9:6** 4820
d they refuse to know Me," **Jer 9:6** 4820
tongue is a deadly arrow; It speaks **d**; **Jer 9:8** 4820
He will cause **d** to succeed by his **Da 8:25** 4820
And the house of Israel with **d**; **Hos 11:12** 4820
of their lord with violence and **d**. **Zph 1:9** 4820
and wickedness, *as well as* **d**, **Mk 7:22** *1388*
in whom there is no **d**!" **Jn 1:47** *1388*
who are full of all **d** and fraud, **Ac 13:10** *1388*
full of envy, murder, strife, **d**, **Ro 1:29** *1388*
that I am, I took you in by **d**. **2Co 12:16** *1388*
in accordance with the lusts of **d**, **Eph 4:22** *539*
error or impurity or by way of **d**; **1Th 2:3** *1388*
putting aside all malice and all **d** **1Pe 2:1** *1388*
COMMITTED NO SIN, NOR WAS ANY **D** **1Pe 2:22** *1388*
EVIL AND HIS LIPS FROM SPEAKING **D**. **1Pe 3:10** *1388*

DECEITFUL
God, And speak what is **d** for Him? **Jb 13:7** 7423a
prayer, which is not from **d** lips. **Ps 17:1** 4820
I do not sit with **d** men, **Ps 26:4** 7723
But they devise **d** words against **Ps 35:20** 4820
me from the **d** and unjust man! **Ps 43:1** 4820
all words that devour, O **d** tongue. **Ps 52:4** 4820
the wicked and **d** mouth against me; **Ps 109:2** 4820
from lying lips, From a **d** tongue. **Ps 120:2** 7423a
be done to you, You **d** tongue? **Ps 120:3** 7423a
Put away from you a **d** mouth And **Pr 4:24** 6143
the counsels of the wicked are **d**. **Pr 12:5** 4820
But **d** are the kisses of an enemy. **Pr 27:6** 6280
Charm is **d** and beauty is vain, *But* **Pr 31:30** 8267
For his molten images are **d**, **Jer 10:14** 8267
"The heart is more **d** than all **Jer 17:9** 6121a
For his molten images are **d**, **Jer 51:17** 8267
not upward, They are like a **d** bow; **Hos 7:16** 7423a
their tongue is **d** in their mouth. **Mi 6:12** 7423a
Nor will a **d** tongue Be found in **Zph 3:13** 8649b
men are false apostles, **d** workers, **2Co 11:13** *1386*
men, by craftiness in **d** scheming; **Eph 4:14** *4106*
paying attention to **d** spirits and **1Tm 4:1** *4108*

DECEITFULLY
"Your brother came **d** and **Gn 27:35** 4820
only do not let Pharaoh deal **d** **Ex 8:29** 8524
He sent messengers to Abimelech **d**, **Jg 9:31** 8649a
brothers have acted **d** like a wadi, **Jb 6:15** 898
to falsehood And has not sworn **d**. **Ps 24:4** 4820
Let death come **d** upon them; **Ps 55:15** 5378

DECEITFULNESS
statutes, For their **d** is useless. **Ps 119:118** 8649b
the **d** of wealth choke the word, **Mt 13:22** *539*
of the world, and the **d** of riches, **Mk 4:19** *539*
you will be hardened by the **d** of sin. **Heb 3:13** *539*

DECEIVE
did you flee secretly and **d** me, **Gn 31:27** 1589
that he came to **d** you and to learn **2Sa 3:25** 6601b
Did I not say, 'Do not **d** me'?" **2Ki 4:28** 7951
'Do not let Hezekiah **d** you, **2Ki 18:29** 5378
in whom you trust **d** you saying, **2Ki 19:10** 5378
do not let Hezekiah **d** you or mislead **2Ch 32:15** 5378
you **d** Him as one deceives a man? **Jb 13:9** 8524
'The enemy will not **d** him, **Ps 89:22** 5377
And do not **d** with your lips. **Pr 24:28** 6601b
'Do not let Hezekiah **d** you, **Is 36:14** 5378
your God in whom you trust **d** you, **Is 37:10** 5378
midst and your diviners **d** you, **Jer 29:8** 5378
'Do not **d** yourselves, saying, **Jer 37:9** 5378
you Will **d** you and overpower you. **Ob 1:7** 5378
put on a hairy robe in order to **d**; **Zch 13:4** 3584
and flattering speech they **d** the hearts **Ro 16:18** *1818*
Let no man **d** himself. **1Co 3:18** *1818*
Let no one **d** you with empty words, **Eph 5:6** *538*
Let no one in any way **d** you, **2Th 2:3** *1818*
those who are trying to **d** you. **1Jn 2:26** *4105*
not **d** the nations any longer, **Rv 20:3** *4105*
and will come out to **d** the nations **Rv 20:8** *4105*

DECEIVED
"The serpent **d** me, and I ate." **Gn 3:13** 5378
Why then have you **d** me?" **Gn 29:25** 7411b
And Jacob **d** Laban the Aramean by **Gn 31:20** 1589
have **d** you in the affair of Peor and **Nu 25:18** 5230
that your hearts are not **d**, **Dt 11:16** 6601b
ban and have both stolen and **d**. **Jos 7:11** 3584
"Why have you **d** us, saying, **Jos 9:22** 7411b
you have **d** me and told me lies; **Jg 16:10** 8524
you have **d** me and told me lies; **Jg 16:13** 8524
You have **d** me these three times **Jg 16:15** 8524
"Why have you **d** me like this and **1Sa 19:17** 7411b
"Why have you **d** me? **1Sa 28:12** 7411b
lord, the king, my servant **d** me; **2Sa 19:26** 7411b
But they **d** Him with their mouth And **Ps 78:36** 6601b
a **d** heart has turned him aside. **Is 44:20** 8524
d this people and Jerusalem, **Jer 4:10** 5378
You have **d** me and I was deceived; **Jer 20:7** 6601b
You have deceived me and I was **d**; **Jer 20:7** 6601b
"Perhaps he will be **d**, **Jer 20:10** 6601b
For you have *only* **d** yourselves; **Jer 42:20** 8582
arrogance of your heart has **d** you, **Jer 49:16** 5378
to my lovers, *but* they **d** me; **La 1:19** 7411b
arrogance of your heart has **d** you, **Ob 1:3** 5378
through the commandment, **d** me and **Ro 7:11** *1818*
Do not be **d**; neither fornicators, nor **1Co 6:9** *4105*
Do not be **d**: "Bad company corrupts **1Co 15:33** *4105*
serpent **d** Eve by his craftiness, **2Co 11:3** *1818*
Do not be **d**, God is not mocked; **Ga 6:7** *4105*
And *it was* not Adam *who* was **d**, **1Tm 2:14** *538*
but the woman being **d**, **1Tm 2:14** *1818*
to worse, deceiving and being **d**. **2Tm 3:13** *4105*
foolish ourselves, disobedient, **d**, **Ti 3:3** *4105*
Do not be **d**, my beloved brethren. **Jas 1:16** *4105*
nations were **d** by *your* sorcery. **Rv 18:23** *4105*
by which he **d** those who had **Rv 19:20** *4105*
And the devil who **d** them was **Rv 20:10** *4105*

DECEIVER
I will be as a **d** in his sight **Gn 27:12** 8591a
when He was still alive that **d** said, **Mt 27:63** *4108*
This is the **d** and the antichrist. **2Jn 1:7** *4108*

DECEIVERS
regarded as **d** and yet true; **2Co 6:8** *4108*
men, empty talkers and **d**, **Ti 1:10** *5423*
d have gone out into the world, **2Jn 1:7** *4108*

DECEIVES
and **d** his companion in regard to a **Lv 6:2** 3584
you deceive Him as one **d** a man? **Jb 13:9** 8524
So is the man who **d** his neighbor, **Pr 26:19** 7411b
"Everyone **d** his neighbor And **Jer 9:5** 8524
when he is nothing, he **d** himself. **Ga 6:3** *5422*
his tongue but **d** his *own* heart, **Jas 1:26** *538*
Little children, make sure no one **d** **1Jn 3:7** *4105*
and Satan, who **d** the whole world; **Rv 12:9** *4105*
And he **d** those who dwell on the **Rv 13:14** *4105*

DECEIVING
"What have you done by **d** me and **Gn 31:26** 1589
'I will go out and be a **d** spirit **1Ki 22:22** 8267
the LORD has put a **d** spirit in the **1Ki 22:23** 8267
'I will go out and be a **d** spirit in **2Ch 18:21** 8267
the LORD has put a **d** spirit in the **2Ch 18:22** 8267
not trust in emptiness, **d** himself; **Jb 15:31** 8582
WITH THEIR TONGUES THEY KEEP **D**," **Ro 3:13** *1387*
to worse, **d** and being deceived. **2Tm 3:13** *4105*
have no sin, we are **d** ourselves and **1Jn 1:8** *4105*

DECEPTION
And their mind prepares **d**." **Jb 15:35** 4820
what is worthless and aim at **d**? **Ps 4:2** 3577
Keep **d** and lies far from me, Give **Pr 30:8** 7723
have concealed ourselves with **d**." **Is 28:15** 8267
all her heart, but rather in **d**," **Jer 3:10** 8267
"Surely, the hills are a **d**, **Jer 3:23** 8267
and the **d** of their own minds. **Jer 14:14** 8649b
of the **d** of their own heart, **Jer 23:26** 8649b
made with him he will practice **d**, **Da 11:23** 4820
There is swearing, **d**, **Hos 4:2** 3584
become a **d** To the kings of Israel. **Mi 1:14** 391
last **d** will be worse than the first." **Mt 27:64** *4106*
through philosophy and empty **d**, **Col 2:8** *539*
and with all the **d** of wickedness **2Th 2:10** *539*

DECEPTIONS
blemishes, reveling in their **d**, **2Pe 2:13** *539*

DECEPTIVE
The wicked earns **d** wages, **Pr 11:18** 8267
his delicacies, For it is **d** food. **Pr 23:3** 3577
"Do not trust in **d** words, saying, **Jer 7:4** 8267
trusting in **d** words to no avail. **Jer 7:8** 8267
You indeed be to me like a **d** *stream* **Jer 15:18** 391
scales And a bag of **d** weights? **Mi 6:11** 4820

DECIDE
that they may **d** between us two. **Gn 31:37** 3198
and he shall pay as the judges **d**. **Ex 21:22**
is too difficult for you to **d**, **Dt 17:8** 4941
and the judges **d** their case, **Dt 25:1** 8199
be judge and **d** between you and me; **1Sa 24:15** 8199
of our fathers look on *it* and **d**." **1Ch 12:17** 3198
And **d** with fairness for the **Is 11:4** 3198
casting lots for them *to* **d** what **Mk 15:24**
to **d** whose it shall be"; *this* **Jn 19:24**
comes down, I will **d** your case." **Ac 24:22** *1231*
be able to **d** between his brethren, **1Co 6:5** *1252*

DECIDED
angry, know that he has **d** on evil. **1Sa 20:7** 3615
d by my father to come upon you, **1Sa 20:9** 3615
had **d** to put David to death. **1Sa 20:33** 3615
I have **d**, 'You and Ziba shall divide **2Sa 19:29** 559
you yourself have **d** *it*." **1Ki 20:40** 2782
Now Solomon **d** to build a house for **2Ch 2:1** 559
Joash **d** to restore the house of the **2Ch 24:4**
1961, 5973, 3820
had **d** to celebrate the Passover in the **2Ch 30:2** 3289
Then the whole assembly **d** to **2Ch 30:23** 3289
he **d** with his officers and his **2Ch 32:3** 3289
when he had **d** to release Him. **Ac 3:13** *2919*
which had been **d** upon by the **Ac 16:4** *2919*
he **d** to return through Macedonia. **Ac 20:3**
1096, 1106
For Paul had **d** to sail past **Ac 20:16** *2919*
having **d** that they should abstain **Ac 21:25** *2919*
to the Emperor, I **d** to send him. **Ac 25:25** *2919*
d that we would sail for Italy, **Ac 27:1** *2919*
I have **d** to deliver such a one to **1Co 5:5**
and has **d** this in his own heart, **1Co 7:37** *2919*
have **d** to spend the winter there. **Ti 3:12** *2919*

DECIDES
And **d** between the mighty ones **Pr 18:18** 6504

DECISION
us his **d** concerning this *matter*." **Ezr 5:17** 7466b
d is in the lips of the king; **Pr 16:10** 7081
But its every **d** is from the LORD. **Pr 16:33** 4941
make a **d** by what His ears hear; **Is 11:3** 3198
"Give *us* advice, make a **d**; **Is 16:3** 6415
d is a command of the holy ones, **Da 4:17** 7595
multitudes in the valley of **d**! **Jl 3:14** 2742b
LORD is near in the valley of **d**. **Jl 3:14** 2742b
Indeed, My **d** is to gather nations, **Zph 3:8** 4941
in custody for the Emperor's **d**, **Ac 25:21** *1233*
a **d** to put out to sea from there, **Ac 27:12** *1012*

DECISIONS
will render **d** for many peoples; **Is 2:4** 3198
who constantly record unjust **d**, **Is 10:1** 5999
They ask Me *for* just **d**, **Is 58:2** 4941
peoples And render **d** for mighty, **Mi 4:3** 3198

DECISIVE
Of **d** destruction on all the earth. **Is 28:22** 2782

DECK
With ivory they have inlaid your **d** **Ezk 27:6** 7175b

DECKS
with lower, second, and third **d**. **Gn 6:16**
d himself with a garland, **Is 61:10** 3547

DECLARATION
And let my **d** *fill* your ears. **Jb 13:17** 262

DECLARE
to **d** to you the word of the LORD; **Dt 5:5** 5046
and they will **d** to you the verdict **Dt 17:9** 5046
the terms of the verdict which they **d** **Dt 17:10** 5046
from the word which they **d** to you, **Dt 17:11** 5046
and she shall **d**, **Dt 25:9**
6030a, 559
'I **d** this day to the LORD my God **Dt 26:3** 5046
I **d** to you today that you shall **Dt 30:18** 5046
am guiltless, He will **d** me guilty. **Jb 9:20** 6140
let the fish of the sea **d** to you. **Jb 12:8** 5608
what I have seen I will also **d**; **Jb 15:17** 5608
from me that I should **d** you right; **Jb 27:5** 6663
d to Him the number of my steps; **Jb 31:37** 5608
Therefore **d** what you know. **Jb 34:33** 1696
D among the peoples His deeds. **Ps 9:11** 5046
They will come and will **d** His **Ps 22:31** 5046
And **d** all Your wonders. **Ps 26:7** 5608
Will it **d** Your faithfulness? **Ps 30:9** 5046
And my tongue shall **d** Your **Ps 35:28** 1897
If I would **d** and speak of them, **Ps 40:5** 5046
the heavens **d** His righteousness, **Ps 50:6** 5046
That my mouth may **d** Your praise. **Ps 51:15** 5046
fear, And they will **d** the work of God, **Ps 64:9** 5046
And I still **d** Your wondrous deeds. **Ps 71:17** 5046
Until I **d** Your strength to *this* **Ps 71:18** 5046
Men **d** Your wondrous works. **Ps 75:1** 5608
as for me, I will **d** *it* forever; **Ps 75:9** 5046
To **d** Your lovingkindness in the **Ps 92:2** 5046
To **d** that the LORD is upright; **Ps 92:15** 5046
The heavens **d** His righteousness, **Ps 97:6** 5046
I **d** my trouble before Him. **Ps 142:2** 5046
And shall **d** Your mighty acts. **Ps 145:4** 5046
Let them bring forth and **d** to us **Is 41:22** 5046
former *events*, **d** what they *were*, **Is 41:22** 5046
D the things that are going to **Is 41:23** 5046
come to pass, Now I **d** new things; **Is 42:9** 5046
d His praise in the coastlands. **Is 42:12** 5046
Who among them can **d** this And **Is 43:9** 5046
for Myself Will **d** My praise. **Is 43:21** 5608
Let him proclaim and **d** it; **Is 44:7** 5046
And let them **d** to them the things **Is 44:7** 5046
"**D** and set forth *your case;* **Is 45:21** 5046
And you, will you not **d** it? **Is 48:6** 5046
D with the sound of joyful **Is 48:20** 5046
"I will **d** your righteousness and **Is 57:12** 5046
And **d** to My people their **Is 58:1** 5046
will **d** My glory among the nations. **Is 66:19** 5046
D in Judah and proclaim in **Jer 4:5** 5046
"**D** this in the house of Jacob And **Jer 5:20** 5046
LORD has spoken, that he may **d** it? **Jer 9:12** 5046
"who use their tongues and **d**, **Jer 23:31** 5001
And **d** in the coastlands afar off, **Jer 31:10** 5046
"**D** in Egypt and proclaim in **Jer 46:14** 5046
D by the Arnon That Moab has been **Jer 48:20** 5046
"**D** and proclaim among the nations. **Jer 50:2** 5046
To **d** in Zion the vengeance of the **Jer 50:28** 5046
Then **d** to them their abominations. **Ezk 23:36** 5046
d to us what you mean by these?" **Ezk 37:18** 5046
My blazing wrath I **d** *that* on that day **Ezk 38:19** 1696
D to the house of Israel all that **Ezk 40:4** 5046
we will **d** the interpretation." **Da 2:4** 2331b
"But if you **d** the dream and its **Da 2:6** 2331b
therefore **d** to me the dream and **Da 2:6** 2331b
we will **d** the interpretation." **Da 2:7** 2331b
can **d** to me its interpretation." **Da 2:9** 2331b
could **d** the matter for the king, **Da 2:10** 2331b
d it to the king except gods, **Da 2:11** 2331b
in order that he might **d** the **Da 2:16** 2331b
and I will **d** the interpretation to **Da 2:24** 2331b
are able to **d** *it* to the king. **Da 2:27** 2331b
"It has seemed good to me to **d** **Da 4:2** 2331b
he will **d** the interpretation." **Da 5:12** 2331b
they could not **d** the interpretation **Da 5:15** 2331b
tribes of Israel I **d** what is sure. **Hos 5:9** 3045
in their mouths They **d** holy war. **Mi 3:5** 6942
"And then I will **d** to them, **Mt 7:23** *3670*
He will **d** all things to us." **Jn 4:25** *312*

DECLARED
So Moses **d** to the sons of Israel **Lv 23:44** 1696
be great, just as You have **d**, **Nu 14:17**
1696, 559
been **d** what should be done to him. **Nu 15:34** 6567a
"So He **d** to you His covenant **Dt 4:13** 5046
today **d** the LORD to be your God, **Dt 26:17** 559
has today **d** you to be His people, **Dt 26:18** 559
"You have **d** today that you **1Sa 24:18** 5046
Then He saw it and **d** it; **Jb 28:27** 5608
"Therefore I have **d** that which I **Jb 42:3** 5046
lovingkindness be **d** in the grave, **Ps 88:11** 5608
been **d** to you from the beginning? **Is 40:21** 5046
Who has **d** *this* from the beginning, **Is 41:26** 5046

Surely there was no one who **d**,	**Is 41:26**	5046
have **d** and saved and proclaimed,	**Is 43:12**	5046
announced *it* to you and **d** *it?*	**Is 44:8**	5046
Who has long since **d** it?	**Is 45:21**	5046
"I **d** the former things long ago	**Is 48:3**	5046
I **d** *them* to you long ago,	**Is 48:5**	5046
Who among them has **d** these things?	**Is 48:14**	5046
'For what reason has the LORD **d**	**Jer 16:10**	1696
calamity that I have **d** against it,	**Jer 19:15**	1696
Micaiah **d** to them all the	**Jer 36:13**	5046
all the calamity that I have **d** to them	**Jer 36:31**	1696
Nebuchadnezzar, to you it is **d**:	**Da 4:31**	560
the LORD God of hosts has **d**:	**Am 6:8**	5002
He had **d** He would bring upon them.	**Jon 3:10**	1696
(*Thus He* **d** all foods clean.)	**Mk 7:19**	*2511*
and **d** in the presence of all the	**Lk 8:47**	*518*
raised his voice and **d** to them:	**Ac 2:14**	*669*
who was **d** the Son of God with	**Ro 1:4**	*3724*

DECLARES

Myself I have sworn, **d** the LORD,	**Gn 22:16**	5002
the LORD God of Israel **d**,	**1Sa 2:30**	5002
but now the LORD **d**,	**1Sa 2:30**	5002
The LORD also **d** to you that the	**2Sa 7:11**	5046
David the son of Jesse **d**,	**2Sa 23:1**	5002
The man who was raised on high **d**,	**2Sa 23:1**	5002
not come to this city," ' **d** the LORD.	**2Ki 19:33**	5002
truly have heard you," **d** the LORD.	**2Ki 22:19**	5002
truly have heard you," **d** the LORD.	**2Ch 34:27**	5002
Then He **d** to them their work And	**Jb 36:9**	5046
"Its noise **d** His presence;	**Jb 36:33**	5046
He **d** His words to Jacob, His	**Ps 147:19**	5046
The man **d** to Ithiel, to Ithiel and	**Pr 30:1**	5002
d, "Ah, I will be relieved of My	**Is 1:24**	5002
D the Lord GOD of hosts.	**Is 3:15**	5002
against them," **d** the LORD of hosts,	**Is 14:22**	5002
and posterity," **d** the LORD.	**Is 14:22**	5002
destruction," **d** the LORD of hosts.	**Is 14:23**	5002
of Israel," **D** the LORD of hosts.	**Is 17:3**	5002
of a fruitful tree, **D** the LORD,	**Is 17:6**	5002
them," **d** the Lord GOD of hosts.	**Is 19:4**	5002
"In that day," **d** the LORD of hosts,	**Is 22:25**	5002
rebellious children," **d** the LORD,	**Is 30:1**	5002
at the standard," **D** the LORD,	**Is 31:9**	5002
not come to this city,' **d** the LORD.	**Is 37:34**	5002
I will help you," **d** the LORD,	**Is 41:14**	5002
"You are My witnesses," **d** the LORD,	**Is 43:10**	5002
you are My witnesses," **d** the LORD,	**Is 43:12**	5002
And he **d** of Jerusalem,	**Is 44:28**	559
As I live," **d** the LORD, "You will	**Is 49:18**	5002
what do I have here," **d** the LORD,	**Is 52:5**	5002
Again the LORD **d**,	**Is 52:5**	5002
is from Me," **d** the LORD.	**Is 54:17**	5002
are your ways My ways," **d** the LORD.	**Is 55:8**	5002
the dispersed of Israel, **d**,	**Is 56:8**	5002
in Jacob," **d** the LORD.	**Is 59:20**	5002
came into being," **d** the LORD.	**Is 66:2**	5002
to an end altogether," **d** the LORD.	**Is 66:17**	5002
will endure before Me," **d** the LORD,	**Is 66:22**	5002
you to deliver you," **d** the LORD.	**Jer 1:8**	5002
kingdoms of the north," **d** the LORD;	**Jer 1:15**	5002
you to deliver you," **d** the LORD.	**Jer 1:19**	5002
came upon them," **d** the LORD.' "	**Jer 2:3**	5002
yet contend with you," **d** the LORD,	**Jer 2:9**	5002
be very desolate," **d** the LORD.	**Jer 2:12**	5002
in you," **d** the Lord GOD of hosts.	**Jer 2:19**	5002
is before Me," **d** the Lord GOD.	**Jer 2:22**	5002
against Me," **d** the LORD.	**Jer 2:29**	5002
Yet you turn to Me," **d** the LORD.	**Jer 3:1**	5002
rather in deception," **d** the LORD.	**Jer 3:10**	5002
faithless Israel,' **d** the LORD;	**Jer 3:12**	5002
For I am gracious,' **d** the LORD;	**Jer 3:12**	5002
not obeyed My voice,' **d** the LORD.	**Jer 3:13**	5002
O faithless sons,' **d** the LORD;	**Jer 3:14**	5002
increased in the land," **d** the LORD,	**Jer 3:16**	5002
Me, O house of Israel," **d** the LORD.	**Jer 3:20**	5002
will return, O Israel," **d** the LORD,	**Jer 4:1**	5002
about in that day," **d** the LORD,	**Jer 4:9**	5002
For a voice **d** from Dan, And	**Jer 4:15**	5046
rebelled against Me,' **d** the LORD.	**Jer 4:17**	5002
punish these *people,*" **d** the LORD,	**Jer 5:9**	5002
treacherously with Me," **d** the LORD.	**Jer 5:11**	5002
O house of Israel," **d** the LORD.	**Jer 5:15**	5002
even in those days," **d** the LORD,	**Jer 5:18**	5002
'Do you not fear Me?' **d** the LORD.	**Jer 5:22**	5002
not punish these *people?*' **d** the LORD,	**Jer 5:29**	5002
of the land," **d** the LORD.	**Jer 6:12**	5002
even I, have seen *it,*" **d** the LORD.	**Jer 7:11**	5002
done all these things," **d** the LORD,	**Jer 7:13**	5002
"Do they spite Me?" **d** the LORD.	**Jer 7:19**	5002
is evil in My sight," **d** the LORD,	**Jer 7:30**	5002
days are coming," **d** the LORD,	**Jer 7:32**	5002
"At that time," **d** the LORD,	**Jer 8:1**	5002
driven them," **d** the LORD of hosts.	**Jer 8:3**	5002
snatch them away," **d** the LORD;	**Jer 8:13**	5002
they will bite you," **d** the LORD.	**Jer 8:17**	5002
they do not know Me," **d** the LORD.	**Jer 9:3**	5002
refuse to know Me," **d** the LORD.	**Jer 9:6**	5002
them for these things?" **d** the LORD.	**Jer 9:9**	5002
in these things," **d** the LORD.	**Jer 9:24**	5002
the days are coming," **d** the LORD,	**Jer 9:25**	5002
uproot and destroy it," **d** the LORD.	**Jer 12:17**	5002
of Judah cling to Me,' **d** the LORD,	**Jer 13:11**	5002
and the sons together," **d** the LORD.	**Jer 13:14**	5002
to you From Me," **d** the LORD,	**Jer 13:25**	5002
four kinds *of doom,*" **d** the LORD:	**Jer 15:3**	5002
who have forsaken Me," **d** the LORD,	**Jer 15:6**	5002
Before their enemies," **d** the LORD.	**Jer 15:9**	5002
you And deliver you," **d** the LORD.	**Jer 15:20**	5002
from this people," **d** the LORD,	**Jer 16:5**	5002
have forsaken Me,' **d** the LORD,	**Jer 16:11**	5002
days are coming," **d** the LORD,	**Jer 16:14**	5002
for many fishermen," **d** the LORD,	**Jer 16:16**	5002
attentively to Me," **d** the LORD,	**Jer 17:24**	5002
you as this potter *does?*" **d** the LORD.	**Jer 18:6**	5002
days are coming," **d** the LORD,	**Jer 19:6**	5002
and its inhabitants," **d** the LORD,	**Jer 19:12**	5002
"Then afterwards," **d** the LORD,	**Jer 21:7**	5002
harm and not for good," **d** the LORD.	**Jer 21:10**	5002
O rocky plain," **d** the LORD,	**Jer 21:13**	5002
results of your deeds," **d** the LORD,	**Jer 21:14**	5002
I swear by Myself," **d** the LORD,	**Jer 22:5**	5002
it means to know Me?" **D** the LORD.	**Jer 22:16**	5002
"As I live," **d** the LORD, "even though	**Jer 22:24**	5002
sheep of My pasture!" **d** the LORD.	**Jer 23:1**	5002
evil of your deeds," **d** the LORD.	**Jer 23:2**	5002
will any be missing," **d** the LORD.	**Jer 23:4**	5002
the days are coming," **d** the LORD,	**Jer 23:5**	5002
the days are coming," **d** the LORD,	**Jer 23:7**	5002
their wickedness," **d** the LORD.	**Jer 23:11**	5002
of their punishment," **d** the LORD.	**Jer 23:12**	5002
I a God who is near," **d** the LORD,	**Jer 23:23**	5002
So I do not see him?" **d** the LORD.	**Jer 23:24**	5002
heavens and the earth?" **d** the LORD.	**Jer 23:24**	5002
in common with grain?" **d** the LORD.	**Jer 23:28**	5002
not My word like fire?" **d** the LORD,	**Jer 23:29**	5002
against the prophets," **d** the LORD,	**Jer 23:30**	5002
against the prophets," **d** the LORD,	**Jer 23:31**	5002
'The Lord **d**.'	**Jer 23:31**	5002
false dreams," **d** the LORD,	**Jer 23:32**	5002
the slightest benefit," **d** the LORD.	**Jer 23:32**	5002
The LORD **d**, 'I will abandon you.'	**Jer 23:33**	5002
not listened to Me," **d** the LORD,	**Jer 25:7**	5002
families of the north,' **d** the LORD,	**Jer 25:9**	5002
and that nation,' **d** the LORD,	**Jer 25:12**	5002
the earth," **d** the LORD of hosts.'	**Jer 25:29**	5002
them to the sword,' **d** the LORD."	**Jer 25:31**	5002
and with pestilence," **d** the LORD,	**Jer 27:8**	5002
remain on its land," **d** the LORD,	**Jer 27:11**	5002
I have not sent them," **d** the LORD,	**Jer 27:15**	5002
the day I visit them,' **d** the LORD.	**Jer 27:22**	5002
who went to Babylon,' **d** the LORD,	**Jer 28:4**	5002
I have not sent them,' **d** the LORD.	**Jer 29:9**	5002
that I have for you,' **d** the LORD,	**Jer 29:11**	5002
will be found by you,' **d** the LORD,	**Jer 29:14**	5002
I have driven you,' **d** the LORD,	**Jer 29:14**	5002
listened to My words,' **d** the LORD,	**Jer 29:19**	5002
you did not listen,' **d** the LORD.	**Jer 29:19**	5002
and am a witness," **d** the LORD.' "	**Jer 29:23**	5002
to do to My people," **d** the LORD,	**Jer 29:32**	5002
days are coming,' **d** the LORD,	**Jer 30:3**	5002
on that day,' **d** the LORD of hosts,	**Jer 30:8**	5002
O Jacob My servant,' **d** the LORD,	**Jer 30:10**	5002
'For I am with you,' **d** the LORD,	**Jer 30:11**	5002
you of your wounds,' **d** the LORD,	**Jer 30:17**	5002
his life to approach Me?' **d** the LORD.	**Jer 30:21**	5002
"At that time," **d** the LORD, "I will	**Jer 31:1**	5002
with My goodness," **d** the LORD.	**Jer 31:14**	5002
will be rewarded," **d** the LORD,	**Jer 31:16**	5002
hope for your future," **d** the LORD,	**Jer 31:17**	5002
have mercy on him," **d** the LORD.	**Jer 31:20**	5002
days are coming," **d** the LORD,	**Jer 31:27**	5002
to build and to plant," **d** the LORD.	**Jer 31:28**	5002
days are coming," **d** the LORD,	**Jer 31:31**	5002
was a husband to them," **d** the LORD.	**Jer 31:32**	5002
after those days," **d** the LORD,	**Jer 31:33**	5002
the greatest of them," **d** the LORD,	**Jer 31:34**	5002
From before Me," **d** the LORD,	**Jer 31:36**	5002
that they have done," **d** the LORD.	**Jer 31:37**	5002
days are coming," **d** the LORD,	**Jer 31:38**	5002
until I visit him," **d** the LORD.	**Jer 32:5**	5002
work of their hands," **d** the LORD.	**Jer 32:30**	5002
their fortunes,' **d** the LORD."	**Jer 32:44**	5002
days are coming,' **d** the LORD,	**Jer 33:14**	5002
have spoken the word," **d** the LORD.	**Jer 34:5**	5002
a release to you,' **d** the LORD,	**Jer 34:17**	5002
I am going to command,' **d** the LORD,	**Jer 34:22**	5002
listening to My words?" **d** the LORD.	**Jer 35:13**	5002
you on that day," **d** the LORD,	**Jer 39:17**	5002
trusted in Me," **d** the LORD.' "	**Jer 39:18**	5002
not be afraid of him,' **d** the LORD,	**Jer 42:11**	5002
be the sign to you,' **d** the LORD,	**Jer 44:29**	5002
disaster on all flesh,' **d** the LORD,	**Jer 45:5**	5002
Terror is on every side!" **D** the LORD.	**Jer 46:5**	5002
d the King Whose name is the LORD	**Jer 46:18**	5002
cut down her forest," **d** the LORD;	**Jer 46:23**	5002
as in the days of old," **d** the LORD.	**Jer 46:26**	5002
servant, do not fear," **d** the LORD,	**Jer 46:28**	5002
the days are coming," **d** the LORD,	**Jer 48:12**	5002
down to the slaughter," **D** the King,	**Jer 48:15**	5002
and his arm broken," **d** the LORD.	**Jer 48:25**	5002
"I know his fury," **d** the LORD,	**Jer 48:30**	5002
make an end of Moab," **d** the LORD,	**Jer 48:35**	5002
an undesirable vessel," **d** the LORD.	**Jer 48:38**	5002
O inhabitant of Moab," **d** the LORD.	**Jer 48:43**	5002
of their punishment," **d** the LORD.	**Jer 48:44**	5002
In the latter days," **d** the LORD.	**Jer 48:47**	5002
the days are coming," **d** the LORD,	**Jer 49:2**	5002
upon you," **D** the Lord GOD of hosts,	**Jer 49:5**	5002
of the sons of Ammon," **D** the LORD.	**Jer 49:6**	5002
have sworn by Myself," **d** the LORD,	**Jer 49:13**	5002
you down from there," **d** the LORD.	**Jer 49:16**	5002
in that day," **d** the LORD of hosts.	**Jer 49:26**	5002
inhabitants of Hazor," **d** the LORD;	**Jer 49:30**	5002
Which lives securely," **d** the LORD.	**Jer 49:31**	5002
from every side," **d** the LORD.	**Jer 49:32**	5002
Even My fierce anger,' **d** the LORD,	**Jer 49:37**	5002
it king and princes,' **D** the LORD.	**Jer 49:38**	5002
the fortunes of Elam,' " **D** the LORD.	**Jer 49:39**	5002
days and at that time," **d** the LORD,	**Jer 50:4**	5002
her will have enough," **d** the LORD.	**Jer 50:10**	5002
days and at that time,' **d** the LORD,	**Jer 50:20**	5002
utterly destroy them," **d** the LORD,	**Jer 50:21**	5002
silenced in that day," **d** the LORD.	**Jer 50:30**	5002
one," **D** the Lord GOD of hosts,	**Jer 50:31**	5002
against the Chaldeans," **d** the LORD,	**Jer 50:35**	5002
with its neighbors," **d** the LORD,	**Jer 50:40**	5002
Zion before your eyes," **d** the LORD.	**Jer 51:24**	5002
the whole earth," **d** the LORD,	**Jer 51:25**	5002
be desolate forever," **d** the LORD.	**Jer 51:26**	5002
sleep And not wake up," **d** the LORD.	**Jer 51:39**	5002
to her from the north," **D** the LORD.	**Jer 51:48**	5002
the days are coming," **d** the LORD,	**Jer 51:52**	5002
will come to her," **d** the LORD.	**Jer 51:53**	5002
sleep and not wake up," **D** the King,	**Jer 51:57**	5002
'So as I live,' **d** the Lord GOD,	**Ezk 5:11**	5002
a sword upon you," the Lord GOD **d**.	**Ezk 11:8**	5002
on their heads," **d** the Lord GOD.	**Ezk 11:21**	5002
perform it," **d** the Lord GOD.' "	**Ezk 12:25**	5002
will be performed," ' " **d** the Lord GOD.	**Ezk 12:28**	5002
'The LORD **d**,' when the LORD has	**Ezk 13:6**	5002
'The LORD **d**,' but it is not I who	**Ezk 13:7**	5002
I am against you," **d** the Lord GOD.	**Ezk 13:8**	5002
there is no peace,' **d** the Lord GOD.	**Ezk 13:16**	5002
be their God," ' **d** the Lord GOD."	**Ezk 14:11**	5002
themselves," **d** the Lord GOD.	**Ezk 14:14**	5002
midst, as I live," **d** the Lord GOD,	**Ezk 14:16**	5002
midst, as I live," **d** the Lord GOD,	**Ezk 14:18**	5002
midst, as I live," **d** the Lord GOD,	**Ezk 14:20**	5002
I did to it," **d** the Lord GOD.	**Ezk 14:23**	5002
unfaithfully,' " **d** the Lord GOD.	**Ezk 15:8**	5002
you became Mine," **d** the Lord GOD.	**Ezk 16:8**	5002
I bestowed on you," **d** the Lord GOD.	**Ezk 16:14**	5002
so it happened," **d** the Lord GOD.	**Ezk 16:19**	5002
('Woe, woe to you!' **d** the Lord GOD),	**Ezk 16:23**	5002
is your heart," **d** the Lord GOD,	**Ezk 16:30**	5002
on your own head," **d** the Lord GOD,	**Ezk 16:43**	5002
"As I live," **d** the Lord GOD, "Sodom,	**Ezk 16:48**	5002
and abominations," the LORD **d**.	**Ezk 16:58**	5002
you have done," the Lord GOD **d**.	**Ezk 16:63**	5002
'As I live,' **d** the Lord GOD,	**Ezk 17:16**	5002
"As I live," **d** the Lord GOD,	**Ezk 18:3**	5002
will surely live," **d** the Lord GOD.	**Ezk 18:9**	5002
of the wicked," **d** the Lord GOD,	**Ezk 18:23**	5002
to his conduct," **d** the Lord GOD.	**Ezk 18:30**	5002
anyone who dies," **d** the Lord GOD.	**Ezk 18:32**	5002
As I live," **d** the Lord GOD, "I will	**Ezk 20:3**	5002
As I live," **d** the Lord GOD, "I will	**Ezk 20:31**	5002
"As I live," **d** the Lord GOD, "surely	**Ezk 20:33**	5002
judgment with you," **d** the Lord GOD.	**Ezk 20:36**	5002
of Israel," **d** the Lord GOD,	**Ezk 20:40**	5002
of Israel," **d** the Lord GOD.' "	**Ezk 20:44**	5002
it will happen,' **d** the Lord GOD."	**Ezk 21:7**	5002
will be no more?" **d** the Lord GOD.	**Ezk 21:13**	5002
have forgotten Me," **d** the Lord GOD.	**Ezk 22:12**	5002
upon their heads," **d** the Lord GOD.	**Ezk 22:31**	5002
for I have spoken,' **d** the Lord GOD.	**Ezk 23:34**	5002
judge you," **d** the Lord GOD.' "	**Ezk 24:14**	5002
know My vengeance," **d** the Lord GOD.	**Ezk 25:14**	5002
for I have spoken,' **d** the Lord GOD,	**Ezk 26:5**	5002
LORD have spoken," **d** the Lord GOD.	**Ezk 26:14**	5002
be found again," **d** the Lord GOD.	**Ezk 26:21**	5002
d the Lord GOD!	**Ezk 28:10**	5002
they acted for Me," **d** the Lord GOD.	**Ezk 29:20**	5002
her by the sword," **D** the Lord GOD.	**Ezk 30:6**	5002
all his hordes!" ' **d** the Lord GOD."	**Ezk 31:18**	5002
on your land," **D** the Lord GOD.	**Ezk 32:8**	5002
to run like oil," **D** the Lord GOD.	**Ezk 32:14**	5002
shall chant it," **d** the Lord GOD.	**Ezk 32:16**	5002
and all his army," **d** the Lord GOD.	**Ezk 32:31**	5002
all his hordes," **d** the Lord GOD.	**Ezk 32:32**	5002
d the Lord GOD, 'I take no pleasure	**Ezk 33:11**	5002
"As I live," **d** the Lord GOD, "surely	**Ezk 34:8**	5002
lead them to rest," **d** the Lord GOD.	**Ezk 34:15**	5002
are My people," **d** the Lord GOD.	**Ezk 34:30**	5002
and I am your God," **d** the Lord GOD.	**Ezk 34:31**	5002
as I live," **d** the Lord GOD,	**Ezk 35:6**	5002
as I live," **d** the Lord GOD,	**Ezk 35:11**	5002
of children,' **d** the Lord GOD.	**Ezk 36:14**	5002
any longer," **d** the Lord GOD.' "	**Ezk 36:15**	5002
I am the LORD," **d** the Lord GOD,	**Ezk 36:23**	5002
for your sake," **d** the Lord GOD,	**Ezk 36:32**	5002
and done it," **d** the LORD.' "	**Ezk 37:14**	5002
land of Israel," **d** the Lord GOD,	**Ezk 38:18**	5002
all My mountains," **d** the Lord GOD.	**Ezk 38:21**	5002
I who have spoken," **d** the Lord GOD.	**Ezk 39:5**	5002
it shall be done," **d** the Lord GOD.	**Ezk 39:8**	5002
plundered them," **d** the Lord GOD.	**Ezk 39:10**	5002
I glorify Myself," **d** the Lord GOD.	**Ezk 39:13**	5002
the men of war," **d** the Lord GOD.	**Ezk 39:20**	5002
house of Israel," **d** the Lord GOD.	**Ezk 39:29**	5002
to minister to Me,' **d** the Lord GOD,	**Ezk 43:19**	5002
will accept you,' **d** the Lord GOD."	**Ezk 43:27**	5002
against them," **d** the Lord GOD,	**Ezk 44:12**	5002
fat and the blood," **d** the Lord GOD.	**Ezk 44:15**	5002
his sin offering," **d** the Lord GOD.	**Ezk 44:27**	5002
from My people," **d** the Lord GOD.	**Ezk 45:9**	5002
for them," **d** the Lord GOD.	**Ezk 45:15**	5002
his inheritance," **d** the Lord GOD.	**Ezk 47:23**	5002
several portions," **d** the Lord GOD.	**Ezk 48:29**	5002
so that she forgot Me," **d** the LORD.	**Hos 2:13**	5002
about in that day," **d** the LORD,	**Hos 2:16**	5002
that I will respond," **d** the LORD.	**Hos 2:21**	5002
them in their houses, **d** the LORD.	**Hos 11:11**	5002
now," **d** the LORD, "Return to Me	**Jl 2:12**	5002
not so, O sons of Israel?" **d** the LORD.	**Am 2:11**	5002
naked in that day," **d** the LORD.	**Am 2:16**	5002
to do what is right," **d** the LORD,	**Am 3:10**	5002

house of Jacob," **D** the Lord GOD, **Am 3:13** 5002
will come to an end," **D** the LORD. **Am 3:15** 5002
be cast to Harmon," **d** the LORD. **Am 4:3** 5002
sons of Israel," **D** the Lord GOD. **Am 4:5** 5002
not returned to Me," **d** the LORD. **Am 4:6** 5002
not returned to Me," **d** the LORD. **Am 4:8** 5002
not returned to Me," **d** the LORD. **Am 4:9** 5002
not returned to Me," **d** the LORD. **Am 4:10** 5002
not returned to Me," **d** the LORD. **Am 4:11** 5002
d to man what are His thoughts, **Am 4:13** 5046
Israel," **d** the LORD God of hosts, **Am 6:14** 5002
in that day," **d** the Lord GOD. **Am 8:3** 5002
about in that day," **d** the Lord GOD, **Am 8:9** 5002
days are coming," **d** the Lord GOD, **Am 8:11** 5002
Me, O sons of Israel?" **d** the LORD. **Am 9:7** 5002
the house of Jacob," **D** the LORD. **Am 9:8** 5002
My name," **D** the LORD who does this. **Am 9:12** 5002
days are coming," **d** the LORD, **Am 9:13** 5002
I will bring you down," **d** the LORD. **Ob 1:4** 5002
I not on that day," **d** the LORD, **Ob 1:8** 5002
d the LORD, "I will assemble **Mi 4:6** 5002
will be in that day," **d** the LORD, **Mi 5:10** 5002
against you," **d** the LORD of hosts. **Na 2:13** 5002
against you," **d** the LORD of hosts; **Na 3:5** 5002
the face of the earth," **d** the LORD. **Zph 1:2** 5002
the face of the earth," **d** the LORD. **Zph 1:3** 5002
"On that day," **d** the LORD, **Zph 1:10** 5002
as I live," **d** the LORD of hosts, **Zph 2:9** 5002
wait for Me," **d** the LORD, **Zph 3:8** 5002
d the LORD of hosts, **Hg 1:9** 5002
"'I am with you,' **d** the LORD." **Hg 1:13** 5002
courage, Zerubbabel,' **d** the LORD, **Hg 2:4** 5002
the land take courage,' **d** the LORD, **Hg 2:4** 5002
d the LORD of hosts. **Hg 2:4** 5002
gold is Mine,' **d** the LORD of hosts. **Hg 2:8** 5002
give peace,' **d** the LORD of hosts." **Hg 2:9** 5002
this nation before Me,' **d** the LORD, **Hg 2:14** 5002
not *come back* to Me,' **d** the LORD. **Hg 2:17** 5002
'On that day,' **d** the LORD of hosts, **Hg 2:23** 5002
Shealtiel, My servant,' **d** the LORD, **Hg 2:23** 5002
chosen you,' " **d** the LORD of hosts. **Hg 2:23** 5002
"Return to Me," **d** the LORD of hosts, **Zch 1:3** 5002
or give heed to Me," **d** the LORD. **Zch 1:4** 5002
built in it," **d** the LORD of hosts, **Zch 1:16** 5002
'For I,' **d** the LORD, **Zch 2:5** 5002
the land of the north," **d** the LORD, **Zch 2:6** 5002
winds of the heavens," **d** the LORD. **Zch 2:6** 5002
dwell in your midst," **d** the LORD. **Zch 2:10** 5002
on it,' **d** the LORD of hosts, **Zch 3:9** 5002
'In that day,' **d** the LORD of **Zch 3:10** 5002
it go forth," **d** the LORD of hosts, **Zch 5:4** 5002
d the LORD of hosts. **Zch 8:6** 5002
former days,' **d** the LORD of hosts. **Zch 8:11** 5002
are what I hate,' **d** the LORD." **Zch 8:17** 5002
name they will walk," **d** the LORD. **Zch 10:12** 5002
of the land," **d** the LORD; **Zch 11:6** 5002
Thus **d** the LORD who stretches out **Zch 12:1** 5002
d the LORD, "I will strike every horse **Zch 12:4** 5002
in that day," **d** the LORD of hosts, **Zch 13:2** 5002
My Associate," **D** the LORD of hosts. **Zch 13:7** 5002
about in all the land," **D** the LORD, **Zch 13:8** 5002
Esau Jacob's brother?" **d** the LORD. **Mal 1:2** 5002

DECLARING
is **d** the work of His hands. **Ps 19:1** 5046
D things that are upright. **Is 45:19** 5046
D the end from the beginning, **Is 46:10** 5046
This very day I am **d** that I will **Zch 9:12** 5046
God is now **d** to men that all **Ac 17:30** *518*
how I did not shrink from **d** to you **Ac 20:20** *312*
"For I did not shrink from **d** to **Ac 20:27** *312*
loudly **d** that he ought not to live **Ac 25:24** *994*
but *kept* **d** both to those of **Ac 26:20** *518*
d that God is certainly among you. **1Co 14:25** *518*

DECLINE
for the shadow to **d** ten steps; **2Ki 20:10** 5186

DECLINED
all our days have **d** in Your fury; **Ps 90:9** 6437

DECLINES
Woe to us, for the day **d**, **Jer 6:4** 6437

DECORATE
Although you **d** *yourself with* **Jer 4:30** 5710b
d *it* with silver and with gold; **Jer 10:4** 3302

DECORATED
and the **d** caps of fine linen, **Ex 39:28** 6287b
and **d** yourselves with ornaments; **Ezk 23:40** 5710b

DECREASE
He does not let their cattle **d**. **Ps 107:38** 4591
and multiply there and do not **d**. **Jer 29:6** 4591
"He must increase, but I must **d**. **Jn 3:30** *1642*

DECREASED
and fifty days the water **d**. **Gn 8:3** 2637
The water **d** steadily until the **Gn 8:5** 2637

DECREE
So they established a **d** to **2Ch 30:5** 1697
"A **d** has been issued by me, **Ezr 4:19** 2942
a **d** to make these men stop *work,* **Ezr 4:21** 2942
rebuilt until a **d** is issued by me. **Ezr 4:21** 2942
"Who issued you a **d** to rebuild **Ezr 5:3** 2942
'Who issued you a **d** to rebuild **Ezr 5:9** 2942
a **d** to rebuild this house of God. **Ezr 5:13** 2942
if it be that a **d** was issued by **Ezr 5:17** 2942
Then King Darius issued a **d**, **Ezr 6:1** 2942
Cyrus, Cyrus the king issued a **d**: **Ezr 6:3** 2942
I issue a **d** concerning what you **Ezr 6:8** 2942
"And I issued a **d** that any man **Ezr 6:11** 2942
I, Darius, have issued *this* **d**, **Ezr 6:12** 2942
their colleagues carried out *the* **d** **Ezr 6:13**
God of Israel and the **d** of Cyrus, **Ezr 6:14** 2942
Now this is the copy of the **d** **Ezr 7:11** 5406
I have issued a **d** that any of the **Ezr 7:13** 2942
issue a **d** to all the treasurers **Ezr 7:21** 2942
the command and **d** of the king were **Es 2:8** 1881
the **d** was issued at the citadel in Susa; **Es 3:15** 1881
command and **d** of the king came, **Es 4:3** 1881
for a **d** which is written in the **Es 8:8** 3791
the **d** was given out at the citadel **Es 8:14** 1881
commandment and his **d** arrived, **Es 8:17** 1881
"You will also **d** a thing, and it **Jb 22:28** 1504
surely tell of the **d** of the LORD: **Ps 2:7** 2706
One which devises mischief by **d**? **Ps 94:20** 2706
made a **d** which will not pass away. **Ps 148:6** 2706
kings reign, And rulers **d** justice. **Pr 8:15** 2710
for the sea, An eternal **d**, **Jer 5:22** 2706
me, there is only one **d** for you. **Da 2:9** 1882
So the **d** went forth that the wise **Da 2:13** 1882
the **d** from the king *so* urgent?" **Da 2:15** 1882
have made a **d** that every man who **Da 3:10** 2942
I make a **d** that any people, **Da 3:29** 2942
by the **d** of the *angelic* watchers And **Da 4:17** 1510
this is the **d** of the Most High, **Da 4:24** 1510
"I make a **d** that in all the **Da 6:26** 2942
a **d** to restore and rebuild Jerusalem **Da 9:25** 1697
the **d** of the king and his nobles: **Jon 3:7** 2940
Before the **d** takes effect **Zph 2:2** 2706
a **d** went out from Caesar Augustus, **Lk 2:1** *1378*

DECREED
and what had been **d** against her. **Es 2:1** 1504
it be **d** that they be destroyed, **Es 3:9** 3789
the heritage **d** to him by God." **Jb 20:29** 561
they will drink and forget what is **d**, **Pr 31:5** 2710
destruction, one that is **d**, **Is 10:23** 2782
"Seventy weeks have been **d** for **Da 9:24** 2852
destruction, one that is **d**, **Da 9:27** 2782
for that which is **d** will be done. **Da 11:36** 2782

DECREES
And many such **d** are with Him. **Jb 23:14**
they were delivering the **d** which **Ac 16:4** *1378*
act contrary to the **d** of Caesar, **Ac 17:7** *1378*
of debt consisting of **d** against us **Col 2:14** *1378*
do you submit yourself to **d**, **Col 2:20** *1379*

DEDAN
sons of Raamah *were* Sheba and **D**. **Gn 10:7** 1719
became the father of Sheba and **D**. **Gn 25:3** 1719
And the sons of **D** were Asshurim **Gn 25:3** 1719
sons of Raamah *were* Sheba and **D**. **1Ch 1:9** 1719
sons of Jokshan *were* Sheba and **D**. **1Ch 1:32** 1719
and **D**, Tema, Buz and all who cut **Jer 25:23** 1719
in the depths, O inhabitants of **D**, **Jer 49:8** 1719
to **D** they will fall by the sword. **Ezk 25:13** 1719
"The sons of **D** were your traders. **Ezk 27:15** 1719
"**D** traded with you in **Ezk 27:20** 1719
"Sheba and **D** and the merchants **Ezk 38:13** 1719

DEDANITES
spend the night, O caravans of **D**. **Is 21:13** 1720

DEDICATE
"**D** yourselves today to the **Ex 32:29** 4390
of Israel, which they **d** to Me, **Lv 22:2** 6942
the sons of Israel **d** to the LORD, **Lv 22:3** 6942
to **d** himself to the LORD, **Nu 6:2** 5144b
and shall **d** to the LORD his days **Nu 6:12** 5144b
the battle and another man would **d** it. **Dt 20:5** 2596
"I wholly **d** the silver from my **Jg 17:3** 6942

DEDICATED
and he defiles his **d** head *of hair,* **Nu 6:9** 5145
Nazirite shall then shave his **d** head **Nu 6:18** 5145
and take the **d** hair of his head **Nu 6:18** 5145
after he has shaved his **d** *hair.* **Nu 6:19** 5145
are a gift to you, **d** to the LORD, **Nu 18:6** 5414
a new house and has not **d** it? **Dt 20:5** 2596
"So I have also **d** him to the LORD; **1Sa 1:28** 7592
as he lives he is **d** to the LORD." **1Sa 1:28** 7592
of the one she **d** to the LORD." **1Sa 2:20** 7596, 7592
David also **d** these to the LORD, **2Sa 8:11** 6942
with the silver and gold that he had **d** **2Sa 8:11** 6942
the things **d** by his father David, **1Ki 7:51** 6944
of Israel **d** the house of the LORD. **1Ki 8:63** 2596
house of the LORD the **d** things of his **1Ki 15:15** 6944
his father and his own **d** things: **1Ki 15:15** 6944
fathers, kings of Judah, had **d**, **2Ki 12:18** 6942
King David also **d** these to the **1Ch 18:11** 6942
of the treasures of the **d** gifts. **1Ch 26:20** 6944
all the treasures of the **d** gifts which **1Ch 26:26** 6944
and the commanders of the army, had **d**. **1Ch 26:26** 6942
They **d** part of the spoil won in **1Ch 26:27** 6942
had **d** and Saul the son of Kish, **1Ch 26:28** 6942
everyone who had **d** *anything,* **1Ch 26:28** 6942
the storehouses of the **d** things; **1Ch 28:12** 6944
that David his father had **d**, **2Ch 5:1** 6944
all the people **d** the house of God. **2Ch 7:5** 2596
into the house of God the **d** things **2Ch 15:18** 6944
his father and his own **d** things: **2Ch 15:18** 6944

DEDICATING
of the LORD my God, **d** it to Him, **2Ch 2:4** 6942

DEDICATION
The leaders offered the **d** **Nu 7:10** 2598
day, for the **d** of the altar." **Nu 7:11** 2598
This *was* the **d** *offering* for the **Nu 7:84** 2598
This *was* the **d** *offering* for the **Nu 7:88** 2598
for the **d** of the altar they **2Ch 7:9** 2598
d of this house of God with joy. **Ezr 6:16** 2597
They offered for the **d** of this **Ezr 6:17** 2597
Now at the **d** of the wall of **Ne 12:27** 2598
celebrate the **d** with gladness, **Ne 12:27** 2598
d of the image that Nebuchadnezzar **Da 3:2** 2597
provinces were assembled for the **d** **Da 3:3** 2597
of the **D** took place at Jerusalem; **Jn 10:22** *1456*

DEDUCTED
it shall be **d** from your valuation. **Lv 27:18** 1639

DEED
"What is this **d** that you have done? **Gn 44:15** 4639
woman who has done this evil **d** to **Dt 17:5** 1697
because by this **d** you have given **2Sa 12:14** 1697
He will repay him for his good **d**. **Pr 19:17** 1576
matter and for every **d** is there. **Ec 3:17** 4639
seen and applied my mind to every **d** **Ec 8:9** 4639
an evil **d** is not executed quickly, **Ec 8:11** 4639
"I signed and sealed the **d**, **Jer 32:10** 5612
and I gave the **d** of purchase to **Jer 32:12** 5612
who signed the **d** of purchase, **Jer 32:12** 5612
deeds, this sealed **d** of purchase and **Jer 32:14** 5612
deed of purchase and this open **d**, **Jer 32:14** 5612
"After I had given the **d** of purchase **Jer 32:16** 5612
great in counsel and mighty in **d**, **Jer 32:19** 5950
For she has done a good **d** to Me. **Mt 26:10** *2041*
She has done a good **d** to Me. **Mk 14:6** *2041*
who was a prophet mighty in **d** and **Lk 24:19** *2041*
"I did one **d**, and you all marvel. **Jn 7:21** *2041*
conceived this **d** in your heart? **Ac 5:4** *4229*
of the Gentiles by word and **d**, **Ro 15:18** *2041*
had done this **d** would be removed **1Co 5:2** *2041*
an abundance for every good **d**; **2Co 9:8** *2041*
we are also in **d** when present. **2Co 10:11** *2041*
Whatever you do in word or **d**, **Col 3:17** *2041*
will rescue me from every evil **d**, **2Tm 4:18** *2041*
and worthless for any good **d**. **Ti 1:16** *2041*
to redeem us from every lawless **d** **Ti 2:14** *458*
to be ready for every good **d**, **Ti 3:1** *2041*
with tongue, but in **d** and truth. **1Jn 3:18** *2041*

DEEDED
of its border, were **d** over **Gn 23:17** 6965
were **d** over to Abraham for a **Gn 23:20** 6965

DEEDS
them, nor do according to their **d**; **Ex 23:24** 4639
has sent me to do all these **d**; **Nu 16:28** 4639
d and publicly defames her, **Dt 22:14** 1697
has charged her with shameful **d**, **Dt 22:17** 1697
on account of the evil of your **d**, **Dt 28:20** 4611
and had known all the **d** of the **Jos 24:31** 4639
the righteous **d** of the LORD, **Jg 5:11** 6666
righteous **d** for His peasantry in Israel. **Jg 5:11** 6666
"Like all the **d** which they have **1Sa 8:8** 4639
and since his **d** *have been* very **1Sa 19:4** 4639
of Kabzeel, who had done mighty **d**, **2Sa 23:20** 6467
his sons came and told him all the **d** **1Ki 13:11** 4639
man of Kabzeel, mighty in **d**, **1Ch 11:22** 6467
known His **d** among the peoples. **1Ch 16:8** 5949
His wonderful **d** which He has done, **1Ch 16:12** 6381
wonderful **d** among all the peoples. **1Ch 16:24** 6381
of Hezekiah and his **d** of devotion, **2Ch 32:32** 2617a
acts of Josiah and his **d** of devotion **2Ch 35:26** 2617a
our evil **d** and our great guilt, **Ezr 9:13** 4639
they were speaking about his good **d** **Ne 6:19** 2899b
did not remember Your wondrous **d** **Ne 9:17** 6381
You or turn from their evil **d**. **Ne 9:35** 4611
and do not blot out my loyal **d** **Ne 13:14** 2617a
Declare among the peoples His **d**. **Ps 9:11** 5949
they have committed abominable **d**; **Ps 14:1** 5949
As for the **d** of men, by the word **Ps 17:4** 6468
according to the **d** of their hands; **Ps 28:4** 4639
the LORD Nor the **d** of His hands, **Ps 28:5** 4639
By awesome **d** You answer us in **Ps 65:5**
in *His* **d** toward the sons of men. **Ps 66:5** 5949
him who goes on in his guilty **d**. **Ps 68:21** 817
with the mighty **d** of the Lord GOD; **Ps 71:16** 1369
I still declare Your wondrous **d**. **Ps 71:17** 6381
Who works **d** of deliverance in the **Ps 74:12** 3444
shall remember the **d** of the LORD; **Ps 77:11** 4611
all Your work And muse on Your **d**. **Ps 77:12** 5949
They forgot His **d** And **Ps 78:11** 5949
are great and do wondrous **d**; **Ps 86:10** 6381
wonderful **d** among all the peoples. **Ps 96:3** 6381
yet an avenger of their *evil* **d**. **Ps 99:8** 5949
The LORD performs righteous **d** And **Ps 103:6** 6666
known His **d** among the peoples. **Ps 105:1** 5949
speak of the mighty **d** of the LORD, **Ps 106:2** 1369
Him to anger with their **d**, **Ps 106:29** 4611
And played the harlot in their **d**. **Ps 106:39** 4611
To practice **d** of wickedness With **Ps 141:4** 5953a
prayer is against their wicked **d**. **Ps 141:5** 7463a
His ways And kind in all His **d**. **Ps 145:17** 4639
Praise Him for His mighty **d**; **Ps 150:2** 1369
And the **d** of a man's hands will **Pr 12:14** 1576
It is by his **d** that a lad **Pr 20:11** 4611
according to the **d** of the wicked. **Ec 8:14** 4639
to the **d** of the righteous. **Ec 8:14** 4639
their **d** are in the hand of God. **Ec 9:1** 5652
the evil of your **d** from My sight. **Is 1:16** 4611
attention to the **d** of the LORD, **Is 5:12** 6467
known His **d** among the peoples; **Is 12:4** 5949
whose **d** are *done* in a dark place, **Is 29:15** 4639
your righteousness and your **d**, **Is 57:12** 4639
According to *their* **d**, **Is 59:18** 1578
are Your zeal and Your mighty **d**? **Is 63:15** 1369
d are like a filthy garment; **Is 64:6** 6666
Because of the evil of your **d**." **Jer 4:4** 4611
"Your ways and your **d** Have **Jer 4:18** 4611
also excel in **d** of wickedness; **Jer 5:28** 1697
"Amend your ways and your **d**, **Jer 7:3** 4611
truly amend your ways and your **d**, **Jer 7:5** 4611
When she has done many vile **d**? **Jer 11:15** 4209
Then You showed me their **d**. **Jer 11:18** 4611

According to the results of his **d**. **Jer 17:10** 4611
reform your ways and your **d**." **Jer 18:11** 4611
Because of the evil of their **d**. **Jer 21:12** 4611
to the results of your **d**," **Jer 21:14** 4611
to you for the evil of your **d**," **Jer 23:2** 4611
way And from the evil of their **d**. **Jer 23:22** 4611
way and from the evil of your **d**, **Jer 25:5** 4611
them according to their **d** and **Jer 25:14** 6467
because of the evil of their **d**.' **Jer 26:3** 4611
amend your ways and your **d** and **Jer 26:13** 4611
"Then I took the **d** of purchase, **Jer 32:11** 5612
"Take these **d**, this sealed deed **Jer 32:14** 5612
according to the fruit of his **d**; **Jer 32:19** 4611
fields for money, sign and seal **d**, **Jer 32:44** 5612
his evil way and amend your **d**, **Jer 35:15** 4611
it, because of the evil of your **d**, **Jer 44:22** 4611
and his righteous **d** which he has **Ezk 3:20** 6666
All his righteous **d** which he has **Ezk 18:24** 6666
remember your ways and all your **d** **Ezk 20:43** 5949
or according to your corrupt **d**, **Ezk 20:44** 5949
so that in all your **d** your sins **Ezk 21:24** 5949
to your **d** I will judge you," **Ezk 24:14** 5949
righteous **d** will be remembered; **Ezk 33:13** 6666
it by their ways and their **d**; **Ezk 36:17** 5949
ways and their **d** I judged them. **Ezk 36:19** 5949
and your **d** that were not good, **Ezk 36:31** 4611
because of their unfaithful **d** **Da 9:7** 4604
to all His **d** which He has done, **Da 9:14** 4639
ways And repay them for their **d**. **Hos 4:9** 4611
Their **d** will not allow them To **Hos 5:4** 4611
And the evil **d** of Samaria, **Hos 7:1** 7463a
Now their **d** are all around them; **Hos 7:2** 4611
Because of the wickedness of their **d** **Hos 9:15** 4611
will repay him according to his **d**. **Hos 12:2** 4611
will never forget any of their **d**. **Am 8:7** 4639
When God saw their **d**, **Jon 3:10** 4639
they have practiced evil **d**. **Mi 3:4** 4611
account of the fruit of their **d**. **Mi 7:13** 4611
were eager to corrupt all their **d**. **Zph 3:7** 5949
all your **d** By which you have rebelled **Zph 3:11** 5949
ways and from your evil **d**." **Zch 1:4** 4611
with our ways and our **d**, **Zch 1:6** 4611
wisdom is vindicated by her **d**." **Mt 11:19** *2041*
EVERY MAN ACCORDING TO HIS **D**. **Mt 16:27** *4234*
do not do according to their **d**; **Mt 23:3** *2041*
all their **d** to be noticed by men; **Mt 23:5** *2041*
d of coveting *and* wickedness, *as* **Mk 7:22** *4124*
"He has done mighty **d** with His arm; **Lk 1:51** *2904*
and approve the **d** of your fathers; **Lk 11:48** *2041*
committed **d** worthy of a flogging, **Lk 12:48**
what we deserve for our **d**; **Lk 23:41**
3739, 4238
for their **d** were evil. **Jn 3:19** *2041*
for fear that his **d** will be exposed. **Jn 3:20** *2041*
that his **d** may be manifested as **Jn 3:21** *2041*
those who did the good **d** to a **Jn 5:29**
those who committed the evil **d** to **Jn 5:29**
of it, that its **d** are evil. **Jn 7:7** *2041*
children, do the **d** of Abraham. **Jn 8:39** *2041*
are doing the **d** of your father." **Jn 8:41** *2041*
speaking of the mighty **d** of God." **Ac 2:11** *3167*
was a man of power in words and **d**. **Ac 7:22** *2041*
with **d** of kindness and charity which **Ac 9:36** *2041*
d appropriate to repentance. **Ac 26:20** *2041*
TO EACH PERSON ACCORDING TO HIS **D**: **Ro 2:6** *2041*
LAWLESS **D** HAVE BEEN FORGIVEN, **Ro 4:7** *458*
to death the **d** of the body, **Ro 8:13** *4234*
Therefore let us lay aside the **d** **Ro 13:12** *2041*
recompensed for his **d** in the body, **2Co 5:10**
end will be according to their **d**. **2Co 11:15** *2041*
the **d** of the flesh are evident, **Ga 5:19** *2041*
in the unfruitful **d** of darkness, **Eph 5:11** *2041*
in mind, *engaged* in evil **d**, **Col 1:21** *2041*
d that are good are quite evident, **1Tm 5:25** *2041*
will repay him according to his **d**. **2Tm 4:14** *2041*
God, but by *their* **d** they deny *Him*, **Ti 1:16** *2041*
to be an example of good **d**, **Ti 2:7** *2041*
possession, zealous for good **d**. **Ti 2:14** *2041*
not on the basis of **d** which we **Ti 3:5** *2041*
be careful to engage in good **d**. **Ti 3:8** *2041*
in good **d** to meet pressing needs, **Ti 3:14** *2041*
D I WILL REMEMBER NO MORE." **Heb 10:17** *458*
one another to love and good **d**, **Heb 10:24** *2041*
his **d** in the gentleness of wisdom. **Jas 3:13** *2041*
may because of your good **d**, **1Pe 2:12** *2041*
after day by *their* lawless **d**), **2Pe 2:8** *2041*
Because his **d** were evil, and his **1Jn 3:12** *2041*
participates in his evil **d**. **2Jn 1:11** *2041*
attention to his **d** which he does, **3Jn 1:10** *2041*
all the ungodly of all their ungodly **d** **Jude 1:15** *2041*
'I know your **d** and your toil and **Rv 2:2** *2041*
and do the **d** you did at first; **Rv 2:5** *2041*
you hate the **d** of the Nicolaitans, **Rv 2:6** *2041*
'I know your **d**, and your love and **Rv 2:19** *2041*
and that your **d** of late are **Rv 2:19** *2041*
unless they repent of her **d**. **Rv 2:22** *2041*
one of you according to your **d**. **Rv 2:23** *2041*
he who keeps My **d** until the end, **Rv 2:26** *2041*
'I know your **d**, that you have a **Rv 3:1** *2041*
for I have not found your **d** **Rv 3:2** *2041*
'I know your **d**. Behold, I have put **Rv 3:8** *2041*
'I know your **d**, that you are **Rv 3:15** *2041*
for their **d** follow with them." **Rv 14:13** *2041*
they did not repent of their **d**. **Rv 16:11** *2041*
to her double according to her **d**; **Rv 18:6** *2041*
the books, according to their **d**. **Rv 20:12** *2041*
one *of them* according to their **d**. **Rv 20:13** *2041*

DEEM
body which we **d** less honorable, **1Co 12:23** *1380*

DEEP
was over the surface of the **d**, **Gn 1:2** 8415
a **d** sleep to fall upon the man, **Gn 2:21** 8639
all the fountains of the great **d** burst **Gn 7:11** 8415
Also the fountains of the **d** and **Gn 8:2** 8415
down, a **d** sleep fell upon Abram; **Gn 15:12** 8639
Blessings of the **d** that lies beneath, **Gn 49:25** 8415
the camp and about two cubits **d** **Nu 11:31**
dew, And from the **d** lying beneath, **Dt 33:13** 8415
Absalom and cast him into a **d** pit **2Sa 18:17** 1419
night, When **d** sleep falls on men, **Jb 4:13** 8639
the land of darkness and **d** shadow, **Jb 10:21** 6757
itself, Of **d** shadow without order, **Jb 10:22** 6757
brings the **d** darkness into light. **Jb 12:22** 6757
And **d** darkness is on my eyelids, **Jb 16:16** 6757
Nor **d** gloom *which* covers me. **Jb 23:17**
The rock in gloom and **d** shadow. **Jb 28:3** 6757
"The **d** says, 'It is not in me'; **Jb 28:14** 8415
"There is no darkness or **d** shadow **Jb 34:22** 6757
walked in the recesses of the **d**? **Jb 38:16** 8415
you seen the gates of **d** darkness? **Jb 38:17** 6757
surface of the **d** is imprisoned. **Jb 38:30** 8415
think the **d** to be gray-haired. **Jb 41:32** 8415
Your judgments are *like* a great **d**. **Ps 36:6** 8415
Your arrows have sunk **d** into me, **Ps 38:2** 5181
D calls to deep at the sound of **Ps 42:7** 8415
Deep calls to **d** at the sound of **Ps 42:7** 8415
and the heart of a man are **d**. **Ps 64:6** 6013
I have sunk in **d** mire, and there **Ps 69:2** 4688
I have come into **d** waters, **Ps 69:2** 4615
my foes and from the **d** waters. **Ps 69:14** 4615
Nor the **d** swallow me up, **Ps 69:15** 4688
took **d** root and filled the land. **Ps 80:9** 8328
Your thoughts are very **d**. **Ps 92:5** 6009
it with the **d** as with a garment; **Ps 104:6** 8415
LORD, And His wonders in the **d**. **Ps 107:24** 4688
Into **d** pits from which they cannot **Ps 140:10** 4113
a circle on the face of the **d**, **Pr 8:27** 8415
the springs of the **d** became fixed, **Pr 8:28** 8415
of a man's mouth are **d** waters; **Pr 18:4** 6013
Laziness casts into a **d** sleep, **Pr 19:15** 8639
heart of a man is *like* **d** water, **Pr 20:5** 6013
mouth of an adulteress is a **d** pit; **Pr 22:14** 6013
For a harlot is a **d** pit And **Pr 23:27** 6013
it **d** as Sheol or high as heaven." **Is 7:11** 6009
over you a spirit of **d** sleep, **Is 29:10** 8639
He has made it **d** and large, A pyre **Is 30:33** 6009
sea, The waters of the great **d**; **Is 51:10** 8415
earth And **d** darkness the peoples; **Is 60:2** 6205
land of drought and of **d** darkness, **Jer 2:6** 6757
light He makes it into **d** darkness, **Jer 13:16** 6757
sister's cup, Which is **d** and wide. **Ezk 23:32** 6013
I bring up the **d** over you **Ezk 26:19** 8415
made it grow, the **d** made it high. **Ezk 31:4** 8415
I closed the **d** over it and held **Ezk 31:15** 8415
I sank into a **d** sleep with my face **Da 8:18** 7290a
I fell into a **d** sleep on my face, **Da 10:9** 7290a
have gone **d** in depravity, **Hos 5:2** 6009
They have gone **d** in depravity As **Hos 9:9** 6009
changes **d** darkness into morning, **Am 5:8** 6757
and it consumed the great **d** and **Am 7:4** 8415
"For You had cast me into the **d**, **Jon 2:3** 4688
The great **d** engulfed me, Weeds **Jon 2:5** 8415
The **d** uttered forth its voice, It **Hab 3:10** 8415
up to heaven with a **d** sigh, **Mk 7:34** *4727*
"Put out into the **d** water and let **Lk 5:4** *899*
who dug **d** and laid a foundation **Lk 6:48** *900*
to draw with and the well is **d**; **Jn 4:11** *901*
sill, sinking into a **d** sleep; **Ac 20:9** *901*
us with groanings too **d** for words; **Ro 8:26** *215*
abundance of joy and their **d** poverty **2Co 8:2** *899*
and a day I have spent in the **d**. **2Co 11:25** *1037*
he has a **d** concern for you and for **Col 4:13** *4183*
not known the **d** things of Satan, **Rv 2:24** *901*

DEEPER
to be **d** than the skin of his body, **Lv 13:3** 6013
not appear to be **d** than the skin, **Lv 13:4** 6013
it appears to be **d** than the skin, **Lv 13:25** 6013
and it is no **d** than the skin, **Lv 13:26** 8217
it appears to be **d** than the skin and **Lv 13:30** 6013
appears to be no **d** than the skin and **Lv 13:31** 6013
the scale is no **d** than the skin, **Lv 13:32** 6013
appears to be no **d** than the skin, **Lv 13:34** 6013
and appears **d** than the surface, **Lv 14:37** 8217
D than Sheol, what can you know? **Jb 11:8** 6013
A rebuke goes **d** into one who has **Pr 17:10** 5181

DEEPLY
He was **d** attracted to Dinah **Gn 34:3** 1692
he was **d** stirred over his brother, **Gn 43:30** 7356
The king was **d** moved and went **2Sa 18:33** 7264
d stirred over her son and said, **1Ki 3:26**
7356, 3648
Drink and imbibe **d**, **SS 5:1** 7937
Woe to those who **d** hide their **Is 29:15** 6009
Him from whom you have **d** defected, **Is 31:6** 6009
he was **d** distressed and set *his* **Da 6:14** 7690
And they were **d** grieved. **Mt 17:23** *4970*
they were **d** grieved and came and **Mt 18:31** *4970*
Being **d** grieved, they each one **Mt 26:22** *4970*
"My soul is **d** grieved, to the **Mt 26:38** *4036*
Sighing **d** in His spirit, He **Mk 8:12** *389*
d grieved to the point of death; **Mk 14:34** *4036*
weeping, He was **d** moved in spirit **Jn 11:33** *1690*
again being **d** moved within, **Jn 11:38** *1690*

DEEPS
"The **d** cover them; **Ex 15:5** 8415
The **d** were congealed in the heart **Ex 15:8** 8415
He lays up the **d** in storehouses. **Ps 33:7** 8415
The **d** also trembled. **Ps 77:16** 8415
And He led them through the **d**, **Ps 106:9** 8415
earth, in the seas and in all **d**. **Ps 135:6** 8415
the earth, Sea monsters and all **d**; **Ps 148:7** 8415
knowledge the **d** were broken up And **Pr 3:20** 8415

DEER
it, as of the gazelle and the **d**. **Dt 12:15** 354
"Just as a gazelle or a **d** is eaten, **Dt 12:22** 354
the **d**, the gazelle, the roebuck, **Dt 14:5** 354
may eat it, as a gazelle or a **d**. **Dt 15:22** 354
oxen, a hundred sheep besides **d**, **1Ki 4:23** 354
you observe the calving of the **d**? **Jb 39:1** 355
of the LORD makes the **d** to calve And **Ps 29:9** 355
the **d** pants for the water brooks, **Ps 42:1** 354
Then the lame will leap like a **d**, **Is 35:6** 354
Her princes have become like **d** That **La 1:6** 354

DEFAMED
he publicly **d** a virgin of Israel. **Dt 22:19**
8034, 7451a, 3318

DEFAMES
shameful deeds and publicly **d** her, **Dt 22:14**
8034, 7451a, 3318

DEFEAT
Then after his return from the **d** **Gn 14:17** 5221
is it the sound of the cry of **d**; **Ex 32:18** 2476
perhaps I may be able to **d** them **Nu 22:6** 5221
before you and you **d** them, **Dt 7:2** 5221
and to **d** your enemies before you, **Dt 23:14** 5414
you shall **d** Midian as one man." **Jg 6:16** 5221
for you will **d** the Arameans at **2Ki 13:17** 5221
then, it is already a **d** for you, **1Co 6:7** *2275*

DEFEATED
came and **d** the Rephaim in **Gn 14:5** 5221
he and his servants, and **d** them, **Gn 14:15** 5221
who **d** Midian in the field of Moab, **Gn 36:35** 5221
after he had **d** Sihon the king of **Dt 1:4** 5221
you will be **d** before your enemies." ' **Dt 1:42** 5062
and we **d** him with his sons and all **Dt 2:33** 5221
d when they came out from Egypt. **Dt 4:46** 5221
up against you to be **d** before you; **Dt 28:7** 5062
you to be **d** before your enemies; **Dt 28:25** 5062
meet us for battle, but we **d** them; **Dt 29:7** 5221
and Joshua **d** him and his people **Jos 10:33** 5221
of Israel, so that they **d** them, **Jos 11:8** 5221
land whom the sons of Israel **d**, **Jos 12:1** 5221
and the sons of Israel **d** them; **Jos 12:6** 5221
whom Joshua and the sons of Israel **d** **Jos 12:7** 5221
they **d** ten thousand men at Bezek. **Jg 1:4** 5221
d the Canaanites and the Perizzites. **Jg 1:5** 5221
and he went and **d** Israel, and they **Jg 3:13** 5221
hand of Israel, and they **d** them; **Jg 11:21** 5221
and the men of Gilead **d** Ephraim, **Jg 12:4** 5221
of Benjamin saw that they were **d**. **Jg 20:36** 5062
"Surely they are **d** before us, as **Jg 20:39** 5062
Israel was **d** before the Philistines **1Sa 4:2** 5062
"Why has the LORD **d** us today **1Sa 4:3** 5062
fought and Israel was **d**, **1Sa 4:10** 5062
valiantly and **d** the Amalekites, **1Sa 14:48** 5221
So Saul **d** the Amalekites, from **1Sa 15:7** 5221
and **d** them with great slaughter, **1Sa 19:8** 5221
to Baal-perazim and **d** them there; **2Sa 5:20** 5221
David **d** the Philistines and subdued **2Sa 8:1** 5221
He **d** Moab, and measured them **2Sa 8:2** 5221
Then David **d** Hadadezer, the son of **2Sa 8:3** 5221
had **d** all the army of Hadadezer, **2Sa 8:9** 5221
against Hadadezer and **d** him; **2Sa 8:10** 5221
that they had been **d** by Israel, **2Sa 10:15** 5062
saw that they were **d** by Israel, **2Sa 10:19** 5062
The people of Israel were **d** **2Sa 18:7** 5062
Israel are **d** before an enemy, **1Ki 8:33** 5062
and Hazael **d** them throughout the **2Ki 10:32** 5221
Three times Joash **d** him and **2Ki 13:25** 5221
"You have indeed **d** Edom, and your **2Ki 14:10** 5221
Judah was **d** by Israel, and **2Ki 14:12** 5062
He **d** the Philistines as far as **2Ki 18:8** 5221
who **d** Midian in the field of Moab, **1Ch 1:46** 5221
and David **d** them there; **1Ch 14:11** 5221
David **d** the Philistines and subdued **1Ch 18:1** 5221
He **d** Moab, and the Moabites **1Ch 18:2** 5221
David also **d** Hadadezer king of **1Ch 18:3** 5221
heard that David had **d** all the army **1Ch 18:9** 5221
against Hadadezer and had **d** him; **1Ch 18:10** 5221
Abishai the son of Zeruiah **d** 18,000 **1Ch 18:12** 5221
that they had been **d** by Israel, **1Ch 19:16** 5062
saw that they were **d** by Israel, **1Ch 19:19** 5062
Israel are **d** before an enemy because **2Ch 6:24** 5062
d them with a great slaughter, **2Ch 13:17** 5221
'Behold, you have **d** Edom.' **2Ch 25:19** 5221
Judah was **d** by Israel, and **2Ch 25:22** 5062
and they **d** him and carried away **2Ch 28:5** 5221
gods of Damascus which had **d** him, **2Ch 28:23** 5221
'For even if you had **d** the entire **Jer 37:10** 5221
Nebuchadnezzar king of Babylon **d** **Jer 46:2** 5221
And their mighty men are **d** And **Jer 46:5** 3807
Nebuchadnezzar king of Babylon **d**. **Jer 49:28** 5221

DEFECT
shall offer it, a male without **d**; **Lv 1:3** 8549
shall offer it a male without **d**. **Lv 1:10** 8549
it without **d** before the LORD. **Lv 3:1** 8549
it, male or female, without **d**. **Lv 3:6** 8549
a bull without **d** as a sin offering **Lv 4:3** 8549
offering a goat, a male without **d**. **Lv 4:23** 8549
a goat, a female without **d**, **Lv 4:28** 8549
bring it, a female without **d**. **Lv 4:32** 8549
a ram without **d** from the flock, **Lv 5:15** 8549
a ram without **d** from the flock, **Lv 5:18** 8549
a ram without **d** from the flock, **Lv 6:6** 8549
a burnt offering, *both* without **d**, **Lv 9:2** 8549

both one year old, without **d**, Lv 9:3 8549
to take two male lambs without **d**, Lv 14:10 8549
and a yearling ewe lamb without **d**, Lv 14:10 8549
who has a **d** shall approach to offer Lv 21:17 4140b
no one who has a **d** shall approach: Lv 21:18 4140b
or *one who has* a **d** in his eye or Lv 21:20 8400
of Aaron the priest who has a **d** Lv 21:21 4140b
since he has a **d**, he shall not Lv 21:21 4140b
near the altar because he has a **d**, Lv 21:23 4140b
a male without **d** from the cattle, Lv 22:19 8549
'Whatever has a **d**, you shall not Lv 22:20 4140b
there shall be no **d** in it. Lv 22:21 4140b
is in them, they have a **d**, Lv 22:25 4140b
a male lamb one year old without **d** Lv 23:12 8549
one year old male lambs without **d**, Lv 23:18 8549
one male lamb a year old without **d** Nu 6:14 8549
one ewe-lamb a year old without **d** Nu 6:14 8549
without **d** for a peace offering, Nu 6:14 8549
red heifer in which is no **d** Nu 19:2 4140b
male lambs one year old without **d** Nu 28:3 8549
male lambs one year old without **d**, Nu 28:9 8549
male lambs one year old without **d**; Nu 28:11 8549
year old, having them without **d**. Nu 28:19 8549
They shall be without **d**. Nu 28:31 8549
male lambs one year old without **d**; Nu 29:2 8549
year old, having them without **d**; Nu 29:8 8549
one year old, which are without **d**; Nu 29:13 8549
male lambs one year old without **d**; Nu 29:17 8549
male lambs one year old without **d**; Nu 29:20 8549
male lambs one year old without **d**; Nu 29:23 8549
male lambs one year old without **d**; Nu 29:26 8549
male lambs one year old without **d**; Nu 29:29 8549
male lambs one year old without **d**; Nu 29:32 8549
male lambs one year old without **d**; Nu 29:36 8549
"But if it has any **d**, Dt 15:21 4140b
or blindness, *or* any serious **d**, Dt 15:21 4140b
which has a blemish *or* any **d**, Dt 17:1 1697, 7451a
His children, because of their **d**; Dt 32:5 4140b
of his head there was no **d** in him. 2Sa 14:25 4140b
he may **d** to his master Saul." 1Ch 12:19 5307
lift up your face without *moral* **d**, Jb 11:15 4140b
youths in whom was no **d**, Da 1:4 3971

DEFECTED
Manasseh also some **d** to David when 1Ch 12:19 5307
there **d** to him from Manasseh: 1Ch 12:20 5307
for many **d** to him from Israel when 2Ch 15:9 5307
Him from whom you have deeply **d**, Is 31:6 5627

DEFEND
'For I will **d** this city to save it 2Ki 19:34 1598
and I will **d** this city for My own 2Ki 20:6 1598
to assemble and to **d** their lives, Es 8:11 5975
to **d** their lives and rid Es 9:16 5975
And **d** the rights of the afflicted Pr 31:9 1777
D the orphan, Plead for the widow. Is 1:17 8199
They do not **d** the orphan, Nor does Is 1:23 8199
'For I will **d** this city to save it Is 37:35 1598
and I will **d** this city." Is 38:6 1598
do not **d** the rights of the poor. Jer 5:28 8199
The LORD of hosts will **d** them. Zch 9:15 1598
d the inhabitants of Jerusalem, Zch 12:8 1598
beforehand to **d** yourselves; Lk 21:14 *626*

DEFENDED
d it and struck the Philistines; 2Sa 23:12 5337
the midst of the plot and **d** it, 1Ch 11:14 5337
he **d** him and took vengeance for Ac 7:24 *292a*

DEFENDING
Now Joram with all Israel was **d** 2Ki 9:14 8104
accusing or else **d** them, Ro 2:15 *626*
that we are **d** ourselves to you. 2Co 12:19 *626*

DEFENSE
keep watch over the house for **d**. 2Ki 11:6 4535
and built cities for **d** in Judah. 2Ch 11:5 4692
The LORD is the **d** of my life; Ps 27:1 4581
He is a saving **d** to His anointed. Ps 28:8 4581
And He removed the **d** of Judah. Is 22:8 4539
have been a **d** for the helpless, Is 25:4 4581
A **d** for the needy in his distress, Is 25:4 4581
which are broken down *to make a* **d** Jer 33:4
what you are to speak in your **d**, Lk 12:11 *626*
to make a **d** to the assembly. Ac 19:33 *626*
my **d** which I now *offer* to you." Ac 22:1 *627*
nation, I cheerfully make my **d**, Ac 24:10 *626*
while Paul said in his own **d**, Ac 25:8 *626*
to make his **d** against the charges. Ac 25:16 *627*
hand and *proceeded* to make his **d**: Ac 26:1 *626*
to make my **d** before you today; Ac 26:2 *626*
Paul was saying this in his **d**, Ac 26:24 *626*
My **d** to those who examine me is 1Co 9:3 *627*
the **d** and confirmation of the gospel Php 1:7 *627*
appointed for the **d** of the gospel; Php 1:16 *627*
At my first **d** no one supported me, 2Tm 4:16 *627*
always *being* ready to make a **d** to 1Pe 3:15 *627*

DEFENSELESS
do not leave me **d**. Ps 141:8 6168, 5315

DEFENSES
Your **d** are defenses of clay. Jb 13:12 1354
Your defenses are **d** of clay. Jb 13:12 1354
When they burst through the **d**, Jl 2:8 7973

DEFER
to the poor nor **d** to the great, Lv 19:15 1921, 6440
of God in truth, and **d** to no one; Mt 22:16 *3199*
You are truthful and **d** to no one; Mk 12:14 *3199*

DEFERRED
Hope **d** makes the heart sick, But Pr 13:12 4900

DEFIANCE
settled in **d** of all his relatives. Gn 25:18 5921, 6440

DEFIANTLY
the person who does *anything* **d**, Nu 15:30 7311, 3027

DEFICIENT
weighed on the scales and found **d**. Da 5:27 2627
what was **d** in your service to me. Php 2:30 *5303*

DEFIED
When he **d** Israel, Jonathan the 2Sa 21:21 2778a
with David when they **d** the Philistines 2Sa 23:9 2778a
Who has **d** Him without harm? Jb 9:4 7185, 413

DEFILE
'Do not **d** yourselves by any of Lv 18:24 2930
not spew you out, should you **d** it, Lv 18:28 2930
as not to **d** yourselves with them; Lv 18:30 2930
so as to **d** My sanctuary and to Lv 20:3 2930
'No one shall **d** himself for a *dead* Lv 21:1 2930
for her he may **d** himself. Lv 21:3 2930
'He shall not **d** himself as a Lv 21:4 2930
nor **d** himself *even* for his father Lv 21:11 2930
so that they will not **d** their camp Nu 5:3 2930
not **d** the land in which you live, Nu 35:34 2930
so that you do not **d** your land Dt 21:23 2930
it, to **d** the pride of all beauty, Is 23:9 2490c
And you will **d** your graven images Is 30:22 2930
is called by My name, to **d** it. Jer 7:30 2930
is called by My name, to **d** it. Jer 32:34 2930
"**D** the temple and fill the courts Ezk 9:7 2930
no longer **d** themselves with all their Ezk 14:11 2930
Israel, or **d** his neighbor's wife or Ezk 18:6 2930
Israel, or **d** his neighbor's wife, Ezk 18:15 2930
and do not **d** yourselves with the Ezk 20:7 2930
or **d** yourselves with their idols. Ezk 20:18 2930
"Will you **d** yourselves after the Ezk 20:30 2930
your wisdom And **d** your splendor. Ezk 28:7 2490c
d themselves with their idols, Ezk 37:23 2930
will not again **d** My holy name, Ezk 43:7 2930
to a dead person to **d** *themselves;* Ezk 44:25 2930
a husband, they may **d** themselves. Ezk 44:25 2930
his mind that he would not **d** himself Da 1:8 1351
that he might not **d** himself. Da 1:8 1351
the heart, and those **d** the man. Mt 15:18 *2840*
are the things which **d** the man; Mt 15:20 *2840*
hands does not **d** the man." Mt 15:20 *2840*
which can **d** him if it goes into him; Mk 7:15 *2840*
out of the man are what **d** the man. Mk 7:15 *2840*
the man from outside cannot **d** him, Mk 7:18 *2840*
from within and **d** the man." Mk 7:23 *2840*
also by dreaming, **d** the flesh, Jude 1:8 *3392*

DEFILED
that he had **d** Dinah his daughter; Gn 34:5 2930
he had **d** Dinah their sister. Gn 34:13 2930
because they had **d** their sister. Gn 34:27 2930
to your father's bed; Then you **d** *it* Gn 49:4 2490c
neighbor's wife, to be **d** with her. Lv 18:20 2930
with any animal to be **d** with it, Lv 18:23 2930
out before you have become **d**. Lv 18:24 2930
'For the land has become **d**, Lv 18:25 2930
and the land has become **d**); Lv 18:27 2930
not seek them out to be **d** by them. Lv 19:31 2930
although she has **d** herself, Nu 5:13 2930
his wife when she has **d** herself, Nu 5:14 2930
wife when she has not **d** herself, Nu 5:14 2930
and if you have **d** yourself and a Nu 5:20 2930
if she has **d** herself and has been Nu 5:27 2930
has not **d** herself and is clean, Nu 5:28 2930
void because his separation was **d**. Nu 6:12 2930
has **d** the sanctuary of the LORD; Nu 19:20 2930
increase of the vineyard will become **d**. Dt 22:9 6942
be his wife, since she has been **d**; Dt 24:4 2930
the shield of the mighty was **d**, 2Sa 1:21 1602
and **d** the high places where the 2Ki 23:8 2930
He also **d** Topheth, which is in the 2Ki 23:10 2930
of the sons of Ammon, the king **d**. 2Ki 23:13 2930
and burned *them* on the altar and **d** it 2Ki 23:16 2930
but because he **d** his father's bed, 1Ch 5:1 2490c
and they **d** the house of the LORD 2Ch 36:14 2930
because they have **d** the priesthood Ne 13:29 1352
They have **d** the dwelling place of Ps 74:7 2490c
They have **d** Your holy temple; Ps 79:1 2930
For your hands are **d** with blood And Is 59:3 1351
But you came and **d** My land, Jer 2:7 2930
'I am not **d**, I have not gone after Jer 2:23 2930
will be **d** like the place Topheth, Jer 19:13 2931
They were **d** with blood So that no La 4:14 1351
Behold, I have never been **d**; Ezk 4:14 2930
because you have **d** My sanctuary Ezk 5:11 2930
with which you have **d** yourselves; Ezk 20:43 2930
and **d** by your idols which you have Ezk 22:4 2930
has lewdly **d** his daughter-in-law. Ezk 22:11 2930
all their idols she **d** herself. Ezk 23:7 2930
"I saw that she had **d** herself; Ezk 23:13 2930
and **d** her with their harlotry. Ezk 23:17 2930
And when she had been **d** by them, Ezk 23:17 2930
have **d** yourself with their idols. Ezk 23:30 2930
they have **d** My sanctuary on the Ezk 23:38 2930
they **d** it by their ways and their Ezk 36:17 2930
they had **d** it with their idols. Ezk 36:18 2930
And they have **d** My holy name by Ezk 43:8 2930
the harlot, Israel has **d** itself. Hos 5:3 2930
is there, Israel has **d** itself. Hos 6:10 2930
All who eat of it will be **d**, Hos 9:4 2930
to her who is rebellious and **d**, Zph 3:1 1351
presenting **d** food upon My altar. Mal 1:7 1351
'How have we **d** You?' Mal 1:7 1351
'The table of the Lord is **d**, Mal 1:12 1351
so that they would not be **d**, Jn 18:28 *3392*
and has **d** this holy place." Ac 21:28 *2840*
their conscience being weak is **d**. 1Co 8:7 *3435*
those who are **d** and unbelieving, Ti 1:15 *3392*
mind and their conscience are **d**. Ti 1:15 *3392*
those who have been **d** sanctify Heb 9:13 *2840*
trouble, and by it many be **d**; Heb 12:15 *3392*
who have not been **d** with women, Rv 14:4 *3435*

DEFILEMENT
contrary to her *interest,* for **d**! Ezk 22:3 2930
from all **d** of flesh and spirit, 2Co 7:1 *3436*

DEFILEMENTS
they have escaped the **d** of the world 2Pe 2:20 *3393*

DEFILES
goes astray and **d** herself, Nu 5:29 2930
he **d** his dedicated head *of hair,* Nu 6:9 2930
d the tabernacle of the LORD; Nu 19:13 2930
shrines, and **d** his neighbor's wife, Ezk 18:11 2930
each of you **d** his neighbor's wife. Ezk 33:26 2930
enters into the mouth *that* **d** the man, Mt 15:11 *2840*
of the mouth, this **d** the man." Mt 15:11 *2840*
the man, that is what **d** the man. Mk 7:20 *2840*
as that which **d** the entire body, Jas 3:6 *4695*

DEFILING
uncleanness by their **d** My tabernacle Lv 15:31 2930
you are **d** yourselves with all your Ezk 20:31 2930

DEFINITE
The LORD set a **d** time, Ex 9:5 4150
send me, and I gave him a **d** time. Ne 2:6 2165
d about him to write to my lord. Ac 25:26 *804*

DEFINITELY
he knew that Saul was **d** coming. 1Sa 26:4 3559
"It is **d** because they have misled Ezk 13:10 3282

DEFORMED
a disfigured *face,* or any **d** *limb,* Lv 21:18 8311

DEFRAUD
And **d** the one in the right with Is 29:21 5186
To **d** a man in his lawsuit La 3:36 5791
NOT BEAR FALSE WITNESS, Do not **d**, Mk 10:19 *650*
you yourselves wrong and **d**. 1Co 6:8 *650*
and that no man transgress and **d** 1Th 4:6 *4122*

DEFRAUDED
have I taken, or whom have I **d**? 1Sa 12:3 6231
"You have not **d** us or oppressed 1Sa 12:4 6231
if I have **d** anyone of anything, Lk 19:8 *4811*
Why not rather be **d**? 1Co 6:7 *650*

DEFRAUDING
Let no one keep **d** you of your Col 2:18 *2603*

DEFY
"I **d** the ranks of Israel this day; 1Sa 17:10 2778a
he is coming up to **d** Israel. 1Sa 17:25 2778a

DEGENERATE
the **d** shoots of a foreign vine? Jer 2:21 5493

DEGRADED
your brother is not **d** in your eyes. Dt 25:3 7034
the glory of Moab will be **d** along Is 16:14 7034

DEGRADING
God gave them over to **d** passions; Ro 1:26 *819*

DEGREE
the standard of a man of high **d**, 1Ch 17:17 4609b
Men of low **d** are only vanity and Ps 62:9 1121, 120
he will destroy to an extraordinary **d** Da 8:24 6381
sorrow not to me, but in some **d** 2Co 2:5 *3313*
but to the **d** that you share the 1Pe 4:13 *2526*
"To the **d** that she glorified Rv 18:7 *3745*
to the same **d** give her torment Rv 18:7 *5118*

DEITIES
seems to be a proclaimer of strange **d**," Ac 17:18 *1140*

DEITY
of **D** dwells in bodily form, Col 2:9 *2320*

DEJECTED
them, behold, they were **d**. Gn 40:6 2196
of white cloth will be utterly **d**. Is 19:9 954

DELAIAH
Pelaiah, Akkub, Johanan, **D** and 1Ch 3:24 1806
the twenty-third for **D**, 1Ch 24:18 1806
the sons of **D**, the sons of Tobiah, Ezr 2:60 1806
house of Shemaiah the son of **D**, Ne 6:10 1806
the sons of **D**, the sons of Tobiah, Ne 7:62 1806
scribe, and **D** the son of Shemaiah, Jer 36:12 1806
Even though Elnathan and **D** and Jer 36:25 1806

DELAY
"Do not **d** me, since the LORD has Gn 24:56 309
man did not **d** to do the thing, Gn 34:19 309
come down to me, do not **d**. Gn 45:9 5975
out of Egypt and could not **d**, Ex 12:39 4102
"You shall not **d** *the offering* Ex 22:29 309
will not **d** with him who hates Him, Dt 7:10 309
God, you shall not **d** to pay it, Dt 23:21 309
'Why does his chariot **d** in coming? Jg 5:28 309
Do not **d** to go, to enter, to Jg 18:9 6101
the River, and that without **d**. Ezr 6:8 989
Do not **d**, O my God. Ps 40:17 309
O LORD, do not **d**. Ps 70:5 309
not **d** To keep Your commandments. Ps 119:60 4102
And My salvation will not **d**. Is 46:13 309
the sake of My name I **d** My wrath, Is 48:9 748
own sake, O my God, do not **d**, Da 9:19 309
d at the opening of the womb. Hos 13:13 5975
for man Or **d** for the sons of men. Mi 5:7 3176
certainly come, it will not **d**. Hab 2:3 309
wondering at his **d** in the temple. Lk 1:21 *5549*
and will He **d** long over them? Lk 18:7 *3114*
"Do not **d** in coming to us." Ac 9:38 *3635*

'Now why do you **d**? **Ac 22:16** *3195*
had assembled here, I did not **d**, **Ac 25:17** *311a*
WILL COME, AND WILL NOT **D**. **Heb 10:37** *5549*
that there will be **d** no longer, **Rv 10:6** *5550*

DELAYED
"For if we had not **d**, **Gn 43:10** 4102
saw that Moses **d** to come down from **Ex 32:1** 954
but he **d** longer than the set time **2Sa 20:5** 309
Be **d** and wait, Blind yourselves and **Is 29:9** 4102
It will no longer be **d**, **Ezk 12:25** 4900
of My words will be **d** any longer. **Ezk 12:28** 4900
but in case I am **d**, **1Tm 3:15** *1019*

DELAYING
Ehud escaped while they were **d**, **Jg 3:26** 4102
"Now while the bridegroom was **d**, **Mt 25:5** *5549*

DELEGATION
sends a **d** and asks for terms of peace. **Lk 14:32** *4242*
hated him and sent a **d** after him, **Lk 19:14** *4242*

DELIBERATING
"Are you **d** together about this, **Jn 16:19** *2212*

DELICACIES
And do not let me eat of their **d**. **Ps 141:4** 4516
Do not desire his **d**, **Pr 23:3** 4303
of a selfish man, Or desire his **d**; **Pr 23:6** 4303
has filled his stomach with my **d**; **Jer 51:34** 5730a
ate **d** Are desolate in the streets; **La 4:5** 4574

DELICATE
"The man who is refined and very **d** **Dt 28:54** 6028
"The refined and **d** woman among **Dt 28:56** 6028
no longer be called tender and **d**. **Is 47:1** 6028

DELICATENESS
the ground for **d** and refinement, **Dt 28:56** 6026

DELIGHT
and that it was a **d** to the eyes, **Gn 3:6** 8378
so the LORD will **d** over you to **Dt 28:63** 7797
"Has the LORD as much **d** in burnt **1Sa 15:22** 2656
'I have no **d** in you,' behold, here **2Sa 15:26** 2654a
lord the king **d** in this thing?" **2Sa 24:3** 2654a
in my **d** in the house of my God, **1Ch 29:3** 7521
the heart and **d** in uprightness, **1Ch 29:17** 7521
servants who **d** to revere Your name, **Ne 1:11** 2655
then you will **d** in the Almighty And **Jb 22:26** 6026
"Will he take **d** in the Almighty? **Jb 27:10** 6026
his **d** is in the law of the LORD, **Ps 1:2** 2656
majestic ones in whom is all my **d**. **Ps 16:3** 2656
D yourself in the LORD; **Ps 37:4** 6026
And will **d** themselves in abundant **Ps 37:11** 6026
I **d** to do Your will, O my God; **Ps 40:8** 2654a
and dishonored Who **d** in my hurt. **Ps 40:14** 2655
For You do not **d** in sacrifice, **Ps 51:16** 2654a
will **d** in righteous sacrifices, **Ps 51:19** 2654a
They **d** in falsehood; **Ps 62:4** 7521
the peoples who **d** in war. **Ps 68:30** 2654a
and dishonored Who **d** in my hurt. **Ps 70:2** 2655
me, Your consolations **d** my soul. **Ps 94:19** 8173b
And he did not **d** in blessing, so **Ps 109:17** 2654a
are studied by all who **d** in them. **Ps 111:2** 2655
I shall **d** in Your statutes; **Ps 119:16** 8173b
Your testimonies also are my **d**; **Ps 119:24** 8191
Your commandments, For I **d** in it. **Ps 119:35** 2654a
I shall **d** in Your commandments, **Ps 119:47** 8173b
with fat, *But* I **d** in Your law. **Ps 119:70** 8173b
I may live, For Your law is my **d**. **Ps 119:77** 8191
If Your law had not been my **d**, **Ps 119:92** 8191
Yet Your commandments are my **d**. **Ps 119:143** 8191
O LORD, And Your law is my **d**. **Ps 119:174** 8191
d in the strength of the horse; **Ps 147:10** 2654a
scoffers **d** themselves in scoffing And **Pr 1:22** 2530
Who **d** in doing evil And rejoice **Pr 2:14** 8056
Let us **d** ourselves with caresses. **Pr 7:18** 5965
And I was daily *His* **d**, **Pr 8:30** 8191
having my **d** in the sons of men. **Pr 8:31** 8191
LORD, But a just weight is His **d**. **Pr 11:1** 7522
blameless in *their* walk are His **d**. **Pr 11:20** 7522
who deal faithfully are His **d**. **Pr 12:22** 7522
prayer of the upright is His **d**. **Pr 15:8** 7522
Righteous lips are the **d** of kings, **Pr 16:13** 7522
fool does not **d** in understanding, **Pr 18:2** 2654a
And let your eyes **d** in my ways. **Pr 23:26** 7521
who rebuke the *wicked* will be **d**, **Pr 24:25** 5276
He will also **d** your soul. **Pr 29:17** 4574
And works with her hands in **d**. **Pr 31:13** 2656
it; for *He takes* no **d** in fools. **Ec 5:4** 2656
time and procedure for every **d**, **Ec 8:6** 2656
"I have no **d** in them"; **Ec 12:1** 2656
shade I took great **d** and sat down, **SS 2:3** 2530
He will **d** in the fear of the LORD, **Is 11:3** 7381a
forever, A **d** for wild donkeys, **Is 32:14** 4885
good, And **d** yourself in abundance. **Is 55:2** 6026
day by day and **d** to know My ways, **Is 58:2** 2654a
They **d** in the nearness of God. **Is 58:2** 2654a
day, And call the sabbath a **d**, **Is 58:13** 6027
Then you will take **d** in the LORD, **Is 58:14** 6026
"My **d** is in her," **Is 62:4** 2656
chose that in which I did not **d**." **Is 65:12** 2654a
chose that in which I did not **d**." **Is 66:4** 2654a
They have no **d** in it. **Jer 6:10** 2654a
for I **d** in these things," **Jer 9:24** 2654a
me a joy and the **d** of my heart; **Jer 15:16** 8057
your eyes and the **d** of your soul; **Ezk 24:21** 4263a
of their eyes and their heart's **d**, **Ezk 24:25** 4853a
For I **d** in loyalty rather than **Hos 6:6** 2654a
the LORD has taken no **d** in them. **Hos 8:13** 7521
do I **d** in your solemn assemblies. **Am 5:21** 7381a
Because of the children of your **d**; **Mi 1:16** 8588
LORD take **d** in thousands of rams, **Mi 6:7** 7521
of the covenant, in whom you **d**, **Mal 3:1** 2655

DELIGHTED
he was **d** with Jacob's daughter. **Gn 34:19** 2654a
LORD **d** over you to prosper you, **Dt 28:63** 7797
Saul's son, greatly **d** in David. **1Sa 19:1** 2654a
He rescued me, because He **d** in me. **2Sa 22:20** 2654a
the LORD your God who **d** in you **1Ki 10:9** 2654a
be the LORD your God who **d** in you, **2Ch 9:8** 2654a
in to the king unless the king **d** in her **Es 2:14** 2654a
He rescued me, because He **d** in me. **Ps 18:19** 2654a
be **d** with her bountiful bosom." **Is 66:11** 6026

DELIGHTFUL
And how **d** is a timely word! **Pr 15:23** 2896a
The Preacher sought to find **d** **Ec 12:10** 2656
"How beautiful and how **d** you are, **SS 7:6** 5276
And the men of Judah His **d** plant. **Is 5:7** 8191
Therefore you plant **d** plants And **Is 17:10** 5282
Ephraim My dear son? Is he a **d** child **Jer 31:20** 8191
for you shall be a **d** land," **Mal 3:12** 2656

DELIGHTING
d in self-abasement and the worship **Col 2:18** *2309*

DELIGHTS
'Behold, the king **d** in you, **1Sa 18:22** 2654a
rescue him, because He **d** in him." **Ps 22:8** 2654a
Who **d** in the prosperity of His **Ps 35:27** 2655
to drink of the river of Your **d**. **Ps 36:8** 5730a
And He **d** in his way. **Ps 37:23** 2654a
Who greatly **d** in His commandments. **Ps 112:1** 2654a
a father *corrects* the son in whom he **d**. **Pr 3:12** 7521
My chosen one *in whom* My soul **d**. **Is 42:1** 7521
For the LORD **d** in you, And *to Him* **Is 62:4** 2654a
soul **d** in their abominations, **Is 66:3** 2654a
Like a vessel in which no one **d**. **Hos 8:8** 2656
Because He **d** in unchanging love. **Mi 7:18** 2654a
of the LORD, and He **d** in them," **Mal 2:17** 2654a
IF HE **D** IN HIM; for He said, **Mt 27:43** *2309*

DELILAH
valley of Sorek, whose name was **D**. **Jg 16:4** 1807
So **D** said to Samson, **Jg 16:6** 1807
Then **D** said to Samson, **Jg 16:10** 1807
So **D** took new ropes and bound him **Jg 16:12** 1807
Then **D** said to Samson, **Jg 16:13** 1807
D took the seven locks of his hair **Jg 16:14** 1807
When **D** saw that he had told her **Jg 16:18** 1807

DELIVER
"**D** me, I pray, from the hand of **Gn 32:11** 5337
"So I have come down to **d** them **Ex 3:8** 5337
you must **d** the quota of bricks." **Ex 5:18** 5414
I will **d** you from their bondage. **Ex 6:6** 5337
for I will **d** the inhabitants of **Ex 23:31** 5414
indeed **d** this people into my hand, **Nu 21:2** 5414
'The congregation shall **d** the **Nu 35:25** 5337
to **d** us into the hand of the Amorites **Dt 1:27** 5414
in order to **d** him into your hand, **Dt 2:30** 5414
I have begun to **d** Sihon and his **Dt 2:31** 5414
the LORD your God will **d** to you; **Dt 7:16** 5414
your God will **d** them before you, **Dt 7:23** 5414
"He will **d** their kings into **Dt 7:24** 5414
d him into the hand of the avenger **Dt 19:12** 5414
to **d** you and to defeat your enemies **Dt 23:14** 5337
comes near to **d** her husband from **Dt 25:11** 5337
LORD will **d** them up before you, **Dt 31:5** 5414
is no one who can **d** from My hand. **Dt 32:39** 5337
and **d** our lives from death." **Jos 2:13** 5337
only to **d** us into the hand of the **Jos 7:7** 5414
your God will **d** it into your hand. **Jos 8:7** 5414
I will **d** all of them slain before Israel; **Jos 11:6** 5414
not **d** the manslayer into his hand, **Jos 20:5** 5462
for the sons of Israel to **d** them, **Jg 3:9** 3467
"Go in this your strength and **d** **Jg 6:14** 3467
"O Lord, how shall I **d** Israel? **Jg 6:15** 3467
for Baal, or will you **d** him? **Jg 6:31** 3467
"If You will **d** Israel through **Jg 6:36** 3467
You will **d** Israel through me, **Jg 6:37** 3467
"I will **d** you with the 300 men **Jg 7:7** 3467
"*Did I* not **d** *you* from **Jg 10:11**
therefore I will no longer **d** you. **Jg 10:13** 3467
let them **d** you in the time of your **Jg 10:14** 3467
only please **d** us this day." **Jg 10:15** 5337
you did not **d** me from their hand. **Jg 12:2** 3467
I saw that you would not **d** *me*, **Jg 12:3** 3467
and he shall begin to **d** Israel **Jg 13:5** 3467
And there was no one to **d** *them*, **Jg 18:28** 5337
"Now then, **d** up the men, the **Jg 20:13** 5414
I will **d** them into your hand." **Jg 20:28** 5414
that it may come among us and **d** us **1Sa 4:3** 3467
Who shall **d** us from the hand of **1Sa 4:8** 5337
and He will **d** you from the hand of **1Sa 7:3** 5337
and he will **d** My people from the **1Sa 9:16** 3467
"How can this one **d** us?" **1Sa 10:27** 3467
Then, if there is no one to **d** us, **1Sa 11:3** 3467
but now **d** us from the hands of our **1Sa 12:10** 5337
things which can not profit or **d**, **1Sa 12:21** 5337
He will **d** me from the hand of this **1Sa 17:37** 5337
LORD will **d** you up into my hands, **1Sa 17:46** 5462
does not **d** by sword or by spear; **1Sa 17:47** 3467
the Philistines and **d** Keilah." **1Sa 23:2** 3467
God did not **d** him into his hand. **1Sa 23:14** 5414
cause and **d** me from your hand." **1Sa 24:15** 8199
may He **d** me from all distress." **1Sa 26:24** 5337
or **d** me into the hands of my master, **1Sa 30:15** 5462
'For the king will hear and **d** his **2Sa 14:16** 5337
them and **d** them to an enemy, **1Ki 8:46** 5414
will **d** them into your hand today, **1Ki 20:13** 5414
come up and **d** me from the hand of **2Ki 16:7** 3467
and He will **d** you from the hand of **2Ki 17:39** 5337
not be able to **d** you from my hand; **2Ki 18:29** 5337
"The LORD will surely **d** us, **2Ki 18:30** 5337
"The LORD will **d** us." **2Ki 18:32** 5337
d Jerusalem from my hand?' " **2Ki 18:35** 5337
birth and there is no strength to **d**. **2Ki 19:3**
which my fathers destroyed **d** them, **2Ki 19:12** 5337
d us from his hand that all the **2Ki 19:19** 3467
and I will **d** you and this city **2Ki 20:6** 5337
d them into the hand of their enemies, **2Ki 21:14** 5414
"Let them **d** it into the hand **2Ki 22:5** 5414
us and **d** us from the nations, **1Ch 16:35** 5337
them and **d** them to an enemy, **2Ch 6:36** 5414
and You will hear and **d** *us*.' **2Ch 20:9** 3467
that He might **d** them into the hand **2Ch 25:20** 5414
"The LORD our God will **d** us from **2Ch 32:11** 5337
all to **d** their land from my hand? **2Ch 32:13** 5337
could **d** his people out of my hand, **2Ch 32:14** 5337
be able to **d** you from my hand? **2Ch 32:14** 5337
able to **d** his people from my hand **2Ch 32:15** 5337
your God **d** you from my hand?' " **2Ch 32:15** 5337
not **d** His people from my hand." **2Ch 32:17** 5337
d in full before the God of **Ezr 7:19** 8000
"From six troubles He will **d** you, **Jb 5:19** 5337
'**D** me from the hand of the **Jb 6:23** 4422
"He will **d** one who is not **Jb 22:30** 4422
'**D** him from going down to the pit, **Jb 33:24** 6308
all those who pursue me, and **d** me, **Ps 7:1** 5337
me away, while there is none to **d**. **Ps 7:2** 5337
D my soul from the wicked with Your **Ps 17:13** 6403
let Him **d** him; Let Him rescue him, **Ps 22:8** 6403
D my soul from the sword, My only **Ps 22:20** 5337
Guard my soul and **d** me; **Ps 25:20** 5337
Do not **d** me over to the desire of **Ps 27:12** 5414
In Your righteousness **d** me. **Ps 31:1** 6403
D me from the hand of my enemies and **Ps 31:15** 5337
it **d** anyone by its great strength. **Ps 33:17** 4422
To **d** their soul from death And to **Ps 33:19** 5337
"**D** me from all my transgressions; **Ps 39:8** 5337
Be pleased, O LORD, to **d** me; **Ps 40:13** 5337
will **d** him in a day of trouble. **Ps 41:1** 4422
O **d** me from the deceitful and **Ps 43:1** 6403
in pieces, and there will be none to **d**. **Ps 50:22** 5337
D me from bloodguiltiness, O God, **Ps 51:14** 5337
D me from my enemies, O my God; **Ps 59:1** 5337
D me from those who do iniquity And **Ps 59:2** 5337
D me from the mire and do not let **Ps 69:14** 5337
O God, *hasten* to **d** me; **Ps 70:1** 5337
In Your righteousness **d** me and **Ps 71:2** 5337
him, for there is no one to **d**." **Ps 71:11** 5337
For he will **d** the needy when he **Ps 72:12** 5337
Do not **d** the soul of Your **Ps 74:19** 5414
And **d** us and forgive our sins **Ps 79:9** 5337
D *them* out of the hand of the **Ps 82:4** 5337
Can he **d** his soul from the power **Ps 89:48** 4422
loved Me, therefore I will **d** him; **Ps 91:14** 6403
Many times He would **d** them; **Ps 106:43** 5337
Your lovingkindness is good, **d** me; **Ps 109:21** 5337
D me according to Your word. **Ps 119:170** 5337
D my soul, O LORD, from lying **Ps 120:2** 5337
D me from my persecutors, For they **Ps 142:6** 5337
D me, O LORD, from my enemies; **Ps 143:9** 5337
me and **d** me out of great waters, **Ps 144:7** 5337
d me out of the hand of aliens, **Ps 144:11** 5337
To **d** you from the way of evil, **Pr 2:12** 5337
To **d** you from the strange woman, **Pr 2:16** 5337
this then, my son, and **d** yourself; **Pr 6:3** 5337
D yourself like a gazelle from *the* **Pr 6:5** 5337
of the upright will **d** them, **Pr 11:6** 5337
mouth of the upright will **d** them. **Pr 12:6** 5337
D those who are being taken away **Pr 24:11** 5337
will not **d** those who practice it. **Ec 8:8** 4422
it off with no one to **d** *it*. **Is 5:29** 5337
I will **d** the Egyptians into the **Is 19:4** 5534a
a Champion, and He will **d** them. **Is 19:20** 5337
He will protect and **d** *it;* **Is 31:5** 5337
for he will not be able to **d** you; **Is 36:14** 5337
"The LORD will surely **d** us, **Is 36:15** 5337
"The LORD will **d** us." **Is 36:18** 5337
d Jerusalem from my hand?' " **Is 36:20** 5337
and there is no strength to **d**. **Is 37:3** 3205
my fathers have destroyed **d** them, **Is 37:12** 5337
d us from his hand that all the **Is 37:20** 3467
"I will **d** you and this city **Is 38:6** 5337
become a prey with none to **d** *them*, **Is 42:22** 5337
is none who can **d** out of My hand; **Is 43:13** 5337
"**D** me, for you are my god." **Is 44:17** 5337
And he cannot **d** himself, nor say, **Is 44:20** 5337
will bear *you* and I will **d** *you*. **Is 46:4** 4422
It cannot **d** him from his distress. **Is 46:7** 3467
They cannot **d** themselves from the **Is 47:14** 5337
Or have I no power to **d**? **Is 50:2** 5337
your collection *of idols* **d** you. **Is 57:13** 5337
For I am with you to **d** you," **Jer 1:8** 5337
you, for I am with you to **d** you," **Jer 1:19** 5337
with you to save you And **d** you," **Jer 15:20** 5337
"So I will **d** you from the hand of **Jer 15:21** 5337
And **d** them up to the power of the **Jer 18:21** 5064
And **d** the *person* who has been **Jer 21:12** 5337
and **d** the one who has been robbed **Jer 22:3** 5337
I will **d** them into the hand of **Jer 29:21** 5414
"But I will **d** you on that day," **Jer 39:17** 5337
save you and **d** you from his hand. **Jer 42:11** 5337
is no one to **d** us from their hand. **La 5:8** 6561
their gold will not be able to **d** them **Ezk 7:19** 5337
and **d** you into the hands **Ezk 11:9** 5414
and **d** My people from your hands, **Ezk 13:21** 5337
will **d** My people out of your hand. **Ezk 13:23** 5337
they could *only* **d** themselves," **Ezk 14:14** 5337
"they could not **d** either *their* **Ezk 14:16** 5337
"they could not **d** either *their* **Ezk 14:18** 5337
"they could not **d** either *their* **Ezk 14:20** 5337
They would **d** only themselves by **Ezk 14:20** 5337

of a righteous man will not **d** him Ezk 33:12 5337
will **d** My flock from their mouth, Ezk 34:10 5337
I will care for My sheep and will **d** Ezk 34:12 5337
therefore, I will **d** My flock, Ezk 34:22 3467
but I will **d** them from all their Ezk 37:23 3467
who can **d** you out of my hands?" Da 3:15 7804
God whom we serve is able to **d** us Da 3:17 7804
and He will **d** us out of your hand, Da 3:17 7804
who is able to **d** in this way." Da 3:29 5338
serve will Himself **d** you." Da 6:16 7804
able to **d** you from the lions?" Da 6:20 7804
and **d** them by the LORD their God, Hos 1:7 3467
God, and will not **d** them by bow, Hos 1:7 3467
away, and there will be none to **d**. Hos 5:14 5337
population To **d** *it* up to Edom. Am 1:6 5462
I will **d** up *the* city and all it Am 6:8 5462
head to **d** him from his discomfort. Jon 4:6 5337
And He will **d** *us* from the Assyrian Mi 5:6 5337
nor their gold Will be able to **d** them Zph 1:18 5337
not **d** *them* from their power." Zch 11:6 5337
temptation, but **d** us from evil. Mt 6:13 *4506*
they will **d** you to tribulation, Mt 24:9 *3860*
for they will **d** you to *the* courts, Mk 13:9 *3860*
so that they *could* **d** Him to the rule and Lk 20:20 *3860*
d him into the hands of the Gentiles.' Ac 21:11 *3860*
they proceeded to **d** Paul and some Ac 27:1 *3860*
I have decided to **d** such a one to 1Co 5:5 *3860*
a *peril of* death, and will **d** *us,* 2Co 1:10 *4506*
And He will yet **d** us, 2Co 1:10 *4506*

DELIVERANCE

to keep you alive by a great **d**. Gn 45:7 6413
d by the hand of Your servant, Jg 15:18 8668
sun is hot, you will have **d**.' " 1Sa 11:9 8668
has accomplished **d** in Israel." 1Sa 11:13 8668
about this great **d** in Israel? 1Sa 14:45 3444
about a great **d** for all Israel; 1Sa 19:5 8668
"*He* is a tower of **d** to His king, 2Sa 22:51 3444
will grant them some *measure* of **d**, 2Ch 12:7 6413
relief and **d** will arise for the Es 4:14 2020
me, And that **d** is driven from me? Jb 6:13 8454
Yet there is no **d** from Your hand. Jb 10:7 5337
"There is no **d** for him in God." Ps 3:2 3444
He gives great **d** to His king, And Ps 18:50 3444
my **d** are the words of my groaning. Ps 22:1 3444
You surround me with songs of **d**. Ps 32:7 6405
For **d** by man is in vain. Ps 60:11 8668
of **d** in the midst of the earth. Ps 74:12 3444
For **d** by man is in vain. Ps 108:12 8668
We could not accomplish **d** for the Is 26:18 3444
was granting them **d** through him, Ac 7:25 *4991*
know that this will turn out for my **d** Php 1:19 *4991*

DELIVERANCES

God is to us a God of **d**; Ps 68:20 4190

DELIVERED

d your enemies into your hand." Gn 14:20 4042
her days to be **d** were fulfilled, Gn 25:24 3205
He **d** *them* into the hand of his Gn 32:16 5414
"An Egyptian **d** us from the hand Ex 2:19 5337
have not **d** Your people at all." Ex 5:23 5337
d me from the sword of Pharaoh." Ex 18:4 5337
and *how* the LORD had **d** them. Ex 18:8 5337
"Blessed be the LORD who **d** you Ex 18:10 5337
and who **d** the people from under Ex 18:10 5337
you shall be **d** into enemy hands. Lv 26:25 5414
Israel and **d** up the Canaanites; Nu 21:3 5414
The LORD our God **d** him over to us Dt 2:33 5414
the LORD our God **d** all over to us. Dt 2:36 5414
for I have **d** him and all his Dt 3:2 5414
"So the LORD our God **d** Og also, Dt 3:3 5414
and **d** them from the hands of the Jos 9:26 5337
when the LORD **d** up the Amorites Jos 10:12 5414
God has **d** them into your hand." Jos 10:19 5414
d them into the hand of Israel, Jos 11:8 5414
now you have **d** the sons of Israel Jos 22:31 5337
you, and I **d** you from his hand. Jos 24:10 5337
LORD raised up judges who **d** them Jg 2:16 3467
LORD was with the judge and **d** them Jg 2:18 3467
'I **d** you from the hands of the Jg 6:9 5337
'My own power has **d** me.' Jg 7:2 3467
d us from the hand of Midian." Jg 8:22 3467
who had **d** them from the hands of Jg 8:34 5337
and **d** you from the hand of Midian; Jg 9:17 5337
Me, and I **d** you from their hands. Jg 10:12 3467
and Israel **d** their territory from 1Sa 7:14 5337
and I **d** you from the hand of the 1Sa 10:18 5337
and **d** you from the hands of your 1Sa 12:11 5337
So the LORD **d** Israel that day, and 1Sa 14:23 3467
and **d** Israel from the hands of 1Sa 14:48 5337
"The LORD who **d** me from the paw 1Sa 17:37 5337
David **d** the inhabitants of Keilah. 1Sa 23:5 3467
"God has **d** him into my hand, for 1Sa 23:7 5235a
that the LORD **d** me into your hand 1Sa 24:18 5462
has **d** your enemy into your hand; 1Sa 26:8 5462
the LORD **d** you into *my* hand today, 1Sa 26:23 5414
who has kept us and **d** into our 1Sa 30:23 5414
not **d** you into the hands of David; 2Sa 3:8 4672
I who **d** you from the hand of Saul. 2Sa 12:7 4672
who has **d** up the men who lifted 2Sa 18:28 5462
"The king **d** us from the hand of 2Sa 19:9 5337
the LORD **d** him from the hand of all 2Sa 22:1 5337
"He **d** me from my strong enemy, 2Sa 22:18 5337
"You have also **d** me from the 2Sa 22:44 6403
and **d** them into the hand of his 1Ki 15:18 5414
d his land from the hand of the king 2Ki 18:33 5337
Have they **d** Samaria from my hand? 2Ki 18:34 5337
have **d** their land from my hand, 2Ki 18:35 5337
for the money **d** into their hands, 2Ki 22:7 5414
and have **d** it into the hand of the 2Ki 22:9 5414
LORD, He **d** them into your hand. 2Ch 16:8 5414
yet the LORD **d** a very great army 2Ch 24:24 5414
who have not **d** their own people from 2Ch 25:15 5337
the LORD his God **d** him into the 2Ch 28:5 5414
And he was also **d** into the hand of 2Ch 28:5 5414
He has **d** them into your hand, 2Ch 28:9 5414
not **d** their people from my hand, 2Ch 32:17 5337
the high priest and **d** the money 2Ch 34:9 5414
and have **d** it into the hands of 2Ch 34:17 5414
and He **d** us from the hand of the Ezr 8:31 5337
Then they **d** the king's edicts to Ezr 8:36 5414
"Therefore You **d** them into the hand Ne 9:27 5414
deliverers who **d** them from the hand Ne 9:27 3467
king's command **d** by the eunuchs. Es 1:12 3027
the command of King Ahasuerus **d** Es 1:15
Then He **d** them into the power of Jb 8:4 7971
And he will be **d** through the Jb 22:30 4422
would be **d** forever from my Judge. Jb 23:7 6403
I **d** the poor who cried for help, Jb 29:12 4422
He **d** me from my strong enemy, And Ps 18:17 5337
You have **d** me from the Ps 18:43 6403
They trusted and You **d** them. Ps 22:4 6403
You they cried out and were **d**; Ps 22:5 4422
A warrior is not **d** by great strength Ps 33:16 5337
me, And **d** me from all my fears. Ps 34:4 5337
For He has **d** me from all trouble, Ps 54:7 5337
You have **d** my soul from death, Ps 56:13 5337
That Your beloved may be **d**, Ps 60:5 2502a
They will be **d** over to the power Ps 63:10 5064
May I be **d** from my foes and from Ps 69:14 5337
He also **d** His people to the sword, Ps 78:62 5462
And You have **d** my soul from the Ps 86:13 5337
He **d** them out of their distresses. Ps 107:6 5337
d *them* from their destructions. Ps 107:20 4422
That Your beloved may be **d**, Ps 108:6 2502a
The righteous is **d** from trouble, Pr 11:8 2502a
knowledge the righteous will be **d**. Pr 11:9 2502a
of the righteous will be **d**. Pr 11:21 4422
who walks blamelessly will be **d**, Pr 28:18 3467
But he who walks wisely will be **d**. Pr 28:26 4422
and he **d** the city by his wisdom. Ec 9:15 4422
to be **d** from the king of Assyria; Is 20:6 5337
d his land from the hand of the king Is 36:18 5337
have they **d** Samaria from my hand? Is 36:19 5337
have **d** their land from my hand, Is 36:20 5337
And have **d** us into the power of Is 64:7 4042
by My name, and say, 'We are **d**!' Jer 7:10 5337
For He has **d** the soul of the needy Jer 20:13 5337
be captured and **d** into his hand; Jer 34:3 5414
He has **d** into the hand of the La 2:7 5462
but you have **d** yourself. Ezk 3:19 5337
and you have **d** yourself." Ezk 3:21 5337
They alone would be **d**, Ezk 14:16 5337
but they alone would be **d**. Ezk 14:18 5337
And I **d** you up to the desire of Ezk 16:27 5414
They are **d** over to the sword with Ezk 21:12 4048
warning, he would have **d** his life. Ezk 33:5 4422
but you have **d** your life. Ezk 33:9 5337
have **d** them from the hand of those Ezk 34:27 5337
have **d** the sons of Israel to the power Ezk 35:5 5064
who has sent His angel and **d** His Da 3:28 7804
Who has *also* **d** Daniel from the Da 6:27 7804
on the name of the LORD Will be **d**; Jl 2:32 4422
Because they **d** up an entire Am 1:9 5462
To be **d** from the hand of calamity! Hab 2:9 5337
to be **d** into the hands of men; Mt 17:22 *3860*
and the Son of Man will be **d** to Mt 20:18 *3860*
d Him to Pilate the governor. Mt 27:2 *3860*
is to be **d** into the hands of men, Mk 9:31 *3860*
and the Son of Man will be **d** to Mk 10:33 *3860*
Him away and **d** Him to Pilate. Mk 15:1 *3860*
to be **d** into the hands of men." Lk 9:44 *3860*
but he **d** Jesus to their will. Lk 23:25 *3860*
be **d** into the hands of sinful men, Lk 24:7 *3860*
d Him to the sentence of death, Lk 24:20 *3860*
would not have **d** Him to you." Jn 18:30 *3860*
the chief priests **d** You to me; Jn 18:35 *3860*
for this reason he who **d** Me to Jn 19:11 *3860*
d over by the predetermined plan and Ac 2:23 *1560*
Jesus, *the one* whom you **d** and Ac 3:13 *3860*
"But God turned away and **d** them Ac 7:42 *3860*
together, they **d** the letter. Ac 15:30 *1929*
and **d** the letter to the governor, Ac 23:33 *325*
yet I was **d** as a prisoner from Ac 28:17 *3860*
He who was **d** over because of our Ro 4:25 *3860*
own Son, but **d** Him over for us all, Ro 8:32 *3860*
just as I **d** them to you. 1Co 11:2 *3860*
Lord that which I also **d** to you, 1Co 11:23 *3860*
For I **d** to you as of first 1Co 15:3 *3860*
who **d** us from so great a *peril of* 2Co 1:10 *4506*
d over to death for Jesus' sake, 2Co 4:11 *3860*

DELIVERER

the LORD raised up a **d** for the Jg 3:9 3467
the LORD raised up a **d** for them, Jg 3:15 3467
my rock and my fortress and my **d**; 2Sa 22:2 6403
The LORD gave Israel a **d**, 2Ki 13:5 3467
in the gate, And there is no **d**. Jb 5:4 5337
my rock and my fortress and my **d**, Ps 18:2 6403
You are my help and my **d**; Ps 40:17 6403
You are my help and my **d**; Ps 70:5 6403
fortress, My stronghold and my **d**, Ps 144:2 6403
God sent *to be* both a ruler and a **d** Ac 7:35 *3086*
"THE **D** WILL COME FROM ZION, HE Ro 11:26 *4506*

DELIVERERS

You gave them **d** who delivered Ne 9:27 3467
The **d** will ascend Mount Zion To Ob 1:21 3467

DELIVERING

in **d** them from the hand of the Ex 18:9 5337
and set *his* mind on **d** Daniel; Da 6:14 7804
d you to the synagogues and Lk 21:12 *3860*
d him to four squads of soldiers Ac 12:4 *3860*
and *began* **d** an address to them. Ac 12:21 *1215*
cities, they were **d** the decrees which Ac 16:4 *3860*

DELIVERS

and when the LORD your God **d** them Dt 7:2 5414
your God **d** them into your hands and Dt 21:10 5414
who **d** you from all your calamities 1Sa 10:19 3467
as the LORD lives, who **d** Israel, 1Sa 14:39 3467
"He **d** the afflicted in their Jb 36:15 2502a
He **d** me from my enemies; Ps 18:48 6403
And **d** them out of all their Ps 34:17 5337
the LORD **d** him out of them all. Ps 34:19 5337
Who **d** the afflicted from him who Ps 35:10 5337
The LORD helps them and **d** them; Ps 37:40 6403
He **d** them from the wicked and Ps 37:40 6403
For it is He who **d** you from the Ps 91:3 5337
He **d** them from the hand of the Ps 97:10 5337
But righteousness **d** from death. Pr 10:2 5337
But righteousness **d** from death. Pr 11:4 5337
He **d** up nations before him And Is 41:2 5414
"He **d** and rescues and performs Da 6:27 7804

DELIVERY

point of birth and not give **d**?" Is 66:9 3205
I who gives **d** shut *the womb?*" Is 66:9 3205

DELUDE

d you with persuasive argument. Col 2:4 *3884*
merely hearers who **d** themselves. Jas 1:22 *3884*

DELUDED

The princes of Memphis are **d**; Is 19:13 5378
your knowledge, they have **d** you; Is 47:10 7725

DELUDING

God will send upon them a **d** influence 2Th 2:11 *4106*

DELUSION

the customs of the peoples are **d**; Jer 10:3 1892
and foolish *In their* discipline of **d** Jer 10:8 1892

DEMAND

the woman's husband may **d** of him, Ex 21:22 7896
you, but I **d** one thing of you, 2Sa 3:13 7592
d the governor's food *allowance,* Ne 5:18 1245
and I will **d** My sheep from them Ezk 34:10 1875
what is yours, do not **d** it back. Lk 6:30 *523*
that their **d** be granted. Lk 23:24 *155*

DEMANDED

"If a ransom is **d** of him, then he Ex 21:30 7896
of his life whatever is **d** of him. Ex 21:30 7896
there our captors **d** of us songs, Ps 137:3 7592
Satan has **d** *permission* to sift you Lk 22:31 *1809*

DEMANDING

were **d** of Him a sign from heaven. Lk 11:16 *2212*
I have found in Him no guilt **d** Lk 23:22

DEMANDS

which the king **d** is difficult, Da 2:11 7593

DEMAS

you his greetings, and *also* **D**. Col 4:14 *1214*
for **D**, having loved this present 2Tm 4:10 *1214*
as do Mark, Aristarchus, **D**, Phm 1:24 *1214*

DEMENTED

is a fool, The inspired man is **d**, Hos 9:7 7696

DEMETRIUS

For a man named **D**, Ac 19:24 *1216*
if **D** and the craftsmen who are Ac 19:38 *1216*
D has received a *good* testimony 3Jn 1:12 *1216*

DEMOLISH

and **d** all their high places; Nu 33:52 8045
Canaan to **d** its strongholds. Is 23:11 8045
They will **d** with the sword your Jer 5:17 7567
your shrines, **d** your high places, Ezk 16:39 5422
And will **d** their gate bars And Hos 11:6 3615

DEMOLISHED

Then he **d** its stones, ground them 2Ki 23:15 7665

DEMON

After the **d** was cast out, the Mt 9:33 *1140*
drinking, and they say, 'He has a **d**!' Mt 11:18 *1140*
him, and the **d** came out of him, Mt 17:18 *1140*
to cast the **d** out of her daughter. Mk 7:26 *1140*
d has gone out of your daughter." Mk 7:29 *1140*
on the bed, the **d** having left. Mk 7:30 *1140*
by the spirit of an unclean **d**, Lk 4:33 *1140*
And when the **d** had thrown him down Lk 4:35 *1140*
no wine, and you say, 'He has a **d**!' Lk 7:33 *1140*
driven by the **d** into the desert. Lk 8:29 *1140*
the **d** slammed him *to the ground* Lk 9:42 *1140*
And He was casting out a **d**, Lk 11:14 *1140*
when the **d** had gone out, Lk 11:14 *1140*
crowd answered, "You have a **d**! Jn 7:20 *1140*
are a Samaritan and have a **d**?" Jn 8:48 *1140*
"I do not have a **d**; Jn 8:49 *1140*
"Now we know that You have a **d**. Jn 8:52 *1140*
"He has a **d** and is insane. Jn 10:20 *1140*
A **d** cannot open the eyes of the Jn 10:21 *1140*

DEMONIACS

various diseases and pains, **d**, Mt 4:24 *1139*
including what had happened to the **d**. Mt 8:33 *1139*

DEMONIC

above, but is earthly, natural, **d**. Jas 3:15 *1141*

DEMON-POSSESSED

brought to Him many who were **d**; Mt 8:16 *1139*
two men who were **d** met Him as they Mt 8:28 *1139*
going out, a mute, **d** man Mt 9:32 *1139*
a **d** man *who was* blind and mute was Mt 12:22 *1139*
my daughter is cruelly **d**." Mt 15:22 *1139*
who were ill and those who were **d**. Mk 1:32 *1139*
man who had been **d** sitting down, Mk 5:15 *1139*

how it had happened to the **d** man, **Mk 5:16** *1139*
the man who had been **d** was **Mk 5:18** *1139*
man who was **d** had been made well. **Lk 8:36** *1139*
are not the sayings of one **d**. **Jn 10:21** *1139*

DEMONS
sacrifice their sacrifices to the goat **d** **Lv 17:7** 8163c
sacrificed to **d** who were not God, **Dt 32:17** 7700
sons and their daughters to the **d**, **Ps 106:37** 7700
name, and in Your name cast out **d**, **Mt 7:22** *1140*
The **d** *began* to entreat Him, **Mt 8:31** *1142*
"He casts out the **d** by the ruler **Mt 9:34** *1140*
demons by the ruler of the **d**." **Mt 9:34** *1140*
cleanse *the* lepers, cast out **d**. **Mt 10:8** *1140*
"This man casts out **d** only by **Mt 12:24** *1140*
by Beelzebul the ruler of the **d**." **Mt 12:24** *1140*
"If I by Beelzebul cast out **d**, **Mt 12:27** *1140*
I cast out **d** by the Spirit of God, **Mt 12:28** *1140*
diseases, and cast out many **d**; **Mk 1:34** *1140*
was not permitting the **d** to speak, **Mk 1:34** *1140*
preaching and casting out the **d**. **Mk 1:39** *1140*
have authority to cast out the **d**. **Mk 3:15** *1140*
d by the ruler of the demons." **Mk 3:22** *1140*
demons by the ruler of the **d**." **Mk 3:22** *1140*
The **d** implored Him, saying, **Mk 5:12**
And they were casting out many **d** **Mk 6:13** *1140*
casting out **d** in Your name, **Mk 9:38** *1140*
from whom He had cast out seven **d**. **Mk 16:9** *1140*
in My name they will cast out **d**, **Mk 16:17** *1140*
D also were coming out of many, **Lk 4:41** *1140*
from whom seven **d** had gone out, **Lk 8:2** *1140*
the city who was possessed with **d**; **Lk 8:27** *1140*
for many **d** had entered him. **Lk 8:30** *1140*
and *the* **d** implored Him to permit **Lk 8:32**
And the **d** came out of the man **Lk 8:33** *1140*
man from whom the **d** had gone out, **Lk 8:35** *1140*
But the man from whom the **d** had **Lk 8:38** *1140*
and authority over all the **d** and **Lk 9:1** *1140*
casting out **d** in Your name; **Lk 9:49** *1140*
even the **d** are subject to us in **Lk 10:17** *1140*
"He casts out **d** by Beelzebul, the **Lk 11:15** *1140*
Beelzebul, the ruler of the **d**." **Lk 11:15** *1140*
that I cast out **d** by Beelzebul. **Lk 11:18** *1140*
"And if I by Beelzebul cast out **d**, **Lk 11:19** *1140*
I cast out **d** by the finger of God, **Lk 11:20** *1140*
I cast out **d** and perform cures **Lk 13:32** *1140*
sacrifice, they sacrifice to **d** and **1Co 10:20** *1140*
want you to become sharers in **d**. **1Co 10:20** *1140*
cup of the Lord and the cup of **d**; **1Co 10:21** *1140*
of the Lord and the table of **d**. **1Co 10:21** *1140*
spirits and doctrines of **d**, **1Tm 4:1** *1140*
the **d** also believe, and shudder. **Jas 2:19** *1140*
hands, so as not to worship **d**, **Rv 9:20** *1140*
for they are spirits of **d**, **Rv 16:14** *1140*
She has become a dwelling place of **d** **Rv 18:2** *1140*

DEMONSTRATE
This was to **d** His righteousness, **Ro 3:25** *1731*
YOU UP, TO **D** MY POWER IN YOU, **Ro 9:17** *1731*
although willing to **d** His wrath **Ro 9:22** *1731*
might **d** His perfect patience as **1Tm 1:16** *1731*

DEMONSTRATED
In everything you **d** yourselves to **2Co 7:11** *4921*

DEMONSTRATES
d to everyone *that* he is a fool. **Ec 10:3** 559
d the righteousness of God, **Ro 3:5** *4921*
But God **d** His own love toward us, **Ro 5:8** *4921*

DEMONSTRATING
d by the Scriptures that Jesus was **Ac 18:28** *1925*

DEMONSTRATION
for the **d**, *I say,* of His **Ro 3:26** *1732*
in **d** of the Spirit and of power, **1Co 2:4** *585*

DEMORALIZED
for they have **d** the builders. **Ne 4:5** 3707, 5048
Egyptians will be **d** within them; **Is 19:3** 1238b

DEN
its lair And remains in its **d**. **Jb 37:8** 4585
will put his hand on the viper's **d**. **Is 11:8** 3975a
a **d** of robbers in your sight? **Jer 7:11** 4631
shall be cast into the lions' **d**. **Da 6:7** 1358
is to be cast into the lions' **d**?" **Da 6:12** 1358
in and cast into the lions' **d**. **Da 6:16** 1358
and laid over the mouth of the **d**; **Da 6:17** 1358
and went in haste to the lions' **d**. **Da 6:19** 1358
he had come near the **d** to Daniel, **Da 6:20** 1358
to be taken up out of the **d**. **Da 6:23** 1358
Daniel was taken up out of the **d** and **Da 6:23** 1358
and their wives into the lions' **d**; **Da 6:24** 1358
not reached the bottom of the **d** **Da 6:24** 1358
Does a young lion growl from his **d** **Am 3:4** 4585
Where is the **d** of the lions And **Na 2:11** 4583
you are making it a ROBBERS' **D**." **Mt 21:13** *4693*
you have made it a ROBBERS' **D**." **Mk 11:17** *4693*
you have made it a ROBBERS' **D**." **Lk 19:46** *4693*

DENARII
slaves who owed him a hundred **d**; **Mt 18:28** *1220*
go and spend two hundred **d** on bread **Mk 6:37** *1220*
sold for over three hundred **d**, **Mk 14:5** *1220*
one owed five hundred **d**, **Lk 7:41** *1220*
two **d** and gave them to the innkeeper **Lk 10:35** *1220*
"Two hundred **d** worth of bread is **Jn 6:7** *1220*
not sold for three hundred **d** and **Jn 12:5** *1220*

DENARIUS
the laborers for a **d** for the day, **Mt 20:2** *1220*
hour came, each one received a **d**. **Mt 20:9** *1220*
each of them also received a **d**. **Mt 20:10** *1220*
did you not agree with me for a **d**? **Mt 20:13** *1220*
And they brought Him a **d**. **Mt 22:19** *1220*
Bring Me a **d** to look at." **Mk 12:15** *1220*
"Show Me a **d**. Whose likeness and **Lk 20:24** *1220*
"A quart of wheat for a **d**, **Rv 6:6** *1220*
three quarts of barley for a **d**; **Rv 6:6** *1220*

DENIAL
and **d** of justice and righteousness **Ec 5:8** 1498

DENIED
Sarah **d** *it* however, saying, **Gn 18:15** 3584
not **d** the words of the Holy One. **Jb 6:10** 3582
For I would have **d** God above. **Jb 31:28** 3584
But he **d** *it* before them all, **Mt 26:70** *720*
And again he **d** *it* with an oath, **Mt 26:72** *720*
But he **d** *it,* saying, **Mk 14:68** *720*
But again he **d** it. And after a **Mk 14:70** *720*
be **d** before the angels of God. **Lk 12:9** *533*
d three times that you know Me." **Lk 22:34** *533*
But he **d** *it,* saying, **Lk 22:57** *720*
He **d** *it,* and said, **Jn 18:25** *720*
Peter then **d** *it* again **Jn 18:27** *720*
his household, he has **d** the faith and **1Tm 5:8** *720*
although they have **d** its power; **2Tm 3:5** *720*
My word, and have not **d** My name. **Rv 3:8** *720*

DENIES
"But whoever **d** Me before men, I **Mt 10:33** *720*
but he who **d** Me before men will **Lk 12:9** *720*
who **d** that Jesus is the Christ? **1Jn 2:22** *720*
one who **d** the Father and the Son. **1Jn 2:22** *720*
Whoever **d** the Son does not have **1Jn 2:23** *720*

DENOTES
d the removing of those things **Heb 12:27** *1213*

DENOUNCE
Jacob for me, And come, **d** Israel!' **Nu 23:7** 2194
And how can I **d** whom the LORD has **Nu 23:8** 2194
D *him;* yes, let us denounce him!" **Jer 20:10** 5046
yes, let us **d** him!" **Jer 20:10** 5046
Then He began to **d** the cities in **Mt 11:20** *3679*

DENOUNCED
denounce whom the LORD has not **d**? **Nu 23:8** 2194

DENS
of Israel made for themselves the **d** **Jg 6:2** 4492
When they crouch in *their* **d** **Jb 38:40** 4585
withdraw And lie down in their **d**. **Ps 104:22** 4585
and Hermon, From the **d** of lions, **SS 4:8** 4585
prey And his **d** with torn flesh. **Na 2:12** 4585

DENSE
is His anger and **d** is *His* smoke; **Is 30:27** 3514

DENY
so that you do not **d** your God." **Jos 24:27** 3584
his place, Then it will **d** him, **Jb 8:18** 3584
That I not be full and **d** *You* and say, **Pr 30:9** 3584
I will also **d** him before My Father **Mt 10:33** *720*
come after Me, he must **d** himself, **Mt 16:24** *533*
you will **d** Me three times." **Mt 26:34** *533*
die with You, I will not **d** You." **Mt 26:35** *533*
you will **d** Me three times." **Mt 26:75** *533*
come after Me, he must **d** himself, **Mk 8:34** *533*
you yourself will **d** Me three times." **Mk 14:30** *533*
die with You, I will not **d** You!" **Mk 14:31** *533*
you will **d** Me three times." **Mk 14:72** *533*
come after Me, he must **d** himself, **Lk 9:23** *720*
you will **d** Me three times." **Lk 22:61** *533*
And he confessed and did not **d**, **Jn 1:20** *720*
crow until you **d** Me three times. **Jn 13:38** *720*
in Jerusalem, and we cannot **d** it. **Ac 4:16** *720*
If we **d** Him, He also will deny us; **2Tm 2:12** *720*
If we deny Him, He also will **d** us; **2Tm 2:12** *720*
for He cannot **d** Himself. **2Tm 2:13** *720*
but by *their* deeds they **d** *Him,* **Ti 1:16** *720*
instructing us to **d** ungodliness **Ti 2:12** *720*
and **d** our only Master and Lord, **Jude 1:4** *720*
My name, and did not **d** My faith even **Rv 2:13** *720*

DENYING
Transgressing and **d** the LORD, **Is 59:13** 3584
And while they were all **d** it, **Lk 8:45** *720*
even **d** the Master who bought them, **2Pe 2:1** *720*

DEPART
I have served you, and let me **d**; **Gn 30:26** 1980
scepter shall not **d** from Judah, **Gn 49:10** 5493
against us and **d** from the land." **Ex 1:10** 5927
"The frogs will **d** from you **Ex 8:11** 5493
of insects may **d** from Pharaoh, **Ex 8:29** 5493
"**D**, go up from here, you and the **Ex 33:1** 1980
man, would not **d** from the tent. **Ex 33:11** 4185
"**D** now from the tents of these **Nu 16:26** 5493
and they do not **d** from your heart **Dt 4:9** 5493
Let him **d** and return to his house, **Dt 20:5** 1980
Let him **d** and return to his house, **Dt 20:6** 1980
Let him **d** and return to his house, **Dt 20:7** 1980
Let him **d** and return to his house, **Dt 20:8** 1980
law shall not **d** from your mouth, **Jos 1:8** 4185
"Please do not **d** from here, until **Jg 6:18** 4185
and **d** from Mount Gilead.' " **Jg 7:3** 6852
"Go, **d**, go down from among the **1Sa 15:6** 5493
the evil spirit would **d** from him. **1Sa 16:23** 5493
d, and go into the land of Judah." **1Sa 22:5** 1980
the morning and have light, **d**." **1Sa 29:10** 1980
and his men, to **d** in the morning to **1Sa 29:11** 1980
they may lead *them* away and **d**." **1Sa 30:22** 1980
shall not **d** from him, **2Sa 7:15** 5493
shall never **d** from your house, **2Sa 12:10** 5493
and I will **d** from the city." **2Sa 20:21** 1980
statutes, I did not **d** from them. **2Sa 22:23** 5493
on the day you **d** and go anywhere, **1Ki 2:42** 3318
"**D** for three days, then return to **1Ki 12:5** 1980
he did not **d** from them. **2Ki 3:3** 5493
sin, from these Jehu did not **d**, **2Ki 10:29** 5493
not **d** from the sins of Jeroboam, **2Ki 10:31** 5493
he did not **d** from all the sins of **2Ki 14:24** 5493
he did not **d** from the sins of **2Ki 15:9** 5493
he did not **d** all his days from the **2Ki 15:18** 5493
he did not **d** from the sins of **2Ki 15:24** 5493
he did not **d** from the sins of **2Ki 15:28** 5493
they did not **d** from them **2Ki 17:22** 5493
he did not **d** from following Him, **2Ki 18:6** 5493
And they did not **d** from the **2Ch 8:15** 5493
father Asa and did not **d** from it, **2Ch 20:32** 5493
not have to **d** from their service, **2Ch 35:15** 5493
"The increase of his house will **d**; **Jb 20:28** 1540
"They say to God, '**D** from us! **Jb 21:14** 5493
"They said to God, '**D** from us!' **Jb 22:17** 5493
d from evil is understanding.' " **Jb 28:28** 5493
D from me, all you who do **Ps 6:8** 5493
D from evil and do good; **Ps 34:14** 5493
D from evil and do good, So you **Ps 37:27** 5493
Before I **d** and am no more." **Ps 39:13** 1980
deceit do not **d** from her streets. **Ps 55:11** 4185
A perverse heart shall **d** from me; **Ps 101:4** 5493
D from me, evildoers, That I may **Ps 119:115** 5493
D from me, therefore, men of **Ps 139:19** 5493
Do not let them **d** from your sight; **Pr 4:21** 3868
not **d** from the words of my mouth. **Pr 5:7** 5493
of the upright is to **d** from evil; **Pr 16:17** 5493
Evil will not **d** from his house. **Pr 17:13** 4185
he is old he will not **d** from it. **Pr 22:6** 5493
Yet his foolishness will not **d** from him. **Pr 27:22** 5493
the jealousy of Ephraim will **d**, **Is 11:13** 5493
and devastators Will **d** from you. **Is 49:17** 3318
D, depart, go out from there, **Is 52:11** 5493
Depart, **d**, go out from there, **Is 52:11** 5493
shall not **d** from your mouth, **Is 59:21** 4185
and he will **d** from there safely. **Jer 43:12** 3318
You who have escaped the sword, **D**! **Jer 51:50** 1980
"**D**! Unclean!" they cried **La 4:15** 5493
"**D**, depart, do not touch!" **La 4:15** 5493
"Depart, **d**, do not touch!" **La 4:15** 5493
and My jealousy will **d** from you, **Ezk 16:42** 5493
to them indeed when I **d** from them! **Hos 9:12** 5493
And the scepter of Egypt will **d**. **Zch 10:11** 5493
D FROM ME, YOU WHO PRACTICE **Mt 7:23** *672*
orders to **d** to the other side **Mt 8:18** *565*
'**D** from Me, accursed ones, into **Mt 25:41** *4198*
Your bond-servant to **d** in peace, **Lk 2:29** *630*
D FROM ME, ALL YOU EVILDOERS.' **Lk 13:27** *868*
His hour had come that He would **d** **Jn 13:1** *3327*
desire to **d** and be with Christ, **Php 1:23** *360*

DEPARTED
years old when he **d** from Haran. **Gn 12:4** 3318
and all their food supply, and **d**. **Gn 14:11** 1980
nephew, and his possessions and **d**, **Gn 14:12** 1980
speaking to Abraham the LORD **d**, **Gn 18:33** 1980
And she **d** and wandered about in **Gn 21:14** 1980
So the servant took Rebekah and **d**. **Gn 24:61** 1980
And Isaac **d** from there and camped **Gn 26:17** 1980
away and they **d** from him in peace. **Gn 26:31** 1980
Then Jacob **d** from Beersheba and **Gn 28:10** 3318
Laban **d** and returned to his place. **Gn 31:55** 1980
that Judah **d** from his brothers and **Gn 38:1** 3381
Then she arose and **d**, **Gn 38:19** 1980
their grain and **d** from there. **Gn 42:26** 1980
his brothers away, and as they **d**, **Gn 45:24** 1980
Then Moses **d** and returned to **Ex 4:18** 1980
of Israel **d** from Moses' presence. **Ex 35:20** 3318
the mark has **d** when you washed it, **Lv 13:58** 5493
LORD burned against them and He **d**. **Nu 12:9** 1980
the elders of Midian **d** with the *fees* **Nu 22:7** 1980
and **d** and returned to his place, **Nu 24:25** 1980
So she sent them away, and they **d**; **Jos 2:21** 1980
d and came to the hill country, **Jos 2:22** 1980
d from the sons of Israel at Shiloh **Jos 22:9** 1980
was dead, each **d** to his home. **Jg 9:55** 1980
know that the LORD had **d** from him. **Jg 16:20** 5493
Then the man **d** from the city, from **Jg 17:8** 1980
Then the five men **d** and came to **Jg 18:7** 1980
Then they turned and **d**, **Jg 18:21** 1980
so he arose and **d** and came to *a* **Jg 19:10** 1980
Israel **d** from there at that time, **Jg 21:24** 1980
d from the place where she was, **Ru 1:7** 3318
So she **d** and went and gleaned in **Ru 2:3** 1980
"The glory has **d** from Israel," **1Sa 4:21** 1540
"The glory has **d** from Israel, for **1Sa 4:22** 1540
the people to go, and they **d**? **1Sa 6:6** 1980
d from among the Amalekites. **1Sa 15:6** 5493
Spirit of the LORD **d** from Saul, **1Sa 16:14** 5493
was with him but had **d** from Saul. **1Sa 18:12** 5493
Then he rose and **d**, while Jonathan **1Sa 20:42** 1980
So David **d** from there and escaped **1Sa 22:1** 1980
So David **d** and went into the **1Sa 22:5** 1980
hundred, arose and **d** from Keilah, **1Sa 23:13** 3318
and God has **d** from me and no **1Sa 28:15** 5493
since the LORD has **d** from you and **1Sa 28:16** 5493
d and came to the house of **2Sa 4:5** 1980
the people **d** each to his house. **2Sa 6:19** 1980
So the messenger **d** and came and **2Sa 11:22** 1980
so the two of them **d** quickly and **2Sa 17:18** 1980
after they had **d** that they came up **2Sa 17:21** 1980
from the day the king **d** until the **2Sa 19:24** 1980
So the people **d**. **1Ki 12:5** 1980
So Israel **d** to their tents. **1Ki 12:16** 1980
arose and **d** and came to Tirzah. **1Ki 14:17** 1980
So he **d** from there and found **1Ki 19:19** 1980
d and brought him word again. **1Ki 20:9** 1980
as soon as you have **d** from me, **1Ki 20:36** 1980
had **d** from him a lion found him and **1Ki 20:36** 1980
So the prophet **d** and waited for **1Ki 20:38** 1980
you shall surely die.' " Then Elijah **d**. **2Ki 1:4** 1980
and they **d** from him and returned **2Ki 3:27** 5265

Context	Reference	Number
He **d** and took with him ten	**2Ki 5:5**	1980
So he **d** from him some distance.	**2Ki 5:19**	1980
he sent the men away, and they **d**.	**2Ki 5:24**	1980
So he **d** from Elisha and returned	**2Ki 8:14**	1980
Then he arose and **d** and	**2Ki 10:12**	935
Now when he had **d** from there, he	**2Ki 10:15**	1980
of Assyria **d** and returned *home,*	**2Ki 19:36**	5265
the people **d** each to his house,	**1Ch 16:43**	1980
Joab **d** and went throughout all	**1Ch 21:4**	3318
again in three days." So the people **d**.	**2Ch 10:5**	1980
So all Israel **d** to their tents.	**2Ch 10:16**	1980
and he **d** with no one's regret, and	**2Ch 21:20**	1980
When they had **d** from him	**2Ch 24:25**	1980
d from the presence of the LORD.	**Jb 1:12**	3318
d from the command of His lips;	**Jb 23:12**	4185
"The **d** spirits tremble Under the	**Jb 26:5**	7496
have not wickedly **d** from my God.	**Ps 18:21**	7561
d spirits rise *and* praise You?	**Ps 88:10**	7496
Egypt was glad when they **d**,	**Ps 105:38**	3318
live, the **d** spirits will not rise;	**Is 26:14**	7496
will give birth to the **d** spirits.	**Is 26:19**	7496
of Assyria **d** and returned *home*	**Is 37:37**	5265
They have turned aside and **d**.	**Jer 5:23**	1980
the smiths had **d** from Jerusalem.)	**Jer 29:2**	3318
Has **d** from the daughter of Zion;	**La 1:6**	3318
Then the glory of the LORD **d** from	**Ezk 10:18**	3318
When the cherubim **d**,	**Ezk 10:19**	3318
its glory, since it has **d** from it.	**Hos 10:5**	1540
He **d** from there to teach and	**Mt 11:1**	*3327*
these parables, He **d** from there.	**Mt 13:53**	*3332*
these words, He **d** from Galilee and	**Mt 19:1**	*3332*
hands on them, He **d** from there.	**Mt 19:15**	*4198*
silver into the temple sanctuary and **d**;	**Mt 27:5**	*402*
And the angel **d** from her.	**Lk 1:38**	*565*
Ananias **d** and entered the house,	**Ac 9:17**	*565*
immediately the angel **d** from him.	**Ac 12:10**	*868*
they encouraged them and **d**.	**Ac 16:40**	*1831*
spoken these words, the Jews **d**,	**Ac 28:29**	*565*
DEPARTING		
It came about as her soul was **d**	**Gn 35:18**	3318
d from their God.	**Hos 4:12**	
D from there, He went into their	**Mt 12:9**	*3327*
D from there, Jesus went along by	**Mt 15:29**	*3327*
D, they *began* going throughout	**Lk 9:6**	*1831*
DEPARTS		
forever overpower him and he **d**;	**Jb 14:20**	1980
His spirit **d**, he returns to the	**Ps 146:4**	3318
treacherously **d** from her lover,	**Jer 3:20**	
fixed order **d** From before Me,"	**Jer 31:36**	4185
Her prey never **d**.	**Na 3:1**	4185
DEPARTURE		
their **d** from the land of Egypt.	**Ex 16:1**	3318
were speaking of His **d** which He	**Lk 9:31**	*1841*
after my **d** savage wolves will come	**Ac 20:29**	*867*
urged you upon my **d** for Macedonia,	**1Tm 1:3**	*4198*
and the time of my **d** has come.	**2Tm 4:6**	*359*
after my **d** you will be able to call	**2Pe 1:15**	*1841*
DEPEND		
you did not **d** on Him who made it,	**Is 22:11**	5027
"On these two commandments **d** the	**Mt 22:40**	*2910*
So then it *does* not **d** on	**Ro 9:16**	
DEPENDED		
In that day you **d** on the weapons	**Is 22:8**	5027
DEPENDENT		
was a certain man without a **d**,	**Ec 4:8**	8145
any woman who is a believer has **d**	**1Tm 5:16**	
DEPENDS		
of everyone **d** on the man you seek;	**2Sa 17:3**	
prosperity **d** upon this business.	**Ac 19:25**	
		1510, 1537
possible, so far as it **d** on you,	**Ro 12:18**	*1537*
DEPLOYED		
the men in ambush also **d** and	**Jg 20:37**	4900
DEPOPULATED		
through the land and they **d** it,	**Ezk 14:15**	7921
DEPORTATION		
at the time of the **d** to Babylon.	**Mt 1:11**	*3350*
After the **d** to Babylon:	**Mt 1:12**	*3350*
from David to the **d** to Babylon	**Mt 1:17**	*3350*
and from the **d** to Babylon to the	**Mt 1:17**	*3350*
DEPORTED		
Osnappar **d** and settled in the city of	**Ezr 4:10**	1541
and **d** the people to Babylon.	**Ezr 5:12**	1541
Because they **d** an entire	**Am 1:6**	1540
DEPOSE		
"I will **d** you from your	**Is 22:19**	1920
DEPOSED		
king of Egypt **d** him at Jerusalem,	**2Ch 36:3**	5493
he was **d** from his royal throne and	**Da 5:20**	5182
DEPOSIT		
a **d** or a security entrusted *to him,*	**Lv 6:2**	6487
the **d** which was entrusted to him or	**Lv 6:4**	6487
"You shall then **d** them in the	**Nu 17:4**	5117
ashes of the heifer and **d** them outside	**Nu 19:9**	5117
year, and shall **d** *it* in your town.	**Dt 14:28**	5117
go *and* **d** them in the temple in	**Ezr 5:15**	5182
DEPOSITED		
So Moses **d** the rods before the	**Nu 17:7**	5117
hand and **d** them in the house,	**2Ki 5:24**	6485
At Michmash he **d** his baggage.	**Is 10:28**	6485
but they had **d** the scroll in the	**Jer 36:20**	6485
DEPRAVED		
God gave them over to a **d** mind,	**Ro 1:28**	*96b*
friction between men of **d** mind and	**1Tm 6:5**	*1311*
oppose the truth, men of **d** mind,	**2Tm 3:8**	*2704*
DEPRAVITY		
The revolters have gone deep in **d**,	**Hos 5:2**	7821a
in **d** As in the days of Gibeah;	**Hos 9:9**	7843
DEPRESSED		
you so **d** morning after morning?	**2Sa 13:4**	1800b
But God, who comforts the **d**,	**2Co 7:6**	*5011*
DEPRESSIONS		
house has greenish or reddish **d** and	**Lv 14:37**	8258
DEPRIVE		
So as to **d** the needy of justice And	**Is 10:2**	5186
To **d** a man of justice In the	**La 3:35**	5186
I am going to **d** the flank of Moab	**Ezk 25:9**	6605a
DEPRIVED		
to be **d** of the rest of my years."	**Is 38:10**	6485
depraved mind and **d** of the truth,	**1Tm 6:5**	*650*
DEPRIVES		
"He **d** the trusted ones of speech And	**Jb 12:20**	5493
"He **d** of intelligence the chiefs	**Jb 12:24**	5493
DEPRIVING		
and **d** myself of pleasure?"	**Ec 4:8**	2637
Stop **d** one another, except by	**1Co 7:5**	*650*
DEPTH		
and its **d** along the front of the	**1Ki 6:3**	7341
for height and the earth for **d**,	**Pr 25:3**	6011
is I who says to the **d** of the sea,	**Is 44:27**	6683
for help from the **d** of Sheol;	**Jon 2:2**	990
up, because they had no **d** of soil.	**Mt 13:5**	*899*
to be drowned in the **d** of the sea.	**Mt 18:6**	*3989*
up because it had no **d** of soil.	**Mk 4:5**	*899*
nor height, nor **d**, nor any other	**Ro 8:39**	*899*
the **d** of the riches both of the	**Ro 11:33**	*899*
and length and height and **d**,	**Eph 3:18**	*899*
DEPTHS		
went down into the **d** like a stone.	**Ex 15:5**	4688
You hurled into the **d**,	**Ne 9:11**	4688
"Can you discover the **d** of God?	**Jb 11:7**	2714
And He covers the **d** of the sea.	**Jb 36:30**	8328
"He makes the **d** boil like a pot;	**Jb 41:31**	4688
Will go into the **d** of the earth.	**Ps 63:9**	8482
them back from the **d** of the sea;	**Ps 68:22**	4688
up again from the **d** of the earth.	**Ps 71:20**	8415
abundant drink like the ocean **d**.	**Ps 78:15**	8415
my soul from the **d** of Sheol.	**Ps 86:13**	8482
pit, In dark places, in the **d**.	**Ps 88:6**	4688
whose hand are the **d** of the earth,	**Ps 95:4**	4278
heavens, they went down to the **d**;	**Ps 107:26**	8415
Out of the **d** I have cried to You,	**Ps 130:1**	4615
wrought in the **d** of the earth;	**Ps 139:15**	8482
were no **d** I was brought forth,	**Pr 8:24**	8415
her guests are in the **d** of Sheol.	**Pr 9:18**	6011
Who made the **d** of the sea a	**Is 51:10**	4615
Who led them through the **d**?	**Is 63:13**	8415
away, turn back, dwell in the **d**,	**Jer 49:8**	6009
Dwell in the **d**, O inhabitants of	**Jer 49:30**	6009
the seas In the **d** of the waters,	**Ezk 27:34**	4615
their sins Into the **d** of the sea.	**Mi 7:19**	4688
all the **d** of the Nile will dry up;	**Zch 10:11**	4688
all things, even the **d** of God.	**1Co 2:10**	*899*
DEPUTIES		
the son of Nathan *was* over the **d**;	**1Ki 4:5**	5324
had twelve **d** over all Israel,	**1Ki 4:7**	5324
Those **d** provided for King	**1Ki 4:27**	5324
besides Solomon's 3,300 chief **d**	**1Ki 5:16**	5324
DEPUTY		
the only **d** who *was* in the land.	**1Ki 4:19**	5333
was no king in Edom; a **d** was king.	**1Ki 22:47**	5324
DERBE		
cities of Lycaonia, Lystra and **D**,	**Ac 14:6**	*1191*
he went away with Barnabas to **D**.	**Ac 14:20**	*1191*
Paul came also to **D** and to Lystra.	**Ac 16:1**	*1191*
and Gaius of **D**, and Timothy,	**Ac 20:4**	*1190b*
DERIDE		
Those who **d** me have used my *name*	**Ps 102:8**	1984b
The arrogant utterly **d** me,	**Ps 119:51**	3917b
DERISION		
to be a **d** among their enemies	**Ex 32:25**	8103
Job, Who drinks up **d** like water,	**Jb 34:7**	3933
and a **d** to those around us.	**Ps 44:13**	7047
scoffing and **d** to those around us.	**Ps 79:4**	7047
In reproach and **d** all day long.	**Jer 20:8**	7047
along the way Clap their hands *in* **d**	**La 2:15**	
will be laughed at and held in **d**;	**Ezk 23:32**	3933
which have become a prey and a **d**	**Ezk 36:4**	3933
be their **d** in the land of Egypt.	**Hos 7:16**	3933
And your inhabitants for **d**,	**Mi 6:16**	8322
DERIVE		
to God, you **d** your benefit,	**Ro 6:22**	*2192*
DERIVED		
of my own **d** from *the* Law,	**Php 3:9**	*1537*
DERIVES		
in heaven and on earth **d** its name,	**Eph 3:15**	*3687*
DERIVING		
what benefit were you then **d** from the	**Ro 6:21**	*2192*
DESCEND		
the pillar of cloud would **d** and	**Ex 33:9**	3381
and they **d** alive into Sheol,	**Nu 16:30**	3381
that **d** from the city of David.	**Ne 3:15**	3381
violence will **d** upon his own pate.	**Ps 7:16**	3381
His glory will not **d** after him.	**Ps 49:17**	3381
jubilant within her, **d** *into it.*	**Is 5:14**	3381
it shall **d** for judgment upon Edom And	**Is 34:5**	3381
You will **d** to Hades;	**Mt 11:23**	*2597*
'WHO WILL **D** INTO THE ABYSS?'	**Ro 10:7**	*2597*
will **d** from heaven with a shout,	**1Th 4:16**	*2597*
DESCENDANT		
also, because he is your **d**."	**Gn 21:13**	2233
I will raise up your **d** after you,	**2Sa 7:12**	2233
chosen, **D** of Abraham My friend,	**Is 41:8**	2233
who was born of a **d** of David	**Ro 1:3**	*4690*
am an Israelite, a **d** of Abraham,	**Ro 11:1**	*4690*
risen from the dead, **d** of David,	**2Tm 2:8**	*4690*
He gives help to the **d** of Abraham.	**Heb 2:16**	*4690*
I am the root and the **d** of David,	**Rv 22:16**	*1085*
DESCENDANTS		
you, and with your **d** after you;	**Gn 9:9**	2233
"To your **d** I will give this land."	**Gn 12:7**	2233
it to you and to your **d** forever.	**Gn 13:15**	2233
your **d** as the dust of the earth,	**Gn 13:16**	2233
then your **d** can also be numbered.	**Gn 13:16**	2233
"So shall your **d** be."	**Gn 15:5**	2233
"Know for certain that your **d**	**Gn 15:13**	2233
"To your **d** I have given this	**Gn 15:18**	2233
"I will greatly multiply your **d**	**Gn 16:10**	2233
between Me and you and your **d** after	**Gn 17:7**	2233
to you and to your **d** after you.	**Gn 17:7**	2233
to you and to your **d** after you,	**Gn 17:8**	2233
you and your **d** after you	**Gn 17:9**	2233
Me and you and your **d** after you:	**Gn 17:10**	2233
foreigner, who is not of your **d**.	**Gn 17:12**	2233
covenant for his **d** after him.	**Gn 17:19**	2233
Isaac your **d** shall be named.	**Gn 21:12**	2233
'To your **d** I will give this land,'	**Gn 24:7**	2233
And may your **d** possess The gate of	**Gn 24:60**	2233
to you and to your **d** I will give all	**Gn 26:3**	2233
your **d** as the stars of heaven,	**Gn 26:4**	2233
will give your **d** all these lands;	**Gn 26:4**	2233
and by your **d** all the nations of	**Gn 26:4**	2233
bless you, and multiply your **d**,	**Gn 26:24**	2233
to you and to your **d** with you,	**Gn 28:4**	2233
will give it to you and to your **d**.	**Gn 28:13**	2233
"Your **d** will also be like the	**Gn 28:14**	2233
and in you and in your **d** shall all	**Gn 28:14**	2233
your **d** as the sand of the sea,	**Gn 32:12**	2233
the land to your **d** after you."	**Gn 35:12**	2233
Jacob and all his **d** with him:	**Gn 46:6**	2233
d he brought with him to Egypt.	**Gn 46:7**	2233
who came to Egypt, his direct **d**,	**Gn 46:26**	3318
will give this land to your **d** after you	**Gn 48:4**	2233
and his **d** shall become a multitude	**Gn 48:19**	2233
to him and to his **d** after him.	**Ex 28:43**	2233
d throughout their generations."	**Ex 30:21**	2233
'I will multiply your **d** as the	**Ex 32:13**	2233
have spoken I will give to your **d**,	**Ex 32:13**	2233
'To your **d** I will give it.'	**Ex 33:1**	2233
among the **d** of Aaron the priest who	**Lv 21:21**	2233
'If any man among all your **d**	**Lv 22:3**	2233
'No man of the **d** of Aaron, who is	**Lv 22:4**	2233
or to the **d** of a stranger's family,	**Lv 25:47**	6133
"Take a census of the **d** of Kohath	**Nu 4:2**	1121
"This is the work of the **d** of	**Nu 4:4**	1121
and Talmai, the **d** of Anak were.	**Nu 13:22**	3211
we saw the **d** of Anak there.	**Nu 13:28**	3211
his **d** shall take possession of it.	**Nu 14:24**	2233
layman who is not of the **d** of Aaron	**Nu 16:40**	2233
LORD to you and your **d** with you."	**Nu 18:19**	2233
be for him and his **d** after him,	**Nu 25:13**	2233
to them and their **d** after them.'	**Dt 1:8**	2233
He chose their **d** after them.	**Dt 4:37**	2233
and He chose their **d** after them,	**Dt 10:15**	2233
to give to them and to their **d**,	**Dt 11:9**	2233
none of his **d**, even to	**Dt 23:2**	
none of their **d**, even to	**Dt 23:3**	
wonder on you and your **d** forever.	**Dt 28:46**	2233
plagues on you and your **d**,	**Dt 28:59**	2233
heart and the heart of your **d**,	**Dt 30:6**	2233
that you may live, you and your **d**,	**Dt 30:19**	2233
from the lips of their **d**);	**Dt 31:21**	2233
Jacob, saying, 'I will give it to your **d**'	**Dt 34:4**	2233
these *were* the male **d** of Manasseh	**Jos 17:2**	1121
his **d** and gave him Isaac.	**Jos 24:3**	2233
The **d** of the Kenite, Moses'	**Jg 1:16**	1121
sons who were his direct **d**,	**Jg 8:30**	3318
between my **d** and your descendants	**1Sa 20:42**	2233
and your **d** forever.' "	**1Sa 20:42**	2233
will not cut off my **d** after me and	**1Sa 24:21**	2233
this day on Saul and his **d**."	**2Sa 4:8**	2233
who was among the **d** of the giant,	**2Sa 21:16**	3211
who was among the **d** of the giant.	**2Sa 21:18**	3211
To David and his **d** forever."	**2Sa 22:51**	2233
and on the head of his **d** forever;	**1Ki 2:33**	2233
but to David and his **d** and	**1Ki 2:33**	2233
their **d** who were left after them	**1Ki 9:21**	1121
afflict the **d** of David for this,	**1Ki 11:39**	2233
to you and to your **d** forever."	**2Ki 5:27**	2233
The LORD rejected all the **d** of	**2Ki 17:20**	2233
The **d** of Shecaniah *were* Shemaiah,	**1Ch 3:22**	1121
set up *one of* your **d** after you,	**1Ch 17:11**	2233
one of the **d** of the giants,	**1Ch 20:4**	3211
of the **d** of Aaron *were these:*	**1Ch 24:1**	1121
men were found from the **d** of Eleazar	**1Ch 24:4**	1121
of Eleazar than the **d** of Ithamar,	**1Ch 24:4**	1121
households of the **d** of Eleazar and	**1Ch 24:4**	1121
and eight of the **d** of Ithamar,	**1Ch 24:4**	1121
both from the **d** of Eleazar and the	**1Ch 24:5**	1121
of Eleazar and the **d** of Ithamar.	**1Ch 24:5**	1121
from their **d** who were left after	**2Ch 8:8**	1121
d of Abraham Your friend forever?	**2Ch 20:7**	2233
fathers' households and their **d**,	**Ezr 2:59**	2233

their fathers' houses or their **d**, **Ne 7:61** 2233
The **d** of Israel separated **Ne 9:2** 2233
To give *it* to his **d**. **Ne 9:8** 2233
and the **d** of Solomon's servants. **Ne 11:3** 1121
for themselves and for their **d** **Es 9:27** 2233
or their memory fade from their **d**. **Es 9:28** 2233
for themselves and for their **d** with **Es 9:31** 2233
also that your **d** will be many, **Jb 5:25** 2233
"Their **d** are established with **Jb 21:8** 2233
And his **d** will not be satisfied **Jb 27:14** 6631
To David and his **d** forever. **Ps 18:50** 2233
d from among the sons of men. **Ps 21:10** 2233
All you **d** of Jacob, glorify Him, **Ps 22:23** 2233
awe of Him, all you **d** of Israel. **Ps 22:23** 2233
And his **d** will inherit the land. **Ps 25:13** 2233
forsaken Or his **d** begging bread. **Ps 37:25** 2233
And his **d** are a blessing. **Ps 37:26** 2233
d of the wicked will be cut off. **Ps 37:28** 2233
The **d** of His servants will **Ps 69:36** 2233
"So I will establish his **d** forever And **Ps 89:29** 2233
"His **d** shall endure forever And **Ps 89:36** 2233
And their **d** will be established **Ps 102:28** 2233
His **d** will be mighty on earth; **Ps 112:2** 2233
But the **d** of the righteous will be **Pr 11:21** 2233
And My blessing on your **d**; **Is 44:3** 6631
d would have been like the sand, **Is 48:19** 2233
And your **d** will possess nations And **Is 54:3** 2233
d in the midst of the peoples. **Is 61:9** 6631
the LORD, And their **d** with them. **Is 65:23** 6631
Why have he and his **d** been hurled **Jer 22:28** 2233
For no man of his **d** will prosper **Jer 22:30** 2233
who brought up and led back the **d** of **Jer 23:8** 2233
Shemaiah the Nehelamite and his **d**; **Jer 29:32** 2233
so I will multiply the **d** of David **Jer 33:22** 2233
I would reject the **d** of Jacob **Jer 33:26** 2233
not taking from his **d** rulers over **Jer 33:26** 2233
rulers over the **d** of Abraham, **Jer 33:26** 2233
"I will also punish him and his **d** **Jer 36:31** 2233
And your **d** from the land of their **Jer 46:27** 2233
swore to the **d** of the house of Jacob **Ezk 20:5** 2233
compass, though not to his *own* **d**, **Da 11:4** 319
"But one of the **d** of her line **Da 11:7** 5342
was Joseph, of the **d** of David; **Lk 1:27** *3624*
To Abraham and his **d** forever." **Lk 1:55** *4690*
said that the Christ comes from the **d** **Jn 7:42** *4690*
"We are Abraham's **d** and have never **Jn 8:33** *4690*
"I know that you are Abraham's **d**; **Jn 8:37** *4690*
SEAT *one* OF HIS **D** ON HIS THRONE, **Ac 2:30** *2590, 3751*
AND TO HIS **D** AFTER HIM. **Ac 7:5** *4690*
that his **D** WOULD BE ALIENS IN A **Ac 7:6** *4690*
"From the **d** of this man, according **Ac 13:23** *4690*
the promise to Abraham or to his **d** **Ro 4:13** *4690*
will be guaranteed to all the **d**, **Ro 4:16** *4690*
"SO SHALL YOUR **D** BE." **Ro 4:18** *4690*
because they are Abraham's **d**, **Ro 9:7** *4690*
ISAAC YOUR **D** WILL BE NAMED." **Ro 9:7** *4690*
of the promise are regarded as **d**. **Ro 9:8** *4690*
Are they **d** of Abraham? **2Co 11:22** *4690*
then you are Abraham's **d**, heirs **Ga 3:29** *4690*
as many **d** AS THE STARS OF **Heb 11:12**
"IN ISAAC YOUR **D** SHALL BE CALLED." **Heb 11:18** *4690*

DESCENDED
These are the chiefs **d** from **Gn 36:16**
These are the chiefs **d** from Reuel **Gn 36:17**
d from Esau's wife Oholibamah, **Gn 36:18**
are the chiefs **d** from the Horites, **Gn 36:21**
are the chiefs **d** from the Horites: **Gn 36:29**
are the chiefs **d** from the Horites, **Gn 36:30**
names of the chiefs **d** from Esau, **Gn 36:40**
the LORD **d** upon it in fire; **Ex 19:18** 3381
The LORD **d** in the cloud and **Ex 34:5** 3381
and he also was **d** from the giants. **1Ch 20:6** 3205
were **d** from the giants in Gath, **1Ch 20:8** 3205
has ascended into heaven and **d**? **Pr 30:4** 3381
That have **d** from Mount Gilead. **SS 4:1** 1570
of goats That have **d** from Gilead. **SS 6:5** 1570
a holy one, **d** from heaven. **Da 4:13** 5182
"I **d** to the roots of the mountains. **Jon 2:6** 3381
for an angel of the Lord **d** from **Mt 28:2** *2597*
and the Holy Spirit **d** upon Him in **Lk 3:22** *2597*
gale of wind **d** on the lake, **Lk 8:23** *2597*
heaven, but He who **d** from heaven: **Jn 3:13** *2597*
they are not all Israel who are **d** **Ro 9:6**
He also had **d** into the lower parts **Eph 4:9** *2597*
He who **d** is Himself also He who **Eph 4:10** *2597*
although these are **d** from Abraham. **Heb 7:5** *1831, 3751*
that our Lord was **d** from Judah, **Heb 7:14** *393*

DESCENDING
of God were ascending and **d** on it. **Gn 28:12** 3381
Sheol, **D** to the chambers of death. **Pr 7:27** 3381
And the **d** of His arm to be seen in **Is 30:30** 5183b
one, **d** from heaven and saying, **Da 4:23** 5182
saw the Spirit of God **d** as a dove **Mt 3:16** *2597*
the Spirit like a dove **d** upon Him; **Mk 1:10** *2597*
Spirit **d** as a dove out of heaven, **Jn 1:32** *2597*
Spirit **d** and remaining upon Him, **Jn 1:33** *2597*
and **d** on the Son of Man." **Jn 1:51** *2597*

DESCENDS
the beast **d** downward to the earth? **Ec 3:21** 3381
that **d** from Jerusalem to Gaza." **Ac 8:26** *2597*

DESCENT
and struck them down on the **d**, **Jos 7:5** 4174
they were at the **d** of Beth-horon, **Jos 10:11** 4174
For at the **d** of Horonaim They have **Jer 48:5** 4174
the son of Ahasuerus, of Median **d**, **Da 9:1** 2233
near the **d** of the Mount of Olives, **Lk 19:37** *2600*
all who were of high-priestly **d**. **Ac 4:6** *1085*

DESCRIBE
d the land in seven divisions, **Jos 18:6** 3789
those who went to **d** the land, **Jos 18:8** 3789
walk through the land and **d** it, **Jos 18:8** 3789
d the temple to the house of **Ezk 43:10** 5046
"Return to your house and **d** what **Lk 8:39** *1334*
SOMEONE SHOULD **D** IT TO YOU.'" **Ac 13:41** *1555*

DESCRIBED
and **d** it by cities in seven **Jos 18:9** 3789
Those who had seen it **d** to **Mk 5:16** *1334*
d to them how he had seen the Lord **Ac 9:27** *1334*
he **d** to them how the Lord had led **Ac 12:17** *1334*

DESCRIBING
d in detail the conversion of the **Ac 15:3** *1555*

DESCRIPTION
walk through the land and write a **d** **Jos 18:4**
and bring *the* **d** here to me. **Jos 18:6**

DESECRATE
arise, **d** the sanctuary fortress, **Da 11:31** 2490c
"And he even tried to **d** the temple; **Ac 24:6** *953*

DESERT
"He found him in a **d** land, **Dt 32:10** 4057b
LORD to the **d** plains of Jericho. **Jos 4:13** 6160
month on the **d** plains of Jericho. **Jos 5:10** 6160
place before the **d** plain. **Jos 8:14** 6160
bread for *their* children in the **d**. **Jb 24:5** 6160
On a **d** without a man in it, **Jb 38:26** 4057b
nomads of the **d** bow before him, **Ps 72:9** 6716b
Nor from the **d** *comes* exaltation; **Ps 75:6** 4057b
against the Most High in the **d**. **Ps 78:17** 6723
And grieved Him in the **d**! **Ps 78:40** 3452
And tempted God in the **d**. **Ps 106:14** 3452
in the wilderness in a **d** region; **Ps 107:4** 3452
It is better to live in a **d** land Than **Pr 21:19** 4057b
d creatures will lie down there, **Is 13:21** 6716b
Assyria appointed it for **d** **Is 23:13** 6716b
forlorn and forsaken like the **d**; **Is 27:10** 4057b
Sharon is like a **d** plain, **Is 33:9** 6160
The **d** creatures will meet **Is 34:14** 6716b
wilderness and the **d** will be glad, **Is 35:1** 6723
in the **d** a highway for our God. **Is 40:3** 6160
I will place the juniper in the **d** **Is 41:19** 6160
the wilderness, Rivers in the **d**. **Is 43:19** 3452
wilderness And rivers in the **d**, **Is 43:20** 3452
her **d** like the garden of the LORD; **Is 51:3** 6160
for them Like an Arab in the **d**, **Jer 3:2** 4057b
the **d** A wayfarers' lodging place; **Jer 9:2** 4057b
land ruined, laid waste like a **d**, **Jer 9:12** 4057b
and all those inhabiting the **d** who **Jer 9:26** 4057b
like drifting straw To the **d** wind. **Jer 13:24** 4057b
"For he will be like a bush in the **d** **Jer 17:6** 6160
foreign people who dwell in the **d**; **Jer 25:24** 4057b
a parched land and a **d**. **Jer 50:12** 6160
"Therefore the **d** creatures will **Jer 50:39** 6716b
of horror, A parched land and a **d**, **Jer 51:43** 6160
wilderness, Make her like **d** land And **Hos 2:3** 6723
be driven by the demon into the **d**. **Lk 8:29** *2048*
(This is a **d** *road.*) **Ac 8:26** *2048*
"I WILL NEVER **D** YOU, NOR WILL I **Heb 13:5** *447*

DESERTED
number so that your roads lie **d**. **Lv 26:22** 8074
days of Jael, the highways were **d**, **Jg 5:6** 2308
the day he **d** *to me* to this day?" **1Sa 29:3** 5307
who had **d** to the king of Babylon **2Ki 25:11** 5307
And **d** she will sit on the ground. **Is 3:26** 5352
the city of praise has not been **d**, **Jer 49:25** 5800a
who had **d** to the king of Babylon and **Jer 52:15** 5307
who had **d** them in Pamphylia **Ac 15:38** *868*
has **d** me and gone to Thessalonica; **2Tm 4:10** *1459*
no one supported me, but all **d** me; **2Tm 4:16** *1459*

DESERTERS
the **d** who had deserted to the king of **2Ki 25:11** 5307
the **d** who had gone over to him and **Jer 39:9** 5307
the **d** who had deserted to the king **Jer 52:15** 5307

DESERTING
amazed that you are so quickly **d** Him **Ga 1:6** *3346a, 575*

DESERTS
for Him who rides through the **d**, **Ps 68:4** 6160
as Jazer *and* wandered to the **d**; **Is 16:8** 4057b
when He led them through the **d**. **Is 48:21** 2723
Through a land of **d** and of pits, **Jer 2:6** 6160
wolf of the **d** will destroy them, **Jer 5:6** 6160
and he lived in the **d** until the **Lk 1:80** *2048*
wandering in **d** and mountains and **Heb 11:38** *2047*

DESERVE
your own field, for you **d** to die; **1Ki 2:26** 376
us less than our iniquities **d**, **Ezr 9:13**
receiving what we **d** for our deeds; **Lk 23:41** *514*
punishment do you think he will **d** **Heb 10:29** *515*
given them blood to drink. They **d** it. **Rv 16:6** *514*

DESERVED
and have dealt with him as he **d** **Jg 9:16** 1576, 3027

DESERVES
if the wicked man **d** to be beaten, **Dt 25:2** 1121
man who has done this **d** to die. **2Sa 12:5** 1121
Answer a fool as his folly **d**, **Pr 26:5**
For what he **d** will be done to him. **Is 3:11** 1576, 3027
They answered, "He **d** death!" **Mt 26:66** *1777*

DESERVING
though he was not **d** of death, **Dt 19:6** 4941
condemned Him to be **d** of death. **Mk 14:64** *1777*
d death has been done by Him. **Lk 23:15** *514*
d death or imprisonment. **Ac 23:29** *514*
statement, **d** full acceptance, **1Tm 1:15** *514*
statement **d** full acceptance. **1Tm 4:9** *514*

DESIGN
in the porch were of lily **d**, **1Ki 7:19** 4639
the top of the pillars was lily **d**. **1Ki 7:22** 4639
This was the **d** of the stands: **1Ki 7:28** 4639
round like the **d** of a pedestal, **1Ki 7:31** 4639
d which may be assigned to him, **2Ch 2:14** 4284
known to them the **d** of the house, **Ezk 43:11** 6699
its whole **d** and all its statutes and **Ezk 43:11** 6699

DESIGNATE
'**D** the cities of refuge, of which **Jos 20:2** 5414
for Me the one whom I **d** to you." **1Sa 16:3** 559
the mouth of the LORD will **d**. **Is 62:2** 5344a

DESIGNATED
her master who **d** her for himself, **Ex 21:8** 3259
these men who had been **d** by name, **Nu 1:17** 5344a
they **d** Bezer in the wilderness on **Jos 20:8** 5414
who were **d** by name to come and **1Ch 12:31** 5344a
were chosen, who were **d** by name, **1Ch 16:41** 5344a
the men who were **d** by name arose, **2Ch 28:15** 5344a
there were men who were **d** by name **2Ch 31:19** 5344a
Levites, all of them **d** by name. **Ezr 8:20** 5344a
to the mountain which Jesus had **d**. **Mt 28:16** *5021*
being **d** by God as a high priest **Heb 5:10** *4316*
and not be **d** according to the **Heb 7:11** *3004*

DESIGNATES
"If he **d** her for his son, he **Ex 21:9** 3259

DESIGNER
and of a **d** and of an embroiderer, **Ex 35:35** 2803

DESIGNS
make artistic **d** for work in gold, **Ex 31:4** 4284
to make **d** for working in gold and **Ex 35:32** 4284
of every work and makers of **d**. **Ex 35:35** 4284
All their deadly **d** against me; **Jer 18:23** 6098
exits, its entrances, all its **d**, **Ezk 43:11** 6699

DESIRABLE
the tree was **d** to make *one* wise, **Gn 3:6** 2530
whom is all that is **d** in Israel? **1Sa 9:20** 2532
whatever is **d** in your eyes, **1Ki 20:6** 4261
They are more **d** than gold, yes, **Ps 19:10** 2530
And all **d** things cannot compare **Pr 8:11** 2656
What is **d** in a man is his kindness, **Pr 19:22** 8378
And he is wholly **d**. **SS 5:16** 4261
all of them **d** young men, **Ezk 23:6** 2531
horses, all of them **d** young men. **Ezk 23:12** 2531
d young men, governors and **Ezk 23:23** 2531
from every kind of **d** object. **Na 2:9** 2532
"It is not **d** for us to neglect **Ac 6:2** *701*

DESIRE
your **d** will be for your husband, **Gn 3:16** 8669
and its **d** is for you, but you must **Gn 4:7** 8669
wife looked with **d** at Joseph, **Gn 39:7** 5375
LORD, for that is what you **d**." **Ex 10:11** 1245
My **d** shall be gratified against **Ex 15:9** 5315
shall not **d** your neighbor's house, **Dt 5:21** 183
any of your gates, whatever you **d**, **Dt 12:15** 185
meat,' because you **d** to eat meat, **Dt 12:20** 183
you may eat meat, whatever you **d**. **Dt 12:20** 185
within your gates whatever you **d**. **Dt 12:21** 185
and have a **d** for her and would **Dt 21:11** 2836a
not **d** to take his brother's wife, **Dt 25:7** 2654a
'I do not **d** to take her,' **Dt 25:8** 2654a
and then take as much as you **d**," **1Sa 2:16** 183
am with you according to your **d**." **1Sa 14:7** 3824
'The king does not **d** any dowry **1Sa 18:25** 2656
all the **d** of your soul to do so; **1Sa 23:20** 185
For all my salvation and all *my* **d**, **2Sa 23:5** 2656
I will do what you **d** concerning **1Ki 5:8** 2656
Then you shall accomplish my **d** by **1Ki 5:9** 2656
and gold according to all his **d** **1Ki 9:11** 2656
all her **d** which she requested, **1Ki 10:13** 2656
shall reign over whatever you **d**, **1Ki 11:37** 183
gave to the queen of Sheba all her **d** **2Ch 9:12** 2656
king **d** to honor more than me?" **Es 6:6** 2654a
And I **d** to argue with God. **Jb 13:3** 2654a
even **d** the knowledge of Your ways. **Jb 21:14** 2654a
I have kept the poor from *their* **d**, **Jb 31:16** 2656
Speak, for I **d** to justify you. **Jb 33:32** 2654a
the wicked boasts of his heart's **d**, **Ps 10:3** 8378
have heard the **d** of the humble; **Ps 10:17** 8378
May He grant you your heart's **d** And **Ps 20:4**
You have given him his heart's **d**, **Ps 21:2** 8378
over to the **d** of my adversaries, **Ps 27:12** 5315
say in their heart, "Aha, our **d**!" **Ps 35:25** 5315
Lord, all my **d** is before You; **Ps 38:9** 8378
him over to the **d** of his enemies. **Ps 41:2** 5315
Then the King will **d** your beauty. **Ps 45:11** 183
d truth in the innermost being, **Ps 51:6** 2654a
And was strong in his *evil* **d**." **Ps 52:7** 1942
You, I **d** nothing on earth. **Ps 73:25** 2654a
asking food according to their **d**. **Ps 78:18** 5315
And their **d** He gave to them. **Ps 78:29** 8378
Before they had satisfied their **d**, **Ps 78:30** 8378
The **d** of the wicked will perish. **Ps 112:10** 8378
the **d** of every living thing. **Ps 145:16** 7522
the **d** of those who fear Him; **Ps 145:19** 7522
nothing you **d** compares with her. **Pr 3:15** 2656
Do not **d** her beauty in your heart, **Pr 6:25** 2530
But the **d** of the righteous will be **Pr 10:24** 8378
d of the righteous is only good, **Pr 11:23** 8378
But the **d** of the treacherous is **Pr 13:2** 5315
But **d** fulfilled is a tree of life. **Pr 13:12** 8378
D realized is sweet to the soul, **Pr 13:19** 8378
separates himself seeks *his own* **d**, **Pr 18:1** 8378

is hope, And do not **d** his death. **Pr 19:18** 5375, 5315
The **d** of the sluggard puts him to **Pr 21:25** 8378
Do not **d** his delicacies, For it is **Pr 23:3** 183
selfish man, Or **d** his delicacies; **Pr 23:6** 183
evil men, Nor **d** to be with them; **Pr 24:1** 183
Or for rulers to **d** strong drink, **Pr 31:4** 177a
my beloved's, And his **d** is for me. **SS 7:10** 8669
Your memory, is the **d** of *our* souls. **Is 26:8** 8378
And he will perform all My **d**.' **Is 44:28** 2656
Without accomplishing what I **d**, **Is 55:11** 2654a
day of your fast you find *your* **d**, **Is 58:3** 2656
satisfy the **d** of the afflicted, **Is 58:10** 5315
satisfy your **d** in scorched places, **Is 58:11** 5315
land to which they **d** to return, **Jer 22:27** 5375, 5315
had set free according to their **d**, **Jer 34:16** 5315
and his **d** will be satisfied in the **Jer 50:19** 5315
up to the **d** of those who hate you, **Ezk 16:27** 5315
the **d** of your eyes with a blow; **Ezk 24:16** 4261
of your power, the **d** of your eyes and **Ezk 24:21** 4261
their pride, the **d** of their eyes and **Ezk 24:25** 4261
his fathers or for the **d** of women, **Da 11:37** 2532
their **d** toward their iniquity. **Hos 4:8** 5315
When it is My **d**, I will chastise **Hos 10:10** 185
man speaks the **d** of his soul; **Mi 7:3** 1942
'I **D** COMPASSION, AND NOT **Mt 9:13** *2309*
'I **D** COMPASSION, AND NOT A **Mt 12:7** *2309*
"Father, I **d** that they also, whom **Jn 17:24** *2309*
"But we **d** to hear from you what **Ac 28:22** *515*
in their **d** toward one another, **Ro 1:27** *3715*
my heart's **d** and my prayer to God **Ro 10:1** *2107*
What do you **d**? Shall I come to you **1Co 4:21** *2309*
But earnestly **d** the greater gifts. **1Co 12:31** *2206*
yet **d** earnestly spiritual *gifts,* **1Co 14:1** *2206*
in the church I **d** to speak five **1Co 14:19** *2309*
If they **d** to learn anything, **1Co 14:35** *2309*
brethren, **d** earnestly to prophesy, **1Co 14:39** *2206*
was not at all *his* **d** to come now, **1Co 16:12** *2307*
do *this,* but also to **d** *to do it.* **2Co 8:10** *2309*
there was the readiness to **d** it, **2Co 8:11** *2309*
cut off opportunity from those who **d** **2Co 11:12** *2309*
d to be enslaved all over again? **Ga 4:9** *2309*
not carry out the **d** of the flesh. **Ga 5:16** *1939*
sets its **d** against the Spirit, **Ga 5:17** *1937*
Those who **d** to make a good showing **Ga 6:12** *2309*
they **d** to have you circumcised so **Ga 6:13** *2309*
d to depart and be with Christ, **Php 1:23** *1939*
impurity, passion, evil **d**, **Col 3:5** *1939*
with great **d** to see your face. **1Th 2:17** *1939*
and fulfill every **d** for goodness **2Th 1:11** *2107*
all who **d** to live godly in Christ **2Tm 3:12** *2309*
And we **d** that each one of you show **Heb 6:11** *1937*
as it is, they **d** a better *country,* **Heb 11:16** *3713*
carried out the **d** of the Gentiles, **1Pe 4:3** *1013*
he forbids those who **d** *to do so* **3Jn 1:10** *1014*
Now I **d** to remind you, though you **Jude 1:5** *1014*
every plague, as often as they **d**. **Rv 11:6** *2309*

DESIRED

"If the LORD had **d** to kill us, He **Jg 13:23** 2654a
the LORD **d** to put them to death. **1Sa 2:25** 2654a
Hiram gave Solomon as much as he **d** **1Ki 5:10** 2656
and all that Solomon **d** to do, **1Ki 9:1** 2837, 2654a
land, To do with them as they **d**. **Ne 9:24** 7522
anything that she **d** was given her **Es 2:13** 559
and meal offering You have not **d**; **Ps 40:6** 2654a
which God has **d** for His abode? **Ps 68:16** 2530
He guided them to their **d** haven. **Ps 107:30** 2656
He has **d** it for His habitation. **Ps 132:13** 183
I will dwell, for I have **d** it. **Ps 132:14** 183
To do righteousness and justice Is **d** **Pr 21:3** 977
is to be more **d** than great wealth, **Pr 22:1** 977
my eyes **d** I did not refuse them. **Ec 2:10** 7592
of the oaks which you have **d**, **Is 1:29** 2530
"Then I **d** to know the exact **Da 7:19** 6634
men **d** to see what you see, **Mt 13:17** *1937*
"I have earnestly **d** to eat this **Lk 22:15** *1937*
them, in the body, just as He **d**. **1Co 12:18** *2309*
AND OFFERING YOU HAVE NOT **D**, **Heb 10:5** *2309*
FOR SIN YOU HAVE NOT **D**, **Heb 10:8** *2309*
when he **d** to inherit the blessing, **Heb 12:17** *2309*

DESIRES

who were among them had greedy **d**; **Nu 11:4** 183, 8378
money for whatever your heart **d**: **Dt 14:26** 183
drink, or whatever your heart **d**; **Dt 14:26** 7592
and comes whenever he **d** to the **Dt 18:6** 185
king over all that your soul **d**." **2Sa 3:21** 183
according to the **d** of each person. **Es 1:8** 7522
that we may do as Esther **d**." **Es 5:5** 1697
man whom the king **d** to honor?" **Es 6:6** 2654a
the man whom the king **d** to honor, **Es 6:7** 2654a
the man whom the king **d** to honor **Es 6:9** 2654a
the man whom the king **d** to honor **Es 6:9** 2654a
man whom the king **d** to honor." **Es 6:11** 2654a
he **d** it and will not let it go, **Jb 20:13** 2550
He does not retain anything he **d**. **Jb 20:20** 2530
And *what* His soul **d**, **Jb 23:13** 183
Who is the man who **d** life And **Ps 34:12** 2655
will give you the **d** of your heart. **Ps 37:4** 4862
O LORD, the **d** of the wicked; **Ps 140:8** 3970
wicked man **d** the booty of evil men, **Pr 12:12** 2530
The soul of the wicked **d** evil; **Pr 21:10** 183
lacks nothing of all that he **d**; **Ec 6:2** 183
is better than what the soul **d**. **Ec 6:9** 1980
your heart and the **d** of your eyes. **Ec 11:9** 4758
d *expressed* by their mouth, **Ezk 33:31** 5690

and the **d** for other things enter **Mk 4:19** *1939*
want to do the **d** of your father. **Jn 8:44** *1939*
So then He has mercy on whom He **d**, **Ro 9:18** *2309*
desires, and He hardens whom He **d**. **Ro 9:18** *2309*
the flesh with its passions and **d**. **Ga 5:24** *1939*
d of the flesh and of the mind, **Eph 2:3** *2307*
who **d** all men to be saved and to **1Tm 2:4** *2309*
it is a fine work he **d** *to do.* **1Tm 3:1** *1937*
sensual **d** in disregard of Christ, **1Tm 5:11** *2691*
and many foolish and harmful **d** **1Tm 6:9** *1939*
in accordance to their own **d**, **2Tm 4:3** *1939*
worldly **d** and to live sensibly, **Ti 2:12** *1939*
the inclination of the pilot **d**. **Jas 3:4** *1014*
"He jealously **d** the Spirit which **Jas 4:5** *1971*
For, "THE ONE WHO **D** LIFE, TO **1Pe 3:10** *2309*
corrupt **d** and despise authority. **2Pe 2:10** *1939*
vanity they entice by fleshly **d**, **2Pe 2:18** *1939*

DESIRING

became hungry and was **d** to eat; **Ac 10:10** *2309*
d even more to show to the heirs **Heb 6:17** *1014*
d to conduct ourselves honorably **Heb 13:18** *2309*

DESIST

"**D** now, let there be no injustice; **Jb 6:29** 7725
Even **d**, my righteousness is yet in **Jb 6:29** 7725

DESISTING

honor it, **d** from your *own* ways, **Is 58:13** 6213a

DESOLATE

and that the land may not be **d**." **Gn 47:19** 3456
that the land may not become **d** and **Ex 23:29** 8077
and will make your sanctuaries **d**, **Lv 26:31** 8074
'I will make the land **d** so **Lv 26:32** 8074
d and your cities become waste. **Lv 26:33** 8077
while it is made **d** without them. **Lv 26:43** 8074
So Tamar remained and was **d** in her **2Sa 13:20** 8074
lies **d** and its gates have been **Ne 2:3** 2720b
is **d** and its gates burned by fire. **Ne 2:17** 2720b
"He has lived in **d** cities, **Jb 15:28** 3582
To satisfy the waste and **d** land And **Jb 38:27** 4875
May their camp be **d**; **Ps 69:25** 8074
Your land is **d**, Your cities are **Is 1:7** 8077
many houses shall become **d**, **Is 5:9** 8047
people And the land is utterly **d**, **Is 6:11** 8077
For the waters of Nimrim are **d**. **Is 15:6** 4923
The highways are **d**, **Is 33:8** 8074
to generation it will be **d**; **Is 34:10** 2717b
make *them* inherit the **d** heritages; **Is 49:8** 8074
"For your waste and **d** places and **Is 49:19** 8074
For the sons of the **d** one *will be* **Is 54:1** 8074
And will resettle the **d** cities. **Is 54:3** 8074
will it any longer be said, "**D**"; **Is 62:4** 8077
at this, And shudder, be very **d**," **Jer 2:12** 2717b
And you, O **d** one, what will you do? **Jer 4:30** 7703
My pleasant field A **d** wilderness. **Jer 12:10** 8077
"It has been made a desolation, **D**, **Jer 12:11** 8076
The whole land has been made **d**, **Jer 12:11** 8074
Shiloh and this city will be **d**, **Jer 26:9** 2717b
streets of Jerusalem that are **d**, **Jer 33:10** 8074
waters of Nimrim will become **d**. **Jer 48:34** 4923
And it will become a **d** heap, **Jer 49:2** 8077
their pasture **d** because of them. **Jer 49:20** 8074
But she will be completely **d**; **Jer 50:13** 8077
their pasture **d** because of them. **Jer 50:45** 8074
But you will be **d** forever," **Jer 51:26** 8077
All her gates are **d**; **La 1:4** 8074
He has made me **d**, Faint all day **La 1:13** 8074
My children are **d** Because the **La 1:16** 8074
He has made me **d**. **La 3:11** 8074
delicacies Are **d** in the streets; **La 4:5** 8074
of Mount Zion which lies **d**, **La 5:18** 8074
"So your altars will become **d** and **Ezk 6:4** 8074
and the high places will be **d**, **Ezk 6:6** 8074
altars may become waste and **d**, **Ezk 6:6** 816
and make the land more **d** and waste **Ezk 6:14** 8077
and it became **d** so that no one **Ezk 14:15** 8077
but the country would be **d**. **Ezk 14:16** 8077
'Thus I will make the land **d**, **Ezk 15:8** 8077
fire so that I might make them **d**, **Ezk 20:26** 8074
land of Israel when it was made **d**, **Ezk 25:3** 8074
"When I make you a **d** city, **Ezk 26:19** 2717b
laid waste, will be **d** forty years; **Ezk 29:12** 8077
"They will be **d** In the midst **Ezk 30:7** 8074
And I will make the land **d** And **Ezk 30:12** 8074
"I will make Pathros **d**, **Ezk 30:14** 8074
the mountains of Israel will be **d** so **Ezk 33:28** 8074
'They are laid **d**; they are given to us **Ezk 35:12** 8074
house of Israel because it was **d**, **Ezk 35:15** 8074
For good reason they have made you **d** **Ezk 36:3** 8074
to the **d** wastes and to the **Ezk 36:4** 8074
"The **d** land will be **Ezk 36:34** 8074
'This **d** land has become like the **Ezk 36:35** 8074
and the waste, **d** and ruined **Ezk 36:35** 8074
and planted that which was **d**; **Ezk 36:36** 8074
Your face shine on Your **d** sanctuary. **Da 9:17** 8076
will come one who makes **d**, **Da 9:27** 8074
out on the one who makes **d**." **Da 9:27** 8074
The storehouses are **d**, **Jl 1:17** 8074
But a **d** wilderness behind them, **Jl 2:3** 8077
it into a parched and **d** land, **Jl 2:20** 8077
Edom will become a **d** wilderness, **Jl 3:19** 8077
all of her images I will make **d**, **Mi 1:7** 8077
d because of her inhabitants, **Mi 7:13** 8077
Yes, she is **d** and waste! **Na 2:10** 4003
plunder And their houses **d**; **Zph 1:13** 8077
I have made their streets **d**, **Zph 3:6** 2717b
houses while this house *lies* **d**?" **Hg 1:4** 2720b
"Because of My house which *lies* **d**, **Hg 1:9** 2720b
they made the pleasant land **d**." **Zch 7:14** 8047
"This place is **d** and the hour is **Mt 14:15** *2048*

we get so many loaves in *this* **d** place **Mt 15:33** *2047*
your house is being left to you **d**! **Mt 23:38** *2048*
is **d** and it is already quite late; **Mk 6:35** *2048*
bread here in *this* **d** place **Mk 8:4** *2047*
for here we are in a **d** place." **Lk 9:12** *2048*
your house is left to you **d**; **Lk 13:35**
'LET HIS HOMESTEAD BE MADE **D**, **Ac 1:20** *2048*
NUMEROUS ARE THE CHILDREN OF THE **D** **Ga 4:27** *2048*
and will make her **d** and naked, **Rv 17:16** *2049*

DESOLATED

in the midst of **d** lands. **Ezk 29:12** 8074
In the midst of the **d** lands; **Ezk 30:7** 8074
"The high places of Isaac will be **d** **Am 7:9** 8074
Thus the land is **d** behind them so **Zch 7:14** 8074

DESOLATING

down, **D** *you* because of your sins. **Mi 6:13** 8074

DESOLATION

sabbaths all the days of the **d**, **Lv 26:34** 8074
'All the days of *its* **d** it will **Lv 26:35** 8074
heap forever, a **d** until this day. **Jos 8:28** 8077
should become a **d** and a curse, **2Ki 22:19** 8047
All the days of its **d** it kept **2Ch 36:21** 8074
ground by night in waste and **d**, **Jb 30:3** 4875
It is **d**, as overthrown by **Is 1:7** 8077
anger, To make the land a **d**; **Is 13:9** 8047
And the land will be a **d**. **Is 17:9** 8077
D is left in the city And the **Is 24:12** 8047
He will stretch over it the line of **d** **Is 34:11** 8414
a wilderness, Jerusalem a **d**. **Is 64:10** 8077
"The whole land shall be a **d**, **Jer 4:27** 8077
And make you a **d**, **Jer 6:8** 8077
will make the cities of Judah a **d**, **Jer 9:11** 8077
To make the cities of Judah A **d**, **Jer 10:22** 8077
"It has been made a **d**, **Jer 12:11** 8077
To make their land a **d**, **Jer 18:16** 8047
city a **d** and an *object of* hissing; **Jer 19:8** 8047
this house will become a **d**. **Jer 22:5** 2723
a hissing, and an everlasting **d**. **Jer 25:9** 2723
land will be a **d** and a horror, **Jer 25:11** 2723
I will make it an everlasting **d**. **Jer 25:12** 8077
"It is a **d**, without man or beast; **Jer 32:43** 8077
Judah a **d** without inhabitant.'" **Jer 34:22** 8077
a ruin and a **d** as it is this day. **Jer 44:6** 8077
For Memphis will become a **d**, **Jer 46:19** 8047
And her cities will become a **d**, **Jer 48:9** 8047
a haunt of jackals, A **d** forever; **Jer 49:33** 8077
Babylon A **d** without inhabitants. **Jer 51:29** 8047
but it will be a perpetual **d**.' **Jer 51:62** 8077
I will make you a **d** and a reproach **Ezk 5:14** 2723
waste and the land will be a **d**. **Ezk 12:20** 8077
sorrow, The cup of horror and **d**, **Ezk 23:33** 8077
Egypt will become a **d** and waste. **Ezk 29:9** 8077
of Egypt an utter waste and **d**, **Ezk 29:10** 8077
So I will make the land of Egypt a **d** **Ezk 29:12** 8077
"When I make the land of Egypt a **d**, **Ezk 32:15** 8077
make the land a **d** and a waste, **Ezk 33:28** 8077
when I make the land a **d** and a **Ezk 33:29** 8077
make you a **d** and a waste. **Ezk 35:3** 8077
cities And you will become a **d**. **Ezk 35:4** 8077
make Mount Seir a waste and a **d** and **Ezk 35:7** 8077
"I will make you an everlasting **d** and **Ezk 35:9** 8077
rejoices, I will make you a **d**. **Ezk 35:14** 8077
You will be a **d**, O Mount Seir, and **Ezk 35:15** 8077
will be cultivated instead of being a **d** **Ezk 36:34** 8077
will set up the abomination of **d**. **Da 11:31** 8074
the abomination of **d** is set up, **Da 12:11** 8074
become a **d** in the day of rebuke; **Hos 5:9** 8047
A day of destruction and **d**, **Zph 1:15** 4875
be abandoned And Ashkelon a **d**; **Zph 2:4** 8077
and salt pits, And a perpetual **d**. **Zph 2:9** 8077
And He will make Nineveh a **d**, **Zph 2:13** 8077
D *will be* on the threshold; **Zph 2:14** 2721b
How she has become a **d**, **Zph 2:15** 8047
and I have made his mountains a **d** and **Mal 1:3** 8077
when you see the ABOMINATION OF **D** **Mt 24:15** *2050*
see the ABOMINATION OF **D** standing **Mk 13:14** *2050*
recognize that her **d** is near. **Lk 21:20** *2050*

DESOLATIONS

Who has wrought **d** in the earth. **Ps 46:8** 8047
cities, The **d** of many generations. **Is 61:4** 8074
completion of the **d** of Jerusalem, **Da 9:2** 2723
Open Your eyes and see our **d** and **Da 9:18** 8074
d are determined. **Da 9:26** 8074

DESPAIR

failing of eyes, and **d** of soul. **Dt 28:65** 1671
Saul then will **d** of searching for **1Sa 27:1** 2976
the words of one in **d** belong to the **Jb 6:26** 2976
He mocks the **d** of the innocent. **Jb 9:23** 4531a
Why are you in **d**, O my soul? **Ps 42:5** 7817
my God, my soul is in **d** within me; **Ps 42:6** 7817
Why are you in **d**, O my soul? **Ps 42:11** 7817
Why are you in **d**, O my soul? **Ps 43:5** 7817

DESPAIRED

I would have **d** unless I had **Ps 27:13**
Therefore I completely **d** of all **Ec 2:20** 2976
so that we **d** even of life; **2Co 1:8** *1820*

DESPAIRING

"For the **d** man *there should be* **Jb 6:14** 4523
perplexed, but not **d**; **2Co 4:8** *1820*

DESPERATELY

than all else And is **d** sick; **Jer 17:9** 605
However, the men rowed **d** to **Jon 1:13**

DESPICABLE

his place a **d** person will arise, **Da 11:21** 959

DESPISE

who **d** Me will be lightly esteemed. **1Sa 2:30** 959
So do not **d** the discipline of the **Jb 5:17** 3988a

not take notice of myself; I **d** my life. **Jb 9:21** 3988a
"Even young children **d** me; **Jb 19:18** 3988a
God is mighty but does not **d** *any;* **Jb 36:5** 3988a
He does not **d** evil. **Ps 36:4** 3988a
heart, O God, You will not **d**. **Ps 51:17** 959
does not **d** His *who are* prisoners. **Ps 69:33** 959
aroused, You will **d** their form. **Ps 73:20** 959
I hate and **d** falsehood, *But* I love **Ps 119:163** 8581
Fools **d** wisdom and instruction. **Pr 1:7** 936
Men do not **d** a thief if he steals **Pr 6:30** 936
will **d** the wisdom of your words. **Pr 23:9** 936
not **d** your mother when she is old. **Pr 23:22** 936
No one would **d** me, either. **SS 8:1** 936
To **d** all the honored of the earth. **Is 23:9** 7043
Your lovers **d** you; **Jer 4:30** 3988a
Do not **d** *us,* for Your own name's **Jer 14:21** 5006
keep saying to those who **d** Me, **Jer 23:17** 5006
Thus they **d** My people, no longer **Jer 33:24** 5006
All who honored her **d** her Because **La 1:8** 2151b
surrounding *you* who **d** you. **Ezk 16:57** 7751c
to you, O priests who **d** My name. **Mal 1:6** 959
be devoted to one and **d** the other. **Mt 6:24** *2706*
do not **d** one of these little ones, **Mt 18:10** *2706*
devoted to one and **d** the other. **Lk 16:13** *2706*
Or do you **d** the church of God and **1Co 11:22** *2706*
So let no one **d** him. **1Co 16:11** *1848*
condition you did not **d** or loathe, **Ga 4:14** *1848*
do not **d** prophetic utterances. **1Th 5:20** *1848*
corrupt desires and **d** authority. **2Pe 2:10** *2706*

DESPISED
her mistress was **d** in her sight. **Gn 16:4** 7043
conceived, I was **d** in her sight. **Gn 16:5** 7043
Thus Esau **d** his birthright. **Gn 25:34** 959
'Because he has **d** the word of the **Nu 15:31** 959
who **d** their lives *even* to death, **Jg 5:18** 2778a
Is this not the people whom you **d**? **Jg 9:38** 3988a
men **d** the offering of the LORD. **1Sa 2:17** 5006
And they **d** him and did not bring **1Sa 10:27** 959
but everything **d** and worthless, **1Sa 15:9** 959
and she **d** him in her heart. **2Sa 6:16** 959
'Why have you **d** the word of the **2Sa 12:9** 959
because you have **d** Me and have **2Sa 12:10** 959
'She has **d** you and mocked you, The **2Ki 19:21** 959
and she **d** him in her heart. **1Ch 15:29** 959
d His words and scoffed at His **2Ch 36:16** 959
they mocked us and **d** us and said, **Ne 2:19** 959
Hear, O our God, how we are **d**! **Ne 4:4** 939
"If I have **d** the claim of my male **Jb 31:13** 3988a
In whose eyes a reprobate is **d**, **Ps 15:4** 959
of men and **d** by the people. **Ps 22:6** 959
For He has not **d** nor abhorred the **Ps 22:24** 959
And has not **d** their prayer. **Ps 102:17** 959
Then they **d** the pleasant land; **Ps 106:24** 3988a
I am small and **d**, *Yet* I do not **Ps 119:141** 959
one of perverse mind will be **d**. **Pr 12:8** 937
is **d** and his words are not heeded. **Ec 9:16** 959
for love, It would be utterly **d**." **SS 8:7** 936
have **d** the Holy One of Israel, **Is 1:4** 5006
And **d** the word of the Holy One of **Is 5:24** 5006
the covenant, he has **d** the cities, **Is 33:8** 3988a
"She has **d** you and mocked you, **Is 37:22** 959
and its Holy One, To the **d** One, **Is 49:7** 960
He was **d** and forsaken of men, A **Is 53:3** 959
men hide their face He was **d**, **Is 53:3** 959
And all those who **d** you will bow **Is 60:14** 5006
"Is this man Coniah a **d**, **Jer 22:28** 959
among the nations, **D** among men. **Jer 49:15** 959
O LORD, and look, For I am **d**. **La 1:11** 2151b
And He has **d** king and priest In **La 2:6** 5006
you who have **d** the oath by **Ezk 16:59** 959
on the throne, whose oath he **d** and **Ezk 17:16** 959
'Now he **d** the oath by breaking the **Ezk 17:18** 959
surely My oath which he **d** and My **Ezk 17:19** 959
"You have **d** My holy things and **Ezk 22:8** 959
You are greatly **d**. **Ob 1:2** 959
who has **d** the day of small things? **Zch 4:10** 936
'How have we **d** Your name?' **Mal 1:6** 959
'The table of the LORD is to be **d**.' **Mal 1:7** 959
its fruit, its food is to be **d**.' **Mal 1:12** 959
"So I also have made you **d** and **Mal 2:9** 959
things of the world and the **d** God **1Co 1:28** *1848*

DESPISES
He who **d** his neighbor lacks sense, **Pr 11:12** 936
The one who **d** the word will be in **Pr 13:13** 936
who is devious in his ways **d** Him. **Pr 14:2** 959
He who **d** his neighbor sins, But **Pr 14:21** 936
But a foolish man **d** his mother. **Pr 15:20** 959
who neglects discipline **d** himself, **Pr 15:32** 3988a
the rod which **d** will be no more?" **Ezk 21:13** 3988a

DESPISING
the rod of My son **d** every tree? **Ezk 21:10** 3988a
endured the cross, **d** the shame, **Heb 12:2** *2706*

DESPITE
d all the signs which I have **Nu 14:11**
His hand is heavy **d** my groaning. **Jb 23:2** 5921

DESPOIL
From the wicked who **d** me, **Ps 17:9** 7703

DESPOILED
and they **d** all the cities, for **2Ch 14:14** 962
laid waste and completely **d**, **Is 24:3** 962
this is a people plundered and **d**; **Is 42:22** 8154
the spoil of those who **d** them and **Ezk 39:10** 7997b

DESPONDENCY
of *their* **d** and cruel bondage. **Ex 6:9** 7115, 7307

DESPONDENT
and needy man, And the **d** in heart, **Ps 109:16** 3512a

DESPONDENTLY
lay in sackcloth and went about **d**. **1Ki 21:27** 328

DESPOT
the hand of a **d** of the nations; **Ezk 31:11** 352c

DESTINE
I will **d** you for the sword, And **Is 65:12** 4487

DESTINED
And he is **d** for the sword. **Jb 15:22** 6822
Which are **d** to become ruins. **Jb 15:28** 6257
many, they are **d** for the sword; **Jb 27:14**
"Those **d** for death, to death; **Jer 15:2**
And those **d** for the sword, to **Jer 15:2**
And those **d** for famine, to **Jer 15:2**
And those **d** for captivity, to **Jer 15:2**
to things **d** to perish with use) **Col 2:22**
know that we have been **d** for this. **1Th 3:3** *2749*
For God has not **d** us for wrath, **1Th 5:9** *5087*
If anyone *is* **d** for captivity, to **Rv 13:10**

DESTINY
fill *cups* with mixed wine for **D**, **Is 65:11** 4507

DESTITUTE
Do justice to the afflicted and **d**. **Ps 82:3** 7326
has regarded the prayer of the **d** And **Ps 102:17** 6199
land is **d** of that which filled it, **Ezk 32:15** 8074
sheepskins, in goatskins, being **d**, **Heb 11:37** *5302*

DESTROY
am about to **d** them with the earth. **Gn 6:13** 7843
to **d** all flesh in which is the **Gn 6:17** 7843
never again **d** every living thing, **Gn 8:21** 5221
again be a flood to **d** the earth." **Gn 9:11** 7843
become a flood to **d** all flesh. **Gn 9:15** 7843
will You **d** the whole city because **Gn 18:28** 7843
d *it* if I find forty-five there." **Gn 18:28** 7843
d *it* on account of the twenty." **Gn 18:31** 7843
not **d** *it* on account of the ten." **Gn 18:32** 7843
for we are about to **d** this place, **Gn 19:13** 7843
the LORD has sent us to **d** it." **Gn 19:13** 7843
for the LORD will **d** the city." **Gn 19:14** 7843
no plague will befall you to **d** *you* **Ex 12:13** 7843
my sword, my hand will **d** them.' **Ex 15:9** 3423
and I will completely **d** them. **Ex 23:23** 3582
them and that I may **d** them; **Ex 32:10** 3615
to **d** them from the face of the earth'? **Ex 32:12** 3615
and I might **d** you on the way." **Ex 33:3** 3615
for one moment, I would **d** you. **Ex 33:5** 3615
I will **d** from among his people. **Lv 23:30** 6
d your cattle and reduce your number **Lv 26:22** 3772
'I then will **d** your high places, **Lv 26:30** 8045
will I so abhor them as to **d** them, **Lv 26:44** 3615
I will utterly **d** their cities." **Nu 21:2** 2763a
d the remnant from the city." **Nu 24:19** 6
so that I did not **d** the sons of **Nu 25:11** 3615
and you will **d** all these people." **Nu 32:15** 7843
and **d** all their figured stones, **Nu 33:52** 6
and **d** all their molten images and **Nu 33:52** 6
the hand of the Amorites to **d** us. **Dt 1:27** 8045
to **d** them from within the camp until **Dt 2:15** 2000
He will not fail you nor **d** you nor **Dt 4:31** 7843
then you shall utterly **d** them. **Dt 7:2** 2763a
you and He will quickly **d** you. **Dt 7:4** 8045
Him to their faces, to **d** them; **Dt 7:10** 6
He will **d** them and He will subdue **Dt 9:3** 8045
drive them out and **d** them quickly, **Dt 9:3** 6
that I may **d** them and blot out **Dt 9:14** 8045
against you in order to **d** you, **Dt 9:19** 8045
angry enough with Aaron to **d** him; **Dt 9:20** 8045
the LORD had said He would **d** you. **Dt 9:25** 8045
'O Lord GOD, do not **d** Your people, **Dt 9:26** 7843
the LORD was not willing to **d** you. **Dt 10:10** 7843
"You shall utterly **d** all the **Dt 12:2** 6
"But you shall utterly **d** them, **Dt 20:17** 2763a
you shall not **d** its trees by **Dt 20:19** 7843
trees you shall **d** and cut down, **Dt 20:20** 7843
you to make you perish and **d** you; **Dt 28:63** 8045
d the watered *land* with the dry.' **Dt 29:19** 5595
will **d** these nations before you, **Dt 31:3** 8045
from before you, And said, '**D**!' **Dt 33:27** 8045
the hand of the Amorites, to **d** us? **Jos 7:7** 6
unless you **d** the things under the ban **Jos 7:12** 8045
and to **d** all the inhabitants of **Jos 9:24** 8045
that he might utterly **d** them, **Jos 11:20** 2763a
mercy, but that he might **d** them, **Jos 11:20** 8045
to **d** the land in which the sons of **Jos 22:33** 7843
camp against them and **d** the produce **Jg 6:4** 7843
you shall utterly **d** every man and **Jg 21:11** 2763a
and utterly **d** all that he has, **1Sa 15:3** 2763a
so that I do not **d** you with them; **1Sa 15:6** 622
not willing to **d** them utterly; **1Sa 15:9** 2763a
'Go and utterly **d** the sinners, the **1Sa 15:18** 2763a
to **d** the city on my account. **1Sa 23:10** 7843
and that you will not **d** my name **1Sa 24:21** 8045
"Do not **d** him, for who can **1Sa 26:9** 7843
came to **d** the king your lord. **1Sa 26:15** 7843
hand to **d** the LORD's anointed?" **2Sa 1:14** 7843
hand and **d** you from the earth?" **2Sa 4:11** 1197a
he killed, and the heir also.' **2Sa 14:7** 8045
of blood will not continue to **d**, **2Sa 14:11** 7843
otherwise they will **d** my son." **2Sa 14:11** 8045
who would **d** both me and my son **2Sa 14:16** 8045
You are seeking to **d** a city, even a **2Sa 20:19** 4191
me that I should swallow up or **d**! **2Sa 20:20** 7843
his hand toward Jerusalem to **d** it, **2Sa 24:16** 7843
Israel were unable to **d** utterly, **1Ki 9:21** 2763a
even to blot *it* out and **d** *it* from **1Ki 13:34** 8045
LORD was not willing to **d** Judah, **2Ki 8:19** 7843
he might **d** the worshipers of Baal. **2Ki 10:19** 6
and would not **d** them or cast them **2Ki 13:23** 7843
against this place to **d** it? **2Ki 18:25** 7843
this land and **d** it. **2Ki 18:25** 7843
sent them against Judah to **d** it, **2Ki 24:2** 6
an angel to Jerusalem to **d** it; **1Ch 21:15** 7843
but as he was about to **d** *it,* **1Ch 21:15** 7843
themselves *so* I will not **d** them, **2Ch 12:7** 7843
so as not to **d** *him* completely; **2Ch 12:12** 7843
from them and did not **d** them), **2Ch 20:10** 8045
they helped to **d** one another. **2Ch 20:23** 4889
Yet the LORD was not willing to **d**, **2Ch 21:7** 7843
that God has planned to **d** you, **2Ch 25:16** 7843
so that He will not **d** you." **2Ch 35:21** 7843
so as to **d** this house of God in **Ezr 6:12** 2255
Haman sought to **d** all the Jews, **Es 3:6** 8045
to all the king's provinces to **d**, **Es 3:13** 8045
which he wrote to **d** the Jews who **Es 8:5** 6
and to defend their lives, to **d**, **Es 8:11** 8045
against the Jews to **d** them and **Es 9:24** 6
lot, to disturb them and **d** them. **Es 9:24** 6
altogether, And would You **d** me? **Jb 10:8** 1104
So You **d** man's hope. **Jb 14:19** 6
You **d** those who speak falsehood; **Ps 5:6** 6
You will **d** from the earth, **Ps 21:10** 6
together Who seek my life to **d** it; **Ps 40:14** 5595
D them in Your faithfulness. **Ps 54:5** 6789
D *them* in wrath, destroy *them* that **Ps 59:13** 3615
Destroy *them* in wrath, **d** *them* that **Ps 59:13** 3615
those who seek my life to **d** it, **Ps 63:9** 7724b
Those who would **d** me are powerful, **Ps 69:4** 6789
From within Your bosom, **d** *them!* **Ps 74:11** 3615
iniquity and did not **d** *them;* **Ps 78:38** 7843
And will **d** them in their evil; **Ps 94:23** 6789
The LORD our God will **d** them. **Ps 94:23** 6789
his neighbor, him I will **d**; **Ps 101:5** 6789
will **d** all the wicked of the land, **Ps 101:8** 6789
He said that He would **d** them, **Ps 106:23** 8045
They did not **d** the peoples, As the **Ps 106:34** 8045
The wicked wait for me to **d** me; **Ps 119:95** 6
d all those who afflict my soul, **Ps 143:12** 6
But all the wicked He will **d**. **Ps 145:20** 8045
complacency of fools will **d** them. **Pr 1:32** 6
He who would **d** himself does it. **Pr 6:32** 7843
of the treacherous will **d** them. **Pr 11:3** 7703
Do not **d** his resting place; **Pr 24:15** 7703
and **d** the work of your hands? **Ec 5:6** 2254b
But rather it is its purpose to **d** And **Is 10:7** 8045
And He will **d** the glory of his **Is 10:18** 3615
hurt or **d** in all My holy mountain, **Is 11:9** 7843
And the LORD will utterly **d** The **Is 11:15** 2763a
indignation, To **d** the whole land. **Is 13:5** 2254b
I will **d** your root with famine, **Is 14:30** 4191
To **d** *the* afflicted with slander, **Is 32:7** 2254b
against this land to **d** it? **Is 36:10** 7843
this land and **d** it. **Is 36:10** 7843
oppressor, As he makes ready to **d**? **Is 51:13** 7843
'Do not **d** it, for there is benefit **Is 65:8** 7843
In order not to **d** all of them. **Is 65:8** 7843
break down, To **d** and to overthrow, **Jer 1:10** 6
wolf of the deserts will **d** them, **Jer 5:6** 7703
"Go up through her vine rows and **d**, **Jer 5:10** 7843
by night And **d** her palaces!" **Jer 6:5** 7843
"Let us **d** the tree with its **Jer 11:19** 7843
that nation, uproot and **d** it," **Jer 12:17** 6
'Just so will I **d** the pride of **Jer 13:9** 7843
so as not to **d** them." ' " **Jer 13:14** 7843
of the earth to devour and **d**. **Jer 15:3** 7843
out My hand against you and **d** you; **Jer 15:6** 7843
of children, I will **d** My people; **Jer 15:7** 6
uproot, to pull down, or to **d** *it;* **Jer 18:7** 6
and I will utterly **d** them and **Jer 25:9** 2763a
For I will **d** completely all the **Jer 30:11** 6213a, 3617
Only I will not **d** you completely. **Jer 30:11** 6213a, 3617
to break down, to overthrow, to **d** and **Jer 31:28** 6
certainly come and **d** this land, **Jer 36:29** 7843
d the city and its inhabitants." **Jer 46:8** 6
coming To **d** all the Philistines, **Jer 47:4** 7703
is going to **d** the Philistines, **Jer 47:4** 7703
d *only* until they had enough. **Jer 49:9** 7843
d out of it king and princes,' **Jer 49:38** 6
Slay and utterly **d** them," **Jer 50:21** 2763a
up like heaps And utterly **d** her, **Jer 50:26** 2763a
is against Babylon to **d** it; **Jer 51:11** 7843
And with you I **d** kingdoms. **Jer 51:20** 7843
the LORD is going to **d** Babylon, **Jer 51:55** 7703
The LORD determined to **d** The wall **La 2:8** 7843
will pursue them in anger and **d** them **La 3:66** 8045
those whom I will send to **d** you, **Ezk 5:16** 7843
and I will **d** your high places. **Ezk 6:3** 6
out My hand against him and **d** him **Ezk 14:9** 8045
against it, **d** its supply of bread, **Ezk 14:13** 7665
the land, so that I would not **d** it; **Ezk 22:30** 7843
perish from the lands; I will **d** you. **Ezk 25:7** 8045
to **d** with everlasting enmity," **Ezk 25:15** 4889
and **d** the remnant of the seacoast. **Ezk 25:16** 6
'They will **d** the walls of Tyre **Ezk 26:4** 7843
walls and **d** your pleasant houses, **Ezk 26:12** 5422
Will be brought in to **d** the land; **Ezk 30:11** 7843
"I will also **d** the idols And make **Ezk 30:13** 6
"I will also **d** all its cattle **Ezk 32:13** 6
the fat and the strong I will **d**. **Ezk 34:16** 8045
I saw when He came to **d** the city. **Ezk 43:3** 7843
to **d** all the wise men of Babylon. **Da 2:12** 7
to **d** the wise men of Babylon; **Da 2:24** 7
"Do not **d** the wise men of Babylon! **Da 2:24** 7
"Chop down the tree and **d** it; **Da 4:23** 2255
And he will **d** to an extraordinary **Da 8:24** 7843
He will **d** mighty men and the holy **Da 8:24** 7843
d many while *they are* at ease. **Da 8:25** 7843

will **d** the city and the sanctuary.	**Da 9:26**	7843
eat his choice food will **d** him,	**Da 11:26**	7665
wrath to **d** and annihilate many.	**Da 11:44**	8045
I will **d** her vines and fig trees,	**Hos 2:12**	8074
And I will **d** your mother.	**Hos 4:5**	1820
altars *And* **d** their *sacred* pillars.	**Hos 10:2**	7703
I will not **d** Ephraim again.	**Hos 11:9**	7843
d it from the face of the earth;	**Am 9:8**	8045
totally **d** the house of Jacob,"	**Am 9:8**	8045
"**D** wise men from Edom And	**Ob 1:8**	6
among you And **d** your chariots.	**Mi 5:10**	6
from among you And **d** your cities.	**Mi 5:14**	8045
And I will **d** you So that there	**Zph 2:5**	6
against the north And **d** Assyria,	**Zph 2:13**	6
and **d** the power of the kingdoms	**Hg 2:22**	8045
I will set about to **d** all the nations	**Zch 12:9**	8045
not **d** the fruits of the ground;	**Mal 3:11**	7843
search for the Child to **d** Him."	**Mt 2:13**	*622*
on earth, where moth and rust **d**,	**Mt 6:19**	*853*
to **d** both soul and body in hell.	**Mt 10:28**	*622*
Him, *as to* how they might **d** Him.	**Mt 12:14**	*622*
'I am able to **d** the temple of God	**Mt 26:61**	*2647*
"You who *are going to* **d** the	**Mt 27:40**	*2647*
Have You come to **d** us?	**Mk 1:24**	*622*
Him, *as to* how they might **d** Him.	**Mk 3:6**	*622*
fire and into the water to **d** him.	**Mk 9:22**	*622*
and *began* seeking how to **d** Him;	**Mk 11:18**	*622*
will come and **d** the vine-growers,	**Mk 12:9**	*622*
d this temple made with hands,	**Mk 14:58**	*2647*
You who *are going to* **d** the temple	**Mk 15:29**	*2647*
Have You come to **d** us?	**Lk 4:34**	*622*
to save a life or to **d** it?"	**Lk 6:9**	*622*
Man did not come to **d** men's lives,	**Lk 9:56**	*622*
the people were trying to **d** Him,	**Lk 19:47**	*622*
"He will come and **d** these	**Lk 20:16**	*622*
"**D** this temple, and in three days	**Jn 2:19**	*3089*
only to steal and kill and **d**;	**Jn 10:10**	*622*
will **d** this place and alter the	**Ac 6:14**	*2647*
Do not **d** with your food him for	**Ro 14:15**	*622*
"I WILL **D** THE WISDOM OF THE WISE,	**1Co 1:19**	*622*
the temple of God, God will **d** him,	**1Co 3:17**	*5351*
beyond measure and tried to **d** it;	**Ga 1:13**	*4199*
faith which he once tried to **d**."	**Ga 1:23**	*4199*
One who is able to save and to **d**;	**Jas 4:12**	*622*
d the works of the devil.	**1Jn 3:8**	*3089*
d those who destroy the earth."	**Rv 11:18**	*1311*
destroy those who **d** the earth."	**Rv 11:18**	*1311*

DESTROYED

this was before the LORD **d** Sodom	**Gn 13:10**	7843
God **d** the cities of the valley,	**Gn 19:29**	7843
me and attack me and I will be **d**,	**Gn 34:30**	8045
be **d** from you and your houses,	**Ex 8:9**	3772
you not realize that Egypt is **d**?"	**Ex 10:7**	6
LORD alone, shall be utterly **d**.	**Ex 22:20**	2763a
this wilderness they shall be **d**,	**Nu 14:35**	8552
utterly **d** them and their cities.	**Nu 21:3**	2763a
in the sight of the LORD was **d**.	**Nu 32:13**	8552
of Esau dispossessed them and **d** them	**Dt 2:12**	8045
but the LORD **d** them before them.	**Dt 2:21**	8045
He **d** the Horites from before them;	**Dt 2:22**	8045
d them and lived in their place.)	**Dt 2:23**	8045
that time and utterly **d** the men,	**Dt 2:34**	2763a
"We utterly **d** them, as we did	**Dt 3:6**	2763a
God has **d** them from among you.	**Dt 4:3**	8045
on it, but will be utterly **d**.	**Dt 4:26**	8045
great confusion until they are **d**.	**Dt 7:23**	8045
before you until you have **d** them.	**Dt 7:24**	8045
with you that He would have **d** you.	**Dt 9:8**	8045
and the LORD completely **d** them;	**Dt 11:4**	6
them, after they are **d** before you,	**Dt 12:30**	8045
d and until you perish quickly,	**Dt 28:20**	8045
come down on you until you are **d**.	**Dt 28:24**	8045
and overtake you until you are **d**,	**Dt 28:45**	8045
on your neck until He has **d** you.	**Dt 28:48**	8045
of your ground until you are **d**,	**Dt 28:51**	8045
will bring on you until you are **d**.	**Dt 28:61**	8045
and to their land, when He **d** them.	**Dt 31:4**	8045
Sihon and Og, whom you utterly **d**.	**Jos 2:10**	2763a
utterly **d** everything in the city,	**Jos 6:21**	2763a
of the sword until they were **d**,	**Jos 8:24**	8552
d all the inhabitants of Ai.	**Jos 8:26**	2763a
captured Ai, and had utterly **d** it	**Jos 10:1**	2763a
slaughter, until they were **d**,	**Jos 10:20**	8552
he utterly **d** it and every person	**Jos 10:28**	2763a
and he utterly **d** that day every	**Jos 10:35**	2763a
And he utterly **d** it and every	**Jos 10:37**	2763a
d every person *who was* in it.	**Jos 10:39**	2763a
but he utterly **d** all who breathed,	**Jos 10:40**	2763a
of the sword, *and* utterly **d** them;	**Jos 11:12**	2763a
the sword, until they had **d** them.	**Jos 11:14**	8045
utterly **d** them with their cities.	**Jos 11:21**	2763a
until He has **d** you from off this	**Jos 23:15**	8045
land when I **d** them before you.	**Jos 24:8**	8045
in Zephath, and utterly **d** it.	**Jg 1:17**	2763a
had **d** Jabin the king of Canaan.	**Jg 4:24**	3772
so that the sons of Israel **d**	**Jg 20:35**	7843
d them in the midst of them.	**Jg 20:42**	7843
the women are **d** out of Benjamin?"	**Jg 21:16**	8045
and utterly **d** all the people with	**1Sa 15:8**	2763a
worthless, that they utterly **d**.	**1Sa 15:9**	2763a
but the rest we have utterly **d**."	**1Sa 15:15**	2763a
and have utterly **d** the Amalekites.	**1Sa 15:20**	2763a
and they **d** the sons of Ammon and	**2Sa 11:1**	7843
people who are with him will be **d**.' "	**2Sa 17:16**	1104
"I pursued my enemies and **d** them,	**2Sa 22:38**	8045
to me, And I **d** those who hated me.	**2Sa 22:41**	6789
to the angel who **d** the people,	**2Sa 24:16**	7843
alive, until he had **d** them,	**1Ki 15:29**	8045
d all the household of Baasha,	**1Ki 16:12**	8045
d the prophets of the LORD,	**1Ki 18:4**	3772
Thus they **d** the cities;	**2Ki 3:25**	2040
in Samaria, until he had **d** him,	**2Ki 10:17**	8045
and **d** all the royal offspring.	**2Ki 11:1**	6
for the king of Aram had **d** them	**2Ki 13:7**	6
at Aphek until you have **d** *them*."	**2Ki 13:17**	3615
Aram until you would have **d** *it*.	**2Ki 13:19**	3615
which my fathers **d** deliver them,	**2Ki 19:12**	7843
So they have **d** them.	**2Ki 19:18**	6
which Hezekiah his father had **d**;	**2Ki 21:3**	6
LORD **d** before the sons of Israel.	**2Ki 21:9**	8045
and **d** them utterly to this day,	**1Ch 4:41**	2763a
They **d** the remnant of the	**1Ch 4:43**	5221
land, whom God had **d** before them.	**1Ch 5:25**	8045
whom the sons of Israel had not **d**,	**2Ch 8:8**	3615
d all the cities around Gerar,	**2Ch 14:14**	5221
the LORD has **d** your works."	**2Ch 20:37**	6555
she rose and **d** all the royal	**2Ch 22:10**	6
d all the officials of the people	**2Ch 24:23**	7843
until they had **d** them all.	**2Ch 31:1**	3615
nations which my fathers utterly **d**	**2Ch 32:14**	2763a
angel who **d** every mighty warrior,	**2Ch 32:21**	3582
LORD **d** before the sons of Israel.	**2Ch 33:9**	8045
and **d** all its valuable articles.	**2Ch 36:19**	7843
who **d** this temple and deported the	**Ezr 5:12**	5642b
let it be decreed that they be **d**,	**Es 3:9**	6
sold, I and my people, to be **d**,	**Es 7:4**	8045
killed and **d** five hundred men,	**Es 9:6**	6
"The Jews have killed and **d** five	**Es 9:12**	6
Or where were the upright **d**?	**Jb 4:7**	3582
"Even after my skin is **d**,	**Jb 19:26**	5362a
You have **d** the wicked;	**Ps 9:5**	6
If the foundations are **d**,	**Ps 11:3**	2040
to me, And I **d** those who hated me.	**Ps 18:40**	6789
will be altogether **d**;	**Ps 37:38**	8045
How they are **d** in a moment!	**Ps 73:19**	8047
You have **d** all those who are	**Ps 73:27**	6789
them, And frogs which **d** them.	**Ps 78:45**	7843
He **d** their vines with hailstones And	**Ps 78:47**	2026
Who were **d** at En-dor, Who became	**Ps 83:10**	8045
Your terrors have **d** me.	**Ps 88:16**	6789
that they might be **d** forevermore.	**Ps 92:7**	8045
They almost **d** me on earth, But as	**Ps 119:87**	3615
The house of the wicked will be **d**,	**Pr 14:11**	8045
ships of Tarshish, For *Tyre* is **d**,	**Is 23:1**	7703
For your stronghold is **d**.	**Is 23:14**	7703
You have punished and **d** them,	**Is 26:14**	8045
O destroyer, While you were not **d**;	**Is 33:1**	7703
finish destroying, you will be **d**;	**Is 33:1**	7703
He has utterly **d** them, He has	**Is 34:2**	2763a
my fathers have **d** deliver them,	**Is 37:12**	7843
So they have **d** them.	**Is 37:19**	6
cut off or **d** from My presence."	**Is 48:19**	8045
and desolate places and your **d** land	**Is 49:19**	2035
His cities have been **d**,	**Jer 2:15**	5327c
My tent is **d**, And all my ropes are	**Jer 10:20**	7703
pestilence upon them until they are **d**	**Jer 24:10**	8552
"until I have **d** it by his hand.	**Jer 27:8**	8552
"Woe to Nebo, for it has been **d**;	**Jer 48:1**	7703
ruined And the plateau will be **d**,	**Jer 48:8**	8045
"Moab has been **d** and men have	**Jer 48:15**	7703
by the Arnon That Moab has been **d**.	**Jer 48:20**	7703
"Moab will be **d** from *being* a	**Jer 48:42**	8045
O Heshbon, for Ai has been **d**!	**Jer 49:3**	7703
His offspring has been **d** along	**Jer 49:10**	7703
Do not be **d** in her punishment, For	**Jer 51:6**	1826a
He has **d** its strongholds And	**La 2:5**	7843
has **d** His appointed meeting place.	**La 2:6**	7843
He has **d** and broken her bars.	**La 2:9**	6
'He **d** their fortified towers	**Ezk 19:7**	7489b
And I have **d** you, O covering	**Ezk 28:16**	6
And all its hordes will be **d**.	**Ezk 32:12**	8045
Daniel and his friends would not be **d**	**Da 2:18**	7
a kingdom which will never be **d**,	**Da 2:44**	2255
is one which will not be **d**,	**Da 6:26**	2255
d and given to the burning fire.	**Da 7:11**	7
is one Which will not be **d**.	**Da 7:14**	2255
away, annihilated and **d** forever.	**Da 7:26**	7
are **d** for lack of knowledge.	**Hos 4:6**	1820
the sin of Israel, will be **d**;	**Hos 10:8**	8045
And all your fortresses will be **d**,	**Hos 10:14**	7703
As Shalman **d** Beth-arbel on the day	**Hos 10:14**	7701
the harvest of the field is **d**.	**Jl 1:11**	6
I who **d** the Amorite before them,	**Am 2:9**	8045
I even **d** his fruit above and his	**Am 2:9**	8045
'We are completely **d**!	**Mi 2:4**	7703
them And **d** their vine branches.	**Na 2:2**	7843
the glorious *trees* have been **d**;	**Zch 11:2**	7703
his armies and **d** those murderers	**Mt 22:7**	*622*
and the flood came and **d** them all.	**Lk 17:27**	*622*
from heaven and **d** them all.	**Lk 17:29**	*622*
utterly **d** from among the people.'	**Ac 3:23**	*1842*
d those who called on this name,	**Ac 9:21**	*4199*
"When He had **d** seven nations	**Ac 13:19**	*2507*
did, and were **d** by the serpents.	**1Co 10:9**	*622*
did, and were **d** by the destroyer.	**1Co 10:10**	*622*
struck down, but not **d**;	**2Co 4:9**	*622*
if I rebuild what I have *once* **d**,	**Ga 2:18**	*2647*
so that he who **d** the firstborn	**Heb 11:28**	*3639*
the beauty of its appearance is **d**;	**Jas 1:11**	*622*
of those creatures also be **d**,	**2Pe 2:12**	*5351*
the world at that time was **d**,	**2Pe 3:6**	*622*
will be **d** with intense heat,	**2Pe 3:10**	*3089*
things are to be **d** in this way,	**2Pe 3:11**	*3089*
the heavens will be **d** by burning,	**2Pe 3:12**	*3089*
d those who did not believe.	**Jude 1:5**	*622*
by these things they are **d**.	**Jude 1:10**	*5351*
and a third of the ships were **d**.	**Rv 8:9**	*1311*

DESTROYER

and will not allow the **d** to come in	**Ex 12:23**	7843
hands, Even the **d** of our country,	**Jg 16:24**	2717b
at peace the **d** comes upon him.	**Jb 15:21**	7703
hiding place to them from the **d**."	**Is 16:4**	7703
and the **d** *still* destroys.	**Is 21:2**	7703
Woe to you, O **d**, While you were	**Is 33:1**	7703
And I have created the **d** to ruin.	**Is 54:16**	7843
And a **d** of nations has set out;	**Jer 4:7**	7843
suddenly the **d** Will come upon us.	**Jer 6:26**	7703
of a young man, A **d** at noonday;	**Jer 15:8**	7703
"A **d** will come to every city,	**Jer 48:8**	7703
For the **d** of Moab has come up	**Jer 48:18**	7703
grape harvest The **d** has fallen.	**Jer 48:32**	7703
of Leb-kamai The spirit of a **d**.	**Jer 51:1**	7843
For the **d** is coming against her,	**Jer 51:56**	7703
did, and were destroyed by the **d**.	**1Co 10:10**	*3644*

DESTROYERS

"The tents of the **d** prosper,	**Jb 12:6**	7703
Your **d** and devastators Will depart	**Is 49:17**	2040
in the wilderness **D** have come,	**Jer 12:12**	7703
I will set apart **d** against you,	**Jer 22:7**	7843
For the **d** will come to her from	**Jer 51:48**	7703
From Me **d** will come to her,"	**Jer 51:53**	7703

DESTROYING

of Heshbon, utterly **d** the men,	**Dt 3:6**	2763a
utterly **d** it and all that is in it	**Dt 13:15**	2763a
edge of the sword, utterly **d** *them;*	**Jos 11:11**	2763a
all the lands, **d** them completely.	**2Ki 19:11**	2763a
and the angel of the LORD **d**	**1Ch 21:12**	7843
calamity, and said to the **d** angel,	**1Ch 21:15**	7843
of Mount Seir **d** *them* completely;	**2Ch 20:23**	2763a
with the sword, killing and **d**;	**Es 9:5**	12
and trouble, A band of **d** angels.	**Ps 78:49**	7451a
turn away His wrath from **d** *them*.	**Ps 106:23**	7843
As soon as you finish **d**,	**Is 33:1**	7703
all the lands, **d** them completely.	**Is 37:11**	2763a
your prophets Like a **d** lion.	**Jer 2:30**	7843
"Woe to the shepherds who are **d**	**Jer 23:1**	6
For the LORD is **d** their pasture,	**Jer 25:36**	7703
I am against you, O **d** mountain,	**Jer 51:25**	7843
not restrained His hand from **d**,	**La 2:8**	1104
with his **d** weapon in his hand."	**Ezk 9:1**	4892
Are You **d** the whole remnant of	**Ezk 9:8**	7843
spared them rather than **d** them,	**Ezk 20:17**	7843
by shedding blood *and* **d** lives in	**Ezk 22:27**	6
We are **d** speculations and every	**2Co 10:5**	*2507*
building you up and not for **d** you,	**2Co 10:8**	*2506*

DESTROYS

male or female slave, and **d** it,	**Ex 21:26**	7843
d the guiltless and the wicked.'	**Jb 9:22**	3615
the nations great, then **d** them;	**Jb 12:23**	6
the godless man **d** his neighbor,	**Pr 11:9**	7843
his work Is brother to him who **d**.	**Pr 18:9**	7843
Is the companion of a man who **d**.	**Pr 28:24**	7843
your ways to that which **d** kings.	**Pr 31:3**	4229a
war, but one sinner **d** much good.	**Ec 9:18**	6
and the destroyer *still* **d**.	**Is 21:2**	7703
Who **d** the whole earth," declares	**Jer 51:25**	7843
where neither moth nor rust **d**,	**Mt 6:20**	*853*
no thief comes near nor moth **d**.	**Lk 12:33**	*1311*
If any man **d** the temple of God,	**1Co 3:17**	*5351*

DESTRUCTION

Anything devoted to **d** is most holy to	**Lv 27:28**	2763a
nations, But his end *shall be* **d**."	**Nu 24:20**	8
So they also *will come* to **d**."	**Nu 24:24**	8
consumed by plague And bitter **d**;	**Dt 32:24**	6986
of the things devoted to **d**,	**1Sa 15:21**	2764a
d in order to topple the wall.	**2Sa 20:15**	7843
The torrents of **d** overwhelmed me;	**2Sa 22:5**	1100
the man whom I had devoted to **d**,	**1Ki 20:42**	2764a
mount of **d** which Solomon the king	**2Ki 23:13**	4889
the death of his father, to his **d**.	**2Ch 22:4**	4889
Now the **d** of Ahaziah was from God,	**2Ch 22:7**	8395
angry with us to the point of **d**,	**Ezr 9:14**	3615
treasuries for the **d** of the Jews.	**Es 4:7**	6
been issued in Susa for their **d**,	**Es 4:8**	8045
to see the **d** of my kindred?"	**Es 8:6**	12
Does God apportion **d** in His anger?	**Jb 21:17**	2256b
up against me their ways of **d**.	**Jb 30:12**	343
up my path, They profit from my **d**;	**Jb 30:13**	1942
Their inward part is **d** *itself.*	**Ps 5:9**	1942
Let **d** come upon him unawares,	**Ps 35:8**	7724b
Into that very **d** let him fall.	**Ps 35:8**	7724b
to injure me have threatened **d**,	**Ps 38:12**	1942
brought me up out of the pit of **d**,	**Ps 40:2**	7588
Your tongue devises **d**,	**Ps 52:2**	1942
D is in her midst;	**Ps 55:11**	1942
bring them down to the pit of **d**;	**Ps 55:23**	7845
take refuge Until **d** passes by.	**Ps 57:1**	1942
You cast them down to **d**.	**Ps 73:18**	4376
of the **d** that lays waste at noon.	**Ps 91:6**	6986
a throne of **d** be allied with You,	**Ps 94:20**	1942
Pride *goes* before **d**,	**Pr 16:18**	7667
He who raises his door seeks **d**.	**Pr 17:19**	7667
d the heart of man is haughty,	**Pr 18:12**	7667
A foolish son is **d** to his father,	**Pr 19:13**	1942
A **d** is determined, overflowing	**Is 10:22**	3631
For a complete **d**, one that is	**Is 10:23**	3617
will be directed to their **d**."	**Is 10:25**	8399
will come as **d** from the Almighty.	**Is 13:6**	7701
sweep it with the broom of **d**,"	**Is 14:23**	8045
has come to an end, **d** has ceased,	**Is 16:4**	7701
one will be called the City of **D**.	**Is 19:18**	2041
d of the daughter of my people."	**Is 22:4**	7701
a storm of hail, a tempest of **d**,	**Is 28:2**	6986
Of decisive **d** on all the earth.	**Is 28:22**	3617
people whom I have devoted to **d**.	**Is 34:5**	4941

And **d** about which you do not know **Is 47:11** 7724b
The devastation and **d**, **Is 51:19** 7667
and **d** are in their highways. **Is 59:7** 7667
or **d** within your borders; **Is 60:18** 7667
evil from the north, And great **d**. **Jer 4:6** 7667
I will not execute a complete **d**. **Jer 4:27** 3617
But do not execute a complete **d**; **Jer 5:10** 3617
"I will not make you a complete **d**. **Jer 5:18** 3617
from the north, And a great **d**. **Jer 6:1** 7667
Violence and **d** are heard in her; **Jer 6:7** 7701
And crush them with twofold **d**! **Jer 17:18** 7670
I proclaim violence and **d**, **Jer 20:8** 7701
'Devastation and great **d**!' **Jer 48:3** 7667
have heard the anguished cry of **d**. **Jer 48:5** 7667
is in the land, And great **d**. **Jer 50:22** 7667
Devote all her army to **d**. **Jer 51:3** 2763a
And of great **d** from the land of **Jer 51:54** 7667
d of the daughter of my people, **La 2:11** 7667
befallen us, Devastation and **d**; **La 3:47** 7667
d of the daughter of my people. **La 3:48** 7667
d of the daughter of my people. **La 4:10** 7667
arrows of famine which were for the **d** **Ezk 5:16** 7843
hand of brutal men, skilled in **d**. **Ezk 21:31** 4889
I bring your **d** among the nations, **Ezk 32:9** 7667
put away violence and **d**, **Ezk 45:9** 7701
desolate, even until a complete **d**, **Da 9:27** 3617
Land, with **d** in his hand. **Da 11:16** 3617
D is theirs, for they have **Hos 7:13** 7701
behold, they will go because of **d**; **Hos 9:6** 7701
It is your **d**, O Israel, That *you* **Hos 13:9** 7843
will come as **d** from the Almighty. **Jl 1:15** 7701
forth *with* **d** upon the strong, **Am 5:9** 7701
So that **d** comes upon the fortress. **Am 5:9** 7701
of Judah In the day of their **d**; **Ob 1:12** 6
the uncleanness that brings on **d**, **Mi 2:10** 2254b
on destruction, A painful **d**. **Mi 2:10** 2256c
I will give you up for **d** And your **Mi 6:16** 8047
Yes, **d** and violence are before me; **Hab 1:3** 7701
A day of **d** and desolation, **Zph 1:15** 7724b
the way is broad that leads to **d**, **Mt 7:13** *684*
D AND MISERY ARE IN THEIR PATHS, **Ro 3:16** *4938*
vessels of wrath prepared for **d**? **Ro 9:22** *684*
to Satan for the **d** of his flesh, **1Co 5:5** *3639*
powerful for the **d** of fortresses. **2Co 10:4** *2506*
is a sign of **d** for them, **Php 1:28** *684*
whose end is **d**, whose god is *their* **Php 3:19** *684*
then **d** will come upon them **1Th 5:3** *3639*
will pay the penalty of eternal **d**, **2Th 1:9** *3639*
is revealed, the son of **d**, **2Th 2:3** *684*
which plunge men into ruin and **d**. **1Tm 6:9** *684*
not of those who shrink back to **d**, **Heb 10:39** *684*
bringing swift **d** upon themselves. **2Pe 2:1** *684*
idle, and their **d** is not asleep. **2Pe 2:3** *684*
to **d** by reducing *them* to ashes, **2Pe 2:6** *2692*
will in the **d** of those creatures **2Pe 2:12** *5356*
of judgment and **d** of ungodly men. **2Pe 3:7** *684*
of the Scriptures, to their own **d**. **2Pe 3:16** *684*
out of the abyss and go to **d**. **Rv 17:8** *684*
of the seven, and he goes to **d**. **Rv 17:11** *684*

DESTRUCTIONS
And delivered *them* from their **d**. **Ps 107:20** 7825

DESTRUCTIVE
liar pays attention to a **d** tongue. **Pr 17:4** 1942
secretly introduce **d** heresies, **2Pe 2:1** *684*

DETAIL
which if they were written in **d**, **Jn 21:25** *1520*
describing in **d** the conversion of **Ac 15:3** *1555*
things we cannot now speak in **d**. **Heb 9:5** *3313*

DETAILS
me, all the **d** of this pattern." **1Ch 28:19** 4399

DETAIN
"Please let us **d** you so that we **Jg 13:15** 6113
"Though you **d** me, I will not eat **Jg 13:16** 6113

DETAINED
your flocks and your herds be **d**. **Ex 10:24** 3322
the girl's father, **d** him; **Jg 19:4** 2388
there that day, **d** before the LORD; **1Sa 21:7** 6113

DETECTED
be **d** that they had devoured them, **Gn 41:21** 3045
But He **d** their trickery and said **Lk 20:23** *2657*

DETERMINE
to **d** whether he laid his hands on **Ex 22:8**
"If He should **d** to do so, If He **Jb 34:14** 7760, 3820
as though you were going to **d** his **Ac 23:15** *1231*
another anymore, but rather **d** this **Ro 14:13** *2919*

DETERMINED
means that the matter is **d** by God, **Gn 41:32** 3559
saw that she was **d** to go with her, **Ru 1:18** 553
been **d** since the day that he violated **2Sa 13:32** 7760
been **d** against him by the king. **Es 7:7** 3615
"Since his days are **d**, **Jb 14:5** 2782
A destruction is **d**, **Is 10:22** 2782
The LORD **d** to destroy The wall of **La 2:8** 2803
desolations are **d**. **Da 9:26** 2782
he was **d** to follow *man's* command. **Hos 5:11** 2974
Herod secretly called the magi and **d** **Mt 2:7** *198b*
according to the time which he had **d** **Mt 2:16** *198b*
He was **d** to go to Jerusalem; **Lk 9:51** *4741*
of Man is going as it has been **d**; **Lk 22:22** *3724*
each of them **d** to send *a* **Ac 11:29** *3724*
the brethren **d** that Paul and **Ac 15:2** *5021*
having **d** *their* appointed times and **Ac 17:26** *3724*
For I **d** to know nothing among you **1Co 2:2** *2919*
But I **d** this for my own sake, that **2Co 2:1** *2919*

DETEST
and their carcasses you shall **d**. **Lv 11:11** 8262
you shall **d** among the birds; **Lv 11:13** 8262
you shall utterly **d** it and you **Dt 7:26** 8262
"You shall not **d** an Edomite, for **Dt 23:7** 8581
you shall not **d** an Egyptian, **Dt 23:7** 8581
of Jacob, And **d** his citadels; **Am 6:8** 8130

DETESTABLE
animal, or any unclean **d** thing, **Lv 7:21** 8263
water, they are **d** things to you, **Lv 11:10** 8263
walk on *all* fours are **d** to you. **Lv 11:20** 8263
which are four-footed are **d** to you. **Lv 11:23** 8263
that swarms on the earth is **d**, **Lv 11:41** 8263
not eat them, for they are **d**. **Lv 11:42** 8263
'Do not render yourselves **d** **Lv 11:43** 8262
of them have committed a **d** act; **Lv 20:13** 8441
shall not make yourselves **d** by animal **Lv 20:25** 8262
"You shall not eat any **d** thing. **Dt 14:3** 8441
is a **d** thing to the LORD your God. **Dt 17:1** 8441
d thing has been done in Israel, **Dt 17:4** 8441
the **d** things of those nations. **Dt 18:9** 8441
these things is **d** to the LORD; **Dt 18:12** 8441
and because of these **d** things the **Dt 18:12** 8441
to do according to all their **d** things **Dt 20:18** 8441
the **d** idol of the Ammonites. **1Ki 11:5** 8251
for Chemosh the **d** idol of Moab, **1Ki 11:7** 8251
the **d** idol of the sons of Ammon. **1Ki 11:7** 8251
less one who is **d** and corrupt, **Jb 15:16** 8581
Who eat swine's flesh, **d** things and **Is 66:17** 8263
"they have set their **d** things in **Jer 7:30** 8251
with the carcasses of their **d** idols **Jer 16:18** 8251
"But they put their **d** things in **Jer 32:34** 8251
defiled My sanctuary with all your **d** **Ezk 5:11** 8251
and their **d** things with it; **Ezk 7:20** 8251
things and beasts *and* **d** things, **Ezk 8:10** 8263
they will remove all its **d** things **Ezk 11:18** 8251
their **d** things and abominations, **Ezk 11:21** 8251
lovers and with all your **d** idols, **Ezk 16:36** 8441
of you, the **d** things of his eyes, **Ezk 20:7** 8251
away the **d** things of their eyes, **Ezk 20:8** 8251
the harlot after their **d** things? **Ezk 20:30** 8251
idols, or with their **d** things, **Ezk 37:23** 8251
as **d** as that which they loved. **Hos 9:10** 8251
And their **d** things from between **Zch 9:7** 8251
men is **d** in the sight of God. **Lk 16:15** *946*
deny *Him*, being **d** and disobedient and **Ti 1:16** *947*

DETESTED
your **d** things from My presence, **Jer 4:1** 8251

DETHRONED
even be **d** from her magnificence." **Ac 19:27** *2507*

DETRIMENT
increase to the **d** of the kings?" **Ezr 4:22** 5142

DEUEL
of Gad, Eliasaph the son of **D**; **Nu 1:14** 1845
Eliasaph the son of **D**, **Nu 2:14** 1845
day *it was* Eliasaph the son of **D**, **Nu 7:42** 1845
offering of Eliasaph the son of **D**. **Nu 7:47** 1845
and Eliasaph the son of **D** was over **Nu 10:20** 1845

DEVASTATE
they came into the land to **d** it. **Jg 6:5** 7843
Kedar And **d** the men of the east. **Jer 49:28** 7703
may winnow her And may **d** her land; **Jer 51:2** 1238b
they will **d** the pride of Egypt, **Ezk 32:12** 7703

DEVASTATED
d the nations and their lands **2Ki 19:17** 2717b
O daughter of Babylon, you **d** one, **Ps 137:8** 7703
are **d** *and* without inhabitant, **Is 6:11** 7582
night Ar of Moab is **d** *and* ruined; **Is 15:1** 7703
night Kir of Moab is **d** *and* ruined. **Is 15:1** 7703
the kings of Assyria have **d** all **Is 37:18** 2717b
For the whole land is **d**; **Jer 4:20** 7703
Suddenly my tents are **d**, **Jer 4:20** 7703
be In the midst of the **d** cities. **Ezk 30:7** 2717b
Even though devastators have **d** **Na 2:2** 1238b
Nineveh is **d**! Who will grieve for her **Na 3:7** 7703

DEVASTATES
LORD lays the earth waste, **d** it, **Is 24:1** 1110

DEVASTATING
and the **d** locust in its kinds, **Lv 11:22** 5556

DEVASTATION
"Because of the **d** of the **Ps 12:5** 7701
the **d** which will come from afar? **Is 10:3** 7724b
The **d** and destruction, famine and **Is 51:19** 7701
D and destruction are in their **Is 59:7** 7701
Nor **d** or destruction within your **Is 60:18** 7701
'**D** and great destruction!' **Jer 48:3** 7701
befallen us, **D** and destruction; **La 3:47** 7612
and **d** in their citadels." **Am 3:10** 7701
And the **d** of *its* beasts by which **Hab 2:17** 7701

DEVASTATIONS
They will raise up the former **d**; **Is 61:4** 8074

DEVASTATORS
and **d** Will depart from you. **Is 49:17** 2717b
Even though **d** have devastated them **Na 2:2** 1238b

DEVELOPING
intent which they are **d** today, **Dt 31:21** 6213a
And as a great dissension was **d**, **Ac 23:10** *1096*

DEVIATE
Nor do they **d** from their paths. **Jl 2:7** 5670

DEVIATED
our steps have not **d** from Your way, **Ps 44:18** 5186

DEVICE
Do not promote his *evil* **d**, **Ps 140:8** 2162

DEVICES
By their own **d** let them fall! **Ps 5:10** 4156
heart, To walk in their own **d**. **Ps 81:12** 4156
And be satiated with their own **d**. **Pr 1:31** 4156
And a man of evil **d** is hated. **Pr 14:17** 4209
but they have sought out many **d**." **Ec 7:29** 2810
And in their **d** you walk. **Mi 6:16** 4156

DEVIL
wilderness to be tempted by the **d**. **Mt 4:1** *1228*
the **d** took Him into the holy city and **Mt 4:5** *1228*
the **d** took Him to a very high **Mt 4:8** *1228*
Then the **d** left Him; **Mt 4:11** *1228*
the enemy who sowed them is the **d**, **Mt 13:39** *1228*
prepared for the **d** and his angels; **Mt 25:41** *1228*
days, being tempted by the **d**. **Lk 4:2** *1228*
And the **d** said to Him, **Lk 4:3** *1228*
And the **d** said to Him, **Lk 4:6** *1228*
d had finished every temptation, **Lk 4:13** *1228*
then the **d** comes and takes away **Lk 8:12** *1228*
and *yet* one of you is a **d**?" **Jn 6:70** *1228*
"You are of *your* father the **d**, **Jn 8:44** *1228*
the **d** having already put into the **Jn 13:2** *1228*
all who were oppressed by the **d**, **Ac 10:38** *1228*
and fraud, you son of the **d**, **Ac 13:10** *1228*
do not give the **d** an opportunity. **Eph 4:27** *1228*
firm against the schemes of the **d**. **Eph 6:11** *1228*
condemnation incurred by the **d**. **1Tm 3:6** *1228*
reproach and the snare of the **d**. **1Tm 3:7** *1228*
escape from the snare of the **d**, **2Tm 2:26** *1228*
power of death, that is, the **d**, **Heb 2:14** *1228*
the **d** and he will flee from you. **Jas 4:7** *1228*
Your adversary, the **d**, **1Pe 5:8** *1228*
one who practices sin is of the **d**; **1Jn 3:8** *1228*
d has sinned from the beginning. **1Jn 3:8** *1228*
to destroy the works of the **d**. **1Jn 3:8** *1228*
the children of the **d** are obvious: **1Jn 3:10** *1228*
when he disputed with the **d** and **Jude 1:9** *1228*
the **d** is about to cast some of you **Rv 2:10** *1228*
old who is called the **d** and Satan, **Rv 12:9** *1228*
the **d** has come down to you, **Rv 12:12** *1228*
of old, who is the **d** and Satan, **Rv 20:2** *1228*
And the **d** who deceived them was **Rv 20:10** *1228*

DEVIOUS
And who are **d** in their ways; **Pr 2:15** 3868
For the **d** are an abomination to the **Pr 3:32** 3868
And put **d** speech far from you. **Pr 4:24** 3891
But he who is **d** in his ways **Pr 14:2** 3868

DEVISE
humiliated who **d** evil against me. **Ps 35:4** 2803
But they **d** deceitful words against **Ps 35:20** 2803
And they **d** treachery all day long. **Ps 38:12** 1897
Against me they **d** my hurt, *saying,* **Ps 41:7** 2803
They **d** injustices, *saying,* **Ps 64:6** 2664
Who **d** evil things in *their* hearts; **Ps 140:2** 2803
not **d** harm against your neighbor, **Pr 3:29** 2790a
in the heart of those who **d** evil, **Pr 12:20** 2790a
they not go astray who **d** evil? **Pr 14:22** 2790a
truth *will be to* those who **d** good. **Pr 14:22** 2790a
eyes *does so* to **d** perverse things; **Pr 16:30** 2803
For their minds **d** violence, And **Pr 24:2** 1897
"**D** a plan, but it will be thwarted; **Is 8:10** 5779
let us **d** plans against Jeremiah. **Jer 18:18** 2803
these are the men who **d** iniquity **Ezk 11:2** 2803
mind and you will **d** an evil plan, **Ezk 38:10** 2803
and he will **d** his schemes against **Da 11:24** 2803
arms, Yet they **d** evil against Me. **Hos 7:15** 2803
Whatever you **d** against the LORD, **Na 1:9** 2803
and do not **d** evil in your hearts **Zch 7:10** 2803
'Also let none of you **d** evil in **Zch 8:17** 2803
AND THE PEOPLES **D** FUTILE THINGS? **Ac 4:25** *3191*

DEVISED
which he had **d** in his own heart; **1Ki 12:33** 908
which he had **d** against the Jews. **Es 8:3** 2803
to revoke the letters **d** by Haman, **Es 8:5** 4284
which he had **d** against the Jews, **Es 9:25** 2803
in the plots which they have **d**. **Ps 10:2** 2803
evil against You *And* **d** a plot, **Ps 21:11** 2803
plan **d** against the whole earth; **Is 14:26** 3289
that they had **d** plots against me, **Jer 11:19** 2803
they have **d** calamity against her: **Jer 48:2** 2803
you And **d** a scheme against you. **Jer 49:30** 2803
for schemes will be **d** against him. **Da 11:25** 2803
"You have **d** a shameful thing for **Hab 2:10** 3289
For we did not follow cleverly **d** **2Pe 1:16** *4679*

DEVISES
Your tongue **d** destruction, Like a **Ps 52:2** 2803
One which **d** mischief by decree? **Ps 94:20** 3335
in his heart continually **d** evil, **Pr 6:14** 2790a
A heart that **d** wicked plans, Feet **Pr 6:18** 2790a
He will condemn a man who **d** evil. **Pr 12:2** 4209
He **d** wicked schemes To destroy *the* **Is 32:7** 3289
But the noble man **d** noble plans; **Is 32:8** 3289

DEVISING
And the peoples **d** a vain thing? **Ps 2:1** 1897
The **d** of folly is sin, And the **Pr 24:9** 2154
you and **d** a plan against you. **Jer 18:11** 2803

DEVOID
man is stupid, **d** of knowledge; **Jer 10:14** 4480
mankind is stupid, **d** of knowledge; **Jer 51:17** 4480
worldly-minded, **d** of the Spirit. **Jude 1:19** *3361, 2192*

DEVOTE
you shall **d** to the LORD the **Ex 13:12** 5674a
that they might **d** themselves to **2Ch 31:4** 2388
D all her army to destruction. **Jer 51:3** 2763a
That you may **d** to the LORD their **Mi 4:13** 2763a
"But we will **d** ourselves to **Ac 6:4** *4342*
you may **d** yourselves to prayer, **1Co 7:5** *4980*
D yourselves to prayer, keeping **Col 4:2** *4342*

DEVOTED
Anything **d** to destruction is most **Lv 27:28** 2764a
"Every **d** thing in Israel shall be **Nu 18:14** 2764a

of the things **d** to destruction, **1Sa 15:21** 2764a
be wholly **d** to the LORD our God, **1Ki 8:61** 8003
not wholly **d** to the LORD his God, **1Ki 11:4** 8003
not wholly **d** to the LORD his God, **1Ki 15:3** 8003
wholly **d** to the LORD all his days. **1Ki 15:14** 8003
man whom I had **d** to destruction, **1Ki 20:42** 2764a
whom I have **d** to destruction. **Is 34:5** 2764a
and every **d** thing in Israel shall **Ezk 44:29** 2764a
and **d** themselves to shame, **Hos 9:10** 5144a
or he will be **d** to one and despise **Mt 6:24** *472*
or else he will be **d** to one **Lk 16:13** *472*
Be **d** to one another in brotherly **Ro 12:10** *5387*
in tribulation, **d** to prayer, **Ro 12:12** *4342*
and that they have **d** themselves **1Co 16:15** *5021*
has **d** herself to every good work. **1Tm 5:10** *1872*

DEVOTING
d themselves to prayer, **Ac 1:14** *4342*
They were continually **d** **Ac 2:42** *4342*
Paul *began* **d** himself completely to **Ac 18:5** *4912*
d themselves to this very thing. **Ro 13:6** *4342*

DEVOTION
of Hezekiah and his deeds of **d**, **2Ch 32:32** 2617a
the acts of Josiah and his deeds of **d** **2Ch 35:26** 2617a
and excessive **d** *to books* is **Ec 12:12** 3854
you the **d** of your youth, **Jer 2:2** 2617a
secure undistracted **d** to the Lord. **1Co 7:35** *2138a*
from the simplicity and purity *of* **d** **2Co 11:3**

DEVOUR
He will **d** the nations *who are* his **Nu 24:8** 398
grapes, for the worm will **d** them. **Dt 28:39** 398
blood, And My sword will **d** flesh, **Dt 32:42** 398
"Shall the sword **d** forever? **2Sa 2:26** 398
command the locust to **d** the land, **2Ch 7:13** 398
"His harvest the hungry **d** And **Jb 5:5** 398
"Nothing remains for him to **d**, **Jb 20:21** 398
And unfanned fire will **d** him; **Jb 20:26** 398
They seize and **d** flocks. **Jb 24:2** 7462a
His wrath, And fire will **d** them. **Ps 21:9** 398
came upon me to **d** my flesh, **Ps 27:2** 398
You love all words that **d**, **Ps 52:4** 1105
To **d** the afflicted from the earth And **Pr 30:14** 398
they **d** Israel with gaping jaws. **Is 9:12** 398
And it will burn and **d** his thorns **Is 10:17** 398
Indeed, fire will **d** Your enemies. **Is 26:11** 398
And a sword not of man will **d** him. **Is 31:8** 398
will **d** your harvest and your food; **Jer 5:17** 398
d your sons and your daughters; **Jer 5:17** 398
will **d** your flocks and your herds; **Jer 5:17** 398
d your vines and your fig trees; **Jer 5:17** 398
and **d** the land and its fullness, **Jer 8:16** 398
of the field, Bring them to **d**! **Jer 12:9** 398
of the earth to **d** and destroy. **Jer 15:3** 398
and it will **d** the palaces of **Jer 17:27** 398
it may **d** all its environs. **Jer 21:14** 398
all who **d** you will be devoured; **Jer 30:16** 398
And the sword will **d** and be **Jer 46:10** 398
And it will **d** the fortified towers **Jer 49:27** 398
And it will **d** all his environs." **Jer 50:32** 398
of the earth will not **d** them; **Ezk 34:28** 398
you will no longer **d** men and **Ezk 36:14** 398
'Arise, **d** much meat!' **Da 7:5** 399
and will **d** the whole earth and **Da 7:23** 399
beasts of the field will **d** them. **Hos 2:12** 398
moon will **d** them with their land. **Hos 5:7** 398
Strangers **d** his strength, Yet he **Hos 7:9** 398
I will also **d** them like a lioness, **Hos 13:8** 398
a sword will **d** your young lions; **Na 2:13** 398
like an eagle swooping *down* to **d**. **Hab 1:8** 398
Who **d** the oppressed in secret. **Hab 3:14** 398
And they will **d** and trample on **Zch 9:15** 398
but will **d** the flesh of the fat **Zch 11:16** 398
because you **d** widows' houses, **Mt 23:14** *2719*
who **d** widows' houses, and for **Mk 12:40** *2719*
who **d** widows' houses, and for **Lk 20:47** *2719*
But if you bite and **d** one another, **Ga 5:15** *2719*
lion, seeking someone to **d**. **1Pe 5:8** *2666*
gave birth he might **d** her child. **Rv 12:4** *2719*

DEVOURED
'A wild beast **d** him.' **Gn 37:20** 398
A wild beast has **d** him; **Gn 37:33** 398
"Yet when they had **d** them, **Gn 41:21**
935, 7130
be detected that they had **d** them, **Gn 41:21**
935, 7130
It **d** Ar of Moab, The dominant **Nu 21:28** 398
died, when the fire **d** 250 men, **Nu 26:10** 398
and the forest **d** more people that **2Sa 18:8** 398
people that day than the sword **d**. **2Sa 18:8** 398
Fire from His mouth **d**; **2Sa 22:9** 398
I have **d** them and shattered them, **2Sa 22:39** 3615
"His skin is **d** by disease, The **Jb 18:13** 398
And fire from His mouth **d**; **Ps 18:8** 398
swarms of flies which **d** them, **Ps 78:45** 398
Fire **d** His young men, **Ps 78:63** 398
For they have **d** Jacob And laid **Ps 79:7** 398
You will be **d** by the sword." **Is 1:20** 398
"It is you who have **d** the vineyard; **Is 3:14** 1197a
Your sword has **d** your prophets **Jer 2:30** 398
For they have **d** Jacob; **Jer 10:25** 398
They have **d** him and consumed him **Jer 10:25** 398
all who devour you will be **d**; **Jer 30:16** 398
the sword has **d** those around you.' **Jer 46:14** 398
And it has **d** the forehead of Moab **Jer 48:45** 398
who came upon them have **d** them; **Jer 50:7** 398
who **d** him was the king of Assyria, **Jer 50:17** 398
Babylon has **d** me *and* crushed me, **Jer 51:34** 398
sacrificed them to idols to be **d**. **Ezk 16:20** 398
learned to tear *his* prey; He **d** men. **Ezk 19:3** 398
learned to tear *his* prey; He **d** men. **Ezk 19:6** 398
They have **d** lives; **Ezk 22:25** 398
I will give to the beasts to be **d**, **Ezk 33:27** 398
It **d** and crushed and trampled **Da 7:7** 399
its claws of bronze, *and which* **d**, **Da 7:19** 399
For fire has **d** the pastures of the **Jl 1:19** 398
And fire has **d** the pastures of the **Jl 1:20** 398
be **d** In the fire of His jealousy, **Zph 1:18** 398
will be **d** By the fire of My zeal. **Zph 3:8** 398
has **d** your wealth with prostitutes, **Lk 15:30** *2719*
came down from heaven and **d** them. **Rv 20:9** *2719*

DEVOURER
"You are a **d** of men and have **Ezk 36:13** 398
"Then I will rebuke the **d** for you, **Mal 3:11** 398

DEVOURING
are **d** them in your presence; **Is 1:7** 398
For a sword of the LORD is **d** From **Jer 12:12** 398
And the caterpillar was **d** Your **Am 4:9** 398

DEVOURS
In the morning he **d** the prey, **Gn 49:27** 398
is a land that **d** its inhabitants; **Nu 13:32** 398
not lie down until it **d** the prey, **Nu 23:24** 398
sword **d** one as well as another; **2Sa 11:25** 398
firstborn of death **d** his limbs. **Jb 18:13** 398
Fire **d** before Him, And it is very **Ps 50:3** 398
Manasseh **d** Ephraim, and Ephraim **Is 9:21** 398
Therefore, a curse **d** the earth, **Is 24:6** 398
enslaves you, anyone **d** you, **2Co 11:20** *2719*
their mouth and **d** their enemies; **Rv 11:5** *2719*

DEVOUT
And **d** men are taken away, while no **Is 57:1** 2617a
and this man was righteous and **d**, **Lk 2:25** *2126*
Jews living in Jerusalem, **d** men from **Ac 2:5** *2126*
Some **d** men buried Stephen, and **Ac 8:2** *2126*
a **d** man and one who feared God **Ac 10:2** *2152*
two of his servants and a **d** soldier **Ac 10:7** *2152*
But the Jews incited the **d** women **Ac 13:50** *4576*
was **d** by the standard of the Law, **Ac 22:12** *2126*
what is good, sensible, just, **d**, **Ti 1:8** *3741*

DEVOUTLY
how **d** and uprightly and **1Th 2:10** *3743*

DEW
God give you of the **d** of heaven, **Gn 27:28** 2919
from the **d** of heaven from above. **Gn 27:39** 2919
was a layer of **d** around the camp. **Ex 16:13** 2919
When the layer of **d** evaporated, **Ex 16:14** 2919
the **d** fell on the camp at night, **Nu 11:9** 2919
rain, My speech distill as the **d**, **Dt 32:2** 2919
things of heaven, with the **d**, **Dt 33:13** 2919
His heavens also drop down **d**. **Dt 33:28** 2919
If there is **d** on the fleece only, **Jg 6:37** 2919
he drained the **d** from the fleece, **Jg 6:38** 2919
there be **d** on all the ground." **Jg 6:39** 2919
and **d** was on all the ground. **Jg 6:40** 2919
Let not **d** or rain be on you, **2Sa 1:21** 2919
him as the **d** falls on the ground; **2Sa 17:12** 2919
be neither **d** nor rain these years, **1Ki 17:1** 2919
And **d** lies all night on my branch. **Jb 29:19** 2919
who has begotten the drops of **d**? **Jb 38:28** 2919
Your youth are to You *as* the **d**. **Ps 110:3** 2919
It is like the **d** of Hermon Coming **Ps 133:3** 2919
up And the skies drip with **d**. **Pr 3:20** 2919
his favor is like **d** on the grass. **Pr 19:12** 2919
For my head is drenched with **d**, **SS 5:2** 2919
of **d** in the heat of harvest." **Is 18:4** 2919
For your **d** is *as* the dew of **Is 26:19** 2919
For your dew is *as* the **d** of **Is 26:19** 2919
be drenched with the **d** of heaven, **Da 4:15** 2920
be drenched with the **d** of heaven, **Da 4:23** 2920
be drenched with the **d** of heaven; **Da 4:25** 2920
was drenched with the **d** of heaven until **Da 4:33** 2920
was drenched with the **d** of heaven until **Da 5:21** 2920
like the **d** which goes away early. **Hos 6:4** 2919
And like **d** which soon disappears, **Hos 13:3** 2919
I will be like the **d** to Israel; **Hos 14:5** 2919
many peoples Like **d** from the LORD, **Mi 5:7** 2919
of you the sky has withheld its **d** and **Hg 1:10** 2919
and the heavens will give their **d**; **Zch 8:12** 2919

DIADEM
d to the remnant of His people; **Is 28:5** 6843
a royal **d** in the hand of your God. **Is 62:3** 6797

DIADEMS
and on his heads *were* seven **d**. **Rv 12:3** *1238*
and on his horns *were* ten **d**, **Rv 13:1** *1238*
and on His head *are* many **d**; **Rv 19:12** *1238*

DIALECT
he spoke to them in the Hebrew **d**, **Ac 21:40** *1258*
addressing them in the Hebrew **d**, **Ac 22:2** *1258*
saying to me in the Hebrew **d**, **Ac 26:14** *1258*

DIAMOND
a turquoise, a sapphire and a **d**; **Ex 28:18** 3095
a turquoise, a sapphire and a **d**; **Ex 39:11** 3095
With a **d** point it is engraved upon **Jer 17:1** 8068
The ruby, the topaz and the **d**; **Ezk 28:13** 3095

DIBLAH
than the wilderness toward **D**; **Ezk 6:14** 1689

DIBLAIM
and took Gomer the daughter of **D**, **Hos 1:3** 1691a

DIBON
Heshbon is ruined as far as **D**, **Nu 21:30** 1769
"Ataroth, **D**, Jazer, Nimrah, **Nu 32:3** 1769
Gad built **D** and Ataroth and Aroer, **Nu 32:34** 1769
the plain of Medeba, as far as **D**; **Jos 13:9** 1769
D and Bamoth-baal and **Jos 13:17** 1769
and its towns, in **D** and its towns, **Ne 11:25** 1769
gone up to the temple and *to* **D**, **Is 15:2** 1769
ground, O daughter dwelling in **D**, **Jer 48:18** 1769
against **D**, Nebo and **Jer 48:22** 1769

DIBON-GAD
from Iyim and camped at **D**. **Nu 33:45**
1769, 1410
They journeyed from **D** and **Nu 33:46**
1769, 1410

DIBRI
was Shelomith, the daughter of **D**, **Lv 24:11** 1704

DICTATED
"He **d** all these words to me, and **Jer 36:18**
4480, 6310, 7121

DICTATION
Baruch wrote on a scroll at the **d** **Jer 36:4** 6310
written at my **d** the words of the LORD **Jer 36:6** 6310
Was it at his **d**?" **Jer 36:17** 6310
had written at the **d** of Jeremiah, **Jer 36:27** 6310
and he wrote on it at the **d** of **Jer 36:32** 6310
words in a book at Jeremiah's **d**, **Jer 45:1** 6310

DID
Noah **d**; according to all that God **Gn 6:22** 6213a
God had commanded him, so he **d**. **Gn 6:22** 6213a
Noah **d** according to all that **Gn 7:5** 6213a
but she **d** not return to him again. **Gn 8:12**
so that they **d** not see their **Gn 9:23**
Why **d** you not tell me that she was **Gn 12:18**
"Why **d** you say, 'She is my sister,' **Gn 12:19**
but he **d** not cut the birds. **Gn 15:10**
"Why **d** Sarah laugh, saying, **Gn 18:13**
it however, saying, "I **d** not laugh"; **Gn 18:15**
"No, but you **d** laugh." **Gn 18:15**
and he **d** not know when she lay **Gn 19:33**
and he **d** not know when she lay **Gn 19:35**
"**D** he not himself say to me, **Gn 20:5**
d I not let you touch her. **Gn 20:6**
d for Sarah as He had promised. **Gn 21:1** 6213a
you **d** not tell me, nor did I hear of **Gn 21:26**
nor **d** I hear of it until today." **Gn 21:26**
How then **d** you say, **Gn 26:9**
and they **d** not quarrel over it; **Gn 26:22**
He **d** not recognize him, **Gn 27:23**
and he forgets what you **d** to him. **Gn 27:45** 6213a
this place, and I **d** not know it." **Gn 28:16**
Jacob **d** so and completed her week, **Gn 29:28** 6213a
and **d** not put them with Laban's **Gn 30:40**
was feeble, he **d** not put *them* in; **Gn 30:42**
God **d** not allow him to hurt me. **Gn 31:7**
"Why **d** you flee secretly and **Gn 31:27**
and deceive me, and **d** not tell me so **Gn 31:27**
and **d** not allow me to kiss my sons **Gn 31:28**
but why **d** you steal my gods?" **Gn 31:30**
For Jacob **d** not know that Rachel **Gn 31:32**
two maids, but he **d** not find *them.* **Gn 31:33**
all the tent but **d** not find *them.* **Gn 31:34**
d not find the household idols. **Gn 31:35**
of beasts I **d** not bring to you; **Gn 31:39**
man **d** not delay to do the thing, **Gn 34:19**
d not pursue the sons of Jacob. **Gn 35:5**
But what he **d** was displeasing in **Gn 38:10** 6213a
for he **d** not know that she was his **Gn 38:16**
woman's hand, he **d** not find her. **Gn 38:20**
"I **d** not find her; **Gn 38:22**
young goat, but you **d** not find her." **Gn 38:23**
d not give her to my son Shelah." **Gn 38:26**
And he **d** not have relations with **Gn 38:26**
that he **d** to prosper in his hand. **Gn 39:3** 6213a
he **d** not concern himself with **Gn 39:6**
he **d** not listen to her to lie **Gn 39:10**
"This is what your slave **d** to me," **Gn 39:19** 6213a
The chief jailer **d** not supervise **Gn 39:23**
and whatever he **d**, the LORD made **Gn 39:23** 6213a
cupbearer **d** not remember Joseph, **Gn 40:23**
But Jacob **d** not send Joseph's **Gn 42:4**
although they **d** not recognize him. **Gn 42:8**
and you will not die." And they **d** so. **Gn 42:20** 6213a
"**D** I not tell you, **Gn 42:22**
They **d** not know, however, that **Gn 42:23**
"Why **d** you treat me so badly by **Gn 43:6**
So the man **d** as Joseph said, and **Gn 43:17** 6213a
And he **d** as Joseph had told *him.* **Gn 44:2** 6213a
Then the sons of Israel **d** so; **Gn 45:21** 6213a
for he **d** not believe them. **Gn 45:26**
land of the priests he **d** not buy, **Gn 47:22**
they **d** not sell their land. **Gn 47:22**
the priests **d** not become Pharaoh's. **Gn 47:26**
Thus his sons **d** for him as he **Gn 50:12** 6213a
all the wrong which we **d** to him!" **Gn 50:15** 1580
sin, for they **d** you wrong." **Gn 50:17** 1580
over Egypt, who **d** not know Joseph. **Ex 1:8**
d not do as the king of Egypt **Ex 1:17**
Why **d** You ever send me? **Ex 5:22**
I **d** not make Myself known to them. **Ex 6:3**
but they **d** not listen to Moses on **Ex 6:9**
So Moses and Aaron **d** *it;* **Ex 7:6** 6213a
LORD commanded them, thus they **d**. **Ex 7:6** 6213a
and thus they **d** just as the LORD **Ex 7:10** 6213a
d the same with their secret arts. **Ex 7:11** 6213a
and he **d** not listen to them, **Ex 7:13**
So Moses and Aaron **d** even as the **Ex 7:20** 6213a
But the magicians of Egypt **d** the **Ex 7:22** 6213a
and he **d** not listen to them. **Ex 7:22**
The magicians **d** the same with **Ex 8:7** 6213a
The LORD **d** according to the **Ex 8:13** 6213a
heart and he **d** not listen to them. **Ex 8:15**
They **d** so; and Aaron stretched out **Ex 8:17** 6213a
and he **d** not listen to them, **Ex 8:19**
Then the LORD **d** so. **Ex 8:24** 6213a
The LORD **d** as Moses asked, and **Ex 8:31** 6213a

and he **d** not let the people go.	Ex 8:32	
LORD **d** this thing on the next	Ex 9:6	6213a
and he **d** not let the people go.	Ex 9:7	
and he **d** not listen to them,	Ex 9:12	
d not let the sons of Israel go,	Ex 9:35	
d not let the sons of Israel go.	Ex 10:20	
They **d** not see one another, nor	Ex 10:23	
nor **d** anyone rise from his place	Ex 10:23	
and he **d** not let the sons of	Ex 11:10	
the sons of Israel went and **d** *so;*	Ex 12:28	6213a
Moses and Aaron, so they **d**.	Ex 12:28	6213a
Then all the sons of Israel **d** *so;*	Ex 12:50	6213a
they **d** just as the LORD had	Ex 12:50	6213a
'It is because of what the LORD **d**	Ex 13:8	6213a
God **d** not lead them by the	Ex 13:17	
He **d** not take away the pillar of	Ex 13:22	
that I am the LORD." And they **d** so.	Ex 14:4	6213a
Thus the one **d** not come near the	Ex 14:20	
For they **d** not know what it was.	Ex 16:15	
The sons of Israel **d** so,	Ex 16:17	6213a
But they **d** not listen to Moses,	Ex 16:20	
ordered, and it **d** not become foul nor	Ex 16:24	
And Moses **d** so in the sight of the	Ex 17:6	6213a
Joshua **d** as Moses told him,	Ex 17:10	6213a
and **d** all that he had said.	Ex 18:24	6213a
seen what I **d** to the Egyptians,	Ex 19:4	6213a
if he **d** not lie in wait *for him,*	Ex 21:13	
Yet He **d** not stretch out His hand	Ex 24:11	
"What **d** this people do to you,	Ex 32:21	6213a
of Levi **d** as Moses instructed,	Ex 32:28	6213a
because of what they **d** with the	Ex 32:35	6213a
he **d** not eat bread or drink water.	Ex 34:28	
that Moses **d** not know that the	Ex 34:29	
so **d** every man who presented an	Ex 35:22	
he **d** likewise on the edge of the	Ex 36:11	6213a
thus he **d** for all the boards of	Ex 36:22	6213a
thus he **d** with both of them for	Ex 36:29	6213a
and the sons of Israel **d** according	Ex 39:32	6213a
had commanded Moses; so they **d**.	Ex 39:32	6213a
So the sons of Israel **d** all the	Ex 39:42	6213a
Thus Moses **d**; according to all that	Ex 40:16	6213a
LORD had commanded him, so he **d**.	Ex 40:16	6213a
then they **d** not set out until the	Ex 40:37	
he **d** with the bull of the sin offering;	Lv 4:20	6213a
unintentionally and **d** not know *it,*	Lv 5:18	
So Moses **d** just as the LORD	Lv 8:4	6213a
Thus Aaron and his sons **d** all the	Lv 8:36	6213a
So they **d** according to the word of	Lv 10:7	6213a
"Why **d** you not eat the sin offering	Lv 10:17	
he **d** with the blood of the bull,	Lv 16:15	6213a
LORD had commanded Moses, *so* he **d**.	Lv 16:34	6213a
you, for they **d** all these things,	Lv 20:23	6213a
Thus the sons of Israel **d**,	Lv 24:23	6213a
it **d** not observe on your sabbaths,	Lv 26:35	
Thus the sons of Israel **d**;	Nu 1:54	6213a
had commanded Moses, so they **d**.	Nu 1:54	6213a
Thus the sons of Israel **d**;	Nu 2:34	6213a
The sons of Israel **d** so and	Nu 5:4	6213a
Moses, thus the sons of Israel **d**.	Nu 5:4	6213a
But he **d** not give *any* to the sons	Nu 7:9	
Aaron therefore **d** so;	Nu 8:3	6213a
Thus **d** Moses and Aaron and all the	Nu 8:20	6213a
so the sons of Israel **d** to them.	Nu 8:20	6213a
the Levites, so they **d** to them.	Nu 8:22	6213a
Moses, so the sons of Israel **d**.	Nu 9:5	6213a
for he **d** not present the offering	Nu 9:13	
remained camped and **d** not set out;	Nu 9:22	
it was lifted, they **d** set out.	Nu 9:22	
"Why **d** we ever leave Egypt?	Nu 11:20	
But they **d** not do *it* again.	Nu 11:25	
and the people **d** not move on until	Nu 12:15	
since they **d** present them before	Nu 16:38	
Thus Moses **d**; just as the LORD had	Nu 17:11	6213a
LORD had commanded him, so he **d**.	Nu 17:11	6213a
So Moses **d** just as the LORD had	Nu 20:27	6213a
shall do to him as you **d** to Sihon,	Nu 21:34	6213a
for I **d** not know that you were	Nu 22:34	
"**D** I not urgently send to you to	Nu 22:37	
Why **d** you not come to me?	Nu 22:37	
Balak **d** just as Balaam had spoken,	Nu 23:2	6213a
"**D** I not tell you,	Nu 23:26	
Balak **d** just as Balaam had said,	Nu 23:30	6213a
he **d** not go as at other times to	Nu 24:1	
"**D** I not tell your messengers	Nu 24:12	
so that I **d** not destroy the sons	Nu 25:11	
sons of Korah, however, **d** not die.	Nu 26:11	
Moses **d** just as the LORD	Nu 27:22	6213a
to her *and* **d** not forbid her,	Nu 30:11	
Moses and Eleazar the priest **d** just	Nu 31:31	6213a
"This is what your fathers **d** when	Nu 32:8	6213a
so that they **d** not go into the land	Nu 32:9	
for they **d** not follow Me fully,	Nu 32:11	
so the daughters of Zelophehad **d**:	Nu 36:10	6213a
just as He **d** for you in Egypt	Dt 1:30	6213a
you **d** not trust the LORD your God,	Dt 1:32	
LORD **d** not listen to your voice nor	Dt 1:45	
just as Israel **d** to the land of	Dt 2:12	6213a
just as He **d** for the sons of Esau,	Dt 2:22	6213a
Moabites who live in Ar **d** for me,	Dt 2:29	6213a
"Only you **d** not go near to the	Dt 2:37	
d to Sihon king of the Amorites,	Dt 3:2	6213a
which we **d** not take from them:	Dt 3:4	
as we **d** to Sihon king of Heshbon,	Dt 3:6	6213a
since you **d** not see any form on	Dt 4:15	
as the LORD your God **d** for you in	Dt 4:34	6213a
"The LORD **d** not make this	Dt 5:3	
fire and **d** not go up the mountain.	Dt 5:5	
cities which you **d** not build,	Dt 6:10	
good things which you **d** not fill,	Dt 6:11	
hewn cisterns which you **d** not dig,	Dt 6:11	
olive trees which you **d** not plant,	Dt 6:11	
"The LORD **d** not set His love on	Dt 7:7	
God **d** to Pharaoh and to all Egypt:	Dt 7:18	6213a
with manna which you **d** not know,	Dt 8:3	
not know, nor **d** your fathers know,	Dt 8:3	
clothing **d** not wear out on you,	Dt 8:4	
nor **d** your foot swell these forty	Dt 8:4	
which your fathers **d** not know,	Dt 8:16	
which I **d** because the LORD had	Dt 9:25	5307
"Yet on your fathers **d** the LORD	Dt 10:15	
His signs and His works which He **d**	Dt 11:3	6213a
and what He **d** to Egypt's army, to	Dt 11:4	6213a
and what He **d** to you in the	Dt 11:5	6213a
what He **d** to Dathan and Abiram,	Dt 11:6	6213a
great work of the LORD which He **d**.	Dt 11:7	6213a
'Our hands **d** not shed this blood,	Dt 21:7	
this blood, nor **d** our eyes see *it.*	Dt 21:7	
her, I **d** not find her a virgin,'	Dt 22:14	
"I **d** not find your daughter a	Dt 22:17	
she **d** not cry out in the city,	Dt 22:24	
because they **d** not meet you with	Dt 23:4	
what the LORD your God **d** to Miriam	Dt 24:9	6213a
"Remember what Amalek **d** to you	Dt 25:17	6213a
and he **d** not fear God.	Dt 25:18	
"Because you **d** not serve the LORD	Dt 28:47	
you **d** not obey the LORD your God.	Dt 28:62	
"You have seen all that the LORD **d**	Dt 29:2	6213a
them just as He **d** to Sihon and Og,	Dt 31:4	6213a
Whom your fathers **d** not dread.	Dt 32:17	
because you **d** not treat Me as holy	Dt 32:51	
'I **d** not consider them';	Dt 33:9	
he **d** not acknowledge his brothers,	Dt 33:9	
Nor **d** he regard his own sons,	Dt 33:9	
listened to him and **d** as the LORD had	Dt 34:9	6213a
I **d** not know where they were from.	Jos 2:4	
and what you **d** to the two kings of	Jos 2:10	6213a
Thus the sons of Israel **d** as	Jos 4:8	6213a
perished because they **d** not listen	Jos 5:6	
standing is holy." And Joshua **d** so.	Jos 5:15	6213a
they **d** so for six days.	Jos 6:14	6213a
why **d** You ever bring this people	Jos 7:7	
of Israel, and this is what I **d**:	Jos 7:20	6213a
as you **d** to Jericho and its king;	Jos 8:2	6213a
But he **d** not know that *there was*	Jos 8:14	
For Joshua **d** not withdraw his hand	Jos 8:26	
which Joshua **d** not read before all	Jos 8:35	
of Him and all that He **d** in Egypt,	Jos 9:9	6213a
and all that He **d** to the two kings	Jos 9:10	6213a
and **d** not ask for the counsel of	Jos 9:14	
The sons of Israel **d** not	Jos 9:18	
Thus he **d** to them, and delivered	Jos 9:26	6213a
Israel, and they **d** not kill them.	Jos 9:26	
and **d** not hasten to go *down* for	Jos 10:13	
They **d** so, and brought these	Jos 10:23	6213a
Thus he **d** to the king of Makkedah	Jos 10:28	6213a
Thus he **d** to its king just as he	Jos 10:30	6213a
so he **d** to Debir and its king,	Jos 10:39	6213a
Joshua **d** to them as the LORD	Jos 11:9	6213a
Israel **d** not burn any cities that	Jos 11:13	
commanded Joshua, and so Joshua **d**;	Jos 11:15	6213a
But the sons of Israel **d** not	Jos 13:13	
Levi he **d** not give an inheritance;	Jos 13:14	
Moses **d** not give an inheritance;	Jos 13:33	
but he **d** not give an inheritance	Jos 14:3	
and they **d** not give a portion to	Jos 14:4	
Thus the sons of Israel **d** just as	Jos 14:5	6213a
But they **d** not drive out the	Jos 16:10	
d not drive them out completely.	Jos 17:13	
and **d** not hate him beforehand.	Jos 20:5	
'**D** not Achan the son of Zerah act	Jos 22:20	
And that man **d** not perish alone in	Jos 22:20	
and they **d** not speak of going up	Jos 22:33	
Egypt by what I **d** in its midst;	Jos 24:5	6213a
own eyes saw what I **d** in Egypt.	Jos 24:7	6213a
groves which you **d** not plant.'	Jos 24:13	
and who **d** these great signs in our	Jos 24:17	6213a
But the sons of Benjamin **d** not	Jg 1:21	
But Manasseh **d** not take possession	Jg 1:27	
d not drive them out completely.	Jg 1:28	
Ephraim **d** not drive out the	Jg 1:29	
Zebulun **d** not drive out the	Jg 1:30	
Asher **d** not drive out the	Jg 1:31	
for they **d** not drive them out.	Jg 1:32	
Naphtali **d** not drive out the	Jg 1:33	
for they **d** not allow them to come	Jg 1:34	
them who **d** not know the LORD,	Jg 2:10	
d evil in the sight of the LORD and	Jg 2:11	6213a
they **d** not listen to their judges,	Jg 2:17	
they **d** not do as *their fathers.*	Jg 2:17	6213a
they **d** not abandon their practices	Jg 2:19	
to walk in it as their fathers **d**,	Jg 2:22	8104
and He **d** not give them into the	Jg 2:23	
The sons of Israel **d** what was	Jg 3:7	6213a
d evil in the sight of the LORD.	Jg 3:12	6213a
for he **d** not draw the sword out of	Jg 3:22	
he **d** not open the doors of the	Jg 3:25	
and **d** not allow anyone to cross.	Jg 3:28	
d evil in the sight of the LORD,	Jg 4:1	6213a
d you sit among the sheepfolds,	Jg 5:16	
And why **d** Dan stay in ships?	Jg 5:17	
Because they **d** not come to the	Jg 5:23	
Then the sons of Israel **d** what was	Jg 6:1	6213a
'**D** not the LORD bring us up from	Jg 6:13	
pour out the broth." And he **d** so.	Jg 6:20	6213a
d as the LORD had spoken to him;	Jg 6:27	6213a
it by day, he **d** it by night.	Jg 6:27	6213a
"Who **d** this thing?"	Jg 6:29	6213a
the son of Joash **d** this thing."	Jg 6:29	6213a
God **d** so that night;	Jg 6:40	6213a
the youth **d** not draw his sword,	Jg 8:20	
and they **d** not lift up their heads	Jg 8:28	
Thus the sons of Israel **d** not	Jg 8:34	
nor **d** they show kindness to the	Jg 8:35	
d evil in the sight of the LORD,	Jg 10:6	6213a
the LORD and **d** not serve Him.	Jg 10:6	
"**D** *I* not *deliver you* from	Jg 10:11	
"**D** you not hate me and drive me	Jg 11:7	
'Israel **d** not take away the land	Jg 11:15	
but they **d** not enter the territory	Jg 11:18	
'But Sihon **d** not trust Israel to	Jg 11:20	
D he ever strive with Israel, or	Jg 11:25	
or **d** he ever fight against them?	Jg 11:25	
why **d** you not recover them within	Jg 11:26	
who **d** to her according to the vow	Jg 11:39	6213a
"Why **d** you cross over to fight	Jg 12:1	
you **d** not deliver me from their	Jg 12:2	
d evil in the sight of the LORD,	Jg 13:1	6213a
And I **d** not ask him where he *came*	Jg 13:6	
from, nor **d** he tell me his name.	Jg 13:6	
For Manoah **d** not know that he was	Jg 13:16	
Now the angel of the LORD **d** not	Jg 13:21	
his father and mother **d** not know	Jg 14:4	
but he **d** not tell his father or	Jg 14:6	
but he **d** not tell them that he had	Jg 14:9	
the young men customarily **d** this.	Jg 14:10	6213a
her father **d** not let him enter.	Jg 15:1	
Philistines said, "Who **d** this?"	Jg 15:6	6213a
to do to him as he **d** to us."	Jg 15:10	6213a
"As they **d** to me, so I have done	Jg 15:11	6213a
But he **d** not know that the LORD	Jg 16:20	
every man **d** what was right in his	Jg 17:6	6213a
d this wickedness take place?"	Jg 20:3	
but Benjamin **d** not know that	Jg 20:34	
tribes of Israel who **d** not come up	Jg 21:5	
him who **d** not come up to the LORD	Jg 21:5	
d not come up to the LORD at Mizpah	Jg 21:8	
because we **d** not take for each man	Jg 21:22	
nor **d** you give *them* to them,	Jg 21:22	
The sons of Benjamin **d** so,	Jg 21:23	6213a
everyone **d** what was right in his	Jg 21:25	6213a
that you **d** not previously know.	Ru 2:11	
"Where **d** you glean today and	Ru 2:19	
glean today and where **d** you work?	Ru 2:19	
to the threshing floor and **d** according	Ru 3:6	6213a
"How **d** it go, my daughter?"	Ru 3:16	
But Hannah **d** not go up, for she	1Sa 1:22	
they **d** not know the LORD	1Sa 2:12	
Thus they **d** in Shiloh to all the	1Sa 2:14	6213a
'**D** I *not* indeed reveal Myself to	1Sa 2:27	
'**D** I *not* choose them from all	1Sa 2:28	
and **d** I *not* give to the house of	1Sa 2:28	
'I **d** indeed say that your house	1Sa 2:30	
"I **d** not call, lie down again."	1Sa 3:5	
"I **d** not call, my son, lie down	1Sa 3:6	
Samuel **d** not yet know the LORD,	1Sa 3:7	
and he **d** not rebuke them.	1Sa 3:13	
"How **d** things go, my son?"	1Sa 4:16	
she **d** not answer or pay attention.	1Sa 4:20	
And the men who **d** not die were	1Sa 5:12	
d they not allow the people to go,	1Sa 6:6	
Then the men **d** so, and took two	1Sa 6:10	6213a
and **d** not turn aside to the right	1Sa 6:12	
Philistines were subdued and they **d**	1Sa 7:13	3254
however, **d** not walk in his ways,	1Sa 8:3	
but they **d** not find *them.*	1Sa 9:4	
but they **d** not find *them.*	1Sa 9:4	
"Where **d** you go?"	1Sa 10:14	
But he **d** not tell him about the	1Sa 10:16	
and **d** not bring him any present.	1Sa 10:27	
He **d** for you and your fathers.	1Sa 12:7	6213a
but Samuel **d** not come to Gilgal;	1Sa 13:8	
and that you **d** not come within the	1Sa 13:11	
But he **d** not tell his father.	1Sa 14:1	
And the people **d** not know that	1Sa 14:3	
He **d** not answer him on that day.	1Sa 14:37	
rescued Jonathan and he **d** not die.	1Sa 14:45	
Amalek *for* what he **d** to Israel,	1Sa 15:2	6213a
"Why then **d** you not obey the	1Sa 15:19	
but rushed upon the spoil and **d**	1Sa 15:19	6213a
"I **d** obey the voice of the LORD,	1Sa 15:20	
Samuel **d** not see Saul again	1Sa 15:35	3254
So Samuel **d** what the LORD said,	1Sa 16:4	6213a
Saul took him that day and **d**	1Sa 18:2	
d not speak anything that day,	1Sa 20:26	
and **d** not eat food on the second	1Sa 20:34	
D they not sing of this one as	1Sa 21:11	
"**D** I *just* begin to inquire of God	1Sa 22:15	
and **d** not reveal it to me."	1Sa 22:17	
d not deliver him into his hand.	1Sa 23:14	
d not allow them to rise up against	1Sa 24:7	
of your robe and **d** not kill you,	1Sa 24:11	
hand and *yet* you **d** not kill me.	1Sa 24:18	
nor **d** we miss anything as long as	1Sa 25:15	
d not tell her husband Nabal.	1Sa 25:19	
but I your maidservant **d** not see	1Sa 25:25	
so she **d** not tell him anything at	1Sa 25:36	
saw or knew *it,* nor **d** any awake,	1Sa 26:12	
because you **d** not guard your lord,	1Sa 26:16	
d not leave a man or a woman alive,	1Sa 27:9	
David **d** not leave a man or a	1Sa 27:11	
LORD, the LORD **d** not answer him,	1Sa 28:6	
face to the ground and **d** homage.	1Sa 28:14	
"As you **d** not obey the LORD and	1Sa 28:18	
and **d** not execute His fierce wrath	1Sa 28:18	
"Because they **d** not go with us,	1Sa 30:22	
David said to him, "How **d** things go	2Sa 1:4	
and *so* also **d** all the men who	2Sa 1:11	

bow of Jonathan **d** not turn back,	**2Sa 1:22**	
sword of Saul **d** not return empty.	**2Sa 1:22**	
Asahel pursued Abner and **d** not	**2Sa 2:19**	
nor **d** they continue to fight	**2Sa 2:28**	
but David **d** not know *it.*	**2Sa 3:26**	
everything the king **d** pleased all	**2Sa 3:36**	6213a
Then David **d** so, just as the LORD	**2Sa 5:25**	6213a
d I speak a word with one of the	**2Sa 7:7**	
and **d** not go down to his house.	**2Sa 11:9**	
d not go down to his house,"	**2Sa 11:10**	
d you not go down to your house?"	**2Sa 11:10**	
but he **d** not go down to his house.	**2Sa 11:13**	
'Why **d** you go so near to the city	**2Sa 11:20**	
D you not know that they would	**2Sa 11:20**	
D not a woman throw an upper	**2Sa 11:21**	
Why **d** you go so near the wall?'	**2Sa 11:21**	
because he **d** this thing and had no	**2Sa 12:6**	6213a
'Indeed you **d** it secretly, but I	**2Sa 12:12**	6213a
and he **d** not listen to our voice.	**2Sa 12:18**	
And thus he **d** to all the cities of	**2Sa 12:31**	6213a
But Absalom **d** not speak to Amnon	**2Sa 13:22**	
The servants of Absalom **d** to	**2Sa 13:29**	6213a
and **d** not see the king's face.	**2Sa 14:24**	
and **d** not see the king's face.	**2Sa 14:28**	
and they **d** not know anything.	**2Sa 15:11**	
d you not go with your friend?"	**2Sa 16:17**	
But a lad **d** see them and told	**2Sa 17:18**	
Why then **d** you not strike him	**2Sa 18:11**	
but I **d** not know what *it was.*"	**2Sa 18:29**	
nor remember what your servant **d**	**2Sa 19:19**	5753b
"Why **d** you not go with me,	**2Sa 19:25**	
then **d** you treat us with contempt?	**2Sa 19:43**	
but **d** not go in to them.	**2Sa 20:3**	
and **d** not *strike* him again,	**2Sa 20:10**	
d all that the king commanded,	**2Sa 21:14**	6213a
I **d** not depart from them.	**2Sa 22:23**	
And I **d** not turn back until they	**2Sa 22:38**	
them, so that they **d** not rise;	**2Sa 22:39**	
LORD, but He **d** not answer them.	**2Sa 22:42**	
things the three mighty men **d**.	**2Sa 23:17**	6213a
he **d** not attain to the three.	**2Sa 23:19**	
Benaiah the son of Jehoiada **d**,	**2Sa 23:22**	6213a
but he **d** not attain to the three.	**2Sa 23:23**	
the king **d** not cohabit with her.	**1Ki 1:4**	
d not invite Nathan the prophet,	**1Ki 1:10**	
Joab the son of Zeruiah **d** to me,	**1Ki 2:5**	6213a
what he **d** to the two commanders of	**1Ki 2:5**	6213a
my father David **d** not know *it:*	**1Ki 2:32**	
"**D** I not make you swear by the	**1Ki 2:42**	
which you **d** to my father David;	**1Ki 2:44**	6213a
and so he **d** for the other capital.	**1Ki 7:18**	6213a
I **d** not choose a city out of all	**1Ki 8:16**	
you **d** well that it was in your	**1Ki 8:18**	2895
him, and they **d** not please him.	**1Ki 9:12**	
But Solomon **d** not make slaves of	**1Ki 9:22**	
which he **d** not explain to her.	**1Ki 10:3**	
I **d** not believe the reports,	**1Ki 10:7**	
Never again **d** such abundance of	**1Ki 10:10**	
Solomon **d** what was evil in the	**1Ki 11:6**	6213a
and **d** not follow the LORD fully,	**1Ki 11:6**	
he **d** for all his foreign wives,	**1Ki 11:8**	6213a
but he **d** not observe what the LORD	**1Ki 11:10**	
along with the evil that Hadad **d**;	**1Ki 11:25**	
My ordinances, as his father David **d**.	**1Ki 11:33**	
as My servant David **d**,	**1Ki 11:38**	6213a
acts of Solomon and whatever he **d**,	**1Ki 11:41**	6213a
king **d** not listen to the people;	**1Ki 12:15**	
the king **d** not listen to them,	**1Ki 12:16**	
thus he **d** in Bethel, sacrificing	**1Ki 12:32**	6213a
and **d** not return by the way which	**1Ki 13:10**	
"Which way **d** he go?"	**1Ki 13:12**	
d not return from his evil way,	**1Ki 13:33**	
Jeroboam's wife **d** so,	**1Ki 14:4**	6213a
d evil in the sight of the LORD,	**1Ki 14:22**	6213a
They **d** according to all the	**1Ki 14:24**	6213a
of Rehoboam and all that he **d**,	**1Ki 14:29**	6213a
because David **d** what was right in	**1Ki 15:5**	6213a
acts of Abijam and all that he **d**,	**1Ki 15:7**	6213a
Asa **d** what was right in the	**1Ki 15:11**	6213a
d and the cities which he built,	**1Ki 15:23**	6213a
d evil in the sight of the LORD,	**1Ki 15:26**	6213a
He **d** not leave to Jeroboam any	**1Ki 15:29**	
acts of Nadab and all that he **d**,	**1Ki 15:31**	6213a
d evil in the sight of the LORD,	**1Ki 15:34**	6213a
and what he **d** and his might,	**1Ki 16:5**	6213a
he **d** in the sight of the LORD,	**1Ki 16:7**	6213a
he **d** not leave a single male,	**1Ki 16:11**	
acts of Elah and all that he **d**,	**1Ki 16:14**	6213a
and in his sin which he **d**,	**1Ki 16:19**	6213a
d evil in the sight of the LORD,	**1Ki 16:25**	6213a
d and his might which he showed,	**1Ki 16:27**	6213a
Ahab the son of Omri **d** evil in	**1Ki 16:30**	6213a
Thus Ahab **d** more to provoke the	**1Ki 16:33**	6213a
So he went and **d** according to the	**1Ki 17:5**	6213a
So she went and **d** according to the	**1Ki 17:15**	6213a
nor **d** the jar of oil become empty,	**1Ki 17:16**	
I **d** when Jezebel killed the prophets	**1Ki 18:13**	6213a
people **d** not answer him a word.	**1Ki 18:21**	
time," and they **d** it a second time.	**1Ki 18:34**	8138
time," and they **d** it a third time.	**1Ki 18:34**	8027
my gold, and I **d** not refuse him."	**1Ki 20:7**	
listened to their voice and **d** so.	**1Ki 20:25**	6213a
d as Jezebel had sent *word* to	**1Ki 21:11**	6213a
"**D** I not tell you that he would	**1Ki 22:18**	
"How **d** the Spirit of the LORD	**1Ki 22:24**	
of the acts of Ahab and all that he **d**	**1Ki 22:39**	6213a
he **d** not turn aside from it, doing	**1Ki 22:43**	
but they **d** not go for the ships	**1Ki 22:48**	
He **d** evil in the sight of the	**1Ki 22:52**	6213a

of the acts of Ahaziah which he **d**,	**2Ki 1:18**	6213a
three days but **d** not find him.	**2Ki 2:17**	
"**D** I not say to you,	**2Ki 2:18**	
d evil in the sight of the LORD,	**2Ki 3:2**	6213a
he **d** not depart from them.	**2Ki 3:3**	
"**D** I ask for a son from my lord?	**2Ki 4:28**	
D I not say, 'Do not deceive me'?"	**2Ki 4:28**	
they **d** not know *what they were.*	**2Ki 4:39**	
"**D** not my heart go *with you,* when	**2Ki 5:26**	
"Where **d** it fall?"	**2Ki 6:6**	
bands of Arameans **d** not come again	**2Ki 6:23**	3254
So the woman arose and **d** according	**2Ki 8:2**	6213a
"What **d** Elisha say to you?"	**2Ki 8:14**	
d evil in the sight of the LORD.	**2Ki 8:18**	6213a
acts of Joram and all that he **d**,	**2Ki 8:23**	6213a
d evil in the sight of the LORD,	**2Ki 8:27**	6213a
d this mad fellow come to you?"	**2Ki 9:11**	
to them, but he **d** not return."	**2Ki 9:18**	
even to them, and he **d** not return;	**2Ki 9:20**	
two kings **d** not stand before him;	**2Ki 10:4**	
But Jehu **d** it in cunning, so	**2Ki 10:19**	6213a
was not a man left who **d** not come.	**2Ki 10:21**	
sin, from these Jehu **d** not depart,	**2Ki 10:29**	
he **d** not depart from the sins of	**2Ki 10:31**	
all that he **d** and all his might,	**2Ki 10:34**	6213a
So the captains of hundreds **d**	**2Ki 11:9**	6213a
Jehoash **d** right in the sight	**2Ki 12:2**	6213a
the hands of those who **d** the work,	**2Ki 12:11**	6213a
gave that to those who **d** the work,	**2Ki 12:14**	6213a
they **d** not require an accounting	**2Ki 12:15**	
to pay to those who **d** the work,	**2Ki 12:15**	6213a
acts of Joash and all that he **d**,	**2Ki 12:19**	6213a
d evil in the sight of the LORD,	**2Ki 13:2**	6213a
he **d** not turn from them.	**2Ki 13:2**	
Nevertheless they **d** not turn away	**2Ki 13:6**	
and all that he **d** and his might,	**2Ki 13:8**	6213a
d evil in the sight of the LORD;	**2Ki 13:11**	6213a
he **d** not turn away from all the	**2Ki 13:11**	
of the acts of Joash and all that he **d**	**2Ki 13:12**	6213a
He **d** right in the sight of the	**2Ki 14:3**	6213a
he **d** according to all that Joash	**2Ki 14:3**	6213a
the slayers he **d** not put to death,	**2Ki 14:6**	
of the acts of Jehoash which he **d**,	**2Ki 14:15**	6213a
d evil in the sight of the LORD;	**2Ki 14:24**	6213a
he **d** not depart from all the sins	**2Ki 14:24**	
The LORD **d** not say that He	**2Ki 14:27**	
and all that he **d** and his might,	**2Ki 14:28**	6213a
He **d** right in the sight of the	**2Ki 15:3**	6213a
acts of Azariah and all that he **d**,	**2Ki 15:6**	6213a
d evil in the sight of the LORD,	**2Ki 15:9**	6213a
he **d** not depart from the sins of	**2Ki 15:9**	
because they **d** not open *to him;*	**2Ki 15:16**	
d evil in the sight of the LORD;	**2Ki 15:18**	6213a
he **d** not depart all his days from	**2Ki 15:18**	
d not remain there in the land.	**2Ki 15:20**	
acts of Menahem and all that he **d**,	**2Ki 15:21**	6213a
d evil in the sight of the LORD;	**2Ki 15:24**	6213a
he **d** not depart from the sins of	**2Ki 15:24**	
of Pekahiah and all that he **d**,	**2Ki 15:26**	6213a
d evil in the sight of the LORD;	**2Ki 15:28**	6213a
he **d** not depart from the sins of	**2Ki 15:28**	
acts of Pekah and all that he **d**,	**2Ki 15:31**	6213a
He **d** what was right in the	**2Ki 15:34**	6213a
he **d** according to all that his	**2Ki 15:34**	6213a
acts of Jotham and all that he **d**,	**2Ki 15:36**	6213a
and he **d** not do what was right in	**2Ki 16:2**	
So Urijah the priest **d** according	**2Ki 16:16**	6213a
of the acts of Ahaz which he **d**,	**2Ki 16:19**	6213a
d evil in the sight of the LORD,	**2Ki 17:2**	6213a
The sons of Israel **d** things secretly	**2Ki 17:9**	2644
the high places as the nations **d**	**2Ki 17:11**	
and they **d** evil things provoking	**2Ki 17:11**	6213a
However, they **d** not listen, but	**2Ki 17:14**	
who **d** not believe in the LORD	**2Ki 17:14**	
Also Judah **d** not keep the	**2Ki 17:19**	
the sins of Jeroboam which he **d**;	**2Ki 17:22**	6213a
they **d** not depart from them	**2Ki 17:22**	
they **d** not fear the LORD;	**2Ki 17:25**	
However, they **d** not listen, but	**2Ki 17:40**	
but they **d** according to their	**2Ki 17:40**	6213a
grandchildren, as their fathers **d**,	**2Ki 17:41**	6213a
He **d** right in the sight of the LORD,	**2Ki 18:3**	6213a
d not depart from following Him,	**2Ki 18:6**	
of Assyria and **d** not serve him.	**2Ki 18:7**	
because they **d** not obey the voice	**2Ki 18:12**	
'**D** the gods of those nations which	**2Ki 19:12**	
'Have you not heard? Long ago I **d** it;	**2Ki 19:25**	6213a
that Hezekiah **d** not show them.	**2Ki 20:13**	
"What **d** these men say, and from	**2Ki 20:14**	
d evil in the sight of the LORD,	**2Ki 21:2**	6213a
He **d** much evil in the sight of the	**2Ki 21:6**	6213a
But they **d** not listen, and	**2Ki 21:9**	
Amorites **d** who *were* before him,	**2Ki 21:11**	6213a
acts of Manasseh and all that he **d**	**2Ki 21:17**	6213a
d evil in the sight of the LORD,	**2Ki 21:20**	6213a
and **d** not walk in the way of the	**2Ki 21:22**	
of the acts of Amon which he **d**,	**2Ki 21:25**	6213a
He **d** right in the sight of the	**2Ki 22:2**	6213a
nor **d** he turn aside to the right	**2Ki 22:2**	
He **d** away with the idolatrous	**2Ki 23:5**	7673a
priests of the high places **d** not go up	**2Ki 23:9**	
He **d** away with the horses	**2Ki 23:11**	7673a
and he **d** to them just as he had	**2Ki 23:19**	6213a
d any like him arise after him.	**2Ki 23:25**	
the LORD **d** not turn from the	**2Ki 23:26**	
acts of Josiah and all that he **d**,	**2Ki 23:28**	6213a
d evil in the sight of the LORD,	**2Ki 23:32**	6213a
d evil in the sight of the LORD,	**2Ki 23:37**	6213a
of Jehoiakim and all that he **d**,	**2Ki 24:5**	6213a

The king of Egypt **d** not come	**2Ki 24:7**	3254
d evil in the sight of the LORD,	**2Ki 24:9**	6213a
d evil in the sight of the LORD,	**2Ki 24:19**	6213a
his brothers **d** not have many sons,	**1Ch 4:27**	
nor **d** all their family multiply	**1Ch 4:27**	
of the LORD which he **d** not keep;	**1Ch 10:13**	
and **d** not inquire of the LORD.	**1Ch 10:14**	
things the three mighty men **d**.	**1Ch 11:19**	6213a
d not attain to the *first* three.	**1Ch 11:21**	
Benaiah the son of Jehoiada **d**,	**1Ch 11:24**	6213a
but he **d** not attain to the three;	**1Ch 11:25**	
But they **d** not help them, for the	**1Ch 12:19**	
for we **d** not seek it in the days	**1Ch 13:3**	
So David **d** not take the ark with	**1Ch 13:13**	
d just as God had commanded him,	**1Ch 14:16**	6213a
you **d** not *carry it* at the first,	**1Ch 15:13**	
for we **d** not seek Him according to	**1Ch 15:13**	
And thus David **d** to all the cities	**1Ch 20:3**	6213a
But he **d** not number Levi and	**1Ch 21:6**	
and Beriah **d** not have many sons,	**1Ch 23:11**	
But David **d** not count those twenty	**1Ch 27:23**	
to count *them,* but **d** not finish;	**1Ch 27:24**	
and bowed low and **d** homage to the	**1Ch 29:20**	7812
in mind, and **d** not ask for riches,	**2Ch 1:11**	
I **d** not choose a city out of all	**2Ch 6:5**	
nor **d** I choose any man for a	**2Ch 6:5**	
you **d** well that it was in your	**2Ch 6:8**	2895
But Solomon **d** not make slaves for	**2Ch 8:9**	
and **d** *so* according to the daily	**2Ch 8:13**	
And they **d** not depart from the	**2Ch 8:15**	
which he **d** not explain to her.	**2Ch 9:2**	
"Nevertheless I **d** not believe	**2Ch 9:6**	
king **d** not listen to the people,	**2Ch 10:15**	
all Israel *saw* that the king **d** not listen	**2Ch 10:16**	
He **d** evil because he did not	**2Ch 12:14**	6213a
He did evil because he **d** not	**2Ch 12:14**	
Jeroboam **d** not again recover	**2Ch 13:20**	
Asa **d** good and right in the	**2Ch 14:2**	6213a
disease he **d** not seek the LORD,	**2Ch 16:12**	
days and **d** not seek the Baals,	**2Ch 17:3**	
and **d** not act as Israel did.	**2Ch 17:4**	
and did not act as Israel **d**.	**2Ch 17:4**	4639
so that they **d** not make war	**2Ch 17:10**	
"**D** I not tell you that he would	**2Ch 18:17**	
"How **d** the Spirit of the LORD	**2Ch 18:23**	
"**D** You not, O our God, drive out	**2Ch 20:7**	
whom You **d** not let Israel invade	**2Ch 20:10**	
from them and **d** not destroy them),	**2Ch 20:10**	
Asa and **d** not depart from it,	**2Ch 20:32**	
just as the house of Ahab **d**	**2Ch 21:6**	6213a
d evil in the sight of the LORD.	**2Ch 21:6**	6213a
He **d** evil in the sight of the	**2Ch 22:4**	6213a
So the Levites and all Judah **d**	**2Ch 23:8**	6213a
for Jehoiada the priest **d** not	**2Ch 23:8**	
Joash **d** what was right in the	**2Ch 24:2**	6213a
But the Levites **d** not act quickly.	**2Ch 24:5**	
Thus they **d** daily and collected	**2Ch 24:11**	6213a
Jehoiada gave it to those who **d**	**2Ch 24:12**	6213a
Thus Joash the king **d** not remember	**2Ch 24:22**	
but they **d** not bury him in the	**2Ch 24:25**	
He **d** right in the sight of the	**2Ch 25:2**	6213a
he **d** not put their children to	**2Ch 25:4**	
but **d** as it is written in the law	**2Ch 25:4**	
He **d** right in the sight of the	**2Ch 26:4**	6213a
He **d** right in the sight of the	**2Ch 27:2**	6213a
however he **d** not enter the temple	**2Ch 27:2**	
and he **d** not do right in the sight	**2Ch 28:1**	
it **d** not help him.	**2Ch 28:21**	
for they **d** not bring him into the	**2Ch 28:27**	
He **d** right in the sight of the	**2Ch 29:2**	6213a
Hezekiah **d** throughout all Judah;	**2Ch 31:20**	6213a
and he **d** what *was* good, right and	**2Ch 31:20**	6213a
he **d** with all his heart and	**2Ch 31:21**	6213a
so that the wrath of the LORD **d**	**2Ch 32:26**	
prospered in all that he **d**.	**2Ch 32:30**	4639
He **d** evil in the sight of the	**2Ch 33:2**	6213a
He **d** much evil in the sight of the	**2Ch 33:6**	6213a
He **d** evil in the sight of the	**2Ch 33:22**	6213a
he **d** not humble himself before the	**2Ch 33:23**	
He **d** right in the sight of the	**2Ch 34:2**	6213a
his father David and **d** not turn aside	**2Ch 34:2**	
The men **d** the work faithfully	**2Ch 34:12**	6213a
Jerusalem **d** according to the covenant	**2Ch 34:32**	6213a
Throughout his lifetime they **d** not	**2Ch 34:33**	
They **d** this also with the bulls.	**2Ch 35:12**	
gatekeepers at each gate **d** not have to	**2Ch 35:15**	
as Josiah **d** with the priests,	**2Ch 35:18**	6213a
nor **d** he listen to the words of	**2Ch 35:22**	
and he **d** evil in the sight of the	**2Ch 36:5**	6213a
and the abominations which he **d**,	**2Ch 36:8**	6213a
d evil in the sight of the LORD.	**2Ch 36:9**	6213a
He **d** evil in the sight of the	**2Ch 36:12**	6213a
he **d** not humble himself before	**2Ch 36:12**	
and they **d** not stop them until a	**Ezr 5:5**	
I **d** not find any Levites there.	**Ezr 8:15**	
he went there, he **d** not eat bread nor	**Ezr 10:6**	
But the exiles **d** so.	**Ezr 10:16**	6213a
I **d** not tell anyone what my God	**Ne 2:12**	
The officials **d** not know where	**Ne 2:16**	
or the rest who **d** the work.	**Ne 2:16**	6213a
but their nobles **d** not support the	**Ne 3:5**	
d according to this promise.	**Ne 5:13**	6213a
But I **d** not do so because of the	**Ne 5:15**	
we **d** not buy any land, and all my	**Ne 5:16**	
Yet for all this I **d** not demand	**Ne 5:18**	
And **d** not remember Your wondrous	**Ne 9:17**	
And You **d** not forsake them.	**Ne 9:17**	
D not forsake them in the	**Ne 9:19**	
of cloud **d** not leave them by day,	**Ne 9:19**	

d not withhold from their mouth, Ne 9:20
Their clothes **d** not wear out, nor Ne 9:21
wear out, nor **d** their feet swell. Ne 9:21
they **d** evil again before You; Ne 9:28 6213a
Yet they acted arrogantly and **d** Ne 9:29
in Your great compassion You **d** not Ne 9:31
D not serve You or turn from Ne 9:35
So **d** I and half of the officials Ne 12:40
because they **d** not meet the sons Ne 13:2
"**D** not your fathers do the same Ne 13:18
on they **d** not come on the sabbath. Ne 13:21
"**D** not Solomon king of Israel sin Ne 13:26
because she **d** not obey the command Es 1:15
his presence, but she **d** not come.' Es 1:17
the king **d** as Memucan proposed. Es 1:21 6213a
the king, and he **d** accordingly. Es 2:4 6213a
Esther **d** not make known her people Es 2:10
she **d** not request anything except Es 2:15
for Esther **d** what Mordecai told Es 2:20 6213a
him, but he **d** not accept *them.* Es 4:4
So Mordecai went away and **d** just Es 4:17 6213a
and that he **d** not stand up or Es 5:9
and they **d** what they pleased to Es 9:5 6213a
but they **d** not lay their hands on Es 9:10
but they **d** not lay their hands on Es 9:15
but they **d** not lay their hands on Es 9:16
Thus Job **d** continually. Jb 1:5 6213a
d not sin nor did he blame God. Jb 1:22
did not sin nor **d** he blame God. Jb 1:22
this Job **d** not sin with his lips. Jb 2:10
distance and **d** not recognize him, Jb 2:12
Because it **d** not shut the opening Jb 3:10
"Why **d** I not die at birth, Come Jb 3:11
"Why **d** the knees receive me, And Jb 3:12
'**D** You not pour me out like milk And Jb 10:10
the case which I **d** not know. Jb 29:16
my words they **d** not speak again, Jb 29:22
on them when they **d** not believe, Jb 29:24
of my face they **d** not cast down. Jb 29:24
"**D** not He who made me in the womb Jb 31:15
silent and **d** not go out of doors? Jb 31:34
that which I **d** not understand, Jb 42:3
for me, which I **d** not know." Jb 42:3
went and **d** as the LORD told them; Jb 42:9 6213a
And I **d** not put away His statutes Ps 18:22
And I **d** not turn back until they Ps 18:37
LORD, but He **d** not answer them. Ps 18:41
And my iniquity I **d** not hide; Ps 32:5
The smiters whom I **d** not know Ps 35:15
work that You **d** in their days, Ps 44:1 6466
sword they **d** not possess the land, Ps 44:3
And their own arm **d** not save them, Ps 44:3
What I **d** not steal, I then have to Ps 69:4
that **d** not prepare its heart And Ps 78:8
d not keep the covenant of God And Ps 78:10
Because they **d** not believe in God And Ps 78:22
And **d** not trust in His salvation. Ps 78:22
Man **d** eat the bread of angels; Ps 78:25
And **d** not believe in His wonderful Ps 78:32
iniquity and **d** not destroy *them;* Ps 78:38
And **d** not arouse all His wrath. Ps 78:38
They **d** not remember His power, The Ps 78:42
He **d** not spare their soul from Ps 78:50
safely, so that they **d** not fear; Ps 78:53
And **d** not keep His testimonies, Ps 78:56
And **d** not choose the tribe of Ps 78:67
a language that I **d** not know: Ps 81:5
people **d** not listen to My voice, Ps 81:11
And Israel **d** not obey Me. Ps 81:11
And all who **d** iniquity flourished, Ps 92:7 6466
d not rebel against His words. Ps 105:28
d not understand Your wonders; Ps 106:7
They **d** not remember Your abundant Ps 106:7
They **d** not wait for His counsel, Ps 106:13
They **d** not believe in His word, Ps 106:24
They **d** not listen to the voice of Ps 106:25
They **d** not destroy the peoples, As Ps 106:34
They **d** not find a way to an Ps 107:4
Because he **d** not remember to show Ps 109:16
And he **d** not delight in blessing, Ps 109:17
I hastened and **d** not delay To keep Ps 119:60
me, I **d** not forsake Your precepts. Ps 119:87
And **d** not want my reproof; Pr 1:25
And **d** not choose the fear of the Pr 1:29
struck me, *but* I **d** not become ill; Pr 23:35
They beat me, *but* I **d** not know *it.* Pr 23:35
"See, we **d** not know this," Pr 24:12
eyes desired I **d** not refuse them. Ec 2:10
I **d** not withhold my heart from any Ec 2:10
in the city where they **d** thus. Ec 8:10 6213a
I sought him but **d** not find him. SS 3:1
I sought him but **d** not find him. SS 3:2
for him but I **d** not find him; SS 5:6
him but he **d** not answer me. SS 5:6
d it produce worthless ones? Is 5:4
my hand and by my wisdom I **d** *this,* Is 10:13 6213a
the way Egypt **d**. Is 10:24
and He will lift it up the way *He* **d** Is 10:26
Who **d** not allow his prisoners to Is 14:17
And he **d** so, going naked and Is 20:2 6213a
sword, Nor **d** they die in battle. Is 22:2
d not depend on Him who made it, Is 22:11
Nor **d** you take into consideration Is 22:11
"He **d** not make me"; Is 29:16
while *others* **d** not deal Is 33:1
'**D** the gods of those nations which Is 37:12
Long ago I **d** it, From ancient Is 37:26 6213a
that Hezekiah **d** not show them. Is 39:2
"What **d** these men say, and from Is 39:3

With whom **d** He consult and *who* Is 40:14
And whose law they **d** not obey? Is 42:24
around, Yet he **d** not recognize *it;* Is 42:25
and **d** not create it a waste place, Is 45:18
I **d** not say to the offspring of Is 45:19
You **d** not show mercy to them, On Is 47:6
These things you **d** not consider Nor Is 47:7
They **d** not thirst when He led Is 48:21
From where **d** these come?' " Is 49:21
whom of My creditors **d** I sell you? Is 50:1
disobedient Nor **d** I turn back. Is 50:5
I **d** not cover My face from Is 50:6
despised, and we **d** not esteem Him. Is 53:3
Yet He **d** not open His mouth; Is 53:7
So He **d** not open His mouth. Is 53:7
of your road, *Yet* you **d** not say, Is 57:10
Therefore you **d** not faint. Is 57:10
you lied, and **d** not remember Me Nor Is 57:11
wilderness, they **d** not stumble; Is 63:13
When You **d** awesome things which Is 64:3 6213a
things which we **d** not expect, Is 64:3
by those who **d** not ask *for Me;* Is 65:1
found by those who **d** not seek Me. Is 65:1
which **d** not call on My name. Is 65:1
I called, but you **d** not answer; Is 65:12
I spoke, but you **d** not hear. Is 65:12
And you **d** evil in My sight And Is 65:12 6213a
that in which I **d** not delight." Is 65:12
I spoke, but they **d** not listen. Is 66:4
And they **d** evil in My sight And Is 66:4 6213a
that in which I **d** not delight." Is 66:4
d your fathers find in Me, Jer 2:5
"They **d** not say, Jer 2:6
"The priests **d** not say, Jer 2:8
who handle the law **d** not know Me; Jer 2:8
after things that **d** not profit. Jer 2:8
You **d** not find them breaking in. Jer 2:34
you seen what faithless Israel **d**? Jer 3:6 6213a
but she **d** not return, and her Jer 3:7
sister Judah **d** not fear; Jer 3:8
sister Judah **d** not return to Me Jer 3:10
them, *But* they **d** not weaken; Jer 5:3
They **d** not even know how to blush. Jer 6:15
and see what I **d** to it because of Jer 7:12 6213a
and speaking, but you **d** not hear, Jer 7:13
I called you but you **d** not answer, Jer 7:13
your fathers, as I **d** to Shiloh. Jer 7:14 6213a
"For I **d** not speak to your Jer 7:22
d not obey or incline their ear, Jer 7:24
"Yet they **d** not listen to Me or Jer 7:26
d more evil than their fathers. Jer 7:26
'This is the nation that **d** not Jer 7:28
the fire, which I **d** not command, Jer 7:31
and it **d** not come into My mind. Jer 7:31
And they **d** not know how to blush; Jer 8:12
"The gods that **d** not make the Jer 10:11
d not obey or incline their ear, Jer 11:8 6213a
them to do, but they **d** not.' " Jer 11:8 6213a
And I **d** not know that they had Jer 11:19
but they **d** not listen.' Jer 13:11
Judah, for what he **d** in Jerusalem. Jer 15:4 6213a
They **d** not repent of their ways. Jer 15:7
I **d** not sit in the circle of Jer 15:17
of merrymakers, Nor **d** I exult. Jer 15:17
"Yet they **d** not listen or incline Jer 17:23
of, nor **d** it *ever* enter My mind; Jer 19:5
he **d** not kill me before birth, Jer 20:17
Why **d** I ever come forth from the Jer 20:18
D not your father eat and drink And Jer 22:15
"I **d** not send *these* prophets, But Jer 23:21
I **d** not speak to them, But they Jer 23:21
I **d** not send them or command them, Jer 23:32
"**D** Hezekiah king of Judah and all Jer 26:19
D he not fear the LORD and entreat Jer 26:19
king of Babylon **d** not take when he Jer 27:20
who **d** not go with you into exile Jer 29:16
but you **d** not listen,' declares Jer 29:19
which I **d** not command them; Jer 29:23
to you, although I **d** not send him, Jer 29:31
but they **d** not obey Your voice or Jer 32:23
your forefathers **d** not obey Me or Jer 34:14
to them but they **d** not listen, Jer 35:17
them but they **d** not answer.' " Jer 35:17
Baruch the son of Neriah **d** Jer 36:8 6213a
how **d** you write all these words? Jer 36:17
nor **d** they rend their garments. Jer 36:24
but they **d** not listen. Jer 36:31
and Jeremiah **d** so. Jer 38:12 6213a
and **d** not listen to His voice, Jer 40:3
son of Ahikam **d** not believe them. Jer 40:14
So he refrained and **d** not put them Jer 41:8
d not obey the voice of the LORD to Jer 43:4
they **d** not obey the voice of the LORD Jer 43:7
'But they **d** not listen or incline Jer 44:5
our kings and our princes **d** in the Jer 44:17 6213a
d not the LORD remember them and Jer 44:21
and **d** not *all this* come into His Jer 44:21
They **d** not stand *their ground.* Jer 46:21
He **d** evil in the sight of the Jer 52:2 6213a
She **d** not consider her future. La 1:9
kings of the earth **d** not believe, La 4:12
Nor **d** any of the inhabitants of La 4:12
They **d** not honor the priests, They La 4:16
They **d** not favor the elders. La 4:16
faces **d** not turn when they moved, Ezk 1:9
I **d** so, as I had been Ezk 12:7 6213a
nor **d** you build the wall around Ezk 13:5
"**D** you not see a false vision and Ezk 13:7
when I **d** not cause him grief, Ezk 13:22

done in vain whatever I **d** to it," Ezk 14:23 6213a
you **d** not remember the days of your Ezk 16:22
she **d** not help the poor and needy. Ezk 16:49
d not commit half of your sins, Ezk 16:51
yet **d** all these things; Ezk 17:18 6213a
d not do any of these things), Ezk 18:11
and **d** what was not good among his Ezk 18:18 6213a
they **d** not cast away the Ezk 20:8
nor **d** they forsake the idols of Ezk 20:8
They **d** not walk in My statutes and Ezk 20:13
statutes, they **d** not walk in them; Ezk 20:16
and I **d** not cause their Ezk 20:17
they **d** not walk in My statutes, Ezk 20:21
"She **d** not forsake her Ezk 23:8
lo, thus they **d** within My house. Ezk 23:39 6213a
She **d** not pour it on the ground To Ezk 24:7
morning I **d** as I was commanded. Ezk 24:18 6213a
trumpet but **d** not take warning; Ezk 33:5
d not search for My flock, Ezk 34:8
and **d** not feed My flock; Ezk 34:8
who **d** not go astray when the sons Ezk 48:11
his face and **d** homage to Daniel, Da 2:46 5457
of the hand that **d** the writing. Da 5:5
"**D** you not sign an injunction Da 6:12
but he **d** as he pleased and Da 8:4 6213a
I **d** not eat any tasty food, nor Da 10:3
nor **d** meat or wine enter my mouth, Da 10:3
nor **d** I use any ointment at all until Da 10:3
were with me **d** not see the vision; Da 10:7
what his fathers never **d**, Da 11:24 6213a
not turn out the way it **d** before. Da 11:29
a god whom his fathers **d** not know; Da 11:38
princes, but I **d** not know *it.* Hos 8:4
d not know that I healed them. Hos 11:3
through Baal he **d** wrong and died. Hos 13:1 816
And **d** not remember *the* covenant Am 1:9
"**D** you present Me with sacrifices Am 5:25
And He **d** not do *it.* Jon 3:10
plant for which you **d** not work and Jon 4:10
and *which* you **d** not cause to grow, Jon 4:10
D the LORD rage against the Hab 3:8
She **d** not trust in the LORD, Zph 3:2
She **d** not draw near to her God. Zph 3:2
yet you **d** not *come back* Hg 2:17
d not listen or give heed to Me," Zch 1:4
d not My words and My statutes, Zch 1:6
And what **d** *that* one *do* while he Mal 2:15
and **d** as the angel of the Lord Mt 1:24 *4160*
I **d** not come to abolish but to Mt 5:17
d we not prophesy in Your name, Mt 7:22
and *yet* it **d** not fall, for it had Mt 7:25
for I **d** not come to call the Mt 9:13
and *so* **d** His disciples. Mt 9:19
I **d** not come to bring peace, but a Mt 10:34
"What **d** you go out into the Mt 11:7
"But what **d** you go out to see? Mt 11:8
"But what **d** you go out Mt 11:9
for you, and you **d** not dance; Mt 11:17
a dirge, and you **d** not mourn.' Mt 11:17
done, because they **d** not repent. Mt 11:20
"Have you not read what David **d** when Mt 12:3 *4160*
where they **d** not have much soil; Mt 13:5
what you see, and **d** not see *it,* Mt 13:17
what you hear, and **d** not hear *it* Mt 13:17
d you not sow good seed in your Mt 13:27
and He **d** not speak to them without Mt 13:34
"Where **d** this man *get* this Mt 13:54
Where then **d** this man *get* all Mt 13:56
And He **d** not do many miracles Mt 13:58
little faith, why **d** you doubt?" Mt 14:31
rightly **d** Isaiah prophesy of you: Mt 15:7
d not plant shall be uprooted. Mt 15:13
But He **d** not answer her a word. Mt 15:23
"*He said that* because we **d** not Mt 16:7
d not speak to you concerning bread? Mt 16:11
Then they understood that He **d** not Mt 16:12
blood **d** not reveal *this* to you, Mt 16:17
and they **d** not recognize him, Mt 17:12
but **d** to him whatever they wished. Mt 17:12 *4160*
he **d** not have *the means* to repay, Mt 18:25
"Why then **d** Moses command Mt 19:7
ninth hour, and **d** the same thing. Mt 20:5 *4160*
d you not agree with me for a Mt 20:13
Son of Man **d** not come to be served, Mt 20:28
The disciples went and **d** just Mt 21:6 *4160*
d the fig tree wither *all* at once?" Mt 21:20
'Then why **d** you not believe him?' Mt 21:25
but he **d** not go. Mt 21:30
two **d** the will of his father?" Mt 21:31 *4160*
and you **d** not believe him; Mt 21:32
and prostitutes **d** believe him; Mt 21:32
d not even feel remorse afterward Mt 21:32
and they **d** the same thing to them. Mt 21:36 *4160*
"**D** you never read in the Mt 21:42
how **d** you come in here without Mt 22:12
nor **d** anyone dare from that day on Mt 22:46
and they **d** not understand until Mt 24:39
man, reaping where you **d** not sow and Mt 25:24
that I reap where I **d** not sow and Mt 25:26
'Lord, when **d** we see You hungry, Mt 25:37
'And when **d** we see You a stranger, Mt 25:38
'When **d** we see You sick, or in Mt 25:39
to the extent that you **d** it to one Mt 25:40 *4160*
least *of them,* you **d** it to Me.' Mt 25:40 *4160*
and you **d** not invite Me in; Mt 25:43
naked, and you **d** not clothe Me; Mt 25:43
prison, and you **d** not visit Me.' Mt 25:43
'Lord, when **d** we see You hungry, Mt 25:44
and **d** not take care of You?' Mt 25:44

Context	Reference	No.
to the extent that you **d** not do it	**Mt 25:45**	*4160*
of these, you **d** not do it to Me.'	**Mt 25:45**	*4160*
she **d** it to prepare Me for burial.	**Mt 26:12**	*4160*
d as Jesus had directed them;	**Mt 26:19**	*4160*
teaching and you **d** not seize Me.	**Mt 26:55**	
They **d** not find *any,* even	**Mt 26:60**	
priests and elders, He **d** not answer.	**Mt 27:12**	
And He **d** not answer him with	**Mt 27:14**	
and **d** as they had been instructed;	**Mt 28:15**	*4160*
I **d** not come to call the	**Mk 2:17**	
"Have you never read what David **d**	**Mk 2:25**	*4160*
where it **d** not have much soil;	**Mk 4:5**	
and He **d** not speak to them without	**Mk 4:34**	
And He **d** not let him, but He said	**Mk 5:19**	
"Where **d** this man *get* these	**Mk 6:2**	
they **d** not even have time to eat.)	**Mk 6:31**	
"Rightly **d** Isaiah prophesy of you	**Mk 7:6**	
and **d** not have more than one loaf	**Mk 8:14**	
of broken pieces **d** you pick up?"	**Mk 8:20**	
For he **d** not know what to answer;	**Mk 9:6**	
d to him whatever they wished,	**Mk 9:13**	*4160*
and He **d** not want anyone to know	**Mk 9:30**	
d not understand *this* statement,	**Mk 9:32**	
"What **d** Moses command you?"	**Mk 10:3**	
of Man **d** not come to be served,	**Mk 10:45**	
'Then why **d** you not believe him?'	**Mk 11:31**	
d not know what to answer Him.	**Mk 14:40**	
teaching, and you **d** not seize Me;	**Mk 14:49**	
But He kept silent and **d** not answer.	**Mk 14:61**	
but He **d** not take it.	**Mk 15:23**	
they **d** not believe them either.	**Mk 16:13**	
you **d** not believe my words,	**Lk 1:20**	
When they **d** not find Him, they	**Lk 2:45**	
D you not know that I had to be in	**Lk 2:49**	
But they **d** not understand the	**Lk 2:50**	
what David **d** when he was hungry,	**Lk 6:3**	*4160*
Stretch out your hand!" And he **d** *so*	**Lk 6:10**	*4160*
I **d** not even consider myself worthy	**Lk 7:7**	
"What **d** you go out into the	**Lk 7:24**	
"But what **d** you go out to see?	**Lk 7:25**	
"But what **d** you go out to see?	**Lk 7:26**	
for you, and you **d** not dance;	**Lk 7:32**	
sang a dirge, and you **d** not weep.'	**Lk 7:32**	
"You **d** not anoint My head with	**Lk 7:46**	
"Someone **d** touch Me, for I was	**Lk 8:46**	
He **d** not allow anyone to enter	**Lk 8:51**	
They **d** so, and had them all	**Lk 9:15**	*4160*
d not understand this statement,	**Lk 9:45**	
But they **d** not receive Him,	**Lk 9:53**	
for the Son of Man **d** not come to	**Lk 9:56**	
which you see, and **d** not see *them,*	**Lk 10:24**	
you hear, and **d** not hear *them.*"	**Lk 10:24**	
d not He who made the outside make	**Lk 11:40**	
you yourselves **d** not enter, and	**Lk 11:52**	
and **d** not get ready or act in accord	**Lk 12:47**	
but the one who **d** not know *it,* and	**Lk 12:48**	
fruit on it and **d** not find any.	**Lk 13:6**	
d the things which were commanded,	**Lk 17:9**	*4160*
was a judge who **d** not fear God	**Lk 18:2**	
fear God and **d** not respect man.	**Lk 18:2**	
and they **d** not comprehend the	**Lk 18:34**	
take up what you **d** not lay down and	**Lk 19:21**	
and reap what you **d** not sow.'	**Lk 19:21**	
D you know that I am an exacting	**Lk 19:22**	
taking up what I **d** not lay down and	**Lk 19:22**	
and reaping what I **d** not sow?	**Lk 19:22**	
'Then why **d** you not put my money	**Lk 19:23**	
who **d** not want me to reign over	**Lk 19:27**	
because you **d** not recognize the	**Lk 19:44**	
'Why **d** you not believe him?'	**Lk 20:5**	
d not know where *it came* from.	**Lk 20:7**	
For they **d** not have courage to	**Lk 20:40**	
sandals, you **d** not lack anything,	**Lk 22:35**	
did not lack anything, **d** you?"	**Lk 22:35**	
temple, you **d** not lay hands on Me;	**Lk 22:53**	
they **d** not find the body of the	**Lk 24:3**	
and **d** not find His body, they	**Lk 24:23**	
but Him they **d** not see."	**Lk 24:24**	
the darkness **d** not comprehend it.	**Jn 1:5**	
Him, and the world **d** not know Him.	**Jn 1:10**	
were His own **d** not receive Him.	**Jn 1:11**	
And he confessed and **d** not deny,	**Jn 1:20**	
"I **d** not recognize Him, but	**Jn 1:31**	
"I **d** not recognize Him, but	**Jn 1:33**	
and **d** not know where it came from	**Jn 2:9**	
signs Jesus **d** in Cana of Galilee,	**Jn 2:11**	*4160*
and because He **d** not need anyone	**Jn 2:25**	
"For God **d** not send the Son into	**Jn 3:17**	
Him *anything* to eat, **d** he?"	**Jn 4:33**	
He **d** in Jerusalem at the feast;	**Jn 4:45**	*4160*
was healed **d** not know who it was,	**Jn 5:13**	
those who **d** the good *deeds* to a	**Jn 5:29**	*4160*
"Rabbi, when **d** You get here?"	**Jn 6:25**	
who they were who **d** not believe,	**Jn 6:64**	
"**D** I Myself not choose you, the	**Jn 6:70**	
"**D** not Moses give you the Law,	**Jn 7:19**	
"I **d** one deed, and you all marvel.	**Jn 7:21**	*4160*
"Why **d** you not bring Him?"	**Jn 7:45**	
D no one condemn you?"	**Jn 8:10**	
They **d** not realize that He had	**Jn 8:27**	
this Abraham **d** not do.	**Jn 8:40**	
then **d** not believe *it* of him,	**Jn 9:18**	
"What **d** He do to you?	**Jn 9:26**	
How **d** He open your eyes?"	**Jn 9:26**	
you already and you **d** not listen;	**Jn 9:27**	
but they **d** not understand what	**Jn 10:6**	
but the sheep **d** not hear them.	**Jn 10:8**	
"**D** I not say to you that if you	**Jn 11:40**	
d not say this on his own initiative	**Jn 11:51**	
d not understand at the first;	**Jn 12:16**	
I **d** not come to judge the world,	**Jn 12:47**	
"For I **d** not speak on My own	**Jn 12:49**	
you also should do as I **d** to you.	**Jn 13:15**	*4160*
"You **d** not choose Me but I chose	**Jn 15:16**	
the works which no one else **d**,	**Jn 15:24**	*4160*
These things I **d** not say to	**Jn 16:4**	
"**D** I not see you in the garden	**Jn 18:26**	
and they themselves **d** not enter	**Jn 18:28**	
or **d** others tell you about Me?"	**Jn 18:34**	
the soldiers **d** these things.	**Jn 19:25**	*4160*
dead, they **d** not break His legs.	**Jn 19:33**	
but he **d** not go in.	**Jn 20:5**	
d not understand the Scripture,	**Jn 20:9**	
and **d** not know that it was Jesus.	**Jn 20:14**	
Blessed *are* they who **d** not see,	**Jn 20:29**	
d not know that it was Jesus.	**Jn 21:4**	
yet Jesus **d** not say to him that he	**Jn 21:23**	
many other things which Jesus **d**,	**Jn 21:25**	*4160*
NOR **D** HIS FLESH SUFFER DECAY.	**Ac 2:31**	
just as your rulers **d** also.	**Ac 3:17**	
'WHY **D** THE GENTILES RAGE,	**Ac 4:25**	
unsold, **d** it not remain your own?	**Ac 5:4**	
d not find them in the prison;	**Ac 5:22**	
but they **d** not understand.	**Ac 7:25**	
are doing just as your fathers **d**.	**Ac 7:51**	
d your fathers not persecute?	**Ac 7:52**	
angels, and *yet* **d** not keep it."	**Ac 7:53**	
he **d** to Your saints at Jerusalem;	**Ac 9:13**	*4160*
charity which she continually **d**.	**Ac 9:36**	*4160*
are witnesses of all the things He **d**	**Ac 10:39**	*4160*
the Holy Spirit just as we **d**,	**Ac 10:47**	
Spirit fell upon them just as *He* **d**	**Ac 11:15**	
And this they **d**, sending it in	**Ac 11:30**	*4160*
put on your sandals." And he **d** so.	**Ac 12:8**	*4160*
and he **d** not know that what was	**Ac 12:9**	
her joy she **d** not open the gate,	**Ac 12:14**	
he **d** not give God the glory,	**Ac 12:23**	
God raised **d** not undergo decay.	**Ac 13:37**	
and yet He **d** not leave Himself	**Ac 14:17**	
in that He **d** good and gave you	**Ac 14:17**	*19a*
Spirit, just as He also **d** to us;	**Ac 15:8**	
Spirit of Jesus **d** not permit them;	**Ac 16:7**	
When they **d** not find them,	**Ac 17:6**	
a longer time, he **d** not consent,	**Ac 18:20**	
"**D** you receive the Holy Spirit	**Ac 19:2**	
and the majority **d** not know for	**Ac 19:32**	
how I **d** not shrink from declaring	**Ac 20:20**	
"For I **d** not shrink from	**Ac 20:27**	
I **d** not cease to admonish each one	**Ac 20:31**	
but **d** not understand the voice of	**Ac 22:9**	
nor in the city *itself* **d** they find	**Ac 24:12**	
I **d** not delay, but on the next day	**Ac 25:17**	
is just what I **d** in Jerusalem;	**Ac 26:10**	*4160*
not only **d** I lock up many of the	**Ac 26:10**	
I **d** not prove disobedient to the	**Ac 26:19**	
d not permit us *to go* farther,	**Ac 27:7**	
but they **d** observe a bay	**Ac 27:39**	
they **d** not agree with one another,	**Ac 28:25**	
God, they **d** not honor Him as God or	**Ro 1:21**	
And just as they **d** not see fit to	**Ro 1:28**	
If some **d** not believe, their	**Ro 3:3**	
God, he **d** not waver in unbelief but	**Ro 4:20**	
much more **d** the grace of God and	**Ro 5:15**	
Therefore **d** that which is good	**Ro 7:13**	
God **d**: sending His own Son in	**Ro 8:3**	
He who **d** not spare His own Son,	**Ro 8:32**	
"Why **d** you make me like this,"	**Ro 9:20**	
And *He* **d** *so* to make known	**Ro 9:23**	
who **d** not pursue righteousness,	**Ro 9:30**	
d not arrive at *that* law.	**Ro 9:31**	
Why? Because *they* **d** not *pursue*	**Ro 9:32**	
they **d** not subject themselves to	**Ro 10:3**	
d not all heed the good news;	**Ro 10:16**	
I say, surely Israel **d** not know,	**Ro 10:19**	
Israel did not know, **d** they?	**Ro 10:19**	
"I WAS FOUND BY THOSE WHO **D** NOT	**Ro 10:20**	
TO THOSE WHO **D** NOT ASK FOR ME."	**Ro 10:20**	
they **d** not stumble so as to fall,	**Ro 11:11**	
not stumble so as to fall, **d** they?	**Ro 11:11**	
for if God **d** not spare the natural	**Ro 11:21**	
even Christ **d** not please Himself;	**Ro 15:3**	
Now I **d** baptize also the household	**1Co 1:16**	
Christ **d** not send me to baptize,	**1Co 1:17**	
its wisdom **d** not *come to* know God,	**1Co 1:21**	
I **d** not come with superiority of	**1Co 2:1**	
you have that you **d** not receive?	**1Co 4:7**	
And if you **d** receive it, why do	**1Co 4:7**	
I **d** not at all *mean* with	**1Co 5:10**	
weep, as though they **d** not weep;	**1Co 7:30**	
as though they **d** not rejoice;	**1Co 7:30**	
buy, as though they **d** not possess;	**1Co 7:30**	
they **d** not make full use of it;	**1Co 7:31**	
we **d** not use this right,	**1Co 9:12**	
act immorally, as some of them **d**,	**1Co 10:8**	*4203*
try the Lord, as some of them **d**,	**1Co 10:9**	*3985*
Nor grumble, as some of them **d**,	**1Co 10:10**	*1111*
I **d** away with childish things.	**1Co 13:11**	*2673*
grace toward me **d** not prove vain;	**1Co 15:10**	
Christ, whom He **d** not raise,	**1Co 15:15**	
as you also partially **d** understand us,	**2Co 1:14**	
that to spare you I **d** not come again	**2Co 1:23**	
I **d** *it* for your sakes in	**2Co 2:10**	
I do not regret it; though I **d** regret it	**2Co 7:8**	
WHO *gathered* MUCH **D** NOT HAVE	**2Co 8:15**	
as if we **d** not reach to you,	**2Co 10:14**	
Or **d** I commit a sin in humbling	**2Co 11:7**	
d not become a burden to you?	**2Co 12:13**	
it may, I **d** not burden you myself;	**2Co 12:16**	
d not take any advantage of you,	**2Co 12:18**	
take any advantage of you, **d** he?	**2Co 12:18**	
D we not conduct ourselves in the	**2Co 12:18**	
I **d** not immediately consult with	**Ga 1:16**	
nor **d** I go up to Jerusalem to	**Ga 1:17**	
But I **d** not see any other of the	**Ga 1:19**	
but *I* **d** *so* in private to those	**Ga 2:2**	
But we **d** not yield in subjection	**Ga 2:5**	
d you receive the Spirit by the	**Ga 3:2**	
D you suffer so many things in	**Ga 3:4**	
time, when you **d** not know God,	**Ga 4:8**	
you **d** not despise or loathe,	**Ga 4:14**	
This persuasion **d** not *come*	**Ga 5:8**	
d not learn Christ in this way,	**Eph 4:20**	
d not regard equality with God a	**Php 2:6**	
I **d** not run in vain nor toil in vain.	**Php 2:16**	
d not come to you in word only,	**1Th 1:5**	
nor **d** we seek glory from men,	**1Th 2:6**	
even as they **d** from the Jews,	**1Th 2:14**	
because they **d** not receive the	**2Th 2:10**	
who **d** not believe the truth,	**2Th 2:12**	
just as *it* **d** also with you;	**2Th 3:1**	
because we **d** not act in an	**2Th 3:7**	
nor **d** we eat anyone's bread	**2Th 3:8**	
the way my forefathers **d**,	**2Tm 1:3**	
the coppersmith **d** me much harm;	**2Tm 4:14**	*1731*
I **d** not want to do anything,	**Phm 1:14**	
which of the angels **d** He ever say,	**Heb 1:5**	
For He **d** not subject to angels the	**Heb 2:5**	
AND THEY **D** NOT KNOW MY WAYS';	**Heb 3:10**	
d not all those who came out of	**Heb 3:16**	
And to whom **d** He swear that they	**Heb 3:18**	
word they heard **d** not profit them,	**Heb 4:2**	
from his works, as God **d** from His.	**Heb 4:10**	
So also Christ **d** not glorify	**Heb 5:5**	
because this He **d** once for all	**Heb 7:27**	*4160*
D NOT CONTINUE IN MY COVENANT,	**Heb 8:9**	
AND I **D** NOT CARE FOR THEM,	**Heb 8:9**	
For Christ **d** not enter a holy	**Heb 9:24**	
By faith Rahab the harlot **d** not	**Heb 11:31**	
d not receive what was promised,	**Heb 11:39**	
For if those **d** not escape when	**Heb 12:25**	
d not God choose the poor of this	**Jas 2:5**	
and the outcry of those who **d** the	**Jas 5:4**	*2325*
and it **d** not rain on the earth for	**Jas 5:17**	
He **d** not revile in return;	**1Pe 2:23**	
For we **d** not follow cleverly	**2Pe 1:16**	
For if God **d** not spare angels when	**2Pe 2:4**	
and **d** not spare the ancient world,	**2Pe 2:5**	
us, because it **d** not know Him.	**1Jn 3:1**	
And for what reason **d** he slay him?	**1Jn 3:12**	
destroyed those who **d** not believe.	**Jude 1:5**	
who **d** not keep their own domain,	**Jude 1:6**	
d not dare pronounce against him a	**Jude 1:9**	
and do the deeds you **d** at first;	**Rv 2:5**	
My name, and **d** not deny My faith even	**Rv 2:13**	
d not repent of the works of their	**Rv 9:20**	
and they **d** not repent of their	**Rv 9:21**	
and they **d** not love their life	**Rv 12:11**	
and they **d** not repent so as to	**Rv 16:9**	
they **d** not repent of their deeds.	**Rv 16:11**	
rest of the dead **d** not come to life	**Rv 20:5**	
DIDYMUS		
Thomas, who is called **D**,	**Jn 11:16**	*1324*
one of the twelve, called **D**,	**Jn 20:24**	*1324*
Simon Peter, and Thomas called **D**,	**Jn 21:2**	*1324*
DIE		
eat from it you will surely **d**."	**Gn 2:17**	4191
it or touch it, or you will **d**.' "	**Gn 3:3**	4191
"You surely will not **d**!	**Gn 3:4**	4191
disaster will overtake me and I will **d**;	**Gn 19:19**	4191
her, know that you shall surely **d**,	**Gn 20:7**	4191
"Do not let me see the boy **d**."	**Gn 21:16**	4194
"Behold, I am about to **d**;	**Gn 25:32**	4191
'I might **d** on account of her.' "	**Gn 26:9**	4191
soul may bless you before I **d**."	**Gn 27:4**	4191
"Give me children, or else I **d**."	**Gn 30:1**	4191
one day, all the flocks will **d**.	**Gn 33:13**	4191
he too may **d** like his brothers."	**Gn 38:11**	4191
so that we may live and not **d**."	**Gn 42:2**	4191
be verified, and you will not **d**."	**Gn 42:20**	4191
go, that we may live and not **d**,	**Gn 43:8**	4191
servants it is found, let him **d**,	**Gn 44:9**	4191
his father, his father would **d**.'	**Gn 44:22**	4191
is not *with us,* he will **d**.	**Gn 44:31**	4191
will go and see him before I **d**."	**Gn 45:28**	4191
"Now let me **d**, since I have seen	**Gn 46:30**	4191
why should we **d** in your presence?	**Gn 47:15**	4191
"Why should we **d** before your	**Gn 47:19**	4191
seed, that we may live and not **d**,	**Gn 47:19**	4191
time for Israel to **d** drew near,	**Gn 47:29**	4191
"Behold, I am about to **d**,	**Gn 48:21**	4191
"Behold, I am about to **d**;	**Gn 50:5**	4191
"I am about to **d**, but God will	**Gn 50:24**	4191
fish that are in the Nile will **d**,	**Ex 7:18**	4191
so that nothing will **d** of all that	**Ex 9:4**	4191
comes down on them, will **d**.	**Ex 9:19**	4191
day you see my face you shall **d**!"	**Ex 10:28**	4191
in the land of Egypt shall **d**,	**Ex 11:5**	4191
us away to **d** in the wilderness?	**Ex 14:11**	4191
than to **d** in the wilderness."	**Ex 14:12**	4191
not God speak to us, or we will **d**."	**Ex 20:19**	4191
even from My altar, that he may **d**.	**Ex 21:14**	4191
he does not **d** but remains in bed,	**Ex 21:18**	4191
the LORD, so that he will not **d**.	**Ex 28:35**	4191
they do not incur guilt and **d**.	**Ex 28:43**	4191
with water, so that they will not **d**;	**Ex 30:20**	4191
their feet, so that they will not **d**;	**Ex 30:21**	4191

of the LORD, so that you will not **d**,	**Lv 8:35**	4191
clothes, so that you will not **d**	**Lv 10:6**	4191
the tent of meeting, or you will **d**;	**Lv 10:7**	4191
so that you will not **d**	**Lv 10:9**	4191
they will not **d** in their uncleanness	**Lv 15:31**	4191
which is on the ark, or he will **d**;	**Lv 16:2**	4191
the testimony, otherwise he will **d**.	**Lv 16:13**	4191
They will **d** childless.	**Lv 20:20**	4191
and **d** thereby because they profane	**Lv 22:9**	4191
not touch the holy *objects* and **d**.	**Nu 4:15**	4191
live and not **d** when they approach	**Nu 4:19**	4191
even for a moment, or they will **d**."	**Nu 4:20**	4191
or for his sister, when they **d**,	**Nu 6:7**	4194
and there they will **d**.' "	**Nu 14:35**	4191
to have us **d** in the wilderness,	**Nu 16:13**	4191
these men **d** the death of all men or	**Nu 16:29**	4191
Me, so that they will not **d**."	**Nu 17:10**	4191
tabernacle of the LORD, must **d**.	**Nu 17:13**	4191
altar, or both they and you will **d**.	**Nu 18:3**	4191
again, or they will bear sin and **d**.	**Nu 18:22**	4191
sons of Israel, or you will **d**.' "	**Nu 18:32**	4191
for us and our beasts to **d** here?	**Nu 20:4**	4191
to his people, and will **d** there."	**Nu 20:26**	4191
of Egypt to **d** in the wilderness?	**Nu 21:5**	4191
Let me **d** the death of the upright,	**Nu 23:10**	4191
sons of Korah, however, did not **d**.	**Nu 26:11**	4191
surely **d** in the wilderness."	**Nu 26:65**	4191
so that the manslayer will not **d**	**Nu 35:12**	4191
in the hand, by which he will **d**,	**Nu 35:17**	4191
in the hand, by which he might **d**,	**Nu 35:18**	4191
"For I will **d** in this land, I	**Dt 4:22**	4191
'Now then why should we **d**?	**Dt 5:25**	4191
God any longer, then we will **d**.	**Dt 5:25**	4191
who is to **d** shall be put to death;	**Dt 17:6**	4191
to the judge, that man shall **d**;	**Dt 17:12**	4191
great fire anymore, or I will **d**.'	**Dt 18:16**	4191
other gods, that prophet shall **d**.'	**Dt 18:20**	4191
avenger of blood, that he may **d**.	**Dt 19:12**	4191
otherwise he might **d** in the battle and	**Dt 20:5**	4191
otherwise he might **d** in the battle and	**Dt 20:6**	4191
otherwise he might **d** in the battle and	**Dt 20:7**	4191
woman, then both of them shall **d**,	**Dt 22:22**	4191
the man who lies with her shall **d**.	**Dt 22:25**	4191
him, then that thief shall **d**;	**Dt 24:7**	4191
the time for you to **d** is near;	**Dt 31:14**	4191
"Then **d** on the mountain where you	**Dt 32:50**	4191
"May Reuben live and not **d**,	**Dt 33:6**	4191
and not **d** by the hand of the	**Jos 20:9**	4191
you shall not **d**."	**Jg 6:23**	4191
"Bring out your son, that he may **d**,	**Jg 6:30**	4191
"We will surely **d**, for we have	**Jg 13:22**	4191
and now shall I **d** of thirst and	**Jg 15:18**	4191
"Let me **d** with the Philistines!"	**Jg 16:30**	4191
"Where you **d**, I will die, and	**Ru 1:17**	4191
"Where you die, I will **d**,	**Ru 1:17**	4191
house will **d** in the prime of life.	**1Sa 2:33**	4191
the same day both of them will **d**.	**1Sa 2:34**	4191
And the men who did not **d** were	**1Sa 5:12**	4191
your God, so that we may not **d**,	**1Sa 12:19**	4191
my son, he shall surely **d**."	**1Sa 14:39**	4191
Here I am, I must **d**!"	**1Sa 14:43**	4191
more also, for you shall surely **d**,	**1Sa 14:44**	4191
"Must Jonathan **d**, who has brought	**1Sa 14:45**	4191
rescued Jonathan and he did not **d**.	**1Sa 14:45**	4191
"Far from it, you shall not **d**.	**1Sa 20:2**	4191
of the LORD, that I may not **d**?	**1Sa 20:14**	4191
him to me, for he must surely **d**."	**1Sa 20:31**	4194
"You shall surely **d**,	**1Sa 22:16**	4191
lives, *all* of you must surely **d**,	**1Sa 26:16**	4194
"Should Abner **d** as a fool dies?	**2Sa 3:33**	4191
he may be struck down and **d**."	**2Sa 11:15**	4191
who has done this deserves to **d**.	**2Sa 12:5**	4194
taken away your sin; you shall not **d**.	**2Sa 12:13**	4191
is born to you shall surely **d**."	**2Sa 12:14**	4191
"For we will surely **d** and are	**2Sa 14:14**	4191
about us; even if half of us **d**,	**2Sa 18:3**	4191
"You shall not **d**."	**2Sa 19:23**	4191
that I may **d** in my own city near	**2Sa 19:37**	4191
is found in him, he will **d**."	**1Ki 1:52**	4191
As David's time to **d** drew near,	**1Ki 2:1**	4191
own field, for you deserve to **d**;	**1Ki 2:26**	4194
"No, for I will **d** here."	**1Ki 2:30**	4191
certain that you shall surely **d**;	**1Ki 2:37**	4191
go anywhere, you shall surely **d**'?	**1Ki 2:42**	4191
"When I **d**, bury me in the grave	**1Ki 13:31**	4191
enter the city the child will **d**.	**1Ki 14:12**	4191
son, that we may eat it and **d**."	**1Ki 17:12**	4191
by causing her son to **d**?"	**1Ki 17:20**	4191
for himself that he might **d**,	**1Ki 19:4**	4191
up, but you shall surely **d**.' "	**2Ki 1:4**	4191
up, but shall surely **d**.	**2Ki 1:6**	4191
gone up, but shall surely **d**.' "	**2Ki 1:16**	4191
"Why do we sit here until we **d**?	**2Ki 7:3**	4191
in the city and we will **d** there;	**2Ki 7:4**	4191
and if we sit here, we **d** also.	**2Ki 7:4**	4191
if they kill us, we will but **d**."	**2Ki 7:4**	4191
me that he will certainly **d**."	**2Ki 8:10**	4191
the illness of which he was to **d**,	**2Ki 13:14**	4191
that you may live and not **d**."	**2Ki 18:32**	4191
for you shall **d** and not live."	**2Ki 20:1**	4191
over to **d** by hunger and by thirst,	**2Ch 32:11**	4191
Curse God and **d**!"	**Jb 2:9**	4191
"Why did I not **d** at birth, Come	**Jb 3:11**	4191
They **d**, yet without wisdom.'	**Jb 4:21**	4191
And with you wisdom will **d**!	**Jb 12:2**	4191
For then I would be silent and **d**.	**Jb 13:19**	1478
Till I **d** I will not put away my	**Jb 27:5**	1478
'I shall **d** in my nest, And I shall	**Jb 29:18**	1478
"In a moment they **d**,	**Jb 34:20**	4191

they will **d** without knowledge.	**Jb 36:12**	1478
"They **d** in youth, And their life	**Jb 36:14**	4191
"When will he **d**, and his name	**Ps 41:5**	4191
For he sees *that even* wise men **d**;	**Ps 49:10**	4191
those who are doomed to **d**.	**Ps 79:11**	8546
"Nevertheless you will **d** like men And	**Ps 82:7**	4191
and about to **d** from my youth on;	**Ps 88:15**	1478
blood And caused their fish to **d**.	**Ps 105:29**	4191
I will not **d**, but live, And tell	**Ps 118:17**	4191
He will **d** for lack of instruction,	**Pr 5:23**	4191
fools **d** for lack of understanding.	**Pr 10:21**	4191
He who hates reproof will **d**.	**Pr 15:10**	4191
is careless of conduct will **d**.	**Pr 19:16**	4191
him with the rod, he will not **d**.	**Pr 23:13**	4191
You, Do not refuse me before I **d**:	**Pr 30:7**	4191
the wise man and the fool alike **d**!	**Ec 2:16**	4191
to give birth and a time to **d**;	**Ec 3:2**	4191
as a man is born, thus will he **d**.	**Ec 5:16**	1980
Why should you **d** before your time?	**Ec 7:17**	4191
For the living know they will **d**;	**Ec 9:5**	4191
sword, Nor did they **d** in battle.	**Is 22:2**	4191
drink, for tomorrow we may **d**."	**Is 22:13**	4191
not be forgiven you Until you **d**,"	**Is 22:14**	4191
There you will **d** And there your	**Is 22:18**	4191
for you shall **d** and not live.' "	**Is 38:1**	4191
lack of water And **d** of thirst.	**Is 50:2**	4191
inhabitants will **d** in like manner;	**Is 51:6**	4191
and will not **d** in the dungeon,	**Is 51:14**	4191
For the youth will **d** at the age of	**Is 65:20**	4191
For their worm will not **d**	**Is 66:24**	4191
you will not **d** at our hand";	**Jer 11:21**	4191
The young men will **d** by the sword,	**Jer 11:22**	4191
and daughters will **d** by famine;	**Jer 11:22**	4191
"They will **d** of deadly diseases,	**Jer 16:4**	4191
men and small will **d** in this land;	**Jer 16:6**	4191
Babylon, and there you will **d** and	**Jer 20:6**	4191
they will **d** of a great pestilence.	**Jer 21:6**	4191
will **d** by the sword and by famine	**Jer 21:9**	4191
d and not see this land again.	**Jer 22:12**	4191
not born, and there you will **d**.	**Jer 22:26**	4191
seized him, saying, "You must **d**!	**Jer 26:8**	4191
"Why will you **d**, you and your	**Jer 27:13**	4191
This year you are going to **d**,	**Jer 28:16**	4191
will **d** for his own iniquity;	**Jer 31:30**	4191
'You will not **d** by the sword.	**Jer 34:4**	4191
'You will **d** in peace;	**Jer 34:5**	4191
scribe, that I may not **d** there."	**Jer 37:20**	4191
'He who stays in this city will **d**	**Jer 38:2**	4191
and he will **d** right where he is	**Jer 38:9**	4191
these words and you will not **d**.	**Jer 38:24**	4191
house of Jonathan to **d** there.' "	**Jer 38:26**	4191
in Egypt, and you will **d** there.	**Jer 42:16**	4191
reside there will **d** by the sword,	**Jer 42:17**	4191
that you will **d** by the sword,	**Jer 42:22**	4191
will **d** by the sword and famine;	**Jer 44:12**	4191
'You will surely **d**,'	**Ezk 3:18**	4191
man shall **d** in his iniquity,	**Ezk 3:18**	4191
way, he shall **d** in his iniquity;	**Ezk 3:19**	4191
obstacle before him, he will **d**;	**Ezk 3:20**	4191
warned him, he shall **d** in his sin,	**Ezk 3:20**	4191
'One third of you will **d** by plague	**Ezk 5:12**	4191
is far off will **d** by the plague,	**Ezk 6:12**	4191
is besieged will **d** by the famine.	**Ezk 6:12**	4191
in the field will **d** by the sword;	**Ezk 7:15**	4191
see it, though he will **d** there.	**Ezk 12:13**	4191
put to death some who should not **d**	**Ezk 13:19**	4191
he broke, in Babylon he shall **d**.	**Ezk 17:16**	4191
The soul who sins will **d**.	**Ezk 18:4**	4191
not **d** for his father's iniquity,	**Ezk 18:17**	4191
he will **d** for his iniquity.	**Ezk 18:18**	4191
"The person who sins will **d**.	**Ezk 18:20**	4191
he shall surely live; he shall not **d**.	**Ezk 18:21**	4191
for them he will **d**.	**Ezk 18:24**	4191
which he has committed he will **d**.	**Ezk 18:26**	4191
he shall surely live; he shall not **d**.	**Ezk 18:28**	4191
For why will you **d**,	**Ezk 18:31**	4191
And you will **d** the death of those	**Ezk 28:8**	4191
'You will **d** the death of the	**Ezk 28:10**	4191
'O wicked man, you will surely **d**,'	**Ezk 33:8**	4191
man shall **d** in his iniquity,	**Ezk 33:8**	4191
way, he will **d** in his iniquity,	**Ezk 33:9**	4191
Why then will you **d**,	**Ezk 33:11**	4191
which he has committed he will **d**.	**Ezk 33:13**	4191
'You will surely **d**,' and he turns	**Ezk 33:14**	4191
he shall surely live; he shall not **d**.	**Ezk 33:15**	4191
iniquity, then he shall **d** in it.	**Ezk 33:18**	4191
in the caves will **d** of pestilence.	**Ezk 33:27**	4191
of their kings when they **d**,	**Ezk 43:7**	4194
And Moab will **d** amid tumult, With	**Am 2:2**	4191
left in one house, they will **d**.	**Am 6:9**	4191
'Jeroboam will **d** by the sword and	**Am 7:11**	4191
yourself will **d** upon unclean soil.	**Am 7:17**	4191
of My people will **d** by the sword,	**Am 9:10**	4191
and begged with *all* his soul to **d**,	**Jon 4:8**	4191
We will not **d**. You, O LORD, have	**Hab 1:12**	4191
What is to **d**, let it die, and what	**Zch 11:9**	4191
What is to die, let it **d**,	**Zch 11:9**	4191
"Even if I have to **d** with You,	**Mt 26:35**	*599*
where THEIR WORM DOES NOT **D**,	**Mk 9:44**	*5053*
where THEIR WORM DOES NOT **D**,	**Mk 9:46**	*5053*
where THEIR WORM DOES NOT **D**,	**Mk 9:48**	*5053*
"*Even* if I have to **d** with You,	**Mk 14:31**	*4880*
by him, was sick and about to **d**.	**Lk 7:2**	*5053*
for they cannot even **d** anymore,	**Lk 20:36**	*599*
that one may eat of it and not **d**.	**Jn 6:50**	*599*
seek Me, and will **d** in your sin;	**Jn 8:21**	*599*
that you will **d** in your sins;	**Jn 8:24**	*599*
am *He,* you will **d** in your sins."	**Jn 8:24**	*599*
also go, so that we may **d** with Him."	**Jn 11:16**	*599*

and believes in Me will never **d**.	**Jn 11:26**	*599*
one man **d** for the people,	**Jn 11:50**	*599*
was going to **d** for the nation,	**Jn 11:51**	*599*
of death by which He was to **d**.	**Jn 12:33**	*599*
man to **d** on behalf of the people.	**Jn 18:14**	*599*
kind of death He was about to **d**.	**Jn 18:32**	*599*
and by that law He ought to **d**	**Jn 19:7**	*599*
that that disciple would not **d**;	**Jn 21:23**	*599*
say to him that he would not **d**,	**Jn 21:23**	*599*
but even to **d** at Jerusalem for the	**Ac 21:13**	*599*
of death, I do not refuse to **d**;	**Ac 25:11**	*599*
will hardly **d** for a righteous man;	**Ro 5:7**	*599*
man someone would dare even to **d**.	**Ro 5:7**	*599*
the dead, is never to **d** again;	**Ro 6:9**	*599*
you also were made to **d** to the Law	**Ro 7:4**	*2289*
to the flesh, you must **d**;	**Ro 8:13**	*599*
we live for the Lord, or if we **d**,	**Ro 14:8**	*599*
or if we die, we **d** for the Lord;	**Ro 14:8**	*599*
therefore whether we live or **d**,	**Ro 14:8**	*599*
better for me to **d** than have any man	**1Co 9:15**	*599*
For as in Adam all **d**,	**1Co 15:22**	*599*
Christ Jesus our Lord, I **d** daily.	**1Co 15:31**	*599*
AND DRINK, FOR TOMORROW WE **D**.	**1Co 15:32**	*599*
d together and to live together.	**2Co 7:3**	*4880*
live is Christ and to **d** is gain.	**Php 1:21**	*599*
as it is appointed for men to **d** once	**Heb 9:27**	*599*
that we might **d** to sin and live to	**1Pe 2:24**	*581*
remain, which were about to **d**;	**Rv 3:2**	*599*
to **d**, and death flees from them.	**Rv 9:6**	*599*
who **d** in the Lord from now on!' "	**Rv 14:13**	*599*

DIED

and thirty years, and he **d**.	**Gn 5:5**	4191
and twelve years, and he **d**.	**Gn 5:8**	4191
hundred and five years, and he **d**.	**Gn 5:11**	4191
hundred and ten years, and he **d**.	**Gn 5:14**	4191
and ninety-five years, and he **d**.	**Gn 5:17**	4191
and sixty-two years, and he **d**.	**Gn 5:20**	4191
and sixty-nine years, and he **d**.	**Gn 5:27**	4191
and seventy-seven years, and he **d**.	**Gn 5:31**	4191
breath of the spirit of life, **d**.	**Gn 7:22**	4191
hundred and fifty years, and he **d**.	**Gn 9:29**	4191
Haran **d** in the presence of his	**Gn 11:28**	4191
and Terah **d** in Haran.	**Gn 11:32**	4191
Sarah **d** in Kiriath-arba	**Gn 23:2**	4191
his last and **d** in a ripe old age,	**Gn 25:8**	4191
and he breathed his last and **d**,	**Gn 25:17**	4191
Now Deborah, Rebekah's nurse, **d**,	**Gn 35:8**	4191
her soul was departing (for she **d**),	**Gn 35:18**	4191
So Rachel **d** and was buried on the	**Gn 35:19**	4191
Isaac breathed his last and **d** and	**Gn 35:29**	4191
Then Bela **d**, and Jobab the son of	**Gn 36:33**	4191
Then Jobab **d**, and Husham of the	**Gn 36:34**	4191
Then Husham **d**, and Hadad the son	**Gn 36:35**	4191
Then Hadad **d**, and Samlah of	**Gn 36:36**	4191
Then Samlah **d**, and Shaul of	**Gn 36:37**	4191
Then Shaul **d**, and Baal-hanan the	**Gn 36:38**	4191
Baal-hanan the son of Achbor **d**,	**Gn 36:39**	4191
daughter, the wife of Judah, **d**;	**Gn 38:12**	4191
and Onan **d** in the land of Canaan).	**Gn 46:12**	4191
when I came from Paddan, Rachel **d**,	**Gn 48:7**	4191
"Your father charged before he **d**,	**Gn 50:16**	4194
Joseph **d** at the age of one hundred	**Gn 50:26**	4191
Joseph **d**, and all his brothers	**Ex 1:6**	4191
days that the king of Egypt **d**;	**Ex 2:23**	4191
The fish that *were* in the Nile **d**,	**Ex 7:21**	4191
and the frogs **d** out of the houses,	**Ex 8:13**	4191
and all the livestock of Egypt **d**;	**Ex 9:6**	4191
of the sons of Israel, not one **d**.	**Ex 9:6**	4191
"Would that we had **d** by the	**Ex 16:3**	4191
them, and they **d** before the LORD.	**Lv 10:2**	4191
the presence of the LORD and **d**.	**Lv 16:1**	4191
But Nadab and Abihu **d** before the	**Nu 3:4**	4191
to the LORD and the fire **d** out.	**Nu 11:2**	8257
we had **d** in the land of Egypt!	**Nu 14:2**	4191
that we had **d** in this wilderness!	**Nu 14:2**	4191
d by a plague before the LORD.	**Nu 14:37**	4191
who **d** by the plague were 14,700,	**Nu 16:49**	4191
those who **d** on account of Korah.	**Nu 16:49**	4191
the body of a man who has **d**,	**Nu 19:13**	4191
a sword or who has **d** *naturally,*	**Nu 19:16**	4191
Miriam **d** there and was buried there.	**Nu 20:1**	4191
Aaron **d** there on the mountain top.	**Nu 20:28**	4191
congregation saw that Aaron had **d**,	**Nu 20:29**	1478
so that many people of Israel **d**.	**Nu 21:6**	4191
who **d** by the plague were 24,000.	**Nu 25:9**	4191
with Korah, when that company **d**,	**Nu 26:10**	4194
and Onan **d** in the land of Canaan.	**Nu 26:19**	4191
But Nadab and Abihu **d** when they	**Nu 26:61**	4191
"Our father **d** in the wilderness,	**Nu 27:3**	4191
but he **d** in his own sin, and he	**Nu 27:3**	4191
command of the LORD, and **d** there in	**Nu 33:38**	4191
years old when he **d** on Mount Hor.	**Nu 33:39**	4194
with an iron object, so that he **d**,	**Nu 35:16**	4191
he will die, and *as a result* he **d**,	**Nu 35:17**	4191
he might die, and *as a result* he **d**,	**Nu 35:18**	4191
in wait and *as a result* he **d**,	**Nu 35:20**	4191
in enmity, and *as a result* he **d**,	**Nu 35:21**	4191
it dropped on him so that he **d**,	**Nu 35:23**	4191
There Aaron **d** and there he was	**Dt 10:6**	4191
as Aaron your brother **d** on Mount	**Dt 32:50**	4191
So Moses the servant of the LORD **d**	**Dt 34:5**	4191
and twenty years old when he **d**,	**Dt 34:7**	4194
d in the wilderness along the way after	**Jos 5:4**	4191
them as far as Azekah, and they **d**;	**Jos 10:11**	4191
there were more who **d** from the	**Jos 10:11**	4191
Nun, the servant of the LORD, **d**,	**Jos 24:29**	4191
and Eleazar the son of Aaron **d**;	**Jos 24:33**	4191
him to Jerusalem and he **d** there.	**Jg 1:7**	4191
d at the age of one hundred and	**Jg 2:8**	4191

it came about when the judge **d**, Jg 2:19 4194
which Joshua left when he **d**, Jg 2:21 4191
And Othniel the son of Kenaz **d**. Jg 3:11 4191
sight of the LORD, after Ehud **d**. Jg 4:1 4191
sound asleep and exhausted. So he **d**. Jg 4:21 4191
And Gideon the son of Joash **d** at a Jg 8:32 4191
of the tower of Shechem also **d**, Jg 9:49 4191
man pierced him through, and he **d**. Jg 9:54 4191
Now after Abimelech **d**, Jg 10:1 4191
he **d** and was buried in Shamir. Jg 10:2 4191
Jair **d** and was buried in Kamon. Jg 10:5 4191
Then Jephthah the Gileadite **d** and Jg 12:7 4191
d and was buried in Bethlehem. Jg 12:10 4191
Then Elon the Zebulunite **d** and was Jg 12:12 4191
the son of Hillel the Pirathonite **d** Jg 12:15 4191
my concubine so that she **d**. Jg 20:5 4191
Then Elimelech, Naomi's husband, **d**; Ru 1:3 4191
both Mahlon and Chilion also **d**, Ru 1:5 4191
of Eli, Hophni and Phinehas, **d**. 1Sa 4:11 4191
and his neck was broken and he **d**, 1Sa 4:18 4191
father-in-law and her husband had **d**, 1Sa 4:19 4191
Samuel **d**; and all Israel gathered 1Sa 25:1 4191
and his heart **d** within him so that 1Sa 25:37 4191
the LORD struck Nabal and he **d**. 1Sa 25:38 4191
fell on his sword and **d** with him. 1Sa 31:5 4191
Thus Saul **d** with his three sons, 1Sa 31:6 4191
So he struck him and he **d**. 2Sa 1:15 4191
he fell there and **d** on the spot. 2Sa 2:23 4191
where Asahel had fallen and **d**, 2Sa 2:23 4191
three hundred and sixty men **d**. 2Sa 2:31 4191
struck him in the belly so that he **d** 2Sa 3:27 4191
heard that Abner had **d** in Hebron, 2Sa 4:1 4191
and he **d** there by the ark of God. 2Sa 6:7 4191
that the king of the Ammonites **d**, 2Sa 10:1 4191
of their army, and he **d** there. 2Sa 10:18 4191
and Uriah the Hittite also **d**. 2Sa 11:17 4191
the wall so that he **d** at Thebez? 2Sa 11:21 4191
the seventh day that the child **d**. 2Sa 12:18 4191
but when the child **d**, you arose 2Sa 12:21 4191
"But now he has **d**; why should I fast? 2Sa 12:23 4191
thus he **d** and was buried in the 2Sa 17:23 4191
Would I had **d** instead of you, O 2Sa 18:33 4191
anointed over us, has **d** in battle. 2Sa 19:10 4191
and he **d**. Then Joab and Abishai 2Sa 20:10 4191
people from Dan to Beersheba **d**. 2Sa 24:15 4191
and he fell upon him so that he **d**. 1Ki 2:25 4191
and fell upon him so that he **d**. 1Ki 2:46 4191
This woman's son **d** in the night, 1Ki 3:19 4191
of the house, the child **d**. 1Ki 14:17 4191
house over him with fire, and **d**, 1Ki 16:18 4191
And Tibni **d** and Omri became king. 1Ki 16:22 4191
of the Arameans, and **d** at evening, 1Ki 22:35 4191
king **d** and was brought to Samaria, 1Ki 22:37 4191
So Ahaziah **d** according to the word 2Ki 1:17 4191
But when Ahab **d**, 2Ki 3:5 4194
on her lap until noon, and *then* **d**. 2Ki 4:20 4191
and he **d** just as the man of God 2Ki 7:17 4191
on him at the gate and he **d**. 2Ki 7:20 4191
it on his face, so that he **d**. 2Ki 8:15 4191
he fled to Megiddo and **d** there. 2Ki 9:27 4191
servants, struck *him* and he **d**; 2Ki 12:21 4191
Elisha **d**, and they buried him. 2Ki 13:20 4191
When Hazael king of Aram **d**, 2Ki 13:24 4191
him to Egypt, and he **d** there. 2Ki 23:34 4191
struck Gedaliah down so that he **d** 2Ki 25:25 4191
When Bela **d**, Jobab the son of 1Ch 1:44 4191
When Jobab **d**, Husham of the land 1Ch 1:45 4191
When Husham **d**, Hadad the son of 1Ch 1:46 4191
When Hadad **d**, Samlah of Masrekah 1Ch 1:47 4191
When Samlah **d**, Shaul of Rehoboth 1Ch 1:48 4191
When Shaul **d**, Baal-hanan the son 1Ch 1:49 4191
When Baal-hanan **d**, Hadad became 1Ch 1:50 4191
Then Hadad **d**. 1Ch 1:51 4191
When Azubah **d**, Caleb married 1Ch 2:19 4191
Appaim, and Seled **d** without sons. 1Ch 2:30 4191
and Jether **d** without sons. 1Ch 2:32 4191
likewise fell on his sword and **d**. 1Ch 10:5 4191
Thus Saul **d** with his three sons, 1Ch 10:6 4191
all *those* of his house **d** together. 1Ch 10:6 4191
So Saul **d** for his trespass which 1Ch 10:13 4191
and he **d** there before God. 1Ch 13:10 4191
the king of the sons of Ammon **d**, 1Ch 19:1 4191
Eleazar **d** and had no sons, but 1Ch 23:22 4191
But Nadab and Abihu **d** before their 1Ch 24:2 4191
Then he **d** in a ripe old age, full 1Ch 29:28 4191
and the LORD struck him and he **d**. 2Ch 13:20 4191
having **d** in the forty-first year 2Ch 16:13 4191
and at sunset he **d**. 2Ch 18:34 4191
sickness and he **d** in great pain. 2Ch 21:19 4191
reached a ripe old age he **d**; 2Ch 24:15 4191
And as he **d** he said, 2Ch 24:22 4194
So he **d**, and they buried him in 2Ch 24:25 4191
brought him to Jerusalem where he **d** 2Ch 35:24 4191
when her father and her mother **d**, Es 2:7 4194
on the young people and they **d**, Jb 1:19 4191
I had **d** and no eye had seen me! Jb 10:18 1478
And Job **d**, an old man and full of Jb 42:17 4191
that King Ahaz **d** this oracle came: Is 14:28 4194
withered, the tender grass **d** out, Is 15:6 3615
So Hananiah the prophet **d** in the Jer 28:17 4191
I have never eaten what **d** of itself or Ezk 4:14 5038
that Pelatiah son of Benaiah **d**. Ezk 11:13 4191
and in the evening my wife **d**. Ezk 24:18 4191
not eat any bird or beast that has **d** a Ezk 44:31 5038
through Baal he did wrong and **d**. Hos 13:1 4191
But when Herod **d**, behold, an angel Mt 2:19 *5053*
"My daughter has just **d**; Mt 9:18 *5053*
for the girl has not **d**, Mt 9:24 *599*
and the first married and **d**, Mt 22:25 *5053*
"Last of all, the woman **d**. Mt 22:27 *599*
And the wind **d** down and it became Mk 4:39 *2869*
"Your daughter has **d**; Mk 5:35 *599*
The child has not **d**, Mk 5:39 *599*
and the first took a wife, and **d** leaving Mk 12:20 *599*
The second one married her, and **d** Mk 12:21 *599*
Last of all the woman **d** also. Mk 12:22 *599*
"Your daughter has **d**; Lk 8:49 *2348*
"Stop weeping, for she has not **d**, Lk 8:52 *599*
at Him, knowing that she had **d**. Lk 8:53 *599*
the poor man **d** and was carried Lk 16:22 *599*
rich man also **d** and was buried. Lk 16:22 *599*
took a wife and **d** childless; Lk 20:29 *599*
and in the same way all seven **d**, Lk 20:31 *599*
"Finally the woman **d** also. Lk 20:32 *599*
in the wilderness, and they **d**. Jn 6:49 *599*
not as the fathers ate and **d**; Jn 6:58 *599*
Abraham **d**, and the prophets *also* Jn 8:52 *599*
than our father Abraham, who **d**? Jn 8:53 *599*
The prophets **d** too; Jn 8:53 *599*
here, my brother would not have **d**. Jn 11:21 *599*
my brother would not have **d**." Jn 11:32 *599*
man who had **d** came forth, bound Jn 11:44 *2348*
that he both **d** and was buried, Ac 2:29 *5053*
From there, after his father **d**, Ac 7:4 *599*
and *there* he and our fathers **d**. Ac 7:15 *5053*
time that she fell sick and **d**; Ac 9:37 *599*
and he was eaten by worms and **d**. Ac 12:23 *1634*
time Christ **d** for the ungodly. Ro 5:6 *599*
were yet sinners, Christ **d** for us. Ro 5:8 *599*
transgression of the one the many **d** Ro 5:15 *599*
we who **d** to sin still live in it? Ro 6:2 *599*
he who has **d** is freed from sin. Ro 6:7 *599*
Now if we have **d** with Christ, we Ro 6:8 *599*
For the death that He **d**, Ro 6:10 *599*
death that He died, He **d** to sin once Ro 6:10 *599*
having **d** to that by which we were Ro 7:6 *599*
came, sin became alive and I **d**; Ro 7:9 *599*
Christ Jesus is He who **d**, Ro 8:34 *599*
this end Christ **d** and lived again, Ro 14:9 *599*
your food him for whom Christ **d**. Ro 14:15 *599*
brother for whose sake Christ **d**. 1Co 8:11 *599*
that Christ **d** for our sins 1Co 15:3 *599*
this, that one **d** for all, 2Co 5:14 *599*
one died for all, therefore all **d**; 2Co 5:14 *599*
and He **d** for all, so that they who 2Co 5:15 *599*
but for Him who **d** and rose again 2Co 5:15 *599*
through the Law I **d** to the Law, Ga 2:19 *599*
Law, then Christ **d** needlessly." Ga 2:21 *599*
If you have **d** with Christ to the Col 2:20 *599*
For you have **d** and your life is Col 3:3 *599*
that Jesus **d** and rose again, 1Th 4:14 *599*
who **d** for us, so that whether we are 1Th 5:10 *599*
For if we **d** with Him, we will 2Tm 2:11 *4880*
All these **d** in faith, without Heb 11:13 *599*
also **d** for sins once for all, 1Pe 3:18 *599*
were in the sea and had life, **d**; Rv 8:9 *599*
and many men **d** from the waters, Rv 8:11 *599*
every living thing in the sea **d**. Rv 16:3 *599*

DIES

He who strikes a man so that he **d** Ex 21:12 4191
with a rod and he **d** at his hand, Ex 21:20 4191
ox hurts another's so that it **d**, Ex 21:35 4191
in and is struck so that he **d**, Ex 22:2 4191
and it **d** or is hurt or is driven Ex 22:10 4191
and it is injured or **d** while its Ex 22:14 4191
'Also the fat of *an animal* which **d** and Lv 7:24 5038
if one of the animals **d** which you Lv 11:39 4191
any person eats *an animal* which **d** or Lv 17:15 5038
which **d** or is torn *by beasts,* Lv 22:8 5038
'But if a man **d** very suddenly Nu 6:9 4191
is the law when a man **d** in a tent: Nu 19:14 4191
'If a man **d** and has no son, then Nu 27:8 4191
eat anything which **d** *of itself.* Dt 14:21 5038
and strikes his friend so that he **d** Dt 19:5 4191
him and strikes him so that he **d**, Dt 19:11 4191
d who took her to be his wife, Dt 24:3 4191
and one of them **d** and has no son, Dt 25:5 4191
or his day will come that he **d**, 1Sa 26:10 4191
"Should Abner die as a fool **d**? 2Sa 3:33 4194
who **d** in the city the dogs will 1Ki 14:11 4191
And he who **d** in the field the 1Ki 14:11 4191
"Anyone of Baasha who **d** in the 1Ki 16:4 4191
and anyone of his who **d** in the 1Ki 16:4 4191
to Ahab, who **d** in the city, 1Ki 21:24 4191
and the one who **d** in the field the 1Ki 21:24 4191
And its stump **d** in the dry soil, Jb 14:8 4191
"But man **d** and lies prostrate. Jb 14:10 4191
"If a man **d**, will he live *again?* Jb 14:14 4191
"One **d** in his full strength, Jb 21:23 4191
another **d** with a bitter soul, Jb 21:25 4191
he **d** he will carry nothing away; Ps 49:17 4194
When a wicked man **d**, Pr 11:7 4194
righteous has a refuge when he **d**. Pr 14:32 4194
As one **d** so dies the other; Ec 3:19 4194
As one dies so **d** the other; Ec 3:19 4194
that you are afraid of man who **d** And Is 51:12 4191
He who eats of their eggs **d**, Is 59:5 4191
from the cistern before he **d**." Jer 38:10 4191
iniquity and **d** because of it, Ezk 18:26 4191
in the death of anyone who **d**," Ezk 18:32 4191
'IF A MAN **D** HAVING NO CHILDREN, Mt 22:24 *599*
for us that IF A MAN'S BROTHER **D** and Mk 12:19 *599*
for us that IF A MAN'S BROTHER **D**, Lk 20:28 *599*
come down before my child **d**." Jn 4:49 *599*
in Me will live even if he **d**, Jn 11:25 *599*
wheat falls into the earth and **d**, Jn 12:24 *599*
but if it **d**, it bears much fruit. Jn 12:24 *599*
but if her husband **d**, Ro 7:2 *599*
but if her husband **d**, Ro 7:3 *599*
and not one **d** for himself; Ro 14:7 *599*
does not come to life unless it **d**; 1Co 15:36 *599*
who has set aside the Law of Moses **d** Heb 10:28 *599*

DIET

his **d** was locusts and wild honey. Mk 1:6 *2068*

DIFFER

Since we have gifts that **d** Ro 12:6 *1313*
he does not **d** at all from a slave Ga 4:1 *1308*

DIFFERENCE

slaves so that they may learn *the* **d** 2Ch 12:8
and they have not taught the **d** Ezk 22:26
shall teach My people *the* **d** Ezk 44:23
120,000 persons who do not know *the* **d** Jon 4:11
(what they were makes no **d** to me; Ga 2:6 *1308*

DIFFERENT

because he has had a **d** spirit and Nu 14:24 312
their laws are **d** from *those* of all Es 3:8 8132
"Thus you are **d** from those women Ezk 16:34 2016
thus you are **d**." Ezk 16:34 2016
from the sea, **d** from one another. Da 7:3 8133
and it was **d** from all the beasts Da 7:7 8133
which was **d** from all the others, Da 7:19 8133
be **d** from all the *other* kingdoms and Da 7:23 8133
and he will be **d** from the previous Da 7:24 8133
He appeared in a **d** form to two of Mk 16:12 *2087*
appearance of His face became **d**, Lk 9:29 *2087*
a **d** law in the members of my body, Ro 7:23 *2087*
or you receive a **d** spirit which 2Co 11:4 *2087*
or a **d** gospel which you have not 2Co 11:4 *2087*
grace of Christ, for a **d** gospel; Ga 1:6 *2087*
in anything you have a **d** attitude, Php 3:15 *2088*
If anyone advocates a **d** doctrine and 1Tm 6:3 *2085*

DIFFERING

not have in your bag **d** weights, Dt 25:13 68
not have in your house **d** measures, Dt 25:14 374
D weights and differing measures, Pr 20:10 68
Differing weights and **d** measures, Pr 20:10 374
D weights are an abomination to Pr 20:23 68

DIFFERS

for star **d** from star in glory. 1Co 15:41 *1308*

DIFFICULT

"Is anything too **d** for the LORD? Gn 18:14 6381
the **d** dispute they would bring to Ex 18:26 7186
'When a man makes a **d** vow, Lv 27:2 6381
case is too **d** for you to decide, Dt 17:8 6381
you today is not too **d** for you, Dt 30:11 6381
sons of Zeruiah are too **d** for me. 2Sa 3:39 7186
came to test him with **d** questions. 1Ki 10:1 2420
to test Solomon with **d** questions. 2Ch 9:1 2420
Or in things too **d** for me. Ps 131:1 6381
Nothing is too **d** for You, Jer 32:17 6381
is anything too **d** for Me?" Jer 32:27 6381
speech or **d** language, Ezk 3:5 3515
speech or **d** language, Ezk 3:6 3515
thing which the king demands is **d**, Da 2:11 3358
and solving of **d** problems were Da 5:12 7001
and solve **d** problems. Da 5:16 7001
'If it is too **d** in the sight of Zch 8:6 6381
it also be too **d** in My sight?' Zch 8:6 6381
"This is a **d** statement; Jn 6:60 *4642*
the last days **d** times will come. 2Tm 3:1 *5467*

DIFFICULTIES

with persecutions, with **d**, 2Co 12:10 *4730*

DIFFICULTY

and the Egyptians will find **d** in Ex 7:18 3811
and He made them drive with **d**; Ex 14:25 3517
one who was deaf and spoke with **d**, Mk 7:32 *3424*
and only with **d** does it leave him, Lk 9:39 *3433*
with **d** they restrained the crowds Ac 14:18 *3433*
and with **d** had arrived off Cnidus, Ac 27:7 *3433*
and with **d** sailing past it we came Ac 27:8 *3433*
D THAT THE RIGHTEOUS IS SAVED, 1Pe 4:18 *3433*

DIG

hewn cisterns which you did not **d**, Dt 6:11 2672
of whose hills you can **d** copper. Dt 8:9 2672
you shall **d** with it and shall turn Dt 23:13 2658
And **d** for it more than for hidden Jb 3:21 2658
"In the dark they **d** into houses, Jb 24:16 2864
of man, now **d** through the wall." Ezk 8:8 2864
"**D** a hole through the wall in Ezk 12:5 2864
They will **d** a hole through the Ezk 12:12 2864
"Though they **d** into Sheol, From Am 9:2 2864
until I **d** around it and put in Lk 13:8 *4626*
I am not strong enough to **d**; Lk 16:3 *4626*

DIGNIFIED

Women *must* likewise *be* **d**, 1Tm 3:11 *4586*
Older men are to be temperate, **d**, Ti 2:2 *4586*
deeds, *with* purity in doctrine, **d**, Ti 2:7 *4587*

DIGNITY

in **d** and preeminent in power. Gn 49:3 7613
"What honor or **d** has been Es 6:3 1420
yourself with eminence and **d**, Jb 40:10 1363
Strength and **d** are her clothing, Pr 31:25 1926
quiet life in all godliness and **d**. 1Tm 2:2 *4587*
children under control with all **d** 1Tm 3:4 *4587*
Deacons likewise *must be* men of **d**, 1Tm 3:8 *4586*

DIGS

or **d** a pit and does not cover it Ex 21:33 3738a
A worthless man **d** up evil, While Pr 16:27 3738a
He who **d** a pit will fall into it, Pr 26:27 3738a
He who **d** a pit may fall into it, Ec 10:8 2658

DIKLAH

and Hadoram and Uzal and **D** Gn 10:27 1853
Hadoram, Uzal, **D**, 1Ch 1:21 1853

DILEAN
and **D** and Mizpeh and Joktheel, **Jos 15:38** 1810
DILIGENCE
it be carried out with all **d**!" **Ezr 6:12** 629
carried out *the decree* with all **d**, **Ezr 6:13** 629
Watch over your heart with all **d**, **Pr 4:23** 4929
precious possession of a man *is* **d**. **Pr 12:27** 2742a
he who leads, with **d**; **Ro 12:8** *4710*
not lagging behind in **d**, **Ro 12:11** *4710*
that each one of you show the same **d** **Heb 6:11** *4710*
very reason also, applying all **d**, **2Pe 1:5** *4710*
DILIGENT
"So take **d** heed to yourselves to **Jos 23:11** 3966
But the hand of the **d** makes rich. **Pr 10:4** 2742a
The hand of the **d** will rule, But **Pr 12:24** 2742a
But the soul of the **d** is made fat. **Pr 13:4** 2742a
of the **d** *lead* surely to advantage, **Pr 21:5** 2742a
tested and found **d** in many things, **2Co 8:22** *4705*
many things, but now even more **d** **2Co 8:22** *4705*
being **d** to preserve the unity of **Eph 4:3** *4704*
Be **d** to present yourself approved **2Tm 2:15** *4704*
us be **d** to enter that rest, **Heb 4:11** *4704*
be all the more **d** to make certain **2Pe 1:10** *4704*
And I will also be **d** that at any **2Pe 1:15** *4704*
be **d** to be found by Him in peace, **2Pe 3:14** *4704*
DILIGENTLY
to yourself and keep your soul **d**, **Dt 4:9** 3966
You shall teach them **d** to your **Dt 6:7** 8150
"You should **d** keep the **Dt 6:17** 8104
that you **d** observe and do **Dt 24:8** 3966
you **d** obey the LORD your God, **Dt 28:1** 8085
therefore, you shall **d** buy bulls, **Ezr 7:17** 629
of you, it shall be done **d**, **Ezr 7:21** 629
returned and searched **d** for God; **Ps 78:34** 7836
That we should keep *them* **d**. **Ps 119:4** 3966
shall **d** consider Your testimonies. **Ps 119:95** 995
They will seek me **d** but **Pr 1:28** 7836
those who **d** seek me will find me. **Pr 8:17** 7836
He who **d** seeks good seeks favor, **Pr 11:27** 7836
who loves him disciplines him **d**. **Pr 13:24** 7836
my spirit within me seeks You **d**; **Is 26:9** 7836
those who **d** labor among you, **1Th 5:12** *2872*
D help Zenas the lawyer and **Ti 3:13** *4709*
DILL
And sow **d** and scatter cummin And **Is 28:25** 7100
For **d** is not threshed with a **Is 28:27** 7100
But **d** is beaten out with a rod, **Is 28:27** 7100
you tithe mint and **d** and cummin, **Mt 23:23** *432*
DILUTED
dross, Your drink **d** with water. **Is 1:22** 4107
DIM
and his eyes were too **d** to see, **Gn 27:1** 3543a
Now the eyes of Israel were *so* **d** **Gn 48:10** 3513
no deeper than the skin, but is **d**, **Lv 13:26** 3544
not spread in the skin, but is **d**, **Lv 13:28** 3544
when he died, his eye was not **d**, **Dt 34:7** 3543a
grow **d** *and* he could not see *well*), **1Sa 3:2** 3544
eyes were **d** because of his age. **1Ki 14:4** 6965
has also grown **d** because of grief, **Jb 17:7** 3543a
grow **d** so that they cannot see, **Ps 69:23** 2821
who look through windows grow **d**; **Ec 12:3** 2821
Their ears dull, And their eyes **d**, **Is 6:10** 8173a
of these things our eyes are **d**; **La 5:17** 2821
DIMINISH
the years you shall **d** its price **Lv 25:16** 4591
you shall **d** their inheritance; **Nu 26:54** 4591
And they will begin to **d** Because **Hos 8:10** 4592
DIMINISHED
When they are **d** and bowed down **Ps 107:39** 4591
them and they will not be **d**; **Jer 30:19** 4591
against you and **d** your rations. **Ezk 16:27** 1639
DIMLY
And a **d** burning wick He will not **Is 42:3** 3544
For now we see in a mirror **d**, **1Co 13:12** *135*
DIMNAH
D with its pasture lands, Nahalal **Jos 21:35** 1829
DIMON
the waters of **D** are full of blood; **Is 15:9** 1775
I will bring added *woes* upon **D**, **Is 15:9** 1775
DIMONAH
and Kinah and **D** and Adadah, **Jos 15:22** 1776
DIN
her multitude, her **d** *of revelry* **Is 5:14** 7588
DINAH
bore a daughter and named her **D**. **Gn 30:21** 1783
Now **D** the daughter of Leah, whom **Gn 34:1** 1783
to **D** the daughter of Jacob, **Gn 34:3** 1783
he had defiled **D** his daughter; **Gn 34:5** 1783
he had defiled **D** their sister. **Gn 34:13** 1783
and took **D** from Shechem's house, **Gn 34:26** 1783
Paddan-aram, with his daughter **D**; **Gn 46:15** 1783
DINAH'S
sons, Simeon and Levi, **D** brothers, **Gn 34:25** 1783
DINE
men are to **d** with me at noon." **Gn 43:16** 398
you sit down to **d** with a ruler, **Pr 23:1** 3898b
was requesting Him to **d** with him, **Lk 7:36** *2068*
in to him and will **d** with him, **Rv 3:20** *1172*
DINHABAH
and the name of his city was **D**. **Gn 36:32** 1838
and the name of his city was **D**. **1Ch 1:43** 1838
DINING
d with Jesus and His disciples. **Mt 9:10** *4873*
d with Jesus and His disciples; **Mk 2:15** *4873*
knowledge, **d** in an idol's temple, **1Co 8:10** *2621*

DINNER
and because of his **d** guests. **Mt 14:9** *4873*
"Behold, I have prepared my **d**; **Mt 22:4** *712*
hall was filled with **d** guests. **Mt 22:10** *345*
came in to look over the **d** guests, **Mt 22:11** *345*
pleased Herod and his **d** guests; **Mk 6:22** *4873*
oaths and because of his **d** guests, **Mk 6:26** *345*
"When you give a luncheon or a **d**, **Lk 14:12** *1173*
"A man was giving a big **d**, **Lk 14:16** *1173*
and at the **d** hour he sent his **Lk 14:17** *1173*
invited shall taste of my **d**.' " **Lk 14:24** *1173*
DIONYSIUS
among whom also were **D** the **Ac 17:34** *1354*
DIOTREPHES
but **D**, who loves to be first among **3Jn 1:9** *1361*
DIP
bunch of hyssop and **d** it in the blood **Ex 12:22** 2881
shall **d** his finger in the blood and **Lv 4:6** 2881
shall **d** his finger in the blood and **Lv 4:17** 2881
and shall **d** them and the live bird **Lv 14:6** 2881
the priest shall then **d** his **Lv 14:16** 2881
and **d** them in the blood of the **Lv 14:51** 2881
take hyssop and **d** *it* in the water, **Nu 19:18** 2881
And may he **d** his foot in oil. **Dt 33:24** 2881
d your piece of bread in the vinegar." **Ru 2:14** 2881
that he may **d** the tip of his **Lk 16:24** *911*
d the morsel and give it to him." **Jn 13:26** *911*
DIPHATH
sons of Gomer *were* Ashkenaz, **D**, **1Ch 1:6** 1784b
DIPPED
and **d** the tunic in the blood; **Gn 37:31** 2881
and he **d** his finger in the blood and **Lv 9:9** 2881
were **d** in the edge of the water **Jos 3:15** 2881
hand and **d** it in the honeycomb, **1Sa 14:27** 2881
So he went down and **d** *himself* **2Ki 5:14** 2881
he took the cover and **d** it in **2Ki 8:15** 2881
"He who **d** his hand with Me in the **Mt 26:23** *1686*
So when He had **d** the morsel, He **Jn 13:26** *911*
is clothed with a robe **d** in blood **Rv 19:13** *911*
DIPS
one who **d** with Me in the bowl. **Mk 14:20** *1686*
DIRECT
came to Egypt, his **d** descendants, **Gn 46:26** 3409
sons who were his **d** descendants, **Jg 8:30** 3409
d your hearts to the LORD and serve **1Sa 7:3** 3559
sea to the place where you **d** me, **1Ki 5:9** 7971
people, and **d** their heart to You; **1Ch 29:18** 3559
"If you would **d** your heart right And **Jb 11:13** 3559
wise, And **d** your heart in the way. **Pr 23:19** 833
in a man who walks to **d** his steps. **Jer 10:23** 3559
D your mind to the highway, The **Jer 31:21** 7896
rams he will **d** against your walls, **Ezk 26:9** 5414
And **d** their desire toward their **Hos 4:8** 5375
and to **d** them to observe the Law **Ac 15:5** *3853*
And so I **d** in all the churches. **1Co 7:17** *1299*
Jesus our Lord **d** our way to you; **1Th 3:11** *2720*
May the Lord **d** your hearts **2Th 3:5** *2720*
we **d** their entire body as well. **Jas 3:3** *3329*
DIRECTED
and the LORD **d** an east wind on the **Ex 10:13** 5090a
and I have **d** the young men to a **1Sa 21:2** 3045
the third day as the king had **d**, **1Ki 12:12** 1696
the third day as the king had **d**, **2Ch 10:12** 1696
the people had not yet **d** their **2Ch 20:33** 3559
and **d** them to the west side of the city **2Ch 32:30** 3474
by His power He **d** the south wind. **Ps 78:26** 5090a
I have **d** you in the way of wisdom; **Pr 4:11** 3384
I **d** my mind to know, to **Ec 7:25** 5437
be spent and My anger *will be* **d** **Is 10:25**
Who has **d** the Spirit of the LORD, **Is 40:13** 8505
And He **d** the people to sit down **Mt 15:35** *3853*
disciples did as Jesus had **d** them; **Mt 26:19** *4929*
POTTER'S FIELD, AS THE LORD **D** ME." **Mt 27:10** *4929*
And He **d** the people to sit down **Mk 8:6** *3853*
just as He who spoke to Moses **d** **Ac 7:44** *1299*
was *divinely* **d** by a holy angel to **Ac 10:22** *5537*
So also the Lord **d** those who **1Co 9:14** *1299*
as I **d** the churches of Galatia, **1Co 16:1** *1299*
Him because of the power of God **d** **2Co 13:4**
elders in every city as I **d** you, **Ti 1:5** *1299*
still **d** by a very small rudder wherever **Jas 3:4** *3329*
DIRECTION
sword which turned every **d** to **Gn 3:24**
duties *shall be* under the **d** of Ithamar **Nu 4:28** 3027
under the **d** of Ithamar the son of **Nu 4:33** 3027
under the **d** of Ithamar the son of **Nu 7:8** 3027
'Then your border shall turn **d** **Nu 34:4**
'The border shall turn **d** from **Nu 34:5**
toward the **d** of the wilderness, **Jg 20:42** 1870
way in the **d** of Beth-shemesh; **1Sa 6:12** 1870
Asaph *were* under the **d** of Asaph, **1Ch 25:2** 3027
under the **d** of the king. **1Ch 25:2** 3027
under the **d** of their father **1Ch 25:3** 3027
All these were under the **d** of **1Ch 25:6** 3027
were under the **d** of the king. **1Ch 25:6** 3027
official, under the **d** of Hananiah, **2Ch 26:11** 3027
d was an elite army of 307,500, **2Ch 26:13** 3027
Valley Gate in the **d** of the Dragon's **Ne 2:13** 6440
"It changes **d**, turning around **Jb 37:12** 4524
And confuse the **d** of your paths. **Is 3:12** 1870
in the **d** of the daughter of My people **Jer 4:11** 1870
turning their faces in its **d**; **Jer 50:5** 2008
to go, they would go in that **d**. **Ezk 1:20** 8033
six men came from the **d** of the **Ezk 9:2** 1870
in the **d** which they faced, **Ezk 10:11** 4725
from every **d** for your harlotries. **Ezk 16:33** 5439
gather them against you from every **d** **Ezk 16:37** 5439

DIRECTIONS
to the **d** of King David of Israel. **Ezr 3:10** 3027
"From all **d** around you; **Jer 49:5**
they moved in any of their four **d** **Ezk 1:17** 7253
d without turning as they went; **Ezk 10:11** 7253
having asked **d** for Simon's house, **Ac 10:17** *1331*
But I am hard-pressed from both **d**, **Php 1:23**
DIRECTLY
"You shall not go **d** up; circle **2Sa 5:23**
At the Fountain Gate they went **d** up **Ne 12:37** 5048
Let your eyes look **d** ahead And **Pr 4:25** 5227
DIRECTOR
For the choir **d**, on my stringed **Hab 3:19** 5329
DIRECTS
his way, But the LORD **d** his steps. **Pr 16:9** 3559
A wise man's heart **d** *him* toward **Ec 10:2**
but the foolish man's heart **d** *him* **Ec 10:2**
DIRGE
pastures of the wilderness a **d**, **Jer 9:10** 7015
And everyone her neighbor a **d**. **Jer 9:20** 7015
which I take up for you as a **d**, **Am 5:1** 7015
we sang a **d**, and you did not mourn.' **Mt 11:17** *2354*
we sang a **d**, and you did not weep.' **Lk 7:32** *2354*
DIRT
sackcloth and with **d** upon them. **Ne 9:1** 127
with worms and a crust of **d**, **Jb 7:5** 6083
the removal of **d** from the flesh, **1Pe 3:21** *4509*
DIRTY
my feet, How can I **d** them *again?* **SS 5:3** 2936
comes in a poor man in **d** clothes, **Jas 2:2** *4508*
DISAGREEABLE
"If it is **d** in your sight to **Jos 24:15** 7489a
DISAGREEMENT
And there occurred such a sharp **d** **Ac 15:39** *3948*
simply had some points of **d** with him **Ac 25:19** *2213*
DISAPPEAR
d from among the sons of men. **Ps 12:1** 6461
city will **d** from Ephraim, **Is 17:3** 7673a
And also the fish of the sea **d**. **Hos 4:3** 622
and growing old is ready to **d**. **Heb 8:13** *854*
DISAPPEARED
Oppressors have completely **d** from **Is 16:4**
DISAPPEARS
When the grass **d**, the new growth **Pr 27:25** 1540
cloud And like dew which soon **d**, **Hos 13:3** 1980
DISAPPOINT
and hope does not **d**, **Ro 5:5** *2617b*
DISAPPOINTED
"They were **d** for they had **Jb 6:20** 954
You they trusted and were not **d**. **Ps 22:5** 954
BELIEVES IN HIM WILL NOT BE **D**." **Ro 9:33** *2617b*
BELIEVES IN HIM WILL NOT BE **D**." **Ro 10:11** *2617b*
BELIEVES IN HIM WILL NOT BE **D**." **1Pe 2:6** *2617b*
DISARMED
had **d** the rulers and authorities, **Col 2:15** *554*
DISASTER
d will overtake me and I will die; **Gn 19:19** 7463a
not know that **d** was close to them. **Jg 20:34** 7463a
they saw that **d** was close to them. **Jg 20:41** 7463a
has proclaimed **d** against you." **1Ki 22:23** 7463a
has proclaimed **d** against you." **2Ch 18:22** 7463a
his **d** therefore cry out for help? **Jb 30:24** 6365
And **d** to those who work iniquity? **Jb 31:3** 5235b
he who flees the report of **d** will fall **Is 24:18** 6343
He also is wise and will bring **d** And **Is 31:2** 7451b
And **d** will fall on you For which **Is 47:11** 1943
D on disaster is proclaimed, For **Jer 4:20** 7667
Disaster on **d** is proclaimed, For **Jer 4:20** 7667
I am bringing **d** on this people, **Jer 6:19** 7463a
"Behold I am bringing **d** on them **Jer 11:11** 7463a
save them in the time of their **d**. **Jer 11:12** 7463a
call to Me because of their **d**. **Jer 11:14** 7463a
flesh take away from you your **d**, **Jer 11:15** 7463a
for I will bring **d** on the men of **Jer 11:23** 7463a
time of **d** and a time of distress. **Jer 15:11** 7463a
are my refuge in the day of **d**. **Jer 17:17** 7463a
Bring on them a day of **d**, **Jer 17:18** 7463a
to destroy and to bring **d**, **Jer 31:28** 7489a
all this great **d** on this people, **Jer 32:42** 7463a
inhabitants of Jerusalem all the **d** that **Jer 35:17** 7463a
city for **d** and not for prosperity; **Jer 39:16** 7463a
am going to bring **d** on all flesh,' **Jer 45:5** 7463a
"The **d** of Moab will soon come, **Jer 48:16** 343
For I will bring the **d** of Esau **Jer 49:8** 343
bring their **d** from every side," **Jer 49:32** 343
would inflict this **d** on them." **Ezk 6:10** 7463a
'A **d**, unique disaster, behold it **Ezk 7:5** 7463a
'A disaster, unique **d**, **Ezk 7:5** 7463a
'**D** will come upon disaster and **Ezk 7:26** 1943
'Disaster will come upon **d** and **Ezk 7:26** 1943
My people In the day of their **d**. **Ob 1:13** 343
calamity In the day of their **d**. **Ob 1:13** 343
wealth In the day of their **d**. **Ob 1:13** 343
You will fear **d** no more. **Zph 3:15** 7451b
angry, they furthered the **d**." **Zch 1:15** 7463a
DISASTERS
and hiss because of all its **d**. **Jer 19:8** 4347
DISBELIEVE
but for those who **d**, **1Pe 2:7** *569*
DISBELIEVED
he who has **d** shall be condemned. **Mk 16:16** *569*
But the Jews who **d** stirred up the **Ac 14:2** *544*
DISCARDED
the utensils which King Ahaz had **d** **2Ch 29:19** 2186a
"Or like a miscarriage which is **d**, **Jb 3:16** 2934

DISCERN

That they would **d** their future!	Dt 32:29	995
lord the king to **d** good and evil.	2Sa 14:17	8085
people to **d** between good and evil.	1Ki 3:9	995
but I could not **d** its appearance;	Jb 4:16	5234
Cannot my palate **d** calamities?	Jb 6:30	995
you may **d** the paths to its home?	Jb 38:20	995
Who can **d** *his* errors?	Ps 19:12	995
To **d** the sayings of understanding,	Pr 1:2	995
you will **d** the fear of the LORD And	Pr 2:5	995
Then you will **d** righteousness and	Pr 2:9	995
you will not **d** words of knowledge.	Pr 14:7	3045
of the hasty will **d** the truth,	Is 32:4	995
and cause them to **d** between the	Ezk 44:23	3045
"So you are to know and **d** *that*	Da 9:25	7919a
to **d** the appearance of the sky,	Mt 16:3	*1252*
but cannot **d** the signs of	Mt 16:3	
senses trained to **d** good and evil.	Heb 5:14	*1253*

DISCERNED

Then Eli **d** that the LORD was	1Sa 3:8	995
the naive, *And* **d** among the youths	Pr 7:7	995

DISCERNING

Pharaoh look for a man **d** and wise,	Gn 41:33	995
no one so **d** and wise as you are.	Gn 41:39	995
'Choose wise and **d** and experienced	Dt 1:13	995
have given you a wise and **d** heart,	1Ki 3:12	995
On the lips of the **d**, wisdom is found	Pr 10:13	995
He who keeps the law is a **d** son,	Pr 28:7	995
to the wise nor wealth to the **d**	Ec 9:11	995
of their **d** men will be concealed.	Is 29:14	995
understanding and **d** knowledge,	Da 1:4	995
Whoever is **d**, let him know them.	Hos 14:9	995

DISCERNMENT

and blessed be your **d**,	1Sa 25:33	2940
yourself **d** to understand justice,	1Ki 3:11	995
very great **d** and breadth of mind,	1Ki 4:29	8394
takes away the **d** of the elders.	Jb 12:20	2940
Now therefore, O kings, show **d**;	Ps 2:10	7919a
Teach me good **d** and knowledge, For	Ps 119:66	2940
For if you cry for **d**,	Pr 2:3	998
For they are not a people of **d**,	Is 27:11	998
And the **d** of their discerning men	Is 29:14	998
with discretion and **d** to Arioch,	Da 2:14	2942
more in real knowledge and all **d**,	Php 1:9	*144*

DISCHARGE

any man has a **d** from his body,	Lv 15:2	2100
from his body, his **d** is unclean.	Lv 15:2	2101
shall be his uncleanness in his **d**:	Lv 15:3	2101
his body allows its **d** to flow or	Lv 15:3	2101
whether his body obstructs its **d**.	Lv 15:3	2101
with the **d** lies becomes unclean,	Lv 15:4	2100
man with the **d** has been sitting,	Lv 15:6	2100
whoever touches the person with the **d**	Lv 15:7	2100
if the man with the **d** spits on one	Lv 15:8	2100
with the **d** rides becomes unclean.	Lv 15:9	2100
whomever the one with the **d**	Lv 15:11	2100
the **d** touches shall be broken,	Lv 15:12	2100
'Now when the man with the **d**	Lv 15:13	2100
becomes cleansed from his **d**,	Lv 15:13	2101
before the LORD because of his **d**.	Lv 15:15	2101
'When a woman has a **d**,	Lv 15:19	2100
if her **d** in her body is blood,	Lv 15:19	2101
has a **d** of her blood many days,	Lv 15:25	2101
if she has a **d** beyond that period,	Lv 15:25	2100
all the days of her impure **d** she	Lv 15:25	2101
which she lies all the days of her **d**	Lv 15:26	2101
'When she becomes clean from her **d**,	Lv 15:28	2101
the LORD because of her impure **d**.'	Lv 15:30	2101
is the law for the one with a **d**,	Lv 15:32	2100
and for the one who has a **d**,	Lv 15:33	2101
who is a leper or who has a **d**,	Lv 22:4	2100
every leper and everyone having a **d**	Nu 5:2	2100
the house of Joab one who has a **d**,	2Sa 3:29	2100
there is no **d** in the time of war,	Ec 8:8	4917
land drink the **d** of your blood As	Ezk 32:6	6824

DISCIPLE

awakens My ear to listen as a **d**.	Is 50:4	3928
"A **d** is not above his teacher,	Mt 10:24	*3101*
d that he become like his teacher,	Mt 10:25	*3101*
"And whoever in the name of a **d**	Mt 10:42	*3101*
every scribe who has become a **d**	Mt 13:52	*3100*
had also become a **d** of Jesus.	Mt 27:57	*3100*
his own life, he cannot be My **d**.	Lk 14:26	*3101*
and come after Me cannot be My **d**.	Lk 14:27	*3101*
none of you can be My **d** who does	Lk 14:33	*3101*
"You are His **d**, but we are	Jn 9:28	*3101*
Jesus, and *so was* another **d**.	Jn 18:15	*3101*
d was known to the high priest,	Jn 18:15	*3101*
So the other **d**, who was known to	Jn 18:16	*3101*
d whom He loved standing nearby,	Jn 19:26	*3101*
Then He said to the **d**,	Jn 19:27	*3101*
From that hour the **d** took her	Jn 19:27	*3101*
of Arimathea, being a **d** of Jesus,	Jn 19:38	*3101*
to the other **d** whom Jesus loved,	Jn 20:2	*3101*
and the other **d** went forth,	Jn 20:3	*3101*
d ran ahead faster than Peter and	Jn 20:4	*3101*
So the other **d** who had first come	Jn 20:8	*3101*
Therefore that **d** whom Jesus loved	Jn 21:7	*3101*
saw the **d** whom Jesus loved	Jn 21:20	*3101*
that that **d** would not die;	Jn 21:23	*3101*
This is the **d** who is testifying to	Jn 21:24	*3101*
there was a **d** at Damascus	Ac 9:10	*3101*
not believing that he was a **d**.	Ac 9:26	*3101*
was a **d** named Tabitha	Ac 9:36	*3102a*
And a **d** was there,	Ac 16:1	*3101*
a **d** of long standing with whom we	Ac 21:16	*3101*

DISCIPLES

seal the law among my **d**.	Is 8:16	3928
GOD has given Me the tongue of **d**,	Is 50:4	3928
He sat down, His **d** came to Him.	Mt 5:1	*3101*
Another of the **d** said to Him,	Mt 8:21	*3101*
into the boat, His **d** followed Him.	Mt 8:23	*3101*
were dining with Jesus and His **d**.	Mt 9:10	*3101*
saw *this*, they said to His **d**,	Mt 9:11	*3101*
Then the **d** of John came to Him,	Mt 9:14	*3101*
fast, but Your **d** do not fast?"	Mt 9:14	*3101*
to follow him, and *so did* His **d**.	Mt 9:19	*3101*
Then He said to His **d**,	Mt 9:37	*3101*
Jesus summoned His twelve **d**	Mt 10:1	*3101*
instructions to His twelve **d**,	Mt 11:1	*3101*
of Christ, he sent *word* by his **d**	Mt 11:2	*3101*
and His **d** became hungry and began	Mt 12:1	*3101*
Your **d** do what is not lawful to do	Mt 12:2	*3101*
out His hand toward His **d**,	Mt 12:49	*3101*
And the **d** came and said to Him,	Mt 13:10	*3101*
And His **d** came to Him and said,	Mt 13:36	*3101*
His **d** came and took away the	Mt 14:12	*3101*
it was evening, the **d** came to Him and	Mt 14:15	*3101*
the loaves He gave them to the **d**,	Mt 14:19	*3101*
and the **d** *gave them* to the crowds,	Mt 14:19	*3101*
He made the **d** get into the boat and	Mt 14:22	*3101*
the **d** saw Him walking on the sea,	Mt 14:26	*3101*
"Why do Your **d** break the	Mt 15:2	*3101*
Then the **d** came and said to Him,	Mt 15:12	*3101*
And His **d** came and implored	Mt 15:23	*3101*
And Jesus called His **d** to Him,	Mt 15:32	*3101*
The **d** said to Him,	Mt 15:33	*3101*
and started giving them to the **d**,	Mt 15:36	*3101*
and the **d** *gave them* to the people.	Mt 15:36	*3101*
And the **d** came to the other side	Mt 16:5	*3101*
Philippi, He was asking His **d**,	Mt 16:13	*3101*
Then He warned the **d** that they	Mt 16:20	*3101*
d that He must go to Jerusalem,	Mt 16:21	*3101*
Then Jesus said to His **d**,	Mt 16:24	*3101*
When the **d** heard *this*, they	Mt 17:6	*3101*
And His **d** asked Him, "	Mt 17:10	*3101*
Then the **d** understood that He had	Mt 17:13	*3101*
"I brought him to Your **d**,	Mt 17:16	*3101*
Then the **d** came to Jesus privately	Mt 17:19	*3101*
At that time the **d** came to Jesus and	Mt 18:1	*3101*
The **d** said to Him,	Mt 19:10	*3101*
and the **d** rebuked them.	Mt 19:13	*3101*
And Jesus said to His **d**,	Mt 19:23	*3101*
When the **d** heard *this*, they	Mt 19:25	*3101*
He took the twelve **d** aside by	Mt 20:17	*3101*
of Olives, then Jesus sent two **d**,	Mt 21:1	*3101*
The **d** went and did just as	Mt 21:6	*3101*
Seeing *this*, the **d** were	Mt 21:20	*3101*
And they sent their **d** to Him,	Mt 22:16	*3101*
to the crowds and to His **d**,	Mt 23:1	*3101*
was going away when His **d** came up	Mt 24:1	*3101*
the **d** came to Him privately,	Mt 24:3	*3101*
all these words, He said to His **d**,	Mt 26:1	*3101*
But the **d** were indignant when they	Mt 26:8	*3101*
Bread the **d** came to Jesus and	Mt 26:17	*3101*
at your house with My **d**.	Mt 26:18	*3101*
The **d** did as Jesus had	Mt 26:19	*3101*
at the table with the twelve **d**.	Mt 26:20	*3101*
He broke *it* and gave *it* to the **d**,	Mt 26:26	*3101*
All the **d** said the same thing too.	Mt 26:35	*3101*
Gethsemane, and said to His **d**,	Mt 26:36	*3101*
to the **d** and found them sleeping,	Mt 26:40	*3101*
Then He came to the **d** and	Mt 26:45	*3101*
Then all the **d** left Him and fled.	Mt 26:56	*3101*
otherwise His **d** may come and steal Him	Mt 27:64	*3101*
"Go quickly and tell His **d**	Mt 28:7	*3101*
joy and ran to report it to His **d**.	Mt 28:8	*3101*
'His **d** came by night and stole Him	Mt 28:13	*3101*
the eleven **d** proceeded to Galilee,	Mt 28:16	*3101*
and make **d** of all the nations,	Mt 28:19	*3100*
were dining with Jesus and His **d**;	Mk 2:15	*3101*
they said to His **d**,	Mk 2:16	*3101*
John's **d** and the Pharisees	Mk 2:18	*3101*
"Why do John's **d** and the	Mk 2:18	*3101*
and the **d** of the Pharisees fast,	Mk 2:18	*3101*
fast, but Your **d** do not fast?"	Mk 2:18	*3101*
and His **d** began to make their way	Mk 2:23	*3101*
withdrew to the sea with His **d**;	Mk 3:7	*3101*
And He told His **d** that a boat	Mk 3:9	*3101*
everything privately to His own **d**.	Mk 4:34	*3101*
And His **d** said to Him,	Mk 5:31	*3101*
and His **d** followed Him.	Mk 6:1	*3101*
When his **d** heard *about this*,	Mk 6:29	*3101*
His **d** came to Him and said,	Mk 6:35	*3101*
them to the **d** to set before them;	Mk 6:41	*3101*
Immediately Jesus made His **d** get	Mk 6:45	*3101*
and had seen that some of His **d**	Mk 7:2	*3101*
"Why do Your **d** not walk according	Mk 7:5	*3101*
His **d** questioned Him about the	Mk 7:17	*3101*
Jesus called His **d** and said to them,	Mk 8:1	*3101*
And His **d** answered Him,	Mk 8:4	*3101*
started giving them to His **d** to serve	Mk 8:6	*3101*
He entered the boat with His **d** and	Mk 8:10	*3101*
Jesus went out, along with His **d**,	Mk 8:27	*3101*
on the way He questioned His **d**,	Mk 8:27	*3101*
turning around and seeing His **d**,	Mk 8:33	*3101*
summoned the crowd with His **d**,	Mk 8:34	*3101*
When they came *back* to the **d**,	Mk 9:14	*3101*
I told Your **d** to cast it out,	Mk 9:18	*3101*
His **d** *began* questioning Him	Mk 9:28	*3101*
teaching His **d** and telling them,	Mk 9:31	*3101*
d *began* questioning Him about this	Mk 10:10	*3101*
but the **d** rebuked them.	Mk 10:13	*3101*
looking around, said to His **d**,	Mk 10:23	*3101*
The **d** were amazed at His words.	Mk 10:24	*3101*
with His **d** and a large crowd,	Mk 10:46	*3101*
of Olives, He sent two of His **d**,	Mk 11:1	*3101*
And His **d** were listening.	Mk 11:14	*3101*
Calling His **d** to Him, He said	Mk 12:43	*3101*
temple, one of His **d** said to Him,	Mk 13:1	*3101*
sacrificed, His **d** said to Him,	Mk 14:12	*3101*
And He sent two of His **d** and	Mk 14:13	*3101*
eat the Passover with My **d**?"	Mk 14:14	*3101*
The **d** went out and came to	Mk 14:16	*3101*
and He said to His **d**,	Mk 14:32	*3101*
"But go, tell His **d** and Peter,	Mk 16:7	*3101*
scribes *began* grumbling at His **d**,	Lk 5:30	*3101*
"The **d** of John often fast and	Lk 5:33	*3101*
the **d** of the Pharisees also do	Lk 5:33	
and His **d** were picking	Lk 6:1	*3101*
day came, He called His **d** to Him and	Lk 6:13	*3101*
was a large crowd of His **d**,	Lk 6:17	*3101*
And turning His gaze toward His **d**,	Lk 6:20	*3101*
His **d** were going along with Him,	Lk 7:11	*3101*
The **d** of John reported to him	Lk 7:18	*3101*
Summoning two of his **d**,	Lk 7:19	*3101*
His **d** *began* questioning Him as	Lk 8:9	*3101*
Jesus and His **d** got into a boat,	Lk 8:22	*3101*
And He said to His **d**,	Lk 9:14	*3101*
the **d** to set before the people.	Lk 9:16	*3101*
alone, the **d** were with Him,	Lk 9:18	*3101*
I begged Your **d** to cast it out,	Lk 9:40	*3101*
He was doing, He said to His **d**,	Lk 9:43	*3101*
His **d** James and John saw *this*,	Lk 9:54	*3101*
Turning to the **d**,	Lk 10:23	*3101*
one of His **d** said to Him,	Lk 11:1	*3101*
just as John also taught his **d**."	Lk 11:1	*3101*
saying to His **d** first *of all*,	Lk 12:1	*3101*
And He said to His **d**,	Lk 12:22	*3101*
Now He was also saying to the **d**,	Lk 16:1	*3101*
He said to His **d**,	Lk 17:1	*3101*
And He said to the **d**,	Lk 17:22	*3101*
touch them, but when the **d** saw it,	Lk 18:15	*3101*
But the **d** understood none of these	Lk 18:34	
Olivet, He sent two of the **d**,	Lk 19:29	*3101*
the whole crowd of the **d** began	Lk 19:37	*3101*
"Teacher, rebuke Your **d**."	Lk 19:39	*3101*
were listening, He said to the **d**,	Lk 20:45	*3101*
eat the Passover with My **d**?"	Lk 22:11	*3101*
and the **d** also followed Him.	Lk 22:39	*3101*
He came to the **d** and found them	Lk 22:45	*3101*
was standing with two of his **d**,	Jn 1:35	*3101*
The two **d** heard him speak, and	Jn 1:37	*3101*
both Jesus and His **d** were invited	Jn 2:2	*3101*
glory, and His **d** believed in Him.	Jn 2:11	*3101*
and *His* brothers and His **d**;	Jn 2:12	*3101*
His **d** remembered that it was	Jn 2:17	*3101*
d remembered that He said this;	Jn 2:22	*3101*
His **d** came into the land of Judea,	Jn 3:22	*3101*
on the part of John's **d** with a Jew	Jn 3:25	*3101*
and baptizing more **d** than John	Jn 4:1	*3101*
not baptizing, but His **d** were),	Jn 4:2	*3101*
For His **d** had gone away into the	Jn 4:8	*3101*
At this point His **d** came,	Jn 4:27	*3101*
the **d** were urging Him,	Jn 4:31	*3101*
So the **d** were saying to one	Jn 4:33	*3101*
and there He sat down with His **d**.	Jn 6:3	*3101*
One of His **d**, Andrew, Simon	Jn 6:8	*3101*
were filled, He said to His **d**,	Jn 6:12	*3101*
came, His **d** went down to the sea,	Jn 6:16	*3101*
entered with His **d** into the boat,	Jn 6:22	*3101*
that His **d** had gone away alone.	Jn 6:22	*3101*
Jesus was not there, nor His **d**,	Jn 6:24	*3101*
Therefore many of His **d**,	Jn 6:60	*3101*
that His **d** grumbled at this,	Jn 6:61	*3101*
of this many of His **d** withdrew and	Jn 6:66	*3101*
that Your **d** also may see Your	Jn 7:3	*3101*
then you are truly **d** of Mine;	Jn 8:31	*3101*
And His **d** asked Him,	Jn 9:2	*3101*
do not want to become His **d** too,	Jn 9:27	*3101*
disciple, but we are **d** of Moses.	Jn 9:28	*3101*
Then after this He said to the **d**,	Jn 11:7	*3101*
The **d** said to Him,	Jn 11:8	*3101*
The **d** then said to Him,	Jn 11:12	*3101*
Didymus, said to *his* fellow **d**,	Jn 11:16	*4827*
and there He stayed with the **d**.	Jn 11:54	*3101*
But Judas Iscariot, one of His **d**,	Jn 12:4	*3101*
These things His **d** did not	Jn 12:16	*3101*
d *began* looking at one another,	Jn 13:22	*3101*
on Jesus' bosom one of His **d**,	Jn 13:23	*3101*
men will know that you are My **d**,	Jn 13:35	*3101*
fruit, and *so* prove to be My **d**.	Jn 15:8	*3101*
d then said to one another,	Jn 16:17	*3101*
His **d** said, "Lo, now You are	Jn 16:29	*3101*
He went forth with His **d** over the	Jn 18:1	*3101*
He entered with His **d**.	Jn 18:1	*3101*
had often met there with His **d**.	Jn 18:2	*3101*
are not also *one* of this man's **d**,	Jn 18:17	*3101*
questioned Jesus about His **d**,	Jn 18:19	*3101*
"You are not also *one* of His **d**,	Jn 18:25	*3101*
So the **d** went away again to their	Jn 20:10	*3101*
came, announcing to the **d**,	Jn 20:18	*3101*
doors were shut where the **d** were,	Jn 20:19	*3101*
The **d** then rejoiced when they	Jn 20:20	*3101*
d were saying to him,	Jn 20:25	*3101*
days His **d** were again inside,	Jn 20:26	*3101*
in the presence of the **d**,	Jn 20:30	*3101*
to the **d** at the Sea of Tiberias,	Jn 21:1	*3101*
Zebedee, and two others of His **d** were	Jn 21:2	*3101*
yet the **d** did not know that it was	Jn 21:4	*3101*
other **d** came in the little boat,	Jn 21:8	*3101*
of the **d** ventured to question Him,	Jn 21:12	*3101*
Jesus was manifested to the **d**,	Jn 21:14	*3101*
the **d** were increasing *in number*,	Ac 6:1	*3101*
congregation of the **d** and said,	Ac 6:2	*3101*
and the number of the **d** continued	Ac 6:7	*3101*

murder against the **d** of the Lord, **Ac 9:1** *3101*
with the **d** who were at Damascus, **Ac 9:19** *3101*
but his **d** took him by night and **Ac 9:25** *3101*
trying to associate with the **d**; **Ac 9:26** *3101*
Since Lydda was near Joppa, the **d**, **Ac 9:38** *3101*
the **d** were first called Christians in **Ac 11:26** *3101*
that any of the **d** had means, **Ac 11:29** *3101*
And the **d** were continually filled **Ac 13:52** *3101*
But while the **d** stood around him, **Ac 14:20** *3101*
to that city and had made many **d**, **Ac 14:21** *3100*
strengthening the souls of the **d**, **Ac 14:22** *3101*
they spent a long time with the **d**. **Ac 14:28** *3101*
placing upon the neck of the **d** a yoke **Ac 15:10** *3101*
Phrygia, strengthening all the **d**. **Ac 18:23** *3101*
and wrote to the **d** to welcome him; **Ac 18:27** *3101*
came to Ephesus, and found some **d**. **Ac 19:1** *3101*
from them and took away the **d**, **Ac 19:9** *3101*
assembly, the **d** would not let him. **Ac 19:30** *3101*
Paul sent for the **d**, and when he **Ac 20:1** *3101*
to draw away the **d** after them. **Ac 20:30** *3101*
After looking up the **d**, **Ac 21:4** *3101*
Some of the **d** from Caesarea **Ac 21:16** *3101*

DISCIPLES'
and began to wash the **d** feet and to **Jn 13:5** *3101*

DISCIPLINE
let you hear His voice to **d** you; **Dt 4:36** 3256
not seen the **d** of the LORD your God **Dt 11:2** 4148
I will **d** you with scorpions.' " **1Ki 12:11** 3256
but I will **d** you with scorpions." **1Ki 12:14** 3256
but I *will* **d** *you* with scorpions.' " **2Ch 10:11**
but I *will* **d** *you* with scorpions." **2Ch 10:14**
not despise the **d** of the Almighty. **Jb 5:17** 4148
"For you hate **d**, And you cast My **Ps 50:17** 4148
do not reject the **d** of the LORD Or **Pr 3:11** 4148
reproofs for **d** are the way of life **Pr 6:23** 4148
one in fetters to the **d** of a fool, **Pr 7:22** 4148
Whoever loves **d** loves knowledge, **Pr 12:1** 4148
A wise son *accepts his* father's **d**, **Pr 13:1** 4148
will come to him who neglects **d**, **Pr 13:18** 4148
A fool rejects his father's **d**, **Pr 15:5** 4148
who neglects **d** despises himself, **Pr 15:32** 4148
it, But the **d** of fools is folly. **Pr 16:22** 4148
D your son while there is hope, **Pr 19:18** 3256
Listen to counsel and accept **d**, **Pr 19:20** 4148
Cease listening, my son, to **d**, **Pr 19:27** 4148
rod of **d** will remove it far from him. **Pr 22:15** 4148
Apply your heart to **d** And **Pr 23:12** 4148
Do not hold back **d** from the child, **Pr 23:13** 4148
and foolish *In their* **d** of delusion **Jer 10:8** 4148
but I **d** my body and make it my slave, **1Co 9:27** *5299*
the **d** and instruction of the Lord. **Eph 6:4** *3809*
rejoicing to see your good **d** and **Col 2:5** *5010*
d yourself for the purpose of **1Tm 4:7** *1128*
bodily **d** is only of little profit, **1Tm 4:8** *1129*
but of power and love and **d**. **2Tm 1:7** *4995*
DO NOT REGARD LIGHTLY THE **D** OF **Heb 12:5** *3809*
It is for **d** that you endure; **Heb 12:7** *3809*
there whom *his* father does not **d**? **Heb 12:7** *3811*
But if you are without **d**, **Heb 12:8** *3809*
we had earthly fathers to **d** us, **Heb 12:9** *3810*
All **d** for the moment seems not to **Heb 12:11** *3809*
whom I love, I reprove and **d**; **Rv 3:19** *3811*

DISCIPLINED
he **d** the men of Succoth with them. **Jg 8:16** 3045
my father **d** you with whips, but I **1Ki 12:11** 3256
my father **d** you with whips, but I **1Ki 12:14** 3256
my father **d** you with whips, but I **2Ch 10:11** 3256
my father **d** you with whips, but I **2Ch 10:14** 3256
The LORD has **d** me severely, But He **Ps 118:18** 3256
we are **d** by the Lord so that **1Co 11:32** *3811*
For they **d** us for a short time as **Heb 12:10** *3811*

DISCIPLINES
you just as a man **d** his son. **Dt 8:5** 3256
he who loves him **d** him diligently. **Pr 13:24** 4148
THOSE WHOM THE LORD LOVES HE **D**, **Heb 12:6** *3811*
but He **d** *us for our* good, so **Heb 12:10**

DISCIPLINING
that the LORD your God was **d** you **Dt 8:5** 3256

DISCLOSE
him and will **d** Myself to him." **Jn 14:21** *1718*
You are going to **d** Yourself to us and **Jn 14:22** *1718*
He will **d** to you what is to come. **Jn 16:13** *312*
of Mine and will **d** *it* to you. **Jn 16:14** *312*
of Mine and will **d** *it* to you. **Jn 16:15** *312*
and **d** the motives of *men's* hearts; **1Co 4:5** *5319*

DISCLOSED
Esther had **d** what he was to her. **Es 8:1** 5046
Joseph's family was **d** to Pharaoh. **Ac 7:13** *5318*
the secrets of his heart are **d**; **1Co 14:25** *5318*
the holy place has not yet been **d** while **Heb 9:8** *5319*

DISCLOSES
there is no one who **d** to me when my **1Sa 22:8** 1540
or **d** to me that my son has stirred up **1Sa 22:8** 1540

DISCLOSING
great or small without **d** it to me. **1Sa 20:2** 1540
confessing and **d** their practices. **Ac 19:18** *312*

DISCOMFORT
head to deliver him from his **d**. **Jon 4:6** 7463a

DISCONTENTED
debt, and everyone who was **d** gathered **1Sa 22:2** 4751, 5315

DISCOURAGED
they **d** the sons of Israel so that **Nu 32:9** 5106, 3820
of the land **d** the people of Judah, **Ezr 4:4** 7503, 3027
"They will become **d** with the work **Ne 6:9** 7503, 3027

DISCOURAGING
"Now why are you **d** the sons of **Nu 32:7** 5106, 3820
inasmuch as he is **d** the men of war **Jer 38:4** 7503, 3027

DISCOURSE
He took up his **d** and said, **Nu 23:7** 4912
Then he took up his **d** and said, **Nu 23:18** 4912
He took up his **d** and said, **Nu 24:3** 4912
He took up his **d** and said, **Nu 24:15** 4912
Amalek and took up his **d** and said, **Nu 24:20** 4912
and took up his **d** and said, **Nu 24:21** 4912
Then he took up his **d** and said, **Nu 24:23** 4912
Then Job continued his **d** and said, **Jb 27:1** 4912
Job again took up his **d** and said, **Jb 29:1** 4912
When He had completed all His **d** **Lk 7:1** *4487*

DISCOVER
you will **d** in the record books and **Ezr 4:15** 7912
"Can you **d** the depths of God? **Jb 11:7** 4672
you **d** the limits of the Almighty? **Jb 11:7** 4672
LORD And **d** the knowledge of God. **Pr 2:5** 4672
So that man will not **d** anything *that* **Ec 7:14** 4672
exceedingly mysterious. Who can **d** it **Ec 7:24** 4672
I concluded that man cannot **d** the **Ec 8:17** 4672
seek laboriously, he will not **d**; **Ec 8:17** 4672
"I know," he cannot **d**. **Ec 8:17** 4672

DISCOVERED
and lies with her and they are **d**, **Dt 22:28** 4672
So his strength was not **d**. **Jg 16:9** 3045
men who were with him had been **d**. **1Sa 22:6** 3045
has been **d** that that city has risen up **Ezr 4:19** 7912
I also **d** that the portions of the **Ne 13:10** 3045
And I **d** more bitter than death the **Ec 7:26** 4672
"Behold, I have **d** this," **Ec 7:27** 4672
the thief is shamed when he is **d**, **Jer 2:26** 4672

DISCOVERY
Concerning the **d** of his iniquity **Ps 36:2** 4672

DISCREDIT
precaution so that no one will **d** us **2Co 8:20** *3469*

DISCREDITED
so that the ministry will not be **d**, **2Co 6:3** *3469*

DISCREET
seven men who can give a **d** answer. **Pr 26:16** 2940

DISCREETLY
proper clothing, modestly and **d**, **1Tm 2:9** *4997*

DISCRETION
LORD give you **d** and understanding, **1Ch 22:12** 7922
endowed with **d** and understanding, **2Ch 2:12** 7922
To the youth knowledge and **d**, **Pr 1:4** 4209
D will guard you, Understanding **Pr 2:11** 4209
Keep sound wisdom and **d**, **Pr 3:21** 4209
That you may observe **d** And **Pr 5:2** 4209
And I find knowledge *and* **d**. **Pr 8:12** 4209
is a beautiful woman who lacks **d**. **Pr 11:22** 2940
A man's **d** makes him slow to anger, **Pr 19:11** 7922
with **d** and discernment to Arioch, **Da 2:14** 5843

DISCUSS
d matters of justice with You: **Jer 12:1** 1696
They began to **d** *this* among themselves, **Mt 16:7** *1260*
why do you **d** among yourselves that **Mt 16:8** *1260*
They *began* to **d** with one **Mk 8:16** *1260*
"Why do you **d** *the fact* that you **Mk 8:17** *1260*
And they began to **d** among **Lk 22:23** *4802*

DISCUSSED
for on the way they had **d** with one **Mk 9:34** *1256*
and **d** together what they might do **Lk 6:11** *1255*
d with the chief priests and officers **Lk 22:4** *4814*

DISCUSSING
d with one another what rising **Mk 9:10** *4802*
"What are you **d** with them?" **Mk 9:16** *4802*
"What were you **d** on the way?" **Mk 9:33** *1260*
While they were talking and **d**, **Lk 24:15** *4802*
But as he was **d** righteousness, **Ac 24:25** *1256*

DISCUSSION
Therefore there arose a **d** on the **Jn 3:25** *2214*
a **d** with anyone or causing a riot. **Ac 24:12** *1256*
have turned aside to fruitless **d**, **1Tm 1:6** *3150*

DISDAINED
looked and saw David, he **d** him; **1Sa 17:42** 959
But he **d** to lay hands on Mordecai **Es 3:6** 959, 5869
Whose fathers I **d** to put with the **Jb 30:1** 3988a

DISDAINFULLY
And you **d** sniff at it," **Mal 1:13** 5301

DISDAINING
place in every square, in **d** money, **Ezk 16:31** 7046

DISEASE
His **d** was severe, yet even in his **2Ch 16:12** 2483
his **d** he did not seek the LORD, **2Ch 16:12** 2483
sickness, a **d** of your bowels, **2Ch 21:15** 4245b
"His skin is devoured by **d**, **Jb 18:13** 905
But sent a wasting **d** among them. **Ps 106:15** 7332
d among his stout warriors; **Is 10:16** 7332
and healing every kind of **d** and **Mt 4:23** *3554*
of **d** and every kind of sickness. **Mt 9:35** *3554*
of **d** and every kind of sickness. **Mt 10:1** *3554*
d with which he was afflicted. **Jn 5:4** *3553*

DISEASED
his old age he was **d** in his feet. **1Ki 15:23** 2470a
reign Asa became **d** in his feet. **2Ch 16:12** 2456
the **d** you have not healed, **Ezk 34:4** 2470a

DISEASES
I will put none of the **d** on you **Ex 15:26** 4245a
d of Egypt which you have known, **Dt 7:15** 4064
He will bring back on you all the **d** **Dt 28:60** 4064
d with which the LORD has afflicted it, **Dt 29:22** 8463
Who heals all your **d**; **Ps 103:3** 8463
the city, Behold, **d** of famine! **Jer 14:18** 8463
"They will die of deadly **d**, **Jer 16:4** 8463
suffering with various **d** and pains, **Mt 4:24** *3554*
AND CARRIED AWAY OUR **D**." **Mt 8:17** *3554*
many who were ill with various **d**, **Mk 1:34** *3554*
various **d** brought them to Him; **Lk 4:40** *3554*
Him and to be healed of their **d**; **Lk 6:18** *3554*
He cured many *people* of **d** and **Lk 7:21** *3554*
all the demons and to heal **d**. **Lk 9:1** *3554*
and the **d** left them and the evil **Ac 19:12** *3554*
people on the island who had **d** were **Ac 28:9** *769*

DISFIGURED
lame man, or he who has a **d** *face*, **Lv 21:18** 2763b

DISGRACE
for that would be a **d** to us. **Gn 34:14** 2781
she sees his nakedness, it is a **d**; **Lv 20:17** 2617b
with **d** and conscious of my misery. **Jb 10:15** 7036
against me And prove my **d** to me, **Jb 19:5** 2781
Wounds and **d** he will find, And his **Pr 6:33** 7036
But sin is a **d** to *any* people. **Pr 14:34** 2617b
Do not **d** the throne of Your glory; **Jer 14:21** 5034a
d that will not be forgotten. **Jer 20:11** 3639
D has covered our faces, For **Jer 51:51** 3639
"Also bear your **d** in that you **Ezk 16:52** 3639
be also ashamed and bear your **d**, **Ezk 16:52** 3639
and bore their **d** with those who **Ezk 32:24** 3639
and they bore their **d** with those **Ezk 32:25** 3639
and bore their **d** with those who go **Ezk 32:30** 3639
d from the peoples any longer, **Ezk 36:15** 2781
the **d** of famine among the nations. **Ezk 36:30** 2781
"They will forget their **d** **Ezk 39:26** 3639
to **d** *and* everlasting contempt. **Da 12:2** 2781
And to the kingdoms your **d**. **Na 3:5** 7036
filled with **d** rather than honor. **Hab 2:16** 7036
utter **d** *will come* upon your glory. **Hab 2:16** 7022
man and not wanting to **d** her, **Mt 1:19** *1165*
me, to take away my **d** among men." **Lk 1:25** *3681*
and then in **d** you proceed to **Lk 14:9** *152*

DISGRACED
helps Me, Therefore, I am not **d**; **Is 50:7** 3637
humiliated, for you will not be **d**; **Is 54:4** 2659

DISGRACEFUL
angry because he had done a **d** thing **Gn 34:7** 5039
committed a **d** thing in Israel.' " **Jos 7:15** 5039
a lewd and **d** act in Israel. **Jg 20:6** 5039
may punish *them* for all the **d** acts **Jg 20:10** 5039
do not do this **d** thing! **2Sa 13:12** 5039
away Is a shameful and **d** son. **Pr 19:26** 2659
but if it is **d** for a woman to have **1Co 11:6** *150*
for it is **d** even to speak of the **Eph 5:12** *150*

DISGRACES
or prophesying **d** his head. **1Co 11:4** *2617b*
or prophesying **d** her head **1Co 11:5** *2617b*

DISGUISE
and **d** yourself so that they will **1Ki 14:2** 8132
d myself and go into the battle, **1Ki 22:30** 2664
will **d** myself and go into battle, **2Ch 18:29** 2664
if his servants also **d** themselves **2Co 11:15** *3345*

DISGUISED
but he **d** himself to them and spoke **Gn 42:7** 5235a
So he **d** his sanity before them, **1Sa 21:13** 8132
Then Saul **d** himself by putting on **1Sa 28:8** 2664
and **d** himself with a bandage over **1Ki 20:38** 2664
So the king of Israel **d** himself **1Ki 22:30** 2664
So the king of Israel **d** himself, **2Ch 18:29** 2664
but **d** himself in order to make war **2Ch 35:22** 2664

DISGUISES
And he **d** his face. **Jb 24:15** 7760, 5643a
He who hates **d** *it* with his lips, **Pr 26:24** 5235a
d himself as an angel of light. **2Co 11:14** *3345*

DISGUISING
d themselves as apostles of Christ. **2Co 11:13** *3345*

DISGUSTED
by them, she became **d** with them. **Ezk 23:17** 3363
then I became **d** with her, as I had **Ezk 23:18** 3363
as I had become **d** with her sister. **Ezk 23:18** 5361

DISGUSTINGLY
wicked man acts **d** and shamefully. **Pr 13:5** 887

DISH
a savory **d** for me such as I love, **Gn 27:4** 4303
and prepare a savory **d** for me, **Gn 27:7** 4303
as a savory **d** for your father, **Gn 27:9** 4303
and his offering *was* one silver **d** **Nu 7:13** 7086
silver **d** whose weight *was* one hundred **Nu 7:19** 7086
his offering *was* one silver **d** **Nu 7:25** 7086
his offering *was* one silver **d** **Nu 7:31** 7086
his offering *was* one silver **d** **Nu 7:37** 7086
his offering *was* one silver **d** **Nu 7:43** 7086
his offering *was* one silver **d** **Nu 7:49** 7086
his offering *was* one silver **d** **Nu 7:55** 7086
his offering *was* one silver **d** **Nu 7:61** 7086
his offering *was* one silver **d** **Nu 7:67** 7086
his offering *was* one silver **d** **Nu 7:73** 7086
his offering *was* one silver **d** **Nu 7:79** 7086
each silver **d** *weighing* one hundred **Nu 7:85** 7086
wipe Jerusalem as one wipes a **d**, **2Ki 21:13** 6747
a **d** of vegetables where love is Than **Pr 15:17** 737
sluggard buries his hand in the **d**, **Pr 19:24** 6747
sluggard buries his hand in the **d**; **Pr 26:15** 6747
outside of the cup and of the **d**, **Mt 23:25** *3953*
inside of the cup and of the **d**, **Mt 23:26** *3953*

DISHAN
and Dishon and Ezer and **D**. Gn 36:21 1789
These are the sons of **D**: Gn 36:28 1789
chief Dishon, chief Ezer, chief **D**. Gn 36:30 1789
Zibeon, Anah, Dishon, Ezer and **D**. 1Ch 1:38 1789
The sons of **D** *were* Uz and Aran. 1Ch 1:42 1789

DISHEARTENED
"He will not be **d** or crushed Until Is 42:4 3543a
have heard bad news; They are **d**. Jer 49:23 4127
"Because you **d** the righteous with Ezk 13:22 3512a
therefore he will be **d** and Da 11:30 3512a

DISHED
the pan and **d** *them* out before him, 2Sa 13:9 3332

DISHES
"You shall make its **d** and its Ex 25:29 7086
its **d** and its pans and its bowls Ex 37:16 7086
a cloth of blue and put on it the **d** Nu 4:7 7086
twelve silver **d**, twelve silver Nu 7:84 7086
30 gold **d**, 1,000 silver dishes, 29 Ezr 1:9 105
30 gold dishes, 1,000 silver **d**, Ezr 1:9 105

DISHON
and **D** and Ezer and Dishan. Gn 36:21 1787
D, and Oholibamah, the daughter of Gn 36:25 1787
These are the sons of **D**: Gn 36:26 1787
chief **D**, chief Ezer, chief Dishan. Gn 36:30 1787
Lotan, Shobal, Zibeon, Anah, **D**, 1Ch 1:38 1787
The son of Anah *was* **D**. 1Ch 1:41 1787
And the sons of **D** *were* Hamran, 1Ch 1:41 1787

DISHONEST
of truth, those who hate **d** gain; Ex 18:21 1215
but turned aside after **d** gain and 1Sa 8:3 1215
to Your testimonies And not to **d** Ps 119:36 1215
intent only upon your own **d** gain, Jer 22:17 1215
I smite My hand at your **d** gain Ezk 22:13 1215
lives in order to get **d** gain. Ezk 22:27 1214
And to cheat with **d** scales, Am 8:5 4820

DISHONOR
fitting for us to see the king's **d**, Ezr 4:14 6173
those be clothed with shame and **d** Ps 35:26 3639
rejected *us* and brought us to **d**, Ps 44:9 3637
All day long my **d** is before me And Ps 44:15 3639
D has covered my face. Ps 69:7 3639
my reproach and my shame and my **d**; Ps 69:19 3639
be covered with reproach and **d**, Ps 71:13 3639
Fill their faces with **d**, Ps 83:16 7036
Let my accusers be clothed with **d**, Ps 109:29 3639
honor, But fools display **d**. Pr 3:35 7036
a scoffer gets **d** for himself, Pr 9:7 7036
When pride comes, then comes **d**, Pr 11:2 7036
But a prudent man conceals **d**. Pr 12:16 7036
comes, And with **d** *comes* scorn. Pr 18:3 7036
out, Even strife and **d** will cease. Pr 22:10 7036
I honor My Father, and you **d** Me. Jn 8:49 *818*
breaking the Law, do you **d** God? Ro 2:23 *818*
has long hair, it is a **d** to him, 1Co 11:14 *819*
it is sown in **d**, it is raised in 1Co 15:43 *819*
by glory and **d**, by evil report and 2Co 6:8 *819*
and some to honor and some to **d**. 2Tm 2:20 *819*

DISHONORED
because his father had **d** him. 1Sa 20:34 3637
be ashamed and **d** who seek my life; Ps 35:4 3637
back and **d** Who delight in my hurt. Ps 40:14 3637
who seek You not be **d** through me, Ps 69:6 3637
back and **d** Who delight in my hurt. Ps 70:2 3637
Let not the oppressed return **d**; Ps 74:21 3637
at you will be shamed and **d**; Is 41:11 3637
bodies would be **d** among them. Ro 1:24 *818*
that the word of God will not be **d**. Ti 2:5 *987*
But you have **d** the poor man. Jas 2:6 *818*

DISHONORS
is he who **d** his father or mother.' Dt 27:16 7034

DISLOCATED
was **d** while he wrestled with him. Gn 32:25 3363

DISMAY
strength, And **d** leaps before him. Jb 41:22 1670
them, or I will **d** you before them. Jer 1:17 2865
I mourn, **d** has taken hold of me. Jer 8:21 8047
bring down on her Anguish and **d**. Jer 15:8 928
on the earth **d** among nations, Lk 21:25 *4928*

DISMAYED
bundles of money, they were **d**. Gn 42:35 3372a
for they were **d** at his presence. Gn 45:3 926
"Then the chiefs of Edom were **d**; Ex 15:15 926
Do not fear or be **d**.' Dt 1:21 2865
Do not fear or be **d**." Dt 31:8 2865
Do not tremble or be **d**, Jos 1:9 2865
"Do not fear or be **d**. Jos 8:1 2865
"Do not fear or be **d**! Jos 10:25 2865
they were **d** and greatly afraid. 1Sa 17:11 2865
They were **d** and put to shame; 2Ki 19:26 2865
courageous, do not fear nor be **d**. 1Ch 22:13 2865
do not fear nor be **d**, 1Ch 28:20 2865
'Do not fear or be **d** because of 2Ch 20:15 2865
Do not fear or be **d**; 2Ch 20:17 2865
do not fear or be **d** because of the 2Ch 32:7 2865
It touches you, and you are **d**. Jb 4:5 926
I would be **d** at His presence; Jb 23:15 926
And the Almighty *who* has **d** me, Jb 23:16 926
"They are **d**, they no longer answer; Jb 32:15 2865
"He laughs at fear and is not **d**; Jb 39:22 2865
me, O LORD, for my bones are **d**. Ps 6:2 926
And my soul is greatly **d**; Ps 6:3 926
will be ashamed and greatly **d**; Ps 6:10 926
You hid Your face, I was **d**. Ps 30:7 926
Let them be ashamed and **d** forever, Ps 83:17 926
And by Your wrath we have been **d**. Ps 90:7 926
You hide Your face, they are **d**; Ps 104:29 926
"Then they will be **d** and ashamed Is 20:5 2865
They were **d** and put to shame; Is 37:27 2865
Nor be **d** at their revilings. Is 51:7 2865
Do not be **d** before them, or I Jer 1:17 2865
to shame, They are **d** and caught; Jer 8:9 2865
"Why are You like a man **d**, Jer 14:9 1724
Let them be **d**, but let me not be Jer 17:18 2865
be dismayed, but let me not be **d**. Jer 17:18 2865
'And do not be **d**, O Israel; Jer 30:10 2865
My servant, do not fear, Nor be **d**, Jer 46:27 2865
words nor be **d** at their presence, Ezk 2:6 2865
of them or be **d** before them, Ezk 3:9 2865
"Then your mighty men will be **d**, Ob 1:9 2865

DISMISS
did not **d** *any of* the divisions. 2Ch 23:8 6362

DISMISSED
Then Joshua **d** the people, each to Jos 24:28 7971
When Joshua had **d** the people, the Jg 2:6 7971
So Solomon **d** Abiathar from being 1Ki 2:27 1644
Then Amaziah **d** them, the troops 2Ch 25:10 914
saying this he **d** the assembly. Ac 19:41 *630*

DISMOUNTED
saw Isaac she **d** from the camel. Gn 24:64 5307
she hurried and **d** from her donkey, 1Sa 25:23 3381

DISOBEDIENCE
man's **d** the many were made sinners, Ro 5:19 *3876*
shown mercy because of their **d**, Ro 11:30 *543*
For God has shut up all in **d** so Ro 11:32 *543*
and we are ready to punish all **d**, 2Co 10:6 *3876*
is now working in the sons of **d**. Eph 2:2 *543*
of God comes upon the sons of **d**. Eph 5:6 *543*
of God will come upon the sons of **d**, Col 3:6 *545*
and **d** received a just penalty, Heb 2:2 *3876*
them failed to enter because of **d**, Heb 4:6 *543*
following the same example of **d**. Heb 4:11 *543*

DISOBEDIENT
d and rebelled against You, Ne 9:26 4784
And I was not **d** Nor did I turn Is 50:5 4784
and the **d** to the attitude of the Lk 1:17 *545*
some were becoming hardened and **d**, Ac 19:9 *544*
prove **d** to the heavenly vision, Ac 26:19 *545*
inventors of evil, **d** to parents, Ro 1:30 *545*
TO A D AND OBSTINATE PEOPLE." Ro 10:21 *544*
just as you once were **d** to God, Ro 11:30 *544*
so these also now have been **d**, Ro 11:31 *544*
from those who are **d** in Judea, Ro 15:31 *544*
arrogant, revilers, **d** to parents, 2Tm 3:2 *545*
deny *Him*, being detestable and **d** and Ti 1:16 *545*
once were foolish ourselves, **d**, Ti 3:3 *545*
His rest, but to those who were **d**? Heb 3:18 *544*
along with those who were **d**, Heb 11:31 *544*
because they are **d** to the word, 1Pe 2:8 *544*
if any *of them* are **d** to the word, 1Pe 3:1 *544*
who once were **d**, when the patience 1Pe 3:20 *544*

DISOBEYED
have **d** the command of the LORD, 1Ki 13:21 4784
who **d** the command of the LORD; 1Ki 13:26 4784

DISORDER
and the crowd in noisy **d**, Mt 9:23 *2350b*
there is **d** and every evil thing. Jas 3:16 *181*

DISORDERLY
to account for this **d** gathering." Ac 19:40 *4963*

DISOWNED
and **d** in the presence of Pilate, Ac 3:13 *720*
you **d** the Holy and Righteous One and Ac 3:14 *720*
"This Moses whom they **d**, Ac 7:35 *720*

DISPATCH
"I will **d** foreigners to Jer 51:2 7971
"Now **d** *some* men to Joppa and Ac 10:5 *3992*

DISPENSE
'**D** true justice and practice Zch 7:9 8199

DISPERSE
I will **d** them in Jacob, And Gn 49:7 2505a
"**D** yourselves among the people 1Sa 14:34 6327a
lifting up of Yourself nations **d**. Is 33:3 5310b
and **d** them among the lands, Ezk 20:23 2219
I will **d** you through the lands, Ezk 22:15 2219
and **d** them among the lands." Ezk 29:12 2219
and **d** them among the lands. Ezk 30:23 2219
and **d** them among the lands, Ezk 30:26 2219

DISPERSED
and they were **d** from the city, 2Sa 20:22 6327a
certain people scattered and **d** among Es 3:8 6504
Should your springs be **d** abroad, Pr 5:16 6327a
And will gather the **d** of Judah Is 11:12 5310b
GOD, who gathers the **d** of Israel, Is 56:8 5080
they were **d** throughout the lands. Ezk 36:19 2219
Ethiopia My worshipers, My **d** ones, Zph 3:10 1323, 6327a
"for I have **d** you as the four Zch 2:6 6566
him were **d** and came to nothing. Ac 5:36 *1262*
twelve tribes who are **d** abroad: Jas 1:1 *1290*

DISPERSES
He **d** the cloud of His lightning. Jb 37:11 6327a
justice **D** all evil with his eyes. Pr 20:8 2219

DISPERSION
to go to the **D** among the Greeks, Jn 7:35 *1290*

DISPERSIONS
slaughter and your **d** have come, Jer 25:34 8600a

DISPIRITED
because they were distressed and **d** Mt 9:36 *4496*

DISPLAY
in order to **d** her beauty to the people Es 1:11 7200
honor, But fools **d** dishonor. Pr 3:35 7311
And they **d** their sin like Sodom; Is 3:9 5046
with them and **d** *great* strength. Da 11:7 2388
will **d** strength and take action. Da 11:32 2388
"I will **d** wonders in the sky Jl 2:30 5414
He made a public **d** of them, Col 2:15 *1165*

DISPLAYED
And he **d** the riches of his royal Es 1:4 7200
Who have **d** Your splendor above the Ps 8:1 5414
it may be **d** because of the truth. Ps 60:4 5264
had **d** His great mercy toward her; Lk 1:58 *3170*
works of God might be **d** in him. Jn 9:3 *5319*
whom God **d** publicly as a Ro 3:25 *4388*

DISPLAYING
of God, **d** himself as being God. 2Th 2:4 *584*

DISPLAYS
knowledge, But a fool **d** folly. Pr 13:16 6566
A wicked man **d** a bold face, But as Pr 21:29 5810

DISPLEASE
d the lords of the Philistines." 1Sa 29:7 6213a, 7451a, 5869
'Do not let this thing **d** you, 2Sa 11:25 7489a, 5869

DISPLEASED
of Canaan **d** his father Isaac; Gn 28:8 7451a
hand on Ephraim's head, it **d** him; Gn 48:17 7489a
kindled greatly, and Moses was **d**. Nu 11:10 7489a, 5869
very angry, for this saying **d** him; 1Sa 18:8 7489a, 5869
God was **d** with this thing, so 1Ch 21:7 7489a, 5869
Or the LORD will see *it* and be **d**, Pr 24:18 7489a, 5869
But it greatly **d** Jonah and he Jon 4:1 7489a

DISPLEASING
was **d** in the sight of the LORD; Gn 38:10 7489a
"If she is **d** in the eyes of her Ex 21:8 7451a
Now then, if it is **d** to you, Nu 22:34 7489a
But the thing was **d** in the sight 1Sa 8:6 7489a
it was very **d** to them that someone Ne 2:10 7489a
It was very **d** to me, so I Ne 13:8 7489a
And it was **d** in His sight that Is 59:15 7489a

DISPLEASURE
I was afraid of the anger and hot **d** Dt 9:19 2534

DISPOSAL
"The land of Egypt is at your **d**; Gn 47:6 6440
"My very own vineyard is at my **d**; SS 8:12 6440
and He will at once put at My **d** Mt 26:53 *3936*

DISPOSED
d to all those who seek Him, Ezr 8:22 2899b

DISPOSSESS
them with pestilence and **d** them, Nu 14:12 3423
how can I **d** them?' Dt 7:17 3423
the Jordan today to go in to **d** nations Dt 9:1 3423
and you will **d** nations greater and Dt 11:23 3423
whom you shall **d** serve their gods, Dt 12:2 3423
which you are going in to **d**, Dt 12:29 3423
d them and dwell in their land, Dt 12:29 3423
those nations, which you shall **d**, Dt 18:14 3423
and you **d** them and settle in their Dt 19:1 3423
before you, and you shall **d** them. Dt 31:3 3423
d from before you the Canaanite, Jos 3:10 3423
But the sons of Israel did not **d** Jos 13:13 3423
the Lord will **d** her And cast her Zch 9:4 3423

DISPOSSESSED
and **d** the Amorites who *were* there. Nu 21:32 3423
and **d** the Amorites who were in it. Nu 32:39 3423
but the sons of Esau **d** them and Dt 2:12 3423
And they **d** them and settled in Dt 2:21 3423
they **d** them and settled in Dt 2:22 3423
for Moses struck them and **d** them. Jos 13:12 3423
and **d** them before you and gave you Jg 6:9 1644
LORD **d** before the sons of Israel. 1Ki 14:24 3423
LORD **d** before the sons of Israel. 2Ki 21:2 3423
LORD **d** before the sons of Israel. 2Ch 33:2 3423

DISPOSSESSING
the LORD is **d** them before you. Dt 9:4 3423
with Joshua upon **d** the nations Ac 7:45 *2697*

DISPUTE
"When they have a **d**, Ex 18:16 1697
major **d** they will bring to you, Ex 18:22 1697
every minor **d** they themselves will Ex 18:22 1697
d they would bring to Moses, Ex 18:26 1697
d they themselves would judge. Ex 18:26 1697
nor shall you testify in a **d** so as Ex 23:2 7379
be partial to a poor man in his **d**. Ex 23:3 7379
to your needy *brother* in his **d**. Ex 23:6 7379
being cases of **d** in your courts, Dt 17:8 7379
the **d** shall stand before the LORD, Dt 19:17 7379
and every **d** and every assault Dt 21:5 7379
"If there is a **d** between men and Dt 25:1 7379
and thus they ended *the* **d**. 2Sa 20:18
"Whenever any **d** comes to you 2Ch 19:10 7379
"If one wished to **d** with Him, Jb 9:3 7378
But the slow to anger calms a **d**. Pr 15:18 7379
for he cannot **d** with him who is Ec 6:10 1777
"In a **d** they shall take their Ezk 44:24 7379
The LORD also has a **d** with Judah, Hos 12:2 7379
Even with Israel He will **d**. Mi 6:2 3198
And there arose also a **d** among Lk 22:24 *5379*
a great **d** among themselves. Ac 28:29 *4803*
confirmation is an end of every **d**. Heb 6:16 *485*
But without any **d** the lesser is Heb 7:7 *485*

DISPUTED
when he **d** with the devil and Jude 1:9 *1252*

DISPUTES
God, and you bring the **d** to God, Ex 18:19 1697

and to judge **d** among the inhabitants **2Ch 19:8** 7379
jealousy, angry tempers, **d**, **2Co 12:20** *2052*
jealousy, outbursts of anger, **d**, **Ga 5:20** *2052*
questions and **d** about words, **1Tm 6:4** *3055*
and strife and **d** about the Law, **Ti 3:9** *3163*

DISPUTING
all things without grumbling or **d**; **Php 2:14** *1261*

DISQUALIFIED
to others, I myself will not be **d**. **1Co 9:27** *96b*

DISQUIETING
"Amid **d** thoughts from the visions **Jb 4:13** 8174b
my **d** thoughts make me respond, **Jb 20:2** 8174b

DISREGARD
should ever **d** that man when he **Lv 20:4** 5956, 5869
yet **d** justice and the love of God; **Lk 11:42** *3928*
sensual desires in **d** of Christ, **1Tm 5:11** *2691*
Let no one **d** you. **Ti 2:15** *4065*

DISREGARDED
d the message which Jephthah sent **Jg 11:28** 3808, 8085
These men, O king, have **d** you; **Da 3:12** 3809, 7761, 5922, 2942

DISREPUTE
this trade of ours fall into **d**, **Ac 19:27** *557*

DISRESPECTFUL
believers as their masters must not be **d** **1Tm 6:2** *2706*

DISSENSION
had great **d** and debate with them, **Ac 15:2** *4714b*
there occurred a **d** between the **Ac 23:7** *4714b*
And as a great **d** was developing, **Ac 23:10** *4714b*
who stirs up **d** among all the Jews **Ac 24:5** *4714b*
holy hands, without wrath and **d**. **1Tm 2:8** *1261*

DISSENSIONS
keep your eye on those who cause **d** **Ro 16:17** *1370*
outbursts of anger, disputes, **d**, **Ga 5:20** *1370*

DISSIPATION
will not be weighted down with **d** **Lk 21:34** *2897*
drunk with wine, for that is **d**, **Eph 5:18** *810*
not accused of **d** or rebellion. **Ti 1:6** *810*
them into the same excesses of **d**, **1Pe 4:4** *810*

DISSOLVE
And You **d** me in a storm. **Jb 30:22** 4127
swim, I **d** my couch with my tears. **Ps 6:6** 4529
because of Him And the hills **d**; **Na 1:5** 4127

DISSOLVED
Everyone is wailing, **d** in tears. **Is 15:3** 3381
wine And all the hills will be **d**. **Am 9:13** 4127
are opened And the palace is **d**. **Na 2:6** 4127

DISTAFF
a leper, or who takes hold of a **d**, **2Sa 3:29** 6418
stretches out her hands to the **d**, **Pr 31:19** 3601

DISTANCE
eyes and saw the place from a **d**. **Gn 22:4** 7350
And he put a **d** *of* three days' **Gn 30:36** 7350
with him and pursued him *a* **d** *of* **Gn 31:23** 7350
was still some **d** to go to Ephrath, **Gn 35:16** 3530, 776
When they saw him from a **d** and **Gn 37:18** 7350
was still some **d** to go to Ephrath; **Gn 48:7** 3530, 776
His sister stood at a **d** to **Ex 2:4** 7350
they trembled and stood at a **d**. **Ex 20:18** 7350
So the people stood at a **d**, **Ex 20:21** 7350
and you shall worship at a **d**. **Ex 24:1** 7350
the camp, a good **d** from the camp, **Ex 33:7** 7368
around the tent of meeting at a **d**. **Nu 2:2** 4480, 5048
"If the **d** is so great for you **Dt 14:24** 1870
shall go out and measure *the* **d** to **Dt 21:2** 7350
"For you shall see the land at a **d**, **Dt 32:52** 4480, 5048
a **d** of about 2,000 cubits by measure. **Jos 3:4** 7350
one heap, a great **d** away at Adam, **Jos 3:16** 7368
some **d** from the house of Micah, **Jg 18:22** 7368
stood on top of the mountain at a **d** **1Sa 26:13** 7350
and stood opposite *them* at a **d**, **2Ki 2:7** 7350
the man of God saw her at a **d**, **2Ki 4:25** 4480, 5048
So he departed from him some **d**. **2Ki 5:19** 3530, 776
they lifted up their eyes at a **d** and **Jb 2:12** 7350
have sent your envoys a great **d** And **Is 57:9** 7350
many swine feeding at a **d** **Mt 8:30** *3112*
But the boat was already a long **d** **Mt 14:24** *4712*
Peter was following Him at a **d** **Mt 26:58** *3113*
were there looking on from a **d**, **Mt 27:55** *3113*
Seeing Jesus from a **d**, **Mk 5:6** *3113*
have come from a great **d**." **Mk 8:3** *3113*
Seeing at a **d** a fig tree in leaf, **Mk 11:13** *3113*
Peter had followed Him at a **d**, **Mk 14:54** *3113*
some women looking on from a **d**, **Mk 15:40** *3113*
men who stood at a **d** met Him; **Lk 17:12** *4207*
tax collector, standing some **d** away, **Lk 18:13** *3113*
but Peter was following at a **d**. **Lk 22:54** *3113*
Galilee were standing at a **d**, **Lk 23:49** *3113*
and having welcomed them from a **d**, **Heb 11:13** *4207*
for a **d** of two hundred miles. **Rv 14:20** *575*
standing at a **d** because of the **Rv 18:10** *3113*
will stand at a **d** because of the **Rv 18:15** *3113*
living by the sea, stood at a **d**, **Rv 18:17** *3113*

DISTANT
dead person, or is on a **d** journey, **Nu 9:10** 7350
foreigner who comes from a **d** land, **Dt 29:22** 7350
servant concerning the **d** future. **2Sa 7:19** 7350
Look also at the **d** stars, **Jb 22:12** 7218
So is good news from a **d** land. **Pr 25:25** 4801
up a standard to the **d** nation, **Is 5:26** 7350
to carry her to colonize **d** places? **Is 23:7** 7350
to the **d** coastlands that have **Is 66:19** 7350
And the sweet cane from a **d** land? **Jer 6:20** 4801
of my people from a **d** land: **Jer 8:19** 4801
to the Sabeans, to a **d** nation," **Jl 3:8** 7350
decisions for mighty, **d** nations. **Mi 4:3** 7350
on a journey into a **d** country, **Lk 15:13** *3117*
"A nobleman went to a **d** **Lk 19:12** *3117*

DISTILL
the rain, My speech **d** as the dew, **Dt 32:2** 5140
water, They **d** rain from the mist, **Jb 36:27** 2212

DISTINCTION
"But the LORD will make a **d** **Ex 9:4** 6395
a **d** between Egypt and Israel.' **Ex 11:7** 6395
and so as to make a **d** between the **Lv 10:10** 914
to make a **d** between the unclean **Lv 11:47** 914
'You are therefore to make a **d** **Lv 20:25** 914
they have made no **d** between the **Ezk 22:26** 914
He made no **d** between us and them, **Ac 15:9** *1252*
for there is no **d**; **Ro 3:22** *1293*
is no **d** between Jew and Greek; **Ro 10:12** *1293*
do not produce a **d** in the tones, **1Co 14:7** *1293*
a renewal in which there is no **d** **Col 3:11**

DISTINCTIONS
you not made **d** among yourselves, **Jas 2:4** *1252*

DISTINCTLY
the words of this law very **d**." **Dt 27:8** 874

DISTINGUISH
Can I **d** between good and bad? **2Sa 19:35** 3045
so that the people could not **d** the **Ezr 3:13** 5234
So you will again **d** between the **Mal 3:18** 7200

DISTINGUISHED
of the one **d** among his brothers. **Gn 49:26** 5139
may be **d** from all the *other* people **Ex 33:16** 6395
and more **d** than the former. **Nu 22:15** 3513
of the one **d** among his brothers. **Dt 33:16** 5139
king of Israel **d** himself today! **2Sa 6:20** 3513
spoken, with them I will be **d**." **2Sa 6:22** 3513
The **d** men of the foremost of **Am 6:1** 5344a
for someone more **d** than you may **Lk 14:8** *1784*
you are **d**, but we are without **1Co 4:10** *1741*

DISTINGUISHES
It is by his deeds that a lad **d** **Pr 20:11** 5234

DISTINGUISHING
So that it became your **d** mark; **Ezk 27:7** 5251
Then this Daniel began **d** himself **Da 6:3** 5330
and to another the **d** of spirits, **1Co 12:10** *1253*
this is a **d** mark in every letter; **2Th 3:17** *4592*

DISTORT
"You shall not **d** justice; **Dt 16:19** 5186
All day long they **d** my words; **Ps 56:5** 6087a
want to **d** the gospel of Christ. **Ga 1:7** *3344*
which the untaught and unstable **d**, **2Pe 3:16** *4761*

DISTORTED
"By a great force my garment is **d**; **Jb 30:18** 2664

DISTORTION
mixed within her a spirit of **d**; **Is 19:14** 5773

DISTORTS
he who **d** the justice due an alien, **Dt 27:19** 5186
devastates it, **d** its surface and **Is 24:1** 5753a

DISTRACTED
in my complaint and am surely **d**, **Ps 55:2** 1949
Martha was **d** with all her **Lk 10:40** *4049*

DISTRESS
answered me in the day of my **d** and **Gn 35:3** 6869a
because we saw the **d** of his soul **Gn 42:21** 6869a
this **d** has come upon us." **Gn 42:21** 6869a
"When you are in **d** and all these **Dt 4:30** 6862b
during the siege and the **d** by **Dt 28:53** 4689
during the siege and the **d** by **Dt 28:55** 4689
during the siege and the **d** by **Dt 28:57** 4689
you in the time of your **d**." **Jg 10:14** 6869a
You will see the **d** of *My* dwelling, **1Sa 2:32** 6862b
Everyone who was in **d**, **1Sa 22:2** 4689
may He deliver me from all **d**. **1Sa 26:24** 6869a
has redeemed my life from all **d**, **2Sa 4:9** 6869a
"In my **d** I called upon the LORD, **2Sa 22:7** 6862b
David said to Gad, "I am in great **d**. **2Sa 24:14** 6887b
has redeemed my life from all **d**, **1Ki 1:29** 6869a
'This day is a day of **d**, **2Ki 19:3** 6869a
David said to Gad, "I am in great **d**; **1Ch 21:13** 6887a
"But in their **d** they turned to **2Ch 15:4** 6862b
them with every kind of **d**. **2Ch 15:6** 6869a
and cry to You in our **d**, **2Ch 20:9** 6869a
Now in the time of his **d** this same **2Ch 28:22** 6887a
When he was in **d**, **2Ch 33:12** 6887a
are in great **d** and reproach, **Ne 1:3** 7463a
to You in the time of their **d**, **Ne 9:27** 6869a
they please, So we are in great **d**. **Ne 9:37** 6869a
"**D** and anguish terrify him, They **Jb 15:24** 6862b
his cry When **d** comes upon him? **Jb 27:9** 6869a
enticed you from the mouth of **d**, **Jb 36:16** 6862b
"Will your riches keep you from **d**, **Jb 36:19** 6862b
I have reserved for the time of **d**, **Jb 38:23** 6862b
You have relieved me in my **d**; **Ps 4:1** 6862b
In my **d** I called upon the LORD, **Ps 18:6** 6862b
to me, O LORD, for I am in **d**; **Ps 31:9** 6887a
altogether who rejoice at my **d**; **Ps 35:26** 7463a
And a refuge in the day of my **d**. **Ps 59:16** 6862b
my mouth spoke when I was in **d**. **Ps 66:14** 6862b
from Your servant, For I am in **d**; **Ps 69:17** 6887a
face from me in the day of my **d**; **Ps 102:2** 6862b
He looked upon their **d** When **Ps 106:44** 6862b
I found **d** and sorrow. **Ps 116:3** 6869a
From *my* **d** I called upon the LORD; **Ps 118:5** 4712
When **d** and anguish come upon you. **Pr 1:27** 6869a
If you are slack in the day of **d**, **Pr 24:10** 6869a
but behold, a cry of **d**. **Is 5:7** 6818
behold, there is darkness *and* **d**; **Is 5:30** 6862b
earth, and behold, **d** and darkness, **Is 8:22** 6869a
raise a cry of **d** over *their* ruin. **Is 15:5** 2201
For the cry of **d** has gone around **Is 15:8** 2201
A defense for the needy in his **d**, **Is 25:4** 6862b
O LORD, they sought You in **d**; **Is 26:16** 6862b
I will bring **d** to Ariel, **Is 29:2** 6693
and her stronghold, and who **d** her, **Is 29:7** 6693
Through a land of **d** and anguish, **Is 30:6** 6869a
salvation also in the time of **d**. **Is 33:2** 6869a
'This day is a day of **d**, **Is 37:3** 6869a
It cannot deliver him from his **d**. **Is 46:7** 6869a
this time, And will cause them **d**, **Jer 10:18** 6887a
Israel, Its Savior in time of **d**, **Jer 14:8** 6869a
time of disaster and a time of **d**. **Jer 15:11** 6869a
And my refuge in the day of **d**, **Jer 16:19** 6869a
and in the **d** with which their enemies **Jer 19:9** 4689
seek their life will **d** them." **Jer 19:9** 6693
And it is the time of Jacob's **d**, **Jer 30:7** 6869a
the earth is full of your cry *of* **d**; **Jer 46:12**
ones have sounded out a cry *of* **d**. **Jer 48:4**
D and pangs have taken hold of her **Jer 49:24** 6869a
D has gripped him, Agony like a **Jer 50:43** 6869a
overtaken her In the midst of **d**. **La 1:3** 4712
"See, O LORD, for I am in **d**; **La 1:20** 6887a
and moat, even in times of **d**. **Da 9:25** 6695a
And there will be a time of **d** such **Da 12:1** 6869a
You who **d** the righteous *and* accept **Am 5:12** 6887c
not boast In the day of *their* **d**. **Ob 1:12** 6869a
survivors In the day of their **d**. **Ob 1:14** 6869a
"I called out of my **d** to the LORD, **Jon 2:2** 6869a
D will not rise up twice. **Na 1:9** 6869a
I saw the tents of Cushan under **d**, **Hab 3:7** 205
wait quietly for the day of **d**, **Hab 3:16** 6869a
that day, A day of trouble and **d**, **Zph 1:15** 4691
I will bring **d** on men So **Zph 1:17** 6887a
they will pass through the sea *of* **d** **Zch 10:11** 6869a
will be great **d** upon the land and **Lk 21:23** *318*
There will be tribulation and **d** **Ro 2:9** *4730*
Will tribulation, or **d**, **Ro 8:35** *4730*
is good in view of the present **d**, **1Co 7:26** *318*
to cause me **d** in my imprisonment. **Php 1:17** *2347*
in all our **d** and affliction we **1Th 3:7** *318*
if she has assisted those in **d**, **1Tm 5:10** *2346*
orphans and widows in their **d**, **Jas 1:27** *2347*

DISTRESSED
The matter **d** Abraham greatly **Gn 21:11** 7489a
"Do not be **d** because of the lad **Gn 21:12** 7489a
Jacob was greatly afraid and **d**; **Gn 32:7** 6887a
so that they were severely **d**. **Jg 2:15** 6887a
so that Israel was greatly **d**. **Jg 10:9** 6887a
She, greatly **d**, prayed to the LORD **1Sa 1:10** 4751
And Samuel was **d** and cried out to **1Sa 15:11** 2734
And Saul answered, "I am greatly **d**; **1Sa 28:15** 6887a
Moreover David was greatly **d** **1Sa 30:6** 6887a
"I am **d** for you, my brother **2Sa 1:26** 6887a
he was deeply **d** and set *his* mind **Da 6:14** 888
Daniel, my spirit was **d** within me, **Da 7:15** 3735
because they were **d** and dispirited **Mt 9:36** *4660*
and began to be grieved and **d**. **Mt 26:37** *85*
began to be very **d** and troubled. **Mk 14:33** *1568*
d I am until it is accomplished! **Lk 12:50** *4912*
he was longing for you all and was **d** **Php 2:26** *85*
you have been **d** by various trials, **1Pe 1:6** *3076*

DISTRESSES
all your calamities and your **d**; **1Sa 10:19** 6869a
Bring me out of my **d**. **Ps 25:17** 4691
have shown me many troubles and **d** **Ps 71:20** 7463a
He delivered them out of their **d**. **Ps 107:6** 4691
He saved them out of their **d**. **Ps 107:13** 4691
He saved them out of their **d**. **Ps 107:19** 4691
He brought them out of their **d**. **Ps 107:28** 4691
And Memphis *will have* **d** daily. **Ezk 30:16** 6862c
afflictions, in hardships, in **d**, **2Co 6:4** *4730*
weaknesses, with insults, with **d**, **2Co 12:10** *318*

DISTRESSING
the LORD showed great and **d** signs **Dt 6:22** 7451a

DISTRIBUTE
to **d** faithfully *their portions* to **2Ch 31:15** 5414
were designated by name to **d** portions **2Ch 31:19** 5414
their task to **d** to their kinsmen. **Ne 13:13** 2505a
he will **d** plunder, booty and **Da 11:24** 967
you possess and **d** it to the poor, **Lk 18:22** *1239*

DISTRIBUTED
d by lot in Shiloh before the LORD at **Jos 19:51** 5157
Further, he **d** to all the people, **2Sa 6:19** 2505a
He **d** to everyone of Israel, **1Ch 16:3** 2505a
He acted wisely and **d** some of **2Ch 11:23** 6555
He **d** to those who were seated; **Jn 6:11** *1239*
and they would be **d** to each as **Ac 4:35** *1239*
He **d** their land as an inheritance **Ac 13:19** *2624*

DISTRIBUTES
he had relied and **d** his plunder. **Lk 11:22** *1239*

DISTRIBUTING
tongues as of fire **d** themselves, **Ac 2:3** *1266*
d to each one individually just as **1Co 12:11** *1244*

DISTRICT
eat Jezebel in the **d** of Jezreel.' **1Ki 21:23** 2426
of half the **d** of Jerusalem, **Ne 3:9** 6418
of half the **d** of Jerusalem, **Ne 3:12** 6418
the official of the **d** of **Ne 3:14** 6418
the official of the **d** of Mizpah, **Ne 3:15** 6418
official of half the **d** of Beth-zur, **Ne 3:16** 6418

official of half the **d** of Keilah, **Ne 3:17** 6418
carried out repairs for his **d**. **Ne 3:17** 6418
the other half of the **d** of Keilah. **Ne 3:18** 6418
from the **d** around Jerusalem, **Ne 12:28** 3603
and all the **d** around the Jordan; **Mt 3:5** *4066*
sent *word* into all that surrounding **d** **Mt 14:35** *4066*
into the **d** of Tyre and Sidon. **Mt 15:21** *3313*
into the **d** of Caesarea Philippi, **Mt 16:13** *3313*
all the surrounding **d** of Galilee. **Mk 1:28** *4066*
and came to the **d** of Dalmanutha. **Mk 8:10** *3313*
into all the **d** around the Jordan, **Lk 3:3** *4066*
through all the surrounding **d**. **Lk 4:14** *4066*
locality in the surrounding **d**. **Lk 4:37** *4066*
and in all the surrounding **d**. **Lk 7:17** *4066*
d asked Him to leave them, **Lk 8:37** *4066*
and drove them out of their **d**. **Ac 13:50** *3725*
city of the **d** of Macedonia, **Ac 16:12** *3310*

DISTRICTS
stood with him from all their **d**. **2Ch 11:13** 1366
and the **d** of Libya around Cyrene, **Ac 2:10** *3313*
When he had gone through those **d** **Ac 20:2** *3313*

DISTURB
let no one **d** his bones." **2Ki 23:18** 5128
lot, to **d** them and destroy them. **Es 9:24** 2000
lie down and none would **d** *you,* **Jb 11:19** 2729
and from the North will **d** him, **Da 11:44** 926
prowled, With nothing to **d** *them?* **Na 2:11** 2729

DISTURBANCE
Jerusalem and to cause a **d** in it. **Ne 4:8** 8442
there was no small **d** among the **Ac 12:18** *5017*
no small **d** concerning the Way. **Ac 19:23** *5017*

DISTURBANCES
for many **d** afflicted all the **2Ch 15:5** 4103
"When you hear of wars and **d**, **Lk 21:9** *181*
slanders, gossip, arrogance, **d**; **2Co 12:20** *181*

DISTURBED
have you **d** me by bringing me up?" **1Sa 28:15** 7264
courage, and all Israel was **d**. **2Sa 4:1** 926
own place and not be **d** again, **2Sa 7:10** 7264
"Even when I remember, I am **d**, **Jb 21:6** 926
why have you become **d** within me? **Ps 42:5** 1993
why have you become **d** within me? **Ps 42:11** 1993
And why are you **d** within me? **Ps 43:5** 1993
When I remember God, then I am **d**; **Ps 77:3** 1993
who believes *in it* will not be **d**. **Is 28:16** 2363a
their voice nor **d** at their noise, **Is 31:4** 6031a
being greatly **d** because they were **Ac 4:2** *1278*
have **d** you with *their* words, **Ac 15:24** *5015*
one would be **d** by these afflictions; **1Th 3:3** *4525*
be **d** either by a spirit or a message **2Th 2:2** *2360*

DISTURBING
only there are some who are **d** you and **Ga 1:7** *5015*
the one who is **d** you will bear his **Ga 5:10** *5015*

DIVERTED
him, and God **d** them from him. **2Ch 18:31** 5496

DIVIDE
should eat, you are to **d** the lamb. **Ex 12:4** 3699
your hand over the sea and **d** it, **Ex 14:16** 1234
will overtake, I will **d** the spoil; **Ex 15:9** 2505a
live ox and **d** its price equally; **Ex 21:35** 2673
and also they shall **d** the dead *ox.* **Ex 21:35** 2673
or among those which **d** the hoof: **Lv 11:4** 6536
chews cud, it does not **d** the hoof, **Lv 11:4** 6536
chews cud, it does not **d** the hoof, **Lv 11:5** 6536
chews cud, it does not **d** the hoof, **Lv 11:6** 6536
all the animals which **d** the hoof but **Lv 11:26** 6536
and **d** the booty between the **Nu 31:27** 2673
those that **d** the hoof in two: **Dt 14:7** 6536
the cud, they do not **d** the hoof; **Dt 14:7** 6536
and **d** into three parts the **Dt 19:3** 8027
shall **d** it into seven portions; **Jos 18:5** 2505a
d the spoil of your enemies with **Jos 22:8** 2505a
"At the sound of those who **d** **Jg 5:11** 2686b
'You and Ziba shall **d** the land.' " **2Sa 19:29** 2505a
"**D** the living child in two, and **1Ki 3:25** 1504
be neither mine nor yours; **d** *him!"* **1Ki 3:26** 1504
the innocent will **d** the silver. **Jb 27:17** 2505a
they **d** him among the merchants? **Jb 41:6** 2673
They **d** my garments among them, And **Ps 22:18** 2505a
Confuse, O Lord, **d** their tongues, **Ps 55:9** 6385
at home will **d** the spoil!" **Ps 68:12** 2505a
to **d** the spoil with the proud. **Pr 16:19** 2505a
D your portion to seven, or even **Ec 11:2** 5414
men rejoice when they **d** the spoil. **Is 9:3** 2505a
nation Whose land the rivers **d**. **Is 18:2** 958
Whose land the rivers **d** **Is 18:7** 958
will **d** the booty with the strong; **Is 53:12** 2505a
to **d** your bread with the hungry And **Is 58:7** 6536
for weighing and **d** the hair. **Ezk 5:1** 2505a
to **d** between the holy and the **Ezk 42:20** 914
"And when you **d** by lot the **Ezk 45:1** 5307
you shall **d** the land for an inheritance **Ezk 47:13** 5157
You shall **d** it for an inheritance, **Ezk 47:14** 5157
"So you shall **d** this land among **Ezk 47:21** 2505a
"You shall **d** it by lot **Ezk 47:22** 5307
"This is the land which you shall **d** **Ezk 48:29** 5307
tell my brother to **d** the *family* **Lk 12:13** *3307*

DIVIDED
there it **d** and became four rivers. **Gn 2:10** 6504
for in his days the earth was **d**; **Gn 10:25** 6385
He **d** his forces against them **Gn 14:15** 2505a
he **d** the people who were with him, **Gn 32:7** 2673
So he **d** the children among Leah **Gn 33:1** 2673
dry land, so the waters were **d**. **Ex 14:21** 1234
"Among these the land shall be **d** **Nu 26:53** 2505a
"But the land shall be **d** by lot. **Nu 26:55** 2505a
their inheritance shall be **d** **Nu 26:56** 2505a
Moses, and they **d** the land. **Jos 14:5** 2505a
who had not **d** their inheritance. **Jos 18:2** 2505a
and there Joshua **d** the land to the **Jos 18:10** 2505a
He **d** the 300 men into three **Jg 7:16** 2673
and **d** them into three companies, **Jg 9:43** 2673
of Israel were **d** into two parts: **1Ki 16:21** 2505a
So they **d** the land between them to **1Ki 18:6** 2505a
and they were **d** here and there, **2Ki 2:8** 2673
they were **d** here and there; **2Ki 2:14** 2673
for in his days the earth was **d**, **1Ch 1:19** 6385
David **d** them into divisions **1Ch 23:6** 2505a
d them according to their offices **1Ch 24:3** 2505a
of Ithamar, they **d** them thus: **1Ch 24:4** 2505a
Thus they were **d** by lot, the one **1Ch 24:5** 2505a
"You **d** the sea before them, So they **Ne 9:11** 1234
is the way that the light is **d**, **Jb 38:24** 2505a
You **d** the sea by Your strength; You **Ps 74:13** 6565b
He **d** the sea and caused them to **Ps 78:13** 1234
To Him who **d** the Red Sea asunder, **Ps 136:13** 1504
of an abundant spoil will be **d**; **Is 33:23** 2505a
His hand has **d** it to them by line. **Is 34:17** 2505a
Who **d** the waters before them to **Is 63:12** 1234
no longer be **d** into two kingdoms. **Ezk 37:22** 2673
of iron, it will be a **d** kingdom; **Da 2:41** 6386
your kingdom has been **d** and given **Da 5:28** 6537a
And they have **d** up My land. **Jl 3:2** 2505a
from you will be **d** among you. **Zch 14:1** 2505a
d against itself is laid waste; **Mt 12:25** *3307*
and any city or house **d** against **Mt 12:25** *3307*
Satan, he is **d** against himself; **Mt 12:26** *3307*
they **d** up His garments among **Mt 27:35** *1266*
If a kingdom is **d** against itself, **Mk 3:24** *3307*
If a house is **d** against itself, **Mk 3:25** *3307*
risen up against himself and is **d**, **Mk 3:26** *3307*
and He **d** up the two fish among **Mk 6:41** *3307*
and **d** up His garments among **Mk 15:24** *1266*
d against itself is laid waste; **Lk 11:17** *1266*
and a house **d** against itself **Lk 11:17**
Satan also is **d** against himself, **Lk 11:18** *1266*
in one household will be **d**, **Lk 12:52** *1266*
"They will be **d**, father against **Lk 12:53** *1266*
So he **d** his wealth between them. **Lk 15:12** *1244*
"THEY D MY OUTER GARMENTS **Jn 19:24** *1266*
the people of the city were **d**; **Ac 14:4** *4977*
and the assembly was **d**. **Ac 23:7** *4977*
Has Christ been **d**? **1Co 1:13** *3307*
and *his interests* are **d**. **1Co 7:34** *3307*

DIVIDES
in the evening he **d** the spoil." **Gn 49:27** 2505a
'Whatever **d** a hoof, thus making **Lv 11:3** 6536
the pig, for though it **d** the hoof, **Lv 11:7** 6536
"Any animal that **d** the hoof **Dt 14:6** 6536
because it **d** the hoof but *does* not **Dt 14:8** 6536

DIVIDING
So they finished **d** the land. **Jos 19:51** 2505a
finding, are they not **d** the spoil? **Jg 5:30** 2505a
d up His garments among themselves. **Lk 23:34** *1266*
down the barrier of the **d** wall, **Eph 2:14** *3320*

DIVINATION
and which he indeed uses for **d**? **Gn 44:5** 5172
man as I can indeed practice **d**?" **Gn 44:15** 5172
nor practice **d** or soothsaying. **Lv 19:26** 5172
with the *fees for* **d** in their hand; **Nu 22:7** 7081
Nor is there any **d** against Israel; **Nu 23:23** 7081
through the fire, one who uses **d**, **Dt 18:10** 7081
"For rebellion is as the sin of **d**, **1Sa 15:23** 7081
and practiced **d** and enchantments, **2Ki 17:17** 7081
practiced witchcraft and used **d**, **2Ki 21:6** 5172
he practiced witchcraft, used **d**, **2Ch 33:6** 5172
to you a false vision, **d**, **Jer 14:14** 7081
d within the house of Israel. **Ezk 12:24** 4738
and lying **d** who are saying, **Ezk 13:6** 7081
and speak a lying **d** when you said, **Ezk 13:7** 4738
see false visions or practice **d**, **Ezk 13:23** 7081
head of the two ways, to use **d**; **Ezk 21:21** 7081
"Into his right hand came the **d**, **Ezk 21:22** 7081
them like a false **d** in their eyes; **Ezk 21:23** 7080
And darkness for you—without **d**. **Mi 3:6** 7080
having a spirit of **d** met us, **Ac 16:16** *4436*

DIVINATIONS
false visions and utter lying **d**. **Ezk 13:9** 7080

DIVINE
this, in whom is a **d** spirit?" **Gn 41:38** 430
"I see a **d** being coming up out of **1Sa 28:13** 430
A **d** decision is in the lips of the **Pr 16:10** 7081
nor the **d** word to the prophet! **Jer 18:18**
while they **d** lies for you **Ezk 21:29** 7080
And her prophets **d** for money. **Mi 3:11** 7080
we ought not to think that the **D** **Ac 17:29** *2304*
His eternal power and **d** nature, **Ro 1:20** *2305*
But what is the **d** response to him? **Ro 11:4** *5538*
covenant had regulations of **d** worship **Heb 9:1** *2999*
performing the **d** worship, **Heb 9:6** *2999*
seeing that His **d** power has **2Pe 1:3** *2304*
become partakers of *the* **d** nature, **2Pe 1:4** *2304*

DIVINED
I have **d** that the LORD has blessed **Gn 30:27** 5172

DIVINELY
was **d** directed by a holy angel to **Ac 10:22**
but **d** powerful for the destruction **2Co 10:4** *2316*

DIVINER
Balaam the son of Beor, the **d**, **Jos 13:22** 7080
the prophet, The **d** and the elder, **Is 3:2** 7080

DIVINER'S
and their **d** wand informs them; **Hos 4:12**

DIVINERS
who practice witchcraft and to **d**, **Dt 18:14** 7080
called for the priests and the **d**, **1Sa 6:2** 7080
to fail, Making fools out of **d**, **Is 44:25** 7080
listen to your prophets, your **d**, **Jer 27:9** 7080
your midst and your **d** deceive you, **Jer 29:8** 7080
nor **d** are able to declare *it* to **Da 2:27** 1505
the Chaldeans and the **d** came in **Da 4:7** 1505
the Chaldeans, Chaldeans and the **d**. **Da 5:7** 1505
conjurers, Chaldeans *and* **d**. **Da 5:11** 1505
And the **d** will be embarrassed. **Mi 3:7** 7080
And the **d** see lying visions And **Zch 10:2** 7080

DIVINERS'
comes by the way of the **d** oak." **Jg 9:37** 6049a

DIVINING
false visions and **d** lies for them, **Ezk 22:28** 7080

DIVISION
"I will put a **d** between My **Ex 8:23** 6304
the year, each **d** *numbering* 24,000: **1Ch 27:1** 4256
the first **d** for the first month; **1Ch 27:2** 4256
and in his **d** *were* 24,000. **1Ch 27:2** 4256
Dodai the Ahohite and his **d** had **1Ch 27:4** 4256
of the **d** for the second month, **1Ch 27:4** 4256
and in his **d** *were* 24,000. **1Ch 27:4** 4256
and in his **d** *were* 24,000. **1Ch 27:5** 4256
over his **d** was Ammizabad his son. **1Ch 27:6** 4256
and in his **d** *were* 24,000. **1Ch 27:7** 4256
and in his **d** *were* 24,000. **1Ch 27:8** 4256
and in his **d** *were* 24,000. **1Ch 27:9** 4256
and in his **d** *were* 24,000. **1Ch 27:10** 4256
and in his **d** *were* 24,000. **1Ch 27:11** 4256
and in his **d** *were* 24,000. **1Ch 27:12** 4256
and in his **d** *were* 24,000. **1Ch 27:13** 4256
and in his **d** *were* 24,000. **1Ch 27:14** 4256
and in his **d** *were* 24,000. **1Ch 27:15** 4256
by **d** of a father's household. **2Ch 35:5** 2515
God, **d** corresponding to division. **Ne 12:24** 4929
God, division corresponding to **d**. **Ne 12:24** 4929
Zacharias, of the **d** of Abijah; **Lk 1:5** *2183*
in the *appointed* order of his **d**, **Lk 1:8** *2183*
I tell you, no, but rather **d**; **Lk 12:51** *1267*
So a **d** occurred in the **Jn 7:43** *4978*
And there was a **d** among them. **Jn 9:16** *4978*
A **d** occurred again among the **Jn 10:19** *4978*
there may be no **d** in the body, **1Co 12:25** *4978*
far as the **d** of soul and spirit, **Heb 4:12** *3311*

DIVISIONS
were the heads of **d** of Israel." **Nu 1:16** 505
the heads of the **d** of Israel, **Nu 10:4** 505
to their **d** by their tribes. **Jos 11:23** 4256
a possession according to their **d**, **Jos 12:7** 4256
describe the land in seven **d**, **Jos 18:6** 2506
it by cities in seven **d** in a book; **Jos 18:9** 2506
of Israel according to their **d**. **Jos 18:10** 4256
Among the **d** of Reuben *There were* **Jg 5:15** 6390
Among the **d** of Reuben *There were* **Jg 5:16** 6390
numbers of the **d** equipped for war, **1Ch 12:23** 7218
d according to the sons of Levi: **1Ch 23:6** 4256
Now the **d** of the descendants of **1Ch 24:1** 4256
For the **d** of the gatekeepers *there* **1Ch 26:1** 4256
To these **d** of the gatekeepers, the **1Ch 26:12** 4256
the **d** of the gatekeepers of the **1Ch 26:19** 4256
the **d** which came in and went out **1Ch 27:1** 4256
of the **d** that served the king, **1Ch 28:1** 4256
also for the **d** of the priests and **1Ch 28:13** 4256
there are the **d** of the priests and **1Ch 28:21** 4256
themselves, without regard to **d**), **2Ch 5:11** 4256
he appointed the **d** of the priests **2Ch 8:14** 4256
by their **d** at every gate; **2Ch 8:14** 4256
did not dismiss *any of* the **d**. **2Ch 23:8** 4256
battle, which entered combat by **d** **2Ch 26:11** 1416
And Hezekiah appointed the **d** of **2Ch 31:2** 4256
and the Levites by their **d**, **2Ch 31:2** 4256
portions to their brothers by **d**, **2Ch 31:15** 4256
their duties according to their **d**; **2Ch 31:16** 4256
by their duties *and* their **d**. **2Ch 31:17** 4256
your fathers' households in your **d**, **2Ch 35:4** 4256
stations and the Levites by their **d** **2Ch 35:10** 4256
they appointed the priests to their **d** **Ezr 6:18** 6392
d in Judah belonged to Benjamin. **Ne 11:36** 4256
opposite them in *their* service **d**. **Ne 12:9** 4931
and that there be no **d** among you, **1Co 1:10** *4978*
I hear that **d** exist among you; **1Co 11:18** *4978*
These are the ones who cause **d**, **Jude 1:19** *592*

DIVORCE
he cannot **d** her all his days. **Dt 22:19** 7971
he cannot **d** her all his days. **Dt 22:29** 7971
writes her a certificate of **d** and puts it **Dt 24:1** 3748
writes her a certificate of **d** and puts *it* **Dt 24:3** 3748
"Where is the certificate of **d** By **Is 50:1** 3748
away and given her a writ of **d**, **Jer 3:8** 3748
"For I hate **d**," says the LORD, **Mal 2:16** 7971
GIVE HER A CERTIFICATE OF D **Mt 5:31** *647*
d his wife for any reason at all?" **Mt 19:3** *630*
GIVE HER A CERTIFICATE OF D **Mt 19:7** *647*
permitted you to **d** your wives; **Mt 19:8** *630*
was lawful for a man to **d** a wife, **Mk 10:2** *630*
OF D AND SEND *her* AWAY." **Mk 10:4** *647*
and that the husband should not **d** his **1Co 7:11** *863*
he must not **d** her. **1Co 7:12** *863*

DIVORCED
take a woman **d** from her husband; **Lv 21:7** 1644
'A widow, or a **d** woman, or one who **Lv 21:14** 1644
daughter becomes a widow or **d**, **Lv 22:13** 1644
vow of a widow or of a **d** woman, **Nu 30:9** 1644
not marry a widow or a **d** woman **Ezk 44:22** 1644
a **d** woman commits adultery. **Mt 5:32** *630*
and he who marries one who is **d** **Lk 16:18** *630*

DIVORCES
“If a husband **d** his wife And she **Jer 3:1** 7971
you that everyone who **d** his wife, **Mt 5:32** *630*
I say to you, whoever **d** his wife, **Mt 19:9** *630*
“Whoever **d** his wife and marries **Mk 10:11** *630*
and if she herself **d** her husband **Mk 10:12** *630*
“Everyone who **d** his wife and **Lk 16:18** *630*

DIZAHAB
and Laban and Hazeroth and **D**. **Dt 1:1** 1774

DO
“If you **d** well, will not *your* **Gn 4:7** 3190
And if you **d** not do well, sin is **Gn 4:7**
And if you do not **d** well, **Gn 4:7** 3190
“I **d** not know. Am I my brother’s **Gn 4:9**
I Myself **d** establish My covenant **Gn 9:9**
And this is what they began to **d**, **Gn 11:6** 6213a
to **d** will be impossible for them. **Gn 11:6** 6213a
“**D** not fear, Abram, I am a shield **Gn 15:1**
d to her what is good in your **Gn 16:6** 6213a
please **d** not pass Your servant by. **Gn 18:3**
“So **d**, as you have said.” **Gn 18:5** 6213a
from Abraham what I am about to **d**, **Gn 18:17** 6213a
be it from You to **d** such a thing, **Gn 18:25** 6213a
d *it* on account of the forty.” **Gn 18:29** 6213a
not **d** *it* if I find thirty there.” **Gn 18:30** 6213a
my brothers, **d** not act wickedly. **Gn 19:7**
and **d** to them whatever you like; **Gn 19:8** 6213a
only **d** nothing to these men, **Gn 19:8** 6213a
D not look behind you, and do not **Gn 19:17**
and **d** not stay anywhere in the **Gn 19:17**
for I cannot **d** anything until you **Gn 19:22** 6213a
But if you **d** not restore *her,* know **Gn 20:7**
“**D** not be distressed because of **Gn 21:12**
“**D** not let me see the boy die.” **Gn 21:16**
D not fear, for God has heard the **Gn 21:17**
“God is with you in all that you **d**; **Gn 21:22** 6213a
“I **d** not know who has done this **Gn 21:26**
“What **d** these seven ewe lambs **Gn 21:29**
“**D** not stretch out your hand **Gn 22:12**
the lad, and **d** nothing to him; **Gn 22:12** 6213a
“Beware that you **d** not take my son **Gn 24:6**
d not take my son back there.” **Gn 24:8**
Why **d** you stand outside since I **Gn 24:31**
and if they **d** not give her to you, **Gn 24:41**
“**D** not delay me, since the LORD **Gn 24:56**
“**D** not go down to Egypt; **Gn 26:2**
D not fear, for I am with you. **Gn 26:24**
that you will **d** us no harm, just **Gn 26:29** 6213a
I **d** not know the day of my death. **Gn 27:2**
Now as for you then, what can I **d**, **Gn 27:37** 6213a
“**D** you have only one blessing, my **Gn 27:38**
“**D** you know Laban the son of **Gn 29:5**
you will **d** this *one* thing for me, **Gn 30:31** 6213a
“**D** we still have any portion or **Gn 31:14**
d whatever God has said to you.” **Gn 31:16** 6213a
“Be careful that you **d** not speak **Gn 31:24**
“It is in my power to **d** you harm, **Gn 31:29** 6213a
But what can I **d** this day to these **Gn 31:43** 6213a
‘To whom **d** you belong, and where **Gn 32:17**
and to whom **d** these *animals* in **Gn 32:17**
the sons of Israel **d** not eat the sinew **Gn 32:32**
“What **d** you mean by all this **Gn 33:8**
“We cannot **d** this thing, to give **Gn 34:14** 6213a
man did not delay to **d** the thing, **Gn 34:19** 6213a
“**D** not fear, for now you have **Gn 35:17**
but **d** not lay hands on him” **Gn 37:22**
then could I **d** this great evil and **Gn 39:9** 6213a
went into the house to **d** his work, **Gn 39:11** 6213a
“**D** not interpretations belong to **Gn 40:8**
and please **d** me a kindness by **Gn 40:14** 6213a
to Pharaoh what He is about to **d**. **Gn 41:25** 6213a
to Pharaoh what He is about to **d**. **Gn 41:28** 6213a
all my people shall **d** homage; **Gn 41:40** 5401a
he says to you, you shall **d**.” **Gn 41:55** 6213a
“**D** this and live, for I fear God: **Gn 42:18** 6213a
“**D** not sin against the boy’; **Gn 42:22**
if I **d** not bring him *back* to you; **Gn 42:37**
“But if you **d** not send *him,* we **Gn 43:5**
If I **d** not bring him *back* to you **Gn 43:9**
“If *it must be* so, then **d** this: **Gn 43:11** 6213a
we **d** not know who put our money in **Gn 43:22**
“Be at ease, **d** not be afraid. **Gn 43:23**
your servants to **d** such a thing.’ **Gn 44:7** 6213a
D you not know that such a man as **Gn 44:15**
“Far be it from me to **d** this. **Gn 44:17** 6213a
and **d** not be angry with your **Gn 44:18**
‘If I **d** not bring him *back* to you, **Gn 44:32**
“Now **d** not be grieved or **Gn 45:5**
come down to me, **d** not delay. **Gn 45:9**
“Say to your brothers, ‘**D** this: **Gn 45:17** 6213a
‘**D** this: take wagons from the land **Gn 45:19** 6213a
‘**D** not concern yourselves with your **Gn 45:20**
“**D** not quarrel on the journey.” **Gn 45:24**
d not be afraid to go down to **Gn 46:3**
Please **d** not bury me in Egypt, **Gn 47:29**
“I will **d** as you have said.” **Gn 47:30** 6213a
“**D** not be afraid, for am I in **Gn 50:19**
“So therefore, **d** not be afraid; **Gn 50:21**
and did not **d** as the king of Egypt **Ex 1:17** 6213a
“**D** not come near here; **Ex 3:5**
I shall **d** in the midst of it; **Ex 3:20** 6213a
will teach you what you are to **d**. **Ex 4:15** 6213a
that He had commanded him *to* **d**. **Ex 4:28**
I **d** not know the LORD, and **Ex 5:2**
why **d** you draw the people away **Ex 5:4**
“Why **d** you deal this way with **Ex 5:15**
see what I will **d** to Pharaoh; **Ex 6:1** 6213a
“For if you **d** not let My people go, **Ex 8:21**

“It is not right to **d** so, **Ex 8:26** 6213a
only **d** not let Pharaoh deal **Ex 8:29**
will **d** this thing in the land.” **Ex 9:5** 6213a
you **d** not yet fear the LORD God.” **Ex 9:30**
D you not realize that Egypt is **Ex 10:7**
we ourselves **d** not know with what **Ex 10:26**
Beware, **d** not see my face again, **Ex 10:28**
‘**D** not eat any of it raw or boiled **Ex 12:9**
lamb, but if you **d** not redeem *it,* **Ex 13:13**
Moses said to the people, “**D** not fear **Ex 14:13**
and **d** what is right in His sight, **Ex 15:26** 6213a
“How long **d** you refuse to keep My **Ex 16:28**
“Why **d** you quarrel with me? **Ex 17:2**
Why **d** you test the LORD?” **Ex 17:2**
“What shall I **d** to this people? **Ex 17:4** 6213a
Why **d** you alone sit *as judge* and **Ex 18:14**
you cannot **d** it alone. **Ex 18:18** 6213a
walk and the work they are to **d**. **Ex 18:20** 6213a
“If you **d** this thing and God *so* **Ex 18:23** 6213a
the LORD has spoken we will **d**!” **Ex 19:8** 6213a
‘Beware that you **d** not go up on **Ex 19:12**
d not go near a woman.” **Ex 19:15**
so that they **d** not break through to **Ex 19:21**
but **d** not let the priests and the **Ex 19:24**
shall labor and **d** all your work, **Ex 20:9** 6213a
in it you shall not **d** any work, **Ex 20:10** 6213a
“**D** not be afraid; for God has come **Ex 20:20**
to go free as the male slaves **d**. **Ex 21:7** 3318
not **d** these three *things* for her, **Ex 21:11** 6213a
“You shall **d** the same with your **Ex 22:30** 6213a
d not join your hand with a wicked **Ex 23:1**
and **d** not kill the innocent or the **Ex 23:7**
You are to **d** the same with your **Ex 23:11** 6213a
“Six days you are to **d** your work, **Ex 23:12** 6213a
and **d** not mention the name of **Ex 23:13**
d not be rebellious toward him, **Ex 23:21**
his voice and **d** all that I say, **Ex 23:22** 6213a
nor **d** according to their deeds; **Ex 23:24** 6213a
the LORD has spoken we will **d**!” **Ex 24:3** 6213a
the LORD has spoken we will **d**, **Ex 24:7** 6213a
thus you shall **d** for all the **Ex 26:17** 6213a
they **d** not incur guilt and die. **Ex 28:43**
“Now this is what you shall **d** to **Ex 29:1** 6213a
shall **d** to Aaron and to his sons, **Ex 29:35** 6213a
we **d** not know what has become of **Ex 32:1**
He said He would **d** to His people. **Ex 32:14** 6213a
“What did this people **d** to you, **Ex 32:21** 6213a
“**D** not let the anger of my lord **Ex 32:22**
we **d** not know what has become of **Ex 32:23**
know what I shall **d** with you.’ ” **Ex 33:5** 6213a
us, **d** not lead us up from here. **Ex 33:15**
“I will also **d** this thing of **Ex 33:17** 6213a
and if you **d** not redeem *it,* then **Ex 34:20**
and he commanded them *to* **d** **Ex 34:32**
the LORD has commanded *you* to **d**: **Ex 35:1** 6213a
‘He shall also **d** with the bull **Lv 4:20** 6213a
thus he shall **d** with it. **Lv 4:20** 6213a
his lips to **d** evil or to do good, **Lv 5:4** 7489a
his lips to do evil or to **d** good, **Lv 5:4** 3190
any one of the things a man may **d**; **Lv 6:3** 6213a
the LORD has commanded to **d**.” **Lv 8:5** 6213a
to **d** as has been done this day, **Lv 8:34** 6213a
the LORD has commanded you to **d**, **Lv 9:6** 6213a
“**D** not uncover your heads nor **Lv 10:6**
“**D** not drink wine or strong **Lv 10:9**
hoof but **d** not make a split *hoof,* **Lv 11:26**
hoof, or which **d** not chew cud, **Lv 11:26**
‘**D** not render yourselves **Lv 11:43**
and **d** with its blood as he did **Lv 16:15** 6213a
and thus he shall **d** for the tent **Lv 16:16** 6213a
your souls and not **d** any work, **Lv 16:29** 6213a
‘You shall not **d** what is done in **Lv 18:3** 6213a
nor are you to **d** what is done in **Lv 18:3** 6213a
‘**D** not defile yourselves by any of **Lv 18:24**
not **d** any of these abominations, **Lv 18:26** 6213a
those persons who **d** *so* shall be **Lv 18:29** 6213a
that you **d** not practice any of the **Lv 18:30**
‘**D** not turn to idols or make for **Lv 19:4**
shall **d** no injustice in judgment; **Lv 19:15** 6213a
‘**D** not profane your daughter by **Lv 19:29**
‘**D** not turn to mediums or **Lv 19:31**
d not seek them out to be defiled **Lv 19:31**
land, you shall not **d** him wrong. **Lv 19:33** 3238
‘You shall **d** no wrong in judgment, **Lv 19:35** 6213a
and all My ordinances and **d** them; **Lv 19:37** 6213a
and all My ordinances and **d** them, **Lv 20:22** 6213a
keep My commandments, and **d** them; **Lv 22:31** 6213a
You shall not **d** any work; **Lv 23:3** 6213a
shall not **d** any laborious work. **Lv 23:7** 6213a
not **d** any laborious work.’ ” **Lv 23:8** 6213a
You shall **d** no laborious work. **Lv 23:21** 6213a
shall not **d** any laborious work, **Lv 23:25** 6213a
not **d** any work on this same day, **Lv 23:28** 6213a
“You shall **d** no work at all. **Lv 23:31** 6213a
d no laborious work of any kind. **Lv 23:35** 6213a
You shall **d** no laborious work. **Lv 23:36** 6213a
we **d** not sow or gather in our crops?” **Lv 25:20**
‘**D** not take usurious interest from **Lv 25:36**
‘But if you **d** not obey Me and do **Lv 26:14**
‘But if you do not obey Me and **d** **Lv 26:14**
I, in turn, will **d** this to you: **Lv 26:16** 6213a
these things you **d** not obey Me, **Lv 26:18**
spite of this you **d** not obey Me, **Lv 26:27**
animal of the kind which men **d** not **Lv 27:11**
d the service of the tabernacle. **Nu 3:7** 5647
d the service of the tabernacle. **Nu 3:8** 5647
who enter the service to **d** the work **Nu 4:3** 6213a
“**D** not let the tribe of the **Nu 4:18**
“But **d** this to them that they may **Nu 4:19** 6213a

to **d** the work in the tent of meeting. **Nu 4:23** 5647
to **d** the work of the tent of meeting. **Nu 4:30** 5647
everyone who could enter to **d** the **Nu 4:47** 5647
so he shall **d** according to the law **Nu 6:21** 6213a
“Thus you shall **d** to them, **Nu 8:7** 6213a
they *themselves* shall **d** no work. **Nu 8:26** 5647
to its ordinance, so he shall **d**; **Nu 9:14** 6213a
with us and we will **d** you good, **Nu 10:29** 3190
“Please **d** not leave us, inasmuch **Nu 10:31**
does for us, we will **d** for you.” **Nu 10:32** 3190
and **d** not let me see my **Nu 11:15**
But they did not **d** *it* again. **Nu 11:25** 3254
you, **d** not account *this* sin to us, **Nu 12:11**
d not let her be like one dead, **Nu 12:12**
“Only **d** not rebel against the LORD; **Nu 14:9**
and **d** not fear the people of the **Nu 14:9**
d not fear them.” **Nu 14:9**
so I will surely **d** to you; **Nu 14:28** 6213a
surely this I will **d** to all this **Nu 14:35** 6213a
“**D** not go up, or you will be struck **Nu 14:42**
so you shall **d** for everyone **Nu 15:12** 6213a
d these things in this manner, **Nu 15:13** 6213a
aroma to the LORD, just as you **d** so **Nu 15:14** 6213a
just as you do so he shall **d**. **Nu 15:14** 6213a
when you unwittingly fail and **d** not **Nu 15:22**
so as to **d** them and not follow **Nu 15:39** 6213a
remember to **d** all My commandments **Nu 15:40** 6213a
so why **d** you exalt yourselves **Nu 16:3**
“**D** this: take censers for yourselves, **Nu 16:6** 6213a
to **d** the service of the tabernacle **Nu 16:9** 5647
“**D** not regard their offering! **Nu 16:15**
has sent me to **d** all these deeds; **Nu 16:28** 6213a
d drink any of your water, **Nu 20:19**
“**D** not fear him, for I have given **Nu 21:34**
d to him as you did to Sihon, **Nu 21:34** 6213a
“**D** not go with them; **Nu 22:12**
I will **d** whatever you say to me. **Nu 22:17** 6213a
and gold, I could not **d** anything, **Nu 22:18** 6213a
I speak to you shall you **d**.” **Nu 22:20** 6213a
been accustomed to **d** so to you?” **Nu 22:30** 6213a
Has He said, and will He not **d** it? **Nu 23:19** 6213a
“**D** not curse them at all nor **Nu 23:25**
the LORD speaks, that I must **d**’?” **Nu 23:26** 6213a
I could not **d** anything contrary to **Nu 24:13** 6213a
what this people will **d** to your people **Nu 24:14** 6213a
you shall **d** no laborious work. **Nu 28:18** 6213a
you shall **d** no laborious work. **Nu 28:25** 6213a
you shall **d** no laborious work. **Nu 28:26** 6213a
you shall **d** no laborious work. **Nu 29:1** 6213a
you shall not **d** any work. **Nu 29:7** 6213a
you shall **d** no laborious work, and **Nu 29:12** 6213a
you shall **d** no laborious work. **Nu 29:35** 6213a
he shall **d** according to all that **Nu 30:2** 6213a
d not take us across the Jordan.” **Nu 32:5**
“If you will **d** this, if you will **Nu 32:20** 6213a
“But if you will not **d** so, **Nu 32:23** 6213a
and **d** what you have promised.” **Nu 32:24** 6213a
will **d** just as my lord commands. **Nu 32:25** 6213a
to your servants, so we will **d**. **Nu 32:31** 6213a
‘But if you **d** not drive out the **Nu 33:55**
as I plan to **d** to them, **Nu 33:56** 6213a
to them, so I will **d** to you.’ ” **Nu 33:56** 6213a
which you have said to **d** is good.’ **Dt 1:14** 6213a
all the things that you should **d**. **Dt 1:18** 6213a
D not fear or be dismayed.’ **Dt 1:21**
‘**D** not be shocked, nor fear them. **Dt 1:29**
‘**D** not go up nor fight, for I am **Dt 1:42**
you and chased you as bees **d**, **Dt 1:44** 6213a
d not provoke them, for I will not **Dt 2:5**
‘**D** not harass Moab, nor provoke **Dt 2:9**
d not harass them nor provoke **Dt 2:19**
‘**D** not fear him, for I have **Dt 3:2**
and you shall **d** to him just as you **Dt 3:2** 6213a
so the LORD shall **d** to all the **Dt 3:21** 6213a
‘**D** not fear them, for the LORD **Dt 3:22**
who can **d** such works and mighty acts **Dt 3:24** 6213a
that you should **d** thus in the land **Dt 4:5** 6213a
“So keep and **d** *them,* for that is **Dt 4:6** 6213a
so that you **d** not forget the things **Dt 4:9**
which your eyes have seen and they **d** **Dt 4:9**
so that you **d** not act corruptly **Dt 4:16**
“So watch yourselves, that you **d** **Dt 4:23**
and **d** that which is evil in the **Dt 4:25** 6213a
shall labor and **d** all your work, **Dt 5:13** 6213a
in it you shall not **d** any work, **Dt 5:14** 6213a
you, and we will hear and **d** *it.’* **Dt 5:27** 6213a
“So you shall observe to **d** just **Dt 5:32** 6213a
that you might **d** *them* in the land **Dt 6:1** 6213a
listen and be careful to **d** *it,* **Dt 6:3** 6213a
then watch yourself, that you **d** not **Dt 6:12**
“You shall **d** what is right **Dt 6:18** 6213a
‘What **d** the testimonies **Dt 6:20**
“But thus you shall **d** to them: **Dt 7:5** 6213a
commanding you today, to **d** them. **Dt 7:11** 6213a
judgments and keep and **d** them, **Dt 7:12** 6213a
So shall the LORD your God **d** to **Dt 7:19** 6213a
today you shall be careful to **d**, **Dt 8:1** 6213a
“Beware that you **d** not forget the **Dt 8:11**
you, to **d** good for you in the end. **Dt 8:16** 3190
“**D** not say in your heart when the **Dt 9:4**
d not forget how you provoked the **Dt 9:7**
GOD, **d** not destroy Your people, **Dt 9:26**
d not look at the stubbornness of **Dt 9:27**
and that you **d** not turn away **Dt 11:16**
I am commanding you to **d**, **Dt 11:22** 6213a
if you **d** not listen to the **Dt 11:28**
and you shall be careful to **d** all **Dt 11:32** 6213a
“You shall not **d** at all what we **Dt 12:8** 6213a
“Be careful that you **d** not offer **Dt 12:13**

shall **d** all that I command you. **Dt 12:14** 6213a
"Be careful that you **d** not **Dt 12:19**
d not inquire after their gods, **Dt 12:30**
'How **d** these nations serve their **Dt 12:30**
gods, that I also may **d** likewise?' **Dt 12:30** 6213a
you, you shall be careful to **d**; **Dt 12:32** 6213a
d such a wicked thing among you. **Dt 13:11** 6213a
cud, they **d** not divide the hoof; **Dt 14:7**
the work of your hand which you **d**. **Dt 14:29** 6213a
d likewise to your maidservant. **Dt 15:17** 6213a
will bless you in whatever you **d**. **Dt 15:18** 6213a
you shall **d** no work *on it*. **Dt 16:8** 6213a
"You shall **d** according to the **Dt 17:10** 6213a
which they tell you, you shall **d**; **Dt 17:11** 6213a
your God has not allowed you *to* **d** **Dt 18:14**
then you shall **d** to him just as he **Dt 19:19** 6213a
had intended to **d** to his brother. **Dt 19:19** 6213a
d such an evil thing among you. **Dt 19:20** 6213a
than you, **d** not be afraid of them; **Dt 20:1**
D not be fainthearted. **Dt 20:3**
D not be afraid, or panic, or **Dt 20:3**
"Thus you shall **d** to all the **Dt 20:15** 6213a
they may not teach you to **d** according **Dt 20:18** 6213a
and **d** not place the guilt of **Dt 21:8**
when you **d** what is right in the **Dt 21:9** 6213a
so that you **d** not defile your land **Dt 21:23**
you, or if you **d** not know him, **Dt 22:2**
Thus you shall **d** with his donkey, **Dt 22:3** 6213a
shall **d** the same with his garment, **Dt 22:3** 6213a
and you shall **d** likewise with **Dt 22:3** 6213a
you shall **d** nothing to the girl; **Dt 22:26** 6213a
d according to all that the Levitical **Dt 24:8** 6213a
so you shall be careful to **d**. **Dt 24:8** 6213a
am commanding you to **d** this thing. **Dt 24:18** 6213a
am commanding you to **d** this thing. **Dt 24:22** 6213a
'I **d** not desire to take her,' **Dt 25:8**
to **d** these statutes and ordinances. **Dt 26:16** 6213a
careful to **d** them with all your heart **Dt 26:16** 6213a
and **d** His commandments and His **Dt 27:10** 6213a
being careful to **d** all His **Dt 28:1** 6213a
and **d** not turn aside from any of **Dt 28:14**
"But it shall come about, if you **d** **Dt 28:15**
to observe to **d** all His **Dt 28:15** 6213a
rebuke, in all you undertake to **d**, **Dt 28:20** 6213a
there will be nothing you can **d**. **Dt 28:32** 3027
"A people whom you **d** not know **Dt 28:33**
words of this covenant to **d** them, **Dt 29:9** 6213a
you may prosper in all that you **d**. **Dt 29:9** 6213a
"The LORD will **d** to them just **Dt 31:4** 6213a
and you shall **d** to them according **Dt 31:5** 6213a
d not be afraid or tremble at **Dt 31:6**
D not fear or be dismayed." **Dt 31:8**
of all the evil which they will **d**, **Dt 31:18** 6213a
for you will **d** that which is evil **Dt 31:29** 6213a
"**D** you thus repay the LORD, O **Dt 32:6**
be careful to **d** according to all **Jos 1:7** 6213a
d not turn from it to the right or **Jos 1:7**
so that you may be careful to **d** **Jos 1:8** 6213a
D not tremble or be dismayed, for **Jos 1:9**
you have commanded us we will **d**, **Jos 1:16** 6213a
I **d** not know where the men went. **Jos 2:5**
"Our life for yours if you **d** not **Jos 2:14**
D not come near it, that you may **Jos 3:4**
LORD will **d** wonders among you." **Jos 3:5** 6213a
'What **d** these stones mean to you?' **Jos 4:6**
You shall **d** so for six days. **Jos 6:3** 6213a
so that you **d** not covet *them* **Jos 6:18**
"**D** not let all the people go up; **Jos 7:3**
d not make all the people toil up **Jos 7:3**
will You **d** for Your great name?" **Jos 7:9** 6213a
D not hide it from me." **Jos 7:19**
"**D** not fear or be dismayed. **Jos 8:1**
"You shall **d** to Ai and its **Jos 8:2** 6213a
D not go very far from the city, **Jos 8:4**
You shall **d** *it* according to the **Jos 8:8** 6213a
you and where **d** you come from?" **Jos 9:8**
"This we will **d** to them, even let **Jos 9:20** 6213a
d as it seems good and right in **Jos 9:25** 6213a
right in your sight to **d** to us." **Jos 9:25** 6213a
"**D** not abandon your servants; **Jos 10:6**
"**D** not fear them, for I have **Jos 10:8**
but **d** not stay *there* yourselves; **Jos 10:19**
D not allow them to enter their **Jos 10:19**
"**D** not fear or be dismayed! **Jos 10:25**
for thus the LORD will **d** to all **Jos 10:25** 6213a
"**D** not be afraid because of them, **Jos 11:6**
"What **d** you want?" **Jos 15:18**
Only **d** not rebel against the LORD, **Jos 22:19**
LORD **d** not save us this day! **Jos 22:22**
"What have you to **d** with the LORD, **Jos 22:24**
to keep and **d** all that is written **Jos 23:6** 6213a
then He will turn and **d** you harm **Jos 24:20** 7489a
so that you **d** not deny your God." **Jos 24:27**
"What **d** you want?" **Jg 1:14**
they did not **d** as *their fathers*. **Jg 2:17** 6213a
D not be afraid." **Jg 4:18**
Why **d** the hoofbeats of his **Jg 5:28**
"Please **d** not depart from here, **Jg 6:18**
"Peace to you, **d** not fear; **Jg 6:23**
men of the city to **d** it by day, **Jg 6:27** 6213a
"**D** not let Your anger burn **Jg 6:39**
"Look at me and **d** likewise. **Jg 7:17** 6213a
outskirts of the camp, **d** as I do. **Jg 7:17** 6213a
outskirts of the camp, do as I **d**. **Jg 7:17** 6213a
to **d** in comparison with you?" **Jg 8:3** 6213a
d to them whatever you can." **Jg 9:33** 6213a
"What you have seen me **d**, **Jg 9:48** 6213a
me do, hurry *and* **d** likewise." **Jg 9:48** 6213a
d to us whatever seems good to **Jg 10:15** 6213a

we will **d** as you have said." **Jg 11:10** 6213a
'**D** you not possess what Chemosh **Jg 11:24**
d to me as you have said, since **Jg 11:36** 6213a
d for the boy who is to be born." **Jg 13:8** 6213a
"Why **d** you ask my name, seeing it **Jg 13:18**
hate me, and you **d** not love me; **Jg 14:16**
Philistines when I **d** them harm." **Jg 15:3** 6213a
to **d** to him as he did to us." **Jg 15:10** 6213a
"**D** you not know that the **Jg 15:11**
"Where **d** you come from?" **Jg 17:9**
And what **d** you have here?" **Jg 18:3**
"What **d** you *report?*" **Jg 18:8**
D not delay to go, to enter, to **Jg 18:9**
"**D** you know that there are in **Jg 18:14**
consider what you should **d**." **Jg 18:14** 6213a
away, and what **d** I have besides? **Jg 18:24**
"**D** not let your voice be heard **Jg 18:25**
and where **d** you come from?" **Jg 19:17**
d not spend the night in the open **Jg 19:20**
please **d** not act so wickedly; **Jg 19:23**
d not commit this act of folly. **Jg 19:23**
and **d** to them whatever you wish. **Jg 19:24** 6213a
But **d** not commit such an act of **Jg 19:24**
thing which we will **d** to Gibeah; **Jg 20:9** 6213a
"What shall we **d** for wives for **Jg 21:7** 6213a
is the thing that you shall **d**: **Jg 21:11** 6213a
"What shall we **d** for wives for **Jg 21:16** 6213a
"**D** not urge me to leave you *or* **Ru 1:16**
Thus may the LORD **d** to me, **Ru 1:17** 6213a
"**D** not call me Naomi; **Ru 1:20**
Why **d** you call me Naomi, since the **Ru 1:21**
D not go to glean in another field; **Ru 2:8**
d not go on from this one, **Ru 2:8**
the sheaves, and **d** not insult her. **Ru 2:15**
may glean, and **d** not rebuke her." **Ru 2:16**
so that *others* **d** not fall upon **Ru 2:22**
but **d** not make yourself known to **Ru 3:3**
will tell you what you shall **d**." **Ru 3:4** 6213a
"All that you say I will **d**." **Ru 3:5** 6213a
"Now, my daughter, **d** not fear. **Ru 3:11**
I will **d** for you whatever you ask, **Ru 3:11** 6213a
'**D** not go to your mother-in-law **Ru 3:17**
why **d** you weep and why do you not **1Sa 1:8**
why do you weep and why **d** you not **1Sa 1:8**
"**D** not consider your maidservant **1Sa 1:16**
"**D** what seems best to you. **1Sa 1:23** 6213a
D not let arrogance come out of **1Sa 2:3**
"Why **d** you do such things, the **1Sa 2:23**
"Why do you **d** such things, the **1Sa 2:23** 6213a
'Why **d** you kick at My sacrifice **1Sa 2:29**
of all the good that I **d** for Israel; **1Sa 2:32** 3190
for Myself a faithful priest who will **d** **1Sa 2:35** 6213a
I am about to **d** a thing in Israel **1Sa 3:11** 6213a
Please **d** not hide it from me. **1Sa 3:17**
May God **d** so to you, and more **1Sa 3:17** 6213a
Him **d** what seems good to Him." **1Sa 3:18** 6213a
"**D** not be afraid, for you have **1Sa 4:20**
"What shall we **d** with the ark of **1Sa 5:8** 6213a
we **d** with the ark of the LORD? **1Sa 6:2** 6213a
of Israel, **d** not send it empty; **1Sa 6:3**
"Why then **d** you harden your **1Sa 6:6**
"**D** not cease to cry to the LORD **1Sa 7:8**
your sons **d** not walk in your ways. **1Sa 8:5**
and *some* to **d** his plowing and to **1Sa 8:12** 2790a
What **d** we have?" **1Sa 9:7**
ago, **d** not set your mind on them, **1Sa 9:20**
d you speak to me in this way?" **1Sa 9:21**
"What shall I **d** about my son?" **1Sa 10:2** 6213a
d for yourself what the occasion **1Sa 10:7** 6213a
and show you what you should **d**." **1Sa 10:8** 6213a
"**D** you see him whom the LORD has **1Sa 10:24**
and you may **d** to us whatever seems **1Sa 11:10** 6213a
the LORD will **d** before your eyes. **1Sa 12:16** 6213a
"**D** not fear. You have committed all **1Sa 12:20**
yet **d** not turn aside from **1Sa 12:20**
"But if you still **d** wickedly, **1Sa 12:25** 7489a
"**D** all that is in your heart; **1Sa 14:7** 6213a
and **d** not sin against the LORD by **1Sa 14:34**
"**D** whatever seems good to you." **1Sa 14:36** 6213a
"**D** what seems good to you." **1Sa 14:40** 6213a
God **d** this *to me* and more also, **1Sa 14:44** 6213a
that he has, and **d** not spare him; **1Sa 15:3**
so that I **d** not destroy you with them; **1Sa 15:6**
I will show you what you shall **d**; **1Sa 16:3** 6213a
"**D** you come in peace?" **1Sa 16:4**
"**D** not look at his appearance or **1Sa 16:7**
"Why **d** you come out to draw up in **1Sa 17:8**
your life, O king, I **d** not know." **1Sa 17:55**
"**D** not let the king sin against **1Sa 19:4**
you **d** not save your life tonight, **1Sa 19:11**
"**D** not let Jonathan know this, **1Sa 20:3**
you say, I will **d** for you." **1Sa 20:4** 6213a
"If it please my father *to* **d** you **1Sa 20:13**
d so to Jonathan and more also, **1Sa 20:13** 6213a
if I **d** not make it known to you **1Sa 20:13**
D I not know that you are choosing **1Sa 20:30**
"Hurry, be quick, **d** not stay!" **1Sa 20:38**
what **d** you have on hand? **1Sa 21:3**
Why **d** you bring him to me? **1Sa 21:14**
"**D** I lack madmen, that you have **1Sa 21:15**
I know what God will **d** for me." **1Sa 22:3** 6213a
"**D** not stay in the stronghold; **1Sa 22:5**
D not let the king impute anything **1Sa 22:15**
"Stay with me; **d** not be afraid, **1Sa 22:23**
"**D** not be afraid, because the **1Sa 23:17**
the desire of your soul to **d** so; **1Sa 23:20** 3381
and you shall **d** to him as it seems **1Sa 24:4** 6213a
I should **d** this thing to my lord, **1Sa 24:6** 6213a
"Why **d** you listen to the words of **1Sa 24:9**

men whose origin I **d** not know?" **1Sa 25:11**
and consider what you should **d**, **1Sa 25:17** 6213a
God **d** so to the enemies of David, **1Sa 25:22** 6213a
"Please **d** not let my lord pay **1Sa 25:25**
"**D** not destroy him, for who can **1Sa 26:9**
d not let my blood fall to the **1Sa 26:20**
know what your servant can **d**." **1Sa 28:2** 6213a
king said to her, "**D** not be afraid; **1Sa 28:13**
but what **d** you see?" **1Sa 28:13**
known to me what I should **d**." **1Sa 28:15** 6213a
"Why then **d** you ask me, since the **1Sa 28:16**
and **d** not let him go down to **1Sa 29:4**
"To whom **d** you belong? **1Sa 30:13**
"You must not **d** so, my brothers, **1Sa 30:23** 6213a
"From where **d** you come?" **2Sa 1:3**
"How **d** you know that Saul and his **2Sa 1:5**
D you not know that it will be **2Sa 2:26**
"May God **d** so to Abner, and more **2Sa 3:9** 6213a
I **d** not accomplish this for him, **2Sa 3:9**
d *it!* For the LORD has spoken **2Sa 3:18** 6213a
"May God **d** so to me, and more **2Sa 3:35** 6213a
"**D** you not know that a prince and **2Sa 3:38**
"Go, **d** all that is in your mind, **2Sa 7:3** 6213a
and to **d** a great thing for You **2Sa 7:23** 6213a
and **d** as You have spoken, **2Sa 7:25** 6213a
"**D** not fear, for I will surely **2Sa 9:7**
servant so your servant will **d**." **2Sa 9:11** 6213a
"**D** you think that David is **2Sa 10:3**
d what is good in His sight." **2Sa 10:12** 6213a
soul, I will not **d** this thing." **2Sa 11:11** 6213a
'**D** not let this thing displease **2Sa 11:25**
d this thing before all Israel, **2Sa 12:12** 6213a
since he might **d** *himself* harm!" **2Sa 12:18** 6213a
to Amnon to **d** anything to her. **2Sa 13:2** 6213a
"No, my brother, **d** not violate **2Sa 13:12**
d not do this disgraceful thing! **2Sa 13:12**
do not **d** this disgraceful thing! **2Sa 13:12** 6213a
d not take this matter to heart." **2Sa 13:20**
D not fear; have not I myself **2Sa 13:28**
"**D** not let my lord suppose they **2Sa 13:32**
d not let my lord the king take **2Sa 13:33**
d not anoint yourself with oil, **2Sa 14:2**
"Please **d** not hide anything from **2Sa 14:18**
now, I will surely **d** this thing; **2Sa 14:21** 6213a
your servants *are ready* to **d** **2Sa 15:15**
d to me as seems good to Him." **2Sa 15:26** 6213a
"Why **d** you have these?" **2Sa 16:2**
"What have I to **d** with you, O **2Sa 16:10**
What shall we **d**?" **2Sa 16:20** 6213a
'**D** not spend the night at the **2Sa 17:16**
seems best to you I will **d**." **2Sa 18:4** 6213a
by the LORD, if you **d** not go out, **2Sa 19:7**
May God **d** so to me, and more also, **2Sa 19:13** 6213a
to **d** what was good in his sight. **2Sa 19:18** 6213a
"What have I to **d** with you, O **2Sa 19:22**
For **d** I not know that I am king **2Sa 19:22**
d what is good in your sight. **2Sa 19:27** 6213a
What right **d** I have yet that I **2Sa 19:28**
"Why **d** you still speak of your **2Sa 19:29**
and **d** for him what is good in your **2Sa 19:37** 6213a
and I will **d** for him what is good **2Sa 19:38** 6213a
require of me, I will **d** for you." **2Sa 19:38** 6213a
Nor **d** we have inheritance in the **2Sa 20:1**
will **d** us more harm than Absalom; **2Sa 20:6** 7489a
"What should I **d** for you? **2Sa 21:3** 6213a
will **d** for you whatever you say." **2Sa 21:4** 6213a
so that you **d** not extinguish the lamp **2Sa 21:17**
me, O LORD, that I should **d** this. **2Sa 23:17** 6213a
them, which I will **d** to you. **2Sa 24:12** 6213a
but **d** not let me fall into the **2Sa 24:14**
"What **d** you wish?" **1Ki 1:16**
lord the king, you **d** not know *it*. **1Ki 1:18**
I will indeed **d** so this day." **1Ki 1:30** 6213a
that you **d** and wherever you turn, **1Ki 2:3** 6213a
and **d** not let his gray hair go **1Ki 2:6**
d not let him go unpunished, **1Ki 2:9**
know what you ought to **d** to him, **1Ki 2:9** 6213a
"**D** you come peacefully?" **1Ki 2:13**
d not refuse me." **1Ki 2:16**
d not refuse me." **1Ki 2:20**
"May God **d** so to me and more **1Ki 2:23** 6213a
"**D** as he has spoken and fall upon **1Ki 2:31** 6213a
and **d** not go out from there to any **1Ki 2:36**
said, so your servant will **d**." **1Ki 2:38** 6213a
I **d** not know how to go out or come **1Ki 3:7**
I will **d** what you desire **1Ki 5:8** 6213a
and **d** according to all for which **1Ki 8:43** 6213a
as **d** Your people Israel, **1Ki 8:43**
and all that Solomon desired to **d**, **1Ki 9:1** 6213a
and **d** not keep My commandments **1Ki 9:6**
to **d** justice and righteousness." **1Ki 10:9** 6213a
"Nevertheless I will not **d** it in **1Ki 11:12** 6213a
and **d** what is right in My sight by **1Ki 11:38** 6213a
"How **d** you counsel *me* to answer **1Ki 12:6**
"What counsel **d** you give that we **1Ki 12:9**
"What portion **d** we have in David? **1Ki 12:16**
d not return by going the way **1Ki 13:17**
why **d** you pretend to be another **1Ki 14:6**
to **d** only that which was right in **1Ki 14:8** 6213a
Then Elijah said to her, "**D** not fear; **1Ki 17:13**
go, **d** as you have said, but make **1Ki 17:13** 6213a
"What **d** I have to do with you, O **1Ki 17:18**
"What do I have to **d** with you, **1Ki 17:18**
will carry you where I **d** not know; **1Ki 18:12**
"**D** it a second time," **1Ki 18:34** 8138
"**D** it a third time," **1Ki 18:34** 8027
d not let one of them escape." **1Ki 18:40**
the gods **d** to me and even more, **1Ki 19:2** 6213a
if I **d** not make your life as the **1Ki 19:2**

Context	Reference	Number
“**D** not listen or consent.”	**1Ki 20:8**	
servant at the first I will **d**,	**1Ki 20:9**	6213a
do, but this thing I cannot **d**.’ ”	**1Ki 20:9**	6213a
the gods **d** so to me and more also,	**1Ki 20:10**	6213a
and see what you have to **d**;	**1Ki 20:22**	6213a
“**D** this thing: remove the kings,	**1Ki 20:24**	6213a
“**D** you now reign over Israel?	**1Ki 21:7**	
d evil in the sight of the LORD.	**1Ki 21:20**	6213a
d evil in the sight of the LORD,	**1Ki 21:25**	6213a
“**D** you see how Ahab has humbled	**1Ki 21:29**	
“**D** you know that Ramoth-gilead	**1Ki 22:3**	
and also prevail. Go and **d** so.’	**1Ki 22:22**	6213a
“**D** not fight with small or great,	**1Ki 22:31**	
d not be afraid of him.”	**2Ki 1:15**	
“**D** you know that the LORD will	**2Ki 2:3**	
“**D** you know that the LORD will	**2Ki 2:5**	
“Ask what I shall **d** for you	**2Ki 2:9**	6213a
“Did I not say to you, ‘**D** not go’?”	**2Ki 2:18**	
“What **d** I have to do with you?	**2Ki 3:13**	
“What do I have to **d** with you?	**2Ki 3:13**	
“What shall I **d** for you?	**2Ki 4:2**	6213a
what **d** you have in the house?”	**2Ki 4:2**	
even empty vessels; **d** not get a few.	**2Ki 4:3**	
what can I **d** for you?	**2Ki 4:13**	6213a
d not lie to your maidservant.”	**2Ki 4:16**	
d not slow down the pace for me	**2Ki 4:24**	
‘**D** not deceive me’?”	**2Ki 4:28**	
meet any man, **d** not salute him,	**2Ki 4:29**	
salutes you, **d** not answer him;	**2Ki 4:29**	
had the prophet told you *to* **d** *some*	**2Ki 5:13**	
that you **d** not pass this place,	**2Ki 6:9**	
What shall we **d**?”	**2Ki 6:15**	6213a
“**D** not fear, for those who are	**2Ki 6:16**	
“May God **d** so to me and more	**2Ki 6:31**	6213a
“**D** you see how this son of a	**2Ki 6:32**	
“Why **d** we sit here until we die?	**2Ki 7:3**	
you will **d** to the sons of Israel:	**2Ki 8:12**	6213a
he should **d** this great thing?”	**2Ki 8:13**	6213a
door and flee and **d** not wait.”	**2Ki 9:3**	
“What have you to **d** with peace?	**2Ki 9:18**	
“What have you to **d** with peace?	**2Ki 9:19**	
all that you say to us we will **d**,	**2Ki 10:5**	6213a
d what is good in your sight.”	**2Ki 10:5**	6213a
is the thing that you shall **d**:	**2Ki 11:5**	6213a
“Why **d** you not repair the damages	**2Ki 12:7**	
and he did not **d** what was right in	**2Ki 16:2**	6213a
“You shall not **d** this thing.”	**2Ki 17:12**	6213a
commanded them not to **d** like them.	**2Ki 17:15**	6213a
d evil in the sight of the LORD,	**2Ki 17:17**	6213a
d not know the custom of the god	**2Ki 17:26**	
they kill them because they **d** not	**2Ki 17:26**	
To this day they **d** according to	**2Ki 17:34**	6213a
they **d** not fear the LORD, nor do	**2Ki 17:34**	
nor **d** they follow their statutes	**2Ki 17:34**	
you shall observe to **d** forever;	**2Ki 17:37**	6213a
did, so they **d** to this day.	**2Ki 17:41**	6213a
would neither listen nor **d** *it*.	**2Ki 18:12**	6213a
Now on whom **d** you rely, that you	**2Ki 18:20**	
and **d** not speak with us in Judean in	**2Ki 18:26**	
‘**D** not let Hezekiah deceive you,	**2Ki 18:29**	
‘**D** not listen to Hezekiah, for	**2Ki 18:31**	
But **d** not listen to Hezekiah when	**2Ki 18:32**	
“**D** not answer him.”	**2Ki 18:36**	
“**D** not be afraid because of the	**2Ki 19:6**	
‘**D** not let your God in whom you	**2Ki 19:10**	
d the thing that He has spoken:	**2Ki 20:9**	6213a
if only they will observe to **d**	**2Ki 21:8**	6213a
and Manasseh seduced them to **d**	**2Ki 21:9**	6213a
to **d** according to all that is	**2Ki 22:13**	6213a
“**D** not be afraid of the servants	**2Ki 25:24**	
my God that I should **d** this.	**1Ch 11:19**	6213a
knowledge of what Israel should **d**,	**1Ch 12:32**	6213a
said that they would **d** so,	**1Ch 13:4**	6213a
“**D** not touch My anointed ones,	**1Ch 16:22**	
ones, And **d** My prophets no harm.”	**1Ch 16:22**	7489a
“**D** all that is in your heart, for	**1Ch 17:2**	6213a
and **d** as You have spoken.	**1Ch 17:23**	6213a
“**D** you think that David is	**1Ch 19:3**	
d what is good in His sight.”	**1Ch 19:13**	6213a
which I will **d** to you.” ’ ”	**1Ch 21:10**	6213a
But **d** not let me fall into the	**1Ch 21:13**	
king **d** what is good in his sight.	**1Ch 21:23**	6213a
d not fear nor be dismayed.	**1Ch 22:13**	
d not fear nor be dismayed, for	**1Ch 28:20**	
Your statutes, and to **d** *them* all,	**1Ch 29:19**	6213a
a house to dwell in, so **d** for me.	**2Ch 2:3**	
and **d** according to all for which	**2Ch 6:33**	6213a
and fear You as **d** Your people	**2Ch 6:33**	
d not turn away the face of Your	**2Ch 6:42**	
your father David walked, even to **d**	**2Ch 7:17**	6213a
to **d** justice and righteousness.”	**2Ch 9:8**	6213a
“How **d** you counsel *me* to answer	**2Ch 10:6**	
“What counsel **d** you give that we	**2Ch 10:9**	
“What portion **d** we have in David?	**2Ch 10:16**	
“**D** you not know that the LORD God	**2Ch 13:5**	
d not fight against the LORD God	**2Ch 13:12**	
be strong and **d** not lose courage,	**2Ch 15:7**	
and prevail also. Go and **d** so.’	**2Ch 18:21**	6213a
“**D** not fight with small or great,	**2Ch 18:30**	
for you **d** not judge for man but	**2Ch 19:6**	
be very careful what you **d**,	**2Ch 19:7**	6213a
shall **d** in the fear of the LORD,	**2Ch 19:9**	6213a
d and you will not be guilty.	**2Ch 19:10**	6213a
nor **d** we know what to do, but our	**2Ch 20:12**	
nor do we know what to **d**,	**2Ch 20:12**	6213a
‘**D** not fear or be dismayed because	**2Ch 20:15**	
D not fear or be dismayed;	**2Ch 20:17**	
was his counselor to **d** wickedly.	**2Ch 22:3**	7561
is the thing which you shall **d**:	**2Ch 23:4**	6213a
you shall **d** the matter quickly.”	**2Ch 24:5**	4116
‘Why **d** you transgress the	**2Ch 24:20**	
of the LORD and **d** not prosper?	**2Ch 24:20**	
d not let the army of Israel go	**2Ch 25:7**	
“But if you **d** go, do *it*, be	**2Ch 25:8**	
“But if you do go, **d** *it*,	**2Ch 25:8**	6213a
“But what *shall we* **d** for the	**2Ch 25:9**	6213a
and he did not **d** right in the	**2Ch 28:1**	6213a
d you not *have* transgressions	**2Ch 28:10**	
“My sons, **d** not be negligent now,	**2Ch 29:11**	
“**D** not be like your fathers and your	**2Ch 30:7**	
“Now **d** not stiffen your neck like	**2Ch 30:8**	
to **d** what the king and the princes	**2Ch 30:12**	6213a
d not fear or be dismayed because	**2Ch 32:7**	
‘**D** you not know what I and my	**2Ch 32:13**	
d not let Hezekiah deceive you or	**2Ch 32:15**	
like this, and **d** not believe him,	**2Ch 32:15**	
if only they will observe to **d** all	**2Ch 33:8**	6213a
to **d** more evil than the nations whom	**2Ch 33:9**	6213a
to **d** according to all that is	**2Ch 34:21**	6213a
d according to the word of the LORD	**2Ch 35:6**	6213a
“What have we to **d** with each	**2Ch 35:21**	
what you are to **d** for these elders	**Ezr 6:8**	5648
d with the rest of the silver and gold,	**Ezr 7:18**	
you may **d** according to the will of	**Ezr 7:18**	5648
‘So now **d** not give your daughters	**Ezr 9:12**	
d according to this proposal;	**Ezr 10:5**	6213a
of your fathers and **d** His will;	**Ezr 10:11**	6213a
so it is our duty to **d**	**Ezr 10:12**	6213a
keep My commandments and **d** them,	**Ne 1:9**	6213a
God was putting into my mind to **d**	**Ne 2:12**	6213a
D not forgive their iniquity and	**Ne 4:5**	
“**D** not be afraid of them;	**Ne 4:14**	
we will **d** exactly as you say.”	**Ne 5:12**	6213a
would **d** according to this promise.	**Ne 5:12**	6213a
d so because of the fear of God.	**Ne 5:15**	6213a
“**D** not let the gates of Jerusalem	**Ne 7:3**	
d not mourn or weep.”	**Ne 8:9**	
D not be grieved, for the joy of	**Ne 8:10**	
d not be grieved.”	**Ne 8:11**	
To **d** with them as they desired.	**Ne 9:24**	6213a
D not let all the hardship seem	**Ne 9:32**	
and **d** not blot out my loyal deeds	**Ne 13:14**	
“Did not your fathers **d** the same	**Ne 13:18**	6213a
“Why **d** you spend the night in	**Ne 13:21**	
If you **d** so again, I will use	**Ne 13:21**	8138
“**D** we then hear about you that	**Ne 13:27**	
he should **d** according to the desires	**Es 1:8**	6213a
they **d** not observe the king’s laws,	**Es 3:8**	
to **d** with them as you please.”	**Es 3:11**	6213a
“**D** not imagine that you in the	**Es 4:13**	
d not eat or drink for three days,	**Es 4:16**	
that we may **d** as Esther desires.”	**Es 5:5**	6213a
my petition and **d** what I request,	**Es 5:8**	6213a
I will **d** as the king says.”	**Es 5:8**	6213a
and **d** so for Mordecai the Jew,	**Es 6:10**	6213a
d not fall short in anything of	**Es 6:10**	
he, who would presume to **d** thus?”	**Es 7:5**	6213a
are in Susa to **d** according to the edict	**Es 9:13**	6213a
what they had started to **d**,	**Es 9:23**	6213a
“From where **d** you come?”	**Jb 1:7**	
only **d** not put forth your hand on	**Jb 1:12**	
“**D** you still hold fast your	**Jb 2:9**	
They **d** not hear the voice of the	**Jb 3:18**	
So **d** not despise the discipline of	**Jb 5:17**	
“**D** you intend to reprove *my*	**Jb 6:26**	
“Why then **d** You not pardon my	**Jb 7:21**	
I **d** not take notice of myself;	**Jb 9:21**	
‘**D** not condemn me;	**Jb 10:2**	
Or **d** You see as a man sees?	**Jb 10:4**	
as the heavens, what can you **d**?	**Jb 11:8**	6466
And **d** not let wickedness dwell in	**Jb 11:14**	
“Only two things **d** not do to me,	**Jb 13:20**	
“Only two things do not **d** to me,	**Jb 13:20**	6213a
“Why **d** You hide Your face And	**Jb 13:24**	
steps, You **d** not observe my sin.	**Jb 14:16**	
“Indeed, you **d** away with	**Jb 15:4**	6565a
“**D** you hear the secret counsel of	**Jb 15:8**	
d you know that we do not know?	**Jb 15:9**	
do you know that we **d** not know?	**Jb 15:9**	
d you understand that we do not?	**Jb 15:9**	
do you understand that we **d** not?	**Jb 15:9**	
And why **d** your eyes flash,	**Jb 15:12**	
“O earth, **d** not cover my blood,	**Jb 16:18**	
I **d** not find a wise man among you.	**Jb 17:10**	
d you persecute me as God *does*,	**Jb 19:22**	
“**D** you know this from of old,	**Jb 20:4**	
“Why **d** the wicked *still* live,	**Jb 21:7**	
We **d** not even desire the knowledge	**Jb 21:14**	
And **d** you not recognize their	**Jb 21:29**	
‘What can the Almighty **d** to them?’	**Jb 22:17**	6466
And why **d** those who know Him not	**Jb 24:1**	
They **d** not want to know its ways Nor	**Jb 24:13**	
They **d** not know the light.	**Jb 24:16**	
d not turn toward the vineyards.	**Jb 24:18**	
Why then **d** you act foolishly?	**Jb 27:12**	
And they **d** not refrain from	**Jb 30:10**	
help, but You **d** not answer me;	**Jb 30:20**	
then could I **d** when God arises?	**Jb 31:14**	6213a
of His majesty I can **d** nothing.	**Jb 31:23**	3201
“**D** not say, ‘We have found wisdom;	**Jb 32:13**	
I wait, because they **d** not speak,	**Jb 32:16**	
“For I **d** not know how to flatter,	**Jb 32:22**	
“Why **d** you complain against Him That	**Jb 33:13**	
be it from God to **d** wickedness,	**Jb 34:10**	
And from the Almighty to **d** wrong.	**Jb 34:10**	
“If He should determine to **d** so,	**Jb 34:14**	
Teach me what I **d** not see;	**Jb 34:32**	
iniquity, I will not **d** it again’?	**Jb 34:32**	3254
“**D** you think this is according to	**Jb 35:2**	
D you say, ‘My righteousness is more	**Jb 35:2**	
what **d** you accomplish against Him?	**Jb 35:6**	
are many, what **d** you do to Him?	**Jb 35:6**	
are many, what do you **d** to Him?	**Jb 35:6**	6213a
righteous, what **d** you give to Him,	**Jb 35:7**	
when you say you **d** not behold Him,	**Jb 35:14**	
“But if they **d** not hear, they	**Jb 36:12**	
They **d** not cry for help when He	**Jb 36:13**	
And **d** not let the greatness of the	**Jb 36:18**	
“**D** not long for the night, When	**Jb 36:20**	
“Be careful, **d** not turn to evil,	**Jb 36:21**	
is exalted, and we **d** not know *Him;*	**Jb 36:26**	
That it may **d** whatever He commands	**Jb 37:12**	6466
“**D** you know how God establishes	**Jb 37:15**	
“**D** you know about the layers of	**Jb 37:16**	
“Now men **d** not see the light	**Jb 37:21**	
And He will not **d** violence to	**Jb 37:23**	6031a
“**D** you know the ordinances of the	**Jb 38:33**	
“**D** you know the time the mountain	**Jb 39:1**	
D you observe the calving of the	**Jb 39:1**	
Or **d** you know the time they give	**Jb 39:2**	
leave and **d** not return to them.	**Jb 39:4**	
“**D** you give the horse *his* might?	**Jb 39:19**	
D you clothe his neck with a mane?	**Jb 39:19**	
“**D** you make him leap like the	**Jb 39:20**	
“Or **d** you have an arm like God,	**Jb 40:9**	
you will not **d** it again!	**Jb 41:8**	3254
know that You can **d** all things,	**Jb 42:2**	
not **d** with you *according to your* folly,	**Jb 42:8**	6213a
D homage to the Son, that He	**Ps 2:12**	5401a
Tremble, and **d** not sin;	**Ps 4:4**	
You hate all who **d** iniquity.	**Ps 5:5**	6466
d not rebuke me in Your anger,	**Ps 6:1**	
from me, all you who **d** iniquity,	**Ps 6:8**	6466
O LORD, **d** not let man prevail;	**Ps 9:19**	
Why **d** You stand afar off,	**Ps 10:1**	
Why **d** You hide *Yourself* in times	**Ps 10:1**	
D not forget the afflicted.	**Ps 10:12**	
What can the righteous **d**?”	**Ps 11:3**	6466
D all the workers of wickedness	**Ps 14:4**	
And **d** not call upon the Lord?	**Ps 14:4**	
cry by day, but You **d** not answer;	**Ps 22:2**	
I trust, **D** not let me be ashamed;	**Ps 25:2**	
D not let my enemies exult over me.	**Ps 25:2**	
D not remember the sins of my	**Ps 25:7**	
D not let me be ashamed, for I	**Ps 25:20**	
I **d** not sit with deceitful men,	**Ps 26:4**	
D not take my soul away *along* with	**Ps 26:9**	
D not hide Your face from me, Do	**Ps 27:9**	
D not turn Your servant away in	**Ps 27:9**	
D not abandon me nor forsake me, O	**Ps 27:9**	
D not deliver me over to the	**Ps 27:12**	
My rock, **d** not be deaf to me,	**Ps 28:1**	
D not drag me away with the wicked	**Ps 28:3**	
Because they **d** not regard the	**Ps 28:5**	
D not be as the horse or as the	**Ps 32:9**	
lions **d** lack and suffer hunger;	**Ps 34:10**	
Depart from evil and **d** good;	**Ps 34:14**	6213a
me of things that I **d** not know.	**Ps 35:11**	
D not let those who are wrongfully	**Ps 35:19**	
For they **d** not speak peace, But	**Ps 35:20**	
it, O LORD, **d** not keep silent;	**Ps 35:22**	
O Lord, **d** not be far from me.	**Ps 35:22**	
d not let them rejoice over me.	**Ps 35:24**	
D not let them say in their heart,	**Ps 35:25**	
D not let them say,	**Ps 35:25**	
ceased to be wise *and* to **d** good.	**Ps 36:3**	3190
D not fret because of evildoers,	**Ps 37:1**	
Trust in the LORD and **d** good;	**Ps 37:3**	6213a
also in Him, and He will **d** it.	**Ps 37:5**	6213a
D not fret because of him who	**Ps 37:7**	
D not fret; *it leads* only to	**Ps 37:8**	
Depart from evil and **d** good,	**Ps 37:27**	6213a
His steps **d** not slip.	**Ps 37:31**	
I, like a deaf man, **d** not hear;	**Ps 38:13**	
D not forsake me, O LORD;	**Ps 38:21**	
O my God, **d** not be far from me!	**Ps 38:21**	
“And now, Lord, for what **d** I wait?	**Ps 39:7**	
mute, I **d** not open my mouth,	**Ps 39:9**	
D not be silent at my tears;	**Ps 39:12**	
I delight to **d** Your will, O my God;	**Ps 40:8**	6213a
D not delay, O my God.	**Ps 40:17**	
And **d** not give him over to the	**Ps 41:2**	
Why **d** I go mourning because of the	**Ps 42:9**	
Why **d** I go mourning because of the	**Ps 43:2**	
And **d** not go out with our armies.	**Ps 44:9**	
Arouse Yourself, why **d** You sleep,	**Ps 44:23**	
Awake, **d** not reject us forever.	**Ps 44:23**	
Why **d** You hide Your face *And*	**Ps 44:24**	
D not be afraid when a man becomes	**Ps 49:16**	
you when you **d** well for yourself	**Ps 49:18**	3190
“I **d** not reprove you for your	**Ps 50:8**	
D not cast me away from Your	**Ps 51:11**	
And **d** not take Your Holy Spirit	**Ps 51:11**	
You **d** not delight in sacrifice,	**Ps 51:16**	
By Your favor **d** good to Zion;	**Ps 51:18**	3190
Why **d** you boast in evil, O mighty	**Ps 52:1**	
And **d** not hide Yourself from my	**Ps 55:1**	
d not depart from her streets.	**Ps 55:11**	
no change, And who **d** not fear God.	**Ps 55:19**	
What can *mere* man **d** to me?	**Ps 56:4**	6213a
What can man **d** to me?	**Ps 56:11**	6213a
D you indeed speak righteousness,	**Ps 58:1**	
D you judge uprightly, O sons of	**Ps 58:1**	
me from those who **d** iniquity And	**Ps 59:2**	6466
D not be gracious to any *who are*	**Ps 59:5**	
D not slay them, or my people	**Ps 59:11**	
Through God we shall **d** valiantly,	**Ps 60:12**	6213a

Context	Reference	Number
D not trust in oppression And do	**Ps 62:10**	
And **d** not vainly hope in robbery;	**Ps 62:10**	
d not set *your* heart *upon them.*	**Ps 62:10**	
tumult of those who **d** iniquity,	**Ps 64:2**	6466
they shoot at him, and **d** not fear.	**Ps 64:4**	
Why **d** *you* look with envy, O	**Ps 68:16**	
the mire and **d** not let me sink;	**Ps 69:14**	
And **d** not hide Your face from Your	**Ps 69:17**	
O LORD, **d** not delay.	**Ps 70:5**	
D not cast me off in the time of	**Ps 71:9**	
D not forsake me when my strength	**Ps 71:9**	
O God, **d** not be far from me;	**Ps 71:12**	
For I **d** not know the sum *of them.*	**Ps 71:15**	
and gray, O God, **d** not forsake me,	**Ps 71:18**	
We **d** not see our signs;	**Ps 74:9**	
Why **d** You withdraw Your hand, even	**Ps 74:11**	
D not deliver the soul of Your	**Ps 74:19**	
D not forget the life of Your	**Ps 74:19**	
D not forget the voice of Your	**Ps 74:23**	
'**D** not boast,' And to the wicked,	**Ps 75:4**	
'**D** not lift up the horn;	**Ps 75:4**	
D not lift up your horn on high,	**Ps 75:5**	
D not speak with insolent pride.' "	**Ps 75:5**	
the nations which **d** not know You,	**Ps 79:6**	
which **d** not call upon Your name.	**Ps 79:6**	
D not remember the iniquities of	**Ps 79:8**	
D justice to the afflicted and	**Ps 82:3**	6663
They **d** not know nor do they	**Ps 82:5**	
do not know nor **d** they understand;	**Ps 82:5**	
O God, **d** not remain quiet;	**Ps 83:1**	
D not be silent and, O God, do not	**Ps 83:1**	
silent and, O God, **d** not be still.	**Ps 83:1**	
are great and **d** wondrous deeds;	**Ps 86:10**	6213a
O LORD, why **d** You reject my soul?	**Ps 88:14**	
Why **d** You hide Your face from me?	**Ps 88:14**	
And **d** not walk in My judgments,	**Ps 89:30**	
And **d** not keep My commandments,	**Ps 89:31**	
D return, O LORD;	**Ps 90:13**	
That you **d** not strike your foot	**Ps 91:12**	
who **d** iniquity will be scattered.	**Ps 92:9**	6466
who **d** wickedness vaunt themselves.	**Ps 94:4**	6466
me against those who **d** wickedness?	**Ps 94:16**	6466
D not harden your hearts, as at	**Ps 95:8**	
And they **d** not know My ways.	**Ps 95:10**	
the LORD all those who **d** iniquity.	**Ps 101:8**	6466
D not hide Your face from me in the	**Ps 102:2**	
d not take me away in the midst of	**Ps 102:24**	
remember His precepts to **d** them.	**Ps 103:18**	6213a
"**D** not touch My anointed ones,	**Ps 105:15**	
ones, And **d** My prophets no harm."	**Ps 105:15**	7489a
Who **d** business on great waters;	**Ps 107:23**	6213a
Through God we will **d** valiantly	**Ps 108:13**	6213a
God of my praise, **D** not be silent!	**Ps 109:1**	
And **d** not let the sin of his	**Ps 109:14**	
all those who **d** *His commandments;*	**Ps 111:10**	6213a
The dead **d** not praise the LORD,	**Ps 115:17**	
Nor **d** any who go down into	**Ps 115:17**	
What can man **d** to me?	**Ps 118:6**	6213a
O LORD, **d** save, we beseech You;	**Ps 118:25**	
beseech You, **d** send prosperity!	**Ps 118:25**	
They also **d** no unrighteousness;	**Ps 119:3**	6466
D not forsake me utterly!	**Ps 119:8**	
D not let me wander from Your	**Ps 119:10**	
D not hide Your commandments from	**Ps 119:19**	
O LORD, **d** not put me to shame!	**Ps 119:31**	
And **d** not take the word of truth	**Ps 119:43**	
I **d** not turn aside from Your law.	**Ps 119:51**	
You are good and **d** good;	**Ps 119:68**	3190
I **d** not forget Your statutes.	**Ps 119:83**	
hand, Yet I **d** not forget Your law.	**Ps 119:109**	
And **d** not let me be ashamed of my	**Ps 119:116**	
D not leave me to my oppressors.	**Ps 119:121**	
D not let the arrogant oppress me.	**Ps 119:122**	
And **d** not let any iniquity have	**Ps 119:133**	
Because they **d** not keep Your law.	**Ps 119:136**	
Yet I **d** not forget Your precepts.	**Ps 119:141**	
me, For I **d** not forget Your law.	**Ps 119:153**	
For they **d** not seek Your statutes.	**Ps 119:155**	
Yet I **d** not turn aside from Your	**Ps 119:157**	
Because they **d** not keep Your word.	**Ps 119:158**	
O LORD, And **d** Your commandments.	**Ps 119:166**	6213a
I **d** not forget Your commandments.	**Ps 119:176**	
put forth their hands to **d** wrong.	**Ps 125:3**	
D good, O LORD, to those who are	**Ps 125:4**	3190
Nor **d** those who pass by say,	**Ps 129:8**	
wait, And in His word **d** I hope.	**Ps 130:5**	
Nor **d** I involve myself in great	**Ps 131:1**	
D not turn away the face of Your	**Ps 132:10**	
have mouths, but they **d** not speak;	**Ps 135:16**	
have eyes, but they **d** not see;	**Ps 135:16**	
have ears, but they **d** not hear,	**Ps 135:17**	
my mouth If I **d** not remember you,	**Ps 137:6**	
If I **d** not exalt Jerusalem Above	**Ps 137:6**	
D not forsake the works of Your	**Ps 138:8**	
D I not hate those who hate You,	**Ps 139:21**	
And **d** I not loathe those who rise	**Ps 139:21**	
"**D** not grant, O LORD, the desires	**Ps 140:8**	
D not promote his *evil* device,	**Ps 140:8**	
D not incline my heart to any evil	**Ps 141:4**	
With men who **d** iniquity;	**Ps 141:4**	6466
And **d** not let me eat of their	**Ps 141:4**	
D not let my head refuse it, For	**Ps 141:5**	
d not leave me defenseless.	**Ps 141:8**	
snares of those who **d** iniquity.	**Ps 141:9**	6466
And **d** not enter into judgment with	**Ps 143:2**	
D not hide Your face from me, Or	**Ps 143:7**	
Teach me to **d** Your will, For You	**Ps 143:10**	6213a
D not trust in princes, In mortal	**Ps 146:3**	
And **d** not forsake your mother's	**Pr 1:8**	
sinners entice you, **D** not consent.	**Pr 1:10**	
d not walk in the way with them.	**Pr 1:15**	
d they reach the paths of life.	**Pr 2:19**	
My son, **d** not forget my teaching,	**Pr 3:1**	
D not let kindness and truth leave	**Pr 3:3**	
And **d** not lean on your own	**Pr 3:5**	
D not be wise in your own eyes;	**Pr 3:7**	
d not reject the discipline of the	**Pr 3:11**	
D not be afraid of sudden fear Nor	**Pr 3:25**	
D not withhold good from those to	**Pr 3:27**	
When it is in your power to **d** *it.*	**Pr 3:27**	6213a
D not say to your neighbor,	**Pr 3:28**	
D not devise harm against your	**Pr 3:29**	
D not contend with a man without	**Pr 3:30**	
D not envy a man of violence And	**Pr 3:31**	
And **d** not choose any of his ways.	**Pr 3:31**	
D not abandon my instruction.	**Pr 4:2**	
D not forget nor turn away from	**Pr 4:5**	
"**D** not forsake her, and she will	**Pr 4:6**	
Take hold of instruction; **d** not let go.	**Pr 4:13**	
D not enter the path of the	**Pr 4:14**	
And **d** not proceed in the way of	**Pr 4:14**	
Avoid it, **d** not pass by it;	**Pr 4:15**	
cannot sleep unless they **d** evil;	**Pr 4:16**	7489a
They **d** not know over what they	**Pr 4:19**	
D not let them depart from your	**Pr 4:21**	
D not turn to the right nor to the	**Pr 4:27**	
And **d** not depart from the words of	**Pr 5:7**	
And **d** not go near the door of her	**Pr 5:8**	
D this then, my son, and deliver	**Pr 6:3**	6213a
And **d** not forsake the teaching of	**Pr 6:20**	
D not desire her beauty in your	**Pr 6:25**	
Men **d** not despise a thief if he	**Pr 6:30**	
Her feet **d** not remain at home;	**Pr 7:11**	
D not let your heart turn aside to	**Pr 7:25**	
ways, **D** not stray into her paths.	**Pr 7:25**	
and be wise, And **d** not neglect *it.*	**Pr 8:33**	
D not reprove a scoffer, or he	**Pr 9:8**	
Ill-gotten gains **d** not profit, But	**Pr 10:2**	
Riches **d** not profit in the day of	**Pr 11:4**	
How much more **d** his friends abandon	**Pr 19:7**	
hope, And **d** not desire his death.	**Pr 19:18**	
you will only have to **d** it again.	**Pr 19:19**	3254
D not love sleep, or you will become	**Pr 20:13**	
d not associate with a gossip.	**Pr 20:19**	
D not say, "I will repay evil";	**Pr 20:22**	
To **d** righteousness and justice Is	**Pr 21:3**	6213a
D not rob the poor because he is	**Pr 22:22**	
D not associate with a man *given*	**Pr 22:24**	
D not be among those who give	**Pr 22:26**	
D not move the ancient boundary	**Pr 22:28**	
D you see a man skilled in his	**Pr 22:29**	
D not desire his delicacies, For	**Pr 23:3**	
D not weary yourself to gain	**Pr 23:4**	
D not eat the bread of a selfish	**Pr 23:6**	
D not speak in the hearing of a	**Pr 23:9**	
D not move the ancient boundary Or	**Pr 23:10**	
D not hold back discipline from	**Pr 23:13**	
D not let your heart envy sinners,	**Pr 23:17**	
D not be with heavy drinkers of	**Pr 23:20**	
And **d** not despise your mother when	**Pr 23:22**	
Buy truth, and **d** not sell *it, Get*	**Pr 23:23**	
D not look on the wine when it is	**Pr 23:31**	
D not be envious of evil men, Nor	**Pr 24:1**	
One who plans to **d** evil, Men will	**Pr 24:8**	7489a
D not lie in wait, O wicked man,	**Pr 24:15**	
D not destroy his resting place;	**Pr 24:15**	
D not rejoice when your enemy	**Pr 24:17**	
And **d** not let your heart be glad	**Pr 24:17**	
D not fret because of evildoers Or	**Pr 24:19**	
D not associate with those who are	**Pr 24:21**	
D not be a witness against your	**Pr 24:28**	
And **d** not deceive with your lips.	**Pr 24:28**	
D not say, "Thus I shall do to him	**Pr 24:29**	6213a
d to him as he has done to me;	**Pr 24:29**	6213a
D not claim honor in the presence	**Pr 25:6**	
And **d** not stand in the place of	**Pr 25:6**	
D not go out hastily to argue *your*	**Pr 25:8**	
what will you **d** in the end,	**Pr 25:8**	6213a
And **d** not reveal the secret of	**Pr 25:9**	
D not answer a fool according to	**Pr 26:4**	
D you see a man wise in his own	**Pr 26:12**	
graciously, **d** not believe him,	**Pr 26:25**	
D not boast about tomorrow, For	**Pr 27:1**	
For you **d** not know what a day may	**Pr 27:1**	
D not forsake your own friend or	**Pr 27:10**	
And **d** not go to your brother's	**Pr 27:10**	
Evil men **d** not understand justice,	**Pr 28:5**	
D you see a man who is hasty in	**Pr 29:20**	
And I **d** not have the understanding	**Pr 30:2**	
Nor **d** I have the knowledge of the	**Pr 30:3**	
D not add to His words Or He	**Pr 30:6**	
D not refuse me before I die:	**Pr 30:7**	
D not slander a slave to his	**Pr 30:10**	
me, Four which I **d** not understand:	**Pr 30:18**	
D not give your strength to women,	**Pr 31:3**	
good there is for the sons of men to **d**	**Ec 2:3**	6213a
for what *will* the man **d** who	**Ec 2:12**	
and to **d** good in one's lifetime;	**Ec 3:12**	6213a
d not know they are doing evil.	**Ec 5:1**	
D not be hasty in word or	**Ec 5:2**	
God, **d** not be late in paying it;	**Ec 5:4**	
D not let your speech cause you to	**Ec 5:6**	
speech cause you to sin and **d** not say	**Ec 5:6**	
d not be shocked at the sight;	**Ec 5:8**	
d not all go to one place?"	**Ec 6:6**	
D not be eager in your heart to be	**Ec 7:9**	
D not say, "Why is it that the former	**Ec 7:10**	
D not be excessively righteous and	**Ec 7:16**	
and **d** not be overly wise.	**Ec 7:16**	
D not be excessively wicked and	**Ec 7:17**	
wicked and **d** not be a fool.	**Ec 7:17**	
d not take seriously all words	**Ec 7:21**	
"**D** not be in a hurry to leave him.	**Ec 8:3**	
D not join in an evil matter, for	**Ec 8:3**	
he will **d** whatever he pleases."	**Ec 8:3**	6213a
them are given fully to **d** evil.	**Ec 8:11**	6213a
but the dead **d** not know anything,	**Ec 9:5**	
Whatever your hand finds to **d**,	**Ec 9:10**	6213a
d it with *all* your might;	**Ec 9:10**	6213a
you, **d** not abandon your position,	**Ec 10:4**	
bedchamber **d** not curse a king,	**Ec 10:20**	
rooms **d** not curse a rich man,	**Ec 10:20**	
for you **d** not know what misfortune	**Ec 11:2**	
Just as you **d** not know the path of	**Ec 11:5**	
so you **d** not know the activity of	**Ec 11:5**	
and **d** not be idle in the evening,	**Ec 11:6**	
for you **d** not know whether morning	**Ec 11:6**	
Rightly **d** they love you."	**SS 1:4**	
"**D** not stare at me because I am	**SS 1:6**	
Where **d** you pasture *your flock,*	**SS 1:7**	
d you make *it* lie down at noon?	**SS 1:7**	
"If you yourself **d** not know, Most	**SS 1:8**	
That you **d** not arouse or awaken *my*	**SS 2:7**	
D not arouse or awaken *my* love Until	**SS 8:4**	
What shall we **d** for our sister On	**SS 8:8**	6213a
My people **d** not understand."	**Is 1:3**	
Cease to **d** evil,	**Is 1:16**	
Learn to **d** good; Seek justice,	**Is 1:17**	3190
They **d** not defend the orphan, Nor	**Is 1:23**	
abased, But **d** not forgive them.	**Is 2:9**	
They **d** not *even* conceal *it.*	**Is 3:9**	
"What **d** you mean by crushing My	**Is 3:15**	
"What more was there to **d** for My	**Is 5:4**	6213a
I am going to **d** to My vineyard:	**Is 5:5**	6213a
But they **d** not pay attention to	**Is 5:12**	
Nor **d** they consider the work of	**Is 5:12**	
on listening, but **d** not perceive;	**Is 6:9**	
on looking, but **d** not understand.'	**Is 6:9**	
d not be fainthearted because of	**Is 7:4**	
If they **d** not speak according to	**Is 8:20**	
Yet the people **d** not turn back to	**Is 9:13**	
Nor **d** they seek the LORD of hosts.	**Is 9:13**	
you **d** in the day of punishment,	**Is 10:3**	6213a
Shall I not **d** to Jerusalem and her	**Is 10:11**	6213a
d not fear the Assyrian who	**Is 10:24**	
"**D** not rejoice, O Philistia, all	**Is 14:29**	
d not betray the fugitive.	**Is 16:3**	
its palm branch or bulrush, may **d**.	**Is 19:15**	6213a
D not try to comfort me concerning	**Is 22:4**	
'What right **d** you have here, And	**Is 22:16**	
here, And whom **d** you have here,	**Is 22:16**	
They **d** not drink wine with song;	**Is 24:9**	
lifted up *yet* they **d** not see it.	**Is 26:11**	
To **d** His task, His unusual task,	**Is 28:21**	6213a
now **d** not carry on as scoffers,	**Is 28:22**	
But they **d** not look to the Holy	**Is 31:1**	
Now on whom **d** you rely, that you	**Is 36:5**	
and **d** not speak with us in Judean in	**Is 36:11**	
'**D** not let Hezekiah deceive you,	**Is 36:14**	
'**D** not listen to Hezekiah,' for	**Is 36:16**	
"**D** not answer him."	**Is 36:21**	
"**D** not be afraid because of the	**Is 37:6**	
'**D** not let your God in whom you	**Is 37:10**	
d this thing that He has spoken:	**Is 38:7**	6213a
give thanks to You, as I **d** today;	**Is 38:19**	
Lift *it* up, **d** not fear.	**Is 40:9**	
D you not know? Have you not heard	**Is 40:21**	
Why **d** you say, O Jacob, and	**Is 40:27**	
D you not know? Have you not heard	**Is 40:28**	
'**D** not fear, for I am with you;	**Is 41:10**	
D not anxiously look about you,	**Is 41:10**	
'**D** not fear, I will help you.'	**Is 41:13**	
"**D** not fear, you worm Jacob, you	**Is 41:14**	
Indeed, **d** good or evil, that we	**Is 41:23**	3190
blind by a way they **d** not know,	**Is 42:16**	
they **d** not know I will guide them.	**Is 42:16**	
These are the things I will **d**,	**Is 42:16**	6213a
but you **d** not observe *them;*	**Is 42:20**	
"**D** not fear, for I have redeemed	**Is 43:1**	
"**D** not fear, for I am with you;	**Is 43:5**	
'**D** not hold *them* back.'	**Is 43:6**	
"**D** not call to mind the former	**Is 43:18**	
"Behold, I will **d** something new,	**Is 43:19**	6213a
'**D** not fear, O Jacob My servant;	**Is 44:2**	
'**D** not tremble and do not be	**Is 44:8**	
not tremble and **d** not be afraid;	**Is 44:8**	
They **d** not know, nor do they	**Is 44:18**	
not know, nor **d** they understand,	**Is 44:18**	
planned *it, surely* I will **d** it.	**Is 46:11**	6213a
destruction about which you **d** not	**Is 47:11**	
D not fear the reproach of man,	**Is 51:7**	
therefore, what **d** I have here,"	**Is 52:5**	
And **d** not feel humiliated, for you	**Is 54:4**	
"Why **d** you spend money for what	**Is 55:2**	
will call a nation you **d** not know,	**Is 55:5**	
And **d** not return there without	**Is 55:10**	
justice and **d** righteousness,	**Is 56:1**	6213a
"Against whom **d** you jest?	**Is 57:4**	
Against whom **d** you open wide your	**Is 57:4**	
a long time So you **d** not fear Me?	**Is 57:11**	
"Cry loudly, **d** not hold back;	**Is 58:1**	
have we fasted and You **d** not see?	**Is 58:3**	
ourselves and You **d** not notice?'	**Is 58:3**	
You **d** not fast like *you do* today	**Is 58:4**	
You do not fast like *you* **d** today	**Is 58:4**	
of water whose waters **d** not fail.	**Is 58:11**	
They **d** not know the way of peace,	**Is 59:8**	

d You cause us to stray from Your **Is 63:17**
D not be angry beyond measure, O **Is 64:9**
to yourself, **d** not come near me, **Is 65:5**
'**D** not destroy it, for there is **Is 65:8**
They will **d** no evil or harm in **Is 65:25** 7489a
Behold, I **d** not know how to speak, **Jer 1:6**
"**D** not say, 'I am a youth,' **Jer 1:7**
"**D** not be afraid of them, For I **Jer 1:8**
"What **d** you see, Jeremiah?" **Jer 1:11**
"What **d** you see?" **Jer 1:13**
D not be dismayed before them, **Jer 1:17**
"Why **d** you contend with Me? **Jer 2:29**
Why **d** My people say, **Jer 2:31**
"Why **d** you go around so much **Jer 2:36**
And **d** not sow among thorns. **Jer 4:3**
Seek refuge, **d** not stand *still,* **Jer 4:6**
They are shrewd to **d** evil, **Jer 4:22** 7489a
But to **d** good they do not know." **Jer 4:22** 3190
But to do good they **d** not know." **Jer 4:22**
O desolate one, what will you **d**? **Jer 4:30** 6213a
d not Your eyes *look* for truth? **Jer 5:3**
For they **d** not know the way of the **Jer 5:4**
But **d** not execute a complete **Jer 5:10**
whose language you **d** not know, **Jer 5:15**
Who have eyes but **d** not see; **Jer 5:21**
Who have ears but **d** not hear. **Jer 5:21**
'**D** you not fear Me?' **Jer 5:22**
'**D** you not tremble in My presence? **Jer 5:22**
'They **d** not say in their heart, **Jer 5:24**
They **d** not plead the cause, The **Jer 5:28**
And they **d** not defend the rights **Jer 5:28**
what will you **d** at the end of it? **Jer 5:31** 6213a
D not go out into the field And **Jer 6:25**
field And **d** not walk on the road, **Jer 6:25**
"**D** not trust in deceptive words, **Jer 7:4**
if you **d** not oppress the alien, **Jer 7:6**
and **d** not shed innocent blood in **Jer 7:6**
you may **d** all these abominations? **Jer 7:10** 6213a
I will **d** to the house which is **Jer 7:14** 6213a
you, **d** not pray for this people, **Jer 7:16**
and **d** not lift up cry or prayer **Jer 7:16**
them, and **d** not intercede with Me; **Jer 7:16**
for I **d** not hear you. **Jer 7:16**
"**D** you not see what they are **Jer 7:17**
"**D** they spite Me?" **Jer 7:19**
"**D** *men* fall and not get up again? **Jer 8:4**
But My people **d** not know The **Jer 8:7**
what kind of wisdom **d** they have? **Jer 8:9**
to evil, And they **d** not know Me," **Jer 9:3**
And **d** not trust any brother; **Jer 9:4**
For what *else* can I **d**, **Jer 9:7** 6213a
"**D** not learn the way of the **Jer 10:2**
And **d** not be terrified by the **Jer 10:2**
D not fear them, For they can do **Jer 10:5**
fear them, For they can **d** no harm, **Jer 10:5** 7489a
harm, Nor can they **d** any good." **Jer 10:5** 3190
the nations that **d** not know You And **Jer 10:25**
families that **d** not call Your name; **Jer 10:25**
and **d** according to all which I **Jer 11:4** 6213a
words of this covenant and **d** them. **Jer 11:6** 6213a
which I commanded *them* to **d**, **Jer 11:8** 6213a
d not pray for this people, **Jer 11:14**
"**D** not prophesy in the name of **Jer 11:21**
d in the thicket of the Jordan? **Jer 12:5** 6213a
D not believe them, although they **Jer 12:6**
but **d** not put it in water." **Jer 13:1**
'**D** we not very well know that **Jer 13:12**
and give heed, **d** not be haughty, **Jer 13:15**
Then you also can **d** good Who are **Jer 13:23** 3190
D not forsake us!" **Jer 14:9**
"**D** not pray for the welfare of **Jer 14:11**
the land that they **d** not know.' " **Jer 14:18**
D not despise *us,* for Your own **Jer 14:21**
D not disgrace the throne of Your **Jer 14:21**
Remember *and* **d** not annul Your **Jer 14:21**
it Into a land you **d** not know; **Jer 15:14**
D not, in view of Your patience, **Jer 15:15**
"**D** not enter a house of mourning, **Jer 16:5**
In the land which you **d** not know; **Jer 17:4**
D not be a terror to me; **Jer 17:17**
and **d** not carry any load on the **Jer 17:21**
on the sabbath day nor **d** any work, **Jer 17:22** 6213a
"But if you **d** not listen to Me to **Jer 17:27**
D give heed to me, O LORD, And **Jer 18:19**
D not forgive their iniquity Or **Jer 18:23**
"**D** justice and righteousness, and **Jer 22:3** 6213a
Also **d** not mistreat *or* do violence **Jer 22:3**
or **d** violence to the stranger, **Jer 22:3** 2554
and **d** not shed innocent blood in **Jer 22:3**
D not weep for the dead or mourn **Jer 22:10**
"**D** you become a king because you **Jer 22:15**
And **d** justice and righteousness? **Jer 22:15** 6213a
And **d** justice and righteousness **Jer 23:5** 6213a
"**D** not listen to the words of the **Jer 23:16**
places So I **d** not see him?" **Jer 23:24**
"**D** I not fill the heavens and the **Jer 23:24**
nor **d** they furnish this people the **Jer 23:32**
"What **d** you see, Jeremiah?" **Jer 24:3**
and **d** not go after other gods to **Jer 25:6**
and **d** not provoke Me to anger with **Jer 25:6**
hands, and I will **d** you no harm.' **Jer 25:6** 7489a
D not omit a word! **Jer 26:2**
calamity which I am planning to **d** **Jer 26:3** 6213a
d with me as is good and right in **Jer 26:14** 6213a
d not listen to your prophets, **Jer 27:9**
"So **d** not listen to the words of **Jer 27:14**
D not listen to the words of your **Jer 27:16**
"**D** not listen to them; **Jer 27:17**
May the LORD **d** so; **Jer 28:6** 6213a

multiply there and **d** not decrease. **Jer 29:6**
'**D** not let your prophets who are **Jer 29:8**
and **d** not listen to the dreams **Jer 29:8**
I am about to **d** to My people," **Jer 29:32** 6213a
Why **d** I see every man *With* his **Jer 30:6**
'And **d** not be dismayed, O Israel; **Jer 30:10**
you, They **d** not seek you; **Jer 30:14**
d you cry out over your injury? **Jer 30:15**
"Why **d** you prophesy, saying, **Jer 32:3**
that You commanded them to **d**; **Jer 32:23** 6213a
they should **d** this abomination, **Jer 32:35** 6213a
away from them, to **d** them good; **Jer 32:40** 3190
rejoice over them to **d** them good and **Jer 32:41** 3190
things, which you **d** not know.' **Jer 33:3**
of all the good that I **d** for them, **Jer 33:9** 6213a
and we **d** not have vineyard or **Jer 35:9**
they **d** not drink *wine* to this day, **Jer 35:14**
and **d** not go after other gods to **Jer 35:15**
and **d** not let anyone know where **Jer 36:19**
'**D** not deceive yourselves, saying, **Jer 37:9**
and **d** not make me return to the **Jer 37:20**
for the king can **d** nothing **Jer 38:5**
d not hide anything from me." **Jer 38:14**
d not hide *it* from us and we will **Jer 38:25**
him, and **d** nothing harmful to him, **Jer 39:12** 6213a
"**D** not be afraid of serving the **Jer 40:9**
"**D** not do this thing, for you are **Jer 40:16**
"Do not **d** this thing, for you are **Jer 40:16** 6213a
"**D** not put us to death; **Jer 41:8**
and the thing that we should **d**." **Jer 42:3** 6213a
if we **d** not act in accordance with **Jer 42:5**
'**D** not be afraid of the king of **Jer 42:11**
d not be afraid of him,' declares **Jer 42:11**
"**D** not go into Egypt!" **Jer 42:19**
tell us so, and we will **d** it." **Jer 42:20** 6213a
d not do this abominable thing **Jer 44:4**
do not **d** this abominable thing **Jer 44:4** 6213a
D not seek *them;* for behold, I am **Jer 45:5**
They **d** not stand because the LORD **Jer 46:15**
O Jacob My servant, **d** not fear, **Jer 46:27**
"O Jacob My servant, **d** not fear," **Jer 46:28**
D not conceal *it but* say, **Jer 50:2**
d not be sparing with *your* arrows, **Jer 50:14**
has done *to others, so* **d** to her. **Jer 50:15** 6213a
"And **d** according to all that I **Jer 50:21** 6213a
that she has done, *so* **d** to her; **Jer 50:29** 6213a
So **d** not spare her young men; **Jer 51:3**
D not be destroyed in her **Jer 51:6**
D not stay! Remember the LORD **Jer 51:50**
"**D** not hide Your ear from my **La 3:56**
You said, "**D** not fear!" **La 3:57**
"Depart, depart, **d** not touch!" **La 4:15**
Why **d** You forget us forever? **La 5:20**
Why **d** You forsake us so long? **La 5:20**
d not be rebellious like that **Ezk 2:8**
D not be afraid of them or be **Ezk 3:9**
and you **d** not warn him or speak **Ezk 3:18**
I will **d** among you what I have not **Ezk 5:9** 6213a
of which I will never **d** again. **Ezk 5:9** 6213a
that I, the LORD, **d** the smiting. **Ezk 7:9**
d you see what they are doing, **Ezk 8:6** 6213a
d you see what the elders of the **Ezk 8:12**
"**D** you see *this,* son of man? **Ezk 8:15**
"**D** you see *this,* son of man? **Ezk 8:17**
d not let your eye have pity and **Ezk 9:5**
eye have pity and **d** not spare. **Ezk 9:5**
but **d** not touch any man on whom is **Ezk 9:6**
keep My ordinances and **d** them. **Ezk 11:20** 6213a
have eyes to see but **d** not see, **Ezk 12:2**
see, ears to hear but **d** not hear; **Ezk 12:2**
to **d** any of these things for you, **Ezk 16:5** 6213a
"while you **d** all these things, **Ezk 16:30** 6213a
no one plays the harlot as you **d**, **Ezk 16:34**
also **d** with you as you have done, **Ezk 16:59** 6213a
'**D** you not know what these things **Ezk 17:12**
"What **d** you mean by using this **Ezk 18:2**
did not **d** any of these things), **Ezk 18:11** 6213a
and observing does not **d** likewise. **Ezk 18:14** 6213a
"**D** I have any pleasure in the **Ezk 18:23**
"**D** you come to inquire of Me? **Ezk 20:3**
and **d** not defile yourselves with **Ezk 20:7**
'**D** not walk in the statutes of **Ezk 20:18**
'Why **d** you groan?' **Ezk 21:7**
and **d** not cover *your* mustache and **Ezk 24:17**
and **d** not eat the bread of men." **Ezk 24:17**
'You will **d** as I have done; **Ezk 24:22** 6213a
all that he has done you will **d**; **Ezk 24:24** 6213a
'Whom **d** you surpass in beauty? **Ezk 32:19**
"Nor **d** they lie beside the fallen **Ezk 32:27**
and you **d** not speak to warn the **Ezk 33:8**
words, but they **d** not do them, **Ezk 33:31**
words, but they do not **d** them, **Ezk 33:31** 6213a
for they **d** the lustful desires **Ezk 33:31** 6213a
but they **d** not practice them. **Ezk 33:32**
was desolate, so I will **d** to you. **Ezk 35:15** 6213a
LORD, have spoken and will **d** it." **Ezk 36:36** 6213a
of Israel ask Me to **d** for them: **Ezk 36:37** 6213a
and all its statutes and **d** them. **Ezk 43:11** 6213a
"Thus you shall **d** on the **Ezk 45:20** 6213a
if you **d** not make known to me the **Da 2:5**
that if you **d** not make the dream **Da 2:9**
"**D** not destroy the wise men of **Da 2:24**
they **d** not serve your gods or **Da 3:12**
that you **d** not serve my gods or **Da 3:14** 383
But if you **d** not worship, you will **Da 3:15**
we **d** not need to give you an **Da 3:16**
d not let the dream or its **Da 4:19**
D not let your thoughts alarm you **Da 5:10**
wood and stone, which **d** not see, **Da 5:23**

own sake, O my God, **d** not delay, **Da 9:19**
"**D** not be afraid, Daniel, for **Da 10:12**
of high esteem, **d** not be afraid. **Da 10:19**
"**D** you understand why I came to **Da 10:20**
authority and **d** as he pleases. **Da 11:3** 6213a
against him will **d** as he pleases, **Da 11:16** 6213a
and **d** away with the regular **Da 11:31** 5493
the king will **d** as he pleases, **Da 11:36** 6213a
D not let Judah become guilty; **Hos 4:15**
Also **d** not go to Gilgal, Or go up **Hos 4:15**
And they **d** not know the LORD. **Hos 5:4**
What shall I **d** with you, O Ephraim? **Hos 6:4** 6213a
What shall I **d** with you, O Judah? **Hos 6:4** 6213a
And they **d** not consider in their **Hos 7:2**
And they **d** not cry to Me from **Hos 7:14**
D not rejoice, O Israel, with **Hos 9:1**
What will you **d** on the day of the **Hos 9:5** 6213a
For we **d** not revere the LORD. **Hos 10:3**
the king, what can he **d** for us?" **Hos 10:3** 6213a
what more have I to **d** with idols? **Hos 14:8**
d they deviate from their paths. **Jl 2:7**
They **d** not crowd each other, **Jl 2:8**
defenses, They **d** not break ranks. **Jl 2:8**
And **d** not make Your inheritance a **Jl 2:17**
D not fear, O land, rejoice and be **Jl 2:21**
D not fear, beasts of the field, **Jl 2:22**
But if you **d** recompense Me, **Jl 3:4**
D two men walk together unless **Am 3:3**
"But they **d** not know how to do **Am 3:10**
not know how to **d** what is right," **Am 3:10** 6213a
For so you love *to* **d**, you sons **Am 4:5**
"Therefore thus I will **d** to you, **Am 4:12** 6213a
Because I will **d** this to you, **Am 4:12** 6213a
"But **d** not resort to Bethel And **Am 5:5**
Bethel And **d** not come to Gilgal, **Am 5:5**
Nor **d** I delight in your solemn **Am 5:21**
D you put off the day of calamity, **Am 6:3**
D horses run on rocks? **Am 6:12**
"What **d** you see, Amos?" **Am 7:8**
and there **d** your prophesying! **Am 7:12**
"What **d** you see, Amos?" **Am 8:2**
to **d** away with the humble of the **Am 8:4** 7673a
"**D** not gloat over your brother's **Ob 1:12**
And **d** not rejoice over the sons of **Ob 1:12**
d not boast In the day of *their* **Ob 1:12**
"**D** not enter the gate of My **Ob 1:13**
d not gloat over their calamity In **Ob 1:13**
And **d** not loot their wealth In the **Ob 1:13**
"**D** not stand at the fork of the road **Ob 1:14**
And **d** not imprison their survivors **Ob 1:14**
And where **d** you come from? **Jon 1:8**
"How could you **d** this?" **Jon 1:10** 6213a
"What should we **d** to you that the **Jon 1:11** 6213a
d not let us perish on account of **Jon 1:14**
d not put innocent blood on us; **Jon 1:14**
D not let man, beast, herd, or **Jon 3:7**
D not let them eat or drink water. **Jon 3:7**
And He did not **d** *it.* **Jon 3:10** 6213a
"**D** you have good reason to be **Jon 4:4**
"**D** you have good reason to be **Jon 4:9**
persons who **d** not know *the difference* **Jon 4:11**
When morning comes, they **d** it, **Mi 2:1** 6213a
'**D** not speak out,' *so* they speak **Mi 2:6**
But if they **d** not speak out **Mi 2:6**
D not My words do good To the one **Mi 2:7**
Do not My words **d** good To the one **Mi 2:7** 3190
"Now, why **d** you cry out loudly? **Mi 4:9**
"But they **d** not know the thoughts **Mi 4:12**
they **d** not understand His purpose; **Mi 4:12**
Which **d** not wait for man **Mi 5:7**
require of you But to **d** justice, **Mi 6:8** 6213a
And what you **d** preserve I will **Mi 6:14**
evil, both hands **d** it well. **Mi 7:3** 3190
D not trust in a neighbor; **Mi 7:5**
D not have confidence in a friend. **Mi 7:5**
D not rejoice over me, O my enemy. **Mi 7:8**
Yet You **d** not save. **Hab 1:2**
Why **d** You make me see iniquity, **Hab 1:3**
Why **d** You look with favor On **Hab 1:13**
'The LORD will not **d** good or evil!' **Zph 1:12** 3190
He will **d** no injustice. **Zph 3:5** 6213a
will **d** no wrong And tell no lies, **Zph 3:13** 6213a
"**D** not be afraid, O Zion; **Zph 3:16**
D not let your hands fall limp. **Zph 3:16**
And how **d** you see it now? **Hg 2:3**
is abiding in your midst; **d** not fear!' **Hg 2:5**
d consider from this day onward: **Hg 2:15**
'**D** consider from this day onward, **Hg 2:18**
"**D** not be like your fathers, to **Zch 1:4**
the prophets, **d** they live forever? **Zch 1:5**
the LORD of hosts purposed to **d** to us **Zch 1:6** 6213a
"What are these coming to **d**?" **Zch 1:21** 6213a
"What **d** you see?" **Zch 4:2**
"**D** you not know what these are?" **Zch 4:5**
"**D** you not know what these are?" **Zch 4:13**
"What **d** you see?" **Zch 5:2**
d you not eat for yourselves and **Zch 7:6**
d you not drink for yourselves? **Zch 7:6**
and **d** not oppress the widow or the **Zch 7:10**
and **d** not devise evil in your **Zch 7:10**
D not fear; let your hands be strong.' **Zch 8:13**
'Just as I purposed to **d** harm to **Zch 8:14** 7489a
purposed in these days to **d** good **Zch 8:15** 3190
to the house of Judah. **D** not fear! **Zch 8:15**
are the things which you should **d**: **Zch 8:16** 6213a
another, and **d** not love perjury; **Zch 8:17**
LORD smites the nations who **d** not go **Zch 14:18**
nations who **d** not go up to celebrate **Zch 14:19**
"If you **d** not listen, and if you **Mal 2:2**

and if you **d** not take it to heart	Mal 2:2	
"**D** we not all have one father?	Mal 2:10	
Why **d** we deal treacherously each	Mal 2:10	
"This is another thing you **d**:	Mal 2:13	6213a
And what did *that* one **d** while	Mal 2:15	
you **d** not deal treacherously."	Mal 2:16	
the alien and **d** not fear Me,"	Mal 3:5	
"For I, the LORD, **d** not change;	Mal 3:6	
d not be afraid to take Mary as	Mt 1:20	
and **d** not suppose that you can say	Mt 3:9	
by You, and **d** You come to me?"	Mt 3:14	
"**D** not think that I came to	Mt 5:17	
and teaches others *to* **d** the same,	Mt 5:19	
you, **d** not resist an evil person;	Mt 5:39	
and **d** not turn away from him who	Mt 5:42	
what reward **d** you have? Do not even	Mt 5:46	4160
D not even the tax collectors do	Mt 5:46	
even the tax collectors **d** the same?	Mt 5:46	4160
D not even the Gentiles do the	Mt 5:47	
not even the Gentiles **d** the same?	Mt 5:47	4160
d not sound a trumpet before you,	Mt 6:2	
as the hypocrites **d** in the	Mt 6:2	4160
d not let your left hand know what	Mt 6:3	
d not use meaningless repetition as	Mt 6:7	
repetition as the Gentiles **d**,	Mt 6:7	
"So **d** not be like them;	Mt 6:8	
'And **d** not lead us into	Mt 6:13	
"But if you **d** not forgive others,	Mt 6:15	
d not put on a gloomy face as the	Mt 6:16	
a gloomy face as the hypocrites **d**,	Mt 6:16	
"**D** not store up for yourselves	Mt 6:19	
thieves **d** not break in or steal;	Mt 6:20	
d not be worried about your life,	Mt 6:25	
of the air, that they **d** not sow,	Mt 6:26	
they **d** not toil nor do they spin,	Mt 6:28	
they do not toil nor **d** they spin,	Mt 6:28	
"**D** not worry then, saying,	Mt 6:31	
d not worry about tomorrow;	Mt 6:34	
"**D** not judge so that you will not	Mt 7:1	
"Why **d** you look at the speck	Mt 7:3	
but **d** not notice the log that is	Mt 7:3	
"**D** not give what is holy to dogs,	Mt 7:6	
and **d** not throw your pearls before	Mt 7:6	
to my slave, '**D** this!' and he does *it*."	Mt 8:9	4160
"What business **d** we have with each	Mt 8:29	
"Why **d** we and the Pharisees fast,	Mt 9:14	
but Your disciples **d** not fast?"	Mt 9:14	
"Nor **d** *people* put new wine into old	Mt 9:17	
"**D** you believe that I am able to	Mt 9:28	
that I am able to **d** this?"	Mt 9:28	4160
"**D** not go in *the* way of *the*	Mt 10:5	
and **d** not enter *any* city of the	Mt 10:5	
"**D** not acquire gold, or silver,	Mt 10:9	
d not worry about how or	Mt 10:19	
"Therefore **d** not fear them, for	Mt 10:26	
"**D** not fear those who kill the body	Mt 10:28	
"So **d** not fear;	Mt 10:31	
"**D** not think that I came to bring	Mt 10:34	
Your disciples **d** what is not	Mt 12:2	4160
is not lawful to **d** on a Sabbath."	Mt 12:2	4160
lawful to **d** good on the Sabbath."	Mt 12:12	4160
by whom **d** your sons cast *them* out?	Mt 12:27	
d You speak to them in parables?"	Mt 13:10	
while seeing they **d** not see,	Mt 13:13	
and while hearing they **d** not hear,	Mt 13:13	
not hear, nor **d** they understand.	Mt 13:13	
'**D** you want us, then, to go and	Mt 13:28	
And He did not **d** many miracles	Mt 13:58	4160
"They **d** not need to go away;	Mt 14:16	
d not be afraid."	Mt 14:27	
"Why **d** Your disciples break	Mt 15:2	
For they **d** not wash their hands	Mt 15:2	
"Why **d** you yourselves	Mt 15:3	
'BUT IN VAIN **D** THEY WORSHIP ME,	Mt 15:9	
"**D** You know that the Pharisees	Mt 15:12	
"**D** you not understand that	Mt 15:17	
and I **d** not want to send them away	Mt 15:32	
"How many loaves **d** you have?"	Mt 15:34	
D you know how to discern the	Mt 16:3	
why **d** you discuss among yourselves	Mt 16:8	
"**D** you not yet understand or	Mt 16:9	
"How is it that you **d** not	Mt 16:11	
"Who **d** people say that the Son of	Mt 16:13	
"But who **d** you say that I am?"	Mt 16:15	
"Get up, and **d** not be afraid."	Mt 17:7	
"Why then **d** the scribes say that	Mt 17:10	
"What **d** you think, Simon?	Mt 17:25	
From whom **d** the kings of the earth	Mt 17:25	
"However, so that we **d** not offend	Mt 17:27	
"See that you **d** not despise one	Mt 18:10	
"What **d** you think?	Mt 18:12	
"I **d** not say to you, up to seven	Mt 18:22	
heavenly Father will also **d** the same	Mt 18:35	4160
and **d** not hinder them from coming	Mt 19:14	
what good thing shall I **d** that I	Mt 19:16	4160
'Is it not lawful for me to **d** what	Mt 20:15	4160
"What **d** you wish?"	Mt 20:21	
"You **d** not know what you are	Mt 20:22	
d you want Me to do for you?"	Mt 20:32	
do you want Me to **d** for you?"	Mt 20:32	4160
"**D** You hear what these *children*	Mt 21:16	
you have faith and **d** not doubt,	Mt 21:21	
d what was done to the fig tree,	Mt 21:21	4160
what authority I **d** these things.	Mt 21:24	4160
they said, "We **d** not know."	Mt 21:27	
what authority I **d** these things.	Mt 21:27	4160
"But what **d** you think?	Mt 21:28	
will he **d** to those vine-growers?"	Mt 21:40	4160
us then, what **d** You think?	Mt 22:17	

"What **d** you think about the	Mt 22:42	
that they tell you, **d** and observe,	Mt 23:3	4160
but **d** not do according to their	Mt 23:3	
do not **d** according to their deeds;	Mt 23:3	4160
say *things* and **d** not do *them*.	Mt 23:3	
say *things* and do not **d** *them*.	Mt 23:3	4160
"But they **d** all their deeds to be	Mt 23:5	4160
"But **d** not be called Rabbi;	Mt 23:8	
"**D** not call *anyone* on earth your	Mt 23:9	
"**D** not be called leaders; for One	Mt 23:10	
for you **d** not enter in yourselves,	Mt 23:13	
nor **d** you allow those who are	Mt 23:13	
"**D** you not see all these things?	Mt 24:2	
'There *He is*,' **d** not believe *him*.	Mt 24:23	
in the wilderness,' **d** not go out,	Mt 24:26	
inner rooms,' **d** not believe *them*.	Mt 24:26	
for you **d** not know which day your	Mt 24:42	
hour when you **d** not think *He will*.	Mt 24:44	
I say to you, I **d** not know you.'	Mt 25:12	
d not know the day nor the hour.	Mt 25:13	
to the extent that you did not **d**	Mt 25:45	4160
of these, you did not **d** it to Me.'	Mt 25:45	4160
"Why **d** you bother the woman?	Mt 26:10	
but you **d** not always have Me.	Mt 26:11	
"Where **d** You want us to prepare	Mt 26:17	
d what you have come for." Then	Mt 26:50	
"Or **d** you think that I cannot	Mt 26:53	
"**D** You not answer?	Mt 26:62	
need **d** we have of witnesses?	Mt 26:65	
what **d** you think?"	Mt 26:66	
"I **d** not know what you are	Mt 26:70	
"I **d** not know the man."	Mt 26:72	
"I **d** not know the man!"	Mt 26:74	
"**D** You not hear how many things	Mt 27:13	
"Whom **d** you want me to release	Mt 27:17	
to **d** with that righteous Man;	Mt 27:19	
"Which of the two **d** you want me	Mt 27:21	
"Then what shall I **d** with Jesus	Mt 27:22	4160
said to the women, "**D** not be afraid;	Mt 28:5	
Jesus said to them, "**D** not be afraid;	Mt 28:10	
"What business **d** we have	Mk 1:24	
"Why **d** John's disciples and the	Mk 2:18	
but Your disciples **d** not fast?"	Mk 2:18	
lawful to **d** good or to do harm	Mk 3:4	4160
lawful to do good or to **d** harm	Mk 3:4	2554
"**D** you not understand this	Mk 4:13	
d You not care that we are	Mk 4:38	
D you still have no faith	Mk 4:40	
"What business **d** we have with each	Mk 5:7	
You by God, **d** not torment me!"	Mk 5:7	
"**D** not be afraid *any longer*, only	Mk 5:36	
And He could **d** no miracle there	Mk 6:5	4160
"**D** not put on two tunics."	Mk 6:9	
to put him to death and could not **d**	Mk 6:19	
"How many loaves **d** you have?	Mk 6:38	
it is I, **d** not be afraid."	Mk 6:50	
Jews **d** not eat unless they carefully	Mk 7:3	
they **d** not eat unless they cleanse	Mk 7:4	
"Why **d** Your disciples not walk	Mk 7:5	
'BUT IN VAIN **D** THEY WORSHIP ME,	Mk 7:7	
you no longer permit him to **d**	Mk 7:12	4160
you **d** many things such as that."	Mk 7:13	4160
D you not understand that whatever	Mk 7:18	
"How many loaves **d** you have?"	Mk 8:5	
"Why **d** you discuss *the fact* that	Mk 8:17	
D you not yet see or understand?	Mk 8:17	
D you have a hardened heart?	Mk 8:17	
"HAVING EYES, **D** YOU NOT SEE?	Mk 8:18	
AND HAVING EARS, **D** YOU NOT HEAR?	Mk 8:18	
And **d** you not remember,	Mk 8:18	
"**D** you not yet understand?"	Mk 8:21	
"**D** you see anything?"	Mk 8:23	
"**D** not even enter the village."	Mk 8:26	
"Who **d** people say that I am?"	Mk 8:27	
"But who **d** you say that I am?"	Mk 8:29	
and they could not **d** *it*."	Mk 9:18	
But if You can **d** anything, take	Mk 9:22	
"I **d** believe; help my unbelief."	Mk 9:24	
him and **d** not enter him again."	Mk 9:25	
"**D** not hinder him, for there is	Mk 9:39	
d not hinder them;	Mk 10:14	
I **d** to inherit eternal life?"	Mk 10:17	4160
"Why **d** you call Me good?	Mk 10:18	
'**D** NOT MURDER, DO NOT COMMIT	Mk 10:19	
D NOT COMMIT ADULTERY,	Mk 10:19	
D NOT STEAL, DO NOT BEAR FALSE	Mk 10:19	
D NOT BEAR FALSE WITNESS,	Mk 10:19	
D not defraud, HONOR YOUR FATHER	Mk 10:19	
d for us whatever we ask of You."	Mk 10:35	4160
d you want Me to do for you?"	Mk 10:36	
do you want Me to **d** for you?"	Mk 10:36	4160
"You **d** not know what you are	Mk 10:38	
d you want Me to do for you?"	Mk 10:51	
do you want Me to **d** for you?"	Mk 10:51	4160
"But if you **d** not forgive,	Mk 11:26	
authority to **d** these things?"	Mk 11:28	4160
what authority I **d** these things.	Mk 11:29	4160
they said, "We **d** not know."	Mk 11:33	
what authority I **d** these things."	Mk 11:33	4160
will the owner of the vineyard **d**?	Mk 12:9	4160
d not understand the Scriptures or	Mk 12:24	
"**D** you see these great buildings?	Mk 13:2	
of wars, **d** not be frightened;	Mk 13:7	
d not worry beforehand about	Mk 13:11	
d not believe *him*;	Mk 13:21	
for you **d** not know when the	Mk 13:33	
for you **d** not know when the master	Mk 13:35	
why **d** you bother her?	Mk 14:6	
you wish you can **d** good to them;	Mk 14:7	4160
but you **d** not always have Me.	Mk 14:7	

"Where **d** You want us to go and	Mk 14:12	
"**D** You not answer?	Mk 14:60	
need **d** we have of witnesses?	Mk 14:63	
"I **d** not know this man you are	Mk 14:71	
"**D** You not answer?	Mk 15:4	
up and began asking him *to* **d**	Mk 15:8	
had been accustomed to **d** for them.	Mk 15:8	4160
"**D** you want me to release for you	Mk 15:9	
"Then what shall I **d** with Him	Mk 15:12	4160
he said to them, "**D** not be amazed;	Mk 16:6	
"**D** not be afraid, Zacharias, for	Lk 1:13	
"**D** not be afraid, Mary;	Lk 1:30	
angel said to them, "**D** not be afraid;	Lk 2:10	
and **d** not begin to say to yourselves,	Lk 3:8	
"Then what shall we **d**?"	Lk 3:10	4160
he who has food is to **d** likewise."	Lk 3:11	4160
"Teacher, what shall we **d**?"	Lk 3:12	4160
what about us, what shall we **d**?"	Lk 3:14	4160
"**D** not take money from anyone by	Lk 3:14	
d here in your hometown as well.'"	Lk 4:23	4160
business **d** we have with each other,	Lk 4:34	
but I will **d** as You say *and* let	Lk 5:5	
"**D** not fear, from now on you will	Lk 5:10	
"Why **d** you eat and drink with the	Lk 5:30	
of the Pharisees also **d** the same,	Lk 5:33	
"Why **d** you do what is not lawful	Lk 6:2	
"Why do you **d** what is not lawful	Lk 6:2	4160
is it lawful to **d** good or to do harm	Lk 6:9	15
to **d** harm on the Sabbath,	Lk 6:9	2554
what they might **d** to Jesus.	Lk 6:11	4160
d good to those who hate you,	Lk 6:27	4160
d not withhold your shirt from him	Lk 6:29	
is yours, **d** not demand it back.	Lk 6:30	
"If you **d** good to those who	Lk 6:33	15
good to those who **d** good to you,	Lk 6:33	15
For even sinners **d** the same.	Lk 6:33	4160
"But love your enemies, and **d** good,	Lk 6:35	15
"**D** not judge, and you will not be	Lk 6:37	
and **d** not condemn, and you will	Lk 6:37	
"Why **d** you look at the speck	Lk 6:41	
but **d** not notice the log that is	Lk 6:41	
when you yourself **d** not see the	Lk 6:42	
men **d** not gather figs from thorns,	Lk 6:44	
nor **d** they pick grapes from a	Lk 6:44	
Why **d** you call Me, 'Lord, Lord,'	Lk 6:46	
Lord,' and **d** not do what I say?	Lk 6:46	
Lord,' and do not **d** what I say?	Lk 6:46	4160
d not trouble Yourself further,	Lk 7:6	
to my slave, '**D** this!' and he does it."	Lk 7:8	4160
and said to her, "**D** not weep."	Lk 7:13	
or **d** we look for someone else?"	Lk 7:19	
or **d** we look for someone else?'"	Lk 7:20	
"**D** you see this woman?	Lk 7:44	
hear the word of God and **d** it."	Lk 8:21	4160
business **d** we have with each other,	Lk 8:28	
I beg You, **d** not torment me."	Lk 8:28	
d not trouble the Teacher anymore."	Lk 8:49	
"**D** not be afraid *any longer*	Lk 8:50	
and **d** not *even* have two tunics	Lk 9:3	
for those who **d** not receive you,	Lk 9:5	
d the people say that I am?"	Lk 9:18	
"But who **d** you say that I am?"	Lk 9:20	
"**D** not hinder *him*;	Lk 9:50	
d You want us to command fire to	Lk 9:54	
"You **d** not know what kind of	Lk 9:55	
D not keep moving from house to	Lk 10:7	
enter and they **d** not receive you,	Lk 10:10	
d not rejoice in this,	Lk 10:20	
I **d** to inherit eternal life?"	Lk 10:25	4160
D THIS AND YOU WILL LIVE."	Lk 10:28	4160
"Which of these three **d** you think	Lk 10:36	
"Go and **d** the same."	Lk 10:37	4160
d You not care that my sister has	Lk 10:40	
me to **d** all the serving alone?	Lk 10:40	1247
'**D** not bother me; the door has	Lk 11:7	
by whom **d** your sons cast them out?	Lk 11:19	
d not be afraid of those who kill	Lk 12:4	
that have no more that they can **d**.	Lk 12:4	4160
D not fear; you are more valuable	Lk 12:7	
d not worry about how or	Lk 12:11	
'What shall I **d**, since I have no	Lk 12:17	4160
'This is what I will **d**:	Lk 12:18	4160
d not worry about *your* life,	Lk 12:22	
cannot **d** even a very little thing,	Lk 12:26	
why **d** you worry about other matters?	Lk 12:26	
"And **d** not seek what you will	Lk 12:29	
drink, and **d** not keep worrying.	Lk 12:29	
"**D** not be afraid, little flock,	Lk 12:32	
belts which **d** not wear out,	Lk 12:33	
an hour that you **d** not expect."	Lk 12:40	
"**D** you suppose that I came to	Lk 12:51	
but why **d** you not analyze this	Lk 12:56	
"And why **d** you not even on your	Lk 12:57	
"**D** you suppose that these	Lk 13:2	
"Or **d** you suppose that those	Lk 13:4	
'I **d** not know where you are from.'	Lk 13:25	
I **d** not know where you are from;	Lk 13:27	
d not take the place of honor,	Lk 14:8	
d not invite your friends or your	Lk 14:12	
since they **d** not have *the means* to	Lk 14:14	
'What shall I **d**, since my master	Lk 16:3	4160
'I know what I shall **d**,	Lk 16:4	4160
'How much **d** you owe my master?'	Lk 16:5	
'And how much **d** you owe?'	Lk 16:7	
'If they **d** not listen to Moses and	Lk 16:31	
when you **d** all the things which	Lk 17:10	4160
D not go away, and do not run after	Lk 17:23	
go away, and **d** not run after *them*.	Lk 17:23	
I **d** not fear God nor respect man,	Lk 18:4	

come to Me, and **d** not hinder them, Lk 18:16
I **d** to inherit eternal life?" Lk 18:18 4160
"Why **d** you call Me good? Lk 18:19
'**D** NOT COMMIT ADULTERY, DO NOT Lk 18:20
ADULTERY, **D** NOT MURDER, DO NOT Lk 18:20
ADULTERY, DO NOT MURDER, **D** NOT Lk 18:20
NOT STEAL, **D** NOT BEAR FALSE WITNESS, Lk 18:20
d you want Me to do for you?" Lk 18:41
do you want Me to **d** for you?" Lk 18:41 4160
'**D** business *with this* until I come Lk 19:13 4231
'We **d** not want this man to reign Lk 19:14
find anything that they might **d**, Lk 19:48 4160
what authority I **d** these things." Lk 20:8 4160
of the vineyard said, 'What shall I **d**? Lk 20:13 4160
owner of the vineyard **d** to them? Lk 20:15 4160
D not go after them. Lk 21:8
disturbances, **d** not be terrified; Lk 21:9
d You want us to prepare it?" Lk 22:9
d this in remembrance of Me." Lk 22:19 4160
be who was going to **d** this thing. Lk 22:23 4238
"Woman, I **d** not know Him." Lk 22:57
I **d** not know what you are talking Lk 22:60
"What further need **d** we have of Lk 22:71
"For if they **d** these things when Lk 23:31 4160
d not know what they are doing." Lk 23:34
"**D** you not even fear God, since Lk 23:40
"Why **d** you seek the living One Lk 24:5
why **d** doubts arise in your hearts? Lk 24:38
What **d** you say about yourself?" Jn 1:22
stands One whom you **d** not know. Jn 1:26
"What **d** you seek?" Jn 1:38
"How **d** You know me?" Jn 1:48
under the fig tree, **d** you believe? Jn 1:50
what does that have to **d** with us? Jn 2:4
"Whatever He says to you, **d** it." Jn 2:5 4160
"What sign **d** You show us Jn 2:18
for no one can **d** these signs that Jn 3:2 4160
You **d** unless God is with him." Jn 3:2 4160
"**D** not be amazed that I said to you, Jn 3:7
but **d** not know where it comes from Jn 3:8
and **d** not understand these things? Jn 3:10
and you **d** not accept our testimony. Jn 3:11
things and you **d** not believe, Jn 3:12
then **d** You get that living water? Jn 4:11
worship what you **d** not know; Jn 4:22
"What **d** You seek?" Jn 4:27
"Why **d** You speak with her?" Jn 4:27
eat that you **d** not know about." Jn 4:32
to **d** the will of Him who sent Me and Jn 4:34 4160
"**D** you not say, Jn 4:35
"**D** you wish to get well?" Jn 5:6
d not sin anymore, so that nothing Jn 5:14
the Son can **d** nothing of Himself, Jn 5:19 4160
"**D** not marvel at this; Jn 5:28
d nothing on My own initiative. Jn 5:30 4160
because I **d** not seek My own will, Jn 5:30
the very works that I **d** Jn 5:36 4160
"You **d** not have His word Jn 5:38
d not believe Him whom He sent. Jn 5:38
"I **d** not receive glory from men; Jn 5:41
that you **d** not have the love of Jn 5:42
name, and you **d** not receive Me; Jn 5:43
and you **d** not seek the glory that Jn 5:44
"**D** not think that I will accuse Jn 5:45
if you **d** not believe his writings, Jn 5:47
knew what He was intending to **d**. Jn 6:6 4160
d not be afraid." Jn 6:20
"**D** not work for the food which Jn 6:27
"What shall we **d**, so that we may Jn 6:28 4160
"What then **d** You do for a sign, Jn 6:30
"What then do You **d** for a sign, Jn 6:30 4160
What work **d** You perform? Jn 6:30
seen Me, and yet **d** not believe. Jn 6:36
from heaven, not to **d** My own will, Jn 6:38 4160
"**D** not grumble among yourselves. Jn 6:43
some of you who **d** not believe." Jn 6:64
"You **d** not want to go away also, Jn 6:67
not want to go away also, **d** you?" Jn 6:67
If You **d** these things, show Jn 7:4 4160
I **d** not go up to this feast Jn 7:8
anyone is willing to **d** His will, Jn 7:17 4160
Why **d** you seek to kill Me?" Jn 7:19
"**D** not judge according to Jn 7:24
The rulers **d** not really know that Jn 7:26
that this is the Christ, **d** they? Jn 7:26
Me is true, whom you **d** not know. Jn 7:28
what then **d** You say?" Jn 8:5
"I **d** not condemn you, either. Jn 8:11
you **d** not know where I come from or Jn 8:14
"But even if I **d** judge, My Jn 8:16
I **d** nothing on My own initiative, Jn 8:28 4160
for I always **d** the things that are Jn 8:29 4160
therefore you also **d** the things Jn 8:38 4160
children, **d** the deeds of Abraham. Jn 8:39 4160
this Abraham did not **d**. Jn 8:40 4160
"Why **d** you not understand what I Jn 8:43
to **d** the desires of your father. Jn 8:44 4160
the truth, you **d** not believe Me. Jn 8:45
truth, why **d** you not believe Me? Jn 8:46
this reason you **d** not hear *them*, Jn 8:47
"**D** we not say rightly that You Jn 8:48
"I **d** not have a demon; Jn 8:49
"But I **d** not seek My glory; Jn 8:50
d You make Yourself out *to be*?" Jn 8:53
if I say that I **d** not know Him, Jn 8:55
a liar like you, but I **d** know Him and Jn 8:55
is He?" He said, "I **d** not know." Jn 9:12
"What **d** you say about Him, since Jn 9:17
how he now sees, we **d** not know; Jn 9:21
opened his eyes, we **d** not know. Jn 9:21
He is a sinner, I **d** not know; Jn 9:25
one thing I **d** know, that though Jn 9:25
"What did He **d** to you? Jn 9:26 4160
why **d** you want to hear *it* again? Jn 9:27
You **d** not want to become His Jn 9:27
become His disciples too, **d** you?" Jn 9:27
we **d** not know where He is from." Jn 9:29
you **d** not know where He is from, Jn 9:30
from God, He could **d** nothing." Jn 9:33 4160
"**D** you believe in the Son of Man?" Jn 9:35
that those who **d** not see may see, Jn 9:39
because they **d** not know the voice Jn 10:5
Why **d** you listen to Him?" Jn 10:20
"I told you, and you **d** not believe; Jn 10:25
works that I **d** in My Father's name, Jn 10:25 4160
"But you **d** not believe because Jn 10:26
a good work we **d** not stone You, Jn 10:33
d you say of Him, whom the Father Jn 10:36
I **d** not do the works of My Father, Jn 10:37
I do not **d** the works of My Father, Jn 10:37 4160
of My Father, **d** not believe Me; Jn 10:37
but if I **d** them, though you do not Jn 10:38 4160
them, though you **d** not believe Me, Jn 10:38
D you believe this?" Jn 11:26
nor **d** you take into account that Jn 11:50
"What **d** you think; Jn 11:56
but you **d** not always have Me." Jn 12:8
not keep them, I **d** not judge him; Jn 12:47
"Lord, **d** You wash my feet?" Jn 13:6
"What I **d** you do not realize now, Jn 13:7 4160
"What I do you **d** not realize now, Jn 13:7
"If I **d** not wash you, you have no Jn 13:8
"**D** you know what I have done to Jn 13:12
you also should **d** as I did to you. Jn 13:15 4160
you are blessed if you **d** them. Jn 13:17 4160
"I **d** not speak of all of you. Jn 13:18
"What you **d**, do quickly." Jn 13:27 4160
"What you do, **d** quickly." Jn 13:27 4160
"**D** not let your heart be troubled; Jn 14:1
we **d** not know where You are going, Jn 14:5
going, how **d** we know the way?" Jn 14:5
"**D** you not believe that I am in Jn 14:10
The words that I say to you I **d** Jn 14:10
the works that I **d**, he will do also; Jn 14:12 4160
he will **d** also; and greater *works* Jn 14:12 4160
works than these he will **d**; Jn 14:12 4160
you ask in My name, that will I **d**, Jn 14:13 4160
anything in My name, I will **d** *it*. Jn 14:14 4160
the world gives **d** I give to you. Jn 14:27
D not let your heart be troubled, Jn 14:27
I **d** exactly as the Father commanded Jn 14:31 4160
apart from Me you can **d** nothing. Jn 15:5 4160
if you **d** what I command you. Jn 15:14 4160
"No longer **d** I call you slaves, Jn 15:15
will **d** to you for My name's sake, Jn 15:21 4160
d not know the One who sent Me. Jn 15:21
"These things they will **d** because Jn 16:3 4160
for if I **d** not go away, the Helper Jn 16:7
because they **d** not believe in Me; Jn 16:9
We **d** not know what He is talking Jn 16:18
and I **d** not say to you that I will Jn 16:26
"**D** you now believe? Jn 16:31
which You have given Me to **d**. Jn 17:4 4160
I **d** not ask on behalf of the Jn 17:9
"I **d** not ask You to take them Jn 17:15
"I **d** not ask on behalf of these Jn 17:20
"Whom **d** you seek?" Jn 18:4
"Whom **d** you seek?" Jn 18:7
"Why **d** you question Me? Jn 18:21
if rightly, why **d** you strike Me?" Jn 18:23
d you bring against this Man?" Jn 18:29
d you wish then that I release for Jn 18:39
"You **d** not speak to me? Jn 19:10
D You not know that I have Jn 19:10
"**D** not write, 'The King of the Jews'; Jn 19:21
and we **d** not know where they have Jn 20:2
and I **d** not know where they have Jn 20:13
and **d** not be unbelieving, but Jn 20:27
"Children, you **d** not have any Jn 21:5
you do not have any fish, **d** you?" Jn 21:5
d you love Me more than these?" Jn 21:15
son of John, **d** you love Me?" Jn 21:16
son of John, **d** you love Me?" Jn 21:17
him the third time, "**D** you love Me?" Jn 21:17
you where you **d** not wish to *go*." Jn 21:18
that Jesus began to **d** and teach, Ac 1:1 4160
why **d** you stand looking into the Ac 1:11
"Brethren, what shall we **d**?" Ac 2:37 4160
"I **d** not possess silver and gold, Ac 3:6
but what I **d** have I give to you: Ac 3:6
at this, or why **d** you gaze at us, Ac 3:12
"What shall we **d** with these men? Ac 4:16 4160
to **d** whatever Your hand and Your Ac 4:28 4160
you propose to **d** with these men. Ac 5:35 4238
why **d** you injure one another?' Ac 7:26
'YOU **D** NOT MEAN TO KILL ME AS Ac 7:28
THE EGYPTIAN YESTERDAY, **D** YOU?' Ac 7:28
WE **D** NOT KNOW WHAT HAPPENED Ac 7:40
d not hold this sin against them!" Ac 7:60
"**D** you understand what you are Ac 8:30
be told you what you must **d**." Ac 9:6 4160
together to **d** away with him, Ac 9:23 337
"**D** not delay in coming to us." Ac 9:38
MY HEART, who will **d** all My will.' Ac 13:22 4160
'What **d** you suppose that I am? Ac 13:25
why **d** you put God to the test by Ac 15:10
is my judgment that we **d** not trouble Ac 15:19
from such things, you will **d** well. Ac 15:29 4238
"**D** not harm yourself, for we are Ac 16:28 4238
"Sirs, what must I **d** to be saved?" Ac 16:30 4160
"**D** not be afraid *any longer*, but Ac 18:9
on speaking and **d** not be silent; Ac 18:9
keep calm and to **d** nothing rash. Ac 19:36 4238
"**D** not be troubled, for his life Ac 20:10
"But I **d** not consider my life of Ac 20:24
"Therefore **d** this that we tell you. Ac 21:23 4160
"**D** you know Greek? Ac 21:37
'What shall I **d**, Lord?' Ac 22:10 4160
has been appointed for you to **d**.' Ac 22:10 4160
'Now why **d** you delay? Ac 22:16
"What are you about to **d**? Ac 22:26 4160
D you sit to try me according to Ac 23:3
"**D** you revile God's high priest?" Ac 23:4
"So **d** not listen to them, for Ac 23:21
I **d** serve the God of our fathers, Ac 24:14
I also **d** my best to maintain Ac 24:16 778
and wishing to **d** the Jews a favor, Ac 24:27 2698
wishing to **d** the Jews a favor, Ac 25:9 2698
of death, I **d** not refuse to die; Ac 25:11
I thought to myself that I had to **d** Ac 26:9 4238
d you believe the Prophets? Ac 26:27
I know that you **d**." Ac 26:27 4100
'**D** not be afraid, Paul; Ac 27:24
I **d** not want you to be unaware, Ro 1:13
to **d** those things which are not Ro 1:28 4160
death, they not only **d** the same, Ro 1:32 4160
But **d** you suppose this, O man, Ro 2:3
things and **d** the same *yourself*, Ro 2:3 4160
Or **d** you think lightly of the Ro 2:4
and **d** not obey the truth, Ro 2:8
For when Gentiles who **d** not have Ro 2:14
d instinctively the things of the Law, Ro 2:14 4160
d you not teach yourself? Ro 2:21
one shall not steal, **d** you steal? Ro 2:21
adultery, **d** you commit adultery? Ro 2:22
abhor idols, **d** you rob temples? Ro 2:22
the Law, **d** you dishonor God? Ro 2:23
us **d** evil that good may come"? Ro 3:8 4160
D we then nullify the Law through Ro 3:31
Or **d** you not know that all of us Ro 6:3
Therefore **d** not let sin reign in Ro 6:12
and **d** not go on presenting the Ro 6:13
D you not know that when you Ro 6:16
Or **d** you not know, brethren Ro 7:1
I am doing, I **d** not understand; Ro 7:15
what I *would* like to **d**, but Ro 7:15
But if I **d** the very thing I do not Ro 7:16 4160
the very thing I **d** not want *to do*, Ro 7:16
the very thing I do not want *to* **d**, Ro 7:16
the good that I want, I **d** not do Ro 7:19
the good that I want, I do not **d** Ro 7:19 4160
the very evil that I **d** not want. Ro 7:19
doing the very thing I **d** not want, Ro 7:20
me, the one who wants to **d** good. Ro 7:21 4160
For what the Law could not **d**, Ro 8:3
who **d** not walk according to the Ro 8:4
for it is not even able *to* **d** *so*, Ro 8:7
if we hope for what we **d** not see, Ro 8:25
for we **d** not know how to pray as Ro 8:26
"**D** NOT SAY IN YOUR HEART, Ro 10:6
Or **d** you not know what the Ro 11:2
d not be arrogant toward the Ro 11:18
D not be conceited, but fear; Ro 11:20
if they **d** not continue in their Ro 11:23
For I **d** not want you, brethren, to Ro 11:25
And **d** not be conformed to this Ro 12:2
d not have the same function, Ro 12:4
bless and **d** not curse. Ro 12:14
d not be haughty in mind, but Ro 12:16
D not be wise in your own Ro 12:16
D not be overcome by evil, but Ro 12:21
D you want to have no fear of Ro 13:3
D what is good and you will have Ro 13:3 4160
But if you **d** what is evil, be Ro 13:4 4160
D this, knowing the time, that Ro 13:11
why **d** you judge your brother? Ro 14:10
why **d** you regard your brother with Ro 14:10
D not destroy with your food him Ro 14:15
Therefore **d** not let what is for Ro 14:16
D not tear down the work of God Ro 14:20
or *to* **d** *anything* by which your Ro 14:21
Yes, they were pleased *to* **d** *so*, Ro 15:27
to whom not only **d** I give thanks, Ro 16:4
and *so* **d** Lucius and Jason Ro 16:21
I **d** not know whether I baptized 1Co 1:16
Yet we **d** speak wisdom among those 1Co 2:6
D you not know that you are a 1Co 3:16
fact, I **d** not even examine myself. 1Co 4:3
Therefore **d** not go on passing 1Co 4:5
What **d** you have that you did not 1Co 4:7
why **d** you boast as if you had not 1Co 4:7
I **d** not write these things to 1Co 4:14
What **d** you desire? 1Co 4:21
D you not know that a little 1Co 5:6
For what have I to **d** with judging 1Co 5:12
D you not judge those who are 1Co 5:12
Or **d** you not know that the saints 1Co 6:2
D you not know that we will judge 1Co 6:3
d you appoint them as judges who 1Co 6:4
You **d** this even to *your* 1Co 6:8
Or **d** you not know that the 1Co 6:9
D not be deceived; 1Co 6:9
God will **d** away with both of them. 1Co 6:13 2673
D you not know that your bodies 1Co 6:15
Or **d** you not know that the one who 1Co 6:16
Or **d** you not know that your body 1Co 6:19
if they **d** not have self-control, 1Co 7:9

For how **d** you know, O wife, 1Co 7:16
Or how **d** you know, O husband, 1Co 7:16
D not worry about it; 1Co 7:21
to become free, rather **d** that. 1Co 7:21 *5530*
d not become slaves of men. 1Co 7:23
D not seek to be released. 1Co 7:27
D not seek a wife. 1Co 7:27
be so, let him **d** what he wishes, 1Co 7:36 *4160*
virgin *daughter,* he will **d** well. 1Co 7:37 *4160*
her in marriage will **d** better. 1Co 7:38 *4160*
neither the worse if we **d** not eat, 1Co 8:8
eat, nor the better if we **d** eat. 1Co 8:8
D we not have a right to eat and 1Co 9:4
D we not have a right to take 1Co 9:5
Or **d** only Barnabas and I not have 1Co 9:6
the right over you, **d** we not more? 1Co 9:12
D you not know that those who 1Co 9:13
me if I **d** not preach the gospel. 1Co 9:16
For if I **d** this voluntarily, I 1Co 9:17 *4238*
I **d** all things for the sake of 1Co 9:23 *4160*
D you not know that those who run 1Co 9:24
They then **d** *it* to receive a 1Co 9:25
I **d** not want you to be unaware, 1Co 10:1
D not be idolaters, as some of them 1Co 10:7
What **d** I mean then? 1Co 10:19
and I **d** not want you to become 1Co 10:20
Or **d** we provoke the Lord to jealousy 1Co 10:22
sacrificed to idols," **d** not eat *it,* 1Co 10:28
eat or drink or whatever you **d**, 1Co 10:31 *4160*
you do, **d** all to the glory of God. 1Co 10:31 *4160*
instruction, I **d** not praise you, 1Co 11:17
D you not have houses in which to 1Co 11:22
d you despise the church of God and 1Co 11:22
d this in remembrance of Me." 1Co 11:24 *4160*
d this, as often as you drink *it,* 1Co 11:25 *4160*
I **d** not want you to be unaware. 1Co 12:1
All **d** not have gifts of healings, 1Co 12:30
have gifts of healings, **d** they? 1Co 12:30
All **d** not speak with tongues, do 1Co 12:30
do not speak with tongues, **d** they? 1Co 12:30
All **d** not interpret, do they? 1Co 12:30
All do not interpret, **d** they? 1Co 12:30
of angels, but **d** not have love, 1Co 13:1
mountains, but **d** not have love, 1Co 13:2
to be burned, but **d** not have love, 1Co 13:3
if they **d** not produce a 1Co 14:7
If then I **d** not know the meaning 1Co 14:11
d not be children in your thinking; 1Co 14:20
and **d** not forbid to speak in 1Co 14:39
how **d** some among you say that 1Co 15:12
d who are baptized for the dead? 1Co 15:29 *4160*
D not be deceived: 1Co 15:33
what kind of body **d** they come?" 1Co 15:35
you **d** not sow the body which is to 1Co 15:37
of Galatia, so **d** you also. 1Co 16:1 *4160*
For I **d** not wish to see you now 1Co 16:7
all that you **d** be done in love. 1Co 16:14
we **d** not want you to be unaware, 2Co 1:8
when I intended to **d** this, 2Co 1:17
d I purpose according to the 2Co 1:17
Or **d** we need, as some, letters of 2Co 3:1
mercy, we **d** not lose heart, 2Co 4:1
For we **d** not preach ourselves but 2Co 4:5
Therefore we **d** not lose heart, but 2Co 4:16
we **d** not want to be unclothed but 2Co 5:4
D not be bound together with 2Co 6:14
D NOT TOUCH WHAT IS UNCLEAN; 2Co 6:17
I **d** not speak to condemn you, 2Co 7:3
by my letter, I **d** not regret it; 2Co 7:8
a year ago not only to **d** *this,* 2Co 8:10 *4160*
but also to desire *to* **d** *it.* 2Co 8:10
Each one *must* **d** just as he has 2Co 9:7
we **d** not war according to the 2Co 10:3
for I **d** not wish to seem as if I 2Co 10:9
to you, and will continue to **d** so. 2Co 11:9
Because I **d** not love you? 2Co 11:11
not love you? God knows *I* **d***!* 2Co 11:11
I am doing I will continue to **d**, 2Co 11:12 *4160*
but if *you* **d**, receive me even as 2Co 11:16
in the body I **d** not know, 2Co 12:2
or out of the body I **d** not know, 2Co 12:2
apart from the body I **d** not know, 2Co 12:3
For if I **d** wish to boast I will 2Co 12:6
for I **d** not seek what is yours, 2Co 12:14
Or **d** you not recognize this about 2Co 13:5
we ourselves **d** not fail the test. 2Co 13:6 *1510*
pray to God that you **d** no wrong; 2Co 13:7 *4160*
but that you may **d** what is right, 2Co 13:7 *4160*
can **d** nothing against the truth, 2Co 13:8
very thing I also was eager to **d**. Ga 2:10 *4160*
"I **d** not nullify the grace of God, Ga 2:21
you, **d** it by the works of the Law, Ga 3:5
law, **d** you not listen to the law? Ga 4:21
and **d** not be subject again to a yoke Ga 5:1
only **d** not *turn* your freedom Ga 5:13
not **d** the things that you please. Ga 5:17 *4160*
D not be deceived, God is not Ga 6:7
will reap if we **d** not grow weary. Ga 6:9
let us **d** good to all people, Ga 6:10 *2038b*
For those who are circumcised **d** Ga 6:13
d not cease giving thanks for you, Eph 1:16
Now to Him who is able to **d** Eph 3:20 *4160*
BE ANGRY, AND *yet* D NOT SIN; Eph 4:26
d not let the sun go down on your Eph 4:26
and **d** not give the devil an Eph 4:27
D not grieve the Holy Spirit of God, Eph 4:30
d not be partakers with them; Eph 5:7
D not participate in the unfruitful Eph 5:11
So then **d** not be foolish, but Eph 5:17
And **d** not get drunk with wine, for Eph 5:18
d not provoke your children to Eph 6:4
d the same things to them, Eph 6:9 *4160*
the latter **d** *it* out of love, Php 1:16
and I **d** not know which to choose. Php 1:22
D nothing from selfishness or Php 2:3
d not *merely* look out for your own Php 2:4
D all things without grumbling or Php 2:14 *4160*
I **d** not regard myself as having Php 3:13
but one thing *I* **d***:* forgetting Php 3:13
I can **d** all things through Him who Php 4:13 *2480*
and in my flesh I **d** my share on Col 1:24
d you submit yourself to decrees, Col 2:20
"**D** not handle, do not taste, do Col 2:21
"Do not handle, **d** not taste, do Col 2:21
do not taste, **d** not touch!" Col 2:21
D not lie to one another, since Col 3:9
Whatever you **d** in word or deed, Col 3:17 *4160*
Whatever you do in word or deed, **d** Col 3:17
and **d** not be embittered against Col 3:19
d not exasperate your children, Col 3:21
Whatever you **d**, do your work Col 3:23 *4160b*
you do, **d** your work heartily, Col 3:23 *2038b*
just as we also **d** for you; 1Th 3:12
(just as you actually **d** walk), 1Th 4:1
the Gentiles who **d** not know God; 1Th 4:5
for indeed you **d** practice it 1Th 4:10
d not want you to be uninformed, 1Th 4:13
as **d** the rest who have no hope. 1Th 4:13
then let us not sleep as others **d**, 1Th 5:6
those who sleep **d** their sleeping at 1Th 5:7 *2518*
D not quench the Spirit; 1Th 5:19
d not despise prophetic utterances. 1Th 5:20
to those who **d** not know God 2Th 1:8
to those who **d** not obey the gospel 2Th 1:8
D you not remember that while I 2Th 2:5
only he who now restrains *will* **d** *so* 2Th 2:7
continue to **d** what we command. 2Th 3:4 *4160*
we **d** not have the right *to this,* 2Th 3:9
d not grow weary of doing good. 2Th 3:13
person and **d** not associate with him, 2Th 3:14
Yet **d** not regard him as an enemy, 2Th 3:15
even though they **d** not understand 1Tm 1:7
But I **d** not allow a woman to teach 1Tm 2:12
it is a fine work he desires *to* **d**. 1Tm 3:1
But have nothing to **d** with worldly 1Tm 4:7 *3868*
D not neglect the spiritual gift 1Tm 4:14
for as you **d** this you will ensure 1Tm 4:16 *4160*
D not sharply rebuke an older man, 1Tm 5:1
D not receive an accusation 1Tm 5:19
D not lay hands upon anyone *too* 1Tm 5:22
Instruct them to **d** good, 1Tm 6:18 *14*
Therefore **d** not be ashamed of the 2Tm 1:8
held captive by him to **d** his will. 2Tm 2:26
d the work of an evangelist, 2Tm 4:5 *4160*
in Christ to order you *to* **d** what Phm 1:8
I did not want to **d** anything, Phm 1:14 *4160*
will **d** even more than what I say. Phm 1:21 *4160*
as **d** Mark, Aristarchus, Demas, Phm 1:24
so that we **d** not drift away *from it.* Heb 2:1
But now we **d** not yet see all Heb 2:8
But we **d** see Him who was made Heb 2:9
D NOT HARDEN YOUR HEARTS Heb 3:8
VOICE, D NOT HARDEN YOUR HEARTS, Heb 3:15
IF YOU HEAR HIS VOICE, D NOT Heb 4:7
of Him with whom we have to **d**. Heb 4:13 *3056*
For we **d** not have a high priest Heb 4:15
And this we will **d**, Heb 6:3 *4160*
TO D YOUR WILL, O GOD.'" Heb 10:7 *4160*
I HAVE COME TO D YOUR WILL." Heb 10:9 *4160*
How much severer punishment **d** you Heb 10:29
d not throw away your confidence, Heb 10:35
D NOT REGARD LIGHTLY THE Heb 12:5
d not refuse Him who is speaking. Heb 12:25
D not neglect to show hospitality Heb 13:2
WHAT WILL MAN D TO ME?" Heb 13:6 *4160*
D not be carried away by varied Heb 13:9
here we **d** not have a lasting city, Heb 13:14
And **d** not neglect doing good and Heb 13:16
Let them **d** this with joy and not Heb 13:17 *4160*
I urge *you* all the more to **d** this, Heb 13:19 *4160*
in every good thing to **d** His will, Heb 13:21 *4160*
D not be deceived, my beloved Jas 1:16
d not hold your faith in our Jas 2:1
D they not blaspheme the fair name Jas 2:7
"D NOT COMMIT ADULTERY," Jas 2:11
"D NOT COMMIT MURDER." Jas 2:11
Now if you **d** not commit adultery, Jas 2:11
adultery, but **d** commit murder, Jas 2:11
and yet you **d** not give them what Jas 2:16
You **d** well; the demons also believe, Jas 2:19 *4160*
d not be arrogant and *so* lie Jas 3:14
You lust and **d** not have; Jas 4:2
You **d** not have because you do not Jas 4:2
do not have because you **d** not ask. Jas 4:2
You ask and **d** not receive, because Jas 4:3
d you not know that friendship Jas 4:4
Or **d** you think that the Scripture Jas 4:5
D not speak against one another, Jas 4:11
Yet you **d** not know what your life Jas 4:14
live and also **d** this or that." Jas 4:15 *4160*
who knows *the* right thing to **d** and Jas 4:17 *4160*
thing to do and does not **d** it, Jas 4:17 *4160*
D not complain, brethren, against Jas 5:9
all, my brethren, **d** not swear, Jas 5:12
and though you **d** not see Him now, 1Pe 1:8
d not be conformed to the former 1Pe 1:14
the praise of those who **d** right. 1Pe 2:14 *15*
and **d** not use your freedom as a 1Pe 2:16
But if when you **d** what is right 1Pe 2:20 *15*
if you **d** what is right without being 1Pe 3:6 *15*
TURN AWAY FROM EVIL AND D GOOD; 1Pe 3:11 *4160*
IS AGAINST THOSE WHO D EVIL." 1Pe 3:12 *4160*
D NOT FEAR THEIR INTIMIDATION, 1Pe 3:14
AND D NOT BE TROUBLED, 1Pe 3:14
they are surprised that you **d** not 1Pe 4:4
Whoever speaks, *is to* **d** *so* as 1Pe 4:11
whoever serves *is to* **d** *so* as 1Pe 4:11
d not be surprised at the fiery 1Pe 4:12
who **d** not obey the gospel of God? 1Pe 4:17 *544*
to which you **d** well to pay 2Pe 1:19 *4160*
they **d** not tremble when they 2Pe 2:10
d not bring a reviling judgment 2Pe 2:11
But **d** not let this one *fact* escape 2Pe 3:8
as *they* **d** also the rest of 2Pe 3:16
lie and **d** not practice the truth; 1Jn 1:6
D not love the world nor the 1Jn 2:15
because you **d** not know the truth, 1Jn 2:21
truth, but because you **d** know it, 1Jn 2:21
D not be surprised, brethren, if the 1Jn 3:13
d the things that are pleasing in His 1Jn 3:22 *4160*
d not believe every spirit, 1Jn 4:1
I **d** not say that he should make 1Jn 5:16
we have received commandment *to* **d** 2Jn 1:4
those who **d** not acknowledge Jesus 2Jn 1:7
Watch yourselves, that you **d** not 2Jn 1:8
d not receive him into *your* house, 2Jn 1:10
and **d** not give him a greeting; 2Jn 1:10
I **d** not want to *do so* with paper 2Jn 1:12
I do not want to **d** *so* with paper 2Jn 1:12
You will **d** well to send them 3Jn 1:6 *4160*
he forbids those who desire *to* **d** *so* 3Jn 1:10
d not imitate what is evil, 3Jn 1:11
which they **d** not understand; Jude 1:10
"**D** not be afraid; I am the first and Rv 1:17
and **d** the deeds you did at first; Rv 2:5 *4160*
'Yet this you **d** have, that you Rv 2:6
'**D** not fear what you are about to Rv 2:10
who **d** not hold this teaching, Rv 2:24
Therefore if you **d** not wake up, I Rv 3:3
and you **d** not know that you are Rv 3:17
and night they **d** not cease to say, Rv 4:8
d not damage the oil and the wine." Rv 6:6
"**D** not harm the earth or the sea Rv 7:3
men who **d** not have the seal of God Rv 9:4
and with them they **d** harm. Rv 9:19 *91*
spoken and **d** not write them." Rv 10:4
the temple and **d** not measure it, Rv 11:2
and cause as many as **d** not worship Rv 13:15
"Why **d** you wonder? Rv 17:7
"**D** not do that; I am a fellow servant Rv 19:10
d that; I am a fellow servant of yours Rv 19:10 *3708*
But he said to me, "**D** not do that Rv 22:9
"Do not **d** that. I am a fellow servant Rv 22:9 *3708*
"**D** not seal up the words of the Rv 22:10
one who does wrong, still **d** wrong; Rv 22:11 *91*

DOCTRINE
carried about by every wind of **d**, Eph 4:14 *1319*
d which you have been following. 1Tm 4:6 *1319*
our **d** will not be spoken against. 1Tm 6:1 *1319*
If anyone advocates a different **d** and 1Tm 6:3 *2085*
the **d** conforming to godliness, 1Tm 6:3 *1319*
when they will not endure sound **d**; 2Tm 4:3 *1319*
be able both to exhort in sound **d** and Ti 1:9 *1319*
which are fitting for sound **d**. Ti 2:1 *1319*
of good deeds, *with* purity in **d**, Ti 2:7 *1319*
will adorn the **d** of God our Savior Ti 2:10 *1319*

DOCTRINES
AS D THE PRECEPTS OF MEN.'" Mt 15:9 *1319*
AS D THE PRECEPTS OF MEN.' Mk 7:7 *1319*
men not to teach strange **d**, 1Tm 1:3 *2085*
deceitful spirits and **d** of demons, 1Tm 4:1 *1319*

DOCUMENT
the **d** which you sent to us has Ezr 4:18 5407
copy of King Artaxerxes' **d** was read Ezr 4:23 5407
d *are the names of* our leaders, Ne 9:38
on the sealed **d** *were the names of:* Ne 10:1
d so that it may not be changed, Da 6:8 3792
King Darius signed the **d**, Da 6:9 3792
Daniel knew that the **d** was signed, Da 6:10 3792

DODAI
D the Ahohite and his division had 1Ch 27:4 1737

DODANIM
and Tarshish, Kittim and **D**. Gn 10:4 1721

DODAVAHU
Then Eliezer the son of **D** of 2Ch 20:37 1735

DODO
the son of Puah, the son of **D**, Jg 10:1 1734
Eleazar the son of **D** the Ahohite, 2Sa 23:9 1734
Elhanan the son of **D** of Bethlehem, 2Sa 23:24 1734
him was Eleazar the son of **D**, 1Ch 11:12 1734
Elhanan the son of **D** of Bethlehem, 1Ch 11:26 1734

DOE
"Naphtali is a **d** let loose, He Gn 49:21 355
As a loving hind and a graceful **d**, Pr 5:19 3280
"For even the **d** in the field has Jer 14:5 355

DOEG
and his name was **D** the Edomite, 1Sa 21:7 1673
Then **D** the Edomite, who was 1Sa 22:9 1673
Then the king said to **D**, 1Sa 22:18 1673
And **D** the Edomite turned around 1Sa 22:18 1673
day, when **D** the Edomite was there, 1Sa 22:22 1673

DOER
And fully recompenses the proud **d**. Ps 31:23 6213a
a hearer of the word and not a **d**, Jas 1:23 *4163*
hearer but an effectual **d**, Jas 1:25 *4163*

law, you are not a **d** of the law but **Jas 4:11** *4163*

DOERS

the **d** of iniquity have fallen; **Ps 36:12** 6466
them away with the **d** of iniquity. **Ps 125:5** 6466
are the **d** of wickedness built up but **Mal 3:15** 6213a
d of the Law will be justified. **Ro 2:13** *4163*
prove yourselves **d** of the word, **Jas 1:22** *4163*

DOES

the woman **d** not follow me.' **Gn 24:39**
my master **d** not concern himself **Gn 39:8**
"Why **d** my lord speak such words **Gn 44:7**
"When Pharaoh **d** not listen to you, **Ex 7:4**
'What **d** this rite mean to you?' **Ex 12:26**
He **d** not have authority to sell **Ex 21:8**
he **d** not die but remains in bed, **Ex 21:18**
warned, yet he **d** not confine it and **Ex 21:29**
a pit and **d** not cover it over, **Ex 21:33**
at all, *and* if he **d** cry out to Me, **Ex 22:23**
for whoever **d** any work on it, that **Ex 31:14** 6213a
whoever **d** any work on the sabbath **Ex 31:15** 6213a
why **d** Your anger burn against Your **Ex 32:11**
"If Your presence **d** not go *with* **Ex 33:15**
whoever **d** any work on it shall be **Ex 35:2** 6213a
leader sins and unintentionally **d** any **Lv 4:22** 6213a
known, if he **d** not tell *it,* **Lv 5:1**
'Now if a person sins and **d** any **Lv 5:17** 6213a
cud, it **d** not divide the hoof, **Lv 11:4**
cud, it **d** not divide the hoof, **Lv 11:5**
cud, it **d** not divide the hoof, **Lv 11:6**
a split hoof, it **d** not chew cud, **Lv 11:7**
in the seas and in the rivers that **d** **Lv 11:10**
'Whatever in the water **d** not have **Lv 11:12**
and it **d** not appear to be deeper **Lv 13:4**
in its place and **d** not spread, **Lv 13:23**
and **d** not bring it to the doorway **Lv 17:9**
"But if he **d** not wash *them* or **Lv 17:16**
which a man may live if he **d** them; **Lv 18:5** 6213a
d any of these abominations, **Lv 18:29** 6213a
who **d** any work on this same day, **Lv 23:30** 6213a
it **d** not revert in the jubilee. **Lv 25:30**
he **d** exchange animal for animal, **Lv 27:10** 4171
or if he **d** exchange it, then both **Lv 27:33** 4171
whatever good the LORD **d** for us, **Nu 10:32** 3190
d flow with milk and honey, **Nu 13:27**
who **d** *anything* unintentionally, **Nu 15:29** 6213a
person who **d** *anything* defiantly, **Nu 15:30** 6213a
but if he **d** not purify himself on **Nu 19:12**
died, and **d** not purify himself, **Nu 19:13**
'But the man who is unclean and **d** **Nu 19:20**
man **d** not live by bread alone, **Dt 8:3**
Levi **d** not have a portion or **Dt 10:9**
what **d** the LORD your God require **Dt 10:12**
God who **d** not show partiality nor **Dt 10:17**
divides the hoof but **d** not **Dt 14:8**
but anything that **d** not have fins **Dt 14:10**
a man or a woman who **d** what is **Dt 17:2** 6213a
"For whoever **d** these things is **Dt 18:12** 6213a
d not come about or come true, **Dt 18:22**
if it **d** not make peace with you, **Dt 20:12**
for whoever **d** these things is an **Dt 22:5** 6213a
so that he **d** not beat him with many **Dt 25:3**
"But if the man **d** not desire to **Dt 25:7**
'Thus it is done to the man who **d** **Dt 25:9**
"For everyone who **d** these things, **Dt 25:16** 6213a
'Cursed is he who **d** not confirm **Dt 27:26**
and **d** not obey your words in all that **Jos 1:18**
'Why **d** his chariot delay in coming? **Jg 5:28**
if he **d** not wish to redeem you, **Ru 3:13**
"What **d** the noise of this great **1Sa 4:6**
"What **d** the noise of this **1Sa 4:14**
"Whoever **d** not come out after **1Sa 11:7**
the LORD **d** not deliver by sword **1Sa 17:47**
'The king **d** not desire any dowry **1Sa 18:25**
my father **d** nothing either great **1Sa 20:2** 6213a
"And when the LORD **d** for my lord **1Sa 25:30** 6213a
in that the king **d** not bring back **2Sa 14:13**
Yet God **d** not take away life, but **2Sa 14:14**
so that he **d** not find for himself **2Sa 20:6**
but why **d** my lord the king delight **2Sa 24:3**
and David our lord **d** not know *it?* **1Ki 1:11**
(for there is no man who **d** not sin) **1Ki 8:46**
heavy shower **d** not stop you.' " **1Ki 18:44**
because he **d** not prophesy good **1Ki 22:8**
"If the LORD **d** not help you, from **2Ki 6:27**
"Why **d** my lord weep?" **2Ki 8:12**
Why **d** my lord seek this thing? **1Ch 21:3**
(for there is no man who **d** not sin) **2Ch 6:36**
who **d** not fulfill this promise; **Ne 5:13**
"Yet all of this **d** not satisfy me **Es 5:13**
"**D** Job fear God for nothing? **Jb 1:9**
d not come from the dust, **Jb 5:6**
Nor **d** trouble sprout from the **Jb 5:6**
d great and unsearchable things, **Jb 5:9** 6213a
"**D** the wild donkey bray over *his* **Jb 6:5**
Or **d** the ox low over his fodder? **Jb 6:5**
So that he **d** not forsake the fear of **Jb 6:14**
But what **d** your argument prove? **Jb 6:25**
goes down to Sheol **d** not come up. **Jb 7:9**
"**D** God pervert justice? Or does **Jb 8:3**
"Does God pervert justice? Or **d** **Jb 8:3**
in his house, but it **d** not stand; **Jb 8:15**
fast to it, but it **d** not endure. **Jb 8:15**
Who **d** great things, unfathomable, **Jb 9:10** 6213a
d not know such things as these? **Jb 12:3**
"Who among all these **d** not know **Jb 12:9**
"**D** not the ear test words, As the **Jb 12:11**
like a shadow and **d** not remain. **Jb 14:2**
So man lies down and **d** not rise. **Jb 14:12**
honor, but he **d** not know *it;* **Jb 14:21**
but he **d** not perceive it. **Jb 14:21**
"Why **d** your heart carry you away? **Jb 15:12**
"He **d** not believe that he will **Jb 15:22**
place of him who **d** not know God." **Jb 18:21**
my servant, but he **d** not answer; **Jb 19:16**
"Why do you persecute me as God **d**, **Jb 19:22**
"He **d** not look at the streams, **Jb 20:17**
He **d** not retain anything he desires. **Jb 20:20**
his prosperity **d** not endure. **Jb 20:21**
His cow calves and **d** not abort. **Jb 21:10**
Or **d** their calamity fall on them? **Jb 21:17**
D God apportion destruction in His **Jb 21:17**
"For what **d** he care for his **Jb 21:21**
'What **d** God know? Can He judge **Jb 22:13**
what His soul desires, that He **d**. **Jb 23:13** 6213a
God **d** not pay attention to folly. **Jb 24:12**
So **d** Sheol *those who* have **Jb 24:19**
And **d** no good for the widow. **Jb 24:21** 3190
upon whom **d** His light not rise? **Jb 25:3**
the cloud **d** not burst under them. **Jb 26:8**
d not reproach any of my days. **Jb 27:6**
"Man **d** not know its value, Nor is **Jb 28:13**
"Where then **d** wisdom come from? **Jb 28:20**
"Yet **d** not one in a heap of ruins **Jb 30:24**
"**D** He not see my ways And number **Jb 31:4**
That He **d** not give an account of **Jb 33:13**
d all these oftentimes with men, **Jb 33:29** 6466
"For He **d** not *need to* consider a **Jb 34:23**
what **d** He receive from your hand? **Jb 35:7**
but He **d** not answer Because of the **Jb 35:12**
is mighty but **d** not despise *any;* **Jb 36:5**
"He **d** not keep the wicked alive, **Jb 36:6**
"He **d** not withdraw His eyes from **Jb 36:7**
"*Beware* that wrath **d** not entice **Jb 36:18**
And He **d** not restrain the **Jb 37:4**
He **d** not regard any who are wise **Jb 37:24**
of the driver he **d** not hear. **Jb 39:7**
he **d** not turn back from the sword. **Jb 39:22**
And he **d** not stand still at the **Jb 39:24**
How blessed is the man who **d** not **Ps 1:1**
season And its leaf **d** not wither; **Ps 1:3**
And in whatever he **d**, he prospers. **Ps 1:3** 6213a
If a man **d** not repent, He will **Ps 7:12**
He **d** not forget the cry of the **Ps 9:12**
his countenance, **d** not seek *Him.* **Ps 10:4**
There is no one who **d** good. **Ps 14:1** 6213a
There is no one who **d** good, **Ps 14:3** 6213a
He **d** not slander with his tongue, **Ps 15:3**
Nor **d** evil to his neighbor, **Ps 15:3** 6213a
to his own hurt and **d** not change; **Ps 15:4**
He **d** not put out his money at **Ps 15:5**
Nor **d** he take a bribe against the **Ps 15:5**
He who **d** these things will never **Ps 15:5** 6213a
the LORD **d** not impute iniquity, **Ps 32:2**
Nor **d** it deliver anyone by its **Ps 33:17**
He **d** not despise evil. **Ps 36:4**
wicked borrows and **d** not pay back, **Ps 37:21**
And **d** not forsake His godly ones; **Ps 37:28**
mute man who **d** not open his mouth. **Ps 38:13**
I am like a man who **d** not hear, **Ps 38:14**
d not know who will gather them. **Ps 39:6**
d not shout in triumph over me. **Ps 41:11**
There is no one who **d** good. **Ps 53:1** 6213a
There is no one who **d** good, **Ps 53:3** 6213a
So that it **d** not hear the voice of **Ps 58:5**
And **d** not allow our feet to slip. **Ps 66:9**
And **d** not despise His *who are* **Ps 69:33**
They say, "How **d** God know? **Ps 73:11**
Why **d** Your anger smoke against **Ps 74:1**
wind that passes and **d** not return. **Ps 78:39**
No good thing **d** He withhold from **Ps 84:11**
d a stupid man understand this: **Ps 92:6**
"The LORD **d** not see, Nor does the **Ps 94:7**
Nor **d** the God of Jacob pay heed." **Ps 94:7**
planted the ear, **d** He not hear? **Ps 94:9**
who formed the eye, **d** He not see? **Ps 94:9**
d not let their cattle decrease. **Ps 107:38**
He **d** whatever He pleases. **Ps 115:3** 6213a
hand of the LORD **d** valiantly. **Ps 118:15** 6213a
hand of the LORD **d** valiantly. **Ps 118:16** 6213a
the reaper **d** not fill his hand, **Ps 129:7**
wait for the LORD, my soul **d** wait, **Ps 130:5**
Whatever the LORD pleases, He **d**, **Ps 135:6** 6213a
To Him who alone **d** great wonders, **Ps 136:4** 6213a
He **d** not delight in the strength **Ps 147:10**
He **d** not take pleasure in the legs **Ps 147:10**
She **d** not ponder the path of life; **Pr 5:6**
are unstable, she **d** not know *it.* **Pr 5:6**
He who would destroy himself **d** it. **Pr 6:32** 6213a
So he **d** not know that it *will cost* **Pr 7:23**
D not wisdom call, And **Pr 8:1**
But he **d** not know that the dead **Pr 9:18**
The merciful man **d** himself good, **Pr 11:17** 1580
But the cruel man **d** himself harm. **Pr 11:17** 5916
lazy man **d** not roast his prey, **Pr 12:27**
a scoffer **d** not listen to rebuke. **Pr 13:1**
a stranger **d** not share its joy. **Pr 14:10**
d not love one who reproves him, **Pr 15:12**
He who winks his eyes **d** *so* to **Pr 16:30**
He who sires a fool **d** *so* to his **Pr 17:21**
d not delight in understanding, **Pr 18:2**
d not plow after the autumn, **Pr 20:4**
gives and **d** not hold back. **Pr 21:26**
He **d** not open his mouth in the **Pr 24:7**
D He not consider *it* who weighs **Pr 24:12**
And **d** He not know *it* who keeps **Pr 24:12**
curse without cause **d** not alight. **Pr 26:2**
So **d** the sluggard on his bed. **Pr 26:14**
Nor **d** a crown *endure* to all **Pr 27:24**
And **d** not know that want will come **Pr 28:22**
d not understand *such* concern. **Pr 29:7**
And **d** not bless his mother. **Pr 30:11**
And **d** not retreat before any, **Pr 30:30**
She **d** him good and not evil All **Pr 31:12** 1580
Her lamp **d** not go out at night. **Pr 31:18**
d not eat the bread of idleness. **Pr 31:27**
What advantage **d** man have in all **Ec 1:3**
his work Which he **d** under the sun? **Ec 1:3** 5998
"What **d** it accomplish?" **Ec 2:2**
For what **d** a man get in all his **Ec 2:22**
even at night his mind **d** not rest. **Ec 2:23**
everything God **d** will remain forever; **Ec 3:14** 6213a
rich man **d** not allow him to sleep. **Ec 5:12**
d not even have a *proper* burial, **Ec 6:3**
and **d** not enjoy good things **Ec 6:6**
For what advantage **d** the wise man **Ec 6:8**
advantage **d** the poor man have, **Ec 6:8**
d good and who never sins. **Ec 7:20** 6213a
Although a sinner **d** evil a hundred **Ec 8:12** 6213a
shadow, because he **d** not fear God. **Ec 8:13**
Man **d** not know whether *it will be* **Ec 9:1**
for the one who **d** not sacrifice. **Ec 9:2**
Moreover, man **d** not know his time: **Ec 9:12**
and he **d** not sharpen *its* edge, **Ec 10:10**
d not *even* know how to go to a city. **Ec 10:15**
manger, *But* Israel **d** not know, **Is 1:3**
Nor **d** the widow's plea come before **Is 1:23**
this, His anger **d** not turn away **Is 9:12**
the Lord **d** not take pleasure in their **Is 9:17**
Nor **d** He have pity on their **Is 9:17**
this, His anger **d** not turn away **Is 9:17**
this, His anger **d** not turn away **Is 9:21**
this, His anger **d** not turn away **Is 10:4**
Yet it **d** not so intend, Nor does it **Is 10:7**
Nor **d** it plan so in its heart, **Is 10:7**
led Egypt astray in all that it **d**, **Is 19:14** 4639
He **d** not learn righteousness; **Is 26:10**
And **d** not perceive the majesty of **Is 26:10**
D the farmer plow continually to **Is 28:24**
D he *continually* turn and harrow **Is 28:24**
D he not level its surface And **Is 28:25**
he **d** not continue to thresh it **Is 28:28**
it, He **d** not thresh it longer. **Is 28:28**
And **d** not retract His words, **Is 31:2**
'*Beware* that Hezekiah **d** not **Is 36:18**
Selects a tree that **d** not rot; **Is 40:20**
earth **D** not become weary or tired. **Is 40:28**
and **d** his work over the coals, **Is 44:12** 6466
I am the LORD who **d** all these. **Is 45:7** 6213a
It **d** not move from its place. **Is 46:7**
your wages for what **d** not satisfy? **Is 55:2**
"How blessed is the man who **d** this, **Is 56:2** 6213a
from you so that He **d** not hear. **Is 59:2**
treads on them **d** not know peace. **Is 59:8**
righteousness **d** not overtake us; **Is 59:9**
though Abraham **d** not know us And **Is 63:16**
us And Israel **d** not recognize us. **Is 63:16**
man who **d** not live out his days; **Is 65:20**
And the one who **d** not reach the age **Is 65:20**
glory For that which **d** not profit. **Jer 2:11**
If there is one who **d** justice, **Jer 5:1** 6213a
"For what purpose **d** frankincense **Jer 6:20**
D one turn away and not repent? **Jer 8:4**
And **d** not speak the truth, **Jer 9:5**
"Cursed is the man who **d** not heed **Jer 11:3**
the LORD **d** not accept them; **Jer 14:10**
deal with you as this potter **d**?" **Jer 18:6**
if it **d** evil in My sight by not **Jer 18:10** 6213a
'**D** the snow of Lebanon forsake the **Jer 18:14**
pay And **d** not give him his wages, **Jer 22:13**
What **d** straw have *in common* with **Jer 23:28**
who **d** the LORD's work negligently, **Jer 48:10** 6213a
"**D** Israel have no sons? **Jer 49:1**
Who **d** not return empty-handed. **Jer 50:9**
"Now so that your heart **d** not grow **Jer 51:46**
For He **d** not afflict willingly Or **La 3:33**
things the Lord **d** not approve. **La 3:36**
and he **d** not turn from his **Ezk 3:19**
should not sin and he **d** not sin, **Ezk 3:21**
'The LORD **d** not see us; **Ezk 8:12**
the land, and the LORD **d** not see!' **Ezk 9:9**
Will he who **d** such things escape? **Ezk 17:15** 6213a
and **d** not eat at the mountain **Ezk 18:6**
if a man **d** not oppress anyone, but **Ezk 18:7**
his pledge, **d** not commit robbery, **Ezk 18:7**
if he **d** not lend *money* on interest **Ezk 18:8**
and who **d** any of these things to a **Ezk 18:10** 6213a
robbery, **d** not restore a pledge, **Ezk 18:12**
and observing **d** not do likewise. **Ezk 18:14**
"He **d** not eat at the mountain **Ezk 18:15**
d not take interest or increase, **Ezk 18:17**
and **d** according to all the **Ezk 18:24** 6213a
abominations that a wicked man **d**, **Ezk 18:24** 6213a
trumpet and **d** not take warning, **Ezk 33:4**
coming and **d** not blow the trumpet and **Ezk 33:6**
and he **d** not turn from his way, **Ezk 33:9**
as he **d** on the sabbath day. **Ezk 46:12** 6213a
iron **d** not combine with pottery. **Da 2:43**
"But whoever **d** not fall down and **Da 3:6**
"But whoever **d** not fall down and **Da 3:11**
"But *even if He* **d** not, let **Da 3:18**
But He **d** according to His will in **Da 4:35** 5648
"For she **d** not know that it was I **Hos 2:8**
strength, Yet he **d** not know *it;* **Hos 7:9**
on him, Yet he **d** not know *it.* **Hos 7:9**
D a lion roar in the forest when **Am 3:4**
D a young lion growl from his den **Am 3:4**

D a bird fall into a trap on the Am 3:5
D a trap spring up from the earth Am 3:5
Surely the Lord GOD **d** nothing Am 3:7 6213a
Or **d** one plow them with oxen? Am 6:12
Declares the LORD who **d** this. Am 9:12 6213a
inhabitant of Zaanan **d** not escape. Mi 1:11
D the LORD take delight in Mi 6:7
And what **d** the LORD require of you Mi 6:8
He **d** not retain His anger forever, Mi 7:18
It will consume you as the locust **d**. Na 3:15
So that he **d** not stay at home. Hab 2:5
His justice to light; He **d** not fail. Zph 3:5
D it not seem to you like nothing Hg 2:3
d not go up to Jerusalem to worship Zch 14:17
of Egypt **d** not go up or enter, Zch 14:18
"*As* for the man who **d** this, Mal 2:12 6213a
"Everyone who **d** evil is good in Mal 2:17 6213a
God and one who **d** not serve Him. Mal 3:18
every tree that **d** not Mt 3:10
nor **d** *anyone* light a lamp Mt 5:15
"Every tree that **d** not bear good Mt 7:19
but he who **d** the will of My Father Mt 7:21 4160
of Mine and **d** not act on them, Mt 7:26
to my slave, 'Do this!' and he **d** *it*." Mt 8:9 4160
"Whoever **d** not receive you, Mt 10:14
"And he who **d** not take his cross Mt 10:38
"And blessed is he who **d** not take Mt 11:6
nor **d** anyone know the Father except Mt 11:27
who **d** not gather with Me scatters. Mt 12:30
seeking rest, and **d** not find *it*. Mt 12:43
"For whoever **d** the will of My Mt 12:50 4160
but whoever **d** not have, even what Mt 13:12
kingdom and **d** not understand it, Mt 13:19
How then **d** it have tares?' Mt 13:27
hands **d** not defile the man." Mt 15:20
"But this kind **d** not go out Mt 17:21
"**D** your teacher not pay the Mt 17:24
d he not leave the ninety-nine on Mt 18:12
"But if he **d** not listen *to you*, Mt 18:16
if each of you **d** not forgive his Mt 18:35
how **d** David in the Spirit call Him Mt 22:43
come on a day when he **d** not expect Mt 24:50
at an hour which he **d** not know, Mt 24:50
but from the one who **d** not have, Mt 25:29
he **d** have shall be taken away. Mt 25:29
"Why **d** this man speak that way? Mk 2:7
"For whoever **d** the will of God, Mk 3:35 4160
and whoever **d** not have, even what Mk 4:25
how, he himself **d** not know. Mk 4:27
"Any place that **d** not receive Mk 6:11
it **d** not go into his heart, Mk 7:19
"Why **d** this generation seek for a Mk 8:12
"For what **d** it profit a man to Mk 8:36
"Elijah **d** first come and restore Mk 9:12
receives Me **d** not receive Me, Mk 9:37
where THEIR WORM **D** NOT DIE, Mk 9:44
where THEIR WORM **D** NOT DIE, Mk 9:46
where THEIR WORM **D** NOT DIE, Mk 9:48
whoever **d** not receive the kingdom Mk 10:15
sea,' and **d** not doubt in his heart, Mk 11:23
how **d** it seem to you?" Mk 14:64
every tree that **d** not Lk 3:9
to my slave, 'Do this!' and he **d** *it*." Lk 7:8 4160
"Blessed is he who **d** not take Lk 7:23
and whoever **d** not have, even what Lk 8:18
and only with difficulty **d** it leave Lk 9:39
he **d** not follow along with us." Lk 9:49
How **d** it read to you?" Lk 10:26
and he who **d** not gather with Me, Lk 11:23
d his life consist of his possessions." Lk 12:15
on a day when he **d** not expect *him* Lk 12:46
him and at an hour he **d** not know, Lk 12:46
Why **d** it even use up the ground?' Lk 13:7
d not each of you on the Sabbath Lk 13:15
and **d** not hate his own father and Lk 14:26
"Whoever **d** not carry his own Lk 14:27
d not first sit down and calculate Lk 14:28
d not give up all his own possessions. Lk 14:33
d not leave the ninety-nine in the Lk 15:4
d not light a lamp and sweep the Lk 15:8
"He **d** not thank the slave because Lk 17:9
things which were commanded, **d** he? Lk 17:9
whoever **d** not receive the kingdom Lk 18:17
but from the one who **d** not have, Lk 19:26
he **d** have shall be taken away. Lk 19:26
and inscription **d** it have?" Lk 20:24
but the end **d** not *follow* Lk 21:9
for a spirit **d** not have flesh and Lk 24:39
what **d** that have to do with us? My Jn 2:4
he who **d** not believe has been Jn 3:18
who **d** evil hates the Light, Jn 3:20 4238
and **d** not come to the Light Jn 3:20
but he who **d** not obey the Son Jn 3:36
for whatever the Father **d**, Jn 5:19 4160
the Son also **d** in like manner. Jn 5:19 4160
He who **d** not honor the Son does Jn 5:23
He who does not honor the Son **d** Jn 5:23
and **d** not come into judgment, Jn 5:24
How **d** He now say, Jn 6:42
"**D** this cause you to stumble? Jn 6:61
"For no one **d** anything in secret when Jn 7:4 4160
"Where **d** this man intend to go Jn 7:35
d not know the Law is accursed." Jn 7:49
"Our Law **d** not judge a man unless Jn 7:51
knows what he is doing, **d** it?" Jn 7:51
"The slave **d** not remain in Jn 8:35
the son **d** remain forever. Jn 8:35
and **d** not stand in the truth because Jn 8:44
He **d** not keep the Sabbath." Jn 9:16
Then how **d** he now see?" Jn 9:19
know that God **d** not hear sinners; Jn 9:31
is God-fearing and **d** His will, Jn 9:31 4160
he who **d** not enter by the door Jn 10:1
in the day, he **d** not stumble, Jn 11:9
darkness **d** not know where he goes. Jn 12:35
in Me, **d** not believe in Me Jn 12:44
My sayings and **d** not keep them, Jn 12:47
Me and **d** not receive My sayings, Jn 12:48
to pass, so that when it **d** occur, Jn 13:19
Father abiding in Me **d** His works. Jn 14:10 4160
it **d** not see Him or know Him, Jn 14:17
"He who **d** not love Me does not Jn 14:24
not love Me **d** not keep My words; Jn 14:24
in Me that **d** not bear fruit, Jn 15:2
"If anyone **d** not abide in Me, he Jn 15:6
for the slave **d** not know what his Jn 15:15
"What **d** this mean?" Ac 2:12
soul that **d** not heed that prophet Ac 3:23
the Most High **d** not dwell in Ac 7:48
SO HE **D** NOT OPEN HIS MOUTH. Ac 8:32
of whom **d** the prophet say this? Ac 8:34
who fears Him and **d** what is right is Ac 10:35 2038b
d not dwell in temples made with Ac 17:24
who **d** not know that the city of the Ac 19:35
people if God **d** raise the dead? Ac 26:8
for every soul of man who **d** evil, Ro 2:9 2716
and peace to everyone who **d** good, Ro 2:10 2038b
THERE IS NONE WHO **D** GOOD, Ro 3:12 4160
For what **d** the Scripture say? Ro 4:3
But to the one who **d** not work, Ro 4:5
into being that which **d** not exist. Ro 4:17
and hope **d** not disappoint, because Ro 5:5
for it **d** not subject itself to the Ro 8:7
d not have the Spirit of Christ, Ro 8:9
of Christ, he **d** not belong to Him. Ro 8:9
So then it **d** not *depend* on Ro 9:16
"Why **d** He still find fault? Ro 9:19
Or **d** not the potter have a right Ro 9:21
But what **d** it say? Ro 10:8
it **d** not bear the sword for nothing; Ro 13:4
Love **d** no wrong to a neighbor; Ro 13:10 2038b
with contempt the one who **d** not eat, Ro 14:3
who **d** not eat is not to judge Ro 14:3
he who eats, **d** so for the Lord, Ro 14:6 2068
not, for the Lord he **d** not eat, Ro 14:6
Happy is he who **d** not condemn Ro 14:22
But a natural man **d** not accept the 1Co 2:14
of God **d** not consist in words but 1Co 4:20
immorality of such a kind as **d** not 1Co 5:1
D any one of you, when he has a 1Co 6:1
The wife **d** not have authority over 1Co 7:4
but the husband **d**; and likewise 1Co 7:4
husband **d** not have authority over 1Co 7:4
his own body, but the wife **d**. 1Co 7:4
(but if she **d** leave, she must 1Co 7:11
do what he wishes, he **d** not sin; 1Co 7:36
daughter in marriage **d** well, 1Co 7:38 4160
he who **d** not give her in marriage 1Co 7:38
care that this liberty of yours **d** not 1Co 8:9
and **d** not eat the fruit of it? 1Co 9:7
and **d** not use the milk of 1Co 9:7
Or **d** not the Law also say these 1Co 9:8
thinks he stands take heed that he **d** 1Co 10:12
if a woman **d** not cover her head, 1Co 11:6
man **d** not originate from woman, 1Co 11:8
D not even nature itself teach you 1Co 11:14
he **d** not judge the body rightly. 1Co 11:29
d not brag *and* is not arrogant, 1Co 13:4
d not act unbecomingly; 1Co 13:5
it **d** not seek its own, is not 1Co 13:5
d not take into account a wrong 1Co 13:5
d not rejoice in unrighteousness, 1Co 13:6
in a tongue **d** not speak to men but 1Co 14:2
he **d** not know what you are saying? 1Co 14:16
if anyone **d** not recognize *this*, 1Co 14:38
at Ephesus, what **d** it profit me? 1Co 15:32
That which you sow **d** not come to 1Co 15:36
nor **d** the perishable inherit the 1Co 15:50
If anyone **d** not love the Lord, he 1Co 16:22
much more **d** the ministry of 2Co 3:9
according to what he **d** not have. 2Co 8:12
So then, **d** He who provides you with Ga 3:5
"CURSED IS EVERYONE WHO **D** NOT Ga 3:10
He **d** not say, "And to seeds," Ga 3:16
d not invalidate a covenant Ga 3:17
he **d** not differ at all from a Ga 4:1
BARREN WOMAN WHO **D** NOT BEAR; Ga 4:27
But what **d** the Scripture say? Ga 4:30
what **d** it mean except that He also Eph 4:9
just as Christ also **d** the church, Eph 5:29
whatever good thing each one **d**, Eph 6:8 4160
For he who **d** wrong will receive Col 3:25 91
For our exhortation **d** not *come* 1Th 2:3
If anyone **d** not obey our 2Th 3:14
(but if a man **d** not know how to 1Tm 3:5
anyone **d** not provide for his own, 1Tm 5:8
and **d** not agree with sound words, 1Tm 6:3
he **d** not win the prize unless he 2Tm 2:5
who **d** not need to be ashamed, 2Tm 2:15
He **d** not give help to angels, Heb 2:16
who **d** not need daily, like those Heb 7:27
whom *his* father **d** not discipline? Heb 12:7
and He Himself **d** not tempt anyone. Jas 1:13
for the anger of man **d** not achieve Jas 1:20
man will be blessed in what he **d**. Jas 1:25 4162
and yet **d** not bridle his tongue Jas 1:26
d not stumble in what he says, Jas 3:2
D a fountain send out from the Jas 3:11
thing to do and **d** not do it, Jas 4:17 4160
he **d** not resist you. Jas 5:6
and *so* **d** my son, Mark. 1Pe 5:13
and **d** not keep His commandments, 1Jn 2:4
and **d** not know where he is going 1Jn 2:11
but the one who **d** the will of God 1Jn 2:17 4160
the Son **d** not have the Father; 1Jn 2:23
reason the world **d** not know us, 1Jn 3:1
anyone who **d** not practice 1Jn 3:10
one who **d** not love his brother. 1Jn 3:10
He who **d** not love abides in death. 1Jn 3:14
d the love of God abide in him? 1Jn 3:17
if our heart **d** not condemn us, 1Jn 3:21
every spirit that **d** not confess Jesus 1Jn 4:3
not from God **d** not listen to us. 1Jn 4:6
who **d** not love does not know God, 1Jn 4:8
who does not love **d** not know God, 1Jn 4:8
for the one who **d** not love his 1Jn 4:20
the one who **d** not believe God has 1Jn 5:10
he who **d** not have the Son of God 1Jn 5:12
Son of God **d** not have the life. 1Jn 5:12
and the evil one **d** not touch him. 1Jn 5:18
d not abide in the teaching of Christ, 2Jn 1:9
of Christ, **d** not have God; 2Jn 1:9
you and **d** not bring this teaching, 2Jn 1:10
them, **d** not accept what we say. 3Jn 1:9
attention to his deeds which he **d**, 3Jn 1:10 4160
he himself **d** not receive the 3Jn 1:10
The one who **d** good is of God; 3Jn 1:11 15
one who **d** evil has not seen God. 3Jn 1:11 2554
and she **d** not want to repent of Rv 2:21
"Let the one who **d** wrong, still Rv 22:11 91

DOG

of Israel a **d** will not *even* bark, Ex 11:7 3611
the wages of a **d** into the house of the Dt 23:18 3611
with his tongue as a **d** laps, Jg 7:5 3611
"Am I a **d**, that you come to me 1Sa 17:43 3611
A dead **d**, a single flea? 1Sa 24:14 3611
should regard a dead **d** like me?" 2Sa 9:8 3611
dead **d** curse my lord the king? 2Sa 16:9 3611
is your servant, *who is but a* **d**, 2Ki 8:13 3611
only *life* from the power of the **d**. Ps 22:20 3611
at evening, they howl like a **d**, Ps 59:6 3611
at evening, they howl like a **d**, Ps 59:14 3611
Like a **d** that returns to its vomit Pr 26:11 3611
Like one who takes a **d** by the ears Pr 26:17 3611
live **d** is better than a dead lion. Ec 9:4 3611
"A **D** RETURNS TO ITS OWN VOMIT," 2Pe 2:22 2965

DOG'S

I a **d** head that belongs to Judah? 2Sa 3:8 3611
like the one who breaks a **d** neck; Is 66:3 3611

DOGS

you shall throw it to the **d**. Ex 22:31 3611
dies in the city the **d** will eat. 1Ki 14:11 3611
dies in the city the **d** will eat, 1Ki 16:4 3611
"In the place where the **d** licked 1Ki 21:19 3611
the **d** will lick up your blood, 1Ki 21:19 3611
'The **d** will eat Jezebel in the 1Ki 21:23 3611
dies in the city, the **d** will eat, 1Ki 21:24 3611
and the **d** licked up his blood 1Ki 22:38 3611
'The **d** shall eat Jezebel in 2Ki 9:10 3611
'In the property of Jezreel the **d** 2Ki 9:36 3611
to put with the **d** of my flock. Jb 30:1 3611
For **d** have surrounded me; Ps 22:16 3611
The tongue of your **d** *may have* its Ps 68:23 3611
of them are mute **d** unable to bark, Is 56:10 3611
And the **d** are greedy, they are not Is 56:11 3611
sword to slay, the **d** to drag off, Jer 15:3 3611
"Do not give what is holy to **d**, Mt 7:6 2965
bread and throw it to the **d**." Mt 15:26 2952
but even the **d** feed on the crumbs Mt 15:27 2952
bread and throw it to the **d**." Mk 7:27 2952
but even the **d** under the table Mk 7:28 2952
even the **d** were coming and licking Lk 16:21 2965
Beware of the **d**, beware of the Php 3:2 2965
Outside are the **d** and the Rv 22:15 2965

DOING

by **d** righteousness and justice, Gn 18:19 6213a
all that Laban has been **d** to you. Gn 31:12 6213a
You have done wrong in **d** this.'" Gn 44:5 6213a
all that he was **d** for the people, Ex 18:14 6213a
that you are **d** for the people? Ex 18:14 6213a
thing that you are **d** is not good. Ex 18:17 6213a
not follow the masses in **d** evil, Ex 23:2
anger and change Your mind about **d** Ex 32:12
sins unintentionally in **d** any of the Lv 4:27 6213a
for this is not my **d**. Nu 16:28 4480, 3820
you had committed in **d** what was evil Dt 9:18 6213a
at all what we are **d** here today, Dt 12:8 6213a
every man **d** whatever is right in Dt 12:8
for you will be **d** what is right in Dt 12:25 6213a
for you will be **d** what is good and Dt 12:28 6213a
and **d** what is right in the sight Dt 13:18 6213a
the words of this law by **d** them.' Dt 27:26 6213a
but you are **d** me wrong by making Jg 11:27 6213a
And what are you **d** in this *place?* Jg 18:3 6213a
"What are you **d**?" Jg 18:18 6213a
his sons were **d** to all Israel, 1Sa 2:22 6213a
so they are **d** to you also. 1Sa 8:8 6213a
are these Hebrews **d** *here?*" 1Sa 29:3
to find out all that you are **d**." 2Sa 3:25 6213a
the LORD by **d** evil in His sight? 2Sa 12:9 6213a
the people who were **d** the work. 1Ki 5:16 6213a
skill for **d** any work in bronze. 1Ki 7:14 6213a
So Hiram finished **d** all the work 1Ki 7:40 6213a
d according to all that I have 1Ki 9:4 6213a
ruled over the people **d** the work. 1Ki 9:23 6213a

d what is right in My sight and **1Ki 11:33** 6213a
d evil in the sight of the LORD, **1Ki 16:19** 6213a
"What are you **d** here, Elijah?" **1Ki 19:9** 6213a
"What are you **d** here, Elijah?" **1Ki 19:13** 6213a
and we are still **d** nothing to take **1Ki 22:3** 2814
d right in the sight of the LORD. **1Ki 22:43** 6213a
"We are not **d** right. **2Ki 7:9** 6213a
d evil in the sight of the LORD. **2Ki 21:16** 6213a
d the work for the service of the **1Ch 23:24** 6213a
So Huram finished **d** the work which **2Ch 4:11** 6213a
planned on **d** in the house of the LORD **2Ch 7:11** 6213a
"Consider what you are **d**, **2Ch 19:6** 6213a
d right in the sight of the LORD. **2Ch 20:32** 6213a
He acted wickedly in so **d**. **2Ch 20:35** 6213a
to your servants they are **d**. **2Ch 34:16** 6213a
"What is this thing you are **d**? **Ne 2:19** 6213a
"What are these feeble Jews **d**? **Ne 4:2** 6213a
one hand **d** the work and the other **Ne 4:17** 6213a
thing which you are **d** is not good; **Ne 5:9** 6213a
"I am **d** a great work and I cannot **Ne 6:3** 6213a
"What is this evil thing you are **d**, **Ne 13:17** 6213a
those who were **d** the king's business **Es 9:3** 6213a
'What are You **d**?' **Jb 9:12** 6213a
D great things which we cannot **Jb 37:5** 6213a
You who serve Him, **d** His will. **Ps 103:21** 6213a
This is the LORD's **d**; **Ps 118:23**
4480, 854
Who delight in **d** evil And rejoice **Pr 2:14** 6213a
D wickedness is like sport to a **Pr 10:23** 6213a
they do not know they are **d** evil. **Ec 5:1** 6213a
"What are you **d**?" **Ec 8:4** 6213a
intent on **d** evil will be cut off; **Is 29:20** 8245
say to the potter, 'What are you **d**?' **Is 45:9** 6213a
keeps his hand from **d** any evil." **Is 56:2** 6213a
you turn your foot From **d** your *own* **Is 58:13** 6213a
who rejoices in **d** righteousness, **Is 64:5** 6213a
are you **d** on the road to Egypt, **Jer 2:18**
are you **d** on the road to Assyria, **Jer 2:18**
"Do you not see what they are **d** **Jer 7:17** 6213a
can do good Who are accustomed to **d** **Jer 13:23** 7489a
day holy by **d** no work on it, **Jer 17:24** 6213a
sons of Judah have been **d** only evil **Jer 32:30** 6213a
you **d** great harm to yourselves, **Jer 44:7** 6213a
man, do you see what they are **d**, **Ezk 8:6** 6213a
said to you, 'What are you **d**?' **Ezk 12:9** 6213a
what these things that you are **d** mean **Ezk 24:19** 6213a
"I am not **d** *this* for your sake," **Ezk 36:32** 6213a
break away now from your sins by **d** **Da 4:27**
God, as he had been **d** previously. **Da 6:10** 5648
Because *I am* **d** something in your **Hab 1:5** 6466
what more are you **d** *than others?* **Mt 5:47** *4160*
know what your right hand is **d** **Mt 6:3** *4160*
'Friend, I am **d** you no wrong; **Mt 20:13** *91*
authority are You **d** these things, **Mt 21:23** *4160*
master finds so **d** when he comes. **Mt 24:46** *4160*
why are they **d** what is not lawful **Mk 2:24** *4160*
all that He was **d** and came to Him. **Mk 3:8** *4160*
'Why are you **d** this?' **Mk 11:3** *4160*
"What are you **d**, untying the colt?" **Mk 11:5** *4160*
authority are You **d** these things, **Mk 11:28** *4160*
out of him without **d** him any harm. **Lk 4:35** *984*
marveling at all that He was **d**, **Lk 9:43** *4160*
master finds so **d** when he comes. **Lk 12:43** *4160*
authority You are **d** these things, **Lk 20:2** *4160*
do not know what they are **d**." **Lk 23:34** *4160*
You show us as your authority for **d** **Jn 2:18** *4160*
His signs which He was **d**. **Jn 2:23** *4160*
was **d** these things on the Sabbath. **Jn 5:16** *4160*
is something He sees the Father **d**; **Jn 5:19** *4160*
all things that He Himself is **d**; **Jn 5:20** *4160*
see Your works which You are **d**. **Jn 7:3** *4160*
from him and knows what he is **d**, **Jn 7:51** *4160*
are **d** the deeds of your father." **Jn 8:41** *4160*
and were saying, "What are we **d**? **Jn 11:47** *4160*
see that you are not **d** any good; **Jn 12:19** *5623*
not know what his master is **d**; **Jn 15:15** *4160*
are **d** just as your fathers did. **Ac 7:51**
and *how* He went about **d** good and **Ac 10:38** *2109*
"Men, why are you **d** these things? **Ac 14:15** *4160*
continued **d** this for many days. **Ac 16:18** *4160*
Jewish chief priest, were **d** this. **Ac 19:14** *4160*
"What are you **d**, weeping and **Ac 21:13** *4160*
"This man is not **d** anything **Ac 26:31** *4238*
those who by perseverance in **d** good **Ro 2:7** *2041*
For what I am **d**, **Ro 7:15** *2716*
but I am **d** the very thing I hate. **Ro 7:15** *4160*
now, no longer am I the one **d** it, **Ro 7:17** *2716*
me, but the **d** of the good *is* not. **Ro 7:18** *2716*
am **d** the very thing I do not want, **Ro 7:20** *4160*
want, I am no longer the one **d** it, **Ro 7:20** *2716*
FOR IN SO **D** YOU WILL HEAP BURNING **Ro 12:20** *4160*
by His **d** you are in Christ Jesus, **1Co 1:30**
and in so **d** he is to eat of the bread **1Co 11:28**
for he is **d** the Lord's work, as I **1Co 16:10** *2038b*
But now finish **d** it also, **2Co 8:11** *4160*
But what I am **d** I will continue **2Co 11:12** *4160*
Let us not lose heart in **d** good, **Ga 6:9** *4160*
d the will of God from the heart. **Eph 6:6** *4160*
my circumstances, how I am **d**, **Eph 6:21** *4238*
even as *it has been* **d** in you also **Col 1:6**
another, just as you also are **d**. **1Th 5:11** *4160*
that you are **d** and will *continue to* **2Th 3:4** *4160*
life, **d** no work at all, **2Th 3:11** *2038b*
do not grow weary of **d** good. **2Th 3:13** *2569*
d nothing in a *spirit of* partiality. **1Tm 5:21** *4160*
do not neglect **d** good and sharing, **Heb 13:16** *2140*
AS YOURSELF," you are **d** well. **Jas 2:8** *4160*
d right you may silence the ignorance **1Pe 2:15** *15*
that you suffer for **d** what is **1Pe 3:17** *15*
rather than for **d** what is wrong. **1Pe 3:17** *2554*
Creator in **d** what is right. **1Pe 4:19** *16*
wrong as the wages of **d** wrong. **2Pe 2:13** *93*

DOINGS
not give an account of all His **d**? **Jb 33:13** 1697
I meditate on all Your **d**; **Ps 143:5** 6467
Are these His **d**?' **Mi 2:7** 4611

DOMAIN
his **d** *will be* a great dominion **Da 11:5** 4475
give You all this **d** and its glory; **Lk 4:6** *1849*
us from the **d** of darkness, **Col 1:13** *1849*
who did not keep their own **d**, **Jude 1:6** *746*

DOME
His vaulted **d** over the earth, **Am 9:6** 92

DOMINANT
Moab, The **d** heights of the Arnon. **Nu 21:28** 1167

DOMINATED
and with severity you have **d** them. **Ezk 34:4** 7287a

DOMINEERED
even their servants **d** the people. **Ne 5:15** 7980

DOMINION
"One from Jacob shall have **d**, **Nu 24:19** 7287a
For he had **d** over everything west **1Ki 4:24** 7287a
in his house nor in all his **d** **2Ki 20:13** 4475
Yours is the **d**, O LORD, and You **1Ch 29:11** 4467
"**D** and awe belong to Him Who **Jb 25:2** 4910
of His, In all places of His **d**; **Ps 103:22** 4475
His sanctuary, Israel, His **d**. **Ps 114:2** 4475
let any iniquity have **d** over me. **Ps 119:133** 7980
And Your **d** *endures* throughout all **Ps 145:13** 4475
in his house nor in all his **d** **Is 39:2** 4475
under his **d** and all the peoples, **Jer 34:1** 4475
And every land of their **d**. **Jer 51:28** 4475
And His **d** is from generation to **Da 4:3** 7985
your **d** to the end of the earth. **Da 4:22** 7985
His **d** is an everlasting dominion, **Da 4:34** 7985
His dominion is an everlasting **d**, **Da 4:34** 7985
"I make a decree that in all the **d** of **Da 6:26** 7985
And His **d** *will be* forever. **Da 6:26** 7985
four heads, and **d** was given to it. **Da 7:6** 7985
beasts, their **d** was taken away, **Da 7:12** 7985
"And to Him was given **d**, **Da 7:14** 7985
His **d** is an everlasting dominion **Da 7:14** 7985
d Which will not pass away; **Da 7:14** 7985
and his **d** will be taken away, **Da 7:26** 7985
'Then the sovereignty, the **d** and **Da 7:27** 7985
ascendancy over him and obtain **d**; **Da 11:5** 4910
domain *will be* a great **d** *indeed.* **Da 11:5** 4475
Even the former **d** will come, **Mi 4:8** 4475
And His **d** will be from sea to sea, **Zch 9:10** 4915a
and from the **d** of Satan to God, **Ac 26:18** *1849*
and authority and power and **d**, **Eph 1:21** *2963*
To Him *be* honor and eternal **d**! **1Tm 6:16** *2904*
the glory and **d** forever and ever. **1Pe 4:11** *2904*
To Him *be* **d** forever and ever. **1Pe 5:11** *2904*
glory, majesty, **d** and authority, **Jude 1:25** *2904*
glory and the **d** forever and ever. **Rv 1:6** *2904*
glory and **d** forever and ever." **Rv 5:13** *2904*

DOMINIONS
the **d** will serve and obey Him.' **Da 7:27** 7985
whether thrones or **d** or rulers or **Col 1:16** *2963*

DONE
completed His work which He had **d**, **Gn 2:2** 6213a
from all His work which He had **d**. **Gn 2:2** 6213a
"What is this you have **d**?" **Gn 3:13** 6213a
"Because you have **d** this, **Gn 3:14** 6213a
He said, "What have you **d**? **Gn 4:10** 6213a
every living thing, as I have **d**. **Gn 8:21** 6213a
his youngest son had **d** to him. **Gn 9:24** 6213a
"What is this you have **d** to me? **Gn 12:18** 6213a
"May the wrong **d** me be upon you. **Gn 16:5**
and see if they have **d** entirely **Gn 18:21** 6213a
of my hands I have **d** this." **Gn 20:5** 6213a
of your heart you have **d** this, **Gn 20:6** 6213a
"What have you **d** to us? **Gn 20:9** 6213a
You have **d** to me things that ought **Gn 20:9** 6213a
things that ought not to be **d**." **Gn 20:9** 6213a
that you have **d** this thing?" **Gn 20:10** 6213a
do not know who has **d** this thing; **Gn 21:26** 6213a
because you have **d** this thing and **Gn 22:16** 6213a
all the things that he had **d**. **Gn 24:66** 6213a
"What is this you have **d** to us? **Gn 26:10** 6213a
have **d** to you nothing but good and **Gn 26:29** 6213a
I have **d** as you told me. **Gn 27:19** 6213a
have **d** what I have promised you." **Gn 28:15** 6213a
"What is this you have **d** to me? **Gn 29:25** 6213a
"What have you **d** by deceiving me **Gn 31:26** 6213a
Now you have **d** foolishly. **Gn 31:28**
5528, 6213a
he had **d** a disgraceful thing in Israel **Gn 34:7** 6213a
such a thing ought not to be **d**. **Gn 34:7** 6213a
so that whatever was **d** there, **Gn 39:22** 6213a
and even here I have **d** nothing **Gn 40:15** 6213a
And thus it was **d** for them. **Gn 42:25** 6213a
is this that God has **d** to us?" **Gn 42:28** 6213a
have **d** wrong in doing this.'" **Gn 44:5** 7489a
"What is this deed that you have **d**? **Gn 44:15** 6213a
"Why have you **d** this thing, and **Ex 1:18** 6213a
what has been **d** to you in Egypt. **Ex 3:16** 6213a
he has **d** harm to this people, **Ex 5:23** 7489a
no work at all shall be **d** on them, **Ex 12:16** 6213a
Now the sons of Israel had **d** **Ex 12:35** 6213a
"What is this we have **d**, **Ex 14:5** 6213a
heard of all that God had **d** for **Ex 18:1** 6213a
all that the LORD had **d** to Pharaoh **Ex 18:8** 6213a
which the LORD had **d** to Israel, **Ex 18:9** 6213a
it shall be **d** to him according to **Ex 21:31** 6213a
'For six days work may be **d**, **Ex 31:15** 6213a
"For six days work may be **d**, **Ex 35:2** 6213a
commanded through Moses to be **d**, **Ex 35:29** 6213a
work and behold, they had **d** it; **Ex 39:43** 6213a
had commanded, this they had **d**. **Ex 39:43** 6213a
LORD has commanded not to be **d**, **Lv 4:2** 6213a
LORD has commanded not to be **d**, **Lv 4:13** 6213a
God has commanded not to be **d**, **Lv 4:22** 6213a
LORD has commanded not to be **d**, **Lv 4:27** 6213a
LORD has commanded not to be **d**, **Lv 5:17** 6213a
he may have **d** to incur guilt." **Lv 6:7** 6213a
to do as has been **d** this day, **Lv 8:34** 6213a
'You shall not do what is **d** in the **Lv 18:3** 4639
nor are you to do what is **d** in the **Lv 18:3** 4639
you have **d** all these abominations, **Lv 18:27** 6213a
'For six days work may be **d**, **Lv 23:3** 6213a
his neighbor, just as he has **d**, **Lv 24:19** 6213a
has done, so it shall be **d** to him: **Lv 24:19** 6213a
and all that is to be **d**, **Nu 4:26** 6213a
'Thus it shall be **d** for each ox, **Nu 15:11** 6213a
be, if it is **d** unintentionally, **Nu 15:24** 6213a
declared what should be **d** to him. **Nu 15:34** 6213a
have I **d** harm to any of them." **Nu 16:15** 7489a
that Israel had **d** to the Amorites. **Nu 22:2** 6213a
"What have I **d** to you, that you **Nu 22:28** 6213a
"What have you **d** to me? **Nu 23:11** 6213a
And to Israel, what God has **d**! **Nu 23:23** 6466
had **d** evil in the sight of the LORD **Nu 32:13** 6213a
you in all that you have **d**; **Dt 2:7** 3027
your God has **d** to these two kings; **Dt 3:21** 6213a
has **d** in the case of Baal-peor, **Dt 4:3** 6213a
Has *anything* been **d** like this great **Dt 4:32** 1961
They have **d** well in all that they **Dt 5:28** 3190
who has **d** these great and awesome **Dt 10:21** 6213a
hates they have **d** for their gods; **Dt 12:31** 6213a
abomination has been **d** among you, **Dt 13:14** 6213a
thing has been **d** in Israel, **Dt 17:4** 6213a
woman who has **d** this evil deed to **Dt 17:5** 6213a
which they have **d** for their gods, **Dt 20:18** 6213a
'Thus it is **d** to the man who does **Dt 25:9** 6213a
I have **d** according to all that **Dt 26:14** 6213a
has the LORD **d** thus to this land? **Dt 29:24** 6213a
the LORD has not **d** all this." **Dt 32:27** 6466
your God had **d** to the Red Sea, **Jos 4:23** 6213a
and tell me now what you have **d**. **Jos 7:19** 6213a
Joshua had **d** to Jericho and to Ai, **Jos 9:3** 6213a
of you, and have **d** this thing. **Jos 9:24** 6213a
he had **d** to Jericho and its king, **Jos 10:1** 6213a
so he had **d** to Ai and its king), **Jos 10:1** 6213a
he had **d** to the king of Jericho. **Jos 10:28** 6213a
he had **d** to the king of Jericho. **Jos 10:30** 6213a
to all that he had **d** to Libnah. **Jos 10:32** 6213a
to all that he had **d** to Lachish. **Jos 10:35** 6213a
to all that he had **d** to Eglon. **Jos 10:37** 6213a
Just as he had **d** to Hebron, so he **Jos 10:39** 6213a
had also **d** to Libnah and its king. **Jos 10:39** 6213a
we have **d** this out of concern, **Jos 22:24** 6213a
your God has **d** to all these nations **Jos 23:3** 6213a
God, as you have **d** to this day. **Jos 23:8** 6213a
you after He has **d** good to you." **Jos 24:20** 3190
LORD which He had **d** for Israel. **Jos 24:31** 6213a
as I have **d**, so God has repaid me." **Jg 1:7** 6213a
what is this you have **d**? **Jg 2:2** 6213a
LORD which He had **d** for Israel. **Jg 2:7** 6213a
work which He had **d** for Israel. **Jg 2:10** 6213a
d evil in the sight of the LORD. **Jg 3:12** 6213a
is this thing you have **d** to us, **Jg 8:1** 6213a
I **d** now in comparison with you? **Jg 8:2** 6213a
the good that he had **d** to Israel. **Jg 8:35** 6213a
so that the violence **d** to **Jg 9:24**
which he had **d** to his father in **Jg 9:56** 6213a
"Let this thing be **d** for me; **Jg 11:37** 6213a
father or mother what he had **d**. **Jg 14:6** 6213a
is this that you have **d** to us?" **Jg 15:11** 6213a
did to me, so I have **d** to them." **Jg 15:11** 6213a
"Thus and so has Micah **d** to me, **Jg 18:4** 6213a
"All that you have **d** for your **Ru 2:11** 6213a
all that the man had **d** for her. **Ru 3:16** 6213a
then He has **d** us this great evil. **1Sa 6:9** 6213a
the deeds which they have **d** since **1Sa 8:8** 6213a
so shall it be **d** to his oxen." **1Sa 11:7** 6213a
wickedness is great which you have **d** **1Sa 12:17** 6213a
great things He has **d** for you. **1Sa 12:24** 1431
"What have you **d**?" **1Sa 13:11** 6213a
"Tell me what you have **d**." **1Sa 14:43** 6213a
"What will be **d** for the man who **1Sa 17:26** 6213a
be **d** for the man who kills him." **1Sa 17:27** 6213a
"What have I **d** now? **1Sa 17:29** 6213a
him all that Saul had **d** to him. **1Sa 19:18** 6213a
said to Jonathan, "What have I **d**? **1Sa 20:1** 6213a
he be put to death? What has he **d**?" **1Sa 20:32** 6213a
today that you have **d** good to me, **1Sa 24:18** 6213a
what you have **d** to me this day. **1Sa 24:19** 6213a
thing that you have **d** is not good. **1Sa 26:16** 6213a
For what have I **d**? **1Sa 26:18** 6213a
'So has David **d** and so *has been* **1Sa 27:11** 6213a
"Behold, you know what Saul has **d**, **1Sa 28:9** 6213a
"The LORD has **d** accordingly **1Sa 28:17** 6213a
the LORD has **d** this thing to you **1Sa 28:18** 6213a
"But what have I **d**? **1Sa 29:8** 6213a
the Philistines had **d** to Saul, **1Sa 31:11** 6213a
because you have **d** this thing. **2Sa 2:6** 6213a
"What have you **d**? Behold, Abner **2Sa 3:24** 6213a
You have **d** all this greatness to **2Sa 7:21** 6213a
But the thing that David had **d** was **2Sa 11:27** 6213a
who has **d** this deserves to die. **2Sa 12:5** 6213a
is this thing that you have **d**? **2Sa 12:21** 6213a
such a thing is not **d** in Israel; **2Sa 13:12** 6213a
the other that you have **d** to me!" **2Sa 13:16** 6213a

servant Joab has **d** this thing. 2Sa 14:20 6213a
'Why have you **d** so?' " 2Sa 16:10 6213a
the concubine of Saul, had **d**, 2Sa 21:11 6213a
Kabzeel, who had **d** mighty deeds, 2Sa 23:20
sinned greatly in what I have **d**. 2Sa 24:10 6213a
and it is I who have **d** wrong; 2Sa 24:17 5753b
but these sheep, what have they **d**? 2Sa 24:17 6213a
"Why have you **d** so?" 1Ki 1:6 6213a
thing been **d** by my lord the king, 1Ki 1:27 1961
I have **d** according to your words. 1Ki 3:12 6213a
'Why has the LORD **d** thus to this 1Ki 9:8 6213a
as David his father *had* **d**. 1Ki 11:6
"Because you have **d** this, 1Ki 11:11
1961, 5973
of God had **d** that day in Bethel; 1Ki 13:11 6213a
you also have **d** more evil than all 1Ki 14:9 6213a
than all that their fathers had **d**, 1Ki 14:22 6213a
d all these things at Your word. 1Ki 18:36 6213a
Jezebel all that Elijah had **d**, 1Ki 19:1 6213a
again, for what have I **d** to you?" 1Ki 19:20 6213a
to all that the Amorites had **d**, 1Ki 21:26 6213a
to all that his father had **d**. 1Ki 22:53 6213a
"What then is to be **d** for her?" 2Ki 4:14 6213a
thing, would you not have **d** *it?* 2Ki 5:13 6213a
what the Arameans have **d** to us. 2Ki 7:12 6213a
great things that Elisha has **d**." 2Ki 8:4 6213a
just as the house of Ahab had **d**, 2Ki 8:18 6213a
like the house of Ahab *had* **d**, 2Ki 8:27
for the LORD has **d** what He spoke 2Ki 10:10 6213a
"Because you have **d** well in 2Ki 10:30 2895
and have **d** to the house of Ahab 2Ki 10:30 6213a
all that Joash his father had **d**. 2Ki 14:3 6213a
all that his father Amaziah had **d**. 2Ki 15:3 6213a
of the LORD, as his fathers had **d**; 2Ki 15:9 6213a
all that his father Uzziah had **d**. 2Ki 15:34 6213a
as his father David *had* **d**. 2Ki 16:2
as *he had* **d** year by year; 2Ki 17:4
all that his father David had **d**. 2Ki 18:3 6213a
at Lachish, saying, "I have **d** wrong. 2Ki 18:14 2398
Assyria have **d** to all the lands, 2Ki 19:11 6213a
d what is good in Your sight." 2Ki 20:3 6213a
as Ahab king of Israel had **d**, 2Ki 21:3 6213a
of Judah has **d** these abominations, 2Ki 21:11 6213a
having **d** wickedly more than all 2Ki 21:11 7489a
they have **d** evil in My sight, 2Ki 21:15 6213a
as Manasseh his father had **d**. 2Ki 21:20 6213a
d against the altar of Bethel." 2Ki 23:17 6213a
them just as he had **d** in Bethel. 2Ki 23:19 6213a
to all that his fathers had **d**. 2Ki 23:32 6213a
to all that his fathers had **d**. 2Ki 23:37 6213a
according to all that he had **d**, 2Ki 24:3 6213a
to all that his father had **d**. 2Ki 24:9 6213a
to all that Jehoiakim had **d**. 2Ki 24:19 6213a
the Philistines had **d** to Saul, 1Ch 10:11 6213a
wonderful deeds which He has **d**, 1Ch 16:12 6213a
in that I have **d** this thing. 1Ch 21:8 6213a
for I have **d** very foolishly." 1Ch 21:8 5528
has sinned and **d** very wickedly, 1Ch 21:17 7489a
but these sheep, what have they **d**? 1Ch 21:17 6213a
and My ordinances, as is **d** now.' 1Ch 28:7
all the work **d** by the craftsmen. 1Ch 29:5 3027
'Why has the LORD **d** thus to this 2Ch 7:21 6213a
because he had **d** well in Israel 2Ch 24:16 6213a
you, because you have **d** this and 2Ch 25:16 6213a
all that his father Amaziah had **d**. 2Ch 26:4 6213a
all that his father Uzziah had **d**; 2Ch 27:2 6213a
LORD as David his father *had* **d**. 2Ch 28:1
all that his father David had **d**. 2Ch 29:2 6213a
have **d** evil in the sight of the LORD 2Ch 29:6 6213a
have **d** to all the peoples of the lands? 2Ch 32:13 6213a
LORD as Manasseh his father had **d**, 2Ch 33:22 6213a
LORD as his father Manasseh had **d**, 2Ch 33:23 3665
of you, it shall be **d** diligently, Ezr 7:21 5648
let it be **d** with zeal for the Ezr 7:23 5648
let it be **d** according to the law. Ezr 10:3 6213a
Nor *can* the task *be* **d** in one Ezr 10:13
where I had gone or what I had **d**; Ne 2:16 6213a
all that I have **d** for this people. Ne 5:19 6213a
as you are saying have not been **d**, Ne 6:8 1961
the work and it will not be **d**." Ne 6:9 6213a
The sons of Israel had indeed not **d** so Ne 8:17 6213a
that Eliashib had **d** for Tobiah, Ne 13:7 6213a
The drinking was **d** according to Es 1:8
what is to be **d** with Queen Vashti, Es 1:15 6213a
Vashti and what she had **d** and what Es 2:1 6213a
as she had **d** when under his care. Es 2:20 1961
learned all that had been **d**, Es 4:1 6213a
of the kingdom it shall be **d**." Es 5:6 6213a
"Nothing has been **d** for him." Es 6:3 6213a
"What is to be **d** for the man whom Es 6:6 6213a
'Thus it shall be **d** to the man Es 6:9 6213a
"Thus it shall be **d** to the man Es 6:11 6213a
of the kingdom it shall be **d**." Es 7:2 6213a
What then have they **d** in the rest Es 9:12 6213a
It shall also be **d**." Es 9:12 6213a
commanded that it should be **d** so; Es 9:14 6213a
This was **d** on the thirteenth day Es 9:17
What have I **d** to You, O watcher Jb 7:20 6466
the hand of the LORD has **d** this, Jb 12:9 6213a
will repay him for what he has **d**? Jb 21:31 6213a
If I have **d** iniquity, I will not do it Jb 34:32 6466
'You have **d** wrong'? Jb 36:23 6466
O LORD my God, if I have **d** this, Ps 7:3 6213a
And all His work is **d** in Ps 33:4
For He spoke, and it was **d**; Ps 33:9 1961
Because it is You who have **d** *it.* Ps 39:9 6213a
are the wonders which You have **d**, Ps 40:5 6213a
"These things you have **d** and Ps 50:21 6213a
And **d** what is evil in Your sight, Ps 51:4 6213a

forever, because You have **d** *it,* Ps 52:9 6213a
And will consider what He has **d**. Ps 64:9 4639
tell of what He has **d** for my soul. Ps 66:16 6213a
You who have **d** great things; Ps 71:19 6213a
His wondrous works that He has **d**. Ps 78:4 6213a
made me glad by what You have **d**, Ps 92:4 6467
For He has **d** wonderful things, Ps 98:1 6213a
His wonders which He has **d**, Ps 105:5 6213a
Who had **d** great things in Egypt, Ps 106:21 6213a
You, LORD, have **d** it. Ps 109:27 6213a
have **d** justice and righteousness; Ps 119:121 6213a
and what more shall be **d** to you, Ps 120:3 3254
has **d** great things for them." Ps 126:2 6213a
LORD has **d** great things for us; Ps 126:3 6213a
cause, If he has **d** you no harm. Pr 3:30 1580
shall do to him as he has **d** to me; Pr 24:29 6213a
"I have **d** no wrong." Pr 30:20 6466
"Many daughters have **d** nobly, Pr 31:29 6213a
been **d** is that which will be done. Ec 1:9 6213a
been done is that which will be **d**. Ec 1:9 6213a
all that has been **d** under heaven. Ec 1:13 6213a
which have been **d** under the sun, Ec 1:14 6213a
my activities which my hands had **d** Ec 2:11 6213a
except what has already been **d**? Ec 2:12 6213a
for the work which had been **d** Ec 2:17 6213a
which God has **d** from the beginning Ec 3:11 6213a
which were being **d** under the sun. Ec 4:1 6213a
activity that is **d** under the sun. Ec 4:3 6213a
skill which is **d** is *the result of* rivalry Ec 4:4 4639
deed that has been **d** under the sun Ec 8:9 6213a
futility which is **d** on the earth, Ec 8:14 6213a
which has been **d** on the earth Ec 8:16 6213a
which has been **d** under the sun. Ec 8:17 6213a
in all that is **d** under the sun, Ec 9:3 6213a
in all that is **d** under the sun. Ec 9:6 6213a
what he deserves will be **d** to him. Is 3:11 6213a
vineyard that I have not **d** in it? Is 5:4 6213a
have **d** to Samaria and her idols?" Is 10:11 6213a
for He has **d** excellent things; Is 12:5 6213a
And whose deeds are **d** in a dark Is 29:15 6213a
are far away, hear what I have **d**; Is 33:13 6213a
Assyria have **d** to all the lands, Is 37:11 6213a
d what is good in Your sight." Is 38:3 6213a
to me, and He Himself has **d** it; Is 38:15 6213a
the hand of the LORD has **d** this, Is 41:20 6213a
O heavens, for the LORD has **d** *it!* Is 44:23 6213a
I have **d** *it,* and I will carry *you;* Is 46:4 6213a
things which have not been **d**, Is 46:10 6213a
'My idol has **d** them, And my graven Is 48:5 6213a
Because He had **d** no violence, Is 53:9 6213a
a nation that has **d** righteousness And Is 58:2 6213a
"Have you not **d** this to yourself By Jer 2:17 6213a
Know what you have **d**! Jer 2:23 6213a
spoken And have **d** evil things, Jer 3:5 6213a
'After she has **d** all these things she Jer 3:7 6213a
Thus it will be **d** to them!" Jer 5:13 6213a
our God **d** all these things to us?' Jer 5:19 6213a
of the abomination they have **d**? Jer 6:15 6213a
you have **d** all these things," Jer 7:13 6213a
"For the sons of Judah have **d** Jer 7:30 6213a
wickedness, Saying, 'What have I **d**?' Jer 8:6 6213a
of the abomination they had **d**? Jer 8:12 6213a
When she has **d** many vile deeds? Jer 11:15 6213a
which they have **d** to provoke Me by Jer 11:17 6213a
one who has **d** all these things. Jer 14:22 6213a
'You too have **d** evil, *even* more Jer 16:12 6213a
Has **d** a most appalling thing. Jer 18:13 6213a
LORD **d** thus to this great city?' Jer 22:8 6213a
I have **d** these things to you. Jer 30:15 6213a
Israel For all that they have **d**," Jer 31:37 6213a
they have **d** nothing of all that Jer 32:23 6213a
they have **d** to provoke Me to anger Jer 32:32 6213a
and **d** what is right in My sight, Jer 34:15 6213a
and have **d** according to all that Jer 35:10 6213a
and **d** according to all that he Jer 35:18 6213a
they have **d** to Jeremiah the prophet Jer 38:9 6213a
it on and **d** just as He promised. Jer 40:3 6213a
the son of Nethaniah had **d**. Jer 41:11 6213a
As she has **d** *to others, so* do to Jer 50:15 6213a
According to all that she has **d**, Jer 50:29 6213a
have **d** in Zion before your eyes," Jer 51:24 6213a
"May the violence **d** to me and to Jer 51:35
like all that Jehoiakim had **d**. Jer 52:2 6213a
They are glad that You have **d** *it.* La 1:21 6213a
The LORD has **d** what He purposed; La 2:17 6213a
he has **d** shall not be remembered; Ezk 3:20 6213a
do among you what I have not **d**, Ezk 5:9 6213a
"I have **d** just as You have Ezk 9:11 6213a
As I have **d**, so it will be done to Ezk 12:11 6213a
done, so it will be **d** to them; Ezk 12:11 6213a
d in vain whatever I did to it," Ezk 14:23 6213a
or **d** according to their abominations; Ezk 16:47 6213a
have not **d** as you and your Ezk 16:48 6213a
as you and your daughters have **d**. Ezk 16:48 6213a
feel ashamed for all that you have **d** Ezk 16:54 6213a
also do with you as you have **d**, Ezk 16:59 6213a
you for all that you have **d**," Ezk 16:63 6213a
all My statutes and **d** them, Ezk 18:19 6213a
All his righteous deeds which he has **d** Ezk 18:24 6213a
the evil things that you have **d**. Ezk 20:43 6213a
"Her priests have **d** violence to Ezk 22:26 2554
'These things will be **d** to you Ezk 23:30 6213a
"Again, they have **d** this to Me: Ezk 23:38 6213a
not commit lewdness as you have **d**. Ezk 23:48
'You will do as I have **d**; Ezk 24:22 6213a
to all that he has **d** you will do; Ezk 24:24 6213a
I, the LORD, have spoken and **d** it," Ezk 37:14 6213a
it is coming and it shall be **d**," Ezk 39:8 1961
ashamed of all that they have **d**, Ezk 43:11 6213a

and of all that shall be **d** in it. Ezk 44:14 6213a
the Most High God has **d** for me. Da 4:2 5648
'What have You **d**?' Da 4:35 5648
heaven there has not been **d** *anything* Da 9:12 6213a
like what was **d** to Jerusalem. Da 9:12 6213a
to all His deeds which He has **d**, Da 9:14 6213a
that which is decreed will be **d**. Da 11:36 6213a
Thus it will be **d** to you at Bethel Hos 10:15 6213a
up, For it has **d** great things." Jl 2:20 6213a
For the LORD has **d** great things. Jl 2:21 6213a
violence **d** to the sons of Judah, Jl 3:19
in a city has not the LORD **d** it? Am 3:6 6213a
As you have **d**, it will be done to Ob 1:15 6213a
have done, it will be **d** to you. Ob 1:15 6213a
have **d** as You have pleased." Jon 1:14 6213a
"My people, what have I **d** to you, Mi 6:3 6213a
and violence **d** to the land, Hab 2:8
"For the violence **d** to Lebanon will Hab 2:17
and violence **d** to the land Hab 2:17
They have **d** violence to the law. Zph 3:4 2554
as I have **d** these many years?" Zch 7:3 6213a
"But not one has **d** *so* who has a Mal 2:15 6213a
and your Father who sees *what is* **d** Mt 6:4
and your Father who sees *what is* **d** Mt 6:6
Your will be **d**, On earth as it is Mt 6:10 *1096*
and your Father who sees *what is* **d** Mt 6:18
d for you as you have believed." Mt 8:13 *1096*
"It shall be **d** to you according to your Mt 9:29 *1096*
which most of His miracles were **d**, Mt 11:20 *1096*
'An enemy has **d** this!' Mt 13:28 *4160*
be **d** for you as you wish." Mt 15:28 *1096*
it shall be **d** for them by My Mt 18:19 *1096*
wonderful things that He had **d**, Mt 21:15 *4160*
do what was **d** to the fig tree, Mt 21:21
d without neglecting the others. Mt 23:23 *4160*
'Well **d**, good and faithful slave. Mt 25:21 *2095*
'Well **d**, good and faithful slave. Mt 25:23 *2095*
For she has **d** a good deed to Me. Mt 26:10 *2038b*
what this woman has **d** will also Mt 26:13 *4160*
I drink it, Your will be **d**." Mt 26:42 *1096*
"Why, what evil has He **d**?" Mt 27:23 *4160*
things the Lord has **d** for you, Mk 5:19 *4160*
great things Jesus had **d** for him; Mk 5:20 *4160*
to see the woman who had **d** this. Mk 5:32 *4160*
all that they had **d** and taught. Mk 6:30 *4160*
"He has **d** all things well; Mk 7:37 *4160*
She has **d** a good deed to Me. Mk 14:6 *2038b*
"She has **d** what she could; Mk 14:8 *4160*
what this woman has **d** Mk 14:9 *4160*
"Why, what evil has He **d**?" Mk 15:14 *4160*
d to me according to your word." Lk 1:38 *1096*
One has **d** great things for me; Lk 1:49 *4160*
has **d** mighty deeds with His arm; Lk 1:51 *4160*
wicked things which Herod had **d**, Lk 3:19 *4160*
we heard was **d** at Capernaum, Lk 4:23 *1096*
When they had **d** this, Lk 5:6 *4160*
great things God has **d** for you." Lk 8:39 *4160*
great things Jesus had **d** for him. Lk 8:39 *4160*
to Him of all that they had **d**. Lk 9:10 *4160*
d without neglecting the others. Lk 11:42 *4160*
days in which work should be **d**; Lk 13:14 *2038b*
glorious things being **d** by Him. Lk 13:17 *1096*
what you commanded has been **d**, Lk 14:22 *1096*
we have **d** *only* that which we ought Lk 17:10 *4160*
that which we ought to have **d**.' Lk 17:10 *4160*
know what business they had **d**. Lk 19:15 *1281*
'Well **d**, good slave, because you Lk 19:17 *2095*
yet not My will, but Yours be **d**." Lk 22:42 *1096*
deserving death has been **d** by Him. Lk 23:15 *4238*
"Why, what evil has this man **d**? Lk 23:22 *4160*
this man has **d** nothing wrong." Lk 23:41 *4238*
me all the things that I *have* **d**; Jn 4:29 *4160*
me all the things that I *have* **d**." Jn 4:39 *4160*
to Mary, and saw what He had **d**, Jn 11:45 *4160*
them the things which Jesus had **d**. Jn 11:46 *4160*
they had **d** these things to Him. Jn 12:16 *4160*
"Do you know what I have **d** to you? Jn 13:12 *4160*
wish, and it will be **d** for you. Jn 15:7 *1096*
"If I had not **d** among them the Jn 15:24 *4160*
"But *they have* **d** *this* to fulfill Jn 15:25
what have You **d**?" Jn 18:35 *4160*
in what name, have you **d** this?" Ac 4:7 *4160*
for a benefit **d** to a sick man, Ac 4:9 *2108*
was being **d** by the angel was real, Ac 12:9 *1096*
and wonders be **d** by their hands. Ac 14:3 *1096*
crowds saw what Paul had **d**, Ac 14:11 *4160*
to report all things that God had **d** Ac 14:27 *4160*
all that God had **d** with them. Ac 15:4 *4160*
wonders God had **d** through them Ac 15:12 *4160*
"The will of the Lord be **d**!" Ac 21:14 *1096*
which God had **d** among the Gentiles Ac 21:19 *4160*
"What, then, is *to be* **d**? They Ac 21:22
who he was and what he had **d**. Ac 21:33 *4160*
I have **d** no wrong to *the* Jews, as Ac 25:10 *91*
this has not been **d** in a corner. Ac 26:26 *4238*
had **d** nothing against our people or Ac 28:17 *4160*
body of sin might be **d** away with, Ro 6:6 *2673*
had not **d** anything good or bad, Ro 9:11 *4238*
the one who had **d** this deed would 1Co 5:2 *4238*
that it will be **d** so in my case; 1Co 9:15 *1096*
of prophecy, they will be **d** away; 1Co 13:8 *2673*
is knowledge, it will be **d** away. 1Co 13:8 *2673*
comes, the partial will be **d** away. 1Co 13:10 *2673*
all things be **d** for edification. 1Co 14:26 *1096*
But all things must be **d** properly 1Co 14:40 *1096*
Let all that you do be **d** in love. 1Co 16:14 *1096*
body, according to what he has **d**, 2Co 5:10 *4238*
You have **d** me no wrong; Ga 4:12 *91*
which are **d** by them in secret. Eph 5:12 *1096*

evil day, and having **d** everything, **Eph 6:13** *2716*
you have **d** well to share *with me* **Php 4:14** *4160*
of the wrong which he has **d**, **Col 3:25** *91*
which we have **d** in righteousness, **Ti 3:5** *4160*
when you have **d** the will of God, **Heb 10:36** *4160*
they have **d** in an ungodly way, **Jude 1:15** *764*
from the throne, saying, "It is **d**." **Rv 16:17** *1096*
"It is **d**. I am the Alpha and the **Rv 21:6** *1096*
man according to what he has **d**. **Rv 22:12** *2041, 1510*

DONKEY
"He will be a wild **d** of a man, **Gn 16:12** 6501
in the morning and saddled his **d**, **Gn 22:3** 2543
"Stay here with the **d**, **Gn 22:5** 2543
his **d** fodder at the lodging place, **Gn 42:27** 2543
and when each man loaded his **d**, **Gn 44:13** 2543
"Issachar is a strong **d**, **Gn 49:14** 2543
his sons and mounted them on a **d**, **Ex 4:20** 2543
a **d** you shall redeem with a lamb, **Ex 13:13** 2543
ox or his **d** or anything that belongs **Ex 20:17** 2543
and an ox or a **d** falls into it, **Ex 21:33** 2543
whether an ox or a **d** or a sheep, **Ex 22:4** 2543
whether it is for ox, for **d**, **Ex 22:9** 2543
"If a man gives his neighbor a **d**, **Ex 22:10** 2543
enemy's ox or his **d** wandering away, **Ex 23:4** 2543
"If you see the **d** of one who **Ex 23:5** 2543
that your ox and your **d** may rest, **Ex 23:12** 2543
lamb the first offspring from a **d**; **Ex 34:20** 2543
not taken a single **d** from them, **Nu 16:15** 2543
in the morning, and saddled his **d** and **Nu 22:21** 860
Now he was riding on his **d** and his **Nu 22:22** 860
When the **d** saw the angel of the **Nu 22:23** 860
the **d** turned off from the way and **Nu 22:23** 860
d to turn her back into the way. **Nu 22:23** 860
the **d** saw the angel of the LORD, **Nu 22:25** 860
the **d** saw the angel of the LORD, **Nu 22:27** 860
and struck the **d** with his stick. **Nu 22:27** 860
LORD opened the mouth of the **d**, **Nu 22:28** 860
Then Balaam said to the **d**, **Nu 22:29** 860
The **d** said to Balaam, **Nu 22:30** 860
"Am I not your **d** on which you **Nu 22:30** 860
struck your **d** these three times? **Nu 22:32** 860
"But the **d** saw me and turned **Nu 22:33** 860
female servant or your ox or your **d** **Dt 5:14** 2543
his ox or his **d** or anything that **Dt 5:21** 2543
"Thus you shall do with his **d**, **Dt 22:3** 2543
not see your countryman's **d** or his ox **Dt 22:4** 2543
plow with an ox and a **d** together. **Dt 22:10** 2543
d shall be torn away from you, **Dt 28:31** 2543
and old, and ox and sheep and **d**, **Jos 6:21** 2543
So she alighted from the **d**, **Jos 15:18** 2543
Then she alighted from her **d**, **Jg 1:14** 2543
as well as no sheep, ox, or **d**. **Jg 6:4** 2543
He found a fresh jawbone of a **d**, **Jg 15:15** 2543
"With the jawbone of a **d**, **Jg 15:16** 2543
With the jawbone of a **d** **Jg 15:16** 2543
Then he placed her on the **d**; **Jg 19:28** 2543
I taken, or whose **d** have I taken, **1Sa 12:3** 2543
ox and sheep, camel and **d**.' " **1Sa 15:3** 2543
Jesse took a **d** *loaded with* **1Sa 16:20** 2543
came about as she was riding on her **d** **1Sa 25:20** 2543
hurried and dismounted from her **d**, **1Sa 25:23** 2543
quickly arose, and rode on a **d**, **1Sa 25:42** 2543
he saddled *his* **d** and arose and **2Sa 17:23** 2543
'I will saddle a **d** for myself that **2Sa 19:26** 2543
Shimei arose and saddled his **d**, **1Ki 2:40** 2543
"Saddle the **d** for me." **1Ki 13:13** 2543
So they saddled the **d** for him and **1Ki 13:13** 2543
that he saddled the **d** for him, **1Ki 13:23** 2543
with the **d** standing beside it; **1Ki 13:24** 2543
"Saddle the **d** for me." **1Ki 13:27** 2543
road with the **d** and the lion standing **1Ki 13:28** 2543
not eaten the body nor torn the **d**. **1Ki 13:28** 2543
man of God and laid it on the **d** and **1Ki 13:29** 2543
a **d** and said to her servant, **2Ki 4:24** 860
the wild **d** bray over *his* grass, **Jb 6:5** 6501
foal of a wild **d** is born a man. **Jb 11:12** 6501
"Who sent out the wild **d** free? **Jb 39:5** 6501
loosed the bonds of the swift **d**, **Jb 39:5** 6171
for the horse, a bridle for the **d**, **Pr 26:3** 2543
owner, And a **d** its master's manger, **Is 1:3** 2543
let out freely the ox and the **d**. **Is 32:20** 2543
d accustomed to the wilderness, **Jer 2:24** 6501
Assyria, *Like* a wild **d** all alone; **Hos 8:9** 6501
Humble, and mounted on a **d**, **Zch 9:9** 2543
Even on a colt, the foal of a **d**. **Zch 9:9** 860
horse, the mule, the camel, the **d** and **Zch 14:15** 2543
you will find a **d** tied *there* and a colt **Mt 21:2** *3688*
GENTLE, AND MOUNTED ON A **D**, **Mt 21:5** *3688*
and brought the **d** and the colt, **Mt 21:7** *3688*
his ox or his **d** from the stall and **Lk 13:15** *3688*
Jesus, finding a young **d**, **Jn 12:14** *3678*
for a mute **d**, speaking with a **2Pe 2:16** *5268*

DONKEY'S
And his **d** colt to the choice vine; **Gn 49:11** 860
until a **d** head was sold for eighty **2Ki 6:25** 2543
"He will be buried with a **d** burial, **Jer 22:19** 2543
IS COMING, SEATED ON A **D** COLT." **Jn 12:15** *3688*

DONKEYS
and gave him sheep and oxen and **d** **Gn 12:16** 2543
servants and female **d** and camels. **Gn 12:16** 860
and maids, and camels and **d**. **Gn 24:35** 2543
male servants and camels and **d**. **Gn 30:43** 2543
I have oxen and **d** *and* flocks **Gn 32:5** 2543
female **d** and ten male donkeys. **Gn 32:15** 860
female donkeys and ten male **d**. **Gn 32:15** 5895
and their herds and their **d**, **Gn 34:28** 2543
the **d** of his father Zibeon. **Gn 36:24** 2543
loaded their **d** with their grain and **Gn 42:26** 2543
take us for slaves with our **d**." **Gn 43:18** 2543
and he gave their **d** fodder. **Gn 43:24** 2543
were sent away, they with their **d**. **Gn 44:3** 2543
ten **d** loaded with the best things **Gn 45:23** 2543
and ten female **d** loaded with grain **Gn 45:23** 860
flocks and the herds and the **d**; **Gn 47:17** 2543
field, on the horses, on the **d**, **Ex 9:3** 2543
and of the **d** and of the sheep; **Nu 31:28** 2543
cattle, of the **d** and of the sheep, **Nu 31:30** 2543
and 61,000 **d**, **Nu 31:34** 2543
and the **d** were 30,500, from which **Nu 31:39** 2543
and 30,500 **d**, **Nu 31:45** 2543
his daughters, his oxen, his **d**, **Jos 7:24** 2543
and took worn-out sacks on their **d**, **Jos 9:4** 2543
"You who ride on white **d**, **Jg 5:10** 860
thirty sons who rode on thirty **d**, **Jg 10:4** 5895
grandsons who rode on seventy **d**; **Jg 12:14** 5895
him his servant and a pair of **d**. **Jg 19:3** 2543
were with him a pair of saddled **d**; **Jg 19:10** 2543
both straw and fodder for our **d**, **Jg 19:19** 2543
his house and gave the **d** fodder, **Jg 19:21** 2543
your best young men and your **d** and **1Sa 8:16** 2543
Now the **d** of Kish, Saul's father, **1Sa 9:3** 860
and arise, go search for the **d**." **1Sa 9:3** 860
cease to be concerned about the **d** **1Sa 9:5** 860
"As for your **d** which were **1Sa 9:20** 860
'The **d** which you went to look for **1Sa 10:2** 860
the **d** and is anxious for you, **1Sa 10:2** 860
"To look for the **d**. **1Sa 10:14** 860
that the **d** had been found." **1Sa 10:16** 860
also oxen, **d**, and sheep *he struck* **1Sa 22:19** 2543
of figs, and loaded *them* on **d**. **1Sa 25:18** 2543
away the sheep, the cattle, the **d**, **1Sa 27:9** 2543
him with a couple of saddled **d**, **2Sa 16:1** 2543
"The **d** are for the king's **2Sa 16:2** 2543
of the servants and one of the **d**, **2Ki 4:22** 860
and their horses and their **d**, **2Ki 7:7** 2543
the horses tied and the **d** tied, **2Ki 7:10** 2543
camels, 250,000 sheep, 2,000 **d**; **1Ch 5:21** 2543
and Naphtali, brought food on **d**, **1Ch 12:40** 2543
Meronothite had charge of the **d**. **1Ch 27:30** 860
led all their feeble ones on **d**, **2Ch 28:15** 2543
their camels, 435; *their* **d**, 6,720. **Ezr 2:67** 2543
their camels, 435; *their* **d**, 6,720. **Ne 7:69** 2543
of grain and loading *them* on **d**, **Ne 13:15** 2543
500 yoke of oxen, 500 female **d**, **Jb 1:3** 860
and the **d** feeding beside them, **Jb 1:14** 860
drive away the **d** of the orphans; **Jb 24:3** 2543
as wild **d** in the wilderness They **Jb 24:5** 6501
yoke of oxen and 1,000 female **d**. **Jb 42:12** 860
The wild **d** quench their thirst. **Ps 104:11** 6501
horsemen in pairs, A train of **d**, **Is 21:7** 2543
their riches on the backs of young **d** **Is 30:6** 5895
Also the oxen and the **d** which work **Is 30:24** 5895
forever, A delight for wild **d**, **Is 32:14** 6501
wild **d** stand on the bare heights; **Jer 14:6** 6501
whose flesh is *like* the flesh of **d** **Ezk 23:20** 2543
place *was* with the wild **d**. **Da 5:21** 6167

DONNING
of fine clothes, a **d** of sackcloth; **Is 3:24** 4228

DOOM
appoint over them four kinds *of* **d**," **Jer 15:3**
'Your **d** has come to you, O **Ezk 7:7** 6843
Your **d** has gone forth; **Ezk 7:10** 6843
A time *of* **d** for the nations. **Ezk 30:3**
and to this **d** they were also **1Pe 2:8**

DOOMED
d to eat their own dung and drink **2Ki 18:27**
preserve those who are **d** to die. **Ps 79:11** 1121
free those who were **d** to death, **Ps 102:20** 1121
d to eat their own dung and drink **Is 36:12**
Because the LORD our God has **d** us **Jer 8:14** 1826a
"Pasture the flock **d** to **Zch 11:4**
So I pastured the flock **d** to **Zch 11:7**

DOOR
well, sin is crouching at the **d**; **Gn 4:7** 6607
d of the ark in the side of it; **Gn 6:16** 6607
the tent **d** in the heat of the day. **Gn 18:1** 6607
ran from the tent **d** to meet them and **Gn 18:2** 6607
Sarah was listening at the tent **d**, **Gn 18:10** 6607
and shut the **d** behind him, **Gn 19:6** 1817
Lot and came near to break the **d**. **Gn 19:9** 1817
house with them, and shut the **d**. **Gn 19:10** 1817
the **d** of his house until morning. **Ex 12:22** 6607
the LORD will pass over the **d** and **Ex 12:23** 6607
him to the **d** or the doorpost. **Ex 21:6** 1817
it through his ear into the **d**, **Dt 15:17** 1817
the house, pounding the **d**; **Jg 19:22** 1817
But Uriah slept at the **d** of the **2Sa 11:9** 6607
and lock the **d** behind her." **2Sa 13:17** 1817
out and locked the **d** behind her. **2Sa 13:18** 1817
of the one **d** turned on pivots, **1Ki 6:34** 1817
of the other **d** turned on pivots. **1Ki 6:34** 1817
the **d** behind you and your sons, **2Ki 4:4** 1817
the **d** behind her and her sons; **2Ki 4:5** 1817
and shut *the* **d** behind him **2Ki 4:21**
and shut the **d** behind them both and **2Ki 4:33** 1817
shut the **d** and hold the door shut **2Ki 6:32** 1817
and hold the **d** shut against him. **2Ki 6:32** 1817
the **d** and flee and do not wait." **2Ki 9:3** 1817
Then he opened the **d** and fled. **2Ki 9:10** 1817
guarded the **d** of the king's house. **2Ch 12:10** 6607
from those who guarded the **d**, **Es 2:21** 5592b
Keep watch over the **d** of my lips. **Ps 141:3** 1800a
do not go near the **d** of her house, **Pr 5:8** 6607
raises his **d** seeks destruction. **Pr 17:19** 6607
As the **d** turns on its hinges, So **Pr 26:14** 1817
But if she is a **d**, We will **SS 8:9** 1817
"Behind the **d** and the **Is 57:8** 1817
from *one* **d** to *the* door opposite. **Ezk 40:13** 6607
from *one* door to *the* **d** opposite. **Ezk 40:13** 6607
the sanctuary each had a double **d**. **Ezk 41:23** 1817
d and two leaves for the other. **Ezk 41:24** 1817
a hundred cubits, *was* the north **d**; **Ezk 42:2** 6607
their **d** post beside My door post, **Ezk 43:8** 4201
their door post beside My **d** post, **Ezk 43:8** 4201
it on the **d** posts of the house, **Ezk 45:19** 4201
me back to the **d** of the house; **Ezk 47:1** 6607
Nebuchadnezzar came near to the **d** **Da 3:26** 8651
valley of Achor as a **d** of hope. **Hos 2:15** 6607
close your **d** and pray **Mt 6:6** *2374*
that He is near, *right* at the **d**. **Mt 24:33** *2374*
and the **d** was shut. **Mt 25:10** *2374*
whole city had gathered at the **d**. **Mk 1:33** *2374*
no longer room, not even near the **d**; **Mk 2:2** *2374*
at the **d**, outside in the street; **Mk 11:4** *2374*
that He is near, *right* at the **d**. **Mk 13:29** *2374*
the **d** has already been shut and my **Lk 11:7** *2374*
they may immediately open *the* **d** **Lk 12:36**
"Strive to enter through the narrow **d**; **Lk 13:24** *2374*
the house gets up and shuts the **d**, **Lk 13:25** *2374*
stand outside and knock on the **d**, **Lk 13:25** *2374*
the **d** into the fold of the sheep, **Jn 10:1** *2374*
the **d** is a shepherd of the sheep. **Jn 10:2** *2374*
to you, I am the **d** of the sheep. **Jn 10:7** *2374*
"I am the **d**; if anyone enters through **Jn 10:9** *2374*
was standing at the **d** outside. **Jn 18:16** *2374*
who kept the **d** said to Peter, **Jn 18:17** *2377*
buried your husband are at the **d**, **Ac 5:9** *2374*
d were watching over the prison. **Ac 12:6** *2374*
he knocked at the **d** of the gate, **Ac 12:13** *2374*
and when they had opened *the* **d**, **Ac 12:16**
a **d** of faith to the Gentiles. **Ac 14:27** *2374*
for a wide **d** for effective *service* **1Co 16:9** *2374*
a **d** was opened for me in the Lord, **2Co 2:12** *2374*
open up to us a **d** for the word, **Col 4:3** *2374*
Judge is standing right at the **d**. **Jas 5:9** *2374*
an open **d** which no one can shut, **Rv 3:8** *2374*
I stand at the **d** and knock; **Rv 3:20** *2374*
hears My voice and opens the **d**, **Rv 3:20** *2374*
a **d** *standing* open in heaven, **Rv 4:1** *2374*

DOORKEEPER
the son of Shallum, the **d**. **Jer 35:4** 8104, 5592b
the **d** to stay on the alert. **Mk 13:34** *2377*
"To him the **d** opens, and the **Jn 10:3** *2377*
went out and spoke to the **d**, **Jn 18:16** *2377*

DOORKEEPERS
d have gathered from the people. **2Ki 22:4** 8104, 5592b
of the second order and the **d**, **2Ki 23:4** 8104, 5592b
of God, which the Levites, the **d**, **2Ch 34:9** 8104, 5592b
the priests, Levites, singers, **d**, **Ezr 7:24** 8652
of the king's eunuchs who were **d**, **Es 6:2** 8104, 5592b

DOORPOST
bring him to the door or the **d**. **Ex 21:6** 4201
the **d** of the temple of the LORD. **1Sa 1:9** 4201
the **d** You have set up your sign; **Is 57:8** 4201
one **d** was like that of the other. **Ezk 41:21** 4201

DOORPOSTS
of the blood and put it on the two **d** **Ex 12:7** 4201
basin to the lintel and the two **d**; **Ex 12:22** 4201
on the lintel and on the two **d**, **Ex 12:23** 4201
write them on the **d** of your house **Dt 6:9** 4201
write them on the **d** of your house **Dt 11:20** 4201
wood, the lintel *and* five-sided **d**. **1Ki 6:31** 4201
nave four-sided **d** of olive wood **1Ki 6:33** 4201
and **d** *had* squared *artistic* frames, **1Ki 7:5** 4201
and *from* the **d** which Hezekiah king **2Ki 18:16** 539
at my gates, Waiting at my **d**. **Pr 8:34** 4201
The **d** of the nave were square; **Ezk 41:21** 4201

DOORS
d of your house into the street, **Jos 2:19** 1817
shut the **d** of the roof chamber behind **Jg 3:23** 1817
the **d** of the roof chamber were **Jg 3:24** 1817
open the **d** of the roof chamber. **Jg 3:25** 1817
comes out of the **d** of my house **Jg 11:31** 1817
he arose and took hold of the **d** **Jg 16:3** 1817
opened the **d** of the house and went **Jg 19:27** 1817
the **d** of the house of the LORD. **1Sa 3:15** 1817
scribbled on the **d** of the gate, **1Sa 21:13** 1817
sanctuary he made **d** of olive wood, **1Ki 6:31** 1817
So *he made* two **d** of olive wood, **1Ki 6:32** 1817
and two **d** of cypress wood; **1Ki 6:34** 1817
both for the **d** of the inner house, **1Ki 7:50** 1817
place, *and* for the **d** of the house, **1Ki 7:50** 1817
the **d** of the temple of the LORD, **2Ki 18:16** 1817
iron to make the nails for the **d** **1Ch 22:3** 1817
and its walls and its **d**; **2Ch 3:7** 1817
great court and **d** for the court, **2Ch 4:9** 1817
and overlaid their **d** with bronze. **2Ch 4:9** 1817
inner **d** for the holy of holies and **2Ch 4:22** 1817
of holies and the **d** of the house, **2Ch 4:22** 1817
the **d** of the house of the LORD and **2Ch 28:24** 1817
he opened the **d** of the house of **2Ch 29:3** 1817
"They have also shut the **d** of the **2Ch 29:7** 1817
consecrated it and hung its **d**. **Ne 3:1** 1817
its **d** with its bolts and bars. **Ne 3:3** 1817
laid its beams and hung its **d** with **Ne 3:6** 1817
its **d** with its bolts and its bars, **Ne 3:13** 1817
its **d** with its bolts and its bars. **Ne 3:14** 1817
its **d** with its bolts and its bars, **Ne 3:15** 1817

had not set up the **d** in the gates, Ne 6:1 1817
let us close the **d** of the temple, Ne 6:10 1817
rebuilt and I had set up the **d**, Ne 7:1 1817
let them shut and bolt the **d**. Ne 7:3 1817
I commanded that the **d** should be Ne 13:19 1817
have opened my **d** to the traveler. Jb 31:32 1817
silent and did not go out of **d**? Jb 31:34 6607
"Or *who* enclosed the sea with **d** When Jb 38:8 1817
on it And set a bolt and **d**, Jb 38:10 1817
"Who can open the **d** of his face? Jb 41:14 1817
And be lifted up, O ancient **d**, Ps 24:7 6607
And lift *them* up, O ancient **d**, Ps 24:9 6607
above And opened the **d** of heaven; Ps 78:23 1817
city, At the entrance of the **d**, Pr 8:3 6607
and the **d** on the street are shut Ec 12:4 1817
over our **d** are all choice *fruits*, SS 7:13 6607
may enter the **d** of the nobles. Is 13:2 6607
And close your **d** behind you; Is 26:20 1802b
To open **d** before him so that gates Is 45:1 1817
I will shatter the **d** of bronze and Is 45:2 1817
Each of the **d** had two leaves, Ezk 41:24 1817
on them, on the **d** of the nave, Ezk 41:25 1817
Open your **d**, O Lebanon, That a Zch 11:1 1817
and when the **d** were shut where the Jn 20:19 *2374*
came, the **d** having been shut, Jn 20:26 *2374*
and the guards standing at the **d**; Ac 5:23 *2374*
immediately all the **d** were opened and Ac 16:26 *2374*
and saw the prison **d** opened, Ac 16:27 *2374*
and immediately the **d** were shut. Ac 21:30 *2374*

DOORWAY
But Lot went out to them at the **d**, Gn 19:6 6607
the **d** of the house with blindness, Gn 19:11 6607
themselves trying to find the **d**. Gn 19:11 6607
make a screen for the **d** of the tent Ex 26:36 6607
to the **d** of the tent of meeting and Ex 29:4 6607
at the **d** of the tent of meeting. Ex 29:11 6607
at the **d** of the tent of meeting. Ex 29:32 6607
at the **d** of the tent of meeting before Ex 29:42 6607
and the screen for the **d** at the Ex 35:15 6607
a screen for the **d** of the tent, Ex 36:37 6607
at the **d** of the tent of meeting, Ex 38:8 6607
to the **d** of the tent of meeting, Ex 38:30 6607
the veil for the **d** of the tent; Ex 39:38 6607
veil for the **d** to the tabernacle. Ex 40:5 6607
in front of the **d** of the tabernacle Ex 40:6 6607
bring Aaron and his sons to the **d** Ex 40:12 6607
veil for the **d** of the tabernacle. Ex 40:28 6607
altar of burnt offering *before* the **d** Ex 40:29 6607
at the **d** of the tent of meeting, Lv 1:3 6607
at the **d** of the tent of meeting. Lv 1:5 6607
at the **d** of the tent of meeting, Lv 3:2 6607
shall bring the bull to the **d** of the tent Lv 4:4 6607
at the **d** of the tent of meeting. Lv 4:7 6607
at the **d** of the tent of meeting. Lv 4:18 6607
at the **d** of the tent of meeting." Lv 8:3 6607
at the **d** of the tent of meeting, Lv 8:4 6607
at the **d** of the tent of meeting, Lv 8:31 6607
shall not go outside the **d** of the tent Lv 8:33 6607
"At the **d** of the tent of meeting, Lv 8:35 6607
from the **d** of the tent of meeting, Lv 10:7 6607
at the **d** of the tent of meeting a Lv 12:6 6607
at the **d** of the tent of meeting, Lv 14:11 6607
at the **d** of the tent of meeting, Lv 14:23 6607
come out of the house, to the **d**, Lv 14:38 6607
to the **d** of the tent of meeting and Lv 15:14 6607
to the **d** of the tent of meeting, Lv 15:29 6607
at the **d** of the tent of meeting. Lv 16:7 6607
and has not brought it to the **d** of Lv 17:4 6607
at the **d** of the tent of meeting to Lv 17:5 6607
at the **d** of the tent of meeting, Lv 17:6 6607
and does not bring it to the **d** of Lv 17:9 6607
to the **d** of the tent of meeting, Lv 19:21 6607
for the **d** of the tent of meeting, Nu 3:25 6607
the screen for the **d** of the court which Nu 3:26 6607
for the **d** of the tent of meeting, Nu 4:25 6607
and the screen for the **d** of the Nu 4:26 6607
to the **d** of the tent of meeting. Nu 6:10 6607
to the **d** of the tent of meeting, Nu 6:13 6607
at the **d** of the tent of meeting, Nu 6:18 6607
at the **d** of the tent of meeting. Nu 10:3 6607
each man at the **d** of his tent; Nu 11:10 6607
and stood at the **d** of the tent, Nu 12:5 6607
at the **d** of the tent of meeting, Nu 16:18 6607
at the **d** of the tent of meeting. Nu 16:19 6607
and stood at the **d** of their tents, Nu 16:27 6607
at the **d** of the tent of meeting, Nu 16:50 6607
to the **d** of the tent of meeting and Nu 20:6 6607
at the **d** of the tent of meeting. Nu 25:6 6607
at the **d** of the tent of meeting, Nu 27:2 6607
to the **d** of her father's house, Dt 22:21 6607
cloud stood at the **d** of the tent. Dt 31:15 6607
at the **d** of the tent of meeting. Jos 19:51 6607
"Stand in the **d** of the tent, and Jg 4:20 6607
woman came and fell down at the **d** Jg 19:26 6607
was lying at the **d** of the house with Jg 19:27 6607
at the **d** of the tent of meeting. 1Sa 2:22 6607
The **d** for the lowest side chamber 1Ki 6:8 6607
sound of her feet coming in the **d**, 1Ki 14:6 6607
guarded the **d** of the king's house. 1Ki 14:27 6607
called her, she stood in the **d**. 2Ki 4:15 6607
at the **d** of the house of Elisha. 2Ki 5:9 6607
from the Angle to the **d** of the Ne 3:20 6607
from the **d** of Eliashib's house Ne 3:21 6607
I have lurked at my neighbor's **d**, Jb 31:9 6607
She sits at the **d** of her house, Pr 9:14 6607
A chamber with its **d** was by Ezk 40:38 6607
each side pillar of the **d**, Ezk 41:3 6607
doorway, two cubits, and the **d**, Ezk 41:3 6607
and the width of the **d**, Ezk 41:3 6607
consisted of one **d** toward the north Ezk 41:11 6607
and another **d** toward the south; Ezk 41:11 6607
shall also worship at the **d** of that gate Ezk 46:3 6607

DOORWAYS
All the **d** and doorposts 1Ki 7:5 6607
walls and in the **d** of the houses, Ezk 33:30 6607
The **d** of the side chambers Ezk 41:11 6607

DOPHKAH
of Sin and camped at **D**. Nu 33:12 1850
They journeyed from **D** and Nu 33:13 1850

DOR
on the heights of **D** on the west Jos 11:2 1756
king of **D** in the heights of Dor, Jos 12:23 1756
king of Dor in the heights of **D**, Jos 12:23 1756
inhabitants of **D** and its towns, Jos 17:11 1756
inhabitants of **D** and its villages, Jg 1:27 1756
in all the height of **D** 1Ki 4:11 1756
with its towns, **D** with its towns. 1Ch 7:29 1756

DORCAS
translated *in Greek* is called **D**); Ac 9:36 *1393*
garments that **D** used to make Ac 9:39 *1393*

DOTHAN
'Let us go to **D**.'" Gn 37:17 1886
his brothers and found them at **D**. Gn 37:17 1886
"Behold, he is in **D**." 2Ki 6:13 1886

DOUBLE
"Take **d** *the* money in your Gn 43:12 4932
took **d** *the* money in their hand, Gn 43:15 4932
donkey or a sheep, he shall pay **d**. Ex 22:4 8147
thief is caught, he shall pay **d**. Ex 22:7 8147
shall pay **d** to his neighbor. Ex 22:9 8147
and you shall **d** over the sixth Ex 26:9 3717
"They shall be **d** beneath, Ex 26:24 8382
"It shall be square *and* folded **d**, Ex 28:16 3717
They were **d** beneath, and Ex 36:29 8382
made the breastpiece folded **d**, Ex 39:9 3717
and a span wide when folded **d**. Ex 39:9 3717
with **d** the service of a hired man; Dt 15:18 4932
a **d** portion of all that he has, Dt 21:17 8147
Dyed work of **d** embroidery on the Jg 5:30 7553
Hannah he would give a **d** portion, 1Sa 1:5 639
a city with **d** gates and bars." 1Sa 23:7
let a **d** portion of your spirit be 2Ki 2:9 8147
Who can come within his **d** mail? Jb 41:13 3718
and with a **d** heart they speak. Ps 12:2 3820
LORD's hand **D** for all her sins." Is 40:2 3718
threshing sledge with **d** edges; Is 41:15 6374
shame *you will have a* **d** *portion*, Is 61:7 4932
possess a **d** *portion* in their land, Is 61:7 4932
The **d** hooks, one handbreadth Ezk 40:43 8240b
the sanctuary each had a **d** door. Ezk 41:23 8147
they are bound for their **d** guilt. Hos 10:10 8147
that I will restore **d** to you. Zch 9:12 4932
and she was bent **d**, Lk 13:11 *4794*
be considered worthy of **d** honor, 1Tm 5:17 *1362*
to her **d** according to her deeds; Rv 18:6 *1363, 1362*

DOUBLED
let the sword be **d** the third time, Ezk 21:14 3717

DOUBLE-MINDED
I hate those who are **d**, Ps 119:113 5588
being a **d** man, unstable in all his Jas 1:8 *1374*
and purify your hearts, you **d**. Jas 4:8 *1374*

DOUBLE-TONGUED
must be men of dignity, not **d**, 1Tm 3:8 *1351*

DOUBLY
"I will first **d** repay their Jer 16:18 4932
trees without fruit, **d** dead, Jude 1:12 *1364*

DOUBT
life shall hang in **d** before you; Dt 28:66
of little faith, why did you **d**?" Mt 14:31 *1365b*
if you have faith and do not **d**, Mt 21:21 *1252*
sea,' and does not **d** in his heart, Mk 11:23 *1252*
"No **d** you will quote this proverb Lk 4:23 *3843*

DOUBTFUL
worshiped *Him;* but some were **d**. Mt 28:17 *1365b*

DOUBTING
must ask in faith without any **d**, Jas 1:6 *1252*
And have mercy on some, who are **d**; Jude 1:22 *1252*

DOUBTS
and why do **d** arise in your hearts? Lk 24:38 *1261*
he who **d** is condemned if he eats, Ro 14:23 *1252*
for the one who **d** is like the surf Jas 1:6 *1252*

DOUGH
their **d** before it was leavened, Ex 12:34 1217
They baked the **d** which they Ex 12:39 1217
'Of the first of your **d** you shall Nu 15:20 6182
'From the first of your **d** you Nu 15:21 6182
And she took **d**, kneaded *it*, made 2Sa 13:8 1217
also bring the first of our **d**, Ne 10:37 6182
and the women knead **d** to make Jer 7:18 1217
give to the priest the first of your **d** Ezk 44:30 6182
of the **d** until it is leavened. Hos 7:4 1217
If the first piece of **d** is holy, Ro 11:16
leavens the whole lump *of* **d**? 1Co 5:6
leaven leavens the whole lump *of* **d**. Ga 5:9

DOVE
Then he sent out a **d** from him, Gn 8:8 3123
but the **d** found no resting place Gn 8:9 3123
he sent out the **d** from the ark. Gn 8:10 3123
The **d** came to him toward evening Gn 8:11 3123
seven days, and sent out the **d**; Gn 8:12 3123
"Oh, that I had wings like a **d**! Ps 55:6 3123
wings of a **d** covered with silver, Ps 68:13 3123
"O my **d**, in the clefts of the SS 2:14 3123
me, my sister, my darling, My **d**, SS 5:2 3123
But my **d**, my perfect one, is SS 6:9 3123
so I twitter; I moan like a **d**; Is 38:14 3123
And be like a **d** that nests Beyond Jer 48:28 3123
Ephraim has become like a silly **d**, Hos 7:11 3123
Spirit of God descending as a **d** Mt 3:16 *4058*
like a **d** descending upon Him; Mk 1:10 *4058*
upon Him in bodily form like a **d**, Lk 3:22 *4058*
descending as a **d** out of heaven, Jn 1:32 *4058*

DOVE'S
and a fourth of a kab of **d** dung 2Ki 6:25 3123

DOVES
Your eyes are *like* **d**." SS 1:15 3123
eyes are *like* **d** behind your veil; SS 4:1 3123
"His eyes are like **d** Beside SS 5:12 3123
like bears, And moan sadly like **d**; Is 59:11 3123
And like the **d** to their lattices? Is 60:8 3123
mountains like **d** of the valleys, Ezk 7:16 3123
like **d** from the land of Assyria; Hos 11:11 3123
are moaning like the sound of **d**, Na 2:7 3123
as serpents and innocent as **d**. Mt 10:16 *4058*
seats of those who were selling **d**. Mt 21:12 *4058*
seats of those who were selling **d**; Mk 11:15 *4058*
were selling oxen and sheep and **d**, Jn 2:14 *4058*
who were selling the **d** He said, Jn 2:16 *4058*

DOWN
The LORD came **d** to see the Gn 11:5 3381
let Us go **d** and there confuse Gn 11:7 3381
went **d** to Egypt to sojourn there, Gn 12:10 3381
of prey came **d** upon the carcasses, Gn 15:11 3381
Now when the sun was going **d**, Gn 15:12
there, and looked **d** toward Sodom; Gn 18:16 8259
"I will go **d** now, and see if they Gn 18:21 3381
d *with his* face to the ground. Gn 19:1 7812
Before they lay **d**, the men of the Gn 19:4 7901
d toward Sodom and Gomorrah, Gn 19:28 8259
when she lay **d** or when she arose. Gn 19:33 7901
when she lay **d** or when she arose. Gn 19:35 7901
she went and sat **d** opposite him, Gn 21:16 3427
He made the camels kneel **d** Gn 24:11 1288
let **d** your jar so that I may drink,' Gn 24:14 5186
and she went **d** to the spring and Gn 24:16 3381
and went **d** to the spring and drew, Gn 24:45 3381
"Do not go **d** to Egypt; Gn 26:2 3381
you, And nations bow **d** to you; Gn 27:29 7812
your mother's sons bow **d** to you. Gn 27:29 7812
his head, and lay **d** in that place. Gn 28:11 7901
bowed **d** to the ground seven times, Gn 33:3 7812
their children, and they bowed **d**. Gn 33:6 7812
her children, and they bowed **d**; Gn 33:7 7812
with Rachel, and they bowed **d**. Gn 33:7 7812
around and bowed **d** to my sheaf." Gn 37:7 7812
stars were bowing **d** to me." Gn 37:9 7812
d before you to the ground?" Gn 37:10 7812
Then they sat **d** to eat a meal. Gn 37:25 3427
way to bring *them* **d** to Egypt. Gn 37:25 3381
"Surely I will go **d** to Sheol in Gn 37:35 3381
Joseph had been taken **d** to Egypt; Gn 39:1 3381
who had taken him **d** there. Gn 39:1 3381
go **d** there and buy *some* for us Gn 42:2 3381
went **d** to buy grain from Egypt. Gn 42:3 3381
Joseph's brothers came and bowed **d** Gn 42:6 7812
"My son shall not go **d** with you; Gn 42:38 3381
gray hair **d** to Sheol in sorrow." Gn 42:38 3381
us, we will go **d** and buy you food. Gn 43:4 3381
do not send *him*, we will not go **d**; Gn 43:5 3381
'Bring your brother **d**'?" Gn 43:7 3381
carry **d** to the man as a present, Gn 43:11 3381
then they arose and went **d** to Gn 43:15 3381
came **d** the first time to buy food, Gn 43:20 3381
"We have also brought **d** other Gn 43:22 3381
They bowed **d** in homage. Gn 43:28 7812
'Bring him **d** to me that I may set Gn 44:21 3381
youngest brother comes **d** with you, Gn 44:23 3381
"But we said, 'We cannot go **d**. Gn 44:26 3381
is with us, then we will go **d**; Gn 44:26 3381
gray hair **d** to Sheol in sorrow.' Gn 44:29 3381
our father **d** to Sheol in sorrow. Gn 44:31 3381
come **d** to me, do not delay. Gn 45:9 3381
and bring my father **d** here." Gn 45:13 3381
do not be afraid to go **d** to Egypt, Gn 46:3 3381
"I will go **d** with you to Egypt, Gn 46:4 3381
but when I lie **d** with my fathers, Gn 47:30 7901
father's sons shall bow **d** to you. Gn 49:8 7812
He couches, he lies **d** as a lion, Gn 49:9 7257
Lying **d** between the sheepfolds. Gn 49:14 7257
and fell **d** before him and said, Gn 50:18 5307
came **d** to bathe at the Nile, Ex 2:5 3381
he struck **d** the Egyptian and hid Ex 2:12 5221
and he sat **d** by a well. Ex 2:15 3427
"So I have come **d** to deliver them Ex 3:8 3381
and throw *it* **d** before Pharaoh, Ex 7:9 7993
and Aaron threw his staff **d** before Ex 7:10 7993
For each one threw **d** his staff and Ex 7:12 7993
when the hail comes **d** on them, Ex 9:19 3381
hail, and fire ran **d** to the earth. Ex 9:23
will come **d** to me and bow themselves Ex 11:8 3381
and will strike **d** all the firstborn in Ex 12:12 5221
the LORD looked **d** on the army Ex 14:24 8259
d into the depths like a stone. Ex 15:5 3381
and when he let his hand **d**, Ex 17:11 5117
and he bowed **d** and kissed him; Ex 18:7 7812
the LORD will come **d** on Mount Sinai Ex 19:11 3381
So Moses went **d** from the mountain Ex 19:14 3381
The LORD came **d** on Mount Sinai, Ex 19:20 3381
"Go **d**, warn the people, so that they Ex 19:21 3381
"Go **d** and come up *again*, you and Ex 19:24 1980
d to the people and told them. Ex 19:25 1980
wrote **d** all the words of the LORD. Ex 24:4 3789

to come **d** from the mountain,	**Ex 32:1**	3381
people sat **d** to eat and to drink,	**Ex 32:6**	3427
"Go **d** at once, for your people,	**Ex 32:7**	1980, 3381
Then Moses turned and went **d** from	**Ex 32:15**	3381
you are to tear **d** their altars and	**Ex 34:13**	5422
pillars and cut **d** their Asherim	**Ex 34:13**	3772
"Write **d** these words, for in	**Ex 34:27**	3789
was coming **d** from Mount Sinai	**Ex 34:29**	3381
was coming **d** from the mountain),	**Ex 34:29**	3381
and he stepped **d** after making the	**Lv 9:22**	3381
shall therefore tear **d** the house,	**Lv 14:45**	5422
whoever lies **d** in the house shall	**Lv 14:47**	7901
stone in your land to bow **d** to it;	**Lv 26:1**	7812
so that you may lie **d** with no one	**Lv 26:6**	7901
be struck **d** before your enemies;	**Lv 26:17**	5062
also break **d** your pride of power;	**Lv 26:19**	7665
and cut **d** your incense altars,	**Lv 26:30**	3772
out, the Levites shall take it **d**;	**Nu 1:51**	3381
on the day that I struck **d** all the	**Nu 3:13**	5221
they shall take **d** the veil of the screen	**Nu 4:5**	3381
on the day that I struck **d** all the	**Nu 8:17**	5221
place where the cloud settled **d**,	**Nu 9:17**	7931
d in the wilderness of Paran.	**Nu 10:12**	7931
Then the tabernacle was taken **d**;	**Nu 10:17**	3381
come **d** and speak with you there,	**Nu 11:17**	3381
d in the cloud and spoke to him;	**Nu 11:25**	3381
Then the LORD came **d** in a pillar	**Nu 12:5**	3381
cut **d** a branch with a single cluster	**Nu 13:23**	3772
sons of Israel cut **d** from there.	**Nu 13:24**	3772
be struck **d** before your enemies,	**Nu 14:42**	5062
lived in that hill country came **d**,	**Nu 14:45**	3381
and beat them **d** as far as Hormah.	**Nu 14:45**	3807
to them went **d** alive to Sheol;	**Nu 16:33**	3381
has no covering tied **d** on it,	**Nu 19:15**	6616
that our fathers went **d** to Egypt,	**Nu 20:15**	3381
Eleazar came **d** from the mountain.	**Nu 20:28**	3381
"But we have cast them **d**,	**Nu 21:30**	3384
the LORD, she lay **d** under Balaam;	**Nu 22:27**	7257
lie **d** until it devours the prey,	**Nu 23:24**	7901
vision of the Almighty, Falling **d**,	**Nu 24:4**	5307
"He couches, he lies **d** as a lion,	**Nu 24:9**	7901
vision of the Almighty, Falling **d**,	**Nu 24:16**	5307
And tear **d** all the sons of Sheth.	**Nu 24:17**	7175a
ate and bowed **d** to their gods.	**Nu 25:2**	7812
the LORD had struck **d** among them.	**Nu 33:4**	5221
and the border shall go **d** from	**Nu 34:11**	3381
and the border shall go **d** and	**Nu 34:11**	3381
'And the border shall go **d** to the	**Nu 34:12**	3381
struck him **d** with an iron object,	**Nu 35:16**	5221
him **d** with a stone in the hand,	**Nu 35:17**	5221
him **d** with his hand in enmity,	**Nu 35:21**	5221
hands and brought it **d** to us;	**Dt 1:25**	3381
you lie **d** and when you rise up.	**Dt 6:7**	7901
you shall tear **d** their altars, and	**Dt 7:5**	5422
pillars, and hew **d** their Asherim,	**Dt 7:5**	1438
'Arise, go **d** from here quickly,	**Dt 9:12**	3381
"So I turned and came **d** from the	**Dt 9:15**	3381
"I fell **d** before the LORD, as	**Dt 9:18**	5307
that came **d** from the mountain.	**Dt 9:21**	3381
"So I fell **d** before the LORD the	**Dt 9:25**	5307
and came **d** from the mountain and	**Dt 10:5**	3381
"Your fathers went **d** to Egypt	**Dt 10:22**	3381
you lie **d** and when you rise up.	**Dt 11:19**	7901
"You shall tear **d** their	**Dt 12:3**	5422
and you shall cut **d** the engraved	**Dt 12:3**	1438
swings the axe to cut **d** the tree,	**Dt 19:5**	3772
and you shall not cut them **d**.	**Dt 20:19**	3772
trees you shall destroy and cut **d**,	**Dt 20:20**	3772
shall bring the heifer **d** to a valley	**Dt 21:4**	3381
or his ox fallen **d** on the way,	**Dt 22:4**	5307
shall be when you sit **d** outside,	**Dt 23:13**	3427
"When the sun goes **d** you shall	**Dt 24:13**	3381
judge shall then make him lie **d** and	**Dt 25:2**	5307
set it **d** before the altar of the LORD	**Dt 26:4**	5117
d to Egypt and sojourned there,	**Dt 26:5**	3381
set it **d** before the LORD your God,	**Dt 26:10**	5117
'Look **d** from Your holy habitation,	**Dt 26:15**	8259
to strike **d** an innocent person.'	**Dt 27:25**	5221
from heaven it shall come **d** on you	**Dt 28:24**	3381
you will go **d** lower and lower.	**Dt 28:43**	3381
the earth, as the eagle swoops **d**,	**Dt 28:49**	1675
come **d** throughout your land,	**Dt 28:52**	3381
about to lie **d** with your fathers;	**Dt 31:16**	7901
He lies **d** as a lion, And tears the	**Dt 33:20**	7931
His heavens also drop **d** dew.	**Dt 33:28**	6201
Now before they lay **d**,	**Jos 2:8**	7901
d by a rope through the window,	**Jos 2:15**	3381
window through which you let us **d**,	**Jos 2:18**	3381
the two men returned and came **d**	**Jos 2:23**	3381
waters which are flowing **d** from above	**Jos 3:13**	3381
the waters which were flowing **d** from	**Jos 3:16**	3381
d toward the sea of the Arabah,	**Jos 3:16**	3381
and lay them **d** in the lodging	**Jos 4:3**	5117
place and put them **d** there.	**Jos 4:8**	5117
face to the earth, and bowed **d**,	**Jos 5:14**	7812
wall of the city will fall **d** flat,	**Jos 6:5**	5307
shout and the wall fell **d** flat,	**Jos 6:20**	5307
d about thirty-six of their men,	**Jos 7:5**	5221
and struck them **d** on the descent,	**Jos 7:5**	5221
took his body **d** from the tree and	**Jos 8:29**	3381
the sky and did not hasten to go **d**	**Jos 10:13**	935
and they took them **d** from the	**Jos 10:27**	3381
them **d** and put them to death.	**Jos 11:17**	5221
and went **d** to Beth-shemesh and	**Jos 15:10**	3381
It went **d** westward to the	**Jos 16:3**	3381
It went **d** from Janoah to	**Jos 16:7**	3381
went **d** to the brook of Kanah,	**Jos 17:9**	3381
the border went **d** to Ataroth-addar,	**Jos 18:13**	3381
The border went **d** to the edge	**Jos 18:16**	3381
it went **d** to the valley of Hinnom,	**Jos 18:16**	3381
southward, and went **d** to En-rogel.	**Jos 18:16**	3381
and it went **d** to the stone of	**Jos 18:17**	3381
and went **d** to the Arabah.	**Jos 18:18**	3381
or serve them, or bow **d** to them.	**Jos 23:7**	7812
other gods and bow **d** to them,	**Jos 23:16**	7812
and his sons went **d** to Egypt.	**Jos 24:4**	3381
sons of Judah went **d** to fight against	**Jg 1:9**	3381
them to come **d** to the valley;	**Jg 1:34**	3381
you shall tear **d** their altars.'	**Jg 2:2**	5422
and bowed themselves **d** to them;	**Jg 2:12**	7812
and bowed themselves **d** to them.	**Jg 2:17**	7812
to serve them and bow **d** to them;	**Jg 2:19**	7812
and the sons of Israel went **d** with	**Jg 3:27**	3381
So they went **d** after him and	**Jg 3:28**	3381
They struck **d** at that time	**Jg 3:29**	5221
who struck **d** six hundred	**Jg 3:31**	5221
So Barak went **d** from Mount Tabor	**Jg 4:14**	3381
of the LORD went **d** to the gates.	**Jg 5:11**	3381
survivors came **d** to the nobles;	**Jg 5:13**	3381
the LORD came **d** to me as warriors.	**Jg 5:13**	3381
whose root is in Amalek *came* **d**,	**Jg 5:14**	
From Machir commanders came **d**,	**Jg 5:14**	3381
and pull **d** the altar of Baal which	**Jg 6:25**	2040
d the Asherah that is beside it;	**Jg 6:25**	3772
Asherah which you shall cut **d**."	**Jg 6:26**	3772
the altar of Baal was torn **d**,	**Jg 6:28**	5422
which was beside it was cut **d**,	**Jg 6:28**	3772
he has torn **d** the altar of Baal,	**Jg 6:30**	5422
he has cut **d** the Asherah which was	**Jg 6:30**	3772
someone has torn **d** his altar."	**Jg 6:31**	5422
because he had torn **d** his altar.	**Jg 6:32**	5422
bring them **d** to the water and I	**Jg 7:4**	3381
brought the people **d** to the water.	**Jg 7:5**	3381
"Arise, go **d** against the camp,	**Jg 7:9**	3381
"But if you are afraid to go **d**,	**Jg 7:10**	3381
Purah your servant **d** to the camp,	**Jg 7:10**	3381
you may go **d** against the camp."	**Jg 7:11**	3381
he went with Purah his servant **d** to	**Jg 7:11**	3381
d so that the tent lay flat."	**Jg 7:13**	4605
"Come **d** against Midian and take	**Jg 7:24**	3381
I will tear **d** this tower."	**Jg 8:9**	5422
Then *the youth* wrote **d** for him the	**Jg 8:14**	3789
He tore **d** the tower of Penuel	**Jg 8:17**	5422
people are coming **d** from the tops	**Jg 9:36**	3381
people are coming **d** from the	**Jg 9:37**	3381
and cut **d** a branch from the trees,	**Jg 9:48**	3772
All the people also cut **d** each	**Jg 9:49**	3772
will burn your house **d** on you."	**Jg 12:1**	
Then Samson went **d** to Timnah and	**Jg 14:1**	3381
Then Samson went **d** to Timnah with	**Jg 14:5**	3381
and he went **d** and talked to the woman;	**Jg 14:7**	3381
his father went **d** to the woman;	**Jg 14:10**	3381
seventh day before the sun went **d**,	**Jg 14:18**	
and he went **d** to Ashkelon and	**Jg 14:19**	3381
and he went **d** and lived in the	**Jg 15:8**	3381
Then 3,000 men of Judah went **d** to	**Jg 15:11**	3381
"We have come **d** to bind you so	**Jg 15:12**	3381
and they brought him **d** to Gaza and	**Jg 16:21**	3381
all his father's household came **d**,	**Jg 16:31**	3381
sat **d** and ate and drank together;	**Jg 19:6**	3427
they sat **d** in the open square of	**Jg 19:15**	3427
the woman came and fell **d** at the	**Jg 19:26**	5307
"They are struck **d** before us, as	**Jg 20:32**	5062
and trod them **d** opposite Gibeah	**Jg 20:43**	1869
and go **d** to the threshing floor;	**Ru 3:3**	3381
"It shall be when he lies **d**,	**Ru 3:4**	7901
go and uncover his feet and lie **d**;	**Ru 3:4**	7901
So she went **d** to the threshing	**Ru 3:6**	3381
he went to lie **d** at the end of the	**Ru 3:7**	7901
and uncovered his feet and lay **d**.	**Ru 3:7**	7901
Lie **d** until morning."	**Ru 3:13**	7901
up to the gate and sat **d** there,	**Ru 4:1**	3427
"Turn aside, friend, sit **d** here."	**Ru 4:1**	3427
And he turned aside and sat **d**.	**Ru 4:1**	3427
elders of the city and said, "Sit **d** here.	**Ru 4:2**	3427
said, "Sit down here." So they sat **d**.	**Ru 4:2**	3427
brings **d** to Sheol and raises up.	**1Sa 2:6**	3381
and bow **d** to him for a piece of silver	**1Sa 2:36**	7812
as Eli was lying **d** in his place	**1Sa 3:2**	7901
and Samuel was lying **d** in the	**1Sa 3:3**	7901
"I did not call, lie **d** again."	**1Sa 3:5**	7901
So he went and lay **d**.	**1Sa 3:5**	7901
not call, my son, lie **d** again."	**1Sa 3:6**	7901
"Go lie **d**, and it shall be if He	**1Sa 3:9**	7901
went and lay **d** in his place.	**1Sa 3:9**	7901
So Samuel lay **d** until morning.	**1Sa 3:15**	7901
she kneeled **d** and gave birth,	**1Sa 4:19**	3766
The Levites took **d** the ark of	**1Sa 6:15**	3381
He struck **d** some of the men of	**1Sa 6:19**	5221
He struck **d** of all the people,	**1Sa 6:19**	5221
come **d** and take it up to you."	**1Sa 6:21**	3381
them **d** as far as below Beth-car.	**1Sa 7:11**	5221
When they came **d** from the high	**1Sa 9:25**	3381
going **d** to the edge of the city,	**1Sa 9:27**	3381
d from the high place with harp,	**1Sa 10:5**	3381
shall go **d** before me to Gilgal;	**1Sa 10:8**	3381
I will come **d** to you to offer	**1Sa 10:8**	3381
and struck **d** the Ammonites until	**1Sa 11:11**	5221
will come **d** against me at Gilgal,	**1Sa 13:12**	3381
Israel went **d** to the Philistines,	**1Sa 13:20**	3381
"Let us go **d** after the	**1Sa 14:36**	3381
I go **d** after the Philistines?	**1Sa 14:37**	3381
go **d** from among the Amalekites,	**1Sa 15:6**	3381
and proceeded on **d** to Gilgal."	**1Sa 15:12**	3381
not sit **d** until he comes here."	**1Sa 16:11**	
and let him come **d** to me.	**1Sa 17:8**	3381
"Why have you come **d**?	**1Sa 17:28**	3381
for you have come **d** in order to	**1Sa 17:28**	3381
d and remove your head from you.	**1Sa 17:46**	5221
and struck **d** two hundred men among	**1Sa 18:27**	5221
let David **d** through a window,	**1Sa 19:12**	3381
prophesied before Samuel and lay **d**	**1Sa 19:24**	5307
to sit **d** to eat with the king.	**1Sa 20:5**	3427
you shall go **d** quickly and come to	**1Sa 20:19**	3381
came, the king sat **d** to eat food.	**1Sa 20:24**	3427
up and Abner sat **d** by Saul's side,	**1Sa 20:25**	3427
his spear at him to strike him **d**;	**1Sa 20:33**	5221
his saliva run **d** into his beard.	**1Sa 21:13**	3381
of it, they went **d** there to him.	**1Sa 22:1**	3381
"Arise, go **d** to Keilah, for I	**1Sa 23:4**	3381
came **d** *with* an ephod in his hand.	**1Sa 23:6**	3381
to go **d** to Keilah to besiege David	**1Sa 23:8**	3381
Will Saul come **d** just as Your	**1Sa 23:11**	3381
"He will come **d**."	**1Sa 23:11**	3381
come **d** according to all the desire	**1Sa 23:20**	3381
and he came **d** to the rock and	**1Sa 23:25**	3381
went **d** to the wilderness of Paran.	**1Sa 25:1**	3381
riding on her donkey and coming **d**	**1Sa 25:20**	3381
his men were coming **d** toward her;	**1Sa 25:20**	3381
went **d** to the wilderness of Ziph,	**1Sa 26:2**	3381
"Who will go **d** with me to	**1Sa 26:6**	3381
"I will go **d** with you."	**1Sa 26:6**	3381
will go **d** into battle and perish.	**1Sa 26:10**	3381
let him go **d** to battle with us,	**1Sa 29:4**	3381
you bring me **d** to this band?"	**1Sa 30:15**	3381
I will bring you **d** to this band."	**1Sa 30:15**	3381
When he had brought him **d**,	**1Sa 30:16**	3381
share is who goes **d** to the battle,	**1Sa 30:24**	3381
men and said, "Go, cut him **d**."	**2Sa 1:15**	6293
and they sat **d**, one on the one	**2Sa 2:13**	3427
so they fell **d** together.	**2Sa 2:16**	5307
and when the sun was going **d**,	**2Sa 2:24**	
servants of David had struck **d** many	**2Sa 2:31**	5221
else before the sun goes **d**."	**2Sa 3:35**	
it, he went **d** to the stronghold.	**2Sa 5:17**	3381
and struck **d** the Philistines from	**2Sa 5:25**	5221
him **d** there for his irreverence;	**2Sa 6:7**	5221
and you lie **d** with your fathers,	**2Sa 7:12**	7901
making them lie **d** on the ground;	**2Sa 8:2**	7901
struck **d** Shobach the commander of	**2Sa 10:18**	5221
"Go **d** to your house, and wash	**2Sa 11:8**	3381
and did not go **d** to his house.	**2Sa 11:9**	3381
"Uriah did not go **d** to his house,"	**2Sa 11:10**	3381
did you not go **d** to your house?"	**2Sa 11:10**	3381
but he did not go **d** to his house.	**2Sa 11:13**	3381
that he may be struck **d** and die."	**2Sa 11:15**	5221
'Who struck **d** Abimelech the son of	**2Sa 11:21**	5221
You have struck **d** Uriah the	**2Sa 12:9**	5221
"Lie **d** on your bed and pretend to	**2Sa 13:5**	7901
lay **d** and pretended to be ill;	**2Sa 13:6**	7901
Amnon's house, and he was lying **d**.	**2Sa 13:8**	7901
has struck **d** all the king's sons,	**2Sa 13:30**	5221
and bring **d** calamity on us and strike	**2Sa 15:14**	5080
And they set **d** the ark of God, and	**2Sa 15:24**	3332
I will strike **d** the king alone,	**2Sa 17:2**	5221
and they went **d** into it.	**2Sa 17:18**	3381
hurried and came **d** with the men of	**2Sa 19:16**	3381
Shimei the son of Gera fell **d** before	**2Sa 19:18**	5307
go **d** to meet my lord the king."	**2Sa 19:20**	3381
of Saul came **d** to meet the king;	**2Sa 19:24**	3381
Gileadite had come **d** from Rogelim;	**2Sa 19:31**	3381
struck **d** Saul in Gilboa.	**2Sa 21:12**	5221
went **d** and his servants with him;	**2Sa 21:15**	3381
the Hushathite struck **d** Saph,	**2Sa 21:18**	5221
David's brother, struck him **d**.	**2Sa 21:21**	5221
and came **d** With thick darkness	**2Sa 22:10**	3381
me, And brings **d** peoples under me,	**2Sa 22:48**	3381
chief men went **d** and came to David	**2Sa 23:13**	3381
He also went **d** and killed a lion	**2Sa 23:20**	3381
but he went **d** to him with a club	**2Sa 23:21**	3381
who was striking **d** the people,	**2Sa 24:17**	5221
Araunah looked **d** and saw the	**2Sa 24:20**	8259
"For he has gone **d** today and has	**1Ki 1:25**	3381
mule, and bring him **d** to Gihon.	**1Ki 1:33**	3381
and the Pelethites went **d** and had	**1Ki 1:38**	3381
they brought him **d** from the altar.	**1Ki 1:53**	3381
gray hair go **d** to Sheol in peace.	**1Ki 2:6**	3381
he came **d** to me at the Jordan,	**1Ki 2:8**	3381, 7122
gray hair **d** to Sheol with blood."	**1Ki 2:9**	3381
which the king had handed **d**,	**1Ki 3:28**	8199
them **d** from Lebanon to the sea;	**1Ki 5:9**	3381
had struck **d** every male in Edom	**1Ki 11:15**	5221
they were sitting **d** at the table,	**1Ki 13:20**	3427
and Asa cut **d** her horrid image and	**1Ki 15:13**	3772
Baasha struck him **d** at Gibbethon,	**1Ki 15:27**	5221
d all the household of Jeroboam.	**1Ki 15:29**	5221
and has also struck **d** the king."	**1Ki 16:16**	5221
and brought him **d** from the upper	**1Ki 17:23**	3381
of the LORD which had been torn **d**.	**1Ki 18:30**	2040
them **d** to the brook Kishon,	**1Ki 18:40**	3381
and he crouched **d** on the earth and	**1Ki 18:42**	1457
'Prepare *your chariot* and go **d**,	**1Ki 18:44**	3381
and sat **d** under a juniper tree;	**1Ki 19:4**	3427
He lay **d** and slept under a	**1Ki 19:5**	7901
he ate and drank and lay **d** again.	**1Ki 19:6**	7901
torn **d** Your altars and killed Your	**1Ki 19:10**	2040
torn **d** Your altars and killed Your	**1Ki 19:14**	2040
And he lay **d** on his bed and turned	**1Ki 21:4**	7901
Ahab arose to go **d** to the	**1Ki 21:16**	3381
go **d** to meet Ahab king of Israel,	**1Ki 21:18**	3381
gone **d** to take possession of it.	**1Ki 21:18**	3381
came **d** to the king of Israel.	**1Ki 22:2**	3381
'You shall not come **d** from the bed	**2Ki 1:4**	3381
Therefore you shall not come **d**	**2Ki 1:6**	3381
man of God, the king says, 'Come **d**.'	**2Ki 1:9**	3381

let fire come **d** from heaven and	**2Ki 1:10**	3381
Then fire came **d** from heaven and	**2Ki 1:10**	3381
'Come **d** quickly.' "	**2Ki 1:11**	3381
let fire come **d** from heaven and	**2Ki 1:12**	3381
Then the fire of God came **d** from	**2Ki 1:12**	3381
d on his knees before Elijah,	**2Ki 1:13**	3766
"Behold fire came **d** from heaven and	**2Ki 1:14**	3381
said to Elijah, "Go **d** with him;	**2Ki 1:15**	3381
and went **d** with him to the king.	**2Ki 1:15**	3381
you shall not come **d** from the bed	**2Ki 1:16**	3381
So they went **d** to Bethel.	**2Ki 2:2**	3381
the king of Edom went **d** to him.	**2Ki 3:12**	3381
do not slow **d** the pace for me	**2Ki 4:24**	6113
So he went **d** and dipped *himself*	**2Ki 5:14**	3381
he came **d** from the chariot to meet	**2Ki 5:21**	5307
to the Jordan, they cut **d** trees.	**2Ki 6:4**	1504
the Arameans are coming **d** there."	**2Ki 6:9**	5185
When they came **d** to him,	**2Ki 6:18**	3381
the messenger came **d** to him and	**2Ki 6:33**	3381
spoke when the king came **d** to him.	**2Ki 7:17**	3381
went **d** to see Joram the son of Ahab	**2Ki 8:29**	3381
of Judah had come **d** to see Joram.	**2Ki 9:16**	3381
three officials looked **d** at him.	**2Ki 9:32**	8259
He said, "Throw her **d**."	**2Ki 9:33**	8058
So they threw her **d**, and some of	**2Ki 9:33**	8058
and we have come **d** to greet the	**2Ki 10:13**	3381
They also broke **d** the *sacred*	**2Ki 10:27**	5422
and broke **d** the house of Baal,	**2Ki 10:27**	5422
the house of Baal, and tore it **d**;	**2Ki 11:18**	5422
king **d** from the house of the LORD,	**2Ki 11:19**	3381
and struck **d** Joash at the house of	**2Ki 12:20**	5221
Millo *as he was* going **d** to Silla.	**2Ki 12:20**	3381
Joash the king of Israel came **d** to	**2Ki 13:14**	3381
and came to Jerusalem and tore **d**	**2Ki 14:13**	6555
he also took **d** the sea from the	**2Ki 16:17**	3381
nor bow **d** yourselves to them nor	**2Ki 17:35**	7812
to Him you shall bow yourselves **d**,	**2Ki 17:36**	7812
and broke **d** the *sacred* pillars and cut	**2Ki 18:4**	7665
pillars and cut **d** the Asherah.	**2Ki 18:4**	3772
And I cut **d** its tall cedars *and*	**2Ki 19:23**	3772
'But I know your sitting **d**,	**2Ki 19:27**	3427
gone **d** on the stairway of Ahaz.	**2Ki 20:11**	3381
wiping it and turning it upside **d**.	**2Ki 21:13**	6440
He also broke **d** the houses of the	**2Ki 23:7**	5422
and he broke **d** the high places of	**2Ki 23:8**	5422
of the LORD, the king broke **d**;	**2Ki 23:12**	5422
and cut **d** the Asherim and filled their	**2Ki 23:14**	3772
and the high place he broke **d**.	**2Ki 23:15**	5422
d the walls around Jerusalem.	**2Ki 25:10**	5422
the king of Babylon struck them **d**	**2Ki 25:21**	5221
with ten men and struck Gedaliah **d**	**2Ki 25:25**	5221
came **d** to take their livestock.	**1Ch 7:21**	3381
the Philistines struck **d** Jonathan,	**1Ch 10:2**	5221
"Whoever strikes **d** a Jebusite	**1Ch 11:6**	5221
it, and struck **d** the Philistines;	**1Ch 11:14**	5221
men went **d** to the rock to David,	**1Ch 11:15**	3381
struck **d** the two *sons of* Ariel of	**1Ch 11:22**	5221
He also went **d** and killed a lion	**1Ch 11:22**	3381
but he went **d** to him with a club	**1Ch 11:23**	3381
so He struck him **d** because he put	**1Ch 13:10**	5221
and they struck **d** the army of the	**1Ch 14:16**	5221
fire came **d** from heaven and	**2Ch 7:1**	3381
seeing the fire come **d** and the	**2Ch 7:3**	3381
bowed **d** on the pavement with their	**2Ch 7:3**	3766
places, tore **d** the *sacred* pillars,	**2Ch 14:3**	7665
sacred pillars, cut **d** the Asherim,	**2Ch 14:3**	1438
d those who owned livestock,	**2Ch 14:15**	5221
and Asa cut **d** her horrid image,	**2Ch 15:16**	3772
went **d** to *visit* Ahab at Samaria.	**2Ch 18:2**	3381
'Tomorrow go **d** against them.	**2Ch 20:16**	3381
Jerusalem fell **d** before the LORD,	**2Ch 20:18**	5307
by night and struck **d** the Edomites	**2Ch 21:9**	5221
went **d** to see Jehoram the son of	**2Ch 22:6**	3381
the house of Baal and tore it **d**,	**2Ch 23:17**	5422
king **d** from the house of the LORD,	**2Ch 23:20**	3381
came and bowed **d** to the king,	**2Ch 24:17**	7812
will bring you **d** before the enemy,	**2Ch 25:8**	3782
power to help and to bring **d**."	**2Ch 25:8**	3782
d 10,000 of the sons of Seir.	**2Ch 25:11**	5221
and threw them **d** from the top of	**2Ch 25:12**	7993
and struck **d** 3,000 of them and	**2Ch 25:13**	5221
as his gods, bowed **d** before them and	**2Ch 25:14**	7812
Why should you be struck **d**?"	**2Ch 25:16**	5221
and tore **d** the wall of Jerusalem	**2Ch 25:23**	6555
and broke **d** the wall of Gath and	**2Ch 26:6**	6555
with him bowed **d** and worshiped.	**2Ch 29:29**	3766
joy, and bowed **d** and worshiped.	**2Ch 29:30**	6915
in pieces, cut **d** the Asherim and	**2Ch 31:1**	1438
and pulled **d** the high places and	**2Ch 31:1**	5422
the wall that had been broken **d** and	**2Ch 32:5**	6555
Hezekiah his father had broken **d**;	**2Ch 33:3**	5422
They tore **d** the altars of the	**2Ch 34:4**	5422
were high above them he chopped **d**;	**2Ch 34:4**	1438
he also tore **d** the altars and beat	**2Ch 34:7**	5422
and chopped **d** all the incense	**2Ch 34:7**	1438
and broke **d** the wall of Jerusalem	**2Ch 36:19**	5422
and that we might write **d** the	**Ezr 5:10**	3790
and my beard, and sat **d** appalled.	**Ezr 9:3**	3427
the wall of Jerusalem is broken **d**	**Ne 1:3**	6555
d and wept and mourned for days;	**Ne 1:4**	3427
of Jerusalem which were broken **d**	**Ne 2:13**	6555
would break their stone wall **d**!"	**Ne 4:3**	6555
a great work and I cannot come **d**.	**Ne 6:3**	3381
I leave it and come **d** to you?"	**Ne 6:3**	3381
heavenly host bows **d** before You.	**Ne 9:6**	7812
You came **d** on Mount Sinai,	**Ne 9:13**	3381
laid **d** for them commandments,	**Ne 9:14**	6680
bowed **d** and paid homage to Haman;	**Es 3:2**	3766
neither bowed **d** nor paid homage.	**Es 3:2**	3766
bowed **d** nor paid homage to him,	**Es 3:5**	3766
the king and Haman sat **d** to drink,	**Es 3:15**	3427
Then they sat **d** on the ground with	**Jb 2:13**	3427
would have lain **d** and been quiet;	**Jb 3:13**	7901
"When I lie **d** I say,	**Jb 7:4**	7901
goes **d** to Sheol does not come up.	**Jb 7:9**	3381
For now I will lie **d** in the dust;	**Jb 7:21**	7901
it is still green *and* not cut **d**,	**Jb 8:12**	6998
tramples **d** the waves of the sea;	**Jb 9:8**	1869
lie **d** and none would disturb *you*,	**Jb 11:19**	7257
"Behold, He tears **d**,	**Jb 12:14**	2040
hope for a tree, When it is cut **d**,	**Jb 14:7**	3772
So man lies **d** and does not rise.	**Jb 14:12**	7901
will not bend **d** to the ground.	**Jb 15:29**	5186
anger has torn me and hunted me **d**,	**Jb 16:9**	7852
"Lay **d**, now, a pledge for me with	**Jb 17:3**	7760
"Will it go **d** with me to Sheol?	**Jb 17:16**	3381
we together go **d** into the dust?"	**Jb 17:16**	5183a
And his own scheme brings him **d**.	**Jb 18:7**	7993
"He breaks me **d** on every side,	**Jb 19:10**	5422
it lies **d** with him in the dust.	**Jb 20:11**	7901
And suddenly they go **d** to Sheol.	**Jb 21:13**	5181
"Together they lie **d** in the dust,	**Jb 21:26**	7901
"When you are cast **d**,	**Jb 22:29**	8213
"He lies **d** rich, but never again;	**Jb 27:19**	7901
of my face they did not cast **d**.	**Jb 29:24**	5307
And let others kneel **d** over her.	**Jb 31:10**	3766
him from going **d** to the pit,	**Jb 33:24**	3381
Which the clouds pour **d**,	**Jb 36:28**	5140
"They kneel **d**, they bring forth	**Jb 39:3**	3766
d the wicked where they stand.	**Jb 40:12**	1915
"Under the lotus plants he lies **d**,	**Jb 40:21**	7901
Or press **d** his tongue with a cord?	**Jb 41:1**	8257
I lay **d** and slept;	**Ps 3:5**	7901
peace I will both lie **d** and sleep,	**Ps 4:8**	7901
trample my life **d** to the ground And	**Ps 7:5**	7429
The nations have sunk **d** in the pit	**Ps 9:15**	2883
He crouches, he bows **d**,	**Ps 10:10**	7817
The LORD has looked **d** from heaven	**Ps 14:2**	8259
eyes to cast *us* **d** to the ground.	**Ps 17:11**	5186
and came **d** With thick darkness	**Ps 18:9**	3381
They have bowed **d** and fallen,	**Ps 20:8**	3766
All those who go **d** to the dust	**Ps 22:29**	3381
makes me lie **d** in green pastures;	**Ps 23:2**	7257
like those who go **d** to the pit.	**Ps 28:1**	3381
tear them **d** and not build them up.	**Ps 28:5**	2040
that I would not go **d** to the pit.	**Ps 30:3**	3381
in my blood, if I go **d** to the pit?	**Ps 30:9**	3381
I bowed **d** mourning, as one who	**Ps 35:14**	7817
been thrust **d** and cannot rise.	**Ps 36:12**	1760
d the afflicted and the needy,	**Ps 37:14**	5307
And Your hand has pressed **d** on me.	**Ps 38:2**	5181
am bent over and greatly bowed **d**;	**Ps 38:6**	7817
out upon him, That when he lies **d**,	**Ps 41:8**	7901
d those who rise up against us.	**Ps 44:5**	947
our soul has sunk **d** into the dust;	**Ps 44:25**	7743
He is your Lord, bow **d** to Him.	**Ps 45:11**	7812
But God will break you **d** forever;	**Ps 52:5**	5422
God has looked **d** from heaven upon	**Ps 53:2**	8259
For they bring **d** trouble upon me And	**Ps 55:3**	4131
Let them go **d** alive to Sheol, For	**Ps 55:15**	3381
them **d** to the pit of destruction;	**Ps 55:23**	3381
forth, In anger put **d** the peoples,	**Ps 56:7**	3381
My soul is bowed **d**;	**Ps 57:6**	3721
by Your power, and bring them **d**,	**Ps 59:11**	3381
who will tread **d** our adversaries.	**Ps 60:12**	947
him **d** from his high position;	**Ps 62:4**	5080
you lie **d** among the sheepfolds,	**Ps 68:13**	7901
d like rain upon the mown grass,	**Ps 72:6**	3381
let all kings bow **d** before him,	**Ps 72:11**	7812
You cast them **d** to destruction.	**Ps 73:18**	5307
He puts **d** one and exalts another.	**Ps 75:7**	8213
must drain *and* drink **d** its dregs.	**Ps 75:8**	8354
waters to run **d** like rivers.	**Ps 78:16**	3381
rained **d** manna upon them to eat	**Ps 78:24**	4305
Why have You broken **d** its hedges,	**Ps 80:12**	6555
Look **d** from heaven and see, and	**Ps 80:14**	5027
is burned with fire, it is cut **d**;	**Ps 80:16**	3683
righteousness looks **d** from heaven.	**Ps 85:11**	8259
among those who go **d** to the pit;	**Ps 88:4**	3381
You have broken **d** all his walls;	**Ps 89:40**	6555
the serpent you will trample **d**.	**Ps 91:13**	7429
Come, let us worship and bow **d**,	**Ps 95:6**	3766
He looked **d** from His holy height;	**Ps 102:19**	8259
the valleys sank **d** To the place	**Ps 104:8**	3381
withdraw And lie **d** in their dens.	**Ps 104:22**	7257
He struck **d** their vines also and	**Ps 105:33**	5221
He also struck **d** all the firstborn in	**Ps 105:36**	5221
cast them **d** in the wilderness,	**Ps 106:26**	5307
And *so* sank **d** in their iniquity.	**Ps 106:43**	4355
who go **d** to the sea in ships,	**Ps 107:23**	3381
they went **d** to the depths;	**Ps 107:26**	3381
and bowed **d** Through oppression,	**Ps 107:39**	7817
who shall tread **d** our adversaries.	**Ps 108:13**	947
Nor *do* any who go **d** into silence;	**Ps 115:17**	3381
the head, Coming **d** upon the beard,	**Ps 133:2**	3381
Coming **d** upon the edge of his	**Ps 133:2**	3381
d upon the mountains of Zion;	**Ps 133:3**	3381
Babylon, There we sat **d** and wept,	**Ps 137:1**	3427
will bow **d** toward Your holy temple	**Ps 138:2**	7812
when I sit **d** and when I rise up;	**Ps 139:2**	3427
scrutinize my path and my lying **d**,	**Ps 139:3**	7250
thrown **d** by the sides of the rock,	**Ps 141:6**	8058
like those who go **d** to the pit.	**Ps 143:7**	3381
Your heavens, O LORD, and come **d**;	**Ps 144:5**	3381
And raises up all who are bowed **d**.	**Ps 145:14**	3721
raises up those who are bowed **d**;	**Ps 146:8**	3721
brings **d** the wicked to the ground.	**Ps 147:6**	8213
as those who go **d** to the pit;	**Pr 1:12**	3381
For her house sinks **d** to death And	**Pr 2:18**	7743
When you lie **d**, you will not be	**Pr 3:24**	7901
When you lie **d**, your sleep will be	**Pr 3:24**	7901
Her feet go **d** to death, Her steps	**Pr 5:5**	3381
How long will you lie **d**,	**Pr 6:9**	7901
are the victims she has cast **d**,	**Pr 7:26**	5307
mouth of the wicked it is torn **d**.	**Pr 11:11**	2040
in a man's heart weighs it **d**,	**Pr 12:25**	7812
tears it **d** with her own hands.	**Pr 14:1**	2040
evil will bow **d** before the good,	**Pr 14:19**	7817
is thrust **d** by his wrongdoing,	**Pr 14:32**	1760
tear **d** the house of the proud,	**Pr 15:25**	5255
And they go **d** into the innermost	**Pr 18:8**	3381
And brings **d** the stronghold in	**Pr 21:22**	3381
you sit **d** to dine with a ruler,	**Pr 23:1**	3427
the cup, When it goes **d** smoothly;	**Pr 23:31**	1980
lies **d** in the middle of the sea,	**Pr 23:34**	7901
who lies **d** on the top of a mast.	**Pr 23:34**	7901
And its stone wall was broken **d**.	**Pr 24:31**	2040
no whisperer, contention quiets **d**.	**Pr 26:20**	8367
And they go **d** into the innermost	**Pr 26:22**	3381
A time to tear **d** and a time to	**Ec 3:3**	6555
two lie **d** together they keep warm,	**Ec 4:11**	7901
do you make *it* lie **d** at noon?	**SS 1:7**	7257
I took great delight and sat **d**,	**SS 2:3**	3427
d from the summit of Amana,	**SS 4:8**	7788
beloved has gone **d** to his garden,	**SS 6:2**	3381
"I went **d** to the orchard of nut	**SS 6:11**	3381
"It goes **d** smoothly for my	**SS 7:9**	
People weighed **d** with iniquity,	**Is 1:4**	3515
I will break **d** its wall and it	**Is 5:5**	6555
against them and struck them **d**.	**Is 5:25**	5221
"The bricks have fallen **d**,	**Is 9:10**	5307
The sycamores have been cut **d**,	**Is 9:10**	1438
them **d** like mud in the streets.	**Is 10:6**	4823
man I brought **d** *their* inhabitants,	**Is 10:13**	3381
That a child could write them **d**.	**Is 10:19**	3789
are tall in stature will be cut **d** And	**Is 10:33**	1438
He will cut **d** the thickets of	**Is 10:34**	5362a
leopard will lie **d** with the young goat,	**Is 11:6**	7257
Their young will lie **d** together,	**Is 11:7**	7257
They will swoop **d** on the	**Is 11:14**	5774a
bows will mow **d** the young men,	**Is 13:18**	7376
make *their flocks* lie **d** there.	**Is 13:20**	7257
desert creatures will lie **d** there,	**Is 13:21**	7257
Have been brought **d** to Sheol;	**Is 14:11**	3381
You have been cut **d** to the earth,	**Is 14:12**	1438
you will be thrust **d** to Sheol,	**Is 14:15**	3381
Who go **d** to the stones of the pit Like	**Is 14:19**	3381
the needy will lie **d** in security;	**Is 14:30**	7257
have trampled **d** its choice clusters	**Is 16:8**	1986
will be for flocks to lie **d** in,	**Is 17:2**	7257
A breaking **d** of walls And a crying	**Is 22:5**	7175a
tore **d** houses to fortify the wall.	**Is 22:10**	5422
will pull you **d** from your station.	**Is 22:19**	2040
The city of chaos is broken **d**;	**Is 24:10**	7665
And Moab will be trodden **d** in his	**Is 25:10**	1758
As straw is trodden **d** in the water	**Is 25:10**	1758
of your walls He will bring **d**,	**Is 25:12**	7817
lie **d** and feed on its branches.	**Is 27:10**	7257
it **d** to the earth with *His* hand.	**Is 28:2**	5117
Who proceed **d** to Egypt Without	**Is 30:2**	3381
those who go **d** to Egypt for help	**Is 31:1**	3381
So will the LORD of hosts come **d**	**Is 31:4**	3381
will hail when the forest comes **d**,	**Is 32:19**	3381
And I cut **d** its tall cedars *and*	**Is 37:24**	3772
"But I know your sitting **d** And	**Is 37:28**	3427
which has gone **d** with the sun on	**Is 38:8**	3381
stairway on which it had gone **d**.	**Is 38:8**	3381
Those who go **d** to the pit cannot	**Is 38:18**	3381
You who go **d** to the sea, and all	**Is 42:10**	3381
bring them all **d** as fugitives,	**Is 43:14**	3381
lie **d** together *and* not rise again;	**Is 43:17**	7901
image and falls **d** before it.	**Is 44:15**	5456
He falls **d** before it and worships;	**Is 44:17**	5456
I fall **d** before a block of wood!"	**Is 44:19**	5456
"Drip **d**, O heavens, from above,	**Is 45:8**	7491
the clouds pour **d** righteousness;	**Is 45:8**	5140
in chains And will bow **d** to you;	**Is 45:14**	7812
Bel has bowed **d**, Nebo stoops over;	**Is 46:1**	3766
over, they have bowed **d** together;	**Is 46:2**	3766
They bow **d**, indeed they worship it.	**Is 46:6**	5456
"Come **d** and sit in the dust, O	**Is 47:1**	3381
arise, Princes will also bow **d**	**Is 49:7**	7812
heat or sun strike them **d**;	**Is 49:10**	5221
They will bow **d** to you with their	**Is 49:23**	7812
You will lie **d** in torment.	**Is 50:11**	7901
'Lie **d** that we may walk over *you*.'	**Is 51:23**	7812
"My people went **d** at the first	**Is 52:4**	3381
and the snow come **d** from heaven,	**Is 55:10**	3381
unable to bark, Dreamers lying **d**,	**Is 56:10**	7901
And made *them* go **d** to Sheol.	**Is 57:9**	8213
I trod **d** the peoples in My anger And	**Is 63:6**	947
cattle which go **d** into the valley,	**Is 63:14**	3381
Look **d** from heaven and see from	**Is 63:15**	5027
Our adversaries have trodden *it* **d**.	**Is 63:18**	947
rend the heavens *and* come **d**,	**Is 64:1**	3381
did not expect, You came **d**,	**Is 64:3**	3381
you will bow **d** to the slaughter.	**Is 65:12**	3766
will come to bow **d** before Me,"	**Is 66:23**	7812
To pluck up and to break **d**,	**Jer 1:10**	5422
tree You have lain **d** as a harlot.	**Jer 2:20**	6808
"Let us lie **d** in our shame, and	**Jer 3:25**	7901
were pulled **d** Before the LORD,	**Jer 4:26**	5422
For evil looks **d** from the north,	**Jer 6:1**	8259
"Cut **d** her trees And cast up a	**Jer 6:6**	3772
them, They shall be cast **d**,"	**Jer 6:15**	3782
they shall be brought **d**,"	**Jer 8:12**	3782
have cast **d** our dwellings.' "	**Jer 9:19**	7993

If you fall **d** in a land of peace,	**Jer 12:5**	982
They have trampled **d** My field;	**Jer 12:10**	947
serve them and to bow **d** to them,	**Jer 13:10**	7812
weep And flow **d** with tears,	**Jer 13:17**	3381
crown Has come **d** from your head."	**Jer 13:18**	3381
flow **d** with tears night and day,	**Jer 14:17**	3381
bring **d** on her Anguish and dismay.	**Jer 15:8**	5307
served them and bowed **d** to them;	**Jer 16:11**	7812
is written **d** with an iron stylus;	**Jer 17:1**	3789
away on earth will be written **d**,	**Jer 17:13**	3789
and go **d** to the potter's house,	**Jer 18:2**	3381
I went **d** to the potter's house,	**Jer 18:3**	3381
a kingdom to uproot, to pull **d**,	**Jer 18:7**	5422
struck **d** by the sword in battle.	**Jer 18:21**	5221
d the inhabitants of this city,	**Jer 21:6**	5221
them **d** with the edge of the sword.	**Jer 21:7**	5221
'Who will come **d** against us?	**Jer 21:13**	5181
"Go **d** to the house of the king of	**Jer 22:1**	3381
And they will cut **d** your choicest	**Jer 22:7**	3772
d to other gods and served them.' "	**Jer 22:9**	7812
'Write this man **d** childless, A man	**Jer 22:30**	3789
into the gloom and fall **d** in it;	**Jer 23:12**	5307
swirl **d** on the head of the wicked.	**Jer 23:19**	2342a
over them to pluck up, to break **d**,	**Jer 31:28**	5422
which are broken **d** *to make a*	**Jer 33:4**	5422
he went **d** to the king's house,	**Jer 36:12**	3381
"Sit **d**, please, and read it to us."	**Jer 36:15**	3427
they let Jeremiah **d** with ropes.	**Jer 38:6**	7971
d by ropes into the cistern to Jeremiah	**Jer 38:11**	7971
in and sat **d** at the Middle Gate:	**Jer 39:3**	3427
broke **d** the walls of Jerusalem.	**Jer 39:8**	5422
d Gedaliah the son of Ahikam,	**Jer 41:2**	5221
Ishmael also struck **d** all the Jews	**Jer 41:3**	5221
had struck **d** because of Gedaliah,	**Jer 41:9**	5221
d Gedaliah the son of Ahikam,	**Jer 41:16**	5221
d Gedaliah the son of Ahikam,	**Jer 41:18**	5221
build you up and not tear you **d**,	**Jer 42:10**	2040
when he had written **d** these words	**Jer 45:1**	3789
I have built I am about to tear **d**,	**Jer 45:4**	2040
of them have fallen **d** together.	**Jer 46:12**	5307
the LORD has thrust them **d**.	**Jer 46:15**	1920
d *and* bereft of inhabitants.	**Jer 46:19**	3341
"They have cut **d** her forest,"	**Jer 46:23**	3772
also gone **d** to the slaughter,"	**Jer 48:15**	3381
"Come **d** from your glory And sit	**Jer 48:18**	3381
I will bring you **d** from there,"	**Jer 49:16**	3381
Her walls have been torn **d**.	**Jer 50:15**	2040
Let them go **d** to the slaughter!	**Jer 50:27**	3381
"They will fall **d** slain in	**Jer 51:4**	5307
And roll you **d** from the crags,	**Jer 51:25**	1556
has set me **d** *like* an empty vessel;	**Jer 51:34**	3322
d like lambs to the slaughter,	**Jer 51:40**	3381
the wall of Babylon has fallen **d**!	**Jer 51:44**	5307
Babylon sink **d** and not rise again	**Jer 51:64**	8257
broke **d** all the walls around Jerusalem	**Jer 52:14**	5422
the king of Babylon struck them **d**	**Jer 52:27**	5221
My eyes run **d** with water;	**La 1:16**	3381
In His wrath He has thrown **d** The	**La 2:2**	2040
has brought *them* **d** to the ground;	**La 2:2**	5060
He has thrown **d** without sparing,	**La 2:17**	2040
run **d** like a river day and night;	**La 2:18**	3381
And is bowed **d** within me.	**La 3:20**	7743
My eyes run **d** with streams of	**La 3:48**	3381
My eyes pour **d** unceasingly,	**La 3:49**	5064
LORD looks **d** And sees from heaven.	**La 3:50**	8259
cause Hunted me **d** like a bird;	**La 3:52**	6679
for you, lie **d** on your left side and	**Ezk 4:4**	7901
you shall lie **d** a second time,	**Ezk 4:6**	7901
your incense altars may be cut **d**,	**Ezk 6:6**	1438
struck **d** *the people* in the city.	**Ezk 9:7**	5221
their conduct **d** on their heads,"	**Ezk 11:21**	5414
nor will they be written **d** in the	**Ezk 13:9**	3789
"So I will tear **d** the wall which	**Ezk 13:14**	2040
and bring it **d** to the ground,	**Ezk 13:14**	5060
of every stature to hunt **d** lives!	**Ezk 13:18**	6679
you hunt **d** the lives of My people,	**Ezk 13:18**	6679
came to me and sat **d** before me.	**Ezk 14:1**	3427
and they will tear **d** your shrines,	**Ezk 16:39**	2040
your conduct **d** on your own head,"	**Ezk 16:43**	5414
I bring **d** the high tree, exalt the	**Ezk 17:24**	8213
She lay **d** among young lions, She	**Ezk 19:2**	7257
It was cast **d** to the ground;	**Ezk 19:12**	7993
and cut them **d** with their swords;	**Ezk 23:47**	1254a
of Tyre and break **d** her towers;	**Ezk 26:4**	2040
axes he will break **d** your towers.	**Ezk 26:9**	5422
pillars will come **d** to the ground.	**Ezk 26:11**	3381
break **d** your walls and destroy	**Ezk 26:12**	2040
sea will go **d** from their thrones,	**Ezk 26:16**	3381
then I will bring you **d** with	**Ezk 26:20**	3381
with those who go **d** to the pit,	**Ezk 26:20**	3381
with those who go **d** to the pit,	**Ezk 26:20**	3381
sea Will come **d** from their ships;	**Ezk 27:29**	3381
'They will bring you **d** to the pit,	**Ezk 28:8**	3381
And her foundations are torn **d**.	**Ezk 30:4**	2040
pride of her power will come **d**;	**Ezk 30:6**	3381
nations have cut it **d** and left it;	**Ezk 31:12**	3772
gone **d** from its shade and left it.	**Ezk 31:12**	3381
with those who go **d** to the pit."	**Ezk 31:14**	3381
"On the day when it went **d** to	**Ezk 31:15**	3381
when I made it go **d** to Sheol	**Ezk 31:16**	3381
with those who go **d** to the pit;	**Ezk 31:16**	3381
"They also went **d** with it to Sheol	**Ezk 31:17**	3381
Yet you will be brought **d** with the	**Ezk 31:18**	3381
of Egypt and bring it **d**,	**Ezk 32:18**	3381
with those who go **d** to the pit;	**Ezk 32:18**	3381
Go **d** and make your bed with the	**Ezk 32:19**	3381
'They have gone **d**, they lie still,	**Ezk 32:21**	3381
who went **d** uncircumcised to the	**Ezk 32:24**	3381
with those who went **d** to the pit.	**Ezk 32:24**	3381
with those who go **d** to the pit;	**Ezk 32:25**	3381
who went **d** to Sheol with their	**Ezk 32:27**	3381
with those who go **d** to the pit.	**Ezk 32:29**	3381
in shame went **d** with the slain.	**Ezk 32:30**	3381
So they lay **d** uncircumcised with	**Ezk 32:30**	7901
with those who go **d** to the pit.	**Ezk 32:30**	3381
yet he will be made to lie **d** among	**Ezk 32:32**	7901
will lie **d** on good grazing ground	**Ezk 34:14**	7257
that you must tread **d** with your	**Ezk 34:18**	7429
what you tread **d** with your feet and	**Ezk 34:19**	4823
showers to come **d** in their season;	**Ezk 34:26**	3381
me **d** in the middle of the valley;	**Ezk 37:1**	5117
mountains also will be thrown **d**,	**Ezk 38:20**	2040
and dash **d** your arrows from your	**Ezk 39:3**	5307
water was flowing **d** from under,	**Ezk 47:1**	3381
region and go **d** into the Arabah;	**Ezk 47:8**	3381
you are to fall **d** and worship the	**Da 3:5**	5308
"But whoever does not fall **d** and	**Da 3:6**	5308
fell **d** *and* worshiped the golden image	**Da 3:7**	5308
d and worship the golden image.	**Da 3:10**	5308
"But whoever does not fall **d** and	**Da 3:11**	5308
to fall **d** and worship the image	**Da 3:15**	5308
"Chop **d** the tree and cut off its	**Da 4:14**	1414
"Chop **d** the tree and destroy it;	**Da 4:23**	1414
then he wrote the dream **d** *and*	**Da 7:1**	3790
d the remainder with its feet;	**Da 7:7**	7512
d the remainder with its feet,	**Da 7:19**	7512
earth and tread it **d** and crush it.	**Da 7:23**	1759
d the saints of the Highest One,	**Da 7:25**	1080
the earth, and it trampled them **d**.	**Da 8:10**	7429
of His sanctuary was thrown **d**.	**Da 8:11**	7993
the vision, but they will fall **d**.	**Da 11:14**	3782
but many will fall **d** slain.	**Da 11:26**	5307
will make them lie **d** in safety.	**Hos 2:18**	7901
them **d** like the birds of the sky.	**Hos 7:12**	3381
The LORD will break **d** their altars	**Hos 10:2**	6202
And I bent **d** *and* fed them.	**Hos 11:4**	5186
desolate, The barns are torn **d**,	**Jl 1:17**	2040
He has poured **d** for you the rain,	**Jl 2:23**	3381
d to the valley of Jehoshaphat.	**Jl 3:2**	3381
Bring **d**, O LORD, Your mighty ones.	**Jl 3:11**	5181
I am weighted **d** beneath you As a	**Am 2:13**	5781
d when filled with sheaves.	**Am 2:13**	5781
Will pull **d** your strength from you	**Am 3:11**	3381
righteousness **d** to the earth."	**Am 5:7**	5117
"But let justice roll **d** like waters	**Am 5:24**	1556
go **d** to Gath of the Philistines.	**Am 6:2**	3381
"That I will make the sun go **d**	**Am 8:9**	3381
From there will I bring them **d**.	**Am 9:2**	3381
'Who will bring me **d** to earth?'	**Ob 1:3**	3381
From there I will bring you **d**,"	**Ob 1:4**	3381
the road To cut **d** their fugitives;	**Ob 1:14**	3772
So he went **d** to Joppa, found a	**Jon 1:3**	3381
and went **d** into it to go with them	**Jon 1:3**	3381
into the hold of the ship, lain **d** and	**Jon 1:5**	7901
and the sun beat **d** on Jonah's head	**Jon 4:8**	5221
He will come **d** and tread on the	**Mi 1:3**	3381
Like water poured **d** a steep place.	**Mi 1:4**	5064
pour her stones **d** into the valley And	**Mi 1:6**	5064
Because a calamity has come **d** from	**Mi 1:12**	3381
The sun will go **d** on the prophets,	**Mi 3:6**	3381
through, Tramples **d** and tears,	**Mi 5:8**	7429
tear **d** all your fortifications.	**Mi 5:11**	2040
bow **d** To the work of your hands.	**Mi 5:13**	7812
make *you* sick, striking you **d**,	**Mi 6:13**	5221
that time she will be trampled **d** Like	**Mi 7:10**	4823
you, The sword will cut you **d**;	**Na 3:15**	3772
Your nobles are lying **d**.	**Na 3:18**	7931
They fly like an eagle swooping **d**	**Hab 1:8**	
"And those who bow **d** on the	**Zph 1:5**	7812
And those who bow **d** *and* swear to	**Zph 1:5**	7812
they will lie **d** at evening;	**Zph 2:7**	7257
of the nations will bow **d** to Him,	**Zph 2:11**	7812
Flocks will lie **d** in her midst,	**Zph 2:14**	7257
For they will feed and lie **d** With	**Zph 3:13**	7257
horses and their riders will go **d**,	**Hg 2:22**	3381
to throw **d** the horns of the	**Zch 1:21**	3034
And he threw her **d** into the middle	**Zch 5:8**	7993
Treading **d** *the enemy* in the mire	**Zch 10:5**	947
of Assyria will be brought **d** And	**Zch 10:11**	3381
impenetrable forest has come **d**.	**Zch 11:2**	3381
"We have been beaten **d**,	**Mal 1:4**	7567
"They may build, but I will tear **d**;	**Mal 1:4**	2040
"You will tread **d** the wicked,	**Mal 4:3**	6072
is cut **d** and thrown into the fire.	**Mt 3:10**	*1581*
the Son of God, throw Yourself **d**;	**Mt 4:6**	*2736*
if You fall **d** and worship me."	**Mt 4:9**	*4098*
and after He sat **d**,	**Mt 5:1**	*2523*
is cut **d** and thrown into the fire.	**Mt 7:19**	*1581*
Jesus came **d** from the mountain,	**Mt 8:1**	*2597*
came to Him and bowed **d** before Him,	**Mt 8:2**	*4352*
the whole herd rushed **d** the steep	**Mt 8:32**	*2596*
official came and bowed **d** before Him,	**Mt 9:18**	*4352*
so He got into a boat and sat **d**,	**Mt 13:2**	*2521*
and they sat **d** and gathered the	**Mt 13:48**	*2523*
Ordering the people to sit **d** on	**Mt 14:19**	*347*
and *began* to bow **d** before Him,	**Mt 15:25**	*4352*
and they laid them **d** at His feet;	**Mt 15:30**	*4496*
people to sit **d** on the ground;	**Mt 15:35**	*377*
they fell face **d** to the ground	**Mt 17:6**	
were coming **d** from the mountain,	**Mt 17:9**	*2597*
to Jesus with her sons, bowing **d**	**Mt 20:20**	*4352*
and the third, **d** to the seventh.	**Mt 22:26**	*2193*
which will not be torn **d**."	**Mt 24:2**	*2647*
on the housetop must not go **d**	**Mt 24:17**	*2597*
'I WILL STRIKE **D** THE SHEPHERD, AND	**Mt 26:31**	*3960*
and sat **d** with the officers to see	**Mt 26:58**	*2521*
d before Him and mocked Him,	**Mt 27:29**	*1120*
And sitting **d**, they *began* to keep	**Mt 27:36**	*2521*
of God, come **d** from the cross."	**Mt 27:40**	*2597*
let Him now come **d** from the cross,	**Mt 27:42**	*2597*
and I am not fit to stoop **d** and	**Mk 1:7**	*2955*
they let **d** the pallet on which the	**Mk 2:4**	*5465*
fall **d** before Him and shout,	**Mk 3:11**	*4363*
came **d** from Jerusalem were saying,	**Mk 3:22**	*2597*
into a boat in the sea and sat **d**;	**Mk 4:1**	*2521*
d and it became perfectly calm.	**Mk 4:39**	*2869*
he ran up and bowed **d** before Him;	**Mk 5:6**	*4352*
d the steep bank into the sea,	**Mk 5:13**	*2596*
had been demon-possessed sitting **d**,	**Mk 5:15**	*2521*
her, came and fell **d** before Him and	**Mk 5:33**	*4363*
And He commanded them all to sit **d** by	**Mk 6:39**	*347*
They sat **d** in groups of hundreds	**Mk 6:40**	*377*
tradition which you have handed **d**;	**Mk 7:13**	*3860*
people to sit **d** on the ground;	**Mk 8:6**	*377*
were coming **d** from the mountain,	**Mk 9:9**	*2597*
Sitting **d**, He called the	**Mk 9:35**	*2523*
He sat **d** opposite the treasury,	**Mk 12:41**	*2523*
which will not be torn **d**."	**Mk 13:2**	*2647*
who is on the housetop must not go **d**,	**Mk 13:15**	*2597*
'I WILL STRIKE **D** THE SHEPHERD, AND	**Mk 14:27**	*3960*
and come **d** from the cross!"	**Mk 15:30**	*2597*
Israel, now come **d** from the cross,	**Mk 15:32**	*2597*
Elijah will come to take Him **d**."	**Mk 15:36**	*2507*
bought a linen cloth, took Him **d**,	**Mk 15:46**	*2507*
sat **d** at the right hand of God.	**Mk 16:19**	*2523*
they were handed **d** to us	**Lk 1:2**	*3860*
brought **d** rulers from *their* thrones,	**Lk 1:52**	*2507*
And He went **d** with them and came	**Lk 2:51**	*2597*
cut **d** and thrown into the fire."	**Lk 3:9**	*1581*
God, throw Yourself **d** from here;	**Lk 4:9**	*2736*
back to the attendant and sat **d**;	**Lk 4:20**	*2523*
in order to throw Him **d** the cliff.	**Lk 4:29**	*2630*
And He came **d** to Capernaum, a city	**Lk 4:31**	*2718*
had thrown him **d** in the midst	**Lk 4:35**	*4496*
And He sat **d** and *began* teaching	**Lk 5:3**	*2523*
and let **d** your nets for a catch."	**Lk 5:4**	*5465*
as You say *and* let **d** the nets."	**Lk 5:5**	*5465*
saw *that*, he fell **d** at Jesus' feet,	**Lk 5:8**	*4363*
and to set him **d** in front of Him.	**Lk 5:18**	*5087*
roof and let him **d** through the tiles	**Lk 5:19**	*2524*
Jesus came **d** with them and stood on a	**Lk 6:17**	*2597*
good measure—pressed **d**,	**Lk 6:38**	*4085*
d the steep bank into the lake and	**Lk 8:33**	*2596*
sitting **d** at the feet of Jesus,	**Lk 8:35**	*2521*
trembling and fell **d** before Him,	**Lk 8:47**	*4363*
"Have them sit **d** *to eat* in	**Lk 9:14**	*2625*
They did so, and had them all sit **d**.	**Lk 9:15**	*2625*
they came **d** from the mountain,	**Lk 9:37**	*2718*
d from heaven and consume them?"	**Lk 9:54**	*2597*
You will be brought **d** to Hades!	**Lk 10:15**	*2597*
going **d** from Jerusalem to Jericho,	**Lk 10:30**	*2597*
priest was going **d** on that road,	**Lk 10:31**	*2597*
men **d** with burdens hard to bear,	**Lk 11:46**	*5412*
I will tear **d** my barns and build	**Lk 12:18**	*2507*
fig tree without finding any. Cut it **d**!	**Lk 13:7**	*1581*
but if not, cut it **d**.' "	**Lk 13:9**	*1581*
sit **d** and calculate the cost to	**Lk 14:28**	*2523*
will not first sit **d** and consider	**Lk 14:31**	*2523*
sit **d** quickly and write fifty.'	**Lk 16:6**	*2523*
immediately and sit **d** to eat'?	**Lk 17:7**	*377*
the house must not go **d** to take	**Lk 17:31**	*2597*
"Zaccheus, hurry and come **d**,	**Lk 19:5**	*2597*
And he hurried and came **d** and	**Lk 19:6**	*2597*
take up what you did not lay **d** and	**Lk 19:21**	*5087*
taking up what I did not lay **d** and	**Lk 19:22**	*5087*
which will not be torn **d**."	**Lk 21:6**	*2647*
your hearts will not be weighted **d**	**Lk 21:34**	*916*
and He knelt **d** and *began* to pray,	**Lk 22:41**	*5087, 1119*
blood, falling **d** upon the ground.	**Lk 22:44**	*2597*
courtyard and had sat **d** together,	**Lk 22:55**	*4776*
And he took it **d** and wrapped it in	**Lk 23:53**	*2507*
After this He went **d** to Capernaum,	**Jn 2:12**	*2597*
Him to come **d** and heal his son;	**Jn 4:47**	*2597*
come **d** before my child dies."	**Jn 4:49**	*2597*
As he was now going **d**,	**Jn 4:51**	*2597*
for an angel of the Lord went **d** at	**Jn 5:4**	*2597*
another steps **d** before me."	**Jn 5:7**	*2597*
and there He sat **d** with His disciples.	**Jn 6:3**	*2521*
"Have the people sit **d**."	**Jn 6:10**	*377*
So the men sat **d**, in number about	**Jn 6:10**	*377*
His disciples went **d** to the sea,	**Jn 6:16**	*2597*
that which comes **d** out of heaven,	**Jn 6:33**	*2597*
"For I have come **d** from heaven,	**Jn 6:38**	*2597*
bread that came **d** out of heaven."	**Jn 6:41**	*2597*
'I have come **d** out of heaven'?"	**Jn 6:42**	*2597*
bread which comes **d** out of heaven,	**Jn 6:50**	*2597*
bread that came **d** out of heaven;	**Jn 6:51**	*2597*
bread which came **d** out of heaven;	**Jn 6:58**	*2597*
He sat **d** and *began* to teach them.	**Jn 8:2**	*2523*
But Jesus stooped **d** and	**Jn 8:6**	*2736*
Again He stooped **d** and	**Jn 8:8**	*2634a*
lays **d** His life for the sheep.	**Jn 10:11**	*5087*
and I lay **d** My life for the sheep.	**Jn 10:15**	*5087*
because I lay **d** My life so that I may	**Jn 10:17**	*5087*
I lay it **d** on My own initiative.	**Jn 10:18**	*5087*
I have authority to lay it **d**,	**Jn 10:18**	*5087*
I will lay **d** my life for You."	**Jn 13:37**	*5087*
"Will you lay **d** your life for Me?	**Jn 13:38**	*5087*
lay **d** his life for his friends.	**Jn 15:13**	*5087*
and sat **d** on the judgment seat at	**Jn 19:13**	*2523*
whom they used to set **d** every day	**Ac 3:2**	*5087*
fell **d** and breathed his last;	**Ac 5:5**	*4098*
which Moses handed **d** to us."	**Ac 6:14**	*3860*
"And Jacob went **d** to Egypt and	**Ac 7:15**	*2597*
by striking **d** the Egyptian.	**Ac 7:24**	*3960*
I HAVE COME **D** TO RESCUE THEM;	**Ac 7:34**	*2597*

Philip went **d** to the city of **Ac 8:5** 2718
who came **d** and prayed for them that **Ac 8:15** 2597
they both went **d** into the water, **Ac 8:38** 2597
and let him **d** through *an opening* **Ac 9:25** 2524
they brought him **d** to Caesarea and **Ac 9:30** 2609
he came **d** also to the saints who **Ac 9:32** 2718
all out and knelt **d** and prayed, **Ac 9:40** 5087, 1119
like a great sheet coming **d**, **Ac 10:11** 2524
Peter went **d** to the men and said, **Ac 10:21** 2597
an object coming **d** like a **Ac 11:5** 2597
and it came right **d** to me, **Ac 11:5**
they heard this, they quieted **d** and **Ac 11:18** 2270
came **d** from Jerusalem to Antioch. **Ac 11:27** 2718
Then he went **d** from Judea to **Ac 12:19** 2718
they went **d** to Seleucia and from **Ac 13:4** 2718
went into the synagogue and sat **d**. **Ac 13:14** 2523
they took Him **d** from the cross and **Ac 13:29** 2507
like men and have come **d** to us." **Ac 14:11** 2597
in Perga, they went **d** to Attalia. **Ac 14:25** 2597
Some men came **d** from Judea and **Ac 15:1** 2718
sent away, they went **d** to Antioch; **Ac 15:30** 2718
by Mysia, they came **d** to Troas. **Ac 16:8** 2597
and we sat **d** and began speaking to **Ac 16:13** 2523
he fell **d** before Paul and Silas, **Ac 16:29** 4363
and Timothy came **d** from Macedonia, **Ac 18:5** 2718
the church, and went **d** to Antioch. **Ac 18:22** 2597
image which fell **d** from heaven? **Ac 19:35** 1356
and fell **d** from the third floor and **Ac 20:9** 2736
But Paul went **d** and fell upon him **Ac 20:10** 2597
knelt **d** and prayed with them all. **Ac 20:36** 5087, 1119
d on the beach and praying, **Ac 21:5** 5087, 1119
named Agabus came **d** from Judea. **Ac 21:10** 2718
and centurions and ran **d** to them; **Ac 21:32** 2701
Paul **d** and set him before them. **Ac 22:30** 2609
ordered the troops to go **d** and take **Ac 23:10** 2597
commander to bring him **d** to you, **Ac 23:15** 2609
Paul **d** tomorrow to the Council, **Ac 23:20** 2609
I brought him **d** to their Council; **Ac 23:28** 2609
Ananias came **d** with some elders, **Ac 24:1** 2597
"When Lysias the commander comes **d**, **Ac 24:22** 2597
among them, he went **d** to Caesarea, **Ac 25:6** 2597
the Jews who had come **d** from **Ac 25:7** 2597
d from the land a violent wind, **Ac 27:14** 2596
Syrtis, they let **d** the sea anchor and **Ac 27:17** 5465
let **d** the *ship's* boat into the sea, **Ac 27:30** 5465
swell up or suddenly fall **d** dead. **Ac 28:6** 2667
(that is, to bring Christ **d**), **Ro 10:6** 2609
THEY HAVE TORN **D** YOUR ALTARS, **Ro 11:3** 2679
TO HEAR NOT, **D** TO THIS VERY DAY." **Ro 11:8** 2193
Do not tear **d** the work of God for **Ro 14:20** 2647
"THE PEOPLE SAT **D** TO EAT AND **1Co 10:7** 2523
struck **d**, but not destroyed; **2Co 4:9** 2598
tent which is our house is torn **d**, **2Co 5:1** 2647
and I was let **d** in a basket **2Co 11:33** 5465
building up and not for tearing **d**. **2Co 13:10** 2506
and broke **d** the barrier of the **Eph 2:14** 3089
let the sun go **d** on your anger, **Eph 4:26** 1931
one look **d** on your youthfulness, **1Tm 4:12** 2706
weak women weighed **d** with sins, **2Tm 3:6** 4987
He sat **d** at the right hand of the **Heb 1:3** 2523
SAT **D** AT THE RIGHT HAND OF GOD **Heb 10:12** 2523
faith the walls of Jericho fell **d** after **Heb 11:30** 4098
and has sat **d** at the right hand of **Heb 12:2** 2523
d from the Father of lights, **Jas 1:17** 2597
there, or sit **d** by my footstool," **Jas 2:3** 2521
not that which comes **d** from above, **Jas 3:15** 2718
that He laid **d** His life for us; **1Jn 3:16** 5087
lay **d** our lives for the brethren. **1Jn 3:16** 5087
faith which was once for all handed **d** **Jude 1:3** 3860
them come and bow **d** at your feet, **Rv 3:9** 4352
comes **d** out of heaven from My God, **Rv 3:12** 2597
him to sit **d** with Me on My throne, **Rv 3:21** 2523
d with My Father on His throne. **Rv 3:21** 2523
the twenty-four elders will fall **d** **Rv 4:10** 4098
elders fell **d** before the Lamb, **Rv 5:8** 4098
the elders fell **d** and worshiped. **Rv 5:14** 4098
will the sun beat **d** on them, **Rv 7:16** 4098
angel coming **d** out of heaven, **Rv 10:1** 2597
And the great dragon was thrown **d**, **Rv 12:9**
he was thrown **d** to the earth, and **Rv 12:9**
his angels were thrown **d** with him. **Rv 12:9**
of our brethren has been thrown **d**, **Rv 12:10**
the devil has come **d** to you, **Rv 12:12** 2597
that he was thrown **d** to the earth, **Rv 12:13**
even makes fire come **d** out of heaven **Rv 13:13** 2597
each, came **d** from heaven upon men; **Rv 16:21** 2597
angel coming **d** from heaven, **Rv 18:1** 2597
city, be thrown **d** with violence, **Rv 18:21**
creatures fell **d** and worshiped God **Rv 19:4** 4098
so that with it He may strike **d** **Rv 19:15** 3960
saw an angel coming **d** from heaven, **Rv 20:1** 2597
d from heaven and devoured them. **Rv 20:9** 2597
coming **d** out of heaven from God, **Rv 21:2** 2597
coming **d** out of heaven from God, **Rv 21:10** 2597
I fell **d** to worship at the feet of **Rv 22:8** 4098

DOWNFALL
they became the **d** of him and all **2Ch 28:23** 3782
quaked at the noise of their **d**. **Jer 49:21** 5307

DOWNPOUR
earth,' And to the **d** and the rain, **Jb 37:6** 1653, 4306
consuming fire In cloudburst, **d** **Is 30:30** 2230
The **d** of waters swept by. **Hab 3:10** 2230

DOWNSTAIRS
"But get up, go **d** and accompany **Ac 10:20** 2597

DOWNWARD
take root **d** and bear fruit upward. **2Ki 19:30** 4295
the beast descends **d** to the earth? **Ec 3:21** 4295
take root **d** and bear fruit upward. **Is 37:31** 4295
and **d** I saw something like fire; **Ezk 1:27** 4295
from His loins and **d** *there was* the **Ezk 8:2** 4295

DOWRY
pay a **d** for her *to be* his wife. **Ex 22:16** 4117
money equal to the **d** for virgins. **Ex 22:17** 4119
'The king does not desire any **d** **1Sa 18:25** 4119
given it *as* a **d** to his daughter, **1Ki 9:16** 7964

DRACHMAS
for the work 61,000 gold **d** and **Ezr 2:69** 1871
gave to the treasury 1,000 gold **d**, **Ne 7:70** 1871
of the work 20,000 gold **d** and **Ne 7:71** 1871
gold **d** and 2,000 silver minas and **Ne 7:72** 1871

DRAG
and we will **d** it into the valley **2Sa 17:13** 5498
Do not **d** me away with the wicked **Ps 28:3** 4900
of the wicked will **d** them away, **Pr 21:7** 1641
Woe to those who **d** iniquity with **Is 5:18** 4900
D them off like sheep for the **Jer 12:3** 5423
sword to slay, the dogs to **d** off, **Jer 15:3** 5498
surely they will **d** them off, **Jer 49:20** 5498
surely they will **d** them off, **Jer 50:45** 5498
hook, **D** them away with their net, **Hab 1:15** 1641
he may not **d** you before the judge, **Lk 12:58** 2694
and personally **d** you into court? **Jas 2:6** 1670

DRAGGED
D off and thrown out beyond the **Jer 22:19** 5498
they came up to him and **d** him away **Ac 6:12** 4884
Paul and **d** him out of the city, **Ac 14:19** 4951
they seized Paul and Silas and **d** **Ac 16:19** 1670
they **d** him out of the temple, **Ac 21:30** 1670

DRAGGING
my soul like a lion, **D** me away, **Ps 7:2** 6561
away, **d** the net *full* of fish. **Jn 21:8** 4951
and **d** off men and women, he would **Ac 8:3** 4951
they *began* **d** Jason and some **Ac 17:6** 4951
d along Gaius and Aristarchus, **Ac 19:29** 4884

DRAGNET
is like a **d** cast into the sea, **Mt 13:47** 4522

DRAGON
kill the **d** who *lives* in the sea. **Is 27:1** 8577
in pieces, Who pierced the **d**? **Is 51:9** 8577
a great red **d** having seven heads **Rv 12:3** 1404
And the **d** stood before the woman **Rv 12:4** 1404
his angels waging war with the **d**. **Rv 12:7** 1404
The **d** and his angels waged war, **Rv 12:7** 1404
And the great **d** was thrown down, **Rv 12:9** 1404
And when the **d** saw that he was **Rv 12:13** 1404
the **d** poured out of his mouth. **Rv 12:16** 1404
the **d** was enraged with the woman, **Rv 12:17** 1404
And the **d** stood on the sand of **Rv 13:1** 1404
And the **d** gave him his power and **Rv 13:2** 1404
they worshiped the **d** because he gave **Rv 13:4** 1404
like a lamb and he spoke as a **d**. **Rv 13:11** 1404
coming out of the mouth of the **d** **Rv 16:13** 1404
And he laid hold of the **d**, **Rv 20:2** 1404

DRAGON'S
in the direction of the **D** Well and **Ne 2:13** 5886

DRAGS
He **d** off the valiant by His power; **Jb 24:22** 4900
the grasshopper **d** himself along, **Ec 12:5** 5445

DRAIN
must **d** *and* drink down its dregs. **Ps 75:8** 4680
'You will drink it and **d** it. **Ezk 23:34** 4680

DRAINED
be **d** out on the side of the altar. **Lv 1:15** 4680
be **d** out at the base of the altar: **Lv 5:9** 4680
he **d** the dew from the fleece, **Jg 6:38** 4680
My vitality was **d** away *as* with the **Ps 32:4** 2015
reeling you have **d** to the dregs. **Is 51:17** 4680

DRANK
He **d** of the wine and became drunk, **Gn 9:21** 8354
so I **d**, and she watered the camels **Gn 24:46** 8354
him ate and **d** and spent the night. **Gn 24:54** 8354
and he ate and **d**, and rose and **Gn 25:34** 8354
them a feast, and they ate and **d**. **Gn 26:30** 8354
he also brought him wine and he **d**. **Gn 27:25** 8354
feasted and **d** freely with him. **Gn 43:34** 7937
saw God, and they ate and **d**. **Ex 24:11** 8354
congregation and their beasts **d**. **Nu 20:11** 8354
I neither ate bread nor **d** water. **Dt 9:9** 8354
I neither ate bread nor **d** water, **Dt 9:18** 8354
of the blood of grapes you **d** wine. **Dt 32:14** 8354
And **d** the wine of their drink offering? **Dt 32:38** 8354
ate and **d** and cursed Abimelech. **Jg 9:27** 8354
When he **d**, his strength returned **Jg 15:19** 8354
they ate and **d** and lodged there. **Jg 19:4** 8354
sat down and ate and **d** together; **Jg 19:6** 8354
washed their feet and ate and **d**. **Jg 19:21** 8354
him, and he ate and **d** before him, **2Sa 11:13** 8354
bread in his house and **d** water. **1Ki 13:19** 8354
he ate and **d** and lay down again. **1Ki 19:6** 8354
So he arose and ate and **d**, **1Ki 19:8** 8354
entered one tent and ate and **d**, **2Ki 7:8** 8354
When he came in, he ate and **d**; **2Ki 9:34** 8354
"I dug *wells* and **d** foreign waters, **2Ki 19:24** 8354
So they ate and **d** that day before **1Ch 29:22** 8354
they **d** their wine at the banquet, **Es 5:6** 4960
they **d** their wine at the banquet, **Es 7:2** 4960
'I dug *wells* and **d** waters, And **Is 37:25** 8354
food and from the wine which he **d**, **Da 1:5** 4960
food or with the wine which he **d**; **Da 1:8** 4960
and his concubines **d** from them. **Da 5:3** 8355
They **d** the wine and praised the **Da 5:4** 8355
just as you **d** on My holy mountain, **Ob 1:16** 8354
and they all **d** from it. **Mk 14:23** 4095
'We ate and **d** in Your presence, **Lk 13:26** 4095
us the well, and **d** of it himself and **Jn 4:12** 4095
sight, and neither ate nor **d**. **Ac 9:9** 4095
who ate and **d** with Him after He **Ac 10:41** 4844a
all **d** the same spiritual drink, **1Co 10:4** 4095
earth opened its mouth and **d** up **Rv 12:16** 2666

DRAW
time when women go out to **d** water. **Gn 24:11** 7579
city are coming out to **d** water; **Gn 24:13** 7579
"I will **d** also for your camels **Gn 24:19** 7579
and ran back to the well to **d**, **Gn 24:20** 7579
the maiden who comes out to **d**, **Gn 24:43** 7579
I will **d** for your camels also"; **Gn 24:44** 7579
and they came to **d** water and **Ex 2:16** 1802a
why do you **d** the people away from **Ex 5:4** 6544a
I will **d** out my sword, my hand **Ex 15:9** 7385a
and will **d** out a sword after you, **Lv 26:33** 7385a
you shall **d** your *border* line from **Nu 34:7** 8376
'You shall **d** a line from Mount Hor **Nu 34:8** 8376
d a line from Hazar-enan to Shepham, **Nu 34:10** 184
d out the abundance of the seas, **Dt 33:19** 3243
not **d** the sword out of his belly; **Jg 3:22** 8025
'I will **d** out to you Sisera, **Jg 4:7** 4900
But the youth did not **d** his sword, **Jg 8:20** 8025
"**D** your sword and kill me, so **Jg 9:54** 8025
26,000 men who **d** the sword, **Jg 20:15** 8025
400,000 men who **d** the sword; **Jg 20:17** 8025
"Shall we again **d** near for battle **Jg 20:23** 5066
"Let us flee that we may **d** them **Jg 20:32** 5423
that day, all who **d** the sword. **Jg 20:35** 8025
were 25,000 men who **d** the sword; **Jg 20:46** 8025
drink from what the servants **d**." **Ru 2:9** 7579
young women going out to **d** water and **1Sa 9:11** 7579
"Let us **d** near to God here." **1Sa 14:36** 7126
"**D** near here, all you chiefs of **1Sa 14:38** 5066
come out to **d** up in battle array? **1Sa 17:8** 6186a
"**D** your sword and pierce me **1Sa 31:4** 8025
he could not **d** it back to himself. **1Ki 13:4** 7725
"**D** your sword and thrust me **1Ch 10:4** 8025
who could **d** up in battle formation **1Ch 12:33** 6186a
could **d** up in battle formation, **1Ch 12:35** 6186a
army to **d** up in battle formation. **1Ch 12:36** 6186a
could **d** up in battle formation, **1Ch 12:38** 6186a
d out Leviathan with a fishhook? **Jb 41:1** 4900
D also the spear and the **Ps 35:3** 7385a
d near to my soul *and* redeem it; **Ps 69:18** 7126
follow after wickedness **d** near; **Ps 119:150** 7126
and **d** near to listen rather than **Ec 5:1** 7126
years **d** near when you will say, **Ec 12:1** 5060
"**D** me after you *and* let us run **SS 1:4** 4900
of Israel **d** near And come to pass, **Is 5:19** 7126
Therefore you will joyously **d** **Is 12:3** 7579
"Because this people **d** near with **Is 29:13** 5066
D near, O nations, to hear; **Is 34:1** 7126
Causing wise men to **d** back And **Is 44:25** 7725
D near together, you fugitives of **Is 45:20** 5066
Let him **d** near to Me. **Is 50:8** 5066
And **d** near for the battle! **Jer 46:3** 5066
And they will **d** up *their* battle **Jer 50:9** 6186a
"**D** up your battle lines against **Jer 50:14** 6186a
"**D** near, O executioners of the **Ezk 9:1** 7126
I will **d** out a sword after them. **Ezk 12:14** 7385a
'The days **d** near as well as the **Ezk 12:23** 7126
and I will **d** My sword out of its **Ezk 21:3** 3318
And they will **d** their swords **Ezk 28:7** 7385a
And they will **d** their swords **Ezk 30:11** 7385a
d near to Me to minister to Me,' **Ezk 43:19** 7126
Let all the soldiers **d** near, **Jl 3:9** 5066
D for yourself water for the siege! **Na 3:14** 7579
She did not **d** near to her God. **Zph 3:2** 7126
the wine vat to **d** fifty measures, **Hg 2:16** 2834
I will **d** near to you for judgment; **Mal 3:5** 7126
"**D** *some* out now and take it to **Jn 2:8** 501
a woman of Samaria to **d** water. **Jn 4:7** 501
to **d** with and the well is deep; **Jn 4:11** 502
nor come all the way here to **d**." **Jn 4:15** 501
earth, will **d** all men to Myself." **Jn 12:32** 1670
d away the disciples after them. **Ac 20:30** 645
Therefore let us **d** near with **Heb 4:16** 4334
through which we **d** near to God. **Heb 7:19** 1448
who **d** near to God through Him, **Heb 7:25** 4334
make perfect those who **d** near. **Heb 10:1** 4334
let us **d** near with a sincere heart **Heb 10:22** 4334
D near to God and He will draw **Jas 4:8** 1448
to God and He will **d** near to you. **Jas 4:8** 1448

DRAWERS
hewers of wood and **d** of water for **Jos 9:21** 7579
both hewers of wood and **d** of water **Jos 9:23** 7579
and **d** of water for the congregation **Jos 9:27** 7579

DRAWING
are terrified, They are **d** back, **Jer 46:5** 5472
your redemption is **d** near." **Lk 21:28** 1448
on the sea and **d** near to the boat; **Jn 6:19** 1096
more as you see the day **d** near. **Heb 10:25** 1448

DRAWN
way with his **d** sword in his hand, **Nu 22:23** 8025
way with his **d** sword in his hand; **Nu 22:31** 8025
you shall take one **d** out of every **Nu 31:30** 270
took one **d** out of every fifty, **Nu 31:47** 270
and be **d** away and worship them and **Dt 4:19** 5080
but are **d** away and worship other **Dt 30:17** 5080
him with his sword **d** in his hand, **Jos 5:13** 8025
we have **d** them away from the city. **Jos 8:6** 5423
and were **d** away from the city. **Jos 8:16** 5423
now, the day has **d** to a close; **Jg 19:9** 7503
and were **d** away from the city, **Jg 20:31** 5423

with his **d** sword in his hand **1Ch 21:16** 8025
a timber shall be **d** from his house **Ezr 6:11** 5256
"It is **d** forth and comes out of **Jb 20:25** 8025
d the sword and bent their bow To **Ps 37:14** 6605a
than oil, Yet they were **d** swords. **Ps 55:21** 6609
And my life has **d** near to Sheol. **Ps 88:3** 5060
from the swords, From the **d** sword, **Is 21:15** 5203
They have **d** near and have come. **Is 41:5** 7126
I have **d** you with lovingkindness. **Jer 31:3** 4900
He has **d** back His right hand From **La 2:3** 7725
have **d** My sword out of its sheath. **Ezk 21:5** 3318
'A sword, a sword is **d**, **Ezk 21:28** 6605a
they have **d** her and all her **Ezk 32:20** 4900
who had **d** the water knew), **Jn 2:9** *501*
was **d** back up into the sky. **Ac 11:10** *385*

DRAWS
wood to the one who **d** your water, **Dt 29:11** 7579
"Then his soul **d** near to the pit, **Jb 33:22** 7126
"For He **d** up the drops of water, **Jb 36:27** 1639
when he **d** him into his net. **Ps 10:9** 4900
a man of understanding **d** it out. **Pr 20:5** 1802a
LORD **d** near on all the nations. **Ob 1:15** 7138
the Father who sent Me **d** him; **Jn 6:44** *1670*

DREAD
were in **d** of the sons of Israel. **Ex 1:12** 6973
"Terror and **d** fall upon them; **Ex 15:16** 6343
was in **d** of the sons of Israel. **Nu 22:3** 6973
I will begin to put the **d** and fear of **Dt 2:25** 6343
"You shall not **d** them, for the **Dt 7:21** 6206
LORD your God will lay the **d** of you **Dt 11:25** 6343
you will be in **d** night and day, **Dt 28:66** 6342
d of your heart which you dread, **Dt 28:67** 6343
dread of your heart which you **d**, **Dt 28:67** 6342
Whom your fathers did not **d**. **Dt 32:17** 8175b
Then the **d** of the LORD fell on the **1Sa 11:7** 6343
for the **d** of the LORD had fallen **2Ch 14:14** 6343
Now the **d** of the LORD was on all **2Ch 17:10** 6343
And the **d** of God was on all the **2Ch 20:29** 6343
for the **d** of the Jews had fallen **Es 8:17** 6343
for the **d** of them had fallen on **Es 9:2** 6343
because the **d** of Mordecai had **Es 9:3** 6343
upon me, And what I **d** befalls me. **Jb 3:25** 3025
D came upon me, and trembling, And **Jb 4:14** 6343
And let not **d** of Him terrify me. **Jb 9:34** 367
you, And the **d** of Him fall on you? **Jb 13:11** 6343
let not the **d** of You terrify me. **Jb 13:21** 367
you, And sudden **d** terrifies you, **Jb 22:10** 6343
There they are in great **d**, **Ps 14:5** 6342
defense of my life; Whom shall I **d**? **Ps 27:1** 6342
object of **d** to my acquaintances; **Ps 31:11** 6343
my life from **d** of the enemy. **Ps 64:1** 6343
d of them had fallen upon them. **Ps 105:38** 6343
Turn away my reproach which I **d**, **Ps 119:39** 3025
I will mock when your **d** comes, **Pr 1:26** 6343
When your **d** comes like a storm And **Pr 1:27** 6343
be at ease from the **d** of evil." **Pr 1:33** 6343
two kings you **d** will be forsaken. **Is 7:16** 6973
what they fear or be in **d** of *it*. **Is 8:12** 6206
your fear, And He shall be your **d**. **Is 8:13** 6206
will tremble and be in **d** because of **Is 19:16** 6342
is mentioned will be in **d** of it, **Is 19:17** 6342
And will bring on them what they **d**. **Is 66:4** 4034
And the **d** of Me is not in you," **Jer 2:19** 6345
LORD is with me like a **d** champion; **Jer 20:11** 6184
into the hand of those whom you **d**, **Jer 22:25** 3016
heard a sound of terror, Of **d**, **Jer 30:5** 6343
"I **d** the Jews who have gone over **Jer 38:19** 1672
the hand of the men whom you **d**. **Jer 39:17** 3016
a great **d** fell on them, **Da 10:7** 2731
LORD our God they will come in **d** And **Mi 7:17** 6342

DREADED
was prospering greatly, he **d** him. **1Sa 18:15** 1481c
"They are **d** and feared; **Hab 1:7** 366

DREADFUL
So that they dwell in **d** valleys, **Jb 30:6** 6178
a fourth beast, **d** and terrifying and **Da 7:7** 1763
all the others, exceedingly **d**, **Da 7:19** 1763

DREAM
to Abimelech in a **d** of the night, **Gn 20:3** 2472
Then God said to him in the **d**, **Gn 20:6** 2472
He had a **d**, and behold, a **Gn 28:12** 2492b
lifted up my eyes and saw in a **d**, **Gn 31:10** 2472
angel of God said to me in the **d**, **Gn 31:11** 2472
the Aramean in a **d** of the night and **Gn 31:24** 2472
Then Joseph had a **d**, **Gn 37:5** 2472
listen to this **d** which I have had; **Gn 37:6** 2472
Now he had still another **d**, **Gn 37:9** 2472
"Lo, I have had still another **d**; **Gn 37:9** 2472
"What is this **d** that you have had? **Gn 37:10** 2472
jail, both had a **d** the same night, **Gn 40:5** 2472
each man with his *own* **d** *and* each **Gn 40:5** 2472
d with its *own* interpretation. **Gn 40:5** 2472
"We have had a **d** and there is no **Gn 40:8** 2472
cupbearer told his **d** to Joseph, **Gn 40:9** 2472
"In my **d**, behold, *there was* a **Gn 40:9** 2472
"I also *saw* in my **d**, **Gn 40:16** 2472
full years that Pharaoh had a **d**, **Gn 41:1** 2492b
awoke, and behold, *it was* a **d**. **Gn 41:7** 2472
"We had a **d** on the same **Gn 41:11** 2472
the interpretation of his *own* **d**. **Gn 41:11** 2472
according to his *own* **d**. **Gn 41:12** 2472
"I have had a **d**, but no one can **Gn 41:15** 2472
hear a **d** you can interpret it." **Gn 41:15** 2472
"In my **d**, behold, I was standing **Gn 41:17** 2472
"I saw also in my **d**, **Gn 41:22** 2472
of the **d** to Pharaoh twice, **Gn 41:32** 2472
I shall speak with him in a **d**. **Nu 12:6** 2472
was relating a **d** to his friend. **Jg 7:13** 2472
"Behold, I had a **d**; **Jg 7:13** 2472
of the **d** and its interpretation, **Jg 7:15** 2472
to Solomon in a **d** at night; **1Ki 3:5** 2472
awoke, and behold, it was a **d**. **1Ki 3:15** 2472
"He flies away like a **d**, **Jb 20:8** 2472
"In a **d**, a vision of the night, **Jb 33:15** 2472
Like a **d** when one awakes, O Lord, **Ps 73:20** 2472
of Zion, We were like those who **d**. **Ps 126:1** 2492b
the **d** comes through much effort and **Ec 5:3** 2472
distress her, will be like a **d**, **Is 29:7** 2472
'I had a **d**, I had a dream!' **Jer 23:25** 2492b
'I had a dream, I had a **d**!' **Jer 23:25** 2492b
who has a **d** may relate *his* dream, **Jer 23:28** 2472
who has a dream may relate *his* **d**, **Jer 23:28** 2472
listen to the dreams which they **d**. **Jer 29:8** 2492b
"I had a **d** and my spirit is **Da 2:3** 2472
is anxious to understand the **d**." **Da 2:3** 2472
Tell the **d** to your servants, and **Da 2:4** 2493
me the **d** and its interpretation, **Da 2:5** 2493
the **d** and its interpretation, **Da 2:6** 2493
me the **d** and its interpretation." **Da 2:6** 2493
king tell the **d** to his servants, **Da 2:7** 2493
you do not make the **d** known to me, **Da 2:9** 2493
therefore tell me the **d**, **Da 2:9** 2493
able to make known to me the **d** **Da 2:26** 2493
This was your **d** and the visions in **Da 2:28** 2493
"This *was* the **d**; now we will tell its **Da 2:36** 2493
so the **d** is true and its **Da 2:45** 2493
"I saw a **d** and it made me fearful; **Da 4:5** 2493
to me the interpretation of the **d**. **Da 4:6** 2493
in and I related the **d** to them **Da 4:7** 2493
and I related the **d** to him, **Da 4:8** 2493
visions of my **d** which I have seen, **Da 4:9** 2493
'This is the **d** *which* I, King **Da 4:18** 2493
do not let the **d** or its **Da 4:19** 2493
the **d** applied to those who hate you **Da 4:19** 2493
Daniel saw a **d** and visions in his **Da 7:1** 2493
then he wrote the **d** down *and* **Da 7:1** 2493
Your old men will **d** dreams, **Jl 2:28** 2492b
the Lord appeared to him in a **d**, **Mt 1:20** *3677*
God in a **d** not to return to Herod, **Mt 2:12** *3677*
Lord appeared to Joseph in a **d** and **Mt 2:13** *3677*
in a **d** to Joseph in Egypt, **Mt 2:19** *3677*
after being warned *by God* in a **d**, **Mt 2:22** *3677*
I suffered greatly in a **d** because of **Mt 27:19** *3677*
YOUR OLD MEN SHALL **D** DREAMS; **Ac 2:17** *1797*

DREAMED
fell asleep and **d** a second time; **Gn 41:5** 2492b
each of us **d** according to the **Gn 41:11** 2492b

DREAMER
"Here comes this **d**! **Gn 37:19** 1167, 2472
"If a prophet or a **d** of dreams **Dt 13:1** 2492b
that prophet or that **d** of dreams; **Dt 13:3** 2492b
"But that prophet or that **d** of **Dt 13:5** 2492b

DREAMERS
dogs unable to bark, **D** lying down, **Is 56:10** 1957
prophets, your diviners, your **d**, **Jer 27:9** 2472

DREAMING
same way these men, also by **d**, **Jude 1:8** *1797*

DREAMS
more for his **d** and for his words. **Gn 37:8** 2472
see what will become of his **d**!" **Gn 37:20** 2472
And Pharaoh told them his **d**, **Gn 41:8** 2472
and he interpreted our **d** for us. **Gn 41:12** 2472
"Pharaoh's **d** are one *and the same;* **Gn 41:25** 2472
the **d** are one *and the same.* **Gn 41:26** 2472
the **d** which he had about them, **Gn 42:9** 2472
"If a prophet or a dreamer of **d** **Dt 13:1** 2472
that prophet or that dreamer of **d**; **Dt 13:3** 2472
of **d** shall be put to death, **Dt 13:5** 2472
by **d** or by Urim or by prophets. **1Sa 28:6** 2472
either through prophets or by **d**; **1Sa 28:15** 2472
with **d** And terrify me by visions; **Jb 7:14** 2472
For in many **d** and in many words **Ec 5:7** 2472
It will be as when a hungry man **d** **Is 29:8** 2492b
Or as when a thirsty man **d** **Is 29:8** 2492b
forget My name by their **d** which **Jer 23:27** 2472
who have prophesied false **d**," **Jer 23:32** 2472
listen to the **d** which they dream. **Jer 29:8** 2472
all *kinds of* visions and **d**. **Da 1:17** 2472
Nebuchadnezzar had **d**; **Da 2:1** 2472
Chaldeans to tell the king his **d**. **Da 2:2** 2472
and insight, interpretation of **d**, **Da 5:12** 2493
Your old men will dream **d**, **Jl 2:28** 2472
lying visions And tell false **d**; **Zch 10:2** 2472
YOUR OLD MEN SHALL DREAM **D**; **Ac 2:17** *1798*

DREGS
must drain *and* drink down its **d**. **Ps 75:8** 8105
reeling you have drained to the **d**. **Is 51:17** 6907
like wine on its **d**, And he has **Jer 48:11** 8105
of the world, the **d** of all things, **1Co 4:13** *4067*

DRENCH
I will **d** you with my tears, O **Is 16:9** 7301

DRENCHED
For my head is **d** with dew, My **SS 5:2** 4390
will be **d** with their blood. **Is 34:3** 4549
him be **d** with the dew of heaven, **Da 4:15** 6647
him be **d** with the dew of heaven, **Da 4:23** 6647
and be **d** with the dew of heaven; **Da 4:25** 6647
body was **d** with the dew of heaven **Da 4:33** 6647
body was **d** with the dew of heaven **Da 5:21** 6647
D like the corners of the altar. **Zch 9:15**

DRESS
"I have taken off my **d**, **SS 5:3** 3801
Although you **d** in scarlet, **Jer 4:30** 3847
and your **d** was of fine linen, **Ezk 16:13** 4403

DRESSED
of the king **d** themselves in robes. **2Sa 13:18** 3847
Joab was **d** in his military attire, **2Sa 20:8** 2296, 3830
D as a harlot and cunning of heart. **Pr 7:10** 7897
the ones near, magnificently **d**, **Ezk 23:12** 3847
was a certain man **d** in linen, **Da 10:5** 3847
one said to the man **d** in linen, **Da 12:6** 3847
I heard the man **d** in linen, **Da 12:7** 3847
The warriors are **d** in scarlet, **Na 2:3** 8529
A man **d** in soft *clothing?* **Mt 11:8** *294*
who was not **d** in wedding clothes, **Mt 22:11** *1746a*
They **d** Him up in purple, and **Mk 15:17** *1737*
A man **d** in soft clothing? **Lk 7:25** *294*
"Be **d** in readiness, and *keep* your **Lk 12:35** *4024*
d in purple and fine linen, **Lk 16:19** *1737*
d Him in a gorgeous robe and sent **Lk 23:11** *4016*
a gold ring and **d** in fine clothes, **Jas 2:2**

DRESSES
gold jewelry, or putting on **d**; **1Pe 3:3** *2440*

DREW
and she **d** for all his camels. **Gn 24:20** 7579
and went down to the spring and **d**, **Gn 24:45** 7579
came about as he **d** back his hand, **Gn 38:29** 7725
the time for Israel to die **d** near, **Gn 47:29** 7126
he **d** his feet into the bed and **Gn 49:33** 622
I **d** him out of the water." **Ex 2:10** 4871
he even **d** the water for us and **Ex 2:19** 1802a
As Pharaoh **d** near, the sons of **Ex 14:10** 7126
went up and **d** near and arrived in **Jos 8:11** 5066
Judah **d** near to Joshua in Gilgal, **Jos 14:6** 5066
foot soldiers who **d** the sword. **Jg 20:2** 8025
all these **d** the sword. **Jg 20:25** 8025
The Philistines **d** up in battle **1Sa 4:2** 6186a
and **d** water and poured it out **1Sa 7:6** 7579
d near to battle against Israel. **1Sa 7:10** 5066
and **d** up in battle array to **1Sa 17:2** 6186a
Philistines **d** up in battle array, **1Sa 17:21** 6186a
and came and **d** near to meet David, **1Sa 17:48** 7126
Philistine and took his sword and **d** it **1Sa 17:51** 8025
d up in battle array at the entrance of **2Sa 10:8** 6186a
people who were with him **d** near to **2Sa 10:13** 5066
He **d** me out of many waters. **2Sa 22:17** 4871
and **d** water from the well of **2Sa 23:16** 7579
valiant men who **d** the sword, **2Sa 24:9** 8025
As David's time to die **d** near, **1Ki 2:1** 7126
And he **d** chains of gold across the **1Ki 6:21** 5674a
Now a certain man **d** his bow at **1Ki 22:34** 4900
with him 700 men who **d** swords, **2Ki 3:26** 8025
And Jehu **d** his bow with his full **2Ki 9:24** 4390
and **d** water from the well of **1Ch 11:18** 7579
came out and **d** up in battle array **1Ch 19:9** 6186a
people who were with him **d** near **1Ch 19:14** 5066
d up in formation against them. **1Ch 19:17** 6186a
And when David **d** up in battle **1Ch 19:17** 6186a
1,100,000 men who **d** the sword; **1Ch 21:5** 8025
was 470,000 men who **d** the sword. **1Ch 21:5** 8025
while Jeroboam **d** up in battle **2Ch 13:3** 6186a
and they **d** up in battle formation **2Ch 14:10** 6186a
A certain man **d** his bow at **2Ch 18:33** 4900
He **d** me out of many waters. **Ps 18:16** 4871
they **d** near to the gates of death. **Ps 107:18** 5060
You **d** near when I called on You; **La 3:57** 7126
Our end **d** near, Our days were **La 4:18** 7126
filled, they **d** it up on the beach; **Mt 13:48** *307*
Jesus reached and **d** out his sword, **Mt 26:51** *645*
of those who stood by **d** his sword, **Mk 14:47** *4685*
"I am *He,*" they **d** back and fell to **Jn 18:6** *565*
having a sword, **d** it **Jn 18:10** *1670*
went up and **d** the net to land, **Jn 21:11** *1670*
And they **d** lots for them, and the **Ac 1:26** *1325*
and **d** away *some* people after him; **Ac 5:37** *868*
he **d** his sword and was about to **Ac 16:27** *4685*

DRIED
the water was **d** up from the earth. **Gn 8:7** 3001
the water was **d** up from the earth. **Gn 8:13** 2717a
surface of the ground was **d** up. **Gn 8:13** 2717a
juice nor eat fresh or **d** grapes. **Nu 6:3** 3002
heard how the LORD **d** up the water **Jos 2:10** 3001
"For the LORD your God **d** up the **Jos 4:23** 3001
which He **d** up before us until we **Jos 4:23** 3001
heard how the LORD had **d** up the **Jos 5:1** 3001
fresh cords that have not been **d**, **Jg 16:7** 2717a
fresh cords that had not been **d**, **Jg 16:8** 2717a
he stretched out against him **d** up, **1Ki 13:4** 3001
a while that the brook **d** up, **1Ki 17:7** 3001
I **d** up All the rivers of Egypt." **2Ki 19:24** 2717a
a river becomes parched and **d** up, **Jb 14:11** 3001
"His roots are **d** below, And his **Jb 18:16** 3001
strength is **d** up like a potsherd, **Ps 22:15** 3001
You **d** up ever-flowing streams. **Ps 74:15** 3001
rebuked the Red Sea and it **d** up, **Ps 106:9** 2717a
I **d** up All the rivers of Egypt.' **Is 37:25** 2717a
to the depth of the sea, 'Be **d** up!' **Is 44:27** 2717a
Was it not You who **d** up the sea, **Is 51:10** 2717a
of the wilderness have **d** up. **Jer 23:10** 3001
her waters, and they will be **d** up! **Jer 50:38** 3001
And the east wind **d** up its fruit. **Ezk 19:12** 3001
'Our bones are **d** up and our hope **Ezk 37:11** 3001
is stricken, their root is **d** up, **Hos 9:16** 3001
dry And his spring will be **d** up; **Hos 13:15** 2717a
torn down, For the grain is **d** up. **Jl 1:17** 3001
For the water brooks are **d** up And **Jl 1:20** 3001
the flow of her blood was **d** up; **Mk 5:29** *3583*
and its water was **d** up, **Rv 16:12** *3583*

DRIES
a broken spirit **d** up the bones. **Pr 17:22** 3001
is ruined, The new wine **d** up, **Jl 1:10** 3001

The vine **d** up And the fig tree **Jl 1:12** 3001
d up From the sons of men. **Jl 1:12** 3001
And the summit of Carmel **d** up." **Am 1:2** 3001
He **d** up all the rivers. **Na 1:4** 2717a
thrown away as a branch and **d** up; **Jn 15:6** *3583*

DRIFT
we do not **d** away *from it.* **Heb 2:1** *3901*

DRIFTING
like **d** straw To the desert wind. **Jer 13:24** 5674a

DRINK
let us make our father **d** wine, **Gn 19:32** 8248
their father **d** wine that night, **Gn 19:33** 8248
us make him **d** wine tonight also; **Gn 19:34** 8248
father **d** wine that night also, **Gn 19:35** 8248
with water and gave the lad a **d**. **Gn 21:19** 8248
let down your jar so that I may **d**,' **Gn 24:14** 8354
'**D**, and I will water your camels **Gn 24:14** 8354
d a little water from your jar." **Gn 24:17** 1572
She said, "**D**, my lord"; **Gn 24:18** 8354
jar to her hand, and gave him a **d**. **Gn 24:18** 8248
she had finished giving him a **d**, **Gn 24:19** 8248
d a little water from your jar"; **Gn 24:43** 8248
"You **d**, and I will draw for your **Gn 24:44** 8354
'Please let me **d**.' **Gn 24:45** 8248
'**D**, and I will water your camels **Gn 24:46** 8354
where the flocks came to **d**; **Gn 30:38** 8354
they mated when they came to **d**. **Gn 30:38** 8354
and he poured out a **d** offering on it; **Gn 35:14** 5262a
could not **d** water from the Nile. **Ex 7:21** 8354
around the Nile for water to **d**, **Ex 7:24** 8354
not **d** of the water of the Nile. **Ex 7:24** 8354
could not **d** the waters of Marah, **Ex 15:23** 8354
"What shall we **d**?" **Ex 15:24** 8354
was no water for the people to **d**. **Ex 17:1** 8354
"Give us water that we may **d**." **Ex 17:2** 8354
of it, that the people may **d**." **Ex 17:6** 8354
with which to pour **d** offerings; **Ex 25:29** 5258a
of a hin of wine for a **d** offering **Ex 29:40** 5262a
grain offering and the same **d** offering **Ex 29:41** 5262a
shall not pour out a **d** offering **Ex 30:9** 5262a
people sat down to eat and to **d**, **Ex 32:6** 8354
and made the sons of Israel **d** *it.* **Ex 32:20** 8248
he did not eat bread or **d** water. **Ex 34:28** 8354
with which to pour out **d** offerings, **Ex 37:16** 5258a
"Do not **d** wine or strong drink, **Lv 10:9** 7941
"Do not drink wine or strong **d**, **Lv 10:9** 8354
with its **d** offering, a fourth of a **Lv 23:13** 5262a
and their **d** offerings, **Lv 23:18** 5262a
sacrifices and **d** offerings, *each* **Lv 23:37** 5262a
bowls and the jars for the **d** offering, **Nu 4:7** 5262a
'Then he shall make the woman **d** **Nu 5:24** 8248
shall make the woman **d** the water. **Nu 5:26** 8248
'When he has made her **d** the water, **Nu 5:27** 8248
abstain from wine and strong **d**; **Nu 6:3** 7941
he shall **d** no vinegar, whether **Nu 6:3** 7941
made from wine or strong **d**, **Nu 6:3** 8354
shall he **d** any grape juice nor **Nu 6:3** 8354
grain offering and their **d** offering. **Nu 6:15** 5262a
grain offering and its **d** offering. **Nu 6:17** 5262a
the Nazirite may **d** wine.' **Nu 6:20** 8354
prepare wine for the **d** offering, **Nu 15:5** 5262a
and for the **d** offering you shall **Nu 15:7** 5262a
and you shall offer as the **d** offering **Nu 15:10** 5262a
offering and its **d** offering, **Nu 15:24** 5262a
nor is there water to **d**." **Nu 20:5** 8354
congregation and their beasts **d**." **Nu 20:8** 8248
not even **d** water from a well. **Nu 20:17** 8354
livestock do **d** any of your water, **Nu 20:19** 8354
we will not **d** water from wells. **Nu 21:22** 8354
'Then the **d** offering with it *shall* **Nu 28:7** 5262a
you shall pour out a **d** offering **Nu 28:7** 5262a
drink offering of strong **d** to the LORD. **Nu 28:7** 7941
of the morning and as its **d** offering, **Nu 28:8** 5262a
offering, and its **d** offering: **Nu 28:9** 5262a
burnt offering and its **d** offering. **Nu 28:10** 5262a
'Their **d** offerings shall be half a **Nu 28:14** 5262a
offered with its **d** offering **Nu 28:15** 5262a
presented with its **d** offering **Nu 28:24** 5262a
them with their **d** offerings. **Nu 28:31** 5262a
and their **d** offerings, according to **Nu 29:6** 5262a
offering, and their **d** offerings. **Nu 29:11** 5262a
its grain offering and its **d** offering. **Nu 29:16** 5262a
offering and their **d** offerings **Nu 29:18** 5262a
offering, and their **d** offering. **Nu 29:19** 5262a
offerings and their **d** offerings **Nu 29:21** 5262a
offering and its **d** offering. **Nu 29:22** 5262a
offering and their **d** offerings **Nu 29:24** 5262a
its grain offering and its **d** offering. **Nu 29:25** 5262a
and their grain offering and their **d** **Nu 29:27** 5262a
offering and its **d** offering. **Nu 29:28** 5262a
offering and their **d** offerings **Nu 29:30** 5262a
offering and its **d** offerings. **Nu 29:31** 5262a
offering and their **d** offerings **Nu 29:33** 5262a
its grain offering and its **d** offering. **Nu 29:34** 5262a
offering and their **d** offerings **Nu 29:37** 5262a
offering and its **d** offering. **Nu 29:38** 5262a
offerings and for your **d** offerings **Nu 29:39** 5262a
that the people had no water to **d**. **Nu 33:14** 8354
them with money so that you may **d**. **Dt 2:6** 8354
water for money so that I may **d**, **Dt 2:28** 8354
or sheep, or wine, or strong **d**, **Dt 14:26** 7941
but you will neither **d** of the **Dt 28:39** 8354
have you drunk wine or strong **d**, **Dt 29:6** 7941
wine of their **d** offering? **Dt 32:38** 5257a
give me a little water to **d**, **Jg 4:19** 8248
a bottle of milk and gave him a **d**; **Jg 4:19** 8248
as everyone who kneels to **d**." **Jg 7:5** 8354
of the people kneeled to **d** water. **Jg 7:6** 8354
not to **d** wine or strong drink, **Jg 13:4** 8354
not to drink wine or strong **d**, **Jg 13:4** 7941
and now you shall not **d** wine or **Jg 13:7** 8354
d nor eat any unclean thing, **Jg 13:7** 7941
vine nor **d** wine or strong drink, **Jg 13:14** 8354
vine nor drink wine or strong **d**, **Jg 13:14** 7941
d from what the servants draw." **Ru 2:9** 8354
drunk neither wine nor strong **d**, **1Sa 1:15** 7941
and they provided him water to **d**. **1Sa 30:11** 8248
then go to my house to eat and to **d** **2Sa 11:11** 8354
It would eat of his bread and **d** of **2Sa 12:3** 8354
is faint in the wilderness to **d**." **2Sa 16:2** 8354
taste what I eat or what I **d**? **2Sa 19:35** 8354
give me water to **d** from the well of **2Sa 23:15** 8248
Nevertheless he would not **d** it, **2Sa 23:16** 8354
Shall I **d** the blood of the men **2Sa 23:17**
Therefore he would not **d** it. **2Sa 23:17** 8354
bread or **d** water in this place. **1Ki 13:8** 8354
shall eat no bread, nor **d** water, **1Ki 13:9** 8354
or **d** water with you in this place. **1Ki 13:16** 8354
eat no bread, nor **d** water there; **1Ki 13:17** 8354
he may eat bread and **d** water.' " **1Ki 13:18** 8354
"Eat no bread and **d** no water"; **1Ki 13:22** 8354
be that you will **d** of the brook, **1Ki 17:4** 8354
and he would **d** from the brook. **1Ki 17:6** 8354
water in a jar, that I may **d**." **1Ki 17:10** 8354
"Go up, eat and **d**; **1Ki 18:41** 8354
So Ahab went up to eat and **d**. **1Ki 18:42** 8354
with water, so that you shall **d**, **2Ki 3:17** 8354
and **d** and go to their master." **2Ki 6:22** 8354
and poured his **d** offering **2Ki 16:13** 5262a
meal offering and their **d** offerings; **2Ki 16:15** 5262a
and **d** their own urine with you?" **2Ki 18:27** 8354
his fig tree and **d** each of the waters **2Ki 18:31** 8354
to **d** from the well of Bethlehem, **1Ch 11:17** 8248
nevertheless David would not **d** it, **1Ch 11:18** 8354
Shall I **d** the blood of these men **1Ch 11:19** 8354
Therefore he would not **d** it. **1Ch 11:19** 8354
with their **d** offerings and sacrifices **1Ch 29:21** 5262a
sandals, fed them and gave them **d**, **2Ch 28:15** 8248
and carpenters, and food, **d** and **Ezr 3:7** 4960
offerings and their **d** offerings **Ezr 7:17** 5261
he did not eat bread nor **d** water, **Ezr 10:6** 8354
eat of the fat, **d** of the sweet, **Ne 8:10** 8354
the people went away to eat, to **d**, **Ne 8:12** 8354
the king and Haman sat down to **d**, **Es 3:15** 8354
do not eat or **d** for three days, **Es 4:16** 8354
to **d** *wine* with Esther the queen. **Es 7:1** 8354
sisters to eat and **d** with them. **Jb 1:4** 8354
d of the wrath of the Almighty. **Jb 21:20** 8354
you have given no water to **d**, **Jb 22:7** 8248
not pour out their **d** offerings **Ps 16:4** 5262a
They **d** their fill of the abundance **Ps 36:8** 8248
to **d** of the river of Your delights. **Ps 36:8** 7301
Or **d** the blood of male goats? **Ps 50:13** 8354
wine to **d** that makes us stagger. **Ps 60:3** 8248
thirst they gave me vinegar to **d**. **Ps 69:21** 8248
must drain *and* **d** down its dregs. **Ps 75:8** 8354
abundant **d** like the ocean depths. **Ps 78:15** 8248
their streams, they could not **d**. **Ps 78:44** 8354
them to **d** tears in large measure. **Ps 80:5** 8248
And mingled my **d** with weeping **Ps 102:9** 8250
They give **d** to every beast of the field **Ps 104:11** 8248
trees of the LORD **d** their fill, **Ps 104:16** 7646
d from the brook by the wayside; **Ps 110:7** 8354
And **d** the wine of violence. **Pr 4:17** 8354
D water from your own cistern And **Pr 5:15** 8354
let us **d** our fill of love until **Pr 7:18** 7301
And **d** of the wine I have mixed. **Pr 9:5** 8354
is a mocker, strong **d** a brawler, **Pr 20:1** 7941
He says to you, "Eat and **d**!" But **Pr 23:7** 8354
I will seek another **d**." **Pr 23:35**
is thirsty, give him water to **d**; **Pr 25:21** 8248
It is not for kings to **d** wine, **Pr 31:4** 8354
Or for rulers to desire strong **d**, **Pr 31:4** 7941
they will **d** and forget what is decreed, **Pr 31:5** 8354
strong **d** to him who is perishing, **Pr 31:6** 7941
Let him **d** and forget his poverty And **Pr 31:7** 8354
for a man *than* to eat and **d** and tell **Ec 2:24** 8354
to **d** and enjoy oneself in all **Ec 5:18** 8354
to eat and to **d** and to be merry, **Ec 8:15** 8354
and **d** your wine with a cheerful **Ec 9:7** 8354
D and imbibe deeply, O lovers." **SS 5:1** 8354
I would give you spiced wine to **d** **SS 8:2** 8248
dross, Your **d** diluted with water. **Is 1:22** 5435
that they may pursue strong **d**, **Is 5:11** 7941
valiant men in mixing strong **d**, **Is 5:22** 7941
out the cloth, they eat, they **d**; **Is 21:5** 8354
"Let us eat and **d**, for tomorrow **Is 22:13** 8354
They do not **d** wine with song; **Is 24:9** 8354
Strong **d** is bitter to those who **Is 24:9** 7941
drink is bitter to those who **d** it. **Is 24:9** 8354
wine and stagger from strong **d**: **Is 28:7** 7941
the prophet reel with strong **d**, **Is 28:7** 7941
wine, they stagger from strong **d**; **Is 28:7** 7941
stagger, but not with strong **d**. **Is 29:9** 7941
to withhold **d** from the thirsty. **Is 32:6** 4945b
and **d** their own urine with you?" **Is 36:12** 8354
and **d** each of the waters of his own **Is 36:16** 8354
To give **d** to My chosen people. **Is 43:20** 8248
anger; You will never **d** it again. **Is 51:22** 8354
let us **d** heavily of strong drink; **Is 56:12** 7941
let us drink heavily of strong **d**; **Is 56:12** 5433a
you have poured out a **d** offering , **Is 57:6** 5262a
will foreigners **d** your new wine for **Is 62:8** 8354
And those who gather it will **d** it **Is 62:9** 8354
Behold, My servants will **d**, **Is 65:13** 8354
To **d** the waters of the Nile? **Jer 2:18** 8354
To **d** the waters of the Euphrates? **Jer 2:18** 8354
and *they* pour out **d** offerings to **Jer 7:18** 5262a
And given us poisoned water to **d**, **Jer 8:14** 8248
and give them poisoned water to **d**. **Jer 9:15** 8248
to **d** for anyone's father or mother. **Jer 16:7** 8248
to sit with them to eat and **d**." **Jer 16:8** 8354
host and poured out **d** offerings **Jer 19:13** 5262a
Did not your father eat and **d** And **Jer 22:15** 8354
And make them **d** poisonous water, **Jer 23:15** 8248
to whom I send you to **d** it. **Jer 25:15** 8248
"They will **d** and stagger and **Jer 25:16** 8354
to whom the LORD sent me **d** it: **Jer 25:17** 8248
of Sheshach shall **d** after them. **Jer 25:26** 8354
"**D**, be drunk, vomit, fall and **Jer 25:27** 8354
take the cup from your hand to **d**, **Jer 25:28** 8354
"You shall surely **d**! **Jer 25:28** 8354
on their roofs and poured out **d** offerings **Jer 32:29** 5262a
and give them wine to **d**." **Jer 35:2** 8248
and I said to them, "**D** wine!" **Jer 35:5** 8354
"We will not **d** wine, for Jonadab **Jer 35:6** 8354
'You shall not **d** wine, you or your **Jer 35:6** 8354
us, not to **d** wine all our days, **Jer 35:8** 8354
commanded his sons not to **d** wine, **Jer 35:14** 8354
So they do not **d** *wine* to this day, **Jer 35:14** 8354
of heaven and pouring out **d** offerings **Jer 44:17** 5262a
of heaven and pouring out **d** offerings **Jer 44:18** 5262a
and were pouring out **d** offerings **Jer 44:19** 5262a
image and poured out **d** offerings **Jer 44:19** 5262a
of heaven and pour out **d** offerings **Jer 44:25** 5262a
And it **d** its fill of their blood; **Jer 46:10** 7301
who were not sentenced to **d** the cup **Jer 49:12** 8354
drink the cup will certainly **d** *it,* **Jer 49:12** 8354
but you will certainly **d** *it.* **Jer 49:12** 8354
the pans and the **d** offering bowls, **Jer 52:19** 4518
"The water you **d** shall be the **Ezk 4:11** 8354
you shall **d** it from time to time. **Ezk 4:11** 8354
and **d** water by measure and in **Ezk 4:16** 8354
and **d** your water with quivering **Ezk 12:18** 8354
and **d** their water with horror, **Ezk 12:19** 8354
they poured out their **d** offerings. **Ezk 20:28** 5262a
'You will **d** your sister's cup, **Ezk 23:32** 8354
'You will **d** it and drain it. **Ezk 23:34** 8354
eat your fruit and **d** your milk. **Ezk 25:4** 8354
d the discharge of your blood As **Ezk 32:6** 8248
you should **d** of the clear waters, **Ezk 34:18** 8354
and **d** what you foul with your feet!' " **Ezk 34:19** 8354
you may eat flesh and **d** blood. **Ezk 39:17** 8354
and **d** the blood of the princes of **Ezk 39:18** 8354
and **d** blood until you are drunk, **Ezk 39:19** 8354
"Nor shall any of the priests **d** **Ezk 44:21** 8354
offerings and the **d** offerings, **Ezk 45:17** 5262a
appointed your food and your **d**; **Da 1:10** 4960
vegetables to eat and water to **d**. **Da 1:12** 8354
food and the wine they were to **d**, **Da 1:16** 4960
his concubines might **d** from them. **Da 5:2** 8355
and my flax, my oil and my **d**.' **Hos 2:5** 8250
They will not pour out **d** offerings of **Hos 9:4** 5258a
The grain offering and the **d** offering **Jl 1:9** 5262a
grain offering and the **d** offering **Jl 1:13** 5262a
grain offering and a **d** offering **Jl 2:14** 5262a
a girl for wine that they may **d**. **Jl 3:3** 8354
house of their God they **d** the wine **Am 2:8** 8354
"But you made the Nazirites **d** wine, **Am 2:12** 8248
"Bring now, that we may **d**!" **Am 4:1** 8354
to another city to **d** water, **Am 4:8** 8354
yet you will not **d** their wine. **Am 5:11** 8354
Who **d** wine from sacrificial bowls **Am 6:6** 8354
plant vineyards and **d** their wine, **Am 9:14** 8354
the nations will **d** continually. **Ob 1:16** 8354
They will **d** and swallow And **Ob 1:16** 8354
Do not let them eat or **d** water. **Jon 3:7** 8354
grapes, but you will not **d** wine. **Mi 6:15** 8354
who are drunken with their **d**, **Na 1:10** 5435
to you who make your neighbors **d**, **Hab 2:15** 8248
d and expose your *own* nakedness. **Hab 2:16** 8354
vineyards but not **d** their wine." **Zph 1:13** 8354
you **d**, but *there is* not *enough* to **Hg 1:6** 8354
'When you eat and **d**, **Zch 7:6** 8354
and do you not **d** for yourselves? **Zch 7:6** 8354
And they will **d** *and* be boisterous **Zch 9:15** 8354
will eat or what you will **d**; **Mt 6:25** *4095*
'What will we **d**?' **Mt 6:31** *4095*
even a cup of cold water to **d**, **Mt 10:42** *4222*
Are you able to **d** the cup that I **Mt 20:22** *4095*
the cup that I am about to **d**?" **Mt 20:22** *4095*
"My cup you shall **d**; **Mt 20:23** *4095*
and eat and **d** with drunkards; **Mt 24:49** *4095*
and you gave Me *something* to **d**; **Mt 25:35** *4222*
thirsty, and give You *something* to **d**? **Mt 25:37** *4222*
and you gave Me nothing to **d**; **Mt 25:42** *4222*
"**D** from it, all of you; **Mt 26:27** *4095*
I will not **d** of this fruit of the **Mt 26:29** *4095*
I **d** it new with you in My Father's **Mt 26:29** *4095*
cannot pass away unless I **d** it, **Mt 26:42** *4095*
Him wine to **d** mixed with gall; **Mt 27:34** *4095*
tasting *it,* He was unwilling to **d**. **Mt 27:34** *4095*
it on a reed, and gave Him a **d**. **Mt 27:48** *4222*
whoever gives you a cup of water to **d** **Mk 9:41** *4222*
able to **d** the cup that I drink, **Mk 10:38** *4095*
able to drink the cup that I **d**, **Mk 10:38** *4095*
"The cup that I **d** you shall drink; **Mk 10:39** *4095*
"The cup that I drink you shall **d**; **Mk 10:39** *4095*
I will never again **d** of the fruit **Mk 14:25** *4095*
d it new in the kingdom of God." **Mk 14:25** *4095*
it on a reed, and gave Him a **d**, **Mk 15:36** *4222*
and if they **d** any deadly *poison,* **Mk 16:18** *4095*
and he will **d** no wine or liquor, **Lk 1:15** *4095*
"Why do you eat and **d** with the **Lk 5:30** *4095*
but Yours eat and **d**." **Lk 5:33** *4095*
ease, eat, **d** *and* be merry." **Lk 12:19** *4095*

will eat and what you will **d**, Lk 12:29 *4095*
and to eat and **d** and get drunk; Lk 12:45 *4095*
and serve me while I eat and **d**; Lk 17:8 *4095*
and afterward you may eat and **d**'? Lk 17:8 *4095*
I will not **d** of the fruit of the Lk 22:18 *4095*
and **d** at My table in My kingdom, Lk 22:30 *4095*
Jesus said to her, "Give Me a **d**." Jn 4:7 *4095*
d since I am a Samaritan woman?" Jn 4:9 *4095*
'Give Me a **d**,' you would have Jn 4:10 *4095*
of the Son of Man and **d** His blood, Jn 6:53 *4095*
true food, and My blood is true **d**. Jn 6:55 *4213*
thirsty, let him come to Me and **d**. Jn 7:37 *4095*
has given Me, shall I not **d** it?" Jn 18:11 *4095*
nor **d** until they had killed Paul. Ac 23:12 *4095*
to eat or **d** until they slay him; Ac 23:21 *4095*
IF HE IS THIRSTY, GIVE HIM A **D**; Ro 12:20 *4222*
good not to eat meat or to **d** wine, Ro 14:21 *4095*
I gave you milk to **d**, 1Co 3:2 *4222*
we not have a right to eat and **d**? 1Co 9:4 *4095*
all drank the same spiritual **d**, 1Co 10:4 *4188*
PEOPLE SAT DOWN TO EAT AND **D**, 1Co 10:7 *4095*
You cannot **d** the cup of the Lord 1Co 10:21 *4095*
you eat or **d** or whatever you do, 1Co 10:31 *4095*
have houses in which to eat and **d**? 1Co 11:22 *4095*
do this, as often as you **d** *it*, 1Co 11:25 *4095*
you eat this bread and **d** the cup, 1Co 11:26 *4095*
eat of the bread and **d** of the cup. 1Co 11:28 *4095*
were all made to **d** of one Spirit. 1Co 12:13 *4222*
are not raised, LET US EAT AND **D**, 1Co 15:32 *4095*
poured out as a **d** offering upon the Php 2:17 *4689*
as your judge in regard to food or **d** Col 2:16 *4213*
No longer **d** water *exclusively,* but 1Tm 5:23 *5202*
being poured out as a **d** offering, 2Tm 4:6 *4689*
food and **d** and various washings, Heb 9:10 *4188*
made all the nations **d** of the wine of Rv 14:8 *4222*
he also will **d** of the wine of the Rv 14:10 *4095*
You have given them blood to **d**. Rv 16:6 *4095*

DRINKER
For the heavy **d** and the glutton Pr 23:21 5433a

DRINKERS
Do not be with heavy **d** of wine, Pr 23:20 5433a
And wail, all you wine **d**, Jl 1:5 8354

DRINKING
until they have finished **d**." Gn 24:19 8354
When the camels had finished **d**, Gn 24:22 8354
difficulty in **d** water from the Nile. Ex 7:18 8354
he has finished eating and **d**. Ru 3:3 8354
rose after eating and **d** in Shiloh. 1Sa 1:9 8354
eating and **d** and dancing because 1Sa 30:16 8354
they are eating and **d** before him; 1Ki 1:25 8354
were eating and **d** and rejoicing. 1Ki 4:20 8354
Solomon's **d** vessels *were* of gold, 1Ki 10:21 4945b
Now he *was* at Tirzah **d** himself 1Ki 16:9 8354
as he was **d** with the kings in the 1Ki 20:12 8354
while Ben-hadad was **d** himself 1Ki 20:16 8354
David three days, eating and **d**, 1Ch 12:39 8354
Solomon's **d** vessels *were* of gold, 2Ch 9:20 4945b
d was *done* according to the law, Es 1:8 8360
king arose in his anger from **d** wine Es 7:7 4960
the place where they were **d** wine, Es 7:8 4960
d wine in their oldest brother's house, Jb 1:13 8354
your daughters were eating and **d** wine Jb 1:18 8354
to those who are heroes in **d** wine And Is 5:22 8354
Eating of meat and **d** of wine: Is 22:13 8354
And behold, he is **d**, Is 29:8 8354
We have to pay for our **d** water, La 5:4 8354
and he was **d** wine in the presence Da 5:1 8355
have been **d** wine from them; Da 5:23 8355
John came neither eating nor **d**, Mt 11:18 *4095*
"The Son of Man came eating and **d**, Mt 11:19 *4095*
the flood they were eating and **d**, Mt 24:38 *4095*
"Why is He eating and **d** with Mk 2:16 *4095*
after **d** old *wine* wishes for new; Lk 5:39 *4095*
eating no bread and **d** no wine, Lk 7:33 *4095*
Son of Man has come eating and **d**, Lk 7:34 *4095*
eating and **d** what they give you; Lk 10:7 *4095*
they were eating, they were **d**, Lk 17:27 *4095*
they were eating, they were **d**, Lk 17:28 *4095*
of God is not eating and **d**, Ro 14:17 *4213*
for they were **d** from a spiritual 1Co 10:4 *4095*
d parties and abominable 1Pe 4:3 *4224*

DRINKS
this the one from which my lord **d** and Gn 44:5 8354
And **d** the blood of the slain." Nu 23:24 8354
d water from the rain of heaven, Dt 11:11 8354
D were served in golden vessels of Es 1:7 8248
Their poison my spirit **d**; Jb 6:4 8354
Man, who **d** iniquity like water! Jb 15:16 8354
Job, Who **d** up derision like water, Jb 34:7 8354
and **d** violence Who sends a message Pr 26:6 8354
that every man who eats and **d** sees Ec 3:13 8354
he **d** no water and becomes weary. Is 44:12 8354
"Everyone who **d** of this water Jn 4:13 *4095*
but whoever **d** of the water that I Jn 4:14 *4095*
and **d** My blood has eternal life, Jn 6:54 *4095*
flesh and **d** My blood abides in Me, Jn 6:56 *4095*
whoever eats the bread or **d** the cup 1Co 11:27 *4095*
For he who eats and **d**, 1Co 11:29 *4095*
eats and **d** judgment to himself if 1Co 11:29 *4095*
For ground that **d** the rain which Heb 6:7 *4095*

DRIP
down, They **d** upon man abundantly. Jb 36:28 7491
And Your paths **d** *with* fatness. Ps 65:11 7491
The pastures of the wilderness **d**, Ps 65:12 7491
up And the skies **d** with dew. Pr 3:20 7491
the lips of an adulteress **d** honey And Pr 5:3 5197
"Your lips, *my* bride, **d** honey; SS 4:11 5197
"**D** down, O heavens, from above, Is 45:8 7491
mountains will **d** with sweet wine, Jl 3:18 5197
the mountains will **d** sweet wine And Am 9:13 5197

DRIPPED
earth quaked, the heavens also **d**, Jg 5:4 5197
dripped, Even the clouds **d** water. Jg 5:4 5197
And my hands **d** with myrrh, And my SS 5:5 5197

DRIPPING
of a wife are a constant **d**. Pr 19:13 1812
A constant **d** on a day of steady rain Pr 27:15 1812
are lilies **D** with liquid myrrh. SS 5:13 5197

DRIPPINGS
honey and the **d** of the honeycomb. Ps 19:10 5317

DRIVE
"**D** out this maid and her son, for Gn 21:10 1644
he will **d** them out of his land." Ex 6:1 1644
d you out from here completely. Ex 11:1 1644
He made them **d** with difficulty; Ex 14:25 5090a
that they will **d** out the Hivites, Ex 23:28 1644
"I will not **d** them out before you Ex 23:29 1644
"I will **d** them out before you Ex 23:30 1644
you will **d** them out before you. Ex 23:31 1644
and I will **d** out the Canaanite, Ex 33:2 1644
to **d** out the Amorite before you, Ex 34:11 1644
"For I will **d** out nations before Ex 34:24 3423
which I will **d** out before you, Lv 20:23 7971
them and **d** them out of the land. Nu 22:6 1644
against them and **d** them out.' " Nu 22:11 1644
then you shall **d** out all the Nu 33:52 3423
'But if you do not **d** out the Nu 33:55 3423
so that you may **d** them out and Dt 9:3 3423
then the LORD will **d** out all these Dt 11:23 3423
God will **d** them out before you. Dt 18:12 3423
I will **d** them out from before the Jos 13:6 3423
and I will **d** them out as the LORD Jos 14:12 3423
of Judah could not **d** them out; Jos 15:63 3423
But they did not **d** out the Jos 16:10 3423
did not **d** them out completely. Jos 17:13 3423
you shall **d** out the Canaanites, Jos 17:18 3423
you and **d** them from before you; Jos 23:5 3423
not continue to **d** these nations out Jos 23:13 3423
but they could not **d** out the Jg 1:19 3423
sons of Benjamin did not **d** out the Jg 1:21 3423
did not **d** them out completely. Jg 1:28 3423
Ephraim did not **d** out the Jg 1:29 3423
not **d** out the inhabitants of Kitron, Jg 1:30 3423
not **d** out the inhabitants of Acco, Jg 1:31 3423
for they did not **d** them out. Jg 1:32 3423
Naphtali did not **d** out the Jg 1:33 3423
'I will not **d** them out before you; Jg 2:3 1644
I also will no longer **d** out before Jg 2:21 3423
me and **d** me from my father's house? Jg 11:7 1644
'**D** and go forward; 2Ki 4:24 5090a
d out the inhabitants of this land 2Ch 20:7 3423
by coming to **d** us out from Your 2Ch 20:11 1644
"They **d** away the donkeys of the Jb 24:3 5090a
the hand of the wicked **d** me away. Ps 36:11 5110
is driven away, *so* **d** *them* away; Ps 68:2 5086
D out the scoffer, and contention Pr 22:10 1644
"I will **d** him *like* a peg in a Is 22:23 8628
And **d** hard all your workers. Is 58:3 5065
and I will **d** you out and you will Jer 27:10 5080
in order that I may **d** you out and Jer 27:15 5080
Go up, you horses, and **d** madly, Jer 46:9 1984b
of soul, to **d** it out for a prey." Ezk 36:5 1644
I will turn you around, **d** you on, Ezk 39:2 8338
I will **d** them out of My house! Hos 9:15 1644
And I will **d** it into a parched and Jl 2:20 5080
"Why could we not **d** it out?" Mt 17:19 *1544b*
"Why could we not **d** it out?" Mk 9:28 *1544b*
He entered the temple and began to **d** Mk 11:15 *1544b*
entered the temple and began to **d** out Lk 19:45 *1544b*
and they resolved to **d** the ship Ac 27:39 *1856*

DRIVEN
You have **d** me this day from the Gn 4:14 1644
And if they are **d** hard one day, Gn 33:13 1849
were **d** out from Pharaoh's presence. Ex 10:11 1644
since they were **d** out of Egypt and Ex 12:39 1644
is **d** away while no one is looking, Ex 22:10 7617
And the sound of a **d** leaf will Lv 26:36 5086
d His enemies out from before Him, Nu 32:21 3423
God has **d** them out before you, Dt 9:4 1920
"You shall be **d** mad by the Dt 28:34 7696
"For the LORD has **d** out great and Jos 23:9 3423
LORD our God has **d** out before us, Jg 11:24 3423
for they have **d** me out today so 1Sa 26:19 1644
nations whom the LORD had **d** out 2Ki 16:3 3423
d out before the sons of Israel, 2Ki 17:8 3423
not **d** out the priests of the LORD, 2Ch 13:9 5080
d out before the sons of Israel. 2Ch 28:3 3423
And that deliverance is **d** from me? Jb 6:13 5080
You cause a **d** leaf to tremble? Jb 13:25 5086
"He is **d** from light into Jb 18:18 1920
"They are **d** from the community; Jb 30:5 1644
As smoke is **d** away, *so* drive *them* Ps 68:2 5086
they will be **d** away into darkness. Is 8:22 5080
Nile Will become dry, be **d** away, Is 19:7 5086
d in a firm place will give way; Is 22:25 8628
is the cartwheel **d** over cummin; Is 28:27 5437
places to which I have **d** them," Jer 8:3 5080
My flock and **d** them away, Jer 23:2 5080
all the countries where I have **d** them Jer 23:3 5080
the countries where I had **d** them.' Jer 23:8 5080
They will be **d** away into the gloom Jer 23:12 1761b
all the places where I have **d** you,' Jer 29:14 5080
the nations where I have **d** them, Jer 29:18 5080
which I have **d** them in My anger, Jer 32:37 5080
places to which they had been **d** away Jer 40:12 5080
to which they had been **d** away, Jer 43:5 5080
the nations Where I have **d** you, Jer 46:28 5080
of you will be **d** out headlong, Jer 49:5 5080
flock, the lions have **d** *them* away. Jer 50:17 5080
He has **d** me and made me walk In La 3:2 5090a
its wickedness I have **d** it away. Ezk 31:11 1644
that you be **d** away from mankind and Da 4:25 2957
you will be **d** away from mankind, Da 4:32 2957
and he was **d** away from mankind and Da 4:33 2957
"He was also **d** away from mankind, Da 5:21 2957
to which You have **d** them, Da 9:7 5080
Ashdod will be **d** out at noon And Zph 2:4 1644
be **d** by the demon into the desert. Lk 8:29 *1643*
they had **d** him out of the city, Ac 7:58 *1544b*
it and let ourselves be **d** along. Ac 27:15 *5342*
let themselves be **d** along. Ac 27:17 *5342*
being **d** about in the Adriatic Sea, Ac 27:27 *1308*
the sea, **d** and tossed by the wind. Jas 1:6 *416*
great and are **d** by strong winds, Jas 3:4 *1643*
water and mists **d** by a storm, 2Pe 2:17 *1643*

DRIVER
he said to the **d** of his chariot, 1Ki 22:34 7395
he said to the **d** of the chariot, 2Ch 18:33 7395
of the **d** he does not hear. Jb 39:7 5065

DRIVES
the nations where the LORD **d** you. Dt 4:27 5090a
all the people where the LORD **d** Dt 28:37 5090a
of Nimshi, for he **d** furiously." 2Ki 9:20 5090a
like chaff which the wind **d** away. Ps 1:4 5086
He who assaults *his* father *and* **d** Pr 19:26 1272
d the *threshing* wheel over them. Pr 20:26 7725
Which the wind of the LORD **d**. Is 59:19 5127

DRIVING
d out from before you nations Dt 4:38 3423
by **d** out all your enemies from Dt 6:19 1920
your God is **d** them out before you, Dt 9:5 3423
to remain, not **d** them out quickly; Jg 2:23 3423
and the **d** is like the driving of 2Ki 9:20 4491
the **d** of Jehu the son of Nimshi, 2Ki 9:20 4491
in **d** out nations from before Your 1Ch 17:21 1644
the angel of the LORD **d** *them* on. Ps 35:5 1760
a **d** rain which leaves no food. Pr 28:3 5502
by banishing them, by **d** them away. Is 27:8 7971
great learning is **d** you mad." Ac 26:24 *4062*

DROP
oil, for your olives will **d** off. Dt 28:40 5394
"Let my teaching **d** as the rain, Dt 32:2 6201
His heavens also **d** down dew. Dt 33:28 6201
"He will **d** off his unripe grape Jb 15:33 2554
are like a **d** from a bucket, Is 40:15 4752

DROPLETS
As the **d** on the fresh grass And as Dt 32:2 8164

DROPPED
it **d** on him so that he died, Nu 35:23 5307
and his bonds **d** from his hands. Jg 15:14 4549
brought in their levies and **d** *them* 2Ch 24:10 7993
again, And my speech **d** on them. Jb 29:22 5197
d *rain* at the presence of God; Ps 68:8 5197
stood still, they **d** their wings. Ezk 1:24 7503
stood still, they **d** their wings. Ezk 1:25 7503

DROPS
"For He draws up the **d** of water, Jb 36:27 5198a
Or who has begotten the **d** of dew? Jb 38:28 96
His sweat became like **d** of blood, Lk 22:44 *2361*

DROPSY
a man suffering from **d**. Lk 14:2 *5203*

DROSS
the wicked of the earth *like* **d**; Ps 119:119 5509
Take away the **d** from the silver, Pr 25:4 5509
earthen vessel overlaid with silver **d** Pr 26:23 5509
Your silver has become **d**, Is 1:22 5509
smelt away your **d** as with lye And Is 1:25 5509
of Israel has become **d** to Me; Ezk 22:18 5509
they are the **d** of silver. Ezk 22:18 5509
'Because all of you have become **d**, Ezk 22:19 5509

DROUGHT
"**D** and heat consume the snow Jb 24:19 6723
Like heat in **d**, You subdue Is 25:5 6724
a land of **d** and of deep darkness, Jer 2:6 6723
to Jeremiah in regard to the **d**: Jer 14:1 1224b
of **d** Nor cease to yield fruit. Jer 17:8 1226
"A **d** on her waters, and they will Jer 50:38 2721a
the wilderness, In the land of **d**. Hos 13:5 8514
"I called for a **d** on the land, Hg 1:11 2721a

DROVE
So He **d** the man out; Gn 3:24 1644
carcasses, and Abram **d** them away. Gn 15:11 5380
and he **d** away all his livestock Gn 31:18 5090a
his servants, every **d** by itself, Gn 32:16 5739
shepherds came and **d** them away, Ex 2:17 1644
and **d** them into the Red Sea; Ex 10:19 8628
d out the enemy from before you, Dt 33:27 1644
Caleb **d** out from there the three Jos 15:14 3423
d out the two kings of the Amorites Jos 24:12 1644
"The LORD **d** out from before Jos 24:18 1644
and he **d** out from there the three Jg 1:20 3423
him and **d** the peg into his temple, Jg 4:21 8628
but Zebul **d** out Gaal and his Jg 9:41 1644
d Jephthah out and said to him, Jg 11:2 1644
d out the Amorites from before His Jg 11:23 3423
d ahead of the *other* livestock, 1Sa 30:20 5090a
Then Jeroboam **d** Israel away from 2Ki 17:21 5067b
His servants **d** his body in a 2Ki 23:30 7392
and Uzza and Ahio **d** the cart. 1Ch 13:7 5090a
Horonite, so I **d** him away from me. Ne 13:28 1272
You with Your own hand **d** out Ps 44:2 3423
d out the nations before them And Ps 78:55 1644
He **d** His adversaries backward; Ps 78:66 5221

You removed a vine from Egypt; You **d** Ps 80:8 1644
And Jesus entered the temple and **d** Mt 21:12 *1544b*
and they got up and **d** Him out of Lk 4:29 *1544b*
and **d** *them* all out of the temple, Jn 2:15 *1544b*
whom God **d** out before our fathers, Ac 7:45 *1856*
and **d** them out of their district. Ac 13:50 *1544b*
And he **d** them away from the Ac 18:16 *556*
and the prophets, and **d** us out. 1Th 2:15 *1559*

DROVES
me, and put a space between **d**." Gn 32:16 5739
and all those who followed the **d**, Gn 32:19 5739

DROWNED
his officers are **d** in the Red Sea. Ex 15:4 2883
to be **d** in the depth of the sea. Mt 18:6 *2670*
and they were **d** in the sea. Mk 5:13 *4155*
bank into the lake and was **d**. Lk 8:33 *638*
when they attempted it, were **d**. Heb 11:29 *2666*

DROWSINESS
And **d** will clothe *one* with rags. Pr 23:21 5124

DROWSY
they all got **d** and *began* to sleep. Mt 25:5 *3573*

DRUNK
He drank of the wine and became **d**, Gn 9:21 7937
and any liquid which may be **d** in Lv 11:34 8354
have you **d** wine or strong drink, Dt 29:6 8354
will make My arrows **d** with blood, Dt 32:42 7937
and **d** and his heart was merry, Ru 3:7 8354
So Eli thought she was **d**. 1Sa 1:13 7910
"How long will you make yourself **d**? 1Sa 1:14 7937
d neither wine nor strong drink, 1Sa 1:15 8354
within him, for he was very **d**; 1Sa 25:36 7910
For he had not eaten bread or **d** 1Sa 30:12 8354
before him, and he made him **d**; 2Sa 11:13 7937
eaten bread and **d** water in the place 1Ki 13:22 8354
eaten bread and after he had **d**, 1Ki 13:23 8354
himself **d** in the house of Arza, 1Ki 16:9 7910
Ben-hadad was drinking himself **d** in 1Ki 20:16 7910
had eaten and **d** he sent them away, 2Ki 6:23 8354
waters of abundance are **d** by them. Ps 73:10 4680
I have **d** my wine and my milk. SS 5:1 8354
They become **d**, but not with wine, Is 29:9 7937
And they will become **d** with their Is 49:26 7937
You who have **d** from the LORD's Is 51:17 8354
this, you afflicted, Who are **d**, Is 51:21 7937
And made them **d** in My wrath, Is 63:6 7937
"Drink, be **d**, vomit, fall and Jer 25:27 7937
"Make him **d**, for he has become Jer 48:26 7937
The nations have **d** of her wine; Jer 51:7 8354
their banquet And make them **d**, Jer 51:39 7937
her princes and her wise men **d**, Jer 51:57 7937
He has made me **d** with wormwood. La 3:15 7301
become **d** and make yourself naked. La 4:21 7937
and drink blood until you are **d**, Ezk 39:19 7943
You too will become **d**, Na 3:11 7937
your venom even to make *them* **d** So Hab 2:15 7937
there is not *enough* to become **d**; Hg 1:6 7937
and to eat and drink and get **d**; Lk 12:45 *3182*
and when *the people* have **d** freely, Jn 2:10 *3184*
"For these men are not **d**, Ac 2:15 *3184*
one is hungry and another is **d**. 1Co 11:21 *3184*
And do not get **d** with wine, for Eph 5:18 *3182*
who get **d** get drunk at night. 1Th 5:7 *3182*
who get drunk get **d** at night. 1Th 5:7 *3184*
were made **d** with the wine of her Rv 17:2 *3184*
d with the blood of the saints, Rv 17:6 *3184*
"For all the nations have **d** of Rv 18:3 *4095*

DRUNKARD
obey us, he is a glutton and a **d**.' Dt 21:20 5433a
which falls into the hand of a **d**, Pr 26:9 7910
earth reels to and fro like a **d** And Is 24:20 7910
'Behold, a gluttonous man and a **d**, Mt 11:19 *3630*
'Behold, a gluttonous man and a **d**, Lk 7:34 *3630*
an idolater, or a reviler, or a **d**, 1Co 5:11 *3183*

DRUNKARDS
me, And I *am* the song of the **d**. Ps 69:12
7941, 8354
proud crown of the **d** of Ephraim, Is 28:1 7910
The proud crown of the **d** of Is 28:3 7910
and **d** were brought from the Ezk 23:42 5433b
Awake, **d**, and weep; Jl 1:5 7910
slaves and eat and drink with **d**; Mt 24:49 *3184*
thieves, nor *the* covetous, nor **d**, 1Co 6:10 *3183*

DRUNKEN
makes them stagger like a **d** man. Jb 12:25 7910
reeled and staggered like a **d** man, Ps 107:27 7910
As a **d** man staggers in his vomit. Is 19:14 7910
I have become like a **d** man, Jer 23:9 7910
those who are **d** with their drink, Na 1:10 5433a

DRUNKENNESS
time—for strength and not for **d**. Ec 10:17 8358
inhabitants of Jerusalem—with **d**! Jer 13:13 7943
will be filled with **d** and sorrow, Ezk 23:33 7943
and **d** and the worries of life, Lk 21:34 *3178*
the day, not in carousing and **d**, Ro 13:13 *3178*
envying, **d**, carousing, and things Ga 5:21 *3178*
a course of sensuality, lusts, **d**, 1Pe 4:3 *3632*

DRUSILLA
days later Felix arrived with **D**, Ac 24:24 *1409*

DRY
and let the **d** land appear"; Gn 1:9 3004
God called the **d** land earth, Gn 1:10 3004
of all that was on the **d** land, Gn 7:22 2724
day of the month, the earth was **d**. Gn 8:14 3001
Nile and pour it on the **d** ground; Ex 4:9 3004
become blood on the **d** ground." Ex 4:9 3006
the midst of the sea on **d** land. Ex 14:16 3004
and turned the sea into **d** land, Ex 14:21 2724
midst of the sea on the **d** land, Ex 14:22 3004
the sons of Israel walked on **d** land Ex 14:29 3004
walked on **d** land through the midst Ex 15:19 3004
offering, mixed with oil or **d**, Lv 7:10 2720a
destroy the watered *land* with the **d**.' Dt 29:19 6771
d ground in the middle of the Jordan Jos 3:17 2724
all Israel crossed on **d** ground, Jos 3:17 2724
were lifted up to the **d** ground, Jos 4:18 2724
crossed this Jordan on **d** ground.' Jos 4:22 3004
was **d** *and* had become crumbled. Jos 9:5 3001
it is **d** and has become crumbled. Jos 9:12 3001
and it is **d** on all the ground, Jg 6:37 2721a
it now be **d** only on the fleece, Jg 6:39 2721a
for it was **d** only on the fleece, Jg 6:40 2721a
of them crossed over on **d** ground. 2Ki 2:8 2724
the midst of the sea on **d** ground; Ne 9:11 3004
the waters, and they **d** up; Jb 12:15 3001
Or will You pursue the **d** chaff? Jb 13:25 3002
And its stump dies in the **d** soil, Jb 14:8 6083
Who gnaw the **d** ground by night Jb 30:3 6723
In a **d** and weary land where there Ps 63:1 6723
He turned the sea into **d** land; Ps 66:6 3004
And His hands formed the **d** land. Ps 95:5 3006
ran in the **d** places *like* a river. Ps 105:41 6723
a **d** land into springs of water; Ps 107:35 6723
Better is a **d** morsel and quietness Pr 17:1 2720a
And **d** grass collapses into the Is 5:24 2842
The waters from the sea will **d** up, Is 19:5 5405
the river will be parched and **d**. Is 19:5 3001
of Egypt will thin out and **d** up; Is 19:6 2717a
fields by the Nile Will become **d**, Is 19:7 3001
When its limbs are **d**, Is 27:11 3001
streams of water in a **d** country, Is 32:2 6724
And the **d** land fountains of water. Is 41:18 6723
coastlands And **d** up the ponds. Is 42:15 3001
land And streams on the **d** ground; Is 44:3 3004
And I will make your rivers **d**. Is 44:27 3001
I **d** up the sea with My rebuke, Is 50:2 2717a
"Behold, I am a **d** tree." Is 56:3 3002
And I will **d** up her sea And make Jer 51:36 2717a
her sea And make her fountain **d**. Jer 51:36 3001
the low tree, **d** up the green tree and Ezk 17:24 3002
and make the **d** tree flourish. Ezk 17:24 3001
In a **d** and thirsty land. Ezk 19:13 6723
in you, as well as every **d** tree; Ezk 20:47 3002
I will make the Nile canals **d** And Ezk 30:12 2724
and lo, *they were* very **d**. Ezk 37:2 3002
'O **d** bones, hear the word of the Ezk 37:4 3002
a miscarrying womb and **d** breasts. Hos 9:14 6784
And his fountain will become **d** And Hos 13:15 954
All the trees of the field **d** up. Jl 1:12 3001
the part not rained on would **d** up. Am 4:7 3001
who made the sea and the **d** land." Jon 1:9 3004
vomited Jonah up onto the **d** land. Jon 2:10 3004
He rebukes the sea and makes it **d**; Na 1:4 3001
the sea also and the **d** land. Hg 2:6 2724
the depths of the Nile will **d** up; Zch 10:11 3001
what will happen when it is **d**?" Lk 23:31 *3584*
they were passing through **d** land; Heb 11:29 *3584*

DRY-SHOD
streams And make *men* walk over **d**. Is 11:15 5275

DUE
"You shall not pervert the justice **d** Ex 23:6
and to his sons as *their* **d** forever Lv 7:34 2706
It is *their* **d** forever throughout Lv 7:36 2708
because it is your **d** and your Lv 10:13 2706
sons' **d** out of the LORD's offerings Lv 10:13 2706
given as your **d** and your sons' due Lv 10:14 2706
given as your due and your sons' **d** Lv 10:14 2706
d you and your sons with you, Lv 10:15 2706
every offering **d** to the LORD, Nu 18:29
be the priests' **d** from the people, Dt 18:3 4941
justice **d** an alien *or* an orphan, Dt 24:17
distorts the justice **d** an alien, Dt 27:19
In **d** time their foot will slip; Dt 32:35
It came about in **d** time, 1Sa 1:20 8622
to the LORD the glory **d** His name; 1Ch 16:29
to give the portion **d** to the priests 2Ch 31:4
Nehemiah gave the portions **d** the Ne 12:47
the LORD the glory **d** to His name; Ps 29:2
Or if **d** to strength, eighty years, Ps 90:10
to the fear that is **d** You? Ps 90:11
give them their food in **d** season. Ps 104:27
give them their food in **d** time. Ps 145:15
good from those to whom it is **d**, Pr 3:27 1167
"I was **d** to offer peace offerings; Pr 7:14 5921
who withholds what is justly **d**, Pr 11:24 3476
And the justice **d** me escapes the Is 40:27
Yet surely the justice **d** to Me is Is 49:4
to whom the stroke *was* **d**? Is 53:8
Indeed it is Your **d**! Jer 10:7 2969
not be eaten **d** to rottenness. Jer 24:2 4480
cannot be eaten **d** to rottenness." Jer 24:3 4480
be eaten **d** to rottenness Jer 24:8 4480
cannot be eaten **d** to rottenness. Jer 29:17 4480
the **d** penalty of their error. Ro 1:27 *1163*
as a favor, but as what is **d**. Ro 4:4 *3783*
Render to all what is **d** them: Ro 13:7 *3782*
tax to whom tax *is* **d**; custom to Ro 13:7
for in **d** time we will reap if we Ga 6:9 *2398*

DUG
to me, that I **d** this well." Gn 21:30 2658
had **d** in the days of Abraham his Gn 26:15 2658
Then Isaac **d** again the wells of Gn 26:18 2658
the wells of water which had been **d** Gn 26:18 2658
But when Isaac's servants **d** in the Gn 26:19 2658
Then they **d** another well, and they Gn 26:21 2658
from there and **d** another well, Gn 26:22 2658
there Isaac's servants **d** a well. Gn 26:25 3738a
about the well which they had **d**, Gn 26:32 2658
in my grave which I **d** for myself Gn 50:5 3738a
So all the Egyptians **d** around the Ex 7:24 2658
Which the nobles of the people **d**, Nu 21:18 3738a
"I **d** *wells* and drank foreign waters, 2Ki 19:24 6979
has **d** a pit and hollowed it out, Ps 7:15 3738a
cause they **d** a pit for my soul. Ps 35:7 2658
They **d** a pit before me; Ps 57:6 3738a
Until a pit is **d** for the wicked. Ps 94:13 3738a
The arrogant have **d** pits for me, Ps 119:85 3738a
He **d** it all around, removed Is 5:2 5823
'I **d** *wells* and drank waters, And Is 37:25 6979
the quarry from which you were **d**. Is 51:1 5365
I went to the Euphrates and **d**, Jer 13:7 2658
For they have **d** a pit for me. Jer 18:20 3738a
For they have **d** a pit to capture Jer 18:22 3738a
So I **d** through the wall, and Ezk 8:8 2864
Then in the evening I **d** through Ezk 12:7 2864
IT AND **D** A WINE PRESS IN IT, Mt 21:33 *3736*
d *a hole* in the ground Mt 25:18 *3736*
and when they had **d** an opening, Mk 2:4 *1846*
AND **D** A VAT UNDER THE WINE PRESS Mk 12:1 *3736*
who **d** deep and laid a foundation Lk 6:48 *4626*

DULL
"His eyes are **d** from wine, And Gn 49:12 2447
If the axe is **d** and he does not Ec 10:10 6949a
people insensitive, Their ears **d**, Is 6:10 3513
His ear so **d** That it cannot hear. Is 59:1 3513
HEART OF THIS PEOPLE HAS BECOME **D**, Mt 13:15 *3975*
HEART OF THIS PEOPLE HAS BECOME **D**, Ac 28:27 *3975*
you have become **d** of hearing. Heb 5:11 *3576*

DUMAH
and Mishma and **D** and Massa, Gn 25:14 1746
Arab and **D** and Eshan, Jos 15:52 1746
Mishma, **D**, Massa, Hadad, Tema, 1Ch 1:30 1746

DUMP
and they shall **d** the plaster that Lv 14:41 8210

DUNG
away **d** until it is all gone. 1Ki 14:10 1557
d for five *shekels* of silver. 2Ki 6:25 1686
corpse of Jezebel will be as **d** on 2Ki 9:37 1828
doomed to eat their own **d** and 2Ki 18:27 2716
Who became as **d** for the ground. Ps 83:10 1828
doomed to eat their own **d** and Is 36:12 2716
be as **d** on the face of the ground. Jer 8:2 1828
fall like **d** on the open field, Jer 9:22 1828
they will be as **d** on the surface Jer 16:4 1828
like **d** on the face of the ground. Jer 25:33 1828
it in their sight over human **d**." Ezk 4:12
1561, 6627
I will give you cow's **d** in place Ezk 4:15 6832
cow's dung in place of human **d** over Ezk 4:15 1561
like dust And their flesh like **d**. Zph 1:17 1557

DUNGEON
should have put me into the **d**." Gn 40:15 953a
brought him out of the **d**; Gn 41:14 953a
of the captive who was in the **d**, Ex 12:29
1004, 953a
together *Like* prisoners in the **d**, Is 24:22 953a
To bring out prisoners from the **d** And Is 42:7 4525
free, and will not die in the **d**, Is 51:14 7845
For Jeremiah had come into the **d**, Jer 37:16
1004, 953a

DUPLICATES
dishes, 1,000 silver dishes, 29 **d**; Ezr 1:9 4252

DURA
of **D** in the province of Babylon. Da 3:1 1757

DURING
will not perish **d** the famine." Gn 41:36
D the seven years of plenty the land Gn 41:47
d the days of their sojourning." Gn 47:9
even **d** plowing time and harvest Ex 34:21
days **d** which he has the infection; Lv 13:46
whoever goes into the house **d** the Lv 14:46 3605
'Everything also on which she lies **d** Lv 15:20
d her menstrual impurity. Lv 18:19
but **d** the seventh year the land Lv 25:4
d the strife of the congregation, Nu 27:14
d the siege and the distress by Dt 28:53
d the siege and the distress by Dt 28:55
d the siege and the distress by Dt 28:57
of the land of Canaan **d** that year. Jos 5:12
for ten years **d** his days. 2Ch 14:1
one at war with him **d** those years, 2Ch 14:6
Ammonites gave him **d** that year 2Ch 27:5
King Ahaz had discarded **d** his reign 2Ch 29:19
should live in booths **d** the feast of Ne 8:14
But **d** all this *time* I was not in Ne 13:6
D that night the king could not Es 6:1
d the harvest and has nothing. Pr 20:4
in which he toils under the sun **d** Ec 5:18
is good for a man **d** *his* lifetime, Ec 6:12
d the few years of his futile Ec 6:12
d my lifetime of futility; Ec 7:15
young man, **d** your childhood, Ec 11:9
d the days of young manhood. Ec 11:9
he saw **d** the reigns of Uzziah, Is 1:1
anytime **d** the day or night, Is 28:19
a woman **d** her menstrual period Ezk 18:6
Jerusalem **d** her appointed feasts, Ezk 36:38
"**D** the seven days of the feast Ezk 45:23
of Beeri, **d** the days of Uzziah, Hos 1:1
and **d** the days of Jeroboam the son Hos 1:1
"Not **d** the festival, otherwise a riot Mt 26:5 *1722*
"Not **d** the festival, otherwise there Mk 14:2 *1722*
And He ate nothing **d** those days, Lk 4:2 *1722*

come **d** them and get healed, **Lk 13:14** *1722*
remember that **d** your life you **Lk 16:25** *1722*
Now **d** the day He was teaching in **Lk 21:37**
at the Passover, **d** the feast, **Jn 2:23** *1722*
D supper, the devil having already **Jn 13:2** *1096*
But **d** the night an angel **Ac 5:19** *1223*
in my house **d** the ninth hour; **Ac 10:30**
d the days of Unleavened Bread. **Ac 12:3**
and made the people great **d** their **Ac 13:17** *1722*
conduct yourselves in fear **d** the **1Pe 1:17**
d the construction of the ark, **1Pe 3:20**
d the days of their prophesying; **Rv 11:6**

DUSKY
feet stumble On the **d** mountains, **Jer 13:16** 5399

DUST
formed man of **d** from the ground, **Gn 2:7** 6083
And **d** you will eat All the days **Gn 3:14** 6083
For you are **d**, And to dust you **Gn 3:19** 6083
dust, And to **d** you shall return." **Gn 3:19** 6083
descendants as the **d** of the earth, **Gn 13:16** 6083
can number the **d** of the earth, **Gn 13:16** 6083
although I am *but* **d** and ashes. **Gn 18:27** 6083
also be like the **d** of the earth, **Gn 28:14** 6083
and strike the **d** of the earth, **Ex 8:16** 6083
and struck the **d** of the earth, **Ex 8:17** 6083
All the **d** of the earth became **Ex 8:17** 6083
fine **d** over all the land of Egypt, **Ex 9:9** 80
and he shall take some of the **d** **Nu 5:17** 6083
"Who can count the **d** of Jacob, **Nu 23:10** 6083
small until it was as fine as **d**; **Dt 9:21** 6083
and I threw its **d** into the brook **Dt 9:21** 6083
rain of your land powder and **d**; **Dt 28:24** 6083
venom of crawling things of the **d**. **Dt 32:24** 6083
and they put **d** on their heads. **Jos 7:6** 6083
"He raises the poor from the **d**, **1Sa 2:8** 6083
clothes torn and **d** on his head. **1Sa 4:12** 127
clothes torn and **d** on his head. **2Sa 1:2** 127
his coat torn and **d** on his head. **2Sa 15:32** 127
cast stones and threw **d** at him. **2Sa 16:13** 6083
them as the **d** of the earth; **2Sa 22:43** 6083
exalted you from the **d** and made **1Ki 16:2** 6083
the wood and the stones and the **d**, **1Ki 18:38** 6083
if the **d** of Samaria will suffice **1Ki 20:10** 6083
made them like the **d** at threshing. **2Ki 13:7** 6083
brook Kidron, and ground *it* to **d**, **2Ki 23:6** 6083
and threw its **d** on the graves of **2Ki 23:6** 6083
their **d** into the brook Kidron. **2Ki 23:12** 6083
its stones, ground them to **d**, **2Ki 23:15** 6083
as numerous as the **d** of the earth. **2Ch 1:9** 6083
and they threw **d** over their heads **Jb 2:12** 6083
Whose foundation is in the **d**, **Jb 4:19** 6083
does not come from the **d**, **Jb 5:6** 6083
For now I will lie down in the **d**; **Jb 7:21** 6083
out of the **d** others will spring. **Jb 8:19** 6083
would You turn me into **d** again? **Jb 10:9** 6083
wash away the **d** of the earth; **Jb 14:19** 6083
skin And thrust my horn in the **d**. **Jb 16:15** 6083
we together go down into the **d**?" **Jb 17:16** 6083
it lies down with him in the **d**. **Jb 20:11** 6083
"Together they lie down in the **d**, **Jb 21:26** 6083
And place *your* gold in the **d**, **Jb 22:24** 6083
"Though he piles up silver like **d** And **Jb 27:16** 6083
"Iron is taken from the **d**, **Jb 28:2** 6083
And its **d** *contains* gold. **Jb 28:6** 6083
I have become like **d** and ashes. **Jb 30:19** 6083
And man would return to **d**. **Jb 34:15** 6083
When the **d** hardens into a mass And **Jb 38:38** 6083
earth And warms them in the **d**, **Jb 39:14** 6083
"Hide them in the **d** together; **Jb 40:13** 6083
And I repent in **d** and ashes." **Jb 42:6** 6083
And lay my glory in the **d**. **Ps 7:5** 6083
fine as the **d** before the wind; **Ps 18:42** 6083
You lay me in the **d** of death. **Ps 22:15** 6083
down to the **d** will bow before Him, **Ps 22:29** 6083
Will the **d** praise You? **Ps 30:9** 6083
our soul has sunk down into the **d**; **Ps 44:25** 6083
And his enemies lick the **d**. **Ps 72:9** 6083
rained meat upon them like the **d**, **Ps 78:27** 6083
make them like the whirling **d**, **Ps 83:13** 1534
have profaned his crown in the **d**. **Ps 89:39** 776
You turn man back into **d** **Ps 90:3** 1793b
stones And feel pity for her **d**. **Ps 102:14** 6083
He is mindful that we are *but* **d**. **Ps 103:14** 6083
expire And return to their **d**. **Ps 104:29** 6083
He raises the poor from the **d** And **Ps 113:7** 6083
My soul cleaves to the **d**; **Ps 119:25** 6083
Nor the first **d** of the world. **Pr 8:26** 6083
the **d** and all return to the dust. **Ec 3:20** 6083
the dust and all return to the **d**. **Ec 3:20** 6083
then the **d** will return to the **Ec 12:7** 6083
Enter the rock and hide in the **d** **Is 2:10** 6083
and their blossom blow away as **d**; **Is 5:24** 80
Or like whirling **d** before a gale. **Is 17:13** 1534
cast to the ground, even to the **d**. **Is 25:12** 6083
the ground, He casts it to the **d**. **Is 26:5** 6083
You who lie in the **d**, **Is 26:19** 6083
the **d** *where* you are prostrate Your **Is 29:4** 6083
speech will whisper from the **d**. **Is 29:4** 6083
enemies will become like fine **d**, **Is 29:5** 80
their **d** become greasy with fat. **Is 34:7** 6083
the **d** of the earth by the measure, **Is 40:12** 6083
as a speck of **d** on the scales; **Is 40:15** 7834
lifts up the islands like fine **d**. **Is 40:15** 1851
makes them like **d** with his sword, **Is 41:2** 6083
"Come down and sit in the **d**, **Is 47:1** 6083
And lick the **d** of your feet; **Is 49:23** 6083
Shake yourself from the **d**, **Is 52:2** 6083
and **d** will be the serpent's food. **Is 65:25** 6083
They have thrown **d** on their heads; **La 2:10** 6083
He has made me cower in the **d**. **La 3:16** 665
Let him put his mouth in the **d**, **La 3:29** 6083
on the ground To cover it with **d**. **Ezk 24:7** 6083
d *raised by* them will cover you; **Ezk 26:10** 80
They will cast **d** on their heads, **Ezk 27:30** 6083
in the **d** of the ground will awake, **Da 12:2** 6083
"These who pant after the *very* **d** **Am 2:7** 6083
roll yourself in the **d**. **Mi 1:10** 6083
will lick the **d** like a serpent, **Mi 7:17** 6083
clouds are the **d** beneath His feet. **Na 1:3** 80
blood will be poured out like **d** And **Zph 1:17** 6083
And piled up silver like **d**, **Zch 9:3** 6083
shake the **d** off your feet. **Mt 10:14** *2868*
it will scatter him like **d**." **Mt 21:44** *3039*
shake the **d** off the soles of **Mk 6:11** *5529b*
shake the **d** off your feet as **Lk 9:5** *2868*
'Even the **d** of your city which **Lk 10:11** *2868*
it will scatter him like **d**." **Lk 20:18** *3039*
But they shook off the **d** of their **Ac 13:51** *2868*
cloaks and tossing **d** into the air, **Ac 22:23** *2868*
"And they threw **d** on their heads **Rv 18:19** *5529b*

DUSTY
d rubble even the burned ones?" **Ne 4:2** 6083

DUTIES
"They shall perform the **d** for **Nu 3:7** 4931
with the **d** of the sons of Israel, **Nu 3:8** 4931
Now the **d** of the sons of Gershon **Nu 3:25** 4931
performing the **d** of the sanctuary. **Nu 3:28** 4931
Now their **d** *involved* the ark, the **Nu 3:31** 4931
perform the **d** of the sanctuary. **Nu 3:32** 4931
Now the appointed **d** of the sons of **Nu 3:36** 4931
performing the **d** of the sanctuary **Nu 3:38** 4931
and their **d** *shall be* under the **Nu 4:28** 4931
They cast lots for their **d**, **1Ch 25:8** 4931
were given **d** like their relatives **1Ch 26:12** 4931
assigned to outside **d** for Israel, **1Ch 26:29** 4399
and the Levites for their **d** of **2Ch 8:14** 4931
d according to their divisions; **2Ch 31:16** 4931
by their **d** *and* their divisions. **2Ch 31:17** 4931
appointed **d** for the priests and the **Ne 13:30** 4931

DUTY
your **d** as a brother-in-law to her, **Gn 38:8** 2992
to them as a **d** all their loads. **Nu 4:27** 4931
"Now this is the **d** of their **Nu 4:31** 4931
army nor be charged with any **d**; **Dt 24:5** 1697
d of a husband's brother to her. **Dt 25:5** 2992
d of a husband's brother to me.' **Dt 25:7** 2992
have said, so it is our **d** to do. **Ezr 10:12** 5921
husband must fulfill his **d** to his wife, **1Co 7:3** *3782*

DWARF
or a hunchback or a **d**, **Lv 21:20** 1851

DWELL
who **d** in tents and *have* livestock. **Gn 4:20** 3427
let him **d** in the tents of Shem; **Gn 9:27** 7931
now my husband will **d** with me, **Gn 30:20** 2082
"Zebulun will **d** at the seashore; **Gn 49:13** 7931
was willing to **d** with the man, **Ex 2:21** 3427
and also the ground on which they **d**. **Ex 8:21**
for Me, that I may **d** among them. **Ex 25:8** 7931
"I will **d** among the sons of **Ex 29:45** 7931
Egypt, that I might **d** among them; **Ex 29:46** 7931
camp where I **d** in their midst." **Nu 5:3** 7931
live, in the midst of which I **d**; **Nu 35:34** 7931
will choose for His name to **d**, **Dt 12:11** 7931
them and **d** in their land, **Dt 12:29** 3427
of the LORD **d** in security by Him, **Dt 33:12** 7931
willing to **d** beyond the Jordan! **Jos 7:7** 3427
so that he may **d** among them. **Jos 20:4** 3427
'He shall **d** in that city until **Jos 20:6** 3427
"**D** with me and be a father and a **Jg 17:10** 3427
"See now, I **d** in a house of **2Sa 7:2** 3427
should build Me a house to **d** in? **2Sa 7:5** 3427
I will **d** among the sons of Israel, **1Ki 6:13** 7931
He would **d** in the thick cloud. **1Ki 8:12** 7931
will God indeed **d** on the earth? **1Ki 8:27** 3427
not build a house for Me to **d** in; **1Ch 17:4** 3427
that they may **d** in their own place **1Ch 17:9** 7931
to build him a house to **d** in, **2Ch 2:3** 3427
He would **d** in the thick cloud. **2Ch 6:1** 7931
d with mankind on the earth? **2Ch 6:18** 3427
"My wife shall not **d** in the house **2Ch 8:11** 3427
God who has caused His name to **d** **Ezr 6:12** 7932
chosen to cause My name to **d**.' **Ne 1:9** 7931
those who **d** in houses of clay, **Jb 4:19** 7931
let wickedness **d** in your tents; **Jb 11:14** 7931
that they **d** in dreadful valleys, **Jb 30:6** 7931
LORD, make me to **d** in safety. **Ps 4:8** 3427
Who may **d** on Your holy hill? **Ps 15:1** 7931
My flesh also will **d** securely. **Ps 16:9** 7931
And I will **d** in the house of the **Ps 23:6** 3427
The world, and those who **d** in it. **Ps 24:1** 3427
That I may **d** in the house of the **Ps 27:4** 3427
D in the land and cultivate **Ps 37:3** 7931
the land And **d** in it forever. **Ps 37:29** 7931
Let me **d** in Your tent forever; **Ps 61:4** 1481a
near *to You* To **d** in Your courts. **Ps 65:4** 7931
They who **d** in the ends *of the* **Ps 65:8** 3427
rebellious **d** in a parched land. **Ps 68:6** 7931
the LORD will **d** *there* forever. **Ps 68:16** 7931
that the LORD God may **d** *there*. **Ps 68:18** 7931
May none **d** in their tents. **Ps 69:25** 3427
they may **d** there and possess it. **Ps 69:35** 3427
who love His name will **d** in it. **Ps 69:36** 7931
earth and all who **d** in it melt; **Ps 75:3** 3427
tribes of Israel **d** in their tents. **Ps 78:55** 7931
are those who **d** in Your house! **Ps 84:4** 3427
Than **d** in the tents of wickedness. **Ps 84:10** 1752
Him, That glory may **d** in our land. **Ps 85:9** 7931
The world and those who **d** in it. **Ps 98:7** 3427
the land, that they may **d** with me; **Ps 101:6** 3427
shall not **d** within my house; **Ps 101:7** 3427
them the birds of the heavens **d**; **Ps 104:12** 7931
wickedness of those who **d** in it. **Ps 107:34** 3427
there He makes the hungry to **d**, **Ps 107:36** 3427
For I **d** among the tents of Kedar! **Ps 120:5** 7931
Here I will **d**, for I have desired **Ps 132:14** 3427
brothers to **d** together in unity! **Ps 133:1** 3427
If I **d** in the remotest part of the **Ps 139:9** 7931
upright will **d** in Your presence. **Ps 140:13** 3427
He has made me **d** in dark places, **Ps 143:3** 3427
"I, wisdom, **d** with prudence, And **Pr 8:12** 7931
the wicked will not **d** in the land. **Pr 10:30** 7931
reproof Will **d** among the wise. **Pr 15:31** 3885a
"O My people who **d** in Zion, do **Is 10:24** 3427
And the wolf will **d** with the lamb, **Is 11:6** 1481a
who **d** in the presence of the LORD. **Is 23:18** 3427
brought low those who **d** on high, **Is 26:5** 3427
justice will **d** in the wilderness And **Is 32:16** 7931
He will **d** on the heights, **Is 33:16** 7931
The people who **d** there will be **Is 33:24** 3427
And owl and raven will **d** in it; **Is 34:11** 7931
to generation they will **d** in it. **Is 34:17** 7931
them out like a tent to **d** in. **Is 40:22** 3427
who **d** in darkness from the prison. **Is 42:7** 3427
islands, and those who **d** on them. **Is 42:10** 3427
"I **d** *on* a high and holy place, **Is 57:15** 7931
of the streets in which to **d**. **Is 58:12** 3427
it, And My servants will **d** there. **Is 65:9** 7931
I will let you **d** in this place. **Jer 7:3** 7931
I will let you **d** in this place, **Jer 7:7** 7931
I made My name **d** at the first, **Jer 7:12** 7931
the ground, You who **d** under siege! **Jer 10:17** 3427
wickedness of those who **d** in it, **Jer 12:4** 3427
"You who **d** in Lebanon, Nested in **Jer 22:23** 3427
saved, And Israel will **d** securely; **Jer 23:6** 7931
ones who **d** in the land of Egypt. **Jer 24:8** 3427
and **d** on the land which the LORD **Jer 25:5** 3427
people who **d** in the desert; **Jer 25:24** 7931
will till it and **d** in it. **Jer 27:11** 3427
all the people who **d** in this city, **Jer 29:16** 3427
its cities will **d** together in it, **Jer 31:24** 3427
place and make them **d** in safety. **Jer 32:37** 3427
and Jerusalem will **d** in safety; **Jer 33:16** 7931
tents you shall **d** all your days, **Jer 35:7** 3427
to build ourselves houses to **d** in; **Jer 35:9** 3427
Then you will **d** in the land which **Jer 35:15** 3427
the cities and **d** among the crags, **Jer 48:28** 7931
away, turn back, **d** in the depths, **Jer 49:8** 3427
D in the depths, O inhabitants of **Jer 49:30** 3427
has no gates or bars; They **d** alone. **Jer 49:31** 7931
O you who **d** by many waters, **Jer 51:13** 7931
In dark places He has made me **d**, **La 3:6** 3427
shall not continue to **d** *with us*." **La 4:15** 1481a
and I will make you **d** in the **Ezk 26:20** 3427
the birds of the heavens will **d**, **Ezk 31:13** 7931
birds of the heavens to **d** on you, **Ezk 32:4** 7931
where I will **d** among the sons of **Ezk 43:7** 7931
and I will **d** among them forever. **Ezk 43:9** 7931
their possession cities to **d** in. **Ezk 45:5**
and wherever the sons of men **d**, **Da 2:38** 1753
And all those who **d** in it mourn, **Am 9:5** 3427
out of the city, **D** in the field, **Mi 4:10** 7931
Though I **d** in darkness, the LORD **Mi 7:8** 3427
to **d** in your paneled houses while **Hg 1:4** 3427
and I will **d** in your midst," **Zch 2:10** 7931
Then I will **d** in your midst, and **Zch 2:11** 7931
will **d** in the midst of Jerusalem. **Zch 8:3** 7931
a mongrel race will **d** in Ashdod, **Zch 9:6** 3427
d on their own sites in Jerusalem. **Zch 12:6** 3427
for Jerusalem will **d** in security. **Zch 14:11** 3427
d on the face of all the earth. **Lk 21:35** *2521*
DESOLATE, AND LET NO ONE **D** IN IT'; **Ac 1:20** *2730*
d in *houses* made by *human* hands; **Ac 7:48** *2730*
not **d** in temples made with hands; **Ac 17:24** *2730*
D IN THEM AND WALK AMONG THEM; **2Co 6:16** *1774*
the power of Christ may **d** in me. **2Co 12:9** *1981*
d in your hearts through faith; **Eph 3:17** *2730*
d on these things. **Php 4:8** *3049*
for all the fullness to **d** in Him, **Col 1:19** *2730*
of Christ richly **d** within you, **Col 3:16** *1774*
which He has made to **d** in us"? **Jas 4:5** *2733b*
'I know where you **d**, **Rv 2:13** *2730*
test those who **d** on the earth. **Rv 3:10** *2730*
on those who **d** on the earth?" **Rv 6:10** *2730*
woe to those who **d** on the earth, **Rv 8:13** *2730*
And those who **d** on the earth *will* **Rv 11:10** *2730*
those who **d** on the earth. **Rv 11:10** *2730*
O heavens and you who **d** in them. **Rv 12:12** *4637*
that is, those who **d** in heaven. **Rv 13:6** *4637*
d on the earth will worship him, **Rv 13:8** *2730*
makes the earth and those who **d** in **Rv 13:12** *2730*
And he deceives those who **d** on the **Rv 13:14** *2730*
telling those who **d** on the earth **Rv 13:14** *2730*
and those who **d** on the earth were **Rv 17:2** *2730*
who **d** on the earth, **Rv 17:8** *2730*
men, and He will **d** among them, **Rv 21:3** *4637*

DWELLER
I am against you, O valley **d**, **Jer 21:13** 3427

DWELLERS
of the world and **d** on earth, **Is 18:3** 7931

DWELLING
not sustain them while **d** together, **Gn 13:6** 3427
Perizzite were **d** then in the land. **Gn 13:7** 3427
of the earth shall be your **d**, **Gn 27:39** 4186
while Israel was **d** in that land, **Gn 35:22** 7931

which You have made for Your **d**, Ex 15:17 3427
his **d** shall be outside the camp. Lv 13:46 4186
generations in all your **d** places. Lv 23:14 4186
'You shall bring in from your **d** Lv 23:17 4186
perpetual statute in all your **d** places Lv 23:21 4186
generations in all your **d** places. Lv 23:31 4186
sells a **d** house in a walled city, Lv 25:29 4186
I will make My **d** among you, Lv 26:11 4908
"Your **d** place is enduring, And Nu 24:21 4186
for I the LORD am **d** in the midst Nu 35:34 7931
His name there for His **d**, Dt 12:5 7931
"The eternal God is a **d** place, Dt 33:27 4585
which I have commanded *in My* **d**, 1Sa 2:29 4583
You will see the distress of *My* **d**, 1Sa 2:32 4583
A place for Your **d** forever." 1Ki 8:13 3427
hear in heaven Your **d** place; 1Ki 8:30 3427
hear in heaven Your **d** place, 1Ki 8:39 3427
hear in heaven Your **d** place, 1Ki 8:43 3427
in heaven Your **d** place, 1Ki 8:49 3427
I am **d** in a house of cedar, 1Ch 17:1 3427
and from *one* **d** place *to another.* 1Ch 17:5 4908
And a place for Your **d** forever." 2Ch 6:2 3427
hear from Your **d** place, 2Ch 6:21 3427
hear from heaven Your **d** place, 2Ch 6:30 3427
from heaven, from Your **d** place, 2Ch 6:33 3427
from heaven, from Your **d** place, 2Ch 6:39 3427
away from the **d** place of the LORD, 2Ch 29:6 4908
prayer came to His holy **d** place, 2Ch 30:27 4583
on His people and on His **d** place; 2Ch 36:15 4583
Israel, whose **d** is in Jerusalem, Ezr 7:15 4907b
tent, the **d** places of the wicked?' Jb 21:28 4908
is the way to the **d** of light? Jb 38:19 7931
And the salt land for his **d** place? Jb 39:6 4908
From His **d** place He looks out On Ps 33:14 3427
holy hill And to Your **d** places. Ps 43:3 4908
holy **d** places of the Most High. Ps 46:4 4908
their **d** places to all generations; Ps 49:11 4908
to Sheol, For evil is in their **d**, Ps 55:15 4033
defiled the **d** place of Your name. Ps 74:7 4908
His **d** place also is in Zion. Ps 76:2 4585
abandoned the **d** place at Shiloh, Ps 78:60 4908
How lovely are Your **d** places, Ps 84:1 4908
all the *other* **d** places of Jacob. Ps 87:2 4908
our **d** place in all generations. Ps 90:1 4583
Even the Most High, your **d** place. Ps 91:9 4583
its **d** With those who hate peace. Ps 120:6 7931
A **d** place for the Mighty One of Ps 132:5 4908
Let us go into His **d** place; Ps 132:7 4908
He blesses the **d** of the righteous. Pr 3:33 5116a
and oil in the **d** of the wise, Pr 21:20 5116a
against the **d** of the righteous; Pr 24:15 5116a
"I will look from My **d** place Is 18:4 4349
"Like a shepherd's tent my **d** is Is 38:12 1755
"Your **d** is in the midst of deceit; Jer 9:6 3427
have compassion on his **d** places; Jer 30:18 4908
for exile, O daughter **d** in Egypt, Jer 46:19 3427
ground, O daughter **d** in Dibon, Jer 48:18 3427
Their **d** places are set on fire, Jer 51:30 4908
there will be nothing **d** in it, Jer 51:62 3427
deliver them from all their **d** places Ezk 37:23 4186
"My **d** place also will be with them; Ezk 37:27 4908
whose **d** place is not with *mortal* Da 2:11 4070
and your **d** place be with the Da 4:25 4070
and your **d** place *will be* with the Da 4:32 4070
and his **d** place *was* with the wild Da 5:21 4070
God, **D** in Zion, My holy mountain. Jl 3:17 7931
So will the sons of Israel **d** in Am 3:12 3427
In the loftiness of your **d** place, Ob 1:3 7931
d places which are not theirs. Hab 1:6 4908
So her **d** will not be cut off Zph 3:7 4583
and he had his **d** among the tombs. Mk 5:3 *2731*
Father's house are many **d** places; Jn 14:2 *3438*
a **d** place for the God of Jacob. Ac 7:46 *4638*
be clothed with our **d** from heaven, 2Co 5:2 *3613*
into a **d** of God in the Spirit. Eph 2:22 *2732*
d in tents with Isaac and Jacob, Heb 11:9 *2730*
as long as I am in this *earthly* **d**, 2Pe 1:13 *4638*
aside of my *earthly* **d** is imminent, 2Pe 1:14 *4638*
She has become a **d** place of Rv 18:2 *2732*

DWELLINGS

of Israel had light in their **d**. Ex 10:23 4186
in all your **d** you shall eat Ex 12:20 4186
of your **d** on the sabbath day." Ex 35:3 4186
your generations in all your **d**: Lv 3:17 4186
bird or animal, in any of your **d**. Lv 7:26 4186
sabbath to the LORD in all your **d**. Lv 23:3 4186
back from around the **d** of Korah, Nu 16:24 4908
back from around the **d** of Korah, Nu 16:27 4908
are your tents, O Jacob, Your **d**, Nu 24:5 4908
your generations in all your **d**. Nu 35:29 4186
such are the **d** of the wicked, Jb 18:21 4908
their camp, Round about their **d**. Ps 78:28 4908
And in secure **d** and in undisturbed Is 32:18 4908
out the curtains of your **d**, Is 54:2 4908
they have cast down our **d**.'" Jer 9:19 4908
"In all your **d**, cities will Ezk 6:6 4186
you and make their **d** among you; Ezk 25:4 4908
city, for **d** and for open spaces; Ezk 48:15 4186
it may consume its palatial **d**. Hos 8:14 759
receive you into the eternal **d**. Lk 16:9 *4633*

DWELLS

Behold, a people *who* **d** apart, Nu 23:9 7931
And he **d** between His shoulders." Dt 33:12 7931
"So Israel **d** in security, The Dt 33:28 7931
of God **d** within tent curtains." 2Sa 7:2 3427
and He **d** in Jerusalem forever. 1Ch 23:25 7931
d in his tent nothing of his; Jb 18:15 7931
And the honorable man **d** in it. Jb 22:8 3427
"On the cliff he **d** and lodges, Jb 39:28 7931
No evil **d** with You. Ps 5:4 1481a
to the LORD, who **d** in Zion; Ps 9:11 3427
And the place where Your glory **d**. Ps 26:8 4908
He who **d** in the shelter of the Ps 91:1 3427
from Zion, Who **d** in Jerusalem. Ps 135:21 7931
of hosts, who **d** on Mount Zion. Is 8:18 7931
LORD is exalted, for He **d** on high; Is 33:5 7931
you sensual one, Who **d** securely, Is 47:8 3427
is forsaken, And no man **d** in them. Jer 4:29 3427
"He who **d** in this city will die Jer 21:9 3427
She **d** among the nations, *But* she La 1:3 3427
of Edom, Who **d** in the land of Uz; La 4:21 3427
who **d** at the entrance to the sea, Ezk 27:3 3427
And the light **d** with Him. Da 2:22 8271
avenged, For the LORD **d** in Zion. Jl 3:21 7931
And everyone who **d** in it mourn? Am 8:8 3427
Which **d** by itself in the woodland, Mi 7:14 7931
exultant city Which **d** securely, Zph 2:15 3427
temple and by Him who **d** within it. Mt 23:21 *2730*
but sin which **d** in me. Ro 7:17 *1774*
I know that nothing good **d** in me, Ro 7:18 *3611*
doing it, but sin which **d** in me. Ro 7:20 *3611*
indeed the Spirit of God **d** in you. Ro 8:9 *3611*
Jesus from the dead **d** in you, Ro 8:11 *3611*
bodies through His Spirit who **d** in Ro 8:11 *3611*
that the Spirit of God **d** in you? 1Co 3:16 *3611*
fullness of Deity **d** in bodily form, Col 2:9 *2730*
and **d** in unapproachable light, 1Tm 6:16 *3611*
the Holy Spirit who **d** in us, 2Tm 1:14 *1774*
earth, in which righteousness **d**. 2Pe 3:13 *2730*
killed among you, where Satan **d**. Rv 2:13 *2730*

DWELT

came and **d** by the oaks of Mamre, Gn 13:18 3427
favor of Him who **d** in the bush. Dt 33:16 7931
"For I have not **d** in a house 2Sa 7:6 3427
Then David **d** in the stronghold; 1Ch 11:7 3427
about, when David **d** in his house, 1Ch 17:1 3427
for I have not **d** in a house since 1Ch 17:5 3427
And **d** as a king among the troops, Jb 29:25 7931
this Mount Zion, where You have **d**. Ps 74:2 7931
have **d** in *the abode of* silence. Ps 94:17 7931
There were those who **d** in darkness Ps 107:10 3427
one crossed And where no man **d**?' Jer 2:6 3427
"We have only **d** in tents, and Jer 35:10 3427
So we have **d** in Jerusalem." Jer 35:11 3427
will never again be inhabited Or **d** in Jer 50:39 7931
of the sky **d** in its branches, Da 4:12 1753
under which the beasts of the field **d** Da 4:21 1753
Word became flesh, and **d** among us, Jn 1:14 *4637*
first **d** in your grandmother Lois and 2Tm 1:5 *1774*

DWINDLE

the luminaries will **d**. Zch 14:6 7087a

DWINDLES

Wealth *obtained* by fraud **d**, Pr 13:11 4591

DYED

rams' skins **d** red, porpoise skins, Ex 25:5 119
for the tent of rams' skins **d** red and Ex 26:14 119
and rams' skins **d** red, and Ex 35:7 119
skins **d** red and porpoise skins, Ex 35:23 119
for the tent of rams' skins **d** red, Ex 36:19 119
the covering of rams' skins **d** red, Ex 39:34 119
To Sisera a spoil of **d** work, Jg 5:30 6648
A spoil of **d** work embroidered, Jg 5:30 6648
D work of double embroidery on the Jg 5:30 6648

DYING

"Behold, we perish, we are **d**, Nu 17:12 6
we are dying, we are all **d**! Nu 17:12 6
the one **d** *naturally* or the grave. Nu 19:18 4191
twelve years old, and she was **d**. Lk 8:42 *599*
but I am **d** here with hunger! Lk 15:17 *622*
have kept this man also from **d**?" Jn 11:37 *599*
about in the body the **d** of Jesus, 2Co 4:10 *3500*
as **d** yet behold, we live; 2Co 6:9 *599*
By faith Jacob, as he was **d**, Heb 11:21 *599*
By faith Joseph, when he was **d**, Heb 11:22 *5053*

DYSENTERY

with *recurrent* fever and **d**; Ac 28:8 *1420*

E

EACH

Thus they separated from **e** other. Gn 13:11 376
laid **e** half opposite the other; Gn 15:10 376
e took his sword and came upon the Gn 34:25 376
e man with his *own* dream *and* each Gn 40:5 376
e dream with its *own* interpretation. Gn 40:5 376
e of us dreamed according to the Gn 41:11 376
To **e** one he interpreted according Gn 41:12 376
e man's money was in the mouth of Gn 43:21 376
and put **e** man's money in the mouth Gn 44:1 376
e man lowered his sack to the Gn 44:11 376
ground, and **e** man opened his sack. Gn 44:11 376
and when **e** man loaded his donkey, Gn 44:13 376
To **e** of them he gave changes of Gn 45:22 3605, 376
came **e** one with his household: Ex 1:1 376
were fighting with **e** other; Ex 2:13 376
For **e** one threw down his staff and Ex 7:12 376
that **e** man ask from his neighbor Ex 11:2 376
and **e** woman from her neighbor Ex 11:2 802
they are **e** one to take a lamb Ex 12:3 376
a lamb for **e** household. Ex 12:3
according to what **e** man should eat, Ex 12:4 376
e of you has in his tent.'" Ex 16:16 376
much bread, two omers for **e** one. Ex 16:22 259
asked **e** other of their welfare and Ex 18:7 376
"If men struggle with **e** other Ex 21:22
"The length of **e** curtain shall be Ex 26:2 259
width of **e** curtain four cubits; Ex 26:2 259
loops shall be opposite **e** other. Ex 26:5 802
"The length of **e** curtain *shall be* Ex 26:8 259
width of **e** curtain four cubits; Ex 26:8 259
shall be the length of **e** board and Ex 26:16
half cubits the width of **e** board. Ex 26:16 259
shall be two tenons for **e** board, Ex 26:17 259
e according to his name for the Ex 28:21 376
"**E** day you shall offer a bull as a Ex 29:36
two one year old lambs **e** day, Ex 29:38
then **e** one of them shall give a Ex 30:12 376
there shall be an equal part of **e**. Ex 30:34 905
e at the entrance of his tent, Ex 33:8 376
e at the entrance of his tent. Ex 33:10 376
e from the work which he was Ex 36:4 376
The length of **e** curtain was Ex 36:9 259
width of **e** curtain four cubits; Ex 36:9 259
the loops were opposite **e** other. Ex 36:12 259
of **e** curtain *was* thirty cubits Ex 36:15 259
cubits the width of **e** curtain; Ex 36:15 259
cubits *was* the length of **e** board Ex 36:21
half cubits the width of **e** board. Ex 36:21 259
There were two tenons for **e** board, Ex 36:22 259
with their faces toward **e** other; Ex 37:9 376
for **e** one who passed over to those Ex 38:26 3605
e with its name for the twelve Ex 39:14 376
e day's matter on its own day Lv 23:37
of an ephah shall be *in* **e** cake. Lv 24:5 259
put pure frankincense on **e** row that Lv 24:7
struggled with **e** other in the camp. Lv 24:10
and **e** of you shall return to his Lv 25:10 376
and **e** of you shall return to his Lv 25:10 376
'On this year of jubilee **e** of you Lv 25:13 376
will therefore stumble over **e** other Lv 26:37 376
there shall be a man of **e** tribe, Nu 1:4 376
e one head of his father's Nu 1:4 376
e of whom was of his father's Nu 1:44 376
shall camp, **e** man by his own camp, Nu 1:52 376
and **e** man by his own standard, Nu 1:52 376
shall camp, **e** by his own standard, Nu 2:2 376
go in and assign **e** of them to his work Nu 4:19 376
and you shall assign **e** *man* by Nu 4:32
the leaders and an ox for **e** one, Nu 7:3
e man according to his service." Nu 7:5 376
their offering, one leader **e** day, Nu 7:11 259
e silver dish *weighing* one hundred Nu 7:85 259
thirty *shekels* and **e** bowl seventy; Nu 7:85 259
e man at the doorway of his tent; Nu 11:10 376
from **e** of their fathers' tribes, Nu 13:2 376, 259
or for the sacrifice, for **e** lamb. Nu 15:5 259
'Thus it shall be done for **e** ox, Nu 15:11 259
be done for each ox, or for **e** ram, Nu 15:11 259
ram, or for **e** of the male lambs, Nu 15:11
tassel of **e** corner a cord of blue. Nu 15:38
"**E** of you take his firepan and put Nu 16:17 376
and **e** of you bring his censer Nu 16:17 376
you and Aaron *shall* **e** *bring* his firepan. Nu 16:17 376
So they **e** took his *own* censer and Nu 16:18 376
a rod for **e** father's household: Nu 17:2
You shall write **e** name on his rod, Nu 17:2 376
there is one rod for the head *of* **e** Nu 17:3
for **e** leader according to their Nu 17:6 259
looked, and **e** man took his rod. Nu 17:9 376
up a bull and a ram on **e** altar. Nu 23:2
up a bull and a ram on **e** altar." Nu 23:4
a bull and a ram on **e** altar. Nu 23:14
a bull and a ram on **e** altar. Nu 23:30
"**E** of you slay his men who have Nu 25:5 376
e shall be given their inheritance Nu 26:54 376
be a fourth of a hin for **e** lamb, Nu 28:7 259
'Then at the beginning of **e** of Nu 28:11
with oil for a grain offering, for **e** bull Nu 28:12 259
for a grain offering for **e** lamb, Nu 28:13 259
this is the burnt offering of **e** Nu 28:14
offer for **e** of the seven lambs; Nu 28:21 259
of an ephah for **e** bull, Nu 28:28 259
a tenth for **e** of the seven lambs; Nu 28:29 259
one-tenth for **e** of the seven lambs. Nu 29:4 259
a tenth for **e** of the seven lambs; Nu 29:10 259
ephah for **e** of the thirteen bulls, Nu 29:14 259
two-tenths for **e** of the two rams, Nu 29:14 259
tenth for **e** of the fourteen lambs; Nu 29:15 259
"A thousand from **e** tribe of all Nu 31:4
Israel, a thousand from **e** tribe, Nu 31:5
them, a thousand from **e** tribe, Nu 31:6
to the LORD what **e** man found, Nu 31:50 376
e shall give some of his cities to Nu 35:8 376
the sons of Israel shall **e** hold to the Nu 36:7 376
the sons of Israel **e** may possess the Nu 36:8 376
e hold to his own inheritance." Nu 36:9 376
of your men, one man for **e** tribe. Dt 1:23
of Israel, one man for **e** tribe. Jos 3:12 376, 259
the people, one man from **e** tribe, Jos 4:2 376, 259
of Israel, one man from **e** tribe; Jos 4:4 376, 259
and **e** of you take up a stone on Jos 4:5 376
from **e** tribe that I may send them, Jos 18:4
These cities **e** had its surrounding Jos 21:42 5892b
one chief for **e** father's household Jos 22:14
from **e** of the tribes of Israel; Jos 22:14 3605
and **e** one of them *was* the head of Jos 22:14 376
the people, **e** to his inheritance. Jos 24:28 376
the sons of Israel went **e** to his Jg 2:6 376
people go, **e** man to his home." Jg 7:7 376
men of Israel, **e** to his tent, Jg 7:8 376
E stood in his place around the camp; Jg 7:21 376

e one resembling the son of a king."	**Jg 8:18**	
that **e** of you give me an earring	**Jg 8:24**	376
people also cut down **e** one his branch	**Jg 9:49**	376
was dead, **e** departed to his home.	**Jg 9:55**	376
Then we will **e** give you eleven	**Jg 16:5**	376
e one could sling a stone at a	**Jg 20:16**	3605
and **e** of you shall catch his wife from	**Jg 21:21**	376
because we did not take for **e** man	**Jg 21:22**	376
and **e** one of them went out from	**Jg 21:24**	376
e of you to her mother's house.	**Ru 1:8**	802
e in the house of her husband."	**Ru 1:9**	802
people away, **e** one to his house.	**1Sa 10:25**	376
rest of the people, **e** to his tent.	**1Sa 13:2**	376
e to sharpen his plowshare,	**1Sa 13:20**	376
'**E** one of you bring me his ox or	**1Sa 14:34**	376
brought **e** one his ox with him and	**1Sa 14:34**	376
kissed **e** other and wept together,	**1Sa 20:41**	376
e other in the name of the LORD,	**1Sa 20:42**	8147
e breaking away from his master.	**1Sa 25:10**	376
"**E** *of you* gird on his sword."	**1Sa 25:13**	376
So **e** man girded on his sword.	**1Sa 25:13**	376
"The LORD will repay **e** man	**1Sa 26:23**	376
and his men, **e** with his household,	**1Sa 27:3**	376
e one because of his sons and his	**1Sa 30:6**	376
with him, **e** with his household;	**2Sa 2:3**	376
E one of them seized his opponent by	**2Sa 2:16**	376
e from following his brother."	**2Sa 2:27**	376
dates and one of raisins to **e** one.	**2Sa 6:19**	376
people departed **e** to his house.	**2Sa 6:19**	376
and **e** mounted his mule and fled.	**2Sa 13:29**	376
who were with him **e** covered his head	**2Sa 15:30**	376
all Israel fled, **e** to his tent.	**2Sa 18:17**	376
Israel had fled, **e** to his tent.	**2Sa 19:8**	376
from the city, **e** to his tent.	**2Sa 20:22**	376
who had six fingers on **e** hand and six	**2Sa 21:20**	
each hand and six toes on **e** foot,	**2Sa 21:20**	
they arose and **e** went on his way.	**1Ki 1:49**	376
e man had to provide for a month	**1Ki 4:7**	259
Solomon's table, **e** in his month;	**1Ki 4:27**	376
be, **e** according to his charge.	**1Ki 4:28**	376
whole house, **e** five cubits high;	**1Ki 6:10**	
of olive wood, **e** ten cubits high.	**1Ki 6:23**	
So their wings were touching **e**	**1Ki 6:27**	3671
on the 45 pillars, 15 in **e** row.	**1Ki 7:3**	
the length of **e** stand was four	**1Ki 7:27**	259
Now **e** stand had four bronze wheels	**1Ki 7:30**	259
supports with wreaths at **e** side.	**1Ki 7:30**	376
at the four corners of **e** stand;	**1Ki 7:34**	259
according to the clear space on **e**,	**1Ki 7:36**	376
e basin *was* four cubits, *and on*	**1Ki 7:38**	259
and on **e** of the ten stands *was* one	**1Ki 7:38**	259
two rows of pomegranates for **e**	**1Ki 7:42**	259
e knowing the affliction of his	**1Ki 8:38**	376
to **e** according to all his ways,	**1Ki 8:39**	376
people Israel, as **e** day requires,	**1Ki 8:59**	3117
shekels of gold on **e** large shield.	**1Ki 10:16**	259
three minas of gold on **e** shield,	**1Ki 10:17**	259
and arms on **e** side of the seat,	**1Ki 10:19**	3117
They killed **e** his man;	**1Ki 20:20**	376
the kings, **e** from his place,	**1Ki 20:24**	376
were sitting **e** on his throne,	**1Ki 22:10**	376
Let **e** of them return to his house	**1Ki 22:17**	376
and **e** one threw a stone on every	**2Ki 3:25**	376
e of us take from there a beam,	**2Ki 6:2**	376
Then they hurried and **e** man took	**2Ki 9:13**	376
Judah went out, **e** in his chariot,	**2Ki 9:21**	376
e with his weapons in his hand;	**2Ki 11:8**	376
And **e** one of them took his men who	**2Ki 11:9**	376
e with his weapons in his hand,	**2Ki 11:11**	376
both the money of **e** man's	**2Ki 12:4**	376
e from his acquaintance;	**2Ki 12:5**	376
but **e** shall be put to death for	**2Ki 14:6**	376
"Come, let us face **e** other."	**2Ki 14:8**	
faced **e** other at Beth-shemesh,	**2Ki 14:11**	
and they fled **e** to his tent.	**2Ki 14:12**	376
from **e** man fifty shekels of silver	**2Ki 15:20**	259
and eat **e** of his vine and each of	**2Ki 18:31**	376
and eat each of his vine and **e** of	**2Ki 18:31**	376
and drink **e** of the waters of his own	**2Ki 18:31**	376
e according to his valuation,	**2Ki 23:35**	376
by the king, a portion for **e** day,	**2Ki 25:30**	3117
people departed **e** to his house,	**1Ch 16:43**	376
six *fingers on* **e** *hand* and six	**1Ch 20:6**	
on each hand and six *toes on* **e**	**1Ch 20:6**	
year, **e** division *numbering* 24,000:	**1Ch 27:1**	259
with the weight of **e** lampstand and	**1Ch 28:15**	
with the weight of **e** lampstand and	**1Ch 28:15**	
to the use of **e** lampstand;	**1Ch 28:15**	4501
tables of showbread, for **e** table;	**1Ch 28:16**	7979
bowls with the weight for **e** bowl;	**1Ch 28:17**	3713a
bowls with the weight for **e** bowl;	**1Ch 28:17**	3713a
on the top of **e** *was* five cubits.	**2Ch 3:15**	
two rows of pomegranates for **e**	**2Ch 4:13**	259
e knowing his own affliction and	**2Ch 6:29**	376
to **e** according to all his ways,	**2Ch 6:30**	376
of beaten gold on **e** large shield.	**2Ch 9:15**	259
shekels of gold on **e** shield,	**2Ch 9:16**	259
and arms on **e** side of the seat,	**2Ch 9:18**	2088
were sitting **e** on his throne,	**2Ch 18:9**	376
Let **e** of them return to his house	**2Ch 18:16**	376
e man with his weapons in his hand;	**2Ch 23:7**	376
And **e** one of them took his men who	**2Ch 23:8**	376
e man with his weapon in his hand,	**2Ch 23:10**	376
but **e** shall be put to death for	**2Ch 25:4**	376
"Come, let us face **e** other."	**2Ch 25:17**	
faced **e** other at Beth-shemesh,	**2Ch 25:21**	
and they fled **e** to his tent.	**2Ch 25:22**	376
their cities, **e** to his possession.	**2Ch 31:1**	376
e according to his service,	**2Ch 31:2**	376
cities, or in **e** and every city,	**2Ch 31:19**	5892b
and the gatekeepers at **e** gate did	**2Ch 35:15**	8179
"What have we to do with **e** other,	**2Ch 35:21**	
and Judah, **e** to his city.	**Ezr 2:1**	376
the ordinance, as **e** day required;	**Ezr 3:4**	3117
the elders and judges of **e** city,	**Ezr 10:14**	5892b
of fathers' *households* for **e**	**Ezr 10:16**	
repairs, **e** in front of his house.	**Ne 3:28**	376
to the wall, **e** one to his work.	**Ne 4:15**	376
e *wore* his sword girded at his	**Ne 4:18**	376
"Let **e** man with his servant spend	**Ne 4:22**	376
e *took* his weapon *even to* the	**Ne 4:23**	376
usury, **e** from his brother!"	**Ne 5:7**	376
Now that which was prepared for **e**	**Ne 5:18**	
of Jerusalem, **e** at his post,	**Ne 7:3**	376
and **e** in front of his own house."	**Ne 7:3**	376
and Judah, **e** to his city,	**Ne 7:6**	376
for themselves, **e** on his roof,	**Ne 8:16**	376
but in the cities of Judah **e** lived	**Ne 11:3**	376
Judah, **e** on his own inheritance.	**Ne 11:20**	376
the gatekeepers as **e** day required,	**Ne 12:47**	3117
had gone away, **e** to his own field.	**Ne 13:10**	376
and the Levites, **e** in his task,	**Ne 13:30**	376
the king had given orders to **e** official	**Es 1:8**	3605
to the desires of **e** person.	**Es 1:8**	376
to **e** province according to its	**Es 1:22**	4082
Now when the turn of **e** young lady	**Es 2:12**	5291
who were over **e** province and	**Es 3:12**	4082
and to the princes of **e** people,	**Es 3:12**	5971a
e province according to its	**Es 3:12**	4082
e people according to its language,	**Es 3:12**	5971a
In **e** and every province where	**Es 4:3**	4082
the Jews who were in **e** and every city	**Es 8:11**	5892b
as law in **e** and every province was	**Es 8:13**	4082
In **e** and every province and	**Es 8:17**	4082
province and in **e** and every city,	**Es 8:17**	5892b
in the house of **e** one on his day,	**Jb 1:4**	376
came **e** one from his own place,	**Jb 2:11**	376
And **e** of them tore his robe and	**Jb 2:12**	376
e other and cannot be separated.	**Jb 41:17**	376
And **e** one gave him one piece of	**Jb 42:11**	376
of money, and **e** a ring of gold.	**Jb 42:11**	376
and peace have kissed **e** other.	**Ps 85:10**	
And **e** *is tested* by the praise	**Pr 27:21**	376
E man has his sword at his side,	**SS 3:8**	376
E one was to bring a thousand	**SS 8:11**	376
be oppressed, **E** one by another,	**Is 3:5**	376
and **e** one by his neighbor;	**Is 3:5**	376
above Him, **e** having six wings:	**Is 6:2**	259
E of them eats the flesh of his	**Is 9:20**	376
will **e** turn to his own people,	**Is 13:14**	376
And **e** one flee to his own land.	**Is 13:14**	376
lie in glory, **E** in his own tomb.	**Is 14:18**	376
will **e** fight against his brother and	**Is 19:2**	376
and **e** against his neighbor,	**Is 19:2**	376
E will be like a refuge from the wind	**Is 32:2**	376
and eat **e** of his vine and each of	**Is 36:16**	376
and eat each of his vine and **e** of	**Is 36:16**	376
and drink **e** of the waters of his own	**Is 36:16**	376
E one helps his neighbor And says	**Is 41:6**	376
E has wandered in his own way;	**Is 47:15**	376
Let us stand up to **e** other;	**Is 50:8**	3162
E of us has turned to his own way;	**Is 53:6**	376
own way, **E** one to his unjust gain,	**Is 56:11**	376
E *one* who walked in his upright	**Is 57:2**	
and they will set **e** one his throne	**Jer 1:15**	376
E one neighing after his	**Jer 5:8**	376
They will pasture **e** in his place.	**Jer 6:3**	376
walked, **e** one, in the stubbornness	**Jer 11:8**	376
e one to his inheritance and each	**Jer 12:15**	376
inheritance and **e** one to his land.	**Jer 12:15**	376
I will dash them against **e** other,	**Jer 13:14**	376
you are **e** one walking according to	**Jer 16:12**	376
to **e** man according to his ways,	**Jer 17:10**	376
back, **e** of you from his evil way,	**Jer 18:11**	376
and **e** of us will act according to	**Jer 18:12**	376
For **e** time I speak, I cry aloud;	**Jer 20:8**	1767
against you, **E** with his weapons;	**Jer 22:7**	376
"who steal My words from **e** other.	**Jer 23:30**	376
"Thus will **e** of you say to his	**Jer 23:35**	376
e man who eats the sour grapes,	**Jer 31:30**	3605
e man his neighbor and each man	**Jer 31:34**	376
neighbor and **e** man his brother,	**Jer 31:34**	376
that **e** man should set free his	**Jer 34:9**	376
and **e** man his female servant,	**Jer 34:9**	376
e man should set free his male servant	**Jer 34:10**	376
and **e** man his female servant,	**Jer 34:10**	376
"At the end of seven years **e** of	**Jer 34:14**	376
e man proclaiming release to his	**Jer 34:15**	376
and **e** man took back his male	**Jer 34:16**	376
and **e** man his female servant whom	**Jer 34:16**	376
release **e** man to his brother and	**Jer 34:17**	376
and **e** man to his neighbor.	**Jer 34:17**	376
among them, **e** man in his tent,	**Jer 37:10**	376
For **e** time you speak about him you	**Jer 48:27**	1767
And **e** of you will be driven out	**Jer 49:5**	376
e turn back to his own people And	**Jer 50:16**	376
they will **e** flee to his own land.	**Jer 50:16**	376
And **e** of you save his life!	**Jer 51:6**	376
let us **e** go to his own country,	**Jer 51:9**	376
And **e** of you save yourselves From	**Jer 51:45**	376
of **e** pillar *was* eighteen cubits,	**Jer 52:21**	259
of **e** capital was five cubits,	**Jer 52:22**	259
E of them had four faces and four	**Ezk 1:6**	259
moved, **e** went straight forward.	**Ezk 1:9**	376
As for the form of their faces, **e**	**Ezk 1:10**	
e had two touching another *being,*	**Ezk 1:11**	376
And **e** went straight forward;	**Ezk 1:12**	376
for **e** *of* the four of them.	**Ezk 1:15**	
e one also had two wings covering	**Ezk 1:23**	376
for forty days, a day for **e** year.	**Ezk 4:6**	
mourning, **e** over his own iniquity.	**Ezk 7:16**	376
e man with his censer in his hand and	**Ezk 8:11**	376
e man in the room of his carved	**Ezk 8:12**	376
e with his destroying weapon in	**Ezk 9:1**	376
e with his shattering weapon in	**Ezk 9:2**	376
one wheel beside **e** cherub;	**Ezk 10:9**	259
And **e** one had four faces.	**Ezk 10:14**	259
E one had four faces and each one	**Ezk 10:21**	259
four faces and **e** one four wings,	**Ezk 10:21**	259
E one went straight ahead.	**Ezk 10:22**	376
e according to his conduct,"	**Ezk 18:30**	376
'Cast away, **e** of you, the	**Ezk 20:7**	376
Israel, **e** according to his power,	**Ezk 22:6**	376
e of you according to his ways."	**Ezk 33:20**	376
and **e** of you defiles his	**Ezk 33:26**	376
to one another, **e** to his brother,	**Ezk 33:30**	376
e *of which was* a cubit and a	**Ezk 40:5**	
the east *numbered* three on **e** side;	**Ezk 40:10**	6311
the same measurement on **e** side.	**Ezk 40:10**	6311
front of the guardrooms on **e** side;	**Ezk 40:12**	6311
were six cubits *square* on **e** side.	**Ezk 40:12**	6311
and on **e** side pillar *were*	**Ezk 40:16**	
It had three guardrooms on **e** side;	**Ezk 40:21**	6311
its side pillars, one on **e** side.	**Ezk 40:26**	6311
on its side pillars, on **e** side,	**Ezk 40:34**	6311
on its side pillars on **e** side,	**Ezk 40:37**	6311
gate *were* two tables on **e** side,	**Ezk 40:39**	6311
were on **e** side next to the gate;	**Ezk 40:41**	6311
porch of the temple and measured **e**	**Ezk 40:48**	
the porch, five cubits on **e** side;	**Ezk 40:48**	6311
gate was three cubits on **e** side.	**Ezk 40:48**	6311
the side pillars, one on **e** side.	**Ezk 40:49**	6311
six cubits wide on **e** side *was* the	**Ezk 41:1**	6311
were five cubits on **e** side.	**Ezk 41:2**	6311
e side pillar of the doorway,	**Ezk 41:3**	
another, and thirty in **e** story;	**Ezk 41:6**	6471
were wider at **e** successive story.	**Ezk 41:7**	
it, with a gallery on **e** side,	**Ezk 41:15**	6311
the sanctuary **e** had a double door.	**Ezk 41:23**	
E of the doors had two leaves, two	**Ezk 41:24**	
a tenth of a bath from **e** kor	**Ezk 45:14**	
and one sheep from **e** flock of two	**Ezk 45:15**	
e one equally with the other;	**Ezk 47:14**	376
and they will speak lies *to* **e** *other*	**Da 11:27**	
And they **e** march in line, Nor do	**Jl 2:7**	376
They do not crowd **e** other,	**Jl 2:8**	376
walls, **E** one straight before her,	**Am 4:3**	802
E man said to his mate, "Come, let	**Jon 1:7**	376
that **e** may turn from his wicked way	**Jon 3:8**	376
E *one* from her pleasant house.	**Mi 2:9**	
E of them will sit under his vine	**Mi 4:4**	376
walk **E** in the name of his god,	**Mi 4:5**	376
E of them hunts the other with a	**Mi 7:2**	376
e of you runs to his own house.	**Hg 1:9**	376
spouts belonging to **e** of the lamps	**Zch 4:2**	
and compassion **e** to his brother;	**Zch 7:9**	376
e man with his staff in his hand	**Zch 8:4**	376
vegetation in the field to **e** man.	**Zch 10:1**	
and **e** *of* those who sell them says,	**Zch 11:5**	
e into another's power and into	**Zch 11:6**	376
the prophets will **e** be ashamed of his	**Zch 13:4**	376
Why do we deal treacherously **e**	**Mal 2:10**	376
E day has enough trouble of its own.	**Mt 6:34**	
"What business do we have with **e**	**Mt 8:29**	
if **e** of you does not forgive his	**Mt 18:35**	*1538*
came, **e** one received a denarius.	**Mt 20:9**	*303*
e of them also received a denarius.	**Mt 20:10**	*303*
e according to his own ability;	**Mt 25:15**	*1538*
they **e** one began to say to Him,	**Mt 26:22**	*1538*
"What business do we have with **e**	**Mk 1:24**	
"What business do we have with **e**	**Mk 5:7**	
assigning to **e** one his task,	**Mk 13:34**	*1538*
to decide what **e** man should take.	**Mk 15:24**	*5101*
e to his own city.	**Lk 2:3**	*1538*
What business do we have with **e** other,	**Lk 4:34**	
and laying His hands on **e** one of them,	**Lk 4:40**	*1538*
"For **e** tree is known by its own	**Lk 6:44**	*1538*
"What business do we have with **e**	**Lk 8:28**	
eat in groups of about fifty **e**."	**Lk 9:14**	*303*
'Give us **e** day our daily bread.	**Lk 11:3**	*2596*
does not **e** of you on the Sabbath	**Lk 13:15**	*1538*
e one of his master's debtors,	**Lk 16:5**	*1538*
had been enemies with **e** other.	**Lk 23:12**	*848*
And they were talking with **e**	**Lk 24:14**	*240*
twenty or thirty gallons **e**.	**Jn 2:6**	*303*
be scattered, **e** to his own *home,*	**Jn 16:32**	*1538*
and they rested on **e** one of them.	**Ac 2:3**	*1538*
because **e** one of them was hearing	**Ac 2:6**	*1538*
"And how is it that we **e** hear	**Ac 2:8**	*1538*
and **e** of you be baptized in	**Ac 2:38**	*1538*
they would be distributed to **e** as	**Ac 4:35**	*1538*
e of them determined to send *a*	**Ac 11:29**	*1538*
He is not far from **e** one of us;	**Ac 17:27**	*1538*
to admonish **e** one with tears.	**Ac 20:31**	*1538*
was offered for **e** one of them.	**Ac 21:26**	*1538*
you, **e** of us by the other's faith,	**Ro 1:12**	*240*
WHO WILL RENDER TO **E** PERSON	**Ro 2:6**	*1538*
allotted to **e** a measure of faith.	**Ro 12:3**	*1538*
e *of us is to exercise them*	**Ro 12:6**	
E person must be fully convinced in	**Ro 14:5**	*1538*
So then **e** one of us will give	**Ro 14:12**	*1538*
E of us is to please his neighbor for	**Ro 15:2**	*1538*
this, that **e** one of you is saying,	**1Co 1:12**	*1538*
Lord gave *opportunity* to **e** one.	**1Co 3:5**	*1538*
but **e** will receive his own reward	**1Co 3:8**	*1538*
But **e** man must be careful how he	**1Co 3:10**	*1538*
e man's work will become evident;	**1Co 3:13**	*1538*

test the quality of **e** man's work. 1Co 3:13 1538
and then **e** man's praise will come 1Co 4:5 1538
e man is to have his own wife, 1Co 7:2 1538
e woman is to have her own husband. 1Co 7:2 1538
e man has his own gift from God, 1Co 7:7 1538
as the Lord has assigned to **e** one, 1Co 7:17 1538
to each one, as God has called **e**, 1Co 7:17 1538
E man must remain in that condition 1Co 7:20 1538
e one is to remain with God in that 1Co 7:24 1538
for in your eating **e** one takes his 1Co 11:21 1538
But to **e** one is given the 1Co 12:7 1538
distributing to **e** one individually 1Co 12:11 1538
placed the members, **e** one of them, 1Co 12:18 1538
you assemble, **e** one has a psalm, 1Co 14:26 1538
and **e** in turn, and one must 1Co 14:27 1538
But **e** in his own order: 1Co 15:23 1538
and to **e** of the seeds a body of 1Co 15:38 1538
e one of you is to put aside and save, 1Co 16:2 1538
that **e** one may be recompensed for 2Co 5:10 1538
E one *must do* just as he has 2Co 9:7 1538
e *one* looking to yourself, so Ga 6:1
e one must examine his own work, Ga 6:4 1538
For **e** one will bear his own load. Ga 6:5 1538
But to **e** one of us grace was given Eph 4:7 1538
working of **e** individual part, Eph 4:16 1538
SPEAK TRUTH **E** ONE *of you* Eph 4:25 1538
tender-hearted, forgiving **e** other, Eph 4:32 1438
Nevertheless, **e** individual Eph 5:33 1538
whatever good thing **e** one does, Eph 6:8 1538
another, and forgiving **e** other, Col 3:13 1438
you should respond to **e** person. Col 4:6 1538
imploring **e** one of you as a father 1Th 2:11 1538
that **e** of you know how to possess 1Th 4:4 1538
and the love of **e** one of you 2Th 1:3 1538
And we desire that **e** one of you Heb 6:11 1538
blessed **e** of the sons of Joseph, Heb 11:21 1538
But **e** one is tempted when he is Jas 1:14 1538
judges according to **e** one's work, 1Pe 1:17 1538
As **e** one has received a *special* 1Pe 4:10 1538
and I will give to **e** one of you Rv 2:23 1538
e one of them having six wings, Rv 4:8 2596
the Lamb, **e** one holding a harp Rv 5:8 1538
given to **e** of them a white robe; Rv 6:11 1538
about one hundred pounds **e**, Rv 16:21
e one of the gates was a single Rv 21:21 1538

EAGER
the schemer is **e** for their wealth. Jb 5:5 7602a
is like a lion that is **e** to tear, Ps 17:12 3700
Do not be **e** in your heart to be Ec 7:9 926
were **e** to corrupt all their deeds. Zph 3:7 7925
e to go to patrol the earth." Zch 6:7 1245
I am **e** to preach the gospel to you Ro 1:15 4289
very thing I also was **e** to do. Ga 2:10 4704
were all the more **e** with great desire 1Th 2:17 4704

EAGERLY
his seat by the road **e** watching, 1Sa 4:13
man who **e** waits for his wages, Jb 7:2 6960a
prayer to You and **e** watch. Ps 5:3
They shall **e** utter the memory of Ps 145:7 5042
I will even look **e** for Him. Is 8:17 6960a
O LORD, We have waited for You **e**; Is 26:8 6960a
the Gentiles **e** seek all these things; Mt 6:32 1934
the nations of the world **e** seek; Lk 12:30 1934
waits **e** for the revealing of the sons Ro 8:19 553
e for *our* adoption as sons, Ro 8:23 553
perseverance we wait **e** for it. Ro 8:25 553
awaiting **e** the revelation of our 1Co 1:7 553
They **e** seek you, not commendably, Ga 4:17 2206
But it is good always to be **e** Ga 4:18 2206
I have sent him all the more **e** so Php 2:28 4709
which also we **e** wait for a Savior, Php 3:20 553
was in Rome, he **e** searched for me and 2Tm 1:17 4709
to sin, to those who **e** await Him. Heb 9:28 553

EAGERNESS
received the word with great **e**, Ac 17:11 4288
not for sordid gain, but with **e**; 1Pe 5:2 4290

EAGLE
the **e** and the vulture and the Lv 11:13 5404
the **e** and the vulture and the Dt 14:12 5404
the earth, as the **e** swoops down, Dt 28:49 5404
"Like an **e** that stirs up its Dt 32:11 5404
Like an **e** that swoops on its prey. Jb 9:26 5404
your command that the **e** mounts up Jb 39:27 5404
your youth is renewed like the **e**. Ps 103:5 5404
e that flies *toward* the heavens. Pr 23:5 5404
The way of an **e** in the sky, The Pr 30:19 5404
one will fly swiftly like an **e** And Jer 48:40 5404
will mount up and swoop like an **e** and Jer 49:22 5404
and all four had the face of an **e**. Ezk 1:10 5404
and the fourth the face of an **e**. Ezk 10:14 5404
"A great **e** with great wings, long Ezk 17:3 5404
"But there was another great **e** Ezk 17:7 5404
a lion and had *the* wings of an **e**. Da 7:4 5403
Like an **e** *the enemy comes* against Hos 8:1 5404
"Though you build high like the **e**, Ob 1:4 5404
Extend your baldness like the **e**, Mi 1:16 5404
like an **e** swooping *down* to devour. Hab 1:8 5404
creature *was* like a flying **e**. Rv 4:7 105
I heard an **e** flying in midheaven, Rv 8:13 105
great **e** were given to the woman, Rv 12:14 105

EAGLE'S
make your nest as high as an **e**, Jer 49:16 5404

EAGLES
They were swifter than **e**, 2Sa 1:23 5404
out, And the young **e** will eat it. Pr 30:17 5404
will mount up *with* wings like **e**, Is 40:31 5404
His horses are swifter than **e**. Jer 4:13 5404
swifter Than the **e** of the sky; La 4:19 5404

EAGLES'
and *how* I bore you on **e** wings, Ex 19:4 5404
until his hair had grown like **e** Da 4:33 5403

EAR
for the barley was in the **e** and the Ex 9:31 24
and give **e** to His commandments, Ex 15:26 238
shall pierce his **e** with an awl; Ex 21:6 241
put *it* on the lobe of Aaron's right **e** Ex 29:20 241
it on the lobe of Aaron's right **e**, Lv 8:23 241
on the lobe of their right **e**, Lv 8:24 241
right **e** of the one to be cleansed, Lv 14:14 241
priest shall put some on the right **e** Lv 14:17 241
and put *it* on the lobe of the right **e** Lv 14:25 241
right **e** of the one to be cleansed, Lv 14:28 241
Give **e** to me, O son of Zippor! Nu 23:18 238
to your voice nor give **e** to you. Dt 1:45 238
it through his **e** into the door, Dt 15:17 241
"Give **e**, O heavens, and let me Dt 32:1 238
give **e**, O rulers! Jg 5:3 238
"Incline Your **e**, O LORD, and 2Ki 19:16 241
let Your **e** now be attentive and Ne 1:6 241
may Your **e** be attentive to the Ne 1:11 241
Yet they would not give **e**. Ne 9:30 238
And my **e** received a whisper of it. Jb 4:12 241
"Does not the **e** test words, As Jb 12:11 241
My **e** has heard and understood it. Jb 13:1 241
"For when the **e** heard, it called Jb 29:11 241
"For the **e** tests words As the Jb 34:3 241
He opens their **e** to instruction, Jb 36:10 241
opens their **e** in *time of* oppression. Jb 36:15 241
of You by the hearing of the **e**; Jb 42:5 241
Give **e** to my words, O LORD, Ps 5:1 238
heart, You will incline Your **e** Ps 10:17 241
Give **e** to my prayer, which is not Ps 17:1 238
Incline Your **e** to me, hear my Ps 17:6 241
Incline Your **e** to me, rescue me Ps 31:2 241
O LORD, and give **e** to my cry; Ps 39:12 238
give attention and incline your **e**: Ps 45:10 241
Give **e**, all inhabitants of the Ps 49:1 238
I will incline my **e** to a proverb; Ps 49:4 241
Give **e** to the words of my mouth. Ps 54:2 238
Give **e** to my prayer, O God; Ps 55:1 238
a deaf cobra that stops up its **e**, Ps 58:4 241
Incline Your **e** to me and save me. Ps 71:2 241
Oh, give **e**, Shepherd of Israel, Ps 80:1 238
Give **e**, O God of Jacob! Ps 84:8 238
Incline Your **e**, O LORD, *and* Ps 86:1 241
Give **e**, O LORD, to my prayer; Ps 86:6 238
Incline Your **e** to my cry! Ps 88:2 241
He who planted the **e**, Ps 94:9 241
Incline Your **e** to me; Ps 102:2 241
He has inclined His **e** to me, Ps 116:2 241
Give **e**, O LORD, to the voice of my Ps 140:6 238
Give **e** to my voice when I call to Ps 141:1 238
LORD, Give **e** to my supplications! Ps 143:1 238
Make your **e** attentive to wisdom, Pr 2:2 241
Incline your **e** to my sayings. Pr 4:20 241
your **e** to my understanding; Pr 5:1 241
inclined my **e** to my instructors! Pr 5:13 241
He whose **e** listens to the Pr 15:31 241
the **e** of the wise seeks knowledge. Pr 18:15 241
The hearing **e** and the seeing eye, Pr 20:12 241
He who shuts his **e** to the cry of Pr 21:13 241
Incline your **e** and hear the words Pr 22:17 241
a wise reprover to a listening **e**. Pr 25:12 241
his **e** from listening to the law, Pr 28:9 241
Nor is the **e** filled with hearing. Ec 1:8 241
Give **e** to the instruction of our God, Is 1:10 238
And give **e**, all remote places of Is 8:9 238
Give **e** and hear my voice, Listen Is 28:23 238
Give **e** to my word, You complacent Is 32:9 238
"Incline Your **e**, O LORD, and Is 37:17 241
Who among you will give **e** to this? Is 42:23 238
long ago your **e** has not been open, Is 48:8 241
My **e** to listen as a disciple. Is 50:4 241
The Lord GOD has opened My **e**; Is 50:5 241
And give **e** to Me, O My nation; Is 51:4 238
"Incline your **e** and come to Me. Is 55:3 241
His **e** so dull That it cannot hear. Is 59:1 241
have not heard or perceived by **e**, Is 64:4 238
did not obey or incline their **e**, Jer 7:24 241
listen to Me or incline their **e**, Jer 7:26 241
e receive the word of His mouth; Jer 9:20 241
did not obey or incline their **e**, Jer 11:8 241
nor inclined your **e** to hear, Jer 25:4 241
obey Me or incline their **e** to Me. Jer 34:14 241
inclined your **e** or listened to Me. Jer 35:15 241
Your **e** from my *prayer for* relief, La 3:56 241
my God, incline Your **e** and hear! Da 9:18 241
couple of legs or a piece of an **e**, Am 3:12 241
what you hear *whispered* in *your* **e**, Mt 10:27 3775
high priest and cut off his **e**. Mt 26:51 5621b
high priest and cut off his **e**. Mk 14:47 5621a
priest and cut off his right **e**. Lk 22:50 3775
He touched his **e** and healed him. Lk 22:51 5621b
slave, and cut off his right **e**; Jn 18:10 5621a
of the one whose **e** Peter cut off, Jn 18:26 5621b
HAS NOT SEEN AND **E** HAS NOT HEARD, 1Co 2:9 3775
And if the **e** says, 1Co 12:16 3775
'He who has an **e**, let him hear Rv 2:7 3775
'He who has an **e**, let him hear Rv 2:11 3775
'He who has an **e**, let him hear Rv 2:17 3775
'He who has an **e**, let him hear Rv 2:29 3775
'He who has an **e**, let him hear Rv 3:6 3775
'He who has an **e**, let him hear Rv 3:13 3775
'He who has an **e**, let him hear Rv 3:22 3775
If anyone has an **e**, Rv 13:9 3775

EARLIER
do according to the **e** customs: 2Ki 17:34 7223
did according to their **e** custom. 2Ki 17:40 7223
example of his father David's **e** days 2Ch 17:3 7223
is no remembrance of **e** things; Ec 1:11 7223
in **e** times He treated the land of Is 9:1 7223
the LORD spoke **e** concerning Moab. Is 16:13 3975b
For whatever was written in **e** Ro 15:4 4270

EARLIEST
from the **e** times of the earth. Pr 8:23 6924a
I saw your forefathers as the **e** Hos 9:10 1063

EARLY
may rise **e** and go on your way." Gn 19:2 7925
Now Abraham arose **e** in the morning Gn 19:27 7925
So Abimelech arose **e** in the Gn 20:8 7925
So Abraham rose **e** in the morning and Gn 21:14 7925
So Abraham rose **e** in the morning Gn 22:3 7925
they arose **e** and exchanged oaths; Gn 26:31 7925
So Jacob rose **e** in the morning, Gn 28:18 7925
E in the morning Laban arose, Gn 31:55 7925
"Rise **e** in the morning and Ex 8:20 7925
"Rise up **e** in the morning and Ex 9:13 7925
Then he arose **e** in the morning, Ex 24:4 7925
e and offered burnt offerings, Ex 32:6 7925
and Moses rose up **e** in the morning Ex 34:4 7925
a grain offering of **e** ripened things Lv 2:14 1061
offering of your **e** ripened things. Lv 2:14 1061
they rose up **e** and went up to the Nu 14:40 7925
its season, the **e** and late rain, Dt 11:14 3138
Then Joshua rose **e** in the morning; Jos 3:1 7925
Now Joshua rose **e** in the morning, Jos 6:12 7925
they rose **e** at the dawning of the day Jos 6:15 7925
So Joshua arose **e** in the morning Jos 7:16 7925
Now Joshua rose **e** in the morning Jos 8:10 7925
rose up **e** and went out to meet Israel Jos 8:14 7925
the city arose **e** in the morning, Jg 6:28 7925
When he arose **e** the next morning Jg 6:38 7925
rose **e** and camped beside the Jg 7:1 7925
rise **e** and rush upon the city; Jg 9:33 7925
day they got up **e** in the morning, Jg 19:5 7925
he arose to go **e** in the morning, Jg 19:8 7925
Then tomorrow you may arise **e** for Jg 19:9 7925
arose **e** and built an altar there and Jg 21:4 7925
Then they arose **e** in the morning 1Sa 1:19 7925
arose **e** the next morning, 1Sa 5:3 7925
they arose **e** the next morning, 1Sa 5:4 7925
And they arose **e**; 1Sa 9:26 7925
e in the morning to meet Saul; 1Sa 15:12 7925
So David arose **e** in the morning 1Sa 17:20 7925
"Now then arise **e** in the morning 1Sa 29:10 7925
e in the morning and have light, 1Sa 29:10 7925
So David arose **e**, he and his men, 1Sa 29:11 7925
Absalom used to rise **e** and 2Sa 15:2 7925
They rose **e** in the morning, 2Ki 3:22 7925
of God had risen **e** and gone out, 2Ki 6:15 7925
when men rose **e** in the morning, 2Ki 19:35 7925
They rose **e** in the morning and 2Ch 20:20 7925
Then King Hezekiah arose **e** and 2Ch 29:20 7925
Gate from **e** morning until midday, Ne 8:3 216
rising up **e** in the morning and Jb 1:5 7925
The **e** rain also covers it with Ps 84:6 4175a
It is vain for you to rise up **e**, Ps 127:2 7925
a loud voice **e** in the morning, Pr 27:14 7925
us rise **e** *and go* to the vineyards; SS 7:12 7925
Woe to those who rise **e** in the Is 5:11 7925
when men arose **e** in the morning, Is 37:36 7925
to you, rising up **e** and speaking, Jer 7:13 7925
daily rising **e** and sending *them*. Jer 7:25 7925
like the dew which goes away **e**. Hos 6:4 7925
the **e** rain for *your* vindication. Jl 2:23 4175a
The **e** and latter rain as before. Jl 2:23 4175a
who went out **e** in the morning to hire Mt 20:1 260
In the **e** morning, while it was Mk 1:35 4404
E in the morning the chief priests Mk 15:1 2117
e on the first day of the week, Mk 16:2 4404
e on the first day of the week, Mk 16:9 4404
And all the people would get up **e** Lk 21:38 3719
first day of the week, at **e** dawn, Lk 24:1 3722
were at the tomb **e** in the morning, Lk 24:22 3720
E in the morning He came again into Jn 8:2 3722
into the Praetorium, and it was **e**; Jn 18:28 4404
Mary Magdalene came **e** to the tomb, Jn 20:1 4404
you know that in the **e** days God Ac 15:7 744
it gets the **e** and late rains. Jas 5:7 4291a

EARNER
oppress the wage **e** in his wages, Mal 3:5 7916

EARNEST
"If you will give **e** heed to the Ex 15:26 8085
appeal, but being himself very **e**, 2Co 8:17 4705
to my **e** expectation and hope, Php 1:20 603

EARNESTLY
"David **e** asked *leave* of me to run 1Sa 20:6 7592
"David **e** asked leave of me *to go* 1Sa 20:28 7592
whole heart and had sought Him **e**, 2Ch 15:15 3605, 7522
I shall seek You **e**; Ps 63:1 7836
meet you, To seek your presence **e**, Pr 7:15 7836
affliction they will seek Me. Hos 5:15 7836
"We **e** pray, O LORD, do not let us Jon 1:14 577
and let men call on God **e** that Jon 3:8 2394
And He **e** warned them not to tell Mk 3:12 4183
And he *began* to implore Him **e** not Mk 5:10 4183
and implored Him **e**, Mk 5:23 4183
to Jesus, they **e** implored Him, Lk 7:4 4709
"I have **e** desired to eat this Lk 22:15 1939
as they **e** serve *God* night and day. Ac 26:7 1722, 1616
But **e** desire the greater gifts. 1Co 12:31 2206

yet desire **e** spiritual *gifts*, 1Co 14:1 2206
my brethren, desire **e** to prophesy, 1Co 14:39 2206
laboring **e** for you in his prayers, Col 4:12 75
most **e** that we may see your face, 1Th 3:10 5238b
prayed **e** that it would not rain Jas 5:17 4335
that you contend **e** for the faith Jude 1:3 1864

EARNESTNESS
For behold what **e** this very thing, 2Co 7:11 4710
but that your **e** on our behalf 2Co 7:12 4710
in all **e** and in the love we inspired 2Co 8:7 4710
but as proving through the **e** of 2Co 8:8 4710
who puts the same **e** on your behalf 2Co 8:16 4710

EARNINGS
From her **e** she plants a vineyard. Pr 31:16 6529, 3709
e on every threshing floor. Hos 9:1 868
of her **e** will be burned with fire And Mi 1:7 868
collected *them* from a harlot's **e**, Mi 1:7 868
e of a harlot they will return. Mi 1:7 868

EARNS
The wicked **e** deceptive wages, But Pr 11:18 6213a
and he who **e**, earns wages *to put* Hg 1:6 7936
e wages *to put* into a purse with Hg 1:6 7936

EARRING
you give me an **e** from his spoil." Jg 8:24 5141
threw an **e** there from his spoil. Jg 8:25 5141
Like an **e** of gold and an ornament Pr 25:12 5141

EARRINGS
came *and* brought brooches and **e** Ex 35:22 5141
signet rings, **e** and necklaces, Nu 31:50 5694
(For they had gold **e**, because they Jg 8:24 5141
The weight of the gold **e** that Jg 8:26 5141
dangling **e**, bracelets, veils, Is 3:19 5188
in your nostril, **e** in your ears and Ezk 16:12 5694
herself with her **e** and jewelry, Hos 2:13 5141

EARS
the rings which were in their **e**, Gn 35:4 241
seven **e** of grain came up on a Gn 41:5 7641
Then behold, seven **e**, Gn 41:6 7641
The thin **e** swallowed up the Gn 41:7 7641
up the seven plump and full **e**. Gn 41:7 7641
in my dream, and behold, seven **e**, Gn 41:22 7641
and lo, seven **e**, withered, thin, Gn 41:23 7641
e swallowed the seven good ears. Gn 41:24 7641
ears swallowed the seven good **e**. Gn 41:24 7641
the seven good **e** are seven years; Gn 41:26 7641
and the seven thin **e** scorched by Gn 41:27 7641
please speak a word in my lord's **e**, Gn 44:18 241
and on the lobes of his sons' right **e** Ex 29:20 241
which are in the **e** of your wives, Ex 32:2 241
gold rings which were in their **e** and Ex 32:3 241
have wept in the **e** of the LORD, Nu 11:18 241
nor eyes to see, nor **e** to hear. Dt 29:4 241
and glean among the **e** of grain Ru 2:2 7641
e of everyone who hears it will tingle. 1Sa 3:11 241
bleating of the sheep in my **e**, 1Sa 15:14 241
all that we have heard with our **e**. 2Sa 7:22 241
my cry for help *came* into His **e**. 2Sa 22:7 241
and fresh **e** of grain in his sack. 2Ki 4:42 3759
arrogance has come up to My **e**, 2Ki 19:28 241
of it, both his **e** will tingle. 2Ki 21:12 241
all that we have heard with our **e**. 1Ch 17:20 241
and Your **e** attentive to the 2Ch 6:40 241
My **e** attentive to the prayer *offered* 2Ch 7:15 241
let my declaration *fill* your **e**. Jb 13:17 241
"Sounds of terror are in his **e**; Jb 15:21 241
e we have heard a report of it.' Jb 28:22 241
Then He opens the **e** of men, Jb 33:16 241
help before Him came into His **e**. Ps 18:6 241
And His **e** are *open* to their cry. Ps 34:15 241
My **e** You have opened; Ps 40:6 241
O God, we have heard with our **e**, Ps 44:1 241
your **e** to the words of my mouth. Ps 78:1 241
My **e** hear of the evildoers who Ps 92:11 241
They have **e**, but they cannot hear; Ps 115:6 241
Let Your **e** be attentive To the Ps 130:2 241
They have **e**, but they do not hear, Ps 135:17 241
And your **e** to words of knowledge. Pr 23:12 241
Like one who takes a dog by the **e** Pr 26:17 241
my **e** the LORD of hosts *has sworn,* Is 5:9 241
people insensitive, Their **e** dull, Is 6:10 241
their eyes, Hear with their **e**, Is 6:10 241
a decision by what His **e** hear; Is 11:3 241
grain, As his arm harvests the **e**, Is 17:5 7641
it will be like one gleaning **e** of grain Is 17:5 7641
e will hear a word behind you, Is 30:21 241
e of those who hear will listen. Is 32:3 241
e from hearing about bloodshed And Is 33:15 241
e of the deaf will be unstopped. Is 35:5 241
arrogance has come up to My **e**, Is 37:29 241
Your **e** are open, but none hears. Is 42:20 241
the deaf, even though they have **e**. Is 43:8 241
bereaved will yet say in your **e**, Is 49:20 241
proclaim in the **e** of Jerusalem, Jer 2:2 241
Who have **e** but do not hear. Jer 5:21 241
Behold, their **e** are closed And Jer 6:10 241
did not listen or incline their **e**, Jer 17:23 241
at which the **e** of everyone that Jer 19:3 241
e to turn from their wickedness, Jer 44:5 241
cry in My **e** with a loud voice, Ezk 8:18 241
see, **e** to hear but do not hear; Ezk 12:2 241
your nostril, earrings in your **e** and Ezk 16:12 241
will remove your nose and your **e**; Ezk 23:25 241
you with information for *your* **e**? Ezk 24:26 241
with your eyes, hear with your **e**, Ezk 40:4 241
and hear with your **e** all that I Ezk 44:5 241
their mouth, Their **e** will be deaf. Mi 7:16 241
and stopped their **e** from hearing. Zch 7:11 241
"He who has **e** to hear, let him Mt 11:15 3775
"He who has **e**, let him hear." Mt 13:9 3775
WITH THEIR **E** THEY SCARCELY HEAR, Mt 13:15 3775
THEIR EYES, HEAR WITH THEIR **E**, Mt 13:15 3775
and your **e**, because they hear. Mt 13:16 3775
He who has **e**, let him hear. Mt 13:43 3775
should come to the governor's **e**, Mt 28:14 191
"He who has **e** to hear, let him Mk 4:9 3775
"If anyone has **e** to hear, let Mk 4:23 3775
["If anyone has **e** to hear, let Mk 7:16 3775
and put His fingers into his **e**, Mk 7:33 3775
And his **e** were opened, and the Mk 7:35 189
AND HAVING **E**, DO YOU NOT HEAR? Mk 8:18 3775
of your greeting reached my **e**, Lk 1:44 3775
"He who has **e** to hear, let him Lk 8:8 3775
"Let these words sink into your **e**; Lk 9:44 3775
He who has **e** to hear, let him hear." Lk 14:35 3775
and uncircumcised in heart and **e** Ac 7:51 3775
a loud voice, and covered their **e** and Ac 7:57 3775
the **e** of the church at Jerusalem, Ac 11:22 3775
some strange things to our **e**; Ac 17:20 189
WITH THEIR **E** THEY SCARCELY HEAR, Ac 28:27 3775
THEIR EYES, AND HEAR WITH THEIR **E**, Ac 28:27 3775
EYES TO SEE NOT AND **E** TO HEAR NOT, Ro 11:8 3775
wanting to have their **e** tickled, 2Tm 4:3 189
turn away their **e** from the truth and 2Tm 4:4 189
the **e** of the Lord of Sabaoth. Jas 5:4 3775
AND HIS **E** ATTEND TO THEIR PRAYER, 1Pe 3:12 3775

EARTH
God created the heavens and the **e**. Gn 1:1 776
The **e** was formless and void, Gn 1:2 776
God called the dry land **e**, Gn 1:10 776
"Let the **e** sprout vegetation, Gn 1:11 776
fruit trees on the **e** bearing fruit Gn 1:11 776
The **e** brought forth vegetation, Gn 1:12 776
heavens to give light on the **e**"; Gn 1:15 776
heavens to give light on the **e**, Gn 1:17 776
and let birds fly above the **e** in Gn 1:20 776
and let birds multiply on the **e**." Gn 1:22 776
"Let the **e** bring forth living Gn 1:24 776
of the **e** after their kind"; Gn 1:24 776
beasts of the **e** after their kind, Gn 1:25 776
the cattle and over all the **e**, Gn 1:26 776
thing that creeps on the **e**." Gn 1:26 776
and multiply, and fill the **e**, Gn 1:28 776
thing that moves on the **e**." Gn 1:28 776
is on the surface of all the **e**, Gn 1:29 776
and to every beast of the **e** and to Gn 1:30 776
moves on the **e** which has life, Gn 1:30 776
heavens and the **e** were completed, Gn 2:1 776
and the **e** when they were created, Gn 2:4 776
the LORD God made **e** and heaven. Gn 2:4 776
of the field was yet in the **e**, Gn 2:5 776
God had not sent rain upon the **e**, Gn 2:5 776
mist used to rise from the **e** and water Gn 2:6 776
vagrant and a wanderer on the **e**." Gn 4:12 776
a vagrant and a wanderer on the **e**, Gn 4:14 776
were on the **e** in those days, Gn 6:4 776
of man was great on the **e**, Gn 6:5 776
that He had made man on the **e**, Gn 6:6 776
Now the **e** was corrupt in the sight Gn 6:11 776
the **e** was filled with violence. Gn 6:11 776
God looked on the **e**, Gn 6:12 776
corrupted their way upon the **e**. Gn 6:12 776
for the **e** is filled with violence Gn 6:13 776
about to destroy them with the **e**. Gn 6:13 776
the flood of water upon the **e**, Gn 6:17 776
that is on the **e** shall perish. Gn 6:17 776
alive on the face of all the **e**. Gn 7:3 776
the **e** forty days and forty nights; Gn 7:4 776
flood of water came upon the **e**. Gn 7:6 776
of the flood came upon the **e**. Gn 7:10 776
The rain fell upon the **e** for Gn 7:12 776
creeps on the **e** after its kind, Gn 7:14 776
came upon the **e** for forty days, Gn 7:17 776
ark, so that it rose above the **e**. Gn 7:17 776
and increased greatly upon the **e**, Gn 7:18 776
more and more upon the **e**, Gn 7:19 776
that moved on the **e** perished, Gn 7:21 776
thing that swarms upon the **e**, Gn 7:21 776
they were blotted out from the **e**; Gn 7:23 776
the **e** one hundred and fifty days. Gn 7:24 776
caused a wind to pass over the **e**, Gn 8:1 776
water receded steadily from the **e**, Gn 8:3 776
the water was dried up from the **e**. Gn 8:7 776
was on the surface of all the **e**. Gn 8:9 776
the water was abated from the **e**. Gn 8:11 776
the water was dried up from the **e**. Gn 8:13 776
day of the month, the **e** was dry. Gn 8:14 776
thing that creeps on the **e**, Gn 8:17 776
may breed abundantly on the **e**, Gn 8:17 776
fruitful and multiply on the **e**." Gn 8:17 776
everything that moves on the **e**, Gn 8:19 776
"While the **e** remains, Seedtime Gn 8:22 776
and multiply, and fill the **e**. Gn 9:1 776
e and on every bird of the sky; Gn 9:2 776
e abundantly and multiply in it." Gn 9:7 776
and every beast of the **e** with you; Gn 9:10 776
ark, even every beast of the **e**. Gn 9:10 776
be a flood to destroy the **e**." Gn 9:11 776
a covenant between Me and the **e**. Gn 9:13 776
when I bring a cloud over the **e**, Gn 9:14 776
of all flesh that is on the **e**." Gn 9:16 776
and all flesh that is on the **e**." Gn 9:17 776
these the whole **e** was populated. Gn 9:19 776
he became a mighty one on the **e**. Gn 10:8 776
for in his days the **e** was divided; Gn 10:25 776
on the **e** after the flood. Gn 10:32 776
Now the whole **e** used the same Gn 11:1 776
over the face of the whole **e**." Gn 11:4 776
over the face of the whole **e**; Gn 11:8 776
the language of the whole **e**; Gn 11:9 776
over the face of the whole **e**. Gn 11:9 776
of the **e** will be blessed." Gn 12:3 127
descendants as the dust of the **e**, Gn 13:16 776
can number the dust of the **e**, Gn 13:16 776
High, Possessor of heaven and **e**; Gn 14:19 776
High, possessor of heaven and **e**, Gn 14:22 776
them and bowed himself to the **e**, Gn 18:2 776
nations of the **e** will be blessed? Gn 18:18 776
Judge of all the **e** deal justly?" Gn 18:25 776
over the **e** when Lot came to Zoar. Gn 19:23 776
and there is not a man on **e** to Gn 19:31 776
to us after the manner of the **e**. Gn 19:31 776
nations of the **e** shall be blessed, Gn 22:18 776
God of heaven and the God of **e**, Gn 24:3 776
nations of the **e** shall be blessed; Gn 26:4 776
stopped up by filling them with **e**. Gn 26:15 6083
And of the fatness of the **e**, Gn 27:28 776
of the **e** shall be your dwelling, Gn 27:39 776
a ladder was set on the **e** with its Gn 28:12 776
also be like the dust of the **e**, Gn 28:14 776
the families of the **e** be blessed. Gn 28:14 127
spread over all the face of the **e**, Gn 41:56 776
The people of all the **e** came Gn 41:57 776
famine was severe in all the **e**. Gn 41:57 776
for you a remnant in the **e**, Gn 45:7 776
multitude in the midst of the **e**." Gn 48:16 776
and strike the dust of the **e**, Ex 8:16 776
and struck the dust of the **e**, Ex 8:17 776
All the dust of the **e** became gnats Ex 8:17 776
is no one like Me in all the **e**. Ex 9:14 776
then have been cut off from the **e**. Ex 9:15 776
My name through all the **e**. Ex 9:16 776
hail, and fire ran down to the **e**. Ex 9:23 776
may know that the **e** is the LORD's. Ex 9:29 776
rain no longer poured on the **e**. Ex 9:33 776
upon the **e** until this day.'" Ex 10:6 127
right hand, The **e** swallowed them. Ex 15:12 776
peoples, for all the **e** is Mine; Ex 19:5 776
on the **e** beneath or in the water under Ex 20:4 776
or in the water under the **e**. Ex 20:4 776
LORD made the heavens and the **e**, Ex 20:11 776
shall make an altar of **e** for Me, Ex 20:24 127
days the LORD made heaven and **e**, Ex 31:17 776
them from the face of the **e**'? Ex 32:12 127
who are upon the face of the **e**?" Ex 33:16 127
bow low toward the **e** and worship. Ex 34:8 776
not been produced in all the **e** nor Ex 34:10 776
all the animals that are on the **e**. Lv 11:2 776
legs with which to jump on the **e**. Lv 11:21 776
things which swarm on the **e**: Lv 11:29 776
swarms on the **e** is detestable, Lv 11:41 776
thing that swarms on the **e**, Lv 11:42 776
things that swarm on the **e**. Lv 11:44 776
everything that swarms on the **e**, Lv 11:46 776
out its blood and cover it with **e**. Lv 17:13 6083
like iron and your **e** like bronze. Lv 26:19 776
man who was on the face of the **e**.) Nu 12:3 127
all the **e** will be filled with the Nu 14:21 776
and the **e** opened its mouth and Nu 16:32 776
and the **e** closed over them, and Nu 16:33 776
"The **e** may swallow us up!" Nu 16:34 776
and the **e** opened its mouth and Nu 26:10 776
what god is there in heaven or on **e** Dt 3:24 776
all the days they live on the **e**, Dt 4:10 127
of any animal that is on the **e**, Dt 4:17 776
that is in the water below the **e**. Dt 4:18 776
e to witness against you today, Dt 4:26 776
day that God created man on the **e**, Dt 4:32 776
e He let you see His great fire, Dt 4:36 776
heaven above and on the **e** below; Dt 4:39 776
in heaven above or on the **e** beneath Dt 5:8 776
or in the water under the **e**. Dt 5:8 776
wipe you off the face of the **e**. Dt 6:15 127
who are on the face of the **e**. Dt 7:6 127
the **e** and all that is in it. Dt 10:14 776
when the **e** opened its mouth and Dt 11:6 776
as the heavens *remain* above the **e**. Dt 11:21 776
as long as you live on the **e**. Dt 12:1 127
end of the **e** to the other end), Dt 13:7 776
who are on the face of the **e**. Dt 14:2 127
above all the nations of the **e**. Dt 28:1 776
"So all the peoples of the **e** Dt 28:10 776
and the **e** which is under you, Dt 28:23 776
to all the kingdoms of the **e**. Dt 28:25 776
sky and to the beasts of the **e**, Dt 28:26 776
from afar, from the end of the **e**, Dt 28:49 776
e to the other end of Dt 28:64 776
e; and there you shall serve Dt 28:64 776
outcasts are at the ends of the **e**, Dt 30:4 8064
e to witness against you today, Dt 30:19 776
and the **e** to witness against them. Dt 31:28 776
the **e** hear the words of my mouth. Dt 32:1 776
ride on the high places of the **e**, Dt 32:13 776
And consumes the **e** with its yield, Dt 32:22 776
things of the **e** and its fullness, Dt 33:16 776
All at once, *to* the ends of the **e**. Dt 33:17 776
in heaven above and on **e** beneath. Jos 2:11 776
covenant of the Lord of all the **e** is Jos 3:11 776
the LORD, the Lord of all the **e**, Jos 3:13 776
that all the peoples of the **e** may Jos 4:24 776
Joshua fell on his face to the **e**, Jos 5:14 776
fell to the **e** on his face before the ark Jos 7:6 776
and cut off our name from the **e**. Jos 7:9 776
they are concealed in the **e** inside Jos 7:21 776
I am going the way of all the **e**, Jos 23:14 776
the field of Edom, The **e** quaked, Jg 5:4 776

produce of the **e** as far as Gaza,	**Jg 6:4**	776
of anything that is on the **e**."	**Jg 18:10**	776
pillars of the **e** are the LORD's,	**1Sa 2:8**	776
LORD will judge the ends of the **e**;	**1Sa 2:10**	776
shout, so that the **e** resounded.	**1Sa 4:5**	776
and the **e** quaked so that it became	**1Sa 14:15**	776
sky and the wild beasts of the **e**,	**1Sa 17:46**	776
that all the **e** may know that there	**1Sa 17:46**	776
of David from the face of the **e**."	**1Sa 20:15**	127
the son of Jesse lives on the **e**,	**1Sa 20:31**	127
being coming up out of the **e**,"	**1Sa 28:13**	776
and destroy you from the **e**?"	**2Sa 4:11**	776
of the great men who are on the **e**.	**2Sa 7:9**	776
the **e** is like Your people Israel,	**2Sa 7:23**	776
remnant on the face of the **e**."	**2Sa 14:7**	127
to know all that is in the **e**."	**2Sa 14:20**	776
left hanging between heaven and **e**,	**2Sa 18:9**	776
"Then the **e** shook and quaked, The	**2Sa 22:8**	776
them as the dust of the **e**;	**2Sa 22:43**	776
tender grass *springs* out of the **e**,	**2Sa 23:4**	776
that the **e** shook at their noise.	**1Ki 1:40**	776
"I am going the way of all the **e**.	**1Ki 2:2**	776
the **e** who had heard of his wisdom.	**1Ki 4:34**	776
in heaven above or on **e** beneath,	**1Ki 8:23**	776
will God indeed dwell on the **e**?	**1Ki 8:27**	776
of the **e** may know Your name,	**1Ki 8:43**	776
of the **e** as Your inheritance,	**1Ki 8:53**	776
e may know that the LORD is God;	**1Ki 8:60**	776
of the **e** in riches and in wisdom.	**1Ki 10:23**	776
All the **e** was seeking the	**1Ki 10:24**	776
it from off the face of the **e**.	**1Ki 13:34**	127
rain on the face of the **e**.' "	**1Ki 17:14**	127
send rain on the face of the **e**."	**1Ki 18:1**	127
and he crouched down on the **e** and	**1Ki 18:42**	776
that there is no God in all the **e**,	**2Ki 5:15**	776
be given two mules' load of **e**;	**2Ki 5:17**	127
shall fall to the **e** nothing of the word	**2Ki 10:10**	776
of all the kingdoms of the **e**.	**2Ki 19:15**	776
You have made heaven and **e**.	**2Ki 19:15**	776
of the **e** may know that You alone,	**2Ki 19:19**	776
began to be a mighty one in the **e**.	**1Ch 1:10**	776
for in his days the **e** was divided,	**1Ch 1:19**	776
His judgments are in all the **e**.	**1Ch 16:14**	776
Sing to the LORD, all the **e**;	**1Ch 16:23**	776
Tremble before Him, all the **e**;	**1Ch 16:30**	776
be glad, and let the **e** rejoice;	**1Ch 16:31**	776
For He is coming to judge the **e**.	**1Ch 16:33**	776
the great ones who are in the **e**.	**1Ch 17:8**	776
the **e** is like Your people Israel,	**1Ch 17:21**	776
standing between **e** and heaven,	**1Ch 21:16**	776
so much blood on the **e** before Me.	**1Ch 22:8**	776
that is in the heavens and the **e**;	**1Ch 29:11**	776
days on the **e** are like a shadow,	**1Ch 29:15**	776
as numerous as the dust of the **e**.	**2Ch 1:9**	776
Israel, who has made heaven and **e**,	**2Ch 2:12**	776
god like You in heaven or on **e**,	**2Ch 6:14**	776
dwell with mankind on the **e**?	**2Ch 6:18**	776
of the **e** may know Your name,	**2Ch 6:33**	776
of the **e** in riches and wisdom.	**2Ch 9:22**	776
And all the kings of the **e** were	**2Ch 9:23**	776
move to and fro throughout the **e**	**2Ch 16:9**	776
the gods of the peoples of the **e**,	**2Ch 32:19**	776
me all the kingdoms of the **e**,	**2Ch 36:23**	776
me all the kingdoms of the **e** and	**Ezr 1:2**	776
servants of the God of heaven and **e**	**Ezr 5:11**	772
host, The **e** and all that is on it,	**Ne 9:6**	776
the **e** and walking around on it."	**Jb 1:7**	776
there is no one like him on the **e**,	**Jb 1:8**	776
"From roaming about on the **e** and	**Jb 2:2**	776
there is no one like him on the **e**,	**Jb 2:3**	776
and *with* counselors of the **e**,	**Jb 3:14**	776
"He gives rain on the **e** And	**Jb 5:10**	776
offspring as the grass of the **e**.	**Jb 5:25**	776
"Is not man forced to labor on **e**,	**Jb 7:1**	776
our days on **e** are as a shadow.	**Jb 8:9**	776
Who shakes the **e** out of its place,	**Jb 9:6**	776
"The **e** is given into the hand of	**Jb 9:24**	776
"Its measure is longer than the **e** And	**Jb 11:9**	776
"Or speak to the **e**, and let it	**Jb 12:8**	776
them out, and they inundate the **e**.	**Jb 12:15**	776
wash away the dust of the **e**;	**Jb 14:19**	776
"O **e**, do not cover my blood, And	**Jb 16:18**	776
sake is the **e** to be abandoned,	**Jb 18:4**	776
"Memory of him perishes from the **e**,	**Jb 18:17**	776
He will take His stand on the **e**.	**Jb 19:25**	6083
the establishment of man on **e**,	**Jb 20:4**	776
the **e** will rise up against him.	**Jb 20:27**	776
the **e** belongs to the mighty man,	**Jb 22:8**	776
Their portion is cursed on the **e**.	**Jb 24:18**	776
space And hangs the **e** on nothing.	**Jb 26:7**	776
"The **e**, from it comes food, And	**Jb 28:5**	776
"For He looks to the ends of the **e** And	**Jb 28:24**	776
holes of the **e** and of the rocks.	**Jb 30:6**	6083
"Who gave Him authority over the **e**?	**Jb 34:13**	776
us more than the beasts of the **e** And	**Jb 35:11**	776
lightning to the ends of the **e**.	**Jb 37:3**	776
'Fall on the **e**,' And to the	**Jb 37:6**	776
it On the face of the inhabited **e**.	**Jb 37:12**	776
I laid the foundation of the **e**?	**Jb 38:4**	776
take hold of the ends of the **e**,	**Jb 38:13**	776
understood the expanse of the **e**?	**Jb 38:18**	776
the east wind scattered on the **e**?	**Jb 38:24**	776
Or fix their rule over the **e**?	**Jb 38:33**	776
she abandons her eggs to the **e** And	**Jb 39:14**	776
"Nothing on **e** is like him, One	**Jb 41:33**	6083
kings of the **e** take their stand And	**Ps 2:2**	776
ends of the **e** as Your possession.	**Ps 2:8**	776
Take warning, O judges of the **e**.	**Ps 2:10**	776
majestic is Your name in all the **e**,	**Ps 8:1**	776

majestic is Your name in all the **e**!	**Ps 8:9**	776
of the **e** will no longer cause terror.	**Ps 10:18**	776
tried in a furnace on the **e**,	**Ps 12:6**	776
for the saints who are in the **e**,	**Ps 16:3**	776
Then the **e** shook and quaked;	**Ps 18:7**	776
has gone out through all the **e**,	**Ps 19:4**	776
You will destroy from the **e**,	**Ps 21:10**	776
All the ends of the **e** will	**Ps 22:27**	776
of the **e** will eat and worship,	**Ps 22:29**	776
The **e** is the LORD's, and all it	**Ps 24:1**	776
The **e** is full of the	**Ps 33:5**	776
Let all the **e** fear the LORD;	**Ps 33:8**	776
On all the inhabitants of the **e**,	**Ps 33:14**	776
off the memory of them from the **e**.	**Ps 34:16**	776
be called blessed upon the **e**;	**Ps 41:2**	776
Our body cleaves to the **e**.	**Ps 44:25**	776
make them princes in all the **e**.	**Ps 45:16**	776
fear, though the **e** should change And	**Ps 46:2**	776
He raised His voice, the **e** melted.	**Ps 46:6**	776
has wrought desolations in the **e**.	**Ps 46:8**	776
wars to cease to the end of the **e**;	**Ps 46:9**	776
I will be exalted in the **e**."	**Ps 46:10**	776
A great King over all the **e**.	**Ps 47:2**	776
For God is the King of all the **e**;	**Ps 47:7**	776
shields of the **e** belong to God;	**Ps 47:9**	776
elevation, the joy of the whole **e**,	**Ps 48:2**	776
Your praise to the ends of the **e**;	**Ps 48:10**	776
And summoned the **e** from the rising	**Ps 50:1**	776
the heavens above, And the **e**,	**Ps 50:4**	776
Let Your glory *be* above all the **e**.	**Ps 57:5**	776
Let Your glory *be* above all the **e**.	**Ps 57:11**	776
On **e** you weigh out the violence of	**Ps 58:2**	776
there is a God who judges on **e**!"	**Ps 58:11**	776
rules in Jacob To the ends of the **e**.	**Ps 59:13**	776
the end of the **e** I call to You when	**Ps 61:2**	776
Will go into the depths of the **e**.	**Ps 63:9**	776
of the **e** and of the farthest sea;	**Ps 65:5**	776
They who dwell in the ends *of the* **e**	**Ps 65:8**	
You visit the **e**	**Ps 65:9**	776
for thus You prepare the **e**.	**Ps 65:9**	
Shout joyfully to God, all the **e**;	**Ps 66:1**	776
"All the **e** will worship You, And	**Ps 66:4**	776
Your way may be known on the **e**,	**Ps 67:2**	776
And guide the nations on the **e**.	**Ps 67:4**	776
The **e** has yielded its produce;	**Ps 67:6**	776
the ends of the **e** may fear Him.	**Ps 67:7**	776
The **e** quaked; The heavens also	**Ps 68:8**	776
Sing to God, O kingdoms of the **e**,	**Ps 68:32**	776
Let heaven and **e** praise Him, The	**Ps 69:34**	776
up again from the depths of the **e**.	**Ps 71:20**	776
Like showers that water the **e**.	**Ps 72:6**	776
the River to the ends of the **e**.	**Ps 72:8**	776
in the **e** on top of the mountains;	**Ps 72:16**	776
flourish like vegetation of the **e**.	**Ps 72:16**	776
whole **e** be filled with His glory.	**Ps 72:19**	776
tongue parades through the **e**.	**Ps 73:9**	776
You, I desire nothing on **e**.	**Ps 73:25**	776
deliverance in the midst of the **e**.	**Ps 74:12**	776
all the boundaries of the **e**;	**Ps 74:17**	776
e and all who dwell in it melt;	**Ps 75:3**	776
Surely all the wicked of the **e**	**Ps 75:8**	776
The **e** feared and was still	**Ps 76:8**	776
To save all the humble of the **e**.	**Ps 76:9**	776
is feared by the kings of the **e**.	**Ps 76:12**	776
The **e** trembled and shook.	**Ps 77:18**	776
e which He has founded forever.	**Ps 78:69**	776
godly ones to the beasts of the **e**.	**Ps 79:2**	776
foundations of the **e** are shaken.	**Ps 82:5**	776
Arise, O God, judge the **e**!	**Ps 82:8**	776
Are the Most High over all the **e**.	**Ps 83:18**	776
Truth springs from the **e**,	**Ps 85:11**	776
are Yours, the **e** also is Yours;	**Ps 89:11**	776
The highest of the kings of the **e**.	**Ps 89:27**	776
gave birth to the **e** and the world,	**Ps 90:2**	776
Rise up, O Judge of the **e**,	**Ps 94:2**	776
hand are the depths of the **e**,	**Ps 95:4**	776
Sing to the LORD, all the **e**.	**Ps 96:1**	776
Tremble before Him, all the **e**.	**Ps 96:9**	776
be glad, and let the **e** rejoice;	**Ps 96:11**	776
For He is coming to judge the **e**.	**Ps 96:13**	776
let the **e** rejoice;	**Ps 97:1**	776
The **e** saw and trembled.	**Ps 97:4**	776
of the Lord of the whole **e**.	**Ps 97:5**	776
the LORD Most High over all the **e**;	**Ps 97:9**	776
All the ends of the **e** have seen	**Ps 98:3**	776
joyfully to the LORD, all the **e**;	**Ps 98:4**	776
for He is coming to judge the **e**;	**Ps 98:9**	776
the cherubim, let the **e** shake!	**Ps 99:1**	776
joyfully to the LORD, all the **e**.	**Ps 100:1**	776
all the kings of the **e** Your glory.	**Ps 102:15**	776
heaven the LORD gazed upon the **e**,	**Ps 102:19**	776
"Of old You founded the **e**,	**Ps 102:25**	776
as the heavens are above the **e**,	**Ps 103:11**	776
the **e** upon its foundations,	**Ps 104:5**	776
will not return to cover the **e**.	**Ps 104:9**	776
The **e** is satisfied with the fruit	**Ps 104:13**	776
may bring forth food from the **e**,	**Ps 104:14**	776
The **e** is full of Your possessions.	**Ps 104:24**	776
He looks at the **e**, and it trembles;	**Ps 104:32**	776
sinners be consumed from the **e** And	**Ps 104:35**	776
His judgments are in all the **e**.	**Ps 105:7**	776
The **e** opened and swallowed up	**Ps 106:17**	776
And Your glory above all the **e**.	**Ps 108:5**	776
cut off their memory from the **e**;	**Ps 109:15**	776
descendants will be mighty on **e**;	**Ps 112:2**	776
that are in heaven and in the **e**?	**Ps 113:6**	776
Tremble, O **e**, before the Lord,	**Ps 114:7**	776
the LORD, Maker of heaven and **e**.	**Ps 115:15**	776
But the **e** He has given to the sons	**Ps 115:16**	776

I am a stranger in the **e**;	**Ps 119:19**	776
e is full of Your lovingkindness,	**Ps 119:64**	776
They almost destroyed me on **e**,	**Ps 119:87**	776
You established the **e**,	**Ps 119:90**	776
the wicked of the **e** *like* dross;	**Ps 119:119**	776
the LORD, Who made heaven and **e**.	**Ps 121:2**	776
the LORD, Who made heaven and **e**.	**Ps 124:8**	776
Zion, He who made heaven and **e**.	**Ps 134:3**	776
He does, In heaven and in **e**,	**Ps 135:6**	776
to ascend from the ends of the **e**;	**Ps 135:7**	776
spread out the **e** above the waters,	**Ps 136:6**	776
of the **e** will give thanks to You,	**Ps 138:4**	776
wrought in the depths of the **e**;	**Ps 139:15**	776
not be established in the **e**;	**Ps 140:11**	776
one plows and breaks open the **e**,	**Ps 141:7**	776
departs, he returns to the **e**;	**Ps 146:4**	127
Who made heaven and **e**,	**Ps 146:6**	776
Who provides rain for the **e**,	**Ps 147:8**	776
sends forth His command to the **e**;	**Ps 147:15**	776
Praise the LORD from the **e**,	**Ps 148:7**	776
Kings of the **e** and all peoples;	**Ps 148:11**	776
Princes and all judges of the **e**;	**Ps 148:11**	776
His glory is above **e** and heaven.	**Ps 148:13**	776
The LORD by wisdom founded the **e**,	**Pr 3:19**	776
from the earliest times of the **e**.	**Pr 8:23**	776
not yet made the **e** and the fields,	**Pr 8:26**	776
out the foundations of the **e**;	**Pr 8:29**	776
Rejoicing in the world, His **e**,	**Pr 8:31**	776
will be rewarded in the **e**,	**Pr 11:31**	776
a fool are on the ends of the **e**.	**Pr 17:24**	776
for height and the **e** for depth,	**Pr 25:3**	776
established all the ends of the **e**?	**Pr 30:4**	776
devour the afflicted from the **e** And	**Pr 30:14**	776
E that is never satisfied with	**Pr 30:16**	776
Under three things the **e** quakes,	**Pr 30:21**	776
Four things are small on the **e**,	**Pr 30:24**	776
comes, But the **e** remains forever.	**Ec 1:4**	776
beast descends downward to the **e**?	**Ec 3:21**	776
is in heaven and you are on the **e**;	**Ec 5:2**	776
there is not a righteous man on **e** who	**Ec 7:20**	776
futility which is done on the **e**,	**Ec 8:14**	776
task which has been done on the **e**	**Ec 8:16**	776
misfortune may occur on the **e**.	**Ec 11:2**	776
they pour out rain upon the **e**;	**Ec 11:3**	776
will return to the **e** as it was,	**Ec 12:7**	776
Listen, O heavens, and hear, O **e**;	**Is 1:2**	776
He arises to make the **e** tremble.	**Is 2:19**	776
He arises to make the **e** tremble.	**Is 2:21**	776
and the fruit of the **e** *will be* the	**Is 4:2**	776
for it from the ends of the **e**;	**Is 5:26**	776
whole **e** is full of His glory."	**Is 6:3**	776
give ear, all remote places of the **e**.	**Is 8:9**	776
Then they will look to the **e**,	**Is 8:22**	776
eggs, I gathered all the **e**;	**Is 10:14**	776
for the afflicted of the **e**;	**Is 11:4**	776
the **e** with the rod of His mouth,	**Is 11:4**	776
For the **e** will be full of the	**Is 11:9**	776
From the four corners of the **e**.	**Is 11:12**	776
this be known throughout the **e**.	**Is 12:5**	776
And the **e** will be shaken from its	**Is 13:13**	776
whole **e** is at rest *and* is quiet;	**Is 14:7**	776
dead, all the leaders of the **e**;	**Is 14:9**	776
You have been cut down to the **e**,	**Is 14:12**	776
the man who made the **e** tremble,	**Is 14:16**	776
not arise and take possession of the **e**	**Is 14:21**	776
plan devised against the whole **e**;	**Is 14:26**	776
of the world and dwellers on **e**,	**Is 18:3**	776
prey, And for the beasts of the **e**;	**Is 18:6**	776
And all the beasts of the **e** will	**Is 18:6**	776
a blessing in the midst of the **e**,	**Is 19:24**	776
traders were the honored of the **e**?	**Is 23:8**	776
despise all the honored of the **e**.	**Is 23:9**	776
the kingdoms on the face of the **e**.	**Is 23:17**	127
Behold, the LORD lays the **e** waste,	**Is 24:1**	776
The **e** will be completely laid	**Is 24:3**	776
The **e** mourns *and* withers, the	**Is 24:4**	776
of the people of the **e** fade away.	**Is 24:4**	776
The **e** is also polluted by its	**Is 24:5**	776
Therefore, a curse devours the **e**,	**Is 24:6**	776
inhabitants of the **e** are burned,	**Is 24:6**	776
The gaiety of the **e** is banished.	**Is 24:11**	776
midst of the **e** among the peoples,	**Is 24:13**	776
the ends of the **e** we hear songs,	**Is 24:16**	776
you, O inhabitant of the **e**.	**Is 24:17**	776
the foundations of the **e** shake.	**Is 24:18**	776
The **e** is broken asunder, The earth	**Is 24:19**	776
asunder, The **e** is split through,	**Is 24:19**	776
The **e** is shaken violently.	**Is 24:19**	776
The **e** reels to and fro like a	**Is 24:20**	776
on high, And the kings of the **e** on	**Is 24:21**	127
And the kings of the earth on **e**.	**Is 24:21**	127
of His people from all the **e**;	**Is 25:8**	776
For when the **e** experiences Your	**Is 26:9**	776
not accomplish deliverance for the **e**	**Is 26:18**	776
And the **e** will give birth to the	**Is 26:19**	776
of the **e** for their iniquity;	**Is 26:21**	776
the **e** will reveal her bloodshed And	**Is 26:21**	776
He has cast *it* down to the **e** with	**Is 28:2**	776
decisive destruction on all the **e**.	**Is 28:22**	776
From the **e** you will speak, And	**Is 29:4**	776
Let the **e** and all it contains hear,	**Is 34:1**	776
And its loose **e** into brimstone,	**Is 34:9**	6083
of all the kingdoms of the **e**.	**Is 37:16**	776
You have made heaven and **e**.	**Is 37:16**	776
of the **e** may know that You alone,	**Is 37:20**	776
the dust of the **e** by the measure,	**Is 40:12**	776
from the foundations of the **e**?	**Is 40:21**	776
who sits above the circle of the **e**,	**Is 40:22**	776
the judges of the **e** meaningless.	**Is 40:23**	776

their stock taken root in the **e**,	Is 40:24	776
the Creator of the ends of the **e**	Is 40:28	776
The ends of the **e** tremble;	Is 41:5	776
have taken from the ends of the **e**,	Is 41:9	776
has established justice in the **e**;	Is 42:4	776
Who spread out the **e** and its	Is 42:5	776
His praise from the end of the **e**!	Is 42:10	776
daughters from the ends of the **e**,	Is 43:6	776
you lower parts of the **e**;	Is 44:23	776
And spreading out the **e** all alone,	Is 44:24	776
Let the **e** open up and salvation	Is 45:8	776
vessel among the vessels of **e**!	Is 45:9	127
"It is I who made the **e**,	Is 45:12	776
God who formed the **e** and made it,	Is 45:18	776
be saved, all the ends of the **e**;	Is 45:22	776
"Surely My hand founded the **e**,	Is 48:13	776
Send it out to the end of the **e**;	Is 48:20	776
may reach to the end of the **e**."	Is 49:6	776
And rejoice, O **e**!	Is 49:13	776
to you with their faces to the **e** And	Is 49:23	776
sky, Then look to the **e** beneath;	Is 51:6	776
And the **e** will wear out like	Is 51:6	776
And laid the foundations of the **e**,	Is 51:13	776
the heavens, to found the **e**,	Is 51:16	776
That all the ends of the **e** may see	Is 52:10	776
is called the God of all the **e**.	Is 54:5	776
Noah Would not flood the **e** again	Is 54:9	776
the heavens are higher than the **e**,	Is 55:9	776
there without watering the **e** And	Is 55:10	776
you ride on the heights of the **e**;	Is 58:14	776
behold, darkness will cover the **e** And	Is 60:2	776
as the **e** brings forth its sprouts,	Is 61:11	776
makes Jerusalem a praise in the **e**.	Is 62:7	776
proclaimed to the end of the **e**,	Is 62:11	776
out their lifeblood on the **e**."	Is 63:6	776
he who is blessed in the **e** will be	Is 65:16	776
And he who swears in the **e** will	Is 65:16	776
I create new heavens and a new **e**;	Is 65:17	776
throne and the **e** is My footstool.	Is 66:1	776
the new **e** Which I make will endure	Is 66:22	776
I looked on the **e**, and behold, *it*	Jer 4:23	776
"For this the **e** shall mourn And	Jer 4:28	776
"Hear, O **e**: behold, I am bringing	Jer 6:19	776
from the remote parts of the **e**.	Jer 6:22	776
sky and for the beasts of the **e**;	Jer 7:33	776
justice and righteousness on **e**;	Jer 9:24	776
At His wrath the **e** quakes,	Jer 10:10	776
the heavens and the **e** will perish	Jer 10:11	778
e and from under the heavens."	Jer 10:11	778
is He who made the **e** by His power,	Jer 10:12	776
to ascend from the end of the **e**;	Jer 10:13	776
of the **e** to devour and destroy.	Jer 15:3	776
of the **e** because of Manasseh,	Jer 15:4	776
sky and for the beasts of the **e**;	Jer 16:4	776
From the ends of the **e** and say,	Jer 16:19	776
away on **e** will be written down,	Jer 17:13	776
the sky and the beasts of the **e**.	Jer 19:7	776
not fill the heavens and the **e**?"	Jer 23:24	776
for all the kingdoms of the **e**,	Jer 24:9	776
and all the kingdoms of the **e**	Jer 25:26	776
all the inhabitants of the **e**,"	Jer 25:29	776
all the inhabitants of the **e**.	Jer 25:30	776
has come to the end of the **e**,	Jer 25:31	776
From the remotest parts of the **e**.	Jer 25:32	776
one end of the **e** to the other.	Jer 25:33	776
all the nations of the **e**.	Jer 26:6	776
"I have made the **e**, the men and	Jer 27:5	776
beasts which are on the face of the **e**	Jer 27:5	776
remove you from the face of the **e**.	Jer 28:16	127
to all the kingdoms of the **e**,	Jer 29:18	776
from the remote parts of the **e**,	Jer 31:8	776
LORD has created a new thing in the **e**	Jer 31:22	776
the foundations of the **e** searched out	Jer 31:37	776
You have made the heavens and the **e**	Jer 32:17	776
says the LORD who made *the* **e**,	Jer 33:2	
before all the nations of the **e** which	Jer 33:9	776
and righteousness on the **e**.	Jer 33:15	776
and **e** I have not established,	Jer 33:25	776
with all the kingdoms of the **e**	Jer 34:1	776
to all the kingdoms of the **e**.	Jer 34:17	776
the sky and the beasts of the **e**.	Jer 34:20	776
among all the nations of the **e**?	Jer 44:8	776
And the **e** is full of your cry *of*	Jer 46:12	776
The **e** has quaked at the noise of	Jer 49:21	776
e Has been cut off and broken!	Jer 50:23	776
that He may bring rest to the **e**,	Jer 50:34	776
from the remote parts of the **e**.	Jer 50:41	776
the **e** is shaken, and an outcry is	Jer 50:46	776
the LORD, Intoxicating all the **e**.	Jer 51:7	776
is He who made the **e** by His power,	Jer 51:15	776
to ascend from the end of the **e**;	Jer 51:16	776
Who destroys the whole **e**,"	Jer 51:25	776
praise of the whole **e** been seized!	Jer 51:41	776
"Then heaven and **e** and all that	Jer 51:48	776
slain of all the **e** have fallen.	Jer 51:49	776
heaven to **e** The glory of Israel,	La 2:1	776
My heart is poured out on the **e** Because	La 2:11	776
of beauty, A joy to all the **e**'?"	La 2:15	776
kings of the **e** did not believe,	La 4:12	776
on the **e** beside the living beings,	Ezk 1:15	776
the living beings rose from the **e**,	Ezk 1:19	776
whenever those rose from the **e**,	Ezk 1:21	776
to the wicked of the **e** as spoil,	Ezk 7:21	776
the Spirit lifted me up between **e** and	Ezk 8:3	776
and rose up from the **e** in my sight	Ezk 10:19	776
dwell in the lower parts of the **e**,	Ezk 26:20	776
You enriched the kings of **e**.	Ezk 27:33	776
I have turned you to ashes on the **e**	Ezk 28:18	776
the **e** and to the birds of the sky.	Ezk 29:5	776

And all the peoples of the **e** have	Ezk 31:12	776
over to death, to the **e** beneath,	Ezk 31:14	776
were comforted in the **e** beneath.	Ezk 31:16	776
trees of Eden to the **e** beneath;	Ezk 31:18	776
beasts of the whole **e** with you.	Ezk 32:4	776
to the lower parts of the **e**,	Ezk 32:24	776
over all the surface of the **e**,	Ezk 34:6	776
and the **e** will yield its increase,	Ezk 34:27	776
of the **e** will not devour them;	Ezk 34:28	776
"As all the **e** rejoices, I will	Ezk 35:14	776
things that creep on the **e**,	Ezk 38:20	127
the **e** will shake at My presence;	Ezk 38:20	127
the blood of the princes of the **e**,	Ezk 39:18	776
and the **e** shone with His glory.	Ezk 43:2	776
"There is not a man on **e** who	Da 2:10	3007
mountain and filled the whole **e**.	Da 2:35	772
which will rule over all the **e**.	Da 2:39	772
language that live in all the **e**:	Da 4:1	772
was a tree in the midst of the **e**	Da 4:10	772
visible to the end of the whole **e**.	Da 4:11	772
the beasts in the grass of the **e**.	Da 4:15	772
sky and was visible to all the **e**	Da 4:20	772
your dominion to the end of the **e**.	Da 4:22	772
of the **e** are accounted as nothing,	Da 4:35	772
And *among* the inhabitants of **e**;	Da 4:35	772
and wonders In heaven and on **e**,	Da 6:27	772
kings *who* will arise from the **e**.	Da 7:17	772
will be a fourth kingdom on the **e**,	Da 7:23	772
and will devour the whole **e** and	Da 7:23	772
e without touching the ground;	Da 8:5	776
of the stars to fall to the **e**,	Da 8:10	776
and they will respond to the **e**,	Hos 2:21	776
the **e** will respond to the grain,	Hos 2:22	776
the spring rain watering the **e**."	Hos 6:3	776
Before them the **e** quakes, The	Jl 2:10	776
wonders in the sky and on the **e**,	Jl 2:30	776
And the heavens and the **e** tremble.	Jl 3:16	776
who pant after the *very* dust of the **e**	Am 2:7	776
among all the families of the **e**;	Am 3:2	127
Does a trap spring up from the **e**	Am 3:5	127
on the high places of the **e**,	Am 4:13	776
righteousness down to the **e**."	Am 5:7	776
them out on the surface of the **e**,	Am 5:8	776
make the **e** dark in broad daylight.	Am 8:9	776
His vaulted dome over the **e**,	Am 9:6	776
them out on the face of the **e**,	Am 9:6	776
destroy it from the face of the **e**;	Am 9:8	127
'Who will bring me down to **e**?'	Ob 1:3	776
The **e** with its bars *was* around me	Jon 2:6	776
Listen, O **e** and all it contains,	Mi 1:2	776
tread on the high places of the **e**.	Mi 1:3	776
wealth to the Lord of all the **e**.	Mi 4:13	776
be great To the ends of the **e**.	Mi 5:4	776
you enduring foundations of the **e**,	Mi 6:2	776
And the **e** will become desolate	Mi 7:13	776
a serpent, Like reptiles of the **e**.	Mi 7:17	776
the **e** is upheaved by His presence,	Na 1:5	776
Who march throughout the **e** To seize	Hab 1:6	776
"For the **e** will be filled With	Hab 2:14	776
all the **e** be silent before Him."	Hab 2:20	776
And the **e** is full of His praise.	Hab 3:3	776
He stood and surveyed the **e**;	Hab 3:6	776
cleaved the **e** with rivers.	Hab 3:9	776
You marched through the **e**;	Hab 3:12	776
things From the face of the **e**,"	Zph 1:2	127
off man from the face of the **e**,"	Zph 1:3	127
And all the **e** will be devoured In	Zph 1:18	776
Of all the inhabitants of the **e**.	Zph 1:18	776
All you humble of the **e** Who have	Zph 2:3	776
will starve all the gods of the **e**;	Zph 2:11	776
For all the **e** will be devoured By	Zph 3:8	776
praise and renown In all the **e**;	Zph 3:19	776
Among all the peoples of the **e**,	Zph 3:20	776
the **e** has withheld its produce.	Hg 1:10	776
to shake the heavens and the **e**,	Hg 2:6	776
to shake the heavens and the **e**.	Hg 2:21	776
LORD has sent to patrol the **e**."	Zch 1:10	776
"We have patrolled the **e**,	Zch 1:11	776
all the **e** is peaceful and quiet."	Zch 1:11	776
to and fro throughout the **e**."	Zch 4:10	776
by the Lord of the whole **e**."	Zch 4:14	776
between the **e** and the heavens.	Zch 5:9	776
before the Lord of all the **e**,	Zch 6:5	776
eager to go to patrol the **e**."	Zch 6:7	776
"Go, patrol the **e**."	Zch 6:7	776
So they patrolled the **e**.	Zch 6:7	776
the River to the ends of the **e**.	Zch 9:10	776
lays the foundation of the **e**,	Zch 12:1	776
the **e** will be gathered against it.	Zch 12:3	776
LORD will be king over all the **e**;	Zch 14:9	776
of the families of the **e** does not go up	Zch 14:17	776
for they shall inherit the **e**.	Mt 5:5	1093
"You are the salt of the **e**;	Mt 5:13	1093
you, until heaven and **e** pass away,	Mt 5:18	1093
or by the **e**, for it is the footstool of	Mt 5:35	1093
be done, On **e** as it is in heaven.	Mt 6:10	1093
for yourselves treasures on **e**,	Mt 6:19	1093
has authority on **e** to forgive sins"	Mt 9:6	1093
I came to bring peace on the **e**;	Mt 10:34	1093
Father, Lord of heaven and **e**,	Mt 11:25	1093
nights in the heart of the **e**.	Mt 12:40	1093
e to hear the wisdom of Solomon;	Mt 12:42	1093
on **e** shall have been bound in heaven,	Mt 16:19	1093
on **e** shall have been loosed in heaven."	Mt 16:19	1093
the **e** collect customs or poll-tax,	Mt 17:25	1093
on **e** shall have been bound in heaven;	Mt 18:18	1093
on **e** shall have been loosed in heaven.	Mt 18:18	1093
that if two of you agree on **e**	Mt 18:19	1093
not call *anyone* on **e** your father;	Mt 23:9	1093

all the righteous blood shed on **e**,	Mt 23:35	1093
the tribes of the **e** will mourn,	Mt 24:30	1093
"Heaven and **e** will pass away, but	Mt 24:35	1093
top to bottom; and the **e** shook	Mt 27:51	1093
given to Me in heaven and on **e**.	Mt 28:18	1093
has authority on **e** to forgive sins"	Mk 2:10	1093
no launderer on **e** can whiten them.	Mk 9:3	1093
from the farthest end of the **e** to	Mk 13:27	1093
"Heaven and **e** will pass away, but	Mk 13:31	1093
be taken of all the inhabited **e**.	Lk 2:1	3625
And on **e** peace among men with whom	Lk 2:14	
has authority on **e** to forgive sins,"	Lk 5:24	1093
O Father, Lord of heaven and **e**,	Lk 10:21	1093
e to hear the wisdom of Solomon;	Lk 11:31	1093
have come to cast fire upon the **e**;	Lk 12:49	1093
that I came to grant peace on **e**?	Lk 12:51	1093
appearance of the **e** and the sky,	Lk 12:56	1093
easier for heaven and **e** to pass away	Lk 16:17	1093
will He find faith on the **e**?"	Lk 18:8	1093
on the **e** dismay among nations,	Lk 21:25	1093
"Heaven and **e** will pass away, but	Lk 21:33	1093
dwell on the face of all the **e**.	Lk 21:35	1093
he who is of the **e** is from the earth	Jn 3:31	1093
the **e** and speaks of the earth.	Jn 3:31	1093
the earth and speaks of the **e**.	Jn 3:31	1093
wheat falls into the **e** and dies,	Jn 12:24	1093
I, if I am lifted up from the **e**,	Jn 12:32	1093
"I glorified You on the **e**,	Jn 17:4	1093
"to the remotest part of the **e**."	Ac 1:8	1093
ABOVE AND SIGNS ON THE **E** BELOW,	Ac 2:19	1093
OF THE **E** SHALL BE BLESSED.'	Ac 3:25	1093
THE HEAVEN AND THE **E** AND THE SEA,	Ac 4:24	1093
KINGS OF THE **E** TOOK THEIR STAND,	Ac 4:26	1093
AND **E** IS THE FOOTSTOOL OF MY FEET	Ac 7:49	1093
HIS LIFE IS REMOVED FROM THE **E**."	Ac 8:33	1093
of the **e** and birds of the air.	Ac 10:12	1093
saw the four-footed animals of the **e**	Ac 11:6	1093
SALVATION TO THE END OF THE **E**.'"	Ac 13:47	1093
THE HEAVEN AND THE **E** AND THE SEA	Ac 14:15	1093
since He is Lord of heaven and **e**,	Ac 17:24	1093
to live on all the face of the **e**,	Ac 17:26	1093
with such a fellow from the **e**,	Ac 22:22	1093
THROUGHOUT THE WHOLE **E**."	Ro 9:17	1093
EXECUTE HIS WORD ON THE **E**,	Ro 9:28	1093
VOICE HAS GONE OUT INTO ALL THE **E**	Ro 10:18	1093
gods whether in heaven or on **e**,	1Co 8:5	1093
FOR THE **E** IS THE LORD'S, AND ALL	1Co 10:26	1093
The first man is from the **e**, earthy;	1Co 15:47	1093
the heavens and things on the **e**.	Eph 1:10	1093
heaven and on **e** derives its name,	Eph 3:15	1093
into the lower parts of the **e**?	Eph 4:9	1093
THAT YOU MAY LIVE LONG ON THE **E**.	Eph 6:3	1093
those who are in heaven and on **e**	Php 2:10	1919
and on earth and under the **e**,	Php 2:10	2709
both in the heavens and on **e**,	Col 1:16	1093
things on **e** or things in heaven.	Col 1:20	1093
not on the things that are on **e**.	Col 3:2	1093
those who are your masters on **e**,	Col 3:22	4561
LAID THE FOUNDATION OF THE **E**,	Heb 1:10	1093
Now if He were on **e**,	Heb 8:4	1093
strangers and exiles on the **e**.	Heb 11:13	1093
refused him who warned *them* on **e**,	Heb 12:25	1093
And His voice shook the **e** then,	Heb 12:26	1093
MORE I WILL SHAKE NOT ONLY THE **E**,	Heb 12:26	1093
You have lived luxuriously on the **e**	Jas 5:5	1093
either by heaven or by **e** or with any	Jas 5:12	1093
and it did not rain on the **e** for	Jas 5:17	1093
and the **e** produced its fruit.	Jas 5:18	1093
during the time of your stay *on* **e**;	1Pe 1:17	
and *the* **e** was formed out of water	2Pe 3:5	1093
His word the present heavens and **e**	2Pe 3:7	1093
and the **e** and its works will be	2Pe 3:10	1093
for new heavens and a new **e**,	2Pe 3:13	1093
the ruler of the kings of the **e**.	Rv 1:5	1093
of the **e** will mourn over Him.	Rv 1:7	1093
test those who dwell on the **e**.	Rv 3:10	1093
And no one in heaven or on the **e**	Rv 5:3	1093
or on the earth or under the **e**	Rv 5:3	1093
of God, sent out into all the **e**.	Rv 5:6	1093
and they will reign upon the **e**."	Rv 5:10	1093
and on the **e** and under the earth	Rv 5:13	1093
and under the **e** and on the sea,	Rv 5:13	1093
granted to take peace from the **e**,	Rv 6:4	1093
to them over a fourth of the **e**,	Rv 6:8	1093
and by the wild beasts of the **e**.	Rv 6:8	1093
on those who dwell on the **e**?"	Rv 6:10	1093
stars of the sky fell to the **e**,	Rv 6:13	1093
Then the kings of the **e** and the	Rv 6:15	1093
at the four corners of the **e**,	Rv 7:1	1093
back the four winds of the **e**,	Rv 7:1	1093
no wind would blow on the **e** or on	Rv 7:1	1093
granted to harm the **e** and the sea,	Rv 7:2	1093
Do not harm the **e** or the sea or the	Rv 7:3	1093
the altar, and threw it to the **e**;	Rv 8:5	1093
and they were thrown to the **e**;	Rv 8:7	1093
a third of the **e** was burned up,	Rv 8:7	1093
woe to those who dwell on the **e**,	Rv 8:13	1093
heaven which had fallen to the **e**;	Rv 9:1	1093
came locusts upon the **e**	Rv 9:3	1093
the scorpions of the **e** have power.	Rv 9:3	1093
not to hurt the grass of the **e**,	Rv 9:4	1093
AND THE **E** AND THE THINGS IN IT,	Rv 10:6	1093
stand before the Lord of the **e**.	Rv 11:4	1093
to strike the **e** with every plague,	Rv 11:6	1093
And those who dwell on the **e** *will*	Rv 11:10	1093
those who dwell on the **e**.	Rv 11:10	1093
destroy those who destroy the **e**."	Rv 11:18	1093
heaven and threw them to the **e**.	Rv 12:4	1093
he was thrown down to the **e**,	Rv 12:9	1093

Woe to the e and the sea, because Rv 12:12 1093
that he was thrown down to the e, Rv 12:13 1093
But the e helped the woman, and Rv 12:16 1093
and the e opened its mouth and Rv 12:16 1093
And the whole e was amazed and Rv 13:3 1093
dwell on the e will worship him, Rv 13:8 1093
beast coming up out of the e; Rv 13:11 1093
And he makes the e and those who Rv 13:12 1093
come down out of heaven to the e Rv 13:13 1093
he deceives those who dwell on the e Rv 13:14 1093
telling those who dwell on the e Rv 13:14 1093
who had been purchased from the e. Rv 14:3 1093
preach to those who live on the e, Rv 14:6 1093
e and sea and springs of waters." Rv 14:7 1093
the harvest of the e is ripe." Rv 14:15 1093
cloud swung His sickle over the e, Rv 14:16 1093
and the e was reaped. Rv 14:16 1093
clusters from the vine of the e, Rv 14:18 1093
angel swung his sickle to the e and Rv 14:19 1093
clusters from the vine of the e, Rv 14:19 1093
on the e the seven bowls of the wrath Rv 16:1 1093
poured out his bowl on the e; Rv 16:2 1093
since man came to be upon the e, Rv 16:18 1093
the kings of the e committed acts of Rv 17:2 1093
and those who dwell on the e were Rv 17:2 1093
THE ABOMINATIONS OF THE E." Rv 17:5 1093
those who dwell on the e, Rv 17:8 1093
reigns over the kings of the e." Rv 17:18 1093
e was illumined with his glory. Rv 18:1 1093
kings of the e have committed acts Rv 18:3 1093
and the merchants of the e have Rv 18:3 1093
"And the kings of the e, Rv 18:9 1093
the merchants of the e weep and Rv 18:11 1093
were the great men of the e, Rv 18:23 1093
who have been slain on the e." Rv 18:24 1093
the e with her immorality, Rv 19:2 1093
kings of the e and their armies Rv 19:19 1093
are in the four corners of the e, Rv 20:8 1093
came up on the broad plain of the e Rv 20:9 1093
presence e and heaven fled away, Rv 20:11 1093
I saw a new heaven and a new e; Rv 21:1 1093
and the first e passed away, Rv 21:1 1093
and the kings of the e will bring Rv 21:24 1093

EARTHEN

Like an e vessel overlaid with Pr 26:23 2789
How they are regarded as e jars, La 4:2 2789
have this treasure in e vessels, 2Co 4:7 3749

EARTHENWARE

the e vessel in which it was boiled Lv 6:28 2789
'As for any e vessel into which Lv 11:33 2789
in an e vessel over running water. Lv 14:5 2789
in an e vessel over running water. Lv 14:50 2789
an e vessel which the person with Lv 15:12 2789
take holy water in an e vessel; Nu 5:17 2789
shall shatter them like e.' " Ps 2:9 3627, 3335
An e vessel among the vessels of earth Is 45:9 2789
"Go and buy a potter's e jar, Jer 19:1 2789
deed, and put them in an e jar, Jer 32:14 2789
but also vessels of wood and of e, 2Tm 2:20 3749

EARTHLY

e things and you do not believe, Jn 3:12 1919
also heavenly bodies and e bodies, 1Co 15:40 1919
and the glory of the e is another. 1Co 15:40 1919
For we know that if the e tent 2Co 5:1 1919
who set their minds on e things. Php 3:19 1919
your e body as dead to immorality, Col 3:5 1093
worship and the e sanctuary. Heb 9:1 2886
we had e fathers to discipline us, Heb 12:9 4561
comes down from above, but is e, Jas 3:15 1919
as long as I am in this e 2Pe 1:13
that the laying aside of my e 2Pe 1:14

EARTHQUAKE

And after the wind an e, 1Ki 19:11 7494
but the LORD was not in the e. 1Ki 19:11 7494
After the e a fire, but the 1Ki 19:12 7494
with thunder and e and loud noise, Is 29:6 7494
a great e in the land of Israel. Ezk 38:19 7494
of Israel, two years before the e. Am 1:1 7494
fled before the e in the days of Uzziah Zch 14:5 7494
when they saw the e and the things Mt 27:54 4578
behold, a severe e had occurred, Mt 28:2 4578
and suddenly there came a great e, Ac 16:26 4578
seal, and there was a great e; Rv 6:12 4578
and flashes of lightning and an e. Rv 8:5 4578
in that hour there was a great e, Rv 11:13 4578
people were killed in the e, Rv 11:13 4578
and an e and a great hailstorm. Rv 11:19 4578
and there was a great e, Rv 16:18 4578
the earth, so great an e was it, Rv 16:18 4578

EARTHQUAKES

there will be famines and e. Mt 24:7 4578
there will be e in various places; Mk 13:8 4578
and there will be great e, Lk 21:11 4578

EARTH'S

the chiefs of the e people And Jb 12:24 776

EARTHY

first man is from the earth, e; 1Co 15:47 5517
As is the e, so also are those who 1Co 15:48 5517
so also are those who are e; 1Co 15:48 5517
we have borne the image of the e, 1Co 15:49 5517

EASE

"Be at e, do not be afraid. Gn 43:23 7965
He will e His hand from you, 1Sa 6:5 7043
'The prisoners are at e together; Jb 3:18 7599
'I am not at e, nor am I quiet, Jb 3:26 7951
me, My couch will e my complaint,' Jb 7:13 5375
at e holds calamity in contempt, Jb 12:5 7600
"I was at e, but He shattered me, Jb 16:12 7961
Being wholly at e and satisfied; Jb 21:23 7600
And always at e, they have Ps 73:12 7961
scoffing of those who are at e, Ps 123:4 7600
be at e from the dread of evil." Pr 1:33 7599
Rise up, you women who are at e, Is 32:9 7600
Tremble, you women who are at e; Is 32:11 7600
those who deal in treachery at e? Jer 12:1 7951
and will be quiet and at e, Jer 30:10 7599
has been at e since his youth; Jer 48:11 7599
up against a nation which is at e, Jer 49:31 7961
abundant food and careless e, Ezk 16:49 7962
was at e in my house and Da 4:4 7954
destroy many while they are at e. Da 8:25 7962
Woe to those who are at e in Zion And Am 6:1 7600
with the nations who are at e; Zch 1:15 7600
take your e, eat, drink and be Lk 12:19 373
this is not for the e of others and 2Co 8:13 425

EASIER

So it will be e for you, and they Ex 18:22 7043
"Which is e, to say, Mt 9:5 2123
it is e for a camel to go through Mt 19:24 2123
"Which is e, to say to the paralytic, Mk 2:9 2123
"It is e for a camel to go Mk 10:25 2123
"Which is e, to say, Lk 5:23 2123
"But it is e for heaven and earth Lk 16:17 2123
"For it is e for a camel to go Lk 18:25 2123

EASILY

might e have lain with your wife, Gn 26:10 4592
the sin which so e entangles us, Heb 12:1 2139

EAST

God planted a garden toward the e, Gn 2:8 6924a
it flows e of Assyria. Gn 2:14 6926
and at the e of the garden of Eden Gn 3:24 6924a
in the land of Nod, e of Eden. Gn 4:16 6926
Sephar, the hill country of the e. Gn 10:30 6924a
It came about as they journeyed e, Gn 11:2 6924a
the mountain on the e of Bethel, Gn 12:8 6924a
on the west and Ai on the e; Gn 12:8 6924a
will live to the e of all his brothers." Gn 16:12 6440
eastward, to the land of the e. Gn 25:6 6924a
Havilah to Shur which is e of Egypt Gn 25:18 5921, 6440
spread out to the west and to the e Gn 28:14 6924b
to the land of the sons of the e. Gn 29:1 6924a
thin and scorched by the e wind, Gn 41:6 6921
thin, and scorched by the e wind, Gn 41:23 6921
seven thin ears scorched by the e wind Gn 41:27 6921
and the LORD directed an e wind on Ex 10:13 6921
the e wind brought the locusts. Ex 10:13 6921
back by a strong e wind all night and Ex 14:21 6921
the e side shall be fifty cubits. Ex 27:13 4217, 6924b
For the e side fifty cubits. Ex 38:13 4217, 6924b
on the mercy seat on the e side; Lv 16:14 6924b
"Now those who camp on the e side Nu 2:3 6924b
on the e side shall set out. Nu 10:5 6924b
which is opposite Moab, to the e. Nu 21:11 4217, 8121
king from the mountains of the E, Nu 23:7 6924a
side of the Jordan toward the e." Nu 32:19 4217
to Riblah on the e side of Ain; Nu 34:11 6924a
e side of the Sea of Chinnereth. Nu 34:11 6924a
on the e side two thousand cubits, Nu 35:5 6924b
of the slopes of Pisgah on the e. Dt 3:17 4217
west and north and south and e, Dt 3:27 4217
cities across the Jordan to the e, Dt 4:41 4217, 8121
were across the Jordan to the e, Dt 4:47 4217, 8121
Arabah across the Jordan to the e, Dt 4:49 4217
is near Beth-aven, e of Bethel, Jos 7:2 6924a
on the e and on the west, Jos 11:3 4217
and the valley of Mizpeh to the e; Jos 11:8 4217
and all the Arabah to the e: Jos 12:1 4217
Sea of Chinneroth toward the e, Jos 12:3 4217
the Shihor which is e of Egypt, Jos 13:3 5921, 6440
and all of Lebanon, toward the e, Jos 13:5 4217, 8121
them beyond the Jordan to the e, Jos 13:8 4217
beyond the Jordan to the e. Jos 13:27 4217
the Jordan at Jericho to the e. Jos 13:32 4217
The e border was the Salt Sea, Jos 15:5 6924b
on the e into the wilderness, Jos 16:1 4217
beyond it to the e of Janoah. Jos 16:6 4217
which was e of Shechem; Jos 17:7 5921, 6440
north and to Issachar on the e. Jos 17:10 4217
was its border on the e side. Jos 18:20 6924b
from Sarid to the e toward the sunrise Jos 19:12 6924b
turned toward the e to Beth-dagon and Jos 19:27 4217, 8121
Judah at the Jordan toward the e. Jos 19:34 4217, 8121
Beyond the Jordan e of Jericho, Jos 20:8 4217
sons of the e and go against them. Jg 6:3 6924a
the sons of the e assembled Jg 6:33 6924a
sons of the e were lying in the valley Jg 7:12 6924a
entire army of the sons of the e; Jg 8:10 6924a
on the e of Nobah and Jogbehah, Jg 8:11 6924a
to the e side of the land of Moab, Jg 11:18 4217, 8121
down opposite Gibeah toward the e. Jg 20:43 4217, 8121
on the e side of the highway that Jg 21:19 4217, 8121
camped in Michmash, e of Beth-aven. 1Sa 13:5 6926
go to Shur, which is e of Egypt. 1Sa 15:7 5921, 6440
the wisdom of all the sons of the e 1Ki 4:30 6924a
facing south, and three facing e; 1Ki 7:25 4217
mountain which is e of Jerusalem, 1Ki 11:7 5921, 6440
Cherith, which is e of the Jordan. 1Ki 17:3 5921, 6440
Cherith, which is e of the Jordan. 1Ki 17:5 5921, 6440
"Open the window toward the e," 2Ki 13:17 6924b
even to the e side of the valley, 1Ch 4:39 4217
To the e he settled as far as 1Ch 5:9 4217
all the land e of Gilead. 1Ch 5:10 4217
on the e side of the Jordan, 1Ch 6:78 4217
its towns, and to the e Naaran, 1Ch 7:28 4217
now at the king's gate to the e). 1Ch 9:18 4217
were on the four sides, to the e, 1Ch 9:24 4217
both to the e and to the west. 1Ch 12:15 4217
lot to the e fell to Shelemiah. 1Ch 26:14 4217
On the e there were six Levites, 1Ch 26:17 4217
facing south and three facing e; 2Ch 4:4 4217
lyres, standing e of the altar, 2Ch 5:12 4217
them into the square on the e. 2Ch 29:4 4217
of the Water Gate toward the e Ne 3:26 4217
the keeper of the E Gate, Ne 3:29 4217
David to the Water Gate on the e. Ne 12:37 4217
greatest of all the men of the e. Jb 1:3 6924a
And fill himself with the e wind? Jb 15:2 6921
in the e are seized with horror. Jb 18:20 6931
"The e wind carries him away, and Jb 27:21 6921
the e wind scattered on the earth? Jb 38:24 6921
With the e wind You break Ps 48:7 6921
not from the e, nor from the west, Ps 75:6 4161
the e wind to blow in the heavens And Ps 78:26 6921
As far as the e is from the west, Ps 103:12 4217
From the e and from the west, Ps 107:3 4217
filled with influences from the e, Is 2:6 6924a
The Arameans on the e and the Is 9:12 6924a
will plunder the sons of the e; Is 11:14 6924a
glorify the LORD in the e, Is 24:15 747a
them on the day of the e wind. Is 27:8 6921
"Who has aroused one from the e Is 41:2 4217
bring your offspring from the e, Is 43:5 4217
Calling a bird of prey from the e, Is 46:11 4217
'Like an e wind I will scatter Jer 18:17 6921
of the Horse Gate toward the e, Jer 31:40 4217
And devastate the men of the e. Jer 49:28 6924a
LORD and their faces toward the e; Ezk 8:16 6924b
of the e gate of the LORD'S house, Ezk 10:19 6931
and brought me to the e gate of the Ezk 11:1 6931
mountain which is e of the city. Ezk 11:23 6924a
wither as soon as the e wind strikes it Ezk 17:10 6921
And the e wind dried up its fruit. Ezk 19:12 6921
sons of the e for a possession, Ezk 25:4 6924a
of Ammon to the sons of the e, Ezk 25:10 6924a
The e wind has broken you In the Ezk 27:26 6921
of those who pass by e of the sea, Ezk 39:11 6926
he went to the gate which faced e, Ezk 40:6 6921
the e numbered three on each side; Ezk 40:10 6921
cubits on the e and on the north. Ezk 40:19 6921
the gate which faced toward the e; Ezk 40:22 6921
as well as the gate on the e; Ezk 40:23 6921
into the inner court toward the e. Ezk 40:32 6921
e side totaled a hundred cubits. Ezk 41:14 6921
was the entrance on the e side, Ezk 42:9 6921
wall of the court toward the e, Ezk 42:10 6921
in front of the wall toward the e, Ezk 42:12 6921
the gate which faced toward the e and Ezk 42:15 6921
He measured on the e side with the Ezk 42:16 6921
the gate facing toward the e; Ezk 43:1 6921
was coming from the way of the e. Ezk 43:2 6921
of the gate facing toward the e. Ezk 43:4 6921
and its steps shall face the e." Ezk 43:17 6921
the sanctuary, which faces the e; Ezk 44:1 6921
and on the e side toward the east, Ezk 45:7 6924b
and on the east side toward the e, Ezk 45:7 6921
the west border to the e border. Ezk 45:7 6921
gate of the inner court facing e shall Ezk 46:1 6921
the gate facing e shall be opened Ezk 46:12 6921
of the house toward the e, Ezk 47:1 6921
the east, for the house faced e. Ezk 47:1 6921
by way of the gate that faces e. Ezk 47:2 6921
the e with a line in his hand, Ezk 47:3 6921
"The e side, from between Ezk 47:18 6921
This is the e side. Ezk 47:18 6921
Hamath, running from e to west, Ezk 48:1 6921
from the e side to the west side, Ezk 48:2 6921
from the e side to the west side, Ezk 48:3 6921
from the e side to the west side, Ezk 48:4 6921
from the e side to the west side, Ezk 48:5 6921
from the e side to the west side, Ezk 48:6 6921
from the e side to the west side, Ezk 48:7 6921
from the e side to the west side, Ezk 48:8 6921
from the e side to the west side; Ezk 48:8 6921
toward the e 10,000 in width, Ezk 48:10 6921
cubits, the e side 4,500 cubits, Ezk 48:16 6921
250 cubits, on the e 250 cubits, Ezk 48:17 6921
be 10,000 cubits toward the e and Ezk 48:18 6921
of the allotment toward the e border Ezk 48:21 6921
from the e side to the west side, Ezk 48:23 6921
from the e side to the west side, Ezk 48:24 6921
from the e side to the west side, Ezk 48:25 6921
from the e side to the west side, Ezk 48:26 6921
from the e side to the west side, Ezk 48:27 6921
"On the e side, 4,500 cubits, Ezk 48:32 6921

toward the south, toward the **e**, Da 8:9 4217
"But rumors from the **E** and from Da 11:44 4217
pursues the **e** wind continually; Hos 12:1 6921
the reeds, An **e** wind will come, Hos 13:15 6921
And from the north even to the **e**; Am 8:12 4217
out from the city and sat **e** of it. Jon 4:5 6924a
God appointed a scorching **e** wind, Jon 4:8 6921
e and from the land of the west; Zch 8:7 4217
is in front of Jerusalem on the **e**; Zch 14:4 6924a
be split in its middle from **e** to west Zch 14:4 4217
magi from the **e** arrived in Jerusalem Mt 2:1 *395*
For we saw His star in the **e** and Mt 2:2 *395*
star, which they had seen in the **e**, Mt 2:9 *395*
many will come from **e** and west, Mt 8:11 *395*
as the lightning comes from the **e** and Mt 24:27 *395*
Himself sent out through them from **e** Mk 16:20
they will come from **e** and west and Lk 13:29 *395*
prepared for the kings from the **e**. Rv 16:12 *395, 2246*
There were three gates on the **e** Rv 21:13 *395*

EASTERN
'For your **e** border you shall also Nu 34:10 6924b
Gilgal on the **e** edge of Jericho. Jos 4:19 4217
Levite, the keeper of the **e** *gate,* 2Ch 31:14 4217
"These waters go out toward the **e** Ezk 47:8 6930
to the **e** sea you shall measure. Ezk 47:18 6931
And its vanguard into the **e** sea, Jl 2:20 6931
half of them toward the **e** sea and Zch 14:8 6931

EASTWARD
and Lot journeyed **e**. Gn 13:11 6924a
and southward and **e** and westward; Gn 13:14 6924b
them away from his son Isaac **e**, Gn 25:6 6924b
and cast it beside the altar **e**, Lv 1:16 6924b
to camp before the tabernacle **e**, Nu 3:38 6924b
from the end of the Salt Sea **e**. Nu 34:3 6924b
Jericho, **e** toward the sunrising." Nu 34:15 6924b
Salt Sea, **e** toward Beth-jeshimoth, Jos 12:3 4217
inheritance **e** was Ataroth-addar, Jos 16:5 4217
turned about **e** to Taanath-shiloh and Jos 16:6 4217
inheritance **e** beyond the Jordan, Jos 18:7 4217
From there it continued **e** Jos 19:13 6924b
of the house **e** toward the south. 1Ki 7:39 6924b
"Go away from here and turn **e**, 1Ki 17:3 6924b
from the Jordan **e**, all the land of 2Ki 10:33 4217
themselves **e** toward the sun. Ezk 8:16 6924b
of the LORD's house which faced **e**. Ezk 11:1 6931

EASY
and regarded it as **e** to go up into Dt 1:41 1951
"It is **e** for the shadow to 2Ki 20:10 7043
is **e** to one who has understanding. Pr 14:6 7043
"For My yoke is **e** and My burden is Mt 11:30 *5543*

EAT
of the garden you may **e** freely; Gn 2:16 398
of good and evil you shall not **e**, Gn 2:17 398
e from it you will surely die." Gn 2:17 398
'You shall not **e** from any tree Gn 3:1 398
the trees of the garden we may **e**; Gn 3:2 398
shall not **e** from it or touch it, Gn 3:3 398
day you **e** from it your eyes will be Gn 3:5 398
which I commanded you not to **e**?" Gn 3:11 398
dust you will **e** All the days of your Gn 3:14 398
'You shall not **e** from it'; Gn 3:17 398
In toil you will **e** of it All the Gn 3:17 398
will **e** the plants of the field; Gn 3:18 398
of your face You will **e** bread, Gn 3:19 398
also from the tree of life, and **e**, Gn 3:22 398
shall not **e** flesh with its life, Gn 9:4 398
when *food* was set before him to **e**, Gn 24:33 398
I will not **e** until I have told my Gn 24:33 398
and bring it to me that I may **e**, Gn 27:4 398
savory dish for me, that I may **e**, Gn 27:7 398
it to your father, that he may **e**, Gn 27:10 398
up, please, sit and **e** of my game, Gn 27:19 398
me, and I will **e** of my son's game, Gn 27:25 398
arise and **e** of his son's game, Gn 27:31 398
me food to **e** and garments to wear, Gn 28:20 398
Israel do not **e** the sinew of the hip Gn 32:32 398
Then they sat down to **e** a meal. Gn 37:25 398
birds will **e** your flesh off you." Gn 40:19 398
that they were to **e** a meal there. Gn 43:25 398
not **e** bread with the Hebrews, Gn 43:32 398
you will **e** the fat of the land.' Gn 45:18 398
Invite him to have something to **e**." Ex 2:20 398
They will also **e** the rest of what Ex 10:5 398
they will **e** every tree which sprouts Ex 10:5 398
and **e** every plant of the land, Ex 10:12 398
to what each man should **e**, Ex 12:4 398
of the houses in which they **e** it. Ex 12:7 398
shall **e** the flesh that *same* night, Ex 12:8 398
they shall **e** it with unleavened bread Ex 12:8 398
'Do not **e** any of it raw or boiled Ex 12:9 398
'Now you shall **e** it in this manner: Ex 12:11 398
and you shall **e** it in haste Ex 12:11 398
days you shall **e** unleavened bread, Ex 12:15 398
you shall **e** unleavened bread, Ex 12:18 398
'You shall not **e** anything leavened; Ex 12:20 398
you shall **e** unleavened bread.' " Ex 12:20 398
no foreigner is to **e** of it; Ex 12:43 398
him, then he may **e** of it. Ex 12:44 398
a hired servant shall not **e** of it. Ex 12:45 398
no uncircumcised person may **e** of it. Ex 12:48 398
days you shall **e** unleavened bread, Ex 13:6 398
you meat to **e** in the evening, Ex 16:8 398
'At twilight you shall **e** meat, Ex 16:12 398
which the LORD has given you to **e**. Ex 16:15 402
every man as much as he should **e**; Ex 16:16 398
gathered as much as he should **e**. Ex 16:18 398
every man as much as he should **e**; Ex 16:21 398

"**E** it today, for today is a Ex 16:25 398
to **e** a meal with Moses' father-in-law Ex 18:12 398
you shall not **e** *any* flesh torn to Ex 22:31 398
the needy of your people may **e**; Ex 23:11 398
the beast of the field may **e**. Ex 23:11 398
you are to **e** unleavened bread, Ex 23:15 398
sons shall **e** the flesh of the ram and Ex 29:32 398
"Thus they shall **e** those things Ex 29:33 398
but a layman shall not **e** *them,* Ex 29:33 398
people sat down to **e** and to drink, Ex 32:6 398
invite you to **e** of his sacrifice, Ex 34:15 398
you are to **e** unleavened bread, Ex 34:18 398
he did not **e** bread or drink water. Ex 34:28 398
not **e** any fat or any blood.' " Lv 3:17 398
of it Aaron and his sons are to **e**. Lv 6:16 398
they are to **e** it in the court of Lv 6:16 398
among the sons of Aaron may **e** it; Lv 6:18 398
who offers it for sin shall **e** it. Lv 6:26 398
among the priests may **e** of it; Lv 6:29 398
among the priests may **e** of it. Lv 7:6 398
who is clean may **e** *such* flesh. Lv 7:19 398
shall not **e** any fat *from* an ox, Lv 7:23 398
but you must certainly not **e** it. Lv 7:24 398
'You are not to **e** any blood, Lv 7:26 398
and **e** it there together with the Lv 8:31 398
'Aaron and his sons shall **e** it.' Lv 8:31 398
and **e** it unleavened beside the altar, Lv 10:12 398
'You shall **e** it, moreover, in a Lv 10:13 398
you may **e** in a clean place, Lv 10:14 398
"Why did you not **e** the sin offering Lv 10:17 398
are the creatures which you may **e** Lv 11:2 398
among the animals, that you may **e**. Lv 11:3 398
you are not to **e** of these, Lv 11:4 398
'You shall not **e** of their flesh Lv 11:8 398
'These you may **e**, whatever is in Lv 11:9 398
seas or in the rivers, you may **e**. Lv 11:9 398
you may not **e** of their flesh, and Lv 11:11 398
'Yet these you may **e** among all the Lv 11:21 398
'These of them you may **e**: Lv 11:22 398
the earth, you shall not **e** them, Lv 11:42 398
'No person among you may **e** blood, Lv 17:12 398
who sojourns among you **e** blood.' Lv 17:12 398
not to **e** the blood of any flesh, Lv 17:14 398
year you are to **e** of its fruit, Lv 19:25 398
not **e** *anything* with the blood, Lv 19:26 398
'He may **e** the food of his God, Lv 21:22 398
may **e** of the holy *gifts* until he Lv 22:4 398
and shall not **e** of the holy *gifts* unless Lv 22:6 398
he shall **e** of the holy *gifts,* Lv 22:7 398
'He shall not **e** *an animal* which Lv 22:8 398
however, is to **e** the holy *gift;* Lv 22:10 398
man shall not **e** of the holy *gift.* Lv 22:10 398
his money, that one may **e** of it, Lv 22:11 398
in his house may **e** of his food. Lv 22:11 398
e of the offering of the *gifts.* Lv 22:12 398
she shall **e** of her father's food; Lv 22:13 398
but no layman shall **e** of it. Lv 22:13 398
days you shall **e** unleavened bread. Lv 23:6 398
you shall **e** neither bread nor Lv 23:14 398
they shall **e** it in a holy place; Lv 24:9 398
shall have all its crops to **e**. Lv 25:7 398
e its crops out of the field. Lv 25:12 398
so that you can **e** your fill and Lv 25:19 398
"What are we going to **e** on the Lv 25:20 398
still **e** old things from the crop, Lv 25:22 398
You will thus **e** your food to the Lv 26:5 398
'You will **e** the old supply and Lv 26:10 398
for your enemies will **e** it up. Lv 26:16 398
you will **e** and not be satisfied. Lv 26:26 398
you will **e** the flesh of your sons Lv 26:29 398
of your daughters you will **e**. Lv 26:29 398
nor **e** fresh or dried grapes. Nu 6:3 398
shall not **e** anything that is produced Nu 6:4 398
they shall **e** it with unleavened Nu 9:11 398
"Who will give us meat to **e**? Nu 11:4 398
which we used to **e** free in Egypt, Nu 11:5 398
'Give us meat that we may **e**!' Nu 11:13 398
tomorrow, and you shall **e** meat; Nu 11:18 398
someone would give us meat to **e**! Nu 11:18 398
give you meat and you shall **e**. Nu 11:18 398
'You shall **e**, not one day, nor two Nu 11:19 398
they may **e** for a whole month.' Nu 11:21 398
you **e** of the food of the land, Nu 15:19 398
most holy *gifts* you shall **e** it; Nu 18:10 398
every male shall **e** it. Nu 18:10 398
household who is clean may **e** it. Nu 18:11 398
household who is clean may **e** it. Nu 18:13 398
'You may **e** it anywhere, you Nu 18:31 398
them with money so that you may **e**, Dt 2:6 398
me food for money so that I may **e**, Dt 2:28 398
see nor hear nor **e** nor smell. Dt 4:28 398
and you **e** and are satisfied, Dt 6:11 398
you will **e** food without scarcity, Dt 8:9 398
you will **e** and be satisfied. Dt 11:15 398
shall **e** before the LORD your God, Dt 12:7 398
e meat within any of your gates, Dt 12:15 398
unclean and the clean may **e** of it, Dt 12:15 398
'Only you shall not **e** the blood; Dt 12:16 398
"You are not allowed to **e** within Dt 12:17 398
you shall **e** them before the LORD Dt 12:18 398
you say, 'I will **e** meat,' because Dt 12:20 398
because you desire to **e** meat, Dt 12:20 398
to eat meat, *then* you may **e** meat, Dt 12:20 398
and you may **e** within your gates Dt 12:21 398
deer is eaten, so you will **e** it; Dt 12:22 398
and the clean alike may **e** of it. Dt 12:22 398
"Only be sure not to **e** the blood, Dt 12:23 398
not **e** the life with the flesh. Dt 12:23 398
"You shall not **e** it; Dt 12:24 398

"You shall not **e** it, so Dt 12:25 398
God, and you shall **e** the flesh. Dt 12:27 398
shall not **e** any detestable thing. Dt 14:3 398
are the animals which you may **e**: Dt 14:4 398
among the animals, that you may **e**. Dt 14:6 398
you are not to **e** of these among Dt 14:7 398
You shall not **e** any of their flesh Dt 14:8 398
may **e** of all that are in water: Dt 14:9 398
has fins and scales you may **e**, Dt 14:9 398
fins and scales you shall not **e**; Dt 14:10 398
"You may **e** any clean bird. Dt 14:11 398
the ones which you shall not **e**: Dt 14:12 398
"You may **e** any clean bird. Dt 14:20 398
You shall not **e** anything which dies Dt 14:21 398
in your town, so that he may **e** it, Dt 14:21 398
"You shall **e** in the presence Dt 14:23 398
you shall **e** in the presence of the Dt 14:26 398
shall come and **e** and be satisfied, Dt 14:29 398
"You and your household shall **e** Dt 15:20 398
"You shall **e** it within your gates; Dt 15:22 398
unclean and the clean alike *may* **e** Dt 15:22
"Only you shall not **e** its blood; Dt 15:23 398
not **e** leavened bread with it; Dt 16:3 398
shall **e** with it unleavened bread, Dt 16:3 398
"You shall cook and **e** *it* in Dt 16:7 398
days you shall **e** unleavened bread, Dt 16:8 398
they shall **e** the LORD's offerings Dt 18:1 398
"They shall **e** equal portions, Dt 18:8 398
for you may **e** from them, and you Dt 20:19 398
then you may **e** grapes until you Dt 23:24 398
that they may **e** in your towns and Dt 26:12 398
peace offerings and **e** there, Dt 27:7 398
eyes, but you will not **e** of it; Dt 28:31 398
shall **e** up the produce of your ground Dt 28:33 398
it shall **e** the offspring of your Dt 28:51 398
"Then you shall **e** the offspring Dt 28:53 398
of his children which he will **e**, Dt 28:55 398
for she will **e** them secretly for Dt 28:57 398
drink, nor **e** any unclean thing. Jg 13:4 398
drink nor **e** any unclean thing, Jg 13:7 398
"She should not **e** anything that Jg 13:14 398
drink, nor **e** any unclean thing; Jg 13:14 398
detain me, I will not **e** your food, Jg 13:16 398
of the eater came something to **e**, Jg 14:14 3978
that you may **e** of the bread and Ru 2:14 398
her; so she wept and would not **e**. 1Sa 1:7 398
not **e** and why is your heart sad? 1Sa 1:8 398
I may **e** a piece of bread. 1Sa 2:36 398
he goes up to the high place to **e**, 1Sa 9:13 398
people will not **e** until he comes, 1Sa 9:13 398
those who are invited will **e**. 1Sa 9:13 398
for you shall **e** with me today; 1Sa 9:19 398
Set *it* before you *and* **e**, 1Sa 9:24 398
and slaughter *it* here and **e**; 1Sa 14:34 398
to sit down to **e** with the king. 1Sa 20:5 398
came, the king sat down to **e** food. 1Sa 20:24 398
and did not **e** food on the second 1Sa 20:34 398
may **e** and have strength when you go 1Sa 28:22 398
he refused and said, "I will not **e**." 1Sa 28:23 398
came to persuade David to **e** bread 2Sa 3:35 1262
shall **e** at my table regularly." 2Sa 9:7 398
shall **e** at my table regularly." 2Sa 9:10 398
Shall I then go to my house to **e** 2Sa 11:11 398
It would **e** of his bread and drink 2Sa 12:3 398
and would not **e** food with them. 2Sa 12:17 1262
come and give me *some* food to **e**, 2Sa 13:5 1262
see *it* and **e** from her hand.' " 2Sa 13:5 398
that I may **e** from her hand." 2Sa 13:6 1262
before him, but he refused to **e**. 2Sa 13:9 398
that I may **e** from your hand." 2Sa 13:10 1262
When she brought *them* to him to **e**, 2Sa 13:11 398
fruit for the young men to **e**, 2Sa 16:2 398
people who *were* with him, to **e**; 2Sa 17:29 398
taste what I **e** or what I drink? 2Sa 19:35 398
among those who **e** at your table; 1Ki 2:7 398
nor would I **e** bread or drink water 1Ki 13:8 398
'You shall **e** no bread, nor drink 1Ki 13:9 398
"Come home with me and **e** bread." 1Ki 13:15 398
nor will I **e** bread or drink water 1Ki 13:16 398
'You shall **e** no bread, nor drink 1Ki 13:17 398
may **e** bread and drink water.' " 1Ki 13:18 398
"**E** no bread and drink no water"; 1Ki 13:22 398
dies in the city the dogs will **e**. 1Ki 14:11 398
the birds of the heavens will **e**; 1Ki 14:11 398
dies in the city the dogs will **e**, 1Ki 16:4 398
the birds of the heavens will **e**." 1Ki 16:4 398
son, that we may **e** it and die." 1Ki 17:12 398
who **e** at Jezebel's table." 1Ki 18:19 398
"Go up, **e** and drink; 1Ki 18:41 398
So Ahab went up to **e** and drink. 1Ki 18:42 398
and he said to him, "Arise, **e**." 1Ki 19:5 398
"Arise, **e**, because the journey is 1Ki 19:7 398
Arise, **e** bread, and let your heart 1Ki 21:7 398
'The dogs will **e** Jezebel in the 1Ki 21:23 398
in the city, the dogs will **e**, 1Ki 21:24 398
the birds of heaven will **e**." 1Ki 21:24 398
and she persuaded him to **e** food. 2Ki 4:8 398
by, he turned in there to **e** food. 2Ki 4:8 398
poured *it* out for the men to **e**. 2Ki 4:40 398
And they were unable to **e**. 2Ki 4:40 398
for the people that they may **e**." 2Ki 4:41 398
to the people that they may **e**." 2Ki 4:42 398
to the people that they may **e**, 2Ki 4:43 398
e and have *some* left over.' " 2Ki 4:43 398
that they may **e** and drink and go 2Ki 6:22 398
your son that we may **e** him today, 2Ki 6:28 398
and we will **e** my son tomorrow.' 2Ki 6:28 398
'Give your son, that we may **e** him'; 2Ki 6:29 398
eyes, but you will not **e** of it." 2Ki 7:2 398

Context	Reference	Number
eyes, but you will not **e** of it."	**2Ki 7:19**	398
'The dogs shall **e** Jezebel in	**2Ki 9:10**	398
dogs shall **e** the flesh of Jezebel;	**2Ki 9:36**	398
doomed to **e** their own dung and	**2Ki 18:27**	398
and **e** each of his vine and each of	**2Ki 18:31**	398
you will **e** this year what grows	**2Ki 19:29**	398
vineyards, and **e** their fruit.	**2Ki 19:29**	398
enough to **e** with plenty left over,	**2Ch 31:10**	398
they should not **e** from the most holy	**Ezr 2:63**	398
that you may be strong and **e** the	**Ezr 9:12**	398
he went there, he did not **e** bread nor	**Ezr 10:6**	398
grain that we may **e** and live."	**Ne 5:2**	398
they should not **e** from the most holy	**Ne 7:65**	398
"Go, **e** of the fat, drink of the	**Ne 8:10**	398
All the people went away to **e**,	**Ne 8:12**	398
to **e** of its fruit and its bounty,	**Ne 9:36**	398
do not **e** or drink for three days,	**Es 4:16**	398
sisters to **e** and drink with them.	**Jb 1:4**	398
Let me sow and another **e**,	**Jb 31:8**	398
Who **e** up my people *as* they eat	**Ps 14:4**	398
eat up my people *as* they **e** bread,	**Ps 14:4**	398
will **e** and be satisfied;	**Ps 22:26**	398
of the earth will **e** and worship,	**Ps 22:29**	398
"Shall I **e** the flesh of bulls Or	**Ps 50:13**	398
Who **e** up My people *as though* they	**Ps 53:4**	398
rained down manna upon them to **e**	**Ps 78:24**	398
Man did **e** the bread of angels;	**Ps 78:25**	398
Indeed, I forget to **e** my bread.	**Ps 102:4**	398
To **e** the bread of painful labors;	**Ps 127:2**	398
e of the fruit of your hands,	**Ps 128:2**	398
not let me **e** of their delicacies.	**Ps 141:4**	3898b
e of the fruit of their own way And	**Pr 1:31**	398
they **e** the bread of wickedness And	**Pr 4:17**	3898b
"Come, **e** of my food And drink of	**Pr 9:5**	3898b
who love it will **e** its fruit.	**Pr 18:21**	398
not **e** the bread of a selfish man,	**Pr 23:6**	3898b
He says to you, "**E** and drink!"	**Pr 23:7**	398
My son, **e** honey, for it is good,	**Pr 24:13**	398
E *only* what you need, That you	**Pr 25:16**	398
is hungry, give him food to **e**;	**Pr 25:21**	398
It is not good to **e** much honey,	**Pr 25:27**	398
He who tends the fig tree will **e** its	**Pr 27:18**	398
And the young eagles will **e** it.	**Pr 30:17**	398
does not **e** the bread of idleness.	**Pr 31:27**	398
nothing better for a man *than* to **e**	**Ec 2:24**	398
For who can **e** and who can have	**Ec 2:25**	398
to **e**, to drink and enjoy oneself	**Ec 5:18**	398
He has also empowered him to **e**	**Ec 5:19**	398
not empowered him to **e** from them,	**Ec 6:2**	398
to **e** and to drink and to be merry,	**Ec 8:15**	398
then, **e** your bread in happiness and	**Ec 9:7**	398
whose princes **e** at the appropriate	**Ec 10:17**	398
garden And **e** its choice fruits!"	**SS 4:16**	398
E, friends; Drink and imbibe deeply,	**SS 5:1**	398
You will **e** the best of the land;	**Is 1:19**	398
will **e** the fruit of their actions.	**Is 3:10**	398
"We will **e** our own bread and wear	**Is 4:1**	398
And strangers will **e** in the waste	**Is 5:17**	398
"He will **e** curds and honey at the	**Is 7:15**	398
the milk produced he will **e** curds,	**Is 7:22**	398
the land will **e** curds and honey.	**Is 7:22**	398
And they **e** *what is* on the left	**Is 9:20**	398
the lion will **e** straw like the ox.	**Is 11:7**	398
who are most helpless will **e**,	**Is 14:30**	7462a
they spread out the cloth, they **e**,	**Is 21:5**	398
"Let us **e** and drink, for tomorrow	**Is 22:13**	398
the ground will **e** salted fodder,	**Is 30:24**	398
doomed to **e** their own dung and	**Is 36:12**	398
and **e** each of his vine and each of	**Is 36:16**	398
you will **e** this year what grows	**Is 37:30**	398
vineyards and **e** their fruit.	**Is 37:30**	398
I roast meat and **e** *it.*	**Is 44:19**	398
The moth will **e** them.	**Is 50:9**	398
moth will **e** them like a garment,	**Is 51:8**	398
the grub will **e** them like wool.	**Is 51:8**	398
who have no money come, buy and **e**.	**Is 55:1**	398
to Me, and **e** what is good,	**Is 55:2**	398
beasts in the forest, Come to **e**.	**Is 56:9**	398
You will **e** the wealth of nations,	**Is 61:6**	398
But those who garner it will **e** it and	**Is 62:9**	398
Who **e** swine's flesh, And the broth	**Is 65:4**	398
"Behold, My servants will **e**,	**Is 65:13**	398
plant vineyards and **e** their fruit.	**Is 65:21**	398
will not plant and another **e**;	**Is 65:22**	398
lion will **e** straw like the ox;	**Is 65:25**	398
in the center, Who **e** swine's flesh,	**Is 66:17**	398
e its fruit and its good things.	**Jer 2:7**	398
to your sacrifices and **e** flesh.	**Jer 7:21**	398
to sit with them to **e** and drink."	**Jer 16:8**	398
I will make them **e** the flesh of their	**Jer 19:9**	398
and they will **e** one another's	**Jer 19:9**	398
Did not your father **e** and drink And	**Jer 22:15**	398
gardens and **e** their produce.	**Jer 29:5**	398
plant gardens and **e** their produce.	**Jer 29:28**	398
Should women **e** their offspring,	**La 2:20**	398
and **e** what I am giving you."	**Ezk 2:8**	398
"Son of man, **e** what you find;	**Ezk 3:1**	398
e this scroll, and go, speak to	**Ezk 3:1**	398
you shall **e** it according to the	**Ezk 4:9**	398
"Your food which you **e** *shall*	**Ezk 4:10**	398
you shall **e** it from time to time.	**Ezk 4:10**	398
You shall **e** it as a barley cake,	**Ezk 4:12**	398
"Thus will the sons of Israel **e**	**Ezk 4:13**	398
and they will **e** bread by weight	**Ezk 4:16**	398
will **e** *their* sons among you,	**Ezk 5:10**	398
and sons will **e** their fathers;	**Ezk 5:10**	398
man, **e** your bread with trembling and	**Ezk 12:18**	398
'They will **e** their bread with	**Ezk 12:19**	398
'The fathers **e** the sour grapes,	**Ezk 18:2**	398
and does not **e** at the mountain	**Ezk 18:6**	398
"He does not **e** at the mountain	**Ezk 18:15**	398
and do not **e** the bread of men."	**Ezk 24:17**	398
you will not **e** the bread of men.	**Ezk 24:22**	398
they will **e** your fruit and drink	**Ezk 25:4**	398
"You **e** *meat* with the blood *in it,*	**Ezk 33:25**	398
"You **e** the fat and clothe	**Ezk 34:3**	398
they must **e** what you tread down	**Ezk 34:19**	7462a
you may **e** flesh and drink blood.	**Ezk 39:17**	398
will **e** the flesh of mighty men	**Ezk 39:18**	398
will **e** fat until you are glutted,	**Ezk 39:19**	398
LORD shall **e** the most holy things.	**Ezk 42:13**	398
prince to **e** bread before the LORD;	**Ezk 44:3**	398
"They shall **e** the grain offering,	**Ezk 44:29**	398
"The priests shall not **e** any bird	**Ezk 44:31**	398
be given some vegetables to **e** and	**Da 1:12**	398
and you be given grass to **e** like	**Da 4:25**	2939
be given grass to **e** like cattle,	**Da 4:32**	2939
was given grass to **e** like cattle,	**Da 5:21**	2939
I did not **e** any tasty food, nor	**Da 10:3**	398
"Those who **e** his choice food	**Da 11:26**	398
They will **e**, but not have	**Hos 4:10**	398
They sacrifice the flesh and **e** *it,*	**Hos 8:13**	398
Assyria they will **e** unclean *food.*	**Hos 9:3**	398
All who **e** of it will be defiled,	**Hos 9:4**	398
have plenty to **e** and be satisfied And	**Jl 2:26**	398
And **e** lambs from the flock And	**Am 6:4**	398
and there **e** bread and there do	**Am 7:12**	398
make gardens and **e** their fruit.	**Am 9:14**	398
They who **e** your bread Will set an	**Ob 1:7**	398
Do not let them **e** or drink water.	**Jon 3:7**	7462a
Who **e** the flesh of my people,	**Mi 3:3**	398
"You will **e**, but you will not be	**Mi 6:14**	398
is not a cluster of grapes to **e**,	**Mi 7:1**	398
you **e**, but *there is* not *enough* to	**Hg 1:6**	398
'When you **e** and drink, do you	**Zch 7:6**	398
do you not **e** for yourselves and do	**Zch 7:6**	398
those who are left **e** one another's	**Zch 11:9**	398
your life, *as to* what you will **e**	**Mt 6:25**	*2068*
'What will we **e**?'	**Mt 6:31**	*2068*
to pick the heads *of grain* and **e**.	**Mt 12:1**	*2068*
which was not lawful for him to **e** nor	**Mt 12:4**	*2068*
you give them *something* to **e**!"	**Mt 14:16**	*2068*
their hands when they **e** bread."	**Mt 15:2**	*2068*
but to **e** with unwashed hands does	**Mt 15:20**	*2068*
three days and have nothing to **e**;	**Mt 15:32**	*2068*
and **e** and drink with drunkards;	**Mt 24:49**	*2068*
and you gave Me *something* to **e**;	**Mt 25:35**	*2068*
and you gave Me *nothing* to **e**;	**Mt 25:42**	*2068*
for You to **e** the Passover?"	**Mt 26:17**	*2068*
said, "Take, **e**; this is My body."	**Mt 26:26**	*2068*
anyone to **e** except the priests,	**Mk 2:26**	*2068*
that they could not even **e** a meal.	**Mk 3:20**	*2068*
should be given her to **e**.	**Mk 5:43**	*2068*
they did not even have time to **e**.)	**Mk 6:31**	*2068*
buy themselves something to **e**."	**Mk 6:36**	*2068*
"You give them *something* to **e**!"	**Mk 6:37**	*2068*
and give them *something* to **e**?"	**Mk 6:37**	*2068*
Jews do not **e** unless they carefully	**Mk 7:3**	*2068*
they do not **e** unless they cleanse	**Mk 7:4**	*2068*
e their bread with impure hands?"	**Mk 7:5**	*2068*
and they had nothing to **e**,	**Mk 8:1**	*2068*
three days and have nothing to **e**	**Mk 8:2**	*2068*
one ever **e** fruit from you again!"	**Mk 11:14**	*2068*
for You to **e** the Passover?"	**Mk 14:12**	*2068*
room in which I may **e** the Passover	**Mk 14:14**	*2068*
"Why do you **e** and drink with the	**Lk 5:30**	*2068*
but Yours **e** and drink."	**Lk 5:33**	*2068*
any to **e** except the priests alone,	**Lk 6:4**	*2068*
something to be given her to **e**.	**Lk 8:55**	*2068*
lodging and get something to **e**;	**Lk 9:12**	*1979*
"You give them *something* to **e**!"	**Lk 9:13**	*2068*
"Have them sit down *to* **e** in	**Lk 9:14**	
you, **e** what is set before you;	**Lk 10:8**	*2068*
take your ease, **e**, drink *and* be	**Lk 12:19**	*2068*
your life, *as to* what you will **e**;	**Lk 12:22**	*2068*
"And do not seek what you will **e**	**Lk 12:29**	*2068*
and to **e** and drink and get drunk;	**Lk 12:45**	*2068*
on *the* Sabbath to **e** bread,	**Lk 14:1**	*2068*
e bread in the kingdom of God!"	**Lk 14:15**	*2068*
it, and let us **e** and celebrate;	**Lk 15:23**	*2068*
immediately and sit down to **e**'?	**Lk 17:7**	
'Prepare something for me to **e**,	**Lk 17:8**	*1172*
yourself and serve me while I **e**	**Lk 17:8**	*1172*
afterward you may **e** and drink'?	**Lk 17:8**	*2068*
for us, so that we may **e** it."	**Lk 22:8**	*2068*
room in which I may **e** the Passover	**Lk 22:11**	*2068*
"I have earnestly desired to **e**	**Lk 22:15**	*2068*
I shall never again **e** it until it	**Lk 22:16**	*2068*
that you may **e** and drink at My	**Lk 22:30**	*2068*
"Have you anything here to **e**?"	**Lk 24:41**	*1034*
urging Him, saying, "Rabbi, **e**."	**Jn 4:31**	*2068*
to **e** that you do not know about."	**Jn 4:32**	*2068*
"No one brought Him *anything* to **e**,	**Jn 4:33**	*2068*
to buy bread, so that these may **e**?"	**Jn 6:5**	*2068*
THEM BREAD OUT OF HEAVEN TO **E**.'"	**Jn 6:31**	*2068*
that one may **e** of it and not die.	**Jn 6:50**	*2068*
this man give us *His* flesh to **e**?"	**Jn 6:52**	*2068*
unless you **e** the flesh of the Son	**Jn 6:53**	*2068*
defiled, but might **e** the Passover.	**Jn 18:28**	*2068*
hungry and was desiring to **e**;	**Ac 10:10**	*1089*
"Get up, Peter, kill and **e**!"	**Ac 10:13**	*2068*
to me, 'Get up, Peter; kill and **e**.'	**Ac 11:7**	*2068*
saying that they would neither **e**	**Ac 23:12**	*2068*
to **e** or drink until they slay him;	**Ac 23:21**	*2068*
and he broke it and began to **e**.	**Ac 27:35**	*2068*
faith that he may **e** all things,	**Ro 14:2**	*2068*
with contempt the one who does not **e**,	**Ro 14:3**	*2068*
who does not **e** is not to judge the one	**Ro 14:3**	*2068*
not, for the Lord he does not **e**,	**Ro 14:6**	*2068*
not to **e** meat or to drink wine,	**Ro 14:21**	*2068*
even to **e** with such a one.	**1Co 5:11**	*4906*
e *food* as if it were sacrificed to	**1Co 8:7**	*2068*
neither the worse if we do not **e**,	**1Co 8:8**	*2068*
eat, nor the better if we do **e**.	**1Co 8:8**	*2068*
to **e** things sacrificed to idols?	**1Co 8:10**	*2068*
I will never **e** meat again,	**1Co 8:13**	*2068*
not have a right to **e** and drink?	**1Co 9:4**	*2068*
and does not **e** the fruit of it?	**1Co 9:7**	*2068*
services **e** the *food* of the temple,	**1Co 9:13**	*2068*
PEOPLE SAT DOWN TO **E** AND DRINK,	**1Co 10:7**	*2068*
are not those who **e** the sacrifices	**1Co 10:18**	*2068*
E anything that is sold in the	**1Co 10:25**	*2068*
e anything that is set before you without	**1Co 10:27**	*2068*
sacrificed to idols," do not **e** *it,*	**1Co 10:28**	*2068*
you **e** or drink or whatever you do,	**1Co 10:31**	*2068*
it is not to **e** the Lord's Supper,	**1Co 11:20**	*2068*
houses in which to **e** and drink?	**1Co 11:22**	*2068*
e this bread and drink the cup,	**1Co 11:26**	*2068*
and in so doing he is to **e** of the bread	**1Co 11:28**	*2068*
when you come together to **e**,	**1Co 11:33**	*2068*
is hungry, let him **e** at home,	**1Co 11:34**	*2068*
not raised, LET US **E** AND DRINK,	**1Co 15:32**	*2068*
he used to **e** with the Gentiles;	**Ga 2:12**	*4906*
nor did we **e** anyone's bread	**2Th 3:8**	*2068*
then he is not to **e**, either.	**2Th 3:10**	*2068*
fashion and **e** their own bread.	**2Th 3:12**	*2068*
the tabernacle have no right to **e**.	**Heb 13:10**	*2068*
grant to **e** of the tree of life which	**Rv 2:7**	*2068*
to **e** things sacrificed to idols and	**Rv 2:14**	*2068*
and **e** things sacrificed to idols.	**Rv 2:20**	*2068*
"Take it and **e** it;	**Rv 10:9**	*2719*
and will **e** her flesh and will burn	**Rv 17:16**	*2068*
so that you may **e** the flesh	**Rv 19:18**	*2068*

EATEN

Context	Reference	Number
Have you **e** from the tree of which	**Gn 3:11**	398
and have **e** from the tree about	**Gn 3:17**	398
except what the young men have **e**,	**Gn 14:24**	398
have I **e** the rams of your flocks.	**Gn 31:38**	398
what must be **e** by every person,	**Ex 12:16**	398
"It is to be **e** in a single house;	**Ex 12:46**	398
And nothing leavened shall be **e**.	**Ex 13:3**	398
be **e** throughout the seven days;	**Ex 13:7**	398
and its flesh shall not be **e**;	**Ex 21:28**	398
it shall not be **e**, because it is	**Ex 29:34**	398
It shall be **e** as unleavened cakes	**Lv 6:16**	398
It shall not be **e**."	**Lv 6:23**	398
It shall be **e** in a holy place, in	**Lv 6:26**	398
in the holy place shall be **e**;	**Lv 6:30**	398
It shall be **e** in a holy place;	**Lv 7:6**	398
be **e** on the day of his offering;	**Lv 7:15**	398
it shall be **e** on the day that he	**Lv 7:16**	398
day what is left of it may be **e**;	**Lv 7:16**	398
should *ever* be **e** on the third day,	**Lv 7:18**	398
anything unclean shall not be **e**;	**Lv 7:19**	398
have **e** it in the sanctuary,	**Lv 10:18**	398
if I had **e** a sin offering today,	**Lv 10:19**	398
they are abhorrent, not to be **e**:	**Lv 11:13**	398
'Any of the food which may be **e**,	**Lv 11:34**	398
earth is detestable, not to be **e**.	**Lv 11:41**	398
the creature which is not to be **e**.	**Lv 11:47**	398
a beast or a bird which may be **e**,	**Lv 17:13**	398
be **e** the same day you offer *it,*	**Lv 19:6**	398
it is **e** at all on the third day,	**Lv 19:7**	398
it shall not be **e**.	**Lv 19:23**	398
"It shall be **e** on the same day,	**Lv 22:30**	398
whose flesh is half **e** away when he	**Nu 12:12**	398
bread *shall be* **e** for seven days.	**Nu 28:17**	398
"When you have **e** and are	**Dt 8:10**	398
when you have **e** and are satisfied,	**Dt 8:12**	398
"Just as a gazelle or a deer is **e**,	**Dt 12:22**	398
they shall not be **e**.	**Dt 14:19**	398
'I have not **e** of it while mourning,	**Dt 26:14**	398
"You have not **e** bread, nor have	**Dt 29:6**	398
and they have **e** and are satisfied	**Dt 31:20**	398
e some of the produce of the land,	**Jos 5:12**	398
When Boaz had **e** and drunk and his	**Ru 3:7**	398
if only the people had **e** freely	**1Sa 14:30**	398
e no food all day and all night.	**1Sa 28:20**	398
For he had not **e** bread or drunk	**1Sa 30:12**	398
we **e** at all at the king's *expense,*	**2Sa 19:42**	398
but have returned and **e** bread and	**1Ki 13:22**	398
e bread and after he had drunk,	**1Ki 13:23**	398
e the body nor torn the donkey.	**1Ki 13:28**	398
had **e** and drunk he sent them away,	**2Ki 6:23**	398
e the governor's food *allowance.*	**Ne 5:14**	398
tasteless be **e** without salt,	**Jb 6:6**	398
Or have **e** my morsel alone, And the	**Jb 31:17**	398
I have **e** its fruit without money,	**Jb 31:39**	398
You give us as sheep to be **e**	**Ps 44:11**	3978
For I have **e** ashes like bread And	**Ps 102:9**	398
And bread **e** in secret is pleasant."	**Pr 9:17**	
vomit up the morsel you have **e**,	**Pr 23:8**	398
have **e** my honeycomb and my honey;	**SS 5:1**	398
could not be **e** due to rottenness.	**Jer 24:2**	398
cannot be **e** due to rottenness."	**Jer 24:3**	398
like the bad figs which cannot be **e**	**Jer 24:8**	398
cannot be **e** due to rottenness.	**Jer 29:17**	398
'The fathers have **e** sour grapes,	**Jer 31:29**	398
I have never **e** what died of itself	**Ezk 4:14**	398
have **e** at the mountain *shrines.*	**Ezk 22:9**	398
unleavened bread shall be **e**.	**Ezk 45:21**	398
You have **e** the fruit of lies.	**Hos 10:13**	398
left, the swarming locust has **e**;	**Jl 1:4**	398
left, the creeping locust has **e**;	**Jl 1:4**	398
left, the stripping locust has **e**.	**Jl 1:4**	398
That the swarming locust has **e**,	**Jl 2:25**	398
He took the cup after they had **e**,	**Lk 22:20**	*1172*

were left over by those who had e. Jn 6:13 *977*
e anything unholy and unclean." Ac 10:14 *2068*
and he was e by worms and died. Ac 12:23 *4662*
and had broken the bread and e, Ac 20:11 *1089*
When they had e enough, Ac 27:38 *2880*
and when I had e it, my stomach Rv 10:10 *2068*

EATER
of the e came something to eat, Jg 14:14 398
to the sower and bread to the e; Is 55:10 398

EATER'S
they fall into the e mouth. Na 3:12 398

EATERS
Or with gluttonous e of meat; Pr 23:20 2151b

EATING
and the birds were e them out of Gn 40:17 398
when they had finished e the grain Gn 43:2 398
whether an e away has produced Lv 13:55 6356
for guilt by e their holy *gifts;* Lv 22:16 398
e *the old* until the ninth year Lv 25:22 398
you are e of vineyards and olive Jos 24:13 398
hands and went on, e as he went. Jg 14:9 398
he has finished e and drinking. Ru 3:3 398
after e and drinking in Shiloh. 1Sa 1:9 398
the LORD by e with the blood." 1Sa 14:33 398
the LORD by e with the blood.' " 1Sa 14:34 398
e and drinking and dancing because 1Sa 30:16 398
are e and drinking before him; 1Ki 1:25 398
him heard *it* as they finished e. 1Ki 1:41 398
were e and drinking and rejoicing. 1Ki 4:20 398
sullen that you are not e food?" 1Ki 21:5 398
And as they were e of the stew, 2Ki 4:40 398
David three days, e and drinking, 1Ch 12:39 398
his sons and his daughters were e and Jb 1:13 398
sons and your daughters were e and Jb 1:18 398
will rain *it* on him while he is e. Jb 20:23 3894
E of meat and drinking of wine: Is 22:13 398
man dreams—And behold, he is e; Is 29:8 398
While they were e bread together Jer 41:1 398
who are e the king's choice food; Da 1:13 398
had been e the king's choice food. Da 1:15 398
and began e grass like cattle, Da 4:33 399
e the vegetation of the land, Am 7:2 398
"Why is your Teacher e with the Mt 9:11 *2068*
John came neither e nor drinking, Mt 11:18 *2068*
Son of Man came e and drinking, Mt 11:19 *2068*
flood they were e and drinking, Mt 24:38 *5176*
As they were e, Mt 26:21 *2068*
While they were e, Mt 26:26 *2068*
saw that He was e with the sinners Mk 2:16 *2068*
"Why is He e and drinking with Mk 2:16 *2068*
e their bread with impure hands, Mk 7:2 *2068*
were reclining *at the table* and e, Mk 14:18 *2068*
one who is e with Me." Mk 14:18 *2068*
While they were e, Mk 14:22 *2068*
and e *the grain.* Lk 6:1 *2068*
e no bread and drinking no wine, Lk 7:33 *2068*
of Man has come e and drinking, Lk 7:34 *2068*
e and drinking what they give you; Lk 10:7 *2068*
the pods that the swine were e, Lk 15:16 *2068*
they were e, they were drinking, Lk 17:27 *2068*
they were e, they were drinking, Lk 17:28 *2068*
watching and going without e, Ac 27:33 *777*
of God is not e and drinking, Ro 14:17 *1035*
because *his* e is not from faith; Ro 14:23
e of things sacrificed to idols, 1Co 8:4 *1035*
for in your e each one takes his 1Co 11:21 *2068*

EATS
for whoever e anything leavened Ex 12:15 398
for whoever e what is leavened, Ex 12:19 398
and the person who e of it will Lv 7:18 398
'But the person who e the flesh of Lv 7:20 398
and e of the flesh of the sacrifice Lv 7:21 398
'For whoever e the fat of the Lv 7:25 398
the person who e shall be cut off Lv 7:25 398
'Any person who e any blood, even Lv 7:27 398
who e some of its carcass shall Lv 11:40 398
and whoever e in the house shall Lv 14:47 398
among them, who e any blood, Lv 17:10 398
against that person who e blood and Lv 17:10 398
whoever e it shall be cut off.' Lv 17:14 398
any person e *an animal* which dies or Lv 17:15 398
who e it will bear his iniquity, Lv 19:8 398
man e a holy *gift* unintentionally, Lv 22:14 398
the man who e food before evening, 1Sa 14:24 398
be the man who e food today.' " 1Sa 14:28 398
He e grass like an ox. Jb 40:15 398
A boar from the forest e it away And Ps 80:13 3765
the image of an ox that e grass. Ps 106:20 398
She e and wipes her mouth, And Pr 30:20 398
that every man who e and drinks Ec 3:13 398
whether he e little or much; Ec 5:12 398
Throughout his life *he* also e in Ec 5:17 398
Each of them e the flesh of his own Is 9:20 398
he e meat as he roasts a roast and Is 44:16 398
He who e of their eggs dies, And Is 59:5 398
each man who e the sour grapes, Jer 31:30 398
he even e at the mountain *shrines,* Ezk 18:11 398
sinners and e with them." Lk 15:2 *4906*
if anyone e of this bread, he Jn 6:51 *2068*
"He who e My flesh and drinks My Jn 6:54 *5176*
"He who e My flesh and drinks My Jn 6:56 *5176*
so he who e Me, he also will live Jn 6:57 *5176*
e this bread will live forever." Jn 6:58 *5176*
'HE WHO E MY BREAD HAS LIFTED UP Jn 13:18 *5176*
he who is weak e vegetables *only.* Ro 14:2 *2068*
The one who e is not to regard Ro 14:3 *2068*
is not to judge the one who e, Ro 14:3 *2068*
he who e, does so for the Lord, for Ro 14:6 *2068*
and he who e not, for the Lord he Ro 14:6 *2068*
the man who e and gives offense. Ro 14:20 *2068*
who doubts is condemned if he e, Ro 14:23 *2068*
Therefore whoever e the bread or 1Co 11:27 *2068*
For he who e and drinks, eats and 1Co 11:29 *2068*
e and drinks judgment to himself if 1Co 11:29 *2068*

EBAL
Alvan and Manahath and E, Gn 36:23 5858a
Gerizim and the curse on Mount E. Dt 11:29 5858c
you shall set up on Mount E, Dt 27:4 5858c
these shall stand on Mount E: Dt 27:13 5858c
the God of Israel, in Mount E, Jos 8:30 5858c
half of them in front of Mount E, Jos 8:33 5858c
E, Abimael, Sheba, 1Ch 1:22 5858b
of Shobal *were* Alian, Manahath, E, 1Ch 1:40 5858a

EBED
son of E came with his relatives, Jg 9:26 5651
Then Gaal the son of E said, Jg 9:28 5651
the words of Gaal the son of E, Jg 9:30 5651
Gaal the son of E and his Jg 9:31 5651
Now Gaal the son of E went out and Jg 9:35 5651
E the son of Jonathan and 50 males Ezr 8:6 5651

EBED-MELECH
But E the Ethiopian, a eunuch, Jer 38:7 5663
and E went out from the king's Jer 38:8 5663
king commanded E the Ethiopian, Jer 38:10 5663
So E took the men under his Jer 38:11 5663
Then E the Ethiopian said to Jer 38:12 5663
"Go and speak to E the Ethiopian, Jer 39:16 5663

EBENEZER
camped beside E while the Philistines 1Sa 4:1 72
and brought it from E to Ashdod. 1Sa 5:1 72
Mizpah and Shen, and named it E, 1Sa 7:12 72

EBER
father of all the children of E, Gn 10:21 5677
and Shelah became the father of E. Gn 10:24 5677
Two sons were born to E; Gn 10:25 5677
years, and became the father of E; Gn 11:14 5677
after he became the father of E, Gn 11:15 5677
E lived thirty-four years, and Gn 11:16 5677
and E lived four hundred and Gn 11:17 5677
Asshur and will afflict E; Nu 24:24 5677
and Shelah became the father of E. 1Ch 1:18 5677
Two sons were born to E, 1Ch 1:19 5677
E, Peleg, Reu, 1Ch 1:25 5677
Sheba, Jorai, Jacan, Zia and E, 1Ch 5:13 5677
The sons of Elpaal *were* E, 1Ch 8:12 5677
Ishpan, E, Eliel, 1Ch 8:22 5677
of Sallai, Kallai; of Amok, E; Ne 12:20 5677

EBEZ
and Rabbith and Kishion and E, Jos 19:20 77

EBIASAPH
Elkanah his son, E his son and 1Ch 6:23 43
the son of Assir, the son of E, 1Ch 6:37 43
the son of Kore, the son of E, 1Ch 9:19 43

EBONY
e they brought as your payment. Ezk 27:15 1894

EBRON
and E and Rehob and Hammon and Jos 19:28 5683

ECBATANA
In E in the fortress, which is Ezr 6:2 307

ECZEMA
it is e that has broken out on the Lv 13:39 933
e or scabs or crushed testicles. Lv 21:20 1618
a running sore or e or scabs, Lv 22:22 1618

EDEN
a garden toward the east, in E; Gn 2:8 5731
out of E to water the garden; Gn 2:10 5731
of E to cultivate it and keep it. Gn 2:15 5731
sent him out from the garden of E, Gn 3:23 5731
of E He stationed the cherubim and Gn 3:24 5731
in the land of Nod, east of E. Gn 4:16 5731
sons of E who *were* in Telassar? 2Ki 19:12 5729
of Zimmah and E the son of Joah; 2Ch 29:12 5730b
Under his authority *were* E, 2Ch 31:15 5730b
sons of E who *were* in Telassar? Is 37:12 5729
wilderness He will make like E, Is 51:3 5731
"Haran, Canneh, E, the traders of Ezk 27:23 5729
"You were in E, the garden of God; Ezk 28:13 5731
branches, And all the trees of E, Ezk 31:9 5731
all the well-watered trees of E, Ezk 31:16 5731
"To which among the trees of E Ezk 31:18 5731
trees of E to the earth beneath; Ezk 31:18 5731
has become like the garden of E; Ezk 36:35 5731
like the garden of E before them But Jl 2:3 5731

EDER
his tent beyond the tower of E. Gn 35:21 4029
were Kabzeel and E and Jagur, Jos 15:21 5740b
Zebadiah, Arad, E, 1Ch 8:15 5738
Mahli, E and Jeremoth. 1Ch 23:23 5740a
Mahli, E and Jerimoth. 1Ch 24:30 5740a

EDGE
Shechem with the e of the sword, Gn 34:26 6310
Etham on the e of the wilderness. Ex 13:20 7097a
people with the e of the sword. Ex 17:13 6310
blue on the e of the outermost curtain Ex 26:4 8193
make *them* on the e of the curtain Ex 26:4 8193
fifty loops on the e of the curtain Ex 26:5 7097a
fifty loops on the e of the curtain Ex 26:10 8193
and fifty loops on the e of the Ex 26:10 8193
the breastpiece, on the e of it, Ex 28:26 8193
blue on the e of the outermost curtain Ex 36:11 8193
he did likewise on the e of the Ex 36:11 8193
he made fifty loops on the e of the Ex 36:12 7097a
he made fifty loops on the e of Ex 36:17 8193
and he made fifty loops on the e Ex 36:17 8193
e which was next to the ephod. Ex 39:19 8193
a town on the e of your territory. Nu 20:16 7097a
him with the e of the sword, Nu 21:24 6310
is on the e of the wilderness. Nu 33:6 7097a
Hor, at the e of the land of Edom. Nu 33:37 7097a
"From Aroer which is on the e of Dt 2:36 8193
on the e of the valley of Arnon, Dt 4:48 8193
that city with the e of the sword, Dt 13:15 6310
cattle with the e of the sword. Dt 13:15 6310
men in it with the e of the sword. Dt 20:13 6310
the e of the waters of the Jordan, Jos 3:8 7097a
were dipped in the e of the water Jos 3:15 7097a
on the eastern e of Jericho. Jos 4:19 7097a
donkey, with the e of the sword. Jos 6:21 6310
were fallen by the e of the sword Jos 8:24 6310
struck it with the e of the sword. Jos 8:24 6310
its king with the e of the sword; Jos 10:28 6310
was in it with the e of the sword. Jos 10:30 6310
was in it with the e of the sword, Jos 10:32 6310
struck it with the e of the sword; Jos 10:35 6310
in it with the e of the sword. Jos 10:37 6310
them with the e of the sword, Jos 10:39 6310
was in it with the e of the sword, Jos 11:11 6310
them with the e of the sword, Jos 11:12 6310
every man with the e of the sword, Jos 11:14 6310
the e of the valley of the Arnon, Jos 12:2 8193
the e of the valley of the Arnon, Jos 13:9 8193
the e of the valley of the Arnon, Jos 13:16 8193
was from the e of Kiriath-jearim, Jos 18:15 7097a
The border went down to the e Jos 18:16 7097a
Then they struck it with the e of Jos 19:47 6310
and struck it with the e of the sword Jg 1:8 6310
the city with the e of the sword, Jg 1:25 6310
the e of the sword before Barak; Jg 4:15 6310
Sisera fell by the e of the sword; Jg 4:16 6310
as far as the e of Abel-meholah, Jg 7:22 8193
them with the e of the sword; Jg 18:27 6310
the city with the e of the sword. Jg 20:37 6310
them with the e of the sword, Jg 20:48 6310
with the e of the sword, Jg 21:10 6310
going down to the e of the city, 1Sa 9:27 7097a
people with the e of the sword. 1Sa 15:8 6310
go, *Saul* seized the e of his robe, 1Sa 15:27 3671
priests with the e of the sword, 1Sa 22:19 6310
he struck with the e of the sword. 1Sa 22:19 6310
cut off the e of Saul's robe secretly. 1Sa 24:4 3671
had cut off the e of Saul's *robe.* 1Sa 24:5 3671
see the e of your robe in my hand! 1Sa 24:11 3671
in that I cut off the e of your robe 1Sa 24:11 3671
city with the e of the sword." 2Sa 15:14 6310
them with the e of the sword; 2Ki 10:25 6310
servants with the e of the sword, Jb 1:15 6310
servants with the e of the sword, Jb 1:17 6310
also turn back the e of his sword And Ps 89:43 6864
down upon the e of his robes. Ps 133:2 6310
and he does not sharpen *its* e, Ec 10:10 6440
by the e of the Nile And all the Is 19:7 6310
them down with the e of the sword. Jer 21:7 6310
And the children's teeth are set on e.' Jer 31:29 6949a
his teeth will be set on e. Jer 31:30 6949a
the children's teeth are set on e'? Ezk 18:2 6949a
wherever your e is appointed. Ezk 21:16 6440
on its e round about one span; Ezk 43:13 8193
boats lying at the e of the lake; Lk 5:2
will fall by the e of the sword, Lk 21:24 *4750*
fire, escaped the e of the sword, Heb 11:34 *4750*

EDGES
nor harm the e of your beard. Lv 19:27 6285
shave off the e of their beards, Lv 21:5 6285
himself a sword which had two e, Jg 3:16 6310
threshing sledge with double e; Is 41:15 6310
bind them in the e of your *robes.* Ezk 5:3 3671

EDIBLE
some of all food which is e, Gn 6:21 398
and between the e creature and the Lv 11:47 398

EDICT
that any man who violates this e, Ezr 6:11 6600
let a royal e be issued by him and Es 1:19 1697
"When the king's e which he Es 1:20 6599
A copy of the e to be issued as Es 3:14 3791
the e which had been issued in Susa Es 4:8 1881
A copy of the e to be issued as Es 8:13 3791
and e were about to be executed, Es 9:1 1881
to do according to the e of today; Es 9:13 1881
and an e was issued in Susa, and Es 9:14 1881
were not afraid of the king's e. Heb 11:23 *1297*

EDICTS
the king's e to the king's satraps and Ezr 8:36 1881

EDIFICATION
neighbor for his good, to his e. Ro 15:2 *3619*
speaks to men for e and exhortation 1Co 14:3 *3619*
to abound for the e of the church. 1Co 14:12 *3619*
Let all things be done for e. 1Co 14:26 *3619*
but only such *a word* as is good for e Eph 4:29 *3619*

EDIFIED
but the other person is not e. 1Co 14:17 *3618*

EDIFIES
makes arrogant, but love e. 1Co 8:1 *3618*
who speaks in a tongue e himself; 1Co 14:4 *3618*
one who prophesies e the church. 1Co 14:4 *3618*

EDIFY
are lawful, but not all things e. 1Co 10:23 *3618*

EDIFYING
so that the church may receive e. 1Co 14:5 *3619*

EDOM
Therefore his name was called E. Gn 25:30 112b
land of Seir, the country of E. Gn 32:3 112b

generations of Esau (that is, **E**). Gn 36:1 112b
in the hill country of Seir; Esau is **E**. Gn 36:8 112b
from Eliphaz in the land of **E**; Gn 36:16 112b
from Reuel in the land of **E**; Gn 36:17 112b
are the sons of Esau (that is, **E**), Gn 36:19 112b
the sons of Seir in the land of **E**. Gn 36:21 112b
kings who reigned in the land of **E** Gn 36:31 112b
Bela the son of Beor reigned in **E**, Gn 36:32 112b
These are the chiefs of **E** Gn 36:43 112b
the chiefs of **E** were dismayed; Ex 15:15 112b
sent messengers to the king of **E**: Nu 20:14 112b
E, however, said to him, Nu 20:18 112b
And **E** came out against him with a Nu 20:20 112b
Thus **E** refused to allow Israel to Nu 20:21 112b
by the border of the land of **E**, Nu 20:23 112b
Sea, to go around the land of **E**; Nu 21:4 112b
"**E** shall be a possession, Nu 24:18 112b
Hor, at the edge of the land of **E**. Nu 33:37 112b
of Zin along the side of **E**, Nu 34:3 112b
families reached the border of **E**, Jos 15:1 112b
border of **E** in the south were Jos 15:21 112b
marched from the field of **E**, Jg 5:4 112b
sent messengers to the king of **E**, Jg 11:17 112b
the king of **E** would not listen. Jg 11:17 112b
land of **E** and the land of Moab, Jg 11:18 112b
Moab, the sons of Ammon, **E**, 1Sa 14:47 112b
He put garrisons in **E**. 2Sa 8:14 112b
In all **E** he put garrisons, and all 2Sa 8:14 112b
of the Red Sea, in the land of **E**. 1Ki 9:26 112b
he was of the royal line in **E**. 1Ki 11:14 112b
came about, when David was in **E**, 1Ki 11:15 112b
had struck down every male in **E** 1Ki 11:15 112b
he had cut off every male in **E**), 1Ki 11:16 112b
Now there was no king in **E**; 1Ki 22:47 112b
"The way of the wilderness of **E**." 2Ki 3:8 112b
king of Judah and the king of **E**; 2Ki 3:9 112b
the king of **E** went down to him. 2Ki 3:12 112b
water came by the way of **E**, 2Ki 3:20 112b
to break through to the king of **E**; 2Ki 3:26 112b
In his days **E** revolted from under 2Ki 8:20 112b
So **E** revolted against Judah to 2Ki 8:22 112b
He killed *of* **E** in the Valley of 2Ki 14:7 112b
"You have indeed defeated **E**, 2Ki 14:10 112b
kings who reigned in the land of **E** 1Ch 1:43 112b
Now the chiefs of **E** were: 1Ch 1:51 112b
These *were* the chiefs of **E**. 1Ch 1:54 112b
from **E**, Moab, the sons of Ammon, 1Ch 18:11 112b
Then he put garrisons in **E**, 1Ch 18:13 112b
on the seashore in the land of **E**. 2Ch 8:17 112b
In his days **E** revolted against the 2Ch 21:8 112b
So **E** revolted against Judah to 2Ch 21:10 112b
'Behold, you have defeated **E**.' 2Ch 25:19 112b
they had sought the gods of **E**. 2Ch 25:20 112b
Over **E** I shall throw My shoe; Ps 60:8 112b
Who will lead me to **E**? Ps 60:9 112b
tents of **E** and the Ishmaelites, Ps 83:6 112b
Over **E** I shall throw My shoe; Ps 108:9 112b
Who will lead me to **E**? Ps 108:10 112b
sons of **E** The day of Jerusalem, Ps 137:7 112b
They will possess **E** and Moab, Is 11:14 112b
The oracle concerning **E**. Is 21:11 112b
shall descend for judgment upon **E** And Is 34:5 112b
great slaughter in the land of **E**. Is 34:6 112b
Who is this who comes from **E**, Is 63:1 112b
Egypt and Judah, and **E** Jer 9:26 112b
E, Moab and the sons of Ammon; Jer 25:21 112b
and send word to the king of **E**, Jer 27:3 112b
among the sons of Ammon and in **E** and Jer 40:11 112b
Concerning **E**. Thus says the LORD Jer 49:7 112b
E will become an object of horror; Jer 49:17 112b
which He has planned against **E**, Jer 49:20 112b
the hearts of the mighty men of **E** in Jer 49:22 112b
and be glad, O daughter of **E**, La 4:21 112b
your iniquity, O daughter of **E**; La 4:22 112b
reproach of the daughters of **E** and Ezk 16:57 112b
"Because **E** has acted against the Ezk 25:12 112b
also stretch out My hand against **E** Ezk 25:13 112b
"I will lay My vengeance on **E** Ezk 25:14 112b
they will act in **E** according to My Ezk 25:14 112b
"There also is **E**, its kings and Ezk 32:29 112b
O Mount Seir, and all **E**, Ezk 35:15 112b
of the nations, and against all **E**, Ezk 36:5 112b
E, Moab and the foremost of the Da 11:41 112b
And **E** will become a desolate Jl 3:19 112b
population To deliver *it* up to **E**. Am 1:6 112b
delivered up an entire population to **E** Am 1:9 112b
"For three transgressions of **E** Am 1:11 112b
bones of the king of **E** to lime. Am 2:1 112b
they may possess the remnant of **E** Am 9:12 112b
says the Lord GOD concerning **E** Ob 1:1 112b
"Destroy wise men from **E** And Ob 1:8 112b
E says, "We have been beaten down, Mal 1:4 112b

EDOMITE
"You shall not detest an **E**, Dt 23:7 130
and his name was Doeg the **E**, 1Sa 21:7 130
Then Doeg the **E**, who was standing 1Sa 22:9 130
And Doeg the **E** turned around and 1Sa 22:18 130
day, when Doeg the **E** was there, 1Sa 22:22 130
Moabite, Ammonite, **E**, 1Ki 11:1 130
adversary to Solomon, Hadad the **E**; 1Ki 11:14 130

EDOMITES
the **E** in the hill country of Seir. Gn 36:9 112b
is, Esau, the father of the **E**), Gn 36:43 112b
the **E** became servants to David. 2Sa 8:14 112b
he and certain **E** of his father's 1Ki 11:17 130
he arose by night and struck the **E** 2Ki 8:21 112b
18,000 **E** in the Valley of Salt. 1Ch 18:12 112b
the **E** became servants to David. 1Ch 18:13 112b
arose by night and struck down the **E** 2Ch 21:9 112b
came from slaughtering the **E** 2Ch 25:14 130
the **E** had come and attacked Judah and 2Ch 28:17 130

EDREI
all his people, for battle at **E**. Nu 21:33 154
who lived in Ashtaroth and **E**. Dt 1:4 154
out to meet us in battle at **E**. Dt 3:1 154
Bashan, as far as Salecah and **E**, Dt 3:10 154
who lived at Ashtaroth and at **E**, Jos 12:4 154
who reigned in Ashtaroth and in **E** Jos 13:12 154
of Gilead, with Ashtaroth and **E**, Jos 13:31 154
and Kedesh and **E** and En-hazor, Jos 19:37 154

EDUCATED
that they should be **e** three years, Da 1:5 1431
learned, having never been **e**?" Jn 7:15 *3129*
"Moses was **e** in all the Ac 7:22 *3811*
up in this city, **e** under Gamaliel, Ac 22:3 *3811*

EFFECT
fire had no **e** on the bodies of these Da 3:27 7981
of peace which he will put into **e**; Da 11:17 6213a
Before the decree takes **e** Zph 2:2 3205
"But God spoke to this **e**, Ac 7:6 *3779*
to the **e** that the day of the Lord 2Th 2:2 *5613*
in **e**, by compulsion but of your own Phm 1:14 *2596*
I WILL **E** A NEW COVENANT WITH Heb 8:8 *4931*

EFFECTING
be shown to be sin by **e** my death Ro 7:13 *2716*
and to another the **e** of miracles, 1Co 12:10 *1755*

EFFECTIVE
for **e** *service* has opened to me, 1Co 16:9 *1756*
which is **e** in the patient enduring 2Co 1:6 *1754*
fellowship of your faith may become **e** Phm 1:6 *1756*
The **e** prayer of a righteous man Jas 5:16 *1754*

EFFECTS
There are varieties of **e**, 1Co 12:6 *1755*

EFFECTUAL
a forgetful hearer but an **e** doer, Jas 1:25 *2041*

EFFECTUALLY
(for He who **e** worked for Peter in Ga 2:8 *1754*
e worked for me also to the Gentiles Ga 2:8 *1754*

EFFEMINATE
idolaters, nor adulterers, nor **e**, 1Co 6:9 *3120*

EFFORT
Make an **e** then to get some of the Nu 13:20 2388
the dream comes through much **e** and Ec 5:3 6045
make an **e** to settle with him, Lk 12:58 *2039*
Make every **e** to come to me soon; 2Tm 4:9 *4704*
every **e** to come before winter. 2Tm 4:21 *4704*
make every **e** to come to me at Ti 3:12 *4704*
while I was making every **e** to Jude 1:3 *4710*

EFFORTS
this Pilate made **e** to release Him, Jn 19:12 *2212*

EGG
any taste in the white of an **e**? Jb 6:6 2495
"Or *if* he is asked for an **e**, Lk 11:12 *5609*

EGGS
the ground, with young ones or **e**, Dt 22:6 1000
sitting on the young or on the **e**, Dt 22:6 1000
she abandons her **e** to the earth And Jb 39:14 1000
And as one gathers abandoned **e**, Is 10:14 1000
snake will make its nest and lay **e** Is 34:15
e and weave the spider's web; Is 59:5 1000
He who eats of their **e** dies, Is 59:5 1000
hatches **e** which it has not laid, Jer 17:11 1716

EGLAH
sixth, Ithream, by David's wife **E**. 2Sa 3:5 5698
sixth *was* Ithream, by his wife **E**. 1Ch 3:3 5698

EGLAIM
Its wail *goes* as far as **E** and its Is 15:8 97

EGLATH-SHELISHIYA
are as far as Zoar *and* **E**, Is 15:5 5700b, 7992
Zoar even to Horonaim *and to* **E**; Jer 48:34 5700b, 7992

EGLON
of Lachish and to Debir king of **E**, Jos 10:3 5700a
of Lachish, *and* the king of **E**, Jos 10:5 5700a
of Lachish, *and* the king of **E**, Jos 10:23 5700a
him passed on from Lachish to **E**, Jos 10:34 5700a
with him went up from **E** to Hebron, Jos 10:36 5700a
to all that he had done to **E**. Jos 10:37 5700a
the king of **E**, one; Jos 12:12 5700a
Lachish and Bozkath and **E**, Jos 15:39 5700a
So the LORD strengthened **E** the Jg 3:12 5700a
The sons of Israel served **E** Jg 3:14 5700a
by him to **E** the king of Moab. Jg 3:15 5700a
the tribute to **E** king of Moab. Jg 3:17 5700a
Now **E** was a very fat man. Jg 3:17 5700a

EGYPT
went down to **E** to sojourn there, Gn 12:10 4714
came about when he came near to **E**, Gn 12:11 4714
came about when Abram came into **E**, Gn 12:14 4714
Abram went up from **E** to the Negev, Gn 13:1 4714
the land of **E** as you go to Zoar. Gn 13:10 4714
of **E** as far as the great river, Gn 15:18 4714
a wife for him from the land of **E**. Gn 21:21 4714
of **E** as one goes toward Assyria; Gn 25:18 4714
"Do not go down to **E**; Gn 26:2 4714
their way to bring *them* down to **E**. Gn 37:25 4714
Thus they brought Joseph into **E**. Gn 37:28 4714
sold him in **E** to Potiphar, Gn 37:36 4714
Joseph had been taken down to **E**; Gn 39:1 4714
the king of **E** offended their lord, Gn 40:1 4714
their lord, the king of **E**. Gn 40:1 4714
and the baker for the king of **E**, Gn 40:5 4714
called for all the magicians of **E**, Gn 41:8 4714
for ugliness in all the land of **E**; Gn 41:19 4714
are coming in all the land of **E**; Gn 41:29 4714
be forgotten in the land of **E**, Gn 41:30 4714
and set him over the land of **E**. Gn 41:33 4714
fifth *of the produce* of the land of **E** Gn 41:34 4714
which will occur in the land of **E**, Gn 41:36 4714
set you over all the land of **E**." Gn 41:41 4714
he set him over all the land of **E**. Gn 41:43 4714
or foot in all the land of **E**." Gn 41:44 4714
went forth over the land of **E**. Gn 41:45 4714
stood before Pharaoh, king of **E**. Gn 41:46 4714
went through all the land of **E**. Gn 41:46 4714
which occurred in the land of **E** and Gn 41:48 4714
in the land of **E** came to an end, Gn 41:53 4714
all the land of **E** there was bread. Gn 41:54 4714
all the land of **E** was famished, Gn 41:55 4714
famine was severe in the land of **E**. Gn 41:56 4714
to **E** to buy grain from Joseph, Gn 41:57 4714
saw that there was grain in **E**, Gn 42:1 4714
heard that there is grain in **E**; Gn 42:2 4714
went down to buy grain from **E**. Gn 42:3 4714
which they had brought from **E**, Gn 43:2 4714
down to **E** and stood before Joseph. Gn 43:15 4714
Joseph, whom you sold into **E**. Gn 45:4 4714
and ruler over all the land of **E**. Gn 45:8 4714
"God has made me lord of all **E**; Gn 45:9 4714
my father of all my splendor in **E**, Gn 45:13 4714
give you the best of the land of **E** Gn 45:18 4714
take wagons from the land of **E** for Gn 45:19 4714
of all the land of **E** is yours.' " Gn 45:20 4714
loaded with the best things of **E**, Gn 45:23 4714
Then they went up from **E**, Gn 45:25 4714
is ruler over all the land of **E**." Gn 45:26 4714
do not be afraid to go down to **E**, Gn 46:3 4714
"I will go down with you to **E**, Gn 46:4 4714
the land of Canaan, and came to **E**, Gn 46:6 4714
he brought with him to **E**. Gn 46:7 4714
Jacob and his sons, who went to **E**: Gn 46:8 4714
Now to Joseph in the land of **E** Gn 46:20 4714
belonging to Jacob, who came to **E**, Gn 46:26 4714
were born to him in **E** were two; Gn 46:27 4714
the house of Jacob, who came to **E**, Gn 46:27 4714
"The land of **E** is at your disposal; Gn 47:6 4714
a possession in the land of **E**, Gn 47:11 4714
so that the land of **E** and the land Gn 47:13 4714
land of **E** and in the land of Canaan Gn 47:14 4714
of **E** and in the land of Pharaoh, Gn 47:15 4714
all the land of **E** for Pharaoh, Gn 47:20 4714
the land of **E** *valid* to this day, Gn 47:26 4714
Now Israel lived in the land of **E**, Gn 47:27 4714
in the land of **E** seventeen years; Gn 47:28 4714
Please do not bury me in **E**, Gn 47:29 4714
you shall carry me out of **E** and Gn 47:30 4714
E before I came to you in Egypt, Gn 48:5 4714
Egypt before I came to you in **E**, Gn 48:5 4714
all the elders of the land of **E**, Gn 50:7 4714
his father, Joseph returned to **E**, Gn 50:14 4714
Now Joseph stayed in **E**, Gn 50:22 4714
and placed in a coffin in **E**. Gn 50:26 4714
Israel who came to **E** with Jacob; Ex 1:1 4714
but Joseph was *already* in **E**. Ex 1:5 4714
Now a new king arose over **E**, Ex 1:8 4714
of **E** spoke to the Hebrew midwives, Ex 1:15 4714
the king of **E** had commanded them, Ex 1:17 4714
king of **E** called for the midwives and Ex 1:18 4714
many days that the king of **E** died. Ex 2:23 4714
of My people who are in **E**, Ex 3:7 4714
the sons of Israel, out of **E**." Ex 3:10 4714
the sons of Israel out of **E**?" Ex 3:11 4714
have brought the people out of **E**, Ex 3:12 4714
what has been done to you in **E**. Ex 3:16 4714
bring you up out of the affliction of **E** Ex 3:17 4714
Israel will come to the king of **E** and Ex 3:18 4714
the king of **E** will not permit you to Ex 3:19 4714
and strike **E** with all My miracles Ex 3:20 4714
to my brethren who are in **E**, Ex 4:18 4714
"Go back to **E**, for all the men Ex 4:19 4714
and returned to the land of **E**. Ex 4:20 4714
"When you go back to **E** see that Ex 4:21 4714
But the king of **E** said to them, Ex 5:4 4714
of **E** to gather stubble for straw. Ex 5:12 4714
tell Pharaoh king of **E** to let the Ex 6:11 4714
Israel and to Pharaoh king of **E**, Ex 6:13 4714
of Israel out of the land of **E**. Ex 6:13 4714
of **E** according to their hosts." Ex 6:26 4714
who spoke to Pharaoh king of **E** Ex 6:27 4714
out the sons of Israel from **E**; Ex 6:27 4714
spoke to Moses in the land of **E**, Ex 6:28 4714
speak to Pharaoh king of **E** all that Ex 6:29 4714
and My wonders in the land of **E**. Ex 7:3 4714
you, then I will lay My hand on **E** and Ex 7:4 4714
the land of **E** by great judgments. Ex 7:4 4714
when I stretch out My hand on **E** Ex 7:5 4714
and they also, the magicians of **E**, Ex 7:11 4714
your hand over the waters of **E**, Ex 7:19 4714
throughout all the land of **E**, Ex 7:19 4714
was through all the land of **E**. Ex 7:21 4714
But the magicians of **E** did the Ex 7:22 4714
come up on the land of **E**.' " Ex 8:5 4714
out his hand over the waters of **E**, Ex 8:6 4714
came up and covered the land of **E**. Ex 8:6 4714
frogs come up on the land of **E**. Ex 8:7 4714
through all the land of **E**.' " Ex 8:16 4714
gnats through all the land of **E**. Ex 8:17 4714
of insects in all the land of **E**. Ex 8:24 4714
of Israel and the livestock of **E**, Ex 9:4 4714
and all the livestock of **E** died; Ex 9:6 4714
fine dust over all the land of **E**, Ex 9:9 4714

beast through all the land of **E**.” **Ex 9:9** 4714
such as has not been *seen* in **E** **Ex 9:18** 4714
may fall on all the land of **E**, **Ex 9:22** 4714
field, throughout the land of **E**.” **Ex 9:22** 4714
LORD rained hail on the land of **E**. **Ex 9:23** 4714
of **E** since it became a nation. **Ex 9:24** 4714
field through all the land of **E**, **Ex 9:25** 4714
not realize that **E** is destroyed?” **Ex 10:7** 4714
the land of **E** for the locusts, **Ex 10:12** 4714
they may come up on the land of **E** and **Ex 10:12** 4714
out his staff over the land of **E**, **Ex 10:13** 4714
locusts came up over all the land of **E** **Ex 10:14** 4714
settled in all the territory of **E**; **Ex 10:14** 4714
field through all the land of **E**. **Ex 10:15** 4714
left in all the territory of **E**. **Ex 10:19** 4714
be darkness over the land of **E**, **Ex 10:21** 4714
all the land of **E** for three days. **Ex 10:22** 4714
I will bring on Pharaoh and on **E**; **Ex 11:1** 4714
greatly esteemed in the land of **E**, **Ex 11:3** 4714
am going out into the midst of **E**, **Ex 11:4** 4714
in the land of **E** shall die, **Ex 11:5** 4714
a great cry in all the land of **E**, **Ex 11:6** 4714
distinction between **E** and Israel.’ **Ex 11:7** 4714
be multiplied in the land of **E**.” **Ex 11:9** 4714
Moses and Aaron in the land of **E**, **Ex 12:1** 4714
the land of **E** on that night, **Ex 12:12** 4714
the firstborn in the land of **E**, **Ex 12:12** 4714
and against all the gods of **E** I **Ex 12:12** 4714
you when I strike the land of **E**. **Ex 12:13** 4714
your hosts out of the land of **E**; **Ex 12:17** 4714
in **E** when He smote the Egyptians, **Ex 12:27** 4714
the firstborn in the land of **E**, **Ex 12:29** 4714
and there was a great cry in **E**, **Ex 12:30** 4714
which they had brought out of **E** into **Ex 12:39** 4714
out of **E** and could not delay, **Ex 12:39** 4714
time that the sons of Israel lived in **E** **Ex 12:40** 4714
LORD went out from the land of **E**. **Ex 12:41** 4714
them out from the land of **E**; **Ex 12:42** 4714
of the land of **E** by their hosts. **Ex 12:51** 4714
day in which you went out from **E**, **Ex 13:3** 4714
did for me when I came out of **E**.’ **Ex 13:8** 4714
the LORD brought you out of **E**. **Ex 13:9** 4714
hand the LORD brought us out of **E**, **Ex 13:14** 4714
every firstborn in the land of **E**, **Ex 13:15** 4714
the LORD brought us out of **E**.” **Ex 13:16** 4714
see war, and return to **E**.” **Ex 13:17** 4714
martial array from the land of **E**. **Ex 13:18** 4714
When the king of **E** was told that **Ex 14:5** 4714
and all the *other* chariots of **E** **Ex 14:7** 4714
the heart of Pharaoh, king of **E**, **Ex 14:8** 4714
because there were no graves in **E** **Ex 14:11** 4714
in this way, bringing us out of **E**? **Ex 14:11** 4714
word that we spoke to you in **E**, **Ex 14:12** 4714
camp of **E** and the camp of Israel; **Ex 14:20** 4714
departure from the land of **E**. **Ex 16:1** 4714
the LORD’s hand in the land of **E**, **Ex 16:3** 4714
brought you out of the land of **E**; **Ex 16:6** 4714
you out of the land of **E**.’ ” **Ex 16:32** 4714
have you brought us up from **E**, **Ex 17:3** 4714
LORD had brought Israel out of **E**. **Ex 18:1** 4714
had gone out of the land of **E**, **Ex 19:1** 4714
brought you out of the land of **E**, **Ex 20:2** 4714
were strangers in the land of **E**. **Ex 22:21** 4714
were strangers in the land of **E**. **Ex 23:9** 4714
Abib, for in it you came out of **E**. **Ex 23:15** 4714
brought them out of the land of **E**, **Ex 29:46** 4714
brought us up from the land of **E**, **Ex 32:1** 4714
you up from the land of **E**.” **Ex 32:4** 4714
you brought up from the land of **E**, **Ex 32:7** 4714
you up from the land of **E**!’ ” **Ex 32:8** 4714
have brought out from the land of **E** **Ex 32:11** 4714
brought us up from the land of **E**, **Ex 32:23** 4714
brought up from the land of **E**, **Ex 33:1** 4714
month of Abib you came out of **E**. **Ex 34:18** 4714
brought you up from the land of **E** to **Lv 11:45** 4714
in the land of **E** where you lived, **Lv 18:3** 4714
you were aliens in the land of **E**; **Lv 19:34** 4714
you out from the land of **E**. **Lv 19:36** 4714
you out from the land of **E**, **Lv 22:33** 4714
them out from the land of **E**. **Lv 23:43** 4714
brought you out of the land of **E** **Lv 25:38** 4714
I brought out from the land of **E**; **Lv 25:42** 4714
I brought out from the land of **E**. **Lv 25:55** 4714
brought you out of the land of **E** so **Lv 26:13** 4714
I brought out of the land of **E** in the **Lv 26:45** 4714
had come out of the land of **E**, **Nu 1:1** 4714
the firstborn in the land of **E**, **Nu 3:13** 4714
of **E** I sanctified them for Myself. **Nu 8:17** 4714
had come out of the land of **E**, **Nu 9:1** 4714
which we used to eat free in **E**, **Nu 11:5** 4714
For we were well-off in **E**.” **Nu 11:18** 4714
“Why did we ever leave **E**?” **Nu 11:20** 4714
seven years before Zoan in **E**.) **Nu 13:22** 4714
that we had died in the land of **E**! **Nu 14:2** 4714
be better for us to return to **E**?” **Nu 14:3** 4714
a leader and return to **E**.” **Nu 14:4** 4714
people, from **E** even until now.” **Nu 14:19** 4714
in **E** and in the wilderness, **Nu 14:22** 4714
from the land of **E** to be your God; **Nu 15:41** 4714
have you made us come up from **E**, **Nu 20:5** 4714
that our fathers went down to **E**, **Nu 20:15** 4714
and we stayed in **E** a long time, **Nu 20:15** 4714
angel and brought us out from **E**; **Nu 20:16** 4714
out of **E** to die in the wilderness? **Nu 21:5** 4714
“Behold, a people came out of **E**; **Nu 22:5** 4714
there is a people who came out of **E** **Nu 22:11** 4714
“God brings them out of **E**, **Nu 23:22** 4714
“God brings him out of **E**, **Nu 24:8** 4714
came out of the land of **E** *were:* **Nu 26:4** 4714

Levi, who was born to Levi in **E**; **Nu 26:59** 4714
of the men who came up from **E**, **Nu 32:11** 4714
the land of **E** by their armies, **Nu 33:1** 4714
Israel had come from the land of **E** **Nu 33:38** 4714
from Azmon to the brook of **E**, **Nu 34:5** 4714
has brought us out of the land of **E**, **Dt 1:27** 4714
did for you in **E** before your eyes, **Dt 1:30** 4714
out of the iron furnace, from **E**, **Dt 4:20** 4714
did for you in **E** before your eyes? **Dt 4:34** 4714
you from **E** by His great power, **Dt 4:37** 4714
Israel, when they came out from **E**, **Dt 4:45** 4714
when they came out from **E**. **Dt 4:46** 4714
brought you out of the land of **E**, **Dt 5:6** 4714
you were a slave in the land of **E**, **Dt 5:15** 4714
brought you from the land of **E**, **Dt 6:12** 4714
‘We were slaves to Pharaoh in **E**, **Dt 6:21** 4714
us from **E** with a mighty hand. **Dt 6:21** 4714
wonders before our eyes against **E**, **Dt 6:22** 4714
the hand of Pharaoh king of **E**. **Dt 7:8** 4714
any of the harmful diseases of **E** **Dt 7:15** 4714
God did to Pharaoh and to all **E**: **Dt 7:18** 4714
you out from the land of **E**, **Dt 8:14** 4714
day that you left the land of **E** until **Dt 9:7** 4714
out of **E** have acted corruptly. **Dt 9:12** 4714
out of **E** with a mighty hand. **Dt 9:26** 4714
you were aliens in the land of **E**. **Dt 10:19** 4714
down to **E** seventy persons *in all,* **Dt 10:22** 4714
He did in the midst of **E** to Pharaoh **Dt 11:3** 4714
the king of **E** and to all his land; **Dt 11:3** 4714
the land of **E** from which you came, **Dt 11:10** 4714
who brought you from the land of **E** **Dt 13:5** 4714
you out from the land of **E**, **Dt 13:10** 4714
you were a slave in the land of **E**, **Dt 15:15** 4714
God brought you out of **E** by night. **Dt 16:1** 4714
out of the land of **E** in haste), **Dt 16:3** 4714
you came out of the land of **E**. **Dt 16:3** 4714
the time that you came out of **E**. **Dt 16:6** 4714
that you were a slave in **E**, **Dt 16:12** 4714
to return to **E** to multiply horses, **Dt 17:16** 4714
brought you up from the land of **E**. **Dt 20:1** 4714
on the way when you came out of **E**, **Dt 23:4** 4714
on the way as you came out of **E**, **Dt 24:9** 4714
that you were a slave in **E**, **Dt 24:18** 4714
you were a slave in the land of **E**; **Dt 24:22** 4714
the way when you came out from **E**, **Dt 25:17** 4714
down to **E** and sojourned there, **Dt 26:5** 4714
and the LORD brought us out of **E** **Dt 26:8** 4714
will smite you with the boils of **E** and **Dt 28:27** 4714
back on you all the diseases of **E** **Dt 28:60** 4714
will bring you back to **E** in ships, **Dt 28:68** 4714
did before your eyes in the land of **E** **Dt 29:2** 4714
how we lived in the land of **E**, **Dt 29:16** 4714
brought them out of the land of **E**. **Dt 29:25** 4714
in the land of **E** against Pharaoh, **Dt 34:11** 4714
before you when you came out of **E**, **Jos 2:10** 4714
who came out of **E** who were males, **Jos 5:4** 4714
the way after they came out of **E**. **Jos 5:4** 4714
out of **E** had not been circumcised. **Jos 5:5** 4714
the men of war who came out of **E**, **Jos 5:6** 4714
away the reproach of **E** from you.” **Jos 5:9** 4714
of Him and all that He did in **E**, **Jos 9:9** 4714
the Shihor which is east of **E**, **Jos 13:3** 4714
and proceeded to the brook of **E**, **Jos 15:4** 4714
the brook of **E** and the Great Sea, **Jos 15:47** 4714
Jacob and his sons went down to **E**. **Jos 24:4** 4714
I plagued **E** by what I did in its **Jos 24:5** 4714
I brought your fathers out of **E**, **Jos 24:6** 4714
and **E** pursued your fathers with **Jos 24:6** 4714
your own eyes saw what I did in **E**. **Jos 24:7** 4714
served beyond the River and in **E**, **Jos 24:14** 4714
fathers up out of the land of **E**, **Jos 24:17** 4714
sons of Israel brought up from **E**, **Jos 24:32** 4714
“I brought you up out of **E** and **Jg 2:1** 4714
brought them out of the land of **E**, **Jg 2:12** 4714
was I who brought you up from **E** and **Jg 6:8** 4714
not the LORD bring us up from **E**?’ **Jg 6:13** 4714
my land when they came up from **E**, **Jg 11:13** 4714
‘For when they came up from **E**, **Jg 11:16** 4714
up from the land of **E** to this day. **Jg 19:30** 4714
in **E** *in bondage* to Pharaoh’s house? **1Sa 2:27** 4714
day that I brought them up from **E** **1Sa 8:8** 4714
‘I brought Israel up from **E**, **1Sa 10:18** 4714
fathers up from the land of **E**. **1Sa 12:6** 4714
“When Jacob went into **E** and your **1Sa 12:8** 4714
fathers out of **E** and settled them **1Sa 12:8** 4714
way while he was coming up from **E**. **1Sa 15:2** 4714
Israel when they came up from **E**.” **1Sa 15:6** 4714
go to Shur, which is east of **E**. **1Sa 15:7** 4714
Shur even as far as the land of **E**. **1Sa 27:8** 4714
“I am a young man of **E**, **1Sa 30:13** 4713
up the sons of Israel from **E**, **2Sa 7:6** 4714
have redeemed for Yourself from **E**, **2Sa 7:23** 4714
alliance with Pharaoh king of **E**, **1Ki 3:1** 4714
and to the border of **E**; **1Ki 4:21** 4714
the east and all the wisdom of **E**. **1Ki 4:30** 4714
Israel came out of the land of **E**, **1Ki 6:1** 4714
they came out of the land of **E**. **1Ki 8:9** 4714
I brought My people Israel from **E**, **1Ki 8:16** 4714
brought them from the land of **E**.” **1Ki 8:21** 4714
You have brought forth from **E**, **1Ki 8:51** 4714
brought our fathers forth from **E**, **1Ki 8:53** 4714
of Hamath to the brook of **E**, **1Ki 8:65** 4714
fathers out of the land of **E**, **1Ki 9:9** 4714
For Pharaoh king of **E** had gone up **1Ki 9:16** 4714
of horses was from **E** and Kue, **1Ki 10:28** 4714
from **E** for 600 *shekels* of silver, **1Ki 10:29** 4714
that Hadad fled to **E**, **1Ki 11:17** 4714
came to **E**, to Pharaoh king of Egypt, **1Ki 11:18** 4714
to Egypt, to Pharaoh king of **E**, **1Ki 11:18** 4714

But when Hadad heard in **E** that **1Ki 11:21** 4714
to **E** to Shishak king of Egypt, **1Ki 11:40** 4714
to Egypt to Shishak king of **E**, **1Ki 11:40** 4714
in **E** until the death of Solomon. **1Ki 11:40** 4714
of it, he was living in **E** **1Ki 12:2** 4714
he was yet in **E**, where he had fled **1Ki 12:2** 4714
you up from the land of **E**.” **1Ki 12:28** 4714
of **E** came up against Jerusalem. **1Ki 14:25** 4714
had sent messengers to So king of **E** **2Ki 17:4** 4714
brought them up from the land of **E** **2Ki 17:7** 4714
the hand of Pharaoh, king of **E**, **2Ki 17:7** 4714
brought you up from the land of **E** **2Ki 17:36** 4714
of this crushed reed, *even* on **E**; **2Ki 18:21** 4714
king of **E** to all who rely on him. **2Ki 18:21** 4714
E for chariots and for horsemen? **2Ki 18:24** 4714
I dried up All the rivers of **E**.” **2Ki 19:24** 4693
the day their fathers came from **E**, **2Ki 21:15** 4714
Pharaoh Neco king of **E** went up **2Ki 23:29** 4714
away and brought *him* to **E**, **2Ki 23:34** 4714
The king of **E** did not come out **2Ki 24:7** 4714
all that belonged to the king of **E** **2Ki 24:7** 4714
brook of **E** to the river Euphrates. **2Ki 24:7** 4714
of the forces arose and went to **E**; **2Ki 25:26** 4714
from the Shihor of **E** even to the **1Ch 13:5** 4714
whom You redeemed out of **E**? **1Ch 17:21** 4714
were imported from **E** and from Kue; **2Ch 1:16** 4714
They imported chariots from **E** **2Ch 1:17** 4714
Israel, when they came out of **E**. **2Ch 5:10** 4714
My people from the land of **E**, **2Ch 6:5** 4714
of Hamath to the brook of **E**. **2Ch 7:8** 4714
brought them from the land of **E**, **2Ch 7:22** 4714
and as far as the border of **E**. **2Ch 9:26** 4714
from **E** and from all countries. **2Ch 9:28** 4714
(for he was in **E** where he had fled **2Ch 10:2** 4714
Jeroboam returned from **E**. **2Ch 10:2** 4714
of **E** came up against Jerusalem **2Ch 12:2** 4714
people who came with him from **E** **2Ch 12:3** 4714
of **E** came up against Jerusalem, **2Ch 12:9** 4714
they came out of the land of **E** **2Ch 20:10** 4714
fame extended to the border of **E**, **2Ch 26:8** 4714
Neco king of **E** came up to make war **2Ch 35:20** 4714
of **E** deposed him at Jerusalem, **2Ch 36:3** 4714
The king of **E** made Eliakim his **2Ch 36:4** 4714
his brother and brought him to **E**. **2Ch 36:4** 4714
affliction of our fathers in **E**, **Ne 9:9** 4714
to return to their slavery in **E**. **Ne 9:17** 4714
God Who brought you up from **E**, **Ne 9:18** 4714
Envoys will come out of **E**; **Ps 68:31** 4714
their fathers In the land of **E**, **Ps 78:12** 4714
When He performed His signs in **E** **Ps 78:43** 4714
And smote all the firstborn in **E**, **Ps 78:51** 4714
You removed a vine from **E**; **Ps 80:8** 4714
he went throughout the land of **E**. **Ps 81:5** 4714
brought you up from the land of **E**; **Ps 81:10** 4714
Israel also came into **E**; **Ps 105:23** 4714
E was glad when they departed, **Ps 105:38** 4714
Our fathers in **E** did not **Ps 106:7** 4714
Who had done great things in **E**, **Ps 106:21** 4714
When Israel went forth from **E**, **Ps 114:1** 4714
He smote the firstborn of **E**, **Ps 135:8** 4714
and wonders into your midst, O **E**, **Ps 135:9** 4714
With colored linens of **E**. **Pr 7:16** 4714
remotest part of the rivers of **E** and **Is 7:18** 4714
staff against you, the way **E** *did.* **Is 10:24** 4714
lift it up the way *He did* in **E**. **Is 10:26** 4714
who will remain, From Assyria, **E**, **Is 11:11** 4714
The tongue of the Sea of **E**; **Is 11:15** 4714
they came up out of the land of **E**. **Is 11:16** 4714
The oracle concerning **E**. **Is 19:1** 4714
cloud and is about to come to **E**; **Is 19:1** 4714
The idols of **E** will tremble at His **Is 19:1** 4714
streams of **E** will thin out and dry up **Is 19:6** 4693
And the pillars *of* **E** will be **Is 19:10** 4714
of hosts Has purposed against **E**. **Is 19:12** 4714
of her tribes Have led **E** astray. **Is 19:13** 4714
led **E** astray in all that it does, **Is 19:14** 4714
work for **E** Which *its* head or tail, **Is 19:15** 4714
Judah will become a terror to **E**; **Is 19:17** 4714
that day five cities in the land of **E** **Is 19:18** 4714
in the midst of the land of **E**, **Is 19:19** 4714
LORD of hosts in the land of **E**; **Is 19:20** 4714
LORD will make Himself known to **E**, **Is 19:21** 4714
The LORD will strike **E**, **Is 19:22** 4714
be a highway from **E** to Assyria, **Is 19:23** 4714
and the Assyrians will come into **E** **Is 19:23** 4714
third *party* with **E** and Assyria, **Is 19:24** 4714
“Blessed is **E** My people, and **Is 19:25** 4714
sign and token against **E** and Cush, **Is 20:3** 4714
of **E** and the exiles of Cush, **Is 20:4** 4714
uncovered, to the shame of **E**. **Is 20:4** 4714
Cush their hope and **E** their boast. **Is 20:5** 4714
When the report *reaches* **E**, **Is 23:5** 4714
the Euphrates to the brook of **E**, **Is 27:12** 4714
who were scattered in the land of **E** **Is 27:13** 4714
Who proceed down to **E** Without **Is 30:2** 4714
seek shelter in the shadow of **E**! **Is 30:2** 4714
the shelter in the shadow of **E**, **Is 30:3** 4714
Even **E**, whose help is vain and **Is 30:7** 4714
those who go down to **E** for help **Is 31:1** 4714
of this crushed reed, *even* on **E**, **Is 36:6** 4714
king of **E** to all who rely on him. **Is 36:6** 4714
E for chariots and for horsemen? **Is 36:9** 4714
I dried up All the rivers of **E**.’ **Is 37:25** 4693
I have given **E** as your ransom, **Is 43:3** 4714
“The products of **E** and the **Is 45:14** 4714
the first into **E** to reside there; **Is 52:4** 4714
us up out of the land of **E**, **Jer 2:6** 4714
are you doing on the road to **E**, **Jer 2:18** 4714
you will be put to shame by **E** As **Jer 2:36** 4714

brought them out of the land of **E**,	**Jer 7:22**	4714
of the land of **E** until this day,	**Jer 7:25**	4714
E and Judah, and Edom and the	**Jer 9:26**	4714
brought them out of the land of **E**,	**Jer 11:4**	4714
them up from the land of **E**,	**Jer 11:7**	4714
of Israel out of the land of **E**,'	**Jer 16:14**	4714
sons of Israel from the land of **E**,'	**Jer 23:7**	4714
ones who dwell in the land of **E**.	**Jer 24:8**	4714
Pharaoh king of **E**, his servants,	**Jer 25:19**	4714
afraid and fled and went to **E**.	**Jer 26:21**	4714
Then King Jehoiakim sent men to **E**:	**Jer 26:22**	4714
certain men with him *went* into **E**.	**Jer 26:22**	4714
And they brought Uriah from **E** and	**Jer 26:23**	4714
bring them out of the land of **E**,	**Jer 31:32**	4714
and wonders in the land of **E**,	**Jer 32:20**	4714
of **E** with signs and with wonders,	**Jer 32:21**	4714
brought them out of the land of **E**,	**Jer 34:13**	4714
Pharaoh's army had set out from **E**;	**Jer 37:5**	4714
to return to its own land of **E**.	**Jer 37:7**	4714
in order to proceed into **E**	**Jer 41:17**	4714
but we will go to the land of **E**,	**Jer 42:14**	4714
really set your mind to enter **E** and	**Jer 42:15**	4714
you there in the land of **E**;	**Jer 42:16**	4714
closely after you there *in* **E**,	**Jer 42:16**	4714
men who set their mind to go to **E**	**Jer 42:17**	4714
out on you when you enter **E**.	**Jer 42:18**	4714
"Do not go into **E**!"	**Jer 42:19**	4714
not to enter **E** to reside there';	**Jer 43:2**	4714
and they entered the land of **E**	**Jer 43:7**	4714
come and strike the land of **E**;	**Jer 43:11**	4714
to the temples of the gods of **E**,	**Jer 43:12**	4714
will wrap himself with the land of **E**	**Jer 43:12**	4714
which is in the land of **E**;	**Jer 43:13**	4714
and the temples of the gods of **E**	**Jer 43:13**	4714
the Jews living in the land of **E**,	**Jer 44:1**	4714
to other gods in the land of **E**,	**Jer 44:8**	4714
the land of **E** to reside there,	**Jer 44:12**	4714
meet their end in the land of **E**;	**Jer 44:12**	4714
those who live in the land of **E**,	**Jer 44:13**	4714
entered the land of **E** to reside there	**Jer 44:14**	4714
in Pathros in the land of **E**,	**Jer 44:15**	4714
Judah who are in the land of **E**,	**Jer 44:24**	4714
who are living in the land of **E**,	**Jer 44:26**	4714
man of Judah in all the land of **E**,	**Jer 44:26**	4714
of Judah who are in the land of **E**	**Jer 44:27**	4714
sword will return out of the land of **E**	**Jer 44:28**	4714
have gone to the land of **E** to reside	**Jer 44:28**	4714
of **E** to the hand of his enemies,	**Jer 44:30**	4714
To **E**, concerning the army of	**Jer 46:2**	4714
army of Pharaoh Neco king of **E**,	**Jer 46:2**	4714
E rises like the Nile, Even like	**Jer 46:8**	4714
balm, O virgin daughter of **E**!	**Jer 46:11**	4714
of Babylon to smite the land of **E**:	**Jer 46:13**	4714
in **E** and proclaim in Migdol,	**Jer 46:14**	4714
king of **E** *is but* a big noise;	**Jer 46:17**	4714
exile, O daughter dwelling in **E**,	**Jer 46:19**	4714
"**E** is a pretty heifer, *But* a	**Jer 46:20**	4714
of **E** has been put to shame,	**Jer 46:24**	4714
and **E** along with her gods and her	**Jer 46:25**	4714
We have submitted to **E** *and* Assyria	**La 5:6**	4714
by sending his envoys to **E**	**Ezk 17:15**	4714
him with hooks To the land of **E**.	**Ezk 19:4**	4714
known to them in the land of **E**,	**Ezk 20:5**	4714
to bring them out from the land of **E**	**Ezk 20:6**	4714
yourselves with the idols of **E**;	**Ezk 20:7**	4714
did they forsake the idols of **E**.	**Ezk 20:8**	4714
in the midst of the land of **E**.	**Ezk 20:8**	4714
them out of the land of **E**.	**Ezk 20:9**	4714
"So I took them out of the land of **E**	**Ezk 20:10**	4714
the wilderness of the land of **E**,	**Ezk 20:36**	4714
and they played the harlot in **E**,	**Ezk 23:3**	4714
her harlotries from *the time in* **E**;	**Ezk 23:8**	4714
the harlot in the land of **E**.	**Ezk 23:19**	4714
harlotry *brought* from the land of **E**	**Ezk 23:27**	4714
to them or remember **E** anymore.'	**Ezk 23:27**	4714
was of fine embroidered linen from **E**	**Ezk 27:7**	4714
face against Pharaoh king of **E**	**Ezk 29:2**	4714
against him and against all **E**.	**Ezk 29:2**	4714
against you, Pharaoh king of **E**,	**Ezk 29:3**	4714
of **E** will know that I am the LORD,	**Ezk 29:6**	4714
land of **E** will become a desolation	**Ezk 29:9**	4714
E an utter waste and desolation,	**Ezk 29:10**	4714
"So I will make the land of **E** a	**Ezk 29:12**	4714
"I will turn the fortunes of **E**	**Ezk 29:14**	4714
of their having turned to **E**.	**Ezk 29:16**	
I will give the land of **E** to	**Ezk 29:19**	4714
"I have given him the land of **E**	**Ezk 29:20**	4714
"A sword will come upon **E**,	**Ezk 30:4**	4714
When the slain fall in **E**,	**Ezk 30:4**	4714
those who support **E** will fall And	**Ezk 30:6**	4714
When I set a fire in **E** And all her	**Ezk 30:8**	4714
be on them as on the day of **E**;	**Ezk 30:9**	4714
also make the hordes of **E** cease	**Ezk 30:10**	4714
they will draw their swords against **E**	**Ezk 30:11**	4714
be a prince in the land of **E**;	**Ezk 30:13**	4714
I will put fear in the land of **E**.	**Ezk 30:13**	4714
wrath on Sin, The stronghold of **E**;	**Ezk 30:15**	4714
"I will set a fire in **E**;	**Ezk 30:16**	4714
I break there the yoke bars of **E**.	**Ezk 30:18**	4714
I will execute judgments on **E**,	**Ezk 30:19**	4714
the arm of Pharaoh king of **E**;	**Ezk 30:21**	4714
king of **E** and will break his arms,	**Ezk 30:22**	4714
it out against the land of **E**.	**Ezk 30:25**	4714
of man, say to Pharaoh king of **E** and	**Ezk 31:2**	4714
over Pharaoh king of **E** and	**Ezk 32:2**	4714
will devastate the pride of **E**,	**Ezk 32:12**	4714
I make the land of **E** a desolation,	**Ezk 32:15**	4714
Over **E** and over all her hordes	**Ezk 32:16**	4714
man, wail for the hordes of **E**	**Ezk 32:18**	4714
to the brook *of* **E** *and* to	**Ezk 47:19**	
to the brook *of* **E**, to the Great	**Ezk 48:28**	
Your people out of the land of **E**	**Da 9:15**	4714
he will take into captivity to **E**,	**Da 11:8**	4714
and the land of **E** will not escape.	**Da 11:42**	4714
over all the precious things of **E**;	**Da 11:43**	4714
she came up from the land of **E**.	**Hos 2:15**	4714
They call to **E**, they go to Assyria.	**Hos 7:11**	4714
their derision in the land of **E**.	**Hos 7:16**	4714
They will return to **E**.	**Hos 8:13**	4714
But Ephraim will return to **E**,	**Hos 9:3**	4714
E will gather them up, Memphis	**Hos 9:6**	4714
him, And out of **E** I called My son.	**Hos 11:1**	4714
will not return to the land of **E**;	**Hos 11:5**	4714
come trembling like birds from **E** And	**Hos 11:11**	4714
Assyria, And oil is carried to **E**.	**Hos 12:1**	4714
LORD your God since the land of **E**;	**Hos 12:9**	4714
the LORD brought Israel from **E**,	**Hos 12:13**	4714
LORD your God Since the land of **E**;	**Hos 13:4**	4714
E will become a waste, And Edom	**Jl 3:19**	4714
brought you up from the land of **E**,	**Am 2:10**	4714
He brought up from the land of **E**:	**Am 3:1**	4714
citadels in the land of **E** and say,	**Am 3:9**	4714
among you after the manner of **E**;	**Am 4:10**	4714
And subside like the Nile of **E**.	**Am 8:8**	4714
And subsides like the Nile of **E**;	**Am 9:5**	4714
up Israel from the land of **E**,	**Am 9:7**	4714
I brought you up from the land of **E**	**Mi 6:4**	4714
From Assyria and the cities of **E**,	**Mi 7:12**	4693
From **E** even to the Euphrates,	**Mi 7:12**	4693
you came out from the land of **E**,	**Mi 7:15**	4714
Ethiopia was *her* might, And **E** too,	**Na 3:9**	4714
I made you when you came out of **E**,	**Hg 2:5**	4714
them back from the land of **E** And	**Zch 10:10**	4714
And the scepter of **E** will depart.	**Zch 10:11**	4714
of **E** does not go up or enter,	**Zch 14:18**	4714
This will be the punishment of **E**,	**Zch 14:19**	4714
and His mother and flee to **E**,	**Mt 2:13**	*125*
while it was still night, and left for **E**.	**Mt 2:14**	*125*
"OUT OF **E** I CALLED MY SON."	**Mt 2:15**	*125*
in a dream to Joseph in **E**,	**Mt 2:19**	*125*
E and the districts of Libya	**Ac 2:10**	*125*
of Joseph and sold him into **E**.	**Ac 7:9**	*125*
the sight of Pharaoh, king of **E**,	**Ac 7:10**	*125*
over **E** and all his household.	**Ac 7:10**	*125*
famine came over all **E** and Canaan,	**Ac 7:11**	*125*
heard that there was grain in **E**,	**Ac 7:12**	*125*
down to **E** and *there* he and our	**Ac 7:15**	*125*
increased and multiplied in **E**,	**Ac 7:17**	*125*
THERE AROSE ANOTHER KING OVER **E**	**Ac 7:18**	*125*
THE OPPRESSION OF MY PEOPLE IN **E**	**Ac 7:34**	*125*
NOW, AND I WILL SEND YOU TO **E**.'	**Ac 7:34**	*125*
wonders and signs in the land of **E**	**Ac 7:36**	*125*
in their hearts turned back to **E**,	**Ac 7:39**	*125*
WHO LED US OUT OF THE LAND OF **E**	**Ac 7:40**	*125*
their stay in the land of **E**,	**Ac 13:17**	*125*
who came out of **E** *led* by Moses?	**Heb 3:16**	*125*
LEAD THEM OUT OF THE LAND OF **E**;	**Heb 8:9**	*125*
riches than the treasures of **E**;	**Heb 11:26**	*125*
By faith he left **E**,	**Heb 11:27**	*125*
a people out of the land of **E**,	**Jude 1:5**	*125*
mystically is called Sodom and **E**,	**Rv 11:8**	*125*

EGYPTIAN

an **E** maid whose name was Hagar.	**Gn 16:1**	4713
wife Sarai took Hagar the **E**,	**Gn 16:3**	4713
Sarah saw the son of Hagar the **E**,	**Gn 21:9**	4713
Abraham's son, whom Hagar the **E**,	**Gn 25:12**	4713
Potiphar, an **E** officer of Pharaoh,	**Gn 39:1**	4713
in the house of his master, the **E**.	**Gn 39:2**	4713
for every **E** sold his field,	**Gn 47:20**	4714
women are not as the **E** women;	**Ex 1:19**	4713
and he saw an **E** beating a Hebrew,	**Ex 2:11**	4713
he struck down the **E** and hid him	**Ex 2:12**	4713
to kill me as you killed the **E**?"	**Ex 2:14**	4713
"An **E** delivered us from the hand	**Ex 2:19**	4713
woman, whose father was an **E**,	**Lv 24:10**	4713
you shall not detest an **E**,	**Dt 23:7**	4713
Now they found an **E** in the field	**1Sa 30:11**	4713
He killed an **E**,	**2Sa 23:21**	4713
Now the **E** *had* a spear in his hand,	**2Sa 23:21**	4713
an **E** servant whose name was Jarha.	**1Ch 2:34**	4713
He killed an **E**,	**1Ch 11:23**	4713
oppressed by striking down the **E**.	**Ac 7:24**	*124*
ME AS YOU KILLED THE **E** YESTERDAY,	**Ac 7:28**	*124*
"Then you are not the **E** who some	**Ac 21:38**	*124*

EGYPTIAN'S

the **E** house on account of Joseph;	**Gn 39:5**	4713
the spear from the **E** hand and	**2Sa 23:21**	4713
Now in the **E** hand *was* a spear like	**1Ch 11:23**	4713
the spear from the **E** hand and	**1Ch 11:23**	4713

EGYPTIANS

when the **E** see you,	**Gn 12:12**	4713
the **E** saw that the woman was very	**Gn 12:14**	4713
and Pharaoh said to all the **E**,	**Gn 41:55**	4714
storehouses, and sold to the **E**;	**Gn 41:56**	4714
and them by themselves, and the **E** who	**Gn 43:32**	4713
because the **E** could not eat bread	**Gn 43:32**	4713
for that is loathsome to the **E**.	**Gn 43:32**	4714
so loudly that the **E** heard *it*,	**Gn 45:2**	4714
shepherd is loathsome to the **E**."	**Gn 46:34**	4714
all the **E** came to Joseph and said,	**Gn 47:15**	4714
the **E** wept for him seventy days.	**Gn 50:3**	4714
a grievous mourning for the **E**."	**Gn 50:11**	4714
The **E** compelled the sons of	**Ex 1:13**	4714
them from the power of the **E**,	**Ex 3:8**	4714
which the **E** are oppressing them.	**Ex 3:9**	4714
favor in the sight of the **E**;	**Ex 3:21**	4714
Thus you will plunder the **E**."	**Ex 3:22**	4714
the **E** are holding them in bondage,	**Ex 6:5**	4714
from under the burdens of the **E**,	**Ex 6:6**	4714
from under the burdens of the **E**.	**Ex 6:7**	4714
E shall know that I am the LORD,	**Ex 7:5**	4714
and the **E** will find difficulty in	**Ex 7:18**	4714
so that the **E** could not drink	**Ex 7:21**	4714
So all the **E** dug around the Nile	**Ex 7:24**	4714
and the houses of the **E** will be	**Ex 8:21**	4714
what is an abomination to the **E**.	**Ex 8:26**	4714
to the **E** before their eyes,	**Ex 8:26**	4714
magicians as well as on all the **E**.	**Ex 9:11**	4714
how I made a mockery of the **E** and	**Ex 10:2**	4714
and the houses of all the **E**,	**Ex 10:6**	4714
favor in the sight of the **E**.	**Ex 11:3**	4714
will pass through to smite the **E**;	**Ex 12:23**	4714
in Egypt when He smote the **E**,	**Ex 12:27**	4714
all his servants and all the **E**,	**Ex 12:30**	4714
The **E** urged the people, to	**Ex 12:33**	4714
requested from the **E** articles of silver	**Ex 12:35**	4714
favor in the sight of the **E**,	**Ex 12:36**	4714
Thus they plundered the **E**.	**Ex 12:36**	4714
E will know that I am the LORD."	**Ex 14:4**	4714
Then the **E** chased after them *with*	**Ex 14:9**	4714
the **E** were marching after them,	**Ex 14:10**	4714
us alone that we may serve the **E**'?	**Ex 14:12**	4714
been better for us to serve the **E**	**Ex 14:12**	4714
the **E** whom you have seen today,	**Ex 14:13**	4714
I will harden the hearts of the **E** so	**Ex 14:17**	4714
E will know that I am the LORD,	**Ex 14:18**	4714
Then the **E** took up the pursuit,	**Ex 14:23**	4714
looked down on the army of the **E**	**Ex 14:24**	4714
the army of the **E** into confusion.	**Ex 14:24**	4714
the **E** said, "Let us flee from Israel,	**Ex 14:25**	4714
fighting for them against the **E**."	**Ex 14:25**	4714
waters may come back over the **E**,	**Ex 14:26**	4714
the **E** were fleeing right into it;	**Ex 14:27**	4714
the **E** in the midst of the sea.	**Ex 14:27**	4714
that day from the hand of the **E**,	**Ex 14:30**	4714
saw the **E** dead on the seashore.	**Ex 14:30**	4714
the LORD had used against the **E**,	**Ex 14:31**	4714
on you which I have put on the **E**;	**Ex 15:26**	4714
and to the **E** for Israel's sake,	**Ex 18:8**	4714
them from the hand of the **E**.	**Ex 18:9**	4714
you from the hand of the **E**	**Ex 18:10**	4714
from under the hand of the **E**.	**Ex 18:10**	4714
have seen what I did to the **E**,	**Ex 19:4**	4714
"Why should the **E** speak, saying,	**Ex 32:12**	4714
"Then the **E** will hear of it, for	**Nu 14:13**	4714
and the **E** treated us and our	**Nu 20:15**	4714
boldly in the sight of all the **E**,	**Nu 33:3**	4714
while the **E** were burying all their	**Nu 33:4**	4714
'And the **E** treated us harshly and	**Dt 26:6**	4713
darkness between you and the **E**,	**Jos 24:7**	4713
you from the hands of the **E**	**Jg 6:9**	4714
"*Did I* not *deliver you* from the **E**,	**Jg 10:11**	4714
These are the gods who smote the **E**	**1Sa 4:8**	4714
do you harden your hearts as the **E**	**1Sa 6:6**	4714
you from the hand of the **E** and	**1Sa 10:18**	4714
Hittites and the kings of the **E**,	**2Ki 7:6**	4714
Ammonites, the Moabites, the **E** and	**Ezr 9:1**	4713
smote the **E** in their firstborn,	**Ps 136:10**	4714
the heart of the **E** will melt within	**Is 19:1**	4714
I will incite **E** against Egyptians;	**Is 19:2**	4714
I will incite Egyptians against **E**;	**Is 19:2**	4714
"Then the spirit of the **E** will be	**Is 19:3**	4714
I will deliver the **E** into the hand	**Is 19:4**	4714
day the **E** will become like women,	**Is 19:16**	4714
and the **E** will know the LORD in	**Is 19:21**	4714
into Egypt and the **E** into Assyria,	**Is 19:23**	4714
and the **E** will worship with the	**Is 19:23**	4714
Now the **E** are men and not God,	**Is 31:3**	4714
also played the harlot with the **E**,	**Ezk 16:26**	4714
when the **E** handled your bosom	**Ezk 23:21**	4714
and I will scatter the **E** among	**Ezk 29:12**	4714
I will gather the **E** from the peoples	**Ezk 29:13**	4714
'I will scatter the **E** among	**Ezk 30:23**	4714
'When I scatter the **E** among the	**Ezk 30:26**	4714
in all the learning of the **E**,	**Ac 7:22**	*124*
and the **E**, when they attempted it,	**Heb 11:29**	*124*

EGYPT'S

one end of **E** border to the other.	**Gn 47:21**	4714
and what He did to **E** army,	**Dt 11:4**	4714

EHI

Gera and Naaman, **E** and Rosh,	**Gn 46:21**	278

EHUD

for them, **E** the son of Gera,	**Jg 3:15**	164
E made himself a sword which	**Jg 3:16**	164
E came to him while he was	**Jg 3:20**	164
E said, "I have a message from God	**Jg 3:20**	164
E stretched out his left hand,	**Jg 3:21**	164
Then **E** went out into the vestibule	**Jg 3:23**	164
Now **E** escaped while they were	**Jg 3:26**	164
sight of the LORD, after **E** died.	**Jg 4:1**	164
of Bilhan *were* Jeush, Benjamin, **E**,	**1Ch 7:10**	164
These are the sons of **E**:	**1Ch 8:6**	261

EIGHT

of Seth were **e** hundred years,	**Gn 5:4**	8083
Then Seth lived **e** hundred and	**Gn 5:7**	8083
Then Enosh lived **e** hundred and	**Gn 5:10**	8083
Then Kenan lived **e** hundred and	**Gn 5:13**	8083
Then Mahalalel lived **e** hundred and	**Gn 5:16**	8083
e hundred and ninety-five years,	**Gn 5:17**	8083
Then Jared lived **e** hundred years	**Gn 5:19**	8083
who is **e** days old shall be circumcised	**Gn 17:12**	8083
son Isaac when he was **e** days old,	**Gn 21:4**	8083
these **e** Milcah bore to Nahor,	**Gn 22:23**	8083
"There shall be **e** boards with	**Ex 26:25**	8083
There were **e** boards with their	**Ex 36:30**	8083

and four carts and **e** oxen he gave Nu 7:8 8083
e bulls, two rams, fourteen male Nu 29:29 8083
served Cushan-rishathaim **e** years. Jg 3:8 8083
and he judged Israel **e** years. Jg 12:14 8083
name was Jesse, and he had **e** sons. 1Sa 17:12 8083
because of **e** hundred slain *by him* 2Sa 23:8 8083
and there were in Israel **e** hundred 2Sa 24:9 8083
ten cubits and stones of **e** cubits. 1Ki 7:10 8083
he reigned **e** years in Jerusalem. 2Ki 8:17 8083
e years old when he became king, 2Ki 22:1 8083
and **e** of the descendants of 1Ch 24:4 8083
he reigned **e** years in Jerusalem. 2Ch 21:5 8083
he reigned in Jerusalem **e** years; 2Ch 21:20 8083
the house of the LORD in **e** days, 2Ch 29:17 8083
e years old when he became king, 2Ch 34:1 8083
e years old when he became king, 2Ch 36:9 8083
portion to seven, or even to **e**, Ec 11:2 8083
escaped from Johanan with **e** men Jer 41:15 8083
the porch of the gate, **e** cubits; Ezk 40:9 8083
and its stairway *had* **e** steps. Ezk 40:31 8083
and its stairway *had* **e** steps. Ezk 40:34 8083
and its stairway had **e** steps. Ezk 40:37 8083
e tables on which they slaughter Ezk 40:41 8083
shepherds and **e** leaders of men. Mi 5:5 8083
And when **e** days had passed, Lk 2:21 *3638*
Some **e** days after these sayings, Lk 9:28 *3638*
After **e** days His disciples were again Jn 20:26 *3638*
who had been bedridden **e** years, Ac 9:33 *3638*
than **e** or ten days among them, Ac 25:6 *3638*
which a few, that is, **e** persons, 1Pe 3:20 *3638*

EIGHTEEN
in his house, three hundred and **e**, Gn 14:14 8083, 6240
Eglon the king of Moab **e** years. Jg 3:14 8083, 6240
for **e** years they *afflicted* all the Jg 10:8 8083, 6240
e cubits was the height of one 1Ki 7:15 8083, 6240
e years old when he became king, 2Ki 24:8 8083, 6240
of the one pillar was **e** cubits, 2Ki 25:17 8083, 6240
For he had taken **e** wives and sixty 2Ch 11:21 8083, 6240
of each pillar *was* **e** cubits, Jer 52:21 8083, 6240
"Or do you suppose that those **e** Lk 13:4 *1178a*
there was a woman who for **e** years Lk 13:11 *1178a*
Satan has bound for **e** long years, Lk 13:16 *1176, 3638*

EIGHTEENTH
in the **e** year of King Jeroboam, 1Ki 15:1 8083, 6240
e year of Jehoshaphat king of Judah, 2Ki 3:1 8083, 6240
in the **e** year of King Josiah, 2Ki 22:3 8083, 6240
But in the **e** year of King Josiah, 2Ki 23:23 8083, 6240
for Hezir, the **e** for Happizzez, 1Ch 24:15 8083, 6240
for the **e** to Hanani, his sons and 1Ch 25:25 8083, 6240
In the **e** year of King Jeroboam, 2Ch 13:1 8083, 6240
Now in the **e** year of his reign, 2Ch 34:8 8083, 6240
In the **e** year of Josiah's reign 2Ch 35:19 8083, 6240
was the **e** year of Nebuchadnezzar. Jer 32:1 8083, 6240
in the **e** year of Nebuchadnezzar Jer 52:29 8083, 6240

EIGHTH
the **e** day you shall give it to Me. Ex 22:30 8066
Now it came about on the **e** day Lv 9:1 8066
'On the **e** day the flesh of his Lv 12:3 8066
"Now on the **e** day he is to take Lv 14:10 8066
"Then the **e** day he shall bring Lv 14:23 8066
'Then on the **e** day he shall take Lv 15:14 8066
'Then on the **e** day she shall take Lv 15:29 8066
and from the **e** day on it shall be Lv 22:27 8066
On the **e** day you shall have a holy Lv 23:36 8066
first day and a rest on the **e** day. Lv 23:39 8066
'When you are sowing the **e** year, Lv 25:22 8066
'Then on the **e** day he shall bring Nu 6:10 8066
On the **e** day *it was* Gamaliel the Nu 7:54 8066
'On the **e** day you shall have a Nu 29:35 8066
of Bul, which is the **e** month, 1Ki 6:38 8066
On the **e** day he sent the people 1Ki 8:66 8066
Jeroboam instituted a feast in the **e** 1Ki 12:32 8066
the fifteenth day in the **e** month, 1Ki 12:33 8066
in the **e** year of his reign. 2Ki 24:12 8083
Johanan the **e**, Elzabad the ninth, 1Ch 12:12 8066
for Hakkoz, the **e** for Abijah, 1Ch 24:10 8066
the **e** to Jeshaiah, his sons and 1Ch 25:15 8066
the seventh *and* Peullethai the **e**; 1Ch 26:5 8066
The **e** for the eighth month *was* 1Ch 27:11 8066
The eighth for the **e** month *was* 1Ch 27:11 8066
On the **e** day they held a 2Ch 7:9 8066
and on the **e** day of the month they 2Ch 29:17 8083
For in the **e** year of his reign 2Ch 34:3 8083
and on the **e** day *there was* a Ne 8:18 8066
be that on the **e** day and onward, Ezk 43:27 8066
In the **e** month of the second year Zch 1:1 8066
And it happened that on the **e** Lk 1:59 *3590*
and circumcised him on the **e** day; Ac 7:8 *3590*
circumcised the **e** day, of the Php 3:5 *3637*
and is not, is himself also an **e** and Rv 17:11 *3590*
the seventh, chrysolite; the **e**, beryl; Rv 21:20 *3590*

EIGHTIETH
in the four hundred and **e** year after 1Ki 6:1 8084

EIGHTY
were one hundred and **e** years. Gn 35:28 8084
Moses was **e** years old and Ex 7:7 8084
land was undisturbed for **e** years. Jg 3:30 8084
was very old, being **e** years old; 2Sa 19:32 8084
"I am now **e** years old. 2Sa 19:35 8084
was sold for **e** *shekels* of silver, 2Ki 6:25 8084
for himself **e** men outside, 2Ki 10:24 8084
with him **e** priests of the LORD, 2Ch 26:17 8084
Or if due to strength, **e** years, Ps 90:10 8084
are sixty queens and **e** concubines, SS 6:8 8084
that **e** men came from Shechem, from Jer 41:5 8084
'Take your bill, and write **e**.' Lk 16:7 *3589*

EIGHTY-FIVE
behold, I am **e** years old today. Jos 14:10 8084
e men who wore the linen ephod. 1Sa 22:18 8084

EIGHTY-FOUR
then as a widow to the age of **e**. Lk 2:37 *3589, 5064*

EIGHTY-SEVEN
lived one hundred and **e** years, Gn 5:25 8084

EIGHTY-SIX
Abram was **e** years old when Gn 16:16 8084

EIGHTY-THREE
was eighty years old and Aaron **e**, Ex 7:7 8084

EIGHTY-TWO
Methuselah lived seven hundred and **e** Gn 5:26 8084
lived one hundred and **e** years, Gn 5:28 8084

EITHER
speak to Jacob **e** good or bad." Gn 31:24 4480
to speak **e** good or bad to Jacob.' Gn 31:29 4480
required amount **e** yesterday or today Ex 5:14 1571
any blood, **e** of bird or animal, Lv 7:26
e in the warp or in the woof, Lv 13:53 176
'The nakedness of your sister, **e** Lv 18:9
shall value it as **e** good or bad; Lv 27:12 996
shall value it as **e** good or bad; Lv 27:14 996
not do anything, **e** small or great, Nu 22:18
of the LORD, **e** good or bad, Nu 24:13
a sacrifice, **e** an ox or a sheep, Dt 18:3 518
LORD has not chosen this one **e**." 1Sa 16:8 1571
LORD has not chosen this one **e**." 1Sa 16:9 1571
my father does nothing **e** great or 1Sa 20:2
the meal, **e** yesterday or today?" 1Sa 20:27 1571
e by dreams or by Urim or by 1Sa 28:6 1571
e through prophets or by dreams; 1Sa 28:15 1571
not speak to Amnon **e** good or bad; 2Sa 13:22 5704
e he is occupied or gone aside, or 1Ki 18:27 3588
e three years of famine, or three 1Ch 21:12 518
The foolish man **e** rages or laughs, Pr 29:9
For if **e** of them falls, the one Ec 4:10
No one would despise me, **e**. SS 8:1 1571
e *their* sons or *their* daughters. Ezk 14:16 518
e *their* sons or *their* daughters, Ezk 14:18
e *their* son or *their* daughter. Ezk 14:20 518
prince shall have *land* on **e** side of Ezk 45:7 2088
make no oath at all, **e** by heaven, Mt 5:34 *3383*
for **e** he will hate the one and Mt 6:24 *2228*
be forgiven him, **e** in this age or Mt 12:32 *3777*
"**E** make the tree good and its Mt 12:33 *2228*
but they did not believe them **e**. Mk 16:13 *3761*
not withhold your shirt from him **e**. Lk 6:29 *2532*
"It is useless **e** for the soil or Lk 14:35 *3777*
for **e** he will hate the one and Lk 16:13 *2228*
e. Go. From now on sin no more."] Jn 8:11 *3761*
Him two other men, one on **e** side, Jn 19:18 *1782*
"I have committed no offense **e** Ac 25:8 *3777*
obey, **e** of sin resulting in death, Ro 6:16 *2273*
spare you, **e**. Ro 11:21 *3761*
Give no offense **e** to Jews or to 1Co 10:32 *2532*
unless I speak to you **e** by way of 1Co 14:6 *2228*
lifeless things, **e** flute or harp, 1Co 14:7 *1535a*
men, **e** from you or from others, 1Th 2:6 *3777*
disturbed **e** by a spirit or a message 2Th 2:2 *3383*
not to eat, **e**. 2Th 3:10 *3366*
not understand **e** what they are saying 1Tm 1:7 *3383*
cannot take anything out of it **e**. 1Tm 6:7 *3761*
e by heaven or by earth or with Jas 5:12 *3383*
e, and he forbids those who desire 3Jn 1:10 *3777*
e the name of the beast or Rv 13:17
On **e** side of the river was the Rv 22:2 *1782*

EKER
were Maaz, Jamin and **E**. 1Ch 2:27 6134

EKRON
as the border of **E** to the north Jos 13:3 6138
to the side of **E** northward. Jos 15:11 6138
E, with its towns and its villages; Jos 15:45 6138
from **E** even to the sea, all that Jos 15:46 6138
and Elon and Timnah and **E**, Jos 19:43 6138
and **E** with its territory. Jg 1:18 6138
So they sent the ark of God to **E**. 1Sa 5:10 6138
to **E** the Ekronites cried out, 1Sa 5:10 6138
it, they returned to **E** that day. 1Sa 6:16 6138
Ashkelon, one for Gath, one for **E**; 1Sa 6:17 6138
to Israel, from **E** even to Gath; 1Sa 7:14 6138
the valley, and to the gates of **E**. 1Sa 17:52 6138
to Shaaraim, even to Gath and **E**. 1Sa 17:52 6138
of Baal-zebub, the god of **E**, 2Ki 1:2 6138
of Baal-zebub, the god of **E**?' 2Ki 1:3 6138
of Baal-zebub, the god of **E**? 2Ki 1:6 6138
inquire of Baal-zebub, the god of **E** 2Ki 1:16 6138
(even Ashkelon, Gaza, **E** and Jer 25:20 6138
will even unleash My power upon **E**, Am 1:8 6138
at noon And **E** will be uprooted. Zph 2:4 6138
Also **E**, for her expectation has Zch 9:5 6138
in Judah, And **E** like a Jebusite. Zch 9:7 6138

EKRONITE
Ashkelonite, the Gittite, the **E**; Jos 13:3 6139

EKRONITES
to Ekron the **E** cried out, 1Sa 5:10 6139

ELA
Shimei the son of **E**, 1Ki 4:18 414

ELAH
chief Oholibamah, chief **E**, Gn 36:41 425
and camped in the valley of **E**, 1Sa 17:2 424
of Israel are in the valley of **E**, 1Sa 17:19 424
you killed in the valley of **E**, 1Sa 21:9 424
and **E** his son became king in his 1Ki 16:6 425
E the son of Baasha became king 1Ki 16:8 425
Baasha and the sins of **E** his son, 1Ki 16:13 425
the acts of **E** and all that he did, 1Ki 16:14 425
And Hoshea the son of **E** made a 2Ki 15:30 425
Hoshea the son of **E** became king 2Ki 17:1 425
the son of **E** king of Israel, 2Ki 18:1 425
of Hoshea the son of **E** king of Israel, 2Ki 18:9 425
chief Oholibamah, chief **E**, 1Ch 1:52 425
of Jephunneh *were* Iru, **E** and Naam; 1Ch 4:15 425
and the son of **E** *was* Kenaz. 1Ch 4:15 425
of Jeroham, and **E** the son of Uzzi, 1Ch 9:8 425

ELAM
The sons of Shem *were* **E** and Asshur Gn 10:22 5867a
Ellasar, Chedorlaomer king of **E**, Gn 14:1 5867a
against Chedorlaomer king of **E** and Gn 14:9 5867a
The sons of Shem *were* **E**, 1Ch 1:17 5867a
Hananiah, **E**, Anthothijah, 1Ch 8:24 5867b
E the fifth, Johanan the sixth, 1Ch 26:3 5867b
the sons of **E**, 1,254; Ezr 2:7 5867b
the sons of the other **E**, Ezr 2:31 5867b
and of the sons of **E**, Ezr 8:7 5867b
of Jehiel, one of the sons of **E**, Ezr 10:2 5867b
and of the sons of **E**: Ezr 10:26 5867b
the sons of **E**, 1,254; Ne 7:12 5867b
the sons of the other **E**, Ne 7:34 5867b
Parosh, Pahath-moab, **E**, Ne 10:14 5867b
Uzzi, Jehohanan, Malchijah, **E** and Ne 12:42 5867b
Assyria, Egypt, Pathros, Cush, **E**, Is 11:11 5867a
Go up, **E**, lay siege, Media; Is 21:2 5867a
E took up the quiver With the Is 22:6 5867a
of Zimri, all the kings of **E** and Jer 25:25 5867a
Jeremiah the prophet concerning **E**, Jer 49:34 5867a
I am going to break the bow of **E**, Jer 49:35 5867a
'I will bring upon **E** the four Jer 49:36 5867a
the outcasts of **E** will not go. Jer 49:36 5867a
'So I will shatter **E** before their Jer 49:37 5867a
'Then I will set My throne in **E** Jer 49:38 5867a
restore the fortunes of **E**,' " Jer 49:39 5867a
"**E** is there and all her hordes Ezk 32:24 5867a
which is in the province of **E**; Da 8:2 5867a

ELAMITES
the men of Susa, that is, the **E**, Ezr 4:9 5962
"Parthians and Medes and **E**, Ac 2:9 *1639*

ELAPSE
seven days shall **e** for him. Ezk 44:26 5608

ELAPSED
Now there **e** an interval of about Ac 5:7 *1096*
When many days had **e**, Ac 9:23 *4137*
Now when several days had **e**, Ac 25:13 *1230*

ELASAH
Ishmael, Nethanel, Jozabad and **E**. Ezr 10:22 501
the hand of **E** the son of Shaphan, Jer 29:3 501

ELATH
away from **E** and from Ezion-geber. Dt 2:8 365a
built **E** and restored it to Judah after 2Ki 14:22 365a
king of Aram recovered **E** for Aram, 2Ki 16:6 365a
the Judeans out of **E** entirely; 2Ki 16:6 359
and the Arameans came to **E** and 2Ki 16:6 365a

EL-BERITH
inner chamber of the temple of **E**. Jg 9:46 410, 1285

EL-BETHEL
there, and called the place **E**, Gn 35:7 416

ELBOW
And my arm be broken off at the **e**. Jb 31:22 7070

ELDAAH
Epher and Hanoch and Abida and **E**. Gn 25:4 420
Epher, Hanoch, Abida and **E**. 1Ch 1:33 420

ELDAD
the name of one was **E** and the name Nu 11:26 419
"**E** and Medad are prophesying in Nu 11:27 419

ELDER
best garments of Esau her **e** son, Gn 27:15 1419
Now when the words of her **e** son Gn 27:42 1419
prophet, The diviner and the **e**, Is 3:2 2205
youth will storm against the **e** And Is 3:5 2205
head is the **e** and honorable man, Is 9:15 2205
the **e** and Oholibah her sister. Ezk 23:4 1419
receive an accusation against an **e** 1Tm 5:19 *4245*
as *your* fellow **e** and witness of 1Pe 5:1 *4850*
The **e** to the chosen lady and her 2Jn 1:1 *4245*
The **e** to the beloved Gaius, whom I 3Jn 1:1 *4245*

ELDERS
the **e** of his household and all the Gn 50:7 2205
all the **e** of the land of Egypt, Gn 50:7 2205
gather the **e** of Israel together and Ex 3:16 2205
and you with the **e** of Israel will Ex 3:18 2205
all the **e** of the sons of Israel; Ex 4:29 2205
called for all the **e** of Israel and Ex 12:21 2205
with you some of the **e** of Israel; Ex 17:5 2205

in the sight of the e of Israel. **Ex 17:6** 2205
and Aaron came with all the e of **Ex 18:12** 2205
and called the e of the people, **Ex 19:7** 2205
and seventy of the e of Israel, **Ex 24:1** 2205
and seventy of the e of Israel, **Ex 24:9** 2205
But to the e he said, **Ex 24:14** 2205
'Then the e of the congregation **Lv 4:15** 2205
and his sons and the e of Israel; **Lv 9:1** 2205
seventy men from the e of Israel, **Nu 11:16** 2205
whom you know to be the e of the **Nu 11:16** 2205
men of the e of the people, **Nu 11:24** 2205
and placed *Him* upon the seventy e. **Nu 11:25** 2205
camp, *both* he and the e of Israel. **Nu 11:30** 2205
the e of Israel following him, **Nu 16:25** 2205
Moab said to the e of Midian, **Nu 22:4** 2205
So the e of Moab and the elders of **Nu 22:7** 2205
So the elders of Moab and the e of **Nu 22:7** 2205
heads of your tribes and your e. **Dt 5:23** 2205
then the e of his city shall send **Dt 19:12** 2205
then your e and your judges shall **Dt 21:2** 2205
man, that is, the e of that city, **Dt 21:3** 2205
and the e of that city shall bring **Dt 21:4** 2205
"All the e of that city which **Dt 21:6** 2205
and bring him out to the e of his **Dt 21:19** 2205
shall say to the e of his city, **Dt 21:20** 2205
to the e of the city at the gate. **Dt 22:15** 2205
girl's father shall say to the e, **Dt 22:16** 2205
garment before the e of the city. **Dt 22:17** 2205
"So the e of that city shall take **Dt 22:18** 2205
up to the gate to the e and say, **Dt 25:7** 2205
'Then the e of his city shall **Dt 25:8** 2205
come to him in the sight of the e, **Dt 25:9** 2205
e of Israel charged the people, **Dt 27:1** 2205
tribes, your e and your officers, **Dt 29:10** 2205
LORD, and to all the e of Israel. **Dt 31:9** 2205
"Assemble to me all the e of your **Dt 31:28** 2205
and he will inform you, Your e, **Dt 32:7** 2205
both he and the e of Israel; **Jos 7:6** 2205
and he went up with the e of **Jos 8:10** 2205
All Israel with their e and **Jos 8:33** 2205
"So our e and all the inhabitants **Jos 9:11** 2205
the hearing of the e of that city; **Jos 20:4** 2205
for their e and their heads and **Jos 23:2** 2205
and called for the e of Israel and **Jos 24:1** 2205
days of the e who survived Joshua, **Jos 24:31** 2205
days of the e who survived Joshua, **Jg 2:7** 2205
the princes of Succoth and its e, **Jg 8:14** 2205
He took the e of the city, and **Jg 8:16** 2205
the e of Gilead went to get Jephthah **Jg 11:5** 2205
Jephthah said to the e of Gilead, **Jg 11:7** 2205
The e of Gilead said to Jephthah, **Jg 11:8** 2205
Jephthah said to the e of Gilead, **Jg 11:9** 2205
The e of Gilead said to Jephthah, **Jg 11:10** 2205
went with the e of Gilead, **Jg 11:11** 2205
the e of the congregation said, **Jg 21:16** 2205
men of the e of the city and said, **Ru 4:2** 2205
and before the e of my people. **Ru 4:4** 2205
said to the e and all the people, **Ru 4:9** 2205
who were in the court, and the e, **Ru 4:11** 2205
the camp, the e of Israel said, **1Sa 4:3** 2205
Then all the e of Israel gathered **1Sa 8:4** 2205
The e of Jabesh said to him, **1Sa 11:3** 2205
please honor me now before the e **1Sa 15:30** 2205
And the e of the city came **1Sa 16:4** 2205
of the spoil to the e of Judah, **1Sa 30:26** 2205
consultation with the e of Israel, **2Sa 3:17** 2205
So all the e of Israel came to the **2Sa 5:3** 2205
The e of his household stood **2Sa 12:17** 2205
Absalom and all the e of Israel. **2Sa 17:4** 2205
Absalom and the e of Israel, **2Sa 17:15** 2205
"Speak to the e of Judah, saying, **2Sa 19:11** 2205
Then Solomon assembled the e of **1Ki 8:1** 2205
Then all the e of Israel came, and **1Ki 8:3** 2205
King Rehoboam consulted with the e **1Ki 12:6** 2205
of the e which they had given him, **1Ki 12:8** 2205
of the e which they had given him, **1Ki 12:13** 2205
all the e of the land and said, **1Ki 20:7** 2205
All the e and all the people **1Ki 20:8** 2205
and sent letters to the e and to **1Ki 21:8** 2205
the e and the nobles who lived in **1Ki 21:11** 2205
and the e were sitting with him. **2Ki 6:32** 2205
came to him, he said to the e, **2Ki 6:32** 2205
to the rulers of Jezreel, the e, **2Ki 10:1** 2205
he who *was* over the city, the e, **2Ki 10:5** 2205
scribe and the e of the priests, **2Ki 19:2** 2205
the e of Judah and of Jerusalem. **2Ki 23:1** 2205
So all the e of Israel came to the **1Ch 11:3** 2205
with the e of Israel and the **1Ch 15:25** 2205
Then David and the e, **1Ch 21:16** 2205
Solomon assembled to Jerusalem the e **2Ch 5:2** 2205
Then all the e of Israel came, and **2Ch 5:4** 2205
King Rehoboam consulted with the e **2Ch 10:6** 2205
But he forsook the counsel of the e **2Ch 10:8** 2205
forsook the counsel of the e. **2Ch 10:13** 2205
all the e of Judah and Jerusalem. **2Ch 34:29** 2205
the eye of their God was on the e of **Ezr 5:5** 7868
those e and said to them thus, **Ezr 5:9** 7868
Jews and the e of the Jews rebuild **Ezr 6:7** 7868
you are to do for these e of Judah **Ezr 6:8** 7868
And the e of the Jews were **Ezr 6:14** 7868
counsel of the leaders and the e, **Ezr 10:8** 2205
the e and judges of each city, **Ezr 10:14** 2205
away the discernment of the e. **Jb 12:20** 2205
Nor may e understand justice. **Jb 32:9** 2205
That he might teach his e wisdom. **Ps 105:22** 2205
praise Him at the seat of the e. **Ps 107:32** 2205
he sits among the e of the land. **Pr 31:23** 2205
the e and princes of His people, **Is 3:14** 2205
His glory will be before His e. **Is 24:23** 2205
scribe and the e of the priests, **Is 37:2** 2205
take some of the e of the people **Jer 19:1** 2205
Then some of the e of the land **Jer 26:17** 2205
to the rest of the e of the exile, **Jer 29:1** 2205
and my e perished in the city While **La 1:19** 2205
The e of the daughter of Zion Sit **La 2:10** 2205
priests, They did not favor the e. **La 4:16** 2205
E were not respected. **La 5:12** 2205
E are gone from the gate, Young **La 5:14** 2205
the priest and counsel from the e. **Ezk 7:26** 2205
the e of Judah sitting before me, **Ezk 8:1** 2205
seventy e of the house of Israel, **Ezk 8:11** 2205
do you see what the e of the house **Ezk 8:12** 2205
the e who *were* before the temple. **Ezk 9:6** 2205
Then some e of Israel came to me **Ezk 14:1** 2205
certain of the e of Israel **Ezk 20:1** 2205
of man, speak to the e of Israel and **Ezk 20:3** 2205
"The e of Gebal and her wise men **Ezk 27:9** 2205
Hear this, O e, And listen, all **Jl 1:2** 2205
Gather the e *And* all the **Jl 1:14** 2205
the congregation, Assemble the e, **Jl 2:16** 2205
break the tradition of the e? **Mt 15:2** *4245*
e and chief priests and scribes, **Mt 16:21** *4245*
and the chief priests and the e of the **Mt 21:23** *4245*
Then the chief priests and the e **Mt 26:3** *4245*
chief priests and e of the people. **Mt 26:47** *4245*
and the e were gathered together. **Mt 26:57** *4245*
all the chief priests and the e of **Mt 27:1** *4245*
silver to the chief priests and e, **Mt 27:3** *4245*
by the chief priests and e, **Mt 27:12** *4245*
But the chief priests and the e **Mt 27:20** *4245*
along with the scribes and e, **Mt 27:41** *4245*
with the e and consulted together, **Mt 28:12** *4245*
observing the traditions of the e; **Mk 7:3** *4245*
to the tradition of the e, **Mk 7:5** *4245*
rejected by the e and the chief priests **Mk 8:31** *4245*
and the scribes and the e came to Him, **Mk 11:27** *4245*
priests and the scribes and the e. **Mk 14:43** *4245*
e and the scribes gathered together **Mk 14:53** *4245*
priests with the e and scribes and **Mk 15:1** *4245*
he sent some Jewish e asking Him **Lk 7:3** *4245*
e and chief priests and scribes, **Lk 9:22** *4245*
scribes with the e confronted *Him*, **Lk 20:1** *4245*
and e who had come against Him, **Lk 22:52** *4245*
of e of the people assembled, **Lk 22:66** *4244*
their rulers and e and scribes **Ac 4:5** *4245*
"Rulers and e of the people, **Ac 4:8** *4245*
and the e had said to them. **Ac 4:23** *4245*
the people, the e and the scribes, **Ac 6:12** *4245*
of Barnabas and Saul to the e. **Ac 11:30** *4245*
e for them in every church, **Ac 14:23** *4245*
and e concerning this issue. **Ac 15:2** *4245*
church and the apostles and the e, **Ac 15:4** *4245*
The apostles and the e came **Ac 15:6** *4245*
good to the apostles and the e, **Ac 15:22** *4245*
and the brethren who are e, **Ac 15:23** *4245*
and e who were in Jerusalem, **Ac 16:4** *4245*
called to him the e of the church. **Ac 20:17** *4245*
James, and all the e were present. **Ac 21:18** *4245*
the Council of the e can testify. **Ac 22:5** *4244*
to the chief priests and the e and **Ac 23:14** *4245*
Ananias came down with some e, **Ac 24:1** *4245*
the chief priests and the e of the **Ac 25:15** *4245*
The e who rule well are to be **1Tm 5:17** *4245*
and appoint e in every city as I **Ti 1:5** *4245*
must call for the e of the church **Jas 5:14** *4245*
I exhort the e among you, **1Pe 5:1** *4245*
likewise, be subject to *your* e; **1Pe 5:5** *4245*
I saw twenty-four e sitting, **Rv 4:4** *4245*
the twenty-four e will fall down **Rv 4:10** *4245*
and one of the e said to me, **Rv 5:5** *4245*
and the e a Lamb standing, as if **Rv 5:6** *4245*
e fell down before the Lamb, **Rv 5:8** *4245*
the living creatures and the e; **Rv 5:11** *4245*
And the e fell down and worshiped. **Rv 5:14** *4245*
e and the four living creatures; **Rv 7:11** *4245*
Then one of the e answered, saying **Rv 7:13** *4245*
And the twenty-four e, **Rv 11:16** *4245*
four living creatures and the e; **Rv 14:3** *4245*
And the twenty-four e and the four **Rv 19:4** *4245*

ELEAD
and Ezer and E whom the men of **1Ch 7:21** 496

ELEADAH
son, Tahath his son, E his son, **1Ch 7:20** 497

ELEALEH
Dibon, Jazer, Nimrah, Heshbon, E, **Nu 32:3** 500
Heshbon and E and Kiriathaim, **Nu 32:37** 500
Heshbon and E also cry out, Their **Is 15:4** 500
with my tears, O Heshbon and E; **Is 16:9** 500
the outcry at Heshbon even to E, **Jer 48:34** 500

ELEASAH
and Helez became the father of E, **1Ch 2:39** 501
and E became the father of Sismai, **1Ch 2:40** 501
Raphah *was* his son, E his son, **1Ch 8:37** 501
and Rephaiah his son, E his son, **1Ch 9:43** 501

ELEAZAR
Nadab and Abihu, E and Ithamar. **Ex 6:23** 499
Aaron's son E married one of **Ex 6:25** 499
Nadab and Abihu, E and Ithamar, **Ex 28:1** 499
and to his sons E and Ithamar, **Lv 10:6** 499
his surviving sons, E and Ithamar, **Lv 10:12** 499
surviving sons E and Ithamar, **Lv 10:16** 499
and Abihu, E and Ithamar. **Nu 3:2** 499
So E and Ithamar served as priests **Nu 3:4** 499
and E the son of Aaron the priest **Nu 3:32** 499
"The responsibility of E the **Nu 4:16** 499
"Say to E, the son of Aaron the **Nu 16:37** 499
So E the priest took the bronze **Nu 16:39** 499
You shall give it to E the priest, **Nu 19:3** 499
'Next E the priest shall take some **Nu 19:4** 499
"Take Aaron and his son E and **Nu 20:25** 499
and put them on his son E. **Nu 20:26** 499
and put them on his son E, **Nu 20:28** 499
and E came down from the mountain. **Nu 20:28** 499
When Phinehas the son of E, **Nu 25:7** 499
"Phinehas the son of E, **Nu 25:11** 499
to E the son of Aaron the priest, **Nu 26:1** 499
So Moses and E the priest spoke **Nu 26:3** 499
Nadab and Abihu, E and Ithamar. **Nu 26:60** 499
by Moses and E the priest, **Nu 26:63** 499
before Moses and before E the priest **Nu 27:2** 499
and have him stand before E the **Nu 27:19** 499
shall stand before E the priest, **Nu 27:21** 499
and set him before E the priest and **Nu 27:22** 499
Phinehas the son of E the priest, **Nu 31:6** 499
and to E the priest and to the **Nu 31:12** 499
Moses and E the priest and all **Nu 31:13** 499
Then E the priest said to the men **Nu 31:21** 499
"You and E the priest and the **Nu 31:26** 499
half and give it to E the priest, **Nu 31:29** 499
Moses and E the priest did **Nu 31:31** 499
LORD's offering to E the priest, **Nu 31:41** 499
Moses and E the priest took **Nu 31:51** 499
So Moses and E the priest took the **Nu 31:54** 499
spoke to Moses and to E the priest **Nu 32:2** 499
concerning them to E the priest, **Nu 32:28** 499
E the priest and Joshua the son of **Nu 34:17** 499
and E his son ministered as priest **Dt 10:6** 499
of Canaan, which E the priest, **Jos 14:1** 499
They came near before E the **Jos 17:4** 499
the inheritances which E the priest **Jos 19:51** 499
the Levites approached E the priest **Jos 21:1** 499
Phinehas the son of E the priest, **Jos 22:13** 499
And Phinehas the son of E the **Jos 22:31** 499
Then Phinehas the son of E the **Jos 22:32** 499
And E the son of Aaron died; **Jos 24:33** 499
and Phinehas the son of E, **Jg 20:28** 499
and consecrated E his son to keep **1Sa 7:1** 499
was E the son of Dodo the Ahohite, **2Sa 23:9** 499
of Aaron *were* Nadab, Abihu, E and **1Ch 6:3** 499
E became the father of Phinehas, **1Ch 6:4** 499
E his son, Phinehas his son, **1Ch 6:50** 499
Phinehas the son of E was **1Ch 9:20** 499
After him was E the son of Dodo, **1Ch 11:12** 499
The sons of Mahli *were* E and Kish. **1Ch 23:21** 499
E died and had no sons, but **1Ch 23:22** 499
of Aaron *were* Nadab, Abihu, E and **1Ch 24:1** 499
E and Ithamar served as priests. **1Ch 24:2** 499
with Zadok of the sons of E and **1Ch 24:3** 499
found from the descendants of E **1Ch 24:4** 499
of the descendants of E and **1Ch 24:4** 499
both from the descendants of E and **1Ch 24:5** 499
for E and one taken for Ithamar. **1Ch 24:6** 499
E, who had no sons. **1Ch 24:28** 499
son of Phinehas, son of E, **Ezr 7:5** 499
him *was* E the son of Phinehas; **Ezr 8:33** 499
Izziah, Malchijah, Mijamin, E, **Ezr 10:25** 499
and Maaseiah, Shemaiah, E, **Ne 12:42** 499
Eliud was the father of E, **Mt 1:15** *1648a*
E the father of Matthan, **Mt 1:15** *1648a*

ELECT
e those days will be cut short. **Mt 24:22** *1588*
mislead, if possible, even the e. **Mt 24:24** *1588*
His e from the four winds, **Mt 24:31** *1588*
the sake of the e, whom He chose, **Mk 13:20** *1588*
to lead astray, if possible, the e. **Mk 13:22** *1588*
His e from the four winds, **Mk 13:27** *1588*
God bring about justice for His e who **Lk 18:7** *1588*
bring a charge against God's e? **Ro 8:33** *1588*

EL-ELOHE-ISRAEL
there an altar and called it E. **Gn 33:20** 415

ELEMENTAL
under the e things of the world. **Ga 4:3** *4747*
the weak and worthless e things, **Ga 4:9** *4747*

ELEMENTARY
to the e principles of the world, **Col 2:8** *4747*
to the e principles of the world, **Col 2:20** *4747*
the e principles of the oracles of God, **Heb 5:12** *4747, 746*
the e teaching about the Christ, **Heb 6:1** *746*

ELEMENTS
e will be destroyed with intense heat, **2Pe 3:10** *4747*
the e will melt with intense heat! **2Pe 3:12** *4747*

ELEVATED
and whomever he wished he e and **Da 5:19** 7313

ELEVATION
Beautiful in e, the joy of the **Ps 48:2** 5131

ELEVEN
his two maids and his e children, **Gn 32:22** 259, 6240
e stars were bowing down to me." **Gn 37:9** 259, 6240
you shall make e curtains in all. **Ex 26:7** 6249, 6240
the e curtains shall have the same **Ex 26:8** 6249, 6240
he made e curtains in all. **Ex 36:14** 6249, 6240
the e curtains had the same **Ex 36:15** 6249, 6240
e bulls, two rams, fourteen male **Nu 29:20** 6249, 6240
It is e days' *journey* from Horeb **Dt 1:2** 259, 6240
e cities with their villages. **Jos 15:51** 259, 6240

you **e** hundred *pieces* of silver." Jg 16:5 505, 3967
"The **e** hundred *pieces* of silver Jg 17:2 505, 3967
He then returned the **e** hundred Jg 17:3 505, 3967
he reigned **e** years in Jerusalem; 2Ki 23:36 259, 6240
he reigned **e** years in Jerusalem; 2Ki 24:18 259, 6240
he reigned **e** years in Jerusalem; 2Ch 36:5 259, 6240
he reigned **e** years in Jerusalem. 2Ch 36:11 259, 6240
he reigned **e** years in Jerusalem; Jer 52:1 259, 6240
cubits and the width **e** cubits; Ezk 40:49 6249, 6240
But the **e** disciples proceeded to Mt 28:16 *1733*
He appeared to the **e** themselves Mk 16:14 *1733*
to the **e** and to all the rest. Lk 24:9 *1733*
e and those who were with them, Lk 24:33 *1733*
was added to the **e** apostles. Ac 1:26 *1733*
taking his stand with the **e**, Ac 2:14 *1733*

ELEVENTH
On the **e** day *it was* Pagiel the son Nu 7:72 6249, 6240
on the first *day* of the **e** month, Dt 1:3 6249, 6240
In the **e** year, in the month of 1Ki 6:38 259, 6240
Now in the **e** year of Joram, the 2Ki 9:29 259, 6240
until the **e** year of King Zedekiah. 2Ki 25:2 6249, 6240
the tenth, Machbannai the **e**. 1Ch 12:13 6249, 6240
the **e** for Eliashib, the twelfth 1Ch 24:12 6249, 6240
the **e** to Azarel, his sons and his 1Ch 25:18 6249, 6240
The **e** for the eleventh month *was* 1Ch 27:14 6249, 6240
The eleventh for the **e** month *was* 1Ch 27:14 6249, 6240
the end of the **e** year of Zedekiah the Jer 1:3 6249, 6240
in the **e** year of Zedekiah, in the Jer 39:2 6249, 6240
until the **e** year of King Zedekiah. Jer 52:5 6249, 6240
Now in the **e** year, Ezk 26:1 6249, 6240
In the **e** year, Ezk 30:20 259, 6240
In the **e** year, Ezk 31:1 259, 6240
twenty-fourth day of the **e** month, Zch 1:7 6249, 6240
"And about the **e** *hour* he went Mt 20:6 *1734*
those *hired* about the **e** hour came, Mt 20:9 *1734*
the tenth, chrysoprase; the **e**, jacinth; Rv 21:20 *1734*

ELHANAN
and **E** the son of Jaare-oregim the 2Sa 21:19 445
E the son of Dodo of Bethlehem, 2Sa 23:24 445
E the son of Dodo of Bethlehem, 1Ch 11:26 445
and **E** the son of Jair killed Lahmi 1Ch 20:5 445

ELI
And the two sons of **E**, 1Sa 1:3 5941
Now **E** the priest was sitting on 1Sa 1:9 5941
that **E** was watching her mouth. 1Sa 1:12 5941
So **E** thought she was drunk. 1Sa 1:13 5941
Then **E** said to her, 1Sa 1:14 5941
Then **E** answered and said, 1Sa 1:17 5941
bull, and brought the boy to **E**. 1Sa 1:25 5941
to the LORD before **E** the priest. 1Sa 2:11 5941
the sons of **E** were worthless men; 1Sa 2:12 5941
Then **E** would bless Elkanah and his 1Sa 2:20 5941
Now **E** was very old; 1Sa 2:22 5941
of God came to **E** and said to him, 1Sa 2:27 5941
ministering to the LORD before **E**. 1Sa 3:1 5941
as **E** was lying down in his place 1Sa 3:2 5941
Then he ran to **E** and said, 1Sa 3:5 5941
So Samuel arose and went to **E** and 1Sa 3:6 5941
And he arose and went to **E** and 1Sa 3:8 5941
Then **E** discerned that the LORD was 1Sa 3:8 5941
And **E** said to Samuel, 1Sa 3:9 5941
I will carry out against **E** all that 1Sa 3:12 5941
I have sworn to the house of **E** that 1Sa 3:14 5941
afraid to tell the vision to **E**. 1Sa 3:15 5941
Then **E** called Samuel and said, 1Sa 3:16 5941
and the two sons of **E**, 1Sa 4:4 5941
and the two sons of **E**, 1Sa 4:11 5941
E was sitting on *his* seat by the 1Sa 4:13 5941
E heard the noise of the outcry, 1Sa 4:14 5941
the man came hurriedly and told **E**. 1Sa 4:14 5941
Now **E** was ninety-eight years old, 1Sa 4:15 5941
The man said to **E**, 1Sa 4:16 5941
E fell off the seat backward beside 1Sa 4:18
the son of Phinehas, the son of **E**, 1Sa 14:3 5941
the house of **E** in Shiloh. 1Ki 2:27 5941
"**E**, ELI, LAMA SABACHTHANI?" Mt 27:46 *2241*
"ELI, **E**, LAMA SABACHTHANI?" Mt 27:46 *2241*
the son of Joseph, the son of **E**, Lk 3:23 *2242*

ELIAB
of Zebulun, **E** the son of Helon; Nu 1:9 446
E the son of Helon, Nu 2:7 446
day *it was* **E** the son of Helon, Nu 7:24 446
offering of **E** the son of Helon. Nu 7:29 446
and **E** the son of Helon over the Nu 10:16 446
Dathan and Abiram, the sons of **E**, Nu 16:1 446
Dathan and Abiram, the sons of **E**; Nu 16:12 446
The son of Pallu: **E**. Nu 26:8 446
The sons of **E**: Nu 26:9 446
Dathan and Abiram, the sons of **E**, Dt 11:6 446
he looked at **E** and thought, 1Sa 16:6 446
the battle were **E** the firstborn, 1Sa 17:13 446
Now **E** his oldest brother heard 1Sa 17:28 446
the father of **E** his firstborn, 1Ch 2:13 446
E his son, Jeroham his son, 1Ch 6:27 446
Obadiah the second, **E** the third, 1Ch 12:9 446
Shemiramoth, Jehiel, Unni, **E**, 1Ch 15:18 446
Shemiramoth, Jehiel, Unni, **E**, 1Ch 15:20 446
Jehiel, Mattithiah, **E**, 1Ch 16:5 446
daughter of **E** the son of Jesse, 2Ch 11:18 446

ELIAB'S
and **E** anger burned against David 1Sa 17:28 446

ELIADA
Elishama, **E** and Eliphelet. 2Sa 5:16 450
to him, Rezon the son of **E**, 1Ki 11:23 450
Elishama, **E** and Eliphelet, nine. 1Ch 3:8 450
of Benjamin, **E** a valiant warrior, 2Ch 17:17 450

ELIAHBA
E the Shaalbonite, the sons of 2Sa 23:32 455
the Baharumite, **E** the Shaalbonite, 1Ch 11:33 455

ELIAKIM
to the king, **E** the son of Hilkiah, 2Ki 18:18 471
Then **E** the son of Hilkiah, and 2Ki 18:26 471
Then **E** the son of Hilkiah, who was 2Ki 18:37 471
Then he sent **E** who was over the 2Ki 19:2 471
Pharaoh Neco made **E** the son of 2Ki 23:34 471
The king of Egypt made **E** his 2Ch 36:4 471
and the priests, **E**, Ne 12:41 471
My servant **E** the son of Hilkiah Is 22:20 471
Then **E** the son of Hilkiah, who was Is 36:3 471
Then **E** and Shebna and Joah said to Is 36:11 471
Then **E** the son of Hilkiah, who was Is 36:22 471
Then he sent **E** who was over the Is 37:2 471
Abihud the father of **E**, Mt 1:13 *1662*
and **E** the father of Azor. Mt 1:13 *1662*
the son of Jonam, the son of **E**, Lk 3:30 *1662*

ELIAM
not Bathsheba, the daughter of **E**, 2Sa 11:3 463
E the son of Ahithophel the 2Sa 23:34 463

ELIASAPH
of Gad, **E** the son of Deuel; Nu 1:14 460
E the son of Deuel, Nu 2:14 460
Gershonites *was* **E** the son of Lael. Nu 3:24 460
day *it was* **E** the son of Deuel, Nu 7:42 460
offering of **E** the son of Deuel. Nu 7:47 460
and **E** the son of Deuel was over Nu 10:20 460

ELIASHIB
sons of Elioenai *were* Hodaviah, **E**, 1Ch 3:24 475
the eleventh for **E**, 1Ch 24:12 475
chamber of Jehohanan the son of **E**. Ezr 10:6 475
Of the singers *there was* **E**; Ezr 10:24 475
Elioenai, **E**, Mattaniah, Jeremoth, Ezr 10:27 475
Vaniah, Meremoth, **E**, Ezr 10:36 475
Then **E** the high priest arose with Ne 3:1 475
of the house of **E** the high priest. Ne 3:20 475
Joiakim became the father of **E**, Ne 12:10 475
and **E** became the father of Joiada, Ne 12:10 475
were registered in the days of **E**, Ne 12:22 475
the days of Johanan the son of **E**. Ne 12:23 475
Now prior to this, **E** the priest, Ne 13:4 475
evil that **E** had done for Tobiah, Ne 13:7 475
the son of **E** the high priest, Ne 13:28 475

ELIASHIB'S
from the doorway of **E** house even Ne 3:21 475

ELIATHAH
and Jerimoth, Hananiah, Hanani, **E**, 1Ch 25:4 448
for the twentieth to **E**, 1Ch 25:27 448

ELIDAD
of Benjamin, **E** the son of Chislon. Nu 34:21 449

ELIEHOENAI
Johanan the sixth, **E** the seventh. 1Ch 26:3 454a
E the son of Zerahiah and 200 Ezr 8:4 454a

ELIEL
households, even Epher, Ishi, **E**, 1Ch 5:24 447
the son of Jeroham, the son of **E**, 1Ch 6:34 447
Elienai, Zillethai, **E**, 1Ch 8:20 447
Ishpan, Eber, **E**, 1Ch 8:22 447
E the Mahavite and Jeribai and 1Ch 11:46 447
E and Obed and Jaasiel the 1Ch 11:47 447
Attai the sixth, **E** the seventh, 1Ch 12:11 447
the sons of Hebron, **E** the chief, 1Ch 15:9 447
Uriel, Asaiah, Joel, Shemaiah, **E** and 1Ch 15:11 447
Asahel, Jerimoth, Jozabad, **E**, 2Ch 31:13 447

ELIENAI
E, Zillethai, Eliel, 1Ch 8:20 462

ELIEZER
of my house is **E** of Damascus?" Gn 15:2 461
The other was named **E**, Ex 18:4 461
of Becher *were* Zemirah, Joash, **E**, 1Ch 7:8 461
Amasai, Zechariah, Benaiah and **E**, 1Ch 15:24 461
sons of Moses *were* Gershom and **E**. 1Ch 23:15 461
son of **E** was Rehabiah the chief; 1Ch 23:17 461
and **E** had no other sons, but the 1Ch 23:17 461
by **E** *were* Rehabiah his son, 1Ch 26:25 461
was **E** the son of Zichri; 1Ch 27:16 461
Then **E** the son of Dodavahu of 2Ch 20:37 461
So I sent for **E**, Ariel, Shemaiah, Ezr 8:16 461
Maaseiah, **E**, Jarib and Gedaliah. Ezr 10:18 461
Pethahiah, Judah and **E**. Ezr 10:23 461
E, Isshijah, Malchijah, Shemaiah, Ezr 10:31 461
the son of Joshua, the son of **E**, Lk 3:29 *1663*

ELIHOREPH
E and Ahijah, the sons of Shisha 1Ki 4:3 456

ELIHU
the son of Jeroham, the son of **E**, 1Sa 1:1 453
Jediael, Michael, Jozabad, **E** and 1Ch 12:20 453
whose brothers, **E** and Semachiah, 1Ch 26:7 453
for Judah, **E**, *one* of David's 1Ch 27:18 453
But the anger of **E** the son of Jb 32:2 453
Now **E** had waited to speak to Job Jb 32:4 453
And when **E** saw that there was no Jb 32:5 453
So **E** the son of Barachel the Jb 32:6 453
Then **E** continued and said, Jb 34:1 453
Then **E** continued and said, Jb 35:1 453
Then **E** continued and said, Jb 36:1 453

ELIJAH
Now **E** the Tishbite, who was of the 1Ki 17:1 452
Then **E** said to her, 1Ki 17:13 452
did according to the word of **E**, 1Ki 17:15 452
the LORD which He spoke through **E**. 1Ki 17:16 452
So she said to **E**, 1Ki 17:18 452
The LORD heard the voice of **E**, 1Ki 17:22 452
E took the child and brought 1Ki 17:23 452
and **E** said, "See, your son is alive." 1Ki 17:23 452
Then the woman said to **E**, 1Ki 17:24 452
LORD came to **E** in the third year, 1Ki 18:1 452
So **E** went to show himself to Ahab. 1Ki 18:2 452
was on the way, behold, **E** met him, 1Ki 18:7 452
"Is this you, **E** my master?" 1Ki 18:7 452
'Behold, **E** *is here*.'" 1Ki 18:8 452
"Behold, **E** *is here*."' 1Ki 18:11 452
"Behold, **E** *is here*" 1Ki 18:14 452
E said, "As the LORD of hosts lives, 1Ki 18:15 452
and Ahab went to meet **E**. 1Ki 18:16 452
Ahab saw **E**, Ahab said to him, 1Ki 18:17 452
E came near to all the people 1Ki 18:21 452
Then **E** said to the people, 1Ki 18:22 452
So **E** said to the prophets of Baal, 1Ki 18:25 452
noon, that **E** mocked them and said, 1Ki 18:27 452
Then **E** said to all the people, 1Ki 18:30 452
E took twelve stones according 1Ki 18:31 452
E the prophet came near and 1Ki 18:36 452
Then **E** said to them, 1Ki 18:40 452
and **E** brought them down to the 1Ki 18:40 452
Now **E** said to Ahab, 1Ki 18:41 452
E went up to the top of Carmel; 1Ki 18:42 452
the hand of the LORD was on **E**, 1Ki 18:46 452
told Jezebel all that **E** had done, 1Ki 19:1 452
Jezebel sent a messenger to **E**, 1Ki 19:2 452
"What are you doing here, **E**?" 1Ki 19:9 452
When **E** heard *it*, 1Ki 19:13 452
"What are you doing here, **E**?" 1Ki 19:13 452
And **E** passed over to him and threw 1Ki 19:19 452
the oxen and ran after **E** and said, 1Ki 19:20 452
followed **E** and ministered to him. 1Ki 19:21 452
the LORD came to **E** the Tishbite, 1Ki 21:17 452
Ahab said to **E**, 1Ki 21:20 452
the LORD came to **E** the Tishbite, 1Ki 21:28 452
the LORD said to **E** the Tishbite, 2Ki 1:3 452
shall surely die.'" Then **E** departed. 2Ki 1:4 452
"It is **E** the Tishbite." 2Ki 1:8 452
E replied to the captain of fifty, 2Ki 1:10 452
E replied to them, 2Ki 1:12 452
bowed down on his knees before **E**, 2Ki 1:13 452
The angel of the LORD said to **E**, 2Ki 1:15 452
of the LORD which **E** had spoken. 2Ki 1:17 452
the LORD was about to take up **E** by 2Ki 2:1 452
E went with Elisha from Gilgal. 2Ki 2:1 452
E said to Elisha, 2Ki 2:2 452
E said to him, 2Ki 2:4 452
Then **E** said to him, 2Ki 2:6 452
E took his mantle and folded 2Ki 2:8 452
over, **E** said to Elisha, 2Ki 2:9 452
And **E** went up by a whirlwind to 2Ki 2:11 452
And he saw **E** no more. Then he took 2Ki 2:12
mantle of **E** that fell from him and 2Ki 2:13 452
mantle of **E** that fell from him and 2Ki 2:14 452
"Where is the LORD, the God of **E**?" 2Ki 2:14 452
"The spirit of **E** rests on Elisha." 2Ki 2:15 452
to pour water on the hands of **E**." 2Ki 3:11 452
by His servant **E** the Tishbite, 2Ki 9:36 452
He spoke through His servant **E**." 2Ki 10:10 452
of the LORD which He spoke to **E**. 2Ki 10:17 452
Jaareshiah, **E** and Zichri *were* the 1Ch 8:27 452
to him from **E** the prophet saying, 2Ch 21:12 452
Maaseiah, **E**, Shemaiah, Jehiel and Ezr 10:21 452
Jehiel, Abdi, Jeremoth and **E**; Ezr 10:26 452
I am going to send you **E** the Mal 4:5
to accept *it*, John himself is **E** Mt 11:14 *2243*
say John the Baptist; and others, **E**; Mt 16:14 *2243*
Moses and **E** appeared to them, Mt 17:3 *2243*
one for Moses, and one for **E**." Mt 17:4 *2243*
say that **E** must come first?" Mt 17:10 *2243*
"**E** is coming and will restore all Mt 17:11 *2243*
I say to you that **E** already came, Mt 17:12 *2243*
"This man is calling for **E**." Mt 27:47 *2243*
whether **E** will come to save Him." Mt 27:49 *2243*
But others were saying, "He is **E**." Mk 6:15 *2243*
and others *say* **E**; Mk 8:28 *2243*
E appeared to them along with Mk 9:4 *2243*
one for Moses, and one for **E**." Mk 9:5 *2243*
say that **E** must come first?" Mk 9:11 *2243*
"**E** does first come and restore Mk 9:12 *2243*
to you that **E** has indeed come, Mk 9:13 *2243*
"Behold, He is calling for **E**." Mk 15:35 *2243*
E will come to take Him down." Mk 15:36 *2243*
Him in the spirit and power of **E**, Lk 1:17 *2243*

widows in Israel in the days of E, Lk 4:25 *2243*
yet E was sent to none of them, Lk 4:26 *2243*
and by some that E had appeared, Lk 9:8 *2243*
the Baptist, and others *say* E; Lk 9:19 *2243*
and they were Moses and E, Lk 9:30 *2243*
and one for Moses, and one for E" Lk 9:33 *2243*
asked him, "What then? Are you E?" Jn 1:21 *2243*
if you are not the Christ, nor E, Jn 1:25 *2243*
says in *the passage about* E, Ro 11:2 *2243*
E was a man with a nature like Jas 5:17 *2243*

ELIKA
the Harodite, E the Harodite, 2Sa 23:25 470

ELIM
Then they came to E where there Ex 15:27 362
Then they set out from E, Ex 16:1 362
Sin, which is between E and Sinai, Ex 16:1 362
from Marah and came to E; Nu 33:9 362
and in E there were twelve springs Nu 33:9 362
They journeyed from E and Nu 33:10 362

ELIMELECH
The name of the man *was* E, Ru 1:2 458
Then E, Naomi's husband, died; Ru 1:3 458
great wealth, of the family of E, Ru 2:1 458
Boaz, who was of the family of E. Ru 2:3 458
which belonged to our brother E, Ru 4:3 458
of Naomi all that belonged to E Ru 4:9 458

ELIMINATE
e harmful beasts from the land, Lv 26:6 7673a
I am going to e from this place, Jer 16:9 7673a
e harmful beasts from the land so Ezk 34:25 7673a

ELIMINATED
passes into the stomach, and is e? Mt 15:17 *1519, 856, 1544b*
but into his stomach, and is e?" Mk 7:19 *1519, 856, 1607*

ELIOENAI
The sons of Neariah *were* E, 1Ch 3:23 454b
The sons of E *were* Hodaviah, 1Ch 3:24 454b
and E, Jaakobah, Jeshohaiah, 1Ch 4:36 454b
were Zemirah, Joash, Eliezer, E, 1Ch 7:8 454b
E, Maaseiah, Ishmael, Nethanel, Ezr 10:22 454b
E, Eliashib, Mattaniah, Jeremoth, Ezr 10:27 454b
Maaseiah, Miniamin, Micaiah, E, Ne 12:41 454b

ELIPHAL
the Hararite, E the son of Ur, 1Ch 11:35 465

ELIPHAZ
Adah bore E to Esau, and Gn 36:4 464
E the son of Esau's wife Adah, Gn 36:10 464
The sons of E were Teman, Gn 36:11 464
was a concubine of Esau's son E Gn 36:12 464
Eliphaz and she bore Amalek to E. Gn 36:12 464
The sons of E, the firstborn of Gn 36:15 464
from E in the land of Edom; Gn 36:16 464
The sons of Esau *were* E, 1Ch 1:35 464
The sons of E *were* Teman, Omar, 1Ch 1:36 464
his own place, E the Temanite, Jb 2:11 464
Then E the Temanite answered, Jb 4:1 464
Then E the Temanite responded, Jb 15:1 464
Then E the Temanite responded, Jb 22:1 464
the LORD said to E the Temanite, Jb 42:7 464
So E the Temanite and Bildad the Jb 42:9 464

ELIPHELEHU
Benaiah, Maaseiah, Mattithiah, E, 1Ch 15:18 466
and Mattithiah, E, Mikneiah, 1Ch 15:21 466

ELIPHELET
Elishama, Eliada and E. 2Sa 5:16 467
E the son of Ahasbai, the son of 2Sa 23:34 467
and Ibhar, Elishama, E, 1Ch 3:6 467
Elishama, Eliada and E, 1Ch 3:8 467
Jeush the second and E the third. 1Ch 8:39 467
Elishama, Beeliada and E. 1Ch 14:7 467
ones, these being their names, E, Ezr 8:13 467
Mattenai, Mattattah, Zabad, E, Ezr 10:33 467

ELI'S
the iniquity of E house shall not be 1Sa 3:14 5941

ELISHA
and E the son of Shaphat of 1Ki 19:16 477
of Jehu, E shall put to death. 1Ki 19:17 477
and found E the son of Shaphat, 1Ki 19:19 477
Elijah went with E from Gilgal. 2Ki 2:1 477
Elijah said to E, 2Ki 2:2 477
But E said, "As the LORD lives and 2Ki 2:2 477
came out to E and said to him, 2Ki 2:3 477
"E, please stay here, for the 2Ki 2:4 477
approached E and said to him, 2Ki 2:5 477
over, Elijah said to E, 2Ki 2:9 477
E said, "Please, let a double portion 2Ki 2:9 477
E saw *it* and cried out, 2Ki 2:12 477
and E crossed over. 2Ki 2:14 477
"The spirit of Elijah rests on E." 2Ki 2:15 477
the men of the city said to E, 2Ki 2:19 477
to the word of E which he spoke. 2Ki 2:22 477
"E the son of Shaphat is here, 2Ki 3:11 477
Now E said to the king of Israel, 2Ki 3:13 477
E said, "As the LORD of hosts lives, 2Ki 3:14 477
of the prophets cried out to E, 2Ki 4:1 477
E said to her, 2Ki 4:2 477
day when E passed over to Shunem, 2Ki 4:8 477
next year, as E had said to her. 2Ki 4:17 477
When E came into the house, behold 2Ki 4:32 477
When E returned to Gilgal, *there* 2Ki 4:38 477
It happened when E the man of 2Ki 5:8 477
at the doorway of the house of E. 2Ki 5:9 477
E sent a messenger to him, 2Ki 5:10 477
the servant of E the man of God, 2Ki 5:20 477
And E said to him, 2Ki 5:25 477
sons of the prophets said to E, 2Ki 6:1 477
but E, the prophet who is in 2Ki 6:12 477
Then E prayed and said, 2Ki 6:17 477
and chariots of fire all around E. 2Ki 6:17 477
E prayed to the LORD and said, 2Ki 6:18 477
according to the word of E. 2Ki 6:18 477
Then E said to them, 2Ki 6:19 477
come into Samaria, E said, 2Ki 6:20 477
when he saw them, said to E, 2Ki 6:21 477
if the head of E the son of 2Ki 6:31 477
Now E was sitting in his house, 2Ki 6:32 477
Then E said, "Listen to the word of 2Ki 7:1 477
Now E spoke to the woman whose son 2Ki 8:1 477
great things that E has done." 2Ki 8:4 477
son, whom E restored to life." 2Ki 8:5 477
Then E came to Damascus. 2Ki 8:7 477
Then E said to him, 2Ki 8:10 477
E answered, "The LORD has shown 2Ki 8:13 477
from E and returned to his master, 2Ki 8:14 477
"What did E say to you?" 2Ki 8:14 477
Now E the prophet called one of 2Ki 9:1 477
When E became sick with the 2Ki 13:14 477
E said to him, 2Ki 13:15 477
then E laid his hands on the 2Ki 13:16 477
Then E said, "Shoot!" And he shot. 2Ki 13:17 477
E died, and they buried him. 2Ki 13:20 477
cast the man into the grave of E. 2Ki 13:21 477
the man touched the bones of E 2Ki 13:21 477
in the time of E the prophet; Lk 4:27 *1666*

ELISHAH
sons of Javan *were* E and Tarshish, Gn 10:4 473
The sons of Javan *were* E, 1Ch 1:7 473
purple from the coastlands of E. Ezk 27:7 473

ELISHAMA
of Ephraim, E the son of Ammihud; Nu 1:10 476
shall be E the son of Ammihud, Nu 2:18 476
day *it was* E the son of Ammihud, Nu 7:48 476
offering of E the son of Ammihud. Nu 7:53 476
with E the son of Ammihud over its Nu 10:22 476
E, Eliada and Eliphelet. 2Sa 5:16 476
son of Nethaniah, the son of E, 2Ki 25:25 476
Jekamiah became the father of E. 1Ch 2:41 476
and Ibhar, E, Eliphelet, 1Ch 3:6 476
E, Eliada and Eliphelet, nine. 1Ch 3:8 476
son, Ammihud his son, E his son, 1Ch 7:26 476
E, Beeliada and Eliphelet. 1Ch 14:7 476
and with them E and Jehoram, the 2Ch 17:8 476
E the scribe, and Delaiah the son of Jer 36:12 476
in the chamber of E the scribe, Jer 36:20 476
of the chamber of E the scribe. Jer 36:21 476
son of Nethaniah, the son of E, Jer 41:1 476

ELISHAPHAT
Adaiah, and E the son of Zichri, 2Ch 23:1 478

ELISHEBA
Aaron married E, Ex 6:23 472

ELISHUA
Ibhar, E, Nepheg, Japhia, 2Sa 5:15 474
Ibhar, E, Elpelet, 1Ch 14:5 474

ELITE
was an e army of 307,500, 2Ch 26:13 2428

ELIUD
and Achim the father of E. Mt 1:14 *1664*
E was the father of Eleazar, Mt 1:15 *1664*

ELIZABETH
of Aaron, and her name was E. Lk 1:5 *1665*
no child, because E was barren, Lk 1:7 *1665*
your wife E will bear you a son, Lk 1:13 *1665*
days E his wife became pregnant, Lk 1:24 *1665*
your relative E has also conceived Lk 1:36 *1665*
house of Zacharias and greeted E. Lk 1:40 *1665*
When E heard Mary's greeting, Lk 1:41 *1665*
E was filled with the Holy Spirit. Lk 1:41 *1665*
time had come for E to give birth, Lk 1:57 *1665*

ELIZAPHAN
families was E the son of Uzziel. Nu 3:30 469
a leader, E the son of Parnach. Nu 34:25 469
of the sons of E, Shemaiah the 1Ch 15:8 469
and from the sons of E, 2Ch 29:13 469

ELIZUR
of Reuben, E the son of Shedeur; Nu 1:5 468
E the son of Shedeur, Nu 2:10 468
day *it was* E the son of Shedeur, Nu 7:30 468
offering of E the son of Shedeur. Nu 7:35 468
set out with E the son of Shedeur, Nu 10:18 468

ELKANAH
Assir and E and Abiasaph; Ex 6:24 511
his name was E the son of Jeroham, 1Sa 1:1 511
the day came that E sacrificed, 1Sa 1:4 511
Then E her husband said to her, 1Sa 1:8 511
And E had relations with Hannah 1Sa 1:19 511
Then the man E went up with all 1Sa 1:21 511
E her husband said to her, 1Sa 1:23 511
Then E went to his home at Ramah. 1Sa 2:11 511
bless E and his wife and say, 1Sa 2:20 511
E his son, Ebiasaph his son and 1Ch 6:23 511
sons of E *were* Amasai and Ahimoth. 1Ch 6:25 511
As for E, the sons of Elkanah *were* 1Ch 6:26 511
the sons of E *were* Zophai his son 1Ch 6:26 511
son, Jeroham his son, E his son. 1Ch 6:27 511
the son of E, the son of Jeroham, 1Ch 6:34 511
the son of Zuph, the son of E, 1Ch 6:35 511
the son of E, the son of Joel, the 1Ch 6:36 511
the son of Asa, the son of E, 1Ch 9:16 511
E, Isshiah, Azarel, Joezer, 1Ch 12:6 511
E *were* gatekeepers for the ark. 1Ch 15:23 511
and E the second to the king. 2Ch 28:7 511

ELKOSHITE
book of the vision of Nahum the E. Na 1:1 512

ELLASAR
king of Shinar, Arioch king of E, Gn 14:1 495
king of Shinar and Arioch king of E Gn 14:9 495

ELMADAM
the son of Cosam, the son of E, Lk 3:28 *1678*

ELNAAM
and Joshaviah, the sons of E, 1Ch 11:46 493

ELNATHAN
the daughter of E of Jerusalem. 2Ki 24:8 494
for Eliezer, Ariel, Shemaiah, E, Ezr 8:16 494
Shemaiah, Elnathan, Jarib, E, Ezr 8:16 494
men, and for Joiarib and E, Ezr 8:16 494
E the son of Achbor and *certain* Jer 26:22 494
Shemaiah, and E the son of Achbor, Jer 36:12 494
Even though E and Delaiah and Jer 36:25 494

ELOI
"E, ELOI, LAMA SABACHTHANI?" Mk 15:34 *1682*
"ELOI, E, LAMA SABACHTHANI?" Mk 15:34 *1682*

ELON
the daughter of E the Hittite; Gn 26:34 356
the daughter of E the Hittite, Gn 36:2 356
Sered and E and Jahleel. Gn 46:14 356
of E, the family of the Elonites; Nu 26:26 356
and E and Timnah and Ekron, Jos 19:43 356
Now E the Zebulunite judged Israel Jg 12:11 356
Then E the Zebulunite died and was Jg 12:12 356

ELONBETH-HANAN
Shaalbim and Beth-shemesh and E; 1Ki 4:9 358

ELONITES
of Elon, the family of the E; Nu 26:26 440

ELOQUENT
"Please, Lord, I have never been e, Ex 4:10 376, 1697
an Alexandrian by birth, an e man, Ac 18:24 *3052*

ELOTH
E on the shore of the Red Sea, 1Ki 9:26 359
Ezion-geber and to E on the seashore 2Ch 8:17 359
He built E and restored it to 2Ch 26:2 359

ELPAAL
became the father of Abitub and E. 1Ch 8:11 508
The sons of E *were* Eber, 1Ch 8:12 508
and Jobab *were* the sons of E. 1Ch 8:18 508

EL-PARAN
in their Mount Seir, as far as E, Gn 14:6 364

ELPELET
Ibhar, Elishua, E, 1Ch 14:5 467

ELSE
"Whom e have you here? Gn 19:12 5750
"Give me children, or e I die." Gn 30:1 518, 369
or e they will multiply and in Ex 1:10 6435
or e the LORD will break out Ex 19:22 6435
What e shall he sleep in? Ex 22:27
in addition to what e he can Nu 6:21
on my feet, nothing e." Nu 20:19
I will find out what e the LORD will Nu 22:19 3254
or e his heart will turn away; nor Dt 17:17 3808
since he has nothing e left, Dt 28:55
secretly for lack of anything e, Dt 28:57
or e fierce men will fall upon you Jg 18:25 6435
e you would now be guilty.'" Jg 21:22
or e my father will cease *to be* 1Sa 9:5 6435
e before the sun goes down." 2Sa 3:35 3605
or e the king and all the people who 2Sa 17:16 6435
the LORD is God; there is no one e. 1Ki 8:60 5750
or e you shall pay a talent of 1Ki 20:39
or e, if it pleases you, I will 1Ki 21:6
or e three days of the sword of 1Ch 21:12
E my Maker would soon take me Jb 32:22
is with you, and there is none e, Is 45:14 5750
am the LORD, and there is none e. Is 45:18 5750
Or e My wrath will go forth like fire Jer 4:4 6435
For what e can I do, because of Jer 9:7
heart is more deceitful than all e Jer 17:9
or e go anywhere it seems right Jer 40:5
no one e who could declare it to the Da 2:11 321
or give your rewards to someone e; Da 5:17 321
"Is anyone e with you?" Am 6:10 5750
or shall we look for someone e?" Mt 11:3 *2087*
somewhere e to the towns nearby, Mk 1:38 *237b*
THERE IS NO ONE E BESIDES HIM; Mk 12:32 *243*
or do we look for someone e?" Lk 7:19 *243*
or do we look for someone e?'" Lk 7:20 *243*
or to everyone e as well?" Lk 12:41
"Or e, while the other is still Lk 14:32 *1490b*
or e he will be devoted to one Lk 16:13 *2228*
or e, that he should give Jn 13:29 *2228*
them the works which no one e did, Jn 15:24 *243*
and someone e will gird you, Jn 21:18 *243*
there is salvation in no one e; Ac 4:12 *243*
or e you may even be found Ac 5:39 *3379*
Of himself or of someone e?" Ac 8:34 *2087*
"Or e let these men themselves Ac 24:20 *2228*
accusing or e defending them, Ro 2:15 *2532*
e be reconciled to her husband), 1Co 7:11 *2228*
of wheat or of something e. 1Co 15:37 *3062*
For we write nothing e to you than 2Co 1:13 *243*
But in whatever respect anyone e 2Co 11:21
guard and to everyone e, Php 1:13 *3062*
For I have no one e of kindred Php 2:20
If anyone e has a mind to put Php 3:4 *243*
whatever e is contrary to sound 1Tm 1:10 *2087*
or e I am coming to you and will Rv 2:5 *1490b*
or e I am coming to you quickly, Rv 2:16 *1490b*

ELTEKE
of Dan, E with its pasture lands, Jos 21:23 514

ELTEKEH
and **E** and Gibbethon and Baalath, **Jos 19:44** 514
ELTEKON
and Maarath and Beth-anoth and **E**; **Jos 15:59** 515
ELTOLAD
and **E** and Chesil and Hormah, **Jos 15:30** 513
and **E** and Bethul and Hormah, **Jos 19:4** 513
ELUDED
seize Him, and He **e** their grasp. **Jn 10:39** *1831*
ELUL
on the twenty-fifth of *the month* **E**, **Ne 6:15** 435
ELUZAI
E, Jerimoth, Bealiah, Shemariah, **1Ch 12:5** 498
ELYMAS
But **E** the magician **Ac 13:8** *1681*
ELZABAD
Johanan the eighth, **E** the ninth, **1Ch 12:12** 443
were Othni, Rephael, Obed and **E**, **1Ch 26:7** 443
ELZAPHAN
Mishael and **E** and Sithri. **Ex 6:22** 469
called also to Mishael and **E**, **Lv 10:4** 469
EMASCULATED
"No one who is **e** or has his male **Dt 23:1** 1795, 6481
EMBALM
the physicians to **e** his father. **Gn 50:2** 2590
EMBALMED
So the physicians **e** Israel. **Gn 50:2** 2590
and he was **e** and placed in a **Gn 50:26** 2590
EMBALMING
such is the period required for **e**. **Gn 50:3** 2591b
EMBARKED
He again **e** and went away to the **Mk 8:13** *1684*
EMBARKING
And **e** in an Adramyttian ship, **Ac 27:2** *1910*
EMBARRASSED
and **e** to lift up my face to You, **Ezr 9:6** 3637
And you will be **e** at the gardens **Is 1:29** 2659
And the diviners will be **e**. **Mi 3:7** 2659
EMBERS
to hot **e** and wood to fire, **Pr 26:21** 1513
EMBITTERED
him, for all the people were **e**, **1Sa 30:6** 4843
the Almighty, who has **e** my soul, **Jb 27:2** 4843
When my heart was **e** And **Ps 73:21** 2556a
I went **e** in the rage of my spirit, **Ezk 3:14** 4751
and **e** them against the brethren. **Ac 14:2** *2559*
and do not be **e** against them. **Col 3:19** *4087*
EMBODIMENT
e of knowledge and of the truth, **Ro 2:20** *3446*
EMBRACE
next year you will **e** a son." **2Ki 4:16** 2263
She will honor you if you **e** her. **Pr 4:8** 2263
And **e** the bosom of a foreigner? **Pr 5:20** 2263
A time to **e** and a time to shun **Ec 3:5** 2263
my head And his right hand **e** me." **SS 2:6** 2263
head And his right hand **e** me." **SS 8:3** 2263
Those reared in purple **E** ash pits. **La 4:5** 2263
EMBRACED
him, and **e** him and kissed him and **Gn 29:13** 2263
Esau ran to meet him and **e** him, **Gn 33:4** 2263
and he kissed them and **e** them. **Gn 48:10** 2263
for him, and ran and **e** him and **Lk 15:20** *1968, 1909, 5137*
began to weep aloud and **e** Paul, **Ac 20:37** *1968, 1909, 5137*
EMBRACING
to embrace and a time to shun **e**. **Ec 3:5** 2263
and fell upon him, and after **e** him, **Ac 20:10** *4843*
EMBROIDERED
dyed work, A spoil of dyed work **e**, **Jg 5:30** 7553
will be led to the King in **e** work; **Ps 45:14** 7553
"I also clothed you with **e** cloth and **Ezk 16:10** 7553
of fine linen, silk and **e** cloth. **Ezk 16:13** 7553
your **e** cloth and covered them, **Ezk 16:18** 7553
and strip off their **e** garments. **Ezk 26:16** 7553
"Your sail was of fine **e** linen **Ezk 27:7** 7553
with emeralds, purple, **e** work, **Ezk 27:16** 7553
in clothes of blue and **e** work, **Ezk 27:24** 7553
EMBROIDERER
and of a designer and of an **e**, **Ex 35:35** 7551
EMBROIDERY
e on the neck of the spoiler?' **Jg 5:30** 7553
EMEK-KEZIZ
were Jericho and Beth-hoglah and **E**, **Jos 18:21** 6010, 7104
EMERALD
be a row of ruby, topaz and **e**; **Ex 28:17** 1304a
was a row of ruby, topaz, and **e**; **Ex 39:10** 1304a
lazuli, the turquoise and the **e**; **Ezk 28:13** 1304b
throne, like an **e** in appearance. **Rv 4:3** *4664*
the third, chalcedony; the fourth, **e**; **Rv 21:19** *4665*
EMERALDS
they paid for your wares with **e**, **Ezk 27:16** 5306
EMERGED
man's hand **e** and began writing **Da 5:5** 5312
EMERY
"Like **e** harder than flint I have **Ezk 3:9** 8068
EMIM
Ham and the **E** in Shaveh-kiriathaim, **Gn 14:5** 368a
(The **E** lived there formerly, a **Dt 2:10** 368a
but the Moabites call them **E**. **Dt 2:11** 368a

EMINENCE
"Adorn yourself with **e** and dignity, **Jb 40:10** 1347b
EMINENT
wealth, nor anything **e** among them. **Ezk 7:11** 5089
inferior to the most **e** apostles. **2Co 11:5** *5244b*
I inferior to the most **e** apostles, **2Co 12:11** *5244b*
EMISSION
'Now if a man has a seminal **e**, **Lv 15:16** 7902
on which there is seminal **e**, **Lv 15:17** 7902
so that there is a seminal **e**, **Lv 15:18** 7902
e so that he is unclean by it, **Lv 15:32** 7902
or if a man has a seminal **e**, **Lv 22:4** 7902
unclean because of a nocturnal **e**, **Dt 23:10** 7137
EMIT
The canals will **e** a stench, **Is 19:6** 2186b
EMMAUS
very day to a village named **E**, **Lk 24:13** *1695*
EMPEROR
he himself appealed to the **E**, **Ac 25:25** *4575*
EMPEROR'S
in custody for the **E** decision, **Ac 25:21** *4575*
EMPIRE
he will arouse the whole **e** **Da 11:2**
EMPLOY
They **e** violence, so that bloodshed **Hos 4:2** 6555
gift, **e** it in serving one another as **1Pe 4:10** *1247*
EMPOWERED
He has also **e** him to eat from them **Ec 5:19** 7980
has not **e** him to eat from them, **Ec 6:2** 7980
EMPTIED
quickly **e** her jar into the trough, **Gn 24:20** 6168
servants have **e** out the money **2Ki 22:9** 5413
"They have also **e** out the money **2Ch 34:17** 5413
thus may he be shaken out and **e**." **Ne 5:13** 7386
I **e** them out as the mire of the **Ps 18:42** 7385a
And he has not been **e** from vessel **Jer 48:11** 7385a
She is **e**! Yes, she is desolate and **Na 2:10** 950
but **e** Himself, taking the form of **Php 2:7** *2758*
EMPTILY
So Job opens his mouth **e**; **Jb 35:16** 1892
EMPTINESS
"Let him not trust in **e**, **Jb 15:31** 7723
For **e** will be his reward. **Jb 15:31** 7723
and in many words there is **e**. **Ec 5:7** 1892
And the plumb line of **e**. **Is 34:11** 922
molten images are wind and **e**. **Is 41:29** 8414
walked after **e** and became empty? **Jer 2:5** 1892
EMPTY
Now the pit was **e**, without any **Gn 37:24** 7386
e the house before the priest goes in **Lv 14:36** 6437
and he put trumpets and **e** pitchers **Jg 7:16** 7386
the LORD has brought me back **e**. **Ru 1:21** 7387
God of Israel, do not send it **e**; **1Sa 6:3** 7387
because your seat will be **e**. **1Sa 20:18** 6485
side, but David's place was **e**. **1Sa 20:25** 6485
new moon, that David's place was **e**; **1Sa 20:27** 6485
sword of Saul did not return **e**. **2Sa 1:22** 7387
nor shall the jar of oil be **e**, **1Ki 17:14** 2637
nor did the jar of oil become **e**, **1Ki 17:16** 2637
your neighbors, *even* **e** vessels; **2Ki 4:3** 7386
(but *they are* only **e** words), **2Ki 18:20** 8193
officer would come, **e** the chest, **2Ch 24:11** 6168
"You have sent widows away **e**, **Jb 22:9** 7387
out the north over **e** space And **Jb 26:7** 8414
God will not listen to an **e** *cry*, **Jb 35:13** 7723
But he who follows **e** *pursuits* will **Pr 28:19** 7386
Egypt, whose help is vain and **e**. **Is 30:7** 7385b
for the war are only **e** words.' **Is 36:5** 8193
It will not return to Me **e**, **Is 55:11** 7387
after emptiness and became **e**? **Jer 2:5** 1891
returned with their vessels **e**; **Jer 14:3** 7387
and they will **e** his vessels and **Jer 48:12** 7385a
has set me down *like* an **e** vessel; **Jer 51:34** 7386
"Then set it **e** on its coals So **Ezk 24:11** 7386
Will they therefore **e** their net **Hab 1:17** 7385a
which **e** the golden *oil* from **Zch 4:12** 7385a
any man make my boast an **e** one. **1Co 9:15** *2758*
may not be made **e** in this case, **2Co 9:3** *2758*
no one deceive you with **e** words, **Eph 5:6** *2756*
from selfishness or **e** conceit, **Php 2:3** *2754*
philosophy and **e** deception, **Col 2:8** *2756*
avoiding worldly *and* **e** chatter *and* **1Tm 6:20** *2757*
But avoid worldly *and* **e** chatter, **2Tm 2:16** *2757*
men, **e** talkers and deceivers, **Ti 1:10** *3151*
EMPTY-HANDED
now you would have sent me away **e**. **Gn 31:42** 7387
when you go, you will not go **e**. **Ex 3:21** 7387
And none shall appear before Me **e**. **Ex 23:15** 7387
None shall appear before Me **e**. **Ex 34:20** 7387
you shall not send him away **e**. **Dt 15:13** 7387
not appear before the LORD **e**. **Dt 16:16** 7387
not go to your mother-in-law **e**.'" **Ru 3:17** 7387
warrior Who does not return **e**. **Jer 50:9** 7387
and beat him and sent him away **e**. **Mk 12:3** *2756*
And sent away the rich **e**. **Lk 1:53** *2756*
beat him and sent him away **e**. **Lk 20:10** *2756*
shamefully and sent him away **e**. **Lk 20:11** *2756*
EMPTYING
about as they were **e** their sacks, **Gn 42:35** 7385a
ENABLED
And the LORD **e** her to conceive, **Ru 4:13** 5414
ENACT
Woe to those who **e** evil statutes And **Is 10:1** 2710
ENACTED
has been **e** on better promises. **Heb 8:6** *3549*

ENAIM
and sat in the gateway of **E**, **Gn 38:14** 5879a
who was by the road at **E**?" **Gn 38:21** 5879a
ENAM
and En-gannim, Tappuah and **E**, **Jos 15:34** 5879b
ENAN
of Naphtali, Ahira the son of **E**. **Nu 1:15** 5881
Ahira the son of **E**, **Nu 2:29** 5881
day *it was* Ahira the son of **E**, **Nu 7:78** 5881
offering of Ahira the son of **E**. **Nu 7:83** 5881
and Ahira the son of **E** over the **Nu 10:27** 5881
ENCAMP
to seek out a place for you to **e**, **Dt 1:33** 2583
Though a host **e** against me, My **Ps 27:3** 2583
E against her on every side, Let **Jer 50:29** 2583
ENCAMPED
came and **e** together at the waters **Jos 11:5** 2583
So they **e** from Beersheba as far as **Ne 11:30** 2583
bones of him who **e** against you; **Ps 53:5** 2583
ENCAMPMENTS
and they will set their **e** among **Ezk 25:4** 2918
ENCAMPS
and when the tabernacle **e**, **Nu 1:51** 2583
LORD **e** around those who fear Him, **Ps 34:7** 2583
ENCHANTER
artisan, And the skillful **e**. **Is 3:3** 3908
ENCHANTMENTS
and practiced divination and **e**, **2Ki 17:17** 5172
ENCIRCLE
Who **e** yourselves with firebrands, **Is 50:11** 247
ENCIRCLED
He **e** him, He cared for him, He **Dt 32:10** 5437
and he **e** the Ophel *with it* and **2Ch 33:14** 5437
Strong *bulls* of Bashan have **e** me. **Ps 22:12** 3803
The cords of the wicked have **e** me, **Ps 119:61** 5749a
they had been **e** for seven days. **Heb 11:30** *2944*
ENCIRCLING
went around **e** it ten to a cubit, **1Ki 7:24** 5437
ten cubits, entirely **e** the sea. **2Ch 4:3** 5362b
I will camp against you **e** *you*, **Is 29:3** 1754
ENCLOSED
"Or *who* **e** the sea with doors When **Jb 38:8** 5480b
You have **e** me behind and before, **Ps 139:5** 6696a
of the court *there were* **e** courts, **Ezk 46:22** 7000
they **e** a great quantity of fish, **Lk 5:6** *4788*
ENCOMPASS
assembly of the peoples **e** You, **Ps 7:7** 5437
A woman will **e** a man." **Jer 31:22** 5437
ENCOMPASSED
"For the waves of death **e** me; **2Sa 22:5** 661
The cords of death **e** me, **Ps 18:4** 661
A band of evildoers has **e** me; **Ps 22:16** 5362b
They have **e** me altogether. **Ps 88:17** 5362b
The cords of death **e** me And **Ps 116:3** 661
He has besieged and **e** me with **La 3:5** 5362b
"Water **e** me to the point of death. **Jon 2:5** 661
ENCOMPASSING
built stories **e** the walls of the house **1Ki 6:5** 5439
ENCOUNTER
came out from the city to **e** them, **Jos 8:22** 7122
battle array to **e** the Philistines. **1Sa 17:2** 7122
I will **e** them like a bear robbed **Hos 13:8** 6298
men to **e** the one coming against him **Lk 14:31** *5221*
when you **e** various trials, **Jas 1:2** *4045*
ENCOUNTERED
"What have you **e**, that you have **Gn 20:10** 7200
ENCOURAGE
e him, for he will cause Israel **Dt 1:38** 2388
and **e** him and strengthen him, **Dt 3:28** 2388
and overthrow it'; and *so* **e** him." **2Sa 11:25** 2388
to **e** them in the work of the house of **Ezr 6:22** 2388, 3027
E the exhausted, and strengthen **Is 35:3** 2388
he rejoiced and *began* to **e** them **Ac 11:23** *3870*
I **e** you to take some food, **Ac 27:34** *3870*
and that he may **e** your hearts; **Col 4:8** *3870*
and **e** you as to your faith, **1Th 3:2** *3870*
Therefore **e** one another and build **1Th 5:11** *3870*
the unruly, **e** the fainthearted, **1Th 5:14** *3888*
that they may **e** the young women to **Ti 2:4** *4994*
But **e** one another day after day, **Heb 3:13** *3870*
ENCOURAGED
e themselves and arrayed for **Jg 20:22** 2388
David at Horesh, and **e** him in God. **1Sa 23:16** 2388, 3027
e them in the service of the house **2Ch 35:2** 2388
e them with articles of silver, **Ezr 1:6** 2388, 3027
but have **e** the wicked not to turn **Ezk 13:22** 2388, 3027
e and strengthened the brethren **Ac 15:32** *3870*
they **e** them and departed. **Ac 16:40** *3870*
the brethren **e** him and wrote to **Ac 18:27** *4389*
All of them were **e** and **Ac 27:36** *2115a*
that I may be **e** together with you **Ro 1:12** *4837*
I **e** him greatly to come to you **1Co 16:12** *3870*
so that I also may be **e** when I **Php 2:19** *2174*
that their hearts may be **e**, **Col 2:2** *3870*
ENCOURAGEMENT
be an **e** and a protection for him. **Da 11:1** 2388
(which translated means Son of **E**), **Ac 4:36** *3874*
they rejoiced because of its **e**. **Ac 15:31** *3874*
and the **e** of the Scriptures we might **Ro 15:4** *3874*
God who gives perseverance and **e** **Ro 15:5** *3874*
Therefore if there is any **e** in Christ, **Php 2:1** *3874*

they have proved to be an **e** to me. **Col 4:11** *3931*
taken refuge would have strong **e** **Heb 6:18** *3874*

ENCOURAGES
So the craftsman **e** the smelter, **Is 41:7** 2388
smooths *metal* with the hammer **e** **Is 41:7**

ENCOURAGING
e them to continue in the faith, **Ac 14:22** *3870*
was **e** them all to take some food, **Ac 27:33** *3870*
were exhorting and **e** and imploring **1Th 2:11** *3888*
habit of some, but **e** *one another;* **Heb 10:25** *3870*

ENCOURAGINGLY
Then Hezekiah spoke **e** to all the **2Ch 30:22** 5921, 3820
city gate, and spoke **e** to them, **2Ch 32:6** 5921, 3824

ENCUMBRANCE
us, let us also lay aside every **e** and **Heb 12:1** *3591*

END
"The **e** of all flesh has come **Gn 6:13** 7093
and at the **e** of one hundred and **Gn 8:3** 7097a
came about at the **e** of forty days, **Gn 8:6** 7093
which is at the **e** of his field; **Gn 23:9** 7097a
happened at the **e** of two full years **Gn 41:1** 7093
in the land of Egypt came to an **e**, **Gn 41:53** 3615
cities from one **e** of Egypt's border **Gn 47:21** 7097a
And at the **e** of four **Ex 12:41** 7093
the Feast of the Ingathering at the **e** **Ex 23:16** 3318
"Make one cherub at one **e** and **Ex 25:19** 7098
end and one cherub at the other **e**; **Ex 25:19** 7098
shall pass through from **e** to end. **Ex 26:28** 7097a
shall pass through from end to **e**. **Ex 26:28** 7097a
of the boards from **e** to end. **Ex 36:33** 7097a
of the boards from end to **e**. **Ex 36:33** 7097a
one cherub at the one **e** and **Ex 37:8** 7098
and one cherub at the other **e**; **Ex 37:8** 7098
the land, at the **e** of forty days, **Nu 13:25** 7093
that you may put an **e** to their **Nu 17:10** 3615
at the extreme **e** of the border. **Nu 22:36** 7097a
And let my **e** be like his!" **Nu 23:10** 319
only see the extreme **e** of them and **Nu 23:13** 7097a
But his **e** *shall be* destruction." **Nu 24:20** 319
the **e** of the Salt Sea eastward. **Nu 34:3** 7097a
one **e** of the heavens to the other. **Dt 4:32** 7097a
able to put an **e** to them quickly, **Dt 7:22** 3615
you, to do good for you in the **e**. **Dt 8:16** 319
"It came about at the **e** of **Dt 9:11** 7093
even to the **e** of the year. **Dt 11:12** 319
e of the earth to the other end), **Dt 13:7** 7097a
end of the earth to the other **e**), **Dt 13:7** 7097a
"At the **e** of every third year you **Dt 14:28** 7097a
"At the **e** of *every* seven years **Dt 15:1** 7093
afar, from the **e** of the earth, **Dt 28:49** 7097a
from one **e** of the earth to the **Dt 28:64** 7097a
earth to the other **e** of the earth; **Dt 28:64** 7097a
"At the **e** of *every* seven years, **Dt 31:10** 7093
I will see what their **e** *shall be;* **Dt 32:20** 319
mourning for Moses came to an **e**. **Dt 34:8** 8552
At the **e** of three days **Jos 3:2** 7097a
came about at the **e** of three days **Jos 9:16** 7097a
as far as the *lower* **e** of the Sea **Jos 13:27** 7097a
from the lower **e** of the Salt Sea, **Jos 15:2** 7097a
which is at the **e** of the valley of **Jos 15:8** 7097a
Sea, at the south **e** of the Jordan. **Jos 18:19** 7097a
the **e** of the staff that was in his hand **Jg 6:21** 7097a
At the **e** of two months **Jg 11:39** 7093
Lo, the day is coming to an **e**; **Jg 19:9** 2583
glean until the **e** of the barley harvest **Ru 2:23** 3615
at the **e** of the heap of grain; **Ru 3:7** 7097a
his house, from beginning to **e**. **1Sa 3:12** 3615
he put out the **e** of the staff that **1Sa 14:27** 7097a
a little honey with the **e** of the staff **1Sa 14:43** 7097a
with the butt **e** of the spear, **2Sa 2:23** 310
that it will be bitter in the **e**? **2Sa 2:26** 314
e of every year that he cut *it,* **2Sa 14:26** 7093
came about at the **e** of forty years **2Sa 15:7** 7093
they came to Jerusalem at the **e** of **2Sa 24:8** 7097a
about at the **e** of three years, **1Ki 2:39** 7093
from the **e** of one wing to the end **1Ki 6:24** 7098
end of one wing to the **e** of the other **1Ki 6:24** 7098
came about at the **e** of twenty years **1Ki 9:10** 7097a
At the **e** of seven years, **2Ki 8:3** 7097a
filled from one **e** to the other. **2Ki 10:21** 6310
At the **e** of three years they **2Ki 18:10** 7097a
Jerusalem from one **e** to another; **2Ki 21:16** 6310
came about at the **e** of the twenty **2Ch 8:1** 7093
and you will find them at the **e** of **2Ch 20:16** 5490
of time, at the **e** of two years, **2Ch 21:19** 7093
which have filled it from **e** to end **Ezr 9:11** 6310
end to **e** *and* with their impurity. **Ezr 9:11** 6310
even as far as the **e** of his house. **Ne 3:21** 8503
make an **e** of them or forsake them, **Ne 9:31** 3617
after the **e** of her twelve months **Es 2:12** 7093
of His anger they come to an **e**. **Jb 4:9** 3615
And what is my **e**, that I should **Jb 6:11** 7093
And come to an **e** without hope. **Jb 7:6** 3615
Yet your **e** will increase greatly. **Jb 8:7** 319
And your iniquities without **e**? **Jb 22:5** 7093
"*Man* puts an **e** to darkness, And **Jb 28:3** 7093
will **e** their days in prosperity **Jb 36:11** 3615
evil of the wicked come to an **e**, **Ps 7:9** 1584
come to an **e** in perpetual ruins, **Ps 9:6** 8552
utterances to the **e** of the world. **Ps 19:4** 7097a
is from one **e** of the heavens, **Ps 19:6** 7097a
circuit to the other **e** of them; **Ps 19:6** 7098
"LORD, make me to know my **e** And **Ps 39:4** 7093
to cease to the **e** of the earth; **Ps 46:9** 7097a
the **e** of the earth I call to You when **Ps 61:2** 7097a
Then I perceived their **e**. **Ps 73:17** 319
His promise come to an **e** forever? **Ps 77:8** 1584
their days to an **e** in futility And **Ps 78:33** 3615
Your years will not come to an **e**. **Ps 102:27** 8552
man, And were at their wits' **e**. **Ps 107:27** 1104
And I shall observe it to the **e**. **Ps 119:33** 6118
statutes Forever, *even* to the **e**. **Ps 119:112** 6118
the **e** she is bitter as wormwood, **Pr 5:4** 319
And you groan at your final **e**, **Pr 5:11** 319
But its **e** is the way of death. **Pr 14:12** 319
And the **e** of joy may be grief. **Pr 14:13** 319
But its **e** is the way of death. **Pr 16:25** 319
The *cast* lot puts an **e** to strife **Pr 18:18** 7673a
Will not be blessed in the **e**. **Pr 20:21** 319
what will you do in the **e**, **Pr 25:8** 319
in the **e** find him to be a son. **Pr 29:21** 319
from the beginning even to the **e**. **Ec 3:11** 5490
there was no **e** to all his labor. **Ec 4:8** 7093
There is no **e** to all the people, **Ec 4:16** 7093
that is the **e** of every man, **Ec 7:2** 5490
The **e** of a matter is better than **Ec 7:8** 319
and the **e** of it is wicked madness. **Ec 10:13** 319
will come to an **e**. **Is 1:28** 3615
there is no **e** to their treasures; **Is 2:7** 7097b
there is no **e** to their chariots. **Is 2:7** 7097b
at the **e** of the conduit of the **Is 7:3** 7097a
There will be no **e** to the increase **Is 9:7** 7093
e to the arrogance of the proud And **Is 13:11** 7673a
the extortioner has come to an **e**, **Is 16:4** 656
I have made an **e** of all the **Is 21:2** 7673a
At the **e** of seventy years it will **Is 23:15** 7093
will come about at the **e** of seventy **Is 23:17** 7093
the ruthless will come to an **e** and **Is 29:20** 656
them will come to an **e** together. **Is 31:3** 3615
night You make an **e** of me. **Is 38:12** 7999a
night You make an **e** of me. **Is 38:13** 7999a
praise from the **e** of the earth! **Is 42:10** 7097a
Declaring the **e** from the beginning **Is 46:10** 319
Send it out to the **e** of the earth; **Is 48:20** 7097a
may reach to the **e** of the earth." **Is 49:6** 7097a
proclaimed to the **e** of the earth, **Is 62:11** 7097a
Will come to an **e** altogether," **Is 66:17** 5486
until the **e** of the eleventh year **Jer 1:3** 8552
Will He be indignant to the **e**?' **Jer 3:5** 5331
what will you do at the **e** of it? **Jer 5:31** 319
to ascend from the **e** of the earth; **Jer 10:13** 7097a
e of the land even to the other; **Jer 12:12** 7097a
to make an **e** of them by the sword, **Jer 14:12** 3615
those prophets shall meet their **e**! **Jer 14:15** 8552
come to an **e** by sword and famine, **Jer 16:4** 3615
And in the **e** he will be a fool." **Jer 17:11** 319
has come to the **e** of the earth, **Jer 25:31** 7097a
one **e** of the earth to the other. **Jer 25:33** 7097a
"At the **e** of seven years each of **Jer 34:14** 7093
at the **e** of ten days the word **Jer 42:7** 7093
meet their **e** in the land of Egypt; **Jer 44:12** 8552
sword *and* meet their **e** by famine. **Jer 44:12** 8552
e by the sword and by famine." **Jer 44:18** 8552
in the land of Egypt will meet their **e** **Jer 44:27** 8552
For I will make a full **e** of all **Jer 46:28** 3617
I will not make a full **e** of you; **Jer 46:28** 3617
"I will make an **e** of Moab," **Jer 48:35** 7673a
in treasures, Your **e** has come, **Jer 51:13** 7093
has come, The measure of your **e**. **Jer 51:13** 1215
to ascend from the **e** of the earth; **Jer 51:16** 7097a
has been captured from **e** *to end;* **Jer 51:31** 7097a
has been captured from end to **e**; **Jer 51:31**
Our **e** drew near, Our days were **La 4:18** 7093
were finished For our **e** had come. **La 4:18** 7093
At the **e** of seven days the word **Ezk 3:16** 7097a
may be broken and brought to an **e**, **Ezk 6:6** 7673a
GOD to the land of Israel, 'An **e**! **Ezk 7:2** 7093
The **e** is coming on the four **Ezk 7:2** 7093
'Now the **e** is upon you, and I **Ezk 7:3** 7093
'An **e** is coming; the end has come! **Ezk 7:6** 7093
'An end is coming; the **e** has come! **Ezk 7:6** 7093
of Israel to a complete **e**?" **Ezk 11:13** 3617
time of the punishment of the **e**,' **Ezk 21:25** 7093
time of the punishment of the **e**. **Ezk 21:29** 7093
"At the **e** of forty years I will **Ezk 29:13** 7093
time of the punishment of the **e**, **Ezk 35:5** 7093
At the **e** of seven months they will **Ezk 39:14** 7097a
at the **e** of which they were to **Da 1:5** 7117
At the **e** of ten days their **Da 1:15** 7117
Then at the **e** of the days which **Da 1:18** 7117
put an **e** to all these kingdoms, **Da 2:44** 5487
to the **e** of the whole earth. **Da 4:11** 5491
dominion to the **e** of the earth. **Da 4:22** 5491
"But at the **e** of that period, **Da 4:34** 7118
your kingdom and put an **e** to it. **Da 5:26** 8000
pertains to the time of the **e**." **Da 8:17** 7093
to the appointed time of the **e**. **Da 8:19** 7093
to make an **e** of sin, **Da 9:24** 8552
And its **e** *will come* with a flood; **Da 9:26** 7093
even to the **e** there will be war; **Da 9:26** 7093
for the **e** is still *to come* at the **Da 11:27** 7093
make them pure until the **e** time; **Da 11:35** 7093
"At the **e** time the king of **Da 11:40** 7093
yet he will come to his **e**, **Da 11:45** 7093
up the book until the **e** of time; **Da 12:4** 7093
be until the **e** of *these* wonders?" **Da 12:6** 7093
and sealed up until the **e** time. **Da 12:9** 7093
as for you, go *your way* to the **e**; **Da 12:13** 7093
portion at the **e** of the age." **Da 12:13** 7093
and I will put an **e** to the kingdom **Hos 1:4** 7673a
also put an **e** to all her gaiety, **Hos 2:11** 7673a
great houses will come to an **e**," **Am 3:15** 5486
e has come for My people Israel. **Am 8:2** 7093
And the **e** of it will be like a **Am 8:10** 319
make a complete **e** of its site, **Na 1:8** 3617
He will make a complete **e** of it. **Na 1:9** 3617
For He will make a complete **e**, **Zph 1:18** 3617
to the **e** that the temple might be **Zch 8:9**
to the **e** who will be saved. **Mt 10:22** *5056*
the harvest is the **e** of the age; **Mt 13:39** *4930*
shall it be at the **e** of the age. **Mt 13:40** *4930*
"So it will be at the **e** of the age; **Mt 13:49** *4930*
those wretches to a wretched **e**, **Mt 21:41** *622*
coming, and of the **e** of the age?" **Mt 24:3** *4930*
place, but *that* is not yet the **e**. **Mt 24:6** *5056*
"But the one who endures to the **e**, **Mt 24:13** *5056*
and then the **e** will come. **Mt 24:14** *5056*
one **e** of the sky to the other. **Mt 24:31** *206*
even to the **e** of the age." **Mt 28:20** *4930*
but *that is* not yet the **e**. **Mk 13:7** *5056*
but the one who endures to the **e**, **Mk 13:13** *5056*
from the farthest **e** of the earth to **Mk 13:27** *206*
to the farthest **e** of heaven. **Mk 13:27** *206*
and His kingdom will have no **e**." **Lk 1:33** *5056*
to the **e** that thoughts from many **Lk 2:35** *3704*
e *does* not *follow* immediately." **Lk 21:9** *5056*
"This sickness is not to **e** in death, **Jn 11:4** *4314*
the world, He loved them to the **e**. **Jn 13:1** *5056*
an **e** to the agony of death, **Ac 2:24** *3089*
TO THE **E** OF THE EARTH.'" **Ac 13:47** *2078*
At the **e** of three months we **Ac 28:11** *3326*
For Christ is the **e** of the law for **Ro 10:4** *5056*
e Christ died and lived again, **Ro 14:9**
will also confirm you to the **e**, **1Co 1:8** *5056*
then *comes* the **e**, when He hands **1Co 15:24** *5056*
you will understand until the **e**; **2Co 1:13** *5056*
For to this **e** also I wrote, **2Co 2:9**
at the **e** of what was fading away. **2Co 3:13** *5056*
whose **e** will be according to **2Co 11:15** *5056*
to the **e** that we who were the **Eph 1:12** *1519*
whose **e** is destruction, whose god **Php 3:19** *5056*
To this **e** also we pray for you **2Th 1:11** *1519*
bring to an **e** by the appearance of **2Th 2:8** *2673*
YOUR YEARS WILL NOT COME TO AN **E**." **Heb 1:12** *1587*
of our hope firm until the **e**. **Heb 3:6** *5056*
of our assurance firm until the **e**, **Heb 3:14** *5056*
assurance of hope until the **e**, **Heb 6:11** *5056*
is an **e** of every dispute. **Heb 6:16** *4009*
beginning of days nor **e** of life, **Heb 7:3** *5056*
The **e** of all things is near; **1Pe 4:7** *5056*
he who keeps My deeds until the **e**, **Rv 2:26** *5056*
Omega, the beginning and the **e**. **Rv 21:6** *5056*
last, the beginning and the **e**." **Rv 22:13** *5056*

ENDANGERED
who splits logs may be **e** by them. **Ec 10:9** 5533

ENDED
when the time of mourning was **e**, **Gn 38:12** 5162
When that year was **e**, **Gn 47:18** 8552
and the border **e** at the sea. **Jos 15:4** 1961, 8444
of En-shemesh and it **e** at En-rogel. **Jos 15:7** 1961, 8444
and the border **e** at the sea. **Jos 15:11** 1961, 8444
to Gezer, and it **e** at the sea. **Jos 16:3** 1961, 8444
of Kanah, and it **e** at the sea. **Jos 16:8** 1961, 8444
of the brook and it **e** at the sea. **Jos 17:9** 1961, 8444
and it **e** at the wilderness of **Jos 18:12** 1961, 8444
and it **e** at Kiriath-baal **Jos 18:14** 1961, 8444
and the border **e** at the north bay **Jos 18:19** 1961, 8444
it **e** at the valley of Iphtahel. **Jos 19:14** 1961, 8444
and their border **e** at the Jordan; **Jos 19:22** 1961, 8444
and it **e** at the sea by the region **Jos 19:29** 1961, 8444
and it **e** at the Jordan. **Jos 19:33** 1961, 8444
Abel,' and thus they **e** *the dispute.* **2Sa 20:18** 8552
The words of Job are **e**. **Jb 31:40** 8552
of David the son of Jesse are **e**. **Ps 72:20** 3615
For the vintage is **e**, **Is 32:10** 3615
to her, that her warfare has **e**, **Is 40:2** 4390
"Harvest is past, summer is **e**, **Jer 8:20** 3615
"At this point the revelation **e**. **Da 7:28** 5491
of his priestly service were **e**, **Lk 1:23** *4092a*
and when they had **e**, **Lk 4:2** *4931*
When our days there were **e**, **Ac 21:5** *1822*

ENDING
oldest and **e** with the youngest, **Gn 44:12** 3615
"He will not see our latter **e**." **Jer 12:4** 319
Now the day was **e**, and the twelve **Lk 9:12** *2827*

ENDLESS
the writing of many books is **e**, **Ec 12:12** 7093, 369
to myths and **e** genealogies, **1Tm 1:4** *562*

EN-DOR
inhabitants of **E** and its towns, **Jos 17:11** 5874
is a woman who is a medium at **E**." **1Sa 28:7** 5874
Who were destroyed at **E**, **Ps 83:10** 5874

ENDOW
e those who love me with wealth, **Pr 8:21** 5157

ENDOWED
"God has **e** me with a good gift; **Gn 30:20** 2064
have **e** with the spirit of wisdom, **Ex 28:3** 4390
e with discretion and **2Ch 2:12** 3045

skilled man, **e** with understanding, 2Ch 2:13 3045
which I have **e** My people Israel, Jer 12:14 5157
of wisdom, **e** with understanding Da 1:4 3045
He is just and **e** with salvation, Zch 9:9 3467

ENDS
at the two **e** of the mercy seat. Ex 25:18 7098
with the mercy seat at its two **e**. Ex 25:19 7098
pieces joined to its two **e**, Ex 28:7 7098
on the two **e** of the breastpiece. Ex 28:23 7098
rings at the **e** of the breastpiece. Ex 28:24 7098
put the *other* two **e** of the two cords Ex 28:25 7098
on the two **e** of the breastpiece, Ex 28:26 7098
at the two **e** of the mercy seat; Ex 37:7 7098
with the mercy seat at the two **e**. Ex 37:8 7098
four rings on the four **e** of the bronze Ex 38:5 7117
was attached at its two *upper* **e**. Ex 39:4 7117
on the two **e** of the breastpiece. Ex 39:16 7098
rings at the **e** of the breastpiece. Ex 39:17 7098
They put the *other* two **e** of Ex 39:18 7098
on the two **e** of the breastpiece, Ex 39:19 7098
are at the **e** of the earth, Dt 30:4 7097a
at once, *to* the **e** of the earth. Dt 33:17 657
LORD will judge the **e** of the earth; 1Sa 2:10 657
the **e** of the poles could be seen from 1Ki 8:8 7218
e of the poles of the ark could be 2Ch 5:9 7218
He looks to the **e** of the earth And Jb 28:24 7098
lightning to the **e** of the earth. Jb 37:3 3671
take hold of the **e** of the earth, Jb 38:13 3671
And the *very* **e** of the earth as Your Ps 2:8 657
All the **e** of the earth will Ps 22:27 657
Your praise to the **e** of the earth; Ps 48:10 7099
To the **e** of the earth. Ps 59:13 657
are the trust of all the **e** of the earth Ps 65:5 7099
They who dwell in the **e** *of the earth* Ps 65:8 7117
the **e** of the earth may fear Him. Ps 67:7 657
the River to the **e** of the earth. Ps 72:8 657
All the **e** of the earth have seen Ps 98:3 657
to ascend from the **e** of the earth; Ps 135:7 7097a
a fool are on the **e** of the earth. Pr 17:24 7097a
all the **e** of the earth? Pr 30:4 657
for it from the **e** of the earth; Is 5:26 7097a
the **e** of the earth we hear songs, Is 24:16 3671
the Creator of the **e** of the earth Is 40:28 7098
The **e** of the earth tremble; Is 41:5 7098
taken from the **e** of the earth, Is 41:9 7098
daughters from the **e** of the earth, Is 43:6 7097a
be saved, all the **e** of the earth; Is 45:22 657
That all the **e** of the earth may Is 52:10 657
From the **e** of the earth and say, Jer 16:19 657
winds From the four **e** of heaven, Jer 49:36 7098
fire has consumed both of its **e** and Ezk 15:4 7098
be great To the **e** of the earth. Mi 5:4 657
the River to the **e** of the earth. Zch 9:10 657
because she came from the **e** of the Mt 12:42 *4009*
because she came from the **e** of the Lk 11:31 *4009*
WORDS TO THE **E** OF THE WORLD." Ro 10:18 *4009*
whom the **e** of the ages have come. 1Co 10:11 *5056*
cursed, and it **e** up being burned. Heb 6:8 *5056*

ENDURANCE
your **e** you will gain your lives. Lk 21:19 *5281*
as servants of God, in much **e**, 2Co 6:4 *5281*
For you have need of **e**, Heb 10:36 *5281*
and let us run with **e** the race Heb 12:1 *5281*
testing of your faith produces **e**. Jas 1:3 *5281*
And let **e** have *its* perfect result, Jas 1:4 *5281*
You have heard of the **e** of Job and Jas 5:11 *5281*

ENDURE
you, then you will be able to **e**, Ex 18:23 5975
"But now your kingdom shall not **e**. 1Sa 13:14 6965
kingdom shall **e** before Me forever; 2Sa 7:16 539
"For how can I **e** to see the Es 8:6 3201
and how can I **e** to see the Es 8:6 3201
what is my end, that I should **e**? Jb 6:11 748, 5315
fast to it, but it does not **e**. Jb 8:15 6965
rich, nor will his wealth **e**; Jb 15:29 6965
his prosperity does not **e**. Jb 20:21 2342b
But man in *his* pomp will not **e**; Ps 49:12 3885a
May his name **e** forever; Ps 72:17 1961
"His descendants shall **e** forever And Ps 89:36 1961
and an arrogant heart will I **e**. Ps 101:5 3201
they will perish, but You **e**; Ps 102:26 5975
the glory of the LORD **e** forever; Ps 104:31 1961
of a man can **e** his sickness, Pr 18:14 3557
Nor does a crown **e** to all Pr 27:24
I cannot **e** iniquity and the solemn Is 1:13 3201
Which I make will **e** before Me," Is 66:22 5975
offspring and your name will **e**. Is 66:22 5975
nations cannot **e** His indignation. Jer 10:10 3557
that for Your sake I **e** reproach. Jer 15:15 5375
holding *it* in, And I cannot **e** *it*. Jer 20:9 3201
LORD was no longer able to **e** *it*, Jer 44:22 5375
"Can your heart **e**, or can your Ezk 22:14 5975
and they will not **e** the insults Ezk 34:29 5375
will themselves **e** their insults. Ezk 36:7 5375
but it will itself **e** forever. Da 2:44 6966
very awesome, And who can **e** it? Jl 2:11 3557
land is unable to **e** all his words. Am 7:10 3557
can **e** the burning of His anger? Na 1:6 6965
who can **e** the day of His coming? Mal 3:2 3557
when we are persecuted, we **e**; 1Co 4:12 *430*
this right, but we **e** all things so 1Co 9:12 *4722*
that you will be able to **e** it. 1Co 10:13 *5297*
when we could **e** it no longer, 1Th 3:1 *4722*
when I could **e** *it* no longer, 1Th 3:5 *4722*
and afflictions which you **e**. 2Th 1:4 *430*
For this reason I **e** all things for 2Tm 2:10 *5278*
If we **e**, we will also reign with 2Tm 2:12 *5278*
they will not **e** sound doctrine; 2Tm 4:3 *430*
sober in all things, **e** hardship, 2Tm 4:5 *2553*
choosing rather to **e** ill-treatment Heb 11:25 *4778*
It is for discipline that you **e**; Heb 12:7 *5278*
treated, you **e** it with patience? 1Pe 2:20 *5278*
suffer *for it* you patiently **e** it, 1Pe 2:20 *5278*

ENDURED
e the insults of the nations.' Ezk 36:6 5375
e to the end who will be saved. Mt 10:22 *5278*
and had **e** much at the hands of Mk 5:26 *3958*
e with much patience vessels of Ro 9:22 *5342*
for you also **e** the same sufferings 1Th 2:14 *3958*
what persecutions I **e**, 2Tm 3:11 *5297*
you **e** a great conflict of Heb 10:32 *5278*
for he **e**, as seeing Him who is Heb 11:27 *2594*
joy set before Him **e** the cross, Heb 12:2 *5278*
For consider Him who has **e** such Heb 12:3 *5278*
We count those blessed who **e**. Jas 5:11 *5278*
and have **e** for My name's sake, Rv 2:3 *941*

ENDURES
The lovingkindness of God **e** all Ps 52:1
them fear You while the sun **e**, Ps 72:5
And His righteousness **e** forever. Ps 111:3 5975
His praise **e** forever. Ps 111:10 5975
And his righteousness **e** forever. Ps 112:3 5975
His righteousness **e** forever; Ps 112:9 5975
And Your dominion **e** throughout Ps 145:13
and knowledge, so it **e**. Pr 28:2 748
And His kingdom **e** from generation Da 4:34
"But the one who **e** to the end, he Mt 24:13 *5278*
but the one who **e** to the end, Mk 13:13 *5278*
the food which **e** to eternal life, Jn 6:27 *3306*
hopes all things, **e** all things. 1Co 13:7 *5278*
HIS RIGHTEOUSNESS **E** FOREVER." 2Co 9:9 *3306*
BUT THE WORD OF THE LORD **E** FOREVER. 1Pe 1:25 *3306*

ENDURING
"Your dwelling place is **e**, Nu 24:21 386
and I will build him an **e** house, 1Sa 2:35 539
make for my lord an **e** house, 1Sa 25:28 539
an **e** house as I built for David, 1Ki 11:38 539
of the LORD is clean, **e** forever; Ps 19:9 5975
me, **E** wealth and righteousness. Pr 8:18 6276
"It is an **e** nation, It is an Jer 5:15 386
is the living God and **e** forever, Da 6:26 7011
you **e** foundations of the earth, Mi 6:2 386
in the patient **e** of the same sufferings 2Co 1:6 *5281*
through the living and **e** word of 1Pe 1:23 *3306*

ENEGLAIM
from Engedi to **E** there will be a Ezk 47:10 5882

ENEMIES
delivered your **e** into your hand." Gn 14:20 6862c
shall possess the gate of their **e**. Gn 22:17 340
shall be on the neck of your **e**; Gn 49:8 340
I will be an enemy to your **e** and Ex 23:22 340
your **e** turn *their* backs to you. Ex 23:27 340
to be a derision among their **e** Ex 32:25 6965
'But you will chase your **e** and Lv 26:7 340
and your **e** will fall before you by Lv 26:8 340
for your **e** will eat it up. Lv 26:16 340
be struck down before your **e**; Lv 26:17 340
e who settle in it will be appalled Lv 26:32 340
hearts in the lands of their **e**. Lv 26:36 340
to stand up before your **e**. Lv 26:37 340
iniquity in the lands of your **e**; Lv 26:39 340
to bring them into the land of their **e** Lv 26:41 340
they are in the land of their **e**, Lv 26:44 340
God, and be saved from your **e**. Nu 10:9 340
And let Your **e** be scattered, And Nu 10:35 340
you will be struck down before your **e**, Nu 14:42 340
I took you to curse my **e**, Nu 23:11 340
"I called you to curse my **e**, Nu 24:10 340
be a possession, Seir, its **e**, Nu 24:18 340
driven His **e** out from before Him, Nu 32:21 340
you will be defeated before your **e**." ' Dt 1:42 340
out all your **e** from before you, Dt 6:19 340
and He gives you rest from all your **e** Dt 12:10 340
you go out to battle against your **e** Dt 20:1 340
the battle against your **e** today. Dt 20:3 340
to fight for you against your **e**, Dt 20:4 340
and you shall use the spoil of your **e** Dt 20:14 340
go out to battle against your **e**, Dt 21:10 340
go out as an army against your **e**, Dt 23:9 340
and to defeat your **e** before you, Dt 23:14 340
rest from all your surrounding **e**, Dt 25:19 340
"The LORD shall cause your **e** who Dt 28:7 340
you to be defeated before your **e**; Dt 28:25 340
sheep shall be given to your **e**, Dt 28:31 340
therefore you shall serve your **e** Dt 28:48 340
your **e** as male and female slaves, Dt 28:68 340
your **e** and on those who hate you, Dt 30:7 340
Even our **e** themselves judge this. Dt 32:31 340
So your **e** will cringe before you, Dt 33:29 340
turned *their* back before their **e**? Jos 7:8 340
cannot stand before their **e**; Jos 7:12 340
turn *their* backs before their **e**, Jos 7:12 340
You cannot stand before your **e** Jos 7:13 340
avenged themselves of their **e**. Jos 10:13 340
e and attack them in the rear. Jos 10:19 340
all your **e** with whom you fight." Jos 10:25 340
of all their **e** stood before them; Jos 21:44 340
gave all their **e** into their hand. Jos 21:44 340
of your **e** with your brothers." Jos 22:8 340
from all their **e** on every side, Jos 23:1 340
the hands of their **e** around *them*, Jg 2:14 340
no longer stand before their **e**. Jg 2:14 340
them from the hand of their **e** Jg 2:18 340
e the Moabites into your hands." Jg 3:28 340
"Thus let all Your **e** perish, Jg 5:31 340
of all their **e** on every side; Jg 8:34 340
LORD has avenged you of your **e**, Jg 11:36 340
mouth speaks boldly against my **e**, 1Sa 2:1 340
deliver us from the power of our **e**." 1Sa 4:3 340
us from the hands of our **e**, 1Sa 12:10 340
the hands of your **e** all around, 1Sa 12:11 340
I have avenged myself on my **e**." 1Sa 14:24 340
spoil of their **e** which they found! 1Sa 14:30 340
against all his **e** on every side, 1Sa 14:47 340
take vengeance on the king's **e**.' " 1Sa 18:25 340
cuts off every one of the **e** of David 1Sa 20:15 340
it at the hands of David's **e**." 1Sa 20:16 340
"May God do so to the **e** of David, 1Sa 25:22 340
own hand, now then let your **e** and 1Sa 25:26 340
but the lives of your **e** He will 1Sa 25:29 340
the **e** of my lord the king?" 1Sa 29:8 340
the spoil of the **e** of the LORD: 1Sa 30:26 340
from the hand of all their **e**.' " 2Sa 3:18 340
"The LORD has broken through my **e** 2Sa 5:20 340
rest on every side from all his **e**, 2Sa 7:1 340
cut off all your **e** from before you; 2Sa 7:9 340
give you rest from all your **e**. 2Sa 7:11 340
to the **e** of the LORD to blaspheme, 2Sa 12:14 340
him from the hand of his **e**." 2Sa 18:19 340
"Let the **e** of my lord the king, 2Sa 18:32 340
delivered us from the hand of our **e** 2Sa 19:9 340
his **e** and from the hand of Saul. 2Sa 22:1 340
And I am saved from my **e**. 2Sa 22:4 340
"I pursued my **e** and destroyed 2Sa 22:38 340
made my **e** turn *their* backs to me, 2Sa 22:41 340
Who also brings me out from my **e**; 2Sa 22:49 340
you asked for the life of your **e**, 1Ki 3:11 340
e who have taken them captive, 1Ki 8:48 340
you from the hand of all your **e**." 2Ki 17:39 340
them into the hand of their **e**, 2Ki 21:14 340
plunder and spoil to all their **e**; 2Ki 21:14 340
broken through my **e** by my hand, 1Ch 14:11 340
cut off all your **e** from before you; 1Ch 17:8 340
And I will subdue all your **e**. 1Ch 17:10 340
the sword of your **e** overtakes *you*, 1Ch 21:12 340
rest from all his **e** on every side; 1Ch 22:9 340
if their **e** besiege them in the 2Ch 6:28 340
go out to battle against their **e**, 2Ch 6:34 340
made them to rejoice over their **e**. 2Ch 20:27 340
fought against the **e** of Israel. 2Ch 20:29 340
Now when the **e** of Judah and Ezr 4:1 6862c
Our **e** said, "They will not know Ne 4:11 6862c
e heard that it was known to us, Ne 4:15 340
reproach of the nations, our **e**? Ne 5:9 340
and to the rest of our **e** that I had Ne 6:1 340
When all our **e** heard *of it*, Ne 6:16 340
them to the hand of their **e**, Ne 9:28 340
to avenge themselves on their **e**. Es 8:13 340
on the day when the **e** of the Jews Es 9:1 340
struck all their **e** with the sword, Es 9:5 340
And rid themselves of their **e**, Es 9:16 340
Jews rid themselves of their **e**, Es 9:22 340
smitten all my **e** on the cheek; Ps 3:7 340
All my **e** will be ashamed and Ps 6:10 340
When my **e** turn back, They stumble Ps 9:3 340
who despoil me, My deadly **e** who Ps 17:9 340
praised, And I am saved from my **e**. Ps 18:3 340
I pursued my **e** and overtook them, Ps 18:37 340
made my **e** turn their backs to me, Ps 18:40 340
He delivers me from my **e**; Ps 18:48 340
hand will find out all your **e**; Ps 21:8 340
before me in the presence of my **e**; Ps 23:5 6887c
Do not let my **e** exult over me. Ps 25:2 340
Look upon my **e**, for they are many, Ps 25:19 340
my flesh, My adversaries and my **e**, Ps 27:2 340
be lifted up above my **e** around me, Ps 27:6 340
have not let my **e** rejoice over me. Ps 30:1 340
Deliver me from the hand of my **e** and Ps 31:15 340
wrongfully my **e** rejoice over me; Ps 35:19 340
And the **e** of the LORD will be like Ps 37:20 340
But my **e** are vigorous *and* strong, Ps 38:19 340
him over to the desire of his **e**. Ps 41:2 340
My **e** speak evil against me, Ps 41:5 340
are in the heart of the King's **e**. Ps 45:5 340
with satisfaction upon my **e**. Ps 54:7 340
Then my **e** will turn back in the Ps 56:9 340
Deliver me from my **e**, Ps 59:1 340
Your **e** will give feigned obedience Ps 66:3 340
God arise, let His **e** be scattered, Ps 68:1 340
will shatter the head of His **e**, Ps 68:21 340
have its portion from *your* **e**." Ps 68:23 340
being wrongfully my **e** Ps 69:4 340
Ransom me because of my **e**! Ps 69:18 340
For my **e** have spoken against me; Ps 71:10 340
And his **e** lick the dust. Ps 72:9 340
But the sea engulfed their **e**. Ps 78:53 340
And our **e** laugh among themselves. Ps 80:6 340
"I would quickly subdue their **e** And Ps 81:14 340
behold, Your **e** make an uproar Ps 83:2 340
Your **e** with Your mighty arm. Ps 89:10 340
You have made all his **e** rejoice. Ps 89:42 340
which Your **e** have reproached, Ps 89:51 340
For, behold, Your **e**, O LORD, Ps 92:9 340
For, behold, Your **e** will perish; Ps 92:9 340
My **e** have reproached me all day Ps 102:8 340
Their **e** also oppressed them, And Ps 106:42 340
e a footstool for Your feet." Ps 110:1 340
"Rule in the midst of Your **e**." Ps 110:2 340
make me wiser than my **e**, Ps 119:98 340
speak with their **e** in the gate. Ps 127:5 340
"His **e** I will clothe with shame, Ps 132:18 340
hand against the wrath of my **e**, Ps 138:7 340
And Your **e** take *Your name* in vain. Ps 139:20 6145
They have become my **e**. Ps 139:22 340

Deliver me, O LORD, from my **e**; Ps 143:9 340
Your lovingkindness, cut off my **e** Ps 143:12 340
his **e** to be at peace with him. Pr 16:7 340
from Rezin And spurs their **e** on, Is 9:11 340
Indeed, fire will devour Your **e**. Is 26:11 6862c
e will become like fine dust, Is 29:5 2114a
He will prevail against His **e**. Is 42:13 340
adversaries, recompense to His **e**; Is 59:18 340
your grain *as* food for your **e**; Is 62:8 340
is rendering recompense to His **e**. Is 66:6 340
will be indignant toward His **e**. Is 66:14 340
of My soul Into the hand of her **e**. Jer 12:7 340
to the sword Before their **e**," Jer 15:9 340
"Then I will cause your **e** to Jer 15:14 340
And I will make you serve your **e** Jer 17:4 340
to fall by the sword before their **e** Jer 19:7 340
in the distress with which their **e** and Jer 19:9 340
will fall by the sword of their **e**. Jer 20:4 340
give over to the hand of their **e**, Jer 20:5 340
give them into the hand of their **e** Jer 34:20 340
give into the hand of their **e** and Jer 34:21 340
of Egypt to the hand of his **e**, Jer 44:30 340
'So I will shatter Elam before their **e** Jer 49:37 340
They have become her **e**. La 1:2 340
become her masters, Her **e** prosper; La 1:5 340
my **e** have heard of my calamity; La 1:21 340
All your **e** Have opened their La 2:16 340
All our **e** have opened their mouths La 3:46 340
My **e** without cause Hunted me down La 3:52 340
them from the lands of their **e**, Ezk 39:27 340
go into captivity before their **e**, Am 9:4 340
you From the hand of your **e**. Mi 4:10 340
And all your **e** will be cut off. Mi 5:9 340
A man's **e** are the men of his own Mi 7:6 340
And He reserves wrath for His **e**. Na 1:2 340
will pursue His **e** into darkness. Na 1:8 340
land are opened wide to your **e**; Na 3:13 340
you, He has cleared away your **e**. Zph 3:15 340
was no peace because of his **e**, Zch 8:10 6862c
"But I say to you, love your **e** and Mt 5:44 *2190*
and A MAN'S **E** WILL BE THE MEMBERS Mt 10:36 *2190*
PUT YOUR **E** BENEATH YOUR FEET"'? Mt 22:44 *2190*
PUT YOUR **E** BENEATH YOUR FEET."' Mk 12:36 *2190*
Salvation FROM OUR **E** Lk 1:71 *2190*
rescued from the hand of our **e**, Lk 1:74 *2190*
say to you who hear, love your **e**, Lk 6:27 *2190*
"But love your **e**, and do good, Lk 6:35 *2190*
"But these **e** of mine, who did not Lk 19:27 *2190*
e will throw up a barricade against you, Lk 19:43 *2190*
E A FOOTSTOOL FOR YOUR FEET."' Lk 20:43 *2190*
for before they had been **e** with each Lk 23:12 *2189b*
E A FOOTSTOOL FOR YOUR FEET."' Ac 2:35 *2190*
For if while we were **e** we Ro 5:10 *2190*
gospel they are **e** for your sake, Ro 11:28 *2190*
has put all His **e** under His feet. 1Co 15:25 *2190*
they are **e** of the cross of Christ, Php 3:18 *2190*
E A FOOTSTOOL FOR YOUR FEET"? Heb 1:13 *2190*
UNTIL HIS **E** BE MADE A FOOTSTOOL Heb 10:13 *2190*
their mouth and devours their **e**; Rv 11:5 *2190*
cloud, and their **e** watched them. Rv 11:12 *2190*

ENEMIES'
while you are in your **e** land; then Lv 26:34 340
and your **e** land will consume you. Lv 26:38 340

ENEMY
hand, O LORD, shatters the **e**. Ex 15:6 340
e said, 'I will pursue, I will overtake, Ex 15:9 340
then I will be an **e** to your Ex 23:22 340
shall be delivered into **e** hands. Lv 26:25 340
not his **e** nor seeking his injury, Nu 35:23 340
by which your **e** will oppress you. Dt 28:53 340
distress by which your **e** will oppress Dt 28:55 340
e will oppress you in your towns Dt 28:57 340
feared the provocation by the **e**, Dt 32:27 340
the long-haired leaders of the **e**.' Dt 32:42 340
drove out the **e** from before you, Dt 33:27 340
Samson our **e** into our hands." Jg 16:23 340
has given our **e** into our hands, Jg 16:24 340
Saul was David's **e** continually. 1Sa 18:29 340
me like this and let my **e** go, 1Sa 19:17 340
to give your **e** into your hand, 1Sa 24:4 340
"For if a man finds his **e**, 1Sa 24:19 340
delivered your **e** into your hand; 1Sa 26:8 340
the son of Saul, your **e**, 2Sa 4:8 340
"He delivered me from my strong **e**, 2Sa 22:18 340
Israel are defeated before an **e**, 1Ki 8:33 340
if their **e** besieges them in the 1Ki 8:37 340
go out to battle against their **e**, 1Ki 8:44 340
and deliver them to an **e**, 1Ki 8:46 340
away captive to the land of the **e**, 1Ki 8:46 340
"Have you found me, O my **e**?" 1Ki 21:20 340
Israel are defeated before an **e** because 2Ch 6:24 340
and deliver them to an **e**, 2Ch 6:36 340
will bring you down before the **e**, 2Ch 25:8 340
to help the king against the **e**. 2Ch 26:13 340
protect us from the **e** on the way, Ezr 8:22 340
the **e** and the ambushes by the way. Ezr 8:31 340
the Agagite, the **e** of the Jews. Es 3:10 6887c
"A foe and an **e** is this wicked Es 7:6 340
house of Haman, the **e** of the Jews, Es 8:1 6887c
son of Hammedatha, the Jews' **e**; Es 9:10 6887c
Your face And consider me Your **e**? Jb 13:24 340
me And considered me as His **e**. Jb 19:11 6862c
"May my **e** be as the wicked And Jb 27:7 340
at the extinction of my **e**, Jb 31:29 8130
He counts me as His **e**. Jb 33:10 340
Let the **e** pursue my soul and Ps 7:5 340
the **e** and the revengeful cease. Ps 8:2 340
The **e** has come to an end in Ps 9:6 340
long will my **e** be exalted over me? Ps 13:2 340
my **e** will say, "I have overcome him," Ps 13:4 340
He delivered me from my strong **e**, Ps 18:17 340
me over into the hand of the **e**; Ps 31:8 340
Because my **e** does not shout in Ps 41:11 340
because of the oppression of the **e**?" Ps 42:9 340
because of the oppression of the **e**? Ps 43:2 340
presence of the **e** and the avenger. Ps 44:16 340
Because of the voice of the **e**, Ps 55:3 340
it is not an **e** who reproaches me, Ps 55:12 340
A tower of strength against the **e**. Ps 61:3 340
my life from dread of the **e**. Ps 64:1 340
The **e** has damaged everything Ps 74:3 340
And the **e** spurn Your name forever? Ps 74:10 340
O LORD, that the **e** has reviled, Ps 74:18 340
"The **e** will not deceive him, Nor Ps 89:22 340
them from the hand of the **e**. Ps 106:10 340
For the **e** has persecuted my soul; Ps 143:3 340
Do not rejoice when your **e** falls, Pr 24:17 340
If your **e** is hungry, give him food Pr 25:21 8130
deceitful are the kisses of an **e**. Pr 27:6 8130
turned Himself to become their **e**, Is 63:10 340
the road, For the **e** has a sword, Jer 6:25 340
Surely I will cause the **e** to make Jer 15:11 340
I will scatter them Before the **e**; Jer 18:17 340
so that *the* **e** will withdraw from Jer 21:2 340
you with the wound of an **e**, Jer 30:14 340
return from the land of the **e**. Jer 31:16 340
e and was seeking his life.'" Jer 44:30 340
For the **e** has magnified himself!" La 1:9 340
Because the **e** has prevailed." La 1:16 340
His right hand From before the **e**. La 2:3 340
He has bent His bow like an **e**; La 2:4 340
The Lord has become like an **e**. La 2:5 340
of the **e** The walls of her palaces. La 2:7 340
caused the **e** to rejoice over you; La 2:17 340
and reared, My **e** annihilated them. La 2:22 340
That the adversary and the **e** Could La 4:12 340
the **e** has spoken against you, Ezk 36:2 340
Like an eagle *the* **e** *comes* against Hos 8:1
The **e** will pursue him. Hos 8:3 340
"An **e**, even one surrounding the Am 3:11 6862c
My people have arisen as an **e** Mi 2:8 340
Do not rejoice over me, O my **e**. Mi 7:8 340
Then my **e** will see, And shame will Mi 7:10 340
search for a refuge from the **e**. Na 3:11 340
Treading down *the* **e** in the mire Zch 10:5
YOUR NEIGHBOR and hate your **e**.' Mt 5:43 *2190*
his **e** came and sowed tares among Mt 13:25 *2190*
'An **e** has done this!' Mt 13:28
2190, 444
the **e** who sowed them is the devil, Mt 13:39 *2190*
and over all the power of the **e**, Lk 10:19 *2190*
devil, you **e** of all righteousness, Ac 13:10 *2190*
"BUT IF YOUR **E** IS HUNGRY, FEED Ro 12:20 *2190*
The last **e** that will be abolished 1Co 15:26 *2190*
your **e** by telling you the truth? Ga 4:16 *2190*
Yet do not regard him as an **e**, 2Th 3:15 *2190*
the **e** no occasion for reproach; 1Tm 5:14 *480*
world makes himself an **e** of God. Jas 4:4 *2190*

ENEMY'S
"If you meet your **e** ox or his Ex 23:4 340

ENFORCE
establish a statute and **e** an injunction Da 6:7 8631

ENGAGE
and Josiah went out to **e** him. 2Ch 35:20 7122
will be careful to **e** in good deeds. Ti 3:8 *4291b*
people must also learn to **e** in good Ti 3:14 *4291b*
e in business and make a profit." Jas 4:13 *1710*

ENGAGED
man seduces a virgin who is not **e**, Ex 22:16 781
'And who is the man that is **e** to a Dt 20:7 781
a girl who is a virgin **e** to a man, Dt 22:23 781
the man finds the girl who is **e**, Dt 22:25 781
the field, the **e** girl cried out, Dt 22:27 781
who is a virgin, who is not **e**, Dt 22:28 781
e in their work day and night. 1Ch 9:33 5921
e in conflict with the LORD." Jer 50:24 1624
to a virgin **e** to a man whose name Lk 1:27 *3423*
along with Mary, who was **e** to him, Lk 2:5 *3423*
"While so **e** as I was journeying Ac 26:12
e in evil deeds, Col 1:21

EN-GANNIM
and Zanoah and **E**, Tappuah and Jos 15:34 5873
and **E** and En-haddah and Beth-pazzez. Jos 19:21 5873
lands, **E** with its pasture lands; Jos 21:29 5873

ENGEDI
and the City of Salt and **E**; Jos 15:62 5872
stayed in the strongholds of **E**. 1Sa 23:29 5872
David is in the wilderness of **E**." 1Sa 24:1 5872
are in Hazazon-tamar (that is **E**)." 2Ch 20:2 5872
blossoms In the vineyards of **E**." SS 1:14 5872
from **E** to Eneglaim there will be a Ezk 47:10 5872

ENGINES
In Jerusalem he made **e** *of war* 2Ch 26:15 2810

ENGRAVE
take two onyx stones and **e** on them Ex 28:9 6605b
you shall **e** the two stones Ex 28:11 6605b
of pure gold and shall **e** on it, Ex 28:36 6605b
I will **e** an inscription on it,' Zch 3:9 6605b

ENGRAVED
was God's writing **e** on the tablets. Ex 32:16 2801
they were **e** *like* the engravings of Ex 39:6 6605b
e *with* the engravings of a signet, Ex 39:14
down the **e** images of their gods and Dt 12:3 6456
gold evenly applied on the **e** work. 1Ki 6:35 2707
He **e** on the plates of its 1Ki 7:36 6605b
They were **e** in the rock forever! Jb 19:24 2672
With a diamond point it is **e** upon Jer 17:1 2790a
of death, in letters **e** on stones, 2Co 3:7 *1795*

ENGRAVER
skill to perform every work of an **e** Ex 35:35 2796
an **e** and a skillful workman and a Ex 38:23 2796

ENGRAVES
"As a jeweler **e** a signet, you Ex 28:11 6603

ENGRAVINGS
shall be *like* the **e** of a seal, Ex 28:21 6603
on it, like the **e** of a seal, Ex 28:36 6603
engraved *like* the **e** of a signet, Ex 39:6 6603
engraved with the **e** of a signet, Ex 39:14 6603
it like the **e** of a signet, Ex 39:30 6603
about with carved **e** of cherubim, 1Ki 6:29 6603
also on its opening *there were* **e**, 1Ki 7:31 4734
and who knows how to make **e**, 2Ch 2:7 6603
who knows how to make all kinds of **e** 2Ch 2:14 6605b

ENGULF
made the water of the Red Sea to **e** Dt 11:4 6687

ENGULFED
But the sea **e** their enemies. Ps 78:53 3680
And **e** the company of Abiram. Ps 106:17 3680
Then the waters would have **e** us, Ps 124:4 7857
been **e** with its tumultuous waves. Jer 51:42 3680
of the seas, And the current **e** me. Jon 2:3 5437
The great deep **e** me, Weeds were Jon 2:5 5437

EN-HADDAH
and En-gannim and **E** and Beth-pazzez. Jos 19:21 5876

EN-HAKKORE
Therefore he named it **E**, Jg 15:19 5875

EN-HAZOR
and Kedesh and Edrei and **E**, Jos 19:37 5877

ENIGMAS
of dreams, explanation of **e** and Da 5:12 280

ENJOY
'Then the land will **e** its sabbaths Lv 26:34 7521
land will rest and **e** its sabbaths. Lv 26:34 7521
E your glory and stay at home; 2Ki 14:10 3513
trading, He cannot even **e** *them.* Jb 20:18 5965
test you with pleasure. So **e** yourself." Ec 2:1
7200, 2896b
to drink and **e** oneself in all Ec 5:18
7200, 2899b
and does not **e** good things Ec 6:6
7200, 2899b
E life with the woman whom you Ec 9:9 7200
will plant And will **e** *them.* Jer 31:5 2490c
but he used to **e** listening to him. Mk 6:20 *2234*
supplies us with all things to **e**. 1Tm 6:17 *619*
to **e** the passing pleasures of sin, Heb 11:25 *619*

ENJOYED
until the land had **e** its sabbaths. 2Ch 36:21 7521
So this Daniel **e** success in the Da 6:28 6744
large crowd **e** listening to Him. Mk 12:37 *2234*
and Galilee and Samaria **e** peace, Ac 9:31 *2192*
first **e** your company for a while Ro 15:24 *1705a*

ENJOYMENT
and who can have **e** without Him? Ec 2:25 2363b
Men prepare a meal for **e**, Ec 10:19 7814

ENJOYS
fruit of a man's mouth he **e** good, Pr 13:2 398
from them, for a foreigner **e** them. Ec 6:2 398

ENLARGE
"May God **e** Japheth, And let him Gn 9:27 6601a
before you and **e** your borders, Ex 34:24 7337
"You **e** my steps under me, 2Sa 22:37 7337
bless me indeed and **e** my border, 1Ch 4:10 7235a
You **e** my steps under me, And Ps 18:36 7337
For You will **e** my heart. Ps 119:32 7337
"**E** the place of your tent; Is 54:2 7337
you **e** your eyes with paint, Jer 4:30 7167
In order to **e** their borders. Am 1:13 7337

ENLARGED
The troubles of my heart are **e**; Ps 25:17 7337
I **e** my works: I built houses Ec 2:4 1431
Therefore Sheol has **e** its throat Is 5:14 7337
our sphere, **e** even more by you, 2Co 10:15 *3170*
because your faith is greatly **e**, 2Th 1:3 *5232*

ENLARGES
LORD your God **e** your territory, Dt 19:8 7337
"Blessed is the one who **e** Gad; Dt 33:20 7337
He **e** the nations, then leads them Jb 12:23 7849
He **e** his appetite like Sheol, And Hab 2:5 7337

ENLIGHTEN
that our God may **e** our eyes and Ezr 9:8 215
E my eyes, or I will sleep the *sleep* Ps 13:3 215

ENLIGHTENED
may be **e** with the light of life. Jb 33:30 215
the eyes of your heart may be **e**, Eph 1:18 *5461*
who have once been **e** and have tasted Heb 6:4 *5461*
former days, when, after being **e**, Heb 10:32 *5461*

ENLIGHTENING
of the LORD is pure, **e** the eyes. Ps 19:8 215

ENLIGHTENS
into the world, **e** every man. Jn 1:9 *5461*

ENLISTED
the one who **e** him as a soldier. 2Tm 2:4 *4758*

EN-MISHPAT
they turned back and came to **E** Gn 14:7 5880

ENMITIES
idolatry, sorcery, **e**, Ga 5:20 *2189b*

ENMITY
put **e** Between you and the woman, Gn 3:15 342

him down with his hand in e, Nu 35:21 342
he pushed him suddenly without e, Nu 35:22 342
having e toward him in time past; Dt 4:42 8130
to destroy with everlasting e," Ezk 25:15 342
"Because you have had everlasting e Ezk 35:5 342
by abolishing in His flesh the e, Eph 2:15 *2189b*
by it having put to death the e. Eph 2:16 *2189b*

ENOCH
conceived, and gave birth to E; Gn 4:17 2585
and called the name of the city E, Gn 4:17 2585
Now to E was born Irad, Gn 4:18 2585
years, and became the father of E. Gn 5:18 2585
after he became the father of E, Gn 5:19 2585
E lived sixty-five years, and Gn 5:21 2585
Then E walked with God three Gn 5:22 2585
So all the days of E were three Gn 5:23 2585
E walked with God; Gn 5:24 2585
E, Methuselah, Lamech, 1Ch 1:3 2585
son of Methuselah, the son of E, Lk 3:37 *1802*
By faith E was taken up so that he Heb 11:5 *1802*
It was also about these men *that* E, Jude 1:14 *1802*

ENOSH
and he called his name E. Gn 4:26 583
years, and became the father of E. Gn 5:6 583
after he became the father of E, Gn 5:7 583
E lived ninety years, and Gn 5:9 583
Then E lived eight hundred and Gn 5:10 583
So all the days of E were nine Gn 5:11 583
Adam, Seth, E, 1Ch 1:1 583
the son of E, the son of Seth, the Lk 3:38 *1800*

ENOUGH
now behold, this town is near e Gn 19:20
the land is large e for them. Gn 34:21 3027
"It is e; my son Joseph is still alive. Gn 45:28 7227a
been e of God's thunder and hail; Ex 9:28 7227a
more than e for the construction work Ex 36:5 1767
and more than e for all the work, Ex 36:7 3498
"You have gone far e, Nu 16:3 7227a
You have gone far e, Nu 16:7 7227a
is it not e for you that the God Nu 16:9 4592
"Is it not e that you have Nu 16:13 4592
stayed long e at this mountain. Dt 1:6 7227a
have circled this mountain long e. Dt 2:3 7227a
and the LORD said to me, 'E! Dt 3:26 7227a
angry e with Aaron to destroy him; Dt 9:20 3966
"The hill country is not e for us, Jos 17:16 4672
not the iniquity of Peor e for us, Jos 22:17 4592
yet they were not e for them. Jg 21:14 3651
e of them for 100 chariots. 2Sa 8:4
"It is e! Now relax your hand!" 2Sa 24:16 7227a
e to hold two measures of seed. 1Ki 18:32
"It is e; now, O LORD, take my life, 1Ki 19:4 7227a
e of them for 100 chariots. 1Ch 18:4
said to the destroying angel, "It is e; 1Ch 21:15 7227a
e to eat with plenty left over, 2Ch 31:10 7646
For my soul has had e troubles, Ps 88:3 7646
has e to satisfy his appetite, Pr 13:25 398
be goats' milk e for your food, Pr 27:27 1767
Four that will not say, "E": Pr 30:15 1952
And fire that never says, "E." Pr 30:16 1952
had e of burnt offerings of rams And Is 1:11 7646
and honey at the time He knows e Is 7:15
"For before the boy will know e Is 7:16
Even Lebanon is not e to burn, Is 40:16 1767
its beasts e for a burnt offering. Is 40:16 1767
destroy *only* until they had e. Jer 49:9 1767
All who plunder her will have e," Jer 50:10 7646
Egypt *and* Assyria to get e bread. La 5:6 7646
"E of all your abominations, O Ezk 44:6 7227a
"E, you princes of Israel; Ezk 45:9 7227a
e water to swim in, a river that Ezk 47:5
They will eat, but not have e; Hos 4:10 7646
not steal *only* until they had e? Ob 1:5 1767
The lion tore e for his cubs, Na 2:12 1767
Killed e for his lionesses, Na 2:12
but *there is* not e to be Hg 1:6
but *there is* not e to become Hg 1:6
but no one is warm e; and he who Hg 1:6
shall be guilty e *to go* into Mt 5:22
Each day has e trouble of its own. Mt 6:34 *713*
"It is e for the disciple that he Mt 10:25 *713*
will not be e for us and you *too* Mt 25:9 *714*
no one was strong e to subdue him. Mk 5:4 *2480*
"Where will anyone be able *to find* e Mk 8:4
It is e; the hour has come; Mk 14:41 *568*
'The old is good e.'" Lk 5:39
to see if he has e to complete it? Lk 14:28
he is strong e with ten thousand *men* Lk 14:31 *1415*
hired men have more than e bread, Lk 15:17 *4052*
I am not strong e to dig; Lk 16:3 *2480*
And He said to them, "It is e." Lk 22:38 *2425*
the Father, and it is e for us." Jn 14:8 *714*
and you have been kind e to come. Ac 10:33 *2573*
When they had eaten e, Ac 27:38
2880, 5160
For you are giving thanks well e, 1Co 14:17 *2573*
though I have e confidence in Phm 1:8 *4183*
and they were not strong e, Rv 12:8 *2480*

ENRAGED
of Aram was e over this thing; 2Ki 6:11 5590
for he was e at him for this. 2Ch 16:10 2197
hand for burning incense, was e; 2Ch 26:19 2196
while he was e with the priests, 2Ch 26:19 2196
they will be e and curse their Is 8:21 7107
but have e Me by all these things, Ezk 16:43 7264
the ram, and he was e at him; Da 8:7 4843
"The king of the South will be e Da 11:11 4843
and will return and become e at Da 11:30 2194
by the magi, he became very e, Mt 2:16 *2373*
king was e, and he sent his armies Mt 22:7 *3710*
and being furiously e at them, Ac 26:11 *1693*
"And the nations were e, Rv 11:18 *3710*
the dragon was e with the woman, Rv 12:17 *3710*

ENRAGES
For jealousy e a man, And he will Pr 6:34 2534

ENRICH
the king will e the man who kills him 1Sa 17:25 6238
You greatly e it; Ps 65:9 6238

ENRICHED
You e the kings of earth. Ezk 27:33 6238
in everything you were e in Him, 1Co 1:5 *4148*
you will be e in everything for 2Co 9:11 *4148*

EN-RIMMON
and in E, in Zorah and in Jarmuth, Ne 11:29 5884

EN-ROGEL
of En-shemesh and it ended at E. Jos 15:7 5883
southward, and went down to E. Jos 18:16 5883
and Ahimaaz were staying at E, 2Sa 17:17 5883
of Zoheleth, which is beside E; 1Ki 1:9 5883

ENROLLED
so that he is not e in the 1Ch 5:1 3187
All of these were e in the 1Ch 5:17 3187
men of valor, e by genealogy, 1Ch 7:5 3187
and were 22,034 e by genealogy. 1Ch 7:7 3187
They were e by genealogy, 1Ch 7:9 3187
And the number of them e by 1Ch 7:40 3187
all Israel was e by genealogies; 1Ch 9:1 3187
These were e by genealogy in their 1Ch 9:22 3187
as well as the priests who were e 2Ch 31:17 3187
e among the Levites. 2Ch 31:19 3187
the people to be e by genealogies. Ne 7:5 3187
the firstborn who are e in heaven, Heb 12:23 *583*

ENROLLMENT
seer, according to genealogical e? 2Ch 12:15 3187
regard to their genealogical e, 2Ch 31:16 3187
The genealogical e *included* 2Ch 31:18 3187
the genealogical e of those who went Ezr 8:1 3187

EN-SHEMESH
continued to the waters of E and Jos 15:7 5885
went to E and went to Geliloth, Jos 18:17 5885

ENSLAVED
where they will be e and oppressed Gn 15:13 5647
service in which you have been e, Is 14:3 5647
from the hand of those who e them. Ezk 34:27 5647
have never yet been e to anyone; Jn 8:33 *1398*
AND THAT THEY WOULD BE E AND Ac 7:6 *1402*
been freed from sin and e to God, Ro 6:22 *1402*
you desire to be e all over again? Ga 4:9 *1398*
gossips nor e to much wine, Ti 2:3 *1402*
e to various lusts and pleasures, Ti 3:3 *1398*
man is overcome, by this he is e. 2Pe 2:19 *1402*

ENSLAVES
you tolerate it if anyone e you, 2Co 11:20 *2615*

ENSNARE
And e him who adjudicates at the Is 29:21 6983

ENSNARED
that you are not e to follow them, Dt 12:30 5367
An evil man is e by the Pr 12:13 4170
By transgression an evil man is e, Pr 29:6 4170
so the sons of men are e at an Ec 9:12 3369

ENSURE
walks by the statutes which e life Ezk 33:15
for as you do this you will e 1Tm 4:16 *4982*

ENTANGLED
again e in them and are overcome, 2Pe 2:20 *1707*

ENTANGLES
No soldier in active service e 2Tm 2:4 *1707*
and the sin which so easily e us, Heb 12:1 *2139*

ENTANGLING
a swift young camel e her ways, Jer 2:23 8308

EN-TAPPUAH
southward to the inhabitants of E. Jos 17:7 5887

ENTER
and you shall e the ark Gn 6:18 935
"E the ark, you and all your Gn 7:1 935
in order to e the land of Canaan; Gn 11:31 1980
my soul not e into their council; Gn 49:6 935
"When you e the land Ex 12:25 935
when they e the tent of meeting, Ex 28:43 935
when they e the tent of meeting, Ex 30:20 935
Moses was not able to e the Ex 40:35 935
thing, nor e the sanctuary until Lv 12:4 935
Now afterward, he may e the camp, Lv 14:8 935
"When you e the land of Canaan, Lv 14:34 935
Aaron that he shall not e at any time Lv 16:2 935
shall e the holy place with this: Lv 16:3 935
'When you e the land and plant Lv 19:23 935
'When you e the land which I am Lv 23:10 935
all who e the service to do the Nu 4:3 935
all who e to perform the service Nu 4:23 935
everyone who could e to do the Nu 4:47 935
they shall e to perform service Nu 8:24 935
'When you e the land where you are Nu 15:2 935
you e the land where I bring you, Nu 15:18 935
for he shall not e the land which Nu 20:24 935
afterward you may e the camp." Nu 31:24 935
'When you e the land of Canaan, Nu 34:2 935
and the cities which we shall e.' Dt 1:22 935
'Not even you shall e there. Dt 1:37 935
before you, he shall e there; Dt 1:38 935
of good or evil, shall e there, Dt 1:39 935
and that I would not e the good Dt 4:21 935
"When you e the land which the Dt 17:14 935
"When you e the land which the Dt 18:9 935
shall e the assembly of the LORD. Dt 23:1 935
shall e the assembly of the LORD; Dt 23:2 935
shall e the assembly of the LORD. Dt 23:2 935
shall e the assembly of the LORD; Dt 23:3 935
ever e the assembly of the LORD, Dt 23:3 935
may e the assembly of the LORD. Dt 23:8 935
you are about to e to possess. Dt 23:20 935
you e your neighbor's vineyard, Dt 23:24 935
"When you e your neighbor's Dt 23:25 935
e his house to take his pledge. Dt 24:10 935
when you e the land which the LORD Dt 26:1 935
so that you may e the land Dt 27:3 935
that you may e into the covenant Dt 29:12 5674a
the Jordan to e and possess it. Dt 30:18 935
not allow them to e their cities, Jos 10:19 935
did not e the territory of Moab, Jg 11:18 935
But her father did not let him e. Jg 15:1 935
Do not delay to go, to e, Jg 18:9 935
"When you e, you will come to a Jg 18:10 935
in order to e *and* lodge in Gibeah. Jg 19:15 935
nor all who e Dagon's house tread on 1Sa 5:5 935
"As soon as you e the city you 1Sa 9:13 935
"David cannot e here." 2Sa 5:6 935
e the city the child will die. 1Ki 14:12 935
when you e an inner room to hide 1Ki 22:25 935
'We will e the city,' then the 2Ki 7:4 935
"You shall not e here." 1Ch 11:5 935
e into the house of the LORD because 2Ch 7:2 935
when you e an inner room to hide 2Ch 18:24 935
"But let no one e the house of 2Ch 23:6 935
they may e, for they are holy. 2Ch 23:6 935
e *who was* in any way unclean. 2Ch 23:19 935
did not e the temple of the LORD. 2Ch 27:2 935
but yield to the LORD and e His 2Ch 30:8 935
And You told them to e in Ne 9:15 935
their fathers to e and possess. Ne 9:23 935
should ever e the assembly of God, Ne 13:1 935
load would e on the sabbath day. Ne 13:19 935
for no one was to e the king's Es 4:2 935
Let no joyful shout e it. Jb 3:7 935
lovingkindness I will e Your house, Ps 5:7 935
sword will e their own heart, Ps 37:15 935
They will e into the King's palace. Ps 45:15 935
they shall not e into My rest." Ps 95:11 935
E His gates with thanksgiving *And* Ps 100:4 935
I shall e through them, I shall Ps 118:19 935
The righteous will e through it. Ps 118:20 935
"Surely I will not e my house, Ps 132:3 935
And do not e into judgment with Ps 143:2 935
For wisdom will e your heart And Pr 2:10 935
Do not e the path of the wicked And Pr 4:14 935
E the rock and hide in the dust Is 2:10 935
may e the doors of the nobles. Is 13:2 935
is shut up so that none may e. Is 24:10 935
that the righteous nation may e, Is 26:2 935
my people, e into your rooms And Is 26:20 935
life I am to e the gates of Sheol; Is 38:10 1980
street, And uprightness cannot e. Is 59:14 935
I will e into judgment with you Jer 2:35 8199
who e by these gates to worship Jer 7:2 935
Or if I e the city, Behold, Jer 14:18 935
"Do not e a house of mourning, or Jer 16:5 935
of, nor did it *ever* e My mind; Jer 19:5 5927
and you will e Babylon, and there Jer 20:6 935
who will e into our habitations?' Jer 21:13 935
and your people who e these gates. Jer 22:2 935
will e the gates of this house, Jer 22:4 935
will e and set this city on fire Jer 32:29 935
really set your mind to e Egypt and Jer 42:15 935
out on you when you e Egypt. Jer 42:18 935
not to e Egypt to reside there'; Jer 43:2 935
seen the nations e her sanctuary, La 1:10 935
not e into Your congregation. La 1:10 935
quiver To e into my inward parts. La 3:13 935
Could e the gates of Jerusalem. La 4:12 935
robbers will e and profane it. Ezk 7:22 935
"E between the whirling wheels Ezk 10:2 935
will they e the land of Israel, Ezk 13:9 935
him to Babylon and e into judgment Ezk 17:20 8199
and there I will e into judgment Ezk 20:35 8199
I will e into judgment with you," Ezk 20:36 8199
will not e the land of Israel. Ezk 20:38 935
as men e a city that is breached. Ezk 26:10 3996
e you that you may come to life. Ezk 37:5 935
I will e into judgment with him; Ezk 38:22 8199
"When the priests e, Ezk 42:14 935
opened, and no one shall e by it, Ezk 44:2 935
he shall e by way of the porch of Ezk 44:3 935
of Israel, shall e My sanctuary. Ezk 44:9 935
"They shall e My sanctuary; Ezk 44:16 935
"It shall be that when they e Ezk 44:17 935
wine when they e the inner court. Ezk 44:21 935
"The prince shall e by way of Ezk 46:2 935
to e the king's personal service. Da 1:5 5975
nor did meat or wine e my mouth, Da 10:3 935
e the fortress of the king of the North, Da 11:7 935
"Then the latter will e the realm Da 11:9 935
he will e the richest *parts* of the realm, Da 11:24 935
and he will e countries, overflow Da 11:40 935
"He will also e the Beautiful Da 11:41 935
then you will e into rest and rise Da 12:13 5117
will not e the house of the LORD. Hos 9:4 935
They e through the windows like a Jl 2:9 935
Then I will e into judgment with Jl 3:2 8199
"E Bethel and transgress; Am 4:4 935
"Do not e the gate of My people Ob 1:13 935
glory of Israel will e Adullam. Mi 1:15 935
"and it will e the house of the Zch 5:4 935

and you go the same day and **e** the Zch 6:10 935
of Egypt does not go up or **e**, Zch 14:18 935
will not **e** the kingdom of heaven. Mt 5:20 1525
"**E** through the narrow gate; Mt 7:13 1525
and there are many who **e** through it. Mt 7:13 1525
will **e** the kingdom of heaven, Mt 7:21 1525
My Father who is in heaven *will* **e**. Mt 7:21
not **e** *any* city of the Samaritans; Mt 10:5 1525
whatever city or village you **e**, Mt 10:11 1525
"As you **e** the house, give it Mt 10:12 1525
"Or how can anyone **e** the strong Mt 12:29 1525
will not **e** the kingdom of heaven. Mt 18:3 1525
you to **e** life crippled or lame, Mt 18:8 1525
for you to **e** life with one eye, Mt 18:9 1525
but if you wish to **e** into life, Mt 19:17 1525
man to **e** the kingdom of heaven. Mt 19:23 1525
man to **e** the kingdom of God." Mt 19:24 1525
for you do not **e** in yourselves, Mt 23:13 1525
e into the joy of your master.' Mt 25:21 1525
e into the joy of your master.' Mt 25:23 1525
you may not **e** into temptation; Mt 26:41 1525
could no longer publicly **e** a city, Mk 1:45 1525
"But no one can **e** the strong Mk 3:27 1525
things **e** in and choke the word, Mk 4:19 1531
the swine so that we may **e** them." Mk 5:12 1525
"Wherever you **e** a house, stay Mk 6:10 1525
"Do not even **e** the village." Mk 8:26 1525
of him and do not **e** him again." Mk 9:25 1525
better for you to **e** life crippled, Mk 9:43 1525
is better for you to **e** life lame, Mk 9:45 1525
it is better for you to **e** the Mk 9:47 1525
a child will not **e** it *at all*." Mk 10:15 1525
wealthy to **e** the kingdom of God!" Mk 10:23 1525
it is to **e** the kingdom of God! Mk 10:24 1525
man to **e** the kingdom of God." Mk 10:25 1525
you, and immediately as you **e** it, Mk 11:2 1531
he was chosen by lot to **e** the Lk 1:9 1525
Him to permit them to **e** the swine. Lk 8:32 1525
not allow anyone to **e** with Him, Lk 8:51 1525
"Whatever house you **e**, Lk 9:4 1525
"Whatever house you **e**, Lk 10:5 1525
"Whatever city you **e** and Lk 10:8 1525
you **e** and they do not receive you, Lk 10:10 1525
those who **e** may see the light. Lk 11:33 1531
you yourselves did not **e**, and Lk 11:52 1525
"Strive to **e** through the narrow door; Lk 13:24 1525
seek to **e** and will not be able. Lk 13:24 1525
a child will not **e** it *at all*." Lk 18:17 1525
wealthy to **e** the kingdom of God! Lk 18:24 1531
man to **e** the kingdom of God." Lk 18:25 1525
as you **e**, you will find a colt tied Lk 19:30 1531
in the country must not **e** the city; Lk 21:21 1525
you may not **e** into temptation." Lk 22:40 1525
you may not **e** into temptation." Lk 22:46 1525
things and to **e** into His glory?" Lk 24:26 1525
He cannot **e** a second time into his Jn 3:4 1525
cannot **e** into the kingdom of God. Jn 3:5 1525
he who does not **e** by the door into Jn 10:1 1525
and they themselves did not **e** into Jn 18:28 1525
but get up and **e** the city, and it Ac 9:6 1525
we must **e** the kingdom of God." Ac 14:22 1525
and ungifted men or unbelievers **e**, 1Co 14:23 1525
For among them are those who **e** 2Tm 3:6 1746a
'THEY SHALL NOT **E** MY REST.' " Heb 3:11 1525
that they would not **e** His rest, Heb 3:18 1525
not able to **e** because of unbelief. Heb 3:19 1525
we who have believed **e** that rest, Heb 4:3 1525
WRATH, THEY SHALL NOT **E** MY REST," Heb 4:3 1525
"THEY SHALL NOT **E** MY REST." Heb 4:5 1525
it remains for some to **e** it, Heb 4:6 1525
to **e** because of disobedience, Heb 4:6 1525
be diligent to **e** that rest, Heb 4:11 1525
e a holy place made with hands, Heb 9:24 1525
we have confidence to **e** the holy Heb 10:19 1529
and no one was able to **e** the Rv 15:8 1525
may **e** by the gates into the city. Rv 22:14 1525

ENTERED

and his sons' wives with him **e** the ark Gn 7:7 935
of his sons with them, **e** the ark, Gn 7:13 935
Those that **e**, male and female Gn 7:16 935
flesh, **e** as God had commanded him; Gn 7:16 935
aside to him and **e** his house; Gn 19:3 935
So the man **e** the house. Gn 24:32 935
of Leah's tent and **e** Rachel's tent. Gn 31:33 935
he **e** his chamber and wept there. Gn 43:30 935
Moses **e** the midst of the cloud Ex 24:18 935
after Moses until he **e** the tent. Ex 33:8 935
Whenever Moses **e** the tent, Ex 33:9 935
When they **e** the tent of meeting, Ex 40:32 935
everyone who **e** the service for Nu 4:35 935
everyone who **e** the service for Nu 4:39 935
everyone who **e** the service for Nu 4:43 935
bring into the land which he **e**, Nu 14:24 935
I have **e** the land which the LORD Dt 26:3 935
to you, who have **e** your house, Jos 2:3 935
and **e** the city and captured it, Jos 8:19 935
them had **e** the fortified cities, Jos 10:20 935
And he **e** with her, and behold Jg 4:22 935
they **e** the inner chamber of the Jg 9:46 935
out the land went up *and* **e** there, Jg 18:17 935
When they **e**, they sat down in the Jg 19:15 935
When he **e** his house, he took a Jg 19:29 935
Now they **e** the land of Moab and Ru 1:2 935
people of the land **e** the forest, 1Sa 14:25 935
When the people **e** the forest, 1Sa 14:26 935
When they **e**, he looked at Eliab 1Sa 16:6 935
and ran to the battle line and **e** 1Sa 17:22 935
When the messengers **e**, 1Sa 19:16 935
before Abishai and **e** the city. 2Sa 10:14 935
the men of Israel, **e** Jerusalem, 2Sa 16:15 935
the king **e** the house of the LORD, 1Ki 14:28 935
So he **e** and shut the door behind 2Ki 4:33 935
they **e** one tent and ate and drank, 2Ki 7:8 935
and they returned and **e** another 2Ki 7:8 935
As Jehu **e** the gate, she said, 2Ki 9:31 935
and **e** the house of the LORD. 2Ki 19:1 935
I **e** its farthest lodging place, 2Ki 19:23 935
the people **e** into the covenant. 2Ki 23:3 5975
his brother and **e** the city. 1Ch 19:15 935
where the ark of the LORD has **e**." 2Ch 8:11 935
the king **e** the house of the LORD, 2Ch 12:11 935
They **e** into the covenant to 2Ch 15:12 935
and they **e** into a covenant with 2Ch 23:1
which **e** combat by divisions according 2Ch 26:11 3318
for he **e** the temple of the LORD to 2Ch 26:16 935
Then Azariah the priest **e** after 2Ch 26:17 935
they **e** the porch of the LORD. 2Ch 29:17 935
everyone who **e** the house of the LORD 2Ch 31:16 935
he had **e** the temple of his god, 2Ch 32:21 935
Then I **e** the Valley Gate again and Ne 2:15 935
When I **e** the house of Shemaiah Ne 6:10 935
sons **e** and possessed the land. Ne 9:24 935
Now Haman had just **e** the outer Es 6:4 935
you **e** into the springs of the sea Or Jb 38:16 935
you **e** the storehouses of the snow, Jb 38:22 935
And it **e** into his body like water And Ps 109:18 935
and **e** the house of the LORD. Is 37:1 935
It has **e** our palaces To cut off Jer 9:21 935
nor had it **e** My mind that they should Jer 32:35 5927
who had **e** into the covenant that Jer 34:10 935
and they **e** the land of Egypt Jer 43:7 935
who have **e** the land of Egypt to reside Jer 44:14 935
For aliens have **e** The holy places Jer 51:51 935
Spirit **e** me and set me on my feet; Ezk 2:2 935
The Spirit then **e** me and made me Ezk 3:24 935
unclean meat ever **e** my mouth." Ezk 4:14 935
So I **e** and looked, and behold, Ezk 8:10 935
And he **e** in my sight. Ezk 10:2 935
side of the temple when the man **e**, Ezk 10:3 935
he **e** and stood beside a wheel. Ezk 10:6 935
and **e** into a covenant with you Ezk 16:8 935
"As I **e** into judgment with your Ezk 20:36 8199
they **e** My sanctuary on the same Ezk 23:39 935
LORD God of Israel has **e** by it; Ezk 44:2 935
he **e** but shall go straight out. Ezk 46:9 935
they **e** the king's personal service. Da 1:19 5975
The queen **e** the banquet hall Da 5:10 5954
was signed, he **e** his house Da 6:10 5954
And foreigners **e** his gate And cast Ob 1:11 935
And when Jesus **e** Capernaum, a Mt 8:5 1525
He **e** and took her by the hand, Mt 9:25 1525
When He **e** the house, the blind men Mt 9:28 2064
how he **e** the house of God, and Mt 12:4 1525
When He had **e** Jerusalem, all Mt 21:10 1525
And Jesus **e** the temple and drove Mt 21:12 1525
When He **e** the temple, the chief Mt 21:23 2064
until the day that Noah **e** the ark, Mt 24:38 1525
of the high priest, and **e** in, Mt 26:58 1525
e the holy city and appeared to many. Mt 27:53 1525
on the Sabbath He **e** the synagogue Mk 1:21 1525
how he **e** the house of God in the Mk 2:26 1525
He **e** again into a synagogue; Mk 3:1 1525
the unclean spirits **e** the swine; Mk 5:13 1525
e *the room* where the child was. Mk 5:40 1531
Wherever He **e** villages, or Mk 6:56 1531
the crowd *and* **e** the house, Mk 7:17 1525
And when He had **e** a house, He Mk 7:24 1525
He **e** the boat with His disciples and Mk 8:10 1684
Jesus **e** Jerusalem *and came* into Mk 11:11 1525
And He **e** the temple and began to Mk 11:15 1525b
and **e** the house of Zacharias and Lk 1:40 1525
He **e** the synagogue on the Sabbath, Lk 4:16 1525
the synagogue, and **e** Simon's home. Lk 4:38 1525
how he **e** the house of God, and Lk 6:4 1525
Sabbath He **e** the synagogue and was Lk 6:6 1525
and He **e** the Pharisee's house and Lk 7:36 1525
e your house; you gave Me no water Lk 7:44 1525
for many demons had **e** him. Lk 8:30 1525
out of the man and **e** the swine; Lk 8:33 1525
were afraid as they **e** the cloud. Lk 9:34 1525
and **e** a village of the Samaritans to Lk 9:52 1525
along, He **e** a village; Lk 10:38 1525
As He **e** a village, ten Lk 17:12 1525
until the day that Noah **e** the ark, Lk 17:27 1525
He **e** Jericho and was passing through Lk 19:1 1525
Jesus **e** the temple and began to Lk 19:45 1525
And Satan **e** into Judas who was Lk 22:3 1525
"When you have **e** the city, Lk 22:10 1525
but when they **e**, they did not find Lk 24:3 1525
and you have **e** into their labor." Jn 4:38 1525
and that Jesus had not **e** with His Jn 6:22 4897
the morsel, Satan then **e** into him. Jn 13:27 1525
a garden, in which He **e** Jn 18:1 1525
and **e** with Jesus into the court of Jn 18:15 4897
e again into the Praetorium, Jn 18:33 1525
he **e** into the Praetorium again and Jn 19:9 1525
following him, and **e** the tomb; Jn 20:6 1525
first come to the tomb then also **e**, Jn 20:8 1525
When they had **e** Ac 1:13 1525
and he **e** the temple with them, Ac 3:8 1525
they **e** into the temple about Ac 5:21 1525
it **e** his mind to visit his Ac 7:23 305
Ananias departed and **e** the house, Ac 9:17 1525
the following day he **e** Caesarea. Ac 10:24 1525
When Peter **e**, Cornelius met him, Ac 10:25 1525
As he talked with him, he **e** and Ac 10:27 1525
or unclean has ever **e** my mouth.' Ac 11:8 1525
with me and we **e** the man's house. Ac 11:12 1525
In Iconium they **e** the synagogue Ac 14:1 1525
him, he got up and **e** the city. Ac 14:20 1525
prison and **e** *the house of* Lydia, Ac 16:40 1525
Now he himself **e** the synagogue and Ac 18:19 1525
And he **e** the synagogue and Ac 19:8 1525
and **e** the barracks and told Paul. Ac 23:16 1525
and **e** the auditorium Ac 25:23 1525
When we **e** Rome, Paul was Ac 28:16 1525
one man sin **e** into the world, Ro 5:12 1525
which HAVE NOT **E** THE HEART OF MAN, 1Co 2:9 305
For the one who has **e** His rest has Heb 4:10 1525
has **e** as a forerunner for us, Heb 6:20 1525
He **e** through the greater and more Heb 9:11
He **e** the holy place once for all, Heb 9:12 1525

ENTERING

where you are **e** to possess it. Dt 4:5 935
where you are **e** to possess it, Dt 7:1 935
which you are **e** to possess it, Dt 11:10 935
where you are **e** to possess it, Dt 11:29 935
where you are **e** to possess it. Dt 28:21 935
where you are **e** to possess it. Dt 28:63 935
where you are **e** to possess it. Dt 30:16 935
"How long will you put off **e** to Jos 18:3 935
for he shut himself in by **e** a city 1Sa 23:7 935
they could not be seen **e** the city. 2Sa 17:17 935
was **e** the threshold of the house, 1Ki 14:17 935
'The land which you are **e** to Ezr 9:11 935
is **e** into judgment with all flesh; Jer 25:31 8199
Egypt, where you are **e** to reside, Jer 44:8 935
set their mind on **e** the land of Egypt Jer 44:12 935
allow those who are **e** to go in. Mt 23:13 1525
And **e** in, He said to them, Mk 5:39 1525
E the tomb, they saw a young man Mk 16:5 1525
you hindered those who were **e**." Lk 11:52 1525
of those who were **e** the temple. Ac 3:2 1531
the church, **e** house after house, Ac 8:3 1531
and **e** the house of Philip the Ac 21:8 1525
a promise remains of **e** His rest, Heb 4:1 1525
e the outer tabernacle performing Heb 9:6 1524

ENTERS

heart when he **e** the holy place, Ex 28:29 935
its tinkling shall be heard when he **e** Ex 28:35 935
shall put them on when he **e** the tent Ex 29:30 935
everyone who **e** the service to do Nu 4:30 935
and whoever **e** the house, let him 2Ch 23:7 935
He **e** into judgment against you? Jb 22:4 935
The LORD **e** into judgment with the Is 3:14 935
He **e** into peace; They rest in their Is 57:2 935
when he **e** your gates as men enter Ezk 26:10 935
one **e** them from the outer court. Ezk 42:9 935
toward the east, as one **e** them. Ezk 42:12 935
"When the prince **e**, Ezk 46:8 935
he who **e** by way of the north gate Ezk 46:9 935
And he who **e** by way of the south Ezk 46:9 935
The thief **e** in, Bandits raid Hos 7:1 935
Decay **e** my bones, And in my place Hab 3:16 935
"*It is* not what **e** into the mouth Mt 15:11 1525
and wherever he **e**, say to the Mk 14:14 1525
him into the house that he **e**. Lk 22:10 1531
"But he who **e** by the door is a Jn 10:2 1525
if anyone **e** through Me, he will Jn 10:9 1525
unbeliever or an ungifted man **e**, 1Co 14:24 1525
and one which **e** within the veil, Heb 6:19 1525
only the high priest **e** once a Heb 9:7
as the high priest **e** the holy Heb 9:25 1525

ENTERTAINED

from the prison, and he **e** them. Jg 16:25 6711, 6440
and **e** us courteously three days. Ac 28:7 3579
have **e** angels without knowing it. Heb 13:2 3579

ENTERTAINMENT

and no **e** was brought before him; Da 6:18 1761a

ENTHRONED

hosts who is **e** *above* the cherubim. 2Sa 6:2 3427
who are **e** *above* the cherubim, 2Ki 19:15 3427
LORD who is **e** *above* the cherubim, 1Ch 13:6 3427
are **e** upon the praises of Israel. Ps 22:3 3427
Even the one who sits **e** from of old Ps 55:19 3427
You who are **e** *above* the cherubim, Ps 80:1 3427
He is **e** *above* the cherubim, let Ps 99:1 3427
LORD our God, Who is **e** on high, Ps 113:5 3427
O You who are **e** in the heavens! Ps 123:1 3427
who is **e** *above* the cherubim, Is 37:16 3427

ENTICE

as your own soul, **e** you secretly, Dt 13:6 5496
"**E** your husband, so that he will tell Jg 14:15 6601b
"**E** him, and see where his great Jg 16:5 6601b
'Who will **e** Ahab to go up and fall 1Ki 22:20 6601b
the LORD and said, 'I will **e** him.' 1Ki 22:21 6601b
'You are to **e** *him* and also prevail. 1Ki 22:22 6601b
'Who will **e** Ahab king of Israel to 2Ch 18:19 6601b
the LORD and said, 'I will **e** him.' 2Ch 18:20 6601b
'You are to **e** *him* and prevail also. 2Ch 18:21 6601b
that wrath does not **e** you to scoffing; Jb 36:18 5496
My son, if sinners **e** you, Pr 1:10 6601b
vanity they **e** by fleshly desires, 2Pe 2:18 1185

ENTICED

"If my heart has been **e** by a woman, Jb 31:9 6601b
And my heart became secretly **e**, Jb 31:27 6601b
He **e** you from the mouth of Jb 36:16 5496
away and **e** by his own lust. Jas 1:14 1185

ENTICES

her many persuasions she **e** him; Pr 7:21 5186
A man of violence **e** his neighbor And Pr 16:29 6601b

ENTICING

cease from sin, **e** unstable souls, 2Pe 2:14 1185

ENTIRE
pass through your e flock today, Gn 30:32 3605
even Pharaoh's e army that had Ex 14:28 3605
the e fat tail which he shall Lv 3:9 8549
angry with the e congregation?" Nu 16:22 3605
until the e generation of those Nu 32:13 3605
e army of the sons of the east; Jg 8:10 3605
through the e tribe of Benjamin, Jg 20:12 3605
both the e city with the cattle Jg 20:48 4974
had finished praying this e prayer 1Ki 8:54 3605
King David said to the e assembly, 1Ch 29:1 3605
The e assembly of those who Ne 8:17 3605
and to annihilate the e army of Es 8:11 3605
The e vision will be to you Is 29:11 3605
your e wall of precious stones. Is 54:12 3605
the e calamity that I have declared Jer 19:15 3605
had defeated the e army of Chaldeans Jer 37:10 3605
forces took the e remnant of Judah Jer 43:5 3605
its e area on the top of the Ezk 43:12 3605
to appoint him over the e kingdom. Da 6:3 3606
been mourning for three e weeks. Da 10:2 3117
the e three weeks were completed. Da 10:3 3117
they deported an e population Am 1:6 8003
they delivered up an e population Am 1:9 8003
against the e family which He Am 3:1 3605
when the e crowd saw Him, Mk 9:15 *3956*
and the e crowd was rejoicing Lk 13:17 *3956*
made an e man well on *the* Sabbath? Jn 7:23 *3650*
of by the e nation of the Jews, Ac 10:22 *3650*
e year they met with the church and Ac 11:26 *3650*
to the head, from whom the e body, Col 2:19 *3956*
instruction with e submissiveness. 1Tm 2:11 *3956*
we direct their e body as well. Jas 3:3 *3650*
as that which defiles the e body, Jas 3:6 *3650*

ENTIRELY
done e according to its outcry, Gn 18:21 3617
e consumed our purchase price. Gn 31:15 398
be e offered up in smoke to the LORD. Lv 6:22 3632
of the priest shall be burned e. Lv 6:23 3632
LORD brings about an e new thing Nu 16:30 1278
the Judeans out of Elath e; 2Ki 16:6
will be e at your command." 1Ch 28:21 3605
ten cubits, e encircling the sea. 2Ch 4:3 5439
"You were born e in sins, and are Jn 9:34 *3650*
of peace Himself sanctify you e; 1Th 5:23 *3651*

ENTRAILS
and its legs along with its e. Ex 12:9 7130
the e and the lobe of the liver, Ex 29:13 7130
and wash its e and its legs, Ex 29:17 7130
the e and the lobe of the liver, Ex 29:22 7130
'Its e, however, and its legs he Lv 1:9 7130
'The e, however, and the legs he Lv 1:13 7130
the fat that covers the e and all Lv 3:3 7130
and all the fat that is on the e, Lv 3:3 7130
and the fat that covers the e and Lv 3:9 7130
and all the fat that is on the e, Lv 3:9 7130
the fat that covers the e and all Lv 3:14 7130
and all the fat that is on the e, Lv 3:14 7130
the fat that covers the e, Lv 4:8 7130
and all the fat which is on the e, Lv 4:8 7130
its legs and its e and its refuse, Lv 4:11 7130
and the fat that covers the e, Lv 7:3 7130
the e and the lobe of the liver, Lv 8:16 7130
the e and the legs with water, Lv 8:21 7130
and all the fat that was on the e, Lv 8:25 7130
He also washed the e and the legs, Lv 9:14 7130

ENTRANCE
to him at the e of the house, Gn 43:19 6607
stand, each at the e of his tent, Ex 33:8 6607
and stand at the e of the tent; Ex 33:9 6607
standing at the e of the tent, Ex 33:10 6607
each at the e of his tent. Ex 33:10 6607
at the e of the tabernacle; Ex 35:15 6607
it at the e of the city gate, Jos 8:29 6607
shall stand at the e of the gate of the Jos 20:4 6607
"Please show us the e to the city Jg 1:24 3996
he showed them the e to the city, Jg 1:25 3996
stood in the e of the city gate; Jg 9:35 6607
wounded up to the e of the gate. Jg 9:40 6607
stood in the e of the city gate; Jg 9:44 6607
and approached the e of the tower Jg 9:52 6607
from Aroer to the e of Minnith, Jg 11:33 935
Dan, stood by the e of the gate. Jg 18:16 6607
while the priest stood by the e of Jg 18:17 6607
battle array at the e of the city, 2Sa 10:8 6607
them as far as the e of the gate. 2Sa 11:23 6607
For the e of the inner 1Ki 6:31 6607
So also he made for the e of the 1Ki 6:33 6607
a great assembly from the e of 1Ki 8:65 935
and stood in the e of the cave. 1Ki 19:13 6607
at the e of the gate of Samaria; 1Ki 22:10 6607
leprous men at the e of the gate; 2Ki 7:3 6607
the e of the gate until morning." 2Ki 10:8 6607
the horses' e of the king's house, 2Ki 11:16 3996
border of Israel from the e of Hamath 2Ki 14:25 935
were at the e of the gate of Joshua 2Ki 23:8 6607
at the e of the house of the LORD, 2Ki 23:11 935
They went to the e of Gedor, 1Ch 4:39 3996
settled as far as the e of the wilderness 1Ch 5:9 935
of the LORD, keepers of the e. 1Ch 9:19 3996
of the e of the tent of meeting. 1Ch 9:21 6607
of Egypt even to the e of Hamath, 1Ch 13:5 935
battle array at the e of the city, 1Ch 19:9 6607
and the e of the house, its inner 2Ch 4:22 6607
who came from the e of Hamath to 2Ch 7:8 935
at the e of the gate of Samaria; 2Ch 18:9 6607
standing by his pillar at the e, 2Ch 23:13 3996
and when she arrived at the e of 2Ch 23:15 3996
even to the e of the Fish Gate; 2Ch 33:14 935
opposite the e to the palace. Es 5:1 6607
At the e of the gates in the city she Pr 1:21 6607
the city, At the e of the doors, Pr 8:3 3996
the e of the gates of Jerusalem, Jer 1:15 6607
is by the e of the potsherd gate, Jer 19:2 6607
and sat in the e of the New Gate Jer 26:10 6607
prophet brought to him at the third e Jer 38:14 3996
e of Pharaoh's palace in Tahpanhes, Jer 43:9 6607
to the e of the north gate of the Ezk 8:3 6607
this idol of jealousy at the e. Ezk 8:5 872
brought me to the e of the court, Ezk 8:7 6607
the wall, and behold, an e. Ezk 8:8 6607
Then He brought me to the e of the Ezk 8:14 6607
the e to the temple of the LORD, Ezk 8:16 6607
and they stood still at the e of Ezk 10:19 6607
men at the e of the gate, Ezk 11:1 6607
who dwells at the e to the sea, Ezk 27:3 3996
From the front of the e gate Ezk 40:15 382b
The width of the e *was* ten cubits Ezk 41:2 6607
and the sides of the e *were* Ezk 41:2 6607
over the e, and to the inner Ezk 41:17 6607
From the ground to above the e Ezk 41:20 6607
was the e on the east side, Ezk 42:9 3996
and mark well the e of the house, Ezk 44:5 3996
Then he brought me through the e, Ezk 46:19 3996
way of Hethlon, to the e of Zedad; Ezk 47:15 935
will afflict you from the e of Hamath Am 6:14 935
the e of the tomb and went away. Mt 27:60 *2374*
a stone against the e of the tomb. Mk 15:46 *2374*
for us from the e of the tomb?" Mk 16:3 *2374*
for in this way the e into the 2Pe 1:11 *1529*

ENTRANCES
its structure, its exits, its e, Ezk 43:11 4126
The land of Nimrod at its e; Mi 5:6 6607

ENTREAT
"E the LORD that He remove the Ex 8:8 6279
when shall I e for you and your Ex 8:9 6279
"Please e the LORD your God, and 1Ki 13:6 2470b
you, And many would e your favor. Jb 11:19 2470b
what would we gain if we e Him?' Jb 21:15 6293
LORD and e the favor of the LORD, Jer 26:19 2470b
let them now e the LORD of hosts that Jer 27:18 6293
once to e the favor of the LORD, Zch 8:21 2470b
and to e the favor of the LORD.' Zch 8:22 2470b
"But now will you not e God's favor, Mal 1:9 2470b
The demons *began* to e Him, Mt 8:31 *3870*

ENTREATED
Then Moses e the LORD his God, and Ex 32:11 2470b
Then Manoah e the LORD and said, Jg 13:8 6279
So the man of God e the LORD, and 1Ki 13:6 2470b
Jehoahaz e the favor of the LORD, 2Ki 13:4 2470b
he e the LORD his God and humbled 2Ch 33:12 2470b
also and *how God* was e by him, 2Ch 33:19 6279

ENTREATIES
then, I urge that e *and* prayers, 1Tm 2:1 *1162*
in e and prayers night and day. 1Tm 5:5 *1162*

ENTREATY
his e and heard his supplication, 2Ch 33:13 6279
matter, and He listened to our e. Ezr 8:23 6279

ENTRUST
I will e him with your authority, Is 22:21 5414, 3027
who will e the true *riches* to you? Lk 16:11 *4100*
This command I e to you, Timothy, 1Tm 1:18 *3908*
e these to faithful men who will be 2Tm 2:2 *3908*
e their souls to a faithful Creator in 1Pe 4:19 *3908*

ENTRUSTED
a deposit or a security e *to him,* Lv 6:2 3027
or the deposit which was e to him or Lv 6:4 6485
"Everything that was e to your 2Ch 34:16 5414, 3027
He e the vineyard to caretakers. SS 8:11 5414
guardhouse and e him to Gedaliah, Jer 39:14 5414
and e his possessions to them. Mt 25:14 *3860*
'Master, you e five talents to me. Mt 25:20 *3860*
'Master, you e two talents to me. Mt 25:22 *3860*
and to whom they e much, Lk 12:48 *3908*
were e with the oracles of God. Ro 3:2 *4100*
I have a stewardship e to me. 1Co 9:17 *4100*
seeing that I had been e with the Ga 2:7 *4100*
by God to be e with the gospel, 1Th 2:4 *4100*
God, with which I have been e. 1Tm 1:11 *4100*
guard what has been e to you, 1Tm 6:20 *3866*
I have e to Him until that day. 2Tm 1:12 *3866*
treasure which has been e to *you.* 2Tm 1:14 *3866*
the proclamation with which I was e Ti 1:3 *4100*

ENTRUSTING
part, was not e Himself to them, Jn 2:24 *4100*
but kept e *Himself* to Him who 1Pe 2:23 *3860*

ENTRY
and the outer e of the king, 2Ki 16:18 3996
at the e of the New Gate of the Jer 36:10 6607

ENUMERATION
is the e of the sons of Israel, 1Ch 27:1 4557

ENVELOPED
The chariots are e in flashing Na 2:3

ENVIED
so that the Philistines e him. Gn 26:14 7065

ENVIOUS
Be not e toward wrongdoers. Ps 37:1 7065
For I was e of the arrogant *As I* Ps 73:3 7065
became e of Moses in the camp, Ps 106:16 7065
Do not be e of evil men, Nor Pr 24:1 7065
evildoers Or be e of the wicked; Pr 24:19 7065
your eye e because I am generous?' Mt 20:15 *4190*
You are e and cannot obtain; Jas 4:2 *2206*

ENVIRONS
Judah and from the e of Jerusalem, Jer 17:26 5439
it may devour all its e. Jer 21:14 5439
Benjamin, in the e of Jerusalem, Jer 32:44 5439
Benjamin, in the e of Jerusalem and Jer 33:13 5439
And it will devour all his e." Jer 50:32 5439

ENVISIONED
which he e in visions concerning Am 1:1 2372

ENVOY
But a faithful e *brings* healing. Pr 13:17 6735a
an e is sent among the nations, Jer 49:14 6735a
And an e has been sent among the Ob 1:1 6735a

ENVOYS
acted craftily and set out as e, Jos 9:4 6737
of the e of the rulers of Babylon, 2Ch 32:31 3917b
E will come out of Egypt; Ps 68:31 2831
Which sends e by the sea, Even in Is 18:2 6735a
have sent your e a great distance And Is 57:9 6735a
against him by sending his e to Egypt Ezk 17:15 4397

ENVY
Why do you look with e, Ps 68:16 7520
Do not e a man of violence And do Pr 3:31 7065
Do not let your heart e sinners, Pr 23:17 7065
according to your e which you showed Ezk 35:11 7068
of e they had handed Him over. Mt 27:18 *5355*
as well as deceit, sensuality, e, Mk 7:22 *3788, 4190*
had handed Him over because of e. Mk 15:10 *5355*
full of e, murder, strife, deceit, Ro 1:29 *5355*
Christ even from e and strife, Php 1:15 *5355*
about words, out of which arise e, 1Tm 6:4 *5355*
spending our life in malice and e, Ti 3:3 *5355*
hypocrisy and e and all slander, 1Pe 2:1 *5355*

ENVYING
e, drunkenness, carousing, and Ga 5:21 *5355*
one another, e one another. Ga 5:26 *5354*

EPAENETUS
Greet E, my beloved, who is the Ro 16:5 *1866*

EPAPHRAS
just as you learned *it* from E, Col 1:7 *1889*
E, who is one of your number, a Col 4:12 *1889*
E, my fellow prisoner in Christ Phm 1:23 *1889*

EPAPHRODITUS
it necessary to send to you E, Php 2:25 *1891*
from E what you have sent, Php 4:18 *1891*

EPHAH
The sons of Midian *were* E and Gn 25:4 5891
(Now an omer is a tenth of an e.) Ex 16:36 374
shall be one-tenth *of an* e of Ex 29:40
he shall bring the tenth of an e Lv 5:11 374
the tenth of an e of fine flour as Lv 6:20 374
and three-tenths *of an* e of Lv 14:10
and one-tenth *of an* e of fine Lv 14:21
balances, just weights, a just e, Lv 19:36 374
shall then be two-tenths *of an* e Lv 23:13
made of two-tenths *of an* e; Lv 23:17
two-tenths *of an* e shall be Lv 24:5
one-tenth of an e of barley meal; Nu 5:15 374
grain offering of one-tenth *of an* e Nu 15:4
a grain offering two-tenths *of an* e Nu 15:6
offering of three-tenths *of an* e Nu 15:9
also a tenth of an e of fine flour Nu 28:5 374
and two-tenths *of an* e of Nu 28:9
and three-tenths *of an* e of Nu 28:12
and a tenth *of an* e of fine Nu 28:13
three-tenths *of an* e for a Nu 28:20
'A tenth *of an* e you shall Nu 28:21
three-tenths *of an* e for each Nu 28:28
three-tenths *of an* e for Nu 29:3
three-tenths *of an* e for Nu 29:9
three-tenths *of an* e for each Nu 29:14
bread from an e of flour; Jg 6:19 374
and it was about an e of barley. Ru 2:17 374
one e of flour and a jug of wine, 1Sa 1:24 374
"Take now for your brothers an e 1Sa 17:17 374
The sons of Midian were E, 1Ch 1:33 5891
E, Caleb's concubine, bore 1Ch 2:46 5891
Regem, Jotham, Geshan, Pelet, E and 1Ch 2:47 5891
will yield *but* an e of grain." Is 5:10 374
The young camels of Midian and E; Is 60:6 5891
have just balances, a just e and Ezk 45:10 374
"The e and the bath shall be the Ezk 45:11 374
and the e a tenth of a homer; Ezk 45:11 374
of an e from a homer of wheat; Ezk 45:13 374
of an e from a homer of barley; Ezk 45:13 374
a grain offering an e with a bull, Ezk 45:24 374
with a bull, an e with a ram and Ezk 45:24 374
a ram and a hin of oil with an e. Ezk 45:24 374
shall be an e with the ram, Ezk 46:5 374
give, and a hin of oil with an e. Ezk 46:5 374
offering, an e with the bull and Ezk 46:7 374
the bull and an e with the ram, Ezk 46:7 374
able, and a hin of oil with an e. Ezk 46:7 374
grain offering shall be an e with a bull Ezk 46:11 374
with a bull and an e with a ram, Ezk 46:11 374
give, and a hin of oil with an e. Ezk 46:11 374
by morning, a sixth of an e and Ezk 46:14 374
"This is the e going forth." Zch 5:6 374
is a woman sitting inside the e." Zch 5:7 374
down into the middle of the e and cast Zch 5:8 374
and they lifted up the e between Zch 5:9 374
"Where are they taking the e?" Zch 5:10 374

EPHAI
the sons of E the Netophathite, Jer 40:8 5778

EPHER
The sons of Midian *were* Ephah and E Gn 25:4 6081

The sons of Midian were Ephah, E, 1Ch 1:33 6081
of Ezrah *were* Jether, Mered, E and 1Ch 4:17 6081
their fathers' households, even E, 1Ch 5:24 6081

EPHES-DAMMIM
between Socoh and Azekah, in E. 1Sa 17:1 658b

EPHESIAN
the E in the city with him, Ac 21:29 *2180*

EPHESIANS
"Great is Artemis of the E!" Ac 19:28 *2180*
"Great is Artemis of the E!" Ac 19:34 *2180*
city of the E is guardian of the temple Ac 19:35 *2180*

EPHESUS
They came to E, Ac 18:19 *2181*
if God wills," he set sail from E. Ac 18:21 *2181*
birth, an eloquent man, came to E; Ac 18:24 *2181*
came to E, and found some Ac 19:1 *2181*
Jews and Greeks, who lived in E; Ac 19:17 *2181*
see and hear that not only in E, Ac 19:26 *2181*
"Men of E, what man is there Ac 19:35 *2181*
For Paul had decided to sail past E Ac 20:16 *2181*
From Miletus he sent to E and Ac 20:17 *2181*
I fought with wild beasts at E, 1Co 15:32 *2181*
will remain in E until Pentecost; 1Co 16:8 *2181*
God, To the saints who are at E Eph 1:1 *2181*
remain on at E so that you 1Tm 1:3 *2181*
what services he rendered at E. 2Tm 1:18 *2181*
But Tychicus I have sent to E. 2Tm 4:12 *2181*
to E and to Smyrna and to Pergamum Rv 1:11 *2181*
angel of the church in E write: Rv 2:1 *2181*

EPHLAL
and Zabad became the father of E, 1Ch 2:37 654
and E became the father of Obed, 1Ch 2:37 654

EPHOD
for the e and for the breastpiece. Ex 25:7 646
a breastpiece and an e and a robe Ex 28:4 646
shall also make the e of gold, Ex 28:6 646
on the shoulder pieces of the e, Ex 28:12 646
work of the e you shall make it: Ex 28:15 646
on the shoulder pieces of the e, Ex 28:25 646
is toward the inner side of the e. Ex 28:26 646
the two shoulder pieces of the e, Ex 28:27 646
skillfully woven band of the e. Ex 28:27 646
rings of the e with a blue cord, Ex 28:28 646
skillfully woven band of the e, Ex 28:28 646
will not come loose from the e. Ex 28:28 646
the robe of the e all of blue. Ex 28:31 646
Aaron the tunic and the robe of the e Ex 29:5 646
and the e and the breastpiece, Ex 29:5 646
skillfully woven band of the e; Ex 29:5 646
for the e and for the breastpiece. Ex 35:9 646
for the e and for the breastpiece; Ex 35:27 646
He made the e of gold, *and* of Ex 39:2 646
shoulder pieces for the e; Ex 39:4 646
on the shoulder pieces of the e, Ex 39:7 646
like the workmanship of the e: Ex 39:8 646
of the e at the front of it. Ex 39:18 646
edge which was next to the e. Ex 39:19 646
the two shoulder pieces of the e, Ex 39:20 646
above the woven band of the e. Ex 39:20 646
rings of the e with a blue cord, Ex 39:21 646
be on the woven band of the e, Ex 39:21 646
would not come loose from the e, Ex 39:21 646
the robe of the e of woven work, Ex 39:22 646
the robe and put the e on him; Lv 8:7 646
with the artistic band of the e, Lv 8:7 646
a leader, Hanniel the son of E. Nu 34:23 641
Gideon made it into an e, Jg 8:27 646
Micah had a shrine and he made an e Jg 17:5 646
there are in these houses an e and Jg 18:14 646
and took the graven image and the e Jg 18:17 646
the e and household idols and the Jg 18:18 646
and he took the e and household Jg 18:20 646
LORD, *as* a boy wearing a linen e. 1Sa 2:18 646
incense, to carry an e before Me; 1Sa 2:28 646
LORD at Shiloh, was wearing an e. 1Sa 14:3 646
wrapped in a cloth behind the e; 1Sa 21:9 646
men who wore the linen e. 1Sa 22:18 646
came down *with* an e in his hand. 1Sa 23:6 646
"Bring the e here." 1Sa 23:9 646
"Please bring me the e." 1Sa 30:7 646
Abiathar brought the e to David. 1Sa 30:7 646
and David was wearing a linen e. 2Sa 6:14 646
David also wore an e of linen. 1Ch 15:27 646
and without e or household idols. Hos 3:4 646

EPHPHATHA
deep sigh, He said to him, "E!" Mk 7:34 *2188*

EPHRAIM
He named the second E, Gn 41:52 669
of Egypt were born Manasseh and E, Gn 46:20 669
two sons Manasseh and E with him. Gn 48:1 669
E and Manasseh shall be mine, as Gn 48:5 669
E with his right hand toward Gn 48:13 669
hand and laid it on the head of E, Gn 48:14 669
make you like E and Manasseh!'" Gn 48:20 669
Thus he put E before Manasseh. Gn 48:20 669
of E, Elishama the son of Ammihud; Nu 1:10 669
Joseph, *namely,* of the sons of E, Nu 1:32 669
numbered men of the tribe of E Nu 1:33 669
of the camp of E by their armies, Nu 2:18 669
and the leader of the sons of E Nu 2:18 669
the numbered men of the camp of E: Nu 2:24 669
Ammihud, leader of the sons of E; Nu 7:48 669
of the camp of the sons of E, Nu 10:22 669
from the tribe of E, Nu 13:8 669
to their families: Manasseh and E. Nu 26:28 669
of E according to their families: Nu 26:35 669
These are the families of the sons of E Nu 26:37 669
tribe of the sons of E a leader, Nu 34:24 669
those are the ten thousands of E, Dt 33:17 669
and the land of E and Manasseh, Dt 34:2 669
were two tribes, Manasseh and E, Jos 14:4 669
sons of Joseph, Manasseh and E, Jos 16:4 669
of E according to their families: Jos 16:5 669
of E according to their families, Jos 16:8 669
which were set apart for the sons of E Jos 16:9 669
in the midst of E to this day, Jos 16:10 669
belonged to the sons of E. Jos 17:8 669
E among the cities of Manasseh), Jos 17:9 669
The south side *belonged* to E and Jos 17:10 669
of E is too narrow for you." Jos 17:15 669
of Joseph, to E and Manasseh, Jos 17:17 669
in the hill country of E. Jos 19:50 669
Shechem in the hill country of E, Jos 20:7 669
from the families of the tribe of E Jos 21:5 669
cities from the tribe of E were allotted Jos 21:20 669
lands, in the hill country of E, Jos 21:21 669
which is in the hill country of E, Jos 24:30 669
him in the hill country of E. Jos 24:33 669
E did not drive out the Jg 1:29 669
in the hill country of E, Jg 2:9 669
trumpet in the hill country of E; Jg 3:27 669
Bethel in the hill country of E; Jg 4:5 669
"From E those whose root is in Jg 5:14 669
all the hill country of E, Jg 7:24 669
So all the men of E were summoned Jg 7:24 669
Then the men of E said to him, Jg 8:1 669
Is not the gleaning *of the grapes* of E Jg 8:2 669
Shamir in the hill country of E. Jg 10:1 669
Benjamin, and the house of E, Jg 10:9 669
Then the men of E were summoned, Jg 12:1 669
the men of Gilead and fought E; Jg 12:4 669
and the men of Gilead defeated E, Jg 12:4 669
"You are fugitives of E, Jg 12:4 669
in the midst of E *and* in the Jg 12:4 669
fords of the Jordan opposite E. Jg 12:5 669
any of the fugitives of E said, Jg 12:5 669
fell at that time 42,000 of E. Jg 12:6 669
at Pirathon in the land of E, Jg 12:15 669
country of E whose name was Micah. Jg 17:1 669
of E to the house of Micah. Jg 17:8 669
came to the hill country of E, Jg 18:2 669
from there to the hill country of E Jg 18:13 669
part of the hill country of E, Jg 19:1 669
was from the hill country of E, Jg 19:16 669
part of the hill country of E, Jg 19:18 669
from the hill country of E, 1Sa 1:1 669
passed through the hill country of E 1Sa 9:4 669
in the hill country of E heard that 1Sa 14:22 669
Ashurites, over Jezreel, over E, 2Sa 2:9 669
in Baal-hazor, which is near E, 2Sa 13:23 669
took place in the forest of E. 2Sa 18:6 669
a man from the hill country of E, 2Sa 20:21 669
Ben-hur, in the hill country of E; 1Ki 4:8 669
Shechem in the hill country of E, 1Ki 12:25 669
to me from the hill country of E. 2Ki 5:22 669
the Gate of E to the Corner Gate, 2Ki 14:13 669
territory from the tribe of E. 1Ch 6:66 669
of E with its pasture lands, 1Ch 6:67 669
The sons of E *were* Shuthelah 1Ch 7:20 669
Their father E mourned many days, 1Ch 7:22 669
and of the sons of E and Manasseh 1Ch 9:3 669
Of the sons of E 20,800, 1Ch 12:30 669
the Pelonite of the sons of E; 1Ch 27:10 669
the Pirathonite of the sons of E; 1Ch 27:14 669
for the sons of E, Hoshea the son 1Ch 27:20 669
which is in the hill country of E, 2Ch 13:4 669
captured in the hill country of E. 2Ch 15:8 669
and Benjamin and those from E, 2Ch 15:9 669
and in the cities of E which Asa 2Ch 17:2 669
Beersheba to the hill country of E 2Ch 19:4 669
nor with any of the sons of E. 2Ch 25:7 669
troops which came to him from E, 2Ch 25:10 669
the Gate of E to the Corner Gate, 2Ch 25:23 669
And Zichri, a mighty man of E, 2Ch 28:7 669
some of the heads of the sons of E, 2Ch 28:12 669
letters also to E and Manasseh, 2Ch 30:1 669
the country of E and Manasseh, 2Ch 30:10 669
even many from E and Manasseh, 2Ch 30:18 669
as well as in E and Manasseh, 2Ch 31:1 669
In the cities of Manasseh, E, 2Ch 34:6 669
had collected from Manasseh and E, 2Ch 34:9 669
in the square at the Gate of E, Ne 8:16 669
and above the Gate of E, Ne 12:39 669
E also is the helmet of My head; Ps 60:7 669
The sons of E were archers Ps 78:9 669
And did not choose the tribe of E, Ps 78:67 669
E and Benjamin and Manasseh, Ps 80:2 669
E also is the helmet of My head; Ps 108:8 669
"The Arameans have camped in E," Is 7:2 669
with E and the son of Remaliah, Is 7:5 669
65 years E will be shattered, Is 7:8 669
and the head of E is Samaria and Is 7:9 669
day that E separated from Judah, Is 7:17 669
E and the inhabitants of Samaria, Is 9:9 669
Manasseh *devours* E, Is 9:21 669
devours Ephraim, and E Manasseh, Is 9:21 669
the jealousy of E will depart, Is 11:13 669
E will not be jealous of Judah, Is 11:13 669
And Judah will not harass E. Is 11:13 669
city will disappear from E, Is 17:3 669
proud crown of the drunkards of E, Is 28:1 669
proud crown of the drunkards of E Is 28:3 669
proclaims wickedness from Mount E. Jer 4:15 669
brothers, all the offspring of E. Jer 7:15 669
On the hills of E call out, Jer 31:6 669
Israel, And E is My firstborn." Jer 31:9 669
"I have surely heard E grieving, Jer 31:18 669
"Is E My dear son? Jer 31:20 669
the hill country of E and Gilead. Jer 50:19 669
of E and all the house of Israel, Ezk 37:16 669
Joseph, which is in the hand of E, Ezk 37:19 669
the east side to the west side, E, Ezk 48:5 669
"Beside the border of E, Ezk 48:6 669
E is joined to idols; Hos 4:17 669
I know E, and Israel is not hidden Hos 5:3 669
For now, O E, you have played the Hos 5:3 669
and E stumble in their iniquity; Hos 5:5 669
E will become a desolation in the Hos 5:9 669
E is oppressed, crushed in Hos 5:11 669
Therefore I am like a moth to E And Hos 5:12 669
When E saw his sickness, And Judah Hos 5:13 669
Then E went to Assyria And sent to Hos 5:13 669
For I *will be* like a lion to E And Hos 5:14 669
What shall I do with you, O E? Hos 6:4 669
The iniquity of E is uncovered, Hos 7:1 669
E mixes himself with the nations; Hos 7:8 669
E has become a cake not turned. Hos 7:8 669
So E has become like a silly dove, Hos 7:11 669
E has hired lovers. Hos 8:9 669
E has multiplied altars for sin, Hos 8:11 669
land, But E will return to Egypt, Hos 9:3 669
E *was* a watchman with my God, a Hos 9:8 669
As for E, their glory will fly Hos 9:11 669
E, as I have seen, Is planted in a Hos 9:13 669
But E will bring out his children Hos 9:13 669
E is stricken, their root is dried Hos 9:16 669
E will be seized with shame And Hos 10:6 669
E is a trained heifer that Hos 10:11 669
I will harness E, Judah will plow, Hos 10:11 669
Yet it is I who taught E to walk, Hos 11:3 669
How can I give you up, O E? Hos 11:8 669
I will not destroy E again. Hos 11:9 669
E surrounds Me with lies And the Hos 11:12 669
E feeds on wind, And pursues the Hos 12:1 669
E said, "Surely I have become rich, Hos 12:8 669
E has provoked to bitter anger; Hos 12:14 669
When E spoke, *there was* trembling. Hos 13:1 669
The iniquity of E is bound up; Hos 13:12 669
O E, what more have I to do with Hos 14:8 669
of E and the territory of Samaria, Ob 1:19 669
I will cut off the chariot from E And Zch 9:10 669
bow, I will fill the bow with E. Zch 9:13 669
"E will be like a mighty man, Zch 10:7 669
wilderness, into a city called E; Jn 11:54 *2187*

EPHRAIMITE
would say to him, "Are you an E?" Jg 12:5 673
of Tohu, the son of Zuph, an E. 1Sa 1:1 673
the son of Nebat, an E of Zeredah, 1Ki 11:26 673

EPHRAIM'S
laid his right hand on E head, Gn 48:17 669
it from E head to Manasseh's head. Gn 48:17 669
the third generation of E sons; Gn 50:23 669
E harlotry is there, Israel has Hos 6:10 669

EPHRATH
still some distance to go to E, Gn 35:16 672
and was buried on the way to E Gn 35:19 672
still some distance to go to E; Gn 48:7 672
buried her there on the way to E Gn 48:7 672
When Azubah died, Caleb married E, 1Ch 2:19 672

EPHRATHAH
and may you achieve wealth in E Ru 4:11 672
sons of Hur, the firstborn of E, 1Ch 2:50 672
sons of Hur, the firstborn of E, 1Ch 4:4 672
Behold, we heard of it in E, Ps 132:6 672
"But as for you, Bethlehem E, Mi 5:2 672

EPHRATHITE
of the E of Bethlehem in Judah, 1Sa 17:12 673

EPHRATHITES
Chilion, E of Bethlehem in Judah. Ru 1:2 673

EPHRON
E the son of Zohar for me, Gn 23:8 6085
Now E was sitting among the sons Gn 23:10 6085
and E the Hittite answered Abraham Gn 23:10 6085
He spoke to E in the hearing Gn 23:13 6085
Then E answered Abraham, saying to Gn 23:14 6085
Abraham listened to E; Gn 23:16 6085
and Abraham weighed out for E the Gn 23:16 6085
of E the son of Zohar the Hittite, Gn 25:9 6085
is in the field of E the Hittite, Gn 49:29 6085
E the Hittite for a burial site. Gn 49:30 6085
a burial site from E the Hittite. Gn 50:13 6085
to the cities of Mount E, Jos 15:9 6085
villages and E with its villages. 2Ch 13:19 6085

EPHRON'S
So E field, which was in Gn 23:17 6085

EPICUREAN
And also some of the E and Stoic Ac 17:18 *1946b*

EPILEPTICS
diseases and pains, demoniacs, e, Mt 4:24 *4583*

EPOCHS
who changes the times and the e; Da 2:21 2166
times or e which the Father has fixed Ac 1:7 *2540*
Now as to the times and the e, 1Th 5:1 *2540*

EQUAL
for you are e to Pharaoh. Gn 44:18
money e to the dowry for virgins. Ex 22:17
there shall be an e part of each. Ex 30:34
"They shall eat e portions, Dt 18:8 2506
he who was least was e to a 1Ch 12:14
"Gold or glass cannot e it, Jb 28:17 6186a
"The topaz of Ethiopia cannot e it, Jb 28:19 6186a
But it is you, a man my e, Ps 55:13 6187
be considered as e with the clay, Is 29:16

Context	Reference	Number
liken Me That I would be *his* **e**?"	**Is 40:25**	7737a
Me And make Me **e** and compare Me,	**Is 46:5**	7737a
you thus **e** in glory and greatness?	**Ezk 31:18**	1819
It even magnified *itself* to be **e**	**Da 8:11**	5704
and you have made them **e** to us who	**Mt 20:12**	*2470*
Father, making Himself **e** with God.	**Jn 5:18**	*2470*
length and width and height are **e**.	**Rv 21:16**	*2470*
EQUALITY		
your affliction, but by way of **e**	**2Co 8:13**	*2471*
your need, that there may be **e**;	**2Co 8:14**	*2471*
did not regard **e** with God a thing	**Php 2:6**	*2470*
EQUALLY		
live ox and divide its price **e**;	**Ex 21:35**	
each one **e** with the other;	**Ezk 47:14**	
EQUIP		
e you in every good thing to do	**Heb 13:21**	*2675*
EQUIPMENT		
the **e** for the service of the tabernacle,	**Ex 39:40**	3627
pillars, its sockets, all its **e**,	**Nu 3:36**	3627
and all the **e** for their service;	**Nu 4:26**	3627
e and with all their service;	**Nu 4:32**	3627
of war and **e** for his chariots.	**1Sa 8:12**	3627
the way was full of clothes and **e** which	**2Ki 7:15**	3627
on with a great army and much **e**.	**Da 11:13**	7399
the **e** of a foolish shepherd.	**Zch 11:15**	3627
EQUIPPED		
about 40,000 **e** for war, crossed	**Jos 4:13**	2502b
They were **e** with bows, using both	**1Ch 12:2**	5401b
of the divisions **e** for war,	**1Ch 12:23**	2502b
and spear *were* 6,800, **e** for war.	**1Ch 12:24**	2502b
and with him 180,000 **e** for war.	**2Ch 17:18**	2502b
Ephraim were archers **e** with bows,	**Ps 78:9**	5401b
adequate, **e** for every good work.	**2Tm 3:17**	*1822*
EQUIPPING		
for the **e** of the saints for the	**Eph 4:12**	*2677*
EQUITY		
judgment for the peoples with **e**.	**Ps 9:8**	4339
Let Your eyes look with **e**.	**Ps 17:2**	4339
time, It is I who judge with **e**.	**Ps 75:2**	4339
will judge the peoples with **e**."	**Ps 96:10**	4339
And the peoples with **e**.	**Ps 98:9**	4339
You have established **e**;	**Ps 99:4**	4339
Righteousness, justice and **e**;	**Pr 1:3**	4339
And **e** *and* every good course.	**Pr 2:9**	4339
ER		
and bore a son and he named him **E**.	**Gn 38:3**	6147
took a wife for **E** his firstborn,	**Gn 38:6**	6147
But **E**, Judah's firstborn, was	**Gn 38:7**	6147
E and Onan and Shelah and Perez	**Gn 46:12**	6147
but **E** and Onan died in the land of	**Gn 46:12**	6147
The sons of Judah *were* **E** and Onan,	**Nu 26:19**	6147
but **E** and Onan died in the land of	**Nu 26:19**	6147
The sons of Judah *were* **E**,	**1Ch 2:3**	6147
And **E**, Judah's firstborn, was	**1Ch 2:3**	6147
E the father of Lecah and Laadah	**1Ch 4:21**	6147
the son of Elmadam, the son of **E**,	**Lk 3:28**	*2262*
ERADICATED		
Thus Jehu **e** Baal out of Israel.	**2Ki 10:28**	8045
ERAN		
of **E**, the family of the Eranites.	**Nu 26:36**	6197
ERANITES		
of Eran, the family of the **E**.	**Nu 26:36**	6198
ERASE		
and I will not **e** his name from the	**Rv 3:5**	*1813*
ERASTUS		
ministered to him, Timothy and **E**,	**Ac 19:22**	*2037*
E, the city treasurer greets you,	**Ro 16:23**	*2037*
E remained at Corinth, but	**2Tm 4:20**	*2037*
ERECH		
Babel and **E** and Accad and Calneh,	**Gn 10:10**	751
the secretaries, the men of **E**,	**Ezr 4:9**	756
ERECT		
my sheaf rose up and also stood **e**;	**Gn 37:7**	5324
"Then you shall **e** the tabernacle	**Ex 26:30**	6965
of your yoke and made you walk **e**.	**Lv 26:13**	6968
e an altar to the LORD on the	**2Sa 24:18**	6965
well-watered mighty ones stand **e**	**Ezk 31:14**	
immediately she was made **e** again and	**Lk 13:13**	*461*
he was about to **e** the tabernacle;	**Heb 8:5**	*2005*
ERECTED		
Then he **e** there an altar and	**Gn 33:20**	5324
month, the tabernacle was **e**.	**Ex 40:17**	6965
Moses **e** the tabernacle and	**Ex 40:18**	6965
its bars and **e** its pillars.	**Ex 40:18**	6965
He **e** the court all around the	**Ex 40:33**	6965
on the day that the tabernacle was **e**	**Nu 9:15**	6965
e over him a very great heap of stones	**2Sa 18:17**	5324
So he **e** an altar for Baal in the	**1Ki 16:32**	6965
and he **e** altars for Baal and made	**2Ki 21:3**	6965
He **e** the pillars in front of	**2Ch 3:17**	6965
broken down and **e** towers on it,	**2Ch 32:5**	5927
he also **e** altars for the Baals and	**2Ch 33:3**	6965
built high places and **e** the Asherim	**2Ch 33:19**	5975
e their siege towers,	**Is 23:13**	6965
ERI		
and Ezbon, **E** and Arodi and Areli.	**Gn 46:16**	6179
of **E**, the family of the Erites;	**Nu 26:16**	6179
ERITES		
of Eri, the family of the **E**;	**Nu 26:16**	6180
ERR		
are a people who **e** in their heart,	**Ps 95:10**	8582
mouth should not **e** in judgment.	**Pr 16:10**	4603
who **e** in mind will know the truth,	**Is 29:24**	8582
ERRED		
And show me how I have **e**.	**Jb 6:24**	7686
"Even if I have truly **e**,	**Jb 19:4**	7686
ERROR		
congregation of Israel commits **e** and	**Lv 4:13**	7686
e in which he sinned unintentionally	**Lv 5:18**	7684
for it was an **e**, and they have	**Nu 15:25**	7684
before the LORD, for their **e**.	**Nu 15:25**	7684
to all the people through **e**.	**Nu 15:26**	7684
and have committed a serious **e**."	**1Sa 26:21**	7686
against His angels He charges **e**.	**Jb 4:18**	8417
truly erred, My **e** lodges with me.	**Jb 19:4**	4879
like an **e** which goes forth from	**Ec 10:5**	7684
and to speak **e** against the LORD,	**Is 32:6**	8442
the due penalty of their **e**.	**Ro 1:27**	*4106*
our exhortation does not *come* from **e**	**1Th 2:3**	*4106*
turns a sinner from the **e** of his way	**Jas 5:20**	*4106*
from the ones who live in **e**,	**2Pe 2:18**	*4106*
away by the **e** of unprincipled men and	**2Pe 3:17**	*4106*
of truth and the spirit of **e**.	**1Jn 4:6**	*4106*
headlong into the **e** of Balaam,	**Jude 1:11**	*4106*
ERRORS		
Who can discern *his* **e**?	**Ps 19:12**	7691
ERRS		
who hurries his footsteps **e**.	**Pr 19:2**	2398
ESARHADDON		
And **E** his son became king in his	**2Ki 19:37**	634
the days of **E** king of Assyria,	**Ezr 4:2**	634
And **E** his son became king in his	**Is 37:38**	634
ESAU		
and they named him **E**.	**Gn 25:25**	6215
up, **E** became a skillful hunter,	**Gn 25:27**	6215
Now Isaac loved **E**, because he had	**Gn 25:28**	6215
and **E** came in from the field and he	**Gn 25:29**	6215
and **E** said to Jacob,	**Gn 25:30**	6215
E said, "Behold, I am about to die;	**Gn 25:32**	6215
gave **E** bread and lentil stew;	**Gn 25:34**	6215
Thus **E** despised his birthright.	**Gn 25:34**	6215
When **E** was forty years old he	**Gn 26:34**	6215
his older son **E** and said to him,	**Gn 27:1**	6215
while Isaac spoke to his son **E**.	**Gn 27:5**	6215
So when **E** went to the field to	**Gn 27:5**	6215
father speak to your brother **E**,	**Gn 27:6**	6215
E my brother is a hairy man and I	**Gn 27:11**	6215
best garments of **E** her elder son,	**Gn 27:15**	6215
"I am **E** your firstborn;	**Gn 27:19**	6215
you are really my son **E** or not."	**Gn 27:21**	6215
the hands are the hands of **E**."	**Gn 27:22**	6215
"Are you really my son **E**?"	**Gn 27:24**	6215
that **E** his brother came in from	**Gn 27:30**	6215
am your son, your firstborn, **E**."	**Gn 27:32**	6215
E heard the words of his father,	**Gn 27:34**	6215
But Isaac replied to **E**,	**Gn 27:37**	6215
E said to his father,	**Gn 27:38**	6215
So **E** lifted his voice and wept.	**Gn 27:38**	6215
So **E** bore a grudge against Jacob	**Gn 27:41**	6215
and **E** said to himself,	**Gn 27:41**	6215
son **E** were reported to Rebekah,	**Gn 27:42**	6215
"Behold your brother **E** is	**Gn 27:42**	6215
the mother of Jacob and **E**.	**Gn 28:5**	6215
Now **E** saw that Isaac had blessed	**Gn 28:6**	6215
So **E** saw that the daughters of	**Gn 28:8**	6215
and **E** went to Ishmael, and	**Gn 28:9**	6215
his brother **E** in the land of Seir,	**Gn 32:3**	6215
"Thus you shall say to my lord **E**:	**Gn 32:4**	6215
"We came to your brother **E**,	**Gn 32:6**	6215
"If **E** comes to the one company	**Gn 32:8**	6215
of my brother, from the hand of **E**;	**Gn 32:11**	6215
him a present for his brother **E**:	**Gn 32:13**	6215
brother **E** meets you and asks you,	**Gn 32:17**	6215
it is a present sent to my lord **E**.	**Gn 32:18**	6215
speak to **E** when you find him;	**Gn 32:19**	6215
looked, and behold, **E** was coming,	**Gn 33:1**	6215
Then **E** ran to meet him and	**Gn 33:4**	6215
E said, "I have plenty, my brother;	**Gn 33:9**	6215
Then **E** said, "Let us take our journey	**Gn 33:12**	6215
E said, "Please let me leave with you	**Gn 33:15**	6215
So **E** returned that day on his way	**Gn 33:16**	6215
you fled from your brother **E**."	**Gn 35:1**	6215
his sons **E** and Jacob buried him.	**Gn 35:29**	6215
records of the generations of **E**	**Gn 36:1**	6215
E took his wives from the	**Gn 36:2**	6215
Adah bore Eliphaz to **E**,	**Gn 36:4**	6215
These are the sons of **E** who were	**Gn 36:5**	6215
Then **E** took his wives and his sons	**Gn 36:6**	6215
So **E** lived in the hill country of	**Gn 36:8**	6215
in the hill country of Seir; **E** is Edom.	**Gn 36:8**	6215
of **E** the father of the Edomites	**Gn 36:9**	6215
she bore to **E**, Jeush and Jalam and	**Gn 36:14**	6215
are the chiefs of the sons of **E**.	**Gn 36:15**	6215
of Eliphaz, the firstborn of **E**,	**Gn 36:15**	6215
These are the sons of **E**	**Gn 36:19**	6215
of the chiefs descended from **E**,	**Gn 36:40**	6215
E, the father of the Edomites	**Gn 36:43**	6215
the sons of **E** who live in Seir;	**Dt 2:4**	6215
Mount Seir to **E** as a possession.	**Dt 2:5**	6215
beyond our brothers the sons of **E**,	**Dt 2:8**	6215
but the sons of **E** dispossessed	**Dt 2:12**	6215
just as He did for the sons of **E**,	**Dt 2:22**	6215
just as the sons of **E** who live in	**Dt 2:29**	6215
'To Isaac I gave Jacob and **E**,	**Jos 24:4**	6215
Esau, and to **E** I gave Mount Seir to	**Jos 24:4**	6215
sons of Isaac *were* **E** and Israel.	**1Ch 1:34**	6215
The sons of **E** *were* Eliphaz, Reuel,	**1Ch 1:35**	6215
I will bring the disaster of **E** upon him	**Jer 49:8**	6215
"But I have stripped **E** bare,	**Jer 49:10**	6215
"O how **E** will be ransacked,	**Ob 1:6**	6215
from the mountain of **E**?	**Ob 1:8**	6215
the mountain of **E** by slaughter.	**Ob 1:9**	6215
the house of **E** *will be* as stubble.	**Ob 1:18**	6215
no survivor of the house of **E**,"	**Ob 1:18**	6215
will possess the mountain of **E**,	**Ob 1:19**	6215
Zion To judge the mountain of **E**,	**Ob 1:21**	6215
"*Was* not **E** Jacob's brother?"	**Mal 1:2**	6215
but I have hated **E**,	**Mal 1:3**	6215
"JACOB I LOVED, BUT **E** I HATED."	**Ro 9:13**	*2269a*
faith Isaac blessed Jacob and **E**,	**Heb 11:20**	*2269a*
immoral or godless person like **E**,	**Heb 12:16**	*2269a*
ESAU'S		
his hand holding on to **E** heel,	**Gn 25:26**	6215
hairy like his brother **E** hands;	**Gn 27:23**	6215
These are the names of **E** sons:	**Gn 36:10**	6215
Eliphaz the son of **E** wife Adah,	**Gn 36:10**	6215
Reuel the son of **E** wife Basemath.	**Gn 36:10**	6215
Timna was a concubine of **E** son	**Gn 36:12**	6215
These are the sons of **E** wife Adah.	**Gn 36:12**	6215
were the sons of **E** wife Basemath.	**Gn 36:13**	6215
the sons of **E** wife Oholibamah,	**Gn 36:14**	6215
are the sons of Reuel, **E** son:	**Gn 36:17**	6215
are the sons of **E** wife Basemath.	**Gn 36:17**	6215
are the sons of **E** wife Oholibamah:	**Gn 36:18**	6215
descended from **E** wife Oholibamah,	**Gn 36:18**	6215
ESCAPE		
"**E** for your life! Do not look behind	**Gn 19:17**	4422
e to the mountains, or you will be	**Gn 19:17**	4422
but I cannot **e** to the mountains,	**Gn 19:19**	4422
Please, let me **e** there	**Gn 19:20**	4422
"Hurry, **e** there, for I cannot do	**Gn 19:22**	4422
company which is left will **e**."	**Gn 32:8**	6413
called that place the Rock of **E**.	**1Sa 23:28**	4256
to **e** into the land of the Philistines.	**1Sa 27:1**	4422
and I will **e** from his hand."	**1Sa 27:1**	4422
none of us will **e** from Absalom.	**2Sa 15:14**	6413
cities and **e** from our sight."	**2Sa 20:6**	5337
do not let one of them **e**."	**1Ki 18:40**	4422
then let no one **e** *or* leave the	**2Ki 9:15**	6412a
whom I bring into your hands to **e** shall	**2Ki 10:24**	4422
there is no remnant nor any who **e**?	**Ezr 9:14**	6413
can **e** any more than all the Jews.	**Es 4:13**	4422
And there will be no **e** for them;	**Jb 11:20**	4498
"He will not **e** from darkness;	**Jb 15:30**	5493
There is no **e** for me;	**Ps 142:4**	4498
the righteous will **e** from trouble.	**Pr 12:13**	3318
And he who tells lies will not **e**.	**Pr 19:5**	4422
pleasing to God will **e** from her,	**Ec 7:26**	4422
and we, how shall we **e**?' "	**Is 20:6**	4422
So he will not **e** the sword, And	**Is 31:8**	5127
which they will not be able to **e**;	**Jer 11:11**	3318
e from the masters of the flock.	**Jer 25:35**	6413
Zedekiah king of Judah will not **e**	**Jer 32:4**	4422
'You will not **e** from his hand,	**Jer 34:3**	4422
will not **e** from their hand.' "	**Jer 38:18**	4422
will not **e** from their hand,	**Jer 38:23**	4422
'Those who **e** the sword will	**Jer 44:28**	6412a
man flee, Nor the mighty man **e**;	**Jer 46:6**	4422
city, So that no city will **e**;	**Jer 48:8**	4422
on every side, Let there be no **e**.	**Jer 50:29**	6413
'Then those of you who **e** will	**Ezk 6:9**	6412a
'Even when their survivors **e**,	**Ezk 7:16**	6403
Will he who does such things **e**?	**Ezk 17:15**	4422
indeed break the covenant and **e**?	**Ezk 17:15**	4422
he shall not **e**.' "	**Ezk 17:18**	4422
and the land of Egypt will not **e**.	**Da 11:42**	6413
There will be those who **e**,	**Jl 2:32**	6413
The swift of foot will not **e**,	**Am 2:15**	4422
flee, Or a refugee who will **e**.	**Am 9:1**	4422
Zion there will be those who **e**,	**Ob 1:17**	6413
inhabitant of Zaanan does not **e**.	**Mi 1:11**	3318
E, you who are living with the	**Zch 2:7**	4422
but they also test God and **e**.' "	**Mal 3:15**	4422
will you **e** the sentence of hell?	**Mt 23:33**	*5343*
yet He could not **e** notice.	**Mk 7:24**	*2990*
may have strength to **e** all these things	**Lk 21:36**	*1628*
none of these things **e** his notice;	**Ac 26:26**	*2990*
were trying to **e** from the ship and	**Ac 27:30**	*5343*
of them would swim away and **e**;	**Ac 27:42**	*1309*
you will **e** the judgment of God?	**Ro 2:3**	*1628*
will provide the way of **e** also,	**1Co 10:13**	*1545*
and they will not **e**.	**1Th 5:3**	*1628*
they may come to their senses *and* **e**	**2Tm 2:26**	
how will we **e** if we neglect so	**Heb 2:3**	*1628*
For if those did not **e** when they	**Heb 12:25**	*1628*
much less *will* we **e** who turn	**Heb 12:25**	
those who barely **e** from the ones	**2Pe 2:18**	*668*
let this one *fact* **e** your notice,	**2Pe 3:8**	*2990*
ESCAPED		
will also eat the rest of what has **e**	**Ex 10:5**	6413
who has **e** from his master to you.	**Dt 23:15**	5337
left of those who survived or **e**.	**Jos 8:22**	6412a
Ehud **e** while they were delaying,	**Jg 3:26**	4422
by the idols and **e** to Seirah.	**Jg 3:26**	4422
robust and valiant men; and no one **e**	**Jg 3:29**	4422
Then Jotham **e** and fled, and went	**Jg 9:21**	5127
I **e** from the battle line today."	**1Sa 4:16**	5127
Saul were taken, but the people **e**.	**1Sa 14:41**	3318
David **e** from his presence twice.	**1Sa 18:11**	5437
And David fled and **e** that night.	**1Sa 19:10**	4422
and he went out and fled and **e**.	**1Sa 19:12**	4422
my enemy go, so that he has **e**?"	**1Sa 19:17**	4422
and **e** and came to Samuel at Ramah,	**1Sa 19:18**	4422
and **e** to the cave of Adullam;	**1Sa 22:1**	4422
Abiathar, **e** and fled after David.	**1Sa 22:20**	4422
Saul that David had **e** from Keilah,	**1Sa 23:13**	4422
and not a man of them **e**,	**1Sa 30:17**	4422
have **e** from the camp of Israel."	**2Sa 1:3**	4422
Rechab and Baanah his brother **e**.	**2Sa 4:6**	4422
Aram **e** on a horse with his horsemen.	**1Ki 20:20**	4422
so that they **e** from under the hand	**2Ki 13:5**	3318

they **e** into the land of Ararat. 2Ki 19:37 4422
remnant of the Amalekites who **e**, 1Ch 4:43 6413
of Aram has **e** out of your hand. 2Ch 16:7 4422
on the ground, and no one had **e**. 2Ch 20:24 6413
He may return to those of you who **e** 2Ch 30:6 6413
Those who had **e** from the sword 2Ch 36:20 7611
to leave us an **e** remnant and to Ezr 9:8 6413
given us an **e** remnant as this, Ezr 9:13 6413
we have been left an **e** remnant, Ezr 9:15 6413
the Jews who had **e** *and* had survived Ne 1:2 6413
and I alone have **e** to tell you." Jb 1:15 4422
and I alone have **e** to tell you." Jb 1:16 4422
and I alone have **e** to tell you." Jb 1:17 4422
and I alone have **e** to tell you." Jb 1:19 4422
e *only* by the skin of my teeth. Jb 19:20 4422
Our soul has **e** as a bird out of Ps 124:7 4422
The snare is broken and we have **e**. Ps 124:7 4422
of the house of Jacob who have **e**, Is 10:20 6413
they **e** into the land of Ararat. Is 37:38 4422
the son of Nethaniah **e** from Johanan Jer 41:15 4422
You who have **e** the sword, Depart! Jer 51:50 6412b
And there was no one who **e** or La 2:22 6412a
for you will have those who **e** the Ezk 6:8 6412a
mouth will be opened to him who **e**, Ezk 24:27 6412a
linen sheet and **e** naked. Mk 14:52 *5343*
saw that she had not **e** notice, Lk 8:47 *2990*
that the prisoners had **e**. Ac 16:27 *1628*
in the wall, and *so* **e** his hands. 2Co 11:33 *1628*
of fire, **e** the edge of the sword, Heb 11:34 *5343*
having **e** the corruption that is in 2Pe 1:4 *668*
For if, after they have **e** the 2Pe 2:20 *668*

ESCAPES

e the notice of the assembly, Lv 4:13 5956
who **e** from the sword of Hazael, 1Ki 19:17 4422
one who **e** from the sword of Jehu, 1Ki 19:17 4422
GOD the Lord belong **e** from death. Ps 68:20 8444
due me **e** the notice of my God"? Is 40:27 5674a
who flees and her who **e** *And* say, Jer 48:19 4422
that on that day he who **e** will Ezk 24:26 6412a
them, And nothing at all **e** them. Jl 2:3 6413
it **e** their notice that by the word 2Pe 3:5 *2990*

ESCORT

the king to **e** him over the Jordan. 2Sa 19:31 7971

ESCORTED

and they **e** him away, with his wife Gn 12:20 7971
Now those who **e** Paul brought him as Ac 17:15 *2525*
e us until *we were* out of the city. Ac 21:5 *4311*

ESEK

So he named the well **E**, Gn 26:20 6230

ESHAN

Arab and Dumah and **E**, Jos 15:52 824

ESHBAAL

Malchi-shua, Abinadab and **E**. 1Ch 8:33 792
Malchi-shua, Abinadab and **E**. 1Ch 9:39 792

ESHBAN

and **E** and Ithran and Cheran. Gn 36:26 790
the sons of Dishon *were* Hamran, **E**, 1Ch 1:41 790

ESHCOL

brother of **E** and brother of Aner, Gn 14:13 812
the men who went with me, Aner, **E**, Gn 14:24 812
Then they came to the valley of **E** Nu 13:23 812
place was called the valley of **E**, Nu 13:24 812
the valley of **E** and saw the land, Nu 32:9 812
and came to the valley of **E** and Dt 1:24 812

ESHEK

The sons of **E** his brother *were* 1Ch 8:39 6232

ESHTAOL

E and Zorah and Ashnah, Jos 15:33 847b
was Zorah and **E** and Ir-shemesh, Jos 19:41 847b
Mahaneh-dan, between Zorah and **E**. Jg 13:25 847b
and buried him between Zorah and **E** Jg 16:31 847b
valiant men from Zorah and **E**, Jg 18:2 847b
to their brothers at Zorah and **E**, Jg 18:8 847b
Danites, from Zorah and from **E**, Jg 18:11 847b

ESHTAOLITES

came the Zorathites and the **E**. 1Ch 2:53 848

ESHTEMOA

and **E** with its pasture lands, Jos 21:14 851
and to those who were in **E**, 1Sa 30:28 851
and Ishbah the father of **E**. 1Ch 4:17 851
the Garmite and **E** the Maacathite. 1Ch 4:19 851
Jattir, **E** with its pasture lands, 1Ch 6:57 851

ESHTEMOH

and Anab and **E** and Anim, Jos 15:50 851

ESHTON

of Mehir, who was the father of **E**. 1Ch 4:11 850
E became the father of Beth-rapha 1Ch 4:12 850

ESPECIALLY

"Go, view the land, **e** Jericho." Jos 2:1 853
a reproach, **E** to my neighbors, Ps 31:11 3966
e of all the tribes of Israel, Zch 9:1
grieving **e** over the word which he Ac 20:38 *3122*
before you *all* and **e** before you, Ac 25:26 *3122*
e because you are an expert in all Ac 26:3 *3122*
but **e** that you may prophesy. 1Co 14:1 *3123*
in the world, and **e** toward you. 2Co 1:12 *4053*
the love which I have **e** for you. 2Co 2:4 *4053*
and **e** to those who are of the Ga 6:10 *3122*
you, **e** those of Caesar's household. Php 4:22 *3122*
Savior of all men, **e** of believers. 1Tm 4:10 *3122*
and **e** for those of his household, 1Tm 5:8 *3122*
e those who work hard at preaching 1Tm 5:17 *3122*
and the books, **e** the parchments. 2Tm 4:13 *3122*
e those of the circumcision, Ti 1:10 *3122*
slave, a beloved brother, **e** to me, Phm 1:16 *3122*
and **e** those who indulge the flesh 2Pe 2:10 *3122*

and **e** *when they are* strangers; 3Jn 1:5 *3778*

ESSENTIAL

and approve the things that are **e**, Ro 2:18 *1308*

ESSENTIALS

no greater burden than these **e**: Ac 15:28 *1876*

ESTABLISH

"But I will **e** My covenant with you; Gn 6:18 6965
Myself do **e** My covenant with you, Gn 9:9 6965
"I **e** My covenant with you; Gn 9:11 6965
"I will **e** My covenant between Gn 17:2 5414
"I will **e** My covenant between Gn 17:7 6965
and I will **e** My covenant with him Gn 17:19 6965
My covenant I will **e** with Isaac, Gn 17:21 6965
and I will **e** the oath which I Gn 26:3 6965
to **e** His name there for His Dt 12:5 7760
where He chooses to **e** His name, Dt 14:23 7931
the LORD chooses to **e** His name. Dt 16:2 7931
your God chooses to **e** His name, Dt 16:6 7931
your God chooses to **e** His name. Dt 16:11 7931
'My husband's brother refuses to **e** Dt 25:7 6965
your God chooses to **e** His name. Dt 26:2 7931
"The LORD will **e** you as a holy Dt 28:9 6965
in order that He may **e** you today Dt 29:13 6965
and to **e** the throne of David over 2Sa 3:10 6965
you, and I will **e** his kingdom. 2Sa 7:12 3559
and I will **e** the throne of his 2Sa 7:13 3559
then I will **e** the throne of your 1Ki 9:5 6965
LORD, that He might **e** His word, 1Ki 12:15 6965
son after him and to **e** Jerusalem; 1Ki 15:4 5975
and I will **e** his kingdom. 1Ch 17:11 3559
and I will **e** his throne forever. 1Ch 17:12 3559
as he went to **e** his rule to the 1Ch 18:3 5324
and I will **e** the throne of his 1Ch 22:10 3559
'I will **e** his kingdom forever if 1Ch 28:7 3559
then I will **e** your royal throne as 2Ch 7:18 6965
that the LORD might **e** His word, 2Ch 10:15 6965
to **e** these days of Purim at their Es 9:31 6965
And **e** His words in your heart. Jb 22:22 7760
to an end, but **e** the righteous; Ps 7:9 3559
God will **e** her forever. Ps 48:8 3559
the Most High Himself will **e** her. Ps 87:5 3559
You will **e** Your faithfulness." Ps 89:2 3559
I will **e** your seed forever And Ps 89:4 3559
I will **e** his descendants forever And Ps 89:29 7760
that they may **e** an inhabited city, Ps 107:36 3559
E Your word to Your servant, As that Ps 119:38 6965
E my footsteps in Your word, And do Ps 119:133 3559
will **e** the boundary of the widow. Pr 15:25 5324
To **e** it and to uphold it with Is 9:7 3559
LORD, You will **e** peace for us, Is 26:12 8239
of My hand, to **e** the heavens, Is 51:16 5193
the LORD who formed it to **e** it, Jer 33:2 3559
and I will **e** an everlasting Ezk 16:60 6965
I will **e** My covenant with you, Ezk 16:62 6965
"I will **e** for them a renowned Ezk 34:29 6965
king should **e** a statute and enforce Da 6:7 6966
e the injunction and sign the Da 6:8 6966
good, And **e** justice in the gate! Am 5:15 3322
On the contrary, we **e** the Law. Ro 3:31 *2476*
and seeking to **e** their own, Ro 10:3 *2476*
Now to Him who is able to **e** you Ro 16:25 *4741*
so that He may **e** your hearts 1Th 3:13 *4741*
first in order to **e** the second. Heb 10:9 *2476*
confirm, strengthen *and* **e** you. 1Pe 5:10 *2311*

ESTABLISHED

sign of the covenant which I have **e** Gn 9:17 6965
He **e** households for them. Ex 1:21 6213a
I also **e** My covenant with them, Ex 6:4 6965
O Lord, which Your hands have **e**. Ex 15:17 3559
LORD **e** between Himself and the sons Lv 26:46 5414
So let the city of Sihon be **e**. Nu 21:27 3559
the matter **e** that this abomination has Dt 13:14 3559
He has made you and **e** you. Dt 32:6 3559
for now the LORD would have **e** your 1Sa 13:13 3559
you nor your kingdom will be **e**. 1Sa 20:31 3559
of Israel will be **e** in your hand. 1Sa 24:20 6965
had **e** him as king over Israel, 2Sa 5:12 3559
throne shall be **e** forever. 2Sa 7:16 3559
"For You have **e** for Yourself Your 2Sa 7:24 3559
servant David be **e** before You. 2Sa 7:26 3559
and his kingdom was firmly **e**. 1Ki 2:12 3559
who has **e** me and set me on the 1Ki 2:24 3559
be **e** before the LORD forever." 1Ki 2:45 3559
was **e** in the hands of Solomon. 1Ki 2:46 3559
had **e** him as king over Israel, 1Ch 14:2 3559
Indeed, the world is firmly **e**, 1Ch 16:30 3559
throne shall be **e** forever. 1Ch 17:14 3559
his house be **e** forever, 1Ch 17:23 539
name be **e** and magnified forever, 1Ch 17:24 539
Your servant is **e** before You.' 1Ch 17:24 3559
Now Solomon the son of David **e** 2Ch 1:1 2388
the kingdom of Rehoboam was **e** and 2Ch 12:1 3559
LORD **e** the kingdom in his control, 2Ch 17:5 3559
LORD your God and you will be **e**. 2Ch 20:20 539
the house of the LORD was **e** *again*. 2Ch 29:35 3559
So they **e** a decree to circulate a 2Ch 30:5 5975
and advanced him and **e** his Es 3:1 7760
the Jews **e** and made a custom for Es 9:27 6965
and Queen Esther had **e** for them, Es 9:31 6965
and just as they had **e** for Es 9:31 6965
Esther **e** these customs for Purim, Es 9:32 6965
are **e** with them in their sight, Jb 21:8 3559
a thing, and it will be **e** for you; Jb 22:28 6965
He **e** it and also searched it out. Jb 28:27 3559
babes You have **e** strength Because Ps 8:2 3245
He has **e** His throne for judgment, Ps 9:7 3559
seas And **e** it upon the rivers. Ps 24:2 3559
steps of a man are **e** by the LORD, Ps 37:23 3559

You have **e** all the boundaries of Ps 74:17 5324
For He **e** a testimony in Jacob And Ps 78:5 6965
He **e** it for a testimony in Joseph When Ps 81:5 7760
With whom My hand will be **e**; Ps 89:21 3559
shall be **e** forever like the moon, Ps 89:37 3559
Indeed, the world is firmly **e**, Ps 93:1 3559
Your throne is **e** from of old; Ps 93:2 3559
Indeed, the world is firmly **e**, Ps 96:10 3559
You have **e** equity; Ps 99:4 3559
will be **e** before You." Ps 102:28 3559
has **e** His throne in the heavens, Ps 103:19 3559
He **e** the earth upon its Ps 104:5 3245
sank down To the place which You **e** Ps 104:8 3245
may be **e** To keep Your statutes! Ps 119:5 3559
You **e** the earth, and it stands. Ps 119:90 3559
a slanderer not be **e** in the earth; Ps 140:11 3559
has also **e** them forever and ever; Ps 148:6 5975
By understanding He **e** the heavens. Pr 3:19 3559
feet And all your ways will be **e**. Pr 4:26 3559
"From everlasting I was **e**, Pr 8:23 5258b
"When He **e** the heavens, I was Pr 8:27 3559
A man will not be **e** by wickedness, Pr 12:3 3559
Truthful lips will be **e** forever, Pr 12:19 3559
LORD And your plans will be **e**. Pr 16:3 3559
a throne is **e** on righteousness. Pr 16:12 3559
And by understanding it is **e**; Pr 24:3 3559
throne will be **e** in righteousness. Pr 25:5 3559
His throne will be **e** forever. Pr 29:14 3559
has **e** all the ends of the earth? Pr 30:4 6965
e as the chief of the mountains, Is 2:2 3559
will even be **e** in lovingkindness, Is 16:5 3559
He has **e** justice in the earth; Is 42:4 7760
time that I **e** the ancient nation. Is 44:7 7760
He **e** it *and* did not create it a Is 45:18 3559
'My purpose will be **e**, Is 46:10 6965
"In righteousness you will be **e**; Is 54:14 3559
Who **e** the world by His wisdom; Jer 10:12 3559
congregation shall be **e** before Me; Jer 30:20 3559
of heaven and earth I have not **e**, Jer 33:25 7760
Who **e** the world by His wisdom, Jer 51:15 3559
e as the chief of the mountains. Mi 4:1 3559
O Rock, have **e** them to correct. Hab 1:12 3245
gift to you, that you may be **e**; Ro 1:11 *4741*
those which exist are **e** by God. Ro 13:1 *5021*
the faith firmly **e** and steadfast, Col 1:23 *2311*
up in Him and **e** in your faith, Col 2:7 *950*
and have been **e** in the truth which 2Pe 1:12 *4741*

ESTABLISHES

to Him Who **e** peace in His heights. Jb 25:2 6213a
"Do you know how God **e** them, Jb 37:15 7760
Who **e** the mountains by His strength, Ps 65:6 3559
And give Him no rest until He **e** Is 62:7 3559
He removes kings and **e** kings; Da 2:21 6966
which the king **e** may be changed." Da 6:15 6966
Now He who **e** us with you in Christ 2Co 1:21 *950*

ESTABLISHING

God loved Israel **e** them forever, 2Ch 9:8 5975
into one new man, *thus* **e** peace, Eph 2:15 *4160*

ESTABLISHMENT

old, From the **e** of man on earth, Jb 20:4 7760

ESTATE

you And restore your righteous **e**. Jb 8:6 5116a
Who remembered us in our low **e**, Ps 136:23 8216
share of the **e** that falls to me.' Lk 15:12 *3776*
he squandered his **e** with loose living. Lk 15:13 *3776*

ESTATES

from the sale of their fathers' **e**. Dt 18:8

ESTEEM

Therefore I **e** right all *Your* precepts Ps 119:128 3474
despised, and we did not **e** Him. Is 53:3 2803
"O Daniel, man of high **e**, Da 10:11 2536b
"O man of high **e**, do not be Da 10:19 2536b
fear the LORD and who **e** His name. Mal 3:16 2803
the people held them in high **e**. Ac 5:13 *3170*
and that you **e** them very highly in 1Th 5:13 *2233*

ESTEEMED

greatly **e** in the land of Egypt, Ex 11:3
who despise Me will be lightly **e**. 1Sa 2:30 7043
I am a poor man and lightly **e**?" 1Sa 18:23 7034
So his name was highly **e**. 1Sa 18:30 3365
"I will be more lightly **e** 2Sa 6:22 7043
is lightly **e** and has a servant Than Pr 12:9 7034
For why should he be **e**? Is 2:22 2803
Yet we ourselves **e** Him stricken, Is 53:4 2803
to tell *you*, for you are highly **e**; Da 9:23 2536b
for that which is highly **e** among Lk 16:15 *5308*

ESTHER

bringing up Hadassah, that is **E**, Es 2:7 635
that **E** was taken to the king's Es 2:8 635
E did not make known her people or Es 2:10 635
learn how **E** was and how she fared. Es 2:11 635
Now when the turn of **E**, Es 2:15 635
And **E** found favor in the eyes of Es 2:15 635
So **E** was taken to King Ahasuerus Es 2:16 635
loved **E** more than all the women, Es 2:17 635
E had not yet made known her Es 2:20 635
for **E** did what Mordecai told her Es 2:20 635
to Mordecai and he told Queen **E**, Es 2:22 635
and **E** informed the king in Es 2:22 635
Then **E** summoned Hathach from the Es 4:5 635
he might show **E** and inform her, Es 4:8 635
and related Mordecai's words to **E**. Es 4:9 635

Then **E** spoke to Hathach and Es 4:10 635
Mordecai told *them* to reply to **E**, Es 4:13 635
Then **E** told *them* to reply to Es 4:15 635
did just as **E** had commanded him. Es 4:17 635
E put on her royal robes and stood in Es 5:1 635
the king saw **E** the queen standing Es 5:2 635
and the king extended to **E** the Es 5:2 635
So **E** came near and touched the top Es 5:2 635
"What is *troubling* you, Queen **E**? Es 5:3 635
E said, "If it pleases the king, Es 5:4 635
that we may do as **E** desires." Es 5:5 635
the banquet which **E** had prepared. Es 5:5 635
the banquet, the king said to **E**, Es 5:6 635
So **E** replied, "My petition Es 5:7 635
"Even **E** the queen let no one but Es 5:12 635
the banquet which **E** had prepared. Es 6:14 635
to drink *wine* with **E** the queen. Es 7:1 635
And the king said to **E** on the Es 7:2 635
"What is your petition, Queen **E**? Es 7:2 635
Then Queen **E** replied, Es 7:3 635
Then King Ahasuerus asked Queen **E**, Es 7:5 635
E said, "A foe and an enemy is Es 7:6 635
to beg for his life from Queen **E**, Es 7:7 635
falling on the couch where **E** was. Es 7:8 635
the enemy of the Jews, to Queen **E**; Es 8:1 635
for **E** had disclosed what he was to Es 8:1 635
And **E** set Mordecai over the house Es 8:2 635
Then **E** spoke again to the king, Es 8:3 635
extended the golden scepter to **E**. Es 8:4 635
So **E** arose and stood before the Es 8:4 635
Queen **E** and to Mordecai the Jew, Es 8:7 635
given the house of Haman to **E**, Es 8:7 635
The king said to Queen **E**, Es 9:12 635
Then said **E**, "If it pleases the king, Es 9:13 635
Then Queen **E**, daughter of Abihail, Es 9:29 635
Queen **E** had established for them, Es 9:31 635
The command of **E** established Es 9:32 635

ESTHER'S
gave a great banquet, **E** banquet, Es 2:18 635
Then **E** maidens and her eunuchs Es 4:4 635
They related **E** words to Mordecai. Es 4:12 635

ESTIMATION
you will not be wise in your own **e** Ro 11:25 *1438*
Do not be wise in your own **e**. Ro 12:16 *1438*

ESTRANGED
are completely **e** from me. Jb 19:13 2114a
The wicked are **e** from the womb; Ps 58:3 2114a
I have become **e** from my brothers And Ps 69:8 2114a
house of Israel who are **e** from Me Ezk 14:5 2114a

ETAM
in the cleft of the rock of **E**. Jg 15:8 5862
the rock of **E** and said to Samson, Jg 15:11 5862
These *were* the sons of **E**: 1Ch 4:3 5862
Their villages *were* **E**, 1Ch 4:32 5862
Thus he built Bethlehem, **E**, 2Ch 11:6 5862

ETERNAL
"The **e** God is a dwelling place, Dt 33:27 6924a
For man goes to his **e** home while Ec 12:5 5769
Counselor, Mighty God, **E** Father, Is 9:6 5703
boundary for the sea, An **e** decree, Jer 5:22 5769
feet and be cast into the **e** fire. Mt 18:8 *166*
I do that I may obtain **e** life?" Mt 19:16 *166*
as much, and will inherit **e** life. Mt 19:29 *166*
into the **e** fire which has been Mt 25:41 *166*
will go away into **e** punishment, Mt 25:46 *166*
but the righteous into **e** life." Mt 25:46 *166*
but is guilty of an **e** sin" Mk 3:29 *166*
what shall I do to inherit **e** life?" Mk 10:17 *166*
and in the age to come, **e** life. Mk 10:30 *166*
proclamation of **e** *salvation.*] Mk 16:20
what shall I do to inherit **e** life?" Lk 10:25 *166*
receive you into the **e** dwellings. Lk 16:9 *166*
what shall I do to inherit **e** life?" Lk 18:18 *166*
and in the age to come, **e** life." Lk 18:30 *166*
believes will in Him have **e** life. Jn 3:15 *166*
not perish, but have **e** life. Jn 3:16 *166*
believes in the Son has **e** life; Jn 3:36 *166*
of water springing up to **e** life." Jn 4:14 *166*
and is gathering fruit for life **e**; Jn 4:36 *166*
Him who sent Me, has **e** life, Jn 5:24 *166*
that in them you have **e** life; Jn 5:39 *166*
the food which endures to **e** life, Jn 6:27 *166*
believes in Him will have **e** life, Jn 6:40 *166*
you, he who believes has **e** life. Jn 6:47 *166*
and drinks My blood has **e** life, Jn 6:54 *166*
You have words of **e** life. Jn 6:68 *166*
and I give **e** life to them, and Jn 10:28 *166*
world will keep it to life **e**. Jn 12:25 *166*
that His commandment is **e** life; Jn 12:50 *166*
given Him, He may give **e** life. Jn 17:2 *166*
"This is **e** life, that they Jn 17:3 *166*
yourselves unworthy of **e** life, Ac 13:46 *166*
been appointed to **e** life believed. Ac 13:48 *166*
His **e** power and divine nature, Ro 1:20 *126*
and honor and immortality, **e** life; Ro 2:7 *166*
reign through righteousness to **e** life Ro 5:21 *166*
and the outcome, **e** life. Ro 6:22 *166*
e life in Christ Jesus our Lord. Ro 6:23 *166*
to the commandment of the **e** God, Ro 16:26 *166*
producing for us an **e** weight of glory 2Co 4:17 *166*
things which are not seen are **e**. 2Co 4:18 *166*
made with hands, **e** in the heavens. 2Co 5:1 *166*
will from the Spirit reap **e** life. Ga 6:8 *166*
This was in accordance with the **e** Eph 3:11 *165*
pay the penalty of **e** destruction, 2Th 1:9 *166*
who has loved us and given us **e** 2Th 2:16 *166*
would believe in Him for **e** life. 1Tm 1:16 *166*
Now to the King **e**, immortal, 1Tm 1:17 *165*
e life to which you were called, 1Tm 6:12 *166*
To Him *be* honor and **e** dominion! 1Tm 6:16 *166*
Christ Jesus *and with it* **e** glory. 2Tm 2:10 *166*
in the hope of **e** life, which God, Ti 1:2 *166*
according to *the* hope of **e** life. Ti 3:7 *166*
Him the source of **e** salvation, Heb 5:9 *166*
of the dead and **e** judgment. Heb 6:2 *166*
all, having obtained **e** redemption. Heb 9:12 *166*
who through the **e** Spirit offered Heb 9:14 *166*
the promise of the **e** inheritance. Heb 9:15 *166*
the blood of the **e** covenant, Heb 13:20 *166*
you to His **e** glory in Christ, 1Pe 5:10 *166*
the entrance into the **e** kingdom of our 2Pe 1:11 *166*
and proclaim to you the **e** life, 1Jn 1:2 *166*
which He Himself made to us: **e** life. 1Jn 2:25 *166*
has **e** life abiding in him. 1Jn 3:15 *166*
that God has given us **e** life, 1Jn 5:11 *166*
you may know that you have **e** life. 1Jn 5:13 *166*
This is the true God and **e** life. 1Jn 5:20 *166*
He has kept in **e** bonds under Jude 1:6 *126*
the punishment of **e** fire. Jude 1:7 *166*
our Lord Jesus Christ to **e** life. Jude 1:21 *166*
having an **e** gospel to preach to Rv 14:6 *166*

ETERNALLY
That he should live on **e**, Ps 49:9 5331

ETERNITY
He has also set **e** in their heart, Ec 3:11 5769
"Even from **e** I am He, Is 43:13 3117
to shame or humiliated To all **e**. Is 45:17 5769
long ago, From the days of **e**." Mi 5:2 5769
us in Christ Jesus from all **e**, 2Tm 1:9 *166*
both now and to the day of **e**. 2Pe 3:18 *165*

ETHAM
E on the edge of the wilderness. Ex 13:20 864a
from Succoth and camped in **E**, Nu 33:6 864a
They journeyed from **E** and Nu 33:7 864a
journey in the wilderness of **E** and Nu 33:8 864a

ETHAN
than all men, than **E** the Ezrahite, 1Ki 4:31 387
The sons of Zerah *were* Zimri, **E**, 1Ch 2:6 387
The son of **E** *was* Azariah. 1Ch 2:8 387
the son of **E**, the son of Zimmah, 1Ch 6:42 387
E the son of Kishi, the son of 1Ch 6:44 387
relatives, **E** the son of Kushaiah, 1Ch 15:17 387
and **E** *were appointed* to sound 1Ch 15:19 387

ETHANIM
at the feast, in the month **E**, 1Ki 8:2 388

ETHBAAL
of **E** king of the Sidonians, 1Ki 16:31 856

ETHER
Libnah and **E** and Ashan, Jos 15:42 6281
Ain, Rimmon and **E** and Ashan; four Jos 19:7 6281

ETHIOPIA
India to **E** over 127 provinces, Es 1:1 3568a
which *extended* from India to **E**, Es 8:9 3568a
"The topaz of **E** cannot equal it, Jb 28:19 3568a
E will quickly stretch out her Ps 68:31 3568a
Behold, Philistia and Tyre with **E**: Ps 87:4 3568a
E and Put, that handle the shield, Jer 46:9 3568a
Syene and even to the border of **E**. Ezk 29:10 3568a
Egypt, And anguish will be in **E**; Ezk 30:4 3568a
"**E**, Put, Lud, all Arabia, Libya Ezk 30:5 3568a
Me in ships to frighten secure **E**; Ezk 30:9 3568a
Persia, **E** and Put with them, all Ezk 38:5 3568a
Are you not as the sons of **E** to Me, Am 9:7 3569
E was *her* might, And Egypt too, Na 3:9 3568a
the rivers of **E** My worshipers, Zph 3:10 3568a

ETHIOPIAN
Now Zerah the **E** came out against 2Ch 14:9 3569
"Can the **E** change his skin Or the Jer 13:23 3569
But Ebed-melech the **E**, Jer 38:7 3569
king commanded Ebed-melech the **E**, Jer 38:10 3569
Ebed-melech the **E** said to Jeremiah, Jer 38:12 3569
"Go and speak to Ebed-melech the **E**, Jer 39:16 3569
and there was an **E** eunuch, Ac 8:27 *128*

ETHIOPIANS
the Lubim, the Sukkiim and the **E**. 2Ch 12:3 3569
the **E** before Asa and before Judah, 2Ch 14:12 3569
and before Judah, and the **E** fled. 2Ch 14:12 3569
and so many **E** fell that they could 2Ch 14:13 3569
"Were not the **E** and the Lubim an 2Ch 16:8 3569
and the Arabs who bordered the **E**; 2Ch 21:16 3569
and **E** *will follow* at his heels. Da 11:43 3569
"You also, O **E**, will be slain by Zph 2:12 3569
of Candace, queen of the **E**, Ac 8:27 *128*

ETH-KAZIN
the sunrise to Gath-hepher, to **E**, Jos 19:13 6278

ETHNAN
of Helah *were* Zereth, Izhar and **E**. 1Ch 4:7 869

ETHNARCH
In Damascus the **e** under Aretas the 2Co 11:32 *1481*

ETHNI
the son of **E**, the son of Zerah, 1Ch 6:41 867

EUBULUS
E greets you, also Pudens and 2Tm 4:21 *2103*

EUNICE
Lois and your mother **E**, 2Tm 1:5 *2131*

EUNUCH
the custody of Hegai, the king's **e**, Es 2:3 5631
the king's **e** who was in charge of Es 2:14 5631
the king's **e** who was in charge of Es 2:15 5631
Nor let the **e** say, Is 56:3 5631
But Ebed-melech the Ethiopian, a **e**, Jer 38:7 5631
there was an Ethiopian **e**, Ac 8:27 *2135*
The **e** answered Philip and said, Ac 8:34 *2135*
came to some water; and the **e** said, Ac 8:36 *2135*
water, Philip as well as the **e**, Ac 8:38 *2135*
and the **e** no longer saw him, but Ac 8:39 *2135*

EUNUCHS
the seven **e** who served in the Es 1:10 5631
king's command delivered by the **e**. Es 1:12 5631
Ahasuerus *delivered* by the **e**?" Es 1:15 5631
and her **e** came and told her, Es 4:4 5631
summoned Hathach from the king's **e**, Es 4:5 5631
the king's **e** who were doorkeepers, Es 6:2 5631
the king's **e** arrived and hastily Es 6:14 5631
e who *were* before the king said, Es 7:9 5631
"To the **e** who keep My sabbaths, Is 56:4 5631
women, *the* children, and *the* **e**, Jer 41:16 5631
"For there are **e** who were born Mt 19:12 *2135*
and there are **e** who were made Mt 19:12 *2135*
eunuchs who were made **e** by men; Mt 19:12 *2134*
and there are *also* **e** who made Mt 19:12 *2135*
also eunuchs who made themselves **e** Mt 19:12 *2134*

EUODIA
I urge **E** and I urge Syntyche to Php 4:2 *2136*

EUPHRATES
And the fourth river is the **E**. Gn 2:14 6578
as the great river, the river **E**: Gn 15:18 6578
and he arose and crossed the **E** Gn 31:21
and Shaul of Rehoboth on the **E** Gn 36:37
from the wilderness to the River **E**; Ex 23:31
as the great river, the river **E**. Dt 1:7 6578
and from the river, the river **E**, Dt 11:24 6578
as the great river, the river **E**, Jos 1:4 6578
and will scatter them beyond the **E** 1Ki 14:15
king of Assyria to the river **E**. 2Ki 23:29 6578
the brook of Egypt to the river **E**. 2Ki 24:7 6578
the wilderness from the river **E**, 1Ch 5:9 6578
establish his rule to the **E** River. 1Ch 18:3 6578
the ruler over all the kings from the **E** 2Ch 9:26 5104
make war at Carchemish on the **E**, 2Ch 35:20 6578
hired from regions beyond the **E** Is 7:20 5104
and abundant waters of the **E**, Is 8:7 5104
of the **E** to the brook of Egypt, Is 27:12 5104
To drink the waters of the **E**? Jer 2:18 5104
go to the **E** and hide it there in a Jer 13:4 6578
So I went and hid it by the **E**, Jer 13:5 6578
go to the **E** and take from there Jer 13:6 6578
Then I went to the **E** and dug, Jer 13:7 6578
was by the **E** River at Carchemish, Jer 46:2 6578
E They have stumbled and fallen. Jer 46:6 6578
land of the north by the river **E**. Jer 46:10 6578
throw it into the middle of the **E**, Jer 51:63 6578
Egypt, From Egypt even to the **E**, Mi 7:12 5104
are bound at the great river **E**." Rv 9:14 *2166*
bowl on the great river, the **E**; Rv 16:12 *2166*

EURAQUILO
the land a violent wind, called **E**; Ac 27:14 *2146b*

EUTYCHUS
E sitting on the window sill, Ac 20:9 *2161*

EVANGELIST
the house of Philip the **e**, Ac 21:8 *2099*
hardship, do the work of an **e**, 2Tm 4:5 *2099*

EVANGELISTS
some *as* prophets, and some *as* **e**, Eph 4:11 *2099*

EVAPORATED
When the layer of dew **e**, Ex 16:14 5927

EVAPORATES
"*As* water **e** from the sea, And a Jb 14:11 235

EVE
the man called his wife's name **E**, Gn 3:20 2332
man had relations with his wife **E**, Gn 4:1 2332
deceived **E** by his craftiness, 2Co 11:3 *2096*
who was first created, *and* then **E**. 1Tm 2:13 *2096*

EVEN
e I am bringing the flood of water Gn 6:17
ark, **e** every beast of the earth. Gn 9:10
"Have I **e** remained alive here Gn 16:13 1571
slay a nation, **e** *though* blameless? Gn 20:4 1571
e of all who went in at the gate Gn 23:10
e between you and us, and let us Gn 26:28
e me also, O my father!" Gn 27:34
e me also, O my father." So Gn 27:38
e in the watering troughs, where Gn 30:38
e all that *was* in the houses. Gn 34:29
brothers, they hated him **e** more. Gn 37:5 5750
So they hated him **e** more for his Gn 37:8 5750
and **e** here I have done nothing Gn 40:15 1571
and behold, it is **e** in my sack." Gn 42:28 1571
from our youth **e** until now, Gn 46:34
he **e** drew the water for us and Ex 2:19 1571
they will not believe **e** these two signs Ex 4:9 1571
"Now then go, and I, **e** I, Ex 4:12
and I, **e** I, will be with your Ex 4:15
did **e** as the LORD had commanded. Ex 7:20 3651
house with no concern **e** for this. Ex 7:23 1571
there was not **e** one of the livestock Ex 9:7 5704
e all that the hail has left." Ex 10:12
e a darkness which may be felt." Ex 10:21
E your little ones may go with you." Ex 10:24 1571
e to the firstborn of the slave Ex 11:5 5704
the sons of Israel a dog will not **e** Ex 11:7
Philistines, **e** though it was near; Ex 13:17 3588
e Pharaoh's entire army that had Ex 14:28
not **e** one of them remained. Ex 14:28 5704
you are to take him **e** from My Ex 21:14
from the loins **e** to the thighs. Ex 28:42
e their heave offering Ex 29:28
e the flocks and the herds may not Ex 34:3 1571
e though the people are so Ex 34:9 3588
e during plowing time and harvest Ex 34:21
e two rings on one side of it, and Ex 37:3

e the gold of the wave offering,	**Ex 38:24**	
and you shall anoint them **e** as you	**Ex 40:15**	3512c
e the person who eats shall be cut	**Lv 7:25**	
e that person shall be cut off	**Lv 7:27**	
"You shall not **e** go out from the	**Lv 10:7**	
from his head **e** to his feet,	**Lv 13:12**	
of the body, **e** white bright spots,	**Lv 13:38**	
e though the mark has not spread,	**Lv 13:55**	
and his eyebrows, **e** all his hair.	**Lv 14:9**	
any mark of leprosy—**e** for a scale,	**Lv 14:54**	
nor defile himself **e** for his	**Lv 21:11**	
e an offering by fire to the	**Lv 24:7**	
'**E** your cattle and the animals	**Lv 25:7**	
'You may **e** bequeath them to your	**Lv 25:46**	
'**E** if he is not redeemed by these	**Lv 25:54**	
and I, **e** I, will strike you seven	**Lv 26:24**	1571
and I, **e** I, will punish you seven	**Lv 26:28**	637
and **e** when no one is pursuing they	**Lv 26:36**	
twenty years **e** to sixty years old,	**Lv 27:3**	
'If it be from five years **e** to	**Lv 27:5**	
a month **e** up to five years old,	**Lv 27:6**	
e all the numbered men were	**Nu 1:46**	
his army, **e** their numbered men,	**Nu 2:4**	
his army, **e** their numbered men,	**Nu 2:6**	
and his army, **e** his numbered men,	**Nu 2:8**	
his army, **e** their numbered men,	**Nu 2:11**	
his army, **e** their numbered men,	**Nu 2:13**	
his army, **e** their numbered men,	**Nu 2:15**	
his army, **e** their numbered men,	**Nu 2:19**	
his army, **e** their numbered men,	**Nu 2:21**	
his army, **e** their numbered men,	**Nu 2:23**	
his army, **e** their numbered men,	**Nu 2:26**	
his army, **e** their numbered men,	**Nu 2:28**	
his army, **e** their numbered men,	**Nu 2:30**	
e their numbered men *were* 7,500.	**Nu 3:22**	
and upward, **e** to fifty years old,	**Nu 4:3**	
the holy *objects* **e** for a moment,	**Nu 4:20**	
and upward **e** to fifty years old,	**Nu 4:30**	
and upward **e** to fifty years old,	**Nu 4:35**	
and upward **e** to fifty years old,	**Nu 4:39**	
and upward **e** to fifty years old,	**Nu 4:43**	
and upward **e** to fifty years old,	**Nu 4:47**	
from *the* seeds **e** to *the* skin.	**Nu 6:4**	
E when the cloud lingered over the	**Nu 9:19**	
I speak mouth to mouth, **E** openly,	**Nu 12:8**	
people, from Egypt **e** until now."	**Nu 14:19**	
e all your numbered men,	**Nu 14:29**	
e forty years, and you will know	**Nu 14:34**	
e those men who brought out the	**Nu 14:37**	
e all that the LORD has	**Nu 15:23**	
e the one whom He will choose, He	**Nu 16:5**	
e all the holy gifts of the sons	**Nu 18:8**	
e every grain offering and every	**Nu 18:9**	
e all the wave offerings of the	**Nu 18:11**	
not **e** drink water from a well.	**Nu 20:17**	
we have laid waste **e** to Nophah,	**Nu 21:30**	5704
him, **e** all the congregation."	**Nu 27:21**	
e *the* land of Canaan according to	**Nu 34:2**	
'Not **e** you shall enter there.	**Dt 1:37**	1571
e *as little as* a footstep because	**Dt 2:5**	5704
in their place **e** to this day.	**Dt 2:22**	5704
is in the valley, **e** to Gilead,	**Dt 2:36**	
e as far as the valley of Arnon,	**Dt 3:16**	
from Chinnereth **e** as far as the	**Dt 3:17**	
of Arnon, **e** as far as Mount Sion	**Dt 4:48**	
e as far as the sea of the Arabah,	**Dt 4:49**	
"**E** at Horeb you provoked the LORD	**Dt 9:8**	
Your people, **e** Your inheritance,	**Dt 9:26**	
Your people, **e** Your inheritance,	**Dt 9:29**	
e you above all peoples, as *it*	**Dt 10:15**	
e to the end of the year.	**Dt 11:12**	
for they **e** burn their sons and	**Dt 12:31**	1571
him, he will not **e** listen to them,	**Dt 21:18**	
e to the tenth generation,	**Dt 23:2**	1571
e to the tenth generation,	**Dt 23:3**	1571
so that he will not give **e** one of	**Dt 28:55**	
e severe and lasting plagues,	**Dt 28:59**	
e all the men of Israel,	**Dt 29:10**	
E our enemies themselves judge	**Dt 32:31**	
e all the words of this law.	**Dt 32:46**	
e as far as the great river,	**Jos 1:4**	
And they have **e** taken some of the	**Jos 7:11**	1571
will do to them, **e** let them live,	**Jos 9:20**	
Kadesh-barnea **e** as far as Gaza,	**Jos 10:41**	
of Goshen **e** as far as Gibeon.	**Jos 10:41**	
e as far as Baal-gad in the valley	**Jos 11:17**	
e as far as the brook Jabbok,	**Jos 12:2**	
e the Salt Sea, eastward toward	**Jos 12:3**	
Lebanon **e** as far as Mount Halak,	**Jos 12:7**	
e as far as the border of Ekron to	**Jos 13:3**	
e all the cities of the plain and	**Jos 13:21**	
at the Great Sea, **e** *its* coastline.	**Jos 15:12**	
from Ekron **e** to the sea, all that	**Jos 15:46**	
the Great Sea, **e** *its* coastline.	**Jos 15:47**	
of lower Beth-horon **e** to Gezer,	**Jos 16:3**	
e though they have chariots of	**Jos 17:18**	3588
e *to* the rest of the sons of	**Jos 21:20**	
e the heads of the families of	**Jos 22:30**	
from the Jordan **e** to the Great Sea	**Jos 23:4**	
e the Amorites who lived in the	**Jos 24:18**	
I will **e** give him my daughter	**Jg 1:12**	
not **e** one was left.	**Jg 4:16**	5704
E the clouds dripped water.	**Jg 5:4**	1571
a people who despised their lives **e**	**Jg 5:18**	
e throughout the whole army;	**Jg 7:22**	
E the destroyer of our country,	**Jg 16:24**	
The chiefs of all the people, **e**	**Jg 20:2**	
their place, **e** out of Maareh-geba.	**Jg 20:33**	
if I should **e** have a husband	**Ru 1:12**	1571
"Let her glean **e** among the	**Ru 2:15**	1571
E the barren gives birth to seven,	**1Sa 2:5**	5704
All Israel from Dan **e** to	**1Sa 3:20**	
to Israel, from Ekron **e** to Gath;	**1Sa 7:14**	
them up from Egypt **e** to this day	**1Sa 8:8**	
you from my youth **e** to this day.	**1Sa 12:2**	5704
"**E** now, take your stand and see	**1Sa 12:16**	1571
E the garrison and the raiders	**1Sa 14:15**	1571
e they also *turned* to be with the	**1Sa 14:21**	1571
e they also pursued them closely	**1Sa 14:22**	1571
bag which he had, **e** in *his* pouch,	**1Sa 17:40**	
to Shaaraim, **e** to Gath and Ekron.	**1Sa 17:52**	
Saul was **e** more afraid of David.	**1Sa 18:29**	3254
not **e** when the LORD cuts off every	**1Sa 20:15**	
as David, **e** the king's son-in-law,	**1Sa 22:14**	
e David with his two wives,	**1Sa 27:3**	
e as far as the land of Egypt.	**1Sa 27:8**	
over Benjamin, **e** over all Israel.	**2Sa 2:9**	
Judah, from Dan **e** to Beersheba."	**2Sa 3:10**	
Israel from Egypt, **e** to this day;	**2Sa 7:6**	
in a tent, **e** in a tabernacle.	**2Sa 7:6**	
e from the day that I commanded	**2Sa 7:11**	
I will **e** take your wives before	**2Sa 12:11**	
e captured the city of waters.	**2Sa 12:27**	1571
"And **e** the one who is valiant,	**2Sa 17:10**	1571
to you, from Dan **e** to Beersheba,	**2Sa 17:11**	
with him, not **e** one will be left.	**2Sa 17:12**	1571
not **e** a small stone is found there."	**2Sa 17:13**	1571
and by dawn not **e** one remained who	**2Sa 17:22**	5704
about us; **e** if half of us die,	**2Sa 18:3**	
"**E** if I should receive a thousand	**2Sa 18:12**	
e to his house?	**2Sa 19:11**	
"Let him **e** take it all, since my	**2Sa 19:30**	1571
from the Jordan **e** to Jerusalem.	**2Sa 20:2**	
of Israel to Abel, **e** Beth-maacah,	**2Sa 20:14**	
a city, **e** a mother in Israel.	**2Sa 20:19**	
E to the LORD, but He did	**2Sa 22:42**	
You **e** lift me above those	**2Sa 22:49**	
"But me, **e** me your servant,	**1Ki 1:26**	
Solomon has **e** taken his seat on	**1Ki 1:46**	1571
e for him, for Abiathar the priest,	**1Ki 2:22**	
the River, from Tiphsah **e** to Gaza,	**1Ki 4:24**	
fig tree, from Dan **e** to Beersheba,	**1Ki 4:25**	
e to the hyssop that grows on the wall	**1Ki 4:33**	
e as the most holy place.	**1Ki 6:16**	
e from the foundation to the	**1Ki 7:9**	
e large stones, stones of ten	**1Ki 7:10**	
cedar beams **e** as the inner court	**1Ki 7:12**	
e above *and* close to the rounded	**1Ki 7:20**	1571
e borders between the frames,	**1Ki 7:28**	
e all these utensils which Hiram	**1Ki 7:45**	
more days, **e** fourteen days.	**1Ki 8:65**	
e the cities for his chariots and	**1Ki 9:19**	
forced laborers, **e** to this day.	**1Ki 9:21**	5704
it to you, **e** ten tribes.	**1Ki 11:35**	
e to Rehoboam king of Judah;	**1Ki 12:27**	
e in the month which he had	**1Ki 12:33**	
e to blot *it* out and destroy *it*	**1Ki 13:34**	
e taking all the shields of gold	**1Ki 14:26**	
may the gods do to me and **e** more,	**1Ki 19:2**	3541
e all the sons of Israel, 7,000.	**1Ki 20:15**	
against him, **e** against Naboth,	**1Ki 21:13**	
will lick up your blood, **e** yours.	**1Ki 21:19**	1571
e empty vessels; do not get a	**2Ki 4:3**	
e the sound of a great army, so	**2Ki 7:6**	
e the camp just as it was,	**2Ki 7:7**	
and it will **e** come on the land	**2Ki 8:1**	1571
she left the land **e** until now."	**2Ki 8:6**	
e every kind of good thing of	**2Ki 8:9**	
the LORD, **e** over Israel.	**2Ki 9:6**	
"He came **e** to them, and he did	**2Ki 9:20**	5704
e the golden calves that *were*	**2Ki 10:29**	
of the Arnon, **e** Gilead and Bashan.	**2Ki 10:33**	
"Two parts of you, **e** all who go	**2Ki 11:7**	
e the arrow of victory over Aram;	**2Ki 13:17**	
so that you, **e** you, would fall,	**2Ki 14:10**	
e with the kings of Israel,	**2Ki 14:29**	
e from all the mighty men of	**2Ki 15:20**	
and **e** made his son pass through	**2Ki 16:3**	1571
e two calves, and made an	**2Ki 17:16**	
e all that Moses the servant of	**2Ki 18:12**	
e on Egypt; on which if a man	**2Ki 18:21**	
e Gozan and Haran and Rezeph	**2Ki 19:12**	
from Egypt, **e** to this day.' "	**2Ki 21:15**	
e all the words of the book which	**2Ki 22:16**	
e that altar and the high place he	**2Ki 23:15**	1571
e every great house he burned with	**2Ki 25:9**	
e sixty cities. All these were	**1Ch 2:23**	
e to the east side of the valley,	**1Ch 4:39**	5704
in Aroer, **e** to Nebo and Baal-meon.	**1Ch 5:8**	
their fathers' households, **e** Epher,	**1Ch 5:24**	
e the spirit of Tilgath-pilneser	**1Ch 5:26**	
e Asaph the son of Berechiah,	**1Ch 6:39**	
e the house of the tent, as	**1Ch 9:23**	
times past, **e** when Saul was king,	**1Ch 11:2**	1571
Millo **e** to the surrounding area;	**1Ch 11:8**	
e as far as Issachar and Zebulun	**1Ch 12:40**	
the hundreds, **e** with every leader.	**1Ch 13:1**	
Egypt **e** to the entrance of Hamath,	**1Ch 13:5**	
e with songs and with lyres,	**1Ch 13:8**	
from Gibeon **e** as far as Gezer.	**1Ch 14:16**	
e to celebrate and to thank and	**1Ch 16:4**	
From everlasting **e** to everlasting.	**1Ch 16:36**	
e according to all that is written	**1Ch 16:40**	
e from the day that I commanded	**1Ch 17:10**	
e a God to Israel; and the house	**1Ch 17:24**	
Israel from Beersheba **e** to Dan,	**1Ch 21:2**	
LORD, **e** pestilence in the land,	**1Ch 21:12**	
e the heads of the fathers' *households*	**1Ch 23:24**	
e the work of the service of the	**1Ch 23:28**	
mighty men, **e** all the valiant men.	**1Ch 28:1**	
e the cherubim that spread out	**1Ch 28:18**	
have you **e** asked for long life,	**2Ch 1:11**	1571
e the golden altar, the tables	**2Ch 4:19**	
e the silver and the gold and all	**2Ch 5:1**	
father David walked, **e** to do according	**2Ch 7:17**	
the Euphrates River **e** to the land of	**2Ch 9:26**	
he **e** took the golden shields which	**2Ch 12:9**	
e he may become a priest of *what*	**2Ch 13:9**	
yet **e** in his disease he did not seek	**2Ch 16:12**	1571
they **e** came from all the cities of	**2Ch 20:4**	1571
e used the holy things of the house of	**2Ch 24:7**	1571
provoke trouble so that you, **e** you,	**2Ch 25:19**	
e all his wars and his acts,	**2Ch 27:7**	
a rage *which* has **e** reached heaven.	**2Ch 28:9**	5704
Israel from Beersheba **e** to Dan,	**2Ch 30:5**	
e according to the command of the	**2Ch 30:6**	
For a multitude of the people, **e**	**2Ch 30:18**	
E *in the matter of* the envoys of	**2Ch 32:31**	3651
e to the entrance of the Fish Gate;	**2Ch 33:14**	
Manasseh **e** his prayer to his God,	**2Ch 33:18**	
Simeon, **e** as far as Naphtali,	**2Ch 34:6**	
e all the curses written in	**2Ch 34:24**	
e everyone whose spirit God had	**Ezr 1:5**	
e until the reign of Darius king	**Ezr 4:5**	
"I, **e** I, King Artaxerxes,	**Ezr 7:21**	
e up to 100 talents of silver,	**Ezr 7:22**	
e all those who know the laws of	**Ezr 7:25**	
e with my garment and my robe	**Ezr 9:5**	
guilt has grown **e** to the heavens.	**Ezr 9:6**	5704
doorway of Eliashib's house **e** as far as	**Ne 3:21**	
dusty rubble **e** the burned ones?"	**Ne 4:2**	
he said, "**E** what they are building	**Ne 4:3**	1571
each *took* his weapon **e** *to*	**Ne 4:23**	
now would you **e** sell your brothers	**Ne 5:8**	1571
e thus may he be shaken out and	**Ne 5:13**	
e their servants domineered the	**Ne 5:15**	1571
"**E** when they made for themselves	**Ne 9:18**	637
e the women and children rejoiced,	**Ne 12:43**	1571
on the sabbath, **e** in Jerusalem.	**Ne 13:16**	
foreign women caused **e** him to sin.	**Ne 13:26**	1571
E one of the sons of Joiada, the	**Ne 13:28**	
e as Mordecai had commanded her;	**Es 2:20**	3512c
E to half of the kingdom it shall	**Es 5:3**	5704
E to half of the kingdom it shall	**Es 5:6**	5704
"**E** Esther the queen let no one	**Es 5:12**	637
E to half of the kingdom it shall	**Es 7:2**	5704
"Will he **e** assault the queen with	**Es 7:8**	1571
E all the princes of the	**Es 9:3**	
It shall **e** be granted you.	**Es 9:12**	
puts no trust **e** in His servants;	**Jb 4:18**	2005
They are **e** oppressed in the gate,	**Jb 5:4**	
E in seven evil will not touch you.	**Jb 5:19**	
would **e** cast *lots* for the orphans And	**Jb 6:27**	637
E desist, my righteousness is yet	**Jb 6:29**	
E the word *spoken* gently with you?	**Jb 15:11**	
"**E** now, behold, my witness is in	**Jb 16:19**	1571
E the wishes of my heart.	**Jb 17:11**	
"**E** if I have truly erred, My	**Jb 19:4**	637
"**E** young children despise me;	**Jb 19:18**	1571
"**E** after my skin is destroyed,	**Jb 19:26**	
E because of my inward agitation.	**Jb 20:2**	
E like a vision of the night he is	**Jb 20:8**	
trading, He cannot **e** enjoy *them.*	**Jb 20:18**	
E the glittering point from his	**Jb 20:25**	
E the heritage decreed to him by	**Jb 20:29**	
"**E** when I remember, I am	**Jb 21:6**	
We do not **e** desire the knowledge	**Jb 21:14**	
Never **e** tasting *anything* good.	**Jb 21:25**	
"**E** today my complaint is	**Jb 23:2**	1571
E like the heads of grain they are	**Jb 24:24**	
"If **e** the moon has no brightness	**Jb 25:5**	5704
"Fools, **e** those without a name,	**Jb 30:8**	1571
I have **e** become a byword to them.	**Jb 30:9**	
"I **e** paid close attention to you;	**Jb 32:12**	
E twice, and I will add nothing more."	**Jb 40:5**	
be laid low **e** at the sight of him?	**Jb 41:9**	1571
E as hard as a lower millstone.	**Jb 41:24**	
The wicked will return to Sheol, **E**	**Ps 9:17**	
no one who does good, not **e** one.	**Ps 14:3**	1571
E to the LORD, but He did	**Ps 18:41**	
E he who cannot keep his soul	**Ps 22:29**	
E though I walk through the valley	**Ps 23:4**	1571
Who seek Your face—**e** Jacob.	**Ps 24:6**	
my eyes, **e** that has gone from me.	**Ps 38:10**	1571
I refrained **e** from good, And my	**Ps 39:2**	
E my close friend in whom I	**Ps 41:9**	1571
E those who trust in their wealth And	**Ps 49:6**	
For he sees *that* **e** wise men die;	**Ps 49:10**	
no one who does good, not **e** one.	**Ps 53:3**	1571
E the one who sits enthroned from of	**Ps 55:19**	
E the sons of men, whose teeth	**Ps 57:4**	
Let them **e** be caught in their pride,	**Ps 59:12**	
men, **E** *among* the rebellious also,	**Ps 68:18**	
Bless God in the congregations, **E**	**Ps 68:26**	
And **e** when *I am* old and gray, O	**Ps 71:18**	1571
E Your truth, O my God; To You	**Ps 71:22**	
Your hand, **e** Your right hand?	**Ps 74:11**	
You, **e** You, are to be feared;	**Ps 76:7**	
e the children *yet* to be born,	**Ps 78:6**	
E winged fowl like the sand of the	**Ps 78:27**	
E the shoot which Your right hand	**Ps 80:15**	
My soul longed and **e** yearned for	**Ps 84:2**	1571
may lay her young, **E** Your altars,	**Ps 84:3**	
E from everlasting to everlasting,	**Ps 90:2**	
E the Most High, your dwelling	**Ps 91:9**	
E He who teaches man knowledge?	**Ps 94:10**	
"**E** they will perish, but You	**Ps 102:26**	

Their land swarmed with frogs **E** Ps 105:30
young locusts, **e** without number, Ps 105:34
They **e** sacrificed their sons and Ps 106:37
From everlasting **e** to everlasting. Ps 106:48
will sing praises, **e** with my soul. Ps 108:1 637
E though princes sit *and* talk Ps 119:23 1571
E those who know Your testimonies. Ps 119:79
Your statutes Forever, **e** to the end. Ps 119:112
tribes go up, **e** the tribes of the LORD Ps 122:4
For He gives to His beloved **e** *in* Ps 127:2
E Aaron's beard, Coming down Ps 133:2
E a heritage to Israel His Ps 136:22
E before there is a word on my Ps 139:4
E there Your hand will lead me, And Ps 139:10 1571
E the darkness is not dark to Ps 139:12 1571
E for the sons of Israel, Ps 148:14
them alive like Sheol, **E** whole, Pr 1:12
loves He reproves, **E** as a father Pr 3:12
is better than gold, **e** pure gold, Pr 8:19
But **e** the compassion of Pr 12:10
E in laughter the heart may be in Pr 14:13 1571
poor is hated **e** by his neighbor, Pr 14:20 1571
E the wicked for the day of evil. Pr 16:4 1571
He makes **e** his enemies to be at Pr 16:7 1571
E a fool, when he keeps silent, is Pr 17:28 1571
not **e** bring it back to his mouth. Pr 19:24 1571
E when he is old he will not Pr 22:6 1571
E strife and dishonor will cease. Pr 22:10
I have taught you today, **e** you. Pr 22:19 637
E his prayer is an abomination. Pr 28:9 1571
E four which are stately when they Pr 30:29
e at night his mind does not rest. Ec 2:23 1571
from the beginning **e** to the end. Ec 3:11
e though he was born poor in his Ec 4:14 1571
and **e** the ones who will come later Ec 4:16 1571
does not **e** have a *proper* burial, Ec 6:3 1571
"**E** if the *other* man lives a Ec 6:6
(**e** though one should never sleep day Ec 8:16 1571
E though man should seek Ec 8:17
E when the fool walks along the Ec 10:3 1571
so wearies him that he does not **e** Ec 10:15
portion to seven, or **e** to eight, Ec 11:2 1571
From the sole of the foot **e** to the Is 1:6 1571
e though you multiply prayers, Is 1:15 1571
They do not **e** conceal *it.* Is 3:9
a cloud by day, **e** smoke, Is 4:5
E great and fine ones, without Is 5:9
E the light is darkened by its Is 5:30
E the king of Assyria and all his Is 8:7
It will reach **e** to the neck; Is 8:8 5704
will **e** be snared and caught." Is 8:15
I will **e** look eagerly for Him. Is 8:17
It **e** sets the thickets of the Is 9:18
have **e** called My mighty warriors, Is 13:3 1571
They will not **e** have compassion on Is 13:18
"**E** the cypress trees rejoice over Is 14:8 1571
"**E** you have been made weak as we, Is 14:10 1571
e to the high places to weep. Is 15:2
and its wailing **e** to Beer-elim. Is 15:8
A throne will **e** be established in Is 16:5
E of his arrogance, pride, Is 16:6
It will be **e** like the reaper Is 17:5
E the Asherim and incense stands. Is 17:8
E in papyrus vessels on the Is 18:2
E from a people feared far and Is 18:7
of hosts, **e** Mount Zion. Is 18:7
They will **e** worship with sacrifice Is 19:21
"**E** as My servant Isaiah has gone Is 20:3 3512c
it will **e** break off and fall, and Is 22:25
e there you will find no rest." Is 23:12 1571
E the veil which is stretched over Is 25:7
cast to the ground, **e** to the dust. Is 25:12 5704
Your name, **e** Your memory, is the Is 26:8
E Leviathan the twisted serpent; Is 27:1 5921
E all who wage war against her and Is 29:7
E Egypt, whose help is vain and Is 30:7
E though *the* needy one speaks what Is 32:7
e on Egypt, on which if a man Is 36:6
e Gozan and Haran and Rezeph Is 37:12
E Lebanon is not enough to burn, Is 40:16
E as the potter treads clay." Is 41:25
have formed, **e** whom I have made." Is 43:7 637
blind, **e** though they have eyes, Is 43:8
the deaf, **e** though they have ears. Is 43:8
"I, **e** I, am the LORD, Is 43:11
"**E** from eternity I am He, Is 43:13 1571
as fugitives, **E** the Chaldeans, Is 43:14
I will **e** make a roadway in the Is 43:19 637
"I, **e** I, am the one who wipes out Is 43:25
e their own witnesses fail to see Is 44:9
be put to shame and **e** humiliated, Is 45:16 1571
E to *your* old age I will be the Is 46:4
And **e** to *your* graying years I Is 46:4 5704
E hidden things which you have not Is 48:6
E from long ago your ear has not Is 48:8 1571
O Jacob, **e** Israel whom I called; Is 48:12
"I, **e** I, have spoken; Is 48:15
E these may forget, but I will not Is 49:15 1571
"**E** the captives of the mighty man Is 49:25 1571
"I, **e** I, am He who comforts you. Is 51:12
e your God Who contends for His Is 51:22
You have **e** made your back like the Is 51:23
E like a wife of *one's* youth when Is 54:6
God, **e** the Holy One of Israel; Is 55:5
E those I will bring to My holy Is 56:7
E to them you have poured out a Is 57:6 1571
Was I not silent **e** for a long time Is 57:11
e an acceptable day to the LORD? Is 58:5
I will **e** repay into their bosom, Is 65:6

E My chosen ones shall inherit it, Is 65:9
Therefore **e** the wicked women You Jer 2:33 1571
from our youth **e** to this day. Jer 3:25
"Yet **e** in those days," Jer 5:18 1571
of them **e** to the greatest of them, Jer 6:13
And from the prophet **e** to the Jer 6:13
They were not **e** ashamed at all; Jer 6:15 1571
They did not **e** know how to blush. Jer 6:15 1571
Behold, I, **e** I, have seen *it,*" Jer 7:11 1571
"**E** the stork in the sky Knows her Jer 8:7 1571
Because from the least **e** to the Jer 8:10
From the prophet **e** to the priest Jer 8:10
the land of Egypt, **e** to this day, Jer 11:7
grow, they have **e** produced fruit. Jer 12:2 1571
"For **e** your brothers and the Jer 12:6 1571
E they have dealt treacherously Jer 12:6 1571
E they have cried aloud after you. Jer 12:6 1571
end of the land **e** to the other; Jer 12:12
e as they taught My people to Jer 12:16 3512c
"For **e** the doe in the field has Jer 14:5 1571
"**E** so they have loved to wander; Jer 14:10 1571
"**E** though Moses and Samuel were Jer 15:1
E for all your sins And within all Jer 15:13
'You too have done evil, **e** more Jer 16:12
And you will, **e** of yourself, let Jer 17:4
E to give to each man according to Jer 17:10
of living water, **e** the LORD. Jer 17:13
e as one breaks a potter's vessel, Jer 19:11 3512c
e all the treasures of the kings Jer 20:5
e in anger and wrath and great Jer 21:5
e those who survive in this city Jer 21:7
e *the king* himself and his Jer 22:4
"**e** though Coniah the son of Jer 22:24 3588
e into the hand of Nebuchadnezzar Jer 22:25
E like a man overcome with wine, Jer 23:9
E in My house I have found their Jer 23:11 1571
in wrath, **E** a whirling tempest; Jer 23:19
e *these* prophets of the deception Jer 23:26
king of Judah, **e** to this day, Jer 25:3
will make slaves of them, **e** them; Jer 25:14 1571
e Ashkelon, Gaza, Ekron and the Jer 25:20
'**E** so will I break within two full Jer 28:11 3602
and **e** to this day both in Israel Jer 32:20
that they built it, **e** to this day, Jer 32:31
the days of Josiah, **e** to this day. Jer 36:2
E though Elnathan and Delaiah and Jer 36:25
'For **e** if you had defeated the Jer 37:10
they **e** sent and took Jeremiah out Jer 39:14
e in whatever He has sent me to Jer 42:21
not become contrite **e** to this day, Jer 44:10
for woe, **e** to cut off all Judah. Jer 44:11
e to all the people who were giving Jer 44:20
E like the rivers whose waters Jer 46:8
It will **e** be burned down *and* Jer 46:19
For **e** they too have turned back Jer 46:21 1571
E though they are *now* more Jer 46:23
e Pharaoh and those who trust in Jer 46:25
e into the hand of Nebuchadnezzar Jer 46:26
E you yourself will be captured; Jer 48:7 1571
E all of you who know his name; Jer 48:17
E for all Moab will I cry out; Jer 48:31
field, **e** from the land of Moab. Jer 48:33
outcry at Heshbon **e** to Elealeh, Jer 48:34
e to Jahaz they have raised their Jer 48:34
from Zoar **e** to Horonaim *and to* Jer 48:34
for **e** the waters of Nimrim will Jer 48:34 1571
e upon Moab, The year of their Jer 48:44
e the little ones of the flock; Jer 49:20
upon them, **E** My fierce anger,' Jer 49:37
of righteousness, **E** the LORD, Jer 50:7
e the little ones of the flock; Jer 50:45
"They will not take from you **e** a Jer 51:26
E the wall of Babylon has fallen Jer 51:44 1571
e every large house he burned with Jer 52:13
E she herself groans and turns La 1:8 1571
E when I cry out and call for La 3:8 1571
E jackals offer the breast, They La 4:3 1571
them, **e** a great rumbling sound. Ezk 3:13
'Behold, I, **e** I, am against you, Ezk 5:8 1571
'**E** when their survivors escape, Ezk 7:16
e through the midst of Jerusalem, Ezk 9:4
e go into exile from your place to Ezk 12:3
e those lives whom you hunt as Ezk 13:20 853
e *though* these three men, Noah, Ezk 14:14
e *though* these three men were in Ezk 14:18
e *though* Noah, Daniel and Job Ezk 14:20
with salt or **e** wrapped in cloths. Ezk 16:4
yet **e** with this you were not Ezk 16:29 1571
e all those whom you loved *and* all Ezk 16:37
he **e** eats at the mountain *shrines,* Ezk 18:11 1571
they **e** profaned My sabbaths, for Ezk 20:16
what if **e** the rod which despises will Ezk 21:13 1571
idols and **e** caused their sons, Ezk 23:37 1571
they have **e** sent for men who come Ezk 23:40 3588
from Teman **e** to Dedan they will Ezk 25:13
e cut off the Cherethites and Ezk 25:16
and **e** to the border of Ethiopia. Ezk 29:10
E the day of the LORD is near; Ezk 30:3
e Pharaoh and all his army," Ezk 32:31
e Pharaoh and all his hordes," Ezk 32:32
My flock has **e** become food for all Ezk 34:8
"Behold, I, **e** I, will judge Ezk 34:20
"**E** all the people of the land Ezk 39:13
e those left on the surface of the Ezk 39:14 853
"And **e** *the* name of *the* city will Ezk 39:16 1571
e My house, when you offered My Ezk 44:7
Daniel **e** understood all *kinds of* Da 1:17
E now You have made known to me Da 2:23
e as iron does not combine with Da 2:43 1888

"But **e** if *He does* not, let Da 3:18
nor had the smell of fire **e** come Da 3:27
his face grew **e** paler, and his Da 5:9
heart, **e** though you knew all this, Da 5:22 1768
and **e** until sunset he kept Da 6:14
It **e** magnified *itself* to be equal Da 8:11 5704
e oppose the Prince of princes, Da 8:25
e turning aside from Your Da 9:5
and moat, **e** in times of distress. Da 9:25
e to the end there will be war; Da 9:26
e until a complete destruction, Da 9:27
not **e** their choicest troops, Da 11:15
e as the LORD loves the sons of Hos 3:1
I, **e** I, will tear to pieces and go Hos 5:14
For from Israel is **e** this! Hos 8:6
E though they hire *allies* among Hos 8:10 1571
E though they bear children, I Hos 9:16 1571
E against the Holy One who is Hos 11:12
E the LORD, the God of hosts, Hos 12:5
E the flocks of sheep suffer. Jl 1:18 1571
E the beasts of the field pant for Jl 1:20 1571
"Yet **e** now," declares the LORD, Jl 2:12 1571
E a grain offering and a drink Jl 2:14
"**E** on the male and female servants I Jl 2:29 1571
E among the survivors whom the Jl 2:32
e unleash My power upon Ekron, Am 1:8
I **e** destroyed his fruit above and Am 2:9
"**E** the bravest among the warriors Am 2:16
enemy, **e** one surrounding the land, Am 3:11
E gloom with no brightness in it? Am 5:20
"**E** though you offer up to Me Am 5:22 3588
And I will not **e** look at Am 5:22
I will not **e** listen to the sound Am 5:23
And from the north **e** to the east; Am 8:12
for the sea was becoming **e** Jon 1:13
reason to be angry, **e** to death." Jon 4:9
of my people, **E** to Jerusalem. Mi 1:9
act, **E** to Israel his sin. Mi 3:8
E the word of the LORD from Mi 4:2
E those whom I have afflicted. Mi 4:6
E the former dominion will come, Mi 4:8
E with Israel He will dispute. Mi 6:2
From Egypt **e** to the Euphrates, Mi 7:12
E from sea to sea and mountain to Mi 7:12
strength and likewise many, **E** so, Na 1:12
E though devastators have Na 2:2
E mockery *and* insinuations against Hab 2:6
Who mix in your venom **e** to make Hab 2:15 637
E at the time when I gather you Zph 3:20
e the time for the house of the Hg 1:2
E including the vine, the fig Hg 2:19 5704
e the inhabitants of many cities. Zch 8:20
mounted on a donkey, **E** on a colt, Zch 9:9
of the sun **e** to its setting, Mal 1:11 5704
e *the* statutes and ordinances Mal 4:4
e the tax collectors do the same? Mt 5:46 *2532*
Do not **e** the Gentiles do the same? Mt 5:47 *2532*
not **e** Solomon in all his glory Mt 6:29 *3761*
that **e** the winds and the sea obey Mt 8:27 *2532*
for *your* journey, or **e** two coats, Mt 10:10 *3366*
and you will **e** be brought before Mt 10:18 *2532*
e a cup of cold water to drink, Mt 10:42 *3441*
e what he has shall be taken away Mt 13:12 *2532*
but **e** the dogs feed on the crumbs Mt 15:27 *2532*
refuses to listen **e** to the church, Mt 18:17 *2532*
MOUNTED ON A DONKEY, **E** ON A COLT, Mt 21:5 *2532*
but **e** if you say to this mountain, Mt 21:21 *2579*
did not **e** feel remorse afterward Mt 21:32 *3761*
mislead, if possible, **e** the elect. Mt 24:24 *2532*
east and flashes **e** to the west, Mt 24:27 *2193*
knows, not **e** the angels of heaven, Mt 24:36 *3761*
e what he does have shall be taken Mt 25:29 *2532*
e the least *of them,* you did Mt 25:40
But Peter said to Him, "**E** Mt 26:33
"**E** if I have to die with You, I Mt 26:35 *2579*
e though many false witnesses came Mt 26:60
for **e** the way you talk gives you away." Mt 26:73 *2532*
with regard to **e** a *single* charge, Mt 27:14 *3761*
always, **e** to the end of the age." Mt 28:20 *2193*
He commands **e** the unclean spirits, Mk 1:27 *2532*
no longer room, not **e** near the door; Mk 2:2 *3366*
of Man is Lord **e** of the Sabbath." Mk 2:28 *2532*
that they could not **e** eat a meal. Mk 3:20 *3366*
e what he has shall be taken away Mk 4:25 *2532*
e the wind and the sea obey Him?" Mk 4:41 *2532*
bind him anymore, **e** with a chain; Mk 5:3 *3761*
they did not **e** have time to eat.) Mk 6:31 *3761*
but **e** the dogs under the table Mk 7:28 *2532*
He makes **e** the deaf to hear and Mk 7:37 *2532*
"Do not **e** enter the village." Mk 8:26 *3366*
They were **e** more astonished Mk 10:26 *4057*
"For **e** the Son of Man did not Mk 10:45 *2532*
"Have you not **e** read this Scripture: Mk 12:10 *3761*
"**E** so, you too, when you see Mk 13:29
knows, not **e** the angels in heaven, Mk 13:32 *3761*
But Peter said to Him, "**E** Mk 14:29
"**E** if I have to die with You, I Mk 14:31
Not **e** in this respect was Mk 14:59 *3761*
e your relative Elizabeth has also Lk 1:36 *2532*
and a sword will pierce **e** your own Lk 2:35 *2532*
about Him was spreading **e** farther, Lk 5:15 *3123*
"Have you not **e** read what David Lk 6:3 *3761*
For **e** sinners love those who love Lk 6:32 *2532*
For **e** sinners do the same. Lk 6:33 *2532*
E sinners lend to sinners in Lk 6:34 *2532*
for this reason I did not **e** Lk 7:7 *3761*
not **e** in Israel have I found such Lk 7:9 *3761*
is this *man* who **e** forgives sins?" Lk 7:49 *2532*
e what he thinks he has shall be Lk 8:18 *2532*

e the winds and the water,	**Lk 8:25**	*2532*
and do not **e** have two tunics	**Lk 9:3**	
'**E** the dust of your city which	**Lk 10:11**	*2532*
e the demons are subject to us in	**Lk 10:17**	*2532*
e though he will not get up and	**Lk 11:8**	*2532*
you yourselves will not **e** touch	**Lk 11:46**	
for not **e** when one has an	**Lk 12:15**	
cannot do **e** a very little thing,	**Lk 12:26**	*3761*
not **e** Solomon in all his glory	**Lk 12:27**	*3761*
second watch, or **e** in the third,	**Lk 12:38**	*2579*
"And why do you not **e** on your own	**Lk 12:57**	*2532*
Why does it **e** use up the ground?'	**Lk 13:7**	*2532*
sisters, yes, and **e** his own life,	**Lk 14:26**	*2532*
if **e** salt has become tasteless,	**Lk 14:34**	*2532*
e the dogs were coming and licking	**Lk 16:21**	*2532*
they will not be persuaded **e** if	**Lk 16:31**	*3761*
'**E** though I do not fear God nor	**Lk 18:4**	*2532*
or **e** like this tax collector.	**Lk 18:11**	*2532*
was **e** unwilling to lift up his	**Lk 18:13**	*3761*
they were bringing **e** their babies	**Lk 18:15**	*2532*
e what he does have shall be taken	**Lk 19:26**	*2532*
you had known in this day, **e** you,	**Lk 19:42**	*2532*
for they cannot **e** die anymore,	**Lk 20:36**	*3761*
dead are raised, **e** Moses showed,	**Lk 20:37**	*2532*
will be betrayed **e** by parents	**Lk 21:16**	*2532*
Galilee **e** as far as this place."	**Lk 23:5**	
And **e** the rulers were sneering at	**Lk 23:35**	*2532*
"Do you not **e** fear God, since you	**Lk 23:40**	*3761*
e to those who believe in His	**Jn 1:12**	
e so must the Son of Man be lifted	**Jn 3:14**	
e so the Son also gives life to	**Jn 5:21**	*2532*
not **e** the Father judges anyone,	**Jn 5:22**	*3761*
Son **e** as they honor the Father.	**Jn 5:23**	*2531a*
e so He gave to the Son also to	**Jn 5:26**	*2532*
For not **e** His brothers were	**Jn 7:5**	*3761*
"**E** if I testify about Myself,	**Jn 8:14**	*2579*
"But **e** if I do judge, My judgment	**Jn 8:16**	*2532*
"**E** in your law it has been	**Jn 8:17**	*2532*
not **e** come on My own initiative,	**Jn 8:42**	*3761*
e as the Father knows Me and I	**Jn 10:15**	*2531a*
"**E** now I know that whatever You	**Jn 11:22**	*2532*
in Me will live **e** if he dies,	**Jn 11:25**	*2579*
e He who comes into the world."	**Jn 11:27**	
THE LORD, **e** the King of Israel."	**Jn 12:13**	*2532*
e of the rulers believed in Him,	**Jn 12:42**	*2532*
another, **e** as I have loved you,	**Jn 13:34**	*2531a*
e as You gave Him authority	**Jn 17:2**	*2531a*
that they may be one **e** as We *are.*	**Jn 17:11**	*2531a*
world, **e** as I am not of the world.	**Jn 17:14**	*2531a*
world, **e** as I am not of the world.	**Jn 17:16**	*2531a*
e as You, Father, *are* in Me and	**Jn 17:21**	*2531a*
them, **e** as You have loved Me.	**Jn 17:23**	*2531a*
he was **e** more afraid;	**Jn 19:8**	
I suppose that **e** the world itself	**Jn 21:25**	*3761*
and **e** to the remotest part of the	**Ac 1:8**	*2193*
E ON MY BONDSLAVES, BOTH MEN	**Ac 2:18**	*2532*
to such an extent that they **e**	**Ac 5:15**	*2532*
e all the Senate of the sons of	**Ac 5:21**	*2532*
e be found fighting against God."	**Ac 5:39**	*2532*
in it, not **e** a foot of ground,	**Ac 7:5**	*3761*
and *yet,* **e** when he had no child,	**Ac 7:5**	
E Simon himself believed; and after	**Ac 8:13**	*2532*
"That is why I came without **e**	**Ac 10:29**	*2532*
E saying these things, with	**Ac 14:18**	
as **e** some of your own poets have	**Ac 17:28**	*2532*
we have not **e** heard whether there	**Ac 19:2**	*3761*
aprons were **e** carried from his body	**Ac 19:12**	*2532*
world worship will **e** be dethroned	**Ac 19:27**	*2532*
but **e** to die at Jerusalem for the	**Ac 21:13**	*2532*
besides he has **e** brought Greeks into	**Ac 21:28**	*2532*
dialect, they became **e** more quiet;	**Ac 22:2**	
Damascus in order to bring **e** those	**Ac 22:5**	*2532*
e tried to desecrate the temple;	**Ac 24:6**	*2532*
pursuing them **e** to foreign cities.	**Ac 26:11**	*2193*
and **e** to the Gentiles, that they	**Ac 26:20**	
since **e** the fast was already over,	**Ac 27:9**	*2532*
e as among the rest of the Gentiles.	**Ro 1:13**	*2531a*
For **e** though they knew God, they	**Ro 1:21**	
IS NONE RIGHTEOUS, NOT **E** ONE;	**Ro 3:10**	*3761*
DOES GOOD, THERE IS NOT **E** ONE."	**Ro 3:12**	*2193*
e *the* righteousness of God through	**Ro 3:22**	*1161*
e God, who gives life to	**Ro 4:17**	
man someone would dare **e** to die.	**Ro 5:7**	*2532*
e over those who had not sinned in	**Ro 5:14**	*2532*
e so through one act of	**Ro 5:18**	*2532*
e so through the obedience of the	**Ro 5:19**	*2532*
e so grace would reign through	**Ro 5:21**	*2532*
E so consider yourselves to be	**Ro 6:11**	*2532*
for it is not **e** able *to do so,*	**Ro 8:7**	*3761*
e we ourselves groan within	**Ro 8:23**	*2532*
e us, whom He also called, not	**Ro 9:24**	
e the righteousness which is by	**Ro 9:30**	*1161*
e Christ did not please Himself;	**Ro 15:3**	*2532*
e as the testimony concerning	**1Co 1:6**	*2531a*
all things, **e** the depths of God.	**1Co 2:10**	*2532*
E so the *thoughts* of God no one	**1Co 2:11**	*2532*
e now you are not yet able,	**1Co 3:2**	*3761*
e as the Lord gave *opportunity* to	**1Co 3:5**	*2532*
fact, I do not **e** examine myself.	**1Co 4:3**	*3761*
of all things, **e** until now.	**1Co 4:13**	
not exist **e** among the Gentiles,	**1Co 5:1**	*3761*
e to eat with such a one.	**1Co 5:11**	*3366*
You do this **e** to *your*	**1Co 6:8**	*2532*
all men were **e** as I myself am.	**1Co 7:7**	*2532*
for them if they remain **e** as I.	**1Co 7:8**	*2532*
For **e** if there are so-called gods	**1Co 8:5**	*2532*
e as the rest of the apostles and	**1Co 9:5**	*2532*
Does not **e** nature itself teach you	**1Co 11:14**	*3761*
For **e** as the body is one and *yet*	**1Co 12:12**	*2509*
but **e** more that you would	**1Co 14:5**	
Yet **e** lifeless things, either	**1Co 14:7**	
E SO THEY WILL NOT LISTEN TO ME,"	**1Co 14:21**	*3761*
I labored **e** more than all of them,	**1Co 15:10**	*4053*
not **e** Christ has been raised;	**1Co 15:13**	*3761*
we are **e** found *to be* false witnesses	**1Co 15:15**	*2532*
not **e** Christ has been raised;	**1Co 15:16**	*3761*
with you, or **e** spend the winter,	**1Co 16:6**	*2532*
so that we despaired **e** of life;	**2Co 1:8**	*2532*
fail to be **e** more with glory?	**2Co 3:8**	
And **e** if our gospel is veiled, it	**2Co 4:3**	*2532*
e though we have known Christ	**2Co 5:16**	*2532*
For **e** when we came into Macedonia	**2Co 7:5**	*2532*
so that I rejoiced **e** more.	**2Co 7:7**	
we rejoiced **e** much more for the	**2Co 7:13**	*4057*
things, but now **e** more diligent because	**2Co 8:22**	*4183*
For **e** if I boast somewhat	**2Co 10:8**	*5037*
measure, to reach **e** as far as you.	**2Co 10:13**	*2532*
for we were the first to come **e** as	**2Co 10:14**	*2532*
sphere, enlarged **e** more by you,	**2Co 10:15**	*1519*
e to the regions beyond you,	**2Co 10:16**	
But **e** if I am unskilled in speech,	**2Co 11:6**	*2532*
for **e** Satan disguises himself as	**2Co 11:14**	*846*
you do, receive me **e** as foolish,	**2Co 11:16**	*2579*
apostles, **e** though I am a nobody.	**2Co 12:11**	*2532*
e though we may appear	**2Co 13:7**	*1161*
But **e** if we, or an angel from	**Ga 1:8**	*2532*
who had set me apart **e** from my	**Ga 1:15**	
But not **e** Titus, who was with me,	**Ga 2:3**	*3761*
subjection to them for **e** an hour,	**Ga 2:5**	*3761*
with the result that **e** Barnabas	**Ga 2:13**	*2532*
e we have believed in Christ	**Ga 2:16**	*2532*
E so Abraham BELIEVED GOD, AND IT	**Ga 3:6**	*2531a*
e though it is *only* a man's	**Ga 3:15**	*3676*
you would **e** mutilate themselves.	**Ga 5:12**	*2532*
e if anyone is caught in any	**Ga 6:1**	*2532*
do not **e** keep the Law themselves,	**Ga 6:13**	*3761*
children of wrath, **e** as the rest.	**Eph 2:3**	*2532*
e when we were dead in our	**Eph 2:5**	*2532*
is the head, **e** Christ,	**Eph 4:15**	
or greed must not **e** be named	**Eph 5:3**	*3366*
but instead **e** expose them;	**Eph 5:11**	*2532*
for it is disgraceful **e** to speak	**Eph 5:12**	*2532*
Jesus Christ to God, **e** the Father;	**Eph 5:20**	*2532*
love his own wife **e** as himself,	**Eph 5:33**	
Christ **e** from envy and strife,	**Php 1:15**	*2532*
all boldness, Christ will **e** now,	**Php 1:20**	*2532*
of death, **e** death on a cross.	**Php 2:8**	*1161*
But **e** if I am being poured out as	**Php 2:17**	*2532*
have confidence **e** in the flesh.	**Php 3:4**	*2532*
you, and now tell you **e** weeping,	**Php 3:18**	*2532*
the power that He has **e** to subject all	**Php 3:21**	*2532*
for **e** in Thessalonica you sent *a*	**Php 4:16**	*2532*
e as *it has been doing* in you also	**Col 1:6**	*2531a*
For **e** though I am absent in body,	**Col 2:5**	*2532*
e though as apostles of Christ we	**1Th 2:6**	
e as they *did* from the Jews,	**1Th 2:14**	*2531a*
Is it not **e** you, in the presence	**1Th 2:19**	*2532*
e so God will bring with Him those	**1Th 4:14**	*2532*
For **e** when we were with you, we	**2Th 3:10**	*2532*
e though they do not understand	**1Tm 1:7**	
e though I was formerly a	**1Tm 1:13**	
is dead **e** while she lives.	**1Tm 5:6**	
see you, **e** as I recall your tears,	**2Tm 1:4**	
e to imprisonment as a criminal;	**2Tm 2:9**	*3360*
e His word, in the proclamation	**Ti 1:3**	
to me **e** your own self as well).	**Phm 1:19**	*2532*
will do **e** more than what I say.	**Phm 1:21**	*2532*
is called by God, **e** as Aaron was.	**Heb 5:4**	*2531b*
desiring **e** more to show to the	**Heb 6:17**	*4053*
to speak, through Abraham **e** Levi,	**Heb 7:9**	*2532*
Now **e** the first *covenant* had	**Heb 9:1**	*2532*
Therefore **e** the first *covenant* was	**Heb 9:18**	*3761*
By faith **e** Sarah herself received	**Heb 11:11**	*2532*
e beyond the proper time of life,	**Heb 11:11**	*2532*
Therefore there was born **e** of one man,	**Heb 11:12**	*2532*
able to raise *people* **e** from the dead	**Heb 11:19**	*2532*
Esau, **e** regarding things to come.	**Heb 11:20**	*2532*
For you know that **e** afterwards,	**Heb 12:17**	*2532*
"IF **E** A BEAST TOUCHES THE	**Heb 12:20**	*2579*
e Jesus our Lord,	**Heb 13:20**	
E so faith, if it has no works, is	**Jas 2:17**	*2532*
e though now for a little while,	**1Pe 1:6**	
e though tested by fire,	**1Pe 1:7**	*1161*
that **e** if any *of them* are disobedient	**1Pe 3:1**	*2532*
But **e** if you should suffer for the	**1Pe 3:14**	*2532*
preached **e** to those who are dead,	**1Pe 4:6**	*2532*
e though you *already* know *them,*	**2Pe 1:12**	*2539*
e denying the Master who bought	**2Pe 2:1**	*2532*
e now many antichrists have appeared;	**1Jn 2:18**	*2532*
hating **e** the garment polluted by	**Jude 1:23**	*2532*
e to all that he saw.	**Rv 1:2**	
see Him, **e** those who pierced Him;	**Rv 1:7**	*2532*
faith **e** in the days of Antipas,	**Rv 2:13**	*2532*
to be killed **e** as they had been,	**Rv 6:11**	*2532*
love their life **e** when faced with death.	**Rv 12:11**	*891*
so that he **e** makes fire come down	**Rv 13:13**	*2532*
the image of the beast would **e** speak	**Rv 13:15**	*2532*
"Pay her back **e** as she has paid,	**Rv 18:6**	*2532*

EVENING

there was **e** and there was morning,	**Gn 1:5**	6153
there was **e** and there was morning,	**Gn 1:8**	6153
There was **e** and there was morning,	**Gn 1:13**	6153
There was **e** and there was morning,	**Gn 1:19**	6153
There was **e** and there was morning,	**Gn 1:23**	6153
there was **e** and there was morning,	**Gn 1:31**	6153
The dove came to him toward **e**,	**Gn 8:11**	6153
angels came to Sodom in the **e** as Lot	**Gn 19:1**	6153
by the well of water at **e** time,	**Gn 24:11**	6153
to meditate in the field toward **e**;	**Gn 24:63**	6153
Now in the **e** he took	**Gn 29:23**	6153
came in from the field in the **e**,	**Gn 30:16**	6153
in the **e** he divides the spoil."	**Gn 49:27**	6153
fourteenth day of the month at **e**,	**Ex 12:18**	6153
twenty-first day of the month at **e**,	**Ex 12:18**	6153
"At **e** you will know that the LORD	**Ex 16:6**	6153
gives you meat to eat in the **e**,	**Ex 16:8**	6153
So it came about at **e** that the	**Ex 16:13**	6153
from the morning until the **e**.	**Ex 18:13**	6153
about you from morning until **e**?"	**Ex 18:14**	6153
from **e** to morning before the LORD;	**Ex 27:21**	6153
morning and half of it in the **e**.	**Lv 6:20**	6153
carcasses becomes unclean until **e**,	**Lv 11:24**	6153
clothes and be unclean until **e**.	**Lv 11:25**	6153
carcasses becomes unclean until **e**,	**Lv 11:27**	6153
clothes and be unclean until **e**;	**Lv 11:28**	6153
are dead becomes unclean until **e**.	**Lv 11:31**	6153
the water and be unclean until **e**,	**Lv 11:32**	6153
carcass becomes unclean until **e**.	**Lv 11:39**	6153
clothes and be unclean until **e**,	**Lv 11:40**	6153
clothes and be unclean until **e**.	**Lv 11:40**	6153
it, becomes unclean until **e**.	**Lv 14:46**	6153
in water and be unclean until **e**;	**Lv 15:5**	6153
in water and be unclean until **e**.	**Lv 15:6**	6153
in water and be unclean until **e**.	**Lv 15:7**	6153
in water and be unclean until **e**.	**Lv 15:8**	6153
him shall be unclean until **e**,	**Lv 15:10**	6153
in water and be unclean until **e**.	**Lv 15:10**	6153
in water and be unclean until **e**.	**Lv 15:11**	6153
in water and be unclean until **e**.	**Lv 15:16**	6153
with water and be unclean until **e**.	**Lv 15:17**	6153
in water and be unclean until **e**.	**Lv 15:18**	6153
her shall be unclean until **e**.	**Lv 15:19**	6153
in water and be unclean until **e**.	**Lv 15:21**	6153
in water and be unclean until **e**.	**Lv 15:22**	6153
it, he shall be unclean until **e**.	**Lv 15:23**	6153
in water and be unclean until **e**.	**Lv 15:27**	6153
water, and remain unclean until **e**;	**Lv 17:15**	6153
any such shall be unclean until **e**,	**Lv 22:6**	6153
on the ninth of the month at **e**,	**Lv 23:32**	6153
from **e** until evening you shall	**Lv 23:32**	6153
e you shall keep your sabbath."	**Lv 23:32**	6153
Aaron shall keep it in order from **e** to	**Lv 24:3**	6153
and in the **e** it was like the	**Nu 9:15**	6153
remained from **e** until morning,	**Nu 9:21**	6153
priest shall be unclean until **e**.	**Nu 19:7**	6153
and shall be unclean until **e**.	**Nu 19:8**	6153
clothes and be unclean until **e**;	**Nu 19:10**	6153
in water and shall be clean by **e**.	**Nu 19:19**	6153
impurity shall be unclean until **e**.	**Nu 19:21**	6153
it shall be unclean until **e**.' "	**Nu 19:22**	6153
the flesh which you sacrifice on the **e**	**Dt 16:4**	6153
the Passover in the **e** at sunset,	**Dt 16:6**	6153
"But it shall be when **e** approaches,	**Dt 23:11**	6153
'Would that it were **e**!'	**Dt 28:67**	6153
And at **e** you shall say,	**Dt 28:67**	6153
Passover on the **e** of the fourteenth	**Jos 5:10**	6153
the ark of the LORD until the **e**,	**Jos 7:6**	6153
the king of Ai on a tree until **e**;	**Jos 8:29**	6153
they hung on the trees until **e**.	**Jos 10:26**	6153
of the field from his work at **e**.	**Jg 19:16**	6153
and wept before the LORD until **e**,	**Jg 20:23**	6153
LORD and fasted that day until **e**.	**Jg 20:26**	6153
and sat there before God until **e**,	**Jg 21:2**	6153
she gleaned in the field until **e**.	**Ru 2:17**	6153
be the man who eats food before **e**,	**1Sa 14:24**	6153
morning and **e** for forty days and	**1Sa 17:16**	6150
in the field until the third **e**.	**1Sa 20:5**	6153
until the **e** of the next day;	**1Sa 30:17**	6153
and fasted until **e** for Saul and his son	**2Sa 1:12**	6153
Now when **e** came David arose from	**2Sa 11:2**	6153
and in the **e** he went out to lie on	**2Sa 11:13**	6153
and bread and meat in the **e**,	**1Ki 17:6**	6153
the time of the offering of the **e**	**1Ki 18:29**	
the time of the offering of the **e**	**1Ki 18:36**	
of the Arameans, and died at **e**,	**1Ki 22:35**	6153
burnt offering and the **e** meal offering	**2Ki 16:15**	6153
continually morning and **e**,	**1Ch 16:40**	6153
the LORD, and likewise at **e**,	**1Ch 23:30**	6153
burnt offerings morning and **e**,	**2Ch 2:4**	6153
"Every morning and **e** they	**2Ch 13:11**	6153
lamps is *ready* to light every **e**;	**2Ch 13:11**	6153
front of the Arameans until the **e**;	**2Ch 18:34**	6153
the morning and **e** burnt offerings,	**2Ch 31:3**	6153
burnt offerings morning and **e**.	**Ezr 3:3**	6153
sat appalled until the **e** offering.	**Ezr 9:4**	6153
But at the **e** offering I arose from	**Ezr 9:5**	6153
In the **e** she would go in and in	**Es 2:14**	6153
'Between morning and **e** they are	**Jb 4:20**	6153
E and morning and at noon, I will	**Ps 55:17**	6153
They return at **e**, they howl like a	**Ps 59:6**	6153
They return at **e**,	**Ps 59:14**	6153
Toward **e** it fades and withers	**Ps 90:6**	6153
his work And to his labor until **e**.	**Ps 104:23**	6153
up of my hands as the **e** offering.	**Ps 141:2**	6153
In the twilight, in the **e**,	**Pr 7:9**	6153, 3117
and do not be idle in the **e**,	**Ec 11:6**	6153
morning or **e** sowing will succeed,	**Ec 11:6**	
the **e** that wine may inflame them!	**Is 5:11**	5399
At **e** time, behold, *there is* terror!	**Is 17:14**	6153
For the shadows of the **e** lengthen!	**Jer 6:4**	6153
will go out at **e** in their sight,	**Ezk 12:4**	6153
Then in the **e** I dug through the	**Ezk 12:7**	6153
and in the **e** my wife died.	**Ezk 24:18**	6153
LORD had been upon me in the **e**,	**Ezk 33:22**	6153
shall not be shut until the **e**.	**Ezk 46:2**	6153
about the time of the **e** offering.	**Da 9:21**	6153

And keener than wolves in the **e**. Hab 1:8 6153
Ashkelon they will lie down at **e**; Zph 2:7 6153
lions, Her judges are wolves at **e**; Zph 3:3 6153
at **e** time there will be light. Zch 14:7 6153
When **e** came, they brought Mt 8:16 *3798*
When it was **e**, the disciples Mt 14:15 *3798*
and when it was **e**, He was there Mt 14:23 *3798*
"When it is **e**, you say, Mt 16:2 *3798*
"When **e** came, the owner Mt 20:8 *3798*
Now when **e** came, Jesus was Mt 26:20 *3798*
When it was **e**, there came a Mt 27:57 *3798*
When **e** came, after the sun Mk 1:32 *3798*
On that day, when **e** came, Mk 4:35 *3798*
When it was **e**, the boat was in Mk 6:47 *3798*
When **e** came, they would go Mk 11:19 *3796*
house is coming, whether in the **e**, Mk 13:35 *3796*
it was **e** He came with the twelve. Mk 14:17 *3798*
When **e** had already come, Mk 15:42 *3798*
but at **e** He would go out and spend Lk 21:37 *3571*
us, for it is *getting* toward **e**, Lk 24:29 *2073*
Now when **e** came, His disciples Jn 6:16 *3798*
So when it was **e** Jn 20:19 *3798*
next day, for it was already **e**. Ac 4:3 *2073*
Prophets, from morning until **e**. Ac 28:23 *2073*

EVENINGS
"For 2,300 **e** *and* mornings; Da 8:14 6153
"The vision of the **e** and Da 8:26 6153

EVENLY
overlaid *them* with gold **e** applied 1Ki 6:35 3474

EVENT
they will multiply and in the **e** of war, Ex 1:10
1961, 3588, 7122
"And you shall observe this **e** as Ex 12:24 1697
After this **e** Jeroboam did not 1Ki 13:33 1697
This **e** became sin to the house 1Ki 13:34 1697
a time for every **e** under heaven Ec 3:1 2656

EVENTFUL
you hid yourself on that **e** day, 1Sa 20:19 4639

EVENTS
It came about after these **e** Gn 39:7 1697
to David all the **e** of the war. 2Sa 11:18 1697
all the **e** of the war to the king, 2Sa 11:19 1697
for it was a turn *of* **e** from the 1Ki 12:15
for it was a turn *of* **e** from God 2Ch 10:15
e King Ahasuerus promoted Haman, Es 3:1 1697
Then Mordecai recorded these **e**, Es 9:20 1697
As for the former **e**, declare Is 41:22
e that are going to take place. Is 44:7
all these **e** will be completed. Da 12:7
the outcome of these **e**?" Da 12:8
a riot in connection with today's **e**, Ac 19:40

EVENTUALLY
of *his* cart and his horses **e** Is 28:28

EVER
"Ask me **e** so much bridal payment Gn 34:12
Why did You **e** send me? Ex 5:22 2088
"**E** since I came to Pharaoh to Ex 5:23
if **e** I let you and your little Ex 10:10 3512c
LORD shall reign forever and **e**." Ex 15:18 5703
"If you **e** take your neighbor's Ex 22:26 2254a
of his peace offerings should **e** Lv 7:18
should **e** disregard that man when Lv 20:4 5956
if he should **e** *wish to* redeem it, Lv 27:13 1350
should **e** wish to redeem the field, Lv 27:19 1350
"Why did we **e** leave Egypt? Nu 11:20 2088
Have I **e** been accustomed to do so Nu 22:30 5532a
if you **e** forget the LORD your God and Dt 8:19 7911
shall **e** enter the assembly of the Dt 23:3 5769
why did You **e** bring this people Jos 7:7 5674a
"For if you **e** go back and cling Jos 23:12 7725
Did he **e** strive with Israel, or Jg 11:25 7378
or did he **e** fight against them? Jg 11:25 3898a
"Nothing like this has **e** Jg 19:30
Israel our father, forever and **e**. 1Ch 29:10 5769
the LORD your God forever and **e**! Ne 9:5 5769
e enter the assembly of God, Ne 13:1 5769
"Remember now, who **e** perished Jb 4:7
'My glory is **e** new with me, Jb 29:20
"Have you **e** in your life Jb 38:12
4480, 3117
be glad, Let them **e** sing for joy; Ps 5:11 5769
out their name forever and **e**. Ps 9:5 5703
The LORD is King forever and **e**; Ps 10:16 5703
him, Length of days forever and **e**. Ps 21:4 5703
throne, O God, is forever and **e**; Ps 45:6 5703
give You thanks forever and **e**. Ps 45:17 5703
is God, Our God forever and **e**; Ps 48:14 5703
And my sin is **e** before me. Ps 51:3 8548
of God forever and **e**. Ps 52:8 5703
They are **e** praising You. Ps 84:4 5750
it will not totter forever and **e**. Ps 104:5 5703
They are upheld forever and **e**; Ps 111:8 5769
law continually, Forever and **e**. Ps 119:44 5703
my enemies, For they are **e** mine. Ps 119:98 5769
will bless Your name forever and **e**. Ps 145:1 5703
praise Your name forever and **e**. Ps 145:2 5703
bless His holy name forever and **e**. Ps 145:21 5703
established them forever and **e**; Ps 148:6 5769
are the eyes of man **e** satisfied. Pr 27:20
pass through it forever and **e**. Is 34:10 5331
and wounds are **e** before Me. Jer 6:7 8548
to your fathers forever and **e**. Jer 7:7 5769
Who **e** heard the like of this? Jer 18:13
a foreign *land* **e** snatched away? Jer 18:14
nor the kings of Judah had **e** Jer 19:4
nor did it **e** enter My mind; Jer 19:5
my grave, And her womb **e** pregnant. Jer 20:17 5769
Why did I **e** come forth from the Jer 20:18 2088
your forefathers forever and **e**. Jer 25:5 5769
unclean meat **e** entered my mouth." Ezk 4:14
as no great king or ruler has **e** Da 2:10
of God be blessed forever and **e**, Da 2:20 5957
like the stars forever and **e**. Da 12:3 5703
that I would **e** forgive them. Hos 1:6 5375
of the LORD our God forever and **e**. Mi 4:5 5703
like this has **e** been seen in Israel." Mt 9:33 *3763*
there **e** be *any* fruit from you." Mt 21:19
1519, 165
the world until now, nor **e** will. Mt 24:21
3756, 3361
on which no one yet has **e** sat; Mk 11:2 *3768*
May no one **e** eat fruit from you Mk 11:14
1519, 165
on which no one yet has **e** sat; Lk 19:30 *4455*
the rock, where no one had **e** lain. Lk 23:53 *3768*
unclean has **e** entered my mouth.' Ac 11:8 *3763*
to all generations forever and **e**. Eph 3:21 *165*
for no one **e** hated his own flesh, Eph 5:29 *4218*
Father *be* the glory forever and **e**. Php 4:20 *165*
of you toward one another grows **e** 2Th 1:3
be honor and glory forever and **e**. 1Tm 1:17 *165*
to Him *be* the glory forever and **e**. 2Tm 4:18 *165*
which of the angels did He **e** say, Heb 1:5 *4218*
THRONE, O GOD, IS FOREVER AND **E**, Heb 1:8 *165*
which of the angels has He **e** said, Heb 1:13 *4218*
YOU, NOR WILL I **E** FORSAKE YOU," Heb 13:5
3756, 3361
whom *be* the glory forever and **e**. Heb 13:21 *165*
glory and dominion forever and **e**. 1Pe 4:11 *165*
To Him *be* dominion forever and **e**. 1Pe 5:11 *165*
e made by an act of human will, 2Pe 1:21 *4218*
For **e** since the fathers fell 2Pe 3:4
and the dominion forever and **e**. Rv 1:6 *165*
to Him who lives forever and **e**, Rv 4:9 *165*
Him who lives forever and **e**, Rv 4:10 *165*
and dominion forever and **e**." Rv 5:13 *165*
be to our God forever and **e**. Rv 7:12 *165*
by Him who lives forever and **e**, Rv 10:6 *165*
and He will reign forever and **e**." Rv 11:15 *165*
torment goes up forever and **e**; Rv 14:11 *165*
of God, who lives forever and **e**. Rv 15:7 *165*
SMOKE RISES UP FOREVER AND **E**." Rv 19:3 *165*
day and night forever and **e**. Rv 20:10 *165*
and lying, shall **e** come into it, Rv 21:27
3756, 3361
they will reign forever and **e**. Rv 22:5 *165*

EVER-FLOWING
You dried up **e** streams. Ps 74:15 386
righteousness like an **e** stream. Am 5:24 386

EVERLASTING
to remember the **e** covenant between Gn 9:16 5769
generations for an **e** covenant, Gn 17:7 5769
of Canaan, for an **e** possession; Gn 17:8 5769
in your flesh for an **e** covenant. Gn 17:13 5769
for an **e** covenant for his descendants Gn 17:19 5769
the name of the LORD, the **E** God. Gn 21:33 5769
after you for an **e** possession.' Gn 48:4 5769
the utmost bound of the **e** hills; Gn 49:26 5769
it is an **e** covenant for the sons Lv 24:8 5769
It is an **e** covenant of salt before Nu 18:19 5769
the choice things of the **e** hills, Dt 33:15 5769
And underneath are the **e** arms; Dt 33:27 5769
He has made an **e** covenant with me, 2Sa 23:5 5769
To Israel as an **e** covenant, 1Ch 16:17 5769
For His lovingkindness is **e**. 1Ch 16:34 5769
From **e** even to everlasting. 1Ch 16:36 5769
From everlasting even to **e**. 1Ch 16:36 5769
because His lovingkindness is **e**. 1Ch 16:41 5769
for His lovingkindness is **e**," 2Ch 5:13 5769
truly His lovingkindness is **e**." 2Ch 7:3 5769
"for His lovingkindness is **e**" 2Ch 7:6 5769
for His lovingkindness is **e**." 2Ch 20:21 5769
God of Israel, From **e** to Ps 41:13 5769
From everlasting to **e**. Amen and Ps 41:13 5769
He put on them an **e** reproach. Ps 78:66 5769
world, Even from **e** to everlasting, Ps 90:2 5769
world, Even from everlasting to **e**, Ps 90:2 5769
You are from **e**. Ps 93:2 5769
His lovingkindness is **e** And Ps 100:5 5769
lovingkindness of the LORD is from **e** Ps 103:17 5769
to **e** on those who fear Him, Ps 103:17 5769
To Israel as an **e** covenant, Ps 105:10 5769
For His lovingkindness is **e**. Ps 106:1 5769
God of Israel, From **e** even Ps 106:48 5769
From everlasting even to **e**. Ps 106:48 5769
For His lovingkindness is **e**. Ps 107:1 5769
And the truth of the LORD is **e**. Ps 117:2 5769
For His lovingkindness is **e**. Ps 118:1 5769
"His lovingkindness is **e**." Ps 118:2 5769
"His lovingkindness is **e**." Ps 118:3 5769
"His lovingkindness is **e**." Ps 118:4 5769
For His lovingkindness is **e**. Ps 118:29 5769
is an **e** righteousness, Ps 119:142 5769
of Your righteous ordinances is **e**. Ps 119:160 5769
Your name, O LORD, is **e**, Ps 135:13 5769
For His lovingkindness is **e**. Ps 136:1 5769
gods, For His lovingkindness is **e**. Ps 136:2 5769
For His lovingkindness is **e**; Ps 136:3 5769
For His lovingkindness is **e**; Ps 136:4 5769
For His lovingkindness is **e**; Ps 136:5 5769
For His lovingkindness is **e**; Ps 136:6 5769
For His lovingkindness is **e**: Ps 136:7 5769
day, For His lovingkindness is **e**, Ps 136:8 5769
For His lovingkindness is **e**. Ps 136:9 5769
For His lovingkindness is **e**, Ps 136:10 5769
For His lovingkindness is **e**, Ps 136:11 5769
arm, For His lovingkindness is **e**. Ps 136:12 5769
For His lovingkindness is **e**, Ps 136:13 5769
it, For His lovingkindness is **e**; Ps 136:14 5769
Sea, For His lovingkindness is **e**. Ps 136:15 5769
For His lovingkindness is **e**; Ps 136:16 5769
For His lovingkindness is **e**; Ps 136:17 5769
For His lovingkindness is **e**: Ps 136:18 5769
For His lovingkindness is **e**, Ps 136:19 5769
For His lovingkindness is **e**, Ps 136:20 5769
For His lovingkindness is **e**, Ps 136:21 5769
For His lovingkindness is **e**. Ps 136:22 5769
For His lovingkindness is **e**, Ps 136:23 5769
For His lovingkindness is **e**; Ps 136:24 5769
For His lovingkindness is **e**. Ps 136:25 5769
For His lovingkindness is **e**. Ps 136:26 5769
Your lovingkindness, O LORD, is **e**; Ps 138:8 5769
in me, And lead me in the **e** way. Ps 139:24 5769
Your kingdom is an **e** kingdom, Ps 145:13 5769
"From **e** I was established, From Pr 8:23 5769
the righteous *has* an **e** foundation. Pr 10:25 5769
statutes, broke the **e** covenant. Is 24:5 5769
GOD the LORD, *we have* an **e** Rock. Is 26:4 5769
Zion, With **e** joy upon their heads. Is 35:10 5769
The **E** God, the LORD, the Creator Is 40:28 5769
by the LORD With an **e** salvation; Is 45:17 5769
And **e** joy *will be* on their heads Is 51:11 5769
But with **e** lovingkindness I will Is 54:8 5769
will make an **e** covenant with you, Is 55:3 5769
For an **e** sign which will not be Is 55:13 5769
I will give them an **e** name which Is 56:5 5769
I will make you an **e** pride, Is 60:15 5769
will have the LORD for an **e** light, Is 60:19 5769
will have the LORD for an **e** light, Is 60:20 5769
their land, **E** joy will be theirs. Is 61:7 5769
And make an **e** covenant with them. Is 61:8 5769
to make for Himself an **e** name, Is 63:12 5769
is the living God and the **e** King. Jer 10:10 5769
With an **e** disgrace that will not Jer 20:11 5769
"I will put an **e** reproach on Jer 23:40 5769
and an **e** humiliation which will not be Jer 23:40 5769
a hissing, and an **e** desolation. Jer 25:9 5769
I will make it an **e** desolation. Jer 25:12 5769
"I have loved you with an **e** love; Jer 31:3 5769
"I will make an **e** covenant Jer 32:40 5769
For His lovingkindness is **e**"; Jer 33:11 5769
to the LORD *in* an **e** covenant Jer 50:5 5769
establish an **e** covenant with you. Ezk 16:60 5769
soul to destroy with **e** enmity," Ezk 25:15 5769
"Because you have had **e** enmity Ezk 35:5 5769
"I will make you an **e** desolation and Ezk 35:9 5769
'The **e** heights have become our Ezk 36:2 5769
will be an **e** covenant with them. Ezk 37:26 5769
His kingdom is an **e** kingdom And Da 4:3 5957
For His dominion is an **e** dominion, Da 4:34 5957
His dominion is an **e** dominion Da 7:14 5957
His kingdom *will be* an **e** kingdom, Da 7:27 5957
to bring in **e** righteousness, Da 9:24 5769
will awake, these to **e** life, Da 12:2 5769
others to disgrace *and* **e** contempt. Da 12:2 5769
Are You not from **e**, Hab 1:12 6924a
His ways are **e**. Hab 3:6 5769

EVERY
and **e** living creature that moves, Gn 1:21 3605
and **e** winged bird after its kind; Gn 1:21 3605
and over **e** creeping thing that Gn 1:26 3605
and over **e** living thing that moves Gn 1:28 3605
I have given you **e** plant yielding Gn 1:29 3605
and **e** tree which has fruit Gn 1:29 3605
and to **e** beast of the earth and to Gn 1:30 3605
and to **e** bird of the sky Gn 1:30 3605
and to **e** thing that moves on the earth Gn 1:30 3605
given **e** green plant for food"; Gn 1:30 3605
the LORD God caused to grow **e** tree Gn 2:9 3605
LORD God formed **e** beast of the field Gn 2:19 3605
the field and **e** bird of the sky, Gn 2:19 3605
sky, and to **e** beast of the field, Gn 2:20 3605
more than **e** beast of the field; Gn 3:14 3605
sword which turned **e** direction to Gn 3:24
and that **e** intent of the thoughts Gn 6:5
of **e** living thing of all flesh, Gn 6:19 3605
bring two of **e** *kind* into the ark, Gn 6:19
of **e** creeping thing of the ground Gn 6:20 3605
two of **e** *kind* will come to you to Gn 6:20 3605
you of **e** clean animal by sevens, Gn 7:2 3605
e living thing that I have made." Gn 7:4 3605
they and **e** beast after its kind, Gn 7:14 3605
and **e** creeping thing that creeps Gn 7:14 3605
kind, and **e** bird after its kind, Gn 7:14 3605
and beasts and **e** swarming thing Gn 7:21 3605
Thus He blotted out **e** living thing Gn 7:23 3605
"Bring out with you **e** living Gn 8:17 3605
birds and animals and **e** creeping Gn 8:17 3605
E beast, every creeping thing, and Gn 8:19 3605
Every beast, **e** creeping thing, and Gn 8:19 3605
every creeping thing, and **e** bird, Gn 8:19 3605
and took of **e** clean animal and of Gn 8:20 3605
and of **e** clean bird and offered burnt Gn 8:20 3605
again destroy **e** living thing, Gn 8:21 3605
the terror of you will be on **e** beast Gn 9:2 3605
earth and on **e** bird of the sky; Gn 9:2 3605
"**E** moving thing that is alive Gn 9:3 3605
from **e** beast I will require it. Gn 9:5
And from **e** man, from every man's Gn 9:5
from **e** man's brother I will Gn 9:5 376
and with **e** living creature that is Gn 9:10 3605
and **e** beast of the earth with you; Gn 9:10 3605
ark, even **e** beast of the earth. Gn 9:10 3605
Me and you and **e** living creature Gn 9:12 3605

Context	Reference	Number
e living creature of all flesh;	Gn 9:15	3605
between God and e living creature	Gn 9:16	3605
e one according to his language,	Gn 10:5	376
e male among you shall be	Gn 17:10	3605
"And e male among you who is	Gn 17:12	3605
e male among the men of Abraham's	Gn 17:23	3605
all the people from e quarter;	Gn 19:4	3605
LORD had blessed Abraham in e way.	Gn 24:1	3605
e speckled and spotted sheep and	Gn 30:32	3605
and e black one among the lambs and	Gn 30:32	3605
E one that is not speckled and	Gn 30:33	3605
goats, e one with white in it,	Gn 30:35	3605
his servants, e drove by itself,	Gn 32:16	5739
that e male of you be circumcised,	Gn 34:15	3605
that e male among us be	Gn 34:22	3605
and e male was circumcised,	Gn 34:24	3605
city unawares, and killed e male.	Gn 34:25	3605
he placed in e city the food from	Gn 41:48	
restore e man's money in his sack,	Gn 42:25	376
e man's bundle of money *was* in his	Gn 42:35	376
for e shepherd is loathsome to the	Gn 46:34	3605
for e Egyptian sold his field,	Gn 47:20	376
e one with the blessing	Gn 49:28	376
"E son who is born you are to	Ex 1:22	3605
and e daughter you are to keep	Ex 1:22	3605
"But e woman shall ask of her	Ex 3:22	
E man and beast that is found in	Ex 9:19	3605
beast and on e plant of the field,	Ex 9:22	3605
the hail also struck e plant of	Ex 9:25	3605
and shattered e tree of the field.	Ex 9:25	3605
and they will eat e tree which sprouts	Ex 10:5	3605
and eat e plant of the land,	Ex 10:12	3605
and they ate e plant of the land	Ex 10:15	3605
what must be eaten by e person,	Ex 12:16	3605
but e man's slave purchased with	Ex 12:44	3605
"Sanctify to Me e firstborn, the	Ex 13:2	3605
e womb among the sons of Israel,	Ex 13:2	3605
the first offspring of e womb,	Ex 13:12	3605
offspring of e beast that you own;	Ex 13:12	3605
"But e first offspring of a	Ex 13:13	3605
and e firstborn of man among your	Ex 13:13	3605
that the LORD killed e firstborn	Ex 13:15	3605
the first offspring of e womb,	Ex 13:15	3605
but e firstborn of my sons I	Ex 13:15	3605
and gather a day's portion e day,	Ex 16:4	
it e man as much as he should eat;	Ex 16:16	376
e man gathered as much as he	Ex 16:18	376
e man as much as he should eat;	Ex 16:21	376
Remain e man in his place;	Ex 16:29	376
and let it be that e major dispute	Ex 18:22	3605
but e minor dispute they	Ex 18:22	3605
but e minor dispute they	Ex 18:26	3605
in e place where I cause My name	Ex 20:24	3605
"For e breach of trust, *whether*	Ex 22:9	3605
from e man whose heart moves him	Ex 25:2	3605
he shall burn it e morning when he	Ex 30:7	
'E man *of you* put his sword upon	Ex 32:27	376
camp, and kill e man his brother,	Ex 32:27	376
his brother, and e man his friend,	Ex 32:27	376
and e man his neighbor.'"	Ex 32:27	376
for e man has been against his son	Ex 32:29	376
from e womb belongs to Me,	Ex 34:19	3605
Let e skillful man among you come,	Ex 35:10	3605
so *did* e man who presented an	Ex 35:22	3605
E man, who had in his possession	Ex 35:23	3605
and e man who had in his	Ex 35:24	3605
as to perform in e inventive work.	Ex 35:33	3605
skill to perform e work of an engraver	Ex 35:35	3605
of e work and makers of designs.	Ex 35:35	3605
and e skillful person in whom the	Ex 36:1	3605
and Oholiab and e skillful person	Ex 36:2	3605
him freewill offerings e morning.	Ex 36:3	1242
sockets, two under e board.	Ex 36:30	259
'E grain offering of yours,	Lv 2:13	3605
shall burn wood on it e morning;	Lv 6:12	1242
'E male among the sons of Aaron	Lv 6:18	3605
"So e grain offering of the	Lv 6:23	3605
'E male among the priests may eat	Lv 6:29	3605
'E male among the priests may eat	Lv 7:6	3605
e grain offering that is baked in	Lv 7:9	3605
'E grain offering, mixed with oil	Lv 7:10	3605
he shall present one of e offering	Lv 7:14	3605
e raven in its kind,	Lv 11:15	3605
in e vessel shall become unclean.	Lv 11:34	3605
'Now e swarming thing that swarms	Lv 11:41	3605
in respect to e swarming thing	Lv 11:42	3605
and e living thing that moves in	Lv 11:46	3605
'E bed on which the person with	Lv 15:4	3605
'E saddle on which the person with	Lv 15:9	3605
and e wooden vessel shall be	Lv 15:12	3605
and e bed on which he lies shall	Lv 15:24	3605
and e thing on which she sits	Lv 15:26	3605
for all their sins once e year."	Lv 16:34	
'E one of you shall reverence his	Lv 19:3	376
'E sabbath day he shall set it in	Lv 24:8	
'Thus for e piece of your	Lv 25:24	3605
'E valuation of yours, moreover,	Lv 27:25	3605
For e tenth part of herd or flock,	Lv 27:32	3605
to the number of names, e male,	Nu 1:2	3605
e male from twenty years old and	Nu 1:20	3605
e male from twenty years old and	Nu 1:22	3605
shall set out, e man in his place by	Nu 2:17	376
they set out, e one by his family	Nu 2:34	376
of Israel instead of e firstborn,	Nu 3:12	3605
e male from a month old and upward	Nu 3:15	3605
in the numbering of e male from a	Nu 3:22	3605
In the numbering of e male from a	Nu 3:28	3605
numbering of e male from a month	Nu 3:34	3605
e male from a month old and	Nu 3:39	3605
"Number e firstborn male of the	Nu 3:40	3605
send away from the camp e leper and	Nu 5:2	3605
'Also e contribution pertaining to	Nu 5:9	3605
'So e man's holy *gifts* shall be his;	Nu 5:10	376
a cart for e two of the leaders	Nu 7:3	
of e first issue of the womb,	Nu 8:16	3605
"For e firstborn among the sons	Nu 8:17	3605
the Levites instead of e firstborn	Nu 8:18	3605
e one a leader among them."	Nu 13:2	3605
for e day you shall bear your	Nu 14:34	3117
are holy, e one of them,	Nu 16:3	3605
e offering of theirs, even every	Nu 18:9	3605
even e grain offering and every	Nu 18:9	3605
even every grain offering and e	Nu 18:9	3605
sin offering and e guilt offering,	Nu 18:9	3605
e male shall eat it.	Nu 18:10	3605
"E devoted thing in Israel shall	Nu 18:14	3605
"E first issue of the womb of all	Nu 18:15	3605
e offering due to the LORD,	Nu 18:29	3605
'E open vessel, which has no	Nu 19:15	3605
e male from a month old and	Nu 26:62	3605
a continual burnt offering e day.	Nu 28:3	
This is the burnt offering of e	Nu 28:10	7676
and e obligation by which she has	Nu 30:4	3605
and e obligation by which she	Nu 30:11	3605
"E vow and every binding oath to	Nu 30:13	3605
"Every vow and e binding oath to	Nu 30:13	3605
Moses, and they killed e male.	Nu 31:7	3605
kill e male among the little ones,	Nu 31:17	3605
and kill e woman who has known man	Nu 31:17	3605
shall purify for yourselves e garment	Nu 31:20	3605
and e article of leather and all the	Nu 31:20	3605
out of e fifty of the persons,	Nu 31:30	
took one drawn out of e fifty,	Nu 31:47	
taken booty, e man for himself.	Nu 31:53	376
until e one of the sons of Israel has	Nu 32:18	376
take one leader of e tribe to apportion	Nu 34:18	
"E daughter who comes into	Nu 36:8	3605
And e man of you girded on his	Dt 1:41	376
men, women and children of e city.	Dt 2:34	3605
men, women and children of e city.	Dt 3:6	3605
return e man to his possession which	Dt 3:20	376
God are alive today, e one of you.	Dt 4:4	3605
and e living thing that followed	Dt 11:6	3605
therefore keep e commandment	Dt 11:8	3605
"E place on which the sole of	Dt 11:24	3605
the hills and under e green tree.	Dt 12:2	3605
e man *doing* whatever is right in	Dt 12:8	376
in e *cultic* place you see,	Dt 12:13	3605
for e abominable act which the	Dt 12:31	3605
and e raven in its kind,	Dt 14:14	3605
comes out of the field e year.	Dt 14:22	8141
"At the end of e third year you	Dt 14:28	
"At the end of e seven years you	Dt 15:1	
e creditor shall release what he	Dt 15:2	3605
shall eat it e year before the LORD	Dt 15:20	8141
"E man shall give as he is able,	Dt 16:17	376
and e dispute and every assault	Dt 21:5	3605
and every dispute and e assault	Dt 21:5	3605
keep yourself from e evil thing.	Dt 23:9	3605
"Also e sickness and every plague	Dt 28:61	3605
every sickness and e plague which,	Dt 28:61	3605
and e curse which is written in	Dt 29:20	3605
to bring upon it e curse which is	Dt 29:27	3605
"At the end of e seven years,	Dt 31:10	
"E place on which the sole of	Jos 1:3	3605
will go up e man straight ahead."	Jos 6:5	376
the city, e man straight ahead,	Jos 6:20	376
it and e person who was in it.	Jos 10:28	3605
and he struck it and e person who	Jos 10:30	3605
and struck it and e person who *was*	Jos 10:32	3605
that day e person who *was* in it,	Jos 10:35	3605
it and e person who *was* in it.	Jos 10:37	3605
destroyed e person *who was* in it.	Jos 10:39	3605
They struck e person who was	Jos 11:11	3605
but they struck e man with the	Jos 11:14	3605
the LORD gave them rest on e side,	Jos 21:44	5439
from all their enemies on e side,	Jos 23:1	5439
maiden, two maidens for e warrior;	Jg 5:30	7218
and e one of them threw an earring	Jg 8:25	376
of all their enemies on e side;	Jg 8:34	5439
e man did what was right in his	Jg 17:6	376
you shall utterly destroy e man	Jg 21:11	3605
e woman who has lain with a man."	Jg 21:11	3605
e man to his tribe and family,	Jg 21:24	376
e offering of My people Israel?'	1Sa 2:29	3605
'Yet I will not cut off e man of	1Sa 2:33	376
and e man fled to his tent;	1Sa 4:10	376
"Go e man to his city."	1Sa 8:22	376
out the right eye of e one of you,	1Sa 11:2	3605
e man's sword was against his	1Sa 14:20	376
against all his enemies on e side,	1Sa 14:47	5439
cuts off e one of the enemies of David	1Sa 20:15	376
brought about *the death* of e person	1Sa 22:22	3605
And Saul sought him e day,	1Sa 23:14	3605
e man his wife and his children,	1Sa 30:22	376
on e side from all his enemies,	2Sa 7:1	5439
David mourned for his son e day.	2Sa 13:37	3605
the end of e year that he cut *it,*	2Sa 14:26	
then e man who has any suit or	2Sa 15:4	3605
E man to his tents, O Israel!"	2Sa 20:1	376
e one of them will be thrust away	2Sa 23:6	3605
e man under his vine and his fig	1Ki 4:25	376
God has given me rest on e side;	1Ki 5:4	5439
once e three years the ships of	1Ki 10:22	
They brought e man his gift,	1Ki 10:25	376
had struck down e male in Edom	1Ki 11:15	3605
he had cut off e male in Edom),	1Ki 11:16	3605
return e man to his house, for	1Ki 12:24	376
off from Jeroboam e male person,	1Ki 14:10	8366
pillars and Asherim on e high hill	1Ki 14:23	3605
hill and beneath e luxuriant tree.	1Ki 14:23	3605
e mouth that has not kissed him."	1Ki 19:18	3605
and will cut off from Ahab e male,	1Ki 21:21	8366
"E man to his city and every man	1Ki 22:36	376
city and e man to his country."	1Ki 22:36	376
'Then you shall strike e fortified	2Ki 3:19	3605
fortified city and e choice city,	2Ki 3:19	3605
and fell e good tree and stop all	2Ki 3:19	3605
and mar e good piece of land with	2Ki 3:19	3605
a stone on e piece of good land	2Ki 3:25	3605
even e kind of good thing of	2Ki 8:9	3605
cut off from Ahab e male person	2Ki 9:8	8366
the hills and under e green tree.	2Ki 16:4	3605
pillars and Asherim on e high hill	2Ki 17:10	3605
high hill and under e green tree,	2Ki 17:10	3605
all His prophets *and* e seer,	2Ki 17:13	3605
But e nation still made gods of	2Ki 17:29	1471
e nation in their cities in which	2Ki 17:29	1471
even e great house he burned with	2Ki 25:9	3605
to come in e seven days from time to	1Ch 9:25	
showbread to prepare it e sabbath.	1Ch 9:32	7676
the hundreds, even with e leader.	1Ch 13:1	3605
as e day's work required;	1Ch 16:37	
from all his enemies on e side;	1Ch 22:9	5439
are skillful in e kind of work.	1Ch 22:15	3605
He not given you rest on e side?	1Ch 22:18	5439
They are to stand e morning to	1Ch 23:30	1242
fathers' households, for e gate.	1Ch 26:13	8179
e intent of the thoughts.	1Ch 28:9	3605
utensils for e kind of service;	1Ch 28:14	3605
utensils for e kind of service;	1Ch 28:14	3605
and e willing man of any skill	1Ch 28:21	3605
and to e leader in all Israel,	2Ch 1:2	3605
by their divisions at e gate;	2Ch 8:14	8179
once e three years the ships of	2Ch 9:21	
They brought e man his gift,	2Ch 9:24	376
E man to your tents, O Israel;	2Ch 10:16	376
return e man to his house, for	2Ch 11:4	376
He put shields and spears in e city	2Ch 11:12	3605
"E morning and evening they burn to	2Ch 13:11	1242
lamps is *ready* to light e evening;	2Ch 13:11	6153
He has given us rest on e side."	2Ch 14:7	5439
them with e kind of distress.	2Ch 15:6	3605
the LORD gave them rest on e side.	2Ch 15:15	5439
E man of Judah and Jerusalem returned	2Ch 20:27	3605
the hills and under e green tree.	2Ch 28:4	3605
himself in e corner of Jerusalem.	2Ch 28:24	3605
In e city of Judah he made	2Ch 28:25	3605
and e unclean thing which they	2Ch 29:16	3605
cities, or in each and e city,	2Ch 31:19	3605
to distribute portions to e male among	2Ch 31:19	3605
E work which he began in the service	2Ch 31:21	3605
who destroyed e mighty warrior,	2Ch 32:21	3605
others, and guided them on e side.	2Ch 32:22	5439
'E survivor, at whatever place he	Ezr 1:4	3605
from e place where you may turn,"	Ne 4:12	3605
"Thus may God shake out e man	Ne 5:13	3605
of houses full of e good thing,	Ne 9:25	3605
year and the exaction of e debt.	Ne 10:31	3605
the first fruits of all the fruit of e tree	Ne 10:35	3605
the fruit of e tree,	Ne 10:37	3605
merchants of e kind of merchandise	Ne 13:20	3605
e people according to their language,	Es 1:22	5971a
that e man should be the master in	Es 1:22	3605
gather e beautiful young virgin to the	Es 2:3	3605
E day Mordecai walked back and forth	Es 2:11	3605
edict to be issued as law in e province	Es 3:14	3605
In each and e province where	Es 4:3	3605
and e *instance* where the king had	Es 5:11	3605
not satisfy me e time I see Mordecai	Es 5:13	3605
to e province according to its	Es 8:9	4082
and to e people according to their	Es 8:9	5971a
the Jews who were in each and e city	Es 8:11	3605
as law in each and e province was	Es 8:13	3605
In each and e province and in	Es 8:17	3605
province and in each and e city,	Es 8:17	3605
throughout e generation,	Es 9:28	1755
every generation, e family,	Es 9:28	4940
every family, e province and	Es 9:28	4082
every province and e city;	Es 9:28	5892b
and all that he has, on e side?	Jb 1:10	5439
You examine him e morning	Jb 7:18	
morning And try him e moment?	Jb 7:18	
is the life of e living thing,	Jb 12:10	3605
him, And harry him at e step.	Jb 18:11	
"He breaks me down on e side,	Jb 19:10	5439
"He seals the hand of e man,	Jb 37:7	3605
And searches after e green thing.	Jb 39:8	3605
E night I make my bed swim,	Ps 6:6	3605
a God who has indignation e day.	Ps 7:11	3605
The wicked strut about on e side When	Ps 12:8	5439
of many, Terror is on e side;	Ps 31:13	5439
Surely e man at his best is a mere	Ps 39:5	3605
e man walks about as a phantom;	Ps 39:6	376
Surely e man is a mere breath.	Ps 39:11	3605
"For e beast of the forest is	Ps 50:10	3605
"I know e bird of the mountains,	Ps 50:11	3605
E one of them has turned aside;	Ps 53:3	3605
day long And chastened e morning.	Ps 73:14	
E *one of them* appears before God	Ps 84:7	
I have called upon You e day,	Ps 88:9	3605
E morning I will destroy all the	Ps 101:8	
drink to e beast of the field;	Ps 104:11	3605
my feet from e evil way,	Ps 119:101	3605
Therefore I hate e false way.	Ps 119:104	3605
everything, I hate e false way.	Ps 119:128	3605
And e one of Your righteous	Ps 119:160	3605

Context	Reference	Number
furnishing **e** kind of produce,	**Ps 144:13**	2177
E day I will bless You, And I	**Ps 145:2**	3605
the desire of **e** living thing.	**Ps 145:16**	3605
And equity *and* **e** good course.	**Pr 2:9**	3605
squares, And lurks by **e** corner.	**Pr 7:12**	3605
E prudent man acts with knowledge,	**Pr 13:16**	3605
eyes of the LORD are in **e** place,	**Pr 15:3**	3605
its **e** decision is from the LORD.	**Pr 16:33**	3605
And **e** man is a friend to him who	**Pr 19:6**	3605
E man's way is right in his own	**Pr 21:2**	3605
E word of God is tested;	**Pr 30:5**	3605
a time for **e** event under heaven	**Ec 3:1**	3605
that **e** man who eats and drinks	**Ec 3:13**	3605
for a time for **e** matter and for	**Ec 3:17**	3605
matter and for **e** deed is there.	**Ec 3:17**	3605
I have seen that **e** labor and	**Ec 4:4**	3605
every labor and **e** skill which is done	**Ec 4:4**	3605
as for **e** man to whom God has given	**Ec 5:19**	3605
Because that is the end of **e** man,	**Ec 7:2**	3605
time and procedure for **e** delight,	**Ec 8:6**	3605
seen and applied my mind to **e** deed	**Ec 8:9**	3605
and I saw **e** work of God, *I*	**Ec 8:17**	3605
because this *applies to* **e** person.	**Ec 12:13**	3605
God will bring **e** act to judgment,	**Ec 12:14**	3605
Against **e** high tower, Against	**Is 2:15**	3605
tower, Against **e** fortified wall,	**Is 2:15**	3605
that **e** place where there used to	**Is 7:23**	3605
For **e** boot of the booted warrior	**Is 9:5**	3605
For **e** one of them is godless and	**Is 9:17**	3605
e mouth is speaking foolishness.	**Is 9:17**	3605
limp, And **e** man's heart will melt.	**Is 13:7**	3605
is bald *and* **e** beard is cut off.	**Is 15:2**	3605
e night at my guard post.	**Is 21:8**	3605
E house is shut up so that none	**Is 24:10**	3605
I water it **e** moment.	**Is 27:3**	
On **e** lofty mountain and on	**Is 30:25**	3605
on **e** high hill there will be streams	**Is 30:25**	3605
e blow of the rod of punishment,	**Is 30:32**	3605
For in that day **e** man will cast	**Is 31:7**	376
Be their strength **e** morning,	**Is 33:2**	
there, **E** one with its kind.	**Is 34:15**	802
"Let **e** valley be lifted up, And	**Is 40:4**	3605
e mountain and hill be made low;	**Is 40:4**	3605
O forest, and **e** tree in it;	**Is 44:23**	3605
back, That to Me **e** knee will bow,	**Is 45:23**	3605
e tongue will swear *allegiance*.	**Is 45:23**	3605
helpless at the head of **e** street,	**Is 51:20**	3605
And **e** tongue that accuses you in	**Is 54:17**	3605
E one who thirsts, come to the	**Is 55:1**	3605
e one who keeps from profaning the	**Is 56:6**	3605
the oaks, Under **e** luxuriant tree,	**Is 57:5**	3605
Remove **e** obstacle out of the way	**Is 57:14**	
go free And break **e** yoke?	**Is 58:6**	3605
For on **e** high hill And under every	**Jer 2:20**	3605
And under **e** green tree You have lain	**Jer 2:20**	3605
She went up on **e** high hill and	**Jer 3:6**	3605
high hill and under **e** green tree,	**Jer 3:6**	3605
the strangers under **e** green tree,	**Jer 3:13**	3605
horseman and bowman **e** city flees;	**Jer 4:29**	3605
E city is forsaken, And no man	**Jer 4:29**	3605
has a sword, Terror is on **e** side.	**Jer 6:25**	5439
Because **e** brother deals craftily,	**Jer 9:4**	3605
And **e** neighbor goes about as a	**Jer 9:4**	3605
E man is stupid, devoid of	**Jer 10:14**	3605
E goldsmith is put to shame by his	**Jer 10:14**	3605
of prey against her on **e** side?	**Jer 12:9**	5439
E jug is to be filled with wine."	**Jer 13:12**	3605
e jug is to be filled with wine?'	**Jer 13:12**	3605
from **e** mountain and every hill and	**Jer 16:16**	3605
from every mountain and **e** hill and	**Jer 16:16**	3605
"Terror on **e** side!	**Jer 20:10**	5439
"Administer justice **e** morning;	**Jer 21:12**	
because **e** man's own word will	**Jer 23:36**	376
LORD over **e** madman who prophesies,	**Jer 29:26**	3605
Why do I see **e** man *With* his hands	**Jer 30:6**	3605
your adversaries, **e** one of them,	**Jer 30:16**	3605
'Turn now **e** man from his evil way and	**Jer 35:15**	376
in order that **e** man will turn from	**Jer 36:3**	376
the king's daughters and **e** person	**Jer 43:6**	3605
we will certainly carry out **e** word that	**Jer 44:17**	3605
Terror is on **e** side!"	**Jer 46:5**	5439
And **e** inhabitant of the land will	**Jer 47:2**	3605
and Sidon **E** ally that is left;	**Jer 47:4**	3605
A destroyer will come to **e** city,	**Jer 48:8**	3605
"For **e** head is bald and every	**Jer 48:37**	3605
is bald and **e** beard cut short;	**Jer 48:37**	3605
'Terror on **e** side!'	**Jer 49:29**	5439
their disaster from **e** side,"	**Jer 49:32**	5439
lines against Babylon on **e** side,	**Jer 50:14**	5439
battle cry against her on **e** side!	**Jer 50:15**	5439
Encamp against her on **e** side,	**Jer 50:29**	5439
For on **e** side they will be opposed	**Jer 51:2**	5439
E goldsmith is put to shame by his	**Jer 51:17**	3605
And **e** land of their dominion.	**Jer 51:28**	3605
even **e** large house he burned with	**Jer 52:13**	3605
hunger At the head of **e** street."	**La 2:19**	3605
feast My terrors on **e** side;	**La 2:22**	5439
They are new **e** morning;	**La 3:23**	
out At the corner of **e** street.	**La 4:1**	3605
all your remnant to **e** wind.	**Ezk 5:10**	3605
third I will scatter to **e** wind,	**Ezk 5:12**	3605
their altars, on **e** high hill,	**Ezk 6:13**	3605
the mountains, under **e** green tree and	**Ezk 6:13**	3605
green tree and under **e** leafy oak	**Ezk 6:13**	3605
e form of creeping things and	**Ezk 8:10**	3605
I will scatter to **e** wind all who are	**Ezk 12:14**	3605
days are long and **e** vision fails'?	**Ezk 12:22**	3605
as the fulfillment of **e** vision.	**Ezk 12:23**	3605
of **e** stature to hunt down lives!	**Ezk 13:18**	3605
out your harlotries on **e** passer-by who	**Ezk 16:15**	3605
yourself a high place in **e** square.	**Ezk 16:24**	3605
high place at the top of **e** street and	**Ezk 16:25**	3605
you spread your legs to **e** passer-by	**Ezk 16:25**	3605
shrine at the beginning of **e** street	**Ezk 16:31**	3605
made your high place in **e** square,	**Ezk 16:31**	3605
e direction for your harlotries.	**Ezk 16:33**	5439
them against you from **e** direction and	**Ezk 16:37**	5439
will be scattered to **e** wind;	**Ezk 17:21**	3605
of **e** kind will nest under it;	**Ezk 17:23**	3605
On **e** side from *their* provinces,	**Ezk 19:8**	5439
then they saw **e** high hill and	**Ezk 20:28**	3605
every high hill and **e** leafy tree,	**Ezk 20:28**	3605
will consume **e** green tree in you,	**Ezk 20:47**	3605
in you, as well as **e** dry tree;	**Ezk 20:47**	3605
and **e** heart will melt, all hands	**Ezk 21:7**	3605
be feeble, **e** spirit will faint and	**Ezk 21:7**	3605
rod of My son despising **e** tree?	**Ezk 21:10**	3605
them against you from **e** side:	**Ezk 23:22**	5439
set themselves against you on **e** side	**Ezk 23:24**	5439
in it the pieces, **E** good piece,	**Ezk 24:4**	3605
on the ground, tremble **e** moment and	**Ezk 26:16**	
E precious stone was your covering:	**Ezk 28:13**	3605
By the sword upon her on **e** side;	**Ezk 28:23**	5439
e head was made bald and every	**Ezk 29:18**	3605
and **e** shoulder was rubbed bare.	**Ezk 29:18**	3605
and they will tremble **e** moment,	**Ezk 32:10**	
moment, **e** man for his own life,	**Ezk 32:10**	376
and they became food for **e** beast	**Ezk 34:5**	3605
the mountains and on **e** high hill;	**Ezk 34:6**	3605
and crushed you from **e** side,	**Ezk 36:3**	5439
and I will gather them from **e** side	**Ezk 37:21**	5439
e wall will fall to the ground.	**Ezk 38:20**	3605
"**E** man's sword will be against	**Ezk 38:21**	376
I will give you as food to **e** kind	**Ezk 39:4**	3605
'Speak to **e** kind of bird and to	**Ezk 39:17**	3605
bird and to **e** beast of the field,	**Ezk 39:17**	3605
gather from **e** side to My sacrifice	**Ezk 39:17**	5439
around about the house on **e** side.	**Ezk 41:5**	5439
all around the temple on **e** side.	**Ezk 41:10**	5439
and **e** cherub had two faces,	**Ezk 41:18**	
and **e** devoted thing in Israel	**Ezk 44:29**	3605
The first of all the first fruits of **e** kind	**Ezk 44:30**	3605
and **e** contribution of every kind,	**Ezk 44:30**	3605
and every contribution of **e** kind,	**Ezk 44:30**	3605
on **e** day of the seven days,	**Ezk 45:23**	3117
in **e** corner of the court *there was*	**Ezk 46:21**	4740
e living creature which swarms in	**Ezk 47:9**	3605
in **e** place where the river goes,	**Ezk 47:9**	3605
They will bear **e** month because	**Ezk 47:12**	
in **e** *branch of* wisdom,	**Da 1:4**	3605
intelligence in **e** *branch of* literature	**Da 1:17**	3605
As for **e** matter of wisdom and	**Da 1:20**	3605
nations and *men of* **e** language,	**Da 3:4**	
nations and *men of* **e** language	**Da 3:7**	
have made a decree that **e** man who	**Da 3:10**	3606
and *men of* **e** language that live	**Da 4:1**	
nations and *men of* **e** language	**Da 5:19**	
nations and *men of* **e** language who	**Da 6:25**	
nations and *men of* **e** language	**Da 7:14**	
and magnify himself above **e** god and	**Da 11:36**	3605
earnings on **e** threshing floor.	**Hos 9:1**	3605
treasury of **e** precious article.	**Hos 13:15**	3605
they stretch out beside **e** altar,	**Am 2:8**	3605
Bring your sacrifices **e** morning,	**Am 4:4**	
morning, Your tithes **e** three days.	**Am 4:4**	
in **e** place they will cast them	**Am 8:3**	3605
loins And baldness on **e** head.	**Am 8:10**	3605
and **e** man cried to his god,	**Jon 1:5**	376
from **e** kind of desirable object.	**Na 2:9**	3605
to pieces At the head of **e** street;	**Na 3:10**	3605
They laugh at **e** fortress And heap	**Hab 1:10**	3605
E morning He brings His justice to	**Zph 3:5**	1242
'and so is **e** work of their hands;	**Hg 2:14**	3605
'I smote you *and* **e** work of your	**Hg 2:17**	3605
'**e** one of you will invite his	**Zch 3:10**	376
From them **e** ruler, *all* of them	**Zch 10:4**	3605
strike **e** horse with bewilderment and	**Zch 12:4**	3605
while I strike **e** horse of the	**Zch 12:4**	3605
will mourn, **e** family by itself;	**Zch 12:12**	4940
that remain, **e** family by itself and	**Zch 12:14**	4940
E cooking pot in Jerusalem and in	**Zch 14:21**	3605
and in **e** place incense is going to	**Mal 1:11**	3605
and **e** evildoer will be chaff;	**Mal 4:1**	3605
e tree that does not	**Mt 3:10**	*3956*
ON **E** WORD THAT PROCEEDS OUT OF	**Mt 4:4**	*3956*
and healing **e** kind of disease and	**Mt 4:23**	*3956*
e kind of sickness among the people.	**Mt 4:23**	*3956*
"So **e** good tree bears good fruit,	**Mt 7:17**	*3956*
"**E** tree that does not bear good	**Mt 7:19**	*3956*
and healing **e** kind of disease and	**Mt 9:35**	*3956*
of disease and **e** kind of sickness.	**Mt 9:35**	*3956*
and to heal **e** kind of disease and	**Mt 10:1**	*3956*
of disease and **e** kind of sickness.	**Mt 10:1**	*3956*
that **e** careless word that people	**Mt 12:36**	*3956*
sea, and gathering *fish* of **e** kind;	**Mt 13:47**	*3956*
"Therefore **e** scribe who has	**Mt 13:52**	*3956*
"**E** plant which My heavenly Father	**Mt 15:13**	*3956*
E MAN ACCORDING TO HIS DEEDS.	**Mt 16:27**	*1538*
WITNESSES **E** FACT MAY BE CONFIRMED.	**Mt 18:16**	*3956*
E day I used to sit in the temple	**Mt 26:55**	*2596*
"**E** day I was with you in the	**Mk 14:49**	*2596*
"**E** *firstborn* MALE THAT OPENS THE	**Lk 2:23**	*3956*
parents went to Jerusalem **e** year	**Lk 2:41**	*2596*
'**E** RAVINE WILL BE FILLED, AND	**Lk 3:5**	*3956*
AND **E** MOUNTAIN AND HILL WILL BE	**Lk 3:5**	*3956*
e tree that does not	**Lk 3:9**	*3956*
devil had finished **e** temptation,	**Lk 4:13**	*3956*
into **e** locality in the surrounding	**Lk 4:37**	*3956*
who had come from **e** village of	**Lk 5:17**	*3956*
in pairs ahead of Him to **e** city	**Lk 10:1**	*3956*
and rue and **e** *kind of* garden herb,	**Lk 11:42**	*3956*
guard against **e** form of greed;	**Lk 12:15**	*3956*
joyously living in splendor **e** day.	**Lk 16:19**	*2596*
you and hem you in on **e** side,	**Lk 19:43**	*3840*
all the people were hanging on to **e**	**Lk 19:48**	*191*
into the world, enlightens **e** man.	**Jn 1:9**	*3956*
"**E** man serves the good wine	**Jn 2:10**	*3956*
"**E** branch in Me that does not	**Jn 15:2**	*3956*
and **e** *branch* that bears fruit, He	**Jn 15:2**	*3956*
to **e** soldier and *also* the tunic;	**Jn 19:23**	*1538*
men from **e** nation under heaven.	**Ac 2:5**	*3956*
whom they used to set down **e** day	**Ac 3:2**	*2596*
'And it will be that **e** soul that	**Ac 3:23**	*3956*
bless you by turning **e** one *of you* from	**Ac 3:26**	*1538*
And **e** day, in the temple and from	**Ac 5:42**	*3956*
but in **e** nation the man who fears	**Ac 10:35**	*3956*
prophets which are read **e** Sabbath,	**Ac 13:27**	*3956*
elders for them in **e** church,	**Ac 14:23**	*2596*
in **e** city those who preach him,	**Ac 15:21**	*2596*
in the synagogues **e** Sabbath."	**Ac 15:21**	*3956*
return and visit the brethren in **e** city	**Ac 15:36**	*3956*
and in the market place **e** day with	**Ac 17:17**	*3956*
e nation of mankind to live on all	**Ac 17:26**	*3956*
reasoning in the synagogue **e** Sabbath	**Ac 18:4**	*3956*
testifies to me in **e** city,	**Ac 20:23**	*2596*
this in **e** way and everywhere,	**Ac 24:3**	*3839*
for **e** soul of man who does evil,	**Ro 2:9**	*3956*
Great in **e** respect.	**Ro 3:2**	*3956*
though **e** man *be found* a liar,	**Ro 3:4**	*3956*
Law, so that **e** mouth may be closed	**Ro 3:19**	*3956*
produced in me coveting of **e** kind;	**Ro 7:8**	*3956*
E person is to be in subjection to	**Ro 13:1**	*3956*
another regards **e** day *alike.*	**Ro 14:5**	*3956*
THE LORD, **E** KNEE SHALL BOW TO ME,	**Ro 14:11**	*3956*
AND **E** TONGUE SHALL GIVE PRAISE TO	**Ro 14:11**	*3956*
with all who in **e** place call on	**1Co 1:2**	*3956*
as I teach everywhere in **e** church.	**1Co 4:17**	*3956*
E *other* sin that a man commits is	**1Co 6:18**	*3956*
that Christ is the head of **e** man,	**1Co 11:3**	*3956*
E man who has *something* on his	**1Co 11:4**	*3956*
But **e** woman who has her head	**1Co 11:5**	*3956*
Why are we also in danger **e** hour?	**1Co 15:30**	*3956*
On the first day of **e** week each	**1Co 16:2**	*2596*
the knowledge of Him in **e** place.	**2Co 2:14**	*3956*
commending ourselves to **e** man's	**2Co 4:2**	*3956*
we are afflicted in **e** way,	**2Co 4:8**	*3956*
but we were afflicted on **e** side:	**2Co 7:5**	*3956*
have an abundance for **e** good deed;	**2Co 9:8**	*3956*
destroying speculations and **e** lofty	**2Co 10:5**	*3956*
and *we are* taking **e** thought	**2Co 10:5**	*3956*
in **e** way we have made *this* evident	**2Co 11:6**	*3956*
E FACT IS TO BE CONFIRMED BY THE	**2Co 13:1**	*3956*
e man who receives circumcision,	**Ga 5:3**	*3956*
who has blessed us with **e**	**Eph 1:3**	*3956*
and **e** name that is named,	**Eph 1:21**	*3956*
from whom **e** family in heaven and	**Eph 3:15**	*3956*
about by **e** wind of doctrine,	**Eph 4:14**	*3956*
by what **e** joint supplies,	**Eph 4:16**	*3956*
for the practice of **e** kind of	**Eph 4:19**	*3956*
joy in my **e** prayer for you all,	**Php 1:4**	*3956*
Only that in **e** way, whether in	**Php 1:18**	*3956*
the name which is above **e** name,	**Php 2:9**	*3956*
name of Jesus **E** KNEE WILL BOW,	**Php 2:10**	*3956*
and that **e** tongue will confess	**Php 2:11**	*3956*
in any and **e** circumstance I have	**Php 4:12**	*3956*
Greet **e** saint in Christ Jesus.	**Php 4:21**	*3956*
bearing fruit in **e** good work and	**Col 1:10**	*3956*
admonishing **e** man and teaching	**Col 1:28**	*3956*
teaching **e** man with all wisdom,	**Col 1:28**	*3956*
present **e** man complete in Christ.	**Col 1:28**	*3956*
but also in **e** place your faith	**1Th 1:8**	*3956*
abstain from **e** form of evil.	**1Th 5:22**	*3956*
and fulfill **e** desire for goodness	**2Th 1:11**	*3956*
exalts himself above **e** so-called god	**2Th 2:4**	*3956*
hearts in **e** good work and word.	**2Th 2:17**	*3956*
that you keep away from **e** brother	**2Th 3:6**	*3956*
grant you peace in **e** circumstance.	**2Th 3:16**	*3956*
a distinguishing mark in **e** letter;	**2Th 3:17**	*3956*
I want the men in **e** place to pray,	**1Tm 2:8**	*3956*
devoted herself to **e** good work.	**1Tm 5:10**	*3956*
Master, prepared for **e** good work.	**2Tm 2:21**	*3956*
equipped for **e** good work.	**2Tm 3:17**	*3956*
Make **e** effort to come to me soon;	**2Tm 4:9**	*4704*
will rescue me from **e** evil deed,	**2Tm 4:18**	*3956*
e effort to come before winter.	**2Tm 4:21**	*4704*
in **e** city as I directed you,	**Ti 1:5**	*2596*
of God our Savior in **e** respect.	**Ti 2:10**	*3956*
to redeem us from **e** lawless deed,	**Ti 2:14**	*3956*
to be ready for **e** good deed,	**Ti 3:1**	*3956*
e consideration for all men.	**Ti 3:2**	*3956*
make **e** effort to come to me at	**Ti 3:12**	*4704*
knowledge of **e** good thing which is in	**Phm 1:6**	*3956*
and **e** transgression and	**Heb 2:2**	*3956*
For **e** house is built by someone,	**Heb 3:4**	*3956*
For **e** high priest taken from among	**Heb 5:1**	*3956*
is an end of **e** dispute.	**Heb 6:16**	*3956*
For **e** high priest is appointed to	**Heb 8:3**	*3956*
For when **e** commandment had been	**Heb 9:19**	*3956*
E priest stands daily ministering	**Heb 10:11**	*3956*
us also lay aside **e** encumbrance and	**Heb 12:1**	*3956*
SCOURGES **E** SON WHOM HE RECEIVES."	**Heb 12:6**	*3956*
in **e** good thing to do His will,	**Heb 13:21**	*3956*
E good thing given and every	**Jas 1:17**	*3956*
and **e** perfect gift is from above,	**Jas 1:17**	*3956*
For **e** species of beasts and birds,	**Jas 3:7**	*3956*
is disorder and **e** evil thing.	**Jas 3:16**	*3956*
Lord's sake to **e** human institution,	**1Pe 2:13**	*3956*

Beloved, do not believe **e** spirit, 1Jn 4:1 *3956*
e spirit that confesses that Jesus 1Jn 4:2 *3956*
and **e** spirit that does not confess 1Jn 4:3 *3956*
while I was making **e** effort to Jude 1:3 *3956*
CLOUDS, and **e** eye will see Him, Rv 1:7 *3956*
with Your blood *men* from **e** tribe and Rv 5:9 *3956*
And **e** created thing which is in Rv 5:13 *3956*
and **e** mountain and island were Rv 6:14 *3956*
strong and **e** slave and free man hid Rv 6:15 *3956*
e tribe of the sons of Israel: Rv 7:4 *3956*
from **e** nation and *all* tribes and Rv 7:9 *3956*
wipe **e** tear from their eyes." Rv 7:17 *3956*
to strike the earth with **e** plague, Rv 11:6 *3956*
and authority over **e** tribe and Rv 13:7 *3956*
and to **e** nation and tribe and Rv 14:6 *3956*
e living thing in the sea died. Rv 16:3 *3956*
And **e** island fled away, and the Rv 16:20 *3956*
and a prison of **e** unclean spirit, Rv 18:2 *3956*
of **e** unclean and hateful bird. Rv 18:2 *3956*
and **e** *kind of* citron wood and Rv 18:12 *3956*
of citron wood and **e** article of ivory Rv 18:12 *3956*
e article *made* from very costly wood Rv 18:12 *3956*
And **e** shipmaster and every Rv 18:17 *3956*
and **e** passenger and sailor, Rv 18:17 *3956*
e one *of them* according to their Rv 20:13 *1538*
wipe away **e** tear from their eyes; Rv 21:4 *3956*
with **e** kind of precious stone. Rv 21:19 *3956*
fruit, yielding its fruit **e** month; Rv 22:2 *2596, 1538*
to render to **e** man according to Rv 22:12 *1538*

EVERYDAY
himself in the affairs of **e** life, 2Tm 2:4 *979*

EVERYONE
a man, His hand *will be* against **e**, Gn 16:12 3605
e who hears will laugh with me." Gn 21:6 3605
"Have **e** go out from me." Gn 45:1 3605
what **e** who is numbered shall give: Ex 30:13 3605
"**E** who is numbered, from twenty Ex 30:14 3605
E who profanes it shall surely be Ex 31:14
And **e** who sought the LORD would Ex 33:7 3605
E whose heart stirred him Ex 35:21 3605, 376
and **e** whose spirit moved him came Ex 35:21 3605, 376
E who could make a contribution of Ex 35:24 3605
skill, **e** whose heart stirred him, Ex 36:2 3605
'**E** who eats it will bear his Lv 19:8
e who enters the service to do the Nu 4:30 3605
e who entered the service for work Nu 4:35 3605
e who was serving in the tent of Nu 4:37 3605
e who entered the service for work Nu 4:39 3605
e who was serving in the tent of Nu 4:41 3605
e who entered the service for work Nu 4:43 3605
e who could enter to do the work Nu 4:47 3605
e by his serving or carrying; Nu 4:49 376
every leper and **e** having a discharge Nu 5:2 3605
e who is unclean because of a Nu 5:2 3605
for **e** according to their number. Nu 15:12 259
"**E** who comes near, who comes near Nu 17:13 3605
E of your household who is clean Nu 18:11 3605
e of your household who is clean Nu 18:13 3605
e who comes into the tent and Nu 19:14 3605
e who is in the tent shall be unclean Nu 19:14 3605
come about, that **e** who is bitten, Nu 21:8 3605
Blessed is **e** who blesses you, And Nu 24:9
And cursed is **e** who curses you." Nu 24:9
servants, **e** who is armed for war, Nu 32:27 3605
Reuben, **e** who is armed for battle, Nu 32:29 3605
e shall be put to death for his Dt 24:16 376
"For **e** who does these things, Dt 25:16 3605
e who acts unjustly is an Dt 25:16 3605
E receives of Your words. Dt 33:3
but **e** of whom I say to you, Jg 7:4 3605
"You shall separate **e** who laps Jg 7:5 3605
well as **e** who kneels to drink." Jg 7:5 3605
e did what was right in his own Jg 21:25 376
'**E** who is left in your house will 1Sa 2:36 3605
ears of **e** who hears it will tingle. 1Sa 3:11 3605
E who was in distress, and everyone 1Sa 22:2 3605
distress, and **e** who was in debt, 1Sa 22:2 3605
and **e** who was discontented gathered 1Sa 22:2 3605
"Have **e** go out from me." 2Sa 13:9 3605, 376
So **e** went out from him. 2Sa 13:9 3605, 376
of **e** depends on the man you seek; 2Sa 17:3 3605
e who came by him stood still. 2Sa 20:12 3605
e who passes by will be astonished 1Ki 9:8 3605
He distributed to **e** of Israel, 1Ch 16:3 3605
to **e** a loaf of bread and a portion 1Ch 16:3 376
e who had dedicated *anything,* 1Ch 26:28 3605
make great and to strengthen **e**. 1Ch 29:12 3605
e who passes by it will be 2Ch 7:21 3605
lambs for **e** who *was* unclean, 2Ch 30:17 3605
e who prepares his heart to seek 2Ch 30:19 3605
e who entered the house of the LORD 2Ch 31:16 3605
to **e** genealogically enrolled among the 2Ch 31:19 3605
even **e** whose spirit God had Ezr 1:5 3605
and from **e** who offered a freewill Ezr 3:5 3605
Then **e** who trembled at the words Ezr 9:4 3605
The hand of **e** who suffers will Jb 20:22 3605
And look on **e** who is proud, and Jb 40:11 3605
"Look on **e** who is proud, *and* Jb 40:12 3605
let **e** who is godly pray to You in Ps 32:6 3605
E who swears by Him will glory, Ps 63:11 3605
like them, **E** who trusts in them. Ps 115:8 3605
blessed is **e** who fears the LORD, Ps 128:1 3605
them, *Yes,* **e** who trusts in them. Ps 135:18 3605
ways of **e** who gains by violence; Pr 1:19 3605
E who is proud in heart is an Pr 16:5 3605
But **e** who is hasty *comes* surely to Pr 21:5 3605
Like an archer who wounds **e**, Pr 26:10 3605
to **e** *that* he is a fool. Ec 10:3 3605
E loves a bribe And chases after Is 1:23 3605
Against **e** who is proud and lofty And Is 2:12 3605
And against **e** who is lifted up, Is 2:12 3605
e who is recorded for life in Jerusalem Is 4:3 3605
for **e** that is left within the land Is 7:22 3605
and in their squares **E** is wailing, Is 15:3 3605
e of Moab will wail. Is 16:7 3605
e to whom it is mentioned will be Is 19:17 3605
"**E** will be ashamed because of a Is 30:5 3605
E who is called by My name, And Is 43:7 3605
E who goes out of them will be Jer 5:6 3605
of them, **E** is greedy for gain, Jer 6:13 3605
to the priest **E** deals falsely. Jer 6:13 3605
E turned to his course, Jer 8:6 3605
the greatest **E** is greedy for gain; Jer 8:10 3605
to the priest **E** practices deceit. Jer 8:10 3605
"Let **e** be on guard against his Jer 9:4 376
"**E** deceives his neighbor And does Jer 9:5 376
And **e** her neighbor a dirge. Jer 9:20 802
lent money to me, *Yet* **e** curses me. Jer 15:10 3605
E who passes by it will be Jer 18:16 3605
ears of **e** that hears of it will tingle. Jer 19:3 3605
e who passes by it will be Jer 19:8 3605
laughingstock all day long; **E** mocks Jer 20:7 3605
And as for **e** who walks in the Jer 23:17 3605
'Turn now **e** from his evil way and Jer 25:5 376
and **e** will turn from his evil way, Jer 26:3 376
and refresh **e** who languishes." Jer 31:25 3605
e will die for his own iniquity; Jer 31:30 376
giving to **e** according to his ways Jer 32:19 376
and **e** will turn from his evil way, Jer 36:7 376
e who passes by it will be Jer 49:17 3605
E who passes by Babylon will be Jer 50:13 3605
e who quotes proverbs will quote Ezk 16:44 3605
"Go, serve **e** his idols; Ezk 20:39 376
in the sight of **e** who passes by. Ezk 36:34 3605
for **e** who goes astray or is naive; Ezk 45:20 376
e who is found written in the Da 12:1 3605
And **e** who lives in it languishes Hos 4:3 3605
They march **e** in his path; Jl 2:8 1397
And **e** who dwells in it mourn? Am 8:8 3605
So that **e** may be cut off Ob 1:9 376
down to Him, **e** from his *own* place. Zph 2:11 376
E who passes by her will hiss *And* Zph 2:15 3605
down, **e** by the sword of another.' Hg 2:22 376
surely **e** who steals will be purged Zch 5:3 3605
and **e** who swears will be purged Zch 5:3 3605
cut off from the tents of Jacob **e** Mal 2:12
"**E** who does evil is good in the Mal 2:17 3605
e who is angry with his brother shall Mt 5:22 *3956*
that **e** who looks at a woman with Mt 5:28 *3956*
you that **e** who divorces his wife, Mt 5:32 *3956*
"For **e** who asks receives, and he Mt 7:8 *3956*
"Not **e** who says to Me, Mt 7:21 *3956*
e who hears these words of Mine and Mt 7:24 *3956*
"**E** who hears these words of Mine Mt 7:26 *3956*
"Therefore **e** who confesses Me before Mt 10:32 *3956*
"And **e** who has left houses or Mt 19:29 *3956*
to **e** who has, *more* shall be given, Mt 25:29 *3956*
"**E** is looking for You." Mk 1:37 *3956*
pallet and went out in the sight of **e**, Mk 2:12 *3956*
things Jesus had done for him; and **e** Mk 5:20 *3956*
"For **e** will be salted with fire. Mk 9:49 *3956*
for **e** considered John to have been a Mk 11:32 *537a*
And **e** was on his way to register for Lk 2:3 *3956*
"Give to **e** who asks of you, and Lk 6:30 *3956*
but **e**, after he has been fully Lk 6:40 *3956*
"**E** who comes to Me and hears My Lk 6:47 *3956*
But while **e** was marveling at all Lk 9:43 *3956*
forgive **e** who is indebted to us. Lk 11:4 *3956*
"For **e** who asks, receives; Lk 11:10 *3956*
"I say to you, **e** who confesses Me before men, Lk 12:8 *3956*
"And **e** who speaks a word Lk 12:10 *3956*
to us, or to **e** *else* as well?" Lk 12:41 *3956*
From **e** who has been given much, Lk 12:48 *3956*
"For **e** who exalts himself will Lk 14:11 *3956*
"Blessed is **e** who will eat bread Lk 14:15 *3748*
and **e** is forcing his way into it. Lk 16:16 *3956*
"**E** who divorces his wife and Lk 16:18 *3956*
for **e** who exalts himself will be Lk 18:14 *3956*
to **e** who has, more shall be given, Lk 19:26 *3956*
"**E** who falls on that stone will Lk 20:18 *3956*
is **e** who is born of the Spirit." Jn 3:8 *3956*
e who does evil hates the Light, Jn 3:20 *3956*
"**E** who drinks of this water will Jn 4:13 *3956*
them, for **e** to receive a little." Jn 6:7 *1538*
that **e** who beholds the Son and Jn 6:40 *3956*
E who has heard and learned from Jn 6:45 *3956*
[**E** went to his home. Jn 7:53 *1538*
e who commits sin is the slave of Jn 8:34 *3956*
and **e** who lives and believes in Me Jn 11:26 *3956*
that **e** who believes in Me will not Jn 12:46 *3956*
but an hour is coming for **e** who Jn 16:2 *3956*
E who is of the truth hears My Jn 18:37 *3956*
e who makes himself out *to be* a Jn 19:12 *3956*
THAT **E** WHO CALLS ON THE NAME OF Ac 2:21 *3956*
E kept feeling a sense of awe; Ac 2:43 *3956*
so that **e** on whom I lay my hands Ac 8:19 *1437*
through His name **e** who believes in Ac 10:43 *3956*
and through Him **e** who believes is Ac 13:39 *3956*
burning them in the sight of **e**; Ac 19:19 *3956*
for salvation to **e** who believes, Ro 1:16 *3956*
Therefore you have no excuse, **e** of Ro 2:1 *444, 3956*
but glory and honor and peace to **e** Ro 2:10 *3956*
righteousness to **e** who believes. Ro 10:4 *3956*
the grace given to me I say to **e** Ro 12:3 *3956*
E who competes in the games exercises 1Co 9:25 *3956*
and to **e** who helps in the work and 1Co 16:16 *3956*
"CURSED IS **E** WHO DOES NOT ABIDE Ga 3:10 *3956*
"CURSED IS **E** WHO HANGS ON A TREE" Ga 3:13 *3956*
But the Scripture has shut up **e** under Ga 3:22 *3956*
praetorian guard and to **e** else, Php 1:13 *3956*
be patient with **e**. 1Th 5:14 *3956*
"**E** who names the name of the Lord is 2Tm 2:19 *3956*
of God He might taste death for **e**. Heb 2:9 *3956*
For **e** who partakes *only* of milk is Heb 5:13 *3956*
NOT TEACH **E** HIS FELLOW CITIZEN, Heb 8:11 *1538*
FELLOW CITIZEN, AND **E** HIS BROTHER, Heb 8:11 *1538*
But **e** must be quick to hear, slow Jas 1:19 *3956*
ready to make a defense to **e** who asks 1Pe 3:15 *3956*
you know that **e** also who practices 1Jn 2:29 *3956*
And **e** who has this hope *fixed* on 1Jn 3:3 *3956*
E who practices sin also practices 1Jn 3:4 *3956*
E who hates his brother is a 1Jn 3:15 *3956*
and **e** who loves is born of God and 1Jn 4:7 *3956*
received a *good* testimony from **e**, 3Jn 1:12 *3956*
e whose name has not been written Rv 13:8
e who loves and practices lying. Rv 22:15 *3956*
I testify to **e** who hears the words Rv 22:18 *3956*

EVERYONE'S
And **e** hand *will be* against him; Gn 16:12 3605
E head is bald *and* every beard is Is 15:2 3605
And I will bring sackcloth on **e** Am 8:10 3605
and **e** chains were unfastened. Ac 16:26 *3956*

EVERYTHING
and **e** that creeps on the ground Gn 1:25 3605
e that is on the earth shall Gn 6:17 3605
and **e** that creeps on the ground, Gn 7:8 3605
bird, **e** that moves on the earth, Gn 8:19 3605
with **e** that creeps on the ground, Gn 9:2 3605
left **e** he owned in Joseph's charge; Gn 39:6 3605
e which I have said to you, Ex 23:13 3605
and he commanded them *to do* **e** that Ex 34:32 3605
and **e** prepared in a pan or on a Lv 7:9 3605
'**E**, moreover, on which part of Lv 11:35 3605
and **e** that swarms on the earth, Lv 11:46 3605
so that **e** in the house need not Lv 14:36 3605
and **e** on which he sits becomes Lv 15:4 3605, 3627
'**E** also on which she lies during Lv 15:20 3605
and **e** on which she sits shall be Lv 15:20 3605
priesthood for **e** concerning the altar Nu 18:7 3605
e by which she has bound herself, Nu 30:9 3605
e that can stand the fire, you Nu 31:23 3605
but man lives by **e** that proceeds Dt 8:3 3605
until **e** was completed that the LORD Jos 4:10 3605
utterly destroyed **e** in the city, Jos 6:21 3605
him **e** and hid nothing from him. 1Sa 3:18 3605
but **e** despised and worthless, that 1Sa 15:9 3605, 4399
just as **e** the king did pleased all 2Sa 3:36 3605, 834
shall send me **e** that you hear." 2Sa 15:36 3605
"**E**, O king, Araunah gives to the 2Sa 24:23 3605
you were afflicted in **e** with which my 1Ki 2:26 3605
dominion over **e** west of the River, 1Ki 4:24 3605
of the king's house, and he took **e**, 1Ki 14:26 3605
indeed **e** that is in the heavens 1Ch 29:11 3605
He took **e**; he even took the golden 2Ch 12:9 3605
"**E** that was entrusted to your 2Ch 34:16 3605
E *was* numbered and weighed, and Ezr 8:34 3605
Thus I purified them from **e** Ne 13:30 3605
e that had happened to him. Es 6:13 3605
low and like **e** gathered up; Jb 24:24 3605
And sees **e** under the heavens. Jb 28:24 3605
"He looks on **e** that is high; Jb 41:34 3605
bare; And in His temple **e** says, Ps 29:9 3605
And **e** that moves in the field is Ps 50:11 2123a
The seas and **e** that moves in them. Ps 69:34 3605
damaged **e** within the sanctuary. Ps 74:3 3605
all *Your* precepts concerning **e**, Ps 119:128 3605
Let **e** that has breath praise the Ps 150:6 3605
The naive believes **e**, Pr 14:15 3605
has made **e** for its own purpose, Pr 16:4 3605
because **e** is futility and striving Ec 2:17 3605
There is an appointed time for **e**. Ec 3:1 3605
made **e** appropriate in its time. Ec 3:11 3605
e God does will remain forever; Ec 3:14 3605, 834
I have seen **e** during my lifetime Ec 7:15 3605
and money is the answer to **e**. Ec 10:19 3605
E that is to come *will be* futility. Ec 11:8 3605
to judgment, **e** which is hidden, Ec 12:14 3605
we have lacked **e** and have met our Jer 44:18 3605
the trumpet and made **e** ready, Ezk 7:14 3605
e which I have brought upon it. Ezk 14:22 3605
so **e** will live where the river Ezk 47:9 3605
e between the border of Judah Ezk 48:22
And twist **e** that is straight, Mi 3:9 3605
"In **e**, therefore, treat people Mt 7:12 *3956*
went to the city and reported **e**, Mt 8:33 *3956*
"Do you not understand that **e** Mt 15:17 *3956*
with me and I will repay you **e**.' Mt 18:26 *3956*
we have left **e** and followed You; Mt 19:27 *3956*
are *all* butchered and **e** is ready; Mt 22:4 *3956*
both by the altar and by **e** on it. Mt 23:20 *3956*
who are outside get **e** in parables, Mk 4:11 *3956*
but He was explaining **e** privately Mk 4:34 *3956*
and *began to* see **e** clearly. Mk 8:25 *537a*
we have left **e** and followed You." Mk 10:28 *3956*
and after looking around at **e**, He Mk 11:11 *3956*
I have told you **e** in advance. Mk 13:23 *3956*
e carefully from the beginning, Lk 1:3 *3956*

When they had performed **e** **Lk 2:39** *3956*
they left **e** and followed Him. **Lk 5:11** *3956*
And he left **e** behind, and got up **Lk 5:28** *3956*
'Come; for **e** is ready now.' **Lk 14:17** *3956*
the younger son gathered **e** **Lk 15:13** *3956*
"Now when he had spent **e**, **Lk 15:14** *3956*
And they left and found **e** just as **Lk 22:13** *3956*
yet **e** John said about this man was **Jn 10:41** *3956*
e You have given Me is from You; **Jn 17:7** *3956*
GIVE HEED to **e** He says to you. **Ac 3:22** *3956*
after he had explained **e** to them, **Ac 10:8** *537a*
and **e** was drawn back up into the **Ac 11:10** *537a*
"In **e** I showed you that by **Ac 20:35** *3956*
believing **e** that is in accordance **Ac 24:14** *3956*
in **e** you were enriched in Him, **1Co 1:5** *3956*
you because you remember me in **e** and **1Co 11:2** *3956*
but in **e** commending ourselves as **2Co 6:4** *3956*
In **e** you demonstrated yourselves **2Co 7:11** *3956*
in **e** I have confidence in you. **2Co 7:16** *3956*
But just as you abound in **e**, **2Co 8:7** *3956*
having all sufficiency in **e**, **2Co 9:8** *3956*
enriched in **e** for all liberality, **2Co 9:11** *3956*
and in **e** I kept myself from being **2Co 11:9** *3956*
a slave although he is owner of **e**, **Ga 4:1** *3956*
e that becomes visible is light. **Eph 5:13** *3956*
to be to their husbands in **e**. **Eph 5:24** *3956*
the evil day, and having done **e**, **Eph 6:13** *537a*
Lord, will make **e** known to you. **Eph 6:21** *3956*
but in **e** by prayer and **Php 4:6** *3956*
But I have received **e** in full and **Php 4:18** *3956*
come to have first place in **e**. **Col 1:18** *3956*
in **e** give thanks; for this is God's **1Th 5:18** *3956*
But examine **e** *carefully;* **1Th 5:21** *3956*
For **e** created by God is good, and **1Tm 4:4** *3956*
will give you understanding in **e**. **2Tm 2:7** *3956*
subject to their own masters in **e**, **Ti 2:9** *3956*
His divine power has granted to us **e** **2Pe 1:3** *3956*

EVERYWHERE
so that all the high mountains **e** **Gn 7:19** 3605
the Jordan, that it was well watered **e** **Gn 13:10** 3605
e we go, say of me, **Gn 20:13** 413, 3605, 4725, 834, 8033
the peoples **e** under the heavens, **Dt 2:25** 3605
let us send **e** to our kinsmen who **1Ch 13:2** 6555
am a youth,' Because **e** I send you, **Jer 1:7** 5921, 3605, 834, 7971
streets there is lamentation **e**; **Jer 48:38** 3605
the news about Him spread **e** **Mk 1:28** *3837*
they were coming to Him from **e**. **Mk 1:45** *3840*
And they went out and preached **e**, **Mk 16:20** *3837*
the gospel and healing **e**. **Lk 9:6** *3837*
proclaim **e** the kingdom of God." **Lk 9:60** *1229*
to men that all *people* **e** should repent, **Ac 17:30** *3837*
to all men **e** against our people and **Ac 21:28** *3836a*
this in every way and **e**, **Ac 24:3** *3837*
us that it is spoken against **e**." **Ac 28:22** *3837*
just as I teach **e** in every church. **1Co 4:17** *3837*

EVI
E and Rekem and Zur and Hur and **Nu 31:8** 189
E and Rekem and Zur and Hur and **Jos 13:21** 189

EVICT
"The women of My people you **e**, **Mi 2:9** 1644

EVIDENCE
to pieces, let him bring it as **e**; **Ex 22:13** 5707
to death at the **e** of witnesses, **Nu 35:30** 6310
"On the **e** of two witnesses or **Dt 17:6** 6310
to death on the **e** of one witness. **Dt 17:6** 6310
on the **e** of two or three witnesses **Dt 19:15** 6310
shall take and bring out the **e** of **Dt 22:15**
the **e** of my daughter's virginity.' **Dt 22:17** 1331
e of their fathers' households and **Ezr 2:59** 5046
find no ground of accusation or **e** **Da 6:4**
explaining and giving **e** that the **Ac 17:3** *3908*

EVIDENT
then the tares became **e** also. **Mt 13:26** *5316*
is hidden that will not become **e**, **Lk 8:17** *5318*
known about God is **e** within them; **Ro 1:19** *5318*
for God made it **e** to them. **Ro 1:19** *5319*
each man's work will become **e**; **1Co 3:13** *5318*
may become **e** among you. **1Co 11:19** *5318*
it is **e** that He is excepted who **1Co 15:27** *1212*
made *this* **e** to you in all things. **2Co 11:6** *5319*
by the Law before God is **e**; **Ga 3:11** *1212*
Now the deeds of the flesh are **e**, **Ga 5:19** *5318*
your progress will be **e** to all. **1Tm 4:15** *5318*
The sins of some men are quite **e**, **1Tm 5:24** *4271*
deeds that are good are quite **e**, **1Tm 5:25** *4271*
For it is **e** that our Lord was **Heb 7:14** *4271*

EVIL
of the knowledge of good and **e**. **Gn 2:9** 7451b
of good and **e** you shall not eat, **Gn 2:17** 7451b
be like God, knowing good and **e**." **Gn 3:5** 7451b
one of Us, knowing good and **e**; **Gn 3:22** 7451b
his heart was only **e** continually. **Gn 6:5** 7451a
of man's heart is **e** from his youth; **Gn 8:21** 7451a
was **e** in the sight of the LORD, **Gn 38:7** 7451a
How then could I do this great **e** and **Gn 39:9** 7463a
'Why have you repaid **e** for good? **Gn 44:4** 7463a
e that would overtake my father?" **Gn 44:34** 7451b
who has redeemed me from all **e**, **Gn 48:16** 7451b
for you, you meant **e** against me, **Gn 50:20** 7463a
Take heed, for **e** is in your mind. **Ex 10:10** 7463a
not follow the masses in doing **e**, **Ex 23:2** 7463a
'With **e** *intent* He brought them out **Ex 32:12** 7463a
that they are prone to **e**. **Ex 32:22** 7451b
his lips to do **e** or to do good, **Lv 5:4** 7489a
shall I bear with this **e** congregation **Nu 14:27** 7451a
this I will do to all this **e** congregation **Nu 14:35** 7451a
had done **e** in the sight of the LORD **Nu 32:13** 7451a
of these men, this **e** generation, **Dt 1:35** 7451a
have no knowledge of good or **e**, **Dt 1:39** 7451b
and do that which is **e** in the **Dt 4:25** 7451a
in doing what was **e** in the sight of the **Dt 9:18** 7451a
shall purge the **e** from among you. **Dt 13:5** 7451b
does what is **e** in the sight of the LORD **Dt 17:2** 7451a
woman who has done this **e** deed to **Dt 17:5** 7451a
shall purge the **e** from your midst. **Dt 17:7** 7451b
you shall purge the **e** from Israel. **Dt 17:12** 7451b
shall purge the **e** from among you. **Dt 19:19** 7451b
do such an **e** thing among you. **Dt 19:20** 7451a
remove the **e** from your midst, **Dt 21:21** 7451b
shall purge the **e** from among you. **Dt 22:21** 7451b
you shall purge the **e** from Israel. **Dt 22:22** 7451b
shall purge the **e** from among you. **Dt 22:24** 7451b
keep yourself from every **e** thing. **Dt 23:9** 7451a
shall purge the **e** from among you. **Dt 24:7** 7451b
on account of the **e** of your deeds, **Dt 28:20** 7455
of all the **e** which they will do, **Dt 31:18** 7463a
and **e** will befall you in the **Dt 31:29** 7463a
is **e** in the sight of the LORD, **Dt 31:29** 7451a
did **e** in the sight of the LORD and **Jg 2:11** 7451a
the LORD was against them for **e**, **Jg 2:15** 7463a
was **e** in the sight of the LORD, **Jg 3:7** 7451a
did **e** in the sight of the LORD. **Jg 3:12** 7451a
done **e** in the sight of the LORD. **Jg 3:12** 7451a
did **e** in the sight of the LORD, **Jg 4:1** 7451a
was **e** in the sight of the LORD; **Jg 6:1** 7451a
Then God sent an **e** spirit between **Jg 9:23** 7451a
did **e** in the sight of the LORD, **Jg 10:6** 7451a
did **e** in the sight of the LORD, **Jg 13:1** 7451a
the **e** things that I hear from all **1Sa 2:23** 7451a
then He has done us this great **e**. **1Sa 6:9** 7463a
we have added to all our sins *this* **e** **1Sa 12:19** 7463a
You have committed all this **e**, **1Sa 12:20** 7463a
was **e** in the sight of the LORD?" **1Sa 15:19** 7451a
and an **e** spirit from the LORD **1Sa 16:14** 7451a
an **e** spirit from God is **1Sa 16:15** 7451a
the **e** spirit from God is on you, **1Sa 16:16** 7451a
So it came about whenever the **e** **1Sa 16:23**
e spirit would depart from him. **1Sa 16:23** 7451a
e spirit from God came mightily upon **1Sa 18:10** 7451a
Now there was an **e** spirit from the **1Sa 19:9** 7451a
know that he has decided on **e**. **1Sa 20:7** 7463a
that **e** has been decided by my father **1Sa 20:9** 7463a
Saul was plotting **e** against him; **1Sa 23:9** 7463a
is no **e** or rebellion in my hands, **1Sa 24:11** 7463a
was harsh and **e** in *his* dealings, **1Sa 25:3** 7451b
for **e** is plotted against our **1Sa 25:17** 7463a
and he has returned me **e** for good. **1Sa 25:21** 7463a
those who seek **e** against my lord, **1Sa 25:26** 7463a
and **e** will not be found in you **1Sa 25:28** 7463a
has kept back His servant from **e**. **1Sa 25:39** 7463a
Or what **e** is in my hand? **1Sa 26:18** 7463a
for I have not found **e** in you from **1Sa 29:6** 7463a
the evildoer according to his **e**." **2Sa 3:39** 7463a
was **e** in the sight of the LORD. **2Sa 11:27** 7489a
the LORD by doing **e** in His sight? **2Sa 12:9** 7451a
I will raise up **e** against you from **2Sa 12:11** 7463a
the king to discern good and **e**. **2Sa 14:17** 7451b
you are *taken* in your own **e**, **2Sa 16:8** 7463a
all who rise up against you for **e**, **2Sa 18:32** 7463a
worse for you than all the **e** that has **2Sa 19:7** 7463a
"You know all the **e** which you **1Ki 2:44** 7463a
return your **e** on your own head. **1Ki 2:44** 7463a
to discern between good and **e**. **1Ki 3:9** 7451b
was **e** in the sight of the LORD, **1Ki 11:6** 7451a
along with the **e** that Hadad *did;* **1Ki 11:25** 7463a
did not return from his **e** way, **1Ki 13:33** 7451a
have done more **e** than all who were **1Ki 14:9** 7489a
did **e** in the sight of the LORD, **1Ki 14:22** 7451a
He did **e** in the sight of the LORD, **1Ki 15:26** 7451a
He did **e** in the sight of the LORD, **1Ki 15:34** 7451a
both because of all the **e** which he **1Ki 16:7** 7463a
doing **e** in the sight of the LORD, **1Ki 16:19** 7451a
did **e** in the sight of the LORD, **1Ki 16:25** 7451a
Ahab the son of Omri did **e** in **1Ki 16:30** 7451a
to do **e** in the sight of the LORD. **1Ki 21:20** 7451a
"Behold, I will bring **e** upon you, **1Ki 21:21** 7463a
to do **e** in the sight of the LORD, **1Ki 21:25** 7451a
will not bring the **e** in his days, **1Ki 21:29** 7463a
but I will bring the **e** upon his **1Ki 21:29** 7463a
good concerning me, but **e**. **1Ki 22:8** 7451b
good concerning me, but **e**?" **1Ki 22:18** 7451b
He did **e** in the sight of the **1Ki 22:52** 7451a
He did **e** in the sight of the LORD, **2Ki 3:2** 7451a
"Behold, this **e** is from the LORD; **2Ki 6:33** 7463a
"Because I know the **e** that you **2Ki 8:12** 7463a
he did **e** in the sight of the LORD. **2Ki 8:18** 7451a
did **e** in the sight of the LORD, **2Ki 8:27** 7451a
He did **e** in the sight of the LORD, **2Ki 13:2** 7451a
He did **e** in the sight of the LORD; **2Ki 13:11** 7451a
He did **e** in the sight of the LORD; **2Ki 14:24** 7451a
He did **e** in the sight of the LORD, **2Ki 15:9** 7451a
He did **e** in the sight of the LORD; **2Ki 15:18** 7451a
He did **e** in the sight of the LORD; **2Ki 15:24** 7451a
He did **e** in the sight of the LORD; **2Ki 15:28** 7451a
He did **e** in the sight of the LORD, **2Ki 17:2** 7451a
did **e** things provoking the LORD. **2Ki 17:11** 7451a
e ways and keep My commandments, **2Ki 17:13** 7451a
to do **e** in the sight of the LORD, **2Ki 17:17** 7451a
He did **e** in the sight of the LORD, **2Ki 21:2** 7451a
He did much **e** in the sight of the **2Ki 21:6** 7451a
and Manasseh seduced them to do **e** **2Ki 21:9** 7451b
they have done **e** in My sight, **2Ki 21:15** 7451b
doing **e** in the sight of the LORD. **2Ki 21:16** 7451a
He did **e** in the sight of the LORD, **2Ki 21:20** 7451a
I bring **e** on this place and on its **2Ki 22:16** 7463a
your eyes will not see all the **e** **2Ki 22:20** 7463a
He did **e** in the sight of the LORD, **2Ki 23:32** 7451a
He did **e** in the sight of the LORD, **2Ki 23:37** 7451a
He did **e** in the sight of the LORD, **2Ki 24:9** 7451a
He did **e** in the sight of the LORD, **2Ki 24:19** 7451a
He did **e** because he did not **2Ch 12:14** 7451b
good concerning me but always **e**. **2Ch 18:7** 7463a
good concerning me, but **e**?" **2Ch 18:17** 7463a
'Should **e** come upon us, the sword, **2Ch 20:9** 7463a
he did **e** in the sight of the LORD. **2Ch 21:6** 7451a
He did **e** in the sight of the **2Ch 22:4** 7451a
have been unfaithful and have done **e** **2Ch 29:6** 7451a
He did **e** in the sight of the **2Ch 33:2** 7451a
much **e** in the sight of the LORD, **2Ch 33:6** 7451a
to do more **e** than the nations whom **2Ch 33:9** 7451b
He did **e** in the sight of the **2Ch 33:22** 7451a
I am bringing **e** on this place and **2Ch 34:24** 7463a
eyes will not see all the **e** which I will **2Ch 34:28** 7463a
and he did **e** in the sight of the **2Ch 36:5** 7451a
he did **e** in the sight of the LORD. **2Ch 36:9** 7451a
He did **e** in the sight of the **2Ch 36:12** 7451a
the rebellious and **e** city and **Ezr 4:12** 873
our **e** deeds and our great guilt, **Ezr 9:13** 7451a
that they might have an **e** report **Ne 6:13** 7451a
they did **e** again before You; **Ne 9:28** 7451b
You or turn from their **e** deeds. **Ne 9:35** 7451a
e that Eliashib had done for Tobiah, **Ne 13:7** 7463a
is this **e** thing you are doing, **Ne 13:17** 7451a
you have committed all this great **e** **Ne 13:27** 7463a
and implored him to avert the **e** **Es 8:3** 7463a
God and turning away from **e**. **Jb 1:1** 7451b
God and turning away from **e**." **Jb 1:8** 7451b
God and turning away from **e**. **Jb 2:3** 7451b
in seven **e** will not touch you. **Jb 5:19** 7451b
"Though **e** is sweet in his mouth **Jb 20:12** 7463a
to depart from **e** is understanding." **Jb 28:28** 7451b
"When I expected good, then **e** came; **Jb 30:26** 7451b
Or exulted when **e** befell him? **Jb 31:29** 7451b
Because of the pride of **e** men. **Jb 35:12** 7451a
commands that they return from **e**. **Jb 36:10** 205
"Be careful, do not turn to **e**, **Jb 36:21** 205
No **e** dwells with You. **Ps 5:4** 7451b
If I have rewarded **e** to my friend, **Ps 7:4** 7451b
e of the wicked come to an end, **Ps 7:9** 7451b
Nor does **e** to his neighbor, **Ps 15:3** 7463a
they intended **e** against You **Ps 21:11** 7463a
the shadow of death, I fear no **e**, **Ps 23:4** 7451b
While **e** is in their hearts. **Ps 28:3** 7463a
to the **e** of their practices; **Ps 28:4** 7455
Keep your tongue from **e** And **Ps 34:13** 7451b
Depart from **e** and do good; **Ps 34:14** 7451b
E shall slay the wicked, **Ps 34:21** 7463a
who devise **e** against me. **Ps 35:4** 7463a
They repay me **e** for good, *To* the **Ps 35:12** 7463a
He does not despise **e**. **Ps 36:4** 7451b
not be ashamed in the time of **e**, **Ps 37:19** 7463a
Depart from **e** and do good, So you **Ps 37:27** 7451b
And those who repay **e** for good, **Ps 38:20** 7463a
My enemies speak **e** against me, **Ps 41:5** 7451b
"You let your mouth loose in **e** And **Ps 50:19** 7463a
And done what is **e** in Your sight, **Ps 51:4** 7451a
Why do you boast in **e**, **Ps 52:1** 7463a
You love **e** more than good, **Ps 52:3** 7451b
riches *And* was strong in his **e** **Ps 52:7**
will recompense the **e** to my foes; **Ps 54:5** 7451b
Sheol, For **e** is in their dwelling, **Ps 55:15** 7451a
thoughts are against me for **e**. **Ps 56:5** 7451b
fast to themselves an **e** purpose; **Ps 64:5** 7451a
us, *And* the years we have seen **e**. **Ps 90:15** 7463a
No **e** will befall you, Nor will any **Ps 91:10** 7463a
And will destroy them in their **e**; **Ps 94:23** 7451a
Hate **e**, you who love the LORD, Who **Ps 97:10** 7451b
And *yet* an avenger of their **e** **Ps 99:8**
I will know no **e**. **Ps 101:4** 7451b
they have repaid me **e** for good And **Ps 109:5** 7463a
those who speak **e** against my soul. **Ps 109:20** 7451b
He will not fear **e** tidings; **Ps 112:7** 7451a
my feet from every **e** way, **Ps 119:101** 7451b
LORD will protect you from all **e**; **Ps 121:7** 7451b
Rescue me, O LORD, from **e** men; **Ps 140:1** 7451a
devise **e** things in *their* hearts; **Ps 140:2** 7451a
Do not promote his **e** device, **Ps 140:8**
e hunt the violent man **Ps 140:11** 7451b
incline my heart to any **e** thing, **Ps 141:4** 7451a
His servant from the **e** sword. **Ps 144:10** 7451a
For their feet run to **e** And **Pr 1:16** 7451b
be at ease from the dread of **e**." **Pr 1:33** 7463a
To deliver you from the way of **e**, **Pr 2:12** 7451b
Who delight in doing **e** And **Pr 2:14** 7451b
rejoice in the perversity of **e**; **Pr 2:14** 7451b
the LORD and turn away from **e**. **Pr 3:7** 7451b
not proceed in the way of **e** men. **Pr 4:14** 7451a
cannot sleep unless they do **e**; **Pr 4:16** 7489a
Turn your foot from **e**. **Pr 4:27** 7451b
his heart continually devises **e**, **Pr 6:14** 7451b
plans, Feet that run rapidly to **e**, **Pr 6:18** 7463a
To keep you from the **e** woman, **Pr 6:24** 7451b
"The fear of the LORD is to hate **e**; **Pr 8:13** 7451b
Pride and arrogance and the **e** way And **Pr 8:13** 7451b
And he who pursues **e** *will bring* **Pr 11:19** 7463a
the **e** man will not go unpunished, **Pr 11:21** 7451a
But he who seeks **e**, **Pr 11:27** 7463a
e will come to him. **Pr 11:27**
will condemn a man who devises **e**. **Pr 12:2** 4209
wicked man desires the booty of **e** men, **Pr 12:12** 7451a
An **e** man is ensnared by the **Pr 12:13** 7451a
the heart of those who devise **e**, **Pr 12:20** 7451b
to fools to turn away from **e**. **Pr 13:19** 7451b
is cautious and turns away from **e**, **Pr 14:16** 7451b

And a man of **e** devices is hated. Pr 14:17 4209
e will bow down before the good, Pr 14:19 7451a
they not go astray who devise **e**? Pr 14:22 7451b
Watching the **e** and the good. Pr 15:3 7451a
E plans are an abomination to the Pr 15:26 7451b
of the wicked pours out **e** things. Pr 15:28 7451a
Even the wicked for the day of **e**. Pr 16:4 7463a
of the LORD one keeps away from **e**. Pr 16:6 7451b
the upright is to depart from **e**; Pr 16:17 7451b
A worthless man digs up **e**, Pr 16:27 7463a
his lips brings **e** to pass. Pr 16:30 7463a
A rebellious man seeks only **e**, Pr 17:11 7451b
He who returns **e** for good, Evil Pr 17:13 7463a
E will not depart from his house. Pr 17:13 7463a
in his language falls into **e**. Pr 17:20 7463a
sleep satisfied, untouched by **e**. Pr 19:23 7451b
Disperses all **e** with his eyes. Pr 20:8 7451b
"I will repay **e**"; Pr 20:22 7451b
Stripes that wound scour away **e**, Pr 20:30 7451b
The soul of the wicked desires **e**; Pr 21:10 7451b
when he brings it with **e** intent! Pr 21:27 2154
sees the **e** and hides himself, Pr 22:3 7463a
Do not be envious of **e** men, Pr 24:1 7463a
One who plans to do **e**, Pr 24:8 7489a
will be no future for the **e** man; Pr 24:20 7451a
And the **e** report about you will Pr 25:10 1681
man sees **e** *and* hides himself, Pr 27:12 7463a
E men do not understand justice, Pr 28:5 7451b
leads the upright astray in an **e** way Pr 28:10 7451b
an **e** eye hastens after wealth And Pr 28:22 7451a
an **e** man is ensnared, Pr 29:6 7451b
yourself Or if you have plotted **e**, Pr 30:32 7451b
not **e** All the days of her life. Pr 31:12 7451b
This too is vanity and a great **e**. Ec 2:21 7463a
who has never seen the **e** activity Ec 4:3 7451a
they do not know they are doing **e**. Ec 5:1 7451a
There is a grievous **e** *which* I have Ec 5:13 7463a
This also is a grievous **e** Ec 5:16 7463a
There is an **e** which I have seen Ec 6:1 7463a
and to know the **e** of folly and the Ec 7:25 7562
Do not join in an **e** matter, Ec 8:3 7451a
and **e** will not deliver those who Ec 8:8 7562
an **e** deed is not executed quickly, Ec 8:11 7451a
them are given fully to do **e**. Ec 8:11 7451a
Although a sinner does **e** a hundred Ec 8:12 7451a
But it will not be well for the **e** Ec 8:13 7563
there are **e** men to whom it happens Ec 8:14 7563
This is an **e** in all that is done Ec 9:3 7451a
of the sons of men are full of **e** and Ec 9:3 7451b
sons of men are ensnared at an **e** time Ec 9:12 7451a
is an **e** I have seen under the sun, Ec 10:5 7463a
before the **e** days come and the Ec 12:1 7463a
hidden, whether it is good or **e**. Ec 12:14 7451a
the **e** of your deeds from My sight. Is 1:16 7455
deeds from My sight. Cease to do **e**, Is 1:16 7489a
they have brought **e** on themselves. Is 3:9 7463a
Woe to those who call **e** good, Is 5:20 7451b
who call evil good, and good **e**; Is 5:20 7451b
has planned **e** against you, Is 7:5 7463a
to refuse **e** and choose good, Is 7:15 7451b
to refuse **e** and choose good, Is 7:16 7451b
Woe to those who enact **e** statutes And Is 10:1 205
I will punish the world for its **e** And Is 13:11 7463a
intent on doing **e** will be cut off; Is 29:20 205
As for a rogue, his weapons are **e**; Is 32:7 7451a
his eyes from looking upon **e**; Is 33:15 7451b
Indeed, do good or **e**, Is 41:23 7489a
"But **e** will come on you Which you Is 47:11 7463a
keeps his hand from doing any **e**." Is 56:2 7451a
man is taken away from **e**, Is 57:1 7463a
Their feet run to **e**, Is 59:7 7451b
aside from **e** makes himself a prey. Is 59:15 7451b
And you did **e** in My sight And Is 65:12 7451a
They will do no **e** or harm in all Is 65:25 7489a
And they did **e** in My sight And Is 66:4 7451a
"Out of the north the **e** will Jer 1:14 7463a
E came upon them," Jer 2:3 7463a
Know therefore and see that it is **e** Jer 2:19 7451a
spoken And have done **e** things, Jer 3:5 7451a
the stubbornness of their **e** heart. Jer 3:17 7451a
Because of the **e** of your deeds." Jer 4:4 7455
I am bringing **e** from the north, Jer 4:6 7463a
Wash your heart from **e**, Jer 4:14 7463a
This is your **e**. How bitter! Jer 4:18 7463a
They are shrewd to do **e**, Jer 4:22 7489a
For **e** looks down from the north, Jer 6:1 7463a
the stubbornness of their **e** heart, Jer 7:24 7451a
did more **e** than their fathers. Jer 7:26 7489a
that which is **e** in My sight," Jer 7:30 7451a
that remains of this **e** family, Jer 8:3 7451a
For they proceed from **e** to evil, Jer 9:3 7463a
For they proceed from evil to **e**, Jer 9:3 7463a
the stubbornness of his **e** heart; Jer 11:8 7451a
has pronounced **e** against you Jer 11:17 7463a
because of the **e** of the house of Israel Jer 11:17 7463a
good Who are accustomed to doing **e**. Jer 13:23 7489a
'You too have done **e**, Jer 16:12 7451a
stubbornness of his own **e** heart, Jer 16:12 7451a
I have spoken turns from its **e**, Jer 18:8 7463a
if it does **e** in My sight by not Jer 18:10 7451a
back, each of you from his **e** way, Jer 18:11 7451a
the stubbornness of his **e** heart.' Jer 18:12 7451a
Should good be repaid with **e**? Jer 18:20 7463a
Because of the **e** of their deeds. Jer 21:12 7455
to you for the **e** of your deeds," Jer 23:2 7455
Their course also is **e** And Jer 23:10 7451a
turned them back from their **e** way Jer 23:22 7451a
way And from the **e** of their deeds. Jer 23:22 7455
I will make them a terror *and an* **e** Jer 24:9 7463a
'Turn now everyone from his **e** way Jer 25:5 7451a
way and from the **e** of your deeds, Jer 25:5 7455
e is going forth From nation to Jer 25:32 7463a
everyone will turn from his **e** way, Jer 26:3 7451a
because of the **e** of their deeds.' Jer 26:3 7455
a great **e** against ourselves." Jer 26:19 7463a
e in My sight from their youth; Jer 32:30 7451a
because of all the **e** of the sons Jer 32:32 7463a
now every man from his **e** way Jer 35:15 7451a
man will turn from his **e** way; Jer 36:3 7451a
everyone will turn from his **e** way, Jer 36:7 7451a
e that Ishmael the son of Nethaniah Jer 41:11 7463a
because of the **e** of your deeds, Jer 44:22 7455
inhabitants of Chaldea for all their **e** Jer 51:24 7463a
He did **e** in the sight of the Jer 52:2 7451a
because of all the **e** abominations Ezk 6:11 7451a
and give **e** advice in this city, Ezk 11:2 7451b
the **e** things that you have done. Ezk 20:43 7451a
not according to your **e** ways or Ezk 20:44 7451a
the land into the hands of **e** men. Ezk 30:12 7451a
back, turn back from your **e** ways! Ezk 33:11 7451a
"Then you will remember your **e** Ezk 36:31 7451a
and you will devise an **e** plan, Ezk 38:10 7451a
their hearts will be *intent* on **e**, Da 11:27 7489a
And the **e** deeds of Samaria, Hos 7:1 7463a
Yet they devise **e** against Me. Hos 7:15 7451b
All their **e** is at Gilgal; Hos 9:15 7463a
lovingkindness And relenting of **e**. Jl 2:13 7463a
keeps silent, for it is an **e** time. Am 5:13 7463a
Seek good and not **e**, Am 5:14 7451b
Hate **e**, love good, And establish Am 5:15 7451b
them for **e** and not for good." Am 9:4 7463a
Who work out **e** on their beds! Mi 2:1 7451b
For it will be an **e** time. Mi 2:3 7463a
"You who hate good and love **e**, Mi 3:2 7451b
they have practiced **e** deeds. Mi 3:4 7489a
Concerning **e**, both hands do it Mi 7:3 7451b
who plotted **e** against the LORD, Na 1:11 7463a
has not your **e** passed continually? Na 3:19 7463a
eyes are too pure to approve **e**, Hab 1:13 7451b
"Woe to him who gets **e** gain for Hab 2:9 7451a
struck the head of the house of the **e** Hab 3:13 7563
'The LORD will not do good or **e**!' Zph 1:12 7489a
"Return now from your **e** ways Zch 1:4 7451a
ways and from your **e** deeds." Zch 1:4 7451a
and do not devise **e** in your hearts Zch 7:10 7463a
e in your heart against another, Zch 8:17 7463a
blind for sacrifice, is it not **e**? Mal 1:8 7451a
the lame and sick, is it not **e**? Mal 1:8 7451a
"Everyone who does **e** is good in Mal 2:17 7451a
kinds of **e** against you because Mt 5:11 *4190*
anything beyond these is of **e**. Mt 5:37 *4190*
you, do not resist an **e** person; Mt 5:39 *4190*
sun to rise on *the* **e** and *the* good, Mt 5:45 *4190*
temptation, but deliver us from **e**. Mt 6:13 *4190*
"If you then, being **e**, Mt 7:11 *4190*
are you thinking **e** in your hearts? Mt 9:4 *4190*
of vipers, how can you, being **e**, Mt 12:34 *4190*
and the **e** man brings out of *his* evil Mt 12:35 *4190*
and the evil man brings out of *his* **e** Mt 12:35 *4190*
of *his* evil treasure what is **e**. Mt 12:35 *4190*
"An **e** and adulterous generation Mt 12:39 *4190*
also be with this **e** generation." Mt 12:45 *4190*
the **e** *one* comes and snatches away Mt 13:19 *4190*
tares are the sons of the **e** *one;* Mt 13:38 *4190*
WHO SPEAKS **E** OF FATHER OR MOTHER Mt 15:4 *2551*
out of the heart come **e** thoughts, Mt 15:19 *4190*
"An **e** and adulterous generation Mt 16:4 *4190*
all they found, both **e** and good; Mt 22:10 *4190*
if that **e** slave says in his heart, Mt 24:48 *2556*
"Why, what **e** has He done?" Mt 27:23 *2556*
WHO SPEAKS **E** OF FATHER OR MOTHER, Mk 7:10 *2551*
of men, proceed the **e** thoughts, Mk 7:21 *2556*
"All these **e** things proceed from Mk 7:23 *4190*
soon afterward to speak **e** of Me. Mk 9:39 *2551*
"Why, what **e** has He done?" Mk 15:14 *2556*
insult you, and scorn your name as **e**, Lk 6:22 *4190*
is kind to ungrateful and **e** *men.* Lk 6:35 *4190*
and the **e** *man* out of the evil Lk 6:45 *4190*
and the evil *man* out of the **e** Lk 6:45 *4190*
treasure brings forth what is **e**; Lk 6:45 *4190*
and afflictions and **e** spirits; Lk 7:21 *4190*
of **e** spirits and sicknesses: Lk 8:2 *4190*
"If you then, being **e**, Lk 11:13 *4190*
other spirits more **e** than itself, Lk 11:26 *4190*
"Why, what **e** has this man done? Lk 23:22 *2556*
for their deeds were **e**. Jn 3:19 *4190*
who does **e** hates the Light, Jn 3:20 *5337*
those who committed the **e** *deeds* to Jn 5:29 *5337*
of it, that its deeds are **e**. Jn 7:7 *4190*
but to keep them from the **e** *one.* Jn 17:15 *4190*
speaking **e** of the Way before the Ac 19:9 *2551*
them and the **e** spirits went out. Ac 19:12 *4190*
name over those who had the **e** spirits Ac 19:13 *4190*
And the **e** spirit answered and said Ac 19:15 *4190*
the man, in whom was the **e** spirit, Ac 19:16 *4190*
E OF A RULER OF YOUR PEOPLE.'" Ac 23:5 *2560*
wickedness, greed, **e**; Ro 1:29 *2549*
boastful, inventors of **e**, Ro 1:30 *2556*
for every soul of man who does **e**, Ro 2:9 *2556*
"Let us do **e** that good may come"? Ro 3:8 *2556*
the very **e** that I do not want. Ro 7:19 *2556*
principle that **e** is present in me, Ro 7:21 *2556*
Abhor what is **e**; cling to what is Ro 12:9 *4190*
pay back **e** for evil to anyone. Ro 12:17 *2556*
pay back evil for **e** to anyone. Ro 12:17 *2556*
Do not be overcome by **e**, Ro 12:21 *2556*
by evil, but overcome **e** with good. Ro 12:21 *2556*
fear for good behavior, but for **e**. Ro 13:3 *2556*
But if you do what is **e**, Ro 13:4 *2556*
on the one who practices **e**. Ro 13:4 *2556*
a good thing be spoken of as **e**; Ro 14:16 *987*
but they are **e** for the man who Ro 14:20 *2556*
good and innocent in what is **e**. Ro 16:19 *2556*
that we would not crave **e** things 1Co 10:6 *2556*
yet in **e** be infants, but in your 1Co 14:20 *2549*
by **e** report and good report; 2Co 6:8 *1426b*
us from this present **e** age, Ga 1:4 *4190*
your time, because the days are **e**. Eph 5:16 *4190*
be able to resist in the **e** day, Eph 6:13 *4190*
the flaming arrows of the **e** *one.* Eph 6:16 *4190*
the dogs, beware of the **e** workers, Php 3:2 *2556*
in mind, *engaged* in **e** deeds, Col 1:21 *4190*
impurity, passion, **e** desire, Col 3:5 *2556*
laid aside the old self with its **e** Col 3:9
repays another with **e** for evil, 1Th 5:15 *2556*
repays another with evil for **e**, 1Th 5:15 *2556*
abstain from every form of **e**. 1Th 5:22 *4190*
rescued from perverse and **e** men; 2Th 3:2 *4190*
and protect you from the **e** *one.* 2Th 3:3 *4190*
abusive language, **e** suspicions, 1Tm 6:4 *4190*
money is a root of all sorts of **e**, 1Tm 6:10 *2556*
But **e** men and impostors will 2Tm 3:13 *4190*
will rescue me from every **e** deed, 2Tm 4:18 *4190*
are always liars, **e** beasts, Ti 1:12 *2556*
not be in any one of you an **e**, Heb 3:12 *4190*
trained to discern good and **e**. Heb 5:14 *2556*
sprinkled *clean* from an **e** conscience Heb 10:22 *4190*
for God cannot be tempted by **e**, Jas 1:13 *2556*
and become judges with **e** motives? Jas 2:4 *4190*
e *and* full of deadly poison. Jas 3:8 *2556*
is disorder and every **e** thing. Jas 3:16 *5337*
all such boasting is **e**. Jas 4:16 *4190*
your freedom as a covering for **e**, 1Pe 2:16 *2549*
not returning **e** for evil or 1Pe 3:9 *2556*
not returning evil for **e** or 1Pe 3:9 *2556*
MUST KEEP HIS TONGUE FROM **E** AND HIS 1Pe 3:10 *2556*
TURN AWAY FROM **E** AND DO GOOD; 1Pe 3:11 *2556*
LORD IS AGAINST THOSE WHO DO **E**." 1Pe 3:12 *2556*
you have overcome the **e** one." 1Jn 2:13 *4190*
and you have overcome the **e** one. 1Jn 2:14 *4190*
not as Cain, *who* was of the **e** one and 1Jn 3:12 *4190*
Because his deeds were **e**, 1Jn 3:12 *4190*
and the **e** one does not touch him. 1Jn 5:18 *4190*
lies in *the power of* the **e** one. 1Jn 5:19 *4190*
participates in his **e** deeds. 2Jn 1:11 *4190*
Beloved, do not imitate what is **e**, 3Jn 1:11 *2556*
one who does **e** has not seen God. 3Jn 1:11 *2554*
and that you cannot tolerate **e** men, Rv 2:2 *2556*

EVILDOER

the **e** according to his evil." 2Sa 3:39 6213a, 7463a
the arm of the wicked and the **e**, Ps 10:15 7451a
An **e** listens to wicked lips; A Pr 17:4 7489a
one of them is godless and an **e**, Is 9:17 7489a
and every **e** will be chaff; Mal 4:1 6213a, 7564
"If this Man were not an **e**, Jn 18:30 *2556*
as a murderer, or thief, or **e**, 1Pe 4:15 *2555*

EVILDOERS

Nor will He support the **e**. Jb 8:20 7489a
A band of **e** has encompassed me; Ps 22:16 7489a
I hate the assembly of **e**, Ps 26:5 7489a
When **e** came upon me to devour my Ps 27:2 7489a
The face of the LORD is against **e**, Ps 34:16 6213a, 7451a
Do not fret because of **e**, Ps 37:1 7489a
For **e** will be cut off, But those Ps 37:9 7489a
me from the secret counsel of **e**, Ps 64:2 7489a
of the **e** who rise up against me. Ps 92:11 7489a
will stand up for me against **e**? Ps 94:16 7489a
Depart from me, **e**, That I may Ps 119:115 7489a
Do not fret because of **e** Or Pr 24:19 7489a
with iniquity, Offspring of **e**, Is 1:4 7489a
of **e** not be mentioned forever. Is 14:20 7489a
will arise against the house of **e** And Is 31:2 7489a
the needy one From the hand of **e**. Jer 20:13 7489a
they strengthen the hands of **e**, Jer 23:14 7489a
DEPART FROM ME, ALL YOU **E**.' Lk 13:27 *93*
in which they slander you as **e**, 1Pe 2:12 *2555*
sent by him for the punishment of **e** 1Pe 2:14 *2555*

EVILDOING

the **e** of Nabal on his own head." 1Sa 25:39 7463a
Do not fret; *it leads* only to **e**. Ps 37:8 7489a

EVIL-MERODACH

the month, that **E** king of Babylon, 2Ki 25:27 192
the month, that **E** king of Babylon, Jer 52:31 192

EVILS

and many **e** and troubles will come Dt 31:17 7463a
that these **e** have come upon us?' Dt 31:17 7463a
when many **e** and troubles have come Dt 31:21 7463a
For **e** beyond number have Ps 40:12 7463a
My people have committed two **e**: Jer 2:13 7451a
the **e** which they have committed, Ezk 6:9 7463a

EWE

Then Abraham set seven **e** lambs of Gn 21:28 3535
"What do these seven **e** lambs mean, Gn 21:29 3535
"You shall take these seven **e** Gn 21:30 3535
a yearling **e** lamb without defect, Lv 14:10 3535
had nothing except one little **e** lamb 2Sa 12:3 3535
Rather he took the poor man's **e** 2Sa 12:4 3535

EWE-LAMB

e a year old without defect for a sin Nu 6:14 3535

EWES

your **e** and your female goats have Gn 31:38 7353
two hundred **e** and twenty rams, Gn 32:14 7353

From the care of the **e** with Ps 78:71 5763
teeth are like a flock of *newly* shorn **e** SS 4:2
"Your teeth are like a flock of **e** SS 6:6 7353
He will gently lead the nursing **e**. Is 40:11

EXACT
and let him **e** a fifth *of the* Gn 41:34 2567
he shall not **e** it of his neighbor Dt 15:2 5065
"From a foreigner you may **e** *it*, Dt 15:3 5065
and the **e** amount of money that Es 4:7 6575
case And **e** full vengeance for you; Jer 51:36 5358
him the **e** meaning of all this. Da 7:16 3330a
the **e** meaning of the fourth beast, Da 7:19 3321
e a tribute of grain from them, Am 5:11 3947
magi and determined from them the **e** Mt 2:7 *5550*
so that you may know the **e** truth Lk 1:4 *803*
a more **e** knowledge about the Way, Ac 24:22 *199*
e representation of His nature, Heb 1:3 *5481*

EXACTED
Menahem **e** the money from Israel, 2Ki 15:20 3318
He **e** the silver and gold from the 2Ki 23:35 5065

EXACTING
"You are **e** usury, each from his Ne 5:7 5377
oil that you are **e** from them." Ne 5:11 5383
of you, because you are an **e** man; Lk 19:21 *840*
Did you know that I am an **e** man, Lk 19:22 *840*

EXACTION
year and the **e** of every debt. Ne 10:31 4855

EXACTLY
"On **e** the tenth day of this Lv 23:27 389
'On **e** the fifteenth day of the Lv 23:39 389
we will do **e** as you say." Ne 5:12 3651
e as a man is born, thus will he die. Ec 5:16 5980
just **e** as the women also had said; Lk 24:24 *3779*
I do **e** as the Father commanded Me. Jn 14:31 *3779*
turn out **e** as I have been told. Ac 27:25
3779, 2596, 5158

EXALT
"Still you **e** yourself against My Ex 9:17 5549
so why do you **e** yourselves above Nu 16:3 5375
"This day I will begin to **e** you Jos 3:7 1431
will **e** the horn of His anointed." 1Sa 2:10 7311
e him according to the words of God, 1Ch 25:5 7311
You **e** Yourself as head over all. 1Ch 29:11 5375
Therefore You will not **e** *them.* Jb 17:4 7311
that you should **e** His work, Jb 36:24 7679
And let us **e** His name together. Ps 34:3 7311
He will **e** you to inherit the land; Ps 37:34 7311
Let not the rebellious **e** themselves. Ps 66:7 7311
E the LORD our God And worship at Ps 99:5 7311
E the LORD our God And worship at Ps 99:9 7311
e Jerusalem Above my chief joy. Ps 137:6 5927
"Prize her, and she will **e** you; Pr 4:8 7311
Is the saw to **e** itself over the Is 10:15 1431
I will **e** You, I will give thanks Is 25:1 7311
the high tree, **e** the low tree, Ezk 17:24 1361b
E that which is low and abase Ezk 21:26 1361b
"Now I, Nebuchadnezzar, praise, **e** Da 4:37 7313
and he will **e** and magnify himself Da 11:36 7311
of the Lord, and He will **e** you. Jas 4:10 *5312*
He may **e** you at the proper time, 1Pe 5:6 *5312*

EXALTATION
west, Nor from the desert *comes* **e**; Ps 75:6 7311

EXALTED
to the LORD, for He is highly **e**; Ex 15:1 1342
to the LORD, for He is highly **e**; Ex 15:21 1342
Agag, And his kingdom shall be **e**. Nu 24:7 5375
On that day the LORD **e** Joshua in Jos 4:14 1431
My horn is **e** in the LORD, My mouth 1Sa 2:1 7311
and that He had **e** his kingdom for 2Sa 5:12 5375
And **e** be God, the rock of my 2Sa 22:47 7311
the son of Haggith **e** himself, 1Ki 1:5 5375
"Because I **e** you from among the 1Ki 14:7 7311
"Inasmuch as I **e** you from the 1Ki 16:2 7311
and that his kingdom was highly **e**, 1Ch 14:2 5375
The LORD highly **e** Solomon in 1Ch 29:25 1431
was with him and **e** him greatly. 2Ch 1:1 1431
"As for this house, which was **e**, 2Ch 7:21 5945a
so that he was **e** in the sight of 2Ch 32:23 5375
e above all blessing and praise! Ne 9:5 7311
"They are **e** a little while, then Jb 24:24 7426a
them forever, and they are **e**. Jb 36:7 1361b
"Behold, God is **e** in His power; Jb 36:22 7682
"Behold, God is **e**, and we do not Jb 36:26 7689
He is **e** in power And Jb 37:23 7689
When vileness is **e** among the sons Ps 12:8 7311
long will my enemy be **e** over me? Ps 13:2 7311
And **e** be the God of my salvation, Ps 18:46 7311
Be **e**, O LORD, in Your strength; Ps 21:13 7311
I will be **e** among the nations, I Ps 46:10 7311
I will be **e** in the earth." Ps 46:10 7311
earth belong to God; He is highly **e**. Ps 47:9 5927
me who has **e** himself against me, Ps 55:12 1431
Be **e** above the heavens, O God; Ps 57:5 7311
Be **e** above the heavens, O God; Ps 57:11 7311
who hate You have **e** themselves. Ps 83:2 5375
is mighty, Your right hand is **e**. Ps 89:13 7311
by Your righteousness they are **e**. Ps 89:16 7311
And by Your favor our horn is **e**. Ps 89:17 7311
have **e** one chosen from the people. Ps 89:19 7311
And in My name his horn will be **e**. Ps 89:24 7311
You have **e** the right hand of his Ps 89:42 7311
But You have **e** my horn like *that* Ps 92:10 7311
You are **e** far above all gods. Ps 97:9 5927
And He is **e** above all the peoples. Ps 99:2 7311
Be **e**, O God, above the heavens, Ps 108:5 7311
His horn will be **e** in honor. Ps 112:9 7311
The right hand of the LORD is **e**; Ps 118:16 7311

For though the LORD is **e**, Ps 138:6 7311
evil device, *that* they *not* be **e**. Ps 140:8 7311
the LORD, For His name alone is **e**; Ps 148:13 7682
blessing of the upright a city is **e**, Pr 11:11 7311
Wisdom is *too* **e** for a fool, He Pr 24:7 7311
who trusts in the LORD will be **e**. Pr 29:25 7682
folly is set in many **e** places Ec 10:6 4791
LORD alone will be **e** in that day. Is 2:11 7682
LORD alone will be **e** in that day. Is 2:17 7682
of hosts will be **e** in judgment, Is 5:16 1361b
sitting on a throne, lofty and **e**, Is 6:1 5375
remember that His name is **e**." Is 12:4 7682
the **e** of the people of the earth Is 24:4 4791
The LORD is **e**, for He dwells on Is 33:5 7682
"Now I will be **e**, now I will be Is 33:10 7426a
high and lifted up and greatly **e**. Is 52:13 1361b
high and **e** One Who lives forever, Is 57:15 5375
e the might of your adversaries. La 2:17 7311
may not be **e** in their stature, Ezk 31:14 1361b
but you have **e** yourself against Da 5:23 7313
He **e** himself in Israel, But Hos 13:1 5375
will not be **e** to heaven, Mt 11:23 *5312*
humbles himself shall be **e**. Mt 23:12 *5312*
And has **e** those who were humble. Lk 1:52 *5312*
will not be **e** to heaven, Lk 10:15 *5312*
who humbles himself will be **e**." Lk 14:11 *5312*
who humbles himself will be **e**." Lk 18:14 *5312*
been **e** to the right hand of God, Ac 2:33 *5312*
"He is the one whom God **e** to His Ac 5:31 *5312*
myself so that you might be **e**, 2Co 11:7 *5312*
now, as always, be **e** in my body, Php 1:20 *3170*
this reason also, God highly **e** Him, Php 2:9 *5251*
sinners and **e** above the heavens; Heb 7:26 *5308*

EXALTING
If you have been foolish in **e** Pr 30:32 5375
be in subjection, not **e** itself, Ezk 17:14 5375
speaking with tongues and **e** God. Ac 10:46 *3170*
reason, to keep me from **e** myself, 2Co 12:7 *5229*
to keep me from **e** myself! 2Co 12:7 *5229*

EXALTS
He brings low, He also **e**. 1Sa 2:7 7311
He puts down one and **e** another. Ps 75:7 7311
he who is quick-tempered **e** folly. Pr 14:29 7311
Righteousness **e** a nation, But sin Pr 14:34 7311
One on high, None at all **e** *Him.* Hos 11:7 7311
Whoever **e** himself shall be humbled; Mt 23:12 *5312*
"My soul **e** the Lord, Lk 1:46 *3170*
who **e** himself will be humbled, Lk 14:11 *5312*
who **e** himself will be humbled, Lk 18:14 *5312*
advantage of you, anyone **e** himself, 2Co 11:20 *1869*
who opposes and **e** himself above 2Th 2:4 *5229*

EXAMINE
please **e** *it* to *see* whether it is Gn 37:32 5234
"Please **e** and see, whose signet Gn 38:25 5234
You **e** him every morning Jb 7:18 6485
E me, O LORD, and try me; Ps 26:2 974
And You **e** my heart's Jer 12:3 974
Let us **e** and probe our ways, And La 3:40 2664
e him immediately let go of him; Ac 22:29 *426*
in fact, I do not even **e** myself. 1Co 4:3 *350*
defense to those who **e** me is this: 1Co 9:3 *350*
But a man must **e** himself, 1Co 11:28 *1381a*
if you are in the faith; **e** yourselves! 2Co 13:5 *1381a*
But each one must **e** his own work, Ga 6:4 *1381a*
But **e** everything *carefully;* 1Th 5:21 *1381a*

EXAMINED
Then he **e** it and said, Gn 37:33 5234
Moses **e** all the work and behold, Ex 39:43 7200
behold, having **e** Him before you, Lk 23:14 *350*
he **e** the guards and ordered that Ac 12:19 *350*
stating that he should be **e** by Ac 22:24 *426*
"And when they had **e** me, Ac 28:18 *350*
thing that I may be **e** by you, 1Co 4:3 *350*

EXAMINES
"Will it be well when He **e** you? Jb 13:9 2713
Until another comes and **e** him. Pr 18:17 2713
but the one who **e** me is the Lord. 1Co 4:4 *350*
men, but God who **e** our hearts. 1Th 2:4 *1381a*

EXAMINING
eagerness, **e** the Scriptures daily Ac 17:11 *350*
and **e** the objects of your worship, Ac 17:23 *333*
By **e** him yourself concerning Ac 24:8 *350*

EXAMPLE
and you will be *an* **e** *of* terror to Dt 28:25
he followed the **e** of his father David's 2Ch 17:3 1870
"For I gave you an **e** that you Jn 13:15 *5262*
things happened to them as an **e**, 1Co 10:11 *5179a*
Brethren, join in following my **e**, Php 3:17 *4831*
so that you became an **e** to all the 1Th 1:7 *5179b*
how you ought to follow our **e**, 2Th 3:7 *3401*
you, so that you would follow our **e**. 2Th 3:9 *3401*
as an **e** for those who would 1Tm 1:16 *5296*
an **e** of those who believe. 1Tm 4:12 *5179b*
yourself to be an **e** of good deeds, Ti 2:7 *5179b*
the same **e** of disobedience. Heb 4:11 *5262*
As an **e**, brethren, of suffering Jas 5:10 *5262*
leaving you an **e** for you to follow 1Pe 2:21 *5261*
having made them an **e** to those who 2Pe 2:6 *5262*
flesh, are exhibited as an **e** in Jude 1:7 *1164*

EXAMPLES
these things happened as **e** for us, 1Co 10:6 *5179b*
but proving to be **e** to the flock. 1Pe 5:3 *5179b*

EXASPERATE
Fathers, do not **e** your children, Col 3:21 *2042*

EXCEED
You **e** *in* wisdom and prosperity the 1Ki 10:7 3254
learn not to **e** what is written, 1Co 4:6 *5228*

EXCEEDING
the altar of God, To God my **e** joy; Ps 43:4 8057
righteousness And **e** faithfulness. Ps 119:138 3966

EXCEEDINGLY
the men of Sodom were wicked **e** Gn 13:13 3966
you, And I will multiply you **e**." Gn 17:2 3966
"I will make you **e** fruitful, Gn 17:6 3966
fruitful and will multiply him **e**. Gn 17:20 3966
great, and their sin is **e** grave. Gn 18:20 3966
with an **e** great and bitter cry, Gn 27:34 3966
So the man became **e** prosperous, Gn 30:43 3966
multiplied, and became **e** mighty, Ex 1:7 3966
to spy out is an **e** good land. Nu 14:7 3966
an **e** large number of livestock. Nu 32:1 3966
the LORD shall be **e** magnificent, 1Ch 22:5 4605
Your commandment is **e** broad. Ps 119:96 3966
I am **e** afflicted; Revive me, O LORD, Ps 119:107
5704, 3966
testimonies, And I love them **e**. Ps 119:167 3966
on the earth, But they are **e** wise: Pr 30:24 2449
been is remote and **e** mysterious. Ec 7:24 6013
Be **e** glad with her, all you who Is 66:10 4885
you *And* are **e** angry with us. La 5:22
5704, 3966
so you were **e** beautiful and Ezk 16:13 3966
on their feet, an **e** great army. Ezk 37:10 3966
from all the others, **e** dreadful, Da 7:19 3493
the male goat magnified *himself* **e**. Da 8:8
5704, 3966
grew **e** great toward the south, Da 8:9 3499a
Now Nineveh was an **e** great city, Jon 3:3 430
"I am **e** jealous for Jerusalem and Zch 1:14 1419
'I am **e** jealous for Zion, yes, Zch 8:2 1419
they rejoiced **e** with great joy. Mt 2:10 *4970*
became radiant and **e** white, Mk 9:3 *3029*

EXCEL
done nobly, But you **e** them all." Pr 31:29 5927
also **e** in deeds of wickedness; Jer 5:28 5674a
that you **e** still more. 1Th 4:1 *4052*
you, brethren, to **e** still more, 1Th 4:10 *4052*

EXCELLENCE
"And in the greatness of Your **e** Ex 15:7 1347b
know that you are a woman of **e**. Ru 3:11 2428
if there is any **e** and if anything Php 4:8 *703*
called us by His own glory and **e**. 2Pe 1:3 *703*
in your faith supply moral **e**, 2Pe 1:5 *703*
excellence, and in *your* moral **e**, 2Pe 1:5 *703*

EXCELLENCIES
that you may proclaim the **e** of Him 1Pe 2:9 *703*

EXCELLENT
Him according to His **e** greatness. Ps 150:2 7230
An **e** wife is the crown of her Pr 12:4 2428
E speech is not fitting for a fool, Pr 17:7 3499a
Have I not written to you **e** things Pr 22:20 7991c
An **e** wife, who can find? Pr 31:10 2428
in song, for He has done **e** things; Is 12:5 1348
order, most **e** Theophilus; Lk 1:3 *2903*
to the most **e** governor Felix, Ac 23:26 *2903*
way and everywhere, most **e** Felix, Ac 24:3 *2903*
not out of my mind, most **e** Festus, Ac 26:25 *2903*
And I show you a still more **e** way. 1Co 12:31 *5236*
may approve the things that are **e**, Php 1:10 *1308*
inherited a more **e** name than they. Heb 1:4 *1313*
He has obtained a more **e** ministry, Heb 8:6 *1313*
behavior **e** among the Gentiles, 1Pe 2:12 *2570*

EXCELS
And I saw that wisdom **e** folly as Ec 2:13 3504
excels folly as light **e** darkness. Ec 2:13 3504

EXCEPT
e what the young men have eaten, Gn 14:24 1107
anything **e** the food which he ate. Gn 39:6
3588, 518
withheld nothing from me **e** you, Gn 39:9
3588, 518
lord **e** our bodies and our lands. Gn 47:18
1115, 518
you to go, **e** under compulsion. Ex 3:19 3808
e what must be eaten by every Ex 12:16 389
e for his relatives who are Lv 21:2
3588, 518
at all to look at **e** this manna." Nu 11:6 1115
e Caleb the son of Jephunneh and Nu 14:30
3588, 518
who can live **e** God has ordained it? Nu 24:23
e Caleb the son of Jephunneh and Nu 26:65
3588, 518
e Caleb the son of Jephunneh the Nu 32:12 1115
e by the blood of him who shed it. Nu 35:33
3588, 518
e Caleb the son of Jephunneh; Dt 1:36 2108
e *what they receive* from the sale Dt 18:8 905
on their mounds, **e** Hazor alone, Jos 11:13 2108
e the Hivites living in Gibeon; Jos 11:19 1115
in the land, **e** cities to live in, Jos 14:4
3588, 518
any dowry **e** a hundred foreskins 1Sa 18:25 3588
For there is no other **e** it here." 1Sa 21:9 2108
e four hundred young men who rode 1Sa 30:17
3588, 518
e to every man his wife and his 1Sa 30:22
3588, 518
"But the poor man had nothing **e** 2Sa 12:3
3588, 518
e he sacrificed and burned incense 1Ki 3:3 7534
There was nothing in the ark **e** the 1Ki 8:9 7534
e in the case of Uriah the Hittite. 1Ki 15:5 7534

rain these years, e by my word." 1Ki 17:1 3588, 518
in the house e a jar of oil." 2Ki 4:2 3588, 518
was left e the tribe of Judah. 2Ki 17:18 7534, 905
None remained e the poorest people 2Ki 24:14 2108
Him, e to burn *incense* before Him? 2Ch 2:6 3588, 518
nothing in the ark e the two tablets 2Ch 5:10 7534
no son was left to him e Jehoahaz, 2Ch 21:17 3588, 518
the house of the LORD e the priests 2Ch 23:6 3588, 518
no animal with me e the animal on Ne 2:12 3588, 518
not request anything e what Hegai, Es 2:15 3588, 518
And who is a rock, e our God, Ps 18:31 2108
do who will come after the king e Ec 2:12
to their owners e to look on? Ec 5:11 3588, 518
e to eat and to drink and to be merry, Ec 8:15 3588, 518
There is none e Me. Is 45:21 2108
none will return e *a few* refugees.' " Jer 44:14 3588, 518
declare it to the king e gods, Da 2:11 3861b
worship any god e their own God. Da 3:28 3861b
forces e Michael your prince. Da 10:21 3588, 518
you were not to know any god e Me, Hos 13:4 2108
e to be thrown out and trampled Mt 5:13 1508
e for *the* reason of unchastity, Mt 5:32 3924
no one knows the Son e the Father; Mt 11:27 1508
anyone know the Father e the Son, Mt 11:27 1508
without honor e in his hometown Mt 13:57 1508
given it, e the sign of Jonah." Mt 16:4 1508
saw no one e Jesus Himself alone. Mt 17:8 1508
go out e by prayer and fasting." Mt 17:21 1508
his wife, e for immorality, Mt 19:9 3361
found nothing on it e leaves only; Mt 21:19 1508
for *anyone* to eat e the priests, Mk 2:26 1508
is hidden, e to be revealed; Mk 4:22 1437, 3361
e Peter and James and John the Mk 5:37 1508
"A prophet is not without honor e Mk 6:4 1508
no miracle there e that He laid His Mk 6:5 1508
for *their* journey, e a mere staff Mk 6:8 1508
with them anymore, e Jesus alone. Mk 9:8 1508
No one is good e God alone. Mk 10:18 1508
any to eat e the priests alone, Lk 6:4 1508
Him, e Peter and John and James, Lk 8:51 1508
knows who the Son is e the Father, Lk 10:22 1508
and who the Father is e the Son, Lk 10:22 1508
glory to God, e this foreigner?" Lk 17:18 1508
No one is good e God alone. Lk 18:19 1508
no other small boat there, e one, Jn 6:22 1508
Father, e the One who is from God; Jn 6:46 1508
Judea and Samaria, e the apostles. Ac 8:1 4133
word to no one e to Jews alone. Ac 11:19 1508
e that the Holy Spirit solemnly Ac 20:23 4133
as I am, e for these chains." Ac 26:29 3924
to know sin e through the Law; Ro 7:7 1508
there is no authority e from God, Ro 13:1 1508
to anyone e to love one another; Ro 13:8 1508
to speak of anything e what Christ has Ro 15:18 3756
none of you e Crispus and Gaius, 1Co 1:14 1508
nothing among you e Jesus Christ, 1Co 2:2 1508
of a man e the spirit of the man which 1Co 2:11 1508
no one knows e the Spirit of God. 1Co 2:11 1508
e by agreement for a time, 1Co 7:5 1509
is Lord," e by the Holy Spirit. 1Co 12:3 1508
e in regard to *my* weaknesses. 2Co 12:5 1508
e that I myself did not become a 2Co 12:13 1508
any other of the apostles e James, Ga 1:19 1508
e in the cross of our Lord Jesus Ga 6:14 1508
what does it mean e that He also Eph 4:9 1508
against an elder e on the basis of two 1Tm 5:19 1622, 1508
sell, e the one who has the mark, Rv 13:17 1508
song e the one hundred and forty-four Rv 14:3 1508
Him which no one knows e Himself. Rv 19:12 1508

EXCEPTED
it is evident that He is e who put 1Co 15:27 1622

EXCESS
he who had gathered much had no e, Ex 16:18 5736
who are in e beyond the Levites, Nu 3:46 5736
of those who are in e among them, Nu 3:48 5736
money from those who were in e, Nu 3:49 5736
you not have it in e and vomit it. Pr 25:16 7646

EXCESSES
not run with *them* into the same e 1Pe 4:4 401

EXCESSIVE
and e devotion *to books* is Ec 12:12 3854
of the pride of Moab, an e pride; Is 16:6 3966
might be overwhelmed by e sorrow. 2Co 2:7 4053

EXCESSIVELY
Do not be e righteous and do not Ec 7:16 7235a
Do not be e wicked and do not be Ec 7:17 7235a
in Asia, that we were burdened e, 2Co 1:8 2596, 5236

EXCHANGE
and Joseph gave them food in e for Gn 47:17
and he fed them with food in e for Gn 47:17
'He shall not replace it or e it, Lv 27:10 4171
or if he does e animal for animal, Lv 27:10 4171
is good or bad, nor shall he e it; Lv 27:33 4171
or if he does e it, then both it Lv 27:33 4171
then you shall e *it* for money, and Dt 14:25 5414
e *of land* to confirm any matter: Ru 4:7 8545
shall give up his life in e." 2Ki 10:24 8478
gold cannot be given in e for it, Jb 28:15 8478
other peoples in e for your life. Is 43:4 8478
shall not sell or e any of it, Ezk 48:14 4171
will a man give in e for his soul? Mt 16:26 465
a man give in e for his soul? Mk 8:37 465
Now in a like e 2Co 6:13 489

EXCHANGED
they arose early and e oaths; Gn 26:31 7650
it be e for articles of fine gold. Jb 28:17 8545
Thus they e their glory For the Ps 106:20 4171
and e the glory of the Ro 1:23 236
they e the truth of God for a lie, Ro 1:25 3337
for their women e the natural Ro 1:26 3337

EXCHANGES
He e the portion of my people; Mi 2:4 4171

EXCHANGING
words that you are e with one another Lk 24:17 474

EXCITED
"Sheol from beneath is e over you Is 14:9 7264

EXCLUDE
you, who e you for My name's sake, Is 66:5 5077

EXCLUDED
for Jeroboam and his sons had e 2Ch 11:14 2186a
they were considered unclean *and* e Ezr 2:62
e from the assembly of the exiles. Ezr 10:8 914
they were considered unclean *and* e Ne 7:64
they e all foreigners from Israel. Ne 13:3 914
Where then is boasting? It is e. Ro 3:27 1576
e from the commonwealth of Israel, Eph 2:12 526
e from the life of God because Eph 4:18 526

EXCLUSIVE
"E of the property of the Levites Ezk 48:22 4480

EXCLUSIVELY
No longer drink water e, but use 1Tm 5:23

EXCREMENT
and shall turn to cover up your e. Dt 23:13 6627

EXCUSE
now they have no e for their sin. Jn 15:22 4392
made, so that they are without e. Ro 1:20 379
Therefore you have no e, Ro 2:1 379

EXCUSED
please consider me e.' Lk 14:18 3868
please consider me e.' Lk 14:19 3868

EXCUSES
they all alike began to make e. Lk 14:18 3868

EXECUTE
the gods of Egypt I will e judgments Ex 12:12 6213a
will e vengeance for the covenant; Lv 26:25 5358
the leaders of the people and e them Nu 25:4 3363
to e the LORD's vengeance on Nu 31:3 5414
not e His fierce wrath on Amalek, 1Sa 28:18 6213a
and e My ordinances and keep all My 1Ki 6:12 6213a
e any design which may be assigned 2Ch 2:14 2803
He will e judgment for the peoples Ps 9:8 1777
When will You e judgment on those Ps 119:84 6213a
To e vengeance on the nations And Ps 149:7 6213a
To e on them the judgment written; Ps 149:9 6213a
the Lord GOD of hosts will e in Is 10:23 6213a
To e My anger. Is 13:3
"Who e a plan, but not Mine, And Is 30:1 6213a
For the LORD will e judgment by Is 66:16 8199
will not e a complete destruction. Jer 4:27 6213a
do not e a complete destruction; Jer 5:10 6213a
and He shall e justice and Jer 33:15 6213a
and I will e judgments among you Ezk 5:8 6213a
for I will e judgments on you and Ezk 5:10 6213a
when I e judgments against you in Ezk 5:15 6213a
and e judgments against you. Ezk 11:9 6213a
and e judgments on you in the sight Ezk 16:41 6213a
"Thus I will e judgments on Moab, Ezk 25:11 6213a
"I will e great vengeance on Ezk 25:17 6213a
LORD when I e judgments in her, Ezk 28:22 6213a
when I e judgments upon all who Ezk 28:26 6213a
Zoan And e judgments on Thebes. Ezk 30:14 6213a
"Thus I will e judgments on Egypt, Ezk 30:19 6213a
I will not e My fierce anger; Hos 11:9 6213a
"And I will e vengeance in anger Mi 5:15 6213a
gave Him authority to e judgment, Jn 5:27 4160
WILL E HIS WORD ON THE EARTH, Ro 9:28 4160
to e judgment upon all, and to Jude 1:15 4160
put it in their hearts to e His purpose Rv 17:17 4160

EXECUTED
also e judgments on their gods. Nu 33:4 6213a
He e the justice of the LORD, And Dt 33:21 6213a
Thus they e judgment on Joash. 2Ch 24:24 6213a
judgment be e upon him strictly, Ezr 7:26 5648
and edict were about to be e, Es 9:1 6213a
He has e judgment. Ps 9:16 6213a
You have e justice and Ps 99:4 6213a
an evil deed is not e quickly, Ec 8:11 6213a
nor have you e My ordinances, Ezk 11:12 6213a
and they e judgments on her. Ezk 23:10 6213a
see My judgment which I have e and Ezk 39:21 6213a
they asked Pilate that He be e. Ac 13:28 337

EXECUTES
"He e justice for the orphan and Dt 10:18 6213a
The God who e vengeance for me, 2Sa 22:48 5414
The God who e vengeance for me, Ps 18:47 5414
Who e justice for the oppressed; Ps 146:7 6213a
and e true justice between man and Ezk 18:8 6213a
or increase, *but* e My ordinances, Ezk 18:17 6213a
my case and e justice for me. Mi 7:9 6213a

EXECUTING
in e what is right in My eyes, 2Ki 10:30 6213a
e judgment on the house of Ahab, 2Ch 22:8 8199

EXECUTION
ordered that they be led away *to* e. Ac 12:19

EXECUTIONER
the king sent an e and commanded Mk 6:27 4688

EXECUTIONERS
"Draw near, O e of the city, each Ezk 9:1 6486

EXEMPT
to all Judah—none was e 1Ki 15:22 5355a
"Then the sons are e. Mt 17:26 1658

EXERCISE
The e of justice is joy for Pr 21:15 6213a
great men e authority over them. Mt 20:25 2715
great men e authority over them. Mk 10:42 2715
each of us is to e them accordingly: Ro 12:6
teach or e authority over a man, 1Tm 2:12 831
In the e of His will He brought us Jas 1:18

EXERCISED
man has e authority over *another* man Ec 8:9 7980

EXERCISES
am the LORD who e lovingkindness, Jer 9:24 6213a
games e self-control in all things. 1Co 9:25 1467
He e all the authority of the Rv 13:12 4160

EXERCISING
e oversight not under compulsion, 1Pe 5:2

EXERT
then he must e more strength. Ec 10:10 1396

EXERTED
done and the labor which I had e, Ec 2:11 6213a

EXERTING
he kept e himself to rescue him. Da 6:14 7712

EXERTION
by the e of the power that He has Php 3:21 1753b

EXHAUSTED
for he was sound asleep and e. Jg 4:21 5888
too e to cross the brook Besor remained 1Sa 30:10 6296
who were too e to follow David, 1Sa 30:21 6296
upon him while he is weary and e 2Sa 17:2 7504b, 3027
'The bowl of flour shall not be e, 1Ki 17:14 3615
The bowl of flour was not e nor 1Ki 17:16 3615
"But now He has e me; Jb 16:7 3811
Encourage the e, and strengthen Is 35:3 3027, 7504b
Their strength is e, Jer 51:30 5405
nations become e *only* for fire." Jer 51:58 3286
and they will become e.' " Jer 51:64 3286
Daniel, was e and sick for days. Da 8:27 1961

EXHIBITED
God has e us apostles last of all, 1Co 4:9 584
flesh, are e as an example in Jude 1:7 4295

EXHILARATED
Be e always with her love. Pr 5:19 7686
my son, be e with an adulteress And Pr 5:20 7686

EXHORT
Now I e you, brethren, by the name 1Co 1:10 3870
I e you, be imitators of 1Co 4:16 3870
and e you in the Lord Jesus, 1Th 4:1 3870
Now such persons we command and e 2Th 3:12 3870
reprove, rebuke, e, 2Tm 4:2 3870
be able both to e in sound doctrine Ti 1:9 3870
These things speak and e and Ti 2:15 3870
I e the elders among you, 1Pe 5:1 3870

EXHORTATION
have any word of e for the people, Ac 13:15 3874
and had given them much e, Ac 20:2 3870, 3056
or he who exhorts, in his e; Ro 12:8 3874
edification and e and consolation. 1Co 14:3 3874
For our e does not *come* from error 1Th 2:3 3874
of Scripture, to e and teaching. 1Tm 4:13 3874
and you have forgotten the e which Heb 12:5 3874
bear with this word of e, Heb 13:22 3874

EXHORTATIONS
So with many other e he Lk 3:18 3870

EXHORTED
the disciples, and when he had e them Ac 20:1 3870
all may learn and all may be e; 1Co 14:31 3870

EXHORTING
testified and kept on e them, Ac 2:40 3870
just as you know how we *were* e and 1Th 2:11 3870
e and testifying that this is the 1Pe 5:12 3870

EXHORTS
or he who e, in his exhortation; Ro 12:8 3870

EXILE
you are a foreigner and also an e; 2Sa 15:19 1540
people of it away into e to Kir, 2Ki 16:9 1540
Israel away into e to Assyria, 2Ki 17:6 1540
had carried away to e before them; 2Ki 17:11 1540
into e from their own land to Assyria 2Ki 17:23 1540
away into e in the cities of Samaria 2Ki 17:26 1540
whom you carried away into e and 2Ki 17:27 1540
had carried away into e from Samaria 2Ki 17:28 1540
they had been carried away into e. 2Ki 17:33 1540
Israel away into e to Assyria, 2Ki 18:11 1540
Then he led away into e all 2Ki 24:14 1540
Jehoiachin away into e to Babylon; 2Ki 24:15 1540
into e from Jerusalem to Babylon. 2Ki 24:15 1473
Babylon brought into e to Babylon. 2Ki 24:16 1473
of the guard carried away into e. 2Ki 25:11 1540
was led away into e from its land. 2Ki 25:21 1540
the e of Jehoiachin king of Judah, 2Ki 25:27 1546
of Assyria carried away into e; 1Ch 5:6 1540
in their place until the e. 1Ch 5:22 1473
and he carried them away into e, 1Ch 5:26 1540
away into e by Nebuchadnezzar. 1Ch 6:15 1540

carried them into e to Manahath, 1Ch 8:6 1540
he carried them into e; 1Ch 8:7 1540
was carried away into e to Babylon 1Ch 9:1 1540
people of the e were building a temple Ezr 4:1 1473
The sons of Israel who returned from e Ezr 6:21 1473
been taken into e from Jerusalem Es 2:6 1540
e for their lack of knowledge; Is 5:13 1540
am barren, an e and a wanderer? Is 49:21 1540
"The e will soon be set free, and Is 51:14 6808
until the e of Jerusalem in the Jer 1:3 1540
All Judah has been carried into e, Jer 13:19 1540
into exile, Wholly carried into e. Jer 13:19 1540
e Jeconiah the son of Jehoiakim, Jer 27:20 1540
the rest of the elders of the e, Jer 29:1 1540
into e from Jerusalem to Babylon. Jer 29:1 1473
into e from Jerusalem to Babylon, Jer 29:4 1540
city where I have sent you into e, Jer 29:7 1540
from where I sent you into e.' Jer 29:14 1540
who did not go with you into e Jer 29:16 1473
'*The* e will be long; build Jer 29:28 1473
carried *them* into e in Babylon. Jer 39:9 1540
us to death or e us to Babylon." Jer 43:3 1540
"Make your baggage ready for e, Jer 46:19 1473
And Chemosh will go off into e Jer 48:7 1473
to vessel, Nor has he gone into e; Jer 48:11 1473
For Malcam will go into e Together Jer 49:3 1473
away into e some of the poorest Jer 52:15 1540
was led away into e from its land. Jer 52:27 1540
carried away into e: Jer 52:28 1540
carried into e 745 Jewish people; Jer 52:30 1540
the e of Jehoiachin king of Judah, Jer 52:31 1546
has gone into e under affliction And La 1:3 1540
He will e you no longer. La 4:22 1540
fifth year of King Jehoiachin's e, Ezk 1:2 1546
prepare for yourself baggage for e Ezk 12:3 1473
go into e by day in their sight; Ezk 12:3 1540
even go into e from your place to Ezk 12:3 1540
in their sight, as baggage for e. Ezk 12:4 1473
sight, as those going into e. Ezk 12:4 1473
baggage like the baggage of an e. Ezk 12:7 1473
they will go into e, Ezk 12:11 1473
of Judah when they went into e, Ezk 25:3 1473
in the twelfth year of our e, Ezk 33:21 1546
Israel went into e for their iniquity Ezk 39:23 1540
them go into e among the nations, Ezk 39:28 1540
In the twenty-fifth year of our e, Ezk 40:1 1546
"Their king will go into e, Am 1:15 1473
you go into e beyond Damascus," Am 5:27 1540
into e at the head of the exiles, Am 6:7 1540
go from its land into e.' Am 7:11 1540
go from its land into e.'" Am 7:17 1540
For they will go from you into e. Mi 1:16 1540
Yet she became an e, Na 3:10 1473
The reproach *of* e is a Zph 3:18

EXILED
e with Jeconiah king of Judah, Es 2:6 1540
the king of Babylon had e. Es 2:6 1540
who were being e to Babylon. Jer 40:1 1540
who had not been e to Babylon. Jer 40:7 1540
people of Aram will go e to Kir," Am 1:5 1540
ravished and half of the city e, Zch 14:2 3318, 1473

EXILES
with the e who went up from Babylon Ezr 1:11 1473
the e whom Nebuchadnezzar the king Ezr 2:1 1473
Levites and the rest of the e, Ezr 6:16 1123, 1547
The e observed the Passover on Ezr 6:19 1121, 1473
the Passover *lamb* for all the e, Ezr 6:20 1121, 1473
The e who had come from the Ezr 8:35 1121, 1473
of the e gathered to me, Ezr 9:4 1473
over the unfaithfulness of the e. Ezr 10:6 1473
Judah and Jerusalem to all the e, Ezr 10:7 1121, 1473
from the assembly of the e. Ezr 10:8 1473
But the e did so. Ezr 10:16 1121, 1473
the e whom Nebuchadnezzar the king Ne 7:6 1473
of Egypt and the e of Cush, Is 20:4 1546
city and will let My e go free, Is 45:13 1546
and he will carry them away as e Jer 20:4 1540
e of Judah who went to Babylon,' Jer 28:4 1546
of the LORD's house and all the e, Jer 28:6 1473
to all the e whom I have sent into Jer 29:4 1473
the word of the LORD, all you e, Jer 29:20 1473
e from Judah who are in Babylon, Jer 29:22 1546
"Send to all the e, saying, Jer 29:31 1473
all the e of Jerusalem and Judah who Jer 40:1 1546
by the river Chebar among the e, Ezk 1:1 1473
"Go to the e, to the sons of Ezk 3:11 1473
Then I came to the e who lived Ezk 3:15 1473
your relatives, your fellow e and Ezk 11:15 1546
Spirit of God to the e in Chaldea. Ezk 11:24 1473
Then I told the e all the things Ezk 11:25 1473
"I have found a man among the e Da 2:25 1123, 1547
who is one of the e from Judah, Da 5:13 1123, 1547
who is one of the e from Judah, Da 6:13 1123, 1547
into exile at the head of the e, Am 6:7 1540
And the e of this host of the sons Ob 1:20 1546
And the e of Jerusalem who are in Ob 1:20 1546
"Take *an offering* from the e, Zch 6:10 1473
were strangers and e on the earth. Heb 11:13 *3927*

EXIST
for in Him we live and move and e, Ac 17:28 *1510*
into being that which does not e. Ro 4:17 *1510*
which e are established by God. Ro 13:1 *1510*
not e even among the Gentiles, 1Co 5:1
from whom are all things and we e 1Co 8:6
and we e through Him. 1Co 8:6
I hear that divisions e among you; 1Co 11:18 *5225*
jealousy and selfish ambition e, Jas 3:16

EXISTED
e for ages Which were before us. Ec 1:10 1961
them is the one who has never e, Ec 4:3 1961
And become as if they had never e. Ob 1:16 1961
than I, for He e before me.'" Jn 1:15 *1510*
rank than I, for He e before me.' Jn 1:30 *1510*
although He e in the form of God, Php 2:6 *5225*
one hand, e in greater numbers because Heb 7:23 *1510, 1096*
by the word of God *the* heavens e 2Pe 3:5 *1510*
and because of Your will they e, Rv 4:11 *1510*

EXISTS
Whatever e has already been named, Ec 6:10 1961
Strife e and contention arises. Hab 1:3 1961
the faith in the Lord Jesus which e Eph 1:15

EXITS
and all their e were both Ezk 42:11 4161
the house, its structure, its e, Ezk 43:11 4161
with all e of the sanctuary. Ezk 44:5 4161
"These are the e of the city: Ezk 48:30 8444

EXODUS
of the e of the sons of Israel, Heb 11:22 *1841*

EXORCISTS
But also some of the Jewish e, Ac 19:13 *1845*

EXPANSE
an e in the midst of the waters, Gn 1:6 7549
God made the e, Gn 1:7 7549
waters which were below the e from Gn 1:7 7549
the waters which were above the e; Gn 1:7 7549
God called the e heaven. Gn 1:8 7549
"Let there be lights in the e of Gn 1:14 7549
be for lights in the e of the heavens Gn 1:15 7549
God placed them in the e of Gn 1:17 7549
in the open e of the heavens." Gn 1:20 7549
And the e of the waters is frozen. Jb 37:10 7341
you understood the e of the earth? Jb 38:18 7338
And their e is declaring the work Ps 19:1 7549
Praise Him in His mighty e. Ps 150:1 7549
there was something like an e, Ezk 1:22 7549
Under the e their wings *were* Ezk 1:23 7549
the e that was over their heads; Ezk 1:25 7549
Now above the e that was over Ezk 1:26 7549
in the e that was over the heads Ezk 10:1 7549
the brightness of the e of heaven, Da 12:3 7549

EXPECT
awesome things which we did not e, Is 64:3 6960a
come on a day when he does not e Mt 24:50 *4328*
those from whom you e to receive, Lk 6:34 *1679*
at an hour that you do not e." Lk 12:40 *1380*
on a day when he does not e *him* Lk 12:46 *4328*
for I e him with the brethren. 1Co 16:11 *1551*
For that man ought not to e Jas 1:7 *3633*

EXPECTANTLY
will wait e for His law." Is 42:4 3176
And for My arm they will wait e. Is 51:5 3176
me, I will watch e for the LORD; Mi 7:7 6822

EXPECTATION
"Behold, your e is false; Jb 41:9 8431
But the e of the wicked perishes. Pr 10:28 8615b
man dies, *his* e will perish, Pr 11:7 8615b
But the e of the wicked is wrath. Pr 11:23 8615b
for her e has been confounded. Zch 9:5 4007
while the people were in a state of e Lk 3:15 *4328*
men fainting from fear and the e Lk 21:26 *4329*
to my earnest e and hope, Php 1:20 *603*
a terrifying e of judgment Heb 10:27 *1561*

EXPECTED
"I never e to see your face, and Gn 48:11 6419
that all Israel e me to be king; 1Ki 2:15 7760, 6440
"When I e good, then evil came; Jb 30:26 6960a
He e *it* to produce *good* grapes, Is 5:2 6960a
when I e *it* to produce *good* grapes Is 5:4 6960a
"Are You the E One, or shall we Mt 11:3 *2064*
"Are You the E One, or do we look Lk 7:19 *2064*
'Are You the E One, or do we look Lk 7:20 *2064*
and *this,* not as we had e, 2Co 8:5 *1679*

EXPECTING
and lend, e nothing in return; Lk 6:35 *560*
e to receive something from them. Ac 3:5 *4328*
that the Jewish people were e." Ac 12:11 *4329*
him not of such crimes as I was e, Ac 25:18 *5282*
But they were e that he was about Ac 28:6 *4328*

EXPEDIENT
it is e for you that one man die Jn 11:50 *4851a*
it was e for one man to die on behalf Jn 18:14 *4851a*

EXPEL
God will e them from his belly. Jb 20:15 3423

EXPELLED
father Asa, he e from the land. 1Ki 22:46 1197a
With His fierce wind He has e *them* Is 27:8 1898
'I have been e from Your sight. Jon 2:4 1644

EXPENDED
spend and be e for your souls. 2Co 12:15 *1550*

EXPENSE
we eaten at all at the king's e, 2Sa 19:42 3899
serves as a soldier at his own e? 1Co 9:7 *3800*

EXPENSES
and pay their e so that they Ac 21:24 *1159*

EXPERIENCE
have made Your people e hardship; Ps 60:3 7200

EXPERIENCED
and e men from your tribes, Dt 1:13 3045
of your tribes, wise and e men, Dt 1:15 3045
not e any of the wars of Canaan; Jg 3:1 3045
those who had not e it formerly). Jg 3:2 3045
others e mockings and scourgings, Heb 11:36 *2983, 3984*

EXPERIENCES
a *royal* command e no trouble, Ec 8:5 3045
For when the earth e Your judgments Is 26:9
They *began* to relate their e Lk 24:35 *3588*
knowing that the same e of 1Pe 5:9 *3588*

EXPERIENCING
e the same conflict which you saw Php 1:30 *2192*

EXPERT
your father is an e in warfare, 2Sa 17:8 376
wielders of the sword, E in war; SS 3:8 3925
The counselor and the e artisan, Is 3:3 2450
Their arrows will be like an e warrior Jer 50:9 7919a
especially because you are an e in Ac 26:3 *1109*

EXPERTS
"You are e at setting aside Mk 7:9 *2573*

EXPIATION
and no e can be made for the land Nu 35:33 3722a

EXPIRE
Come forth from the womb and e? Jb 3:11 1478
take away their spirit, they e And Ps 104:29 1478

EXPIRED
Before the days had e 1Sa 18:26 4390

EXPIRES
Man e, and where is he? Jb 14:10 1478

EXPLAIN
was no one who could e it to me." Gn 41:24 5046
king which he did not e to her. 1Ki 10:3 5046
Solomon which he did not e to her. 2Ch 9:2 5046
e it that righteous men, wise men, Ec 9:1 952
and e its interpretation to me shall be Da 5:7 2331b
and there was none to e *it.* Da 8:27 995
"E to us the parable of the tares Mt 13:36 *1285*
"E the parable to us." Mt 15:15 *5419*
to e to them in orderly sequence, Ac 11:4 *1620*
much to say, and *it is* hard to e, Heb 5:11 *1421*

EXPLAINED
e the law to the people while the Ne 8:7 995
He e to them the things concerning Lk 24:27 *1329*
bosom of the Father, He has e *Him.* Jn 1:18 *1834*
after he had e everything to them, Ac 10:8 *1834*
they took him aside and e to him Ac 18:26 *1620*

EXPLAINING
but He was e everything privately Mk 4:34 *1956*
He was e the Scriptures to us?" Lk 24:32 *1272*
e and giving evidence that the Ac 17:3 *1272*
and he was e to them by solemnly Ac 28:23 *1620*

EXPLANATION
and to seek wisdom and an e, Ec 7:25 2808
one thing to another to find an e, Ec 7:27 2808
of dreams, e of enigmas and Da 5:12 263

EXPLICITLY
the Spirit e says that in later times 1Tm 4:1 *4490*

EXPLOIT
they will e you with false words; 2Pe 2:3 *1710*

EXPLORE
And I set my mind to seek and e by Ec 1:13 8446

EXPLORED
I e with my mind *how* to stimulate Ec 2:3 8446

EXPLORES
e the mountains for his pasture And Jb 39:8 8446

EXPORTED
and by the same means they e them 1Ki 10:29 3318
and by the same means they e them 2Ch 1:17 3318

EXPOSE
He will e your sins! La 4:22 1540
and e your nakedness to them that Ezk 16:37 1540
Or I will strip her naked And e her Hos 2:3 3322
drink and e your *own* nakedness. Hab 2:16 6188
so that they would e their infants Ac 7:19 *4160, 1570*
darkness, but instead even e them; Eph 5:11 *1651*

EXPOSED
nakedness will not be e on it.' Ex 20:26 1540
she has e the flow of her blood; Lv 20:18 1540
behind the wall, the e places, Ne 4:13 6706
Your shame also will be e; Is 47:3 7200
And your heels have been e. Jer 13:22 2554
were ninety-six e pomegranates; Jer 52:23 7307
And they have not e your iniquity La 2:14 1540
Light for fear that his deeds will be e. Jn 3:20 *1651*
when they are e by the light, Eph 5:13 *1651*

EXPOSING
e the white which *was* in the rods. Gn 30:37 4286

EXPOSURE
often without food, in cold and e. 2Co 11:27 *1132*

EXPOUND
Moses undertook to e this law, Dt 1:5 874

EXPRESS
I will e my riddle on the harp. Ps 49:4 6605a

EXPRESSED
whose spirit was e through you? Jb 26:4 3318
for they do the lustful desires e Ezk 33:31

EXPRESSION
The **e** of their faces bears witness **Is 3:9** 1971
e was altered toward Shadrach, **Da 3:19** 6755
(Now this **e**, "He ascended," **Eph 4:9**
This **e**, "Yet once more," **Heb 12:27**
EXPRESSLY
LORD came **e** to Ezekiel the priest, **Ezk 1:3** 1961
EXPROPRIATIONS
Stop your **e** from My people," **Ezk 45:9** 1646
EXTEND
'Your southern sector shall **e** from **Nu 34:3** 1961
and your southern border shall **e** **Nu 34:3** 1961
shall give to the Levites *shall* **e** **Nu 35:4**
none to **e** lovingkindness to him, **Ps 109:12** 4900
I **e** peace to her like a river, **Is 66:12** 5186
hearth shall **e** upwards four horns. **Ezk 43:15**
"The boundary shall **e** from **Ezk 47:17** 1961
south side toward the south *shall* **e** **Ezk 47:19**
E your baldness like the eagle, **Mi 1:16** 7337
You **e** Your hand to heal, **Ac 4:30** *1614*
EXTENDED
The territory of the Canaanite **e** from **Gn 10:19** 1961
Now their settlement **e** from Mesha **Gn 10:30** 1961
with Joseph and **e** kindness to him, **Gn 39:21** 5186
The border **e** *from there* and **Jos 18:14** 8388a
It **e** northward and went to **Jos 18:17** 8388a
of these cherubim **e** twenty cubits, **2Ch 3:13** 6566
his fame **e** to the border of Egypt, **2Ch 26:8** 1980
and has **e** lovingkindness to me **Ezr 7:28** 5186
but has **e** lovingkindness to us in **Ezr 9:9** 5186
and the king **e** to Esther the **Es 5:2** 3447
e the golden scepter to Esther. **Es 8:4** 3447
princes of the provinces which **e** **Es 8:9**
Or **e** our hands to a strange god, **Ps 44:20** 6566
e his hand through the opening, **SS 5:4** 7971
e all the borders of the land. **Is 26:15** 7368
behold, a hand was **e** to me; **Ezk 2:9** 7971
e all around its planting place, **Ezk 31:4** 1980
For its roots **e** to many waters. **Ezk 31:7** 1961
the gate **e** round about to **Ezk 40:14**
and the side chambers **e** to the **Ezk 41:6** 935
that day will your boundary be **e**. **Mi 7:11** 7368
EXTENDS
wadis That **e** to the site of Ar, **Nu 21:15** 5186
"When the LORD your God **e** your **Dt 12:20** 7337
O LORD, **e** to the heavens, **Ps 36:5**
She **e** her hand to the poor, **Pr 31:20** 6566
wood, he **e** a measuring line; **Is 44:13** 5186
That **e** its roots by a stream And **Jer 17:8** 7971
EXTENSION
but an **e** of life was granted to **Da 7:12** 754
EXTENSIVE
"The work is great and **e**, **Ne 4:19** 7342
EXTENSIVELY
and he built **e** the wall of Ophel. **2Ch 27:3** 7230
EXTENT
'In proportion to the **e** of the **Lv 25:16** 7230
end And what is the **e** of my days **Ps 39:4** 4060a
to the **e** that you did it to one of **Mt 25:40** *1909, 3745*
to the **e** that you did not do it to **Mt 25:45** *1909, 3745*
to such an **e** that Jesus could no **Mk 1:45** *5620*
to such an **e** that they could not **Mk 3:20** *5620*
to such an **e** that they even **Ac 5:15** *5620*
EXTERIOR
front of the **e** of the inner court, **Ezk 40:19** 2351
EXTERMINATE
and who planned to **e** us from **2Sa 21:5** 8045
And He will **e** its sinners from it. **Is 13:9** 8045
EXTERMINATED
against them until they are **e**.' **1Sa 15:18** 3615
"Rahab who has been **e**." **Is 30:7** 7674
EXTERNAL
Apart from *such* **e** things, there is **2Co 11:28** *3924*
on earth, not with **e** service, **Col 3:22** *3787*
Your adornment must not be *merely* **e** **1Pe 3:3** *1855*
EXTINCTION
I rejoiced at the **e** of my enemy, **Jb 31:29** 6365
EXTINGUISH
they will **e** my coal which is left, **2Sa 14:7** 3518
do not **e** the lamp of Israel." **2Sa 21:17** 3518
dimly burning wick He will not **e**; **Is 42:3** 3518
fire And burn with none to **e** *it*, **Jer 21:12** 3518
"And when *I* **e** you, I will cover **Ezk 32:7** 3518
be able to **e** all the flaming arrows **Eph 6:16** *4570*
EXTINGUISHED
spirit is broken, my days are **e**, **Jb 17:1** 2193
They were **e** as a fire of thorns; **Ps 118:12** 1846
been quenched *and* **e** like a wick): **Is 43:17** 3518
EXTOL
My father's God, and I will **e** Him. **Ex 15:2** 7311
I will **e** You, O LORD, for You **Ps 30:1** 7311
Let them **e** Him also in the **Ps 107:32** 7311
You are my God, I **e** You. **Ps 118:28** 7311
I will **e** You, my God, O King, **Ps 145:1** 7311
will **e** your love more than wine. **SS 1:4** 2142
EXTOLLED
And He was **e** with my tongue. **Ps 66:17** 7311
EXTORTED
or *if* he has **e** from his companion, **Lv 6:2** 6231
EXTORTION
by robbery or what he got by **e**, **Lv 6:4** 6233
on practicing oppression and **e**." **Jer 22:17** 4835
father, because he practiced **e**, **Ezk 18:18** 6233

EXTORTIONER
For the **e** has come to an end, **Is 16:4** 4671a
EXTRACT
And if you **e** the precious from the **Jer 15:19** 3318
EXTRAORDINARY
then the LORD will bring **e** plagues **Dt 28:59** 6381
And to work His work, His **e** work. **Is 28:21** 5237
which was large and of **e** splendor, **Da 2:31** 3493
"*This was* because an **e** spirit, **Da 5:12** 3493
e wisdom have been found in you. **Da 5:14** 3493
because he possessed an **e** spirit, **Da 6:3** 3493
And he will destroy to an **e** degree **Da 8:24** 6381
e miracles by the hands of Paul, **Ac 19:11** *5177*
The natives showed us **e** kindness; **Ac 28:2** *5177*
EXTREME
at the **e** end of the border. **Nu 22:36** 7097a
will only see the **e** end of them and **Nu 23:13** 7097a
wilderness of Zin at the **e** south. **Jos 15:1** 7097a
at the **e** rear toward the west. **Ezk 46:19** 3411
came to me in *my* **e** weariness about **Da 9:21** 3286
EXTREMELY
Why then have I been **e** wise?" **Ec 2:15** 3148
the furnace had been made **e** hot, **Da 3:22** 3493
and terrifying and **e** strong; **Da 7:7** 3493
e large and mighty army for war; **Da 11:25** 5704, 3966
Then the men became **e** frightened **Jon 1:10** 3374, 1419
Jonah was **e** happy about the plant. **Jon 4:6** 8057, 1419
They were so **e** violent that no **Mt 8:28** *3029*
away, although it was **e** large. **Mk 16:4** *4970*
for he was **e** rich. **Lk 18:23** *4970*
being more **e** zealous for my **Ga 1:14** *4053*
because its plague was **e** severe. **Rv 16:21** *4970*
EXTREMITY
Now the cities at the **e** of the **Jos 15:21** 7097a
from the northern **e**, **Ezk 48:1** 7097a
EXULT
daughters of the uncircumcised will **e**. **2Sa 1:20** 5937
Let the field **e**, and all that is **1Ch 16:32** 5970
e when they find the grave? **Jb 3:22** 7797
who love Your name may **e** in You. **Ps 5:11** 5970
I will be glad and **e** in You; **Ps 9:2** 5970
Do not let my enemies **e** over me. **Ps 25:2** 5970
It shall **e** in His salvation. **Ps 35:9** 7797
"I will **e**, I will portion out **Ps 60:6** 5937
let them **e** before God; **Ps 68:3** 5970
is the LORD, and **e** before Him. **Ps 68:4** 5937
LORD, How long shall the wicked **e**? **Ps 94:3** 5937
Let the field **e**, and all that is **Ps 96:12** 5937
"I will **e**, I will portion out **Ps 108:7** 5937
Let the godly ones **e** in glory; **Ps 149:5** 5937
"You shall **e** no more, O crushed **Is 23:12** 5937
LORD, My soul will **e** in my God; **Is 61:10** 1523
of merrymakers, Nor did I **e**. **Jer 15:17** 5937
Yet I will **e** in the LORD, I will **Hab 3:18** 5937
Rejoice and **e** with all *your* heart, **Zph 3:14** 5937
He will **e** over you with joy, He **Zph 3:17** 7797
we **e** in hope of the glory of God. **Ro 5:2** *2744*
but we also **e** in our tribulations, **Ro 5:3** *2744*
but we also **e** in God through our **Ro 5:11** *2744*
EXULTANT
You boisterous town, you **e** city; **Is 22:2** 5947
the **e** city Which dwells securely, **Zph 2:15** 5947
EXULTANTLY
And my eye has looked **e** upon my **Ps 92:11**
EXULTATION
O Israel, with **e** like the nations! **Hos 9:1** 1524a
Their **e** *was* like those Who devour **Hab 3:14** 5951
is our hope or joy or crown of **e**? **1Th 2:19** *2746a*
His glory you may rejoice with **e**. **1Pe 4:13** *21*
EXULTED
enemy, Or **e** when evil befell him? **Jb 31:29** 5782
HEART WAS GLAD AND MY TONGUE **E**; **Ac 2:26** *21*
EXULTING
warriors, My proudly **e** ones, **Is 13:3** 5947
your midst Your proud, **e** ones, **Zph 3:11** 5947
EXULTS
"My heart **e** in the LORD; **1Sa 2:1** 5970
Therefore my heart **e**, **Ps 28:7** 5937
EYE
e for eye, tooth for tooth, hand **Ex 21:24** 5869
eye for **e**, tooth for tooth, hand **Ex 21:24** 5869
the **e** of his male or female slave, **Ex 21:26** 5869
him go free on account of his **e**. **Ex 21:26** 5869
or *one who has* a defect in his **e** **Lv 21:20** 5869
fracture for fracture, **e** for eye, **Lv 24:20** 5869
fracture for fracture, eye for **e**, **Lv 24:20** 5869
You, O LORD, are seen **e** to eye, **Nu 14:14** 5869
You, O LORD, are seen eye to **e**, **Nu 14:14** 5869
of the man whose **e** is opened; **Nu 24:3** 5869
of the man whose **e** is opened, **Nu 24:15** 5869
your **e** shall not pity them, **Dt 7:16** 5869
and your **e** shall not pity him, nor **Dt 13:8** 5869
and your **e** is hostile toward your **Dt 15:9** 5869
life for life, **e** for eye, tooth **Dt 19:21** 5869
life for life, eye for **e**, **Dt 19:21** 5869
guarded him as the pupil of His **e**. **Dt 32:10** 5869
when he died, his **e** was not dim, **Dt 34:7** 5869
the right **e** of every one of you, **1Sa 11:2** 5869
but my **e** had pity on you; and I **1Sa 24:10** 5869
that Your **e** may be open toward this **2Ch 6:20** 5869
But the **e** of their God was on the **Ezr 5:5** 5870a
My **e** will not again see good. **Jb 7:7** 5869
"The **e** of him who sees me will **Jb 7:8** 5869

I had died and no **e** had seen me! **Jb 10:18** 5869
"Behold, my **e** has seen all *this*, **Jb 13:1** 5869
My **e** weeps to God. **Jb 16:20** 5869
my **e** gazes on their provocation. **Jb 17:2** 5869
"My **e** has also grown dim because **Jb 17:7** 5869
"The **e** which saw him sees him no **Jb 20:9** 5869
"The **e** of the adulterer waits **Jb 24:15** 5869
'No **e** will see me.' **Jb 24:15** 5869
the falcon's **e** caught sight of it. **Jb 28:7** 5869
And his **e** sees anything precious. **Jb 28:10** 5869
And when the **e** saw, it gave **Jb 29:11** 5869
But now my **e** sees You; **Jb 42:5** 5869
My **e** has wasted away with grief; **Ps 6:7** 5869
Keep me as the apple of the **e**; **Ps 17:8** 5869
My **e** is wasted away from grief, my **Ps 31:9** 5869
counsel you with My **e** upon you. **Ps 32:8** 5869
the **e** of the LORD is on those who **Ps 33:18** 5869
my **e** has looked *with satisfaction* **Ps 54:7** 5869
Their **e** bulges from fatness; **Ps 73:7** 5869
My **e** has wasted away because of **Ps 88:9** 5869
And my **e** has looked *exultantly* **Ps 92:11** 5869
He who formed the **e**, **Ps 94:9** 5869
teaching as the apple of your **e**. **Pr 7:2** 5869
He who winks the **e** causes trouble, **Pr 10:10** 5869
The hearing ear and the seeing **e**, **Pr 20:12** 5869
an evil **e** hastens after wealth And **Pr 28:22** 5869
The **e** that mocks a father And **Pr 30:17** 5869
e is not satisfied with seeing, **Ec 1:8** 5869
Nor will their **e** pity children. **Is 13:18** 5869
has the **e** seen a God besides You, **Is 64:4** 5869
to face and see him **e** to eye; **Jer 32:4** 5869
to face and see him eye to **e**; **Jer 32:4** 5869
see the king of Babylon **e** to eye, **Jer 34:3** 5869
see the king of Babylon eye to **e**, **Jer 34:3** 5869
all that were pleasant to the **e**; **La 2:4** 5869
and My **e** will have no pity and I **Ezk 5:11** 5869
'For My **e** will have no pity on **Ezk 7:4** 5869
'My **e** will show no pity nor **Ezk 7:9** 5869
My **e** will have no pity nor will I **Ezk 8:18** 5869
do not let your **e** have pity and **Ezk 9:5** 5869
My **e** will have no pity nor will I **Ezk 9:10** 5869
"No **e** looked with pity on you to **Ezk 16:5** 5869
"Yet My **e** spared them rather than **Ezk 20:17** 5869
you, touches the apple of His **e**. **Zch 2:8** 5869
be on his arm And on his right **e**! **Zch 11:17** 5869
And his right **e** will be blind." **Zch 11:17** 5869
If your right **e** makes you stumble, **Mt 5:29** *3788*
'AN **E** FOR AN EYE, AND A TOOTH FOR **Mt 5:38** *3788*
'AN EYE FOR AN **E**, AND A TOOTH FOR **Mt 5:38** *3788*
"The **e** is the lamp of the body; **Mt 6:22** *3788*
if your **e** is clear, **Mt 6:22** *3788*
"But if your **e** is bad, your whole **Mt 6:23** *3788*
speck that is in your brother's **e**, **Mt 7:3** *3788*
the log that is in your own **e**? **Mt 7:3** *3788*
me take the speck out of your **e**,' **Mt 7:4** *3788*
behold, the log is in your own **e**? **Mt 7:4** *3788*
take the log out of your own **e**, **Mt 7:5** *3788*
the speck out of your brother's **e**. **Mt 7:5** *3788*
If your **e** causes you to stumble, **Mt 18:9** *3788*
for you to enter life with one **e**, **Mt 18:9** *3442*
to go through the **e** of a needle, **Mt 19:24** *5144a*
e envious because I am generous?' **Mt 20:15** *3788*
If your **e** causes you to stumble, **Mk 9:47** *3788*
the kingdom of God with one **e**, **Mk 9:47** *3442*
camel to go through the **e** of a needle **Mk 10:25** *5168*
speck that is in your brother's **e**, **Lk 6:41** *3788*
the log that is in your own **e**? **Lk 6:41** *3788*
out the speck that is in your **e**,' **Lk 6:42** *3788*
see the log that is in your own **e**? **Lk 6:42** *3788*
take the log out of your own **e**, **Lk 6:42** *3788*
speck that is in your brother's **e**. **Lk 6:42** *3788*
"The **e** is the lamp of your body; **Lk 11:34** *3788*
when your **e** is clear, your whole **Lk 11:34** *3788*
to go through the **e** of a needle than **Lk 18:25** *5144a*
keep your **e** on those who cause **Ro 16:17** *4648*
"THINGS WHICH **E** HAS NOT SEEN AND **1Co 2:9** *3788*
"Because I am not an **e**, **1Co 12:16** *3788*
If the whole body were an **e**, **1Co 12:17** *3788*
And the **e** cannot say to the hand, **1Co 12:21** *3788*
moment, in the twinkling of an **e**, **1Co 15:52** *3788*
CLOUDS, and every **e** will see Him, **Rv 1:7** *3788*
and **e** salve to anoint your eyes so **Rv 3:18** *2854*
EYEBROWS
his head and his beard and his **e**, **Lv 14:9** 5869, 1354
EYELIDS
And deep darkness is on my **e**, **Jb 16:16** 6079
are like the **e** of the morning. **Jb 41:18** 6079
His **e** test the sons of men. **Ps 11:4** 6079
You have held my **e** *open*; **Ps 77:4** 5869, 8109
to my eyes Or slumber to my **e** **Ps 132:4** 6079
your eyes, Nor slumber to your **e**; **Pr 6:4** 6079
Nor let her capture you with her **e**. **Pr 6:25** 6079
And his **e** are raised *in arrogance*. **Pr 30:13** 6079
tears And our **e** flow with water. **Jer 9:18** 6079
EYES
eat from it your **e** will be opened, **Gn 3:5** 5869
that it was a delight to the **e**, **Gn 3:6** 5869
the **e** of both of them were opened, **Gn 3:7** 5869
found favor in the **e** of the LORD. **Gn 6:8** 5869
Lot lifted up his **e** and saw **Gn 13:10** 5869
"Now lift up your **e** and look from **Gn 13:14** 5869
he lifted up his **e** and looked, **Gn 18:2** 5869
her **e** and she saw a well of water; **Gn 21:19** 5869
the third day Abraham raised his **e** **Gn 22:4** 5869
Abraham raised his **e** and looked, **Gn 22:13** 5869
and he lifted up his **e** and looked, **Gn 24:63** 5869

Rebekah lifted up her **e**,	**Gn 24:64**	5869
and his **e** were too dim to see,	**Gn 27:1**	5869
And Leah's **e** were weak, but Rachel	**Gn 29:17**	5869
lifted up my **e** and saw in a dream,	**Gn 31:10**	5869
your **e** and see *that* all the male	**Gn 31:12**	5869
and my sleep fled from my **e**.	**Gn 31:40**	5869
Jacob lifted his **e** and looked,	**Gn 33:1**	5869
He lifted his **e** and saw the	**Gn 33:5**	5869
as they raised their **e** and looked,	**Gn 37:25**	5869
them and bound him before their **e**.	**Gn 42:24**	5869
e and saw his brother Benjamin,	**Gn 43:29**	5869
me that I may set my **e** on him.'	**Gn 44:21**	5869
"Behold, your **e** see,	**Gn 45:12**	5869
the **e** of my brother Benjamin *see,*	**Gn 45:12**	5869
and Joseph will close your **e**."	**Gn 46:4**	5869
"Why should we die before your **e**,	**Gn 47:19**	5869
Now the **e** of Israel were *so* dim	**Gn 48:10**	5869
"His **e** are dull from wine, And	**Gn 49:12**	5869
to the Egyptians before their **e**,	**Ex 8:26**	5869
"If she is displeasing in the **e**	**Ex 21:8**	5869
And to the **e** of the sons of Israel	**Ex 24:17**	5869
e the infection has not changed	**Lv 13:5**	5869
fever that will waste away the **e**	**Lv 26:16**	5869
it is hidden from the **e** of her husband	**Nu 5:13**	5869
and you will be as **e** for us.	**Nu 10:31**	5869
your own heart and your own **e**,	**Nu 15:39**	5869
you put out the **e** of these men?	**Nu 16:14**	5869
speak to the rock before their **e**,	**Nu 20:8**	5869
the LORD opened the **e** of Balaam,	**Nu 22:31**	5869
And Balaam lifted up his **e** and saw	**Nu 24:2**	5869
down, yet having his **e** uncovered,	**Nu 24:4**	5869
down, yet having his **e** uncovered.	**Nu 24:16**	5869
before their **e** at the water."	**Nu 27:14**	5869
e and as thorns in your sides,	**Nu 33:55**	5869
for you in Egypt before your **e**,	**Dt 1:30**	5869
'Your **e** have seen all that the	**Dt 3:21**	5869
lift up your **e** to the west and north	**Dt 3:27**	5869
and east, and see *it* with your **e**,	**Dt 3:27**	5869
"Your **e** have seen what the LORD	**Dt 4:3**	5869
the things which your **e** have seen and	**Dt 4:9**	5869
not to lift up your **e** to heaven	**Dt 4:19**	5869
for you in Egypt before your **e**?	**Dt 4:34**	5869
before our **e** against Egypt,	**Dt 6:22**	5869
the great trials which your **e** saw	**Dt 7:19**	5869
and smashed them before your **e**.	**Dt 9:17**	5869
for you which your **e** have seen.	**Dt 10:21**	5869
but your own **e** have seen all the	**Dt 11:7**	5869
the **e** of the LORD your God are	**Dt 11:12**	5869
whatever is right in his own **e**;	**Dt 12:8**	5869
for a bribe blinds the **e** of the	**Dt 16:19**	5869
this blood, nor did our **e** see *it.*	**Dt 21:7**	5869
is right in the **e** of the LORD.	**Dt 21:9**	5869
she finds no favor in his **e** because he	**Dt 24:1**	5869
brother is not degraded in your **e**.	**Dt 25:3**	5869
be slaughtered before your **e**,	**Dt 28:31**	5869
while your **e** look on and	**Dt 28:32**	5869
a trembling heart, failing of **e**,	**Dt 28:65**	5869
of your **e** which you will see.	**Dt 28:67**	5869
did before your **e** in the land of Egypt	**Dt 29:2**	5869
trials which your **e** have seen,	**Dt 29:3**	5869
you a heart to know, nor **e** to see,	**Dt 29:4**	5869
I have let you see *it* with your **e**,	**Dt 34:4**	5869
he lifted up his **e** and looked,	**Jos 5:13**	5869
your sides and thorns in your **e**,	**Jos 23:13**	5869
own **e** saw what I did in Egypt.	**Jos 24:7**	5869
seized him and gouged out his **e**;	**Jg 16:21**	5869
of the Philistines for my two **e**."	**Jg 16:28**	5869
did what was right in his own **e**.	**Jg 17:6**	5869
And he lifted up his **e** and saw the	**Jg 19:17**	5869
did what was right in his own **e**.	**Jg 21:25**	5869
"Let your **e** be on the field which	**Ru 2:9**	5869
that your **e** will fail *from weeping* and	**1Sa 2:33**	5869
and his **e** were set so that he	**1Sa 4:15**	5869
and they raised their **e** and saw	**1Sa 6:13**	5869
a bribe to blind my **e** with it?	**1Sa 12:3**	5869
the LORD will do before your **e**.	**1Sa 12:16**	5869
his mouth, and his **e** brightened.	**1Sa 14:27**	5869
how my **e** have brightened because I	**1Sa 14:29**	5869
you were little in your own **e**,	**1Sa 15:17**	5869
e and a handsome appearance.	**1Sa 16:12**	5869
this day your **e** have seen that the	**1Sa 24:10**	5869
my young men find favor in your **e**,	**1Sa 25:8**	5869
uncovered himself today in the **e** of	**2Sa 6:20**	5869
and will be humble in my own **e**,	**2Sa 6:22**	5869
this was insignificant in Your **e**,	**2Sa 7:19**	5869
take your wives before your **e** and	**2Sa 12:11**	5869
watchman raised his **e** and looked,	**2Sa 13:34**	5869
wall, and raised his **e** and looked,	**2Sa 18:24**	5869
to my cleanness before His **e**.	**2Sa 22:25**	5869
But Your **e** are on the haughty	**2Sa 22:28**	5869
e of my lord the king *still* see;	**2Sa 24:3**	5869
the **e** of all Israel are on you,	**1Ki 1:20**	5869
today while my own **e** see *it.*' "	**1Ki 1:48**	5869
that Your **e** may be open toward	**1Ki 8:29**	5869
that Your **e** may be open to the	**1Ki 8:52**	5869
and My **e** and My heart will be	**1Ki 9:3**	5869
until I came and my **e** had seen it.	**1Ki 10:7**	5869
his **e** were dim because of his age.	**1Ki 14:4**	5869
whatever is desirable in your **e**,	**1Ki 20:6**	5869
himself with a bandage over his **e**.	**1Ki 20:38**	5869
took the bandage away from his **e**,	**1Ki 20:41**	5869
on his mouth and his **e** on his eyes	**2Ki 4:34**	5869
his **e** and his hands on his hands,	**2Ki 4:34**	5869
times and the lad opened his **e**.	**2Ki 4:35**	5869
open his **e** that he may see."	**2Ki 6:17**	5869
the LORD opened the servant's **e** and	**2Ki 6:17**	5869
"O LORD, open the **e** of these *men,*	**2Ki 6:20**	5869
So the LORD opened their **e** and	**2Ki 6:20**	5869
you will see it with your own **e**,	**2Ki 7:2**	5869
you will see it with your own **e**,	**2Ki 7:19**	5869
her **e** and adorned her head and	**2Ki 9:30**	5869
executing what is right in My **e**,	**2Ki 10:30**	5869
open Your **e**, O LORD, and see;	**2Ki 19:16**	5869
And haughtily lifted up your **e**?	**2Ki 19:22**	5869
your **e** will not see all the	**2Ki 22:20**	5869
the sons of Zedekiah before his **e**,	**2Ki 25:7**	5869
then put out the **e** of Zedekiah and	**2Ki 25:7**	5869
right in the **e** of all the people.	**1Ch 13:4**	5869
"This was a small thing in Your **e**,	**1Ch 17:17**	5869
Then David lifted up his **e** and saw	**1Ch 21:16**	5869
I pray, let Your **e** be open	**2Ch 6:40**	5869
"Now My **e** will be open and My	**2Ch 7:15**	5869
and My **e** and My heart will be	**2Ch 7:16**	5869
until I came and my **e** had seen it.	**2Ch 9:6**	5869
"For the **e** of the LORD move to	**2Ch 16:9**	5869
to do, but our **e** are on You."	**2Ch 20:12**	5869
as you see with your own **e**.	**2Ch 29:8**	5869
so your **e** will not see all the	**2Ch 34:28**	5869
house was laid before their **e**,	**Ezr 3:12**	5869
that our God may enlighten our **e**	**Ezr 9:8**	5869
and Your **e** open to hear the prayer	**Ne 1:6**	5869
favor in the **e** of all who saw her.	**Es 2:15**	5869
lifted up their **e** at a distance and	**Jb 2:12**	5869
womb, Or hide trouble from my **e**.	**Jb 3:10**	5869
A form *was* before my **e**;	**Jb 4:16**	5869
Your **e** *will be* on me, but I will	**Jb 7:8**	5869
'Have You **e** of flesh?	**Jb 10:4**	5869
And I am innocent in your **e**.'	**Jb 11:4**	5869
"But the **e** of the wicked will	**Jb 11:20**	5869
also open Your **e** on him	**Jb 14:3**	5869
And why do your **e** flash,	**Jb 15:12**	5869
The **e** of his children also will	**Jb 17:5**	5869
as beasts, As stupid in your **e**?	**Jb 18:3**	5869
my **e** will see and not another.	**Jb 19:27**	5869
their offspring before their **e**,	**Jb 21:8**	5869
"Let his own **e** see his decay, And	**Jb 21:20**	5869
And His **e** are on their ways.	**Jb 24:23**	5869
He opens his **e**, and it is no longer.	**Jb 27:19**	5869
hidden from the **e** of all living And	**Jb 28:21**	5869
"I was **e** to the blind And feet	**Jb 29:15**	5869
"I have made a covenant with my **e**;	**Jb 31:1**	5869
way, Or my heart followed my **e**,	**Jb 31:7**	5869
caused the **e** of the widow to fail,	**Jb 31:16**	5869
he was righteous in his own **e**.	**Jb 32:1**	5869
His **e** are upon the ways of a man,	**Jb 34:21**	5869
withdraw His **e** from the righteous;	**Jb 36:7**	5869
His **e** see *it* from afar.	**Jb 39:29**	5869
And his **e** are like the eyelids of	**Jb 41:18**	5869
shall not stand before Your **e**;	**Ps 5:5**	5869
His **e** stealthily watch for the	**Ps 10:8**	5869
His **e** behold, His eyelids test the	**Ps 11:4**	5869
Enlighten my **e**, or I will sleep the	**Ps 13:3**	5869
whose **e** a reprobate is despised,	**Ps 15:4**	5869
Let Your **e** look with equity.	**Ps 17:2**	5869
e to cast *us* down to the ground.	**Ps 17:11**	5869
cleanness of my hands in His **e**.	**Ps 18:24**	5869
But haughty **e** You abase.	**Ps 18:27**	5869
LORD is pure, enlightening the **e**.	**Ps 19:8**	5869
My **e** are continually toward the	**Ps 25:15**	5869
Your lovingkindness is before my **e**,	**Ps 26:3**	5869
am cut off from before Your **e**";	**Ps 31:22**	5869
The **e** of the LORD are toward the	**Ps 34:15**	5869
"Aha, aha, our **e** have seen it!"	**Ps 35:21**	5869
is no fear of God before his **e**.	**Ps 36:1**	5869
flatters him in his *own* **e** Concerning	**Ps 36:2**	5869
And the light of my **e**,	**Ps 38:10**	5869
the case in order before your **e**.	**Ps 50:21**	5869
His **e** keep watch on the nations;	**Ps 66:7**	5869
My **e** fail while I wait for my God.	**Ps 69:3**	5869
May their **e** grow dim so that they	**Ps 69:23**	5869
You will only look on with your **e** And	**Ps 91:8**	5869
no worthless thing before my **e**;	**Ps 101:3**	5869
My **e** shall be upon the faithful of	**Ps 101:6**	5869
They have **e**, but they cannot see;	**Ps 115:5**	5869
soul from death, My **e** from tears,	**Ps 116:8**	5869
It is marvelous in our **e**.	**Ps 118:23**	5869
Open my **e**, that I may behold	**Ps 119:18**	5869
away my **e** from looking at vanity,	**Ps 119:37**	5869
My **e** fail *with longing* for Your	**Ps 119:82**	5869
My **e** fail *with longing* for Your	**Ps 119:123**	5869
My **e** shed streams of water,	**Ps 119:136**	5869
My **e** anticipate the night watches,	**Ps 119:148**	5869
lift up my **e** to the mountains;	**Ps 121:1**	5869
To You I lift up my **e**,	**Ps 123:1**	5869
as the **e** of servants *look* to the	**Ps 123:2**	5869
As the **e** of a maid to the hand of	**Ps 123:2**	5869
So our **e** *look* to the LORD our God,	**Ps 123:2**	5869
is not proud, nor my **e** haughty;	**Ps 131:1**	5869
I will not give sleep to my **e** Or	**Ps 132:4**	5869
They have **e**, but they do not see;	**Ps 135:16**	5869
Your **e** have seen my unformed	**Ps 139:16**	5869
For my **e** are toward You, O GOD,	**Ps 141:8**	5869
The **e** of all look to You, And	**Ps 145:15**	5869
The LORD opens *the* **e** *of*	**Ps 146:8**	5869
Do not be wise in your own **e**;	**Pr 3:7**	5869
Let your **e** look directly ahead And	**Pr 4:25**	5869
man are before the **e** of the LORD,	**Pr 5:21**	5869
Give no sleep to your **e**,	**Pr 6:4**	5869
Who winks with his **e**,	**Pr 6:13**	5869
Haughty **e**, a lying tongue, And	**Pr 6:17**	5869
to the teeth and smoke to the **e**,	**Pr 10:26**	5869
of a fool is right in his own **e**,	**Pr 12:15**	5869
The **e** of the LORD are in every	**Pr 15:3**	5869
Bright **e** gladden the heart;	**Pr 15:30**	5869
He who winks his **e** *does so* to	**Pr 16:30**	5869
But the **e** of a fool are on the	**Pr 17:24**	5869
Disperses all evil with his **e**.	**Pr 20:8**	5869
Open your **e**, *and* you will be	**Pr 20:13**	5869
man's way is right in his own **e**,	**Pr 21:2**	5869
Haughty **e** and a proud heart, The	**Pr 21:4**	5869
neighbor finds no favor in his **e**.	**Pr 21:10**	5869
The **e** of the LORD preserve	**Pr 22:12**	5869
When you set your **e** on it,	**Pr 23:5**	5869
And let your **e** delight in my ways.	**Pr 23:26**	5869
Who has redness of **e**?	**Pr 23:29**	5869
Your **e** will see strange things And	**Pr 23:33**	5869
the prince, Whom your **e** have seen.	**Pr 25:7**	5869
That he not be wise in his own **e**.	**Pr 26:5**	5869
you see a man wise in his own **e**?	**Pr 26:12**	5869
sluggard is wiser in his own **e** Than	**Pr 26:16**	5869
Nor are the **e** of man ever satisfied.	**Pr 27:20**	5869
The rich man is wise in his own **e**,	**Pr 28:11**	5869
shuts his **e** will have many curses.	**Pr 28:27**	5869
LORD gives light to the **e** of both.	**Pr 29:13**	5869
a kind who is pure in his own **e**,	**Pr 30:12**	5869
oh how lofty are his **e**!	**Pr 30:13**	5869
e desired I did not refuse them.	**Ec 2:10**	5869
The wise man's **e** are in his head,	**Ec 2:14**	5869
his **e** were not satisfied with	**Ec 4:8**	5869
What the **e** see is better than what	**Ec 6:9**	5869
is good for the **e** to see the sun.	**Ec 11:7**	5869
heart and the desires of your **e**.	**Ec 11:9**	5869
Your **e** are *like* doves."	**SS 1:15**	5869
Your **e** are *like* doves behind your	**SS 4:1**	5869
with a single *glance* of your **e**,	**SS 4:9**	5869
"His **e** are like doves Beside	**SS 5:12**	5869
"Turn your **e** away from me, For	**SS 6:5**	5869
Your **e** *like* the pools in Heshbon	**SS 7:4**	5869
in his **e** as one who finds peace.	**SS 8:10**	5869
prayer, I will hide My **e** from you	**Is 1:15**	5869
heads held high and seductive **e**,	**Is 3:16**	5869
The **e** of the proud also will be	**Is 5:15**	5869
those who are wise in their own **e** And	**Is 5:21**	5869
For my **e** have seen the King, the	**Is 6:5**	5869
Their ears dull, And their **e** dim,	**Is 6:10**	5869
they might see with their **e**,	**Is 6:10**	5869
will not judge by what His **e** see,	**Is 11:3**	5869
dashed to pieces Before their **e**;	**Is 13:16**	5869
And his **e** will look to the Holy	**Is 17:7**	5869
"Turn your **e** away from me, Let me	**Is 22:4**	8159
of deep sleep, He has shut your **e**,	**Is 29:10**	5869
the **e** of the blind will see.	**Is 29:18**	5869
your **e** will behold your Teacher.	**Is 30:20**	5869
Then the **e** of those who see will	**Is 32:3**	5869
his **e** from looking upon evil;	**Is 33:15**	5869
Your **e** will see the King in His	**Is 33:17**	5869
Your **e** will see Jerusalem, an	**Is 33:20**	5869
the **e** of the blind will be opened And	**Is 35:5**	5869
open Your **e**, O LORD, and see;	**Is 37:17**	5869
And haughtily lifted up your **e**?	**Is 37:23**	5869
e look wistfully to the heights;	**Is 38:14**	5869
Lift up your **e** on high And see who	**Is 40:26**	5869
To open blind **e**, To bring out	**Is 42:7**	5869
blind, even though they have **e**,	**Is 43:8**	5869
for He has smeared over their **e** so	**Is 44:18**	5869
"Lift up your **e** and look around;	**Is 49:18**	5869
"Lift up your **e** to the sky, Then	**Is 51:6**	5869
own **e** When the LORD restores Zion.	**Is 52:8**	5869
We grope like those who have no **e**;	**Is 59:10**	5869
"Lift up your **e** round about and	**Is 60:4**	5869
e to the bare heights and see;	**Jer 3:2**	5869
you enlarge your **e** with paint,	**Jer 4:30**	5869
do not Your **e** *look* for truth?	**Jer 5:3**	5869
and senseless people, Who have **e** but	**Jer 5:21**	5869
And my **e** a fountain of tears,	**Jer 9:1**	5869
for us, That our **e** may shed tears And	**Jer 9:18**	5869
And my **e** will bitterly weep And	**Jer 13:17**	5869
"Lift up your **e** and see Those	**Jer 13:20**	5869
Their **e** fail For there is no	**Jer 14:6**	5869
'Let my **e** flow down with tears	**Jer 14:17**	5869
before your **e** and in your time,	**Jer 16:9**	5869
"For My **e** are on all their ways;	**Jer 16:17**	5869
iniquity concealed from My **e**.	**Jer 16:17**	5869
and while your **e** look on, they	**Jer 20:4**	5869
"But your **e** and your heart Are	**Jer 22:17**	5869
I will set My **e** on them for good,	**Jer 24:6**	5869
he will slay them before your **e**.	**Jer 29:21**	5869
weeping And your **e** from tears;	**Jer 31:16**	5869
whose **e** are open to all the ways	**Jer 32:19**	5869
Zedekiah before his **e** at Riblah;	**Jer 39:6**	5869
He then blinded Zedekiah's **e** and	**Jer 39:7**	5869
of many, as your own **e** *now* see us,	**Jer 42:2**	5869
have done in Zion before your **e**,"	**Jer 51:24**	5869
the sons of Zedekiah before his **e**,	**Jer 52:10**	5869
Then he blinded the **e** of Zedekiah;	**Jer 52:11**	5869
My **e** run down with water;	**La 1:16**	5869
My **e** fail because of tears, My	**La 2:11**	5869
Let your **e** have no rest.	**La 2:18**	5869
My **e** run down with streams of	**La 3:48**	5869
My **e** pour down unceasingly,	**La 3:49**	5869
My **e** bring pain to my soul Because	**La 3:51**	5869
Yet our **e** failed,	**La 4:17**	5869
of these things our **e** are dim;	**La 5:17**	5869
them were full of **e** round about.	**Ezk 1:18**	5869
away from Me, and by their **e** which	**Ezk 6:9**	5869
"Son of man, raise your **e** now	**Ezk 8:5**	5869
So I raised my **e** toward the north,	**Ezk 8:5**	5869
wheels were full of **e** all around,	**Ezk 10:12**	5869
who have **e** to see but do not see,	**Ezk 12:2**	5869
can not see the land with *his* **e**.	**Ezk 12:12**	5869
lift up his **e** to the idols of the house	**Ezk 18:6**	5869
but lifts up his **e** to the idols	**Ezk 18:12**	5869
or lift up his **e** to the idols of the	**Ezk 18:15**	5869
the detestable things of his **e**,	**Ezk 20:7**	5869
the detestable things of their **e**,	**Ezk 20:8**	5869
and their **e** were on the idols of	**Ezk 20:24**	5869
a false divination in their **e**;	**Ezk 21:23**	5869

hide their **e** from My sabbaths, **Ezk 22:26** 5869
you will not lift up your **e** to them **Ezk 23:27** 5869
whom you bathed, painted your **e** and **Ezk 23:40** 5869
the desire of your **e** with a blow; **Ezk 24:16** 5869
your power, the desire of your **e** and **Ezk 24:21** 5869
pride, the desire of their **e** and **Ezk 24:25** 5869
earth In the **e** of all who see you. **Ezk 28:18** 5869
lift up your **e** to your idols as **Ezk 33:25** 5869
be in your hand before their **e**. **Ezk 37:20** 5869
through you before their **e**, **Ezk 38:16** 5869
"Son of man, see with your **e**, **Ezk 40:4** 5869
man, mark well, see with your **e** and **Ezk 44:5** 5869
raised my **e** toward heaven and **Da 4:34** 5870a
e like the eyes of a man and **Da 7:8** 5870a
eyes like the **e** of a man and **Da 7:8** 5870a
that horn which had **e** and a mouth **Da 7:20** 5870a
Then I lifted my **e** and looked, **Da 8:3** 5869
a conspicuous horn between his **e**. **Da 8:5** 5869
between his **e** is the first king. **Da 8:21** 5869
Open Your **e** and see our **Da 9:18** 5869
I lifted my **e** and looked, and **Da 10:5** 5869
his **e** were like flaming torches, **Da 10:6** 5869
food been cut off before our **e**, **Jl 1:16** 5869
And I will set My **e** against them **Am 9:4** 5869
the **e** of the Lord GOD are on the **Am 9:8** 5869
And let our **e** gloat over Zion.' **Mi 4:11** 5869
My **e** will look on her; **Mi 7:10** 5869
e are too pure to approve evil, **Hab 1:13** 5869
your fortunes before your **e**," **Zph 3:20** 5869
Then I lifted up my **e** and looked, **Zch 1:18** 5869
Then I lifted up my **e** and looked, **Zch 2:1** 5869
on one stone are seven **e**. **Zch 3:9** 5869
these are the **e** of the LORD which **Zch 4:10** 5869
I lifted up my **e** again and looked, **Zch 5:1** 5869
"Lift up now your **e** and **Zch 5:5** 5869
Then I lifted up my **e** and looked, **Zch 5:9** 5869
I lifted up my **e** again and looked, **Zch 6:1** 5869
(for the **e** of men, especially of all the **Zch 9:1** 5869
For now I have seen with My **e**. **Zch 9:8** 5869
their **e** will rot in their sockets, **Zch 14:12** 5869
Your **e** will see this and you **Mal 1:5** 5869
Then He touched their **e**, **Mt 9:29** *3788*
And their **e** were opened. **Mt 9:30** *3788*
THEY HAVE CLOSED THEIR **E**, OTHERWISE **Mt 13:15** *3788*
OTHERWISE THEY WOULD SEE WITH THEIR **E**, **Mt 13:15** *3788*
"But blessed are your **e**, **Mt 13:16** *3788*
And lifting up their **e**, **Mt 17:8** *3788*
with one eye, than to have two **e** **Mt 18:9** *3788*
we want our **e** to be opened." **Mt 20:33** *3788*
compassion, Jesus touched their **e**; **Mt 20:34** *3659*
AND IT IS MARVELOUS IN OUR **E**'? **Mt 21:42** *3788*
sleeping, for their **e** were heavy. **Mt 26:43** *3788*
"HAVING **E**, DO YOU NOT SEE? **Mk 8:18** *3788*
and after spitting on his **e** and **Mk 8:23** *3659*
He laid His hands on his **e**; **Mk 8:25** *3788*
with one eye, than, having two **e**, **Mk 9:47** *3788*
AND IT IS MARVELOUS IN OUR **E**'?" **Mk 12:11** *3788*
for their **e** were very heavy; **Mk 14:40** *3788*
For my **e** have seen Your salvation, **Lk 2:30** *3788*
and the **e** of all in the synagogue **Lk 4:20** *3788*
e which see the things you see, **Lk 10:23** *3788*
"In Hades he lifted up his **e**, **Lk 16:23** *3788*
to lift up his **e** to heaven, **Lk 18:13** *3788*
they have been hidden from your **e**. **Lk 19:42** *3788*
But their **e** were prevented from **Lk 24:16** *3788*
Then their **e** were opened and they **Lk 24:31** *3788*
I say to you, lift up your **e** and **Jn 4:35** *3788*
Jesus, lifting up His **e** **Jn 6:5** *3788*
and applied the clay to his **e**, **Jn 9:6** *3788*
"How then were your **e** opened?" **Jn 9:10** *3788*
made clay, and anointed my **e**, **Jn 9:11** *3788*
made the clay and opened his **e**. **Jn 9:14** *3788*
"He applied clay to my **e**, **Jn 9:15** *3788*
Him, since He opened your **e**?" **Jn 9:17** *3788*
or who opened his **e**, **Jn 9:21** *3788*
How did He open your **e**?" **Jn 9:26** *3788*
is from, and *yet* He opened my **e**. **Jn 9:30** *3788*
the **e** of a person born blind. **Jn 9:32** *3788*
cannot open the **e** of the blind, **Jn 10:21** *3788*
opened the **e** of the blind man, **Jn 11:37** *3788*
Then Jesus raised His **e**, **Jn 11:41** *3788*
"HE HAS BLINDED THEIR **E** AND **Jn 12:40** *3788*
SO THAT THEY WOULD NOT SEE WITH THEIR **E** **Jn 12:40** *3788*
and lifting up His **e** to heaven, **Jn 17:1** *3788*
and though his **e** were open, **Ac 9:8** *3788*
from his **e** something like scales, **Ac 9:18** *3788*
And she opened her **e**, **Ac 9:40** *3788*
to open their **e** so that they may **Ac 26:18** *3788*
AND THEY HAVE CLOSED THEIR **E**; **Ac 28:27** *3788*
OTHERWISE THEY MIGHT SEE WITH THEIR **E**, **Ac 28:27** *3788*
NO FEAR OF GOD BEFORE THEIR **E**." **Ro 3:18** *3788*
E TO SEE NOT AND EARS TO HEAR NOT, **Ro 11:8** *3788*
THEIR **E** BE DARKENED TO SEE NOT, **Ro 11:10** *3788*
before whose **e** Jesus Christ was **Ga 3:1** *3788*
out your **e** and given them to me. **Ga 4:15** *3788*
I pray that the **e** of your heart **Eph 1:18** *3788*
open and laid bare to the **e** of Him **Heb 4:13** *3788*
fixing our **e** on Jesus, the author **Heb 12:2** *872*
"FOR THE **E** OF THE LORD ARE TOWARD **1Pe 3:12** *3788*
having **e** full of adultery that **2Pe 2:14** *3788*
what we have seen with our **e**, **1Jn 1:1** *3788*
the darkness has blinded his **e**. **1Jn 2:11** *3788*
lust of the flesh and the lust of the **e** **1Jn 2:16** *3788*
His **e** were like a flame of fire. **Rv 1:14** *3788*
who has **e** like a flame of fire, **Rv 2:18** *3788*
and eye salve to anoint your **e** so **Rv 3:18** *3788*
full of **e** in front and behind. **Rv 4:6** *3788*
are full of **e** around and within; **Rv 4:8** *3788*
having seven horns and seven **e**, **Rv 5:6** *3788*
wipe every tear from their **e**." **Rv 7:17** *3788*
His **e** *are* a flame of fire, and **Rv 19:12** *3788*
wipe away every tear from their **e**; **Rv 21:4** *3788*

EYESERVICE
not by way of **e**, as men-pleasers, **Eph 6:6** *3787*

EYESIGHT
now his **e** had begun to grow dim **1Sa 3:2** 5869

EYEWITNESSES
from the beginning were **e** and servants **Lk 1:2** *845*
but we were **e** of His majesty. **2Pe 1:16** *2030*

EZBAI
Carmelite, Naarai the son of **E**, **1Ch 11:37** 229

EZBON
Ziphion and Haggi, Shuni and **E**, **Gn 46:16** 675
E, Uzzi, Uzziel, Jerimoth and Iri. **1Ch 7:7** 675

EZEKIEL
came expressly to **E** the priest, **Ezk 1:3** 3168
'Thus **E** will be a sign to you; **Ezk 24:24** 3168

EZEL
you shall remain by the stone **E**. **1Sa 20:19** 237

EZEM
Baalah and Iim and **E**, **Jos 15:29** 6107
and Hazar-shual and Balah and **E**, **Jos 19:3** 6107
at Bilhah, **E**, Tolad, **1Ch 4:29** 6107

EZER
and Dishon and **E** and Dishan. **Gn 36:21** 687
These are the sons of **E**: **Gn 36:27** 687
chief Dishon, chief **E**, **Gn 36:30** 687
Shobal, Zibeon, Anah, Dishon, **E** and **1Ch 1:38** 687
The sons of **E** *were* Bilhan, Zaavan **1Ch 1:42** 687
Gedor, and **E** the father of Hushah. **1Ch 4:4** 5829
and **E** and Elead whom the men of **1Ch 7:21** 5827
E *was* the first, Obadiah the **1Ch 12:9** 5829
Next to him **E** the son of Jeshua, **Ne 3:19** 5829
Jehohanan, Malchijah, Elam and **E**. **Ne 12:42** 5827

EZION-GEBER
from Abronah and camped at **E**. **Nu 33:35** 6100
They journeyed from **E** and **Nu 33:36** 6100
road, away from Elath and from **E**. **Dt 2:8** 6100
also built a fleet of ships in **E**, **1Ki 9:26** 6100
go for the ships were broken at **E**. **1Ki 22:48** 6100
Then Solomon went to **E** and to **2Ch 8:17** 6100
and they made the ships in **E**. **2Ch 20:36** 6100

EZNITE
he was *called* Adino the **E**, **2Sa 23:8** 6112

EZRA
there went up **E** son of Seraiah, **Ezr 7:1** 5830
This **E** went up from Babylon, and **Ezr 7:6** 5830
For **E** had set his heart to study **Ezr 7:10** 5830
Artaxerxes gave to **E** the priest, **Ezr 7:11** 5830
king of kings, to **E** the priest, **Ezr 7:12** 5831
River, that whatever **E** the priest, **Ezr 7:21** 5831
"You, **E**, according to the **Ezr 7:25** 5831
Now while **E** was praying and making **Ezr 10:1** 5830
of Elam, said to **E**, **Ezr 10:2** 5830
Then **E** rose and made the leading **Ezr 10:5** 5830
Then **E** rose from before the house **Ezr 10:6** 5830
Then **E** the priest stood up and **Ezr 10:10** 5830
And **E** the priest selected men *who* **Ezr 10:16** 5830
and they asked **E** the scribe to **Ne 8:1** 5830
Then **E** the priest brought the law **Ne 8:2** 5830
E the scribe stood at a wooden **Ne 8:4** 5830
E opened the book in the sight **Ne 8:5** 5830
Then **E** blessed the LORD the great **Ne 8:6** 5830
and **E** the priest *and* scribe, **Ne 8:9** 5830
Levites were gathered to **E** the scribe **Ne 8:13** 5830
Seraiah, Jeremiah, **E**, **Ne 12:1** 5830
of **E**, Meshullam; of Amariah, **Ne 12:13** 5830
and of **E** the priest *and* scribe. **Ne 12:26** 5830
with Azariah, **E**, Meshullam, **Ne 12:33** 5830
And **E** the scribe went before them. **Ne 12:36** 5830

EZRAH
The sons of **E** *were* Jether, **1Ch 4:17** 5834

EZRAHITE
than all men, than Ethan the **E**, **1Ki 4:31** 250

EZRI
E the son of Chelub had charge **1Ch 27:26** 5836

F

FABLES
worldly **f** fit only for old women. **1Tm 4:7** *3454*

FABRIC
of gold *And* its seat of purple **f**, **SS 3:10** 713

FABRICS
crimson and violet **f**, and who **2Ch 2:7**
violet, linen and crimson **f**, **2Ch 2:14**
of Thyatira, a seller of purple **f**, **Ac 16:14** *4211*

FACE
By the sweat of your **f** You will eat **Gn 3:19** 639
this day from the **f** of the ground; **Gn 4:14** 6440
and from Your **f** I will be hidden, **Gn 4:14** 6440
to multiply on the **f** of the land, **Gn 6:1** 6440
created from the **f** of the land, **Gn 6:7** 6440
alive on the **f** of all the earth. **Gn 7:3** 6440
and I will blot out from the **f** of **Gn 7:4** 6440
that was upon the **f** of the land, **Gn 7:23** 6440
was abated from the **f** of the land; **Gn 8:8** 6440
over the **f** of the whole earth." **Gn 11:4** 6440
over the **f** of the whole earth; **Gn 11:8** 6440
over the **f** of the whole earth. **Gn 11:9** 6440
Abram fell on his **f**, **Gn 17:3** 6440
Abraham fell on his **f** and laughed, **Gn 17:17** 6440
down *with his* **f** to the ground. **Gn 19:1** 639
was beautiful of form and **f**. **Gn 29:17** 4758
and made the flocks **f** toward the **Gn 30:40** 6440
and set his **f** toward the hill **Gn 31:21** 6440
Then afterward I will see his **f**; **Gn 32:20** 6440
"I have seen God **f** to face, yet **Gn 32:30** 6440
"I have seen God face to **f**, **Gn 32:30** 6440
f as one sees the face of God, **Gn 33:10** 6440
face as one sees the **f** of God, **Gn 33:10** 6440
harlot, for she had covered her **f**. **Gn 38:15** 6440
over all the **f** of the earth, **Gn 41:56** 6440
'You shall not see my **f** unless **Gn 43:3** 6440
'You will not see my **f** unless **Gn 43:5** 6440
Then he washed his **f** and **Gn 43:31** 6440
you will not see my **f** again.' **Gn 44:23** 6440
for we cannot see the man's **f** **Gn 44:26** 6440
me die, since I have seen your **f**, **Gn 46:30** 6440
"I never expected to see your **f**, **Gn 48:11** 6440
bowed with his **f** to the ground. **Gn 48:12** 639
Then Joseph fell on his father's **f**, **Gn 50:1** 6440
Then Moses hid his **f**, **Ex 3:6** 6440
Beware, do not see my **f** again, **Ex 10:28** 6440
day you see my **f** you shall die!" **Ex 10:28** 6440
I shall never see your **f** again!" **Ex 10:29** 6440
them from the **f** of the earth'? **Ex 32:12** 6440
used to speak to Moses **f** to face, **Ex 33:11** 6440
used to speak to Moses face to **f**, **Ex 33:11** 6440
who are upon the **f** of the earth?" **Ex 33:16** 6440
"You cannot see My **f**, **Ex 33:20** 6440
but My **f** shall not be seen." **Ex 33:23** 6440
his **f** shone because of his speaking **Ex 34:29** 6440
behold, the skin of his **f** shone, **Ex 34:30** 6440
them, he put a veil over his **f**. **Ex 34:33** 6440
Israel would see the **f** of Moses, **Ex 34:35** 6440
that the skin of Moses' **f** shone. **Ex 34:35** 6440
would replace the veil over his **f** **Ex 34:35** 6440
I will set My **f** against that **Lv 17:10** 6440
'I will also set My **f** against that **Lv 20:3** 6440
then I Myself will set My **f** **Lv 20:5** 6440
I will also set My **f** against that **Lv 20:6** 6440
or he who has a disfigured **f**, **Lv 21:18**
'I will set My **f** against you **Lv 26:17** 6440
The LORD make His **f** shine on you, **Nu 6:25** 6440
who was on the **f** of the earth.) **Nu 12:3** 6440
her father had but spit in her **f**, **Nu 12:14** 6440
heard *this*, he fell on his **f**; **Nu 16:4** 6440
set his **f** toward the wilderness. **Nu 24:1** 6440
'The LORD spoke to you **f** to face **Dt 5:4** 6440
"The LORD spoke to you face to **f** **Dt 5:4** 6440
wipe you off the **f** of the earth. **Dt 6:15** 6440
who are on the **f** of the earth. **Dt 7:6** 6440
Him, He will repay him to his **f**. **Dt 7:10** 6440
who are on the **f** of the earth. **Dt 14:2** 6440
off his foot and spit in his **f**; **Dt 25:9** 6440
them and hide My **f** from them, **Dt 31:17** 6440
"But I will surely hide My **f** in **Dt 31:18** 6440
'I will hide My **f** from them, I **Dt 32:20** 6440
whom the LORD knew **f** to face, **Dt 34:10** 6440
whom the LORD knew face to **f**, **Dt 34:10** 6440
Joshua fell on his **f** to the earth, **Jos 5:14** 6440
fell to the earth on his **f** before the **Jos 7:6** 6440
it that you have fallen on your **f**? **Jos 7:10** 6440
the angel of the LORD **f** to face." **Jg 6:22** 6440
the angel of the LORD face to **f**." **Jg 6:22** 6440
Then she fell on her **f**, **Ru 2:10** 6440
ate, and her **f** was no longer *sad*. **1Sa 1:18** 6440
Dagon had fallen on his **f** to the **1Sa 5:3** 6440
Dagon had fallen on his **f** to the **1Sa 5:4** 6440
he fell on his **f** to the ground. **1Sa 17:49** 6440
David from the **f** of the earth." **1Sa 20:15** 6440
and fell on his **f** to the ground, **1Sa 20:41** 639
David bowed with his **f** to the **1Sa 24:8** 639
and fell on her **f** before David and **1Sa 25:23** 6440
with her **f** to the ground and said, **1Sa 25:41** 639
f to the ground and did homage. **1Sa 28:14** 639
up my **f** to your brother Joab?" **2Sa 2:22** 6440
f unless you first bring Michal, **2Sa 3:13** 6440
on his **f** and prostrated himself. **2Sa 9:6** 6440
she fell on her **f** to the ground **2Sa 14:4** 639
remnant on the **f** of the earth." **2Sa 14:7** 6440
Joab fell on his **f** to the ground, **2Sa 14:22** 6440
house, and let him not see my **f**." **2Sa 14:24** 6440
house and did not see the king's **f**. **2Sa 14:24** 6440
and did not see the king's **f**. **2Sa 14:28** 6440
therefore, let me see the king's **f**, **2Sa 14:32** 6440
f to the ground before the king, **2Sa 14:33** 639
the king with his **f** to the ground. **2Sa 18:28** 639
The king covered his **f** and **2Sa 19:4** 6440
f to the ground before the king. **2Sa 24:20** 639
the king with his **f** to the ground. **1Ki 1:23** 639
bowed with her **f** to the ground, **1Ki 1:31** 639
it from off the **f** of the earth. **1Ki 13:34** 6440
rain on the **f** of the earth.' " **1Ki 17:14** 6440
send rain on the **f** of the earth." **1Ki 18:1** 6440
him and fell on his **f** and said, **1Ki 18:7** 6440
and put his **f** between his knees. **1Ki 18:42** 6440
he wrapped his **f** in his mantle and **1Ki 19:13** 6440
turned away his **f** and ate no food. **1Ki 21:4** 6440
and lay my staff on the lad's **f**." **2Ki 4:29** 6440
and laid the staff on the lad's **f**, **2Ki 4:31** 6440
in water and spread it on his **f**, **2Ki 8:15** 6440
he lifted up his **f** to the window **2Ki 9:32** 6440
will be as dung on the **f** of the field **2Ki 9:37** 6440
set his **f** to go up to Jerusalem. **2Ki 12:17** 6440
"Come, let us **f** each other." **2Ki 14:8**
7200, 6440
Then he turned his **f** to the wall and **2Ki 20:2** 6440
Seek His **f** continually. **1Ch 16:11** 6440

David with his f to the ground. 1Ch 21:21 639
turn away the f of Your anointed; 2Ch 6:42 6440
and seek My f and turn from their 2Ch 7:14 6440
tomorrow go out to f them, 2Ch 20:17 6440
his head with *his* f to the ground, 2Ch 20:18 639
"Come, let us f each other." 2Ch 25:17 7200, 6440
and will not turn *His* f away from 2Ch 30:9 6440
to lift up my f to You, Ezr 9:6 6440
f sad though you are not sick? Ne 2:2 6440
my f not be sad when the city, Ne 2:3 6440
lady was beautiful of form and f, Es 2:7 4758
mouth, they covered Haman's f. Es 7:8 6440
will surely curse You to Your f." Jb 1:11 6440
he will curse You to Your f." Jb 2:5 6440
"Then a spirit passed by my f; Jb 4:15 6440
at me, And *see* if I lie to your f. Jb 6:28 6440
up your f without *moral* defect, Jb 11:15 6440
Then I will not hide from Your f: Jb 13:20 6440
"Why do You hide Your f And Jb 13:24 6440
he has covered his f with his fat And Jb 15:27 6440
against me, It testifies to my f. Jb 16:8 6440
"My f is flushed from weeping, Jb 16:16 6440
And lift up your f to God. Jb 22:26 6440
And he disguises his f. Jb 24:15 6440
obscures the f of the full moon And Jb 26:9 6440
of my f they did not cast down. Jb 29:24 6440
not refrain from spitting at my f. Jb 30:10 6440
That he may see His f with joy, Jb 33:26 6440
And when He hides His f, Jb 34:29 6440
On the f of the inhabited earth. Jb 37:12 6440
"Who can open the doors of his f? Jb 41:14 6440
He has hidden His f; Ps 10:11 6440
The upright will behold His f. Ps 11:7 6440
long will You hide Your f from me? Ps 13:1 6440
behold Your f in righteousness; Ps 17:15 6440
has He hidden His f from him; Ps 22:24 6440
who seek Him, Who seek Your f Ps 24:6 6440
When You said, "Seek My f," Ps 27:8 6440
"Your f, O LORD, I shall seek." Ps 27:8 6440
Do not hide Your f from me, Do not Ps 27:9 6440
You hid Your f, Ps 30:7 6440
Your f to shine upon Your servant; Ps 31:16 6440
The f of the LORD is against Ps 34:16 6440
Why do You hide Your f Ps 44:24 6440
Hide Your f from my sins And blot Ps 51:9 6440
And cause His f to shine upon us Ps 67:1 6440
Dishonor has covered my f. Ps 69:7 6440
not hide Your f from Your servant, Ps 69:17 6440
And cause Your f to shine *upon us,* Ps 80:3 6440
And cause Your f to shine *upon us,* Ps 80:7 6440
Cause Your f to shine *upon us,* and Ps 80:19 6440
look upon the f of Your anointed. Ps 84:9 6440
Why do You hide Your f from me? Ps 88:14 6440
Do not hide Your f from me in the Ps 102:2 6440
may make *his* f glisten with oil, Ps 104:15 6440
You hide Your f, Ps 104:29 6440
You renew the f of the ground. Ps 104:30 6440
Seek His f continually. Ps 105:4 6440
Make Your f shine upon Your servant, Ps 119:135 6440
turn away the f of Your anointed. Ps 132:10 6440
Do not hide Your f from me, Or I Ps 143:7 6440
with a brazen f she says to him: Pr 7:13 6440
a circle on the f of the deep, Pr 8:27 6440
A joyful heart makes a cheerful f, Pr 15:13 6440
In the light of a king's f is life, Pr 16:15 6440
A wicked man displays a bold f, Pr 21:29 6440
As in water f *reflects* face, So Pr 27:19 6440
As in water face *reflects* f, Pr 27:19 6440
a f is sad a heart may be happy. Ec 7:3 6440
and causes his stern f to beam. Ec 8:1 6440
And grinding the f of the poor?" Is 3:15 6440
with two he covered his f, Is 6:2 6440
His f from the house of Jacob; Is 8:17 6440
and their God as they f upward. Is 8:21 6437
the f of the world with cities." Is 14:21 6440
kingdoms on the f of the earth. Is 23:17 6440
nor shall his f now turn pale; Is 29:22 6440
Hezekiah turned his f to the wall and Is 38:2 6440
f from humiliation and spitting. Is 50:6 6440
I have set My f like flint, Is 50:7 6440
one from whom men hide their f He Is 53:3 6440
I hid My f from you for a moment, Is 54:8 6440
I hid *My* f and was angry, And he Is 57:17 6440
sins have hidden *His* f from you so Is 59:2 6440
You have hidden Your f from us And Is 64:7 6440
continually provoke Me to My f, Is 65:3 6440
their back to Me, And not *their* f; Jer 2:27 6440
be as dung on the f of the ground. Jer 8:2 6440
your skirts off over your f, Jer 13:26 6440
they are not hidden from My f, Jer 16:17 6440
show them My back and not *My* f Jer 18:17 6440
"For I have set My f against this Jer 21:10 6440
are upon the f of the ground, Jer 25:26 6440
like dung on the f of the ground. Jer 25:33 6440
which are on the f of the earth Jer 27:5 6440
you from the f of the earth. Jer 28:16 6440
he will speak with him f to face Jer 32:4 6310
he will speak with him face to f Jer 32:4 6310
be removed from before My f, Jer 32:31 6440
their back to Me and not *their* f; Jer 32:33 6440
and I have hidden My f from this Jer 33:5 6440
he will speak with you f to face, Jer 34:3 6310
he will speak with you face to f, Jer 34:3 6310
to set My f against you for woe, Jer 44:11 6440
faces, *each* had the f of a man; Ezk 1:10 6440
all four had the f of a lion on Ezk 1:10 6440
and the f of a bull on the left, Ezk 1:10 6440
all four had the f of an eagle. Ezk 1:10 6440

my f and heard a voice speaking. Ezk 1:28 6440
your f as hard as their faces and Ezk 3:8 6440
river Chebar, and I fell on my f. Ezk 3:23 6440
and set your f toward it so that Ezk 4:3 6440
"Then you shall set your f toward Ezk 4:7 6440
set your f toward the mountains of Ezk 6:2 6440
'I will also turn My f from them, Ezk 7:22 6440
fell on my f and cried out saying, Ezk 9:8 6440
first f *was* the face of a cherub, Ezk 10:14 6440
first face *was* the f of a cherub, Ezk 10:14 6440
second f *was* the face of a man, Ezk 10:14 6440
second face *was* the f of a man, Ezk 10:14 6440
a man, the third the f of a lion, Ezk 10:14 6440
and the fourth the f of an eagle. Ezk 10:14 6440
Then I fell on my f and cried out Ezk 11:13 6440
You shall cover your f so that you Ezk 12:6 6440
He will cover his f so that he can Ezk 12:12 6440
set your f against the daughters Ezk 13:17 6440
puts right before his f the Ezk 14:4 6440
puts right before his f the Ezk 14:7 6440
I will set My f against that man Ezk 14:8 6440
and I set My f against them. Ezk 15:7 6440
when I set My f against them. Ezk 15:7 6440
into judgment with you f to face. Ezk 20:35 6440
into judgment with you face to f. Ezk 20:35 6440
of man, set your f toward Teman, Ezk 20:46 6440
man, set your f toward Jerusalem, Ezk 21:2 6440
your f toward the sons of Ammon and Ezk 25:2 6440
of man, set your f toward Sidon, Ezk 28:21 6440
man, set your f against Pharaoh king Ezk 29:2 6440
set your f against Mount Seir, Ezk 35:2 6440
set your f toward Gog of the land Ezk 38:2 6440
men who are on the f of the earth Ezk 38:20 6440
Me, and I hid My f from them; Ezk 39:23 6440
and I hid My f from them. Ezk 39:24 6440
I will not hide My f from them any Ezk 39:29 6440
a man's f toward the palm tree on Ezk 41:19 6440
and a young lion's f toward the Ezk 41:19 6440
and I fell on my f. Ezk 43:3 6440
and its steps shall f the east." Ezk 43:17 6437
of the LORD, and I fell on my f. Ezk 44:4 6440
on his f and did homage to Daniel, Da 2:46 600
Then the king's f grew pale and Da 5:6 2122
alarmed, his f grew *even* paler, Da 5:9 2122
alarm you or your f be pale. Da 5:10 2122
alarming me and my f grew pale, Da 7:28 2122
I was frightened and fell on my f; Da 8:17 6440
sleep with my f to the ground; Da 8:18 6440
let Your f shine on Your desolate Da 9:17 6440
his f had the appearance of Da 10:6 6440
I fell into a deep sleep on my f, Da 10:9 6440
my face, with my f to the ground. Da 10:9 6440
I turned my f toward the ground Da 10:15 6440
"He will set his f to come Da 11:17 6440
"Then he will turn his f to the Da 11:18 6440
"So he will turn his f toward the Da 11:19 6440
put away her harlotry from her f And Hos 2:2 6440
their guilt and seek My f; Hos 5:15 6440
They are before My f. Hos 7:2 6440
them out on the f of the earth, Am 9:6 6440
it from the f of the earth; Am 9:8 6440
hide His f from them at that time Mi 3:4 6440
lift up your skirts over your f, Na 3:5 6440
things From the f of the earth," Zph 1:2 6440
cut off man from the f of the earth, Zph 1:3 6440
over the f of the whole land; Zch 5:3 6440
a gloomy f as the hypocrites *do,* Mt 6:16 4659
your head and wash your f Mt 6:17 4383
and His f shone like the sun, and Mt 17:2 4383
they fell f down to the ground Mt 17:6 4383
f of My Father who is in heaven. Mt 18:10 4383
and fell on His f and prayed, Mt 26:39 4383
f and beat Him with their fists; Mt 26:67 4383
received Him with slaps *in the* f. Mk 14:65
he fell on his f and implored Him, Lk 5:12 4383
of His f became different, Lk 9:29 4383
and he fell on his f at His feet, Lk 17:16 4383
dwell on the f of all the earth. Lk 21:35 4383
and his f was wrapped around with Jn 11:44 3799
and to give Him slaps *in the* f. Jn 19:3
his f like the face of an angel. Ac 6:15 4383
his face like the f of an angel. Ac 6:15 4383
to live on all the f of the earth, Ac 17:26 4383
kingdom, will no longer see my f. Ac 20:25 4383
they would not see his f again. Ac 20:38 4383
meets his accusers f to face and Ac 25:16 4383
meets his accusers face to f and Ac 25:16 4383
in it and could not f the wind, Ac 27:15 503
mirror dimly, but then f to face; 1Co 13:12 4383
mirror dimly, but then face to f; 1Co 13:12 4383
fall on his f and worship God, 1Co 14:25 4383
not look intently at the f of Moses 2Co 3:7 4383
because of the glory of his f, 2Co 3:7 4383
who used to put a veil over his f 2Co 3:13 4383
with unveiled f, beholding as in a 2Co 3:18 4383
glory of God in the f of Christ. 2Co 4:6 4383
am meek when f to face with you, 2Co 10:1 4383
am meek when face to f with you, 2Co 10:1 4383
himself, anyone hits you in the f. 2Co 11:20 4383
Antioch, I opposed him to his f, Ga 2:11 4383
who have not personally seen my f, Col 2:1 4383
with great desire to see your f. 1Th 2:17 4383
earnestly that we may see your f, 1Th 3:10 4383
at his natural f in a mirror; Jas 1:23 4383
BUT THE F OF THE LORD IS AGAINST 1Pe 3:12 4383
come to you and speak f to face, 2Jn 1:12 4750
come to you and speak face to f, 2Jn 1:12 4750
and we will speak f to face. 3Jn 1:14 4750
and we will speak face to f. 3Jn 1:14 4750

and His f was like the sun shining Rv 1:16 3799
had a f like that of a man, Rv 4:7 4383
head, and his f was like the sun, Rv 10:1 4383
they will see His f, Rv 22:4 4383

FACE-CLOTH

and the f which had been on His Jn 20:7 4676

FACED

was in Machpelah, which f Mamre, Gn 23:17 6440
Then the king f about and blessed 1Ki 8:14 5437, 6440
Judah f each other at Beth-shemesh, 2Ki 14:11 7200, 6440
Then the king f about and blessed 2Ch 6:3 5437, 6440
Judah f each other at Beth-shemesh, 2Ch 25:21 7200, 6440
in the direction which they f, Ezk 10:11 6437, 7218
the LORD's house which f eastward. Ezk 11:1 6437
he went to the gate which f east, Ezk 40:6 6440
porch of the gate was f inward. Ezk 40:9 1004
thirty chambers f the pavement. Ezk 40:17 413
the outer court which f the north, Ezk 40:20 6440
the gate which f toward the east; Ezk 40:22 6440
the gate which f toward the east and Ezk 42:15 6440
for the priests, which f north; Ezk 46:19 6437
the east, for the house f east. Ezk 47:1 6440
did not love their life even when f Rv 12:11

FACES

and their f were turned away, so Gn 9:23 6440
"Why are your f so sad today?" Gn 40:7 6440
to him with *their* f to the ground. Gn 42:6 639
the f of the cherubim are to be Ex 25:20 6440
with their f toward each other; Ex 37:9 6440
the f of the cherubim were toward Ex 37:9 6440
they shouted and fell on their f. Lv 9:24 6440
Moses and Aaron fell on their f Nu 14:5 6440
But they fell on their f and Nu 16:22 6440
Then they fell on their f. Nu 16:45 6440
of meeting and fell on their f. Nu 20:6 6440
to Pi-hahiroth, which f Baal-zephon, Nu 33:7 5921, 6440
those who hate Him to their f, Dt 7:10 6440
fell on their f to the ground. Jg 13:20 6440
shame the f of all your servants, 2Sa 19:5 6440
saw it, they fell on their f; 1Ki 18:39 6440
f were like the faces of lions, 1Ch 12:8 6440
faces were like the f of lions, 1Ch 12:8 6440
with sackcloth, fell on their f. 1Ch 21:16 6440
with their f to the ground, 2Ch 7:3 639
forsaken Him and turned their f 2Ch 29:6 6440
LORD with *their* f to the ground. Ne 8:6 639
He covers the f of its judges. Jb 9:24 6440
with Your bowstrings at their f. Ps 21:12 6440
their f will never be ashamed. Ps 34:5 6440
Fill their f with dishonor, That Ps 83:16 6440
Lebanon, Which f toward Damascus. SS 7:4 6440
f bears witness against them, Is 3:9 6440
in astonishment, Their f aflame. Is 13:8 6440
will wipe tears away from all f, Is 25:8 6440
to you with their f to the earth And Is 49:23 639
made their f harder than rock; Jer 5:3 6440
And *why* have all f turned pale? Jer 30:6 6440
turning their f in its direction; Jer 50:5 6440
Disgrace has covered our f, Jer 51:51 6440
of them had four f and four wings. Ezk 1:6 6440
f and wings of the four of them, Ezk 1:8 6440
their f did not turn when they Ezk 1:9
As for the form of their f, Ezk 1:10 6440
Such were their f. Ezk 1:11 6440
made your face as hard as their f and Ezk 3:8 6440
and shame *will be* on all f and Ezk 7:18 6440
LORD and their f toward the east; Ezk 8:16 6440
of the upper gate which f north, Ezk 9:2 6437
And each one had four f. Ezk 10:14 6440
four f and each one four wings, Ezk 10:21 6440
As for the likeness of their f, Ezk 10:22 6440
they were the same f whose Ezk 10:22 6440
have put right before their f the Ezk 14:3 6440
and turn your f away from all your Ezk 14:6 6440
chamber which f toward the south, Ezk 40:45 6440
but the chamber which f toward the Ezk 40:46 6440
and every cherub had two f, Ezk 41:18 6440
the sanctuary, which f the east; Ezk 44:1 6437
by way of *the gate* that f east. Ezk 47:2 6437
for why should he see your f Da 1:10 6440
are in anguish; All f turn pale. Jl 2:6 6440
And all their f are grown pale! Na 2:10 6440
Their horde of f *moves* forward. Hab 1:9 6440
I will spread refuse on your f, Mal 2:3 6440
and bowed their f to the ground, Lk 24:5 4383
and they fell on their f before Rv 7:11 4383
f were like the faces of men. Rv 9:7 4383
faces were like the f of men. Rv 9:7 4383
fell on their f and worshiped God, Rv 11:16 4383

FACIAL

and his f expression was altered Da 3:19 600

FACING

of the field at Machpelah f Mamre Gn 23:19 6440
son of Zohar the Hittite, f Mamre, Gn 25:9 5921, 6440
their wings and f one another; Ex 25:20 6440, 413
on twelve oxen, three f north, 1Ki 7:25 6437
three facing north, three f west, 1Ki 7:25 6437
three facing west, three f south, 1Ki 7:25 6437
facing south, and three f east; 1Ki 7:25 6437
on their feet f the *main* room. 2Ch 3:13 6440

Context	Reference	Number
on twelve oxen, three f the north,	2Ch 4:4	6437
facing the north, three f west,	2Ch 4:4	6437
three facing west, three f south and	2Ch 4:4	6437
facing south and three f east;	2Ch 4:4	6437
pot, f away from the north."	Jer 1:13	6440
refuge in flight, Without f back;	Jer 46:5	6437
of the gate f inward *was* one rod.	Ezk 40:7	4480
the porch of the gate f inward,	Ezk 40:8	4480
the south gate f toward the north.	Ezk 40:44	6440
the outer court f the chambers,	Ezk 42:7	6440
the length of those f the temple	Ezk 42:8	6440
f the separate area and facing the	Ezk 42:10	413, 6440
separate area and f the building,	Ezk 42:10	413, 6440
gate, the gate f toward the east;	Ezk 43:1	6437
way of the gate f toward the east.	Ezk 43:4	6440
"The gate of the inner court f	Ezk 46:1	6437
f east shall be opened for him.	Ezk 46:12	6437
Crete, f southwest and northwest,	Ac 27:12	*991*
FACT		
"For I was in f kidnapped from	Gn 40:15	1589
EVERY F MAY BE CONFIRMED.	Mt 18:16	*4487*
to discuss with one another *the* f	Mk 8:16	
"Why do you discuss *the* f that	Mk 8:17	
the f that the dead rise again,	Mk 12:26	*3754*
a f to which we are witnesses.	Ac 3:15	
the f that a noteworthy miracle has	Ac 4:16	*3754*
"*As for the* f that He raised Him	Ac 13:34	
since you can take note of the f	Ac 24:11	*3754*
in f, I do not even examine myself.	1Co 4:3	*235*
just as you are *in* f unleavened.	1Co 5:7	
if in f the dead are not raised.	1Co 15:15	*686*
in f, in every way we have made	2Co 11:6	*235*
EVERY F IS TO BE CONFIRMED BY THE	2Co 13:1	*4487*
realizing the f that law is not	1Tm 1:9	*3778*
You are aware of the f that all	2Tm 1:15	*3778*
But do not let this one f escape	2Pe 3:8	
FACTIONS		
there must also be f among you,	1Co 11:19	*139*
anger, disputes, dissensions, f,	Ga 5:20	*139*
FACTIOUS		
Reject a f man after a first and	Ti 3:10	*141*
FACTS		
"So, since these are undeniable f,	Ac 19:36	*368*
the f because of the uproar,	Ac 21:34	*804*
FADE		
memory f from their descendants.	Es 9:28	5486
Foreigners f away, And come	Ps 18:45	5034b
grass And f like the green herb.	Ps 37:2	5034b
that day the glory of Jacob will f,	Is 17:4	1809
of the people of the earth f away.	Is 24:4	535
midst of his pursuits will f away.	Jas 1:11	*3133*
and undefiled and will not f away,	1Pe 1:4	*263*
FADED		
and if the infection has f and	Lv 13:6	3544
not lower than the skin and is f,	Lv 13:21	3544
has f after it has been washed,	Lv 13:56	3544
FADES		
Toward evening it f and	Ps 90:6	4448c
be like an oak whose leaf f away Or	Is 1:30	5034b
withers, the world f *and* withers,	Is 24:4	535
The grass withers, the flower f,	Is 40:7	5034b
The grass withers, the flower f,	Is 40:8	5034b
that which f away *was* with glory,	2Co 3:11	*2673*
FADING		
f flower of its glorious beauty,	Is 28:1	5034b
f flower of its glorious beauty,	Is 28:4	5034b
glory of his face, f *as* it was,	2Co 3:7	*2673*
at the end of what was f away.	2Co 3:13	*2673*
FAIL		
'But when you unwittingly f and do	Nu 15:22	7368
He will not f you nor destroy you	Dt 4:31	7503
will not f you or forsake you."	Dt 31:6	7503
He will not f you or forsake you.	Dt 31:8	7503
I will not f you or forsake you.	Jos 1:5	7503
that your eyes will f *from weeping*	1Sa 2:33	3615
him and let none of his words f.	1Sa 3:19	5307, 776
no man's heart f on account of him;	1Sa 17:32	5307
and may there not f from the house	2Sa 3:29	3772
He will not f you nor forsake you	1Ch 28:20	7503
be given to them daily without f,	Ezr 6:9	7960
so that they would not f to	Es 9:27	5674a
were not to f from among the Jews,	Es 9:28	5674a
"But the eyes of the wicked will f,	Jb 11:20	3615
again, And its shoots will not f.	Jb 14:7	2308
"His ox mates without f;	Jb 21:10	1602
caused the eyes of the widow to f,	Jb 31:16	3615
My eyes f while I wait for my God.	Ps 69:3	3615
My flesh and my heart may f,	Ps 73:26	3615
eyes f *with longing* for Your word,	Ps 119:82	3615
My eyes f *with longing* for Your	Ps 119:123	3615
own witnesses f to see or know,	Is 44:9	1077
Causing the omens of boasters to f,	Is 44:25	6565a
of water whose waters do not f.	Is 58:11	3576
the heart of the princes will f;	Jer 4:9	6
eyes f For there is no vegetation.	Jer 14:6	3615
He has made my strength f.	La 1:14	3782
My eyes f because of tears, My	La 2:11	3615
For His compassions never f.	La 3:22	3615
and their fruit will not f.	Ezk 47:12	8552
And the new wine will f them.	Hos 9:2	3584
the goal and it will not f.	Hab 2:3	3576
the yield of the olive should f And	Hab 3:17	3584
His justice to light; He does not f.	Zph 3:5	5737c
of a letter of the Law to f.	Lk 16:17	*4098*
you, that your faith may not f;	Lk 22:32	*1587*
f to be even more with glory?	2Co 3:8	*3780*
unless indeed you f the test?	2Co 13:5	*96b*
we ourselves do not f the test.	2Co 13:6	*96b*
will f me if I tell of Gideon,	Heb 11:32	*1952a*
FAILED		
had made to the house of Israel f;	Jos 21:45	5307
God spoke concerning you has f;	Jos 23:14	5307
for you, not one of them has f.	Jos 23:14	5307
has f of all His good promise,	1Ki 8:56	5307
"My relatives have f,	Jb 19:14	2308
Words have f them.	Jb 32:15	6275
has f because of my iniquity,	Ps 31:10	3782
And my heart has f me.	Ps 40:12	5800a
ashamed, because they have f,	Jer 20:11	3808, 7919a
eyes f, *Looking* for help was useless;	La 4:17	3615
as though the word of God has f.	Ro 9:6	*1601b*
f to enter because of disobedience,	Heb 4:6	*3756*
FAILING		
you a trembling heart, f of eyes,	Dt 28:65	3631
of the burden bearers is f,	Ne 4:10	3782
FAILS		
My heart throbs, my strength f me;	Ps 38:10	5800a
not forsake me when my strength f.	Ps 71:9	3615
me quickly, O LORD, my spirit f;	Ps 143:7	3615
gets hungry and his strength f;	Is 44:12	369
days are long and every vision f'?	Ezk 12:22	6
new wine dries up, Fresh oil f.	Jl 1:10	535
vine dries up And the fig tree f;	Jl 1:12	535
that when it f, they will receive	Lk 16:9	*1587*
Love never f; but if *there are gifts*	1Co 13:8	*4098*
FAILURE		
and their f is riches for the Gentiles,	Ro 11:12	*2275*
FAINT		
of their bodies are a f white,	Lv 13:39	3544
rear when you were f and weary;	Dt 25:18	5889
is f in the wilderness to drink."	2Sa 16:2	3287
"*It is* God *who* has made my heart f,	Jb 23:16	7401
And how f a word we hear of Him!	Jb 26:14	8102
call to You when my heart is f;	Ps 61:2	5848c
I sigh, then my spirit grows f.	Ps 77:3	5848c
is sick And the whole heart is f.	Is 1:5	1742
when he awakens, behold, he is f And	Is 29:8	5889
strength, Therefore you did not f.	Is 57:10	2470a
the spirit would grow f before Me,	Is 57:16	5848c
is me, for I f before murderers."	Jer 4:31	5888
healing, My heart is f *within me!*	Jer 8:18	1742
so that your heart does not grow f,	Jer 51:46	7401
made me desolate, F all day long.	La 1:13	1739
are many and my heart is f."	La 1:22	1742
f In the streets of the city.	La 2:11	5848c
As they f like a wounded man In	La 2:12	5848c
little ones Who are f because of	La 2:19	5848c
Because of this our heart is f,	La 5:17	1739
be feeble, every spirit will f and	Ezk 21:7	3543a
the young men will f from thirst.	Am 8:13	5968
on Jonah's head so that he became f	Jon 4:8	5968
hungry, for they might f on the way."	Mt 15:32	*1590*
homes, they will f on the way;	Mk 8:3	*1590*
F WHEN YOU ARE REPROVED BY HIM;	Heb 12:5	*1590*
FAINTED		
Their soul f within them.	Ps 107:5	5848c
Your sons have f, They lie	Is 51:20	5968
FAINTHEARTED		
Do not be f. Do not be afraid,	Dt 20:3	7401, 3824
is the man that is afraid and f?	Dt 20:8	7401, 3824
have no fear and do not be f	Is 7:4	7401, 3824
the unruly, encourage the f,	1Th 5:14	*3642*
FAINTING		
praise instead of a spirit of f.	Is 61:3	3544
"While I was f away, I remembered	Jon 2:7	5848c
men f from fear and the	Lk 21:26	*674*
FAINTS		
My heart f within me!	Jb 19:27	3615
FAIR		
How f are your tents, O Jacob,	Nu 24:5	2895
cross over and see the f land that	Dt 3:25	2896a
were found so f as Job's daughters;	Jb 42:15	3303
come over her f neck *with a yoke;*	Hos 10:11	2898
'*It will be* f weather, for the sky	Mt 16:2	*2105*
a place called F Havens,	Ac 27:8	*2568*
Do they not blaspheme the f name	Jas 2:7	*2570*
FAIRER		
You are f than the sons of men;	Ps 45:2	3302
FAIRLY		
you are to judge your neighbor f.	Lv 19:15	6664
FAIRNESS		
And decide with f for the	Is 11:4	4334
to your slaves justice and f,	Col 4:1	*2471*
FAITH		
because you broke f with Me in the	Dt 32:51	4603
"Will you have f in him that he	Jb 39:12	539
Who keeps f forever;	Ps 146:6	571
the righteous will live by his f.	Hab 2:4	530
clothe you? You of little f!	Mt 6:30	*3640b*
great f with anyone in Israel.	Mt 8:10	*4102*
you afraid, you men of little f?"	Mt 8:26	*3640b*
Seeing their f, Jesus said to the	Mt 9:2	*4102*
your f has made you well."	Mt 9:22	*4102*
done to you according to your f."	Mt 9:29	*4102*
"You of little f, why did you	Mt 14:31	*3640b*
"O woman, your f is great;	Mt 15:28	*4102*
"You men of little f,	Mt 16:8	*3640b*
of the littleness of your f;	Mt 17:20	*3640a*
f the size of a mustard seed,	Mt 17:20	*4102*
"Truly I say to you, if you have f and	Mt 21:21	*4102*
Jesus seeing their f said to the	Mk 2:5	*4102*
Do you still have no f?"	Mk 4:40	*4102*
your f has made you well;	Mk 5:34	*4102*
your f has made you well."	Mk 10:52	*4102*
saying to them, "Have f in God.	Mk 11:22	*4102*
Seeing their f,	Lk 5:20	*4102*
have I found such great f."	Lk 7:9	*4102*
"Your f has saved you;	Lk 7:50	*4102*
"Where is your f?"	Lk 8:25	*4102*
your f has made you well;	Lk 8:48	*4102*
He clothe you? You men of little f!	Lk 12:28	*3640b*
said to the Lord, "Increase our f!"	Lk 17:5	*4102*
"If you had f like a mustard	Lk 17:6	*4102*
your f has made you well."	Lk 17:19	*4102*
will He find f on the earth?"	Lk 18:8	*4102*
your f has made you well."	Lk 18:42	*4102*
for you, that your f may not fail;	Lk 22:32	*4102*
"And on the basis of f in His name,	Ac 3:16	*4102*
and the f which *comes* through Him	Ac 3:16	*4102*
full of f and of the Holy Spirit,	Ac 6:5	*4102*
were becoming obedient to the f.	Ac 6:7	*4102*
full of the Holy Spirit and of f.	Ac 11:24	*4102*
the proconsul away from the f.	Ac 13:8	*4102*
that he had f to be made well,	Ac 14:9	*4102*
them to continue in the f,	Ac 14:22	*4102*
a door of f to the Gentiles.	Ac 14:27	*4102*
them, cleansing their hearts by f.	Ac 15:9	*4102*
were being strengthened in the f,	Ac 16:5	*4102*
and f in our Lord Jesus Christ.	Ac 20:21	*4102*
him *speak* about f in Christ Jesus.	Ac 24:24	*4102*
have been sanctified by f in Me.'	Ac 26:18	*4102*
of f among all the Gentiles for	Ro 1:5	*4102*
because your f is being proclaimed	Ro 1:8	*4102*
you, each of us by the other's f,	Ro 1:12	*4102*
God is revealed from f to faith;	Ro 1:17	*4102*
God is revealed from faith to f;	Ro 1:17	*4102*
RIGHTEOUS *man* SHALL LIVE BY F."	Ro 1:17	*4102*
righteousness of God through f in	Ro 3:22	*4102*
in His blood through f.	Ro 3:25	*4102*
of the one who has f in Jesus.	Ro 3:26	*4102*
No, but by a law of f.	Ro 3:27	*4102*
by f apart from works of the Law.	Ro 3:28	*4102*
who will justify the circumcised by f	Ro 3:30	*4102*
uncircumcised through f is one.	Ro 3:30	*4102*
we then nullify the Law through f?	Ro 3:31	*4102*
f is credited as righteousness,	Ro 4:5	*4102*
"F WAS CREDITED TO ABRAHAM AS	Ro 4:9	*4102*
f which he had while uncircumcised,	Ro 4:11	*4102*
steps of the f of our father Abraham	Ro 4:12	*4102*
through the righteousness of f.	Ro 4:13	*4102*
f is made void and the promise is	Ro 4:14	*4102*
For this reason *it is* by f,	Ro 4:16	*4102*
those who are of the f of Abraham,	Ro 4:16	*4102*
in f he contemplated his own body,	Ro 4:19	*4102*
in unbelief but grew strong in f,	Ro 4:20	*4102*
having been justified by f,	Ro 5:1	*4102*
our introduction by f into this grace	Ro 5:2	*4102*
the righteousness which is by f;	Ro 9:30	*4102*
they did not *pursue it* by f,	Ro 9:32	*4102*
based on f speaks as	Ro 10:6	*4102*
word of f which we are preaching,	Ro 10:8	*4102*
So f *comes* from hearing, and	Ro 10:17	*4102*
unbelief, but you stand by your f.	Ro 11:20	*4102*
allotted to each a measure of f.	Ro 12:3	*4102*
to the proportion of his f;	Ro 12:6	*4102*
accept the one who is weak in f,	Ro 14:1	*4102*
has f that he may eat all things,	Ro 14:2	*4100*
The f which you have, have as your	Ro 14:22	*4102*
because *his eating is* not from f;	Ro 14:23	*4102*
and whatever is not from f is sin.	Ro 14:23	*4102*
leading to obedience of f;	Ro 16:26	*4102*
that your f would not rest on the	1Co 2:5	*4102*
to another f by the same Spirit,	1Co 12:9	*4102*
and if I have all f,	1Co 13:2	*4102*
But now f, hope, love, abide these	1Co 13:13	*4102*
is vain, your f also is vain.	1Co 15:14	*4102*
been raised, your f is worthless;	1Co 15:17	*4102*
on the alert, stand firm in the f,	1Co 16:13	*4102*
Not that we lord it over your f,	2Co 1:24	*4102*
in your f you are standing firm.	2Co 1:24	*4102*
But having the same spirit of f,	2Co 4:13	*4102*
for we walk by f, not by sight	2Co 5:7	*4102*
in f and utterance and knowledge	2Co 8:7	*4102*
the hope that as your f grows,	2Co 10:15	*4102*
to see if you are in the f;	2Co 13:5	*4102*
now preaching the f which he once	Ga 1:23	*4102*
Law but through f in Christ Jesus,	Ga 2:16	*4102*
may be justified by f in Christ and	Ga 2:16	*4102*
I live by f in the Son of God,	Ga 2:20	*4102*
of the Law, or by hearing with f?	Ga 3:2	*4102*
of the Law, or by hearing with f?	Ga 3:5	*4102*
are of f who are sons of Abraham.	Ga 3:7	*4102*
would justify the Gentiles by f,	Ga 3:8	*4102*
are of f are blessed with Abraham,	Ga 3:9	*4102*
RIGHTEOUS MAN SHALL LIVE BY F."	Ga 3:11	*4102*
However, the Law is not of f;	Ga 3:12	*4102*
promise of the Spirit through f.	Ga 3:14	*4102*
that the promise by f in Jesus	Ga 3:22	*4102*
But before f came, we were kept in	Ga 3:23	*4102*
being shut up to the f which was	Ga 3:23	*4102*
that we may be justified by f.	Ga 3:24	*4102*
But now that f has come, we are no	Ga 3:25	*4102*
of God through f in Christ Jesus.	Ga 3:26	*4102*
For we through the Spirit, by f,	Ga 5:5	*4102*
but f working through love.	Ga 5:6	*4102*

who are of the household of the f. Ga 6:10 4102
having heard of the f in the Lord Eph 1:15 4102
you have been saved through f; Eph 2:8 4102
confident access through f in Him. Eph 3:12 4102
dwell in your hearts through f; Eph 3:17 4102
one Lord, one f, one baptism, Eph 4:5 4102
all attain to the unity of the f, Eph 4:13 4102
taking up the shield of f with Eph 6:16 4102
to the brethren, and love with f, Eph 6:23 4102
your progress and joy in the f, Php 1:25 4102
together for the f of the gospel; Php 1:27 4102
sacrifice and service of your f, Php 2:17 4102
that which is through f in Christ, Php 3:9 4102
comes from God on the basis of f, Php 3:9 4102
since we heard of your f in Christ Col 1:4 4102
if indeed you continue in the f Col 1:23 4102
the stability of your f in Christ. Col 2:5 4102
in Him and established in your f, Col 2:7 4102
through f in the working of God, Col 2:12 4102
your work of f and labor of love 1Th 1:3 4102
your f toward God has gone forth, 1Th 1:8 4102
and encourage you as to your f, 1Th 3:2 4102
sent to find out about your f, 1Th 3:5 4102
us good news of your f and love, 1Th 3:6 4102
about you through your f; 1Th 3:7 4102
what is lacking in your f? 1Th 3:10 4102
on the breastplate of f and love, 1Th 5:8 4102
your f is greatly enlarged, 2Th 1:3 4102
perseverance and f in the midst of 2Th 1:4 4102
and the work of f with power, 2Th 1:11 4102
by the Spirit and f in the truth. 2Th 2:13 4102
for not all have f. 2Th 3:2 4102
Timothy, *my* true child in *the* f: 1Tm 1:2 4102
administration of God which is by f. 1Tm 1:4 4102
a good conscience and a sincere f. 1Tm 1:5 4102
with the f and love which are 1Tm 1:14 4102
keeping f and a good conscience, 1Tm 1:19 4102
shipwreck in regard to their f. 1Tm 1:19 4102
of the Gentiles in f and truth. 1Tm 2:7 4102
continue in f and love and sanctity 1Tm 2:15 4102
of the f with a clear conscience. 1Tm 3:9 4102
in the f that is in Christ Jesus. 1Tm 3:13 4102
some will fall away from the f, 1Tm 4:1 4102
nourished on the words of the f 1Tm 4:6 4102
conduct, love, f *and* purity, 1Tm 4:12 4102
household, he has denied the f and 1Tm 5:8 4102
it have wandered away from the f and 1Tm 6:10 4102
righteousness, godliness, f, 1Tm 6:11 4102
Fight the good fight of f; 1Tm 6:12 4102
and thus gone astray from the f. 1Tm 6:21 4102
of the sincere f within you, 2Tm 1:5 4102
in the f and love which are in 2Tm 1:13 4102
and they upset the f of some. 2Tm 2:18 4102
and pursue righteousness, f, 2Tm 2:22 4102
mind, rejected in regard to the f. 2Tm 3:8 4102
my teaching, conduct, purpose, f, 2Tm 3:10 4102
f which is in Christ Jesus. 2Tm 3:15 4102
the course, I have kept the f; 2Tm 4:7 4102
for the f of those chosen of God Ti 1:1 4102
my true child in a common f: Ti 1:4 4102
that they may be sound in the f, Ti 1:13 4102
dignified, sensible, sound in f, Ti 2:2 4102
but showing all good f so that they Ti 2:10 4102
Greet those who love us in *the* f. Ti 3:15 4102
and of the f which you have toward Phm 1:5 4102
the fellowship of your f may become Phm 1:6 4102
united by f in those who heard. Heb 4:2 4102
dead works and of f toward God, Heb 6:1 4102
who through f and patience inherit Heb 6:12 4102
heart in full assurance of f, Heb 10:22 4102
MY RIGHTEOUS ONE SHALL LIVE BY F; Heb 10:38 4102
f to the preserving of the soul. Heb 10:39 4102
Now f is the assurance of *things* Heb 11:1 4102
By f we understand that the worlds Heb 11:3 4102
By f Abel offered to God a better Heb 11:4 4102
about his gifts, and through f, Heb 11:4
By f Enoch was taken up so that he Heb 11:5 4102
And without f it is impossible to Heb 11:6 4102
By f Noah, being warned *by God* Heb 11:7 4102
righteousness which is according to f. Heb 11:7 4102
By f Abraham, when he was called, Heb 11:8 4102
By f he lived as an alien in the Heb 11:9 4102
By f even Sarah herself received Heb 11:11 4102
All these died in f, Heb 11:13 4102
By f Abraham, when he was tested, Heb 11:17 4102
By f Isaac blessed Jacob and Esau, Heb 11:20 4102
By f Jacob, as he was dying, Heb 11:21 4102
By f Joseph, when he was dying, Heb 11:22 4102
By f Moses, when he was born, was Heb 11:23 4102
By f Moses, when he had grown up, Heb 11:24 4102
By f he left Egypt, not fearing Heb 11:27 4102
By f he kept the Passover and the Heb 11:28 4102
By f they passed through the Red Heb 11:29 4102
By f the walls of Jericho fell Heb 11:30 4102
By f Rahab the harlot did not Heb 11:31 4102
who by f conquered kingdoms, Heb 11:33 4102
gained approval through their f, Heb 11:39 4102
the author and perfecter of f, Heb 12:2 4102
of their conduct, imitate their f. Heb 13:7 4102
of your f produces endurance. Jas 1:3 4102
must ask in f without any doubting, Jas 1:6 4102
do not hold your f in our glorious Jas 2:1 4102
poor of this world *to be* rich in f Jas 2:5 4102
brethren, if someone says he has f Jas 2:14 4102
Can that f save him? Jas 2:14 4102
Even so f, if it has no works, is Jas 2:17 4102
"You have f and I have works; Jas 2:18 4102
show me your f without the works, Jas 2:18 4102
will show you my f by my works." Jas 2:18 4102
that f without works is useless? Jas 2:20 4102
that f was working with his works, Jas 2:22 4102
of the works, f was perfected; Jas 2:22 4102
by works and not by f alone. Jas 2:24 4102
so also f without works is dead. Jas 2:26 4102
and the prayer offered in f will Jas 5:15 4102
by the power of God through f for a 1Pe 1:5 4102
that the proof of your f, 1Pe 1:7 4102
f the salvation of your souls. 1Pe 1:9 4102
that your f and hope are in God. 1Pe 1:21 4102
But resist him, firm in *your* f, 1Pe 5:9 4102
a f of the same kind as ours, 2Pe 1:1 4102
in your f supply moral excellence, 2Pe 1:5 4102
that has overcome the world—our f. 1Jn 5:4 4102
that you contend earnestly for the f Jude 1:3 4102
yourselves up on your most holy f, Jude 1:20 4102
My name, and did not deny My f even Rv 2:13 4102
f and service and perseverance, Rv 2:19 4102
and the f of the saints. Rv 13:10 4102
of God and their f in Jesus. Rv 14:12 4102

FAITHFUL

He is f in all My household; Nu 12:7 539
your God, He is God, the f God, Dt 7:9 539
I will raise up for Myself a f priest 1Sa 2:35 539
your servants is as f as David, 1Sa 22:14 539
who are peaceable *and* f in Israel. 2Sa 20:19 539
for he was a f man and feared God Ne 7:2 571
found his heart f before You, Ne 9:8 539
For the f disappear from among the Ps 12:1 539
The LORD preserves the f And Ps 31:23 539
And whose spirit was not f to God. Ps 78:8 539
Nor were they f in His covenant. Ps 78:37 539
And the witness in the sky is f." Ps 89:37 539
shall be upon the f of the land, Ps 101:6 539
I have chosen the f way; Ps 119:30 530
All Your commandments are f; Ps 119:86 530
But a f envoy *brings* healing. Pr 13:17 529
a f messenger to those who send him Pr 25:13 539
F are the wounds of a friend, But Pr 27:6 539
A f man will abound with blessings, Pr 28:20 530
the f city has become a harlot, Is 1:21 539
city of righteousness, A f city." Is 1:26 539
I will take to Myself f witnesses Is 8:2 539
may enter, The One that remains f. Is 26:2 529
Because of the LORD who is f, Is 49:7 539
to the f mercies shown to David. Is 55:3 539
choice vine, A completely f seed. Jer 2:21 571
a true and f witness against us if Jer 42:5 539
corruption, inasmuch as he was f, Da 6:4 540
against the Holy One who is f. Hos 11:12 539
"Who then is the f and sensible Mt 24:45 4103
'Well done, good and f slave. Mt 25:21 4103
You were f with a few things, I Mt 25:21 4103
'Well done, good and f slave. Mt 25:23 4103
You were f with a few things, I Mt 25:23 4103
is the f and sensible steward, Lk 12:42 4103
"He who is f in a very little Lk 16:10 4103
little thing is f also in much; Lk 16:10 4103
"Therefore if you have not been f Lk 16:11 4103
"And if you have not been f in Lk 16:12 4103
been f in a very little thing, Lk 19:17 4103
judged me to be f to the Lord, Ac 16:15 4103
God is f, through whom you were 1Co 1:9 4103
beloved and f child in the Lord, 1Co 4:17 4103
and God is f, who will not allow 1Co 10:13 4103
But as God is f, our word to you 2Co 1:18 4103
and *who are* f in Christ Jesus: Eph 1:1 4103
and f minister in the Lord, Eph 6:21 4103
To the saints and f brethren in Col 1:2 4103
who is a f servant of Christ on Col 1:7 4103
our beloved brother and f servant Col 4:7 4103
our f and beloved brother, Col 4:9 4103
F is He who calls you, and He also 1Th 5:24 4103
But the Lord is f, and He will 2Th 3:3 4103
me, because He considered me f, 1Tm 1:12 4103
but temperate, f in all things. 1Tm 3:11 4103
witnesses, entrust these to f men 2Tm 2:2 4103
If we are faithless, He remains f, 2Tm 2:13 4103
holding fast the f word which is Ti 1:9 4103
become a merciful and f high priest Heb 2:17 4103
He was f to Him who appointed Him, Heb 3:2 4103
f in all His house as a servant, Heb 3:5 4103
but Christ *was* f as a Son over Heb 3:6
for He who promised is f; Heb 10:23 4103
considered Him f who had promised. Heb 11:11 4103
entrust their souls to a f Creator 1Pe 4:19 4103
Through Silvanus, our f brother 1Pe 5:12 4103
He is f and righteous to forgive 1Jn 1:9 4103
from Jesus Christ, the f witness, Rv 1:5 4103
Be f until death, and I will give Rv 2:10 4103
of Antipas, My witness, My f one, Rv 2:13 4103
The Amen, the f and true Witness, Rv 3:14 4103
are the called and chosen and f." Rv 17:14 4103
sat on it *is* called F and True Rv 19:11 4103
for these words are f and true." Rv 21:5 4103
"These words are f and true"; Rv 22:6 4103

FAITHFULLY

will deal kindly and f with you." Jos 2:14 571
did the work, for they dealt f. 2Ki 12:15 530
their hands, for they deal f." 2Ki 22:7 530
of the LORD, f and wholeheartedly. 2Ch 19:9 530
They f brought in the 2Ch 31:12 530
to distribute f *their portions* to 2Ch 31:15 530
consecrated themselves f in holiness. 2Ch 31:18 530
The men did the work f with 2Ch 34:12 530
For You have dealt f, Ne 9:33 571
those who deal f are His delight. Pr 12:22 530
He will f bring forth justice. Is 42:3 571
will f give them their recompense And Is 61:8 571
and will f plant them in this Jer 32:41 571
and My ordinances so as to deal f Ezk 18:9 571
you are acting f in whatever you 3Jn 1:5 4103

FAITHFULNESS

the f which You have shown to Your Gn 32:10 571
deal with me in kindness and f. Gn 47:29 571
A God of f and without injustice, Dt 32:4 530
generation, Sons in whom is no f. Dt 32:20 529
for his righteousness and his f; 1Sa 26:23 530
After these acts of f Sennacherib 2Ch 32:1 571
Will it declare Your f? Ps 30:9 571
And all His work is *done* in f. Ps 33:4 530
Your f *reaches* to the skies. Ps 36:5 530
Dwell in the land and cultivate f. Ps 37:3 530
spoken of Your f and Your salvation; Ps 40:10 530
Destroy them in Your f. Ps 54:5 571
in the grave, Your f in Abaddon? Ps 88:11 530
make known Your f with my mouth. Ps 89:1 530
You will establish Your f." Ps 89:2 530
Your f also in the assembly of the Ps 89:5 530
Your f also surrounds You. Ps 89:8 530
"My f and My lovingkindness Ps 89:24 530
him, Nor deal falsely in My f. Ps 89:33 530
swore to David in Your f? Ps 89:49 530
His f is a shield and bulwark. Ps 91:4 571
the morning And Your f by night, Ps 92:2 530
And the peoples in His f. Ps 96:13 530
and His f to the house of Israel; Ps 98:3 530
And His f to all generations. Ps 100:5 530
that in f You have afflicted me. Ps 119:75 530
Your f *continues* throughout all Ps 119:90 530
in righteousness And exceeding f. Ps 119:138 530
Answer me in Your f, Ps 143:1 530
And f the belt about His waist. Is 11:5 530
on it in f in the tent of David; Is 16:5 571
formed long ago, with perfect f. Is 25:1 544
to the pit cannot hope for Your f. Is 38:18 571
father tells his sons about Your f. Is 38:19 571
new every morning; Great is Your f. La 3:23 530
And I will betroth you to Me in f. Hos 2:20 530
Because there is no f or kindness Hos 4:1 571
regard vain idols Forsake their f, Jon 2:8 2617a
justice and mercy and f; Mt 23:23 4102
will not nullify the f of God, Ro 3:3 4102
patience, kindness, goodness, f, Ga 5:22 4102

FAITHLESS

And increases the f among men. Pr 23:28 898
in a f man in time of trouble. Pr 25:19 898
"Have you seen what f Israel did? Jer 3:6 4878
all the adulteries of f Israel, Jer 3:8 4878
"F Israel has proved herself more Jer 3:11 4878
'Return, f Israel,' declares the Jer 3:12 4878
'Return, O f sons,' declares the Jer 3:14 7726
"Return, O f sons, I will heal Jer 3:22 7726
go here and there, O f daughter? Jer 31:22 7728
Their heart is f; Hos 10:2 2505b
If we are f, He remains faithful, 2Tm 2:13 *569*

FAITHLESSNESS

O faithless sons, I will heal your f." Jer 3:22 4878

FALCON

the kite and the f in its kind, Lv 11:14 344
and the red kite, the f, Dt 14:13 344

FALCON'S

has the f eye caught sight of it. Jb 28:7 344

FALL

a deep sleep to f upon the man, Gn 2:21 5307
occasion against us and f upon us, Gn 43:18 5307
He will f upon us with pestilence Ex 5:3 6293
may f on all the land of Egypt, Ex 9:22 1961
"Terror and dread f upon them; Ex 15:16 5307
but God let *him* f into his hand, Ex 21:13 579
of them may f when they are dead Lv 11:32 5307
into which one of them may f, Lv 11:33 5307
carcass may f becomes unclean; Lv 11:35 5307
the land will not f to harlotry Lv 19:29 2181
will f before you by the sword; Lv 26:7 5307
will f before you by the sword. Lv 26:8 5307
from the sword, and they will f. Lv 26:36 5307
night, the manna would f with it. Nu 11:9 3381
and let *them* f beside the camp, Nu 11:31 5203
into this land, to f by the sword? Nu 14:3 5307
will f in this wilderness, Nu 14:29 5307
will f in this wilderness. Nu 14:32 5307
you, and you will f by the sword, Nu 14:43 5307
shall f to you as an inheritance, Nu 34:2 5307
wall of the city will f down flat, Jos 6:5 5307
and wrath f on all the Jos 22:20 1961
"Rise up yourself, and f on us; Jg 8:21 6293
f into the hands of the uncircumcised Jg 15:18 5307
or else fierce men will f upon you Jg 18:25 6293
f upon you in another field." Ru 2:22 6293
hair of his head shall f to the ground, 1Sa 14:45 5307
Now Saul planned to make David f 1Sa 18:25 5307
do not let my blood f to the 1Sa 26:20 5307
"May it f on the head of Joab and 2Sa 3:29 2342a
your son shall f to the ground." 2Sa 14:11 5307
and we will f on him as the dew 2Sa 17:12 5307
Let us now f into the hand of the 2Sa 24:14 5307
let me f into the hand of man." 2Sa 24:14 5307
of his hairs will f to the ground; 1Ki 1:52 5307
"Go, f upon him." 1Ki 2:29 6293
and f upon him and bury him, 1Ki 2:31 6293
to go up and f at Ramoth-gilead?' 1Ki 22:20 5307
man of God said, "Where did it f?" 2Ki 6:6 5307
"Know then that there shall f to 2Ki 10:10 5307
so that you, even you, would f, 2Ki 14:10 5307
f by the sword in his own land. 2Ki 19:7 5307

me f into the hand of the LORD, 1Ch 21:13 5307
let me f into the hand of man." 1Ch 21:13 5307
to go up and f at Ramoth-gilead?' 2Ch 18:19 5307
would f and Judah with you?" 2Ch 25:19 5307
do not f short in anything of all Es 6:10 5307
before whom you have begun to f, Es 6:13 5307
but will surely f before him." Es 6:13 5307
And the dread of Him f on you? Jb 13:11 5307
Or does their calamity f on them? Jb 21:17 935
Let my shoulder f from the socket, Jb 31:22 5307
'F on the earth,' And to the Jb 37:6 1933a
By their own devices let them f! Ps 5:10 5307
unfortunate f by his mighty ones. Ps 10:10 5307
that very destruction let him f. Ps 35:8 5307
For I am ready to f, Ps 38:17 6761
The peoples f under You; Ps 45:5 5307
them f in the midst of their camp, Ps 78:28 5307
f like *any* one of the princes." Ps 82:7 5307
away like a flood, they f asleep; Ps 90:5 1961
A thousand may f at your side And Ps 91:7 5307
hate the work of those who f away; Ps 101:3 7846
"May burning coals f upon them; Ps 140:10 4131
the wicked f into their own nets, Ps 141:10 5307
The LORD sustains all who f And Ps 145:14 5307
will f by his own wickedness. Pr 11:5 5307
is no guidance the people f, Pr 11:14 5307
who trusts in his riches will f, Pr 11:28 5307
cursed of the LORD will f into it. Pr 22:14 5307
He who digs a pit will f into it, Pr 26:27 5307
Will himself f into his own pit, Pr 28:10 5307
his heart will f into calamity. Pr 28:14 5307
he who is crooked will f all at once. Pr 28:18 5307
the righteous will see their f. Pr 29:16 4658
He who digs a pit may f into it, Ec 10:8 5307
the lips of those who f asleep. SS 7:9 3463
Your men will f by the sword And Is 3:25 5307
Then they will f and be broken; Is 8:15 5307
the captives Or f among the slain. Is 10:4 5307
Lebanon will f by the Mighty One. Is 10:34 5307
Therefore all hands will f limp, Is 13:7 7503
is captured will f by the sword. Is 13:15 5307
it will even break off and f, Is 22:25 5307
of disaster will f into the pit, Is 24:18 5307
is heavy upon it, And it will f, Is 24:20 5307
to you Like a breach about to f, Is 30:13 5307
slaughter, when the towers f. Is 30:25 5307
And he who is helped will f, Is 31:3 5307
will f by a sword not of man, Is 31:8 5307
Wild oxen will also f with them Is 34:7 3381
f by the sword in his own land. Is 37:7 5307
I f down before a block of wood!" Is 44:19 5456
And disaster will f on you For Is 47:11 5307
iniquity of us all To f on Him. Is 53:6 6293
assails you will f because of you. Is 54:15 5307
they shall f among those who fall; Jer 6:15 5307
they shall fall among those who f; Jer 6:15 5307
"Do *men* f and not get up again? Jer 8:4 5307
they shall f among those who fall; Jer 8:12 5307
they shall fall among those who f; Jer 8:12 5307
f like dung on the open field, Jer 9:22 5307
If you f down in a land of peace, Jer 12:5 982
and I will cause them to f by the Jer 19:7 5307
f by the sword of their enemies. Jer 20:4 5307
friends, Watching for my f, Jer 20:10 6761
into the gloom and f down in it; Jer 23:12 5307
"Drink, be drunk, vomit, f and Jer 25:27 5307
you will f like a choice vessel. Jer 25:34 5307
and you will not f by the sword; Jer 39:18 5307
they will f by the sword *and* meet Jer 44:12 5307
the terror Will f into the pit, Jer 48:44 5307
young men will f in her streets, Jer 49:26 5307
young men will f in her streets, Jer 50:30 5307
and f With no one to raise him up; Jer 50:32 5307
"They will f down slain in Jer 51:4 5307
all her slain will f in her midst. Jer 51:47 5307
is to f *for* the slain of Israel, Jer 51:49 5307
will f by the sword around you, Ezk 5:12 5307
slain f in front of your idols. Ezk 6:4 5307
"The slain will f among you, Ezk 6:7 5307
of Israel, which will f by sword, Ezk 6:11 5307
who is near will f by the sword, Ezk 6:12 5307
"You will f by the sword. Ezk 11:10 5307
with whitewash, that it will f. Ezk 13:11 5307
and you, O hailstones, will f; Ezk 13:11 5307
his troops will f by the sword, Ezk 17:21 5307
and many f at all their gates. Ezk 21:15 4383
survivors will f by the sword. Ezk 23:25 5307
left behind will f by the sword. Ezk 24:21 5307
to Dedan they will f by the sword. Ezk 25:13 5307
shake at the sound of your f when Ezk 26:15 4658
will tremble On the day of your f; Ezk 26:18 4658
Will f into the heart of the seas Ezk 27:27 5307
And the wounded will f in her Ezk 28:23 5307
You will f on the open field; Ezk 29:5 5307
When the slain f in Egypt, Ezk 30:4 5307
will f with them by the sword." Ezk 30:5 5307
those who support Egypt will f And Ezk 30:6 5307
will f within her by the sword," Ezk 30:6 5307
of Pi-beseth Will f by the sword, Ezk 30:17 5307
make the sword f from his hand. Ezk 30:22 5307
but the arms of Pharaoh will f. Ezk 30:25 5307
nations quake at the sound of its f Ezk 31:16 4658
own life, on the day of your f." Ezk 32:10 4658
I will cause your hordes to f; Ezk 32:12 5307
"They shall f in the midst of Ezk 32:20 5307
waste places will f by the sword, Ezk 33:27 5307
those slain by the sword will f. Ezk 35:8 5307
every wall will f to the ground. Ezk 38:20 5307
f on the mountains of Israel, Ezk 39:4 5307
"You will f on the open field; Ezk 39:5 5307
shall f to you as an inheritance. Ezk 47:14 5307
you are to f down and worship the Da 3:5 5308
"But whoever does not f down and Da 3:6 5308
is to f down and worship the Da 3:10 5308
"But whoever does not f down and Da 3:11 5308
to f down and worship the image Da 3:15 5308
of the stars to f to the earth, Da 8:10 5307
will cause tens of thousands to f; Da 11:12 5307
the vision, but they will f down. Da 11:14 3782
and f and be found no more. Da 11:19 5307
but many will f down slain. Da 11:26 5307
they will f by sword and by flame, Da 11:33 3782
"Now when they f they will be Da 11:34 3782
of those who have insight will f, Da 11:35 3782
Land, and many *countries* will f; Da 11:41 3782
Their princes will f by the sword Hos 7:16 5307
And to the hills, "F on us!" Hos 10:8 5307
They will f by the sword, Their Hos 13:16 5307
Does a bird f into a trap on the Am 3:5 5307
And they will f to the ground. Am 3:14 5307
daughters will f by the sword, Am 7:17 5307
They will f and not rise again." Am 8:14 5307
not a kernel will f to the ground. Am 9:9 5307
Though I f I will rise; Mi 7:8 5307
they f into the eater's mouth. Na 3:12 5307
Do not let your hands f limp. Zph 3:16 7503
I will cause the men to f, Zch 11:6 4672
panic from the LORD will f on them Zch 14:13 1961
then no *rain will* f on them; Zch 14:18
if You f down and worship me." Mt 4:9 4098
and *yet* it did not f, Mt 7:25 4098
it fell—and great was its f." Mt 7:27 4431
And *yet* not one of them will f to Mt 10:29 4098
man, both will f into a pit." Mt 15:14 4098
f from their masters' table." Mt 15:27 4098
that upon you may f *the guilt of* Mt 23:35 2064
"At that time many will f Mt 24:10 4624
AND THE STARS WILL F from the sky, Mt 24:29 4098
f away because of Me this night, Mt 26:31 4624
all may f away because of You, Mt 26:33 4624
of You, I will never f away." Mt 26:33 4624
f down before Him and shout, Mk 3:11 4363
the word, immediately they f away. Mk 4:17 4624
"You will all f away, because it Mk 14:27 4624
"*Even* though all may f away, Mk 14:29 4624
the f and rise of many in Israel, Lk 2:34 4431
Will they not both f into a pit? Lk 6:39 1706
and in time of temptation f away. Lk 8:13 868
f from heaven like lightning. Lk 10:18 4098
have a son or an ox f into a well, Lk 14:5 4098
will f by the edge of the sword, Lk 21:24 4098
'F ON US,' AND TO THE HILLS, Lk 23:30 4098
shadow might f on any one of them. Ac 5:15 1982
trade of ours f into disrepute, Ac 19:27 2064
the *ship's* boat and let it f away. Ac 27:32 1601b
swell up or suddenly f down dead. Ac 28:6 2667
and f short of the glory of God, Ro 3:23 5302
they did not stumble so as to f, Ro 11:11 4098
he stands take heed that he does not f. 1Co 10:12 4098
f on his face and worship God, 1Co 14:25 4098
he will not become conceited and f 1Tm 3:6 1706
so that he will not f into reproach 1Tm 3:7 1706
some will f away from the faith, 1Tm 4:1 868
But those who want to get rich f 1Tm 6:9 1706
so that no one will f, through *following* Heb 4:11 4098
It is a terrifying thing to f into Heb 10:31 1706
that you may not f under judgment. Jas 5:12 4098
and f from your own steadfastness, 2Pe 3:17 1601b
the twenty-four elders will f down Rv 4:10 4098
"F on us and hide us from the Rv 6:16 4098
so that rain will not f Rv 11:6 1026

FALLEN

And why has your countenance f? Gn 4:6 5307
gather the f fruit of your vineyard; Lv 19:10 6528
because our inheritance has f to Nu 32:19 935
or his ox f down on the way, Dt 22:4 5307
the terror of you has f on us, Jos 2:9 5307
it that you have f on your face? Jos 7:10 5307
and all of them were f by the edge Jos 8:24 5307
master had f to the floor dead. Jg 3:25 5307
for the f were 120,000 swordsmen. Jg 8:10 5307
Dagon had f on his face to the 1Sa 5:3 5307
Dagon had f on his face to the 1Sa 5:4 5307
sleep from the LORD had f on them. 1Sa 26:12 5307
his three sons f on Mount Gilboa. 1Sa 31:8 5307
of the people have f and are dead; 2Sa 1:4 5307
he could not live after he had f. 2Sa 1:10 5307
because they had f by the sword. 2Sa 1:12 5307
How have the mighty f! 2Sa 1:19 5307
f in the midst of the battle! 2Sa 1:25 5307
"How have the mighty f, 2Sa 1:27 5307
place where Asahel had f and died, 2Sa 2:23 5307
before the wicked, you have f." 2Sa 3:34 5307
man has f this day in Israel? 2Sa 3:38 5307
and his sons f on Mount Gilboa. 1Ch 10:8 5307
dread of the LORD had f on them; 2Ch 14:14 1961
our fathers have f by the sword, 2Ch 29:9 5307
dread of the Jews had f on them. Es 8:17 5307
of them had f on all the peoples. Es 9:2 5307
dread of Mordecai had f on them. Es 9:3 5307
has f into the hole which he made. Ps 7:15 5307
have f to me in pleasant places; Ps 16:6 5307
They have bowed down and f, Ps 20:8 5307
the doers of iniquity have f; Ps 36:12 5307
terrors of death have f upon me. Ps 55:4 5307
themselves have f into the midst of it. Ps 57:6 5307
who reproach You have f on me. Ps 69:9 5307
the dread of them had f upon them. Ps 105:38 5307
has stumbled and Judah has f, Is 3:8 5307
"The bricks have f down, But we Is 9:10 5307
"How you have f from heaven, O Is 14:12 5307
and your harvest has f away. Is 16:9 5307
city And will become a f ruin. Is 17:1 4654a
"F, fallen is Babylon; Is 21:9 5307
"Fallen, f is Babylon; Is 21:9 5307
They have stumbled and f. Jer 46:6 5307
both of them have f down together. Jer 46:12 5307
they have f one against another. Jer 46:16 5307
grape harvest The destroyer has f. Jer 48:32 5307
herself up, her pillars have f, Jer 50:15 5307
Babylon has f and been broken; Jer 51:8 5307
the wall of Babylon has f down! Jer 51:44 5307
the slain of all the earth have f. Jer 51:49 5307
Therefore she has f astonishingly; La 1:9 3381
my young men Have f by the sword. La 2:21 5307
The crown has f from our head; La 5:16 5307
"Behold, when the wall has f, Ezk 13:12 5307
Have f in the midst of you. Ezk 27:34 5307
the valleys its branches have f and Ezk 31:12 5307
will be on its f branches Ezk 31:13
of them are slain, f by the sword, Ezk 32:22 5307
of them are slain, f by the sword, Ezk 32:23 5307
all of them slain, f by the sword, Ezk 32:24 5307
the f heroes of the uncircumcised, Ezk 32:27 5307
All their kings have f. Hos 7:7 5307
She has f, she will not rise Am 5:2 5307
raise up the f booth of David, Am 9:11 5307
lain down and f sound asleep. Jon 1:5 7290a
O cypress, for the cedar has f, Zch 11:2 5307
who had f asleep were raised; Mt 27:52 2837
"Our friend Lazarus has f asleep; Jn 11:11 2837
"Lord, if he has f asleep, he Jn 11:12 2837
He had not yet f upon any of them; Ac 8:16 1968
TABERNACLE OF DAVID WHICH HAS F, Ac 15:16 4098
when we had all f to the ground, Ac 26:14 2667
until now, but some have f asleep; 1Co 15:6 2837
Then those also who have f asleep 1Co 15:18 2837
you have f from grace. Ga 5:4 1601b
those who have f asleep in Jesus. 1Th 4:14 2837
precede those who have f asleep. 1Th 4:15 2837
and *then* have f away, it is Heb 6:6 3895
remember from where you have f, Rv 2:5 4098
heaven which had f to the earth; Rv 9:1 4098
"F, fallen is Babylon the great, Rv 14:8 4098
"Fallen, f is Babylon the great, Rv 14:8 4098
five have f, one is, the other has Rv 17:10 4098
"F, fallen is Babylon the great! Rv 18:2 4098
"Fallen, f is Babylon the great! Rv 18:2 4098

FALLING

vision of the Almighty, F down, Nu 24:4 5307
vision of the Almighty, F down, Nu 24:16 5307
f on the couch where Esther was. Es 7:8 5307
"But the f mountain crumbles Jb 14:18 5307
me violently so that I was f, Ps 118:13 5307
to Jesus, f on his knees before Him Mt 17:14 1120
Him and f on his knees before Him, Mk 1:40 1120
a convulsion, and f to the ground, Mk 9:20 4098
THE STARS WILL BE F from heaven, Mk 13:25 4098
words which were f from His lips; Lk 4:22 1607
were f from the rich man's table; Lk 16:21 4098
of blood, f down upon the ground. Lk 22:44 2597
and f headlong, he burst open in Ac 1:18 1096
Then f on his knees, he cried out Ac 7:60 5087

FALLOW

you shall let it rest and lie f, Ex 23:11 5203
is in the f ground of the poor, Pr 13:23 5215b
"Break up your f ground, And do Jer 4:3 5215b
Break up your f ground, For it is Hos 10:12 5215b

FALLS

So that his rider f backward. Gn 49:17 5307
and an ox or a donkey f into it, Ex 21:33 5307
'If a part of their carcass f Lv 11:37 5307
a part of their carcass f on it, Lv 11:38 5307
Wherever the lot f to anyone, Nu 33:54 3318
is making war with you until it f. Dt 20:20 3381
on your house if anyone f from it. Dt 22:8 5307
a distaff, or who f by the sword, 2Sa 3:29 5307
As one f before the wicked, you 2Sa 3:34 5307
he f on them at the first attack, 2Sa 17:9 5307
on him as the dew f on the ground; 2Sa 17:12 5307
night, When deep sleep f on men, Jb 4:13 5307
night, When sound sleep f on men, Jb 33:15 5307
When he f, he will not be hurled Ps 37:24 5307
wicked messenger f into adversity, Pr 13:17 5307
in his language f into evil. Pr 17:20 5307
For a righteous man f seven times, Pr 24:16 5307
Do not rejoice when your enemy f, Pr 24:17 5307
f into the hand of a drunkard, Pr 26:9 5927
For if either of them f, Ec 4:10 5307
But woe to the one who f when Ec 4:10 5307
time when it suddenly f on them. Ec 9:12 5307
and whether a tree f toward the Ec 11:3 5307
the north, wherever the tree f, Ec 11:3 5307
against Jacob, And it f on Israel. Is 9:8 5307
image and f down before it. Is 44:15 5456
He f down before it and worships; Is 44:17 5456
but he who goes out and f away to Jer 21:9 5307
and when it f, you will be Ezk 13:14 5307
if it f into a pit on the Sabbath, Mt 12:11 1706
the word, immediately he f away. Mt 13:21 4624
for he often f into the fire and Mt 17:15 4098
"And he who f on this stone will Mt 21:44 4098
but on whomever it f, Mt 21:44 4098
a house *divided* against itself f. Lk 11:17 4098
share of the estate that f to me.' Lk 15:12 1911
"Everyone who f on that stone Lk 20:18 4098

but on whomever it **f**, **Lk 20:18** *4098*
wheat **f** into the earth and dies, **Jn 12:24** *4098*
judgment of God rightly **f** upon those **Ro 2:2** *1510*
To his own master he stands or **f**; **Ro 14:4** *4098*
unbelieving heart that **f** away from **Heb 3:12** *868*
drinks the rain which often **f** on it **Heb 6:7** *2064*
and its flower **f** off and the **Jas 1:11** *1601b*
WITHERS, AND THE FLOWER **F** OFF, **1Pe 1:24** *1601b*

FALSE
will pay no attention to **f** words." **Ex 5:9** 8267
f witness against your neighbor. **Ex 20:16** 8267
"You shall not bear a **f** report; **Ex 23:1** 7723
"Keep far from a **f** charge, and do **Ex 23:7** 8267
f witness against your neighbor. **Dt 5:20** 7723
and if the witness is a **f** witness **Dt 19:18** 8267
"For He knows **f** men, And He sees **Jb 11:11** 7723
"For truly my words are not **f**; **Jb 36:4** 8267
"Behold, your expectation is **f**; **Jb 41:9** 3576
For **f** witnesses have risen against **Ps 27:12** 8267
A horse is a **f** hope for victory; **Ps 33:17** 8267
Remove the **f** way from me, And **Ps 119:29** 8267
Therefore I hate every **f** way. **Ps 119:104** 8267
everything, I hate every **f** way. **Ps 119:128** 8267
A **f** witness *who* utters lies, And **Pr 6:19** 8267
A **f** balance is an abomination to **Pr 11:1** 4820
what is right, But a **f** witness, **Pr 12:17** 8267
lie, But a **f** witness utters lies. **Pr 14:5** 8267
A **f** witness will not go **Pr 19:5** 8267
A **f** witness will not go **Pr 19:9** 8267
LORD, And a **f** scale is not good. **Pr 20:23** 4820
A **f** witness will perish, But the **Pr 21:28** 3577
f witness against his neighbor. **Pr 25:18** 8267
His idle boasts are **f**. **Is 16:6** 3808, 3653
is a rebellious people, **f** sons, **Is 30:9** 3586
"Behold, all of them are **f**; **Is 41:29** 205
are prophesying to you a **f** vision, **Jer 14:14** 8267
who have prophesied **f** dreams," **Jer 23:32** 8267
for you **F** and foolish *visions;* **La 2:14** 7723
for you **f** and misleading oracles. **La 2:14** 7723
there will no longer be any **f** vision **Ezk 12:24** 7723
"Did you not see a **f** vision and **Ezk 13:7** 7723
the prophets who see **f** visions **Ezk 13:9** 7723
you women will no longer see **f** **Ezk 13:23** 7723
like a **f** divination in their eyes; **Ezk 21:23** 7723
while they see for you **f** visions, **Ezk 21:29** 7723
seeing **f** visions and divining lies **Ezk 22:28** 7723
in whose hands are **f** balances, **Hos 12:7** 4820
lying visions And tell **f** dreams; **Zch 10:2** 7723
'YOU SHALL NOT MAKE **F** VOWS, **Mt 5:33** *1964*
"Beware of the **f** prophets, who **Mt 7:15** *5578*
fornications, thefts, **f** witness, **Mt 15:19** *5577a*
YOU SHALL NOT BEAR **F** WITNESS; **Mt 19:18** *5576*
"Many **f** prophets will arise and **Mt 24:11** *5578*
"For **f** Christs and false prophets **Mt 24:24** *5580*
"For false Christs and **f** prophets **Mt 24:24** *5578*
obtain **f** testimony against Jesus, **Mt 26:59** *5577a*
many **f** witnesses came forward. **Mt 26:60** *5577b*
NOT STEAL, DO NOT BEAR **F** WITNESS, **Mk 10:19** *5576*
for **f** Christs and false prophets **Mk 13:22** *5580*
Christs and **f** prophets will arise, **Mk 13:22** *5578*
giving **f** testimony against Him, **Mk 14:56** *5576*
to give **f** testimony against Him, **Mk 14:57** *5576*
used to treat the **f** prophets in **Lk 6:26** *5578*
NOT STEAL, DO NOT BEAR **F** WITNESS, **Lk 18:20** *5576*
put forward **f** witnesses who said, **Ac 6:13** *5571*
a Jewish **f** prophet whose name was **Ac 13:6** *5578*
found *to be* **f** witnesses of God, **1Co 15:15** *5577b*
For such men are **f** apostles, **2Co 11:13** *5570*
the sea, dangers among **f** brethren; **2Co 11:26** *5569*
But *it was* because of the **f** **Ga 2:4** *5569*
beware of the **f** circumcision; **Php 3:2** *2699*
all power and signs and **f** wonders, **2Th 2:9** *5579*
that they will believe what is **f**, **2Th 2:11** *5579*
But **f** prophets also arose among **2Pe 2:1** *5578*
will also be **f** teachers among you, **2Pe 2:1** *5572*
will exploit you with **f** words; **2Pe 2:3** *4112*
because many **f** prophets have gone **1Jn 4:1** *5578*
not, and you found them *to be* **f**; **Rv 2:2** *5571*
out of the mouth of the **f** prophet, **Rv 16:13** *5578*
and with him the **f** prophet who **Rv 19:20** *5578*
beast and the **f** prophet are also; **Rv 20:10** *5578*

FALSEHOOD
your answers remain *full of* **f**?" **Jb 21:34** 4604
"If I have walked with **f**, **Jb 31:5** 7723
You destroy those who speak **f**; **Ps 5:6** 3577
mischief and brings forth **f**. **Ps 7:14** 8267
They speak **f** to one another; **Ps 12:2** 7723
has not lifted up his soul to **f** And **Ps 24:4** 7723
nor to those who lapse into **f**. **Ps 40:4** 3577
he comes to see *me,* he speaks **f**; **Ps 41:6** 7723
F more than speaking what is right. **Ps 52:3** 8267
They delight in **f**; **Ps 62:4** 3577
He who speaks **f** shall not maintain **Ps 101:7** 8267
I hate and despise **f**, **Ps 119:163** 8267
right hand is a right hand of **f**. **Ps 144:8** 8267
right hand is a right hand of **f**. **Ps 144:11** 8267
A righteous man hates **f**, **Pr 13:5** 8267
obtained by **f** is sweet to a man, **Pr 20:17** 8267
If a ruler pays attention to **f**, **Pr 29:12** 8267
drag iniquity with the cords of **f**, **Is 5:18** 7723
prophet who teaches **f** is the tail. **Is 9:15** 8267
For we have made **f** our refuge and **Is 28:15** 3577
Your lips have spoken **f**, **Is 59:3** 8267
forgotten Me And trusted in **f**. **Jer 13:25** 8267
are prophesying **f** in My name. **Jer 14:14** 8267
have inherited nothing but **f**, **Jer 16:19** 8267
of adultery and walking in **f**; **Jer 23:14** 8267
of the prophets who prophesy **f**, **Jer 23:26** 8267
"They see **f** and lying divination **Ezk 13:6** 7723
you have spoken **f** and seen a lie, **Ezk 13:8** 7723
disheartened the righteous with **f** **Ezk 13:22** 8267
wind and **f** Had told lies *and said,* **Mi 2:11** 8267
it, *Or* an image, a teacher of **f**? **Hab 2:18** 8267
Therefore, laying aside **f**, **Eph 4:25** *5579*

FALSEHOODS
by their **f** and reckless boasting; **Jer 23:32** 8267

FALSELY
that you will not deal **f** with me or **Gn 21:23** 8266
and lied about it and sworn **f**, **Lv 6:3** 8267
anything about which he swore **f**; **Lv 6:5** 8267
'You shall not steal, nor deal **f**, **Lv 19:11** 8266
You shall not swear **f** by My name, **Lv 19:12** 8267
and he has accused his brother **f**, **Dt 19:18** 8267
not dealt **f** with Your covenant. **Ps 44:17** 8266
Nor deal **f** in My faithfulness. **Ps 89:33** 8266
a man who boasts of his gifts **f**. **Pr 25:14** 8267
Sons who will not deal **f**." **Is 63:8** 8266
LORD lives,' Surely they swear **f**." **Jer 5:2** 8267
The prophets prophesy **f**, **Jer 5:31** 8267
to the priest Everyone deals **f**. **Jer 6:13** 8267
and commit adultery and swear **f**, **Jer 7:9** 8267
to whom you have **f** prophesied.'" **Jer 20:6** 8267
said who prophesy **f** in My name, **Jer 23:25** 8267
"but they prophesy **f** in My name, **Jer 27:15** 8267
they prophesy **f** to you in My name; **Jer 29:9** 8267
prophesying to you **f** in My name, **Jer 29:21** 8267
have spoken words in My name **f**, **Jer 29:23** 8267
deeds of Samaria, For they deal **f**; **Hos 7:1** 8267
the one who swears **f** by My name; **Zch 5:4** 8267
spoken **f** in the name of the LORD'; **Zch 13:3** 8267
and against those who swear **f**, **Mal 3:5** 8267
and **f** say all kinds of evil against **Mt 5:11** *5574*
by force, or accuse *anyone* **f**, **Lk 3:14** *4811*
arguments of what is **f** called **1Tm 6:20** *5581*

FALTER
his means with regard to you **f**, **Lv 25:35** 4131

FAME
who have heard of Your **f** will say, **Nu 14:15** 8088
which He has made, for praise, **f**, **Dt 26:19** 8034
and his **f** was in all the land. **Jos 6:27** 8089
of the **f** of the LORD your God; **Jos 9:9** 8034
and his **f** was *known* in all the **1Ki 4:31** 8034
heard about the **f** of Solomon **1Ki 10:1** 8088
Then the **f** of David went out into **1Ch 14:17** 8034
Sheba heard of the **f** of Solomon, **2Ch 9:1** 8088
and his **f** extended to the border **2Ch 26:8** 8034
Hence his **f** spread afar, for he **2Ch 26:15** 8034
and his **f** spread throughout all **Es 9:4** 8089
heard My **f** nor seen My glory. **Is 66:19** 8088
"Then your **f** went forth among the **Ezk 16:14** 8034
the harlot because of your **f**, **Ezk 16:15** 8034
whose **f** in *the things of* the gospel **2Co 8:18** *1868*

FAMILIAR
For he is **f** with the terrors of **Jb 24:17** 5234
My companion and my **f** friend; **Ps 55:13** 3045

FAMILIES
went out by their **f** from the ark. **Gn 8:19** 4940
language, according to their **f**, **Gn 10:5** 4940
and afterward the **f** of the **Gn 10:18** 4940
sons of Ham, according to their **f**, **Gn 10:20** 4940
of Shem, according to their **f**, **Gn 10:31** 4940
are the **f** of the sons of Noah, **Gn 10:32** 4940
f of the earth will be blessed." **Gn 12:3** 4940
all the **f** of the earth be blessed. **Gn 28:14** 4940
to their **f** *and* their localities, **Gn 36:40** 4940
these are the **f** of Reuben. **Ex 6:14** 4940
these are the **f** of Simeon. **Ex 6:15** 4940
and Shimei, according to their **f**. **Ex 6:17** 4940
These are the **f** of the Levites **Ex 6:19** 4940
these are the **f** of the Korahites. **Ex 6:24** 4940
the Levites according to their **f**. **Ex 6:25** 4940
lambs according to your **f**, **Ex 12:21** 4940
out of their **f** who are with you, **Lv 25:45** 4940
of the sons of Israel, by their **f**, **Nu 1:2** 4940
registered by ancestry in their **f**, **Nu 1:18** 4940
registration by their **f**, **Nu 1:20** 4940
registration by their **f**, **Nu 1:22** 4940
registration by their **f**, **Nu 1:24** 4940
registration by their **f**, **Nu 1:26** 4940
registration by their **f**, **Nu 1:28** 4940
registration by their **f**, **Nu 1:30** 4940
registration by their **f**, **Nu 1:32** 4940
registration by their **f**, **Nu 1:34** 4940
registration by their **f**, **Nu 1:36** 4940
registration by their **f**, **Nu 1:38** 4940
registration by their **f**, **Nu 1:40** 4940
registration by their **f**, **Nu 1:42** 4940
fathers' households, by their **f**; **Nu 3:15** 4940
of the sons of Gershon by their **f**: **Nu 3:18** 4940
and the sons of Kohath by their **f**: **Nu 3:19** 4940
and the sons of Merari by their **f**: **Nu 3:20** 4940
These are the **f** of the Levites **Nu 3:20** 4940
were the **f** of the Gershonites. **Nu 3:21** 4940
The **f** of the Gershonites were to **Nu 3:23** 4940
were the **f** of the Kohathites. **Nu 3:27** 4940
The **f** of the sons of Kohath were **Nu 3:29** 4940
of the Kohathite **f** was Elizaphan **Nu 3:30** 4940
these *were* the **f** of Merari. **Nu 3:33** 4940
of the **f** of Merari *was* Zuriel the son **Nu 3:35** 4940
command of the LORD by their **f**, **Nu 3:39** 4940
the sons of Levi, by their **f**, **Nu 4:2** 4940
the tribe of the **f** of the Kohathites **Nu 4:18** 4940
fathers' households, by their **f**; **Nu 4:22** 4940
of the **f** of the Gershonites, **Nu 4:24** 4940
the **f** of the sons of the Gershonites **Nu 4:28** 4940
you shall number them by their **f**, **Nu 4:29** 4940
of the **f** of the sons of Merari, **Nu 4:33** 4940
sons of the Kohathites by their **f** and **Nu 4:34** 4940
men by their **f** were 2,750. **Nu 4:36** 4940
numbered men of the Kohathite **f**, **Nu 4:37** 4940
of the sons of Gershon by their **f** and **Nu 4:38** 4940
Their numbered men by their **f**, **Nu 4:40** 4940
of the **f** of the sons of Gershon, **Nu 4:41** 4940
The numbered men of the **f** of **Nu 4:42** 4940
of the sons of Merari by their **f**, **Nu 4:42** 4940
men by their **f** were 3,200. **Nu 4:44** 4940
of the **f** of the sons of Merari, **Nu 4:45** 4940
by their **f** and by their fathers' **Nu 4:46** 4940
people weeping throughout their **f**, **Nu 11:10** 4940
These are the **f** of the Reubenites, **Nu 26:7** 4940
of Simeon according to their **f**: **Nu 26:12** 4940
These are the **f** of the Simeonites, **Nu 26:14** 4940
sons of Gad according to their **f**: **Nu 26:15** 4940
These are the **f** of the sons of Gad **Nu 26:18** 4940
Judah according to their **f** were: **Nu 26:20** 4940
These are the **f** of Judah according **Nu 26:22** 4940
of Issachar according to their **f**: **Nu 26:23** 4940
These are the **f** of Issachar **Nu 26:25** 4940
of Zebulun according to their **f**: **Nu 26:26** 4940
These are the **f** of the Zebulunites **Nu 26:27** 4940
of Joseph according to their **f**: **Nu 26:28** 4940
These are the **f** of Manasseh; **Nu 26:34** 4940
of Ephraim according to their **f**: **Nu 26:35** 4940
are the **f** of the sons of Ephraim **Nu 26:37** 4940
of Joseph according to their **f**. **Nu 26:37** 4940
of Benjamin according to their **f**: **Nu 26:38** 4940
of Benjamin according to their **f**; **Nu 26:41** 4940
sons of Dan according to their **f**: **Nu 26:42** 4940
These are the **f** of Dan according **Nu 26:42** 4940
of Dan according to their **f**. **Nu 26:42** 4940
All the **f** of the Shuhamites, **Nu 26:43** 4940
of Asher according to their **f**: **Nu 26:44** 4940
These are the **f** of the sons of **Nu 26:47** 4940
of Naphtali according to their **f**: **Nu 26:48** 4940
These are the **f** of Naphtali **Nu 26:50** 4940
of Naphtali according to their **f**; **Nu 26:50** 4940
the Levites according to their **f**: **Nu 26:57** 4940
These are the **f** of Levi: **Nu 26:58** 4940
f of Manasseh the son of Joseph, **Nu 27:1** 4940
land by lot according to your **f**; **Nu 33:54** 4940
of the **f** of the sons of Joseph, **Nu 36:1** 4940
from the **f** of the sons of Manasseh **Nu 36:12** 4940
takes *by lot* shall come near by **f**, **Jos 7:14** 4940
of Reuben according to their **f**. **Jos 13:15** 4940
of Reuben according to their **f**, **Jos 13:23** 4940
sons of Gad, according to their **f**. **Jos 13:24** 4940
sons of Gad according to their **f**, **Jos 13:28** 4940
of Manasseh according to their **f**. **Jos 13:29** 4940
of Machir according to their **f**. **Jos 13:31** 4940
f reached the border of Edom, **Jos 15:1** 4940
of Judah according to their **f**. **Jos 15:12** 4940
of Judah according to their **f**. **Jos 15:20** 4940
of Ephraim according to their **f**: **Jos 16:5** 4940
of Ephraim according to their **f**, **Jos 16:8** 4940
of Manasseh according to their **f**: **Jos 17:2** 4940
of Joseph according to their **f**. **Jos 17:2** 4940
came up according to their **f**, **Jos 18:11** 4940
according to their **f** *and* according **Jos 18:20** 4940
of Benjamin according to their **f** **Jos 18:21** 4940
of Benjamin according to their **f**. **Jos 18:28** 4940
of Simeon according to their **f**, **Jos 19:1** 4940
of Simeon according to their **f**. **Jos 19:8** 4940
of Zebulun according to their **f**. **Jos 19:10** 4940
of Zebulun according to their **f**, **Jos 19:16** 4940
of Issachar according to their **f**, **Jos 19:17** 4940
of Issachar according to their **f**, **Jos 19:23** 4940
of Asher according to their **f**. **Jos 19:24** 4940
of Asher according to their **f**, **Jos 19:31** 4940
of Naphtali according to their **f**. **Jos 19:32** 4940
of Naphtali according to their **f**, **Jos 19:39** 4940
sons of Dan according to their **f**. **Jos 19:40** 4940
sons of Dan according to their **f**, **Jos 19:48** 4940
out for the **f** of the Kohathites. **Jos 21:4** 4940
from the **f** of the tribe of Ephraim **Jos 21:5** 4940
from the **f** of the tribe of Issachar **Jos 21:6** 4940
sons of Merari according to their **f** **Jos 21:7** 4940
one of the **f** of the Kohathites, **Jos 21:10** 4940
to the **f** of the sons of Kohath, **Jos 21:20** 4940
f of the rest of the sons of Kohath **Jos 21:26** 4940
one of the **f** of the Levites, **Jos 21:27** 4940
the Gershonites according to their **f** **Jos 21:33** 4940
To the **f** of the sons of Merari, **Jos 21:34** 4940
of Merari according to their **f**, **Jos 21:40** 4940
the rest of the **f** of the Levites; **Jos 21:40** 4940
to the heads of the **f** of Israel. **Jos 22:21** 505
the **f** of Israel who *were* with him, **Jos 22:30** 505
the **f** of the tribe of Benjamin? **1Sa 9:21** 4940
tribe of Benjamin near by its **f**, **1Sa 10:21** 4940
and the **f** of Kiriath-jearim: **1Ch 2:53** 4940
The **f** of scribes who lived at **1Ch 2:55** 4940
were the **f** of the Zorathites. **1Ch 4:2** 4940
the **f** of Aharhel the son of Harum. **1Ch 4:8** 4940
f of the house of the linen workers **1Ch 4:21** 4940
by name *were* leaders in their **f**; **1Ch 4:38** 4940
His kinsmen by their **f**, **1Ch 5:7** 4940
And these are the **f** of the Levites **1Ch 6:19** 4940
Aaron of the **f** of the Kohathites **1Ch 6:54** 4940
their **f** were thirteen cities. **1Ch 6:60** 4940
of Gershom, according to their **f**, **1Ch 6:62** 4940
by lot, according to their **f**, **1Ch 6:63** 4940
some of the **f** of the sons of Kohath **1Ch 6:66** 4940
relatives among all the **f** of Issachar **1Ch 7:5** 4940
to the LORD, O **f** of the peoples, **1Ch 16:28** 4940
the people in **f** with their swords **Ne 4:13** 4940

the contempt of **f** terrified me,	**Jb 31:34**	4940
And all the **f** of the nations will	**Ps 22:27**	4940
to the LORD, O **f** of the peoples,	**Ps 96:7**	4940
And makes *his* **f** like a flock.	**Ps 107:41**	4940
f of the kingdoms of the north,"	**Jer 1:15**	4940
all the **f** of the house of Israel.	**Jer 2:4**	4940
the **f** that do not call Your name;	**Jer 10:25**	4940
and take all the **f** of the north,'	**Jer 25:9**	4940
be the God of all the **f** of Israel,	**Jer 31:1**	4940
'The two **f** which the LORD chose,	**Jer 33:24**	4940
among all the **f** of the earth;	**Am 3:2**	4940
harlotries And **f** by her sorceries.	**Na 3:4**	4940
all the **f** that remain, every	**Zch 12:14**	4940
whichever of the **f** of the earth does	**Zch 14:17**	4940
F OF THE EARTH SHALL BE BLESSED.'	**Ac 3:25**	*3965*
they are upsetting whole **f**,	**Ti 1:11**	*3624*
FAMILY		
our **f** through our father."	**Gn 19:32**	2233
our **f** through our father."	**Gn 19:34**	2233
that man and against his **f**,	**Lv 20:5**	4940
each of you shall return to his **f**.	**Lv 25:10**	4940
him, and shall go back to his **f**,	**Lv 25:41**	4940
the descendants of a stranger's **f**,	**Lv 25:47**	4940
relatives from his **f** may redeem	**Lv 25:49**	4940
they set out, every one by his **f**	**Nu 2:34**	4940
Of Gershon *was* the **f** of the Libnites	**Nu 3:21**	4940
and the **f** of the Shimeites;	**Nu 3:21**	4940
Kohath *was* the **f** of the Amramites	**Nu 3:27**	4940
Amramites and the **f** of the Izharites	**Nu 3:27**	4940
and the **f** of the Hebronites and the	**Nu 3:27**	4940
and the **f** of the Uzzielites;	**Nu 3:27**	4940
Of Merari *was* the **f** of the Mahlites	**Nu 3:33**	4940
and the **f** of the Mushites;	**Nu 3:33**	4940
Hanoch, the **f** of the Hanochites;	**Nu 26:5**	4940
of Pallu, the **f** of the Palluites;	**Nu 26:5**	4940
Hezron, the **f** of the Hezronites;	**Nu 26:6**	4940
of Carmi, the **f** of the Carmites.	**Nu 26:6**	4940
Nemuel, the **f** of the Nemuelites;	**Nu 26:12**	4940
of Jamin, the **f** of the Jaminites;	**Nu 26:12**	4940
Jachin, the **f** of the Jachinites;	**Nu 26:12**	4940
of Zerah, the **f** of the Zerahites;	**Nu 26:13**	4940
of Shaul, the **f** of the Shaulites.	**Nu 26:13**	4940
Zephon, the **f** of the Zephonites;	**Nu 26:15**	4940
of Haggi, the **f** of the Haggites;	**Nu 26:15**	4940
of Shuni, the **f** of the Shunites;	**Nu 26:15**	4940
of Ozni, the **f** of the Oznites;	**Nu 26:16**	4940
of Eri, the **f** of the Erites;	**Nu 26:16**	4940
of Arod, the **f** of the Arodites;	**Nu 26:17**	4940
of Areli, the **f** of the Arelites.	**Nu 26:17**	4940
Shelah, the **f** of the Shelanites;	**Nu 26:20**	4940
of Perez, the **f** of the Perezites;	**Nu 26:20**	4940
of Zerah, the **f** of the Zerahites.	**Nu 26:20**	4940
Hezron, the **f** of the Hezronites;	**Nu 26:21**	4940
of Hamul, the **f** of the Hamulites.	**Nu 26:21**	4940
of Tola, the **f** of the Tolaites;	**Nu 26:23**	4940
of Puvah, the **f** of the Punites;	**Nu 26:23**	4940
Jashub, the **f** of the Jashubites;	**Nu 26:24**	4940
Shimron, the **f** of the Shimronites.	**Nu 26:24**	4940
of Sered, the **f** of the Seredites;	**Nu 26:26**	4940
of Elon, the **f** of the Elonites;	**Nu 26:26**	4940
Jahleel, the **f** of the Jahleelites.	**Nu 26:26**	4940
Machir, the **f** of the Machirites;	**Nu 26:29**	4940
Gilead, the **f** of the Gileadites.	**Nu 26:29**	4940
of Iezer, the **f** of the Iezerites;	**Nu 26:30**	4940
of Helek, the **f** of the Helekites;	**Nu 26:30**	4940
Asriel, the **f** of the Asrielites;	**Nu 26:31**	4940
Shechem, the **f** of the Shechemites;	**Nu 26:31**	4940
Shemida, the **f** of the Shemidaites;	**Nu 26:32**	4940
Hepher, the **f** of the Hepherites.	**Nu 26:32**	4940
the **f** of the Shuthelahites;	**Nu 26:35**	4940
Becher, the **f** of the Becherites;	**Nu 26:35**	4940
of Tahan, the **f** of the Tahanites.	**Nu 26:35**	4940
of Eran, the **f** of the Eranites.	**Nu 26:36**	4940
of Bela, the **f** of the Belaites;	**Nu 26:38**	4940
Ashbel, the **f** of the Ashbelites;	**Nu 26:38**	4940
Ahiram, the **f** of the Ahiramites;	**Nu 26:38**	4940
the **f** of the Shuphamites;	**Nu 26:39**	4940
Hupham, the **f** of the Huphamites.	**Nu 26:39**	4940
of Ard, the **f** of the Ardites;	**Nu 26:40**	4940
of Naaman, the **f** of the Naamites.	**Nu 26:40**	4940
Shuham, the **f** of the Shuhamites.	**Nu 26:42**	4940
of Imnah, the **f** of the Imnites;	**Nu 26:44**	4940
of Ishvi, the **f** of the Ishvites;	**Nu 26:44**	4940
of Beriah, the **f** of the Berites.	**Nu 26:44**	4940
of Heber, the **f** of the Heberites;	**Nu 26:45**	4940
the **f** of the Malchielites.	**Nu 26:45**	4940
Jahzeel, the **f** of the Jahzeelites;	**Nu 26:48**	4940
of Guni, the **f** of the Gunites;	**Nu 26:48**	4940
of Jezer, the **f** of the Jezerites;	**Nu 26:49**	4940
Shillem, the **f** of the Shillemites.	**Nu 26:49**	4940
Gershon, the **f** of the Gershonites;	**Nu 26:57**	4940
Kohath, the **f** of the Kohathites;	**Nu 26:57**	4940
of Merari, the **f** of the Merarites.	**Nu 26:57**	4940
the **f** of the Libnites, the family	**Nu 26:58**	4940
Libnites, the **f** of the Hebronites,	**Nu 26:58**	4940
Hebronites, the **f** of the Mahlites,	**Nu 26:58**	4940
Mahlites, the **f** of the Mushites,	**Nu 26:58**	4940
Mushites, the **f** of the Korahites.	**Nu 26:58**	4940
be withdrawn from among his **f**	**Nu 27:4**	4940
his nearest relative in his own **f**,	**Nu 27:11**	4940
of the **f** of the sons of Gilead,	**Nu 36:1**	4940
f of the tribe of their father.'	**Nu 36:6**	4940
the **f** of the tribe of her father,	**Nu 36:8**	4940
tribe of the **f** of their father.	**Nu 36:12**	4940
not be *married* outside *the* **f**	**Dt 25:5**	
you a man or woman, or **f** or tribe,	**Dt 29:18**	4940
and the **f** which the LORD takes	**Jos 7:14**	4940
He brought the **f** of Judah near,	**Jos 7:17**	4940
he took the **f** of the Zerahites;	**Jos 7:17**	4940
he brought the **f** of the Zerahites	**Jos 7:17**	4940
let the man and all his **f** go free.	**Jg 1:25**	4940
my **f** is the least in Manasseh,	**Jg 6:15**	505
he gave in marriage outside *the* **f**,	**Jg 12:9**	
of Zorah, of the **f** of the Danites,	**Jg 13:2**	4940
in Judah, of the **f** of Judah,	**Jg 17:7**	4940
sons of Dan sent from their **f** five	**Jg 18:2**	4940
Then from the **f** of the Danites,	**Jg 18:11**	4940
to a tribe and a **f** in Israel?"	**Jg 18:19**	4940
every man to his tribe and **f**,	**Jg 21:24**	4940
wealth, of the **f** of Elimelech,	**Ru 2:1**	4940
who was of the **f** of Elimelech.	**Ru 2:3**	4940
my **f** the least of all the families	**1Sa 9:21**	4940
and the Matrite **f** was taken.	**1Sa 10:21**	4940
my life *or* my father's **f** in Israel,	**1Sa 18:18**	4940
sacrifice there for the whole **f**.'	**1Sa 20:6**	4940
our **f** has a sacrifice in the city,	**1Sa 20:29**	4940
the whole **f** has risen against your	**2Sa 14:7**	4940
a man of the **f** of the house of Saul	**2Sa 16:5**	4940
for he alone of Jeroboam's **f** will	**1Ki 14:13**	
son of Elishama, of the royal **f**,	**2Ki 25:25**	2233
nor did all their **f** multiply like	**1Ch 4:27**	4940
by lot, from the **f** of the tribe,	**1Ch 6:61**	4940
of the **f** of the sons of Kohath.	**1Ch 6:70**	4940
f of the half-tribe of Manasseh:	**1Ch 6:71**	4940
ark of God remained with the **f** of	**1Ch 13:14**	1004
LORD blessed the **f** of Obed-edom	**1Ch 13:14**	1004
killed your brothers, your own **f**,	**2Ch 21:13**	1004, 1
every generation, every **f**,	**Es 9:28**	4940
Buzite, of the **f** of Ram burned;	**Jb 32:2**	4940
one from a city and two from a **f**,	**Jer 3:14**	4940
that remains of this evil **f**,	**Jer 8:3**	4940
of the royal **f** and *one* of the	**Jer 41:1**	2233
He took one of the royal **f** and made	**Ezk 17:13**	2233
of the royal **f** and of the nobles,	**Da 1:3**	2233
against the entire **f** which He	**Am 3:1**	4940
I am planning against this **f** a	**Mi 2:3**	4940
will mourn, every **f** by itself;	**Zch 12:12**	4940
the **f** of the house of David by	**Zch 12:12**	4940
the **f** of the house of Nathan by	**Zch 12:12**	4940
the **f** of the house of Levi by	**Zch 12:13**	4940
the **f** of the Shimeites by itself and	**Zch 12:13**	4940
that remain, every **f** by itself and	**Zch 12:14**	4940
If the **f** of Egypt does not go	**Zch 14:18**	4940
was of the house and **f** of David,	**Lk 2:4**	*3965*
tell my brother to divide the **f**	**Lk 12:13**	
Joseph's **f** was disclosed to Pharaoh.	**Ac 7:13**	*1085*
"Brethren, sons of Abraham's **f**,	**Ac 13:26**	*1085*
from whom every **f** in heaven and on	**Eph 3:15**	*3965*
piety in regard to their own **f** and	**1Tm 5:4**	*3624*
FAMINE		
Now there was a **f** in the land;	**Gn 12:10**	7458
for the **f** was severe in the land.	**Gn 12:10**	7458
Now there was a **f** in the land,	**Gn 26:1**	7458
besides the previous **f** that had	**Gn 26:1**	7458
wind will be seven years of **f**.	**Gn 41:27**	7458
them seven years of **f** will come,	**Gn 41:30**	7458
and the **f** will ravage the land.	**Gn 41:30**	7458
land because of that subsequent **f**;	**Gn 41:31**	7458
the seven years of **f** which will occur	**Gn 41:36**	7458
will not perish during the **f**."	**Gn 41:36**	7458
Now before the year of **f** came,	**Gn 41:50**	7458
seven years of **f** began to come,	**Gn 41:54**	7458
then there was **f** in all the lands,	**Gn 41:54**	7458
When the **f** was *spread* over all the	**Gn 41:56**	7458
and the **f** was severe in the land	**Gn 41:56**	7458
the **f** was severe in all the earth.	**Gn 41:57**	7458
for the **f** was in the land of	**Gn 42:5**	7458
for the **f** of your households,	**Gn 42:19**	7459
for the **f** of your households,	**Gn 42:33**	7459
Now the **f** was severe in the land.	**Gn 43:1**	7458
"For the **f** *has been* in the land	**Gn 45:6**	7458
are still five years of **f** *to come,*	**Gn 45:11**	7458
for the **f** is severe in the land of	**Gn 47:4**	7458
because the **f** was very severe,	**Gn 47:13**	7458
languished because of the **f**.	**Gn 47:13**	7458
the **f** was severe upon them.	**Gn 47:20**	7458
'*They will be* wasted by **f**,	**Dt 32:24**	7458
that there was a **f** in the land.	**Ru 1:1**	7458
Now there was a **f** in the days of	**2Sa 21:1**	7458
Shall seven years of **f** come to you	**2Sa 24:13**	7458
"If there is **f** in the land, if	**1Ki 8:37**	7458
Now the **f** *was* severe in Samaria.	**1Ki 18:2**	7458
Gilgal, *there was* a **f** in the land.	**2Ki 4:38**	7458
There was a great **f** in Samaria;	**2Ki 6:25**	7458
then the **f** is in the city and we	**2Ki 7:4**	7458
for the LORD has called for a **f**,	**2Ki 8:1**	7458
the **f** was so severe in the city that	**2Ki 25:3**	7458
either three years of **f**,	**1Ch 21:12**	7458
"If there is **f** in the land, if	**2Ch 6:28**	7458
or judgment, or pestilence, or **f**,	**2Ch 20:9**	7458
get grain because of the **f**."	**Ne 5:3**	7458
f He will redeem you from death,	**Jb 5:20**	7458
"You will laugh at violence and **f**,	**Jb 5:22**	3720
"From want and **f** they are gaunt	**Jb 30:3**	3720
And to keep them alive in **f**.	**Ps 33:19**	7458
of **f** they will have abundance.	**Ps 37:19**	7459
He called for a **f** upon the land;	**Ps 105:16**	7458
I will destroy your root with **f**,	**Is 14:30**	7458
and destruction, **f** and sword;	**Is 51:19**	7458
And we will not see sword or **f**.	**Jer 5:12**	7458
sons and daughters will die by **f**;	**Jer 11:22**	7458
by the sword, **f** and pestilence."	**Jer 14:12**	7458
see the sword nor will you have **f**,	**Jer 14:13**	7458
'There will be no sword or **f** in	**Jer 14:15**	7458
by sword and **f** those prophets shall	**Jer 14:15**	7458
because of the **f** and the sword;	**Jer 14:16**	7458
the city, Behold, diseases of **f**!	**Jer 14:18**	7458
And those *destined* for **f**, to famine;	**Jer 15:2**	7458
those *destined* for famine, to **f**;	**Jer 15:2**	7458
and come to an end by sword and **f**,	**Jer 16:4**	7458
give their children over to **f** And	**Jer 18:21**	7458
pestilence, the sword and the **f**,	**Jer 21:7**	7458
sword and by **f** and by pestilence;	**Jer 21:9**	7458
'I will send the sword, the **f** and	**Jer 24:10**	7458
nation with the sword, with **f** and	**Jer 27:8**	7458
and your people, by the sword, **f** and	**Jer 27:13**	7458
am sending upon them the sword, **f** and	**Jer 29:17**	7458
sword, with **f** and with pestilence;	**Jer 29:18**	7458
it, because of the sword, the **f** and	**Jer 32:24**	7458
king of Babylon by sword, by **f** and	**Jer 32:36**	7458
to the pestilence and to the **f**;	**Jer 34:17**	7458
sword and by **f** and by pestilence,	**Jer 38:2**	7458
where he is because of the **f**,	**Jer 38:9**	7458
and the **f**, about which you are	**Jer 42:16**	7458
there will die by the sword, by **f** and	**Jer 42:17**	7458
you will die by the sword, by **f** and	**Jer 42:22**	7458
the sword *and* meet their end by **f**.	**Jer 44:12**	7458
great will die by the sword and **f**;	**Jer 44:12**	7458
Jerusalem, with the sword, with **f** and	**Jer 44:13**	7458
our end by the sword and by **f**."	**Jer 44:18**	7458
meet their end by the sword and by **f**	**Jer 44:27**	7458
the **f** was so severe in the city that	**Jer 52:6**	7458
Because of the burning heat of **f**.	**La 5:10**	7458
or be consumed by **f** among you,	**Ezk 5:12**	7458
against them the deadly arrows of **f**	**Ezk 5:16**	7458
also intensify the **f** upon you and	**Ezk 5:16**	7458
send on you **f** and wild beasts,	**Ezk 5:17**	7458
which will fall by sword, **f** and	**Ezk 6:11**	7458
and is besieged will die by the **f**.	**Ezk 6:12**	7458
the plague and the **f** are within.	**Ezk 7:15**	7458
f and the plague will also consume	**Ezk 7:15**	7458
few of them from the sword, the **f** and	**Ezk 12:16**	7458
of bread, send **f** against it and	**Ezk 14:13**	7458
sword, **f**, wild beasts and plague	**Ezk 14:21**	7458
again be victims of **f** in the land,	**Ezk 34:29**	7458
and I will not bring a **f** on you.	**Ezk 36:29**	7458
disgrace of **f** among the nations.	**Ezk 36:30**	7458
"When I will send a **f** on the land,	**Am 8:11**	7458
Not a **f** for bread or a thirst for	**Am 8:11**	7458
a great **f** came over all the land;	**Lk 4:25**	*3042*
severe **f** occurred in that country,	**Lk 15:14**	*3042*
"Now a **f** came over all Egypt and	**Ac 7:11**	*3042*
be a great **f** all over the world.	**Ac 11:28**	*3042*
or distress, or persecution, or **f**,	**Ro 8:35**	*3042*
to kill with sword and with **f** and	**Rv 6:8**	*3042*
pestilence and mourning and **f**,	**Rv 18:8**	*3042*
FAMINES		
there will be **f** and earthquakes.	**Mt 24:7**	*3042*
there will *also* be **f**.	**Mk 13:8**	*3042*
in various places plagues and **f**;	**Lk 21:11**	*3042*
FAMISHED		
in from the field and he was **f**;	**Gn 25:29**	5889
red stuff there, for I am **f**."	**Gn 25:30**	5889
when all the land of Egypt was **f**,	**Gn 41:55**	7456
"His strength is **f**, And calamity	**Jb 18:12**	7457
a **f** man any bitter thing is sweet.	**Pr 27:7**	7457
And their honorable men are **f**,	**Is 5:13**	7458
the land hard-pressed and **f**,	**Is 8:21**	7457
FAMOUS		
and become **f** in Bethlehem.	**Ru 4:11**	7121, 8034
may his name become **f** in Israel.	**Ru 4:14**	7121
mighty men of valor, **f** men,	**1Ch 5:24**	8034
f men in their fathers' households.	**1Ch 12:30**	8034
f and glorious throughout all	**1Ch 22:5**	8034
FANGS		
Break out the **f** of the young lions,	**Ps 58:6**	4973
And it has the **f** of a lioness.	**Jl 1:6**	4973
FANTASIES		
and *these* **f** *as I lay* on my bed and	**Da 4:5**	2031
FAR		
you go toward Gerar, as **f** as Gaza;	**Gn 10:19**	5704
Admah and Zeboiim, as **f** as Lasha.	**Gn 10:19**	5704
and they went as **f** as Haran,	**Gn 11:31**	5704
land as **f** as the site of Shechem,	**Gn 12:6**	5704
from the Negev as **f** as Bethel,	**Gn 13:3**	5704
and moved his tents as **f** as Sodom.	**Gn 13:12**	5704
their Mount Seir, as **f** as El-paran,	**Gn 14:6**	5704
and went in pursuit as **f** as Dan.	**Gn 14:14**	5704
and pursued them as **f** as Hobah,	**Gn 14:15**	5704
of Egypt as **f** as the great river,	**Gn 15:18**	5704
"**F** be it from You to do such a	**Gn 18:25**	2486
F be it from You!	**Gn 18:25**	2486
of the city, *and* were not **f** off,	**Gn 44:4**	7368
F be it from your servants to do	**Gn 44:7**	2486
"**F** be it from me to do this.	**Gn 44:17**	2486
only you shall not go very **f** away.	**Ex 8:28**	7368
"Keep **f** from a false charge, and	**Ex 23:7**	7368
feet, as **f** as the priest can see,	**Lv 13:12**	3605
wilderness of Zin as **f** as Rehob,	**Nu 13:21**	5704
and beat them down as **f** as Hormah.	**Nu 14:45**	5704
"You have gone **f** enough, for all	**Nu 16:3**	7227a
You have gone **f** enough, you sons	**Nu 16:7**	7227a
Jabbok, as **f** as the sons of Ammon;	**Nu 21:24**	5704
of his hand, as **f** as the Arnon.	**Nu 21:26**	5704
Heshbon is ruined as **f** as Dibon,	**Nu 21:30**	5704
from Beth-jeshimoth as **f** as	**Nu 33:49**	5704
Lebanon, as **f** as the great river,	**Dt 1:7**	5704
lived in villages as **f** as Gaza,	**Dt 2:23**	5704
Bashan, as **f** as Salecah and Edrei,	**Dt 3:10**	5704
as **f** as the border of the Geshurites	**Dt 3:14**	5704
even as **f** as the valley of Arnon,	**Dt 3:16**	5704
and as **f** as the river Jabbok,	**Dt 3:16**	5704
as **f** as the sea of the Arabah,	**Dt 3:17**	5704
of Arnon, even as **f** as Mount Sion	**Dt 4:48**	5704
as **f** as the sea of the Arabah,	**Dt 4:49**	5704

as **f** as the western sea. Dt 11:24 5704
to put His name is too **f** from you, Dt 12:21 7368
you, near you or **f** from you, Dt 13:7 7350
too **f** away from you when the LORD Dt 14:24 7368
cities that are very **f** from you, Dt 20:15 7350
all the land, Gilead as **f** as Dan, Dt 34:1 5704
of Judah as **f** as the western sea, Dt 34:2 5704
city of palm trees, as **f** as Zoar. Dt 34:3 5704
even as **f** as the great river, Jos 1:4 5704
and as **f** as the Great Sea toward Jos 1:4 5704
from the gate as **f** as Shebarim and Jos 7:5 5704
Do not go very **f** from the city, Jos 8:4 7368
"We have come from a **f** country; Jos 9:6 7350
have come from a very **f** country Jos 9:9 7350
'We are very **f** from you,' when you Jos 9:22 7350
them as **f** as Azekah and Makkedah. Jos 10:10 5704
heaven on them as **f** as Azekah, Jos 10:11 5704
Kadesh-barnea even as **f** as Gaza, Jos 10:41 5704
of Goshen even as **f** as Gibeon. Jos 10:41 5704
and pursued them as **f** as Great Jos 11:8 5704
even as **f** as Baal-gad in the Jos 11:17 5704
of the Arnon as **f** as Mount Hermon, Jos 12:1 5704
even as **f** as the brook Jabbok, Jos 12:2 5704
and the Arabah as **f** as the Sea of Jos 12:3 5704
and as **f** as the sea of the Arabah, Jos 12:3 5704
as **f** as the border of the Jos 12:5 5704
as f as the border of Sihon king Jos 12:5
Lebanon even as **f** as Mount Halak, Jos 12:7 5704
even as **f** as the border of Ekron Jos 13:3 5704
to the Sidonians, as **f** as Aphek, Jos 13:4 5704
Mount Hermon as **f** as Lebo-hamath. Jos 13:5 5704
Lebanon as **f** as Misrephoth-maim, Jos 13:6 5704
plain of Medeba, as **f** as Dibon; Jos 13:9 5704
as **f** as the border of the sons of Jos 13:10 5704
and all Bashan as **f** as Salecah; Jos 13:11 5704
as **f** as Aroer which is before Jos 13:25 5704
as **f** as Ramath-mizpeh and Betonim, Jos 13:26 5704
as **f** as the border of Debir; Jos 13:26 5704
as **f** as the *lower* end of the Sea Jos 13:27 5704
as **f** as the mouth of the Jordan. Jos 15:5 5704
as **f** as the brook of Egypt and the Jos 15:47 5704
as **f** as the territory of lower Jos 16:3 5704
as **f** as upper Beth-horon. Jos 16:5 5704
the LORD has thus **f** blessed?" Jos 17:14 5704
these cities as **f** as Baalath-beer, Jos 19:8 5704
inheritance was as **f** as Sarid. Jos 19:10 5704
as **f** as the border of Chisloth-tabor, Jos 19:12 5921
and Kanah, as **f** as Great Sidon. Jos 19:28 5704
and Jabneel, as **f** as Lakkum, Jos 19:33 5704
"**F** be it from us that we should Jos 22:29 2486
"**F** be it from us that we should Jos 24:16 2486
Baal-hermon as **f** as Lebo-hamath. Jg 3:3 5704
as **f** away as the oak in Zaanannim, Jg 4:11 5704
the army as **f** as Harosheth-hagoyim, Jg 4:16 5704
produce of the earth as **f** as Gaza, Jg 6:4 5704, 935
and the army fled as **f** as Jg 7:22 5704
as **f** as the edge of Abel-meholah, Jg 7:22 5704
as **f** as Beth-barah and the Jordan. Jg 7:24 5704
as **f** as Beth-barah and the Jordan. Jg 7:24 5704
as **f** as the Jabbok and the Jordan; Jg 11:13 5704
from the Arnon as **f** as the Jabbok, Jg 11:22 5704
the wilderness as **f** as the Jordan. Jg 11:22 5704
cities, and as **f** as Abel-keramim. Jg 11:33 5704
as **f** as the vineyards of Timnah; Jg 14:5 5704
and they were **f** from the Sidonians Jg 18:7 7350
because it was **f** from Sidon and Jg 18:28 7350
we will go on as **f** as Gibeah." Jg 19:12 5704
the LORD declares, '**F** be it from Me 1Sa 2:30 2486
them down as **f** as below Beth-car. 1Sa 7:11 5704
"Thus **f** the LORD has helped us." 1Sa 7:12 5704
come as **f** as the oak of Tabor, 1Sa 10:3 5704
f be it from me that I should sin 1Sa 12:23 2486
great deliverance in Israel? **F** from it! 1Sa 14:45 2486
Philistines as **f** as the valley, 1Sa 17:52 5704
and came as **f** as the large well 1Sa 19:22 5704
"**F** from it, you shall not die. 1Sa 20:2 2486
"**F** be it from you! 1Sa 20:9 2486
F be it from me! Do not let the king 1Sa 22:15 2486
"**F** be it from me because of the 1Sa 24:6 2486
even as **f** as the land of Egypt. 1Sa 27:8 5704
and followed her as **f** as Bahurim. 2Sa 3:16 5704
from Geba as **f** as Gezer. 2Sa 5:25 5704
that You have brought me this **f**? 2Sa 7:18 1988
in the middle as **f** as their hips, 2Sa 10:4 5704
as **f** as the entrance of the gate. 2Sa 11:23 5704
and came as **f** as the Jordan. 2Sa 19:15 5704
"**F** be it, far be it from me that 2Sa 20:20 2486
f be it from me that I should 2Sa 20:20 2486
"Be it **f** from me, O LORD, that I 2Sa 23:17 2486
as **f** as the other side of Jokmeam; 1Ki 4:12 5704
a **f** country for Your name's sake 1Ki 8:41 7350
land of the enemy, **f** off or near; 1Ki 8:46 7350
before the one as **f** as Dan. 1Ki 12:30 5704
LORD has sent me as **f** as Bethel." 2Ki 2:2 5704
as **f** as the Sea of the Arabah, 2Ki 14:25 5704
as **f** as Gaza and its territory, 2Ki 18:8 5704
"They have come from a **f** country, 2Ki 20:14 7350
the same cities as **f** as Baal. 1Ch 4:33 5704
To the east he settled as **f** as 1Ch 5:9 5704
land of Bashan as **f** as Salecah. 1Ch 5:11 5704
of Sharon, as **f** as their borders. 1Ch 5:16 5921
as **f** as Ayyah with its towns, 1Ch 7:28 5704
"Be it **f** from me before my God 1Ch 11:19 2486
even as **f** as Issachar and Zebulun 1Ch 12:40 5704
from Gibeon even as **f** as Gezer. 1Ch 14:16 5704
that You have brought me this **f**? 1Ch 17:16 1988
Hadadezer king of Zobah *as f as* 1Ch 18:3
in the middle as **f** as their hips, 1Ch 19:4 5704
when he comes from a **f** country for 2Ch 6:32 7350

captive to a land **f** off or near, 2Ch 6:36 7350
and as **f** as the border of Egypt. 2Ch 9:26 5704
Judah and came as **f** as Jerusalem. 2Ch 12:4 5704
him pursued them as **f** as Gerar; 2Ch 14:13 5704
and Manasseh, and as **f** as Zebulun, 2Ch 30:10 5704
Simeon, even as **f** as Naphtali, 2Ch 34:6 5704
and the sound was heard **f** away. Ezr 3:13 7350
Jerusalem as **f** as the Broad Wall. Ne 3:8 5704
at the king's garden as **f** as the steps Ne 3:15 5704
made repairs as **f** as *a point* Ne 3:16 5704
and as **f** as the artificial pool Ne 3:16 5704
even as **f** as the end of his house. Ne 3:21 5704
from the house of Azariah as **f** as Ne 3:24 5704
the Angle and as **f** as the corner. Ne 3:24 5704
as **f** as the front of the Water Gate Ne 3:26 5704
and as **f** as the wall of Ophel. Ne 3:27 5704
as **f** as the house of the temple Ne 3:31 5704
as **f** as the upper room of the corner. Ne 3:31 5704
on the wall **f** from one another. Ne 4:19 7350
as **f** as the valley of Hinnom. Ne 11:30 5704
Hundred, as **f** as the Sheep Gate; Ne 12:39 5704
He went as **f** as the king's gate, Es 4:2 5704
King Ahasuerus, both near and **f**, Es 9:20 7350
"His sons are **f** from safety, They Jb 5:4 7368
is in your hand, put it **f** away, Jb 11:14 7368
has removed my brothers **f** from me, Jb 19:13 7368
of the wicked is **f** from me. Jb 21:16 7368
of the wicked is **f** from me. Jb 22:18 7368
unrighteousness **f** from your tent, Jb 22:23 7368
"**F** be it from me that I should Jb 27:5 2486
sinks a shaft **f** from habitation, Jb 28:4
and swing to and fro **f** from men. Jb 28:4
F be it from God to do wickedness, Jb 34:10 2486
'Thus **f** you shall come, but no Jb 38:11 5704
F from my deliverance are the Ps 22:1 7350
Be not **f** from me, for trouble is Ps 22:11 7368
But You, O LORD, be not **f** off; Ps 22:19 7368
O Lord, do not be **f** from me. Ps 35:22 7368
O my God, do not be **f** from me! Ps 38:21 7368
Is Mount Zion *in* the **f** north, Ps 48:2 3411
"Behold, I would wander **f** away, Ps 55:7 7368
O God, do not be **f** from me; Ps 71:12 7368
who are **f** from You will perish; Ps 73:27 7369
my acquaintances **f** from me; Ps 88:8 7368
lover and friend **f** from me; Ps 88:18 7368
You are exalted **f** above all gods. Ps 97:9 3966
As **f** as the east is from the west, Ps 103:12 7368
So **f** has He removed our Ps 103:12 7368
f from their ruined homes. Ps 109:10
in blessing, so it was **f** from him. Ps 109:17 7368
They are **f** from Your law. Ps 119:150 7368
Salvation is **f** from the wicked, Ps 119:155 7350
And put devious speech **f** from you. Pr 4:24 7368
Keep your way **f** from her And do Pr 5:8 7368
The LORD is **f** from the wicked, But Pr 15:29 7368
himself will be **f** from them. Pr 22:5 7368
will remove it **f** from him. Pr 22:15 7368
who is near than a brother **f** away. Pr 27:10 7350
Keep deception and lies **f** from me, Pr 30:8 7368
For her worth is **f** above jewels. Pr 31:10 7350
be wise," but it was **f** from me. Ec 7:23 7350
"The LORD has removed men **f** away, Is 6:12 7368
They are coming from a **f** country Is 13:5 4801
His fugitives are as **f** as Zoar *and* Is 15:5 5704
Its wail *goes* as **f** as Eglaim and Is 15:8 5704
clusters Which reached as **f** as Jazer Is 16:8 5704
them and they will flee **f** away, Is 17:13 4801
To a people feared **f** and wide, Is 18:2 4480, 1931
from a people feared **f** and wide, Is 18:7 4480, 1931
"Watchman, how **f** gone is the night? Is 21:11
how **f** gone is the night?" Is 21:11
Though they had fled **f** away. Is 22:3 7350
remove their hearts **f** from Me, Is 29:13 7368
"You who are **f** away, hear what I Is 33:13 7350
have come to me from a **f** country, Is 39:3 7350
of My purpose from a **f** country. Is 46:11 4801
Who are **f** from righteousness. Is 46:12 7350
My righteousness, it is not **f** off; Is 46:13 7368
who swallowed you will be **f** away. Is 49:19 7368
You will be **f** from oppression, for Is 54:14 7368
Indeed, **f** removed from Me, you Is 57:8
who is **f** and to him who is near," Is 57:19 7350
Therefore justice is **f** from us, Is 59:9 7368
salvation, *but* it is **f** from us. Is 59:11 7368
And righteousness stands **f** away; Is 59:14 7368
That they went **f** from Me And Jer 2:5 7368
'Besiegers come from a **f** country, Jer 4:16 4801
their lips But **f** from their mind. Jer 12:2 7350
"And not a God **f** off? Jer 23:23 7350
kings of the north, near and **f**, Jer 25:26 7350
to remove you **f** from your land; Jer 27:10 7368
fields as **f** as the brook Kidron, Jer 31:40 5704
and went in as **f** as Tahpanhes. Jer 43:7 5704
of the land of Moab, **f** and near. Jer 48:24 7350
Thus **f** the judgment on Moab. Jer 48:47 5704
Thus **f** are the words of Jeremiah. Jer 51:64 5704
Because **f** from me is a comforter, La 1:16 7368
is **f** off will die by the plague, Ezk 6:12 7350
I would be **f** from My sanctuary? Ezk 8:6 7368
was heard as **f** as the outer court, Ezk 10:5 5704
'Go **f** from the LORD; Ezk 11:15 7368
them **f** away among the nations and Ezk 11:16 7368
and he prophesies of times **f** off.' Ezk 12:27 7350
who are **f** from you will mock you, Ezk 22:5 7350
your blood As **f** as the mountains, Ezk 32:6 413
corpses of their kings **f** from Me; Ezk 43:9 7368
the Levites who went **f** from Me when Ezk 44:10 7368

as **f** as the waters of Meribath-kadesh Ezk 47:19 5704
as f as Hazar-enan *at* Ezk 48:1
are nearby and those who are **f** away Da 9:7 7350
f more riches than all *of them;* Da 11:2 1419
the northern *army* **f** from you, Jl 2:20 7368
them **f** from their territory, Jl 3:6 7368
the Canaanites as **f** as Zarephath, Ob 1:20 5704
Those who are **f** off will come and Zch 6:15 7350
will remember Me in **f** countries, Zch 10:9 4801
Benjamin's Gate as **f** as the place of Zch 14:10 5704
THEIR HEART IS **F** AWAY FROM ME. Mt 15:8 *4206*
as **f** as the courtyard of the high Mt 26:58 *2193*
so **f** as they were able to hear it; Mk 4:33
THEIR HEART IS **F** AWAY FROM ME. Mk 7:6 *4206*
not **f** from the kingdom of God." Mk 12:34 *3112*
was not **f** from the house, Lk 7:6 *3112*
while the other is still **f** away, Lk 14:32 *4206*
torment, and saw Abraham **f** away and Lk 16:23 *3113*
even as **f** as this place." Lk 23:5 *2193*
He led them out as **f** as Bethany, Lk 24:50 *2193*
for they were not **f** from the land, Jn 21:8 *3112*
and for all who are **f** off, Ac 2:39 *3112*
the whole island as **f** as Paphos, Ac 13:6 *891*
Paul out to go as **f** as the sea; Ac 17:14 *2193*
Paul brought him as **f** as Athens; Ac 17:15 *2193*
He is not **f** from each one of us; Ac 17:27 *3112*
you **f** away to the Gentiles.' " Ac 22:21 *3112*
came from there as **f** as the Market Ac 28:15 *891*
(and have been prevented so **f**) Ro 1:13 *891*
so **f** as it depends on you, Ro 12:18 *3588*
f as Illyricum I have fully preached Ro 15:19 *3360*
of glory **f** beyond all comparison, 2Co 4:17 *5236*
to reach even as **f** as you. 2Co 10:13 *891*
the first to come even as **f** as you 2Co 10:14 *891*
in **f** more labors, in far more 2Co 11:23 *4057*
labors, in **f** more imprisonments, 2Co 11:23 *4057*
f above all rule and authority and Eph 1:21 *5231*
you who formerly were **f** off have Eph 2:13 *3112*
PEACE TO YOU WHO WERE **F** AWAY, Eph 2:17 *3112*
Now to Him who is able to do **f** more Eph 3:20 *5238b*
ascended **f** above all the heavens, Eph 4:10 *5231*
have **f** more courage to speak the Php 1:14 *4057*
confidence in the flesh, I **f** more: Php 3:4
and piercing as **f** as the division Heb 4:12 *891*
Anyone who goes too **f** and does not 2Jn 1:9 *4254*

FAR-DISTANT

They will behold a **f** land. Is 33:17 4801

FARE

was going to Tarshish, paid the **f** and Jon 1:3 7939

FARED

how your cattle have **f** with me. Gn 30:29 1961
how Esther was and how she **f**. Es 2:11 6213a

FARES

since he **f** well with you; Dt 15:16

FAREWELL

Then Moses bade his father-in-law **f**, Ex 18:27 7971
After bidding them **f**, Mk 6:46 *657*
things, you will do well. **F**." Ac 15:29 *4517*
praying, we said **f** to one another. Ac 21:5 *537b*

FARM

and began to consume the **f** land. Am 7:4 2506
went their way, one to his own **f**, Mt 22:5 *68*

FARMER

Does the **f** plow continually to Is 28:24 2790a
the **f** and they who go about with Jer 31:24 406
you I shatter the **f** and his team, Jer 51:23 406
They also call the **f** to mourning Am 5:16 406
The hard-working **f** ought to be the 2Tm 2:6 *1092*
The **f** waits for the precious Jas 5:7 *1092*

FARMERS

be your **f** and your vinedressers. Is 61:5 406
The **f** have been put to shame, They Jer 14:4 406
Be ashamed, O **f**, Wail, O Jl 1:11 406

FARMING

began **f** and planted a vineyard. Gn 9:20 376, 127

FARMS

children or **f** for My name's sake, Mt 19:29 *68*
mother or father or children or **f**, Mk 10:29 *68*
and mothers and children and **f**, Mk 10:30 *68*

FARTHER

if the scab spreads **f** on the skin after Lv 13:7 6581
leprosy breaks out **f** on the skin, Lv 13:12 6524a
and if it spreads **f** on the skin, Lv 13:22 6581
If it spreads **f** in the skin, then Lv 13:27 6581
"But if the scale spreads **f** in Lv 13:35 6581
'Thus far you shall come, but no **f**; Jb 38:11 3254
measuring line will go out **f** straight Jer 31:39 5750
Going on a little **f**, Mk 1:19 *4260*
about Him was spreading even **f**, Lk 5:15 *3123*
He acted as though He were going **f**. Lk 24:28 *4206*
wind did not permit us *to go* **f**, Ac 27:7 *4330*
and a little **f** on they took Ac 27:28 *1339*

FARTHEST

its **f** borders it shall be yours; Jos 17:18 8444
And I entered its **f** lodging place, 2Ki 19:23 7093
And to the **f** limit he searches out Jb 28:3 3605
of the earth and of the **f** sea; Ps 65:5 7350
a far country, From the **f** horizons, Is 13:5 7093
Come to her from the **f** border; Jer 50:26 7093
from the **f** end of the earth to Mk 13:27 *206*
the earth to the **f** end of heaven. Mk 13:27 *206*

FASHION

And the same one **f** us in the womb? Jb 31:15 3559
Those who **f** a graven image are all Is 44:9 3335
quiet **f** and eat their own bread. 2Th 3:12 *2271*

FASHIONED
The LORD God **f** into a woman **Gn 2:22** 1129
and **f** it with a graving tool and **Ex 32:4** 6696c
He **f** the two pillars of bronze; **1Ki 7:15** 6696c
hands **f** and made me altogether, **Jb 10:8** 6087b
Your hands made me and **f** me; **Ps 119:73** 3559
corner pillars **f** as for a palace; **Ps 144:12** 2404
Who has **f** a god or cast an idol to **Is 44:10** 3335

FASHIONING
over the coals, **f** it with hammers and **Is 44:12** 3335
I am **f** calamity against you and **Jer 18:11** 3335

FASHIONS
He who **f** the hearts of them all, **Ps 33:15** 3335
And a silversmith **f** chains of **Is 40:19**
When he **f** speechless idols. **Hab 2:18** 6213a

FAST
the LORD had closed **f** all the wombs **Gn 20:18** 6113
"But you who held **f** to the LORD **Dt 4:4** 1695
in all His ways and hold **f** to Him, **Dt 11:22** 1692
voice, and by holding **f** to Him; **Dt 30:20** 1692
hold **f** to Him and serve Him with **Jos 22:5** 1692
but we will bind you **f** and give you **Jg 15:13** 631
now he has died; why should I **f**? **2Sa 12:23** 6684
And his head caught **f** in the oak, **2Sa 18:9** 2388
Solomon held **f** to these in love. **1Ki 11:2** 1692
"Proclaim a **f** and seat Naboth at **1Ki 21:9** 6685
They proclaimed a **f** and seated **1Ki 21:12** 6685
proclaimed a **f** throughout all Judah. **2Ch 20:3** 6685
I proclaimed a **f** there at the river **Ezr 8:21** 6685
are found in Susa, and **f** for me; **Es 4:16** 6684
also will **f** in the same way. **Es 4:16** 6684
he still holds **f** his integrity, **Jb 2:3** 2388
you still hold **f** your integrity? **Jb 2:9** 2388
He holds **f** to it, but it does not **Jb 8:15** 2388
"My foot has held **f** to His path; **Jb 23:11** 270
"I hold **f** my righteousness and **Jb 27:6** 2388
My steps have held **f** to Your paths. **Ps 17:5** 8551
He commanded, and it stood **f**. **Ps 33:9**
hold **f** to themselves an evil purpose; **Ps 64:5** 2388
And happy are all who hold her **f**. **Pr 3:18** 8551
"Let your heart hold **f** my words; **Pr 4:4** 8551
"Stand **f** now in your spells **Is 47:12**
Me, And hold **f** My covenant, **Is 56:4** 2388
sabbath And holds **f** My covenant; **Is 56:6** 2388
on the day of your **f** you find *your* **Is 58:3** 6685
you **f** for contention and strife **Is 58:4** 6684
You do not **f** like *you do* today to **Is 58:4** 6684
it a **f** like this which I choose, **Is 58:5** 6685
Will you call this a **f**, **Is 58:5** 6685
"Is this not the **f** which I **Is 58:6** 6685
They hold **f** to deceit, They refuse **Jer 8:5** 2388
"When they **f**, I am not going to **Jer 14:12** 6684
in the LORD's house on a **f** day. **Jer 36:6** 6685
proclaimed a **f** before the LORD. **Jer 36:9** 6685
them captive have held them **f**, **Jer 50:33** 2388
Consecrate a **f**, Proclaim a solemn **Jl 1:14** 6685
a trumpet in Zion, Consecrate a **f**, **Jl 2:15** 6685
and they called a **f** and put on **Jon 3:5** 6685
'The **f** of the fourth, the fast of **Zch 8:19** 6685
of the fourth, the **f** of the fifth, **Zch 8:19** 6685
the fifth, the **f** of the seventh and **Zch 8:19** 6685
and the **f** of the tenth *months* will **Zch 8:19** 6685
"Whenever you **f**, **Mt 6:16** *3522*
"But you, when you **f**, **Mt 6:17** *3522*
"Why do we and the Pharisees **f**, **Mt 9:14** *3522*
but Your disciples do not **f**?" **Mt 9:14** *3522*
from them, and then they will **f**. **Mt 9:15** *3522*
the disciples of the Pharisees **f**, **Mk 2:18** *3522*
but Your disciples do not **f**?" **Mk 2:18** *3522*
of the bridegroom cannot **f**, **Mk 2:19** *3522*
with them, they cannot **f**. **Mk 2:19** *3522*
and then they will **f** in that day. **Mk 2:20** *3522*
of John often **f** and offer prayers, **Lk 5:33** *3522*
attendants of the bridegroom **f** while **Lk 5:34** *3522*
then they will **f** in those days." **Lk 5:35** *3522*
and good heart, and hold it **f**, **Lk 8:15** *2722*
'I **f** twice a week; **Lk 18:12** *3522*
since even the **f** was already over, **Ac 27:9** *3521*
stuck **f** and remained immovable, **Ac 27:41** *2043*
if you hold **f** the word which I **1Co 15:2** *2722*
holding **f** the word of life, so **Php 2:16** *1907*
and not holding **f** to the head, **Col 2:19** *2902*
hold **f** to that which is good; **1Th 5:21** *2722*
holding **f** the faithful word which **Ti 1:9** *472*
if we hold **f** our confidence and **Heb 3:6** *2722*
if we hold **f** the beginning of our **Heb 3:14** *2722*
God, let us hold **f** our confession. **Heb 4:14** *2902*
Let us hold **f** the confession of **Heb 10:23** *2722*
and you hold **f** My name, and did **Rv 2:13** *2902*
you have, hold **f** until I come. **Rv 2:25** *2902*
hold **f** what you have, so **Rv 3:11** *2902*

FASTED
LORD and **f** that day until evening. **Jg 20:26** 6684
the LORD, and **f** on that day and **1Sa 7:6** 6684
tree at Jabesh, and **f** seven days. **1Sa 31:13** 6684
They mourned and wept and **f** **2Sa 1:12** 6684
and David **f** and went and lay all **2Sa 12:16** 6684, 6685
child was alive, you **f** and wept; **2Sa 12:21** 6684
was *still* alive, I **f** and wept; **2Sa 12:22** 6684
and put on sackcloth and **f**, **1Ki 21:27** 6684
oak in Jabesh, and **f** seven days. **1Ch 10:12** 6684
So we **f** and sought our God **Ezr 8:23** 6684
have we **f** and You do not see? **Is 58:3** 6684
'When you **f** and mourned in the **Zch 7:5** 6684
was it actually for Me that you **f**? **Zch 7:5** 6684
had **f** forty days and forty nights, **Mt 4:2** *3522*
when they had **f** and prayed and **Ac 13:3** *3522*

FASTEN
it and **f** them on its four feet, **Ex 25:12** 5414
"You shall **f** it on a blue **Ex 28:37** 7760
it, to **f** it on the turban above, **Ex 39:31** 5414
f it with a pin, then I will become **Jg 16:13** 8628
It shall not **f** its grip on me. **Ps 101:3** 1692
They **f** it with nails and with **Jer 10:4** 2388

FASTENED
They **f** a blue cord to it, to **Ex 39:31** 5414
And she **f** *it* with the pin and **Jg 16:14** 8628
and they **f** his body to the wall of **1Sa 31:10** 8628
in its sheath **f** at his waist; **2Sa 20:8** 6775
and they were **f** to the house with **1Ki 6:10** 270
f his head in the house of Dagon. **1Ch 10:10** 8628
all around, that they might be **f**, **Ezk 41:6** 270
and not be **f** into the wall of the **Ezk 41:6** 270
and **f** their feet in the stocks. **Ac 16:24** *805*
f itself on his hand. **Ac 28:3** *2510*

FASTENS
he **f** it with nails, *So that* it **Is 41:7** 2388

FASTER
"You have made my heart beat **f**, **SS 4:9** 3823a
You have made my heart beat **f** with **SS 4:9** 3823a
disciple ran ahead **f** than Peter and **Jn 20:4** *5036*

FASTING
and I was **f** and praying before the **Ne 1:4** 6684
sons of Israel assembled with **f**, **Ne 9:1** 6685
mourning among the Jews, with **f**, **Es 4:3** 6685
times of **f** and their lamentations. **Es 9:31** 6685
I humbled my soul with **f**, **Ps 35:13** 6685
When I wept in my soul with **f**, **Ps 69:10** 6685
My knees are weak from **f**, **Ps 109:24** 6685
his palace and spent the night **f**, **Da 6:18** 2908
prayer and supplications, with **f**, **Da 9:3** 6685
with all your heart, And with **f**, **Jl 2:12** 6685
noticed by men when they are **f**. **Mt 6:16** *3522*
your **f** will not be noticed by men, **Mt 6:18** *3522*
go out except by prayer and **f**." **Mt 17:21** *3521*
and the Pharisees were **f**; **Mk 2:18** *3522*
ministering to the Lord and **f**, **Ac 13:2** *3522*
church, having prayed with **f**, **Ac 14:23** *3521*

FASTINGS
night and day with **f** and prayers. **Lk 2:37** *3521*

FAT
his flock and of their **f** portions. **Gn 4:4** 2459
came up seven cows, sleek and **f**; **Gn 41:2** 1277
ate up the seven sleek and **f** cows. **Gn 41:4** 1277
f and sleek came up out of the **Gn 41:18** 1277
ate up the first seven **f** cows. **Gn 41:20** 1277
you will eat the **f** of the land.' **Gn 45:18** 2459
nor is the **f** of My feast to remain **Ex 23:18** 2459
"You shall take all the **f** **Ex 29:13** 2459
kidneys and the **f** that is on them, **Ex 29:13** 2459
f from the ram and the fat tail, **Ex 29:22** 2459
fat from the ram and the **f** tail, **Ex 29:22** 451
and the **f** that covers the entrails **Ex 29:22** 2459
and the two kidneys and the **f** that **Ex 29:22** 2459
the **f** that covers the entrails and **Lv 3:3** 2459
all the **f** that is on the entrails, **Lv 3:3** 2459
with the **f** that is on them, **Lv 3:4** 2459
by fire to the LORD, its **f**, **Lv 3:9** 2459
the entire **f** tail which he shall **Lv 3:9** 451
and the **f** that covers the entrails **Lv 3:9** 2459
all the **f** that is on the entrails, **Lv 3:9** 2459
with the **f** that is on them, **Lv 3:10** 2459
the **f** that covers the entrails **Lv 3:14** 2459
all the **f** that is on the entrails, **Lv 3:14** 2459
with the **f** that is on them, **Lv 3:15** 2459
all **f** is the LORD's. **Lv 3:16** 2459
not eat any **f** or any blood.' " **Lv 3:17** 2459
remove from it all the **f** of the bull **Lv 4:8** 2459
the **f** that covers the entrails, **Lv 4:8** 2459
the **f** which is on the entrails, **Lv 4:8** 2459
with the **f** that is on them, **Lv 4:9** 2459
'He shall remove all its **f** **Lv 4:19** 2459
'All its **f** he shall offer up **Lv 4:26** 2459
f of the sacrifice of peace offerings. **Lv 4:26** 2459
'Then he shall remove all its **f**, **Lv 4:31** 2459
just as the **f** was removed from the **Lv 4:31** 2459
'Then he shall remove all its **f**, **Lv 4:35** 2459
just as the **f** of the lamb is **Lv 4:35** 2459
and offer up in smoke the **f** **Lv 6:12** 2459
he shall offer from it all its **f**: **Lv 7:3** 2459
the **f** tail and the fat that covers **Lv 7:3** 451
the **f** that covers the entrails, **Lv 7:3** 2459
with the **f** that is on them, **Lv 7:4** 2459
shall not eat any **f** *from* an ox, **Lv 7:23** 2459
the **f** of *an animal* which dies and **Lv 7:24** 2459
the **f** of an animal torn *by beasts* may **Lv 7:24** 2459
'For whoever eats the **f** of the **Lv 7:25** 2459
shall bring the **f** with the breast, **Lv 7:30** 2459
up the **f** in smoke on the altar, **Lv 7:31** 2459
of the peace offerings and the **f**, **Lv 7:33** 2459
He also took all the **f** that was on **Lv 8:16** 2459
and the two kidneys and their **f**; **Lv 8:16** 2459
He took the **f**, and the fat **Lv 8:25** 2459
He took the fat, and the **f** tail, **Lv 8:25** 451
the **f** that was on the entrails, **Lv 8:25** 2459
and their **f** and the right thigh. **Lv 8:25** 2459
of **f** and on the right thigh. **Lv 8:26** 2459
The **f** and the kidneys and the lobe **Lv 9:10** 2459
of **f** from the ox and from the ram, **Lv 9:19** 2459
ox and from the ram, the **f** tail, **Lv 9:19** 451
and the **f** covering, **Lv 9:19**
the portions of **f** on the breasts; **Lv 9:20** 2459
the portions of **f** on the altar; **Lv 9:24** 2459
by fire of the portions of **f**, **Lv 10:15** 2459
offer up in smoke the **f** of the sin **Lv 16:25** 2459
and offer up the **f** in smoke as a **Lv 17:6** 2459
How is the land, is it **f** or lean? **Nu 13:20** 8082a
and shall offer up their **f** in smoke **Nu 18:17** 2459
of the flock, With **f** of lambs, **Dt 32:14** 2459
"But Jeshurun grew **f** and kicked **Dt 32:15** 8080
You are grown **f**, thick, and sleek **Dt 32:15** 8080
'Who ate the **f** of their **Dt 32:38** 2459
Now Eglon was a very **f** man. **Jg 3:17** 1277
and the **f** closed over the blade, **Jg 3:22** 2459
Also, before they burned the **f**, **1Sa 2:15** 2459
"They must surely burn the **f** first, **1Sa 2:16** 2459
by making yourselves **f** with the **1Sa 2:29** 1254b
And to heed than the **f** of rams. **1Sa 15:22** 2459
slain, from the **f** of the mighty, **2Sa 1:22** 2459
ten **f** oxen, twenty pasture-fed **1Ki 4:23** 1277
and the **f** of the peace offerings; **1Ki 8:64** 2459
and the **f** of the peace offerings. **1Ki 8:64** 2459
and the **f** of the peace offerings because **2Ch 7:7** 2459
the grain offering and the **f**. **2Ch 7:7** 2459
with the **f** of the peace offerings and **2Ch 29:35** 2459
offerings and the **f** until night; **2Ch 35:14** 2459
"Go, eat of the **f**, drink of the **Ne 8:10** 4924b
they ate, were filled and grew **f**, **Ne 9:25** 8080
has covered his face with his **f** And **Jb 15:27** 2459
His sides are filled out with **f**, **Jb 21:24** 2459
You burnt offerings of **f** beasts, **Ps 66:15** 4220
And their body is **f**. **Ps 73:4** 1277
Their heart is covered with **f**, **Ps 119:70** 2459
soul of the diligent is made **f**. **Pr 13:4** 1878
Good news puts **f** on the bones. **Pr 15:30** 1878
of rams And the **f** of fed cattle; **Is 1:11** 2459
with blood, It is sated with **f**, **Is 34:6** 2459
With the **f** of the kidneys of rams. **Is 34:6** 2459
their dust become greasy with **f**. **Is 34:7** 2459
Me with the **f** of your sacrifices; **Is 43:24** 2459
'They are **f**, they are sleek, They **Jer 5:28** 8080
"You eat the **f** and clothe **Ezk 34:3** 2459
you slaughter the **f** *sheep* without **Ezk 34:3** 1277
f and the strong I will destroy. **Ezk 34:16** 8082a
the **f** sheep and the lean sheep. **Ezk 34:20** 1277
will eat **f** until you are glutted, **Ezk 39:19** 2459
My food, the **f** and the blood; **Ezk 44:7** 2459
to offer Me the **f** and the blood," **Ezk 44:15** 2459
will devour the flesh of the **f** *sheep* **Zch 11:16** 1277

FATAL
slain, and his **f** wound was healed. **Rv 13:3** *2288*
beast, whose **f** wound was healed. **Rv 13:12** *2288*

FATE
if they suffer the **f** of all men, **Nu 16:29** 6486
in the west are appalled at his **f**, **Jb 18:20** 3117
know that one **f** befalls them both. **Ec 2:14** 4745
"As is the **f** of the fool, it will **Ec 2:15** 4745
For the **f** of the sons of men and **Ec 3:19** 4745
and the **f** of beasts is the same. **Ec 3:19** 4745
There is one **f** for the righteous **Ec 9:2** 4745
that there is one **f** for all men. **Ec 9:3** 4745
because they suffered this **f**? **Lk 13:2**

FATEFUL
Her **f** time also will soon come **Is 13:22**

FATHER
shall leave his **f** and his mother, **Gn 2:24** 1
and Irad became the **f** of Mehujael, **Gn 4:18** 3205
became the **f** of Methushael, **Gn 4:18** 3205
Methushael became the **f** of Lamech. **Gn 4:18** 3205
he was the **f** of those who dwell in **Gn 4:20** 1
he was the **f** of all those who play **Gn 4:21** 1
f of *a son* in his own likeness, **Gn 5:3** 3205
Adam after he became the **f** of Seth **Gn 5:4** 3205
years, and became the **f** of Enosh. **Gn 5:6** 3205
after he became the **f** of Enosh, **Gn 5:7** 3205
years, and became the **f** of Kenan. **Gn 5:9** 3205
after he became the **f** of Kenan, **Gn 5:10** 3205
and became the **f** of Mahalalel. **Gn 5:12** 3205
he became the **f** of Mahalalel, **Gn 5:13** 3205
years, and became the **f** of Jared. **Gn 5:15** 3205
after he became the **f** of Jared, **Gn 5:16** 3205
years, and became the **f** of Enoch. **Gn 5:18** 3205
after he became the **f** of Enoch, **Gn 5:19** 3205
and became the **f** of Methuselah. **Gn 5:21** 3205
he became the **f** of Methuselah, **Gn 5:22** 3205
years, and became the **f** of Lamech. **Gn 5:25** 3205
after he became the **f** of Lamech, **Gn 5:26** 3205
years, and became the **f** of a son. **Gn 5:28** 3205
after he became the **f** of Noah, **Gn 5:30** 3205
and Noah became the **f** of Shem, **Gn 5:32** 3205
Noah became the **f** of three sons: **Gn 6:10** 3205
and Ham was the **f** of Canaan. **Gn 9:18** 1
Ham, the **f** of Canaan, saw the **Gn 9:22** 1
saw the nakedness of his **f**, **Gn 9:22** 1
covered the nakedness of their **f**; **Gn 9:23** 1
Now Cush became the **f** of Nimrod; **Gn 10:8** 3205
Mizraim became the **f** of Ludim **Gn 10:13** 3205
Canaan became the **f** of Sidon, **Gn 10:15** 3205
the **f** of all the children of Eber, **Gn 10:21** 1
Arpachshad became the **f** of Shelah; **Gn 10:24** 3205
and Shelah became the **f** of Eber. **Gn 10:24** 3205
Joktan became the **f** of Almodad **Gn 10:26** 3205
and became the **f** of Arpachshad two **Gn 11:10** 3205
he became the **f** of Arpachshad, **Gn 11:11** 3205
years, and became the **f** of Shelah; **Gn 11:12** 3205
after he became the **f** of Shelah, **Gn 11:13** 3205
years, and became the **f** of Eber; **Gn 11:14** 3205
after he became the **f** of Eber, **Gn 11:15** 3205
years, and became the **f** of Peleg; **Gn 11:16** 3205
after he became the **f** of Peleg, **Gn 11:17** 3205
years, and became the **f** of Reu; **Gn 11:18** 3205
after he became the **f** of Reu, **Gn 11:19** 3205
years, and became the **f** of Serug; **Gn 11:20** 3205

after he became the **f** of Serug,	**Gn 11:21**	3205
years, and became the **f** of Nahor;	**Gn 11:22**	3205
after he became the **f** of Nahor,	**Gn 11:23**	3205
years, and became the **f** of Terah;	**Gn 11:24**	3205
after he became the **f** of Terah,	**Gn 11:25**	3205
years, and became the **f** of Abram,	**Gn 11:26**	3205
Terah became the **f** of Abram,	**Gn 11:27**	3205
and Haran became the **f** of Lot.	**Gn 11:27**	3205
Haran died in the presence of his **f**	**Gn 11:28**	1
Haran, the **f** of Milcah and Iscah.	**Gn 11:29**	1
the **f** of a multitude of nations.	**Gn 17:4**	1
the **f** of a multitude of nations.	**Gn 17:5**	1
become the **f** of twelve princes,	**Gn 17:20**	3205
"Our **f** is old, and there is not a	**Gn 19:31**	1
let us make our **f** drink wine,	**Gn 19:32**	1
our family through our **f**."	**Gn 19:32**	1
their **f** drink wine that night,	**Gn 19:33**	1
went in and lay with her **f**;	**Gn 19:33**	1
I lay last night with my **f**;	**Gn 19:34**	1
our family through our **f**."	**Gn 19:34**	1
f drink wine that night also,	**Gn 19:35**	1
of Lot were with child by their **f**.	**Gn 19:36**	1
the **f** of the Moabites to this day.	**Gn 19:37**	1
he is the **f** of the sons of Ammon	**Gn 19:38**	1
my sister, the daughter of my **f**,	**Gn 20:12**	1
spoke to Abraham his **f** and said,	**Gn 22:7**	1
Abraham his father and said, "My **f**!"	**Gn 22:7**	1
brother and Kemuel the **f** of Aram	**Gn 22:21**	1
Bethuel became the **f** of Rebekah;	**Gn 22:23**	3205
became the **f** of Sheba and Dedan.	**Gn 25:3**	3205
Abraham became the **f** of Isaac;	**Gn 25:19**	3205
which I swore to your **f** Abraham.	**Gn 26:3**	1
dug in the days of Abraham his **f**,	**Gn 26:15**	1
dug in the days of his **f** Abraham,	**Gn 26:18**	1
names which his **f** had given them.	**Gn 26:18**	1
"I am the God of your **f** Abraham;	**Gn 26:24**	1
your **f** speak to your brother Esau,	**Gn 27:6**	1
them *as* a savory dish for your **f**,	**Gn 27:9**	1
"Then you shall bring *it* to your **f**,	**Gn 27:10**	1
"Perhaps my **f** will feel me, then	**Gn 27:12**	1
savory food such as his **f** loved.	**Gn 27:14**	1
Then he came to his **f** and said,	**Gn 27:18**	1
came to his father and said, "My **f**."	**Gn 27:18**	1
Jacob said to his **f**,	**Gn 27:19**	1
Jacob came close to Isaac his **f**,	**Gn 27:22**	1
Then his **f** Isaac said to him,	**Gn 27:26**	1
from the presence of Isaac his **f**,	**Gn 27:30**	1
food, and brought it to his **f**;	**Gn 27:31**	1
and he said to his **f**,	**Gn 27:31**	1
"Let my **f** arise and eat of his	**Gn 27:31**	1
Isaac his **f** said to him,	**Gn 27:32**	1
Esau heard the words of his **f**,	**Gn 27:34**	1
and bitter cry, and said to his **f**,	**Gn 27:34**	1
"Bless me, *even* me also, O my **f**!"	**Gn 27:34**	1
Esau said to his **f**,	**Gn 27:38**	1
you have only one blessing, my **f**?	**Gn 27:38**	1
Bless me, *even* me also, O my **f**."	**Gn 27:38**	1
his **f** answered and said to him,	**Gn 27:39**	1
with which his **f** had blessed him;	**Gn 27:41**	1
of mourning for my **f** are near;	**Gn 27:41**	1
house of Bethuel your mother's **f**;	**Gn 28:2**	1
and that Jacob had obeyed his **f**	**Gn 28:7**	1
of Canaan displeased his **f** Isaac;	**Gn 28:8**	1
f Abraham and the God of Isaac;	**Gn 28:13**	1
Rachel that he was a relative of her **f**	**Gn 29:12**	1
son, and she ran and told her **f**.	**Gn 29:12**	1
f he has made all this wealth."	**Gn 31:1**	1
the God of my **f** has been with me.	**Gn 31:5**	1
your **f** with all my strength.	**Gn 31:6**	1
"Yet your **f** has cheated me and	**Gn 31:7**	1
God has taken away from our **f**	**Gn 31:16**	1
the land of Canaan to his **f** Isaac.	**Gn 31:18**	1
of your **f** spoke to me last night,	**Gn 31:29**	1
She said to her **f**,	**Gn 31:35**	1
"If the God of my **f**,	**Gn 31:42**	1
God of Nahor, the God of their **f**,	**Gn 31:53**	1
swore by the fear of his **f** Isaac.	**Gn 31:53**	1
"O God of my **f** Abraham and God of	**Gn 32:9**	1
Abraham and God of my **f** Isaac,	**Gn 32:9**	1
of the sons of Hamor, Shechem's **f**,	**Gn 33:19**	1
So Shechem spoke to his **f** Hamor,	**Gn 34:4**	1
Then Hamor the **f** of Shechem went	**Gn 34:6**	1
said to her **f** and to her brothers,	**Gn 34:11**	1
answered Shechem and his **f** Hamor	**Gn 34:13**	1
than all the household of his **f**.	**Gn 34:19**	1
but his **f** called him Benjamin.	**Gn 35:18**	1
Jacob came to his **f** Isaac at	**Gn 35:27**	1
Esau the **f** of the Edomites in the hill	**Gn 36:9**	1
the donkeys of his **f** Zibeon.	**Gn 36:24**	1
is, Esau, the **f** of the Edomites),	**Gn 36:43**	1
land where his **f** had sojourned,	**Gn 37:1**	1
bad report about them to their **f**.	**Gn 37:2**	1
His brothers saw that their **f**	**Gn 37:4**	1
it to his **f** and to his brothers;	**Gn 37:10**	1
his **f** rebuked him and said to him,	**Gn 37:10**	1
but his **f** kept the saying *in mind*.	**Gn 37:11**	1
hands, to restore him to his **f**.	**Gn 37:22**	1
brought it to their **f** and said,	**Gn 37:32**	1
So his **f** wept for him.	**Gn 37:35**	1
the youngest is with our **f** today,	**Gn 42:13**	1
f Jacob in the land of Canaan,	**Gn 42:29**	1
twelve brothers, sons of our **f**;	**Gn 42:32**	1
the youngest is with our **f** today in	**Gn 42:32**	1
f saw their bundles of money,	**Gn 42:35**	1
Their **f** Jacob said to them,	**Gn 42:36**	1
Then Reuben spoke to his **f**,	**Gn 42:37**	1
Egypt, that their **f** said to them,	**Gn 43:2**	1
'Is your **f** still alive?	**Gn 43:7**	1
Judah said to his **f** Israel,	**Gn 43:8**	1
Then their **f** Israel said to them,	**Gn 43:11**	1
Your God and the God of your **f** has	**Gn 43:23**	1
"Is your old **f** well, of whom you	**Gn 43:27**	1
"Your servant our **f** is well;	**Gn 43:28**	1
you, go up in peace to your **f**."	**Gn 44:17**	1
'Have you a **f** or a brother?'	**Gn 44:19**	1
'We have an old **f** and a little	**Gn 44:20**	1
his mother, and his **f** loves him.'	**Gn 44:20**	1
'The lad cannot leave his **f**,	**Gn 44:22**	1
for if he should leave his **f**,	**Gn 44:22**	1
his father, his **f** would die.'	**Gn 44:22**	1
we went up to your servant my **f**,	**Gn 44:24**	1
"Our **f** said,	**Gn 44:25**	1
"Your servant my **f** said to us,	**Gn 44:27**	1
when I come to your servant my **f**,	**Gn 44:30**	1
our **f** down to Sheol in sorrow.	**Gn 44:31**	1
became surety for the lad to my **f**,	**Gn 44:32**	1
the blame before my **f** forever.'	**Gn 44:32**	1
to my **f** if the lad is not with me	**Gn 44:34**	1
evil that would overtake my **f**?"	**Gn 44:34**	1
Is my **f** still alive?"	**Gn 45:3**	1
and He has made me a **f** to Pharaoh	**Gn 45:8**	1
"Hurry and go up to my **f**,	**Gn 45:9**	1
my **f** of all my splendor in Egypt,	**Gn 45:13**	1
hurry and bring my **f** down here."	**Gn 45:13**	1
and take your **f** and your	**Gn 45:18**	1
wives, and bring your **f** and come.	**Gn 45:19**	1
To his **f** he sent as follows:	**Gn 45:23**	1
for his **f** on the journey.	**Gn 45:23**	1
land of Canaan to their **f** Jacob.	**Gn 45:25**	1
spirit of their **f** Jacob revived.	**Gn 45:27**	1
to the God of his **f** Isaac.	**Gn 46:1**	1
"I am God, the God of your **f**;	**Gn 46:3**	1
sons of Israel carried their **f** Jacob	**Gn 46:5**	1
up to Goshen to meet his **f** Israel;	**Gn 46:29**	1
"My **f** and my brothers and their	**Gn 47:1**	1
"Your **f** and your brothers have	**Gn 47:5**	1
settle your **f** and your brothers in	**Gn 47:6**	1
Then Joseph brought his **f** Jacob	**Gn 47:7**	1
settled his **f** and his brothers and	**Gn 47:11**	1
Joseph provided his **f** and his	**Gn 47:12**	1
"Behold, your **f** is sick."	**Gn 48:1**	1
Joseph said to his **f**,	**Gn 48:9**	1
When Joseph saw that his **f** laid	**Gn 48:17**	1
Joseph said to his **f**,	**Gn 48:18**	1
"Not so, my **f**, for this one is	**Gn 48:18**	1
But his **f** refused and said,	**Gn 48:19**	1
And listen to Israel your **f**.	**Gn 49:2**	1
the God of your **f** who helps you,	**Gn 49:25**	1
"The blessings of your **f** Have	**Gn 49:26**	1
and this is what their **f** said to	**Gn 49:28**	1
the physicians to embalm his **f**.	**Gn 50:2**	1
'My **f** made me swear, saying,	**Gn 50:5**	1
please let me go up and bury my **f**;	**Gn 50:5**	1
"Go up and bury your **f**,	**Gn 50:6**	1
So Joseph went up to bury his **f**,	**Gn 50:7**	1
seven days mourning for his **f**.	**Gn 50:10**	1
After he had buried his **f**,	**Gn 50:14**	1
gone up with him to bury his **f**.	**Gn 50:14**	1
saw that their **f** was dead,	**Gn 50:15**	1
"Your **f** charged before he died,	**Gn 50:16**	1
servants of the God of your **f**."	**Gn 50:17**	1
When they came to Reuel their **f**,	**Ex 2:18**	1
"I am the God of your **f**,	**Ex 3:6**	1
"The God of my **f** was my help, and	**Ex 18:4**	1
"Honor your **f** and your mother,	**Ex 20:12**	1
"He who strikes his **f** or his	**Ex 21:15**	1
"He who curses his **f** or his	**Ex 21:17**	1
"If her **f** absolutely refuses to	**Ex 22:17**	1
even as you have anointed their **f**,	**Ex 40:15**	1
uncover the nakedness of your **f**,	**Lv 18:7**	1
wife's daughter, born to your **f**,	**Lv 18:11**	1
reverence his mother and his **f**,	**Lv 19:3**	1
who curses his **f** or his mother,	**Lv 20:9**	1
he has cursed his **f** or his mother,	**Lv 20:9**	1
his mother and his **f** and his son	**Lv 21:2**	1
by harlotry, she profanes her **f**;	**Lv 21:9**	1
even for his **f** or his mother,	**Lv 21:11**	1
woman, whose **f** was an Egyptian,	**Lv 24:10**	1121, 376
in the lifetime of their **f** Aaron.	**Nu 3:4**	1
for his **f** or for his mother,	**Nu 6:7**	1
"If her **f** had but spit in her	**Nu 12:14**	1
of Levi, the tribe of your **f**,	**Nu 18:2**	1
and Machir became the **f** of Gilead:	**Nu 26:29**	3205
Kohath became the **f** of Amram.	**Nu 26:58**	3205
"Our **f** died in the wilderness,	**Nu 27:3**	1
"Why should the name of our **f** be	**Nu 27:4**	1
inheritance of their **f** to them.	**Nu 27:7**	1
'If his **f** has no brothers,	**Nu 27:11**	1
and her **f** hears her vow and her	**Nu 30:4**	1
and her **f** says nothing to her,	**Nu 30:4**	1
"But if her **f** should forbid her	**Nu 30:5**	1
because her **f** had forbidden her.	**Nu 30:5**	1
as between a **f** and his daughter,	**Nu 30:16**	1
family of the tribe of their **f**.'	**Nu 36:6**	1
the family of the tribe of her **f**	**Nu 36:8**	1
tribe of the family of their **f**.	**Nu 36:12**	1
"When you become the **f** of	**Dt 4:25**	3205
'Honor your **f** and your mother, as	**Dt 5:16**	1
her **f** and mother a full month;	**Dt 21:13**	1
will not obey his **f** or his mother,	**Dt 21:18**	1
his **f** and mother shall seize him,	**Dt 21:19**	1
then the girl's **f** and her mother	**Dt 22:15**	1
girl's **f** shall say to the elders,	**Dt 22:16**	1
silver and give it to the girl's **f**,	**Dt 22:19**	1
girl's **f** fifty *shekels* of silver,	**Dt 22:29**	1
'My **f** was a wandering Aramean, and	**Dt 26:5**	1
he who dishonors his **f** or mother.'	**Dt 27:16**	1
of his **f** or of his mother.'	**Dt 27:22**	1
not He your **F** who has bought you?	**Dt 32:6**	1
Ask your **f**, and he will inform	**Dt 32:7**	1
Who said of his **f** and his mother,	**Dt 33:9**	1
and spare my **f** and my mother and	**Jos 2:13**	1
the house your **f** and your mother	**Jos 2:18**	1
brought out Rahab and her **f** and	**Jos 6:23**	1
Arba being the **f** of Anak	**Jos 15:13**	1
him to ask her **f** for a field.	**Jos 15:18**	1
of Manasseh, the **f** of Gilead,	**Jos 17:1**	1
Dan after the name of Dan their **f**.	**Jos 19:47**	1
Arba being the **f** of Anak	**Jos 21:11**	1
the **f** of Abraham and the father of	**Jos 24:2**	1
of Abraham and the **f** of Nahor,	**Jos 24:2**	1
f Abraham from beyond the River,	**Jos 24:3**	1
the sons of Hamor the **f** of Shechem	**Jos 24:32**	1
him to ask her **f** for a field.	**Jg 1:14**	1
of Baal which belongs to your **f**,	**Jg 6:25**	1
buried in the tomb of his **f** Joash,	**Jg 8:32**	1
of the household of his mother's **f**,	**Jg 9:1**	1
for my **f** fought for you and risked	**Jg 9:17**	1
the men of Hamor the **f** of Shechem;	**Jg 9:28**	1
which he had done to his **f** in	**Jg 9:56**	1
And Gilead was the **f** of Jephthah.	**Jg 11:1**	3205
"My **f**, you have given your word	**Jg 11:36**	1
She said to her **f**,	**Jg 11:37**	1
months she returned to her **f**,	**Jg 11:39**	1
back and told his **f** and mother,	**Jg 14:2**	1
his **f** and his mother said to him,	**Jg 14:3**	1
But Samson said to his **f**,	**Jg 14:3**	1
his **f** and mother did not know that	**Jg 14:4**	1
to Timnah with his **f** and mother,	**Jg 14:5**	1
his **f** or mother what he had done.	**Jg 14:6**	1
When he came to his **f** and mother,	**Jg 14:9**	1
Then his **f** went down to the woman;	**Jg 14:10**	1
not told *it* to my **f** or mother;	**Jg 14:16**	1
But her **f** did not let him enter.	**Jg 15:1**	1
Her **f** said, "I really thought that you	**Jg 15:2**	1
burned her and her **f** with fire.	**Jg 15:6**	1
in the tomb of Manoah his **f**.	**Jg 16:31**	1
me and be a **f** and a priest to me,	**Jg 17:10**	1
us, and be to us a **f** and a priest.	**Jg 18:19**	1
their **f** who was born in Israel;	**Jg 18:29**	1
and when the girl's **f** saw him,	**Jg 19:3**	1
His father-in-law, the girl's **f**,	**Jg 19:4**	1
the girl's **f** said to his son-in-law,	**Jg 19:5**	1
and the girl's **f** said to the man,	**Jg 19:6**	1
the morning, and the girl's **f** said,	**Jg 19:8**	1
his father-in-law, the girl's **f**,	**Jg 19:9**	1
and how you left your **f** and your	**Ru 2:11**	1
He is the **f** of Jesse, the father	**Ru 4:17**	1
father of Jesse, the **f** of David.	**Ru 4:17**	1
listen to the voice of their **f**,	**1Sa 2:25**	1
reveal Myself to the house of your **f**	**1Sa 2:27**	1
give to the house of your **f** all the fire	**1Sa 2:28**	1
house of your **f** should walk before	**1Sa 2:30**	1
Now the donkeys of Kish, Saul's **f**,	**1Sa 9:3**	1
or else my **f** will cease *to be concerned*	**1Sa 9:5**	1
your **f** has ceased to be concerned	**1Sa 10:2**	1
"Now, who is their **f**?"	**1Sa 10:12**	1
But he did not tell his **f**.	**1Sa 14:1**	1
his **f** put the people under oath;	**1Sa 14:27**	1
"Your **f** strictly put the people	**1Sa 14:28**	1
"My **f** has troubled the land.	**1Sa 14:29**	1
Kish *was* the **f** of Saul,	**1Sa 14:51**	1
the **f** of Abner *was* the son	**1Sa 14:51**	1
"Saul my **f** is seeking to put you	**1Sa 19:2**	1
my **f** in the field where you are,	**1Sa 19:3**	1
I will speak with my **f** about you;	**1Sa 19:3**	1
spoke well of David to Saul his **f** and	**1Sa 19:4**	1
And what is my sin before your **f**,	**1Sa 20:1**	1
my **f** does nothing either great or	**1Sa 20:2**	1
my **f** hide this thing from me?	**1Sa 20:2**	1
"Your **f** knows well that I have	**1Sa 20:3**	1
"If your **f** misses me at all, then	**1Sa 20:6**	1
should you bring me to your **f**?"	**1Sa 20:8**	1
decided by my **f** to come upon you,	**1Sa 20:9**	1
if your **f** answers you harshly?"	**1Sa 20:10**	1
When I have sounded out my **f**	**1Sa 20:12**	1
"If it please my **f** *to do* you	**1Sa 20:13**	1
with you as He has been with my **f**.	**1Sa 20:13**	1
Saul his **f** and said to him,	**1Sa 20:32**	1
so Jonathan knew that his **f** had	**1Sa 20:33**	1
because his **f** had dishonored him.	**1Sa 20:34**	1
"Please let my **f** and my mother	**1Sa 22:3**	1
to any of the household of my **f**,	**1Sa 22:15**	1
of Saul my **f** will not find you,	**1Sa 23:17**	1
and Saul my **f** knows that also."	**1Sa 23:17**	1
"Now, my **f**, see!	**1Sa 24:11**	1
to the house of Saul your **f**,	**2Sa 3:8**	1
your **f** and above all his house,	**2Sa 6:21**	1
"I will be a **f** to him and he will	**2Sa 7:14**	1
for the sake of your **f** Jonathan,	**2Sa 9:7**	1
as his **f** showed kindness to me."	**2Sa 10:2**	1
to console him concerning his **f**.	**2Sa 10:2**	1
think that David is honoring your **f**	**2Sa 10:3**	1
when your **f** comes to see you, say	**2Sa 13:5**	1
the kingdom of my **f** to me.' "	**2Sa 16:3**	1
made yourself odious to your **f**.	**2Sa 16:21**	1
"You know your **f** and his men,	**2Sa 17:8**	1
your **f** is an expert in warfare,	**2Sa 17:8**	1
for all Israel knows that your **f**	**2Sa 17:10**	1
was buried in the grave of his **f**.	**2Sa 17:23**	1
the grave of my **f** and my mother.	**2Sa 19:37**	1
Zela, in the grave of Kish his **f**;	**2Sa 21:14**	1
His **f** had never crossed him at	**1Ki 1:6**	1
sat on the throne of David his **f**,	**1Ki 2:12**	1
me on the throne of David my **f**, and	**1Ki 2:24**	1
of the Lord God before my **f** David,	**1Ki 2:26**	1

with which my **f** was afflicted.”	1Ki 2:26	1
while my **f** David did not know *it:*	1Ki 2:32	1
which you did to my **f** David;	1Ki 2:44	1
in the statutes of his **f** David,	1Ki 3:3	1
to Your servant David my **f**,	1Ki 3:6	1
king in place of my **f** David,	1Ki 3:7	1
as your **f** David walked,	1Ki 3:14	1
him king in place of his **f**,	1Ki 5:1	1
“You know that David my **f** was	1Ki 5:3	1
as the LORD spoke to David my **f**,	1Ki 5:5	1
you which I spoke to David your **f**.	1Ki 6:12	1
and his **f** was a man of Tyre,	1Ki 7:14	1
things dedicated by his **f** David,	1Ki 7:51	1
who spoke with His mouth to my **f**	1Ki 8:15	1
“Now it was in the heart of my **f**	1Ki 8:17	1
“But the LORD said to my **f** David,	1Ki 8:18	1
I have risen in place of my **f** David	1Ki 8:20	1
kept with Your servant, my **f** David,	1Ki 8:24	1
keep with Your servant David my **f**	1Ki 8:25	1
spoken to Your servant, my **f** David.	1Ki 8:26	1
before Me as your **f** David walked,	1Ki 9:4	1
as I promised to your **f** David,	1Ki 9:5	1
the heart of David his **f** *had been.*	1Ki 11:4	1
fully, as David his **f** *had done.*	1Ki 11:6	1
days for the sake of your **f** David,	1Ki 11:12	1
breach of the city of his **f** David.	1Ki 11:27	1
My ordinances, as his **f** David *did.*	1Ki 11:33	1
buried in the city of his **f** David,	1Ki 11:43	1
“Your **f** made our yoke hard;	1Ki 12:4	1
lighten the hard service of your **f** and	1Ki 12:4	1
elders who had served his **f** Solomon	1Ki 12:6	1
yoke which your **f** put on us’?”	1Ki 12:9	1
‘Your **f** made our yoke heavy, now	1Ki 12:10	1
my **f** loaded you with a heavy yoke,	1Ki 12:11	1
my **f** disciplined you with whips,	1Ki 12:11	1
“My **f** made your yoke heavy, but I	1Ki 12:14	1
my **f** disciplined you with whips,	1Ki 12:14	1
also they related to their **f**.	1Ki 13:11	1
Their **f** said to them,	1Ki 13:12	1
He walked in all the sins of his **f**	1Ki 15:3	1
like the heart of his **f** David.	1Ki 15:3	1
of the LORD, like David his **f**.	1Ki 15:11	1
f and his own dedicated things:	1Ki 15:15	1
as between my **f** and your father.	1Ki 15:19	1
as between my father and your **f**.	1Ki 15:19	1
in the city of David his **f**;	1Ki 15:24	1
and walked in the way of his **f** and	1Ki 15:26	1
let me kiss my **f** and my mother,	1Ki 19:20	1
“The cities which my **f** took from	1Ki 20:34	1
took from your **f** I will restore,	1Ki 20:34	1
as my **f** made in Samaria.”	1Ki 20:34	1
in all the way of Asa his **f**;	1Ki 22:43	1
remained in the days of his **f** Asa,	1Ki 22:46	1
in the city of his **f** David,	1Ki 22:50	1
and walked in the way of his **f**	1Ki 22:52	1
to all that his **f** had done.	1Ki 22:53	1
“My **f**, my father, the chariots of	2Ki 2:12	1
“My father, my **f**, the chariots of	2Ki 2:12	1
not like his **f** and his mother;	2Ki 3:2	1
of Baal which his **f** had made.	2Ki 3:2	1
Go to the prophets of your **f** and	2Ki 3:13	1
went out to his **f** to the reapers.	2Ki 4:18	1
He said to his **f**, “My head, my	2Ki 4:19	1
“My **f**, had the prophet told you	2Ki 5:13	1
“My **f**, shall I kill them?	2Ki 6:21	1
riding together after Ahab his **f**,	2Ki 9:25	1
“My **f**, my father, the chariots of	2Ki 13:14	1
“My father, my **f**, the chariots of	2Ki 13:14	1
from the hand of Jehoahaz his **f**.	2Ki 13:25	1
LORD, yet not like David his **f**;	2Ki 14:3	1
to all that Joash his **f** had done.	2Ki 14:3	1
who had slain the king his **f**.	2Ki 14:5	1
in the place of his **f** Amaziah.	2Ki 14:21	1
all that his **f** Amaziah had done.	2Ki 15:3	1
to all that his **f** Uzziah had done.	2Ki 15:34	1
in the city of David his **f**;	2Ki 15:38	1
his God, as his **f** David *had done.*	2Ki 16:2	1
to all that his **f** David had done.	2Ki 18:3	1
the LORD, the God of your **f** David,	2Ki 20:5	1
Hezekiah his **f** had destroyed;	2Ki 21:3	1
LORD, as Manasseh his **f** had done.	2Ki 21:20	1
all the way that his **f** had walked,	2Ki 21:21	1
f had served and worshiped them.	2Ki 21:21	1
in all the way of his **f** David,	2Ki 22:2	1
made him king in place of his **f**.	2Ki 23:30	1
king in the place of Josiah his **f**,	2Ki 23:34	1
to all that his **f** had done.	2Ki 24:9	1
Cush became the **f** of Nimrod;	1Ch 1:10	3205
became the **f** of the people of Lud,	1Ch 1:11	3205
Canaan became the **f** of Sidon,	1Ch 1:13	3205
Arpachshad became the **f** of Shelah	1Ch 1:18	3205
and Shelah became the **f** of Eber.	1Ch 1:18	3205
Joktan became the **f** of Almodad,	1Ch 1:20	3205
Abraham became the **f** of Isaac.	1Ch 1:34	3205
Ram became the **f** of Amminadab,	1Ch 2:10	3205
Amminadab became the **f** of Nahshon,	1Ch 2:10	3205
Nahshon became the **f** of Salma,	1Ch 2:11	3205
Salma, Salma became the **f** of Boaz,	1Ch 2:11	3205
Boaz became the **f** of Obed, and	1Ch 2:12	3205
and Obed became the **f** of Jesse;	1Ch 2:12	3205
the **f** of Eliab his firstborn,	1Ch 2:13	3205
and the **f** of Amasa was Jether the	1Ch 2:17	1
Hur became the **f** of Uri,	1Ch 2:20	3205
and Uri became the **f** of Bezalel.	1Ch 2:20	3205
of Machir the **f** of Gilead,	1Ch 2:21	1
Segub became the **f** of Jair,	1Ch 2:22	3205
sons of Machir, the **f** of Gilead.	1Ch 2:23	1
bore him Ashhur the **f** of Tekoa.	1Ch 2:24	1
Attai became the **f** of Nathan,	1Ch 2:36	3205
and Nathan became the **f** of Zabad,	1Ch 2:36	3205
and Zabad became the **f** of Ephlal,	1Ch 2:37	3205
and Ephlal became the **f** of Obed,	1Ch 2:37	3205
and Obed became the **f** of Jehu,	1Ch 2:38	3205
and Jehu became the **f** of Azariah,	1Ch 2:38	3205
and Azariah became the **f** of Helez,	1Ch 2:39	3205
and Helez became the **f** of Eleasah,	1Ch 2:39	3205
Eleasah became the **f** of Sismai,	1Ch 2:40	3205
Sismai became the **f** of Shallum,	1Ch 2:40	3205
Shallum became the **f** of Jekamiah,	1Ch 2:41	3205
Jekamiah became the **f** of Elishama.	1Ch 2:41	3205
firstborn, who was the **f** of Ziph;	1Ch 2:42	1
son was Mareshah, the **f** of Hebron.	1Ch 2:42	1
Shema became the **f** of Raham,	1Ch 2:44	3205
father of Raham, the **f** of Jorkeam;	1Ch 2:44	1
and Rekem became the **f** of Shammai.	1Ch 2:44	3205
and Maon *was* the **f** of Bethzur.	1Ch 2:45	1
and Haran became the **f** of Gazez.	1Ch 2:46	3205
bore Shaaph the **f** of Madmannah,	1Ch 2:49	1
Sheva the **f** of Machbena and the	1Ch 2:49	1
of Machbena and the **f** of Gibea;	1Ch 2:49	1
Shobal the **f** of Kiriath-jearim,	1Ch 2:50	1
Salma the **f** of Bethlehem *and*	1Ch 2:51	1
and Hareph the **f** of Beth-gader.	1Ch 2:51	1
the **f** of Kiriath-jearim had sons:	1Ch 2:52	1
the **f** of the house of Rechab.	1Ch 2:55	1
of Shobal became the **f** of Jahath,	1Ch 4:2	3205
became the **f** of Ahumai and Lahad.	1Ch 4:2	3205
Penuel *was* the **f** of Gedor,	1Ch 4:4	1
Gedor, and Ezer the **f** of Hushah.	1Ch 4:4	1
of Ephrathah, the **f** of Bethlehem.	1Ch 4:4	1
Ashhur, the **f** of Tekoa, had	1Ch 4:5	1
became the **f** of Anub and Zobebah,	1Ch 4:8	3205
of Shuhah became the **f** of Mehir,	1Ch 4:11	3205
of Mehir, who was the **f** of Eshton.	1Ch 4:11	1
the **f** of Beth-rapha and Paseah,	1Ch 4:12	3205
and Tehinnah the **f** of Ir-nahash.	1Ch 4:12	1
Meonothai became the **f** of Ophrah,	1Ch 4:14	3205
and Seraiah became the **f** of Joab	1Ch 4:14	3205
of Joab the **f** of Ge-harashim,	1Ch 4:14	1
and Ishbah the **f** of Eshtemoa.	1Ch 4:17	1
wife bore Jered the **f** of Gedor,	1Ch 4:18	1
of Gedor, and Heber the **f** of Soco,	1Ch 4:18	1
and Jekuthiel the **f** of Zanoah.	1Ch 4:18	1
Er the **f** of Lecah and Laadah the	1Ch 4:21	1
and Laadah the **f** of Mareshah,	1Ch 4:21	1
Eleazar became the **f** of Phinehas,	1Ch 6:4	3205
Phinehas became the **f** of Abishua,	1Ch 6:4	3205
and Abishua became the **f** of Bukki,	1Ch 6:5	3205
and Bukki became the **f** of Uzzi,	1Ch 6:5	3205
and Uzzi became the **f** of Zerahiah,	1Ch 6:6	3205
Zerahiah became the **f** of Meraioth,	1Ch 6:6	3205
Meraioth became the **f** of Amariah,	1Ch 6:7	3205
Amariah became the **f** of Ahitub,	1Ch 6:7	3205
and Ahitub became the **f** of Zadok,	1Ch 6:8	3205
and Zadok became the **f** of Ahimaaz,	1Ch 6:8	3205
Ahimaaz became the **f** of Azariah,	1Ch 6:9	3205
Azariah became the **f** of Johanan,	1Ch 6:9	3205
Johanan became the **f** of Azariah	1Ch 6:10	3205
Azariah became the **f** of Amariah,	1Ch 6:11	3205
Amariah became the **f** of Ahitub,	1Ch 6:11	3205
and Ahitub became the **f** of Zadok,	1Ch 6:12	3205
and Zadok became the **f** of Shallum,	1Ch 6:12	3205
Shallum became the **f** of Hilkiah,	1Ch 6:13	3205
Hilkiah became the **f** of Azariah,	1Ch 6:13	3205
Azariah became the **f** of Seraiah,	1Ch 6:14	3205
Seraiah became the **f** of Jehozadak;	1Ch 6:14	3205
she bore Machir the **f** of Gilead.	1Ch 7:14	1
Their **f** Ephraim mourned many days,	1Ch 7:22	1
who was the **f** of Birzaith.	1Ch 7:31	1
Heber became the **f** of Japhlet,	1Ch 7:32	3205
the **f** of Bela his firstborn,	1Ch 8:1	3205
became the **f** of Uzza and Ahihud.	1Ch 8:7	3205
Shaharaim became the **f** of children	1Ch 8:8	3205
his wife he became the **f** of Jobab,	1Ch 8:9	3205
became the **f** of Abitub and Elpaal.	1Ch 8:11	3205
Jeiel, the **f** of Gibeon lived,	1Ch 8:29	1
Mikloth became the **f** of Shimeah.	1Ch 8:32	3205
Ner became the **f** of Kish,	1Ch 8:33	3205
and Kish became the **f** of Saul,	1Ch 8:33	3205
and Saul became the **f** of Jonathan,	1Ch 8:33	3205
Merib-baal became the **f** of Micah.	1Ch 8:34	3205
Ahaz became the **f** of Jehoaddah,	1Ch 8:36	3205
Jehoaddah became the **f** of Alemeth,	1Ch 8:36	3205
and Zimri became the **f** of Moza.	1Ch 8:36	3205
Moza became the **f** of Binea;	1Ch 8:37	3205
Jeiel the **f** of Gibeon lived,	1Ch 9:35	1
Mikloth became the **f** of Shimeam.	1Ch 9:38	3205
Ner became the **f** of Kish,	1Ch 9:39	3205
and Kish became the **f** of Saul,	1Ch 9:39	3205
and Saul became the **f** of Jonathan,	1Ch 9:39	3205
Merib-baal became the **f** of Micah.	1Ch 9:40	3205
Ahaz became the **f** of Jarah,	1Ch 9:42	3205
and Jarah became the **f** of Alemeth,	1Ch 9:42	3205
and Zimri became the **f** of Moza,	1Ch 9:42	3205
f of Binea and Rephaiah his son,	1Ch 9:43	3205
the **f** of more sons and daughters.	1Ch 14:3	3205
“I will be his **f** and he shall be	1Ch 17:13	1
his **f** showed kindness to me.”	1Ch 19:2	1
to console him concerning his **f**.	1Ch 19:2	1
that David is honoring your **f**,	1Ch 19:3	1
be My son and I will be his **f**;	1Ch 22:10	1
before their **f** and had no sons.	1Ch 24:2	1
to them through Aaron their **f**,	1Ch 24:19	1
of their **f** Jeduthun with the harp,	1Ch 25:3	1
under the direction of their **f** to sing	1Ch 25:6	1
ruled over the house of their **f**,	1Ch 26:6	1
firstborn, his **f** made him first),	1Ch 26:10	1
chose me from all the house of my **f**	1Ch 28:4	1
and among the sons of my **f** He took	1Ch 28:4	1
to Me, and I will be a **f** to him.	1Ch 28:6	1
Solomon, know the God of your **f**,	1Ch 28:9	1
You, O LORD God of Israel our **f**,	1Ch 29:10	1
as king instead of David his **f**;	1Ch 29:23	1
“You have dealt with my **f** David	2Ch 1:8	1
to my **f** David is fulfilled,	2Ch 1:9	1
“As you dealt with David my **f** and	2Ch 2:3	1
whom David my **f** provided.	2Ch 2:7	1
of a Danite woman and a Tyrian **f**,	2Ch 2:14	1
those of my lord David your **f**.	2Ch 2:14	1
which his **f** David had taken;	2Ch 2:17	1
LORD had appeared to his **f** David,	2Ch 3:1	1
that David his **f** had dedicated,	2Ch 5:1	1
who spoke with His mouth to my **f**	2Ch 6:4	1
it was in the heart of my **f** David	2Ch 6:7	1
“But the LORD said to my **f** David,	2Ch 6:8	1
have risen in the place of my **f** David	2Ch 6:10	1
kept with Your servant David, my **f**,	2Ch 6:15	1
keep with Your servant David, my **f**,	2Ch 6:16	1
if you walk before Me as your **f**	2Ch 7:17	1
as I covenanted with your **f** David,	2Ch 7:18	1
to the ordinance of his **f** David,	2Ch 8:14	1
buried in the city of his **f** David;	2Ch 9:31	1
“Your **f** made our yoke hard;	2Ch 10:4	1
lighten the hard service of your **f** and	2Ch 10:4	1
elders who had served his **f** Solomon	2Ch 10:6	1
yoke which your **f** put on us’?”	2Ch 10:9	1
‘Your **f** made our yoke heavy, but	2Ch 10:10	1
my **f** loaded you with a heavy yoke,	2Ch 10:11	1
my **f** disciplined you with whips,	2Ch 10:11	1
“My **f** made your yoke heavy, but I	2Ch 10:14	1
my **f** disciplined you with whips,	2Ch 10:14	1
and became the **f** of twenty-two	2Ch 13:21	3205
f and his own dedicated things:	2Ch 15:18	1
as between my **f** and your father.	2Ch 16:3	1
as between my father and your **f**.	2Ch 16:3	1
which Asa his **f** had captured.	2Ch 17:2	1
followed the example of his **f** David’s	2Ch 17:3	1
but sought the God of his **f**,	2Ch 17:4	1
He walked in the way of his **f**	2Ch 20:32	1
Their **f** gave them many gifts	2Ch 21:3	1
of his **f** and made himself secure,	2Ch 21:4	1
says the LORD God of your **f** David,	2Ch 21:12	1
in the ways of Jehoshaphat your **f**	2Ch 21:12	1
after the death of his **f**,	2Ch 22:4	1
the **f** of sons and daughters.	2Ch 24:3	3205
his **f** Jehoiada had shown him,	2Ch 24:22	1
who had slain his **f** the king.	2Ch 25:3	1
in the place of his **f** Amaziah.	2Ch 26:1	1
all that his **f** Amaziah had done.	2Ch 26:4	1
to all that his **f** Uzziah had done;	2Ch 27:2	1
the LORD as David his **f** *had done.*	2Ch 28:1	1
to all that his **f** David had done.	2Ch 29:2	1
Hezekiah his **f** had broken down;	2Ch 33:3	1
LORD as Manasseh his **f** had done,	2Ch 33:22	1
which his **f** Manasseh had made,	2Ch 33:22	1
LORD as his **f** Manasseh had done,	2Ch 33:23	1
walked in the ways of his **f** David	2Ch 34:2	1
to seek the God of his **f** David;	2Ch 34:3	1
in place of his **f** in Jerusalem.	2Ch 36:1	1
Jeshua became the **f** of Joiakim,	Ne 12:10	3205
Joiakim became the **f** of Eliashib,	Ne 12:10	3205
Eliashib became the **f** of Joiada,	Ne 12:10	
Joiada became the **f** of Jonathan,	Ne 12:11	3205
Jonathan became the **f** of Jaddua.	Ne 12:11	3205
for she had no **f** or mother.	Es 2:7	1
when her **f** and her mother died,	Es 2:7	1
are among us, Older than your **f**.	Jb 15:10	1
If I call to the pit, ‘You are my **f**’;	Jb 17:14	1
“I was a **f** to the needy, And I	Jb 29:16	1
he grew up with me as with a **f**,	Jb 31:18	1
“Has the rain a **f**?	Jb 38:28	1
and their **f** gave them inheritance	Jb 42:15	1
For my **f** and my mother have	Ps 27:10	1
A **f** of the fatherless and a judge	Ps 68:5	1
‘You are my **F**, My God, and the	Ps 89:26	1
Just as a **f** has compassion on *his*	Ps 103:13	1
Even as a **f** *corrects* the son	Pr 3:12	1
O sons, the instruction of a **f**,	Pr 4:1	1
When I was a son to my **f**,	Pr 4:3	1
observe the commandment of your **f**	Pr 6:20	1
A wise son makes a **f** glad,	Pr 10:1	1
A wise son makes a **f** glad,	Pr 15:20	1
And the **f** of a fool has no joy.	Pr 17:21	1
A foolish son is a grief to his **f** And	Pr 17:25	1
son is destruction to his **f**,	Pr 19:13	1
He who assaults *his* **f** *and* drives	Pr 19:26	1
He who curses his **f** or his mother,	Pr 20:20	1
Listen to your **f** who begot you,	Pr 23:22	1
The **f** of the righteous will	Pr 23:24	1
your **f** and your mother be glad,	Pr 23:25	1
of gluttons humiliates his **f**.	Pr 28:7	1
He who robs his **f** or his mother And	Pr 28:24	1
who loves wisdom makes his **f** glad,	Pr 29:3	1
is a kind of *man* who curses his **f** And	Pr 30:11	1
The eye that mocks a **f** And	Pr 30:17	1
the boy knows how to cry out ‘My **f**	Is 8:4	1
Counselor, Mighty God, Eternal **F**,	Is 9:6	1
And he will become a **f** to the	Is 22:21	1
the LORD, the God of your **f** David,	Is 38:5	1
A **f** tells his sons about Your	Is 38:19	1
“Woe to him who says to a **f**,	Is 45:10	1
“Look to Abraham your **f** And	Is 51:2	1
with the heritage of Jacob your **f**,	Is 58:14	1
For You are our **F**,	Is 63:16	1
You, O LORD, are our **F**,	Is 63:16	1
But now, O LORD, You are our **F**,	Is 64:8	1
‘You are my **f**,’ And to a stone,	Jer 2:27	1

'My **F**, You are the friend of my	**Jer 3:4**	1
'You shall call Me, My **F**,	**Jer 3:19**	1
and the household of your **f**,	**Jer 12:6**	1
to drink for anyone's **f** or mother.	**Jer 16:7**	1
man who brought the news To my **f**,	**Jer 20:15**	1
king in the place of Josiah his **f**,	**Jer 22:11**	1
Did not your **f** eat and drink And	**Jer 22:15**	1
For I am a **f** to Israel, And	**Jer 31:9**	1
Jonadab the son of Rechab, our **f**,	**Jer 35:6**	1
Jonadab the son of Rechab, our **f**,	**Jer 35:8**	1
that Jonadab our **f** commanded us.	**Jer 35:10**	1
their **f** which he commanded them,	**Jer 35:16**	1
the command of Jonadab your **f**,	**Jer 35:18**	1
have become orphans without a **f**,	**La 5:3**	1
your **f** was an Amorite and your	**Ezk 16:3**	1
a Hittite and your **f** an Amorite.	**Ezk 16:45**	1
the soul of the **f** as well as the	**Ezk 18:4**	1
"As for his **f**, because he	**Ezk 18:18**	1
nor will the **f** bear the punishment	**Ezk 18:20**	1
have treated **f** and mother lightly	**Ezk 22:7**	1
however, for **f**, for mother, for	**Ezk 44:25**	1
Nebuchadnezzar his **f** had taken out	**Da 5:2**	2
and in the days of your **f**,	**Da 5:11**	2
And King Nebuchadnezzar, your **f**,	**Da 5:11**	2
your father, your **f** the king,	**Da 5:11**	2
my **f** the king brought from Judah?	**Da 5:13**	2
majesty to Nebuchadnezzar your **f**.	**Da 5:18**	2
And a man and his **f** resort to the	**Am 2:7**	1
For son treats **f** contemptuously,	**Mi 7:6**	1
then his **f** and mother who gave	**Zch 13:3**	1
and his **f** and mother who gave	**Zch 13:3**	1
"'A son honors *his* **f**,	**Mal 1:6**	1
Then if I am a **f**, where is My	**Mal 1:6**	1
"Do we not all have one **f**?	**Mal 2:10**	1
Abraham was the **f** of Isaac, Isaac	**Mt 1:2**	*1080*
Isaac the **f** of Jacob, and Jacob	**Mt 1:2**	*1080*
and Jacob the **f** of Judah and his	**Mt 1:2**	*1080*
Judah was the **f** of Perez and Zerah by	**Mt 1:3**	*1080*
Perez was the **f** of Hezron,	**Mt 1:3**	*1080*
and Hezron the **f** of Ram.	**Mt 1:3**	*1080*
Ram was the **f** of Amminadab,	**Mt 1:4**	*1080*
Amminadab the **f** of Nahshon,	**Mt 1:4**	*1080*
and Nahshon the **f** of Salmon.	**Mt 1:4**	*1080*
Salmon was the **f** of Boaz by Rahab,	**Mt 1:5**	*1080*
Boaz was the **f** of Obed by Ruth,	**Mt 1:5**	*1080*
and Obed the **f** of Jesse.	**Mt 1:5**	*1080*
Jesse was the **f** of David the king.	**Mt 1:6**	*1080*
David was the **f** of Solomon by	**Mt 1:6**	*1080*
Solomon was the **f** of Rehoboam,	**Mt 1:7**	*1080*
Rehoboam the **f** of Abijah, and Abijah	**Mt 1:7**	*1080*
and Abijah the **f** of Asa.	**Mt 1:7**	*1080*
Asa was the **f** of Jehoshaphat,	**Mt 1:8**	*1080*
Jehoshaphat the **f** of Joram,	**Mt 1:8**	*1080*
and Joram the **f** of Uzziah.	**Mt 1:8**	*1080*
Uzziah was the **f** of Jotham, Jotham	**Mt 1:9**	*1080*
Jotham the **f** of Ahaz, and Ahaz	**Mt 1:9**	*1080*
and Ahaz the **f** of Hezekiah.	**Mt 1:9**	*1080*
Hezekiah was the **f** of Manasseh,	**Mt 1:10**	*1080*
Manasseh the **f** of Amon, and Amon	**Mt 1:10**	*1080*
and Amon the **f** of Josiah.	**Mt 1:10**	*1080*
Josiah became the **f** of Jeconiah and his	**Mt 1:11**	*1080*
Jeconiah became the **f** of Shealtiel,	**Mt 1:12**	*1080*
and Shealtiel the **f** of Zerubbabel.	**Mt 1:12**	*1080*
Zerubbabel was the **f** of Abihud,	**Mt 1:13**	*1080*
Abihud the **f** of Eliakim, and Eliakim	**Mt 1:13**	*1080*
and Eliakim the **f** of Azor.	**Mt 1:13**	*1080*
Azor was the **f** of Zadok, Zadok	**Mt 1:14**	*1080*
Zadok the **f** of Achim, and Achim	**Mt 1:14**	*1080*
and Achim the **f** of Eliud.	**Mt 1:14**	*1080*
Eliud was the **f** of Eleazar, Eleazar	**Mt 1:15**	*1080*
Eleazar the **f** of Matthan,	**Mt 1:15**	*1080*
and Matthan the **f** of Jacob.	**Mt 1:15**	*1080*
Jacob was the **f** of Joseph the husband	**Mt 1:16**	*1080*
Judea in place of his **f** Herod,	**Mt 2:22**	*3962*
'We have Abraham for our **f**';	**Mt 3:9**	*3962*
in the boat with Zebedee their **f**,	**Mt 4:21**	*3962*
left the boat and their **f**,	**Mt 4:22**	*3962*
glorify your **F** who is in heaven.	**Mt 5:16**	*3962*
sons of your **F** who is in heaven;	**Mt 5:45**	*3962*
as your heavenly **F** is perfect.	**Mt 5:48**	*3962*
with your **F** who is in heaven.	**Mt 6:1**	*3962*
your **F** who sees *what is done* in secret	**Mt 6:4**	*3962*
pray to your **F** who is in secret,	**Mt 6:6**	*3962*
your **F** who sees *what is done* in secret	**Mt 6:6**	*3962*
for your **F** knows what you need before	**Mt 6:8**	*3962*
'Our **F** who is in heaven, Hallowed	**Mt 6:9**	*3962*
heavenly **F** will also forgive you.	**Mt 6:14**	*3962*
then your **F** will not forgive your	**Mt 6:15**	*3962*
but by your **F** who is in secret;	**Mt 6:18**	*3962*
your **F** who sees *what is done* in secret	**Mt 6:18**	*3962*
yet your heavenly **F** feeds them.	**Mt 6:26**	*3962*
for your heavenly **F** knows that you	**Mt 6:32**	*3962*
how much more will your **F** who is	**Mt 7:11**	*3962*
the will of My **F** who is in heaven	**Mt 7:21**	*3962*
me first to go and bury my **f**."	**Mt 8:21**	*3962*
of your **F** who speaks in you.	**Mt 10:20**	*3962*
brother to death, and a **f** *his* child;	**Mt 10:21**	*3962*
to the ground apart from your **F**.	**Mt 10:29**	*3962*
I will also confess him before My **F**	**Mt 10:32**	*3962*
I will also deny him before My **F**	**Mt 10:33**	*3962*
I came to SET A MAN AGAINST HIS **F**,	**Mt 10:35**	*3962*
"He who loves **f** or mother more	**Mt 10:37**	*3962*
"I praise You, **F**,	**Mt 11:25**	*3962*
"Yes, **F**, for this way was well-pleasing	**Mt 11:26**	*3962*
been handed over to Me by My **F**;	**Mt 11:27**	*3962*
one knows the Son except the **F**;	**Mt 11:27**	*3962*
nor does anyone know the **F** except	**Mt 11:27**	*3962*
the will of My **F** who is in heaven,	**Mt 12:50**	*3962*
THE SUN in the kingdom of their **F**.	**Mt 13:43**	*3962*

'HONOR YOUR **F** AND MOTHER,' and,	**Mt 15:4**	*3962*
WHO SPEAKS EVIL OF **F** OR MOTHER	**Mt 15:4**	*3962*
says to *his* **f** or mother,	**Mt 15:5**	*3962*
not to honor his **f** or his mother.'	**Mt 15:6**	*3962*
"Every plant which My heavenly **F**	**Mt 15:13**	*3962*
to you, but My **F** who is in heaven.	**Mt 16:17**	*3962*
glory of His **F** with His angels,	**Mt 16:27**	*3962*
the face of My **F** who is in heaven.	**Mt 18:10**	*3962*
the will of your **F** who is in heaven	**Mt 18:14**	*3962*
for them by My **F** who is in heaven.	**Mt 18:19**	*3962*
"My heavenly **F** will also do the same	**Mt 18:35**	*3962*
MAN SHALL LEAVE HIS **F** AND MOTHER	**Mt 19:5**	*3962*
HONOR YOUR **F** AND MOTHER	**Mt 19:19**	*3962*
or brothers or sisters or **f** or mother	**Mt 19:29**	*3962*
it has been prepared by My **F**."	**Mt 20:23**	*3962*
the two did the will of his **f**?"	**Mt 21:31**	*3962*
not call *anyone* on earth your **f**;	**Mt 23:9**	*3962*
for One is your **F**, He who is in	**Mt 23:9**	*3962*
nor the Son, but the **F** alone.	**Mt 24:36**	*3962*
'Come, you who are blessed of My **F**,	**Mt 25:34**	*3962*
"My **F**, if it is possible, let	**Mt 26:39**	*3962*
"My **F**, if this cannot pass away	**Mt 26:42**	*3962*
that I cannot appeal to My **F**,	**Mt 26:53**	*3962*
baptizing them in the name of the **F**	**Mt 28:19**	*3962*
and they left their **f** Zebedee in	**Mk 1:20**	*3962*
He took along the child's **f** and	**Mk 5:40**	*3962*
'HONOR YOUR **F** AND YOUR MOTHER';	**Mk 7:10**	*3962*
WHO SPEAKS EVIL OF **F** OR MOTHER,	**Mk 7:10**	*3962*
a man says to *his* **f** or *his* mother,	**Mk 7:11**	*3962*
anything for *his* **f** or *his* mother;	**Mk 7:12**	*3962*
of His **F** with the holy angels."	**Mk 8:38**	*3962*
And He asked his **f**,	**Mk 9:21**	*3962*
boy's **f** cried out and said,	**Mk 9:24**	*3962*
MAN SHALL LEAVE HIS **F** AND MOTHER,	**Mk 10:7**	*3962*
HONOR YOUR **F** AND MOTHER.' "	**Mk 10:19**	*3962*
mother or **f** or children or farms,	**Mk 10:29**	*3962*
the coming kingdom of our **f** David;	**Mk 11:10**	*3962*
so that your **F** who is in	**Mk 11:25**	*3962*
neither will your **F** who is in	**Mk 11:26**	*3962*
to death, and a **f** *his* child;	**Mk 13:12**	*3962*
nor the Son, but the **F** *alone.*	**Mk 13:32**	*3962*
And He was saying, "Abba! **F**!	**Mk 14:36**	*3962*
(the **f** of Alexander and Rufus),	**Mk 15:21**	*3962*
Him the throne of His **f** David;	**Lk 1:32**	*3962*
call him Zacharias, after his **f**.	**Lk 1:59**	*3962*
And they made signs to his **f**,	**Lk 1:62**	*3962*
And his **f** Zacharias was filled	**Lk 1:67**	*3962*
which He swore to Abraham our **f**,	**Lk 1:73**	*3962*
And His **f** and mother were amazed	**Lk 2:33**	*3962*
Your **f** and I have been anxiously	**Lk 2:48**	*3962*
'We have Abraham for our **f**,'	**Lk 3:8**	*3962*
just as your **F** is merciful.	**Lk 6:36**	*3962*
James, and the girl's **f** and mother.	**Lk 8:51**	*3962*
of the **F** and of the holy angels.	**Lk 9:26**	*3962*
boy and gave him back to his **f**.	**Lk 9:42**	*3962*
me first to go and bury my **f**."	**Lk 9:59**	*3962*
"I praise You, O **F**,	**Lk 10:21**	*3962*
Yes, **F**, for this way was	**Lk 10:21**	*3962*
been handed over to Me by My **F**,	**Lk 10:22**	*3962*
knows who the Son is except the **F**,	**Lk 10:22**	*3962*
and who the **F** is except the Son,	**Lk 10:22**	*3962*
'**F**, hallowed be Your name.	**Lk 11:2**	*3962*
your heavenly **F** give the Holy Spirit	**Lk 11:13**	*3962*
but your **F** knows that you need	**Lk 12:30**	*3962*
for your **F** has chosen gladly to	**Lk 12:32**	*3962*
will be divided, **f** against son and	**Lk 12:53**	*3962*
against son and son against **f**	**Lk 12:53**	*3962*
and does not hate his own **f** and	**Lk 14:26**	*3962*
"The younger of them said to his **f**,	**Lk 15:12**	*3962*
'**F**, give me the share of the	**Lk 15:12**	*3962*
'I will get up and go to my **f**,	**Lk 15:18**	*3962*
"**F**, I have sinned against heaven,	**Lk 15:18**	*3962*
"So he got up and came to his **f**.	**Lk 15:20**	*3962*
a long way off, his **f** saw him and	**Lk 15:20**	*3962*
'**F**, I have sinned against heaven	**Lk 15:21**	*3962*
"But the **f** said to his slaves,	**Lk 15:22**	*3962*
f has killed the fattened calf because	**Lk 15:27**	*3962*
and his **f** came out and *began*	**Lk 15:28**	*3962*
"But he answered and said to his **f**,	**Lk 15:29**	*3962*
'**F** Abraham, have mercy on me, and	**Lk 16:24**	*3962*
"And he said, 'Then I beg you, **f**,	**Lk 16:27**	*3962*
"But he said, 'No, **f** Abraham,	**Lk 16:30**	*3962*
HONOR YOUR **F** AND MOTHER.' "	**Lk 18:20**	*3962*
as My **F** has granted Me a kingdom,	**Lk 22:29**	*3962*
"**F**, if You are willing, remove	**Lk 22:42**	*3962*
"**F**, forgive them; for they do not	**Lk 23:34**	*3962*
"**F**, INTO YOUR HANDS I COMMIT MY	**Lk 23:46**	*3962*
the promise of My **F** upon you;	**Lk 24:49**	*3962*
of the only begotten from the **F**,	**Jn 1:14**	*3962*
God who is in the bosom of the **F**,	**Jn 1:18**	*3962*
"The **F** loves the Son and has	**Jn 3:35**	*3962*
are not greater than our **f** Jacob,	**Jn 4:12**	*3962*
will you worship the **F**.	**Jn 4:21**	*3962*
worship the **F** in spirit and truth;	**Jn 4:23**	*3962*
the **F** seeks to be His worshipers.	**Jn 4:23**	*3962*
So the **f** knew that *it was* at that	**Jn 4:53**	*3962*
"My **F** is working until now, and I	**Jn 5:17**	*3962*
also was calling God His own **F**,	**Jn 5:18**	*3962*
is something He sees the **F** doing;	**Jn 5:19**	*3962*
for whatever the **F** does, these	**Jn 5:19**	*3962*
"For the **F** loves the Son, and	**Jn 5:20**	*3962*
and *the* **F** will show Him greater	**Jn 5:20**	
"For just as the **F** raises the	**Jn 5:21**	*3962*
"For not even the **F** judges anyone,	**Jn 5:22**	*3962*
the Son even as they honor the **F**.	**Jn 5:23**	*3962*
does not honor the **F** who sent Him.	**Jn 5:23**	*3962*
just as the **F** has life in Himself,	**Jn 5:26**	*3962*
the **F** has given Me to accomplish	**Jn 5:36**	*3962*
about Me, that the **F** has sent Me.	**Jn 5:36**	*3962*

"And the **F** who sent Me, He has	**Jn 5:37**	*3962*
I will accuse you before the **F**;	**Jn 5:45**	*3962*
give to you, for on Him the **F**,	**Jn 6:27**	*3962*
but it is My **F** who gives you the	**Jn 6:32**	*3962*
the **F** gives Me will come to Me,	**Jn 6:37**	*3962*
"For this is the will of My **F**,	**Jn 6:40**	*3962*
whose **f** and mother we know?	**Jn 6:42**	*3962*
the **F** who sent Me draws him;	**Jn 6:44**	*3962*
has heard and learned from the **F**,	**Jn 6:45**	*3962*
"Not that anyone has seen the **F**,	**Jn 6:46**	*3962*
He has seen the **F**.	**Jn 6:46**	*3962*
"As the living **F** sent Me, and I	**Jn 6:57**	*3962*
Me, and I live because of the **F**,	**Jn 6:57**	*3962*
has been granted him from the **F**."	**Jn 6:65**	*3962*
but I and the **F** who sent Me.	**Jn 8:16**	
and the **F** who sent Me testifies	**Jn 8:18**	*3962*
"Where is Your **F**?"	**Jn 8:19**	*3962*
"You know neither Me nor My **F**;	**Jn 8:19**	*3962*
Me, you would know My **F** also."	**Jn 8:19**	*3962*
been speaking to them about the **F**.	**Jn 8:27**	*3962*
these things as the **F** taught Me.	**Jn 8:28**	*3962*
which I have seen with *My* **F**;	**Jn 8:38**	*3962*
which you heard from *your* **f**."	**Jn 8:38**	*3962*
"Abraham is our **f**."	**Jn 8:39**	*3962*
are doing the deeds of your **f**."	**Jn 8:41**	*3962*
we have one **F**: God."	**Jn 8:41**	*3962*
"If God were your **F**,	**Jn 8:42**	*3962*
"You are of *your* **f** the devil, and	**Jn 8:44**	*3962*
want to do the desires of your **f**.	**Jn 8:44**	*3962*
he is a liar and the **f** of lies.	**Jn 8:44**	*3962*
but I honor My **F**, and you dishonor	**Jn 8:49**	*3962*
not greater than our **f** Abraham,	**Jn 8:53**	*3962*
it is My **F** who glorifies Me, of	**Jn 8:54**	*3962*
"Your **f** Abraham rejoiced to see	**Jn 8:56**	*3962*
even as the **F** knows Me and I know	**Jn 10:15**	*3962*
Father knows Me and I know the **F**;	**Jn 10:15**	*3962*
"For this reason the **F** loves Me,	**Jn 10:17**	*3962*
I received from My **F**."	**Jn 10:18**	*3962*
"My **F**, who has given *them* to Me,	**Jn 10:29**	*3962*
"I and the **F** are one."	**Jn 10:30**	*3962*
you many good works from the **F**;	**Jn 10:32**	*3962*
whom the **F** sanctified and sent	**Jn 10:36**	*3962*
"If I do not do the works of My **F**,	**Jn 10:37**	*3962*
understand that the **F** is in Me,	**Jn 10:38**	*3962*
Father is in Me, and I in the **F**."	**Jn 10:38**	*3962*
"**F**, I thank You that You	**Jn 11:41**	*3962*
serves Me, the **F** will honor him.	**Jn 12:26**	*3962*
'**F**, save Me from this hour'?	**Jn 12:27**	*3962*
"**F**, glorify Your name."	**Jn 12:28**	*3962*
but the **F** Himself who sent Me has	**Jn 12:49**	*3962*
speak just as the **F** has told Me."	**Jn 12:50**	*3962*
depart out of this world to the **F**,	**Jn 13:1**	*3962*
knowing that the **F** had given all	**Jn 13:3**	*3962*
no one comes to the **F** but	**Jn 14:6**	*3962*
you would have known My **F** also;	**Jn 14:7**	*3962*
"Lord, show us the **F**,	**Jn 14:8**	*3962*
He who has seen Me has seen the **F**;	**Jn 14:9**	*3962*
how *can* you say, 'Show us the **F**'?	**Jn 14:9**	*3962*
not believe that I am in the **F**,	**Jn 14:10**	*3962*
in the Father, and the **F** is in Me?	**Jn 14:10**	*3962*
F abiding in Me does His works.	**Jn 14:10**	*3962*
"Believe Me that I am in the **F** and	**Jn 14:11**	*3962*
Me that I am in the Father and the **F**	**Jn 14:11**	*3962*
because I go to the **F**.	**Jn 14:12**	*3962*
the **F** may be glorified in the Son.	**Jn 14:13**	*3962*
"I will ask the **F**,	**Jn 14:16**	*3962*
you will know that I am in My **F**,	**Jn 14:20**	*3962*
loves Me will be loved by My **F**,	**Jn 14:21**	*3962*
and My **F** will love him, and We	**Jn 14:23**	*3962*
whom the **F** will send in My name,	**Jn 14:26**	*3962*
rejoiced because I go to the **F**	**Jn 14:28**	*3962*
for the **F** is greater than I.	**Jn 14:28**	*3962*
world may know that I love the **F**,	**Jn 14:31**	*3962*
I do exactly as the **F** commanded Me.	**Jn 14:31**	*3962*
vine, and My **F** is the vinedresser.	**Jn 15:1**	*3962*
"My **F** is glorified by this, that	**Jn 15:8**	*3962*
"Just as the **F** has loved Me, I	**Jn 15:9**	*3962*
My **F** I have made known to you.	**Jn 15:15**	*3962*
you ask of the **F** in My name He	**Jn 15:16**	*3962*
"He who hates Me hates My **F** also.	**Jn 15:23**	*3962*
and hated Me and My **F** as well.	**Jn 15:24**	*3962*
I will send to you from the **F**,	**Jn 15:26**	*3962*
of truth who proceeds from the **F**,	**Jn 15:26**	*3962*
because they have not known the **F** or	**Jn 16:3**	*3962*
because I go to the **F** and	**Jn 16:10**	*3962*
things that the **F** has are Mine;	**Jn 16:15**	*3962*
'because I go to the **F**'?"	**Jn 16:17**	*3962*
you ask the **F** for anything	**Jn 16:23**	*3962*
will tell you plainly of the **F**.	**Jn 16:25**	*3962*
will request of the **F** on your behalf;	**Jn 16:26**	*3962*
for the **F** Himself loves you,	**Jn 16:27**	*3962*
that I came forth from the **F**.	**Jn 16:27**	*3962*
"I came forth from the **F** and	**Jn 16:28**	*3962*
world again and going to the **F**."	**Jn 16:28**	*3962*
alone, because the **F** is with Me.	**Jn 16:32**	*3962*
"**F**, the hour has come;	**Jn 17:1**	*3962*
F, glorify Me together with Yourself,	**Jn 17:5**	*3962*
Holy **F**, keep them in Your name, *the*	**Jn 17:11**	*3962*
even as You, **F**, *are* in Me and I	**Jn 17:21**	*3962*
"**F**, I desire that they also, whom	**Jn 17:24**	*3962*
"O righteous **F**, although the	**Jn 17:25**	*3962*
the cup which the **F** has given Me,	**Jn 18:11**	*3962*
I have not yet ascended to the **F**;	**Jn 20:17**	*3962*
'I ascend to My **F** and your Father,	**Jn 20:17**	*3962*
'I ascend to My Father and your **F**,	**Jn 20:17**	*3962*
as the **F** has sent Me, I also send	**Jn 20:21**	*3962*
wait for what the **F** had promised,	**Ac 1:4**	*3962*
the **F** has fixed by His own authority;	**Ac 1:7**	*3962*
and having received from the **F** the	**Ac 2:33**	*3962*

mouth of our f David Your servant, Ac 4:25 3962
of glory appeared to our f Abraham Ac 7:2 3962
From there, after his f died, Ac 7:4 3962
so *Abraham* became the f of Isaac, Ac 7:8 1080
and Isaac *became the f of* Jacob, Ac 7:8
sent *word* and invited Jacob his f Ac 7:14 3962
where he became the f of two sons. Ac 7:29 1080
a believer, but his f was a Greek, Ac 16:1 3962
all knew that his f was a Greek. Ac 16:3 3962
And it happened that the f of Ac 28:8 3962
our F and the Lord Jesus Christ. Ro 1:7 3962
that he might be the f of all who Ro 4:11 3962
and the f of circumcision to those Ro 4:12 3962
steps of the faith of our f Abraham Ro 4:12 3962
Abraham, who is the f of us all, Ro 4:16 3962
"A F OF MANY NATIONS HAVE I MADE Ro 4:17 3962
might become a f of many nations Ro 4:18 3962
dead through the glory of the F, Ro 6:4 3962
by which we cry out, "Abba! F!" Ro 8:15 3962
twins by one man, our f Isaac; Ro 9:10 3962
and F of our Lord Jesus Christ. Ro 15:6 3962
our F and the Lord Jesus Christ. 1Co 1:3 3962
became your f through the gospel. 1Co 4:15 1080
us there is *but* one God, the F, 1Co 8:6 3962
over the kingdom to the God and F, 1Co 15:24 3962
our F and the Lord Jesus Christ. 2Co 1:2 3962
and F of our Lord Jesus Christ, 2Co 1:3 3962
the F of mercies and God of all 2Co 1:3 3962
"And I will be a f to you, 2Co 6:18 3962
The God and F of the Lord Jesus, 2Co 11:31 3962
Jesus Christ and God the F, Ga 1:1 3962
to you and peace from God our F and Ga 1:3 3962
to the will of our God and F, Ga 1:4 3962
until the date set by the f. Ga 4:2 3962
into our hearts, crying, "Abba! F!" Ga 4:6 3962
our F and the Lord Jesus Christ. Eph 1:2 3962
and F of our Lord Jesus Christ, Eph 1:3 3962
Lord Jesus Christ, the F of glory, Eph 1:17 3962
our access in one Spirit to the F. Eph 2:18 3962
I bow my knees before the F, Eph 3:14 3962
one God and F of all who is over Eph 4:6 3962
Jesus Christ to God, even the F; Eph 5:20 3962
MAN SHALL LEAVE HIS F AND MOTHER Eph 5:31 3962
HONOR YOUR F AND MOTHER Eph 6:2 3962
the F and the Lord Jesus Christ. Eph 6:23 3962
our F and the Lord Jesus Christ. Php 1:2 3962
Lord, to the glory of God the F. Php 2:11 3962
gospel like a child *serving* his f. Php 2:22 3962
to our God and F *be* the glory Php 4:20 3962
to you and peace from God our F. Col 1:2 3962
the F of our Lord Jesus Christ, Col 1:3 3962
giving thanks to the F, Col 1:12 3962
thanks through Him to God the F. Col 3:17 3962
in God the F and the Lord Jesus 1Th 1:1 3962
in the presence of our God and F, 1Th 1:3 3962
you as a f *would* his own children, 1Th 2:11 3962
Now may our God and F Himself and 1Th 3:11 3962
in holiness before our God and F 1Th 3:13 3962
in God our F and the Lord Jesus 2Th 1:1 3962
from God the F and the Lord Jesus 2Th 1:2 3962
Christ Himself and God our F, 2Th 2:16 3962
peace from God the F and Christ 1Tm 1:2 3962
but *rather* appeal to *him* as a f, 1Tm 5:1 3962
peace from God the F and Christ 2Tm 1:2 3962
peace from God the F and Christ Ti 1:4 3962
from God our F and the Lord Jesus Phm 1:3 3962
"I WILL BE A F TO HIM AND HE SHALL Heb 1:5 3962
are sanctified are all from one F; Heb 2:11
Without f, without mother, without Heb 7:3 540
of his f when Melchizedek met him. Heb 7:10 3962
whom *his* f does not discipline? Heb 12:7 3962
be subject to the F of spirits, Heb 12:9 3962
coming down from the F of lights, Jas 1:17 3962
in the sight of *our* God and F is Jas 1:27 3962
Abraham our f justified by works when Jas 2:21 3962
With it we bless *our* Lord and F, Jas 3:9 3962
to the foreknowledge of God the F, 1Pe 1:2 3962
and F of our Lord Jesus Christ, 1Pe 1:3 3962
If you address as F the One 1Pe 1:17 3962
honor and glory from God the F, 2Pe 1:17 3962
the F and was manifested to us 1Jn 1:2 3962
our fellowship is with the F, 1Jn 1:3 3962
we have an Advocate with the F, 1Jn 2:1 3962
children, because you know the F. 1Jn 2:13 3962
the love of the F is not in him. 1Jn 2:15 3962
pride of life, is not from the F, 1Jn 2:16 3962
one who denies the F and the Son. 1Jn 2:22 3962
the Son does not have the F; 1Jn 2:23 3962
confesses the Son has the F also. 1Jn 2:23 3962
abide in the Son and in the F. 1Jn 2:24 3962
a love the F has bestowed on us, 1Jn 3:1 3962
F has sent the Son *to be* the Savior 1Jn 4:14 3962
the F loves the *child* born of Him. 1Jn 5:1 1080
God the F and from Jesus Christ, 2Jn 1:3 3962
Jesus Christ, the Son of the F, 2Jn 1:3 3962
commandment *to do* from the F. 2Jn 1:4 3962
he has both the F and the Son. 2Jn 1:9 3962
the called, beloved in God the F, Jude 1:1 3962
kingdom, priests to His God and F Rv 1:6 3962
have received *authority* from My F; Rv 2:27 3962
will confess his name before My F and Rv 3:5 3962
sat down with My F on His throne. Rv 3:21 3962
the name of His F written on their Rv 14:1 3962

FATHERED

and f twenty-eight sons and sixty 2Ch 11:21 3205
bad investment and he had f a son, Ec 5:14 3205

FATHER-IN-LAW

your f is going up to Timnah to Gn 38:13 2524
out that she sent to her f, Gn 38:25 2524
the flock of Jethro his f, Ex 3:1 2860b
and returned to Jethro his f and Ex 4:18 2860b
the priest of Midian, Moses' f, Ex 18:1 2860b
Jethro, Moses' f, Ex 18:2 2860b
Then Jethro, Moses' f, Ex 18:5 2860b
"I, your f Jethro, am coming to Ex 18:6 2860b
Then Moses went out to meet his f, Ex 18:7 2860b
Moses told his f all that the Ex 18:8 2860b
Then Jethro, Moses' f, Ex 18:12 2860b
a meal with Moses' f before God. Ex 18:12 2860b
Now when Moses' f saw all that he Ex 18:14 2860b
Moses said to his f, Ex 18:15 2860b
Moses' f said to him, Ex 18:17 2860b
So Moses listened to his f and Ex 18:24 2860b
Then Moses bade his f farewell, Ex 18:27 2860b
of Reuel the Midianite, Moses' f, Nu 10:29 2860b
of the Kenite, Moses' f, Jg 1:16 2860b
the sons of Hobab the f of Moses, Jg 4:11 2860b
His f, the girl's father, Jg 19:4 2860b
but his f urged him so that he Jg 19:7 2860b
his concubine and servant, his f, Jg 19:9 2860b
her f and her husband had died, 1Sa 4:19 2524
because of her f and her husband. 1Sa 4:21 2524
for he was f of Caiaphas, who was Jn 18:13 3995

FATHERLESS

become widows and your children f. Ex 22:24 3490
the f and a judge for the widows, Ps 68:5 3490
Vindicate the weak and f; Ps 82:3 3490
Let his children be f And Ps 109:9 3490
to be gracious to his f children. Ps 109:12 3490
He supports the f and the widow, Ps 146:9 3490
Or go into the fields of the f, Pr 23:10 3490
the f and the widow they have Ezk 22:7 3490

FATHER'S

they did not see their f nakedness. Gn 9:23 1
relatives And from your f house, Gn 12:1 1
me to wander from my f house, Gn 20:13 1
who took me from my f house and Gn 24:7 1
for us to lodge in your f house?" Gn 24:23 1
but you shall go to my f house and Gn 24:38 1
my relatives and from my f house; Gn 24:40 1
wells which his f servants had dug Gn 26:15 1
I return to my f house in safety, Gn 28:21 1
Rachel came with her f sheep, Gn 29:9 1
has taken away all that was our f, Gn 31:1 1
"I see your f attitude, that it Gn 31:5 1
God has taken away your f livestock Gn 31:9 1
or inheritance in our f house? Gn 31:14 1
household idols that were her f. Gn 31:19 1
longed greatly for your f house; Gn 31:30 1
lay with Bilhah his f concubine; Gn 35:22 1
the sons of Zilpah, his f wives. Gn 37:2 1
pasture their f flock in Shechem. Gn 37:12 1
"Remain a widow in your f house Gn 38:11 1
went and lived in her f house. Gn 38:11 1
trouble and all my f household." Gn 41:51 1
brothers and to his f household, Gn 46:31 1
'My brothers and my f household, Gn 46:31 1
and all his f household with food, Gn 47:12 1
and he grasped his f hand to Gn 48:17 1
Because you went up to your f bed; Gn 49:4 1
Your f sons shall bow down to you. Gn 49:8 1
Then Joseph fell on his f face, Gn 50:1 1
his brothers and his f household; Gn 50:8 1
in Egypt, he and his f household, Gn 50:22 1
troughs to water their f flock. Ex 2:16 1
married his f sister Jochebed, Ex 6:20 1733
My f God, and I will extol Him. Ex 15:2 1
his f place shall make atonement: Lv 16:32 1
the nakedness of your f wife; Lv 18:8 1
it is your f nakedness. Lv 18:8 1
either your f daughter or your Lv 18:9 1
of your f wife's daughter, Lv 18:11 1
the nakedness of your f sister; Lv 18:12 1
she is your f blood relative. Lv 18:12 1
the nakedness of your f brother; Lv 18:14 1
is a man who lies with his f wife, Lv 20:11 1
he has uncovered his f nakedness; Lv 20:11 1
his f daughter or his mother's Lv 20:17 1
sister or of your f sister, Lv 20:19 1
to her f house as in her youth, Lv 22:13 1
she shall eat of her f food; Lv 22:13 1
each one head of his f household. Nu 1:4 1
of whom was of his f household. Nu 1:44 1
according to his f household. Nu 2:34 1
them a rod for each f household: Nu 17:2 1
and your sons and your f household Nu 18:1 1
a leader of a f household among Nu 25:14 1
people of a f household in Midian. Nu 25:15 1
possession among our f brothers." Nu 27:4 1
possession among their f brothers, Nu 27:7 1
his inheritance to his f brothers. Nu 27:10 1
in her f house in her youth, Nu 30:3 1
is in her youth in her f house. Nu 30:16 1
to the doorway of her f house, Dt 22:21 1
playing the harlot in her f house; Dt 22:21 1
"A man shall not take his f wife Dt 22:30 1
he will not uncover his f skirt. Dt 22:30 1
is he who lies with his f wife, Dt 27:20 1
he has uncovered his f skirt.' Dt 27:20 1
deal kindly with my f household, Jos 2:12 1
brothers and all your f household. Jos 2:18 1
her f household and all she had, Jos 6:25 1
among their f brothers. Jos 17:4 1
one chief for each f household Jos 22:14 1
was the head of his f household Jos 22:14 1
I am the youngest in my f house." Jg 6:15 1
"Take your f bull and a second Jg 6:25 1
he was too afraid of his f household Jg 6:27 1
he went to his f house at Ophrah and Jg 9:5 1
you have risen against my f house Jg 9:18 1
an inheritance in our f house, Jg 11:2 1
me and drive me from my f house? Jg 11:7 1
you and your f house with fire. Jg 14:15 1
and he went up to his f house. Jg 14:19 1
and all his f household came down, Jg 16:31 1
her f house in Bethlehem in Judah, Jg 19:2 1
she brought him into her f house, Jg 19:3 1
and the strength of your f house 1Sa 2:31 1
and for all your f household?" 1Sa 9:20 1
to tend his f flock at Bethlehem. 1Sa 17:15 1
make his f house free in Israel." 1Sa 17:25 1
servant was tending his f sheep. 1Sa 17:34 1
not let him return to his f house. 1Sa 18:2 1
my life *or* my f family in Israel, 1Sa 18:18 1
all his f household heard *of it,* 1Sa 22:1 1
Ahitub, and all his f household, 1Sa 22:11 1
you and all your f household!" 1Sa 22:16 1
every person in your f household. 1Sa 22:22 1
my name from my f household." 1Sa 24:21 1
his f tomb which was in Bethlehem. 2Sa 2:32 1
you gone in to my f concubine?" 2Sa 3:7 1
of Joab and on all his f house; 2Sa 3:29 1
iniquity is on me and my f house, 2Sa 14:9 1
been your f servant in time past, 2Sa 15:34 1
I have served in your f presence, 2Sa 16:19 1
"Go in to your f concubines, whom 2Sa 16:21 1
Absalom went in to his f concubines 2Sa 16:22 1
"For all my f household was 2Sa 19:28 1
me and against my f house." 2Sa 24:17 1
remove from me and from my f house 1Ki 2:31 1
certain Edomites of his f servants 1Ki 11:17 1
finger is thicker than my f loins! 1Ki 12:10 1
but you and your f house *have,* 1Ki 18:18 1
sons, and set *him* on his f throne, 2Ki 10:3 1
but because he defiled his f bed, 1Ch 5:1 1
and his relatives of his f house, 1Ch 9:19 1
of his f house twenty-two captains. 1Ch 12:28 1
be against me and my f household, 1Ch 21:17 1
so they became a f household, 1Ch 23:11 1
one f household taken for Eleazar 1Ch 24:6 1
in the house of Judah, my f house, 1Ch 28:4 1
finger is thicker than my f loins! 2Ch 10:10 1
by division of a f household. 2Ch 35:5 1
for *each of* their f households, Ezr 10:16 1
I and my f house have sinned. Ne 1:6 1
you and your f house will perish. Es 4:14 1
your people and your f house; Ps 45:10 1
Hear, my son, your f instruction And Pr 1:8 1
wise son *accepts his* f discipline, Pr 13:1 1
A fool rejects his f discipline, Pr 15:5 1
your own friend or your f friend, Pr 27:10 1
of his brother in his f house, Is 3:6 1
and on your f house such days as Is 7:17 1
a throne of glory to his f house. Is 22:23 1
him all the glory of his f house, Is 22:24 1
they have obeyed their f command. Jer 35:14 1
all his f sins which he committed, Ezk 18:14 1
will not die for his f iniquity, Ezk 18:17 1
punishment for the f iniquity?' Ezk 18:19 1
the punishment for the f iniquity, Ezk 18:20 1
his sister, his f daughter. Ezk 22:11 1
it new with you in My F kingdom." Mt 26:29 3962
that I had to be in My F *house?*" Lk 2:49 3962
'How many of my f hired men have Lk 15:17 3962
that you send him to my f house Lk 16:27 3962
F house a place of business." Jn 2:16 3962
"I have come in My F name, Jn 5:43 3962
the works that I do in My F name, Jn 10:25 3962
to snatch *them* out of the F hand. Jn 10:29 3962
"In My F house are many dwelling Jn 14:2 3962
not Mine, but the F who sent Me. Jn 14:24 3962
as I have kept My F commandments Jn 15:10 3962
three months in his f home. Ac 7:20 3962
that someone has his f wife. 1Co 5:1 3962
For it was the F good pleasure Col 1:19

FATHERS

you shall go to your f in peace; Gn 15:15 1
Return to the land of your f and to Gn 31:3 1
even until now, both we and our f,' Gn 46:34 1
shepherds, both we and our f." Gn 47:3 1
they attained the years that my f lived Gn 47:9 1
but when I lie down with my f, Gn 47:30 1
my f Abraham and Isaac walked, Gn 48:15 1
names of my f Abraham and Isaac; Gn 48:16 1
you back to the land of your f. Gn 48:21 1
bury me with my f in the cave that Gn 49:29 1
God of your f has sent me to you.' Ex 3:13 1
'The LORD, the God of your f, Ex 3:15 1
'The LORD, the God of your f, Ex 3:16 1
that the LORD, the God of their f, Ex 4:5 1
something which neither your f nor Ex 10:6 1
He swore to your f to give you, Ex 13:5 1
as He swore to you and to your f, Ex 13:11 1
iniquity of the f on the children, Ex 20:5 1
visiting the iniquity of f on the Ex 34:7 1
You swore to their f'? Nu 11:12 1
visiting the iniquity of the f on Nu 14:18 1
the land which I swore to their f, Nu 14:23 1
that our f went down to Egypt, and Nu 20:15 1
treated us and our f badly. Nu 20:15 1
names of the tribes of their f. Nu 26:55 1
"This is what your f did when I Nu 32:8 1
according to the tribes of your f. Nu 33:54 1
from the inheritance of our f and will Nu 36:3 1
the inheritance of the tribe of our f." Nu 36:4 1

inheritance of the tribe of his **f**.	Nu 36:7	1
possess the inheritance of his **f**.	Nu 36:8	1
the LORD swore to give to your **f**,	Dt 1:8	1
'May the LORD, the God of your **f**,	Dt 1:11	1
as the LORD, the God of your **f**,	Dt 1:21	1
land which I swore to give your **f**,	Dt 1:35	1
which the LORD, the God of your **f**,	Dt 4:1	1
your **f** which He swore to them.	Dt 4:31	1
"Because He loved your **f**,	Dt 4:37	1
not make this covenant with our **f**,	Dt 5:3	1
iniquity of the **f** on the children,	Dt 5:9	1
as the LORD, the God of your **f**,	Dt 6:3	1
the land which He swore to your **f**,	Dt 6:10	1
the LORD swore to *give* your **f**,	Dt 6:18	1
land which He had sworn to our **f**.'	Dt 6:23	1
did not know, nor did your **f** know,	Dt 8:3	1
manna which your **f** did not know,	Dt 8:16	1
covenant which He swore to your **f**,	Dt 8:18	1
which the LORD swore to your **f**,	Dt 9:5	1
I swore to their **f** to give them.'	Dt 10:11	1
"Yet on your **f** did the LORD set	Dt 10:15	1
"Your **f** went down to Egypt	Dt 10:22	1
LORD swore to your **f** to give to them	Dt 11:9	1
LORD swore to your **f** to give them,	Dt 11:21	1
which the LORD, the God of your **f**,	Dt 12:1	1
neither you nor your **f** have known,	Dt 13:6	1
just as He has sworn to your **f**,	Dt 13:17	1
just as He has sworn to your **f**,	Dt 19:8	1
which He promised to give your **f**	Dt 19:8	1
"**F** shall not be put to death for	Dt 24:16	1
sons be put to death for *their* **f**;	Dt 24:16	1
LORD swore to our **f** to give us.'	Dt 26:3	1
to the LORD, the God of our **f**,	Dt 26:7	1
as You swore to our **f**.'	Dt 26:15	1
as the LORD, the God of your **f**,	Dt 27:3	1
LORD swore to your **f** to give you.	Dt 28:11	1
neither you nor your **f** have known,	Dt 28:36	1
you or your **f** have not known.	Dt 28:64	1
to you and as He swore to your **f**,	Dt 29:13	1
of the LORD, the God of their **f**,	Dt 29:25	1
the land which your **f** possessed,	Dt 30:5	1
and multiply you more than your **f**.	Dt 30:5	1
just as He rejoiced over your **f**;	Dt 30:9	1
which the LORD swore to your **f**,	Dt 30:20	1
has sworn to their **f** to give them,	Dt 31:7	1
are about to lie down with your **f**;	Dt 31:16	1
honey, which I swore to their **f**,	Dt 31:20	1
lately, Whom your **f** did not dread.	Dt 32:17	1
I swore to their **f** to give them.	Jos 1:6	1
ask their **f** in time to come,	Jos 4:21	1
had sworn to their **f** to give us,	Jos 5:6	1
which the LORD, the God of your **f**,	Jos 18:3	1
He had sworn to give to their **f**,	Jos 21:43	1
all that He had sworn to their **f**,	Jos 21:44	1
of the LORD which our **f** made,	Jos 22:28	1
your **f** lived beyond the River,	Jos 24:2	1
'I brought your **f** out of Egypt,	Jos 24:6	1
and Egypt pursued your **f** with	Jos 24:6	1
put away the gods which your **f** served	Jos 24:14	1
the gods which your **f** served	Jos 24:15	1
our **f** up out of the land of Egypt,	Jos 24:17	1
land which I have sworn to your **f**;	Jg 2:1	1
also were gathered to their **f**;	Jg 2:10	1
the LORD, the God of their **f**,	Jg 2:12	1
the way in which their **f** had walked	Jg 2:17	1
they did not do as *their* **f**.	Jg 2:17	1
act more corruptly than their **f**,	Jg 2:19	1
which I commanded their **f** and	Jg 2:20	1
LORD to walk in it as their **f** did,	Jg 2:22	1
commanded their **f** through Moses.	Jg 3:4	1
which our **f** told us about,	Jg 6:13	1
when their **f** or their brothers	Jg 21:22	1
your **f** up from the land of Egypt.	1Sa 12:6	1
which He did for you and your **f**.	1Sa 12:7	1
and your **f** cried out to the LORD,	1Sa 12:8	1
who brought your **f** out of Egypt	1Sa 12:8	1
you, *as it was* against your **f**.	1Sa 12:15	1
and you lie down with your **f**,	2Sa 7:12	1
lord the king sleeps with his **f**,	1Ki 1:21	1
Then David slept with his **f** and	1Ki 2:10	1
which He made with our **f** when He	1Ki 8:21	1
which You gave to their **f**.	1Ki 8:34	1
which You have given to our **f**.	1Ki 8:40	1
which You have given to their **f**,	1Ki 8:48	1
brought our **f** forth from Egypt,	1Ki 8:53	1
be with us, as He was with our **f**;	1Ki 8:57	1
which He commanded our **f**.	1Ki 8:58	1
their **f** out of the land of Egypt,	1Ki 9:9	1
Egypt that David slept with his **f** and	1Ki 11:21	1
And Solomon slept with his **f** and	1Ki 11:43	1
come to the grave of your **f**.' "	1Ki 13:22	1
land which He gave to their **f**,	1Ki 14:15	1
and he slept with his **f**,	1Ki 14:20	1
than all that their **f** had done,	1Ki 14:22	1
And Rehoboam slept with his **f** and	1Ki 14:31	1
with his **f** in the city of David;	1Ki 14:31	1
And Abijam slept with his **f** and	1Ki 15:8	1
the idols which his **f** had made.	1Ki 15:12	1
And Asa slept with his **f** and was	1Ki 15:24	1
buried with his **f** in the city of David	1Ki 15:24	1
his **f** and was buried in Tirzah,	1Ki 16:6	1
So Omri slept with his **f** and	1Ki 16:28	1
for I am not better than my **f**."	1Ki 19:4	1
you the inheritance of my **f**."	1Ki 21:3	1
you the inheritance of my **f**."	1Ki 21:4	1
So Ahab slept with his **f**,	1Ki 22:40	1
And Jehoshaphat slept with his **f**	1Ki 22:50	1
and was buried with his **f** in the city	1Ki 22:50	1
So Joram slept with his **f** and	2Ki 8:24	1
with his **f** in the city of David;	2Ki 8:24	1
with his **f** in the city of David.	2Ki 9:28	1
And Jehu slept with his **f**,	2Ki 10:35	1
and Jehoram and Ahaziah, his **f**,	2Ki 12:18	1
with his **f** in the city of David,	2Ki 12:21	1
And Jehoahaz slept with his **f**,	2Ki 13:9	1
So Joash slept with his **f**,	2Ki 13:13	1
"The **f** shall not be put to death	2Ki 14:6	1
sons be put to death for the **f**;	2Ki 14:6	1
So Jehoash slept with his **f** and	2Ki 14:16	1
with his **f** in the city of David.	2Ki 14:20	1
after the king slept with his **f**.	2Ki 14:22	1
And Jeroboam slept with his **f**,	2Ki 14:29	1
And Azariah slept with his **f**,	2Ki 15:7	1
with his **f** in the city of David,	2Ki 15:7	1
of the LORD, as his **f** had done;	2Ki 15:9	1
And Menahem slept with his **f**,	2Ki 15:22	1
And Jotham slept with his **f**,	2Ki 15:38	1
and he was buried with his **f** in	2Ki 15:38	1
So Ahaz slept with his **f**,	2Ki 16:20	1
with his **f** in the city of David;	2Ki 16:20	1
the law which I commanded your **f**,	2Ki 17:13	1
stiffened their neck like their **f**,	2Ki 17:14	1
which He made with their **f** and	2Ki 17:15	1
grandchildren, as their **f** did,	2Ki 17:41	1
which my **f** destroyed deliver them,	2Ki 19:12	1
and all that your **f** have laid up	2Ki 20:17	1
So Hezekiah slept with his **f**,	2Ki 20:21	1
the land which I gave their **f**,	2Ki 21:8	1
the day their **f** came from Egypt,	2Ki 21:15	1
And Manasseh slept with his **f** and	2Ki 21:18	1
the LORD, the God of his **f**,	2Ki 21:22	1
because our **f** have not listened to	2Ki 22:13	1
I will gather you to your **f**,	2Ki 22:20	1
to all that his **f** had done.	2Ki 23:32	1
to all that his **f** had done.	2Ki 23:37	1
So Jehoiakim slept with his **f**,	2Ki 24:6	1
were the **f** of Keilah the Garmite	1Ch 4:19	1
against the God of their **f** and	1Ch 5:25	1
and their **f** had been over the camp	1Ch 9:19	1
of our **f** look on *it* and decide."	1Ch 12:17	1
you must go *to be* with your **f**,	1Ch 17:11	2
and tenants, as all our **f** were;	1Ch 29:15	1
Abraham, Isaac and Israel, our **f**,	1Ch 29:18	1
the LORD, the God of their **f**,	1Ch 29:20	1
have given to them and to their **f**.	2Ch 6:25	1
which You have given to our **f**.	2Ch 6:31	1
which You have given to their **f** and	2Ch 6:38	1
the LORD, the God of their **f** who	2Ch 7:22	1
And Solomon slept with his **f** and	2Ch 9:31	1
to the LORD God of their **f**.	2Ch 11:16	1
And Rehoboam slept with his **f** and	2Ch 12:16	1
against the LORD God of your **f**,	2Ch 13:12	1
in the LORD, the God of their **f**.	2Ch 13:18	1
So Abijah slept with his **f**,	2Ch 14:1	1
to seek the LORD God of their **f**	2Ch 14:4	1
to seek the LORD God of their **f**	2Ch 15:12	1
So Asa slept with his **f**,	2Ch 16:13	1
to the LORD, the God of their **f**.	2Ch 19:4	1
"O LORD, the God of our **f**,	2Ch 20:6	1
hearts to the God of their **f**.	2Ch 20:33	1
Then Jehoshaphat slept with his **f**	2Ch 21:1	1
with his **f** in the city of David,	2Ch 21:1	1
forsaken the LORD God of his **f**.	2Ch 21:10	1
for him like the fire for his **f**.	2Ch 21:19	1
of the LORD, the God of their **f**,	2Ch 24:18	1
the LORD, the God of their **f**.	2Ch 24:24	1
"**F** shall not be put to death for	2Ch 25:4	1
nor sons be put to death for **f**,	2Ch 25:4	1
with his **f** in the city of Judah.	2Ch 25:28	1
after the king slept with his **f**.	2Ch 26:2	1
So Uzziah slept with his **f**,	2Ch 26:23	1
and they buried him with his **f** in	2Ch 26:23	1
And Jotham slept with his **f**,	2Ch 27:9	1
forsaken the LORD God of their **f**.	2Ch 28:6	1
the LORD, the God of your **f**,	2Ch 28:9	1
the LORD, the God of his **f**,	2Ch 28:25	1
So Ahaz slept with his **f**,	2Ch 28:27	1
of the LORD, the God of your **f**,	2Ch 29:5	1
"For our **f** have been unfaithful	2Ch 29:6	1
our **f** have fallen by the sword,	2Ch 29:9	1
be like your **f** and your brothers,	2Ch 30:7	1
to the LORD God of their **f**.	2Ch 30:7	1
not stiffen your neck like your **f**,	2Ch 30:8	1
seek God, the LORD God of his **f**,	2Ch 30:19	1
thanks to the LORD God of their **f**.	2Ch 30:22	1
what I and my **f** have done to all	2Ch 32:13	1
nations which my **f** utterly destroyed	2Ch 32:14	1
my hand or from the hand of my **f**.	2Ch 32:15	1
So Hezekiah slept with his **f**,	2Ch 32:33	1
which I have appointed for your **f**,	2Ch 33:8	1
greatly before the God of his **f**.	2Ch 33:12	1
So Manasseh slept with his **f**,	2Ch 33:20	1
our **f** have not observed the word	2Ch 34:21	1
I will gather you to your **f** and	2Ch 34:28	1
of God, the God of their **f**.	2Ch 34:32	1
following the LORD God of their **f**.	2Ch 34:33	1
was buried in the tombs of his **f**.	2Ch 35:24	1
The LORD, the God of their **f**,	2Ch 36:15	1
in the record books of your **f**.	Ezr 4:15	2
'But because our **f** had provoked	Ezr 5:12	2
be the LORD, the God of our **f**,	Ezr 7:27	1
to the LORD God of your **f**.	Ezr 8:28	1
"Since the days of our **f** to this	Ezr 9:7	1
to the LORD God of your **f** and	Ezr 10:11	1
and the iniquities of their **f**.	Ne 9:2	1
the affliction of our **f** in Egypt,	Ne 9:9	1
"But they, our **f**, acted arrogantly	Ne 9:16	1
told their **f** to enter and possess.	Ne 9:23	1
our priests, our prophets, our **f** and	Ne 9:32	1
and our **f** have not kept Your law Or	Ne 9:34	1
land which You gave to our **f**	Ne 9:36	1
"Did not your **f** do the same,	Ne 13:18	1
things searched out by their **f**.	Jb 8:8	1
have not concealed from their **f**,	Jb 15:18	1
Whose **f** I disdained to put with	Jb 30:1	1
In You our **f** trusted;	Ps 22:4	1
You, A sojourner like all my **f**.	Ps 39:12	1
with our ears, Our **f** have told us The	Ps 44:1	1
place of your **f** will be your sons;	Ps 45:16	1
go to the generation of his **f**;	Ps 49:19	1
and known, And our **f** have told us.	Ps 78:3	1
Israel, Which He commanded our **f** That	Ps 78:5	1
And not be like their **f**,	Ps 78:8	1
He wrought wonders before their **f** In	Ps 78:12	1
acted treacherously like their **f**;	Ps 78:57	1
"When your **f** tested Me, They	Ps 95:9	1
We have sinned like our **f**,	Ps 106:6	1
Our **f** in Egypt did not understand	Ps 106:7	1
f be remembered before the LORD,	Ps 109:14	1
And the glory of sons is their **f**.	Pr 17:6	1
wealth are an inheritance from **f**,	Pr 19:14	1
boundary Which your **f** have set.	Pr 22:28	1
If a man **f** a hundred *children* and	Ec 6:3	3205
of the iniquity of their **f**.	Is 14:21	1
my **f** have destroyed deliver them,	Is 37:12	1
and all that your **f** have laid up	Is 39:6	1
house, Where our **f** praised You,	Is 64:11	1
iniquities of their **f** together,"	Is 65:7	1
injustice did your **f** find in Me,	Jer 2:5	1
I gave your **f** as an inheritance.	Jer 3:18	1
labor of our **f** since our youth,	Jer 3:24	1
the LORD our God, we and our **f**,	Jer 3:25	1
against them, **F** and sons together;	Jer 6:21	1
I gave to your **f** forever and ever.	Jer 7:7	1
place which I gave you and your **f**,	Jer 7:14	1
wood, and the **f** kindle the fire,	Jer 7:18	1
"For I did not speak to your **f**,	Jer 7:22	1
"Since the day that your **f** came	Jer 7:25	1
they did more evil than their **f**.	Jer 7:26	1
Baals, as their **f** taught them,"	Jer 9:14	1
they nor their **f** have known;	Jer 9:16	1
'For I solemnly warned your **f** in	Jer 11:7	1
covenant which I made with their **f**."	Jer 11:10	1
the **f** and the sons together,"	Jer 13:14	1
O LORD, The iniquity of our **f**,	Jer 14:20	1
f who beget them in this land:	Jer 16:3	1
not known, neither you nor your **f**;	Jer 16:13	1
own land which I gave to their **f**.	Jer 16:15	1
"Our **f** have inherited nothing but	Jer 16:19	1
just as their **f** forgot My name	Jer 23:27	1
city which I gave you and your **f**.	Jer 23:39	1
the **f** of sons and daughters,	Jer 29:6	3205
'The **f** have eaten sour grapes, And	Jer 31:29	1
covenant which I made with their **f**	Jer 31:32	1
but repays the iniquity of **f**	Jer 32:18	1
as *spices* were burned for your **f**,	Jer 34:5	1
neither they, you, nor your **f**.	Jer 44:3	1
the wickedness of your **f**,	Jer 44:9	1
before you and before your **f**,"	Jer 44:10	1
The **f** have not turned back for	Jer 47:3	1
the LORD, the hope of their **f**.'	Jer 50:7	1
Our **f** sinned, *and* are no more;	La 5:7	1
they and their **f** have transgressed	Ezk 2:3	1
f will eat *their* sons among you,	Ezk 5:10	1
you, and sons will eat their **f**;	Ezk 5:10	1
'The **f** eat the sour grapes, But	Ezk 18:2	1
know the abominations of their **f**;	Ezk 20:4	1
walk in the statutes of your **f** or	Ezk 20:18	1
eyes were on the idols of their **f**.	Ezk 20:24	1
"Yet in this your **f** have blasphemed	Ezk 20:27	1
after the manner of your **f** and play	Ezk 20:30	1
I entered into judgment with your **f**	Ezk 20:36	1
My servant, in which your **f** lived;	Ezk 37:25	1
"To You, O God of my **f**,	Da 2:23	2
to our kings, our princes, our **f** and	Da 9:6	1
our kings, our princes and our **f**,	Da 9:8	1
sins and the iniquities of our **f**,	Da 9:16	1
accomplish what his **f** never did,	Da 11:24	1
his **f** or for the desire of women,	Da 11:37	1
a god whom his **f** did not know;	Da 11:38	1
Those after which their **f** walked.	Am 2:4	1
LORD was very angry with your **f**.	Zch 1:2	1
"Do not be like your **f**,	Zch 1:4	1
"Your **f**, where are they?	Zch 1:5	1
the prophets, overtake your **f**?	Zch 1:6	1
when your **f** provoked Me to wrath,'	Zch 8:14	1
to profane the covenant of our **f**?	Mal 2:10	1
"From the days of your **f** you have	Mal 3:7	1
hearts of the **f** to *their* children and	Mal 4:6	1
hearts of the children to their **f**,	Mal 4:6	1
been *living* in the days of our **f**,	Mt 23:30	*3962*
measure *of the guilt* of your **f**.	Mt 23:32	*3962*
OF THE **F** BACK TO THE CHILDREN,	Lk 1:17	*3962*
As He spoke to our **f**,	Lk 1:55	*3962*
To show mercy toward our **f**,	Lk 1:72	*3962*
f used to treat the prophets.	Lk 6:23	*3962*
their **f** used to treat the false prophets in	Lk 6:26	*3962*
"Now suppose one of you **f** is	Lk 11:11	*3962*
and *it was* your **f** *who* killed them.	Lk 11:47	*3962*
and approve the deeds of your **f**;	Lk 11:48	*3962*
"Our **f** worshiped in this	Jn 4:20	*3962*
"Our **f** ate the manna in the	Jn 6:31	*3962*
"Your **f** ate the manna in the	Jn 6:49	*3962*
not as the **f** ate and died; he who	Jn 6:58	*3962*
it is from Moses, but from the **f**),	Jn 7:22	*3962*
and Jacob, the God of our **f**,	Ac 3:13	*3962*
which God made with your **f**,	Ac 3:25	*3962*

“The God of our **f** raised up Ac 5:30 *3962*
“Hear me, brethren and **f**! Ac 7:2 *3962*
and our **f** could find no food. Ac 7:11 *3962*
sent our **f** *there* the first time. Ac 7:12 *3962*
there he and our **f** died. Ac 7:15 *3962*
and mistreated our **f** so that they Ac 7:19 *3962*
‘I AM THE GOD OF YOUR F, Ac 7:32 *3962*
Sinai, and *who was* with our **f**; Ac 7:38 *3962*
Our **f** were unwilling to be obedient Ac 7:39 *3962*
“Our **f** had the tabernacle of Ac 7:44 *3962*
our **f** brought it in with Joshua Ac 7:45 *3962*
whom God drove out before our **f**, Ac 7:45 *3962*
you are doing just as your **f** did. Ac 7:51 *3962*
prophets did your **f** not persecute? Ac 7:52 *3962*
of this people Israel chose our **f** and Ac 13:17 *3962*
news of the promise made to the **f**, Ac 13:32 *3962*
asleep, and was laid among his **f** and Ac 13:36 *3962*
f nor we have been able to bear? Ac 15:10 *3962*
“Brethren and **f**, hear my defense Ac 22:1 *3962*
according to the law of our **f**, Ac 22:3 *3971*
‘The God of our **f** has appointed Ac 22:14 *3962*
sect I do serve the God of our **f**, Ac 24:14 *3971*
the promise made by God to our **f**; Ac 26:6 *3962*
people or the customs of our **f**, Ac 28:17 *3971*
Isaiah the prophet to your **f**, Ac 28:25 *3962*
whose are the **f**, and from whom is Ro 9:5 *3962*
are beloved for the sake of the **f**; Ro 11:28 *3962*
the promises *given* to the **f**, Ro 15:8 *3962*
yet *you would* not *have* many **f**, 1Co 4:15 *3962*
our **f** were all under the cloud and 1Co 10:1 *3962*
F, do not provoke your children to Eph 6:4 *3962*
F, do not exasperate your Col 3:21 *3962*
those who kill their **f** or mothers, 1Tm 1:9 *3970a*
after He spoke long ago to the **f** Heb 1:1 *3962*
YOUR F TRIED *Me* BY TESTING *Me*, Heb 3:9 *3962*
WHICH I MADE WITH THEIR F ON THE Heb 8:9 *3962*
we had earthly **f** to discipline us, Heb 12:9 *3962*
For *ever* since the **f** fell asleep, 2Pe 3:4 *3962*
I am writing to you, **f**, 1Jn 2:13 *3962*
I have written to you, **f**, 1Jn 2:14 *3962*

FATHERS'

heads of their **f** households. Ex 6:14 1
heads of the **f** *households* Ex 6:25 1
according to their **f** households, a Ex 12:3 1
by their **f** households, according Nu 1:2 1
the leaders of their **f** tribes; Nu 1:16 1
by their **f** households, according Nu 1:18 1
by their **f** households, according Nu 1:20 1
by their **f** households, their Nu 1:22 1
by their **f** households, according Nu 1:24 1
by their **f** households, according Nu 1:26 1
by their **f** households, according Nu 1:28 1
by their **f** households, according Nu 1:30 1
by their **f** households, according Nu 1:32 1
by their **f** households, according Nu 1:34 1
by their **f** households, according Nu 1:36 1
by their **f** households, according Nu 1:38 1
by their **f** households, according Nu 1:40 1
by their **f** households, according Nu 1:42 1
of Israel by their **f** households, Nu 1:45 1
among them by their **f** tribe. Nu 1:47 1
banners of their **f** households; Nu 2:2 1
of Israel by their **f** households; Nu 2:32 1
sons of Levi by their **f** households, Nu 3:15 1
according to their **f** households. Nu 3:20 1
and the leader of the **f** households Nu 3:24 1
and the leader of the **f** households Nu 3:30 1
The leader of the **f** households of Nu 3:35 1
by their **f** households, Nu 4:2 1
by their **f** households, by their Nu 4:22 1
by their **f** households; Nu 4:29 1
and by their **f** households, Nu 4:34 1
and by their **f** households, Nu 4:38 1
by their **f** households, were 2,630. Nu 4:40 1
by their **f** households, Nu 4:42 1
and by their **f** households, Nu 4:46 1
the heads of their **f** households, Nu 7:2 1
send a man from each of their **f** tribes, Nu 13:2 1
according to their **f** households. Nu 17:2 1
of each of their **f** households. Nu 17:3 1
according to their **f** households, Nu 17:6 1
by their **f** households, whoever is Nu 26:2 1
the heads of the **f** *households* Nu 31:26 1
you have risen up in your **f** place, Nu 32:14 1
and to the heads of the **f** Nu 32:28 1
to their **f** households, Nu 34:14 1
to their **f** households, Nu 34:14 1
And the heads of the **f** *households* Nu 36:1 1
the heads of the **f** *households* Nu 36:1 1
receive from the sale of their **f** Dt 18:8 1
the leaders of the **f** *households* 1Ki 8:1 1
and their **f** houses increased 1Ch 4:38 1
Their kinsmen of their **f** households 1Ch 5:13 1
was head of their **f** households. 1Ch 5:15 1
heads of their **f** households, 1Ch 5:24 1
heads of their **f** households. 1Ch 5:24 1
according to their **f** *households*. 1Ch 6:19 1
heads of their **f** households. *The* 1Ch 7:2 1
according to their **f** households 1Ch 7:4 1
They *were* heads of **f** households, 1Ch 7:7 1
heads of their **f** households, 20,200 1Ch 7:9 1
the heads of their **f** households, 1Ch 7:11 1
heads of the **f** houses, choice 1Ch 7:40 1
these are the heads of **f** *households* 1Ch 8:6 1
heads of **f** *households*. 1Ch 8:10 1
who were heads of **f** *households* 1Ch 8:13 1
heads of the **f** *households* 1Ch 8:28 1
were heads of **f** *households* 1Ch 9:9 1
according to their **f** houses. 1Ch 9:9 1
heads of their **f** households, 1,760 1Ch 9:13 1
heads of **f** *households* of 1Ch 9:33 1
These were heads of **f** *households* 1Ch 9:34 1
famous men in their **f** households. 1Ch 12:30 1
heads of the **f** *households* 1Ch 15:12 1
the heads of the **f** *households* 1Ch 23:9 1
according to their **f** households, 1Ch 23:24 1
heads of the **f** *households* 1Ch 23:24 1
sixteen heads of **f** households 1Ch 24:4 1
according to their **f** households. 1Ch 24:4 1
and the heads of the **f** *households* 1Ch 24:6 1
according to their **f** households. 1Ch 24:30 1
and the heads of the **f** *households* 1Ch 24:31 1
Levites—the head of **f** *households* 1Ch 24:31 1
according to their **f** households, 1Ch 26:13 1
heads of the **f** *households*, 1Ch 26:21 1
and the heads of the **f** *households*, 1Ch 26:26 1
their genealogies and **f** *households*, 1Ch 26:31 1
heads of **f** *households*. 1Ch 26:32 1
the heads of **f** *households*, 1Ch 27:1 1
rulers of the **f** *households*, 1Ch 29:6 1
the heads of the **f** *households*. 2Ch 1:2 1
the leaders of the **f** *households* 2Ch 5:2 1
muster according to their **f** households: 2Ch 17:14 1
the heads of the **f** *households* 2Ch 19:8 1
and the heads of the **f** *households* 2Ch 23:2 1
to *their* **f** households 2Ch 25:5 1
according to their **f** households, 2Ch 31:17 1
yourselves by your **f** households 2Ch 35:4 1
the sections of the **f** households 2Ch 35:5 1
to the sections of the **f** households 2Ch 35:12 1
Then the heads of **f** *households* Ezr 1:5 1
give evidence of their **f** households Ezr 2:59 1
Some of the heads of **f** *households*, Ezr 2:68 1
Levites and heads of **f** *households*, Ezr 3:12 1
heads of **f** *households*, Ezr 4:2 1
rest of the heads of **f** *households* Ezr 4:3 1
the heads of their **f** *households* Ezr 8:1 1
the heads of the **f** *households* Ezr 8:29 1
who were heads of **f** *households* Ezr 10:16 1
the place of my **f** tombs, lies Ne 2:3 1
to the city of my **f** tombs, that I Ne 2:5 1
could not show their **f** houses Ne 7:61 1
the heads of **f** *households* Ne 7:70 1
Some of the heads of **f** *households* Ne 7:71 1
the heads of **f** *households* Ne 8:13 1
according to our **f** households, at Ne 10:34 1
heads of **f** *households*, Ne 11:13 1
the heads of **f** *households* were: Ne 12:12 1
Levites, the heads of **f** *households* Ne 12:22 1
Levi, the heads of **f** *households*, Ne 12:23 1
have uncovered *their* **f** nakedness; Ezk 22:10 1
in your days Or in your **f** days? Jl 1:2 1

FATHOMS

and found *it to be* twenty **f**; Ac 27:28 *3712*
and found *it to be* fifteen **f**. Ac 27:28 *3712*

FATLING

he sacrificed an ox and a **f**. 2Sa 6:13 4806
the young lion and the **f** together; Is 11:6 4806

FATLINGS

of the sheep, the oxen, the **f**, 1Sa 15:9 4932
and **f** by the stone of Zoheleth, 1Ki 1:9 4806
oxen and **f** and sheep in abundance, 1Ki 1:19 4806
oxen and **f** and sheep in abundance, 1Ki 1:25 4806
bulls, all of them **f** of Bashan. Ezk 39:18 4806
at the peace offerings of your **f**. Am 5:22 4806

FATNESS

heaven, And of the **f** of the earth, Gn 27:28 8082b
‘Shall I leave my **f** with which God Jg 9:9 1880
set on your table was full of **f**. Jb 36:16 1880
is satisfied as with marrow and **f**, Ps 63:5 1880
bounty, And Your paths drip *with* **f**. Ps 65:11 1880
Their eye bulges from **f**; Ps 73:7 2459
flesh has grown lean, without **f**. Ps 109:24 8081
yoke will be broken because of **f**. Is 10:27 8081
f of his flesh will become lean. Is 17:4 4924a

FATTENED

woman had a **f** calf in the house, 1Sa 28:24 4770
gazelles, roebucks, and **f** fowl. 1Ki 4:23 75
Than a **f** ox *served* with hatred. Pr 15:17 75
in her midst Are like **f** calves, Jer 46:21 4770
my oxen and my **f** livestock are *all* Mt 22:4 *4619b*
and bring the **f** calf, kill it, and Lk 15:23 *4618b*
your father has killed the **f** calf because Lk 15:27 *4618b*
you killed the **f** calf for him.’ Lk 15:30 *4618b*
you have **f** your hearts in a day of Jas 5:5 *5142*

FATTER

and they were **f** than all the youths Da 1:15 1277, 1320

FAULT

it is the **f** of your *own* people.” Ex 5:16 2398
and I have found no **f** in him from 1Sa 29:3 3972
Yet let no one find **f**, Hos 4:4 7378
go and show him his **f** in private; if Mt 18:15 *1651*
“Why does He still find **f**? Ro 9:19 *3201*
For finding **f** with them, He says, Heb 8:8 *3201*
These are grumblers, finding **f**, Jude 1:16 *3202*

FAULTFINDER

the **f** contend with the Almighty? Jb 40:2 3250

FAULTLESS

if that first *covenant* had been **f**, Heb 8:7 *273*

FAULTS

Acquit me of hidden **f**. Ps 19:12

FAVOR

found **f** in the eyes of the LORD. Gn 6:8 2580
now I have found **f** in Your sight, Gn 18:3 2580
servant has found **f** in your sight, Gn 19:19 2580
I may find **f** in your sight. Gn 32:5 2580
find **f** in the sight of my lord.” Gn 33:8 2580
now I have found **f** in your sight, Gn 33:10 2580
find **f** in the sight of my lord.” Gn 33:15 2580
“If I find **f** in your sight, then Gn 34:11 2580
So Joseph found **f** in his sight and Gn 39:4 2580
and gave him **f** in the sight of the Gn 39:21 2580
us find **f** in the sight of my lord, Gn 47:25 2580
if I have found **f** in your sight, Gn 47:29 2580
now I have found **f** in your sight, Gn 50:4 2580
f in the sight of the Egyptians; Ex 3:21 2580
f in the sight of the Egyptians. Ex 11:3 2580
f in the sight of the Egyptians, Ex 12:36 2580
have also found **f** in My sight.’ Ex 33:12 2580
if I have found **f** in Your sight, Ex 33:13 2580
so that I may find **f** in Your sight. Ex 33:13 2580
that I have found **f** in Your sight, Ex 33:16 2580
for you have found **f** in My sight and Ex 33:17 2580
now I have found **f** in Your sight, Ex 34:9 2580
have I not found **f** in Your sight, Nu 11:11 2580
if I have found **f** in Your sight, Nu 11:15 2580
“If we have found **f** in your sight, Nu 32:5 2580
with them and show no **f** to them. Dt 7:2 2603a
happens that she finds no **f** in his eyes Dt 24:1 2580
the old, nor show **f** to the young. Dt 28:50 2603a
f of Him who dwelt in the bush. Dt 33:16 7522
“O Naphtali, satisfied with **f**, Dt 33:23 7522
now I have found **f** in Your sight, Jg 6:17 2580
one in whose sight I may find **f**.” Ru 2:2 2580
“Why have I found **f** in your sight Ru 2:10 2580
“I have found **f** in your sight, my Ru 2:13 2580
maidservant find **f** in your sight.” 1Sa 1:18 2580
in **f** both with the LORD and with men 1Sa 2:26 2896a
have not asked the **f** of the LORD.’ 1Sa 13:12 6440
for he has found **f** in my sight.” 1Sa 16:22 2580
that I have found **f** in your sight, 1Sa 20:3 2580
if I have found **f** in your sight, 1Sa 20:29 2580
my young men find **f** in your eyes, 1Sa 25:8 2580
now I have found **f** in your sight, 1Sa 27:5 2580
that I have found **f** in your sight, 2Sa 14:22 2580
I find **f** in the sight of the LORD, 2Sa 15:25 2580
let me find **f** in your sight, O my 2Sa 16:4 2580
found great **f** before Pharaoh, 1Ki 11:19 2580
entreated the **f** of the LORD, 2Ki 13:4 6440
servant has found **f** before you, Ne 2:5 3190
pleased him and found **f** with him. Es 2:9 2617a
And Esther found **f** in the eyes of Es 2:15 2580
and she found **f** and kindness with Es 2:17 2580
to go in to the king to implore his **f** Es 4:8 2603a
she obtained **f** in his sight; Es 5:2 2580
found **f** in the sight of the king, Es 5:8 2580
“If I have found **f** in your sight, Es 7:3 2580
if I have found **f** before him and the Es 8:5 2580
and in **f** with his many kinsmen, Es 10:3 7521
And many would entreat your **f**. Jb 11:19 6440
“His sons **f** the poor, And his Jb 20:10 7521
You surround him with **f** as Ps 5:12 7522
a moment, His **f** is for a lifetime; Ps 30:5 7522
by Your **f** You have made my Ps 30:7 7522
and rejoice, who **f** my vindication; Ps 35:27 2655
the people will seek your **f**. Ps 45:12 6440
By Your **f** do good to Zion; Ps 51:18 7522
You showed **f** to Your land; Ps 85:1 7521
And by Your **f** our horn is exalted. Ps 89:17 7522
Let the **f** of the Lord our God Ps 90:17 5278
LORD, in *Your* **f** toward Your people; Ps 106:4 7522
sought Your **f** with all *my* heart; Ps 119:58 6440
So you will find **f** and good repute Pr 3:4 2580
life And obtains **f** from the LORD. Pr 8:35 7522
who diligently seeks good seeks **f**, Pr 11:27 7522
man will obtain **f** from the LORD, Pr 12:2 7522
Good understanding produces **f**, Pr 13:15 2580
The king's **f** is toward a servant Pr 14:35 7522
And his **f** is like a cloud with the Pr 16:15 7522
And obtains **f** from the LORD. Pr 18:22 7522
seek the **f** of a generous man, Pr 19:6 6440
his **f** is like dew on the grass. Pr 19:12 7522
neighbor finds no **f** in his eyes. Pr 21:10 2603a
F is better than silver and gold. Pr 22:1 2580
find *more* **f** Than he who flatters Pr 28:23 2580
Many seek the ruler's **f**, Pr 29:26 6440
nor **f** to men of ability; Ec 9:11 2580
Though the wicked is shown **f**, Is 26:10 2603a
My **f** I have had compassion on you. Is 60:10 7522
for I will grant you no **f**.’ Jer 16:13 2594
and entreat the **f** of the LORD, Jer 26:19 6440
showed **f** to Jehoiachin king of Jer 52:31 5375, 7218
They did not **f** the elders. La 4:16 2603a
Now God granted Daniel **f** and Da 1:9 2617a
and judgment was passed in **f** of Da 7:22
yet we have not sought the **f** of Da 9:13 2470b, 6440
He wept and sought His **f**. Hos 12:4 2603a
can not look on wickedness *with* **f**. Hab 1:13
Why do You look with **f** On those Hab 1:13
men to seek the **f** of the LORD, Zch 7:2 2470b
once to entreat the **f** of the LORD, Zch 8:21 2470b, 6440
and to entreat the **f** of the LORD.’ Zch 8:22 2470b, 6440
the one I called **F** and Zch 11:7 5278
I took my staff **F** Zch 11:10 5278
now will you not entreat God's **f**, Mal 1:9 6440
accepts *it with* **f** from your hand. Mal 2:13 7522
in the days when He looked *with* **f** Lk 1:25
for you have found **f** with God. Lk 1:30 *5485*
and in **f** with God and men. Lk 2:52 *5485*
and having **f** with all the people. Ac 2:47 *5485*

and granted him f and wisdom in Ac 7:10 5485
"*David* found f in God's sight, Ac 7:46 5485
and wishing to do the Jews a f, Ac 24:27 5485
wishing to do the Jews a f, Ac 25:9 5485
his wage is not credited as a f, Ro 4:4 5485
the f bestowed on us through 2Co 1:11 5486
urging for the f of participation in 2Co 8:4 5485
For am I now seeking the f of men, Ga 1:10 3982
For this *finds* f, if for the sake 1Pe 2:19 5485
endure it, this *finds* f with God. 1Pe 2:20 5485

FAVORABLE
will give Pharaoh a f answer." Gn 41:16 7965
are uniformly f to the king. 1Ki 22:13 2896a
are uniformly f to the king. 2Ch 18:12 2896a
hand of my God had been f to me and Ne 2:18 2896a
And will He never be f again? Ps 77:7 7521
"In a f time I have answered You, Is 49:8 7522
proclaim the f year of the LORD And Is 61:2 7522
made judgment f for your sisters. Ezk 16:52 6419
PROCLAIM THE F YEAR OF THE LORD." Lk 4:19 *1184*

FAVORABLY
God, and you have received me f. Gn 33:10 7521
saw that he had interpreted f, Gn 40:16 2896a
of one of them, and speak f." 1Ki 22:13 2896a
be like one of them and speak f." 2Ch 18:12 2896a
"The hand of our God is f disposed Ezr 8:22 2899b
look f on the schemes of the wicked? Jb 10:3 3313

FAVORED
May he be f by his brothers, And Dt 33:24 7521
presence, For You f them. Ps 44:3 7521
"Greetings, f one! The Lord *is* with Lk 1:28 *5487*

FAVORITE
bread, And his soul f food. Jb 33:20 8378

FAVORITISM
with *an attitude of* personal f. Jas 2:1 *4382*

FAVORS
f Joab and whoever is for David, 2Sa 20:11 2654a
The LORD f those who fear Him, Ps 147:11 7521
have scattered your f to the strangers Jer 3:13 1870

FAWNS
"Your two breasts are like two f, SS 4:5 6082
"Your two breasts are like two f, SS 7:3 6082

FEAR
"The f of you and the terror Gn 9:2 4172
for f you would say, 'I have made Gn 14:23
"Do not f, Abram, I am a shield Gn 15:1 3372a
is no f of God in this place, Gn 20:11 3374
Do not f, for God has heard the Gn 21:17 3372a
for now I know that you f God, Gn 22:12 3372a
Do not f, for I am with you. Gn 26:24 3372a
of Abraham, and the f of Isaac, Gn 31:42 6343
by the f of his father Isaac. Gn 31:53 6343
for I f him, that he will come and Gn 32:11 3372a
"Do not f, for now you have Gn 35:17 3372a
"Do this and live, for I f God: Gn 42:18 3372a
if the lad is not with me—for I f Gn 44:34 6435
you do not yet f the LORD God." Ex 9:30 3372a
Moses said to the people, "Do not f! Ex 14:13 3372a
all the people able men who f God, Ex 18:21 3372a
the f of Him may remain with you, Ex 20:20 3374
another, but you shall f your God; Lv 25:17 3372a
do not f the people of the land, Nu 14:9 3372a
the LORD is with us; do not f them." Nu 14:9 3372a
"Do not f him, for I have given Nu 21:34 3372a
in great f because of the people, Nu 22:3 1481c
You shall not f man, for the Dt 1:17 1481c
Do not f or be dismayed.' Dt 1:21 3372a
'Do not be shocked, nor f them. Dt 1:29 3372a
put the dread and f of you upon the Dt 2:25 3374
'Do not f him, for I have Dt 3:2 3372a
'Do not f them, for the LORD your Dt 3:22 3372a
hear My words so they may learn to f Dt 4:10 3372a
in them, that they would f Me and Dt 5:29 3372a
might f the LORD your God, Dt 6:2 3372a
shall f *only* the LORD your God; Dt 6:13 3372a
to f the LORD our God for our good Dt 6:24 3372a
to walk in His ways and to f Him. Dt 8:6 3372a
you, but to f the LORD your God, Dt 10:12 3372a
"You shall f the LORD your God; Dt 10:20 3372a
and the f of you on all the land Dt 11:25 4172
the LORD your God and f Him; Dt 13:4 3372a
to f the LORD your God always. Dt 14:23 3372a
may learn to f the LORD his God, Dt 17:19 3372a
all Israel will hear *of it* and f. Dt 21:21 3372a
and he did not f God. Dt 25:18 3372a
f this honored and awesome name, Dt 28:58 3372a
Do not f or be dismayed." Dt 31:8 3372a
and learn and f the LORD your God, Dt 31:12 3372a
and learn to f the LORD your God, Dt 31:13 3372a
may f the LORD your God forever." Jos 4:24 3372a
"Do not f or be dismayed. Jos 8:1 3372a
"Do not f them, for I have given Jos 10:8 3372a
"Do not f or be dismayed! Jos 10:25 3372a
heart of the people melt with f; Jos 14:8 4529
f the LORD and serve Him in Jos 24:14 3372a
you shall not f the gods of the Jg 6:10 3372a
"Peace to you, do not f; Jg 6:23 3372a
"Now, my daughter, do not f. Ru 3:11 3372a
you will f the LORD and serve Him, 1Sa 12:14 3372a
Samuel said to the people, "Do not f. 1Sa 12:20 3372a
"Only f the LORD and serve Him in 1Sa 12:24 3372a
"Do not f, for I will surely show 2Sa 9:7 3372a
Do not f; have not I myself 2Sa 13:28 3372a
Who rules in the f of God, 2Sa 23:3 3374
that they may f You all the days 1Ki 8:40 3372a
may know Your name, to f You, 1Ki 8:43 3372a
Then Elijah said to her, "Do not f; 1Ki 17:13 3372a

"Do not f, for those who are with 2Ki 6:16 3372a
they did not f the LORD; 2Ki 17:25 3372a
them how they should f the LORD. 2Ki 17:28 3372a
they do not f the LORD, nor do 2Ki 17:34 3372a
"You shall not f other gods, nor 2Ki 17:35 3372a
outstretched arm, Him you shall f, 2Ki 17:36 3372a
and you shall not f other gods. 2Ki 17:37 3372a
nor shall you f other gods. 2Ki 17:38 3372a
"But the LORD your God you shall f; 2Ki 17:39 3372a
the f of him on all the nations. 1Ch 14:17 6343
do not f nor be dismayed. 1Ch 22:13 3372a
do not f nor be dismayed, for the 1Ch 28:20 3372a
that they may f You, to walk in 2Ch 6:31 3372a
may know Your name, and f You as 2Ch 6:33 3372a
let the f of the LORD be upon you; 2Ch 19:7 6343
you shall do in the f of the LORD, 2Ch 19:9 3374
'Do not f or be dismayed because 2Ch 20:15 3372a
Do not f or be dismayed; 2Ch 20:17 3372a
do not f or be dismayed because of 2Ch 32:7 3372a
When I saw *their* f, I rose Ne 4:14
should you not walk in the f of Ne 5:9 3374
not do so because of the f of God. Ne 5:15 3374
"Does Job f God for nothing? Jb 1:9 3372a
"For what I f comes upon me, And Jb 3:25 6342
not your f *of God* your confidence, Jb 4:6 3374
visit your abode and f no loss. Jb 5:24 2398
not forsake the f of the Almighty. Jb 6:14 3374
"*Then* I would speak and not f Him; Jb 9:35 3372a
you would be steadfast and not f. Jb 11:15 3372a
Their houses are safe from f, Jb 21:9 6343
'Behold, the f of the Lord, that Jb 28:28 3374
no f of me should terrify you, Jb 33:7 367
"Therefore men f Him; Jb 37:24 3372a
laughs at f and is not dismayed; Jb 39:22 6343
raises himself up, the mighty f; Jb 41:25 1481c
is like him, One made without f. Jb 41:33 2844a
Put them in f, O LORD; Ps 9:20 4177b
who honors those who f the LORD; Ps 15:4 3372a
The f of the LORD is clean, Ps 19:9 3374
You who f the LORD, praise Him; Ps 22:23 3372a
my vows before those who f Him. Ps 22:25 3372a
the shadow of death, I f no evil, Ps 23:4 3372a
the LORD is for those who f Him, Ps 25:14 3372a
and my salvation; Whom shall I f? Ps 27:1 3372a
against me, My heart will not f; Ps 27:3 3372a
stored up for those who f You, Ps 31:19 3372a
Let all the earth f the LORD; Ps 33:8 3372a
of the LORD is on those who f Him, Ps 33:18 3372a
encamps around those who f Him, Ps 34:7 3372a
O f the LORD, you His saints; Ps 34:9 3372a
For to those who f Him there Ps 34:9 3372a
will teach you the f of the LORD. Ps 34:11 3374
is no f of God before his eyes. Ps 36:1 6343
Many will see and f And Ps 40:3 3372a
Therefore we will not f, Ps 46:2 3372a
should I f in days of adversity, Ps 49:5 3372a
The righteous will see and f, Ps 52:6 3372a
in great f *where* no fear had been; Ps 53:5 6343
in great fear *where* no f had been; Ps 53:5 6343
F and trembling come upon me, Ps 55:5 3374
no change, And who do not f God. Ps 55:19 3372a
a banner to those who f You, Ps 60:4 3372a
of those who f Your name. Ps 61:5 3372a
they shoot at him, and do not f. Ps 64:4 3372a
Then all men will f, Ps 64:9 3372a
Come *and* hear, all who f God, Ps 66:16 3372a
the ends of the earth may f Him. Ps 67:7 3372a
them f You while the sun *endures*, Ps 72:5 3372a
safely, so that they did not f; Ps 78:53 6342
is near to those who f Him, Ps 85:9 3372a
Unite my heart to f Your name. Ps 86:11 3372a
to the f that is due You? Ps 90:11 3374
will f the name of the LORD And Ps 102:15 3372a
toward those who f Him. Ps 103:11 3372a
has compassion on those who f Him. Ps 103:13 3372a
to everlasting on those who f Him, Ps 103:17 3372a
has given food to those who f Him; Ps 111:5 3372a
The f of the LORD is the beginning Ps 111:10 3374
He will not f evil tidings; Ps 112:7 3372a
heart is upheld, he will not f, Ps 112:8 3372a
You who f the LORD, trust in the Ps 115:11 3372a
will bless those who f the LORD, Ps 115:13 3372a
Oh let those who f the LORD say, Ps 118:4 3372a
The LORD is for me; I will not f; Ps 118:6 3372a
companion of all those who f You, Ps 119:63 3372a
who f You see me and be glad, Ps 119:74 3372a
May those who f You turn to me, Ps 119:79 3372a
My flesh trembles for f of You, Ps 119:120 6343
the desire of those who f Him; Ps 145:19 3372a
The LORD favors those who f Him, Ps 147:11 3372a
The f of the LORD is the beginning Pr 1:7 3374
did not choose the f of the LORD. Pr 1:29 3374
will discern the f of the LORD And Pr 2:5 3374
F the LORD and turn away from evil. Pr 3:7 3372a
Do not be afraid of sudden f Nor Pr 3:25 6343
"The f of the LORD is to hate evil; Pr 8:13 3374
The f of the LORD is the beginning Pr 9:10 3374
The f of the LORD prolongs life, Pr 10:27 3374
In the f of the LORD there is Pr 14:26 3374
The f of the LORD is a fountain of Pr 14:27 3374
a little with the f of the LORD Than Pr 15:16 3374
The f of the LORD is the Pr 15:33 3374
And by the f of the LORD one keeps Pr 16:6 3374
The f of the LORD *leads* to life, Pr 19:23 3374
and the f of the LORD Are riches, Pr 22:4 3374
live in the f of the LORD always. Pr 23:17 3374
My son, f the LORD and the king; Pr 24:21 3372a
The f of man brings a snare, But Pr 29:25 2731
so worked that men should f Him. Ec 3:14 3372a

there is emptiness. Rather, f God. Ec 5:7 3372a
will be well for those who f God, Ec 8:12 3372a
who fear God, who f Him openly. Ec 8:12 3372a
shadow, because he does not f God. Ec 8:13 3372a
f God and keep His commandments, Ec 12:13 3372a
be calm, have no f and do not be Is 7:4 3372a
there for f of briars and thorns; Is 7:25 3374
you are not to f what they fear or Is 8:12 3372a
what they f or be in dread of *it*. Is 8:12 4172
And He shall be your f, Is 8:13 4172
do not f the Assyrian who strikes Is 10:24 3372a
knowledge and the f of the LORD. Is 11:2 3374
will delight in the f of the LORD, Is 11:3 3374
The f of the LORD is his treasure. Is 33:6 3374
"Take courage, f not. Is 35:4 3372a
Lift *it* up, do not f. Is 40:9 3372a
'Do not f, for I am with you; Is 41:10 3372a
'Do not f, I will help you.' Is 41:13 3372a
"Do not f, you worm Jacob, you Is 41:14 3372a
look about us and f together. Is 41:23 3372a
"Do not f, for I have redeemed Is 43:1 3372a
"Do not f, for I am with you; Is 43:5 3372a
'Do not f, O Jacob My servant; Is 44:2 3372a
Do not f the reproach of man, Is 51:7 3372a
That you f continually all day Is 51:13 6342
"F not, for you will not be put Is 54:4 3372a
oppression, for you will not f; Is 54:14 3372a
a long time So you do not f Me? Is 57:11 3372a
So they will f the name of the Is 59:19 3372a
sister Judah did not f; Jer 3:8 3372a
'Do you not f Me?' Jer 5:22 3372a
"Let us now f the LORD our God, Jer 5:24 3372a
Do not f them, For they can do no Jer 10:5 3372a
Who would not f You, O King of Jer 10:7 3372a
will not f when the heat comes; Jer 17:8 3372a
Did he not f the LORD and entreat Jer 26:19 3372a
'F not, O Jacob My servant,' Jer 30:10 3372a
way, that they may f Me always, Jer 32:39 3372a
and I will put the f of Me in Jer 32:40 3374
and they will f and tremble Jer 33:9 6342
they turned in f one to another Jer 36:16 6342
you, O Jacob My servant, do not f, Jer 46:27 3372a
"O Jacob My servant, do not f," Jer 46:28 3372a
You said, "Do not f!" La 3:57 3372a
f them nor fear their words, Ezk 2:6 3372a
fear them nor f their words, Ezk 2:6 3372a
neither f their words nor be Ezk 2:6 3372a
I will put f in the land of Egypt. Ezk 30:13 3374
men are to f and tremble before the Da 6:26 1763
will f For the calf of Beth-aven. Hos 10:5 1481c
Do not f, O land, rejoice and be Jl 2:21 3372a
Do not f, beasts of the field, For Jl 2:22 3372a
A lion has roared! Who will not f? Am 3:8 3372a
and I f the LORD God of heaven who Jon 1:9 3372a
it is sound wisdom to f Your name: Mi 6:9 3372a
the report about You *and* I f. Hab 3:2 3372a
You will f disaster no more. Zph 3:15 3372a
is abiding in your midst; do not f! Hg 2:5 3372a
Do not f; let your hands be strong.' Zch 8:13 3372a
and to the house of Judah. Do not f! Zch 8:15 3372a
the alien and do not f Me," Mal 3:5 3372a
those who f the LORD and who esteem Mal 3:16 3372a
"But for you who f My name, Mal 4:2 3372a
"Therefore do not f them, Mt 10:26 *5399*
Do not f those who kill the body Mt 10:28 *5399*
but rather f Him who is able to Mt 10:28 *5399*
"So do not f; Mt 10:31 *5399*
And they cried out in f. Mt 14:26 *5401*
'From men,' we f the people; Mt 21:26 *5399*
The guards shook for f of him Mt 28:4 *5401*
the tomb quickly with f and great joy Mt 28:8 *5401*
he saw *the angel*, and f gripped him. Lk 1:12 *5401*
TOWARD THOSE WHO F HIM. Lk 1:50 *5399*
F came on all those living around Lk 1:65 *5401*
Might serve Him without f, Lk 1:74 *870*
"Do not f, from now on you will Lk 5:10 *5399*
and they were filled with f, Lk 5:26 *5401*
F gripped them all, and they *began* Lk 7:16 *5401*
they were gripped with great f; Lk 8:37 *5401*
"But I will warn you whom to f: Lk 12:5 *5399*
f the One who, after He has killed Lk 12:5 *5399*
yes, I tell you, f Him! Lk 12:5 *5399*
Do not f; you are more valuable than Lk 12:7 *5399*
was a judge who did not f God Lk 18:2 *5399*
I do not f God nor respect man, Lk 18:4 *5399*
men fainting from f and the Lk 21:26 *5401*
"Do you not even f God, since you Lk 23:40 *5399*
and does not come to the Light for f Jn 3:20 *2443, 3361*
openly of Him for f of the Jews. Jn 7:13 *5401*
"F NOT, DAUGHTER OF ZION; Jn 12:15 *5399*
for f that they would be put out of Jn 12:42 *2443, 3361*
a secret *one* for f of the Jews, Jn 19:38 *5401*
disciples were, for f of the Jews, Jn 20:19 *5401*
f came over all who heard of it. Ac 5:5 *5401*
f came over the whole church, Ac 5:11 *5401*
Moses shook with f and would not Ac 7:32 *1790*
going on in the f of the Lord and Ac 9:31 *5401*
"Men of Israel, and you who f God, Ac 13:16 *5399*
and those among you who f God, Ac 13:26 *5399*
rushed in, and trembling with f Ac 16:29 *1790*
and f fell upon them all and the Ac 19:17 *5401*
NO F OF GOD BEFORE THEIR EYES." Ro 3:18 *5401*
of slavery leading to f again, Ro 8:15 *5401*
Do not be conceited, but f; Ro 11:20 *5399*
a cause of f for good behavior, Ro 13:3 *5401*
want to have no f of authority? Ro 13:3 *5399*
to whom custom; f to whom fear; Ro 13:7 *5401*

fear to whom **f**; honor to whom Ro 13:7 5401
and in **f** and in much trembling, 1Co 2:3 5401
knowing the **f** of the Lord, 2Co 5:11 5401
holiness in the **f** of God. 2Co 7:1 5401
what indignation, what **f**, 2Co 7:11 5401
received him with **f** and trembling. 2Co 7:15 5401
for **f** that I might be running, Ga 2:2 3381
I **f** for you, that perhaps I have Ga 4:11 5399
to one another in the **f** of Christ. Eph 5:21 5401
the flesh, with **f** and trembling, Eph 6:5 5401
speak the word of God without **f**. Php 1:14 870
salvation with **f** and trembling; Php 2:12 5401
for **f** that the tempter might have 1Th 3:5 3381
free those who through **f** of death Heb 2:15 5401
Therefore, let us **f** if, Heb 4:1 5399
"I AM FULL OF **F** and trembling." Heb 12:21 1630
conduct yourselves in **f** during the 1Pe 1:17 5401
love the brotherhood, **f** God, 1Pe 2:17 5399
without being frightened by any **f**. 1Pe 3:6 4423
AND DO NOT **F** THEIR INTIMIDATION, 1Pe 3:14 5399
There is no **f** in love; 1Jn 4:18 5401
but perfect love casts out **f**, 1Jn 4:18 5401
because **f** involves punishment, 1Jn 4:18 5401
they feast with you without **f**, Jude 1:12 870
and on some have mercy with **f**, Jude 1:23 5401
f what you are about to suffer. Rv 2:10 5399
and great **f** fell upon those who Rv 11:11 5401
and those who **f** Your name, Rv 11:18 5399
"**F** God, and give Him glory, Rv 14:7 5399
"Who will not **f**, O Lord, and Rv 15:4 5399
because of the **f** of her torment, Rv 18:10 5401
because of the **f** of her torment, Rv 18:15 5401
His bond-servants, you who **f** Him, Rv 19:5 5399

FEARED

But the midwives **f** God, Ex 1:17 3372a
Because the midwives **f** God, Ex 1:21 3372a
servants of Pharaoh who **f** the word Ex 9:20 3372a
Egyptians, the people **f** the LORD, Ex 14:31 3372a
f the provocation by the enemy, Dt 32:27 1481c
therefore we **f** greatly for our Jos 9:24 3372a
that he **f** greatly, because Gibeon Jos 10:2 3372a
greatly **f** the LORD and Samuel. 1Sa 12:18 3372a
mouth, for the people **f** the oath. 1Sa 14:26 3372a
because I **f** the people and 1Sa 15:24 3372a
and greatly **f** Achish king of Gath. 1Sa 21:12 3372a
So the Arameans **f** to help the sons 2Sa 10:19 3372a
had handed down, they **f** the king, 1Ki 3:28 3372a
(Now Obadiah **f** the LORD greatly; 1Ki 18:3 3372a
have **f** the LORD from my youth. 1Ki 18:12 3372a
know that your servant **f** the LORD; 2Ki 4:1 3372a
But they **f** greatly and said, 2Ki 10:4 3372a
Egypt, and they had **f** other gods 2Ki 17:7 3372a
They also **f** the LORD and appointed 2Ki 17:32 3372a
They **f** the LORD and served their 2Ki 17:33 3372a
So while these nations **f** the LORD, 2Ki 17:41 3372a
He also is to be **f** above all gods. 1Ch 16:25 3372a
man and **f** God more than many. Ne 7:2 3372a
Because I **f** the great multitude, Jb 31:34 6206
For the LORD Most High is to be **f**, Ps 47:2 3372a
You, even You, are to be **f**; Ps 76:7 3372a
The earth **f** and was still Ps 76:8 3372a
bring gifts to Him who is to be **f**. Ps 76:11 4172
He is **f** by the kings of the earth. Ps 76:12 3372a
A God greatly **f** in the council of Ps 89:7 6206
He is to be **f** above all gods. Ps 96:4 3372a
with You, That You may be **f**. Ps 130:4 3372a
To a people **f** far and wide, Is 18:2 3372a
Even from a people **f** far and wide, Is 18:7 3372a
nor have they **f** nor walked in My Jer 44:10 3372a
"You have **f** a sword; Ezk 11:8 3372a
f and trembled before him; Da 5:19 1763
Then the men **f** the LORD greatly, Jon 1:16 3372a
"They are dreaded and **f**; Hab 1:7 3372a
My name is **f** among the nations." Mal 1:14 3372a
f the LORD spoke to one another, Mal 3:16 3372a
him to death, he **f** the crowd, Mt 14:5 5399
seize Him, they **f** the people, Mt 21:46 5399
and *yet* they **f** the people Mk 12:12 5399
very hour, and they **f** the people; Lk 20:19 5399
who **f** God with all his household, Ac 10:2 5399

FEARFUL

for it is a **f** thing that I am Ex 34:10 3372a
"Of whom were you worried and **f** Is 57:11 3372a
"I saw a dream and it made me **f**; Da 4:5 1763
and those who followed were **f**. Mk 10:32 5399
They were **f** and amazed, saying Lk 8:25 5399
be troubled, nor let it be **f**. Jn 14:27 1168
the rest also will be **f** *of sinning*. 1Tm 5:20 5401

FEARFULLY

for I am **f** and wonderfully made; Ps 139:14 3372a
f tormented." Mt 8:6 1171

FEARING

make our sons stop **f** the LORD.' Jos 22:25 3372a
man was blameless, upright, **f** God and Jb 1:1 3372a
f God and turning away from evil." Jb 1:8 3372a
a blameless and upright man **f** God Jb 2:3 3372a
And harden our heart from **f** You? Is 63:17 3374
of Babylon, whom you are *now* **f**; Jer 42:11 3372a
But the woman **f** and trembling, Mk 5:33 5399
and **f** that they might run aground Ac 27:17 5399
F that we might run aground somewhere Ac 27:29 5399
f the party of the circumcision. Ga 2:12 5399
sincerity of heart, **f** the Lord. Col 3:22 5399
not **f** the wrath of the king; Heb 11:27 5399

FEARS

Who is the man who **f** the LORD? Ps 25:12 3372a
And delivered me from all my **f**. Ps 34:4 4034
blessed is the man who **f** the LORD, Ps 112:1 3372a
is everyone who **f** the LORD, Ps 128:1 3372a
the man be blessed Who **f** the LORD. Ps 128:4 3372a
What the wicked **f** will come upon Pr 10:24 4034
But the one who **f** the commandment Pr 13:13 3372a
in his uprightness **f** the LORD, Pr 14:2 3372a
blessed is the man who **f** always, Pr 28:14 6342
vain, *But* a woman who **f** the LORD, Pr 31:30 3372a
for the one who **f** God comes forth Ec 7:18 3372a
Who is among you that **f** the LORD, Is 50:10 3372a
who **f** Him and does what is right is Ac 10:35 5399
conflicts without, **f** within. 2Co 7:5 5401
who **f** is not perfected in love. 1Jn 4:18 5399

FEARSOME

And they are mad over **f** idols. Jer 50:38 367

FEAST

and he prepared a **f** for them, Gn 19:3 4960
and Abraham made a great **f** on the Gn 21:8 4960
Then he made them a **f**, Gn 26:30 4960
men of the place and made a **f**. Gn 29:22 4960
he made a **f** for all his servants; Gn 40:20 4960
a **f** to Me in the wilderness.'" Ex 5:1 2287
we must hold a **f** to the LORD." Ex 10:9 2282
celebrate it *as* a **f** to the LORD; Ex 12:14 2282
'You shall also observe the **F** *of* Ex 12:17
there shall be a **f** to the LORD. Ex 13:6 2282
you shall celebrate a **f** to Me. Ex 23:14 2287
observe the **F** of Unleavened Bread; Ex 23:15 2282
"Also *you shall observe* the **F** of Ex 23:16 2282
also the **F** of the Ingathering at Ex 23:16 2282
nor is the fat of My **f** to remain Ex 23:18 2282
"Tomorrow *shall be* a **f** to the LORD." Ex 32:5 2282
observe the **F** of Unleavened Bread. Ex 34:18 2282
shall celebrate the **F** of Weeks, Ex 34:22 2282
and the **F** of Ingathering at the Ex 34:22 2282
sacrifice of the **F** of the Passover Ex 34:25 2282
there is the **F** of Unleavened Bread Lv 23:6 2282
is the **F** of Booths for seven days Lv 23:34 2282
the **f** of the LORD for seven days, Lv 23:39 2282
thus celebrate it *as* a **f** to the LORD Lv 23:41 2282
day of this month *shall be* a **f**, Nu 28:17 2282
offering to the LORD in your **F** Nu 28:26
a **f** to the LORD for seven days. Nu 29:12 2282
you shall celebrate the **F** of Weeks Dt 16:10 2282
"You shall celebrate the **F** of Booths Dt 16:13 2282
and you shall rejoice in your **f**, Dt 16:14 2282
celebrate a **f** to the LORD your God Dt 16:15 2287
at the **F** of Unleavened Bread and Dt 16:16 2282
at the **F** of Weeks and at the Feast Dt 16:16 2282
of Weeks and at the **F** of Booths, Dt 16:16 2282
of debts, at the **F** of Booths, Dt 31:10 2282
and Samson made a **f** there, Jg 14:10 4960
me within the seven days of the **f**, Jg 14:12 4960
seven days while their **f** lasted. Jg 14:17 4960
there is a **f** of the LORD from year Jg 21:19 2282
he was holding a **f** in his house, 1Sa 25:36 4960
his house, like the **f** of a king. 1Sa 25:36 4960
And David made a **f** for Abner and 2Sa 3:20 4960
and made a **f** for all his servants. 1Ki 3:15 4960
to King Solomon at the **f**, 1Ki 8:2 2282
observed the **f** at that time, 1Ki 8:65 2282
Jeroboam instituted a **f** in the 1Ki 12:32 2282
like the **f** which is in Judah, 1Ki 12:32 2282
a **f** for the sons of Israel and 1Ki 12:33 2282
So he prepared a great **f** for them; 2Ki 6:23 3740
themselves to the king at the **f**, 2Ch 5:3 2282
the **f** at that time for seven days, 2Ch 7:8 2282
seven days and the **f** seven days. 2Ch 7:9 2282
the **F** of Unleavened Bread, 2Ch 8:13 2282
Unleavened Bread, the **F** of Weeks and 2Ch 8:13 2282
of Weeks and the **F** of Booths. 2Ch 8:13 2282
celebrate the **F** of Unleavened Bread 2Ch 30:13 2282
celebrated the **F** of Unleavened Bread 2Ch 30:21 2282
assembly decided to celebrate *the* **f** 2Ch 30:23 2282
and the **F** of Unleavened Bread 2Ch 35:17 2282
They celebrated the **F** of Booths, Ezr 3:4 2282
observed the **F** of Unleavened Bread Ezr 6:22 2282
during the **f** of the seventh month. Ne 8:14 2282
they celebrated the **f** seven days, Ne 8:18 2282
for the Jews, a **f** and a holiday. Es 8:17 4960
and hold a **f** in the house of each one Jb 1:4 4960
Like godless jesters at a **f**, Ps 35:16 4580
At the full moon, on our **f** day. Ps 81:3 2282
cheerful heart *has* a continual **f**. Pr 15:15 4960
whose princes **f** in the morning. Ec 10:16 398
appointed **f** and sabbath in Zion, La 2:6 4150
As in the day of an appointed **f**. La 2:7 4150
called as in the day of an appointed **f** La 2:22 4150
the Passover, a **f** of seven days; Ezk 45:21 2282
During the seven days of the **f** he shall Ezk 45:23 2282
day of the month, at the **f**, Ezk 45:25 2282
f for a thousand of his nobles, Da 5:1 3900
on the day of the **f** of the LORD? Hos 9:5 2282
and to celebrate the **F** of Booths. Zch 14:16 2282
up to celebrate the **F** of Booths. Zch 14:18 2282
up to celebrate the **F** of Booths. Zch 14:19 2282
who gave a wedding **f** for his son. Mt 22:2 1062
had been invited to the wedding **f**, Mt 22:3 1062
come to the wedding **f**." Mt 22:4 1062
there, invite to the wedding **f**.' Mt 22:9 1062
went in with him to the wedding **f**; Mt 25:10 1062
Now at *the* **f** the governor was Mt 27:15 1859
Now at *the* **f** he used to release Mk 15:6 1859
year at the **F** of the Passover. Lk 2:41 1859
according to the custom of the **F**; Lk 2:42 1859
he returns from the wedding **f**, Lk 12:36 1062
invited by someone to a wedding **f**, Lk 14:8 1062
Now the **F** of Unleavened Bread, Lk 22:1 1859
release to them at the **f** one prisoner. Lk 23:17 1859
at the Passover, during the **f**, Jn 2:23 1859
that He did in Jerusalem at the **f**; Jn 4:45 1859
themselves also went to the **f**. Jn 4:45 1859
things there was a **f** of the Jews, Jn 5:1 1859
the Passover, the **f** of the Jews, Jn 6:4 1859
Now the **f** of the Jews, the Feast Jn 7:2 1859
of the Jews, the **F** of Booths, Jn 7:2 4634
"Go up to the **f** yourselves; Jn 7:8 1859
I do not go up to this **f** because Jn 7:8 1859
His brothers had gone up to the **f**, Jn 7:10 1859
were seeking Him at the **f** and Jn 7:11 1859
when it was now the midst of the **f** Jn 7:14 1859
last day, the great *day* of the **f**, Jn 7:37 1859
the **F** of the Dedication took place Jn 10:22 1456
will not come to the **f** at all?" Jn 11:56 1859
crowd who had come to the **f**, Jn 12:12 1859
were going up to worship at the **f**; Jn 12:20 1859
Now before the **F** of the Passover, Jn 13:1 1859
things we have need of for the **f**'; Jn 13:29 1859
Therefore let us celebrate the **f**, 1Co 5:8 1858b
when they **f** with you without fear, Jude 1:12 4910

FEASTED

they **f** and drank freely with him. Gn 43:34 8354

FEASTING

made it a day of **f** and rejoicing. Es 9:17 4960
made it a day of **f** and rejoicing. Es 9:18 4960
a holiday for rejoicing and **f** and Es 9:19 4960
make them days of **f** and rejoicing Es 9:22 4960
days of **f** had completed their cycle, Jb 1:5 4960
a house full of **f** with strife. Pr 17:1 2077
Than to go to a house of **f**, Ec 7:2 4960
shall not go into a house of **f** to sit Jer 16:8 4960

FEASTS

gladness and in your appointed **f**, Nu 10:10 4150
appointed **f** of the LORD our God, 2Ch 2:4 4150
new moons and the three annual **f** 2Ch 8:13 4150
festivals and your appointed **f**, Is 1:14 4150
year, observe *your* **f** on schedule. Is 29:1 2282
Zion, the city of our appointed **f**; Is 33:20 4150
no one comes to the appointed **f**. La 1:4 4150
Jerusalem during her appointed **f**, Ezk 36:38 4150
My statutes in all My appointed **f** and Ezk 44:24 4150
and the drink offerings, at the **f**, Ezk 45:17 2282
f of the house of Israel; Ezk 45:17 4150
the LORD at the appointed **f**, Ezk 46:9 4150
At the festivals and the appointed **f** Ezk 46:11 4150
an end to all her gaiety, Her **f**, Hos 2:11 2282
Celebrate your **f**, O Judah; Na 1:15 2282
who grieve about the appointed **f** Zph 3:18 4150
cheerful **f** for the house of Judah; Zch 8:19 4150
your faces, the refuse of your **f**; Mal 2:3 2282
who are hidden reefs in your love **f** Jude 1:12 26

FEATHERS

take away its crop with its **f** and Lv 1:16 5133
his hair had grown like eagles' **f** Da 4:33

FED

Jacob **f** the rest of Laban's flocks. Gn 30:36 7462a
and he **f** them with food in Gn 47:17 5095
that I **f** you in the wilderness, Ex 16:32 398
and **f** you with manna which you did Dt 8:3 398
"In the wilderness He **f** you manna Dt 8:16 398
f them and gave them drink, 2Ch 28:15 398
f them with the bread of tears, Ps 80:5 398
of rams And the fat of **f** cattle; Is 1:11 4806
When I had **f** them to the full, Jer 5:7 7646
my mouth, and He **f** me this scroll. Ezk 3:2 398
oil and honey with which I **f** you, Ezk 16:19 398
rather the shepherds **f** themselves Ezk 34:8 7462a
creatures **f** themselves from it. Da 4:12 2110
And I bent down *and* **f** them. Hos 11:4 398
and longing to be **f** with the Lk 16:21 5526
was **f** by the king's country. Ac 12:20 5142

FEEBLE

but when the flock was **f**, Gn 30:42 5848c
But the **f** gird on strength. 1Sa 2:4 3782
led all their **f** ones on donkeys, 2Ch 28:15 3782
"What are these **f** Jews doing? Ne 4:2 537
And you have strengthened **f** knees. Jb 4:4 3766
exhausted, and strengthen the **f**. Is 35:3
3782, 1290
will melt, all hands will be **f**, Ezk 21:7 7503
and the one who is **f** among them in Zch 12:8 3782
are weak and the knees that are **f**, Heb 12:12 3886

FEEBLER

so the **f** were Laban's and the Gn 30:42 5848c

FEED

have plenty of both straw and **f**, Gn 24:25 4554
he gave straw and **f** to the camels, Gn 24:32 4554
and **f** him sparingly with bread and 1Ki 22:27 398
and **f** him sparingly with bread and 2Ch 18:26 398
I would **f** you with the finest of the Ps 81:16 398
The lips of the righteous **f** many, Pr 10:21 7462a
F me with the food that is my Pr 30:8 2963
gazelle Which **f** among the lilies. SS 4:5 7462a
lie down and **f** on its branches. Is 27:10 3615
Along the roads they will **f**, Is 49:9 7462a
"I will **f** your oppressors Is 49:26 398
And I will **f** you *with* the heritage Is 58:14 398
who will **f** you on knowledge and Jer 3:15 7462a
"behold, I will **f** them, this Jer 9:15 398
I am going to **f** them wormwood And Jer 23:15 398
"Son of man, **f** your stomach and Ezk 3:3 398
Should not the shepherds **f** the flock? Ezk 34:2 7462a
themselves and did not **f** My flock; Ezk 34:8 7462a
will not **f** themselves anymore, Ezk 34:10 7462a
and I will **f** them on the mountains Ezk 34:13 7462a
"I will **f** them in a good pasture, Ezk 34:14 7462a

and f in rich pasture on	Ezk 34:14	7462a
"I will f My flock and I will	Ezk 34:15	7462a
I will f them with judgment.	Ezk 34:16	7462a
you should f in the good pasture,	Ezk 34:18	7462a
servant David, and he will f them;	Ezk 34:23	7462a
he will f them himself and be	Ezk 34:23	7462a
They f on the sin of My people And	Hos 4:8	398
and wine press will not f them,	Hos 9:2	7462a
Let them f in Bashan and Gilead As	Mi 7:14	7462a
For they will f and lie down With	Zph 3:13	7462a
That a fire may f on your cedars.	Zch 11:1	398
but even the dogs f on the crumbs	Mt 15:27	*2068*
did we see You hungry, and f You,	Mt 25:37	*5142*
the dogs under the table f on the	Mk 7:28	*2068*
him into his fields to f swine.	Lk 15:15	*1006*
IF YOUR ENEMY IS HUNGRY, F HIM,	Ro 12:20	*5595*
all my possessions to f *the poor,*	1Co 13:3	*5595*
FEEDING		
and the donkeys f beside them,	Jb 1:14	7462a
of prey will spend the summer f	Is 18:6	
Israel who have been f themselves!	Ezk 34:2	7462a
the fat *sheep* without f the flock.	Ezk 34:3	7462a
and make them cease from f sheep.	Ezk 34:10	7462a
the f place of the young lions,	Na 2:11	4829
a herd of many swine f	Mt 8:30	*1006*
of swine f nearby on the mountain.	Mk 5:11	*1006*
swine f there on the mountain;	Lk 8:32	*1006*
FEEDS		
The worm f sweetly till he is	Jb 24:20	4985
whatever moves in the field f on it.	Ps 80:13	7462a
But the mouth of fools f on folly.	Pr 15:14	7462a
He f on ashes; a deceived heart has	Is 44:20	7462a
Ephraim f on wind, And pursues the	Hos 12:1	7462a
yet your heavenly Father f them.	Mt 6:26	*5142*
and *yet* God f them;	Lk 12:24	*5142*
FEEL		
"Perhaps my father will f me,	Gn 27:12	4959
come close, that I may f you,	Gn 27:21	4184
"Let me f the pillars on which	Jg 16:26	4184
pots can f *the fire of* thorns He	Ps 58:9	995
stones And f pity for her dust.	Ps 102:14	2603a
have hands, but they cannot f;	Ps 115:7	4184
not f humiliated, for you will	Is 54:4	3637
and f ashamed for all that you	Ezk 16:54	3637
at ease in Zion And to those who f	Am 6:1	
"In that day you will f no shame	Zph 3:11	954
"I f compassion for the	Mt 15:32	*4697*
did not even f remorse afterward	Mt 21:32	*3338*
"I f compassion for the people	Mk 8:2	*4697*
f indignant with James and John.	Mk 10:41	*23*
me to f this way about you all,	Php 1:7	*5426*
for when they f sensual desires in	1Tm 5:11	*2691*
FEELING		
if there is good f toward David,	1Sa 20:12	
Everyone kept f a sense of awe;	Ac 2:43	*1096*
FEELINGS		
know the f of a stranger,	Ex 23:9	5315
And my f were aroused for him.	SS 5:4	4578
And my inward f for Kir-hareseth.	Is 16:11	7130
Who tries the f and the heart,	Jer 11:20	3629
FEES		
of Midian departed with the f *for*	Nu 22:7	
FEET		
water be brought and wash your f,	Gn 18:4	7272
spend the night, and wash your f;	Gn 19:2	7272
and water to wash his f and the	Gn 24:32	7272
f of the men who were with him.	Gn 24:32	7272
water, and they washed their f;	Gn 43:24	7272
ruler's staff from between his f,	Gn 49:10	7272
he drew his f into the bed and	Gn 49:33	7272
remove your sandals from your f,	Ex 3:5	7272
foreskin and threw it at Moses' f,	Ex 4:25	7272
girded, your sandals on your f,	Ex 12:11	7272
and under His f there appeared to	Ex 24:10	7272
it and fasten them on its four f,	Ex 25:12	6471
corners which are on its four f.	Ex 25:26	7272
on the big toes of their right f,	Ex 29:20	7272
their hands and their f from it;	Ex 30:19	7272
wash their hands and their f,	Ex 30:21	7272
four rings of gold for it on its four f;	Ex 37:3	6471
corners that were on its four f.	Ex 37:13	7272
washed their hands and their f.	Ex 40:31	7272
those which have above their f	Lv 11:21	7272
on *all* fours, whatever has many f,	Lv 11:42	7272
from his head even to his f,	Lv 13:12	7272
Let me only pass through on my f,	Nu 20:19	7272
when the soles of the f of the priests	Jos 3:13	7272
the f of the priests carrying the ark	Jos 3:15	7272
the priests' f are standing firm,	Jos 4:3	7272
the f of the priests who carried the ark	Jos 4:9	7272
and the soles of the priests' f	Jos 4:18	7272
"Remove your sandals from your f,	Jos 5:15	7272
and patched sandals on their f,	Jos 9:5	7272
f on the necks of these kings."	Jos 10:24	7272
and put their f on their necks.	Jos 10:24	7272
"Between her f he bowed, he fell,	Jg 5:27	7272
Between her f he bowed, he fell;	Jg 5:27	7272
washed their f and ate and drank.	Jg 19:21	7272
go and uncover his f and lie down;	Ru 3:4	4772
and uncovered his f and lay down.	Ru 3:7	4772
a woman was lying at his f.	Ru 3:8	4772
So she lay at his f until morning	Ru 3:14	4772
"He keeps the f of His godly	1Sa 2:9	7272
climbed up on his hands and f,	1Sa 14:13	7272
She fell at his f and said,	1Sa 25:24	7272
wash the f of my lord's servants."	1Sa 25:41	7272
bound, nor your f put in fetters;	2Sa 3:34	7272
son, had a son crippled in his f.	2Sa 4:4	7272
and cut off their hands and f and	2Sa 4:12	7272
who is crippled in both f."	2Sa 9:3	7272
Now he was lame in both f.	2Sa 9:13	7272
to your house, and wash your f."	2Sa 11:8	7272
he had neither cared for his f,	2Sa 19:24	7272
With thick darkness under His f.	2Sa 22:10	7272
"He makes my f like hinds' *feet,*	2Sa 22:34	7272
"He makes my feet like hinds' f,	2Sa 22:34	
me, And my f have not slipped.	2Sa 22:37	7166
And they fell under my f.	2Sa 22:39	7272
and on his sandals on his f.	1Ki 2:5	7272
put them under the soles of his f.	1Ki 5:3	7272
and its four f had supports;	1Ki 7:30	6471
of her f coming in the doorway,	1Ki 14:6	7272
When your f enter the city the	1Ki 14:12	7272
old age he was diseased in his f.	1Ki 15:23	7272
hill, she caught hold of his f.	2Ki 4:27	7272
Then she went in and fell at his f	2Ki 4:37	7272
sound of his master's f behind him?"	2Ki 6:32	7272
the f and the palms of her hands.	2Ki 9:35	7272
he revived and stood up on his f.	2Ki 13:21	7272
And with the sole of my f I dried	2Ki 19:24	6471
"And I will not make the f of	2Ki 21:8	7272
King David rose to his f and said,	1Ch 28:2	7272
on their f facing the *main* room.	2Ch 3:13	7272
Asa became diseased in his f.	2Ch 16:12	7272
wear out, nor did their f swell.	Ne 9:21	7272
again to the king, fell at his f,	Es 8:3	7272
prepared for those whose f slip.	Jb 12:5	7272
"You put my f in the stocks	Jb 13:27	7272
set a limit for the soles of my f,	Jb 13:27	7272
thrown into the net by his own f,	Jb 18:8	7272
to the blind And f to the lame.	Jb 29:15	7272
They thrust aside my f and build	Jb 30:12	7272
'He puts my f in the stocks;	Jb 33:11	7272
have put all things under his f,	Ps 8:6	7272
My f have not slipped.	Ps 17:5	6471
With thick darkness under His f.	Ps 18:9	7272
He makes my f like hinds' *feet,*	Ps 18:33	7272
He makes my feet like hinds' f,	Ps 18:33	
me, And my f have not slipped.	Ps 18:36	7166
They fell under my f.	Ps 18:38	7272
They pierced my hands and my f.	Ps 22:16	7272
He will pluck my f out of the net.	Ps 25:15	7272
have set my f in a large place.	Ps 31:8	7272
And He set my f upon a rock making	Ps 40:2	7272
under us And nations under our f.	Ps 47:3	7272
death, Indeed my f from stumbling,	Ps 56:13	7272
his f in the blood of the wicked.	Ps 58:10	6471
And does not allow our f to slip.	Ps 66:9	7272
me, my f came close to stumbling,	Ps 73:2	7272
They afflicted his f with fetters,	Ps 105:18	7272
enemies a footstool for Your f."	Ps 110:1	7272
They have f, but they cannot walk;	Ps 115:7	7272
from tears, My f from stumbling.	Ps 116:8	7272
turned my f to Your testimonies.	Ps 119:59	7272
restrained my f from every evil way,	Ps 119:101	7272
Your word is a lamp to my f And	Ps 119:105	7272
Our f are standing Within your	Ps 122:2	7272
Who have purposed to trip up my f.	Ps 140:4	6471
Keep your f from their path,	Pr 1:15	7272
For their f run to evil And they	Pr 1:16	7272
Watch the path of your f And	Pr 4:26	7272
Her f go down to death, Her steps	Pr 5:5	7272
his eyes, who signals with his f,	Pr 6:13	7272
plans, F that run rapidly to evil,	Pr 6:18	7272
coals And his f not be scorched?	Pr 6:28	7272
Her f do not remain at home;	Pr 7:11	7272
He cuts off *his own* f	Pr 26:6	7272
I have washed my f,	SS 5:3	7272
beautiful are your f in sandals,	SS 7:1	6471
And tinkle the bangles on their f,	Is 3:16	7272
and with two he covered his f,	Is 6:2	7272
and take your shoes off your f."	Is 20:2	7272
Whose f used to carry her to	Is 23:7	7272
it, The f of the afflicted,	Is 26:6	7272
And with the sole of my f I dried	Is 37:25	6471
calls in righteousness to His f?	Is 41:2	7272
not been traversing with his f.	Is 41:3	7272
And lick the dust of your f;	Is 49:23	7272
the f of him who brings good news,	Is 52:7	7272
Their f run to evil, And they	Is 59:7	7272
make the place of My f glorious.	Is 60:13	7272
themselves at the soles of your f;	Is 60:14	7272
"Keep your f from being unshod	Jer 2:25	7272
before your f stumble On the dusky	Jer 13:16	7272
have not kept their f in check.	Jer 14:10	7272
me And hidden snares for my f.	Jer 18:22	7272
your f were sunk in the mire,	Jer 38:22	7272
He has spread a net for my f;	La 1:13	7272
To crush under His f All the	La 3:34	7272
their f were like a calf's hoof,	Ezk 1:7	7272
stand on your f that I may speak	Ezk 2:1	7272
entered me and set me on my f;	Ezk 2:2	7272
me and made me stand on my f,	Ezk 3:24	7272
of porpoise skin on your f;	Ezk 16:10	
and put your shoes on your f,	Ezk 24:17	7272
heads and your shoes on your f.	Ezk 24:23	7272
stamped your f and rejoiced with all	Ezk 25:6	7272
muddied the waters with your f And	Ezk 32:2	7272
tread down with your f the rest of	Ezk 34:18	7272
must foul the rest with your f?	Ezk 34:18	7272
what you tread down with your f and	Ezk 34:19	7272
what you foul with your f!'"	Ezk 34:19	7272
to life and stood on their f,	Ezk 37:10	7272
the place of the soles of My f,	Ezk 43:7	7272
its f partly of iron and partly of	Da 2:33	7271
statue on its f of iron and clay and	Da 2:34	7271
In that you saw the f and toes,	Da 2:41	7271
"*As* the toes of the f *were*	Da 2:42	7271
made to stand on two f like a man;	Da 7:4	7271
down the remainder with its f;	Da 7:7	7271
down the remainder with its f,	Da 7:19	7271
his arms and f like the gleam of	Da 10:6	4772
clouds are the dust beneath His f.	Na 1:3	7272
the f of him who brings good news,	Na 1:15	7272
He has made my f like hinds' *feet,*	Hab 3:19	7272
He has made my feet like hinds' f,	Hab 3:19	
In that day His f will stand	Zch 14:4	7272
rot while they stand on their f,	Zch 14:12	7272
be ashes under the soles of your f	Mal 4:3	7272
for it is the footstool of His f,	Mt 5:35	*4228*
they will trample them under their f,	Mt 7:6	*4228*
shake the dust off your f.	Mt 10:14	*4228*
and they laid them down at His f;	Mt 15:30	*4228*
than to have two hands or two f	Mt 18:8	*4228*
YOUR ENEMIES BENEATH YOUR F" '?	Mt 22:44	*4228*
hold of His f and worshiped Him.	Mt 28:9	*4228*
on seeing Him, fell at His f	Mk 5:22	*4228*
the dust off the soles of your f	Mk 6:11	*4228*
came and fell at His f.	Mk 7:25	*4228*
than, having your two f, to be cast	Mk 9:45	*4228*
YOUR ENEMIES BENEATH YOUR F." '	Mk 12:36	*4228*
our f into the way of peace."	Lk 1:79	*4228*
saw *that,* he fell down at Jesus' f,	Lk 5:8	*1119*
and standing behind *Him* at His f,	Lk 7:38	*4228*
began to wet His f with her tears,	Lk 7:38	*4228*
kissing His f and anointing them	Lk 7:38	*4228*
you gave Me no water for My f,	Lk 7:44	*4228*
she has wet My f with her tears and	Lk 7:44	*4228*
in, has not ceased to kiss My f.	Lk 7:45	*4228*
she anointed My f with perfume.	Lk 7:46	*4228*
sitting down at the f of Jesus,	Lk 8:35	*4228*
and he fell at Jesus' f,	Lk 8:41	*4228*
shake the dust off your f as a	Lk 9:5	*4228*
of your city which clings to our f we	Lk 10:11	*4228*
seated at the Lord's f,	Lk 10:39	*4228*
on his hand and sandals on his f;	Lk 15:22	*4228*
and he fell on his face at His f,	Lk 17:16	*4228*
ENEMIES A FOOTSTOOL FOR YOUR F."	Lk 20:43	*4228*
"See My hands and My f,	Lk 24:39	*4228*
showed them His hands and His f.	Lk 24:40	*4228*
and wiped His f with her hair,	Jn 11:2	*4228*
she saw Him, and fell at His f,	Jn 11:32	*4228*
nard, and anointed the f of Jesus and	Jn 12:3	*4228*
and wiped His f with her hair;	Jn 12:3	*4228*
and began to wash the disciples' f and	Jn 13:5	*4228*
"Lord, do You wash my f?"	Jn 13:6	*4228*
"Never shall You wash my f!"	Jn 13:8	*4228*
"Lord, *then wash* not only my f, but	Jn 13:9	*4228*
bathed needs only to wash his f,	Jn 13:10	*4228*
So when He had washed their f,	Jn 13:12	*4228*
and the Teacher, washed your f,	Jn 13:14	*4228*
also ought to wash one another's f.	Jn 13:14	*4228*
one at the head and one at the f,	Jn 20:12	*4228*
ENEMIES A FOOTSTOOL FOR YOUR F." '	Ac 2:35	*4228*
and immediately his f and his	Ac 3:7	*939*
and lay them at the apostles' f,	Ac 4:35	*4228*
and laid it at the apostles' f.	Ac 4:37	*4228*
it, he laid it at the apostles' f.	Ac 5:2	*4228*
the f of those who have buried	Ac 5:9	*4228*
And immediately she fell at his f	Ac 5:10	*4228*
OFF THE SANDALS FROM YOUR F,	Ac 7:33	*4228*
EARTH IS THE FOOTSTOOL OF MY F;	Ac 7:49	*4228*
the f of a young man named Saul.	Ac 7:58	*4228*
fell at his f and worshiped *him.*	Ac 10:25	*4228*
sandals of whose f I am not worthy	Ac 13:25	*4228*
shook off the dust of their f *in protest*	Ac 13:51	*4228*
who had no strength in his f,	Ac 14:8	*4228*
"Stand upright on your f."	Ac 14:10	*4228*
fastened their f in the stocks.	Ac 16:24	*4228*
and bound his own f and hands,	Ac 21:11	*4228*
'But get up and stand on your f;	Ac 26:16	*4228*
"THEIR F ARE SWIFT TO SHED BLOOD,	Ro 3:15	*4228*
HOW BEAUTIFUL ARE THE F OF THOSE	Ro 10:15	*4228*
soon crush Satan under your f.	Ro 16:20	*4228*
or again the head to the f,	1Co 12:21	*4228*
put all His enemies under His f.	1Co 15:25	*4228*
THINGS IN SUBJECTION UNDER HIS F.	1Co 15:27	*4228*
things in subjection under His f,	Eph 1:22	*4228*
and having shod YOUR F WITH THE	Eph 6:15	*4228*
if she has washed the saints' f,	1Tm 5:10	*4228*
ENEMIES A FOOTSTOOL FOR YOUR F"?	Heb 1:13	*4228*
IN SUBJECTION UNDER HIS F."	Heb 2:8	*4228*
BE MADE A FOOTSTOOL FOR HIS F.	Heb 10:13	*4228*
make straight paths for your f,	Heb 12:13	*4228*
in a robe reaching to the f,	Rv 1:13	*4158*
His f *were* like burnished bronze,	Rv 1:15	*4228*
I fell at His f like a dead man.	Rv 1:17	*4228*
His f are like burnished bronze,	Rv 2:18	*4228*
them come and bow down at your f,	Rv 3:9	*4228*
and his f like pillars of fire;	Rv 10:1	*4228*
them, and they stood on their f;	Rv 11:11	*4228*
the sun, and the moon under her f,	Rv 12:1	*4228*
his f were like *those* of a bear,	Rv 13:2	*4228*
I fell at his f to worship him.	Rv 19:10	*4228*
I fell down to worship at the f of	Rv 22:8	*4228*
FEIGNED		
will give f obedience to You.	Ps 66:3	3584
FELIX		
him safely to F the governor.	Ac 23:24	*5344*
to the most excellent governor F,	Ac 23:26	*5344*
and everywhere, most excellent F,	Ac 24:3	*5344*
But F, having a more exact	Ac 24:22	*5344*
later F arrived with Drusilla,	Ac 24:24	*5344*
F became frightened and said,	Ac 24:25	*5344*

F was succeeded by Porcius Festus, Ac 24:27 5344
a favor, F left Paul imprisoned. Ac 24:27 5344
left as a prisoner by F; Ac 25:14 5344

FELL

very angry and his countenance f. Gn 4:5 5307
The rain f upon the earth for Gn 7:12 1961
fled, and they f into them. Gn 14:10 5307
down, a deep sleep f upon Abram; Gn 15:12 5307
and great darkness f upon him. Gn 15:12 5307
Abram f on his face, and God Gn 17:3 5307
Abraham f on his face and laughed, Gn 17:17 5307
and f on his neck and kissed him, Gn 33:4 5307
He f asleep and dreamed a Gn 41:5 3462
they f to the ground before him. Gn 44:14 5307
he f on his brother Benjamin's neck Gn 45:14 5307
he f on his neck and wept on his Gn 46:29 5307
Then Joseph f on his father's Gn 50:1 5307
and f down before him and said, Gn 50:18 5307
men of the people f that day. Ex 32:28 5307
they shouted and f on their faces. Lv 9:24 5307
on which the lot for the LORD f, Lv 16:9 5927
which the lot for the scapegoat f shall Lv 16:10 5927
the dew f on the camp at night, Nu 11:9 3381
Then Moses and Aaron f on their Nu 14:5 5307
heard *this*, he f on his face; Nu 16:4 5307
But they f on their faces and Nu 16:22 5307
Then they f on their faces. Nu 16:45 5307
of meeting and f on their faces. Nu 20:6 5307
"I f down before the LORD, as Dt 9:18 5307
"So I f down before the LORD the Dt 9:25 5307
Joshua f on his face to the earth, Jos 5:14 5307
shout and the wall f down flat, Jos 6:20 5307
Then Joshua tore his clothes and f to Jos 7:6 5307
All who f that day, both men Jos 8:25 5307
there f ten portions to Manasseh, Jos 17:5 5307
Then the second lot f to Simeon, Jos 19:1 3318
The fourth lot f to Issachar, to Jos 19:17 3318
Now the fifth lot f to the tribe Jos 19:24 3318
lot f to the sons of Naphtali; Jos 19:32 3318
The seventh lot f to the tribe of Jos 19:40 3318
Sisera f by the edge of the sword; Jg 4:16 5307
"Between her feet he bowed, he f, Jg 5:27 5307
Between her feet he bowed, he f; Jg 5:27 5307
Where he bowed, there he f dead. Jg 5:27 5307
tent and struck it so that it f, Jg 7:13 5307
many f wounded up to the entrance Jg 9:40 5307
Thus there f at that time 42,000 Jg 12:6 5307
f on their faces to the ground. Jg 13:20 5307
so that the house f on the lords and Jg 16:30 5307
the woman came and f down at the Jg 19:26 5307
Thus 18,000 men of Benjamin f; Jg 20:44 5307
So all of Benjamin who f that day Jg 20:46 5307
Then she f on her face, bowing to Ru 2:10 5307
there f of Israel thirty thousand 1Sa 4:10 5307
Eli f off the seat backward beside the 1Sa 4:18 5307
dread of the LORD f on the people, 1Sa 11:7 5307
and they f before Jonathan, and 1Sa 14:13 5307
he f on his face to the ground. 1Sa 17:49 5307
and f on his face to the ground, 1Sa 20:41 5307
and f on her face before David and 1Sa 25:23 5307
She f at his feet and said, 1Sa 25:24 5307
Then Saul immediately f full 1Sa 28:20 5307
when I f sick three days ago. 1Sa 30:13 2470a
and f slain on Mount Gilboa. 1Sa 31:1 5307
Saul took his sword and f on it. 1Sa 31:4 5307
he also f on his sword and died 1Sa 31:5 5307
came to David that he f to the ground 2Sa 1:2 5307
so they f down together. 2Sa 2:16 5307
he f there and died on the spot. 2Sa 2:23 5307
to flee, he f and became lame. 2Sa 4:4 5307
came to David and f on his face 2Sa 9:6 5307
people among David's servants f; 2Sa 11:17 5307
she f on her face to the ground 2Sa 14:4 5307
Joab f on his face to the ground, 2Sa 14:22 5307
And Shimei the son of Gera f down 2Sa 19:18 5307
and as he went forward, it f out. 2Sa 20:8 5307
that the seven of them f together; 2Sa 21:9 5307
and they f by the hand of David 2Sa 21:22 5307
And they f under my feet. 2Sa 22:39 5307
and he f upon him so that he died. 1Ki 2:25 6293
because he f upon two men more 1Ki 2:32 6293
f upon him and put him to death, 1Ki 2:34 6293
and f upon him so that he died. 1Ki 2:46 6293
him and f on his face and said, 1Ki 18:7 5307
Then the fire of the LORD f and 1Ki 18:38 5307
saw it, they f on their faces; 1Ki 18:39 5307
wall f on 27,000 men who were left. 1Ki 20:30 5307
And Ahaziah f through the lattice 2Ki 1:2 5307
mantle of Elijah that f from him and 2Ki 2:13 5307
mantle of Elijah that f from him and 2Ki 2:14 5307
and f every good tree and stop all 2Ki 3:19 5307
Then she went in and f at his feet 2Ki 4:37 5307
the axe head f into the water; 2Ki 6:5 5307
the Hagrites, who f by their hand, 1Ch 5:10 5307
For many f slain, because the war 1Ch 5:22 5307
and f slain on Mount Gilboa. 1Ch 10:1 5307
Saul took his sword and f on it. 1Ch 10:4 5307
likewise f on his sword and died. 1Ch 10:5 5307
and they f by the hand of David 1Ch 20:8 5307
70,000 men of Israel f. 1Ch 21:14 5307
with sackcloth, f on their faces. 1Ch 21:16 5307
lot to the east f to Shelemiah. 1Ch 26:14 5307
For Obed-edom *it* f to the south, 1Ch 26:15
chosen men of Israel f slain. 2Ch 13:17 5307
and so many Ethiopians f that they 2Ch 14:13 5307
Jerusalem f down before the LORD, 2Ch 20:18 5307
and I f on my knees and stretched Ezr 9:5 3766
again to the king, f at his feet, Es 8:3 5307
"The fire of God f from heaven Jb 1:16 5307
and it f on the young people and Jb 1:19 5307
he f to the ground and worshiped. Jb 1:20 5307
They f under my feet. Ps 18:38 5307
my enemies, they stumbled and f. Ps 27:2 5307
His priests f by the sword, Ps 78:64 5307
The chastening for our well-being f Is 53:5
When her people f into the hand of La 1:7 5307
I f on my face and heard a voice Ezk 1:28 5307
river Chebar, and I f on my face. Ezk 3:23 5307
the hand of the Lord GOD f on me Ezk 8:1 5307
I f on my face and cried out Ezk 9:8 5307
the Spirit of the LORD f upon me, Ezk 11:5 5307
Then I f on my face and cried out Ezk 11:13 5307
and all of them f by the sword. Ezk 39:23 5307
and I f on my face. Ezk 43:3 5307
of the LORD, and I f on my face. Ezk 44:4 5307
Then King Nebuchadnezzar f on his Da 2:46 5308
f down *and* worshiped the golden Da 3:7 5308
f into the midst of the furnace of Da 3:23 5308
and before which three *of them* f, Da 7:20 5308
I was frightened and f on my face; Da 8:17 5307
a great dread f on them, Da 10:7 5307
I f into a deep sleep on my face, Da 10:9 7290a
cast lots and the lot f on Jonah. Jon 1:7 5307
they f to the ground and worshiped Him. Mt 2:11 4098
"And the rain f, and the floods Mt 7:25 2597
"The rain f, and the floods came, Mt 7:27 4098
and it f—and great was its fall." Mt 7:27 4098
some *seeds* f beside the road, Mt 13:4 4098
"Others f on the rocky places, Mt 13:5 4098
"Others f among the thorns, Mt 13:7 4098
"And others f on the good soil and Mt 13:8 4098
they f face down to the ground Mt 17:6 4098
"So the slave f *to the ground* Mt 18:26 4098
"So his fellow slave f *to* Mt 18:29 4098
and f on His face and prayed, Mt 26:39 4098
sixth hour darkness f upon all the land Mt 27:45 1096
some *seed* f beside the road, Mk 4:4 4098
"Other *seed* f on the rocky Mk 4:5 4098
"Other *seed* f among the Mk 4:7 4098
"Other *seeds* f into the good Mk 4:8 4098
on seeing Him, f at His feet Mk 5:22 4098
her, came and f down before Him and Mk 5:33 4363
came and f at His feet. Mk 7:25 4363
beyond *them*, and f to the ground and Mk 14:35 4098
darkness f over the whole land Mk 15:33 1096
saw *that*, he f down at Jesus' feet, Lk 5:8 4363
he f on his face and implored Him, Lk 5:12 4098
he sowed, some f beside the road, Lk 8:5 4098
"Other *seed* f on rocky *soil*, Lk 8:6 2667
"Other *seed* f among the thorns; Lk 8:7 4098
Other *seed* f into the good soil, Lk 8:8 4098
The *seed* which f among the thorns, Lk 8:14 4098
were sailing along He f asleep; Lk 8:23 879a
he cried out and f before Him, Lk 8:28 4363
and he f at Jesus' feet, and *began* Lk 8:41 4098
trembling and f down before Him, Lk 8:47 4363
and f among robbers, and they Lk 10:30 4045
who f into the robbers' *hands?*" Lk 10:36 1706
tower in Siloam f and killed them were Lk 13:4 4098
and he f on his face at His feet, Lk 17:16 4098
and darkness f over the whole land Lk 23:44 1096
she saw Him, and f at His feet, Jn 11:32 4098
drew back and f to the ground. Jn 18:6 4098
them, and the lot f to Matthias; Ac 1:26 4098
Ananias f down and breathed his last Ac 5:5 4098
And immediately she f at his feet Ac 5:10 4098
Having said this, he f asleep. Ac 7:60 2837
and he f to the ground and heard Ac 9:4 4098
And immediately there f from his Ac 9:18 634
time that she f sick and died; Ac 9:37 770
preparations, he f into a trance; Ac 10:10 1096
f at his feet and worshiped *him*. Ac 10:25 4098
the Holy Spirit f upon all those Ac 10:44 1968
the Holy Spirit f upon them just Ac 11:15 1968
And his chains f off his hands. Ac 12:7 1601b
a mist and a darkness f upon him, Ac 13:11 4098
in his own generation, f asleep, Ac 13:36 2837
he f down before Paul and Silas, Ac 16:29 4363
and fear f upon them all and the Ac 19:17 1968
image which f down from heaven? Ac 19:35 1356
and f down from the third floor and Ac 20:9 4098
But Paul went down and f upon him Ac 20:10 1968
not be persuaded, we f silent, Ac 21:14 2270
and I f to the ground and heard a Ac 22:7 4098
temple, that I f into a trance, Ac 22:17 1096
to those who f, severity, but to Ro 11:22 4098
WHO REPROACHED YOU F ON ME." Ro 15:3 1968
twenty-three thousand f in one day. 1Co 10:8 4098
the woman being deceived, f 1Tm 2:14 1096
whose bodies f in the wilderness? Heb 3:17 4098
faith the walls of Jericho f down after Heb 11:30 4098
ever since the fathers f asleep, 2Pe 3:4 2837
I f at His feet like a dead man. Rv 1:17 4098
elders f down before the Lamb, Rv 5:8 4098
the elders f down and worshiped. Rv 5:14 4098
stars of the sky f to the earth, Rv 6:13 4098
and they f on their faces before Rv 7:11 4098
and a great star f from heaven, Rv 8:10 4098
and it f on a third of the rivers Rv 8:10 4098
and great fear f upon those who Rv 11:11 1968
and a tenth of the city f; Rv 11:13 4098
f on their faces and worshiped Rv 11:16 4098
and the cities of the nations f. Rv 16:19 4098
creatures f down and worshiped God Rv 19:4 4098
I f at his feet to worship him. Rv 19:10 4098
I f down to worship at the feet of Rv 22:8 4098

FELLED

f to the ground on that day 22,000 Jg 20:21 7843
and f to the ground again 18,000 men Jg 20:25 7843
of water and f all the good trees, 2Ki 3:25 5307
Whose stump remains when it is f. Is 6:13 7995

FELLING

But as one was f a beam, the axe 2Ki 6:5 5307

FELLOW

shall not hate your f countryman Lv 19:17 251
'If a f countryman of yours Lv 25:25 251
I Myself have taken your f Levites Nu 18:6 251
cases between your f countrymen, Dt 1:16 251
a man and his f countryman, Dt 1:16 251
gives rest to your f countrymen as Dt 3:20 251
like all his f Levites who stand Dt 18:7 251
man's sword was against his f, 1Sa 14:20 7453
man of bloodshed, and worthless f! 2Sa 16:7 376
Now a worthless f happened to be 2Sa 20:1 376
Why did this mad f come to you?" 2Ki 9:11 7696
your relatives, your f exiles and Ezk 11:15 376
of man, say to your f citizens, Ezk 33:12 1121, 5971a
"Yet your f citizens say, Ezk 33:17 1121, 5971a
your f citizens who talk about you Ezk 33:30 1121, 5971a
"This f blasphemes." Mt 9:3
found one of his f slaves who owed Mt 18:28 4889
"So his f slave fell *to the ground* Mt 18:29 4889
f slaves saw what had happened, Mt 18:31 4889
have had mercy on your f slave, Mt 18:33 4889
and begins to beat his f slaves Mt 24:49 4889
Didymus, said to *his* f disciples, Jn 11:16 4827
"Away with such a f from the earth, Ac 22:22 5108
pest and a f who stirs up dissension Ac 24:5
of God and f heirs with Christ, Ro 8:17 4789
move to jealousy my f countrymen Ro 11:14 4561
my f workers in Christ Jesus, Ro 16:3 4904
my kinsmen and my f prisoners, Ro 16:7 4869
Urbanus, our f worker in Christ, Ro 16:9 4904
Timothy my f worker greets you, Ro 16:21 4904
For we are God's f workers; 1Co 3:9 4904
I may become a f partaker of it. 1Co 9:23 4791
my partner and f worker among you; 2Co 8:23 4904
nevertheless, crafty f that I am, 2Co 12:16
are f citizens with the saints, Eph 2:19 4847
that the Gentiles are f heirs and Eph 3:6 4789
heirs and f members of the body, Eph 3:6 4954
and f partakers of the promise in Eph 3:6 4830
and f worker and fellow soldier, Php 2:25 4904
and fellow worker and f soldier, Php 2:25 4961
and the rest of my f workers, Php 4:3 4904
our beloved f bond-servant, Col 1:7 4889
and f bond-servant in the Lord, Col 4:7 4889
Aristarchus, my f prisoner, sends Col 4:10 4869
the only f workers for the kingdom Col 4:11 4904
our brother and God's f worker in 1Th 3:2 4904
our beloved *brother* and f worker, Phm 1:1 4904
and to Archippus our f soldier, Phm 1:2 4961
my f prisoner in Christ Jesus, Phm 1:23 4869
Demas, Luke, my f workers. Phm 1:24 4904
NOT TEACH EVERYONE HIS F CITIZEN, Heb 8:11 4177
f heirs of the same promise; Heb 11:9 4789
to recognize, you foolish f, Jas 2:20 444
as a f heir of the grace of life, 1Pe 3:7 4789
as *your* f elder and witness of the 1Pe 5:1 4850
may be f workers with the truth. 3Jn 1:8 4904
your brother and f partaker in the Rv 1:9 4791
until *the number of* their f servants Rv 6:11 4889
I am a f servant of yours and your Rv 19:10 4889
I am a f servant of yours and of Rv 22:9 4889

FELLOWS

hired worthless and reckless f, Jg 9:4 376
and worthless f gathered Jg 11:3 376
of the city, certain worthless f, Jg 19:22 1121
"No, my f, please do not act so Jg 19:23 251
men, the worthless f in Gibeah, Jg 20:13 1121
With the oil of joy above Your f. Ps 45:7 2270

FELLOWSHIP

We who had sweet f together Ps 55:14 5475
to the apostles' teaching and to f, Ac 2:42 2842
were called into f with His Son, 1Co 1:9 2842
or what f has light with darkness? 2Co 6:14 2842
God, and the f of the Holy Spirit, 2Co 13:14 2842
and Barnabas the right hand of f, Ga 2:9 2842
if there is any f of the Spirit, Php 2:1 2842
and the f of His sufferings, Php 3:10 2842
and I pray that the f of your Phm 1:6 2842
that you too may have f with us; 1Jn 1:3 2842
indeed our f is with the Father, 1Jn 1:3 2842
If we say that we have f with Him 1Jn 1:6 2842
Light, we have f with one another, 1Jn 1:7 2842

FELT

his father, and he f him and said, Gn 27:22 4959
And Laban f through all the tent but Gn 31:34 4959
you have f through all my goods, Gn 31:37 4959
even a darkness which may be f." Ex 10:21 4959
You f secure in your wickedness Is 47:10 982
He f compassion for them, Mt 9:36 4697
and f compassion for them and Mt 14:14 4697
"And the lord of that slave f Mt 18:27 4697
he f remorse and returned the Mt 27:3 3338
and she f in her body that she was Mk 5:29 1097
and He f compassion for them Mk 6:34 4697
at him, Jesus f a love for him and Mk 10:21 25
saw her, He f compassion for her, Lk 7:13 4697
when he saw him, he f compassion, Lk 10:33 4697
saw him and f compassion *for him*, Lk 15:20 4697
f *his* righteous soul tormented day 2Pe 2:8 928
I f the necessity to write to you Jude 1:3 2192

FEMALE
male and **f** He created them. Gn 1:27 5347
He created them male and **f**, Gn 5:2 5347
they shall be male and **f**. Gn 6:19 5347
by sevens, a male and his **f**; Gn 7:2 802
not clean two, a male and his **f**; Gn 7:2 802
of the sky, by sevens, male and **f**, Gn 7:3 5347
ark to Noah by twos, male and **f**, Gn 7:9 5347
entered, male and **f** of all flesh, Gn 7:16 5347
and donkeys and male and **f** servants Gn 12:16 8198
servants and **f** donkeys and camels. Gn 12:16 860
and a three year old **f** goat, Gn 15:9 5795
and oxen and male and **f** servants, Gn 20:14 8198
the speckled and spotted **f** goats, Gn 30:35 5795
and had large flocks and **f** and Gn 30:43 8198
your **f** goats have not miscarried, Gn 31:38 5795
flocks and male and **f** servants; Gn 32:5 8198
f goats and twenty male goats, Gn 32:14 5795
f donkeys and ten male donkeys. Gn 32:15 860
and ten **f** donkeys loaded with Gn 45:23 860
your male or your **f** servant or Ex 20:10 519
or his male servant or his **f** servant Ex 20:17 519
sells his daughter as a **f** slave, Ex 21:7 519
strikes his male or **f** slave with a rod Ex 21:20 519
the eye of his male or **f** slave, Ex 21:26 519
a tooth of his male or **f** slave, Ex 21:27 519
"If the ox gores a male or **f** slave, Ex 21:32 519
rest, and the son of your **f** slave, Ex 23:12 519
of the herd, whether male or **f**, Lv 3:1 5347
he shall offer it, male or **f**, Lv 3:6 5347
a goat, a **f** without defect, Lv 4:28 5347
bring it, a **f** without defect. Lv 4:32 5347
has committed, a **f** from the flock, Lv 5:6 5347
'But if she bears a **f** *child,* Lv 12:5 5347
a child, whether a male or a **f**. Lv 12:7 5347
discharge, whether a male or a **f**, Lv 15:33 5347
with a male as one lies with a **f**; Lv 18:22 802
and your male and **f** slaves, Lv 25:6 519
'As for your male and **f** slaves Lv 25:44 519
you may acquire male and **f** slaves Lv 25:44 519
'Or if it is a **f**, then your Lv 27:4 5347
and for the **f** ten shekels. Lv 27:5 5347
and for the **f** your valuation shall Lv 27:6 5347
and for the **f** ten shekels. Lv 27:7 5347
shall send away both male and **f**; Nu 5:3 5347
he shall offer a one year old **f** goat Nu 15:27 5795
figure, the likeness of male or **f**, Dt 4:16 5347
or your male servant or your **f** servant Dt 5:14 519
your **f** servant may rest as well as you. Dt 5:14 519
his male servant or his **f** servant, Dt 5:21 519
there will be no male or **f** barren Dt 7:14
your male and **f** servants, Dt 12:12 519
and your male and **f** servants, Dt 12:18 519
male and **f** servants and the Levite Dt 16:11 519
male and **f** servants and the Levite Dt 16:14 519
your enemies as male and **f** slaves, Dt 28:68 8198
male servants and your **f** servants 1Sa 8:16 8198
Then two **f** bears came out of the 2Ki 2:24
and oxen and male and **f** servants? 2Ki 5:26 8198
Jerusalem for male and **f** slaves. 2Ch 28:10 8198
And all the male and **f** singers 2Ch 35:25
besides their male and **f** servants who Ezr 2:65 519
their male and their **f** servants, Ne 7:67 519
they had 245 male and **f** singers. Ne 7:67
500 yoke of oxen, 500 **f** donkeys, Jb 1:3 860
the claim of my male or **f** slaves Jb 31:13 519
yoke of oxen and 1,000 **f** donkeys. Jb 42:12 860
I bought male and **f** slaves and Ec 2:7 8198
I provided for myself male and **f** Ec 2:8
as male servants and **f** servants; Is 14:2 8198
and each man his **f** servant, Jer 34:9 8198
and each man his **f** servant, Jer 34:10 8198
male servants and the **f** servants whom Jer 34:11 8198
male servants and for **f** servants. Jer 34:11 8198
and each man his **f** servant whom Jer 34:16 8198
male servants and **f** servants." Jer 34:16 8198
"Even on the male and **f** Jl 2:29 8198
beginning MADE THEM MALE AND **F** Mt 19:4 *2338*
God MADE THEM MALE AND **F**. Mk 10:6 *2338*
man, there is neither male nor **f**; Ga 3:28 *2338*

FENCE
leaning wall, like a tottering **f**? Ps 62:3 1447
plant *it* you carefully **f** *it* in, Is 17:11 5473

FENCED
heap of wheat **F** about with lilies. SS 7:2 5473

FERTILE
the hill country and the **f** fields, 2Ch 26:10 3759
fortified cities and a **f** land. Ne 9:25 8082a
had a vineyard on a **f** hill. Is 5:1
1121, 8081
Which is at the head of the **f** valley Is 28:1 8081
is at the head of the **f** valley, Is 28:4 8081
will be turned into a **f** field, Is 29:17 3759
And the **f** field will be considered Is 29:17 3759
And the wilderness becomes a **f** Is 32:15 3759
the **f** field is considered as a forest. Is 32:15 3759
will abide in the **f** field. Is 32:16 3759
the land and planted it in **f** soil. Ezk 17:5 2233

FERTILITY
away from the **f** of the earth shall Gn 27:39 8082b

FERTILIZER
I dig around it and put in **f**; Lk 13:8 *2874b*

FERVENT
and being **f** in spirit, he was Ac 18:25 *2204*
f in spirit, serving the Lord; Ro 12:11 *2204*
f in your love for one another, 1Pe 4:8 *1618*

FERVENTLY
in agony He was praying very **f**; Lk 22:44 *1619*
prayer for him was being made **f** Ac 12:5 *1619*
f love one another from the heart, 1Pe 1:22 *1619*

FESTAL
f robes, outer tunics, cloaks, Is 3:22 4254
And all her **f** assemblies. Hos 2:11 4150
will clothe you with **f** robes." Zch 3:4 4254

FESTER
My wounds grow foul *and* **f** Because Ps 38:5 4743

FESTIVAL
and trod *them,* and held a **f**; Jg 9:27 1974
and to celebrate a great **f**, Ne 8:12 8057
a multitude keeping **f**. Ps 42:4 2287
Bind the **f** sacrifice with cords to Ps 118:27 2282
in the night when you keep the **f**, Is 30:29 2282
you do on the day of the appointed **f** Hos 9:5 4150
As in the days of the appointed **f**. Hos 12:9 4150
"Not during the **f**, otherwise a riot Mt 26:5 *1859*
during the **f**, otherwise there might be Mk 14:2 *1859*
or in respect to a **f** or a new moon Col 2:16 *1859*

FESTIVALS
the new moons and the fixed **f** in 1Ch 23:31 4150
the new moons and for the fixed **f**, 2Ch 31:3 4150
and for all the fixed **f** of the LORD Ezr 3:5 4150
"I hate your new moon **f** and your Is 1:14
"At the **f** and the appointed Ezk 46:11 2282
"I hate, I reject your **f**, Am 5:21 2282
"Then I will turn your **f** into Am 8:10 2282

FESTIVE
eyes, for we have come on a **f** day. 1Sa 25:8 2896a

FESTUS
Felix was succeeded by Porcius **F**, Ac 24:27 *5347*
F then, having arrived in the Ac 25:1 *5347*
F then answered that Paul was Ac 25:4 *5347*
But **F**, wishing to do the Jews a Ac 25:9 *5347*
Then when **F** had conferred with his Ac 25:12 *5347*
and paid their respects to **F**. Ac 25:13 *5347*
F laid Paul's case before the Ac 25:14 *5347*
Then Agrippa *said* to **F**, Ac 25:22 *5347*
of the city, at the command of **F**, Ac 25:23 *5347*
F said, "King Agrippa, and all you Ac 25:24 *5347*
defense, **F** said in a loud voice, Ac 26:24 *5347*
out of my mind, most excellent **F**, Ac 26:25 *5347*
And Agrippa said to **F**, Ac 26:32 *5347*

FETCH
"I will **f** my knowledge from afar, Jb 36:3 5375

FETTERS
not bound, nor your feet put in **f**; 2Sa 3:34 5178
f and brought him to Babylon. 2Ki 25:7 5178
"And if they are bound in **f**, Jb 36:8 2203b
"Let us tear their **f** apart And Ps 2:3 4147
They afflicted his feet with **f**, Ps 105:18 3525
And their nobles with **f** of iron, Ps 149:8 3525
in **f** to the discipline of a fool, Pr 7:22 5914
Or your **f** will be made stronger; Is 28:22 4147
bound him in **f** of bronze to bring Jer 39:7 5178
f and brought him to Babylon and Jer 52:11 5178
her great men were bound with **f**. Na 3:10 2203b

FEVER
consumption and **f** that will waste Lv 26:16 6920
and with **f** and with inflammation Dt 28:22 6920
on me, And my bones burn with **f**. Jb 30:30 2721a
away *as* with the **f** heat of summer. Ps 32:4 2725
lying sick in bed with a **f**. Mt 8:14 *4445*
her hand, and the **f** left her; Mt 8:15 *4446*
was lying sick with a **f**; Mk 1:30 *4445*
by the hand, and the **f** left her, Mk 1:31 *4446*
was suffering from a high **f**, Lk 4:38 *4446*
over her, He rebuked the **f**, Lk 4:39 *4446*
the seventh hour the **f** left him." Jn 4:52 *4446*
with *recurrent* **f** and dysentery; Ac 28:8 *4446*

FEW
"Let the girl stay with us *a* **f** Gn 24:55
"Stay with him a **f** days, Gn 27:44 259
and they seemed to him but a **f** days Gn 29:20 259
and my men being **f** in number, Gn 34:30 4962
f and unpleasant have been the Gn 47:9 4592
and if **f** years remain until the Lv 25:52 4592
a **f** days over the tabernacle, Nu 9:20 4557
weak, whether they are **f** or many. Nu 13:18 4592
f in number among the nations where Dt 4:27 4962
and sojourned there, **f** in number; Dt 26:5 4962
you shall be left **f** in number, Dt 28:62 4592
and not die, Nor his men be **f**." Dt 33:6 4557
toil up there, for they are **f**." Jos 7:3 4592
to save by many or by **f**." 1Sa 14:6 4592
those **f** sheep in the wilderness? 1Sa 17:28 4592
I am gathering a **f** sticks that I 1Ki 17:12 8147
even empty vessels; do not get a **f**. 2Ki 4:3 4591
When they were only a **f** in number, 1Ch 16:19 4962
were only a few in number, Very **f**, 1Ch 16:19 4592
But the priests were too **f**, 2Ch 29:34 4592
the night, I and a **f** men with me. Ne 2:12 4592
f and the houses were not built. Ne 7:4 4592
"Would He not let my **f** days alone? Jb 10:20 4592
"For when a **f** years are past, I Jb 16:22 4557
they were only a **f** men in number, Ps 105:12 4962
only a few men in number, Very **f**, Ps 105:12 4592
Let his days be **f**; Ps 109:8 4592
heaven the **f** years of their lives. Ec 2:3 4557
therefore let your words be **f**. Ec 5:2 4592
under the sun *during* the **f** years of his Ec 5:18 4557
the **f** years of his futile life? Ec 6:12 4557
There was a small city with **f** men Ec 9:14 4592
stand idle because they are **f**, Ec 12:3 4591
hosts Had left us a **f** survivors, Is 1:9 4592
of the sons of Kedar, will be **f**; Is 21:17 4591
are burned, and **f** men are left. Is 24:6 4213
Within a year and *a* **f** days You Is 32:10
in it an infant *who lives but a* **f** Is 65:20
we are left *but* a **f** out of many, Jer 42:2 4592
for none will return except *a* **f** Jer 44:14
to the land of Judah **f** in number. Jer 44:28 4962
"Take also a **f** in number from Ezk 5:3 4592
spare a **f** of them from the sword, Ezk 12:16 4557
a **f** days he will be shattered, Da 11:20 259
life, and there are **f** who find it. Mt 7:14 *3641*
plentiful, but the workers are **f**. Mt 9:37 *3641*
"Seven, and a **f** small fish." Mt 15:34 *3641*
are called, but **f** *are* chosen." Mt 22:14 *3641*
You were faithful with a **f** things, Mt 25:21 *3641*
You were faithful with a **f** things, Mt 25:23 *3641*
a **f** sick people and healed them. Mk 6:5 *3641*
They also had a **f** small fish; Mk 8:7 *3641*
plentiful, but the laborers are **f**; Lk 10:2 *3641*
of a flogging, will receive but **f**. Lk 12:48 *3641*
just a **f** who are being saved?" Lk 13:23 *3641*
and they stayed there a **f** days. Jn 2:12
3756, 4183
asked him to stay on for a **f** days. Ac 10:48 *5100*
of the ark, in which a **f**, 1Pe 3:20 *3641*
'But I have a **f** things against Rv 2:14 *3641*
'But you have a **f** people in Sardis Rv 3:4 *3641*

FEWEST
for you were the **f** of all peoples, Dt 7:7 4592

FEWNESS
proportion to the **f** of the years you Lv 25:16 4591

FIELD
no shrub of the **f** was yet in the Gn 2:5 7704
plant of the **f** had yet sprouted, Gn 2:5 7704
the **f** and every bird of the sky, Gn 2:19 7704
sky, and to every beast of the **f**, Gn 2:20 7704
the **f** which the LORD God had made. Gn 3:1 7704
more than every beast of the **f**; Gn 3:14 7704
you will eat the plants of the **f**; Gn 3:18 7704
about when they were in the **f**, Gn 4:8 7704
which is at the end of his **f**; Gn 23:9 7704
I give you the **f**, and I give you Gn 23:11 7704
I will give the price of the **f**, Gn 23:13 7704
So Ephron's **f**, which was in Gn 23:17 7704
the **f** and cave which was in it, Gn 23:17 7704
all the trees which were in the **f**, Gn 23:17 7704
the **f** at Machpelah facing Mamre Gn 23:19 7704
So the **f** and the cave that is in Gn 23:20 7704
meditate in the **f** toward evening; Gn 24:63 7704
man walking in the **f** to meet us?" Gn 24:65 7704
in the **f** of Ephron the son of Gn 25:9 7704
the **f** which Abraham purchased from Gn 25:10 7704
a skillful hunter, a man of the **f**, Gn 25:27 7704
in from the **f** and he was famished; Gn 25:29 7704
out to the **f** and hunt game for me; Gn 27:3 7704
So when Esau went to the **f** to hunt Gn 27:5 7704
of a **f** which the LORD has blessed; Gn 27:27 7704
looked, and saw a well in the **f**, Gn 29:2 7704
went and found mandrakes in the **f**, Gn 30:14 7704
came in from the **f** in the evening, Gn 30:16 7704
and Leah to his flock in the **f**, Gn 31:4 7704
were with his livestock in the **f**, Gn 34:5 7704
in from the **f** when they heard *it;* Gn 34:7 7704
city and that which was in the **f**; Gn 34:28 7704
defeated Midian in the **f** of Moab, Gn 36:35 7704
we were binding sheaves in the **f**, Gn 37:7 7704
behold, he was wandering in the **f**; Gn 37:15 7704
owned, in the house and in the **f**. Gn 39:5 7704
for every Egyptian sold his **f**, Gn 47:20 7704
for seed of the **f** and for your food Gn 47:24 7704
is in the **f** of Ephron the Hittite, Gn 49:29 7704
that is in the **f** of Machpelah, Gn 49:30 7704
Abraham bought along with the **f** Gn 49:30 7704
the **f** and the cave that is in it, Gn 49:32 7704
the **f** of Machpelah before Mamre, Gn 50:13 7704
Abraham had bought along with the **f** Gn 50:13 7704
at all *kinds* of labor in the **f**, Ex 1:14 7704
your livestock which are in the **f**, Ex 9:3 7704
whatever you have in the **f** to safety. Ex 9:19 7704
in the **f** and is not brought home, Ex 9:19 7704
and his livestock in the **f**. Ex 9:21 7704
beast and on every plant of the **f**, Ex 9:22 7704
The hail struck all that was in the **f** Ex 9:25 7704
hail also struck every plant of the **f** Ex 9:25 7704
and shattered every tree of the **f**. Ex 9:25 7704
sprouts for you out of the **f**. Ex 10:5 7704
f through all the land of Egypt. Ex 10:15 7704
you will not find it in the **f**. Ex 16:25 7704
"If a man lets a **f** or vineyard be Ex 22:5 7704
that it grazes in another man's **f**, Ex 22:5 7704
restitution from the best of his own **f** Ex 22:5 7704
grain or the **f** *itself* is consumed, Ex 22:6 7704
any flesh torn to pieces in the **f**; Ex 22:31 7704
leave the beast of the **f** may eat. Ex 23:11 7704
labors *from* what you sow in the **f**; Ex 23:16 7704
fruit of your labors from the **f**. Ex 23:16 7704
beasts of the **f** become too numerous Ex 23:29 7704
live bird go free over the open **f**. Lv 14:7 7704
outside the city into the open **f**. Lv 14:53 7704
were sacrificing in the open **f**, Lv 17:5 7704
to the very corners of your **f**, Lv 19:9 7704
sow your **f** with two kinds of seed, Lv 19:19 7704
to the very corners of your **f** nor Lv 23:22 7704
'Six years you shall sow your **f**, Lv 25:3 7704
your **f** nor prune your vineyard. Lv 25:4 7704
shall eat its crops out of the **f**. Lv 25:12 7704
of the **f** will bear their fruit. Lv 26:4 7704
among you the beasts of the **f**, Lv 26:22 7704

his f as of the year of jubilee,	Lv 27:17	7704
his f after the jubilee,	Lv 27:18	7704
should ever wish to redeem the f,	Lv 27:19	7704
'Yet if he will not redeem the f,	Lv 27:20	7704
but has sold the f to another man,	Lv 27:20	7704
the f shall be holy to the LORD,	Lv 27:21	7704
to the LORD, like a f set apart;	Lv 27:21	7704
if he consecrates to the LORD a f	Lv 27:22	7704
part of the f of his own property,	Lv 27:22	7704
'In the year of jubilee the f	Lv 27:24	7704
anyone who in the open f touches	Nu 19:16	7704
through f or through vineyard;	Nu 20:17	7704
not turn off into f or vineyard;	Nu 21:22	7704
ox licks up the grass of the f."	Nu 22:4	7704
from the way and went into the f;	Nu 22:23	7704
So he took him to the f of Zophim,	Nu 23:14	7704
his f or his male servant or his	Dt 5:21	7704
comes out of the f every year.	Dt 14:22	7704
For is the tree of the f a man,	Dt 20:19	7704
"But if in the f the man finds	Dt 22:25	7704
"When he found her in the f,	Dt 22:27	7704
"When you reap your harvest in your f	Dt 24:19	7704
have forgotten a sheaf in the f,	Dt 24:19	7704
shall bring out much seed to the f	Dt 28:38	7704
And he ate the produce of the f;	Dt 32:13	7706a
all the inhabitants of Ai in the f in	Jos 8:24	7704
him to ask her father for a f.	Jos 15:18	7704
him to ask her father for a f.	Jg 1:14	7704
marched from the f of Edom,	Jg 5:4	7704
also, on the high places of the f.	Jg 5:18	7704
They went out into the f and	Jg 9:27	7704
you, and lie in wait in the f.	Jg 9:32	7704
that the people went out to the f,	Jg 9:42	7704
and lay in wait in the f;	Jg 9:43	7704
who *were* in the f and slew them.	Jg 9:44	7704
woman as she was sitting in the f,	Jg 13:9	7704
of the f from his work at evening.	Jg 19:16	7704
the other to Gibeah, *and* in the f,	Jg 20:31	7704
"Please let me go to the f and	Ru 2:2	7704
in the f after the reapers;	Ru 2:3	7704
of the f belonging to Boaz,	Ru 2:3	7704
Do not go to glean in another f;	Ru 2:8	7704
eyes be on the f which they reap,	Ru 2:9	7704
gleaned in the f until evening.	Ru 2:17	7704
fall upon you in another f."	Ru 2:22	7704
buy the f from the hand of Naomi,	Ru 4:5	7704
The cart came into the f of	1Sa 6:14	7704
the f of Joshua the Beth-shemite.	1Sa 6:18	7704
Saul was coming from the f behind	1Sa 11:5	7704
a trembling in the camp, in the f,	1Sa 14:15	7704
the sky and the beasts of the f."	1Sa 17:44	7704
my father in the f where you are,	1Sa 19:3	7704
in the f until the third evening.	1Sa 20:5	7704
and let us go out into the f."	1Sa 20:11	7704
So both of them went out to the f.	1Sa 20:11	7704
So David hid in the f;	1Sa 20:24	7704
Jonathan went out into the f for the	1Sa 20:35	7704
in the f and brought him to David,	1Sa 30:11	7704
of the gazelles which is in the f.	2Sa 2:18	7704
were by themselves in the f.	2Sa 10:8	7704
my lord are camping in the open f.	2Sa 11:11	7704
and came out against us in the f,	2Sa 11:23	7704
them struggled together in the f,	2Sa 14:6	7704
"See, Joab's f is next to mine,	2Sa 14:30	2513a
servants set the f on fire.	2Sa 14:30	2513a
your servants set my f on fire?"	2Sa 14:31	2513a
bear robbed of her cubs in the f.	2Sa 17:8	7704
out into the f against Israel,	2Sa 18:6	7704
Amasa from the highway into the f	2Sa 20:12	7704
nor the beasts of the f by night.	2Sa 21:10	7704
"Go to Anathoth to your own f,	1Ki 2:26	7704
both of them were alone in the f.	1Ki 11:29	7704
And he who dies in the f the birds	1Ki 14:11	7704
and anyone of his who dies in the f	1Ki 16:4	7704
f the birds of heaven will eat."	1Ki 21:24	7704
out into the f to gather herbs,	2Ki 4:39	7704
camp to hide themselves in the f,	2Ki 7:12	7704
king for her house and for her f.	2Ki 8:3	7704
king for her house and for her f.	2Ki 8:5	7704
was hers and all the produce of the f	2Ki 8:6	7704
of the f of Naboth the Jezreelite,	2Ki 9:25	7704
the f in the property of Jezreel,	2Ki 9:37	7704
on the highway of the fuller's f.	2Ki 18:17	7704
They were as the vegetation of the f	2Ki 19:26	7704
defeated Midian in the f of Moab,	1Ch 1:46	7704
Let the f exult, and all that is	1Ch 16:32	7704
come were by themselves in the f.	1Ch 19:9	7704
buried him with his fathers in the f	2Ch 26:23	7704
and of all the produce of the f;	2Ch 31:5	7704
had gone away, each to his own f.	Ne 13:10	7704
league with the stones of the f,	Jb 5:23	7704
the f will be at peace with you.	Jb 5:23	7704
harvest their fodder in the f And	Jb 24:6	7704
they grow up in the open f;	Jb 39:4	1253b
the beasts of the f play there.	Jb 40:20	7704
And also the beasts of the f,	Ps 8:7	7706a
that moves in the f is Mine.	Ps 50:11	7706a
land of Egypt, in the f of Zoan.	Ps 78:12	7704
And His marvels in the f of Zoan,	Ps 78:43	7704
moves in the f feeds on it.	Ps 80:13	7706a
Let the f exult, and all that is	Ps 96:12	7706a
As a flower of the f,	Ps 103:15	7704
drink to every beast of the f;	Ps 104:11	7706a
We found it in the f of Jaar.	Ps 132:6	7704
it ready for yourself in the f;	Pr 24:27	7704
I passed by the f of the sluggard And	Pr 24:30	7704
goats *will bring* the price of a f,	Pr 27:26	7704
She considers a f and buys it;	Pr 31:16	7704
the f is an advantage to the land.	Ec 5:9	7704
gazelles or by the hinds of the f,	SS 2:7	7704
gazelles or by the hinds of the f,	SS 3:5	7704
a watchman's hut in a cucumber f,	Is 1:8	4750
to house *and* join f to field,	Is 5:8	7704
to house *and* join field to f,	Is 5:8	7704
on the highway to the fuller's f,	Is 7:3	7704
taken away from the fruitful f;	Is 16:10	3759
will be turned into a fertile f,	Is 29:17	3759
And the fertile f will be	Is 29:17	3759
And the wilderness becomes a fertile f	Is 32:15	3759
the fertile f is considered as a forest.	Is 32:15	3759
will abide in the fertile f.	Is 32:16	3759
on the highway of the fuller's f.	Is 36:2	7704
They were *as* the vegetation of the f	Is 37:27	7704
is like the flower of the f.	Is 40:6	7704
beasts of the f will glorify Me,	Is 43:20	7704
of the f will clap *their* hands.	Is 55:12	7704
All you beasts of the f,	Is 56:9	7706a
'Like watchmen of a f they are	Jer 4:17	7706a
Do not go out into the f And	Jer 6:25	7704
on the trees of the f and on the fruit	Jer 7:20	7704
will fall like dung on the open f,	Jer 9:22	7704
"Like a scarecrow in a cucumber f	Jer 10:5	4750
gather all the beasts of the f,	Jer 12:9	7704
They have trampled down My f;	Jer 12:10	2513a
pleasant f A desolate wilderness.	Jer 12:10	2513a
On the hills in the f,	Jer 13:27	7704
"For even the doe in the f has	Jer 14:5	7704
'Zion will be plowed *as* a f,	Jer 26:18	7704
animals of the f to serve him.	Jer 27:6	7704
him the beasts of the f.	Jer 28:14	7704
my f which is at Anathoth,	Jer 32:7	7704
'Buy my f, please, that is at	Jer 32:8	7704
"I bought the f which was at	Jer 32:9	7704
"Buy for yourself the f with money and	Jer 32:25	7704
do not have vineyard or f or seed.	Jer 35:9	7704
of the forces that were in the f,	Jer 40:7	7704
of the forces that were in the f came	Jer 40:13	7704
oil and honey hidden in the f."	Jer 41:8	7704
taken away From the fruitful f,	Jer 48:33	3759
For lack of the fruits of the f.	La 4:9	7706a
is in the f will die by the sword;	Ezk 7:15	7704
were thrown out into the open f,	Ezk 16:5	7704
you numerous like plants of the f.	Ezk 16:7	7704
f will know that I am the LORD;	Ezk 17:24	7704
You will fall on the open f;	Ezk 29:5	7704
to all the trees of the f.	Ezk 31:4	7704
was loftier than all the trees of the f	Ezk 31:5	7704
the beasts of the f gave birth,	Ezk 31:6	7704
and all the beasts of the f will	Ezk 31:13	7704
all the trees of the f wilted away	Ezk 31:15	7704
I will cast you on the open f.	Ezk 32:4	7704
and whoever is in the open f I	Ezk 33:27	7704
beast of the f and were scattered.	Ezk 34:5	7704
of the f for lack of a shepherd,	Ezk 34:8	7704
the tree of the f will yield its fruit and	Ezk 34:27	7704
the tree and the produce of the f,	Ezk 36:30	7704
the heavens, the beasts of the f,	Ezk 38:20	7704
predatory bird and beast of the f.	Ezk 39:4	7704
"You will fall on the open f;	Ezk 39:5	7704
They will not take wood from the f	Ezk 39:10	7704
bird and to every beast of the f,	Ezk 39:17	7704
men dwell, *or* the beasts of the f,	Da 2:38	1251
of the f found shade under it,	Da 4:12	1251
it In the new grass of the f;	Da 4:15	1251
under which the beasts of the f	Da 4:21	1251
it in the new grass of the f,	Da 4:23	1251
let him share with the beasts of the f	Da 4:23	1251
place be with the beasts of the f	Da 4:25	1251
will be with the beasts of the f.	Da 4:32	1251
beasts of the f will devour them.	Hos 2:12	7704
for them With the beasts of the f,	Hos 2:18	7704
of the f and the birds of the sky,	Hos 4:3	7704
them Like a lamb in a large f?	Hos 4:16	4800
weeds in the furrows of the f.	Hos 10:4	7706a
heaps Beside the furrows of the f.	Hos 12:11	7706a
The f is ruined, The land mourns;	Jl 1:10	7704
the harvest of the f is destroyed.	Jl 1:11	7704
All the trees of the f dry up.	Jl 1:12	7704
burned up all the trees of the f.	Jl 1:19	7704
the beasts of the f pant for You;	Jl 1:20	7704
Do not fear, beasts of the f,	Jl 2:22	7706a
you Zion will be plowed as a f,	Mi 3:12	7704
out of the city, Dwell in the f,	Mi 4:10	7704
In the midst of a fruitful f.	Mi 7:14	3759
vegetation in the f to *each* man.	Zch 10:1	7704
vine in the f cast *its grapes*,"	Mal 3:11	7704
how the lilies of the f grow;	Mt 6:28	*68*
God so clothes the grass of the f,	Mt 6:30	*68*
man who sowed good seed in his f.	Mt 13:24	*68*
you not sow good seed in your f?	Mt 13:27	*68*
a man took and sowed in his f;	Mt 13:31	*68*
parable of the tares of the f."	Mt 13:36	*68*
and the f is the world;	Mt 13:38	*68*
like a treasure hidden in the f,	Mt 13:44	*68*
all that he has and buys that f.	Mt 13:44	*68*
"Whoever is in the f must not	Mt 24:18	*68*
there will be two men in the f;	Mt 24:40	*68*
bought the Potter's F as a burial place	Mt 27:7	*68*
For this reason that f has been	Mt 27:8	*68*
called the F of Blood to this day.	Mt 27:8	*68*
GAVE THEM FOR THE POTTER'S F,	Mt 27:10	*68*
the one who is in the f must not	Mk 13:16	*68*
God so clothes the grass in the f,	Lk 12:28	*68*
"Now his older son was in the f,	Lk 15:25	*68*
when he has come in from the f,	Lk 17:7	*68*
one who is in the f must not turn back.	Lk 17:31	*68*
"Two men will be in the f;	Lk 17:36	*68*
(Now this man acquired a f with	Ac 1:18	*5564*
that f was called Hakeldama,	Ac 1:19	*5564*
Hakeldama, that is, F of Blood.)	Ac 1:19	*5564*
you are God's f, God's building.	1Co 3:9	*1091*

FIELDS

food from its own surrounding f.	Gn 41:48	7704
the houses, the courts, and the f.	Ex 8:13	7704
shall be considered as open f;	Lv 25:31	7704
'But pasture f of their cities	Lv 25:34	7704
part of the f of his own property,	Lv 27:16	7704
or of the f of his own property,	Lv 27:28	7704
an inheritance of f and vineyards.	Nu 16:14	7704
grass in your f for your cattle,	Dt 11:15	7704
Sodom, And from the f of Gomorrah;	Dt 32:32	7709
f of the city and its villages they	Jos 21:12	7704
He will take the best of your f and	1Sa 8:14	7704
to all of you f and vineyards?	1Sa 22:7	7704
with them, while we were in the f.	1Sa 25:15	7704
be on you, nor f of offerings;	2Sa 1:21	7704
Jerusalem in the f of the Kidron,	2Ki 23:4	7709
f of the city and its villages,	1Ch 6:56	7704
hill country and the fertile f,	2Ch 26:10	3759
"We are mortgaging our f,	Ne 5:3	7704
tax *on* our f and our vineyards.	Ne 5:4	7704
we are helpless because our f and	Ne 5:5	7704
to them this very day their f,	Ne 5:11	7704
as for the villages with their f,	Ne 11:25	7704
their villages, Lachish and its f,	Ne 11:30	7704
from *their* f in Geba and Azmaveth,	Ne 12:29	7704
to gather into them from the f of	Ne 12:44	7704
earth And sends water on the f,	Jb 5:10	2351
And sow f and plant vineyards,	Ps 107:37	7704
and ten thousands in our f;	Ps 144:13	2351
not yet made the earth and the f,	Pr 8:26	2351
go into the f of the fatherless,	Pr 23:10	7704
Your f—strangers are devouring	Is 1:7	127
the f of Heshbon have withered,	Is 16:8	7709
f by the Nile Will become dry,	Is 19:7	4218
Beat your breasts for the pleasant f,	Is 32:12	7704
Their f and their wives together;	Jer 6:12	7704
to others, Their f to new owners;	Jer 8:10	7704
the f as far as the brook Kidron,	Jer 31:40	7709
"Houses and f and vineyards will	Jer 32:15	7704
'F will be bought in this land of	Jer 32:43	7704
'Men will buy f for money, sign	Jer 32:44	7704
them vineyards and f at that time.	Jer 39:10	3010
They covet f and then seize *them*,	Mi 2:2	7704
the apostate He apportions our f.'	Mi 2:4	7704
fail And the f produce no food,	Hab 3:17	7709
which they had cut from the f.	Mk 11:8	*68*
shepherds staying out in the f and	Lk 2:8	*63*
sent him into his f to feed swine.	Lk 15:15	*68*
up your eyes and look on the f,	Jn 4:35	*5561*
of the laborers who mowed your f,	Jas 5:4	*5561*

FIERCE

be their anger, for it is f;	Gn 49:7	5794
so that the f anger of the LORD	Nu 25:4	2740
a nation of f countenance who	Dt 28:50	5794
or else f men will fall upon you	Jg 18:25	4751, 5315
Gibeah, the battle became f;	Jg 20:34	3513
arose from the table in f anger,	1Sa 20:34	2750
not execute His f wrath on Amalek,	1Sa 28:18	2740
are mighty men and they are f,	2Sa 17:8	4751, 5315
that the battle was too f for him,	2Ki 3:26	2388
and they returned home in f anger.	2Ch 25:10	2750
until the f anger of our God on	Ezr 10:14	2740
of the lion and the voice of the f	Jb 4:10	
God will send His f anger on him	Jb 20:23	2740
Nor has the f lion passed over it.	Jb 28:8	
so f that he dares to arouse him;	Jb 41:10	393
F men launch an attack against me,	Ps 59:3	5794
Wrath is f and anger is a flood,	Pr 27:4	395
of the f anger of Rezin and Aram and	Is 7:4	2750
His f and great and mighty sword,	Is 27:1	7186
With His f wind He has expelled	Is 27:8	7186
of His arm to be seen in f anger,	Is 30:30	2197
You will no longer see a f people,	Is 33:19	3267
For the f anger of the LORD Has	Jer 4:8	2740
the LORD, before His f anger.	Jer 4:26	2740
of the f anger of the LORD."	Jer 12:13	2740
of the f anger of the LORD.	Jer 25:37	2740
And because of His f anger."	Jer 25:38	2740
The f anger of the LORD will not	Jer 30:24	2740
upon them, Even My f anger,'	Jer 49:37	2740
From the f anger of the LORD.	Jer 51:45	2740
on the day of His f anger.	La 1:12	2740
In f anger He has cut off All the	La 2:3	2750
He has poured out His f anger;	La 4:11	2740
I will not execute My f anger;	Hos 11:9	2740
That f and impetuous people Who	Hab 1:6	4751
And there arose a f gale of wind,	Mk 4:37	*3173*
and a f gale of wind descended	Lk 8:23	*2978*
Men were scorched with f heat;	Rv 16:9	*3173*
cup of the wine of His f wrath.	Rv 16:19	*2372*
wine press of the f wrath of God,	Rv 19:15	*2372*

FIERCELY

"If anyone f assails *you* it will	Is 54:15	1481b
The bellows blow f,	Jer 6:29	2787

FIERCENESS

turned from the f of His anger.	Jos 7:26	2740
the LORD did not turn from the f	2Ki 23:26	2740
of His anger And the f of battle;	Is 42:25	5807
of the f of the oppressing *sword*	Jer 25:38	2740

FIERCEST

f battle and withdraw from him,	2Sa 11:15	2389

FIERY

The LORD sent f serpents among	Nu 21:6	8314a

"Make a **f** *serpent*, and set it on **Nu 21:8** 8314a
with its **f** serpents and scorpions **Dt 8:15** 8314a
with inflammation and with **f** heat **Dt 28:22** 2746
He makes His arrows **f** shafts. **Ps 7:13** 1814
You will make them as a **f** oven in **Ps 21:9** 784
enough to go into the **f** hell. **Mt 5:22** *4442*
eyes and be cast into the **f** hell. **Mt 18:9** *4442*
at the **f** ordeal among you, **1Pe 4:12** *4451*

FIFTEEN
Enosh lived eight hundred and **f** years **Gn 5:10** 2568, 6240
water prevailed **f** cubits higher, **Gn 7:20** 2568, 6240
one side *of the gate shall be* **f** cubits **Ex 27:14** 2568, 6240
other side *shall be* hangings of **f** cubits **Ex 27:15** 2568, 6240
side *of the gate were* **f** cubits, **Ex 38:14** 2568, 6240
court *were* hangings of **f** cubits, **Ex 38:15** 2568, 6240
your valuation shall be **f** shekels, **Lv 27:7** 2568, 6240
Ziba had **f** sons and twenty servants. **2Sa 9:10** 2568, 6240
his **f** sons and his twenty servants **2Sa 19:17** 2568, 6240
son of Joash king of Judah lived **f** **2Ki 14:17** 2568, 6240
I will add **f** years to your life, **2Ki 20:6** 2568, 6240
lived **f** years after the death of **2Ch 25:25** 2568, 6240
I will add **f** years to your life. **Is 38:5** 2568, 6240
and **f** shekels shall be your maneh. **Ezk 45:12** 2568, 6235
So I bought her for myself for **f** **Hos 3:2** 2568, 6240
and found *it to be* **f** fathoms. **Ac 27:28** *1178b*
and stayed with him **f** days. **Ga 1:18** *1178b*
with the rod, **f** hundred miles; **Rv 21:16** *1178b*

FIFTEENTH
on the **f** day of the second month **Ex 16:1** 2568, 6240
'Then on the **f** day of the same **Lv 23:6** 2568, 6240
'On the **f** of this seventh month is **Lv 23:34** 2568, 6240
the **f** day of the seventh month, **Lv 23:39** 2568, 6240
'On the **f** day of this month **Nu 28:17** 2568, 6240
'Then on the **f** day of the seventh **Nu 29:12** 2568, 6240
on the **f** day of the first month; **Nu 33:3** 2568, 6240
month on the **f** day of the month, **1Ki 12:32** 2568, 6240
on the **f** day in the eighth month, **1Ki 12:33** 2568, 6240
In the **f** year of Amaziah the son **2Ki 14:23** 2568, 6240
the **f** for Bilgah, the sixteenth **1Ch 24:14** 2568, 6240
for the **f** to Jeremoth, his sons **1Ch 25:22** 2568, 6240
month of the **f** year of Asa's reign. **2Ch 15:10** 2568, 6240
and they rested on the **f** day and **Es 9:18** 2568, 6240
and the **f** day of the same month, **Es 9:21** 2568, 6240
year, on the **f** of the month, **Ezk 32:17** 2568, 6240
month, on the **f** day of the month, **Ezk 45:25** 2568, 6240
Now in the **f** year of the reign of **Lk 3:1** *4003*

FIFTH
and there was morning, a **f** day. **Gn 1:23** 2549
conceived and bore Jacob a **f** son. **Gn 30:17** 2549
let him exact a **f** *of the produce* of **Gn 41:34** 2567
you shall give a **f** to Pharaoh, **Gn 47:24** 2549
that Pharaoh should have the **f**; **Gn 47:26** 2569
shall add to it a **f** part of it and **Lv 5:16** 2549
'In the **f** year you are to eat **Lv 19:25** 2549
then he shall add to it a **f** of it **Lv 22:14** 2549
On the **f** day *it was* Shelumiel the **Nu 7:36** 2549
'Then on the **f** day: **Nu 29:26** 2549
on the first *day* in the **f** month. **Nu 33:38** 2549
Now the **f** lot fell to the tribe of **Jos 19:24** 2549
On the **f** day he arose to go **Jg 19:8** 2549
and the **f**, Shephatiah the son of **2Sa 3:4** 2549
in the **f** year of King Rehoboam, **1Ki 14:25** 2549
Now in the **f** year of Joram the son **2Ki 8:16** 2568
on the seventh day of the **f** month, **2Ki 25:8** 2549
Nethanel the fourth, Raddai the **f**, **1Ch 2:14** 2549
the **f** *was* Shephatiah, by Abital; **1Ch 3:3** 2549
Nohah the fourth and Rapha the **f**. **1Ch 8:2** 2549
the fourth, Jeremiah the **f**, **1Ch 12:10** 2549
the **f** for Malchijah, the sixth for **1Ch 24:9** 2549
the **f** to Nethaniah, his sons and **1Ch 25:12** 2549
Elam the **f**, Johanan the sixth, **1Ch 26:3** 2549
Sacar the fourth, Nethanel the **f**, **1Ch 26:4** 2549
The **f** for the fifth month *was* the **1Ch 27:8** 2549
The fifth for the **f** month *was* the **1Ch 27:8** 2549
about in King Rehoboam's **f** year, **2Ch 12:2** 2549
came to Jerusalem in the **f** month, **Ezr 7:8** 2549
the **f** month he came to Jerusalem, **Ezr 7:9** 2549
to me in the same manner a **f** time **Ne 6:5** 2549
exile of Jerusalem in the **f** month. **Jer 1:3** 2549
the fourth year, in the **f** month, **Jer 28:1** 2549
Now in the **f** year of Jehoiakim **Jer 36:9** 2549
on the tenth *day* of the **f** month, **Jer 52:12** 2549
on the **f** *day* of the fourth month, **Ezk 1:1** 2568
(On the **f** of the month in the **Ezk 1:2** 2568
the **f** year of King Jehoiachin's exile, **Ezk 1:2** 2549
on the **f** *day* of the sixth month, **Ezk 8:1** 2568
the seventh year, in the **f** *month,* **Ezk 20:1** 2549
on the **f** of the tenth month, **Ezk 33:21** 2568
I weep in the **f** month and abstain, **Zch 7:3** 2549
mourned in the **f** and seventh months **Zch 7:5** 2549
of the fourth, the fast of the **f**, **Zch 8:19** 2549
When the Lamb broke the **f** seal, **Rv 6:9** *3991*
Then the **f** angel sounded, and I saw **Rv 9:1** *3991*
Then the **f** *angel* poured out his **Rv 16:10** *3991*
the **f**, sardonyx; the sixth, sardius; **Rv 21:20** *3991*

FIFTIES
of hundreds, of **f** and of tens. **Ex 18:21** 2572
of hundreds, of **f** and of tens. **Ex 18:25** 2572
and of hundreds, of **f** and of tens, **Dt 1:15** 2572
commanders of thousands and of **f**, **1Sa 8:12** 2572
and hid them by **f** in a cave, **1Ki 18:4** 2572
of the LORD by **f** in a cave, **1Ki 18:13** 2572
captains of fifty with their **f**; **2Ki 1:14** 2572
in groups of hundreds and of **f**. **Mk 6:40** *4004*

FIFTIETH
'You shall thus consecrate the **f** **Lv 25:10** 2572
have the **f** year as a jubilee; **Lv 25:11** 2572
f year of Azariah king of Judah, **2Ki 15:23** 2572

FIFTY
cubits, its breadth **f** cubits, **Gn 6:15** 2572
the earth one hundred and **f** days. **Gn 7:24** 2572
and **f** days the water decreased. **Gn 8:3** 2572
and **f** years after the flood. **Gn 9:28** 2572
were nine hundred and **f** years, **Gn 9:29** 2572
are **f** righteous within the city; **Gn 18:24** 2572
for the sake of the **f** righteous who **Gn 18:24** 2572
"If I find in Sodom **f** righteous **Gn 18:26** 2572
the **f** righteous are lacking five, **Gn 18:28** 2572
make **f** loops in the one curtain, **Ex 26:5** 2572
you shall make **f** loops on the edge **Ex 26:5** 2572
You shall make **f** clasps of gold, **Ex 26:6** 2572
"You shall make **f** loops on **Ex 26:10** 2572
and **f** loops on the edge of the **Ex 26:10** 2572
You shall make **f** clasps of bronze, **Ex 26:11** 2572
west side *shall be* hangings of **f** cubits **Ex 27:12** 2572
the east side *shall be* **f** cubits. **Ex 27:13** 2572
and the width **f** throughout, **Ex 27:18** 2572
half as much, two hundred and **f**, **Ex 30:23** 2572
fragrant cane two hundred and **f**, **Ex 30:23** 2572
He made **f** loops in the one curtain **Ex 36:12** 2572
he made **f** loops on the edge of the **Ex 36:12** 2572
He made **f** clasps of gold and **Ex 36:13** 2572
he made **f** loops on the edge of the **Ex 36:17** 2572
and he made **f** loops on the edge of **Ex 36:17** 2572
He made **f** clasps of bronze to **Ex 36:18** 2572
there were hangings of **f** cubits **Ex 38:12** 2572
For the east side **f** cubits. **Ex 38:13** 2572
'You shall count **f** days to the day **Lv 23:16** 2572
shall be **f** shekels of silver, **Lv 27:3** 2572
seed at **f** shekels of silver. **Lv 27:16** 2572
and upward, even to **f** years old, **Nu 4:3** 2572
years and upward to **f** years old, **Nu 4:23** 2572
and upward even to **f** years old, **Nu 4:30** 2572
and upward even to **f** years old, **Nu 4:35** 2572
and upward even to **f** years old, **Nu 4:39** 2572
and upward even to **f** years old, **Nu 4:43** 2572
and upward even to **f** years old, **Nu 4:47** 2572
"But at the age of **f** years they **Nu 8:25** 2572
and **f** leaders of the congregation, **Nu 16:2** 2572
LORD, two hundred and **f** firepans; **Nu 16:17** 2572
consumed the two hundred and **f** men **Nu 16:35** 2572
out of every **f** of the persons, **Nu 31:30** 2572
took one drawn out of every **f**, **Nu 31:47** 2572
girl's father **f** *shekels* of silver, **Dt 22:29** 2572
a bar of gold **f** shekels in weight, **Jos 7:21** 2572
and **f** men as runners before him. **2Sa 15:1** 2572
the oxen for **f** shekels of silver. **2Sa 24:24** 2572
with **f** men to run before him. **1Ki 1:5** 2572
Solomon's work, five hundred and **f**, **1Ki 9:23** 2572
him a captain of **f** with his fifty. **2Ki 1:9** 2572
him a captain of fifty with his **f**. **2Ki 1:9** 2572
replied to the captain of **f**, **2Ki 1:10** 2572
and consume you and your **f**." **2Ki 1:10** 2572
heaven and consumed him and his **f**. **2Ki 1:10** 2572
captain of **f** with his fifty. **2Ki 1:11** 2572
captain of fifty with his **f**. **2Ki 1:11** 2572
and consume you and your **f**." **2Ki 1:12** 2572
heaven and consumed him and his **f**. **2Ki 1:12** 2572
of a third **f** with his fifty. **2Ki 1:13** 2572
of a third fifty with his **f**. **2Ki 1:13** 2572
the third captain of **f** went up, **2Ki 1:13** 2572
the lives of these **f** servants of yours **2Ki 1:13** 2572
captains of **f** with their fifties; **2Ki 1:14** 2572
Now **f** men of the sons of the **2Ki 2:7** 2572
with your servants **f** strong men, **2Ki 2:16** 2572
They sent therefore **f** men; **2Ki 2:17** 2572
not more than **f** horsemen and ten **2Ki 13:7** 2572
from each man **f** shekels of silver **2Ki 15:20** 2572
him were **f** men of the Gileadites, **2Ki 15:25** 2572
the nails was **f** shekels of gold. **2Ch 3:9** 2572
two hundred and **f** who ruled over **2Ch 8:10** 2572
hundred and **f** talents of gold and **2Ch 8:18** 2572
hundred and **f** Jews and officials, **Ne 5:17** 2572
"Have a gallows **f** cubits high **Es 5:14** 2572
at Haman's house **f** cubits high, **Es 7:9** 2572
The captain of **f** and the honorable **Is 3:3** 2572
porch of the gate *was* **f** cubits. **Ezk 40:15** 2572
Its length *was* **f** cubits and the **Ezk 40:21** 2572
the length *was* **f** cubits and the **Ezk 40:25** 2572
it *was* **f** cubits long and **Ezk 40:29** 2572
it *was* **f** cubits long and **Ezk 40:33** 2572
the length *was* **f** cubits and the **Ezk 40:36** 2572
the width *was* **f** cubits. **Ezk 42:2** 2572
chambers, its length *was* **f** cubits. **Ezk 42:7** 2572
in the outer court *was* **f** cubits; **Ezk 42:8** 2572
and **f** cubits for its open space **Ezk 45:2** 2572
the wine vat to draw **f** measures, **Hg 2:16** 2572
hundred denarii, and the other **f**. **Lk 7:41** *4004*
eat in groups of about **f** each." **Lk 9:14** *4004*
and sit down quickly and write **f**.' **Lk 16:6** *4004*
"You are not yet **f** years old, and **Jn 8:57** *4004*
about four hundred and **f** years. **Ac 13:19** *4004*
it **f** thousand pieces of silver. **Ac 19:19** *3461, 4002*

FIFTY-FIVE
he reigned **f** years in Jerusalem; **2Ki 21:1** 2572
he reigned **f** years in Jerusalem. **2Ch 33:1** 2572

FIFTY-SECOND
f year of Azariah king of Judah, **2Ki 15:27** 2572

FIFTY-THREE
of large fish, a hundred and **f**; **Jn 21:11** *4004, 5140*

FIFTY-TWO
he reigned **f** years in Jerusalem; **2Ki 15:2** 2572
he reigned **f** years in Jerusalem; **2Ch 26:3** 2572
of *the month* Elul, in **f** days. **Ne 6:15** 2572

FIG
and they sewed **f** leaves together **Gn 3:7** 8384
and **f** trees and pomegranates, **Dt 8:8** 8384
"Then the trees said to the **f** tree, **Jg 9:10** 8384
"But the **f** tree said to them, **Jg 9:11** 8384
They gave him a piece of **f** cake **1Sa 30:12** 1690
man under his vine and his **f** tree, **1Ki 4:25** 8384
each of his vine and each of his **f** tree **2Ki 18:31** 8384
f cakes and bunches of raisins, **1Ch 12:40** 1690
vines also and their **f** trees, **Ps 105:33** 8384
He who tends the **f** tree will eat its **Pr 27:18** 8384
'The **f** tree has ripened its figs, **SS 2:13** 8384
the first-ripe **f** prior to summer, **Is 28:4** 1063
Or as *one* withers from the **f** tree. **Is 34:4** 8384
each of his vine and each of his **f** tree **Is 36:16** 8384
your vines and your **f** trees; **Jer 5:17** 8384
vine And no figs on the **f** tree, **Jer 8:13** 8384
destroy her vines and **f** trees, **Hos 2:12** 8384
on the **f** tree in its first *season.* **Hos 9:10** 8384
a waste And my **f** tree splinters. **Jl 1:7** 8384
dries up And the **f** tree fails; **Jl 1:12** 8384
The **f** tree and the vine have **Jl 2:22** 8384
f trees and olive trees; **Am 4:9** 8384
his vine And under his **f** tree, **Mi 4:4** 8384
Or a first-ripe **f** *which* I crave. **Mi 7:1** 1063
All your fortifications are **f** trees **Na 3:12** 8384
the **f** tree should not blossom And **Hab 3:17** 8384
including the vine, the **f** tree, **Hg 2:19** 8384
his vine and under *his* **f** tree.' " **Zch 3:10** 8384
Seeing a lone **f** tree by the road, **Mt 21:19** *4808*
And at once the **f** tree withered. **Mt 21:19** *4808*
did the **f** tree wither *all* at once?" **Mt 21:20** *4808*
do what was done to the **f** tree, **Mt 21:21** *4808*
learn the parable from the **f** tree: **Mt 24:32** *4808*
at a distance a **f** tree in leaf, **Mk 11:13** *4808*
they saw the **f** tree withered from **Mk 11:20** *4808*
the **f** tree which You cursed has **Mk 11:21** *4808*
learn the parable from the **f** tree: **Mk 13:28** *4808*
"A man had a **f** tree which **Lk 13:6** *4808*
come looking for fruit on this **f** tree **Lk 13:7** *4808*
the **f** tree and all the trees; **Lk 21:29** *4808*
when you were under the **f** tree, **Jn 1:48** *4808*
that I saw you under the **f** tree, **Jn 1:50** *4808*
Can a **f** tree, my brethren, produce **Jas 3:12** *4808*
as a **f** tree casts its unripe figs **Rv 6:13** *4808*

FIGHT
who hate us, and **f** against us and **Ex 1:10** 3898a
f for you while you keep silent." **Ex 14:14** 3898a
us and go out, **f** against Amalek. **Ex 17:9** 3898a
I may be able to **f** against them and **Nu 22:11** 3898a
you will Himself **f** on your behalf, **Dt 1:30** 3898a
we will indeed go up and **f**, **Dt 1:41** 3898a
"Do not go up nor **f**, **Dt 1:42** 3898a
to **f** for you against your enemies, **Dt 20:4** 3898a
approach a city to **f** against it, **Dt 20:10** 3898a
to **f** with Joshua and with Israel. **Jos 9:2** 3898a
your enemies with whom you **f**." **Jos 10:25** 3898a
of Merom, to **f** against Israel. **Jos 11:5** 3898a
Canaanites, to **f** against them?" **Jg 1:1** 3898a
we may **f** against the Canaanites; **Jg 1:3** 3898a
sons of Judah went down to **f** against **Jg 1:9** 3898a
you went to **f** against Midian?" **Jg 8:1** 3898a
Go out now and **f** with them!" **Jg 9:38** 3898a
Jordan to **f** also against Judah, **Jg 10:9** 3898a
to **f** against the sons of Ammon? **Jg 10:18** 3898a
may **f** against the sons of Ammon." **Jg 11:6** 3898a
that you may go with us and **f** with **Jg 11:8** 3898a
"If you take me back to **f** against **Jg 11:9** 3898a
come to me to **f** against my land?" **Jg 11:12** 3898a
or did he ever **f** against them? **Jg 11:25** 3898a
sons of Ammon to **f** against them; **Jg 11:32** 3898a
"Why did you cross over to **f** **Jg 12:1** 3898a
to me this day to **f** against me?" **Jg 12:3** 3898a
therefore, be men and **f**." **1Sa 4:9** 3898a
out before us and **f** our battles." **1Sa 8:20** 3898a
assembled to **f** with Israel, **1Sa 13:5** 3898a

and f against them until they are 1Sa 15:18 3898a
is able to f with me and kill me, 1Sa 17:9 3898a
me a man that we may f together." 1Sa 17:10 3898a
go and f with this Philistine." 1Sa 17:32 3898a
this Philistine to f with him; 1Sa 17:33 3898a
for me and f the LORD's battles." 1Sa 18:17 3898a
for war, to f against Israel. 1Sa 28:1 3898a
that I may not go and f against 1Sa 29:8 3898a
did they continue to f anymore. 2Sa 2:28 3898a
you go so near to the city to f? 2Sa 11:20 3898a
to f against the house of Israel 1Ki 12:21 3898a
"You must not go up and f against 1Ki 12:24 3898a
us f against them in the plain, 1Ki 20:23 3898a
will f against them in the plain, 1Ki 20:25 3898a
up to Aphek to f against Israel. 1Ki 20:26 4421
"Do not f with small or great, 1Ki 22:31 3898a
turned aside to f against him, 1Ki 22:32 3898a
around and take me out of the f; 1Ki 22:34 4264
go with me to f against Moab?" 2Ki 3:7 4421
had come up to f against them. 2Ki 3:21 3898a
and f for your master's house." 2Ki 10:3 3898a
has come out to f against you," 2Ki 19:9 3898a
to f against Israel to restore the 2Ch 11:1 3898a
not go up or f against your relatives; 2Ch 11:4 3898a
do not f against the LORD God of 2Ch 13:12 3898a
"Do not f with small or great, 2Ch 18:30 3898a
turned aside to f against him. 2Ch 18:31 3898a
around and take me out of the f 2Ch 18:33 4264
'You *need* not f in this *battle;* 2Ch 20:17 3898a
to help us and to f our battles." 2Ch 32:8 3898a
to come *and* f against Jerusalem Ne 4:8 3898a
awesome, and f for your brothers, Ne 4:14 3898a
Our God will f for us." Ne 4:20 3898a
F against those who fight against Ps 35:1 3898a
against those who f against me. Ps 35:1 3898a
are many who f proudly against me. Ps 56:2 3898a
will each f against his brother and Is 19:2 3898a
weapons, He will f them. Is 30:32 3898a
has come out to f against you," Is 37:9 3898a
"They will f against you, but Jer 1:19 3898a
And though they f against you, Jer 15:20 3898a
"If you f against the Chaldeans, Jer 32:5 3898a
of the Chaldeans who f against it, Jer 32:24 3898a
coming to f with the Chaldeans and Jer 33:5 3898a
and they will f against it and Jer 34:22 3898a
return and f against this city, Jer 37:8 3898a
the men and went to f with Ishmael Jer 41:12 3898a
to f against the prince of Persia; Da 10:20 3898a
and f with the king of the North. Da 11:11 3898a
And they will f, for the LORD *will* Zch 10:5 3898a
forth and f against those nations, Zch 14:3 3898a
Judah also will f at Jerusalem; Zch 14:14 3898a
by them you f the good fight, 1Tm 1:18 *4754*
by them you fight the good f, 1Tm 1:18 *4752*
F the good fight of faith; 1Tm 6:12 *75*
Fight the good f of faith; 1Tm 6:12 *73*
I have fought the good f, 2Tm 4:7 *73*
so you f and quarrel. Jas 4:2 *3164*

FIGHTING

Hebrews were f with each other; Ex 2:13 5327b
for the LORD is f for them against Ex 14:25 3898a
your God is the one f for you.' Dt 3:22 3898a
God is He who has been f for you. Jos 23:3 3898a
of Elah, f with the Philistines." 1Sa 17:19 3898a
Philistines are f against Keilah and 1Sa 23:1 3898a
lord is f the battles of the LORD, 1Sa 25:28 3898a
Philistines were f against Israel, 1Sa 31:1 3898a
Then Joab returned from f against 2Sa 10:14 3898a
king of Assyria f against Libnah, 2Ki 19:8 3898a
F all day long he oppresses me. Ps 56:1 3898a
king of Assyria f against Libnah, Is 37:8 3898a
"The Chaldeans who are f Jer 32:29 3898a
were f against Jerusalem and Jer 34:1 3898a
of Babylon was f against Jerusalem Jer 34:7 3898a
Chaldeans who were f against you, Jer 37:10 3898a
men of Babylon have ceased f, Jer 51:30 3898a
then My servants would be f so Jn 18:36 *75*
may even be found f against God." Ac 5:39 *2314*
to them as they were f together, Ac 7:26 *3164*

FIGHTS

LORD your God is He who f for you, Jos 23:10 3898a
as when He f on a day of battle. Zch 14:3 3898a

FIGS

of the pomegranates and the f. Nu 13:23 8384
or f or vines or pomegranates, Nu 20:5 8384
and two hundred cakes of f, 1Sa 25:18 1690
Isaiah said, "Take a cake of f." 2Ki 20:7 8384
as well as wine, grapes, f and Ne 13:15 8384
'The fig tree has ripened its f, SS 2:13 6291
"Let them take a cake of f and Is 38:21 8384
vine And no f on the fig tree, Jer 8:13 8384
two baskets of f set before the Jer 24:1 8384
One basket had very good f, Jer 24:2 8384
very good figs, like first-ripe f, Jer 24:2 8384
the other basket had very bad f which Jer 24:2 8384
"F, the good figs, very good; Jer 24:3 8384
'Figs, the good f, very good; Jer 24:3 8384
and the bad f, very bad, which Jer 24:3
'Like these good f, so I will Jer 24:5 8384
'But like the bad f which cannot Jer 24:8 8384
I will make them like split-open f Jer 29:17 8384
and a grower of sycamore f. Am 7:14 1103
thorn *bushes* nor f from thistles, Mt 7:16 *4810*
for it was not the season for f. Mk 11:13 *4810*
men do not gather f from thorns, Lk 6:44 *4810*
olives, or a vine produce f? Jas 3:12 *4810*
f when shaken by a great wind. Rv 6:13 *3653*

FIGURATIVE

have spoken to you in f language; Jn 16:25 *3942*
no longer speak to you in f language, Jn 16:25 *3942*

FIGURATIVELY

I have f applied to myself and 1Co 4:6 *3345*

FIGURE

yourselves in the form of any f, Dt 4:16 5566
To understand a proverb and a f, Pr 1:6 4426
a f with the appearance of a man. Ezk 1:26 1823
f of speech Jesus spoke to them, Jn 10:6 *3942*
and are not using a f of speech. Jn 16:29 *3942*

FIGURED

nor shall you place a f stone in Lv 26:1 4906
and destroy all their f stones, Nu 33:52 4906

FIGUREHEAD

had the Twin Brothers for its f. Ac 28:11 *3902*

FIGURES

Now f like oxen *were* under it *and* 2Ch 4:3 1823
f resembling four living beings. Ezk 1:5 1823

FILED

they f a complaint against me, Jb 31:13 7378

FILIGREE

set them in f *settings* of gold. Ex 28:11 4865
You shall make f *settings* of gold, Ex 28:13 4865
corded chains on the f *settings.* Ex 28:14 4865
they shall be set in gold f. Ex 28:20 4396
two cords on the two f *settings,* Ex 28:25 4865
stones, set in gold f *settings;* Ex 39:6 4865
They were set in gold f *settings* Ex 39:13 4865
f *settings* and two gold rings, Ex 39:16 4865
two cords on the two f *settings,* Ex 39:18 4865

FILL

and f the waters in the seas, Gn 1:22 4390
and multiply, and f the earth, Gn 1:28 4390
and multiply, and f the earth. Gn 9:1 4390
Then Joseph gave orders to f their Gn 42:25 4390
"F the men's sacks with food, as Gn 44:1 4390
so that you can eat your f and live Lv 25:19 7648
good things which you did not f, Dt 6:11 4390
F your horn with oil and go; 1Sa 16:1 4390
"F four pitchers with water and 1Ki 18:34 4390
yet f your mouth with laughter And Jb 8:21 4390
And let my declaration f your Jb 13:17
f himself with the east wind? Jb 15:2 4390
Him And f my mouth with arguments. Jb 23:4 4390
"Can you f his skin with harpoons, Jb 41:7 4390
You f with Your treasure; Ps 17:14 4390
f of the abundance of Your house; Ps 36:8 7301
your mouth wide and I will f it. Ps 81:10 4390
F their faces with dishonor, That Ps 83:16 4390
trees of the LORD drink their f, Ps 104:16 7646
He will f *them* with corpses, Ps 110:6 4390
the reaper does not f his hand, Ps 129:7 4390
We will f our houses with spoil; Pr 1:13 4390
drink our f of love until morning; Pr 7:18 7301
That I may f their treasuries. Pr 8:21 4390
will have his f of his own ways, Pr 14:14 7646
will f the breadth of your land, Is 8:8 4393
f the face of the world with cities." Is 14:21 4390
will f the whole world with fruit. Is 27:6 4390
And who f *cups* with mixed wine for Is 65:11 4390
I am about to f all the inhabitants Jer 13:13 4390
not f the heavens and the earth?" Jer 23:24 4390
"I will f the soul of the Jer 31:14 7301
and to f them with the corpses of Jer 33:5 4390
And drink its f of their blood; Jer 46:10 7301
Sharpen the arrows, f the quivers! Jer 51:11 4390
"Surely I will f you with a Jer 51:14 4390
and f your body with this scroll Ezk 3:3 4390
nor can they f their stomachs, Ezk 7:19 4390
and f the courts with the slain. Ezk 9:7 4390
and f your hands with coals of Ezk 10:2 4390
F *it* with choice bones. Ezk 24:4 4390
And f the land with the slain. Ezk 30:11 4390
f the valleys with your refuse. Ezk 32:5 4390
f its mountains with its slain; Ezk 35:8 4390
Who f the house of their lord with Zph 1:9 4390
I will f this house with glory,' Hg 2:7 4390
I will f the bow with Ephraim. Zch 9:13 4390
"F up, then, the measure *of the guilt* Mt 23:32 *4137*
"F the waterpots with water." Jn 2:7 *1072*
Now may the God of hope f you with Ro 15:13 *4137*
that He might f all things.) Eph 4:10 *4137*
f up the measure of their sins. 1Th 2:16 *378*

FILLED

and the earth was f with violence. Gn 6:11 4390
f with violence because of them; Gn 6:13 4390
went and f the skin with water and Gn 21:19 4390
down to the spring and f her jar and Gn 24:16 4390
so that the land was f with them. Ex 1:7 4390
and f the troughs to water their Ex 2:16 4390
'Then your houses shall be f and Ex 10:6 4390
morning you shall be f with bread; Ex 16:12 7646
"I have f him with the Spirit Ex 31:3 4390
has f him with the Spirit of God, Ex 35:31 4390
"He has f them with skill to Ex 35:35 4390
of the LORD f the tabernacle. Ex 40:34 4390
of the LORD f the tabernacle. Ex 40:35 4390
and f his hand with some of it and Lv 9:17 4390
be f with the glory of the LORD. Nu 14:21 4390
was f with the spirit of wisdom, Dt 34:9 4390
wineskins which we f were new, Jos 9:13 4390
and he was f with wisdom and 1Ki 7:14 4390
the cloud f the house of the LORD, 1Ki 8:10 4390
the LORD f the house of the LORD. 1Ki 8:11 4390
he also f the trench with water. 1Ki 18:35 4390
but the Arameans f the country. 1Ki 20:27 4390
that valley shall be f with water, 2Ki 3:17 4390
and the country was f with water. 2Ki 3:20 4390
every piece of good land and f it. 2Ki 3:25 4390
was f from one end to the other. 2Ki 10:21 4390
until he had f Jerusalem from one end 2Ki 21:16 4390
f their places with human bones. 2Ki 23:14 4390
f Jerusalem with innocent blood; 2Ki 24:4 4390
of the LORD, was f with a cloud, 2Ch 5:13 4390
of the LORD f the house of God. 2Ch 5:14 4390
the glory of the LORD f the house. 2Ch 7:1 4390
the glory of the LORD f the LORD's 2Ch 7:2 4390
place which he had f with spices 2Ch 16:14 4390
their abominations which have f it Ezr 9:11 4390
So they ate, were f and Ne 9:25 7646
to him, Haman was f with rage. Es 3:5 4390
was f with anger against Mordecai. Es 5:9 4390
His sides are f out with fat, And Jb 21:24 4390
f their houses with good *things;* Jb 22:18 4390
For my loins are f with burning, Ps 38:7 4390
My mouth is f with Your praise And Ps 71:8 4390
whole earth be f with His glory. Ps 72:19 4390
So they ate and were well f, Ps 78:29 7646
God heard, He was f with wrath And Ps 78:59 5674b
f with wrath at His inheritance. Ps 78:62 5674b
it took deep root and f the land. Ps 80:9 4390
soul He has f with what is good. Ps 107:9 4390
we are greatly f with contempt. Ps 123:3 7646
Our soul is greatly f With the Ps 123:4 7646
our mouth was f with laughter And Ps 126:2 4390
your barns will be f with plenty And Pr 3:10 4390
strangers will be f with your strength Pr 5:10 7646
But the wicked are f with trouble. Pr 12:21 4390
his mouth will be f with gravel. Pr 20:17 4390
And by knowledge the rooms are f Pr 24:4 4390
Nor is the ear f with hearing. Ec 1:8 4390
f *with influences* from the east, Is 2:6 4390
also been f with silver and gold Is 2:7 4390
land has also been f with horses And Is 2:7 4390
land has also been f with idols; Is 2:8 4390
His lips are f with indignation And Is 30:27 4390
He has f Zion with justice and Is 33:5 4390
sword of the LORD is f with blood, Is 34:6 4390
Nor have you f Me with the fat Is 43:24 7301
jug is to be f with wine." Jer 13:12 4390
every jug is to be f with wine?' Jer 13:12 4390
For You f me with indignation. Jer 15:17 4390
they have f My inheritance with Jer 16:18 4390
and *because* they have f this place Jer 19:4 4390
of Nethaniah f it with the slain. Jer 41:9 4390
He has f his stomach with my Jer 51:34 4390
He has f me with bitterness, He La 3:15 7646
Let him be f with reproach. La 3:30 7646
that they have f the land with Ezk 8:17 4390
and the land is f with blood and Ezk 9:9 4390
and the cloud f the inner court. Ezk 10:3 4390
the temple was f with the cloud and Ezk 10:4 4390
and the court was f with the Ezk 10:4 4390
be f with drunkenness and sorrow, Ezk 23:33 4390
I shall be f, *now that* she is laid Ezk 26:2 4390
And you were f and were very Ezk 27:25 4390
were internally f with violence, Ezk 28:16 4390
is destitute of that which f it, Ezk 32:15 4393
cities be f with flocks of men. Ezk 36:38 4392
the glory of the LORD f the house. Ezk 43:5 4390
the glory of the LORD f the house Ezk 44:4 4390
mountain and f the whole earth. Da 2:35 4391
Nebuchadnezzar was f with wrath, Da 3:19 4391
weighted down when f with sheaves. Am 2:13 4392
I am f with power—With the Spirit Mi 3:8 4390
And f his lairs with prey And his Na 2:12 4390
earth will be f With the knowledge Hab 2:14 4390
"You will be f with disgrace Hab 2:16 7646
the city will be f with boys and girls Zch 8:5 4390
be f like a *sacrificial* basin, Zch 9:15 4390
and when it was f, they drew it up Mt 13:48 *4137*
hall was f with dinner guests. Mt 22:10 *4092a*
a sponge, he f it with sour wine and Mt 27:48 *4092a*
ran and f a sponge with sour wine, Mk 15:36 *1072*
he will be f with the Holy Spirit while Lk 1:15 *4092a*
was f with the Holy Spirit. Lk 1:41 *4092a*
F THE HUNGRY WITH GOOD THINGS; Lk 1:53 *1705a*
was f with the Holy Spirit, Lk 1:67 *4092a*
'EVERY RAVINE WILL BE F, Lk 3:5 *4137*
all *the people* in the synagogue were f Lk 4:28 *4092a*
came and f both of the boats, Lk 5:7 *4092a*
and they were f with fear, saying, Lk 5:26 *4092a*
they themselves were f with rage, Lk 6:11 *4092a*
come in, so that my house may be f. Lk 14:23 *1072*
"And he would have gladly f his Lk 15:16 *1072*
So they f them up to the brim. Jn 2:7 *1072*
When they were f, Jn 6:12 *1705a*
and f twelve baskets with Jn 6:13 *1072*
you ate of the loaves and were f. Jn 6:26 *5526*
and the house was f with the Jn 12:3 *4137*
to you, sorrow has f your heart. Jn 16:6 *4137*
and it f the whole house where Ac 2:2 *4137*
And they were all f with the Holy Ac 2:4 *4092a*
and they were f with wonder and Ac 3:10 *4092a*
Peter, f with the Holy Spirit, Ac 4:8 *4092a*
were all f with the Holy Spirit and Ac 4:31 *4092a*
why has Satan f your heart to lie Ac 5:3 *4137*
and they were f with jealousy. Ac 5:17 *4092a*
f Jerusalem with your teaching and Ac 5:28 *4137*
and be f with the Holy Spirit." Ac 9:17 *4092a*
as Paul, f with the Holy Spirit, Ac 13:9 *4092a*
crowds, they were f with jealousy and Ac 13:45 *4092a*
disciples were continually f with joy Ac 13:52 *4137*
heard *this* and were f with rage, Ac 19:28 *4134*
The city was f with the confusion, Ac 19:29 *4092a*

being f with all unrighteousness, Ro 1:29 4137
of goodness, f with all knowledge and Ro 15:14 4137
You are already f, you have 1Co 4:8 2880
I am f with comfort; 2Co 7:4 4137
be f up to all the fullness of God. Eph 3:19 4137
but be f with the Spirit, Eph 5:18 4137
having been f with the fruit of Php 1:11 4137
of being f and going hungry, Php 4:12 5526
be f with the knowledge of His will Col 1:9 4137
so that I may be f with joy. 2Tm 1:4 4137
"Go in peace, be warmed and be f," Jas 2:16 5526
and f it with the fire of the Rv 8:5 1072
And the temple was f with smoke Rv 15:8 1072
the birds were f with their flesh. Rv 19:21 5526

FILLING

stopped up by f them with earth. Gn 26:15 4390
were f their houses *with* silver. Jb 3:15 4390
train of His robe f the temple. Is 6:1 4390
while the temple was f with smoke. Is 6:4 4390
city, f its streets with them." Ezk 11:6 4390
that the boat was already f up. Mk 4:37 1072
in f up what is lacking in Col 1:24 466

FILLS

"When he f his belly, *God* will Jb 20:23 4390
out of that which f the heart. Mt 12:34 4051
from that which f his heart. Lk 6:45 4051
how will the one who f the place 1Co 14:16 378
fullness of Him who f all in all. Eph 1:23 4137

FILTH

the f of the daughters of Zion and Is 4:4 6675
throw f on you And make you vile, Na 3:6 8251

FILTHINESS

Yet is not washed from his f. Pr 30:12 6675
And its f may be melted in it, Ezk 24:11 2932a
"In your f is lewdness. Ezk 24:13 2932a
not be cleansed from your f again Until Ezk 24:13 2932a
your f and from all your idols. Ezk 36:25 2932a
there must be no f and silly talk, Eph 5:4 151
Therefore, putting aside all f and Jas 1:21 4507b

FILTHY

the tables are full of f vomit, Is 28:8 6675
deeds are like a f garment; Is 64:6 5713c
Joshua was clothed with f garments Zch 3:3 6674
"Remove the f garments from him." Zch 3:4 6674
and the one who is f, still be Rv 22:11 4508
the one who is filthy, still be f; Rv 22:11 4507a

FINAL

And you groan at your f end, When Pr 5:11 319
the f period of the indignation, Da 8:19 319

FINALLY

all the men of war had f perished Dt 2:16 8552
"F all the trees said to the bramble, Jg 9:14
F his servants conspired against 2Ch 33:24
"But f Daniel came in before me, Da 4:8 318b
"F the woman died also. Lk 20:32 5306
F, brethren, rejoice, be made 2Co 13:11 3062
F, be strong in the Lord and in Eph 6:10 3062
F, my brethren, rejoice in the Php 3:1 3062
F, brethren, whatever is true, Php 4:8 3062
F then, brethren, we request and 1Th 4:1 3062
F, brethren, pray for us that the 2Th 3:1 3062

FIND

"If I f in Sodom fifty righteous Gn 18:26 4672
it if I f forty-five there." Gn 18:28 4672
not do *it* if I f thirty there." Gn 18:30 4672
trying to f the doorway. Gn 19:11 4672
you f your gods shall not live; Gn 31:32 4672
two maids, but he did not f *them.* Gn 31:33 4672
all the tent but did not f *them.* Gn 31:34 4672
but did not f the household idols. Gn 31:35 4672
may f favor in your sight. Gn 32:5 4672
speak to Esau when you f him; Gn 32:19 4672
f favor in the sight of my lord." Gn 33:8 4672
f favor in the sight of my lord." Gn 33:15 4672
"If I f favor in your sight, then Gn 34:11 4672
the woman's hand, he did not f her. Gn 38:20 4672
to Judah, and said, "I did not f her; Gn 38:22 4672
this young goat, but you did not f her." Gn 38:23 4672
"Can we f a man like this, in Gn 41:38 4672
f favor in the sight of my lord, Gn 47:25 4672
to f out what would happen to him. Ex 2:4 3045
yourselves wherever you can f *it,* Ex 5:11 4672
and the Egyptians will f difficulty Ex 7:18 3811
you will not f it in the field. Ex 16:25 4672
that I may f favor in Your sight. Ex 33:13 4672
f sufficient for its redemption, Lv 25:26 4672
and I will f out what else the Nu 22:19 3045
be sure your sin will f you out. Nu 32:23 4672
and you will f *Him* if you search Dt 4:29 4672
God is testing you to f out if you love Dt 13:3 3045
her, I did not f her a virgin,' Dt 22:14 4672
not f your daughter a virgin." Dt 22:17 4672
those nations you shall f no rest, Dt 28:65 7280b
to f out if they would obey the Jg 3:4 3045
days of the feast, and f it out, Jg 14:12 4672
stay wherever he might f *a place;* Jg 17:8 4672
stay wherever I may f *a place.*" Jg 17:9 4672
LORD grant that you may f rest, Ru 1:9 4672
in whose sight I may f favor." Ru 2:2 4672
f favor in your sight." 1Sa 1:18 4672
but they did not f *them.* 1Sa 9:4 4672
but they did not f *them.* 1Sa 9:4 4672
as you enter the city you will f him 1Sa 9:13 4672
up for you will f him at once." 1Sa 9:13 4672
then you will f two men close to 1Sa 10:2 4672
if I f out anything, then I will 1Sa 19:3 7200
'Go, f the arrows.' 1Sa 20:21 4672
f now the arrows which I am about 1Sa 20:36 4672
of Saul my father will not f you, 1Sa 23:17 4672
my young men f favor in your eyes, 1Sa 25:8 4672
Please give whatever you f at hand 1Sa 25:8 4672
to f out all that you are doing." 2Sa 3:25 3045
If I f favor in the sight of the 2Sa 15:25 4672
let me f favor in your sight, O my 2Sa 16:4 4672
searched and could not f *them,* 2Sa 17:20 4672
does not f for himself fortified cities 2Sa 20:6 4672
perhaps we will f grass and keep 1Ki 18:5 4672
swear that they could not f you. 1Ki 18:10 4672
and tell Ahab and he cannot f you, 1Ki 18:12 4672
three days but did not f him. 2Ki 2:17 4672
seek Him, He will let you f Him; 1Ch 28:9 4672
seek Him, He will let you f Him; 2Ch 15:2 4672
sought Him, and He let them f Him. 2Ch 15:4 4672
earnestly, and He let them f Him. 2Ch 15:15 4672
and you will f them at the end of 2Ch 20:16 4672
your brothers and your sons *will* f 2Ch 30:9
come and f abundant water?" 2Ch 32:4 4672
the silver and gold which you f Ezr 7:16 7912
I did not f any Levites there. Ezr 8:15 4672
and could not f a word *to say.* Ne 5:8 4672
exult when they f the grave? Jb 3:22 4672
I do not f a wise man among you. Jb 17:10 4672
for a case against him can we f?' Jb 19:28 4672
a dream, and they cannot f him; Jb 20:8 4672
that I knew where I might f Him, Jb 23:3 4672
'Who can f one who has not been Jb 31:31 5414
him f it according to his way. Jb 34:11 4672
"The Almighty—we cannot f Him; Jb 37:23 4672
wickedness until You f none. Ps 10:15 4672
have tested me and You f nothing; Ps 17:3 4672
And f your burnt offering Ps 20:3 1878
hand will f out all your enemies; Ps 21:8 4672
will f out those who hate you. Ps 21:8 4672
Would not God f this out? Ps 44:21 2713
servants f pleasure in her stones And Ps 102:14 7521
not f a way to an inhabited city. Ps 107:4 4672
Until I f a place for the LORD, A Ps 132:5 4672
f all *kinds* of precious wealth, Pr 1:13 4672
but they will not f me, Pr 1:28 4672
So you will f favor and good Pr 3:4 4672
they are life to those who f them And Pr 4:22 4672
Wounds and disgrace he will f, Pr 6:33 4672
right to those who f knowledge. Pr 8:9 4672
And I f knowledge *and* discretion. Pr 8:12 4672
who diligently seek me will f me. Pr 8:17 4672
to the word will f good, Pr 16:20 4672
keeps understanding will f good. Pr 19:8 4672
But who can f a trustworthy man? Pr 20:6 4672
ways And f a snare for yourself. Pr 22:25 3947
If you f *it,* then there will be a Pr 24:14 4672
forsakes *them* will f compassion. Pr 28:13 7355
f *more* favor Than he who flatters Pr 28:23 4672
Will in the end f him to be a son. Pr 29:21
An excellent wife, who can f? Pr 31:10 4672
yet so that man will not f out the Ec 3:11 4672
to another to f an explanation, Ec 7:27 4672
for you will f it after many days. Ec 11:1 4672
Preacher sought to f delightful words Ec 12:10 4672
I sought him but did not f him. SS 3:1 4672
I sought him but did not f him. SS 3:2 4672
for him but I did not f him; SS 5:6 4672
of Jerusalem, If you f my beloved, SS 5:8 4672
even there you will f no rest." Is 23:12 5117
will f herself a resting place. Is 34:14 4672
They will f gladness and joy, And Is 35:10 5381
with you, but will not f them, Is 41:12 4672
of your fast you f *your* desire, Is 58:3 4672
did your fathers f in Me, Jer 2:5 4672
In her month they will f her. Jer 2:24 4672
You did not f them breaking in. Jer 2:34 4672
open squares, If you can f a man, Jer 5:1 4672
you will f rest for your souls. Jer 6:16 4672
'You will seek Me and f *Me* Jer 29:13 4672
when it went to f its rest." Jer 31:2 7280b
f No vision from the LORD. La 2:9 4672
"Son of man, eat what you f; Ezk 3:1 4672
trying to f a ground of accusation Da 6:4 7912
but they could f no ground of Da 6:4 7912
"We will not f any ground of Da 6:5 7912
against this Daniel unless we f *it* Da 6:5 7912
so that she cannot f her paths. Hos 2:6 4672
seek them, but will not f *them.* Hos 2:7 4672
Yet let no one f fault, and let Hos 4:4 7378
the LORD, but they will not f *Him;* Hos 5:6 4672
they will f in me No iniquity, Hos 12:8 4672
the LORD, But they will not f *it.* Am 8:12 4672
seek, and you will f; Mt 7:7 2147
life, and there are few who f it. Mt 7:14 2147
his life for My sake will f it. Mt 10:39 2147
YOU WILL F REST FOR YOUR SOULS. Mt 11:29 2147
seeking rest, and does not f *it.* Mt 12:43 2147
his life for My sake will f it. Mt 16:25 2147
its mouth, you will f a shekel. Mt 17:27 2147
you will f a donkey tied *there* and Mt 21:2 2147
and as many as you f *there,* Mt 22:9 2147
They did not f *any,* Mt 26:60 2147
"Where will anyone be able *to* f Mk 8:4
it, you will f a colt tied *there,* Mk 11:2 2147
perhaps He would f anything on it; Mk 11:13 2147
he should come suddenly and f you Mk 13:36 2147
will f a baby wrapped in cloths and Lk 2:12 2147
When they did not f Him, Lk 2:45 2147
they might f *reason* to accuse Him. Lk 6:7 2147
f lodging and get something to eat; Lk 9:12 2647
seek, and you will f; Lk 11:9 2147
f on the alert when he comes; Lk 12:37 2147
fruit on it and did not f any. Lk 13:6 2147
will He f faith on the earth?" Lk 18:8 2147
you enter, you will f a colt tied Lk 19:30 2147
not f anything that they might do, Lk 19:48 2147
"I f no guilt in this man." Lk 23:4 2147
not f the body of the Lord Jesus. Lk 24:3 2147
and did not f His body, they came, Lk 24:23 2147
will seek Me, and will not f Me; Jn 7:34 2147
to go that we will not f Him? Jn 7:35 2147
will seek Me, and will not f Me; Jn 7:36 2147
go in and out and f pasture. Jn 10:9 2147
"I f no guilt in Him. Jn 18:38 2147
know that I f no guilt in Him." Jn 19:4 2147
Him, for I f no guilt in Him." Jn 19:6 2147
boat and you will f *a catch.*" Jn 21:6 2147
came did not f them in the prison; Ac 5:22 2147
and our fathers could f no food. Ac 7:11 2147
that he might f a dwelling place Ac 7:46 2147
When they did not f them, Ac 17:6 2147
might grope for Him and f Him, Ac 17:27 2147
when he could not f out the facts Ac 21:34 1097
so that he might f out the reason why Ac 22:24 1921
"We f nothing wrong with this man; Ac 23:9 2147
nor in the city *itself* did they f me Ac 24:12 2147
the present, and when I f time I Ac 24:25 3335
I f then the principle that evil Ro 7:21 2147
"Why does He still f fault? Ro 9:19 3201
and f *refreshing* rest in your company. Ro 15:32 4875
the Lord wills, and I shall f out, 1Co 4:19 1097
come with me and f you unprepared, 2Co 9:4 2147
I may f you to be not what I wish 2Co 12:20 2147
thing I want to f out from you: Ga 3:2 3129
sent to f out about your faith, 1Th 3:5 1097
the Lord grant to him to f mercy 2Tm 1:18 2147
f grace to help in time of need. Heb 4:16 2147
I was very glad to f *some* of your 2Jn 1:4 2147
will seek death and will not f it; Rv 9:6 2147
you and *men* will no longer f them. Rv 18:14 2147

FINDING

no one f him would slay him. Gn 4:15 4672
'Are they not f, are they not Jg 5:30 4672
upon f one pearl of great value, Mt 13:46 2147
and they were not f any. Mk 14:55 2147
But not f any *way* to bring him in Lk 5:19 2147
seeking rest, and not f any, Lk 11:24 2147
on this fig tree without f any. Lk 13:7 2147
and f him, He said, Jn 9:35 2147
Jesus, f a young donkey, sat Jn 12:14 2147
(f no basis on which to punish Ac 4:21 2147
my spirit, not f Titus my brother; 2Co 2:13 2147
For f fault with them, He says, Heb 8:8 3201
These are grumblers, f fault, Jude 1:16 3202

FINDS

and whoever f me will kill me." Gn 4:14 4672
and the blood avenger f him Nu 35:27 4672
and *another* man f her in the city Dt 22:23 4672
the man f the girl who is engaged, Dt 22:25 4672
"If a man f a girl who is a virgin, Dt 22:28 4672
and it happens that she f no favor Dt 24:1 4672
"For if a man f his enemy, will 1Sa 24:19 4672
word, As one who f great spoil. Ps 119:162 4672
blessed is the man who f wisdom And Pr 3:13 4672
"For he who f me finds life And Pr 8:35 4672
"For he who finds me f life And Pr 8:35 4672
A scoffer seeks wisdom and f none, Pr 14:6
who has a crooked mind f no good, Pr 17:20 4672
who f a wife finds a good thing And Pr 18:22 4672
who finds a wife f a good thing And Pr 18:22 4672
neighbor f no favor in his eyes. Pr 21:10 2603a
righteousness and loyalty F life, Pr 21:21 4672
Whatever your hand f to do, Ec 9:10 4672
in his eyes as one who f peace. SS 8:10 4672
For in You the orphan f mercy." Hos 14:3 7355
asks receives, and he who seeks f, Mt 7:8 2147
when it comes, it f it unoccupied, Mt 12:44 2147
"If it turns out that he f it, Mt 18:13 2147
master f so doing when he comes. Mt 24:46 2147
and he who seeks, f; Lk 11:10 2147
it f it swept and put in order. Lk 11:25 2147
even in the third, and f *them* so, Lk 12:38 2147
master f so doing when he comes. Lk 12:43 2147
one which is lost until he f it? Lk 15:4 2147
search carefully until she f it? Lk 15:8 2147
For this f favor, if for 1Pe 2:19
this f favor with God. 1Pe 2:20

FINE

prepare three measures of f flour, Gn 18:6 5560
him in garments of f linen and Gn 41:42 8336
"It will become f dust over Ex 9:9
there was a f flake-like thing, Ex 16:14 1851
f as the frost on the ground. Ex 16:14 1851
and scarlet *material,* f linen, Ex 25:4 8336
with ten curtains of f twisted linen Ex 26:1 8336
material and f twisted linen; Ex 26:31 8336
material and f twisted linen, Ex 26:36 8336
hangings for the court of f twisted Ex 27:9 8336
material and f twisted linen, Ex 27:16 8336
five cubits of f twisted linen, Ex 27:18 8336
scarlet *material* and the f linen. Ex 28:5 8336
material and f twisted linen, Ex 28:6 8336
material and f twisted linen. Ex 28:8 8336
and f twisted linen you shall make it. Ex 28:15 8336
of checkered work of f linen, Ex 28:39 8336
shall make a turban of f linen, Ex 28:39 8336
shall make them of f wheat flour. Ex 29:2 5560
one-tenth *of an ephah* of f flour mixed Ex 29:40 5560
You shall beat some of it very f, Ex 30:36 1854
and scarlet *material,* f linen, Ex 35:6 8336

f linen and goats' *hair* and rams' skins	Ex 35:23	8336
scarlet *material* and in **f** linen.	Ex 35:25	8336
scarlet *material,* and in **f** linen,	Ex 35:35	8336
of **f** twisted linen and blue and	Ex 36:8	8336
material, and **f** twisted linen;	Ex 36:35	8336
material, and **f** twisted linen,	Ex 36:37	8336
the court were of **f** twisted linen.	Ex 38:9	8336
around *were* of **f** twisted linen.	Ex 38:16	8336
material and **f** twisted linen.	Ex 38:18	8336
in scarlet *material,* and **f** linen.	Ex 38:23	8336
material, and **f** twisted linen.	Ex 39:2	8336
scarlet *material,* and the **f** linen,	Ex 39:3	8336
material, and **f** twisted linen,	Ex 39:5	8336
material and **f** twisted linen.	Ex 39:8	8336
and the turban of **f** linen,	Ex 39:28	8336
and the decorated caps of **f** linen,	Ex 39:28	8336
linen breeches of **f** twisted linen,	Ex 39:28	8336
and the sash of **f** twisted linen,	Ex 39:29	8336
his offering shall be of **f** flour,	Lv 2:1	5560
take from it his handful of its **f** flour	Lv 2:2	5560
cakes of **f** flour mixed with oil,	Lv 2:4	5560
griddle, *it shall be* of **f** flour,	Lv 2:5	5560
shall be made of **f** flour with oil.	Lv 2:7	5560
of **f** flour for a sin offering;	Lv 5:11	5560
the **f** flour of the grain offering,	Lv 6:15	5560
the tenth of an ephah of **f** flour	Lv 6:20	5560
stirred **f** flour mixed with oil.	Lv 7:12	5560
three-tenths *of an ephah* of **f** flour	Lv 14:10	5560
and one-tenth *of an ephah* of **f** flour	Lv 14:21	5560
ephah of **f** flour mixed with oil,	Lv 23:13	5560
they shall be of a **f** flour,	Lv 23:17	5560
"Then you shall take **f** flour and	Lv 24:5	5560
basket of unleavened cakes of **f** flour	Nu 6:15	5560
both of them full of **f** flour mixed	Nu 7:13	5560
both of them full of **f** flour mixed	Nu 7:19	5560
both of them full of **f** flour mixed	Nu 7:25	5560
both of them full of **f** flour mixed	Nu 7:31	5560
both of them full of **f** flour mixed	Nu 7:37	5560
both of them full of **f** flour mixed	Nu 7:43	5560
both of them full of **f** flour mixed	Nu 7:49	5560
both of them full of **f** flour mixed	Nu 7:55	5560
both of them full of **f** flour mixed	Nu 7:61	5560
both of them full of **f** flour mixed	Nu 7:67	5560
both of them full of **f** flour mixed	Nu 7:73	5560
both of them full of **f** flour mixed	Nu 7:79	5560
offering, **f** flour mixed with oil;	Nu 8:8	5560
one-tenth *of an ephah* of **f** flour mixed	Nu 15:4	5560
two-tenths *of an ephah* of **f** flour	Nu 15:6	5560
three-tenths *of an ephah* of **f** flour	Nu 15:9	5560
of **f** flour for a grain offering,	Nu 28:5	5560
and two-tenths *of an ephah* of **f** flour	Nu 28:9	5560
of **f** flour mixed with oil	Nu 28:12	5560
of **f** flour mixed with oil	Nu 28:12	5560
and a tenth *of an ephah* of **f** flour	Nu 28:13	5560
offer **f** flour mixed with oil:	Nu 28:20	5560
offering, **f** flour mixed with oil:	Nu 28:28	5560
offering, **f** flour mixed with oil:	Nu 29:3	5560
offering, **f** flour mixed with oil:	Nu 29:9	5560
offering, **f** flour mixed with oil:	Nu 29:14	5560
small until it was as **f** as dust;	Dt 9:21	1854
and they shall **f** him a hundred	Dt 22:19	6064
of **f** flour and sixty kors of meal,	1Ki 4:22	5560
a measure of **f** flour will be *sold* for a	2Ki 7:1	5560
Then a measure of **f** flour *was sold*	2Ki 7:16	5560
a measure of **f** flour for a shekel,	2Ki 7:18	5560
and he imposed on the land a **f** of	2Ki 23:33	6066
f gold and what was fine silver.	2Ki 25:15	3701
fine gold and what was **f** silver.	2Ki 25:15	3701
over the **f** flour and the wine	1Ch 9:29	5560
was clothed with a robe of **f** linen	1Ch 15:27	948
the **f** flour for a grain offering,	1Ch 23:29	5560
wood and overlaid it with **f** gold,	2Ch 3:5	2896a
and he overlaid it with **f** gold,	2Ch 3:8	2896a
purple, crimson and **f** linen,	2Ch 3:14	948
and kinsmen, clothed in **f** linen,	2Ch 5:12	948
and imposed on the land a **f** of one	2Ch 36:3	6064
two utensils of **f** shiny bronze,	Ezr 8:27	2896a
There were hangings of **f** white and	Es 1:6	3768
held by cords of **f** purple linen	Es 1:6	948
a garment of **f** linen and purple;	Es 8:15	948
exchanged for articles of **f** gold.	Jb 28:17	6337
gold, And called **f** gold my trust,	Jb 31:24	3800
f as the dust before the wind;	Ps 18:42	7833
than gold, yes, than much **f** gold;	Ps 19:10	6337
set a crown of **f** gold on his head.	Ps 21:3	6337
Above gold, yes, above **f** gold.	Ps 119:127	6337
silver And her gain better than **f** gold.	Pr 3:14	
also not good to **f** the righteous,	Pr 17:26	6064
and an ornament of **f** gold	Pr 25:12	3800
clothing is **f** linen and purple.	Pr 31:22	8336
Instead of **f** clothes, a donning of	Is 3:24	6614
desolate, *Even* great and **f** ones,	Is 5:9	2896a
enemies will become like **f** dust,	Is 29:5	1851
lifts up the islands like **f** dust.	Is 40:15	1851
f gold and what was fine silver.	Jer 52:19	3701
fine gold and what was **f** silver.	Jer 52:19	3701
of Zion, Weighed against **f** gold,	La 4:2	6337
reached the age for **f** ornaments;	Ezk 16:7	5716
and I wrapped you with **f** linen and	Ezk 16:10	8336
and your dress was of **f** linen,	Ezk 16:13	8336
You ate **f** flour, honey and oil;	Ezk 16:13	5560
bread which I gave you, **f** flour,	Ezk 16:19	5560
"Your sail was of **f** embroidered	Ezk 27:7	8336
purple, embroidered work, **f** linen,	Ezk 27:16	948
hin of oil to moisten the **f** flour,	Ezk 46:14	5560
of that statue *was made* of **f** gold,	Da 2:32	2869
like a merchant seeking **f** pearls,	Mt 13:45	*2570*
and if it bears fruit next year, **f**	Lk 13:9	
dressed in purple and **f** linen,	Lk 16:19	*1040*
it is a **f** work he desires *to do.*	1Tm 3:1	*2570*
ring and dressed in **f** clothes,	Jas 2:2	*2986*
one who is wearing the **f** clothes,	Jas 2:3	*2986*
precious stones and pearls and **f** linen	Rv 18:12	*1039*
and olive oil and **f** flour and wheat	Rv 18:13	*4585*
in **f** linen and purple and scarlet,	Rv 18:16	*1039*
her to clothe herself in **f** linen,	Rv 19:8	*1039*
for the **f** linen is the righteous	Rv 19:8	*1039*
are in heaven, clothed in **f** linen,	Rv 19:14	*1039*
FINED		
he shall surely be **f** as the	Ex 21:22	6064
the wine of those who have been **f**.	Am 2:8	6064
FINELY		
they made **f** woven garments for	Ex 39:1	8278
made the tunics of **f** woven linen	Ex 39:27	8336
of **f** ground sweet incense,	Lv 16:12	1851
FINEST		
also for yourself the **f** of spices:	Ex 30:23	7218
With the **f** of the wheat	Dt 32:14	2459, 3629
feed you with the **f** of the wheat,	Ps 81:16	2459
you with the **f** of the wheat.	Ps 147:14	2459
along with all the **f** spices.	SS 4:14	7218
bow of Elam, The **f** of their might.	Jer 49:35	7225
themselves with the **f** of oils,	Am 6:6	7225
FINGER		
"This is the **f** of God."	Ex 8:19	676
horns of the altar with your **f**;	Ex 29:12	676
of stone, written by the **f** of God.	Ex 31:18	676
shall dip his **f** in the blood and	Lv 4:6	676
shall dip his **f** in the blood and	Lv 4:17	676
of the sin offering with his **f** and	Lv 4:25	676
shall take some of its blood with his **f**	Lv 4:30	676
blood of the sin offering with his **f**	Lv 4:34	676
took the blood and with his **f** put	Lv 8:15	676
and he dipped his **f** in the blood and	Lv 9:9	676
then dip his right-hand **f** into the oil	Lv 14:16	676
and with his **f** sprinkle some of	Lv 14:16	676
and with his right-hand **f** the	Lv 14:27	676
sprinkle *it* with his **f** on the mercy seat	Lv 16:14	676
the blood with his **f** seven times.	Lv 16:14	676
"With his **f** he shall sprinkle	Lv 16:19	676
take some of its blood with his **f** and	Nu 19:4	676
of stone written by the **f** of God;	Dt 9:10	676
'My little **f** is thicker than my	1Ki 12:10	6995
'My little **f** is thicker than my	2Ch 10:10	6995
f rings, nose rings,	Is 3:21	2885
your midst, The pointing of the **f** and	Is 58:9	676
to move them with *so much as* a **f**.	Mt 23:4	*1147*
I cast out demons by the **f** of God,	Lk 11:20	*1147*
that he may dip the tip of his **f**	Lk 16:24	*1147*
with His **f** wrote on the ground.	Jn 8:6	*1147*
my **f** into the place of the nails,	Jn 20:25	*1147*
"Reach here with your **f**, and see My	Jn 20:27	*1147*
FINGERS		
man of *great* stature who had six **f** on	2Sa 21:20	676
who had twenty-four **f** and toes,	1Ch 20:6	676
six **f** *on each hand* and six *toes*	1Ch 20:6	676
Your heavens, the work of Your **f**,	Ps 8:3	676
for war, *And* my **f** for battle;	Ps 144:1	676
his feet, Who points with his **f**;	Pr 6:13	676
Bind them on your **f**;	Pr 7:3	676
myrrh, And my **f** with liquid myrrh,	SS 5:5	676
That which their **f** have made.	Is 2:8	676
to that which his **f** have made,	Is 17:8	676
blood And your **f** with iniquity;	Is 59:3	676
and four **f** in thickness,	Jer 52:21	676
Suddenly the **f** of a man's hand	Da 5:5	677
and put His **f** into his ears,	Mk 7:33	*1147*
the burdens with one of your **f**.	Lk 11:46	*1147*
FINISH		
and **f** it to a cubit from the top;	Gn 6:16	3615
to count *them,* but did not **f**;	1Ch 27:24	3615
temple and to **f** this structure?"	Ezr 5:3	3635
temple and to **f** this structure?'	Ezr 5:9	3635
Can they **f** in a day?	Ne 4:2	3615
As soon as you **f** destroying,	Is 33:1	8552
soon as you **f** reading this scroll,	Jer 51:63	3615
holy city, to **f** the transgression,	Da 9:24	3615
and as soon as they **f** shattering	Da 12:7	3615
house, and his hands will **f** *it.*	Zch 4:9	1214
you will not **f** *going through* the	Mt 10:23	*5055*
foundation and is not able to **f**,	Lk 14:29	*1615*
to build and was not able to **f**.'	Lk 14:30	*1615*
so that I may **f** my course	Ac 20:24	*5048*
But now **f** doing it also,	2Co 8:11	*2005*
FINISHED		
When He **f** talking with him,	Gn 17:22	3615
As soon as He had **f** speaking	Gn 18:33	3615
Before he had **f** speaking,	Gn 24:15	3615
when she had **f** giving him a drink,	Gn 24:19	3615
until they have **f** drinking."	Gn 24:19	3615
When the camels had **f** drinking,	Gn 24:22	3615
I had **f** speaking in my heart,	Gn 24:45	3615
as Isaac had **f** blessing Jacob,	Gn 27:30	3615
when they had **f** eating the grain	Gn 43:2	3615
When Jacob **f** charging his sons, he	Gn 49:33	3615
When He had **f** speaking with	Ex 31:18	3615
Moses had **f** speaking with them,	Ex 34:33	3615
Thus Moses **f** the work.	Ex 40:33	3615
sons have **f** covering the holy *objects*	Nu 4:15	3615
had **f** setting up the tabernacle,	Nu 7:1	3615
As he **f** speaking all these words,	Nu 16:31	3615
have **f** speaking to the people,	Dt 20:9	3615
"When you have **f** paying all the	Dt 26:12	3615
when Moses **f** writing the words of	Dt 31:24	3615
When Moses had **f** speaking all	Dt 32:45	3615
nation had **f** crossing the Jordan.	Jos 3:17	8552
nation had **f** crossing the Jordan,	Jos 4:1	8552
all the people had **f** crossing,	Jos 4:11	8552
had **f** circumcising all the nation,	Jos 5:8	8552
Israel had **f** killing all the inhabitants	Jos 8:24	3615
the sons of Israel had **f** slaying them	Jos 10:20	3615
When they **f** apportioning the land	Jos 19:49	3615
So they **f** dividing the land.	Jos 19:51	3615
he had **f** presenting the tribute,	Jg 3:18	3615
When he had **f** speaking,	Jg 15:17	3615
they have **f** all my harvest.' "	Ru 2:21	3615
he has **f** eating and drinking.	Ru 3:3	3615
When he had **f** prophesying, he came	1Sa 10:13	3615
he **f** offering the burnt offering,	1Sa 13:10	3615
when he had **f** speaking to Saul,	1Sa 18:1	3615
f speaking these words to Saul,	1Sa 24:16	3615
When David had **f** offering the	2Sa 6:18	3615
"When you have **f** telling all the	2Sa 11:19	3615
As soon as he had **f** speaking,	2Sa 13:36	3615
had **f** passing from the city.	2Sa 15:24	8552
him heard *it* as they **f** eating.	1Ki 1:41	3615
until he had **f** building his own	1Ki 3:1	3615
So he built the house and **f** it;	1Ki 6:9	3615
Solomon built the house and **f** it.	1Ki 6:14	3615
gold, until all the house was **f**.	1Ki 6:22	8552
the house was **f** throughout all its	1Ki 6:38	3615
years, and he **f** all his house.	1Ki 7:1	3615
So the work of the pillars was **f**.	1Ki 7:22	8552
So Hiram **f** doing all the work	1Ki 7:40	3615
in the house of the LORD was **f**.	1Ki 7:51	7999a
When Solomon had **f** praying this	1Ki 8:54	3615
Solomon had **f** building the house of	1Ki 9:1	3615
So he **f** the house.	1Ki 9:25	7999a
had **f** offering the burnt offering,	2Ki 10:25	3615
When David had **f** offering the	1Ch 16:2	3615
of the house of the LORD is **f**.	1Ch 28:20	3615
So Huram **f** doing the work which he	2Ch 4:11	3615
for the house of the LORD was **f**.	2Ch 5:1	7999a
Now when Solomon had **f** praying,	2Ch 7:1	3615
Thus Solomon **f** the house of the	2Ch 7:11	3615
of the LORD, and until it was **f**.	2Ch 8:16	3615
f with the inhabitants of Seir,	2Ch 20:23	3615
into the chest until they had **f**.	2Ch 24:10	3615
When they had **f**,	2Ch 24:14	3615
and **f** on the sixteenth day of the	2Ch 29:17	3615
until the burnt offering was **f**.	2Ch 29:28	3615
Now when all this was **f**,	2Ch 31:1	3615
and **f** *them* by the seventh month.	2Ch 31:7	3615
is rebuilt and the walls are **f**,	Ezr 4:13	3635
city is rebuilt and the walls **f**,	Ezr 4:16	3635
great king of Israel built and **f**.	Ezr 5:11	3635
And they **f** building according to	Ezr 6:14	3635
They **f** *investigating* all the	Ezr 10:17	3615
We have **f** our years like a sigh.	Ps 90:9	3615
an end and the scorner will be **f**,	Is 29:20	3615
When Jeremiah **f** speaking all	Jer 26:8	3615
had **f** telling all the people all	Jer 43:1	3615
days were **f** For our end had come.	La 4:18	4390
had **f** measuring the inner house,	Ezk 42:15	3615
'When you have **f** cleansing *it,* you	Ezk 43:23	3615
until the indignation is **f**,	Da 11:36	3615
when it had **f** eating the vegetation	Am 7:2	3615
When Jesus had **f** these words,	Mt 7:28	*5055*
When Jesus had **f** giving instructions	Mt 11:1	*5055*
When Jesus had **f** these parables,	Mt 13:53	*5055*
When Jesus had **f** these words,	Mt 19:1	*5055*
When Jesus had **f** all these words,	Mt 26:1	*5055*
he cannot stand, but he is **f**!	Mk 3:26	*5056*
the devil had **f** every temptation,	Lk 4:13	*4931*
When He had **f** speaking, He	Lk 5:4	*3973*
a certain place, after He had **f**,	Lk 11:1	*3973*
He said, "It is **f**!"	Jn 19:30	*5055*
So when they had **f** breakfast,	Jn 21:15	*709*
Now after these things were **f**,	Ac 19:21	*4137*
we had **f** the voyage from Tyre,	Ac 21:7	*1274*
Therefore, when I have **f** this,	Ro 15:28	*2005*
good fight, I have **f** the course,	2Tm 4:7	*5055*
although His works were **f** from the	Heb 4:3	*1096*
then the mystery of God is **f**,	Rv 10:7	*5055*
When they have **f** their testimony,	Rv 11:7	*5055*
in them the wrath of God is **f**.	Rv 15:1	*5055*
of the seven angels were **f**.	Rv 15:8	*5055*
FINISHES		
he **f** atoning for the holy place and	Lv 16:20	3615
FINISHING		
and are **f** the walls and repairing	Ezr 4:12	3635
FINS		
all that have **f** and scales, those	Lv 11:9	5579
that does not have **f** and scales	Lv 11:10	5579
does not have **f** and scales is abhorrent	Lv 11:12	5579
that has **f** and scales you may eat,	Dt 14:9	5579
f and scales you shall not eat;	Dt 14:10	5579
FIR		
of *instruments made of* **f** wood,	2Sa 6:5	1265
stork, whose home is the **f** trees.	Ps 104:17	1265
He plants a **f**, and the rain makes	Is 44:14	766
your planks of **f** trees from Senir;	Ezk 27:5	1265
FIRE		
and **f** from the LORD out of heaven,	Gn 19:24	784
in his hand the **f** and the knife.	Gn 22:6	784
"Behold, the **f** and the wood, but	Gn 22:7	784
f from the midst of a bush;	Ex 3:2	784
the bush was burning with **f**,	Ex 3:2	784
hail, and **f** ran down to the earth.	Ex 9:23	784
and **f** flashing continually in the	Ex 9:24	784
that *same* night, roasted with **f**,	Ex 12:8	784
water, but rather roasted with **f**,	Ex 12:9	784
morning, you shall burn with **f**.	Ex 12:10	784

of f by night to give them light, Ex 13:21 784
day, nor the pillar of f by night, Ex 13:22 784
through the pillar of f and cloud Ex 14:24 784
the LORD descended upon it in f; Ex 19:18 784
"If a f breaks out and spreads to Ex 22:6 784
f shall surely make restitution. Ex 22:6 1200
a consuming f on the mountain top. Ex 24:17 784
burn with f outside the camp; Ex 29:14 784
an offering by f to the LORD. Ex 29:18 801
is an offering by f to the LORD. Ex 29:25 801
shall burn the remainder with f; Ex 29:34 784
an offering by f to the LORD. Ex 29:41 801
smoke a f *sacrifice* to the LORD. Ex 30:20 801
had made and burned *it* with f, Ex 32:20 784
to me, and I threw it into the f, Ex 32:24 784
"You shall not kindle a f in any Ex 35:3 784
and there was f in it by night, Ex 40:38 784
the priest shall put f on the altar Lv 1:7 784
altar and arrange wood on the f. Lv 1:7 784
is on the f that is on the altar. Lv 1:8 784
an offering by f of a soothing Lv 1:9 801
is on the f that is on the altar. Lv 1:12 784
an offering by f of a soothing Lv 1:13 801
on the wood which is on the f; Lv 1:17 784
an offering by f of a soothing Lv 1:17 801
an offering by f of a soothing Lv 2:2 801
of the offerings to the LORD by f. Lv 2:3 801
smoke on the altar *as* an offering by f Lv 2:9 801
of the offerings to the LORD by f. Lv 2:10 801
as an offering by f to the LORD. Lv 2:11 801
heads of grain roasted in the f, Lv 2:14 784
as an offering by f to the LORD. Lv 2:16 801
an offering by f to the LORD, Lv 3:3 801
is on the wood that is on the f; Lv 3:5 784
it is an offering by f of a Lv 3:5 801
as an offering by f to the LORD, Lv 3:9 801
an offering by f to the LORD. Lv 3:11 801
as an offering by f to the LORD, Lv 3:14 801
by f for a soothing aroma; Lv 3:16 801
out, and burn it on wood with f; Lv 4:12 784
on the offerings by f to the LORD. Lv 4:35 801
the offerings of the LORD by f: Lv 5:12 801
f on the altar is to be kept burning Lv 6:9 784
ashes *to* which the f reduces the burnt Lv 6:10 784
f on the altar shall be kept burning Lv 6:12 784
'F shall be kept burning Lv 6:13 784
share from My offerings by f; Lv 6:17 801
the offerings by f to the LORD. Lv 6:18 801
it shall be burned with f. Lv 6:30 784
as an offering by f to the LORD; Lv 7:5 801
third day shall be burned with f. Lv 7:17 784
it shall be burned with f. Lv 7:19 784
by f is offered to the LORD, Lv 7:25 801
bring offerings by f to the LORD. Lv 7:30 801
the offerings by f to the LORD, Lv 7:35 801
burned in the f outside the camp, Lv 8:17 784
was an offering by f to the LORD, Lv 8:21 801
was an offering by f to the LORD. Lv 8:28 801
the bread you shall burn in the f. Lv 8:32 784
he burned with f outside the camp. Lv 9:11 784
Then f came out from before the Lv 9:24 784
and after putting f in them, Lv 10:1 784
offered strange f before the LORD, Lv 10:1 784
And f came out from the presence Lv 10:2 784
over from the LORD's offerings by f Lv 10:12 801
out of the LORD's offerings by f; Lv 10:13 801
by f of the portions of fat, Lv 10:15 801
sustains in its skin a burn by f, Lv 13:24 784
it shall be burned in the f. Lv 13:52 784
you shall burn it in the f, Lv 13:55 784
the mark shall be burned in the f. Lv 13:57 784
full of coals of f from upon the altar Lv 16:12 784
incense on the f before the LORD, Lv 16:13 784
flesh, and their refuse in the f. Lv 16:27 784
third day shall be burned with f. Lv 19:6 784
and they shall be burned with f, Lv 20:14 784
the offerings by f to the LORD, Lv 21:6 801
she shall be burned with f. Lv 21:9 784
to offer the LORD's offerings by f; Lv 21:21 801
by f on the altar to the LORD. Lv 22:22 801
of an offering by f to the LORD. Lv 22:27 801
an offering by f to the LORD. Lv 23:8 801
an offering by f to the LORD *for* a Lv 23:13 801
an offering by f of a soothing Lv 23:18 801
an offering by f to the LORD.' " Lv 23:25 801
an offering by f to the LORD. Lv 23:27 801
an offering by f to the LORD. Lv 23:36 801
an offering by f to the LORD; Lv 23:36 801
to present offerings by f to the LORD Lv 23:37 801
even an offering by f to the LORD. Lv 24:7 801
him from the LORD's offerings by f, Lv 24:9 801
they offered strange f before the LORD Nu 3:4 784
hair of his head and put *it* on the f Nu 6:18 784
of f over the tabernacle, Nu 9:15 784
and the appearance of f by night. Nu 9:16 784
and the f of the LORD burned among Nu 11:1 784
to the LORD and the f died out. Nu 11:2 784
f of the LORD burned among them. Nu 11:3 784
day and in a pillar of f by night. Nu 14:14 784
make an offering by f to the LORD, Nu 15:3 801
a hin of wine as an offering by f, Nu 15:10 801
in presenting an offering by f, Nu 15:13 801
wishes to make an offering by f, Nu 15:14 801
an offering by f to the LORD, Nu 15:25 801
and put f in them, and lay incense Nu 16:7 784
his *own* censer and put f on it, Nu 16:18 784
F also came forth from the LORD Nu 16:35 784
and put in it f from the altar, Nu 16:46 784
holy *gifts reserved* from the f; Nu 18:9 784

fat in smoke *as* an offering by f, Nu 18:17 801
"For a f went forth from Heshbon, Nu 21:28 784
died, when the f devoured 250 men, Nu 26:10 784
offered strange f before the LORD. Nu 26:61 784
My food for My offerings by f, Nu 28:2 801
'This is the offering by f which Nu 28:3 801
an offering by f to the LORD. Nu 28:6 801
shall offer it, an offering by f, Nu 28:8 801
an offering by f to the LORD. Nu 28:13 801
shall present an offering by f, Nu 28:19 801
the food of the offering by f, Nu 28:24 801
an offering by f to the LORD. Nu 29:6 801
an offering by f as a soothing Nu 29:13 801
burnt offering, an offering by f, Nu 29:36 801
lived and all their camps with f. Nu 31:10 784
everything that can stand the f, Nu 31:23 784
you shall pass through the f, Nu 31:23 784
But whatever cannot stand the f Nu 31:23 784
in f by night and cloud by day, Dt 1:33 784
and the mountain burned with f to Dt 4:11 784
to you from the midst of the f; Dt 4:12 784
at Horeb from the midst of the f, Dt 4:15 784
LORD your God is a consuming f, Dt 4:24 784
speaking from the midst of the f, Dt 4:33 784
earth He let you see His great f, Dt 4:36 784
His words from the midst of the f. Dt 4:36 784
mountain from the midst of the f, Dt 5:4 784
for you were afraid because of the f Dt 5:5 784
mountain from the midst of the f, Dt 5:22 784
the mountain was burning with f, Dt 5:23 784
His voice from the midst of the f; Dt 5:24 784
For this great f will consume us; Dt 5:25 784
speaking from the midst of the f, Dt 5:26 784
burn their graven images with f. Dt 7:5 784
their gods you are to burn with f; Dt 7:25 784
over before you as a consuming f. Dt 9:3 784
the f on the day of the assembly. Dt 9:10 784
the mountain was burning with f, Dt 9:15 784
burned it with f and crushed it, Dt 9:21 784
the f on the day of the assembly; Dt 10:4 784
and burn their Asherim with f, Dt 12:3 784
daughters in the f to their gods. Dt 12:31 784
burn the city and all its booty with f Dt 13:16 784
offerings by f and His portion. Dt 18:1 801
his daughter pass through the f, Dt 18:10 784
me not see this great f anymore, Dt 18:16 784
For a f is kindled in My anger, Dt 32:22 784
And sets on f the foundations of Dt 32:22 3857
They burned the city with f, Jos 6:24 784
the ban shall be burned with f, Jos 7:15 784
and they burned them with f after Jos 7:25 784
that you shall set the city on f. Jos 8:8 784
they quickly set the city on f. Jos 8:19 784
and burn their chariots with f." Jos 11:6 784
and burned their chariots with f. Jos 11:9 784
And he burned Hazor with f. Jos 11:11 784
the offerings by f to the LORD, Jos 13:14 801
the sword and set the city on f. Jg 1:8 784
and f sprang up from the rock and Jg 6:21 784
may f come out from the bramble Jg 9:15 784
let f come out from Abimelech and Jg 9:20 784
and let f come out from the men of Jg 9:20 784
chamber on f over those *inside,* Jg 9:49 784
of the tower to burn it with f. Jg 9:52 784
you and your father's house with f. Jg 14:15 784
When he had set f to the torches, Jg 15:5 784
burned her and her father with f. Jg 15:6 784
as flax that is burned with f, Jg 15:14 784
of tow snaps when it touches f. Jg 16:9 784
and they burned the city with f. Jg 18:27 784
they also set on f all the cities Jg 20:48 784
all the f *offerings* of the sons of Israel 1Sa 2:28 801
Ziklag and burned it with f; 1Sa 30:1 784
behold, it was burned with f, 1Sa 30:3 784
and we burned Ziklag with f." 1Sa 30:14 784
go and set it on f." 2Sa 14:30 784
servants set the field on f. 2Sa 14:30 784
your servants set my field on f?" 2Sa 14:31 784
F from His mouth devoured; 2Sa 22:9 784
Him Coals of f were kindled. 2Sa 22:13 784
burned with f in *their* place." 2Sa 23:7 784
Gezer and burned it with f, 1Ki 9:16 784
the king's house over him with f, 1Ki 16:18 784
the wood, but put no f *under it;* 1Ki 18:23 784
and I will not put a f *under it.* 1Ki 18:23 784
and the God who answers by f, 1Ki 18:24 784
your god, but put no f *under it.*" 1Ki 18:25 784
Then the f of the LORD fell and 1Ki 18:38 784
After the earthquake a f, 1Ki 19:12 784
but the LORD *was* not in the f; 1Ki 19:12 784
the f a sound of a gentle blowing. 1Ki 19:12 784
let f come down from heaven and 2Ki 1:10 784
Then f came down from heaven and 2Ki 1:10 784
let f come down from heaven and 2Ki 1:12 784
Then the f of God came down from 2Ki 1:12 784
"Behold f came down from heaven and 2Ki 1:14 784
there appeared a chariot of f and 2Ki 2:11 784
a chariot of fire and horses of f which 2Ki 2:11 784
chariots of f all around Elisha. 2Ki 6:17 784
strongholds you will set on f, 2Ki 8:12 784
made his son pass through the f, 2Ki 16:3 784
daughters pass through the f, 2Ki 17:17 784
burned their children in the f 2Ki 17:31 784
have cast their gods into the f, 2Ki 19:18 784
made his son pass through the f, 2Ki 21:6 784
pass through the f for Molech. 2Ki 23:10 784
the chariots of the sun with f. 2Ki 23:11 784
great house he burned with f. 2Ki 25:9 784
order and they were burned with f. 1Ch 14:12 784

He answered him with f from heaven 1Ch 21:26 784
f came down from heaven and 2Ch 7:1 784
seeing the f come down and the 2Ch 7:3 784
they made a very great f for him. 2Ch 16:14 8316
And his people made no f for him 2Ch 21:19 8316
him like the f for his fathers. 2Ch 21:19 8316
and burned his sons in f, 2Ch 28:3 784
the f in the valley of Ben-hinnom; 2Ch 33:6 784
the f according to the ordinance, 2Ch 35:13 784
its fortified buildings with f and 2Ch 36:19 784
and its gates are burned with f." Ne 1:3 784
gates have been consumed by f?" Ne 2:3 784
gates which were consumed by f. Ne 2:13 784
and its gates burned by f. Ne 2:17 784
And with a pillar of f by night To Ne 9:12 784
way, Nor the pillar of f by night, Ne 9:19 784
"The f of God fell from heaven Jb 1:16 784
And f consumes the tents of the Jb 15:34 784
the flame of his f gives no light. Jb 18:5 784
And unfanned f will devour him; Jb 20:26 784
abundance the f has consumed.' Jb 22:20 784
underneath it is turned up as f. Jb 28:5 784
be f that consumes to Abaddon, Jb 31:12 784
Sparks of f leap forth. Jb 41:19 784
F and brimstone and burning wind Ps 11:6 784
And f from His mouth devoured; Ps 18:8 784
clouds, Hailstones and coals of f. Ps 18:12 784
voice, Hailstones and coals of f. Ps 18:13 784
His wrath, And f will devour them. Ps 21:9 784
of the LORD hews out flames of f. Ps 29:7 784
While I was musing the f burned; Ps 39:3 784
He burns the chariots with f. Ps 46:9 784
F devours before Him, And it is Ps 50:3 784
among those who breathe forth f, Ps 57:4 3857
Before your pots can feel *the* f *of* Ps 58:9
went through f and through water, Ps 66:12 784
As wax melts before the f, Ps 68:2 784
all the night with a light of f. Ps 78:14 784
And a f was kindled against Jacob And Ps 78:21 784
F devoured His young men, Ps 78:63 784
Will Your jealousy burn like f? Ps 79:5 784
It is burned with f, Ps 80:16 784
Like f that burns the forest And Ps 83:14 784
that sets the mountains on f, Ps 83:14 3857
Will Your wrath burn like f? Ps 89:46 784
F goes before Him And burns up Ps 97:3 784
Flaming f His ministers. Ps 104:4 784
rain, *And* flaming f in their land. Ps 105:32 784
And f to illumine by night. Ps 105:39 784
a f blazed up in their company; Ps 106:18 784
extinguished as a f of thorns; Ps 118:12 784
May they be cast into the f, Ps 140:10 784
F and hail, snow and clouds; Ps 148:8 784
Can a man take f in his bosom And Pr 6:27 784
his words are like scorching f. Pr 16:27 784
For lack of wood the f goes out, Pr 26:20 784
to hot embers and wood to f, Pr 26:21 784
with water, And f that never says, Pr 30:16 784
Its flashes are flashes of f, SS 8:6 784
Your cities are burned with f, Is 1:7 784
of a flaming f by night; Is 4:5 784
as a tongue of f consumes stubble And Is 5:24 784
be for burning, fuel for the f. Is 9:5 784
For wickedness burns like a f; Is 9:18 784
people are like fuel for the f; Is 9:19 784
And under his glory a f will be Is 10:16 3350
a f and his Holy One a flame, Is 10:17 784
f will devour Your enemies. Is 26:11 784
Women come *and* make a f with them, Is 27:11 215
and the flame of a consuming f. Is 29:6 784
pieces To take f from a hearth Or Is 30:14 784
His tongue is like a consuming f; Is 30:27 784
And *in* the flame of a consuming f In Is 30:30 784
A pyre of f with plenty of wood; Is 30:33 784
whose f is in Zion and whose Is 31:9 217
breath will consume you like a f. Is 33:11 784
thorns which are burned in the f. Is 33:12 784
us can live with the consuming f? Is 33:14 784
have cast their gods into the f, Is 37:19 784
When you walk through the f, Is 43:2 784
he also makes a f to bake bread. Is 44:15 8026b
Half of it he burns in the f; Is 44:16 784
I am warm, I have seen the f." Is 44:16 217
"I have burned half of it in the f and Is 44:19 784
become like stubble, F burns them; Is 47:14 784
to warm by *Nor* a f to sit before! Is 47:14 217
Behold, all you who kindle a f, Is 50:11 784
Walk in the light of your f And Is 50:11 784
smith who blows the f of coals And Is 54:16 784
As f kindles the brushwood, *as* Is 64:2 784
as f causes water to boil Is 64:2 784
You, Has been burned *by* f; Is 64:11 784
A f that burns all the day. Is 65:5 784
the LORD will come in f And His Is 66:15 784
And His rebuke with flames of f. Is 66:15 784
f And by His sword on all flesh, Is 66:16 784
And their f will not be quenched; Is 66:24 784
My wrath will go forth like f Jer 4:4 784
making My words in your mouth f Jer 5:14 784
The lead is consumed by the f; Jer 6:29 800
and the fathers kindle the f, Jer 7:18 784
sons and their daughters in the f, Jer 7:31 784
tumult He has kindled f on it, Jer 11:16 784
a f has been kindled in My anger, Jer 15:14 784
For you have kindled a f in My Jer 17:4 784
I will kindle a f in its gates Jer 17:27 784
the f as burnt offerings to Baal, Jer 19:5 784
a burning f Shut up in my bones; Jer 20:9 784
and he will burn it with f." Jer 21:10 784

My wrath may not go forth like **f**	**Jer 21:12**	784
"And I will kindle a **f** in its forest	**Jer 21:14**	784
cedars And throw *them* on the **f**.	**Jer 22:7**	784
"Is not My word like **f**?"	**Jer 23:29**	784
king of Babylon roasted in the **f**,	**Jer 29:22**	784
set this city on **f** and burn it,	**Jer 32:29**	784
daughters to pass through *the* **f**	**Jer 32:35**	
and he will burn it with **f**.	**Jer 34:2**	784
it and take it and burn it with **f**;	**Jer 34:22**	784
with *a* **f** burning in the brazier	**Jer 36:22**	
the **f** that was in the brazier,	**Jer 36:23**	784
in the **f** that was in the brazier.	**Jer 36:23**	784
king of Judah had burned in the **f**,	**Jer 36:32**	784
capture it and burn it with **f**."	**Jer 37:8**	784
up and burn this city with **f**.' "	**Jer 37:10**	784
city will not be burned with **f**,	**Jer 38:17**	784
and they will burn it with **f**,	**Jer 38:18**	784
city will be burned with **f**.' "	**Jer 38:23**	784
The Chaldeans also burned with **f**	**Jer 39:8**	784
"And I shall set **f** to the temples	**Jer 43:12**	784
Egypt he will burn with **f**.	**Jer 43:13**	784
a **f** has gone forth from Heshbon And	**Jer 48:45**	784
And her towns will be set on **f**.	**Jer 49:2**	784
set **f** to the wall of Damascus,	**Jer 49:27**	784
And I will set **f** to his cities	**Jer 50:32**	784
dwelling places are set on **f**;	**Jer 51:30**	3341
have burned the marshes with **f**,	**Jer 51:32**	784
her high gates will be set on **f**;	**Jer 51:58**	784
become exhausted *only* for **f**."	**Jer 51:58**	784
large house he burned with **f**.	**Jer 52:13**	784
on high He sent **f** into my bones,	**La 1:13**	784
a flaming **f** Consuming round about.	**La 2:3**	784
has poured out His wrath like **f**.	**La 2:4**	784
And He has kindled a **f** in Zion	**La 4:11**	784
a great cloud with **f** flashing	**Ezk 1:4**	784
metal in the midst of the **f**.	**Ezk 1:4**	784
looked like burning coals of **f**,	**Ezk 1:13**	784
The **f** was bright, and lightning	**Ezk 1:13**	784
lightning was flashing from the **f**.	**Ezk 1:13**	784
like **f** all around within it,	**Ezk 1:27**	784
downward I saw something like **f**;	**Ezk 1:27**	784
the **f** at the center of the city,	**Ezk 5:2**	217
of them and throw them into the **f** and	**Ezk 5:4**	784
the fire and burn them in the **f**;	**Ezk 5:4**	784
from it a **f** will spread to all the	**Ezk 5:4**	784
there was the appearance of **f**,	**Ezk 8:2**	784
of **f** from between the cherubim and	**Ezk 10:2**	784
"Take **f** from between the whirling	**Ezk 10:6**	784
the **f** which was between the cherubim,	**Ezk 10:7**	784
has been put into the **f** for fuel,	**Ezk 15:4**	784
the **f** has consumed both of its ends	**Ezk 15:4**	784
when the **f** has consumed it and it	**Ezk 15:5**	784
I have given to the **f** for fuel,	**Ezk 15:6**	784
they have come out of the **f**,	**Ezk 15:7**	784
fire, yet the **f** will consume them.	**Ezk 15:7**	784
causing them to pass through *the* **f**.	**Ezk 16:21**	
They will burn your houses with **f**	**Ezk 16:41**	784
The **f** consumed it.	**Ezk 19:12**	784
f has gone out from *its* branch;	**Ezk 19:14**	784
firstborn to pass through *the* **f**	**Ezk 20:26**	
your sons to pass through the **f**,	**Ezk 20:31**	784
I am about to kindle a **f** in you,	**Ezk 20:47**	784
on you with the **f** of My wrath,	**Ezk 21:31**	784
'You will be fuel for the **f**;	**Ezk 21:32**	784
blow **f** on it in order to melt *it*,	**Ezk 22:20**	784
on you with the **f** of My wrath,	**Ezk 22:21**	784
them with the **f** of My wrath;	**Ezk 22:31**	784
will be consumed by the **f**.	**Ezk 23:25**	784
to pass through *the* **f** to them as	**Ezk 23:37**	
and burn their houses with **f**.	**Ezk 23:47**	784
"Heap on the wood, kindle the **f**,	**Ezk 24:10**	784
Let her rust *be* in the **f**!	**Ezk 24:12**	784
in the midst of the stones of **f**.	**Ezk 28:14**	784
From the midst of the stones of **f**.	**Ezk 28:16**	784
brought **f** from the midst of you;	**Ezk 28:18**	784
When I set a **f** in Egypt And all	**Ezk 30:8**	784
Pathros desolate, Set a **f** in Zoan And	**Ezk 30:14**	784
"I will set a **f** in Egypt;	**Ezk 30:16**	784
"Surely in the **f** of My jealousy I	**Ezk 36:5**	784
rain, with hailstones, **f** and	**Ezk 38:22**	784
"And I will send **f** upon Magog	**Ezk 39:6**	784
midst of a furnace of blazing **f**."	**Da 3:6**	5135
midst of a furnace of blazing **f**;	**Da 3:11**	5135
midst of a furnace of blazing **f**;	**Da 3:15**	5135
us from the furnace of blazing **f**;	**Da 3:17**	5135
into the furnace of blazing **f**.	**Da 3:20**	5135
midst of the furnace of blazing **f**.	**Da 3:21**	5135
the flame of the **f** slew those men	**Da 3:22**	5135
of blazing **f** *still* tied up.	**Da 3:23**	5135
bound into the midst of the **f**?"	**Da 3:24**	5135
the midst of the **f** without harm,	**Da 3:25**	5135
door of the furnace of blazing **f**;	**Da 3:26**	5135
came out of the midst of the **f**.	**Da 3:26**	5135
f had no effect on the bodies of these	**Da 3:27**	5135
smell of **f** *even* come upon them.	**Da 3:27**	5135
Its wheels *were* a burning **f**.	**Da 7:9**	5135
"A river of **f** was flowing And	**Da 7:10**	5135
and given to the burning **f**.	**Da 7:11**	785
baker Who ceases to stir up *the* **f**	**Hos 7:4**	
morning it burns like a flaming **f**.	**Hos 7:6**	784
But I will send a **f** on its cities	**Hos 8:14**	784
For **f** has devoured the pastures of	**Jl 1:19**	784
And **f** has devoured the pastures of	**Jl 1:20**	784
A **f** consumes before them And	**Jl 2:3**	784
flame of **f** consuming the stubble,	**Jl 2:5**	784
Blood, **f** and columns of smoke.	**Jl 2:30**	784
send **f** upon the house of Hazael And	**Am 1:4**	784
will send **f** upon the wall of Gaza And	**Am 1:7**	784
will send **f** upon the wall of Tyre And	**Am 1:10**	784
"So I will send **f** upon Teman And	**Am 1:12**	784
kindle a **f** on the wall of Rabbah And	**Am 1:14**	784
"So I will send **f** upon Moab And	**Am 2:2**	784
"So I will send **f** upon Judah And	**Am 2:5**	784
Or He will break forth like a **f**,	**Am 5:6**	784
calling to contend *with them* by **f**,	**Am 7:4**	784
"Then the house of Jacob will be a **f**	**Ob 1:18**	784
set them on **f** and consume them,	**Ob 1:18**	1814
be split, Like wax before the **f**,	**Mi 1:4**	784
earnings will be burned with **f** And	**Mi 1:7**	784
His wrath is poured out like **f** And	**Na 1:6**	784
F consumes your gate bars.	**Na 3:13**	784
There **f** will consume you, The	**Na 3:15**	784
of hosts That peoples toil for **f**,	**Hab 2:13**	784
devoured In the **f** of His jealousy,	**Zph 1:18**	784
be devoured By the **f** of My zeal.	**Zph 3:8**	784
'will be a wall of **f** around her,	**Zch 2:5**	784
not a brand plucked from the **f**?"	**Zch 3:2**	784
And she will be consumed with **f**.	**Zch 9:4**	784
That a **f** may feed on your cedars.	**Zch 11:1**	784
the third part through the **f**,	**Zch 13:9**	784
you might not uselessly kindle **f** *on*	**Mal 1:10**	
For He is like a refiner's **f** and like	**Mal 3:2**	784
is cut down and thrown into the **f**.	**Mt 3:10**	*4442*
you with the Holy Spirit and **f**.	**Mt 3:11**	*4442*
the chaff with unquenchable **f**."	**Mt 3:12**	*4442*
is cut down and thrown into the **f**.	**Mt 7:19**	*4442*
are gathered up and burned with **f**,	**Mt 13:40**	*4442*
throw them into the furnace of **f**;	**Mt 13:42**	*4442*
throw them into the furnace of **f**;	**Mt 13:50**	*4442*
for he often falls into the **f** and	**Mt 17:15**	*4442*
and be cast into the eternal **f**.	**Mt 18:8**	*4442*
and set their city on **f**.	**Mt 22:7**	*1705b*
into the eternal **f** which has been	**Mt 25:41**	*4442*
thrown him both into the **f** and into	**Mk 9:22**	*4442*
hell, into the unquenchable **f**,	**Mk 9:43**	*4442*
DIE, AND THE **F** IS NOT QUENCHED.	**Mk 9:44**	*4442*
DIE, AND THE **F** IS NOT QUENCHED.	**Mk 9:46**	*4442*
DIE, AND THE **F** IS NOT QUENCHED.	**Mk 9:48**	*4442*
everyone will be salted with **f**.	**Mk 9:49**	*4442*
and warming himself at the **f**.	**Mk 14:54**	*5457*
cut down and thrown into the **f**."	**Lk 3:9**	*4442*
you with the Holy Spirit and **f**.	**Lk 3:16**	*4442*
the chaff with unquenchable **f**."	**Lk 3:17**	*4442*
do You want us to command **f** to	**Lk 9:54**	*4442*
come to cast **f** upon the earth;	**Lk 12:49**	*4442*
it rained **f** and brimstone from heaven	**Lk 17:29**	*4442*
After they had kindled a **f** in	**Lk 22:55**	*4442*
them, and cast them into the **f** and	**Jn 15:6**	*4442*
there, having made a charcoal **f**,	**Jn 18:18**	*439*
saw a charcoal **f** *already* laid and	**Jn 21:9**	*439*
as of **f** distributing themselves,	**Ac 2:3**	*4442*
THE EARTH BELOW, BLOOD, AND **F**,	**Ac 2:19**	*4442*
kindled a **f** and received us all.	**Ac 28:2**	*4443*
of sticks and laid them on the **f**,	**Ac 28:3**	*4443*
into the **f** and suffered no harm.	**Ac 28:5**	*4442*
it is *to be* revealed with **f**,	**1Co 3:13**	*4442*
f itself will test the quality of each	**1Co 3:13**	*4442*
be saved, yet so as through **f**.	**1Co 3:15**	*4442*
His mighty angels in flaming **f**,	**2Th 1:7**	*4442*
AND HIS MINISTERS A FLAME OF **F**."	**Heb 1:7**	*4442*
and THE FURY OF A **F** WHICH WILL	**Heb 10:27**	*4442*
quenched the power of **f**,	**Heb 11:34**	*4442*
can be touched and to a blazing **f**,	**Heb 12:18**	*4442*
for our God is a consuming **f**.	**Heb 12:29**	*4442*
is set aflame by such a small **f**!	**Jas 3:5**	*4442*
And the tongue is a **f**,	**Jas 3:6**	*4442*
sets on **f** the course of *our* life,	**Jas 3:6**	*5394*
our life, and is set on **f** by hell.	**Jas 3:6**	*5394*
will consume your flesh like **f**.	**Jas 5:3**	*4442*
even though tested by **f**,	**1Pe 1:7**	*4442*
earth are being reserved for **f**,	**2Pe 3:7**	*4442*
the punishment of eternal **f**.	**Jude 1:7**	*4442*
snatching them out of the **f**;	**Jude 1:23**	*4442*
His eyes were like a flame of **f**.	**Rv 1:14**	*4442*
who has eyes like a flame of **f**,	**Rv 2:18**	*4442*
to buy from Me gold refined by **f** so	**Rv 3:18**	*4442*
of **f** burning before the throne,	**Rv 4:5**	*4442*
and filled it with the **f** of the altar	**Rv 8:5**	*4442*
and there came hail and **f**,	**Rv 8:7**	*4442*
with **f** was thrown into the sea;	**Rv 8:8**	*4442*
riders had breastplates *the color* of **f**	**Rv 9:17**	*4447*
proceed **f** and smoke and brimstone.	**Rv 9:17**	*4442*
by the **f** and the smoke and the	**Rv 9:18**	*4442*
and his feet like pillars of **f**;	**Rv 10:1**	*4442*
f flows out of their mouth and	**Rv 11:5**	*4442*
so that he even makes **f** come down	**Rv 13:13**	*4442*
and he will be tormented with **f**	**Rv 14:10**	*4442*
the one who has power over **f**,	**Rv 14:18**	*4442*
like a sea of glass mixed with **f**,	**Rv 15:2**	*4442*
given to it to scorch men with **f**.	**Rv 16:8**	*4442*
flesh and will burn her up with **f**.	**Rv 17:16**	*4442*
and she will be burned up with **f**;	**Rv 18:8**	*4442*
His eyes *are* a flame of **f**,	**Rv 19:12**	*4442*
of **f** which burns with brimstone.	**Rv 19:20**	*4442*
and **f** came down from heaven and	**Rv 20:9**	*4442*
into the lake of **f** and brimstone,	**Rv 20:10**	*4442*
were thrown into the lake of **f**.	**Rv 20:14**	*4442*
the second death, the lake of **f**.	**Rv 20:14**	*4442*
he was thrown into the lake of **f**.	**Rv 20:15**	*4442*
that burns with **f** and brimstone,	**Rv 21:8**	*4442*

FIREBRAND

like a **f** snatched from a blaze;	**Am 4:11**	181

FIREBRANDS

Like a madman who throws **F**,	**Pr 26:18**	2131
these two stubs of smoldering **f**,	**Is 7:4**	181
Who encircle yourselves with **f**,	**Is 50:11**	2131

FIRELIGHT

seeing him as he sat in the **f** and	**Lk 22:56**	*5457*

FIREPAN

"He shall take a **f** full of	**Lv 16:12**	4289
take his **f** and put incense on it,	**Nu 16:17**	4289
Aaron *shall* each *bring* his **f**."	**Nu 16:17**	4289

FIREPANS

basins and its forks and its **f**;	**Ex 27:3**	4289
basins, the flesh hooks and the **f**;	**Ex 38:3**	4289
of Aaron, took their respective **f**,	**Lv 10:1**	4289
the **f**, the forks and shovels and	**Nu 4:14**	4289
the LORD, two hundred and fifty **f**;	**Nu 16:17**	4289
bowls and the spoons and the **f**,	**1Ki 7:50**	4289
took away the **f** and the basins,	**2Ki 25:15**	4289
spoons and the **f** of pure gold;	**2Ch 4:22**	4289
also took away the bowls, the **f**,	**Jer 52:19**	4289

FIREPOT

will make the clans of Judah like a **f**	**Zch 12:6**	3595

FIRES

and make **f** with the weapons and	**Ezk 39:9**	1197a
years they will make **f** of them.	**Ezk 39:9**	784
they will make **f** with the weapons;	**Ezk 39:10**	784

FIREWOOD

or gather **f** from the forests,	**Ezk 39:10**	2404

FIRM

But his bow remained **f**,	**Gn 49:24**	386
covenant of the LORD stood **f** on dry	**Jos 3:17**	5975
the priests' feet are standing **f**,	**Jos 4:3**	3559
"Be very **f**, then, to keep and do	**Jos 23:6**	2388
made his position over Israel **f**.	**2Ch 17:1**	2388
a **f** regulation for the song leaders	**Ne 11:23**	548
together, **F** on him and immovable.	**Jb 41:23**	3332
upon a rock making my footsteps **f**.	**Ps 40:2**	3559
When He made **f** the skies above,	**Pr 8:28**	553
drive him *like* a peg in a **f** place,	**Is 22:23**	539
peg driven in a **f** place will give way;	**Is 22:25**	539
floor At the time it is stamped **f**;	**Jer 51:33**	1869
"The command from me is **f**:	**Da 2:5**	230
that the command from me is **f**,	**Da 2:8**	230
"And he will make a **f** covenant	**Da 9:27**	1396
yet he has no **f** root in himself,	**Mt 13:21**	
and they have no **f** root in	**Mk 4:17**	
and these have no **f** root; they	**Lk 8:13**	
But he who stands **f** in his heart,	**1Co 7:37**	*1476*
the alert, stand **f** in the faith,	**1Co 16:13**	*4739*
in your faith you are standing **f**.	**2Co 1:24**	*2476*
therefore keep standing **f** and do	**Ga 5:1**	*4739*
that you will be able to stand **f**	**Eph 6:11**	*2476*
done everything, to stand **f**.	**Eph 6:13**	*2476*
Stand **f** therefore, HAVING GIRDED	**Eph 6:14**	*2476*
you are standing **f** in one spirit,	**Php 1:27**	*4739*
in this way stand **f** in the Lord,	**Php 4:1**	*4739*
live, if you stand **f** in the Lord.	**1Th 3:8**	*4739*
stand **f** and hold to the traditions	**2Th 2:15**	*4739*
the **f** foundation of God stands,	**2Tm 2:19**	*4731*
boast of our hope **f** until the end.	**Heb 3:6**	*949*
of our assurance **f** until the end,	**Heb 3:14**	*949*
But resist him, **f** in *your* faith,	**1Pe 5:9**	*4731*
the true grace of God. Stand **f** in it!	**1Pe 5:12**	*2476*

FIRMLY

and his kingdom was **f** established.	**1Ki 2:12**	3966
as the kingdom was **f** in his hand,	**2Ki 14:5**	2388
the world is **f** established,	**1Ch 16:30**	3559
as the kingdom was **f** in his grasp,	**2Ch 25:3**	2388
He will be like a tree **f** planted	**Ps 1:3**	
It is I who have **f** set its pillars.	**Ps 75:3**	8505
the world is **f** established,	**Ps 93:1**	3559
the world is **f** established,	**Ps 96:10**	3559
And He is about to grasp you **f**	**Is 22:17**	5844b
for the foundation, **f** placed.	**Is 28:16**	3245
hold the base of its mast **f**,	**Is 33:23**	2388
Yet there is no one who stands **f**	**Da 10:21**	2388
and hold **f** to the traditions,	**1Co 11:2**	*2722*
our hope for you is **f** grounded,	**2Co 1:7**	*949*
faith **f** established and steadfast,	**Col 1:23**	*2311*
having been **f** rooted *and now* being	**Col 2:7**	*4492*

FIRST

The name of the **f** is Pishon;	**Gn 2:11**	259
month, on the **f** day of the month,	**Gn 8:5**	259
in the six hundred and **f** year,	**Gn 8:13**	259
and first year, in the **f** *month,*	**Gn 8:13**	7223
month, on the **f** of the month,	**Gn 8:13**	259
Now the **f** came forth red, all over	**Gn 25:25**	7223
"**F** sell me your birthright."	**Gn 25:31**	3117
And Jacob said, "**F** swear to me";	**Gn 25:33**	3117
"This one came out **f**."	**Gn 38:28**	7223
cows ate up the **f** seven fat cows.	**Gn 41:20**	7223
was returned in our sacks the **f** time	**Gn 43:18**	8462
came down the **f** time to buy food,	**Gn 43:20**	8462
or heed the witness of the **f** sign,	**Ex 4:8**	7223
be the **f** month of the year to you.	**Ex 12:2**	7223
but on the **f** day you shall remove	**Ex 12:15**	7223
the **f** day until the seventh day,	**Ex 12:15**	7223
'On the **f** day you shall have a	**Ex 12:16**	7223
'In the **f** *month,* on the fourteenth	**Ex 12:18**	7223
the **f** offspring of every womb	**Ex 13:2**	6363a
the **f** offspring of every womb,	**Ex 13:12**	6363a
and the **f** offspring of every beast	**Ex 13:12**	6363a
every **f** offspring of a donkey you	**Ex 13:13**	6363a
the **f** offspring of every womb,	**Ex 13:15**	6363a
the Feast of the Harvest *of* the **f** fruits	**Ex 23:16**	1061
bring the choice **f** fruits of your soil	**Ex 23:19**	1061
"A bulb shall be under the **f**	**Ex 25:35**	
of the outermost curtain in the **f**	**Ex 26:4**	
curtain that is outermost in the **f**	**Ex 26:10**	
complete to its top to the **f** ring;	**Ex 26:24**	259
the **f** row *shall be* a row of ruby,	**Ex 28:17**	259

“The **f** offspring from every womb Ex 34:19 6363a
the **f** offspring from cattle and Ex 34:19 6363a
the **f** offspring from a donkey; Ex 34:20 6363a
the **f** fruits of the wheat harvest, Ex 34:22 1061
bring the very **f** of the first fruits of Ex 34:26 7225
shall bring the very first of the **f** fruits Ex 34:26 1061
outermost curtain in the **f** set; Ex 36:11 259
curtain that was outermost in the **f** Ex 36:17 259
complete to its top to the **f** ring; Ex 36:29 259
and a bulb was under the **f** pair Ex 37:21
The **f** row *was* a row of ruby, Ex 39:10 259
“On the **f** day of the first month Ex 40:2 7223
“On the first day of the **f** month Ex 40:2 259
in the **f** month of the second year, Ex 40:17 7223
year, on the **f** *day* of the month, Ex 40:17 259
‘As an offering of **f** fruits you Lv 2:12 7225
burn it as he burned the **f** bull; Lv 4:21 7223
who shall offer **f** that which is Lv 5:8 7223
offered it for sin, like the **f**. Lv 9:15 7223
‘In the **f** month, on the fourteenth Lv 23:5 7223
‘On the **f** day you shall have a Lv 23:7 7223
shall bring in the sheaf of the **f** fruits Lv 23:10 7225
leaven as **f** fruits to the LORD. Lv 23:17 1061
with the bread of the **f** fruits Lv 23:20 1061
month on the **f** of the month you Lv 23:24 259
the **f** day is a holy convocation; Lv 23:35 7223
with a rest on the **f** day and a Lv 23:39 7223
‘Now on the **f** day you shall take Lv 23:40 7223
on the **f** of the second month, Nu 1:1 259
on the **f** of the second month. Nu 1:18 259
They shall set out **f**. Nu 2:9 7223
the **f** issue of the womb among the Nu 3:12 6363a
offering on the **f** day was Nahshon Nu 7:12 7223
of every **f** issue of the womb, Nu 8:16 6363b
in the **f** month of the second year Nu 9:1 7223
the Passover in the **f** *month,* Nu 9:5 7223
and on the **f** *days* of your months, Nu 10:10 7218
So they moved out for the **f** time Nu 10:13 7223
to their armies, set out **f**, Nu 10:14 7223
was the time of the **f** ripe grapes. Nu 13:20 1061
‘Of the **f** of your dough you shall Nu 15:20 7225
‘From the **f** of your dough you Nu 15:21 7225
the **f** fruits of those which they Nu 18:12 7225
“The **f** ripe fruits of all that is Nu 18:13 1061
“Every **f** issue of the womb of all Nu 18:15 6363a
wilderness of Zin in the **f** month; Nu 20:1 7223
“Amalek was the **f** of the nations, Nu 24:20 7225
on the fourteenth day of the **f** month Nu 28:16 7223
‘On the **f** day *shall be* a holy Nu 28:18 7223
‘Also on the day of the **f** fruits, Nu 28:26 1061
month, on the **f** day of the month, Nu 29:1 259
from Rameses in the **f** month, Nu 33:3 7223
the fifteenth day of the **f** month; Nu 33:3 7223
on the **f** *day* in the fifth month. Nu 33:38 259
the **f** *day* of the eleventh month, Dt 1:3 259
down before the LORD, as at the **f**, Dt 9:18 7223
and forty nights like the **f** time, Dt 10:10 7223
your hand shall be **f** against him Dt 13:9 7223
sacrifice on the evening of the **f** day Dt 16:4 7223
of the witnesses shall be **f** against him Dt 17:7 7223
him the **f** fruits of your grain, Dt 18:4 7225
and the **f** shearing of your sheep. Dt 18:4 7225
that you shall take some of the **f** Dt 26:2 7225
I have brought the **f** of the Dt 26:10 7225
provided the **f** *part* for himself, Dt 33:21 7225
Jordan on the tenth of the **f** month Jos 4:19 7223
come out to meet us as at the **f**, Jos 8:5 7223
fleeing before us as at the **f**.’ Jos 8:6 7223
f to bless the people of Israel. Jos 8:33 7223
of Levi, for the lot was theirs **f**. Jos 21:10 7223
f for us against the Canaanites, Jg 1:1 8462
“Who shall go up **f** for us to Jg 20:18 8462
“Judah *shall go up* **f**.” Jg 20:18 8462
had arrayed themselves the **f** day. Jg 20:22 7223
down before us, as at the **f**.” Jg 20:32 7223
before us, as in the **f** battle.” Jg 20:39 7223
last kindness to be better than the **f** Ru 3:10 7223
“They must surely burn the fat **f**, 1Sa 2:16 3117
That **f** slaughter which 1Sa 14:14 7223
it was the **f** altar that he built 1Sa 14:35 2490c
my face unless you **f** bring Michal, 2Sa 3:13 6440
he falls on them at the **f** attack, 2Sa 17:9 8462
“I think the running of the **f** one 2Sa 18:27 7223
the **f** of all the house of Joseph 2Sa 19:20 7223
advice **f** to bring back our king?” 2Sa 19:43 7223
put to death in the **f** days of harvest 2Sa 21:9 7223
But the **f** woman said, 1Ki 3:22 2088
“Give the **f** woman the living child, 1Ki 3:27
me a little bread cake from it **f** and 1Ki 17:13 7223
and prepare it **f** for you are many, 1Ki 18:25 7223
your servant at the **f** I will do, 1Ki 20:9 7223
of the provinces went out **f**; 1Ki 20:17 7223
f for the word of the LORD.” 1Ki 22:5 3117
and consumed the **f** two captains of 2Ki 1:14 7223
man of God bread of the **f** fruits, 2Ki 4:42 1061
Kohathites (for theirs was the **f** 1Ch 6:54
Now the **f** who lived in their 1Ch 9:2 7223
f shall be chief and commander.” 1Ch 11:6 7223
Joab the son of Zeruiah went up **f**, 1Ch 11:6 7223
he did not attain to the **f** three. 1Ch 11:21
Ezer *was* the **f**, Obadiah the 1Ch 12:9 7218
who crossed the Jordan in the **f** month 1Ch 12:15 7223
you did not *carry it* at the **f**, 1Ch 15:13 7223
Then on that day David **f** assigned 1Ch 16:7 7218
Jehiel the **f** and Zetham and Joel, 1Ch 23:8 7218
Jahath was the **f** and 1Ch 23:11 7218
sons of Hebron *were* Jeriah the **f**, 1Ch 23:19 7218
the **f** and Isshiah the second. 1Ch 23:20 7218
the **f** lot came out for Jehoiarib, 1Ch 24:7 7223
sons of Rehabiah, Isshiah the **f**. 1Ch 24:21 7218
Jeriah *the* **f**, Amariah 1Ch 24:23
Now the **f** lot came out for Asaph 1Ch 25:9 7223
sons of Merari had sons: Shimri the **f** 1Ch 26:10 7218
firstborn, his father made him **f**), 1Ch 26:10 7218
f division for the first month; 1Ch 27:2 7223
first division for the **f** month; 1Ch 27:2 7223
of the army for the **f** month. 1Ch 27:3 7223
of King David, from **f** to last, 1Ch 29:29 7223
to the wing of the **f** cherub. 2Ch 3:12 312
acts of Solomon, from **f** to last, 2Ch 9:29 7223
acts of Rehoboam, from **f** to last, 2Ch 12:15 7223
the acts of Asa from **f** to last, 2Ch 16:11 7223
f for the word of the LORD.” 2Ch 18:4 3117
acts of Jehoshaphat, **f** to last, 2Ch 20:34 7223
acts of Amaziah, from **f** to last, 2Ch 25:26 7223
of the acts of Uzziah, **f** to last, 2Ch 26:22 7223
and all his ways, from **f** to last, 2Ch 28:26 7223
In the **f** year of his reign, in the 2Ch 29:3 7223
year of his reign, in the **f** month, 2Ch 29:3 7223
on the **f** *day* of the first month, 2Ch 29:17 259
on the first *day* of the **f** month, 2Ch 29:17 7223
the sixteenth day of the **f** month. 2Ch 29:17 7223
abundance the **f** fruits of grain, 2Ch 31:5 7225
the fourteenth *day* of the **f** month. 2Ch 35:1 7223
and his acts, **f** to last, behold, 2Ch 35:27 7223
Now in the **f** year of Cyrus king of 2Ch 36:22 259
f year of Cyrus king of Persia, Ezr 1:1 259
From the **f** day of the seventh Ezr 3:6 259
old men who had seen the **f** temple, Ezr 3:12 7223
f year of Cyrus king of Babylon, Ezr 5:13 2298
“In the **f** year of King Cyrus, Ezr 6:3 2298
on the fourteenth of the **f** month. Ezr 6:19 7223
For on the **f** of the first month he Ezr 7:9 259
For on the first of the **f** month he Ezr 7:9 7223
and on the **f** of the fifth month he Ezr 7:9 259
of the **f** month to go to Jerusalem; Ezr 8:31 7223
So they convened on the **f** day of Ezr 10:16 259
wives by the **f** day of the first month. Ezr 10:17 259
wives by the first day of the **f** month. Ezr 10:17 7223
the genealogy of those who came up **f** Ne 7:5 7223
on the **f** day of the seventh month. Ne 8:2 259
from the **f** day to the last day. Ne 8:18 7223
might bring the **f** fruits of our ground Ne 10:35 1061
the **f** fruits of all the fruit of every tree Ne 10:35 1061
also bring the **f** of our dough, Ne 10:37 7225
the **f** proceeding to the right on Ne 12:31
the contributions, the **f** fruits and Ne 12:44 7225
times and for the **f** fruits. Ne 13:31 1061
sat in the **f** place in the kingdom Es 1:14 7223
In the **f** month, which is the month Es 3:7 7223
the thirteenth day of the **f** month, Es 3:12 7223
“Were you the **f** man to be born, Jb 15:7 7223
“He is the **f** of the ways of God; Jb 40:19 7225
He named the **f** Jemimah, Jb 42:14 259
The **f** *issue* of their virility in Ps 78:51 7225
The **f** fruits of all their vigor. Ps 105:36 7225
from the **f** of all your produce; Pr 3:9 7225
Nor the **f** dust of the world. Pr 8:26 7218
f to plead his case *seems* right, Pr 18:17 7223
restore your judges as at the **f**, Is 1:26 7223
‘I, the LORD, am the **f**, Is 41:4 7223
“Your **f** forefather sinned, And Is 43:27 7223
‘I am the **f** and I am the last, And Is 44:6 7223
I am He, I am the **f**, Is 48:12 7223
the **f** I have not spoken in secret, Is 48:16 7218
the **f** into Egypt to reside there; Is 52:4 7223
the ships of Tarshish *will come* **f**, Is 60:9 7223
to the LORD, The **f** of His harvest. Jer 2:3 7225
one giving birth to her **f** child, Jer 4:31 1069
I made My name dwell at the **f**, Jer 7:12 7223
“I will **f** doubly repay their Jer 16:18 7223
was the **f** year of Nebuchadnezzar Jer 25:1 7224
rebuild them as they were at **f**. Jer 33:7 7223
of the land as they were at **f**,’ Jer 33:11 7223
from the day I **f** spoke to you, Jer 36:2
the **f** scroll which Jehoiakim the king Jer 36:28 7223
The **f** one *who* devoured him was the Jer 50:17 7223
in the **f** year of his reign, Jer 52:31
f face *was* the face of a cherub, Ezk 10:14 259
year, on the **f** of the month, Ezk 26:1 259
year, in the **f** *month,* Ezk 29:17 7223
month, on the **f** of the month, Ezk 29:17 259
the eleventh year, in the **f** *month,* Ezk 30:20 7223
month, on the **f** of the month, Ezk 31:1 259
month, on the **f** of the month, Ezk 32:1 259
treat you better than at the **f**. Ezk 36:11 7221
same measurement as the **f** gate. Ezk 40:21 7223
“The **f** of all the first Ezk 44:30 7225
“The first of all the **f** Ezk 44:30 1061
give to the priest the **f** of your dough Ezk 44:30 7225
“In the **f** *month,* on the first of Ezk 45:18 7223
month, on the **f** of the month, Ezk 45:18 259
“In the **f** *month,* on the Ezk 45:21 7223
the **f** year of Cyrus the king. Da 1:21 259
In the **f** year of Belshazzar king Da 7:1 2298
“The **f** *was* like a lion and had Da 7:4 6933
and three of the **f** horns were Da 7:8 6933
is between his eyes is the **f** king. Da 8:21 7223
In the **f** year of Darius the son of Da 9:1 259
in the **f** year of his reign, Da 9:2 259
twenty-fourth day of the **f** month, Da 10:4 7223
for from the **f** day that you set Da 10:12 7223
In the **f** year of Darius the Mede, Da 11:1 259
the LORD **f** spoke through Hosea, Hos 1:2 8462
‘I will go back to my **f** husband, Hos 2:7 7223
on the fig tree in its **f** *season.* Hos 9:10 7225
on the **f** day of the sixth month, Hg 1:1 259
the **f** chariot *were* red horses, Zch 6:2 7223
will save the tents of Judah **f**, so Zch 12:7 7223
of the **F** Gate to the Corner Gate, Zch 14:10 7223
f be reconciled to your brother, Mt 5:24 4413
“But seek **f** His kingdom and His Mt 6:33 4413
f take the log out of your own Mt 7:5 4413
Lord, permit me **f** to go and bury Mt 8:21 4413
The **f**, Simon, who is called Peter, Mt 10:2 4413
unless he **f** binds the strong *man?* Mt 12:29 4413
that man becomes worse than the **f**. Mt 12:45 4413
“**F** gather up the tares and bind Mt 13:30 4413
say that Elijah must come **f**?” Mt 17:10 4413
the house, Jesus spoke to him **f**, Mt 17:25 4399
and take the **f** fish that comes up; Mt 17:27 4413
“But many *who are* **f** will be last; Mt 19:30 4413
are first will be last; and the last, **f**. Mt 19:30 4413
with the last *group* to the **f**.’ Mt 20:8 4413
“When those *hired* **f** came, Mt 20:10 4413
“So the last shall be **f**, Mt 20:16 4413
shall be first, and the **f** last.” Mt 20:16 4413
f among you shall be your slave; Mt 20:27 4413
and he came to the **f** and said, Mt 21:28 4413
“The **f**.” Jesus said to them, Mt 21:31 4413
group of slaves larger than the **f**; Mt 21:36 4413
and the **f** married and died, and Mt 22:25 4413
f clean the inside of the cup and Mt 23:26 4413
Now on the **f** *day* of Unleavened Mt 26:17 4413
will be worse than the **f**.” Mt 27:64 4413
dawn toward the **f** *day* of the week, Mt 28:1 1520
unless he **f** binds the strong man, Mk 3:27 4413
f the blade, then the head, then Mk 4:28 4413
“Let the children be satisfied **f**, Mk 7:27 4413
say that Elijah must come **f**?” Mk 9:11 4413
f come and restore all things. Mk 9:12 4413
“If anyone wants to be **f**, Mk 9:35 4413
“But many *who are* **f** will Mk 10:31 4413
and the last, **f**.” Mk 10:31 4413
and whoever wishes to be **f** among Mk 10:44 4413
and the **f** took a wife, and died leaving Mk 12:20 4413
“The gospel must **f** be Mk 13:10 4413
On the **f** day of Unleavened Bread, Mk 14:12 4413
early on the **f** day of the week, Mk 16:2 1520
early on the **f** day of the week, Mk 16:9
He **f** appeared to Mary Magdalene, Mk 16:9 4413
This was the **f** census taken while Lk 2:2 4413
f take the log out of your own Lk 6:42 4413
me **f** to go and bury my father.” Lk 9:59 4413
but **f** permit me to say good-bye to Lk 9:61 4413
Whatever house you enter, **f** say, Lk 10:5 4413
man becomes worse than the **f**.” Lk 11:26 4413
He had not **f** ceremonially washed Lk 11:38 4413
saying to His disciples **f** *of all,* Lk 12:1 4413
some are last who will be **f** and Lk 13:30 4413
and *some* are **f** who will be last.” Lk 13:30 4413
The **f** one said to him, Lk 14:18 4413
does not **f** sit down and calculate Lk 14:28 4413
will not **f** sit down and consider Lk 14:31 4413
and he *began* saying to the **f**, Lk 16:5 4413
“But **f** He must suffer many things Lk 17:25 4413
“The **f** appeared, saying, Lk 19:16 4413
and the **f** took a wife and died Lk 20:29 4413
these things must take place **f**, Lk 21:9 4413
Then came the **f** day of Unleavened Lk 22:7
But on the **f** day of the week, at Lk 24:1 1520
He found **f** his own brother Simon and Jn 1:41 4413
“Every man serves the good wine **f**, Jn 2:10 4413
whoever then **f**, after the stirring Jn 5:4 4413
unless it **f** hears from him and Jn 7:51 4413
the **f** to throw a stone at her.” Jn 8:7 4413
place where John was **f** baptizing, Jn 10:40 4413
did not understand at the **f**; Jn 12:16 4413
and led Him to Annas **f**; Jn 18:13 4413
and broke the legs of the **f** man and Jn 19:32 4413
who had **f** come to Him by night, Jn 19:39 4413
Now on the **f** *day* of the week Mary Jn 20:1 1520
Peter and came to the tomb **f**; Jn 20:4 4413
So the other disciple who had **f** Jn 20:8 4413
that day, the **f** *day* of the week, Jn 20:19 1520
The **f** account I composed, Ac 1:1 4413
“For you **f**, God raised up His Ac 3:26 4413
sent our fathers *there* the **f** time. Ac 7:12 4413
f called Christians in Antioch. Ac 11:26 4416b
had passed the **f** and second guard, Ac 12:10 4413
of God be spoken to you **f**; Ac 13:46 4413
“Simeon has related how God **f** Ac 15:14 4413
On the **f** day of the week, when Ac 20:7 1520
the **f** day that I set foot in Asia, Ac 20:18 4413
both to those of Damascus **f**, Ac 26:20 4413
He would be the **f** to proclaim light Ac 26:23 4413
jump overboard **f** and get to land, Ac 27:43 4413
F, I thank my God through Jesus Ro 1:8 4413
the Jew **f** and also to the Greek. Ro 1:16 4413
of the Jew **f** and also of the Greek, Ro 2:9 4413
the Jew **f** and also to the Greek. Ro 2:10 4413
F of all, that they were entrusted Ro 3:2 4413
having the **f** fruits of the Spirit, Ro 8:23 536
F Moses says, “I WILL MAKE YOU Ro 10:19 4413
If the **f** piece *of dough* is holy, Ro 11:16 536
OR WHO HAS **F** GIVEN TO HIM THAT IT Ro 11:35 4272
when I have **f** enjoyed your company Ro 15:24 4413
the **f** convert to Christ from Asia. Ro 16:5 536
For, in the **f** place, when you come 1Co 11:18 4413
each one takes his own supper **f**; 1Co 11:21 4301
appointed in the church, **f** apostles, 1Co 12:28 4413
is seated, the **f** one must keep silent. 1Co 14:30 4413
it from you that the word of God **f** 1Co 14:36
delivered to you as of **f** importance 1Co 15:3 4413
the **f** fruits of those who are 1Co 15:20 536
Christ the **f** fruits, after that 1Co 15:23 536
“The **f** MAN, Adam, BECAME A LIVING 1Co 15:45 4413

However, the spiritual is not f,	1Co 15:46	4413
The f man is from the earth,	1Co 15:47	4413
On the f day of every week each	1Co 16:2	1520
they were the f fruits of Achaia,	1Co 16:15	536
I intended at f to come to you,	2Co 1:15	4387
they f gave themselves to the Lord	2Co 8:5	4413
who were the f to begin a year ago	2Co 8:10	4278
for we were the f to come even as	2Co 10:14	5348
the gospel to you the f time;	Ga 4:13	4387
to the end that we who were the f	Eph 1:12	4276
the f commandment with a promise),	Eph 6:2	4413
gospel from the f day until now.	Php 1:5	4413
at the f preaching of the gospel,	Php 4:15	746
to have f place in everything.	Col 1:18	4409
the dead in Christ will rise f.	1Th 4:16	4413
come unless the apostasy comes f,	2Th 2:3	4413
F of all, then, I urge that	1Tm 2:1	4413
For it was Adam who was f created,	1Tm 2:13	4413
These men must also f be tested;	1Tm 3:10	4413
they must f learn to practice piety	1Tm 5:4	4413
which f dwelt in your grandmother	2Tm 1:5	4413
farmer ought to be the f to receive his	2Tm 2:6	4413
my f defense no one supported me,	2Tm 4:16	4413
man after a f and second warning,	Ti 3:10	1520
at the f spoken through the Lord,	Heb 2:3	746
of all *the spoils,* was f of all,	Heb 7:2	4413
up sacrifices, f for His own sins and	Heb 7:27	4387
f *covenant* had been faultless,	Heb 8:7	4413
He has made the f obsolete.	Heb 8:13	4413
Now even the f *covenant* had	Heb 9:1	4413
committed under the f covenant,	Heb 9:15	4413
Therefore even the f *covenant* was	Heb 9:18	4413
He takes away the f in order to	Heb 10:9	4413
of f fruits among His creatures.	Jas 1:18	536
the wisdom from above is f pure,	Jas 3:17	4413
and if *it begins* with us f,	1Pe 4:17	4413
But know this f of all, that no	2Pe 1:20	4413
become worse for them than the f.	2Pe 2:20	4413
Know this f of all, that in the	2Pe 3:3	4413
We love, because He f loved us.	1Jn 4:19	4413
who loves to be f among them,	3Jn 1:9	5383
I am the f and the last,	Rv 1:17	4413
that you have left your f love.	Rv 2:4	4413
and do the deeds you did at f;	Rv 2:5	4413
The f and the last, who was dead,	Rv 2:8	4413
of late are greater than at f.	Rv 2:19	4413
and the f voice which I had heard,	Rv 4:1	4413
The f creature *was* like a lion,	Rv 4:7	4413
The f sounded, and there came	Rv 8:7	4413
The f woe is past;	Rv 9:12	1520
of the f beast in his presence.	Rv 13:12	4413
in it to worship the f beast,	Rv 13:12	4413
f fruits to God and to the Lamb.	Rv 14:4	536
So the f *angel* went and poured	Rv 16:2	4413
This is the f resurrection.	Rv 20:5	4413
has a part in the f resurrection;	Rv 20:6	4413
for the f heaven and the first	Rv 21:1	4413
and the f earth passed away,	Rv 21:1	4413
the f things have passed away."	Rv 21:4	4413
The f foundation stone was jasper;	Rv 21:19	4413
and the Omega, the f and the last,	Rv 22:13	4413

FIRSTBORN

his f, and Heth	Gn 10:15	1060
Then the f said to the younger,	Gn 19:31	1067
and the f went in and lay with her	Gn 19:33	1067
On the following day, the f said to	Gn 19:34	1067
The f bore a son, and called his	Gn 19:37	1067
Uz his f and Buz his brother	Gn 22:21	1060
the f of Ishmael, and Kedar	Gn 25:13	1060
"I am Esau your f; I have done as	Gn 27:19	1060
your f, Esau."	Gn 27:32	1060
to marry off the younger before the f.	Gn 29:26	1067
the sons of Leah: Reuben, Jacob's f,	Gn 35:23	1060
the f of Esau, are chief Teman,	Gn 36:15	1060
Now Judah took a wife for Er his f,	Gn 38:6	1060
But Er, Judah's f, was evil in	Gn 38:7	1060
Joseph named the f Manasseh, "For,"	Gn 41:51	1060
the f according to his birthright	Gn 43:33	1060
Jacob's f.	Gn 46:8	1060
although Manasseh was the f.	Gn 48:14	1060
for this one is the f. Place your	Gn 48:18	1060
"Reuben, you are my f; My might	Gn 49:3	1060
My son, My f.	Ex 4:22	1060
your son, your f."'"	Ex 4:23	1060
Israel's f: Hanoch and Pallu,	Ex 6:14	1060
and all the f in the land of Egypt	Ex 11:5	1060
from the f of the Pharaoh who sits on	Ex 11:5	1060
even to the f of the slave girl who	Ex 11:5	1060
all the f of the cattle as well.	Ex 11:5	1060
and will strike down all the f in	Ex 12:12	1060
that the LORD struck all the f in	Ex 12:29	1060
from the f of Pharaoh who sat on his	Ex 12:29	1060
who sat on his throne to the f of	Ex 12:29	1060
and all the f of cattle.	Ex 12:29	1060
"Sanctify to Me every f, the first	Ex 13:2	1060
and every f of man among your sons	Ex 13:13	1060
that the LORD killed every f in	Ex 13:15	1060
both the f of man and the firstborn	Ex 13:15	1060
the f of beast.	Ex 13:15	1060
but every f of my sons I redeem.'	Ex 13:15	1060
The f of your sons you shall give to	Ex 22:29	1060
You shall redeem all the f of your	Ex 34:20	1060
'However, a f among animals, which	Lv 27:26	1060
which as a f belongs to the LORD,	Lv 27:26	1069
Now the sons of Reuben, Israel's f,	Nu 1:20	1060
Nadab the f, and Abihu, Eleazar	Nu 3:2	1060
the sons of Israel instead of every f,	Nu 3:12	1060
"For all the f are Mine; on the day	Nu 3:13	1060
the day that I struck down all the f	Nu 3:13	1060
I sanctified to Myself all the f in	Nu 3:13	1060
"Number every f male of the sons of	Nu 3:40	1060
instead of all the f among the sons	Nu 3:41	1060
of the Levites instead of all the f	Nu 3:41	1060
So Moses numbered all the f among	Nu 3:42	1060
and all the f males by the number of	Nu 3:43	1060
"Take the Levites instead of all the f	Nu 3:45	1060
the ransom of the 273 of the f of	Nu 3:46	1060
from the f of the sons of Israel he	Nu 3:50	1060
the f of all the sons of Israel.	Nu 8:16	1060
"For every f among the sons of	Nu 8:17	1060
the day that I struck down all the f	Nu 8:17	1060
taken the Levites instead of every f	Nu 8:18	1060
nevertheless the f of man you shall	Nu 18:15	1060
and the f of unclean animals you	Nu 18:15	1060
"But the f of an ox or the firstborn	Nu 18:17	1060
"But the firstborn of an ox or the f	Nu 18:17	1060
or the firstborn of a sheep or the f	Nu 18:17	1060
Reuben, Israel's f, the sons of	Nu 26:5	1060
Egyptians were burying all their f	Nu 33:4	1060
and the f of your herd and of your	Dt 12:6	1060
or the f of your herd or flock, or	Dt 12:17	1060
and the f of your herd and your flock,	Dt 14:23	1060
to the LORD your God all the f	Dt 15:19	1060
you shall not work with the f of your	Dt 15:19	1060
nor shear the f of your flock.	Dt 15:19	1060
if the f son belongs to the unloved,	Dt 21:15	1060
make the son of the loved the f	Dt 21:16	1069
unloved, who is the f.	Dt 21:16	1060
"But he shall acknowledge the f,	Dt 21:17	1060
to him belongs the right of the f.	Dt 21:17	1060
"It shall be that the f whom she	Dt 25:6	1060
"As the f of his ox, majesty is his,	Dt 33:17	1060
with *the loss of* his f he shall	Jos 6:26	1060
for he was the f of Joseph.	Jos 17:1	1060
To Machir the f of Manasseh,	Jos 17:1	1060
So he said to Jether his f, "Rise,	Jg 8:20	1060
Now the name of his f was Joel,	1Sa 8:2	1060
the name of the f Merab	1Sa 14:49	1067
went to the battle were Eliab the f,	1Sa 17:13	1060
his f was Amnon, by Ahinoam	2Sa 3:2	1060
with the *loss of* Abiram his f,	1Ki 16:34	1060
of Sidon, his f, Heth,	1Ch 1:13	1060
their genealogies: the f of Ishmael	1Ch 1:29	1060
Judah's f, was wicked in the sight	1Ch 2:3	1060
became the father of Eliab his f,	1Ch 2:13	1060
Now the sons of Jerahmeel the f of	1Ch 2:25	1060
of Hezron *were* Ram the f, then	1Ch 2:25	1060
The sons of Ram, the f of Jerahmeel,	1Ch 2:27	1060
were Mesha his f, who was	1Ch 2:42	1060
the f of Ephrathah, *were* Shobal	1Ch 2:50	1060
the f *was* Amnon, by Ahinoam	1Ch 3:1	1060
sons of Josiah *were* Johanan the f,	1Ch 3:15	1060
the f of Ephrathah, the father of	1Ch 4:4	1060
Now the sons of Reuben the f of	1Ch 5:1	1060
of Israel (for he was the f,	1Ch 5:1	1060
the sons of Reuben the f of Israel	1Ch 5:3	1060
sons of Samuel *were* Joel the f,	1Ch 6:28	1060
became the father of Bela his f,	1Ch 8:1	1060
and his f son *was* Abdon, then	1Ch 8:30	1060
Eshek his brother *were* Ulam his f,	1Ch 8:39	1060
the Shilonites *were* Asaiah the f	1Ch 9:5	1060
who was the f of Shallum the Korahite,	1Ch 9:31	1060
and his f son *was* Abdon, then	1Ch 9:36	1060
Zechariah the f, Jediael the second,	1Ch 26:2	1060
Obed-edom had sons: Shemaiah the f,	1Ch 26:4	1060
the first (although he was not the f,	1Ch 26:10	1060
to Jehoram because he was the f.	2Ch 21:3	1060
bring to the house of our God the f	Ne 10:36	1062
and the f of our herds and our flocks	Ne 10:36	1060
The f of death devours his limbs.	Jb 18:13	1060
And smote all the f in Egypt,	Ps 78:51	1060
"I also shall make him *My* f,	Ps 89:27	1060
He also struck down all the f in	Ps 105:36	1060
He smote the f of Egypt, Both of man	Ps 135:8	1060
who smote the Egyptians in their f,	Ps 136:10	1060
And Ephraim is My f."	Jer 31:9	1060
in that they caused all their f to	Ezk 20:26	1060
Shall I present my f *for* my	Mi 6:7	1060
Him like the bitter weeping over a f.	Zch 12:10	1060
And she gave birth to her f son;	Lk 2:7	4416a
"EVERY f MALE THAT OPENS	Lk 2:23	
so that He would be the f among many	Ro 8:29	4416a
the f of all creation.	Col 1:15	4416a
the f from the dead, so that He	Col 1:18	4416a
And when He again brings the f into	Heb 1:6	4416a
so that he who destroyed the f would	Heb 11:28	4416a
general assembly and church of the f	Heb 12:23	4416a
the f of the dead, and the ruler of	Rv 1:5	4416a

FIRSTLINGS

also brought of the f of his flock	Gn 4:4	1060

FIRST-RIPE

be like the f fig prior to summer,	Is 28:4	1063
had very good figs, like f figs,	Jer 24:2	1063
to eat, *Or* a f fig *which* I crave.	Mi 7:1	1063

FISH

and let them rule over the f of	Gn 1:26	1710
and rule over the f of the sea and	Gn 1:28	1710
ground, and all the f of the sea,	Gn 9:2	1709
f that are in the Nile will die,	Ex 7:18	1710
The f that *were* in the Nile died,	Ex 7:21	1710
"We remember the f which we used	Nu 11:5	1710
Or should all the f of the sea be	Nu 11:22	1709
the likeness of any f that is in	Dt 4:18	1710
birds and creeping things and f.	1Ki 4:33	1709
to the entrance of the F Gate;	2Ch 33:14	1709
of Hassenaah built the F Gate;	Ne 3:3	1709
by the Old Gate, by the F Gate,	Ne 12:39	1709
f and all kinds of merchandise,	Ne 13:16	1710
the f of the sea declare to you.	Jb 12:8	1709
the heavens and the f of the sea,	Ps 8:8	1709
blood And caused their f to die.	Ps 105:29	1710
f caught in a treacherous net and	Ec 9:12	1709
Their f stink for lack of water And	Is 50:2	1710
"and they will f for them;	Jer 16:16	1770
And make the f of your	Ezk 29:4	1710
And all the f of your rivers will	Ezk 29:4	1710
you and all the f of your rivers;	Ezk 29:5	1710
"The f of the sea, the birds	Ezk 38:20	1709
And there will be very many f,	Ezk 47:9	1710
Their f will be according to their	Ezk 47:10	1710
like the f of the Great Sea,	Ezk 47:10	1710
also the f of the sea disappear.	Hos 4:3	1709
And the last of you with f hooks.	Am 4:2	1729
a great f to swallow Jonah,	Jon 1:17	1709
the f three days and three nights.	Jon 1:17	1709
his God from the stomach of the f,	Jon 2:1	1710
Then the LORD commanded the f,	Jon 2:10	1709
made men like the f of the sea,	Hab 1:14	1709
of the sky And the f of the sea,	Zph 1:3	1709
sound of a cry from the F Gate,	Zph 1:10	1709
"Or if he asks for a f,	Mt 7:10	2486
and gathering f of every kind;	Mt 13:47	
sat down and gathered the good f	Mt 13:48	
here only five loaves and two f."	Mt 14:17	2486
the five loaves and the two f,	Mt 14:19	2486
"Seven, and a few small f."	Mt 15:34	2485
took the seven loaves and the f;	Mt 15:36	2486
take the first f that comes up;	Mt 17:27	2486
"Five, and two f."	Mk 6:38	2486
the five loaves and the two f,	Mk 6:41	2486
He divided up the two f among them	Mk 6:41	2486
broken pieces, and also of the f.	Mk 6:43	2486
They also had a few small f;	Mk 8:7	2485
enclosed a great quantity of f;	Lk 5:6	2486
catch of f which they had taken;	Lk 5:9	2486
more than five loaves and two f,	Lk 9:13	2486
the five loaves and the two f,	Lk 9:16	2486
is asked by his son for a f;	Lk 11:11	2486
give him a snake instead of a f,	Lk 11:11	2486
gave Him a piece of a broiled f;	Lk 24:42	2486
has five barley loaves and two f,	Jn 6:9	3795
of the f as much as they wanted.	Jn 6:11	3795
"Children, you do not have any f,	Jn 21:5	4371
because of the great number of f.	Jn 21:6	2486
away, dragging the net *full* of f.	Jn 21:8	2486
already laid and f placed on it,	Jn 21:9	3795
the f which you have now caught."	Jn 21:10	3795
the net to land, full of large f,	Jn 21:11	2486
gave *it* to them, and the f likewise.	Jn 21:13	3795
flesh of birds, and another of f.	1Co 15:39	2486

FISHERMEN

And the f will lament, And all	Is 19:8	1728
I am going to send for many f,"	Jer 16:16	1728
about that f will stand beside it;	Ezk 47:10	1728
a net into the sea; for they were f.	Mt 4:18	231
a net in the sea; for they were f.	Mk 1:16	231
but the f had gotten out of them and	Lk 5:2	231

FISHERS

and I will make you f of men."	Mt 4:19	231
I will make you become f of men."	Mk 1:17	231

FISHHOOK

you draw out Leviathan with a f?	Jb 41:1	2443

FISHING

Or his head with f spears?	Jb 41:7	1709
them together in their f net.	Hab 1:15	4365a
And burn incense to their f net;	Hab 1:16	4365a
Peter said to them, "I am going f."	Jn 21:3	232

FIST

other with a stone or with *his* f,	Ex 21:18	106
He shakes his f at the mountain of	Is 10:32	3027
and to strike with a wicked f.	Is 58:4	106

FISTS

has gathered the wind in His f?	Pr 30:4	2651
rest is better than two f full of labor	Ec 4:6	2651
face and beat Him with their f;	Mt 26:67	2852
Him, and to beat Him with their f,	Mk 14:65	2852

FIT

all strong and f for war,	2Ki 24:16	6213a
write to the Jews as you see f,	Es 8:8	2896a
'And it had strong branches f	Ezk 19:11	
I am not f to remove His sandals;	Mt 3:11	2425
and I am not f to stoop down and	Mk 1:7	2425
and I am not f to untie the thong	Lk 3:16	2425
is f for the kingdom of God."	Lk 9:62	2111
f to acknowledge God any longer,	Ro 1:28	1381a
and not f to be called an apostle,	1Co 15:9	2425
fables f only for old women.	1Tm 4:7	1126

FITTED

for each board, f to one another;	Ex 26:17	7947
for each board, f to one another;	Ex 36:22	7947
With its interior lovingly f out	SS 3:10	7528
being f together, is growing into a	Eph 2:21	4883
being f and held together by what	Eph 4:16	4883

FITTEST

best and f of your master's sons,	2Ki 10:3	3477

FITTING

and it is not f for us to see the	Ezr 4:14	749
speech is not f for a fool,	Pr 17:7	5000
Luxury is not f for a fool;	Pr 19:10	5000
So honor is not f for a fool.	Pr 26:1	5000
what I have seen to be good and f:	Ec 5:18	3303
f for us to fulfill all righteousness.	Mt 3:15	4241
it seemed f for me as well, having	Lk 1:3	1380
and if it is f for me to go also,	1Co 16:4	514

coarse jesting, which are not f,	Eph 5:4	*433*
husbands, as is f in the Lord.	Col 3:18	*433*
for you, brethren, as is *only* f,	2Th 1:3	*514*
which are f for sound doctrine.	Ti 2:1	*4241*
For it was f for Him, for whom are	Heb 2:10	*4241*
For it was f for us to have	Heb 7:26	*4241*
FIVE		
lived one hundred and f years,	Gn 5:6	2568
were nine hundred and f years,	Gn 5:11	2568
Then Lamech lived f hundred and	Gn 5:30	2568
Noah was f hundred years old,	Gn 5:32	2568
and Shem lived f hundred years	Gn 11:11	2568
were two hundred and f years;	Gn 11:32	2568
four kings against f.	Gn 14:9	2568
the fifty righteous are lacking f,	Gn 18:28	2568
the whole city because of f?"	Gn 18:28	2568
but Benjamin's portion was f times	Gn 43:34	2568
and there are still f years in	Gn 45:6	2568
still f years of famine *to come,*	Gn 45:11	2568
silver and f changes of garments.	Gn 45:22	2568
f men from among his brothers and	Gn 47:2	2568
he shall pay f oxen for the ox and	Ex 22:1	2568
"F curtains shall be joined to	Ex 26:3	2568
and *the other* f curtains *shall be*	Ex 26:3	2568
join f curtains by themselves and	Ex 26:9	2568
f for the boards of one side of	Ex 26:26	2568
and f bars for the boards of the	Ex 26:27	2568
and f bars for the boards of the	Ex 26:27	2568
"You shall make f pillars of	Ex 26:37	2568
cast f sockets of bronze for them.	Ex 26:37	2568
f cubits long and five cubits wide;	Ex 27:1	2568
cubits long and f cubits wide;	Ex 27:1	2568
f cubits of fine twisted linen,	Ex 27:18	2568
flowing myrrh f hundred *shekels,*	Ex 30:23	2568
and of cassia f hundred, according	Ex 30:24	2568
joined f curtains to one another and	Ex 36:10	2568
and *the other* f curtains he joined	Ex 36:10	2568
joined f curtains by themselves and	Ex 36:16	2568
f for the boards of one side of	Ex 36:31	2568
and f bars for the boards of the	Ex 36:32	2568
and f bars for the boards of the	Ex 36:32	2568
its f pillars with their hooks,	Ex 36:38	2568
their f sockets were of bronze.	Ex 36:38	2568
of acacia wood, f cubits long,	Ex 38:1	2568
cubits long, and f cubits wide,	Ex 38:1	2568
and the height *was* f cubits,	Ex 38:18	2568
f of you will chase a hundred, and	Lv 26:8	2568
'If it be from f years even to	Lv 27:5	2568
a month even up to f years old,	Lv 27:6	2568
then your valuation shall be f	Lv 27:6	2568
you shall take f shekels apiece,	Nu 3:47	2568
peace offerings, two oxen, f rams,	Nu 7:17	2568
two oxen, five rams, f male goats,	Nu 7:17	2568
goats, f male lambs one year old.	Nu 7:17	2568
peace offerings, two oxen, f rams,	Nu 7:23	2568
two oxen, five rams, f male goats,	Nu 7:23	2568
goats, f male lambs one year old.	Nu 7:23	2568
peace offerings, two oxen, f rams,	Nu 7:29	2568
two oxen, five rams, f male goats,	Nu 7:29	2568
goats, f male lambs one year old.	Nu 7:29	2568
peace offerings, two oxen, f rams,	Nu 7:35	2568
two oxen, five rams, f male goats,	Nu 7:35	2568
goats, f male lambs one year old.	Nu 7:35	2568
peace offerings, two oxen, f rams,	Nu 7:41	2568
two oxen, five rams, f male goats,	Nu 7:41	2568
goats, f male lambs one year old.	Nu 7:41	2568
peace offerings, two oxen, f rams,	Nu 7:47	2568
two oxen, five rams, f male goats,	Nu 7:47	2568
goats, f male lambs one year old.	Nu 7:47	2568
peace offerings, two oxen, f rams,	Nu 7:53	2568
two oxen, five rams, f male goats,	Nu 7:53	2568
goats, f male lambs one year old.	Nu 7:53	2568
peace offerings, two oxen, f rams,	Nu 7:59	2568
two oxen, five rams, f male goats,	Nu 7:59	2568
goats, f male lambs one year old.	Nu 7:59	2568
peace offerings, two oxen, f rams,	Nu 7:65	2568
two oxen, five rams, f male goats,	Nu 7:65	2568
goats, f male lambs one year old.	Nu 7:65	2568
peace offerings, two oxen, f rams,	Nu 7:71	2568
two oxen, five rams, f male goats,	Nu 7:71	2568
goats, f male lambs one year old.	Nu 7:71	2568
peace offerings, two oxen, f rams,	Nu 7:77	2568
two oxen, five rams, f male goats,	Nu 7:77	2568
goats, f male lambs one year old.	Nu 7:77	2568
peace offerings, two oxen, f rams,	Nu 7:83	2568
two oxen, five rams, f male goats,	Nu 7:83	2568
goats, f male lambs one year old.	Nu 7:83	2568
one day, nor two days, nor f days,	Nu 11:19	2568
valuation, f shekels in silver,	Nu 18:16	2568
and Reba, the f kings of Midian;	Nu 31:8	2568
one in f hundred of the persons	Nu 31:28	2568
So the f kings of the Amorites,	Jos 10:5	2568
Now these f kings had fled and	Jos 10:16	2568
"The f kings have been found	Jos 10:17	2568
f kings out to me from the cave."	Jos 10:22	2568
and brought these f kings out to	Jos 10:23	2568
and he hanged them on f trees;	Jos 10:26	2568
the f lords of the Philistines:	Jos 13:3	2568
the f lords of the Philistines and	Jg 3:3	2568
f men out of their whole number,	Jg 18:2	2568
Then the f men departed and came	Jg 18:7	2568
Then the f men who went to spy out	Jg 18:14	2568
Now the f men who went to spy out	Jg 18:17	2568
"F golden tumors and five golden	1Sa 6:4	2568
"Five golden tumors and f golden	1Sa 6:4	2568
When the f lords of the	1Sa 6:16	2568
belonging to the f lords,	1Sa 6:18	2568
f thousand shekels of bronze.	1Sa 17:5	2568
f smooth stones from the brook,	1Sa 17:40	2568
Give me f loaves of bread, or	1Sa 21:3	2568
and f sheep already prepared	1Sa 25:18	2568
and f measures of roasted grain	1Sa 25:18	2568
her f maidens who attended her;	1Sa 25:42	2568
He was f years old when the report	2Sa 4:4	2568
and the f sons of Merab the	2Sa 21:8	2568
Judah were f hundred thousand men.	2Sa 24:9	2568
lowest story *was* f cubits wide,	1Ki 6:6	2568
whole house, each f cubits high;	1Ki 6:10	2568
F cubits *was* the one wing of	1Ki 6:24	2568
f cubits the other wing of the cherub;	1Ki 6:24	2568
height of the one capital was f cubits	1Ki 7:16	2568
of the other capital was f cubits.	1Ki 7:16	2568
form, and its height was f cubits,	1Ki 7:23	2568
f on the right side of the house	1Ki 7:39	2568
f on the left side of the house;	1Ki 7:39	2568
f on the right side and five on	1Ki 7:49	2568
the right side and f on the left,	1Ki 7:49	2568
work, f hundred and fifty,	1Ki 9:23	2568
dung for f *shekels* of silver.	2Ki 6:25	2568
take f of the horses which remain,	2Ki 7:13	2568
should have struck f or six times,	2Ki 13:19	2568
and f of the king's advisers who	2Ki 25:19	2568
Judah had f sons in all.	1Ch 2:4	2568
f of them in all.	1Ch 2:6	2568
Hasadiah and Jushab-hesed, f.	1Ch 3:20	2568
Tochen and Ashan, f cities;	1Ch 4:32	2568
f hundred men went to Mount Seir,	1Ch 4:42	2568
all f of them *were* chief men.	1Ch 7:3	2568
The sons of Bela were f:	1Ch 7:7	2568
of *great* stature f cubits tall.	1Ch 11:23	2568
the wing of one, of f cubits,	2Ch 3:11	2568
and *its* other wing, of f cubits,	2Ch 3:11	2568
of the other cherub, of f cubits,	2Ch 3:12	2568
and *its* other wing of f cubits was	2Ch 3:12	2568
on the top of each *was* f cubits.	2Ch 3:15	2568
and its height *was* f cubits and	2Ch 4:2	2568
and he set f on the right side and	2Ch 4:6	2568
the right side and f on the left to	2Ch 4:6	2568
f on the right side and five on	2Ch 4:7	2568
the right side and f on the left.	2Ch 4:7	2568
f on the right side and five on	2Ch 4:8	2568
the right side and f on the left.	2Ch 4:8	2568
a bronze platform, f cubits long,	2Ch 6:13	2568
five cubits long, f cubits wide and	2Ch 6:13	2568
and destroyed f hundred men,	Es 9:6	2568
killed and destroyed f hundred men	Es 9:12	2568
Four *or* f on the branches of a	Is 17:6	2568
In that day f cities in the land	Is 19:18	2568
You will flee at the threat of f	Is 30:17	2568
of each capital was f cubits,	Jer 52:22	2568
f cubits between the guardrooms.	Ezk 40:7	2568
cubits long and f cubits wide.	Ezk 40:30	2568
the porch, f cubits on each side;	Ezk 40:48	2568
were f cubits on each side.	Ezk 41:2	2568
of the side chambers *was* f cubits.	Ezk 41:9	2568
space *was* f cubits all around.	Ezk 41:11	2568
was f cubits thick all around,	Ezk 41:12	2568
measuring reed f hundred reeds by	Ezk 42:16	2568
He measured on the north side f	Ezk 42:17	2568
On the south side he measured f	Ezk 42:18	2568
and measured f hundred reeds with	Ezk 42:19	2568
the length f hundred and the width	Ezk 42:20	2568
hundred and the width f hundred,	Ezk 42:20	2568
a square round about f hundred by	Ezk 45:2	2568
five hundred by f hundred *cubits,*	Ezk 45:2	2568
here only f loaves and two fish."	Mt 14:17	*4002*
the f loaves and the two fish,	Mt 14:19	*4002*
were about f thousand men who ate,	Mt 14:21	*4000*
the f loaves of the five thousand,	Mt 16:9	*4002*
the five loaves of the f thousand,	Mt 16:9	*4000*
"F of them were foolish, and five	Mt 25:2	*4002*
were foolish, and f were prudent.	Mt 25:2	*4002*
"To one he gave f talents,	Mt 25:15	*4002*
the one who had received the f talents	Mt 25:16	*4002*
them, and gained f more talents.	Mt 25:16	*4002*
The one who had received the f talents	Mt 25:20	*4002*
up and brought f more talents,	Mt 25:20	*4002*
you entrusted f talents to me.	Mt 25:20	*4002*
I have gained f more talents.'	Mt 25:20	*4002*
"F, and two fish."	Mk 6:38	*4002*
the f loaves and the two fish,	Mk 6:41	*4002*
There were f thousand men who	Mk 6:44	*4000*
f loaves for the five thousand,	Mk 8:19	*4000*
five loaves for the f thousand,	Mk 8:19	*4000*
herself in seclusion for f months,	Lk 1:24	*4002*
one owed f hundred denarii, and	Lk 7:41	*4001*
more than f loaves and two fish,	Lk 9:13	*4002*
there were about f thousand men.)	Lk 9:14	*4000*
the f loaves and the two fish,	Lk 9:16	*4002*
not f sparrows sold for two cents?	Lk 12:6	*4002*
for from now on f *members* in one	Lk 12:52	*4002*
'I have bought f yoke of oxen, and	Lk 14:19	*4002*
for I have f brothers	Lk 16:28	*4002*
mina, master, has made f minas.'	Lk 19:18	*4002*
'And you are to be over f cities.'	Lk 19:19	*4002*
for you have had f husbands,	Jn 4:18	*4002*
Bethesda, having f porticoes.	Jn 5:2	*4002*
has f barley loaves and two fish,	Jn 6:9	*4002*
down, in number about f thousand.	Jn 6:10	*4000*
from the f barley loaves which	Jn 6:13	*4002*
men came to be about f thousand.	Ac 4:4	*4002*
to them at Troas within f days;	Ac 20:6	*4002*
After f days the high priest	Ac 24:1	*4002*
to speak f words with my mind so	1Co 14:19	*4002*
f hundred brethren at one time,	1Co 15:6	*4001*
F times I received from the Jews	2Co 11:24	*3999*
but to torment for f months;	Rv 9:5	*4002*
power to hurt men for f months.	Rv 9:10	*4002*
f have fallen, one is, the other	Rv 17:10	*4002*
FIVE-SIDED		
wood, the lintel *and* f doorposts.	1Ki 6:31	2549
FIX		
"I will f your boundary from	Ex 23:31	7896
and the axes, and to f the hoes.	1Sa 13:21	5324
Or f their rule over the earth?	Jb 38:33	7760
not to be conceited or to f their hope	1Tm 6:17	*1679*
f your hope completely on the	1Pe 1:13	*1679*
FIXED		
He f his gaze steadily *on him*	2Ki 8:11	5975
the new moons and the f festivals	1Ch 23:31	4150
Judah and from Jerusalem the levy f	2Ch 24:6	
to bring to the LORD the levy f	2Ch 24:9	
new moons and for the f festivals,	2Ch 31:3	4150
and *offered* the f number of burnt	Ezr 3:4	
and for all the f festivals of the LORD	Ezr 3:5	4150
households, at f times annually,	Ne 10:34	2163
be f straight in front of you.	Pr 4:25	3474
the springs of the deep became f,	Pr 8:28	5810
took up f positions at the gate.	Is 22:7	7896
And the f order of the moon and	Jer 31:35	2708
f order departs From before Me,"	Jer 31:36	2706
and the f patterns of heaven and	Jer 33:25	2708
It is f: She is stripped, she is carried	Na 2:7	5324
in the synagogue were f on Him.	Lk 4:20	*816*
and you there is a great chasm f,	Lk 16:26	*4741*
Father has f by His own authority;	Ac 1:7	*5087*
f his gaze on him and said,	Ac 3:4	*816*
and when I had f my gaze on it	Ac 11:6	*816*
Holy Spirit, f his gaze on him,	Ac 13:9	*816*
when he had f his gaze on him	Ac 14:9	*816*
because He has f a day in which He	Ac 17:31	*2476*
have f our hope on the living God,	1Tm 4:10	*1679*
left alone, has f her hope on God	1Tm 5:5	*1679*
And everyone who has this hope f	1Jn 3:3	
FIXES		
He again f a certain day,	Heb 4:7	*3724*
FIXING		
And f their gaze on him, all who	Ac 6:15	*816*
And f his gaze on him and being	Ac 10:4	*816*
f our eyes on Jesus, the author	Heb 12:2	*872*
FLAG		
are left as a f on a mountain top And	Is 30:17	8650
FLAGRANT		
for the land commits f harlotry,	Hos 1:2	2181
FLAKE-LIKE		
there was a fine f thing,	Ex 16:14	2636
FLAME		
A f from the town of Sihon;	Nu 21:28	3852
For it came about when the f went	Jg 13:20	3851
ascended in the f of the altar.	Jg 13:20	3851
The f will wither his shoots, And	Jb 15:30	7957
the f of his fire gives no light.	Jb 18:5	7632
And a f goes forth from his mouth.	Jb 41:21	3851
And like a f that sets the	Ps 83:14	3852
The f consumed the wicked.	Ps 106:18	3852
of fire, The *very* f of the LORD.	SS 8:6	7957
dry grass collapses into the f,	Is 5:24	3852
will be kindled like a burning f.	Is 10:16	784
a fire and his Holy One a f,	Is 10:17	3852
and the f of a consuming fire.	Is 29:6	3851
And *in* the f of a consuming fire In	Is 30:30	3851
scorched, Nor will the f burn you.	Is 43:2	3852
from the power of the f;	Is 47:14	3852
And a f from the midst of Sihon,	Jer 48:45	3852
blazing f will not be quenched and	Ezk 20:47	3852
the f of the fire slew those men	Da 3:22	7631
they will fall by sword and by f,	Da 11:33	3852
And the f has burned up all the	Jl 1:19	3852
them And behind them a f burns.	Jl 2:3	3852
a f of fire consuming the stubble,	Jl 2:5	3851
fire And the house of Joseph a f;	Ob 1:18	3852
for I am in agony in this f.'	Lk 16:24	*5395*
IN THE F OF A BURNING THORN BUSH	Ac 7:30	*5395*
AND HIS MINISTERS A F OF FIRE."	Heb 1:7	*5395*
His eyes were like a f of fire.	Rv 1:14	*5395*
who has eyes like a f of fire,	Rv 2:18	*5395*
His eyes *are* a f of fire,	Rv 19:12	*5395*
FLAMES		
of the LORD hews out f of fire.	Ps 29:7	3852
And His rebuke with f of fire.	Is 66:15	3851
His throne *was* ablaze with f,	Da 7:9	7631
FLAMING		
and the f sword which turned every	Gn 3:24	3858a
appeared a smoking oven and a f torch	Gn 15:17	784
There He broke the f arrows,	Ps 76:3	7565
messengers, F fire His ministers.	Ps 104:4	3857
rain, *And* f fire in their land.	Ps 105:32	3852
brightness of a f fire by night;	Is 4:5	3852
a f fire Consuming round about.	La 2:3	3852
his eyes were like f torches,	Da 10:6	784
morning it burns like a f fire.	Hos 7:6	3852
wood and a f torch among sheaves,	Zch 12:6	784
the f arrows of the evil *one.*	Eph 6:16	*4448*
with His mighty angels in f fire,	2Th 1:7	*5395*
FLANK		
And his f *shall be* toward Sidon.	Gn 49:13	3411
the f of Moab of *its* cities,	Ezk 25:9	3802
FLAP		
'The ostriches' wings f joyously	Jb 39:13	5965
FLAPPED		
not one that f its wing or opened *its*	Is 10:14	5074
FLASH		
And why do your eyes f,	Jb 15:12	7335
"His sneezes f forth light, And	Jb 41:18	1984a

f forth lightning and scatter them; Ps 144:6 1299
Will not f forth their light; Is 13:10 1984a
Polished to f like lightning!' Ezk 21:10 1300

FLASHED
Your arrows f here and there. Ps 77:17 1980
a light from heaven f around him; Ac 9:3 *4015b*
f from heaven all around me, Ac 22:6 *4015b*

FLASHES
there were thunder and lightning f Ex 19:16 1300
the thunder and the lightning f Ex 20:18 3940
And lightning f in abundance, Ps 18:14 1300
Its f are flashes of fire, The SS 8:6 7565
Its flashes are f of fire, The SS 8:6 7565
is He who f forth *with* destruction Am 5:9 1082
dash to and fro like lightning f. Na 2:4 1300
the east and f even to the west, Mt 24:27 *5316*
it f out of one part of the sky, Lk 17:24 *797*
Out from the throne come f of Rv 4:5 *796*
thunder and sounds and f of lightning Rv 8:5 *796*
and there were f of lightning and Rv 11:19 *796*
And there were f of lightning and Rv 16:18 *796*

FLASHING
and fire f continually in the Ex 9:24 3947
If I sharpen My f sword, And My Dt 32:41 1300
there was f lightning for them. Dt 33:2 799
him, The f spear and javelin. Jb 39:23 3851
a great cloud with fire f forth Ezk 1:4 3947
and lightning was f from the fire. Ezk 1:13 3318
The chariots are *enveloped* in f Na 2:3 784
Horsemen charging, Swords f Na 3:3 3851
He has rays f from His hand, Hab 3:4

FLASK
Then Samuel took the f of oil, 1Sa 10:1 6378
take this f of oil in your hand and 2Ki 9:1 6378
"Then take the f of oil and pour 2Ki 9:3 6378

FLASKS
oil in f along with their lamps. Mt 25:4 *30*

FLAT
wall of the city will fall down f, Jos 6:5 8478
shout and the wall fell down f, Jos 6:20 8478
down so that the tent lay f." Jg 7:13 5307

FLATTER
be partial to no one, Nor f *any* man. Jb 32:21 3655
"For I do not know how to f, Jb 32:22 3655
They f with their tongue. Ps 5:9 2505b

FLATTERING
With f lips and with a double Ps 12:2 2513b
May the LORD cut off all f lips, Ps 12:3 2513b
With her f lips she seduces him. Pr 7:21 2507b
crushes, And a f mouth works ruin. Pr 26:28 2509
be any false vision or f divination Ezk 12:24 2509
and by their smooth and f speech Ro 16:18 *2129*
For we never came with f speech, 1Th 2:5 *2850*
f people for the sake of *gaining* Jude 1:16 *2296*

FLATTERS
For it f him in his *own* eyes Concerning Ps 36:2 2505b
adulteress who f with her words; Pr 2:16 2505b
foreigner who f with her words. Pr 7:5 2505b
Than he who f with the tongue. Pr 28:23 2505b
A man who f his neighbor Is Pr 29:5 2505b

FLAVOR
Therefore he retains his f, Jer 48:11 2940

FLAX
the f and the barley were ruined, Ex 9:31 6594
in the ear and the f was in bud. Ex 9:31 6594
and hidden them in the stalks of f Jos 2:6 6593
as f that is burned with fire, Jg 15:14 6593
She looks for wool and f And Pr 31:13 6593
linen made from combed f Is 19:9 6593
with a line of f and a measuring Ezk 40:3 6593
and my water, My wool and my f, Hos 2:5 6593
My f *Given* to cover her nakedness. Hos 2:9 6593

FLEA
A dead dog, a single f? 1Sa 24:14 6550
come out to search for a single f, 1Sa 26:20 6550

FLED
the kings of Sodom and Gomorrah f, Gn 14:10 5127
survived f to the hill country. Gn 14:10 5127
and she f from her presence. Gn 16:6 1272
So he f with all that he had; Gn 31:21 1272
on the third day that Jacob had f, Gn 31:22 1272
and my sleep f from my eyes. Gn 31:40 5074
you f from your brother Esau." Gn 35:1 1272
him when he f from his brother. Gn 35:7 1272
his garment in her hand and f, Gn 39:12 5127
in her hand and had f outside, Gn 39:13 5127
left his garment beside me and f and Gn 39:15 5127
garment beside me and f outside." Gn 39:18 5127
But Moses f from the presence of Ex 2:15 1272
and Moses f from it. Ex 4:3 5127
was told that the people had f, Ex 14:5 1272
around them f at their outcry, Nu 16:34 5127
his city of refuge to which he f; Nu 35:25 5127
who has f to his city of refuge, Nu 35:32 5127
but they f from the men of Ai. Jos 7:4 5127
f by the way of the wilderness. Jos 8:15 5127
As they f from before Israel, Jos 10:11 5127
Now these five kings had f and Jos 10:16 5127
to the city from which he f.'" Jos 20:6 5127
But Adoni-bezek f; Jg 1:6 5127
his chariot and f away on foot. Jg 4:15 5127
Now Sisera f away on foot to the Jg 4:17 5127
army ran, crying out as they f. Jg 7:21 5127
and the army f as far as Jg 7:22 5127
When Zebah and Zalmunna f, Jg 8:12 5127
Then Jotham escaped and f, Jg 9:21 1272
chased him, and he f before him; Jg 9:40 5127
f there and shut themselves in; Jg 9:51 5127
So Jephthah f from his brothers Jg 11:3 1272
The rest turned and f toward the Jg 20:45 5127
But 600 men turned and f toward Jg 20:47 5127
and every man f to his tent; 1Sa 4:10 5127
"Israel has f before the 1Sa 4:17 5127
heard that the Philistines had f, 1Sa 14:22 5127
they f from him and were greatly 1Sa 17:24 5127
their champion was dead, they f. 1Sa 17:51 5127
so that they f before him. 1Sa 19:8 5127
David f and escaped that night. 1Sa 19:10 5127
and he went out and f and escaped. 1Sa 19:12 1272
Now David f and escaped and came 1Sa 19:18 1272
Then David f from Naioth in Ramah, 1Sa 20:1 1272
arose and f that day from Saul, 1Sa 21:10 1272
escaped and f after David. 1Sa 22:20 1272
of Ahimelech f to David at Keilah, 1Sa 23:6 1272
Saul that David had f to Gath, 1Sa 27:4 1272
men who rode on camels and f. 1Sa 30:17 5127
and the men of Israel f from 1Sa 31:1 5127
saw that the men of Israel had f 1Sa 31:7 5127
they abandoned the cities and f; 1Sa 31:7 5127
"The people have f from the 2Sa 1:4 5127
and the Beerothites f to Gittaim and 2Sa 4:3 1272
and his nurse took him up and f. 2Sa 4:4 5127
Arameans, and they f before him. 2Sa 10:13 5127
of Ammon saw that the Arameans f, 2Sa 10:14 5127
they *also* f before Abishai and 2Sa 10:14 5127
But the Arameans f before Israel, 2Sa 10:18 5127
and each mounted his mule and f. 2Sa 13:29 5127
Now Absalom had f. 2Sa 13:34 1272
Now Absalom f and went to Talmai 2Sa 13:37 1272
Absalom had f and gone to Geshur, 2Sa 13:38 1272
And all Israel f, each to his tent. 2Sa 18:17 5127
Now Israel had f, each to his tent. 2Sa 19:8 5127
f out of the land from Absalom. 2Sa 19:9 1272
the people f from the Philistines. 2Sa 23:11 5127
I f from Absalom your brother. 1Ki 2:7 1272
And Joab f to the tent of the LORD 1Ki 2:28 5127
had f to the tent of the LORD, 1Ki 2:29 5127
that Hadad f to Egypt, he and 1Ki 11:17 1272
who had f from his lord Hadadezer 1Ki 11:23 1272
but Jeroboam arose and f to Egypt 1Ki 11:40 1272
where he had f from the presence 1Ki 12:2 1272
and the Arameans f and 1Ki 20:20 5127
the rest f to Aphek into the city, 1Ki 20:30 5127
And Ben-hadad f and came into the 1Ki 20:30 5127
so that they f before them; 2Ki 3:24 5127
they arose and f in the twilight, 2Ki 7:7 5127
as it was, and f for their life. 2Ki 7:7 5127
but *his* army f to their tents. 2Ki 8:21 5127
Then he opened the door and f. 2Ki 9:10 5127
about and f and said to Ahaziah, 2Ki 9:23 5127
he f by the way of the garden 2Ki 9:27 5127
he f to Megiddo and died there. 2Ki 9:27 5127
and they f each to his tent. 2Ki 14:12 5127
in Jerusalem, and he f to Lachish; 2Ki 14:19 5127
and all the men of war f by night 2Ki 25:4
Israel f before the Philistines and 1Ch 10:1 5127
in the valley saw that they had f, 1Ch 10:7 5127
they forsook their cities and f; 1Ch 10:7 5127
people f before the Philistines. 1Ch 11:13 5127
Arameans, and they f before him. 1Ch 19:14 5127
of Ammon saw that the Arameans f, 1Ch 19:15 5127
also f before Abshai his brother and 1Ch 19:15 5127
The Arameans f before Israel, 1Ch 19:18 5127
(for he was in Egypt where he had f 2Ch 10:2 1272
the sons of Israel f before Judah, 2Ch 13:16 5127
Judah, and the Ethiopians f. 2Ch 14:12 5127
and they f each to his tent. 2Ch 25:22 5127
in Jerusalem, and he f to Lachish; 2Ch 25:27 5127
were terrified, they f in alarm. Ps 48:5 2648
At Your rebuke they f, Ps 104:7 5127
The sea looked and f; Ps 114:3 5127
and Gibeah of Saul has f away. Is 10:29 5127
Madmenah has f. Is 10:31 5074
where we f for help to be Is 20:6 5127
For they have f from the swords, Is 21:15 5074
All your rulers have f together, Is 22:3 5074
Though they had f far away. Is 22:3 1272
the birds of the heavens had f. Jer 4:25 5074
of the sky and the beasts have f; Jer 9:10 5074
heard *it*, and he was afraid and f and Jer 26:21 1272
they f and went out of the Jer 39:4 1272
back *and* have f away together; Jer 46:21 5127
and all the men of war f and went Jer 52:7 1272
And they have f without strength La 1:6 1980
So they f and wandered; La 4:15 5327a
and his sleep f from him. Da 6:18 5075
Now Jacob f to the land of Aram, Hos 12:12 1272
to forestall this I f to Tarshish, Jon 4:2 1272
you will flee just as you f before Zch 14:5 5127
all the disciples left Him and f. Mt 26:56 *5343*
And they all left Him and f. Mk 14:50 *5343*
They went out and f from the tomb, Mk 16:8 *5343*
"At this remark, MOSES F Ac 7:29 *5343*
and f to the cities of Lycaonia, Ac 14:6 *2703*
so that they f out of that house Ac 19:16 *1628*
Then the woman f into the Rv 12:6 *5343*
And every island f away, Rv 16:20 *5343*
presence earth and heaven f away, Rv 20:11 *5343*

FLEE
this town is near *enough* to f to, Gn 19:20 5127
f to Haran, to my brother Laban! Gn 27:43 1272
did you f secretly and deceive me, Gn 31:27 1272
his livestock f into the houses; Ex 9:20 5127
"Let us f from Israel, for the Ex 14:25 5127
you a place to which he may f. Ex 21:13 5127
f when no one is pursuing you. Lv 26:17 5127
will f as though from the sword, Lv 26:36 5127
who hate You f before You." Nu 10:35 5127
"Therefore, f to your place now. Nu 24:11 1272
give for the manslayer to f to; Nu 35:6 5127
unintentionally may f there. Nu 35:11 5127
unintentionally may f there. Nu 35:15 5127
city of refuge to which he may f, Nu 35:26 5127
that a manslayer might f there, Dt 4:42 5127
so that any manslayer may f there. Dt 19:3 5127
who may f there and live: Dt 19:4 5127
he may f to one of these cities and live Dt 19:5 5127
and will f before you seven ways. Dt 28:7 5127
will f seven ways before them, Dt 28:25 5127
first, we will f before them. Jos 8:5 5127
So we will f before them. Jos 8:6 5127
no place to f this way or that, Jos 8:20 5127
premeditation, may f there, Jos 20:3 5127
He shall f to one of these cities, Jos 20:4 5127
unintentionally may f there, Jos 20:9 5127
"Let us f that we may draw them Jg 20:32 5127
happened that in her hurry to f, 2Sa 4:4 5127
"Arise and let us f, 2Sa 15:14 1272
people who are with him will f. 2Sa 17:2 5127
for if we indeed f, 2Sa 18:3 5127
steal away when they f in battle. 2Sa 19:3 5127
Or will you f three months before 2Sa 24:13 5127
his chariot to f to Jerusalem. 1Ki 12:18 5127
the door and f and do not wait." 2Ki 9:3 5127
his chariot to f to Jerusalem. 2Ch 10:18 5127
"Should a man like me f? Ne 6:11 1272
They f away, they see no good. Jb 9:25 1272
"He may f from the iron weapon, Jb 20:24 1272
surely try to f from its power. Jb 27:22 1272
"The arrow cannot make him f; Jb 41:28 1272
"F *as* a bird to your mountain; Ps 11:1 5110
see me in the street f from me. Ps 31:11 5074
those who hate Him f before Him. Ps 68:1 5127
"Kings of armies f, they flee, Ps 68:12 5074
"Kings of armies flee, they f, Ps 68:12 5074
What ails you, O sea, that you f? Ps 114:5 5127
where can I f from Your presence? Ps 139:7 1272
wicked f when no one is pursuing, Pr 28:1 5127
the day when the shadows f away, SS 2:17 5127
the day When the shadows f away, SS 4:6 5127
To whom will you f for help? Is 10:3 5127
And each one f to his own land. Is 13:14 5127
them and they will f far away, Is 17:13 5127
"No, for we will f on horses," Is 30:16 5127
on horses," Therefore you shall f! Is 30:16 5127
One thousand *will* f at the threat Is 30:17
You will f at the threat of five Is 30:17 5127
the sound of the tumult peoples f; Is 33:3 5074
sorrow and sighing will f away. Is 35:10 5127
F from the Chaldeans! Is 48:20 1272
sorrow and sighing will f away. Is 51:11 5127
"F for safety, O sons of Benjamin, Jer 6:1 5756
Let not the swift man f, Jer 46:6 5127
"F, save your lives, That you may Jer 48:6 5127
to Moab, For she will f away; Jer 48:9 3318
"F away, turn back, dwell in the Jer 49:8 5127
She has turned away to f, Jer 49:24 5127
"Run away, f! Dwell in the depths, Jer 49:30 5110
they will each f to his own land. Jer 50:16 5127
F from the midst of Babylon, And Jer 51:6 5127
Let the beasts f from under it And Da 4:14 5111
will f naked in that day," Am 2:16 5127
seer, f away to the land of Judah and Am 7:12 1272
not have a fugitive who will f, Am 9:1 5127
But Jonah rose up to f to Tarshish Jon 1:3 1272
The sun rises and they f, Na 3:17 5074
F from the land of the north," Zch 2:6 5127
You will f by the valley of My Zch 14:5 5127
you will f just as you fled before Zch 14:5 5127
and His mother and f to Egypt, Mt 2:13 *5343*
you to f from the wrath to come? Mt 3:7 *5343*
you in one city, f to the next; Mt 10:23 *5343*
are in Judea must f to the mountains. Mt 24:16 *5343*
are in Judea must f to the mountains. Mk 13:14 *5343*
you to f from the wrath to come? Lk 3:7 *5343*
are in Judea must f to the mountains, Lk 21:21 *5343*
not follow, but will f from him, Jn 10:5 *5343*
F immorality. Every *other* sin that a 1Co 6:18 *5343*
my beloved, f from idolatry. 1Co 10:14 *5343*
But f from these things, you man 1Tm 6:11 *5343*
Now f from youthful lusts and 2Tm 2:22 *5343*
the devil and he will f from you. Jas 4:7 *5343*

FLEECE
I will put a f of wool on the Jg 6:37 1492
If there is dew on the f only, Jg 6:37 1492
next morning and squeezed the f, Jg 6:38 1492
he drained the dew from the f, Jg 6:38 1492
make a test once more with the f, Jg 6:39 1492
let it now be dry only on the f, Jg 6:39 1492
for it was dry only on the f, Jg 6:40 1492
warmed with the f of my sheep, Jb 31:20 1488

FLEEING
"I am f from the presence of my Gn 16:8 1272
by not telling him that he was f. Gn 31:20 1272
Egyptians were f right into it; Ex 14:27 5127
and by f to one of these cities he Dt 4:42 5127
are f before us as at the first.' Jos 8:6 5127
for the people who had been f to Jos 8:20 5127
f and did not reveal it to me." 1Sa 22:17 1272
hand has pierced the f serpent. Jb 26:13 1281
f birds *or* scattered nestlings, Is 16:2 5074
punish Leviathan the f serpent, Is 27:1 1281
f from the presence of the LORD, Jon 1:10 1272

her days, Now they are f; Na 2:8 5127

FLEES

and he f to one of these cities, Dt 19:11 5127
He also f like a shadow and does Jb 14:2 1272
he who f the report of disaster will Is 24:18 5127
horseman and bowman every city f; Jer 4:29 1272
Ask him who f and her who escapes Jer 48:19 5127
"The one who f from the terror Jer 48:44 5127
As when a man f from a lion And a Am 5:19 5127
and leaves the sheep and f, Jn 10:12 5343
"He f because he is a hired hand Jn 10:13
long to die, and death f from them. Rv 9:6 5343

FLEET

built a f of ships in Ezion-geber, 1Ki 9:26 590
sent his servants with the f, 1Ki 9:27 590

FLEETING

by a lying tongue Is a f vapor, Pr 21:6 5086
all the days of your f life which He Ec 9:9 1892
and the prime of life are f. Ec 11:10 1892

FLESH

and closed up the f at that place. Gn 2:21 1320
of my bones, And f of my flesh; Gn 2:23 1320
of my bones, And flesh of my f; Gn 2:23 1320
and they shall become one f. Gn 2:24 1320
man forever, because he also is f; Gn 6:3 1320
for all f had corrupted their way Gn 6:12 1320
end of all f has come before Me; Gn 6:13 1320
to destroy all f in which is the Gn 6:17 1320
of every living thing of all f, Gn 6:19 1320
by twos of all f in which was the Gn 7:15 1320
entered, male and female of all f, Gn 7:16 1320
All f that moved on the earth Gn 7:21 1320
thing of all f that is with you, Gn 8:17 1320
you shall not eat f with its life, Gn 9:4 1320
and all f shall never again be cut Gn 9:11 1320
every living creature of all f; Gn 9:15 1320
become a flood to destroy all f. Gn 9:15 1320
of all f that is on the earth." Gn 9:16 1320
and all f that is on the earth." Gn 9:17 1320
in the f of your foreskin, Gn 17:11 1320
f for an everlasting covenant. Gn 17:13 1320
in the f of his foreskin, Gn 17:14 1320
and circumcised the f of their Gn 17:23 1320
in the f of his foreskin. Gn 17:24 1320
in the f of his foreskin. Gn 17:25 1320
"Surely you are my bone and my f." Gn 29:14 1320
he is our brother, our own f." Gn 37:27 1320
birds will eat your f off you." Gn 40:19 1320
restored like the rest of his f. Ex 4:7 1320
shall eat the f that same night, Ex 12:8 1320
any of the f outside of the house, Ex 12:46 1320
and its f shall not be eaten; Ex 21:28 1320
any f torn to pieces in the field; Ex 22:31 1320
breeches to cover their bare f; Ex 28:42 1320
"But the f of the bull and its Ex 29:14 1320
and boil its f in a holy place. Ex 29:31 1320
sons shall eat the f of the ram and Ex 29:32 1320
"If any of the f of Ex 29:34 1320
the f hooks and the firepans; Ex 38:3 4207b
hide of the bull and all its f with its Lv 4:11 1320
on undergarments next to his f; Lv 6:10 1320
its f will become consecrated; Lv 6:27 1320
'Now as for the f of the sacrifice Lv 7:15 1320
but what is left over from the f Lv 7:17 1320
'So if any of the f of the Lv 7:18 1320
'Also the f that touches anything Lv 7:19 1320
As for other f, anyone who is Lv 7:19 1320
who is clean may eat such f. Lv 7:19 1320
'But the person who eats the f of Lv 7:20 1320
and eats of the f of the sacrifice Lv 7:21 1320
its hide and its f and its refuse he Lv 8:17 1320
"Boil the f at the doorway of the Lv 8:31 1320
"The remainder of the f and Lv 8:32 1320
The f and the skin, however, he Lv 9:11 1320
their f nor touch their carcasses; Lv 11:8 1320
you may not eat of their f, Lv 11:11 1320
'On the eighth day the f of Lv 12:3 1320
is quick raw f in the swelling, Lv 13:10 1320
"But whenever raw f appears on him, Lv 13:14 1320
priest shall look at the raw f, Lv 13:15 1320
the raw f is unclean, it is Lv 13:15 1320
"Or if the raw f turns again and Lv 13:16 1320
and the raw f of the burn becomes Lv 13:24 1320
shall burn their hides, their f, Lv 16:27 1320
the life of the f is in the blood, Lv 17:11 1320
"For as for the life of all f, Lv 17:14 1320
are not to eat the blood of any f, Lv 17:14 1320
the life of all f is its blood; Lv 17:14 1320
nor make any cuts in their f. Lv 21:5 1320
you will eat the f of your sons Lv 26:29 1320
the f of your daughters you will eat. Lv 26:29 1320
whose f is half eaten away when he Nu 12:12 1320
God of the spirits of all f, Nu 16:22 1320
first issue of the womb of all f, Nu 18:15 1320
its hide and its f and its blood, Nu 19:5 1320
the God of the spirits of all f, Nu 27:16 1320
'For who is there of all f who Dt 5:26 1320
shall not eat the life with the f. Dt 12:23 1320
offerings, the f and the blood, Dt 12:27 1320
your God, and you shall eat the f. Dt 12:27 1320
their f nor touch their carcasses. Dt 14:8 1320
and none of the f which you Dt 16:4 1320
the f of your sons and of your Dt 28:53 1320
any of the f of his children which he Dt 28:55 1320
And My sword will devour f, Dt 32:42 1320
that I am your bone and your f." Jg 9:2 1320
and I will give your f to the 1Sa 17:44 1320
we are your bone and your f. 2Sa 5:1 1320
you are my bone and my f. 2Sa 19:12 1320
'Are you not my bone and my f? 2Sa 19:13 1320
and sacrificed them and boiled their f 1Ki 19:21 1320
the f of the child became warm. 2Ki 4:34 1320
and your f will be restored to 2Ki 5:10 1320
and his f was restored like the 2Ki 5:14 1320
like the f of a little child and 2Ki 5:14 1320
dogs shall eat the f of Jezebel; 2Ki 9:36 1320
we are your bone and your f. 1Ch 11:1 1320
"With him is only an arm of f, 2Ch 32:8 1320
"Now our f is like the flesh Ne 5:5 1320
is like the f of our brothers, Ne 5:5 1320
now, and touch his bone and his f; Jb 2:5 1320
The hair of my f bristled up. Jb 4:15 1320
of stones, Or is my f bronze? Jb 6:12 1320
"My f is clothed with worms and a Jb 7:5 1320
'Have You eyes of f? Jb 10:4 1320
Clothe me with skin and f, Jb 10:11 1320
should I take my f in my teeth And Jb 13:14 1320
And made his thighs heavy with f. Jb 15:27 6371b
bone clings to my skin and my f, Jb 19:20 1320
And are not satisfied with my f? Jb 19:22 1320
Yet from my f I shall see God; Jb 19:26 1320
And horror takes hold of my f. Jb 21:6 1320
"His f wastes away from sight, Jb 33:21 1320
f become fresher than in youth, Jb 33:25 1320
All f would perish together, And Jb 34:15 1320
of his f are joined together, Jb 41:23 1320
My f also will dwell securely. Ps 16:9 1320
came upon me to devour my f, Ps 27:2 1320
my f because of Your indignation; Ps 38:3 1320
And there is no soundness in my f. Ps 38:7 1320
"Shall I eat the f of bulls Or Ps 50:13 1320
for You, my f yearns for You, Ps 63:1 1320
My f and my heart may fail, But Ps 73:26 7607
remembered that they were but f, Ps 78:39 1320
The f of Your godly ones to the Ps 79:2 1320
My heart and my f sing for joy to Ps 84:2 1320
groaning My bones cling to my f. Ps 102:5 1320
And my f has grown lean, without Ps 109:24 1320
My f trembles for fear of You, Ps 119:120 1320
Who gives food to all f, Ps 136:25 1320
And all f will bless His holy name Ps 145:21 1320
your f and your body are consumed; Pr 5:11 1320
his hands and consumes his own f. Ec 4:5 1320
of them eats the f of his own arm. Is 9:20 1320
fatness of his f will become lean. Is 17:4 1320
their horses are f and not spirit; Is 31:3 1320
And all f will see it together; Is 40:5 1320
All f is grass, and all its Is 40:6 1320
your oppressors with their own f, Is 49:26 1320
And all f will know that I, the Is 49:26 1320
to hide yourself from your own f? Is 58:7 1320
Who eat swine's f, And the broth Is 65:4 1320
by fire And by His sword on all f, Is 66:16 1320
in the center, Who eat swine's f, Is 66:17 1320
to your sacrifices and eat f. Jer 7:21 1320
Can the sacrificial f take away Jer 11:15 1320
mankind And makes f his strength, Jer 17:5 1320
"I will make them eat the f Jer 19:9 1320
sons and the f of their daughters, Jer 19:9 1320
and they will eat one another's f Jer 19:9 1320
entering into judgment with all f; Jer 25:31 1320
I am the LORD, the God of all f; Jer 32:27 1320
going to bring disaster on all f,' Jer 45:5 1320
me and to my f be upon Babylon," Jer 51:35 7607
my f and my skin to waste away, La 3:4 1320
city is the pot and we are the f.' Ezk 11:3 1320
the midst of the city are the f and Ezk 11:7 1320
will you be f in the midst of it, Ezk 11:11 1320
take the heart of stone out of their f Ezk 11:19 1320
flesh and give them a heart of f, Ezk 11:19 1320
"All f will see that I, the Ezk 20:48 1320
against all f from south to north. Ezk 21:4 1320
"Thus all f will know that I, the Ezk 21:5 1320
whose f is like the flesh of Ezk 23:20 1320
whose flesh is like the f of Ezk 23:20 1320
kindle the fire, Boil the f well And Ezk 24:10 1320
will lay your f on the mountains And Ezk 32:5 1320
f and give you a heart of flesh. Ezk 36:26 1320
flesh and give you a heart of f. Ezk 36:26 1320
on you, make f grow back on you, Ezk 37:6 1320
sinews were on them, and f grew and Ezk 37:8 1320
you may eat f and drink blood. Ezk 39:17 1320
"You will eat the f of mighty men Ezk 39:18 1320
tables was the f of the offering. Ezk 40:43 1320
in heart and uncircumcised in f, Ezk 44:7 1320
in heart and uncircumcised in f, Ezk 44:9 1320
place is not with mortal f." Da 2:11 1321
They sacrifice the f and eat it, Hos 8:13 1320
them And their f from their bones, Mi 3:2 7607
Who eat the f of my people, Mi 3:3 7607
prey And his dens with torn f. Na 2:12 2966
like dust And their f like dung. Zph 1:17 3894
"Be silent, all f, before the LORD; Zch 2:13 1320
who are left eat one another's f." Zch 11:9 1320
but will devour the f of the fat Zch 11:16 1320
their f will rot while they stand Zch 14:12 1320
because f and blood did not reveal Mt 16:17 4561
AND THE TWO SHALL BECOME ONE F'? Mt 19:5 4561
they are no longer two, but one f. Mt 19:6 4561
is willing, but the f is weak." Mt 26:41 4561
AND THE TWO SHALL BECOME ONE F Mk 10:8 4561
they are no longer two, but one f. Mk 10:8 4561
is willing, but the f is weak." Mk 14:38 4561
AND ALL F WILL SEE THE SALVATION Lk 3:6 4561
for a spirit does not have f and Lk 24:39 4561
blood nor of the will of the f Jn 1:13 4561
And the Word became f, Jn 1:14 4561
which is born of the f is flesh, Jn 3:6 4561
which is born of the flesh is f, Jn 3:6 4561
the life of the world is My f." Jn 6:51 4561
this man give us His f to eat?" Jn 6:52 4561
unless you eat the f of the Son of Jn 6:53 4561
"He who eats My f and drinks My Jn 6:54 4561
"For My f is true food, and My Jn 6:55 4561
"He who eats My f and drinks My Jn 6:56 4561
the f profits nothing; Jn 6:63 4561
You judge according to the f; Jn 8:15 4561
as You gave Him authority over all f, Jn 17:2 4561
MY F ALSO WILL LIVE IN HOPE; Ac 2:26 4561
HADES, NOR DID His F SUFFER DECAY. Ac 2:31 4561
of David according to the f, Ro 1:3 4561
that which is outward in the f. Ro 2:28 4561
works of the Law no f will be justified Ro 3:20 4561
our forefather according to the f, Ro 4:1 4561
because of the weakness of your f. Ro 6:19 4561
For while we were in the f, Ro 7:5 4561
but I am of f, sold into bondage Ro 7:14 4560
dwells in me, that is, in my f; Ro 7:18 4561
other, with my f the law of sin. Ro 7:25 4561
do, weak as it was through the f, Ro 8:3 4561
f and as an offering for sin, Ro 8:3 4561
sin, He condemned sin in the f, Ro 8:3 4561
do not walk according to the f but Ro 8:4 4561
those who are according to the f set Ro 8:5 4561
minds on the things of the f, Ro 8:5 4561
the mind set on the f is death, Ro 8:6 4561
on the f is hostile toward God; Ro 8:7 4561
are in the f cannot please God. Ro 8:8 4561
not in the f but in the Spirit, Ro 8:9 4561
under obligation, not to the f, Ro 8:12 4561
flesh, to live according to the f Ro 8:12 4561
you are living according to the f, Ro 8:13 4561
my kinsmen according to the f, Ro 9:3 4561
is the Christ according to the f, Ro 9:5 4561
of the f who are children of God, Ro 9:8 4561
for the f in regard to its lusts. Ro 13:14 4561
not many wise according to the f, 1Co 1:26 4561
spiritual men, but as to men of f, 1Co 3:1 4560
for the destruction of his f, 1Co 5:5 4561
"THE TWO SHALL BECOME ONE F." 1Co 6:16 4561
All f is not the same flesh, but 1Co 15:39 4561
All flesh is not the same f, 1Co 15:39 4561
but there is one f of men, 1Co 15:39
of men, and another f of beasts, 1Co 15:39 4561
of beasts, and another f of birds, 1Co 15:39 4561
that f and blood cannot inherit 1Co 15:50 4561
do I purpose according to the f, 2Co 1:17 4561
may be manifested in our mortal f. 2Co 4:11 4561
no one according to the f; 2Co 5:16 4561
known Christ according to the f, 2Co 5:16 4561
all defilement of f and spirit, 2Co 7:1 4561
into Macedonia our f had no rest, 2Co 7:5 4561
if we walked according to the f. 2Co 10:2 4561
For though we walk in the f, 2Co 10:3 4561
we do not war according to the f, 2Co 10:3 4561
of our warfare are not of the f, 2Co 10:4 4559
many boast according to the f, 2Co 11:18 4561
was given me a thorn in the f, 2Co 12:7 4561
consult with f and blood, Ga 1:16 4561
the Law no f will be justified. Ga 2:16 4561
life which I now live in the f I live by Ga 2:20 4561
you now being perfected by the f? Ga 3:3 4561
was born according to the f, Ga 4:23 4561
he who was born according to the f Ga 4:29 4561
into an opportunity for the f, Ga 5:13 4561
not carry out the desire of the f. Ga 5:16 4561
For the f sets its desire against Ga 5:17 4561
and the Spirit against the f; Ga 5:17 4561
the deeds of the f are evident, Ga 5:19 4561
f with its passions and desires. Ga 5:24 4561
For the one who sows to his own f Ga 6:8 4561
will from the f reap corruption, Ga 6:8 4561
to make a good showing in the f try Ga 6:12 4561
that they may boast in your f. Ga 6:13 4561
lived in the lusts of our f, Eph 2:3 4561
desires of the f and of the mind, Eph 2:3 4561
you, the Gentiles in the f, Eph 2:11 4561
performed in the f by human hands Eph 2:11 4561
by abolishing in His f the enmity, Eph 2:15 4561
for no one ever hated his own f, Eph 5:29 4561
AND THE TWO SHALL BECOME ONE F. Eph 5:31 4561
your masters according to the f, Eph 6:5 4561
is not against f and blood, Eph 6:12 4561
But if I am to live on in the f, Php 1:22 4561
yet to remain on in the f is more Php 1:24 4561
and put no confidence in the f, Php 3:3 4561
have confidence even in the f. Php 3:4 4561
a mind to put confidence in the f, Php 3:4 4561
and in my f I do my share on Col 1:24 4561
f by the circumcision of Christ; Col 2:11 4561
and the uncircumcision of your f, Col 2:13 4561
He who was revealed in the f, 1Tm 3:16 4561
both in the f and in the Lord. Phm 1:16 4561
the children share in f and blood, Heb 2:14 4561
In the days of His f, Heb 5:7 4561
for the cleansing of the f, Heb 9:13 4561
through the veil, that is, His f, Heb 10:20 4561
and will consume your f like fire. Jas 5:3 4561
"ALL F IS LIKE GRASS, AND ALL ITS 1Pe 1:24 4561
having been put to death in the f, 1Pe 3:18 4561
the removal of dirt from the f, 1Pe 3:21 4561
Christ has suffered in the f, 1Pe 4:1 4561
in the f has ceased from sin, 1Pe 4:1 4561
to live the rest of the time in the f 1Pe 4:2 4561
they are judged in the f as men, 1Pe 4:6 4561
those who indulge the f in its corrupt 2Pe 2:10 4561

the lust of the **f** and the lust of 1Jn 2:16 4561
has come in the **f** is from God; 1Jn 4:2 4561
Jesus Christ *as* coming in the **f**. 2Jn 1:7 4561
and went after strange **f**, Jude 1:7 4561
also by dreaming, defile the **f**, Jude 1:8 4561
the garment polluted by the **f**. Jude 1:23 4561
and will eat her **f** and will burn Rv 17:16 4561
so that you may eat the **f** of Rv 19:18 4561
and the **f** of commanders and the flesh Rv 19:18 4561
and the **f** of mighty men and the flesh Rv 19:18 4561
the **f** of horses and of those who sit Rv 19:18 4561
sit on them and the **f** of all men, Rv 19:18 4561
birds were filled with their **f**. Rv 19:21 4561

FLESHLY
for you are still **f**. 1Co 3:3 4559
strife among you, are you not **f**, 1Co 3:3 4559
not in **f** wisdom but in the grace 2Co 1:12 4559
you in His **f** body through death, Col 1:22 4561
without cause by his **f** mind, Col 2:18 4561
of no value against **f** indulgence. Col 2:23 4561
strangers to abstain from **f** lusts which 1Pe 2:11 4559
vanity they entice by **f** desires, 2Pe 2:18 4561

FLEW
and it **f** here and there until the Gn 8:7 3318
"And He rode on a cherub and **f**; 2Sa 22:11 5774a
He rode upon a cherub and **f**; Ps 18:10 5774a
his feet, and with two he **f**. Is 6:2 5774a
Then one of the seraphim **f** to me with Is 6:6 5774a

FLIES
any winged bird that **f** in the sky, Dt 4:17 5774a
"He **f** away like a dream, and they Jb 20:8 5774a
He sent among them swarms of **f** which Ps 78:45 6157
Or of the arrow that **f** by day; Ps 91:5 5774a
and there came a swarm of **f** *And* Ps 105:31 6157
eagle that **f** *toward* the heavens. Pr 23:5 5774a
Dead **f** make a perfumer's oil Ec 10:1 2070
creeping locust strips and **f** away. Na 3:16 5774a

FLIGHT
And two put ten thousand to **f**, Dt 32:30 5127
of your men puts to **f** a thousand, Jos 23:10 7291
put to **f** the inhabitants of Gath; 1Ch 8:13 1272
put to **f** all those in the valleys, 1Ch 12:15 1272
"**F** will perish from the shepherds, Jer 25:35 4498
And have taken refuge in **f**, Jer 46:5 4498
"**F** will perish from the swift, Am 2:14 4498
your **f** will not be in the winter, Mt 24:20 5437
in war, put foreign armies to **f**. Heb 11:34 2827

FLING
f their silver into the streets and Ezk 7:19 7993
and it will **f** truth to the ground Da 8:12 7993

FLINT
Then Zipporah took a **f** and cut off Ex 4:25 6864
for you out of the rock of **f**. Dt 8:15 2496
"Make for yourself **f** knives and Jos 5:2 6864
So Joshua made himself **f** knives Jos 5:3 6864
"He puts his hand on the **f**; Jb 28:9 2496
The **f** into a fountain of water. Ps 114:8 2496
hoofs of its horses seem like **f** and Is 5:28 6862d
I have set My face like **f**, Is 50:7 2496
than **f** I have made your forehead. Ezk 3:9 6864
"They made their hearts *like* **f** so Zch 7:12 8068

FLINTY
the rock, And oil from the **f** rock, Dt 32:13 2496

FLITTING
Like a sparrow in *its* **f**, Pr 26:2 5110

FLOAT
it in there, and made the iron **f**. 2Ki 6:6 6687

FLOATED
ark **f** on the surface of the water. Gn 7:18 1980

FLOCK
his **f** and of their fat portions. Gn 4:4 6629
ewe lambs of the **f** by themselves. Gn 21:28 6629
"Go now to the **f** and bring me two Gn 27:9 6629
f of Laban his mother's brother. Gn 29:10 6629
again pasture *and* keep your **f**: Gn 30:31 6629
pass through your entire **f** today, Gn 30:32 6629
all the black in the **f** of Laban; Gn 30:40 6629
did not put them with Laban's **f**. Gn 30:40 6629
the stronger of the **f** were mating, Gn 30:41 6629
the sight of the **f** in the gutters, Gn 30:41 6629
but when the **f** was feeble, he did Gn 30:42 6629
and Leah to his **f** in the field, Gn 31:4 6629
all the **f** brought forth speckled; Gn 31:8 6629
all the **f** brought forth striped. Gn 31:8 6629
at the time when the **f** were mating Gn 31:10 6629
Laban had gone to shear his **f**, Gn 31:19 6629
and six years for your **f**, Gn 31:41 6629
was pasturing the **f** with his Gn 37:2 6629
their father's **f** in Shechem. Gn 37:12 6629
not your brothers pasturing *the* **f** Gn 37:13
brothers and the welfare of the **f**, Gn 37:14 6629
me where they are pasturing *the* **f**." Gn 37:16
will send you a young goat from the **f**." Gn 38:17 6629
troughs to water their father's **f**. Ex 2:16 6629
helped them and watered their **f**. Ex 2:17 6629
water for us and watered the **f**." Ex 2:19 6629
the **f** of Jethro his father-in-law, Ex 3:1 6629
and he led the **f** to the west side Ex 3:1 6629
of animals from the herd or the **f**. Lv 1:2 6629
'But if his offering is from the **f**, Lv 1:10 6629
offerings to the LORD is from the **f**, Lv 3:6 6629
committed, a female from the **f**, Lv 5:6 6629
a ram without defect from the **f**, Lv 5:15 6629
a ram without defect from the **f**, Lv 5:18 6629
a ram without defect from the **f**, Lv 6:6 6629
offering, of the herd or of the **f**, Lv 22:21 6629
For every tenth part of herd or **f**, Lv 27:32 6629
LORD, from the herd or from the **f**. Nu 15:3 6629
your herd and the young of your **f**, Dt 7:13 6629
of your herd and of your **f**. Dt 12:6 6629
the firstborn of your herd or **f**, Dt 12:17 6629
f which the LORD has given you, Dt 12:21 6629
firstborn of your herd and your **f**, Dt 14:23 6629
shall furnish him liberally from your **f** Dt 15:14 6629
born of your herd and of your **f**; Dt 15:19 6629
nor shear the firstborn of your **f**. Dt 15:19 6629
your God from the **f** and the herd, Dt 16:2 6629
your herd and the young of your **f**. Dt 28:4 6629
your herd and the young of your **f**. Dt 28:18 6629
of your herd or the young of your **f** Dt 28:51 6629
Curds of cows, and milk of the **f**, Dt 32:14 6629
son David who is with the **f**." 1Sa 16:19 6629
tend his father's **f** at Bethlehem. 1Sa 17:15 6629
and left the **f** with a keeper and took 1Sa 17:20 6629
came and took a lamb from the **f**, 1Sa 17:34 5739
from his own **f** or his own herd, 2Sa 12:4 6629
a ram of the **f** for their offense. Ezr 10:19 6629
their little ones like the **f**, Jb 21:11 6629
to put with the dogs of my **f**. Jb 30:1 6629
led Your people like a **f** Ps 77:20 6629
them in the wilderness like a **f**; Ps 78:52 5739
who lead Joseph like a **f**; Ps 80:1 6629
And makes *his* families like a **f**. Ps 107:41 6629
Where do you pasture *your* **f**, SS 1:7
Go forth on the trail of the **f** And SS 1:8 6629
He pastures *his* **f** among SS 2:16
Your hair is like a **f** of goats SS 4:1 5739
"Your teeth are like a **f** of *newly* SS 4:2 5739
To pasture *his* **f** in the gardens SS 6:2
He who pastures *his* **f** among SS 6:3
Your hair is like a **f** of goats SS 6:5 5739
"Your teeth are like a **f** of ewes SS 6:6 5739
a shepherd He will tend His **f**, Is 40:11 5739
sea with the shepherds of His **f**? Is 63:11 6629
And all their **f** is scattered. Jer 10:21 4830
Because the **f** of the LORD has been Jer 13:17 5739
Where is the **f** that was given you, Jer 13:20 5739
My **f** and driven them away, Jer 23:2 6629
will gather the remnant of My **f** Jer 23:3 6629
in ashes, you masters of the **f**; Jer 25:34 6629
escape from the masters of the **f**. Jer 25:35 6629
wailing of the masters of the **f**! Jer 25:36 6629
him as a shepherd keeps his **f**." Jer 31:10 5739
the young of the **f** and the herd; Jer 31:12 6629
even the little ones of the **f**; Jer 49:20 6629
male goats at the head of the **f**. Jer 50:8 6629
"Israel is a scattered **f**, Jer 50:17 7716
even the little ones of the **f**; Jer 50:45 6629
I shatter the shepherd and his **f**, Jer 51:23 5739
"Take the choicest of the **f**, Ezk 24:5 6629
not the shepherds feed the **f**? Ezk 34:2 6629
fat *sheep* without feeding the **f**. Ezk 34:3 6629
"My **f** wandered through all the Ezk 34:6 6629
My **f** was scattered over all Ezk 34:6 6629
because My **f** has become a prey, Ezk 34:8 6629
My **f** has even become food for all Ezk 34:8 6629
shepherds did not search for My **f**, Ezk 34:8 6629
themselves and did not feed My **f**; Ezk 34:8 6629
deliver My **f** from their mouth, Ezk 34:10 6629
f and I will lead them to rest," Ezk 34:15 6629
"As for you, My **f**, Ezk 34:17 6629
'As for My **f**, they must eat Ezk 34:19 6629
therefore, I will deliver My **f**, Ezk 34:22 6629
will increase their men like a **f**. Ezk 36:37 6629
"Like the **f** for sacrifices, like Ezk 36:38 6629
like the **f** at Jerusalem during her Ezk 36:38 6629
a ram without blemish from the **f**. Ezk 43:23 6629
a young bull and a ram from the **f**, Ezk 43:25 6629
and one sheep from *each* **f** of two Ezk 45:15 6629
And eat lambs from the **f** And Am 6:4 6629
the **f** and the LORD said to me, Am 7:15 6629
beast, herd, or **f** taste a thing. Jon 3:7 6629
Like a **f** in the midst of its Mi 2:12 5739
"As for you, tower of the **f**, Mi 4:8 5739
He will arise and shepherd *His* **f** Mi 5:4
The **f** of Your possession Which Mi 7:14 6629
Though the **f** should be cut off Hab 3:17 6629
that day As the **f** of His people; Zch 9:16 6629
LORD of hosts has visited His **f**, Zch 10:3 5739
"Pasture the **f** *doomed* to slaughter. Zch 11:4 6629
the **f** *doomed* to slaughter, Zch 11:7 6629
hence the afflicted of the **f**. Zch 11:7 6629
so I pastured the **f**. Zch 11:7 6629
and thus the afflicted of the **f** Zch 11:11 6629
shepherd Who leaves the **f**! Zch 11:17 6629
swindler who has a male in his **f** and Mal 1:14 6629
SHEEP OF THE F SHALL BE SCATTERED.' Mt 26:31 4167
watch over their **f** by night. Lk 2:8 4167
"Do not be afraid, little **f**, Lk 12:32 4168
become one **f** *with* one shepherd. Jn 10:16 4167
for yourselves and for all the **f**, Ac 20:28 4168
in among you, not sparing the **f**; Ac 20:29 4168
Or who tends a **f** and does not use 1Co 9:7 4167
does not use the milk of the **f**? 1Co 9:7 4167
shepherd the **f** of God among you, 1Pe 5:2 4168
proving to be examples to the **f**. 1Pe 5:3 4168

FLOCKS
And Abel was a keeper of **f**, Gn 4:2 6629
also had **f** and herds and tents. Gn 13:5 6629
and He has given him **f** and herds, Gn 24:35 6629
for he had possessions of **f** and Gn 26:14 6629
three **f** of sheep were lying there Gn 29:2 5739
from that well they watered the **f**. Gn 29:2 5739
all the **f** were gathered there, Gn 29:3 5739
until all the **f** are gathered, Gn 29:8 5739
Jacob fed the rest of Laban's **f**. Gn 30:36 6629
in front of the **f** in the gutters, Gn 30:38 6629
where the **f** came to drink; Gn 30:38 6629
So the **f** mated by the rods, and Gn 30:39 6629
and the **f** brought forth striped, Gn 30:39 6629
and made the **f** face toward the Gn 30:40 6629
and had large **f** and female and Gn 30:43 6629
have I eaten the rams of your **f**. Gn 31:38 6629
children, and the **f** are my flocks, Gn 31:43 6629
children, and the flocks are my **f**, Gn 31:43 6629
f and male and female servants; Gn 32:5 6629
f and the herds and the camels, Gn 32:7 6629
the **f** and herds which are nursing are Gn 33:13 6629
hard one day, all the **f** will die. Gn 33:13 6629
They took their **f** and their herds Gn 34:28 6629
your **f** and your herds and all that Gn 45:10 6629
and they have brought their **f** and Gn 46:32 6629
father and my brothers and their **f** Gn 47:1 6629
is no pasture for your servants' **f**, Gn 47:4 6629
f and the herds and the donkeys; Gn 47:17 6629
little ones and their **f** and their herds Gn 50:8 6629
on the herds, and on the **f**. Ex 9:3 6629
our **f** and our herds we shall go, Ex 10:9 6629
your **f** and your herds be detained. Ex 10:24 6629
"Take both your **f** and your herds, Ex 12:32 6629
with them, along with **f** and herds, Ex 12:38 6629
even the **f** and the herds may not Ex 34:3 6629
"Should **f** and herds be Nu 11:22 6629
all their **f** and all their goods they Nu 31:9 4735
your herds and your **f** multiply, Dt 8:13 6629
"At the sound of those who divide **f** Jg 5:11
To hear the piping for the **f**? Jg 5:16 5739
"He will take a tenth of your **f**, 1Sa 8:17 6629
man had a great many **f** and herds. 2Sa 12:2 6629
them like two little **f** of goats, 1Ki 20:27 2835
to seek pasture for their **f**. 1Ch 4:39 6629
there was pasture there for their **f**. 1Ch 4:41 6629
the Hagrite had charge of the **f**. 1Ch 27:31 6629
the Arabians also brought him **f**, 2Ch 17:11 6629
cattle and sheepfolds for the **f**. 2Ch 32:28 5739
acquired **f** and herds in abundance, 2Ch 32:29 6629
present, **f** of lambs and young goats, 2Ch 35:7 6629
2,600 *from the* **f** and 300 bulls. 2Ch 35:8
5,000 *from the* **f** and 500 bulls. 2Ch 35:9
our **f** as it is written in the law, Ne 10:36 6629
They seize and devour **f**. Jb 24:2 5739
The meadows are clothed with **f** And Ps 65:13 6629
And our **f** bring forth thousands Ps 144:13 6629
Know well the condition of your **f**, Pr 27:23 6629
Also I possessed **f** and herds Ec 2:7 6629
Beside the **f** of your companions?" SS 1:7 5739
Nor will shepherds make *their* **f** Is 13:20
They will be for **f** to lie down in, Is 17:2 5739
for wild donkeys, a pasture for **f**; Is 32:14 5739
"All the **f** of Kedar will be Is 60:7 6629
will stand and pasture your **f**, Is 61:5 6629
will be a pasture land for **f**, Is 65:10 6629
youth, their **f** and their herds, Jer 3:24 6629
will devour your **f** and your herds; Jer 5:17 6629
and their **f** will come to her, Jer 6:3 5739
and they who go about with **f**. Jer 31:24 5739
of shepherds who rest their **f**. Jer 33:12 6629
the **f** will again pass under the Jer 33:13 6629
take away their tents and their **f**; Jer 49:29 6629
of Ammon a resting place for **f**. Ezk 25:5 6629
cities be filled with **f** of men. Ezk 36:38 6629
f and herds To seek the LORD, Hos 5:6 6629
Even the **f** of sheep suffer. Jl 1:18 5739
a young lion among **f** of sheep, Mi 5:8 5739
for shepherds and folds for **f**. Zph 2:6 6629
F will lie down in her midst, All Zph 2:14 5739

FLOGGED
you will be **f** in *the* synagogues, Mk 13:9 1194
they **f** them and ordered them not Ac 5:40 1194

FLOGGING
and committed deeds worthy of a **f**, Lk 12:48 4127

FLOOD
the **f** of water upon the earth, Gn 6:17 3999
f of water came upon the earth. Gn 7:6 3999
ark because of the water of the **f**. Gn 7:7 3999
of the **f** came upon the earth. Gn 7:10 3999
Then the **f** came upon the earth for Gn 7:17 3999
be cut off by the water of the **f**, Gn 9:11 3999
be a **f** to destroy the earth." Gn 9:11 3999
become a **f** to destroy all flesh. Gn 9:15 3999
and fifty years after the **f**. Gn 9:28 3999
were born to them after the **f**. Gn 10:1 3999
on the earth after the **f**. Gn 10:32 3999
Arpachshad two years after the **f**; Gn 11:10 3999
"Terrors overtake him like a **f**; Jb 27:20 4325
"Who has cleft a channel for the **f**, Jb 38:25 7858
The LORD sat *as King* at the **f**; Ps 29:10 3999
Surely in a **f** of great waters they Ps 32:6 7858
deep waters, and a **f** overflows me. Ps 69:2 7642b
the **f** of water not overflow me Nor Ps 69:15 7642b
have swept them away like a **f**; Ps 90:5 2229
Wrath is fierce and anger is a **f**, Pr 27:4 7858
Noah Would not **f** the earth again Is 54:9 5674a
And its end *will come* with a **f**; Da 9:26 7858
But with an overflowing **f** He will Na 1:8 7858
before the **f** they were eating and Mt 24:38 2627
the **f** came and took them all away; Mt 24:39 2627
and when a **f** occurred, the torrent Lk 6:48 4132
the **f** came and destroyed them all. Lk 17:27 2627
a **f** upon the world of the ungodly; 2Pe 2:5 2627
her to be swept away with the **f**. Rv 12:15 4216

FLOODED
overflowing forces will be **f** away Da 11:22 7857
was destroyed, being **f** with water. 2Pe 3:6 2626

FLOODGATES
and the f of the sky were opened. Gn 7:11 699
and the f of the sky were closed, Gn 8:2 699

FLOODING
A f rain will come, and you, O Ezk 13:11 7857
be in My anger a f rain and hailstones Ezk 13:13 7857

FLOODS
The f have lifted up, O LORD, The Ps 93:3 5104
The f have lifted up their voice, Ps 93:3 5104
f lift up their pounding waves. Ps 93:3 5104
rain fell, and the f came, Mt 7:25 *4215*
rain fell, and the f came, Mt 7:27 *4215*

FLOOR
came to the threshing f of Atad, Gn 50:10 1637
at the threshing f of Atad, Gn 50:11 1637
dust that is on the f of the tabernacle Nu 5:17 7172
the offering of the threshing f, Nu 15:20 1637
as the grain from the threshing f Nu 18:27 1637
as the product of the threshing f, Nu 18:30 1637
f and from your wine vat; Dt 15:14 1637
threshing f and your wine vat; Dt 16:13 1637
master had fallen to the f dead. Jg 3:25 776
fleece of wool on the threshing f. Jg 6:37 1637
barley at the threshing f tonight. Ru 3:2 1637
and go down to the threshing f; Ru 3:3 1637
So she went down to the threshing f Ru 3:6 1637
woman came to the threshing f." Ru 3:14 1637
came to the threshing f of Nacon, 2Sa 6:6 1637
f of Araunah the Jebusite. 2Sa 24:16 1637
f of Araunah the Jebusite." 2Sa 24:18 1637
"To buy the threshing f from you, 2Sa 24:21 1637
So David bought the threshing f 2Sa 24:24 1637
from the f of the house to the 1Ki 6:15 7172
and he overlaid the f of the house 1Ki 6:15 7172
cedar from the f to the ceiling; 1Ki 6:16 7172
the f of the house with gold, 1Ki 6:30 7172
with cedar from f to floor. 1Ki 7:7 7172
with cedar from floor to f. 1Ki 7:7 7172
at the threshing f at the entrance 1Ki 22:10 1637
From the threshing f, 2Ki 6:27 1637
came to the threshing f of Chidon, 1Ch 13:9 1637
threshing f of Ornan the Jebusite. 1Ch 21:15 1637
threshing f of Ornan the Jebusite. 1Ch 21:18 1637
and went out from the threshing f and 1Ch 21:21 1637
me the site of *this* threshing f, 1Ch 21:22 1637
threshing f of Ornan the Jebusite, 1Ch 21:28 1637
threshing f of Ornan the Jebusite. 2Ch 3:1 1637
they were sitting at the threshing f 2Ch 18:9 1637
gather *it from* your threshing f? Jb 39:12 1637
my afflicted of the threshing f! Is 21:10 1637
of Babylon is like a threshing f Jer 51:33 1637
earnings on every threshing f. Hos 9:1 1637
Threshing f and wine press will Hos 9:2 1637
blown away from the threshing f And Hos 13:3 1637
from My sight on the f of the sea, Am 9:3 7172
like sheaves to the threshing f. Mi 4:12 1637
thoroughly clear His threshing f; Mt 3:12 *257*
thoroughly clear His threshing f, Lk 3:17 *257*
and fell down from the third f and Ac 20:9 *5152*

FLOORS
are plundering the threshing f." 1Sa 23:1 1637
chaff from the summer threshing f; Da 2:35 147
threshing f will be full of grain, Jl 2:24 1637

FLOUR
prepare three measures of fine f, Gn 18:6 7058, 5560
shall make them of fine wheat f. Ex 29:2 5560
one-tenth *of an ephah* of fine f mixed Ex 29:40 5560
his offering shall be of fine f, Lv 2:1 5560
take from it his handful of its fine f Lv 2:2 5560
cakes of fine f mixed with oil, Lv 2:4 5560
griddle, *it shall be* of fine f, Lv 2:5 5560
shall be made of fine f with oil. Lv 2:7 5560
of fine f for a sin offering; Lv 5:11 5560
the fine f of the grain offering, Lv 6:15 5560
f as a regular grain offering, Lv 6:20 5560
stirred fine f mixed with oil. Lv 7:12 5560
and three-tenths *of an ephah* of fine f Lv 14:10 5560
one-tenth *of an ephah* of fine f Lv 14:21 5560
an ephah of fine f mixed with oil, Lv 23:13 5560
they shall be of a fine f, Lv 23:17 5560
f and bake twelve cakes with it; Lv 24:5 5560
basket of unleavened cakes of fine f Nu 6:15 5560
both of them full of fine f mixed Nu 7:13 5560
both of them full of fine f mixed Nu 7:19 5560
both of them full of fine f mixed Nu 7:25 5560
both of them full of fine f mixed Nu 7:31 5560
both of them full of fine f mixed Nu 7:37 5560
both of them full of fine f mixed Nu 7:43 5560
both of them full of fine f mixed Nu 7:49 5560
both of them full of fine f mixed Nu 7:55 5560
both of them full of fine f mixed Nu 7:61 5560
both of them full of fine f mixed Nu 7:67 5560
both of them full of fine f mixed Nu 7:73 5560
both of them full of fine f mixed Nu 7:79 5560
offering, fine f mixed with oil; Nu 8:8 5560
one-tenth *of an ephah* of fine f mixed Nu 15:4 5560
two-tenths *of an ephah* of fine f mixed Nu 15:6 5560
of three-tenths *of an ephah* of fine f Nu 15:9 5560
of fine f for a grain offering, Nu 28:5 5560
two-tenths *of an ephah* of fine f mixed Nu 28:9 5560
of fine f mixed with oil Nu 28:12 5560
of fine f mixed with oil Nu 28:12 5560
and a tenth *of an ephah* of fine f Nu 28:13 5560
shall offer fine f mixed with oil: Nu 28:20 5560
offering, fine f mixed with oil: Nu 28:28 5560
offering, fine f mixed with oil: Nu 29:3 5560
offering, fine f mixed with oil: Nu 29:9 5560
offering, fine f mixed with oil: Nu 29:14 5560
bread from an ephah of f; Jg 6:19 7058
one ephah of f and a jug of wine, 1Sa 1:24 7058
and she took f, kneaded it and 1Sa 28:24 7058
basins, pottery, wheat, barley, f, 2Sa 17:28 7058
of fine f and sixty kors of meal, 1Ki 4:22 5560
only a handful of f in the bowl 1Ki 17:12 7058
bowl of f shall not be exhausted, 1Ki 17:14 7058
The bowl of f was not exhausted 1Ki 17:16 7058
fine f will be *sold* for a shekel, 2Ki 7:1 5560
Then a measure of fine f *was sold* 2Ki 7:16 5560
a measure of fine f for a shekel, 2Ki 7:18 5560
and over the fine f and the wine and 1Ch 9:29 5560
oxen, great quantities of f cakes, 1Ch 12:40 7058
the fine f for a grain offering, 1Ch 23:29 5560
You ate fine f, honey and oil; Ezk 16:13 5560
My bread which I gave you, fine f, Ezk 16:19 5560
hin of oil to moisten the fine f, Ezk 46:14 5560
took and hid in three pecks of f Mt 13:33 *224*
took and hid in three pecks of f Lk 13:21 *224*
and olive oil and fine f and wheat Rv 18:13 *4585*

FLOURISH
At the scent of water it will f Jb 14:9 6524a
In his days may the righteous f, Ps 72:7 6524a
f like vegetation of the earth. Ps 72:16 6692a
man will f like the palm tree, Ps 92:12 6524a
will f in the courts of our God. Ps 92:13 6524a
will f like the *green* leaf. Pr 11:28 6524a
the tent of the upright will f. Pr 14:11 6524a
bones will f like the new grass; Is 66:14 6524a
tree and make the dry tree f. Ezk 17:24 6524a
Grain will make the young men f, Zch 9:17 5107

FLOURISHED
grass And all who did iniquity f, Ps 92:7 6692a

FLOURISHES
In the morning it f and Ps 90:6 6692a
As a flower of the field, so he f. Ps 103:15 6692a
Though he f among the reeds, An Hos 13:15 6509

FLOURISHING
in my house and f in my palace. Da 4:4 7487b

FLOW
cleansed from the f of her blood. Lv 12:7 4726
body allows its discharge to f or Lv 15:3 7388a
nakedness, he has laid bare her f, Lv 20:18 4726
has exposed the f of her blood; Lv 20:18 4726
does f with milk and honey, Nu 13:27 2100
"Water will f from his buckets, Nu 24:7 5140
behold, *there was* a f of honey; 1Sa 14:26 1982
f away in the day of His anger. Jb 20:28 5064
f away like water that runs off; Ps 58:7 3988b
They f between the mountains; Ps 104:10 1980
wind to blow and the waters to f. Ps 147:18 5140
For from it f the springs of life. Pr 4:23
All the rivers f into the sea, Yet Ec 1:7 1980
To the place where the rivers f, Ec 1:7 1980
rivers flow, There they f again. Ec 1:7 1980
water f out of the rock for them; Is 48:21 5140
And our eyelids f with water. Jer 9:18 5140
weep And f down with tears, Jer 13:17 3381
f down with tears night and day, Jer 14:17 3381
sea, being made to f into the sea, Ezk 47:8 3318
And the hills will f with milk, Jl 3:18 1980
brooks of Judah will f with water; Jl 3:18 1980
waters will f out of Jerusalem, Zch 14:8 3318
the f of her blood was dried up; Mk 5:29 *4077*
f rivers of living water.' " Jn 7:38 *4482*

FLOWED
Now a river f out of Eden to water Gn 2:10 3318
The water f around the altar and 1Ki 18:35 1980
stream which f through the region, 2Ch 32:4 7857
opened the rock and water f out; Ps 105:41 2100
Waters f over my head; La 3:54 6687

FLOWER
in the one branch, a bulb and a f, Ex 25:33 6525
in the other branch, a bulb and a f Ex 25:33 6525
a bulb and a f in one branch, Ex 37:19 6525
a bulb and a f in the other Ex 37:19 6525
a f he comes forth and withers. Jb 14:2 6731b
will cast off his f like the olive tree. Jb 15:33 5328
As a f of the field, so he Ps 103:15 6731b
the f becomes a ripening grape, Is 18:5 5328
fading f of its glorious beauty, Is 28:1 6731b
fading f of its glorious beauty, Is 28:4 6731b
is like the f of the field. Is 40:6 6731b
The grass withers, the f fades, Is 40:7 6731b
The grass withers, the f fades, Is 40:8 6731b
and its f falls off and the Jas 1:11 *438*
ALL ITS GLORY LIKE THE F OF GRASS. 1Pe 1:24 *438*
WITHERS, AND THE F FALLS OFF, 1Pe 1:24 *438*

FLOWERING
like f grass he will pass away. Jas 1:10 *438*

FLOWERS
f shall be *of one piece* with it. Ex 25:31 6525
blossoms, its bulbs and its f. Ex 25:34 6525
its f were *of one piece* with it. Ex 37:17 6525
blossoms, its bulbs and its f; Ex 37:20 6525
from its base to its f it Nu 8:4 6525
in the shape of gourds and open f; 1Ki 6:18 6731b
cherubim, palm trees, and open f, 1Ki 6:29 6731b
cherubim, palm trees, and open f, 1Ki 6:32 6731b
cherubim, palm trees, and open f; 1Ki 6:35 6731b
the f and the lamps and the tongs, 1Ki 7:49 6525
the f, the lamps, and the tongs of 2Ch 4:21 6525
'The f have *already* appeared in SS 2:12 5339

FLOWING
and found there a well of f water, Gn 26:19 2416a
to a land f with milk and honey, Ex 3:8 2100
a land f with milk and honey." Ex 3:17 2100
you, a land f with milk and honey, Ex 13:5 2100
The f waters stood up like a heap; Ex 15:8 5140
of f myrrh five hundred *shekels,* Ex 30:23 1865
to a land f with milk and honey; Ex 33:3 2100
a land f with milk and honey." Lv 20:24 2100
out of a land f with milk and honey Nu 16:13 2100
into a land f with milk and honey, Nu 16:14 2100
and f water shall be added to them Nu 19:17 2416a
in a land f with milk and honey. Dt 6:3 2100
f forth in valleys and hills; Dt 8:7 3318
a land f with milk and honey. Dt 11:9 2100
a land f with milk and honey. Dt 26:9 2100
us, a land f with milk and honey, Dt 26:15 2100
you, a land f with milk and honey, Dt 27:3 2100
the land f with milk and honey, Dt 31:20 2100
and the waters which are f down Jos 3:13 3381
the waters which were f down Jos 3:16 3381
and those which were f down toward Jos 3:16 3381
us, a land f with milk and honey. Jos 5:6 2100
The rivers f with honey and curds. Jb 20:17 5158a
"He dams up the streams from f, Jb 28:11 1065
And streams f from Lebanon." SS 4:15
And the f locks of your head are SS 7:5 1803a
F gently *through* the lips of those SS 7:9 1680
the gently f waters of Shiloah And Is 8:6 1980
from the f stream of the Euphrates to Is 27:12 7642b
them a land f with milk and honey, Jer 11:5 2100
Or is the cold f water *from* a Jer 18:14 5140
a land f with milk and honey. Jer 32:22 2100
Your valley is f *away,* O Jer 49:4 2100
for them, f with milk and honey, Ezk 20:6 2100
given them, f with milk and honey, Ezk 20:15 2100
with f turbans on their heads, Ezk 23:15 5628
water was f from under the Ezk 47:1 3318
the water was f down from under, Ezk 47:1 3381
"A river of fire was f And coming Da 7:10 5047

FLOWS
it f around the whole land of Gn 2:11 5437
f around the whole land of Cush. Gn 2:13 5437
it f east of Assyria. Gn 2:14 1980
land which f with milk and honey. Nu 14:8 2100
of the righteous f with wisdom, Pr 10:31 5107
their water f from the sanctuary, Ezk 47:12 3318
fire f out of their mouth and devours Rv 11:5 *1607*

FLUENTLY
I know that he speaks f. Ex 4:14 1696

FLUSHED
"My face is f from weeping, And Jb 16:16 2560c

FLUTE
place with harp, tambourine, f, 1Sa 10:5 2485
And rejoice at the sound of the f. Jb 21:12 5748
And my f to the sound of those who Jb 30:31 5748
and harp, by tambourine and f, Is 5:12 2485
one marches to *the sound of* the f, Is 30:29 2485
you hear the sound of the horn, f, Da 3:5 4953
heard the sound of the horn, f, Da 3:7 4953
hears the sound of the horn, f, Da 3:10 4953
you hear the sound of the horn, f, Da 3:15 4953
'We played the f for you, and you Mt 11:17 *832*
'We played the f for you, and you Lk 7:32 *832*
lifeless things, either f or harp, 1Co 14:7 *836*
is played on the f or on the harp? 1Co 14:7 *832*

FLUTE-PLAYERS
official's house, and saw the f and Mt 9:23 *834*
sound of harpists and musicians and f Rv 18:22 *834*

FLUTES
on f and rejoicing with great joy, 1Ki 1:40 2485
as those who play the f *shall say,* Ps 87:7 2490b
My heart wails for Moab like f; Jer 48:36 2485
like f for the men of Kir-heres. Jer 48:36 2485

FLY
and let birds f above the earth in Gn 1:20 5774a
for trouble, As sparks f upward. Jb 5:7 5774a
I would f away and be at rest. Ps 55:6 5774a
For soon it is gone and we f away. Ps 90:10 5774a
the LORD will whistle for the f that is Is 7:18 2070
"Who are these who f like a cloud And Is 60:8 5774a
one will f swiftly like an eagle And Jer 48:40 1675
their glory will f away like a bird Hos 9:11 5774a
They f like an eagle swooping *down* Hab 1:8 5774a
so that she could f into the Rv 12:14 *4072*
the birds which f in midheaven, Rv 19:17 *4072*

FLYING
flitting, like a swallow in *its* f, Pr 26:2 5774a
And its fruit will be a f serpent. Is 14:29 5774a
and lion, viper and f serpent, Is 30:6 5774a
Like f birds so the LORD of hosts Is 31:5 5774a
and behold, *there was* a f scroll. Zch 5:1 5774a
"I see a f scroll; Zch 5:2 5774a
creature *was* like a f eagle. Rv 4:7 *4072*
I heard an eagle f in midheaven, Rv 8:13 *4072*
saw another angel f in midheaven, Rv 14:6 *4072*

FOAL
"He ties *his* f to the vine, And Gn 49:11 5895
When the f of a wild donkey is born Jb 11:12 5895
Even on a colt, the f of a donkey. Zch 9:9 1121
THE F OF A BEAST OF BURDEN.' " Mt 21:5 *5207*

FOAM
Though its waters roar *and* f, Ps 46:3 2560a
casting up their own shame like f; Jude 1:13 *1890*

FOAMING
rolling around and f *at the mouth.* Mk 9:20 *875*
a convulsion with f *at the mouth* Lk 9:39 *876*

FOAMS
hand of the LORD, and the wine f; Ps 75:8 2560a
the ground and he f *at the mouth,* Mk 9:18 *875*

FODDER
his donkey **f** at the lodging place, **Gn 42:27** 4554
and he gave their donkeys **f**. **Gn 43:24** 4554
both straw and **f** for our donkeys, **Jg 19:19** 4554
his house and gave the donkeys **f**, **Jg 19:21** 1101b
Or does the ox low over his **f**? **Jb 6:5** 1098
"They harvest their **f** in the field And **Jb 24:6** 1098
work the ground will eat salted **f**, **Is 30:24** 1098
FOE
"A **f** and an enemy is this wicked **Es 7:6** 6862c
FOES
your **f** while they pursue you? **2Sa 24:13** 6862c
to be swept away before your **f**, **1Ch 21:12** 6862c
Your righteousness because of my **f**; **Ps 5:8** 7796b
in a level path Because of my **f**. **Ps 27:11** 7796b
the iniquity of my **f** surrounds me, **Ps 49:5** 6120
will recompense the evil to my **f**; **Ps 54:5** 7796b
My **f** have trampled upon me all day **Ps 56:2** 7796b
me look *triumphantly* upon my **f**. **Ps 59:10** 7796b
May I be delivered from my **f** and **Ps 69:14** 8130
has looked *exultantly* upon my **f**, **Ps 92:11** 7790
And avenge Myself on My **f**. **Is 1:24** 340
and into the hand of their **f** and **Jer 21:7** 340
so as to avenge Himself on His **f**; **Jer 46:10** 6862c
FOLD
will roar mightily against His **f**. **Jer 25:30** 5116a
them together like sheep in the **f**; **Mi 2:12** 1223
should be cut off from the **f** And **Hab 3:17** 4356
holy meat in the **f** of his garment, **Hg 2:12** 3671
and touches bread with this **f**, **Hg 2:12** 3671
the door into the **f** of the sheep, **Jn 10:1** *833*
sheep, which are not of this **f**; **Jn 10:16** *833*
FOLDED
"It shall be square *and* **f** double, **Ex 28:16** 3717
made the breastpiece **f** double, **Ex 39:9** 3717
and a span wide when **f** double. **Ex 39:9** 3717
Elijah took his mantle and **f** **2Ki 2:8** 1563
A tent which will not be **f** **Is 33:20** 6813
FOLDING
A little **f** of the hands to rest" **Pr 6:10** 2264
A little **f** of the hands to rest," **Pr 24:33** 2264
FOLDS
"The **f** of his flesh are joined **Jb 41:23** 4651
Nor male goats out of your **f**. **Ps 50:9** 4356
The fool **f** his hands and consumes **Ec 4:5** 2263
"And the peaceful **f** are made **Jer 25:37** 5116c
for shepherds and **f** for flocks. **Zph 2:6** 1448
FOLIAGE
the **f** of beautiful trees, **Lv 23:40** 6529
And Bashan and Carmel lose *their* **f**. **Is 33:9**
'Its **f** *was* beautiful and its fruit **Da 4:12** 6074a
off its **f** and scatter its fruit; **Da 4:14** 6074a
and whose **f** *was* beautiful and its **Da 4:21** 6074a
FOLLOW
not willing to **f** me to this land; **Gn 24:5** 1980, 310
the woman is not willing to **f** you, **Gn 24:8** 1980, 310
'Suppose the woman does not **f** me.' **Gn 24:39** 1980, 310
to his house steward, "Up, **f** the men; **Gn 44:4** 7291, 310
you and all the people who **f** you,' **Ex 11:8** 7272
not **f** the masses in doing evil, **Ex 23:2** 1961, 310
you shall not **f** the customs of the **Lv 20:23** 1980
so as to **f** and not **f** after **Nu 15:39** 8446
for they did not **f** Me fully, **Nu 32:11** 310
"You shall not **f** other gods, any **Dt 6:14** 1980, 310
you are not ensnared to **f** them, **Dt 12:30** 310
"You shall **f** the LORD your God **Dt 13:4** 310, 1980
were called together to **f** him. **Jg 6:34** 310
were called together to **f** him; **Jg 6:35** 310
they were inclined to **f** Abimelech, **Jg 9:3** 310
over you will **f** the LORD your God. **1Sa 12:14** 310
who were too exhausted to **f** David, **1Sa 30:21** 1980, 310
among the people who **f** Absalom.' **2Sa 17:9** 310
is for David, *let him* **f** Joab." **2Sa 20:11** 310
and did not **f** the LORD fully, **1Ki 11:6** 310
If the LORD is God, **f** Him; **1Ki 18:21** 1980, 310
but if Baal, **f** him." **1Ki 18:21** 1980, 310
my mother, then I will **f** you." **1Ki 19:20** 1980, 310
for all the people who **f** me." **1Ki 20:10** 7272
f me and I will bring you to the **2Ki 6:19** 1980, 310
nor do they **f** their statutes or **2Ki 17:34** 6213a
all men will **f** after him, **Jb 21:33** 4900
will **f** me all the days of my life, **Ps 23:6** 7291
me, because I **f** what is good. **Ps 38:20** 7291
virgins, her companions who **f** her, **Ps 45:14** 310
the upright in heart will **f** it. **Ps 94:15** 310
who **f** after wickedness draw near; **Ps 119:150** 7291
And **f** the impulses of your heart **Ec 11:9** 1980
we are going to **f** our own plans, **Jer 18:12** 310, 1980
will **f** closely after you there *in* **Jer 42:16** 1692
The sword will **f** after you. **Jer 48:2** 310, 1980
and Libyans and Ethiopians *will* **f** **Da 11:43**
and jewelry, And **f** her lovers, **Hos 2:13** 1980, 310
was determined to **f** *man's* command. **Hos 5:11** 1980, 310
"**F** Me, and I will make you **Mt 4:19** *1205, 3694*
I will **f** You wherever You go." **Mt 8:19** *190*
But Jesus said to him, "**F** Me, **Mt 8:22** *190*
and He said to him, "**F** Me!" **Mt 9:9** *190*
Jesus got up and *began* to **f** him, **Mt 9:19** *190*
f after Me is not worthy of Me. **Mt 10:38** *190*
and take up his cross and **f** Me. **Mt 16:24** *190*
and come, **f** Me." **Mt 19:21** *190*
"**F** Me, and I will make you become **Mk 1:17** *1205, 3694*
servants, and went away to **f** Him. **Mk 1:20** *3694*
tax booth, and He said to him, "**F** Me **Mk 2:14** *190*
and take up his cross and **f** Me. **Mk 8:34** *190*
and come, **f** Me." **Mk 10:21** *190*
carrying a pitcher of water; **f** him; **Mk 14:13** *190*
used to **f** Him and minister to Him; **Mk 15:41** *190*
tax booth, and He said to him, "**F** Me **Lk 5:27** *190*
and got up and *began* to **f** Him. **Lk 5:28** *190*
take up his cross daily and **f** Me. **Lk 9:23** *190*
he does not **f** along with us." **Lk 9:49** *190*
"I will **f** You wherever You go." **Lk 9:57** *190*
And He said to another, "**F** Me." **Lk 9:59** *190*
"I will **f** You, Lord; **Lk 9:61** *190*
and come, **f** Me." **Lk 18:22** *190*
but the end *does* not **f** **Lk 21:9**
f him into the house that he **Lk 22:10** *190*
And Jesus said to him, "**F** Me." **Jn 1:43** *190*
and the sheep **f** him because they **Jn 10:4** *190*
A stranger they simply will not **f**, **Jn 10:5** *190*
and I know them, and they **f** Me; **Jn 10:27** *190*
"If anyone serves Me, he must **f** Me; **Jn 12:26** *190*
"Where I go, you cannot **f** Me now; **Jn 13:36** *190*
but you will **f** later." **Jn 13:36** *190*
why can I not **f** You right now? **Jn 13:37** *190*
He said to him, "**F** Me!" **Jn 21:19** *190*
what *is that* to you? You **f** Me!" **Jn 21:22** *190*
your cloak around you and **f** me." **Ac 12:8** *190*
he went out and continued to **f**, **Ac 12:9** *190*
and the rest *should* **f**, some on **Ac 27:44**
but who also **f** in the steps of the **Ro 4:12** *4748*
how you ought to **f** our example, **2Th 3:7** *3401*
you, so that you would **f** our example. **2Th 3:9** *3401*
already turned aside to **f** Satan. **1Tm 5:15** *3694*
for others, their *sins* **f** after. **1Tm 5:24** *1872*
of Christ and the glories to **f**. **1Pe 1:11** *3326, 3778*
example for you to **f** in His steps, **1Pe 2:21** *1872*
For we did not **f** cleverly devised **2Pe 1:16** *1811*
Many will **f** their sensuality, **2Pe 2:2** *1811*
who **f** the Lamb wherever He goes. **Rv 14:4** *190*
for their deeds **f** with them." **Rv 14:13** *190*
FOLLOWED
mounted the camels and **f** the man. **Gn 24:61** 1980, 310
and all those who **f** the droves, **Gn 32:19** 1980, 310
spirit and has **f** Me fully, **Nu 14:24** 310
for they have **f** the LORD fully.' **Nu 32:12** 310
because he has **f** the LORD fully.' **Dt 1:36** 310
for all the men who **f** Baal-peor, **Dt 4:3** 1980, 310
every living thing that **f** them, **Dt 11:6** 7272
Your hand, And they **f** in Your steps; **Dt 33:3** 8497
the covenant of the LORD **f** them. **Jos 6:8** 1980, 310
but I **f** the LORD my God fully. **Jos 14:8** 310
you have **f** the LORD my God fully.' **Jos 14:9** 310
he **f** the LORD God of Israel fully. **Jos 14:14** 310
and **f** other gods from *among* the **Jg 2:12** 1980, 310
reckless fellows, and they **f** him. **Jg 9:4** 1980, 310
one his branch and **f** Abimelech, **Jg 9:49** 1980, 310
Then Manoah arose and **f** his wife, **Jg 13:11** 1980, 310
the Philistines **f** them to the border **1Sa 6:12** 1980, 310
all the people **f** him trembling. **1Sa 13:7** 310
Now the three oldest **f** Saul, **1Sa 17:14** 1980, 310
and she **f** the messengers of David and **1Sa 25:42** 1980, 310
house of Judah, however, **f** David. **2Sa 2:10** 310
went, and **f** her as far as Bahurim. **2Sa 3:16** 310
saw that his counsel was not **f**, **2Sa 17:23** 6213a
and **f** Sheba the son of Bichri; **2Sa 20:2** 310
to Joab, for Joab had **f** Adonijah, **1Ki 2:28** 5186, 310
although he had not **f** Absalom. **1Ki 2:28** 310, 5186
of Judah **f** the house of David. **1Ki 12:20** 310
and who **f** Me with all his heart, **1Ki 14:8** 1980, 310
people **f** Tibni the son of Ginath, **1Ki 16:21** 1961, 310
the *other* half **f** Omri. **1Ki 16:21** 310
But the people who **f** Omri **1Ki 16:22** 310
who **f** Tibni the son of Ginath. **1Ki 16:22** 310
LORD and you have **f** the Baals. **1Ki 18:18** 1980, 310
f Elijah and ministered to him. **1Ki 19:21** 1980, 310
and the army which **f** them. **1Ki 20:19** 310
or for the cattle that **f** them. **2Ki 3:9** 7272
And he arose and **f** her. **2Ki 4:30** 1980, 310
and **f** the sins of Jeroboam the son **2Ki 13:2** 1980, 310
And they **f** vanity and became vain, **2Ki 17:15** 1980, 310
f them to Jerusalem, to sacrifice **2Ch 11:16** 935
he **f** the example of his father David's **2Ch 17:3** 1980
of his father, **f** His commandments, **2Ch 17:4** 1980
nor the men of the guard who **f** me, **Ne 4:23** 310
of the leaders of Judah **f** them, **Ne 12:32** 1980, 310
while I **f** them with half of the **Ne 12:38** 310
the way, Or my heart **f** my eyes, **Jb 31:7** 310, 1980
'and have **f** other gods and served **Jer 16:11** 1980, 310
but they **f** in the direction which **Ezk 10:11** 310, 1980
left their nets and **f** Him. **Mt 4:20** *190*
boat and their father, and **f** Him. **Mt 4:22** *190*
Large crowds **f** Him from **Mt 4:25** *190*
mountain, large crowds **f** Him. **Mt 8:1** *190*
the boat, His disciples **f** Him. **Mt 8:23** *190*
And he got up and **f** Him. **Mt 9:9** *190*
from there, two blind men **f** Him, **Mt 9:27** *190*
Many **f** Him, and He healed them **Mt 12:15** *190*
f Him on foot from the cities. **Mt 14:13** *190*
and large crowds **f** Him, **Mt 19:2** *190*
we have left everything and **f** You; **Mt 19:27** *190*
to you, that you who have **f** Me, **Mt 19:28** *190*
Jericho, a large crowd **f** Him. **Mt 20:29** *190*
regained their sight and **f** Him. **Mt 20:34** *190*
those who **f**, were shouting, **Mt 21:9** *190*
who had **f** Jesus from Galilee while **Mt 27:55** *190*
left their nets and **f** Him. **Mk 1:18** *190*
And he got up and **f** Him. **Mk 2:14** *190*
a great multitude from Galilee **f**; **Mk 3:7** *190*
and His disciples **f** Him. **Mk 6:1** *190*
have left everything and **f** You." **Mk 10:28** *190*
and those who **f** were fearful. **Mk 10:32** *190*
in front and those who **f** **Mk 11:9** *190*
Peter had **f** Him at a distance, **Mk 14:54** *190*
the word by the signs that **f**. **Mk 16:20** *1872*
they left everything and **f** Him. **Lk 5:11** *190*
were aware of this and **f** Him; **Lk 9:11** *190*
left our own *homes* and **f** You." **Lk 18:28** *190*
and the disciples also **f** Him. **Lk 22:39** *190*
with Him out of Galilee **f**, **Lk 23:55** *2628*
heard him speak, and they **f** Jesus. **Jn 1:37** *190*
who heard John *speak* and **f** Him, **Jn 1:40** *190*
A large crowd **f** Him, because they **Jn 6:2** *190*
up quickly and went out, they **f** her, **Jn 11:31** *190*
and all who **f** him were dispersed **Ac 5:36** *3982*
those who **f** him were scattered. **Ac 5:37** *3982*
proselytes **f** Paul and Barnabas, **Ac 13:43** *190*
you ought to have **f** my advice and **Ac 27:21** *3980*
a spiritual rock which **f** them; **1Co 10:4** *190*
Now you **f** my teaching, conduct, **2Tm 3:10** *3877*
having **f** the way of Balaam, **2Pe 2:15** *1811*
and there **f** peals of thunder and **Rv 8:5** *1096*
the whole earth was amazed *and* **f** **Rv 13:3**
another angel, a second one, **f**, **Rv 14:8** *190*
angel, a third one, **f** them, **Rv 14:9** *190*
FOLLOWERS
As soon as He was alone, His **f**, **Mk 4:10** *3588, 4012*
to drink because of your name as **f** **Mk 9:41**
FOLLOWING
On the **f** day, the firstborn said to **Gn 19:34** 4283
have turned back from **f** the LORD. **Nu 14:43** 310
with the elders of Israel **f** him, **Nu 16:25** 1980, 310
"For if you turn away from **f** Him, **Nu 32:15** 310
from **f** Me to serve other gods; **Dt 7:4** 310
by **f** other gods which you have not **Dt 11:28** 1980, 310
away from **f** the LORD this day, **Jos 22:16** 310
away this day from **f** the LORD? **Jos 22:18** 310
to turn away from **f** the LORD, **Jos 22:23** 310
away from **f** the LORD this day, **Jos 22:29** 310
in **f** other gods to serve them and **Jg 2:19** 1980, 310
Tabor with ten thousand men **f** him. **Jg 4:14** 310
is in Amalek *came down*, **f** you, **Jg 5:14** 310
bread to the people who are **f** me, **Jg 8:5** 7272
leave you *or* turn back from **f** you; **Ru 1:16** 310
do not turn aside from **f** the LORD, **1Sa 12:20** 310
for he has turned back from **f** Me and **1Sa 15:11** 310
So Samuel went back **f** Saul, **1Sa 15:31** 310
right or to the left from **f** Abner. **2Sa 2:19** 310
willing to turn aside from **f** him. **2Sa 2:21** 310
"Turn aside from **f** me. **2Sa 2:22** 310
turn back from **f** their brothers?" **2Sa 2:26** 310
each from **f** his brother." **2Sa 2:27** 310
Then Joab returned from **f** Abner; **2Sa 2:30** 310
the pasture, from **f** the sheep, **2Sa 7:8** 310
of Israel withdrew from **f** David **2Sa 20:2** 310
and **f** Adonijah they helped him. **1Ki 1:7** 310
sons indeed turn away from **f** Me, **1Ki 9:6** 310
So he returned from **f** him, **1Ki 19:21** 310
acted very abominably in **f** idols, **1Ki 21:26** 1980, 310
On the **f** day, he took the cover **2Ki 8:15** 4283
drove Israel away from **f** the LORD and **2Ki 17:21** 310
he did not depart from **f** Him, **2Ki 18:6** 310
the sons of Aaron they gave the **f** **1Ch 6:57**
They gave to them the **f** cities of **1Ch 6:67**
the pasture, from **f** the sheep, **1Ch 17:7** 310
f the census which his father **2Ch 2:17** 310
Amaziah turned away from **f** the LORD **2Ch 25:27** 310
f the LORD God of their fathers. **2Ch 34:33** 310

the people were very unfaithful **f** 2Ch 36:14
in which I found the **f** record: Ne 7:5
they turned aside from **f** Him, Jb 34:27 310
In a **f** generation let their name Ps 109:13 312
Indeed, *while* **f** the way of Your Is 26:8
is not good, **f** their own thoughts, Is 65:2 310
the gardens, **F** one in the center, Is 66:17 310
Your **f** after Me in the wilderness, Jer 2:2 1980
And not turn away from **f** Me.' Jer 3:19 310
prophets who are **f** their own spirit Ezk 13:3 1980, 310
dream down *and* related the **f** Da 7:1
the LORD took me from **f** the flock Am 7:15 310
have turned back from **f** the LORD, Zph 1:6 310
and said to those who were **f**, Mt 8:10 *190*
But Peter was **f** Him at a Mt 26:58 *190*
many of them, and they were **f** Him. Mk 2:15 *190*
was **f** Him and pressing in on Him. Mk 5:24 *190*
him because he was not **f** us." Mk 9:38 *190*
sight and *began* **f** Him on the road. Mk 10:52 *190*
A young man was **f** Him, Mk 14:51 *4870*
to the crowd that was **f** Him, Lk 7:9 *190*
his sight and *began* **f** Him, Lk 18:43 *190*
but Peter was **f** at a distance. Lk 22:54 *190*
And **f** Him was a large Lk 23:27 *190*
Jesus turned and saw them **f**, Jn 1:38 *190*
Simon Peter was **f** Jesus, Jn 18:15 *190*
Peter also came, **f** him, Jn 20:6 *190*
disciple whom Jesus loved **f** *them* Jn 21:20 *190*
"On the **f** day he appeared to Ac 7:26 *1897a*
On the **f** day he entered Caesarea. Ac 10:24 *1887*
and on the day **f** to Neapolis; Ac 16:11 *1897a*
F after Paul and us, she kept Ac 16:17 *2628*
arrived the **f** day opposite Chios; Ac 20:15 *1897a*
and the day **f** we came to Miletus. Ac 20:15 *2192*
And the **f** day Paul went in Ac 21:18 *1897a*
the multitude of the people kept **f** Ac 21:36 *190*
But on the night *immediately* **f**, Ac 23:11 *1897a*
Brethren, join in **f** my example, Php 3:17 *4831*
doctrine which you have been **f**. 1Tm 4:6 *3877*
through **f** the same example of Heb 4:11
mocking, **f** after their own lusts, 2Pe 3:3 *4198*
fault, **f** after their *own* lusts; Jude 1:16 *4198*
f after their own ungodly lusts." Jude 1:18 *4198*
and Hades was **f** with him. Rv 6:8 *190*
clean, were **f** Him on white horses. Rv 19:14 *190*

FOLLOWS

To his father he sent as **f**: Gn 45:23 2088
was *as* **f**: the number of sheep Nu 31:36
and whoever **f** her put to death 2Ki 11:15 935, 310
and whoever **f** her, put to death 2Ch 23:14 935, 310
to King Artaxerxes, as **f** Ezr 4:8 3660
and there was written in it as **f**: Ezr 6:2 3652
beautification were completed as **f**: Es 2:12 3651
Suddenly he **f** her As an ox goes Pr 7:22 1980, 310
But he who **f** empty *pursuits* will Pr 28:19 7291
"You shall say to Zedekiah as **f**: Jer 21:3 3541
of hosts, the God of Israel, as **f**: Jer 44:25 559
he went and spoke to him as **f**: Da 2:24 3652
presence and spoke to him as **f**: Da 2:25 3652
'He shouted out and spoke as **f**: Da 4:14 3652
to the king and spoke to him as **f**: Da 6:6 3652
so that bloodshed **f** bloodshed. Hos 4:2 5060
Berechiah, the son of Iddo, as **f**: Zch 1:7 559
birth of Jesus Christ was as **f**: Mt 1:18 *3779*
for a tablet and wrote as **f**, Lk 1:63 *3004*
he who **f** Me will not walk in the Jn 8:12 *190*
based on faith speaks as **f**: "Do Ro 10:6 *3779*

FOLLY

committed an act of **f** in Israel by Dt 22:21 5039
do not commit this act of **f**. Jg 19:23 5039
an act of **f** against this man." Jg 19:24 5039
is his name and **f** is with him; 1Sa 25:25 5039
God does not pay attention to **f**. Jb 24:12 8604
do with you *according to your* **f**, Jb 42:8 5039
and fester Because of my **f** Ps 38:5 200
it is You who knows my **f**, Ps 69:5 200
But let them not turn back to **f**. Ps 85:8 3690
of his **f** he will go astray. Pr 5:23 200
"Forsake *your* **f** and live, And Pr 9:6 6612a
The woman of **f** is boisterous, *She* Pr 9:13 3687
the heart of fools proclaims **f**. Pr 12:23 200
knowledge, But a fool displays **f**. Pr 13:16 200
But the **f** of fools is foolishness. Pr 14:24 200
he who is quick-tempered exalts **f**. Pr 14:29 200
But the mouth of fools spouts **f**. Pr 15:2 200
But the mouth of fools feeds on **f**. Pr 15:14 200
F is joy to him who lacks sense, Pr 15:21 200
But the discipline of fools is **f**. Pr 16:22 200
cubs, Rather than a fool in his **f**. Pr 17:12 200
hears, It is **f** and shame to him. Pr 18:13 200
The devising of **f** is sin, And the Pr 24:9 200
answer a fool according to his **f**, Pr 26:4 200
Answer a fool as his **f** *deserves*, Pr 26:5 200
vomit Is a fool who repeats his **f**. Pr 26:11 200
wisdom and to know madness and **f**; Ec 1:17 5531
wisely, and how to take hold of **f**, Ec 2:3 5531
to consider wisdom, madness and **f**; Ec 2:12 5531
excels **f** as light excels darkness. Ec 2:13 5531
and to know the evil of **f** and the Ec 7:25 3689
f is set in many exalted places Ec 10:6 5529
the beginning of his talking is **f** and Ec 10:13 5531
their **f** will be obvious to all, 2Tm 3:9 *454*
just as Jannes's and Jambres's **f** was 2Tm 3:9 *454*

FOND

Having so **f** an affection for you, 1Th 2:8 *3655b*
to much wine or **f** of sordid gain, 1Tm 3:8 *146*
pugnacious, not **f** of sordid gain, Ti 1:7 *146*

FONDLED

on the hip and **f** on the knees. Is 66:12 8173b

FOOD

it shall be **f** for you; Gn 1:29 402
given every green plant for **f**"; Gn 1:30 402
to the sight and good for **f**; Gn 2:9 3978
saw that the tree was good for **f**, Gn 3:6 3978
some of all **f** which is edible, Gn 6:21 3978
be for **f** for you and for them." Gn 6:21 402
that is alive shall be **f** for you; Gn 9:3 402
Gomorrah and all their **f** supply, Gn 14:11 400
But when **f** was set before him to Gn 24:33
savory **f** such as his father loved. Gn 27:14 4303
gave the savory **f** and the bread, Gn 27:17 4303
Then he also made savory **f**, Gn 27:31 4303
me **f** to eat and garments to wear, Gn 28:20 3899
except the **f** which he ate. Gn 39:6 3899
all sorts of baked **f** for Pharaoh, Gn 40:17 3978
"Then let them gather all the **f** Gn 41:35 3978
and store up the grain for **f** in Gn 41:35 400
"Let the **f** become as a Gn 41:36 400
So he gathered all the **f** of *these* Gn 41:48 400
and placed the **f** in the cities; Gn 41:48 400
he placed in every city the **f** from Gn 41:48 400
the land of Canaan, to buy **f**." Gn 42:7 400
your servants have come to buy **f**. Gn 42:10 400
"Go back, buy us a little **f**." Gn 43:2 400
us, we will go down and buy you **f**. Gn 43:4 400
came down the first time to buy **f**, Gn 43:20 400
other money in our hand to buy **f**; Gn 43:22 400
"Fill the men's sacks with **f**, Gn 44:1 400
'Go back, buy us a little **f**.' Gn 44:25 400
all his father's household with **f**, Gn 47:12 3899
there was no **f** in all the land, Gn 47:13 3899
"Give us **f**, for why should we die Gn 47:15 3899
and I will give you **f** for your Gn 47:16
and Joseph gave them **f** in exchange Gn 47:17 3899
and he fed them with **f** in exchange Gn 47:17 3899
Buy us and our land for **f**, Gn 47:19 3899
for seed of the field and for your **f** Gn 47:24 400
and as **f** for your little ones." Gn 47:24 398
"As for Asher, his **f** shall be rich, Gn 49:20 3899
woman, he may not reduce her **f**, Ex 21:10 7607
it up in smoke on the altar *as* **f**, Lv 3:11 3899
up in smoke on the altar *as* **f**, Lv 3:16 3899
'Any of the **f** which may be eaten, Lv 11:34 400
animals dies which you have for **f**, Lv 11:39 402
plant all kinds of trees for **f**, Lv 19:23 3978
the **f** of their God; so they shall Lv 21:6 3899
for he offers the **f** of your God; he Lv 21:8 3899
defect shall approach to offer the **f** Lv 21:17 3899
he shall not come near to offer the **f** Lv 21:21 3899
'He may eat the **f** of his God, Lv 21:22 3899
the holy *gifts*, for it is his **f**. Lv 22:7 3899
in his house may eat of his **f**. Lv 22:11 3899
she shall eat of her father's **f**; Lv 22:13 3899
for offering as the **f** of your God; Lv 22:25 3899
products of the land for **f**; Lv 25:6 402
at interest, nor your **f** for gain. Lv 25:37 400
You will thus eat your **f** to the Lv 26:5 3899
when you eat of the **f** of the land, Nu 15:19 3899
For there is no **f** and no water, Nu 21:5 3899
and we loathe this miserable **f**." Nu 21:5 3899
My **f** for My offerings by fire, Nu 28:2 3899
the **f** of the offering by fire, Nu 28:24 3899
"You shall buy **f** from them with Dt 2:6 400
me **f** for money so that I may eat, Dt 2:28 400
you will eat **f** without scarcity, Dt 8:9 3899
by giving him **f** and clothing. Dt 10:18 3899
did not meet you with **f** and water Dt 23:4 3899
interest on money, **f**, Dt 23:19 400
"Your carcasses will be **f** to Dt 28:26 3978
detain me, I will not eat your **f**, Jg 13:16 3899
10,000 to supply **f** for the people, Jg 20:10 6720
His people in giving them **f**. Ru 1:6 3899
the man who eats **f** before evening, 1Sa 14:24 3899
So none of the people tasted **f**. 1Sa 14:24 3899
be the man who eats **f** today.' " 1Sa 14:28 3899
came, the king sat down to eat **f**. 1Sa 20:24 3899
and did not eat **f** on the second 1Sa 20:34 3899
eaten no **f** all day and all night. 1Sa 28:20 3899
your master's grandson may have **f**; 2Sa 9:10 3899
and would not eat **f** with them. 2Sa 12:17 3899
they set **f** before him and he ate. 2Sa 12:20 3899
child died, you arose and ate **f**." 2Sa 12:21 3899
come and give me *some* **f** to eat, 2Sa 13:5 3899
let her prepare the **f** in my sight, 2Sa 13:5 1279
house, and prepare **f** for him." 2Sa 13:7 1279
"Bring the **f** into the bedroom, 2Sa 13:10 1279
by giving **f** to my household." 1Ki 5:9 3899
of wheat as **f** for his household, 1Ki 5:11 4361
the **f** of his table, the seating of 1Ki 10:5 3978
assigned him **f** and gave him land. 1Ki 11:18 3899
went in the strength of that **f** forty 1Ki 19:8 396
turned away his face and ate no **f**. 1Ki 21:4 3899
that you are not eating **f**?" 1Ki 21:5 3899
and she persuaded him to eat **f**. 2Ki 4:8 3899
by, he turned in there to eat **f**. 2Ki 4:8 3899
no **f** for the people of the land. 2Ki 25:3 3899
Naphtali, brought **f** on donkeys, 1Ch 12:40 3899
the **f** at his table, the seating of 2Ch 9:4 3978
officers in them and stores of **f**, 2Ch 11:11 3978
and he gave them **f** in abundance. 2Ch 11:23 4202
f, drink and oil to the Sidonians Ezr 3:7 3978
eaten the governor's **f** *allowance*. Ne 5:14 3899
demand the governor's **f** *allowance*, Ne 5:18 3899
them on the day they sold **f**. Ne 13:15 6718b
her with her cosmetics and **f**, Es 2:9 4490
feasting and sending portions *of* **f** Es 9:19
rejoicing and sending portions *of* **f** Es 9:22
comes at the sight of my **f**, Jb 3:24 3899
They are like loathsome **f** to me. Jb 6:7 3899
words, As the palate tastes its **f**? Jb 12:11 400
"He wanders about for **f**, Jb 15:23 3899
Yet his **f** in his stomach is Jb 20:14 3899
mouth more than my necessary **f**. Jb 23:12 2706
forth seeking **f** in their activity, Jb 24:5 2964
"The earth, from it comes **f**, Jb 28:5 3899
And whose **f** is the root of the Jb 30:4 3899
bread, And his soul favorite **f**. Jb 33:20 3978
words As the palate tastes **f**. Jb 34:3 398
He gives **f** in abundance. Jb 36:31 400
God And wander about without **f**? Jb 38:41 400
"From there he spies out **f**; Jb 39:29 400
"Surely the mountains bring him **f**, Jb 40:20 944
have been my **f** day and night, Ps 42:3 3899
They wander about for **f** And Ps 59:15 398
They also gave me gall for my **f** And Ps 69:21 1267
You gave him as **f** for the Ps 74:14 3978
f according to their desire. Ps 78:18 3978
eat And gave them **f** from heaven. Ps 78:24 1715
He sent them **f** in abundance. Ps 78:25 6720
While their **f** was in their mouths, Ps 78:30 400
for **f** to the birds of the heavens, Ps 79:2 3978
may bring forth **f** from the earth, Ps 104:14 3899
And **f** which sustains man's heart. Ps 104:15 3899
prey And seek their **f** from God. Ps 104:21 400
give them their **f** in due season. Ps 104:27 400
soul abhorred all kinds of **f**, Ps 107:18 400
has given **f** to those who fear Him; Ps 111:5 2964
Who gives **f** to all flesh, For His Ps 136:25 3899
give them their **f** in due time. Ps 145:15 400
Who gives **f** to the hungry. Ps 146:7 3899
He gives to the beast its **f**, Ps 147:9 3899
Prepares her **f** in the summer *And* Pr 6:8 3899
She has prepared her **f**, Pr 9:2 2874
"Come, eat of my **f** And drink of Pr 9:5 3899
Abundant **f** *is in* the fallow ground Pr 13:23 400
and you will be satisfied with **f**. Pr 20:13 3899
gives some of his **f** to the poor. Pr 22:9 3899
delicacies, For it is deceptive **f**. Pr 23:3 3899
is hungry, give him **f** to eat; Pr 25:21 3899
be goats' milk enough for your **f**, Pr 27:27 3899
food, For the **f** of your household, Pr 27:27 3899
a driving rain which leaves no **f**. Pr 28:3 3899
his land will have plenty of **f**, Pr 28:19 3899
me with the **f** that is my portion, Pr 30:8 3899
fool when he is satisfied with **f**, Pr 30:22 3899
prepare their **f** in the summer; Pr 30:25 3899
She brings her **f** from afar. Pr 31:14 3899
And gives **f** to her household And Pr 31:15 2964
but her gain will become sufficient **f** Is 23:18 398
your grain *as* **f** for your enemies; Is 62:8 3978
and dust will be the serpent's **f**. Is 65:25 3899
devour your harvest and your **f**; Jer 5:17 3899
be **f** for the birds of the sky and Jer 7:33 3978
carcasses will become **f** for the birds Jer 16:4 3978
carcasses as **f** for the birds of the sky Jer 19:7 3978
And their dead bodies will be **f** Jer 34:20 3978
for *then* we had plenty of **f** and Jer 44:17 3899
no **f** for the people of the land. Jer 52:6 3899
have given their precious things for **f** La 1:11 400
While they sought **f** to restore La 1:19 400
They became **f** for them Because of La 4:10 1262
"Your **f** which you eat *shall* Ezk 4:10 3978
had arrogance, abundant **f** and Ezk 16:49 3899
through *the fire* to them as **f**. Ezk 23:37 402
I have given you for **f** to the Ezk 29:5 402
and they became **f** for every beast Ezk 34:5 402
My flock has even become **f** for all Ezk 34:8 402
they will not be **f** for them. Ezk 34:10 402
they are given to us for **f**.' Ezk 35:12 402
I will give you as **f** to every Ezk 39:4 402
My house, when you offered My **f**, Ezk 44:7 3899
grow all *kinds of* trees for **f**. Ezk 47:12 3978
and their fruit will be for **f** Ezk 47:12 3978
be **f** for the workers of the city. Ezk 48:18 3899
daily ration from the king's choice **f** Da 1:5 6598
defile himself with the king's choice **f** Da 1:8 6598
appointed your **f** and your drink; Da 1:10 3978
who are eating the king's choice **f**; Da 1:13 6598
been eating the king's choice **f**. Da 1:15 6598
continued to withhold their choice **f** Da 1:16 6598
abundant, And in it *was* **f** for all. Da 4:12 4203
and in which *was* **f** for all, Da 4:21 4203
I did not eat any tasty **f**, Da 10:3 3899
eat his choice **f** will destroy him, Da 11:26 6598
in Assyria they will eat unclean **f**. Hos 9:3
f been cut off before our eyes, Jl 1:16 400
large, And their **f** is plentiful. Hab 1:16 3978
fail And the fields produce no **f**, Hab 3:17 400
bread with this fold, or cooked **f**, Hg 2:12 5138
food, wine, oil, or any *other* **f**, Hg 2:12 3978
defiled **f** upon My altar. Mal 1:7 3899
fruit, its **f** is to be despised.' Mal 1:12 400
that there may be **f** in My house, Mal 3:10 2964
his **f** was locusts and wild honey. Mt 3:4 *5160*
Is not life more than **f**, Mt 6:25 *5160*
and buy **f** for themselves." Mt 14:15 *1033*
He blessed *the* **f**, and breaking Mt 14:19
them their **f** at the proper time? Mt 24:45 *5160*
He blessed *the* **f** and broke Mk 6:41
he who has **f** is to do likewise." Lk 3:11 *1033*

and buy f for all these people." **Lk 9:13** *1033*
"For life is more than f, **Lk 12:23** *5160*
gone away into the city to buy f. **Jn 4:8** *5160*
"I have f to eat that you do not **Jn 4:32** *1035*
"My f is to do the will of Him **Jn 4:34** *1033*
not work for the f which perishes, **Jn 6:27** *1035*
f which endures to eternal life, **Jn 6:27** *1035*
"For My flesh is true f, **Jn 6:55** *1035*
in the daily serving *of* f. **Ac 6:1**
and our fathers could find no f. **Ac 7:11** *5527*
he took f and was strengthened. **Ac 9:19** *5160*
your hearts with f and gladness." **Ac 14:17** *5160*
his house and set f before them, **Ac 16:34** *5132*
had gone a long time without f, **Ac 27:21** *776*
them all to take some f, **Ac 27:33** *5160*
I encourage you to take some f, **Ac 27:34** *5160*
and they themselves also took f. **Ac 27:36** *5160*
because of f your brother is hurt, **Ro 14:15** *1033*
Do not destroy with your f him for **Ro 14:15** *1033*
the work of God for the sake of f. **Ro 14:20** *1033*
you milk to drink, not solid f; **1Co 3:2** *1033*
F is for the stomach and the **1Co 6:13** *1033*
stomach and the stomach is for f **1Co 6:13** *1033*
eat f as if it were sacrificed to **1Co 8:7**
But f will not commend us to God; **1Co 8:8** *1033*
if f causes my brother to stumble, **1Co 8:13** *1033*
perform sacred services eat the f **1Co 9:13**
and all ate the same spiritual f; **1Co 10:3** *1033*
seed to the sower and bread for f will **2Co 9:10** *1035*
and thirst, often without f, **2Co 11:27** *3521*
to act as your judge in regard to f or **Col 2:16** *1035*
If we have f and covering, **1Tm 6:8** *1305*
come to need milk and not solid f. **Heb 5:12** *5160*
But solid f is for the mature, who **Heb 5:14** *5160*
since they *relate* only to f and **Heb 9:10** *1033*
clothing and in need of daily f, **Jas 2:15** *5160*

FOODS

(*Thus He* declared all f clean.) **Mk 7:19** *1033*
and advocate abstaining from f which **1Tm 4:3** *1033*
strengthened by grace, not by f, **Heb 13:9** *1033*

FOOL

I have played the f and have **1Sa 26:21** 5528
"Should Abner die as a f dies? **2Sa 3:33** 5036
The f has said in his heart, **Ps 14:1** 5036
The f has said in his heart, **Ps 53:1** 5036
fetters to the discipline of a f, **Pr 7:22** 191
a babbling f will be ruined. **Pr 10:8** 191
a babbling f will be ruined. **Pr 10:10** 191
And he who spreads slander is a f. **Pr 10:18** 3684
wickedness is like sport to a f, **Pr 10:23** 3684
of a f is right in his own eyes, **Pr 12:15** 191
knowledge, But a f displays folly. **Pr 13:16** 3684
Leave the presence of a f, **Pr 14:7** 3684
But a f is arrogant and careless. **Pr 14:16** 3684
A f rejects his father's discipline, **Pr 15:5** 191
speech is not fitting for a f, **Pr 17:7** 5036
Than a hundred blows into a f. **Pr 17:10** 3684
Rather than a f in his folly. **Pr 17:12** 3684
in the hand of a f to buy wisdom, **Pr 17:16** 3684
sires a f *does so* to his sorrow, **Pr 17:21** 3684
And the father of a f has no joy. **Pr 17:21** 5036
a f are on the ends of the earth. **Pr 17:24** 3684
Even a f, when he keeps silent, is **Pr 17:28** 191
A f does not delight in **Pr 18:2** 3684
is perverse in speech and is a f. **Pr 19:1** 3684
Luxury is not fitting for a f; **Pr 19:10** 3684
for a man, But any f will quarrel. **Pr 20:3** 191
not speak in the hearing of a f, **Pr 23:9** 3684
Wisdom is *too* exalted for a f, **Pr 24:7** 191
So honor is not fitting for a f. **Pr 26:1** 3684
answer a f according to his folly, **Pr 26:4** 3684
Answer a f as his folly *deserves*, **Pr 26:5** 3684
a message by the hand of a f. **Pr 26:6** 3684
So is he who gives honor to a f. **Pr 26:8** 3684
So is he who hires a f or who **Pr 26:10** 3684
Is a f who repeats his folly. **Pr 26:11** 3684
is more hope for a f than for him. **Pr 26:12** 3684
a f is heavier than both of them. **Pr 27:3** 191
Though you pound a f in a mortar **Pr 27:22** 191
trusts in his own heart is a f, **Pr 28:26** 3684
A f always loses his temper, But a **Pr 29:11** 3684
is more hope for a f than for him. **Pr 29:20** 3684
And a f when he is satisfied with **Pr 30:22** 5036
head, but the f walks in darkness. **Ec 2:14** 3684
"As is the fate of the f, **Ec 2:15** 3684
of the wise man *as* with the f, **Ec 2:16** 3684
the wise man and the f alike die! **Ec 2:16** 3684
he will be a wise man or a f? **Ec 2:19** 5530
The f folds his hands and consumes **Ec 4:5** 3684
voice of a f through many words. **Ec 5:3** 3684
does the wise man have over the f? **Ec 6:8** 3684
pot, So is the laughter of the f; **Ec 7:6** 3684
wicked and do not be a f. **Ec 7:17** 5530
Even when the f walks along the **Ec 10:3** 5530
to everyone *that* he is a f. **Ec 10:3** 5530
while the lips of a f consume him; **Ec 10:12** 3684
Yet the f multiplies words. **Ec 10:14** 5530
The toil of a f *so* wearies him **Ec 10:15** 3684
longer will the f be called noble, **Is 32:5** 5036
For a f speaks nonsense, And his **Is 32:6** 5036
And in the end he will be a f." **Jer 17:11** 5036
The prophet is a f, **Hos 9:7** 191
'You f,' shall be guilty *enough to* **Mt 5:22** *3474*
"But God said to him, 'You f! **Lk 12:20** *878*
You f! That which you sow does not **1Co 15:36** *878*

FOOLISH

the LORD, O f and unwise people? **Dt 32:6** 5036
them to anger with a f nation, **Dt 32:21** 5036
one of the f ones shamelessly uncovers **2Sa 6:20** 7386
as one of the f women speaks. **Jb 2:10** 5036
"For anger slays the f man, **Jb 5:2** 191
"I have seen the f taking root, **Jb 5:3** 191
Make me not the reproach of the f. **Ps 39:8** 5036
is the way of those who are f, **Ps 49:13** 3689
a f people has spurned Your name. **Ps 74:18** 5036
Remember how the f man reproaches **Ps 74:22** 5036
a f son is a grief to his mother. **Pr 10:1** 3684
But with the mouth of the f, **Pr 10:14** 191
And the f will be servant to the **Pr 11:29** 191
But the f tears it down with her **Pr 14:1** 200
of the f is a rod for *his* back, **Pr 14:3** 191
But a f man despises his mother. **Pr 15:20** 3684
A f son is a grief to his father And **Pr 17:25** 3684
A f son is destruction to his **Pr 19:13** 3684
wise, But a f man swallows it up. **Pr 21:20** 3684
has a controversy with a f man, **Pr 29:9** 191
The f man either rages or laughs, **Pr 29:9**
If you have been f in exalting **Pr 30:32** 5034a
lad is better than an old and f king **Ec 4:13** 3684
but the f man's heart *directs him* **Ec 10:2** 3684
"For My people are f, **Jer 4:22** 191
are only the poor, They are f; **Jer 5:4** 2973
this, O f and senseless people, **Jer 5:21** 5530
they are altogether stupid and f **Jer 10:8** 3688
seen for you False and f *visions;* **La 2:14** 8602a
"Woe to the f prophets who are **Ezk 13:3** 5036
the equipment of a f shepherd. **Zch 11:15** 196
on them, will be like a f man **Mt 7:26** *3474*
"Five of them were f, **Mt 25:2** *3474*
"For when the f took their lamps, **Mt 25:3** *3474*
"The f said to the prudent, **Mt 25:8** *3474*
"You f ones, did not He who made **Lk 11:40** *878*
"O f men and slow of heart to **Lk 24:25** *453*
both to the wise and to the f. **Ro 1:14** *453*
and their f heart was darkened. **Ro 1:21** *801*
a corrector of the f, **Ro 2:20** *878*
made f the wisdom of the world? **1Co 1:20** *3471*
but God has chosen the f things of **1Co 1:27** *3474*
become f, so that he may become wise. **1Co 3:18** *3474*
I say, let no one think me f; **2Co 11:16** *878*
if *you do,* receive me even as f, **2Co 11:16** *878*
so wise, tolerate the f gladly. **2Co 11:19** *878*
do wish to boast I will not be f, **2Co 12:6** *878*
I have become f; **2Co 12:11** *878*
You f Galatians, who has bewitched **Ga 3:1** *453*
Are you so f? Having begun by the **Ga 3:3** *453*
So then do not be f, **Eph 5:17** *878*
many f and harmful desires which **1Tm 6:9** *453*
f and ignorant speculations, **2Tm 2:23** *3474*
For we also once were f ourselves, **Ti 3:3** *453*
But avoid f controversies and **Ti 3:9** *3474*
to recognize, you f fellow, **Jas 2:20** *2756*
silence the ignorance of f men. **1Pe 2:15** *878*

FOOLISHLY

Now you have done f. **Gn 31:28** 5528
f and in which we have sinned. **Nu 12:11** 2973
"You have acted f; **1Sa 13:13** 5528
for I have acted very f." **2Sa 24:10** 5528
servant, for I have done very f." **1Ch 21:8** 5528
You have acted f in this. **2Ch 16:9** 5528
Why then do you act f? **Jb 27:12** 1891
A quick-tempered man acts f, **Pr 14:17** 200
The princes of Zoan have acted f, **Is 19:13** 2973
they have acted f in Israel, **Jer 29:23** 5039

FOOLISHNESS

the counsel of Ahithophel f." **2Sa 15:31** 5528
But the f of fools is deceit. **Pr 14:8** 200
The naive inherit f, **Pr 14:18** 200
But the folly of fools is f. **Pr 14:24** 200
The f of man ruins his way, And **Pr 19:3** 200
F is bound up in the heart of a **Pr 22:15** 200
Yet his f will not depart from **Pr 27:22** 200
of folly and the f of madness. **Ec 7:25** 3689
so a little f is weightier than **Ec 10:1** 5531
And every mouth is speaking f. **Is 9:17** 5039
turning their knowledge into f, **Is 44:25** 5528
envy, slander, pride *and* f. **Mk 7:22** *877*
is f to those who are perishing, **1Co 1:18** *3472*
through the f of the message preached **1Co 1:21** *3472*
block and to Gentiles f, **1Co 1:23** *3472*
the f of God is wiser than men, **1Co 1:25** *3474*
for they are f to him; and he **1Co 2:14** *3472*
of this world is f before God. **1Co 3:19** *3472*
would bear with me in a little f; **2Co 11:1** *877*
as the Lord would, but as in f, **2Co 11:17** *877*
I speak in f **2Co 11:21** *877*

FOOL'S

A f anger is known at once, But **Pr 12:16** 191
A f lips bring strife, And his **Pr 18:6** 3684
A f mouth is his ruin, And his **Pr 18:7** 3684

FOOLS

be like one of the f in Israel. **2Sa 13:13** 5036
barefoot And makes f of judges. **Jb 12:17** 1984b
"F, even those without a name, **Jb 30:8**
1121, 5036
F, because of their rebellious **Ps 107:17** 191
F despise wisdom and instruction. **Pr 1:7** 191
in scoffing And f hate knowledge? **Pr 1:22** 3684
of f will destroy them. **Pr 1:32** 3684
honor, But f display dishonor. **Pr 3:35** 3684
And, O f, understand wisdom. **Pr 8:5** 3684
f die for lack of understanding. **Pr 10:21** 191
the heart of f proclaims folly. **Pr 12:23** 3684
to f to turn away from evil. **Pr 13:19** 3684
companion of f will suffer harm. **Pr 13:20** 3684
way, But the foolishness of f is deceit. **Pr 14:8** 3684
F mock at sin, But among the **Pr 14:9** 191
But the folly of f is foolishness. **Pr 14:24** 3684
the hearts of f it is made known. **Pr 14:33** 3684
But the mouth of f spouts folly. **Pr 15:2** 3684
But the hearts of f are not so. **Pr 15:7** 3684
But the mouth of f feeds on folly. **Pr 15:14** 3684
But the discipline of f is folly. **Pr 16:22** 191
And blows for the back of f. **Pr 19:29** 3684
And a rod for the back of f. **Pr 26:3** 3684
So is a proverb in the mouth of f. **Pr 26:7** 3684
So is a proverb in the mouth of f. **Pr 26:9** 3684
than to offer the sacrifice of f; **Ec 5:1** 3684
it; for *He takes* no delight in f. **Ec 5:4** 3684
of f is in the house of pleasure. **Ec 7:4** 3684
one to listen to the song of f. **Ec 7:5** 3684
anger resides in the bosom of f. **Ec 7:9** 3684
the shouting of a ruler among f. **Ec 9:17** 3684
The princes of Zoan are mere f; **Is 19:11** 191
way, And f will not wander *on it.* **Is 35:8** 191
to fail, Making f out of diviners, **Is 44:25** 1984b
priests, and they will become f! **Jer 50:36** 2973
"You f and blind men! **Mt 23:17** *3474*
to be wise, they became f, **Ro 1:22** *3471*
We are f for Christ's sake, but **1Co 4:10** *3474*

FOOT

place for the sole of her f, **Gn 8:9** 7272
or f in all the land of Egypt." **Gn 41:44** 7272
six hundred thousand men on f, **Ex 12:37** 7273
stood at the f of the mountain. **Ex 19:17** 8482
tooth, hand for hand, f for foot, **Ex 21:24** 7272
tooth, hand for hand, foot for f, **Ex 21:24** 7272
and built an altar at the f of the **Ex 24:4** 8478
them at the f of the mountain. **Ex 32:19** 8478
and on the big toe of his right f. **Lv 8:23** 7272
on the big toe of their right f. **Lv 8:24** 7272
and on the big toe of his right f. **Lv 14:14** 7272
and on the big toe of his right f. **Lv 14:17** 7272
and on the big toe of his right f. **Lv 14:25** 7272
and on the big toe of his right f. **Lv 14:28** 7272
who has a broken f or broken hand, **Lv 21:19** 7272
among whom I am, are 600,000 on f; **Nu 11:21** 7273
Balaam's f against the wall, **Nu 22:25** 7272
the land on which he has set f, **Dt 1:36** 1869
only let me pass through on f, **Dt 2:28** 7272
at the f of the slopes of Pisgah **Dt 3:17** 8478
stood at the f of the mountain, **Dt 4:11** 8478
at the f of the slopes of Pisgah. **Dt 4:49** 8478
your f swell these forty years. **Dt 8:4** 7272
your f like a vegetable garden. **Dt 11:10** 7272
which the sole of your f treads **Dt 11:24** 7272
all the land on which you set f, **Dt 11:25** 1869
tooth, hand for hand, f for foot. **Dt 19:21** 7272
tooth, hand for hand, foot for f. **Dt 19:21** 7272
off his f and spit in his face; **Dt 25:9** 7272
your f to the crown of your head. **Dt 28:35** 7272
not venture to set the sole of her f on **Dt 28:56** 7272
place for the sole of your f; **Dt 28:65** 7272
sandal has not worn out on your f. **Dt 29:5** 7272
In due time their f will slip; **Dt 32:35** 7272
And may he dip his f in oil. **Dt 33:24** 7272
which the sole of your f treads, **Jos 1:3** 7272
and the Hivite at the f of Hermon **Jos 11:3** 8478
Lebanon at the f of Mount Hermon. **Jos 11:17** 8478
at the f of the slopes of Pisgah; **Jos 12:3** 8478
'Surely the land on which your f **Jos 14:9** 7272
his chariot and fled away on f. **Jg 4:15** 7272
Now Sisera fled away on f to the **Jg 4:17** 7272
f soldiers who drew the sword. **Jg 20:2** 7273
Israel thirty thousand f soldiers. **1Sa 4:10** 7273
200,000 f soldiers and 10,000 men **1Sa 15:4** 7273
horsemen and 20,000 f soldiers; **2Sa 8:4** 7273
of Zobah, 20,000 f soldiers, **2Sa 10:6** 7273
from the sole of his f to the **2Sa 14:25** 7272
each hand and six toes on each f, **2Sa 21:20** 7272
100,000 f soldiers in one day. **1Ki 20:29** 7273
and he trampled her under f. **2Ki 9:33**
horsemen and 20,000 f soldiers, **1Ch 18:4** 7273
charioteers and 40,000 f soldiers, **1Ch 19:18** 7273
each hand and six *toes on each* f; **1Ch 20:6**
and I will not again remove the f **2Ch 33:8** 7272
of his f to the crown of his head. **Jb 2:7** 7272
"My f has held fast to His path; **Jb 23:11** 7272
habitation, Forgotten by the f; **Jb 28:4** 7272
my f has hastened after deceit, **Jb 31:5** 7272
forgets that a f may crush them, **Jb 39:15** 7272
hid, their own f has been caught. **Ps 9:15** 7272
My f stands on a level place; **Ps 26:12** 7272
not the f of pride come upon me, **Ps 36:11** 7272
over me, *Who,* when my f slips, **Ps 38:16** 7272
passed through the river on f; **Ps 66:6** 7272
your f may shatter *them* in blood, **Ps 68:23** 7272
under f the pieces of silver; **Ps 68:30** 7511
not strike your f against a stone. **Ps 91:12** 7272
"My f has slipped," **Ps 94:18** 7272
He will not allow your f to slip; **Ps 121:3** 7272
And your f will not stumble. **Pr 3:23** 7272
keep your f from being caught. **Pr 3:26** 7272
Turn your f from evil. **Pr 4:27** 7272
Let your f rarely be in your **Pr 25:17** 7272
Like a bad tooth and an unsteady f **Pr 25:19** 7272
From the sole of the f even to the **Is 1:6** 7272
"The f will trample it, The feet **Is 26:6** 7272
of Ephraim is trodden under f. **Is 28:3** 7272
you turn your f From doing your **Is 58:13** 7272
'Clap your hand, stamp your f and **Ezk 6:11** 7272
"A man's f will not pass through **Ezk 29:11** 7272
and the f of a beast will not pass **Ezk 29:11** 7272
And the f of man will not muddy **Ezk 32:13** 7272
The swift of f will not escape, **Am 2:15** 7272

will tread our iniquities under f. Mi 7:19 3533
STRIKE YOUR F AGAINST A STONE.' " Mt 4:6 *4228*
out and trampled under f by men. Mt 5:13 *2662*
followed Him on f from the cities. Mt 14:13 *3979a*
or your f causes you to stumble, Mt 18:8 *4228*
'Bind him hand and f, Mt 22:13 *4228*
together on f from all the cities, Mk 6:33 *3979a*
If your f causes you to stumble, Mk 9:45 *4228*
STRIKE YOUR F AGAINST A STONE.' " Lk 4:11 *4228*
and it was trampled under f and Lk 8:5 *2662*
Jerusalem will be trampled under f by Lk 21:24 *3961*
bound hand and f with wrappings, Jn 11:44 *4228*
in it, not even a f of ground, Ac 7:5 *4228*
first day that I set f in Asia, Ac 20:18 *1910*
Spirit not to set f in Jerusalem. Ac 21:4 *1910*
If the f says, 1Co 12:15 *4228*
trampled under f the Son of God, Heb 10:29 *2662*
He placed his right f on the Rv 10:2 *4228*
and they will tread under f the Rv 11:2 *3961*

FOOTHILLS
and the f were inhabited?' " Zch 7:7 8219

FOOTHOLD
in deep mire, and there is no f; Ps 69:2 4613

FOOTMEN
and ten chariots and 10,000 f, 2Ki 13:7 7273
f and they have tired you out, Jer 12:5 7273

FOOTPRINTS
And Your f may not be known. Ps 77:19 6119
Tracked with bloody f. Hos 6:8

FOOTSTEP
even *as little as* a f because I Dt 2:5
4096, 3709, 7272

FOOTSTEPS
feet upon a rock making my f firm. Ps 40:2 804a
Your f toward the perpetual ruins; Ps 74:3 6471
And will make His f into a way. Ps 85:13 6471
the f of Your anointed. Ps 89:51 6119
Establish my f in Your word, And do Ps 119:133 6471
And he who hurries his f errs. Pr 19:2 7272

FOOTSTOOL
the LORD and for the f of our God. 1Ch 28:2
1916, 7272
six steps to the throne and a f in gold 2Ch 9:18 3534
our God And worship at His f; Ps 99:5
1916, 7272
Your enemies a f for Your feet." Ps 110:1
1916, 7272
Let us worship at His f. Ps 132:7
1916, 7272
My throne and the earth is My f. Is 66:1
1916, 7272
His f In the day of His anger. La 2:1
1916, 7272
for it is the f of His feet, Mt 5:35 *5286*
ENEMIES A F FOR YOUR FEET." ' Lk 20:43 *5286*
ENEMIES A F FOR YOUR FEET." ' Ac 2:35 *5286*
AND EARTH IS THE F OF MY FEET; Ac 7:49 *5286*
ENEMIES A F FOR YOUR FEET"? Heb 1:13 *5286*
ENEMIES BE MADE A F FOR HIS FEET. Heb 10:13 *5286*
over there, or sit down by my f," Jas 2:3 *5286*

FORASMUCH
"F as you are sent by the king Ezr 7:14
3606, 6903, 1768

FORBEARANCE
By f a ruler may be persuaded, And Pr 25:15
753, 639
because in the f of God He passed Ro 3:25 *463*

FORBID
f her on the day he hears *of it*, Nu 30:5 5106
nothing to her *and* did not f her, Nu 30:11 5106
"The LORD f that I should stretch 1Sa 26:11 2486
"The LORD f me that I should give 1Ki 21:3 2486
"God f *it*, Lord! Mt 16:22 *2436*
and do not f to speak in tongues. 1Co 14:39 *2967*
men who f marriage *and advocate* 1Tm 4:3 *2967*

FORBIDDEN
you shall count their fruit as f. Lv 19:23 6190
Three years it shall be f to you; Lv 19:23 6189
her because her father had f her. Nu 30:5 5106
having been f by the Holy Spirit Ac 16:6 *2967*

FORBIDDING
and f to pay taxes to Caesar, Lk 23:2 *2967*

FORBIDS
her husband hears *of it*, he f her, Nu 30:8 5106
he f those who desire *to do so* 3Jn 1:10 *2967*

FORCE
take your daughters from me by f. Gn 31:31 1497
he took her and lay with her by f. Gn 34:2 6031a
out against him with a heavy f and Nu 20:20 5971a
and if not, I will take it by f." 1Sa 2:16 2394
and stopped them by f of arms. Ezr 4:23 153
again, I will use f against you." Ne 13:21 3027
a great f my garment is distorted; Jb 30:18 3581b
but with f and with severity you Ezk 34:4 2394
go up and gain power with a small f Da 11:23
and violent men take it by f. Mt 11:12 *726*
not take money from anyone by f, Lk 3:14 *1286*
to come and take Him by f to Jn 6:15 *726*
and take him away from them by f, Ac 23:10 *726*
I tried to f them to blaspheme; Ac 26:11 *315*
broken up by the f *of the waves*. Ac 27:41 *970*
for it is never in f while the one Heb 9:17 *2480*

FORCED
And became a slave at f labor. Gn 49:15 4522
shall become your f labor and shall Dt 20:11 4522
day, and they became f laborers. Jos 16:10 4522
put the Canaanites to f labor, Jos 17:13 4522
put the Canaanites to f labor, Jg 1:28 4522
and became subject to f labor. Jg 1:30 4522
Beth-anath became f labor for them. Jg 1:33 4522
Then the Amorites f the sons of Jg 1:34 3905
grew strong, they became f labor. Jg 1:35 4522
So I f myself and offered the 1Sa 13:12 662
and Adoram was over the f labor, 2Sa 20:24 4522
over the men subject to f labor. 1Ki 4:6 4522
levied f laborers from all Israel; 1Ki 5:13 4522
f laborers numbered 30,000 men. 1Ki 5:13 4522
Adoniram *was* over the f laborers. 1Ki 5:14 4522
f labor which King Solomon levied 1Ki 9:15 4522
them Solomon levied f laborers, 1Ki 9:21 4522
f labor of the house of Joseph. 1Ki 11:28 5447
Adoram, who was over the f labor, 1Ki 12:18 4522
raised as f laborers to this day. 2Ch 8:8 4522
Hadoram, who was over the f labor, 2Ch 10:18 4522
are f into bondage *already*, Ne 5:5 3533
"Is not man f to labor on earth, Jb 7:1 6635
slack *hand* will be put to f labor. Pr 12:24 4522
young men will become f laborers. Is 31:8 4522
provinces Has become a f laborer! La 1:1 4522
I was f to appeal to Caesar, Ac 28:19 *315*

FORCES
his f against them by night, Gn 14:15
the man f her and lies with her, Dt 22:25 2388
When all the captains of the f, 2Ki 25:23 2428
of the f arose and went to Egypt; 2Ki 25:26 2428
Lachish with all his f with him, 2Ch 32:9 4475
Or all the f of *your* strength? Jb 36:19 3981
of the f that were in the field, Jer 40:7 2428
all the commanders of the f that were Jer 40:13 2428
all the commanders of the f that were Jer 41:11 2428
of the f that were with him, Jer 41:13 2428
commanders of the f that were with Jer 41:16 2428
Then all the commanders of the f, Jer 42:1 2428
of the f that were with him, Jer 42:8 2428
and all the commanders of the f, Jer 43:4 2428
the f took the entire remnant of Judah Jer 43:5 2428
firmly with me against these f Da 10:21
assemble a multitude of great f; Da 11:10 2428
and the f of the South will not Da 11:15 2220
"The overflowing f will be Da 11:22 2220
"F from him will arise, desecrate Da 11:31 2220
"Whoever f you to go one mile, go Mt 5:41 *29*
the world f of this darkness, Eph 6:12 *2888*
against the spiritual f of Eph 6:12

FORCING
we are f our sons and our Ne 5:5 3533
and everyone is f his way into it. Lk 16:16 *971*

FORD
and crossed the f of the Jabbok. Gn 32:22 4569a
Then they kept crossing the f to 2Sa 19:18 5679
it was a river that I could not f, Ezk 47:5 5674a

FORDED
in, a river that could not be f. Ezk 47:5 5674a

FORDS
the road to the Jordan to the f; Jos 2:7 4569b
the f of the Jordan opposite Moab, Jg 3:28 4569b
The Gileadites captured the f Jg 12:5 4569b
slew him at the f of the Jordan. Jg 12:6 4569b
I am going to wait at the f of the 2Sa 15:28 5679
night at the f of the wilderness, 2Sa 17:16 6160
will be at the f of the Arnon. Is 16:2 4569b
The f also have been seized, And Jer 51:32 4569b

FOREFATHER
"Your first f sinned, And your Is 43:27 1
our f according to the flesh, Ro 4:1 *4310b*

FOREFATHERS
return to the property of his f. Lv 25:41 1
because of the iniquities of their f Lv 26:39 1
and the iniquity of their f, Lv 26:40 1
the oath which He swore to your f, Dt 7:8 1
which He swore to your f. Dt 7:12 1
He swore to your f to give you. Dt 7:13 1
the LORD swore *to give* to your f. Dt 8:1 1
iniquities of *our* f against us; Ps 79:8 7223
which I commanded your f in the Jer 11:4 1
the oath which I swore to your f, Jer 11:5 1
because your f have forsaken Me,' Jer 16:11 1
done evil, *even* more than your f; Jer 16:12 1
day holy, as I commanded your f. Jer 17:22 1
they nor their f nor the kings of Judah Jer 19:4 1
I gave to them and their f.' " Jer 24:10 1
you and your f forever and ever; Jer 25:5 1
the land that I gave to their f and Jer 30:3 1
swore to their f to give them, Jer 32:22 1
'I made a covenant with your f in Jer 34:13 1
but your f did not obey Me or Jer 34:14 1
I have given to you and to your f; Jer 35:15 1
her, just as we ourselves, our f, Jer 44:17 1
of Jerusalem, you and your f, Jer 44:21 1
which I swore to give to your f Ezk 20:42 1
in the land that I gave to your f; Ezk 36:28 1
for I swore to give it to your f, Ezk 47:14 1
I saw your f as the earliest fruit Hos 9:10 1
to our f From the days of old. Mi 7:20 1
clear conscience the way my f did, 2Tm 1:3 *4269*
way of life inherited from your f, 1Pe 1:18 *3970b*

FOREGO
and we will f *the crops* the Ne 10:31 5203

FOREHEAD
hand, and as a reminder on your f, Ex 13:9
996, 5869
and as phylacteries on your f, Ex 13:16
996, 5869
"It shall be on Aaron's f, Ex 28:38 4696
and it shall always be on his f, Ex 28:38 4696
and sides, he is bald on the f; Lv 13:41 1371
if on the bald head or the bald f, Lv 13:42 1372
on his bald head or on his bald f, Lv 13:42 1372
on his bald head or on his bald f. Lv 13:43 1372
shall crush through the f of Moab, Nu 24:17 6285
shall be as frontals on your f. Dt 6:8 996, 5869
shall be as frontals on your f. Dt 11:18
996, 5869
your f for the sake of the dead. Dt 14:1
996, 5869
struck the Philistine on his f. 1Sa 17:49 4696
And the stone sank into his f, 1Sa 17:49 4696
the leprosy broke out on his f 2Ch 26:19 4696
behold, he *was* leprous on his f; 2Ch 26:20 4696
an iron sinew And your f bronze, Is 48:4 4696
Yet you had a harlot's f; Jer 3:3 4696
And it has devoured the f of Moab Jer 48:45 6285
your f as hard as their foreheads. Ezk 3:8 4696
than flint I have made your f. Ezk 3:9 4696
their right hand or on their f, Rv 13:16 *3359*
a mark on his f or on his hand, Rv 14:9 *3359*
and on her f a name *was* written, Rv 17:5 *3359*
on their f and on their hand; Rv 20:4 *3359*

FOREHEADS
the LORD will make their f bare." Is 3:17 6596
your forehead as hard as their f. Ezk 3:8 4696
and put a mark on the f of the men Ezk 9:4 4696
of our God on their f." Rv 7:3 *3359*
have the seal of God on their f. Rv 9:4 *3359*
of His Father written on their f. Rv 14:1 *3359*
and His name *will be* on their f. Rv 22:4 *3359*

FOREIGN
the f gods which are among you, Gn 35:2 5236
all the f gods which they had and Gn 35:4 5236
been a sojourner in a f land." Ex 2:22 5237
been a sojourner in a f land." Ex 18:3 5237
have authority to sell her to a f people Ex 21:8 5237
hired man and your f resident, Lv 25:6 8453
And there was no f god with him. Dt 32:12 5236
forsake the LORD and serve f gods, Jos 24:20 5236
f gods which are in your midst, Jos 24:23 5236
away the f gods from among them and Jg 10:16 5236
remove the f gods and the 1Sa 7:3 5236
Solomon loved many f women 1Ki 11:1 5237
also he did for all his f wives, 1Ki 11:8 5237
"I dug *wells* and drank f waters, 2Ki 19:24 2114a
the f altars and high places, 2Ch 14:3 5236
He also removed the f gods and the 2Ch 33:15 5236
and have married f women from the Ezr 10:2 5237
married f wives adding to the guilt of Ezr 10:10 5237
the land and from the f wives." Ezr 10:11 5237
who have married f wives come at Ezr 10:14 5237
all the men who had married f wives Ezr 10:17 5237
of the priests who had married f wives Ezr 10:18 5237
All these had married f wives, Ezr 10:44 5237
f women caused even him to sin. Ne 13:26 5237
our God by marrying f women?" Ne 13:27 5237
I purified them from everything f Ne 13:30 5236
Nor shall you worship any f god. Ps 81:9 5236
sing the LORD's song In a f land? Ps 137:4 5236
stammering lips and a f tongue, Is 28:11 312
the degenerate shoots of a f vine? Jer 2:21 5237
Me and served f gods in your land, Jer 5:19 5236
graven images, with f idols?" Jer 8:19 5236
from a f *land* ever snatched away? Jer 18:14 2114a
and all the f people, all the Jer 25:20 6154a
kings of the f people who dwell in the Jer 25:24 6154a
with *the help of* a f god; Da 11:39 5236
clothe themselves with f garments. Zph 1:8 5237
married the daughter of a f god. Mal 2:11 5236
WOULD BE ALIENS IN A F LAND, Ac 7:6 *245*
pursuing them even to f cities. Ac 26:11 *1854*
land of promise, as in a f *land*, Heb 11:9 *245*
in war, put f armies to flight. Heb 11:34 *245*

FOREIGNER
is bought with money from any f, Gn 17:12
1121, 5236
or bought with money from a f, Gn 17:27
1121, 5236
no f is to eat of it; Ex 12:43
1121, 5236
accept any such from the hand of a f Lv 22:25
1121, 5236
eat it, or you may sell it to a f, Dt 14:21 5237
"From a f you may exact *it*, but Dt 15:3 5237
you may not put a f over Dt 17:15 5237
"You may charge interest to a f, Dt 23:20 5237
f who comes from a distant land, Dt 29:22 5237
notice of me, since I am a f?" Ru 2:10 5237
for you are a f and also an exile; 2Sa 15:19 5237
"Also concerning the f who is not 1Ki 8:41 5237
all for which the f calls to You, 1Ki 8:43 5237
"Also concerning the f who is not 2Ch 6:32 5237
all for which the f calls to You, 2Ch 6:33 5237
I am a f in their sight. Jb 19:15 5237
And embrace the bosom of a f? Pr 5:20 5237
the f who flatters with her words. Pr 7:5 5237
from them, for a f enjoys them. Ec 6:2 5237
Let not the f who has joined Is 56:3
1121, 5236
"No f uncircumcised in heart and Ezk 44:9
1121, 5236
glory to God, except this f?" Lk 17:18 *241*
who is a Jew to associate with a f Ac 10:28 *246*

FOREIGNERS
"Are we not reckoned by him as f? Gn 31:15 5237

will not turn aside into the city of **f**	**Jg 19:12**	5237
"**F** pretend obedience to me;	**2Sa 22:45**	1121, 5236
"**F** lose heart, And come trembling	**2Sa 22:46**	1121, 5236
So David gave orders to gather the **f**	**1Ch 22:2**	1616
separated themselves from all **f**,	**Ne 9:2**	1121, 5236
they excluded all **f** from Israel.	**Ne 13:3**	6154a
they obey me; **F** submit to me.	**Ps 18:44**	1121, 5236
F fade away, And come trembling	**Ps 18:45**	1121, 5236
And for **f**, hold him in pledge.	**Pr 20:16**	5237
bargains with the children of **f**.	**Is 2:6**	5237
"Also the **f** who join themselves	**Is 56:6**	1121, 5236
"**F** will build up your walls,	**Is 60:10**	1121
And **f** will be your farmers and	**Is 61:5**	1121, 5236
Nor will **f** drink your new wine for	**Is 62:8**	1121, 5236
the **f** who are in the midst of her,	**Jer 50:37**	6154a
I will dispatch **f** to Babylon that	**Jer 51:2**	2114a
it into the hands of the **f** as plunder	**Ezk 7:21**	2114a
when you brought in **f**,	**Ezk 44:7**	1121, 5236
but you have set **f** to keep charge	**Ezk 44:8**	
of all the **f** who are among the	**Ezk 44:9**	1121, 5236
And **f** entered his gate And cast	**Ob 1:11**	5237
FOREKNEW		
those whom He **f**, He also predestined	**Ro 8:29**	*4267*
not rejected His people whom He **f**.	**Ro 11:2**	*4267*
FOREKNOWLEDGE		
predetermined plan and **f** of God,	**Ac 2:23**	*4268*
to the **f** of God the Father,	**1Pe 1:2**	*4268*
FOREKNOWN		
For He was **f** before the foundation	**1Pe 1:20**	*4267*
FOREMAN		
of the vineyard said to his **f**,	**Mt 20:8**	*2012*
FOREMEN		
over the people and their **f**,	**Ex 5:6**	7860
f went out and spoke to the people,	**Ex 5:10**	7860
the **f** of the sons of Israel,	**Ex 5:14**	7860
Then the **f** of the sons of Israel	**Ex 5:15**	7860
The **f** of the sons of Israel	**Ex 5:19**	7860
with **f** over them to supervise:	**2Ch 34:12**	6485
FOREMOST		
been **f** in this unfaithfulness."	**Ezr 9:2**	7223
and the **f** of the sons of Ammon.	**Da 11:41**	7225
men of the **f** of nations,	**Am 6:1**	7225
is the great and **f** commandment.	**Mt 22:38**	*4413*
commandment is the **f** of all?"	**Mk 12:28**	*4413*
Jesus answered, "The **f** is, 'HEAR,	**Mk 12:29**	*4413*
sinners, among whom I am **f** *of all.*	**1Tm 1:15**	*4413*
so that in me as the **f**,	**1Tm 1:16**	*4413*
FORERUNNER		
"It is he who will go *as a* **f**	**Lk 1:17**	
Jesus has entered as a **f** for us,	**Heb 6:20**	*4274*
FORESAIL		
and hoisting the **f** to the wind,	**Ac 27:40**	*736*
FORESEEING		
f that God would justify the	**Ga 3:8**	*4275a*
FORESKIN		
in the flesh of your **f**,	**Gn 17:11**	6190
circumcised in the flesh of his **f**,	**Gn 17:14**	6190
circumcised the flesh of their **f**	**Gn 17:23**	6190
circumcised in the flesh of his **f**.	**Gn 17:24**	6190
circumcised in the flesh of his **f**.	**Gn 17:25**	6190
son's **f** and threw it at Moses' feet,	**Ex 4:25**	6190
of his **f** shall be circumcised.	**Lv 12:3**	6190
FORESKINS		
a hundred **f** of the Philistines,	**1Sa 18:25**	6190
Then David brought their **f**,	**1Sa 18:27**	6190
a hundred **f** of the Philistines."	**2Sa 3:14**	6190
And remove the **f** of your heart,	**Jer 4:4**	6190
FOREST		
man goes into the **f** with his friend	**Dt 19:5**	3293a
go up to the **f** and clear a place	**Jos 17:15**	3293a
though it is a **f**, you shall clear it,	**Jos 17:18**	3293a
people of the land entered the **f**,	**1Sa 14:25**	3293a
When the people entered the **f**,	**1Sa 14:26**	3293a
and went into the **f** of Hereth.	**1Sa 22:5**	3293a
took place in the **f** of Ephraim.	**2Sa 18:6**	3293a
and the **f** devoured more people	**2Sa 18:8**	3293a
and cast him into a deep pit in the **f**	**2Sa 18:17**	3293a
the house of the **f** of Lebanon;	**1Ki 7:2**	3293a
in the house of the **f** of Lebanon.	**1Ki 10:17**	3293a
the house of the **f** of Lebanon	**1Ki 10:21**	3293a
lodging place, its thickest **f**.	**2Ki 19:23**	3293a
Then the trees of the **f** will sing	**1Ch 16:33**	3293a
in the house of the **f** of Lebanon.	**2Ch 9:16**	3293a
the house of the **f** of Lebanon	**2Ch 9:20**	3293a
Asaph the keeper of the king's **f**,	**Ne 2:8**	6508
"For every beast of the **f** is Mine,	**Ps 50:10**	3293a
lifted up *His* axe in a **f** of trees.	**Ps 74:5**	5441
A boar from the **f** eats it away And	**Ps 80:13**	3293a
Like fire that burns the **f** And	**Ps 83:14**	3293a
trees of the **f** will sing for joy	**Ps 96:12**	3293a
the beasts of the **f** prowl about.	**Ps 104:20**	3293a
to irrigate a **f** of growing trees.	**Ec 2:6**	3293a
tree among the trees of the **f**,	**SS 2:3**	3293a
of the **f** shake with the wind.	**Is 7:2**	3293a
sets the thickets of the **f** aflame And	**Is 9:18**	3293a
He will destroy the glory of his **f**	**Is 10:18**	3293a
the trees of his **f** will be so small in	**Is 10:19**	3293a
of the **f** with an iron *axe*,	**Is 10:34**	3293a
be like forsaken places in the **f**,	**Is 17:9**	2793
the weapons of the house of the **f**,	**Is 22:8**	3293a
field will be considered as a **f**?	**Is 29:17**	3293a
field is considered as a **f**.	**Is 32:15**	3293a
will hail when the **f** comes down,	**Is 32:19**	3293a
its highest peak, its thickest **f**.	**Is 37:24**	3293a
himself among the trees of the **f**.	**Is 44:14**	3293a
shout of joy, you mountains, O **f**,	**Is 44:23**	3293a
field, All you beasts in the **f**,	**Is 56:9**	3293a
a lion from the **f** will slay them,	**Jer 5:6**	3293a
Because it is wood cut from the **f**,	**Jer 10:3**	3293a
become to Me Like a lion in the **f**;	**Jer 12:8**	3293a
"And I will kindle a fire in its **f**	**Jer 21:14**	3293a
as the high places of a **f**."	**Jer 26:18**	3293a
"They have cut down her **f**,"	**Jer 46:23**	3293a
which is among the trees of the **f**?	**Ezk 15:2**	3293a
the vine among the trees of the **f**,	**Ezk 15:6**	3293a
against the **f** land of the Negev,	**Ezk 20:46**	3293a
and say to the **f** of the Negev,	**Ezk 20:47**	3293a
beautiful branches and **f** shade,	**Ezk 31:3**	2793
And I will make them a **f**,	**Hos 2:12**	3293a
roar in the **f** when he has no prey?	**Am 3:4**	3293a
will become high places of a **f**.	**Mi 3:12**	3293a
a lion among the beasts of the **f**,	**Mi 5:8**	3293a
the impenetrable **f** has come down.	**Zch 11:2**	3293a
how great a **f** is set aflame by	**Jas 3:5**	*5208*
FORESTALL		
to **f** this I fled to Tarshish,	**Jon 4:2**	6923
FORESTS		
to calve And strips the **f** bare	**Ps 29:9**	3293a
or gather firewood from the **f**,	**Ezk 39:10**	3293a
FORETOLD		
which the Holy Spirit **f** by the	**Ac 1:16**	*4275b*
And just as Isaiah **f**,	**Ro 9:29**	*4275b*
FOREVER		
the tree of life, and eat, and live **f**"	**Gn 3:22**	5769
shall not strive with man **f**,	**Gn 6:3**	5769
to you and to your descendants **f**.	**Gn 13:15**	5704, 5769
me bear the blame before you **f**.	**Gn 43:9**	3605, 3117
the blame before my father **f**.'	**Gn 44:32**	3605, 3117
This is My name **f**, and this is My	**Ex 3:15**	5769
for you and your children **f**.	**Ex 12:24**	5704, 5769
you will never see them again **f**.	**Ex 14:13**	5704, 5769
"The LORD shall reign **f** and ever."	**Ex 15:18**	5769
and may also believe in you **f**."	**Ex 19:9**	5769
It *shall be* a statute **f** to him and	**Ex 28:43**	5769
portion **f** from the sons of Israel,	**Ex 29:28**	5769
Me and the sons of Israel **f**;	**Ex 31:17**	5769
and they shall inherit *it* **f**.'"	**Ex 32:13**	5769
due **f** from the sons of Israel.	**Lv 7:34**	5769
It is *their* due **f** throughout their	**Lv 7:36**	5769
by fire, *his* portion **f**."	**Lv 24:9**	5769
with them and with their sons **f**!	**Dt 5:29**	5769
you and your sons after you **f**,	**Dt 12:28**	5704, 5769
and it shall be a ruin **f**.	**Dt 13:16**	5769
and he shall be your servant **f**.	**Dt 15:17**	5769
serve in the name of the LORD **f**.	**Dt 18:5**	3605, 3117
on you and your descendants **f**.	**Dt 28:46**	5704, 5769
belong to us and to our sons **f**,	**Dt 29:29**	5704, 5769
to heaven, And say, as I live **f**,	**Dt 32:40**	5769
to the sons of Israel **f**."	**Jos 4:7**	5704, 5769
may fear the LORD your God **f**."	**Jos 4:24**	3605, 3117
burned Ai and made it a heap **f**,	**Jos 8:28**	5769
to you and to your children **f**,	**Jos 14:9**	5704, 5769
the LORD and stay there **f**."	**1Sa 1:22**	5704, 5769
your father should walk before Me **f**	**1Sa 2:30**	5704, 5769
man will not be in your house **f**.	**1Sa 2:32**	3605, 3117
to judge his house **f** for the iniquity	**1Sa 3:13**	5704, 5769
for by sacrifice or offering **f**."	**1Sa 3:14**	5704, 5769
your kingdom over Israel **f**.	**1Sa 13:13**	5704, 5769
lovingkindness from my house **f**,	**1Sa 20:15**	5704, 5769
LORD is between you and me **f**."	**1Sa 20:23**	5704, 5769
and your descendants **f**.'"	**1Sa 20:42**	5704, 5769
he will become my servant **f**."	**1Sa 27:12**	5769
"Shall the sword devour **f**?	**2Sa 2:26**	5331
innocent before the LORD **f** of the	**2Sa 3:28**	5704, 5769
the throne of his kingdom **f**.	**2Sa 7:13**	5704, 5769
kingdom shall endure before Me **f**;	**2Sa 7:16**	5704, 5769
shall be established **f**.	**2Sa 7:16**	5704, 5769
Israel as Your own people **f**,	**2Sa 7:24**	5704, 5769
and his house, confirm *it* **f**,	**2Sa 7:25**	5704, 5769
that Your name may be magnified **f**,	**2Sa 7:26**	5704, 5769
it may continue **f** before You.	**2Sa 7:29**	5769
of Your servant be blessed **f**."	**2Sa 7:29**	5769
To David and his descendants **f**."	**2Sa 22:51**	5704, 5769
"May my lord King David live **f**."	**1Ki 1:31**	5769
on the head of his descendants **f**;	**1Ki 2:33**	5769
there be peace from the LORD **f**."	**1Ki 2:33**	5704, 5769
established before the LORD **f**."	**1Ki 2:45**	5704, 5769
A place for Your dwelling **f**."	**1Ki 8:13**	5769
built by putting My name there **f**,	**1Ki 9:3**	5704, 5769
of your kingdom over Israel **f**,	**1Ki 9:5**	5769
because the LORD loved Israel **f**,	**1Ki 10:9**	5769
they will be your servants **f**."	**1Ki 12:7**	3605, 3117
you and to your descendants **f**."	**2Ki 5:27**	5769
you, you shall observe to do **f**;	**2Ki 17:37**	3605, 3117
of Israel, I will put My name **f**.	**2Ki 21:7**	5769
God and to minister to Him **f**."	**1Ch 15:2**	5704, 5769
Remember His covenant **f**,	**1Ch 16:15**	5769
and I will establish his throne **f**.	**1Ch 17:12**	5704, 5769
in My house and in My kingdom **f**,	**1Ch 17:14**	5704, 5769
shall be established **f**.	**1Ch 17:14**	5704, 5769
made Your own people **f**,	**1Ch 17:22**	5704, 5769
his house be established **f**,	**1Ch 17:23**	5704, 5769
be established and magnified **f**,	**1Ch 17:24**	5704, 5769
it may continue **f** before You;	**1Ch 17:27**	5769
blessed, and it is blessed **f**."	**1Ch 17:27**	5769
of his kingdom over Israel **f**.'	**1Ch 22:10**	5704, 5769
as most holy, he and his sons **f**,	**1Ch 23:13**	5704, 5769
to Him and to bless in His name **f**.	**1Ch 23:13**	5704, 5769
and He dwells in Jerusalem **f**.	**1Ch 23:25**	5704, 5769
father to be king over Israel **f**.	**1Ch 28:4**	5769
I will establish his kingdom **f** if	**1Ch 28:7**	5704, 5769
it to your sons after you **f**.	**1Ch 28:8**	5704, 5769
forsake Him, He will reject you **f**.	**1Ch 28:9**	5703
of Israel our father, **f** and ever.	**1Ch 29:10**	5769
preserve this **f** in the intentions	**1Ch 29:18**	5769
this *being required* **f** in Israel.	**2Ch 2:4**	5769
And a place for Your dwelling **f**."	**2Ch 6:2**	5769
house that My name may be there **f**,	**2Ch 7:16**	5704, 5769
loved Israel establishing them **f**,	**2Ch 9:8**	5769
they will be your servants **f**."	**2Ch 10:7**	3605, 3117
gave the rule over Israel **f** to David	**2Ch 13:5**	5769
of Abraham Your friend **f**?	**2Ch 20:7**	5769
give a lamp to him and his sons **f**.	**2Ch 21:7**	3605, 3117
which He has consecrated **f**,	**2Ch 30:8**	5769
"My name shall be in Jerusalem **f**."	**2Ch 33:4**	5769
of Israel, I will put My name **f**;	**2Ch 33:7**	5769
lovingkindness is upon Israel **f**."	**Ezr 3:11**	5769
as an inheritance to your sons **f**.'	**Ezr 9:12**	5704, 5769
"Let the king live **f**.	**Ne 2:3**	5769
the LORD your God **f** and ever!	**Ne 9:5**	4480, 5769
Unobserved, they perish **f**.	**Jb 4:20**	5331
I will not live **f**.	**Jb 7:16**	5769
f overpower him and he departs;	**Jb 14:20**	5331
They were engraved in the rock **f**!	**Jb 19:24**	5703
He perishes **f** like his refuse;	**Jb 20:7**	5331
be delivered **f** from my Judge.	**Jb 23:7**	5331
the throne He has seated them **f**,	**Jb 36:7**	5331
Will you take him for a servant **f**?	**Jb 41:4**	5769
blotted out their name **f** and ever.	**Ps 9:5**	5769
But the LORD abides **f**;	**Ps 9:7**	5769
hope of the afflicted perish **f**.	**Ps 9:18**	5703
The LORD is King **f** and ever;	**Ps 10:16**	5769
him from this generation **f**.	**Ps 12:7**	5769
Will You forget me **f**?	**Ps 13:1**	5331
right hand there are pleasures **f**.	**Ps 16:11**	5331
To David and his descendants **f**.	**Ps 18:50**	5704, 5769
of the LORD is clean, enduring **f**;	**Ps 19:9**	5703
to him, Length of days **f** and ever.	**Ps 21:4**	5769
You make him most blessed **f**;	**Ps 21:6**	5703
Let your heart live **f**!	**Ps 22:26**	5703
dwell in the house of the LORD **f**.	**Ps 23:6**	753, 3117
shepherd also, and carry them **f**.	**Ps 28:9**	5704, 5769
Yes, the LORD sits as King **f**.	**Ps 29:10**	5769
God, I will give thanks to You **f**.	**Ps 30:12**	5769
The counsel of the LORD stands **f**,	**Ps 33:11**	5769
And their inheritance will be **f**.	**Ps 37:18**	5769
and do good, So you will abide **f**.	**Ps 37:27**	5769
They are preserved **f**,	**Ps 37:28**	5769

the land And dwell in it **f**. **Ps 37:29** 5703
You set me in Your presence **f**. **Ps 41:12** 5769
we will give thanks to Your name **f**. **Ps 44:8** 5769
Awake, do not reject us **f**. **Ps 44:23** 5331
Therefore God has blessed You **f**. **Ps 45:2** 5769
Your throne, O God, is **f** and ever; **Ps 45:6** 5769
will give You thanks **f** and ever. **Ps 45:17** 5769
God will establish her **f**. **Ps 48:8** 5704, 5769
such is God, Our God **f** and ever; **Ps 48:14** 5769
And he should cease *trying* **f** **Ps 49:8** 5769
is *that* their houses are **f** **Ps 49:11** 5769
But God will break you down **f**; **Ps 52:5** 5331
lovingkindness of God **f** and ever. **Ps 52:8** 5769
I will give You thanks **f**, **Ps 52:9** 5769
Let me dwell in Your tent **f**; **Ps 61:4** 5769
He will abide before God **f**; **Ps 61:7** 5769
I will sing praise to Your name **f**, **Ps 61:8** 5703
He rules by His might **f**; **Ps 66:7** 5769
the LORD will dwell *there* **f**. **Ps 68:16** 5331
May his name endure **f**; **Ps 72:17** 5769
blessed be His glorious name **f**; **Ps 72:19** 5769
of my heart and my portion **f**. **Ps 73:26** 5769
God, why have You rejected *us* **f**? **Ps 74:1** 5331
And the enemy spurn Your name **f**? **Ps 74:10** 5331
the life of Your afflicted **f**. **Ps 74:19** 5331
as for me, I will declare *it* **f**, **Ps 75:9** 5769
Will the Lord reject **f**? **Ps 77:7** 5769
Has His lovingkindness ceased **f**? **Ps 77:8** 5331
Has *His* promise come to an end **f**? **Ps 77:8** 1755
the earth which He has founded **f**. **Ps 78:69** 5769
Will You be angry **f**? **Ps 79:5** 5331
Will give thanks to You **f**; **Ps 79:13** 5769
time *of punishment* would be **f**. **Ps 81:15** 5769
them be ashamed and dismayed **f**, **Ps 83:17** 5703
Will You be angry with us **f**? **Ps 85:5** 5769
And will glorify Your name **f**. **Ps 86:12** 5769
the lovingkindness of the LORD **f**; **Ps 89:1** 5769
"Lovingkindness will be built up **f**; **Ps 89:2** 5769
I will establish your seed **f** And **Ps 89:4** 5704, 5769
I will keep for him **f**, **Ps 89:28** 5769
will establish his descendants **f** And **Ps 89:29** 5703
"His descendants shall endure **f** And **Ps 89:36** 5769
be established **f** like the moon, **Ps 89:37** 5769
Will You hide Yourself **f**? **Ps 89:46** 5331
Blessed be the LORD **f**! **Ps 89:52** 5769
But You, O LORD, are on high **f**. **Ps 92:8** 5769
But You, O LORD, abide **f** **Ps 102:12** 5769
Nor will He keep *His anger* **f**. **Ps 103:9** 5769
it will not totter **f** and ever. **Ps 104:5** 5769
the glory of the LORD endure **f**; **Ps 104:31** 5769
He has remembered His covenant **f**, **Ps 105:8** 5769
To all generations **f**. **Ps 106:31** 5704, 5769
"You are a priest **f** According to **Ps 110:4** 5769
And His righteousness endures **f**. **Ps 111:3** 5703
He will remember His covenant **f**. **Ps 111:5** 5769
They are upheld **f** and ever; **Ps 111:8** 5703
He has ordained His covenant **f**; **Ps 111:9** 5769
His praise endures **f**. **Ps 111:10** 5703
And his righteousness endures **f**. **Ps 112:3** 5703
righteous will be remembered **f**. **Ps 112:6** 5769
His righteousness endures **f**; **Ps 112:9** 5703
LORD From this time forth and **f**. **Ps 113:2** 5704, 5769
LORD From this time forth and **f**. **Ps 115:18** 5704, 5769
Your law continually, **F** and ever. **Ps 119:44** 5769
F, O LORD, Your word is settled in **Ps 119:89** 5769
have inherited Your testimonies **f** **Ps 119:111** 5769
heart to perform Your statutes **F**, **Ps 119:112** 5769
Your testimonies are righteous **f**; **Ps 119:144** 5769
That You have founded them **f**. **Ps 119:152** 5769
in From this time forth and **f**. **Ps 121:8** 5704, 5769
cannot be moved but abides **f**. **Ps 125:1** 5769
people From this time forth and **f**. **Ps 125:2** 5704, 5769
LORD From this time forth and **f**. **Ps 131:3** 5704, 5769
shall sit upon your throne **f**." **Ps 132:12** 5703
"This is My resting place **f**; **Ps 132:14** 5703
LORD commanded the blessing—life **f**. **Ps 133:3** 5704, 5769
I will bless Your name **f** and ever. **Ps 145:1** 5769
I will praise Your name **f** and ever. **Ps 145:2** 5769
bless His holy name **f** and ever. **Ps 145:21** 5769
Who keeps faith **f**; **Ps 146:6** 5769
The LORD will reign **f**, **Ps 146:10** 5769
also established them **f** and ever; **Ps 148:6** 5703
Truthful lips will be established **f**, **Pr 12:19** 5703
listens *to the truth* will speak **f**. **Pr 21:28** 5331
For riches are not **f**, **Pr 27:24** 5769
His throne will be established **f**. **Pr 29:14** 5703
comes, But the earth remains **f**. **Ec 1:4** 5769
everything God does will remain **f**; **Ec 3:14** 5769
of evildoers not be mentioned **f**. **Is 14:20** 5769
"Trust in the LORD **f**, **Is 26:4** 5703
does not continue to thresh it **f**. **Is 28:28** 5331
the time to come As a witness **f**. **Is 30:8** 5704, 5769
watch-tower have become caves **f**, **Is 32:14** 5704, 5769
quietness and confidence **f**. **Is 32:17** 5704, 5769
Its smoke will go up **f** **Is 34:10** 5769
will pass through it **f** and ever. **Is 34:10** 5331
They shall possess it **f**; **Is 34:17** 5704, 5769
But the word of our God stands **f**. **Is 40:8** 5769
'I will be a queen **f**.' **Is 47:7** 5703, 5769
But My salvation will be **f**, **Is 51:6** 5769
But My righteousness will be **f**, **Is 51:8** 5769
high and exalted One Who lives **f**, **Is 57:15** 5703
"For I will not contend **f**, **Is 57:16** 5769
says the LORD, "from now and **f**." **Is 59:21** 5704, 5769
They will possess the land **f**, **Is 60:21** 5769
LORD, Nor remember iniquity **f**; **Is 64:9** 5703
and rejoice **f** in what I create; **Is 65:18** 5703
'Will He be angry **f**? **Jer 3:5** 5769
'I will not be angry **f**. **Jer 3:12** 5769
I gave to your fathers **f** and ever. **Jer 7:7** 4480, 5769
in My anger Which will burn **f**. **Jer 17:4** 5704, 5769
and this city will be inhabited **f**. **Jer 17:25** 5769
and your forefathers **f** and ever; **Jer 25:5** 4480, 5769
From being a nation before Me **f**." **Jer 31:36** 3605, 3117
up or overthrown anymore **f**." **Jer 31:40** 5769
drink wine, you or your sons, **f**. **Jer 35:6** 5704, 5769
haunt of jackals, A desolation **f**; **Jer 49:33** 5704, 5769
But you will be desolate **f**," **Jer 51:26** 5769
For the Lord will not reject **f**, **La 3:31** 5769
You, O LORD, rule **f**; **La 5:19** 5769
Why do You forget us **f**? **La 5:20** 5331
you will cease to be **f**.' " ' " **Ezk 27:36** 5704, 5769
terrified And you will cease to be **f**." ' " **Ezk 28:19** 5704, 5769
sons and their sons' sons, **f**; **Ezk 37:25** 5704, 5769
servant will be their prince **f**. **Ezk 37:25** 5769
set My sanctuary in their midst **f**. **Ezk 37:26** 5769
is in their midst **f**. **Ezk 37:28** 5769
dwell among the sons of Israel **f**. **Ezk 43:7** 5769
and I will dwell among them **f**. **Ezk 43:9** 5769
O king, live **f**! Tell the dream to your **Da 2:4** 5957
name of God be blessed **f** and ever, **Da 2:20** 5957
but it will itself endure **f**. **Da 2:44** 5957
"O king, live **f**! **Da 3:9** 5957
and honored Him who lives **f**; **Da 4:34** 5957
queen spoke and said, "O king, live **f**! **Da 5:10** 5957
"King Darius, live **f**! **Da 6:6** 5957
spoke to the king, "O king, live **f**! **Da 6:21** 5957
is the living God and enduring **f**, **Da 6:26** 5957
And His dominion *will be* **f**. **Da 6:26** 5491
kingdom and possess the kingdom **f**, **Da 7:18** 5957
away, annihilated and destroyed **f**. **Da 7:26** 5491
like the stars **f** and ever. **Da 12:3** 5769
and swore by Him who lives **f** **Da 12:7** 5769
"I will betroth you to Me **f**; **Hos 2:19** 5769
But Judah will be inhabited **f** And **Jl 3:20** 5769
And he maintained his fury **f**. **Am 1:11** 5331
shame, And you will be cut off **f**. **Ob 1:10** 5769
with its bars *was* around me **f**, **Jon 2:6** 5769
children you take My splendor **f**. **Mi 2:9** 5769
of the LORD our God **f** and ever. **Mi 4:5** 5769
in Mount Zion From now on and **f**. **Mi 4:7** 5704, 5769
He does not retain His anger **f**, **Mi 7:18** 5703
And the prophets, do they live **f**? **Zch 1:5** 5769
whom the LORD is indignant **f**." **Mal 1:4** 5704, 5769
and the power and the glory **f**. **Mt 6:13** *165*
reign over the house of Jacob **f**, **Lk 1:33** *165*
To Abraham and his descendants **f**." **Lk 1:55** *165*
of this bread, he will live **f**; **Jn 6:51** *165*
eats this bread will live **f**." **Jn 6:58** *165*
does not remain in the house **f**; **Jn 8:35** *165*
the son does remain **f**. **Jn 8:35** *165*
that the Christ is to remain **f**; **Jn 12:34** *165*
Helper, that He may be with you **f**; **Jn 14:16** *165*
the Creator, who is blessed **f**. **Ro 1:25** *165*
who is over all, God blessed **f**. **Ro 9:5** *165*
SEE NOT, AND BEND THEIR BACKS **F**." **Ro 11:10** *1223, 3956*
To Him *be* the glory **f**. **Ro 11:36** *165*
Jesus Christ, be the glory **f**. **Ro 16:27** *165*
HIS RIGHTEOUSNESS ENDURES **F**. **2Co 9:9** *165*
Lord Jesus, He who is blessed **f**, **2Co 11:31** *165*
to all generations **f** and ever. **Eph 3:21** *165*
Father *be* the glory **f** and ever. **Php 4:20** *165*
be honor and glory **f** and ever. **1Tm 1:17** *165*
to Him *be* the glory **f** and ever. **2Tm 4:18** *165*
that you would have him back **f**, **Phm 1:15** *166*
"YOUR THRONE, O GOD, IS **F** AND EVER **Heb 1:8** *165*
YOU ARE A PRIEST **F** ACCORDING TO **Heb 5:6** *165*
having become a high priest **f** **Heb 6:20** *165*
YOU ARE A PRIEST **F** ACCORDING TO **Heb 7:17** *165*
'YOU ARE A PRIEST **F**' **Heb 7:21** *165*
other hand, because He continues **f**, **Heb 7:24** *165*
He is able also to save **f** those who **Heb 7:25** *1519, 3838*
appoints a Son, made perfect **f**. **Heb 7:28** *165*
yesterday and today and **f**. **Heb 13:8** *165*
to whom *be* the glory **f** and ever. **Heb 13:21** *165*
THE WORD OF THE LORD ENDURES **F**." **1Pe 1:25** *165*
the glory and dominion **f** and ever. **1Pe 4:11** *165*
To Him *be* dominion **f** and ever. **1Pe 5:11** *165*
who does the will of God lives **f**. **1Jn 2:17** *165*
in us and will be with us **f**: **2Jn 1:2** *165*
darkness has been reserved **f**. **Jude 1:13** *165*
before all time and now and **f**. **Jude 1:25** *165*
glory and the dominion **f** and ever. **Rv 1:6** *165*
to Him who lives **f** and ever, **Rv 4:9** *165*
worship Him who lives **f** and ever, **Rv 4:10** *165*
glory and dominion **f** and ever." **Rv 5:13** *165*
might, *be* to our God **f** and ever. **Rv 7:12** *165*
swore by Him who lives **f** and ever, **Rv 10:6** *165*
and He will reign **f** and ever." **Rv 11:15** *165*
their torment goes up **f** and ever; **Rv 14:11** *165*
of God, who lives **f** and ever. **Rv 15:7** *165*
HER SMOKE RISES UP **F** AND EVER." **Rv 19:3** *165*
day and night **f** and ever. **Rv 20:10** *165*
and they will reign **f** and ever. **Rv 22:5** *165*

FOREVERMORE
that they might be destroyed **f**. **Ps 92:7** 5704, 5703
befits Your house, O LORD, **f**. **Ps 93:5** 753, 3117
righteousness From then on and **f**. **Is 9:7** 5703, 5769
to whom *be* the glory **f**. **Ga 1:5** *165*
dead, and behold, I am alive **f**, **Rv 1:18** *165*

FOREWARN
of which I **f** you, just as I have **Ga 5:21** *4302*

FOREWARNED
I have **f** you, that those who practice **Ga 5:21** *4275b*

FORFEIT
make me **f** my head to the king." **Da 1:10** 2325
the whole world, and **f** his soul? **Mk 8:36** *2210*

FORFEITED
all his possessions should be **f** **Ezr 10:8** 2763a

FORFEITS
him to anger **f** his own life. **Pr 20:2** 2398
the whole world and **f** his soul? **Mt 16:26** *2210*
world, and loses or **f** himself? **Lk 9:25** *2210*

FORGAVE
And You **f** the guilt of my sin. Selah. **Ps 32:5** 5375
compassionate, **f** *their* iniquity and **Ps 78:38** 3722a
You **f** the iniquity of Your people; **Ps 85:2** 5375
released him and **f** him the debt. **Mt 18:27** *863*
I **f** you all that debt because you **Mt 18:32** *863*
repay, he graciously **f** them both. **Lk 7:42** *5483*
suppose the one whom he **f** more." **Lk 7:43** *5483*
just as the Lord **f** you, **Col 3:13** *5483*

FORGED
arrogant have **f** a lie against me; **Ps 119:69** 2950

FORGER
the **f** of all implements of bronze **Gn 4:22** 3913

FORGET
"God has made me **f** all my trouble **Gn 41:51** 5382
you do not **f** the things which your **Dt 4:9** 7911
that you do not **f** the covenant of the **Dt 4:23** 7911
nor **f** the covenant with your fathers **Dt 4:31** 7911
that you do not **f** the LORD who brought **Dt 6:12** 7911
"Beware that you do not **f** the LORD **Dt 8:11** 7911
and you will **f** the LORD your God who **Dt 8:14** 7911
if you ever **f** the LORD your God and **Dt 8:19** 7911
do not **f** how you provoked the LORD **Dt 9:7** 7911
from under heaven; you must not **f**. **Dt 25:19** 7911
me, and not **f** Your maidservant, **1Sa 1:11** 7911
made with you, you shall not **f**, **2Ki 17:38** 7911
"So are the paths of all who **f** God; **Jb 8:13** 7911
'I will **f** my complaint, I will **Jb 9:27** 7911
"For you would **f** *your* trouble, As **Jb 11:16** 7911
"A mother will **f** him; **Jb 24:20** 7911
Because God has made her **f** wisdom, **Jb 39:17** 5382
not **f** the cry of the afflicted. **Ps 9:12** 7911
Even all the nations who **f** God. **Ps 9:17** 7913
Do not **f** the afflicted. **Ps 10:12** 7911
Will You **f** me forever? **Ps 13:1** 7911
And **f** our affliction and our **Ps 44:24** 7911
F your people and your father's **Ps 45:10** 7911
"Now consider this, you who **f** God, **Ps 50:22** 7911
not slay them, or my people will **f**; **Ps 59:11** 7911
Do not **f** the life of Your **Ps 74:19** 7911
Do not **f** the voice of Your **Ps 74:23** 7911
God And not **f** the works of God, **Ps 78:7** 7911
away, Indeed, I **f** to eat my bread. **Ps 102:4** 7911
soul, And **f** none of His benefits; **Ps 103:2** 7911
I shall not **f** Your word. **Ps 119:16** 7911
smoke, I do not **f** Your statutes. **Ps 119:83** 7911
I will never **f** Your precepts, For **Ps 119:93** 7911
my hand, Yet I do not **f** Your law. **Ps 119:109** 7911
Yet I do not **f** Your precepts. **Ps 119:141** 7911
rescue me, For I do not **f** Your law. **Ps 119:153** 7911
For I do not **f** Your commandments. **Ps 119:176** 7911
If I **f** you, O Jerusalem, May my **Ps 137:5** 7911
May my right hand **f** *her skill*. **Ps 137:5** 7911
My son, do not **f** my teaching, But **Pr 3:1** 7911
Do not **f** nor turn away from the **Pr 4:5** 7911
they will drink and **f** what is decreed, **Pr 31:5** 7911
Let him drink and **f** his poverty And **Pr 31:7** 7911
"Can a woman **f** her nursing child And **Is 49:15** 7911
Even these may **f**, but I will not **Is 49:15** 7911
may forget, but I will not **f** you. **Is 49:15** 7911
will **f** the shame of your youth, **Is 54:4** 7911
the LORD, Who **f** My holy mountain, **Is 65:11** 7913
"Can a virgin **f** her ornaments, Or **Jer 2:32** 7911
who intend to make My people **f** My **Jer 23:27** 7911
I will surely **f** you and cast you **Jer 23:39** 5382
Why do You **f** us forever? **La 5:20** 7911
"They will **f** their disgrace **Ezk 39:26** 5375
God, I also will **f** your children. **Hos 4:6** 7911
I will never **f** any of their deeds. **Am 8:7** 7911
For God is not unjust so as to **f** **Heb 6:10** *1950*

FORGETFUL
a f hearer but an effectual doer, Jas 1:25 *1953*
FORGETFULNESS
righteousness in the land of f? Ps 88:12 5388
FORGETS
and he f what you did to him. Gn 27:45 7911
God f a part of your iniquity. Jb 11:6 5382
she f that a foot may crush them, Jb 39:15 7911
And f the covenant of her God; Pr 2:17 7911
FORGETTING
f what *lies* behind and reaching Php 3:13 *1950*
FORGIVE
"Please f, I beg you, the transgression Gn 50:17 5375
please f the transgression of the Gn 50:17 5375
please f my sin only this once, Ex 10:17 5375
"But now, if You will, f their sin Ex 32:32 5375
and the LORD will f her because Nu 30:5 5545
and the LORD will f her. Nu 30:8 5545
them, and the LORD will f her. Nu 30:12 5545
'F Your people Israel whom You Dt 21:8 3722a
shall never be willing to f him, Dt 29:20 5545
He will not f your transgression Jos 24:19 5375
"Please f the transgression of 1Sa 25:28 5375
Your dwelling place; hear and f. 1Ki 8:30 5545
f the sin of Your people Israel, 1Ki 8:34 5545
then hear in heaven and f the 1Ki 8:36 5545
and f and act and render to each 1Ki 8:39 5545
and f Your people who have sinned 1Ki 8:50 5545
and the LORD would not f. 2Ki 24:4 5545
from heaven; hear and f. 2Ch 6:21 5545
f the sin of Your people Israel, 2Ch 6:25 5545
then hear in heaven and f the 2Ch 6:27 5545
heaven Your dwelling place, and f, 2Ch 6:30 5545
and f Your people who have sinned 2Ch 6:39 5545
from heaven, will f their sin and 2Ch 7:14 5545
Do not f their iniquity and let Ne 4:5 3680
and my trouble, And f all my sins. Ps 25:18 5375
transgressions, You f them. Ps 65:3 3722a
And deliver us and f our sins Ps 79:9 3722a
Lord, are good, and ready to f, Ps 86:5 5546a
been abased, But do not f them. Is 2:9 5375
Do not f their iniquity Or blot Jer 18:23 3722a
"for I will f their iniquity, and Jer 31:34 5545
f their iniquity and their sin." Jer 36:3 5545
O Lord, f! O Lord, listen and take Da 9:19 5545
Israel, that I would ever f them. Hos 1:6 5375
'And f us our debts, as we also Mt 6:12 *863*
f others for their transgressions, Mt 6:14 *863*
heavenly Father will also f you. Mt 6:14 *863*
"But if you do not f others, Mt 6:15 *863*
will not f your transgressions. Mt 6:15 *863*
has authority on earth to f sins" Mt 9:6 *863*
brother sin against me and I f him? Mt 18:21 *863*
f his brother from your heart." Mt 18:35 *863*
who can f sins but God alone?" Mk 2:7 *863*
has authority on earth to f sins" Mk 2:10 *863*
"Whenever you stand praying, f, Mk 11:25 *863*
also f you your transgressions. Mk 11:25 *863*
"But if you do not f, Mk 11:26 *863*
heaven f your transgressions." Mk 11:26 *863*
Who can f sins, but God alone?" Lk 5:21 *863*
has authority on earth to f sins," Lk 5:24 *863*
'And f us our sins, For we Lk 11:4 *863*
For we ourselves also f everyone Lk 11:4 *863*
and if he repents, f him. Lk 17:3 *863*
seven times, saying, 'I repent,' f him Lk 17:4 *863*
Jesus was saying, "Father, f them; Lk 23:34 *863*
"If you f the sins of any, *their* Jn 20:23 *863*
should rather f and comfort *him,* 2Co 2:7 *5483*
But one whom you f anything, I *forgive* 2Co 2:10 *5483*
I f also; for indeed what I have 2Co 2:10
a burden to you? F me this wrong! 2Co 12:13 *5483*
faithful and righteous to f us our sins 1Jn 1:9 *863*
FORGIVEN
for them, and they will be f. Lv 4:20 5545
to his sin, and he will be f. Lv 4:26 5545
for him, and he will be f. Lv 4:31 5545
has committed, and he will be f. Lv 4:35 5545
committed, and it will be f him. Lv 5:10 5545
of these, and it will be f him; Lv 5:13 5545
offering, and it will be f him. Lv 5:16 5545
know *it,* and it will be f him. Lv 5:18 5545
and he will be f for any one of Lv 6:7 5545
he has committed will be f him. Lv 19:22 5545
as You also have f this people, Nu 14:19 5375
of Israel, and they will be f; Nu 15:25 5545
of the sons of Israel will be f, Nu 15:26 5545
for him that he may be f. Nu 15:28 5545
bloodguiltiness shall be f them. Dt 21:8 3722a
is he whose transgression is f, Ps 32:1 5375
taken away and your sin is f." Is 6:7 3722a
not be f you Until you die," Is 22:14 3722a
this Jacob's iniquity will be f; Is 27:9 3722a
there will be f *their* iniquity. Is 33:24 5375
when I have f you for all that you Ezk 16:63 3722a
as we also have f our debtors. Mt 6:12 *863*
son; your sins are f." Mt 9:2 *863*
'Your sins are f,' or to say, Mt 9:5 *863*
sin and blasphemy shall be f people, Mt 12:31 *863*
against the Spirit shall not be f. Mt 12:31 *863*
the Son of Man, it shall be f him; Mt 12:32 *863*
Spirit, it shall not be f him, Mt 12:32 *863*
"Son, your sins are f." Mk 2:5 *863*
say to the paralytic, 'Your sins are f'; Mk 2:9 *863*
sins shall be f the sons of men, Mk 3:28 *863*
OTHERWISE THEY MIGHT RETURN AND BE F." Mk 4:12 *863*
"Friend, your sins are f you." Lk 5:20 *863*
'Your sins have been f you,' Lk 5:23 *863*
sins, which are many, have been f, Lk 7:47 *863*
but he who is f little, loves Lk 7:47 *863*
"Your sins have been f." Lk 7:48 *863*
the Son of Man, it will be f him; Lk 12:10 *863*
Spirit, it will not be f him. Lk 12:10 *863*
any, *their sins* have been f them; Jn 20:23 *863*
of your heart may be f you. Ac 8:22 *863*
WHOSE LAWLESS DEEDS HAVE BEEN F, Ro 4:7 *863*
for indeed what I have f, 2Co 2:10 *5483*
forgiven, if I have f anything, 2Co 2:10 *5483*
as God in Christ also has f you. Eph 4:32 *5483*
f us all our transgressions, Col 2:13 *5483*
sins, they will be f him. Jas 5:15 *863*
have been f you for His name's sake. 1Jn 2:12 *863*
FORGIVENESS
But You are a God of f, Ne 9:17 5547
But there is f with You, That Ps 130:4 5547
our God *belong* compassion and f, Da 9:9 5547
poured out for many for f of sins. Mt 26:28 *859*
of repentance for the f of sins. Mk 1:4 *859*
against the Holy Spirit never has f, Mk 3:29 *859*
salvation By the f of their sins, Lk 1:77 *859*
of repentance for the f of sins; Lk 3:3 *859*
and that repentance for f of sins Lk 24:47 *859*
Christ for the f of your sins; Ac 2:38 *859*
to Israel, and f of sins. Ac 5:31 *859*
in Him receives f of sins." Ac 10:43 *859*
f of sins is proclaimed to you, Ac 13:38 *859*
that they may receive f Ac 26:18 *859*
blood, the f of our trespasses, Eph 1:7 *859*
we have redemption, the f of sins. Col 1:14 *859*
shedding of blood there is no f. Heb 9:22 *859*
where there is f of these things, Heb 10:18 *859*
FORGIVES
who f iniquity, transgression and sin Ex 34:7 5375
"Who is this *man* who even f sins?" Lk 7:49 *863*
FORGIVING
f iniquity and transgression; Nu 14:18 5375
You were a f God to them, And *yet* Ps 99:8 5375
tender-hearted, f each other, Eph 4:32 *5483*
one another, and f each other, Col 3:13 *5483*
FORGOT
not remember Joseph, but f him. Gn 40:23 7911
And f the God who gave you birth. Dt 32:18 7911
LORD, and f the LORD their God and Jg 3:7 7911
"But they f the LORD their God, 1Sa 12:9 7911
They f His deeds And His Ps 78:11 7911
They quickly f His works; Ps 106:13 7911
They f God their Savior, Who had Ps 106:21 7911
fathers f My name because of Baal? Jer 23:27 7911
her lovers, so that she f Me," Hos 2:13 7911
Therefore they f Me. Hos 13:6 7911
FORGOTTEN
will be f in the land of Egypt, Gn 41:30 7911
and have f a sheaf in the field, Dt 24:19 7911
or f any of Your commandments. Dt 26:13 7911
it shall not be f from the lips of their Dt 31:21 7911
And my intimate friends have f me. Jb 19:14 7911
from habitation, F by the foot; Jb 28:4 7911
the needy will not always be f, Ps 9:18 7911
"God has f; He has hidden His face; Ps 10:11 7911
I am f as a dead man, out of mind; Ps 31:12 7911
"Why have You f me? Ps 42:9 7911
upon us, but we have not f You, Ps 44:17 7911
If we had f the name of our God Or Ps 44:20 7911
Has God f to be gracious, Ps 77:9 7911
me, *But* I have not f Your law. Ps 119:61 7911
my adversaries have f Your words. Ps 119:139 7911
in the coming days all will be f. Ec 2:16 7911
and they are *soon* f in the city Ec 8:10 7911
a reward, for their memory is f. Ec 9:5 7911
For you have f the God of your Is 17:10 7911
Tyre will be f for seventy years Is 23:15 7911
walk about the city, O f harlot; Is 23:16 7911
O Israel, you will not be f by Me. Is 44:21 5382
me, And the Lord has f me." Is 49:14 7911
you have f the LORD your Maker, Is 51:13 7911
Because the former troubles are f, Is 65:16 7911
have f Me Days without number. Jer 2:32 7911
They have f the LORD their God. Jer 3:21 7911
f Me And trusted in falsehood. Jer 13:25 7911
'For My people have f Me, Jer 18:15 7911
disgrace that will not be f. Jer 20:11 7911
humiliation which will not be f." Jer 23:40 7911
'All your lovers have f you, Jer 30:14 7911
"Have you f the wickedness of Jer 44:9 7911
covenant that will not be f. Jer 50:5 7911
And have f their resting place. Jer 50:6 7911
The LORD has caused to be f The La 2:6 7911
I have f happiness. La 3:17 5382
oppression, and you have f Me," Ezk 22:12 7911
'Because you have f Me and cast Me Ezk 23:35 7911
you have f the law of your God, Hos 4:6 7911
has f his Maker and built palaces; Hos 8:14 7911
side *of the sea,* but they had f Mt 16:5 *1950*
And they had f to take bread, Mk 8:14 *1950*
not one of them is f before God. Lk 12:6 *1950*
and you have f the exhortation Heb 12:5 *1585*
f what kind of person he was. Jas 1:24 *1950*
having f *his* purification from his 2Pe 1:9
2983, 3024
FORK
with a three-pronged f in his hand. 1Sa 2:13 4207a
all that the f brought up the 1Sa 2:14 4207a
been winnowed with shovel and f. Is 30:24 4214
winnow them with a winnowing f Jer 15:7 4214
Do not stand at the f of the road Ob 1:14 6563
His winnowing f is in His hand, Mt 3:12 *4425*
"His winnowing f is in His Lk 3:17 *4425*
FORKS
basins and its f and its firepans; Ex 27:3 4207b
the f and shovels and the basins, Nu 4:14 4207b
plowshares, the mattocks, the f, 1Sa 13:21
7969, 7053
and the f, the basins, and the 1Ch 28:17 4207b
The pails, the shovels, the f and 2Ch 4:16 4207b
FORLORN
f and forsaken like the desert; Is 27:10 7971
FORM
Rachel was beautiful of f and face. Gn 29:17 8389
was handsome in f and appearance. Gn 39:6 8389
they shall f the two corners. Ex 26:24 1961
And he beholds the f of the LORD. Nu 12:8 8544
but you saw no f—only a voice. Dt 4:12 8544
since you did not see any f on the Dt 4:15 8544
yourselves in the f of any figure, Dt 4:16 8544
a graven image in the f of anything Dt 4:23 8544
make an idol in the f of anything, Dt 4:25 8544
He said to her, "What is his f?" 1Sa 28:14 8389
the same measure and the same f. 1Ki 6:25 7095
from brim to brim, circular in f, 1Ki 7:23 5439
a circular f half a cubit high, 1Ki 7:35 5439
casting, one measure and one f. 1Ki 7:37 7095
from brim to brim, circular in f, 2Ch 4:2 5437
lady was beautiful of f and face, Es 2:7 8389
A f *was* before my eyes; Jb 4:16 8544
f shall be for Sheol to consume So Ps 49:14 6736
You will despise their f. Ps 73:20 6754
steep pathway, Let me see your f, SS 2:14 4758
is sweet, And your f is lovely." SS 2:14 4758
and makes it like the f of a man, Is 44:13 8403
His f more than the sons of men. Is 52:14 8389
He has no *stately* f or majesty Is 53:2 8389
tree, beautiful in fruit and f'; Jer 11:16 8389
they had human f. Ezk 1:5 1823
As for the f of their faces, *each* Ezk 1:10 1823
all four of them had the same f, Ezk 1:16 1823
He stretched out the f of a hand Ezk 8:3 8403
every f of creeping things and Ezk 8:10 8403
cherubim appeared to have the f of a Ezk 10:8 8403
wings *was* the f of human hands. Ezk 10:21 1823
years they will f an alliance, Da 11:6 2266
in a different f to two of them while Mk 16:12 *3444*
upon Him in bodily f like a dove, Lk 3:22 *1491b*
guard against every f of greed; Lk 12:15 *3956*
voice at any time nor seen His f. Jn 5:37 *1491b*
he wrote a letter having this f: Ac 23:25 *5179b*
image in the f of corruptible man and Ro 1:23 *3667*
from the heart to that f of teaching Ro 6:17 *5179b*
f of this world is passing away. 1Co 7:31 *4976*
He existed in the f of God, Php 2:6 *3444*
taking the f of a bond-servant, Php 2:7 *3444*
of Deity dwells in bodily f, Col 2:9 *4985*
abstain from every f of evil. 1Th 5:22 *1491b*
holding to a f of godliness, 2Tm 3:5 *3446*
come *and* not the very f of things, Heb 10:1 *1504*
FORMATION
who could draw up in battle f with 1Ch 12:33 6186a
who could draw up in battle f, 1Ch 12:35 6186a
the army to draw up in battle f. 1Ch 12:36 6186a
who could draw up in battle f, 1Ch 12:38 4634
and drew up in f against them. 1Ch 19:17 6186a
Jeroboam drew up in battle f against 2Ch 13:3 6186a
and they drew up in battle f in 2Ch 14:10 6186a
FORMED
God f man of dust from the ground, Gn 2:7 3335
He placed the man whom He had f. Gn 2:8 3335
LORD God f every beast of the field Gn 2:19 3335
which f the rear guard for all Nu 10:25
Then Solomon f a marriage alliance 1Ki 3:1 2859
"The Chaldeans f three bands and Jb 1:17 7760
I too have been f out of the clay. Jb 33:6 7169
He who f the eye, does He not see? Ps 94:9 3335
And His hands f the dry land. Ps 95:5 3335
which You have f to sport in it. Ps 104:26 3336
For You f my inward parts; You wove Ps 139:13 7069
of the wind and how bones *are* f Ec 11:5
Plans f long ago, with perfect Is 25:1
is f say to him who formed it, Is 29:16 3335
is formed say to him who f it, Is 29:16 3335
O Jacob, And He who f you, Is 43:1 3335
for My glory, Whom I have f, Is 43:7 3335
Before Me there was no God f, Is 43:10 3335
"The people whom I f for Myself Will Is 43:21 3335
made you And f you from the womb, Is 44:2 3335
I have f you, you are My servant, Is 44:21 3335
the one who f you from the womb, Is 44:24 3335
God who f the earth and made it, Is 45:18 3335
place, *But* f it to be inhabited), Is 45:18 3335
who f Me from the womb to be His Is 49:5 3335
is f against you will prosper; Is 54:17 3335
I f you in the womb I knew you, Jer 1:5 3335
the LORD who f it to establish it, Jer 33:2 3335
king of Babylon has f a plan against Jer 49:30 3289
your breasts were f and your hair Ezk 16:7 3559
Then a cloud f, overshadowing Mk 9:7 *1096*
a cloud f and *began* to overshadow Lk 9:34 *1096*
f a mob and set the city in an Ac 17:5 *3792*
f by the art and thought of man. Ac 17:29 *5480*
and when a plot was f against him Ac 20:3 *1096*
the Jews f a conspiracy and bound Ac 23:12 *4160*
more than forty who f this plot. Ac 23:13 *4160*
in labor until Christ is f in you Ga 4:19 *3445*
earth was f out of water and by 2Pe 3:5 *4921*
FORMER
his hand according to your f custom Gn 40:13 7223

two stone tablets like the **f** ones, **Ex 34:1** 7223
the **f** tablets which you shattered. **Ex 34:1** 7223
two stone tablets like the **f** ones, **Ex 34:4** 7223
but the **f** days will be void **Nu 6:12** 7223
who had fought against the **f** king **Nu 21:26** 7223
and more distinguished than the **f**. **Nu 22:15** 428
the **f** days which were before you, **Dt 4:32** 7223
tablets of stone like the **f** ones, **Dt 10:1** 7223
the **f** tablets which you shattered, **Dt 10:2** 7223
tablets of stone like the **f** ones, **Dt 10:3** 7223
the tablets, like the **f** writing, **Dt 10:4** 7223
then her **f** husband who sent her **Dt 24:4** 7223
Now this was *the custom* in **f** times **Ru 4:7** 6440
But the **f** governors who were **Ne 5:15** 7223
Where are Your **f** lovingkindnesses, **Ps 89:49** 7223
f days were better than these?" **Ec 7:10** 7223
As for the **f** *events,* declare what **Is 41:22** 7223
Or from **f** times, that we may say, **Is 41:26** 6440
the **f** things have come to pass, **Is 42:9** 7223
And proclaim to us the **f** things? **Is 43:9** 7223
"Do not call to mind the **f** things, **Is 43:18** 7223
"Remember the **f** things long past, **Is 46:9** 7223
"I declared the **f** things long ago **Is 48:3** 7223
will raise up the **f** devastations; **Is 61:4** 7223
their **f** work into their bosom." **Is 65:7** 7223
the **f** troubles are forgotten, **Is 65:16** 7223
And the **f** things will not be **Is 65:17** 7223
F companions to be head over you? **Jer 13:21**
the **f** kings who were before you, **Jer 34:5** 7223
write on it all the **f** words that were **Jer 36:28** 7223
will return to their **f** state, **Ezk 16:55** 6927
will *also* return to your **f** state. **Ezk 16:55** 6927
the one of whom I spoke in **f** days **Ezk 38:17** 6931
be given into the hand of the **f**. **Da 11:11**
a greater multitude than the **f**, **Da 11:13** 7223
Even the **f** dominion will come, **Mi 4:8** 7223
saw this temple in its **f** glory? **Hg 2:3** 7223
house will be greater than the **f**,' **Hg 2:9** 7223
to whom the **f** prophets proclaimed, **Zch 1:4** 7223
LORD proclaimed by the **f** prophets, **Zch 7:7** 7223
His Spirit through the **f** prophets; **Zch 7:12** 7223
of this people as in the **f** days,' **Zch 8:11** 7223
the days of old and as in **f** years. **Mal 3:4** 6931
of my **f** manner of life in Judaism, **Ga 1:13** *4218*
to your **f** manner of life, **Eph 4:22** *4387*
the **f** proclaim Christ out of **Php 1:17**
3588, 1161
setting aside of a **f** commandment **Heb 7:18** *4254*
The **f** priests, on the one hand, **Heb 7:23**
But remember the **f** days, **Heb 10:32** *4387*
do not be conformed to the **f** lusts **1Pe 1:14** *4387*
in **f** times the holy women also, **1Pe 3:5** *4218*
his purification from his **f** sins. **2Pe 1:9** *3819*

FORMERLY
altar which he had made there **f**; **Gn 13:4** 7223
was not *friendly* toward him as **f**. **Gn 31:2** 8543
it is not *friendly* toward me as **f**, **Gn 31:5** 8543
(The Emim lived there **f**, **Dt 2:10** 6440
The Horites **f** lived in Seir, but **Dt 2:12** 6440
for Rephaim **f** lived in it, **Dt 2:20** 6440
for Hazor **f** was the head of all **Jos 11:10** 6440
name of Hebron was **f** Kiriath-arba; **Jos 14:15** 6440
name of Debir **f** was Kiriath-sepher. **Jos 15:15** 6440
name of Hebron **f** *was* Kiriath-arba); **Jg 1:10** 6440
of Debir **f** *was* Kiriath-sepher). **Jg 1:11** 6440
the name of the city was **f** Luz). **Jg 1:23** 6440
who had not experienced it **f**). **Jg 3:2** 6440
the name of the city **f** was Laish. **Jg 18:29** 7223
(**F** in Israel, when a man went to **1Sa 9:9** 6440
prophet now was **f** called a seer.) **1Sa 9:9** 6440
and he was in his presence as **f**. **1Sa 19:7**
8032a, 865a
wicked afflict them any more as **f**, **2Sa 7:10** 7223
"**F** they used to say, **2Sa 20:18** 7223
Israel lived in their tents as **f**. **2Ki 13:5**
8032a, 8543
who lived there **f** *were* Hamites. **1Ch 4:40** 6440
not waste them anymore as **f**, **1Ch 17:9** 7223
f they put the grain offerings, **Ne 13:5** 6440
"**F** *I said* to Zion, **Is 41:27** 7223
'Their children also will be as **f**, **Jer 30:20** 6924a
to be inhabited as you were **f** and **Ezk 36:11** 6927
the Pharisees the man who was **f** blind. **Jn 9:13** *4218*
who **f** was practicing magic in the **Ac 8:9** *4391*
in which you **f** walked according to **Eph 2:2** *4218*
all **f** lived in the lusts of our flesh, **Eph 2:3** *4218*
that **f** you, the Gentiles in the flesh, **Eph 2:11** *4218*
But now in Christ Jesus you who **f** **Eph 2:13** *4218*
for you were **f** darkness, but now **Eph 5:8** *4218*
f alienated and hostile in mind, **Col 1:21** *4218*
even though I was **f** a blasphemer **1Tm 1:13** *4387*
who **f** was useless to you, but now **Phm 1:11** *4218*
and those who **f** had good news **Heb 4:6** *4387*

FORMING
One **f** light and creating darkness, **Is 45:7** 3335
He was **f** a locust-swarm when the **Am 7:1** 3335

FORMLESS
The earth was **f** and void, **Gn 1:2** 8414
and behold, *it was* **f** and void; **Jer 4:23** 8414

FORMS
He who **f** mountains and creates the **Am 4:13** 3335
f the spirit of man within him, **Zch 12:1** 3335
plants and **f** large branches; **Mk 4:32** *4160*

FORNICATION
"We were not born of **f**; **Jn 8:41** *4202*
and from **f** and from what is strangled **Ac 15:20** *4202*
from things strangled and from **f**; **Ac 15:29** *4202*
what is strangled and from **f**." **Ac 21:25** *4202*

FORNICATIONS
thoughts, murders, adulteries, **f**, **Mt 15:19** *4202*
men, proceed the evil thoughts, **f**, **Mk 7:21** *4202*

FORNICATORS
neither **f**, nor idolaters, nor **1Co 6:9** *4205*
f and adulterers God will judge. **Heb 13:4** *4205*

FORSAKE
do not **f** the Levite as long as you **Dt 12:19** 5800a
He will not fail you or **f** you." **Dt 31:6** 5800a
He will not fail you or **f** you. **Dt 31:8** 5800a
and will **f** Me and break My **Dt 31:16** 5800a
and I will **f** them and hide My face **Dt 31:17** 5800a
I will not fail you or **f** you. **Jos 1:5** 5800a
f the LORD to serve other gods; **Jos 24:16** 5800a
"If you **f** the LORD and serve **Jos 24:20** 5800a
and will not **f** My people Israel." **1Ki 6:13** 5800a
may He not leave us or **f** us, **1Ki 8:57** 5203
but if you **f** Him, He will reject **1Ch 28:9** 5800a
He will not fail you nor **f** you **1Ch 28:20** 5800a
"But if you turn away and **f** My **2Ch 7:19** 5800a
but if you **f** Him, He will forsake **2Ch 15:2** 5800a
if you forsake Him, He will **f** you. **2Ch 15:2** 5800a
are against all those who **f** Him." **Ezr 8:22** 5800a
And You did not **f** them. **Ne 9:17** 5800a
not **f** them in the wilderness; **Ne 9:19** 5800a
not make an end of them or **f** them, **Ne 9:31** 5800a
So that he does not **f** **Jb 6:14** 5800a
Do not abandon me nor **f** me, **Ps 27:9** 5800a
Cease from anger and **f** wrath; **Ps 37:8** 5800a
And does not **f** His godly ones; **Ps 37:28** 5800a
Do not **f** me, O LORD; **Ps 38:21** 5800a
not **f** me when my strength fails. **Ps 71:9** 5800a
old and gray, O God, do not **f** me, **Ps 71:18** 5800a
"If his sons **f** My law And do not **Ps 89:30** 5800a
Nor will He **f** His inheritance. **Ps 94:14** 5800a
Do not **f** me utterly! **Ps 119:8** 5800a
of the wicked, Who **f** Your law. **Ps 119:53** 5800a
for me, I did not **f** Your precepts. **Ps 119:87** 5800a
Do not **f** the works of Your hands. **Ps 138:8** 7503
do not **f** your mother's teaching; **Pr 1:8** 5203
"Do not **f** her, and she will guard **Pr 4:6** 5800a
not **f** the teaching of your mother; **Pr 6:20** 5203
"**F** *your* folly and live, And **Pr 9:6** 5800a
Do not **f** your own friend or your **Pr 27:10** 5800a
who **f** the law praise the wicked, **Pr 28:4** 5800a
f the LORD will come to an end. **Is 1:28** 5800a
God of Israel I will not **f** them. **Is 41:17** 5800a
Let the wicked **f** his way And the **Is 55:7** 5800a
"But you who **f** the LORD, Who **Is 65:11** 5800a
For you to **f** the LORD your God, **Jer 2:19** 5800a
called by Your name; Do not **f** us!" **Jer 14:9** 5117
midst of his days it will **f** him, **Jer 17:11** 5800a
who **f** You will be put to shame. **Jer 17:13** 5800a
f the rock of the open country? **Jer 18:14** 5800a
F her and let us each go to his **Jer 51:9** 5800a
Why do You **f** us so long? **La 5:20** 5800a
nor did they **f** the idols of Egypt. **Ezk 20:8** 5800a
"She did not **f** her harlotries **Ezk 23:8** 5800a
for those who **f** the holy covenant. **Da 11:30** 5800a
vain idols **F** their faithfulness, **Jon 2:8** 5800a
are among the Gentiles to **f** Moses, **Ac 21:21** *646*
YOU, NOR WILL I EVER **F** YOU," **Heb 13:5** *1459*

FORSAKEN
who has not **f** His lovingkindness **Gn 24:27** 5800a
your deeds, because you have **f** Me. **Dt 28:20** 5800a
"You have not **f** your brothers **Jos 22:3** 5800a
f our God and served the Baals." **Jg 10:10** 5800a
have **f** Me and served other gods; **Jg 10:13** 5800a
they have **f** Me and served other gods **1Sa 8:8** 5800a
'We have sinned because we have **f** **1Sa 12:10** 5800a
because they have **f** Me, **1Ki 11:33** 5800a
f the commandments of the LORD and **1Ki 18:18** 5800a
of Israel have **f** Your covenant, **1Ki 19:10** 5800a
of Israel have **f** Your covenant, **1Ki 19:14** 5800a
"Because they have **f** Me and have **2Ki 22:17** 5800a
'You have **f** Me, so I also have **2Ch 12:5** 5800a
I also have **f** you to Shishak.' " **2Ch 12:5** 5800a
is our God, and we have not **f** Him; **2Ch 13:10** 5800a
LORD our God, but you have **f** Him. **2Ch 13:11** 5800a
had **f** the LORD God of his fathers. **2Ch 21:10** 5800a
Because you have **f** the LORD, **2Ch 24:20** 5800a
the LORD, He has also **f** you.' " **2Ch 24:20** 5800a
because they had **f** the LORD, **2Ch 24:24** 5800a
f the LORD God of their fathers. **2Ch 28:6** 5800a
and have **f** Him and turned their **2Ch 29:6** 5800a
"Because they have **f** Me and have **2Ch 34:25** 5800a
our bondage our God has not **f** us, **Ezr 9:9** 5800a
For we have **f** Your commandments, **Ezr 9:10** 5800a
"Why is the house of God **f**?" **Ne 13:11** 5800a
he has oppressed *and* **f** the poor; **Jb 20:19** 5800a
have not **f** those who seek You. **Ps 9:10** 5800a
God, my God, why have You **f** me? **Ps 22:1** 5800a
my father and my mother have **f** me, **Ps 27:10** 5800a
I have not seen the righteous **f** Or **Ps 37:25** 5800a
God has **f** him; Pursue and seize him, **Ps 71:11** 5800a
F among the dead, Like the slain **Ps 88:5** 2670
And the **f** places are many in the **Is 6:12** 5805
two kings you dread will be **f**. **Is 7:16** 5800a
"The cities of Aroer are **f**; **Is 17:2** 5800a
be like **f** places in the forest, **Is 17:9** 5805
forlorn and **f** like the desert; **Is 27:10** 5800a
abandoned, the populated city **f**. **Is 32:14** 5800a
"The LORD has **f** me, And the Lord **Is 49:14** 5800a
He was despised and **f** of men, **Is 53:3** 2310
a wife **f** and grieved in spirit, **Is 54:6** 5800a
not **f** the ordinance of their God. **Is 58:2** 5800a
"Whereas you have been **f** and **Is 60:15** 5800a
no longer be said to you, "**F**," **Is 62:4** 5800a
"Sought out, a city not **f**." **Is 62:12** 5800a
whereby they have **f** Me and have **Jer 1:16** 5800a
They have **f** Me, The fountain of **Jer 2:13** 5800a
Every city is **f**, And no man dwells **Jer 4:29** 5800a
Your sons have **f** Me And sworn by **Jer 5:7** 5800a
'As you have **f** Me and served **Jer 5:19** 5800a
f The generation of His wrath.' **Jer 7:29** 5203
"Because they have **f** My law which **Jer 9:13** 5800a
"I have **f** My house, I have **Jer 12:7** 5800a
"You who have **f** Me," **Jer 15:6** 5203
your forefathers have **f** Me,' **Jer 16:11** 5800a
have **f** and have not kept My law. **Jer 16:11** 5800a
f the fountain of living water, **Jer 17:13** 5800a
"Because they have **f** Me and have **Jer 19:4** 5800a
nor Judah has been **f** By his God, **Jer 51:5** 488
the LORD has **f** the land.' " **Ezk 8:12** 5800a
'The LORD has **f** the land, and the **Ezk 9:9** 5800a
wastes and to the **f** cities which **Ezk 36:4** 5800a
MY GOD, WHY HAVE YOU **F** ME?" **Mt 27:46** *1459*
MY GOD, WHY HAVE YOU **F** ME?" **Mk 15:34** *1459*
persecuted, but not **f**; **2Co 4:9** *1459*

FORSAKES
is for him who **f** the way; **Pr 15:10** 5800a
and **f** *them* will find compassion. **Pr 28:13** 5800a

FORSAKING
By your **f** the LORD your God When **Jer 2:17** 5800a
flagrant harlotry, **f** the LORD." **Hos 1:2** 4480, 310
played the harlot, **f** your God. **Hos 9:1**
4480, 5921
not **f** our own assembling together, **Heb 10:25** *1459*
f the right way, they have gone **2Pe 2:15** *2641*

FORSOOK
they **f** the covenant of the LORD, **Dt 29:25** 5800a
Then he **f** God who made him, **Dt 32:15** 5203
and they **f** the LORD, the God of **Jg 2:12** 5800a
So they **f** the LORD and served Baal **Jg 2:13** 5800a
thus they **f** the LORD and did not **Jg 10:6** 5800a
'Because they **f** the LORD their **1Ki 9:9** 5800a
But he **f** the counsel of the elders **1Ki 12:8** 5800a
for he **f** the advice of the elders **1Ki 12:13** 5800a
They **f** all the commandments of **2Ki 17:16** 5800a
So he **f** the LORD, the God of his **2Ki 21:22** 5800a
they **f** their cities and fled; **1Ch 10:7** 5800a
'Because they **f** the LORD, the God **2Ch 7:22** 5800a
But he **f** the counsel of the elders **2Ch 10:8** 5800a
f the counsel of the elders. **2Ch 10:13** 5800a
with him **f** the law of the LORD. **2Ch 12:1** 5800a
"For a brief moment I **f** you, **Is 54:7** 5800a
'Because they **f** the covenant of **Jer 22:9** 5800a

FORTH
The earth brought **f** vegetation, **Gn 1:12** 3318
"Let the earth bring **f** living **Gn 1:24** 3318
pain you will bring **f** children; **Gn 3:16** 3205
that land he went **f** into Assyria, **Gn 10:11** 3318
"Go **f** from your country, And from **Gn 12:1**
So Abram went **f** as the LORD had **Gn 12:4**
will come **f** from your own body, **Gn 15:4** 3318
and kings will come **f** from you. **Gn 17:6** 3318
Now the first came **f** red, **Gn 25:25** 3318
Afterward his brother came **f** **Gn 25:26** 3318
and the flocks brought **f** striped, **Gn 30:39** 3205
all the flock brought **f** speckled; **Gn 31:8** 3205
all the flock brought **f** striped. **Gn 31:8** 3205
from Shechem's house, and went **f**. **Gn 34:26** 3318
And kings shall come **f** from you. **Gn 35:11** 3318
went **f** over the land of Egypt. **Gn 41:45** 3318
the land brought **f** abundantly. **Gn 41:47** 6213a
secret arts to bring **f** gnats, **Ex 8:18** 3318
if by now I had put **f** My hand **Ex 9:15** 7971
you are not to bring **f** any of the **Ex 12:46** 3318
of Abib, you are about to go **f**. **Ex 13:4** 3318
You send **f** Your burning anger, **Ex 15:7**
LORD, or He will break **f** upon them." **Ex 19:24** 6555
f from gate to gate in the camp, **Ex 32:27** 5674a
and come **f** and offer his burnt **Lv 16:24** 3318
bring **f** the crop for three years. **Lv 25:21** 6213a
Was it I who brought them **f**, **Nu 11:12** 3205
there went **f** a wind from the LORD and **Nu 11:31** 5265
Fire also came **f** from the LORD and **Nu 16:35** 3318
wrath has gone **f** from the LORD, **Nu 16:46** 3318
put **f** buds and produced blossoms, **Nu 17:8** 3318
You shall thus bring **f** water for **Nu 20:8** 3318
shall we bring **f** water for you out **Nu 20:10** 3318
and water came **f** abundantly, and **Nu 20:11** 3318
"For a fire went **f** from Heshbon, **Nu 21:28** 3318
A star shall come **f** from Jacob, **Nu 24:17**
flowing **f** in valleys and hills; **Dt 8:7** 3318
He shone **f** from Mount Paran, And **Dt 33:2** 3313
"Rejoice, Zebulun, in your going **f**, **Dt 33:18** 3318
whelp, That leaps **f** from Bashan." **Dt 33:22**
went **f** to anoint a king over them, **Jg 9:8** 1980
the LORD has gone **f** against me." **Ru 1:13** 3318
but David went back and **f** from **1Sa 17:15**
were not willing to put **f** their hands **1Sa 22:17** 7971
of the wicked comes **f** wickedness'; **1Sa 24:13** 3318
you, who will come **f** from you, **2Sa 7:12** 3318
brought me **f** into a broad place; **2Sa 22:20** 3318
You have brought **f** from Egypt, **1Ki 8:51** 3318
brought our fathers **f** from Egypt, **1Ki 8:53** 3318
"Go **f** and stand on the mountain **1Ki 19:11** 3318
in the house once back and **f**, **2Ki 4:35** 2008
of Jerusalem will go **f** a remnant, **2Ki 19:31** 3318
came **f** from the holy place **2Ch 5:11** 3318
himself and led his people **f**, **2Ch 25:11** 5090a
You brought **f** water from a **Ne 9:15** 3318
Mordecai walked back and **f** in front **Es 2:11**
"But put **f** Your hand now and touch **Jb 1:11** 7971
do not put **f** your hand on him." **Jb 1:12** 7971

“However, put **f** Your hand now, Jb 2:5 7971
Come **f** from the womb and expire? Jb 3:11 3318
bring **f** words from their minds? Jb 8:10 3318
a flower he comes **f** and withers. Jb 14:2 3318
And put **f** sprigs like a plant. Jb 14:9 6213a
you brought **f** before the hills? Jb 15:7 2342a
mischief and bring **f** iniquity, Jb 15:35 3205
drawn **f** and comes out of his back, Jb 20:25 8025
“They send **f** their little ones Jb 21:11 3318
will be led **f** at the day of fury. Jb 21:30 2986
tried me, I shall come **f** as gold. Jb 23:10 3318
They go **f** seeking food in their Jb 24:5 3318
When, bursting **f**, it went out from Jb 38:8 1518
And they stand **f** like a garment. Jb 38:14 3320
Can you lead **f** a constellation in its Jb 38:32 3318
“Can you send **f** lightnings that Jb 38:35 3318
down, they bring **f** their young, Jb 39:3 6398
“His sneezes flash **f** light, Jb 41:18 1984a
Sparks of fire leap **f**. Jb 41:19 4422
“Out of his nostrils smoke goes **f** As Jb 41:20 3318
And a flame goes **f** from his mouth. Jb 41:21 3318
mischief and brings **f** falsehood. Ps 7:14 3205
judgment come **f** from Your presence; Ps 17:2 3318
me **f** also into a broad place; Ps 18:19 3318
Day to day pours **f** speech, Ps 19:2 5042
brought me **f** from the womb; Ps 22:9 1518
He will bring **f** your Ps 37:6 3318
led **f** with gladness and rejoicing; Ps 45:15 2986
of beauty, God has shone **f**. Ps 50:2 3313
I was brought **f** in iniquity, Ps 51:5 2342a
He has put **f** his hands against Ps 55:20 7971
of wickedness, cast them **f**, Ps 56:7 6405
God will send **f** His lovingkindness Ps 57:3 3318
among those who breathe **f** fire, Ps 57:4 3857
they belch **f** with their mouth; Ps 59:7 5042
You not go **f** with our armies, Ps 60:10 3318
You went **f** before Your people, Ps 68:7 3318
He speaks **f** with His voice, Ps 68:33 5414
The skies gave **f** a sound; Ps 77:17
f streams also from the rock And Ps 78:16 3318
led **f** His own people like sheep And Ps 78:52 5265
above the cherubim, shine **f**! Ps 80:1 3313
God of vengeance, shine **f**! Ps 94:1 3313
They pour **f** *words,* they speak Ps 94:4 5042
Break **f** and sing for joy and sing Ps 98:4 6476
He sends **f** springs in the valleys; Ps 104:10 3318
may bring **f** food from the earth, Ps 104:14 3318
Man goes **f** to his work And to his Ps 104:23 3318
You send **f** Your Spirit, they Ps 104:30 3318
He brought **f** His people with joy, Ps 105:43 3318
Or can show **f** all His praise? Ps 106:2
You not go **f** with our armies, Ps 108:11 3318
is judged, let him come **f** guilty, Ps 109:7 3318
The LORD will stretch **f** Your strong Ps 110:2 7971
LORD From this time **f** and forever. Ps 113:2
When Israel went **f** from Egypt, Ps 114:1 3318
LORD From this time **f** and forever. Ps 115:18
in From this time **f** and forever. Ps 121:8
From this time **f** and forever. Ps 125:2
not put **f** their hands to do wrong. Ps 125:3 7971
LORD From this time **f** and forever. Ps 131:3
the horn of David to spring **f**; Ps 132:17 6779
Who brings **f** the wind from His Ps 135:7 3318
You will stretch **f** Your hand Ps 138:7 7971
f lightning and scatter them; Ps 144:6 1299
Stretch **f** Your hand from on high; Ps 144:7 7971
And our flocks bring **f** thousands Ps 144:13 503
sends **f** His command to the earth; Ps 147:15
He casts **f** His ice as fragments; Ps 147:17
sends **f** His word and melts them; Ps 147:18
were no depths I was brought **f**, Pr 8:24 2342a
Before the hills I was brought **f**; Pr 8:25 2342a
bring **f** what is acceptable, Pr 10:32 3045
The north wind brings **f** rain, Pr 25:23 2342a
not know what a day may bring **f**. Pr 27:1 3205
pressing the nose brings **f** blood; Pr 30:33 3318
God comes **f** with both of them. Ec 7:18 3318
error which goes **f** from the ruler Ec 10:5 3318
Go **f** on the trail of the flock And SS 1:8 3318
My perfume gave **f** its fragrance. SS 1:12
have given **f** *their* fragrance. SS 2:13
“Go **f**, O daughters of Zion, And SS 3:11 3318
mandrakes have given **f** fragrance; SS 7:13
For the law will go **f** from Zion And Is 2:3 3318
Will not flash **f** their light; Is 13:10 1984a
They break **f** into shouts of joy. Is 14:7 6476
the nations back and **f** in a sieve, Is 30:28 1234
For waters will break **f** in Is 35:6 1234
of Jerusalem will go **f** a remnant Is 37:32 3318
who leads **f** their host by number, Is 40:26 3318
Calling **f** the generations from the Is 41:4
Let them bring **f** and declare to us Is 41:22 5066
bring **f** justice to the nations. Is 42:1 3318
will faithfully bring **f** justice. Is 42:3 3318
Before they spring **f** I proclaim *them* Is 42:9 6779
The LORD will go **f** like a warrior, Is 42:13 3318
f the chariot and the horse, Is 43:17 3318
new, Now it will spring **f**; Is 43:19 6779
Break **f** into a shout of joy, you Is 44:23 6476
in Israel He shows **f** His glory. Is 44:23
“Declare and set **f** *your case;* Is 45:21 5066
The word has gone **f** from My mouth Is 45:23 3318
came **f** from the loins of Judah, Is 48:1 3318
ago And they went **f** from My mouth, Is 48:3 3318
Go **f** from Babylon! Is 48:20 3318
the rock and the water gushed **f**. Is 48:21
to those who are bound, ‘Go **f**,’ Is 49:9 3318
Break **f** into joyful shouting, O Is 49:13 6476
For a law will go **f** from Me, Is 51:4 3318
is near, My salvation has gone **f**, Is 51:5 3318
Break **f**, shout joyfully together, Is 52:9 6476
Break **f** into joyful shouting and Is 54:1 6476
be which goes **f** from My mouth; Is 55:11 3318
with joy And be led **f** with peace; Is 55:12 2986
hills will break **f** into shouts of joy Is 55:12 6476
recovery will speedily spring **f**; Is 58:8 6779
mischief and bring **f** iniquity. Is 59:4 3205
which is crushed a snake breaks **f**. Is 59:5 1234
as the earth brings **f** its sprouts, Is 61:11 3318
righteousness goes **f** like brightness, Is 62:1 3318
will bring **f** offspring from Jacob, Is 65:9 3318
she travailed, she brought **f**; Is 66:7 3205
a nation be brought **f** all at once? Is 66:8 3205
she also brought **f** her sons. Is 66:8 3205
“Then they will go **f** and look On Is 66:24 3318
“Out of the north the evil will break **f** Jer 1:14 6605a
Or else My wrath will go **f** like fire Jer 4:4 3318
For to You I have set **f** my cause. Jer 20:12 1540
Why did I ever come **f** from the Jer 20:18 3318
That My wrath may not go **f** like Jer 21:12 3318
who went **f** from this place, Jer 22:11 3318
has gone **f** into all the land.’ ” Jer 23:15 3318
of the LORD has gone **f** in wrath, Jer 23:19 3318
is going **f** From nation to nation, Jer 25:32 3318
shall come **f** from their midst; Jer 30:21 3318
Wrath has gone **f**, A sweeping Jer 30:23 3318
And go **f** to the dances of the Jer 31:4 3318
Branch of David to spring **f**; Jer 33:15 6779
a fire has gone **f** from Heshbon And Jer 48:45 3318
rush back and **f** inside the walls; Jer 49:3 7751a
And go **f** from the land of the Jer 50:8 3318
And has brought **f** the weapons of His Jer 50:25 3318
f the wind from His storehouses. Jer 51:16 3318
“Come **f** from her midst, My Jer 51:45 3318
tumult of their voices sounds **f**. Jer 51:55 5414
fled and went **f** from the city at night Jer 52:7 3318
High That both good and ill go **f**? La 3:38 3318
a great cloud with fire flashing **f** Ezk 1:4 3947
and **f** among the living beings. Ezk 1:13
Your doom has gone **f**; Ezk 7:10 3318
they are going to come **f** to you Ezk 14:22 3318
“Then your fame went **f** among the Ezk 16:14 3318
may bring **f** boughs and bear fruit and Ezk 17:23 5375
therefore My sword will go **f** from Ezk 21:4 3318
they set **f** your splendor. Ezk 27:10
“On that day messengers will go **f** Ezk 30:9 3318
And you burst **f** in your rivers And Ezk 32:2 1518
is which comes **f** from the LORD.’ Ezk 33:30 3318
you will put **f** your branches and Ezk 36:8
who bring **f** sons in your midst. Ezk 47:22 3205
So the decree went **f** that the wise Da 2:13 5312
who had gone **f** to slay the wise Da 2:14 5312
came **f** a rather small horn which Da 8:9 3318
I have now come **f** to give you Da 9:22 3318
so I am going **f**, and behold, the Da 10:20 3318
South will be enraged and go **f** and Da 11:11 3318
and he will go **f** with great wrath Da 11:44 3318
many will go back and **f**, Da 12:4 7751a
going **f** is as certain as the dawn; Hos 6:3 4161
are *like* the light that goes **f**. Hos 6:5 3318
“The city which goes **f** a thousand Am 5:3 3318
And the one which goes **f** a hundred Am 5:3 3318
live, Or He will break **f** like a fire, Am 5:6 6743a
It is He who flashes **f** *with* Am 5:9 1082
will cast them **f** in silence.” Am 8:3
you Will send you **f** to the border, Ob 1:7
LORD is coming **f** from His place. Mi 1:3 3318
For from Zion will go **f** the law, Mi 4:2 3318
go **f** for Me to be ruler in Israel. Mi 5:2 3318
His goings **f** are from long ago, Mi 5:2 4163
From you has gone **f** One who Na 1:11 3318
The deep uttered **f** its voice, Hab 3:10 5414
You went **f** for the salvation Hab 3:13 3318
bring **f** the top stone with shouts of Zch 4:7 3318
“This is the curse that is going **f** Zch 5:3 3318
“I will make it go **f**,” Zch 5:4 3318
and see what this is going **f**.” Zch 5:5 3318
“This is the ephah going **f**.” Zch 5:6 3318
four chariots were coming **f** from Zch 6:1 3318
the four spirits of heaven, going **f** Zch 6:5 3318
are going **f** to the north country; Zch 6:6 3318
the white ones go **f** after them, Zch 6:6 3318
ones go **f** to the south country. Zch 6:6 3318
so that no one went back and **f**, Zch 7:14 5674a
arrow will go **f** like lightning; Zch 9:14 3318
Then the LORD will go **f** and fight Zch 14:3 3318
and you will go **f** and skip about Mal 4:2 3318
OUT OF YOU SHALL COME **F** A RULER Mt 2:6 *1831*
indeed bears fruit and brings **f**, Mt 13:23 *4160*
Son of Man will send **f** His angels, Mt 13:41 *649*
“Then THE RIGHTEOUS WILL SHINE **F** Mt 13:43 *1584*
the angels will come **f** Mt 13:49 *1831*
“And He will send **f** His angels Mt 24:31 *649*
tender and puts **f** its leaves, Mt 24:32 *1631*
proceeding from Him had gone **f**, Mk 5:30 *1831*
then He will send **f** the angels, Mk 13:27 *649*
tender and puts **f** its leaves, Mk 13:28 *1631*
his heart brings **f** what is good; Lk 6:45 *4393*
treasure brings **f** what is evil; Lk 6:45 *4393*
as soon as they put **f** *leaves,* Lk 21:30 *4261*
I am sending **f** the promise of My Lk 24:49 *1821*
He went **f** from there into Galilee. Jn 4:43 *1831*
and will come **f**; Jn 5:29 *1607*
I proceeded **f** and have come from Jn 8:42 *1831*
“When he puts **f** all his own, he Jn 10:4 *1544b*
“Lazarus, come **f**.” Jn 11:43 *1854*
man who had died came **f**, Jn 11:44 *1831*
and that He had come **f** from God and Jn 13:3 *1831*
that I came **f** from the Father. Jn 16:27 *1831*
“I came **f** from the Father and Jn 16:28 *1831*
that I came **f** from You, Jn 17:8 *1831*
He went **f** with His disciples over Jn 18:1 *1831*
that were coming upon Him, went **f** and Jn 18:4 *1831*
So Peter and the other disciple went **f**, Jn 20:3 *1831*
F OF MY SPIRIT ON ALL MANKIND; Ac 2:17 *1632a*
I WILL IN THOSE DAYS POUR **F** OF MY Ac 2:18 *1632a*
He has poured **f** this which you Ac 2:33 *1632a*
Lord has sent **f** His angel and rescued Ac 12:11 *1821*
that the word of God *first* went **f**? 1Co 14:36 *1831*
the time came, God sent **f** His Son, Ga 4:4 *1821*
God has sent **f** the Spirit of His Ga 4:6 *1821*
BREAK **F** AND SHOUT, YOU WHO ARE Ga 4:27 *4486*
may speak **f** the mystery of Christ, Col 4:3 *2980*
the Lord has sounded **f** from you, 1Th 1:8 *1837*
your faith toward God has gone **f**, 1Th 1:8 *1831*
falls on it and brings **f** vegetation Heb 6:7 *5088*
accomplished, it brings **f** death. Jas 1:15 *616*
brought us **f** by the word of truth, Jas 1:18 *616*

FORTIETH
in the **f** year after the sons of Nu 33:38 705
In the **f** year, Dt 1:3 705
in the **f** year of David's reign, 1Ch 26:31 705

FORTIFICATIONS
they like *open* camps or with **f**? Nu 13:19 4013
The unassailable **f** of your Is 25:12 4013
land And tear down all your **f**. Mi 5:11 4013
All your **f** are fig trees with ripe Na 3:12 4013
Strengthen your **f**! Na 3:14 4013

FORTIFIED
the cities are **f** *and* very large; Nu 13:28 1219
while our little ones live in the **f** cities Nu 32:17 4013
and Beth-haran as **f** cities, Nu 32:36 4013
cities are large and **f** to heaven. Dt 1:28 1219
were cities **f** with high walls, Dt 3:5 1219
you, great cities **f** to heaven, Dt 9:1 1219
high and **f** walls in which you trusted Dt 28:52 1219
of them had entered the **f** cities, Jos 10:20 4013
were there, with great **f** cities; Jos 14:12 1219
Ramah and to the **f** city of Tyre; Jos 19:29 4013
The **f** cities *were* Ziddim, Zer Jos 19:35 4013
both of **f** cities and of country 1Sa 6:18 4013
does not find for himself **f** cities 2Sa 20:6 1219
went up against Judah and **f** Ramah 1Ki 15:17 1129
f city and every choice city, 2Ki 3:19 4013
and a **f** city and the weapons, 2Ki 10:2 4013
towns, from watchtower to **f** city. 2Ki 17:9 4013
from watchtower to **f** city. 2Ki 18:8 4013
Assyria came up against all the **f** cities 2Ki 18:13 1219
turn **f** cities into ruinous heaps. 2Ki 19:25 1219
Beth-horon, **f** cities *with* walls, 2Ch 8:5 4692
which are **f** cities in Judah and in 2Ch 11:10 4694
and Benjamin to all the **f** cities, 2Ch 11:23 4694
He captured the **f** cities of 2Ch 12:4 4694
He built **f** cities in Judah, 2Ch 14:6 4694
f Ramah in order to prevent *anyone* 2Ch 16:1 1129
with them he **f** Geba and Mizpah. 2Ch 16:6 1129
in all the **f** cities of Judah, 2Ch 17:2 1219
in the **f** cities through all Judah. 2Ch 17:19 4013
land in all the **f** cities of Judah, 2Ch 19:5 1219
things, with **f** cities in Judah, 2Ch 21:3 4694
at the corner buttress and **f** them. 2Ch 26:9 2388
Judah and besieged the **f** cities, 2Ch 32:1 1219
in all the **f** cities of Judah. 2Ch 33:14 1219
all its **f** buildings with fire and 2Ch 36:19 759
f cities and a fertile land. Ne 9:25 1219
high tower, Against every **f** wall, Is 2:15 1219
Hyenas will howl in their **f** towers Is 13:22 490
“The **f** city will disappear from Is 17:3 4013
into a heap, A **f** city into a ruin; Is 25:2 1219
For the **f** city is isolated, A Is 27:10 1219
will come up in its **f** towers, Is 34:13 4013
and thistles in its **f** cities; Is 34:13 4013
Assyria came up against all the **f** cities Is 36:1 1219
turn **f** cities into ruinous heaps. Is 37:26 1219
I have made you today as a **f** city and Jer 1:18 4013
and let us go Into the **f** cities.’ Jer 4:5 4013
your **f** cities in which you trust. Jer 5:17 4013
and let us go into the **f** cities And Jer 8:14 4013
to this people A **f** wall of bronze; Jer 15:20 1219
for they *alone* remained as **f** cities Jer 34:7 4013
devour the **f** towers of Ben-hadad.” Jer 49:27 759
‘He destroyed their **f** towers Ezk 19:7 490
and to Judah into **f** Jerusalem. Ezk 21:20 1219
cities are **f** *and* inhabited.’ Ezk 36:35 1219
And Judah has multiplied **f** cities, Hos 8:14 1219
Against the **f** cities And the high Zph 1:16 1219

FORTIFY
tore down houses to **f** the wall. Is 22:10 1219
she should **f** her lofty stronghold, Jer 51:53 1219

FORTIFYING
of it, he ceased **f** Ramah 1Ki 15:21 1129
f Ramah and stopped his work. 2Ch 16:5 1129

FORTRESS
my rock and my **f** and my deliverer; 2Sa 22:2 4686b
“God is my strong **f**; 2Sa 22:33 4581
and came to the **f** of Tyre and to 2Sa 24:7 4013
In Ecbatana in the **f**, Ezr 6:2 1003b
of the **f** which is by the temple, Ne 2:8 1002
Hananiah the commander of the **f**, Ne 7:2 1002
my rock and my **f** and my deliverer, Ps 18:2 4686b
For You are my rock and my **f**; Ps 31:3 4686b
me, For You are my rock and my **f**. Ps 71:3 4686b
“My refuge and my **f**, Ps 91:2 4686b
My lovingkindness and my **f**, Ps 144:2 4686b
The rich man's wealth is his **f**, Pr 10:15 7151, 5797

the **f** of the king of the North, **Da 11:7** 4581
again wage war up to his *very* **f**. **Da 11:10** 4581
arise, desecrate the sanctuary **f**, **Da 11:31** 4581
that destruction comes upon the **f**. **Am 5:9** 4013
Man the **f**, watch the road; **Na 2:1** 4694
They laugh at every **f** And **Hab 1:10** 4013
a **f** And piled up silver like dust, **Zch 9:3** 4692

FORTRESSES
And come trembling out of their **f**. **2Sa 22:46** 4526
He also strengthened the **f** and put **2Ch 11:11** 4694
built **f** and store cities in Judah. **2Ch 17:12** 1003a
and he built **f** and towers on the **2Ch 27:4** 1003a
And come trembling out of their **f**. **Ps 18:45** 4526
face toward the **f** of his own land, **Da 11:19** 4581
instead he will honor a god of **f**, **Da 11:38** 4581
take action against the strongest of **f** **Da 11:39** 4581
And all your **f** will be destroyed, **Hos 10:14** 4013
come trembling out of their **f**; **Mi 7:17** 4526
powerful for the destruction of **f**. **2Co 10:4** *3794*

FORTUNATE
Then Leah said, "How **f**!" **Gn 30:11** 1409
by the Jews, I consider myself **f**, **Ac 26:2** *3107*

FORTUNATUS
of Stephanas and **F** and Achaicus, **1Co 16:17** *5415*

FORTUNE
mountain, Who set a table for **F**, **Is 65:11** 1409
not laid, *So* is he who makes a **f**, **Jer 17:11** 6239
care for them And restore their **f**. **Zph 2:7** 7622

FORTUNES
The LORD restored the **f** of Job **Jb 42:10** 7622
'and I will restore your **f** and **Jer 29:14** 7622
f of My people Israel and Judah.' **Jer 30:3** 7622
I will restore the **f** of the tents **Jer 30:18** 7622
cities when I restore their **f**, **Jer 31:23** 7622
for I will restore their **f**,' **Jer 32:44** 7622
'I will restore the **f** of Judah **Jer 33:7** 7622
of Judah and the **f** of Israel and **Jer 33:7** 7622
For I will restore the **f** of the **Jer 33:11** 7622
I will restore their **f** and will have **Jer 33:26** 7622
f of Moab In the latter days," **Jer 48:47** 7622
The **f** of the sons of Ammon," **Jer 49:6** 7622
I will restore the **f** of Elam,' " **Jer 49:39** 7622
"I will turn the **f** of Egypt **Ezk 29:14** 7622
I will restore the **f** of Jacob **Ezk 39:25** 7622
When I restore the **f** of My people. **Hos 6:11** 7622
the **f** of Judah and Jerusalem, **Jl 3:1** 7622
restore your **f** before your eyes," **Zph 3:20** 7622

FORTUNE-TELLERS
And you will have **f** no more. **Mi 5:12** 6049a

FORTUNE-TELLING
bringing her masters much profit by **f**. **Ac 16:16** *3132*

FORTY
Kenan lived eight hundred and **f** years **Gn 5:13** 705
the earth **f** days and forty nights. **Gn 7:4** 705
the earth forty days and **f** nights; **Gn 7:4** 705
earth for **f** days and forty nights. **Gn 7:12** 705
earth for forty days and **f** nights. **Gn 7:12** 705
came upon the earth for **f** days, **Gn 7:17** 705
came about at the end of **f** days, **Gn 8:6** 705
"Suppose **f** are found there?" **Gn 18:29** 705
not do *it* on account of the **f**." **Gn 18:29** 705
and Isaac was **f** years old when he **Gn 25:20** 705
When Esau was **f** years old he **Gn 26:34** 705
their colts, **f** cows and ten bulls, **Gn 32:15** 705
Now **f** days were required for it, **Gn 50:3** 705
of Israel ate the manna **f** years, **Ex 16:35** 705
mountain **f** days and forty nights. **Ex 24:18** 705
mountain forty days and **f** nights. **Ex 24:18** 705
"You shall make **f** sockets of **Ex 26:19** 705
and their **f** sockets of silver; **Ex 26:21** 705
the LORD **f** days and forty nights; **Ex 34:28** 705
the LORD forty days and **f** nights; **Ex 34:28** 705
and he made **f** sockets of silver **Ex 36:24** 705
and their **f** sockets of silver; **Ex 36:26** 705
the land, at the end of **f** days, **Nu 13:25** 705
for **f** years in the wilderness, **Nu 14:33** 705
you spied out the land, **f** days, **Nu 14:34** 705
your guilt a year, *even* **f** years, **Nu 14:34** 705
wander in the wilderness **f** years, **Nu 32:13** 705
These **f** years the LORD your God **Dt 2:7** 705
in the wilderness these **f** years, **Dt 8:2** 705
did your foot swell these **f** years. **Dt 8:4** 705
on the mountain **f** days and nights; **Dt 9:9** 705
It came about at the end of **f** days **Dt 9:11** 705
at the first, **f** days and nights; **Dt 9:18** 705
the LORD the **f** days and nights, **Dt 9:25** 705
stayed on the mountain **f** days and **Dt 10:10** 705
and **f** nights like the first time, **Dt 10:10** 705
may beat him **f** times *but* no more, **Dt 25:3** 705
led you **f** years in the wilderness; **Dt 29:5** 705
walked **f** years in the wilderness, **Jos 5:6** 705
"I was **f** years old when Moses the **Jos 14:7** 705
Then the land had rest **f** years. **Jg 3:11** 705
seen Among **f** thousand in Israel. **Jg 5:8** 705
land was undisturbed for **f** years. **Jg 5:31** 705
for **f** years in the days of Gideon. **Jg 8:28** 705
He had **f** sons and thirty **Jg 12:14** 705
hands of the Philistines **f** years. **Jg 13:1** 705
Thus he judged Israel **f** years. **1Sa 4:18** 705
and he reigned **f** two years over **1Sa 13:1**
morning and evening for **f** days and **1Sa 17:16** 705
was **f** years old when he became **2Sa 2:10** 705
king, *and* he reigned **f** years. **2Sa 5:4** 705
at the end of **f** years that Absalom **2Sa 15:7** 705
reigned over Israel *were* **f** years: **1Ki 2:11** 705
sanctuary, was **f** cubits *long*. **1Ki 6:17** 705
of bronze, one basin held **f** baths; **1Ki 7:38** 705
over all Israel was **f** years. **1Ki 11:42** 705
in the strength of that food **f** days and **1Ki 19:8** 705
forty days and **f** nights to Horeb, **1Ki 19:8** 705
thing of Damascus, **f** camels' loads; **2Ki 8:9** 705
he reigned **f** years in Jerusalem; **2Ki 12:1** 705
reigned over Israel *was* **f** years; **1Ch 29:27** 705
Solomon reigned **f** years in **2Ch 9:30** 705
he reigned **f** years in Jerusalem; **2Ch 24:1** 705
wine besides **f** shekels of silver; **Ne 5:15** 705
f years You provided for **Ne 9:21** 705
"For **f** years I loathed *that* **Ps 95:10** 705
assigned it to you for **f** days, **Ezk 4:6** 705
will not be inhabited for **f** years. **Ezk 29:11** 705
waste, will be desolate **f** years; **Ezk 29:12** 705
"At the end of **f** years I will **Ezk 29:13** 705
the length of the nave, **f** cubits, **Ezk 41:2** 705
f *cubits* long and thirty wide; **Ezk 46:22** 705
I led you in the wilderness **f** years **Am 2:10** 705
in the wilderness for **f** years, **Am 5:25** 705
"Yet **f** days and Nineveh will be **Jon 3:4** 705
fasted **f** days and forty nights, **Mt 4:2** *5065b*
fasted forty days and **f** nights, **Mt 4:2** *5065b*
f days being tempted by Satan; **Mk 1:13** *5065b*
for **f** days, being tempted by the **Lk 4:2** *5065b*
to them over a *period of* **f** days and **Ac 1:3** *5065b*
for the man was more than **f** years **Ac 4:22** *5065b*
he was approaching the age of **f**, **Ac 7:23** *5066a*
"After **f** years had passed, AN **Ac 7:30** *5065b*
and in the wilderness for **f** years. **Ac 7:36** *5065b*
F YEARS IN THE WILDERNESS, **Ac 7:42** *5065b*
"For a period of about **f** **Ac 13:18** *5066a*
tribe of Benjamin, for **f** years. **Ac 13:21** *5065b*
more than **f** who formed this plot. **Ac 23:13** *5065b*
for more than **f** of them are lying **Ac 23:21** *5065b*
AND SAW MY WORKS FOR F YEARS **Heb 3:9** *5065b*
whom was He angry for **f** years? **Heb 3:17** *5065b*

FORTY-EIGHT
to the Levites *shall be* **f** cities, **Nu 35:7**
705, 8083
of the sons of Israel were **f** cities **Jos 21:41**
705, 8083

FORTY-FIRST
died in the **f** year of his reign. **2Ch 16:13**
705, 259

FORTY-FIVE
destroy *it* if I find **f** there." **Gn 18:28**
705, 2568
just as He spoke, these **f** years, **Jos 14:10**
705, 2568

FORTY-FOUR
one hundred and **f** thousand sealed **Rv 7:4**
5065b, 5064
Him one hundred and **f** thousand, **Rv 14:1**
5065b, 5064
one hundred and **f** thousand who had **Rv 14:3**
5065b, 5064

FORTY-NINE
of years, *namely*, **f** years. **Lv 25:8**
705, 8672

FORTY-ONE
Rehoboam was **f** years old when he **1Ki 14:21**
705, 259
He reigned **f** years in Jerusalem; **1Ki 15:10**
705, 259
in Samaria, *and reigned* **f** years. **2Ki 14:23**
705, 259
Now Rehoboam was **f** years old when **2Ch 12:13**
705, 259

FORTY-SEVEN
life was one hundred and **f** years. **Gn 47:28**
705, 7651

FORTY-SIX
took **f** years to build this temple, **Jn 2:20**
5065b, 2532, 1803

FORTY-TWO
to them you shall give **f** cities. **Nu 35:6**
705, 8147
tore up **f** lads of their number. **2Ki 2:24**
705, 8147
at the pit of Beth-eked, **f** men; **2Ki 10:14**
705, 8147
foot the holy city for **f** months. **Rv 11:2**
5065b, 1417
act for **f** months was given to him. **Rv 13:5**
5065b, 1417

FORWARD
Tell the sons of Israel to go **f**. **Ex 14:15** 5265
"Come **f**, carry your relatives **Lv 10:4** 7126
So they came **f** and carried them **Lv 10:5** 7126
When they had both come **f**, **Nu 12:5** 3318
"Go **f**, and march around the city, **Jos 6:7** 5674a
LORD went **f** and blew the trumpets; **Jos 6:8** 5674a
company who was with him dashed **f** **Jg 9:44**
the man was startled and bent **f**; **Ru 3:8** 3943
upon David from that day **f**. **1Sa 16:13** 4605
The Philistine came **f** morning **1Sa 17:16** 5066
So it has been from that day **f**, **1Sa 30:25** 4605
and as he went **f**, it fell out. **2Sa 20:8** 3318
"Then a spirit came **f** and stood **1Ki 22:21** 3318
and they went **f** into the land, **2Ki 3:24**
said to her servant, "Drive and go **f**; **2Ki 4:24**
shall the shadow go **f** ten steps or **2Ki 20:9**
"Then a spirit came **f** and stood **2Ch 18:20** 3318
I go **f** but He is not *there*, **Jb 23:8** 6924a
Let them come **f**, then let them **Is 41:1** 5066
"Bring **f** your strong *arguments*," **Is 41:21** 5066
and went backward and not **f**. **Jer 7:24** 6440
That the mighty men may march **f**: **Jer 46:9** 3318
they moved, each went straight **f**. **Ezk 1:9** 6440
And each went straight **f**; **Ezk 1:12** 6440
Chaldeans came **f** and brought charges **Da 3:8** 7127
Their horde of faces *moves* **f**. **Hab 1:9** 6921
many false witnesses came **f**. **Mt 26:60** *4334*
But later on two came **f**, **Mt 26:60** *4334*
"Get up and come **f**!" **Mk 3:3**
1519, 3319
and came **f** and questioned Jesus, **Mk 14:60**
1519, 3319
"Get up and come **f**!" **Lk 6:8**
1519, 3319
And he got up and came **f**. **Lk 6:8**
So they put **f** two men, Joseph **Ac 1:23** *2476*
put **f** false witnesses who said, **Ac 6:13** *2476*
Herod was about to bring him **f**, **Ac 12:6** *4254*
since the Jews had put him **f**; **Ac 19:33** *4261*
and reaching **f** to what *lies* ahead, **Php 3:13** *1901*

FOUGHT
and **f** against Israel at Rephidim. **Ex 17:8** 3898a
told him, and **f** against Amalek; **Ex 17:10** 3898a
Atharim, then he **f** against Israel and **Nu 21:1** 3898a
to Jahaz and **f** against Israel. **Nu 21:23** 3898a
who had **f** against the former king **Nu 21:26** 3898a
camped by Gibeon and **f** against it. **Jos 10:5** 3898a
for the LORD **f** for Israel. **Jos 10:14** 3898a
to Libnah, and **f** against Libnah. **Jos 10:29** 3898a
camped by it and **f** against it. **Jos 10:31** 3898a
camped by it and **f** against it. **Jos 10:34** 3898a
to Hebron, and they **f** against it. **Jos 10:36** 3898a
to Debir, and they **f** against it. **Jos 10:38** 3898a
the God of Israel, **f** for Israel. **Jos 10:42** 3898a
and **f** with Leshem and captured it. **Jos 19:47** 3898a
the Jordan, and they **f** with you; **Jos 24:8** 3898a
Moab, arose and **f** against Israel, **Jos 24:9** 3898a
citizens of Jericho **f** against you, **Jos 24:11** 3898a
found Adoni-bezek in Bezek and **f** **Jg 1:5** 3898a
sons of Judah **f** against Jerusalem **Jg 1:8** 3898a
"The kings came *and* **f**; **Jg 5:19** 3898a
Then **f** the kings of Canaan At **Jg 5:19** 3898a
"The stars **f** from heaven, From **Jg 5:20** 3898a
courses they **f** against Sisera. **Jg 5:20** 3898a
for my father **f** for you and risked **Jg 9:17** 3898a
of Shechem and **f** with Abimelech. **Jg 9:39** 3898a
f against the city all that day, **Jg 9:45** 3898a
to the tower and **f** against it, **Jg 9:52** 3898a
sons of Ammon **f** against Israel. **Jg 11:4** 3898a
the sons of Ammon **f** against Israel **Jg 11:5** 3898a
in Jahaz and **f** with Israel. **Jg 11:20** 3898a
the men of Gilead and **f** Ephraim; **Jg 12:4** 3898a
f and Israel was defeated, **1Sa 4:10** 3898a
of Moab, and they **f** against them. **1Sa 12:9** 3898a
he **f** against all his enemies on **1Sa 14:47** 3898a
out and **f** with the Philistines and **1Sa 19:8** 3898a
Keilah and **f** with the Philistines; **1Sa 23:5** 3898a
because he had **f** against Hadadezer **2Sa 8:10** 3898a
to meet David and **f** against him. **2Sa 10:17** 3898a
city went out and **f** against Joab, **2Sa 11:17** 3898a
Now Joab **f** against Rabbah of the **2Sa 12:26** 3898a
"I have **f** against Rabbah, I have **2Sa 12:27** 3898a
and went to Rabbah, **f** against it and **2Sa 12:29** 3898a
as they **f** against the Philistines, **2Sa 21:15** 3898a
Samaria and **f** against it. **1Ki 20:1** 3898a
the kings have surely **f** together, **2Ki 3:23** 2717c
he **f** against Hazael king of Aram. **2Ki 8:29** 3898a
he **f** with Hazael king of Aram. **2Ki 9:15** 3898a
f against Gath and captured it, **2Ki 12:17** 3898a
f against Amaziah king of Judah, **2Ki 13:12** 3898a
he **f** with Amaziah king of Judah, **2Ki 14:15** 3898a
how he **f** and how he recovered for **2Ki 14:28** 3898a
the Philistines **f** against Israel; **1Ch 10:1** 3898a
because he had **f** against Hadadezer **1Ch 18:10** 3898a
the Arameans, they **f** against him. **1Ch 19:17** 3898a
f against the enemies of Israel. **2Ch 20:29** 3898a
he **f** against Hazael king of Aram. **2Ch 22:6** 3898a
He **f** also with the king of the **2Ch 27:5** 3898a
And **f** against me without cause. **Ps 109:3** 3898a
he **f** against Ashdod and captured it, **Is 20:1** 3898a
their enemy, He **f** against them. **Is 63:10** 3898a
I **f** with wild beasts at Ephesus, **1Co 15:32** *2341*
I have **f** the good fight, I have **2Tm 4:7** *75*

FOUL
die, and the Nile will become **f**, **Ex 7:18** 887
Nile died, and the Nile became **f**, **Ex 7:21** 887
in heaps, and the land became **f**. **Ex 8:14** 887
and it bred worms and became **f**; **Ex 16:20** 887
ordered, and it did not become **f** nor **Ex 16:24** 887
My wounds grow **f** *and* fester Because **Ps 38:5** 887
must **f** the rest with your feet? **Ezk 34:18** 7511
what you **f** with your feet!' " **Ezk 34:19** 4833
and its **f** smell will come up, **Jl 2:20** 6709

FOULED
your feet And **f** their rivers.' " **Ezk 32:2** 7511

FOUND
not **f** a helper suitable for him. **Gn 2:20** 4672
f favor in the eyes of the LORD. **Gn 6:8** 4672
but the dove **f** no resting place **Gn 8:9** 4672
they **f** a plain in the land of Shinar **Gn 11:2** 4672
Now the angel of the LORD **f** her by **Gn 16:7** 4672
now I have **f** favor in Your sight, **Gn 18:3** 4672
"Suppose forty are **f** there?" **Gn 18:29** 4672
suppose thirty are **f** there?" **Gn 18:30** 4672
suppose twenty are **f** there?" **Gn 18:31** 4672
suppose ten are **f** there?" **Gn 18:32** 4672
servant has **f** favor in your sight, **Gn 19:19** 4672
f there a well of flowing water, **Gn 26:19** 4672
"We have **f** water." **Gn 26:32** 4672

went and f mandrakes in the field,	Gn 30:14	4672
if f with me, will be considered	Gn 30:33	
you f of all your household goods?	Gn 31:37	4672
now I have f favor in your sight,	Gn 33:10	4672
he is the Anah who f the hot springs	Gn 36:24	4672
A man f him, and behold, he	Gn 37:15	4672
his brothers and f them at Dothan.	Gn 37:17	4672
"We f this; please examine *it* to *see*	Gn 37:32	4672
So Joseph f favor in his sight and	Gn 39:4	4672
the money which we f in the mouth	Gn 44:8	4672
whomever of your servants it is f,	Gn 44:9	4672
whom it is f shall be my slave,	Gn 44:10	4672
the cup was f in Benjamin's sack.	Gn 44:12	4672
God has f out the iniquity of your	Gn 44:16	4672
possession the cup has been f."	Gn 44:16	4672
possession the cup has been f,	Gn 44:17	4672
money that was f in the land of Egypt	Gn 47:14	4672
if I have f favor in your sight,	Gn 47:29	4672
now I have f favor in your sight,	Gn 50:4	4672
Every man and beast that is f in	Ex 9:19	4672
be no leaven f in your houses;	Ex 12:19	4672
in the wilderness and f no water.	Ex 15:22	4672
out to gather, but they f none.	Ex 16:27	4672
him or he is f in his possession,	Ex 21:16	4672
f alive in his possession,	Ex 22:4	4672
have also f favor in My sight.'	Ex 33:12	4672
if I have f favor in Your sight,	Ex 33:13	4672
that I have f favor in Your sight,	Ex 33:16	4672
for you have f favor in My sight and	Ex 33:17	4672
now I have f favor in Your sight,	Ex 34:9	4672
or has f what was lost and lied	Lv 6:3	4672
him or the lost thing which he f,	Lv 6:4	4672
'But if he has not f sufficient	Lv 25:28	4672
have I not f favor in Your sight,	Nu 11:11	4672
if I have f favor in Your sight,	Nu 11:15	4672
they f a man gathering wood on the	Nu 15:32	4672
Those who f him gathering wood	Nu 15:33	4672
to the LORD what each man f,	Nu 31:50	4672
"If we have f favor in your	Nu 32:5	4672
"If there is f in your midst, in	Dt 17:2	4672
"There shall not be f among you	Dt 18:10	4672
all the people who are f in it shall	Dt 20:11	4672
"If a slain person is f lying in	Dt 21:1	4672
which he has lost and you have f,	Dt 22:3	4672
that the girl was not f a virgin,	Dt 22:20	4672
is f lying with a married woman,	Dt 22:22	4672
"When he f her in the field, the	Dt 22:27	4672
he has f some indecency in her,	Dt 24:1	4672
"He f him in a desert land, And	Dt 32:10	4672
the road, but had not f *them.*	Jos 2:22	4672
"The five kings have been f	Jos 10:17	4672
They f Adoni-bezek in Bezek	Jg 1:5	4672
now I have f favor in Your sight,	Jg 6:17	4672
would not have f out my riddle."	Jg 14:18	4672
He f a fresh jawbone of a donkey,	Jg 15:15	4672
the cattle and all that they f;	Jg 20:48	4672
fire all the cities which they f.	Jg 20:48	4672
And they f among the inhabitants	Jg 21:12	4672
"Why have I f favor in your sight	Ru 2:10	4672
"I have f favor in your sight, my	Ru 2:13	4672
they f young women going out to	1Sa 9:11	4672
on them, for they have been f.	1Sa 9:20	4672
you went to look for have been f.	1Sa 10:2	4672
we saw that they could not be f,	1Sa 10:14	369
that the donkeys had been f."	1Sa 10:16	4672
looked for him, he could not be f.	1Sa 10:21	4672
you have f nothing in my hand."	1Sa 12:5	4672
be f in all the land of Israel,	1Sa 13:19	4672
neither sword nor spear was f in the	1Sa 13:22	4672
but they were f with Saul and his	1Sa 13:22	4672
of their enemies which they f!	1Sa 14:30	4672
for he has f favor in my sight."	1Sa 16:22	4672
that I have f favor in your sight,	1Sa 20:3	4672
if I have f favor in your sight,	1Sa 20:29	4672
of bread, or whatever can be f."	1Sa 21:3	4672
not be f in you all your days.	1Sa 25:28	4672
now I have f favor in your sight,	1Sa 27:5	4672
and I have f no fault in him from	1Sa 29:3	4672
for I have not f evil in you from	1Sa 29:6	4672
what have you f in your servant	1Sa 29:8	4672
Now they f an Egyptian in the	1Sa 30:11	4672
that they f Saul and his three	1Sa 31:8	4672
Your servant has f courage to pray	2Sa 7:27	4672
that I have f favor in your sight,	2Sa 14:22	4672
of the places where he can be f,	2Sa 17:12	4672
even a small stone is f there."	2Sa 17:13	4672
and f Abishag the Shunammite,	1Ki 1:3	4672
but if wickedness is f in him,	1Ki 1:52	4672
f great favor before Pharaoh,	1Ki 11:19	4672
the Shilonite f him on the road.	1Ki 11:29	4672
and f him sitting under an oak;	1Ki 13:14	4672
He went and f his body thrown	1Ki 13:28	4672
in him something good was f toward	1Ki 14:13	4672
and f Elisha the son of Shaphat,	1Ki 19:19	4672
departed from him a lion f him and	1Ki 20:36	4672
Then he f another man and said,	1Ki 20:37	4672
"Have you f me, O my enemy?"	1Ki 21:20	4672
"I have f *you,* because you have	1Ki 21:20	4672
and f a wild vine and gathered	2Ki 4:39	4672
they went out to meet Jehu and f him	2Ki 9:21	4672
but they f nothing more of her than the	2Ki 9:35	4672
wherever any damage may be f.	2Ki 12:5	4672
was f in the house of the LORD.	2Ki 12:10	4672
gold that was f among the treasuries	2Ki 12:18	4672
were f in the house of the LORD,	2Ki 14:14	4672
silver and gold that was f in the house	2Ki 16:8	4672
of Assyria f conspiracy in Hoshea,	2Ki 17:4	4672
the silver which was f in the house	2Ki 18:15	4672
Then Rabshakeh returned and f the	2Ki 19:8	4672
all that was f in his treasuries.	2Ki 20:13	4672
"I have f the book of the law in	2Ki 22:8	4672
the money that was f in the house,	2Ki 22:9	4672
of this book that has been f,	2Ki 22:13	4672
was f in the house of the LORD.	2Ki 23:2	4672
priest f in the house of the LORD.	2Ki 23:24	4672
advisers who were f in the city;	2Ki 25:19	4672
the land who were f in the city.	2Ki 25:19	4672
They f rich and good pasture,	1Ch 4:40	4672
and the Meunites who were f there,	1Ch 4:41	4672
that they f Saul and his sons	1Ch 10:8	4672
f *courage* to pray before You.	1Ch 17:25	4672
he f it to weigh a talent of gold,	1Ch 20:2	4672
Since more chief men were f from	1Ch 24:4	4672
f among them at Jazer of Gilead)	1Ch 26:31	4672
and 153,600 were f.	2Ch 2:17	4672
of the bronze could not be f out.	2Ch 4:18	2713
spoil, they f much among them,	2Ch 20:25	4672
the possessions f in the king's house	2Ch 21:17	4672
he f the princes of Judah and the	2Ch 22:8	4672
f them to be 300,000 choice men,	2Ch 25:5	4672
utensils which were f in the house of	2Ch 25:24	4672
and every unclean thing which they f	2Ch 29:16	4672
Hilkiah the priest f the book of	2Ch 34:14	4672
"I have f the book of the law in	2Ch 34:15	4672
was f in the house of the LORD,	2Ch 34:17	4672
of the book which has been f;	2Ch 34:21	4672
was f in the house of the LORD.	2Ch 34:30	4672
did, and what was f against him,	2Ch 36:8	4672
a scroll was f and there was	Ezr 6:2	7912
who had married foreign wives were f	Ezr 10:18	4672
servant has f favor before you,	Ne 2:5	3190
Then I f the book of the genealogy	Ne 7:5	4672
in which I f the following record:	Ne 7:5	4672
They f written in the law how	Ne 8:14	4672
"You f his heart faithful before You,	Ne 9:8	4672
and there was f written in it that	Ne 13:1	4672
pleased him and f favor with him.	Es 2:9	5375
And Esther f favor in the eyes of	Es 2:15	5375
and she f favor and kindness with	Es 2:17	5375
plot was investigated and f *to be so,*	Es 2:23	4672
all the Jews who are f in Susa,	Es 4:16	4672
if I have f favor in the sight of	Es 5:8	4672
It was f written what Mordecai	Es 6:2	4672
"If I have f favor in your sight,	Es 7:3	4672
and if I have f favor before him	Es 8:5	4672
"But where can wisdom be f?	Jb 28:12	4672
is it f in the land of the living.	Jb 28:13	4672
because they had f no answer,	Jb 32:3	4672
'We have f wisdom;	Jb 32:13	4672
to the pit, I have f a ransom';	Jb 33:24	4672
were f so fair as Job's daughters;	Jb 42:15	4672
in a time when You may be f;	Ps 32:6	4672
for him, but he could not be f.	Ps 37:36	4672
And for comforters, but I f none.	Ps 69:20	4672
The bird also has f a house,	Ps 84:3	4672
"I have f David My servant;	Ps 89:20	4672
I f distress and sorrow.	Ps 116:3	4672
We f it in the field of Jaar.	Ps 132:6	4672
But when he is f, he must repay	Pr 6:31	4672
earnestly, and I have f you.	Pr 7:15	4672
perverts his ways will be f out.	Pr 10:9	3045
of the discerning, wisdom is f,	Pr 10:13	4672
is f in the way of righteousness.	Pr 16:31	4672
Have you f honey?	Pr 25:16	4672
curse you and you will be f guilty.	Pr 30:10	816
I am still seeking but have not f.	Ec 7:28	4672
I have f one man among a thousand,	Ec 7:28	4672
not f a woman among all these.	Ec 7:28	4672
"Behold, I have f only this, that	Ec 7:29	4672
But there was f in it a poor wise	Ec 9:15	4672
make the rounds in the city f me,	SS 3:3	4672
When I f him whom my soul loves;	SS 3:4	4672
make the rounds in the city f me,	SS 5:7	4672
If I f you outdoors, I would kiss	SS 8:1	4672
who is f will be thrust through,	Is 13:15	4672
f were taken captive together,	Is 22:3	4672
a sherd will not be f among its pieces	Is 30:14	4672
These will not be f there.	Is 35:9	4672
Then Rabshakeh returned and f the	Is 37:8	4672
all that was f in his treasuries.	Is 39:2	4672
Joy and gladness will be f in her,	Is 51:3	4672
the heavens, to f the earth,	Is 51:16	3245
Seek the LORD while He may be f;	Is 55:6	4672
You f renewed strength, Therefore	Is 57:10	4672
be f by those who did not seek Me.	Is 65:1	4672
the new wine is f in the cluster,	Is 65:8	4672
on your skirts is f The lifeblood of	Jer 2:34	4672
wicked men are f among My people,	Jer 5:26	4672
distress, That they may be f."	Jer 10:18	4672
"A conspiracy has been f among	Jer 11:9	4672
to the cisterns and f no water.	Jer 14:3	4672
Your words were f and I ate them,	Jer 15:16	4672
house I have f their wickedness,"	Jer 23:11	4672
'I will be f by you,' declares	Jer 29:14	4672
who survived the sword F grace	Jer 31:2	4672
the Chaldeans who were f there,	Jer 41:3	4672
were f among them said to Ishmael,	Jer 41:8	4672
they f him by the great pool that is in	Jer 41:12	4672
groaning and have f no rest."	Jer 45:3	4672
"Surely it will no *more* be f,	Jer 46:23	2713
of Judah, but they will not be f;	Jer 50:20	4672
You have been f and also seized	Jer 50:24	4672
advisers who were f in the city,	Jer 52:25	4672
were f in the midst of the city.	Jer 52:25	4672
nations, *But* she has f no rest;	La 1:3	4672
like deer That have f no pasture;	La 1:6	4672
would not destroy it; but I f no one.	Ezk 22:30	4672
you will never be f again,"	Ezk 26:21	4672
unrighteousness was f in you.	Ezk 28:15	4672
all not one was f like Daniel,	Da 1:19	4672
he f them ten times better than	Da 1:20	4672
"I have f a man among the exiles	Da 2:25	7912
so that not a trace of them was f.	Da 2:35	7912
beasts of the field f shade under it,	Da 4:12	2927
wisdom of the gods were f in him.	Da 5:11	7912
problems were f in this Daniel,	Da 5:12	7912
wisdom have been f in you.	Da 5:14	7912
on the scales and f deficient.	Da 5:27	7912
or corruption was *to be* f in him.	Da 6:4	7912
men came by agreement and f Daniel	Da 6:11	7912
as I was f innocent before Him;	Da 6:22	7912
no injury whatever was f on him,	Da 6:23	7912
stumble and fall and be f no more.	Da 11:19	4672
who is f written in the book,	Da 12:1	4672
I f Israel like grapes in the	Hos 9:10	4672
He f Him at Bethel And there He	Hos 12:4	4672
rich, I have f wealth for myself;	Hos 12:8	4672
f a ship which was going to	Jon 1:3	4672
f The rebellious acts of Israel.	Mi 1:13	4672
tongue Be f in their mouths;	Zph 3:13	4672
Until no *room* can be f for them.	Zch 10:10	4672
was not f on his lips;	Mal 2:6	4672
she was f to be with child by the Holy	Mt 1:18	2147
when you have f *Him,* report to me,	Mt 2:8	2147
I have not f such great faith with	Mt 8:10	2147
who has f his life will lose it,	Mt 10:39	2147
the field, which a man f and hid	Mt 13:44	2147
"But that slave went out and f	Mt 18:28	2147
went out and f others standing	Mt 20:6	2147
and f nothing on it except leaves	Mt 21:19	2147
and gathered together all they f,	Mt 22:10	2147
the disciples and f them sleeping,	Mt 26:40	2147
Again He came and f them sleeping,	Mt 26:43	2147
f a man of Cyrene named Simon,	Mt 27:32	2147
they f Him, and said to Him,	Mk 1:37	2147
And when they f out, they said,	Mk 6:38	1097
she f the child lying on the bed,	Mk 7:30	2147
They went away and f a colt	Mk 11:4	2147
to it, He f nothing but leaves,	Mk 11:13	2147
and f *it* just as He had told them;	Mk 14:16	2147
And He came and f them sleeping,	Mk 14:37	2147
again He came and f them sleeping,	Mk 14:40	2147
for you have f favor with God.	Lk 1:30	2147
f their way to Mary and Joseph,	Lk 2:16	429
days they f Him in the temple,	Lk 2:46	2147
and f the place where it was written,	Lk 4:17	2147
have I f such great faith."	Lk 7:9	2147
they f the slave in good health.	Lk 7:10	2147
clothed and live in luxury are f	Lk 7:25	
and f the man from whom the demons	Lk 8:35	2147
had spoken, Jesus was f alone.	Lk 9:36	2147
"When he has f it, he lays it	Lk 15:5	2147
I have f my sheep which was lost!'	Lk 15:6	2147
When she has f it, she calls together	Lk 15:9	2147
have f the coin which I had lost!'	Lk 15:9	2147
he was lost and has been f.'	Lk 15:24	2147
and *was* lost and has been f.' "	Lk 15:32	2147
"Was no one f who returned to	Lk 17:18	2147
and f it just as He had told them.	Lk 19:32	2147
And they left and f *everything*	Lk 22:13	2147
and f them sleeping from sorrow,	Lk 22:45	2147
"We f this man misleading our	Lk 23:2	2147
I have f no guilt in this man	Lk 23:14	2147
I have f in Him no guilt *demanding*	Lk 23:22	2147
And they f the stone rolled away	Lk 24:2	2147
went to the tomb and f it just exactly	Lk 24:24	2147
and f gathered together the eleven	Lk 24:33	2147
He f first his own brother Simon and	Jn 1:41	2147
"We have f the Messiah"	Jn 1:41	2147
into Galilee, and He f Philip.	Jn 1:43	2147
f Nathanael and said to him,	Jn 1:45	2147
"We have f Him of whom Moses in	Jn 1:45	2147
And He f in the temple those who	Jn 2:14	2147
Jesus f him in the temple and	Jn 5:14	2147
When they f Him on the other	Jn 6:25	2147
He f that he had already been in	Jn 11:17	2147
young men came in and f her dead,	Ac 5:10	2147
"We f the prison house locked	Ac 5:23	2147
opened up, we f no one inside."	Ac 5:23	2147
even be f fighting against God."	Ac 5:39	2147
The statement f approval with	Ac 6:5	700
"*David* f favor in God's	Ac 7:46	2147
But Philip f himself at Azotus,	Ac 8:40	2147
if he f any belonging to the Way,	Ac 9:2	2147
he f a man named Aeneas,	Ac 9:33	2147
and f many people assembled.	Ac 10:27	2147
and when he had f him, he brought	Ac 11:26	2147
for him and had not f him,	Ac 12:19	2147
Paphos, they f a magician,	Ac 13:6	2147
'I HAVE F DAVID the son of Jesse,	Ac 13:22	2147
"And though they f no ground for	Ac 13:28	2147
Jews of Thessalonica f out that the	Ac 17:13	1097
I also f an altar with this	Ac 17:23	2147
he f a Jew named Aquila,	Ac 18:2	2147
to Ephesus, and f some disciples.	Ac 19:1	2147
counted up the price of them and f it	Ac 19:19	2147
and having f a ship crossing over	Ac 21:2	2147
when he f out that he was a Roman,	Ac 22:29	1921
and I f him to be accused over	Ac 23:29	2147
"For we have f this man a real pest	Ac 24:5	2147
they f me *occupied* in the temple,	Ac 24:18	2147
tell what misdeed they f when I stood	Ac 24:20	2147
"But I f that he had committed	Ac 25:25	2638
the centurion f an Alexandrian ship	Ac 27:6	2147
and f *it to be* twenty fathoms;	Ac 27:28	2147
and f *it to be* fifteen fathoms.	Ac 27:28	2147
then we f out that the island was	Ac 28:1	1921

There we **f** *some* brethren, and were Ac 28:14 2147
Rather, let God be **f** true, Ro 3:4 *1096*
though every man *be* **f** a liar, as Ro 3:4 2147
according to the flesh, has **f**? Ro 4:1 2147
WAS **F** BY THOSE WHO DID NOT SEEK ME, Ro 10:20 2147
in Christ Jesus I have **f** reason for Ro 15:17 2147
that one be **f** trustworthy. 1Co 4:2 2147
f *to be* false witnesses of God, 1Co 15:15 2147
put it on, will not be **f** naked. 2Co 5:3 2147
and **f** diligent in many things, 2Co 8:22 1510
be **f** by you to be not what you wish; 2Co 12:20 2147
have also been **f** sinners, Ga 2:17 2147
Being **f** in appearance as a man, Php 2:8 2147
which is in the Law, **f** blameless. Php 3:6 *1096*
and may be **f** in Him, not having a Php 3:9 2147
with the faith and love which are **f** 1Tm 1:14 *1722*
Yet for this reason I **f** mercy, 1Tm 1:16 *1653*
eagerly searched for me and **f** me 2Tm 1:17 2147
NOT **F** BECAUSE GOD TOOK HIM UP; Heb 11:5 2147
for he **f** no place for repentance, Heb 12:17 2147
may be **f** to result in praise and 1Pe 1:7 2147
NOR WAS ANY DECEIT **F** IN HIS MOUTH 1Pe 2:22 2147
diligent to be **f** by Him in peace, 2Pe 3:14 2147
not, and you **f** them *to be* false; Rv 2:2 2147
for I have not **f** your deeds Rv 3:2 2147
one was **f** worthy to open the book or Rv 5:4 2147
a place **f** for them in heaven. Rv 12:8 2147
And no lie was **f** in their mouth; Rv 14:5 2147
and the mountains were not **f**. Rv 16:20 2147
and will not be **f** any longer. Rv 18:21 2147
craft will be **f** in you any longer; Rv 18:22 2147
in her was **f** the blood of prophets Rv 18:24 2147
away, and no place was **f** for them. Rv 20:11 2147
not **f** written in the book of life, Rv 20:15 2147

FOUNDATION

his firstborn he shall lay its **f**, Jos 6:26 3245
f of the house with cut stones. 1Ki 5:17 3245
In the fourth year the **f** of the 1Ki 6:37 3245
even from the **f** to the coping, and 1Ki 7:9 4527
The **f** was of costly stones, 1Ki 7:10 3245
of the **f** of the house of the LORD, 2Ch 8:16 4143
and a third at the Gate of the **F**; 2Ch 23:5 3247
of God to restore it on its **f**. Ezr 2:68 4349
So they set up the altar on its **f**, Ezr 3:3 4350
but the **f** of the temple of the Ezr 3:6 3245
the **f** of the temple of the LORD, Ezr 3:10 3245
praised the LORD because the **f** of the Ezr 3:11 3245
wept with a loud voice when the **f** of Ezr 3:12 3245
of clay, Whose **f** is in the dust, Jb 4:19 3247
when I laid the **f** of the earth? Jb 38:4 3245
His **f** is in the holy mountains. Ps 87:1 3248
justice are the **f** of Your throne; Ps 89:14 4349
justice are the **f** of His throne. Ps 97:2 4349
"Raze it, raze it To its very **f**." Ps 137:7 3247
righteous *has* an everlasting **f**. Pr 10:25 3247
A costly cornerstone *for* the **f**, Is 28:16 4143
'Your **f** will be laid.' " Is 44:28 3245
so that its **f** is laid bare; Ezk 13:14 3247
have laid the **f** of this house, Zch 4:9 3245
day that the **f** of the house of the Zch 8:9 3245
heavens, lays the **f** of the earth, Zch 12:1 3245
HIDDEN SINCE THE **F** OF THE WORLD." Mt 13:35 2602
for you from the **f** of the world. Mt 25:34 2602
deep and laid a **f** on the rock; Lk 6:48 2310b
on the ground without any **f**; Lk 6:49 2310b
shed since the **f** of the world, Lk 11:50 2602
"Otherwise, when he has laid a **f** and Lk 14:29 2310b
loved Me before the **f** of the world. Jn 17:24 2602
not build on another man's **f**; Ro 15:20 2310b
a wise master builder I laid a **f**, 1Co 3:10 2310b
For no man can lay a **f** other than 1Co 3:11 2310b
man builds on the **f** with gold, 1Co 3:12 2310b
in Him before the **f** of the world, Eph 1:4 2602
f of the apostles and prophets, Eph 2:20 2310b
of a good **f** for the future, 1Tm 6:19 2310b
the firm **f** of God stands, 2Tm 2:19 2310b
LAID THE **F** OF THE EARTH, Heb 1:10 2311
finished from the **f** of the world. Heb 4:3 2602
not laying again a **f** of repentance Heb 6:1 2310b
often since the **f** of the world; Heb 9:26 2602
before the **f** of the world, 1Pe 1:20 2602
been written from the **f** of the world Rv 13:8 2602
of life from the **f** of the world, Rv 17:8 2602
of the city had twelve **f** stones, Rv 21:14 2310b
The **f** stones of the city wall were Rv 21:19 2310b
The first **f** stone was jasper; Rv 21:19 2310b

FOUNDATIONS

on fire the **f** of the mountains. Dt 32:22 4144
The **f** of heaven were trembling And 2Sa 22:8 4144
The **f** of the world were laid bare By 2Sa 22:16 4144
he laid its **f** with the *loss of* 1Ki 16:34 3245
Now these are the **f** which Solomon 2Ch 3:3 3245
the walls and repairing the **f**. Ezr 4:12 787
Sheshbazzar came *and* laid the **f** of the Ezr 5:16 787
rebuilt and let its **f** be retained, Ezr 6:3 787
f were washed away by a river? Jb 22:16 3247
If the **f** are destroyed, What can Ps 11:3 8356
And the **f** of the mountains were Ps 18:7 4144
And the **f** of the world were laid Ps 18:15 4144
All the **f** of the earth are shaken. Ps 82:5 4144
established the earth upon its **f**, Ps 104:5 4349
He marked out the **f** of the earth; Pr 8:29 4144
And the **f** of the thresholds Is 6:4 522c
and the **f** of the earth shake. Is 24:18 4144
from the **f** of the earth? Is 40:21 4144
And laid the **f** of the earth, Is 51:13 3245
your **f** I will lay in sapphires. Is 54:11 3245
You will raise up the age-old **f**; Is 58:12 4144
f of the earth searched out below, Jer 31:37 4144
for a corner Nor a stone for **f**, Jer 51:26 4144
in Zion Which has consumed its **f**. La 4:11 3247
wealth, And her **f** are torn down. Ezk 30:4 3247
the **f** of the side chambers were a Ezk 41:8 4145
valley And will lay bare her **f**. Mi 1:6 3247
And you enduring **f** of the earth, Mi 6:2 4144
f of the prison house were shaken; Ac 16:26 *2310a*
looking for the city which has **f**, Heb 11:10 *2310b*

FOUNDED

from the day it was **f** until now. Ex 9:18 3245
For He has **f** it upon the seas And Ps 24:2 3245
the earth which He has **f** forever. Ps 78:69 3245
all it contains, You have **f** them. Ps 89:11 3245
"Of old You **f** the earth, Ps 102:25 3245
That You have **f** them forever. Ps 119:152 3245
The LORD by wisdom **f** the earth, Pr 3:19 3245
That the LORD has **f** Zion, Is 14:32 3245
"Surely My hand **f** the earth, And Is 48:13 3245
And has **f** His vaulted dome over Am 9:6 3245
when the temple of the LORD was **f**, Hg 2:18 3245
for it had been **f** on the rock. Mt 7:25 *2311*

FOUNDS

And **f** a town with violence! Hab 2:12 3559

FOUNTAIN

security, The **f** of Jacob secluded, Dt 33:28 5871a
the **f** of the waters of Nephtoah. Jos 18:15 4599
to the **F** Gate and the King's Pool, Ne 2:14 5871a
of Mizpah, repaired the **F** Gate. Ne 3:15 5871a
At the **F** Gate they went Ne 12:37 5871a
For with You is the **f** of life; Ps 36:9 4726
you who are of the **f** of Israel. Ps 68:26 4726
The flint into a **f** of water. Ps 114:8 4599
Let your **f** be blessed, And rejoice Pr 5:18 4726
of the righteous is a **f** of life, Pr 10:11 4726
of the wise is a **f** of life, Pr 13:14 4726
fear of the LORD is a **f** of life, Pr 14:27 4726
is a **f** of life to one who has it, Pr 16:22 4726
f of wisdom is a bubbling brook. Pr 18:4 4726
Me, The **f** of living waters, Jer 2:13 4726
waters And my eyes a **f** of tears, Jer 9:1 4726
forsaken the **f** of living water, Jer 17:13 4726
dry up her sea And make her **f** dry. Jer 51:36 4726
And his **f** will become dry And his Hos 13:15 4726
"In that day a **f** will be opened Zch 13:1 4726
Does a **f** send out from the same Jas 3:11 *4077*

FOUNTAINS

f of the great deep burst open, Gn 7:11 4599
Also the **f** of the deep and the Gn 8:2 4599
brooks of water, of **f** and springs, Dt 8:7 5871a
And the dry land **f** of water. Is 41:18 4161

FOUR

it divided and became **f** rivers. Gn 2:10 702
and Arpachshad lived **f** hundred and Gn 11:13 702
and Shelah lived **f** hundred and Gn 11:15 702
and Eber lived **f** hundred and Gn 11:17 702
f kings against five. Gn 14:9 702
and oppressed **f** hundred years. Gn 15:13 702
worth **f** hundred shekels of silver, Gn 23:15 702
Heth, **f** hundred shekels of silver, Gn 23:16 702
and **f** hundred men are with him." Gn 32:6 702
and **f** hundred men with him. Gn 33:1 702
was **f** hundred and thirty years. Ex 12:40 702
end of **f** hundred and thirty years, Ex 12:41 702
the ox and **f** sheep for the sheep. Ex 22:1 702
shall cast **f** gold rings for it and Ex 25:12 702
it and fasten them on its **f** feet, Ex 25:12 702
"You shall make **f** gold rings Ex 25:26 702
put rings on the **f** corners which are Ex 25:26 702
corners which are on its **f** feet. Ex 25:26 702
f cups shaped like almond *blossoms,* Ex 25:34 702
width of each curtain **f** cubits; Ex 26:2 702
width of each curtain **f** cubits; Ex 26:8 702
shall hang it on **f** pillars of acacia Ex 26:32 702
of gold, on **f** sockets of silver. Ex 26:32 702
make its horns on its **f** corners; Ex 27:2 702
you shall make **f** bronze rings at its Ex 27:4 702
bronze rings at its **f** corners. Ex 27:4 702
with their **f** pillars and their Ex 27:16 702
four pillars and their **f** sockets. Ex 27:16 702
mount on it **f** rows of stones; Ex 28:17 702
width of each curtain **f** cubits; Ex 36:9 702
and **f** cubits the width of each Ex 36:15 702
made **f** pillars of acacia for it, Ex 36:36 702
cast **f** sockets of silver for them. Ex 36:36 702
He cast **f** rings of gold for it Ex 37:3 702
of gold for it on its **f** feet; Ex 37:3 702
He cast **f** gold rings for it Ex 37:13 702
put the rings on the **f** corners that Ex 37:13 702
corners that were on its **f** feet. Ex 37:13 702
f cups shaped like almond *blossoms,* Ex 37:20 702
made its horns on its **f** corners, Ex 38:2 702
He cast **f** rings on the four Ex 38:5 702
f ends of the bronze grating Ex 38:5 702
Their **f** pillars and their four Ex 38:19 702
their **f** sockets *were* of bronze; Ex 38:19 702
mounted **f** rows of stones on it. Ex 39:10 702
Two carts and **f** oxen he gave to Nu 7:7 702
and **f** carts and eight oxen he gave Nu 7:8 702
width **f** cubits by ordinary cubit.) Dt 3:11 702
make yourself tassels on the **f** corners Dt 22:12 702
f cities with their villages; Jos 19:7 702
Almon with its pasture lands; **f** cities. Jos 21:18 702
with its pasture lands; **f** cities. Jos 21:22 702
with its pasture lands; **f** cities. Jos 21:24 702
with its pasture lands; **f** cities. Jos 21:29 702
Rehob with its pasture lands; **f** cities. Jos 21:31 702
with its pasture lands; **f** cities Jos 21:35 702
with its pasture lands; **f** cities. Jos 21:37 702
with its pasture lands; **f** cities in all. Jos 21:39 702
against Shechem in **f** companies. Jg 9:34 702
the Gileadite **f** days in the year. Jg 11:40 702
there for a period of **f** months. Jg 19:2 702
at the rock of Rimmon **f** months. Jg 20:47 702
Philistines who killed about **f** thousand 1Sa 4:2 702
were about **f** hundred men with him. 1Sa 22:2 702
and about **f** hundred men went up 1Sa 25:13 702
was a year and **f** months. 1Sa 27:7 702
pursued, he and **f** hundred men, 1Sa 30:10 702
except **f** hundred young men who 1Sa 30:17 702
These **f** were born to the giant in 2Sa 21:22 702
in the **f** hundred and eightieth year 1Ki 6:1 702
on **f** rows of cedar pillars with 1Ki 7:2 702
were of lily design, **f** cubits. 1Ki 7:19 702
length of each stand was **f** cubits 1Ki 7:27 702
its width **f** cubits and its height three 1Ki 7:27 702
Now each stand had **f** bronze wheels 1Ki 7:30 702
and its **f** feet had supports; 1Ki 7:30 702
The **f** wheels *were* underneath 1Ki 7:32 702
Now *there were* **f** supports at the 1Ki 7:34 702
at the **f** corners of each stand; 1Ki 7:34 702
each basin *was* **f** cubits, *and* on 1Ki 7:38 702
and the **f** hundred pomegranates for 1Ki 7:42 702
and took **f** hundred and twenty 1Ki 9:28 702
"Fill **f** pitchers with water and 1Ki 18:34 702
together, about **f** hundred men, 1Ki 22:6 702
Now there were **f** leprous men at 2Ki 7:3 702
Shobab, Nathan and Solomon, **f**, 1Ch 3:5 702
Now the sons of Issachar *were* **f**: 1Ch 7:1 702
gatekeepers were on the **f** sides, 1Ch 9:24 702
for the **f** chief gatekeepers who 1Ch 9:26 702
and his **f** sons *who were* with him 1Ch 21:20 702
These **f** *were* the sons of Shimei. 1Ch 23:10 702
The sons of Kohath were **f**: 1Ch 23:12 702
six Levites, on the north **f** daily, 1Ch 26:17 702
four daily, on the south **f** daily, 1Ch 26:17 702
At the Parbar on the west *there were* **f** 1Ch 26:18 702
and the **f** hundred pomegranates for 2Ch 4:13 702
and took from there **f** hundred and 2Ch 8:18 702
the prophets, **f** hundred men, 2Ch 18:5 702
to me **f** times in this manner, Ne 6:4 702
struck the **f** corners of the house, Jb 1:19 702
and his grandsons, **f** generations. Jb 42:16 702
F that will not say, "Enough": Pr 30:15 702
me, **F** which I do not understand: Pr 30:18 702
And under **f**, it cannot bear up: Pr 30:21 702
F things are small on the earth, Pr 30:24 702
Even **f** which are stately when they Pr 30:29 702
From the **f** corners of the earth. Is 11:12 702
F *or* five on the branches of a Is 17:6 702
over them **f** kinds *of doom,*" Jer 15:3 702
had read three or **f** columns, Jer 36:23 702
will bring upon Elam the **f** winds Jer 49:36 702
winds From the **f** ends of heaven, Jer 49:36 702
and **f** fingers in thickness, Jer 52:21 702
resembling **f** living beings. Ezk 1:5 702
them had **f** faces and four wings. Ezk 1:6 702
them had four faces and **f** wings. Ezk 1:6 702
on their **f** sides *were* human hands. Ezk 1:8 702
faces and wings of the **f** of them, Ezk 1:8 702
all **f** had the face of a lion on Ezk 1:10 702
all **f** had the face of an eagle. Ezk 1:10 702
beings, for *each of* the **f** of them. Ezk 1:15 702
all **f** of them had the same form, Ezk 1:16 702
in any of their **f** directions without Ezk 1:17 702
rims of all **f** of them were full of Ezk 1:18 702
on the **f** corners of the land. Ezk 7:2 702
f wheels beside the cherubim, Ezk 10:9 702
f of them had the same likeness, Ezk 10:10 702
they went in *any of* their **f** directions Ezk 10:11 702
wheels belonging to all **f** of them. Ezk 10:12 702
And each one had **f** faces. Ezk 10:14 702
f faces and each one four wings, Ezk 10:21 702
four faces and each one **f** wings, Ezk 10:21 702
when I send My **f** severe judgments Ezk 14:21 702
"Come from the **f** winds, O breath, Ezk 37:9 702
F tables *were* on each side next to Ezk 40:41 702
there were **f** tables of hewn stone, Ezk 40:42 702
of the side chambers, **f** cubits, Ezk 41:5 702
He measured it on the **f** sides; Ezk 42:20 702
larger ledge *shall be* **f** cubits and Ezk 43:14 702
altar hearth *shall be* **f** cubits; Ezk 43:15 702
shall extend upwards **f** horns. Ezk 43:15 702
wide, square in its **f** sides. Ezk 43:16 702
by fourteen wide in its **f** sides, Ezk 43:17 702
blood and put it on its **f** horns Ezk 43:20 702
and on the **f** corners of the ledge and Ezk 43:20 702
on the **f** corners of the ledge of Ezk 45:19 702
to the **f** corners of the court; Ezk 46:21 702
In the **f** corners of the court Ezk 46:22 702
these **f** in the corners *were* the Ezk 46:22 702
in them, around the **f** of them, Ezk 46:23 702
As for these **f** youths, Da 1:17 702
I see **f** men loosed *and* walking Da 3:25 703
the **f** winds of heaven were Da 7:2 703
"And **f** great beasts were coming Da 7:3 703
had on its back **f** wings of a bird; Da 7:6 703
the beast also had **f** heads, Da 7:6 703
beasts, which are **f** *in number,* Da 7:17 703
are **f** kings *who* will arise from Da 7:17 703
there came up **f** conspicuous *horns* Da 8:8 702
toward the **f** winds of heaven. Da 8:8 702
the **f** *horns that* arose in its place Da 8:22 702
represent **f** kingdoms *which* will arise Da 8:22 702
the **f** points of the compass, Da 11:4 702
for **f** I will not revoke its *punishment,* Am 1:3 702
for **f** I will not revoke its *punishment,* Am 1:6 702

for **f** I will not revoke its *punishment*, Am 1:9 702
for **f** I will not revoke its *punishment*, Am 1:11 702
for **f** I will not revoke its *punishment*, Am 1:13 702
for **f** I will not revoke its *punishment*, Am 2:1 702
for **f** I will not revoke its *punishment*, Am 2:4 702
for **f** I will not revoke its *punishment*, Am 2:6 702
and behold, *there were* **f** horns. Zch 1:18 702
the LORD showed me **f** craftsmen. Zch 1:20 702
as the **f** winds of the heavens," Zch 2:6 702
f chariots were coming forth from Zch 6:1 702
"These are the **f** spirits of Zch 6:5 702
those who ate were **f** thousand men, Mt 15:38 *5070*
seven loaves of the **f** thousand, Mt 16:10 *5070*
His elect from the **f** winds, Mt 24:31 *5064*
Him a paralytic, carried by **f** men. Mk 2:3 *5064*
About **f** thousand were *there* Mk 8:9 *5070*
the seven for the **f** thousand, Mk 8:20 *5070*
His elect from the **f** winds, Mk 13:27 *5064*
will give back **f** times as much." Lk 19:8 *5073*
'There are yet **f** months, and *then* Jn 4:35 *5072*
had rowed about three or **f** miles, Jn 6:19
already been in the tomb **f** days. Jn 11:17 *5064*
for he has been *dead* **f** days." Jn 11:39 *5066b*
outer garments and made **f** parts, Jn 19:23 *5064*
and a group of about **f** hundred men Ac 5:36 *5071*
MISTREATED FOR **F** HUNDRED YEARS. Ac 7:6 *5071*
by **f** corners to the ground, Ac 10:11 *5064*
"**F** days ago to this hour, I was Ac 10:30 *5067a*
lowered by **f** corners from the sky; Ac 11:5 *5064*
delivering him to **f** squads of Ac 12:4 *5064*
about **f** hundred and fifty years. Ac 13:19 *5071*
this man had **f** virgin daughters Ac 21:9 *5064*
We have **f** men who are under a vow; Ac 21:23 *5064*
a revolt and led the **f** thousand men Ac 21:38 *5070*
they cast **f** anchors from the stern Ac 27:29 *5064*
f hundred and thirty years later, Ga 3:17 *5071*
f living creatures full of eyes in Rv 4:6 *5064*
And the **f** living creatures, each Rv 4:8 *5064*
(with the **f** living creatures) Rv 5:6 *5064*
the **f** living creatures and the Rv 5:8 *5064*
f living creatures kept saying, Rv 5:14 *5064*
and I heard one of the **f** living Rv 6:1 *5064*
of the **f** living creatures saying, Rv 6:6 *5064*
After this I saw **f** angels standing Rv 7:1 *5064*
at the **f** corners of the earth, Rv 7:1 *5064*
back the **f** winds of the earth, Rv 7:1 *5064*
out with a loud voice to the **f** angels Rv 7:2 *5064*
elders and the **f** living creatures; Rv 7:11 *5064*
from the **f** horns of the golden altar Rv 9:13 *5064*
"Release the **f** angels who are Rv 9:14 *5064*
And the **f** angels, who had been Rv 9:15 *5064*
and before the **f** living creatures Rv 14:3 *5064*
Then one of the **f** living creatures Rv 15:7 *5064*
and the **f** living creatures fell down Rv 19:4 *5064*
are in the **f** corners of the earth, Rv 20:8 *5064*

FOUR-FIFTHS
and **f** shall be your own for seed Gn 47:24 702, 3027

FOURFOLD
make restitution for the lamb **f**, 2Sa 12:6 706

FOUR-FOOTED
which are **f** are detestable to you. Lv 11:23 702, 7272
there were in it all *kinds of* **f** animals Ac 10:12 *5074*
I saw the **f** animals of the earth Ac 11:6 *5074*
man and of birds and **f** animals and Ro 1:23 *5074*

FOURS
on *all* **f** are detestable to you. Lv 11:20 702
insects which walk on *all* **f**: Lv 11:21 702
the creatures that walk on *all* **f**, Lv 11:27 702
and whatever walks on *all* **f**, Lv 11:42 702

FOUR-SIDED
nave **f** doorposts of olive wood 1Ki 6:33 7243

FOURTEEN
f years for your two daughters and Gn 31:41 702, 6240
there were **f** persons in all. Gn 46:22 702, 6240
rams, **f** male lambs one year old, Nu 29:13 702, 6240
a tenth for each of the **f** lambs; Nu 29:15 702, 6240
f male lambs one year old without Nu 29:17 702, 6240
f male lambs one year old without Nu 29:20 702, 6240
f male lambs one year old without Nu 29:23 702, 6240
f male lambs one year old without Nu 29:26 702, 6240
f male lambs one year old without Nu 29:29 702, 6240
f male lambs one year old without Nu 29:32 702, 6240
f cities with their villages. Jos 15:36 702, 6240
f cities with their villages. Jos 18:28 702, 6240
and seven *more* days, *even* **f** days. 1Ki 8:65 702, 6240
for God gave **f** sons and three 1Ch 25:5 702, 6240
and took **f** wives to himself, 2Ch 13:21 702, 6240
"The ledge *shall be* **f** *cubits* Ezk 43:17 702, 6240
long by **f** wide in its four sides, Ezk 43:17 702, 6240
to David are **f** generations; Mt 1:17 *1180*
to Babylon, **f** generations; Mt 1:17 *1180*
the Messiah, **f** generations. Mt 1:17 *1180*
I know a man in Christ who **f** years 2Co 12:2 *1180*
Then after an interval of **f** years Ga 2:1 *1180*

FOURTEENTH
In the **f** year Chedorlaomer and Gn 14:5 702, 6240
until the **f** day of the same month, Ex 12:6 702, 6240
the **f** day of the month at evening, Ex 12:18 702, 6240
on the **f** day of the month at Lv 23:5 702, 6240
"On the **f** day of this month, at Nu 9:3 702, 6240
month, on the **f** day of the month, Nu 9:5 702, 6240
month on the **f** day at twilight, Nu 9:11 702, 6240
'Then on the **f** day of the first Nu 28:16 702, 6240
Passover on the evening of the **f** day Jos 5:10 702, 6240
in the **f** year of King Hezekiah, 2Ki 18:13 702, 6240
for Huppah, the **f** for Jeshebeab, 1Ch 24:13 702, 6240
for the **f**, Mattithiah, his sons 1Ch 25:21 702, 6240
on the **f** of the second month. 2Ch 30:15 702, 6240
on the **f** *day* of the first month. 2Ch 35:1 702, 6240
on the **f** of the first month. Ezr 6:19 702, 6240
assembled also on the **f** day of the Es 9:15 702, 6240
and on the **f** day they rested and Es 9:17 702, 6240
and the **f** of the same month, Es 9:18 702, 6240
make the **f** day of the month Adar *a* Es 9:19 702, 6240
the **f** day of the month Adar, Es 9:21 702, 6240
in the **f** year of King Hezekiah, Is 36:1 702, 6240
f year after the city was taken, Ezk 40:1 702, 6240
month, on the **f** day of the month, Ezk 45:21 702, 6240
But when the **f** night came, as Ac 27:27 *5065a*
"Today is the **f** day that you have Ac 27:33 *5065a*

FOURTH
and there was morning, a **f** day. Gn 1:19 7243
And the **f** river is the Euphrates. Gn 2:14 7243
"Then in the **f** generation they Gn 15:16 7243
on the third and the **f** generations Ex 20:5 7256
and the **f** row a beryl and an onyx Ex 28:20 7243
to the third and **f** generations." Ex 34:7 7256
and the **f** row, a beryl, an onyx, Ex 39:13 7243
'But in the **f** year all its fruit Lv 19:24 7243
drink offering, a **f** of a hin of wine. Lv 23:13 7243
On the **f** day *it was* Elizur the son Nu 7:30 7243
the third and the **f** *generations*.' Nu 14:18 7256
Or number the **f** part of Israel? Nu 23:10 7255
with a **f** of a hin of beaten oil. Nu 28:5 7243
be a **f** of a hin for each lamb, Nu 28:7 7243
ram and a **f** of a hin for a lamb; Nu 28:14 7243
'Then on the **f** day: Nu 29:23 7243
on the third and the **f** *generations* Dt 5:9 7256
The **f** lot fell to Issachar, to the Jos 19:17 7243
Then it came about on the **f** day Jg 14:15 7637
Now on the **f** day Jg 19:5 7243
my hand a **f** of a shekel of silver; 1Sa 9:8 7253
and the **f**, Adonijah the son of 2Sa 3:4 7243
in the **f** year of Solomon's reign 1Ki 6:1 7243
In the **f** year the foundation of 1Ki 6:37 7243
the **f** year of Ahab king of Israel. 1Ki 22:41 702
and a **f** of a kab of dove's dung 2Ki 6:25 7255
your sons of the **f** generation 2Ki 10:30 7243
"Your sons to the **f** generation 2Ki 15:12 7243
in the **f** year of King Hezekiah, 2Ki 18:9 7243
On the ninth day of the **f** month 2Ki 25:3
Nethanel the **f**, Raddai the fifth, 1Ch 2:14 7243
the **f** *was* Adonijah the son of 1Ch 3:2 7243
the third Zedekiah, the **f** Shallum. 1Ch 3:15 7243
Nohah the **f** and Rapha the fifth. 1Ch 8:2 7243
Mishmannah the **f**, Jeremiah the 1Ch 12:10 7243
the third and Jekameam the **f**. 1Ch 23:19 7243
third for Harim, the **f** for Seorim, 1Ch 24:8 7243
the third, Jekameam the **f**. 1Ch 24:23 7243
the **f** to Izri, his sons and his 1Ch 25:11 7243
Zebadiah the third, Jathniel the **f**, 1Ch 26:2 7243
Joah the third, Sacar the **f**, 1Ch 26:4 7243
the third, Zechariah the **f**; 1Ch 26:11 7243
The **f** for the fourth month *was* 1Ch 27:7 7243
The fourth for the **f** month *was* 1Ch 27:7 7243
month of the **f** year of his reign. 2Ch 3:2 702
Then on the **f** day they assembled 2Ch 20:26 7243
On the **f** day the silver and Ezr 8:33 7243
LORD their God for a **f** of the day; Ne 9:3 7243
and for *another* **f** they confessed Ne 9:3 7243
in the **f** year of Jehoiakim the son Jer 25:1 7243
king of Judah, in the **f** year, Jer 28:1 7243
In the **f** year of Jehoiakim Jer 36:1 7243
year of Zedekiah, in the **f** month, Jer 39:2 7243
in the **f** year of Jehoiakim the son Jer 45:1 7243
king of Babylon defeated in the **f** year Jer 46:2 7243
in the **f** year of his reign. Jer 51:59 7243
On the ninth *day* of the **f** month Jer 52:6 7243
on the fifth *day* of the **f** month, Ezk 1:1 7243
and the **f** the face of an eagle. Ezk 10:14 7243
be a **f** kingdom as strong as iron; Da 2:40 7244
the **f** is like a son of *the* gods!" Da 3:25 7244
visions, and behold, a **f** beast, Da 7:7 7244
the exact meaning of the **f** beast, Da 7:19 7244
'The **f** beast will be a fourth Da 7:23 7244
will be a **f** kingdom on the earth, Da 7:23 7244
Then a **f** will gain far more riches Da 11:2 7243
f chariot strong dappled horses. Zch 6:3 7243
In the **f** year of King Darius, Zch 7:1 702
on the **f** *day* of the ninth month, Zch 7:1 702
'The fast of the **f**, the fast of Zch 8:19 7243
And in the **f** watch of the night He Mt 14:25 *5067a*
at about the **f** watch of the night He Mk 6:48 *5067a*
and the **f** creature *was* like a Rv 4:7 *5067a*
When the Lamb broke the **f** seal, Rv 6:7 *5067a*
of the **f** living creature saying, Rv 6:7 *5067a*
to them over a **f** of the earth, Rv 6:8 *5067a*
The **f** angel sounded, and a Rv 8:12 *5067a*
The **f** *angel* poured out his Rv 16:8 *5067a*
the third, chalcedony; the **f**, emerald; Rv 21:19 *5067a*

FOWL
roebucks, and fattened **f**. 1Ki 4:23 1257
f like the sand of the seas, Ps 78:27 5775
Creeping things and winged **f**; Ps 148:10 6833

FOWLER
a bird from the hand of the **f**. Pr 6:5 3353

FOWLERS
They watch like **f** lying in wait; Jer 5:26 3353

FOX
if a **f** should jump on *it*, Ne 4:3 7776
"Go and tell that **f**, Lk 13:32 *258*

FOXES
went and caught three hundred **f**, Jg 15:4 7776
and turned *the* **f** tail to tail Jg 15:4
he released the **f** into the Jg 15:5
They will be a prey for **f**. Ps 63:10 7776
"Catch the **f** for us, The little SS 2:15 7776
The little **f** that are ruining the SS 2:15 7776
lies desolate, **F** prowl in it. La 5:18 7776
have been like **f** among ruins. Ezk 13:4 7776
"The **f** have holes and the birds Mt 8:20 *258*
"The **f** have holes and the birds Lk 9:58 *258*

FRACTURE
f for fracture, eye for eye, tooth Lv 24:20 7667
fracture for **f**, eye for eye, tooth Lv 24:20 7667
LORD binds up the **f** of His people Is 30:26 7667

FRACTURED
'Those *that are* blind or **f** or Lv 22:22 7665

FRAGILE
Whose confidence is **f**, Jb 8:14 6962b

FRAGMENTS
He casts forth His ice as **f**; Ps 147:17 6595
handfuls of barley and **f** of bread, Ezk 13:19 6604b
gnaw its **f** And tear your breasts; Ezk 23:34 2789
pieces and the small house to **f**. Am 6:11 1233
f so that nothing will be lost." Jn 6:12 *2801*
f from the five barley loaves which Jn 6:13 *2801*

FRAGRANCE
"Your oils have a pleasing **f**, SS 1:3 7381b
My perfume gave forth its **f**. SS 1:12 7381b
blossom have given forth *their* **f**. SS 2:13 7381b
And the **f** of your oils Than all SS 4:10 7381b
And the **f** of your garments is like SS 4:11 7381b
garments is like the **f** of Lebanon. SS 4:11 7381b
Make my garden breathe out **f**, SS 4:16
the **f** of your breath like apples, SS 7:8 7381b
"The mandrakes have given forth **f**; SS 7:13 7381b
and the **f** of the cloud of incense Ezk 8:11 6282b
his **f** like *the cedars of* Lebanon. Hos 14:6 7381b
filled with the **f** of the perfume. Jn 12:3 *3744*
For we are a **f** of Christ to God 2Co 2:15 *2175*

FRAGRANT
oil and for the **f** incense, Ex 25:6 5561
Aaron shall burn **f** incense on it; Ex 30:7 5561
and of **f** cinnamon half as much, Ex 30:23 1314
of **f** cane two hundred and fifty, Ex 30:23 1314
the **f** incense for the holy place, Ex 31:11 5561
oil, and for the **f** incense, Ex 35:8 5561
anointing oil and the **f** incense, Ex 35:15 5561
oil and for the **f** incense. Ex 35:28 5561
and the pure, **f** incense of spices, Ex 37:29 5561
anointing oil and the **f** incense, Ex 39:38 5561
and he burned **f** incense on it, Ex 40:27 5561
on the horns of the altar of **f** incense Lv 4:7 5561
oil for the light and the **f** incense Nu 4:16 5561
Him, to burn **f** incense before Him and 2Ch 2:4 5561
burnt offerings and **f** incense, 2Ch 13:11 5561
All Your garments are **f** *with* Ps 45:8
to him an offering and **f** incense. Da 2:46 5208
a sacrifice to God as a **f** aroma. Eph 5:2 *2175*
what you have sent, a **f** aroma, Php 4:18 *2175*

FRAIL
"My lord knows that the children are **f** Gn 33:13 7390

FRAME
mighty strength, or his orderly **f**. Jb 41:12 6187
For He Himself knows our **f**; Ps 103:14 3336
My **f** was not hidden from You, Ps 139:15 6108

FRAMES
involved the **f** of the tabernacle, Nu 3:36 7175b
he made windows with *artistic* **f**. 1Ki 6:4 8261
artistic window **f** in three rows, 1Ki 7:4 8261
doorposts *had* squared *artistic* **f**, 1Ki 7:5 8260

even borders between the **f**, 1Ki 7:28 7948
were between the **f** *were* lions, 1Ki 7:29 7948
the **f** there *was* a pedestal above, 1Ki 7:29 7948
in evil And your tongue **f** deceit. Ps 50:19 6775

FRAMEWORK

rafter will answer it from the **f**. Hab 2:11 6086

FRANKINCENSE

and galbanum, spices with pure **f**; Ex 30:34 3828
pour oil on it and put **f** on it. Lv 2:1 3828
and of its oil with all of its **f**. Lv 2:2 3828
You shall put pure **f** on each row Lv 24:7 3828
pour oil on it nor put **f** on it, Nu 5:15 3828
the oil and the **f** and the spices. 1Ch 9:29 3828
put the grain offerings, the **f**, Ne 13:5 3828
the grain offerings and the **f**. Ne 13:9 3828
smoke, Perfumed with myrrh and **f**, SS 3:6 3828
of myrrh And to the hill of **f**. SS 4:6 3828
cinnamon, With all the trees of **f**, SS 4:14 3828
They will bring gold and **f**, Is 60:6 3828
does **f** come to Me from Sheba And Jer 6:20 3828
Him gifts of gold, **f**, and myrrh. Mt 2:11 *3030*
incense and perfume and **f** and wine Rv 18:13 *3030*

FRAUD

Wealth *obtained* by **f** dwindles, Pr 13:11 1892
who are full of all deceit and **f**, Ac 13:10 *4468*

FREE

you will be **f** from this my oath; Gn 24:8 5352
then you will be **f** from my oath, Gn 24:41 5352
you, you will be **f** from my oath.' Gn 24:41 5355a
go out as a **f** man without payment. Ex 21:2 2670
'I will not go out as a **f** man,' Ex 21:5 2670
not to go **f** as the male slaves do. Ex 21:7 3318
him go **f** on account of his eye. Ex 21:26 2670
him go **f** on account of his tooth. Ex 21:27 2670
bird go **f** over the open field. Lv 14:7 7971
he shall let the live bird go **f** Lv 14:53 7971
to death, because she was not **f**. Lv 19:20 2666
then be **f** and conceive children. Nu 5:28 5352
the man will be **f** from guilt, Nu 5:31 5352
which we used to eat **f** in Egypt, Nu 11:5 2600
you shall return and be **f** of obligation Nu 32:22 5355a
seventh year you shall set him **f**. Dt 15:12 2670
"When you set him **f**, Dt 15:13 2670
hard to you when you set him **f**, Dt 15:18 2670
he shall be **f** at home one year and Dt 24:5 5355a
is none *remaining*, bond or **f**. Dt 32:36 5800a
"We *shall be* **f** from this oath to Jos 2:17 5355a
his own head, and we *shall be* **f**; Jos 2:19 5355a
then we shall be **f** from the oath Jos 2:20 5355a
the man and all his family go **f**. Jg 1:25 7971
other times and shake myself **f**." Jg 16:20 5287
his father's house **f** in Israel." 1Sa 17:25 2670
person, both bond and **f** in Israel, 1Ki 14:10 5800a
male, both bond and **f** in Israel; 1Ki 21:21 5800a
person both bond and **f** in Israel. 2Ki 9:8 5800a
for there was neither bond nor **f**, 2Ki 14:26 5800a
the temple **f** *from other service;* 1Ch 9:33 6362
the slave is **f** from his master. Jb 3:19 2670
"Who sent out the wild donkey **f**? Jb 39:5 2670
To set **f** those who were doomed to Ps 102:20 6605a
ruler of peoples, and set him **f**. Ps 105:20 6605a
The LORD sets the prisoners **f**. Ps 146:7 6605a
city and will let My exiles go **f**, Is 45:13 7971
"The exile will soon be set **f**, Is 51:14 6605a
And to let the oppressed go **f** And Is 58:6 2670
'We *are* **f** *to* roam; We will no Jer 2:31 7300
set you **f** for *purposes of* good; Jer 15:11 8281
be completely **f** from punishment? Jer 25:29 5352
You will not be **f** from punishment; Jer 25:29 5352
man should set **f** his male servant Jer 34:9 2670
man should set **f** his male servant Jer 34:10 2670
they obeyed, and set *them* **f**. Jer 34:10 7971
servants whom they had set **f**, Jer 34:11 2670
shall set **f** his Hebrew brother who Jer 34:14 7971
you shall send him out **f** from you; Jer 34:14 2670
set **f** according to their desire, Jer 34:16 2670
But the **f** space between the side Ezk 41:9 5117
the side chambers toward the **f** space Ezk 41:11 5117
and the width of the **f** space Ezk 41:11 5117
and I will grant you **f** access Zch 3:7 4109
I have set your prisoners **f** from Zch 9:11 7971
But he pulled **f** of the linen sheet Mk 14:52 *2641*
SET **F** THOSE WHO ARE OPPRESSED, Lk 4:18 *1722, 859*
and the truth will make you **f**." Jn 8:32 *1659*
'You will become **f**'?" Jn 8:33 *1658*
the Son makes you **f**, Jn 8:36 *1659*
you free, you will be **f** indeed. Jn 8:36 *1658*
yourselves **f** from such things, Ac 15:29 *1301*
"This man might have been set **f** Ac 26:32 *630*
But the **f** gift is not like the Ro 5:15 *5486*
but on the other hand the **f** gift Ro 5:16 *5486*
were **f** in regard to righteousness. Ro 6:20 *1658*
but the **f** gift of God is eternal Ro 6:23 *5486*
dies, she is **f** from the law, Ro 7:3 *1658*
me **f** from the body of this death? Ro 7:24 *4506*
Jesus has set you **f** from the law of sin Ro 8:2 *1659*
the creation itself also will be set **f** Ro 8:21 *1659*
if you are able also to become **f**, 1Co 7:21 *1658*
he who was called while **f**, 1Co 7:22 *1658*
I want you to be **f** from concern. 1Co 7:32 *275*
she is **f** to be married to whom she 1Co 7:39 *1658*
Am I not **f**? Am I not an apostle? 1Co 9:1 *1658*
For though I am **f** from all *men*, I 1Co 9:19 *1658*
or Greeks, whether slaves or **f**, 1Co 12:13 *1658*
there is neither slave nor **f** man, Ga 3:28 *1658*
bondwoman and one by the **f** woman. Ga 4:22 *1658*
the **f** woman through the promise. Ga 4:23 *1658*
But the Jerusalem above is **f**; Ga 4:26 *1658*
WITH THE SON OF THE **F** WOMAN." Ga 4:30 *1658*
a bondwoman, but of the **f** woman. Ga 4:31 *1658*
for freedom that Christ set us **f**; Ga 5:1 *1659*
from the Lord, whether slave or **f**. Eph 6:8 *1658*
f from the love of money. 1Tm 3:3 *866*
keep yourself **f** from sin. 1Tm 5:22 *53*
but of your own **f** will. Phm 1:14 *1595*
and might **f** those who through fear of Heb 2:15 *525*
is **f** from the love of money, Heb 13:5 *866*
Act as **f** men, and do not use your 1Pe 2:16 *1658*
strong and every slave and **f** man hid Rv 6:15 *1658*
and the **f** men and the slaves, Rv 13:16 *1658*
of all men, both **f** men and slaves, Rv 19:18 *1658*

FREED

LORD has **f** him from the hand of his 2Sa 18:19 8199
for the LORD has **f** you this day 2Sa 18:31 8199
His hands were **f** from the basket. Ps 81:6 5674a
you are **f** from your sickness." Lk 13:12 *630*
who believes is **f** from all things, Ac 13:39 *1344*
not be **f** through the Law of Moses. Ac 13:39 *1344*
for he who has died is **f** from sin. Ro 6:7 *1344*
and having been **f** from sin, you Ro 6:18 *1659*
f from sin and enslaved to God, Ro 6:22 *1659*

FREEDMAN

while a slave, is the Lord's **f**; 1Co 7:22 *558*

FREEDMEN

was called the Synagogue of the **F**, Ac 6:9 *3032*

FREEDOM

been redeemed nor given her **f**, Lv 19:20 2668
to captives And **f** to prisoners; Is 61:1 6495
in custody and *yet* have *some* **f**, Ac 24:23 *425*
f of the glory of the children of God. Ro 8:21 *1657*
for why is my **f** judged by 1Co 10:29 *1657*
was for **f** that Christ set us free; Ga 5:1 *1657*
For you were called to **f**, Ga 5:13 *1657*
not *turn* your **f** into an opportunity Ga 5:13 *1657*
use your **f** as a covering for evil, 1Pe 2:16 *1657*
promising them **f** while they 2Pe 2:19 *1657*

FREEING

I am **f** you today from the chains Jer 40:4 6605a

FREELY

tree of the garden you may eat **f**; Gn 2:16 398
they feasted and drank **f** with him. Gn 43:34 7937
you shall **f** open your hand to him, Dt 15:8 6605a
'You shall **f** open your hand to Dt 15:11 6605a
if only the people had eaten **f** 1Sa 14:30 398
f offered to the God of Israel, Ezr 7:15 5069
f in the day of Your power; Ps 110:3 5071
He has given **f** to the poor, Ps 112:9 6340
let out **f** the ox and the donkey. Is 32:20 7971
apostasy, I will love them **f**, Hos 14:4 5071
F you received, freely give. Mt 10:8 *1432*
Freely you received, **f** give. Mt 10:8 *1431*
it **f** and to spread the news around, Mk 1:45 *4183*
first, and when *the people* have drunk **f**, Jn 2:10 *3184*
them, moving about **f** in Jerusalem, Ac 9:28 *1531, 2532, 1607*
with Him **f** give us all things? Ro 8:32 *5483*
the things **f** given to us by God, 1Co 2:12 *5483*
Our mouth has spoken **f** to you, 2Co 6:11 *455*
f bestowed on us in the Beloved. Eph 1:6 *5487*

FREEMAN

barbarian, Scythian, slave and **f**, Col 3:11 *1658*

FREEWILL

brought a **f** offering to the LORD. Ex 35:29 5071
to him **f** offerings every morning. Ex 36:3 5071
is a votive or a **f** offering, Lv 7:16 5071
or any of their **f** offerings, Lv 22:18 5071
special vow or for a **f** offering, Lv 22:21 5071
may present it for a **f** offering, Lv 22:23 5071
all your votive and **f** offerings, Lv 23:38 5071
or as a **f** offering or in your Nu 15:3 5071
offerings and your **f** offerings, Nu 29:39 5071
offerings, your **f** offerings, Dt 12:6 5071
you vow, or your **f** offerings, Dt 12:17 5071
of a **f** offering of your hand, Dt 16:10 5071
was over the **f** offerings of God, 2Ch 31:14 5071
a **f** offering to the people, 2Ch 35:8 5071
together with a **f** offering for the Ezr 1:4 5071
that was given as a **f** offering. Ezr 1:6 5068
offered a **f** offering to the LORD. Ezr 3:5 5071
along with the **f** offering of the Ezr 7:16 5069
silver and the gold are a **f** offering to Ezr 8:28 5071
the **f** offerings of my mouth, Ps 119:108 5071
the prince provides a **f** offering, Ezk 46:12 5071
as a **f** offering to the LORD, Ezk 46:12 5071
And proclaim **f** offerings, Am 4:5 5071

FREQUENT

I have been on **f** journeys, in 2Co 11:26 *4178*
your stomach and your **f** ailments. 1Tm 5:23 *4437*

FRESH

Then Jacob took **f** rods of poplar Gn 30:37 3892
you shall bring **f** heads of grain Lv 2:14 24
juice nor eat **f** or dried grapes. Nu 6:3 3892
"All the best of the **f** oil and Nu 18:12 3323
of the **f** wine and of the grain, Nu 18:12 8492
As the droplets on the **f** grass And Dt 32:2 1877
He found a **f** jawbone of a donkey, Jg 15:15 2961
"If they bind me with seven **f** cords Jg 16:7 3892
f cords that had not been dried, Jg 16:8 3892
and **f** ears of grain in his sack. 2Ki 4:42 3759
I have been anointed with **f** oil. Ps 92:10 7488
And **f** water from your own well. Pr 5:15 5140
garden spring, A well of **f** water, SS 4:15 2416a
"As a well keeps its waters **f**, Jer 6:7 7174b
So she keeps **f** her wickedness. Jer 6:7 7174b
the waters *of the sea* become **f**. Ezk 47:8 7495
go there and *the others* become **f**; Ezk 47:9 7495
and marshes will not become **f**; Ezk 47:11 7495
new wine dries up, **F** oil fails. Jl 1:10 3323
put new wine into **f** wineskins, Mt 9:17 *2537*
puts new wine into **f** wineskins." Mk 2:22 *2537*
wine must be put into **f** wineskins. Lk 5:38 *2537*
opening *both* **f** and bitter *water?* Jas 3:11 *1099*
Nor *can* salt water produce **f**. Jas 3:12 *1099*

FRESHER

his flesh become **f** than in youth, Jb 33:25 7375

FRESHLY

in her beak was a **f** picked olive leaf. Gn 8:11 2965

FRET

Do not **f** because of evildoers, Be Ps 37:1 2734
Do not **f** because of him who Ps 37:7 2734
Do not **f**; *it leads* only to Ps 37:8 2734
Do not **f** because of evildoers Or Pr 24:19 2734

FRICTION

and constant **f** between men of 1Tm 6:5 *1275*

FRIEND

he and his **f** Hirah the Adullamite. Gn 38:12 7453
the young goat by his **f** the Adullamite, Gn 38:20 7453
his brother, and every man his **f**, Ex 32:27 7453
just as a man speaks to his **f**. Ex 33:11 7453
make a sale, moreover, to your **f** or Lv 25:14 5997
you shall buy from your **f**; Lv 25:15 5997
or your **f** who is as your own soul, Dt 13:6 7453
he kills his **f** unintentionally, Dt 19:4 7453
the forest with his **f** to cut wood, Dt 19:5 7453
and strikes his **f** so that he dies Dt 19:5 7453
man was relating a dream to his **f**. Jg 7:13 7453
His **f** replied, Jg 7:14 7453
his companion who had been his **f**. Jg 14:20 7462c
"Turn aside, **f**, sit down here." Ru 4:1 6423, 492
had a **f** whose name was Jonadab, 2Sa 13:3 7453
So Hushai, David's **f**, 2Sa 15:37 7463b
when Hushai the Archite, David's **f**, 2Sa 16:16 7463b
"Is this your loyalty to your **f**? 2Sa 16:17 7453
Why did you not go with your **f**?" 2Sa 16:17 7453
Nathan, a priest, *was* the king's **f**; 1Ki 4:5 7463b
had always been a **f** of David. 1Ki 5:1 157
the Archite *was* the king's **f**. 1Ch 27:33 7453
of Abraham Your **f** forever? 2Ch 20:7 157
should be kindness from his **f**; Jb 6:14 7453
orphans And barter over your **f**. Jb 6:27 7453
If I have rewarded evil to my **f**, Ps 7:4 7999b
takes up a reproach against his **f**; Ps 15:3 7453
as though it were my **f** or brother; Ps 35:14 7453
Even my close **f** in whom I trusted, Ps 41:9 376, 7965
My companion and my familiar **f**; Ps 55:13 3045
removed lover and **f** far from me; Ps 88:18 7453
understanding *your* intimate **f**; Pr 7:4 4129
A **f** loves at all times, And a Pr 17:17 7453
But there is a **f** who sticks closer Pr 18:24 157
poor man is separated from his **f**. Pr 19:4 7453
man is a **f** to him who gives gifts. Pr 19:6 7453
is gracious, the king is his **f**. Pr 22:11 7453
Faithful are the wounds of a **f**, Pr 27:6 157
a man's counsel is sweet to his **f**. Pr 27:9 7453
your own **f** or your father's friend, Pr 27:10 7453
your own friend or your father's **f**, Pr 27:10 7453
who blesses his **f** with a loud voice Pr 27:14 7453
is my beloved and this is my **f**, SS 5:16 7453
Descendant of Abraham My **f**, Is 41:8 157
You are the **f** of my youth? Jer 3:4 441a
Neighbor and **f** will perish." Jer 6:21 7453
Do not have confidence in a **f**. Mi 7:5 7453
a **f** of tax collectors and sinners!' Mt 11:19 *5384*
'**F**, I am doing you no wrong; Mt 20:13 *2083*
'**F**, how did you come in here Mt 22:12 *2083*
"**F**, *do* what you have come for." Mt 26:50 *2083*
"**F**, your sins are forgiven you." Lk 5:20 *444*
a **f** of tax collectors and sinners!' Lk 7:34 *5384*
"Suppose one of you has a **f**, Lk 11:5 *5384*
'**F**, lend me three loaves; Lk 11:5 *5384*
for a **f** of mine has come to me Lk 11:6 *5384*
give him *anything* because he is his **f**, Lk 11:8 *5384*
'**F**, move up higher'; Lk 14:10 *5384*
but the **f** of the bridegroom, who Jn 3:29 *5384*
"Our **f** Lazarus has fallen asleep; Jn 11:11 *5384*
this Man, you are no **f** of Caesar; Jn 19:12 *5384*
and he was called the **f** of God. Jas 2:23 *5384*
whoever wishes to be a **f** of the world Jas 4:4 *5384*

FRIENDLY

it was not **f** toward him as Gn 31:2
that it is not **f** toward me as Gn 31:5
"These men are **f** with us; Gn 34:21 8003
could not speak to him on **f** terms. Gn 37:4 7965

FRIEND'S

commits adultery with his **f** wife, Lv 20:10 7453
friend or buy from your **f** hand, Lv 25:14 5997

FRIENDS

to the elders of Judah, to his **f**, 1Sa 30:26 7453
to his brothers and to his **f**, 2Sa 3:8 4828
of his relatives nor of his **f**, 1Ki 16:11 7453
for his **f** and his wife Zeresh. Es 5:10 157
wife and all his **f** said to him, Es 5:14 157
wife and all his **f** everything that had Es 6:13 157
Now when Job's three **f** heard of Jb 2:11 7453
"I am a joke to my **f**, Jb 12:4 7453
"My **f** are my scoffers; Jb 16:20 7453
"He who informs against **f** for a Jb 17:5 7453
my intimate **f** have forgotten me. Jb 19:14 3045
"Pity me, pity me, O you my **f**, Jb 19:21 7453
his anger burned against his three **f** Jb 32:3 7453

answer you, And your f with you. Jb 35:4 7453
you and against your two f, Jb 42:7 7453
of Job when he prayed for his f, Jb 42:10 7453
my f stand aloof from my plague; Ps 38:11 7453
the sake of my brothers and my f, Ps 122:8 7453
a slanderer separates intimate f. Pr 16:28 441a
a matter separates intimate f. Pr 17:9 441a
A man of *too many* f *comes* to ruin, But Pr 18:24 7453
Wealth adds many f, Pr 19:4 7453
more do his f abandon him! Pr 19:7 4828
Eat, f; Drink and imbibe deeply, SS 5:1 7453
to yourself and to all your f; Jer 20:4 157
you and all your f to whom you Jer 20:6 157
All my trusted f, Watching for my Jer 20:10 582, 7965
"Your close f Have misled and Jer 38:22 376, 7965
All her f have dealt treacherously La 1:2 7453
for Daniel and his f to kill *them.* Da 2:13 2269
to his house and informed his f, Da 2:17 2269
so that Daniel and his f would not Da 2:18 2269
you and your f who are sitting in Zch 3:8 7453
was wounded in the house of my f.' Zch 13:6 157
"Make f quickly with your Mt 5:25 *2132*
the house, the centurion sent f, Lk 7:6 *5384*
"I say to you, My f, Lk 12:4 *5384*
do not invite your f or your Lk 14:12 *5384*
together his f and his neighbors, Lk 15:6 *5384*
together her f and neighbors, Lk 15:9 *5384*
that I might celebrate with my f; Lk 15:29 *5384*
make f for yourselves by means of Lk 16:9 *5384*
and brothers and relatives and f, Lk 21:16 *5384*
Now Herod and Pilate became f with Lk 23:12 *5384*
one lay down his life for his f. Jn 15:13 *5384*
"You are My f if you do what I Jn 15:14 *5384*
but I have called you f, Jn 15:15 *5384*
his relatives and close f. Ac 10:24 *5384*
Asiarchs who were f of his sent to him Ac 19:31 *5384*
of his f from ministering to him. Ac 24:23 *2398*
to go to his f and receive care. Ac 27:3 *5384*
Peace *be* to you. The f greet you. 3Jn 1:15 *5384*
Greet the f by name. 3Jn 1:15 *5384*

FRIENDSHIP
the f of God *was* over my tent; Jb 29:4 5475
f with the world is hostility toward Jas 4:4 *5373*

FRIGHTEN
will be no one to f *them* away. Dt 28:26 2729
the wall, to f and terrify them, 2Ch 32:18 3372a
all of them were *trying* to f us, Ne 6:9 3372a
prophets who were *trying* to f me. Ne 6:14 3372a
Then Tobiah sent letters to f me. Ne 6:19 3372a
Then You f me with dreams Jb 7:14 2865
"All around terrors f him, Jb 18:11 1204
there will be no one to f *them.* Is 17:2 2729
and no one will f *them away.* Jer 7:33 2729
Me in ships to f secure Ethiopia; Ezk 30:9 2729

FRIGHTENED
and the men were greatly f. Gn 20:8 3372a
them, and they became very f; Ex 14:10 3372a
Judah, and f them from building, Ezr 4:4 1089
f and act accordingly and sin, Ne 6:13 3372a
came I was f and fell on my face; Da 8:17 1204
extremely f and they said to him, Jon 1:10 3372a
But seeing the wind, he became f, Mt 14:30 *5399*
See that you are not f, Mt 24:6 *2360*
happening, became very f and said, Mt 27:54 *5399*
and they became f. Mk 5:15 *5399*
and rumors of wars, do not be f; Mk 13:7 *2360*
and they were terribly f. Lk 2:9 *5399*
and they became f. Lk 8:35 *5399*
But they were startled and f and Lk 24:37 *1719*
near to the boat; and they were f. Jn 6:19 *5399*
to come, Felix became f and said, Ac 24:25 *1719*
right without being f by any fear. 1Pe 3:6 *5399*

FRINGE
and touched the f of His cloak; Mt 9:20 *2899*
just touch the f of His cloak; Mt 14:36 *2899*
just touch the f of His cloak; Mk 6:56 *2899*
and touched the f of His cloak, Lk 8:44 *2899*

FRINGES
these are the f of His ways; Jb 26:14 7098

FRO
the eyes of the LORD move to and f 2Ch 16:9 7751a
and swing to and f far from men. Jb 28:4 5128
He who goes to and f weeping, Ps 126:6 1980
reels to and f like a drunkard And Is 24:20 5128
And all the hills moved to and f. Jer 4:24 7043
"Roam to and f through the Jer 5:1 7751a
to and f like bolts of lightning. Ezk 1:14 7725
go to and f to seek the word of the Am 8:12 7751a
to and f like lightning flashes. Na 2:4 7323
to and f throughout the earth." Zch 4:10 7751a

FROGS
smite your whole territory with f. Ex 8:2 6854
"The Nile will swarm with f, Ex 8:3 6854
"So the f will come up on you and Ex 8:4 6854
make f come up on the land of Egypt. Ex 8:5 6854
and the f came up and covered the Ex 8:6 6854
f come up on the land of Egypt. Ex 8:7 6854
that He remove the f from me and Ex 8:8 6854
that the f be destroyed from you Ex 8:9 6854
"The f will depart from you Ex 8:11 6854
cried to the LORD concerning the f Ex 8:12 6854
and the f died out of the houses, Ex 8:13 6854
them, And f which destroyed them. Ps 78:45 6854
Their land swarmed with f *Even* in Ps 105:30 6854
three unclean spirits like f; Rv 16:13 *944*

FROLIC
and shaggy goats will f there. Is 13:21 7540

FRONT
in f of the flocks in the gutters, Gn 30:38 5227
He commanded the one in f, Gn 32:17 7223
these *animals* in f of you belong?' Gn 32:17 6440
the maids and their children in f, Gn 33:2 7223
there was a vine in f of me; Gn 40:9 6440
you shall camp in f of Baal-zephon, Ex 14:2 6440
Pi-hahiroth, in f of Baal-zephon. Ex 14:9 6440
camped in f of the mountain. Ex 19:2 5048
light on the space in f of it. Ex 25:37 6440
curtain at the f of the tent. Ex 26:9 6440
of the ephod, at the f of it. Ex 28:25 6440
on the f of it close to the place Ex 28:27 6440
shall be at the f of the turban. Ex 28:37 6440
You shall put this altar in f of the veil Ex 30:6 6440
in f of the mercy seat that is Ex 30:6 6440
not graze in f of that mountain." Ex 34:3 4136
the LORD passed by in f of him Ex 34:6 6440
of the ephod at the f of it. Ex 39:18 6440
of the ephod, on the f of it, Ex 39:20 6440
set the altar of burnt offering in f of Ex 40:6 6440
tent of meeting in f of the veil; Ex 40:26 6440
in f of the veil of the sanctuary. Lv 4:6 6440
before the LORD, in f of the veil. Lv 4:17 6440
nip its head at the f of its neck, Lv 5:8 4136
before the LORD in f of the altar. Lv 6:14 6440
head, and on the turban, at its f, Lv 8:9 6440
to the f of the tent of meeting, Lv 9:5 6440
away from the f of the sanctuary Lv 10:4 6440
becomes bald at the f and sides, Lv 13:41 6440
on the top or on the f of it. Lv 13:55 1372
also in f of the mercy seat he Lv 16:14 6440
seat and in f of the mercy seat. Lv 16:15 6440
in the f of the lampstand.' " Nu 8:2 6440
lamps at the f of the lampstand, Nu 8:3 6440
in f of them for the three days, Nu 10:33 6440
will be there in f of you, Nu 14:43 6440
to the f of the tent of meeting, Nu 16:43 6440
of meeting in f of the testimony, Nu 17:4 6440
of its blood toward the f of the tent Nu 19:4 6440
you shall read this law in f of Dt 31:11 5048
near and arrived in f of the city, Jos 8:11 5048
Half of them *stood* in f of Mount Jos 8:33 4136
half of them in f of Mount Ebal, Jos 8:33 4136
side in f of the Arabah northward and Jos 18:18 4136
country, and he *was* in f of them. Jg 3:27 6440
and the valuables in f of them. Jg 18:21 6440
with the shield-bearer in f of him. 1Sa 17:41 6440
to seek David and his men in f of the 1Sa 24:2 6440
which is in f of Giah by the way 2Sa 2:24 6440
at them in f of the balsam trees. 2Sa 5:23 4136
against him in f and in the rear, 2Sa 10:9 6440
"Place Uriah in the f line of the 2Sa 11:15 6440
The porch in f of the nave of 1Ki 6:3 6440
the f of the house *was* ten cubits. 1Ki 6:3 6440
nave in f of *the inner sanctuary,* 1Ki 6:17 6440
the f of the inner sanctuary, 1Ki 6:21 6440
and a porch *was* in f of them and 1Ki 7:6 6440
and a threshold in f of them. 1Ki 7:6 6440
left, in f of the inner sanctuary, 1Ki 7:49 6440
his chariot in f of the Arameans, 1Ki 22:35 5227
brought from the f of the house, 2Ki 16:14 6440
at them in f of the balsam trees. 1Ch 14:14 4136
against him in f and in the rear, 1Ch 19:10 6440
The porch which was in f of 2Ch 3:4 6440
pillars for the f of the house, 2Ch 3:15 6440
the pillars in f of the temple, 2Ch 3:17 6440
to burn in f of the inner 2Ch 4:20 6440
seen in f of the inner sanctuary, 2Ch 5:9 6440
so that *Israel* was in f of Judah and 2Ch 13:13 6440
were attacked both f and rear; 2Ch 13:14 6440
was in f of the porch of the LORD. 2Ch 15:8 6440
propped himself up in his chariot in f 2Ch 18:34 5227
in f of the wilderness of Jeruel. 2Ch 20:16 6440
in f of the ascent of the armory Ne 3:19 5048
out repairs in f of their house. Ne 3:23 5048
of Uzai *made repairs* in f of the Angle Ne 3:25 5048
as far as the f of the Water Gate Ne 3:26 5048
Tekoites repaired another section in f Ne 3:27 5048
repairs, each in f of his house. Ne 3:28 5048
out repairs in f of his house. Ne 3:29 5048
repairs in f of his own quarters. Ne 3:30 5048
in f of the Inspection Gate and as Ne 3:31 5048
out the f of my garment and said, Ne 5:13 2684
and each in f of his own house." Ne 7:3 5048
which was in f of the Water Gate, Ne 8:1 6440
square which was in f of the Water Ne 8:3 6440
spend the night in f of the wall? Ne 13:21 5048
Mordecai walked back and forth in f Es 2:11 6440
square in f of the king's gate. Es 4:6 6440
palace in f of the king's rooms, Es 5:1 5227
be fixed straight in f of you. Pr 4:25 5048
it was written on the f and back, Ezk 2:10 6440
slain fall in f of your idols. Ezk 6:4 6440
of Israel in f of their idols; Ezk 6:5 6440
Standing in f of them were Ezk 8:11 6440
one cubit *wide* in f of the guardrooms Ezk 40:12 6440
From the f of the entrance Ezk 40:15 6440
to the f of the inner porch of the gate Ezk 40:15 6440
width from the f of the lower gate Ezk 40:19 6440
to the f of the exterior of the inner Ezk 40:19 6440
and its porch *was* in f of them. Ezk 40:22 6440
and its porches *were* in f of them; Ezk 40:26 6440
gate, with its f toward the south, Ezk 40:44 6440
the altar was in f of the temple. Ezk 40:47 6440
The building that *was* in f of Ezk 41:12 6440
Also the width of the f of the Ezk 41:14 6440
the length of the building along the f Ezk 41:15 6440
as for the f of the sanctuary, the Ezk 41:21 6440
on the f of the porch outside. Ezk 41:25 6440
The way in f of them *was* like Ezk 42:11 6440
in f of the wall toward the east, Ezk 42:12 6440
north gate to the f of the house; Ezk 44:4 6440
in f of the 25,000 *cubits* of the Ezk 48:21 6440
westward in f of the 25,000 toward Ezk 48:21 6440
was standing in f of you, Da 2:31 6903
was standing in f of the canal. Da 8:3 6440
seen standing in f of the canal, Da 8:6 6440
friends who are sitting in f of you Zch 3:8 6440
is in f of Jerusalem on the east; Zch 14:4 6440
his hands in f of the crowd, Mt 27:24 *2713*
Those who went in f and those who Mk 11:9 *4254*
was standing right in f of Him, Mk 15:39 *1727*
and to set him down in f of Him. Lk 5:18 *1799*
middle *of the crowd,* in f of Jesus. Lk 5:19 *1715*
in f of Him was a man Lk 14:2 *1715*
and guards in f of the door were Ac 12:6 *4253*
was standing in f of the gate. Ac 12:14 *4253*
him in f of the judgment seat. Ac 18:17 *1715*
full of eyes in f and behind. Rv 4:6 *1715*

FRONTALS
shall be as f on your forehead. Dt 6:8 2903
shall be as f on your forehead. Dt 11:18 2903

FRONTIER
at the f of the land of Canaan, Jos 22:11 4136

FRONTIERS
of its cities which are on its f, Ezk 25:9 7097a

FROST
consumed me and the f by night, Gn 31:40 7140
fine as the f on the ground. Ex 16:14 3713b
And the f of heaven, who has given Jb 38:29 3713b
And their sycamore trees with f. Ps 78:47 2602
He scatters the f like ashes. Ps 147:16 3713b
of the day and the f of the night. Jer 36:30 7140

FROZEN
the expanse of the waters is f. Jb 37:10 4164

FRUIT
and f trees on the earth bearing Gn 1:11 6529
earth bearing f after their kind Gn 1:11 6529
their kind, and trees bearing f with Gn 1:12 6529
tree which has f yielding seed; Gn 1:29 6529
"From the f of the trees of the Gn 3:2 6529
but from the f of the tree which Gn 3:3 6529
wise, she took from its f and ate; Gn 3:6 6529
the LORD of the f of the ground. Gn 4:3 6529
from you the f of the womb?" Gn 30:2 6529
the f of the trees that the hail had left. Ex 10:15 6529
the year when you gather in *the* f Ex 23:16
the fallen f of your vineyard; Lv 19:10 6528
shall count their f as forbidden. Lv 19:23 6529
year all its f shall be holy, Lv 19:24 6529
year you are to eat of its f, Lv 19:25 6529
of the field will bear their f. Lv 26:4 6529
the land will not yield their f. Lv 26:20 6529
the land or of the f of the tree, Lv 27:30 6529
get some of the f of the land." Nu 13:20 6529
and showed them the f of the land. Nu 13:26 6529
milk and honey, and this is its f. Nu 13:27 6529
"Then they took *some* of the f of Dt 1:25 6529
He will also bless the f of your Dt 7:13 6529
womb and the f of your ground, Dt 7:13 6529
the ground will not yield its f; Dt 11:17 2981
and has not begun to use its f? Dt 20:6 2490c
another man would begin to use its f. Dt 20:6 2490c
trees which you know are not f trees Dt 20:20 3978
but you will not use its f. Dt 28:30 2490c
bearing poisonous f and wormwood. Dt 29:18 6509
leave my sweetness and my good f, Jg 9:11 8570
summer f for the young men to eat, 2Sa 16:2 7019c
plant vineyards, and eat their f. 2Ki 19:29 6529
root downward and bear f upward. 2Ki 19:30 6529
groves, F trees in abundance. Ne 9:25 3978
to eat of its f and its bounty, Ne 9:36 6529
the first fruits of all the f of every tree Ne 10:35 6529
the f of every tree, Ne 10:37 6529
I have eaten its f without money, Jb 31:39 3581b
Which yields its f in its season And Ps 1:3 6529
Its f will wave like *the cedars of* Ps 72:16 6529
who pass *that* way pick its f? Ps 80:12
will still yield f in old age; Ps 92:14 5107
satisfied with the f of His works. Ps 104:13 6529
And ate up the f of their ground. Ps 105:35 6529
they might take possession of *the* f Ps 105:44
The f of the womb is a reward. Ps 127:3 6529
shall eat of the f of your hands, Ps 128:2 3018
"Of the f of your body I will set Ps 132:11 6529
F trees and all cedars; Ps 148:9 6529
eat of the f of their own way And Pr 1:31 6529
"My f is better than gold, even Pr 8:19 6529
The f of the righteous is a tree Pr 11:30 6529
the root of the righteous yields f. Pr 12:12
with good by the f of his words, Pr 12:14 6529
From the f of a man's mouth he Pr 13:2 6529
With the f of a man's mouth his Pr 18:20 6529
those who love it will eat its f. Pr 18:21 6529
tends the fig tree will eat its f, Pr 27:18 6529
in them all kinds of f trees; Ec 2:5 6529
Thus I hated all the f of my labor Ec 2:18 5999
control over all the f of my labor Ec 2:19 5999
despaired of all the f of my labor Ec 2:20 5999
He will take nothing from the f of Ec 5:15 5999
And his f was sweet to my taste. SS 2:3 6529
I will take hold of its f stalks.' SS 7:8 5577
shekels of silver for its f. SS 8:11 6529
those who take care of its f." SS 8:12 6529

will eat the **f** of their actions. Is 3:10 6529
the **f** of the earth *will be* Is 4:2 6529
punish the **f** of the arrogant heart Is 10:12 6529
branch from his roots will bear **f**. Is 11:1 6509
compassion on the **f** of the womb, Is 13:18 6529
its **f** will be a flying serpent. Is 14:29 6529
will fill the whole world with **f**. Is 27:6 8570
And the **f** gathering will not Is 32:10
plant vineyards and eat their **f**. Is 37:30 6529
root downward and bear **f** upward. Is 37:31 6529
open up and salvation bear **f**, Is 45:8 6509
plant vineyards and eat their **f**. Is 65:21 6529
To eat its **f** and its good things. Jer 2:7 6529
this people, The **f** of their plans, Jer 6:19 6529
field and on the **f** of the ground; Jer 7:20 6529
tree, beautiful in **f** and form"; Jer 11:16 6529
us destroy the tree with its **f**, Jer 11:19 3899
grow, they have even produced **f**. Jer 12:2 6529
of drought Nor cease to yield **f**. Jer 17:8 6529
according to the **f** of his deeds; Jer 32:19 6529
in wine and summer **f** and oil and Jer 40:10 7019c
and summer **f** in great abundance. Jer 40:12 7019c
might yield branches and bear **f** Ezk 17:8 6529
and cut off its **f**, so that it withers Ezk 17:9 6529
may bring forth boughs and bear **f** and Ezk 17:23 6529
And the east wind dried up its **f**. Ezk 19:12 6529
It has consumed its shoots *and* **f**, Ezk 19:14 6529
eat your **f** and drink your milk. Ezk 25:4 6529
of the field will yield its **f** and Ezk 34:27 6529
bear your **f** for My people Israel; Ezk 36:8 6529
"I will multiply the **f** of the Ezk 36:30 6529
wither and their **f** will not fail. Ezk 47:12 6529
and their **f** will be for food and Ezk 47:12 6529
was beautiful and its **f** abundant, Da 4:12 4
off its foliage and scatter its **f**; Da 4:14 4
was beautiful and its **f** abundant, Da 4:21 4
forefathers as the earliest **f** on the fig Hos 9:10 1063
is dried up, They will bear no **f**. Hos 9:16 6529
He produces **f** for himself. Hos 10:1 6529
The more his **f**, The more altars he Hos 10:1 6529
You have eaten the **f** of lies. Hos 10:13 6529
we may present the **f** of our lips. Hos 14:2 6499
From Me comes your **f**. Hos 14:8 6529
For the tree has borne its **f**, Jl 2:22 6529
his **f** above and his root below. Am 2:9 6529
And the **f** of righteousness into Am 6:12 6529
there was a basket of summer **f**. Am 8:1 7019c
"A basket of summer **f**." Am 8:2 7019c
And make gardens and eat their **f**. Am 9:14 6529
The **f** of my body for the sin of my Mi 6:7 6529
For I am Like the **f** pickers, Mi 7:1 7019c
account of the **f** of their deeds. Mi 7:13 6529
fortifications are fig trees with ripe **f** Na 3:12 1061
And there be no **f** on the vines, Hab 3:17 2981
it has not borne **f**. Yet from Hg 2:19
the vine will yield its **f**, Zch 8:12 6529
Lord is defiled, and as for its **f**, Mal 1:12 5204b
f in keeping with repentance; Mt 3:8 *2590*
that does not bear good **f** is cut down Mt 3:10 *2590*
"So every good tree bears good **f**, Mt 7:17 *2590*
but the bad tree bears bad **f**. Mt 7:17 *2590*
"A good tree cannot produce bad **f**, Mt 7:18 *2590*
nor can a bad tree produce good **f**. Mt 7:18 *2590*
tree that does not bear good **f** is cut Mt 7:19 *2590*
the tree good and its **f** good Mt 12:33 *2590*
make the tree bad and its **f** bad; Mt 12:33 *2590*
for the tree is known by its **f**. Mt 12:33 *2590*
who indeed bears **f** and Mt 13:23 *2592*
there ever be *any* **f** from you." Mt 21:19 *2590*
to a people, producing the **f** of it. Mt 21:43 *2590*
I will not drink of this **f** of the Mt 26:29 *1079b*
word and accept it and bear **f**, Mk 4:20 *2592*
one ever eat **f** from you again!" Mk 11:14 *2590*
never again drink of the **f** of the vine Mk 14:25 *1079b*
and blessed *is* the **f** of your womb! Lk 1:42 *2590*
that does not bear good **f** is cut down Lk 3:9 *2590*
no good tree which produces bad **f**, Lk 6:43 *2590*
a bad tree which produces good **f**. Lk 6:43 *2590*
each tree is known by its own **f**. Lk 6:44 *2590*
life, and bring no **f** to maturity. Lk 8:14 *5052*
and bear **f** with perseverance. Lk 8:15 *2592*
and he came looking for **f** on it and Lk 13:6 *2590*
three years I have come looking for **f** Lk 13:7 *2590*
and if it bears **f** next year, *fine* Lk 13:9 *2590*
I will not drink of the **f** of the Lk 22:18 *1079b*
is gathering **f** for life eternal; Jn 4:36 *2590*
but if it dies, it bears much **f**. Jn 12:24 *2590*
branch in Me that does not bear **f**, Jn 15:2 *2590*
and every *branch* that bears **f**, Jn 15:2 *2590*
it so that it may bear more **f**. Jn 15:2 *2590*
branch cannot bear **f** of itself unless Jn 15:4 *2590*
Me and I in him, he bears much **f** Jn 15:5 *2590*
this, that you bear much **f**, Jn 15:8 *2590*
that you would go and bear **f**, Jn 15:16 *2590*
and *that* your **f** would remain, Jn 15:16 *2590*
obtain some **f** among you also, Ro 1:13 *2590*
that we might bear **f** for God. Ro 7:4 *2592*
of our body to bear **f** for death. Ro 7:5 *2592*
put my seal on this **f** of theirs, Ro 15:28 *2590*
and does not eat the **f** of it? 1Co 9:7 *2590*
But the **f** of the Spirit is love, Ga 5:22 *2590*
(for the **f** of the Light *consists* Eph 5:9 *2590*
having been filled with the **f** of Php 1:11 *2590*
bearing **f** and increasing, Col 1:6 *2592*
bearing **f** in every good work and Col 1:10 *2592*
the peaceful **f** of righteousness. Heb 12:11 *2590*
the **f** of lips that give thanks to Heb 13:15 *2590*
And the seed whose **f** is Jas 3:18 *2590*
and the earth produced its **f**. Jas 5:18 *2590*
autumn trees without **f**, Jude 1:12 *175*
"The **f** you long for has gone Rv 18:14 *3703*
life, bearing twelve *kinds of* **f**, Rv 22:2 *2590*
fruit, yielding its **f** every month; Rv 22:2 *2590*

FRUITFUL

"Be **f** and multiply, and fill the Gn 1:22 6509
"Be **f** and multiply, and fill the Gn 1:28 6509
be **f** and multiply on the earth." Gn 8:17 6509
"Be **f** and multiply, and fill the Gn 9:1 6509
"As for you, be **f** and multiply; Gn 9:7 6509
"I will make you exceedingly **f**, Gn 17:6 6509
bless him, and will make him **f** and Gn 17:20 6509
and we will be **f** in the land." Gn 26:22 6509
and make you **f** and multiply you, Gn 28:3 6509
Be **f** and multiply; Gn 35:11 6509
f in the land of my affliction." Gn 41:52 6509
were **f** and became very numerous. Gn 47:27 6509
I will make you **f** and numerous, Gn 48:4 6509
"Joseph is a **f** bough, A fruitful Gn 49:22 6509
bough, A **f** bough by a spring; Gn 49:22 6509
were **f** and increased greatly, Ex 1:7 6509
until you become **f** and take Ex 23:30 6509
and make you **f** and multiply you, Lv 26:9 6509
He caused His people to be very **f**, Ps 105:24 6509
A **f** land into a salt waste, Ps 107:34 6529
vineyards, And gather a **f** harvest. Ps 107:37 6529
Your wife shall be like a **f** vine Within Ps 128:3 6509
of his forest and of his **f** garden, Is 10:18 3759
are taken away from the **f** field; Is 16:10 3759
five on the branches of a **f** tree, Is 17:6 6509
pleasant fields, for the **f** vine, Is 32:12 6509
"I brought you into the **f** land To Jer 2:7 3759
the **f** land was a wilderness, Jer 4:26 3759
and they will be **f** and multiply. Jer 23:3 6509
are taken away From the **f** field, Jer 48:33 3759
It was **f** and full of branches Ezk 19:10 6509
and they will increase and be **f**; Ezk 36:11 6509
In the midst of a **f** field. Mi 7:14 3759
rains from heaven and **f** seasons, Ac 14:17 *2593*
this *will mean* **f** labor for me; Php 1:22 *2590*

FRUITLESS

have turned aside to **f** discussion, 1Tm 1:6 *3150*

FRUITS

the Feast of the Harvest *of* the first **f** Ex 23:16 1061
bring the choice first **f** of your soil Ex 23:19 1061
the first **f** of the wheat harvest, Ex 34:22 1061
shall bring the very first of the first **f** Ex 34:26 1061
'As an offering of first **f** you Lv 2:12 7225
f of your harvest to the priest. Lv 23:10 7225
leaven as first **f** to the LORD. Lv 23:17 1061
bread of the first **f** for a wave offering Lv 23:20 1061
the first **f** of those which they Nu 18:12 7225
f of all that is in their land, Nu 18:13 1061
'Also on the day of the first **f**, Nu 28:26 1061
him the first **f** of your grain, Dt 18:4 7225
of raisins, a hundred summer **f**, 2Sa 16:1 7019c
man of God bread of the first **f**, 2Ki 4:42 1061
in abundance the first **f** of grain, 2Ch 31:5 7225
might bring the first **f** of our ground Ne 10:35 1061
the first **f** of all the fruit of every tree Ne 10:35 1061
the contributions, the first **f** and Ne 12:44 7225
times and for the first **f**. Ne 13:31 1061
The first **f** of all their vigor. Ps 105:36 7225
of pomegranates With choice **f**, SS 4:13 4022, 6529
his garden And eat its choice **f**!" SS 4:16 6529
And over our doors are all choice **f**, SS 7:13
the shouting over your summer **f** and Is 16:9 7019c
Upon your summer **f** and your grape Jer 48:32 7019c
For lack of the **f** of the field. La 4:9 8570
"The first of all the first **f** Ezk 44:30 1061
not destroy the **f** of the ground; Mal 3:11 6529
"You will know them by their **f**. Mt 7:16 *2590*
you will know them by their **f**. Mt 7:20 *2590*
f in keeping with repentance, Lk 3:8 *2590*
having the first **f** of the Spirit, Ro 8:23 *536*
first **f** of those who are asleep. 1Co 15:20 *536*
Christ the first **f**, 1Co 15:23 *536*
they were the first **f** of Achaia, 1Co 16:15 *536*
of first **f** among His creatures. Jas 1:18 *536*
full of mercy and good **f**, Jas 3:17 *2590*
as first **f** to God and to the Lamb. Rv 14:4 *536*

FRUSTRATE

hired counselors against them to **f** Ezr 4:5 6565a
has planned, and who can **f** *it?* Is 14:27 6565a

FRUSTRATED

Amnon was so **f** because of his 2Sa 13:2 6887a
us, and that God had **f** their plan, Ne 4:15 6565a
Without consultation, plans are **f**, Pr 15:22 6565a

FRUSTRATES

"He **f** the plotting of the shrewd, Jb 5:12 6565a
He **f** the plans of the peoples. Ps 33:10 5106

FUEL

be for burning, **f** for the fire. Is 9:5 3980
people are like **f** for the fire; Is 9:19 3980
has been put into the fire for **f**, Ezk 15:4 402
I have given to the fire for **f**, Ezk 15:6 402
'You will be **f** for the fire; Ezk 21:32 402

FUGITIVE

Then a **f** came and told Abram the Gn 14:13 6412a
blood Will be a **f** until death; Pr 28:17 5127
the outcasts, do not betray the **f**. Is 16:3 5074
of Tema, Meet the **f** with bread. Is 21:14 5074
will not have a **f** who will flee, Am 9:1 5127

FUGITIVES

He has given his sons as **f**, Nu 21:29 6412b
"You are **f** of Ephraim, O Jg 12:4 6412a
when *any of* the **f** of Ephraim said, Jg 12:5 6412a
His **f** are as far as Zoar *and* Is 15:5 1281
A lion upon the **f** of Moab and upon Is 15:9 6413
And will bring them all down as **f**, Is 43:14 1281
together, you **f** of the nations; Is 45:20 6412a
in haste, Nor will you go as **f**; Is 52:12 4499
The **f** stand without strength; Jer 48:45 5127
no one to gather the **f** together. Jer 49:5 5074
There is a sound of **f** and refugees Jer 50:28 5127
of the road To cut down their **f**; Ob 1:14 6412a

FULFILL

I will **f** the number of your days. Ex 23:26 4390
to the LORD to **f** a special vow or Lv 22:21 6381
or a sacrifice to **f** a special vow, Nu 15:3 6381
a sacrifice, to **f** a special vow, Nu 15:8 6381
order to **f** the word of the LORD, 1Ki 2:27 4390
to **f** the word of the LORD by the 2Ch 36:21 4390
in order to **f** the word of the LORD 2Ch 36:22 3615
in order to **f** the word of the LORD Ezr 1:1 3615
who does not **f** this promise; Ne 5:13 6965
"Can you count the months they **f**, Jb 39:2 4390
desire And **f** all your counsel! Ps 20:4 4390
May the LORD **f** all your petitions. Ps 20:5 4390
to the LORD your God and **f** *them;* Ps 76:11 7999a
He will **f** the desire of those who Ps 145:19 6213a
you and **f** My good word to you, Jer 29:10 6965
'when I will **f** the good word which Jer 33:14 6965
up in order to **f** the vision, Da 11:14 5975
Now all this took place to **f** what was Mt 1:22 *4137*
This was to **f** what had been Mt 2:15 *4137*
This was to **f** what was spoken Mt 2:23 *4137*
for us to **f** all righteousness." Mt 3:15 *4137*
This was to **f** what was spoken Mt 4:14 *4137*
did not come to abolish but to **f**. Mt 5:17 *4137*
SHALL **F** YOUR VOWS TO THE LORD.' Mt 5:33 *591*
This was to **f** what was spoken Mt 8:17 *4137*
This was to **f** what was spoken Mt 12:17 *4137*
This was to **f** what was spoken Mt 13:35 *4137*
This took place to **f** what was spoken Mt 21:4 *4137*
"But all this has taken place to **f** Mt 26:56 *4137*
but *this has taken place* to **f** Mk 14:49 *4137*
This was to **f** the word of Isaiah Jn 12:38 *4137*
"But *they have done this* to **f** Jn 15:25 *4137*
to **f** the word which He spoke, "Of Jn 18:9 *4137*
to **f** the word of Jesus which He spoke, Jn 18:32 *4137*
this was to **f** the Scripture: Jn 19:24 *4137*
to **f** the Scripture, said, "I am Jn 19:28 *5048*
For these things came to pass to **f** Jn 19:36 *4137*
husband must **f** his duty to his wife, 1Co 7:3 *591*
and thereby **f** the law of Christ. Ga 6:2 *378*
in the Lord, that you may **f** it." Col 4:17 *4137*
and **f** every desire for goodness 2Th 1:11 *4137*
of an evangelist, **f** your ministry. 2Tm 4:5 *4135*

FULFILLED

her days to be delivered were **f**, Gn 25:24 4390
period of your ordination is **f**; Lv 8:33 4390
He shall be holy until the days are **f** Nu 6:5 4390
the days of his separation are **f**, Nu 6:13 4390
all have been **f** for you, not one Jos 23:14 935
David and has **f** *it* with His hand, 1Ki 8:15 4390
has **f** His word which He spoke; 1Ki 8:20 6965
spoken with Your mouth and have **f** it 1Ki 8:24 4390
"When your days are **f** 1Ch 17:11 4390
promise to my father David is **f**, 2Ch 1:9 539
David and has **f** *it* with His hands, 2Ch 6:4 4390
has **f** His word which He spoke; 2Ch 6:10 6965
and have **f** it with Your hand, 2Ch 6:15 4390
And You have **f** Your promise, For Ne 9:8 6965
But desire **f** is a tree of life. Pr 13:12 935
who have not **f** the words of the Jer 34:18 6965
mouths and **f** *it* with your hands, Jer 44:25 4390
concerning Nebuchadnezzar was **f**; Da 4:33 5487
Jeremiah the prophet was **f**: Mt 2:17 *4137*
the prophecy of Isaiah is being **f**, Mt 13:14 *378*
then will the Scriptures be **f**, Mt 26:54 *4137*
Jeremiah the prophet was **f**: Mt 27:9 *4137*
"The time is **f**, and the kingdom Mk 1:15 *4137*
these things are going to be **f**?" Mk 13:4 *4931*
the Scripture was **f** which says, Mk 15:28 *4137*
will be **f** in their proper time." Lk 1:20 *4137*
has been **f** in your hearing." Lk 4:21 *4137*
things which are written will be **f**. Lk 21:22 *4092a*
the times of the Gentiles are **f**. Lk 21:24 *4137*
it is **f** in the kingdom of God." Lk 22:16 *4137*
which is written must be **f** in Me, Lk 22:37 *5055*
and the Psalms must be **f**." Lk 24:44 *4137*
it is that the Scripture may be **f**, Jn 13:18 *4137*
that the Scripture would be **f**. Jn 17:12 *4137*
the Scripture had to be **f**, Ac 1:16 *4137*
would suffer, He has thus **f**. Ac 3:18 *4137*
when they had **f** their mission, Ac 12:25 *4137*
f *these* by condemning *Him*. Ac 13:27 *4137*
that God has **f** this *promise* to our Ac 13:33 *1603*
of the Law might be **f** in us, Ro 8:4 *4137*
loves his neighbor has **f** *the* law. Ro 13:8 *4137*
the whole Law is **f** in one word, Ga 5:14 *4137*
the Scripture was **f** which says, Jas 2:23 *4137*
the words of God will be **f**. Rv 17:17 *5055*

FULFILLING

Stormy wind, **f** His word; Ps 148:8 6213a
you are **f** the royal law according Jas 2:8 *5055*

FULFILLMENT

as well as the **f** of every vision. Ezk 12:23 1697
they hope for the **f** of *their* word. Ezk 13:6 6965
believed that there would be a **f** of Lk 1:45 *5050*
which refers to Me has *its* **f**." Lk 22:37 *5056*
how much more will their **f** be! Ro 11:12 *4138*
therefore love is the **f** of *the* law. Ro 13:10 *4138*

FULFILLS
he **f** his day like a hired man. **Jb 14:6** 7521

FULL
of Siddim was **f** of tar pits; **Gn 14:10**
for the **f** price let him give it to **Gn 23:9** 4392
at the end of two **f** years that Pharaoh **Gn 41:1** 3117
up the seven plump and **f** ears. **Gn 41:7** 4392
behold, seven ears, **f** and good, **Gn 41:22** 4392
mouth of his sack, our money in **f**. **Gn 43:21** 4948
pays us back in **f** for all the wrong **Gn 50:15** 7725
will be **f** of swarms of insects, **Ex 8:21** 4390
meat, when we ate bread to the **f**; **Ex 16:3** 7648
and bread to the **f** in the morning; **Ex 16:8** 7646
it, he shall make **f** restitution. **Ex 22:14** 7999a
make restitution for it in **f** and **Lv 6:5** 7218
"He shall take a firepan **f** of **Lv 16:12** 4393
and the land become **f** of lewdness. **Lv 19:29** 4390
until a **f** year from its sale; **Lv 25:29** 8552
of redemption lasts a **f** year. **Lv 25:29** 3117
him within the space of a **f** year, **Lv 25:30** 8549
You will thus eat your food to the **f** **Lv 26:5** 7648
restitution in **f** for his wrong and **Nu 5:7** 7218
both of them **f** of fine flour mixed **Nu 7:13** 4392
pan of ten *shekels,* **f** of incense; **Nu 7:14** 4392
both of them **f** of fine flour mixed **Nu 7:19** 4392
pan of ten *shekels,* **f** of incense; **Nu 7:20** 4392
both of them **f** of fine flour mixed **Nu 7:25** 4392
pan of ten *shekels,* **f** of incense; **Nu 7:26** 4392
both of them **f** of fine flour mixed **Nu 7:31** 4392
pan of ten *shekels,* **f** of incense; **Nu 7:32** 4392
both of them **f** of fine flour mixed **Nu 7:37** 4392
pan of ten *shekels,* **f** of incense; **Nu 7:38** 4392
both of them **f** of fine flour mixed **Nu 7:43** 4392
pan of ten *shekels,* **f** of incense; **Nu 7:44** 4392
both of them **f** of fine flour mixed **Nu 7:49** 4392
pan of ten *shekels,* **f** of incense; **Nu 7:50** 4392
both of them **f** of fine flour mixed **Nu 7:55** 4392
pan of ten *shekels,* **f** of incense; **Nu 7:56** 4392
both of them **f** of fine flour mixed **Nu 7:61** 4392
pan of ten *shekels,* **f** of incense; **Nu 7:62** 4392
both of them **f** of fine flour mixed **Nu 7:67** 4392
pan of ten *shekels,* **f** of incense; **Nu 7:68** 4392
both of them **f** of fine flour mixed **Nu 7:73** 4392
pan of ten *shekels,* **f** of incense; **Nu 7:74** 4392
both of them **f** of fine flour mixed **Nu 7:79** 4392
pan of ten *shekels,* **f** of incense; **Nu 7:80** 4392
twelve gold pans, **f** of incense, **Nu 7:86** 4392
the **f** produce from the wine vat. **Nu 18:27** 4395
me his house **f** of silver and gold, **Nu 22:18** 4393
me his house **f** of silver and gold, **Nu 24:13** 4393
"Take **f** vengeance for the sons of **Nu 31:2** 5360
and houses **f** of all good things **Dt 6:11** 4392
her father and mother a **f** month; **Dt 21:13** 3117
shall have a **f** and just weight; **Dt 25:15** 8003
shall have a **f** and just measure, **Dt 25:15** 8003
And **f** of the blessing of the LORD, **Dt 33:23** 4392
the fleece, a bowl **f** of water. **Jg 6:38** 4393
the house was **f** of men and women, **Jg 16:27** 4390
her master was, until **f** daylight. **Jg 19:26**
"I went out **f**, but the LORD has **Ru 1:21** 4392
and your wages be **f** from the LORD, **Ru 2:12** 8003
Those who were **f** hire themselves **1Sa 2:5** 7649
gave them in **f** number to the king, **1Sa 18:27** 4390
Then Saul immediately fell **f** **1Sa 28:20** 4393
and one **f** line to keep alive. **2Sa 8:2** 4393
Now it came about after two **f** **2Sa 13:23** 3117
lived two **f** years in Jerusalem, **2Sa 14:28** 3117
was a plot of ground **f** of lentils, **2Sa 23:11** 4392
'Make this valley **f** of trenches.' **2Ki 3:16** 1356a
you shall set aside what is **f**." **2Ki 4:4** 4392
When the vessels were **f**, **2Ki 4:6** 4390
from it his lap **f** of wild gourds, **2Ki 4:39** 4393
the mountain was **f** of horses and **2Ki 6:17** 4390
was **f** of clothes and equipment which **2Ki 7:15** 4392
And Jehu drew his bow with his **f** **2Ki 9:24** 4390
was a plot of ground **f** of barley; **1Ch 11:13** 4392
f price you shall give it to me, **1Ch 21:22** 4392
surely buy *it* for the **f** price; **1Ch 21:24** 4392
died in a ripe old age, **f** of days, **1Ch 29:28** 7649
the **f** cost is to be paid to these **Ezr 6:8** 629
in **f** before the God of Jerusalem. **Ezr 7:19** 8000
of houses **f** of every good thing, **Ne 9:25** 4392
wrote with **f** authority to confirm **Es 9:29** 3605
and the **f** account of the greatness **Es 10:2** 6575
will come to the grave in **f** vigor, **Jb 5:26** 3624
will give **f** vent to my complaint; **Jb 10:1**
5800a, 5921
Is short-lived and **f** of turmoil. **Jb 14:1** 7649
bones are **f** of his youthful vigor, **Jb 20:11** 4390
"One dies in his **f** strength, **Jb 21:23** 8537
For your answers remain **f** *of* **Jb 21:34**
obscures the face of the **f** moon And **Jb 26:9** 3677
"For I am **f** of words; **Jb 32:18** 4390
on your table was **f** of fatness. **Jb 36:16** 4390
were **f** of judgment on the wicked; **Jb 36:17** 4390
died, an old man and **f** of days. **Jb 42:17** 7649
His mouth is **f** of curses and **Ps 10:7** 4390
whose right hand is **f** of bribes. **Ps 26:10** 4390
The earth is **f** of the **Ps 33:5** 4390
am **f** of anxiety because of my sin. **Ps 38:18** 1672
right hand is **f** of righteousness. **Ps 48:10** 4390
The stream of God is **f** of water; **Ps 65:9** 4390
the dark places of the land are **f** of **Ps 74:20** 4390
the LORD heard and was **f** of wrath; **Ps 78:21** 5674b
at the new moon, At the **f** moon, **Ps 81:3** 3677
You have been **f** of wrath against **Ps 89:38** 5674b
shall be **f** of sap and very green, **Ps 92:14** 1879
The earth is **f** of Your possessions. **Ps 104:24** 4390
earth is **f** of Your lovingkindness, **Ps 119:64** 4390
the man whose quiver is **f** of them; **Ps 127:5** 4390
Let our garners be **f**, **Ps 144:13** 4392
and brighter until the **f** day. **Pr 4:18** 3559
At the **f** moon he will come home." **Pr 7:20** 3677
a house **f** of feasting with strife. **Pr 17:1** 4392
That I not be **f** and deny *You* **Pr 30:9** 7646
the sea, Yet the sea is not **f**. **Ec 1:7** 4392
One hand **f** of rest is better than **Ec 4:6** 4393
rest is better than two fists **f** of labor **Ec 4:6** 4393
but the **f** stomach of the rich man **Ec 5:12** 7647
of the sons of men are **f** of evil and **Ec 9:3** 4392
If the clouds are **f**, they pour out **Ec 11:3** 4390
"His mouth is **f** *of* sweetness. **SS 5:16**
dawn, As beautiful as the **f** moon, **SS 6:10** 3842
harlot, She *who* was **f** of justice! **Is 1:21** 4392
whole earth is **f** of His glory." **Is 6:3** 4393
earth will be **f** of the knowledge of **Is 11:9** 4390
their houses will be **f** of owls; **Is 13:21** 4390
waters of Dimon are **f** of blood; **Is 15:9** 4390
reason my loins are **f** of anguish; **Is 21:3** 4390
You who were **f** of noise, You **Is 22:2** 4392
valleys were **f** of chariots, **Is 22:7** 4390
And this will be the **f** price of **Is 27:9** 3605
the tables are **f** of filthy vomit, **Is 28:8** 4390
They will come on you in **f** **Is 47:9** 8537
a net, **F** of the wrath of the LORD, **Is 51:20** 4392
When I had fed them to the **f**, **Jer 5:7** 7646
'Like a cage **f** of birds, So their **Jer 5:27** 4392
So their houses are **f** of deceit; **Jer 5:27** 4392
I am **f** of the wrath of the LORD; **Jer 6:11** 4390
For the land is **f** of adulterers; **Jer 23:10** 4390
will I break within two **f** years the **Jer 28:11** 3117
the Rechabites pitchers **f** of wine and **Jer 35:5** 4392
is **f** of your cry *of distress;* **Jer 46:12** 4390
For I will make a **f** end of all **Jer 46:28** 3617
I will not make a **f** end of you; **Jer 46:28** 3617
Although their land is **f** of guilt **Jer 51:5** 4390
And exact **f** vengeance for you; **Jer 51:36** 5360
the city That was **f** of people! **La 1:1** 7227a
them were **f** of eyes round about. **Ezk 1:18** 4392
the land is **f** of bloody crimes and **Ezk 7:23** 4390
and the city is **f** of violence. **Ezk 7:23** 4390
and the city is **f** of perversion; **Ezk 9:9** 4390
wheels were **f** of eyes all around, **Ezk 10:12** 4392
and a **f** plumage of many colors came **Ezk 17:3** 4392
It was fruitful and **f** of branches **Ezk 19:10** 6058
you of ill repute, **f** of turmoil. **Ezk 22:5** 7227a
F of wisdom and perfect in beauty. **Ezk 28:12** 4392
And the ravines will be **f** of you. **Ezk 32:6** 4390
and it was **f** of bones. **Ezk 37:1** 4392
chambers were a **f** rod of six long **Ezk 41:8** 4393
And you will be satisfied *in* **f** **Jl 2:19**
and the vine have yielded in **f**. **Jl 2:22** 2428
floors will be **f** of grain, **Jl 2:24** 4390
tread, for the wine press is **f**; **Jl 3:13** 4390
men of *the* city are **f** of violence, **Mi 6:12** 4390
at **f** *strength* and likewise many, **Na 1:12** 8003
completely **f** of lies *and* pillage; **Na 3:1** 4392
And the earth is **f** of His praise. **Hab 3:3** 4390
you, they have their reward in **f**. **Mt 6:2** *568*
you, they have their reward in **f**. **Mt 6:5** *568*
you, they have their reward in **f**. **Mt 6:16** *568*
whole body will be **f** of light. **Mt 6:22** *5460*
whole body will be **f** of darkness. **Mt 6:23** *4652*
but when it is **f** grown, it is **Mt 13:32** *837*
broken pieces, twelve **f** baskets. **Mt 14:20** *4134*
pieces, seven large baskets **f**. **Mt 15:37** *4134*
and how many baskets **f** you picked **Mt 16:9**
and how many large baskets **f** you **Mt 16:10**
but inside they are **f** of robbery **Mt 23:25** *1073*
but inside they are **f** of dead **Mt 23:27** *1073*
f of hypocrisy and lawlessness. **Mt 23:28** *3324*
f baskets of the broken pieces, **Mk 6:43** *4138*
seven large baskets **f** of what was left **Mk 8:8** *4051*
how many baskets **f** of broken **Mk 8:19** *4134*
how many large baskets **f** of broken **Mk 8:20** *4138*
spending the **f** number of days, **Lk 2:43** *5048*
Jesus, **f** of the Holy Spirit, **Lk 4:1** *4134*
are receiving your comfort in **f**. **Lk 6:24** *568*
were picked up, twelve baskets **f**. **Lk 9:17**
whole body also is **f** of light; **Lk 11:34** *5460*
your body also is **f** of darkness. **Lk 11:34** *4652*
your whole body is **f** of light, **Lk 11:36** *5460*
are **f** of robbery and wickedness. **Lk 11:39** *1073*
the Father, **f** of grace and truth. **Jn 1:14** *4134*
this joy of mine has been made **f**. **Jn 3:29** *4137*
and *that* your joy may be made **f**. **Jn 15:11** *4137*
that your joy may be made **f**. **Jn 16:24** *4137*
have My joy made **f** in themselves. **Jn 17:13** *4137*
A jar **f** of sour wine was standing **Jn 19:29** *3324*
so they put a sponge **f** of the sour **Jn 19:29** *3324*
dragging the net **f** of fish. **Jn 21:8**
the net to land, **f** of large fish, **Jn 21:11** *3324*
"They are **f** of sweet wine." **Ac 2:13** *3325*
F OF GLADNESS WITH YOUR PRESENCE.' **Ac 2:28** *4137*
of Solomon, **f** of amazement. **Ac 3:11** *1569a*
with his wife's **f** knowledge, **Ac 5:2** *4924a*
f of the Spirit and of wisdom, **Ac 6:3** *4134*
a man **f** of faith and of the Holy **Ac 6:5** *4134*
And Stephen, **f** of grace and power, **Ac 6:8** *4134*
But being **f** of the Holy Spirit, he **Ac 7:55** *4134*
and **f** of the Holy Spirit and of **Ac 11:24** *4134*
who are **f** of all deceit and fraud, **Ac 13:10** *4134*
was observing the city **f** of idols. **Ac 17:16** *2712*
And he stayed two **f** years in his **Ac 28:30** *3650*
f of envy, murder, strife, deceit, **Ro 1:29** *3324*
IS **F** OF CURSING AND BITTERNESS"; **Ro 3:14** *1073*
you yourselves are **f** of goodness, **Ro 15:14** *3324*
they did not make **f** use of it; **1Co 7:31** *2710*
f use of my right in the gospel. **1Co 9:18** *2710*
Put on the **f** armor of God, so **Eph 6:11** *3833*
take up the **f** armor of God, **Eph 6:13** *3833*
I have received everything in **f** and **Php 4:18** *568*
the **f** assurance of understanding, **Col 2:2** *4136*
Holy Spirit and with **f** conviction; **1Th 1:5** *4183*
For you yourselves know **f** well **1Th 5:2** *199*
statement, deserving **f** acceptance, **1Tm 1:15** *3956*
statement deserving **f** acceptance. **1Tm 4:9** *3956*
as to realize the **f** assurance of hope **Heb 6:11** *4136*
heart in **f** assurance of faith, **Heb 10:22** *4136*
"I AM **F** OF FEAR and trembling." **Heb 12:21** *1630*
evil *and* **f** of deadly poison. **Jas 3:8** *3324*
f of mercy and good fruits, **Jas 3:17** *3324*
f of compassion and *is* merciful. **Jas 5:11** *4184*
joy inexpressible and **f** of glory, **1Pe 1:8** *1392*
having eyes **f** of adultery that **2Pe 2:14** *3324*
that you may receive a **f** reward. **2Jn 1:8** *4134*
face, so that your joy may be made **f**. **2Jn 1:12** *4137*
f of eyes in front and behind. **Rv 4:6** *1073*
are **f** of eyes around and within; **Rv 4:8** *1073*
and golden bowls **f** of incense, **Rv 5:8** *1073*
which is mixed in **f** strength in **Rv 14:10** *194*
bowls **f** of the wrath of God, **Rv 15:7** *1073*
beast, **f** of blasphemous names, **Rv 17:3** *1073*
having in her hand a gold cup **f** of **Rv 17:4** *1073*
bowls **f** of the seven last plagues came **Rv 21:9** *1073*

FULLER'S
is on the highway of the **f** field. **2Ki 18:17** 3526
on the highway to the **f** field, **Is 7:3** 3526
on the highway of the **f** field. **Is 36:2** 3526

FULLERS'
a refiner's fire and like **f** soap. **Mal 3:2** 3526

FULLEST
and peace be yours in the **f** measure. **1Pe 1:2** *4129*

FULLNESS
choice things of the earth and its **f**, **Dt 33:16** 4393
"In the **f** of his plenty he will be **Jb 20:22** 4390
In Your presence is **f** of joy; **Ps 16:11** 7648
come and devour the land and its **f**, **Jer 8:16** 4393
And overflow the land and all its **f**, **Jer 47:2** 4393
their land will be stripped of its **f** **Ezk 12:19** 4393
And the land and its **f** were appalled **Ezk 19:7** 4393
For of His **f** we have all received, **Jn 1:16** *4138*
has happened to Israel until the **f** of **Ro 11:25** *4138*
I will come in the **f** of the blessing **Ro 15:29** *4138*
But when the **f** of the time came, God **Ga 4:4** *4138*
an administration suitable to the **f** **Eph 1:10** *4138*
which is His body, the **f** of Him who **Eph 1:23** *4138*
you may be filled up to all the **f** of **Eph 3:19** *4138*
of the stature which belongs to the **f** **Eph 4:13** *4138*
good pleasure for all the **f** to **Col 1:19** *4138*
For in Him all the **f** of Deity dwells **Col 2:9** *4138*

FULLY
spirit and has followed Me **f**, **Nu 14:24** 4390
for they did not follow Me **f**, **Nu 32:11** 4390
they have followed the LORD **f**.' **Nu 32:12** 4390
he has followed the LORD **f**.' **Dt 1:36** 4390
grapes until you are **f** satisfied, **Dt 23:24** 7648
but I followed the LORD my God **f**. **Jos 14:8** 4390
have followed the LORD my God **f**.' **Jos 14:9** 4390
followed the LORD God of Israel **f**. **Jos 14:14** 4390
husband has been **f** reported to me, **Ru 2:11** 5046
and did not follow the LORD **f**, **1Ki 11:6** 4390
And **f** recompenses the proud doer. **Ps 31:23**
5921, 3499a
Your testimonies are **f** confirmed; **Ps 93:5** 3966
among them are given **f** to do evil. **Ec 8:11** 4390
of recompense, He will **f** repay. **Jer 51:56** 7999a
after he has been **f** trained, **Lk 6:40** *2675*
but when they were **f** awake, **Lk 9:32** *1235*
"When a strong *man,* **f** armed, **Lk 11:21** *2528*
My time has not yet **f** come." **Jn 7:8** *4137*
and being **f** assured that what God **Ro 4:21** *4135*
be **f** convinced in his own mind. **Ro 14:5** *4135*
f preached the gospel of Christ. **Ro 15:19** *4137*
but then I will know **f** just as I **1Co 13:12** *1921*
just as I also have been **f** known. **1Co 13:12** *1921*
this service is not only **f** supplying the **2Co 9:12** *4322*
they **f** supplied my need, **2Co 11:9** *4322*
that I might **f** carry out the **Col 1:25** *4137*
that you may stand perfect and **f** **Col 4:12** *4135*
might be **f** accomplished, **2Tm 4:17** *4135*

FUNCTION
f for that which is unnatural, **Ro 1:26** *5540*
men abandoned the natural **f** of the **Ro 1:27** *5540*
members do not have the same **f**, **Ro 12:4** *4234*

FURIOUS
was **f** with his two officials, **Gn 40:2** 7107
"Pharaoh was **f** with his servants, **Gn 41:10** 7107
was **f** and went away and said, **2Ki 5:11** 7107
he became **f** and very angry and **Ne 4:1** 2734
king became indignant and very **f** and **Da 2:12** 7108

FURIOUSLY
son of Nimshi, for he drives **f**." **2Ki 9:20** 7697
and being **f** enraged at them, I **Ac 26:11** *4057*

FURNACE
ascended like the smoke of a **f**. **Gn 19:28** 3536
ascended like the smoke of a **f**, **Ex 19:18** 3536
and brought you out of the iron **f**, **Dt 4:20** 3564a
from the midst of the iron **f**), **1Ki 8:51** 3564a
silver tried in a **f** on the earth, **Ps 12:6** 5948
is for silver and the **f** for gold, **Pr 17:3** 3564a
is for silver and the **f** for gold, **Pr 27:21** 3564a
Zion and whose **f** is in Jerusalem. **Is 31:9** 8574
tested you in the **f** of affliction. **Is 48:10** 3564a
land of Egypt, from the iron **f**, **Jer 11:4** 3564a

tin and iron and lead in the f; Ezk 22:18 3564a
and tin into the f to blow fire on it Ezk 22:20 3564a
'As silver is melted in the f, Ezk 22:22 3564a
midst of a f of blazing fire." Da 3:6 861
the midst of a f of blazing fire. Da 3:11 861
the midst of a f of blazing fire; Da 3:15 861
us from the f of blazing fire; Da 3:17 861
giving orders to heat the f seven times Da 3:19 861
them into the f of blazing fire. Da 3:20 861
midst of the f of blazing fire. Da 3:21 861
the f had been made extremely hot, Da 3:22 861
the midst of the f of blazing fire Da 3:23 861
the door of the f of blazing fire; Da 3:26 861
day is coming, burning like a f; Mal 4:1 8574
and tomorrow is thrown into the f, Mt 6:30 *2823*
will throw them into the f of fire; Mt 13:42 *2575*
will throw them into the f of fire; Mt 13:50 *2575*
and tomorrow is thrown into the f, Lk 12:28 *2823*
it has been made to glow in a f, Rv 1:15 *2575*
pit, like the smoke of a great f; Rv 9:2 *2575*

FURNACES
section and the Tower of F. Ne 3:11 8574
on the wall, above the Tower of F, Ne 12:38 8574

FURNISH
"You shall f him liberally from Dt 15:14 6059
nor do they f this people the Jer 23:32 3276

FURNISHED
pillars around the court shall be f Ex 27:17 2836b
court were f with silver bands. Ex 38:17 2836b
f from the thousands of Israel, Nu 31:5 4560
ten days all sorts of wine *were* f Ne 5:18
a large upper room f *and* ready; Mk 14:15 *4766*
show you a large, f upper room; Lk 22:12 *4766*
having f proof to all men by Ac 17:31 *3930*

FURNISHING
be full, f every kind of produce, Ps 144:13 6329
And f seed to the sower and bread Is 55:10 5414

FURNISHINGS
to Moses, the tent and all its f: Ex 39:33 3627
shall consecrate it and all its f; Ex 40:9 3627
and over all its f and over all Nu 1:50 3627
the tabernacle and all its f, Nu 1:50 3627
all the f of the tent of meeting, Nu 3:8 3627
and all the f of the sanctuary, Nu 4:15 3627
with the sanctuary and its f." Nu 4:16 3627
and consecrated it with all its f Nu 7:1 3627
they shall not come near to the f of Nu 18:3 3627
sprinkle *it* on the tent and on all the f Nu 19:18 3627

FURNITURE
and the pattern of all its f, Ex 25:9 3627
it, and all the f of the tent, Ex 31:7 3627
Solomon made all the f which 1Ki 7:48 3627
also were appointed over the f and 1Ch 9:29 3627

FURROW
about half a f in an acre of land. 1Sa 14:14 4618
the wild ox in a f with ropes, Jb 39:10 8525

FURROWS
me, And its f weep together; Jb 31:38 8525
You water its f abundantly Ps 65:10 8525
They lengthened their f." Ps 129:3 4618
weeds in the f of the field. Hos 10:4 8525
heaps Beside the f of the field. Hos 12:11 8525

FURTHER
angel of the LORD said to her f, Gn 16:11
God said f to Abraham, Gn 17:9
Reuben f said to them, Gn 37:22
spoke f to Moses and said to him, Ex 6:2
"But if there is *any* f injury, Ex 21:23
f spoke to Moses and to Aaron, Lv 14:33
'F, you will eat the flesh of Lv 26:29
The LORD spoke f to Moses, saying, Nu 10:1
The angel of the LORD went f, Nu 22:26 3254
"F, you shall speak to the sons Nu 27:8
"The LORD spoke f to me, saying, Dt 9:13
shall speak f to the people and Dt 20:8 3254
"Then you will go on f from there, 1Sa 10:3 1973
they inquired f of the LORD, 1Sa 10:22 5750
F, he distributed to all the 2Sa 6:19
F, he adorned the house with 2Ch 3:6
His servants spoke f against 2Ch 32:16 5750
and reported f word to the king, 2Ch 34:16 5750
And what is your f request? Es 9:12 5750
does not *need to* consider a man f, Jb 34:23 5750
Again the LORD spoke to me f, Is 8:5 5750
f need do we have of witnesses? Mt 26:65 *2089*
f need do we have of witnesses? Mk 14:63 *2089*
But Jesus made no f answer; Mk 15:5 *3765*
"Lord, do not trouble Yourself f, Lk 7:6
f need do we have of testimony? Lk 22:71 *2089*
not spread any f among the people, Ac 4:17
1909, 4183
When they had threatened them f, Ac 4:21 *4324*
that I may not weary you any f, Ac 24:4
1909, 4183
resulting in f lawlessness, so Ro 6:19
f place for me in these regions, Ro 15:23 *3371*
if I boast somewhat f about 2Co 10:8 *4053*
for it will lead to f ungodliness, 2Tm 2:16 *4183*
But they will not make f progress; 2Tm 3:9
1909, 4183
what f need *was there* for another Heb 7:11 *2089*
f word be spoken to them. Heb 12:19 *4369*

FURTHERANCE
served with me in the f of the gospel Php 2:22

FURTHERED
angry, they f the disaster." Zch 1:15 5826

FURTHERING
to mere speculation rather than f 1Tm 1:4

FURTHERMORE
F, they said, "This one came in as Gn 19:9
and f he is coming to meet you, Gn 32:6 1571
and f, the men of the place said, Gn 38:22 1571
f, I have seen the oppression with Ex 3:9 1571
God, f, said to Moses, Ex 3:15 5750
The LORD f said to him, Ex 4:6 5750
"F I have heard the groaning of Ex 6:5 1571
F, the man Moses *himself* was Ex 11:3 1571
"F, you shall select out of all Ex 18:21
F, they made two gold rings and Ex 39:20
'F, anything that the unclean Nu 19:22
"F, you shall not intermarry with Dt 7:3
f, do not go on from this one, but Ru 2:8 1571
"F, he said to me, Ru 2:21 1571
F, Ahithophel said to Absalom, 2Sa 17:1
F, the altar that *was* at Bethel 2Ki 23:15 1571
F, all the officials of the 2Ch 36:14 1571
F, I have seen under the sun *that* Ec 3:16 5750
F, if two lie down together they Ec 4:11 1571
F, as for every man to whom God Ec 5:19 1571
F, the hearts of the sons of men Ec 9:3 1571
F, in your bedchamber do not curse Ec 10:20 1571
F, men are afraid of a high place Ec 12:5 1571
F, the word of the LORD came to me Ezk 12:26
"F, Samaria did not commit half Ezk 16:51
"F, they have even sent for men Ezk 23:40 637
"F, I withheld the rain from you Am 4:7 1571
"F, wine betrays the haughty man, Hab 2:5 637
F, we had earthly fathers to Heb 12:9 *1534*

FURY
until your brother's f subsides, Gn 27:44 2534
anger and in f and in great wrath, Dt 29:28 2534
will be led forth at the day of f. Jb 21:30 5678
anger And terrify them in His f, Ps 2:5 2740
upon them His burning anger, F and Ps 78:49 5678
You withdrew all Your f; Ps 85:3 5678
our days have declined in Your f; Ps 90:9 5678
power of Your anger And Your f, Ps 90:11 5678
The f of a king is *like* Pr 16:14 2534
And the rod of his f will perish. Pr 22:8 5678
By the f of the LORD of hosts the Is 9:19 5678
against the people of My f Is 10:6 5678
Cruel, with f and burning anger, Is 13:9 5678
be shaken from its place At the f of Is 13:13 5678
has ceased, *And how* f has ceased! Is 14:4 4787b
used to strike the peoples in f with Is 14:6 5678
of his arrogance, pride, and f; Is 16:6 5678
because of the f of the oppressor, Is 51:13 2534
where is the f of the oppressor? Is 51:13 2534
To render His anger with f, Is 66:15 2534
"I know his f," declares the LORD, Jer 48:30 5678
"So I will calm My f against you Ezk 16:42 2534
'But it was plucked up in f; Ezk 19:12 2534
My f will mount up in My anger. Ezk 38:18 2534
And he maintained his f forever. Am 1:11 5678
THE F OF A FIRE WHICH WILL CONSUME Heb 10:27 *2205b*

FUTILE
after f things which can not profit 1Sa 12:21 8414
or deliver, because they are f. 1Sa 12:21 8414
the few years of his f life? Ec 6:12 1892
a graven image are all of them f, Is 44:9 8414
"But it is f; His idle boasts have Jer 48:30
3808, 3653a
AND THE PEOPLES DEVISE F THINGS? Ac 4:25 *2756*
became f in their speculations, Ro 1:21 *3154*
silver or gold from your f way of life 1Pe 1:18 *3152*

FUTILITY
brought their days to an end in f And Ps 78:33 1892
And behold, it too was f. Ec 2:1 1892
is f and striving after wind. Ec 2:17 1892
in f and goes into obscurity; Ec 6:4 1892
is f and a striving after wind. Ec 6:9 1892
are many words which increase f. Ec 6:11 1892
of the fool; And this too is f. Ec 7:6 1892
during my lifetime of f; Ec 7:15 1892
where they did thus. This too is f. Ec 8:10 1892
is f which is done on the earth, Ec 8:14 1892
I say that this too is f. Ec 8:14 1892
that is to come *will be* f. Ec 11:8 1892
f and the deception of their own Jer 14:14 457
F and things of no profit." Jer 16:19 1892
They are leading you into f; Jer 23:16 1891
the creation was subjected to f, Ro 8:20 *3153*
also walk, in the f of their mind, Eph 4:17 *3153*

FUTURE
That they would discern their f! Dt 32:29 319
servant concerning the distant f. 2Sa 7:19 7350
Surely there is a f, Pr 23:18 319
find *it*, then there will be a f, Pr 24:14 319
will be no f for the evil man; Pr 24:20 319
clothing, And she smiles at the f. Pr 31:25
314, 3117
to give you a f and a hope. Jer 29:11 319
"There is hope for your f," Jer 31:17 319
She did not consider her f. La 1:9 319
to what would take place in the f; Da 2:29 311
what will take place in the f; Da 2:45 311
pertains to many days *in the* f." Da 8:26
vision pertains to the days yet f." Da 10:14
of a good foundation for the f, 1Tm 6:19 *3195*
in the f there is laid up for me 2Tm 4:8 *3062*

G

GAAL
Now G the son of Ebed came with Jg 9:26 1603
Then G the son of Ebed said, Jg 9:28 1603
the words of G the son of Ebed, Jg 9:30 1603
G the son of Ebed and his Jg 9:31 1603
Now G the son of Ebed went out and Jg 9:35 1603
When G saw the people, he said Jg 9:36 1603
G spoke again and said, Jg 9:37 1603
So G went out before the leaders Jg 9:39 1603
but Zebul drove out G and his Jg 9:41 1603

GAASH
Ephraim, on the north of Mount G. Jos 24:30 1608
of Ephraim, north of Mount G. Jg 2:9 1608
Hiddai of the brooks of G, 2Sa 23:30 1608
Hurai of the brooks of G, 1Ch 11:32 1608

GABBAI
and after him G *and* Sallai, 928. Ne 11:8 1373a

GABBATHA
The Pavement, but in Hebrew, G. Jn 19:13 *1042*

GABRIEL
"G, give this *man* an Da 8:16 1403
in prayer, then the man G, Da 9:21 1403
"I am G, who stands in the Lk 1:19 *1043*
angel G was sent from God to a city Lk 1:26 *1043*

GAD
So she named him G. Gn 30:11 1410
of Zilpah, Leah's maid: G and Asher. Gn 35:26 1410
The sons of G: Gn 46:16 1410
"As for G, raiders shall raid Gn 49:19 1410
Dan and Naphtali, G and Asher. Ex 1:4 1410
of G, Eliasaph the son of Deuel; Nu 1:14 1410
Of the sons of G, their Nu 1:24 1410
numbered men of the tribe of G Nu 1:25 1410
"Then *comes* the tribe of G, Nu 2:14 1410
and the leader of the sons of G: Nu 2:14 1410
of Deuel, leader of the sons of G; Nu 7:42 1410
the tribal army of the sons of G, Nu 10:20 1410
from the tribe of G, Nu 13:15 1410
of G according to their families: Nu 26:15 1410
These are the families of the sons of G Nu 26:18 1410
sons of G had an exceedingly large Nu 32:1 1410
the sons of G and the sons of Nu 32:2 1410
of G and to the sons of Reuben, Nu 32:6 1410
The sons of G and the sons of Nu 32:25 1410
sons of G and the sons of Reuben, Nu 32:29 1410
The sons of G and the sons of Nu 32:31 1410
to the sons of G and to the sons Nu 32:33 1410
The sons of G built Dibon and Nu 32:34 1410
and the tribe of the sons of G Nu 34:14 1410
Reuben, G, Asher, Zebulun, Dan, Dt 27:13 1410
Of G he said, Dt 33:20 1410
"Blessed is the one who enlarges G; Dt 33:20 1410
The sons of Reuben and the sons of G Jos 4:12 1410
an inheritance to the tribe of G, Jos 13:24 1410
tribe of Gad, to the sons of G, Jos 13:24 1410
of G according to their families, Jos 13:28 1410
G and Reuben and the half-tribe of Jos 18:7 1410
in Gilead from the tribe of G, Jos 20:8 1410
G and from the tribe of Zebulun. Jos 21:7 1410
From the tribe of G, Jos 21:38 1410
sons of Reuben and the sons of G Jos 22:9 1410
the sons of Reuben and the sons of G Jos 22:10 1410
the sons of Reuben and the sons of G Jos 22:11 1410
sons of Reuben and to the sons of G Jos 22:13 1410
sons of Reuben and to the sons of G Jos 22:15 1410
the sons of Reuben and the sons of G Jos 22:21 1410
you sons of Reuben and sons of G; Jos 22:25 1410
sons of G and the sons of Manasseh Jos 22:30 1410
of G and to the sons of Manasseh, Jos 22:31 1410
of Reuben and from the sons of G, Jos 22:32 1410
and the sons of G were living. Jos 22:33 1410
of G called the altar *Witness;* Jos 22:34 1410
into the land of G and Gilead. 1Sa 13:7 1410
The prophet G said to David, 1Sa 22:5 1410
in the middle of the valley of G and 2Sa 24:5 1410
of the LORD came to the prophet G, 2Sa 24:11 1410
So G came to David and told him, 2Sa 24:13 1410
Then David said to G, 2Sa 24:14 1410
So G came to David that day and 2Sa 24:18 1410
up according to the word of G, 2Sa 24:19 1410
Joseph, Benjamin, Naphtali, G and 1Ch 2:2 1410
Now the sons of G lived opposite 1Ch 5:11 1410
tribe of Reuben, the tribe of G and 1Ch 6:63 1410
and from the tribe of G: 1Ch 6:80 1410
of G were captains of the army; 1Ch 12:14 1410
The LORD spoke to G, 1Ch 21:9 1410
G came to David and said to him, 1Ch 21:11 1410
David said to G, 1Ch 21:13 1410
LORD commanded G to say to David, 1Ch 21:18 1410
So David went up at the word of G, 1Ch 21:19 1410
in the chronicles of G the seer, 1Ch 29:29 1410
of David and of G the king's seer, 2Ch 29:25 1410
has Malcam taken possession of G Jer 49:1 1410
the east side to the west side, G, Ezk 48:27 1410
"And beside the border of G, Ezk 48:28 1410
the gate of G, one; Ezk 48:34 1410
the tribe of G twelve thousand, Rv 7:5 *1045*

GADARENES
side into the country of the G, Mt 8:28 *1046*

GADDI
of Manasseh, G the son of Susi; Nu 13:11 3426

GADDIEL
of Zebulun, G the son of Sodi; Nu 13:10 1427

GADI
Then Menahem son of **G** went up from **2Ki 15:14** 1424
Menahem son of **G** became king over **2Ki 15:17** 1424
GADITE
of Nathan of Zobah, Bani the **G**, **2Sa 23:36** 1425
GADITES
to the Reubenites and to the **G**. **Dt 3:12** 1425
To the Reubenites and to the **G** **Dt 3:16** 1425
and Ramoth in Gilead for the **G**, **Dt 4:43** 1425
to the Reubenites, the **G**, **Dt 29:8** 1425
To the Reubenites and to the **G** **Jos 1:12** 1425
it to the Reubenites and the **G** and **Jos 12:6** 1425
the Reubenites and the **G** received **Jos 13:8** 1425
summoned the Reubenites and the **G** **Jos 22:1** 1425
the **G** and the Reubenites and the **2Ki 10:33** 1425
The sons of Reuben and the **G** and **1Ch 5:18** 1425
namely the Reubenites, the **G** and **1Ch 5:26** 1425
From the **G** there came over to **1Ch 12:8** 1425
of the Reubenites and the **G** and of **1Ch 12:37** 1425
the **G** and the half-tribe of the **1Ch 26:32** 1425
GAHAM
Tebah and **G** and Tahash and Maacah. **Gn 22:24** 1514
GAHAR
the sons of Giddel, the sons of **G**, **Ezr 2:47** 1515
the sons of Giddel, the sons of **G**, **Ne 7:49** 1515
GAIETY
Instead, there is **g** and gladness, **Is 22:13** 8342
The **g** of tambourines ceases, The **Is 24:8** 4885
stops, The **g** of the harp ceases. **Is 24:8** 4885
The **g** of the earth is banished. **Is 24:11** 4885
will also put an end to all her **g**, **Hos 2:11** 4885
GAIN
truth, those who hate dishonest **g**; **Ex 18:21** 1215
at interest, nor your food for **g**. **Lv 25:37** 4768
you that you may **g** acquisition, **Lv 25:45** 7069
but turned aside after dishonest **g** **1Sa 8:3** 1215
they might **g** insight into the words **Ne 8:13** 7919a
hoped to **g** the mastery over them, **Es 9:1** 7980
would we **g** if we entreat Him?' **Jb 21:15** 3276
And not to *dishonest* **g**. **Ps 119:36** 1215
silver And her **g** better than fine gold. **Pr 3:14** 8393
that you may **g** understanding, **Pr 4:1** 3045
and he will **g** knowledge. **Pr 19:25** 995
Do not weary yourself to **g** wealth, **Pr 23:4** 6238
unjust **g** will prolong *his* days. **Pr 28:16** 1215
And he will have no lack of **g**. **Pr 31:11** 7998
She senses that her **g** is good; **Pr 31:18** 5504
Her **g** and her harlot's wages **Is 23:18** 5504
but her **g** will become sufficient **Is 23:18** 5504
He who rejects unjust **g** And **Is 33:15** 1215
for the LORD Will **g** new strength; **Is 40:31** 2498
let the peoples **g** new strength; **Is 41:1** 2498
consider and **g** insight as well, **Is 41:20** 7919a
own way, Each one to his unjust **g**, **Is 56:11** 1215
iniquity of his unjust **g** I was angry **Is 57:17** 1215
of them, Everyone is greedy for **g**, **Jer 6:13** 1215
greatest Everyone is greedy for **g**; **Jer 8:10** 1215
only upon your own dishonest **g**, **Jer 22:17** 1215
neighbors for **g** by oppression, **Ezk 22:12** 1214
I smite My hand at your dishonest **g** **Ezk 22:13** 1215
lives in order to get dishonest **g**. **Ezk 22:27** 1215
their heart goes after their **g**. **Ezk 33:31** 1215
and **g** understanding of the vision. **Da 9:23** 995
Then a fourth will **g** far more **Da 11:2** 6238
princes who will **g** ascendancy over **Da 11:5** 2388
and he will go up and **g** power with **Da 11:23** 6105a
"But he will **g** control over the **Da 11:43** 4910
may devote to the LORD their unjust **g** **Mi 4:13** 1215
"Woe to him who gets evil **g** for **Hab 2:9** 1215
profit a man to **g** the whole world, **Mk 8:36** *2770*
endurance you will **g** your lives. **Lk 21:19** *2932*
live is Christ and to die is **g**. **Php 1:21** *2771*
But whatever things were **g** to me, **Php 3:7** *2771*
so that I may **g** Christ, **Php 3:8** *2770*
that you may **g** the glory of our **2Th 2:14** *4047*
to much wine or fond of sordid **g**, **1Tm 3:8** *146*
that godliness is a means of **g**. **1Tm 6:5** *4200*
actually is a means of great **g** when **1Tm 6:6** *4200*
pugnacious, not fond of sordid **g**, **Ti 1:7** *146*
teach for the sake of sordid **g**. **Ti 1:11** *2771*
and not for sordid **g**, **1Pe 5:2** *147*
GAINED
Jews themselves **g** the mastery over **Es 9:1** 7980
which His right hand had **g**. **Ps 78:54** 7069
arm have **g** the victory for Him. **Ps 98:1** 3467
An inheritance **g** hurriedly at the **Pr 20:21** 973b
them, and **g** five more talents. **Mt 25:16** *2770*
the two *talents* **g** two more. **Mt 25:17** *2770*
See, I have **g** five more talents.' **Mt 25:20** *2770*
See, I have **g** two more talents.' **Mt 25:22** *2770*
for they had not **g** any insight **Mk 6:52** *4920*
by it the men of old **g** approval. **Heb 11:2** *3140*
g approval through their faith, **Heb 11:39** *3140*
GAINING
flattering people for the sake of **g** **Jude 1:16**
GAINS
of everyone who **g** by violence; **Pr 1:19** 1214
And the man who **g** understanding. **Pr 3:13** 6329
Ill-gotten **g** do not profit, But **Pr 10:2** 214
profit a man if he **g** the whole world **Mt 16:26** *2770*
profited if he **g** the whole world, **Lk 9:25** *2770*
GAIUS
dragging along **G** and Aristarchus, **Ac 19:29** *1050*
and **G** of Derbe, and Timothy, **Ac 20:4** *1050*
G, host to me and to the whole **Ro 16:23** *1050*
none of you except Crispus and **G**, **1Co 1:14** *1050*
The elder to the beloved **G**, **3Jn 1:1** *1050*

GALAL
G and Mattaniah the son of Mica, **1Ch 9:15** 1559
the son of Shemaiah, the son of **G**, **1Ch 9:16** 1559
the son of Shammua, the son of **G**, **Ne 11:17** 1559
GALATIA
as I directed the churches of **G**, **1Co 16:1** *1053*
are with me, To the churches of **G**: **Ga 1:2** *1053*
Crescens *has gone* to **G**, **2Tm 4:10** *1053*
scattered throughout Pontus, **G**, **1Pe 1:1** *1053*
GALATIAN
through the Phrygian and **G** region, **Ac 16:6** *1054*
through the **G** region and Phrygia, **Ac 18:23** *1054*
GALATIANS
You foolish **G**, who has bewitched **Ga 3:1** *1052*
GALBANUM
spices, stacte and onycha and **g**, **Ex 30:34** 2464
GALE
Or like whirling dust before a **g**. **Is 17:13** 5492a
there arose a fierce **g** of wind, **Mk 4:37** *2978*
and a fierce **g** of wind descended **Lk 8:23** *2978*
GALEED
but Jacob called it **G**. **Gn 31:47** 1567
Therefore it was named **G**, **Gn 31:48** 1567
GALILEAN
"You too were with Jesus the **G**." **Mt 26:69** *1057*
of them, for you are a **G** too." **Mk 14:70** *1057*
was with Him, for he is a **G** too." **Lk 22:59** *1057*
he asked whether the man was a **G**. **Lk 23:6** *1057*
GALILEANS
who reported to Him about the **G** whose **Lk 13:1** *1057*
"Do you suppose that these **G** were **Lk 13:2** *1057*
greater sinners than all *other* **G** because **Lk 13:2** *1057*
to Galilee, the **G** received Him, **Jn 4:45** *1057*
not all these who are speaking **G**? **Ac 2:7** *1057*
GALILEE
So they set apart Kedesh in **G** in **Jos 20:7** 1551
Naphtali, *they gave* Kedesh in **G**, **Jos 21:32** 1551
twenty cities in the land of **G**. **1Ki 9:11** 1551
Kedesh and Hazor and Gilead and **G**, **2Ki 15:29** 1552
in **G** with its pasture lands, **1Ch 6:76** 1551
side of Jordan, **G** of the Gentiles. **Is 9:1** 1551
he left for the regions of **G**, **Mt 2:22** *1056*
G at the Jordan *coming* to John, **Mt 3:13** *1056*
into custody, He withdrew into **G**; **Mt 4:12** *1056*
THE JORDAN, **G** OF THE GENTILES **Mt 4:15** *1056*
was walking by the Sea of **G**, **Mt 4:18** *1056*
Jesus was going throughout all **G**, **Mt 4:23** *1056*
crowds followed Him from **G** **Mt 4:25** *1056*
Jesus went along by the Sea of **G**, **Mt 15:29** *1056*
they were gathering together in **G**, **Mt 17:22** *1056*
these words, He departed from **G** and **Mt 19:1** *1056*
Jesus, from Nazareth in **G**." **Mt 21:11** *1056*
I will go ahead of you to **G**." **Mt 26:32** *1056*
who had followed Jesus from **G** while **Mt 27:55** *1056*
He is going ahead of you into **G**, **Mt 28:7** *1056*
to My brethren to leave for **G**, **Mt 28:10** *1056*
eleven disciples proceeded to **G**, **Mt 28:16** *1056*
Jesus came from Nazareth in **G** and **Mk 1:9** *1056*
into custody, Jesus came into **G**, **Mk 1:14** *1056*
was going along by the Sea of **G**, **Mk 1:16** *1056*
all the surrounding district of **G**. **Mk 1:28** *1056*
their synagogues throughout all **G**, **Mk 1:39** *1056*
a great multitude from **G** followed; **Mk 3:7** *1056*
and the leading men of **G**; **Mk 6:21** *1056*
through Sidon to the Sea of **G**, **Mk 7:31** *1056*
out and *began* to go through **G**, **Mk 9:30** *1056*
I will go ahead of you to **G**." **Mk 14:28** *1056*
When He was in **G**, **Mk 15:41** *1056*
'He is going ahead of you to **G**; **Mk 16:7** *1056*
was sent from God to a city in **G** called **Lk 1:26** *1056*
Joseph also went up from **G**, **Lk 2:4** *1056*
of the Lord, they returned to **G**, **Lk 2:39** *1056*
and Herod was tetrarch of **G**, **Lk 3:1** *1056*
to **G** in the power of the Spirit, **Lk 4:14** *1056*
down to Capernaum, a city of **G**, **Lk 4:31** *1056*
of **G** and Judea and *from* Jerusalem; **Lk 5:17** *1056*
Gerasenes, which is opposite **G**. **Lk 8:26** *1056*
was passing between Samaria and **G**. **Lk 17:11** *1056*
all over Judea, starting from **G** even **Lk 23:5** *1056*
accompanied Him from **G** were **Lk 23:49** *1056*
with Him out of **G** followed, **Lk 23:55** *1056*
to you while He was still in **G**, **Lk 24:6** *1056*
He purposed to go into **G**, **Jn 1:43** *1056*
there was a wedding in Cana of **G**, **Jn 2:1** *1056*
His signs Jesus did in Cana of **G**, **Jn 2:11** *1056*
Judea and went away again into **G**. **Jn 4:3** *1056*
He went forth from there into **G**. **Jn 4:43** *1056*
So when He came to **G**, **Jn 4:45** *1056*
He came again to Cana of **G** **Jn 4:46** *1056*
had come out of Judea into **G**, **Jn 4:47** *1056*
He had come out of Judea into **G**. **Jn 4:54** *1056*
to the other side of the Sea of **G** **Jn 6:1** *1056*
things Jesus was walking in **G**, **Jn 7:1** *1056*
things to them, He stayed in **G**. **Jn 7:9** *1056*
is not going to come from **G**, **Jn 7:41** *1056*
"You are not also from **G**, are you? **Jn 7:52** *1056*
that no prophet arises out of **G**." **Jn 7:52** *1056*
who was from Bethsaida of **G**, **Jn 12:21** *1056*
and Nathanael of Cana in **G**, **Jn 21:2** *1056*
"Men of **G**, why do you stand **Ac 1:11** *1057*
"After this man, Judas of **G** rose **Ac 5:37** *1057*
and **G** and Samaria enjoyed peace, **Ac 9:31** *1056*
all Judea, starting from **G**, **Ac 10:37** *1056*
up with Him from **G** to Jerusalem, **Ac 13:31** *1056*
GALL
He pours out my **g** on the ground. **Jb 16:13** 4845
the glittering point from his **g**. **Jb 20:25** 4845

They also gave me **g** for my food And **Ps 69:21** 7219
Him wine to drink mixed with **g**; **Mt 27:34** *5521*
"For I see that you are in the **g** **Ac 8:23** *5521*
GALLERIES
the **g** round about their three stories **Ezk 41:16** 863b
the **g** took more *space* away from them **Ezk 42:5** 863b
GALLERY
behind it, with a **g** on each side, **Ezk 41:15** 862a
was **g** corresponding to gallery in **Ezk 42:3** 863b
to **g** in three stories. **Ezk 42:3** 863b
GALLIM
the son of Laish, who was from **G**. **1Sa 25:44** 1554
with your voice, O daughter of **G**! **Is 10:30** 1554
GALLIO
while **G** was proconsul of Achaia, **Ac 18:12** *1058*
his mouth, **G** said to the Jews, **Ac 18:14** *1058*
But **G** was not concerned about any **Ac 18:17** *1058*
GALLONS
twenty or thirty **g** each. **Jn 2:6** *3355*
GALLOPING
of the **g** hoofs of his stallions, **Jer 47:3** 8161
rattling of the wheel, **G** horses And **Na 3:2** 1725
Their horsemen come **g**, **Hab 1:8** 6335a
GALLOWS
so, they were both hanged on a **g**; **Es 2:23** 6086
"Have a **g** fifty cubits high made **Es 5:14** 6086
Haman, so he had the **g** made. **Es 5:14** 6086
g which he had prepared for him. **Es 6:4** 6086
the **g** standing at Haman's house **Es 7:9** 6086
So they hanged Haman on the **g** **Es 7:10** 6086
and him they have hanged on the **g** **Es 8:7** 6086
ten sons be hanged on the **g**." **Es 9:13** 6086
sons should be hanged on the **g**. **Es 9:25** 6086
GAMALIEL
Manasseh, **G** the son of Pedahzur; **Nu 1:10** 1583
G the son of Pedahzur, **Nu 2:20** 1583
day *it was* **G** the son of Pedahzur, **Nu 7:54** 1583
offering of **G** the son of Pedahzur. **Nu 7:59** 1583
and **G** the son of Pedahzur over the **Nu 10:23** 1583
But a Pharisee named **G**, **Ac 5:34** *1059*
up in this city, educated under **G**, **Ac 22:3** *1059*
GAME
because he had a taste for **g**, **Gn 25:28** 6718a
to the field and hunt **g** for me; **Gn 27:3** 6718a
field to hunt for **g** to bring *home*, **Gn 27:5** 6718a
'Bring me *some* **g** and prepare a **Gn 27:7** 6718a
up, please, sit and eat of my **g**, **Gn 27:19** 6718a
me, and I will eat of my son's **g**, **Gn 27:25** 6718a
arise and eat of his son's **g**, **Gn 27:31** 6718a
hunted **g** and brought *it* to me, **Gn 27:33** 6718a
GAMES
Everyone who competes in the **g** **1Co 9:25** *75*
GAMMADIM
and the **G** were in your towers. **Ezk 27:11** 1575
GAMUL
Jachin, the twenty-second for **G**, **1Ch 24:17** 1577
GANGRENE
and their talk will spread like **g**. **2Tm 2:17** *1044*
GAP
in the **g** before Me for the land, **Ezk 22:30** 6556
GAPED
have **g** at me with their mouth, **Jb 16:10** 6473
GAPING
they devour Israel with **g** jaws. **Is 9:12** 3605
GARDEN
God planted a **g** toward the east, **Gn 2:8** 1588
life also in the midst of the **g**, **Gn 2:9** 1588
flowed out of Eden to water the **g**; **Gn 2:10** 1588
put him into the **g** of Eden to cultivate **Gn 2:15** 1588
"From any tree of the **g** you may eat **Gn 2:16** 1588
eat from any tree of the **g**'?" **Gn 3:1** 1588
of the trees of the **g** we may eat; **Gn 3:2** 1588
which is in the middle of the **g**, **Gn 3:3** 1588
in the **g** in the cool of the day, **Gn 3:8** 1588
LORD God among the trees of the **g**. **Gn 3:8** 1588
heard the sound of You in the **g**, **Gn 3:10** 1588
sent him out from the **g** of Eden, **Gn 3:23** 1588
and at the east of the **g** of Eden **Gn 3:24** 1588
like the **g** of the LORD, like the land **Gn 13:10** 1588
with your foot like a vegetable **g**. **Dt 11:10** 1588
that I may have it for a vegetable **g** **1Ki 21:2** 1588
he fled by the way of the **g** house. **2Ki 9:27** 1588
buried in the **g** of his own house, **2Ki 21:18** 1588
his own house, in the **g** of Uzza, **2Ki 21:18** 1588
in his grave in the **g** of Uzza, **2Ki 21:26** 1588
the two walls beside the king's **g**, **2Ki 25:4** 1588
of the Pool of Shelah at the king's **g** **Ne 3:15** 1588
of the **g** of the king's palace. **Es 1:5** 1593
wine *and went* into the palace **g**; **Es 7:7** 1593
the king returned from the palace **g** **Es 7:8** 1593
his shoots spread out over his **g**. **Jb 8:16** 1593
"A **g** locked is my sister, *my* **SS 4:12** 1588
sister, *my* bride, A rock **g** locked, **SS 4:12** 1530
"*You are* a **g** spring, A well of **SS 4:15** 1588
Make my **g** breathe out *fragrance*, **SS 4:16** 1588
his **g** And eat its choice fruits!" **SS 4:16** 1588
"I have come into my **g**, **SS 5:1** 1588
"My beloved has gone down to his **g**, **SS 6:2** 1588
away Or as a **g** that has no water. **Is 1:30** 1593
his forest and of his fruitful **g**, **Is 10:18** 3759
her desert like the **g** of the LORD; **Is 51:3** 1588

And you will be like a watered **g**, **Is 58:11** 1588
And as a **g** causes the things sown **Is 61:11** 1593
life will be like a watered **g**, **Jer 31:12** 1588
by way of the king's **g** through the **Jer 39:4** 1588
walls which *was* by the king's **g**, **Jer 52:7** 1588
His tabernacle like a **g** *booth;* **La 2:6** 1588
"You were in Eden, the **g** of God; **Ezk 28:13** 1588
in God's **g** could not match it; **Ezk 31:8** 1588
No tree in God's **g** could compare **Ezk 31:8** 1588
Eden, which were in the **g** of God, **Ezk 31:9** 1588
has become like the **g** of Eden; **Ezk 36:35** 1588
is like the **g** of Eden before them But **Jl 2:3** 1588
it is larger than the **g** plants and **Mt 13:32** *3001*
becomes larger than all the **g** plants **Mk 4:32** *3001*
and rue and every *kind of* **g** herb, **Lk 11:42** *3001*
man took and threw into his own **g**; **Lk 13:19** *2779*
the Kidron, where there was a **g**, **Jn 18:1** *2779*
I not see you in the **g** with Him?" **Jn 18:26** *2779*
He was crucified there was a **g**, **Jn 19:41** *2779*
and in the **g** a new tomb in which **Jn 19:41** *2779*

GARDENER
Supposing Him to be the **g**, **Jn 20:15** *2780*

GARDENS
out, Like **g** beside the river, **Nu 24:6** 1593
I made **g** and parks for myself and **Ec 2:5** 1593
flock in the **g** And gather lilies. **SS 6:2** 1588
"O you who sit in the **g**, **SS 8:13** 1588
at the **g** which you have chosen. **Is 1:29** 1593
g and burning incense on bricks; **Is 65:3** 1593
purify themselves *to go* to the **g**, **Is 66:17** 1593
and plant **g** and eat their produce. **Jer 29:5** 1593
and plant **g** and eat their produce; **Jer 29:28** 1593
Your many **g** and vineyards, **Am 4:9** 1593
And make **g** and eat their fruit. **Am 9:14** 1593

GAREB
Ira the Ithrite, **G** the Ithrite, **2Sa 23:38** 1619
Ira the Ithrite, **G** the Ithrite, **1Ch 11:40** 1619
straight ahead to the hill **G**; **Jer 31:39** 1619

GARLAND
place on your head a **g** of grace; **Pr 4:9** 3880
Giving them a **g** instead of ashes, **Is 61:3** 6287b
bridegroom decks himself with a **g**, **Is 61:10** 6287b

GARLANDS
brought oxen and **g** to the gates, **Ac 14:13** *4725*

GARLIC
leeks and the onions and the **g**, **Nu 11:5** 7762a

GARMENT
But Shem and Japheth took a **g** and **Gn 9:23** 8071
red, all over like a hairy **g**; **Gn 25:25** 155
She caught him by his **g**, **Gn 39:12** 899b
left his **g** in her hand and fled, **Gn 39:12** 899b
he had left his **g** in her hand and **Gn 39:13** 899b
he left his **g** beside me and fled and **Gn 39:15** 899b
So she left his **g** beside her until **Gn 39:16** 899b
g beside me and fled outside." **Gn 39:18** 899b
any of its blood splashes on a **g**, **Lv 6:27** 899b
a **g** has a mark of leprosy in it, **Lv 13:47** 899b
it is a wool **g** or a linen garment, **Lv 13:47** 899b
it is a wool garment or a linen **g**, **Lv 13:47** 899b
in the **g** or in the leather, **Lv 13:49** 899b
if the mark has spread in the **g**, **Lv 13:51** 899b
"So he shall burn the **g**, **Lv 13:52** 899b
the mark has not spread in the **g**, **Lv 13:53** 899b
of the **g** or out of the leather, **Lv 13:56** 899b
and if it appears again in the **g**, **Lv 13:57** 899b
"The **g**, whether the warp or **Lv 13:58** 899b
leprosy in a **g** of wool or linen, **Lv 13:59** 899b
and for the leprous **g** or house, **Lv 14:55** 899b
'As for any **g** or any leather on **Lv 15:17** 899b
nor wear a **g** upon you of two kinds **Lv 19:19** 899b
You shall purify for yourselves every **g** **Nu 31:20** 899b
you shall do the same with his **g**, **Dt 22:3** 8071
g with which you cover yourself. **Dt 22:12** 3682
g before the elders of the city. **Dt 22:17** 8071
nor take a widow's **g** in pledge. **Dt 24:17** 899b
So they spread out a **g**, **Jg 8:25** 8071
Now she had on a long-sleeved **g**; **2Sa 13:18** 3801
long-sleeved **g** which *was* on her; **2Sa 13:19** 3801
threw a **g** over him when he saw that **2Sa 20:12** 899b
each man took his **g** and placed it **2Ki 9:13** 899b
matter, I tore my **g** and my robe, **Ezr 9:3** 899b
even with my **g** and my robe torn, **Ezr 9:5** 899b
out the front of my **g** and said, **Ne 5:13** 2684
and a **g** of fine linen and purple; **Es 8:15** 8509
thing, Like a **g** that is moth-eaten. **Jb 13:28** 899b
a great force my **g** is distorted; **Jb 30:18** 3830
When I made a cloud its **g** And **Jb 38:9** 3830
And they stand forth like a **g**. **Jb 38:14** 3830
The **g** of violence covers them. **Ps 73:6** 7897
of them will wear out like a **g**; **Ps 102:26** 899b
it with the deep as with a **g**; **Ps 104:6** 3830
with cursing as with his **g**, **Ps 109:18** 4055
a **g** with which he covers himself, **Ps 109:19** 899b
Take his **g** when he becomes surety **Pr 20:16** 899b
who takes off a **g** on a cold day, **Pr 25:20** 899b
Take his **g** when he becomes surety **Pr 27:13** 899b
has wrapped the waters in His **g**? **Pr 30:4** 8071
they will all wear out like a **g**; **Is 50:9** 899b
the earth will wear out like a **g** And **Is 51:6** 899b
the moth will eat them like a **g**, **Is 51:8** 899b
deeds are like a filthy **g**; **Is 64:6** 899b
shepherd wraps himself with his **g**, **Jer 43:12** 899b
You strip the robe off the **g** From **Mi 2:8** 8008
holy meat in the fold of his **g**, **Hg 2:12** 899b
will grasp the **g** of a Jew, **Zch 8:23** 3671
him who covers his **g** with wrong," **Mal 2:16** 3830
himself had a **g** of camel's hair and **Mt 3:4** *1742*
of unshrunk cloth on an old **g**; **Mt 9:16** *2440*
the patch pulls away from the **g**, **Mt 9:16** *2440*
"If I only touch His **g**, **Mt 9:21** *2440*
of unshrunk cloth on an old **g**; **Mk 2:21** *2440*
g and puts it on an old garment; **Lk 5:36** *2440*
garment and puts it on an old **g**; **Lk 5:36** *2440*
the Lord, he put his outer **g** on **Jn 21:7** *1903*
THEY ALL WILL BECOME OLD LIKE A **G**, **Heb 1:11** *2440*
LIKE A **G** THEY WILL ALSO BE CHANGED. **Heb 1:12** *2440*
even the **g** polluted by the flesh. **Jude 1:23** *5509*

GARMENTS
g of skin for Adam and his wife, **Gn 3:21** 3801
and articles of gold, and **g**, **Gn 24:53** 899b
the best **g** of Esau her elder son, **Gn 27:15** 899b
he smelled the smell of his **g**, **Gn 27:27** 899b
give me food to eat and **g** to wear, **Gn 28:20** 899b
yourselves and change your **g**; **Gn 35:2** 8071
so he tore his **g**. **Gn 37:29** 899b
So she removed her widow's **g** and **Gn 38:14** 899b
her veil and put on her widow's **g**. **Gn 38:19** 899b
clothed him in **g** of fine linen and **Gn 41:42** 899b
each of them he gave changes of **g**, **Gn 45:22** 8071
of silver and five changes of **g**. **Gn 45:22** 8071
He washes his **g** in wine, And his **Gn 49:11** 3830
and let them wash their **g**; **Ex 19:10** 8071
people, and they washed their **g**. **Ex 19:14** 8071
holy **g** for Aaron your brother, **Ex 28:2** 899b
make Aaron's **g** to consecrate him, **Ex 28:3** 899b
are the **g** which they shall make: **Ex 28:4** 899b
and they shall make holy **g** for **Ex 28:4** 899b
"You shall take the **g**, **Ex 29:5** 899b
sprinkle *it* on Aaron and on his **g** and **Ex 29:21** 899b
sons and on his sons' **g** with him; **Ex 29:21** 899b
he and his **g** shall be consecrated, **Ex 29:21** 899b
his sons and his sons' **g** with him. **Ex 29:21** 899b
"The holy **g** of Aaron shall be **Ex 29:29** 899b
the woven **g** as well, and the holy **Ex 31:10** 899b
the holy **g** for Aaron the priest, **Ex 31:10** 899b
the priest, and the **g** of his sons, **Ex 31:10** 899b
the woven **g** for ministering in **Ex 35:19** 899b
the holy **g** for Aaron the priest and **Ex 35:19** 899b
the priest and the **g** of his sons, **Ex 35:19** 899b
its service and for the holy **g**. **Ex 35:21** 899b
they made finely woven **g** for **Ex 39:1** 899b
the holy **g** which were for Aaron, **Ex 39:1** 899b
the woven **g** for ministering in the **Ex 39:41** 899b
the holy **g** for Aaron the priest and **Ex 39:41** 899b
the priest and the **g** of his sons, **Ex 39:41** 899b
You shall put the holy **g** on Aaron **Ex 40:13** 899b
his **g** and put on other garments, **Lv 6:11** 899b
his garments and put on other **g**, **Lv 6:11** 899b
and the **g** and the anointing oil **Lv 8:2** 899b
sprinkled it on Aaron, on his **g**, **Lv 8:30** 899b
and on the **g** of his sons with him; **Lv 8:30** 899b
and he consecrated Aaron, his **g**, **Lv 8:30** 899b
and the **g** of his sons with him. **Lv 8:30** 899b
(these are holy **g**). **Lv 16:4** 899b
and take off the linen **g** which he **Lv 16:23** 899b
he shall thus put on the linen **g**, **Lv 16:32** 899b
on the linen garments, the holy **g**, **Lv 16:32** 899b
been consecrated to wear the **g**, **Lv 21:10** 899b
g throughout their generations, **Nu 15:38** 899b
and strip Aaron of his **g** and put **Nu 20:26** 899b
Moses had stripped Aaron of his **g** **Nu 20:28** 899b
Then Saul clothed David with his **g** **1Sa 17:38** 4055
and cut off their **g** in the middle **2Sa 10:4** 4063
and put on mourning **g** now, **2Sa 14:2** 899b
articles of silver and gold, **g**, **1Ki 10:25** 8008
"Bring out **g** for all the worshipers **2Ki 10:22** 3830
So he brought out **g** for them. **2Ki 10:22** 4403
and cut off their **g** in the middle **1Ch 19:4** 4063
articles of silver and gold, **g**, **2Ch 9:24** 8008
among them, *including* goods, **g** and **2Ch 20:25** 899b
silver minas and 100 priestly **g**. **Ezr 2:69** 3801
50 basins, 530 priests' **g**. **Ne 7:70** 3801
silver minas and 67 priests' **g**. **Ne 7:72** 3801
And she sent **g** to clothe Mordecai **Es 4:4** 899b
And prepares **g** as *plentiful as* the clay, **Jb 27:16** 4403
You whose **g** are hot, When the land **Jb 37:17** 899b
They divide my **g** among them, And **Ps 22:18** 899b
All Your **g** are *fragrant with* myrrh **Ps 45:8** 899b
She makes linen **g** and sells *them*, **Pr 31:24** 5466
And the fragrance of your **g** is **SS 4:11** 8008
yourself in your beautiful **g**, **Is 52:1** 899b
put on **g** of vengeance for clothing And **Is 59:17** 899b
clothed me with **g** of salvation, **Is 61:10** 899b
g of glowing colors from Bozrah, **Is 63:1** 899b
And Your **g** like the one who treads **Is 63:2** 899b
lifeblood is sprinkled on My **g**, **Is 63:3** 899b
afraid, nor did they rend their **g**. **Jer 36:24** 899b
that no one could touch their **g**. **La 4:14** 3830
and strip off their embroidered **g**. **Ezk 26:16** 899b
"They traded with you in choice **g**, **Ezk 27:24** 4360
their **g** in which they minister, **Ezk 42:14** 899b
They shall put on other **g**; **Ezk 42:14** 899b
shall be clothed with linen **g**; **Ezk 44:17** 899b
they shall put off their **g** in **Ezk 44:19** 899b
then they shall put on other **g** **Ezk 44:19** 899b
to the people with their **g**. **Ezk 44:19** 899b
rend your heart and not your **g**." **Jl 2:13** 899b
"On **g** taken as pledges they **Am 2:8** 899b
clothe themselves with foreign **g**. **Zph 1:8** 4403
Joshua was clothed with filthy **g** **Zch 3:3** 899b
"Remove the filthy **g** from him." **Zch 3:4** 899b
his head and clothed him with **g**, **Zch 3:5** 899b
silver and **g** in great abundance. **Zch 14:14** 899b
His **g** became as white as light. **Mt 17:2** *2440*
and lengthen the tassels *of their* **g**. **Mt 23:5**
and put His *own* **g** back on Him, **Mt 27:31** *2440*
divided up His **g** among themselves by **Mt 27:35** *2440*
"If I just touch His **g**, **Mk 5:28** *2440*
"Who touched My **g**?" **Mk 5:30** *2440*
and His **g** became radiant and **Mk 9:3** *2440*
off Him and put His *own* **g** on Him. **Mk 15:20** *2440*
divided up His **g** among themselves, **Mk 15:24** *2440*
dividing up His **g** among themselves **Lk 23:34** *2440*
from supper, and laid aside His **g**; **Jn 13:4** *2440*
their feet, and taken His **g** and **Jn 13:12** *2440*
His outer **g** and made four parts, **Jn 19:23** *2440*
DIVIDED MY OUTER **G** AMONG THEM, **Jn 19:24** *2440*
and showing all the tunics and **g** **Ac 9:39** *2440*
man stood before me in shining **g**, **Ac 10:30** *2066*
shook out his **g** and said to them, **Ac 18:6** *2440*
and gold or pearls or costly **g**, **1Tm 2:9** *2441*
and your **g** have become moth-eaten. **Jas 5:2** *2440*
who have not soiled their **g**; **Rv 3:4** *2440*
will thus be clothed in white **g**; **Rv 3:5** *2440*
you may become rich, and white **g** so **Rv 3:18** *2440*
sitting, clothed in white **g**, **Rv 4:4** *2440*

GARMITE
the **G** and Eshtemoa the Maacathite. **1Ch 4:19** 1636

GARNER
But those who **g** it will eat it and **Is 62:9** 622

GARNERS
Let our **g** be full, furnishing **Ps 144:13** 4200

GARRISON
of God where the Philistine **g** is; **1Sa 10:5** 5333
Jonathan smote the **g** of the **1Sa 13:3** 5333
smitten the **g** of the Philistines, **1Sa 13:4** 5333
And the **g** of the Philistines went **1Sa 13:23** 4673
let us cross over to the Philistines' **g** **1Sa 14:1** 4673
cross over to the Philistines' **g**, **1Sa 14:4** 4673
to the **g** of these uncircumcised; **1Sa 14:6** 4673
to the **g** of the Philistines, **1Sa 14:11** 4673
the men of the **g** hailed Jonathan **1Sa 14:12** 4673
the **g** and the raiders trembled, **1Sa 14:15** 4673
while the **g** of the Philistines was **2Sa 23:14** 4673
while the **g** of the Philistines *was* **1Ch 11:16** 5333

GARRISONS
Then David put **g** among the **2Sa 8:6** 5333
He put **g** in Edom. **2Sa 8:14** 5333
In all Edom he put **g**, **2Sa 8:14** 5333
Then David put **g** among **1Ch 18:6** 5333
Then he put **g** in Edom, and all the **1Ch 18:13** 5333
and set **g** in the land of Judah and **2Ch 17:2** 5333

GASH
nor will anyone **g** himself or shave **Jer 16:6** 1413
How long will you **g** yourself? **Jer 47:5** 1413

GASHED
clothes torn and their bodies **g**, **Jer 41:5** 1413

GASHES
there are **g** on all the hands and **Jer 48:37** 1417

GASHING
and **g** himself with stones. **Mk 5:5** *2629*

GASHMU
among the nations, and **G** says, **Ne 6:6** 1654

GASP
groan, I will both **g** and pant. **Is 42:14** 5395

GASPING
the daughter of Zion **g** for breath, **Jer 4:31** 3306

GATAM
Omar, Zepho and **G** and Kenaz. **Gn 36:11** 1609
chief Korah, chief **G**, **Gn 36:16** 1609
were Teman, Omar, Zephi, **G**, **1Ch 1:36** 1609

GATE
Lot was sitting in the **g** of Sodom. **Gn 19:1** 8179
possess the **g** of their enemies. **Gn 22:17** 8179
who went in at the **g** of his city, **Gn 23:10** 8179
who went in at the **g** of his city. **Gn 23:18** 8179
The **g** of those who hate them." **Gn 24:60** 8179
and this is the **g** of heaven." **Gn 28:17** 8179
came to the **g** of their city and **Gn 34:20** 8179
All who went out of the **g** of **Gn 34:24** 8179
who went out of the **g** of his city. **Gn 34:24** 8179
for the *one* side *of the* **g** *shall* **Ex 27:14**
"For the **g** of the court **Ex 27:16** 8179
Moses stood in the **g** of the camp, **Ex 32:26** 8179
forth from **g** to gate in the camp, **Ex 32:27** 8179
forth from gate to **g** in the camp, **Ex 32:27** 8179
the screen for the **g** of the court; **Ex 35:17** 8179
for the *one* side *of the* **g** *were* **Ex 38:14**
On both sides of the **g** of the **Ex 38:15** 8179
The screen of the **g** of the **Ex 38:18** 8179
the sockets of the **g** of the court, **Ex 38:31** 8179
the screen for the **g** of the court, **Ex 39:40** 8179
the doorway of the **g** of the court **Nu 4:26** 8179
the elders of the city at the **g**. **Dt 22:15** 8179
you shall bring them both out to the **g** **Dt 22:24** 8179
up to the **g** to the elders and say, **Dt 25:7** 8179
when *it was time* to shut the **g** at **Jos 2:5** 8179
had gone out, they shut the **g**. **Jos 2:7** 8179
from the **g** as far as Shebarim and **Jos 7:5** 8179
it at the entrance of the city **g**, **Jos 8:29** 8179
shall stand at the entrance of the **g** of **Jos 20:4** 8179
in the entrance of the city **g**; **Jg 9:35** 8179
up to the entrance of the **g**. **Jg 9:40** 8179
in the entrance of the city **g**; **Jg 9:44** 8179
all night at the **g** of the city. **Jg 16:2** 8179
took hold of the doors of the city **g** **Jg 16:3** 8179
stood by the entrance of the **g**. **Jg 18:16** 8179
priest stood by the entrance of the **g** **Jg 18:17** 8179
up to the **g** and sat down there, **Ru 4:1** 8179
the seat backward beside the **g**, **1Sa 4:18** 8179
Saul approached Samuel in the **g** and **1Sa 9:18** 8179
scribbled on the doors of the **g**, **1Sa 21:13** 8179

the **g** to speak with him privately, **2Sa 3:27** 8179
as far as the entrance of the **g**. **2Sa 11:23** 8179
and stand beside the way to the **g**; **2Sa 15:2** 8179
So the king stood beside the **g**, **2Sa 18:4** 8179
to the roof of the **g** by the wall, **2Sa 18:24** 8179
the chamber over the **g** and wept. **2Sa 18:33** 8179
the king arose and sat in the **g**. **2Sa 19:8** 8179
the king is sitting in the **g**," **2Sa 19:8** 8179
of Bethlehem which is by the **g**!" **2Sa 23:15** 8179
of Bethlehem which was by the **g**, **2Sa 23:16** 8179
when he came to the **g** of the city, **1Ki 17:10** 6607
the entrance of the **g** of Samaria; **1Ki 22:10** 8179
a shekel, in the **g** of Samaria.' " **2Ki 7:1** 8179
men at the entrance of the **g**; **2Ki 7:3** 8179
he leaned to have charge of the **g**; **2Ki 7:17** 8179
people trampled on him at the **g**, **2Ki 7:17** 8179
this time at the **g** of Samaria." **2Ki 7:18** 8179
people trampled on him at the **g** and **2Ki 7:20** 8179
As Jehu entered the **g**, **2Ki 9:31** 8179
entrance of the **g** until morning." **2Ki 10:8** 8179
third also *shall be* at the **g** Sur, **2Ki 11:6** 8179
third at the **g** behind the guards), **2Ki 11:6** 8179
and came by the way of the **g** of **2Ki 11:19** 8179
G of Ephraim to the Corner Gate, **2Ki 14:13** 8179
Gate of Ephraim to the Corner **G**, **2Ki 14:13** 8179
upper **g** of the house of the LORD. **2Ki 15:35** 8179
at the entrance of the **g** of Joshua **2Ki 23:8** 8179
were on one's left at the city **g**. **2Ki 23:8** 8179
by way of the **g** between the two walls **2Ki 25:4** 8179
now at the king's **g** to the east). **1Ch 9:18** 8179
of Bethlehem, which is by the **g**!" **1Ch 11:17** 8179
of Bethlehem which *was* by the **g**, **1Ch 11:18** 8179
the sons of Jeduthun for the **g**. **1Ch 16:42** 8179
fathers' households, for every **g**. **1Ch 26:13** 8179
the west, by the **g** of Shallecheth, **1Ch 26:16** 8179
by their divisions at every **g**; **2Ch 8:14** 8179
the entrance of the **g** of Samaria; **2Ch 18:9** 8179
third at the **G** of the Foundation; **2Ch 23:5** 8179
of the Horse **G** of the king's house, **2Ch 23:15** 8179
the upper **g** to the king's house. **2Ch 23:20** 8179
by the **g** of the house of the LORD. **2Ch 24:8** 8179
G of Ephraim to the Corner Gate, **2Ch 25:23** 8179
Gate of Ephraim to the Corner **G**, **2Ch 25:23** 8179
towers in Jerusalem at the Corner **G** **2Ch 26:9** 8179
and at the Valley **G** and at the corner **2Ch 26:9** 8179
upper **g** of the house of the LORD, **2Ch 27:3** 8179
the keeper of the eastern **g**, *was* **2Ch 31:14** 8179
him in the square at the city **g**, **2Ch 32:6** 8179
to the entrance of the Fish **G**; **2Ch 33:14** 8179
and the gatekeepers at each **g** did **2Ch 35:15** 8179
I went out at night by the Valley **G** **Ne 2:13** 8179
Well and *on* to the Refuse **G**, **Ne 2:13** 8179
the Fountain **G** and the King's Pool, **Ne 2:14** 8179
the Valley **G** again and returned. **Ne 2:15** 8179
the priests and built the Sheep **G**; **Ne 3:1** 8179
of Hassenaah built the Fish **G**; **Ne 3:3** 8179
of Besodeiah repaired the Old **G**; **Ne 3:6** 8179
of Zanoah repaired the Valley **G**. **Ne 3:13** 8179
of the wall to the Refuse **G**. **Ne 3:13** 8179
repaired the Refuse **G**. **Ne 3:14** 8179
Mizpah, repaired the Fountain **G**. **Ne 3:15** 8179
as far as the front of the Water **G** **Ne 3:26** 8179
Above the Horse **G** the priests **Ne 3:28** 8179
the keeper of the East **G**, **Ne 3:29** 8179
in front of the Inspection **G** and **Ne 3:31** 8179
room of the corner and the Sheep **G** **Ne 3:32** 8179
which was in front of the Water **G**, **Ne 8:1** 8179
which was in front of the Water **G** **Ne 8:3** 8179
and in the square at the Water **G** and **Ne 8:16** 8179
in the square at the **G** of Ephraim. **Ne 8:16** 8179
of the wall toward the Refuse **G**. **Ne 12:31** 8179
At the Fountain **G** they went **Ne 12:37** 8179
David to the Water **G** on the east. **Ne 12:37** 8179
and above the **G** of Ephraim, by the **Ne 12:39** 8179
the Gate of Ephraim, by the Old **G**, **Ne 12:39** 8179
by the Old Gate, by the Fish **G**, **Ne 12:39** 8179
Hundred, as far as the Sheep **G**; **Ne 12:39** 8179
stopped at the **G** of the Guard. **Ne 12:39** 8179
Mordecai was sitting at the king's **g** **Es 2:19** 8179
Mordecai was sitting at the king's **g**, **Es 2:21** 8179
servants who were at the king's **g** **Es 3:2** 8179
servants who were at the king's **g** **Es 3:3** 8179
He went as far as the king's **g**, **Es 4:2** 8179
the king's **g** clothed in sackcloth. **Es 4:2** 8179
square in front of the king's **g**. **Es 4:6** 8179
Haman saw Mordecai in the king's **g** **Es 5:9** 8179
the Jew sitting at the king's **g**." **Es 5:13** 8179
who is sitting at the king's **g**; **Es 6:10** 8179
Mordecai returned to the king's **g**. **Es 6:12** 8179
They are even oppressed in the **g**, **Jb 5:4** 8179
I went out to the **g** of the city, **Jb 29:7** 8179
I saw I had support in the **g**, **Jb 31:21** 8179
who sit in the **g** talk about me, **Ps 69:12** 8179
This is the **g** of the LORD; **Ps 118:20** 8179
speak with their enemies in the **g**. **Ps 127:5** 8179
Or crush the afflicted at the **g**; **Pr 22:22** 8179
does not open his mouth in the **g**. **Pr 24:7** 8179
in Heshbon By the **g** of Bath-rabbim; **SS 7:4** 8179
"Wail, O **g**; cry, O city; Melt away, **Is 14:31** 8179
took up fixed positions at the **g**. **Is 22:7** 8179
And the **g** is battered to ruins. **Is 24:12** 8179
who repel the onslaught at the **g**. **Is 28:6** 8179
him who adjudicates at the **g**, **Is 29:21** 8179
"Stand in the **g** of the LORD's **Jer 7:2** 8179
"Go and stand in the public **g**, **Jer 17:19** 8179
by the entrance of the potsherd **g**, **Jer 19:2** 8179
that were at the upper Benjamin **G**, **Jer 20:2** 8179
of the New **G** of the LORD's *house*. **Jer 26:10** 8179
Tower of Hananel to the Corner **G**. **Jer 31:38** 8179
of the Horse **G** toward the east, **Jer 31:40** 8179
of the New **G** of the LORD's house, **Jer 36:10** 8179
While he was at the **G** of Benjamin, **Jer 37:13** 8179
was sitting in the **G** of Benjamin; **Jer 38:7** 8179
in and sat down at the Middle **G**: **Jer 39:3** 8179
the **g** between the two walls; **Jer 39:4** 8179
city at night by way of the **g** between **Jer 52:7** 8179
Elders are gone from the **g**, **La 5:14** 8179
of the north **g** of the inner *court*, **Ezk 8:3** 8179
to the north of the altar **g** *was* **Ezk 8:5** 8179
entrance of the **g** of the LORD's house **Ezk 8:14** 8179
of the upper **g** which faces north, **Ezk 9:2** 8179
of the east **g** of the LORD's house, **Ezk 10:19** 8179
brought me to the east **g** of the LORD's **Ezk 11:1** 8179
men at the entrance of the **g**, **Ezk 11:1** 8179
he went to the **g** which faced east, **Ezk 40:6** 8179
measured the threshold of the **g**, **Ezk 40:6** 8179
And the threshold of the **g** by the **Ezk 40:7** 8179
the **g** facing inward *was* one rod. **Ezk 40:7** 8179
the porch of the **g** facing inward, **Ezk 40:8** 8179
He measured the porch of the **g**, **Ezk 40:9** 8179
porch of the **g** was faced inward. **Ezk 40:9** 8179
The guardrooms of the **g** toward **Ezk 40:10** 8179
cubits, and the length of the **g**, **Ezk 40:11** 8179
He measured the **g** from the **Ezk 40:13** 8179
the **g** *extended* round about to the **Ezk 40:14** 8179
From the front of the entrance **g** **Ezk 40:15** 8179
porch of the **g** *was* fifty cubits. **Ezk 40:15** 8179
pillars within the **g** all around, **Ezk 40:16** 8179
width from the front of the lower **g** to **Ezk 40:19** 8179
As for the **g** of the outer **Ezk 40:20** 8179
same measurement as the first **g**. **Ezk 40:21** 8179
the **g** which faced toward the east; **Ezk 40:22** 8179
The inner court had a **g** **Ezk 40:23** 8179
had a gate opposite the **g** on the north **Ezk 40:23** 8179
gate on the north as well as *the* **g** **Ezk 40:23**
a hundred cubits from **g** to gate. **Ezk 40:23** 8179
a hundred cubits from gate to **g**. **Ezk 40:23** 8179
there was a **g** toward the south; **Ezk 40:24** 8179
The **g** and its porches had **Ezk 40:25**
court had a **g** toward the south; **Ezk 40:27** 8179
from **g** to gate toward the south, **Ezk 40:27** 8179
from gate to **g** toward the south, **Ezk 40:27** 8179
to the inner court by the south **g**; **Ezk 40:28** 8179
and he measured the south **g** **Ezk 40:28** 8179
And the **g** and its porches had **Ezk 40:29**
And he measured the **g** according to **Ezk 40:32** 8179
And the **g** and its porches had **Ezk 40:33**
Then he brought me to the north **g**; **Ezk 40:35** 8179
And the **g** had windows all around; **Ezk 40:36**
g *were* two tables on each side, **Ezk 40:39** 8179
porch of the **g** *were* two tables. **Ezk 40:40** 8179
were on each side next to the **g**; **Ezk 40:41** 8179
From the outside to the inner **g** were **Ezk 40:44** 8179
was at the side of the north **g**, **Ezk 40:44** 8179
south **g** facing toward the north. **Ezk 40:44** 8179
g was three cubits on each side. **Ezk 40:48** 8179
the **g** which faced toward the east and **Ezk 42:15** 8179
Then he led me to the **g**, **Ezk 43:1** 8179
the **g** facing toward the east; **Ezk 43:1** 8179
of the **g** facing toward the east. **Ezk 43:4** 8179
of the outer **g** of the sanctuary, **Ezk 44:1** 8179
"This **g** shall be shut; **Ezk 44:2** 8179
by way of the porch of the **g** and **Ezk 44:3** 8179
north **g** to the front of the house; **Ezk 44:4** 8179
posts of the **g** of the inner court. **Ezk 45:19** 8179
"The **g** of the inner court facing **Ezk 46:1** 8179
enter by way of the porch of the **g** **Ezk 46:2** 8179
and stand by the post of the **g**. **Ezk 46:2** 8179
of the **g** and then go out; **Ezk 46:2** 8179
but the **g** shall not be shut until **Ezk 46:2** 8179
worship at the doorway of that **g** **Ezk 46:3** 8179
the **g** and go out by the same way. **Ezk 46:8** 8179
he who enters by way of the north **g** **Ezk 46:9** 8179
go out by way of the south **g**, **Ezk 46:9** 8179
he who enters by way of the south **g** **Ezk 46:9** 8179
go out by way of the north **g**. **Ezk 46:9** 8179
No one shall return by way of the **g** **Ezk 46:9** 8179
the **g** facing east shall be opened **Ezk 46:12** 8179
and the **g** shall be shut after he **Ezk 46:12** 8179
which *was* at the side of the **g**, **Ezk 46:19** 8179
brought me out by way of the north **g** **Ezk 47:2** 8179
around on the outside to the outer **g** **Ezk 47:2** 8179
to the outer gate by way of *the* **g** **Ezk 47:2**
the **g** of Reuben, one; **Ezk 48:31** 8179
the **g** of Judah, one; **Ezk 48:31** 8179
the **g** of Levi, one. **Ezk 48:31** 8179
the **g** of Joseph, one; **Ezk 48:32** 8179
the **g** of Benjamin, one; **Ezk 48:32** 8179
the **g** of Dan, one. **Ezk 48:32** 8179
the **g** of Simeon, one; **Ezk 48:33** 8179
the **g** of Issachar, one; **Ezk 48:33** 8179
the **g** of Zebulun, one. **Ezk 48:33** 8179
the **g** of Gad, one; **Ezk 48:34** 8179
the **g** of Asher, one; **Ezk 48:34** 8179
the **g** of Naphtali, one. **Ezk 48:34** 8179
And will demolish their **g** bars And **Hos 11:6**
"I will also break the **g** bar of **Am 1:5**
hate him who reproves in the **g**, **Am 5:10** 8179
And turn aside the poor in the **g**. **Am 5:12** 8179
And establish justice in the **g**! **Am 5:15** 8179
And foreigners entered his **g** And **Ob 1:11** 8179
"Do not enter the **g** of My people **Ob 1:13** 8179
It has reached the **g** of my people, **Mi 1:9** 8179
the LORD To the **g** of Jerusalem. **Mi 1:12** 8179
break out, pass through the **g** and **Mi 2:13** 8179
Fire consumes your **g** bars. **Na 3:13**
sound of a cry from the Fish **G**, **Zph 1:10** 8179
from Benjamin's **G** as far as the place **Zch 14:10** 8179
of the First **G** to the Corner Gate, **Zch 14:10** 8179
of the First Gate to the Corner **G**, **Zch 14:10** 8179
"Enter through the narrow **g**; **Mt 7:13** *4439*
for the **g** is wide and the way is **Mt 7:13** *4439*
"For the **g** is small and the way **Mt 7:14** *4439*
He approached the **g** of the city, **Lk 7:12** *4439*
named Lazarus was laid at his **g**, **Lk 16:20** *4440*
is in Jerusalem by the sheep **g** a **Jn 5:2**
at the **g** of the temple which is called **Ac 3:2** *2374*
G of the temple to *beg* alms, **Ac 3:10** *4439*
Simon's house, appeared at the **g**; **Ac 10:17** *4440*
iron **g** that leads into the city, **Ac 12:10** *4439*
he knocked at the door of the **g**, **Ac 12:13** *4440*
of her joy she did not open the **g**, **Ac 12:14** *4440*
was standing in front of the **g**. **Ac 12:14** *4440*
went outside the **g** to a riverside, **Ac 16:13** *4439*
own blood, suffered outside the **g**. **Heb 13:12** *4439*

GATEKEEPER

watchman called to the **g** and said, **2Sa 18:26** 7778
the son of Meshelemiah was **g** of the **1Ch 9:21** 7778

GATEKEEPERS

and called to the **g** of the city, **2Ki 7:10** 7778
The **g** called and told *it* **2Ki 7:11** 7778
Now the **g** *were* Shallum and Akkub **1Ch 9:17** 7778
These *were* the **g** for the camp of **1Ch 9:18** 7778
be **g** at the thresholds were 212. **1Ch 9:22** 7778
The **g** were on the four sides, to **1Ch 9:24** 7778
the four chief **g** who *were* Levites, **1Ch 9:26** 7778
Obed-edom and Jeiel, the **g**. **1Ch 15:18** 7778
and Elkanah were **g** for the ark. **1Ch 15:23** 7778
Jehiah also *were* **g** for the ark. **1Ch 15:24** 7778
son of Jeduthun, and Hosah as **g**. **1Ch 16:38** 7778
and 4,000 *were* **g**, and 4,000 *were* **1Ch 23:5** 7778
the **g** *there were* of the Korahites, **1Ch 26:1** 7778
To these divisions of the **g**, **1Ch 26:12** 7778
These were the divisions of the **g** **1Ch 26:19** 7778
and the **g** by their divisions at **2Ch 8:14** 7778
in on the sabbath, *shall be* **g**, **2Ch 23:4**
7778, 5592b
the **g** of the house of the LORD, **2Ch 23:19** 7778
were scribes and officials and **g**. **2Ch 34:13** 7778
and the **g** at each gate did not **2Ch 35:15** 7778
The sons of the **g**: **Ezr 2:42** 7778
of the people, the singers, the **g** and **Ezr 2:70** 7778
the Levites, the singers, the **g** and **Ezr 7:7** 7778
of the **g**: Shallum, Telem and Uri. **Ezr 10:24** 7778
and the **g** and the singers and the **Ne 7:1** 7778
The **g**: the sons of Shallum, the sons **Ne 7:45** 7778
the priests, the Levites, the **g**, **Ne 7:73** 7778
the priests, the Levites, the **g**, **Ne 10:28** 7778
who are ministering, the **g** and **Ne 10:39** 7778
Also the **g**, Akkub, Talmon and **Ne 11:19** 7778
and Akkub *were* **g** keeping watch at **Ne 12:25** 7778
together with the singers and the **g** **Ne 12:45** 7778
and the **g** as each day required, **Ne 12:47** 7778
Levites, the singers and the **g**, **Ne 13:5** 7778
as **g** to sanctify the sabbath day. **Ne 13:22**
8104, 8179

GATES

with high walls, **g** and bars, **Dt 3:5** 1817
of your house and on your **g**. **Dt 6:9** 8179
of your house and on your **g**, **Dt 11:20** 8179
the Levite who is within your **g**, **Dt 12:12** 8179
and eat meat within any of your **g**, **Dt 12:15** 8179
your **g** the tithe of your grain or **Dt 12:17** 8179
the Levite who is within your **g**; **Dt 12:18** 8179
within your **g** whatever you desire. **Dt 12:21** 8179
"You shall eat it within your **g**; **Dt 15:22** 8179
done this evil deed to your **g**, **Dt 17:5** 8179
son he shall set up its **g**." **Jos 6:26** 1817
Then war *was* in the **g**. **Jg 5:8** 8179
of the LORD went down to the **g**. **Jg 5:11** 8179
the valley, and to the **g** of Ekron. **1Sa 17:52** 8179
a city with double **g** and bars." **1Sa 23:7** 1817
was sitting between the two **g**; **2Sa 18:24** 8179
and set up its **g** with the *loss of* **1Ki 16:34** 1817
broke down the high places of the **g** **2Ki 23:8** 8179
of the **g** of the house of the LORD, **1Ch 9:23** 8179
doors of the **g** and for the clamps, **1Ch 22:3** 8179
fortified cities *with* walls, **g** and **2Ch 8:5** 1817
with walls and towers, **g** and bars. **2Ch 14:7** 1817
in the **g** of the camp of the LORD. **2Ch 31:2** 8179
and its **g** are burned with fire." **Ne 1:3** 8179
g have been consumed by fire?" **Ne 2:3** 8179
make beams for the **g** of the fortress **Ne 2:8** 8179
its **g** which were consumed by fire. **Ne 2:13** 8179
desolate and its **g** burned by fire. **Ne 2:17** 8179
had not set up the doors in the **g**, **Ne 6:1** 8179
"Do not let the **g** of Jerusalem be **Ne 7:3** 8179
brethren who kept watch at the **g**, **Ne 11:19** 8179
watch at the storehouses of the **g**. **Ne 12:25** 8179
also purified the people, the **g** and **Ne 12:30** 8179
as it grew dark at the **g** of Jerusalem **Ne 13:19** 8179
stationed some of my servants at the **g** **Ne 13:19** 8179
"Have the **g** of death been **Jb 38:17** 8179
you seen the **g** of deep darkness? **Jb 38:17** 8179
lift me up from the **g** of death, **Ps 9:13** 8179
That in the **g** of the daughter of **Ps 9:14** 8179
Lift up your heads, O **g**, **Ps 24:7** 8179
Lift up your heads, O **g**, **Ps 24:9** 8179
The LORD loves the **g** of Zion More **Ps 87:2** 8179
Enter His **g** with thanksgiving *And* **Ps 100:4** 8179
For He has shattered **g** of bronze And **Ps 107:16** 1817
they drew near to the **g** of death. **Ps 107:18** 8179
Open to me the **g** of righteousness; **Ps 118:19** 8179
feet are standing Within your **g**, **Ps 122:2** 8179
strengthened the bars of your **g**; **Ps 147:13** 8179
the entrance of the **g** in the city she **Pr 1:21** 8179

Beside the **g**, at the opening to Pr 8:3 8179
to me, Watching daily at my **g**, Pr 8:34 1817
wicked at the **g** of the righteous. Pr 14:19 8179
Her husband is known in the **g**, Pr 31:23 8179
let her works praise her in the **g**. Pr 31:31 8179
And her **g** will lament and mourn, Is 3:26 6607
"Open the **g**, that the righteous Is 26:2 8179
life I am to enter the **g** of Sheol; Is 38:10 8179
him so that **g** will not be shut: Is 45:1 8179
of rubies, And your **g** of crystal, Is 54:12 8179
Your **g** will be open continually; Is 60:11 8179
salvation, and your **g** praise. Is 60:18 8179
Go through, go through the **g**, Is 62:10 8179
entrance of the **g** of Jerusalem, Jer 1:15 8179
these **g** to worship the LORD!' " Jer 7:2 8179
And her **g** languish; They sit on the Jer 14:2 8179
fork At the **g** of the land; Jer 15:7 8179
well as in all the **g** of Jerusalem; Jer 17:19 8179
who come in through these **g**: Jer 17:20 8179
in through the **g** of Jerusalem. Jer 17:21 8179
"to bring no load in through the **g** of Jer 17:24 8179
will come in through the **g** of this city Jer 17:25 8179
coming in through the **g** of Jerusalem Jer 17:27 8179
I will kindle a fire in its **g** Jer 17:27 8179
and your people who enter these **g**. Jer 22:2 8179
will enter the **g** of this house, Jer 22:4 8179
out beyond the **g** of Jerusalem. Jer 22:19 8179
"It has no **g** or bars; Jer 49:31 1817
The bars of her **g** are broken. Jer 51:30
her high **g** will be set on fire; Jer 51:58 8179
All her **g** are desolate; La 1:4 8179
Her **g** have sunk into the ground, La 2:9 8179
Could enter the **g** of Jerusalem. La 4:12 8179
and many fall at all their **g**. Ezk 21:15 8179
set battering rams against the **g**, Ezk 21:22 8179
when he enters your **g** as men enter Ezk 26:10 8179
walls and having no bars or **g**, Ezk 38:11 1817
was by the side of the **g**, Ezk 40:18 8179
corresponding to the length of the **g**. Ezk 40:18 8179
was by the side pillars at the **g**; Ezk 40:38 8179
having oversight at the **g** of the Ezk 44:11 8179
enter at the **g** of the inner court, Ezk 44:17 8179
ministering in the **g** of the inner court Ezk 44:17 8179
shall be the **g** of the city, named Ezk 48:31 8179
Israel, three **g** toward the north: Ezk 48:31 8179
4,500 *cubits,* shall be three **g**: Ezk 48:32 8179
by measurement, shall be three **g**: Ezk 48:33 8179
4,500 *cubits, shall be* three **g**: Ezk 48:34 8179
The **g** of the rivers are opened And Na 2:6 8179
The **g** of your land are opened wide Na 3:13 8179
and judgment for peace in your **g**. Zch 8:16 8179
among you who would shut the **g**, Mal 1:10 1817
and the **g** of Hades will not Mt 16:18 *4439*
Lord opened the **g** of the prison, Ac 5:19 *2374*
also watching the **g** day and night Ac 9:24 *4439*
oxen and garlands to the **g**, Ac 14:13 *4440*
and high wall, with twelve **g**, Rv 21:12 *4440*
gates, and at the **g** twelve angels; Rv 21:12 *4440*
There were three **g** on the east and Rv 21:13 *4440*
and three **g** on the north and three Rv 21:13 *4440*
and three **g** on the south and three Rv 21:13 *4440*
the south and three **g** on the west. Rv 21:13 *4440*
the city, and its **g** and its wall. Rv 21:15 *4440*
the twelve **g** were twelve pearls; Rv 21:21 *4440*
one of the **g** was a single pearl. Rv 21:21 *4440*
its **g** will never be closed; Rv 21:25 *4440*
may enter by the **g** into the city. Rv 22:14 *4440*

GATEWAY

and sat in the **g** of Enaim, Gn 38:14 6607
the veil for the **g** of the court. Ex 40:8 8179
the veil for the **g** of the court. Ex 40:33 8179
city at the **g** of his hometown. Dt 21:19 8179
the **g** of the peoples is broken; Ezk 26:2 1817
and he was standing in the **g**. Ezk 40:3 8179
he measured the width of the **g**, Ezk 40:11 6607, 8179
went up to the **g** toward the north, Ezk 40:40 6607, 8179
When he had gone out to the **g**, Mt 26:71 *4440*

GATH

only in Gaza, in **G**, Jos 11:22 1661
Israel be brought around to **G**." 1Sa 5:8 1661
Gaza, one for Ashkelon, one for **G**, 1Sa 6:17 1661
to Israel, from Ekron even to **G**; 1Sa 7:14 1661
Philistines named Goliath, from **G**, 1Sa 17:4 1661
Philistine from **G** named Goliath, 1Sa 17:23 1661
to Shaaraim, even to **G** and Ekron. 1Sa 17:52 1661
and went to Achish king of **G**. 1Sa 21:10 1661
greatly feared Achish king of **G**. 1Sa 21:12 1661
the son of Maoch, king of **G**. 1Sa 27:2 1661
And David lived with Achish at **G**, 1Sa 27:3 1661
Saul that David had fled to **G**, 1Sa 27:4 1661
or a woman alive to bring to **G**, 1Sa 27:11 1661
"Tell *it* not in **G**, Proclaim it 2Sa 1:20 1661
men who had come with him from **G**, 2Sa 15:18 1661
There was war at **G** again, 2Sa 21:20 1661
four were born to the giant in **G**, 2Sa 21:22 1661
Achish son of Maacah, king of **G**. 1Ki 2:39 1661
"Behold, your servants are in **G**." 1Ki 2:39 1661
and went to **G** to Achish to look 1Ki 2:40 1661
and brought his servants from **G**. 1Ki 2:40 1661
had gone from Jerusalem to **G**, 1Ki 2:41 1661
fought against **G** and captured it, 2Ki 12:17 1661
men of **G** who were born in the land 1Ch 7:21 1661
put to flight the inhabitants of **G**; 1Ch 8:13 1661
and subdued them and took **G** and its 1Ch 18:1 1661
Again there was war at **G**, 1Ch 20:6 1661
descended from the giants in **G**, 1Ch 20:8 1661
G, Mareshah, Ziph, 2Ch 11:8 1661
and broke down the wall of **G** and 2Ch 26:6 1661
go down to **G** of the Philistines. Am 6:2 1661
Tell it not in **G**, Weep not at all. Mi 1:10 1661

GATHER

is edible, and **g** *it* to yourself; Gn 6:21 622
Jacob said to his kinsmen, "**G** stones. Gn 31:46 3950
they will **g** together against me Gn 34:30 622
"Then let them **g** all the food of Gn 41:35 6908
"**G** together and hear, O sons of Gn 49:2 6908
g the elders of Israel together and Ex 3:16 622
go and **g** straw for themselves. Ex 5:7 7197a
of Egypt to **g** stubble for straw. Ex 5:12 7197a
and **g** a day's portion every day, Ex 16:4 3950
twice as much as they **g** daily." Ex 16:5 3950
'**G** of it every man as much as he Ex 16:16 3950
"Six days you shall **g** it, Ex 16:26 3950
some of the people went out to **g**, Ex 16:27 3950
for six years and **g** in its yield, Ex 23:10 622
when you **g** in *the fruit of* your labors Ex 23:16 622
g the gleanings of your harvest. Lv 19:9 3950
nor shall you **g** the fallen fruit Lv 19:10 3950
g the gleaning of your harvest; Lv 23:22 3950
your vineyard and **g** in its crop, Lv 25:3 622
untrimmed vines you shall not **g**; Lv 25:5 1219
nor **g** in *from* its untrimmed vines. Lv 25:11 1219
we do not sow or **g** in our crops?" Lv 25:20 622
you **g** together into your cities, Lv 26:25 622
all the congregation shall **g** Nu 10:3 3259
The people would go about and **g** *it* Nu 11:8 3950
"**G** for Me seventy men from the Nu 11:16 622
'Now a man who is clean shall **g** up Nu 19:9 622
that you may **g** in your grain and Dt 11:14 622
"Then you shall **g** all its booty Dt 13:16 6908
you **g** the grapes of your vineyard, Dt 24:21 1219
field but you will **g** in little, Dt 28:38 622
of the wine nor **g** *the grapes,* Dt 28:39 103
g you again from all the peoples Dt 30:3 6908
the LORD your God will **g** you, Dt 30:4 6908
and **g** to yourself into the house Jos 2:18 622
to **g** up *scraps* under my table; Jg 1:7 3950
'Please let me glean and **g** after Ru 2:7 622
"**G** all Israel to Mizpah and I 1Sa 7:5 6908
and **g** all Israel to my lord the 2Sa 3:21 6908
g the rest of the people together 2Sa 12:28 622
g to me all Israel at Mount Carmel, 1Ki 18:19 6908
out into the field to **g** herbs, 2Ki 4:39 3950
I will **g** you to your fathers, 2Ki 22:20 622
And **g** us and deliver us from the 1Ch 16:35 6908
So David gave orders to **g** the 1Ch 22:2 3664
I will **g** you to your fathers and 2Ch 34:28 622
I will **g** them from there and will Ne 1:9 6908
to **g** into them from the fields of Ne 12:44 3664
g every beautiful young virgin to the Es 2:3 6908
If He should **g** to Himself His Jb 34:14 622
g *it from* your threshing floor? Jb 39:12 622
and does not know who will **g** them. Ps 39:6 622
"**G** My godly ones to Me, Those who Ps 50:5 622
You give to them, they **g** *it* up; Ps 104:28 3950
And **g** us from among the nations, Ps 106:47 6908
And **g** a fruitful harvest. Ps 107:37 6213a
stones and a time to **g** stones; Ec 3:5 3664
flock in the gardens And **g** lilies. SS 6:2 3950
And will **g** the dispersed of Judah Is 11:12 6908
Or like sheep with none to **g** *them,* Is 13:14 6908
and **g** *them* under its protection. Is 34:15 1716
In His arm He will **g** the lambs And Is 40:11 6908
the east, And **g** you from the west. Is 43:5 6908
"**G** yourselves and come; Is 45:20 6908
All of them **g** together, they come Is 49:18 6908
great compassion I will **g** you. Is 54:7 6908
"Yet *others* I will **g** to them, Is 56:8 6908
They all **g** together, they come to Is 60:4 6908
And those who **g** it will drink it Is 62:9 6908
to **g** all nations and tongues. Is 66:18 6908
"The children **g** wood, and the Jer 7:18 3950
But no one will **g** *them.*' " Jer 9:22 622
Go, **g** all the beasts of the field, Jer 12:9 622
and I will **g** them into the center Jer 21:4 622
I Myself will **g** the remnant of My Jer 23:3 6908
will **g** you from all the nations Jer 29:14 6908
And I will **g** them from the remote Jer 31:8 6908
who scattered Israel will **g** him And Jer 31:10 6908
I will **g** them out of all the lands Jer 32:37 6908
g in wine and summer fruit and Jer 40:10 622
one to **g** the fugitives together. Jer 49:5 6908
"**G** yourselves together and come Jer 49:14 6908
"I will **g** you from the peoples Ezk 11:17 6908
I will **g** all your lovers with Ezk 16:37 6908
So I will **g** them against you from Ezk 16:37 6908
g you from the lands where you are Ezk 20:34 6908
g you from the lands where you are Ezk 20:41 6908
I am going to **g** you into the midst Ezk 22:19 6908
'As they **g** silver and bronze and Ezk 22:20 6910
so I will **g** *you* in My anger and Ezk 22:20 6908
'I will **g** you and blow on you Ezk 22:21 3664
"When I **g** the house of Israel Ezk 28:25 6908
I will **g** the Egyptians from the Ezk 29:13 6908
and **g** them from the countries Ezk 34:13 6908
nations, **g** you from all the lands and Ezk 36:24 6908
and I will **g** them from every side Ezk 37:21 6908
or **g** firewood from the forests, Ezk 39:10 2404
g from every side to My sacrifice Ezk 39:17 622
g them from the lands of their enemies Ezk 39:27 6908
the nations, Now I will **g** them up; Hos 8:10 6908
Egypt will **g** them up, Memphis will Hos 9:6 6908
G the elders *And* all the inhabitants Jl 1:14 622
G the people, sanctify the Jl 2:16 622
G the children and the nursing Jl 2:16 622
I will **g** all the nations And Jl 3:2 6908
nations, And **g** yourselves there. Jl 3:11 6908
surely **g** the remnant of Israel. Mi 2:12 6908
the lame And **g** the outcasts, Mi 4:6 6908
g them together in their fishing net. Hab 1:15 622
G yourselves together, yes, Zph 2:1 7197b
yourselves together, yes, **g**, Zph 2:1 7197b
My decision is to **g** nations, Zph 3:8 622
"I will **g** those who grieve about Zph 3:18 622
save the lame And **g** the outcast, Zph 3:19 6908
at the time when I **g** you together; Zph 3:20 6908
"I will whistle for them to **g** them Zch 10:8 6908
of Egypt And **g** them from Assyria; Zch 10:10 6908
For I will **g** all the nations Zch 14:2 622
He will **g** His wheat into the barn, Mt 3:12 *4863*
reap nor **g** into barns, Mt 6:26 *4863*
who does not **g** with Me scatters. Mt 12:30 *4863*
us, then, to go and **g** them up?' Mt 13:28 *4816*
"First **g** up the tares and bind Mt 13:30 *4816*
g the wheat into my barn.' Mt 13:30 *4863*
and they will **g** out of His kingdom Mt 13:41 *4816*
to **g** your children together, Mt 23:37 *1996*
is, there the vultures will **g**. Mt 24:28 *4863*
THEY WILL G TOGETHER His elect from Mt 24:31 *1996*
and **g** where I scattered no *seed.* Mt 25:26 *4863*
and will **g** together His elect from Mk 13:27 *1996*
and to **g** the wheat into His barn, Lk 3:17 *4863*
For men do not **g** figs from thorns, Lk 6:44 *4816*
and he who does not **g** with Me, Lk 11:23 *4863*
to **g** your children together, Lk 13:34 *1996*
"**G** up the leftover fragments so Jn 6:12 *4863*
order that He might also **g** together Jn 11:52 *4863*
and they **g** them, and cast them Jn 15:6 *4863*
and **g** the clusters from the vine Rv 14:18 *5166*
to **g** them together for the war of Rv 16:14 *4863*
to **g** them together for the war; Rv 20:8 *4863*

GATHERED

the heavens be **g** into one place, Gn 1:9 6960b
and he was **g** to his people. Gn 25:8 622
and died, and was **g** to his people. Gn 25:17 622
When all the flocks were **g** there, Gn 29:3 622
time for the livestock to be **g**. Gn 29:7 622
until all the flocks are **g**, Gn 29:8 622
Laban **g** all the men of the place and Gn 29:22 622
all his property which he had **g**, Gn 31:18 7408
which he had **g** in Paddan-aram, Gn 31:18 7408
and died and was **g** to his people, Gn 35:29 622
your sheaves **g** around and bowed Gn 37:7 5437
So he **g** all the food of *these* Gn 41:48 6908
Joseph **g** all the money that Gn 47:14 3950
"I am about to be **g** to my people; Gn 49:29 622
his last, and was **g** to his people. Gn 49:33 622
and *some* **g** much and *some* little. Ex 16:17 3950
he who had **g** much had no excess, Ex 16:18
he who had **g** little had no lack; Ex 16:18
man **g** as much as he should eat. Ex 16:18 3950
They **g** it morning by morning, Ex 16:21 3950
day they **g** twice as much bread, Ex 16:22 3950
sons of Levi **g** together to him. Ex 32:26 622
have **g** in the crops of the land, Lv 23:39 622
of the sea be **g** together for them, Nu 11:22 622
he **g** seventy men of the elders of Nu 11:24 622
all the next day, and **g** the quail Nu 11:32 622
who **g** least gathered ten homers) Nu 11:32
who gathered least **g** ten homers) Nu 11:32 622
who are **g** together against Me. Nu 14:35 3259
are **g** together against the LORD; Nu 16:11 3259
g the assembly before the rock. Nu 20:10 6950
"Aaron will be **g** to his people; Nu 20:24 622
So Aaron will be **g** *to his people,* Nu 20:26 622
So Sihon **g** all his people and went Nu 21:23 622
those who **g** themselves together Nu 27:3 3259
you too will be **g** to your people, Nu 27:13 622
you will be **g** to your people." Nu 31:2 622
seven days after you have **g** in from Dt 16:13 622
ascend, and be **g** to your people, Dt 32:50 622
Mount Hor and was **g** to his people, Dt 32:50 622
the heads of the people were **g**, Dt 33:5 622
that they **g** themselves together Jos 9:2 6908
of Eglon, **g** together and went up, Jos 10:5 622
of Israel **g** themselves at Shiloh to Jos 22:12 6950
Then Joshua **g** all the tribes of Jos 24:1 622
also were **g** to their fathers; Jg 2:10 622
And he **g** to himself the sons of Jg 3:13 622
and **g** *the grapes of* their vineyards Jg 9:27 1219
tower of Shechem were **g** together. Jg 9:47 6908
And the sons of Israel **g** together and Jg 10:17 622
g themselves about Jephthah, Jg 11:3 3950
so Sihon **g** all his people and Jg 11:20 622
Then Jephthah **g** all the men of Jg 12:4 6908
of Israel were **g** against the city, Jg 20:11 622
g from the cities to Gibeah, Jg 20:14 622
So they sent and **g** all the lords 1Sa 5:8 622
g all the lords of the Philistines 1Sa 5:11 622
They **g** to Mizpah, and drew 1Sa 7:6 6908
sons of Israel had **g** to Mizpah, 1Sa 7:7 6908
Then all the elders of Israel **g** 1Sa 8:4 6908
g their armies for battle; 1Sa 17:1 622
and they were **g** at Socoh which 1Sa 17:1 622
Saul and the men of Israel were **g** and 1Sa 17:2 622
who was discontented **g** to him; 1Sa 22:2 6908
g together and mourned for him, 1Sa 25:1 6908
g their armed camps for war, 1Sa 28:1 6908
So the Philistines **g** together and 1Sa 28:4 6908
and Saul **g** all Israel together and 1Sa 28:4 6908
Now the Philistines **g** together all 1Sa 29:1 6908
The sons of Benjamin **g** 2Sa 2:25 6908
he had **g** all the people together, 2Sa 2:30 6908
g all the chosen men of Israel, 2Sa 6:1 622

they **g** themselves together.	2Sa 10:15	622
he **g** all Israel together and	2Sa 10:17	622
So David **g** all the people and went	2Sa 12:29	622
ground which cannot be **g** up again.	2Sa 14:14	622
all Israel be surely **g** to you,	2Sa 17:11	622
men who carried Joab's armor **g**	2Sa 18:15	5437
and they were **g** together and also	2Sa 20:14	6950
and they **g** the bones of those who	2Sa 21:13	622
Philistines who were **g** there to battle	2Sa 23:9	622
Philistines were **g** into a troop where	2Sa 23:11	622
Solomon **g** chariots and horsemen;	1Ki 10:26	622
He **g** men to himself and became	1Ki 11:24	6908
king of Aram **g** all his army,	1Ki 20:1	6908
of Israel **g** the prophets together,	1Ki 22:6	6908
and found a wild vine and **g** from	2Ki 4:39	3950
that Ben-hadad king of Aram **g** all	2Ki 6:24	6908
Then Jehu **g** all the people and	2Ki 10:18	6908
doorkeepers have **g** from the people.	2Ki 22:4	622
will be **g** to your grave in peace,	2Ki 22:20	622
and they **g** to him all the elders	2Ki 23:1	622
g to David at Hebron and said,	1Ch 11:1	6908
were **g** together there to battle,	1Ch 11:13	622
g together the sons of Aaron and	1Ch 15:4	622
And the sons of Ammon **g** together	1Ch 19:7	622
he **g** all Israel together and	1Ch 19:17	622
And he **g** together all the leaders	1Ch 23:2	622
and the princes of Judah who had **g**	2Ch 12:5	622
and worthless men **g** about him,	2Ch 13:7	6908
He **g** all Judah and Benjamin	2Ch 15:9	6908
So Judah **g** together to seek help	2Ch 20:4	6908
throughout Judah and **g** the Levites	2Ch 23:2	6908
He **g** the priests and Levites and	2Ch 24:5	6908
when Ahaz **g** together the utensils	2Ch 28:24	622
and **g** them into the square on the	2Ch 29:4	622
the people been **g** to Jerusalem.	2Ch 30:3	622
many people were **g** at Jerusalem	2Ch 30:13	622
and **g** them to him in the square at	2Ch 32:6	6908
shall be **g** to your grave in peace,	2Ch 34:28	622
Then the king sent and **g** all the	2Ch 34:29	622
the people **g** together as one man	Ezr 3:1	622
and I **g** leading men from Israel to	Ezr 7:28	6908
of the exiles **g** to me,	Ezr 9:4	622
children, **g** to him from Israel;	Ezr 10:1	6908
were **g** there for the work.	Ne 5:16	6908
And all the people **g** as one man at	Ne 8:1	622
and the Levites were **g** to Ezra the	Ne 8:13	622
Then I **g** them together and	Ne 13:11	6908
many young ladies were **g** to the	Es 2:8	6908
were **g** together the second time,	Es 2:19	6908
low and like everything **g** up;	Jb 24:24	7092
the nettles they are **g** together.	Jb 30:7	5596
and **g** themselves together;	Ps 35:15	622
smiters whom I did not know **g**	Ps 35:15	622
When the peoples are **g** together,	Ps 102:22	6908
And **g** from the lands, From the	Ps 107:3	6908
herbs of the mountains are **g** in,	Pr 27:25	622
Who has **g** the wind in His fists?	Pr 30:4	622
g my myrrh along with my balsam.	SS 5:1	717
abandoned eggs, I **g** all the earth;	Is 10:14	622
kingdoms, Of nations **g** together!	Is 13:4	622
They will be **g** together *Like*	Is 24:22	622
and you will be **g** up one by one, O	Is 27:12	3950
is **g** *as* the caterpillar gathers;	Is 33:4	622
Yes, the hawks will be **g** there,	Is 34:15	6908
And His Spirit has **g** them.	Is 34:16	6908
All the nations have **g** together So	Is 43:9	6908
that Israel might be **g** to Him	Is 49:5	622
to them, to those *already* **g**."	Is 56:8	6908
Kedar will be **g** together to you,	Is 60:7	6908
all the nations will be **g** to it,	Jer 3:17	6960b
They will not be **g** or buried;	Jer 8:2	622
They will not be lamented, **g**	Jer 25:33	622
And all the people **g** about	Jer 26:9	6950
and **g** in wine and summer fruit in	Jer 40:12	622
so that all the Jews who are **g** to	Jer 40:15	6908
will not be brought together or **g**.	Ezk 29:5	6908
whose inhabitants have been **g** from	Ezk 38:8	6908
people who are **g** from the nations,	Ezk 38:12	622
g them *again* to their own land;	Ezk 39:28	3664
and the king's high officials **g** around	Da 3:27	3673
sons of Israel will be **g** together,	Hos 1:11	6908
And the peoples will be **g** against	Hos 10:10	622
For He has **g** them like sheaves to	Mi 4:12	6908
of the earth will be **g** against it.	Zch 12:3	622
the surrounding nations will be **g**,	Zch 14:14	622
Grapes are not **g** from thorn *bushes*	Mt 7:16	4816
And large crowds **g** to Him,	Mt 13:2	4863
are **g** up and burned with fire,	Mt 13:40	4816
g the good *fish* into containers,	Mt 13:48	4816
three have **g** together in My name,	Mt 18:20	4863
and **g** together all they found,	Mt 22:10	4863
they **g** themselves together.	Mt 22:34	4863
the Pharisees were **g** together,	Mt 22:41	4863
the nations will be **g** before Him;	Mt 25:32	4863
elders of the people were **g** together	Mt 26:3	4863
and the elders were **g** together.	Mt 26:57	4863
So when the people **g** together,	Mt 27:17	4863
g the whole *Roman* cohort around	Mt 27:27	4863
Pharisees **g** together with Pilate,	Mt 27:62	4863
the whole city had **g** at the door.	Mk 1:33	1996
And many were **g** together, so that	Mk 2:2	4863
home, and the crowd **g** again,	Mk 3:20	4905
such a very large crowd **g** to Him	Mk 4:1	4863
a large crowd **g** around Him;	Mk 5:21	4863
apostles **g** together with Jesus;	Mk 6:30	4863
the scribes **g** around Him	Mk 7:1	4863
crowds **g** around Him again,	Mk 10:1	4848
elders and the scribes **g** together.	Mk 14:53	4905
and he **g** up courage and went in	Mk 15:43	5111
thousands of people had **g**	Lk 12:1	1996
the younger son **g** everything	Lk 15:13	4863
also the vultures will be **g**."	Lk 17:37	1996
and found **g** together the eleven	Lk 24:33	120a
So they **g** them up, and filled	Jn 6:13	4863
The Jews then **g** around Him,	Jn 10:24	2944
were **g** together in Jerusalem;	Ac 4:5	4863
WERE **G** TOGETHER AGAINST THE LORD	Ac 4:26	4863
"For truly in this city there were **g**	Ac 4:27	4863
the place where they had **g** together	Ac 4:31	4863
were **g** together and were praying.	Ac 12:12	4867
arrived and **g** the church together,	Ac 14:27	4863
g the congregation together,	Ac 15:30	4863
he **g** together with the workmen of	Ac 19:25	4867
we were **g** together to break bread,	Ac 20:7	4863
room where we were **g** together.	Ac 20:8	4863
But when Paul had **g** a bundle of	Ac 28:3	4962
as it is written, "HE WHO **G**	2Co 8:15	
AND HE WHO **G** LITTLE HAD NO	2Co 8:15	
and **g** *the clusters from* the vine	Rv 14:19	5166
And they **g** them together to the	Rv 16:16	4863

GATHERER

a grape-**g** Over the branches."	Jer 6:9	1219

GATHERERS

"If grape **g** came to you, Would	Jer 49:9	1219
If grape **g** came to you, Would they	Ob 1:5	1219
the fruit pickers, like the grape **g**.	Mi 7:1	5955

GATHERING

g of the waters He called seas;	Gn 1:10	4723b
will last for you until grape **g**,	Lv 26:5	1210
and grape **g** will last until	Lv 26:5	1210
a man **g** wood on the sabbath day.	Nu 15:32	7197a
Those who found him **g** wood	Nu 15:33	7197a
a widow was there **g** sticks;	1Ki 17:10	7197a
I am **g** a few sticks that I may go	1Ki 17:12	7197a
He has given the task of **g** and	Ec 2:26	622
the reaper **g** the standing grain,	Is 17:5	7105a
And the fruit **g** will not come.	Is 32:10	625
on the **g** of young men together;	Jer 6:11	5475
G together all the chief priests	Mt 2:4	4863
for while you are **g** up the tares,	Mt 13:29	4816
the sea, and **g** *fish* of every kind;	Mt 13:47	4863
they were **g** together in Galilee,	Mt 17:22	4962
and **g** where you scattered no *seed.*	Mt 25:24	4863
saw that a crowd was rapidly **g**,	Mk 9:25	1998
and large crowds were **g** to	Lk 5:15	4905
and is **g** fruit for life eternal;	Jn 4:36	4863
G them together, He commanded them	Ac 1:4	4871a
a **g** of about one hundred and twenty	Ac 1:15	3793
account for this disorderly **g**."	Ac 19:40	4963
Christ and our **g** together to Him,	2Th 2:1	1997

GATHERS

one who **g** the ashes of the heifer	Nu 19:10	622
He **g** the waters of the sea	Ps 33:7	3664
His heart **g** wickedness to itself;	Ps 41:6	6908
He **g** the outcasts of Israel.	Ps 147:2	3664
g her provision in the harvest.	Pr 6:8	103
He who **g** in summer is a son who	Pr 10:5	103
one who **g** by labor increases *it.*	Pr 13:11	6908
G it for him who is gracious to	Pr 28:8	6908
nest, And as one **g** abandoned eggs,	Is 10:14	622
is gathered *as* the caterpillar **g**;	Is 33:4	625
who **g** the dispersed of Israel,	Is 56:8	6908
He also **g** to himself all nations	Hab 2:5	622
hen **g** her chicks under her wings,	Mt 23:37	1996
just as a hen **g** her brood under	Lk 13:34	

GATH-HEPHER

eastward toward the sunrise to **G**,	Jos 19:13	1662
the prophet, who was of **G**.	2Ki 14:25	1662

GATH-RIMMON

and Jehud and Bene-berak and **G**,	Jos 19:45	1667
lands, **G** with its pasture lands;	Jos 21:24	1667
and **G** with its pasture lands;	Jos 21:25	1667
and **G** with its pasture lands;	1Ch 6:69	1667

GAUNT

them from the Nile, ugly and **g**,	Gn 41:3	1851, 1320
The ugly and **g** cows ate up the	Gn 41:4	1851, 1320
them, poor and very ugly and **g**,	Gn 41:19	7534, 1320
"From want and famine they are **g**	Jb 30:3	1565

GAVE

The man **g** names to all the cattle,	Gn 2:20	7121
she **g** also to her husband with her,	Gn 3:6	5414
woman whom You **g** *to be* with me,	Gn 3:12	5414
with me, she **g** me from the tree,	Gn 3:12	5414
she conceived and **g** birth to Cain,	Gn 4:1	3205
she **g** birth to his brother Abel.	Gn 4:2	3205
conceived, and **g** birth to Enoch;	Gn 4:17	3205
Adah **g** birth to Jabal;	Gn 4:20	3205
she also **g** birth to Tubal-cain,	Gn 4:22	3205
and she **g** birth to a son, and	Gn 4:25	3205
as *I* **g** the green plant.	Gn 9:3	
and **g** him sheep and oxen and	Gn 12:16	1961
He **g** him a tenth of all.	Gn 14:20	5414
and **g** her to her husband Abram as	Gn 16:3	5414
I **g** my maid into your arms,	Gn 16:5	5414
calf and **g** *it* to the servant	Gn 18:7	5414
servants, and **g** them to Abraham,	Gn 20:14	5414
of water and **g** *them* to Hagar,	Gn 21:14	5414
and **g** *her* the boy, and sent her	Gn 21:14	
with water and **g** the lad a drink.	Gn 21:19	8248
and oxen and **g** them to Abimelech	Gn 21:27	5414
to her hand, and **g** him a drink.	Gn 24:18	8248
he **g** straw and feed to the camels,	Gn 24:32	5414
garments, and **g** them to Rebekah;	Gn 24:53	5414
he also **g** precious things to her	Gn 24:53	5414
g all that he had to Isaac;	Gn 25:5	5414
Abraham **g** gifts while he was still	Gn 25:6	5414
old when she **g** birth to them.	Gn 25:26	3205
g Esau bread and lentil stew;	Gn 25:34	5414
and he **g** them the same names which	Gn 26:18	7121
g the savory food and the bread,	Gn 27:17	5414
which God **g** to Abraham."	Gn 28:4	5414
Laban also **g** his maid Zilpah to	Gn 29:24	5414
and he **g** him his daughter Rachel	Gn 29:28	5414
Laban also **g** his maid Bilhah to	Gn 29:29	5414
g him her maid Bilhah as a wife,	Gn 30:4	5414
and **g** her to Jacob as a wife.	Gn 30:9	5414
God **g** heed to Leah, and she	Gn 30:17	8085
I **g** my maid to my husband."	Gn 30:18	5414
and God **g** heed to her and opened	Gn 30:22	8085
and **g** them into the care of his	Gn 30:35	5414
So they **g** to Jacob all the foreign	Gn 35:4	5414
which I **g** to Abraham and Isaac,	Gn 35:12	5414
So he **g** *them* to her and went in	Gn 38:18	5414
and **g** him favor in the sight of	Gn 39:21	5414
and he **g** him Asenath, the daughter	Gn 41:45	5414
Then Joseph **g** orders to fill their	Gn 42:25	6680
Joseph's house and **g** them water,	Gn 43:24	5414
and he **g** their donkeys fodder.	Gn 43:24	5414
and Joseph **g** them wagons according	Gn 45:21	5414
and **g** them provisions for the	Gn 45:21	5414
of them he **g** changes of garments,	Gn 45:22	5414
but to Benjamin he **g** three hundred	Gn 45:22	5414
whom Laban **g** to his daughter Leah;	Gn 46:18	5414
Laban **g** to his daughter Rachel,	Gn 46:25	5414
and **g** them a possession in the	Gn 47:11	5414
and Joseph **g** them food in exchange	Gn 47:17	5414
allotment which Pharaoh **g** them.	Gn 47:22	5414
and he **g** his daughter Zipporah to	Ex 2:21	5414
Then she **g** birth to a son, and he	Ex 2:22	3205
and **g** them a charge to the sons of	Ex 6:13	6680
The LORD **g** the people favor in	Ex 11:3	5414
darkness, yet it **g** light at night.	Ex 14:20	215
He **g** Moses the two tablets of the	Ex 31:18	5414
So they **g** *it* to me, and I threw it	Ex 32:24	5414
and He **g** it to you to bear away	Lv 10:17	5414
Then Moses **g** the ransom money to	Nu 3:51	5414
oxen and **g** them to the Levites.	Nu 7:6	5414
oxen he **g** to the sons of Gershon,	Nu 7:7	5414
oxen he **g** to the sons of Merari,	Nu 7:8	5414
So they **g** out to the sons of Israel	Nu 13:32	3318
when the LORD **g** commandment	Nu 15:23	6680
their leaders **g** him a rod apiece,	Nu 17:6	5414
Moses **g** the levy *which was* the	Nu 31:41	5414
and **g** them to the Levites,	Nu 31:47	5414
So Moses **g** command concerning them	Nu 32:28	6680
So Moses **g** to them, to the sons of	Nu 32:33	5414
and they **g** *other* names to the cities	Nu 32:38	7121
So Moses **g** Gilead to Machir the	Nu 32:40	5414
which the LORD **g** to them.)	Dt 2:12	5414
I **g** to the Reubenites and to the	Dt 3:12	5414
I **g** to the half-tribe of Manasseh,	Dt 3:13	5414
"To Machir I **g** Gilead.	Dt 3:15	5414
I **g** from Gilead even as far as the	Dt 3:16	5414
tablets of stone and **g** them to me.	Dt 5:22	5414
LORD **g** me the two tablets of stone	Dt 9:10	5414
g me the two tablets of stone,	Dt 9:11	5414
and the LORD **g** them to me.	Dt 10:4	5414
'I **g** my daughter to this man for a	Dt 22:16	5414
and we took their land and **g** it as	Dt 29:8	5414
this law and **g** it to the priests,	Dt 31:9	5414
g the nations their inheritance,	Dt 32:8	5157
forgot the God who **g** you birth.	Dt 32:18	2342a
Moses **g** you beyond the Jordan,	Jos 1:14	5414
Moses the servant of the LORD **g** you	Jos 1:15	5414
and at sunset Joshua **g** command and	Jos 8:29	6680
It came about at sunset that Joshua **g**	Jos 10:27	6680
LORD **g** it also with its king into	Jos 10:30	5414
The LORD **g** Lachish into the	Jos 10:32	5414
and Joshua **g** it for an inheritance	Jos 11:23	5414
Moses the servant of the LORD **g** it to	Jos 12:6	5414
and Joshua **g** it to the tribes of	Jos 12:7	5414
their inheritance which Moses **g** them	Jos 13:8	5414
the servant of the LORD **g** to them;	Jos 13:8	5414
So Moses **g** *an inheritance* to the	Jos 13:15	5414
Moses also **g** *an inheritance* to the	Jos 13:24	5414
Moses also **g** *an inheritance* to the	Jos 13:29	5414
and **g** Hebron to Caleb the son of	Jos 14:13	5414
Now he **g** to Caleb the son of	Jos 15:13	5414
so he **g** him Achsah his daughter as	Jos 15:17	5414
So he **g** her the upper springs and	Jos 15:19	5414
he **g** them an inheritance among their	Jos 17:4	5414
the servant of the LORD **g** them."	Jos 18:7	5414
the sons of Israel **g** an inheritance	Jos 19:49	5414
they **g** him the city for which he asked	Jos 19:50	5414
So the sons of Israel **g** the	Jos 21:3	5414
Now the sons of Israel **g** by lot to	Jos 21:8	5414
They **g** these cities which are	Jos 21:9	5414
Thus they **g** them Kiriath-arba,	Jos 21:11	5414
they **g** to Caleb the son of	Jos 21:12	5414
of Aaron the priest they **g** Hebron,	Jos 21:13	5414
They **g** them Shechem, the city	Jos 21:21	5414
they **g** Golan in Bashan, the city	Jos 21:27	
From the tribe of Issachar, *they* **g**	Jos 21:28	
From the tribe of Asher, *they* **g**	Jos 21:30	
From the tribe of Naphtali, *they* **g**	Jos 21:32	
they **g** from the tribe of Zebulun,	Jos 21:34	
From the tribe of Reuben, *they* **g**	Jos 21:36	
From the tribe of Gad, *they* **g**	Jos 21:38	
So the LORD **g** Israel all the land	Jos 21:43	5414
LORD **g** them rest on every side,	Jos 21:44	5117
the LORD **g** all their enemies into	Jos 21:44	5414
the LORD **g** you beyond the Jordan.	Jos 22:4	5414

the other half Joshua g *a possession* Jos 22:7 5414
his descendants and g him Isaac. Jos 24:3 5414
'To Isaac I g Jacob and Esau, Jos 24:4 5414
Esau, and to Esau I g Mount Seir to Jos 24:4 5414
and I g them into your hand, and Jos 24:8 5414
Thus I g them into your hand. Jos 24:11 5414
'I g you a land on which you Jos 24:13 5414
and the LORD g the Canaanites and Jg 1:4 5414
so he g him his daughter Achsah Jg 1:13 5414
So Caleb g her the upper springs Jg 1:15 5414
Then they g Hebron to Caleb, as Jg 1:20 5414
and He g them into the hands of Jg 2:14 5414
and g their own daughters to their Jg 3:6 5414
the LORD g Cushan-rishathaim king Jg 3:10 5414
bottle of milk and g him a drink; Jg 4:19 8248
for water *and* she g him milk; Jg 5:25 5414
and the LORD g them into the hands Jg 6:1 5414
before you and g you their land, Jg 6:9 5414
They g him seventy *pieces* of Jg 9:4 5414
g Sihon and all his people into Jg 11:21 5414
and the LORD g them into his hand. Jg 11:32 5414
and the LORD g them into my hand. Jg 12:3 5414
and thirty daughters *whom* he g in Jg 12:9 7971
so that the LORD g them into the Jg 13:1 5414
Then the woman g birth to a son Jg 13:24 3205
he g *some* to them and they ate *it;* Jg 14:9 5414
and g the changes *of clothes* to Jg 14:19 5414
so I g her to your companion. Jg 15:2 5414
wife and g her to his companion." Jg 15:6 5414
of silver and g them to the silversmith Jg 17:4 5414
house and g the donkeys fodder, Jg 19:21 1101b
When the men of Israel g ground to Jg 20:36 5414
and they g them the women whom Jg 21:14 5414
She also took *it* out and g Naomi Ru 2:18 5414
six *measures* of barley he g to me, Ru 3:17 5414
his sandal and g it to another; Ru 4:7 5414
and she g birth to a son. Ru 4:13 3205
The neighbor women g him a name, Ru 4:17 7121
that she g birth to a son; 1Sa 1:20 3205
and she conceived and g birth to 1Sa 2:21 3205
she kneeled down and g birth, 1Sa 4:19 3205
and g them a place at the head of 1Sa 9:22 5414
"Bring the portion that I g you, 1Sa 9:23 5414
that was on him and g it to David, 1Sa 18:4 5414
and they g them in full number to 1Sa 18:27 4390
So Saul g him Michal his daughter 1Sa 18:27 5414
Then Jonathan g his weapons to his 1Sa 20:40 5414
priest g him consecrated *bread;* 1Sa 21:6 5414
LORD for him, g him provisions, 1Sa 22:10 5414
and g him the sword of Goliath the 1Sa 22:10 5414
from Keilah, he g up the pursuit. 1Sa 23:13 2308
So Achish g him Ziklag that day; 1Sa 27:6 5414
David, and g him bread and he ate, 1Sa 30:11 5414
They g him a piece of fig cake 1Sa 30:12 5414
the reward I g him for *his* news. 2Sa 4:10 5414
'I also g you your master's house 2Sa 12:8 5414
and I g you the house of Israel 2Sa 12:8 5414
and she g birth to a son, and he 2Sa 12:24 3205
advice of Ahithophel, which he g 2Sa 16:23 3289
Then he g them into the hands of 2Sa 21:9 5414
And Joab g the number of the 2Sa 24:9 5414
and I g birth to a child while she 1Ki 3:17 3205
on the third day after I g birth, 1Ki 3:18 3205
woman also g birth to a child, 1Ki 3:18 3205
Now God g Solomon wisdom and very 1Ki 4:29 5414
So Hiram g Solomon as much as he 1Ki 5:10 5414
Solomon then g Hiram 20,000 kors 1Ki 5:11 5414
The LORD g wisdom to Solomon, 1Ki 5:12 5414
them back to the land which You g to 1Ki 8:34 5414
then King Solomon g Hiram twenty 1Ki 9:11 5414
She g the king a hundred and 1Ki 10:10 5414
the queen of Sheba g King Solomon. 1Ki 10:10 5414
King Solomon g to the queen of 1Ki 10:13 5414
what he g her according to his royal 1Ki 10:13 5414
who g him a house and assigned him 1Ki 11:18 5414
assigned him food and g him land. 1Ki 11:18 5414
so that he g him in marriage the 1Ki 11:19 5414
Then he g a sign the same day, 1Ki 13:3 5414
the house of David and g it to you 1Ki 14:8 5414
land which He g to their fathers, 1Ki 14:15 5414
his God g him a lamp in Jerusalem, 1Ki 15:4 5414
the house and g him to his mother; 1Ki 17:23 5414
g *it* to the people and they ate. 1Ki 19:21 5414
and g them to two of his servants; 2Ki 5:23 5414
And he g him his hand, and he took 2Ki 10:15 5414
The priest g to the captains 2Ki 11:10 5414
out and put the crown on him and g 2Ki 11:12 5414
They g the money which was 2Ki 12:11 5414
for they g that to those who did 2Ki 12:14 5414
into whose hand they g the money 2Ki 12:15 5414
and He g them continually into the 2Ki 13:3 5414
The LORD g Israel a deliverer, 2Ki 13:5 5414
and Menahem g Pul a thousand 2Ki 15:19 5414
g them into the hand of plunderers 2Ki 17:20 5414
Hezekiah g *him* all the silver 2Ki 18:15 5414
and g it to the king of Assyria. 2Ki 18:16 5414
the land which I g their fathers, 2Ki 21:8 5414
And Hilkiah g the book to Shaphan 2Ki 22:8 5414
So Jehoiakim g the silver and gold 2Ki 23:35 5414
Sheshan g his daughter to 1Ch 2:35 5414
g Hebron in the land of Judah and 1Ch 6:55 5414
g to Caleb the son of Jephunneh. 1Ch 6:56 5414
To the sons of Aaron they g 1Ch 6:57 5414
the sons of Israel g to the Levites 1Ch 6:64 5414
They g by lot from the tribe 1Ch 6:65 5414
They g to them the *following* 1Ch 6:67 5414
who g him strong support in his 1Ch 11:10 2388
so David g the order and they were 1Ch 14:12 559
he g instruction in singing 1Ch 15:22 3256

Joab g the number of the 1Ch 21:5 5414
So David g Ornan 600 shekels of 1Ch 21:25 5414
So David g orders to gather the 1Ch 22:2 559
for God g fourteen sons and three 1Ch 25:5 5414
Then David g to his son Solomon 1Ch 28:11 5414
they g 5,000 talents and 10,000 darics 1Ch 29:7 5414
possessed *precious* stones g them 1Ch 29:8 5414
and g praise to the LORD, 2Ch 7:3 3034
he g praise by their means, 2Ch 7:6 3034
Then she g the king one hundred 2Ch 9:9 5414
queen of Sheba g to King Solomon. 2Ch 9:9 5414
King Solomon g to the queen of 2Ch 9:12 5414
and he g them food in abundance. 2Ch 11:23 5414
g the rule over Israel forever to David 2Ch 13:5 5414
Judah, God g them into their hand. 2Ch 13:16 5414
LORD g them rest on every side. 2Ch 15:15 5117
his God g him rest on all sides. 2Ch 20:30 5117
g them many gifts of silver, 2Ch 21:3 5414
but he g the kingdom to Jehoram 2Ch 21:3 5414
Then Jehoiada the priest g to the 2Ch 23:9 5414
and g *him* the testimony and made 2Ch 23:11
The king and Jehoiada g it to 2Ch 24:12 5414
also g tribute to Uzziah, 2Ch 26:8 5414
Ammonites g him during that year one 2Ch 27:5 5414
they g them clothes and sandals, 2Ch 28:15 3847
fed them and g them drink, 2Ch 28:15 8248
and g *it* to the king of Assyria 2Ch 28:21 5414
Then Hezekiah g the order to offer 2Ch 29:27 559
spoke to him and g him a sign. 2Ch 32:24 5414
But Hezekiah g no return for the 2Ch 32:25 7725
Then they g *it* into the hands of 2Ch 34:10 5414
They in turn g *it* to the 2Ch 34:11 5414
And Hilkiah g the book to Shaphan. 2Ch 34:15 5414
"Hilkiah the priest g me a book." 2Ch 34:18 5414
g to the priests for the Passover 2Ch 35:8 5414
He g *them* all into his hand. 2Ch 36:17 5414
According to their ability they g Ezr 2:69 5414
Then they g money to the masons Ezr 3:7 5414
He g them into the hand of Ezr 5:12 3052
Artaxerxes g to Ezra the priest, Ezr 7:11 5414
up the wine and g it to the king. Ne 2:1 5414
me, and I g him a definite time. Ne 2:6 5414
and g them the king's letters. Ne 2:9 5414
fathers' *households* g to the work. Ne 7:70 5414
The governor g to the treasury Ne 7:70 5414
heads of fathers' *households* g into the Ne 7:71 5414
rest of the people g was 20,000 gold Ne 7:72 5414
And g him the name Abraham. Ne 9:7 7760
You g them just ordinances and true Ne 9:13 5414
"You g Your good Spirit to instruct Ne 9:20 5414
And You g them water for their thirst. Ne 9:20 5414
"You also g them kingdoms Ne 9:22 5414
And You g them into their hand, with Ne 9:24 5414
to Your great compassion You g them Ne 9:27 5414
Therefore You g them into the hand of Ne 9:30 5414
With Your great goodness which You g Ne 9:35 5414
And as to the land which You g to our Ne 9:36 5414
g the portions due the singers and the Ne 12:47 5414
Then I g an order and they Ne 13:9 559
he g a banquet for all his princes Es 1:3 6213a
the king g a banquet lasting seven Es 1:5 6213a
Queen Vashti also g a banquet for Es 1:9 6213a
g her seven choice maids from the Es 2:9 5414
Then the king g a great banquet, Es 2:18 6213a
a holiday for the provinces and g gifts Es 2:18 5414
from his hand and g it to Haman, Es 3:10 5414
He also g him a copy of the text Es 4:8 5414
king could not sleep so he g an order Es 6:1 559
Ahasuerus g the house of Haman, Es 8:1 5414
from Haman, and g it to Mordecai. Es 8:2 5414
g and the LORD has taken away. Jb 1:21 5414
the eye saw, it g witness of me, Jb 29:11 5749b
g Him authority over the earth? Jb 34:13 6485
I g the wilderness for a home And Jb 39:6 7760
each one g him one piece of money, Jb 42:11 5414
and their father g them Jb 42:15 5414
He asked life of You, You g it to Ps 21:4 5414
They also g me gall for my food And Ps 69:21 5414
for my thirst they g me vinegar Ps 69:21 8248
You g him as food for the creatures Ps 74:14 5414
The skies g forth a sound; Ps 77:17 5414
And g *them* abundant drink like the Ps 78:15 8248
eat And g them food from heaven. Ps 78:24 5414
And their desire He g to them. Ps 78:29 935
He g also their crops to the Ps 78:46 5414
He g over their cattle also to the Ps 78:48 5462
g over their life to the plague, Ps 78:50 5462
g up His strength to captivity And Ps 78:61 5414
"So I g them over to the Ps 81:12 7971
the mountains were born Or You g Ps 90:2 2342a
And the statute that He g them. Ps 99:7 5414
He g them hail for rain, *And* Ps 105:32 5414
He g them also the lands of the Ps 105:44 5414
So He g them their request, But Ps 106:15 5414
Then He g them into the hand of Ps 106:41 5414
And He g their land as a heritage, Ps 135:12 5414
And g their land as a heritage, Ps 136:21 5414
let her rejoice who g birth to you. Pr 23:25 3205
When I g my heart to know wisdom Ec 8:16 5414
will return to God who g it. Ec 12:7 5414
My perfume g forth its fragrance. SS 1:12 5414
she was in labor *and* g you birth. SS 8:5 3205
conceived and g birth to a son. Is 8:3 3205
we writhed *in labor,* We g birth, Is 26:18 3205
and *who* g Him understanding? Is 40:14 995
Who g Jacob up for spoil, and Is 42:24 5414
And g them into your hand. Is 47:6 5414
I g My back to those who strike Is 50:6 5414
Sarah who g birth to you in pain; Is 51:2 2342a

Spirit of the LORD g them rest. Is 63:14 5117
pain came, she g birth to a boy. Is 66:7 4422
And to a stone, 'You g me birth.' Jer 2:27 3205
to the land that I g your fathers as an Jer 3:18 5157
in the land that I g to your Jer 7:7 5414
which I g you and your fathers, Jer 7:14 5414
land which I g to their fathers. Jer 16:15 5414
of your inheritance That I g you; Jer 17:4 5414
which I g you and your fathers. Jer 23:39 5414
g to them and their forefathers.' " Jer 24:10 5414
that I g to their forefathers and Jer 30:3 5414
and I g the deed of purchase to Jer 32:12 5414
and g them this land, which You Jer 32:22 5414
Jeremiah took another scroll and g it Jer 36:32 5414
Then King Zedekiah g commandment, Jer 37:21 6680
and g him a loaf of bread daily Jer 37:21 5414
and g them vineyards and fields at Jer 39:10 5414
king of Babylon g orders about Jer 39:11 6680
captain of the bodyguard g him a Jer 40:5 5414
just as I g over Zedekiah king of Jer 44:30 5414
g you birth will be humiliated. Jer 50:12 3205
"Also My bread which I g you, Ezk 16:19 5414
of your sons which you g to idols, Ezk 16:36 5414
"I g them My statutes and Ezk 20:11 5414
"Also I g them My sabbaths to Ezk 20:12 5414
"I also g them statutes that Ezk 20:25 5414
I g her into the hand of her Ezk 23:9 5414
"Those from Beth-togarmah g Ezk 27:14 5414
which I g to My servant Jacob. Ezk 28:25 5414
the beasts of the field g birth, Ezk 31:6 3205
land that I g to your forefathers; Ezk 36:28 5414
land that I g to Jacob My servant, Ezk 37:25 5414
so I g them into the hand of their Ezk 39:23 5414
The Lord g Jehoiakim king of Da 1:2 5414
God g them knowledge and Da 1:17 5414
Then the king g orders to call in Da 2:2 559
and g orders to destroy all the Da 2:12 560
and g orders to present to him an Da 2:46 560
Daniel and g him many great gifts, Da 2:48 3052
anger g orders to bring Shadrach, Da 3:13 560
"So I g orders to bring into my Da 4:6 7761
he g orders to bring the gold and Da 5:2 560
Then Belshazzar g orders, and they Da 5:29 560
Then the king g orders, and Daniel Da 6:16 560
king was very pleased and g orders Da 6:23 560
The king then g orders, and they Da 6:24 560
So I g my attention to the Lord Da 9:3 5414
He g *me* instruction and talked Da 9:22 995
again and g birth to a daughter. Hos 1:6 3205
conceived and g birth to a son. Hos 1:8 3205
that it was I who g her the grain, Hos 2:8 5414
And I g numerous visions, Hos 12:10 7235a
through the prophets I g parables. Hos 12:10 1819
I g you a king in My anger And Hos 13:11 5414
"But I g you also cleanness of Am 4:6 5414
then his father and mother who g Zch 13:3 3205
and his father and mother who g Zch 13:3 3205
and I g them to him *as an object* Mal 2:5 5414
the LORD g attention and heard *it,* Mal 3:16 7181
virgin until she g birth to a Son; Mt 1:25 *5088*
He g orders to depart to the other Mt 8:18 *2753*
and g them authority over unclean Mt 10:1 *1325*
loaves He g them to the disciples, Mt 14:19 *1325*
and the disciples g *them* to Mt 14:19
and the disciples g *them* to Mt 15:36
and who g You this authority?" Mt 21:23 *1325*
who g a wedding feast for his son. Mt 22:2 *4160*
"To one he g five talents, to Mt 25:15 *1325*
and you g Me *something* to eat; Mt 25:35 *1325*
I was thirsty, and you g Me Mt 25:35 *4222*
and you g Me *nothing* to eat; Mt 25:42 *1325*
and you g Me nothing to drink; Mt 25:42 *4222*
it and g *it* to the disciples, Mt 26:26 *1325*
and given thanks, He g *it* to them, Mt 26:27 *1325*
was betraying Him g them a sign, Mt 26:48 *1325*
THEY G THEM FOR THE POTTER'S FIELD Mt 27:10 *1325*
they g Him wine to drink mixed Mt 27:34 *1325*
it on a reed, and g Him a drink. Mt 27:48 *4222*
they g a large sum of money to the Mt 28:12 *1325*
and he also g it to those who were Mk 2:26 *1325*
(to whom He g the name Peter), Mk 3:16 *2007*
(to them He g the name Boanerges, Mk 3:17 *2007*
Jesus g them permission. Mk 5:13 *2010*
And He g them strict orders that Mk 5:43 *1291*
and g them authority over the unclean Mk 6:7 *1325*
Herod on his birthday g a banquet Mk 6:21 *4160*
a platter, and g it to the girl; Mk 6:28 *1325*
and the girl g it to her mother. Mk 6:28 *1325*
And He g them orders not to tell Mk 7:36 *1291*
He g thanks and broke them, Mk 8:6 *2168*
He g them orders not to relate to Mk 9:9 *1291*
them, and they g them permission. Mk 11:6 *863*
or who g You this authority to do Mk 11:28 *1325*
and g *it* to them, and said, Mk 14:22 *1325*
and given thanks, He g *it* to them, Mk 14:23 *1325*
it on a reed, and g Him a drink, Mk 15:36 *4222*
and she g birth to a son. Lk 1:57 *1080*
she g birth to her firstborn son; Lk 2:7 *5088*
g it back to the attendant Lk 4:20 *591*
And Levi g a big reception for Him Lk 5:29 *4160*
and g it to his companions?" Lk 6:4 *1325*
Jesus g him back to his mother. Lk 7:15 *1325*
and He g sight to many *who were* Lk 7:21 *5483*
you g Me no water for My feet, but Lk 7:44 *1325*
"You g Me no kiss; Lk 7:45 *1325*
And He g them permission. Lk 8:32 *2010*
and He g orders for *something* to Lk 8:55 *1299*
and g them power and authority Lk 9:1 *1325*
they g an account to Him of all Lk 9:10 *1334*

boy and **g** him back to his father. Lk 9:42 *591*
he took out two denarii and **g** them to Lk 10:35 *1325*
saw it, they **g** praise to God. Lk 18:43 *1325*
his slaves, and **g** them ten minas and Lk 19:13 *1325*
one who **g** You this authority?" Lk 20:2 *1325*
He broke it and **g** it to them, Lk 22:19 *1325*
g Him a piece of a broiled fish; Lk 24:42 *1929*
to them He **g** the right to become Jn 1:12 *1325*
that He **g** His only begotten Son, Jn 3:16 *1325*
that Jacob **g** to his son Joseph; Jn 4:5 *1325*
Jacob, are You, who **g** us the well, Jn 4:12 *1325*
even so He **g** to the Son also to Jn 5:26 *1325*
and He **g** Him authority to execute Jn 5:27 *1325*
'HE G THEM BREAD OUT OF HEAVEN TO Jn 6:31 *1325*
"For I **g** you an example that you Jn 13:15 *1325*
morsel, He took and **g** it to Judas, Jn 13:26 *1325*
even as You **g** Him authority over Jn 17:2 *1325*
whom You **g** Me out of the world; Jn 17:6 *1325*
they were Yours and You **g** them to Me, Jn 17:6 *1325*
You **g** Me I have given to them; Jn 17:8 *1325*
But Jesus **g** him no answer. Jn 19:9 *1325*
His head and **g** up His spirit. Jn 19:30 *3860*
took the bread and **g** *it* to them, Jn 21:13 *1325*
"We **g** you strict orders not to Ac 5:28 *3853*
stood up in the Council and **g** Ac 5:34 *2753*
"But He **g** him no inheritance in Ac 7:5 *1325*
"And He **g** him the covenant of Ac 7:8 *1325*
And he **g** her his hand and raised Ac 9:41 *1325*
and **g** many alms to the *Jewish* Ac 10:2 *4160*
them in and **g** them lodging. Ac 10:23 *3579*
"Therefore if God **g** to them the Ac 11:17 *1325*
gave to them the same gift as *He* **g** Ac 11:17
He **g** *them* judges until Samuel Ac 13:20 *1325*
God **g** them Saul the son of Kish, Ac 13:21 *1325*
in that He did good and **g** you Ac 14:17 *1325*
number to whom we **g** no instruction Ac 15:24 *1291*
Then he **g** orders to the centurion Ac 24:23 *1299*
not face the wind, we **g** way *to it* Ac 27:15 *1929*
he took bread and **g** thanks to God Ac 27:35 *2168*
Therefore God **g** them over in the Ro 1:24 *3860*
For this reason God **g** them over to Ro 1:26 *3860*
g them over to a depraved mind, Ro 1:28 *3860*
"GOD G THEM A SPIRIT OF STUPOR, Ro 11:8 *1325*
I **g** you milk to drink, not solid 1Co 3:2 *4222*
Lord **g** *opportunity* to each one. 1Co 3:5 *1325*
also sealed us and **g** *us* the Spirit 2Co 1:22 *1325*
g to us the Spirit as a pledge. 2Co 5:5 *1325*
g us the ministry of reconciliation, 2Co 5:18 *1325*
they **g** of their own accord, 2Co 8:3
but they first **g** themselves to the 2Co 8:5 *1325*
ABROAD, HE G TO THE POOR, 2Co 9:9 *1325*
which the Lord **g** for building you 2Co 10:8 *1325*
the authority which the Lord **g** me for 2Co 13:10 *1325*
who **g** Himself for our sins so that Ga 1:4 *1325*
g to me and Barnabas the right Ga 2:9 *1325*
who loved me and **g** Himself up for me. Ga 2:20 *3860*
and **g** Him as head over all things Eph 1:22 *1325*
CAPTIVES, AND HE G GIFTS TO MEN." Eph 4:8 *1325*
And He **g** some *as* apostles, and Eph 4:11 *1325*
you and **g** Himself up for us, Eph 5:2 *3860*
church and **g** Himself up for her, Eph 5:25 *3860*
know what commandments we **g** you 1Th 4:2 *1325*
who **g** Himself as a ransom for all, 1Tm 2:6 *1325*
who **g** Himself for us Ti 2:14 *1325*
g a tenth of the choicest spoils. Heb 7:4 *1325*
and **g** orders concerning his bones. Heb 11:22 *1781*
Him from the dead and **g** Him glory, 1Pe 1:21 *1325*
which God **g** Him to show to His Rv 1:1 *1325*
'I **g** her time to repent, Rv 2:21 *1325*
and **g** glory to the God of heaven. Rv 11:13 *1325*
when she **g** birth he might devour Rv 12:4 *5088*
And she **g** birth to a son, a male Rv 12:5 *5088*
who **g** birth to the male *child.* Rv 12:13 *5088*
And the dragon **g** him his power and Rv 13:2 *1325*
he **g** his authority to the beast; Rv 13:4 *1325*
Then one of the four living creatures **g** Rv 15:7 *1325*
g up the dead which were in it, Rv 20:13 *1325*
and death and Hades **g** up the dead Rv 20:13 *1325*

GAZA
you go toward Gerar, as far as **G**; Gn 10:19 5804a
who lived in villages as far as **G**, Dt 2:23 5804a
Kadesh-barnea even as far as **G**, Jos 10:41 5804a
only in **G**, in Gath, and in Ashdod Jos 11:22 5804a
G, its towns and its villages; Jos 15:47 5804a
And Judah took **G** with its Jg 1:18 5804a
produce of the earth as far as **G**, Jg 6:4 5804a
went to **G** and saw a harlot there, Jg 16:1 5804a
and they brought him down to **G** and Jg 16:21 5804a
one for Ashdod, one for **G**, 1Sa 6:17 5804a
the River, from Tiphsah even to **G**, 1Ki 4:24 5804a
as far as **G** and its territory, 2Ki 18:8 5804a
Ashkelon, **G**, Ekron and the remnant Jer 25:20 5804a
before Pharaoh conquered **G**. Jer 47:1 5804a
"Baldness has come upon **G**; Jer 47:5 5804a
"For three transgressions of **G** Am 1:6 5804a
will send fire upon the wall of **G** And Am 1:7 5804a
For **G** will be abandoned And Zph 2:4 5804a
G too will writhe in great pain; Zch 9:5 5804a
the king will perish from **G**, Zch 9:5 5804a
descends from Jerusalem to **G**." Ac 8:26 *1048*

GAZE
break through to the LORD to **g**, Ex 19:21 7200
and **g** after Moses until he entered Ex 33:8 5027
He fixed his **g** steadily *on him* 2Ki 8:11 6440
never turn Your **g** away from me, Jb 7:19 8159
Your **g** from him that he may rest, Jb 14:6 8159
How then could I **g** at a virgin? Jb 31:1 995
"Turn Your **g** away from me, that I Ps 39:13 8159
And let your **g** be fixed straight Pr 4:25 6079
And **g** on King Solomon with the SS 3:11 7200
come back, that we may **g** at you!" SS 6:13 2372
should you **g** at the Shulammite, SS 6:13 2372
"Those who see you will **g** at you, Is 14:16 7688
turning His **g** toward His disciples, Lk 6:20 *3788*
fixed his **g** on him and said, Ac 3:4 *816*
at this, or why do you **g** at us, Ac 3:12 *816*
And fixing their **g** on him, Ac 6:15 *816*
And fixing his **g** on him and Ac 10:4 *816*
and when I had fixed my **g** on it Ac 11:6 *816*
Holy Spirit, fixed his **g** on him, Ac 13:9 *816*
when he had fixed his **g** on him Ac 14:9 *816*

GAZED
heaven the LORD **g** upon the earth, Ps 102:19 5027
he **g** intently into heaven and saw Ac 7:55 *816*

GAZELLE
of it, as of the **g** and the deer. Dt 12:15 6643b
"Just as a **g** or a deer is eaten, Dt 12:22 6643b
the deer, the **g**, the roebuck, the Dt 14:5 6643b
may eat it, as a **g** or a deer. Dt 15:22 6643b
like a **g** from *the hunter's* hand And Pr 6:5 6643b
is like a **g** or a young stag. SS 2:9 6643b
and be like a **g** Or a young stag on SS 2:17 6643b
are like two fawns, Twins of a **g** Which SS 4:5 6646
are like two fawns, Twins of a **g**. SS 7:3 6646
And be like a **g** or a young stag On SS 8:14 6643b
it will be that like a hunted **g**, Is 13:14 6643b

GAZELLES
of the **g** which is in the field. 2Sa 2:18 6643b
a hundred sheep besides deer, **g**, 1Ki 4:23 6643b
swift as the **g** on the mountains. 1Ch 12:8 6643b
g or by the hinds of the field, SS 2:7 6643b
g or by the hinds of the field, SS 3:5 6643b

GAZES
And my eye **g** on their provocation. Jb 17:2 3885a

GAZEZ
bore Haran, Moza and **G**; 1Ch 2:46 1495
and Haran became the father of **G**. 1Ch 2:46 1495

GAZING
the man was **g** at her in silence, Gn 24:21 7583
And as they were **g** intently into Ac 1:10 *816*

GAZITE
the **G**, the Ashdodite, the Jos 13:3 5841

GAZITES
When it was told to the **G**, Jg 16:2 5841

GAZZAM
the sons of Nekoda, the sons of **G**, Ezr 2:48 1502
the sons of **G**, the sons of Uzza, Ne 7:51 1502

GEAR
"Now then, please take your **g**, Gn 27:3 3627

GEBA
Chephar-ammoni and Ophni and **G** Jos 18:24 1387
lands, **G** with its pasture lands, Jos 21:17 1387
of the Philistines that was in **G**, 1Sa 13:3 1387
were staying in **G** of Benjamin 1Sa 13:16 1387
the other on the south opposite **G**. 1Sa 14:5 1387
from **G** as far as Gezer. 2Sa 5:25 1387
them **G** of Benjamin and Mizpah. 1Ki 15:22 1387
incense, from **G** to Beersheba; 2Ki 23:8 1387
G with its pasture lands, Allemeth 1Ch 6:60 1387
of the inhabitants of **G**, 1Ch 8:6 1387
them he fortified **G** and Mizpah. 2Ch 16:6 1387
the sons of Ramah and **G**, Ezr 2:26 1387
the men of Ramah and **G**, Ne 7:30 1387
Benjamin also *lived* from **G** *onward,* Ne 11:31 1387
their fields in **G** and Azmaveth, Ne 12:29 1387
"**G** will be our lodging place." Is 10:29 1387
G to Rimmon south of Jerusalem; Zch 14:10 1387

GEBAL
G and Ammon and Amalek, Ps 83:7 1381
"The elders of **G** and her wise men Ezk 27:9 1380

GEBALITE
and the land of the **G**, Jos 13:5 1382

GEBALITES
builders and the **G** cut them, 1Ki 5:18 1382

GEBER
G the son of Uri, in the land of 1Ki 4:19 1398

GEBIM
of **G** have sought refuge. Is 10:31 1374

GECKO
and the **g**, and the crocodile, and Lv 11:30 604

GEDALIAH
he appointed **G** the son of Ahikam, 2Ki 25:22 1436b
Babylon had appointed **G** *governor,* 2Ki 25:23 1436b
they came to **G** to Mizpah, 2Ki 25:23 1436b
G swore to them and their men 2Ki 25:24 1436b
came with ten men and struck **G** 2Ki 25:25 1436b
G, Zeri, Jeshaiah, Shimei, 1Ch 25:3 1436b
Asaph to Joseph, the second for **G**, 1Ch 25:9 1436b
Maaseiah, Eliezer, Jarib and **G**. Ezr 10:18 1436a
Mattan, and **G** the son of Pashhur, Jer 38:1 1436b
guardhouse and entrusted him to **G**, Jer 39:14 1436b
back then to **G** the son of Ahikam, Jer 40:5 1436a
Then Jeremiah went to Mizpah to **G** Jer 40:6 1436b
king of Babylon had appointed **G** Jer 40:7 1436b
So they came to **G** at Mizpah, along Jer 40:8 1436a
Then **G** the son of Ahikam, the son Jer 40:9 1436b
over them **G** the son of Ahikam, Jer 40:11 1436b
the land of Judah, to **G** at Mizpah, Jer 40:12 1436b
in the field came to **G** at Mizpah Jer 40:13 1436b
But **G** the son of Ahikam did not Jer 40:14 1436b
spoke secretly to **G** in Mizpah, Jer 40:15 1436b
But **G** the son of Ahikam said to Jer 40:16 1436b
to Mizpah to **G** the son of Ahikam. Jer 41:1 1436b
struck down **G** the son of Ahikam, Jer 41:2 1436b
him, *that is* with **G** at Mizpah, Jer 41:3 1436b
next day after the killing of **G**, Jer 41:4 1436b
"Come to **G** the son of Ahikam!" Jer 41:6 1436b
he had struck down because of **G**, Jer 41:9 1436b
the charge of **G** the son of Ahikam; Jer 41:10 1436b
struck down **G** the son of Ahikam, Jer 41:16 1436a
struck down **G** the son of Ahikam, Jer 41:18 1436b
had left with **G** the son of Ahikam Jer 43:6 1436b
Zephaniah son of Cushi, son of **G**, Zph 1:1 1436a

GEDER
the king of **G**, one; Jos 12:13 1445

GEDERAH
Adithaim and **G** and Gederothaim; Jos 15:36 1449
the inhabitants of Netaim and **G**; 1Ch 4:23 1448

GEDERATHITE
Jahaziel, Johanan, Jozabad the **G**, 1Ch 12:4 1452

GEDERITE
Baal-hanan the **G** had charge of 1Ch 27:28 1451

GEDEROTH
and **G**, Beth-dagon and Naamah and Jos 15:41 1450
had taken Beth-shemesh, Aijalon, **G**, 2Ch 28:18 1450

GEDEROTHAIM
and Adithaim and Gederah and **G**; Jos 15:36 1453

GEDOR
Halhul, Beth-zur and **G**, Jos 15:58 1446
Penuel *was* the father of **G**, 1Ch 4:4 1446
wife bore Jered the father of **G**, 1Ch 4:18 1446
They went to the entrance of **G**, 1Ch 4:39 1446
G, Ahio and Zecher. 1Ch 8:31 1446
G, Ahio, Zechariah and Mikloth. 1Ch 9:37 1446
the sons of Jeroham of **G**. 1Ch 12:7 1446

GE-HARASHIM
father of Joab the father of **G**, 1Ch 4:14 1516, 2798

GEHAZI
Then he said to **G** his servant, 2Ki 4:12 1522
G answered, "Truly she has no son 2Ki 4:14 1522
he said to **G** his servant, 2Ki 4:25 1522
And **G** came near to push her away; 2Ki 4:27 1522
he said to **G**, "Gird up your loins 2Ki 4:29 1522
Then **G** passed on before them and 2Ki 4:31 1522
He called **G** and said, 2Ki 4:36 1522
But **G**, the servant of Elisha the 2Ki 5:20 1522
So **G** pursued Naaman. 2Ki 5:21 1522
"Where have you been, **G**?" 2Ki 5:25 1522
Now the king was talking with **G**, 2Ki 8:4 1522
And **G** said, "My lord, O king, this is 2Ki 8:5 1522

GELILOTH
went to En-shemesh and went to **G**, Jos 18:17 1553

GEMALLI
tribe of Dan, Ammiel the son of **G**; Nu 13:12 1582

GEMARIAH
Shaphan, and **G** the son of Hilkiah, Jer 29:3 1587
G the son of Shaphan the scribe, Jer 36:10 1587
Now when Micaiah the son of **G**, Jer 36:11 1587
Achbor, and **G** the son of Shaphan, Jer 36:12 1587
G pleaded with the king not to burn the Jer 36:25 1587

GENEALOGICAL
their **g** registration by their Nu 1:20 8435
their **g** registration by their Nu 1:22 8435
their **g** registration by their Nu 1:24 8435
their **g** registration by their Nu 1:26 8435
their **g** registration by their Nu 1:28 8435
their **g** registration by their Nu 1:30 8435
their **g** registration by their Nu 1:32 8435
their **g** registration by their Nu 1:34 8435
their **g** registration by their Nu 1:36 8435
their **g** registration by their Nu 1:38 8435
their **g** registration by their Nu 1:40 8435
their **g** registration by their Nu 1:42 8435
seer, according to **g** enrollment? 2Ch 12:15 3187
regard to their **g** enrollment, 2Ch 31:16 3187
The **g** enrollment *included* all 2Ch 31:18 3187
g enrollment of those who went up Ezr 8:1 3187
150 males *who were in* the **g** list; Ezr 8:3 3187

GENEALOGICALLY
well as the priests who were enrolled **g** 2Ch 31:17 3187
g enrolled among the Levites. 2Ch 31:19 3187

GENEALOGIES
of Noah, according to their **g**, Gn 10:32 8435
These are their **g**: 1Ch 1:29 8435
enrolled in the **g** in the days of Jotham 1Ch 5:17 3187
So all Israel was enrolled by **g**; 1Ch 9:1 3187
to their **g** and fathers' *households,* 1Ch 26:31 8435
the people to be enrolled by **g**. Ne 7:5 3187
attention to myths and endless **g**, 1Tm 1:4 *1076*
But avoid foolish controversies and **g** Ti 3:9 *1076*

GENEALOGY
and they have their **g**. 1Ch 4:33 3187
the **g** according to the birthright. 1Ch 5:1 3187
in the **g** of their generations, 1Ch 5:7 3187
men of valor, enrolled by **g**, 1Ch 7:5 3187
and were 22,034 enrolled by **g**. 1Ch 7:7 3187
They were enrolled by **g**, 1Ch 7:9 3187
them enrolled by **g** for service in war 1Ch 7:40 3187
enrolled by **g** in their villages, 1Ch 9:22 3187
Then I found the book of the **g** of Ne 7:5 3188
The record of the **g** of Jesus the Messiah, Mt 1:1 *1078*
father, without mother, without **g**, Heb 7:3 *35*
But the one whose **g** is not traced Heb 7:6 *1075*

GENERAL
to the **g** assembly and church of Heb 12:23 *3831*

GENERATION
fourth **g** they will return here, Gn 15:16 1755

saw the third **g** of Ephraim's sons; **Gn 50:23** 1755
all his brothers and all that **g**. **Ex 1:6** 1755
will have war against Amalek from **g** **Ex 17:16** 1755
against Amalek from generation to **g**." **Ex 17:16** 1755
until the entire **g** of those who had **Nu 32:13** 1755
'Not one of these men, this evil **g**, **Dt 1:35** 1755
until all the **g** of the men of war **Dt 2:14** 1755
His lovingkindness to a thousandth **g** **Dt 7:9** 1755
even to the tenth **g**, shall enter **Dt 23:2** 1755
even to the tenth **g**, shall ever **Dt 23:3** 1755
"The sons of the third **g** who are **Dt 23:8** 1755
"Now the **g** to come, your sons who **Dt 29:22** 1755
But are a perverse and crooked **g**. **Dt 32:5** 1755
For they are a perverse **g**, Sons in **Dt 32:20** 1755
All that **g** also were gathered to **Jg 2:10** 1755
and there arose another **g** after them **Jg 2:10** 1755
your sons of the fourth **g** shall sit **2Ki 10:30** 1755
"Your sons to the fourth **g** shall **2Ki 15:12** 1755
and celebrated throughout every **g**, **Es 9:28** 1755
preserve him from this **g** forever. **Ps 12:7** 1755
For God is with the righteous **g**. **Ps 14:5** 1755
told of the Lord to the *coming* **g**. **Ps 22:30** 1755
is the **g** of those who seek Him, **Ps 24:6** 1755
of His heart from **g** to generation. **Ps 33:11** 1755
of His heart from generation to **g**. **Ps 33:11** 1755
you may tell *it* to the next **g**. **Ps 48:13** 1755
shall go to the **g** of his fathers; **Ps 49:19** 1755
I declare Your strength to *this* **g**, **Ps 71:18** 1755
betrayed the **g** of Your children. **Ps 73:15** 1755
But tell to the **g** to come the **Ps 78:4** 1755
That the **g** to come might know, **Ps 78:6** 1755
A stubborn and rebellious **g**, **Ps 78:8** 1755
A **g** that did not prepare its heart And **Ps 78:8** 1755
"For forty years I loathed *that* **g**, **Ps 95:10** 1755
will be written for the **g** to come, **Ps 102:18** 1755
g let their name be blotted out. **Ps 109:13** 1755
The **g** of the upright will be **Ps 112:2** 1755
One **g** shall praise Your works to **Ps 145:4** 1755
A **g** goes and a generation comes, **Ec 1:4** 1755
A generation goes and a **g** comes, **Ec 1:4** 1755
or lived in from **g** to generation; **Is 13:20** 1755
or lived in from generation to **g**; **Is 13:20** 1755
From **g** to generation it will be **Is 34:10** 1755
to **g** it will be desolate; **Is 34:10** 1755
From **g** to generation they will **Is 34:17** 1755
to **g** they will dwell in it. **Is 34:17** 1755
And as for His **g**, who considered **Is 53:8** 1755
pride, A joy from **g** to generation. **Is 60:15** 1755
pride, A joy from generation to **g**. **Is 60:15** 1755
"O **g**, heed the word of the LORD. **Jer 2:31** 1755
and forsaken The **g** of His wrath.' **Jer 7:29** 1755
Or dwelt in from **g** to generation. **Jer 50:39** 1755
Or dwelt in from generation to **g**. **Jer 50:39** 1755
throne is from **g** to generation. **La 5:19** 1755
throne is from generation to **g**. **La 5:19** 1755
dominion is from **g** to generation. **Da 4:3** 1859
dominion is from generation to **g**. **Da 4:3** 1859
endures from **g** to generation. **Da 4:34** 1859
endures from generation to **g**. **Da 4:34** 1859
sons, And their sons the next **g**. **Jl 1:3** 1755
to what shall I compare this **g**? **Mt 11:16** *1074*
adulterous **g** craves for a sign; **Mt 12:39** *1074*
stand up with this **g** at the judgment **Mt 12:41** *1074*
rise up with this **g** at the judgment **Mt 12:42** *1074*
will also be with this evil **g**." **Mt 12:45** *1074*
adulterous **g** seeks after a sign; **Mt 16:4** *1074*
"You unbelieving and perverted **g**, **Mt 17:17** *1074*
things will come upon this **g**. **Mt 23:36** *1074*
this **g** will not pass away until **Mt 24:34** *1074*
"Why does this **g** seek for a sign? **Mk 8:12** *1074*
no sign will be given to this **g**." **Mk 8:12** *1074*
in this adulterous and sinful **g**, **Mk 8:38** *1074*
"O unbelieving **g**, how long shall **Mk 9:19** *1074*
this **g** will not pass away until **Mk 13:30** *1074*
"AND HIS MERCY IS UPON **G** AFTER **Lk 1:50** *1074*
AFTER **G** TOWARD THOSE WHO FEAR HIM. **Lk 1:50** *1074*
shall I compare the men of this **g**, **Lk 7:31** *1074*
"You unbelieving and perverted **g**, **Lk 9:41** *1074*
"This **g** is a wicked generation; **Lk 11:29** *1074*
"This generation is a wicked **g**; **Lk 11:29** *1074*
will the Son of Man be to this **g**. **Lk 11:30** *1074*
will rise up with the men of this **g** **Lk 11:31** *1074*
stand up with this **g** at the judgment **Lk 11:32** *1074*
may be charged against this **g**, **Lk 11:50** *1074*
shall be charged against this **g**.' **Lk 11:51** *1074*
things and be rejected by this **g**. **Lk 17:25** *1074*
this **g** will not pass away until **Lk 21:32** *1074*
"Be saved from this perverse **g**!" **Ac 2:40** *1074*
WHO WILL RELATE HIS **G**? **Ac 8:33** *1074*
the purpose of God in his own **g**, **Ac 13:36** *1074*
midst of a crooked and perverse **g**, **Php 2:15** *1074*
I WAS ANGRY WITH THIS **G**, **Heb 3:10** *1074*
in the seventh **g** from Adam, **Jude 1:14**

GENERATIONS

This is the book of the **g** of Adam. **Gn 5:1** 8435
are *the records of* the **g** of Noah. **Gn 6:9** 8435
is with you, for all successive **g**; **Gn 9:12** 1755
are *the records of* the **g** of Shem, **Gn 10:1** 8435
are *the records of* the **g** of Shem. **Gn 11:10** 8435
are *the records of* the **g** of Terah. **Gn 11:27** 8435
g for an everlasting covenant, **Gn 17:7** 1755
after you throughout their **g**. **Gn 17:9** 1755
be circumcised throughout your **g**, **Gn 17:12** 1755
the records of the **g** of Ishmael, **Gn 25:12** 8435
are *the records of* the **g** of Isaac, **Gn 25:19** 8435
are *the records of* the **g** of Esau **Gn 36:1** 8435
the records of the **g** of Esau the father **Gn 36:9** 8435
are *the records of* the **g** of Jacob. **Gn 37:2** 8435
this is My memorial-name to all **g**. **Ex 3:15** 1755
sons of Levi according to their **g**: **Ex 6:16** 8435
the Levites according to their **g**. **Ex 6:19** 8435
throughout your **g** you are to **Ex 12:14** 1755
your **g** as a permanent ordinance. **Ex 12:17** 1755
sons of Israel throughout their **g**. **Ex 12:42** 1755
of it be kept throughout your **g**, **Ex 16:32** 1755
to be kept throughout your **g**." **Ex 16:33** 1755
the fourth **g** of those who hate Me, **Ex 20:5**
perpetual statute throughout their **g** **Ex 27:21** 1755
burnt offering throughout your **g** **Ex 29:42** 1755
before the LORD throughout your **g**. **Ex 30:8** 1755
once a year throughout your **g**. **Ex 30:10** 1755
descendants throughout their **g**." **Ex 30:21** 1755
oil to Me throughout your **g**. **Ex 30:31** 1755
Me and you throughout your **g**, **Ex 31:13** 1755
their **g** as a perpetual covenant.' **Ex 31:16** 1755
to the third and fourth **g**." **Ex 34:7**
priesthood throughout their **g**." **Ex 40:15** 1755
perpetual statute throughout your **g** **Lv 3:17** 1755
ordinance throughout your **g**, **Lv 6:18** 1755
forever throughout their **g**.' " **Lv 7:36** 1755
statute throughout your **g** **Lv 10:9** 1755
to them throughout their **g**." **Lv 17:7** 1755
your offspring throughout their **g** who **Lv 21:17** 1755
your descendants throughout your **g** **Lv 22:3** 1755
perpetual statute throughout your **g** **Lv 23:14** 1755
dwelling places throughout your **g**. **Lv 23:21** 1755
perpetual statute throughout your **g** **Lv 23:31** 1755
statute throughout your **g**; **Lv 23:41** 1755
so that your **g** may know that I had **Lv 23:43** 1755
statute throughout your **g**. **Lv 24:3** 1755
to its purchaser throughout his **g**; **Lv 25:30** 1755
records of the **g** of Aaron and Moses **Nu 3:1** 8435
'If any one of you or of your **g** **Nu 9:10** 1755
statute throughout your **g**. **Nu 10:8** 1755
to the third and the fourth **g**.' **Nu 14:18**
be among you throughout your **g**, **Nu 15:14** 1755
statute throughout your **g**; **Nu 15:15** 1755
an offering throughout your **g**. **Nu 15:21** 1755
and onward throughout your **g**, **Nu 15:23** 1755
their garments throughout their **g**, **Nu 15:38** 1755
statute throughout your **g**, **Nu 18:23** 1755
ordinance to you throughout your **g** **Nu 35:29** 1755
and on the third and the fourth **g** **Dt 5:9**
old, Consider the years of all **g**. **Dt 32:7** 1755
you and between our **g** after us, **Jos 22:27** 1755
to us or to our **g** in time to come, **Jos 22:28** 1755
the **g** of the sons of Israel might **Jg 3:2** 1755
Now these are the **g** of Perez: **Ru 4:18** 8435
in the genealogy of their **g**, **1Ch 5:7** 8435
mighty men of valor in their **g**; **1Ch 7:2** 8435
With them by their **g** according **1Ch 7:4** 8435
genealogy, according to their **g**, **1Ch 7:9** 8435
households according to their **g**, **1Ch 8:28** 8435
relatives according to their **g**, **1Ch 9:9** 8435
the Levites according to their **g**, **1Ch 9:34** 8435
He commanded to a thousand **g**, **1Ch 16:15** 1755
"Please inquire of past **g**, **Jb 8:8** 1755
sons and his grandsons, four **g**. **Jb 42:16** 1755
g I will not be in adversity." **Ps 10:6** 1755
name to be remembered in all **g**; **Ps 45:17** 1755
their dwelling places to all **g**; **Ps 49:11** 1755
His years will be as many **g**. **Ps 61:6** 1755
as the moon, throughout all **g**. **Ps 72:5** 1755
all **g** we will tell of Your praise. **Ps 79:13** 1755
You prolong Your anger to all **g**? **Ps 85:5** 1755
To all **g** I will make known Your **Ps 89:1** 1755
build up your throne to all **g**." **Ps 89:4** 1755
been our dwelling place in all **g**. **Ps 90:1** 1755
And His faithfulness to all **g**. **Ps 100:5** 1755
And Your name to all **g**. **Ps 102:12** 1755
Your years are throughout all **g**. **Ps 102:24** 1755
He commanded to a thousand **g**, **Ps 105:8** 1755
righteousness, To all **g** forever. **Ps 106:31** 1755
continues throughout all **g**; **Ps 119:90** 1755
O LORD, throughout all **g**. **Ps 135:13** 1755
dominion *endures* throughout all **g**. **Ps 145:13** 1755
Your God, O Zion, to all **g**. **Ps 146:10** 1755
Nor does a crown *endure* to all **g**. **Pr 27:24** 1755
forth the **g** from the beginning? **Is 41:4** 1755
And My salvation to all **g**." **Is 51:8** 1755
days of old, the **g** of long ago. **Is 51:9** 1755
cities, The desolations of many **g**. **Is 61:4** 1755
after it To the years of many **g**. **Jl 2:2** 1755
forever And Jerusalem for all **g**. **Jl 3:20** 1755
So all the **g** from Abraham **Mt 1:17** *1074*
Abraham to David are fourteen **g**; **Mt 1:17** *1074*
deportation to Babylon, fourteen **g**; **Mt 1:17** *1074*
to the Messiah, fourteen **g**. **Mt 1:17** *1074*
on all **g** will count me blessed. **Lk 1:48** *1074*
"In the **g** gone by He **Ac 14:16** *1074*
"For Moses from ancient **g** has in **Ac 15:21** *1074*
in other **g** was not made known to **Eph 3:5** *1074*
Jesus to all **g** forever and ever. **Eph 3:21** *1074*
hidden from the *past* ages and **g**, **Col 1:26** *1074*

GENEROUS

The **g** man will be prosperous, And **Pr 11:25** 1293
will seek the favor of a **g** man, **Pr 19:6** 5081
He who is **g** will be blessed, For **Pr 22:9** 2896a, 5869
Or the rogue be spoken of *as* **g**. **Is 32:5** 7771a
your eye envious because I am **g**?' **Mt 20:15** *18*
our administration of this **g** gift; **2Co 8:20** *100*
works, to be **g** and ready to share, **1Tm 6:18** *2130*

GENEROUSLY

and shall **g** lend him sufficient **Dt 15:8** 5670
"You shall **g** give to him, and **Dt 15:10** 5414
be able to offer as **g** as this? **1Ch 29:14**
to all **g** and without reproach, **Jas 1:5** *574*

GENITALS

out her hand and seizes his **g**, **Dt 25:11** 4016

GENNESARET

over, they came to land at **G**. **Mt 14:34** *1082*
over they came to land at **G**, **Mk 6:53** *1082*
He was standing by the lake of **G**; **Lk 5:1** *1082*

GENTILE

to you as a **G** and a tax collector. **Mt 18:17** *1482*
Now the woman was a **G**, **Mk 7:26** *1674*

GENTILES

side of Jordan, Galilee of the **G**. **Is 9:1** 1471
THE JORDAN, GALILEE OF THE **G** **Mt 4:15** *1484*
Do not even the **G** do the same? **Mt 5:47** *1482*
repetition as the **G** do, **Mt 6:7** *1482*
the **G** eagerly seek all these things; **Mt 6:32** *1484*
"Do not go in *the* way of *the* **G**, **Mt 10:5** *1484*
a testimony to them and to the **G**. **Mt 10:18** *1484*
SHALL PROCLAIM JUSTICE TO THE **G**. **Mt 12:18** *1484*
AND IN HIS NAME THE **G** WILL HOPE. **Mt 12:21** *1484*
and will hand Him over to the **G** to **Mt 20:19** *1484*
rulers of the **G** lord it over them, **Mt 20:25** *1484*
and will hand Him over to the **G**. **Mk 10:33** *1484*
rulers of the **G** lord it over them; **Mk 10:42** *1484*
A LIGHT OF REVELATION TO THE **G**, **Lk 2:32** *1484*
"For He will be handed over to the **G**, **Lk 18:32** *1484*
will be trampled under foot by the **G** **Lk 21:24** *1484*
the times of the **G** are fulfilled. **Lk 21:24** *1484*
kings of the **G** lord it over them; **Lk 22:25** *1484*
'WHY DID THE **G** RAGE, AND THE **Ac 4:25** *1484*
the **G** and the peoples of Israel, **Ac 4:27** *1484*
to bear My name before the **G** and **Ac 9:15** *1484*
been poured out on the **G** also. **Ac 10:45** *1484*
G also had received the word of God. **Ac 11:1** *1484*
God has granted to the **G** also the **Ac 11:18** *1484*
behold, we are turning to the **G**. **Ac 13:46** *1484*
PLACED YOU AS A LIGHT FOR THE **G**, **Ac 13:47** *1484*
When the **G** heard this, they **Ac 13:48** *1484*
stirred up the minds of the **G** and **Ac 14:2** *1484*
an attempt was made by both the **G** **Ac 14:5** *1484*
opened a door of faith to the **G**. **Ac 14:27** *1484*
in detail the conversion of the **G**, **Ac 15:3** *1484*
that by my mouth the **G** would hear **Ac 15:7** *1484*
had done through them among the **G**. **Ac 15:12** *1484*
among the **G** a people for His name. **Ac 15:14** *1484*
G WHO ARE CALLED BY MY NAME,' **Ac 15:17** *1484*
turning to God from among the **G**, **Ac 15:19** *1484*
and Cilicia who are from the **G**, **Ac 15:23** *1484*
with the Jews and the God-fearing **G**, **Ac 17:17**
From now on I will go to the **G**." **Ac 18:6** *1484*
him into the hands of the **G**.' " **Ac 21:11** *1484*
among the **G** through his ministry. **Ac 21:19** *1484*
are among the **G** to forsake Moses, **Ac 21:21** *1484*
the **G** who have believed, **Ac 21:25** *1484*
send you far away to the **G**.' " **Ac 22:21** *1484*
the *Jewish* people and from the **G**, **Ac 26:17** *1484*
of Judea, and *even* to the **G**, **Ac 26:20** *1484*
the *Jewish* people and to the **G**." **Ac 26:23** *1484*
of God has been sent to the **G**; **Ac 28:28** *1484*
of faith among all the **G** for **Ro 1:5** *1484*
even as among the rest of the **G**. **Ro 1:13** *1484*
For when **G** who do not have the Law **Ro 2:14** *1484*
GOD IS BLASPHEMED AMONG THE **G** **Ro 2:24** *1484*
Is He not *the God of* **G** also? **Ro 3:29** *1484*
God of Gentiles also? Yes, of **G** also, **Ro 3:29** *1484*
Jews only, but also from among **G**. **Ro 9:24** *1484*
That **G**, who did not pursue **Ro 9:30** *1484*
salvation *has come* to the **G**, **Ro 11:11** *1484*
their failure is riches for the **G**, **Ro 11:12** *1484*
I am speaking to you who are **G**. **Ro 11:13** *1484*
then as I am an apostle of **G**, **Ro 11:13** *1484*
the fullness of the **G** has come in; **Ro 11:25** *1484*
for the **G** to glorify God **Ro 15:9** *1484*
GIVE PRAISE TO YOU AMONG THE **G**, **Ro 15:9** *1484*
"REJOICE, O **G**, WITH HIS PEOPLE." **Ro 15:10** *1484*
"PRAISE THE LORD ALL YOU **G**, **Ro 15:11** *1484*
HE WHO ARISES TO RULE OVER THE **G**, **Ro 15:12** *1484*
IN HIM SHALL THE **G** HOPE." **Ro 15:12** *1484*
minister of Christ Jesus to the **G**, **Ro 15:16** *1484*
of the **G** may become acceptable, **Ro 15:16** *1484*
of the **G** by word and deed, **Ro 15:18** *1484*
For if the **G** have shared in their **Ro 15:27** *1484*
also all the churches of the **G**; **Ro 16:4** *1484*
block and to **G** foolishness, **1Co 1:23** *1484*
does not exist even among the **G**, **1Co 5:1** *1484*
the things which the **G** sacrifice, **1Co 10:20** *1484*
my countrymen, dangers from the **G**, **2Co 11:26** *1484*
I might preach Him among the **G**, **Ga 1:16** *1484*
gospel which I preach among the **G**, **Ga 2:2** *1484*
worked for me also to the **G**), **Ga 2:8** *1484*
that we *might go* to the **G** **Ga 2:9** *1484*
James, he used to eat with the **G**; **Ga 2:12** *1484*
like the **G** and not like the Jews, **Ga 2:14** *1483*
compel the **G** to live like Jews? **Ga 2:14** *1484*
and not sinners from among the **G**; **Ga 2:15** *1484*
God would justify the **G** by faith, **Ga 3:8** *1484*
of Abraham might come to the **G**, **Ga 3:14** *1484*
formerly you, the **G** in the flesh, **Eph 2:11** *1484*
Jesus for the sake of you **G** **Eph 3:1** *1484*
that the **G** are fellow heirs and **Eph 3:6** *1484*
to preach to the **G** the **Eph 3:8** *1484*
no longer just as the **G** also walk, **Eph 4:17** *1484*
glory of this mystery among the **G**, **Col 1:27** *1484*
to the **G** so that they may be saved; **1Th 2:16** *1484*
like the **G** who do not know God; **1Th 4:5** *1484*
of the **G** in faith and truth. **1Tm 2:7** *1484*
and that all the **G** might hear; **2Tm 4:17** *1484*
behavior excellent among the **G**, **1Pe 2:12** *1484*

carried out the desire of the G, 1Pe 4:3 1484
accepting nothing from the G. 3Jn 1:7 1482

GENTLE
the fire a sound of a g blowing. 1Ki 19:12 1851
A g answer turns away wrath, But a Pr 15:1 7390
a g lamb led to the slaughter; Jer 11:19 441a
"Blessed are the g, for they Mt 5:5 4239b
for I am g and humble in heart, Mt 11:29 4239b
YOUR KING IS COMING TO YOU, G, Mt 21:5 4239b
Let your g *spirit* be known to all Php 4:5 1933
But we proved to be g among you, 1Th 2:7 2261
to wine or pugnacious, but g, 1Tm 3:3 1933
no one, to be peaceable, g, Ti 3:2 1933
is first pure, then peaceable, g, Jas 3:17 1933
only to those who are good and g, 1Pe 2:18 1933
quality of a g and quiet spirit, 1Pe 3:4 4239b

GENTLEMEN
all you g here present with us, Ac 25:24 435

GENTLENESS
And Your g makes me great. Ps 18:35 6038
or with love and a spirit of g? 1Co 4:21 4240
by the meekness and g of Christ 2Co 10:1 1932
g, self-control; against such things Ga 5:23 4240
such a one in a spirit of g; Ga 6:1 4240
with all humility and g, Eph 4:2 4240
humility, g and patience; Col 3:12 4240
faith, love, perseverance *and* g. 1Tm 6:11 4239a
with g correcting those who are in 2Tm 2:25 4240
his deeds in the g of wisdom. Jas 3:13 4240
in you, yet with g and reverence; 1Pe 3:15 4240

GENTLY
"*Deal* g for my sake with the 2Sa 18:5 328
Even the word *spoken* g with you? Jb 15:11 328
of the valley will g cover him; Jb 21:33 4985
Flowing g *through* the lips of SS 7:9 1680
the g flowing waters of Shiloah And Is 8:6 328
He will g lead the nursing *ewes*. Is 40:11 5095
he can deal g with the ignorant Heb 5:2 3356

GENUBATH
sister of Tahpenes bore his son G, 1Ki 11:20 1592
and G was in Pharaoh's house among 1Ki 11:20 1592

GENUINE
in the Holy Spirit, in g love, 2Co 6:6 505

GENUINELY
g be concerned for your welfare. Php 2:20 1104

GERA
Becher and Ashbel, G and Naaman, Gn 46:21 1617
for them, Ehud the son of G, Jg 3:15 1617
name was Shimei, the son of G; 2Sa 16:5 1617
Then Shimei the son of G, 2Sa 19:16 1617
And Shimei the son of G fell down 2Sa 19:18 1617
Shimei the son of G the Benjamite, 1Ki 2:8 1617
Addar, G, Abihud, 1Ch 8:3 1617
G, Shephuphan and Huram. 1Ch 8:5 1617
namely, Naaman, Ahijah and G 1Ch 8:7 1617

GERAHS
(the shekel is twenty g), Ex 30:13 1626
The shekel shall be twenty g. Lv 27:25 1626
(the shekel is twenty g), Nu 3:47 1626
the sanctuary, which is twenty g. Nu 18:16 1626
"The shekel shall be twenty g; Ezk 45:12 1626

GERAR
from Sidon as you go toward G, Gn 10:19 1642
then he sojourned in G. Gn 20:1 1642
king of G sent and took Sarah. Gn 20:2 1642
So Isaac went to G, Gn 26:1 1642
So Isaac lived in G. Gn 26:6 1642
and camped in the valley of G, Gn 26:17 1642
the herdsmen of G quarreled with Gn 26:20 1642
from G with his adviser Ahuzzath and Gn 26:26 1642
with him pursued them as far as G; 2Ch 14:13 1642
destroyed all the cities around G, 2Ch 14:14 1642

GERASENES
sea, into the country of the G. Mk 5:1 1086
sailed to the country of the G, Lk 8:26 1086
all the people of the country of the G Lk 8:37 1086

GERIZIM
G and the curse on Mount Ebal. Dt 11:29 1630
on Mount G to bless the people: Dt 27:12 1630
stood in front of Mount G and half Jos 8:33 1630
and stood on the top of Mount G, Jg 9:7 1630

GERSHOM
to a son, and he named him G, Ex 2:22 1647
two sons, of whom one was named G, Ex 18:3 1647
and Jonathan, the son of G, Jg 18:30 1647
The sons of Levi *were* G, 1Ch 6:16 1647
are the names of the sons of G: 1Ch 6:17 1647
Of G: Libni his son, Jahath his son, 1Ch 6:20 1647
the son of Jahath, the son of G, 1Ch 6:43 1647
To the sons of G, 1Ch 6:62 1647
To the sons of G *were given*, from 1Ch 6:71 1647
of the sons of G, Joel the chief, 1Ch 15:7 1647
sons of Moses *were* G and Eliezer. 1Ch 23:15 1647
son of G *was* Shebuel the chief. 1Ch 23:16 1647
Shebuel the son of G, 1Ch 26:24 1647
of the sons of Phinehas, G; Ezr 8:2 1647

GERSHON
G, Kohath, and Merari. Gn 46:11 1648
G and Kohath and Merari; Ex 6:16 1648
The sons of G: Libni and Shimei, Ex 6:17 1648
G and Kohath and Merari. Nu 3:17 1648
the sons of G by their families: Nu 3:18 1648
Of G *was* the family of the Nu 3:21 1648
Now the duties of the sons of G in Nu 3:25 1648
a census of the sons of G also, Nu 4:22 1648
the sons of G by their families and Nu 4:38 1648
of the families of the sons of G, Nu 4:41 1648
oxen he gave to the sons of G, Nu 7:7 1648
sons of G and the sons of Merari, Nu 10:17 1648
of G, the family of the Nu 26:57 1648
The sons of G received Jos 21:6 1648
To the sons of G, Jos 21:27 1648
The sons of Levi *were* G, 1Ch 6:1 1648
G, Kohath, and Merari. 1Ch 23:6 1648

GERSHONITE
belonging to Ladan the G. 1Ch 26:21 1649
the LORD, in care of Jehiel the G. 1Ch 29:8 1649

GERSHONITES
these *were* the families of the G. Nu 3:21 1649
The families of the G were to camp Nu 3:23 1649
G *was* Eliasaph the son of Lael. Nu 3:24 1649
service of the families of the G, Nu 4:24 1649
the service of the sons of the G, Nu 4:27 1649
of the G in the tent of meeting, Nu 4:28 1649
of Gershon, the family of the G; Nu 26:57 1649
All the cities of the G according Jos 21:33 1649
Of the G *were* Ladan and Shimei. 1Ch 23:7 1649
sons of the G belonging to Ladan, 1Ch 26:21 1649
and from the G, Joah the son of 2Ch 29:12 1649

GERUTH
they went and stayed in G Chimham, Jer 41:17 1628

GESHAN
of Jahdai *were* Regem, Jotham, G, 1Ch 2:47 1529

GESHEM
official, and G the Arab heard *it*, Ne 2:19 1654
Sanballat, Tobiah, to G the Arab and Ne 6:1 1654
and G sent *a message* to me, Ne 6:2 1654

GESHUR
for G and Maacath live among Jos 13:13 1650
the daughter of Talmai, king of G; 2Sa 3:3 1650
the son of Ammihud, the king of G. 2Sa 13:37 1650
So Absalom had fled and gone to G, 2Sa 13:38 1650
So Joab arose and went to G and 2Sa 14:23 1650
"Why have I come from G? 2Sa 14:32 1650
while I was living at G in Aram, 2Sa 15:8 1650
But G and Aram took the towns of 1Ch 2:23 1650
the daughter of Talmai king of G; 1Ch 3:2 1650

GESHURITES
of the G and the Maacathites, Dt 3:14 1651
of the G and the Maacathites, Jos 12:5 1651
and all *those of* the G; Jos 13:2 1651
of the G and Maacathites, Jos 13:11 1651
the G or the Maacathites; Jos 13:13 1651
and raided the G and the Girzites 1Sa 27:8 1651

GESTURED
Simon Peter g to him, Jn 13:24 3506

GET
"Up, g out of this place, for the Gn 19:14 3318
my voice, and go, g *them* for me." Gn 27:13 3947
G up, please, sit and eat of my Gn 27:19 6965
I will send and g you from there. Gn 27:45 3947
"G me this young girl for a wife." Gn 34:4 3947
and g me out of this house. Gn 40:14 3318
of you that he may g your brother, Gn 42:16 3947
before the midwife can g to them." Ex 1:19 935
G *back* to your labors!" Ex 5:4 1980
'You go *and* g straw for yourselves Ex 5:11 3947
Pharaoh said to him, "G away from Ex 10:28 1980
up, g out from among my people, Ex 12:31 3318
Aaron had let them g out of control Ex 32:25 6544a
not found sufficient means to g it Lv 25:28 7725
"Where am I to g meat to give to Nu 11:13
g some of the fruit of the land." Nu 13:20 3947
'G back from around the dwellings Nu 16:24 5927
'G away from among this Nu 16:45 7426a
and g from them a rod for each Nu 17:2 3947
you shall not go back to g it; Dt 24:19 3947
go up to heaven for us to g it for us Dt 30:12 3947
cross the sea for us to g it for us Dt 30:13 3947
g Jephthah from the land of Tob; Jg 11:5 3947
g her for me as a wife." Jg 14:2 3947
"G her for me, for she looks good Jg 14:3 3947
"G up and let us go," Jg 19:28 6965
"G up, that I may send you away." 1Sa 9:26 6965
are on this side of you, g them,' 1Sa 20:21 3947
please let me g away that I may 1Sa 20:29 4422
was hurrying to g away from Saul, 1Sa 23:26 1980
of the house as if to g wheat, 2Sa 4:6 3947
could I g rid of my reproach? 2Sa 13:13 1980
"G up, go away!" 2Sa 13:15 6965
"G out, get out, you man of 2Sa 16:7 3318
"Get out, g out, you man of 2Sa 16:7 3318
The king said, "G me a sword." 1Ki 3:24 3947
g me a little water in a jar, 1Ki 17:10 3947
As she was going to g *it*, 1Ki 17:11 3947
even empty vessels; do not g a few. 2Ki 4:3 4591
alive and g into the city.'" 2Ki 7:12 935
Then Joram said, "G ready." 2Ki 9:21 631
G out of the sanctuary, for you 2Ch 26:18 3318
and he himself also hastened to g out 2Ch 26:20 3318
therefore let us g grain that we Ne 5:2 3947
g grain because of the famine." Ne 5:3 3947
will not allow me to g my breath, Jb 9:18 7725
I cry, 'Violence!' but I g no answer Jb 19:7 6030a
"Let me speak that I may g relief; Jb 32:20 7304
They g rid of their labor pains. Jb 39:3 7971
Your precepts I g understanding; Ps 119:104 995
your acquiring, g understanding. Pr 4:7 7069
better it is to g wisdom than gold! Pr 16:16 7069
And to g understanding is to be Pr 16:16 7069
G wisdom and instruction Pr 23:23
For what does a man g in all his Ec 2:22 1933b
"G out of the way, turn aside Is 30:11 5493
G yourself up on a high mountain, Is 40:9 5927
They will run and not g tired, Is 40:31 3021
"let us g wine, and let us drink Is 56:12 3947
"Do *men* fall and not g up again? Jer 8:4 6965
king sent Jehudi to g the scroll, Jer 36:21 3947
going to send and g Nebuchadnezzar Jer 43:10 3947
your stand and g yourself ready, Jer 46:14 3559
G up! And let us go back To our own Jer 46:16 6965
and Assyria to g enough bread. La 5:6 7646
We g our bread at the risk of our La 5:9 935
"G up, go out to the plain, and Ezk 3:22 6965
son of man, g yourself a brick, Ezk 4:1 3947
"Then g yourself an iron plate Ezk 4:3 3947
in order to g dishonest gain. Ezk 22:27 1214
G up, call on your god. Jon 1:6 6965
"G up! Take the Child and His Mt 2:13 1453
"G up, take the Child and His Mt 2:20 1453
'G up, and walk'? Mt 9:5 1453
"G up, pick up your bed and go home." Mt 9:6 1453
His garment, I will g well." Mt 9:21 4982
"Where *did* this man g this Mt 13:54
Where then *did* this man g all Mt 13:56
the disciples g into the boat and Mt 14:22 1684
"Where would we g so many loaves Mt 15:33
"G behind Me, Satan! Mt 16:23 5217
"G up, and do not be afraid." Mt 17:7 1452
g into the kingdom of God before you Mt 21:31 4254
not go down to g the things out that Mt 24:17 142
not turn back to g his cloak. Mt 24:18 142
"G up, let us be going; behold, Mt 26:46 1453
to g to Him because of the crowd, Mk 2:4 4374
'G up, and pick up your pallet Mk 2:9 1453
"I say to you, g up, pick up your Mk 2:11 1453
"G up and come forward!" Mk 3:3 1453
outside g everything in parables, Mk 4:11 1096
that she will g well and live." Mk 5:23 4982
His garments, I will g well." Mk 5:28 4982
say to you, g up!"). Mk 5:41 1453
"Where did this man g these Mk 6:2
Jesus made His disciples g into the boat Mk 6:45 1684
"G behind Me, Satan; Mk 8:33 5217
to g anything out of his house; Mk 13:15 142
not turn back to g his coat. Mk 13:16 142
"G up, let us be going; behold, Mk 14:42 1453
'G up and walk'? Lk 5:23 1453
g up, and pick up your stretcher Lk 5:24 1453
"G up and come forward!" And he Lk 6:8 1453
to g to Him because of the crowd. Lk 8:19 4940
lodging and g something to eat; Lk 9:12 2147
I cannot g up and give you *anything*.' Lk 11:7 450
even though he will not g up and Lk 11:8 450
he will g up and give him as much as Lk 11:8 1453
and to eat and drink and g drunk; Lk 12:45 3182
did not g ready or act in accord with Lk 12:47 2090
you will not g out of there until Lk 12:59 1831
come during them and g healed, Lk 13:14 2323
'I will g up and go to my father, Lk 15:18 450
I pay tithes of all that I g.' Lk 18:12 2932
And all the people would g up Lk 21:38 3719
G up and pray that you may not enter Lk 22:46 450
then do You g that living water? Jn 4:11 2192
hour when he began to g better. Jn 4:52 2192
"Do you wish to g well?" Jn 5:6 1096
Jesus said to him, "G up, pick up Jn 5:8 1453
"Rabbi, when did You g here?" Jn 6:25 1096
G up, let us go from here. Jn 14:31 1453
"G up and go south to the road that Ac 8:26 450
but g up and enter the city, and it Ac 9:6 450
And the Lord *said* to him, "G up Ac 9:11 450
g up and make your bed." Ac 9:34 450
A voice came to him, "G up, Peter, Ac 10:13 450
"But g up, go downstairs Ac 10:20 450
'G up, Peter; kill and eat.' Ac 11:7 450
woke him up, saying, "G up quickly." Ac 12:7 450
'G up and go on into Damascus, Ac 22:10 450
'Now why do you delay? G up and be Ac 22:16 450
and g out of Jerusalem quickly, Ac 22:18 1831
"G two hundred soldiers ready by Ac 23:23 2090
'But g up and stand on your feet; Ac 26:16 450
to g the *ship's* boat under control. Ac 27:16 1096
overboard first and g to land, Ac 27:43 1826
to g their living from the gospel. 1Co 9:14 2198
And do not g drunk with wine, for Eph 5:18 3182
how to g along with humble means, Php 4:12 5013
who g drunk get drunk at night. 1Th 5:7 3182
who get drunk g drunk at night. 1Th 5:7 3184
of Christ, they want to g married, 1Tm 5:11 1060
want younger *widows* to g married, 1Tm 5:14 1060
But those who want to g rich fall 1Tm 6:9 4147
"G up and measure the temple of God Rv 11:1 1453

GETHER
were Uz and Hul and G and Mash. Gn 10:23 1666
Arpachshad, Lud, Aram, Uz, Hul, G 1Ch 1:17 1666

GETHSEMANE
with them to a place called G, Mt 26:36 1068
They came to a place named G; Mk 14:32 1068

GETS
if he g up and walks around Ex 21:19 6965
a scoffer g dishonor for himself, Pr 9:7 3947
And he who reproves a wicked man g Pr 9:7
But he who sows righteousness g a Pr 11:18
soul of the sluggard craves and g Pr 13:4
who g wisdom loves his own soul; Pr 19:8 7069
But a child who g his own way Pr 29:15 7971
woman when she g a husband, Pr 30:23 1166
g hungry and his strength fails; Is 44:12 7456
"Woe to him who g evil gain for Hab 2:9 1214
to bed at night and g up by day, Mk 4:27 1453

head of the house **g** up and shuts **Lk 13:25** *1453*
it **g** the early and late rains. **Jas 5:7** *2983*

GETTING
G into a boat, Jesus crossed over **Mt 9:1** *1684*
As He was **g** into the boat, the **Mk 5:18** *1684*
G up, He went from there to **Mk 10:1** *450*
for it is **g** toward evening, **Lk 24:29** *1684*
and after **g** into a boat, they **Jn 6:17** *1684*
were coming to him and **g** cured. **Ac 28:9** *2323*

GEUEL
tribe of Gad, **G** the son of Machi. **Nu 13:15** 1345

GEZER
king of **G** came up to help Lachish, **Jos 10:33** 1507
the king of **G**, one; **Jos 12:12** 1507
of lower Beth-horon even to **G**, **Jos 16:3** 1507
out the Canaanites who lived in **G**, **Jos 16:10** 1507
and **G** with its pasture lands, **Jos 21:21** 1507
Canaanites who were living in **G**; **Jg 1:29** 1507
Canaanites lived in **G** among them. **Jg 1:29** 1507
Philistines from Geba as far as **G**. **2Sa 5:25** 1507
Jerusalem, Hazor, Megiddo, and **G**. **1Ki 9:15** 1507
Egypt had gone up and captured **G** and **1Ki 9:16** 1507
rebuilt **G** and the lower Beth-horon **1Ki 9:17** 1507
G also with its pasture lands, **1Ch 6:67** 1507
and to the west **G** with its towns, **1Ch 7:28** 1507
from Gibeon even as far as **G**. **1Ch 14:16** 1507
out at **G** with the Philistines; **1Ch 20:4** 1507

GHOST
were terrified, and said, "It is a **g**!" **Mt 14:26** *5326*
they supposed that it was a **g**, **Mk 6:49** *5326*

GHOSTS
resort to idols and **g** of the dead And **Is 19:3** 330b

GIAH
which is in front of **G** by the way **2Sa 2:24** 1520

GIANT
among the descendants of the **g**, **2Sa 21:16** 7498b
among the descendants of the **g**. **2Sa 21:18** 7498b
he also had been born to the **g**. **2Sa 21:20** 7498b
four were born to the **g** in Gath, **2Sa 21:22** 7498b

GIANTS
one of the descendants of the **g**, **1Ch 20:4** 7498b
he also was descended from the **g**. **1Ch 20:6** 7498b
were descended from the **g** in Gath, **1Ch 20:8** 7498b

GIBBAR
the sons of **G**, 95; **Ezr 2:20** 1402

GIBBETHON
and Eltekeh and **G** and Baalath, **Jos 19:44** 1405
lands, **G** with its pasture lands, **Jos 21:23** 1405
and Baasha struck him down at **G**, **1Ki 15:27** 1405
all Israel were laying siege to **G**. **1Ki 15:27** 1405
the people were camped against **G**, **1Ki 16:15** 1405
Israel with him went up from **G** and **1Ki 16:17** 1405

GIBEA
of Machbena and the father of **G**; **1Ch 2:49** 1388

GIBEAH
Kain, **G** and Timnah; **Jos 15:57** 1390
G, Kiriath; fourteen cities with their **Jos 18:28** 1390
him at **G** of Phinehas his son, **Jos 24:33** 1390
but we will go on as far as **G**." **Jg 19:12** 1390
spend the night in **G** or Ramah." **Jg 19:13** 1390
near **G** which belongs to Benjamin. **Jg 19:14** 1390
in order to enter *and* lodge in **G**. **Jg 19:15** 1390
Ephraim, and he was staying in **G**, **Jg 19:16** 1390
at **G** which belongs to Benjamin. **Jg 20:4** 1390
"But the men of **G** rose up against **Jg 20:5** 1390
the thing which we will do to **G**; **Jg 20:9** 1390
when they come to **G** of Benjamin, **Jg 20:10** 1390
men, the worthless fellows in **G**, **Jg 20:13** 1390
gathered from the cities to **G**, **Jg 20:14** 1390
of **G** who were numbered, **Jg 20:15** 1390
the morning and camped against **G**. **Jg 20:19** 1390
for battle against them at **G**. **Jg 20:20** 1390
the sons of Benjamin came out of **G** **Jg 20:21** 1390
against them from **G** the second day **Jg 20:25** 1390
Israel set men in ambush around **G**. **Jg 20:29** 1390
and arrayed themselves against **G** as **Jg 20:30** 1390
up to Bethel and the other to **G**, **Jg 20:31** 1390
from all Israel came against **G**, **Jg 20:34** 1390
whom they had set against **G**, **Jg 20:36** 1390
hurried and rushed against **G**; **Jg 20:37** 1390
down opposite **G** toward the east. **Jg 20:43** 1390
Saul also went to his house at **G**; **1Sa 10:26** 1390
Then the messengers came to **G** of **1Sa 11:4** 1390
with Jonathan at **G** of Benjamin. **1Sa 13:2** 1390
up from Gilgal to **G** of Benjamin. **1Sa 13:15** 1390
Saul was staying in the outskirts of **G** **1Sa 14:2** 1390
watchmen in **G** of Benjamin looked, **1Sa 14:16** 1390
went up to his house at **G** of Saul. **1Sa 15:34** 1390
Now Saul was sitting in **G**, **1Sa 22:6** 1390
Ziphites came up to Saul at **G**, **1Sa 23:19** 1390
the Ziphites came to Saul at **G**, **1Sa 26:1** 1390
them before the LORD in **G** of Saul, **2Sa 21:6** 1390
of **G** of the sons of Benjamin, **2Sa 23:29** 1390
of **G** of the sons of Benjamin, **1Ch 11:31** 1390
the daughter of Uriel of **G**. **2Ch 13:2** 1390
and **G** of Saul has fled away. **Is 10:29** 1390
Blow the horn in **G**, **Hos 5:8** 1390
in depravity As in the days of **G**; **Hos 9:9** 1390
the days of **G** you have sinned, **Hos 10:9** 1390
of iniquity overtake them in **G**? **Hos 10:9** 1390

GIBEATH-HAARALOTH
the sons of Israel at **G**. **Jos 5:3** 1389, 6190

GIBEATHITE
Joash, the sons of Shemaah the **G**; **1Ch 12:3** 1395

GIBEON
When the inhabitants of **G** heard **Jos 9:3** 1391
Now their cities *were* **G** and **Jos 9:17** 1391
and that the inhabitants of **G** had **Jos 10:1** 1391
because **G** *was* a great city, **Jos 10:2** 1391
and help me, and let us attack **G**, **Jos 10:4** 1391
camped by **G** and fought against it. **Jos 10:5** 1391
Then the men of **G** sent *word* to **Jos 10:6** 1391
them with a great slaughter at **G**, **Jos 10:10** 1391
"O sun, stand still at **G**, **Jos 10:12** 1391
of Goshen even as far as **G**. **Jos 10:41** 1391
except the Hivites living in **G**; **Jos 11:19** 1391
G and Ramah and Beeroth, **Jos 18:25** 1391
G with its pasture lands, **Jos 21:17** 1391
went out from Mahanaim to **G** with **2Sa 2:12** 1391
out and met them by the pool of **G**; **2Sa 2:13** 1391
Helkath-hazzurim, which is in **G**. **2Sa 2:16** 1391
by the way of the wilderness of **G**. **2Sa 2:24** 1391
to death in the battle at **G**. **2Sa 3:30** 1391
at the large stone which is in **G**, **2Sa 20:8** 1391
king went to **G** to sacrifice there, **1Ki 3:4** 1391
In **G** the LORD appeared to Solomon **1Ki 3:5** 1391
as He had appeared to him at **G**. **1Ki 9:2** 1391
Now in **G**, *Jeiel*, the father of **1Ch 8:29** 1391
Jeiel, the father of **G** lived, **1Ch 8:29** 1391
In **G** Jeiel the father of **1Ch 9:35** 1391
Jeiel the father of **G** lived, **1Ch 9:35** 1391
from **G** even as far as Gezer. **1Ch 14:16** 1391
in the high place which *was* at **G**, **1Ch 16:39** 1391
the high place at **G** at that time. **1Ch 21:29** 1391
to the high place which was at **G**, **2Ch 1:3** 1391
the high place which was at **G**, **2Ch 1:13** 1391
the men of **G** and of Mizpah, **Ne 3:7** 1391
the sons of **G**, 95; **Ne 7:25** 1391
stirred up as in the valley of **G**, **Is 28:21** 1391
the prophet, who was from **G**, **Jer 28:1** 1391
by the great pool that is in **G**. **Jer 41:12** 1391
whom he had brought back from **G**. **Jer 41:16** 1391

GIBEONITE
and Ishmaiah the **G**, **1Ch 12:4** 1393
the **G** and Jadon the Meronothite, **Ne 3:7** 1393

GIBEONITES
because he put the **G** to death." **2Sa 21:1** 1393
called the **G** and spoke to them **2Sa 21:2** 1393
the **G** were not of the sons of Israel **2Sa 21:2** 1393
Thus David said to the **G**, **2Sa 21:3** 1393
Then the **G** said to him, **2Sa 21:4** 1393
gave them into the hands of the **G**, **2Sa 21:9** 1393

GIDDALTI
Eliathah, **G** and Romamti-ezer, **1Ch 25:4** 1437
for the twenty-second to **G**, **1Ch 25:29** 1437

GIDDEL
the sons of **G**, the sons of Gahar, **Ezr 2:47** 1435
the sons of Darkon, the sons of **G**, **Ezr 2:56** 1435
the sons of Hanan, the sons of **G**, **Ne 7:49** 1435
the sons of Darkon, the sons of **G**, **Ne 7:58** 1435

GIDEON
G was beating out wheat in the wine **Jg 6:11** 1439
Then **G** said to him, **Jg 6:13** 1439
So **G** said to Him, **Jg 6:17**
G went in and prepared a young goat **Jg 6:19** 1439
When **G** saw that he was the angel **Jg 6:22** 1439
Then **G** built an altar there to the **Jg 6:24** 1439
Then **G** took ten men of his **Jg 6:27** 1439
"**G** the son of Joash did this **Jg 6:29** 1439
Spirit of the LORD came upon **G**; **Jg 6:34** 1439
Then **G** said to God, **Jg 6:36** 1439
Then **G** said to God, **Jg 6:39** 1439
Then Jerubbaal (that is, **G**) **Jg 7:1** 1439
The LORD said to **G**, **Jg 7:2** 1439
Then the LORD said to **G**, **Jg 7:4** 1439
And the LORD said to **G**, **Jg 7:5** 1439
The LORD said to **G**, **Jg 7:7** 1439
And **G** sent all the *other* men of **Jg 7:8**
When **G** came, behold, a man was **Jg 7:13** 1439
the sword of **G** the son of Joash, **Jg 7:14** 1439
When **G** heard the **Jg 7:15** 1439
'For the LORD and for **G**.' " **Jg 7:18** 1439
So **G** and the hundred men who were **Jg 7:19** 1439
"A sword for the LORD and for **G**!" **Jg 7:20** 1439
G sent messengers throughout **Jg 7:24** 1439
Zeeb to **G** from across the Jordan. **Jg 7:25** 1439
Then **G** and the 300 men who were **Jg 8:4** 1439
G said, "All right, when the LORD **Jg 8:7** 1439
G went up by the way of those **Jg 8:11** 1439
Then **G** the son of Joash returned **Jg 8:13** 1439
So **G** arose and killed Zebah and **Jg 8:21** 1439
Then the men of Israel said to **G**, **Jg 8:22** 1439
But **G** said to them, **Jg 8:23** 1439
Yet **G** said to them, **Jg 8:24** 1439
G made it into an ephod, and **Jg 8:27** 1439
a snare to **G** and his household. **Jg 8:27** 1439
for forty years in the days of **G**. **Jg 8:28** 1439
Now **G** had seventy sons who were **Jg 8:30** 1439
And **G** the son of Joash died at a **Jg 8:32** 1439
came about, as soon as **G** was dead, **Jg 8:33** 1439
of Jerubbaal (*that is*, **G**) in **Jg 8:35** 1439
time will fail me if I tell of **G**, **Heb 11:32** *1066*

GIDEONI
of Benjamin, Abidan the son of **G**; **Nu 1:11** 1441
Abidan the son of **G**, **Nu 2:22** 1441
day *it was* Abidan the son of **G**, **Nu 7:60** 1441
offering of Abidan the son of **G**. **Nu 7:65** 1441
and Abidan the son of **G** over the **Nu 10:24** 1441

GIDOM
at **G** and killed 2,000 of them. **Jg 20:45** 1440

GIFT
"God has endowed me with a good **g**; **Gn 30:20** 2065
g which has been brought to you, **Gn 33:11** 1293
ever so much bridal payment and **g**, **Gn 34:12** 4976
is to eat the holy **g**; **Lv 22:10**
man shall not eat of the holy **g**. **Lv 22:10**
'But if a man eats a holy **g** **Lv 22:14**
of it and shall give the holy **g** **Lv 22:14**
have given the Levites as a **g** to Aaron **Nu 8:19** 5414
they are a **g** to you, dedicated to **Nu 18:6** 4979
is yours, the offering of their **g**, **Nu 18:11** 4976
let this **g** which your maidservant **1Sa 25:27** 1293
a **g** for you from the spoil of the **1Sa 30:26** 1293
They brought every man his **g**, **1Ki 10:25** 4503
"Take a **g** in your hand and go to **2Ki 8:8** 4503
meet him and took a **g** in his hand, **2Ki 8:9** 4503
They brought every man his **g**, **2Ch 9:24** 4503
of Tyre *will come* with a **g**; **Ps 45:12** 4503
children are a **g** of the LORD, **Ps 127:3** 5159
A man's **g** makes room for him And **Pr 18:16** 4976
A **g** in secret subdues anger, And a **Pr 21:14** 4976
all his labor—it is the **g** of God. **Ec 3:13** 4991
this is the **g** of God. **Ec 5:19** 4991
At that time a **g** of homage will be **Is 18:7** 7862
a ration and a **g** and let him go. **Jer 40:5** 4864
"If the prince gives a **g** *out of* **Ezk 46:16** 4979
if he gives a **g** from his inheritance **Ezk 46:17** 4979
"If you knew the **g** of God, and **Jn 4:10** *1431*
receive the **g** of the Holy Spirit. **Ac 2:38** *1431*
obtain the **g** of God with money! **Ac 8:20** *1431*
because the **g** of the Holy Spirit **Ac 10:45** *1431*
to them the same **g** as *He gave* to us **Ac 11:17** *1431*
impart some spiritual **g** to you, **Ro 1:11** *5486*
being justified as a **g** by His grace **Ro 3:24** *1431*
g is not like the transgression. **Ro 5:15** *5486*
the **g** by the grace of the one Man, **Ro 5:15** *1431*
The **g** is not like *that which* **Ro 5:16** *1434*
free **g** *arose* from many transgressions **Ro 5:16** *5486*
of grace and of the **g** of righteousness **Ro 5:17** *1431*
but the free **g** of God is eternal **Ro 6:23** *5486*
that you are not lacking in any **g**, **1Co 1:7** *5486*
each man has his own **g** from God, **1Co 7:7** *5486*
If I have *the* **g** *of* prophecy, **1Co 13:2**
to carry your **g** to Jerusalem; **1Co 16:3** *5485*
administration of this generous **g**; **2Co 8:20** *100*
previously promised bountiful **g**, **2Co 9:5** *2129*
would be ready as a bountiful **g** **2Co 9:5** *2129*
be to God for His indescribable **g**! **2Co 9:15** *1431*
of yourselves, *it is* the **g** of God; **Eph 2:8** *1435*
according to the **g** of God's grace **Eph 3:7** *1431*
to the measure of Christ's **g**. **Eph 4:7** *1431*
even in Thessalonica you sent *a* **g** **Php 4:16**
Not that I seek the **g** itself, **Php 4:17** *1390*
the spiritual **g** within you, **1Tm 4:14** *5486*
kindle afresh the **g** of God which is in **2Tm 1:6** *5486*
and have tasted of the heavenly **g** **Heb 6:4** *1431*
and every perfect **g** is from above, **Jas 1:17** *1434*
each one has received a *special* **g**, **1Pe 4:10** *5486*

GIFTS
gave **g** while he was still living, **Gn 25:6** 4979
with regard to all their holy **g**; **Ex 28:38** 4979
sons to be careful with the holy **g** **Lv 22:2**
generations approaches the holy **g** **Lv 22:3**
may eat of the holy **g** until he is **Lv 22:4**
and shall not eat of the holy **g** **Lv 22:6**
he shall eat of the holy **g**, for **Lv 22:7**
not eat of the offering of the **g**. **Lv 22:12**
'They shall not profane the holy **g** **Lv 22:15**
for guilt by eating their holy **g**; **Lv 22:16**
of the LORD, and besides your **g** and **Lv 23:38** 4979
pertaining to all the holy **g** of **Nu 5:9**
'So every man's holy **g** shall be **Nu 5:10**
the holy **g** of the sons of Israel I **Nu 18:8**
shall be yours from the most holy **g** **Nu 18:9**
"As the most holy **g** you shall **Nu 18:10**
"All the offerings of the holy **g**, **Nu 18:19**
'Out of all your **g** you shall **Nu 18:29** 4979
sacred **g** of the sons of Israel, **Nu 18:32** 6944
the treasures of the dedicated **g**. **1Ch 26:20** 6944
the treasures of the dedicated **g** which **1Ch 26:26** 6944
Some of the Philistines brought **g** **2Ch 17:11** 4503
father gave them many **g** of silver, **2Ch 21:3** 4979
and the tithe of sacred **g** which **2Ch 31:6** 6944
And many were bringing **g** to the **2Ch 32:23** 4503
gave **g** according to the king's bounty. **Es 2:18** 4864
to one another and **g** to the poor. **Es 9:22** 4979
You have received **g** among men, **Ps 68:18** 4979
Kings will bring **g** to You. **Ps 68:29** 7862
kings of Sheba and Seba offer **g**. **Ps 72:10** 814
g to Him who is to be feared. **Ps 76:11** 7862
be satisfied though you give many **g**. **Pr 6:35** 7810
is a friend to him who gives **g**. **Pr 19:6** 4976
a man who boasts of his **g** falsely. **Pr 25:14** 4991
"Men give **g** to all harlots, but **Ezk 16:33** 5078
but you give your **g** to all your **Ezk 16:33** 5083
them unclean because of their **g**, **Ezk 20:26** 4979
"When you offer your **g**, **Ezk 20:31** 4979
with your **g** and with your idols. **Ezk 20:39** 4979
and the choicest of your **g**, **Ezk 20:40** 4864
me **g** and a reward and great honor; **Da 2:6** 4978
Daniel and gave him many great **g**, **Da 2:48** 4978
"Keep your **g** for yourself or **Da 5:17** 4978
As for My sacrificial **g**, **Hos 8:13** 1890
g On behalf of Moresheth-gath; **Mi 1:14** 7964
they presented to Him **g** of gold, **Mt 2:11** *1435*
to give good **g** to your children, **Mt 7:11** *1390*
to give good **g** to your children, **Lk 11:13** *1390*
putting their **g** into the treasury. **Lk 21:1** *1435*
beautiful stones and votive **g**, **Lk 21:5** *334*

for the **g** and the calling of God **Ro 11:29** *5486*
Since we have **g** that differ **Ro 12:6** *5486*
Now concerning spiritual **g**, **1Co 12:1**
Now there are varieties of **g**, **1Co 12:4** *5486*
g of healing by the one Spirit, **1Co 12:9** *5486*
then miracles, then **g** of healings, **1Co 12:28** *5486*
All do not have **g** of healings, do **1Co 12:30** *5486*
earnestly desire the greater **g**. **1Co 12:31** *5486*
but if *there are* **g** *of* prophecy, **1Co 13:8**
yet desire earnestly spiritual **g**, **1Co 14:1**
you are zealous of spiritual **g**, **1Co 14:12**
CAPTIVES, AND HE GAVE **G** TO MEN." **Eph 4:8** *1390*
miracles and by **g** of the Holy Spirit **Heb 2:4** *3311*
both **g** and sacrifices for sins; **Heb 5:1** *1435*
to offer both **g** and sacrifices; **Heb 8:3** *1435*
offer the **g** according to the Law; **Heb 8:4** *1435*
Accordingly both **g** and sacrifices **Heb 9:9** *1435*
God testifying about his **g**, **Heb 11:4** *1435*
they will send **g** to one another, **Rv 11:10** *1435*

GIHON
The name of the second river is **G**; **Gn 2:13** 1521
own mule, and bring him down to **G**. **1Ki 1:33** 1521
David's mule, and brought him to **G**. **1Ki 1:38** 1521
have anointed him king in **G**, **1Ki 1:45** 1521
waters of **G** and directed them to the **2Ch 32:30** 1521
of David on the west side of **G**, **2Ch 33:14** 1521

GILALAI
Shemaiah, Azarel, Milalai, **G**, **Ne 12:36** 1562

GILBOA
together and they camped in **G**. **1Sa 28:4** 1533
and fell slain on Mount **G**. **1Sa 31:1** 1533
his three sons fallen on Mount **G**. **1Sa 31:8** 1533
I happened to be on Mount **G**, **2Sa 1:6** 1533
"O mountains of **G**, Let not dew or **2Sa 1:21** 1533
Philistines struck down Saul in **G**. **2Sa 21:12** 1533
and fell slain on Mount **G**. **1Ch 10:1** 1533
and his sons fallen on Mount **G**. **1Ch 10:8** 1533

GILEAD
face toward the hill country of **G**. **Gn 31:21** 1568
him in the hill country of **G**. **Gn 31:23** 1568
camped in the hill country of **G**. **Gn 31:25** 1568
of Ishmaelites was coming from **G**, **Gn 37:25** 1568
and Machir became the father of **G**: **Nu 26:29** 1568
of **G**, the family of the Gileadites. **Nu 26:29** 1568
These are the sons of **G**: **Nu 26:30** 1568
the son of Hepher, the son of **G**, **Nu 27:1** 1568
land of Jazer and the land of **G**, **Nu 32:1** 1568
remain there in the cities of **G**; **Nu 32:26** 1568
the land of **G** for a possession; **Nu 32:29** 1568
of Manasseh went to **G** and took it, **Nu 32:39** 1568
G to Machir the son of Manasseh, **Nu 32:40** 1568
of the family of the sons of **G**, **Nu 36:1** 1568
which is in the valley, even to **G**, **Dt 2:36** 1568
and all **G** and all Bashan, **Dt 3:10** 1568
hill country of **G** and its cities I **Dt 3:12** 1568
"The rest of **G** and all **Dt 3:13** 1568
"To Machir I gave **G**. **Dt 3:15** 1568
I gave from **G** even as far as the **Dt 3:16** 1568
and Ramoth in **G** for the Gadites, **Dt 4:43** 1568
him all the land, **G** as far as Dan, **Dt 34:1** 1568
of the valley and half of **G**, **Jos 12:2** 1568
the Maacathites, and half of **G**, **Jos 12:5** 1568
and **G**, and the territory of the **Jos 13:11** 1568
Jazer, and all the cities of **G**, **Jos 13:25** 1568
also half of **G**, with Ashtaroth and **Jos 13:31** 1568
of Manasseh, the father of **G**, **Jos 17:1** 1568
Gilead, were allotted **G** and Bashan, **Jos 17:1** 1568
the son of Hepher, the son of **G**, **Jos 17:3** 1568
besides the land of **G** and Bashan, **Jos 17:5** 1568
And the land of **G** belonged to the **Jos 17:6** 1568
Ramoth in **G** from the tribe of Gad, **Jos 20:8** 1568
of Gad, *they gave* Ramoth in **G**, **Jos 21:38** 1568
of Canaan, to go to the land of **G**, **Jos 22:9** 1568
of Manasseh, into the land of **G**, **Jos 22:13** 1568
of Manasseh, to the land of **G**, **Jos 22:15** 1568
sons of Gad, from the land of **G** to **Jos 22:32** 1568
"**G** remained across the Jordan; **Jg 5:17** 1568
and depart from Mount **G**.'" **Jg 7:3** 1568
they had thirty cities in the land of **G** **Jg 10:4** 1568
in **G** in the land of the Amorites. **Jg 10:8** 1568
summoned and they camped in **G**. **Jg 10:17** 1568
The people, the leaders of **G**, **Jg 10:18** 1568
over all the inhabitants of **G**." **Jg 10:18** 1568
And **G** was the father of Jephthah. **Jg 11:1** 1568
the elders of **G** went to get Jephthah **Jg 11:5** 1568
Jephthah said to the elders of **G**, **Jg 11:7** 1568
The elders of **G** said to Jephthah, **Jg 11:8** 1568
over all the inhabitants of **G**." **Jg 11:8** 1568
Jephthah said to the elders of **G**, **Jg 11:9** 1568
The elders of **G** said to Jephthah, **Jg 11:10** 1568
went with the elders of **G**, **Jg 11:11** 1568
he passed through **G** and Manasseh; **Jg 11:29** 1568
he passed through Mizpah of **G**, **Jg 11:29** 1568
and from Mizpah of **G** he went on to **Jg 11:29** 1568
the men of **G** and fought Ephraim; **Jg 12:4** 1568
and the men of **G** defeated Ephraim, **Jg 12:4** 1568
the men of **G** would say to him, **Jg 12:5** 1568
buried in *one of* the cities of **G**. **Jg 12:7** 1568
including the land of **G**, **Jg 20:1** 1568
Jordan into the land of Gad and **G**. **1Sa 13:7** 1568
He made him king over **G**, **2Sa 2:9** 1568
Absalom camped in the land of **G**. **2Sa 17:26** 1568
Then they came to **G** and to the **2Sa 24:6** 1568
Manasseh, which are in **G** were his: **1Ki 4:13** 1568
the son of Uri, in the land of **G**, **1Ki 4:19** 1568
who was of the settlers of **G**, **1Ki 17:1** 1568
eastward, all the land of **G**, **2Ki 10:33** 1568
of the Arnon, even **G** and Bashan. **2Ki 10:33** 1568
and Hazor and **G** and Galilee, **2Ki 15:29** 1568
of Machir the father of **G**, **1Ch 2:21** 1568
cities in the land of **G**. **1Ch 2:22** 1568
sons of Machir, the father of **G**. **1Ch 2:23** 1568
had increased in the land of **G**. **1Ch 5:9** 1568
throughout all the land east of **G**. **1Ch 5:10** 1568
the son of Jaroah, the son of **G**, **1Ch 5:14** 1568
They lived in **G**, **1Ch 5:16** 1568
Ramoth in **G** with its pasture lands, **1Ch 6:80** 1568
she bore Machir the father of **G**. **1Ch 7:14** 1568
the sons of **G** the son of Machir, **1Ch 7:17** 1568
found among them at Jazer of **G**) **1Ch 26:31** 1568
the half-tribe of Manasseh in **G**, **1Ch 27:21** 1568
"**G** is Mine, and Manasseh is Mine; **Ps 60:7** 1568
"**G** is Mine, Manasseh is Mine; **Ps 108:8** 1568
That have descended from Mount **G**. **SS 4:1** 1568
goats That have descended from **G**. **SS 6:5** 1568
Is there no balm in **G**? **Jer 8:22** 1568
"You are *like* **G** to Me, *Like* the **Jer 22:6** 1568
Go up to **G** and obtain balm, O **Jer 46:11** 1568
the hill country of Ephraim and **G**. **Jer 50:19** 1568
from between Hauran, Damascus, **G** and **Ezk 47:18** 1568
G is a city of wrongdoers, Tracked **Hos 6:8** 1568
Is there iniquity *in* **G**? **Hos 12:11** 1568
G with *implements* of sharp iron. **Am 1:3** 1568
ripped open the pregnant women of **G** **Am 1:13** 1568
And Benjamin *will possess* **G**. **Ob 1:19** 1568
and **G** As in the days of old. **Mi 7:14** 1568
into the land of **G** and Lebanon Until **Zch 10:10** 1568

GILEADITE
After him, Jair the **G** arose and **Jg 10:3** 1569
the **G** was a valiant warrior, **Jg 11:1** 1569
the **G** four days in the year. **Jg 11:40** 1569
Then Jephthah the **G** died and was **Jg 12:7** 1569
and Barzillai the **G** from Rogelim, **2Sa 17:27** 1569
the **G** had come down from Rogelim; **2Sa 19:31** 1569
to the sons of Barzillai the **G**, **1Ki 2:7** 1569
the daughters of Barzillai the **G**, **Ezr 2:61** 1569
the daughters of Barzillai, the **G**, **Ne 7:63** 1569

GILEADITES
of Gilead, the family of the **G**. **Nu 26:29** 1569
"You are fugitives of Ephraim, O **G**, **Jg 12:4** 1568
The **G** captured the fords of **Jg 12:5** 1568
with him were fifty men of the **G**, **2Ki 15:25** 1121, 1569

GILEAD'S
G wife bore him sons; **Jg 11:2** 1568

GILGAL
live in the Arabah, opposite **G**, **Dt 11:30** 1537
and camped at **G** on the eastern edge **Jos 4:19** 1537
the Jordan, Joshua set up at **G**. **Jos 4:20** 1537
place is called **G** to this day. **Jos 5:9** 1537
the sons of Israel camped at **G** they **Jos 5:10** 1537
went to Joshua to the camp at **G** and **Jos 9:6** 1537
word to Joshua to the camp at **G**, **Jos 10:6** 1537
So Joshua went up from **G**, **Jos 10:7** 1537
by marching all night from **G**. **Jos 10:9** 1537
him returned to the camp to **G**. **Jos 10:15** 1537
him returned to the camp at **G**. **Jos 10:43** 1537
the king of Goiim in **G**, **Jos 12:23** 1537
of Judah drew near to Joshua in **G**, **Jos 14:6** 1537
and turned northward toward **G** **Jos 15:7** 1537
the LORD came up from **G** to Bochim. **Jg 2:1** 1537
from the idols which were at **G**, **Jg 3:19** 1537
to Bethel and **G** and Mizpah, **1Sa 7:16** 1537
you shall go down before me to **G**; **1Sa 10:8** 1537
G and renew the kingdom there." **1Sa 11:14** 1537
So all the people went to **G**, **1Sa 11:15** 1537
Saul king before the LORD in **G**. **1Sa 11:15** 1537
were then summoned to Saul at **G**. **1Sa 13:4** 1537
as for Saul, he *was* still in **G**, **1Sa 13:7** 1537
but Samuel did not come to **G**; **1Sa 13:8** 1537
will come down against me at **G**, **1Sa 13:12** 1537
up from **G** to Gibeah of Benjamin. **1Sa 13:15** 1537
and proceeded on down to **G**." **1Sa 15:12** 1537
to the LORD your God at **G**." **1Sa 15:21** 1537
to pieces before the LORD at **G**. **1Sa 15:33** 1537
And Judah came to **G** in order to go **2Sa 19:15** 1537
Now the king went on to **G**, **2Sa 19:40** 1537
Elijah went with Elisha from **G**. **2Ki 2:1** 1537
When Elisha returned to **G**, **2Ki 4:38** 1537
Also do not go to **G**, **Hos 4:15** 1537
All their evil is at **G**; **Hos 9:15** 1537
In **G** they sacrifice bulls, Yes, **Hos 12:11** 1537
In **G** multiply transgression! **Am 4:4** 1537
to Bethel And do not come to **G**, **Am 5:5** 1537
For **G** will certainly go into **Am 5:5** 1537
him, *And* from Shittim to **G**, **Mi 6:5** 1537

GILOH
and Goshen and Holon and **G**; **Jos 15:51** 1542
David's counselor, from his city **G**, **2Sa 15:12** 1542

GILONITE
Absalom sent for Ahithophel the **G**, **2Sa 15:12** 1526
Eliam the son of Ahithophel the **G**, **2Sa 23:34** 1526

GIMZO
villages, and **G** with its villages, **2Ch 28:18** 1579

GINATH
followed Tibni the son of **G**, **1Ki 16:21** 1527
who followed Tibni the son of **G**. **1Ki 16:22** 1527

GINNETHOI
Iddo, **G**, Abijah, **Ne 12:4** 1599

GINNETHON
Daniel, **G**, Baruch, **Ne 10:6** 1599
of Iddo, Zechariah; of **G**, Meshullam; **Ne 12:16** 1599

GIRD
and **g** him with the skillfully **Ex 29:5** 640
"You shall **g** them with **Ex 29:9** 2296
But the feeble **g** on strength. **1Sa 2:4** 247
"Each *of you* **g** on his sword." **1Sa 25:13** 2296
"Tear your clothes and **g** on **2Sa 3:31** 2296
"**G** up your loins and take my **2Ki 4:29** 2296
"**G** up your loins, and take this **2Ki 9:1** 2296
"Now **g** up your loins like a man, **Jb 38:3** 247
"Now **g** up your loins like a man; **Jb 40:7** 247
G Your sword on *Your* thigh, O Mighty **Ps 45:3** 2296
hills **g** themselves with rejoicing. **Ps 65:12** 2296
of wrath You will **g** Yourself. **Ps 76:10** 2296
G yourselves, yet be shattered; **Is 8:9** 247
G yourselves, yet be shattered. **Is 8:9** 247
I will **g** you, though you have not **Is 45:5** 247
"Now, **g** up your loins and arise, **Jer 1:17** 247
G yourselves with sackcloth and **Jer 49:3** 2296
will **g** themselves with sackcloth and **Ezk 7:18** 2296
And **g** themselves with sackcloth; **Ezk 27:31** 2296
they shall not **g** themselves with **Ezk 44:18** 2296
G yourselves *with sackcloth* And **Jl 1:13** 2296
that he will **g** himself *to serve*, **Lk 12:37** *4024*
younger, you used to **g** yourself and **Jn 21:18** *2224*
and someone else will **g** you, **Jn 21:18** *2224*
"**G** yourself and put on your **Ac 12:8** *2224*

GIRDED
with your loins **g**, your sandals on **Ex 12:11** 2296
on him and **g** him with the sash, **Lv 8:7** 2296
and he **g** him with the artistic **Lv 8:7** 2296
tunics, and **g** them with sashes and **Lv 8:13** 2296
he shall be **g** with the linen sash and **Lv 16:4** 2296
every man of you **g** on his weapons **Dt 1:41** 2296
David **g** his sword over his **1Sa 17:39** 2296
So each man **g** on his sword. **1Sa 25:13** 2296
And David also **g** on his sword, and **1Sa 25:13** 2296
in weight, was **g** with a new *sword*, **2Sa 21:16** 2296
g me with strength for battle; **2Sa 22:40** 247
and he **g** up his loins and outran **1Ki 18:46** 8151
So they **g** sackcloth on their loins **1Ki 20:32** 2296
sword **g** at his side as he built, **Ne 4:18** 631
g me with strength for battle; **Ps 18:39** 247
sackcloth and **g** me with gladness, **Ps 30:11** 247
His strength, Being **g** with might; **Ps 65:6** 247
and **g** Himself with strength; **Ps 93:1** 247
have **g** themselves with sackcloth; **Is 15:3** 2296
have **g** themselves with sackcloth. **La 2:10** 2296
g with belts on their loins, with **Ezk 23:15** 2289
whose waist was **g** with *a belt of* **Da 10:5** 2296
Wail like a virgin **g** with **Jl 1:8** 2296
a towel, He **g** Himself. **Jn 13:4** *1241*
the towel with which He was **g**. **Jn 13:5** *1241*
HAVING **G** YOUR LOINS WITH TRUTH, **Eph 6:14** *4024*
and **g** across His chest with a **Rv 1:13** *4024*
and **g** around their chests with **Rv 15:6** *4024*

GIRDLE
leather **g** bound about his loins." **2Ki 1:8** 232
And binds their loins with a **g**. **Jb 12:18** 232

GIRDS
'Let not him who **g** on *his armor* **1Ki 20:11** 2296
The God who **g** me with strength And **Ps 18:32** 247
which he constantly **g** himself. **Ps 109:19** 2296
She **g** herself with strength And **Pr 31:17** 2296

GIRGASHITE
Jebusite and the Amorite and the **G** **Gn 10:16** 1622
and the **G** and the Jebusite." **Gn 15:21** 1622
the Hivite, the Perizzite, the **G**, **Jos 3:10** 1622
and the Hittite and the **G**, **Jos 24:11** 1622
the Perizzite, the Jebusite and the **G** **Ne 9:8** 1622

GIRGASHITES
the Hittites and the **G** and the **Dt 7:1** 1622
Jebusites, the Amorites, the **G**, **1Ch 1:14** 1622

GIRL
it be that the **g** to whom I say, **Gn 24:14** 5291
The **g** was very beautiful, a **Gn 24:16** 5291
Then the **g** ran and told her **Gn 24:28** 5291
"Let the **g** stay with us *a few* **Gn 24:55** 5291
"We will call the **g** and consult her **Gn 24:57** 5291
he loved the **g** and spoke tenderly **Gn 34:3** 5291
"Get me this young **g** for a wife." **Gn 34:4** 3207
but give me the **g** in marriage." **Gn 34:12** 5291
So the **g** went and called the **Ex 2:8** 5959
g who is behind the millstones; **Ex 11:5** 8198
that the **g** was not found a virgin, **Dt 22:20** 5291
then they shall bring out the **g** to **Dt 22:21** 5291
"If there is a **g** who is a virgin **Dt 22:23** 5291
the **g**, because she did not cry out **Dt 22:24** 5291
man finds the **g** who is engaged, **Dt 22:25** 5291
"But you shall do nothing to the **g**; **Dt 22:26** 5291
no sin in the **g** worthy of death, **Dt 22:26** 5291
field, the engaged **g** cried out, **Dt 22:27** 5291
a man finds a **g** who is a virgin, **Dt 22:28** 5291
So they searched for a beautiful **g** **1Ki 1:3** 5291
The **g** was very beautiful; **1Ki 1:4** 5291
little **g** from the land of Israel; **2Ki 5:2** 5291
spoke the **g** who is from the land **2Ki 5:4** 5291
a **g** for wine that they may drink. **Jl 3:3** 3207
and his father resort to the same **g** **Am 2:7** 5291
for the **g** has not died, but is **Mt 9:24** 2877
her by the hand, and the **g** got up. **Mt 9:25** 2877
on a platter and given to the **g**, **Mt 14:11** 2877
"Little **g**, I say to you, get up!"). **Mk 5:41** *2877*
the **g** got up and *began* to walk, **Mk 5:42** 2877
and the king said to the **g**, **Mk 6:22** 2877
a platter, and gave it to the **g**; **Mk 6:28** 2877
and the **g** gave it to her mother. **Mk 6:28** *2877*

GIRL'S
then the **g** father and her mother **Dt 22:15** 5291
out the *evidence* of the **g** virginity **Dt 22:15** 5291
"The **g** father shall say to **Dt 22:16** 5291

and give it to the **g** father, Dt 22:19 5291
shall give to the **g** father fifty *shekels* Dt 22:29 5291
and when the **g** father saw him, Jg 19:3 5291
His father-in-law, the **g** father, Jg 19:4 5291
the **g** father said to his son-in-law, Jg 19:5 5291
and the **g** father said to the man, Jg 19:6 5291
morning, and the **g** father said, Jg 19:8 5291
his father-in-law, the **g** father, Jg 19:9 5291
and the **g** father and mother. Lk 8:51 *3816*

GIRLS
"But all the **g** who have not known Nu 31:18 2945, 802
and **g** playing in its streets.' Zch 8:5 3207

GIRZITES
and the **G** and the Amalekites; 1Sa 27:8 1629b

GISHPA
and Ziha and **G** were in charge of Ne 11:21 1658

GITTAIM
and the Beerothites fled to **G** and 2Sa 4:3 1664
Hazor, Ramah, **G**, Ne 11:33 1664

GITTITE
Ashdodite, the Ashkelonite, the **G**, Jos 13:3 1663
to the house of Obed-edom the **G**. 2Sa 6:10 1663
of Obed-edom the **G** three months, 2Sa 6:11 1663
Then the king said to Ittai the **G**, 2Sa 15:19 1663
So Ittai the **G** passed over with 2Sa 15:22 1663
under the command of Ittai the **G**. 2Sa 18:2 1663
Bethlehemite killed Goliath the **G**, 2Sa 21:19 1663
to the house of Obed-edom the **G**. 1Ch 13:13 1663
the brother of Goliath the **G**, 1Ch 20:5 1663

GITTITES
all the Pelethites and all the **G**, 2Sa 15:18 1663

GIVE
heavens to **g** light on the earth"; Gn 1:15 215
heavens to **g** light on the earth, Gn 1:17 215
of Lamech, **G** heed to my speech, Gn 4:23 238
"This one will **g** us rest from Gn 5:29 5162
I **g** all to you, as *I gave* the Gn 9:3 5414
descendants I will **g** this land." Gn 12:7 5414
I will **g** it to you and to your Gn 13:15 5414
for I will **g** it to you." Gn 13:17 5414
"**G** the people to me and take the Gn 14:21 5414
"O Lord GOD, what will You **g** me, Gn 15:2 5414
g you this land to possess it." Gn 15:7 5414
"I will **g** to you and to your Gn 17:8 5414
indeed I will **g** you a son by her. Gn 17:16 5414
g me a burial site among you that Gn 23:4 5414
that he may **g** me the cave of Gn 23:9 5414
for the full price let him **g** it to Gn 23:9 5414
I **g** you the field, and I give you Gn 23:11 5414
I **g** you the cave that is in it. Gn 23:11 5414
sons of my people I **g** it to you; Gn 23:11 5414
I will **g** the price of the field, Gn 23:13 5414
descendants I will **g** this land,' Gn 24:7 5414
and if they do not **g** her to you, Gn 24:41 5414
I will **g** all these lands, Gn 26:3 5414
and will **g** your descendants all Gn 26:4 5414
God **g** you of the dew of heaven, Gn 27:28 5414
g you the blessing of Abraham, Gn 28:4 5414
I will **g** it to you and to your Gn 28:13 5414
and will **g** me food to eat and Gn 28:20 5414
and of all that You **g** me I Gn 28:22 5414
I will surely **g** a tenth to You." Gn 28:22 6237
"It is better that I **g** her to you Gn 29:19 5414
g her to another man; Gn 29:19 5414
"**G** *me* my wife, for my time is Gn 29:21 3051
and we will **g** you the other also Gn 29:27 5414
"**G** me children, or else I die." Gn 30:1 3051
"Please **g** me some of your son's Gn 30:14 5414
"May the LORD **g** me another son." Gn 30:24 3254
"**G** *me* my wives and my children Gn 30:26 5414
me your wages, and I will **g** it." Gn 30:28 5414
"What shall I **g** you?" Gn 30:31 5414
"You shall not **g** me anything. Gn 30:31 5414
please **g** her to him in marriage. Gn 34:8 5414
g your daughters to us and take Gn 34:9 5414
I will **g** whatever you say to me. Gn 34:11 5414
will **g** according as you say to me; Gn 34:12 5414
but **g** me the girl in marriage." Gn 34:12 5414
to **g** our sister to one who is Gn 34:14 5414
we will **g** our daughters to you, Gn 34:16 5414
and **g** our daughters to them. Gn 34:21 5414
and Isaac, I will **g** it to you, Gn 35:12 5414
And I will **g** the land to your Gn 35:12 5414
Rachel began to **g** birth and she Gn 35:16 3205
not to **g** offspring to his brother. Gn 38:9 5414
"What will you **g** me, that you may Gn 38:16 5414
"Will you **g** a pledge until you send Gn 38:17 5414
"What pledge shall I **g** you?" Gn 38:18 5414
did not **g** her to my son Shelah." Gn 38:26 5414
g Pharaoh a favorable answer." Gn 41:16 6030a
and to **g** them provisions for the Gn 42:25 5414
opened his sack to **g** his donkey fodder Gn 42:27 5414
I will **g** your brother to you, and Gn 42:34 5414
and I will **g** you the best of the Gn 45:18 5414
"**G** us food, for why should we die Gn 47:15 3051
"**G** up your livestock, and I will Gn 47:16 3051
g you *food* for your livestock, Gn 47:16 5414
So **g** us seed, that we may live and Gn 47:19 5414
you shall **g** a fifth to Pharaoh, Gn 47:24 5414
and will **g** this land to your Gn 48:4 5414
"I **g** you one portion more Gn 48:22 5414
helping the Hebrew women to **g** birth Ex 1:16 3205
and **g** birth before the midwife can Ex 1:19 3205
me and I will **g** *you* your wages." Ex 2:9 5414
are no longer to **g** the people straw Ex 5:7 5414
'I am not going to **g** you *any* straw. Ex 5:10 5414
to **g** them the land of Canaan, Ex 6:4 5414
which I swore to **g** to Abraham, Ex 6:8 5414
will **g** it to you *for* a possession; Ex 6:8 5414
land which the LORD will **g** you, Ex 12:25 5414
He swore to your fathers to **g** you, Ex 13:5 5414
of fire by night to **g** them light, Ex 13:21 215
"If you will **g** earnest heed to Ex 15:26 8085
and **g** ear to His commandments, Ex 15:26 238
"**G** us water that we may drink." Ex 17:2 5414
I will **g** you counsel, and God be Ex 18:19 3289
then he shall **g** for the redemption Ex 21:30 5414
the owner shall **g** his *or her* master Ex 21:32 5414
he shall **g** money to its owner, and Ex 21:34 7725
refuses to **g** her to him, Ex 22:17 5414
of your sons you shall **g** to Me. Ex 22:29 5414
eighth day you shall **g** it to Me. Ex 22:30 5414
and I will **g** you the stone tablets Ex 24:12 5414
the testimony which I shall **g** you. Ex 25:16 5414
testimony which I will **g** to you. Ex 25:21 5414
all that I will **g** you in commandment Ex 25:22 6680
each one of them shall **g** a ransom Ex 30:12 5414
everyone who is numbered shall **g**: Ex 30:13 5414
g the contribution to the LORD. Ex 30:14 5414
when you **g** the contribution to the Ex 30:15 5414
and shall **g** it for the service of Ex 30:16 5414
I will **g** to your descendants, Ex 32:13 5414
'To your descendants I will **g** it.' Ex 33:1 5414
with you, and I will **g** you rest." Ex 33:14 5117
of it and **g** it to the priest. Lv 5:16 5414
He shall **g** it to the one to whom Lv 6:5 5414
'You shall **g** the right thigh Lv 7:32 5414
then the priest shall **g** orders to Lv 14:4 6680
"The priest shall also **g** orders Lv 14:5 6680
which I **g** you for a possession, Lv 14:34 5414
meeting and **g** them to the priest; Lv 15:14 5414
'You shall not **g** any of your Lv 18:21 5414
will **g** it to you to possess it, Lv 20:24 5414
g the holy *gift* to the priest. Lv 22:14 5414
to **g** to you and reap its harvest, Lv 23:10 5414
which you **g** to the LORD. Lv 23:38 5414
into the land which I shall **g** you, Lv 25:2 5414
not **g** him your silver at interest, Lv 25:37 5414
of Egypt to **g** you the land of Canaan Lv 25:38 5414
shall **g** you rains in their season, Lv 26:4 5414
shall on that day **g** your valuation Lv 27:23 5414
"You shall thus **g** the Levites to Nu 3:9 5414
and **g** the money, the ransom of Nu 3:48 5414
g *it* to him whom he has wronged. Nu 5:7 5414
on you, And **g** you peace.' Nu 6:26 7760
you shall **g** them to the Levites, Nu 7:5 5414
But he did not **g** *any* to the sons Nu 7:9 5414
the seven lamps will **g** light in Nu 8:2 215
'I will **g** it to you'; Nu 10:29 5414
"Who will **g** us meat to eat? Nu 11:4
get meat to **g** to all this people? Nu 11:13 5414
'**G** us meat that we may eat!' Nu 11:13 5414
someone would **g** us meat to eat! Nu 11:18
will **g** you meat and you shall eat. Nu 11:18 5414
'I will **g** them meat, so that Nu 11:21 5414
going to **g** to the sons of Israel; Nu 13:2 5414
bring us into this land and **g** it to us Nu 14:8 5414
of your dough you shall **g** to the LORD Nu 15:21 5414
of those which they **g** to the LORD, Nu 18:12 5414
give to the LORD, I **g** them to you. Nu 18:12 5414
and from it you shall **g** the LORD's Nu 18:28 5414
shall **g** it to Eleazar the priest, Nu 19:3 5414
people, that I may **g** them water." Nu 21:16 5414
'Though Balak were to **g** me his Nu 22:18 5414
G ear to me, O son of Zippor! Nu 23:18 238
'Though Balak were to **g** me his Nu 24:13 5414
I **g** him My covenant of peace; Nu 25:12 5414
G us a possession among our Nu 27:4 5414
surely **g** them a hereditary possession Nu 27:7 5414
then you shall **g** his inheritance Nu 27:9 5414
then you shall **g** his inheritance Nu 27:10 5414
then you shall **g** his inheritance Nu 27:11 5414
and **g** it to Eleazar the priest, Nu 31:29 5414
and **g** them to the Levites who keep Nu 31:30 5414
then you shall **g** them the land of Nu 32:29 5414
you shall **g** more inheritance, Nu 33:54 7235a
you shall **g** less inheritance. Nu 33:54 4591
g to the nine and a half tribes. Nu 34:13 5414
of Israel that they **g** to the Levites Nu 35:2 5414
and you shall **g** to the Levites Nu 35:2 5414
cities which you shall **g** to the Levites Nu 35:4 5414
"The cities which you shall **g** Nu 35:6 5414
g for the manslayer to flee to; Nu 35:6 5414
them you shall **g** forty-two cities. Nu 35:6 5414
"All the cities which you shall **g** Nu 35:7 5414
the cities which you shall **g** from the Nu 35:8 5414
each shall **g** some of his cities to Nu 35:8 5414
"The cities which you are to **g** Nu 35:13 5414
'You shall **g** three cities across Nu 35:14 5414
"The LORD commanded my lord to **g** Nu 36:2 5414
to **g** the inheritance of Zelophehad Nu 36:2 5414
the LORD had commanded him *to* **g** Dt 1:3
LORD swore to **g** to your fathers, Dt 1:8 5414
the LORD our God is about to **g** us. Dt 1:20 5414
LORD our God is about to **g** us.' Dt 1:25 5414
which I swore to **g** your fathers, Dt 1:35 5414
him and to his sons I will **g** the land Dt 1:36 5414
there, and I will **g** it to them and Dt 1:39 5414
to your voice nor **g** ear to you. Dt 1:45 238
will not **g** you any of their land, Dt 2:5 5414
for I will not **g** you any of their Dt 2:9 5414
for I will not **g** you any of the Dt 2:19 5414
and **g** me water for money so that I Dt 2:28 5414
God will **g** them beyond the Jordan. Dt 3:20 5414
he will **g** them as an inheritance Dt 3:28 5159
"Only **g** heed to yourself and keep Dt 4:9 8104
g you their land for an inheritance, Dt 4:38 5414
land which I **g** them to possess.' Dt 5:31 5414
Isaac and Jacob, to **g** you, Dt 6:10 5414
land which the LORD swore to **g** Dt 6:18
to **g** us the land which He had Dt 6:23 5414
not **g** your daughters to their sons, Dt 7:3 5414
to your forefathers to **g** you. Dt 7:13 5414
land which the LORD swore *to* **g** Dt 8:1
swore to their fathers to **g** them.' Dt 10:11 5414
LORD swore to your fathers to **g** to Dt 11:9 5414
that He will **g** the rain for your Dt 11:14 5414
"He will **g** grass in your Dt 11:15 5414
swore to your fathers to **g** them, Dt 11:21 5414
You may **g** it to the alien who is Dt 14:21 5414
brother, and you **g** him nothing; Dt 15:9 5414
"You shall generously **g** to him, Dt 15:10 5414
not be grieved when you **g** to him, Dt 15:10 5414
you shall **g** to him as the LORD Dt 15:14 5414
which you shall **g** just as the LORD Dt 16:10 5414
"Every man shall **g** as he is able, Dt 16:17 4979
shall **g** to the priest the shoulder Dt 18:3 5414
"You shall **g** him the first fruits Dt 18:4 5414
God will **g** you as a possession, Dt 19:3 5157
He promised to **g** your fathers Dt 19:8 5414
and **g** it to the girl's father, Dt 22:19 5414
shall **g** to the girl's father fifty *shekels* Dt 22:29 5414
shall **g** happiness to his wife whom he Dt 24:5 8055
"You shall **g** him his wages on his Dt 24:15 5414
swore to our fathers to **g** us.' Dt 26:3 5414
then you shall **g** it to the Levite, Dt 26:12 5414
swore to your fathers to **g** you. Dt 28:11 5414
to **g** rain to your land in its Dt 28:12 5414
so that he will not **g** *even* one of Dt 28:55 5414
LORD will **g** you a trembling heart, Dt 28:65 5414
Isaac, and Jacob, to **g** them." Dt 30:20 5414
sworn to their fathers to **g** them, Dt 31:7 5414
g it to them as an inheritance. Dt 31:7 5157
"**G** ear, O heavens, and let me Dt 32:1 238
is I who put to death and **g** life. Dt 32:39 2421a
'I will **g** it to your descendants'; Dt 34:4 5414
for you shall **g** this people Jos 1:6 5157
swore to their fathers to **g** them. Jos 1:6 5414
rest and will **g** you this land.' Jos 1:13 5414
and **g** me a pledge of truth, Jos 2:12 5414
sworn to their fathers to **g** us, Jos 5:6 5414
implore you, **g** glory to the LORD, Jos 7:19 7760
of Israel, and **g** praise to Him; Jos 7:19 5414
for I will **g** it into your hand." Jos 8:18 5414
Moses to **g** you all the land, Jos 9:24 5414
Levi he did not **g** an inheritance; Jos 13:14 5414
Moses did not **g** an inheritance; Jos 13:33 5414
but he did not **g** an inheritance to Jos 14:3 5414
and they did not **g** a portion to Jos 14:4 5414
g me this hill country about which Jos 14:12 5414
I will **g** him Achsah my daughter as Jos 15:16 5414
Then she said, "**G** me a blessing; Jos 15:19 5414
g me also springs of water." Jos 15:19 5414
"The LORD commanded Moses to **g** us Jos 17:4 5414
city to them and **g** him a place, Jos 20:4 5414
Moses to **g** us cities to live in, Jos 21:2 5414
had sworn to **g** to their fathers, Jos 21:43 5414
I will even **g** him my daughter Jg 1:12 5414
"**G** me a blessing, since you have Jg 1:15 3051
g me also springs of water." Jg 1:15 5414
g them into the hand of Joshua. Jg 2:23 5414
I will **g** him into your hand.' " Jg 4:7 5414
g me a little water to drink, Jg 4:19 8248
"Hear, O kings; **g** ear, O rulers! Jg 5:3 238
Me to **g** Midian into their hands, Jg 7:2 5414
will **g** the Midianites into your hands; Jg 7:7 5414
"Please **g** loaves of bread to the Jg 8:5 5414
we should **g** bread to your army?" Jg 8:6 5414
that we should **g** bread to your men Jg 8:15 5414
g me an earring from his spoil." Jg 8:24 5414
"We will surely **g** *them.*" Jg 8:25 5414
"If You will indeed **g** the sons Jg 11:30 5414
conceive and **g** birth to a son. Jg 13:3 3205
conceive and **g** birth to a son, Jg 13:5 3205
conceive and **g** birth to a son, Jg 13:7 3205
then I will **g** you thirty linen Jg 14:12 5414
then you shall **g** me thirty linen Jg 14:13 5414
g you into the hands of the Philistines Jg 15:12 5414
fast and **g** you into their hands; Jg 15:13 5414
we will each **g** you eleven hundred Jg 16:5 5414
and I will **g** you ten *pieces* of Jg 17:10 5414
g your advice and counsel here." Jg 20:7 3051
"None of us shall **g** his daughter Jg 21:1 5414
sworn by the LORD not to **g** them any Jg 21:7 5414
"But we cannot **g** them wives of our Jg 21:18 5414
'**G** them to us voluntarily, because Jg 21:22 2603a
nor did you **g** *them* to them, Jg 21:22 5414
"**G** me the cloak that is on you Ru 3:15 3051
will **g** you by this young woman." Ru 4:12 5414
he would **g** portions to Peninnah 1Sa 1:4 5414
he would **g** a double portion, 1Sa 1:5 5414
but will **g** Your maidservant a son, 1Sa 1:11 5414
then I will **g** him to the LORD all 1Sa 1:11 5414
He will **g** strength to His king, 1Sa 2:10 5414
"**G** the priest meat for roasting, 1Sa 2:15 5414
"No, but you shall **g** *it to me* now; 1Sa 2:16 5414
"May the LORD **g** you children from 1Sa 2:20 7760
and did I *not* **g** to the house of 1Sa 2:28 5414
was pregnant and about to **g** birth; 1Sa 4:19 3205
g glory to the God of Israel; 1Sa 6:5 5414
"**G** us a king to judge us." 1Sa 8:6 5414
and **g** *them* to his servants. 1Sa 8:14 5414
and **g** to his officers and to his 1Sa 8:15 5414
I will **g** *it* to the man of God and 1Sa 9:8 5414

you and **g** you two *loaves* of bread,	**1Sa 10:4**	5414
g them into the hand of Israel?"	**1Sa 14:37**	5414
"**G** a perfect *lot.*"	**1Sa 14:41**	3051
g me a man that we may fight	**1Sa 17:10**	5414
and will **g** him his daughter and make	**1Sa 17:25**	5414
and I will **g** your flesh to the	**1Sa 17:44**	5414
And I will **g** the dead bodies of	**1Sa 17:46**	5414
He will **g** you into our hands."	**1Sa 17:47**	5414
I will **g** her to you as a wife,	**1Sa 18:17**	5414
"I will **g** her to him that she may	**1Sa 18:21**	5414
G me five loaves of bread, or	**1Sa 21:3**	5414
"There is none like it; **g** it to me."	**1Sa 21:9**	5414
Will the son of Jesse also **g** to	**1Sa 22:7**	5414
for I will **g** the Philistines into	**1Sa 23:4**	5414
to **g** your enemy into your hand,	**1Sa 24:4**	5414
Please **g** whatever you find at hand	**1Sa 25:8**	5414
and **g** it to men whose origin I do	**1Sa 25:11**	5414
let them **g** me a place in one of	**1Sa 27:5**	5414
"Moreover the LORD will also **g**	**1Sa 28:19**	5414
Indeed the LORD will **g** over the	**1Sa 28:19**	5414
we will not **g** them any of the	**1Sa 30:22**	5414
"**G** me my wife Michal, to whom I	**2Sa 3:14**	5414
Will You **g** them into my hand?"	**2Sa 5:19**	5414
for I will certainly **g** the Philistines	**2Sa 5:19**	5414
and I will **g** you rest from all	**2Sa 7:11**	5117
and **g** *them* to your companion,	**2Sa 12:11**	5414
come and **g** me *some* food to eat,	**2Sa 13:5**	5414
I will **g** orders concerning you."	**2Sa 14:8**	6680
me and I would **g** him justice."	**2Sa 15:4**	6663
said to Ahithophel, "**G** your advice.	**2Sa 16:20**	3051
And the king said, "I will **g** *them.*"	**2Sa 21:6**	5414
"Therefore I will **g** thanks to You,	**2Sa 22:50**	3034
"Oh that someone would **g** me water	**2Sa 23:15**	8248
please let me **g** you counsel and	**1Ki 1:12**	3289
that he may **g** me Abishag the	**1Ki 2:17**	5414
"Ask what *you wish* me to **g** you."	**1Ki 3:5**	5414
"So **g** Your servant an	**1Ki 3:9**	5414
and **g** half to the one and half to	**1Ki 3:25**	5414
my lord, **g** her the living child,	**1Ki 3:26**	5414
"**G** the first woman the living	**1Ki 3:27**	5414
and I will **g** you wages for your	**1Ki 5:6**	5414
would **g** Hiram year by year.	**1Ki 5:11**	5414
and will **g** it to your servant.	**1Ki 11:11**	5414
but I will **g** one tribe to your son	**1Ki 11:13**	5414
of Solomon and **g** you ten tribes	**1Ki 11:31**	5414
his son's hand and **g** it to you,	**1Ki 11:35**	5414
'But to his son I will **g** one tribe,	**1Ki 11:36**	5414
David, and I will **g** Israel to you.	**1Ki 11:38**	5414
"What counsel do you **g** that we	**1Ki 12:9**	3289
and I will **g** you a reward."	**1Ki 13:7**	5414
"If you were to **g** me half your	**1Ki 13:8**	5414
"He will **g** up Israel on	**1Ki 14:16**	5414
He said to her, "**G** me your son."	**1Ki 17:19**	5414
"Now let them **g** us two oxen;	**1Ki 18:23**	5414
"You shall **g** me your silver and	**1Ki 20:5**	5414
therefore I will **g** all this great	**1Ki 20:28**	5414
"**G** me your vineyard, that I may	**1Ki 21:2**	5414
and I will **g** you a better vineyard	**1Ki 21:2**	5414
I will **g** you the price of it in	**1Ki 21:2**	5414
LORD forbid me that I should **g** you	**1Ki 21:3**	5414
"I will not **g** you the inheritance	**1Ki 21:4**	5414
'**G** me your vineyard for money;	**1Ki 21:6**	5414
g you a vineyard in its place.'	**1Ki 21:6**	5414
'I will not **g** you my vineyard.' "	**1Ki 21:6**	5414
I will **g** you the vineyard of	**1Ki 21:7**	5414
he refused to **g** you for money;	**1Ki 21:15**	5414
g *it* into the hand of the king."	**1Ki 22:6**	5414
g *it* into the hand of the king."	**1Ki 22:12**	5414
g *it* into the hand of the king."	**1Ki 22:15**	5414
to **g** them into the hand of Moab."	**2Ki 3:10**	5414
to **g** them into the hand of Moab."	**2Ki 3:13**	5414
g the Moabites into your hand.	**2Ki 3:18**	5414
"**G** *them* to the people that they	**2Ki 4:42**	5414
"**G** *them* to the people that they	**2Ki 4:43**	5414
Please **g** them a talent of silver	**2Ki 5:22**	5414
'**G** your son that we may eat him	**2Ki 6:28**	5414
'**G** your son, that we may eat him';	**2Ki 6:29**	5414
He had promised him to **g** a lamp	**2Ki 8:19**	5414
"If it is, **g** *me* your hand."	**2Ki 10:15**	5414
shall **g** up his life in exchange."	**2Ki 10:24**	
'**G** your daughter to my son in	**2Ki 14:9**	5414
I will **g** you two thousand horses,	**2Ki 18:23**	5414
and let them **g** it to the workmen	**2Ki 22:5**	5414
taxed the land in order to **g** the money	**2Ki 23:35**	5414
to **g** it to Pharaoh Neco.	**2Ki 23:35**	5414
"Oh that someone would **g** me water	**1Ch 11:17**	8248
will You **g** them into my hand?"	**1Ch 14:10**	5414
I will **g** them into your hand."	**1Ch 14:10**	5414
relatives to **g** thanks to the LORD.	**1Ch 16:7**	3034
Oh **g** thanks to the LORD, call upon	**1Ch 16:8**	3034
you I will **g** the land of Canaan,	**1Ch 16:18**	5414
O **g** thanks to the LORD, for *He is*	**1Ch 16:34**	3034
To **g** thanks to Your holy name,	**1Ch 16:35**	3034
by name, to **g** thanks to the LORD,	**1Ch 16:41**	3034
"**G** me the site of *this* threshing	**1Ch 21:22**	5414
full price you shall **g** it to me,	**1Ch 21:22**	5414
I will **g** the oxen for burnt	**1Ch 21:23**	5414
for the grain offering; I will **g** *it* all	**1Ch 21:23**	5414
and I will **g** him rest from all his	**1Ch 22:9**	5117
and I will **g** peace and quiet to	**1Ch 22:9**	5414
"Only the LORD **g** you discretion	**1Ch 22:12**	5414
and **g** you charge over Israel,	**1Ch 22:12**	6680
I **g** to the house of my God,	**1Ch 29:3**	5414
and **g** to my son Solomon a	**1Ch 29:19**	5414
"Ask what I shall **g** you."	**2Ch 1:7**	5414
"**G** me now wisdom and knowledge,	**2Ch 1:10**	5414
And I will **g** you riches and wealth	**2Ch 1:12**	5414
behold, I will **g** to your servants,	**2Ch 2:10**	5414
"What counsel do you **g** that we	**2Ch 10:9**	3289
g *it* into the hand of the king."	**2Ch 18:5**	5414
g *it* into the hand of the king."	**2Ch 18:11**	5414
and **g** it to the descendants of	**2Ch 20:7**	5414
"**G** thanks to the LORD, for His	**2Ch 20:21**	3034
since He had promised to **g** a lamp	**2Ch 21:7**	5414
"The LORD has much more to **g** you	**2Ch 25:9**	5414
'**G** your daughter to my son in	**2Ch 25:18**	5414
also on Judah to **g** them one heart	**2Ch 30:12**	5414
to minister and to **g** thanks and to	**2Ch 31:2**	3034
to **g** the portion due to the priests	**2Ch 31:4**	5414
to **g** yourselves over to die by hunger	**2Ch 32:11**	5414
offerings that *they* might **g** them	**2Ch 35:12**	5414
they were not able to **g** evidence of	**Ezr 2:59**	5046
to **g** us a peg in His holy place,	**Ezr 9:8**	5414
to **g** us reviving to raise up the	**Ezr 9:9**	5414
and to **g** us a wall in Judah and	**Ezr 9:9**	5414
'So now do not **g** your daughters to	**Ezr 9:12**	5414
that he may **g** me timber to make	**Ne 2:8**	5414
God of heaven will **g** us success;	**Ne 2:20**	6743b
g them up for plunder in a land of	**Ne 4:4**	5414
g back to them this very day their	**Ne 5:11**	7725
"We will **g** *it* back and will	**Ne 5:12**	7725
translating to **g** the sense so that	**Ne 8:8**	7760
You **g** life to all of them	**Ne 9:6**	2421a
g *him* the land of the Canaanite,	**Ne 9:8**	5414
To **g** *it* to his descendants.	**Ne 9:8**	5414
which You swore to **g** them.	**Ne 9:15**	5414
Yet they would not **g** ear.	**Ne 9:30**	238
we will not **g** our daughters to the	**Ne 10:30**	5414
them, to praise *and* **g** thanks,	**Ne 12:24**	3034
g your daughters to their sons,	**Ne 13:25**	5414
let the king **g** her royal position to	**Es 1:19**	5414
will **g** honor to their husbands,	**Es 1:20**	5414
a man has he will **g** for his life.	**Jb 2:4**	5414
'**G** me *something,*' Or,	**Jb 6:22**	3051
will **g** full vent to my complaint;	**Jb 10:1**	5800a
And his hands **g** back his wealth.	**Jb 20:10**	7725
g an account of all His doings?	**Jb 33:13**	6030a
righteous, what do you **g** to Him,	**Jb 35:7**	5414
time the mountain goats **g** birth?	**Jb 39:1**	3205
do you know the time they **g** birth?	**Jb 39:2**	3205
"Do you **g** the horse *his* might?	**Jb 39:19**	5414
and I will surely **g** the nations as	**Ps 2:8**	5414
G ear to my words, O LORD,	**Ps 5:1**	238
In Sheol who will **g** You thanks?	**Ps 6:5**	3034
I will **g** thanks to the LORD	**Ps 7:17**	3034
I will **g** thanks to the LORD with	**Ps 9:1**	3034
cause, O LORD, **g** heed to my cry;	**Ps 17:1**	7181
G ear to my prayer, which is not	**Ps 17:1**	238
Therefore I will **g** thanks to You	**Ps 18:49**	3034
will **g** strength to His people;	**Ps 29:11**	5414
And **g** thanks to His holy name.	**Ps 30:4**	3034
I will **g** thanks to You forever.	**Ps 30:12**	3034
G thanks to the LORD with the lyre;	**Ps 33:2**	3034
I will **g** You thanks in the great	**Ps 35:18**	3034
And You **g** them to drink of	**Ps 36:8**	8248
g you the desires of your heart.	**Ps 37:4**	5414
O LORD, and **g** ear to my cry;	**Ps 39:12**	238
And do not **g** him over to the	**Ps 41:2**	5414
will **g** thanks to Your name forever.	**Ps 44:8**	3034
You **g** us as sheep to be eaten	**Ps 44:11**	5414
g attention and incline your ear:	**Ps 45:10**	7200
g You thanks forever and ever.	**Ps 45:17**	3034
G ear, all inhabitants of the	**Ps 49:1**	238
Or **g** to God a ransom for him	**Ps 49:7**	5414
sacrifice, otherwise I would **g** it;	**Ps 51:16**	5414
I will **g** You thanks forever,	**Ps 52:9**	3034
G ear to the words of my mouth.	**Ps 54:2**	238
I will **g** thanks to Your name, O	**Ps 54:6**	3034
G ear to my prayer, O God;	**Ps 55:1**	238
G heed to me and answer me;	**Ps 55:2**	7181
I will **g** thanks to You, O Lord,	**Ps 57:9**	3034
O **g** us help against the adversary,	**Ps 60:11**	3051
G heed to my prayer.	**Ps 61:1**	7181
will **g** feigned obedience to You.	**Ps 66:3**	3584
G the king Your judgments, O God,	**Ps 72:1**	5414
We **g** thanks to You, O God, we	**Ps 75:1**	3034
to You, O God, we **g** thanks,	**Ps 75:1**	3034
Can He **g** bread also?	**Ps 78:20**	5414
Will **g** thanks to You forever;	**Ps 79:13**	3034
Oh, **g** ear, Shepherd of Israel,	**Ps 80:1**	238
G ear, O God of Jacob!	**Ps 84:8**	238
the LORD will **g** what is good,	**Ps 85:12**	5414
G ear, O LORD, to my prayer;	**Ps 86:6**	238
And **g** heed to the voice of my	**Ps 86:6**	7181
I will **g** thanks to You, O Lord my	**Ps 86:12**	3034
For He will **g** His angels charge	**Ps 91:11**	6680
is good to **g** thanks to the LORD And	**Ps 92:1**	3034
And **g** thanks to His holy name.	**Ps 97:12**	3034
G thanks to Him, bless His name.	**Ps 100:4**	3034
will **g** heed to the blameless way.	**Ps 101:2**	7919a
They **g** drink to every beast of the	**Ps 104:11**	8248
g them their food in due season.	**Ps 104:27**	5414
You **g** to them, they gather	**Ps 104:28**	5414
Oh **g** thanks to the LORD, call upon	**Ps 105:1**	3034
"To you I will **g** the land of	**Ps 105:11**	5414
Oh **g** thanks to the LORD, for He is	**Ps 106:1**	3034
To **g** thanks to Your holy name And	**Ps 106:47**	3034
Oh **g** thanks to the LORD, for He is	**Ps 107:1**	3034
Let them **g** thanks to the LORD for	**Ps 107:8**	3034
Let them **g** thanks to the LORD for	**Ps 107:15**	3034
Let them **g** thanks to the LORD for	**Ps 107:21**	3034
Let them **g** thanks to the LORD for	**Ps 107:31**	3034
Let him **g** heed to these things,	**Ps 107:43**	8104
I will **g** thanks to You, O LORD,	**Ps 108:3**	3034
g us help against the adversary,	**Ps 108:12**	3051
g thanks abundantly to the LORD;	**Ps 109:30**	3034
I will **g** thanks to the LORD with	**Ps 111:1**	3034
But to Your name **g** glory Because of	**Ps 115:1**	5414
May the LORD **g** you increase, You	**Ps 115:14**	3254
G thanks to the LORD, for He is	**Ps 118:1**	3034
I shall **g** thanks to the LORD.	**Ps 118:19**	3034
I shall **g** thanks to You, for You	**Ps 118:21**	3034
my God, and I **g** thanks to You;	**Ps 118:28**	3034
G thanks to the LORD, for He is	**Ps 118:29**	3034
I shall **g** thanks to You with	**Ps 119:7**	3034
G me understanding, that I may	**Ps 119:34**	995
At midnight I shall rise to **g** thanks	**Ps 119:62**	3034
G me understanding, that I may	**Ps 119:73**	995
g me understanding, That I may	**Ps 119:125**	995
G me understanding that I may live.	**Ps 119:144**	995
G me understanding according to	**Ps 119:169**	995
To **g** thanks to the name of the LORD.	**Ps 122:4**	3034
I will not **g** sleep to my eyes Or	**Ps 132:4**	5414
G thanks to the LORD, for He is	**Ps 136:1**	3034
G thanks to the God of gods, For	**Ps 136:2**	3034
G thanks to the Lord of lords, For	**Ps 136:3**	3034
G thanks to the God of heaven, For	**Ps 136:26**	3034
g You thanks with all my heart;	**Ps 138:1**	3034
And **g** thanks to Your name for Your	**Ps 138:2**	3034
the earth will **g** thanks to You,	**Ps 138:4**	3034
I will **g** thanks to You, for I am	**Ps 139:14**	3034
G ear, O LORD, to the voice of my	**Ps 140:6**	238
will **g** thanks to Your name;	**Ps 140:13**	3034
G ear to my voice when I call to	**Ps 141:1**	238
"**G** heed to my cry, For I am	**Ps 142:6**	7181
that I may **g** thanks to Your name;	**Ps 142:7**	3034
O LORD, **G** ear to my supplications!	**Ps 143:1**	238
Your works shall **g** thanks to You,	**Ps 145:10**	3034
g them their food in due time.	**Ps 145:15**	5414
To **g** prudence to the naive, To the	**Pr 1:4**	5414
back, And tomorrow I will **g** *it,*"	**Pr 3:28**	5414
And **g** attention that you may gain	**Pr 4:1**	7181
For I **g** you sound teaching;	**Pr 4:2**	5414
My son, **g** attention to my words;	**Pr 4:20**	7181
My son, **g** attention to my wisdom,	**Pr 5:1**	7181
Or you will **g** your vigor to others	**Pr 5:9**	5414
G no sleep to your eyes, Nor slumber	**Pr 6:4**	5414
He must **g** all the substance of his	**Pr 6:31**	5414
satisfied though you **g** many gifts.	**Pr 6:35**	7235a
G *instruction* to a wise man and	**Pr 9:9**	5414
not be among those who **g** pledges,	**Pr 22:26**	8628, 3709
G me your heart, my son, And let	**Pr 23:26**	5414
is hungry, **g** him food to eat;	**Pr 25:21**	398
is thirsty, **g** him water to drink;	**Pr 25:21**	8248
men who can **g** a discreet answer.	**Pr 26:16**	7725
The rod and reproof **g** wisdom,	**Pr 29:15**	5414
son, and he will **g** you comfort;	**Pr 29:17**	5117
G me neither poverty nor riches;	**Pr 30:8**	5414
leech has two daughters, "**G**,"	**Pr 30:15**	3051
has two daughters, "Give," "**G**."	**Pr 30:15**	3051
Do not **g** your strength to women,	**Pr 31:3**	5414
G strong drink to him who is	**Pr 31:6**	5414
G her the product of her hands,	**Pr 31:31**	5414
he may **g** to one who is good in	**Ec 2:26**	5414
A time to **g** birth and a time to	**Ec 3:2**	3205
and a time to **g** up as lost;	**Ec 3:6**	6
There I will **g** you my love.	**SS 7:12**	5414
I would **g** you spiced wine to drink	**SS 8:2**	8248
If a man were to **g** all the riches	**SS 8:7**	5414
G ear to the instruction of our	**Is 1:10**	238
There will be a shelter to **g**	**Is 4:6**	
Lord Himself will **g** you a sign:	**Is 7:14**	5414
And **g** ear, all remote places of the	**Is 8:9**	238
"I will **g** thanks to You, O LORD;	**Is 12:1**	3034
"**G** thanks to the LORD, call on	**Is 12:4**	3034
"**G** *us* advice, make a decision;	**Is 16:3**	935
driven in a firm place will **g** way;	**Is 22:25**	4185
You, I will **g** thanks to Your name;	**Is 25:1**	3034
approaches *the time* to **g** birth,	**Is 26:17**	3205
g birth to the departed spirits.	**Is 26:19**	5307
Should someone **g** Me briars *and*	**Is 27:4**	5414
is rest, **g** rest to the weary,"	**Is 28:12**	5117
G ear and hear my voice, Listen	**Is 28:23**	238
g it to the one who is literate,	**Is 29:11**	5414
Then He will **g** *you* rain for the	**Is 30:23**	5414
G ear to my word, You complacent	**Is 32:9**	238
you will **g** birth to stubble;	**Is 33:11**	3205
corpses will **g** off their stench,	**Is 34:3**	5927
I will **g** you two thousand horses,	**Is 36:8**	5414
the living who **g** thanks to You,	**Is 38:19**	3034
will **g** a messenger of good news.'	**Is 41:27**	5414
Who, if I ask, can **g** an answer.	**Is 41:28**	7725
I will not **g** My glory to another,	**Is 42:8**	5414
Let them **g** glory to the LORD And	**Is 42:12**	7760
with none to say, "**G** *them* back!"	**Is 42:22**	7725
Who among you will **g** ear to this?	**Is 42:23**	238
will **g** heed and listen hereafter?	**Is 42:23**	7181
I will **g** *other* men in your place	**Is 43:4**	5414
I will say to the north, '**G** *them* up!'	**Is 43:6**	5414
To **g** drink to My chosen people.	**Is 43:20**	8248
g you the treasures of darkness And	**Is 45:3**	5414
My glory I will not **g** to another.	**Is 48:11**	5414
And I will keep You and **g** You for	**Is 49:8**	5414
And **g** ear to Me, O My nation;	**Is 51:4**	238
To them I will **g** in My house and	**Is 56:5**	5414
I will **g** them an everlasting name	**Is 56:5**	5414
remember Me Nor **g** *Me* a thought?	**Is 57:11**	7760
if you **g** yourself to the hungry And	**Is 58:10**	6329
And **g** strength to your bones;	**Is 58:11**	2502b
will the moon **g** you light;	**Is 60:19**	215
g them their recompense And	**Is 61:8**	5414
And **g** Him no rest until He	**Is 62:7**	5414
"I will never again **g** your grain	**Is 62:8**	5414
point of birth and not **g** delivery?"	**Is 66:9**	3205
"Then I will **g** you shepherds	**Jer 3:15**	5414
sons And **g** you a pleasant land,	**Jer 3:19**	5414

whom shall I speak and **g** warning That Jer 6:10 5749b
I will **g** their wives to others, Jer 8:10 5414
g them poisoned water to drink. Jer 9:15 8248
to **g** them a land flowing with milk Jer 11:5 5414
Listen and **g** heed, do not be Jer 13:15 238
G glory to the LORD your God, Jer 13:16 5414
but I will **g** you lasting peace in Jer 14:13 5414
idols of the nations who **g** rain? Jer 14:22 1652
So I will **g** over their survivors Jer 15:9 5414
I will **g** for booty without cost, Jer 15:13 5414
nor **g** them a cup of consolation to Jer 16:7 8248
I will **g** over your wealth and all Jer 17:3 5414
Even to **g** to each man according to Jer 17:10 5414
g no heed to any of his words." Jer 18:18 7181
Do **g** heed to me, O LORD, And Jer 18:19 7181
g their children over to famine And Jer 18:21 5414
and I will **g** over their carcasses Jer 19:7 5414
So I will **g** over all Judah to the Jer 20:4 5414
'I will also **g** over all the wealth Jer 20:5 5414
I will **g** over to the hand of their Jer 20:5 5414
"I will **g** over Zedekiah king of Jer 21:7 5414
pay And does not **g** him his wages, Jer 22:13 5414
and I will **g** you over into the Jer 22:25 5414
I will **g** them a heart to know Me, Jer 24:7 5414
and I will **g** it to the one who is Jer 27:5 5414
and **g** your daughters to husbands, Jer 29:6 5414
to **g** you a future and a hope. Jer 29:11 5414
and see If a male can **g** birth. Jer 30:6 3205
prey upon you I will **g** for prey. Jer 30:16 5414
Proclaim, **g** praise and say, Jer 31:7 1984b
and **g** them joy for their sorrow. Jer 31:13 8055
I am about to **g** this city into the Jer 32:3 5414
to their forefathers to **g** them, Jer 32:22 5414
I am about to **g** this city into the Jer 32:28 5414
will **g** them one heart and one way, Jer 32:39 5414
"**G** thanks to the LORD of hosts, Jer 33:11 3034
'I will **g** the men who have Jer 34:18 5414
I will **g** them into the hand of Jer 34:20 5414
I will **g** into the hand of their enemies Jer 34:21 5414
and **g** them wine to drink." Jer 35:2 8248
Besides, if I **g** you advice, you Jer 38:15 3289
nor will I **g** you over to the hand of Jer 38:16 5414
for they may **g** me over into their Jer 38:19 5414
"They will not **g** you over. Jer 38:20 5414
Neriah is inciting you against us to **g** Jer 43:3 5414
I am going to **g** over Pharaoh Jer 44:30 5414
'but I will **g** your life to you as Jer 45:5 5414
"I shall **g** them over to the Jer 46:26 5414
"**G** wings to Moab, For she will Jer 48:9 5414
G yourself no relief, La 2:18 5414
Let him **g** his cheek to the smiter, La 3:30 5414
will **g** them hardness of heart, La 3:65 5414
I will **g** you cow's dung in place Ezk 4:15 5414
'I will **g** it into the hands Ezk 7:21 5414
and **g** evil advice in this city, Ezk 11:2 3289
g you the land of Israel." Ezk 11:17 5414
"And I will **g** them one heart, Ezk 11:19 5414
flesh and **g** them a heart of flesh, Ezk 11:19 5414
will be brought to **g** him an answer Ezk 14:4 6030a
"Men **g** gifts to all harlots, but Ezk 16:33 5414
but you **g** your gifts to all your Ezk 16:33 5414
because you **g** money and no money Ezk 16:34 5414
"I will also **g** you into the Ezk 16:39 5414
I will **g** them to you as daughters, Ezk 16:61 5414
g him horses and many troops. Ezk 17:15 5414
land which I swore to **g** to them, Ezk 20:28 5414
I swore to **g** to your forefathers. Ezk 20:42 5414
to **g** it into the hand of the slayer. Ezk 21:11 5414
and I will **g** it *to Him*.' Ezk 21:27 5414
g you into the hand of brutal men, Ezk 21:31 5414
I will **g** you into the hand of Ezk 23:28 5414
I will **g** her cup into your hand.' Ezk 23:31 5414
and **g** them over to terror and Ezk 23:46 5414
I am going to **g** you to the sons of Ezk 25:4 5414
g you for spoil to the nations. Ezk 25:7 5414
and I will **g** it for a possession along Ezk 25:10 5414
I will **g** the land of Egypt to Ezk 29:19 5414
I will **g** it into the hand of a despot Ezk 31:11 5414
the moon will not **g** its light. Ezk 32:7 215
mouth and **g** them warning from Me. Ezk 33:7 2094b
g to the beasts to be devoured, Ezk 33:27 5414
"I will **g** you over to bloodshed, Ezk 35:6 6213a
I will **g** you a new heart and put a Ezk 36:26 5414
flesh and **g** you a heart of flesh. Ezk 36:26 5414
I will **g** you as food to every Ezk 39:4 5414
I will **g** Gog a burial ground there Ezk 39:11 5414
and **g** attention to all that I am Ezk 40:4 7760
'You shall **g** to the Levitical Ezk 43:19 5414
and you shall **g** them no possession Ezk 44:28 5414
you shall also **g** to the priest the Ezk 44:30 5414
g the city possession of *an area* Ezk 45:6 5414
but they shall **g** *the rest of* the Ezk 45:8 5414
the people of the land shall **g** to this Ezk 45:16 1961
lambs as much as he is able to **g**, Ezk 46:5 4991
lambs as much as one is able to **g**, Ezk 46:11 4991
he shall **g** his sons inheritance Ezk 46:18 5157
swore to **g** it to your forefathers, Ezk 47:14 5414
you shall **g** *him* his inheritance," Ezk 47:23 5414
the king that he would **g** him time, Da 2:16 5415
my fathers, I **g** thanks and praise, Da 2:23 3029
g you an answer concerning this Da 3:16 8421
able to **g** interpretations and solve Da 5:16 6590
or **g** your rewards to someone else; Da 5:17 3052
g this *man* an understanding of the Da 8:16 995
I have now come forth to **g** you Da 9:22 7919a
so **g** heed to the message and gain Da 9:23 995
come to **g** you an understanding of Da 10:14 995
he will also **g** him the daughter of Da 11:17 5414
will **g** understanding to the many; Da 11:33 995
he will **g** great honor to those who Da 11:39 7235a
Who **g** *me* my bread and my water, Hos 2:5 5414
g her her vineyards from there, Hos 2:15 5414
G heed, O house of Israel! Hos 5:1 7181
G them, O LORD—what will You Hos 9:14 5414
O LORD—what will You **g**? Hos 9:14 5414
G them a miscarrying womb and dry Hos 9:14 5414
How can I **g** you up, O Ephraim? Hos 11:8 5414
"**G** me a king and princes"? Hos 13:10 5414
you will **g** parting gifts On behalf Mi 1:14 5414
"Writhe and labor to **g** birth, Mi 4:10 1518
He will **g** them *up* until the time Mi 5:3 5414
do preserve I will **g** to the sword. Mi 6:14 5414
I will **g** you up for destruction Mi 6:16 5414
You will **g** truth to Jacob *And* Mi 7:20 5414
g to the peoples purified lips, Zph 3:9 2015
I will **g** you renown and praise Zph 3:20 5414
'and in this place I will **g** peace,' Hg 2:9 5414
did not listen or **g** heed to Me," Zch 1:4 7181
and the heavens will **g** their dew; Zch 8:12 5414
He will **g** them showers of rain, Zch 10:1 5414
good in your sight, **g** *me* my wages; Zch 11:12 3051
to heart to **g** honor to My name," Mal 2:2 5414
"All these things I will **g** You, Mt 4:9 *1325*
LET HIM **G** HER A CERTIFICATE OF Mt 5:31 *1325*
"**G** to him who asks of you, and do Mt 5:42 *1325*
"So when you **g** to the poor, Mt 6:2 *4160*
when you **g** to the poor, do not Mt 6:3 *4160*
'**G** us this day our daily bread. Mt 6:11 *1325*
"Do not **g** what is holy to dogs, Mt 7:6 *1325*
for a loaf, will **g** him a stone? Mt 7:9 *1929*
a fish, he will not **g** him a snake, Mt 7:10 *1929*
to **g** good gifts to your children, Mt 7:11 *1325*
g what is good to those who ask Him! Mt 7:11 *1325*
Freely you received, freely **g**. Mt 10:8 *1325*
the house, **g** it your greeting. Mt 10:12 *782*
"If the house is worthy, **g** it your Mt 10:13 *2064*
heavy-laden, and I will **g** you rest. Mt 11:28 *373*
they shall **g** an accounting for it in Mt 12:36 *591*
oath to **g** her whatever she asked. Mt 14:7 *1325*
"**G** me here on a platter the head Mt 14:8 *1325*
you **g** them *something* to eat!" Mt 14:16 *1325*
"I will **g** you the keys of the Mt 16:19 *1325*
a man **g** in exchange for his soul? Mt 16:26 *1325*
and **g** it to them for you and Me." Mt 17:27 *1325*
G HER A CERTIFICATE OF DIVORCE Mt 19:7 *1325*
possessions and **g** to *the* poor, Mt 19:21 *1325*
whatever is right I will **g** you.' Mt 20:4 *1325*
but I wish to **g** to this last man Mt 20:14 *1325*
on *My* left, this is not Mine to **g**, Mt 20:23 *1325*
to **g** His life a ransom for many." Mt 20:28 *1325*
lawful to **g** a poll-tax to Caesar, Mt 22:17 *1325*
AND THE MOON WILL NOT **G** ITS LIGHT, Mt 24:29 *1325*
g them their food at the proper time? Mt 24:45 *1325*
'**G** us some of your oil, for our Mt 25:8 *1325*
and **g** it to the one who has the Mt 25:28 *1325*
or thirsty, and **g** You *something* to drink? Mt 25:37 *4222*
willing to **g** me to betray Him Mt 26:15 *1325*
g orders for the grave to be made Mt 27:64 *2753*
you want and I will **g** it to you." Mk 6:22 *1325*
you ask of me, I will **g** it to you; Mk 6:23 *1325*
"I want you to **g** me at once Mk 6:25 *1325*
"You **g** them *something* to eat!" Mk 6:37 *1325*
and **g** them *something* to eat?" Mk 6:37 *1325*
a man **g** in exchange for his soul? Mk 8:37 *1325*
you possess and **g** to the poor, Mk 10:21 *1325*
on *My* left, this is not Mine to **g**; Mk 10:40 *1325*
to **g** His life a ransom for many." Mk 10:45 *1325*
and will **g** the vineyard to others. Mk 12:9 *1325*
AND THE MOON WILL NOT **G** ITS LIGHT, Mk 13:24 *1325*
this, and promised to **g** him money. Mk 14:11 *1325*
to **g** false testimony against Him, Mk 14:57 *5576*
to **g** Him wine mixed with myrrh; Mk 15:23 *1325*
and you will **g** him the name John. Lk 1:13 *2564*
and the Lord God will **g** Him the Lk 1:32 *1325*
had come for Elizabeth to **g** birth, Lk 1:57 *5088*
To **g** to His people *the* knowledge Lk 1:77 *1325*
were completed for her to **g** birth. Lk 2:6 *5088*
"I will **g** You all this domain and Lk 4:6 *1325*
me, and I **g** it to whomever I wish. Lk 4:6 *1325*
"**G** to everyone who asks of you, Lk 6:30 *1325*
"**G**, and it will be given to you. Lk 6:38 *1325*
"You **g** them *something* to eat!" Lk 9:13 *1325*
and drinking what they **g** you; Lk 10:7 *3844*
'**G** us each day our daily bread. Lk 11:3 *1325*
cannot get up and **g** you *anything.*' Lk 11:7 *1325*
he will not get up and **g** him *anything* Lk 11:8 *1325*
up and **g** him as much as he needs. Lk 11:8 *1325*
g him a snake instead of a fish, Lk 11:11 *1929*
egg, he will not **g** him a scorpion, Lk 11:12 *1929*
to **g** good gifts to your children, Lk 11:13 *1325*
heavenly Father **g** the Holy Spirit Lk 11:13 *1325*
"But **g** that which is within as Lk 11:41 *1325*
gladly to **g** you the kingdom. Lk 12:32 *1325*
your possessions and **g** to charity; Lk 12:33 *1325*
to **g** them their rations at the Lk 12:42 *1325*
'**G** *your* place to this man,' and then in Lk 14:9 *1325*
"When you **g** a luncheon or a Lk 14:12 *4160*
"But when you **g** a reception, Lk 14:13 *4160*
not **g** up all his own possessions. Lk 14:33 *657*
g me the share of the estate that Lk 15:12 *1325*
G an accounting of your management, Lk 16:2 *591*
will **g** you that which is your own? Lk 16:12 *1325*
who returned to **g** glory to God, Lk 17:18 *1325*
'**G** me legal protection from my Lk 18:3 *1556*
me, I will **g** her legal protection, Lk 18:5 *1556*
possessions I will **g** to the poor, Lk 19:8 *1325*
will **g** back four times as much." Lk 19:8 *591*
and **g** it to the one who has the Lk 19:24 *1325*
would **g** him *some* of the produce Lk 20:10 *1325*
will **g** the vineyard to others." Lk 20:16 *1325*
for I will **g** you utterance and Lk 21:15 *1325*
glad and agreed to **g** him money. Lk 22:5 *1325*
so that we may **g** an answer to Jn 1:22 *1325*
Jesus said to her, "**G** Me a drink." Jn 4:7 *1325*
'**G** Me a drink,' you would have Jn 4:10 *1325*
I will **g** him shall never thirst; Jn 4:14 *1325*
but the water that I will **g** him Jn 4:14 *1325*
"Sir, **g** me this water, so I will Jn 4:15 *1325*
the Son of Man will **g** to you, Jn 6:27 *1325*
"Lord, always **g** us this bread." Jn 6:34 *1325*
bread also which I will **g** for the life Jn 6:51 *1325*
this man **g** us *His* flesh to eat?" Jn 6:52 *1325*
"Did not Moses **g** you the Law, and Jn 7:19 *1325*
and said to him, "**G** glory to God; Jn 9:24 *1325*
and I **g** eternal life to them, and Jn 10:28 *1325*
You ask of God, God will **g** You." Jn 11:22 *1325*
dip the morsel and **g** it to him." Jn 13:26 *1325*
he should **g** something to the poor. Jn 13:29 *1325*
"A new commandment I **g** to you, Jn 13:34 *1325*
and He will **g** you another Helper, Jn 14:16 *1325*
My peace I **g** to you; Jn 14:27 *1325*
as the world gives do I **g** to you. Jn 14:27 *1325*
in My name He may **g** to you. Jn 15:16 *1325*
in My name, He will **g** it to you. Jn 16:23 *1325*
given Him, He may **g** eternal life. Jn 17:2 *1325*
and to **g** Him slaps *in the face.* Jn 19:3 *1325*
to you and **g** heed to my words. Ac 2:14 *1801*
he *began* to **g** them his attention, Ac 3:5 *1907*
but what I do have I **g** to you: Ac 3:6 *1325*
TO HIM YOU SHALL **G** HEED TO Ac 3:22 *191*
right in the sight of God to **g** heed to Ac 4:19 *191*
WOULD **G** IT TO HIM AS A POSSESSION, Ac 7:5 *1325*
"**G** this authority to me as well, Ac 8:19 *1325*
he did not **g** God the glory, Ac 12:23 *1325*
'I WILL **G** YOU THE HOLY *and* SURE Ac 13:34 *1325*
is able to build *you* up and to **g** *you* Ac 20:32 *1325*
more blessed to **g** than to receive. Ac 20:35 *1325*
"I will **g** you a hearing after Ac 23:35 *1251*
not honor Him as God or **g** thanks Ro 1:21 *2168*
but also **g** hearty approval to Ro 1:32 *4909*
will also **g** life to your mortal bodies Ro 8:11 *2227*
with Him freely **g** us all things? Ro 8:32 *5483*
g preference to one another in Ro 12:10 *4285*
IF HE IS THIRSTY, **G** HIM A DRINK; Ro 12:20 *4222*
TONGUE SHALL **G** PRAISE TO GOD." Ro 14:11 *1843*
will **g** an account of himself to God. Ro 14:12 *1325*
"THEREFORE I WILL **G** PRAISE TO Ro 15:9 *1843*
to whom not only do I **g** thanks, Ro 16:4 *2168*
to the married I **g** instructions, 1Co 7:10 *3853*
but I **g** an opinion as one who by 1Co 7:25 *1325*
he who does not **g** her in marriage 1Co 7:38 *1061a*
that for which I **g** thanks? 1Co 10:30 *2168*
G no offense either to Jews or to 1Co 10:32 *1096*
And if I **g** all my possessions to 1Co 13:3 *5595*
has shone in our hearts to **g** the Light 2Co 4:6 *1325*
I **g** *my* opinion in this matter, 2Co 8:10 *1325*
may **g** to you a spirit of wisdom Eph 1:17 *1325*
do not **g** the devil an opportunity. Eph 4:27 *1325*
it will **g** grace to those who hear. Eph 4:29 *1325*
to them, and **g** up threatening, Eph 6:9 *447*
We **g** thanks to God, the Father of Col 1:3 *2168*
We **g** thanks to God always for all 1Th 1:2 *2168*
in the Lord and **g** you instruction, 1Th 5:12 *3560*
in everything **g** thanks; 1Th 5:18 *2168*
always to **g** thanks to God for you, 2Th 1:3 *2168*
and *to* **g** relief to you who are 2Th 1:7
always **g** thanks to God for you, 2Th 2:13 *2168*
you, we used to **g** you this order: 2Th 3:10 *3853*
which **g** rise to mere speculation 1Tm 1:4 *3930*
g attention to the *public* reading 1Tm 4:13 *4337*
and **g** the enemy no occasion for 1Tm 5:14 *1325*
the Lord will **g** you understanding 2Tm 2:7 *1325*
able to **g** you the wisdom that leads to 2Tm 3:15 *4679*
He does not **g** help to angels, Heb 2:16 *1949*
of lips that **g** thanks to His name. Heb 13:15 *3670*
as those who will **g** an account. Heb 13:17 *591*
do not **g** them what is necessary Jas 2:16 *1325*
asks you to **g** an account for the hope 1Pe 3:15
but they will **g** account to Him 1Pe 4:5 *591*
God will for him **g** life to those who 1Jn 5:16 *1325*
and do not **g** him a greeting; 2Jn 1:10 *3004*
I will **g** you the crown of life. Rv 2:10 *1325*
I will **g** *some* of the hidden manna, Rv 2:17 *1325*
and I will **g** him a white stone, Rv 2:17 *1325*
and I will **g** to each one of you Rv 2:23 *1325*
WILL **G** AUTHORITY OVER THE NATIONS Rv 2:26 *1325*
and I will **g** him the morning star. Rv 2:28 *1325*
living creatures **g** glory and honor Rv 4:9 *1325*
him to **g** me the little book. Rv 10:9 *1325*
"We **g** You thanks, O Lord God, Rv 11:17 *2168*
in labor and in pain to **g** birth. Rv 12:2 *5088*
woman who was about to **g** birth, Rv 12:4 *5088*
g breath to the image of the beast, Rv 13:15 *1325*
"Fear God, and **g** Him glory, Rv 14:7 *1325*
not repent so as to **g** Him glory. Rv 16:9 *1325*
to **g** her the cup of the wine of Rv 16:19 *1325*
they **g** their power and authority to Rv 17:13 *1325*
and **g** back *to her* double according Rv 18:6 *1363*
degree **g** her torment and mourning; Rv 18:7 *1325*
"**G** praise to our God, all you His Rv 19:5 *134*
be glad and **g** the glory to Him, Rv 19:7 *1325*
I will **g** to the one who thirsts Rv 21:6 *1325*

GIVEN

I have **g** you every plant yielding Gn 1:29 5414
I have **g** every green plant for Gn 1:30
sea, into your hand they are **g**. Gn 9:2 5414
You have **g** no offspring to me, Gn 15:3 5414

descendants I have **g** this land,	**Gn 15:18**	5414
has **g** heed to your affliction.	**Gn 16:11**	8085
I have **g** your brother a thousand	**Gn 20:16**	5414
and He has **g** him flocks and herds,	**Gn 24:35**	5414
and he has **g** him all that he has.	**Gn 24:36**	5414
names which his father had **g** them.	**Gn 26:18**	7121
I have **g** to him as servants;	**Gn 27:37**	5414
therefore **g** me this *son* also."	**Gn 29:33**	5414
my voice and has **g** me a son."	**Gn 30:6**	5414
"God has **g** me my wages because I	**Gn 30:18**	5414
livestock and **g** *them* to me.	**Gn 31:9**	5414
has graciously **g** your servant."	**Gn 33:5**	2603a
had not been **g** to him as a wife.	**Gn 38:14**	5414
has **g** you treasure in your sacks;	**Gn 43:23**	5414
my sons, whom God has **g** me here."	**Gn 48:9**	5414
and have **g** heed to their cry	**Ex 3:7**	8085
is no straw **g** to your servants,	**Ex 5:16**	5414
for you will be **g** no straw,	**Ex 5:18**	5414
the LORD had **g** the people favor	**Ex 12:36**	5414
which the LORD has **g** you to eat.	**Ex 16:15**	5414
the LORD has **g** you the sabbath;	**Ex 16:29**	5414
I have **g** it as their share from My	**Lv 6:17**	5414
and have **g** them to Aaron the	**Lv 7:34**	5414
LORD had commanded to be **g** them	**Lv 7:36**	5414
for they have been **g** as your due	**Lv 10:14**	5414
and I have **g** it to you on the	**Lv 17:11**	5414
been redeemed nor **g** her freedom,	**Lv 19:20**	5414
he has **g** some of his offspring to	**Lv 20:3**	5414
they are wholly **g** to him from	**Nu 3:9**	5414
for they are wholly **g** to Me from	**Nu 8:16**	5414
"I have **g** the Levites as a	**Nu 8:19**	5414
nor have you **g** us an inheritance	**Nu 16:14**	5414
have **g** you charge of My offerings,	**Nu 18:8**	5414
I have **g** them to you as a portion and	**Nu 18:8**	5414
I have **g** them to you and to your	**Nu 18:11**	5414
I have **g** to you and your sons and	**Nu 18:19**	5414
I have **g** all the tithe in Israel	**Nu 18:21**	5414
I have **g** to the Levites for an	**Nu 18:24**	5414
tithe which I have **g** you from them	**Nu 18:26**	5414
the land which I have **g** them."	**Nu 20:12**	5414
I have **g** to the sons of Israel,	**Nu 20:24**	5414
He has **g** his sons as fugitives,	**Nu 21:29**	5414
for I have **g** him into your hand,	**Nu 21:34**	5414
each shall be **g** their inheritance	**Nu 26:54**	5414
since no inheritance was **g** to them	**Nu 26:62**	5414
I have **g** to the sons of Israel.	**Nu 27:12**	5414
let this land be **g** to your	**Nu 32:5**	5414
land which the LORD has **g** them?	**Nu 32:7**	5414
land which the LORD had **g** them.	**Nu 32:9**	5414
g the land to you to possess it.	**Nu 33:53**	5414
because I have **g** Mount Seir to Esau	**Dt 2:5**	5414
because I have **g** Ar to the sons of	**Dt 2:9**	5414
because I have **g** it to the sons of	**Dt 2:19**	5414
I have **g** Sihon the Amorite, king	**Dt 2:24**	5414
has **g** you this land to possess it;	**Dt 3:18**	5414
in your cities which I have **g** you,	**Dt 3:19**	5414
possession which I have **g** you.'	**Dt 3:20**	5414
the good land which He has **g** you.	**Dt 8:10**	5414
the land which I have **g** you,'	**Dt 9:23**	5414
has **g** you to possess as long as	**Dt 12:1**	5414
LORD your God which He has **g** you;	**Dt 12:15**	5414
flock which the LORD has **g** you,	**Dt 12:21**	5414
for he has **g** you six years *with*	**Dt 15:18**	5647
LORD your God which He has **g** you.	**Dt 16:17**	5414
which the LORD your God has **g** you.	**Dt 20:14**	5414
your God has **g** you rest from all your	**Dt 25:19**	5117
place and has **g** us this land,	**Dt 26:9**	5414
which You, O LORD have **g** me.'	**Dt 26:10**	5414
God has **g** you and your household.	**Dt 26:11**	5414
and also have **g** it to the Levite	**Dt 26:13**	5414
the ground which You have **g** us,	**Dt 26:15**	5414
sheep shall be **g** to your enemies,	**Dt 28:31**	5414
shall be **g** to another people,	**Dt 28:32**	5414
which the LORD your God has **g** you.	**Dt 28:52**	5414
whom the LORD your God has **g** you,	**Dt 28:53**	5414
has not **g** you a heart to know,	**Dt 29:4**	5414
them, And the LORD had **g** them up?	**Dt 32:30**	5462
foot treads, I have **g** it to you,	**Jos 1:3**	5414
that the LORD has **g** you the land,	**Jos 2:9**	5414
has **g** all the land into our hands;	**Jos 2:24**	5414
I have **g** Jericho into your hand,	**Jos 6:2**	5414
For the LORD has **g** you the city.	**Jos 6:16**	5414
g into your hand the king of Ai,	**Jos 8:1**	5414
Moses the servant of the LORD had **g**	**Jos 8:33**	6680
for I have **g** them into your hands;	**Jos 10:8**	5414
For Moses had **g** the inheritance of	**Jos 14:3**	5414
have **g** me the land of the Negev,	**Jos 15:19**	5414
"Why have you **g** me only one lot	**Jos 17:14**	5414
God of your fathers, has **g** you?	**Jos 18:3**	5414
God has **g** rest to your brothers,	**Jos 22:4**	5117
had **g** *a possession* in Bashan,	**Jos 22:7**	5414
when the LORD had **g** rest to Israel	**Jos 23:1**	5117
which the LORD your God has **g** you.	**Jos 23:13**	5414
which the LORD your God has **g** you.	**Jos 23:15**	5414
good land which He has **g** you."	**Jos 23:16**	5414
which was **g** him in the hill country	**Jos 24:33**	5414
I have **g** the land into his hand."	**Jg 1:2**	5414
have **g** me the land of the Negev,	**Jg 1:15**	5414
for the LORD has **g** your enemies	**Jg 3:28**	5414
LORD has **g** Sisera into your hands;	**Jg 4:14**	5414
g us into the hand of Midian."	**Jg 6:13**	5414
for I have **g** it into your hands.	**Jg 7:9**	5414
God has **g** Midian and all the camp	**Jg 7:14**	5414
for the LORD has **g** the camp of	**Jg 7:15**	5414
"God has **g** the leaders of Midian,	**Jg 8:3**	5414
when the LORD has **g** Zebah and	**Jg 8:7**	5414
for I have **g** my word to the LORD,	**Jg 11:35**	6475
you have **g** your word to the LORD;	**Jg 11:36**	6475
But Samson's wife was **g** to his	**Jg 14:20**	5414
"You have **g** this great deliverance	**Jg 15:18**	5414
"Our god has **g** Samson our enemy	**Jg 16:23**	5414
has **g** our enemy into our hands,	**Jg 16:24**	5414
for God has **g** it into your hand, a	**Jg 18:10**	5414
seven sons, has **g** birth to him."	**Ru 4:15**	3205
and the LORD has **g** me my petition	**1Sa 1:27**	5414
for you have **g** birth to a son."	**1Sa 4:20**	3205
LORD has **g** them into our hands;	**1Sa 14:10**	5414
g them into the hands of Israel."	**1Sa 14:12**	5414
and has **g** it to your neighbor,	**1Sa 15:28**	5414
should have been **g** to David,	**1Sa 18:19**	5414
that she was **g** to Adriel the	**1Sa 18:19**	5414
in that you have **g** him bread and a	**1Sa 22:13**	5414
LORD had **g** you today into my hand	**1Sa 24:10**	5414
brought to my lord be **g** to the young	**1Sa 25:27**	5414
Saul had **g** Michal his daughter,	**1Sa 25:44**	5414
hand and **g** it to your neighbor,	**1Sa 28:17**	5414
with what the LORD has **g** us,	**1Sa 30:23**	5414
thus the LORD has **g** my lord the	**2Sa 4:8**	5414
and the LORD had **g** him rest on	**2Sa 7:1**	5117
I have **g** to your master's grandson.	**2Sa 9:9**	5414
you have **g** occasion to the enemies	**2Sa 12:14**	5006
and the LORD has **g** the kingdom	**2Sa 16:8**	5414
Ahithophel has **g** is not good."	**2Sa 17:7**	3289
And I would have **g** you ten *pieces*	**2Sa 18:11**	5414
men from his sons be **g** to us,	**2Sa 21:6**	5414
"You have also **g** me the shield	**2Sa 22:36**	5414
"Let Abishag the Shunammite be **g**	**1Ki 2:21**	5414
that You have **g** him a son to sit	**1Ki 3:6**	5414
I have **g** you a wise and discerning	**1Ki 3:12**	5414
g you what you have not asked,	**1Ki 3:13**	5414
God has **g** me rest on every side;	**1Ki 5:4**	5117
who has **g** to David a wise son over	**1Ki 5:7**	5414
g Your people for an inheritance.	**1Ki 8:36**	5414
which You have **g** to our fathers.	**1Ki 8:40**	5414
You have **g** to their fathers,	**1Ki 8:48**	5414
has **g** rest to His people Israel,	**1Ki 8:56**	5414
from the land which I have **g** them,	**1Ki 9:7**	5414
cities which Solomon had **g** him,	**1Ki 9:12**	5414
these cities which you have **g** me,	**1Ki 9:13**	5414
g it *as* a dowry to his daughter,	**1Ki 9:16**	5414
the elders which they had **g** him,	**1Ki 12:8**	3289
the elders which they had **g** him,	**1Ki 12:13**	3289
God had **g** by the word of the LORD.	**1Ki 13:5**	5414
the LORD has **g** him to the lion,	**1Ki 13:26**	5414
Then they took the ox which was **g**	**1Ki 18:26**	5414
the LORD had **g** victory to Aram.	**2Ki 5:1**	5414
be **g** two mules' load of earth;	**2Ki 5:17**	5414
and this city will not be **g** into	**2Ki 18:30**	5414
"Jerusalem will not be **g** into	**2Ki 19:10**	5414
the priest has **g** me a book."	**2Ki 22:10**	5414
kings of Judah had **g** to the sun,	**2Ki 23:11**	5414
allowance was **g** him by the king,	**2Ki 25:30**	5414
his birthright was **g** to the sons	**1Ch 5:1**	5414
with them were **g** into their hand;	**1Ch 5:20**	5414
rest of the sons of Kohath *were* **g**	**1Ch 6:61**	
were **g** from the tribe of Issachar	**1Ch 6:62**	
To the sons of Merari *were* **g** by	**1Ch 6:63**	
To the sons of Gershom *were* **g**	**1Ch 6:71**	
were **g** from the tribe of	**1Ch 6:77**	
were **g** *them,* from the tribe of	**1Ch 6:78**	
He not **g** you rest on every side?	**1Ch 22:18**	5117
For He has **g** the inhabitants of	**1Ch 22:18**	5414
Israel has **g** rest to His people,	**1Ch 23:25**	5117
LORD according to the ordinance **g**	**1Ch 24:19**	
were **g** duties like their	**1Ch 26:12**	
(for the LORD has **g** me many sons),	**1Ch 28:5**	5414
and from Your hand we have **g** You.	**1Ch 29:14**	5414
who has **g** King David a wise son,	**2Ch 2:12**	5414
the land which You have **g** to them	**2Ch 6:25**	5414
which You have **g** to Your people	**2Ch 6:27**	5414
which You have **g** to our fathers.	**2Ch 6:31**	5414
You have **g** to their fathers and	**2Ch 6:38**	5414
from My land which I have **g** you,	**2Ch 7:20**	5414
cities which Huram had **g** to him,	**2Ch 8:2**	5414
the elders which they had **g** him,	**2Ch 10:8**	3289
because the LORD had **g** him rest.	**2Ch 14:6**	5117
He has **g** us rest on every side."	**2Ch 14:7**	5117
they will be **g** into your hand."	**2Ch 18:14**	5414
You have **g** us as an inheritance.	**2Ch 20:11**	3423
have **g** to the troops of Israel?"	**2Ch 25:9**	5414
God had **g** him very great wealth.	**2Ch 32:29**	5414
the statutes and the ordinances **g**	**2Ch 33:8**	
book of the law of the LORD **g**	**2Ch 34:14**	
has **g** me all the kingdoms of the	**2Ch 36:23**	5414
has **g** me all the kingdoms of the	**Ezr 1:2**	5414
that was **g** as a freewill offering.	**Ezr 1:6**	5068
and they were **g** to one whose name	**Ezr 5:14**	3052
be **g** to them daily without fail,	**Ezr 6:9**	3052
the LORD God of Israel had **g**;	**Ezr 7:6**	5414
"Also the utensils which are **g** to	**Ezr 7:19**	3052
whom David and the princes had **g**	**Ezr 8:20**	5414
our priests have been **g** into the hand	**Ezr 9:7**	5414
g us an escaped remnant as this,	**Ezr 9:13**	5414
let letters be **g** me for the	**Ne 2:7**	5414
which the LORD had **g** to Israel.	**Ne 8:1**	6680
law, which was **g** through Moses,	**Ne 10:29**	5414
because God had **g** them great joy,	**Ne 12:43**	8055
the Levites had not been **g** *them,*	**Ne 13:10**	5414
for so the king had **g** orders to	**Es 1:8**	3245
and let their cosmetics be **g** *them.*	**Es 2:3**	5414
anything that she desired was **g**	**Es 2:13**	5414
the kingdom it shall be **g** to you."	**Es 5:3**	5414
my life be **g** me as my petition,	**Es 7:3**	5414
g the house of Haman to Esther,	**Es 8:7**	5414
was **g** out at the citadel in Susa.	**Es 8:14**	5414
"Why is light **g** to him who suffers,	**Jb 3:20**	5414
"*Why is light* **g** to a man whose	**Jb 3:23**	
is **g** into the hand of the wicked;	**Jb 9:24**	5414
To whom alone the land was **g**,	**Jb 15:19**	5414
you have **g** no water to drink,	**Jb 22:7**	8248
you have **g** to *one* without wisdom!	**Jb 26:3**	3289
"Pure gold cannot be **g** in exchange	**Jb 28:15**	5414
of heaven, who has **g** it birth?	**Jb 38:29**	3205
Or **g** understanding to the mind?	**Jb 38:36**	5414
g her a share of understanding.	**Jb 39:17**	2505a
g to Me that I should repay *him?*	**Jb 41:11**	6923
You have also **g** me the shield of	**Ps 18:35**	5414
You have **g** him his heart's desire,	**Ps 21:2**	5414
And You have not **g** me over into	**Ps 31:8**	5462
You have **g** us wine to drink that	**Ps 60:3**	8248
You have **g** a banner to those who	**Ps 60:4**	5414
You have **g** *me* the inheritance of	**Ps 61:5**	5414
He has **g** heed to the voice of my	**Ps 66:19**	7181
have **g** commandment to save me,	**Ps 71:3**	6680
may the gold of Sheba be **g** to him;	**Ps 72:15**	5414
They have **g** the dead bodies of Your	**Ps 79:2**	5414
have **g** help to one who is mighty;	**Ps 89:19**	7737b
has **g** food to those who fear Him;	**Ps 111:5**	5414
He has **g** freely to the poor,	**Ps 112:9**	5414
earth He has **g** to the sons of men.	**Ps 115:16**	5414
But He has not **g** me over to death.	**Ps 118:18**	5414
is God, and He has **g** us light;	**Ps 118:27**	215
What shall be **g** to you, and what	**Ps 120:3**	5414
g us to be torn by their teeth.	**Ps 124:6**	5414
Have **g** a pledge for a stranger,	**Pr 6:1**	8628
Do not associate with a man **g** to	**Pr 22:24**	
with those who are **g** to change,	**Pr 24:21**	8132
grievous task *which* God has **g** to the	**Ec 1:13**	5414
He has **g** wisdom and knowledge	**Ec 2:26**	5414
while to the sinner He has **g** the	**Ec 2:26**	5414
task which God has **g** the sons of men	**Ec 3:10**	5414
of his life which God has **g** him;	**Ec 5:18**	5414
whom God has **g** riches and wealth,	**Ec 5:19**	5414
a man to whom God has **g** riches and	**Ec 6:2**	5414
among them are **g** fully to do evil.	**Ec 8:11**	4390
which God has **g** him under the sun.	**Ec 8:15**	5414
He has **g** to you under the sun;	**Ec 9:9**	5414
they are **g** by one Shepherd.	**Ec 12:11**	5414
have **g** forth *their* fragrance.	**SS 2:13**	5414
mandrakes have **g** forth fragrance;	**SS 7:13**	5414
children whom the LORD has **g** me	**Is 8:18**	5414
born to us, a son will be **g** to us;	**Is 9:6**	5414
neither travailed nor **g** birth,	**Is 23:4**	3205
The LORD has **g** a command	**Is 23:11**	6680
be **g** to the one who is illiterate,	**Is 29:12**	5414
Although the Lord has **g** you bread	**Is 30:20**	5414
His bread will be **g** *him,*	**Is 33:16**	5414
He has **g** them over to slaughter.	**Is 34:2**	5414
glory of Lebanon will be **g** to it,	**Is 35:2**	5414
this city will not be **g** into the	**Is 36:15**	5414
'Jerusalem will not be **g** into the	**Is 37:10**	5414
I have **g** Egypt as your ransom,	**Is 43:3**	5414
Because I have **g** waters in the	**Is 43:20**	5414
I have **g** you a title of honor	**Is 45:4**	3655
has **g** Me the tongue of disciples,	**Is 50:4**	5414
away and **g** her a writ of divorce,	**Jer 3:8**	5414
what I have **g** them will pass away	**Jer 8:13**	5414
And **g** us poisoned water to drink,	**Jer 8:14**	8248
I have **g** the beloved of My soul	**Jer 12:7**	5414
Where is the flock that was **g** you,	**Jer 13:20**	5414
the doe in the field has **g** birth only to	**Jer 14:5**	3205
"It will be **g** into the hand of	**Jer 21:10**	5414
g heed to His word and listened?	**Jer 23:18**	7181
the land which the LORD has **g** to you	**Jer 25:5**	5414
He has **g** them to the sword,'	**Jer 25:31**	5414
not **g** into the hands of the people	**Jer 26:24**	5414
"Now I have **g** all these lands	**Jer 27:6**	5414
and I have **g** him also the wild	**Jer 27:6**	5414
g him the beasts of the field.	**Jer 28:14**	5414
be **g** into the hand of the king	**Jer 32:4**	5414
"After I had **g** the deed of	**Jer 32:16**	5414
and the city is **g** into the hand of	**Jer 32:24**	5414
the city is **g** into the hand of the	**Jer 32:25**	5414
'It is **g** into the hand of the king	**Jer 32:36**	5414
g into the hand of the Chaldeans."	**Jer 32:43**	5414
dwell in the land which I have **g** to	**Jer 35:15**	5414
"You will be **g** into the hand of	**Jer 37:17**	5414
'This city will certainly be **g**	**Jer 38:3**	5414
then this city will be **g** over to	**Jer 38:18**	5414
"and you will not be **g** into the	**Jer 39:17**	5414
are *meant* for death *will be* **g**	**Jer 43:11**	
G over to the power of the people	**Jer 46:24**	5414
When the LORD has **g** it an order?	**Jer 47:7**	6680
She has **g** herself up, her pillars	**Jer 50:15**	5414
was **g** him by the king of Babylon,	**Jer 52:34**	5414
They have **g** their precious things	**La 1:11**	5414
The Lord has **g** me into the hands	**La 1:14**	5414
has been **g** us as a possession.'	**Ezk 11:15**	5414
I have **g** to the fire for fuel,	**Ezk 15:6**	5414
so have I **g** up the inhabitants of	**Ezk 15:6**	5414
of My silver, which I had **g** you,	**Ezk 16:17**	5414
give money and no money is **g** you;	**Ezk 16:34**	5414
into the land which I had **g** them,	**Ezk 20:15**	5414
"It is **g** to be polished, that	**Ezk 21:11**	5414
I have **g** the glittering sword.	**Ezk 21:15**	5414
I have **g** you for food to the	**Ezk 29:5**	5414
"I have **g** him the land of Egypt	**Ezk 29:20**	5414
have all been **g** over to death,	**Ezk 31:14**	5414
She is **g** over to the sword;	**Ezk 32:20**	5414
land has been **g** as a possession.'	**Ezk 33:24**	5414
they are **g** to us for food.'	**Ezk 35:12**	5414
and let us be **g** some vegetables to	**Da 1:12**	5414
You have **g** me wisdom and power;	**Da 2:23**	3052
God of heaven has **g** the kingdom,	**Da 2:37**	3052
He has **g** *them* into your hand and	**Da 2:38**	3052
"To you the command is **g**,	**Da 3:4**	560
And let a beast's mind be **g** to him,	**Da 4:16**	3052

and you be **g** grass to eat like	**Da 4:25**	2939
be **g** grass to eat like cattle,	**Da 4:32**	2939
He was **g** grass to eat like cattle,	**Da 5:21**	2939
kingdom has been divided and **g** over	**Da 5:28**	3052
a human mind also was **g** to it.	**Da 7:4**	3052
heads, and dominion was **g** to it.	**Da 7:6**	3052
and **g** to the burning fire.	**Da 7:11**	3052
"And to Him was **g** dominion, Glory	**Da 7:14**	3052
be **g** into his hand for a time,	**Da 7:25**	3052
will be **g** to the people of the saints	**Da 7:27**	3052
the host will be **g** over *to the horn*	**Da 8:12**	5414
sovereignty will be uprooted and **g**	**Da 11:4**	
his power, but she will be **g** up,	**Da 11:6**	5414
be **g** into the hand of the *former.*	**Da 11:11**	5414
take away My wool and My flax **G**	**Hos 2:9**	
wages Which my lovers have **g** me.'	**Hos 2:12**	5414
For He has **g** you the early rain	**Jl 2:23**	5414
their land Which I have **g** them,"	**Am 9:15**	5414
"Ask, and it will be **g** to you;	**Mt 7:7**	*1325*
who had **g** such authority to men.	**Mt 9:8**	*1325*
for it will be **g** you in that hour	**Mt 10:19**	*1325*
and *yet* no sign will be **g** to it	**Mt 12:39**	*1325*
has, to him *more* shall be **g**,	**Mt 13:12**	*1325*
it to be **g** because of his oaths,	**Mt 14:9**	*1325*
on a platter and **g** to the girl,	**Mt 14:11**	*1325*
help you has been **g** *to God,*"	**Mt 15:5**	*1435*
and a sign will not be **g** it,	**Mt 16:4**	*1325*
only those to whom it has been **g**.	**Mt 19:11**	*1325*
and **g** to a people, producing the	**Mt 21:43**	*1325*
marry nor are **g** in marriage,	**Mt 22:30**	*1061a*
everyone who has, *more* shall be **g**,	**Mt 25:29**	*1325*
and *the money* **g** to the poor."	**Mt 26:9**	*1325*
He had taken a cup and **g** thanks,	**Mt 26:27**	*1325*
ordered it to be **g** *to him.*	**Mt 27:58**	*591*
g to Me in heaven and on earth.	**Mt 28:18**	*1325*
"To you has been **g** the mystery of	**Mk 4:11**	*1325*
and more will be **g** you besides.	**Mk 4:24**	*4369*
has, to him *more* shall be **g**;	**Mk 4:25**	*1325*
something should be **g** her to eat.	**Mk 5:43**	*1325*
and what is *this* wisdom **g** to Him,	**Mk 6:2**	*1325*
(that is to say, **g** *to God*),"	**Mk 7:11**	*1435*
will be **g** to this generation."	**Mk 8:12**	*1325*
marry nor are **g** in marriage,	**Mk 12:25**	*1061a*
whatever is **g** you in that hour;	**Mk 13:11**	*1325*
and *the money* **g** to the poor."	**Mk 14:5**	*1325*
He had taken a cup *and* **g** thanks,	**Mk 14:23**	*2168*
betraying Him had **g** them a signal,	**Mk 14:44**	*1325*
has **g** help to Israel His servant,	**Lk 1:54**	*482*
the name **g** by the angel before He	**Lk 2:21**	*2564*
"Give, and it will be **g** to you.	**Lk 6:38**	*1325*
has, to him *more* shall be **g**;	**Lk 8:18**	*1325*
for *something* to be **g** her to eat.	**Lk 8:55**	*1325*
I have **g** you authority to tread	**Lk 10:19**	*1325*
ask, and it will be **g** to you;	**Lk 11:9**	*1325*
be **g** to it but the sign of Jonah.	**Lk 11:29**	*1325*
g much, much will be required;	**Lk 12:48**	*1325*
you have never **g** me a young goat,	**Lk 15:29**	*1325*
they were being **g** in marriage,	**Lk 17:27**	*1061a*
to whom he had **g** the money,	**Lk 19:15**	*1325*
everyone who has, more shall be **g**,	**Lk 19:26**	*1325*
age marry and are **g** in marriage,	**Lk 20:34**	*1061b*
marry nor are **g** in marriage;	**Lk 20:35**	*1061a*
He had taken a cup *and* **g** thanks,	**Lk 22:17**	*2168*
had taken *some* bread *and* **g** thanks,	**Lk 22:19**	*2168*
is My body which is **g** for you;	**Lk 22:19**	*1325*
For the Law was **g** through Moses;	**Jn 1:17**	*1325*
it has been **g** him from heaven.	**Jn 3:27**	*1325*
has **g** all things into His hand.	**Jn 3:35**	*1325*
would have **g** you living water."	**Jn 4:10**	*1325*
He has **g** all judgment to the Son,	**Jn 5:22**	*1325*
the Father has **g** Me to accomplish	**Jn 5:36**	*1325*
and having **g** thanks, He	**Jn 6:11**	*2168*
bread after the Lord had **g** thanks.	**Jn 6:23**	*2168*
has **g** you the bread out of heaven,	**Jn 6:32**	*1325*
that He has **g** Me I lose nothing,	**Jn 6:39**	*1325*
Moses has **g** you circumcision	**Jn 7:22**	*1325*
for the Spirit was not yet **g**.	**Jn 7:39**	*1325*
"My Father, who has **g** *them* to Me,	**Jn 10:29**	*1325*
Pharisees had **g** orders that if anyone	**Jn 11:57**	*1325*
denarii and **g** to poor *people?*"	**Jn 12:5**	*1325*
who sent Me has **g** Me a	**Jn 12:49**	*1325*
had **g** all things into His hands,	**Jn 13:3**	*1325*
that to all whom You have **g** Him,	**Jn 17:2**	*1325*
work which You have **g** Me to do.	**Jn 17:4**	*1325*
You have **g** Me is from You;	**Jn 17:7**	*1325*
You gave Me I have **g** to them;	**Jn 17:8**	*1325*
but of those whom You have **g** Me;	**Jn 17:9**	*1325*
the name which You have **g** Me,	**Jn 17:11**	*1325*
in Your name which You have **g** Me;	**Jn 17:12**	*1325*
"I have **g** them Your word;	**Jn 17:14**	*1325*
have **g** Me I have given to them,	**Jn 17:22**	*1325*
have given Me I have **g** to them,	**Jn 17:22**	*1325*
they also, whom You have **g** Me,	**Jn 17:24**	*1325*
My glory which You have **g** Me	**Jn 17:24**	*1325*
You have **g** Me I lost not one."	**Jn 18:9**	*1325*
the cup which the Father has **g** Me,	**Jn 18:11**	*1325*
it had been **g** you from above;	**Jn 19:11**	*1325*
He had by the Holy Spirit **g** orders	**Ac 1:2**	*1781*
faith which *comes* through Him has **g**	**Ac 3:16**	*1325*
heaven that has been **g** among men by	**Ac 4:12**	*1325*
God has **g** to those who obey Him."	**Ac 5:32**	*1325*
and had **g** them much exhortation,	**Ac 20:2**	*3870*
When he had **g** him permission,	**Ac 21:40**	*2010*
that money would be **g** him by Paul;	**Ac 24:26**	*1325*
the Holy Spirit who was **g** to us.	**Ro 5:5**	*1325*
OR WHO HAS FIRST **G** TO HIM THAT IT	**Ro 11:35**	*4272*
For through the grace **g** to me I	**Ro 12:3**	*1325*
according to the grace **g** to us,	**Ro 12:6**	*1325*
of God to confirm the promises **g**	**Ro 15:8**	
the grace that was **g** me from God,	**Ro 15:15**	*1325*
which was **g** you in Christ Jesus,	**1Co 1:4**	*1325*
the things freely **g** to us by God,	**1Co 2:12**	*5483*
grace of God which was **g** to me,	**1Co 3:10**	*1325*
hair is **g** to her for a covering.	**1Co 11:15**	*1325*
and when He had **g** thanks, He broke	**1Co 11:24**	*2168*
to each one is **g** the manifestation	**1Co 12:7**	*1325*
For to one is **g** the word of wisdom	**1Co 12:8**	*1325*
that thanks may be **g** by many	**2Co 1:11**	*2168*
g in the churches of Macedonia,	**2Co 8:1**	*1325*
Because of the proof **g** by this	**2Co 9:13**	
was **g** me a thorn in the flesh,	**2Co 12:7**	*1325*
the grace that had been **g** to me,	**Ga 2:9**	*1325*
g which was able to impart life,	**Ga 3:21**	*1325*
might be **g** to those who believe.	**Ga 3:22**	*1325*
out your eyes and **g** them to me.	**Ga 4:15**	*1325*
who is **g** as a pledge of our	**Eph 1:14**	*728*
grace which was **g** to me for you;	**Eph 3:2**	*1325*
gift of God's grace which was **g** to me	**Eph 3:7**	*1325*
of all saints, this grace was **g**,	**Eph 3:8**	*1325*
But to each one of us grace was **g**	**Eph 4:7**	*1325*
g themselves over to sensuality for	**Eph 4:19**	*3860*
that utterance may be **g** to me in	**Eph 6:19**	*1325*
who has loved us and **g** us eternal	**2Th 2:16**	*1325*
the testimony **g** at the proper	**1Tm 2:6**	
has not **g** us a spirit of timidity,	**2Tm 1:7**	*1325*
your prayers I will be **g** to you.	**Phm 1:22**	*5483*
THE CHILDREN WHOM GOD HAS **G** ME."	**Heb 2:13**	*1325*
For if Joshua had **g** them rest,	**Heb 4:8**	*2664*
and with them an oath **g** as	**Heb 6:16**	
reproach, and it will be **g** to him.	**Jas 1:5**	*1325*
Every good thing **g** and every perfect	**Jas 1:17**	*1394*
according to the wisdom **g** him,	**2Pe 3:15**	*1325*
by the Spirit whom He has **g** us.	**1Jn 3:24**	*1325*
because He has **g** us of His Spirit.	**1Jn 4:13**	*1325*
in the testimony that God has **g**	**1Jn 5:10**	*3140*
that God has **g** us eternal life,	**1Jn 5:11**	*1325*
come, and has **g** us understanding so	**1Jn 5:20**	*1325*
and a crown was **g** to him,	**Rv 6:2**	*1325*
and a great sword was **g** to him.	**Rv 6:4**	*1325*
Authority was **g** to them over a	**Rv 6:8**	*1325*
g to each of them a white robe;	**Rv 6:11**	*1325*
and seven trumpets were **g** to them.	**Rv 8:2**	*1325*
and much incense was **g** to him,	**Rv 8:3**	*1325*
the bottomless pit was **g** to him.	**Rv 9:1**	*1325*
and power was **g** them, as the	**Rv 9:3**	*1325*
Then there was **g** me a measuring rod	**Rv 11:1**	*1325*
for it has been **g** to the nations;	**Rv 11:2**	*1325*
great eagle were **g** to the woman,	**Rv 12:14**	*1325*
There was **g** to him a mouth	**Rv 13:5**	*1325*
for forty-two months was **g** to him.	**Rv 13:5**	*1325*
It was also **g** to him to make war	**Rv 13:7**	*1325*
tongue and nation was **g** to him.	**Rv 13:7**	*1325*
signs which it was **g** him to perform	**Rv 13:14**	*1325*
it was **g** to him to give breath	**Rv 13:15**	*1325*
be **g** a mark on their right hand or	**Rv 13:16**	*1325*
You have **g** them blood to drink.	**Rv 16:6**	*1325*
g to it to scorch men with fire.	**Rv 16:8**	*1325*
It was **g** to her to clothe	**Rv 19:8**	*1325*
them, and judgment was **g** to them.	**Rv 20:4**	*1325*

GIVER

for God loves a cheerful **g**.	**2Co 9:7**	*1395*

GIVES

let loose, He **g** beautiful words.	**Gn 49:21**	5414
to your fathers, and **g** it to you,	**Ex 13:11**	5414
when the LORD **g** you meat to eat	**Ex 16:8**	5414
therefore He **g** you bread for two	**Ex 16:29**	5414
which the LORD your God **g** you.	**Ex 20:12**	5414
"If his master **g** him a wife, and	**Ex 21:4**	5414
child so that she **g** birth prematurely,	**Ex 21:22**	3205
"If a man **g** his neighbor money or	**Ex 22:7**	5414
"If a man **g** his neighbor a	**Ex 22:10**	5414
g birth and bears a male *child,*	**Lv 12:2**	2232
who **g** any of his offspring to	**Lv 20:2**	5414
he **g** any of his offspring to Molech,	**Lv 20:4**	5414
one **g** to the LORD shall be holy.	**Lv 27:9**	5414
whatever any man **g** to the priest,	**Nu 5:10**	5414
until the LORD **g** rest to your	**Dt 3:20**	5117
which the LORD your God **g** you.	**Dt 5:16**	5414
and He **g** you rest from all your	**Dt 12:10**	5117
you and **g** you a sign or a wonder,	**Dt 13:1**	5414
which the LORD your God **g** you,	**Dt 17:14**	5414
which the LORD your God **g** you,	**Dt 18:9**	5414
land the LORD your God **g** you,	**Dt 19:1**	5414
LORD your God **g** you to possess.	**Dt 19:2**	5414
and **g** you all the land which He	**Dt 19:8**	5414
your God **g** you as an inheritance,	**Dt 19:10**	5414
LORD your God **g** you to possess.	**Dt 19:14**	5414
LORD your God **g** it into your hand,	**Dt 20:13**	5414
LORD your God **g** you to possess,	**Dt 21:1**	5414
your God **g** you as an inheritance,	**Dt 21:23**	5414
your God **g** you as an inheritance.	**Dt 24:4**	5414
which the LORD your God **g** you.	**Dt 25:15**	5414
land which the LORD your God **g** you	**Dt 25:19**	5414
your God **g** you as an inheritance,	**Dt 26:1**	5414
land that the LORD your God **g** you,	**Dt 26:2**	5414
which the LORD your God **g** you,	**Dt 27:2**	5414
which the LORD your God **g** you,	**Dt 27:3**	5414
which the LORD your God **g** you.	**Dt 28:8**	5414
'The LORD your God **g** you rest and	**Jos 1:13**	5117
the LORD **g** your brothers rest,	**Jos 1:15**	5117
as *He* **g** you, and they also	**Jos 1:15**	
when the LORD **g** us the land that we	**Jos 2:14**	5414
and the LORD **g** them up to me,	**Jg 11:9**	5414
Chemosh your god **g** you to possess?	**Jg 11:24**	3423
is he who **g** a wife to Benjamin."	**Jg 21:18**	5414
Even the barren **g** birth to seven,	**1Sa 2:5**	3205
O king, Araunah **g** to the king."	**2Sa 24:23**	5414
"He **g** rain on the earth And	**Jb 5:10**	5414
He inflicts pain, and **g** relief;	**Jb 5:18**	2280
the flame of his fire **g** no light.	**Jb 18:5**	5050
the Almighty **g** them understanding.	**Jb 32:8**	995
breath of the Almighty **g** me life.	**Jb 33:4**	2421a
Maker, Who **g** songs in the night,	**Jb 35:10**	5414
But **g** justice to the afflicted.	**Jb 36:6**	5414
He **g** food in abundance.	**Jb 36:31**	5414
g great deliverance to His king,	**Ps 18:50**	
the righteous is gracious and **g**.	**Ps 37:21**	5414
The Lord **g** the command;	**Ps 68:11**	5414
The God of Israel Himself **g**	**Ps 68:35**	5414
The LORD **g** grace and glory;	**Ps 84:11**	5414
unfolding of Your words **g** light;	**Ps 119:130**	215
It **g** understanding to the simple.	**Ps 119:130**	995
For He **g** to His beloved *even in*	**Ps 127:2**	5414
Who **g** food to all flesh, For His	**Ps 136:25**	5414
Who **g** salvation to kings, Who	**Ps 144:10**	5414
Who **g** food to the hungry.	**Ps 146:7**	5414
He **g** names to all of them.	**Ps 147:4**	7121
He **g** to the beast its food, *And* to	**Ps 147:9**	5414
He **g** snow like wool;	**Ps 147:16**	5414
For the LORD **g** wisdom;	**Pr 2:6**	5414
Yet He **g** grace to the afflicted.	**Pr 3:34**	5414
He who **g** attention to the word	**Pr 16:20**	7919a
who **g** an answer before he hears,	**Pr 18:13**	7725
is a friend to him who **g** gifts.	**Pr 19:6**	
g and does not hold back.	**Pr 21:26**	5414
he **g** some of his food to the poor.	**Pr 22:9**	5414
for himself Or who **g** to the rich,	**Pr 22:16**	5414
the lips Who **g** a right answer.	**Pr 24:26**	7725
man who **g** way before the wicked.	**Pr 25:26**	4131
So is he who **g** honor to a fool.	**Pr 26:8**	5414
who **g** to the poor will never want,	**Pr 28:27**	5414
The king **g** stability to the land	**Pr 29:4**	5975
LORD **g** light to the eyes of both.	**Pr 29:13**	215
And **g** food to her household And	**Pr 31:15**	5414
then he **g** his legacy to one who	**Ec 2:21**	5414
the LORD **g** you rest from your pain	**Is 14:3**	5117
He **g** strength to the weary, And to	**Is 40:29**	5414
Who **g** breath to the people on it And	**Is 42:5**	5414
I who **g** delivery shut *the womb?*"	**Is 66:9**	3205
our God, Who **g** rain in its season,	**Jer 5:24**	5414
Who **g** the sun for light by day And	**Jer 31:35**	5414
but **g** his bread to the hungry and	**Ezk 18:7**	5414
but he **g** his bread to the hungry and	**Ezk 18:16**	5414
"If the prince **g** a gift *out of*	**Ezk 46:16**	5414
"But if he **g** a gift from his	**Ezk 46:17**	5414
He **g** wisdom to wise men And	**Da 2:21**	3052
and it **g** light to all who are in	**Mt 5:15**	*2989*
g to one of these little ones even a cup	**Mt 10:42**	*4222*
for even the way you talk **g** you away."	**Mt 26:73**	*4160*
"For whoever **g** you a cup of water	**Mk 9:41**	*4222*
He **g** the Spirit without measure.	**Jn 3:34**	*1325*
raises the dead and **g** them life,	**Jn 5:21**	*2227*
Son also **g** life to whom He wishes.	**Jn 5:21**	*2227*
I know that the testimony which He **g**	**Jn 5:32**	*3140*
but it is My Father who **g** you the	**Jn 6:32**	*1325*
heaven, and **g** life to the world."	**Jn 6:33**	*1325*
the Father **g** Me will come to Me,	**Jn 6:37**	*1325*
"It is the Spirit who **g** life;	**Jn 6:63**	*2227*
not as the world **g** do I give to you	**Jn 14:27**	*1325*
but when she **g** birth to the child,	**Jn 16:21**	*1080*
since He Himself **g** to all *people* life and	**Ac 17:25**	*1325*
who **g** life to the dead and calls	**Ro 4:17**	*2227*
he who **g**, with liberality;	**Ro 12:8**	*3330*
the Lord, for he **g** thanks to God;	**Ro 14:6**	*2168*
does not eat, and **g** thanks to God.	**Ro 14:6**	*2168*
the man who eats and **g** offense.	**Ro 14:20**	*1223*
Now may the God who **g** perseverance	**Ro 15:5**	*1325*
So then both he who **g** his own	**1Co 7:38**	*1061a*
God **g** it a body just as He wished,	**1Co 15:38**	*1325*
who **g** us the victory through our	**1Co 15:57**	*1325*
kills, but the Spirit **g** life.	**2Co 3:6**	*2227*
God who **g** His Holy Spirit to you.	**1Th 4:8**	*1325*
But she who **g** herself to wanton	**1Tm 5:6**	*4684*
of God, who **g** life to all things,	**1Tm 6:13**	*2225*
but He **g** help to the descendant of	**Heb 2:16**	*1949*
who **g** to all generously and	**Jas 1:5**	*1325*
has conceived, it **g** birth to sin;	**Jas 1:15**	*5088*
But He **g** a greater grace.	**Jas 4:6**	*1325*
BUT **G** GRACE TO THE HUMBLE."	**Jas 4:6**	*1325*
PROUD, BUT **G** GRACE TO THE HUMBLE.	**1Pe 5:5**	*1325*
for the one who **g** him a greeting	**2Jn 1:11**	*3004*

GIVING

she had finished **g** him a drink,	**Gn 24:19**	8248
about at the time she was **g** birth,	**Gn 38:27**	3205
took place while she was **g** birth,	**Gn 38:28**	3205
you are to live, which I am **g** you,	**Nu 15:2**	5414
I am **g** you the priesthood as a	**Nu 18:7**	5414
the LORD our God is **g** to us.'	**Dt 2:29**	5414
the God of your fathers, is **g** you.	**Dt 4:1**	5414
God is **g** you as an inheritance.	**Dt 4:21**	5414
which I am **g** you today,	**Dt 4:40**	6680
your God is **g** you for all time."	**Dt 4:40**	5414
who is **g** you power to make wealth,	**Dt 8:18**	5414
g you this good land to possess,	**Dt 9:6**	5414
alien by **g** him food and clothing.	**Dt 10:18**	5414
good land which the LORD is **g** you.	**Dt 11:17**	5414
which the LORD your God is **g** you,	**Dt 11:31**	5414
which the LORD your God is **g** you.	**Dt 12:9**	5414
LORD your God is **g** you to inherit,	**Dt 12:10**	
LORD your God is **g** you to live in,	**Dt 13:12**	5414
land which the LORD your God is **g**	**Dt 15:4**	5414
which the LORD your God is **g** you;	**Dt 15:7**	5414
which the LORD your God is **g** you;	**Dt 16:5**	5414
which the LORD your God is **g** you,	**Dt 16:18**	5414
which the LORD your God is **g** you,	**Dt 16:20**	5414
which the LORD your God is **g** you,	**Dt 17:2**	5414

God is **g** you as an inheritance, **Dt 20:16** 5414
by **g** him a double portion of all **Dt 21:17** 5414
which I am **g** to the sons of Israel **Dt 32:49** 5414
which I am **g** the sons of Israel." **Dt 32:52** 5414
to the land which I am **g** to them, **Jos 1:2** 5414
which the LORD your God is **g** you, **Jos 1:11** 5414
which the LORD your God is **g** them. **Jos 1:15** 5414
visited His people in **g** them food. **Ru 1:6** 5414
by **g** food to my household." **1Ki 5:9** 5414
and justifying the righteous by **g** him **1Ki 8:32** 5414
that you are **g** your servant into **1Ki 18:9** 5414
which David made for **g** praise. **1Ch 23:5** 1984b
in **g** thanks and praising the LORD. **1Ch 25:3** 3034
and justifying the righteous by **g** him **2Ch 6:23** 5414
David had made for **g** praise to the **2Ch 7:6** 3034
and **g** thanks to the LORD God **2Ch 30:22** 3034
praising and **g** thanks to the LORD, **Ezr 3:11** 3034
In **g** them the heritage of the **Ps 111:6** 5414
has the advantage of **g** success. **Ec 10:10** 3787
'To what are you **g** birth?' " **Is 45:10** 2342a
G them a garland instead of ashes, **Is 61:3** 5414
of one **g** birth to her first child, **Jer 4:31** 1069
g to everyone according to his **Jer 32:19** 5414
I am **g** this city into the hand of **Jer 34:2** 5414
who were **g** him *such* an answer **Jer 44:20** 6030a
mouth and eat what I am **g** you." **Ezk 2:8** 5414
this scroll which I am **g** you." **Ezk 3:3** 5414
drink, and kept **g** them vegetables. **Da 1:16** 5414
He answered by **g** orders to heat **Da 3:19** 560
and **g** thanks before his God, **Da 6:10** 3029
and **g** attention to Your truth. **Da 9:13** 7919a
have stopped **g** heed to the LORD. **Hos 4:10** 8104
so that your **g** will be in secret; **Mt 6:4** *1654*
When Jesus had finished **g** instructions **Mt 11:1** *1299*
and **g** thanks, He broke them and **Mt 15:36** *2168*
started **g** them to the disciples, **Mt 15:36** *1325*
marrying and **g** in marriage, **Mt 24:38** *1061a*
broke the loaves and He kept **g** *them* **Mk 6:41** *1325*
and started **g** them to His **Mk 8:6** *1325*
And He was **g** orders to them, **Mk 8:15** *1291*
g false testimony against Him, **Mk 14:56** *5576*
came up and *began* **g** thanks to God, **Lk 2:38** *437*
and kept **g** *them* to the disciples **Lk 9:16** *1325*
"A man was **g** a big dinner, **Lk 14:16** *4160*
and no one was **g** *anything* to him. **Lk 15:16** *1325*
face at His feet, **g** thanks to Him. **Lk 17:16** *2168*
it, He *began* **g** *it* to them. **Lk 24:30** *1929*
the Spirit was **g** them utterance. **Ac 2:4** *1325*
were **g** testimony to the resurrection **Ac 4:33** *591*
g attention to what was said by Philip, **Ac 8:6** *4337*
greatest, were **g** attention to him, **Ac 8:10** *4337*
And they were **g** him attention **Ac 8:11** *4337*
to them **g** them the Holy Spirit, **Ac 15:8** *1325*
explaining and **g** evidence that the **Ac 17:3** *3908*
g notice of the completion of the **Ac 21:26** *1229*
g orders for him to be kept in **Ac 23:35** *2753*
strong in faith, **g** glory to God, **Ro 4:20** *1325*
the covenants and the **g** of the Law **Ro 9:4** *3548*
But in **g** this instruction, I do **1Co 11:17** *3853*
g more abundant honor to that **1Co 12:24** *1325*
"Amen" at your **g** of thanks, **1Co 14:16** *2169*
For you are **g** thanks well enough, **1Co 14:17** *2168*
people may cause the **g** of thanks **2Co 4:15** *2169*
g you an occasion to be proud of us, **2Co 5:12** *1325*
g no cause for offense in **2Co 6:3** *1325*
do not cease **g** thanks for you, **Eph 1:16** *2168*
fitting, but rather **g** of thanks. **Eph 5:4** *2169*
always **g** thanks for all things in **Eph 5:20** *2168*
of **g** and receiving but you alone; **Php 4:15** *1394*
g thanks to the Father, who has **Col 1:12** *2168*
g thanks through Him to God the **Col 3:17** *2168*
insult, but **g** a blessing instead; **1Pe 3:9** *2127*
by **g** their kingdom to the beast, **Rv 17:17** *1325*

GIZONITE
the sons of Hashem the **G**, **1Ch 11:34** 1493

GLAD
you, he will be **g** in his heart. **Ex 4:14** 8055
your God with joy and a **g** heart, **Dt 28:47** 2898
The priest's heart was **g**, **Jg 18:20** 3190
saw him, he was **g** to meet him. **Jg 19:3** 8055
saw the ark and were **g** to see *it.* **1Sa 6:13** 8055
the men of Jabesh; and they were **g**. **1Sa 11:9** 8055
they went to their tents joyful and **g** **1Ki 8:66** 2896a
of those who seek the LORD be **g**. **1Ch 16:10** 8055
Let the heavens be **g**, **1Ch 16:31** 8055
that day and **g** and pleased of heart; **Es 5:9** 8056
"The righteous see and are **g**, **Jb 22:19** 8055
all who take refuge in You be **g**, **Ps 5:11** 8055
I will be **g** and exult in You; **Ps 9:2** 8055
Jacob will rejoice, Israel will be **g**. **Ps 14:7** 8055
Therefore my heart is **g** and **Ps 16:9** 8055
Your strength the king will be **g**, **Ps 21:1** 8055
and be **g** in Your lovingkindness, **Ps 31:7** 8055
Be **g** in the LORD and rejoice, **Ps 32:11** 8055
I have proclaimed **g** tidings of **Ps 40:9** 1319
You rejoice and be **g** in You; **Ps 40:16** 8055
instruments have made You **g**. **Ps 45:8** 8055
streams make **g** the city of God, **Ps 46:4** 8055
Let Mount Zion be **g**, **Ps 48:11** 8055
Jacob rejoice, let Israel be **g**. **Ps 53:6** 8055
man will be **g** in the LORD and **Ps 64:10** 8055
the nations be **g** and sing for joy; **Ps 67:4** 8055
But let the righteous be **g**; **Ps 68:3** 8055
The humble have seen *it and* are **g**; **Ps 69:32** 8055
You rejoice and be **g** in You; **Ps 70:4** 8055
Make **g** the soul of Your servant, **Ps 86:4** 8055
for joy and be **g** all our days. **Ps 90:14** 8055
Make us **g** according to the days **Ps 90:15** 8055
made me **g** by what You have done, **Ps 92:4** 8055
Let the heavens be **g**, **Ps 96:11** 8055
Let the many islands be **g**. **Ps 97:1** 8055
Zion heard *this* and was **g**, **Ps 97:8** 8055
Be **g** in the LORD, you righteous **Ps 97:12** 8055
And wine which makes man's heart **g**, **Ps 104:15** 8055
Let the LORD be **g** in His works; **Ps 104:31** 8055
for me, I shall be **g** in the LORD. **Ps 104:34** 8055
of those who seek the LORD be **g**. **Ps 105:3** 8055
Egypt was **g** when they departed, **Ps 105:38** 8055
were **g** because they were quiet, **Ps 107:30** 8055
The upright see it and are **g**; **Ps 107:42** 8055
But Your servant shall be **g**. **Ps 109:28** 8055
Let us rejoice and be **g** in it. **Ps 118:24** 8055
who fear You see me and be **g**, **Ps 119:74** 8055
I was **g** when they said to me, **Ps 122:1** 8055
done great things for us; We are **g**. **Ps 126:3** 8056
Let Israel be **g** in his Maker; **Ps 149:2** 8055
A wise son makes a father **g**, **Pr 10:1** 8055
down, But a good word makes it **g**. **Pr 12:25** 8055
A wise son makes a father **g**, **Pr 15:20** 8055
wise, My own heart also will be **g**; **Pr 23:15** 8055
a wise son will be **g** in him. **Pr 23:24** 8055
your father and your mother be **g**, **Pr 23:25** 8055
your heart be **g** when he stumbles; **Pr 24:17** 1523
Oil and perfume make the heart **g**, **Pr 27:9** 8055
wise, my son, and make my heart **g**, **Pr 27:11** 8055
loves wisdom makes his father **g**, **Pr 29:3** 8055
"We will rejoice in you and be **g**; **SS 1:4** 8055
They will be **g** in Your presence As **Is 9:3** 8055
rejoice and be **g** in His salvation." **Is 25:9** 8055
wilderness and the desert will be **g**, **Is 35:1** 1523
shout joyfully with a **g** heart, **Is 65:14** 2898
"But be **g** and rejoice forever in **Is 65:18** 7797
Jerusalem and be **g** in My people; **Is 65:19** 7797
Be exceedingly **g** with her, all you **Is 66:10** 7797
this, and your heart will be **g**, **Is 66:14** 7797
that were with him, they were **g**. **Jer 41:13** 8055
"Because you are **g**, because you **Jer 50:11** 8055
They are **g** that You have done *it.* **La 1:21** 7797
Rejoice and be **g**, O daughter of **La 4:21** 8055
wickedness they make the king **g**, **Hos 7:3** 8055
fear, O land, rejoice and be **g**, **Jl 2:21** 8055
And be **g** in the LORD your God; **Jl 2:23** 8055
Therefore they rejoice and are **g**. **Hab 1:15** 1523
"Sing for joy and be **g**, **Zch 2:10** 8055
But these seven will be **g** when **Zch 4:10** 8055
heart will be **g** as if *from* wine; **Zch 10:7** 8055
children will see *it* and be **g**, **Zch 10:7** 8055
"Rejoice and be **g**, for your **Mt 5:12** *21*
They were **g** when they heard *this,* **Mk 14:11** *5463*
"Be **g** in that day and leap *for* **Lk 6:23** *5463*
They were **g** and agreed to **Lk 22:5** *5463*
was very **g** when he saw Jesus; **Lk 23:8** *5463*
My day, and he saw *it* and was **g**." **Jn 8:56** *5463*
and I am **g** for your sakes that I **Jn 11:15** *5463*
MY HEART WAS **G** AND MY TONGUE **Ac 2:26** *2165*
who then makes me **g** but the one **2Co 2:2** *2165*
I was very **g** to find *some* of your **2Jn 1:4** *5463*
For I was very **g** when brethren **3Jn 1:3** *5463*
be **g** and give the glory to Him, **Rv 19:7** *21*

GLADDEN
Bright eyes **g** the heart; **Pr 15:30** 8055

GLADLY
chosen **g** to give you the kingdom. **Lk 12:32** *2106*
"And he would have **g** filled his **Lk 15:16** *1937*
and came down and received Him **g**. **Lk 19:6** *5463*
the brethren received us **g**. **Ac 21:17** *780*
so wise, tolerate the foolish **g**. **2Co 11:19** *2234*
Most **g**, therefore, I will rather **2Co 12:9** *2234*
I will most **g** spend and be **2Co 12:15** *2234*

GLADNESS
g and in your appointed feasts, **Nu 10:10** 8057
into the city of David with **g**. **2Sa 6:12** 8057
day before the LORD with great **g**. **1Ch 29:22** 8057
celebrate the dedication with **g**, **Ne 12:27** 8057
was light and **g** and joy and honor. **Es 8:16** 8057
there was **g** and joy for the Jews, **Es 8:17** 8057
turned for them from sorrow into **g** **Es 9:22** 8057
You have put **g** in my heart, More **Ps 4:7** 8057
him joyful with **g** in Your presence. **Ps 21:6** 8057
my sackcloth and girded me with **g**, **Ps 30:11** 8057
be led forth with **g** and rejoicing; **Ps 45:15** 8057
Make me to hear joy and **g**, **Ps 51:8** 8057
Yes, let them rejoice with **g**. **Ps 68:3** 8057
And **g** for the upright in heart. **Ps 97:11** 8057
Serve the LORD with **g**; **Ps 100:2** 8057
rejoice in the **g** of Your nation, **Ps 106:5** 8057
The hope of the righteous is **g**, **Pr 10:28** 8057
occupied with the **g** of his heart. **Ec 5:20** 8057
on the day of his **g** of heart." **SS 3:11** 8057
You shall increase their **g**; **Is 9:3** 8057
presence As with the **g** of harvest, **Is 9:3** 8057
G and joy are taken away from **Is 16:10** 8057
Instead, there is gaiety and **g**, **Is 22:13** 8057
increase their **g** in the LORD, **Is 29:19** 8057
And **g** of heart as when one marches **Is 30:29** 8057
They will find **g** and joy, And **Is 35:10** 8342
Joy and **g** will be found in her, **Is 51:3** 8057
They will obtain **g** and joy, **Is 51:11** 8342
The oil of **g** instead of mourning, **Is 61:3** 8342
rejoicing And her people *for* **g**. **Is 65:18** 4885
voice of joy and the voice of **g**, **Jer 7:34** 8057
of rejoicing and the voice of **g**, **Jer 16:9** 8057
voice of joy and the voice of **g**, **Jer 25:10** 8057
"Sing aloud with **g** for Jacob, And **Jer 31:7** 8057
voice of joy and the voice of **g**, **Jer 33:11** 8057
"So **g** and joy are taken away From **Jer 48:33** 8057
G and joy from the house of our **Jl 1:16** 8057
tenth *months* will become joy, **g**, **Zch 8:19** 8057
"You will have joy and **g**, **Lk 1:14** *20*
ME FULL OF **G** WITH YOUR PRESENCE.' **Ac 2:28** *2167*
with **g** and sincerity of heart, **Ac 2:46** *20*
your hearts with food and **g**." **Ac 14:17** *2167*
OIL OF **G** ABOVE YOUR COMPANIONS." **Heb 1:9** *20*

GLANCE
heart beat faster with a single **g** **SS 4:9**

GLARES
My adversary **g** at me. **Jb 16:9** 3913, 5869

GLASS
"Gold or **g** cannot equal it, Nor **Jb 28:17** 2137
like a sea of **g**, like crystal; **Rv 4:6** *5193*
like a sea of **g** mixed with fire, **Rv 15:2** *5193*
name, standing on the sea of **g**, **Rv 15:2** *5193*
city was pure gold, like clear **g**. **Rv 21:18** *5194*
was pure gold, like transparent **g**. **Rv 21:21** *5194*

GLEAM
like the awesome **g** of crystal, **Ezk 1:22** 5869
like the **g** of a Tarshish stone. **Ezk 10:9** 5869
like the **g** of polished bronze, **Da 10:6** 5869

GLEAMED
and they **g** like burnished bronze. **Ezk 1:7** 5340a

GLEAMING
Swords flashing, spears **g**, **Na 3:3** 1300
At the radiance of Your **g** spear. **Hab 3:11** 1300
His clothing *became* white *and* **g**. **Lk 9:29** *1823*

GLEAN
'Nor shall you **g** your vineyard, **Lv 19:10** 5953b
let me go to the field and **g** among the **Ru 2:2** 3950
'Please let me **g** and gather after **Ru 2:7** 3950
Do not go to **g** in another field; **Ru 2:8** 3950
When she rose to **g**, **Ru 2:15** 3950
"Let her **g** even among the **Ru 2:15** 3950
and leave *it* that she may **g**, **Ru 2:16** 3950
"Where did you **g** today and where **Ru 2:19** 3950
to **g** until the end of the barley harvest **Ru 2:23** 3950
And **g** the vineyard of the wicked. **Jb 24:6** 3953
"They will thoroughly **g** as the **Jer 6:9** 5953b

GLEANED
So she departed and went and **g** in **Ru 2:3** 3950
she **g** in the field until evening. **Ru 2:17** 3950
Then she beat out what she had **g**, **Ru 2:17** 3950
mother-in-law saw what she had **g**. **Ru 2:18** 3950

GLEANING
nor gather the **g** of your harvest; **Lv 23:22** 3951
Is not the **g** *of the grapes of* **Jg 8:2** 5955
Or it will be like one **g** ears of **Is 17:5** 3950

GLEANINGS
you gather the **g** of your harvest. **Lv 19:9** 3951
Yet **g** will be left in it like the **Is 17:6** 5955
As the **g** when the grape harvest is **Is 24:13** 5955
to you, Would they not leave **g**? **Jer 49:9** 5955
you, Would they not leave *some* **g**? **Ob 1:5** 5955

GLISTEN
he may make *his* face **g** with oil, **Ps 104:15** 6670b

GLISTENING
And its pinions with **g** gold. **Ps 68:13** 3422

GLITTERING
Even the **g** point from his gall. **Jb 20:25** 1300
I have given the **g** sword. **Ezk 21:15** 19

GLOAT
"Do not **g** over your brother's **Ob 1:12** 7200
do not **g** over their calamity In **Ob 1:13** 7200
And let our eyes **g** over Zion.' **Mi 4:11** 2372

GLOATED
g because my wealth was great, **Jb 31:25** 8055

GLOOM
darkness, cloud and thick **g**. **Dt 4:11** 6205
of the cloud and *of* the thick **g**, **Dt 5:22** 6205
"Let darkness and black **g** claim it; **Jb 3:5** 6757
of utter **g** as darkness *itself,* **Jb 10:22** 5890
Nor deep **g** *which* covers me. **Jb 23:17** 652
he searches out The rock in **g** and **Jb 28:3** 652
and darkness, the **g** of anguish; **Is 8:22** 4588
more **g** for her who was in anguish; **Is 9:1** 4155
All joy turns to **g**. **Is 24:11** 6150
And out of *their* **g** and darkness **Is 29:18** 652
your **g** *will become* like midday. **Is 58:10** 653
For brightness, but we walk in **g**. **Is 59:9** 653
darkness, *And* turns *it* into **g**. **Jer 13:16** 6205
into the **g** and fall down in it; **Jer 23:12** 653
A day of darkness and **g**, **Jl 2:2** 653
Even **g** with no brightness in it? **Am 5:20** 651
A day of darkness and **g**, **Zph 1:15** 653
to darkness and **g** and whirlwind, **Heb 12:18** *2217*
into mourning and your joy to **g**. **Jas 4:9** *2726*

GLOOMY
scattered on a cloudy and **g** day. **Ezk 34:12** 6205
on a **g** face as the hypocrites *do,* **Mt 6:16** *4659*

GLORIES
of Christ and the **g** to follow. **1Pe 1:11** *1391*

GLORIFIED
increased the nation, You are **g**; **Is 26:15** 3513
For He has **g** you." **Is 55:5** 6286
of Israel because He has **g** you. **Is 60:9** 6286
work of My hands, That I may be **g**. **Is 60:21** 6286
of the LORD, that He may be **g**. **Is 61:3** 6286
'Let the LORD be **g**, that we may **Is 66:5** 3513
And I will be **g** in your midst. **Ezk 28:22** 3513
and your ways, you have not **g**. **Da 5:23** 1922
may be pleased with it and be **g**," **Hg 1:8** 3513
were awestruck, and **g** God, **Mt 9:8** *1392*

and they g the God of Israel. Mt 15:31 1392
because Jesus was not yet g. Jn 7:39 1392
the Son of God may be g by it." Jn 11:4 1392
but when Jesus was g, Jn 12:16 1392
come for the Son of Man to be g. Jn 12:23 1392
"I have both g it, and will Jn 12:28 1392
"Now is the Son of Man g, Jn 13:31 1392
glorified, and God is g in Him; Jn 13:31 1392
if God is g in Him, God will also Jn 13:32 1392
the Father may be g in the Son. Jn 14:13 1392
"My Father is g by this, Jn 15:8 1392
"I g You on the earth, having Jn 17:4 1392
and I have been g in them. Jn 17:10 1392
fathers, has g His servant Jesus, Ac 3:13 1392
they quieted down and g God, Ac 11:18 1392
that we may also be g with *Him.* Ro 8:17 4888
He justified, He also g. Ro 8:30 1392
to be g in His saints on that day, 2Th 1:10 1740
of our Lord Jesus will be g in you, 2Th 1:12 1740
Lord will spread rapidly and be g, 2Th 3:1 1392
God may be g through Jesus Christ, 1Pe 4:11 1392
g herself and lived sensuously, Rv 18:7 1392

GLORIFIES

it is My Father who g Me, Jn 8:54 1392

GLORIFY

voice to praise and to g the LORD, 2Ch 5:13 3034
you descendants of Jacob, g Him, Ps 22:23 3513
And they shall g Your name. Ps 86:9 3513
And will g Your name forever. Ps 86:12 3513
Therefore g the LORD in the east, Is 24:15 3513
a strong people will g You; Is 25:3 3513
"The beasts of the field will g Me, Is 43:20 3513
And I shall g My glorious house. Is 60:7 6286
on the day that I g Myself," Ezk 39:13 3513
g your Father who is in heaven. Mt 5:16 1392
"If I g Myself, My glory is Jn 8:54 1392
"Father, g Your name." Jn 12:28 1392
it, and will g it again." Jn 12:28 1392
God will also g Him in Himself, Jn 13:32 1392
and will g Him immediately. Jn 13:32 1392
"He will g Me, for He will take of Jn 16:14 1392
g Your Son, that the Son may Jn 17:1 1392
Your Son, that the Son may g You, Jn 17:1 1392
g Me together with Yourself, Jn 17:5 1392
what kind of death he would g God. Jn 21:19 1392
with one voice g the God and Father Ro 15:6 1392
Gentiles to g God for His mercy; Ro 15:9 1392
therefore g God in your body. 1Co 6:20 1392
they will g God for *your* obedience 2Co 9:13 1392
So also Christ did not g Himself Heb 5:5 1392
g God in the day of visitation. 1Pe 2:12 1392
but is to g God in this name. 1Pe 4:16 1392
not fear, O Lord, and g Your name? Rv 15:4 1392

GLORIFYING

were all amazed and were g God, Mk 2:12 1392
g and praising God for all that Lk 2:20 1392
lying on, and went home g God. Lk 5:25 1392
with astonishment and *began* g God; Lk 5:26 1392
them all, and they *began* g God, Lk 7:16 1392
made erect again and *began* g God. Lk 13:13 1392
back, g God with a loud voice, Lk 17:15 1392
and *began* following Him, g God; Lk 18:43 1392
all g God for what had happened; Ac 4:21 1392
and g the word of the Lord; Ac 13:48 1392
they heard it they *began* g God; Ac 21:20 1392
And they were g God because of me. Ga 1:24 1392

GLORIOUS

famous and g throughout all lands. 1Ch 22:5 8597
thank You, and praise Your g name. 1Ch 29:13 8597
O may Your g name be blessed And Ne 9:5 3519b
King's daughter is all g within; Ps 45:13 3519a
Make His praise g. Ps 66:2 3519b
And blessed be His g name forever; Ps 72:19 3519b
G things are spoken of you, O city Ps 87:3 3513
On the g splendor of Your majesty And Ps 145:5 3519b
To rebel against His g presence. Is 3:8 3519b
the LORD will be beautiful and g, Is 4:2 3519b
but later on He shall make *it* g, Is 9:1 3513
And His resting place will be g. Is 11:10 3519b
the fading flower of its g beauty, Is 28:1 6643a
the fading flower of its g beauty, Is 28:4 6643a
a g diadem to the remnant of His Is 28:5 8597
sake To make the law great and g. Is 42:21 142
And I shall glorify My g house. Is 60:7 8597
shall make the place of My feet g. Is 60:13 3513
Who caused His g arm to go at the Is 63:12 8597
To make for Yourself a g name. Is 63:14 8597
from Your holy and g habitation; Is 63:15 8597
A g throne on high from the Jer 17:12 3519b
very g In the heart of the seas. Ezk 27:25 3513
the g *trees* have been destroyed; Zch 11:2 117
of Man will sit on His g throne, Mt 19:28 1391
then He will sit on His g throne. Mt 25:31 1391
the g things being done by Him. Lk 13:17 1741
AND G DAY OF THE LORD SHALL COME Ac 2:20 2016
power, according to His g might, Col 1:11 1391
the g gospel of the blessed God, 1Tm 1:11 1391
do not hold your faith in our g Jas 2:1 1391

GLORY

Let not my g be united with their Gn 49:6 3519b
you will see the g of the LORD, Ex 16:7 3519b
the g of the LORD appeared in the Ex 16:10 3519b
The g of the LORD rested on Ex 24:16 3519b
the appearance of the g of the LORD Ex 24:17 3519b
brother, for g and for beauty. Ex 28:2 3519b
for them, for g and for beauty. Ex 28:40 3519b
it shall be consecrated by My g. Ex 29:43 3519b
"I pray You, show me Your g!" Ex 33:18 3519b
about, while My g is passing by, Ex 33:22 3519b
and the g of the LORD filled the Ex 40:34 3519b
and the g of the LORD filled the Ex 40:35 3519b
g of the LORD may appear to you." Lv 9:6 3519b
the g of the LORD appeared to all Lv 9:23 3519b
Then the g of the LORD appeared in Nu 14:10 3519b
be filled with the g of the LORD. Nu 14:21 3519b
who have seen My g and My signs Nu 14:22 3519b
And the g of the LORD appeared to Nu 16:19 3519b
it and the g of the LORD appeared. Nu 16:42 3519b
g of the LORD appeared to them; Nu 20:6 3519b
shown us His g and His greatness, Dt 5:24 3519b
I implore you, give g to the LORD, Jos 7:19 3519b
"The g has departed from Israel," 1Sa 4:21 3519b
"The g has departed from Israel, 1Sa 4:22 3519b
shall give g to the God of Israel; 1Sa 6:5 3519b
"Also the G of Israel will 1Sa 15:29 5331
for the g of the LORD filled the 1Ki 8:11 3519b
Enjoy your g and stay at home; 2Ki 14:10 3513
G in His holy name; 1Ch 16:10 1984b
Tell of His g among the nations, 1Ch 16:24 3519b
Ascribe to the LORD g and strength 1Ch 16:28 3519b
to the LORD the g due His name; 1Ch 16:29 3519b
holy name, And g in Your praise." 1Ch 16:35 7623b
the power and the g and the victory 1Ch 29:11 8597
for the g of the LORD filled the 2Ch 5:14 3519b
g of the LORD filled the house. 2Ch 7:1 3519b
because the g of the LORD filled 2Ch 7:2 3519b
the g of the LORD upon the house, 2Ch 7:3 3519b
he displayed the riches of his royal g Es 1:4 3519b
to them the g of his riches, Es 5:11 3519b
'My g is *ever* new with me, And my Jb 29:20 3519b
LORD, are a shield about me, My g, Ps 3:3 3519b
And lay my g in the dust. Ps 7:5 3519b
You crown him with g and majesty! Ps 8:5 3519b
heart is glad and my g rejoices; Ps 16:9 3519b
are telling of the g of God; Ps 19:1 3519b
His g is great through Your Ps 21:5 3519b
That the King of g may come in! Ps 24:7 3519b
Who is the King of g? Ps 24:8 3519b
That the King of g may come in! Ps 24:9 3519b
Who is this King of g? Ps 24:10 3519b
of hosts, He is the King of g. Ps 24:10 3519b
And the place where Your g dwells. Ps 26:8 3519b
to the LORD g and strength. Ps 29:1 3519b
to the LORD the g due to His name; Ps 29:2 3519b
The God of g thunders, The LORD is Ps 29:3 3519b
His temple everything says, "G!" Ps 29:9 3519b
be like the g of the pastures, Ps 37:20 3368
The g of Jacob whom He loves. Ps 47:4 1347b
the g of his house is increased; Ps 49:16 3519b
His g will not descend after him. Ps 49:17 3519b
Let Your g *be* above all the earth. Ps 57:5 3519b
Awake, my g! Awake, harp and lyre Ps 57:8 3519b
Let Your g *be* above all the earth. Ps 57:11 3519b
On God my salvation and my g *rest;* Ps 62:7 3519b
To see Your power and Your g. Ps 63:2 3519b
Everyone who swears by Him will g, Ps 63:11 1984b
all the upright in heart will g. Ps 64:10 1984b
Sing the g of His name; Ps 66:2 3519b
And with Your g all day long. Ps 71:8 8597
whole earth be filled with His g. Ps 72:19 3519b
me, And afterward receive me to g. Ps 73:24 3519b
And His g into the hand of the Ps 78:61 8597
salvation, for the g of Your name; Ps 79:9 3519b
The LORD gives grace and g; Ps 84:11 3519b
Him, That g may dwell in our land. Ps 85:9 3519b
You are the g of their strength, Ps 89:17 8597
Tell of His g among the nations, Ps 96:3 3519b
to the LORD g and strength. Ps 96:7 3519b
to the LORD the g of His name; Ps 96:8 3519b
all the peoples have seen His g. Ps 97:6 3519b
all the kings of the earth Your g. Ps 102:15 3519b
He has appeared in His g. Ps 102:16 3519b
the g of the LORD endure forever; Ps 104:31 3519b
G in His holy name; Ps 105:3 1984b
I may g with Your inheritance. Ps 106:5 1984b
Thus they exchanged their g For Ps 106:20 3519b
holy name And g in Your praise. Ps 106:47 7623b
And Your g above all the earth. Ps 108:5 3519b
His g is above the heavens. Ps 113:4 3519b
g Because of Your lovingkindness, Ps 115:1 3519b
For great is the g of the LORD. Ps 138:5 3519b
speak of the g of Your kingdom And Ps 145:11 3519b
g of the majesty of Your kingdom. Ps 145:12 3519b
His g is above earth and heaven. Ps 148:13 1935
Let the godly ones exult in g; Ps 149:5 3519b
multitude of people is a king's g, Pr 14:28 1927a
A gray head is a crown of g; Pr 16:31 8597
the g of sons is their fathers. Pr 17:6 8597
his g to overlook a transgression. Pr 19:11 8597
The g of young men is their Pr 20:29 8597
the g of God to conceal a matter, Pr 25:2 3519b
But the g of kings is to search Pr 25:2 3519b
Nor is it g to search out one's own Pr 25:27 3519b
it glory to search out one's own g. Pr 25:27 3519b
triumph, there is great g, Pr 28:12 8597
over all the g will be a canopy. Is 4:5 3519b
whole earth is full of His g." Is 6:3 3519b
the king of Assyria and all his g; Is 8:7 3519b
And under his g a fire will be Is 10:16 3519b
And He will destroy the g of his Is 10:18 3519b
the g of the Chaldeans' pride, Is 13:19 8597
the kings of the nations lie in g, Is 14:18 3519b
the g of Moab will be degraded Is 16:14 3519b
the g of the sons of Israel," Is 17:3 3519b
day the g of Jacob will fade, Is 17:4 3519b
throne of g to his father's house. Is 22:23 3519b
all the g of his father's house, Is 22:24 3519b
"G to the Righteous One," Is 24:16 6643a
His g will be before His elders. Is 24:23 3519b
The g of Lebanon will be given to Is 35:2 3519b
They will see the g of the LORD, Is 35:2 3519b
g of the LORD will be revealed, Is 40:5 3519b
will g in the Holy One of Israel. Is 41:16 1984b
I will not give My g to another, Is 42:8 3519b
Let them give g to the LORD And Is 42:12 3519b
And whom I have created for My g, Is 43:7 3519b
in Israel He shows forth His g. Is 44:23 6286
Will be justified and will g." Is 45:25 1984b
in Zion, *And* My g for Israel. Is 46:13 8597
My g I will not give to another. Is 48:11 3519b
In Whom I will show My g." Is 49:3 6286
The g of the LORD will be your Is 58:8 3519b
His g from the rising of the sun, Is 59:19 3519b
And the g of the LORD has risen Is 60:1 3519b
And His g will appear upon you. Is 60:2 3519b
"The g of Lebanon will come to Is 60:13 3519b
light, And your God for your g. Is 60:19 8597
And all kings your g; Is 62:2 3519b
And the g of the nations like an Is 66:12 3519b
And they shall come and see My g. Is 66:18 3519b
heard My fame nor seen My g. Is 66:19 3519b
declare My g among the nations. Is 66:19 3519b
But My people have changed their g Jer 2:11 3519b
in Him, And in Him they will g." Jer 4:2 1984b
for renown, for praise and for g; Jer 13:11 8597
Give g to the LORD your God, Jer 13:16 3519b
not disgrace the throne of Your g; Jer 14:21 3519b
and g before all the nations of Jer 33:9 8597
"Come down from your g And sit Jer 48:18 3519b
heaven to earth The g of Israel, La 2:1 8597
the likeness of the g of the LORD. Ezk 1:28 3519b
the g of the LORD in His place." Ezk 3:12 3519b
the g of the LORD was standing Ezk 3:23 3519b
like the g which I saw by the Ezk 3:23 3519b
the g of the God of Israel *was* Ezk 8:4 3519b
Then the g of the God of Israel Ezk 9:3 3519b
Then the g of the LORD went up Ezk 10:4 3519b
brightness of the g of the LORD. Ezk 10:4 3519b
Then the g of the LORD departed Ezk 10:18 3519b
and the g of the God of Israel Ezk 10:19 3519b
and the g of the God of Israel Ezk 11:22 3519b
The g of the LORD went up from Ezk 11:23 3519b
which is the g of all lands. Ezk 20:6 6643a
which is the g of all lands, Ezk 20:15 6643a
its frontiers, the g of the land, Ezk 25:9 6643a
set g in the land of the living. Ezk 26:20 6643a
you thus equal in g and greatness? Ezk 31:18 3519b
will set My g among the nations; Ezk 39:21 3519b
the g of the God of Israel was Ezk 43:2 3519b
and the earth shone with His g. Ezk 43:2 3519b
And the g of the LORD came into Ezk 43:4 3519b
g of the LORD filled the house. Ezk 43:5 3519b
the g of the LORD filled the house Ezk 44:4 3519b
power, the strength and the g; Da 2:37 3367
and for the g of my majesty?' Da 4:30 3367
to me for the g of my kingdom, Da 4:36 3367
granted sovereignty, grandeur, g and Da 5:18 3367
and *his* g was taken away from him. Da 5:20 3367
given dominion, G and a kingdom, Da 7:14 3367
I will change their g into shame. Hos 4:7 3519b
their g will fly away like a bird Hos 9:11 3519b
will cry out over it, Over its g, Hos 10:5 3519b
g of Israel will enter Adullam. Mi 1:15 3519b
knowledge of the g of the LORD, Hab 2:14 3519b
disgrace *will come* upon your g. Hab 2:16 3519b
saw this temple in its former g? Hg 2:3 3519b
and I will fill this house with g,' Hg 2:7 3519b
'The latter g of this house will Hg 2:9 3519b
I will be the g in her midst.' " Zch 2:5 3519b
"After g He has sent Me against Zch 2:8 3519b
wail, For their g is ruined; Zch 11:3 155
that the g of the house of David Zch 12:7 8597
the g of the inhabitants of Jerusalem Zch 12:7 8597
of the world and their g; Mt 4:8 1391
kingdom and the power and the g Mt 6:13 1391
not even Solomon in all his g clothed Mt 6:29 1391
g of His Father with His angels, Mt 16:27 1391
OF THE SKY with power and great g. Mt 24:30 1391
the Son of Man comes in His g, Mt 25:31 1391
when He comes in the g of His Father Mk 8:38 1391
right and one on *Your* left, in Your g." Mk 10:37 1391
IN CLOUDS with great power and g. Mk 13:26 1391
g of the Lord shone around them; Lk 2:9 1391
"G to God in the highest, And on Lk 2:14 1391
And the g of Your people Israel." Lk 2:32 1391
You all this domain and its g; Lk 4:6 1391
him when He comes in His g, Lk 9:26 1391
and *the* g of the Father and of Lk 9:26
who, appearing in g, were speaking Lk 9:31 1391
they saw His g and the two men Lk 9:32 1391
not even Solomon in all his g, Lk 12:27 1391
who returned to give g to God, Lk 17:18 1391
in heaven and g in the highest!" Lk 19:38 1391
IN A CLOUD with power and great g. Lk 21:27 1391
things and to enter into His g?" Lk 24:26 1391
among us, and we saw His g, Jn 1:14 1391
g as of the only begotten from the Jn 1:14 1391
of Galilee, and manifested His g, Jn 2:11 1391
"I do not receive g from men; Jn 5:41 1391
you receive g from one another and Jn 5:44 1391
not seek the g that is from the *one* Jn 5:44 1391
from himself seeks his own g; Jn 7:18 1391
the g of the One who sent Him, Jn 7:18 1391
"But I do not seek My g; Jn 8:50 1391
I glorify Myself, My g is nothing; Jn 8:54 1391
and said to him, "Give g to God; Jn 9:24 1391

in death, but for the **g** of God, **Jn 11:4** *1391*
you will see the **g** of God?" **Jn 11:40** *1391*
Isaiah said because he saw His **g**, **Jn 12:41** *1391*
with the **g** which I had with You **Jn 17:5** *1391*
"The **g** which You have given **Jn 17:22** *1391*
so that they may see My **g** **Jn 17:24** *1391*
The God of **g** appeared to our **Ac 7:2** *1391*
into heaven and saw the **g** of God, **Ac 7:55** *1391*
because he did not give God the **g**, **Ac 12:23** *1391*
and exchanged the **g** of the **Ro 1:23** *1391*
for **g** and honor and immortality, **Ro 2:7** *1391*
but **g** and honor and peace to every **Ro 2:10** *1391*
truth of God abounded to His **g**, **Ro 3:7** *1391*
and fall short of the **g** of God, **Ro 3:23** *1391*
strong in faith, giving **g** to God, **Ro 4:20** *1391*
we exult in hope of the **g** of God. **Ro 5:2** *1391*
dead through the **g** of the Father, **Ro 6:4** *1391*
g that is to be revealed to us. **Ro 8:18** *1391*
of the **g** of the children of God. **Ro 8:21** *1391*
the **g** and the covenants and the giving **Ro 9:4** *1391*
of His **g** upon vessels of mercy, **Ro 9:23** *1391*
He prepared beforehand for **g**, **Ro 9:23** *1391*
To Him *be* the **g** forever. **Ro 11:36** *1391*
also accepted us to the **g** of God. **Ro 15:7** *1391*
Jesus Christ, be the **g** forever. **Ro 16:27** *1391*
before the ages to our **g**; **1Co 2:7** *1391*
not have crucified the Lord of **g**; **1Co 2:8** *1391*
you do, do all to the **g** of God. **1Co 10:31** *1391*
he is the image and **g** of God; **1Co 11:7** *1391*
but the woman is the **g** of man. **1Co 11:7** *1391*
has long hair, it is a **g** to her? **1Co 11:15** *1391*
but the **g** of the heavenly is one, **1Co 15:40** *1391*
and the **g** of the earthly is **1Co 15:40**
There is one **g** of the sun, and **1Co 15:41** *1391*
sun, and another **g** of the moon, **1Co 15:41** *1391*
moon, and another **g** of the stars; **1Co 15:41** *1391*
for star differs from star in **g**. **1Co 15:41** *1391*
in dishonor, it is raised in **g**; **1Co 15:43** *1391*
Amen to the **g** of God through us. **2Co 1:20** *1391*
engraved on stones, came with **g**, **2Co 3:7** *1391*
because of the **g** of his face, **2Co 3:7** *1391*
fail to be even more with **g**? **2Co 3:8** *1391*
ministry of condemnation has **g**, **2Co 3:9** *1391*
of righteousness abound in **g**. **2Co 3:9** *1391*
For indeed what had **g**, **2Co 3:10** *1392*
in this case has no **g** because **2Co 3:10** *1392*
of the **g** that surpasses *it*. **2Co 3:10** *1391*
that which fades away *was* with **g**, **2Co 3:11** *1391*
more that which remains *is* in **g**. **2Co 3:11** *1391*
as in a mirror the **g** of the Lord, **2Co 3:18** *1391*
the same image from **g** to glory, **2Co 3:18** *1391*
the same image from glory to **g**, **2Co 3:18** *1391*
of the gospel of the **g** of Christ, **2Co 4:4** *1391*
g of God in the face of Christ. **2Co 4:6** *1391*
thanks to abound to the **g** of God. **2Co 4:15** *1391*
of **g** far beyond all comparison, **2Co 4:17** *1391*
by **g** and dishonor, by evil report **2Co 6:8** *1391*
us for the **g** of the Lord Himself, **2Co 8:19** *1391*
of the churches, a **g** to Christ. **2Co 8:23** *1391*
to whom *be* the **g** forevermore. **Ga 1:5** *1391*
the praise of the **g** of His grace, **Eph 1:6** *1391*
would be to the praise of His **g**. **Eph 1:12** *1391*
to the praise of His **g**. **Eph 1:14** *1391*
Jesus Christ, the Father of **g**, **Eph 1:17** *1391*
what are the riches of the **g** of **Eph 1:18** *1391*
your behalf, for they are your **g**. **Eph 3:13** *1391*
according to the riches of His **g**, **Eph 3:16** *1391*
to Him *be* the **g** in the church and **Eph 3:21** *1391*
Himself the church in all her **g**, **Eph 5:27** *1741*
to the **g** and praise of God. **Php 1:11** *1391*
Lord, to the **g** of God the Father. **Php 2:11** *1391*
day of Christ I will have reason to **g** **Php 2:16** *2745*
and **g** in Christ Jesus and put no **Php 3:3** *2744*
and *whose* **g** is in their shame, **Php 3:19** *1391*
conformity with the body of His **g**, **Php 3:21** *1391*
His riches in **g** in Christ Jesus. **Php 4:19** *1391*
Father *be* the **g** forever and ever. **Php 4:20** *1391*
the riches of the **g** of this mystery **Col 1:27** *1391*
is Christ in you, the hope of **g**. **Col 1:27** *1391*
will be revealed with Him in **g**. **Col 3:4** *1391*
nor did we seek **g** from men, either **1Th 2:6** *1391*
you into His own kingdom and **g**. **1Th 2:12** *1391*
For you are our **g** and joy. **1Th 2:20** *1391*
Lord and from the **g** of His power, **2Th 1:9** *1391*
the **g** of our Lord Jesus Christ. **2Th 2:14** *1391*
be honor and **g** forever and ever. **1Tm 1:17** *1391*
on in the world, Taken up in **g**. **1Tm 3:16** *1391*
Jesus *and with it* eternal **g**. **2Tm 2:10** *1391*
to Him *be* the **g** forever and ever. **2Tm 4:18** *1391*
the **g** of our great God and Savior, **Ti 2:13** *1391*
And He is the radiance of His **g** **Heb 1:3** *1391*
CROWNED HIM WITH **G** AND HONOR, **Heb 2:7** *1391*
of death crowned with **g** and honor, **Heb 2:9** *1391*
in bringing many sons to **g**, **Heb 2:10** *1391*
worthy of more **g** than Moses, **Heb 3:3** *1391*
of **g** overshadowing the mercy seat; **Heb 9:5** *1391*
to whom *be* the **g** forever and ever. **Heb 13:21** *1391*
g in his high position; **Jas 1:9** *2744*
and the rich man *is to* **g** in his **Jas 1:10**
may be found to result in praise and **g** **1Pe 1:7** *1391*
joy inexpressible and full of **g**, **1Pe 1:8** *1392*
Him from the dead and gave Him **g**, **1Pe 1:21** *1391*
ITS **G** LIKE THE FLOWER OF GRASS. **1Pe 1:24** *1391*
g and dominion forever and ever. **1Pe 4:11** *1391*
also at the revelation of His **g** you **1Pe 4:13** *1391*
of **g** and of God rests on you. **1Pe 4:14** *1391*
of the **g** that is to be revealed, **1Pe 5:1** *1391*
receive the unfading crown of **g**. **1Pe 5:4** *1391*
you to His eternal **g** in Christ, **1Pe 5:10** *1391*

us by His own **g** and excellence. **2Pe 1:3** *1391*
honor and **g** from God the Father, **2Pe 1:17** *1391*
was made to Him by the Majestic **G**, **2Pe 1:17** *1391*
To Him *be* the **g**, both now and to **2Pe 3:18** *1391*
of His **g** blameless with great joy, **Jude 1:24** *1391*
Jesus Christ our Lord, *be* **g**, **Jude 1:25** *1391*
to Him *be* the **g** and the dominion **Rv 1:6** *1391*
creatures give **g** and honor and thanks **Rv 4:9** *1391*
to receive **g** and honor and power; **Rv 4:11** *1391*
and honor and **g** and blessing." **Rv 5:12** *1391*
g and dominion forever and ever." **Rv 5:13** *1391*
blessing and **g** and wisdom and **Rv 7:12** *1391*
and gave **g** to the God of heaven. **Rv 11:13** *1391*
"Fear God, and give Him **g**, **Rv 14:7** *1391*
the **g** of God and from His power; **Rv 15:8** *1391*
not repent so as to give Him **g**. **Rv 16:9** *1391*
earth was illumined with his **g**. **Rv 18:1** *1391*
and **g** and power belong to our God; **Rv 19:1** *1391*
and be glad and give the **g** to Him, **Rv 19:7** *1391*
having the **g** of God. **Rv 21:11** *1391*
for the **g** of God has illumined it, **Rv 21:23** *1391*
earth will bring their **g** into it. **Rv 21:24** *1391*
and they will bring the **g** and the **Rv 21:26** *1391*

GLOW
may be hot And its bronze may **g** **Ezk 24:11** 2787
has been made to **g** in a furnace, **Rv 1:15** *4448*

GLOWING
garments of **g** colors from Bozrah, **Is 63:1** 2556b
like **g** metal in the midst of the fire. **Ezk 1:4** 2830
something like **g** metal that looked like **Ezk 1:27** 2830
like the appearance of **g** metal. **Ezk 8:2** 2830

GLUTTED
you will eat fat until you are **g**, **Ezk 39:19** 7654
"You will be **g** at My table **Ezk 39:20** 7646

GLUTTON
us, he is a **g** and a drunkard.' **Dt 21:20** 2151b
and the **g** will come to poverty, **Pr 23:21** 2151b

GLUTTONOUS
of wine, *Or* with **g** eaters of meat; **Pr 23:20** 2151b
'Behold, a **g** man and a drunkard, a **Mt 11:19** *5314*
'Behold, a **g** man and a drunkard, **Lk 7:34** *5314*

GLUTTONS
who is a companion of **g** humiliates **Pr 28:7** 2151b
liars, evil beasts, lazy **g**." **Ti 1:12** *1064*

GNASH
He will **g** his teeth and melt away; **Ps 112:10** 2786
They hiss and **g** *their* teeth. **La 2:16** 2786

GNASHED
He has **g** at me with His teeth; **Jb 16:9** 2786
They **g** at me with their teeth. **Ps 35:16** 2786

GNASHES
And **g** at him with his teeth. **Ps 37:12** 2786

GNASHING
will be weeping and **g** of teeth." **Mt 8:12** *1030*
will be weeping and **g** of teeth. **Mt 13:42** *1030*
will be weeping and **g** of teeth. **Mt 13:50** *1030*
will be weeping and **g** of teeth.' **Mt 22:13** *1030*
there will be weeping and **g** of teeth. **Mt 24:51** *1030*
will be weeping and **g** of teeth. **Mt 25:30** *1030*
there will be weeping and **g** of **Lk 13:28** *1030*
they *began* **g** their teeth at him. **Ac 7:54** *1031*

GNAT
strain out a **g** and swallow a camel **Mt 23:24** *2971*

GNATS
g through all the land of Egypt.' " **Ex 8:16** 3654
and there were **g** on man and beast. **Ex 8:17** 3654
g through all the land of Egypt. **Ex 8:17** 3654
secret arts to bring forth **g**, **Ex 8:18** 3654
so there were **g** on man and beast. **Ex 8:18** 3654
And **g** in all their territory. **Ps 105:31** 3654

GNAW
they are gaunt Who **g** the dry ground **Jb 30:3** 6207
Then you will **g** its fragments And **Ezk 23:34** 1633b

GNAWED
g their tongues because of pain, **Rv 16:10** *3145*

GNAWING
me, And my **g** *pains* take no rest. **Jb 30:17** 6207
What the **g** locust has left, the **Jl 1:4** 1501
locust and the **g** locust, **Jl 2:25** 1501

GO
On your belly you will **g**, **Gn 3:14** 1980
"**G** out of the ark, you and your **Gn 8:16** 3318
from Sidon as you **g** toward Gerar, **Gn 10:19** 935
as you **g** toward Sodom and Gomorrah **Gn 10:19** 935
from Mesha as you **g** toward Sephar, **Gn 10:30** 935
let Us **g** down and there confuse **Gn 11:7** 3381
"**G** forth from your country, And **Gn 12:1** 1980
may **g** well with me because of you, **Gn 12:13** 3190
is your wife, take her and **g**." **Gn 12:19** 1980
left, then I will **g** to the right; **Gn 13:9** 3231
then I will **g** to the left." **Gn 13:9** 8041
land of Egypt as you **g** to Zoar. **Gn 13:10** 935
shall **g** to your fathers in peace; **Gn 15:15** 935
Please **g** in to my maid; **Gn 16:2** 935
after that you may **g** on, **Gn 18:5** 5674a
"I will **g** down now, and see if **Gn 18:21** 3381
rise early and **g** on your way." **Gn 19:2** 1980
then you **g** in and lie with him, **Gn 19:34** 935
everywhere we **g**, say of me, **Gn 20:13** 935
and **g** to the land of Moriah, **Gn 22:2** 1980
and I and the lad will **g** over **Gn 22:5** 1980
but you will **g** to my country and **Gn 24:4** 1980
when women **g** out to draw water. **Gn 24:11** 3318
you shall **g** to my father's house and **Gn 24:38** 1980
journey on which I **g** successful; **Gn 24:42** 1980
is Rebekah before you, take *her* and **g**, **Gn 24:51** 1980

afterward she may **g**." **Gn 24:55** 1980
away that I may **g** to my master." **Gn 24:56** 1980
"Will you **g** with this man?" **Gn 24:58** 1980
this man?" And she said, "I will **g**." **Gn 24:58** 1980
"Do not **g** down to Egypt; **Gn 26:2** 3381
"**G** away from us, for you are too **Gn 26:16** 1980
and **g** out to the field and hunt **Gn 27:3** 3318
"**G** now to the flock and bring me **Gn 27:9** 1980
only obey my voice, and **g**, **Gn 27:13** 1980
"Arise, **g** to Paddan-aram, to the **Gn 28:2** 1980
and will keep you wherever you **g**, **Gn 28:15** 1980
Water the sheep, and **g**, **Gn 29:7** 1980
that I may **g** in to her." **Gn 29:21** 935
is my maid Bilhah, **g** in to her that **Gn 30:3** 935
that I may **g** to my own place and **Gn 30:25** 1980
to **g** to the land of Canaan to his **Gn 31:18** 935
"Let me **g**, for the dawn is **Gn 32:26** 7971
let you **g** unless you bless me." **Gn 32:26** 7971
"Let us take our journey and **g**, **Gn 33:12** 1980
and go, and I will **g** before you." **Gn 33:12** 1980
we will take our daughter and **g**." **Gn 34:17** 1980
"Arise, **g** up to Bethel and live **Gn 35:1** 5927
let us arise and **g** up to Bethel, **Gn 35:3** 5927
some distance to **g** to Ephrath, **Gn 35:16** 935
And he said to him, "I will **g**." **Gn 37:13** 2009
"**G** now and see about the welfare **Gn 37:14** 1980
'Let us **g** to Dothan.' " **Gn 37:17** 1980
as for me, where am I to **g**?" **Gn 37:30** 935
"Surely I will **g** down to Sheol in **Gn 37:35** 3381
"**G** in to your brother's wife, and **Gn 38:8** 935
g to Joseph; whatever he says to you, **Gn 41:55** 1980
g down there and buy *some* for us **Gn 42:2** 3381
you shall not **g** from this place **Gn 42:15** 3318
but as for *the rest of* you, **g**, **Gn 42:19** 1980
famine of your households, and **g**. **Gn 42:33** 1980
"My son shall not **g** down with you; **Gn 42:38** 3381
"**G** back, buy us a little food." **Gn 43:2** 7725
we will **g** down and buy you food. **Gn 43:4** 3381
not send *him*, we will not **g** down; **Gn 43:5** 3381
with me and we will arise and **g**, **Gn 43:8** 1980
g up in peace to your father." **Gn 44:17** 5927
'**G** back, buy us a little food.' **Gn 44:25** 7725
"But we said, 'We cannot **g** down. **Gn 44:26** 3381
is with us, then we will **g** down; **Gn 44:26** 3381
the lad **g** up with his brothers. **Gn 44:33** 5927
"For how shall I **g** up to my **Gn 44:34** 5927
"Have everyone **g** out from me." **Gn 45:1** 3318
"Hurry and **g** up to my father, and **Gn 45:9** 5927
and **g** to the land of Canaan, **Gn 45:17** 1980, 935
will **g** and see him before I die." **Gn 45:28** 1980
not be afraid to **g** down to Egypt, **Gn 46:3** 3381
"I will **g** down with you to Egypt, **Gn 46:4** 3381
"I will **g** up and tell Pharaoh, **Gn 46:31** 5927
some distance to **g** to Ephrath; **Gn 48:7** 935
let me **g** up and bury my father; **Gn 50:5** 5927
"**G** up and bury your father, as he **Gn 50:6** 5927
"Shall I **g** and call a nurse for **Ex 2:7** 1980
daughter said to her, "**G** *ahead*." **Ex 2:8** 1980
am I, that I should **g** to Pharaoh, **Ex 3:11** 1980
"**G** and gather the elders of **Ex 3:16** 1980
let us **g** a three days' journey **Ex 3:18** 1980
of Egypt will not permit you to **g**, **Ex 3:19** 1980
and after that he will let you **g**. **Ex 3:20** 7971
and it shall be that when you **g**, **Ex 3:21** 1980
go, you will not **g** empty-handed. **Ex 3:21** 1980
"Now then **g**, and I, even I, will **Ex 4:12** 1980
"Please, let me **g**, that I may **Ex 4:18** 1980
Jethro said to Moses, "**G** in peace." **Ex 4:18** 1980
"**G** back to Egypt, for all the men **Ex 4:19** 1980
"When you **g** back to Egypt see **Ex 4:21** 1980
that he will not let the people **g**. **Ex 4:21** 7971
'Let My son **g** that he may serve **Ex 4:23** 7971
but you have refused to let him **g**. **Ex 4:23** 7971
"**G** to meet Moses in the **Ex 4:27** 1980
'Let My people **g** that they may **Ex 5:1** 7971
obey His voice to let Israel **g**? **Ex 5:2** 7971
I will not let Israel **g**." **Ex 5:2** 7971
let us **g** a three days' journey **Ex 5:3** 1980
let them **g** and gather straw for **Ex 5:7** 1980
'Let us **g** and sacrifice to our God.' **Ex 5:8** 1980
'You **g** *and* get straw for **Ex 5:11** 1980
'Let us **g** *and* sacrifice to the LORD.' **Ex 5:17** 1980
"So **g** now *and* work; **Ex 5:18** 1980
compulsion he will let them **g**, **Ex 6:1** 7971
"**G**, tell Pharaoh king of Egypt to **Ex 6:11** 935
let the sons of Israel **g** out of his **Ex 6:11** 7971
sons of Israel **g** out of his land. **Ex 7:2** 7971
he refuses to let the people **g**. **Ex 7:14** 7971
"**G** to Pharaoh in the morning as **Ex 7:15** 1980
"Let My people **g**, that they may **Ex 7:16** 7971
"**G** to Pharaoh and say to him, **Ex 8:1** 935
"Let My people **g**, that they may **Ex 8:1** 7971
"But if you refuse to let *them* **g**, **Ex 8:2** 7971
which will come up and **g** into your **Ex 8:3** 935
and I will let the people **g**, **Ex 8:8** 7971
"Let My people **g**, that they may **Ex 8:20** 7971
if you do not let My people **g**, **Ex 8:21** 7971
"**G**, sacrifice to your God within **Ex 8:25** 1980
"We must **g** a three days' journey **Ex 8:27** 1980
"I will let you **g**, that you may **Ex 8:28** 7971
you shall not **g** very far away. **Ex 8:28** 1980
g to sacrifice to the LORD." **Ex 8:29** 7971
and he did not let the people **g**. **Ex 8:32** 7971
"**G** to Pharaoh and speak to him, **Ex 9:1** 935
"Let My people **g**, that they may **Ex 9:1** 7971
"For if you refuse to let *them* **g** and **Ex 9:2** 7971
and he did not let the people **g**. **Ex 9:7** 7971
"Let My people **g**, that they may **Ex 9:13** 7971

My people by not letting them **g**. **Ex 9:17** 7971
and I will let you **g**, **Ex 9:28** 7971
"As soon as I **g** out of the city, **Ex 9:29** 3318
did not let the sons of Israel **g**, **Ex 9:35** 7971
"**G** to Pharaoh, for I have **Ex 10:1** 935
Let My people **g**, that they may **Ex 10:3** 7971
if you refuse to let My people **g**, **Ex 10:4** 7971
Let the men **g**, that they may serve **Ex 10:7** 7971
"**G**, serve the LORD your God! **Ex 10:8** 1980
"We shall **g** with our young **Ex 10:9** 1980
flocks and our herds we shall **g**, **Ex 10:9** 1980
I let you and your little ones **g**! **Ex 10:10** 7971
G now, the men *among you,* and **Ex 10:11** 1980
did not let the sons of Israel **g**. **Ex 10:20** 7971
"**G**, serve the LORD; **Ex 10:24** 1980
your little ones may **g** with you." **Ex 10:24** 1980
livestock too shall **g** with us; **Ex 10:26** 1980
he was not willing to let them **g**. **Ex 10:27** 7971
that he will let you **g** from here. **Ex 11:1** 7971
When he lets you **g**, **Ex 11:1** 7971
'**G** out, you and all the people who **Ex 11:8** 3318
and after that I will **g** out." **Ex 11:8** 3318
sons of Israel **g** out of his land. **Ex 11:10** 7971
'For I will **g** through the land of **Ex 12:12** 5674a
"**G** and take for yourselves lambs **Ex 12:21** 4900
and none of you shall **g** outside **Ex 12:22** 3318
and **g**, worship the LORD, as you **Ex 12:31** 1980
herds, as you have said, and **g**, **Ex 12:32** 1980
of Abib, you are about to **g** forth. **Ex 13:4** 3318
was stubborn about letting us **g**, **Ex 13:15** 7971
when Pharaoh had let the people **g**, **Ex 13:17** 7971
let Israel **g** from serving us?" **Ex 14:5** 7971
Tell the sons of Israel to **g** forward **Ex 14:15** 5265
and the sons of Israel shall **g** **Ex 14:16** 935
so that they will **g** in after them; **Ex 14:17** 935
and the people shall **g** out and **Ex 16:4** 3318
let no man **g** out of his place on **Ex 16:29** 3318
which you struck the Nile, and **g**. **Ex 17:5** 1980
"Choose men for us and **g** out, **Ex 17:9** 3318
will **g** to their place in peace." **Ex 18:23** 935
"**G** to the people and consecrate **Ex 19:10** 1980
do not **g** up on the mountain or **Ex 19:12** 5927
do not **g** near a woman." **Ex 19:15** 5066
"**G** down, warn the people, so **Ex 19:21** 3381
"**G** down and come up *again,* you **Ex 19:24**
1980, 3381
not **g** up by steps to My altar, **Ex 20:26** 5927
but on the seventh he shall **g** out **Ex 21:2** 3318
comes alone, he shall **g** out alone; **Ex 21:3** 3318
his wife shall **g** out with him. **Ex 21:3** 3318
master, and he shall **g** out alone. **Ex 21:4** 3318
I will not **g** out as a free man,' **Ex 21:5** 3318
to **g** free as the male slaves do. **Ex 21:7** 3318
then she shall **g** out for nothing, **Ex 21:11** 3318
who struck him shall **g** unpunished; **Ex 21:19** 5352
him **g** free on account of his eye. **Ex 21:26** 7971
g free on account of his tooth. **Ex 21:27** 7971
owner of the ox shall **g** unpunished. **Ex 21:28** 5355a
"For My angel will **g** before you **Ex 23:23** 1980
shall **g** out from its sides; **Ex 25:32** 3318
us a god who will **g** before us; **Ex 32:1** 1980
"**G** down at once, for your people, **Ex 32:7** 1980
a god for us who will **g** before us; **Ex 32:23** 1980
and **g** back and forth from gate to **Ex 32:27**
5674a, 7725
"But **g** now, lead the people where **Ex 32:34** 1980
My angel shall **g** before you; **Ex 32:34** 1980
"Depart, **g** up from here, you and **Ex 33:1** 5927
"**G** *up* to a land flowing with **Ex 33:3**
for I will not **g** up in your midst, **Ex 33:3** 5927
should I **g** up in your midst for **Ex 33:5** 5927
who sought the LORD would **g** out to **Ex 33:7** 3318
"My presence shall **g** *with you,* **Ex 33:14** 1980
Your presence does not **g** *with us,* **Ex 33:15** 1980
let the Lord **g** along in our midst, **Ex 34:9** 1980
when you **g** up three times a year to **Ex 34:24** 5927
It shall not **g** out, but the priest **Lv 6:12** 3518
it is not to **g** out. **Lv 6:13** 3518
"You shall not **g** outside the **Lv 8:33** 3318
"You shall not even **g** out from **Lv 10:7** 3318
and the priest shall **g** out to the **Lv 14:3** 3318
bird **g** free over the open field. **Lv 14:7** 7971
shall **g** in to look at the house. **Lv 14:36** 935
he shall let the live bird **g** free **Lv 14:53** 7971
'Then he shall **g** out to the altar **Lv 16:18** 3318
not **g** about as a slanderer among **Lv 19:16** 1980
shall he **g** out of the sanctuary nor **Lv 21:12** 3318
only he shall not **g** in to the veil **Lv 21:23** 935
'He shall then **g** out from you, he **Lv 25:41** 3318
and shall **g** back to his family, **Lv 25:41** 7725
g out in the year of jubilee, **Lv 25:54** 3318
is able to **g** out to war in Israel, **Nu 1:3** 3318
whoever *was able to* **g** out to war, **Nu 1:20** 3318
whoever *was able to* **g** out to war, **Nu 1:22** 3318
whoever *was able to* **g** out to war, **Nu 1:24** 3318
whoever *was able to* **g** out to war, **Nu 1:26** 3318
whoever *was able to* **g** out to war, **Nu 1:28** 3318
whoever *was able to* **g** out to war, **Nu 1:30** 3318
whoever *was able to* **g** out to war, **Nu 1:32** 3318
whoever *was able to* **g** out to war, **Nu 1:34** 3318
whoever *was able to* **g** out to war, **Nu 1:36** 3318
whoever *was able to* **g** out to war, **Nu 1:38** 3318
whoever *was able to* **g** out to war, **Nu 1:40** 3318
whoever *was able to* **g** out to war, **Nu 1:42** 3318
able to **g** out to war in Israel, **Nu 1:45** 3318
Aaron and his sons shall **g** in and **Nu 4:5** 935
Aaron and his sons shall **g** in and **Nu 4:19** 935
but they shall not **g** in to see the **Nu 4:20** 935
which is made for the wrong *must* **g** **Nu 5:8**
hair of the woman's head **g** loose, **Nu 5:18** 6544a
a curse shall **g** into your stomach, **Nu 5:22** 935
g into her and *cause* bitterness. **Nu 5:24** 935
g into her and *cause* bitterness, **Nu 5:27** 935
shall not **g** near to a dead person. **Nu 6:6** 935
Levites may **g** in to serve the tent of **Nu 8:15** 935
"When you **g** to war in your **Nu 10:9** 935
to **g** to my *own* land and relatives." **Nu 10:30** 1980
"So it will be, if you **g** with us, **Nu 10:32** 1980
The people would **g** about and **Nu 11:8** 7751a
"**G** up there into the Negev; **Nu 13:17** 5927
then **g** up into the hill country. **Nu 13:17** 5927
g up and take possession of it, **Nu 13:30** 5927
able to **g** up against the people, **Nu 13:31** 5927
and You **g** before them in a **Nu 14:14** 1980
but we will **g** up to the place **Nu 14:40** 5927
"Do not **g** up, or you will be struck **Nu 14:42** 5927
will **g** along the king's highway, **Nu 20:17** 1980
"We will **g** up by the highway, **Nu 20:19** 5927
Sea, to **g** around the land of Edom; **Nu 21:4** 5437
We will **g** by the king's highway **Nu 21:22** 1980
"Do not **g** with them; **Nu 22:12** 1980
"**G** back to your land, for the **Nu 22:13** 1980
refused to let me **g** with you." **Nu 22:13** 1980
call you, rise up *and* **g** with them; **Nu 22:20** 1980
"**G** with the men, but you shall **Nu 22:35** 1980
your burnt offering, and I will **g**; **Nu 23:3** 1980
he did not **g** as at other times to **Nu 24:1** 1980
able to **g** out to war in Israel." **Nu 26:2** 3318
"**G** up to this mountain of Abarim, **Nu 27:12** 5927
g out and come in before them, **Nu 27:17** 3318
At his command they shall **g** out **Nu 27:21** 3318
that they may **g** against Midian to **Nu 31:3** 1961
"Shall your brothers **g** to war **Nu 32:6** 935
they did not **g** into the land which the **Nu 32:9** 935
ourselves will be armed ready *to* **g** **Nu 32:17**
and the border shall **g** down from **Nu 34:11** 3381
and the border shall **g** down and **Nu 34:11** 3381
'And the border shall **g** down to **Nu 34:12** 3381
and **g** to the hill country of the **Dt 1:7** 935
g in and possess the land which **Dt 1:8** 935
g up, take possession, as the **Dt 1:21** 5927
the way by which we should **g** up and **Dt 1:22** 5927
"Yet you were not willing to **g** up, **Dt 1:26** 5927
'Where can we **g** up? **Dt 1:28** 5927
you the way in which you should **g**, **Dt 1:33** 1980
we will indeed **g** up and fight, **Dt 1:41** 5927
to **g** up into the hill country. **Dt 1:41** 5927
'Do not **g** up nor fight, for I am **Dt 1:42** 5927
"Only you did not **g** near to the **Dt 2:37** 7126
'**G** up to the top of Pisgah and **Dt 3:27** 5927
for he shall **g** across at the head **Dt 3:28** 5674a
so that you may live and **g** **Dt 4:1** 935
"Or has a god tried to **g** to take **Dt 4:34** 935
that it may **g** well with you and **Dt 4:40** 3190
and did not **g** up the mountain. **Dt 5:5** 5927
and that it may **g** well with you on **Dt 5:16** 3190
'**G** near and hear all that the LORD **Dt 5:27** 7126
'**G**, say to them, "Return to your **Dt 5:30** 1980
may **g** in and possess the good land **Dt 6:18** 935
and **g** in and possess the land **Dt 8:1** 935
and **g** after other gods and serve **Dt 8:19** 1980
crossing over the Jordan today to **g** in **Dt 9:1** 935
'Arise, **g** down from here quickly, **Dt 9:12** 3381
'**G** up and possess the land which I **Dt 9:23** 5927
that they may **g** in and possess the **Dt 10:11** 935
so that you may be strong and **g** in **Dt 11:8** 935
cross the Jordan to **g** in to possess the **Dt 11:31** 935
you shall take and **g** to the place **Dt 12:26** 935
'Let us **g** after other gods **Dt 13:2** 1980
'Let us **g** and serve other gods' **Dt 13:6** 1980
'Let us **g** and serve other gods' **Dt 13:13** 1980
bind the money in your hand and **g** **Dt 14:25** 1980
'I will not **g** out from you,' **Dt 15:16** 3318
then you shall arise and **g** up to **Dt 17:8** 5927
that it may **g** well with you. **Dt 19:13** 2895
"When you **g** out to battle against **Dt 20:1** 3318
your judges shall **g** out and measure **Dt 21:2** 3318
"When you **g** out to battle against **Dt 21:10** 3318
and after that you may **g** in to her **Dt 21:13** 935
let her **g** wherever she wishes; **Dt 21:14** 7971
shall certainly let the mother **g**, **Dt 22:7** 7971
"When you **g** out as an army **Dt 23:9** 3318
then he must **g** outside the camp; **Dt 23:10** 3318
outside the camp and **g** out there, **Dt 23:12** 3318
he shall not **g** out with the army nor **Dt 24:5** 3318
you shall not **g** back to get it; **Dt 24:19** 7725
shall not **g** over the boughs again; **Dt 24:20** 6287a
you shall not **g** over it again; **Dt 24:21** 5953b
between men and they **g** to court, **Dt 25:1** 5066
Her husband's brother shall **g** in **Dt 25:5** 935
then his brother's wife shall **g** up **Dt 25:7** 5927
put *it* in a basket and **g** to the place **Dt 26:2** 1980
"You shall **g** to the priest **Dt 26:3** 935
blessed *shall you be* when you **g** out. **Dt 28:6** 3318
to **g** after other gods to serve **Dt 28:14** 1980
cursed *shall you be* when you **g** out. **Dt 28:19** 3318
will **g** out one way against them, **Dt 28:25** 3318
for they will **g** into captivity. **Dt 28:41** 1980
you will **g** down lower and lower. **Dt 28:43** 3381
to **g** and serve the gods of those **Dt 29:18** 1980
'Who will **g** up to heaven for us to **Dt 30:12** 5927
I am no longer able to come and **g**, **Dt 31:2** 935
for you shall **g** with this people **Dt 31:7** 935
"**G** up to this mountain of the **Dt 32:49** 5927
but you shall not **g** there, **Dt 32:52** 935
but you shall not **g** over there." **Dt 34:4** 5674a
may have success wherever you **g**. **Jos 1:7** 1980
God is with you wherever you **g**." **Jos 1:9** 1980
to **g** in to possess the land which **Jos 1:11** 935
wherever you send us we will **g**. **Jos 1:16** 1980
"**G**, view the land, especially **Jos 2:1** 1980
"**G** to the hill country, so that the **Jos 2:16** 1980
afterward you may **g** on your way." **Jos 2:16** 1980
from your place and **g** after it. **Jos 3:3** 1980
know the way by which you shall **g**, **Jos 3:4** 1980
g up every man straight ahead." **Jos 6:5** 5927
"**G** forward, and march around the **Jos 6:7** 5674a
g on before the ark of the LORD." **Jos 6:7** 5674a
g into the treasury of the LORD." **Jos 6:19** 935
"**G** into the harlot's house and **Jos 6:22** 935
"**G** up and spy out the land." **Jos 7:2** 5927
"Do not let all the people **g** up; **Jos 7:3** 5927
thousand men need **g** up to Ai; **Jos 7:3** 5927
with you and arise, **g** up to Ai; **Jos 8:1** 5927
the people of war to **g** up to Ai; **Jos 8:3** 5927
Do not **g** very far from the city, **Jos 8:4** 7368
to **g** to meet them and say to them, **Jos 9:11** 1980
to **g** *down* for about a whole day. **Jos 10:13** 935
g up to the forest and clear a **Jos 17:15** 5927
"**G** and walk through the land and **Jos 18:8** 1980
turn now and **g** to your tents, **Jos 22:4** 1980
to **g** to the land of Gilead, **Jos 22:9** 1980
to **g** up against them in war. **Jos 22:12** 5927
"For if you ever **g** back and cling **Jos 23:12** 7725
you, and **g** and serve other gods and **Jos 23:16** 1980
"Who shall **g** up first for us **Jg 1:1** 5927
The LORD said, "Judah shall **g** up; **Jg 1:2** 5927
and I in turn will **g** with you into **Jg 1:3** 1980
the man and all his family **g** free. **Jg 1:25** 7971
'**G** and march to Mount Tabor, and **Jg 4:6** 1980
"If you will **g** with me, then I **Jg 4:8** 1980
will go with me, then I will **g**; **Jg 4:8** 1980
but if you will not **g** with me, **Jg 4:8** 1980
not go with me, I will not **g**." **Jg 4:8** 1980
"I will surely **g** with you; **Jg 4:9** 1980
sons of the east and **g** against them. **Jg 6:3** 5927
'**G** in this your strength and **Jg 6:14** 1980
'This one shall **g** with you,' he **Jg 7:4** 1980
go with you,' he shall **g** with you; **Jg 7:4** 1980
'This one shall not **g** with you,' **Jg 7:4** 1980
not go with you,' he shall not **g**." **Jg 7:4** 1980
so let all the *other* people **g**, **Jg 7:7** 1980
"Arise, **g** down against the camp, **Jg 7:9** 3381
"But if you are afraid to **g** down, **Jg 7:10** 3381
g with Purah your servant down to **Jg 7:10** 3381
you may **g** down against the camp." **Jg 7:11** 3381
and **g** to wave over the trees?' **Jg 9:9** 1980
and **g** to wave over the trees?' **Jg 9:11** 1980
and **g** to wave over the trees?' **Jg 9:13** 1980
G out now and fight with them!" **Jg 9:38** 3318
"**G** and cry out to the gods which **Jg 10:14** 1980
that you may **g** with us and fight **Jg 11:8** 1980
that I may **g** to the mountains and **Jg 11:37**
1980, 3381
Then he said, "**G**." **Jg 11:38** 1980
without calling us to **g** with you? **Jg 12:1** 1980
that you **g** to take a wife from the **Jg 14:3** 1980
g in to my wife in *her* room." **Jg 15:1** 935
"I will **g** out as at other times **Jg 16:20** 3318
"**G**, search the land." **Jg 18:2** 1980
The priest said to them, "**G** in peace; **Jg 18:6** 1980
and let us **g** up against them; **Jg 18:9** 5927
Do not delay to **g**, to enter, to **Jg 18:9** 1980
the morning, and he prepared to **g**; **Jg 19:5** 1980
bread, and afterward you may **g**." **Jg 19:5** 1980
Then the man arose to **g**, **Jg 19:7** 1980
arose to **g** early in the morning, **Jg 19:8** 1980
When the man arose to **g** along with **Jg 19:9** 1980
journey so that you may **g** home." **Jg 19:9** 1980
we will **g** on as far as Gibeah." **Jg 19:12** 5674a
let her **g** at the approach of dawn. **Jg 19:25** 7971
and went out to **g** on his way, **Jg 19:27** 1980
"Get up and let us **g**," **Jg 19:28** 1980
"Not one of us will **g** to his tent, **Jg 20:8** 1980
we will **g** *up* against it by lot. **Jg 20:9**
to **g** out to battle against the **Jg 20:14** 3318
"Who shall **g** up first for us to **Jg 20:18** 5927
"Judah *shall* **g** *up* first." **Jg 20:18**
"**G** up against him." **Jg 20:23** 5927
"Shall I yet again **g** out to **Jg 20:28** 3318
"**G** up, for tomorrow I will **Jg 20:28** 5927
"**G** and strike the inhabitants of **Jg 21:10** 1980
"**G** and lie in wait in the **Jg 21:20** 1980
and **g** to the land of Benjamin. **Jg 21:21** 1980
"**G**, return each of you to her **Ru 1:8** 1980
Why should you **g** with me? **Ru 1:11** 1980
G, for I am too old to have a **Ru 1:12** 1980
for where you **g**, I will go, and **Ru 1:16** 1980
for where you go, I will **g**, **Ru 1:16** 1980
she was determined to **g** with her, **Ru 1:18** 1980
"Please let me **g** to the field and **Ru 2:2** 1980
"**G**, my daughter." **Ru 2:2** 1980
not **g** to glean in another field; **Ru 2:8** 1980
do not **g** on from this one, **Ru 2:8** 5674a
which they reap, and **g** after them. **Ru 2:9** 1980
g to the water jars and drink from **Ru 2:9** 1980
that you **g** out with his maids, **Ru 2:22** 3318
and **g** down to the threshing floor; **Ru 3:3** 3381
and you shall **g** and uncover his **Ru 3:4** 935
"How did it **g**, my daughter?" **Ru 3:16**
'Do not **g** to your mother-in-law **Ru 3:17** 935
Now this man would **g** up from his **1Sa 1:3** 5927
Eli answered and said, "**G** in peace; **1Sa 1:17** 1980
But Hannah did not **g** up, **1Sa 1:22** 5927
"*I will not* **g** *up* until the child **1Sa 1:22**
My priests, to **g** up to My altar, **1Sa 2:28** 5927
"**G** lie down, and it shall be if **1Sa 3:9** 1980

"How did things **g**, my son?"	**1Sa 4:16**	1961
they not allow the people to **g**,	**1Sa 6:6**	7971
Then send it away that it may **g**.	**1Sa 6:8**	1980
to whom shall He **g** up from us?"	**1Sa 6:20**	5927
He used to **g** annually on	**1Sa 7:16**	1980
that our king may judge us and **g**	**1Sa 8:20**	3318
"**G** every man to his city."	**1Sa 8:22**	1980
arise, **g** search for the donkeys."	**1Sa 9:3**	1980
Now let us **g** there, perhaps he can	**1Sa 9:6**	1980
if we **g**, what shall we bring the	**1Sa 9:7**	1980
"Come, and let us **g** to the seer";	**1Sa 9:9**	1980
come, let us **g**."	**1Sa 9:10**	1980
g up for you will find him at once."	**1Sa 9:13**	5927
them to **g** up to the high place.	**1Sa 9:14**	5927
G up before me to the high place,	**1Sa 9:19**	5927
in the morning I will let you **g**,	**1Sa 9:19**	7971
might **g** ahead of us and pass on,	**1Sa 9:27**	5674a
"When you **g** from me today, then	**1Sa 10:2**	1980
you will **g** on further from there,	**1Sa 10:3**	2498
shall **g** down before me to Gilgal;	**1Sa 10:8**	3381
"Where did you **g**?"	**1Sa 10:14**	1980
"Come and let us **g** to Gilgal and	**1Sa 11:14**	1980
for *then you would* **g** after futile	**1Sa 12:21**	
in our place and not **g** up to them.	**1Sa 14:9**	5927
'Come up to us,' then we will **g** up,	**1Sa 14:10**	5927
"Let us **g** down after the	**1Sa 14:36**	3381
I **g** down after the Philistines?	**1Sa 14:37**	3381
'Now **g** and strike Amalek and	**1Sa 15:3**	1980
"**G**, depart, go down from among	**1Sa 15:6**	1980
g down from among the Amalekites,	**1Sa 15:6**	3381
from Havilah as you **g** to Shur,	**1Sa 15:7**	935
'**G** and utterly destroy the sinners,	**1Sa 15:18**	1980
As Samuel turned to **g**,	**1Sa 15:27**	1980
before Israel, and **g** back with me,	**1Sa 15:30**	7725
Fill your horn with oil and **g**;	**1Sa 16:1**	1980
But Samuel said, "How can I **g**?	**1Sa 16:2**	1980
your servant will **g** and fight with	**1Sa 17:32**	1980
"You are not able to **g** against	**1Sa 17:33**	1980
"**G**, and may the LORD be with you."	**1Sa 17:37**	1980
"I cannot **g** with these, for I	**1Sa 17:39**	1980
"I will **g** out and stand	**1Sa 19:3**	3318
me like this and let my enemy **g**,	**1Sa 19:17**	7971
'Let me **g**! Why should I put you to	**1Sa 19:17**	7971
But let me **g**, that I may hide	**1Sa 20:5**	7971
and let us **g** out into the field."	**1Sa 20:11**	3318
away, that you may **g** in safety.	**1Sa 20:13**	1980
you shall **g** down quickly and come	**1Sa 20:19**	3381
'**G**, find the arrows.'	**1Sa 20:21**	1980
the arrows are beyond you,' **g**,	**1Sa 20:22**	1980
earnestly asked leave of me *to* **g**	**1Sa 20:28**	
'Please let me **g**, since our family	**1Sa 20:29**	7971
"**G**, bring *them* to the city."	**1Sa 20:40**	1980
"**G** in safety, inasmuch as we have	**1Sa 20:42**	1980
and **g** into the land of Judah."	**1Sa 22:5**	935
g and attack these Philistines?"	**1Sa 23:2**	1980
"**G** and attack the Philistines and	**1Sa 23:2**	1980
How much more then if we **g** to	**1Sa 23:3**	1980
"Arise, **g** down to Keilah, for I	**1Sa 23:4**	3381
to **g** down to Keilah to besiege	**1Sa 23:8**	3381
they went wherever they could **g**.	**1Sa 23:13**	1980
"**G** now, make more sure, and	**1Sa 23:22**	1980
certainty, and I will **g** with you;	**1Sa 23:23**	1980
will he let him **g** away safely?	**1Sa 24:19**	7971
"**G** up to Carmel, visit Nabal and	**1Sa 25:5**	5927
She said to her young men, "**G** on	**1Sa 25:19**	5674a
"**G** up to your house in peace.	**1Sa 25:35**	5927
"Who will **g** down with me to Saul	**1Sa 26:6**	3381
"I will **g** down with you."	**1Sa 26:6**	3381
g down into battle and perish.	**1Sa 26:10**	3381
the jug of water, and let us **g**."	**1Sa 26:11**	1980
'**G**, serve other gods.'	**1Sa 26:19**	1980
will **g** out with me in the camp,	**1Sa 28:1**	3318
may **g** to her and inquire of her."	**1Sa 28:7**	1980
strength when you **g** on *your* way."	**1Sa 28:22**	1980
"Make the man **g** back, that he may	**1Sa 29:4**	7725
let him **g** down to battle with us,	**1Sa 29:4**	3381
therefore return and **g** in peace,	**1Sa 29:7**	1980
that I may not **g** and fight against	**1Sa 29:8**	935
not **g** up with us to the battle.'	**1Sa 29:9**	5927
"Because they did not **g** with us,	**1Sa 30:22**	1980
his men were accustomed to **g**."	**1Sa 30:31**	1980
"How did things **g**? Please tell me."	**2Sa 1:4**	1961
"**G**, cut him down."	**2Sa 1:15**	5066
"Shall I **g** up to one of the	**2Sa 2:1**	5927
And the LORD said to him, "**G** up."	**2Sa 2:1**	5927
"Where shall I **g** up?"	**2Sa 2:1**	5927
Then Abner said to him, "**G**, return."	**2Sa 3:16**	1980
"Let me arise and **g** and	**2Sa 3:21**	1980
I **g** up against the Philistines?	**2Sa 5:19**	5927
"**G** up, for I will certainly give	**2Sa 5:19**	5927
"You shall not **g** *directly* up;	**2Sa 5:23**	5927
"**G**, do all that is in your mind,	**2Sa 7:3**	1980
"**G** and say to My servant David,	**2Sa 7:5**	1980
time when kings **g** out *to battle,*	**2Sa 11:1**	3318
"**G** down to your house, and wash	**2Sa 11:8**	3381
and did not **g** down to his house.	**2Sa 11:9**	3381
"Uriah did not **g** down to his house	**2Sa 11:10**	3381
you not **g** down to your house?"	**2Sa 11:10**	3381
Shall I then **g** to my house to eat	**2Sa 11:11**	935
and tomorrow I will let you **g**."	**2Sa 11:12**	7971
he did not **g** down to his house.	**2Sa 11:13**	3381
g so near to the city to fight?	**2Sa 11:20**	5066
Why did you **g** so near the wall?'	**2Sa 11:21**	5066
I will **g** to him, but he will not	**2Sa 12:23**	1980
"**G** now to your brother Amnon's	**2Sa 13:7**	1980
"Have everyone **g** out from me."	**2Sa 13:9**	3318
"Get up, **g** away!"	**2Sa 13:15**	1980
servants **g** with your servant."	**2Sa 13:24**	1980
"No, my son, we should not all **g**,	**2Sa 13:25**	1980

he urged him, he would not **g**,	**2Sa 13:25**	1980
let my brother Amnon **g** with us."	**2Sa 13:26**	1980
"Why should he **g** with you?"	**2Sa 13:26**	1980
and all the king's sons **g** with him.	**2Sa 13:27**	7971
David longed to **g** out to Absalom;	**2Sa 13:39**	3318
then **g** to the king and speak to	**2Sa 14:3**	935
"**G** to your house, and I will give	**2Sa 14:8**	1980
g therefore, bring back the young	**2Sa 14:21**	1980
g and set it on fire."	**2Sa 14:30**	1980
"Please let me **g** and pay my vow	**2Sa 15:7**	1980
The king said to him, "**G** in peace."	**2Sa 15:9**	1980
G in haste, or he will overtake us	**2Sa 15:14**	1980
"Why will you also **g** with us?	**2Sa 15:19**	1980
with us, while I **g** where I will?	**2Sa 15:20**	1980
"**G** and pass over."	**2Sa 15:22**	1980
Let me **g** over now and cut off his	**2Sa 16:9**	5674a
did you not **g** with your friend?"	**2Sa 16:17**	1980
"**G** in to your father's concubines,	**2Sa 16:21**	935
that you personally **g** into battle.	**2Sa 17:11**	1980
maidservant would **g** and tell them,	**2Sa 17:17**	1980
they would **g** and tell King David,	**2Sa 17:17**	1980
will surely **g** out with you also."	**2Sa 18:2**	3318
"You should not **g** out;	**2Sa 18:3**	3318
"**G**, tell the king what you have	**2Sa 18:21**	1980
g out and speak kindly to your	**2Sa 19:7**	3318
by the LORD, if you do not **g** out,	**2Sa 19:7**	3318
in order to **g** to meet the king,	**2Sa 19:15**	1980
g down to meet my lord the king."	**2Sa 19:20**	3381
"Why did you not **g** with me,	**2Sa 19:25**	1980
ride on it and **g** with the king,'	**2Sa 19:26**	1980
g up with the king to Jerusalem?	**2Sa 19:34**	5927
but did not **g** in to them.	**2Sa 20:3**	935
not **g** out again with us to battle,	**2Sa 21:17**	3318
"**G**, number Israel and Judah."	**2Sa 24:1**	1980
"**G** about now through all the	**2Sa 24:2**	7751a
"**G** and speak to David,	**2Sa 24:12**	1980
"**G** up, erect an altar to the LORD	**2Sa 24:18**	5927
"**G** at once to King David and say	**1Ki 1:13**	1980
"**G** to your house."	**1Ki 1:53**	1980
do not let his gray hair **g** down to	**1Ki 2:6**	3381
do not let him **g** unpunished,	**1Ki 2:9**	5352
"**G** to Anathoth to your own field,	**1Ki 2:26**	1980
"**G**, fall upon him."	**1Ki 2:29**	1980
not **g** out from there to any place.	**1Ki 2:36**	3318
g out and cross over the brook Kidron	**1Ki 2:37**	3318
the day you depart and **g** anywhere,	**1Ki 2:42**	1980
not know how to **g** out or come in.	**1Ki 3:7**	3318
I will make them into rafts *to* **g**	**1Ki 5:9**	
they would **g** up by winding stairs	**1Ki 6:8**	5927
"When Your people **g** out to battle	**1Ki 8:44**	3318
g and serve other gods and worship	**1Ki 9:6**	1980
he should not **g** after other gods;	**1Ki 11:10**	1980
that I may **g** to my own country."	**1Ki 11:21**	1980
to **g** to your own country?"	**1Ki 11:22**	1980
you must surely let me **g**."	**1Ki 11:22**	7971
"You must not **g** up and fight	**1Ki 12:24**	5927
"If this people **g** up to offer	**1Ki 12:27**	5927
much for you to **g** up to Jerusalem;	**1Ki 12:28**	5927
your house I would not **g** with you,	**1Ki 13:8**	935
"Which way did he **g**?"	**1Ki 13:12**	1980
return with you, nor **g** with you,	**1Ki 13:16**	935
wife of Jeroboam, and **g** to Shiloh;	**1Ki 14:2**	1980
and a jar of honey, and **g** to him.	**1Ki 14:3**	935
"**G**, say to Jeroboam,	**1Ki 14:7**	1980
"Now you, arise, **g** to your house.	**1Ki 14:12**	1980
g, break your treaty with Baasha	**1Ki 15:19**	1980
"**G** away from here and turn	**1Ki 17:3**	1980
"Arise, **g** to Zarephath, which	**1Ki 17:9**	1980
I may **g** in and prepare for me and my	**1Ki 17:12**	935
g, do as you have said, but make	**1Ki 17:13**	935
"**G**, show yourself to Ahab, and I	**1Ki 18:1**	1980
"**G** through the land to all the	**1Ki 18:5**	1980
G, say to your master,	**1Ki 18:8**	1980
'**G**, say to your master,	**1Ki 18:11**	1980
'**G**, say to your master,	**1Ki 18:14**	1980
"**G** up, eat and drink;	**1Ki 18:41**	5927
"**G** up now, look toward the sea."	**1Ki 18:43**	5927
And he said, "**G** back" seven times.	**1Ki 18:43**	7725
"**G** up, say to Ahab,	**1Ki 18:44**	5927
'Prepare *your chariot* and **g** down,	**1Ki 18:44**	3381
"**G** forth and stand on the	**1Ki 19:11**	3318
"**G**, return on your way to the	**1Ki 19:15**	1980
"**G** back again, for what have I	**1Ki 19:20**	1980
"**G**, strengthen yourself and	**1Ki 20:22**	1980
and **g** out to the king of Israel;	**1Ki 20:31**	3318
"**G**, bring him."	**1Ki 20:33**	935
let you **g** with this covenant."	**1Ki 20:34**	7971
a covenant with him and let him **g**.	**1Ki 20:34**	7971
you have let **g** out of *your* hand	**1Ki 20:42**	7971
your life shall **g** for his life,	**1Ki 20:42**	1961
Ahab arose to **g** down to the	**1Ki 21:16**	3381
g down to meet Ahab king of	**1Ki 21:18**	3381
"Will you **g** with me to battle at	**1Ki 22:4**	1980
"Shall I **g** against Ramoth-gilead	**1Ki 22:6**	1980
"**G** up, for the Lord will give *it*	**1Ki 22:6**	5927
"**G** up to Ramoth-gilead and	**1Ki 22:12**	5927
we **g** to Ramoth-gilead to battle,	**1Ki 22:15**	1980
"**G** up and succeed, and the LORD	**1Ki 22:15**	5927
to **g** up and fall at Ramoth-gilead?'	**1Ki 22:20**	5927
'I will **g** out and be a deceiving	**1Ki 22:22**	3318
and also prevail. **G** and do so.'	**1Ki 22:22**	3318
myself and **g** into the battle,	**1Ki 22:30**	935
Tarshish to **g** to Ophir for gold,	**1Ki 22:48**	1980
but they did not **g** for the ships	**1Ki 22:48**	1980
"Let my servants **g** with your	**1Ki 22:49**	1980
"**G**, inquire of Baal-zebub, the	**2Ki 1:2**	1980
g up to meet the messengers of the	**2Ki 1:3**	5927
'**G**, return to the king who sent	**2Ki 1:6**	1980
said to Elijah, "**G** down with him;	**2Ki 1:15**	3381

them **g** and search for your master;	**2Ki 2:16**	1980
"Did I not say to you, 'Do not **g**'?"	**2Ki 2:18**	1980
"**G** up, you baldhead;	**2Ki 2:23**	5927
g up, you baldhead!"	**2Ki 2:23**	5927
g with me to fight against Moab?"	**2Ki 3:7**	1980
"I will **g** up; I am as you are, my	**2Ki 3:7**	5927
"Which way shall we **g** up?"	**2Ki 3:8**	5927
G to the prophets of your father	**2Ki 3:13**	1980
"**G**, borrow vessels at large for	**2Ki 4:3**	1980
"And you shall **g** in and shut the	**2Ki 4:4**	935
"**G**, sell the oil and pay your	**2Ki 4:7**	1980
"Why will you **g** to him today?	**2Ki 4:23**	1980
"Drive and **g** forward;	**2Ki 4:24**	1980
in your hand, and **g** your way;	**2Ki 4:29**	1980
"**G** now, and I will send a letter	**2Ki 5:5**	1980
"**G** and wash in the Jordan seven	**2Ki 5:10**	1980
He said to him, "**G** in peace."	**2Ki 5:19**	1980
"Did not my heart **g** *with you,*	**2Ki 5:26**	1980
"Please let us **g** to the Jordan and	**2Ki 6:2**	1980
where we may live." So he said, "**G**."	**2Ki 6:2**	1980
willing to **g** with your servants."	**2Ki 6:3**	1980
And he answered, "I shall **g**."	**2Ki 6:3**	1980
"**G** and see where he is, that I	**2Ki 6:13**	1980
and drink and **g** to their master."	**2Ki 6:22**	1980
and let us **g** over to the camp of	**2Ki 7:4**	5307
to **g** to the camp of the Arameans;	**2Ki 7:5**	935
g and tell the king's household."	**2Ki 7:9**	935
of the Arameans, saying, "**G** and see.	**2Ki 7:14**	1980
"Arise and **g** with your household,	**2Ki 8:1**	1980
hand and **g** to meet the man of God,	**2Ki 8:8**	1980
"**G**, say to him, 'You will surely	**2Ki 8:10**	1980
your hand and **g** to Ramoth-gilead.	**2Ki 9:1**	1980
and **g** in and bid him arise from	**2Ki 9:2**	935
city to **g** tell *it* in Jezreel."	**2Ki 9:15**	1980
"**G** in, kill them; let none come out."	**2Ki 10:25**	935
even all who **g** out on the sabbath,	**2Ki 11:7**	3318
who were to **g** out on the sabbath,	**2Ki 11:9**	3318
set his face to **g** up to Jerusalem.	**2Ki 12:17**	5927
and let him **g** and live there;	**2Ki 17:27**	1980
g into his hand and pierce it.	**2Ki 18:21**	935
'**G** up against this land and	**2Ki 18:25**	5927
Jerusalem will **g** forth a remnant,	**2Ki 19:31**	3318
g up to the house of the LORD.	**2Ki 20:5**	5927
and that I shall **g** up to the house	**2Ki 20:8**	5927
shall the shadow **g** forward ten	**2Ki 20:9**	1980
ten steps or **g** back ten steps?"	**2Ki 20:9**	7725
"**G** up to Hilkiah the high priest	**2Ki 22:4**	5927
"**G**, inquire of the LORD for me	**2Ki 22:13**	1980
did not **g** up to the altar of the LORD	**2Ki 23:9**	5927
to **g** out with the army to war.	**1Ch 7:11**	3318
when he was about to **g** to battle	**1Ch 12:19**	935
I **g** up against the Philistines?	**1Ch 14:10**	5927
"**G** up, for I will give them into	**1Ch 14:10**	5927
"You shall not **g** up after them;	**1Ch 14:14**	5927
then you shall **g** out to battle,	**1Ch 14:15**	3318
"**G** and tell David My servant,	**1Ch 17:4**	1980
must **g** *to be* with your fathers,	**1Ch 17:11**	1980
time when kings **g** out *to battle,*	**1Ch 20:1**	3318
"**G**, number Israel from Beersheba	**1Ch 21:2**	1980
"**G** and speak to David, saying,	**1Ch 21:10**	1980
that David should **g** up and build	**1Ch 21:18**	5927
not **g** before it to inquire of God,	**1Ch 21:30**	1980
that I may **g** out and come in	**2Ch 1:10**	3318
"When Your people **g** out to battle	**2Ch 6:34**	3318
and **g** and serve other gods and	**2Ch 7:19**	1980
"You shall not **g** up or fight	**2Ch 11:4**	5927
g, break your treaty with Baasha	**2Ch 16:3**	1980
him to **g** up against Ramoth-gilead.	**2Ch 18:2**	5927
g with me *against* Ramoth-gilead?"	**2Ch 18:3**	1980
"Shall we **g** against Ramoth-gilead	**2Ch 18:5**	1980
"**G** up, for God will give *it* into	**2Ch 18:5**	5927
"**G** up to Ramoth-gilead and	**2Ch 18:11**	5927
we **g** to Ramoth-gilead to battle,	**2Ch 18:14**	1980
"**G** up and succeed, for they will	**2Ch 18:14**	5927
to **g** up and fall at Ramoth-gilead?'	**2Ch 18:19**	5927
'I will **g** and be a deceiving	**2Ch 18:21**	3318
and prevail also. **G** and do so.'	**2Ch 18:21**	3318
disguise myself and **g** into battle,	**2Ch 18:29**	935
'Tomorrow **g** down against them.	**2Ch 20:16**	3381
tomorrow **g** out to face them, for	**2Ch 20:17**	3318
to make ships to **g** to Tarshish,	**2Ch 20:36**	1980
and could not **g** to Tarshish.	**2Ch 20:37**	1980
who were to **g** out on the sabbath,	**2Ch 23:8**	3318
"**G** out to the cities of Judah and	**2Ch 24:5**	3318
able to **g** to war *and* handle spear	**2Ch 25:5**	3318
let the army of Israel **g** with you,	**2Ch 25:7**	935
"But if you do **g**, do *it,* be	**2Ch 25:8**	935
to him from Ephraim, to **g** home;	**2Ch 25:10**	1980
kings of Judah had let **g** to ruin.	**2Ch 34:11**	7843
"**G**, inquire of the LORD for me	**2Ch 34:21**	1980
be with him, and let him **g** up!'"	**2Ch 36:23**	5927
Let him **g** up to Jerusalem which is	**Ezr 1:3**	5927
God had stirred to **g** up and rebuild	**Ezr 1:5**	5927
g *and* deposit them in the temple	**Ezr 5:15**	236
he began to **g** up from Babylon;	**Ezr 7:9**	4609b
who are willing to **g** to Jerusalem,	**Ezr 7:13**	1981
go to Jerusalem, may **g** with you.	**Ezr 7:13**	1981
men from Israel to **g** up with me.	**Ezr 7:28**	5927
the first month to **g** to Jerusalem;	**Ezr 8:31**	1980
for the house to which I will **g**."	**Ne 2:8**	935
one such as I **g** into the temple to	**Ne 6:11**	935
I will not **g** in."	**Ne 6:11**	935
"**G**, eat of the fat, drink of the	**Ne 8:10**	1980
"**G** out to the hills, and bring	**Ne 8:15**	3318
the way In which they were to **g**.	**Ne 9:12**	1980
the way in which they were to **g**.	**Ne 9:19**	1980
came to **g** in to King Ahasuerus,	**Es 2:12**	935
g in to the king in this way:	**Es 2:13**	935
In the evening she would **g** in and	**Es 2:14**	935

She would not again **g** in to the **Es 2:14** 935
came to **g** in to the king, **Es 2:15** 935
and ordered him *to* **g** to Mordecai **Es 4:5**
and to order her to **g** in to the **Es 4:8** 935
"**G**, assemble all the Jews who are **Es 4:16** 1980
And thus I will **g** in to the king, **Es 4:16** 935
then **g** joyfully with the king to **Es 5:14** 935
His sons used to **g** and hold a feast **Jb 1:4** 1980
They **g** up into nothing and perish. **Jb 6:18** 5927
That we may **g** to court together. **Jb 9:32** 935
Before I **g**—and I shall not return **Jb 10:21** 1980
a multitude of words **g** unanswered, **Jb 11:2** 6030a
such words to **g** out of your mouth? **Jb 15:13** 3318
Of His mouth he will **g** away. **Jb 15:30** 5493
I shall **g** the way of no return. **Jb 16:22** 1980
"Will it **g** down with me to Sheol? **Jb 17:16** 3381
together **g** down into the dust?" **Jb 17:16** 5183a
desires it and will not let it **g**, **Jb 20:13** 5800a
And suddenly they **g** down to Sheol. **Jb 21:13** 5181
While countless ones **g** before him. **Jb 21:33**
I **g** forward but He is not *there*, **Jb 23:8** 1980
They **g** forth seeking food in their **Jb 24:5** 3318
to **g** about naked without clothing, **Jb 24:10** 1980
and will not let it **g**. **Jb 27:6** 7503
"I **g** about mourning without **Jb 30:28** 1980
silent and did not **g** out of doors? **Jb 31:34** 3318
should **g** before God in judgment. **Jb 34:23** 1980
that they may **g** And say to you, **Jb 38:35** 1980
Out of his mouth **g** burning torches **Jb 41:19** 1980
rams, and **g** to My servant Job, **Jb 42:8** 1980
All those who **g** down to the dust **Ps 22:29** 3381
men, Nor will I **g** with pretenders. **Ps 26:4** 935
And I will **g** about Your altar, **Ps 26:6** 5437
like those who **g** down to the pit. **Ps 28:1** 3381
I would not **g** down to the pit. **Ps 30:3** 3381
my blood, if I **g** down to the pit? **Ps 30:9** 3381
you in the way which you should **g**; **Ps 32:8** 1980
I **g** mourning all day long. **Ps 38:6** 1980
I used to **g** along with the throng **Ps 42:4** 5674a
Why do I **g** mourning because of the **Ps 42:9** 1980
Why do I **g** mourning because of the **Ps 43:2** 1980
Then I will **g** to the altar of God, **Ps 43:4** 935
do not **g** out with our armies. **Ps 44:9** 3318
Walk about Zion and **g** around her; **Ps 48:12** 5362b
G through her palaces, **Ps 48:13** 6448
He shall **g** to the generation of **Ps 49:19** 935
they **g** around her upon her walls, **Ps 55:10** 5437
Let them **g** down alive to Sheol, **Ps 55:15** 3381
speak lies **g** astray from birth. **Ps 58:3** 8582
like a dog, And **g** around the city. **Ps 59:6** 5437
like a dog, And **g** around the city. **Ps 59:14** 5437
You not **g** forth with our armies, **Ps 60:10** 3318
In the balances they **g** up; **Ps 62:9** 5927
g into the depths of the earth. **Ps 63:9** 935
They **g** from strength to strength, **Ps 84:7** 1980
Righteousness will **g** before Him And **Ps 85:13** 1980
among those who **g** down to the pit; **Ps 88:4** 3381
I am shut up and cannot **g** out. **Ps 88:8** 3318
and truth **g** before You. **Ps 89:14** 6923
way, To **g** to an inhabited city. **Ps 107:7** 1980
who **g** down to the sea in ships, **Ps 107:23** 3381
You not **g** forth with our armies, **Ps 108:11** 3318
Nor *do* any who **g** down into silence **Ps 115:17** 3381
us **g** to the house of the LORD." **Ps 122:1** 1980
To which the tribes **g** up, **Ps 122:4** 5927
Let us **g** into His dwelling place; **Ps 132:7** 935
Where can I **g** from Your Spirit? **Ps 139:7** 1980
like those who **g** down to the pit. **Ps 143:7** 3381
as those who **g** down to the pit; **Pr 1:12** 3381
None who **g** to her return again, **Pr 2:19** 935
"**G**, and come back, And tomorrow I **Pr 3:28** 1980
Take hold of instruction; do not let **g**. **Pr 4:13** 7503
Her feet **g** down to death, Her **Pr 5:5** 3381
not **g** near the door of her house, **Pr 5:8** 7126
And your hard-earned goods *will* **g** **Pr 5:10**
of his folly he will **g** astray. **Pr 5:23** 7686
G, humble yourself, and importune **Pr 6:3** 1980
G to the ant, O sluggard, Observe **Pr 6:6** 1980
touches her will not **g** unpunished. **Pr 6:29** 5352
evil man will not **g** unpunished, **Pr 11:21** 5352
they not **g** astray who devise evil? **Pr 14:22** 8582
him, He will not **g** to the wise. **Pr 15:12** 1980
at calamity will not **g** unpunished. **Pr 17:5** 5352
And they **g** down into the innermost **Pr 18:8** 3381
witness will not **g** unpunished, **Pr 19:5** 5352
witness will not **g** unpunished, **Pr 19:9** 5352
will **g** out in time of darkness. **Pr 20:20** 1846
hides himself, But the naive **g** on, **Pr 22:3** 5674a
up a child in the way he should **g**, **Pr 22:6**
and contention will **g** out, **Pr 22:10** 3318
Or **g** with a hot-tempered man, **Pr 22:24** 935
Or **g** into the fields of the **Pr 23:10** 935
Those who **g** to taste mixed wine. **Pr 23:30** 935
Do not **g** out hastily to argue *your* **Pr 25:8** 3318
And they **g** down into the innermost **Pr 26:22** 3381
And do not **g** to your brother's **Pr 27:10** 935
to be rich will not **g** unpunished. **Pr 28:20** 5352
Yet all of them **g** out in ranks; **Pr 30:27** 3318
Her lamp does not **g** out at night. **Pr 31:18** 3518
All **g** to the same place. **Ec 3:20** 1980
as you **g** to the house of God and **Ec 5:1** 1980
do not all **g** to one place?" **Ec 6:6** 1980
It is better to **g** to a house of **Ec 7:2** 1980
Than to **g** to a house of feasting, **Ec 7:2** 1980
and also not let **g** of the other; **Ec 7:18**
5117, 3027
those who used to **g** in and out **Ec 8:10** 935
Afterwards they **g** to the dead. **Ec 9:3**
G *then*, eat your bread in **Ec 9:7** 1980
not *even* know how to **g** to a city. **Ec 10:15** 1980
mourners **g** about in the street. **Ec 12:5** 5437
G forth on the trail of the flock And **SS 1:8** 3318
arise now and **g** about the city; **SS 3:2** 5437
on to him and would not let him **g** Until **SS 3:4** 7503
"**G** forth, O daughters of Zion, **SS 3:11** 3318
I will **g** my way to the mountain of **SS 4:6** 1980
let us **g** out into the country, **SS 7:11** 3318
"Let us rise early *and* **g** to **SS 7:12**
let us **g** up to the mountain of the **Is 2:3** 5927
the law will **g** forth from Zion And **Is 2:3** 3318
will **g** into caves of the rocks And **Is 2:19** 935
In order to **g** into the caverns of **Is 2:21** 935
Say to the righteous that *it will* **g** **Is 3:10**
Woe to the wicked! *It will* **g** **Is 3:11**
And **g** along with mincing steps And **Is 3:16** 1980
Therefore My people **g** into exile **Is 5:13** 1540
I send, and who will **g** for Us?" **Is 6:8** 1980
"**G**, and tell this people: **Is 6:9** 1980
"**G** out now to meet Ahaz, you and **Is 7:3** 3318
"Let us **g** up against Judah and **Is 7:6** 5927
you will not **g** there for fear of **Is 7:25** 935
channels and **g** over all its banks. **Is 8:7** 1980
did not allow his prisoners to **g** **Is 14:17**
g down to the stones of the pit Like **Is 14:19** 3381
For they **g** up the ascent of Luhith **Is 15:5** 5927
G, swift messengers, to a nation **Is 18:2** 1980
"**G** and loosen the sackcloth from **Is 20:2** 1980
G up, Elam, lay siege, Media; **Is 21:2** 5927
"**G**, station the lookout, let him **Is 21:6** 1980
"Come, **g** to this steward, To **Is 22:15** 935
will **g** back to her harlot's wages and **Is 23:17** 7725
they may **g** and stumble backward, **Is 28:13** 1980
Now **g**, write it on a tablet before **Is 30:8** 935
To **g** to the mountain of the LORD, **Is 30:29** 935
who **g** down to Egypt for help **Is 31:1** 3381
which no boat with oars will **g**, **Is 33:21** 1980
Its smoke will **g** up forever **Is 34:10** 5927
will any vicious beast **g** up on it; **Is 35:9** 5927
g into his hand and pierce it. **Is 36:6** 935
'**G** up against this land and **Is 36:10** 5927
And I will **g** to its highest peak, **Is 37:24** 935
Jerusalem will **g** forth a remnant **Is 37:32** 3318
"**G** and say to Hezekiah, **Is 38:5** 1980
of Ahaz, to **g** back ten steps." **Is 38:8** 7725
Those who **g** down to the pit cannot **Is 38:18** 3381
g up to the house of the LORD?" **Is 38:22** 5927
You who **g** down to the sea, and all **Is 42:10** 3381
LORD will **g** forth like a warrior, **Is 42:13** 3318
"I will **g** before you and make the **Is 45:2** 1980
and will let My exiles **g** free, **Is 45:13** 7971
g away together in humiliation. **Is 45:16** 1980
"Sit silently, and **g** into darkness, **Is 47:5** 935
leads you in the way you should **g**. **Is 48:17** 1980
G forth from Babylon! **Is 48:20** 3318
'**G** forth,' To those who are in **Is 49:9** 3318
For a law will **g** forth from Me, **Is 51:4** 3318
Depart, depart, **g** out from there, **Is 52:11** 3318
G out of the midst of her, purify **Is 52:11** 3318
But you will not **g** out in haste, **Is 52:12** 3318
Nor will you **g** as fugitives; **Is 52:12** 1980
For the LORD will **g** before you, **Is 52:12** 1980
"For you will **g** out with joy And **Is 55:12** 3318
And made *them* **g** down to Sheol. **Is 57:9** 8213
And to let the oppressed **g** free And **Is 58:6** 7971
righteousness will **g** before you; **Is 58:8** 1980
They will **g** up with acceptance on **Is 60:7** 5927
G through, go through the gates, **Is 62:10** 5674a
Go through, **g** through the gates, **Is 62:10** 5674a
to **g** at the right hand of Moses, **Is 63:12** 1980
which **g** down into the valley, **Is 63:14** 3381
sanctify and purify themselves *to* **g** **Is 66:17**
"Then they will **g** forth and look **Is 66:24** 3318
I send you, you shall **g**, **Jer 1:7** 1980
"**G** and proclaim in the ears of **Jer 2:2** 1980
"Why do you **g** around so much **Jer 2:36** 235
"From this *place* also you will **g** **Jer 2:37** 3318
"**G** and proclaim these words **Jer 3:12** 1980
Or else My wrath will **g** forth like fire **Jer 4:4** 3318
us **g** Into the fortified cities.' **Jer 4:5** 935
They **g** into the thickets and climb **Jer 4:29** 935
"I will **g** to the great And will **Jer 5:5** 1980
"**G** up through her vine rows and **Jer 5:10** 5927
Do not **g** out into the field And **Jer 6:25** 3318
"But **g** now to My place which was **Jer 7:12** 1980
us **g** into the fortified cities And **Jer 8:14** 935
leave my people And **g** from them! **Jer 9:2** 1980
inhabitants of Jerusalem will **g** and cry **Jer 11:12** 1980
G, gather all the beasts of the **Jer 12:9** 1980
"**G** and buy yourself a linen **Jer 13:1** 1980
g to the Euphrates and hide it **Jer 13:4** 1980
g to the Euphrates and take from **Jer 13:6** 1980
'If I **g** out to the country, **Jer 14:18** 3318
from My presence and let them **g**! **Jer 15:1** 3318
'Where should we **g**?' **Jer 15:2** 3318
or **g** to lament or to console them; **Jer 16:5** 1980
"Moreover you shall not **g** into a **Jer 16:8** 935
let **g** of your inheritance That I **Jer 17:4** 8058
"**G** and stand in the public gate, **Jer 17:19** 1980
kings of Judah come in and **g** out, **Jer 17:19** 3318
and **g** down to the potter's house, **Jer 18:2** 3381
"**G** and buy a potter's earthenware **Jer 19:1** 1980
"Then **g** out to the valley of **Jer 19:2** 3318
your house will **g** into captivity; **Jer 20:6** 1980
That My wrath may not **g** forth like **Jer 21:12** 3318
"**G** down to the house of the king **Jer 22:1** 3381
"**G** up to Lebanon and cry out, And **Jer 22:20** 5927
your lovers will **g** into captivity; **Jer 22:22** 1980
and do not **g** after other gods to **Jer 25:6** 1980
will drink and stagger and **g** mad **Jer 25:16** 1984b
"Command them *to* **g** to their **Jer 27:4**
Jerusalem may not **g** to Babylon. **Jer 27:18** 935
"**G** and speak to Hananiah, saying, **Jer 28:13** 1980
who did not **g** with you into exile **Jer 29:16** 3318
of them, will **g** into captivity; **Jer 30:16** 1980
And **g** forth to the dances of the **Jer 31:4** 3318
'Arise, and let us **g** up *to* Zion, **Jer 31:6** 5927
long will you **g** here and there, **Jer 31:22** 2559
and they who **g** about with flocks. **Jer 31:24** 5265
"The measuring line will **g** **Jer 31:39** 3318
'**G** and speak to Zedekiah king of **Jer 34:2** 1980
and you will **g** to Babylon. **Jer 34:3** 935
"**G** to the house of the Rechabites and **Jer 35:2** 1980
'Come and let us **g** to Jerusalem **Jer 35:11** 935
'**G** and say to the men of Judah and **Jer 35:13** 1980
and do not **g** after other gods to **Jer 35:15** 1980
g into the house of the LORD. **Jer 36:5** 935
"So you **g** and read from the **Jer 36:6** 935
"**G**, hide yourself, you and **Jer 36:19** 1980
will surely **g** away from us," **Jer 37:9** 1980
away from us," for they will not **g**. **Jer 37:9** 1980
out from Jerusalem to **g** to the land **Jer 37:12** 1980
'If you will indeed **g** out to the **Jer 38:17** 3318
'But if you will not **g** out to the **Jer 38:18** 3318
that it may **g** well with you and **Jer 38:20** 3190
"But if you keep refusing to **g** out, **Jer 38:21** 3318
"**G** and speak to Ebed-melech the **Jer 39:16** 1980
g wherever it seems good and right **Jer 40:4** 1980
good and right for you to **g**." **Jer 40:4** 1980
"**G** on back then to Gedaliah the **Jer 40:5** 7725
or else **g** anywhere it seems right **Jer 40:5** 1980
it seems right for you to **g**." **Jer 40:5** 1980
a ration and a gift and let him **g**. **Jer 40:5** 7971
that it may **g** well with you. **Jer 40:9** 3190
"Let me **g** and kill Ishmael the **Jer 40:15** 1980
so that it may **g** well with **Jer 42:6** 3190
we will **g** to the land of Egypt, **Jer 42:14** 935
Egypt and **g** in to reside there, **Jer 42:15** 935
men who set their mind to **g** to Egypt **Jer 42:17** 935
"Do not **g** into Egypt!" **Jer 42:19** 935
where you wish to **g** to reside. **Jer 42:22** 935
G ahead and confirm your vows, **Jer 44:25** 6965
the places where you may **g**.' " **Jer 45:5** 1980
G up, you horses, and drive madly, **Jer 46:9** 5927
G up to Gilead and obtain balm, O **Jer 46:11** 5927
And let us **g** back To our own **Jer 46:16** 7725
And Chemosh will **g** off into exile **Jer 48:7** 3318
For Malcam will **g** into exile **Jer 49:3** 1980
g up to Kedar And devastate the **Jer 49:28** 5927
g up against a nation which is at **Jer 49:31** 5927
the outcasts of Elam will not **g**. **Jer 49:36** 935
will **g** along weeping as they go, **Jer 50:4** 1980
will go along weeping as they **g**, **Jer 50:4** 1980
And **g** forth from the land of the **Jer 50:8** 3318
of Merathaim, **g** up against it, **Jer 50:21** 5927
Let them **g** down to the slaughter! **Jer 50:27** 3381
They have refused to let them **g**. **Jer 50:33** 7971
let us each **g** to his own country, **Jer 51:9** 1980
me in so that I cannot **g** out; **La 3:7** 3318
That both good and ill **g** forth? **La 3:38** 3318
the spirit was about to **g**, **Ezk 1:12** 1980
was about to go, they would **g**, **Ezk 1:12** 1980
the spirit was about to **g**, **Ezk 1:20** 1980
they would **g** in that direction. **Ezk 1:20** 1980
eat this scroll, and **g**, **Ezk 3:1** 1980
g to the house of Israel and speak **Ezk 3:4** 1980, 935
"**G** to the exiles, to the sons of **Ezk 3:11** 1980
"Get up, **g** out to the plain, and **Ezk 3:22** 3318
"**G**, shut yourself up in your house **Ezk 3:24** 935
that you cannot **g** out among them. **Ezk 3:25** 3318
"**G** in and see the wicked **Ezk 8:9** 935
"**G** through the midst of the city, **Ezk 9:4** 5674a
"**G** through the city after him and **Ezk 9:5** 5674a
G out!" Thus they went out and **Ezk 9:7** 3318
the wheels would **g** beside them; **Ezk 10:16** 1980
'**G** far from the LORD; **Ezk 11:15** 7368
"But as for those whose hearts **g** **Ezk 11:21** 1980
and **g** into exile by day in their sight; **Ezk 12:3** 1540
even **g** into exile from your place **Ezk 12:3** 1540
g out at evening in their sight, **Ezk 12:4** 3318
their sight and **g** out through it. **Ezk 12:5** 3318
they will **g** into exile, into **Ezk 12:11** 1980
shoulder in the dark and **g** out. **Ezk 12:12** 3318
among the nations where they **g**, **Ezk 12:16** 935
and I will let them **g**, **Ezk 13:20** 7971
is the high place to which you **g**?' **Ezk 20:29** 935
"**G**, serve everyone his idols; **Ezk 20:39** 1980
therefore My sword will **g** forth **Ezk 21:4** 3318
yourself sharp, **g** to the right; **Ezk 21:16** 3231
g to the left, wherever your edge **Ezk 21:16** 8041
of them will **g** out of one land. **Ezk 21:19** 3318
as they would **g** in to a harlot. **Ezk 23:44** 935
will **g** down from their thrones, **Ezk 26:16** 3381
with those who **g** down to the pit, **Ezk 26:20** 3381
with those who **g** down to the pit, **Ezk 26:20** 3381
"On that day messengers will **g** **Ezk 30:9** 3318
the women will **g** into captivity. **Ezk 30:17** 1980
daughters will **g** into captivity. **Ezk 30:18** 1980
those who **g** down to the pit." **Ezk 31:14** 3381
I made it **g** down to Sheol with those **Ezk 31:16** 3381
with those who **g** down to the pit; **Ezk 31:16** 3381
with those who **g** down to the pit; **Ezk 32:18** 3381
G down and make your bed with the **Ezk 32:19** 3381
with those who **g** down to the pit; **Ezk 32:25** 3381
with those who **g** down to the pit. **Ezk 32:29** 3381
with those who **g** down to the pit. **Ezk 32:30** 3381
"You will **g** up, you will come **Ezk 38:9** 5927
'I will **g** up against the land of **Ezk 38:11** 5927

I will **g** against those who are	**Ezk 38:11**	5927
the cities of Israel will **g** out and	**Ezk 39:9**	3318
g into exile among the nations,	**Ezk 39:28**	1540
then they shall not **g** out into the	**Ezk 42:14**	3318
and shall **g** out by the same way."	**Ezk 44:3**	3318
they **g** out into the outer court,	**Ezk 44:19**	3318
They shall not **g** to a dead person	**Ezk 44:25**	935
of the gate and then **g** out;	**Ezk 46:2**	3318
he shall **g** in by way of the porch	**Ezk 46:8**	935
gate and **g** out by the same way.	**Ezk 46:8**	3318
gate to worship shall **g** out by	**Ezk 46:9**	3318
of the south gate shall **g** out by	**Ezk 46:9**	3318
entered but shall **g** straight out.	**Ezk 46:9**	3318
"When they **g** in, the prince	**Ezk 46:10**	935
the prince shall **g** in among them;	**Ezk 46:10**	935
and when they **g** out, he shall go	**Ezk 46:10**	3318
when they go out, he shall **g** out.	**Ezk 46:10**	3318
Then he shall **g** out, and the gate	**Ezk 46:12**	3318
"These waters **g** out toward the	**Ezk 47:8**	3318
region and **g** down into the Arabah;	**Ezk 47:8**	3381
then they **g** toward the sea, being	**Ezk 47:8**	935
fish, for these waters **g** there and	**Ezk 47:9**	935
who did not **g** astray when the sons	**Ezk 48:11**	8582
the South will be enraged and **g** forth	**Da 11:11**	3318
and he will **g** up and gain power	**Da 11:23**	5927
and he will **g** forth with great	**Da 11:44**	3318
many will **g** back and forth, and	**Da 12:4**	7751a
"**G** *your way,* Daniel, for *these*	**Da 12:9**	1980
as for you, **g** *your way* to the end;	**Da 12:13**	1980
"**G**, take to yourself a wife of	**Hos 1:2**	1980
And they will **g** up from the land,	**Hos 1:11**	5927
'I will **g** after my lovers, Who	**Hos 2:5**	1980
'I will **g** back to my first husband,	**Hos 2:7**	1980
"**G** again, love a woman *who* is	**Hos 3:1**	1980
For the *men* themselves **g** apart	**Hos 4:14**	6504
Also do not **g** to Gilgal, Or go up	**Hos 4:15**	935
go to Gilgal, Or **g** up to Beth-aven	**Hos 4:15**	5927
They will **g** with their flocks and	**Hos 5:6**	1980
I, will tear to pieces and **g** away,	**Hos 5:14**	1980
I will **g** away *and* return to My	**Hos 5:15**	1980
call to Egypt, they **g** to Assyria.	**Hos 7:11**	1980
When they **g**, I will spread My net	**Hos 7:12**	1980
will **g** because of destruction;	**Hos 9:6**	1980
And a spring will **g** out from the	**Jl 3:18**	3318
of Aram will **g** exiled to Kir,"	**Am 1:5**	1540
"Their king will **g** into exile, He	**Am 1:15**	1980
"You will **g** out *through* breaches	**Am 4:3**	3318
will certainly **g** into captivity And	**Am 5:5**	1540
g into exile beyond Damascus,"	**Am 5:27**	1540
G over to Calneh and look, And go	**Am 6:2**	5674a
And **g** from there to Hamath the	**Am 6:2**	1980
Then **g** down to Gath of the	**Am 6:2**	3381
they will now **g** into exile at the	**Am 6:7**	1540
g from its land into exile.' "	**Am 7:11**	1540
"**G**, you seer, flee away to the	**Am 7:12**	1980
'**G** prophesy to My people Israel.'	**Am 7:15**	1980
g from its land into exile.' "	**Am 7:17**	1540
"That I will make the sun **g** down	**Am 8:9**	935
They will **g** to and fro to seek the	**Am 8:12**	7751a
"And though they **g** into captivity	**Am 9:4**	1980
let us **g** against her for battle"	**Ob 1:1**	6965
g to Nineveh the great city and	**Jon 1:2**	1980
and went down into it to **g** with	**Jon 1:3**	935
g to Nineveh the great city and	**Jon 3:2**	1980
Then Jonah began to **g** through the	**Jon 3:4**	935
wail, I must **g** barefoot and naked;	**Mi 1:8**	1980
G on your way, inhabitant of	**Mi 1:11**	5674a
they will **g** from you into exile.	**Mi 1:16**	1540
"Arise and **g**, For this is no	**Mi 2:10**	1980
through the gate and **g** out by it.	**Mi 2:13**	3318
sun will **g** down on the prophets,	**Mi 3:6**	935
"Come and let us **g** up to the	**Mi 4:2**	5927
from Zion will **g** forth the law,	**Mi 4:2**	3318
now you will **g** out of the city,	**Mi 4:10**	3318
in the field, And **g** to Babylon.	**Mi 4:10**	935
From you One will **g** forth for Me	**Mi 5:2**	3318
G into the clay and tread the	**Na 3:14**	935
"**G** up to the mountains, bring	**Hg 1:8**	5927
and their riders will **g** down,	**Hg 2:22**	3381
"I will make it **g** forth,"	**Zch 5:4**	3318
the white ones **g** forth after them,	**Zch 6:6**	3318
ones **g** forth to the south country.	**Zch 6:6**	3318
eager to **g** to patrol the earth."	**Zch 6:7**	1980
"**G**, patrol the earth."	**Zch 6:7**	1980
and you **g** the same day and enter	**Zch 6:10**	935
of one will **g** to another,	**Zch 8:21**	1980
"Let us **g** at once to entreat the	**Zch 8:21**	1980
seek the LORD of hosts; I will also **g**."	**Zch 8:21**	1980
"Let us **g** with you, for we have	**Zch 8:23**	1980
arrow will **g** forth like lightning;	**Zch 9:14**	3318
them slay them and **g** unpunished,	**Zch 11:5**	816
Then the LORD will **g** forth and	**Zch 14:3**	3318
will **g** up from year to year to worship	**Zch 14:16**	5927
does not **g** up to Jerusalem to worship	**Zch 14:17**	5927
of Egypt does not **g** up or enter,	**Zch 14:18**	5927
nations who do not **g** up to celebrate	**Zch 14:18**	5927
nations who do not **g** up to celebrate	**Zch 14:19**	5927
and you will **g** forth and skip	**Mal 4:2**	3318
"**G** and search carefully for	**Mt 2:8**	*4198*
and **g** into the land of Israel;	**Mt 2:20**	*4198*
Herod, he was afraid to **g** there.	**Mt 2:22**	*565*
Then Jesus said to him, "**G**, Satan!	**Mt 4:10**	*5217*
shall be guilty *enough to* **g**	**Mt 5:22**	
before the altar and **g**;	**Mt 5:24**	*5217*
your whole body to **g** into hell.	**Mt 5:30**	*565*
forces you to **g** one mile,	**Mt 5:41**	
to go one mile, **g** with him two.	**Mt 5:41**	*5217*
you pray, **g** into your inner room,	**Mt 6:6**	*1525*
but **g**, show yourself to the	**Mt 8:4**	*5217*

and I say to this one, '**G**!'	**Mt 8:9**	*4198*
said to the centurion, "**G**;	**Mt 8:13**	*5217*
will follow You wherever You **g**."	**Mt 8:19**	*565*
first to **g** and bury my father."	**Mt 8:21**	*565*
And He said to them, "**G**!" And	**Mt 8:32**	*5217*
pick up your bed and **g** home."	**Mt 9:6**	*5217*
"But **g** and learn what this means:	**Mt 9:13**	*4198*
not **g** in *the* way of the Gentiles,	**Mt 10:5**	*565*
but rather **g** to the lost sheep of	**Mt 10:6**	*4198*
"And as you **g**, preach, saying,	**Mt 10:7**	*4198*
as you **g** out of that house or that	**Mt 10:14**	*1831*
"**G** and report to John what you	**Mt 11:4**	*4198*
"What did you **g** out into the	**Mt 11:7**	*1831*
"But what did you **g** out to see?	**Mt 11:8**	*1831*
"But what did you **g** out to see?	**Mt 11:9**	*1831*
and they **g** in and live there;	**Mt 12:45**	*1525*
then, to **g** and gather them up?"	**Mt 13:28**	*565*
that they may **g** into the villages	**Mt 14:15**	*565*
"They do not need to **g** away;	**Mt 14:16**	*565*
and **g** ahead of Him to the other	**Mt 14:22**	*4254*
that He must **g** to Jerusalem,	**Mt 16:21**	*565*
"But this kind does not **g** out	**Mt 17:21**	*1607*
do not offend them, **g** to the sea	**Mt 17:27**	*4198*
and **g** and search for the one that is	**Mt 18:12**	*4198*
g and show him his fault in private;	**Mt 18:15**	*5217*
g *and* sell your possessions and	**Mt 19:21**	*5217*
to **g** through the eye of a needle,	**Mt 19:24**	
'You also **g** into the vineyard, and	**Mt 20:4**	*5217*
'You **g** into the vineyard too.'	**Mt 20:7**	*5217*
'Take what is yours and **g**,	**Mt 20:14**	*5217*
was about to **g** up to Jerusalem,	**Mt 20:17**	*305*
"**G** into the village opposite you,	**Mt 21:2**	*4198*
g work today in the vineyard.'	**Mt 21:28**	*5217*
but he did not **g**.	**Mt 21:30**	*565*
'**G** therefore to the main highways,	**Mt 22:9**	*4198*
those who are entering to **g** in.	**Mt 23:13**	*1525*
on the housetop must not **g** down	**Mt 24:17**	*2597*
in the wilderness,' do not **g** out,	**Mt 24:26**	*1831*
g instead to the dealers and buy	**Mt 25:9**	*4198*
a man *about* to **g** on a journey,	**Mt 25:14**	*589*
g away into eternal punishment,	**Mt 25:46**	*565*
"**G** into the city to a certain	**Mt 26:18**	*5217*
"The Son of Man *is to* **g**,	**Mt 26:24**	*5217*
I will **g** ahead of you to Galilee."	**Mt 26:32**	*4254*
while I **g** over there and pray."	**Mt 26:36**	*565*
g, make it *as* secure as you know	**Mt 27:65**	*5217*
"**G** quickly and tell His disciples	**Mt 28:7**	*4198*
g and take word to My brethren to	**Mt 28:10**	*5217*
"**G** therefore and make disciples	**Mt 28:19**	*4198*
the Spirit impelled Him *to* **g**	**Mk 1:12**	*1544*
"Let us **g** somewhere else to the	**Mk 1:38**	*71*
but **g**, show yourself to the priest	**Mk 1:44**	*5217*
pick up your pallet and **g** home."	**Mk 2:11**	*5217*
"Let us **g** over to the other side."	**Mk 4:35**	*1330*
"**G** home to your people and report	**Mk 5:19**	*5217*
g in peace and be healed of your	**Mk 5:34**	*5217*
to you, as you **g** out from there,	**Mk 6:11**	*1607*
send them away so that they may **g**	**Mk 6:36**	*565*
"Shall we **g** and spend two hundred	**Mk 6:37**	*565*
many loaves do you have? **G** look!"	**Mk 6:38**	*5217*
disciples get into the boat and **g** ahead	**Mk 6:45**	*4254*
it does not **g** into his heart,	**Mk 7:19**	*1531*
"Because of this answer **g**;	**Mk 7:29**	*5217*
and *began to* **g** through Galilee,	**Mk 9:30**	*3899*
your two hands, to **g** into hell,	**Mk 9:43**	*565*
g and sell all you possess and	**Mk 10:21**	*5217*
"It is easier for a camel to **g**	**Mk 10:25**	*1330*
"**G**; your faith has made you	**Mk 10:52**	*5217*
"**G** into the village opposite you,	**Mk 11:2**	*5217*
they would **g** out of the city.	**Mk 11:19**	*1607*
on the housetop must not **g** down,	**Mk 13:15**	*2597*
or **g** in to get anything out	**Mk 13:15**	*2597*
"Where do You want us to **g** and	**Mk 14:12**	*565*
"**G** into the city, and a man will	**Mk 14:13**	*5217*
"For the Son of Man *is to* **g** just	**Mk 14:21**	*5217*
I will **g** ahead of you to Galilee."	**Mk 14:28**	*4254*
"But **g**, tell His disciples and	**Mk 16:7**	*5217*
"**G** into all the world and preach	**Mk 16:15**	*4198*
"It is he who will **g** *as a*	**Lk 1:17**	*4281*
For you will **g** on BEFORE THE LORD	**Lk 1:76**	*4313*
Let us **g** straight to Bethlehem then	**Lk 2:15**	*1330*
"**G** away from me Lord, for I am a	**Lk 5:8**	*1831*
"But **g** and show yourself to the	**Lk 5:14**	*565*
up your stretcher and **g** home."	**Lk 5:24**	*4198*
and I say to this one, '**G**!'	**Lk 7:8**	*4198*
"**G** and report to John what you	**Lk 7:22**	*4198*
"What did you **g** out into the	**Lk 7:24**	*1831*
"But what did you **g** out to see?	**Lk 7:25**	*1831*
"But what did you **g** out to see?	**Lk 7:26**	*1831*
Your faith has saved you; **g** in peace.	**Lk 7:50**	*4198*
and as they **g** on their way they	**Lk 8:14**	*4198*
"Let us **g** over to the other side	**Lk 8:22**	*1330*
Him not to command them to **g** away	**Lk 8:31**	*565*
faith has made you well; **g** in peace."	**Lk 8:48**	*4198*
you, as you **g** out from that city,	**Lk 9:5**	*1831*
they may **g** into the surrounding	**Lk 9:12**	*4198*
unless perhaps we **g** and buy food	**Lk 9:13**	*4198*
He was determined to **g** to Jerusalem;	**Lk 9:51**	*4198*
will follow You wherever You **g**."	**Lk 9:57**	*565*
first to **g** and bury my father."	**Lk 9:59**	*565*
g and proclaim everywhere the	**Lk 9:60**	*565*
"**G**; behold, I send you out	**Lk 10:3**	*5217*
g out into its streets and say,	**Lk 10:10**	*1831*
"**G** and do the same."	**Lk 10:37**	*4198*
and they **g** in and live there;	**Lk 11:26**	*1525*
"**G** away, leave here, for	**Lk 13:31**	*1831*
"**G** and tell that fox,	**Lk 13:32**	*4198*
g and recline at the last place,	**Lk 14:10**	*4198*
I need to **g** out and look at it;	**Lk 14:18**	*1831*

'**G** out at once into the streets	**Lk 14:21**	*1831*
'**G** out into the highways and along	**Lk 14:23**	*1831*
and **g** after the one which is lost until	**Lk 15:4**	*4198*
I will get up and **g** to my father,	**Lk 15:18**	*4198*
and was not willing to **g** in;	**Lk 15:28**	*1525*
"**G** and show yourselves to the	**Lk 17:14**	*4198*
"Stand up and **g**;	**Lk 17:19**	*4198*
Do not **g** away, and do not run	**Lk 17:23**	*565*
house must not **g** down to take them out;	**Lk 17:31**	*2597*
to **g** through the eye of a needle than	**Lk 18:25**	*1525*
"**G** into the village ahead of *you;*	**Lk 19:30**	*5217*
Do not **g** after them.	**Lk 21:8**	*4198*
but at evening He would **g** out and	**Lk 21:37**	*1831*
"**G** and prepare the Passover for	**Lk 22:8**	*4198*
g both to prison and to death!"	**Lk 22:33**	*4198*
purposed to **g** into Galilee,	**Jn 1:43**	*1831*
"**G**, call your husband and come	**Jn 4:16**	*5217*
"**G**; your son lives."	**Jn 4:50**	*4198*
"You do not want to **g** away also,	**Jn 6:67**	*5217*
"Lord, to whom shall we **g**?	**Jn 6:68**	*565*
here and **g** into Judea,	**Jn 7:3**	*5217*
"**G** up to the feast yourselves;	**Jn 7:8**	*305*
I do not **g** up to this feast	**Jn 7:8**	*305*
you, then I **g** to Him who sent Me.	**Jn 7:33**	*5217*
"Where does this man intend to **g**	**Jn 7:35**	*4198*
He is not intending to **g** to the	**Jn 7:35**	*4198*
they *began to* **g** out one by one,	**Jn 8:9**	*1831*
G. From now on sin no more."]	**Jn 8:11**	*4198*
"I **g** away, and you will seek Me,	**Jn 8:21**	*5217*
"**G**, wash in the pool of Siloam"	**Jn 9:7**	*5217*
'**G** to Siloam and wash';	**Jn 9:11**	*5217*
be saved, and will **g** in and out	**Jn 10:9**	
		1525, 1831
"Let us **g** to Judea again."	**Jn 11:7**	*71*
but I **g**, so that I may awaken him out	**Jn 11:11**	*4198*
but let us **g** to him."	**Jn 11:15**	*71*
"Let us also **g**, so that we may die	**Jn 11:16**	*71*
"Unbind him, and let him **g**."	**Jn 11:44**	*5217*
"If we let Him **g** *on* like this,	**Jn 11:48**	
"Where I **g**, you cannot follow Me	**Jn 13:36**	*5217*
I **g** to prepare a place for you.	**Jn 14:2**	*4198*
I **g** and prepare a place for you,	**Jn 14:3**	*4198*
because I **g** to the Father.	**Jn 14:12**	*4198*
'I **g** away, and I will come to you.'	**Jn 14:28**	*5217*
because I **g** to the Father,	**Jn 14:28**	*4198*
up, let us **g** from here.	**Jn 14:31**	*71*
that you would **g** and bear fruit,	**Jn 15:16**	*5217*
to your advantage that I **g** away;	**Jn 16:7**	*565*
for if I do not **g** away, the Helper	**Jn 16:7**	*565*
but if I **g**, I will send Him to you.	**Jn 16:7**	*4198*
because I **g** to the Father and	**Jn 16:10**	*5217*
'because I **g** to the Father'?"	**Jn 16:17**	*5217*
seek Me, let these **g** their way,"	**Jn 18:8**	*5217*
but he did not **g** in.	**Jn 20:5**	*1525*
but **g** to My brethren and say to	**Jn 20:17**	*4198*
you where you do not wish to **g**."	**Jn 21:18**	
have watched Him **g** into heaven."	**Ac 1:11**	*4198*
aside to **g** to his own place."	**Ac 1:25**	*4198*
John about to **g** into the temple,	**Ac 3:3**	*1524*
them further, they let them **g**	**Ac 4:21**	*630*
"**G**, stand and speak to	**Ac 5:20**	*4198*
FOR US GODS WHO WILL **G** BEFORE US;	**Ac 7:40**	*4313*
"Get up and **g** south to the road	**Ac 8:26**	*4198*
"**G** up and join this chariot."	**Ac 8:29**	*4334*
g to the street called Straight,	**Ac 9:11**	*4198*
"**G**, for he is a chosen instrument	**Ac 9:15**	*4198*
"But get up, **g** downstairs and	**Ac 10:20**	*2597*
to **g** with them without misgivings.	**Ac 11:12**	*4905*
the nations to **g** their own ways;	**Ac 14:16**	*4198*
g up to Jerusalem to the apostles	**Ac 15:2**	*305*
Paul wanted this man to **g** with him;	**Ac 16:3**	*1831*
were trying to **g** into Bithynia,	**Ac 16:7**	*4198*
we sought to **g** into Macedonia,	**Ac 16:10**	*1831*
come out now and **g** in peace."	**Ac 16:36**	*4198*
Paul out to **g** as far as the sea;	**Ac 17:14**	*4198*
on I will **g** to the Gentiles."	**Ac 18:6**	*4198*
but **g** on speaking and do not be	**Ac 18:9**	
he wanted to **g** across to Achaia,	**Ac 18:27**	*1330*
Paul purposed in the Spirit to **g**	**Ac 19:21**	*4198*
wanted to **g** into the assembly,	**Ac 19:30**	*1525*
he left to **g** to Macedonia.	**Ac 20:1**	*4198*
intending himself to **g** by land.	**Ac 20:13**	*3978*
him not to **g** up to Jerusalem.	**Ac 21:12**	*305*
'Get up and **g** on into Damascus,	**Ac 22:10**	*4198*
"And He said to me, '**G**!	**Ac 22:21**	*4198*
him immediately let **g** of him;	**Ac 22:29**	*868*
ordered the troops to **g** down and take	**Ac 23:10**	*2597*
the commander let the young man **g**,	**Ac 23:22**	*630*
the horsemen to **g** on with him,	**Ac 23:32**	*565*
"**G** away for the present, and when	**Ac 24:25**	*4198*
influential men among you **g** there	**Ac 25:5**	*4782*
willing to **g** up to Jerusalem and	**Ac 25:9**	*305*
Caesar, to Caesar you shall **g**."	**Ac 25:12**	*4198*
I asked whether he was willing to **g** to	**Ac 25:20**	*4198*
and allowed him to **g** to his friends	**Ac 27:3**	*4198*
the wind did not permit us *to* **g**	**Ac 27:7**	
'**G** TO THIS PEOPLE AND SAY	**Ac 28:26**	*4198*
and do not **g** on presenting the	**Ro 6:13**	
whenever I **g** to Spain	**Ro 15:24**	*4198*
will **g** on by way of you to Spain.	**Ro 15:28**	*565*
Therefore do not **g** on passing	**1Co 4:5**	
would have to **g** out of the world.	**1Co 5:10**	*1831*
g to law before the unrighteous and	**1Co 6:1**	*2919*
invites you and you want to **g**,	**1Co 10:27**	*4198*
if it is fitting for me to **g** also,	**1Co 16:4**	*4198*
to go also, they will **g** with me.	**1Co 16:4**	*4198*
you after I **g** through Macedonia,	**1Co 16:5**	*1330*
me on my way wherever I may **g**.	**1Co 16:6**	*4198*
that they would **g** on ahead to you	**2Co 9:5**	*4281*

but I will **g** on to visions and **2Co 12:1** *2064*
I urged Titus *to* **g**, and I sent **2Co 12:18**
nor did I **g** up to Jerusalem to **Ga 1:17** *424*
so that we *might* **g** to **Ga 2:9**
let the sun **g** down on your anger, **Eph 4:26** *1931*
as soon as I see how things **g** **Php 2:23**
they **g** around from house to house; **1Tm 5:13** *4022*
ALWAYS **G** ASTRAY IN THEIR HEART **Heb 3:10** *4105*
For if we **g** on sinning willfully **Heb 10:26**
us **g** out to Him outside the camp, **Heb 13:13** *1831*
"**G** in peace, be warmed and be **Jas 2:16** *5217*
will **g** to such and such a city, **Jas 4:13** *4198*
he will not **g** out from it anymore; **Rv 3:12** *1831*
"**G**, take the book which is open **Rv 10:8** *5217*
"**G** and pour out on the earth **Rv 16:1** *5217*
which **g** out to the kings of the **Rv 16:14** *1607*
the abyss and **g** to destruction. **Rv 17:8** *5217*

GOADS
The words of wise men are like **g**, **Ec 12:11** 1861b
for you to kick against the **g**.' **Ac 26:14** *2759*

GOAH
then it will turn to **G**. **Jer 31:39** 1601

GOAL
It hastens toward the **g** and **Hab 2:3** 7093
and the third *day* I reach My **g**.' **Lk 13:32** *5048*
I press on toward the **g** for the **Php 3:14** *4649*
But the **g** of our instruction is **1Tm 1:5** *5056*

GOAT
and a three year old female **g**, **Gn 15:9** 5795
tunic, and slaughtered a male **g** and **Gn 37:31** 8163b
"I will send you a young **g** from **Gn 38:17** 1423, 5795
When Judah sent the young **g** by his **Gn 38:20** 1423, 5795
I sent this young **g**, but you did not **Gn 38:23** 1423
You are not to boil a young **g** in **Ex 23:19** 1423
material, fine linen, **g** *hair*, **Ex 25:4** 5795
"You shall not boil a young **g** in its **Ex 34:26** 1423
'Moreover, if his offering is a **g**, **Lv 3:12** 5795
shall bring for his offering a **g**, **Lv 4:23** 8163b, 5795
hand on the head of the male **g** and **Lv 4:24** 8163b
shall bring for his offering a **g**, **Lv 4:28** 8166
a lamb or a **g** as a sin offering. **Lv 5:6** 8166, 5795
fat *from* an ox, a sheep or a **g**. **Lv 7:23** 5795
'Take a male **g** for a sin offering, **Lv 9:3** 5795
and took the **g** of the sin offering **Lv 9:15** 5795
for the **g** of the sin offering, **Lv 10:16** 5795
"Then Aaron shall offer the **g** on **Lv 16:9** 5795
g on which the lot for the scapegoat **Lv 16:10** 5795
"Then he shall slaughter the **g** of **Lv 16:15** 5795
bull and of the blood of the **g** and **Lv 16:18** 5795
altar, he shall offer the live **g**. **Lv 16:20** 5795
hands on the head of the live **g**, **Lv 16:21** 5795
he shall lay them on the head of the **g** **Lv 16:21** 5795
"The **g** shall bear on itself **Lv 16:22** 5795
release the **g** in the wilderness. **Lv 16:22** 8163b
"The one who released the **g** **Lv 16:26** 8163b
and the **g** of the sin offering, **Lv 16:27** 8163b
ox or a lamb or a **g** in the camp, **Lv 17:3** 5795
their sacrifices to the **g** demons **Lv 17:7** 8163b
an ox or a sheep or a **g** is born, **Lv 22:27** 5795
'You shall also offer one male **g** **Lv 23:19** 8163b
one male **g** for a sin offering; **Nu 7:16** 5795
one male **g** for a sin offering; **Nu 7:22** 5795
one male **g** for a sin offering; **Nu 7:28** 5795
one male **g** for a sin offering; **Nu 7:34** 5795
one male **g** for a sin offering; **Nu 7:40** 5795
one male **g** for a sin offering; **Nu 7:46** 5795
one male **g** for a sin offering; **Nu 7:52** 5795
one male **g** for a sin offering; **Nu 7:58** 5795
one male **g** for a sin offering; **Nu 7:64** 5795
one male **g** for a sin offering; **Nu 7:70** 5795
one male **g** for a sin offering; **Nu 7:76** 5795
one male **g** for a sin offering; **Nu 7:82** 5795
and one male **g** for a sin offering. **Nu 15:24** 5795
old female **g** for a sin offering. **Nu 15:27** 5795
a sheep or the firstborn of a **g**, **Nu 18:17** 5795
'And one male **g** for a sin offering **Nu 28:15** 5795
and one male **g** for a sin offering to **Nu 28:22** 8163b
male **g** to make atonement for you. **Nu 28:30** 5795
one male **g** for a sin offering, **Nu 29:5** 5795
one male **g** for a sin offering, **Nu 29:11** 5795
and one male **g** for a sin offering, **Nu 29:16** 5795
and one male **g** for a sin offering, **Nu 29:19** 5795
and one male **g** for a sin offering, **Nu 29:22** 8163b
and one male **g** for a sin offering, **Nu 29:25** 5795
and one male **g** for a sin offering, **Nu 29:28** 8163b
and one male **g** for a sin offering, **Nu 29:31** 8163b
and one male **g** for a sin offering, **Nu 29:34** 8163b
and one male **g** for a sin offering, **Nu 29:38** 8163b
the ox, the sheep, the **g**, **Dt 14:4** 5795
gazelle, the roebuck, the wild **g**, **Dt 14:5** 689
You shall not boil a young **g** in its **Dt 14:21** 1423
Gideon went in and prepared a young **g** **Jg 6:19** 1423, 5795
you so that we may prepare a young **g** **Jg 13:15** 1423, 5795
So Manoah took the young **g** with **Jg 13:19** 1423, 5795
he tore him as one tears a young **g** **Jg 14:6** 1423
visited his wife with a young **g**, **Jg 15:1** 5795
and a jug of wine and a young **g**, **1Sa 16:20** 5795
strutting rooster, the male **g** also, **Pr 30:31** 8495
will lie down with the young **g**, **Is 11:6** 1423
g also will cry to its kind; **Is 34:14** 8163b
second day you shall offer a male **g** **Ezk 43:22** 5795
daily a **g** for a sin offering; **Ezk 43:25** 8163b
a male **g** daily for a sin offering. **Ezk 45:23** 5795
a male **g** was coming from the west **Da 8:5** 6842
and the **g** *had* a conspicuous horn **Da 8:5** 6842
g magnified *himself* exceedingly. **Da 8:8** 5795
"The shaggy **g** *represents* the **Da 8:21** 5795
you have never given me a young **g**, **Lk 15:29** *2056*

GOATS
flock and bring me two choice young **g** **Gn 27:9** 1423, 5795
And she put the skins of the young **g** **Gn 27:16** 1423, 5795
spotted and speckled among the **g**; **Gn 30:32** 5795
the **g** and black among the lambs, **Gn 30:33** 5795
the striped and spotted male **g** and all **Gn 30:35** 8495
the speckled and spotted female **g**, **Gn 30:35** 5795
the male **g** which were mating *were* **Gn 31:10** 6260
g which are mating are striped, **Gn 31:12** 6260
your female **g** have not miscarried, **Gn 31:38** 5795
female **g** and twenty male goats, **Gn 32:14** 5795
female goats and twenty male **g**, **Gn 32:14** 8495
it from the sheep or from the **g**. **Ex 12:5** 5795
flock, of the sheep or of the **g**, **Lv 1:10** 5795
two male **g** for a sin offering and one **Lv 16:5** 5795
"He shall take the two **g** and **Lv 16:7** 8163b
shall cast lots for the two **g**, **Lv 16:8** 8163b
the cattle, the sheep, or the **g**. **Lv 22:19** 5795
two oxen, five rams, five male **g**, **Nu 7:17** 6260
two oxen, five rams, five male **g**, **Nu 7:23** 6260
two oxen, five rams, five male **g**, **Nu 7:29** 6260
two oxen, five rams, five male **g**, **Nu 7:35** 6260
two oxen, five rams, five male **g**, **Nu 7:41** 6260
two oxen, five rams, five male **g**, **Nu 7:47** 6260
two oxen, five rams, five male **g**, **Nu 7:53** 6260
two oxen, five rams, five male **g**, **Nu 7:59** 6260
two oxen, five rams, five male **g**, **Nu 7:65** 6260
two oxen, five rams, five male **g**, **Nu 7:71** 6260
two oxen, five rams, five male **g**, **Nu 7:77** 6260
two oxen, five rams, five male **g**, **Nu 7:83** 6260
male **g** for a sin offering twelve; **Nu 7:87** 5795
all the rams 60, the male **g** 60, **Nu 7:88** 6260
of the male lambs, or of the **g**. **Nu 15:11** 5795
rams, the breed of Bashan, and **g**, **Dt 32:14** 6260
one carrying three young **g**, another **1Sa 10:3** 1423
front of the Rocks of the Wild **G**. **1Sa 24:2** 3277
thousand sheep and a thousand **g**. **1Sa 25:2** 5795
them like two little flocks of **g**, **1Ki 20:27** 5795
7,700 rams and 7,700 male **g**. **2Ch 17:11** 8495
and seven male **g** for a sin **2Ch 29:21** 5795
Then they brought the male **g** of **2Ch 29:23** 8163b
flocks of lambs and young **g**, all for **2Ch 35:7** 1121, 5795
offering for all Israel 12 male **g**, **Ezr 6:17** 5796
12 male **g** for a sin offering, **Ezr 8:35** 6842
time the mountain **g** give birth? **Jb 39:1** 3277
Nor male **g** out of your folds. **Ps 50:9** 6260
Or drink the blood of male **g**? **Ps 50:13** 6260
an offering of bulls with male **g**. **Ps 66:15** 6260
high mountains are for the wild **g**; **Ps 104:18** 3277
And the **g** *will bring* the price of **Pr 27:26** 6260
g By the tents of the shepherds. **SS 1:8** 1429
Your hair is like a flock of **g** **SS 4:1** 5795
Your hair is like a flock of **g** **SS 6:5** 5795
the blood of bulls, lambs or **g**. **Is 1:11** 6260
and shaggy **g** will frolic there. **Is 13:21** 8163b
with the blood of lambs and **g**, **Is 34:6** 6260
male **g** at the head of the flock. **Jer 50:8** 6260
Like rams together with male **g**. **Jer 51:40** 6260
customers for lambs, rams and **g**; **Ezk 27:21** 6260
between the rams and the male **g**. **Ezk 34:17** 6260
though they were rams, lambs, **g** and **Ezk 39:18** 6260
And I will punish the male **g**; **Zch 10:3** 6260
separates the sheep from the **g**; **Mt 25:32** *2056*
His right, and the **g** on the left. **Mt 25:33** *2055*
through the blood of **g** and calves, **Heb 9:12** *5131*
For if the blood of **g** and bulls **Heb 9:13** *5131*
the blood of the calves and the **g**, **Heb 9:19** *5131*
of bulls and **g** to take away sins. **Heb 10:4** *5131*

GOATS'
shall make curtains of **g** *hair* **Ex 26:7** 5795
linen, **g** *hair*, **Ex 35:6** 5795
and fine linen and **g** *hair* **Ex 35:23** 5795
with a skill spun the **g** *hair* **Ex 35:26** 5795
Then he made curtains of **g** *hair* **Ex 36:14** 5795
and all the work of **g** *hair*, **Nu 31:20** 5795
and put a quilt of **g** *hair* at **1Sa 19:13** 5795
bed with the quilt of **g** *hair* **1Sa 19:16** 5795
And *there will be* **g** milk enough **Pr 27:27** 5795

GOATSKINS
went about in sheepskins, in **g**, **Heb 11:37** *122, 1192*

GOB
again with the Philistines at **G**; **2Sa 21:18** 1359
with the Philistines again at **G**, **2Sa 21:19** 1359

GOBLET
"Your navel is *like* a round **g** Which **SS 7:2** 101

GOD
In the beginning **G** created the **Gn 1:1** 430
and the Spirit of **G** was moving **Gn 1:2** 430
Then **G** said, "Let there be light"; **Gn 1:3** 430
G saw that the light was good; **Gn 1:4** 430
and **G** separated the light from the **Gn 1:4** 430
G called the light day, and **Gn 1:5** 430
G said, "Let there be an expanse in **Gn 1:6** 430
G made the expanse, and **Gn 1:7** 430
G called the expanse heaven. **Gn 1:8** 430
Then **G** said, "Let the waters below **Gn 1:9** 430
G called the dry land earth, **Gn 1:10** 430
and **G** saw that it was good. **Gn 1:10** 430
Then **G** said, "Let the earth sprout **Gn 1:11** 430
and **G** saw that it was good. **Gn 1:12** 430
Then **G** said, "Let there be lights in **Gn 1:14** 430
G made the two great lights, **Gn 1:16** 430
G placed them in the expanse **Gn 1:17** 430
and **G** saw that it was good. **Gn 1:18** 430
Then **G** said, "Let the waters teem **Gn 1:20** 430
G created the great sea monsters and **Gn 1:21** 430
and **G** saw that it was good. **Gn 1:21** 430
G blessed them, saying, **Gn 1:22** 430
Then **G** said, "Let the earth bring **Gn 1:24** 430
G made the beasts of the earth **Gn 1:25** 430
and **G** saw that it was good. **Gn 1:25** 430
G said, "Let Us make man in Our **Gn 1:26** 430
G created man in His own image, **Gn 1:27** 430
in the image of **G** He created him; **Gn 1:27** 430
G blessed them; **Gn 1:28** 430
and **G** said to them, **Gn 1:28** 430
G said, "Behold, I have given you **Gn 1:29** 430
G saw all that He had made, **Gn 1:31** 430
By the seventh day **G** completed **Gn 2:2** 430
Then **G** blessed the seventh day and **Gn 2:3** 430
work which **G** had created and made. **Gn 2:3** 430
the LORD **G** made earth and heaven. **Gn 2:4** 430
for the LORD **G** had not sent rain **Gn 2:5** 430
Then the LORD **G** formed man of dust **Gn 2:7** 430
The LORD **G** planted a garden **Gn 2:8** 430
Out of the ground the LORD **G** **Gn 2:9** 430
Then the LORD **G** took the man and **Gn 2:15** 430
The LORD **G** commanded the man, **Gn 2:16** 430
Then the LORD **G** said, **Gn 2:18** 430
Out of the ground the LORD **G** **Gn 2:19** 430
So the LORD **G** caused a deep sleep **Gn 2:21** 430
G fashioned into a woman the rib **Gn 2:22** 430
field which the LORD **G** had made. **Gn 3:1** 430
"Indeed, has **G** said, **Gn 3:1** 430
middle of the garden, **G** has said, **Gn 3:3** 430
"For **G** knows that in the day you **Gn 3:5** 430
be opened, and you will be like **G**, **Gn 3:5** 430
the sound of the LORD **G** walking in **Gn 3:8** 430
from the presence of the LORD **G** **Gn 3:8** 430
Then the LORD **G** called to the man, **Gn 3:9** 430
Then the LORD **G** said to the woman, **Gn 3:13** 430
The LORD **G** said to the serpent, **Gn 3:14** 430
The LORD **G** made garments of **Gn 3:21** 430
Then the LORD **G** said, **Gn 3:22** 430
therefore the LORD **G** sent him out **Gn 3:23** 430
"**G** has appointed me another **Gn 4:25** 430
In the day when **G** created man, He **Gn 5:1** 430
He made him in the likeness of **G**. **Gn 5:1** 430
Then Enoch walked with **G** three **Gn 5:22** 430
Enoch walked with **G**; **Gn 5:24** 430
and he was not, for **G** took him. **Gn 5:24** 430
sons of **G** saw that the daughters **Gn 6:2** 430
sons of **G** came in to the daughters **Gn 6:4** 430
Noah walked with **G**. **Gn 6:9** 430
was corrupt in the sight of **G**, **Gn 6:11** 430
G looked on the earth, and **Gn 6:12** 430
Then **G** said to Noah, **Gn 6:13** 430
to all that **G** had commanded him, **Gn 6:22** 430
female, as **G** had commanded Noah. **Gn 7:9** 430
entered as **G** had commanded him; **Gn 7:16** 430
But **G** remembered Noah and all the **Gn 8:1** 430
and **G** caused a wind to pass over **Gn 8:1** 430
Then **G** spoke to Noah, saying, **Gn 8:15** 430
And **G** blessed Noah and his sons **Gn 9:1** 430
For in the image of **G** He made man. **Gn 9:6** 430
Then **G** spoke to Noah and to his **Gn 9:8** 430
G said, "This is the sign of the **Gn 9:12** 430
covenant between **G** and every living **Gn 9:16** 430
And **G** said to Noah, **Gn 9:17** 430
be the LORD, The **G** of Shem; **Gn 9:26** 430
"May **G** enlarge Japheth, And let **Gn 9:27** 430
he was a priest of **G** Most High. **Gn 14:18** 410
"Blessed be Abram of **G** Most High, **Gn 14:19** 430
And blessed be **G** Most High, Who **Gn 14:20** 430
sworn to the LORD **G** Most High, **Gn 14:22** 430
"O Lord **G**, what will You give **Gn 15:2** 3068
"O Lord **G**, how may I know that I **Gn 15:8** 3068
G said to Abram, "Know for **Gn 15:13** 430
"You are a **G** who sees"; **Gn 16:13** 410
"I am **G** Almighty; Walk before Me, **Gn 17:1** 410
his face, and **G** talked with him, **Gn 17:3** 430
to be **G** to you and to your **Gn 17:7** 430
and I will be their **G**." **Gn 17:8** 430
G said further to Abraham, **Gn 17:9** 430
Then **G** said to Abraham, **Gn 17:15** 430
And Abraham said to **G**, **Gn 17:18** 430
But **G** said, "No, but Sarah your wife **Gn 17:19** 430
with him, **G** went up from Abraham. **Gn 17:22** 430
same day, as **G** had said to him. **Gn 17:23** 430
when **G** destroyed the cities of the **Gn 19:29** 430
valley, that **G** remembered Abraham, **Gn 19:29** 430
But **G** came to Abimelech in a dream **Gn 20:3** 430
Then **G** said to him in the dream, **Gn 20:6** 430
is no fear of **G** in this place, **Gn 20:11** 430
when **G** caused me to wander from my **Gn 20:13** 430
Abraham prayed to **G**, **Gn 20:17** 430
and **G** healed Abimelech and his **Gn 20:17** 430
time of which **G** had spoken to him. **Gn 21:2** 430
days old, as **G** had commanded him. **Gn 21:4** 430
"**G** has made laughter for me; **Gn 21:6** 430
But **G** said to Abraham, **Gn 21:12** 430
G heard the lad crying; **Gn 21:17** 430
of **G** called to Hagar from heaven and **Gn 21:17** 430
for **G** has heard the voice of the **Gn 21:17** 430
Then **G** opened her eyes and she saw **Gn 21:19** 430
G was with the lad, and he **Gn 21:20** 430

“**G** is with you in all that you do;	Gn 21:22	430
swear to me here by **G** that you	Gn 21:23	430
of the LORD, the Everlasting **G**.	Gn 21:33	410
things, that **G** tested Abraham,	Gn 22:1	430
the place of which **G** had told him.	Gn 22:3	430
“**G** will provide for Himself the	Gn 22:8	430
the place of which **G** had told him;	Gn 22:9	430
for now I know that you fear **G**,	Gn 22:12	430
the **G** of heaven and the God of	Gn 24:3	430
God of heaven and the **G** of earth,	Gn 24:3	430
“The LORD, the **G** of heaven, who	Gn 24:7	430
LORD, the **G** of my master Abraham,	Gn 24:12	430
LORD, the **G** of my master Abraham,	Gn 24:27	430
LORD, the **G** of my master Abraham,	Gn 24:42	430
LORD, the **G** of my master Abraham,	Gn 24:48	430
that **G** blessed his son Isaac;	Gn 25:11	430
“I am the **G** of your father Abraham;	Gn 26:24	430
G caused *it* to happen to me.”	Gn 27:20	430
G give you of the dew of heaven,	Gn 27:28	430
“May **G** Almighty bless you and	Gn 28:3	410
which **G** gave to Abraham.”	Gn 28:4	430
the angels of **G** were ascending and	Gn 28:12	430
the **G** of your father Abraham and	Gn 28:13	430
father Abraham and the **G** of Isaac;	Gn 28:13	430
is none other than the house of **G**,	Gn 28:17	430
“If **G** will be with me and will	Gn 28:20	430
then the LORD will be my **G**.	Gn 28:21	430
“Am I in the place of **G**,	Gn 30:2	430
“**G** has vindicated me, and has	Gn 30:6	430
G gave heed to Leah, and she	Gn 30:17	430
“**G** has given me my wages because	Gn 30:18	430
“**G** has endowed me with a good	Gn 30:20	430
Then **G** remembered Rachel, and God	Gn 30:22	430
and **G** gave heed to her and opened	Gn 30:22	430
“**G** has taken away my reproach.”	Gn 30:23	430
G of my father has been with me.	Gn 31:5	430
G did not allow him to hurt me.	Gn 31:7	430
“Thus **G** has taken away your	Gn 31:9	430
of **G** said to me in the dream,	Gn 31:11	430
‘I am the **G** *of* Bethel, where you	Gn 31:13	410
“Surely all the wealth which **G**	Gn 31:16	430
do whatever **G** has said to you.”	Gn 31:16	430
G came to Laban the Aramean in	Gn 31:24	430
but the **G** of your father spoke to	Gn 31:29	430
“If the **G** of my father, the God	Gn 31:42	430
of my father, the **G** of Abraham,	Gn 31:42	430
G has seen my affliction and the	Gn 31:42	430
G is witness between you and me.”	Gn 31:50	430
“The **G** of Abraham and the God of	Gn 31:53	430
God of Abraham and the **G** of Nahor,	Gn 31:53	430
of Nahor, the **G** of their father,	Gn 31:53	430
his way, the angels of **G** met him.	Gn 32:1	430
“O **G** of my father Abraham and God	Gn 32:9	430
Abraham and **G** of my father Isaac,	Gn 32:9	430
for you have striven with **G** and	Gn 32:28	430
“I have seen **G** face to face, yet	Gn 32:30	430
“The children whom **G** has	Gn 33:5	430
face as one sees the face of **G**,	Gn 33:10	430
G has dealt graciously with me and	Gn 33:11	430
Then **G** said to Jacob,	Gn 35:1	430
and make an altar there to **G**,	Gn 35:1	410
I will make an altar there to **G**,	Gn 35:3	410
G had revealed Himself to him when	Gn 35:7	430
Then **G** appeared to Jacob again	Gn 35:9	430
G said to him,	Gn 35:10	430
G also said to him,	Gn 35:11	430
“I am **G** Almighty; Be fruitful and	Gn 35:11	410
Then **G** went up from him in the	Gn 35:13	430
place where **G** had spoken with him,	Gn 35:15	430
great evil and sin against **G**?”	Gn 39:9	430
“Do not interpretations belong to **G**?	Gn 40:8	430
G will give Pharaoh a favorable	Gn 41:16	430
G has told to Pharaoh what He is	Gn 41:25	430
G has shown to Pharaoh what He is	Gn 41:28	430
the matter is determined by **G**,	Gn 41:32	430
and **G** will quickly bring it about.	Gn 41:32	430
G has informed you of all this,	Gn 41:39	430
“**G** has made me forget all my	Gn 41:51	430
“**G** has made me fruitful in the	Gn 41:52	430
“Do this and live, for I fear **G**:	Gn 42:18	430
What is this that **G** has done to us?	Gn 42:28	430
and may **G** Almighty grant you	Gn 43:14	410
Your **G** and the God of your father	Gn 43:23	430
Your God and the **G** of your father	Gn 43:23	430
“May **G** be gracious to you, my son.”	Gn 43:29	430
G has found out the iniquity of	Gn 44:16	430
for **G** sent me before you to	Gn 45:5	430
“**G** sent me before you to	Gn 45:7	430
not you who sent me here, but **G**;	Gn 45:8	430
“**G** has made me lord of all Egypt;	Gn 45:9	430
to the **G** of his father Isaac.	Gn 46:1	430
G spoke to Israel in visions	Gn 46:2	430
“I am **G**, the God of your father;	Gn 46:3	410
“I am God, the **G** of your father;	Gn 46:3	430
“**G** Almighty appeared to me at Luz	Gn 48:3	410
sons, whom **G** has given me here.”	Gn 48:9	430
G has let me see your children as	Gn 48:11	430
“The **G** before whom my fathers	Gn 48:15	430
The **G** who has been my shepherd all	Gn 48:15	430
‘May **G** make you like Ephraim and	Gn 48:20	430
to die, but **G** will be with you,	Gn 48:21	430
G of your father who helps you,	Gn 49:25	410
of the **G** of your father.”	Gn 50:17	430
but **G** meant it for good in order	Gn 50:20	430
G will surely take care of you and	Gn 50:24	430
“**G** will surely take care of you,	Gn 50:25	430
But the midwives feared **G**,	Ex 1:17	430
So **G** was good to the midwives, and	Ex 1:20	430
Because the midwives feared **G**,	Ex 1:21	430
of *their* bondage rose up to **G**.	Ex 2:23	430
So **G** heard their groaning;	Ex 2:24	430
and **G** remembered His covenant with	Ex 2:24	430
G saw the sons of Israel, and	Ex 2:25	430
Israel, and **G** took notice *of them*.	Ex 2:25	430
came to Horeb, the mountain of **G**.	Ex 3:1	430
G called to him from the midst of	Ex 3:4	430
“I am the **G** of your father, the	Ex 3:6	430
of your father, the **G** of Abraham,	Ex 3:6	430
God of Abraham, the **G** of Isaac,	Ex 3:6	430
of Isaac, and the **G** of Jacob.”	Ex 3:6	430
for he was afraid to look at **G**.	Ex 3:6	430
But Moses said to **G**,	Ex 3:11	430
worship **G** at this mountain.”	Ex 3:12	430
Then Moses said to **G**,	Ex 3:13	430
‘The **G** of your fathers has sent me	Ex 3:13	430
G said to Moses,	Ex 3:14	430
G, furthermore, said to Moses,	Ex 3:15	430
‘The LORD, the **G** of your fathers,	Ex 3:15	430
of your fathers, the **G** of Abraham,	Ex 3:15	430
God of Abraham, the **G** of Isaac,	Ex 3:15	430
God of Isaac, and the **G** of Jacob,	Ex 3:15	430
‘The LORD, the **G** of your fathers,	Ex 3:16	430
of your fathers, the **G** of Abraham,	Ex 3:16	430
‘The LORD, the **G** of the Hebrews,	Ex 3:18	430
may sacrifice to the LORD our **G**.’	Ex 3:18	430
the LORD, the **G** of their fathers,	Ex 4:5	430
their fathers, the **G** of Abraham,	Ex 4:5	430
God of Abraham, the **G** of Isaac,	Ex 4:5	430
God of Isaac, and the **G** of Jacob,	Ex 4:5	430
you and you will be as **G** to him.	Ex 4:16	430
took the staff of **G** in his hand.	Ex 4:20	430
and met him at the mountain of **G** and	Ex 4:27	430
says the LORD, the **G** of Israel,	Ex 5:1	430
“The **G** of the Hebrews has met	Ex 5:3	430
may sacrifice to the LORD our **G**,	Ex 5:3	430
‘Let us go and sacrifice to our **G**.’	Ex 5:8	430
G spoke further to Moses and said	Ex 6:2	430
Isaac, and Jacob, as **G** Almighty,	Ex 6:3	410
My people, and I will be your **G**;	Ex 6:7	430
know that I am the LORD your **G**,	Ex 6:7	430
“See, I make you *as* **G** to Pharaoh,	Ex 7:1	430
‘The LORD, the **G** of the Hebrews,	Ex 7:16	430
is no one like the LORD our **G**.	Ex 8:10	430
“This is the finger of **G**.”	Ex 8:19	430
to your **G** within the land.”	Ex 8:25	430
we will sacrifice to the LORD our **G**	Ex 8:26	430
LORD our **G** as He commands us.”	Ex 8:27	430
the LORD your **G** in the wilderness;	Ex 8:28	430
the LORD, the **G** of the Hebrews,	Ex 9:1	430
the LORD, the **G** of the Hebrews,	Ex 9:13	430
you do not yet fear the LORD **G**.”	Ex 9:30	430
the LORD, the **G** of the Hebrews,	Ex 10:3	430
they may serve the LORD their **G**.	Ex 10:7	430
“Go, serve the LORD your **G**!	Ex 10:8	430
the LORD your **G** and against you.	Ex 10:16	430
supplication to the LORD your **G**,	Ex 10:17	430
sacrifice *them* to the LORD our **G**.	Ex 10:25	430
of them to serve the LORD our **G**.	Ex 10:26	430
G did not lead them by the	Ex 13:17	430
for **G** said, “The people might change	Ex 13:17	430
Hence **G** led the people around by	Ex 13:18	430
“**G** will surely take care of you	Ex 13:19	430
The angel of **G**,	Ex 14:19	430
This is my **G**, and I will praise	Ex 15:2	410
My father’s **G**, and I will extol	Ex 15:2	430
to the voice of the LORD your **G**,	Ex 15:26	430
that I am the LORD your **G**.’ ”	Ex 16:12	430
with the staff of **G** in my hand.”	Ex 17:9	430
heard of all that **G** had done for	Ex 18:1	430
“The **G** of my father was my help,	Ex 18:4	430
he was camped, at the mount of **G**.	Ex 18:5	430
offering and sacrifices for **G**,	Ex 18:12	430
with Moses’ father-in-law before **G**.	Ex 18:12	430
people come to me to inquire of **G**.	Ex 18:15	430
the statutes of **G** and His laws.”	Ex 18:16	430
you counsel, and **G** be with you.	Ex 18:19	430
people’s representative before **G**,	Ex 18:19	430
and you bring the disputes to **G**,	Ex 18:19	430
able men who fear **G**, men of truth	Ex 18:21	430
this thing and **G** *so* commands you,	Ex 18:23	430
Moses went up to **G**,	Ex 19:3	430
people out of the camp to meet **G**,	Ex 19:17	430
and **G** answered him with thunder.	Ex 19:19	430
Then **G** spoke all these words,	Ex 20:1	430
“I am the LORD your **G**,	Ex 20:2	430
for I, the LORD your **G**,	Ex 20:5	430
the LORD your God, am a jealous **G**,	Ex 20:5	410
name of the LORD your **G** in vain,	Ex 20:7	430
is a sabbath of the LORD your **G**;	Ex 20:10	430
which the LORD your **G** gives you.	Ex 20:12	430
but let not **G** speak to us, or we	Ex 20:19	430
G has come in order to test you,	Ex 20:20	430
the thick cloud where **G** *was*.	Ex 20:21	430
his master shall bring him to **G**,	Ex 21:6	430
but **G** let *him* fall into his hand,	Ex 21:13	430
“He who sacrifices to any **g**,	Ex 22:20	430
“You shall not curse **G**,	Ex 22:28	430
shall appear before the Lord **G**.	Ex 23:17	3068
into the house of the LORD your **G**.	Ex 23:19	430
you shall serve the LORD your **G**,	Ex 23:25	430
and they saw the **G** of Israel;	Ex 24:10	430
and they saw **G**, and they ate	Ex 24:11	430
went up to the mountain of **G**.	Ex 24:13	430
of Israel and will be their **G**.	Ex 29:45	430
know that I am the LORD their **G**	Ex 29:46	430
I am the LORD their **G**.	Ex 29:46	430
have filled him with the Spirit of **G**	Ex 31:3	430
stone, written by the finger of **G**.	Ex 31:18	430
make us a **g** who will go before us;	Ex 32:1	430
“This is your **g**, O Israel, who	Ex 32:4	430
‘This is your **g**, O Israel, who	Ex 32:8	430
Moses entreated the LORD his **G**,	Ex 32:11	430
a **g** for us who will go before us;	Ex 32:23	430
says the LORD, the **G** of Israel,	Ex 32:27	430
made a **g** of gold for themselves.	Ex 32:31	430
“The LORD, the LORD **G**,	Ex 34:6	410
G said, “Behold, I am going to make	Ex 34:10	
you shall not worship any other **g**,	Ex 34:14	410
name is Jealous, is a jealous **G**	Ex 34:14	410
are to appear before the Lord **G**,	Ex 34:23	3068
the Lord GOD, the **G** of Israel.	Ex 34:23	430
to appear before the LORD your **G**,	Ex 34:24	430
into the house of the LORD your **G**.	Ex 34:26	430
filled him with the Spirit of **G**,	Ex 35:31	430
salt of the covenant of your **G** shall	Lv 2:13	430
G has commanded not to be done,	Lv 4:22	430
‘For I am the LORD your **G**.	Lv 11:44	430
the land of Egypt to be your **G**;	Lv 11:45	430
‘I am the LORD your **G**.	Lv 18:2	430
I am the LORD your **G**.	Lv 18:4	430
you profane the name of your **G**;	Lv 18:21	430
I am the LORD your **G**.’ ”	Lv 18:30	430
for I the LORD your **G** am holy.	Lv 19:2	430
I am the LORD your **G**.	Lv 19:3	430
I am the LORD your **G**.	Lv 19:4	430
I am the LORD your **G**.	Lv 19:10	430
as to profane the name of your **G**;	Lv 19:12	430
but you shall revere your **G**;	Lv 19:14	430
I am the LORD your **G**.	Lv 19:25	430
I am the LORD your **G**.	Lv 19:31	430
aged, and you shall revere your **G**;	Lv 19:32	430
I am the LORD your **G**.	Lv 19:34	430
I am the LORD your **G**,	Lv 19:36	430
be holy, for I am the LORD your **G**.	Lv 20:7	430
I am the LORD your **G**,	Lv 20:24	430
‘They shall be holy to their **G** and	Lv 21:6	430
not profane the name of their **G**,	Lv 21:6	430
to the LORD, the food of their **G**;	Lv 21:6	430
for he is holy to his **G**.	Lv 21:7	430
for he offers the food of your **G**;	Lv 21:8	430
profane the sanctuary of his **G**,	Lv 21:12	430
anointing oil of his **G** is on him;	Lv 21:12	430
to offer the food of his **G**.	Lv 21:17	430
near to offer the food of his **G**.	Lv 21:21	430
‘He may eat the food of his **G**,	Lv 21:22	430
offering as the food of your **G**;	Lv 22:25	430
the land of Egypt, to be your **G**;	Lv 22:33	430
brought in the offering of your **G**,	Lv 23:14	430
I am the LORD your **G**.’ ”	Lv 23:22	430
behalf before the LORD your **G**.	Lv 23:28	430
the LORD your **G** for seven days.	Lv 23:40	430
I am the LORD your **G**.’ ”	Lv 23:43	430
‘If anyone curses his **G**,	Lv 24:15	430
for I am the LORD your **G**.’ ”	Lv 24:22	430
but you shall fear your **G**;	Lv 25:17	430
for I am the LORD your **G**.	Lv 25:17	430
from him, but revere your **G**,	Lv 25:36	430
‘I am the LORD your **G**,	Lv 25:38	430
land of Canaan *and* to be your **G**.	Lv 25:38	430
but are to revere your **G**.	Lv 25:43	430
I am the LORD your **G**.	Lv 25:55	430
for I am the LORD your **G**.	Lv 26:1	430
also walk among you and be your **G**,	Lv 26:12	430
‘I am the LORD your **G**,	Lv 26:13	430
for I am the LORD their **G**.	Lv 26:44	430
nations, that I might be their **G**.	Lv 26:45	430
separation to **G** is on his head.	Nu 6:7	430
remembered before the LORD your **G**,	Nu 10:9	430
a reminder of you before your **G**.	Nu 10:10	430
I am the LORD your **G**.”	Nu 10:10	430
“O **G**, heal her, I pray!”	Nu 12:13	410
and be holy to your **G**.	Nu 15:40	430
“I am the LORD your **G** who brought	Nu 15:41	430
the land of Egypt to be your **G**;	Nu 15:41	430
I am the LORD your **G**.”	Nu 15:41	430
the **G** of Israel has separated you	Nu 16:9	430
“O **G**, God of the spirits of	Nu 16:22	410
G of the spirits of all flesh,	Nu 16:22	430
people spoke against **G** and Moses,	Nu 21:5	430
Then **G** came to Balaam and said,	Nu 22:9	430
Balaam said to **G**,	Nu 22:10	430
G said to Balaam,	Nu 22:12	430
to the command of the LORD my **G**.	Nu 22:18	430
G came to Balaam at night and	Nu 22:20	430
But **G** was angry because he was	Nu 22:22	430
The word that **G** puts in my mouth,	Nu 22:38	430
Now **G** met Balaam, and he said to	Nu 23:4	430
I curse whom **G** has not cursed?	Nu 23:8	410
“**G** is not a man, that He should	Nu 23:19	410
The LORD his **G** is with him, And	Nu 23:21	430
“**G** brings them out of Egypt, He	Nu 23:22	410
And to Israel, what **G** has done!	Nu 23:23	410
agreeable with **G** that you curse them	Nu 23:27	430
and the Spirit of **G** came upon him.	Nu 24:2	430
of him who hears the words of **G**,	Nu 24:4	410
“**G** brings him out of Egypt, He is	Nu 24:8	410
of him who hears the words of **G**,	Nu 24:16	410
can live except **G** has ordained it?	Nu 24:23	410
because he was jealous for his **G** and	Nu 25:13	430
the **G** of the spirits of all flesh,	Nu 27:16	430
LORD our **G** spoke to us at Horeb,	Dt 1:6	430
LORD your **G** has multiplied you,	Dt 1:10	430
the LORD, the **G** of your fathers,	Dt 1:11	430
the LORD our **G** had commanded us;	Dt 1:19	430
LORD our **G** is about to give us.	Dt 1:20	430
the LORD your **G** has placed the	Dt 1:21	430
the LORD, the **G** of your fathers,	Dt 1:21	430

LORD our G is about to give us.'	Dt 1:25	430
the command of the LORD your G;	Dt 1:26	430
'The LORD your G who goes before	Dt 1:30	430
how the LORD your G carried you,	Dt 1:31	430
you did not trust the LORD your G,	Dt 1:32	430
as the LORD our G commanded us.'	Dt 1:41	430
"For the LORD your G has blessed	Dt 2:7	430
the LORD your G has been with you;	Dt 2:7	430
the LORD our G is giving to us.'	Dt 2:29	430
for the LORD your G hardened his	Dt 2:30	430
our G delivered him over to us,	Dt 2:33	430
our G delivered all over to us.	Dt 2:36	430
the LORD our G had commanded us.	Dt 2:37	430
the LORD our G delivered Og also,	Dt 3:3	430
'The LORD your G has given you	Dt 3:18	430
land which the LORD your G will give	Dt 3:20	430
G has done to these two kings;	Dt 3:21	430
G is the one fighting for you.'	Dt 3:22	430
'O Lord G, You have begun to show	Dt 3:24	3068
for what g is there in heaven or	Dt 3:24	410
the LORD, the G of your fathers,	Dt 4:1	430
LORD your G which I command you.	Dt 4:2	430
the LORD your G has destroyed them	Dt 4:3	430
who held fast to the LORD your G	Dt 4:4	430
as the LORD my G commanded me,	Dt 4:5	430
nation is there that has a g so near to	Dt 4:7	430
our G whenever we call on Him?	Dt 4:7	430
before the LORD your G at Horeb,	Dt 4:10	430
those which the LORD your G has	Dt 4:19	430
land which the LORD your G is giving	Dt 4:21	430
the covenant of the LORD your G which	Dt 4:23	430
the LORD your G has commanded you.	Dt 4:23	430
LORD your G is a consuming fire,	Dt 4:24	430
is a consuming fire, a jealous G.	Dt 4:24	410
G *so as* to provoke Him to anger,	Dt 4:25	430
you will seek the LORD your G,	Dt 4:29	430
your G and listen to His voice.	Dt 4:30	430
your G is a compassionate God;	Dt 4:31	430
your God is a compassionate G;	Dt 4:31	410
that G created man on the earth,	Dt 4:32	430
people heard the voice of G speaking	Dt 4:33	430
"Or has a g tried to go to take	Dt 4:34	430
as the LORD your G did for you in	Dt 4:34	430
might know that the LORD, He is G;	Dt 4:35	430
He is G in heaven above and on the	Dt 4:39	430
G is giving you for all time."	Dt 4:40	430
"The LORD our G made a covenant	Dt 5:2	430
'I am the LORD your G who	Dt 5:6	430
for I, the LORD your G,	Dt 5:9	430
the LORD your God, am a jealous G,	Dt 5:9	410
name of the LORD your G in vain,	Dt 5:11	430
as the LORD your G commanded you.	Dt 5:12	430
is a sabbath of the LORD your G;	Dt 5:14	430
and the LORD your G brought you	Dt 5:15	430
therefore the LORD your G	Dt 5:15	430
the LORD your G has commanded you,	Dt 5:16	430
which the LORD your G gives you.	Dt 5:16	430
the LORD our G has shown us His	Dt 5:24	430
seen today that G speaks with man,	Dt 5:24	430
of the LORD our G any longer,	Dt 5:25	430
G speaking from the midst of the fire,	Dt 5:26	430
hear all that the LORD our G says;	Dt 5:27	430
the LORD our G speaks to you,	Dt 5:27	430
the LORD your G has commanded you;	Dt 5:32	430
the LORD your G has commanded you,	Dt 5:33	430
G has commanded *me* to teach you,	Dt 6:1	430
might fear the LORD your G,	Dt 6:2	430
the LORD, the G of your fathers,	Dt 6:3	430
The LORD is our G, the LORD is one!	Dt 6:4	430
love the LORD your G with all your	Dt 6:5	430
your G brings you into the land	Dt 6:10	430
shall fear *only* the LORD your G;	Dt 6:13	430
for the LORD your G in the midst	Dt 6:15	430
the midst of you is a jealous G;	Dt 6:15	410
the anger of the LORD your G will	Dt 6:15	430
put the LORD your G to the test,	Dt 6:16	430
commandments of the LORD your G,	Dt 6:17	430
which the LORD our G commanded you	Dt 6:20	430
to fear the LORD our G for our	Dt 6:24	430
commandment before the LORD our G,	Dt 6:25	430
"When the LORD your G brings	Dt 7:1	430
G delivers them before you	Dt 7:2	430
a holy people to the LORD your G;	Dt 7:6	430
the LORD your G has chosen you to	Dt 7:6	430
therefore that the LORD your G,	Dt 7:9	430
that the LORD your God, He is G,	Dt 7:9	430
God, He is God, the faithful G,	Dt 7:9	410
that the LORD your G will keep	Dt 7:12	430
LORD your G will deliver to you;	Dt 7:16	430
what the LORD your G did to Pharaoh	Dt 7:18	430
the LORD your G brought you out.	Dt 7:19	430
So shall the LORD your G do to all	Dt 7:19	430
the LORD your G will send the	Dt 7:20	430
the LORD your G is in your midst,	Dt 7:21	430
your midst, a great and awesome G.	Dt 7:21	410
'The LORD your G will clear	Dt 7:22	430
G will deliver them before you,	Dt 7:23	430
an abomination to the LORD your G.	Dt 7:25	430
your G has led you in the wilderness	Dt 8:2	430
the LORD your G was disciplining you	Dt 8:5	430
commandments of the LORD your G,	Dt 8:6	430
"For the LORD your G is bringing	Dt 8:7	430
you shall bless the LORD your G	Dt 8:10	430
that you do not forget the LORD your G	Dt 8:11	430
and you will forget the LORD your G	Dt 8:14	430
shall remember the LORD your G,	Dt 8:18	430
you ever forget the LORD your G and	Dt 8:19	430
to the voice of the LORD your G.	Dt 8:20	430
it is the LORD your G who is crossing	Dt 9:3	430
the LORD your G has driven them out	Dt 9:4	430
the LORD your G is driving them out	Dt 9:5	430
your G is giving you this good land	Dt 9:6	430
your G to wrath in the wilderness;	Dt 9:7	430
stone written by the finger of G;	Dt 9:10	430
sinned against the LORD your G.	Dt 9:16	430
the command of the LORD your G;	Dt 9:23	430
'O Lord G, do not destroy Your	Dt 9:26	3068
as the LORD your G spoke to him.)	Dt 10:9	430
the LORD your G require from you,	Dt 10:12	430
you, but to fear the LORD your G,	Dt 10:12	430
and to serve the LORD your G with	Dt 10:12	430
to the LORD your G belong heaven	Dt 10:14	430
"For the LORD your G is the God	Dt 10:17	430
G of gods and the Lord of lords,	Dt 10:17	430
G who does not show partiality nor	Dt 10:17	410
"You shall fear the LORD your G;	Dt 10:20	430
is your praise and He is your G,	Dt 10:21	430
and now the LORD your G has made	Dt 10:22	430
therefore love the LORD your G,	Dt 11:1	430
the discipline of the LORD your G	Dt 11:2	430
for which the LORD your G cares;	Dt 11:12	430
the eyes of the LORD your G are	Dt 11:12	430
to love the LORD your G and to	Dt 11:13	430
to do, to love the LORD your G,	Dt 11:22	430
the LORD your G will lay the	Dt 11:25	430
commandments of the LORD your G,	Dt 11:27	430
commandments of the LORD your G,	Dt 11:28	430
when the LORD your G brings you	Dt 11:29	430
the LORD your G is giving you,	Dt 11:31	430
the LORD, the G of your fathers,	Dt 12:1	430
like this toward the LORD your G.	Dt 12:4	430
place which the LORD your G will	Dt 12:5	430
shall eat before the LORD your G,	Dt 12:7	430
the LORD your G has blessed you.	Dt 12:7	430
the LORD your G is giving you.	Dt 12:9	430
your G is giving you to inherit,	Dt 12:10	430
place in which the LORD your G will	Dt 12:11	430
rejoice before the LORD your G,	Dt 12:12	430
your G which He has given you;	Dt 12:15	430
eat them before the LORD your G	Dt 12:18	430
which the LORD your G will choose,	Dt 12:18	430
your G in all your undertakings.	Dt 12:18	430
"When the LORD your G extends	Dt 12:20	430
place which the LORD your G chooses	Dt 12:21	430
on the altar of the LORD your G;	Dt 12:27	430
on the altar of the LORD your G,	Dt 12:27	430
in the sight of the LORD your G.	Dt 12:28	430
"When the LORD your G cuts off	Dt 12:29	430
thus toward the LORD your G,	Dt 12:31	430
for the LORD your G is testing you	Dt 13:3	430
if you love the LORD your G with all	Dt 13:3	430
the LORD your G and fear Him;	Dt 13:4	430
rebellion against the LORD your G	Dt 13:5	430
LORD your G commanded you to walk.	Dt 13:5	430
to seduce you from the LORD your G	Dt 13:10	430
your G is giving you to live in,	Dt 13:12	430
burnt offering to the LORD your G;	Dt 13:16	430
to the voice of the LORD your G,	Dt 13:18	430
in the sight of the LORD your G.	Dt 13:18	430
are the sons of the LORD your G;	Dt 14:1	430
a holy people to the LORD your G,	Dt 14:2	430
a holy people to the LORD your G.	Dt 14:21	430
the presence of the LORD your G,	Dt 14:23	430
to fear the LORD your G always.	Dt 14:23	430
place where the LORD your G chooses	Dt 14:24	430
when the LORD your G blesses you,	Dt 14:24	430
which the LORD your G chooses.	Dt 14:25	430
of the LORD your G and rejoice,	Dt 14:26	430
in order that the LORD your G may	Dt 14:29	430
land which the LORD your G is giving	Dt 15:4	430
to the voice of the LORD your G,	Dt 15:5	430
"For the LORD your G will bless	Dt 15:6	430
the LORD your G is giving you,	Dt 15:7	430
your G will bless you in all your work	Dt 15:10	430
the LORD your G has blessed you.	Dt 15:14	430
and the LORD your G redeemed you;	Dt 15:15	430
so the LORD your G will bless you	Dt 15:18	430
consecrate to the LORD your G all the	Dt 15:19	430
every year before the LORD your G	Dt 15:20	430
sacrifice it to the LORD your G.	Dt 15:21	430
the Passover to the LORD your G,	Dt 16:1	430
G brought you out of Egypt by night.	Dt 16:1	430
the Passover to the LORD your G	Dt 16:2	430
the LORD your G is giving you;	Dt 16:5	430
G chooses to establish His name,	Dt 16:6	430
which the LORD your G chooses.	Dt 16:7	430
assembly to the LORD your G;	Dt 16:8	430
Feast of Weeks to the LORD your G	Dt 16:10	430
as the LORD your G blesses you;	Dt 16:10	430
rejoice before the LORD your G,	Dt 16:11	430
your G chooses to establish His name.	Dt 16:11	430
celebrate a feast to the LORD your G	Dt 16:15	430
because the LORD your G will bless	Dt 16:15	430
G in the place which He chooses,	Dt 16:16	430
your G which He has given you.	Dt 16:17	430
the LORD your G is giving you,	Dt 16:18	430
the LORD your G is giving you.	Dt 16:20	430
the altar of the LORD your G,	Dt 16:21	430
which the LORD your G hates.	Dt 16:22	430
not sacrifice to the LORD your G an	Dt 17:1	430
detestable thing to the LORD your G	Dt 17:1	430
the LORD your G is giving you,	Dt 17:2	430
in the sight of the LORD your G,	Dt 17:2	430
which the LORD your G chooses.	Dt 17:8	430
there to serve the LORD your G,	Dt 17:12	430
which the LORD your G gives you,	Dt 17:14	430
you whom the LORD your G chooses,	Dt 17:15	430
may learn to fear the LORD his G,	Dt 17:19	430
"For the LORD your G has chosen	Dt 18:5	430
in the name of the LORD his G,	Dt 18:7	430
which the LORD your G gives you,	Dt 18:9	430
the LORD your G will drive them out	Dt 18:12	430
blameless before the LORD your G.	Dt 18:13	430
G has not allowed you *to do* so.	Dt 18:14	430
"The LORD your G will raise up	Dt 18:15	430
asked of the LORD your G in Horeb	Dt 18:16	430
again the voice of the LORD my G,	Dt 18:16	430
LORD your G cuts off the nations,	Dt 19:1	430
land the LORD your G gives you,	Dt 19:1	430
LORD your G gives you to possess.	Dt 19:2	430
G will give you as a possession,	Dt 19:3	430
your G enlarges your territory,	Dt 19:8	430
today, to love the LORD your G,	Dt 19:9	430
G gives you as an inheritance,	Dt 19:10	430
LORD your G gives you to possess.	Dt 19:14	430
for the LORD your G,	Dt 20:1	430
G is the one who goes with you,	Dt 20:4	430
your G gives it into your hand,	Dt 20:13	430
the LORD your G has given you.	Dt 20:14	430
peoples that the LORD your G is giving	Dt 20:16	430
the LORD your G has commanded you,	Dt 20:17	430
would sin against the LORD your G.	Dt 20:18	430
LORD your G gives you to possess,	Dt 21:1	430
for the LORD your G has chosen	Dt 21:5	430
G delivers them into your hands and	Dt 21:10	430
who is hanged is accursed of G),	Dt 21:23	430
G gives you as an inheritance.	Dt 21:23	430
an abomination to the LORD your G.	Dt 22:5	430
the LORD your G was not willing to	Dt 23:5	430
but the LORD your G turned the	Dt 23:5	430
because the LORD your G loves you.	Dt 23:5	430
"Since the LORD your G walks in	Dt 23:14	430
your G for any votive offering,	Dt 23:18	430
an abomination to the LORD your G.	Dt 23:18	430
so that the LORD your G may bless	Dt 23:20	430
you make a vow to the LORD your G,	Dt 23:21	430
G will surely require it of you.	Dt 23:21	430
vowed to the LORD your G,	Dt 23:23	430
G gives you as an inheritance.	Dt 24:4	430
"Remember what the LORD your G	Dt 24:9	430
for you before the LORD your G.	Dt 24:13	430
your G redeemed you from there;	Dt 24:18	430
in order that the LORD your G may	Dt 24:19	430
which the LORD your G gives you.	Dt 25:15	430
an abomination to the LORD your G.	Dt 25:16	430
and he did not fear G.	Dt 25:18	430
the LORD your G has given you rest	Dt 25:19	430
land which the LORD your G gives	Dt 25:19	430
G gives you as an inheritance,	Dt 26:1	430
that the LORD your G gives you,	Dt 26:2	430
your G chooses to establish His name.	Dt 26:2	430
'I declare this day to the LORD my G	Dt 26:3	430
the altar of the LORD your G.	Dt 26:4	430
and say before the LORD your G,	Dt 26:5	430
to the LORD, the G of our fathers,	Dt 26:7	430
it down before the LORD your G,	Dt 26:10	430
worship before the LORD your G;	Dt 26:10	430
the good which the LORD your G has	Dt 26:11	430
shall say before the LORD your G,	Dt 26:13	430
to the voice of the LORD my G;	Dt 26:14	430
"This day the LORD your G	Dt 26:16	430
declared the LORD to be your G,	Dt 26:17	430
people to the LORD your G,	Dt 26:19	430
which the LORD your G gives you,	Dt 27:2	430
which the LORD your G gives you,	Dt 27:3	430
the LORD, the G of your fathers,	Dt 27:3	430
there an altar to the LORD your G,	Dt 27:5	430
build the altar of the LORD your G	Dt 27:6	430
offerings to the LORD your G;	Dt 27:6	430
rejoice before the LORD your G.	Dt 27:7	430
a people for the LORD your G.	Dt 27:9	430
therefore obey the LORD your G,	Dt 27:10	430
diligently obey the LORD your G,	Dt 28:1	430
the LORD your G will set you high	Dt 28:1	430
if you obey the LORD your G:	Dt 28:2	430
which the LORD your G gives you.	Dt 28:8	430
commandments of the LORD your G	Dt 28:9	430
commandments of the LORD your G,	Dt 28:13	430
you do not obey the LORD your G,	Dt 28:15	430
you would not obey the LORD your G	Dt 28:45	430
your G with joy and a glad heart,	Dt 28:47	430
the LORD your G has given you.	Dt 28:52	430
the LORD your G has given you,	Dt 28:53	430
and awesome name, the LORD your G,	Dt 28:58	430
you did not obey the LORD your G.	Dt 28:62	430
know that I am the LORD your G.	Dt 29:6	430
of you, before the LORD your G:	Dt 29:10	430
the covenant with the LORD your G,	Dt 29:12	430
His oath which the LORD your G is	Dt 29:12	430
people and that He may be your G,	Dt 29:13	430
in the presence of the LORD our G	Dt 29:15	430
away today from the LORD our G,	Dt 29:18	430
the LORD, the G of their fathers,	Dt 29:25	430
things belong to the LORD our G,	Dt 29:29	430
the LORD your G has banished you,	Dt 30:1	430
and you return to the LORD your G	Dt 30:2	430
then the LORD your G will restore	Dt 30:3	430
the LORD your G has scattered you.	Dt 30:3	430
the LORD your G will gather you,	Dt 30:4	430
"The LORD your G will bring	Dt 30:5	430
"Moreover the LORD your G will	Dt 30:6	430
to love the LORD your G with all	Dt 30:6	430
"The LORD your G will inflict	Dt 30:7	430
"Then the LORD your G will	Dt 30:9	430
if you obey the LORD your G to	Dt 30:10	430
G with all your heart and soul.	Dt 30:10	430
you today to love the LORD your G,	Dt 30:16	430

and that the LORD your **G** may bless **Dt 30:16** 430
by loving the LORD your **G**, **Dt 30:20** 430
G who will cross ahead of you; **Dt 31:3** 430
G is the one who goes with you. **Dt 31:6** 430
to appear before the LORD your **G** **Dt 31:11** 430
learn and fear the LORD your **G**, **Dt 31:12** 430
and learn to fear the LORD your **G**, **Dt 31:13** 430
because our **G** is not among us **Dt 31:17** 430
the covenant of the LORD your **G**, **Dt 31:26** 430
Ascribe greatness to our **G**! **Dt 32:3** 430
A **G** of faithfulness and without **Dt 32:4** 410
there was no foreign **g** with him. **Dt 32:12** 410
Then he forsook **G** who made him, **Dt 32:15** 433
to demons who were not **G**, **Dt 32:17** 433
forgot the **G** who gave you birth. **Dt 32:18** 410
Me jealous with *what* is not **G**; **Dt 32:21** 410
He, And there is no **g** besides Me; **Dt 32:39** 430
Moses the man of **G** blessed the sons **Dt 33:1** 430
is none like the **G** of Jeshurun, **Dt 33:26** 410
"The eternal **G** is a dwelling place, **Dt 33:27** 430
G is with you wherever you go." **Jos 1:9** 430
the LORD your **G** is giving you, **Jos 1:11** 430
'The LORD your **G** gives you rest and **Jos 1:13** 430
the LORD your **G** is giving them. **Jos 1:15** 430
may the LORD your **G** be with you as **Jos 1:17** 430
LORD your **G**, He is God in heaven **Jos 2:11** 430
He is **G** in heaven above and on **Jos 2:11** 430
of the covenant of the LORD your **G** **Jos 3:3** 430
the words of the LORD your **G**." **Jos 3:9** 430
that the living **G** is among you, **Jos 3:10** 410
G into the middle of the Jordan, **Jos 4:5** 430
"For the LORD your **G** dried up the **Jos 4:23** 430
your **G** had done to the Red Sea, **Jos 4:23** 430
fear the LORD your **G** forever." **Jos 4:24** 430
"Alas, O Lord **G**, why did You **Jos 7:7** 3068
thus the LORD, the **G** of Israel, **Jos 7:13** 430
to the LORD, the **G** of Israel, **Jos 7:19** 430
against the LORD, the **G** of Israel, **Jos 7:20** 430
for the LORD your **G** will deliver **Jos 8:7** 430
to the LORD, the **G** of Israel, **Jos 8:30** 430
of the fame of the LORD your **G**; **Jos 9:9** 430
them by the LORD the **G** of Israel. **Jos 9:18** 430
them by the LORD, the **G** of Israel, **Jos 9:19** 430
of water for the house of my **G**." **Jos 9:23** 430
G had commanded His servant Moses **Jos 9:24** 430
for the LORD your **G** has delivered **Jos 10:19** 430
just as the LORD, the **G** of Israel, **Jos 10:40** 430
because the LORD, the **G** of Israel, **Jos 10:42** 430
fire to the LORD, the **G** of Israel, **Jos 13:14** 430
the LORD, the **G** of Israel, is **Jos 13:33** 430
LORD spoke to Moses the man of **G** **Jos 14:6** 430
I followed the LORD my **G** fully. **Jos 14:8** 430
followed the LORD my **G** fully.' **Jos 14:9** 430
the LORD **G** of Israel fully. **Jos 14:14** 430
the LORD, the **G** of your fathers, **Jos 18:3** 430
you here before the LORD our **G**. **Jos 18:6** 430
commandment of the LORD your **G**. **Jos 22:3** 430
"And now the LORD your **G** has **Jos 22:4** 430
to love the LORD your **G** and walk **Jos 22:5** 430
committed against the **G** of Israel, **Jos 22:16** 430
the altar of the LORD our **G**. **Jos 22:19** 430
"The Mighty One, **G**, the LORD, the **Jos 22:22** 430
God, the LORD, the Mighty One, **G**, **Jos 22:22** 430
do with the LORD, the **G** of Israel? **Jos 22:24** 430
besides the altar of the LORD our **G** **Jos 22:29** 430
and the sons of Israel blessed **G**; **Jos 22:33** 430
between us that the LORD is **G**." **Jos 22:34** 430
all that the LORD your **G** has done **Jos 23:3** 430
for the LORD your **G** is He who has **Jos 23:3** 430
"The LORD your **G**, **Jos 23:5** 430
as the LORD your **G** promised you. **Jos 23:5** 430
are to cling to the LORD your **G**, **Jos 23:8** 430
your **G** is He who fights for you, **Jos 23:10** 430
to love the LORD your **G**. **Jos 23:11** 430
the LORD your **G** will not continue to **Jos 23:13** 430
the LORD your **G** has given you. **Jos 23:13** 430
words which the LORD your **G** spoke **Jos 23:14** 430
words which the LORD your **G** spoke **Jos 23:15** 430
the LORD your **G** has given you. **Jos 23:15** 430
the covenant of the LORD your **G**, **Jos 23:16** 430
presented themselves before **G**. **Jos 24:1** 430
says the LORD, the **G** of Israel, **Jos 24:2** 430
for the LORD our **G** is He who **Jos 24:17** 430
serve the LORD, for He is our **G**." **Jos 24:18** 430
the LORD, for He is a holy **G**. **Jos 24:19** 430
He is a jealous **G**; **Jos 24:19** 410
to the LORD, the **G** of Israel." **Jos 24:23** 430
G and we will obey His voice." **Jos 24:24** 430
words in the book of the law of **G**; **Jos 24:26** 430
so that you do not deny your **G**." **Jos 24:27** 430
I have done, so **G** has repaid me." **Jg 1:7** 430
the LORD, the **G** of their fathers, **Jg 2:12** 430
LORD, and forgot the LORD their **G** and **Jg 3:7** 430
"I have a message from **G** for you." **Jg 3:20** 430
"Behold, the LORD, the **G** of Israel, **Jg 4:6** 430
So **G** subdued on that day Jabin the **Jg 4:23** 430
to the LORD, the **G** of Israel. **Jg 5:3** 430
of the LORD, the **G** of Israel. **Jg 5:5** 430
says the LORD, the **G** of Israel, **Jg 6:8** 430
"I am the LORD your **G**; **Jg 6:10** 430
The angel of **G** said to him, **Jg 6:20** 430
"Alas, O Lord **G**! For now I have **Jg 6:22** 3068
build an altar to the LORD your **G** **Jg 6:26** 430
If he is a **g**, let him contend for **Jg 6:31** 430
Then Gideon said to **G**, **Jg 6:36** 430
Then Gideon said to **G**, **Jg 6:39** 430
G did so that night; **Jg 6:40** 430
G has given Midian and all the **Jg 7:14** 430
"**G** has given the leaders of **Jg 8:3** 430

and made Baal-berith their **g**. **Jg 8:33** 430
did not remember the LORD their **G**, **Jg 8:34** 430
Shechem, that **G** may listen to you. **Jg 9:7** 430
with which **G** and men are honored, **Jg 9:9** 430
new wine, which cheers **G** and men, **Jg 9:13** 430
Then **G** sent an evil spirit between **Jg 9:23** 430
went into the house of their **g**, **Jg 9:27** 430
Thus **G** repaid the wickedness of **Jg 9:56** 430
Also **G** returned all the wickedness **Jg 9:57** 430
our **G** and served the Baals." **Jg 10:10** 430
'The LORD, the **G** of Israel, **Jg 11:21** 430
now the LORD, the **G** of Israel, **Jg 11:23** 430
your **g** gives you to possess? **Jg 11:24** 430
our **G** has driven out before us, **Jg 11:24** 430
be a Nazirite to **G** from the womb; **Jg 13:5** 430
"A man of **G** came to me and his **Jg 13:6** 430
the appearance of the angel of **G**, **Jg 13:6** 430
the boy shall be a Nazirite to **G** from **Jg 13:7** 430
please let the man of **G** whom You **Jg 13:8** 430
G listened to the voice of **Jg 13:9** 430
and the angel of **G** came again to **Jg 13:9** 430
surely die, for we have seen **G**." **Jg 13:22** 430
But **G** split the hollow place that **Jg 15:19** 430
to **G** from my mother's womb. **Jg 16:17** 430
great sacrifice to Dagon their **g**, **Jg 16:23** 430
"Our **g** has given Samson our enemy **Jg 16:23** 430
saw him, they praised their **g**, **Jg 16:24** 430
"Our **g** has given our enemy into **Jg 16:24** 430
"O Lord **G**, please remember me and **Jg 16:28** 3068
strengthen me just this time, O **G**, **Jg 16:28** 430
"Inquire of **G**, please, that we **Jg 18:5** 430
for **G** has given it into your hand, **Jg 18:10** 430
that the house of **G** was at Shiloh. **Jg 18:31** 430
the assembly of the people of **G**, **Jg 20:2** 430
up to Bethel, and inquired of **G** and **Jg 20:18** 430
of **G** *was* there in those days, **Jg 20:27** 430
sat there before **G** until evening, **Jg 21:2** 430
"Why, O LORD, **G** of Israel, has **Jg 21:3** 430
shall be my people, and your **G**, **Ru 1:16** 430
be my people, and your God, my **G**. **Ru 1:16** 430
from the LORD, the **G** of Israel, **Ru 2:12** 430
and may the **G** of Israel grant your **1Sa 1:17** 430
Nor is there any rock like our **G**. **1Sa 2:2** 430
For the LORD is a **G** of knowledge, **1Sa 2:3** 410
another, **G** will mediate for him; **1Sa 2:25** 430
of **G** came to Eli and said to him, **1Sa 2:27** 430
the LORD **G** of Israel declares, **1Sa 2:30** 430
lamp of **G** had not yet gone out, **1Sa 3:3** 430
the LORD where the ark of **G** *was,* **1Sa 3:3** 430
May **G** do so to you, and more also, **1Sa 3:17** 430
with the ark of the covenant of **G** **1Sa 4:4** 430
"**G** has come into the camp." **1Sa 4:7** 430
And the ark of **G** was taken; **1Sa 4:11** 430
was trembling for the ark of **G**. **1Sa 4:13** 430
and the ark of **G** has been taken." **1Sa 4:17** 430
When he mentioned the ark of **G** **1Sa 4:18** 430
the news that the ark of **G** was taken **1Sa 4:19** 430
because the ark of **G** was taken and **1Sa 4:21** 430
for the ark of **G** was taken." **1Sa 4:22** 430
Now the Philistines took the ark of **G** **1Sa 5:1** 430
the Philistines took the ark of **G** and **1Sa 5:2** 430
"The ark of the **G** of Israel must **1Sa 5:7** 430
severe on us and on Dagon our **g**." **1Sa 5:7** 430
with the ark of the **G** of Israel?" **1Sa 5:8** 430
"Let the ark of the **G** of Israel **1Sa 5:8** 430
the ark of the **G** of Israel *around.* **1Sa 5:8** 430
they sent the ark of **G** to Ekron. **1Sa 5:10** 430
And as the ark of **G** **1Sa 5:10** 430
of the **G** of Israel around to us, **1Sa 5:10** 430
away the ark of the **G** of Israel, **1Sa 5:11** 430
hand of **G** was very heavy there. **1Sa 5:11** 430
away the ark of the **G** of Israel, **1Sa 6:3** 430
give glory to the **G** of Israel; **1Sa 6:5** 430
before the LORD, this holy **G**? **1Sa 6:20** 430
to cry to the LORD our **G** for us, **1Sa 7:8** 430
there is a man of **G** in this city, **1Sa 9:6** 430
present to bring to the man of **G**. **1Sa 9:7** 430
G and he will tell us our way." **1Sa 9:8** 430
when a man went to inquire of **G**, **1Sa 9:9** 430
the city where the man of **G** was. **1Sa 9:10** 430
proclaim the word of **G** to you." **1Sa 9:27** 430
three men going up to **G** at Bethel **1Sa 10:3** 430
you will come to the hill of **G** where **1Sa 10:5** 430
for **G** is with you. **1Sa 10:7** 430
leave Samuel, **G** changed his heart; **1Sa 10:9** 430
of **G** came upon him mightily, **1Sa 10:10** 430
says the LORD, the **G** of Israel, **1Sa 10:18** 430
"But you have today rejected your **G**, **1Sa 10:19** 430
men whose hearts **G** had touched **1Sa 10:26** 430
Then the Spirit of **G** came upon **1Sa 11:6** 430
"But they forgot the LORD their **G**, **1Sa 12:9** 430
the LORD your **G** *was* your king. **1Sa 12:12** 430
you will follow the LORD your **G**. **1Sa 12:14** 430
your servants to the LORD your **G**, **1Sa 12:19** 430
commandment of the LORD your **G**, **1Sa 13:13** 430
"Bring the ark of **G** here." **1Sa 14:18** 430
For the ark of **G** was at that time **1Sa 14:18** 430
"Let us draw near to **G** here." **1Sa 14:36** 430
Saul inquired of **G**, **1Sa 14:37** 430
said to the LORD, the **G** of Israel, **1Sa 14:41** 430
"May **G** do this *to me* and more **1Sa 14:44** 430
he has worked with **G** this day." **1Sa 14:45** 430
to sacrifice to the LORD your **G**; **1Sa 15:15** 430
to the LORD your **G** at Gilgal." **1Sa 15:21** 430
I may worship the LORD your **G**." **1Sa 15:30** 430
for **G** *sees* not as man sees, for **1Sa 16:7** 430
spirit from **G** is terrorizing you. **1Sa 16:15** 430
the evil spirit from **G** is on you, **1Sa 16:16** 430
evil spirit from **G** came to Saul, **1Sa 16:23** 430

the armies of the living **G**?" **1Sa 17:26** 430
the armies of the living **G**." **1Sa 17:36** 430
the **G** of the armies of Israel, **1Sa 17:45** 430
know that there is a **G** in Israel, **1Sa 17:46** 430
from **G** came mightily upon Saul, **1Sa 18:10** 430
the Spirit of **G** came upon the **1Sa 19:20** 430
Spirit of **G** came upon him also, **1Sa 19:23** 430
"The LORD, the **G** of Israel, *be* **1Sa 20:12** 430
I know what **G** will do for me." **1Sa 22:3** 430
and have inquired of **G** for him, **1Sa 22:13** 430
to inquire of **G** for him today? **1Sa 22:15** 430
"**G** has delivered him into my **1Sa 23:7** 430
"O LORD **G** of Israel, Your servant **1Sa 23:10** 430
O LORD **G** of Israel, I pray, tell **1Sa 23:11** 430
but **G** did not deliver him into his **1Sa 23:14** 430
Horesh, and encouraged him in **G**. **1Sa 23:16** 430
G do so to the enemies of David, **1Sa 25:22** 430
the living with the LORD your **G**; **1Sa 25:29** 430
"Blessed be the LORD **G** of Israel, **1Sa 25:32** 430
as the LORD **G** of Israel lives, **1Sa 25:34** 430
"Today **G** has delivered your enemy **1Sa 26:8** 430
and **G** has departed from me and **1Sa 28:15** 430
in my sight, like an angel of **G**; **1Sa 29:9** 430
himself in the LORD his **G**. **1Sa 30:6** 430
"Swear to me by **G** that you will **1Sa 30:15** 430
"As **G** lives, if you had not **2Sa 2:27** 430
"May **G** do so to Abner, and more **2Sa 3:9** 430
"May **G** do so to me, and more **2Sa 3:35** 430
the LORD **G** of hosts was with him. **2Sa 5:10** 430
of **G** which is called by the Name, **2Sa 6:2** 430
They placed the ark of **G** on a **2Sa 6:3** 430
of **G** from the house of Abinadab, **2Sa 6:4** 430
the ark of **G** and took hold of it, **2Sa 6:6** 430
and **G** struck him down there for **2Sa 6:7** 430
and he died there by the ark of **G**. **2Sa 6:7** 430
him, on account of the ark of **G**." **2Sa 6:12** 430
went and brought up the ark of **G** **2Sa 6:12** 430
G dwells within tent curtains." **2Sa 7:2** 430
"Who am I, O Lord **G**, **2Sa 7:18** 3068
in Your eyes, O Lord **G**, **2Sa 7:19** 3068
is the custom of man, O Lord **G**. **2Sa 7:19** 3068
know Your servant, O Lord **G**! **2Sa 7:20** 3068
reason You are great, O Lord **G**; **2Sa 7:22** 3068
and there is no **G** besides You, **2Sa 7:22** 430
whom **G** went to redeem for Himself **2Sa 7:23** 430
You, O LORD, have become their **G**. **2Sa 7:24** 430
"Now therefore, O LORD **G**, **2Sa 7:25** 430
LORD of hosts is **G** over Israel'; **2Sa 7:26** 430
O LORD of hosts, the **G** of Israel, **2Sa 7:27** 430
"Now, O Lord **G**, You are God, **2Sa 7:28** 3068
"Now, O Lord GOD, You are **G**, **2Sa 7:28** 430
For You, O Lord **G**, have spoken; **2Sa 7:29** 3068
I may show the kindness of **G**?" **2Sa 9:3** 430
and for the cities of our **G**; **2Sa 10:12** 430
Thus says the LORD **G** of Israel, **2Sa 12:7** 430
inquired of **G** for the child; **2Sa 12:16** 430
the king remember the LORD your **G**, **2Sa 14:11** 430
a thing against the people of **G**? **2Sa 14:13** 430
Yet **G** does not take away life, but **2Sa 14:14** 430
my son from the inheritance of **G**.' **2Sa 14:16** 430
comforting, for as the angel of **G**, **2Sa 14:17** 430
the LORD your **G** be with you.' " **2Sa 14:17** 430
like the wisdom of the angel of **G**, **2Sa 14:20** 430
the ark of the covenant of **G**. **2Sa 15:24** 430
And they set down the ark of **G**, **2Sa 15:24** 430
"Return the ark of **G** to the city. **2Sa 15:25** 430
and Abiathar returned the ark of **G** to **2Sa 15:29** 430
the summit, where **G** was worshiped, **2Sa 15:32** 430
if one inquired of the word of **G**; **2Sa 16:23** 430
"Blessed is the LORD your **G**, **2Sa 18:28** 430
May **G** do so to me, and more also, **2Sa 19:13** 430
the king is like the angel of **G**, **2Sa 19:27** 430
and after that **G** was moved by **2Sa 21:14** 430
My **G**, my rock, in whom I take **2Sa 22:3** 430
the LORD, Yes, I cried to my **G**; **2Sa 22:7** 430
not acted wickedly against my **G**. **2Sa 22:22** 430
By my **G** I can leap over a wall. **2Sa 22:30** 430
"As for **G**, His way is blameless; **2Sa 22:31** 410
"For who is **G**, besides the LORD? **2Sa 22:32** 410
And who is a rock, besides our **G**? **2Sa 22:32** 430
"**G** is my strong fortress; **2Sa 22:33** 410
And exalted be **G**, the rock of my **2Sa 22:47** 430
G who executes vengeance for me, **2Sa 22:48** 410
The anointed of the **G** of Jacob, **2Sa 23:1** 430
"The **G** of Israel said, The Rock **2Sa 23:3** 430
Who rules in the fear of **G**, **2Sa 23:3** 430
"Truly is not my house so with **G**? **2Sa 23:5** 410
"Now may the LORD your **G** add to **2Sa 24:3** 430
"May the LORD your **G** accept you." **2Sa 24:23** 430
LORD my **G** which cost me nothing." **2Sa 24:24** 430
maidservant by the LORD your **G**, **1Ki 1:17** 430
you by the LORD the **G** of Israel, **1Ki 1:30** 430
LORD, the **G** of my lord the king, **1Ki 1:36** 430
'May your **G** make the name of **1Ki 1:47** 430
'Blessed be the LORD, the **G** of Israel **1Ki 1:48** 430
the charge of the LORD your **G**, **1Ki 2:3** 430
"May **G** do so to me and more also, **1Ki 2:23** 430
the Lord **G** before my father David, **1Ki 2:26** 3068
and **G** said, "Ask what *you wish* me **1Ki 3:5** 430
"Now, O LORD my **G**, **1Ki 3:7** 430
G said to him, **1Ki 3:11** 430
saw that the wisdom of **G** was in him **1Ki 3:28** 430
Now **G** gave Solomon wisdom and very **1Ki 4:29** 430
house for the name of the LORD his **G** **1Ki 5:3** 430
"But now the LORD my **G** has given **1Ki 5:4** 430
for the name of the LORD my **G**, **1Ki 5:5** 430
Blessed be the LORD, the **G** of Israel **1Ki 8:15** 430
name of the LORD, the **G** of Israel. **1Ki 8:17** 430
name of the LORD, the **G** of Israel. **1Ki 8:20** 430

“O LORD, the **G** of Israel, there **1Ki 8:23** 430
there is no **G** like You in heaven **1Ki 8:23** 430
O LORD, the **G** of Israel, **1Ki 8:25** 430
“Now therefore, O **G** of Israel, **1Ki 8:26** 430
will **G** indeed dwell on the earth? **1Ki 8:27** 430
to his supplication, O LORD my **G**, **1Ki 8:28** 430
forth from Egypt, O Lord **G**.” **1Ki 8:53** 3068
“May the LORD our **G** be with us, **1Ki 8:57** 430
to the LORD our **G** day and night, **1Ki 8:59** 430
earth may know that the LORD is **G**; **1Ki 8:60** 430
wholly devoted to the LORD our **G**, **1Ki 8:61** 430
of Egypt, before the LORD our **G**, **1Ki 8:65** 430
they forsook the LORD their **G**, **1Ki 9:9** 430
“Blessed be the LORD your **G** who **1Ki 10:9** 430
which **G** had put in his heart. **1Ki 10:24** 430
wholly devoted to the LORD his **G**, **1Ki 11:4** 430
from the LORD, the **G** of Israel, **1Ki 11:9** 430
G also raised up *another* adversary **1Ki 11:23** 430
says the LORD, the **G** of Israel, **1Ki 11:31** 430
Sidonians, Chemosh the **g** of Moab, **1Ki 11:33** 430
Milcom the **g** of the sons of Ammon; **1Ki 11:33** 430
But the word of **G** came to Shemaiah **1Ki 12:22** 430
God came to Shemaiah the man of **G**, **1Ki 12:22** 430
there came a man of **G** from Judah **1Ki 13:1** 430
heard the saying of the man of **G**, **1Ki 13:4** 430
sign which the man of **G** had given **1Ki 13:5** 430
said to the man of **G**, **1Ki 13:6** 430
“Please entreat the LORD your **G**, **1Ki 13:6** 430
the man of **G** entreated the LORD, **1Ki 13:6** 430
the king said to the man of **G**, **1Ki 13:7** 430
But the man of **G** said to the king, **1Ki 13:8** 430
of **G** had done that day in Bethel; **1Ki 13:11** 430
seen the way which the man of **G** **1Ki 13:12** 430
So he went after the man of **G** and **1Ki 13:14** 430
man of **G** who came from Judah?” **1Ki 13:14** 430
the man of **G** who came from Judah, **1Ki 13:21** 430
the LORD your **G** commanded you, **1Ki 13:21** 430
“It is the man of **G**, **1Ki 13:26** 430
took up the body of the man of **G** **1Ki 13:29** 430
in which the man of **G** is buried; **1Ki 13:31** 430
‘Thus says the LORD **G** of Israel, **1Ki 14:7** 430
good was found toward the LORD **G** **1Ki 14:13** 430
wholly devoted to the LORD his **G**, **1Ki 15:3** 430
G gave him a lamp in Jerusalem, **1Ki 15:4** 430
the LORD **G** of Israel to anger. **1Ki 15:30** 430
provoking the LORD **G** of Israel to **1Ki 16:13** 430
LORD **G** of Israel with their idols. **1Ki 16:26** 430
did more to provoke the LORD **G** **1Ki 16:33** 430
the LORD, the **G** of Israel lives, **1Ki 17:1** 430
“As the LORD your **G** lives, **1Ki 17:12** 430
thus says the LORD **G** of Israel, **1Ki 17:14** 430
I have to do with you, O man of **G**? **1Ki 17:18** 430
“O LORD my **G**, have You also **1Ki 17:20** 430
“O LORD my **G**, I pray You, let **1Ki 17:21** 430
I know that you are a man of **G** and **1Ki 17:24** 430
“As the LORD your **G** lives, **1Ki 18:10** 430
If the LORD is **G**, follow Him; **1Ki 18:21** 430
you call on the name of your **g**, **1Ki 18:24** 430
and the **G** who answers by fire, **1Ki 18:24** 430
who answers by fire, He is **G**.” **1Ki 18:24** 430
and call on the name of your **g**, **1Ki 18:25** 430
with a loud voice, for he is a **g**; **1Ki 18:27** 430
“O LORD, the **G** of Abraham, Isaac **1Ki 18:36** 430
known that You are **G** in Israel and **1Ki 18:36** 430
may know that You, O LORD, are **G**, **1Ki 18:37** 430
“The LORD, He is **G**; **1Ki 18:39** 430
the LORD, He is **G**.” **1Ki 18:39** 430
to Horeb, the mountain of **G**. **1Ki 19:8** 430
for the LORD, the **G** of hosts; **1Ki 19:10** 430
for the LORD, the **G** of hosts; **1Ki 19:14** 430
Then a man of **G** came near and **1Ki 20:28** 430
“The LORD is a **g** of *the* **1Ki 20:28** 430
He is not a **g** of *the* valleys,” **1Ki 20:28** 430
‘You cursed **G** and the king.’ **1Ki 21:10** 430
“Naboth cursed **G** and the king.” **1Ki 21:13** 430
provoked the LORD **G** of Israel to **1Ki 22:53** 430
of Baal-zebub, the **g** of Ekron, **2Ki 1:2** 430
‘Is it because there is no **G** in **2Ki 1:3** 430
of Baal-zebub, the **g** of Ekron?’ **2Ki 1:3** 430
‘Is it because there is no **G** in **2Ki 1:6** 430
of Baal-zebub, the **g** of Ekron? **2Ki 1:6** 430
“O man of **G**, the king says, **2Ki 1:9** 430
“If I am a man of **G**, **2Ki 1:10** 430
“O man of **G**, thus says the king, **2Ki 1:11** 430
“If I am a man of **G**, **2Ki 1:12** 430
Then the fire of **G** came down from **2Ki 1:12** 430
“O man of **G**, please let my life **2Ki 1:13** 430
inquire of Baal-zebub, the **g** of Ekron **2Ki 1:16** 430
is it because there is no **G** in Israel **2Ki 1:16** 430
is the LORD, the **G** of Elijah?” **2Ki 2:14** 430
she came and told the man of **G**. **2Ki 4:7** 430
this is a holy man of **G** passing by **2Ki 4:9** 430
“No, my lord, O man of **G**, **2Ki 4:16** 430
him on the bed of the man of **G**, **2Ki 4:21** 430
run to the man of **G** and return.” **2Ki 4:22** 430
to the man of **G** to Mount Carmel. **2Ki 4:25** 430
man of **G** saw her at a distance, **2Ki 4:25** 430
came to the man of **G** to the hill, **2Ki 4:27** 430
but the man of **G** said, **2Ki 4:27** 430
“O man of **G**, there is death in **2Ki 4:40** 430
brought the man of **G** bread of the **2Ki 4:42** 430
“Am I **G**, to kill and to make **2Ki 5:7** 430
when Elisha the man of **G** heard that **2Ki 5:8** 430
on the name of the LORD his **G**, **2Ki 5:11** 430
to the word of the man of **G**; **2Ki 5:14** 430
the man of **G** with all his company, **2Ki 5:15** 430
there is no **G** in all the earth, **2Ki 5:15** 430
servant of Elisha the man of **G**, **2Ki 5:20** 430
Then the man of **G** said, **2Ki 6:6** 430

The man of **G** sent *word* to the **2Ki 6:9** 430
which the man of **G** had told him; **2Ki 6:10** 430
of **G** had risen early and gone out, **2Ki 6:15** 430
“May **G** do so to me and more also, **2Ki 6:31** 430
answered the man of **G** and said, **2Ki 7:2** 430
just as the man of **G** had said, **2Ki 7:17** 430
man of **G** had spoken to the king, **2Ki 7:18** 430
answered the man of **G** and said, **2Ki 7:19** 430
to the word of the man of **G**, **2Ki 8:2** 430
the servant of the man of **G**, **2Ki 8:4** 430
“The man of **G** has come here.” **2Ki 8:7** 430
hand and go to meet the man of **G**, **2Ki 8:8** 430
ashamed, and the man of **G** wept. **2Ki 8:11** 430
says the LORD, the **G** of Israel, **2Ki 9:6** 430
law of the LORD, the **G** of Israel, **2Ki 10:31** 430
the man of **G** was angry with him **2Ki 13:19** 430
word of the LORD, the **G** of Israel, **2Ki 14:25** 430
in the sight of the LORD his **G**, **2Ki 16:2** 430
sinned against the LORD their **G**, **2Ki 17:7** 430
right against the LORD their **G**. **2Ki 17:9** 430
not believe in the LORD their **G**. **2Ki 17:14** 430
commandments of the LORD their **G** **2Ki 17:16** 430
commandments of the LORD their **G**, **2Ki 17:19** 430
the custom of the **g** of the land; **2Ki 17:26** 430
the custom of the **g** of the land.” **2Ki 17:26** 430
the custom of the **g** of the land.” **2Ki 17:27** 430
the LORD your **G** you shall fear; **2Ki 17:39** 430
in the LORD, the **G** of Israel; **2Ki 18:5** 430
the voice of the LORD their **G**, **2Ki 18:12** 430
‘We trust in the LORD our **G**,’ **2Ki 18:22** 430
‘Perhaps the LORD your **G** will hear **2Ki 19:4** 430
has sent to reproach the living **G**, **2Ki 19:4** 430
which the LORD your **G** has heard. **2Ki 19:4** 430
‘Do not let your **G** in whom you **2Ki 19:10** 430
“O LORD, the **G** of Israel, who are **2Ki 19:15** 430
the cherubim, You are the **G**, **2Ki 19:15** 430
has sent to reproach the living **G**. **2Ki 19:16** 430
“Now, O LORD our **G**, **2Ki 19:19** 430
that You alone, O LORD, are **G**.” **2Ki 19:19** 430
says the LORD, the **G** of Israel, **2Ki 19:20** 430
in the house of Nisroch his **g**, **2Ki 19:37** 430
LORD, the **G** of your father David, **2Ki 20:5** 430
says the LORD, the **G** of Israel, **2Ki 21:12** 430
the LORD, the **G** of his fathers, **2Ki 21:22** 430
“Thus says the LORD **G** of Israel, **2Ki 22:15** 430
‘Thus says the LORD **G** of Israel, **2Ki 22:18** 430
which the man of **G** proclaimed, **2Ki 23:16** 430
“It is the grave of the man of **G** **2Ki 23:17** 430
the Passover to the LORD your **G** **2Ki 23:21** 430
Jabez called on the **G** of Israel, **1Ch 4:10** 430
G granted him what he requested. **1Ch 4:10** 430
they cried out to **G** in the battle, **1Ch 5:20** 430
slain, because the war *was* of **G**. **1Ch 5:22** 430
against the **G** of their fathers and **1Ch 5:25** 430
whom **G** had destroyed before them. **1Ch 5:25** 430
So the **G** of Israel stirred up the **1Ch 5:26** 430
the tabernacle of the house of **G**. **1Ch 6:48** 430
the servant of **G** had commanded. **1Ch 6:49** 430
chief officer of the house of **G**; **1Ch 9:11** 430
of the service of the house of **G**. **1Ch 9:13** 430
the treasuries in the house of **G**. **1Ch 9:26** 430
the night around the house of **G**, **1Ch 9:27** 430
and the LORD your **G** said to you, **1Ch 11:2** 430
before my **G** that I should do this. **1Ch 11:19** 430
may the **G** of our fathers look on **1Ch 12:17** 430
Indeed, your **G** helps you!” **1Ch 12:18** 430
a great army like the army of **G**. **1Ch 12:22** 430
and if it is from the LORD our **G**, **1Ch 13:2** 430
bring back the ark of our **G** to us, **1Ch 13:3** 430
the ark of **G** from Kiriath-jearim. **1Ch 13:5** 430
bring up from there the ark of **G**, **1Ch 13:6** 430
They carried the ark of **G** on a **1Ch 13:7** 430
before **G** with all *their* might, **1Ch 13:8** 430
and he died there before **G**. **1Ch 13:10** 430
David was afraid of **G** that day, **1Ch 13:12** 430
I bring the ark of **G** *home* to me?” **1Ch 13:12** 430
Thus the ark of **G** remained with **1Ch 13:14** 430
David inquired of **G**, **1Ch 14:10** 430
“**G** has broken through my enemies **1Ch 14:11** 430
David inquired again of **G**, **1Ch 14:14** 430
again of God, and **G** said to him, **1Ch 14:14** 430
for **G** will have gone out before **1Ch 14:15** 430
did just as **G** had commanded him, **1Ch 14:16** 430
prepared a place for the ark of **G** and **1Ch 15:1** 430
No one is to carry the ark of **G** but **1Ch 15:2** 430
chose them to carry the ark of **G** and **1Ch 15:2** 430
the ark of the LORD **G** of Israel to **1Ch 15:12** 430
LORD our **G** made an outburst on us, **1Ch 15:13** 430
the ark of the LORD **G** of Israel. **1Ch 15:14** 430
the ark of **G** on their shoulders with **1Ch 15:15** 430
the trumpets before the ark of **G**. **1Ch 15:24** 430
Because **G** was helping the Levites **1Ch 15:26** 430
And they brought in the ark of **G** **1Ch 16:1** 430
and peace offerings before **G**. **1Ch 16:1** 430
and praise the LORD **G** of Israel: **1Ch 16:4** 430
the ark of the covenant of **G**. **1Ch 16:6** 430
He is the LORD our **G**; **1Ch 16:14** 430
“Save us, O **G** of our salvation, **1Ch 16:35** 430
be the LORD, the **G** of Israel, **1Ch 16:36** 430
instruments *for* the songs of **G**, **1Ch 16:42** 430
your heart, for **G** is with you.” **1Ch 17:2** 430
that the word of **G** came to Nathan, **1Ch 17:3** 430
“Who am I, O LORD **G**, **1Ch 17:16** 430
a small thing in Your eyes, O **G**; **1Ch 17:17** 430
of a man of high degree, O LORD **G**. **1Ch 17:17** 430
is there any **G** besides You, **1Ch 17:20** 430
whom **G** went to redeem for Himself **1Ch 17:21** 430
O LORD, became their **G**. **1Ch 17:22** 430
LORD of hosts is the **G** of Israel, **1Ch 17:24** 430

God of Israel, *even* a **G** to Israel; **1Ch 17:24** 430
“For You, O my **G**, have revealed **1Ch 17:25** 430
“Now, O LORD, You are **G**, **1Ch 17:26** 430
and for the cities of our **G**; **1Ch 19:13** 430
G was displeased with this **1Ch 21:7** 430
David said to **G**, **1Ch 21:8** 430
And **G** sent an angel to Jerusalem **1Ch 21:15** 430
David said to **G**, **1Ch 21:17** 430
O LORD my **G**, please let Your hand **1Ch 21:17** 430
not go before it to inquire of **G**, **1Ch 21:30** 430
“This is the house of the LORD **G**, **1Ch 22:1** 430
stones to build the house of **G**. **1Ch 22:2** 430
a house for the LORD **G** of Israel. **1Ch 22:6** 430
to the name of the LORD my **G**. **1Ch 22:7** 430
build the house of the LORD your **G** **1Ch 22:11** 430
keep the law of the LORD your **G**. **1Ch 22:12** 430
“Is not the LORD your **G** with you? **1Ch 22:18** 430
your soul to seek the LORD your **G**; **1Ch 22:19** 430
build the sanctuary of the LORD **G**, **1Ch 22:19** 430
and the holy vessels of **G** into the **1Ch 22:19** 430
But *as for* Moses the man of **G**, **1Ch 23:14** 430
“The LORD **G** of Israel has given **1Ch 23:25** 430
of the service of the house of **G**, **1Ch 23:28** 430
the sanctuary and officers of **G**, **1Ch 24:5** 430
G of Israel had commanded him. **1Ch 24:19** 430
him according to the words of **G**, **1Ch 25:5** 430
for **G** gave fourteen sons and three **1Ch 25:5** 430
for the service of the house of **G**. **1Ch 25:6** 430
G had indeed blessed him. **1Ch 26:5** 430
the treasures of the house of **G** and **1Ch 26:20** 430
the affairs of **G** and of the king. **1Ch 26:32** 430
and for the footstool of our **G**. **1Ch 28:2** 430
“But **G** said to me, **1Ch 28:3** 430
“Yet, the LORD, the **G** of Israel, **1Ch 28:4** 430
LORD, and in the hearing of our **G**, **1Ch 28:8** 430
commandments of the LORD your **G** **1Ch 28:8** 430
know the **G** of your father, **1Ch 28:9** 430
the storehouses of the house of **G** and **1Ch 28:12** 430
nor be dismayed, for the LORD **G**, **1Ch 28:20** 430
the LORD God, my **G**, is with you. **1Ch 28:20** 430
all the service of the house of **G**, **1Ch 28:21** 430
Solomon, whom alone **G** has chosen, **1Ch 29:1** 430
not for man, but for the LORD **G**. **1Ch 29:1** 430
have provided for the house of my **G** **1Ch 29:2** 430
my delight in the house of my **G**, **1Ch 29:3** 430
I give to the house of my **G**, **1Ch 29:3** 430
for the house of **G** they gave 5,000 **1Ch 29:7** 430
O LORD **G** of Israel our father, **1Ch 29:10** 430
our **G**, we thank You, and praise **1Ch 29:13** 430
“O LORD our **G**, all this abundance **1Ch 29:16** 430
“Since I know, O my **G**, **1Ch 29:17** 430
“O LORD, the **G** of Abraham, Isaac and **1Ch 29:18** 430
“Now bless the LORD your **G**.” **1Ch 29:20** 430
the LORD, the **G** of their fathers, **1Ch 29:20** 430
and the LORD his **G** *was* with him **2Ch 1:1** 430
David had brought up the ark of **G** **2Ch 1:4** 430
In that night **G** appeared to **2Ch 1:7** 430
Solomon said to **G**, **2Ch 1:8** 430
“Now, O LORD **G**, Your promise to my **2Ch 1:9** 430
G said to Solomon, **2Ch 1:11** 430
for the name of the LORD my **G**, **2Ch 2:4** 430
feasts of the LORD our **G**, **2Ch 2:4** 430
is our **G** than all the gods. **2Ch 2:5** 430
be the LORD, the **G** of Israel, **2Ch 2:12** 430
laid for building the house of **G**. **2Ch 3:3** 430
King Solomon in the house of **G**: **2Ch 4:11** 430
that *were* in the house of **G**: **2Ch 4:19** 430
the treasuries of the house of **G**. **2Ch 5:1** 430
of the LORD filled the house of **G**. **2Ch 5:14** 430
be the LORD, the **G** of Israel, **2Ch 6:4** 430
name of the LORD, the **G** of Israel. **2Ch 6:7** 430
name of the LORD, the **G** of Israel. **2Ch 6:10** 430
“O LORD, the **G** of Israel, there **2Ch 6:14** 430
there is no **g** like You in heaven **2Ch 6:14** 430
O LORD, the **G** of Israel, **2Ch 6:16** 430
O LORD, the **G** of Israel, **2Ch 6:17** 430
“But will **G** indeed dwell with **2Ch 6:18** 430
to his supplication, O LORD my **G**, **2Ch 6:19** 430
“Now, O my **G**, I pray, let **2Ch 6:40** 430
“Now therefore arise, O LORD **G**, **2Ch 6:41** 430
let Your priests, O LORD **G**, **2Ch 6:41** 430
“O LORD **G**, do not turn away the **2Ch 6:42** 430
people dedicated the house of **G**. **2Ch 7:5** 430
the LORD, the **G** of their fathers who **2Ch 7:22** 430
the man of **G** had so commanded. **2Ch 8:14** 430
LORD your **G** who delighted in you, **2Ch 9:8** 430
as king for the LORD your **G**; **2Ch 9:8** 430
because your **G** loved Israel **2Ch 9:8** 430
which **G** had put in his heart. **2Ch 9:23** 430
it was a turn *of events* from **G** that **2Ch 10:15** 430
came to Shemaiah the man of **G**, **2Ch 11:2** 430
seeking the LORD **G** of Israel followed **2Ch 11:16** 430
to the LORD **G** of their fathers. **2Ch 11:16** 430
the LORD **G** of Israel gave the rule **2Ch 13:5** 430
“But as for us, the LORD is our **G**, **2Ch 13:10** 430
keep the charge of the LORD our **G**, **2Ch 13:11** 430
G is with us at *our* head and His **2Ch 13:12** 430
the LORD **G** of your fathers, **2Ch 13:12** 430
then it was that **G** routed Jeroboam **2Ch 13:15** 430
G gave them into their hand. **2Ch 13:16** 430
the LORD, the **G** of their fathers. **2Ch 13:18** 430
in the sight of the LORD his **G**, **2Ch 14:2** 430
Judah to seek the LORD **G** of their **2Ch 14:4** 430
we have sought the LORD our **G**; **2Ch 14:7** 430
Then Asa called to the LORD his **G** and **2Ch 14:11** 430
so help us, O LORD our **G**, **2Ch 14:11** 430
O LORD, You are our **G**; **2Ch 14:11** 430
Now the Spirit of **G** came on **2Ch 15:1** 430
Israel was without the true **G** and **2Ch 15:3** 430

turned to the LORD **G** of Israel,	**2Ch 15:4**	430
for **G** troubled them with every	**2Ch 15:6**	430
that the LORD his **G** was with him.	**2Ch 15:9**	430
to seek the LORD **G** of their fathers	**2Ch 15:12**	430
whoever would not seek the LORD **G**	**2Ch 15:13**	430
He brought into the house of **G** the	**2Ch 15:18**	430
not relied on the LORD your **G**,	**2Ch 16:7**	430
but sought the **G** of his father,	**2Ch 17:4**	430
for **G** will give *it* into the hand	**2Ch 18:5**	430
what my **G** says, that I will speak.	**2Ch 18:13**	430
him, and **G** diverted them from him.	**2Ch 18:31**	430
have set your heart to seek **G**."	**2Ch 19:3**	430
the LORD, the **G** of their fathers.	**2Ch 19:4**	430
for the LORD our **G** will have no	**2Ch 19:7**	430
"O LORD, the **G** of our fathers,	**2Ch 20:6**	430
are You not **G** in the heavens?	**2Ch 20:6**	430
"Did You not, O our **G**,	**2Ch 20:7**	430
"O our **G**, will You not judge	**2Ch 20:12**	430
up to praise the LORD **G** of Israel,	**2Ch 20:19**	430
put your trust in the LORD your **G** and	**2Ch 20:20**	430
And the dread of **G** was on all the	**2Ch 20:29**	430
his **G** gave him rest on all sides.	**2Ch 20:30**	430
hearts to the **G** of their fathers.	**2Ch 20:33**	430
the LORD **G** of his fathers.	**2Ch 21:10**	430
the LORD **G** of your father David,	**2Ch 21:12**	430
destruction of Ahaziah was from **G**,	**2Ch 22:7**	430
hidden with them in the house of **G**	**2Ch 22:12**	430
with the king in the house of **G**.	**2Ch 23:3**	430
which were in the house of **G**.	**2Ch 23:9**	430
the house of your **G** annually,	**2Ch 24:5**	430
had broken into the house of **G** and	**2Ch 24:7**	430
of **G** on Israel in the wilderness.	**2Ch 24:9**	430
and they restored the house of **G**	**2Ch 24:13**	430
in Israel and to **G** and His house.	**2Ch 24:16**	430
the LORD, the **G** of their fathers,	**2Ch 24:18**	430
the Spirit of **G** came on Zechariah	**2Ch 24:20**	430
"Thus **G** has said,	**2Ch 24:20**	430
the LORD, the **G** of their fathers.	**2Ch 24:24**	430
the rebuilding of the house of **G**,	**2Ch 24:27**	430
But a man of **G** came to him saying,	**2Ch 25:7**	430
yet **G** will bring you down before	**2Ch 25:8**	430
for **G** has power to help and to	**2Ch 25:8**	430
Amaziah said to the man of **G**,	**2Ch 25:9**	430
And the man of **G** answered,	**2Ch 25:9**	430
that **G** has planned to destroy you,	**2Ch 25:16**	430
not listen, for it was from **G**,	**2Ch 25:20**	430
in the house of **G** with Obed-edom,	**2Ch 25:24**	430
seek **G** in the days of Zechariah,	**2Ch 26:5**	430
through the vision of **G**;	**2Ch 26:5**	430
sought the LORD, **G** prospered him.	**2Ch 26:5**	430
G helped him against the	**2Ch 26:7**	430
was unfaithful to the LORD his **G**,	**2Ch 26:16**	430
have no honor from the LORD **G**."	**2Ch 26:18**	430
his ways before the LORD his **G**.	**2Ch 27:6**	430
the LORD his **G** delivered him into	**2Ch 28:5**	430
the LORD **G** of their fathers.	**2Ch 28:6**	430
the LORD, the **G** of your fathers,	**2Ch 28:9**	430
your own against the LORD your **G**?	**2Ch 28:10**	430
the utensils of the house of **G**,	**2Ch 28:24**	430
cut the utensils of the house of **G**	**2Ch 28:24**	430
the LORD, the **G** of his fathers,	**2Ch 28:25**	430
the LORD, the **G** of your fathers,	**2Ch 29:5**	430
in the sight of the LORD our **G**,	**2Ch 29:6**	430
the holy place to the **G** of Israel.	**2Ch 29:7**	430
with the LORD **G** of Israel,	**2Ch 29:10**	430
G had prepared for the people,	**2Ch 29:36**	430
Passover to the LORD **G** of Israel.	**2Ch 30:1**	430
the LORD **G** of Israel at Jerusalem.	**2Ch 30:5**	430
return to the LORD **G** of Abraham,	**2Ch 30:6**	430
to the LORD **G** of their fathers,	**2Ch 30:7**	430
and serve the LORD your **G**,	**2Ch 30:8**	430
G is gracious and compassionate,	**2Ch 30:9**	430
The hand of **G** was also on Judah to	**2Ch 30:12**	430
to the law of Moses the man of **G**;	**2Ch 30:16**	430
who prepares his heart to seek **G**,	**2Ch 30:19**	430
God, the LORD **G** of his fathers,	**2Ch 30:19**	430
to the LORD **G** of their fathers.	**2Ch 30:22**	430
consecrated to the LORD their **G**,	**2Ch 31:6**	430
chief officer of the house of **G**.	**2Ch 31:13**	430
over the freewill offerings of **G**,	**2Ch 31:14**	430
and true before the LORD his **G**.	**2Ch 31:20**	430
in the service of the house of **G**	**2Ch 31:21**	430
and in commandment, seeking his **G**,	**2Ch 31:21**	430
but with us is the LORD our **G** to	**2Ch 32:8**	430
"The LORD our **G** will deliver us	**2Ch 32:11**	430
that your **G** should be able to	**2Ch 32:14**	430
for no **g** of any nation or kingdom	**2Ch 32:15**	433
G deliver you from my hand?' "	**2Ch 32:15**	430
spoke further against the LORD **G**	**2Ch 32:16**	430
to insult the LORD **G** of Israel,	**2Ch 32:17**	430
so the **G** of Hezekiah will not	**2Ch 32:17**	430
They spoke of the **G** of	**2Ch 32:19**	430
had entered the temple of his **g**,	**2Ch 32:21**	430
for **G** had given him very great	**2Ch 32:29**	430
G left him *alone only* to test him,	**2Ch 32:31**	430
he had made in the house of **G**,	**2Ch 33:7**	430
of which **G** had said to David and	**2Ch 33:7**	430
he entreated the LORD his **G** and	**2Ch 33:12**	430
before the **G** of his fathers.	**2Ch 33:12**	430
Manasseh knew that the LORD *was* **G**.	**2Ch 33:13**	430
to serve the LORD **G** of Israel.	**2Ch 33:16**	430
although only to the LORD their **G**.	**2Ch 33:17**	430
Manasseh even his prayer to his **G**,	**2Ch 33:18**	430
the name of the LORD **G** of Israel,	**2Ch 33:18**	430
His prayer also and *how* **G** was	**2Ch 33:19**	
to seek the **G** of his father David;	**2Ch 34:3**	430
the house of the LORD his **G**.	**2Ch 34:8**	430
was brought into the house of **G**,	**2Ch 34:9**	430
says the LORD, the **G** of Israel,	**2Ch 34:23**	430
'Thus says the LORD **G** of Israel	**2Ch 34:26**	430
and you humbled yourself before **G**	**2Ch 34:27**	430
according to the covenant of **G**,	**2Ch 34:32**	430
of God, the **G** of their fathers.	**2Ch 34:32**	430
Israel to serve the LORD their **G**.	**2Ch 34:33**	430
the LORD **G** of their fathers.	**2Ch 34:33**	430
LORD your **G** and His people Israel.	**2Ch 35:3**	430
the officials of the house of **G**,	**2Ch 35:8**	430
and **G** has ordered me to hurry.	**2Ch 35:21**	430
interfering with **G** who is with me,	**2Ch 35:21**	430
words of Neco from the mouth of **G**,	**2Ch 35:22**	430
in the sight of the LORD his **G**.	**2Ch 36:5**	430
in the sight of the LORD his **G**;	**2Ch 36:12**	430
made him swear *allegiance* by **G**.	**2Ch 36:13**	430
turning to the LORD **G** of Israel.	**2Ch 36:13**	430
The LORD, the **G** of their fathers,	**2Ch 36:15**	430
mocked the messengers of **G**,	**2Ch 36:16**	430
the articles of the house of **G**,	**2Ch 36:18**	430
Then they burned the house of **G** and	**2Ch 36:19**	430
'The LORD, the **G** of heaven, has	**2Ch 36:23**	430
may the LORD his **G** be with him,	**2Ch 36:23**	430
'The LORD, the **G** of heaven, has	**Ezr 1:2**	430
His people, may his **G** be with him!	**Ezr 1:3**	430
of the LORD, the **G** of Israel;	**Ezr 1:3**	430
He is the **G** who is in Jerusalem.	**Ezr 1:3**	430
of **G** which is in Jerusalem.' "	**Ezr 1:4**	430
whose spirit **G** had stirred to go up	**Ezr 1:5**	430
offered willingly for the house of **G**	**Ezr 2:68**	430
the altar of the **G** of Israel to	**Ezr 3:2**	430
in the law of Moses, the man of **G**.	**Ezr 3:2**	430
coming to the house of **G** at Jerusalem	**Ezr 3:8**	430
the workmen in the temple of **G**.	**Ezr 3:9**	430
a temple to the LORD **G** of Israel,	**Ezr 4:1**	430
for we, like you, seek your **G**;	**Ezr 4:2**	430
us in building a house to our **G**;	**Ezr 4:3**	430
build to the LORD **G** of Israel,	**Ezr 4:3**	430
Then work on the house of **G** in	**Ezr 4:24**	426
in the name of the **G** of Israel,	**Ezr 5:1**	426
house of **G** which is in Jerusalem;	**Ezr 5:2**	426
and the prophets of **G** were with	**Ezr 5:2**	426
the eye of their **G** was on the elders	**Ezr 5:5**	426
to the house of the great **G**,	**Ezr 5:8**	426
'We are the servants of the **G** of	**Ezr 5:11**	426
provoked the **G** of heaven to wrath,	**Ezr 5:12**	426
decree to rebuild this house of **G**.	**Ezr 5:13**	426
silver utensils of the house of **G** which	**Ezr 5:14**	426
let the house of **G** be rebuilt in its	**Ezr 5:15**	426
of the house of **G** in Jerusalem;	**Ezr 5:16**	426
this house of **G** at Jerusalem;	**Ezr 5:17**	426
the house of **G** at Jerusalem,	**Ezr 6:3**	426
utensils of the house of **G**,	**Ezr 6:5**	426
shall put *them* in the house of **G**.'	**Ezr 6:5**	426
Leave this work on the house of **G**	**Ezr 6:7**	426
this house of **G** on its site.	**Ezr 6:7**	426
the rebuilding of this house of **G**:	**Ezr 6:8**	426
burnt offering to the **G** of heaven,	**Ezr 6:9**	426
offer acceptable sacrifices to the **G** of	**Ezr 6:10**	426
"May the **G** who has caused His	**Ezr 6:12**	426
this house of **G** in Jerusalem.	**Ezr 6:12**	426
according to the command of the **G**	**Ezr 6:14**	426
of this house of **G** with joy.	**Ezr 6:16**	426
the dedication of this temple of **G**	**Ezr 6:17**	426
for the service of **G** in Jerusalem,	**Ezr 6:18**	426
to seek the LORD **G** of Israel,	**Ezr 6:21**	426
in the work of the house of **G**,	**Ezr 6:22**	430
the house of God, the **G** of Israel.	**Ezr 6:22**	430
the LORD **G** of Israel had given;	**Ezr 7:6**	430
of the LORD his **G** *was* upon him.	**Ezr 7:6**	430
good hand of his **G** *was* upon him.	**Ezr 7:9**	430
of the law of the **G** of heaven,	**Ezr 7:12**	426
according to the law of your **G**	**Ezr 7:14**	426
freely offered to the **G** of Israel,	**Ezr 7:15**	426
of their **G** which is in Jerusalem;	**Ezr 7:16**	426
of your **G** which is in Jerusalem.	**Ezr 7:17**	426
according to the will of your **G**.	**Ezr 7:18**	426
service of the house of your **G**,	**Ezr 7:19**	426
in full before the **G** of Jerusalem.	**Ezr 7:19**	426
the needs for the house of your **G**,	**Ezr 7:20**	426
of the law of the **G** of heaven,	**Ezr 7:21**	426
is commanded by the **G** of heaven,	**Ezr 7:23**	426
for the house of the **G** of heaven,	**Ezr 7:23**	426
or servants of this house of **G**.	**Ezr 7:24**	426
according to the wisdom of your **G**	**Ezr 7:25**	426
those who know the laws of your **G**;	**Ezr 7:25**	426
of your **G** and the law of the king,	**Ezr 7:26**	426
be the LORD, the **G** of our fathers,	**Ezr 7:27**	430
the hand of the LORD my **G** upon me,	**Ezr 7:28**	430
to us for the house of our **G**.	**Ezr 8:17**	430
According to the good hand of our **G**	**Ezr 8:18**	430
humble ourselves before our **G** to seek	**Ezr 8:21**	430
"The hand of our **G** is favorably	**Ezr 8:22**	430
our **G** concerning this *matter*,	**Ezr 8:23**	430
the offering for the house of our **G**	**Ezr 8:25**	430
to the LORD **G** of your fathers.	**Ezr 8:28**	430
Jerusalem to the house of our **G**.	**Ezr 8:30**	430
and the hand of our **G** was over us,	**Ezr 8:31**	430
weighed out in the house of our **G**	**Ezr 8:33**	430
offerings to the **G** of Israel:	**Ezr 8:35**	430
the people and the house of **G**.	**Ezr 8:36**	430
who trembled at the words of the **G** of	**Ezr 9:4**	430
out my hands to the LORD my **G**;	**Ezr 9:5**	430
"O my **G**, I am ashamed and	**Ezr 9:6**	430
to lift up my face to You, my **G**,	**Ezr 9:6**	430
been *shown* from the LORD our **G**,	**Ezr 9:8**	430
that our **G** may enlighten our eyes	**Ezr 9:8**	430
our **G** has not forsaken us,	**Ezr 9:9**	430
to raise up the house of our **G**,	**Ezr 9:9**	430
"Now, our **G**, what shall we	**Ezr 9:10**	430
since You our **G** have requited *us*	**Ezr 9:13**	430
"O LORD **G** of Israel, You are	**Ezr 9:15**	430
himself before the house of **G**,	**Ezr 10:1**	430
"We have been unfaithful to our **G** and	**Ezr 10:2**	430
let us make a covenant with our **G** to	**Ezr 10:3**	430
at the commandment of our **G**;	**Ezr 10:3**	430
Ezra rose from before the house of **G**	**Ezr 10:6**	430
open square *before* the house of **G**,	**Ezr 10:9**	430
to the LORD **G** of your fathers and	**Ezr 10:11**	430
until the fierce anger of our **G** on	**Ezr 10:14**	430
praying before the **G** of heaven.	**Ne 1:4**	430
beseech You, O LORD **G** of heaven,	**Ne 1:5**	430
heaven, the great and awesome **G**,	**Ne 1:5**	410
So I prayed to the **G** of heaven.	**Ne 2:4**	430
the good hand of my **G** *was* on me.	**Ne 2:8**	430
I did not tell anyone what my **G**	**Ne 2:12**	430
hand of my **G** had been favorable	**Ne 2:18**	430
"The **G** of heaven will give us	**Ne 2:20**	430
Hear, O our **G**, how we are despised!	**Ne 4:4**	430
But we prayed to our **G**,	**Ne 4:9**	430
that **G** had frustrated their plan,	**Ne 4:15**	430
Our **G** will fight for us."	**Ne 4:20**	430
you not walk in the fear of our **G**	**Ne 5:9**	430
"Thus may **G** shake out every man	**Ne 5:13**	430
do so because of the fear of **G**.	**Ne 5:15**	430
Remember me, O my **G**,	**Ne 5:19**	430
O **G**, strengthen my hands.	**Ne 6:9**	
meet together in the house of **G**,	**Ne 6:10**	430
that surely **G** had not sent him,	**Ne 6:12**	430
Remember, O my **G**, Tobiah and	**Ne 6:14**	430
with the help of our **G**.	**Ne 6:16**	430
man and feared **G** more than many.	**Ne 7:2**	430
Then my **G** put it into my heart to	**Ne 7:5**	430
Ezra blessed the LORD the great **G**.	**Ne 8:6**	430
from the book, from the law of **G**,	**Ne 8:8**	430
day is holy to the LORD your **G**;	**Ne 8:9**	430
in the courts of the house of **G**,	**Ne 8:16**	430
read from the book of the law of **G**	**Ne 8:18**	430
their **G** for a fourth of the day;	**Ne 9:3**	430
and worshiped the LORD their **G**.	**Ne 9:3**	430
a loud voice to the LORD their **G**.	**Ne 9:4**	430
bless the LORD your **G** forever and	**Ne 9:5**	430
"You are the LORD **G**,	**Ne 9:7**	430
But You are a **G** of forgiveness,	**Ne 9:17**	433
G Who brought you up from Egypt,'	**Ne 9:18**	430
a gracious and compassionate **G**.	**Ne 9:31**	410
"Now therefore, our **G**,	**Ne 9:32**	430
the mighty, and the awesome **G**,	**Ne 9:32**	410
of the lands to the law of **G**,	**Ne 10:28**	430
the commandments of **G** our Lord,	**Ne 10:29**	3068
the service of the house of our **G**:	**Ne 10:32**	430
the work of the house of our **G**.	**Ne 10:33**	430
bring it to the house of our **G**,	**Ne 10:34**	430
burn on the altar of the LORD our **G**	**Ne 10:34**	430
and bring to the house of our **G**	**Ne 10:36**	430
ministering in the house of our **G**,	**Ne 10:36**	430
chambers of the house of our **G**,	**Ne 10:37**	430
the tithes to the house of our **G**,	**Ne 10:38**	430
not neglect the house of our **G**.	**Ne 10:39**	430
the leader of the house of **G**,	**Ne 11:11**	430
outside work of the house of **G**;	**Ne 11:16**	430
for the service of the house of **G**.	**Ne 11:22**	430
prescribed by David the man of **G**,	**Ne 12:24**	430
instruments of David the man of **G**,	**Ne 12:36**	430
their stand in the house of **G**.	**Ne 12:40**	430
G had given them great joy,	**Ne 12:43**	430
they performed the worship of their **G**	**Ne 12:45**	430
and hymns of thanksgiving to **G**.	**Ne 12:46**	430
ever enter the assembly of **G**,	**Ne 13:1**	430
G turned the curse into a blessing.	**Ne 13:2**	430
chambers of the house of our **G**,	**Ne 13:4**	430
in the courts of the house of **G**.	**Ne 13:7**	430
there the utensils of the house of **G**	**Ne 13:9**	430
"Why is the house of **G** forsaken?"	**Ne 13:11**	430
Remember me for this, O my **G**,	**Ne 13:14**	430
house of my **G** and its services.	**Ne 13:14**	430
G brought on us and on this city	**Ne 13:18**	430
For this also remember me, O my **G**,	**Ne 13:22**	430
hair, and made them swear by **G**,	**Ne 13:25**	430
him, and he was loved by his **G**,	**Ne 13:26**	430
G made him king over all Israel;	**Ne 13:26**	430
acting unfaithfully against our **G**	**Ne 13:27**	430
Remember them, O my **G**,	**Ne 13:29**	430
Remember me, O my **G**,	**Ne 13:31**	430
was blameless, upright, fearing **G** and	**Jb 1:1**	430
and cursed **G** in their hearts."	**Jb 1:5**	430
sons of **G** came to present themselves	**Jb 1:6**	430
fearing **G** and turning away from	**Jb 1:8**	430
"Does Job fear **G** for nothing?	**Jb 1:9**	430
"The fire of **G** fell from heaven	**Jb 1:16**	430
Job did not sin nor did he blame **G**.	**Jb 1:22**	430
sons of **G** came to present themselves	**Jb 2:1**	430
fearing **G** and turning away from	**Jb 2:3**	430
Curse **G** and die!"	**Jb 2:9**	430
from **G** and not accept adversity?"	**Jb 2:10**	430
Let not **G** above care for it, Nor	**Jb 3:4**	433
hidden, And whom **G** has hedged in?	**Jb 3:23**	433
"Is not your fear *of* **G** your	**Jb 4:6**	
"By the breath of **G** they perish,	**Jb 4:9**	433
'Can mankind be just before **G**?	**Jb 4:17**	433
"But as for me, I would seek **G**,	**Jb 5:8**	410
I would place my cause before **G**;	**Jb 5:8**	430
happy is the man whom **G** reproves,	**Jb 5:17**	433
terrors of **G** are arrayed against me	**Jb 6:4**	433
And that **G** would grant my longing!	**Jb 6:8**	433
that **G** were willing to crush me,	**Jb 6:9**	433
"Does **G** pervert justice? Or does	**Jb 8:3**	410
"If you would seek **G** And implore	**Jb 8:5**	410
are the paths of all who forget **G**;	**Jb 8:13**	410
G will not reject *a man of*	**Jb 8:20**	410

a man be in the right before **G**?	**Jb 9:2**	410
"*It is* **G** who removes	**Jb 9:5**	
"**G** will not turn back His anger;	**Jb 9:13**	433
"I will say to **G**,	**Jb 10:2**	433
"But would that **G** might speak,	**Jb 11:5**	433
Know then that **G** forgets a part of	**Jb 11:6**	433
"Can you discover the depths of **G**?	**Jb 11:7**	433
The one who called on **G** and	**Jb 12:4**	433
those who provoke **G** are secure,	**Jb 12:6**	410
Whom **G** brings into their power.	**Jb 12:6**	433
And I desire to argue with **G**.	**Jb 13:3**	410
you speak what is unjust for **G**,	**Jb 13:7**	410
Will you contend for **G**?	**Jb 13:8**	410
And hinder meditation before **G**.	**Jb 15:4**	410
you hear the secret counsel of **G**,	**Jb 15:8**	433
Are the consolations of **G** too small	**Jb 15:11**	410
should turn your spirit against **G** And	**Jb 15:13**	410
stretched out his hand against **G** And	**Jb 15:25**	410
"**G** hands me over to ruffians And	**Jb 16:11**	410
My eye weeps to **G**.	**Jb 16:20**	433
with **G** As a man with his neighbor!	**Jb 16:21**	433
of him who does not know **G**."	**Jb 18:21**	410
Know then that **G** has wronged me And	**Jb 19:6**	433
For the hand of **G** has struck me.	**Jb 19:21**	433
"Why do you persecute me as **G** *does,*	**Jb 19:22**	410
Yet from my flesh I shall see **G**;	**Jb 19:26**	433
G will expel them from his belly.	**Jb 20:15**	410
"When he fills his belly, **G**	**Jb 20:23**	
is the wicked man's portion from **G**,	**Jb 20:29**	430
heritage decreed to him by **G**."	**Jb 20:29**	410
the rod of **G** is not on them.	**Jb 21:9**	433
"They say to **G**,	**Jb 21:14**	410
Does **G** apportion destruction in	**Jb 21:17**	
'**G** stores away a man's iniquity	**Jb 21:19**	433
Let **G** repay him so that he may	**Jb 21:19**	
"Can anyone teach **G** knowledge,	**Jb 21:22**	410
"Can a vigorous man be of use to **G**,	**Jb 22:2**	410
"Is not **G** *in* the height of heaven?	**Jb 22:12**	433
'What does **G** know?	**Jb 22:13**	410
'They said to **G**,	**Jb 22:17**	410
And lift up your face to **G**.	**Jb 22:26**	433
is **G** *who* has made my heart faint,	**Jb 23:16**	410
Yet **G** does not pay attention to	**Jb 24:12**	433
"How then can a man be just with **G**?	**Jb 25:4**	410
"As **G** lives, who has taken away	**Jb 27:2**	410
the breath of **G** is in my nostrils,	**Jb 27:3**	433
cut off, When **G** requires his life?	**Jb 27:8**	433
"Will **G** hear his cry When	**Jb 27:9**	410
Will he call on **G** at all times?	**Jb 27:10**	433
instruct you in the power of **G**;	**Jb 27:11**	410
portion of a wicked man from **G**,	**Jb 27:13**	410
"**G** understands its way,	**Jb 28:23**	430
the days when **G** watched over me;	**Jb 29:2**	433
friendship of **G** *was* over my tent;	**Jb 29:4**	433
"And what is the portion of **G**	**Jb 31:2**	433
And let **G** know my integrity.	**Jb 31:6**	433
then could I do when **G** arises?	**Jb 31:14**	410
calamity from **G** is a terror to me,	**Jb 31:23**	410
For I would have denied **G** above.	**Jb 31:28**	410
he justified himself before **G**.	**Jb 32:2**	430
G will rout him, not man.'	**Jb 32:13**	410
"The Spirit of **G** has made me, And	**Jb 33:4**	410
"Behold, I belong to **G** like you;	**Jb 33:6**	410
this, For **G** is greater than man.	**Jb 33:12**	433
"Indeed **G** speaks once, Or twice,	**Jb 33:14**	410
Then he will pray to **G**,	**Jb 33:26**	433
G does all these oftentimes with	**Jb 33:29**	410
But **G** has taken away my right;	**Jb 34:5**	410
When he is pleased with **G**.'	**Jb 34:9**	430
Far be it from **G** to do wickedness,	**Jb 34:10**	410
"Surely, **G** will not act wickedly,	**Jb 34:12**	410
he should go before **G** in judgment.	**Jb 34:23**	410
"For has anyone said to **G**,	**Jb 34:31**	410
his words against **G**.' "	**Jb 34:37**	410
'Where is **G** my Maker, Who gives	**Jb 35:10**	433
"Surely **G** will not listen to an	**Jb 35:13**	410
G is mighty but does not despise	**Jb 36:5**	410
"Behold, **G** is exalted in His power;	**Jb 36:22**	410
"Behold, **G** is exalted, and we do	**Jb 36:26**	410
"**G** thunders with His voice	**Jb 37:5**	410
"From the breath of **G** ice is made,	**Jb 37:10**	410
and consider the wonders of **G**.	**Jb 37:14**	410
you know how **G** establishes them,	**Jb 37:15**	433
Around **G** is awesome majesty.	**Jb 37:22**	433
all the sons of **G** shouted for joy?	**Jb 38:7**	430
When its young cry to **G** And	**Jb 38:41**	410
G has made her forget wisdom,	**Jb 39:17**	433
Let him who reproves **G** answer it."	**Jb 40:2**	433
"Or do you have an arm like **G**,	**Jb 40:9**	410
"He is the first of the ways of **G**;	**Jb 40:19**	410
is no deliverance for him in **G**."	**Ps 3:2**	430
Arise, O LORD; save me, O my **G**!	**Ps 3:7**	430
I call, O **G** of my righteousness!	**Ps 4:1**	430
my cry for help, my King and my **G**,	**Ps 5:2**	430
For You are not a **G** who takes	**Ps 5:4**	410
Hold them guilty, O **G**;	**Ps 5:10**	430
Lord my **G**, in You I have taken	**Ps 7:1**	430
O LORD my **G**, if I have done this,	**Ps 7:3**	430
G tries the hearts and minds.	**Ps 7:9**	430
My shield is with **G**,	**Ps 7:10**	430
G is a righteous judge, And a God	**Ps 7:11**	430
a **G** who has indignation every day.	**Ps 7:11**	410
made him a little lower than **G**,	**Ps 8:5**	430
Even all the nations who forget **G**.	**Ps 9:17**	430
All his thoughts are, "There is no **G**."	**Ps 10:4**	430
He says to himself, "**G** has forgotten;	**Ps 10:11**	410
O **G**, lift up Your hand.	**Ps 10:12**	410
Why has the wicked spurned **G**?	**Ps 10:13**	430
and answer me, O LORD my **G**;	**Ps 13:3**	430
said in his heart, "There is no **G**."	**Ps 14:1**	430
who understand, Who seek after **G**.	**Ps 14:2**	430
For **G** is with the righteous	**Ps 14:5**	430
Preserve me, O **G**, for I take	**Ps 16:1**	410
who have bartered for another **g**	**Ps 16:4**	
for You will answer me, O **G**;	**Ps 17:6**	410
fortress and my deliverer, My **G**,	**Ps 18:2**	410
LORD, And cried to my **G** for help;	**Ps 18:6**	430
not wickedly departed from my **G**.	**Ps 18:21**	430
LORD my **G** illumines my darkness.	**Ps 18:28**	430
by my **G** I can leap over a wall.	**Ps 18:29**	430
As for **G**, His way is blameless;	**Ps 18:30**	410
For who is **G**, but the LORD?	**Ps 18:31**	433
And who is a rock, except our **G**,	**Ps 18:31**	430
The **G** who girds me with strength And	**Ps 18:32**	410
exalted be the **G** of my salvation,	**Ps 18:46**	430
G who executes vengeance for me,	**Ps 18:47**	410
are telling of the glory of **G**;	**Ps 19:1**	410
May the name of the **G** of Jacob set	**Ps 20:1**	430
in the name of our **G** we will set up	**Ps 20:5**	430
in the name of the LORD, our **G**.	**Ps 20:7**	430
My **G**, my God, why have You	**Ps 22:1**	410
My God, my **G**, why have You	**Ps 22:1**	410
O my **G**, I cry by day, but You	**Ps 22:2**	430
been my **G** from my mother's womb.	**Ps 22:10**	410
from the **G** of his salvation.	**Ps 24:5**	430
O my **G**, in You I trust, Do not	**Ps 25:2**	430
You are the **G** of my salvation;	**Ps 25:5**	430
Redeem Israel, O **G**,	**Ps 25:22**	430
forsake me, O **G** of my salvation!	**Ps 27:9**	430
The **G** of glory thunders, The LORD	**Ps 29:3**	410
O LORD my **G**, I cried to You for	**Ps 30:2**	430
O LORD my **G**, I will give thanks to	**Ps 30:12**	430
ransomed me, O LORD, **G** of truth.	**Ps 31:5**	410
O LORD, I say, "You are my **G**."	**Ps 31:14**	430
is the nation whose **G** is the LORD,	**Ps 33:12**	430
And to my cause, my **G** and my Lord.	**Ps 35:23**	430
Judge me, O LORD my **G**,	**Ps 35:24**	430
is no fear of **G** before his eyes.	**Ps 36:1**	430
is like the mountains of **G**;	**Ps 36:6**	410
is Your lovingkindness, O **G**!	**Ps 36:7**	430
The law of his **G** is in his heart;	**Ps 37:31**	430
You will answer, O Lord my **G**.	**Ps 38:15**	430
O my **G**, do not be far from me!	**Ps 38:21**	430
mouth, a song of praise to our **G**;	**Ps 40:3**	430
Many, O LORD my **G**, are the wonders	**Ps 40:5**	430
I delight to do Your will, O my **G**;	**Ps 40:8**	430
Do not delay, O my **G**.	**Ps 40:17**	430
be the LORD, the **G** of Israel,	**Ps 41:13**	430
So my soul pants for You, O **G**.	**Ps 42:1**	430
My soul thirsts for **G**,	**Ps 42:2**	430
thirsts for God, for the living **G**;	**Ps 42:2**	410
shall I come and appear before **G**?	**Ps 42:2**	430
"Where is your **G**?"	**Ps 42:3**	430
in procession to the house of **G**,	**Ps 42:4**	430
Hope in **G**, for I shall again	**Ps 42:5**	430
O my **G**, my soul is in despair	**Ps 42:6**	430
A prayer to the **G** of my life.	**Ps 42:8**	410
I will say to **G** my rock,	**Ps 42:9**	410
"Where is your **G**?"	**Ps 42:10**	430
Hope in **G**, for I shall yet praise	**Ps 42:11**	430
help of my countenance and my **G**.	**Ps 42:11**	430
Vindicate me, O **G**, and plead my	**Ps 43:1**	430
For You are the **G** of my strength;	**Ps 43:2**	430
Then I will go to the altar of **G**,	**Ps 43:4**	430
of God, To **G** my exceeding joy;	**Ps 43:4**	410
the lyre I shall praise You, O **G**,	**Ps 43:4**	430
I shall praise You, O God, my **G**.	**Ps 43:4**	430
Hope in **G**, for I shall again	**Ps 43:5**	430
help of my countenance and my **G**.	**Ps 43:5**	430
O **G**, we have heard with our ears,	**Ps 44:1**	430
You are my King, O **G**;	**Ps 44:4**	430
In **G** we have boasted all day long,	**Ps 44:8**	430
had forgotten the name of our **G** Or	**Ps 44:20**	430
extended our hands to a strange **g**,	**Ps 44:20**	410
Would not **G** find this out?	**Ps 44:21**	430
G has blessed You forever.	**Ps 45:2**	430
Your throne, O **G**, is forever and	**Ps 45:6**	430
Therefore **G**, Your God, has anointed	**Ps 45:7**	430
Therefore God, Your **G**,	**Ps 45:7**	430
G is our refuge and strength, A	**Ps 46:1**	430
streams make glad the city of **G**,	**Ps 46:4**	430
G is in the midst of her, she will	**Ps 46:5**	430
G will help her when morning dawns.	**Ps 46:5**	430
G of Jacob is our stronghold.	**Ps 46:7**	430
striving and know that I am **G**;	**Ps 46:10**	430
G of Jacob is our stronghold.	**Ps 46:11**	430
Shout to **G** with the voice of joy.	**Ps 47:1**	430
G has ascended with a shout, The	**Ps 47:5**	430
Sing praises to **G**, sing praises;	**Ps 47:6**	430
G is the King of all the earth;	**Ps 47:7**	430
G reigns over the nations, God	**Ps 47:8**	430
G sits on His holy throne.	**Ps 47:8**	430
as the people of the **G** of Abraham,	**Ps 47:9**	430
shields of the earth belong to **G**;	**Ps 47:9**	430
be praised, In the city of our **G**,	**Ps 48:1**	430
G, in her palaces, Has made	**Ps 48:3**	430
of hosts, in the city of our **G**;	**Ps 48:8**	430
G will establish her forever.	**Ps 48:8**	430
on Your lovingkindness, O **G**,	**Ps 48:9**	430
As is Your name, O **G**,	**Ps 48:10**	430
For such is **G**, Our God forever and	**Ps 48:14**	430
is God, Our **G** forever and ever;	**Ps 48:14**	430
Or give to **G** a ransom for him	**Ps 49:7**	430
But **G** will redeem my soul from the	**Ps 49:15**	430
The Mighty One, **G**, the LORD, has	**Ps 50:1**	430
of beauty, **G** has shone forth.	**Ps 50:2**	430
our **G** come and not keep silence;	**Ps 50:3**	430
For **G** Himself is judge.	**Ps 50:6**	430
I am **G**, your God.	**Ps 50:7**	430
I am God, your **G**.	**Ps 50:7**	430
to **G** a sacrifice of thanksgiving And	**Ps 50:14**	430
But to the wicked **G** says,	**Ps 50:16**	430
consider this, you who forget **G**,	**Ps 50:22**	433
I shall show the salvation of **G**."	**Ps 50:23**	430
Be gracious to me, O **G**,	**Ps 51:1**	430
Create in me a clean heart, O **G**,	**Ps 51:10**	430
me from bloodguiltiness, O **G**,	**Ps 51:14**	430
O God, the **G** of my salvation;	**Ps 51:14**	430
sacrifices of **G** are a broken spirit;	**Ps 51:17**	430
broken and a contrite heart, O **G**,	**Ps 51:17**	430
of **G** *endures* all day long.	**Ps 52:1**	410
But **G** will break you down forever;	**Ps 52:5**	410
who would not make **G** his refuge,	**Ps 52:7**	430
olive tree in the house of **G**;	**Ps 52:8**	430
I trust in the lovingkindness of **G**	**Ps 52:8**	430
said in his heart, "There is no **G**,"	**Ps 53:1**	430
G has looked down from heaven upon	**Ps 53:2**	430
understands, Who seeks after **G**.	**Ps 53:2**	430
bread And have not called upon **G**?	**Ps 53:4**	430
For **G** scattered the bones of him	**Ps 53:5**	430
because **G** had rejected them.	**Ps 53:5**	430
G restores His captive people,	**Ps 53:6**	430
Save me, O **G**, by Your name, And	**Ps 54:1**	430
Hear my prayer, O **G**;	**Ps 54:2**	430
They have not set **G** before them.	**Ps 54:3**	430
Behold, **G** is my helper;	**Ps 54:4**	430
Give ear to my prayer, O **G**;	**Ps 55:1**	430
Walked in the house of **G** in the	**Ps 55:14**	430
As for me, I shall call upon **G**,	**Ps 55:16**	430
G will hear and answer them	**Ps 55:19**	410
no change, And who do not fear **G**.	**Ps 55:19**	430
But You, O **G**, will bring them	**Ps 55:23**	430
Be gracious to me, O **G**, for man has	**Ps 56:1**	430
In **G**, whose word I praise, In God	**Ps 56:4**	430
praise, In **G** I have put my trust;	**Ps 56:4**	430
anger put down the peoples, O **G**!	**Ps 56:7**	430
This I know, that **G** is for me.	**Ps 56:9**	430
In **G**, *whose* word I praise, In the	**Ps 56:10**	430
In **G** I have put my trust, I shall	**Ps 56:11**	430
Your vows are *binding* upon me, O **G**;	**Ps 56:12**	430
I may walk before **G** In the light	**Ps 56:13**	430
Be gracious to me, O **G**,	**Ps 57:1**	430
I will cry to **G** Most High, To God	**Ps 57:2**	430
To **G** who accomplishes *all things*	**Ps 57:2**	410
G will send forth His	**Ps 57:3**	430
Be exalted above the heavens, O **G**;	**Ps 57:5**	430
My heart is steadfast, O **G**,	**Ps 57:7**	430
Be exalted above the heavens, O **G**;	**Ps 57:11**	430
O **G**, shatter their teeth in their	**Ps 58:6**	430
is a **G** who judges on earth!"	**Ps 58:11**	430
me from my enemies, O my **G**;	**Ps 59:1**	430
You, O LORD **G** of hosts,	**Ps 59:5**	430
God of hosts, the **G** of Israel,	**Ps 59:5**	430
for You, For **G** is my stronghold.	**Ps 59:9**	430
My **G** in His lovingkindness will	**Ps 59:10**	430
G will let me look *triumphantly*	**Ps 59:10**	430
may know that **G** rules in Jacob To	**Ps 59:13**	430
For **G** is my stronghold, the God	**Ps 59:17**	430
the **G** who shows me lovingkindness.	**Ps 59:17**	430
O **G**, You have rejected us.	**Ps 60:1**	430
G has spoken in His holiness:	**Ps 60:6**	430
Have not You Yourself, O **G**,	**Ps 60:10**	430
not go forth with our armies, O **G**?	**Ps 60:10**	430
Through **G** we shall do valiantly,	**Ps 60:12**	430
Hear my cry, O **G**;	**Ps 61:1**	430
For You have heard my vows, O **G**;	**Ps 61:5**	430
He will abide before **G** forever;	**Ps 61:7**	430
soul *waits* in silence for **G** only;	**Ps 62:1**	430
soul, wait in silence for **G** only,	**Ps 62:5**	430
On **G** my salvation and my glory	**Ps 62:7**	430
of my strength, my refuge is in **G**.	**Ps 62:7**	430
G is a refuge for us.	**Ps 62:8**	430
Once **G** has spoken;	**Ps 62:11**	430
That power belongs to **G**;	**Ps 62:11**	430
O **G**, You are my God;	**Ps 63:1**	430
O God, You are my **G**;	**Ps 63:1**	410
But the king will rejoice in **G**;	**Ps 63:11**	430
Hear my voice, O **G**,	**Ps 64:1**	430
G will shoot at them with an arrow	**Ps 64:7**	430
And they will declare the work of **G**,	**Ps 64:9**	430
You, *and* praise in Zion, O **G**,	**Ps 65:1**	430
O **G** of our salvation,	**Ps 65:5**	430
The stream of **G** is full of water;	**Ps 65:9**	430
Shout joyfully to **G**,	**Ps 66:1**	430
to **G**, "How awesome are Your works!	**Ps 66:3**	430
Come and see the works of **G**,	**Ps 66:5**	430
Bless our **G**, O peoples, And sound	**Ps 66:8**	430
For You have tried us, O **G**;	**Ps 66:10**	430
Come *and* hear, all who fear **G**,	**Ps 66:16**	430
But certainly **G** has heard;	**Ps 66:19**	430
Blessed be **G**, Who has not turned	**Ps 66:20**	430
G be gracious to us and bless us,	**Ps 67:1**	430
Let the peoples praise You, O **G**;	**Ps 67:3**	430
Let the peoples praise You, O **G**;	**Ps 67:5**	430
G, our God, blesses us.	**Ps 67:6**	430
God, our **G**, blesses us.	**Ps 67:6**	430
G blesses us, That all the ends of	**Ps 67:7**	430
Let **G** arise, let His enemies be	**Ps 68:1**	430
So let the wicked perish before **G**.	**Ps 68:2**	430
let them exult before **G**;	**Ps 68:3**	430
Sing to **G**, sing praises to His	**Ps 68:4**	430
Is **G** in His holy habitation.	**Ps 68:5**	430
G makes a home for the lonely;	**Ps 68:6**	430
O **G**, when You went forth	**Ps 68:7**	430
dropped *rain* at the presence of **G**;	**Ps 68:8**	430
quaked at the presence of **G**,	**Ps 68:8**	430
presence of God, the **G** of Israel.	**Ps 68:8**	430

shed abroad a plentiful rain, O **G**; Ps 68:9 430
in Your goodness for the poor, O **G**. Ps 68:10 430
of **G** is the mountain of Bashan; Ps 68:15 430
which **G** has desired for His abode? Ps 68:16 430
The chariots of **G** are myriads, Ps 68:17 430
that the LORD **G** may dwell *there.* Ps 68:18 430
The **G** *who* is our salvation. Ps 68:19 410
G is to us a God of deliverances; Ps 68:20 410
God is to us a **G** of deliverances; Ps 68:20 410
And to **G** the Lord belong escapes Ps 68:20 3068
Surely **G** will shatter the head of Ps 68:21 430
have seen Your procession, O **G**, Ps 68:24 430
O God, The procession of my **G**, Ps 68:24 410
Bless **G** in the congregations, *Even* Ps 68:26 430
G has commanded your strength; Ps 68:28 430
Show Yourself strong, O **G**, Ps 68:28 430
stretch out her hands to **G**. Ps 68:31 430
Sing to **G**, O kingdoms of the earth, Ps 68:32 430
Ascribe strength to **G**; Ps 68:34 430
O **G**, *You are* awesome from Your Ps 68:35 430
The **G** of Israel Himself gives Ps 68:35 410
Blessed be **G**! Ps 68:35 430
Save me, O **G**, For the waters have Ps 69:1 430
eyes fail while I wait for my **G**. Ps 69:3 430
O **G**, it is You who knows my Ps 69:5 430
through me, O Lord **G** of hosts; Ps 69:6 3068
through me, O **G** of Israel, Ps 69:6 430
O **G**, in the greatness of Your Ps 69:13 430
May Your salvation, O **G**, Ps 69:29 430
praise the name of **G** with song And Ps 69:30 430
You who seek **G**, let your heart Ps 69:32 430
For **G** will save Zion and build the Ps 69:35 430
O **G**, *hasten* to deliver me; Ps 70:1 430
"Let **G** be magnified." Ps 70:4 430
Hasten to me, O **G**! Ps 70:5 430
Rescue me, O my **G**, out of the hand Ps 71:4 430
O Lord **G**, *You are* my confidence Ps 71:5 3068
"**G** has forsaken him; Ps 71:11 430
O **G**, do not be far from me; Ps 71:12 430
O my **G**, hasten to my help! Ps 71:12 430
the mighty deeds of the Lord **G**; Ps 71:16 3068
O **G**, You have taught me from my Ps 71:17 430
even when *I am* old and gray, O **G**, Ps 71:18 430
For Your righteousness, O **G**, Ps 71:19 430
O **G**, who is like You? Ps 71:19 430
a harp, *Even* Your truth, O my **G**; Ps 71:22 430
Give the king Your judgments, O **G**, Ps 72:1 430
Blessed be the LORD **G**, Ps 72:18 430
be the LORD God, the **G** of Israel, Ps 72:18 430
Surely **G** is good to Israel, To Ps 73:1 430
They say, "How does **G** know? Ps 73:11 410
I came into the sanctuary of **G**; Ps 73:17 410
But **G** is the strength of my heart Ps 73:26 430
me, the nearness of **G** is my good; Ps 73:28 430
I have made the Lord **G** my refuge, Ps 73:28 3068
O **G**, why have You rejected *us* Ps 74:1 430
meeting places of **G** in the land. Ps 74:8 410
How long, O **G**, will the adversary Ps 74:10 430
Yet **G** is my king from of old, Who Ps 74:12 430
Arise, O **G**, *and* plead Your own Ps 74:22 430
We give thanks to You, O **G**, Ps 75:1 430
But **G** is the Judge; Ps 75:7 430
sing praises to the **G** of Jacob. Ps 75:9 430
G is known in Judah; Ps 76:1 430
At Your rebuke, O **G** of Jacob, Ps 76:6 430
When **G** arose to judgment, To save Ps 76:9 430
Make vows to the LORD your **G** Ps 76:11 430
My voice *rises* to **G**, Ps 77:1 430
My voice *rises* to **G**, Ps 77:1 430
When I remember **G**, then I am Ps 77:3 430
Has **G** forgotten to be gracious, Ps 77:9 410
Your way, O **G**, is holy; Ps 77:13 430
What **g** is great like our God? Ps 77:13 410
What god is great like our **G**? Ps 77:13 430
are the **G** who works wonders; Ps 77:14 410
The waters saw You, O **G**; Ps 77:16 430
should put their confidence in **G** And Ps 78:7 430
And not forget the works of **G**, Ps 78:7 410
spirit was not faithful to **G**. Ps 78:8 410
did not keep the covenant of **G** And Ps 78:10 430
in their heart they put **G** to the test Ps 78:18 410
Then they spoke against **G**; Ps 78:19 430
"Can **G** prepare a table in the Ps 78:19 410
Because they did not believe in **G** And Ps 78:22 430
The anger of **G** rose against them And Ps 78:31 430
and searched diligently for **G**; Ps 78:34 410
remembered that **G** was their rock, Ps 78:35 430
the Most High **G** their Redeemer. Ps 78:35 410
Again and again they tempted **G**, Ps 78:41 410
rebelled against the Most High **G** And Ps 78:56 430
When **G** heard, He was filled with Ps 78:59 430
O **G**, the nations have invaded Ps 79:1 430
Help us, O **G** of our salvation, for Ps 79:9 430
"Where is their **G**?" Ps 79:10 430
O **G**, restore us And cause Your Ps 80:3 430
O LORD **G** *of* hosts, How long will Ps 80:4 430
O **G** *of* hosts, restore us And Ps 80:7 430
the cedars of **G** with its boughs. Ps 80:10 410
O **G** *of* hosts, turn again now, we Ps 80:14 430
O LORD **G** of hosts, restore us; Ps 80:19 430
Sing for joy to **G** our strength; Ps 81:1 430
Shout joyfully to the **G** of Jacob. Ps 81:1 430
An ordinance of the **G** of Jacob. Ps 81:4 430
there be no strange **g** among you; Ps 81:9 410
shall you worship any foreign **g**. Ps 81:9 410
"I, the LORD, am your **G**, Ps 81:10 430
G takes His stand in His own Ps 82:1 430
Arise, O **G**, judge the earth! Ps 82:8 430
O **G**, do not remain quiet; Ps 83:1 430
Do not be silent and, O **G**, Ps 83:1 410
for ourselves The pastures of **G**." Ps 83:12 430
O my **G**, make them like the Ps 83:13 430
sing for joy to the living **G**. Ps 84:2 410
O LORD of hosts, My King and my **G**. Ps 84:3 430
of them appears before **G** in Zion. Ps 84:7 430
O LORD **G** of hosts, hear my prayer; Ps 84:8 430
Give ear, O **G** of Jacob! Ps 84:8 430
Behold our shield, O **G**, Ps 84:9 430
threshold of the house of my **G** Than Ps 84:10 430
the LORD **G** is a sun and shield; Ps 84:11 430
Restore us, O **G** of our salvation, Ps 85:4 430
hear what **G** the LORD will say; Ps 85:8 410
O You my **G**, save Your servant who Ps 86:2 430
You alone are **G**. Ps 86:10 430
give thanks to You, O Lord my **G**, Ps 86:12 430
O **G**, arrogant men have risen up Ps 86:14 430
are a **G** merciful and gracious, Ps 86:15 410
things are spoken of you, O city of **G**. Ps 87:3 430
O Lord, the **G** of my salvation, I Ps 88:1 430
A **G** greatly feared in the council Ps 89:7 410
O LORD **G** of hosts, who is like Ps 89:8 430
'You are my Father, My **G**, Ps 89:26 410
to everlasting, You are **G**. Ps 90:2 410
of the Lord our **G** be upon us; Ps 90:17 430
"My refuge and my fortress, My **G**, Ps 91:2 430
flourish in the courts of our **G**. Ps 92:13 430
O Lord, **G** of vengeance, Ps 94:1 410
G of vengeance, shine forth! Ps 94:1 410
does the **G** of Jacob pay heed." Ps 94:7 430
And my **G** the rock of my refuge. Ps 94:22 430
The LORD our **G** will destroy them. Ps 94:23 430
For the LORD is a great **G** And Ps 95:3 410
For He is our **G**, And we are the Ps 95:7 430
have seen the salvation of our **G**. Ps 98:3 430
Exalt the LORD our **G** And Ps 99:5 430
O LORD our **G**, You answered Ps 99:8 430
You were a forgiving **G** to them, Ps 99:8 410
Exalt the LORD our **G** And Ps 99:9 430
For holy is the LORD our **G**. Ps 99:9 430
Know that the LORD Himself is **G**; Ps 100:3 430
"O my **G**, do not take me away in Ps 102:24 410
O LORD my **G**, You are very great; Ps 104:1 430
prey And seek their food from **G**. Ps 104:21 410
to my **G** while I have my being. Ps 104:33 430
He is the LORD our **G**; Ps 105:7 430
And tempted **G** in the desert. Ps 106:14 410
They forgot **G** their Savior, Who Ps 106:21 410
Save us, O LORD our **G**, Ps 106:47 430
be the LORD, the **G** of Israel, Ps 106:48 430
rebelled against the words of **G** And Ps 107:11 410
My heart is steadfast, O **G**; Ps 108:1 430
Be exalted, O **G**, above the Ps 108:5 430
G has spoken in His holiness: Ps 108:7 430
Have not You Yourself, O **G**, Ps 108:11 430
not go forth with our armies, O **G**? Ps 108:11 430
Through **G** we will do valiantly Ps 108:13 430
O **G** of my praise, Do not be silent! Ps 109:1 430
But You, O **G**, the Lord, deal Ps 109:21 3068
Help me, O LORD my **G**; Ps 109:26 430
Who is like the LORD our **G**, Ps 113:5 430
the Lord, Before the **G** of Jacob, Ps 114:7 433
"Where, now, is their **G**?" Ps 115:2 430
But our **G** is in the heavens; Ps 115:3 430
Yes, our **G** is compassionate. Ps 116:5 430
The LORD is **G**, and He has given us Ps 118:27 410
You are my **G**, and I give thanks Ps 118:28 410
You are my **G**, I extol You. Ps 118:28 430
observe the commandments of my **G**. Ps 119:115 430
LORD our **G**, I will seek your good. Ps 122:9 430
so our eyes *look* to the LORD our **G**, Ps 123:2 430
the courts of the house of our **G**! Ps 135:2 430
Give thanks to the **G** of gods, Ps 136:2 430
Give thanks to the **G** of heaven, Ps 136:26 410
also are Your thoughts to me, O **G**! Ps 139:17 410
You would slay the wicked, O **G**; Ps 139:19 433
Search me, O **G**, and know my heart; Ps 139:23 410
I said to the LORD, "You are my **G**; Ps 140:6 410
"O **G** the Lord, the strength of my Ps 140:7 3068
For my eyes are toward You, O **G**, Ps 141:8 3068
to do Your will, For You are my **G**; Ps 143:10 430
will sing a new song to You, O **G**; Ps 144:9 430
the people whose **G** is the LORD! Ps 144:15 430
I will extol You, my **G**, Ps 145:1 430
I will sing praises to my **G** while I Ps 146:2 430
he whose help is the **G** of Jacob, Ps 146:5 410
Whose hope is in the LORD his **G**, Ps 146:5 430
LORD will reign forever, Your **G**, Ps 146:10 430
is good to sing praises to our **G**; Ps 147:1 430
Sing praises to our **G** on the lyre, Ps 147:7 430
Praise your **G**, O Zion! Ps 147:12 430
praises of **G** *be* in their mouth, Ps 149:6 410
Praise **G** in His sanctuary; Ps 150:1 410
And discover the knowledge of **G**. Pr 2:5 430
And forgets the covenant of her **G**; Pr 2:17 430
repute In the sight of **G** and man. Pr 3:4 430
glory of **G** to conceal a matter, Pr 25:2 430
Every word of **G** is tested; Pr 30:5 433
And profane the name of my **G**. Pr 30:9 430
It is a grievous task *which* **G** has Ec 1:13 430
that it is from the hand of **G**. Ec 2:24 430
I have seen the task which **G** has Ec 3:10 430
the work which **G** has done from the Ec 3:11 430
it is the gift of **G**. Ec 3:13 430
that everything **G** does will remain Ec 3:14 430
for **G** has *so* worked that men Ec 3:14 430
for **G** seeks what has passed by. Ec 3:15 430
"**G** will judge both the righteous Ec 3:17 430
"**G** has surely tested them in Ec 3:18 430
steps as you go to the house of **G** and Ec 5:1 430
up a matter in the presence of **G**. Ec 5:2 430
For **G** is in heaven and you are on Ec 5:2 430
When you make a vow to **G**, Ec 5:4 430
the presence of the messenger *of* **G** Ec 5:6
Why should **G** be angry on account Ec 5:6 430
there is emptiness. Rather, fear **G**. Ec 5:7 430
of his life which **G** has given him; Ec 5:18 430
G has given riches and wealth, Ec 5:19 430
this is the gift of **G**. Ec 5:19 430
because **G** keeps him occupied with Ec 5:20 430
a man to whom **G** has given riches Ec 6:2 430
yet **G** has not empowered him to eat Ec 6:2 430
Consider the work of **G**, Ec 7:13 430
G has made the one as well as the Ec 7:14 430
G comes forth with both of them. Ec 7:18 430
who is pleasing to **G** will escape Ec 7:26 430
this, that **G** made men upright, Ec 7:29 430
king because of the oath before **G**. Ec 8:2 430
will be well for those who fear **G**, Ec 8:12 430
because he does not fear **G**. Ec 8:13 430
days of his life which **G** has given Ec 8:15 430
and I saw every work of **G**, Ec 8:17 430
their deeds are in the hand of **G**. Ec 9:1 430
for **G** has already approved your Ec 9:7 430
of **G** who makes all things. Ec 11:5 430
G will bring you to judgment for Ec 11:9 430
will return to **G** who gave it. Ec 12:7 430
fear **G** and keep His commandments, Ec 12:13 430
For **G** will bring every act to Ec 12:14 430
Give ear to the instruction of our **G**, Is 1:10 430
Therefore the Lord **G** of hosts, Is 1:24 3068
To the house of the **G** of Jacob; Is 2:3 430
the Lord **G** of hosts is going to Is 3:1 3068
Declares the Lord **G** of hosts. Is 3:15 3068
And the holy **G** will show Himself Is 5:16 410
thus says the Lord **G**: Is 7:7 3068
for yourself from the LORD your **G**; Is 7:11 430
try the patience of my **G** as well? Is 7:13 430
not stand, For **G** is with us." Is 8:10 410
should not a people consult their **G**? Is 8:19 430
and their **G** as they face upward. Is 8:21 430
Wonderful Counselor, Mighty **G**, Is 9:6 410
the Lord, the **G** of hosts, Is 10:16 3068
remnant of Jacob, to the mighty **G**. Is 10:21 410
the Lord **G** of hosts will execute Is 10:23 3068
thus says the Lord **G** of hosts, Is 10:24 3068
Behold, the Lord, the **G** of hosts, Is 10:33 3068
"Behold, **G** is my salvation, I Is 12:2 410
LORD **G** is my strength and song, Is 12:2 3068
G overthrew Sodom and Gomorrah. Is 13:19 430
my throne above the stars of **G**, Is 14:13 410
the LORD, the **G** of Israel. Is 17:6 430
For you have forgotten the **G** of Is 17:10 430
them with vine slips of a strange **g**. Is 17:10
declares the Lord **G** of hosts. Is 19:4 3068
LORD of hosts, The **G** of Israel, Is 21:10 430
the LORD **G** of Israel has spoken." Is 21:17 430
G of hosts has a day of panic, Is 22:5 3068
in that day the Lord **G** of hosts called Is 22:12 3068
you die," says the Lord **G** of hosts. Is 22:14 3068
Thus says the Lord **G** of hosts, Is 22:15 3068
the **G** of Israel, In the coastlands Is 24:15 430
O Lord, You are my **G**; Is 25:1 430
And the Lord **G** will wipe tears Is 25:8 3068
this is our **G** for whom we have Is 25:9 430
For in **G** the LORD, *we have* an Is 26:4 3050
O LORD our **G**, other masters Is 26:13 430
Therefore thus says the Lord **G**, Is 28:16 3068
heard from the Lord **G** of hosts Of Is 28:22 3068
For his **G** instructs and teaches Is 28:26 430
stand in awe of the **G** of Israel. Is 29:23 430
For thus the Lord **G**, Is 30:15 3068
For the LORD is a **G** of justice; Is 30:18 430
the Egyptians are men and not **G**, Is 31:3 410
of the LORD, The majesty of our **G**. Is 35:2 430
your **G** will come *with* vengeance; Is 35:4 430
The recompense of **G** will come, Is 35:4 430
'We trust in the LORD our **G**,' Is 36:7 430
'Perhaps the LORD your **G** will hear Is 37:4 430
has sent to reproach the living **G**, Is 37:4 430
which the LORD your **G** has heard. Is 37:4 430
G in whom you trust deceive you, Is 37:10 430
"O LORD of hosts, the **G** of Israel, Is 37:16 430
the cherubim, You are the **G**, Is 37:16 430
them to reproach the living **G**. Is 37:17 430
"Now, O LORD our **G**, Is 37:20 430
that You alone, LORD, are **G**." Is 37:20 430
says the LORD, the **G** of Israel, Is 37:21 430
in the house of Nisroch his **g**, Is 37:38 430
LORD, the **G** of your father David, Is 38:5 430
O comfort My people," says your **G**. Is 40:1 430
in the desert a highway for our **G**. Is 40:3 430
the word of our **G** stands forever. Is 40:8 430
"Here is your **G**!" Is 40:9 430
the Lord **G** will come with might, Is 40:10 3068
To whom then will you liken **G**? Is 40:18 410
me escapes the notice of my **G**"? Is 40:27 430
The Everlasting **G**, the LORD, the Is 40:28 430
look about you, for I am your **G**. Is 41:10 430
"For I am the LORD your **G**, Is 41:13 430
As the **G** of Israel I will not Is 41:17 430
Thus says **G** the LORD, Who created Is 42:5 410
"For I am the LORD your **G**, Is 43:3 430
Before Me there was no **G** formed, Is 43:10 410
And there was no strange **g** among Is 43:12
declares the LORD, "And I am **G**. Is 43:12 410
And there is no **G** besides Me. Is 44:6 430
Is there any **G** besides Me, Or is Is 44:8 433

Who has fashioned a **g** or cast an Is 44:10 410
He also makes a **g** and worships it; Is 44:15 410
the rest of it he makes into a **g**, Is 44:17 410
"Deliver me, for you are my **g**." Is 44:17 410
is I, The LORD, the **G** of Israel, Is 45:3 430
Besides Me there is no **G**. Is 45:5 430
'Surely, **G** is with you, and there Is 45:14 410
is none else, No other **G**.' " Is 45:14 430
You are a **G** who hides Himself, Is 45:15 410
who hides Himself, O **G** of Israel, Is 45:15 430
He is the **G** who formed the earth and Is 45:18 430
And pray to a **g** who cannot save. Is 45:20 410
there is no other **G** besides Me, Is 45:21 430
Me, A righteous **G** and a Savior; Is 45:21 410
For I am **G**, and there is no other. Is 45:22 410
and he makes it *into* a **g**; Is 46:6 410
things long past, For I am **G**, Is 46:9 410
I am **G**, and there is no one like Is 46:9 430
LORD And invoke the **G** of Israel, Is 48:1 430
city And lean on the **G** of Israel; Is 48:2 430
And now the Lord **G** has sent Me, Is 48:16 3068
"I am the LORD your **G**, Is 48:17 430
LORD, And My reward with My **G**." Is 49:4 430
LORD, And My **G** is My strength), Is 49:5 430
Thus says the Lord **G**, Is 49:22 3068
The Lord **G** has given Me the tongue Is 50:4 3068
The Lord **G** has opened My ear; Is 50:5 3068
For the Lord **G** helps Me, Is 50:7 3068
Behold, the Lord **G** helps Me; Is 50:9 3068
of the LORD and rely on his **G**. Is 50:10 430
"For I am the LORD your **G**, Is 51:15 430
of the LORD, The rebuke of your **G**. Is 51:20 430
G Who contends for His people, Is 51:22 430
For thus says the Lord **G**, Is 52:4 3068
And says to Zion, "Your **G** reigns!" Is 52:7 430
may see The salvation of our **G**. Is 52:10 430
And the **G** of Israel *will be* your Is 52:12 430
Him stricken, Smitten of **G**, Is 53:4 430
is called the **G** of all the earth. Is 54:5 430
when she is rejected," Says your **G**. Is 54:6 430
you, Because of the LORD your **G**, Is 55:5 430
And to our **G**, For He will Is 55:7 430
Lord **G**, who gathers the dispersed Is 56:8 3068
"There is no peace," says my **G**, Is 57:21 430
forsaken the ordinance of their **G**. Is 58:2 430
They delight in the nearness of **G**. Is 58:2 430
separation between you and your **G**, Is 59:2 430
LORD, And turning away from our **G**, Is 59:13 430
For the name of the LORD your **G**, Is 60:9 430
light, And your **G** for your glory. Is 60:19 430
Spirit of the Lord **G** is upon me, Is 61:1 3068
And the day of vengeance of our **G**; Is 61:2 430
spoken of *as* ministers of our **G**. Is 61:6 430
LORD, My soul will exult in my **G**; Is 61:10 430
So the Lord **G** will cause Is 61:11 3068
diadem in the hand of your **G**. Is 62:3 430
So your **G** will rejoice over you. Is 62:5 430
has the eye seen a **G** besides You, Is 64:4 430
Therefore, thus says the Lord **G**, Is 65:13 3068
And the Lord **G** will slay you. Is 65:15 3068
be blessed by the **G** of truth; Is 65:16 430
will swear by the **G** of truth; Is 65:16 430
shut *the womb?*" says your **G**. Is 66:9 430
Alas, Lord **G**! Behold, I do not know Jer 1:6 3068
By your forsaking the LORD your **G** Jer 2:17 430
you to forsake the LORD your **G**, Jer 2:19 430
you," declares the Lord **G** of hosts. Jer 2:19 3068
is before Me," declares the Lord **G**. Jer 2:22 3068
G says, "If a husband divorces his Jer 3:1
transgressed against the LORD your **G** Jer 3:13 430
have forgotten the LORD their **G**. Jer 3:21 430
For You are the LORD our **G**. Jer 3:22 430
our **G** Is the salvation of Israel. Jer 3:23 430
sinned against the LORD our **G**, Jer 3:25 430
the voice of the LORD our **G**." Jer 3:25 430
Then I said, "Ah, Lord **G**! Surely Jer 4:10 3068
LORD *Or* the ordinance of their **G**. Jer 5:4 430
And the ordinance of their **G**." Jer 5:5 430
says the LORD, the **G** of hosts, Jer 5:14 430
G done all these things to us?' Jer 5:19 430
"Let us now fear the LORD our **G**, Jer 5:24 430
LORD of hosts, the **G** of Israel, Jer 7:3 430
Therefore thus says the Lord **G**, Jer 7:20 3068
LORD of hosts, the **G** of Israel, Jer 7:21 430
My voice, and I will be your **G**, Jer 7:23 430
obey the voice of the LORD their **G** Jer 7:28 430
Because the LORD our **G** has doomed Jer 8:14 430
LORD of hosts, the **G** of Israel, Jer 9:15 430
But the LORD is the true **G**; Jer 10:10 430
living **G** and the everlasting King. Jer 10:10 430
says the LORD, the **G** of Israel, Jer 11:3 430
My people, and I will be your **G**,' Jer 11:4 430
says the LORD, the **G** of Israel, Jer 13:12 430
Give glory to the LORD your **G**, Jer 13:16 430
Lord **G**!" I said, "Look, the prophets Jer 14:13 3068
Is it not You, O LORD our **G**? Jer 14:22 430
by Your name, O LORD **G** of hosts. Jer 15:16 430
LORD of hosts, the **G** of Israel: Jer 16:9 430
committed against the LORD our **G**?' Jer 16:10 430
LORD of hosts, the **G** of Israel, Jer 19:3 430
LORD of hosts, the **G** of Israel, Jer 19:15 430
'Thus says the LORD **G** of Israel, Jer 21:4 430
the covenant of the LORD their **G** and Jer 22:9 430
Therefore thus says the LORD **G** of Jer 23:2 430
"Am I a **G** who is near," Jer 23:23 430
"And not a **G** far off? Jer 23:23 430
the words of the living **G**, Jer 23:36 430
God, the LORD of hosts, our **G**. Jer 23:36 430
"Thus says the LORD **G** of Israel, Jer 24:5 430
My people, and I will be their **G**, Jer 24:7 430
thus the LORD, the **G** of Israel, Jer 25:15 430
LORD of hosts, the **G** of Israel, Jer 25:27 430
obey the voice of the LORD your **G**; Jer 26:13 430
in the name of the LORD our **G**." Jer 26:16 430
LORD of hosts, the **G** of Israel, Jer 27:4 430
LORD of hosts, the **G** of Israel, Jer 27:21 430
LORD of hosts, the **G** of Israel, Jer 28:2 430
LORD of hosts, the **G** of Israel, Jer 28:14 430
LORD of hosts, the **G** of Israel, Jer 29:4 430
LORD of hosts, the **G** of Israel, Jer 29:8 430
LORD of hosts, the **G** of Israel, Jer 29:21 430
LORD of hosts, the **G** of Israel, Jer 29:25 430
says the LORD, the **G** of Israel, Jer 30:2 430
they shall serve the LORD their **G** and Jer 30:9 430
people, And I will be your **G**.' " Jer 30:22 430
G of all the families of Israel, Jer 31:1 430
up *to* Zion, To the LORD our **G**.' " Jer 31:6 430
For You are the LORD my **G**. Jer 31:18 430
LORD of hosts, the **G** of Israel, Jer 31:23 430
and I will be their **G**, Jer 31:33 430
LORD of hosts, the **G** of Israel, Jer 32:14 430
LORD of hosts, the **G** of Israel, Jer 32:15 430
'Ah Lord **G**! Behold, You have made Jer 32:17 3068
after them, O great and mighty **G**. Jer 32:18 410
You have said to me, O Lord **G**, Jer 32:25 3068
I am the LORD, the **G** of all flesh; Jer 32:27 430
says the LORD **G** of Israel concerning Jer 32:36 430
My people, and I will be their **G**; Jer 32:38 430
"For thus says the LORD **G** of Jer 33:4 430
"Thus says the LORD **G** of Israel, Jer 34:2 430
"Thus says the LORD **G** of Israel, Jer 34:13 430
the son of Igdaliah, the man of **G**, Jer 35:4 430
LORD of hosts, the **G** of Israel, Jer 35:13 430
says the LORD, the **G** of hosts, Jer 35:17 430
the God of hosts, the **G** of Israel, Jer 35:17 430
LORD of hosts, the **G** of Israel, Jer 35:18 430
LORD of hosts, the **G** of Israel, Jer 35:19 430
to the LORD our **G** on our behalf." Jer 37:3 430
"Thus says the LORD **G** of Israel, Jer 37:7 430
"Thus says the LORD **G** of hosts, Jer 38:17 430
God of hosts, the **G** of Israel, Jer 38:17 430
LORD of hosts, the **G** of Israel, Jer 39:16 430
"The LORD your **G** promised this Jer 40:2 430
pray for us to the LORD your **G**, Jer 42:2 430
that the LORD your **G** may tell us Jer 42:3 430
going to pray to the LORD your **G** Jer 42:4 430
LORD your **G** will send you to us. Jer 42:5 430
our **G** to whom we are sending you, Jer 42:6 430
to the voice of the LORD our **G**." Jer 42:6 430
says the LORD the **G** of Israel, Jer 42:9 430
to the voice of the LORD your **G**, Jer 42:13 430
LORD of hosts, the **G** of Israel, Jer 42:15 430
LORD of hosts, the **G** of Israel, Jer 42:18 430
who sent me to the LORD your **G**, Jer 42:20 430
"Pray for us to the LORD our **G**; Jer 42:20 430
and whatever the LORD our **G** says, Jer 42:20 430
have not obeyed the LORD your **G**, Jer 42:21 430
whom the LORD their **G** had sent, Jer 43:1 430
all the words of the LORD their **G** Jer 43:1 430
our **G** has not sent you to say, Jer 43:2 430
LORD of hosts, the **G** of Israel, Jer 43:10 430
LORD of hosts, the **G** of Israel, Jer 44:2 430
thus says the LORD **G** of hosts, Jer 44:7 430
God of hosts, the **G** of Israel, Jer 44:7 430
LORD of hosts, the **G** of Israel, Jer 44:11 430
LORD of hosts, the **G** of Israel Jer 44:25 430
"As the Lord **G** lives." Jer 44:26 3068
the LORD the **G** of Israel to you, Jer 45:2 430
belongs to the Lord **G** of hosts, Jer 46:10 3068
slaughter for the Lord **G** of hosts, Jer 46:10 3068
LORD of hosts, the **G** of Israel, Jer 46:25 430
LORD of hosts, the **G** of Israel, Jer 48:1 430
you," Declares the Lord **G** of hosts, Jer 49:5 3068
the LORD their **G** they will seek. Jer 50:4 430
LORD of hosts, the **G** of Israel: Jer 50:18 430
For it is a work of the Lord **G** of Jer 50:25 3068
the vengeance of the LORD our **G**, Jer 50:28 430
one," Declares the Lord **G** of hosts, Jer 50:31 3068
"As when **G** overthrew Sodom And Jer 50:40 430
Judah has been forsaken By his **G**, Jer 51:5 430
Zion The work of the LORD our **G**! Jer 51:10 430
LORD of hosts, the **G** of Israel: Jer 51:33 430
For the LORD is a **G** of recompense, Jer 51:56 410
and hands Toward **G** in heaven; La 3:41 410
opened and I saw visions of **G**. Ezk 1:1 430
'Thus says the Lord **G**.' Ezk 2:4 3068
'Thus says the Lord **G**.' " Ezk 3:11 3068
'Thus says the Lord **G**.' Ezk 3:27 3068
But I said, "Ah, Lord **G**! Behold, Ezk 4:14 3068
'Thus says the Lord **G**, Ezk 5:5 3068
'Therefore, thus says the Lord **G**, Ezk 5:7 3068
therefore, thus says the Lord **G**, Ezk 5:8 3068
'So as I live,' declares the Lord **G**, Ezk 5:11 3068
listen to the word of the Lord **G**! Ezk 6:3 3068
says the Lord **G** to the mountains, Ezk 6:3 3068
'Thus says the Lord **G**, Ezk 6:11 3068
the Lord **G** to the land of Israel, Ezk 7:2 3068
'Thus says the Lord **G**, Ezk 7:5 3068
the hand of the Lord **G** fell on me Ezk 8:1 3068
in the visions of **G** to Jerusalem, Ezk 8:3 430
of the **G** of Israel *was* there, Ezk 8:4 430
Then the glory of the **G** of Israel Ezk 9:3 430
"Alas, Lord **G**! Are You destroying Ezk 9:8 3068
of **G** Almighty when He speaks. Ezk 10:5 410
the **G** of Israel hovered over them. Ezk 10:19 430
G of Israel by the river Chebar; Ezk 10:20 430
'Therefore, thus says the Lord **G**, Ezk 11:7 3068
upon you," the Lord **G** declares. Ezk 11:8 3068
a loud voice and said, "Alas, Lord **G**! Ezk 11:13 3068
'Thus says the Lord **G**, Ezk 11:16 3068
'Thus says the Lord **G**, Ezk 11:17 3068
My people, and I shall be their **G**. Ezk 11:20 430
their heads," declares the Lord **G**. Ezk 11:21 3068
the **G** of Israel hovered over them. Ezk 11:22 430
me in a vision by the Spirit of **G** Ezk 11:24 430
'Thus says the Lord **G**, Ezk 12:10 3068
'Thus says the Lord **G** concerning Ezk 12:19 3068
'Thus says the Lord **G**, Ezk 12:23 3068
it," declares the Lord **G**.' " Ezk 12:25 3068
'Thus says the Lord **G**, Ezk 12:28 3068
performed," ' " declares the Lord **G**. Ezk 12:28 3068
'Thus says the Lord **G**, Ezk 13:3 3068
Therefore, thus says the Lord **G**, Ezk 13:8 3068
against you," declares the Lord **G**. Ezk 13:8 3068
you may know that I am the Lord **G**. Ezk 13:9 3068
Therefore, thus says the Lord **G**, Ezk 13:13 3068
is no peace,' declares the Lord **G**. Ezk 13:16 3068
'Thus says the Lord **G**, Ezk 13:18 3068
Therefore, thus says the Lord **G**, Ezk 13:20 3068
'Thus says the Lord **G**, Ezk 14:4 3068
'Thus says the Lord **G**, Ezk 14:6 3068
and I shall be their **G**," Ezk 14:11 430
declares the Lord **G**." Ezk 14:11 3068
themselves," declares the Lord **G**. Ezk 14:14 3068
as I live," declares the Lord **G**, Ezk 14:16 3068
as I live," declares the Lord **G**, Ezk 14:18 3068
as I live," declares the Lord **G**, Ezk 14:20 3068
For thus says the Lord **G**, Ezk 14:21 3068
I did to it," declares the Lord **G**. Ezk 14:23 3068
"Therefore, thus says the Lord **G**, Ezk 15:6 3068
unfaithfully,' " declares the Lord **G**. Ezk 15:8 3068
'Thus says the Lord **G** to Jerusalem, Ezk 16:3 3068
became Mine," declares the Lord **G**. Ezk 16:8 3068
on you," declares the Lord **G**. Ezk 16:14 3068
it happened," declares the Lord **G**. Ezk 16:19 3068
woe to you!' declares the Lord **G**), Ezk 16:23 3068
your heart," declares the Lord **G**, Ezk 16:30 3068
Thus says the Lord **G**, Ezk 16:36 3068
own head," declares the Lord **G**, Ezk 16:43 3068
"As I live," declares the Lord **G**, Ezk 16:48 3068
For thus says the Lord **G**, Ezk 16:59 3068
have done," the Lord **G** declares. Ezk 16:63 3068
'Thus says the Lord **G**, Ezk 17:3 3068
'Thus says the Lord **G**, Ezk 17:9 3068
'As I live,' declares the Lord **G**, Ezk 17:16 3068
Therefore, thus says the Lord **G**, Ezk 17:19 3068
Thus says the Lord **G**, Ezk 17:22 3068
"As I live," declares the Lord **G**, Ezk 18:3 3068
surely live," declares the Lord **G**. Ezk 18:9 3068
the wicked," declares the Lord **G**, Ezk 18:23 3068
his conduct," declares the Lord **G**. Ezk 18:30 3068
who dies," declares the Lord **G**. Ezk 18:32 3068
'Thus says the Lord **G**, Ezk 20:3 3068
As I live," declares the Lord **G**, Ezk 20:3 3068
'Thus says the Lord **G**, Ezk 20:5 3068
saying, I am the LORD your **G**, Ezk 20:5 430
I am the LORD your **G**.' Ezk 20:7 430
'I am the LORD your **G**; Ezk 20:19 430
know that I am the LORD your **G**.' Ezk 20:20 430
'Thus says the Lord **G**, Ezk 20:27 3068
'Thus says the Lord **G**, Ezk 20:30 3068
As I live," declares the Lord **G**, Ezk 20:31 3068
"As I live," declares the Lord **G**, Ezk 20:33 3068
with you," declares the Lord **G**. Ezk 20:36 3068
of Israel," thus says the Lord **G**, Ezk 20:39 3068
of Israel," declares the Lord **G**, Ezk 20:40 3068
Israel," declares the Lord **G**.' " Ezk 20:44 3068
thus says the Lord **G**, Ezk 20:47 3068
"Ah Lord **G**! They are saying of me, Ezk 20:49 3068
happen,' declares the Lord **G**." Ezk 21:7 3068
declares the Lord **G**. Ezk 21:13 3068
"Therefore, thus says the Lord **G**, Ezk 21:24 3068
thus says the Lord **G**, Ezk 21:26 3068
'Thus says the Lord **G** concerning Ezk 21:28 3068
'Thus says the Lord **G**, Ezk 22:3 3068
forgotten Me," declares the Lord **G**. Ezk 22:12 3068
'Therefore, thus says the Lord **G**, Ezk 22:19 3068
'Thus says the Lord **G**,' Ezk 22:28 3068
their heads," declares the Lord **G**. Ezk 22:31 3068
O Oholibah, thus says the Lord **G**, Ezk 23:22 3068
"For thus says the Lord **G**, Ezk 23:28 3068
'Thus says the Lord **G**, Ezk 23:32 3068
have spoken,' declares the Lord **G**. Ezk 23:34 3068
"Therefore, thus says the Lord **G**, Ezk 23:35 3068
"For thus says the Lord **G**, Ezk 23:46 3068
know that I am the Lord **G**.' " Ezk 23:49 3068
'Thus says the Lord **G**, Ezk 24:3 3068
'Therefore, thus says the Lord **G**, Ezk 24:6 3068
'Therefore, thus says the Lord **G**, Ezk 24:9 3068
you," declares the Lord **G**.' " Ezk 24:14 3068
'Thus says the Lord **G**, Ezk 24:21 3068
will know that I am the Lord **G**. Ezk 24:24 3068
'Hear the word of the Lord **G**! Ezk 25:3 3068
Thus says the Lord **G**, Ezk 25:3 3068
'For thus says the Lord **G**, Ezk 25:6 3068
'Thus says the Lord **G**, Ezk 25:8 3068
'Thus says the Lord **G**, Ezk 25:12 3068
therefore thus says the Lord **G**, Ezk 25:13 3068
My vengeance," declares the Lord **G**. Ezk 25:14 3068
'Thus says the Lord **G**, Ezk 25:15 3068
therefore thus says the Lord **G**, Ezk 25:16 3068
therefore thus says the Lord **G**, Ezk 26:3 3068
have spoken,' declares the Lord **G**, Ezk 26:5 3068
For thus says the Lord **G**, Ezk 26:7 3068
have spoken," declares the Lord **G**. Ezk 26:14 3068
Thus says the Lord **G** to Tyre, Ezk 26:15 3068
For thus says the Lord **G**, Ezk 26:19 3068

found again," declares the Lord **G**.	**Ezk 26:21**	3068
'Thus says the Lord **G**,	**Ezk 27:3**	3068
'Thus says the Lord **G**,	**Ezk 28:2**	3068
'I am a **g**, I sit in the seat of	**Ezk 28:2**	410
Yet you are a man and not **G**,	**Ezk 28:2**	410
your heart like the heart of **G**	**Ezk 28:2**	430
Therefore thus says the Lord **G**,	**Ezk 28:6**	3068
your heart Like the heart of **G**,	**Ezk 28:6**	430
'Will you still say, "I am a **g**,"	**Ezk 28:9**	430
Though you are a man and not **G**,	**Ezk 28:9**	410
declares the Lord **G**!	**Ezk 28:10**	3068
'Thus says the Lord **G**,	**Ezk 28:12**	3068
"You were in Eden, the garden of **G**;	**Ezk 28:13**	430
were on the holy mountain of **G**;	**Ezk 28:14**	430
as profane From the mountain of **G**.	**Ezk 28:16**	430
'Thus says the Lord **G**,	**Ezk 28:22**	3068
will know that I am the Lord **G**."	**Ezk 28:24**	3068
'Thus says the Lord **G**,	**Ezk 28:25**	3068
that I am the LORD their **G**.	**Ezk 28:26**	430
'Thus says the Lord **G**,	**Ezk 29:3**	3068
'Therefore thus says the Lord **G**,	**Ezk 29:8**	3068
'For thus says the Lord **G**,	**Ezk 29:13**	3068
know that I am the Lord **G**.	**Ezk 29:16**	3068
Therefore thus says the Lord **G**,	**Ezk 29:19**	3068
acted for Me," declares the Lord **G**.	**Ezk 29:20**	3068
'Thus says the Lord **G**,	**Ezk 30:2**	3068
by the sword," Declares the Lord **G**.	**Ezk 30:6**	3068
'Thus says the Lord **G**,	**Ezk 30:10**	3068
'Thus says the Lord **G**,	**Ezk 30:13**	3068
"Therefore thus says the Lord **G**,	**Ezk 30:22**	3068
which were in the garden of **G**,	**Ezk 31:9**	430
'Therefore thus says the Lord **G**,	**Ezk 31:10**	3068
'Thus says the Lord **G**,	**Ezk 31:15**	3068
declares the Lord **G**."	**Ezk 31:18**	3068
Thus says the Lord **G**,	**Ezk 32:3**	3068
on your land," Declares the Lord **G**.	**Ezk 32:8**	3068
For thus says the Lord **G**,	**Ezk 32:11**	3068
run like oil," Declares the Lord **G**.	**Ezk 32:14**	3068
chant it," declares the Lord **G**.	**Ezk 32:16**	3068
all his army," declares the Lord **G**.	**Ezk 32:31**	3068
hordes," declares the Lord **G**.	**Ezk 32:32**	3068
declares the Lord **G**,	**Ezk 33:11**	3068
'Thus says the Lord **G**,	**Ezk 33:25**	3068
'Thus says the Lord **G**,	**Ezk 33:27**	3068
'Thus says the Lord **G**,	**Ezk 34:2**	3068
"As I live," declares the Lord **G**,	**Ezk 34:8**	3068
'Thus says the Lord **G**,	**Ezk 34:10**	3068
For thus says the Lord **G**,	**Ezk 34:11**	3068
them to rest," declares the Lord **G**.	**Ezk 34:15**	3068
My flock, thus says the Lord **G**,	**Ezk 34:17**	3068
thus says the Lord **G** to them,	**Ezk 34:20**	3068
"And I, the LORD, will be their **G**,	**Ezk 34:24**	430
know that I, the LORD their **G**,	**Ezk 34:30**	430
My people," declares the Lord **G**.	**Ezk 34:30**	3068
you are men, and I am your **G**,"	**Ezk 34:31**	430
am your God," declares the Lord **G**.	**Ezk 34:31**	3068
'Thus says the Lord **G**,	**Ezk 35:3**	3068
as I live," declares the Lord **G**,	**Ezk 35:6**	3068
as I live," declares the Lord **G**,	**Ezk 35:11**	3068
'Thus says the Lord **G**,	**Ezk 35:14**	3068
'Thus says the Lord **G**,	**Ezk 36:2**	3068
'Thus says the Lord **G**,	**Ezk 36:3**	3068
hear the word of the Lord **G**.	**Ezk 36:4**	3068
Thus says the Lord **G** to the	**Ezk 36:4**	3068
therefore thus says the Lord **G**,	**Ezk 36:5**	3068
'Thus says the Lord **G**,	**Ezk 36:6**	3068
'Therefore thus says the Lord **G**,	**Ezk 36:7**	3068
'Thus says the Lord **G**,	**Ezk 36:13**	3068
of children,' declares the Lord **G**.	**Ezk 36:14**	3068
longer," declares the Lord **G**.' "	**Ezk 36:15**	3068
'Thus says the Lord **G**,	**Ezk 36:22**	3068
am the LORD," declares the Lord **G**,	**Ezk 36:23**	3068
My people, and I will be your **G**.	**Ezk 36:28**	430
your sake," declares the Lord **G**,	**Ezk 36:32**	3068
'Thus says the Lord **G**,	**Ezk 36:33**	3068
'Thus says the Lord **G**,	**Ezk 36:37**	3068
"O Lord **G**, You know."	**Ezk 37:3**	3068
says the Lord **G** to these bones,	**Ezk 37:5**	3068
'Thus says the Lord **G**,	**Ezk 37:9**	3068
'Thus says the Lord **G**,	**Ezk 37:12**	3068
'Thus says the Lord **G**,	**Ezk 37:19**	3068
'Thus says the Lord **G**,	**Ezk 37:21**	3068
My people, and I will be their **G**.	**Ezk 37:23**	430
and I will be their **G**,	**Ezk 37:27**	430
'Thus says the Lord **G**,	**Ezk 38:3**	3068
'Thus says the Lord **G**,	**Ezk 38:10**	3068
'Thus says the Lord **G**,	**Ezk 38:14**	3068
'Thus says the Lord **G**,	**Ezk 38:17**	3068
of Israel," declares the Lord **G**,	**Ezk 38:18**	3068
My mountains," declares the Lord **G**.	**Ezk 38:21**	3068
'Thus says the Lord **G**,	**Ezk 39:1**	3068
have spoken," declares the Lord **G**.	**Ezk 39:5**	3068
be done," declares the Lord **G**.	**Ezk 39:8**	3068
them," declares the Lord **G**.	**Ezk 39:10**	3068
Myself," declares the Lord **G**.	**Ezk 39:13**	3068
son of man, thus says the Lord **G**,	**Ezk 39:17**	3068
men of war," declares the Lord **G**.	**Ezk 39:20**	3068
LORD their **G** from that day onward.	**Ezk 39:22**	430
Therefore thus says the Lord **G**,	**Ezk 39:25**	3068
will know that I am the LORD their **G**	**Ezk 39:28**	430
of Israel," declares the Lord **G**.	**Ezk 39:29**	3068
In the visions of **G** He brought me	**Ezk 40:2**	430
the glory of the **G** of Israel was	**Ezk 43:2**	430
"Son of man, thus says the Lord **G**,	**Ezk 43:18**	3068
to Me,' declares the Lord **G**,	**Ezk 43:19**	3068
accept you,' declares the Lord **G**."	**Ezk 43:27**	3068
G of Israel has entered by it;	**Ezk 44:2**	430
'Thus says the Lord **G**,	**Ezk 44:6**	3068
'Thus says the Lord **G**,	**Ezk 44:9**	3068

against them," declares the Lord **G**,	**Ezk 44:12**	3068
the blood," declares the Lord **G**.	**Ezk 44:15**	3068
sin offering," declares the Lord **G**.	**Ezk 44:27**	3068
'Thus says the Lord **G**,	**Ezk 45:9**	3068
My people," declares the Lord **G**.	**Ezk 45:9**	3068
for them," declares the Lord **G**.	**Ezk 45:15**	3068
'Thus says the Lord **G**,	**Ezk 45:18**	3068
'Thus says the Lord **G**,	**Ezk 46:1**	3068
'Thus says the Lord **G**,	**Ezk 46:16**	3068
Thus says the Lord **G**,	**Ezk 47:13**	3068
inheritance," declares the Lord **G**.	**Ezk 47:23**	3068
portions," declares the Lord **G**.	**Ezk 48:29**	3068
of the vessels of the house of **G**;	**Da 1:2**	430
of Shinar, to the house of his **g**,	**Da 1:2**	430
into the treasury of his **g**.	**Da 1:2**	430
Now **G** granted Daniel favor and	**Da 1:9**	430
G gave them knowledge and	**Da 1:17**	430
might request compassion from the **G**	**Da 2:18**	426
Daniel blessed the **G** of heaven;	**Da 2:19**	426
"Let the name of **G** be blessed	**Da 2:20**	426
"To You, O **G** of my fathers, I	**Da 2:23**	426
there is a **G** in heaven who reveals	**Da 2:28**	426
to whom the **G** of heaven has given	**Da 2:37**	426
the **G** of heaven will set up a kingdom	**Da 2:44**	426
the great **G** has made known to the	**Da 2:45**	426
"Surely your **G** is a God of gods	**Da 2:47**	426
"Surely your God is a **G** of gods	**Da 2:47**	426
and what **g** is there who can	**Da 3:15**	426
our **G** whom we serve is able to	**Da 3:17**	426
you servants of the Most High **G**,	**Da 3:26**	426
"Blessed be the **G** of Shadrach,	**Da 3:28**	426
any **g** except their own God.	**Da 3:28**	426
any god except their own **G**.	**Da 3:28**	426
against the **G** of Shadrach,	**Da 3:29**	426
inasmuch as there is no other **g**	**Da 3:29**	426
the Most High **G** has done for me.	**Da 4:2**	426
according to the name of my **g**,	**Da 4:8**	426
house of **G** which *was* in Jerusalem;	**Da 5:3**	426
Most High **G** granted sovereignty,	**Da 5:18**	426
the Most High **G** is ruler over	**Da 5:21**	426
But the **G** in whose hand are your	**Da 5:23**	426
G has numbered your kingdom	**Da 5:26**	426
with regard to the law of his **G**."	**Da 6:5**	426
to any **g** or man besides you,	**Da 6:7**	426
and giving thanks before his **G**,	**Da 6:10**	426
and supplication before his **G**.	**Da 6:11**	426
to any **g** or man besides you,	**Da 6:12**	426
"Your **G** whom you constantly serve	**Da 6:16**	426
"Daniel, servant of the living **G**,	**Da 6:20**	426
your **G**, whom you constantly serve,	**Da 6:20**	426
"My **G** sent His angel and shut the	**Da 6:22**	426
because he had trusted in his **G**.	**Da 6:23**	426
tremble before the **G** of Daniel;	**Da 6:26**	426
the living **G** and enduring forever,	**Da 6:26**	426
I gave my attention to the Lord **G**	**Da 9:3**	430
LORD my **G** and confessed and said,	**Da 9:4**	430
O Lord, the great and awesome **G**,	**Da 9:4**	410
"To the Lord our **G**	**Da 9:9**	430
the voice of the LORD our **G**,	**Da 9:10**	430
the law of Moses the servant of **G**,	**Da 9:11**	430
sought the favor of the LORD our **G**	**Da 9:13**	430
for the LORD our **G** is righteous	**Da 9:14**	430
"And now, O Lord our **G**,	**Da 9:15**	430
"So now, our **G**, listen to the	**Da 9:17**	430
"O my **G**, incline Your ear and	**Da 9:18**	430
For Your own sake, O my **G**,	**Da 9:19**	430
supplication before the LORD my **G**	**Da 9:20**	430
of the holy mountain of my **G**,	**Da 9:20**	430
humbling yourself before your **G**,	**Da 10:12**	430
but the people who know their **G**	**Da 11:32**	430
and magnify himself above every **g** and	**Da 11:36**	410
things against the **G** of gods;	**Da 11:36**	410
he show regard for any *other* **g**;	**Da 11:37**	433
he will honor a **g** of fortresses,	**Da 11:38**	433
a **g** whom his fathers did not know;	**Da 11:38**	433
with *the help of* a foreign **g**;	**Da 11:39**	433
deliver them by the LORD their **G**,	**Hos 1:7**	430
My people and I am not your **G**."	**Hos 1:9**	
are the sons of the living **G**."	**Hos 1:10**	410
'*You are* my **G**!'	**Hos 2:23**	430
LORD their **G** and David their king;	**Hos 3:5**	430
Or knowledge of **G** in the land.	**Hos 4:1**	430
have forgotten the law of your **G**,	**Hos 4:6**	430
harlot, *departing* from their **G**.	**Hos 4:12**	430
allow them To return to their **G**.	**Hos 5:4**	430
of **G** rather than burnt offerings.	**Hos 6:6**	430
returned to the LORD their **G**,	**Hos 7:10**	430
"My **G**, we of Israel know You!"	**Hos 8:2**	430
craftsman made it, so it is not **G**;	**Hos 8:6**	430
the harlot, forsaking your **G**.	**Hos 9:1**	430
Ephraim *was* a watchman with my **G**,	**Hos 9:8**	430
hostility in the house of his **G**.	**Hos 9:8**	430
My **G** will cast them away Because	**Hos 9:17**	430
For I am **G** and not man, the Holy	**Hos 11:9**	410
Judah is also unruly against **G**,	**Hos 11:12**	410
his maturity he contended with **G**.	**Hos 12:3**	430
Even the LORD, the **G** of hosts,	**Hos 12:5**	430
Therefore, return to your **G**,	**Hos 12:6**	430
And wait for your **G** continually.	**Hos 12:6**	430
your **G** since the land of Egypt;	**Hos 12:9**	430
your **G** Since the land of Egypt;	**Hos 13:4**	430
were not to know any **g** except Me,	**Hos 13:4**	430
she has rebelled against her **G**.	**Hos 13:16**	430
O Israel, to the LORD your **G**,	**Hos 14:1**	430
'Our **g**,' To the work of our hands;	**Hos 14:3**	430
in sackcloth O ministers of my **G**,	**Jl 1:13**	430
withheld from the house of your **G**.	**Jl 1:13**	430
To the house of the LORD your **G**,	**Jl 1:14**	430
and joy from the house of our **G**?	**Jl 1:16**	430

Now return to the LORD your **G**,	**Jl 2:13**	430
a drink offering For the LORD your **G**?	**Jl 2:14**	430
'Where is their **G**?' "	**Jl 2:17**	430
And be glad in the LORD your **G**;	**Jl 2:23**	430
the name of the LORD your **G**,	**Jl 2:26**	430
LORD your **G**, And there is no other;	**Jl 2:27**	430
know that I am the LORD your **G**,	**Jl 3:17**	430
will perish," Says the Lord **G**.	**Am 1:8**	3068
And in the house of their **G** they	**Am 2:8**	430
Surely the Lord **G** does nothing	**Am 3:7**	3068
The Lord **G** has spoken!	**Am 3:8**	3068
Therefore, thus says the Lord **G**,	**Am 3:11**	3068
of Jacob," Declares the Lord **G**,	**Am 3:13**	3068
the Lord GOD, the **G** of hosts.	**Am 3:13**	430
Lord **G** has sworn by His holiness,	**Am 4:2**	3068
of Israel," Declares the Lord **G**.	**Am 4:5**	3068
as **G** overthrew Sodom and Gomorrah,	**Am 4:11**	430
to you, Prepare to meet your **G**,	**Am 4:12**	430
The LORD **G** of hosts is His name.	**Am 4:13**	430
For thus says the Lord **G**,	**Am 5:3**	3068
the LORD **G** of hosts be with you,	**Am 5:14**	430
Perhaps the LORD **G** of hosts May be	**Am 5:15**	430
thus says the LORD **G** of hosts,	**Am 5:16**	430
whose name is the **G** of hosts.	**Am 5:27**	430
The Lord **G** has sworn by Himself,	**Am 6:8**	3068
the LORD **G** of hosts has declared:	**Am 6:8**	430
declares the LORD **G** of hosts,	**Am 6:14**	430
Thus the Lord **G** showed me, and	**Am 7:1**	3068
"Lord **G**, please pardon!	**Am 7:2**	3068
Thus the Lord **G** showed me, and	**Am 7:4**	3068
the Lord **G** was calling to contend	**Am 7:4**	3068
"Lord **G**, please stop!	**Am 7:5**	3068
too shall not be," said the Lord **G**.	**Am 7:6**	3068
Thus the Lord **G** showed me, and	**Am 8:1**	3068
in that day," declares the Lord **G**.	**Am 8:3**	3068
in that day," declares the Lord **G**,	**Am 8:9**	3068
are coming," declares the Lord **G**,	**Am 8:11**	306
'As your **g** lives, O Dan,' And,	**Am 8:14**	430
The Lord **G** of hosts, The One	**Am 9:5**	3068
eyes of the Lord **G** are on the sinful	**Am 9:8**	3068
given them," Says the LORD your **G**.	**Am 9:15**	430
Thus says the Lord **G** concerning	**Ob 1:1**	3068
and every man cried to his **g**,	**Jon 1:5**	430
Get up, call on your **g**.	**Jon 1:6**	430
Perhaps *your* **g** will be concerned	**Jon 1:6**	430
and I fear the LORD **G** of heaven	**Jon 1:9**	430
Jonah prayed to the LORD his **G**	**Jon 2:1**	430
my life from the pit, O LORD my **G**.	**Jon 2:6**	430
people of Nineveh believed in **G**;	**Jon 3:5**	430
and let men call on **G** earnestly	**Jon 3:8**	430
"Who knows, **G** may turn and	**Jon 3:9**	430
When **G** saw their deeds, that they	**Jon 3:10**	430
then **G** relented concerning the	**Jon 3:10**	430
a gracious and compassionate **G**,	**Jon 4:2**	410
So the LORD **G** appointed a plant	**Jon 4:6**	430
But **G** appointed a worm when dawn	**Jon 4:7**	430
G appointed a scorching east wind,	**Jon 4:8**	430
Then **G** said to Jonah,	**Jon 4:9**	430
Lord **G** be a witness against you,	**Mi 1:2**	3068
Because there is no answer from **G**.	**Mi 3:7**	430
to the house of the **G** of Jacob,	**Mi 4:2**	430
walk Each in the name of his **g**,	**Mi 4:5**	430
the LORD our **G** forever and ever.	**Mi 4:5**	430
of the name of the LORD His **G**.	**Mi 5:4**	430
bow myself before the **G** on high?	**Mi 6:6**	430
And to walk humbly with your **G**?	**Mi 6:8**	430
wait for the **G** of my salvation.	**Mi 7:7**	430
My **G** will hear me.	**Mi 7:7**	430
"Where is the LORD your **G**?"	**Mi 7:10**	430
To the LORD our **G** they will come	**Mi 7:17**	430
Who is a **G** like You, who pardons	**Mi 7:18**	410
and avenging **G** is the LORD;	**Na 1:2**	410
They whose strength is their **g**."	**Hab 1:11**	433
from everlasting, O LORD, my **G**,	**Hab 1:12**	430
G comes from Teman, And the Holy	**Hab 3:3**	433
rejoice in the **G** of my salvation.	**Hab 3:18**	430
The Lord **G** is my strength, And He	**Hab 3:19**	3068
Be silent before the Lord **G**!	**Zph 1:7**	3068
For the LORD their **G** will care for	**Zph 2:7**	430
LORD of hosts, The **G** of Israel,	**Zph 2:9**	430
She did not draw near to her **G**.	**Zph 3:2**	430
"The LORD your **G** is in your	**Zph 3:17**	430
obeyed the voice of the LORD their **G**	**Hg 1:12**	430
as the LORD their **G** had sent him.	**Hg 1:12**	430
of the LORD of hosts, their **G**,	**Hg 1:14**	430
completely obey the LORD your **G**.	**Zch 6:15**	430
G in truth and righteousness.'	**Zch 8:8**	430
we have heard that **G** is with you.	**Zch 8:23**	430
also will be a remnant for our **G**,	**Zch 9:7**	430
the Lord **G** will blow the trumpet,	**Zch 9:14**	3068
And the LORD their **G** will save	**Zch 9:16**	430
them, For I am the LORD their **G** and	**Zch 10:6**	430
Thus says the LORD my **G**,	**Zch 11:4**	430
the LORD of hosts, their **G**.'	**Zch 12:5**	430
the house of David *will be* like **G**,	**Zch 12:8**	430
'The LORD is my **G**.' "	**Zch 13:9**	430
Then the LORD, my **G**,	**Zch 14:5**	430
Has not one **G** created us?	**Mal 2:10**	410
the daughter of a foreign **g**.	**Mal 2:11**	410
says the LORD, the **G** of Israel,	**Mal 2:16**	430
"Where is the **G** of justice?"	**Mal 2:17**	430
"Will a man rob **G**?	**Mal 3:8**	430
'It is vain to serve **G**;	**Mal 3:14**	430
they also test **G** and escape.' "	**Mal 3:15**	430
between one who serves **G** and one	**Mal 3:18**	430
translated means, "**G** WITH US."	**Mt 1:23**	*2316*
And having been warned *by* **G** in a	**Mt 2:12**	
Then after being warned *by* **G** in a	**Mt 2:22**	
that from these stones **G** is able	**Mt 3:9**	*2316*

Spirit of **G** descending as a dove	**Mt 3:16**	*2316*
"If You are the Son of **G**,	**Mt 4:3**	*2316*
OUT OF THE MOUTH OF **G**.' "	**Mt 4:4**	*2316*
the Son of **G**, throw Yourself down;	**Mt 4:6**	*2316*
THE LORD YOUR **G** TO THE TEST.' "	**Mt 4:7**	*2316*
SHALL WORSHIP THE LORD YOUR **G**,	**Mt 4:10**	*2316*
in heart, for they shall see **G**.	**Mt 5:8**	*2316*
they shall be called sons of **G**.	**Mt 5:9**	*2316*
heaven, for it is the throne of **G**,	**Mt 5:34**	*2316*
You cannot serve **G** and wealth.	**Mt 6:24**	*2316*
"But if **G** so clothes the grass of	**Mt 6:30**	*2316*
we have with each other, Son of **G**?	**Mt 8:29**	*2316*
awestruck, and glorified **G**,	**Mt 9:8**	*2316*
how he entered the house of **G**,	**Mt 12:4**	*2316*
out demons by the Spirit of **G**,	**Mt 12:28**	*2316*
kingdom of **G** has come upon you.	**Mt 12:28**	*2316*
transgress the commandment of **G** for	**Mt 15:3**	*2316*
"For **G** said, 'HONOR YOUR FATHER	**Mt 15:4**	*2316*
has been given *to* **G**,"	**Mt 15:5**	
by this you invalidated the word of **G**	**Mt 15:6**	*2316*
they glorified the **G** of Israel.	**Mt 15:31**	*2316*
Christ, the Son of the living **G**."	**Mt 16:16**	*2316*
"**G** forbid *it*, Lord!	**Mt 16:22**	*2436*
What therefore **G** has joined	**Mt 19:6**	
man to enter the kingdom of **G**."	**Mt 19:24**	*2316*
with **G** all things are possible."	**Mt 19:26**	*2316*
into the kingdom of **G** before you.	**Mt 21:31**	*2316*
kingdom of **G** will be taken away	**Mt 21:43**	*2316*
and teach the way of **G** in truth,	**Mt 22:16**	*2316*
to **G** the things that are God's."	**Mt 22:21**	*2316*
the Scriptures nor the power of **G**.	**Mt 22:29**	*2316*
what was spoken to you by **G**:	**Mt 22:31**	*2316*
'I AM THE **G** OF ABRAHAM, AND THE	**Mt 22:32**	*2316*
OF ABRAHAM, AND THE **G** OF ISAAC,	**Mt 22:32**	*2316*
GOD OF ISAAC, AND THE **G** OF JACOB	**Mt 22:32**	*2316*
He is not the **G** of the dead but of	**Mt 22:32**	*2316*
LORD YOUR **G** WITH ALL YOUR HEART,	**Mt 22:37**	*2316*
of **G** and by Him who sits upon it.	**Mt 23:22**	*2316*
'I am able to destroy the temple of **G**	**Mt 26:61**	*2316*
"I adjure You by the living **G**,	**Mt 26:63**	*2316*
are the Christ, the Son of **G**."	**Mt 26:63**	*2316*
If You are the Son of **G**,	**Mt 27:40**	*2316*
"HE TRUSTS IN **G**; LET GOD RESCUE	**Mt 27:43**	*2316*
"HE TRUSTS IN GOD; LET **G** RESCUE	**Mt 27:43**	*2316*
for He said, 'I am the Son of **G**.' "	**Mt 27:43**	*2316*
"MY **G**, MY GOD, WHY HAVE YOU	**Mt 27:46**	*2316*
"MY GOD, MY **G**, WHY HAVE YOU	**Mt 27:46**	*2316*
"Truly this was the Son of **G**!"	**Mt 27:54**	*2316*
of Jesus Christ, the Son of **G**.	**Mk 1:1**	*2316*
preaching the gospel of **G**,	**Mk 1:14**	*2316*
and the kingdom of **G** is at hand;	**Mk 1:15**	*2316*
the Holy One of **G**!"	**Mk 1:24**	*2316*
can forgive sins but **G** alone?"	**Mk 2:7**	*2316*
all amazed and were glorifying **G**,	**Mk 2:12**	*2316*
how he entered the house of **G** in	**Mk 2:26**	*2316*
"You are the Son of **G**!"	**Mk 3:11**	*2316*
"For whoever does the will of **G**,	**Mk 3:35**	*2316*
the mystery of the kingdom of **G**,	**Mk 4:11**	*2316*
"The kingdom of **G** is like a man	**Mk 4:26**	*2316*
shall we picture the kingdom of **G**,	**Mk 4:30**	*2316*
Jesus, Son of the Most High **G**?	**Mk 5:7**	*2316*
I implore You by **G**,	**Mk 5:7**	
"Neglecting the commandment of **G**,	**Mk 7:8**	*2316*
setting aside the commandment of **G**	**Mk 7:9**	*2316*
is to say, given *to* **G**),"	**Mk 7:11**	
thus invalidating the word of **G** by	**Mk 7:13**	*2316*
until they see the kingdom of **G**	**Mk 9:1**	*2316*
enter the kingdom of **G** with one eye,	**Mk 9:47**	*2316*
G MADE THEM MALE AND FEMALE.	**Mk 10:6**	
therefore **G** has joined together,	**Mk 10:9**	*2316*
the kingdom of **G** belongs to such	**Mk 10:14**	*2316*
does not receive the kingdom of **G** like	**Mk 10:15**	*2316*
No one is good except **G** alone.	**Mk 10:18**	*2316*
to enter the kingdom of **G**!"	**Mk 10:23**	*2316*
it is to enter the kingdom of **G**!	**Mk 10:24**	*2316*
man to enter the kingdom of **G**."	**Mk 10:25**	*2316*
it is impossible, but not with **G**;	**Mk 10:27**	*2316*
all things are possible with **G**."	**Mk 10:27**	*2316*
saying to them, "Have faith in **G**.	**Mk 11:22**	*2316*
but teach the way of **G** in truth.	**Mk 12:14**	*2316*
to **G** the things that are God's."	**Mk 12:17**	*2316*
the Scriptures or the power of **G**?	**Mk 12:24**	*2316*
burning bush, how **G** spoke to him,	**Mk 12:26**	*2316*
'I AM THE **G** OF ABRAHAM, AND THE	**Mk 12:26**	*2316*
OF ABRAHAM, AND THE **G** OF ISAAC,	**Mk 12:26**	*2316*
GOD OF ISAAC, and the **G** of Jacob'?	**Mk 12:26**	*2316*
"He is not the **G** of the dead, but	**Mk 12:27**	*2316*
THE LORD OUR **G** IS ONE LORD;	**Mk 12:29**	*2316*
LORD YOUR **G** WITH ALL YOUR HEART,	**Mk 12:30**	*2316*
not far from the kingdom of **G**."	**Mk 12:34**	*2316*
of the creation which **G** created until	**Mk 13:19**	*2316*
I drink it new in the kingdom of **G**."	**Mk 14:25**	*2316*
"MY **G**, MY GOD, WHY HAVE YOU	**Mk 15:34**	*2316*
"MY GOD, MY **G**, WHY HAVE YOU	**Mk 15:34**	*2316*
"Truly this man was the Son of **G**!"	**Mk 15:39**	*2316*
was waiting for the kingdom of **G**;	**Mk 15:43**	*2316*
sat down at the right hand of **G**.	**Mk 16:19**	*2316*
both righteous in the sight of **G**,	**Lk 1:6**	*2316*
his priestly service before **G** in the	**Lk 1:8**	*2316*
of Israel back to the Lord their **G**.	**Lk 1:16**	*2316*
who stands in the presence of **G**,	**Lk 1:19**	*2316*
sent from **G** to a city in Galilee called	**Lk 1:26**	*2316*
for you have found favor with **G**.	**Lk 1:30**	*2316*
and the Lord **G** will give Him the	**Lk 1:32**	*2316*
shall be called the Son of **G**.	**Lk 1:35**	*2316*
will be impossible with **G**."	**Lk 1:37**	*2316*
has rejoiced in **G** my Savior.	**Lk 1:47**	*2316*
he *began* to speak in praise of **G**.	**Lk 1:64**	*2316*
"Blessed *be* the Lord **G** of Israel,	**Lk 1:68**	*2316*

of the tender mercy of our **G**,	**Lk 1:78**	*2316*
of the heavenly host praising **G** and	**Lk 2:13**	*2316*
"Glory to **G** in the highest, And	**Lk 2:14**	*2316*
glorifying and praising **G** for all	**Lk 2:20**	*2316*
Him into his arms, and blessed **G**,	**Lk 2:28**	*2316*
up and *began* giving thanks to **G**,	**Lk 2:38**	*2316*
and the grace of **G** was upon Him.	**Lk 2:40**	*2316*
and in favor with **G** and men.	**Lk 2:52**	*2316*
the word of **G** came to John,	**Lk 3:2**	*2316*
WILL SEE THE SALVATION OF **G**.' "	**Lk 3:6**	*2316*
from these stones **G** is able	**Lk 3:8**	*2316*
the son of Adam, the son of **G**.	**Lk 3:38**	*2316*
"If You are the Son of **G**,	**Lk 4:3**	*2316*
SHALL WORSHIP THE LORD YOUR **G**	**Lk 4:8**	*2316*
"If You are the Son of **G**,	**Lk 4:9**	*2316*
THE LORD YOUR **G** TO THE TEST.' "	**Lk 4:12**	*2316*
who You are—the Holy One of **G**!"	**Lk 4:34**	*2316*
"You are the Son of **G**!"	**Lk 4:41**	*2316*
"I must preach the kingdom of **G**	**Lk 4:43**	*2316*
and listening to the word of **G**,	**Lk 5:1**	*2316*
can forgive sins, but **G** alone?"	**Lk 5:21**	*2316*
on, and went home glorifying **G**.	**Lk 5:25**	*2316*
and *began* glorifying **G**;	**Lk 5:26**	*2316*
how he entered the house of **G**,	**Lk 6:4**	*2316*
the whole night in prayer to **G**.	**Lk 6:12**	*2316*
for yours is the kingdom of **G**.	**Lk 6:20**	*2316*
all, and they *began* glorifying **G**,	**Lk 7:16**	*2316*
"**G** has visited His people!"	**Lk 7:16**	*2316*
kingdom of **G** is greater than he."	**Lk 7:28**	*2316*
and preaching the kingdom of **G**.	**Lk 8:1**	*2316*
the mysteries of the kingdom of **G**,	**Lk 8:10**	*2316*
the seed is the word of **G**.	**Lk 8:11**	*2316*
hear the word of **G** and do it."	**Lk 8:21**	*2316*
Jesus, Son of the Most High **G**?	**Lk 8:28**	*2316*
great things **G** has done for you."	**Lk 8:39**	*2316*
out to proclaim the kingdom of **G** and	**Lk 9:2**	*2316*
about the kingdom of **G** and curing	**Lk 9:11**	*2316*
"The Christ of **G**."	**Lk 9:20**	*2316*
until they see the kingdom of **G**."	**Lk 9:27**	*2316*
all amazed at the greatness of **G**.	**Lk 9:43**	*2316*
everywhere the kingdom of **G**."	**Lk 9:60**	*2316*
is fit for the kingdom of **G**."	**Lk 9:62**	*2316*
kingdom of **G** has come near to you.'	**Lk 10:9**	*2316*
the kingdom of **G** has come near.'	**Lk 10:11**	*2316*
LOVE THE LORD YOUR **G** WITH ALL	**Lk 10:27**	*2316*
out demons by the finger of **G**,	**Lk 11:20**	*2316*
kingdom of **G** has come upon you.	**Lk 11:20**	*2316*
hear the word of **G** and observe it."	**Lk 11:28**	*2316*
justice and the love of **G**;	**Lk 11:42**	*2316*
reason also the wisdom of **G** said,	**Lk 11:49**	*2316*
the altar and the house *of* **G**;	**Lk 11:51**	
one of them is forgotten before **G**.	**Lk 12:6**	*2316*
him also before the angels of **G**;	**Lk 12:8**	*2316*
be denied before the angels of **G**.	**Lk 12:9**	*2316*
"But **G** said to him,	**Lk 12:20**	*2316*
and is not rich toward **G**."	**Lk 12:21**	*2316*
and *yet* **G** feeds them;	**Lk 12:24**	*2316*
"But if **G** so clothes the grass in	**Lk 12:28**	*2316*
again and *began* glorifying **G**.	**Lk 13:13**	*2316*
"What is the kingdom of **G** like,	**Lk 13:18**	*2316*
shall I compare the kingdom of **G**?	**Lk 13:20**	*2316*
the prophets in the kingdom of **G**,	**Lk 13:28**	*2316*
at the table in the kingdom of **G**.	**Lk 13:29**	*2316*
eat bread in the kingdom of **G**!"	**Lk 14:15**	*2316*
in the presence of the angels of **G**	**Lk 15:10**	*2316*
You cannot serve **G** and wealth."	**Lk 16:13**	*2316*
of men, but **G** knows your hearts;	**Lk 16:15**	*2316*
is detestable in the sight of **G**.	**Lk 16:15**	*2316*
of the kingdom of **G** has been preached,	**Lk 16:16**	*2316*
glorifying **G** with a loud voice,	**Lk 17:15**	*2316*
returned to give glory to **G**,	**Lk 17:18**	*2316*
when the kingdom of **G** was coming,	**Lk 17:20**	*2316*
"The kingdom of **G** is not coming	**Lk 17:20**	*2316*
kingdom of **G** is in your midst."	**Lk 17:21**	*2316*
was a judge who did not fear **G**	**Lk 18:2**	*2316*
I do not fear **G** nor respect man,	**Lk 18:4**	*2316*
will not **G** bring about justice for	**Lk 18:7**	*2316*
'**G**, I thank You that I am not	**Lk 18:11**	*2316*
'**G**, be merciful to me, the sinner!'	**Lk 18:13**	*2316*
of **G** belongs to such as these.	**Lk 18:16**	*2316*
does not receive the kingdom of **G** like	**Lk 18:17**	*2316*
No one is good except **G** alone.	**Lk 18:19**	*2316*
wealthy to enter the kingdom of **G**!	**Lk 18:24**	*2316*
man to enter the kingdom of **G**."	**Lk 18:25**	*2316*
with people are possible with **G**."	**Lk 18:27**	*2316*
for the sake of the kingdom of **G**,	**Lk 18:29**	*2316*
began following Him, glorifying **G**;	**Lk 18:43**	*2316*
saw it, they gave praise to **G**.	**Lk 18:43**	*2316*
supposed that the kingdom of **G** was	**Lk 19:11**	*2316*
disciples began to praise **G** joyfully	**Lk 19:37**	*2316*
but teach the way of **G** in truth.	**Lk 20:21**	*2316*
to **G** the things that are God's."	**Lk 20:25**	*2316*
like angels, and are sons of **G**,	**Lk 20:36**	*2316*
calls the Lord THE **G** OF ABRAHAM,	**Lk 20:37**	*2316*
OF ABRAHAM, AND THE **G** OF ISAAC,	**Lk 20:37**	*2316*
GOD OF ISAAC, AND THE **G** OF JACOB.	**Lk 20:37**	*2316*
"Now He is not the **G** of the dead but	**Lk 20:38**	*2316*
that the kingdom of **G** is near.	**Lk 21:31**	*2316*
fulfilled in the kingdom of **G**."	**Lk 22:16**	*2316*
on until the kingdom of **G** comes."	**Lk 22:18**	*2316*
RIGHT HAND of the power OF **G**."	**Lk 22:69**	*2316*
"Are You the Son of **G**,	**Lk 22:70**	*2316*
if this is the Christ of **G**,	**Lk 23:35**	*2316*
"Do you not even fear **G**,	**Lk 23:40**	*2316*
had happened, he *began* praising **G**,	**Lk 23:47**	*2316*
was waiting for the kingdom of **G**;	**Lk 23:51**	*2316*
the sight of **G** and all the people,	**Lk 24:19**	*2316*
in the temple praising **G**.	**Lk 24:53**	*2316*
the Word, and the Word was with **G**,	**Jn 1:1**	*2316*

was with God, and the Word was **G**.	**Jn 1:1**	*2316*
He was in the beginning with **G**.	**Jn 1:2**	*2316*
There came a man sent from **G**,	**Jn 1:6**	*2316*
the right to become children of **G**,	**Jn 1:12**	*2316*
nor of the will of man, but of **G**.	**Jn 1:13**	*2316*
No one has seen **G** at any time;	**Jn 1:18**	*2316*
the only begotten **G** who	**Jn 1:18**	*2316*
the Lamb of **G** who takes away the	**Jn 1:29**	*2316*
that this is the Son of **G**."	**Jn 1:34**	*2316*
"Behold, the Lamb of **G**!"	**Jn 1:36**	*2316*
"Rabbi, You are the Son of **G**;	**Jn 1:49**	*2316*
and the angels of **G** ascending and	**Jn 1:51**	*2316*
You have come from **G** *as* a teacher;	**Jn 3:2**	*2316*
You do unless **G** is with him."	**Jn 3:2**	*2316*
he cannot see the kingdom of **G**."	**Jn 3:3**	*2316*
enter into the kingdom of **G**.	**Jn 3:5**	*2316*
"For **G** so loved the world, that	**Jn 3:16**	*2316*
"For **G** did not send the Son into	**Jn 3:17**	*2316*
of the only begotten Son of **G**.	**Jn 3:18**	*2316*
as having been wrought in **G**."	**Jn 3:21**	*2316*
his seal to *this,* that **G** is true.	**Jn 3:33**	*2316*
"For He whom **G** has sent speaks	**Jn 3:34**	*2316*
has sent speaks the words of **G**;	**Jn 3:34**	*2316*
the wrath of **G** abides on him."	**Jn 3:36**	*2316*
"If you knew the gift of **G**,	**Jn 4:10**	*2316*
"**G** is spirit, and those who	**Jn 4:24**	*2316*
also was calling **G** His own Father,	**Jn 5:18**	*2316*
making Himself equal with **G**.	**Jn 5:18**	*2316*
hear the voice of the Son of **G**,	**Jn 5:25**	*2316*
have the love of **G** in yourselves.	**Jn 5:42**	*2316*
that is from the *one and* only **G**?	**Jn 5:44**	*2316*
for on Him the Father, **G**,	**Jn 6:27**	*2316*
that we may work the works of **G**?"	**Jn 6:28**	*2316*
"This is the work of **G**,	**Jn 6:29**	*2316*
"For the bread of **G** is that which	**Jn 6:33**	*2316*
THEY SHALL ALL BE TAUGHT OF **G**.'	**Jn 6:45**	*2316*
except the One who is from **G**;	**Jn 6:46**	*2316*
that You are the Holy One of **G**."	**Jn 6:69**	*2316*
the teaching, whether it is of **G** or	**Jn 7:17**	*2316*
the truth, which I heard from **G**;	**Jn 8:40**	*2316*
we have one Father: **G**."	**Jn 8:41**	*2316*
"If **G** were your Father, you would	**Jn 8:42**	*2316*
forth and have come from **G**,	**Jn 8:42**	*2316*
is of **G** hears the words of God;	**Jn 8:47**	*2316*
is of God hears the words of **G**;	**Jn 8:47**	*2316*
them, because you are not of **G**."	**Jn 8:47**	*2316*
of whom you say, 'He is our **G**';	**Jn 8:54**	*2316*
works of **G** might be displayed	**Jn 9:3**	*2316*
"This man is not from **G**,	**Jn 9:16**	*2316*
and said to him, "Give glory to **G**;	**Jn 9:24**	*2316*
know that **G** has spoken to Moses,	**Jn 9:29**	*2316*
know that **G** does not hear sinners;	**Jn 9:31**	*2316*
"If this man were not from **G**,	**Jn 9:33**	*2316*
man, make Yourself out *to be* **G**."	**Jn 10:33**	*2316*
gods, to whom the word of **G** came	**Jn 10:35**	*2316*
'I am the Son of **G**'?	**Jn 10:36**	*2316*
death, but for the glory of **G**,	**Jn 11:4**	*2316*
Son of **G** may be glorified by it."	**Jn 11:4**	*2316*
I know that whatever You ask of **G**,	**Jn 11:22**	*2316*
You ask of God, **G** will give You."	**Jn 11:22**	*2316*
You are the Christ, the Son of **G**,	**Jn 11:27**	*2316*
you will see the glory of **G**?"	**Jn 11:40**	*2316*
together into one the children of **G**	**Jn 11:52**	*2316*
men rather than the approval of **G**.	**Jn 12:43**	*2316*
and that He had come forth from **G** and	**Jn 13:3**	*2316*
from God and was going back to **G**,	**Jn 13:3**	*2316*
and **G** is glorified in Him;	**Jn 13:31**	*2316*
if **G** is glorified in Him, God will	**Jn 13:32**	*2316*
G will also glorify Him in	**Jn 13:32**	*2316*
believe in **G**, believe also in Me.	**Jn 14:1**	*2316*
that he is offering service to **G**.	**Jn 16:2**	*2316*
we believe that You came from **G**."	**Jn 16:30**	*2316*
may know You, the only true **G**,	**Jn 17:3**	*2316*
Himself out *to be* the Son of **G**."	**Jn 19:7**	*2316*
Father, and My **G** and your God.' "	**Jn 20:17**	*2316*
Father, and My God and your **G**.' "	**Jn 20:17**	*2316*
"My Lord and my **G**!"	**Jn 20:28**	*2316*
Jesus is the Christ, the Son of **G**;	**Jn 20:31**	*2316*
kind of death he would glorify **G**.	**Jn 21:19**	*2316*
concerning the kingdom of **G**.	**Ac 1:3**	*2316*
of the mighty deeds of **G**."	**Ac 2:11**	*2316*
SHALL BE IN THE LAST DAYS,' **G** says,	**Ac 2:17**	*2316*
a man attested to you by **G** with	**Ac 2:22**	*2316*
signs which **G** performed through Him	**Ac 2:22**	*2316*
plan and foreknowledge of **G**,	**Ac 2:23**	*2316*
"But **G** raised Him up again,	**Ac 2:24**	*2316*
and knew that **G** HAD SWORN TO HIM	**Ac 2:30**	*2316*
"This Jesus **G** raised up again, to	**Ac 2:32**	*2316*
exalted to the right hand of **G**,	**Ac 2:33**	*2316*
G has made Him both Lord and	**Ac 2:36**	*2316*
our **G** will call to Himself."	**Ac 2:39**	*2316*
praising **G** and having favor with	**Ac 2:47**	*2316*
and leaping and praising **G**.	**Ac 3:8**	*2316*
saw him walking and praising **G**;	**Ac 3:9**	*2316*
"The **G** of Abraham, Isaac and	**Ac 3:13**	*2316*
and Jacob, the **G** of our fathers,	**Ac 3:13**	*2316*
one whom **G** raised from the dead,	**Ac 3:15**	*2316*
"But the things which **G** announced	**Ac 3:18**	*2316*
all things about which **G** spoke by the	**Ac 3:21**	*2316*
LORD **G** WILL RAISE UP FOR YOU	**Ac 3:22**	*2316*
which **G** made with your fathers,	**Ac 3:25**	*2316*
first, **G** raised up His Servant and	**Ac 3:26**	*2316*
whom **G** raised from the dead	**Ac 4:10**	*2316*
is right in the sight of **G** to give heed	**Ac 4:19**	*2316*
give heed to you rather than to **G**,	**Ac 4:19**	*2316*
glorifying **G** for what had happened;	**Ac 4:21**	*2316*
to **G** with one accord and said,	**Ac 4:24**	*2316*
speak the word of **G** with boldness.	**Ac 4:31**	*2316*
have not lied to men but to **G**."	**Ac 5:4**	*2316*

“We must obey **G** rather than men. **Ac 5:29** *2316*
“The **G** of our fathers raised up **Ac 5:30** *2316*
“He is the one whom **G** exalted to **Ac 5:31** *2316*
whom **G** has given to those who obey **Ac 5:32** *2316*
but if it is of **G**, you will not be **Ac 5:39** *2316*
be found fighting against **G**.” **Ac 5:39** *2314*
for us to neglect the word of **G** in **Ac 6:2** *2316*
The word of **G** kept on spreading; **Ac 6:7** *2316*
against Moses and *against* **G**.” **Ac 6:11** *2316*
The **G** of glory appeared to our **Ac 7:2** *2316*
G had him move to this country in **Ac 7:4**
“But **G** spoke to this effect, that **Ac 7:6** *2316*
I MYSELF WILL JUDGE,’ said **G**, **Ac 7:7** *2316*
Yet **G** was with him, **Ac 7:9** *2316*
which **G** had assured to Abraham, **Ac 7:17** *2316*
he was lovely in the sight of **G**, **Ac 7:20** *2316*
G was granting them deliverance **Ac 7:25** *2316*
‘I AM THE **G** OF YOUR FATHERS, THE **Ac 7:32** *2316*
THE **G** OF ABRAHAM AND ISAAC AND **Ac 7:32** *2316*
is the one whom **G** sent *to be* both **Ac 7:35** *2316*
‘**G** WILL RAISE UP FOR YOU A **Ac 7:37** *2316*
“But **G** turned away and delivered **Ac 7:42** *2316*
AND THE STAR OF THE **G** ROMPHA, **Ac 7:43** *2316*
G drove out before our fathers, **Ac 7:45** *2316*
dwelling place for the **G** of Jacob. **Ac 7:46** *2316*
heaven and saw the glory of **G**, **Ac 7:55** *2316*
standing at the right hand of **G**; **Ac 7:55** *2316*
standing at the right hand of **G**.” **Ac 7:56** *2316*
is called the Great Power of **G**.” **Ac 8:10** *2316*
of **G** and the name of Jesus Christ, **Ac 8:12** *2316*
had received the word of **G**, **Ac 8:14** *2316*
obtain the gift of **G** with money! **Ac 8:20** *2316*
your heart is not right before **G**. **Ac 8:21** *2316*
Jesus Christ is the Son of **G**.” **Ac 8:37** *2316*
“He is the Son of **G**.” **Ac 9:20** *2316*
feared **G** with all his household, **Ac 10:2** *2316*
and prayed to **G** continually. **Ac 10:2** *2316*
of **G** who had *just* come in **Ac 10:3** *2316*
ascended as a memorial before **G**. **Ac 10:4** *2316*
“What **G** has cleansed, no *longer* **Ac 10:15** *2316*
and *yet* **G** has shown me that I **Ac 10:28** *2316*
have been remembered before **G**. **Ac 10:31** *2316*
we are all here present before **G** **Ac 10:33** *2316*
G is not one to show partiality, **Ac 10:34** *2316*
how **G** anointed Him with the Holy **Ac 10:38** *2316*
for **G** was with Him. **Ac 10:38** *2316*
“**G** raised Him up on the third **Ac 10:40** *2316*
who were chosen beforehand by **G**, **Ac 10:41** *2316*
One who has been appointed by **G** **Ac 10:42** *2316*
with tongues and exalting **G**. **Ac 10:46** *2316*
also had received the word of **G**. **Ac 11:1** *2316*
‘What **G** has cleansed, no longer **Ac 11:9** *2316*
“Therefore if **G** gave to them the **Ac 11:17** *2316*
quieted down and glorified **G**, **Ac 11:18** *2316*
G has granted to the Gentiles also **Ac 11:18** *2316*
arrived and witnessed the grace of **G**, **Ac 11:23** *2316*
made fervently by the church to **G**. **Ac 12:5** *2316*
voice of a **g** and not of a man!” **Ac 12:22** *2316*
he did not give **G** the glory, **Ac 12:23** *2316*
G in the synagogues of the Jews; **Ac 13:5** *2316*
and sought to hear the word of **G**. **Ac 13:7** *2316*
“Men of Israel, and you who fear **G**, **Ac 13:16** *2316*
“The **G** of this people Israel **Ac 13:17** *2316*
and **G** gave them Saul the son of **Ac 13:21** *2316*
G has brought to Israel a Savior, **Ac 13:23** *2316*
and those among you who fear **G**, **Ac 13:26** *2316*
“But **G** raised Him from the dead; **Ac 13:30** *2316*
that **G** has fulfilled this *promise* **Ac 13:33** *2316*
of **G** in his own generation, **Ac 13:36** *2316*
G raised did not undergo decay. **Ac 13:37** *2316*
to continue in the grace of **G**. **Ac 13:43** *2316*
G be spoken to you first; **Ac 13:46** *2316*
these vain things to a living **G**, **Ac 14:15** *2316*
we must enter the kingdom of **G**.” **Ac 14:22** *2316*
been commended to the grace of **G** **Ac 14:26** *2316*
to report all things that **G** had done **Ac 14:27** *2316*
all that **G** had done with them. **Ac 15:4** *2316*
days **G** made a choice among you, **Ac 15:7** *2316*
“And **G**, who knows the heart, testified **Ac 15:8** *2316*
“Now therefore why do you put **G** **Ac 15:10** *2316*
what signs and wonders **G** had done **Ac 15:12** *2316*
“Simeon has related how **G** first **Ac 15:14** *2316*
to **G** from among the Gentiles, **Ac 15:19** *2316*
concluding that **G** had called us to **Ac 16:10** *2316*
purple fabrics, a worshiper of **G**, **Ac 16:14** *2316*
bond-servants of the Most High **G**, **Ac 16:17** *2316*
and singing hymns of praise to **G**, **Ac 16:25** *2316*
in **G** with his whole household. **Ac 16:34** *2316*
the word of **G** had been proclaimed **Ac 17:13** *2316*
‘TO AN UNKNOWN **G**.’ **Ac 17:23** *2316*
“The **G** who made the world and all **Ac 17:24** *2316*
that they would seek **G**, **Ac 17:27** *2316*
“Being then the children of **G**, **Ac 17:29** *2316*
G is now declaring to men that all **Ac 17:30** *2316*
Titius Justus, a worshiper of **G**, **Ac 18:7** *2316*
teaching the word of **G** among them. **Ac 18:11** *2316*
worship **G** contrary to the law.” **Ac 18:13** *2316*
return to you again if **G** wills,” **Ac 18:21** *2316*
explained to him the way of **G** more **Ac 18:26** *2316*
them about the kingdom of **G**. **Ac 19:8** *2316*
G was performing extraordinary **Ac 19:11** *2316*
repentance toward **G** and faith in our **Ac 20:21** *2316*
of the gospel of the grace of **G**. **Ac 20:24** *2316*
to you the whole purpose of **G**. **Ac 20:27** *2316*
to shepherd the church of **G** which **Ac 20:28** *2316*
to **G** and to the word of His grace, **Ac 20:32** *2316*
the things which **G** had done among **Ac 21:19** *2316*
heard it they *began* glorifying **G**; **Ac 21:20** *2316*
our fathers, being zealous for **G** just **Ac 22:3** *2316*

‘The **G** of our fathers has **Ac 22:14** *2316*
before **G** up to this day.” **Ac 23:1** *2316*
“**G** is going to strike you, you **Ac 23:3** *2316*
I do serve the **G** of our fathers, **Ac 24:14** *2316*
having a hope in **G**, **Ac 24:15** *2316*
both before **G** and before men. **Ac 24:16** *2316*
promise made by **G** to our fathers; **Ac 26:6** *2316*
as they earnestly serve **G** night **Ac 26:7**
people if **G** does raise the dead? **Ac 26:8** *2316*
from the dominion of Satan to **G**, **Ac 26:18** *2316*
they should repent and turn to **G**, **Ac 26:20** *2316*
So, having obtained help from **G**, **Ac 26:22** *2316*
“I would wish to **G**, that whether in a **Ac 26:29** *2316*
an angel of the **G** to whom I belong **Ac 27:23** *2316*
G has granted you all those who **Ac 27:24** *2316*
courage, men, for I believe **G** that **Ac 27:25** *2316*
to **G** in the presence of all, **Ac 27:35** *2316*
and *began* to say that he was a **g**. **Ac 28:6** *2316*
he thanked **G** and took courage. **Ac 28:15** *2316*
testifying about the kingdom of **G** and **Ac 28:23** *2316*
G has been sent to the Gentiles; **Ac 28:28** *2316*
preaching the kingdom of **G** and **Ac 28:31** *2316*
set apart for the gospel of **G**, **Ro 1:1** *2316*
who was declared the Son of **G** with **Ro 1:4** *2316*
all who are beloved of **G** in Rome, **Ro 1:7** *2316*
Grace to you and peace from **G** our **Ro 1:7** *2316*
I thank my **G** through Jesus Christ **Ro 1:8** *2316*
For **G**, whom I serve in my spirit **Ro 1:9** *2316*
at last by the will of **G** I may succeed **Ro 1:10** *2316*
for it is the power of **G** for **Ro 1:16** *2316*
the righteousness of **G** is revealed **Ro 1:17** *2316*
For the wrath of **G** is revealed **Ro 1:18** *2316*
which is known about **G** is evident **Ro 1:19** *2316*
for **G** made it evident to them. **Ro 1:19** *2316*
For even though they knew **G**, **Ro 1:21** *2316*
God, they did not honor Him as **G** or **Ro 1:21** *2316*
the glory of the incorruptible **G** for an **Ro 1:23** *2316*
Therefore **G** gave them over in the **Ro 1:24** *2316*
exchanged the truth of **G** for a lie, **Ro 1:25** *2316*
For this reason **G** gave them over **Ro 1:26** *2316*
fit to acknowledge **G** any longer, **Ro 1:28** *2316*
G gave them over to a depraved **Ro 1:28** *2316*
slanderers, haters of **G**, **Ro 1:30** *2319*
they know the ordinance of **G**, **Ro 1:32** *2316*
judgment of **G** rightly falls upon those **Ro 2:2** *2316*
you will escape the judgment of **G**? **Ro 2:3** *2316*
that the kindness of **G** leads you to **Ro 2:4** *2316*
of the righteous judgment of **G**, **Ro 2:5** *2316*
For there is no partiality with **G**. **Ro 2:11** *2316*
of the Law *who* are just before **G**, **Ro 2:13** *2316*
G will judge the secrets of men **Ro 2:16** *2316*
rely upon the Law and boast in **G**, **Ro 2:17** *2316*
the Law, do you dishonor **G**? **Ro 2:23** *2316*
“THE NAME OF **G** IS BLASPHEMED **Ro 2:24** *2316*
is not from men, but from **G**. **Ro 2:29** *2316*
entrusted with the oracles of **G**. **Ro 3:2** *2316*
not nullify the faithfulness of **G**, **Ro 3:3** *2316*
Rather, let **G** be found true, **Ro 3:4** *2316*
the righteousness of **G**, **Ro 3:5** *2316*
The **G** who inflicts wrath is not **Ro 3:5** *2316*
how will **G** judge the world? **Ro 3:6** *2316*
truth of **G** abounded to His glory, **Ro 3:7** *2316*
THERE IS NONE WHO SEEKS FOR **G**; **Ro 3:11** *2316*
NO FEAR OF **G** BEFORE THEIR EYES.” **Ro 3:18** *2316*
world may become accountable to **G**; **Ro 3:19** *2316*
of **G** has been manifested, **Ro 3:21** *2316*
even *the* righteousness of **G** **Ro 3:22** *2316*
and fall short of the glory of **G**, **Ro 3:23** *2316*
whom **G** displayed publicly as a **Ro 3:25** *2316*
because in the forbearance of **G** He **Ro 3:25** *2316*
Or is **G** *the God* of Jews only? **Ro 3:29** *2316*
Or is God *the* **G** of Jews only? **Ro 3:29**
Is He not *the* **G** of Gentiles also? **Ro 3:29**
since indeed **G** who will justify **Ro 3:30** *2316*
but not before **G**. **Ro 4:2** *2316*
“ABRAHAM BELIEVED **G**, **Ro 4:3** *2316*
man to whom **G** credits righteousness **Ro 4:6** *2316*
of Him whom he believed, *even* **G**, **Ro 4:17** *2316*
with respect to the promise of **G**, **Ro 4:20** *2316*
in faith, giving glory to **G**, **Ro 4:20** *2316*
and being fully assured that what **G** **Ro 4:21**
peace with **G** through our Lord **Ro 5:1** *2316*
exult in hope of the glory of **G**. **Ro 5:2** *2316*
because the love of **G** has been **Ro 5:5** *2316*
But **G** demonstrates His own love **Ro 5:8** *2316*
shall be saved from the wrath *of* **G** **Ro 5:9**
to **G** through the death of His Son, **Ro 5:10** *2316*
G through our Lord Jesus Christ, **Ro 5:11** *2316*
much more did the grace of **G** and **Ro 5:15** *2316*
life that He lives, He lives to **G**. **Ro 6:10** *2316*
but alive to **G** in Christ Jesus. **Ro 6:11** *2316*
to **G** as those alive from the dead, **Ro 6:13** *2316*
instruments of righteousness to **G**. **Ro 6:13** *2316*
But thanks be to **G** that though you **Ro 6:17** *2316*
freed from sin and enslaved to **G**, **Ro 6:22** *2316*
but the free gift of **G** is eternal **Ro 6:23** *2316*
that we might bear fruit for **G**. **Ro 7:4** *2316*
the law of **G** in the inner man, **Ro 7:22** *2316*
G through Jesus Christ our Lord! **Ro 7:25** *2316*
my mind am serving the law of **G**, **Ro 7:25** *2316*
it was through the flesh, **G** *did* **Ro 8:3** *2316*
on the flesh is hostile toward **G**; **Ro 8:7** *2316*
subject itself to the law of **G**, **Ro 8:7** *2316*
are in the flesh cannot please **G**. **Ro 8:8** *2316*
the Spirit of **G** dwells in you. **Ro 8:9** *2316*
are being led by the Spirit of **G**, **Ro 8:14** *2316*
of God, these are sons of **G**. **Ro 8:14** *2316*
spirit that we are children of **G**, **Ro 8:16** *2316*
if children, heirs also, heirs of **G** **Ro 8:17** *2316*

the revealing of the sons of **G**. **Ro 8:19** *2316*
of the glory of the children of **G**. **Ro 8:21** *2316*
saints according to *the will of* **G**. **Ro 8:27** *2316*
And we know that **G** causes all **Ro 8:28** *2316*
for good to those who love **G**, **Ro 8:28** *2316*
If **G** *is* for us, who *is* against us? **Ro 8:31** *2316*
G is the one who justifies; **Ro 8:33** *2316*
who is at the right hand of **G**, **Ro 8:34** *2316*
to separate us from the love of **G**, **Ro 8:39** *2316*
is over all, **G** blessed forever. **Ro 9:5** *2316*
though the word of **G** has failed. **Ro 9:6** *2316*
the flesh who are children of **G**, **Ro 9:8** *2316*
There is no injustice with **G**, **Ro 9:14** *2316*
who runs, but on **G** who has mercy. **Ro 9:16** *2316*
you, O man, who answers back to **G**? **Ro 9:20** *2316*
What if **G**, although willing to **Ro 9:22** *2316*
BE CALLED SONS OF THE LIVING **G**.” **Ro 9:26** *2316*
my prayer to **G** for them is for *their* **Ro 10:1** *2316*
that they have a zeal for **G**, **Ro 10:2** *2316*
to the righteousness of **G**. **Ro 10:3** *2316*
that **G** raised Him from the dead, **Ro 10:9** *2316*
G has not rejected His people, **Ro 11:1** *2316*
G has not rejected His people whom **Ro 11:2** *2316*
he pleads with **G** against Israel? **Ro 11:2** *2316*
“**G** GAVE THEM A SPIRIT OF STUPOR, **Ro 11:8** *2316*
for if **G** did not spare the natural **Ro 11:21** *2316*
the kindness and severity of **G**; **Ro 11:22** *2316*
for **G** is able to graft them in **Ro 11:23** *2316*
the calling of **G** are irrevocable. **Ro 11:29** *2316*
as you once were disobedient to **G**, **Ro 11:30** *2316*
For **G** has shut up all in **Ro 11:32** *2316*
of the wisdom and knowledge of **G**! **Ro 11:33** *2316*
brethren, by the mercies of **G**, **Ro 12:1** *2316*
holy sacrifice, acceptable to **G**, **Ro 12:1** *2316*
may prove what the will of **G** is, **Ro 12:2** *2316*
as **G** has allotted to each a **Ro 12:3** *2316*
but leave room for the wrath *of* **G**, **Ro 12:19**
is no authority except from **G**, **Ro 13:1** *2316*
which exist are established by **G**. **Ro 13:1** *2316*
has opposed the ordinance of **G**; **Ro 13:2** *2316*
a minister of **G** to you for good. **Ro 13:4** *2316*
for it is a minister of **G**, **Ro 13:4** *2316*
for *rulers* are servants of **G**, **Ro 13:6** *2316*
who eats, for **G** has accepted him. **Ro 14:3** *2316*
Lord, for he gives thanks to **G**; **Ro 14:6** *2316*
not eat, and gives thanks to **G**. **Ro 14:6** *2316*
before the judgment seat of **G**. **Ro 14:10** *2316*
TONGUE SHALL GIVE PRAISE TO **G**.” **Ro 14:11** *2316*
give an account of himself to **G**. **Ro 14:12** *2316*
the kingdom of **G** is not eating and **Ro 14:17** *2316*
is acceptable to **G** and approved by **Ro 14:18** *2316*
work of **G** for the sake of food. **Ro 14:20** *2316*
as your own conviction before **G**. **Ro 14:22** *2316*
may the **G** who gives perseverance **Ro 15:5** *2316*
glorify the **G** and Father of our Lord **Ro 15:6** *2316*
accepted us to the glory of **G**. **Ro 15:7** *2316*
the truth of **G** to confirm the promises **Ro 15:8** *2316*
to glorify **G** for His mercy; **Ro 15:9** *2316*
Now may the **G** of hope fill you **Ro 15:13** *2316*
grace that was given me from **G**, **Ro 15:15** *2316*
as a priest the gospel of **G**, **Ro 15:16** *2316*
in things pertaining to **G**. **Ro 15:17** *2316*
me in your prayers to **G** for me, **Ro 15:30** *2316*
come to you in joy by the will of **G** **Ro 15:32** *2316*
the **G** of peace be with you all. **Ro 15:33** *2316*
G of peace will soon crush Satan **Ro 16:20** *2316*
the commandment of the eternal **G**, **Ro 16:26** *2316*
to the only wise **G**, **Ro 16:27** *2316*
of Jesus Christ by the will of **G**, **1Co 1:1** *2316*
church of **G** which is at Corinth, **1Co 1:2** *2316*
Grace to you and peace from **G** our **1Co 1:3** *2316*
thank my **G** always concerning you for **1Co 1:4** *2316*
for the grace of **G** which was given **1Co 1:4** *2316*
G is faithful, through whom you **1Co 1:9** *2316*
I thank **G** that I baptized none of **1Co 1:14** *2316*
being saved it is the power of **G**. **1Co 1:18** *2316*
Has not **G** made foolish the wisdom **1Co 1:20** *2316*
For since in the wisdom of **G** the **1Co 1:21** *2316*
its wisdom did not *come to* know **G**, **1Co 1:21** *2316*
G was well-pleased through the **1Co 1:21** *2316*
power of **G** and the wisdom of God. **1Co 1:24** *2316*
power of God and the wisdom of **G**. **1Co 1:24** *2316*
of **G** is wiser than men, **1Co 1:25** *2316*
of **G** is stronger than men. **1Co 1:25** *2316*
but **G** has chosen the foolish **1Co 1:27** *2316*
and **G** has chosen the weak things **1Co 1:27** *2316*
and the despised **G** has chosen, **1Co 1:28** *2316*
that no man may boast before **G**. **1Co 1:29** *2316*
who became to us wisdom from **G**, **1Co 1:30** *2316*
to you the testimony of **G**. **1Co 2:1** *2316*
of men, but on the power of **G**. **1Co 2:5** *2316*
which **G** predestined before the **1Co 2:7** *2316*
ALL THAT **G** HAS PREPARED FOR THOSE WHO **1Co 2:9** *2316*
For to us **G** revealed *them* through **1Co 2:10** *2316*
all things, even the depths of **G**. **1Co 2:10** *2316*
Even so the *thoughts* of **G** no one **1Co 2:11** *2316*
one knows except the Spirit of **G**. **1Co 2:11** *2316*
but the Spirit who is from **G**, **1Co 2:12** *2316*
things freely given to us by **G**, **1Co 2:12** *2316*
the things of the Spirit of **G**, **1Co 2:14** *2316*
but **G** was causing the growth. **1Co 3:6** *2316*
but **G** who causes the growth. **1Co 3:7** *2316*
grace of **G** which was given to me, **1Co 3:10** *2316*
know that you are a temple of **G** and **1Co 3:16** *2316*
the Spirit of **G** dwells in you? **1Co 3:16** *2316*
any man destroys the temple of **G**, **1Co 3:17** *2316*
temple of God, **G** will destroy him, **1Co 3:17** *2316*
him, for the temple of **G** is holy, **1Co 3:17** *2316*
world is foolishness before **G**. **1Co 3:19** *2316*

and Christ belongs to **G**.	1Co 3:23	*2316*
stewards of the mysteries of **G**.	1Co 4:1	*2316*
praise will come to him from **G**.	1Co 4:5	*2316*
G has exhibited us apostles last	1Co 4:9	*2316*
of **G** does not consist in words but	1Co 4:20	*2316*
those who are outside, **G** judges.	1Co 5:13	*2316*
not inherit the kingdom of **G**?	1Co 6:9	*2316*
will inherit the kingdom of **G**.	1Co 6:10	*2316*
and in the Spirit of our **G**.	1Co 6:11	*2316*
but **G** will do away with both of	1Co 6:13	*2316*
G has not only raised the Lord,	1Co 6:14	*2316*
is in you, whom you have from **G**,	1Co 6:19	*2316*
therefore glorify **G** in your body.	1Co 6:20	*2316*
each man has his own gift from **G**,	1Co 7:7	*2316*
but **G** has called us to peace.	1Co 7:15	*2316*
to each one, as **G** has called each,	1Co 7:17	*2316*
keeping of the commandments of **G**.	1Co 7:19	*2316*
each one is to remain with **G** in that	1Co 7:24	*2316*
that I also have the Spirit of **G**.	1Co 7:40	*2316*
but if anyone loves **G**,	1Co 8:3	*2316*
and that there is no **G** but one.	1Co 8:4	*2316*
yet for us there is *but* one **G**,	1Co 8:6	*2316*
But food will not commend us to **G**;	1Co 8:8	*2316*
G is not concerned about oxen,	1Co 9:9	*2316*
of **G** but under the law of Christ,	1Co 9:21	*2316*
of them **G** was not well-pleased;	1Co 10:5	*2316*
and **G** is faithful, who will not	1Co 10:13	*2316*
sacrifice to demons and not to **G**;	1Co 10:20	*2316*
you do, do all to the glory of **G**.	1Co 10:31	*2316*
to Greeks or to the church of **G**;	1Co 10:32	*2316*
and **G** is the head of Christ.	1Co 11:3	*2316*
he is the image and glory of **G**;	1Co 11:7	*2316*
and all things originate from **G**.	1Co 11:12	*2316*
to pray to **G** *with her head* uncovered?	1Co 11:13	*2316*
nor have the churches of **G**.	1Co 11:16	*2316*
Or do you despise the church of **G** and	1Co 11:22	*2316*
speaking by the Spirit of **G** says,	1Co 12:3	*2316*
but the same **G** who works all	1Co 12:6	*2316*
But now **G** has placed the members,	1Co 12:18	*2316*
But **G** has *so* composed the body,	1Co 12:24	*2316*
And **G** has appointed in the church,	1Co 12:28	*2316*
does not speak to men but to **G**;	1Co 14:2	*2316*
I thank **G**, I speak in tongues more	1Co 14:18	*2316*
fall on his face and worship **G**,	1Co 14:25	*2316*
that **G** is certainly among you.	1Co 14:25	*2316*
let him speak to himself and to **G**.	1Co 14:28	*2316*
for **G** is not *a God* of confusion	1Co 14:33	*2316*
for God is not *a* **G** of confusion	1Co 14:33	*2316*
the word of **G** *first* went forth?	1Co 14:36	*2316*
I persecuted the church of **G**.	1Co 15:9	*2316*
by the grace of **G** I am what I am,	1Co 15:10	*2316*
not I, but the grace of **G** with me.	1Co 15:10	*2316*
found *to be* false witnesses of **G**,	1Co 15:15	*2316*
against **G** that He raised Christ,	1Co 15:15	*2316*
the kingdom to the **G** and Father,	1Co 15:24	*2316*
to Him, so that **G** may be all in all.	1Co 15:28	*2316*
for some have no knowledge of **G**.	1Co 15:34	*2316*
But **G** gives it a body just as He	1Co 15:38	*2316*
cannot inherit the kingdom of **G**;	1Co 15:50	*2316*
but thanks be to **G**,	1Co 15:57	*2316*
of Christ Jesus by the will of **G**,	2Co 1:1	*2316*
To the church of **G** which is at	2Co 1:1	*2316*
Grace to you and peace from **G** our	2Co 1:2	*2316*
Blessed *be* the **G** and Father of our	2Co 1:3	*2316*
of mercies and **G** of all comfort,	2Co 1:3	*2316*
we ourselves are comforted by **G**.	2Co 1:4	*2316*
but in **G** who raises the dead;	2Co 1:9	*2316*
wisdom but in the grace of **G**,	2Co 1:12	*2316*
But as **G** is faithful, our word to	2Co 1:18	*2316*
For the Son of **G**, Christ Jesus,	2Co 1:19	*2316*
many as are the promises of **G**,	2Co 1:20	*2316*
Amen to the glory of **G** through us.	2Co 1:20	*2316*
in Christ and anointed us is **G**,	2Co 1:21	*2316*
I call **G** as witness to my soul,	2Co 1:23	*2316*
But thanks be to **G**,	2Co 2:14	*2316*
For we are a fragrance of Christ to **G**	2Co 2:15	*2316*
like many, peddling the word of **G**,	2Co 2:17	*2316*
as from sincerity, but as from **G**,	2Co 2:17	*2316*
speak in Christ in the sight of **G**.	2Co 2:17	*2316*
with the Spirit of the living **G**,	2Co 3:3	*2316*
we have through Christ toward **G**.	2Co 3:4	*2316*
but our adequacy is from **G**,	2Co 3:5	*2316*
or adulterating the word of **G**,	2Co 4:2	*2316*
man's conscience in the sight of **G**.	2Co 4:2	*2316*
in whose case the **g** of this world	2Co 4:4	*2316*
of Christ, who is the image of **G**.	2Co 4:4	*2316*
G, who said, "Light shall shine out	2Co 4:6	*2316*
glory of **G** in the face of Christ.	2Co 4:6	*2316*
be of **G** and not from ourselves;	2Co 4:7	*2316*
to abound to the glory of **G**.	2Co 4:15	*2316*
down, we have a building from **G**,	2Co 5:1	*2316*
us for this very purpose is **G**,	2Co 5:5	*2316*
but we are made manifest to **G**;	2Co 5:11	*2316*
are beside ourselves, it is for **G**;	2Co 5:13	*2316*
Now all *these* things are from **G**,	2Co 5:18	*2316*
that **G** was in Christ reconciling	2Co 5:19	*2316*
G were making an appeal through us;	2Co 5:20	*2316*
of Christ, be reconciled to **G**.	2Co 5:20	*2316*
the righteousness of **G** in Him.	2Co 5:21	*2316*
to receive the grace of **G** in vain	2Co 6:1	*2316*
ourselves as servants of **G**,	2Co 6:4	*2316*
word of truth, in the power of **G**;	2Co 6:7	*2316*
has the temple of **G** with idols?	2Co 6:16	*2316*
we are the temple of the living **G**;	2Co 6:16	*2316*
just as **G** said, "I WILL DWELL IN THEM	2Co 6:16	*2316*
AND I WILL BE THEIR **G**,	2Co 6:16	*2316*
holiness in the fear of **G**.	2Co 7:1	*2316*
But **G**, who comforts the depressed,	2Co 7:6	*2316*
according to *the will of* **G**,	2Co 7:9	*2316*
is according to *the will of* **G** produces	2Co 7:10	*2316*
known to you in the sight of **G**.	2Co 7:12	*2316*
the grace of **G** which has been given	2Co 8:1	*2316*
Lord and to us by the will of **G**.	2Co 8:5	*2316*
But thanks be to **G** who	2Co 8:16	*2316*
for **G** loves a cheerful giver.	2Co 9:7	*2316*
And **G** is able to make all grace	2Co 9:8	*2316*
us is producing thanksgiving to **G**.	2Co 9:11	*2316*
through many thanksgivings to **G**.	2Co 9:12	*2316*
by this ministry, they will glorify **G**	2Co 9:13	*2316*
the surpassing grace of **G** in you.	2Co 9:14	*2316*
to **G** for His indescribable gift!	2Co 9:15	*2316*
up against the knowledge of **G**,	2Co 10:5	*2316*
the sphere which **G** apportioned to us	2Co 10:13	*2316*
gospel of **G** to you without charge?	2Co 11:7	*2316*
I do not love you? **G** knows *I do!*	2Co 11:11	*2316*
G and Father of the Lord Jesus,	2Co 11:31	*2316*
of the body I do not know, **G** knows	2Co 12:2	*2316*
the body I do not know, **G** knows	2Co 12:3	*2316*
it is in the sight of **G** that we	2Co 12:19	*2316*
my **G** may humiliate me before you,	2Co 12:21	*2316*
lives because of the power of **G**.	2Co 13:4	*2316*
power of **G** *directed* toward you.	2Co 13:4	*2316*
we pray to **G** that you do no wrong;	2Co 13:7	*2316*
and the **G** of love and peace will	2Co 13:11	*2316*
Jesus Christ, and the love of **G**,	2Co 13:14	*2316*
Jesus Christ and **G** the Father,	Ga 1:1	*2316*
you and peace from **G** our Father and	Ga 1:3	*2316*
to the will of our **G** and Father,	Ga 1:4	*2316*
seeking the favor of men, or of **G**?	Ga 1:10	*2316*
the church of **G** beyond measure and	Ga 1:13	*2316*
But when **G**, who had set me apart	Ga 1:15	
you before **G** that I am not lying.)	Ga 1:20	*2316*
were glorifying **G** because of me.	Ga 1:24	*2316*
G shows no partiality)	Ga 2:6	*2316*
the Law, so that I might live to **G**.	Ga 2:19	*2316*
I live by faith in the Son of **G**,	Ga 2:20	*2316*
"I do not nullify the grace of **G**,	Ga 2:21	*2316*
Even so Abraham BELIEVED **G**,	Ga 3:6	*2316*
foreseeing that **G** would justify	Ga 3:8	*2316*
by the Law before **G** is evident;	Ga 3:11	*2316*
covenant previously ratified by **G**,	Ga 3:17	*2316*
but **G** has granted it to Abraham by	Ga 3:18	*2316*
whereas **G** is *only* one.	Ga 3:20	*2316*
contrary to the promises of **G**?	Ga 3:21	*2316*
G through faith in Christ Jesus.	Ga 3:26	*2316*
time came, **G** sent forth His Son,	Ga 4:4	*2316*
G has sent forth the Spirit of His	Ga 4:6	*2316*
if a son, then an heir through **G**.	Ga 4:7	*2316*
time, when you did not know **G**,	Ga 4:8	*2316*
now that you have come to know **G**,	Ga 4:9	*2316*
God, or rather to be known by **G**,	Ga 4:9	*2316*
you received me as an angel of **G**,	Ga 4:14	*2316*
not inherit the kingdom of **G**.	Ga 5:21	*2316*
not be deceived, **G** is not mocked;	Ga 6:7	*2316*
them, and upon the Israel of **G**.	Ga 6:16	*2316*
of Christ Jesus by the will of **G**,	Eph 1:1	*2316*
Grace to you and peace from **G** our	Eph 1:2	*2316*
Blessed *be* the **G** and Father of our	Eph 1:3	*2316*
the **G** of our Lord Jesus Christ,	Eph 1:17	*2316*
But **G**, being rich in mercy,	Eph 2:4	*2316*
yourselves, *it is* the gift of **G**;	Eph 2:8	*2316*
which **G** prepared beforehand so	Eph 2:10	*2316*
hope and without **G** in the world.	Eph 2:12	*112*
one body to **G** through the cross,	Eph 2:16	*2316*
a dwelling of **G** in the Spirit.	Eph 2:22	*2316*
for ages has been hidden in **G** who	Eph 3:9	*2316*
manifold wisdom of **G** might now be	Eph 3:10	*2316*
filled up to all the fullness of **G**.	Eph 3:19	*2316*
one **G** and Father of all who is	Eph 4:6	*2316*
of the knowledge of the Son of **G**,	Eph 4:13	*2316*
excluded from the life of **G** because	Eph 4:18	*2316*
which in *the likeness of* **G** has	Eph 4:24	*2316*
not grieve the Holy Spirit of **G**,	Eph 4:30	*2316*
just as **G** in Christ also has	Eph 4:32	*2316*
Therefore be imitators of **G**,	Eph 5:1	*2316*
to **G** as a fragrant aroma.	Eph 5:2	*2316*
in the kingdom of Christ and **G**.	Eph 5:5	*2316*
the wrath of **G** comes upon the sons	Eph 5:6	*2316*
of our Lord Jesus Christ to **G**,	Eph 5:20	*2316*
the will of **G** from the heart.	Eph 6:6	*2316*
Put on the full armor of **G**,	Eph 6:11	*2316*
take up the full armor of **G**,	Eph 6:13	*2316*
Spirit, which is the word of **G**.	Eph 6:17	*2316*
from **G** the Father and the Lord	Eph 6:23	*2316*
Grace to you and peace from **G** our	Php 1:2	*2316*
my **G** in all my remembrance of you,	Php 1:3	*2316*
For **G** is my witness, how I long	Php 1:8	*2316*
to the glory and praise of **G**.	Php 1:11	*2316*
speak the word of **G** without fear.	Php 1:14	*2316*
for you, and that *too*, from **G**.	Php 1:28	*2316*
He existed in the form of **G**,	Php 2:6	*2316*
with **G** a thing to be grasped,	Php 2:6	*2316*
also, **G** highly exalted Him,	Php 2:9	*2316*
to the glory of **G** the Father.	Php 2:11	*2316*
for it is **G** who is at work in you,	Php 2:13	*2316*
children of **G** above reproach in	Php 2:15	*2316*
of death, but **G** had mercy on him,	Php 2:27	*2316*
who worship in the Spirit of **G** and	Php 3:3	*2316*
from **G** on the basis of faith,	Php 3:9	*2316*
upward call of **G** in Christ Jesus.	Php 3:14	*2316*
G will reveal that also to you;	Php 3:15	*2316*
whose **g** is *their* appetite,	Php 3:19	*2316*
your requests be made known to **G**.	Php 4:6	*2316*
And the peace of **G**,	Php 4:7	*2316*
the **G** of peace will be with you.	Php 4:9	*2316*
sacrifice, well-pleasing to **G**.	Php 4:18	*2316*
And my **G** will supply all your	Php 4:19	*2316*
Now to our **G** and Father *be* the	Php 4:20	*2316*
of Jesus Christ by the will of **G**,	Col 1:1	*2316*
you and peace from **G** our Father.	Col 1:2	*2316*
We give thanks to **G**,	Col 1:3	*2316*
the grace of **G** in truth;	Col 1:6	*2316*
increasing in the knowledge of **G**;	Col 1:10	*2316*
is the image of the invisible **G**,	Col 1:15	*2316*
according to the stewardship from **G**	Col 1:25	*2316*
the *preaching of* the word of **G**,	Col 1:25	*2316*
to whom **G** willed to make known	Col 1:27	*2316*
through faith in the working of **G**,	Col 2:12	*2316*
with a growth which is from **G**.	Col 2:19	*2316*
is, seated at the right hand of **G**.	Col 3:1	*2316*
life is hidden with Christ in **G**.	Col 3:3	*2316*
that the wrath of **G** will come upon	Col 3:6	*2316*
those who have been chosen of **G**,	Col 3:12	*2316*
thankfulness in your hearts to **G**.	Col 3:16	*2316*
through Him to **G** the Father.	Col 3:17	*2316*
that **G** will open up to us a door	Col 4:3	*2316*
G who are from the circumcision,	Col 4:11	*2316*
assured in all the will of **G**.	Col 4:12	*2316*
in **G** the Father and the Lord Jesus	1Th 1:1	*2316*
thanks to **G** always for all of you,	1Th 1:2	*2316*
the presence of our **G** and Father,	1Th 1:3	*2316*
knowing, brethren beloved by **G**,	1Th 1:4	*2316*
faith toward **G** has gone forth,	1Th 1:8	*2316*
and how you turned to **G** from idols	1Th 1:9	*2316*
to serve a living and true **G**,	1Th 1:9	*2316*
we had the boldness in our **G** to	1Th 2:2	*2316*
gospel of **G** amid much opposition.	1Th 2:2	*2316*
just as we have been approved by **G**	1Th 2:4	*2316*
speak, not as pleasing men, but **G**	1Th 2:4	*2316*
G is witness	1Th 2:5	*2316*
of **G** but also our own lives,	1Th 2:8	*2316*
proclaimed to you the gospel of **G**.	1Th 2:9	*2316*
You are witnesses, and *so is* **G**,	1Th 2:10	*2316*
walk in a manner worthy of the **G**	1Th 2:12	*2316*
constantly thank **G** that when you	1Th 2:13	*2316*
that when you received the word of **G**	1Th 2:13	*2316*
what it really is, the word of **G**,	1Th 2:13	*2316*
became imitators of the churches of **G**	1Th 2:14	*2316*
They are not pleasing to **G**,	1Th 2:15	*2316*
what thanks can we render to **G** for	1Th 3:9	*2316*
before our **G** on your account,	1Th 3:9	*2316*
Now may our **G** and Father Himself	1Th 3:11	*2316*
blame in holiness before our **G**	1Th 3:13	*2316*
you ought to walk and please **G**	1Th 4:1	*2316*
For this is the will of **G**,	1Th 4:3	*2316*
the Gentiles who do not know **G**;	1Th 4:5	*2316*
For **G** has not called us for the	1Th 4:7	*2316*
is not rejecting man but the **G** who	1Th 4:8	*2316*
taught by **G** to love one another;	1Th 4:9	*2312*
even so **G** will bring with Him	1Th 4:14	*2316*
and with the trumpet of **G**,	1Th 4:16	*2316*
G has not destined us for wrath,	1Th 5:9	*2316*
Now may the **G** of peace Himself	1Th 5:23	*2316*
in **G** our Father and the Lord Jesus	2Th 1:1	*2316*
Grace to you and peace from **G** the	2Th 1:2	*2316*
to give thanks to **G** for you,	2Th 1:3	*2316*
among the churches of **G** for your	2Th 1:4	*2316*
worthy of the kingdom of **G**,	2Th 1:5	*2316*
only just for **G** to repay with affliction	2Th 1:6	*2316*
to those who do not know **G** and to	2Th 1:8	*2316*
that our **G** will count you worthy of	2Th 1:11	*2316*
our **G** and *the* Lord Jesus Christ.	2Th 1:12	*2316*
so-called **g** or object of worship,	2Th 2:4	*2316*
takes his seat in the temple of **G**,	2Th 2:4	*2316*
displaying himself as being **G**.	2Th 2:4	*2316*
For this reason **G** will send	2Th 2:11	*2316*
always give thanks to **G** for you,	2Th 2:13	*2316*
because **G** has chosen you from the	2Th 2:13	*2316*
Christ Himself and **G** our Father,	2Th 2:16	*2316*
direct your hearts into the love of **G**	2Th 3:5	*2316*
the commandment of **G** our Savior,	1Tm 1:1	*2316*
mercy *and* peace from **G** the Father	1Tm 1:2	*2316*
furthering the administration of **G**	1Tm 1:4	*2316*
glorious gospel of the blessed **G**,	1Tm 1:11	*2316*
immortal, invisible, the only **G**,	1Tm 1:17	*2316*
in the sight of **G** our Savior,	1Tm 2:3	*2316*
For there is one **G**,	1Tm 2:5	*2316*
mediator also between **G** and men,	1Tm 2:5	*2316*
he take care of the church of **G**?),	1Tm 3:5	*2316*
himself in the household of **G**,	1Tm 3:15	*2316*
is the church of the living **G**,	1Tm 3:15	*2316*
which **G** has created to be	1Tm 4:3	*2316*
everything created by **G** is good,	1Tm 4:4	*2316*
means of the word of **G** and prayer.	1Tm 4:5	*2316*
fixed our hope on the living **G**,	1Tm 4:10	*2316*
is acceptable in the sight of **G**.	1Tm 5:4	*2316*
alone, has fixed her hope on **G**	1Tm 5:5	*2316*
charge you in the presence of **G** and	1Tm 5:21	*2316*
so that the name of **G** and *our*	1Tm 6:1	*2316*
from these things, you man of **G**,	1Tm 6:11	*2316*
I charge you in the presence of **G**,	1Tm 6:13	*2316*
uncertainty of riches, but on **G**,	1Tm 6:17	*2316*
of Christ Jesus by the will of **G**,	2Tm 1:1	*2316*
mercy *and* peace from **G** the Father	2Tm 1:2	*2316*
I thank **G**, whom I serve with a	2Tm 1:3	*2316*
kindle afresh the gift of **G** which is in	2Tm 1:6	*2316*
For **G** has not given us a spirit of	2Tm 1:7	*2316*
according to the power of **G**,	2Tm 1:8	*2316*
the word of **G** is not imprisoned.	2Tm 2:9	*2316*
charge *them* in the presence of **G**	2Tm 2:14	*2316*
to present yourself approved to **G**	2Tm 2:15	*2316*
the firm foundation of **G** stands,	2Tm 2:19	*2316*
if perhaps **G** may grant them	2Tm 2:25	*2316*
pleasure rather than lovers of **G**,	2Tm 3:4	*5377*
All Scripture is inspired by **G** and	2Tm 3:16	*2315*
that the man of **G** may be adequate,	2Tm 3:17	*2316*
presence of **G** and of Christ Jesus,	2Tm 4:1	*2316*

Paul, a bond-servant of **G** and Ti 1:1 2316
for the faith of those chosen of **G** Ti 1:1 2316
the hope of eternal life, which **G**, Ti 1:2 2316
the commandment of **G** our Savior, Ti 1:3 2316
Grace and peace from **G** the Father Ti 1:4 2316
They profess to know **G**, Ti 1:16 2316
word of **G** will not be dishonored. Ti 2:5 2316
of **G** our Savior in every respect. Ti 2:10 2316
For the grace of **G** has appeared, Ti 2:11 2316
glory of our great **G** and Savior, Ti 2:13 2316
But when the kindness of **G** our Ti 3:4 2316
those who have believed **G** will be Ti 3:8 2316
Grace to you and peace from **G** our Phm 1:3 2316
I thank my **G** always, making Phm 1:4 2316
G, after He spoke long ago to the Heb 1:1 2316
ALL THE ANGELS OF **G** WORSHIP HIM." Heb 1:6 2316
"YOUR THRONE, O **G**, IS FOREVER AND Heb 1:8 2316
THEREFORE **G**, YOUR GOD, HAS Heb 1:9 2316
THEREFORE GOD, YOUR **G**, Heb 1:9 2316
G also testifying with them, Heb 2:4 2316
that by the grace of **G** He might Heb 2:9 2316
CHILDREN WHOM **G** HAS GIVEN ME." Heb 2:13 2316
priest in things pertaining to **G**, Heb 2:17 2316
the builder of all things is **G**. Heb 3:4 2316
that falls away from the living **G**. Heb 3:12 2316
"AND **G** RESTED ON THE SEVENTH DAY Heb 4:4 2316
Sabbath rest for the people of **G**. Heb 4:9 2316
from his works, as **G** did from His. Heb 4:10 2316
For the word of **G** is living and Heb 4:12 2316
the heavens, Jesus the Son of **G**, Heb 4:14 2316
of men in things pertaining to **G**, Heb 5:1 2316
it when he is called by **G**, Heb 5:4 2316
being designated by **G** as a high Heb 5:10 2316
principles of the oracles of **G**, Heb 5:12 2316
dead works and of faith toward **G**, Heb 6:1 2316
this we will do, if **G** permits. Heb 6:3 2316
and have tasted the good word of **G** Heb 6:5 2316
to themselves the Son of **G** and Heb 6:6 2316
receives a blessing from **G**; Heb 6:7 2316
For **G** is not unjust so as to Heb 6:10 2316
G made the promise to Abraham, Heb 6:13 2316
In the same way **G**, desiring even Heb 6:17 2316
it is impossible for **G** to lie, Heb 6:18 2316
Salem, priest of the Most High **G**, Heb 7:1 2316
life, but made like the Son of **G**, Heb 7:3 2316
through which we draw near to **G**. Heb 7:19 2316
who draw near to **G** through Him, Heb 7:25 2316
just as Moses was warned *by* **G** Heb 8:5
AND I WILL BE THEIR **G**, Heb 8:10 2316
Himself without blemish to **G**, Heb 9:14 2316
dead works to serve the living **G**? Heb 9:14 2316
COVENANT WHICH **G** COMMANDED Heb 9:20 2316
in the presence of **G** for us; Heb 9:24 2316
TO DO YOUR WILL, O **G**.' " Heb 10:7 2316
SAT DOWN AT THE RIGHT HAND OF **G** Heb 10:12 2316
great priest over the house of **G**, Heb 10:21 2316
trampled under foot the Son of **G**, Heb 10:29 2316
into the hands of the living **G**. Heb 10:31 2316
when you have done the will of **G**, Heb 10:36 2316
were prepared by the word of **G**, Heb 11:3 2316
to **G** a better sacrifice than Cain, Heb 11:4 2316
G testifying about his gifts, Heb 11:4 2316
NOT FOUND BECAUSE **G** TOOK HIM UP; Heb 11:5 2316
taken up he was pleasing to **G**. Heb 11:5 2316
to **G** must believe that He is and Heb 11:6 2316
By faith Noah, being warned *by* **G** Heb 11:7
whose architect and builder is **G**. Heb 11:10 2316
Therefore **G** is not ashamed to be Heb 11:16 2316
not ashamed to be called their **G**; Heb 11:16 2316
He considered that **G** is able to Heb 11:19 2316
ill-treatment with the people of **G** than Heb 11:25 2316
G had provided something better Heb 11:40 2316
the right hand of the throne of **G**. Heb 12:2 2316
G deals with you as with sons; Heb 12:7 2316
one comes short of the grace of **G**; Heb 12:15 2316
and to the city of the living **G**, Heb 12:22 2316
to **G**, the Judge of all, and to the Heb 12:23 2316
by which we may offer to **G** an Heb 12:28 2316
for our **G** is a consuming fire. Heb 12:29 2316
and adulterers **G** will judge. Heb 13:4 2316
who spoke the word of **G** to you; Heb 13:7 2316
offer up a sacrifice of praise to **G**, Heb 13:15 2316
with such sacrifices **G** is pleased. Heb 13:16 2316
Now the **G** of peace, who brought up Heb 13:20 2316
of **G** and of the Lord Jesus Christ, Jas 1:1 2316
lacks wisdom, let him ask of **G**, Jas 1:5 2316
"I am being tempted by **G**"; Jas 1:13 2316
for **G** cannot be tempted by evil, Jas 1:13 2316
achieve the righteousness of **G**. Jas 1:20 2316
in the sight of *our* **G** and Father is Jas 1:27 2316
did not **G** choose the poor of this Jas 2:5 2316
You believe that **G** is one. Jas 2:19 2316
"AND ABRAHAM BELIEVED **G**, Jas 2:23 2316
and he was called the friend of **G**. Jas 2:23 2316
been made in the likeness of **G**; Jas 3:9 2316
the world is hostility toward **G**? Jas 4:4 2316
world makes himself an enemy of **G**. Jas 4:4 2316
"**G** IS OPPOSED TO THE PROUD, BUT Jas 4:6 2316
Submit therefore to **G**. Jas 4:7 2316
to **G** and He will draw near to you. Jas 4:8 2316
the foreknowledge of **G** the Father, 1Pe 1:2 2316
Blessed be the **G** and Father of our 1Pe 1:3 2316
protected by the power of **G** through 1Pe 1:5 2316
through Him are believers in **G**, 1Pe 1:21 2316
that your faith and hope are in **G**. 1Pe 1:21 2316
the living and enduring word of **G**. 1Pe 1:23 2316
and precious in the sight of **G**, 1Pe 2:4 2316
to **G** through Jesus Christ. 1Pe 2:5 2316
but now you are THE PEOPLE OF **G**; 1Pe 2:10 2316
G in the day of visitation. 1Pe 2:12 2316
For such is the will of **G** that by 1Pe 2:15 2316
but *use it* as bondslaves of **G**. 1Pe 2:16 2316
love the brotherhood, fear **G**, 1Pe 2:17 2316
if for the sake of conscience toward **G** 1Pe 2:19 2316
it, this *finds* favor with **G**. 1Pe 2:20 2316
is precious in the sight of **G**. 1Pe 3:4 2316
holy women also, who hoped in **G**, 1Pe 3:5 2316
is better, if **G** should will it so, 1Pe 3:17 2316
so that He might bring us to **G**, 1Pe 3:18 2316
the patience of **G** kept waiting in 1Pe 3:20 2316
but an appeal to **G** for a good 1Pe 3:21 2316
who is at the right hand of **G**, 1Pe 3:22 2316
of men, but for the will of **G**. 1Pe 4:2 2316
spirit according to *the will of* **G**. 1Pe 4:6 2316
of the manifold grace of **G**. 1Pe 4:10 2316
who is speaking the utterances of **G**; 1Pe 4:11 2316
by the strength which **G** supplies; 1Pe 4:11 2316
so that in all things **G** may be 1Pe 4:11 2316
of glory and of **G** rests on you. 1Pe 4:14 2316
is to glorify **G** in this name. 1Pe 4:16 2316
to begin with the household of **G**; 1Pe 4:17 2316
who do not obey the gospel of **G**? 1Pe 4:17 2316
who suffer according to the will of **G** 1Pe 4:19 2316
shepherd the flock of **G** among you, 1Pe 5:2 2316
according to *the will of* **G**; 1Pe 5:2 2316
for **G** IS OPPOSED TO THE PROUD, 1Pe 5:5 2316
under the mighty hand of **G**, 1Pe 5:6 2316
little while, the **G** of all grace, 1Pe 5:10 2316
that this is the true grace of **G**. 1Pe 5:12 2316
righteousness of our **G** and Savior, 2Pe 1:1 2316
of **G** and of Jesus our Lord; 2Pe 1:2 2316
honor and glory from **G** the Father, 2Pe 1:17 2316
by the Holy Spirit spoke from **G**. 2Pe 1:21 2316
For if **G** did not spare angels when 2Pe 2:4 2316
by the word of **G** *the* heavens existed 2Pe 3:5 2316
the coming of the day of **G**, 2Pe 3:12 2316
announce to you, that **G** is Light, 1Jn 1:5 2316
of **G** has truly been perfected. 1Jn 2:5 2316
and the word of **G** abides in you, 1Jn 2:14 2316
does the will of **G** lives forever. 1Jn 2:17 2316
we would be called children of **G**; 1Jn 3:1 2316
Beloved, now we are children of **G**, 1Jn 3:2 2316
Son of **G** appeared for this purpose, 1Jn 3:8 2316
No one who is born of **G** practices 1Jn 3:9 2316
cannot sin, because he is born of **G**. 1Jn 3:9 2316
By this the children of **G** and the 1Jn 3:10 2316
not practice righteousness is not of **G**, 1Jn 3:10 2316
does the love of **G** abide in him? 1Jn 3:17 2316
for **G** is greater than our heart and 1Jn 3:20 2316
us, we have confidence before **G**; 1Jn 3:21 2316
to see whether they are from **G**, 1Jn 4:1 2316
By this you know the Spirit of **G**: 1Jn 4:2 2316
has come in the flesh is from **G**; 1Jn 4:2 2316
not confess Jesus is not from **G**; 1Jn 4:3 2316
You are from **G**, little children, 1Jn 4:4 2316
We are from **G**; he who knows God 1Jn 4:6 2316
he who knows **G** listens to us; 1Jn 4:6 2316
not from **G** does not listen to us. 1Jn 4:6 2316
love one another, for love is from **G**; 1Jn 4:7 2316
everyone who loves is born of **G** 1Jn 4:7 2316
loves is born of God and knows **G**. 1Jn 4:7 2316
who does not love does not know **G**, 1Jn 4:8 2316
does not know God, for **G** is love. 1Jn 4:8 2316
love of **G** was manifested in us, 1Jn 4:9 2316
that **G** has sent His only begotten 1Jn 4:9 2316
this is love, not that we loved **G**, 1Jn 4:10 2316
Beloved, if **G** so loved us, we also 1Jn 4:11 2316
No one has seen **G** at any time; 1Jn 4:12 2316
love one another, **G** abides in us, 1Jn 4:12 2316
that Jesus is the Son of **G**, 1Jn 4:15 2316
the Son of God, **G** abides in him, 1Jn 4:15 2316
God abides in him, and he in **G**. 1Jn 4:15 2316
the love which **G** has for us. 1Jn 4:16 2316
G is love, and the one who abides 1Jn 4:16 2316
who abides in love abides in **G**, 1Jn 4:16 2316
in God, and **G** abides in him. 1Jn 4:16 2316
If someone says, "I love **G**," 1Jn 4:20 2316
cannot love **G** whom he has not 1Jn 4:20 2316
who loves **G** should love his brother 1Jn 4:21 2316
Jesus is the Christ is born of **G**, 1Jn 5:1 2316
that we love the children of **G**, 1Jn 5:2 2316
G and observe His commandments. 1Jn 5:2 2316
For this is the love of **G**, 1Jn 5:3 2316
is born of **G** overcomes the world; 1Jn 5:4 2316
that Jesus is the Son of **G**? 1Jn 5:5 2316
men, the testimony of **G** is greater; 1Jn 5:9 2316
for the testimony of **G** is this, 1Jn 5:9 2316
who believes in the Son of **G** has 1Jn 5:10 2316
not believe **G** has made Him a liar, 1Jn 5:10 2316
G has given concerning His Son. 1Jn 5:10 2316
that **G** has given us eternal life, 1Jn 5:11 2316
Son of **G** does not have the life. 1Jn 5:12 2316
in the name of the Son of **G**, 1Jn 5:13 2316
he shall ask and **G** will for him 1Jn 5:16 2316
that no one who is born of **G** sins; 1Jn 5:18 2316
but He who was born of **G** keeps him 1Jn 5:18 2316
We know that we are of **G**, 1Jn 5:19 2316
know that the Son of **G** has come, 1Jn 5:20 2316
is the true **G** and eternal life. 1Jn 5:20 2316
from **G** the Father and from Jesus 2Jn 1:3 2316
of Christ, does not have **G**; 2Jn 1:9 2316
their way in a manner worthy of **G**. 3Jn 1:6 2316
The one who does good is of **G**; 3Jn 1:11 2316
one who does evil has not seen **G**. 3Jn 1:11 2316
called, beloved in **G** the Father, Jude 1:1 2316
who turn the grace of our **G** into Jude 1:4 2316
keep yourselves in the love of **G**, Jude 1:21 2316
to the only **G** our Savior, through Jude 1:25 2316
which **G** gave Him to show to His Rv 1:1 2316
who testified to the word of **G** Rv 1:2 2316
priests to His **G** and Father Rv 1:6 2316
and the Omega," says the Lord **G**, Rv 1:8 2316
the word of **G** and the testimony of Rv 1:9 2316
which is in the Paradise of **G**.' Rv 2:7 2316
The Son of **G**, who has eyes like a Rv 2:18 2316
He who has the seven Spirits of **G** and Rv 3:1 2316
completed in the sight of My **G**. Rv 3:2 2316
a pillar in the temple of My **G**, Rv 3:12 2316
write on him the name of My **G**, Rv 3:12 2316
and the name of the city of My **G**, Rv 3:12 2316
down out of heaven from My **G**, Rv 3:12 2316
Beginning of the creation of **G**, Rv 3:14 2316
which are the seven Spirits of **G**; Rv 4:5 2316
"HOLY, HOLY, HOLY *is* THE LORD **G**, Rv 4:8 2316
are You, our Lord and our **G**, Rv 4:11 2316
which are the seven Spirits of **G**, Rv 5:6 2316
and purchased for **G** with Your Rv 5:9 2316
be a kingdom and priests to our **G**; Rv 5:10 2316
slain because of the word of **G**, Rv 6:9 2316
having the seal of the living **G**; Rv 7:2 2316
of our **G** on their foreheads." Rv 7:3 2316
to our **G** who sits on the throne, Rv 7:10 2316
before the throne and worshiped **G**, Rv 7:11 2316
be to our **G** forever and ever. Rv 7:12 2316
they are before the throne of **G**; Rv 7:15 2316
and **G** will wipe every tear from Rv 7:17 2316
seven angels who stand before **G**, Rv 8:2 2316
before **G** out of the angel's hand. Rv 8:4 2316
the seal of **G** on their foreheads. Rv 9:4 2316
golden altar which is before **G**, Rv 9:13 2316
then the mystery of **G** is finished, Rv 10:7 2316
"Get up and measure the temple of **G** Rv 11:1 2316
the breath of life from **G** came into Rv 11:11 2316
and gave glory to the **G** of heaven. Rv 11:13 2316
who sit on their thrones before **G**, Rv 11:16 2316
fell on their faces and worshiped **G**, Rv 11:16 2316
"We give You thanks, O Lord **G**, Rv 11:17 2316
temple of **G** which is in heaven was Rv 11:19 2316
caught up to **G** and to His throne. Rv 12:5 2316
she had a place prepared by **G**, Rv 12:6 2316
and the kingdom of our **G** and the Rv 12:10 2316
them before our **G** day and night. Rv 12:10 2316
who keep the commandments of **G** and Rv 12:17 2316
mouth in blasphemies against **G**, Rv 13:6 2316
first fruits to **G** and to the Lamb. Rv 14:4 2316
"Fear **G**, and give Him glory, Rv 14:7 2316
drink of the wine of the wrath of **G**, Rv 14:10 2316
of **G** and their faith in Jesus. Rv 14:12 2316
wine press of the wrath of **G**. Rv 14:19 2316
them the wrath of **G** is finished. Rv 15:1 2316
sea of glass, holding harps of **G**. Rv 15:2 2316
of **G**, and the song of the Lamb, Rv 15:3 2316
marvelous are Your works, O Lord **G**, Rv 15:3 2316
bowls full of the wrath of **G**, Rv 15:7 2316
the glory of **G** and from His power; Rv 15:8 2316
the seven bowls of the wrath of **G**." Rv 16:1 2316
"Yes, O Lord **G**, the Almighty, Rv 16:7 2316
and they blasphemed the name of **G** Rv 16:9 2316
they blasphemed the **G** of heaven Rv 16:11 2316
for the war of the great day of **G**, Rv 16:14 2316
the great was remembered before **G**, Rv 16:19 2316
and men blasphemed **G** because of Rv 16:21 2316
"For **G** has put it in their hearts Rv 17:17 2316
words of **G** will be fulfilled. Rv 17:17 2316
G has remembered her iniquities. Rv 18:5 2316
Lord **G** who judges her is strong. Rv 18:8 2316
because **G** has pronounced judgment Rv 18:20 2316
glory and power belong to our **G**; Rv 19:1 2316
G who sits on the throne saying, Rv 19:4 2316
"Give praise to our **G**, Rv 19:5 2316
Lord our **G**, the Almighty, reigns. Rv 19:6 2316
"These are true words of **G**." Rv 19:9 2316
the testimony of Jesus; worship **G**. Rv 19:10 2316
His name is called The Word of **G**. Rv 19:13 2316
press of the fierce wrath of **G**, Rv 19:15 2316
for the great supper of **G**, Rv 19:17 2316
and because of the word of **G**, Rv 20:4 2316
but they will be priests of **G** and Rv 20:6 2316
coming down out of heaven from **G**, Rv 21:2 2316
the tabernacle of **G** is among men, Rv 21:3 2316
and **G** Himself will be among them, Rv 21:3 2316
be his **G** and he will be My son. Rv 21:7 2316
coming down out of heaven from **G**, Rv 21:10 2316
having the glory of **G**. Rv 21:11 2316
no temple in it, for the Lord **G** the Rv 21:22 2316
the glory of **G** has illumined it, Rv 21:23 2316
the throne of **G** and of the Lamb, Rv 22:1 2316
and the throne of **G** and of the Rv 22:3 2316
the Lord **G** will illumine them; Rv 22:5 2316
the **G** of the spirits of the prophets, Rv 22:6 2316
the words of this book. Worship **G**." Rv 22:9 2316
G will add to him the plagues Rv 22:18 2316
G will take away his part from Rv 22:19 2316

GODDESS

Ashtoreth the **g** of the Sidonians 1Ki 11:5 430
Ashtoreth the **g** of the Sidonians, 1Ki 11:33 430
the temple of the great **g** Artemis be Ac 19:27 2299
temples nor blasphemers of our **g**. Ac 19:37 2299

GOD-FEARING

but if anyone is **G** and Jn 9:31 2318
a righteous and **G** man well spoken Ac 10:22 2316
many of the Jews and of the **G** Ac 13:43 4576
a large number of the **G** Greeks Ac 17:4 4576
with the Jews and the **G** *Gentiles*, Ac 17:17 4576

GODLESS

And the hope of the **g** will perish, Jb 8:13 2611

For a **g** man may not come before **Jb 13:16** 2611
the company of the **g** is barren, **Jb 15:34** 2611
stir up himself against the **g**. **Jb 17:8** 2611
And the joy of the **g** momentary? **Jb 20:5** 2611
hope of the **g** when he is cut off, **Jb 27:8** 2611
So that **g** men would not rule Nor **Jb 34:30** 2611
"But the **g** in heart lay up anger; **Jb 36:13** 2611
Like **g** jesters at a feast, They **Ps 35:16** 2611
the **g** man destroys his neighbor, **Pr 11:9** 2611
one of them is **g** and an evildoer, **Is 9:17** 2611
I send it against a **g** nation And **Is 10:6** 2611
Trembling has seized the **g**. **Is 33:14** 2611
of **g** men and put *Him* to death. **Ac 2:23** *459*
no immoral or **g** person like Esau, **Heb 12:16** *952*
OF THE **G** MAN AND THE SINNER? **1Pe 4:18** *765*

GODLESSNESS

By smooth *words* he will turn to **g** **Da 11:32** 2610

GODLINESS

quiet life in all **g** and dignity. **1Tm 2:2** *2150*
for women making a claim to **g**. **1Tm 2:10** *2317*
great is the mystery of **g**: **1Tm 3:16** *2150*
yourself for the purpose of **g**; **1Tm 4:7** *2150*
g is profitable for all things, **1Tm 4:8** *2150*
with the doctrine conforming to **g**, **1Tm 6:3** *2150*
suppose that **g** is a means of gain. **1Tm 6:5** *2150*
But **g** *actually* is a means of great **1Tm 6:6** *2150*
and pursue righteousness, **g**, **1Tm 6:11** *2150*
holding to a form of **g**, **2Tm 3:5** *2150*
the truth which is according to **g**, **Ti 1:1** *2150*
pertaining to life and **g**, **2Pe 1:3** *2150*
and in *your* perseverance, **g**, **2Pe 1:6** *2150*
and in *your* **g**, brotherly kindness, **2Pe 1:7** *2150*
you to be in holy conduct and **g**, **2Pe 3:11** *2150*

GODLY

and Your Urim *belong* to Your **g** man, **Dt 33:8** 2623
"He keeps the feet of His **g** ones, **1Sa 2:9** 2623
g ones rejoice in what is good. **2Ch 6:41** 2623
set apart the **g** man for Himself; **Ps 4:3** 2623
LORD, for the **g** man ceases to be, **Ps 12:1** 2623
praise to the LORD, you His **g** ones, **Ps 30:4** 2623
love the LORD, all you His **g** ones! **Ps 31:23** 2623
let everyone who is **g** pray to You **Ps 32:6** 2623
And does not forsake His **g** ones; **Ps 37:28** 2623
"Gather My **g** ones to Me, Those **Ps 50:5** 2623
in the presence of Your **g** ones. **Ps 52:9** 2623
The flesh of Your **g** ones to the **Ps 79:2** 2623
peace to His people, to His **g** ones; **Ps 85:8** 2623
Preserve my soul, for I am a **g** man; **Ps 86:2** 2623
spoke in vision to Your **g** ones, **Ps 89:19** 2623
preserves the souls of His **g** ones; **Ps 97:10** 2623
LORD Is the death of His **g** ones. **Ps 116:15** 2623
And let Your **g** ones sing for joy. **Ps 132:9** 2623
g ones will sing aloud for joy. **Ps 132:16** 2623
And Your **g** ones shall bless You. **Ps 145:10** 2623
people, Praise for all His **g** ones; **Ps 148:14** 2623
in the congregation of the **g** ones. **Ps 149:1** 2623
Let the **g** ones exult in glory; **Ps 149:5** 2623
is an honor for all His **g** ones. **Ps 149:9** 2623
preserves the way of His **g** ones. **Pr 2:8** 2623
The **g** person has perished from the **Mi 7:2** 2623
he was seeking a **g** offspring? **Mal 2:15** 430
that in holiness and **g** sincerity, **2Co 1:12** *2316*
this very thing, this **g** sorrow, **2Co 7:11** *2596, 2316*
jealous for you with a **g** jealousy; **2Co 11:2** *2316*
all who desire to live **g** in Christ **2Tm 3:12** *2153*
and **g** in the present age, **Ti 2:12** *2153*
to rescue the **g** from temptation, **2Pe 2:9** *2152*

GOD'S

up as a pillar, will be **G** house, **Gn 28:22** 430
"This is **G** camp." **Gn 32:2** 430
be afraid, for am I in **G** place? **Gn 50:19** 430
been enough of **G** thunder and hail; **Ex 9:28** 430
The tablets were **G** work, **Ex 32:16** 430
and the writing was **G** writing **Ex 32:16** 430
fear man, for the judgment is **G**. **Dt 1:17** 430
for **G** tent of meeting was there, **2Ch 1:3** 430
for the battle is not yours but **G**. **2Ch 20:15** 430
and an oath to walk in **G** law, **Ne 10:29** 430
given through Moses, **G** servant, **Ne 10:29** 430
'My righteousness is more than **G**'? **Jb 35:2** 410
yet more to be said in **G** behalf. **Jb 36:2** 433
to one who is good in **G** sight. **Ec 2:26** 430
in **G** garden could not match it; **Ezk 31:8** 430
No tree in **G** garden could compare **Ezk 31:8** 430
now will you not entreat **G** favor, **Mal 1:9** 410
"You are certainly **G** Son!" **Mt 14:33** *2316*
setting your mind on **G** interests, **Mt 16:23** *2316*
to God the things that are **G**." **Mt 22:21** *2316*
setting your mind on **G** interests, **Mk 8:33** *2316*
to God the things that are **G**." **Mk 12:17** *2316*
this, they acknowledged **G** justice, **Lk 7:29** *2316*
rejected **G** purpose for themselves, **Lk 7:30** *2316*
to God the things that are **G**." **Lk 20:25** *2316*
"*David* found favor in **G** sight, **Ac 7:46** *2316*
I that I could stand in **G** way?" **Ac 11:17** *2316*
"Do you revile **G** high priest?" **Ac 23:4** *2316*
bring a charge against **G** elect? **Ro 8:33** *2316*
so that **G** purpose according **Ro 9:11** *2316*
not knowing about **G** righteousness and **Ro 10:3** *2316*
according to **G** gracious choice. **Ro 11:5**
severity, but to you, **G** kindness, **Ro 11:22** *2316*
from the standpoint of **G** choice **Ro 11:28**
we speak **G** wisdom in a mystery, **1Co 2:7** *2316*
For we are **G** fellow workers; **1Co 3:9** *2316*
you are **G** field, God's building. **1Co 3:9** *2316*
you are God's field, **G** building. **1Co 3:9** *2316*
the redemption of **G** *own* possession, **Eph 1:14**
saints, and are of **G** household, **Eph 2:19** *2316*
the stewardship of **G** grace which was **Eph 3:2** *2316*
according to the gift of **G** grace **Eph 3:7** *2316*
in a true knowledge of **G** mystery, **Col 2:2** *2316*
our brother and **G** fellow worker in **1Th 3:2** *2316*
is **G** will for you in Christ Jesus. **1Th 5:18** *2316*
This is a plain indication of **G** **2Th 1:5** *2316*
be above reproach as **G** steward, **Ti 1:7** *2316*
A PEOPLE FOR **G** OWN POSSESSION, **1Pe 2:9**

GODS

but why did you steal my **g**?" **Gn 31:30** 430
you find your **g** shall not live; **Gn 31:32** 430
"Put away the foreign **g** which are **Gn 35:2** 430
all the foreign **g** which they had and **Gn 35:4** 430
and against all the **g** of Egypt I **Ex 12:12** 430
"Who is like You among the **g**, **Ex 15:11** 410
LORD is greater than all the **g**; **Ex 18:11** 430
shall have no other **g** before Me. **Ex 20:3** 430
'You shall not make *other* **g** **Ex 20:23**
g of silver or gods of gold, you **Ex 20:23** 430
gods of silver or **g** of gold, **Ex 20:23** 430
not mention the name of other **g**, **Ex 23:13** 430
"You shall not worship their **g**, **Ex 23:24** 430
with them or with their **g**. **Ex 23:32** 430
for *if* you serve their **g**, **Ex 23:33** 430
they would play the harlot with their **g** **Ex 34:15** 430
gods and sacrifice to their **g**, **Ex 34:15** 430
play the harlot with their **g** and **Ex 34:16** 430
to play the harlot with their **g**. **Ex 34:16** 430
make for yourself no molten **g**. **Ex 34:17** 430
or make for yourselves molten **g**; **Lv 19:4** 430
to the sacrifices of their **g**, **Nu 25:2** 430
ate and bowed down to their **g**. **Nu 25:2** 430
executed judgments on their **g**. **Nu 33:4** 430
"There you will serve **g**, **Dt 4:28** 430
shall have no other **g** before Me. **Dt 5:7** 430
"You shall not follow other **g**, **Dt 6:14** 430
any of the **g** of the peoples who **Dt 6:14** 430
following Me to serve other **g**; **Dt 7:4** 430
nor shall you serve their **g**, **Dt 7:16** 430
their **g** you are to burn with fire; **Dt 7:25** 430
and go after other **g** and serve **Dt 8:19** 430
God of **g** and the Lord of lords, **Dt 10:17** 430
serve other **g** and worship them. **Dt 11:16** 430
other **g** which you have not known. **Dt 11:28** 430
serve their **g**, on the high mountains **Dt 12:2** 430
the engraved images of their **g** and **Dt 12:3** 430
you do not inquire after their **g**, **Dt 12:30** 430
do these nations serve their **g**, **Dt 12:30** 430
hates they have done for their **g**; **Dt 12:31** 430
daughters in the fire to their **g**. **Dt 12:31** 430
'Let us go after other **g** **Dt 13:2** 430
'Let us go and serve other **g**' **Dt 13:6** 430
of the **g** of the peoples who are **Dt 13:7** 430
'Let us go and serve other **g**' **Dt 13:13** 430
served other **g** and worshiped them, **Dt 17:3** 430
speaks in the name of other **g**, **Dt 18:20** 430
which they have done for their **g**, **Dt 20:18** 430
to go after other **g** to serve them. **Dt 28:14** 430
and there you shall serve other **g**, **Dt 28:36** 430
and there you shall serve other **g**, **Dt 28:64** 430
and serve the **g** of those nations; **Dt 29:18** 430
served other **g** and worshiped them, **Dt 29:26** 430
g whom they have not known and **Dt 29:26** 430
worship other **g** and serve them, **Dt 30:17** 430
with the strange **g** of the land, **Dt 31:16** 430
do, for they will turn to other **g**. **Dt 31:18** 430
turn to other **g** and serve them, **Dt 31:20** 430
made Him jealous with strange **g**; **Dt 32:16**
To **g** whom they have not known, **Dt 32:17** 430
New **g** who came lately, Whom your **Dt 32:17** 430
'Where are their **g**, The rock in **Dt 32:37** 430
or mention the name of their **g**, **Jos 23:7** 430
you, and go and serve other **g** and **Jos 23:16** 430
of Nahor, and they served other **g**. **Jos 24:2** 430
and put away the **g** which your **Jos 24:14** 430
whether the **g** which your fathers **Jos 24:15** 430
or the **g** of the Amorites in whose **Jos 24:15** 430
forsake the LORD to serve other **g**; **Jos 24:16** 430
the LORD and serve foreign **g**, **Jos 24:20** 430
foreign **g** which are in your midst, **Jos 24:23** 430
g will be a snare to you.'" **Jg 2:3** 430
and followed other **g** from *among* **Jg 2:12** 430
gods from *among* the **g** of the peoples **Jg 2:12** 430
they played the harlot after other **g** **Jg 2:17** 430
in following other **g** to serve them **Jg 2:19** 430
to their sons, and served their **g**. **Jg 3:6** 430
"New **g** were chosen; **Jg 5:8** 430
you shall not fear the **g** of the **Jg 6:10** 430
and the Ashtaroth, the **g** of Aram, **Jg 10:6** 430
the gods of Aram, the **g** of Sidon, **Jg 10:6** 430
the gods of Sidon, the **g** of Moab, **Jg 10:6** 430
Moab, the **g** of the sons of Ammon, **Jg 10:6** 430
and the **g** of the Philistines; **Jg 10:6** 430
forsaken Me and served other **g**; **Jg 10:13** 430
to the **g** which you have chosen; **Jg 10:14** 430
the foreign **g** from among them and **Jg 10:16** 430
have taken away my **g** which I made, **Jg 18:24** 430
gone back to her people and her **g**; **Ru 1:15** 430
from the hand of these mighty **g**? **1Sa 4:8** 430
These are the **g** who smote the **1Sa 4:8** 430
ease His hand from you, your **g**, **1Sa 6:5** 430
remove the foreign **g** and the **1Sa 7:3** 430
have forsaken Me and served other **g** **1Sa 8:8** 430
Philistine cursed David by his **g**. **1Sa 17:43** 430
'Go, serve other **g**.' **1Sa 26:19** 430
Egypt, *from* nations and their **g**? **2Sa 7:23** 430
serve other **g** and worship them, **1Ki 9:6** 430
and adopted other **g** and worshiped **1Ki 9:9** 430
turn your heart away after their **g**." **1Ki 11:2** 430
turned his heart away after other **g**; **1Ki 11:4** 430
incense and sacrificed to their **g**. **1Ki 11:8** 430
he should not go after other **g**; **1Ki 11:10** 430
behold your **g**, O Israel, that **1Ki 12:28** 430
gone and made for yourself other **g** **1Ki 14:9** 430
may the **g** do to me and even more, **1Ki 19:2** 430
the **g** do so to me and more also, **1Ki 20:10** 430
"Their **g** are gods of the **1Ki 20:23** 430
"Their gods are **g** of the **1Ki 20:23** 430
nor will he sacrifice to other **g**, **2Ki 5:17** 430
and they had feared other **g** **2Ki 17:7** 430
But every nation still made **g** of **2Ki 17:29** 430
Anammelech the **g** of Sepharvaim. **2Ki 17:31** 430
and served their own **g** according to **2Ki 17:33** 430
"You shall not fear other **g**, **2Ki 17:35** 430
and you shall not fear other **g**. **2Ki 17:37** 430
nor shall you fear other **g**. **2Ki 17:38** 430
'Has any one of the **g** of **2Ki 18:33** 430
are the **g** of Hamath and Arpad? **2Ki 18:34** 430
Where are the **g** of Sepharvaim, **2Ki 18:34** 430
'Who among all the **g** of the lands **2Ki 18:35** 430
'Did the **g** of those nations which **2Ki 19:12** 430
have cast their **g** into the fire, **2Ki 19:18** 430
not **g** but the work of men's hands, **2Ki 19:18** 430
have burned incense to other **g** **2Ki 22:17** 430
the **g** of the peoples of the land, **1Ch 5:25** 430
put his armor in the house of their **g** **1Ch 10:10** 430
They abandoned their **g** there; **1Ch 14:12** 430
also is to be feared above all **g**. **1Ch 16:25** 430
the **g** of the peoples are idols, **1Ch 16:26** 430
greater is our God than all the **g**. **2Ch 2:5** 430
serve other **g** and worship them, **2Ch 7:19** 430
and they adopted other **g** and **2Ch 7:22** 430
which Jeroboam made for **g** for you. **2Ch 13:8** 430
become a priest of *what are* no **g**. **2Ch 13:9** 430
brought the **g** of the sons of Seir, **2Ch 25:14** 430
of Seir, set them up as his **g**, **2Ch 25:14** 430
"Why have you sought the **g** of the **2Ch 25:15** 430
they had sought the **g** of Edom. **2Ch 25:20** 430
For he sacrificed to the **g** of **2Ch 28:23** 430
"Because the **g** of the kings of **2Ch 28:23** 430
places to burn incense to other **g**, **2Ch 28:25** 430
Were the **g** of the nations of the **2Ch 32:13** 430
'Who *was there* among all the **g** of **2Ch 32:14** 430
'As the **g** of the nations of the **2Ch 32:17** 430
the **g** of the peoples of the earth, **2Ch 32:19** 430
He also removed the foreign **g** and **2Ch 33:15** 430
have burned incense to other **g**, **2Ch 34:25** 430
and put in the house of his **g**; **Ezr 1:7** 430
indeed speak righteousness, O **g**? **Ps 58:1** 410
"You are **g**, And all of you are **Ps 82:6** 430
is no one like You among the **g**, **Ps 86:8** 430
God And a great King above all **g**, **Ps 95:3** 430
He is to be feared above all **g**. **Ps 96:4** 430
the **g** of the peoples are idols, **Ps 96:5** 430
Worship Him, all you **g**. **Ps 97:7** 430
You are exalted far above all **g**. **Ps 97:9** 430
And that our Lord is above all **g**. **Ps 135:5** 430
Give thanks to the God of **g**, **Ps 136:2** 430
sing praises to You before the **g**. **Ps 138:1** 430
g are shattered on the ground." **Is 21:9** 430
Has any one of the **g** of the **Is 36:18** 430
are the **g** of Hamath and Arpad? **Is 36:19** 430
Where are the **g** of Sepharvaim? **Is 36:19** 430
'Who among all the **g** of these **Is 36:20** 430
'Did the **g** of those nations which **Is 37:12** 430
have cast their **g** into the fire, **Is 37:19** 430
not **g** but the work of men's hands, **Is 37:19** 430
That we may know that you are **g**; **Is 41:23** 430
say to molten images, "You are our **g** **Is 42:17** 430
offered sacrifices to other **g**, **Jer 1:16** 430
"Has a nation changed **g** When **Jer 2:11** 430
gods When they were not **g**? **Jer 2:11** 430
g Which you made for yourself? **Jer 2:28** 430
number of your cities Are your **g**, **Jer 2:28** 430
And sworn by those who are not **g**. **Jer 5:7** 430
and served foreign **g** in your land, **Jer 5:19** 430
after other **g** to your own ruin, **Jer 7:6** 430
other **g** that you have not known, **Jer 7:9** 430
to other **g** in order to spite Me. **Jer 7:18** 430
"The **g** that did not make the **Jer 10:11** 426
gone after other **g** to serve them; **Jer 11:10** 430
the **g** to whom they burn incense, **Jer 11:12** 430
your **g** are as many as your cities, **Jer 11:13** 430
have gone after other **g** to serve them **Jer 13:10** 430
'and have followed other **g** and **Jer 16:11** 430
will serve other **g** day and night, **Jer 16:13** 430
Can man make **g** for himself? **Jer 16:20** 430
Yet they are not **g**! **Jer 16:20** 430
They burn incense to worthless **g** **Jer 18:15**
have burned sacrifices in it to other **g** **Jer 19:4** 430
drink offerings to other **g**."'" **Jer 19:13** 430
to other **g** and served them.'" **Jer 22:9** 430
and do not go after other **g** to **Jer 25:6** 430
to other **g** to provoke Me to anger. **Jer 32:29** 430
go after other **g** to worship them. **Jer 35:15** 430
to the temples of the **g** of Egypt, **Jer 43:12** 430
and the temples of the **g** of Egypt **Jer 43:13** 430
other **g** whom they had not known, **Jer 44:3** 430
not to burn sacrifices to other **g**. **Jer 44:5** 430
to other **g** in the land of Egypt, **Jer 44:8** 430
burning sacrifices to other **g**, **Jer 44:15** 430
along with her **g** and her kings, **Jer 46:25** 430
one who burns incense to his **g**. **Jer 48:35** 430
am a god, I sit in the seat of **g** **Ezk 28:2** 430
declare it to the king except **g**, In **Da 2:11** 426
"Surely your God is a God of **g** **Da 2:47** 426
they do not serve your **g** or **Da 3:12** 426

that you do not serve my g or Da 3:14 426
we are not going to serve your g Da 3:18 426
fourth is like a son of *the* g!" Da 3:25 426
in whom is a spirit of the holy g; Da 4:8 426
I know that a spirit of the holy g is in Da 4:9 426
a spirit of the holy g is in you.' Da 4:18 426
praised the g of gold and silver, Da 5:4 426
in whom is a spirit of the holy g; Da 5:11 426
wisdom of the g were found in him. Da 5:11 426
that a spirit of the g is in you, Da 5:14 426
praised the g of silver and gold, Da 5:23 426
"Also their g with their Da 11:8 430
things against the God of g; Da 11:36 410
show no regard for the g of his fathers Da 11:37 430
though they turn to other g and Hos 3:1 430
g which you made for yourselves. Am 5:26 430
image From the house of your g. Na 1:14 430
starve all the g of the earth; Zph 2:11 430
'I SAID, YOU ARE G'? Jn 10:34 *2316*
"If he called them g, Jn 10:35 *2316*
FOR US G WHO WILL GO BEFORE US; Ac 7:40 *2316*
"The g have become like men and Ac 14:11 *2316*
saying that g made with hands are Ac 19:26
made with hands are no g *at all*. Ac 19:26 *2316*
g whether in heaven or on earth, 1Co 8:5 *2316*
there are many g and many lords, 1Co 8:5 *2316*
to those which by nature are no g. Ga 4:8 *2316*

GOES

of Egypt as one g toward Assyria; Gn 25:18 935
with the present that g before me. Gn 32:20 1980
in mind when it g well with you, Gn 40:14 3190
when he g in before the LORD; Ex 28:30 935
priest g in to look at the mark, Lv 14:36 935
whoever g into the house during Lv 14:46 935
"When he g in to make atonement Lv 16:17 935
'If any man's wife g astray and is Nu 5:12 7847
g astray and defiles herself, Nu 5:29 7847
the person who g astray when he sins Nu 15:28 7683
'But if the manslayer at any time g Nu 35:26 3318
'The LORD your God who g before Dt 1:30 1980
who g before you on *your* way, to Dt 1:33 1980
as when *a man* g into the forest Dt 19:5 935
God is the one who g with you, Dt 20:4 1980
"If any man takes a wife and g in Dt 22:13 935
perform what g out from your lips, Dt 23:23 4161
and she leaves his house and g and Dt 24:2 1980
"When the sun g down you shall Dt 24:13 935
God is the one who g with you. Dt 31:6 1980
is the one who g ahead of you; Dt 31:8 1980
anyone who g out of the doors of Jos 2:19 3318
"My heart g *out* to Jg 5:9
one of which g up to Bethel and Jg 20:31 5927
that g up from Bethel to Shechem, Jg 21:19 5927
if it g up by the way of its own 1Sa 6:9 5927
he g up to the high place to eat, 1Sa 9:13 5927
share is who g down to the battle, 1Sa 30:24 3381
else before the sun g down." 2Sa 3:35 935
when my master g into the house of 2Ki 5:18 935
he g out and when he comes in." 2Ki 11:8 3318
he comes in and when he g out." 2Ch 23:7 3318
So he who g down to Sheol does not Jb 7:9 3381
the light of the wicked g out, Jb 18:5 1846
And his lamp g out above him. Jb 18:6 1846
Who g in company with the workers Jb 34:8 732
that g out from His mouth. Jb 37:2 3318
"Then the beast g into its lair And Jb 37:8 935
He g out to meet the weapons. Jb 39:21 3318
"Out of his nostrils smoke g forth As Jb 41:20 3318
a flame g forth from his mouth. Jb 41:21 3318
When he g outside, he tells it. Ps 41:6 3318
which melts away as it g along, Ps 58:8 1980
him who g on in his guilty deeds. Ps 68:21 1980
Fire g before Him And burns up Ps 97:3 1980
Man g forth to his work And to his Ps 104:23 3318
He who g to and fro weeping, Ps 126:6 1980
who g in to his neighbor's wife; Pr 6:29 935
her As an ox g to the slaughter, Pr 7:22 935
he who ignores reproof g astray. Pr 10:17 8582
When it g well with the righteous, Pr 11:10
He who g about as a talebearer Pr 11:13 1980
But the lamp of the wicked g out. Pr 13:9 1846
Pride g before destruction, Pr 16:18
A rebuke g deeper into one who has Pr 17:10 5181
But humility g before honor. Pr 18:12
But when he g his way, then he Pr 20:14 235
He who g about as a slanderer Pr 20:19 1980
the cup, When it g down smoothly; Pr 23:31 1980
For lack of wood the fire g out, Pr 26:20 3518
g and a generation comes, Ec 1:4 1980
in futility and g into obscurity; Ec 6:4 1980
which g forth from the ruler Ec 10:5 3318
For man g to his eternal home Ec 12:5 1980
"It g *down* smoothly for my SS 7:9 1980
Its wail g as far as Eglaim Is 15:8
So will My word be which g forth Is 55:11 3318
g forth like brightness, Is 62:1 3318
his wife And she g from him Jer 3:1 1980
"Behold, he g up like clouds, And Jer 4:13 5927
Everyone who g out of them will Jer 5:6 3318
In vain the refining g on, Jer 6:29 6884
neighbor g about as a slanderer. Jer 9:4 1980
but he who g out and falls away to Jer 21:9 3318
for the one who g away; Jer 22:10 1980
but he who g out to the Chaldeans Jer 38:2 3318
their heart g after their gain. Ezk 33:31 1980
day that he g into the sanctuary, Ezk 44:27 935
everyone who g astray or is naive; Ezk 45:20 7686
gate shall be shut after he g out. Ezk 46:12 3318
in every place where the river g, Ezk 47:9 935
will live where the river g. Ezk 47:9 935
like the dew which g away early. Hos 6:4 1980
are *like* the light that g forth. Hos 6:5 3318
"The city which g forth a Am 5:3 3318
And the one which g forth a Am 5:3 3318
And a bear meets him, Or g home, Am 5:19 935
"The breaker g up before them; Mi 2:13 5927
So their king g on before them, Mi 2:13 5674a
Before Him g pestilence, And Hab 3:5 1980
and he g, and to another, Mt 8:9 *4198*
the unclean spirit g out of a man, Mt 12:43 *1831*
"Then it g and takes along with Mt 12:45 *4198*
from joy over it he g and sells all Mt 13:44 *5217*
everything that g into the mouth Mt 15:17 *1531*
and he g to bed at night and gets up Mk 4:27 *2518*
the man which can defile him if it g Mk 7:15 *1531*
whatever g into the man from outside Mk 7:18 *1531*
and I say to this one, 'Go!' and he g, Lk 7:8 *4198*
and g to him at midnight and says to Lk 11:5 *4198*
the unclean spirit g out of a man, Lk 11:24 *1831*
"Then it g and takes *along* seven Lk 11:26 *4198*
someone g to them from the dead, Lk 16:30 *4198*
all his own, he g ahead of them, Jn 10:4 *4198*
darkness does not know where he g. Jn 12:35 *5217*
but brother g to law with brother, 1Co 6:6 *2919*
Anyone who g too far and does not 2Jn 1:9 *4254*
for captivity, to captivity he g; Rv 13:10 *5217*
who follow the Lamb wherever He g. Rv 14:4 *5217*
smoke of their torment g up forever Rv 14:11 *305*
seven, and he g to destruction. Rv 17:11 *5217*

GOG

were Shemaiah his son, G his son, 1Ch 5:4 1463
toward G of the land of Magog, Ezk 38:2 1463
"Behold, I am against you, O G, Ezk 38:3 1463
son of man, and say to G, Ezk 38:14 1463
you before their eyes, O G." Ezk 38:16 1463
when G comes against the land of Ezk 38:18 1463
son of man, prophesy against G and Ezk 39:1 1463
"Behold, I am against you, O G, Ezk 39:1 1463
I will give G a burial ground there Ezk 39:11 1463
they will bury G there with all his Ezk 39:11 1463
corners of the earth, G and Magog, Rv 20:8 *1136*

GOIIM

king of Elam, and Tidal king of G, Gn 14:1 1472b
Tidal king of G and Amraphel king Gn 14:9 1472b
the king of G in Gilgal, one; Jos 12:23 1471

GOING

Now when the sun was g down, Gn 15:12 935
come from and where are you g?" Gn 16:8 1980
"So now if you are g to deal Gn 24:49 3426
had come from g to Beer-lahai-roi; Gn 24:62 935
you belong, and where are you g, Gn 32:17 1980
you actually g to reign over us? Gn 37:8
you really g to rule over us?" Gn 37:8
your father-in-law is g up to Gn 38:13 5927
I am g to the sons of Israel, Ex 3:13 935
'I am not g to give you *any* straw. Ex 5:10
as he is g out to the water, Ex 7:15 3318
"Behold, I am g out from you, and Ex 8:29 3318
Who are the ones that are g?" Ex 10:8 1980
am g out into the midst of Egypt, Ex 11:4 3318
The LORD was g before them in Ex 13:21 1980
sons of Israel were g out boldly. Ex 14:8 3318
been g before the camp of Israel, Ex 14:19 1980
I am g to send an angel before you Ex 23:20
to all that I am g to show you, Ex 25:9
branches g out from the lampstand; Ex 25:33 3318
and now I am g up to the LORD, Ex 32:30 5927
Is it not by Your g with us, Ex 33:16 1980
"Behold, I am g to make a covenant. Ex 34:10
that I am g to perform with you. Ex 34:10
I am g to drive out the Amorite Ex 34:11
of the land into which you are g, Ex 34:12 935
six branches g out of its sides; Ex 37:18 3318
branches g out of the lampstand. Ex 37:19 3318
he is g to offer out of the herd, Lv 3:1
'If he is g to offer a lamb for Lv 3:7
the land which I am g to give to you Lv 23:10
"What are we g to eat on the Lv 25:20
You are g to deal thus with me, Nu 11:15
g to give to the sons of Israel; Nu 13:2
God was angry because he was g, Nu 22:22 1980
now, behold, I am g to my people; Nu 24:14 1980
you are g over to possess it. Dt 4:14 5674a
g over the Jordan to possess it. Dt 4:26 5674a
you are g over to possess it, Dt 6:1 5674a
you are g to possess their land, Dt 9:5 935
which you are g in to dispossess, Dt 12:29 935
the midst of which they are g, Dt 31:16 935
"Rejoice, Zebulun, in your g forth, Dt 33:18 3318
you are g to ambush the city from Jos 8:4
war and for g out and coming in. Jos 14:11 3318
g up from Jericho through the hill Jos 16:1 5927
speak of g up against them in war to Jos 22:33 5927
I am g the way of all the earth, Jos 23:14 1980
and I am g to stay wherever I may Jg 17:9 1980
we are g will be prosperous." Jg 18:5 1980
are g has the LORD's approval." Jg 18:6 1980
"Where are you g, and where do Jg 19:17 1980
But I am *now* g to my house, and no Jg 19:18 1980
city was g up *in smoke* to heaven. Jg 20:40 5927
first by not g after young men, Ru 3:10 1980
young women g out to draw water and 1Sa 9:11 3318
g down to the edge of the city, 1Sa 9:27 3381
and there three men g up to God at 1Sa 10:3 5927
the army was g out in battle array 1Sa 17:20 3318
g out against the Philistine, 1Sa 17:55 3318
and your g out and your coming in 1Sa 29:6 3318
and when the sun was g down, 2Sa 2:24 935
learn of your g out and coming in and 2Sa 3:25 4161
I am g to wait at the fords of the 2Sa 15:28
mule that was under him kept g. 2Sa 18:9 5674a
you will have no reward for g?" 2Sa 18:22 4672
"I am g the way of all the earth. 1Ki 2:2 1980
by g the way which you came.' " 1Ki 13:17 1980
order to prevent *anyone* from g out 1Ki 15:17 3318
As she was g to get *it*, he 1Ki 17:11 1980
you are g to inquire of Baal-zebub, 2Ki 1:3 1980
As they were g along and talking, 2Ki 2:11 1980
and as he was g up by the way, 2Ki 2:23 5927
Millo *as he was* g down to Silla. 2Ki 12:20 3381
And your g out and your coming in, 2Ki 19:27 3318
returned from g against Jeroboam. 2Ch 11:4 1980
prevent *anyone* from g out or coming 2Ch 16:1 3318
LORD is g to strike your people, 2Ch 21:14
back from g with him to battle, 2Ch 25:13 1980
and this work is g on with great Ezr 5:8 5648
g to restore *it* for themselves? Ne 4:2
shone Or the moon g in splendor, Jb 31:26 1980
'Deliver him from g down to the pit, Jb 33:24 3381
redeemed my soul from g to the pit, Jb 33:28 5674a
The LORD will guard your g out and Ps 121:8 3318
wisdom in Sheol where you are g. Ec 9:10 1980
the Lord GOD of hosts is g to Is 3:1
what I am g to do to My vineyard: Is 5:5
I am g to stir up the Medes Is 13:17
which He is g to wave over them. Is 19:16
he did so, g naked and barefoot. Is 20:2 1980
And your g out and your coming in Is 37:28 3318
to us what is g to take place; Is 41:22
that are g to come afterward, Is 41:23
events that are g to take place. Is 44:7
G about as a talebearer. Jer 6:28 1980
I am not g to listen to their cry; Jer 14:12
I am not g to accept them. Jer 14:12
Rather I am g to make an end of Jer 14:12
"You keep g backward. Jer 15:6 1980
am g to eliminate from this place, Jer 16:9
am g to send for many fishermen," Jer 16:16
behold, I am g to make them know Jer 16:21
we are g to follow our own plans, Jer 18:12 1980
is not g to be lost to the priest, Jer 18:18
I am g to make you a terror to Jer 20:4
I am g to feed them wormwood Jer 23:15
is g forth From nation to nation, Jer 25:32 3318
'Within two years I am g to bring Jer 28:3
'I am also g to bring back to this Jer 28:4
This year you are g to die, Jer 28:16
so I am g to bring on them all the Jer 32:42
'Behold, I am g to command,' Jer 34:22
in and g out among the people, Jer 37:4 3318
is g to return to its own land of Egypt. Jer 37:7
"You are g over to the Chaldeans!" Jer 37:13 5307
am not g over to the Chaldeans"; Jer 37:14 5307
"I am g to ask you something; Jer 38:14
are g to be brought out to the officers Jer 38:22
As Jeremiah was still not g back, Jer 40:5 7725
I am g to stay at Mizpah to stand Jer 40:10
I am g to pray to the LORD your Jer 42:4
'But if you are g to say, Jer 42:13
I am g to bring on them. Jer 42:17
I am g to send and get Jer 43:10
and I am g to set his throne *right* Jer 43:10
I am g to set My face against you Jer 44:11
we are not g to listen to you! Jer 44:16
am g to punish you in this place, Jer 44:29
I am g to give over Pharaoh Hophra Jer 44:30
I am g to bring disaster on all Jer 45:5
I am g to punish Amon of Thebes, Jer 46:25
see, I am g to save you from afar, Jer 46:27
waters are g to rise from the Jer 47:2
LORD is g to destroy the Philistines, Jer 47:4
I am g to bring terror upon you," Jer 49:5
I am g to break the bow of Elam, Jer 49:35
I am g to arouse and bring up Jer 50:9
I am g to punish the king of Jer 50:18
I am g to arouse against Babylon Jer 51:1
is g to render recompense to her. Jer 51:6
Therefore the nations are g mad. Jer 51:7 1984b
I am g to plead your case And Jer 51:36
the LORD is g to destroy Babylon, Jer 51:55
that I am g to bring upon her; Jer 51:64
I am g to break the staff of bread Ezk 4:16
am g to bring a sword on you, Ezk 6:3
but no one is g to the battle, Ezk 7:14 1980
sight, as those g into exile. Ezk 12:4 4161
they are g to come forth to you Ezk 14:22
"you are surely not g to use this Ezk 18:3
I am g to gather you into the Ezk 22:19
I am g to give you to the sons of Ezk 25:4
I am g to deprive the flank of Ezk 25:9
which I am g to sacrifice for you, Ezk 39:17
to all that I am g to show you; Ezk 40:4
There were seven steps g up to it, Ezk 40:26 5927
that we are not g to serve your Da 3:18
I am g to let you know what will Da 8:19
so I am g forth, and behold, the Da 10:20 3318
kings are g to arise in Persia. Da 11:2
His g forth is as certain as the Hos 6:3 4161
"Behold, I am g to send you Jl 2:19
I am g to arouse them from the Jl 3:7
the LORD is g to command that the Am 6:11
I am g to raise up a nation Am 6:14
a ship which was g to Tarshish, Jon 1:3 935
which I am g to tell you." Jon 3:2
I am g to deal at that time With Zph 3:19
I am g to shake the heavens and Hg 2:6

‘I am **g** to shake the heavens and	Hg 2:21	
“Where are you **g**?”	Zch 2:2	1980
was speaking with me was **g** out,	Zch 2:3	3318
I am **g** to bring in My servant the	Zch 3:8	
“This is the curse that is **g**	Zch 5:3	3318
and see what this is **g** forth.”	Zch 5:5	3318
“This is the ephah **g** forth.”	Zch 5:6	3318
g forth after standing before the	Zch 6:5	3318
are **g** forth to the north country;	Zch 6:6	3318
those who are **g** to the land of the	Zch 6:8	3318
I am **g** to save My people from the	Zch 8:7	
I am **g** to raise up a shepherd in	Zch 11:16	
I am **g** to make Jerusalem a cup	Zch 12:2	
is **g** to be offered to My name,	Mal 1:11	
I am **g** to rebuke your offspring,	Mal 2:3	
I am **g** to send My messenger,	Mal 3:1	
I am **g** to send you Elijah the	Mal 4:5	
for Herod is **g** to search for the	Mt 2:13	*3195*
Then Jerusalem was **g** out to him,	Mt 3:5	*1607*
G on from there He saw two other	Mt 4:21	*4260*
Jesus was **g** throughout all Galilee,	Mt 4:23	*4013*
“If You *are* **g** *to* cast us out,	Mt 8:31	
As they were **g** out,	Mt 9:32	*1831*
Jesus was **g** through all the	Mt 9:35	*4013*
you will not finish **g** *through*	Mt 10:23	
As these men were **g** *away,*	Mt 11:7	*4198*
“For the Son of Man is **g** to come	Mt 16:27	*3195*
is **g** to suffer at their hands.”	Mt 17:12	*3195*
“The Son of Man is **g** to be	Mt 17:22	*3195*
“Behold, we are **g** up to Jerusalem;	Mt 20:18	*305*
The crowds **g** ahead of Him,	Mt 21:9	*4254*
was **g** away when His disciples came	Mt 24:1	*4198*
oil, for our lamps are **g** out.’	Mt 25:8	*4570*
were **g** away to make the purchase,	Mt 25:10	*565*
“Get up, let us be **g**;	Mt 26:46	*71*
and saying, “You who *are* **g** *to*	Mt 27:40	
He is **g** ahead of you into Galilee,	Mt 28:7	*4254*
country of Judea was **g** out to him,	Mk 1:5	*1607*
was **g** along by the Sea of Galilee,	Mk 1:16	*3855*
G on a little farther, He saw James	Mk 1:19	*4260*
g around the villages teaching.	Mk 6:6	*4013*
were many *people* coming and **g**,	Mk 6:31	*5217*
The people saw them **g**,	Mk 6:33	*5217*
And **g** back to her home, she found	Mk 7:30	*565*
on the road **g** up to Jerusalem,	Mk 10:32	*305*
them what was **g** to happen to Him,	Mk 10:32	*3195*
“Behold, we are **g** up to Jerusalem,	Mk 10:33	*305*
that what he says is **g** to happen,	Mk 11:23	
As He was **g** out of the temple,	Mk 13:1	*1607*
things are **g** to be fulfilled?”	Mk 13:4	*3195*
“Get up, let us be **g**;	Mk 14:42	*71*
You who *are* **g** *to* destroy	Mk 15:29	
‘He is **g** ahead of you to Galilee;	Mk 16:7	*4254*
they were **g** to call him Zacharias,	Lk 1:59	
were **g** out to be baptized by him,	Lk 3:7	*1607*
to keep Him from **g** away from them.	Lk 4:42	*4198*
disciples were **g** along with Him,	Lk 7:11	*4848*
He *began* **g** around from one	Lk 8:1	*1353*
began **g** throughout the villages,	Lk 9:6	*1330*
for the Son of Man is **g** to be	Lk 9:44	*3195*
As they were **g** along the road,	Lk 9:57	*4198*
where He Himself was **g** to come.	Lk 10:1	*3195*
“A man was **g** down from	Lk 10:30	*2597*
priest was **g** down on that road,	Lk 10:31	*2597*
“For while you are **g** with your	Lk 12:58	*5217*
oxen, and I am **g** to try them out;	Lk 14:19	*4198*
crowds were **g** along with Him;	Lk 14:25	*4848*
as they were **g**, they were cleansed.	Lk 17:14	*5217*
“Behold, we are **g** up to	Lk 18:31	*305*
Now hearing a crowd **g** by,	Lk 18:36	*1279*
God was **g** to appear immediately.	Lk 19:11	*3195*
these things, He was **g** on ahead,	Lk 19:28	*4198*
g up to Jerusalem.	Lk 19:28	*4198*
As He was **g**, they were	Lk 19:36	*4198*
is **g** as it has been determined;	Lk 22:22	*4198*
be who was **g** to do this thing.	Lk 22:23	*3195*
Him saw what was **g** to happen,	Lk 22:49	
two of them were **g** that very day	Lk 24:13	*4198*
was He who was **g** to redeem Israel.	Lk 24:21	*3195*
the village where they were **g**,	Lk 24:28	*4198*
and He acted as though He were **g**	Lk 24:28	*4198*
it comes from and where it is **g**;	Jn 3:8	*5217*
As he was now **g** down,	Jn 4:51	*2597*
at the land to which they were **g**.	Jn 6:21	*5217*
the twelve, was **g** to betray Him.	Jn 6:71	*3195*
is not **g** to come from Galilee,	Jn 7:41	
I came from and where I am **g**;	Jn 8:14	*5217*
I come from or where I am **g**.	Jn 8:14	*5217*
where I am **g**, you cannot come.”	Jn 8:21	*5217*
‘Where I am **g**, you cannot come’?”	Jn 8:22	*5217*
You, and are You **g** there again?”	Jn 11:8	*5217*
was **g** to the tomb to weep there.	Jn 11:31	*5217*
Jesus was **g** to die for the nation,	Jn 11:51	*3195*
him many of the Jews were **g** away and	Jn 12:11	*5217*
were **g** up to worship at the feast;	Jn 12:20	*305*
from God and was **g** back to God,	Jn 13:3	*5217*
‘Where I am **g**, you cannot come.’	Jn 13:33	*5217*
“Lord, where are You **g**?”	Jn 13:36	*5217*
you know the way where I am **g**.”	Jn 14:4	*5217*
we do not know where You are **g**,	Jn 14:5	*5217*
are **g** to disclose Yourself to us and	Jn 14:22	*3195*
“But now I am **g** to Him who sent Me;	Jn 16:5	*5217*
‘Where are You **g**?’	Jn 16:5	*5217*
again and **g** to the Father.”	Jn 16:28	*4198*
and they were **g** to the tomb.	Jn 20:3	*2064*
“I am **g** fishing.”	Jn 21:3	*5217*
intently into the sky while He was **g**,	Ac 1:10	*4198*
Now Peter and John were **g** up to	Ac 3:1	*305*
g on in the fear of the Lord and	Ac 9:31	*4198*
But **g** on from Perga, they arrived	Ac 13:14	*1330*
As Paul and Barnabas were **g** out,	Ac 13:42	*1826*
we were **g** to the place of prayer,	Ac 16:16	*4198*
But we, **g** ahead to the ship, set	Ac 20:13	*4281*
“God is **g** to strike you, you	Ac 23:3	*3195*
as though you were **g** to determine	Ac 23:15	*3195*
as though they were **g** to inquire	Ac 23:20	*3195*
Moses said was **g** to take place;	Ac 26:22	*3195*
watching and **g** without eating,	Ac 27:33	
I am **g** to Jerusalem serving the	Ro 15:25	*4198*
for I am **g** through Macedonia;	1Co 16:5	*1330*
of being filled and **g** hungry,	Php 4:12	*3983*
we were **g** to suffer affliction;	1Th 3:4	*3195*
g before them to judgment;	1Tm 5:24	*4254*
obeyed by **g** out to a place which	Heb 11:8	*1831*
out, not knowing where he was **g**.	Heb 11:8	*2064*
and does not know where he is **g**	1Jn 2:11	*5217*

GOINGS

His **g** forth are from long ago,	Mi 5:2	4163

GOLAN

G in Bashan for the Manassites.	Dt 4:43	1474
and **G** in Bashan from the tribe of	Jos 20:8	1474
Manasseh, *they gave* **G** in Bashan,	Jos 21:27	1474
G in Bashan with its pasture lands	1Ch 6:71	1474

GOLD

land of Havilah, where there is **g**.	Gn 2:11	2091
The **g** of that land is good;	Gn 2:12	2091
in livestock, in silver and in **g**.	Gn 13:2	2091
the man took a **g** ring	Gn 24:22	2091
wrists weighing ten shekels in **g**,	Gn 24:22	2091
and herds, and silver and **g**,	Gn 24:35	2091
of silver and articles of **g**,	Gn 24:53	2091
the **g** necklace around his neck.	Gn 41:42	2091
silver or **g** from your lord’s house?	Gn 44:8	2091
of silver and articles of **g**,	Ex 3:22	2091
of silver and articles of **g**.”	Ex 11:2	2091
of silver and articles of **g**,	Ex 12:35	2091
gods of silver or gods of **g**,	Ex 20:23	2091
g, silver and bronze,	Ex 25:3	2091
You shall overlay it with pure **g**,	Ex 25:11	2091
shall make a **g** molding around it.	Ex 25:11	2091
shall cast four **g** rings for it and	Ex 25:12	2091
wood and overlay them with **g**.	Ex 25:13	2091
shall make a mercy seat of pure **g**,	Ex 25:17	2091
“You shall make two cherubim of **g**,	Ex 25:18	2091
“You shall overlay it with pure **g**	Ex 25:24	2091
and make a **g** border around it.	Ex 25:24	2091
a **g** border for the rim around it.	Ex 25:25	2091
“You shall make four **g** rings	Ex 25:26	2091
wood and overlay them with **g**,	Ex 25:28	2091
you shall make them of pure **g**.	Ex 25:29	2091
shall make a lampstand of pure **g**.	Ex 25:31	2091
piece of hammered work of pure **g**.	Ex 25:36	2091
their trays *shall be* of pure **g**.	Ex 25:38	2091
be made from a talent of pure **g**,	Ex 25:39	2091
You shall make fifty clasps of **g**,	Ex 26:6	2091
“You shall overlay the boards with **g**	Ex 26:29	2091
rings of **g** *as* holders for the bars;	Ex 26:29	2091
you shall overlay the bars with **g**.	Ex 26:29	2091
pillars of acacia overlaid with **g**,	Ex 26:32	2091
gold, their hooks *also being of* **g**,	Ex 26:32	2091
screen and overlay them with **g**,	Ex 26:37	2091
gold, their hooks *also being of* **g**;	Ex 26:37	2091
“They shall take the **g** and	Ex 28:5	2091
shall also make the ephod of **g**,	Ex 28:6	2091
of **g**, of blue and purple and	Ex 28:8	2091
them in filigree *settings* of **g**.	Ex 28:11	2091
shall make filigree *settings* of **g**,	Ex 28:13	2091
and two chains of pure **g**;	Ex 28:14	2091
of **g**, of blue and purple and	Ex 28:15	2091
they shall be set in **g** filigree.	Ex 28:20	2091
of twisted cordage work in pure **g**.	Ex 28:22	2091
on the breastpiece two rings of **g**,	Ex 28:23	2091
You shall put the two cords of **g** on	Ex 28:24	2091
“You shall make two rings of **g**	Ex 28:26	2091
“You shall make two rings of **g**	Ex 28:27	2091
bells of **g** between them all around:	Ex 28:33	2091
shall also make a plate of pure **g**	Ex 28:36	2091
You shall overlay it with pure **g**,	Ex 30:3	2091
a **g** molding all around for it.	Ex 30:3	2091
“You shall make two **g** rings	Ex 30:4	2091
wood and overlay them with **g**.	Ex 30:5	2091
artistic designs for work in **g**,	Ex 31:4	2091
and the pure **g** lampstand with all	Ex 31:8	
“Tear off the **g** rings which are	Ex 32:2	2091
people tore off the **g** rings which were	Ex 32:3	2091
‘Whoever has any **g**, let them tear	Ex 32:24	2091
made a god of **g** for themselves.	Ex 32:31	2091
g, silver, and bronze,	Ex 35:5	2091
and bracelets, all articles of **g**;	Ex 35:22	2091
an offering of **g** to the LORD.	Ex 35:22	2091
in **g** and in silver and in bronze,	Ex 35:32	2091
He made fifty clasps of **g** and	Ex 36:13	2091
He overlaid the boards with **g**	Ex 36:34	2091
made their rings of **g** *as* holders for	Ex 36:34	2091
and overlaid the bars with **g**.	Ex 36:34	2091
for it, and overlaid them with **g**,	Ex 36:36	2091
with gold, with their hooks of **g**;	Ex 36:36	2091
their tops and their bands with **g**;	Ex 36:38	2091
it with pure **g** inside and out,	Ex 37:2	2091
a **g** molding for it all around.	Ex 37:2	2091
He cast four rings of **g** for it on its	Ex 37:3	2091
wood and overlaid them with **g**.	Ex 37:4	2091
He made a mercy seat of pure **g**,	Ex 37:6	2091
He made two cherubim of **g**;	Ex 37:7	2091
He overlaid it with pure **g**,	Ex 37:11	2091
a **g** molding for it all around.	Ex 37:11	2091
and made a **g** molding for its rim	Ex 37:12	2091
He cast four **g** rings for it	Ex 37:13	2091
wood and overlaid them with **g**,	Ex 37:15	2091
to pour out drink offerings, of pure **g**.	Ex 37:16	2091
he made the lampstand of pure **g**.	Ex 37:17	2091
a single hammered work of pure **g**.	Ex 37:22	2091
snuffers and its trays of pure **g**.	Ex 37:23	2091
utensils from a talent of pure **g**.	Ex 37:24	2091
He overlaid it with pure **g**,	Ex 37:26	2091
a **g** molding for it all around.	Ex 37:26	2091
wood and overlaid them with **g**.	Ex 37:28	2091
the **g** that was used for the work,	Ex 38:24	2091
even the **g** of the wave offering,	Ex 38:24	2091
He made the ephod of **g**,	Ex 39:2	2091
Then they hammered out **g** sheets	Ex 39:3	2091
of **g** *and* of blue and purple and	Ex 39:5	2091
set in **g** filigree *settings;*	Ex 39:6	2091
of **g** *and* of blue and purple and	Ex 39:8	2091
They were set in **g** filigree	Ex 39:13	2091
of twisted cordage work in pure **g**.	Ex 39:15	2091
They made two **g** filigree	Ex 39:16	2091
filigree *settings* and two **g** rings,	Ex 39:16	2091
Then they put the two **g** cords in	Ex 39:17	2091
They made two **g** rings and	Ex 39:19	2091
they made two **g** rings and placed	Ex 39:20	2091
They also made bells of pure **g**,	Ex 39:25	2091
plate of the holy crown of pure **g**,	Ex 39:30	2091
the pure **g** lampstand, with its	Ex 39:37	
and the **g** altar, and the anointing	Ex 39:38	2091
you shall set the **g** altar of	Ex 40:5	2091
Then he placed the **g** altar in the	Ex 40:26	2091
the lamps in order on the pure **g**	Lv 24:4	
on the pure **g** table before the	Lv 24:6	
one **g** pan of ten *shekels,* full of	Nu 7:14	2091
one **g** pan of ten *shekels,* full of	Nu 7:20	2091
one **g** pan of ten *shekels,* full of	Nu 7:26	2091
one **g** pan of ten *shekels,* full of	Nu 7:32	2091
one **g** pan of ten *shekels,* full of	Nu 7:38	2091
one **g** pan of ten *shekels,* full of	Nu 7:44	2091
one **g** pan of ten *shekels,* full of	Nu 7:50	2091
one **g** pan of ten *shekels,* full of	Nu 7:56	2091
one **g** pan of ten *shekels,* full of	Nu 7:62	2091
one **g** pan of ten *shekels,* full of	Nu 7:68	2091
one **g** pan of ten *shekels,* full of	Nu 7:74	2091
one **g** pan of ten *shekels,* full of	Nu 7:80	2091
silver bowls, twelve **g** pans,	Nu 7:84	2091
the twelve **g** pans, full of	Nu 7:86	2091
all the **g** of the pans 120 *shekels;*	Nu 7:86	2091
the lampstand, hammered work of **g**;	Nu 8:4	2091
me his house full of silver and **g**,	Nu 22:18	2091
me his house full of silver and **g**,	Nu 24:13	2091
only the **g** and the silver, the	Nu 31:22	2091
each man found, articles of **g**,	Nu 31:50	2091
the priest took the **g** from them,	Nu 31:51	2091
All the **g** of the offering	Nu 31:52	2091
the priest took the **g** from the captains	Nu 31:54	2091
shall not covet the silver or the **g**	Dt 7:25	2091
and your silver and **g** multiply,	Dt 8:13	2091
increase silver and **g** for himself.	Dt 17:17	2091
of wood, stone, silver, and **g**,	Dt 29:17	2091
“But all the silver and **g** and	Jos 6:19	2091
Only the silver and **g**, and articles	Jos 6:24	2091
bar of **g** fifty shekels in weight,	Jos 7:21	2091
silver, the mantle, the bar of **g**,	Jos 7:24	2091
much livestock, with silver, **g**,	Jos 22:8	2091
(For they had **g** earrings, because	Jg 8:24	2091
The weight of the **g** earrings	Jg 8:26	2091
requested was 1,700 *shekels* of **g**,	Jg 8:26	2091
and put the articles of **g** which	1Sa 6:8	2091
in which were the articles of **g**,	1Sa 6:15	2091
ornaments of **g** on your apparel.	2Sa 1:24	2091
David took the shields of **g**	2Sa 8:7	2091
of silver, of **g** and of bronze.	2Sa 8:10	2091
with the silver and **g** that he had	2Sa 8:11	2091
and its weight *was* a talent of **g**,	2Sa 12:30	2091
no *concern* of silver or **g** with Saul	2Sa 21:4	2091
and he overlaid it with pure **g**.	1Ki 6:20	2091
inside of the house with pure **g**.	1Ki 6:21	2091
And he drew chains of **g** across the	1Ki 6:21	2091
and he overlaid it with **g**.	1Ki 6:21	2091
overlaid the whole house with **g**,	1Ki 6:22	2091
sanctuary he overlaid with **g**.	1Ki 6:22	2091
also overlaid the cherubim with **g**.	1Ki 6:28	2091
the floor of the house with **g**,	1Ki 6:30	2091
flowers, and overlaid them with **g**;	1Ki 6:32	2091
and he spread the **g** on the	1Ki 6:32	2091
and he overlaid *them* with **g** evenly	1Ki 6:35	2091
of the inner sanctuary, of pure **g**;	1Ki 7:49	2091
and the lamps and the tongs, of **g**;	1Ki 7:49	2091
and the firepans, of pure **g**;	1Ki 7:50	2091
house, *that is,* of the nave, of **g**.	1Ki 7:50	2091
silver and the **g** and the utensils,	1Ki 7:51	2091
g according to all his desire),	1Ki 9:11	2091
sent to the king 120 talents of **g**.	1Ki 9:14	2091
twenty talents of **g** from there,	1Ki 9:28	2091
very much **g** and precious stones.	1Ki 10:2	2091
a hundred and twenty talents of **g**,	1Ki 10:10	2091
Hiram, which brought **g** from Ophir,	1Ki 10:11	2091
Now the weight of **g** which came in	1Ki 10:14	2091
in one year was 666 talents of **g**,	1Ki 10:14	2091
200 large shields of beaten **g**,	1Ki 10:16	2091
shekels of **g** on each large shield.	1Ki 10:16	2091
He made 300 shields of beaten **g**,	1Ki 10:17	2091
three minas of **g** on each shield,	1Ki 10:17	2091
and overlaid it with refined **g**.	1Ki 10:18	2091
drinking vessels *were* of **g**,	1Ki 10:21	2091
forest of Lebanon *were* of pure **g**.	1Ki 10:21	2091
came bringing **g** and silver,	1Ki 10:22	2091
gift, articles of silver and **g**,	1Ki 10:25	2091
all the shields of **g** which Solomon	1Ki 14:26	2091

silver and **g** and utensils. **1Ki 15:15** 2091
Asa took all the silver and the **g** **1Ki 15:18** 2091
you a present of silver and **g**; **1Ki 15:19** 2091
'Your silver and your **g** are mine; **1Ki 20:3** 2091
shall give me your silver and your **g** **1Ki 20:5** 2091
children and my silver and my **g**, **1Ki 20:7** 2091
of Tarshish to go to Ophir for **g**, **1Ki 22:48** 2091
six thousand *shekels* of **g** and ten **2Ki 5:5** 2091
there silver and **g** and clothes, **2Ki 7:8** 2091
bowls, trumpets, any vessels of **g**, **2Ki 12:13** 2091
g that was found among the treasuries **2Ki 12:18** 2091
He took all the **g** and silver **2Ki 14:14** 2091
Ahaz took the silver and **g** **2Ki 16:8** 2091
of silver and thirty talents of **g**. **2Ki 18:14** 2091
At that time Hezekiah cut off *the* **g** **2Ki 18:16** 2091
the silver and the **g** and the **2Ki 20:13** 2091
of silver and a talent of **g**. **2Ki 23:33** 2091
gave the silver and **g** to Pharaoh, **2Ki 23:35** 2091
He exacted the silver and **g** from **2Ki 23:35** 2091
and cut in pieces all the vessels of **g** **2Ki 24:13** 2091
what was fine **g** and what was fine **2Ki 25:15** 2091
David took the shields of **g** **1Ch 18:7** 2091
all kinds of articles of **g** and silver **1Ch 18:10** 2091
and the **g** which he had carried away **1Ch 18:11** 2091
found it to weigh a talent of **g**, **1Ch 20:2** 2091
David gave Ornan 600 shekels of **g** **1Ch 21:25** 2091
house of the LORD 100,000 talents of **g** **1Ch 22:14** 2091
"Of the **g**, the silver and the **1Ch 22:16** 2091
the weight of **g** for all utensils **1Ch 28:14** 2091
and the weight *of* **g** for **1Ch 28:15**
and the **g** by weight for the tables **1Ch 28:16** 2091
and the pitchers of pure **g**; **1Ch 28:17** 2091
of incense refined **g** by weight; **1Ch 28:18** 2091
g for the model of the chariot, **1Ch 28:18** 2091
God the **g** for the *things of* gold, **1Ch 29:2** 2091
God the gold for the *things of* **g**, **1Ch 29:2** 2091
treasure I have of **g** and silver, **1Ch 29:3** 2091
namely, 3,000 talents of **g**, **1Ch 29:4** 2091
of gold, of the **g** of Ophir, **1Ch 29:4** 2091
of **g** for the *things of* gold and **1Ch 29:5** 2091
of gold for the *things of* **g** and **1Ch 29:5** 2091
talents and 10,000 darics of **g**, **1Ch 29:7** 2091
king made silver and **g** as plentiful **2Ch 1:15** 2091
me a skilled man to work in **g**, **2Ch 2:7** 2091
who knows how to work in **g**, **2Ch 2:14** 2091
inside he overlaid it with pure **g**. **2Ch 3:4** 2091
wood and overlaid it with fine **g**, **2Ch 3:5** 2091
and the **g** was gold from Parvaim. **2Ch 3:6** 2091
and the gold was **g** from Parvaim. **2Ch 3:6** 2091
He also overlaid the house with **g** **2Ch 3:7** 2091
and he overlaid it with fine **g**, **2Ch 3:8** 2091
the nails was fifty shekels of **g**. **2Ch 3:9** 2091
overlaid the upper rooms with **g**. **2Ch 3:9** 2091
holies and overlaid them with **g**. **2Ch 3:10** 2091
with their lamps of pure **g**, **2Ch 4:20** 2091
the lamps, and the tongs of **g**, **2Ch 4:21** 2091
the tongs of gold, of purest **g**; **2Ch 4:21** 2091
and the firepans of pure **g**; **2Ch 4:22** 2091
house, *that is,* of the nave, of **g**. **2Ch 4:22** 2091
and the **g** and all the utensils, **2Ch 5:1** 2091
hundred and fifty talents of **g** and **2Ch 8:18** 2091
a large amount of **g** and precious **2Ch 9:1** 2091
hundred and twenty talents of **g** and **2Ch 9:9** 2091
Solomon who brought **g** from Ophir, **2Ch 9:10** 2091
Now the weight of **g** which came to **2Ch 9:13** 2091
in one year was 666 talents of **g**, **2Ch 9:13** 2091
brought **g** and silver to Solomon. **2Ch 9:14** 2091
200 large shields of beaten **g**, **2Ch 9:15** 2091
using 600 *shekels of* beaten **g** on **2Ch 9:15** 2091
He made 300 shields of beaten **g**, **2Ch 9:16** 2091
shekels of **g** on each shield, **2Ch 9:16** 2091
ivory and overlaid it with pure **g**. **2Ch 9:17** 2091
footstool in **g** attached to the throne, **2Ch 9:18** 2091
drinking vessels *were* of **g**, **2Ch 9:20** 2091
forest of Lebanon *were* of pure **g**; **2Ch 9:20** 2091
came bringing **g** and silver, **2Ch 9:21** 2091
gift, articles of silver and **g**, **2Ch 9:24** 2091
silver and **g** and utensils. **2Ch 15:18** 2091
Then Asa brought out silver and **g** **2Ch 16:2** 2091
I have sent you silver and **g**; **2Ch 16:3** 2091
of silver, **g** and precious things, **2Ch 21:3** 2091
pans and utensils of **g** and silver. **2Ch 24:14** 2091
He took all the **g** and silver **2Ch 25:24** 2091
himself treasuries for silver, **g**, **2Ch 32:27** 2091
of silver and one talent of **g**. **2Ch 36:3** 2091
support him with silver and **g**, **Ezr 1:4** 2091
with articles of silver, with **g**, **Ezr 1:6** 2091
30 **g** dishes, 1,000 silver dishes, **Ezr 1:9** 2091
30 **g** bowls, 410 silver bowls of a **Ezr 1:10** 2091
the articles of **g** and silver *numbered* **Ezr 1:11** 2091
for the work 61,000 **g** drachmas and **Ezr 2:69** 2091
g and silver utensils of the house **Ezr 5:14** 1722
g and silver utensils of the house **Ezr 6:5** 1722
and to bring the silver and **g**, **Ezr 7:15** 1722
with all the silver and **g** which **Ezr 7:16** 1722
with the rest of the silver and **g**, **Ezr 7:18** 1722
out to them the silver, the **g** and **Ezr 8:25** 2091
worth 100 talents, *and* 100 **g** talents, **Ezr 8:26** 2091
and 20 **g** bowls *worth* 1,000 darics **Ezr 8:27** 2091
fine shiny bronze, precious as **g**. **Ezr 8:27** 2091
and the **g** are a freewill offering to **Ezr 8:28** 2091
out silver and **g** and the utensils, **Ezr 8:30** 2091
the **g** and the utensils were weighed **Ezr 8:33** 2091
to the treasury 1,000 **g** drachmas, **Ne 7:70** 2091
of the work 20,000 **g** drachmas and **Ne 7:71** 2091
people gave was 20,000 **g** drachmas **Ne 7:72** 2091
and couches of **g** and silver on a **Es 1:6** 2091
with a large crown of **g** and a **Es 8:15** 2091
Or with princes who had **g**, **Jb 3:15** 2091
And place *your* **g** in the dust, And **Jb 22:24** 1220
And *the* **g** *of* Ophir among **Jb 22:24**
Then the Almighty will be your **g** **Jb 22:25** 1220
tried me, I shall come forth as **g**. **Jb 23:10** 2091
And a place where they refine **g**. **Jb 28:1** 2091
And its dust *contains* **g**. **Jb 28:6** 2091
"Pure **g** cannot be given in **Jb 28:15** 5458
be valued in the **g** of Ophir, **Jb 28:16** 3800
"**G** or glass cannot equal it, Nor **Jb 28:17** 2091
exchanged for articles of fine **g**. **Jb 28:17** 6337
Nor can it be valued in pure **g**. **Jb 28:19** 3800
"If I have put my confidence *in* **g**, **Jb 31:24** 2091
gold, And called fine **g** my trust, **Jb 31:24** 3800
of money, and each a ring of **g**. **Jb 42:11** 2091
They are more desirable than **g**, **Ps 19:10** 2091
than gold, yes, than much fine **g**; **Ps 19:10** 6337
set a crown of fine **g** on his head. **Ps 21:3** 6337
stands the queen in **g** from Ophir. **Ps 45:9** 3800
Her clothing is interwoven with **g**. **Ps 45:13** 2091
And its pinions with glistening **g**. **Ps 68:13** 2742d
the **g** of Sheba be given to him; **Ps 72:15** 2091
them out with silver and **g**, **Ps 105:37** 2091
Their idols are silver and **g**, **Ps 115:4** 2091
thousands of **g** and silver *pieces.* **Ps 119:72** 2091
I love Your commandments Above **g**, **Ps 119:127** 2091
Above gold, yes, above fine **g**. **Ps 119:127** 6337
the nations are *but* silver and **g**, **Ps 135:15** 2091
silver And her gain better than fine **g**. **Pr 3:14** 2742d
knowledge rather than choicest **g**. **Pr 8:10** 2742d
"My fruit is better than **g**, **Pr 8:19** 2742d
is better than gold, even pure **g**, **Pr 8:19** 6337
As a ring of **g** in a swine's snout **Pr 11:22** 2091
better it is to get wisdom than **g**! **Pr 16:16** 2742d
for silver and the furnace for **g**, **Pr 17:3** 2091
There is **g**, and an abundance of **Pr 20:15** 2091
Favor is better than silver and **g**. **Pr 22:1** 2091
Like apples of **g** in settings of **Pr 25:11** 2091
Like an earring of **g** and an **Pr 25:12** 2091
and an ornament of fine **g** Is a wise **Pr 25:12** 3800
for silver and the furnace for **g**, **Pr 27:21** 2091
collected for myself silver and **g** and **Ec 2:8** 2091
ornaments of **g** With beads of silver." **SS 1:11** 2091
Its back of **g** *And* its seat of purple **SS 3:10** 2091
"His head is *like* **g**, **SS 5:11** 3800
"His head is *like* gold, pure **g**; **SS 5:11** 6337
hands are rods of **g** Set with beryl; **SS 5:14** 2091
Set on pedestals of pure **g**; **SS 5:15** 6337
been filled with silver and **g** **Is 2:7** 2091
of silver and their idols of **g**, **Is 2:20** 2091
mortal man scarcer than pure **g** And **Is 13:12** 6337
And mankind than the **g** of Ophir. **Is 13:12** 3800
silver or take pleasure in **g**. **Is 13:17** 2091
your molten images plated with **g**. **Is 30:22** 2091
his silver idols and his **g** idols, **Is 31:7** 2091
the silver and the **g** and the **Is 39:2** 2091
it, A goldsmith plates it with **g**, **Is 40:19** 2091
"Those who lavish **g** from the **Is 46:6** 2091
will bring **g** and frankincense, **Is 60:6** 2091
silver and their **g** with them, **Is 60:9** 2091
"Instead of bronze I will bring **g**, **Is 60:17** 2091
yourself with ornaments of **g**, **Jer 4:30** 2091
decorate *it* with silver and with **g**; **Jer 10:4** 2091
from Tarshish, And **g** from Uphaz, **Jer 10:9** 2091
what was fine **g** and what was fine **Jer 52:19** 2091
How dark the **g** has become, *How* the **La 4:1** 2091
How the pure **g** has changed! **La 4:1** 3800
of Zion, Weighed against fine **g**, **La 4:2** 6337
their **g** will become an abhorrent **Ezk 7:19** 2091
their **g** will not be able to deliver **Ezk 7:19** 2091
were adorned with **g** and silver, **Ezk 16:13** 2091
made of My **g** and of My silver, **Ezk 16:17** 2091
kinds of precious stones and **g**. **Ezk 27:22** 2091
And have acquired **g** and silver for **Ezk 28:4** 2091
And the **g**, the workmanship of your **Ezk 28:13** 2091
to carry away silver and **g**, **Ezk 38:13** 2091
of that statue *was made* of fine **g**, **Da 2:32** 1722
the silver and the **g** were crushed **Da 2:35** 1722
You are the head of **g**. **Da 2:38** 1722
the clay, the silver and the **g**, **Da 2:45** 1722
the king made an image of **g**, **Da 3:1** 1722
he gave orders to bring the **g** and **Da 5:2** 1722
Then they brought the **g** vessels **Da 5:3** 1722
praised the gods of **g** and silver, **Da 5:4** 1722
a necklace of **g** around his neck, **Da 5:7** 1722
a necklace of **g** around your neck, **Da 5:16** 1722
praised the gods of silver and **g**, **Da 5:23** 1722
a necklace of **g** around his neck, **Da 5:29** 1722
with *a belt of* pure **g** of Uphaz. **Da 10:5** 3800
precious vessels of silver and **g** he will **Da 11:8** 2091
he will honor *him* with **g**, **Da 11:38** 2091
hidden treasures of **g** and silver and **Da 11:43** 2091
And lavished on her silver and **g**, **Hos 2:8** 2091
With their silver and **g** they have **Hos 8:4** 2091
you have taken My silver and My **g**, **Jl 3:5** 2091
Plunder the silver! Plunder the **g**! **Na 2:9** 2091
it is overlaid with **g** and silver, **Hab 2:19** 2091
Neither their silver nor their **g** **Zph 1:18** 2091
silver is Mine and the **g** is Mine,' **Hg 2:8** 2091
a lampstand all of **g** with its bowl **Zch 4:2** 2091
"Take silver and **g**, **Zch 6:11** 2091
g like the mire of the streets. **Zch 9:3** 2742d
And test them as **g** is tested. **Zch 13:9** 2091
g and silver and garments in great **Zch 14:14** 2091
and refine them like **g** and silver, **Mal 3:3** 2091
to Him gifts of **g**, frankincense **Mt 2:11** *5557*
"Do not acquire **g**, or silver, or **Mt 10:9** *5557*
swears by the **g** of the temple is **Mt 23:16** *5557*
Which is more important, the **g** **Mt 23:17** *5557*
the temple that sanctified the **g**? **Mt 23:17** *5557*
"I do not possess silver and **g**, **Ac 3:6** *5553*
is like **g** or silver or stone, **Ac 17:29** *5557*
no one's silver or **g** or clothes. **Ac 20:33** *5553*
builds on the foundation with **g**, **1Co 3:12** *5553*
g or pearls or costly garments, **1Tm 2:9** *5553*
are not only **g** and silver vessels, **2Tm 2:20** *5552*
covered on all sides with **g**, **Heb 9:4** *5553*
with a **g** ring and dressed in fine **Jas 2:2** *5554*
g and your silver have rusted; **Jas 5:3** *5557*
than **g** which is perishable, **1Pe 1:7** *5553*
with perishable things like silver or **g** **1Pe 1:18** *5553*
the hair, and wearing **g** jewelry, **1Pe 3:3** *5553*
to buy from Me **g** refined by fire so **Rv 3:18** *5553*
heads appeared to be crowns like **g**, **Rv 9:7** *5557*
and the idols of **g** and of silver **Rv 9:20** *5552*
and adorned with **g** and precious **Rv 17:4** *5553*
having in her hand a **g** cup full of **Rv 17:4** *5552*
cargoes of **g** and silver and **Rv 18:12** *5557*
and adorned with **g** and precious **Rv 18:16** *5553*
g measuring rod to measure the city, **Rv 21:15** *5552*
and the city was pure **g**, **Rv 21:18** *5553*
the street of the city was pure **g**, **Rv 21:21** *5553*

GOLDEN
a **g** bell and a pomegranate, a **Ex 28:34** 2091
a **g** bell and a pomegranate, **Ex 28:34** 2091
He made two **g** rings for it **Ex 37:27** 2091
its front, he placed the **g** plate, **Lv 8:9** 2091
"Over the **g** altar they shall **Nu 4:11** 2091
"Five **g** tumors and five golden **1Sa 6:4** 2091
"Five golden tumors and five **g** mice **1Sa 6:4** 2091
and the box with the **g** mice and **1Sa 6:11** 2091
These are the **g** tumors which **1Sa 6:17** 2091
and the **g** mice, *according* to the **1Sa 6:18** 2091
the **g** altar and the golden table **1Ki 7:48** 2091
the golden altar and the **g** table **1Ki 7:48** 2091
consulted, and made two **g** calves, **1Ki 12:28** 2091
even the **g** calves that *were* at **2Ki 10:29** 2091
for the **g** *utensils,* the weight of **1Ch 28:14** 2091
weight *of gold* for the **g** lampstands **1Ch 28:15** 2091
lampstands and their **g** lamps, **1Ch 28:15** 2091
and for the **g** bowls with the **1Ch 28:17** 2091
Then he made the ten **g** lampstands **2Ch 4:7** 2091
And he made one hundred **g** bowls. **2Ch 4:8** 2091
even the **g** altar, the tables with **2Ch 4:19** 2091
he even took the **g** shields which **2Ch 12:9** 2091
the **g** calves which Jeroboam made **2Ch 13:8** 2091
and the **g** lampstand with its lamps **2Ch 13:11** 2091
in **g** vessels of various kinds, **Es 1:7** 2091
the **g** scepter so that he may live. **Es 4:11** 2091
g scepter which *was* in his hand. **Es 5:2** 2091
extended the **g** scepter to Esther. **Es 8:4** 2091
"Out of the north comes **g** *splendor;* **Jb 37:22** 2091
broken and the **g** bowl is crushed, **Ec 12:6** 2091
a **g** cup in the hand of the LORD, **Jer 51:7** 2091
fall down and worship the **g** image **Da 3:5** 1722
fell down *and* worshiped the **g** image **Da 3:7** 1722
fall down and worship the **g** image. **Da 3:10** 1722
g image which you have set up." **Da 3:12** 1722
the **g** image that I have set up? **Da 3:14** 1722
g image that you have set up." **Da 3:18** 1722
which are beside the two **g** pipes, **Zch 4:12** 2091
empty the **g** *oil* from themselves?" **Zch 4:12** 2091
having a **g** altar of incense and **Heb 9:4** *5552*
was a **g** jar holding the manna, **Heb 9:4** *5552*
turned I saw seven **g** lampstands; **Rv 1:12** *5552*
across His chest with a **g** sash. **Rv 1:13** *5552*
hand, and the seven **g** lampstands: **Rv 1:20** *5552*
among the seven **g** lampstands, **Rv 2:1** *5552*
and **g** crowns on their heads. **Rv 4:4** *5552*
harp and **g** bowls full of incense, **Rv 5:8** *5552*
at the altar, holding a **g** censer; **Rv 8:3** *5552*
on the **g** altar which was before **Rv 8:3** *5552*
the **g** altar which is before God, **Rv 9:13** *5552*
man, having a **g** crown on His head **Rv 14:14** *5552*
their chests with **g** sashes. **Rv 15:6** *5552*
gave to the seven angels seven **g** bowls **Rv 15:7** *5552*

GOLDSMITH
casts it, A **g** plates it with gold, **Is 40:19** 6884
Hire a **g**, and he makes it *into* a god; **Is 46:6** 6884
craftsman and of the hands of a **g**; **Jer 10:9** 6884
g is put to shame by his idols; **Jer 10:14** 6884
g is put to shame by his idols, **Jer 51:17** 6884

GOLDSMITHS
of Harhaiah of the **g** made repairs. **Ne 3:8** 6884
After him Malchijah, one of the **g**, **Ne 3:31** 6885
the **g** and the merchants carried out **Ne 3:32** 6884

GOLGOTHA
they came to a place called **G**, **Mt 27:33** *1115*
they brought Him to the place **G**, **Mk 15:22** *1115*
which is called in Hebrew, **G**. **Jn 19:17** *1115*

GOLIATH
armies of the Philistines named **G**, **1Sa 17:4** 1555
the Philistine from Gath named **G**, **1Sa 17:23** 1555
"The sword of **G** the Philistine, **1Sa 21:9** 1555
the sword of **G** the Philistine." **1Sa 22:10** 1555
Bethlehemite killed **G** the Gittite, **2Sa 21:19** 1555
the brother of **G** the Gittite, **1Ch 20:5** 1555

GOMER
The sons of Japheth *were* **G** and **Gn 10:2** 1586
The sons of **G** *were* Ashkenaz **Gn 10:3** 1586
The sons of Japheth *were* **G**, **1Ch 1:5** 1586
The sons of **G** *were* Ashkenaz, **1Ch 1:6** 1586
G with all its troops; **Ezk 38:6** 1586
took **G** the daughter of Diblaim, **Hos 1:3** 1586

GOMORRAH
Sodom and **G** and Admah and Zeboiim, **Gn 10:19** 6017
the LORD destroyed Sodom and **G** **Gn 13:10** 6017

Sodom, and with Birsha king of **G**, **Gn 14:2** 6017
the king of Sodom and the king of **G** **Gn 14:8** 6017
and the kings of Sodom and **G** fled, **Gn 14:10** 6017
took all the goods of Sodom and **G** **Gn 14:11** 6017
The outcry of Sodom and **G** is indeed **Gn 18:20** 6017
rained on Sodom and **G** brimstone **Gn 19:24** 6017
he looked down toward Sodom and **G**, **Gn 19:28** 6017
like the overthrow of Sodom and **G**, **Dt 29:23** 6017
Sodom, And from the fields of **G**; **Dt 32:32** 6017
be like Sodom, We would be like **G**. **Is 1:9** 6017
of our God, You people of **G**. **Is 1:10** 6017
as when God overthrew Sodom and **G**. **Is 13:19** 6017
Sodom, And her inhabitants like **G**. **Jer 23:14** 6017
Sodom and **G** with its neighbors," **Jer 49:18** 6017
Sodom And **G** with its neighbors," **Jer 50:40** 6017
you, as God overthrew Sodom and **G**, **Am 4:11** 6017
And the sons of Ammon like **G** **Zph 2:9** 6017
and **G** in the day of judgment than **Mt 10:15** *1116*
AND WOULD HAVE RESEMBLED **G**." **Ro 9:29** *1116*
condemned the cities of Sodom and **G** **2Pe 2:6** *1116*
and **G** and the cities around them, **Jude 1:7** *1116*

GONE

and Jacob had hardly **g** out from **Gn 27:30** 3318
mother and had **g** to Paddan-aram. **Gn 28:7** 1980
Laban had **g** to shear his flock, **Gn 31:19** 1980
"Now you have indeed **g** away **Gn 31:30** 1980
been with me wherever I have **g**." **Gn 35:3** 1980
They had *just* **g** out of the city, **Gn 44:4** 3318
For *our* money is **g**." **Gn 47:15** 656
since *your* money is **g**." **Gn 47:16** 656
the prey, my son, you have **g** up. **Gn 49:9** 5927
and all who had **g** up with him to **Gn 50:14** 5927
had **g** into the sea after them; **Ex 14:28** 935
had **g** out of the land of Egypt, **Ex 19:1** 3318
not **g** astray into uncleanness, **Nu 5:19** 7847
if you, however, have **g** astray, **Nu 5:20** 7847
but now our appetite is **g**. **Nu 11:6** 3002
but had not **g** out to the tent), **Nu 11:26** 3318
When they had **g** up into the Negev, **Nu 13:22** 5927
men who had **g** up with him said, **Nu 13:31** 5927
"The land through which we have **g**, **Nu 13:32** 5674a
"You have **g** far enough, for all **Nu 16:3**
You have **g** far enough, you sons of **Nu 16:7**
wrath has **g** forth from the LORD, **Nu 16:46** 3318
men of war who had **g** to battle, **Nu 31:21** 935
from the men who had **g** to war **Nu 31:42** 6633
some worthless men have **g** out from **Dt 13:13** 3318
and has **g** and served other gods **Dt 17:3** 1980
He sees that *their* strength is **g**, **Dt 32:36** 235
who were pursuing them had **g** out, **Jos 2:7** 3318
who had not **g** out after Israel, **Jos 8:17** 3318
the men of war who had **g** with him, **Jos 10:24** 1980
When he had **g** out, his servants **Jg 3:24** 3318
Abinoam had **g** up to Mount Tabor. **Jg 4:12** 5927
the LORD has **g** out before you." **Jg 4:14** 3318
When they had **g** some distance from **Jg 18:22** 7368
and the priest, and have **g** away, **Jg 18:24** 1980
near Jebus, the day was almost **g**; **Jg 19:11** 7286
of Israel had **g** up to Mizpah.) **Jg 20:3** 5927
the LORD has **g** forth against me." **Ru 1:13** 3318
your sister-in-law has **g** back to **Ru 1:15** 7725
the lamp of God had not yet **g** out, **1Sa 3:3** 3518
For the bread is **g** from our sack **1Sa 9:7** 235
did not know that Jonathan had **g**. **1Sa 14:3** 1980
now and see who has **g** from us." **1Sa 14:17** 1980
had **g** after Saul to the battle. **1Sa 17:13** 1980
When the lad was **g**, **1Sa 20:41** 935
when the wine had **g** out of Nabal, **1Sa 25:37** 3318
would have **g** away in the morning, **2Sa 2:27** 5927
g in to my father's concubine?" **2Sa 3:7** 935
him away, and he had **g** in peace. **2Sa 3:22** 1980
him away, and he has **g** in peace." **2Sa 3:23** 1980
sent him away and he is already **g**? **2Sa 3:24** 1980
for then the LORD will have **g** out **2Sa 5:24** 3318
ark of the LORD had **g** six paces, **2Sa 6:13** 6805
g with all the sons of Israel, **2Sa 7:7** 1980
been with you wherever you have **g** **2Sa 7:9** 1980
Absalom had fled and **g** to Geshur, **2Sa 13:38** 1980
g about through the whole land, **2Sa 24:8** 7751a
"For he has **g** down today and has **1Ki 1:25** 3381
had **g** from Jerusalem to Gath, **1Ki 2:41** 1980
Egypt had **g** up and captured Gezer and **1Ki 9:16** 5927
army had **g** up to bury the slain, **1Ki 11:15** 5927
of God who came from Judah had **g**. **1Ki 13:12** 1980
Now when he had **g**, a lion met him **1Ki 13:24** 1980
and have **g** and made for yourself **1Ki 14:9** 1980
sweeps away dung until it is all **g**. **1Ki 14:10** 8552
either he is occupied or **g** aside, **1Ki 18:27** 5509
busy here and there, he was **g**." **1Ki 20:40** 369
g down to take possession of it. **1Ki 21:18** 3381
from the bed where you have **g** up, **2Ki 1:4** 5927
from the bed where you have **g** up, **2Ki 1:6** 5927
from the bed where you have **g** up, **2Ki 1:16** 5927
the Arameans had **g** out in bands and **2Ki 5:2** 3318
of God had risen early and **g** out, **2Ki 6:15** 3318
therefore they have **g** from the **2Ki 7:12** 3318
had **g** out of the middle court, **2Ki 20:4** 3318
g down on the stairway of Ahaz. **2Ki 20:11** 3381
for God will have **g** out before you **1Ch 14:15** 3318
but I have **g** from tent to tent and **1Ch 17:5** 1961
been with you wherever you have **g**, **1Ch 17:8** 1980
have **g** to the province of Judah, **Ezr 5:8** 236
where I had **g** or what I had done; **Ne 2:16** 1980
of Babylon I had **g** to the king. **Ne 13:6** 935
performed the service had **g** away, **Ne 13:10** 1272
"When a cloud vanishes, it is **g**, **Jb 7:9** 1980
me down on every side, and I am **g**; **Jb 19:10** 1980
a little while, then they are **g**; **Jb 24:24** 369
carries him away, and he is **g**, **Jb 27:21** 1980

"Oh that I were as in months **g** by, **Jb 29:2** 6924a
has **g** out through all the earth, **Ps 19:4** 3318
my iniquities are **g** over my head; **Ps 38:4** 5674a
my eyes, even that has **g** from me. **Ps 38:10** 369
For soon it is **g** and we fly away. **Ps 90:10** 1468
not **g** astray from Your precepts. **Ps 119:110** 8582
I have **g** astray like a lost sheep; **Ps 119:176** 8582
home, He has **g** on a long journey; **Pr 7:19** 1980
them with words, *but* they are **g**. **Pr 19:7** 3808
you set your eyes on it, it is **g**. **Pr 23:5** 369
is past, The rain is over *and* **g**. **SS 2:11** 1980
beloved had turned away *and* had **g**! **SS 5:6** 5674a
"Where has your beloved **g**, **SS 6:1** 1980
beloved has **g** down to his garden, **SS 6:2** 3381
They have **g** through the pass, **Is 10:29** 5674a
g up to the temple and *to* Dibon, **Is 15:2** 5927
g around the territory of Moab, **Is 15:8** 5362b
"Even as My servant Isaiah has **g** **Is 20:3** 1980
"Watchman, how far **g** is the night? **Is 21:11** 4480
how far **g** is the night?" **Is 21:11** 4480
have all **g** up to the housetops? **Is 22:1** 5927
and say to them, "Be **g**!" **Is 30:22** 3318
which has **g** down with the sun on **Is 38:8** 3381
stairway on which it had **g** down. **Is 38:8** 3381
The word has **g** forth from My mouth **Is 45:23** 3318
have themselves **g** into captivity. **Is 46:2** 1980
is near, My salvation has **g** forth, **Is 51:5** 3318
of us like sheep have **g** astray, **Is 53:6** 8582
have **g** up and made your bed wide. **Is 57:8** 5927
I have not **g** after the Baals'? **Jer 2:23** 1980
"A lion has **g** up from his **Jer 4:7** 5927
He has **g** out from his place To **Jer 4:7** 3318
and which they have **g** after and **Jer 8:2** 1980
and the beasts have fled; they are **g**. **Jer 9:10** 1980
have **g** from me and are no more. **Jer 10:20** 3318
and they have **g** after other gods **Jer 11:10** 1980
have **g** after other gods to serve them **Jer 13:10** 1980
both prophet and priest Have **g** roving **Jer 14:18**
has **g** forth into all the land.'" **Jer 23:15** 3318
of the LORD has **g** forth in wrath, **Jer 23:19** 3318
Wrath has **g** forth, A sweeping **Jer 30:23** 3318
Babylon which has **g** away from you. **Jer 34:21** 5927
all the bread in the city was **g**. **Jer 37:21** 8552
who have **g** over to the Chaldeans, **Jer 38:19** 5307
the deserters who had **g** over to **Jer 39:9** 5307
until they are completely **g**. **Jer 44:27** 3615
all the remnant of Judah who have **g** **Jer 44:28** 935
vessel, Nor has he **g** into exile. **Jer 48:11** 1980
and men have **g** up to his cities; **Jer 48:15** 5927
also **g** down to the slaughter," **Jer 48:15** 3381
a fire has **g** forth from Heshbon And **Jer 48:45** 3318
wandered off, they have **g** away! **Jer 50:3** 1980
They have **g** along from mountain to **Jer 50:6** 1980
has **g** into exile under affliction And **La 1:3** 1540
Her little ones have **g** away As **La 1:5** 1980
young men Have **g** into captivity. **La 1:18** 1980
Elders are **g** from the gate, Young **La 5:14** 7673a
Your doom has **g** forth; **Ezk 7:10** 3318
countries where they had **g**." **Ezk 11:16** 935
have not **g** up into the breaches, **Ezk 13:5** 5927
is **g** and its plasterers are gone, **Ezk 13:15** 369
is gone and its plasterers are **g**, **Ezk 13:15** 369
fire has **g** out from *its* branch; **Ezk 19:14** 3318
whose rust has not **g** out of it! **Ezk 24:6** 3318
her great rust has not **g** from her; **Ezk 24:12** 3318
the peoples of the earth have **g** down **Ezk 31:12** 3381
'They have **g** down, they lie still, **Ezk 32:21** 3381
the nations where they have **g**, **Ezk 37:21** 1980
who had **g** forth to slay the wise **Da 2:14** 5312
Their liquor **g**, They play the **Hos 4:18** 5493
have **g** deep in depravity, **Hos 5:2** 6009
For they have **g** up to Assyria, **Hos 8:9** 5927
They have **g** deep in depravity As **Hos 9:9** 6009
But Jonah had **g** below into the **Jon 1:5** 3381
From you has **g** forth One who **Na 1:11** 3318
have **g** to war against Jerusalem; **Zch 14:12** 6633
Now when they had **g**, behold, an **Mt 2:13** *402*
and having **g** up on the mountain, **Mt 15:29** *305*
and one of them has **g** astray, **Mt 18:12** *4105*
which have not **g** astray. **Mt 18:13** *4105*
When he had **g** out to the gateway, **Mt 26:71** *1831*
proceeding from Him had **g** forth, **Mk 5:30** *1831*
demon has **g** out of your daughter." **Mk 7:29** *1831*
had **g** away from them into heaven, **Lk 2:15** *565*
from whom seven demons had **g** out, **Lk 8:2** *1831*
from whom the demons had **g** out, **Lk 8:35** *1831*
man from whom the demons had **g** **Lk 8:38** *1831*
that power had **g** out of Me." **Lk 8:46** *1831*
when the demon had **g** out, **Lk 11:14** *1831*
"He has **g** to be the guest of a **Lk 19:7** *1525*
For His disciples had **g** away into **Jn 4:8** *565*
His disciples had **g** away alone. **Jn 6:22** *565*
brothers had **g** up to the feast, **Jn 7:10** *305*
look, the world has **g** after Him." **Jn 12:19** *565*
Therefore when he had **g** out, **Jn 13:31** *1831*
When they had **g** through the **Ac 13:6** *1330*
"In the generations **g** by He **Ac 14:16** *3944*
had not **g** with them to the work. **Ac 15:38** *4905*
that their hope of profit was **g**, **Ac 16:19** *1831*
When he had **g** through those **Ac 20:2** *1330*
But these had **g** on ahead and were **Ac 20:5** *4281*
When he had **g** *back* up and had **Ac 20:11** *305*
and when they had **g** aside, they **Ac 26:31** *402*
had **g** a long time without food, **Ac 27:21** *5225*
HAS **G** OUT INTO ALL THE EARTH, **Ro 10:18** *1831*
The night is almost **g**, **Ro 13:12** *4298*
he has **g** to you of his own accord. **2Co 8:17** *1831*
your faith toward God has **g** forth, **1Th 1:8** *1831*
and thus **g** astray from the faith. **1Tm 6:21** *795*

men who have **g** astray from the **2Tm 2:18** *795*
deserted me and **g** to Thessalonica; **2Tm 4:10** *4198*
Crescens *has* **g** to Galatia, Titus **2Tm 4:10**
has looked at himself and **g** away, **Jas 1:24** *565*
hand of God, having **g** into heaven, **1Pe 3:22** *4198*
the right way, they have **g** astray, **2Pe 2:15** *4105*
have **g** out into the world. **1Jn 4:1** *1831*
have **g** out into the world, **2Jn 1:7** *1831*
For they have **g** the way of Cain, **Jude 1:11** *4198*
fruit you long for has **g** from you, **Rv 18:14** *565*

GONG

a noisy **g** or a clanging cymbal. **1Co 13:1** *5475*

GOOD

God saw that the light was **g**; **Gn 1:4** 2896a
and God saw that it was **g**. **Gn 1:10** 2896a
and God saw that it was **g**. **Gn 1:12** 2896a
and God saw that it was **g**. **Gn 1:18** 2896a
and God saw that it was **g**. **Gn 1:21** 2896a
and God saw that it was **g**. **Gn 1:25** 2896a
made, and behold, it was very **g**. **Gn 1:31** 2896a
to the sight and **g** for food; **Gn 2:9** 2896a
tree of the knowledge of **g** and evil. **Gn 2:9** 2896b
The gold of that land is **g**; **Gn 2:12** 2896a
of **g** and evil you shall not eat, **Gn 2:17** 2896b
is not **g** for the man to be alone; **Gn 2:18** 2896a
be like God, knowing **g** and evil." **Gn 3:5** 2896b
saw that the tree was **g** for food, **Gn 3:6** 2896a
one of Us, knowing **g** and evil; **Gn 3:22** 2896b
will be buried at a **g** old age. **Gn 15:15** 2896a
to her what is **g** in your sight." **Gn 16:6** 2896a
and set out with a variety of **g** **Gn 24:10** 2898
we cannot speak to you bad or **g**. **Gn 24:50** 2896a
have done to you nothing but **g** and **Gn 26:29** 2896b
what **g** will my life be to me?" **Gn 27:46**
"God has endowed me with a **g** gift; **Gn 30:20** 2896a
"**G**, let it be according to your **Gn 30:34** 2005
speak to Jacob either **g** or bad." **Gn 31:24** 2896a
speak either **g** or bad to Jacob.' **Gn 31:29** 2896a
up on a single stalk, plump and **g**. **Gn 41:5** 2896a
behold, seven ears, full and **g**, **Gn 41:22** 2896a
ears swallowed the seven **g** ears. **Gn 41:24** 2896a
"The seven **g** cows are seven years; **Gn 41:26** 2896a
the seven **g** ears are seven years; **Gn 41:26** 2896a
of these **g** years that are coming, **Gn 41:35** 2896a
Now the proposal seemed **g** to **Gn 41:37** 3190
'Why have you repaid evil for **g**? **Gn 44:4** 2899b
he saw that a resting place was **g** **Gn 49:15** 2896a
but God meant it for **g** in order to **Gn 50:20** 2899b
So God was **g** to the midwives, and **Ex 1:20** 3190
land to a **g** and spacious land, **Ex 3:8** 2896a
thing that you are doing is not **g**. **Ex 18:17** 2896a
camp, a **g** distance from the camp, **Ex 33:7** 7368
his lips to do evil or to do **g**, **Lv 5:4** 3190
been **g** in the sight of the LORD?" **Lv 10:19** 3190
that, it seemed **g** in his sight. **Lv 10:20** 3190
life of an animal shall make it **g**, **Lv 24:18** 7999a
kills an animal shall make it **g**, **Lv 24:21** 7999a
it or exchange it, a **g** for a bad, **Lv 27:10** 2896a
good for a bad, or a bad for a **g**; **Lv 27:10** 2896a
shall value it as either **g** or bad; **Lv 27:12** 2896a
shall value it as either **g** or bad; **Lv 27:14** 2896a
concerned whether *it is* **g** or bad, **Lv 27:33** 2896a
come with us and we will do you **g**, **Nu 10:29** 3190
promised **g** concerning Israel." **Nu 10:29** 2896a
whatever **g** the LORD does for us, **Nu 10:32** 2896b
which they live, is it **g** or bad? **Nu 13:19** 2896a
spy out is an exceedingly **g** land. **Nu 14:7** 2896a
spoken, and will He not make it **g**? **Nu 23:19** 6965
of the LORD, either **g** or bad, **Nu 24:13** 2899b
which you have said to do is **g**.' **Dt 1:14** 2896a
'It is a **g** land which the LORD our **Dt 1:25** 2896a
shall see the **g** land which I swore **Dt 1:35** 2896a
have no knowledge of **g** or evil, **Dt 1:39** 2896b
that **g** hill country and Lebanon.' **Dt 3:25** 2896a
I would not enter the **g** land which **Dt 4:21** 2896a
take possession of this **g** land. **Dt 4:22** 2896a
g things which you did not fill, **Dt 6:11** 2898
and **g** in the sight of the LORD, **Dt 6:18** 2896a
you may go in and possess the **g** land **Dt 6:18** 2896a
fear the LORD our God for our **g** **Dt 6:24** 2896b
God is bringing you into a **g** land, **Dt 8:7** 2896a
the **g** land which He has given you. **Dt 8:10** 2896a
built **g** houses and lived *in them*, **Dt 8:12** 2896a
you, to do **g** for you in the end. **Dt 8:16** 3190
giving you this **g** land to possess, **Dt 9:6** 2896a
commanding you today for your **g**? **Dt 10:13** 2896b
will perish quickly from the **g** land **Dt 11:17** 2896a
for you will be doing what is **g** **Dt 12:28** 2896a
rejoice in all the **g** which the LORD **Dt 26:11** 2896b
open for you His **g** storehouse, **Dt 28:12** 2896a
will again rejoice over you for **g**, **Dt 30:9** 2896b
do as it seems **g** and right in your **Jos 9:25** 2896a
Not one of the **g** promises which **Jos 21:45** 2896a
until you perish from off this **g** land **Jos 23:13** 2896a
not one word of all the **g** words which **Jos 23:14** 2896a
just as all the **g** words which the LORD **Jos 23:15** 2896a
has destroyed you from off this **g** land **Jos 23:15** 2896a
g land which He has given you." **Jos 23:16** 2896a
you after He has done **g** to you." **Jos 24:20** 3190
the **g** that he had done to Israel. **Jg 8:35** 2899b
leave my sweetness and my **g** fruit, **Jg 9:11** 2896a
do to us whatever seems **g** to You; **Jg 10:15** 2896a
for me, for she looks **g** to me." **Jg 14:3** 3474
and she looked **g** to Samson. **Jg 14:7** 3474
land, and behold, it is very **g**. **Jg 18:9** 2896a
"It is **g**, my daughter, that you **Ru 2:22** 2896a
comes, if he will redeem you, **g**; **Ru 3:13** 2896a
for the report is not **g** which I **1Sa 2:24** 2896a

of all the **g** that I do for Israel;	**1Sa 2:32**	3190
let Him do what seems **g** to Him."	**1Sa 3:18**	2896a
do to us whatever seems **g** to you."	**1Sa 11:10**	2896a
instruct you in the **g** and right way.	**1Sa 12:23**	2896a
"Do whatever seems **g** to you."	**1Sa 14:36**	2896a
"Do what seems **g** to you."	**1Sa 14:40**	2896a
the lambs, and all that was **g**,	**1Sa 15:9**	2896b
'It is **g**,' your servant *will be*	**1Sa 20:7**	2896a
there is **g** *feeling* toward David,	**1Sa 20:12**	2895
to him as it seems **g** to you.' "	**1Sa 24:4**	3190
today that you have done **g** to me,	**1Sa 24:18**	2899b
the LORD therefore reward you with **g**	**1Sa 24:19**	2899b
"Yet the men were very **g** to us,	**1Sa 25:15**	2896a
and he has returned me evil for **g**.	**1Sa 25:21**	2899b
g that He has spoken concerning you,	**1Sa 25:30**	2899b
thing that you have done is not **g**.	**1Sa 26:16**	2896a
to carry the **g** news to the house	**1Sa 31:9**	
He said, "**G**!	**2Sa 3:13**	2896a
all that seemed **g** to Israel and to the	**2Sa 3:19**	2895
thought he was bringing **g** news,	**2Sa 4:10**	
this **g** thing to Your servant.	**2Sa 7:28**	2899b
LORD do what is **g** in His sight."	**2Sa 10:12**	2896a
speak to Amnon either **g** or bad;	**2Sa 13:22**	2896a
the king to discern **g** and evil.	**2Sa 14:17**	2896b
"See, your claims are **g** and right,	**2Sa 15:3**	2896a
Him do to me as seems **g** to Him."	**2Sa 15:26**	2895
will look on my affliction and return **g**	**2Sa 16:12**	2899b
Ahithophel has given is not **g**."	**2Sa 17:7**	2896a
the **g** counsel of Ahithophel,	**2Sa 17:14**	2896a
there is **g** news in his mouth."	**2Sa 18:25**	
one also is bringing **g** news."	**2Sa 18:26**	
"This is a **g** man and comes with	**2Sa 18:27**	2896a
good man and comes with **g** news."	**2Sa 18:27**	2896a
my lord the king receive **g** news,	**2Sa 18:31**	
and to do what was **g** in his sight.	**2Sa 19:18**	2896a
do what is **g** in your sight.	**2Sa 19:27**	2896a
I distinguish between **g** and bad?	**2Sa 19:35**	2896b
for him what is **g** in your sight."	**2Sa 19:37**	2895
for him what is **g** in your sight;	**2Sa 19:38**	2896a
offer up what is **g** in his sight.	**2Sa 24:22**	2896a
a valiant man and bring **g** news."	**1Ki 1:42**	2896b
then said to the king, "The word is **g**.	**1Ki 2:38**	2896a
'The word which I have heard is **g**.'	**1Ki 2:42**	2896a
to discern between **g** and evil.	**1Ki 3:9**	2896b
g way in which they should walk.	**1Ki 8:36**	2896a
has failed of all His **g** promise,	**1Ki 8:56**	2896a
and speak **g** words to them,	**1Ki 12:7**	2896a
because in him something **g** was	**1Ki 14:13**	2896a
He will uproot Israel from this **g** land	**1Ki 14:15**	2896a
"That is a **g** idea."	**1Ki 18:24**	2896a
does not prophesy **g** concerning me,	**1Ki 22:8**	2896a
not prophesy **g** concerning me,	**1Ki 22:18**	2896a
and fell every **g** tree and stop all	**2Ki 3:19**	2896a
and mar every **g** piece of land	**2Ki 3:19**	2896a
piece of **g** land and filled it.	**2Ki 3:25**	2896a
water and felled all the **g** trees,	**2Ki 3:25**	2896a
This day is a day of **g** news,	**2Ki 7:9**	
every kind of **g** thing of Damascus,	**2Ki 8:9**	2898
do what is **g** in your sight."	**2Ki 10:5**	2896a
done what is **g** in Your sight."	**2Ki 20:3**	2896a
LORD which you have spoken is **g**."	**2Ki 20:19**	2896a
They found rich and **g** pasture,	**1Ch 4:40**	2896a
to carry the **g** news to their idols	**1Ch 10:9**	
"If it seems **g** to you, and if it	**1Ch 13:2**	2895
Proclaim **g** tidings of His	**1Ch 16:23**	
thanks to the LORD, for *He is* **g**;	**1Ch 16:34**	2896a
have promised this **g** thing to Your	**1Ch 17:26**	2899b
LORD do what is **g** in His sight."	**1Ch 19:13**	2896a
king do what is **g** in his sight.	**1Ch 21:23**	2896a
so that you may possess the **g** land	**1Ch 28:8**	2896a
"*He* indeed is **g** for His	**2Ch 5:13**	2896a
g way in which they should walk.	**2Ch 6:27**	2896a
godly ones rejoice in what is **g**.	**2Ch 6:41**	2896b
"Truly He is **g**, truly His	**2Ch 7:3**	2896a
them and speak **g** words to them,	**2Ch 10:7**	2896a
also conditions were **g** in Judah.	**2Ch 12:12**	2896a
Asa did **g** and right in the	**2Ch 14:2**	2896a
g concerning me but always evil.	**2Ch 18:7**	2899b
not prophesy **g** concerning me,	**2Ch 18:17**	2896a
"But there is *some* **g** in you,	**2Ch 19:3**	2896a
"May the **g** LORD pardon	**2Ch 30:18**	2896a
all the Levites who showed **g** insight	**2Ch 30:22**	2896a
and he did what *was* **g**,	**2Ch 31:20**	2896a
"For He is **g**, for His	**Ezr 3:11**	2896a
g hand of his God *was* upon him.	**Ezr 7:9**	2896a
"Whatever seems **g** to you and	**Ezr 7:18**	3191
According to the **g** hand of our	**Ezr 8:18**	2896a
may be strong and eat the **g** *things*	**Ezr 9:12**	2898
the **g** hand of my God *was* on me.	**Ne 2:8**	2896a
put their hands to the **g** *work*.	**Ne 2:18**	2899b
which you are doing is not **g**;	**Ne 5:9**	2896a
Remember me, O my God, for **g**,	**Ne 5:19**	2899b
they were speaking about his **g**	**Ne 6:19**	2899b
laws, **G** statutes and commandments.	**Ne 9:13**	2896a
Your **g** Spirit to instruct them,	**Ne 9:20**	2896a
of houses full of every **g** thing,	**Ne 9:25**	2898
Remember me, O my God, for **g**.	**Ne 13:31**	2899b
spoke **g** on behalf of the king!"	**Es 7:9**	2896a
one who sought the **g** of his people	**Es 10:3**	2896b
Shall we indeed accept **g** from God	**Jb 2:10**	2896b
My eye will not again see **g**.	**Jb 7:7**	2896b
They flee away, they see no **g**.	**Jb 9:25**	2899b
Never even tasting *anything* **g**.	**Jb 21:25**	2899b
filled their houses with **g** *things;*	**Jb 22:18**	2896b
Thereby **g** will come to you.	**Jb 22:21**	2899b
And does no **g** for the widow.	**Jb 24:21**	3190
"Indeed, what **g** *was*	**Jb 30:2**	
"When I expected **g**, then evil	**Jb 30:26**	2896b
us know among ourselves what is **g**.	**Jb 34:4**	2896a
"Who will show us *any* **g**?"	**Ps 4:6**	2896b
There is no one who does **g**.	**Ps 14:1**	2896b
There is no one who does **g**,	**Ps 14:3**	2896b
I have no **g** besides You."	**Ps 16:2**	2899b
with the blessings of **g** things;	**Ps 21:3**	2896b
G and upright is the LORD;	**Ps 25:8**	2896a
taste and see that the LORD is **g**;	**Ps 34:8**	2896a
not be in want of any **g** thing.	**Ps 34:10**	2896b
length of days that he may see **g**?	**Ps 34:12**	2896b
Depart from evil and do **g**;	**Ps 34:14**	2896b
They repay me evil for **g**,	**Ps 35:12**	2899b
has ceased to be wise *and* to do **g**.	**Ps 36:3**	3190
himself on a path that is not **g**;	**Ps 36:4**	2896a
Trust in the LORD and do **g**;	**Ps 37:3**	2896b
Depart from evil and do **g**,	**Ps 37:27**	2896b
And those who repay evil for **g**,	**Ps 38:20**	2899b
me, because I follow what is **g**.	**Ps 38:20**	2896b
silent, I refrained *even* from **g**,	**Ps 39:2**	2896b
My heart overflows with a **g** theme;	**Ps 45:1**	2896a
By Your favor do **g** to Zion;	**Ps 51:18**	3190
You love evil more than **g**,	**Ps 52:3**	2896b
wait on Your name, for *it is* **g**,	**Ps 52:9**	2896a
There is no one who does **g**.	**Ps 53:1**	2896b
There is no one who does **g**,	**Ps 53:3**	2896b
to Your name, O LORD, for it is **g**.	**Ps 54:6**	2896a
The women who proclaim the **g**	**Ps 68:11**	
LORD, for Your lovingkindness is **g**;	**Ps 69:16**	2896a
Surely God is **g** to Israel, To	**Ps 73:1**	2896a
me, the nearness of God is my **g**;	**Ps 73:28**	2896a
No **g** thing does He withhold from	**Ps 84:11**	2896b
the LORD will give what is **g**,	**Ps 85:12**	2896b
For You, Lord, are **g**,	**Ps 86:5**	2896a
Show me a sign for **g**,	**Ps 86:17**	2899b
is **g** to give thanks to the LORD And	**Ps 92:1**	2896a
Proclaim **g** tidings of His	**Ps 96:2**	
For the LORD is **g**;	**Ps 100:5**	2896a
your years with **g** things,	**Ps 103:5**	2896b
hand, they are satisfied with **g**.	**Ps 104:28**	2896b
thanks to the LORD, for He is **g**;	**Ps 106:1**	2896a
thanks to the LORD, for He is **g**,	**Ps 107:1**	2896a
soul He has filled with what is **g**.	**Ps 107:9**	2896b
they have repaid me evil for **g** And	**Ps 109:5**	2899b
Because Your lovingkindness is **g**,	**Ps 109:21**	2896a
A **g** understanding have all those	**Ps 111:10**	2896a
thanks to the LORD, for He is **g**;	**Ps 118:1**	2896a
thanks to the LORD, for He is **g**;	**Ps 118:29**	2896a
dread, For Your ordinances are **g**.	**Ps 119:39**	2896a
Teach me **g** discernment and	**Ps 119:66**	2898
You are **g** and do good;	**Ps 119:68**	2896a
You are good and do **g**;	**Ps 119:68**	3190
is **g** for me that I was afflicted,	**Ps 119:71**	2895
Be surety for Your servant for **g**;	**Ps 119:122**	2896b
LORD our God, I will seek your **g**.	**Ps 122:9**	2896b
Do **g**, O LORD, to those who are	**Ps 125:4**	3190
good, O LORD, to those who are **g** And	**Ps 125:4**	2896a
how **g** and how pleasant it is For	**Ps 133:1**	2896a
the LORD, for the LORD is **g**;	**Ps 135:3**	2896a
thanks to the LORD, for He is **g**,	**Ps 136:1**	2896a
Let Your **g** Spirit lead me on level	**Ps 143:10**	2896a
The LORD is **g** to all, And His	**Ps 145:9**	2896a
is **g** to sing praises to our God;	**Ps 147:1**	2896a
And equity *and* every **g** course.	**Pr 2:9**	2896a
you will walk in the way of **g** men And	**Pr 2:20**	2896a
So you will find favor and **g**	**Pr 3:4**	2896a
g from those to whom it is due,	**Pr 3:27**	2896b
The merciful man does himself **g**,	**Pr 11:17**	2617a
desire of the righteous is only **g**,	**Pr 11:23**	2896b
diligently seeks **g** seeks favor,	**Pr 11:27**	2896b
A **g** man will obtain favor from the	**Pr 12:2**	2896a
A man will be satisfied with **g**	**Pr 12:14**	2896b
down, But a **g** word makes it glad.	**Pr 12:25**	2896a
fruit of a man's mouth he enjoys **g**,	**Pr 13:2**	2896b
G understanding produces favor,	**Pr 13:15**	2896a
A **g** man leaves an inheritance to	**Pr 13:22**	2896a
among the upright there is **g** will.	**Pr 14:9**	7522
But a **g** man will *be satisfied* with	**Pr 14:14**	2896a
evil will bow down before the **g**,	**Pr 14:19**	2896a
will be to those who devise **g**.	**Pr 14:22**	2896b
Watching the evil and the **g**.	**Pr 15:3**	2896a
G news puts fat on the bones.	**Pr 15:30**	2896a
to the word will find **g**,	**Pr 16:20**	2896b
leads him in a way that is not **g**.	**Pr 16:29**	2896a
He who returns evil for **g**,	**Pr 17:13**	2899b
who has a crooked mind finds no **g**,	**Pr 17:20**	2896b
A joyful heart is **g** medicine,	**Pr 17:22**	3190
also not **g** to fine the righteous,	**Pr 17:26**	2896a
partiality to the wicked is not **g**,	**Pr 18:5**	2896a
who finds a wife finds a **g** thing And	**Pr 18:22**	2896b
Also it is not **g** for a person to	**Pr 19:2**	2896a
keeps understanding will find **g**.	**Pr 19:8**	2896b
He will repay him for his **g** deed.	**Pr 19:17**	1576
LORD, And a false scale is not **g**.	**Pr 20:23**	2896a
A **g** name is to be more desired	**Pr 22:1**	
My son, eat honey, for it is **g**,	**Pr 24:13**	2896a
partiality in judgment is not **g**.	**Pr 24:23**	2896a
a **g** blessing will come upon them.	**Pr 24:25**	2896b
So is **g** news from a distant land.	**Pr 25:25**	2896a
It is not **g** to eat much honey, Nor	**Pr 25:27**	2896a
But the blameless will inherit **g**.	**Pr 28:10**	2896b
To show partiality is not **g**,	**Pr 28:21**	2896a
She does him **g** and not evil All	**Pr 31:12**	2896b
She senses that her gain is **g**;	**Pr 31:18**	2896a
until I could see what **g** there is	**Ec 2:3**	2896a
tell himself that his labor is **g**.	**Ec 2:24**	2896b
For to a person who is **g** in His	**Ec 2:26**	2896a
to one who is **g** in God's sight.	**Ec 2:26**	2896a
and to do **g** in one's lifetime;	**Ec 3:12**	2896b
eats and drinks sees **g** in all his labor	**Ec 3:13**	2896b
have a **g** return for their labor.	**Ec 4:9**	2896a
When **g** things increase, those who	**Ec 5:11**	2899b
I have seen to be **g** and fitting:	**Ec 5:18**	2896a
is not satisfied with **g** things and	**Ec 6:3**	2899b
and does not enjoy **g** things	**Ec 6:6**	2899b
g for a man during *his* lifetime,	**Ec 6:12**	2896a
A **g** name is better than a good	**Ec 7:1**	2896a
name is better than a **g** ointment,	**Ec 7:1**	2896a
Wisdom along with an inheritance is **g**	**Ec 7:11**	2896a
It is **g** that you grasp one thing and	**Ec 7:18**	2896a
does **g** and who never sins.	**Ec 7:20**	2896b
for there is nothing **g** for a man	**Ec 8:15**	2896a
for the **g**, for the clean and for	**Ec 9:2**	2896a
As the **g** man is, so is the sinner;	**Ec 9:2**	2896a
but one sinner destroys much **g**.	**Ec 9:18**	2899b
both of them alike will be **g**.	**Ec 11:6**	2896a
is **g** for the eyes to see the sun.	**Ec 11:7**	2896a
hidden, whether it is **g** or evil.	**Ec 12:14**	2896a
Learn to do **g**; Seek justice,	**Is 1:17**	3190
He expected *it* to produce **g**	**Is 5:2**	
when I expected *it* to produce **g**	**Is 5:4**	
Woe to those who call evil **g**,	**Is 5:20**	2896b
who call evil good, and **g** evil;	**Is 5:20**	2896b
to refuse evil and choose **g**.	**Is 7:15**	2896b
to refuse evil and choose **g**,	**Is 7:16**	2896b
done what is **g** in Your sight."	**Is 38:3**	2896a
LORD which you have spoken is **g**."	**Is 39:8**	2896a
O Zion, bearer of **g** news,	**Is 40:9**	
O Jerusalem, bearer of **g** news;	**Is 40:9**	
Saying of the soldering, "It is **g**";	**Is 41:7**	2896a
Indeed, do **g** or evil, that we may	**Is 41:23**	3190
will give a messenger of **g** news.'	**Is 41:27**	
accomplish all My **g** pleasure';	**Is 46:10**	2656
out His **g** pleasure on Babylon,	**Is 48:14**	2656
the feet of him who brings **g** news,	**Is 52:7**	
And brings **g** news of happiness,	**Is 52:7**	
And the **g** pleasure of the LORD	**Is 53:10**	2656
to Me, and eat what is **g**,	**Is 55:2**	2896b
And will bear **g** news of the	**Is 60:6**	
To bring **g** news to the afflicted;	**Is 61:1**	
walk *in* the way which is not **g**,	**Is 65:2**	2896a
To eat its fruit and its **g** things.	**Jer 2:7**	2898
But to do **g** they do not know."	**Jer 4:22**	3190
sins have withheld **g** from you.	**Jer 5:25**	2896b
ancient paths, Where the **g** way is,	**Jer 6:16**	2896a
waited for peace, but no **g** *came;*	**Jer 8:15**	2896b
no harm, Nor can they do any **g**."	**Jer 10:5**	3190
g Who are accustomed to doing evil.	**Jer 13:23**	3190
for peace, but nothing **g** *came;*	**Jer 14:19**	2896b
set you free for *purposes of* **g**;	**Jer 15:11**	2896b
I will think better of the **g** with which	**Jer 18:10**	2899b
Should **g** be repaid with evil?	**Jer 18:20**	2899b
You To speak **g** on their behalf,	**Jer 18:20**	2899b
city for harm and not for **g**,"	**Jer 21:10**	2899b
One basket had very **g** figs,	**Jer 24:2**	2896a
"Figs, the **g** figs, very good;	**Jer 24:3**	2896a
"Figs, the good figs, very **g**;	**Jer 24:3**	2896a
'Like these **g** figs, so I will	**Jer 24:5**	2896a
regard as **g** the captives of Judah,	**Jer 24:5**	2899b
I will set My eyes on them for **g**,	**Jer 24:6**	2899b
as is **g** and right in your sight.	**Jer 26:14**	2896a
you and fulfill My **g** word to you,	**Jer 29:10**	2896a
and he will not see the **g** that I	**Jer 29:32**	2896b
fear Me always, for their own **g** and	**Jer 32:39**	2896b
for their own good and for *the* **g** *of*	**Jer 32:39**	
turn away from them, to do them **g**;	**Jer 32:40**	3190
rejoice over them to do them **g** and	**Jer 32:41**	3190
the **g** that I am promising them.	**Jer 32:42**	2899b
of all the **g** that I do for them,	**Jer 33:9**	2899b
fear and tremble because of all the **g**	**Jer 33:9**	2899b
LORD of hosts, For the LORD is **g**,	**Jer 33:11**	2896a
'when I will fulfill the **g** word	**Jer 33:14**	2896a
seems **g** and right for you to go."	**Jer 40:4**	2896a
over them for harm and not for **g**,	**Jer 44:27**	2899b
Has **g** counsel been lost to the	**Jer 49:7**	
is **g** to those who wait for Him,	**La 3:25**	2896a
It is **g** that he waits silently For	**La 3:26**	2896a
It is **g** for a man that he should	**La 3:27**	2896a
High That both **g** and ill go forth?	**La 3:38**	2896a
in **g** soil beside abundant waters,	**Ezk 17:8**	2896a
what was not **g** among his people,	**Ezk 18:18**	2896a
gave them statutes that were not **g**	**Ezk 20:25**	2896a
in it the pieces, Every **g** piece,	**Ezk 24:4**	2896a
"I will feed them in a **g** pasture,	**Ezk 34:14**	2896a
will lie down on **g** grazing ground	**Ezk 34:14**	2896a
you should feed in the **g** pasture,	**Ezk 34:18**	2896a
"For **g** reason they have made you	**Ezk 36:3**	
and your deeds that were not **g**,	**Ezk 36:31**	2896a
"It has seemed **g** to me to declare	**Da 4:2**	8232
It seemed **g** to Darius to appoint	**Da 6:1**	8232
Israel has rejected the **g**;	**Hos 8:3**	2896b
Seek **g** and not evil, that you may	**Am 5:14**	2896b
Hate evil, love **g**, And establish	**Am 5:15**	2896b
them for evil and not for **g**."	**Am 9:4**	2899b
you have **g** reason to be angry?"	**Jon 4:4**	3190
"Do you have **g** reason to be angry	**Jon 4:9**	3190
"I have **g** reason to be angry,	**Jon 4:9**	3190
Maroth Becomes weak waiting for **g**,	**Mi 1:12**	2896b
do **g** To the one walking uprightly?	**Mi 2:7**	3190
"You who hate **g** and love evil,	**Mi 3:2**	2896b
He has told you, O man, what is **g**;	**Mi 6:8**	2896a
The LORD is **g**, A stronghold in the	**Na 1:7**	2896a
the feet of him who brings **g** news,	**Na 1:15**	
'The LORD will not do **g** or evil!'	**Zph 1:12**	3190
do **g** to Jerusalem and to the house of	**Zch 8:15**	3190
"If it is **g** in your sight, give	**Zch 11:12**	2896a
is **g** in the sight of the LORD,	**Mal 2:17**	2896a
that does not bear **g** fruit is cut down	**Mt 3:10**	*2570*
It is no longer **g** for anything,	**Mt 5:13**	*2480*
that they may see your **g** works,	**Mt 5:16**	*2570*

sun to rise on *the* evil and *the* **g**, Mt 5:45 *18*
to give **g** gifts to your children, Mt 7:11 *18*
what is **g** to those who ask Him! Mt 7:11 *18*
"So every **g** tree bears good fruit, Mt 7:17 *18*
"So every good tree bears **g** fruit, Mt 7:17 *2570*
"A **g** tree cannot produce bad Mt 7:18 *18*
can a bad tree produce **g** fruit. Mt 7:18 *2570*
"Every tree that does not bear **g** fruit Mt 7:19 *2570*
lawful to do **g** on the Sabbath." Mt 12:12 *2573*
"Either make the tree **g** and Mt 12:33 *2570*
the tree good and its fruit **g** Mt 12:33 *2570*
you, being evil, speak what is **g**? Mt 12:34 *18*
"The **g** man brings out of *his* good Mt 12:35 *18*
good man brings out of *his* **g** treasure Mt 12:35 *18*
of *his* good treasure what is **g**; Mt 12:35 *18*
"And others fell on the **g** soil and Mt 13:8 *2570*
whom seed was sown on the **g** soil, Mt 13:23 *2570*
man who sowed **g** seed in his field. Mt 13:24 *2570*
you not sow **g** seed in your field? Mt 13:27 *2570*
sows the **g** seed is the Son of Man, Mt 13:37 *2570*
and *as for* the **g** seed, these are Mt 13:38 *2570*
the **g** *fish* into containers, Mt 13:48 *2570*
"It is not **g** to take the Mt 15:26 *2570*
"Lord, it is **g** for us to be here; Mt 17:4 *2570*
what **g** thing shall I do that I may Mt 19:16 *18*
are you asking Me about what is **g**? Mt 19:17 *18*
There is *only* One who is **g**; Mt 19:17 *18*
all they found, both evil and **g**; Mt 22:10 *18*
'Well done, **g** and faithful slave. Mt 25:21 *18*
'Well done, **g** and faithful slave. Mt 25:23 *18*
For she has done a **g** deed to Me. Mt 26:10 *2570*
for a **g** opportunity to betray Jesus. Mt 26:16 *2120*
It would have been **g** for that man Mt 26:24 *2570*
to do **g** or to do harm on the Sabbath, Mk 3:4 *18*
"Other *seeds* fell into the **g** soil Mk 4:8 *2570*
whom seed was sown on the **g** soil; Mk 4:20 *2570*
for it is not **g** to take the Mk 7:27 *2570*
"Rabbi, it is **g** for us to be here; Mk 9:5 *2570*
"Salt is **g**; but if the salt becomes Mk 9:50 *2570*
"**G** Teacher, what shall I do to Mk 10:17 *18*
"Why do you call Me **g**? Mk 10:18 *18*
No one is **g** except God alone. Mk 10:18 *18*
She has done a **g** deed to Me. Mk 14:6 *2570*
you wish you can do **g** to them; Mk 14:7 *2095*
It would have been **g** for that man Mk 14:21 *2570*
you and to bring you this **g** news. Lk 1:19 *2097*
FILLED THE HUNGRY WITH **G** THINGS; Lk 1:53 *18*
I bring you **g** news of great joy Lk 2:10 *2097*
that does not bear **g** fruit is cut down Lk 3:9 *2570*
'The old is **g** *enough*.' " Lk 5:39 *5543*
it lawful to do **g** or to do harm on Lk 6:9 *15*
do **g** to those who hate you, Lk 6:27 *2573*
do **g** to those who do good to you, Lk 6:33 *15*
do good to those who do **g** to you, Lk 6:33 *15*
"But love your enemies, and do **g**, Lk 6:35 *15*
g measure—pressed down, shaken Lk 6:38 *2570*
g tree which produces bad fruit, Lk 6:43 *2570*
a bad tree which produces **g** fruit. Lk 6:43 *2570*
"The **g** man out of the good Lk 6:45 *18*
"The good man out of the **g** Lk 6:45 *18*
his heart brings forth what is **g**; Lk 6:45 *18*
they found the slave in **g** health. Lk 7:10 *5198*
Other *seed* fell into the **g** soil, Lk 8:8 *18*
"But the *seed* in the **g** soil, Lk 8:15 *2570*
the word in an honest and **g** heart, Lk 8:15 *18*
"Master, it is **g** for us to be here; Lk 9:33 *2570*
for Mary has chosen the **g** part, Lk 10:42 *18*
to give **g** gifts to your children, Lk 11:13 *18*
"Therefore, salt is **g**; Lk 14:34 *2570*
life you received your **g** things, Lk 16:25 *18*
"**G** Teacher, what shall I do to Lk 18:18 *18*
"Why do you call Me **g**? Lk 18:19 *18*
No one is **g** except God alone. Lk 18:19 *18*
'Well done, **g** slave, because you Lk 19:17 *18*
and *began* seeking a **g** opportunity Lk 22:6 *2120*
Council, a **g** and righteous man Lk 23:50 *18*
g thing come out of Nazareth?" Jn 1:46 *18*
"Every man serves the **g** wine first, Jn 2:10 *2570*
have kept the **g** wine until now." Jn 2:10 *2570*
those who did the **g** *deeds* to a Jn 5:29 *18*
some were saying, "He is a **g** man"; Jn 7:12 *18*
"I am the **g** shepherd; Jn 10:11 *2570*
the **g** shepherd lays down His life Jn 10:11 *2570*
"I am the **g** shepherd, Jn 10:14 *2570*
you many **g** works from the Father; Jn 10:32 *2570*
"For a **g** work we do not stone Jn 10:33 *2570*
see that you are not doing any **g**; Jn 12:19 *5623*
here before you in **g** health. Ac 4:10 *5199*
seven men of **g** reputation, Ac 6:3 *3140*
believed Philip preaching the **g** news Ac 8:12 *2097*
and *how* He went about doing **g** and Ac 10:38 *2109*
for he was a **g** man, and full of Ac 11:24 *18*
"And we preach to you the **g** news Ac 13:32 *2097*
in that He did **g** and gave you Ac 14:17 *19a*
Then it seemed **g** to the apostles Ac 15:22 *1380*
it seemed **g** to us, having become Ac 15:25 *1380*
"For it seemed **g** to the Holy Ac 15:28 *1380*
g to Silas to remain there. Ac 15:34 *1380*
a perfectly **g** conscience before God Ac 23:1 *18*
sailed slowly for a **g** many days, Ac 27:7 *2425*
in doing **g** seek for glory and honor Ro 2:7 *18*
and peace to everyone who does **g**, Ro 2:10 *18*
"Let us do evil that **g** may come"? Ro 3:8 *18*
THERE IS NONE WHO DOES **G**, Ro 3:12 *5544*
now as **g** as dead since he was Ro 4:19
though perhaps for the **g** man Ro 5:7 *18*
is holy and righteous and **g**. Ro 7:12 *18*
Therefore did that which is **g** Ro 7:13 *18*
my death through that which is **g**, Ro 7:13 *18*
the Law, *confessing* that the Law is **g**. Ro 7:16 *2570*
know that nothing **g** dwells in me, Ro 7:18 *18*
me, but the doing of the **g** *is* not. Ro 7:18 *2570*
For the **g** that I want, I do not do Ro 7:19 *18*
in me, the one who wants to do **g**. Ro 7:21 *2570*
for **g** to those who love God, Ro 8:28 *18*
had not done anything **g** or bad, Ro 9:11 *18*
ARE THE FEET OF THOSE WHO BRING **G** Ro 10:15 *2097*
OF THOSE WHO BRING GOOD NEWS OF **G** Ro 10:15 *18*
However, they did not all heed the **g** Ro 10:16 *2098*
is **g** and acceptable and perfect. Ro 12:2 *18*
cling to what is **g**. Ro 12:9 *18*
by evil, but overcome evil with **g**. Ro 12:21 *18*
a cause of fear for **g** behavior, Ro 13:3 *18*
Do what is **g** and you will have Ro 13:3 *18*
is a minister of God to you for **g**. Ro 13:4 *18*
a **g** thing be spoken of as evil; Ro 14:16 *18*
It is **g** not to eat meat or to Ro 14:21 *2570*
to please his neighbor for his **g**, Ro 15:2 *18*
want you to be wise in what is **g** and Ro 16:19 *18*
Your boasting is not **g**. 1Co 5:6 *2570*
it is **g** for a man not to touch a 1Co 7:1 *2570*
it is **g** for them if they remain even as 1Co 7:8 *2570*
I think then that this is **g** in 1Co 7:26 *2570*
is **g** for a man to remain as he is. 1Co 7:26 *2570*
Let no one seek his own **g**, but 1Co 10:24
of the Spirit for the common **g**. 1Co 12:7 *4851a*
"Bad company corrupts **g** morals." 1Co 15:33 *5543*
being always of **g** courage, 2Co 5:6 *2292*
we are of **g** courage, I say, and 2Co 5:8 *2292*
he has done, whether **g** or bad. 2Co 5:10 *18*
by evil report and **g** report; 2Co 6:8 *2162*
an abundance for every **g** deed; 2Co 9:8 *18*
But it is **g** always to be eagerly Ga 4:18 *2570*
all **g** things with the one who teaches Ga 6:6 *18*
Let us not lose heart in doing **g**, Ga 6:9 *2570*
let us do **g** to all people, Ga 6:10 *18*
to make a **g** showing in the flesh Ga 6:12 *2146a*
in Christ Jesus for **g** works, Eph 2:10 *18*
with his own hands what is **g**, Eph 4:28 *18*
but only such a *word* as is **g** for Eph 4:29 *18*
With **g** will render service, as to Eph 6:7 *2133*
whatever **g** thing each one does, Eph 6:8 *18*
that He who began a **g** work in you Php 1:6 *18*
strife, but some also from **g** will; Php 1:15 *2107*
and to work for *His* **g** pleasure. Php 2:13 *2107*
lovely, whatever is of **g** repute, Php 4:8 *2163*
bearing fruit in every **g** work and Col 1:10 *18*
For it was the *Father's* **g** pleasure Col 1:19 *2106*
rejoicing to see your **g** discipline Col 2:5 *5010*
us **g** news of your faith and love, 1Th 3:6 *2097*
but always seek after that which is **g** 1Th 5:15 *18*
hold fast to that which is **g**; 1Th 5:21 *2570*
comfort and **g** hope by grace, 2Th 2:16 *18*
hearts in every **g** work and word. 2Th 2:17 *18*
do not grow weary of doing **g**. 2Th 3:13 *2569*
a pure heart and a **g** conscience and 1Tm 1:5 *18*
But we know that the Law is **g**, 1Tm 1:8 *2570*
by them you fight the **g** fight, 1Tm 1:18 *2570*
keeping faith and a **g** conscience, 1Tm 1:19 *18*
This is **g** and acceptable in the 1Tm 2:3 *2570*
but rather by means of **g** works, 1Tm 2:10 *18*
And he must have a **g** reputation 1Tm 3:7 *2570*
and **g** managers of *their* children 1Tm 3:12 *2573*
everything created by God is **g**, 1Tm 4:4 *2570*
be a **g** servant of Christ Jesus, 1Tm 4:6 *2570*
having a reputation for **g** works; 1Tm 5:10 *2570*
devoted herself to every **g** work. 1Tm 5:10 *18*
deeds that are **g** are quite evident, 1Tm 5:25 *2570*
Fight the **g** fight of faith; 1Tm 6:12 *2570*
and you made the **g** confession in 1Tm 6:12 *2570*
who testified the **g** confession 1Tm 6:13 *2570*
Instruct them to do **g**, 1Tm 6:18 *14*
to do good, to be rich in **g** works, 1Tm 6:18 *2570*
of a **g** foundation for the future, 1Tm 6:19 *2570*
as a **g** soldier of Christ Jesus. 2Tm 2:3 *2570*
Master, prepared for every **g** work. 2Tm 2:21 *18*
self-control, brutal, haters of **g**, 2Tm 3:3 *865*
equipped for every **g** work. 2Tm 3:17 *18*
I have fought the **g** fight, 2Tm 4:7 *2570*
but hospitable, loving what is **g**, Ti 1:8 *5358*
and worthless for any **g** deed. Ti 1:16 *18*
to much wine, teaching what is **g**, Ti 2:3 *2567*
to be an example of **g** deeds, Ti 2:7 *2570*
but showing all **g** faith so that they Ti 2:10 *18*
possession, zealous for **g** deeds. Ti 2:14 *2570*
to be ready for every **g** deed, Ti 3:1 *18*
be careful to engage in **g** deeds. Ti 3:8 *2570*
are **g** and profitable for men. Ti 3:8 *2570*
learn to engage in **g** deeds to meet Ti 3:14 *2570*
knowledge of every **g** thing which is in Phm 1:6 *18*
we have had **g** news preached to us, Heb 4:2 *2097*
and those who formerly had **g** news Heb 4:6 *2097*
trained to discern **g** and evil. Heb 5:14 *2570*
and have tasted the **g** word of God Heb 6:5 *2570*
priest of the **g** things to come, Heb 9:11 *18*
it has *only* a shadow of the **g** things Heb 10:1 *18*
one another to love and **g** deeds, Heb 10:24 *2570*
man, and him as **g** as dead at that, Heb 11:12
but He *disciplines us* for *our* **g**, Heb 12:10 *4851a*
for it is **g** for the heart to be Heb 13:9 *2570*
not neglect doing **g** and sharing, Heb 13:16 *2140*
sure that we have a **g** conscience, Heb 13:18 *2570*
in every **g** thing to do His will, Heb 13:21 *18*
Every **g** thing given and every Jas 1:17 *18*
"You sit here in a **g** place," Jas 2:3 *2573*
Let him show by his **g** behavior his Jas 3:13 *2570*
full of mercy and **g** fruits, Jas 3:17 *18*
may because of your **g** deeds, 1Pe 2:12 *2570*
to those who are **g** and gentle, 1Pe 2:18 *18*
DESIRES LIFE, TO LOVE AND SEE **G** DAYS, 1Pe 3:10 *18*
MUST TURN AWAY FROM EVIL AND DO **G**; 1Pe 3:11 *18*
you prove zealous for what is **g**? 1Pe 3:13 *18*
and keep a **g** conscience so that in 1Pe 3:16 *18*
those who revile your **g** behavior 1Pe 3:16 *18*
appeal to God for a **g** conscience 1Pe 3:21 *18*
as **g** stewards of the manifold 1Pe 4:10 *2570*
may prosper and be in **g** health, 3Jn 1:2 *5198*
what is evil, but what is **g**. 3Jn 1:11 *18*
The one who does **g** is of God; 3Jn 1:11 *15*
Demetrius has received a **g** 3Jn 1:12

GOOD-BYE

me to say **g** to those at home." Lk 9:61 *657*

GOOD-FOR-NOTHING

'You **g**,' shall be guilty before Mt 5:22 *4469*

GOOD-LOOKING

in whom was no defect, who were **g**, Da 1:4 2896a, 4758

GOODNESS

Jethro rejoiced over all the **g** which Ex 18:9 2899b
make all My **g** pass before you, Ex 33:19 2898
I also will show this **g** to you, 2Sa 2:6 2899b
glad of heart for all the **g** that the 1Ki 8:66 2899b
happy of heart because of the **g** that 2Ch 7:10 2899b
fat, And reveled in Your great **g**. Ne 9:25 2898
g which You gave them, Ne 9:35 2898
Surely **g** and lovingkindness will Ps 23:6 2896b
that I would see the **g** of the LORD Ps 27:13 2898
How great is Your **g**, Ps 31:19 2898
satisfied with the **g** of Your house, Ps 65:4 2898
provided in Your **g** for the poor, Ps 68:10 2899b
the memory of Your abundant **g** Ps 145:7 2898
g toward the house of Israel, Is 63:7 2898
will be satisfied with My **g**," Jer 31:14 2898
and to His **g** in the last days. Hos 3:5 2898
that you yourselves are full of **g**, Ro 15:14 *19b*
joy, peace, patience, kindness, **g**, Ga 5:22 *19b*
all **g** and righteousness and truth), Eph 5:9 *19b*
and fulfill every desire for **g** and 2Th 1:11 *19b*
that your **g** would not be, Phm 1:14 *18*

GOODNESS'

For Your **g** sake, O LORD. Ps 25:7 2898

GOODS

Then they took all the **g** of Sodom Gn 14:11 7399
He brought back all the **g**, Gn 14:16 7399
me and take the **g** for yourself." Gn 14:21 7399
you have felt through all my **g**, Gn 31:37 3627
you found of all your household **g**? Gn 31:37 3627
and all his **g** which he had acquired Gn 36:6 7075
concern yourselves with your **g**, Gn 45:20 3627
money or **g** to keep *for him* Ex 22:7 3627
all their flocks and all their **g** they Nu 31:9 2428
much among them, *including* **g**, 2Ch 20:25 7399
king's portion of his **g** for the burnt 2Ch 31:3 7399
and gold, with **g** and cattle, Ezr 1:4 7399
of silver, with gold, with **g**, Ezr 1:6 7399
banishment or for confiscation of **g** Ezr 7:26 5232
household **g** out of the room. Ne 13:8 3627
g *will go* to the house of an alien; Pr 5:10 6089a
Their tent curtains, all their **g** and Jer 49:29 3627
of the abundance of your **g**; Ezk 27:16 4639
of the abundance of your **g**, Ezk 27:18 4639
who have acquired cattle and **g**, Ezk 38:12 7075
gold, to take away cattle and **g**, Ezk 38:13 7075
will store all my grain and my **g**. Lk 12:18 *18*
you have many **g** laid up for many Lk 12:19 *18*
whose **g** are in the house Lk 17:31 *4632*
But whoever has the world's **g**, 1Jn 3:17 *979*

GOPHER

for yourself an ark of **g** wood; Gn 6:14 1613

GORE

you will **g** the Arameans until 1Ki 22:11 5055
these you shall **g** the Arameans until 2Ch 18:10 5055

GORES

an ox **g** a man or a woman to death, Ex 21:28 5055
"Whether it **g** a son or a Ex 21:31 5055
the ox **g** a male or female slave, Ex 21:32 5055

GORGEOUS

dressed Him in a **g** robe and sent Lk 23:11 *2986*

GORING

ox was previously in the habit of **g** and Ex 21:29 5056
ox was previously in the habit of **g**, Ex 21:36 5056

GOSHEN

You shall live in the land of **G**, Gn 45:10 1657
point out *the way* before him to **G**; Gn 46:28 1657
and they came into the land of **G**. Gn 46:28 1657
up to **G** to meet his father Israel; Gn 46:29 1657
you may live in the land of **G**; Gn 46:34 1657
they are in the land of **G**." Gn 47:1 1657
servants live in the land of **G**." Gn 47:4 1657
let them live in the land of **G**; Gn 47:6 1657
lived in the land of Egypt, in **G**, Gn 47:27 1657
and their herds in the land of **G**. Gn 50:8 1657
I will set apart the land of **G**, Ex 8:22 1657
Only in the land of **G**, Ex 9:26 1657
of **G** even as far as Gibeon. Jos 10:41 1657
all the Negev, all that land of **G**, Jos 11:16 1657
and **G** and Holon and Giloh; Jos 15:51 1657

GOSPEL

proclaiming the **g** of the kingdom, Mt 4:23 *2098*
proclaiming the **g** of the kingdom, Mt 9:35 *2098*
POOR HAVE THE **G** PREACHED TO THEM. Mt 11:5 *2097*
"This **g** of the kingdom shall Mt 24:14 *2098*
wherever this **g** is preached in the Mt 26:13 *2098*
of the **g** of Jesus Christ, Mk 1:1 *2098*

Galilee, preaching the **g** of God, Mk 1:14 *2098*
repent and believe in the **g**." Mk 1:15 *2098*
"The **g** must first be preached Mk 13:10 *2098*
wherever the **g** is preached in the Mk 14:9 *2098*
and preach the **g** to all creation. Mk 16:15 *2098*
he preached the **g** to the people. Lk 3:18 *2097*
ME TO PREACH THE **G** TO THE POOR. Lk 4:18 *2097*
POOR HAVE THE **G** PREACHED TO THEM. Lk 7:22 *2097*
the villages, preaching the **g** and Lk 9:6 *2097*
since that time the **g** of the kingdom of Lk 16:16 *2097*
in the temple and preaching the **g**, Lk 20:1 *2097*
and were preaching the **g** to many Ac 8:25 *2097*
preaching the **g** to all the cities until Ac 8:40 *2097*
they continued to preach the **g**. Ac 14:7 *2097*
and preach the **g** to you Ac 14:15 *2097*
After they had preached the **g** Ac 14:21 *2097*
the word of the **g** and believe. Ac 15:7 *2098*
called us to preach the **g** to them. Ac 16:10 *2097*
of the **g** of the grace of God. Ac 20:24 *2098*
set apart for the **g** of God, Ro 1:1 *2098*
the *preaching of the* **g** of His Son, Ro 1:9 *2098*
the **g** to you also who are in Rome. Ro 1:15 *2097*
For I am not ashamed of the **g**, Ro 1:16 *2098*
the day when, according to my **g**, Ro 2:16 *2098*
From the standpoint of the **g** they Ro 11:28 *2098*
as a priest the **g** of God, Ro 15:16 *2098*
fully preached the **g** of Christ. Ro 15:19 *2098*
thus I aspired to preach the **g**, Ro 15:20 *2097*
establish you according to my **g** Ro 16:25 *2098*
to baptize, but to preach the **g**, 1Co 1:17 *2097*
became your father through the **g**. 1Co 4:15 *2098*
no hindrance to the **g** of Christ. 1Co 9:12 *2098*
directed those who proclaim the **g** 1Co 9:14 *2098*
to get their living from the **g**. 1Co 9:14 *2098*
For if I preach the **g**, 1Co 9:16 *2097*
woe is me if I do not preach the **g**. 1Co 9:16 *2097*
That, when I preach the **g**, 1Co 9:18 *2097*
I may offer the **g** without charge, 1Co 9:18 *2098*
full use of my right in the **g**. 1Co 9:18 *2098*
all things for the sake of the **g**, 1Co 9:23 *2098*
the **g** which I preached to you, 1Co 15:1 *2098*
I came to Troas for the **g** of Christ 2Co 2:12 *2098*
And even if our **g** is veiled, it is 2Co 4:3 *2098*
light of the **g** of the glory of Christ, 2Co 4:4 *2098*
whose fame in *the things of* the **g** *has* 2Co 8:18 *2098*
confession of the **g** of Christ and 2Co 9:13 *2098*
as far as you in the **g** of Christ; 2Co 10:14 *2098*
so as to preach the **g** even to the 2Co 10:16 *2097*
g which you have not accepted, 2Co 11:4 *2098*
g of God to you without charge? 2Co 11:7 *2098*
of Christ, for a different **g**; Ga 1:6 *2098*
want to distort the **g** of Christ. Ga 1:7 *2098*
should preach to you a **g** contrary Ga 1:8 *2097*
if any man is preaching to you a **g** Ga 1:9 *2097*
that the **g** which was preached by Ga 1:11 *2098*
and I submitted to them the **g** Ga 2:2 *2098*
of the **g** would remain with you. Ga 2:5 *2098*
with the **g** to the uncircumcised, Ga 2:7 *2098*
about the truth of the **g**, Ga 2:14 *2098*
the **g** beforehand to Abraham, Ga 3:8 *4283*
preached the **g** to you the first time; Ga 4:13 *2097*
the **g** of your salvation Eph 1:13 *2098*
in Christ Jesus through the **g**, Eph 3:6 *2098*
THE PREPARATION OF THE **G** OF PEACE; Eph 6:15 *2098*
boldness the mystery of the **g**, Eph 6:19 *2098*
g from the first day until now. Php 1:5 *2098*
defense and confirmation of the **g**, Php 1:7 *2098*
for the greater progress of the **g**, Php 1:12 *2098*
for the defense of the **g**; Php 1:16 *2098*
manner worthy of the **g** of Christ, Php 1:27 *2098*
together for the faith of the **g**; Php 1:27 *2098*
with me in the furtherance of the **g** Php 2:22 *2098*
my struggle in *the cause of* the **g**, Php 4:3 *2098*
at the first preaching of the **g**, Php 4:15 *2098*
heard in the word of truth, the **g** Col 1:5 *2098*
hope of the **g** that you have heard, Col 1:23 *2098*
for our **g** did not come to you in 1Th 1:5 *2098*
the **g** of God amid much opposition. 1Th 2:2 *2098*
by God to be entrusted with the **g**, 1Th 2:4 *2098*
not only the **g** of God but also our 1Th 2:8 *2098*
we proclaimed to you the **g** of God. 1Th 2:9 *2098*
fellow worker in the **g** of Christ, 1Th 3:2 *2098*
not obey the **g** of our Lord Jesus. 2Th 1:8 *2098*
this He called you through our **g**, 2Th 2:14 *2098*
the glorious **g** of the blessed God, 1Tm 1:11 *2098*
g according to the power of God, 2Tm 1:8 *2098*
immortality to light through the **g**, 2Tm 1:10 *2098*
of David, according to my **g**, 2Tm 2:8 *2098*
me in my imprisonment for the **g**; Phm 1:13 *2098*
those who preached the **g** to you 1Pe 1:12 *2097*
For the **g** has for this purpose 1Pe 4:6 *2097*
who do not obey the **g** of God? 1Pe 4:17 *2098*
having an eternal **g** to preach to Rv 14:6 *2098*

GOSPEL'S
My sake and the **g** will save it. Mk 8:35 *2098*
for My sake and for the **g** sake, Mk 10:29 *2098*

GOSSIP
do not associate with a **g**. Pr 20:19 6601a, 8193
tempers, disputes, slanders, **g**, 2Co 12:20 *5587*

GOSSIPS
strife, deceit, malice; *they are* **g**, Ro 1:29 *5588*
be dignified, not malicious **g**, 1Tm 3:11 *1228*
idle, but also **g** and busybodies, 1Tm 5:13 *5397*
irreconcilable, malicious **g**, 2Tm 3:3 *1228*
their behavior, not malicious **g** nor Ti 2:3 *1228*

GOT
So he went and **g** *them,* and brought Gn 27:14 3947
she **g** him a wicker basket and Ex 2:3 3947
or what he **g** by extortion, Lv 6:4 6231
So they **g** back from around the Nu 16:27 5927
they **g** up early in the morning, Jg 19:5 7925
I **g** up and went out to the plain; Ezk 3:23 6965
Then I **g** up *again* and carried on Da 8:27 6965
So Joseph **g** up and took the Child Mt 2:14 *1453*
So Joseph **g** up, took the Child Mt 2:21 *1453*
and she **g** up and waited on Him. Mt 8:15 *1453*
When He **g** into the boat, His Mt 8:23 *1684*
Then He **g** up and rebuked the winds Mt 8:26 *1453*
And he **g** up and went home. Mt 9:7 *1453*
And he **g** up and followed Him. Mt 9:9 *450*
Jesus **g** up and *began* to follow Mt 9:19 *1453*
and the girl **g** up. Mt 9:25 *1453*
He **g** into a boat and sat down, Mt 13:2 *1684*
And Peter **g** out of the boat, and Mt 14:29 *2597*
When they **g** into the boat, the Mt 14:32 *305*
crowds, Jesus **g** into the boat Mt 15:39 *1684*
all **g** drowsy and *began* to sleep. Mt 25:5 *3573*
Jesus **g** up, left *the house,* Mk 1:35 *450*
And he **g** up and immediately picked up Mk 2:12 *1453*
And he **g** up and followed Him. Mk 2:14 *450*
He **g** into a boat in the sea and sat Mk 4:1 *1684*
And He **g** up and rebuked the wind Mk 4:39 *1326*
When He **g** out of the boat, Mk 5:2 *1831*
Immediately the girl **g** up and *began* Mk 5:42 *450*
cities, and **g** there ahead of them. Mk 6:33 *4281*
Then He **g** into the boat with them, Mk 6:51 *305*
When they **g** out of the boat, Mk 6:54 *1831*
Jesus **g** up and went away from there Mk 7:24 *450*
hand and raised him; and he **g** up. Mk 9:27 *450*
and they **g** up and drove Him out of Lk 4:29 *450*
Then He **g** up and *left* Lk 4:38 *450*
and she immediately **g** up and waited Lk 4:39 *450*
And He **g** into one of the boats, Lk 5:3 *1684*
Immediately he **g** up before them, Lk 5:25 *450*
he left everything behind, and **g** up Lk 5:28 *450*
And he **g** up and came forward. Lk 6:8 *450*
and His disciples **g** into a boat, Lk 8:22 *1684*
And He **g** up and rebuked the wind Lk 8:24 *1326*
and He **g** into a boat and returned. Lk 8:37 *1684*
her spirit returned, and she **g** up Lk 8:55 *450*
he **g** up and came to his father. Lk 15:20 *450*
Then the whole body of them **g** up Lk 23:1 *450*
But Peter **g** up and ran to the tomb; Lk 24:12 *450*
And they **g** up that very hour Lk 24:33 *450*
themselves **g** into the small boats, Jn 6:24 *1684*
And when she heard it, she **g** up Jn 11:29 *1453*
when they saw that Mary **g** up quickly Jn 11:31 *450*
g up from supper, and laid aside His Jn 13:4 *1453*
went out and **g** into the boat; Jn 21:3 *1684*
So when they **g** out on the land, Jn 21:9 *576*
young men **g** up and covered him up, Ac 5:6 *450*
So he **g** up and went; and there was Ac 8:27 *450*
Saul **g** up from the ground, and Ac 9:8 *1453*
and he **g** up and was baptized; Ac 9:18 *450*
Immediately he **g** up. Ac 9:34 *450*
And on the next day he **g** up and went Ac 10:23 *450*
he **g** up and entered the city. Ac 14:20 *450*
After these days we **g** ready Ac 21:15 *1980b*
When he **g** to the stairs, Ac 21:35 *1096*

GOTTEN
"I have **g** a manchild with *the* Gn 4:1 7069
the fishermen had **g** out of them and Lk 5:2 *576*

GOUGE
that I will **g** out the right eye of 1Sa 11:2 5365

GOUGED
seized him and **g** out his eyes; Jg 16:21 5365

GOURDS
the shape of **g** and open flowers; 1Ki 6:18 6497
Under its brim **g** went around 1Ki 7:24 6497
the **g** were in two rows, cast with 1Ki 7:24 6497
from it his lap full of wild **g**, 2Ki 4:39 6498

GOVERN
the greater light to **g** the day, Gn 1:16 4475
the lesser light to **g** the night; Gn 1:16 4475
and to **g** the day and the night, Gn 1:18 4910
then you will also **g** My house and Zch 3:7 1777

GOVERNED
in the days when the judges **g**, Ru 1:1 8199

GOVERNING
g all *the provinces* beyond the Ezr 4:20 7990
subjection to the **g** authorities. Ro 13:1 *5242*

GOVERNMENT
the **g** will rest on His shoulders; Is 9:6 4951
the increase of *His* **g** or of peace, Is 9:7 4951
Daniel in regard to **g** affairs; Da 6:4 4437

GOVERNOR
return him to Amon the **g** of the city 1Ki 22:26 8269
gate of Joshua the **g** of the city, 2Ki 23:8 8269
of Babylon had appointed Gedaliah **g**, 2Ki 25:23
him to Amon the **g** of the city and 2Ch 18:25 8269
The **g** said to them that they Ezr 2:63 8660
the **g** of *the province* beyond the Ezr 5:3 6347
the **g** of *the province* beyond the Ezr 5:6 6347
whom he had appointed **g**. Ezr 5:14 6347
g of *the province* beyond the Ezr 6:6 6347
let the **g** of the Jews and the Ezr 6:7 6347
the **g** of *the province* beyond the Ezr 6:13 6347
repairs for the official seat of the **g** Ne 3:7 6346
be their **g** in the land of Judah, Ne 5:14 6346
The **g** said to them that they Ne 7:65 8660
The **g** gave to the treasury 1,000 Ne 7:70 8660
Then Nehemiah, who was the **g**, Ne 8:9 8660
Nehemiah the **g**, the son of Ne 10:1 8660
and in the days of Nehemiah the **g** Ne 12:26 6346
the son of Shealtiel, **g** of Judah, Hg 1:1 6346
the son of Shealtiel, **g** of Judah, Hg 1:14 6346
the son of Shealtiel, **g** of Judah, Hg 2:2 6346
to Zerubbabel **g** of Judah, Hg 2:21 6346
Why not offer it to your **g**? Mal 1:8 6346
delivered Him to Pilate the **g**. Mt 27:2 *2232*
Now Jesus stood before the **g**, Mt 27:11 *2232*
and the **g** questioned Him, Mt 27:11 *2232*
so the **g** was quite amazed. Mt 27:14 *2232*
Now at *the* feast the **g** was Mt 27:15 *2232*
the **g** said to them, Mt 27:21 *2232*
Then the soldiers of the **g** took Mt 27:27 *2232*
while Quirinius was **g** of Syria. Lk 2:2 *2230*
Pontius Pilate was **g** of Judea, Lk 3:1 *2230*
rule and the authority of the **g**. Lk 20:20 *2232*
and he made him **g** over Egypt and Ac 7:10 *2233*
bring him safely to Felix the **g**. Ac 23:24 *2232*
to the most excellent **g** Felix, Ac 23:26 *2232*
and delivered the letter to the **g**, Ac 23:33 *2232*
charges to the **g** against Paul. Ac 24:1 *2232*
saying *to the* **g**, "Since we have Ac 24:2
the **g** had nodded for him to speak, Ac 24:10 *2232*
king stood up and the **g** and Bernice, Ac 26:30 *2232*

GOVERNOR'S
have eaten the **g** food *allowance.* Ne 5:14 6346
not demand the **g** food *allowance,* Ne 5:18 6346
if this should come to the **g** ears, Mt 28:14 *2232*

GOVERNORS
Arabs and the **g** of the country. 1Ki 10:15 6346
the **g** of the country brought gold 2Ch 9:14 6346
the judges and the lesser **g**, Ezr 4:9 671b
and to the **g** *in the provinces* Ezr 8:36 6346
let letters be given me for the **g** *of the* Ne 2:7 6346
Then I came to the **g** *of the* Ne 2:9 6346
But the former **g** who were before Ne 5:15 6346
the **g** who were over each province and Es 3:12 6346
to the Jews, the satraps, the **g** and Es 8:9 6346
the provinces, the satraps, the **g** and Es 9:3 6346
with you I shatter **g** and prefects. Jer 51:23 6346
Their **g** and all their prefects, Jer 51:28 6346
and her wise men drunk, Her **g**, Jer 51:57 6346
in purple, **g** and officials, Ezk 23:6 6346
the Assyrians, **g** and officials, Ezk 23:12 6346
men, **g** and officials all of them, Ezk 23:23 6346
satraps, the prefects and the **g**, Da 3:2 6347
satraps, the prefects and the **g**, Da 3:3 6347
the **g** and the king's high Da 3:27 6347
the high officials and the **g** have Da 6:7 6347
before **g** and kings for My sake, Mt 10:18 *2232*
before **g** and kings for My sake, Mk 13:9 *2232*
kings and **g** for My name's sake. Lk 21:12 *2232*
or to **g** as sent by him for the 1Pe 2:14 *2232*

GOZAN
and Habor, *on* the river of **G**, 2Ki 17:6 1470
and on the Habor, the river of **G**, 2Ki 18:11 1470
even **G** and Haran and Rezeph and 2Ki 19:12 1470
Hara and to the river of **G**, 1Ch 5:26 1470
even **G** and Haran and Rezeph and Is 37:12 1470

GRACE
g has been *shown* from the LORD Ezr 9:8 8467
G is poured upon Your lips; Ps 45:2 2580
The LORD gives **g** and glory; Ps 84:11 2580
Yet He gives **g** to the afflicted. Pr 3:34 2580
place on your head a garland of **g**; Pr 4:9 2580
Found **g** in the wilderness Jer 31:2 2580
shouts of "**G**, grace to it!" Zch 4:7 2580
shouts of "Grace, **g** to it!" Zch 4:7 2580
Spirit of **g** and of supplication, Zch 12:10 2580
and the **g** of God was upon Him. Lk 2:40 *5485*
the Father, full of **g** and truth. Jn 1:14 *5485*
all received, and **g** upon grace. Jn 1:16 *5485*
all received, and grace upon **g**. Jn 1:16 *5485*
g and truth were realized through Jn 1:17 *5485*
and abundant **g** was upon them all. Ac 4:33 *5485*
And Stephen, full of **g** and power, Ac 6:8 *5485*
arrived and witnessed the **g** of God, Ac 11:23 *5485*
them to continue in the **g** of God. Ac 13:43 *5485*
testifying to the word of His **g**, Ac 14:3 *5485*
had been commended to the **g** of God Ac 14:26 *5485*
through the **g** of the Lord Jesus, Ac 15:11 *5485*
the brethren to the **g** of the Lord. Ac 15:40 *5485*
those who had believed through **g**, Ac 18:27 *5485*
of the gospel of the **g** of God. Ac 20:24 *5485*
to God and to the word of His **g**, Ac 20:32 *5485*
through whom we have received **g** Ro 1:5 *5485*
G to you and peace from God our Ro 1:7 *5485*
being justified as a gift by His **g** Ro 3:24 *5485*
it may be in accordance with **g**, Ro 4:16 *5485*
into this **g** in which we stand; Ro 5:2 *5485*
much more did the **g** of God and the Ro 5:15 *5485*
the gift by the **g** of the one Man, Ro 5:15 *5485*
those who receive the abundance of **g** Ro 5:17 *5485*
g abounded all the more, Ro 5:20 *5485*
even so **g** would reign through Ro 5:21 *5485*
in sin so that **g** may increase? Ro 6:1 *5485*
are not under law but under **g**. Ro 6:14 *5485*
we are not under law but under **g**? Ro 6:15 *5485*
But if it is by **g**, it is no longer Ro 11:6 *5485*
otherwise **g** is no longer grace. Ro 11:6 *5485*
otherwise grace is no longer **g**. Ro 11:6 *5485*
For through the **g** given to me I Ro 12:3 *5485*
according to the **g** given to us, Ro 12:6 *5485*
the **g** that was given me from God, Ro 15:15 *5485*
g of our Lord Jesus be with you. Ro 16:20 *5485*
The **g** of our Lord Jesus Christ be Ro 16:24 *5485*
G to you and peace from God our 1Co 1:3 *5485*
for the **g** of God which was given 1Co 1:4 *5485*
g of God which was given to me, 1Co 3:10 *5485*

by the **g** of God I am what I am, **1Co 15:10** *5485*
g toward me did not prove vain; **1Co 15:10** *5485*
not I, but the **g** of God with me. **1Co 15:10** *5485*
g of the Lord Jesus be with you. **1Co 16:23** *5485*
G to you and peace from God our **2Co 1:2** *5485*
wisdom but in the **g** of God, **2Co 1:12** *5485*
that the **g** which is spreading to **2Co 4:15** *5485*
to receive the **g** of God in vain **2Co 6:1** *5485*
to make known to you the **g** of God **2Co 8:1** *5485*
the **g** of our Lord Jesus Christ, **2Co 8:9** *5485*
able to make all **g** abound to you, **2Co 9:8** *5485*
of the surpassing **g** of God in you. **2Co 9:14** *5485*
"My **g** is sufficient for you, for **2Co 12:9** *5485*
The **g** of the Lord Jesus Christ, **2Co 13:14** *5485*
G to you and peace from God our **Ga 1:3** *5485*
who called you by the **g** of Christ, **Ga 1:6** *5485*
womb and called me through His **g**, **Ga 1:15** *5485*
the **g** that had been given to me, **Ga 2:9** *5485*
"I do not nullify the **g** of God, **Ga 2:21** *5485*
you have fallen from **g**. **Ga 5:4** *5485*
The **g** of our Lord Jesus Christ be **Ga 6:18** *5485*
G to you and peace from God our **Eph 1:2** *5485*
the praise of the glory of His **g**, **Eph 1:6** *5485*
according to the riches of His **g** **Eph 1:7** *5485*
(by **g** you have been saved), **Eph 2:5** *5485*
show the surpassing riches of His **g** **Eph 2:7** *5485*
For by **g** you have been saved **Eph 2:8** *5485*
g which was given to me for you; **Eph 3:2** *5485*
according to the gift of God's **g** **Eph 3:7** *5485*
of all saints, this **g** was given, **Eph 3:8** *5485*
But to each one of us **g** was given **Eph 4:7** *5485*
it will give **g** to those who hear. **Eph 4:29** *5485*
G be with all those who love our **Eph 6:24** *5485*
G to you and peace from God our **Php 1:2** *5485*
all are partakers of **g** with me. **Php 1:7** *5485*
The **g** of the Lord Jesus Christ be **Php 4:23** *5485*
G to you and peace from God our **Col 1:2** *5485*
understood the **g** of God in truth; **Col 1:6** *5485*
Let your speech always be with **g**, **Col 4:6** *5485*
G be with you. **Col 4:18** *5485*
G to you and peace. **1Th 1:1** *5485*
The **g** of our Lord Jesus Christ be **1Th 5:28** *5485*
G to you and peace from God the **2Th 1:2** *5485*
according to the **g** of our God and **2Th 1:12** *5485*
comfort and good hope by **g**, **2Th 2:16** *5485*
The **g** of our Lord Jesus Christ be **2Th 3:18** *5485*
G, mercy *and* peace from God the **1Tm 1:2** *5485*
and the **g** of our Lord was more **1Tm 1:14** *5485*
astray from the faith. **G** be with you. **1Tm 6:21** *5485*
G, mercy *and* peace from God the **2Tm 1:2** *5485*
according to His own purpose and **g** **2Tm 1:9** *5485*
in the **g** that is in Christ Jesus. **2Tm 2:1** *5485*
be with your spirit. **G** be with you. **2Tm 4:22** *5485*
G and peace from God the Father **Ti 1:4** *5485*
For the **g** of God has appeared, **Ti 2:11** *5485*
that being justified by His **g** we **Ti 3:7** *5485*
G be with you all. **Ti 3:15** *5485*
G to you and peace from God our **Phm 1:3** *5485*
The **g** of the Lord Jesus Christ be **Phm 1:25** *5485*
that by the **g** of God He might **Heb 2:9** *5485*
confidence to the throne of **g**, **Heb 4:16** *5485*
find **g** to help in time of need. **Heb 4:16** *5485*
and has insulted the Spirit of **g**? **Heb 10:29** *5485*
one comes short of the **g** of God; **Heb 12:15** *5485*
the heart to be strengthened by **g**, **Heb 13:9** *5485*
G be with you all. **Heb 13:25** *5485*
But He gives a greater **g**. **Jas 4:6** *5485*
BUT GIVES **G** TO THE HUMBLE." **Jas 4:6** *5485*
May **g** and peace be yours in **1Pe 1:2** *5485*
prophets who prophesied of the **g** that **1Pe 1:10** *5485*
fix your hope completely on the **g** to **1Pe 1:13** *5485*
as a fellow heir of the **g** of life, **1Pe 3:7** *5485*
stewards of the manifold **g** of God. **1Pe 4:10** *5485*
PROUD, BUT GIVES **G** TO THE HUMBLE. **1Pe 5:5** *5485*
a little while, the God of all **g**, **1Pe 5:10** *5485*
that this is the true **g** of God. **1Pe 5:12** *5485*
G and peace be multiplied to you **2Pe 1:2** *5485*
but grow in the **g** and knowledge of **2Pe 3:18** *5485*
G, mercy *and* peace will be with **2Jn 1:3** *5485*
ungodly persons who turn the **g** of **Jude 1:4** *5485*
G to you and peace, from Him who **Rv 1:4** *5485*
g of the Lord Jesus be with all. **Rv 22:21** *5485*

GRACEFUL
they are a **g** wreath to your head And **Pr 1:9** 2580
As a loving hind and a **g** doe, **Pr 5:19** 2580

GRACIOUS
"May God be **g** to you, my son." **Gn 43:29** 2603a
Me, I will hear *him*, for I am **g**. **Ex 22:27** 2587
be **g** to whom I will be gracious, **Ex 33:19** 2603a
be gracious to whom I will be **g**, **Ex 33:19** 2603a
the LORD God, compassionate and **g**, **Ex 34:6** 2587
shine on you, And be **g** to you; **Nu 6:25** 2603a
knows, the LORD may be **g** to me, **2Sa 12:22** 2603a
But the LORD was **g** to them and had **2Ki 13:23** 2603a
your God is **g** and compassionate, **2Ch 30:9** 2587
forgiveness, **G** and compassionate, **Ne 9:17** 2587
are a **g** and compassionate God. **Ne 9:31** 2587
Then let him be **g** to him, and say, **Jb 33:24** 2603a
Be **g** to me and hear my prayer. **Ps 4:1** 2603a
Be **g** to me, O LORD, for I *am* **Ps 6:2** 2603a
Be **g** to me, O LORD; **Ps 9:13** 2603a
Turn to me and be **g** to me, **Ps 25:16** 2603a
Redeem me, and be **g** to me. **Ps 26:11** 2603a
And be **g** to me and answer me. **Ps 27:7** 2603a
"Hear, O LORD, and be **g** to me; **Ps 30:10** 2603a
Be **g** to me, O LORD, for I am in **Ps 31:9** 2603a
But the righteous is **g** and gives. **Ps 37:21** 2603a
All day long he is **g** and lends, **Ps 37:26** 2603a
"O LORD, be **g** to me; **Ps 41:4** 2603a
But You, O LORD, be **g** to me and **Ps 41:10** 2603a
Be **g** to me, O God, according to **Ps 51:1** 2603a
Be **g** to me, O God, for man **Ps 56:1** 2603a
Be **g** to me, O God, be gracious to **Ps 57:1** 2603a
gracious to me, O God, be **g** to me, **Ps 57:1** 2603a
Do not be **g** to any *who are* **Ps 59:5** 2603a
God be **g** to us and bless us, *And* **Ps 67:1** 2603a
Has God forgotten to be **g**, **Ps 77:9** 2603a
Be **g** to me, O Lord, For to You I **Ps 86:3** 2603a
O Lord, are a God merciful and **g**, **Ps 86:15** 2587
Turn to me, and be **g** to me; **Ps 86:16** 2603a
For it is time to be **g** to her, **Ps 102:13** 2603a
The LORD is compassionate and **g**, **Ps 103:8** 2587
be **g** to his fatherless children. **Ps 109:12** 2603a
The LORD is **g** and compassionate. **Ps 111:4** 2587
He is **g** and compassionate and **Ps 112:4** 2587
with the man who is **g** and lends; **Ps 112:5** 2603a
G is the LORD, and righteous; **Ps 116:5** 2587
Be **g** to me according to Your word. **Ps 119:58** 2603a
Turn to me and be **g** to me, **Ps 119:132** 2603a
God, Until He is **g** to us. **Ps 123:2** 2603a
Be **g** to us, O LORD, be gracious to **Ps 123:3** 2603a
to us, O LORD, be **g** to us, **Ps 123:3** 2603a
The LORD is **g** and merciful; **Ps 145:8** 2587
A **g** woman attains honor, And **Pr 11:16** 2580
happy is he who is **g** to the poor. **Pr 14:21** 2603a
who is **g** to the needy honors Him. **Pr 14:31** 2603a
One who is **g** to a poor man lends to **Pr 19:17** 2603a
of heart *And* whose speech is **g**, **Pr 22:11** 2580
it for him who is **g** to the poor. **Pr 28:8** 2603a
the mouth of a wise man are **g**, **Ec 10:12** 2580
Creator will not be **g** to them. **Is 27:11** 2603a
the LORD longs to be **g** to you, **Is 30:18** 2603a
He will surely be **g** to you at the **Is 30:19** 2603a
O LORD, be **g** to us; **Is 33:2** 2603a
For I am **g**,' declares the LORD; **Jer 3:12** 2623
For He is **g** and compassionate, **Jl 2:13** 2587
May be **g** to the remnant of Joseph. **Am 5:15** 2603a
are a **g** and compassionate God, **Jon 4:2** 2587
was speaking with me with **g** words, **Zch 1:13** 2896a
favor, that He may be **g** to us? **Mal 1:9** 2603a
and wondering at the **g** words which **Lk 4:22** *5485*
according to *God's* **g** choice. **Ro 11:5** *5485*
also complete in you this **g** work **2Co 8:6** *5485*
you abound in this **g** work also. **2Co 8:7** *5485*
to travel with us in this **g** work, **2Co 8:19** *5485*

GRACIOUSLY
God has **g** given your servant." **Gn 33:5** 2603a
because God has dealt **g** with me and **Gn 33:11** 2603a
from me, And **g** grant me Your law. **Ps 119:29** 2603a
When he speaks **g**, do not believe **Pr 26:25** 2603a
all iniquity And receive *us* **g**, **Hos 14:2** 2896b
to repay, he **g** forgave them both. **Lk 7:42** *5483*

GRADUALLY
our being saved was **g** abandoned. **Ac 27:20**

GRAFT
God is able to **g** them in again. **Ro 11:23** *1461b*

GRAFTED
you, being a wild olive, were **g** in **Ro 11:17** *1461b*
off so that I might be **g** in." **Ro 11:19** *1461b*
in their unbelief, will be **g** in, **Ro 11:23** *1461b*
and were **g** contrary to nature into **Ro 11:24** *1461b*
be **g** into their own olive tree? **Ro 11:24** *1461b*

GRAIN
an abundance of **g** and new wine; **Gn 27:28** 1715
and with **g** and new wine I have **Gn 27:37** 1715
seven ears of **g** came up on a single **Gn 41:5** 7641
and store up the **g** for food in the **Gn 41:35** 1250
Thus Joseph stored up **g** in great **Gn 41:49** 1250
to Egypt to buy **g** from Joseph, **Gn 41:57** 7666
saw that there was **g** in Egypt, **Gn 42:1** 7668
heard that there is **g** in Egypt; **Gn 42:2** 7668
went down to buy **g** from Egypt. **Gn 42:3** 1250
sons of Israel came to buy **g** among **Gn 42:5** 7666
carry **g** for the famine of your **Gn 42:19** 7668
gave orders to fill their bags with **g** **Gn 42:25** 1250
loaded their donkeys with their **g** and **Gn 42:26** 7668
of your brothers with me and take **g** **Gn 42:33**
when they had finished eating the **g** **Gn 43:2** 7668
and his money for the **g**." **Gn 44:2** 7668
and ten female donkeys loaded with **g** **Gn 45:23** 1250
for the **g** which they bought, **Gn 47:14** 7668
stacked **g** or the standing grain or **Ex 22:6**
or the standing **g** or the field *itself* **Ex 22:6** 7054
shall offer with it the same **g** offering **Ex 29:41**
when anyone presents a **g** offering **Lv 2:1**
remainder of the **g** offering belongs **Lv 2:3**
of a **g** offering baked in an oven, **Lv 2:4**
a **g** offering *made* on the griddle, **Lv 2:5**
it is a **g** offering. **Lv 2:6**
is a **g** offering *made* in a pan, **Lv 2:7**
'When you bring in the **g** offering **Lv 2:8**
g offering its memorial portion, **Lv 2:9**
remainder of the **g** offering belongs **Lv 2:10**
'No **g** offering, which you bring to **Lv 2:11**
'Every **g** offering of yours, **Lv 2:13**
be lacking from your **g** offering; **Lv 2:13**
'Also if you bring a **g** offering of **Lv 2:14**
heads of **g** roasted in the fire, **Lv 2:14** 24
for the **g** offering of your early **Lv 2:14**
it is a **g** offering. **Lv 2:15**
priest's, like the **g** offering.' " **Lv 5:13**
this is the law of the **g** offering: **Lv 6:14**
the fine flour of the **g** offering, **Lv 6:15**
incense that is on the **g** offering, **Lv 6:15**
flour as a regular **g** offering, **Lv 6:20**
You shall present the **g** offering **Lv 6:21**
every **g** offering of the priest shall **Lv 6:23**
every **g** offering that is baked in **Lv 7:9**
'Every **g** offering, mixed with oil **Lv 7:10**
the **g** offering and the sin **Lv 7:37**
and a **g** offering mixed with oil; **Lv 9:4**
Next he presented the **g** offering, **Lv 9:17**
"Take the **g** offering that is left **Lv 10:12**
mixed with oil for a **g** offering, **Lv 14:10**
and the **g** offering on the altar. **Lv 14:20**
mixed with oil for a **g** offering, **Lv 14:21**
together with the **g** offering. **Lv 14:31**
'Its **g** offering shall then be **Lv 23:13**
nor roasted **g** nor new growth. **Lv 23:14** 7039
a new **g** offering to the LORD. **Lv 23:16**
g offering and their drink **Lv 23:18**
offerings and **g** offerings, **Lv 23:37**
continual **g** offering and the anointing **Nu 4:16**
it is a **g** offering of jealousy, **Nu 5:15**
a **g** offering of memorial, **Nu 5:15**
place the **g** offering of memorial in **Nu 5:18**
is the **g** offering of jealousy, **Nu 5:18**
shall take the **g** offering of jealousy **Nu 5:25**
and he shall wave the **g** offering **Nu 5:25**
priest shall take a handful of the **g** **Nu 5:26**
g offering and their drink offering. **Nu 6:15**
its **g** offering and its drink offering. **Nu 6:17**
mixed with oil for a **g** offering; **Nu 7:13**
mixed with oil for a **g** offering; **Nu 7:19**
mixed with oil for a **g** offering; **Nu 7:25**
mixed with oil for a **g** offering; **Nu 7:31**
mixed with oil for a **g** offering; **Nu 7:37**
mixed with oil for a **g** offering; **Nu 7:43**
mixed with oil for a **g** offering; **Nu 7:49**
mixed with oil for a **g** offering; **Nu 7:55**
mixed with oil for a **g** offering; **Nu 7:61**
mixed with oil for a **g** offering; **Nu 7:67**
mixed with oil for a **g** offering; **Nu 7:73**
mixed with oil for a **g** offering; **Nu 7:79**
old with their **g** offering twelve, **Nu 7:87**
take a bull with its **g** offering, **Nu 8:8**
shall present to the LORD a **g** offering **Nu 15:4**
prepare as a **g** offering two-tenths **Nu 15:6**
shall offer with the bull a **g** offering **Nu 15:9**
to the LORD, with its **g** offering and **Nu 15:24**
even every **g** offering and every **Nu 18:9**
of the fresh wine and of the **g**, **Nu 18:12** 1715
as the **g** from the threshing floor or **Nu 18:27** 1715
It is not a place of **g** or figs or **Nu 20:5** 2233
of fine flour for a **g** offering, **Nu 28:5**
as the **g** offering of the morning **Nu 28:8**
mixed with oil as a **g** offering, **Nu 28:9**
flour mixed with oil for a **g** offering, **Nu 28:12**
flour mixed with oil for a **g** offering, **Nu 28:12**
of a **g** offering for each lamb, **Nu 28:13**
'For their **g** offering, you **Nu 28:20**
when you present a new **g** offering **Nu 28:26**
and their **g** offering, fine flour **Nu 28:28**
burnt offering and its **g** offering, **Nu 28:31**
also their **g** offering, fine flour **Nu 29:3**
the new moon and its **g** offering, **Nu 29:6**
burnt offering and its **g** offering, **Nu 29:6**
and their **g** offering, fine flour **Nu 29:9**
burnt offering and its **g** offering, **Nu 29:11**
and their **g** offering, fine flour **Nu 29:14**
its **g** offering and its drink offering. **Nu 29:16**
and their **g** offering and their **Nu 29:18**
burnt offering and its **g** offering, **Nu 29:19**
and their **g** offering and their **Nu 29:21**
its **g** offering and its drink offering. **Nu 29:22**
their **g** offering and their **Nu 29:24**
its **g** offering and its drink offering. **Nu 29:25**
and their **g** offering and their **Nu 29:27**
its **g** offering and its drink offering. **Nu 29:28**
and their **g** offering and their **Nu 29:30**
its **g** offering and its drink offerings. **Nu 29:31**
and their **g** offering and their **Nu 29:33**
its **g** offering and its drink offering. **Nu 29:34**
their **g** offering and their **Nu 29:37**
its **g** offering and its drink offering. **Nu 29:38**
and for your **g** offerings and for your **Nu 29:39**
your **g** and your new wine and your **Dt 7:13** 1715
that you may gather in your **g** and **Dt 11:14** 1715
your gates the tithe of your **g** or **Dt 12:17** 1715
His name, the tithe of your **g**, **Dt 14:23** 1715
put the sickle to the standing **g**. **Dt 16:9** 7054
him the first fruits of your **g**, **Dt 18:4** 1715
enter your neighbor's standing **g**, **Dt 23:25** 7054
in your neighbor's standing **g**. **Dt 23:25** 7054
who also leaves you no **g**, **Dt 28:51** 1715
In a land of **g** and new wine; **Dt 33:28** 1715
unleavened cakes and parched **g**. **Jos 5:11**
offering or **g** offering on it, **Jos 22:23**
for **g** offering or for sacrifice, **Jos 22:29**
Manoah took the young goat with the **g** **Jg 13:19**
and a **g** offering from our hands, **Jg 13:23**
the standing **g** of the Philistines, **Jg 15:5** 7054
the shocks and the standing **g**, **Jg 15:5** 7054
field and glean among the ears of **g** **Ru 2:2** 7641
and he served her roasted **g**, **Ru 2:14** 7039
purposely pull out for her *some* **g** **Ru 2:16**
down at the end of the heap of **g**; **Ru 3:7** 6194
roasted **g** and these ten loaves and **1Sa 17:17** 7039
and five measures of roasted **g** and a **1Sa 25:18** 7039
well's mouth and scattered **g** on it, **2Sa 17:19** 7383
parched **g**, beans, lentils, **2Sa 17:28**
the burnt offering and the **g** offering **1Ki 8:64**
the **g** offering and the fat of the peace **1Ki 8:64**
and fresh ears of **g** in his sack. **2Ki 4:42** 3759
land, a land of **g** and new wine, **2Ki 18:32** 1715

and the wheat for the g offering; 1Ch 21:23
the fine flour for a g offering, 1Ch 23:29
burnt offering, the g offering and 2Ch 7:7
abundance the first fruits of g, 2Ch 31:5 1715
also for the produce of g, 2Ch 32:28 1715
with their g offerings and their Ezr 7:17
get g that we may eat and live." Ne 5:2 1715
get g because of the famine." Ne 5:3 1715
are lending them money and g. Ne 5:10 1715
part of the money and of the g, Ne 5:11 1715
any g on the sabbath day to sell, Ne 10:31 7668
for the continual g offering, Ne 10:33
bring the contribution of the g, Ne 10:39 1715
formerly they put the g offerings, Ne 13:5
the utensils and the tithes of g, Ne 13:5 1715
the g offerings and the frankincense. Ne 13:9
then brought the tithe of the g, Ne 13:12 1715
bringing in sacks of g and loading Ne 13:15 6194
the stacking of g in its season. Jb 5:26 1430a
And his g will not bend down to Jb 15:29 4512
the heads of g they are cut off. Jb 24:24 7641
in him that he will return your g And Jb 39:12 2233
when their g and new wine abound. Ps 4:7 1715
You prepare their g, Ps 65:9 1715
the valleys are covered with g; Ps 65:13 1250
May there be abundance of g in the Ps 72:16 1250
He who withholds g, Pr 11:26 1250
a pestle along with crushed g, Pr 27:22 7383
will yield *but* an ephah of g." Is 5:10
reaper gathering the standing g, Is 17:5 7054
of g In the valley of Rephaim. Is 17:5 7641
The g of the Nile, the harvest of Is 23:3 2233
G *for* bread is crushed, Indeed, Is 28:28
land, a land of g and new wine, Is 36:17 1715
You have made a g offering. Is 57:6
your g *as* food for your enemies; Is 62:8 1715
He who offers a g offering *is like* Is 66:3
as a g offering to the LORD, Is 66:20
bring their g offering in a clean vessel Is 66:20
burnt offering and g offering, Jer 14:12
g offerings and incense, Jer 17:26
straw have *in common* with g?" Jer 23:28 1250
Over the g and the new wine Jer 31:12 1715
offerings, to burn g offerings and Jer 33:18
having g offerings and incense in Jer 41:5
"Where is g and wine?" La 2:12 1715
call for the g and multiply it, Ezk 36:29 1715
most holy things, the g offering, Ezk 42:13
"They shall eat the g offering, Ezk 44:29
for a g offering, for a burnt offering and Ezk 45:15
burnt offerings, the g offerings and Ezk 45:17
the sin offering, the g offering, Ezk 45:17
provide as a g offering an ephah Ezk 45:24
burnt offering, the g offering and Ezk 45:25
and the g offering shall be an Ezk 46:5
and the g offering with the lambs Ezk 46:5
"And he shall provide a g offering, Ezk 46:7
the g offering shall be an ephah with Ezk 46:11
shall provide a g offering with it Ezk 46:14
a g offering to the LORD Ezk 46:14
provide the lamb, the g offering and Ezk 46:15
they shall bake the g offering, Ezk 46:20
stop to sacrifice and g offering; Da 9:27
that it was I who gave her the g, Hos 2:8 1715
I will take back My g at harvest Hos 2:9 1715
the earth will respond to the g, Hos 2:22 1715
For the sake of g and new wine Hos 7:14 1715
The standing g has no heads; Hos 8:7 7054
grain has no heads; It yields no g. Hos 8:7 7058
in his shadow Will again raise g, Hos 14:7 1715
The g offering and the drink offering Jl 1:9
land mourns; For the g is ruined, Jl 1:10 1715
For the g offering and the Jl 1:13
torn down, For the g is dried up. Jl 1:17 1715
Even a g offering and a drink offering Jl 2:14
"Behold, I am going to send you g, Jl 2:19 1715
threshing floors will be full of g, Jl 2:24 1250
exact a tribute of g from them, Am 5:11 1250
offerings and your g offerings, Am 5:22
you present Me with sacrifices and g Am 5:25
be over, So that we may sell g, Am 8:5 7668
of Israel among all nations As g Am 9:9
land, on the mountains, on the g, Hg 1:11 1715
that time *when* one came to a g Hg 2:16
G will make the young men flourish, Zch 9:17 1715
and a g offering *that is* pure; Mal 1:11
and began to pick the heads *of* g Mt 12:1
the wheat sprouted and bore g, Mt 13:26 *2590*
along while picking the heads *of* g. Mk 2:23
then the mature g in the head. Mk 4:28 *4621*
disciples were picking the heads of g, Lk 6:1 *4719*
their hands, and eating *the* g. Lk 6:1
will store all my g and my goods. Lk 12:18 *4621*
unless a g of wheat falls into the Jn 12:24 *2848*
heard that there was g in Egypt, Ac 7:12 *4619a*
a bare g, perhaps of wheat or of 1Co 15:37 *2848*

GRAINFIELDS
went through the g on the Sabbath, Mt 12:1 *4702*
through the g on the Sabbath, Mk 2:23 *4702*
He was passing through *some* g on Lk 6:1 *4702*

GRAINS
And your offspring like its g; Is 48:19 4579

GRANDCHILDREN
on the children and on the g to the Ex 34:7 1121
children likewise and their g, 2Ki 17:41 1121
G are the crown of old men, And Pr 17:6 1121
if any widow has children or g, 1Tm 5:4 *1549*

GRANDDAUGHTER
and the g of Zibeon the Hivite; Gn 36:2 1323
of Anah and the g of Zibeon: Gn 36:14 1323
the g of Omri king of Israel. 2Ki 8:26 1323
name was Athaliah, the g of Omri. 2Ch 22:2 1323

GRANDDAUGHTERS
with him, his daughters and his g, Gn 46:7 1323, 1121

GRANDEUR
High God granted sovereignty, g, Da 5:18 7238
of the g which He bestowed on him, Da 5:19 7238

GRANDFATHER
you all the land of your g Saul; 2Sa 9:7 1

GRANDFATHERS
your fathers nor your g have seen, Ex 10:6 1

GRANDMOTHER
which first dwelt in your g Lois and 2Tm 1:5 *3125*

GRANDSON
and Lot the son of Haran, his g, Gn 11:31 1121
of your son, and of your g, Ex 10:2 1121
g might fear the LORD your God, Dt 6:2 1121
I have given to your master's g. 2Sa 9:9 1121
that your master's g may have food; 2Sa 9:10 1121
Mephibosheth your master's g shall 2Sa 9:10 1121
serve him and his son and his g Jer 27:7 1121
son of Ahikam and g of Shaphan, Jer 43:6 1121
son of Neriah, the g of Mahseiah, Jer 51:59 1121

GRANDSONS
his sons and his g with him, Gn 46:7 1121
known to your sons and your g. Dt 4:9 1121
g who rode on seventy donkeys; Jg 12:14 1121
archers, and had many sons and g, 1Ch 8:40 1121
and saw his sons and his g, Jb 42:16 1121

GRANT
"Behold, I g you this request Gn 19:21 5375
please g me success today, Gn 24:12 7136a
and may God Almighty g you Gn 43:14 5414
"I will g this people favor Ex 3:21 5414
'I shall also g peace in the land, Lv 26:6 5414
you shall g a remission *of debts.* Dt 15:1 6213a
the LORD g that you may find rest, Ru 1:9 5414
the God of Israel g your petition 1Sa 1:17 5414
serve them and g them their petition, 1Ki 12:7 6030a
but I will g them some *measure* of 2Ch 12:7 5414
God may enlighten our eyes and g us Ezr 9:8 5414
g him compassion before this man. Ne 1:11 5414
and if it pleases the king to g my Es 5:8 5414
And that God would g my longing! Jb 6:8 5414
May He g you your heart's desire And Ps 20:4 5414
O LORD, And g us Your salvation. Ps 85:7 5414
Oh g Your strength to Your servant, Ps 86:16 5414
That You may g him relief from Ps 94:13 8252
me, And graciously g me Your law. Ps 119:29 2603a
"Do not g, O LORD, the desires of Ps 140:8 5414
And I will g salvation in Zion, Is 46:13 5414
To g those who mourn *in* Zion, Is 61:3 7760
Or can the heavens g showers? Jer 14:22 5414
for I will g you no favor.' Jer 16:13 5414
and I will g you free access among Zch 3:7 5414
"G that we may sit, Mk 10:37 *1325*
To g us that we, being rescued Lk 1:74 *1325*
worthy for You to g this to him; Lk 7:4 *3930*
that I came to g peace on earth? Lk 12:51 *1325*
has granted Me a kingdom, I g you Lk 22:29 *1303*
I WILL G WONDERS IN THE SKY ABOVE Ac 2:19 *1325*
and g that Your bond-servants may Ac 4:29 *1325*
Savior, to g repentance to Israel, Ac 5:31 *1325*
any further, I beg you to g us, Ac 24:4 *191*
g you to be of the same mind with Ro 15:5 *1325*
that He would g you, according to Eph 3:16 *1325*
g to your slaves justice and Col 4:1 *3930*
Lord of peace Himself continually g 2Th 3:16 *1325*
The Lord g mercy to the house of 2Tm 1:16 *1325*
the Lord g to him to find mercy 2Tm 1:18 *1325*
if perhaps God may g them 2Tm 2:25 *1325*
will g to eat of the tree of life which Rv 2:7 *1325*
I will g to him to sit down with Rv 3:21 *1325*
g *authority* to my two witnesses, Rv 11:3 *1325*

GRANTED
to you and g your request." 1Sa 25:35 5375
who has g one to sit on my throne 1Ki 1:48 5414
And God g him what he requested. 1Ch 4:10 935
and knowledge have been g to you. 2Ch 1:12 5414
the king g him all he requested Ezr 7:6 5414
And the king g *them* to me because Ne 2:8 5414
for it shall be g to you. Es 5:6 5414
It shall be g you. Es 7:2 5414
In them the king g the Jews who Es 8:11 5414
It shall even be g you. Es 9:12 5414
let tomorrow also be g to the Jews Es 9:13 5414
have g me life and lovingkindness; Jb 10:12 6213a
desire of the righteous will be g. Pr 10:24 5414
to all that the LORD has g us, Is 63:7 1580
Which He has g them according to Is 63:7 1580
Now God g Daniel favor and Da 1:9 5414
the Most High God g sovereignty, Da 5:18 3052
but an extension of life was g to Da 7:12 3052
fall they will be g a little help, Da 11:34 5826
"To you it has been g to know the Mt 13:11 *1325*
but to them it has not been g. Mt 13:11 *1325*
it will be g him. Mk 11:23
and they will be g you. Mk 11:24
he g the body to Joseph. Mk 15:45 *1433*
"To you it has been g to know the Lk 8:10 *1325*
as My Father has g Me a kingdom, Lk 22:29 *1303*
that their demand be g. Lk 23:24 *1096*
has been g him from the Father." Jn 6:65 *1325*
and Pilate g permission. Jn 19:38 *2010*
for a murderer to be g to you, Ac 3:14 *5483*
and g him favor and wisdom in the Ac 7:10 *1325*
g that He become visible, Ac 10:40 *1325*
God has g to the Gentiles also the Ac 11:18 *1325*
God has g you all those who are Ac 27:24 *5483*
but God has g it to Abraham by Ga 3:18 *5483*
it has been g for Christ's sake, Php 1:29 *5483*
grace which was g us in Christ Jesus 2Tm 1:9 *1325*
divine power has g to us everything 2Pe 1:3 *1433*
For by these He has g to us His 2Pe 1:4 *1433*
g to take peace from the earth, Rv 6:4 *1325*
g to harm the earth and the sea, Rv 7:2 *1325*

GRANTING
g them deliverance through him, Ac 7:25 *1325*
g that signs and wonders be done Ac 14:3 *1325*

GRAPE
last for you until g gathering, Lv 26:5 1210
and g gathering will last until Lv 26:5 1210
shall he drink any g juice nor Nu 6:3 6025
that is produced by the g vine, Nu 6:4 3196
drop off his unripe g like the vine, Jb 15:33 1155
the flower becomes a ripening g, Is 18:5 1155
when the g harvest is over. Is 24:13 1210
a g gatherer Over the branches." Jer 6:9
summer fruits and your g harvest Jer 48:32 1210
"If g gatherers came to you, Jer 49:9
If g gatherers came to you, Would Ob 1:5
fruit pickers, like the g gatherers. Mi 7:1 1210

GRAPES
and its clusters produced ripe g. Gn 40:10 6025
so I took the g and squeezed them Gn 40:11 6025
And his robes in the blood of g. Gn 49:11 6025
and your g of untrimmed vines you Lv 25:5 6025
juice nor eat fresh or dried g. Nu 6:3 6025
was the time of the first ripe g. Nu 13:20 6025
branch with a single cluster of g; Nu 13:23 6025
g until you are fully satisfied, Dt 23:24 6025
you gather the g of your vineyard, Dt 24:21
drink of the wine nor gather *the* g, Dt 28:39
of the blood of g you drank wine. Dt 32:14 6025
Their g are grapes of poison, Dt 32:32 6025
Their grapes are g of poison, Dt 32:32 6025
Is not the gleaning *of the* g of Jg 8:2
into the field and gathered *the* g Jg 9:27
wine, g, figs and all kinds of loads, Ne 13:15 6025
He expected *it* to produce *good* g, Is 5:2 6025
I expected *it* to produce *good* g Is 5:4 6025
"There will be no g on the vine And Jer 8:13 6025
shout like those who tread *the* g, Jer 25:30
'The fathers have eaten sour g, Jer 31:29 1155
each man who eats the sour g, Jer 31:30 1155
'The fathers eat the sour g, Ezk 18:2 1155
Israel like g in the wilderness; Hos 9:10 6025
treader of g him who sows seed; Am 9:13 6025
And the g, but you will not drink Mi 6:15 8492
is not a cluster of g to eat, Mi 7:1
in the field cast *its* g," Mal 3:11
G are not gathered from thorn Mt 7:16 *4718*
do they pick g from a briar bush. Lk 6:44 *4718*
earth, because her g are ripe." Rv 14:18 *4718*

GRASP
out your hand and g *it* by its tail" Ex 4:4 270
the kingdom was firmly in his g, 2Ch 25:3 2388
Out of the g of the wrongdoer and Ps 71:4 3709
lizard you may g with the hands, Pr 30:28 8610
And her hands g the spindle. Pr 31:19 8551
It is good that you g one thing and Ec 7:18 270
And He is about to g you firmly Is 22:17 5844b
you from the g of the violent." Jer 15:21 3709
g the garment of a Jew, Zch 8:23 2388
seize Him, and He eluded their g. Jn 10:39 *5495*

GRASPED
and he g his father's hand to Gn 48:17 8551
Samson g the two middle pillars Jg 16:29 3943
And He has g me by the neck and Jb 16:12 270
equality with God a thing to be g, Php 2:6 *725*

GRASPS
rock pile, He g a house of stones. Jb 8:17 270
And g oil with his right hand. Pr 27:16 7121
"He who g the bow will not stand Am 2:15 8610

GRASS
and they grazed in the marsh g. Gn 41:2 260
and they grazed in the marsh g. Gn 41:18 260
ox licks up the g of the field." Nu 22:4 3418
"He will give g in your fields Dt 11:15 6212a
and no g grows in it, Dt 29:23 6212a
As the droplets on the fresh g And Dt 32:2 1877
tender g *springs* out of the earth, 2Sa 23:4 1877
perhaps we will find g and keep 1Ki 18:5 2682
As g on the housetops is scorched 2Ki 19:26 2682
offspring as the g of the earth. Jb 5:25 6212a
the wild donkey bray over *his* g, Jb 6:5 1877
to make the seeds of g to sprout? Jb 38:27 1877
He eats g like an ox. Jb 40:15 2682
will wither quickly like the g And Ps 37:2 2682
down like rain upon the mown g, Ps 72:6
are like g which sprouts anew. Ps 90:5 2682
the wicked sprouted up like g And Ps 92:7 6212a
like g and has withered away, Ps 102:4 6212a
And I wither away like g. Ps 102:11 6212a
As for man, his days are like g; Ps 103:15 2682
the g to grow for the cattle, Ps 104:14 2682
the image of an ox that eats g. Ps 106:20 6212a
them be like g upon the housetops, Ps 129:6 2682
makes g to grow on the mountains. Ps 147:8 2682
his favor is like dew on the g. Pr 19:12 6212a

When the **g** disappears, the new Pr 27:25 2682
dry **g** collapses into the flame, Is 5:24 2842
Surely the **g** is withered, the Is 15:6 2682
withered, the tender **g** died out, Is 15:6 1877
place, **G** *becomes* reeds and rushes. Is 35:7 2682
As **g** on the housetops is scorched Is 37:27 2682
All flesh is **g**, and all its Is 40:6 2682
The **g** withers, the flower fades, Is 40:7 2682
Surely the people are **g**. Is 40:7 2682
The **g** withers, the flower fades, Is 40:8 2682
spring up among the **g** Like poplars Is 44:4 2682
the son of man who is made like **g**, Is 51:12 2682
will flourish like the new **g**; Is 66:14 1877
her young, Because there is no **g**. Jer 14:5 1877
it In the new **g** of the field; Da 4:15 1883
the beasts in the **g** of the earth. Da 4:15 6212b
it in the new **g** of the field, Da 4:23 1883
and you be given **g** to eat like Da 4:25 6212b
be given **g** to eat like cattle, Da 4:32 6212b
and began eating **g** like cattle, Da 4:33 6212b
He was given **g** to eat like cattle, Da 5:21 6212b
God so clothes the **g** of the field, Mt 6:30 *5528*
people to sit down on the **g**, Mt 14:19 *5528*
down by groups on the green **g**. Mk 6:39 *5528*
God so clothes the **g** in the field, Lk 12:28 *5528*
Now there was much **g** in the place. Jn 6:10 *5528*
flowering **g** he will pass away. Jas 1:10 *5528*
scorching wind and withers the **g**; Jas 1:11 *5528*
"ALL FLESH IS LIKE **G**, 1Pe 1:24 *5528*
ITS GLORY LIKE THE FLOWER OF **G**. 1Pe 1:24 *5528*
THE **G** WITHERS, AND THE FLOWER 1Pe 1:24 *5528*
and all the green **g** was burned up. Rv 8:7 *5528*
not to hurt the **g** of the earth, Rv 9:4 *5528*

GRASSHOPPER
its kinds, and the **g** in its kinds. Lv 11:22 2284
is blight *or* mildew, locust *or* **g**, 1Ki 8:37 2625
mildew, if there is locust or **g**, 2Ch 6:28 2625
He gave also their crops to the **g** And Ps 78:46 2625
the **g** drags himself along, Ec 12:5 2284

GRASSHOPPERS
we became like **g** in our own sight, Nu 13:33 2284
And its inhabitants are like **g**, Is 40:22 2284
marshals are like hordes of **g** Settling Na 3:17 1462

GRATEFULLY
God has created to be **g** shared in 1Tm 4:3 *3326, 2169*

GRATIFIED
My desire shall be **g** against them; Ex 15:9 4390

GRATING
for it a **g** of network of bronze, Ex 27:4 4346
burnt offering with its bronze **g**, Ex 35:16 4346
a **g** of bronze network beneath, Ex 38:4 4346
bronze **g** *as* holders for the poles. Ex 38:5 4346
the bronze altar and its bronze **g**, Ex 38:30 4346
the bronze altar and its bronze **g**, Ex 39:39 4346

GRATITUDE
and overflowing with **g**. Col 2:7 *2169*
if it is received with **g**; 1Tm 4:4 *2169*
cannot be shaken, let us show **g**, Heb 12:28 *5485*

GRAVE
and their sin is exceedingly **g**. Gn 18:20 3513
you his **g** for burying your dead." Gn 23:6 6913
Jacob set up a pillar over her **g**; Gn 35:20 6900
pillar of Rachel's **g** to this day. Gn 35:20 6900
in my **g** which I dug for myself in Gn 50:5 6913
naturally, or a human bone or a **g**, Nu 19:16 6913
the one dying *naturally* or the **g**. Nu 19:18 6913
voice and wept at the **g** of Abner, 2Sa 3:32 6913
it in the **g** of Abner in Hebron. 2Sa 4:12 6913
was buried in the **g** of his father. 2Sa 17:23 6913
the **g** of my father and my mother. 2Sa 19:37 6913
Zela, in the **g** of Kish his father; 2Sa 21:14 6913
come to the **g** of your fathers.'" 1Ki 13:22 6913
He laid his body in his own **g**, 1Ki 13:30 6913
"When I die, bury me in the **g** in 1Ki 13:31 6913
family will come to the **g**, 1Ki 14:13 6913
and buried him in his **g** with his 2Ki 9:28 6900
cast the man into the **g** of Elisha. 2Ki 13:21 6913
in his **g** in the garden of Uzza, 2Ki 21:26 6900
be gathered to your **g** in peace, 2Ki 22:20 6913
"It is the **g** of the man of God 2Ki 23:17 6913
the **g** which belonged to the kings, 2Ch 26:23 6900
be gathered to your **g** in peace, 2Ch 34:28 6913
exult when they find the **g**? Jb 3:22 6913
will come to the **g** in full vigor, Jb 5:26 6913
The **g** is *ready* for me. Jb 17:1 6913
"While he is carried to the **g**, Jb 21:32 6913
Their throat is an open **g**; Ps 5:9 6913
Like the slain who lie in the **g**, Ps 88:5 6913
lovingkindness be declared in the **g**, Ps 88:11 6913
His **g** was assigned with wicked men, Is 53:9 6913
"Their quiver is like an open **g**, Jer 5:16 6913
my mother would have been my **g**, Jer 20:17 6913
her company is round about her **g**. Ezk 32:23 6900
all her hordes around her **g**; Ezk 32:24 6900
I will prepare your **g**, Na 1:14 6913
Mary, sitting opposite the **g**. Mt 27:61 *5028*
orders for the **g** to be made secure Mt 27:64 *5028*
they went and made the **g** secure, Mt 27:66 *5028*
other Mary came to look at the **g**. Mt 28:1 *5028*
"THEIR THROAT IS AN OPEN **G**, Ro 3:13 *5028*

GRAVEL
his mouth will be filled with **g**. Pr 20:17 2687
He has broken my teeth with **g**; La 3:16 2687

GRAVEN
not act corruptly and make a **g** image Dt 4:16 6459
and make for yourselves a **g** image Dt 4:23 6459
and burn their **g** images with fire. Dt 7:5 6456
"The **g** images of their gods you Dt 7:25 6456
make a **g** image and a molten image; Jg 17:3 6459
into a **g** image and a molten image, Jg 17:4 6459
and a **g** image and a molten image? Jg 18:14 6459
and took the **g** image and the ephod Jg 18:17 6459
Micah's house and took the **g** image, Jg 18:18 6459
household idols and the **g** image and Jg 18:20 6459
set up for themselves the **g** image; Jg 18:30 6459
Micah's **g** image which he had made, Jg 18:31 6459
His jealousy with their **g** images. Ps 78:58 6456
be ashamed who serve **g** images, Ps 97:7 6459
Whose **g** images *were* greater than Is 10:10 6456
And you will defile your **g** images Is 30:22 6456
Nor My praise to **g** images. Is 42:8 6456
Those who fashion a **g** image are Is 44:9 6459
he makes it a **g** image and falls Is 44:15 6459
he makes into a god, his **g** image. Is 44:17 6459
And my **g** image and my molten image Is 48:5 6459
provoked Me with their **g** images, Jer 8:19 6456

GRAVES
dead in the choicest of our **g**; Gn 23:6 6913
because there were no **g** in Egypt Ex 14:11 6913
on the **g** of the common people. 2Ki 23:6 6913
he saw the **g** that *were* there on 2Ki 23:16 6913
took the bones from the **g** and burned 2Ki 23:16 6913
scattered *it* on the **g** of those who had 2Ch 34:4 6913
Who sit among **g** and spend the Is 65:4 6913
of Jerusalem from their **g**. Jer 8:1 6913
her **g** are round about her. Ezk 32:22 6913
whose **g** are set in the remotest Ezk 32:23 6913
Her **g** are around it, they are all Ezk 32:25 6913
their **g** surround them. Ezk 32:26 6913
I will open your **g** and cause you Ezk 37:12 6913
you to come up out of your **g**, Ezk 37:12 6913
when I have opened your **g** and Ezk 37:13 6913
you to come up out of your **g**, Ezk 37:13 6913

GRAVING
and fashioned it with a **g** tool and Ex 32:4 2747

GRAY
g hair down to Sheol in sorrow." Gn 42:38 7872
g hair down to Sheol in sorrow.' Gn 44:29 7872
servants will bring the **g** hair of your Gn 44:31 7872
nursling with the man of **g** hair. Dt 32:25 7872
before you, but I am old and **g**, 1Sa 12:2 7867
and do not let his **g** hair go down 1Ki 2:6 7872
g hair down to Sheol with blood." 1Ki 2:9 7872
And even when *I am* old and **g**, Ps 71:18 7872
A **g** head is a crown of glory; Pr 16:31 7872
honor of old men is their **g** hair. Pr 20:29 7872
G hairs also are sprinkled on him, Hos 7:9 7872

GRAY-HAIRED
the **g** and the aged are among us, Jb 15:10 7867
One would think the deep to be **g**. Jb 41:32 7872

GRAYHEADED
'You shall rise up before the **g** and Lv 19:32 7872

GRAYING
to *your* **g** years I will bear *you!* Is 46:4 7872

GRAZE
not **g** in front of that mountain." Ex 34:3 7462a
lambs will **g** as in their pasture, Is 5:17 7462a
Also the cow and the bear will **g**, Is 11:7 7462a
There the calf will **g**, Is 27:10 7462a
will **g** in a roomy pasture. Is 30:23 7462a
and the lamb will **g** together, Is 65:25 7462a
he will **g** on Carmel and Bashan, Jer 50:19 7462a

GRAZED
and they **g** in the marsh grass. Gn 41:2 7462a
and they **g** in the marsh grass. Gn 41:18 7462a
man lets a field or vineyard be **g** *bare* Ex 22:5 1197b

GRAZES
that it **g** in another man's field, Ex 22:5 1197b

GRAZING
the cattle which were **g** in Sharon; 1Ch 27:29 7462a
and their **g** ground will be on the Ezk 34:14 5116a
will lie down on good **g** ground Ezk 34:14 5116a

GREASY
And their dust become **g** with fat. Is 34:7 1878

GREAT
God made the two **g** lights, Gn 1:16 1419
God created the **g** sea monsters and Gn 1:21 1419
"My punishment is too **g** to bear! Gn 4:13 1419
wickedness of man was **g** on Gn 6:5 7227a
all the fountains of the **g** deep burst Gn 7:11 7227a
that is the **g** city. Gn 10:12 1419
And I will make you a **g** nation, Gn 12:2 1419
bless you, And make your name **g**; Gn 12:2 1431
with **g** plagues because of Sarai, Gn 12:17 1419
for their possessions were so **g** Gn 13:6 7227a
Your reward shall be very **g**." Gn 15:1 7235a
and **g** darkness fell upon him. Gn 15:12 1419
of Egypt as far as the **g** river, Gn 15:18 1419
and I will make him a **g** nation. Gn 17:20 1419
become a **g** and mighty nation, Gn 18:18 1419
of Sodom and Gomorrah is indeed **g**, Gn 18:20 7231
with blindness, both small and **g**, Gn 19:11 1419
outcry has become so **g** before the Gn 19:13 1431
on me and on my kingdom a **g** sin? Gn 20:9 1419
and Abraham made a **g** feast on the Gn 21:8 1419
I will make a **g** nation of him." Gn 21:18 1419
and herds and a **g** household, Gn 26:14 7227a
an exceedingly **g** and bitter cry, Gn 27:34 1419
which is too **g** to be numbered.'" Gn 32:12 7230
there was a **g** terror upon the Gn 35:5 430
too **g** for them to live together, Gn 36:7 7227a
How then could I do this **g** evil and Gn 39:9 1419
seven years of **g** abundance are Gn 41:29 1419
stored up grain in **g** abundance Gn 41:49 3966
keep you alive by a **g** deliverance. Gn 45:7 1419
I will make you a **g** nation there. Gn 46:3 1419
a people and he also will be **g**. Gn 48:19 1431
and it was a very **g** company. Gn 50:9 3515
very **g** and sorrowful lamentation; Gn 50:10 1419
arm and with **g** judgments. Ex 6:6 1419
the land of Egypt by **g** judgments. Ex 7:4 1419
And there came **g** swarms of insects Ex 8:24 3515
a **g** cry in all the land of Egypt, Ex 11:6 1419
and there was a **g** cry in Egypt, Ex 12:30 1419
When Israel saw the **g** power Ex 14:31 1419
I will make of you a **g** nation." Ex 32:10 1419
g power and with a mighty hand? Ex 32:11 1419
brought *such* **g** sin upon them?" Ex 32:21 1419
yourselves have committed a **g** sin; Ex 32:30 1419
this people has committed a **g** sin, Ex 32:31 1419
and the cormorant and the **g** owl, Lv 11:17 3244
and the **g** lizard in its kinds, Lv 11:29 6632b
to the poor nor defer to the **g**, Lv 19:15 1419
whom we saw in it are men of **g** Nu 13:32 4060
let the power of the Lord be **g**, Nu 14:17 1431
in **g** fear because of the people, Nu 22:3 3966
do anything, either small or **g**, Nu 22:18 1419
border, you shall have the **G** Sea, Nu 34:6 1419
line from the **G** Sea to Mount Hor. Nu 34:7 1419
Lebanon, as far as the **g** river, Dt 1:7 1419
hear the small and the **g** alike. Dt 1:17 1419
and went through all that **g** and Dt 1:19 1419
through this **g** wilderness. Dt 2:7 1419
there formerly, a people as **g**, Dt 2:10 1419
a people as **g**, numerous, and tall Dt 2:21 1419
besides a **g** many unwalled towns. Dt 3:5 3966
'Surely this **g** nation is a wise Dt 4:6 1419
"For what **g** nation is there that Dt 4:7 1419
"Or what **g** nation is there that Dt 4:8 1419
been done like this **g** thing, Dt 4:32 1419
outstretched arm and by **g** terrors, Dt 4:34 1419
earth He let you see His **g** fire, Dt 4:36 1419
you from Egypt by His **g** power, Dt 4:37 1419
the thick gloom, with a **g** voice, Dt 5:22 1419
For this **g** fire will consume us; Dt 5:25 1419
g and splendid cities which you Dt 6:10 1419
the LORD showed **g** and distressing Dt 6:22 1419
the **g** trials which your eyes saw Dt 7:19 1419
your midst, a **g** and awesome God. Dt 7:21 1419
throw them into **g** confusion until Dt 7:23 1419
the **g** and terrible wilderness, Dt 8:15 1419
you, **g** cities fortified to heaven, Dt 9:1 1419
a people **g** and tall, the sons of Dt 9:2 1419
have brought out by Your **g** power and Dt 9:29 1419
gods and the Lord of lords, the **g**, Dt 10:17 1419
who has done these **g** and awesome Dt 10:21 1419
g work of the LORD which He did. Dt 11:7 1419
the little owl, the **g** owl, Dt 14:16 3244
"If the distance is so **g** for Dt 14:24 7235a
me not see this **g** fire anymore, Dt 18:16 1419
a **g**, mighty and populous nation. Dt 26:5 1419
and with **g** terror and with signs and Dt 26:8 1419
the **g** trials which your eyes have Dt 29:3 1419
seen, those **g** signs and wonders. Dt 29:3 1419
Why this **g** outburst of anger?' Dt 29:24 1419
anger and in fury and in **g** wrath, Dt 29:28 1419
the **g** terror which Moses performed Dt 34:12 1419
even as far as the **g** river, Jos 1:4 1419
and as far as the **G** Sea toward the Jos 1:4 1419
heap, a **g** distance away at Adam, Jos 3:16 3966
people shall shout with a **g** shout; Jos 6:5 1419
the people shouted with a **g** shout Jos 6:20 1419
will You do for Your **g** name?" Jos 7:9 1419
They raised over him a **g** heap Jos 7:26 1419
and raised over it a **g** heap of Jos 8:29 1419
coast of the **G** Sea toward Lebanon, Jos 9:1 1419
because Gibeon *was* a **g** city, Jos 10:2 1419
them with a **g** slaughter at Gibeon, Jos 10:10 1419
them with a very **g** slaughter, Jos 10:20 1419
and pursued them as far as **G** Sidon Jos 11:8 7227a
there, with **g** fortified cities; Jos 14:12 1419
The west border *was* at the **G** Sea, Jos 15:12 1419
the brook of Egypt and the **G** Sea, Jos 15:47 1419
numerous people and have **g** power; Jos 17:17 1419
and Kanah, as far as **G** Sidon. Jos 19:28 7227a
"Return to your tents with **g** riches Jos 22:8 7227a
from the Jordan even to the **G** Sea Jos 23:4 1419
driven out **g** and strong nations Jos 23:9 1419
and who did these **g** signs in our Jos 24:17 1419
seen all the **g** work of the LORD Jg 2:7 1419
There were **g** resolves of heart. Jg 5:15 1419
There were **g** searchings of heart. Jg 5:16 1419
struck them with a very **g** slaughter Jg 11:33 1419
g strife with the sons of Ammon; Jg 12:2 3966
ruthlessly with a **g** slaughter; Jg 15:8 1419
"You have given this **g** deliverance Jg 15:18 1419
and see where his **g** strength *lies* Jg 16:5 1419
tell me where your **g** strength is Jg 16:6 1419
me where your **g** strength is." Jg 16:15 1419
a **g** sacrifice to Dagon their god, Jg 16:23 1419
they would make a **g** cloud of smoke Jg 20:38 7235a
For they had taken a **g** oath Jg 21:5 1419
of her husband, a man of **g** wealth, Ru 2:1 1368
of my **g** concern and provocation." 1Sa 1:16 7230
sin of the young men was very **g** 1Sa 2:17 1419
all Israel shouted with a **g** shout, 1Sa 4:5 1419
noise of this **g** shout in the camp 1Sa 4:6 1419
and the slaughter was very **g**, 1Sa 4:10 1419
a **g** slaughter among the people, 1Sa 4:17 1419
the city with very **g** confusion; 1Sa 5:9 1419
then He has done us this **g** evil. 1Sa 6:9 1419
the people with a **g** slaughter. 1Sa 6:19 1419

LORD thundered with a **g** thunder	**1Sa 7:10**	1419
see this **g** thing which the LORD	**1Sa 12:16**	1419
and see that your wickedness is **g**	**1Sa 12:17**	7227a
people on account of His **g** name,	**1Sa 12:22**	1419
what **g** things He has done for you.	**1Sa 12:24**	1431
so that it became a **g** trembling.	**1Sa 14:15**	430
and there was very **g** confusion.	**1Sa 14:20**	1419
the Philistines has not been **g**."	**1Sa 14:30**	7235a
roll a **g** stone to me today."	**1Sa 14:33**	1419
this **g** deliverance in Israel?	**1Sa 14:45**	1419
enrich the man who kills him with **g**	**1Sa 17:25**	1419
a **g** deliverance for all Israel;	**1Sa 19:5**	1419
defeated them with **g** slaughter,	**1Sa 19:8**	1419
my father does nothing either **g** or	**1Sa 20:2**	1419
struck them with a **g** slaughter.	**1Sa 23:5**	1419
who were in it, both small and **g**,	**1Sa 30:2**	1419
dancing because of all the **g** spoil that	**1Sa 30:16**	1419
was missing, whether small or **g**,	**1Sa 30:19**	1419
a prince and a **g** man has fallen	**2Sa 3:38**	1419
and I will make you a **g** name,	**2Sa 7:9**	1419
of the **g** men who are on the earth.	**2Sa 7:9**	1419
"For this reason You are **g**,	**2Sa 7:22**	1431
and to do a **g** thing for You and	**2Sa 7:23**	1420
man had a **g** many flocks and herds.	**2Sa 12:2**	3966
spoil of the city in **g** amounts.	**2Sa 12:30**	3966
hated her with a very **g** hatred;	**2Sa 13:15**	1419
slaughter there that day was **g**,	**2Sa 18:7**	1419
the thick branches of a **g** oak.	**2Sa 18:9**	1419
over him a very **g** heap of stones.	**2Sa 18:17**	1419
your servant, I saw a **g** tumult,	**2Sa 18:29**	1419
Mahanaim, for he was a very **g** man.	**2Sa 19:32**	1419
where there was a man of **g**	**2Sa 21:20**	
And Your help makes me **g**.	**2Sa 22:36**	7235a
about a **g** victory that day;	**2Sa 23:10**	1419
LORD brought about a **g** victory.	**2Sa 23:12**	1419
"I am in **g** distress.	**2Sa 24:14**	3966
of the LORD for His mercies are **g**,	**2Sa 24:14**	7227a
flutes and rejoicing with **g** joy,	**1Ki 1:40**	1419
for that was the **g** high place;	**1Ki 3:4**	1419
"You have shown **g** lovingkindness	**1Ki 3:6**	1419
for him this **g** lovingkindness,	**1Ki 3:6**	1419
a **g** people who are too many	**1Ki 3:8**	7227a
to judge this **g** people of Yours?"	**1Ki 3:9**	3515
sixty **g** cities with walls and	**1Ki 4:13**	1419
wisdom and very **g** discernment and	**1Ki 4:29**	7235a
a wise son over this **g** people."	**1Ki 5:7**	7227a
and they quarried **g** stones,	**1Ki 5:17**	1419
so on the outside to the **g** court.	**1Ki 7:9**	1419
So the **g** court all around *had*	**1Ki 7:12**	1419
of Your **g** name and Your mighty hand,	**1Ki 8:42**	1419
a **g** assembly from the entrance of	**1Ki 8:65**	1419
and a very **g** *amount* of spices and	**1Ki 10:10**	7235a
a very **g** *number of* almug trees	**1Ki 10:11**	7235a
the king made a **g** throne of ivory	**1Ki 10:18**	1419
found **g** favor before Pharaoh,	**1Ki 11:19**	3966
the journey is too **g** for you."	**1Ki 19:7**	7227a
And a **g** and strong wind was	**1Ki 19:11**	1419
you seen all this **g** multitude?	**1Ki 20:13**	1419
the Arameans with a **g** slaughter.	**1Ki 20:21**	1419
this **g** multitude into your hand,	**1Ki 20:28**	1419
"Do not fight with small or **g**,	**1Ki 22:31**	1419
there came **g** wrath against Israel,	**2Ki 3:27**	1419
Aram, was a **g** man with his master,	**2Ki 5:1**	1419
told you *to do some* **g** thing,	**2Ki 5:13**	1419
and chariots and a **g** army there,	**2Ki 6:14**	3515
So he prepared a **g** feast for them;	**2Ki 6:23**	1419
There was a **g** famine in Samaria;	**2Ki 6:25**	1419
even the sound of a **g** army,	**2Ki 7:6**	1419
g things that Elisha has done."	**2Ki 8:4**	1419
that he should do this **g** thing?"	**2Ki 8:13**	1419
were with the **g** men of the city,	**2Ki 10:6**	1419
and all his **g** men and his	**2Ki 10:11**	1419
for I have a **g** sacrifice for Baal;	**2Ki 10:19**	1419
"Upon the **g** altar burn the	**2Ki 16:15**	1419
and made them commit a **g** sin.	**2Ki 17:21**	1419
from the land of Egypt with **g** power	**2Ki 17:36**	1419
'Thus says the **g** king, the king of	**2Ki 18:19**	1419
"Hear the word of the **g** king,	**2Ki 18:28**	1419
for **g** is the wrath of the LORD	**2Ki 22:13**	1419
all the people, both small and **g**;	**2Ki 23:2**	1419
turn from the fierceness of His **g** wrath	**2Ki 23:26**	1419
every **g** house he burned with fire.	**2Ki 25:9**	1419
all the people, both small and **g**,	**2Ki 25:26**	1419
LORD saved them by a **g** victory.	**1Ch 11:14**	1419
He killed an Egyptian, a man of **g**	**1Ch 11:23**	
was a **g** army like the army of God.	**1Ch 12:22**	1419
oxen, **g** quantities of flour cakes,	**1Ch 12:40**	7230
For **g** is the LORD, and greatly to	**1Ch 16:25**	1419
the **g** ones who are in the earth.	**1Ch 17:8**	1419
house for a **g** while to come,	**1Ch 17:17**	7350
to make known all these **g** things.	**1Ch 17:19**	1420
a name by **g** and terrible things,	**1Ch 17:21**	1420
of the city, a very **g** amount.	**1Ch 20:2**	7235a
was a man of **g** stature	**1Ch 20:6**	
"I am in **g** distress;	**1Ch 21:13**	3966
LORD, for His mercies are very **g**.	**1Ch 21:13**	7227a
much blood and have waged **g** wars;	**1Ch 22:8**	1419
with **g** pains I have prepared for	**1Ch 22:14**	6040a
for they are in **g** quantity;	**1Ch 22:14**	7230
alike, the small as well as the **g**,	**1Ch 25:8**	1419
lots, the small and the **g** alike,	**1Ch 26:13**	1419
inexperienced and the work is **g**;	**1Ch 29:1**	1419
and it lies in Your hand to make **g** and	**1Ch 29:12**	1431
before the LORD with **g** gladness.	**1Ch 29:22**	1419
David with **g** lovingkindness,	**2Ch 1:8**	1419
can rule this **g** people of Yours?"	**2Ch 1:10**	1419
I am about to build *will be* **g**,	**2Ch 2:5**	1419
to build *will be* **g** and wonderful.	**2Ch 2:9**	1419
g court and doors for the court,	**2Ch 4:9**	1419
these utensils in **g** quantities,	**2Ch 4:18**	3966
a far country for Your **g** name's sake	**2Ch 6:32**	1419
with him, a very **g** assembly	**2Ch 7:8**	1419
and a very **g** *amount of* spices and	**2Ch 9:9**	7230
the king made a **g** throne of ivory	**2Ch 9:17**	1419
being a **g** multitude and *having*	**2Ch 13:8**	7227a
defeated them with a **g** slaughter,	**2Ch 13:17**	7227a
put to death, whether small or **g**,	**2Ch 15:13**	1419
they made a very **g** fire for him.	**2Ch 16:14**	1419
and he had **g** riches and honor.	**2Ch 17:5**	7230
He took **g** pride in the ways of	**2Ch 17:6**	1361b
Jehoshaphat had **g** riches and honor;	**2Ch 18:1**	7230
"Do not fight with small or **g**,	**2Ch 18:30**	1419
"A **g** multitude is coming against	**2Ch 20:2**	7227a
are powerless before this **g** multitude	**2Ch 20:12**	7227a
because of this **g** multitude,	**2Ch 20:15**	7227a
possessions with a **g** calamity;	**2Ch 21:14**	1419
sickness and he died in **g** pain.	**2Ch 21:19**	7451a
a very **g** army into their hands,	**2Ch 24:24**	7230
who could wage war with **g** power,	**2Ch 26:13**	2428
of shooting arrows and **g** stones.	**2Ch 26:15**	1419
from him a **g** number of captives and	**2Ch 28:5**	1419
also a **g** deal of spoil from them,	**2Ch 28:8**	7227a
for our guilt is **g** so that *His*	**2Ch 28:13**	7227a
in **g** numbers as it was prescribed.	**2Ch 30:5**	7230
Bread *for* seven days with **g** joy,	**2Ch 30:21**	1419
So there was **g** joy in Jerusalem,	**2Ch 30:26**	1419
this **g** quantity is left over."	**2Ch 31:10**	1995
by divisions, whether **g** or small,	**2Ch 31:15**	1419
weapons and shields in **g** number.	**2Ch 32:5**	7230
God had given him very **g** wealth.	**2Ch 32:29**	7227a
for **g** is the wrath of the LORD	**2Ch 34:21**	1419
of the house of God, **g** and small,	**2Ch 36:18**	1419
all the people shouted with a **g** shout	**Ezr 3:11**	1419
g and honorable Osnappar deported	**Ezr 4:10**	7229
Judah, to the house of the **g** God,	**Ezr 5:8**	7229
this work is going on with **g** care	**Ezr 5:8**	629
which a **g** king of Israel built and	**Ezr 5:11**	7229
this day we *have been* in **g** guilt,	**Ezr 9:7**	1419
our evil deeds and our **g** guilt,	**Ezr 9:13**	1419
are in **g** distress and reproach,	**Ne 1:3**	1419
of heaven, the **g** and awesome God,	**Ne 1:5**	1419
g power and by Your strong hand.	**Ne 1:10**	1419
in front of the **g** projecting tower	**Ne 3:27**	1419
the Lord who is **g** and awesome,	**Ne 4:14**	1419
"The work is **g** and extensive, and	**Ne 4:19**	7235a
Now there was a **g** outcry of the	**Ne 5:1**	1419
I held a **g** assembly against them.	**Ne 5:7**	1419
a **g** work and I cannot come down.	**Ne 6:3**	1419
Ezra blessed the LORD the **g** God.	**Ne 8:6**	1419
and to celebrate a **g** festival,	**Ne 8:12**	1419
And there was **g** rejoicing.	**Ne 8:17**	1419
And committed **g** blasphemies,	**Ne 9:18**	1419
You, in Your **g** compassion, Did	**Ne 9:19**	7227a
And reveled in Your **g** goodness.	**Ne 9:25**	1419
and they committed **g** blasphemies.	**Ne 9:26**	1419
and according to Your **g** compassion	**Ne 9:27**	7227a
in Your **g** compassion You did not	**Ne 9:31**	7227a
"Now therefore, our God, the **g**,	**Ne 9:32**	1419
With Your **g** goodness which You	**Ne 9:35**	7227a
please, So we are in **g** distress.	**Ne 9:37**	1419
and I appointed two **g** choirs,	**Ne 12:31**	1419
offered **g** sacrifices and rejoiced	**Ne 12:43**	1419
because God had given them **g** joy,	**Ne 12:43**	1419
you have committed all this **g** evil	**Ne 13:27**	1419
of his **g** majesty for many days,	**Es 1:4**	1420
all his kingdom, **g** as it is,	**Es 1:20**	7227a
to their husbands, **g** and small."	**Es 1:20**	1419
Then the king gave a **g** banquet,	**Es 2:18**	1419
was **g** mourning among the Jews,	**Es 4:3**	1419
the queen writhed in **g** anguish.	**Es 4:4**	3966
Mordecai was **g** in the king's house,	**Es 9:4**	1419
Ahasuerus, and **g** among the Jews	**Es 10:3**	1419
a **g** wind came from across the	**Jb 1:19**	1419
they saw that *his* pain was very **g**.	**Jb 2:13**	1431
"The small and the **g** are there,	**Jb 3:19**	1419
does **g** and unsearchable things,	**Jb 5:9**	1419
Who does **g** things, unfathomable,	**Jb 9:10**	1419
"He makes the nations **g**,	**Jb 12:23**	7679
"Is not your wickedness **g**,	**Jb 22:5**	7227a
a **g** force my garment is distorted;	**Jb 30:18**	7230
gloated because my wealth was **g**,	**Jb 31:25**	7227a
Because I feared the **g** multitude,	**Jb 31:34**	7227a
Doing **g** things which we cannot	**Jb 37:5**	1419
And the number of your days is **g**!	**Jb 38:21**	7227a
trust him because his strength is **g**	**Jb 39:11**	7227a
The tongue that speaks **g** things;	**Ps 12:3**	1419
There they are in **g** dread,	**Ps 14:5**	6343
And Your gentleness makes me **g**.	**Ps 18:35**	7235a
gives **g** deliverance to His king,	**Ps 18:50**	1431
In keeping them there is **g** reward.	**Ps 19:11**	7227a
be acquitted of **g** transgression.	**Ps 19:13**	7227a
glory is **g** through Your salvation,	**Ps 21:5**	1419
comes my praise in the **g** assembly;	**Ps 22:25**	7227a
Pardon my iniquity, for it is **g**.	**Ps 25:11**	7227a
How **g** is Your goodness, Which You	**Ps 31:19**	7227a
Surely in a flood of **g** waters they	**Ps 32:6**	7227a
is not delivered by **g** strength.	**Ps 33:16**	7230
deliver anyone by its **g** strength.	**Ps 33:17**	7230
You thanks in the **g** congregation;	**Ps 35:18**	7227a
Your judgments are *like* a **g** deep.	**Ps 36:6**	7227a
in the **g** congregation;	**Ps 40:9**	7227a
Your truth from the **g** congregation.	**Ps 40:10**	7227a
A **g** King over all the earth.	**Ps 47:2**	1419
G is the LORD, and greatly to be	**Ps 48:1**	1419
far north, The city of the **g** King.	**Ps 48:2**	7227a
in **g** fear *where* no fear had been;	**Ps 53:5**	6343
For Your lovingkindness is **g** to the	**Ps 57:10**	1419
the *good* tidings are a **g** host:	**Ps 68:11**	7227a
You who have done **g** things;	**Ps 71:19**	1419
His name is **g** in Israel.	**Ps 76:1**	1419
What god is **g** like our God?	**Ps 77:13**	1419
are **g** and do wondrous deeds;	**Ps 86:10**	1419
Your lovingkindness toward me is **g**,	**Ps 86:13**	1419
How **g** are Your works, O LORD!	**Ps 92:5**	1431
For the LORD is a **g** God And	**Ps 95:3**	1419
God And a **g** King above all gods,	**Ps 95:3**	1419
For **g** is the LORD and greatly to	**Ps 96:4**	1419
The LORD is **g** in Zion, And He is	**Ps 99:2**	1419
praise Your **g** and awesome name;	**Ps 99:3**	1419
So **g** is His lovingkindness toward	**Ps 103:11**	1396
O LORD my God, You are very **g**;	**Ps 104:1**	1431
There is the sea, **g** and broad,	**Ps 104:25**	1419
number, Animals both small and **g**.	**Ps 104:25**	1419
Who had done **g** things in Egypt,	**Ps 106:21**	1419
Who do business on **g** waters;	**Ps 107:23**	7227a
For Your lovingkindness is **g** above	**Ps 108:4**	1419
G are the works of the LORD;	**Ps 111:2**	1419
The small together with the **g**.	**Ps 115:13**	1419
His lovingkindness is **g** toward us,	**Ps 117:2**	1396
G are Your mercies, O LORD;	**Ps 119:156**	7227a
word, As one who finds **g** spoil.	**Ps 119:162**	7227a
who love Your law have **g** peace,	**Ps 119:165**	7227a
LORD has done **g** things for them."	**Ps 126:2**	1431
The LORD has done **g** things for us;	**Ps 126:3**	1431
do I involve myself in **g** matters,	**Ps 131:1**	1419
For I know that the LORD is **g** And	**Ps 135:5**	1419
To Him who alone does **g** wonders,	**Ps 136:4**	1419
To Him who made *the* **g** lights,	**Ps 136:7**	1419
To Him who smote **g** kings,	**Ps 136:17**	1419
For **g** is the glory of the LORD.	**Ps 138:5**	1419
me and deliver me out of **g** waters,	**Ps 144:7**	7227a
G is the LORD, and highly to be	**Ps 145:3**	1419
to anger and **g** in lovingkindness.	**Ps 145:8**	1419
G is our Lord and abundant in	**Ps 147:5**	1419
to be poor, but has **g** wealth.	**Pr 13:7**	7227a
slow to anger has **g** understanding,	**Pr 14:29**	7227a
G wealth is *in* the house of	**Pr 15:6**	7227a
g treasure and turmoil with it.	**Pr 15:16**	7227a
Than **g** income with injustice.	**Pr 16:8**	7230
him And brings him before **g** men.	**Pr 18:16**	1419
of **g** anger will bear the penalty,	**Pr 19:19**	1419
to be more desired than **g** wealth,	**Pr 22:1**	7227a
If you are a man of **g** appetite.	**Pr 23:2**	
not stand in the place of **g** men;	**Pr 25:6**	1419
triumph, there is **g** glory,	**Pr 28:12**	7227a
a **g** oppressor lacks understanding,	**Pr 28:16**	7227a
Then I became **g** and increased more	**Ec 2:9**	1431
This too is vanity and a **g** evil.	**Ec 2:21**	7227a
eats in darkness with **g** vexation,	**Ec 5:17**	7235a
a **g** king came to it, surrounded it and	**Ec 9:14**	1419
composure allays **g** offenses.	**Ec 10:4**	1419
I took **g** delight and sat down,	**SS 2:3**	
desolate, *Even* **g** and fine ones,	**Is 5:9**	1419
in darkness Will see a **g** light;	**Is 9:2**	1419
For **g** in your midst is the Holy	**Is 12:6**	1419
along with all *his* **g** population,	**Is 16:14**	7227a
His fierce and **g** and mighty sword,	**Is 27:1**	1419
that a **g** trumpet will be blown,	**Is 27:13**	1419
wonderful and *His* wisdom **g**.	**Is 28:29**	1431
on the day of the **g** slaughter,	**Is 30:25**	7227a
a **g** slaughter in the land of Edom.	**Is 34:6**	1419
'Thus says the **g** king, the king of	**Is 36:4**	1419
"Hear the words of the **g** king,	**Is 36:13**	1419
my own welfare I had **g** bitterness;	**Is 38:17**	4751
To make the law **g** and glorious.	**Is 42:21**	1431
of the **g** power of your spells.	**Is 47:9**	3966
the sea, The waters of the **g** deep;	**Is 51:10**	7227a
allot Him a portion with the **g**,	**Is 53:12**	7227a
g compassion I will gather you.	**Is 54:7**	1419
well-being of your sons will be **g**.	**Is 54:13**	7227a
sent your envoys a **g** distance And	**Is 57:9**	
And the **g** goodness toward the	**Is 63:7**	7227a
from the north, And **g** destruction.	**Jer 4:6**	1419
"I will go to the **g** And will speak	**Jer 5:5**	1419
they have become **g** and rich.	**Jer 5:27**	1431
the north, And a **g** destruction.	**Jer 6:1**	1419
And a **g** nation will be aroused	**Jer 6:22**	1419
We are put to **g** shame, For we have	**Jer 9:19**	3966
You are **g**, and great is Your name	**Jer 10:6**	1419
great, and **g** is Your name in might.	**Jer 10:6**	1419
A **g** commotion out of the land of the	**Jer 10:22**	1419
With the noise of a **g** tumult He	**Jer 11:16**	1419
and the **g** pride of Jerusalem.	**Jer 13:9**	7227a
"Both **g** men and small will die in	**Jer 16:6**	1419
all this **g** calamity against us?	**Jer 16:10**	1419
anger and wrath and **g** indignation.	**Jer 21:5**	1419
they will die of a **g** pestilence.	**Jer 21:6**	1419
LORD done thus to this **g** city?'	**Jer 22:8**	1419
'(For many nations and **g** kings	**Jer 25:14**	1419
And a **g** storm is being stirred up	**Jer 25:32**	1419
a **g** evil against ourselves."	**Jer 26:19**	1419
the face of the earth by My **g** power	**Jer 27:5**	1419
then many nations and **g** kings will	**Jer 27:7**	1419
many lands and against **g** kingdoms,	**Jer 28:8**	1419
for that day is **g**, There is none	**Jer 30:7**	1419
your iniquity is **g** *And* your sins	**Jer 30:14**	7230
your iniquity is **g** *And* your sins	**Jer 30:15**	7230
A **g** company, they will return	**Jer 31:8**	1419
heavens and the earth by Your **g** power	**Jer 32:17**	1419
after them, O **g** and mighty God.	**Jer 32:18**	1419
g in counsel and mighty in deed,	**Jer 32:19**	1419
outstretched arm and with **g** terror;	**Jer 32:21**	1419
in My wrath and in **g** indignation;	**Jer 32:37**	1419
this **g** disaster on this people,	**Jer 32:42**	1419
will tell you **g** and mighty things,	**Jer 33:3**	1419
for **g** is the anger and the wrath	**Jer 36:7**	1419
and summer fruit in **g** abundance.	**Jer 40:12**	3966

by the **g** pool that is in Gibeon.	**Jer 41:12**	7227a
both small and **g** approached	**Jer 42:1**	1419
all the people both small and **g**,	**Jer 42:8**	1419
you doing **g** harm to yourselves,	**Jer 44:7**	1419
Both small and **g** will die by the	**Jer 44:12**	1419
'Behold, I have sworn by My **g** name,'	**Jer 44:26**	1419
seeking **g** things for yourself?	**Jer 45:5**	1419
'Devastation and **g** destruction!'	**Jer 48:3**	1419
against Babylon A horde of **g** nations	**Jer 50:9**	1419
is in the land, And **g** destruction.	**Jer 50:22**	1419
And a **g** nation and many kings Will	**Jer 50:41**	1419
And of **g** destruction from the land	**Jer 51:54**	1419
Who was *once* **g** among the nations!	**La 1:1**	7227a
G is Your faithfulness.	**La 3:23**	7227a
a **g** cloud with fire flashing forth	**Ezk 1:4**	1419
a **g** rumbling sound behind me,	**Ezk 3:12**	1419
them, even a **g** rumbling sound.	**Ezk 3:13**	1419
the **g** abominations which the house	**Ezk 8:6**	1419
Israel and Judah is very, very **g**,	**Ezk 9:9**	1419
"A **g** eagle with great wings, long	**Ezk 17:3**	1419
"A great eagle with **g** wings,	**Ezk 17:3**	1419
"But there was another **g** eagle	**Ezk 17:7**	1419
with **g** wings and much plumage;	**Ezk 17:7**	1419
And neither by **g** strength nor by	**Ezk 17:9**	1419
with *his* mighty army and **g** company	**Ezk 17:17**	1419
is the sword for the **g** one slain,	**Ezk 21:14**	1419
I also will make the pile **g**.	**Ezk 24:9**	1431
her **g** rust has not gone from her;	**Ezk 24:12**	7227a
"I will execute **g** vengeance	**Ezk 25:17**	1419
chariots, cavalry and a **g** army.	**Ezk 26:7**	7227a
and the **g** waters cover you,	**Ezk 26:19**	7227a
have brought you Into **g** waters;	**Ezk 27:26**	7227a
"By your **g** wisdom, by your trade	**Ezk 28:5**	7230
The **g** monster that lies in the	**Ezk 29:3**	1419
g nations lived under its shade.	**Ezk 31:6**	7227a
vindicate the holiness of My **g** name	**Ezk 36:23**	1419
their feet, an exceedingly **g** army.	**Ezk 37:10**	1419
a **g** company *with* buckler and	**Ezk 38:4**	7227a
goods, to capture **g** spoil?	**Ezk 38:13**	1419
a **g** assembly and a mighty army;	**Ezk 38:15**	1419
there will surely be a **g** earthquake	**Ezk 38:19**	1419
as a **g** sacrifice on the mountains	**Ezk 39:17**	1419
kinds, like the fish of the **G** Sea,	**Ezk 47:10**	1419
the **G** Sea *by* the way of Hethlon,	**Ezk 47:15**	1419
brook *of Egypt and* to the **G** Sea.	**Ezk 47:19**	1419
The west side *shall be* the **G** Sea,	**Ezk 47:20**	1419
the brook *of Egypt,* to the **G** Sea.	**Ezk 48:28**	1419
me gifts and a reward and **g** honor;	**Da 2:6**	7690
inasmuch as no **g** king or ruler has	**Da 2:10**	7229
there was a single **g** statue;	**Da 2:31**	7690
became a **g** mountain and filled the	**Da 2:35**	7229
the **g** God has made known to the	**Da 2:45**	7229
Daniel and gave him many **g** gifts,	**Da 2:48**	7229
"How **g** are His signs And how	**Da 4:3**	7229
the earth and its height *was* **g**.	**Da 4:10**	7690
have become **g** and grown strong,	**Da 4:22**	7236
and your majesty has become **g** and	**Da 4:22**	7236
'Is this not Babylon the **g**,	**Da 4:30**	7229
Belshazzar the king held a **g** feast	**Da 5:1**	7229
heaven were stirring up the **g** sea.	**Da 7:2**	7229
"And four **g** beasts were coming up	**Da 7:3**	7229
and a mouth uttering **g** *boasts.*	**Da 7:8**	7229
'These **g** beasts, which are four *in*	**Da 7:17**	7229
and a mouth uttering **g** *boasts*	**Da 7:20**	7229
exceedingly **g** toward the south,	**Da 8:9**	1431
O Lord, the **g** and awesome God,	**Da 9:4**	1419
us, to bring on us **g** calamity;	**Da 9:12**	1419
on account of Your **g** compassion.	**Da 9:18**	7227a
was true and *one of* **g** conflict,	**Da 10:1**	1419
I was by the bank of the **g** river,	**Da 10:4**	1419
a **g** dread fell on them,	**Da 10:7**	1419
left alone and saw this **g** vision;	**Da 10:8**	1419
and he will rule with **g** authority	**Da 11:3**	7227a
will be a **g** dominion *indeed.*	**Da 11:5**	7227a
with them and display **g** strength.	**Da 11:7**	
assemble a multitude of **g** forces;	**Da 11:10**	7227a
latter will raise a **g** multitude,	**Da 11:11**	7227a
with a **g** army and much equipment.	**Da 11:13**	1419
he will give **g** honor to those who	**Da 11:39**	7235a
and he will go forth with **g** wrath	**Da 11:44**	1419
the **g** prince who stands *guard* over	**Da 12:1**	1419
For **g** will be the day of Jezreel.	**Hos 1:11**	1419
because your hostility is *so* **g**.	**Hos 9:7**	7227a
because of your **g** wickedness.	**Hos 10:15**	7463a
So there is a **g** and mighty people;	**Jl 2:2**	7227a
Surely His camp is very **g**,	**Jl 2:11**	7227a
LORD is indeed **g** and very awesome,	**Jl 2:11**	1419
up, For it has done **g** things."	**Jl 2:20**	1431
For the LORD has done **g** things.	**Jl 2:21**	1431
My **g** army which I sent among you.	**Jl 2:25**	1419
Before the **g** and awesome day of	**Jl 2:31**	1419
for their wickedness is **g**.	**Jl 3:13**	7227a
and see *the* **g** tumults within her	**Am 3:9**	7227a
g houses will come to an end,"	**Am 3:15**	7227a
are many and your sins are **g**,	**Am 5:12**	6099
And go from there to Hamath the **g**,	**Am 6:2**	7227a
command that the **g** house be smashed	**Am 6:11**	1419
and it consumed the **g** deep and	**Am 7:4**	7227a
"Arise, go to Nineveh the **g** city and	**Jon 1:2**	1419
The LORD hurled a **g** wind on	**Jon 1:4**	1419
there was a **g** storm on the sea so that	**Jon 1:4**	1419
this **g** storm *has come* upon you."	**Jon 1:12**	1419
a **g** fish to swallow Jonah,	**Jon 1:17**	1419
The **g** deep engulfed me, Weeds were	**Jon 2:5**	
go to Nineveh the **g** city and	**Jon 3:2**	1419
Nineveh was an exceedingly **g** city,	**Jon 3:3**	1419
the **g** city in which there are more	**Jon 4:11**	1419
be **g** To the ends of the earth.	**Mi 5:4**	1431
And a **g** man speaks the desire of	**Mi 7:3**	1419
is slow to anger and **g** in power,	**Na 1:3**	1419
her **g** men were bound with fetters.	**Na 3:10**	1419
Near is the **g** day of the LORD,	**Zph 1:14**	1419
'What are you, O **g** mountain?	**Zch 4:7**	1419
therefore **g** wrath came from the	**Zch 7:12**	1419
g wrath I am jealous for her.'	**Zch 8:2**	1419
Gaza too will writhe in **g** pain;	**Zch 9:5**	3966
will be **g** mourning in Jerusalem,	**Zch 12:11**	1431
a **g** panic from the LORD will fall on	**Zch 14:13**	7227a
and garments in **g** abundance.	**Zch 14:14**	3966
name *will be* **g** among the nations,	**Mal 1:11**	1419
will be **g** among the nations,"	**Mal 1:11**	1419
to the Lord, for I am a **g** King,"	**Mal 1:14**	1419
g and terrible day of the LORD.	**Mal 4:5**	1419
rejoiced exceedingly with **g** joy.	**Mt 2:10**	*3173*
RAMAH, WEEPING AND **G** MOURNING,	**Mt 2:18**	*4183*
SITTING IN DARKNESS SAW A **G** LIGHT,	**Mt 4:16**	*3173*
for your reward in heaven is **g**;	**Mt 5:12**	*4183*
called **g** in the kingdom of heaven.	**Mt 5:19**	*3173*
for it is THE CITY OF THE **G** KING.	**Mt 5:35**	*3173*
darkness, how **g** is the darkness!	**Mt 6:23**	*4214*
and it fell—and **g** was its fall."	**Mt 7:27**	*3173*
g faith with anyone in Israel.	**Mt 8:10**	*5118*
there arose a **g** storm on the sea,	**Mt 8:24**	*3173*
upon finding one pearl of **g** value,	**Mt 13:46**	*4186*
"O woman, your faith is **g**;	**Mt 15:28**	*3173*
and *their* **g** men exercise authority	**Mt 20:25**	*3173*
but whoever wishes to become **g**	**Mt 20:26**	*3173*
is the **g** commandment in the Law?"	**Mt 22:36**	*3173*
is the **g** and foremost commandment.	**Mt 22:38**	*3173*
there will be a **g** tribulation,	**Mt 24:21**	*3173*
and will show **g** signs and wonders,	**Mt 24:24**	*3173*
OF THE SKY with power and **g** glory.	**Mt 24:30**	*4183*
send forth His angels with A **G** TRUMPET	**Mt 24:31**	*3173*
left the tomb quickly with fear and **g** joy	**Mt 28:8**	*3173*
and a **g** multitude from Galilee	**Mk 3:7**	*4183*
a **g** number of people heard of all	**Mk 3:8**	*4183*
report to them what **g** things the Lord	**Mk 5:19**	*3745*
g things Jesus had done for him;	**Mk 5:20**	*3745*
and some of them have come from a **g**	**Mk 8:3**	*3113*
and their **g** men exercise authority	**Mk 10:42**	*3173*
but whoever wishes to become **g**	**Mk 10:43**	*3173*
"Do you see these **g** buildings?	**Mk 13:2**	*3173*
IN CLOUDS with **g** power and glory.	**Mk 13:26**	*4183*
be **g** in the sight of the Lord;	**Lk 1:15**	*3173*
"He will be **g** and will be called	**Lk 1:32**	*3173*
One has done **g** things for me;	**Lk 1:49**	*3173*
displayed His **g** mercy toward her;	**Lk 1:58**	*3170*
I bring you good news of **g** joy	**Lk 2:10**	*3173*
a **g** famine came over all the land;	**Lk 4:25**	*3173*
enclosed a **g** quantity of fish,	**Lk 5:6**	*4183*
g crowd of tax collectors and other	**Lk 5:29**	*4183*
and a **g** throng of people from all	**Lk 6:17**	*4183*
your reward is **g** in heaven.	**Lk 6:23**	*4183*
and your reward will be **g**,	**Lk 6:35**	*4183*
the ruin of that house was **g**."	**Lk 6:49**	*3173*
have I found such **g** faith."	**Lk 7:9**	*5118*
"A **g** prophet has arisen among us!"	**Lk 7:16**	*3173*
a crop a hundred times as **g**."	**Lk 8:8**	*1542*
for they were gripped with **g** fear;	**Lk 8:37**	*3173*
g things God has done for you."	**Lk 8:39**	*3745*
g things Jesus had done for him.	**Lk 8:39**	*3745*
you, this is the one who is **g**."	**Lk 9:48**	*3173*
and you there is a **g** chasm fixed,	**Lk 16:26**	*3173*
and there will be **g** earthquakes,	**Lk 21:11**	*3173*
terrors and **g** signs from heaven.	**Lk 21:11**	*3173*
will be **g** distress upon the land and	**Lk 21:23**	*3173*
IN A CLOUD with power and **g** glory.	**Lk 21:27**	*4183*
returned to Jerusalem with **g** joy,	**Lk 24:52**	*3173*
last day, the **g** *day* of the feast,	**Jn 7:37**	*3173*
because of the **g** number of fish.	**Jn 21:6**	*4128*
in amazement and **g** perplexity,	**Ac 2:12**	*1280*
BEFORE THE **G** AND GLORIOUS DAY OF	**Ac 2:20**	*3173*
And with **g** power the apostles were	**Ac 4:33**	*3173*
and **g** fear came over all who heard	**Ac 5:5**	*3173*
And **g** fear came over the whole	**Ac 5:11**	*3173*
and a **g** many of the priests were	**Ac 6:7**	*4183*
was performing **g** wonders and signs	**Ac 6:8**	*3173*
Canaan, and **g** affliction *with it,*	**Ac 7:11**	*3173*
And on that day a **g** persecution	**Ac 8:1**	*3173*
Samaria, claiming to be someone **g**;	**Ac 8:9**	*3173*
is called the **G** Power of God."	**Ac 8:10**	*3173*
signs and **g** miracles taking place,	**Ac 8:13**	*3173*
object like a **g** sheet coming down,	**Ac 10:11**	*3173*
object coming down like a **g** sheet	**Ac 11:5**	*3173*
be a **g** famine all over the world.	**Ac 11:28**	*3173*
and made the people **g** during their	**Ac 13:17**	*5312*
Paul and Barnabas had **g** dissension	**Ac 15:2**	*3756, 3641*
g joy to all the brethren.	**Ac 15:3**	*3173*
there came a **g** earthquake,	**Ac 16:26**	*3173*
the word with **g** eagerness,	**Ac 17:11**	*3956*
the temple of the **g** goddess Artemis	**Ac 19:27**	*3173*
"**G** is Artemis of the Ephesians!"	**Ac 19:28**	*3173*
"**G** is Artemis of the Ephesians!"	**Ac 19:34**	*3173*
of the temple of the **g** Artemis and	**Ac 19:35**	*3173*
and when there was a **g** hush,	**Ac 21:40**	*4183*
And there occurred a **g** uproar;	**Ac 23:9**	*3173*
as a **g** dissension was developing,	**Ac 23:10**	*4183*
with Bernice amid **g** pomp,	**Ac 25:23**	*4183*
testifying both to small and **g**,	**Ac 26:22**	*3173*
g learning is driving you mad."	**Ac 26:24**	*4183*
with damage and **g** loss,	**Ac 27:10**	*4183*
a **g** dispute among themselves.	**Ac 28:29**	*4183*
G in every respect.	**Ro 3:2**	*4183*
that I have **g** sorrow and unceasing	**Ro 9:2**	*3173*
a **g** many kinds of languages in the	**1Co 14:10**	*5118*
us from so **g** a *peril of* death,	**2Co 1:10**	*5082*
we use **g** boldness in *our* speech,	**2Co 3:12**	*4183*
G is my confidence in you; great	**2Co 7:4**	*4183*
g is my boasting on your behalf.	**2Co 7:4**	*4183*
that in a **g** ordeal of affliction	**2Co 8:2**	*4183*
of *his* **g** confidence in you.	**2Co 8:22**	*4183*
His **g** love with which He loved us,	**Eph 2:4**	*4183*
This mystery is **g**;	**Eph 5:32**	*3173*
how **g** a struggle I have on your	**Col 2:1**	*2245*
with **g** desire to see your face.	**1Th 2:17**	*4183*
and **g** confidence in the faith that is in	**1Tm 3:13**	*4183*
and **g** is the mystery of godliness:	**1Tm 3:16**	*3173*
actually is a means of **g** gain when	**1Tm 6:6**	*3173*
with **g** patience and instruction.	**2Tm 4:2**	*3956*
the glory of our **g** God and Savior,	**Ti 2:13**	*3173*
if we neglect so **g** a salvation?	**Heb 2:3**	*5082*
Therefore, since we have a **g** high priest	**Heb 4:14**	*3173*
g this man was to whom Abraham,	**Heb 7:4**	*4080*
a **g** priest over the house of God,	**Heb 10:21**	*3173*
a **g** conflict of sufferings,	**Heb 10:32**	*4183*
confidence, which has a **g** reward.	**Heb 10:35**	*3173*
since we have so **g** a cloud of	**Heb 12:1**	*5118*
from the dead the **g** Shepherd of the	**Heb 13:20**	*3173*
though they are so **g** and are	**Jas 3:4**	*5082*
and *yet* it boasts of **g** things.	**Jas 3:5**	*3173*
how **g** a forest is set aflame by	**Jas 3:5**	*2245*
who according to His **g** mercy has	**1Pe 1:3**	*4183*
See how **g** a love the Father has	**1Jn 3:1**	*4217*
for the judgment of the **g** day,	**Jude 1:6**	*3173*
of His glory blameless with **g** joy,	**Jude 1:24**	*20*
with her into **g** tribulation,	**Rv 2:22**	*3173*
and a **g** sword was given to him.	**Rv 6:4**	*3173*
and there was a **g** earthquake;	**Rv 6:12**	*3173*
figs when shaken by a **g** wind.	**Rv 6:13**	*3173*
the kings of the earth and the **g** men	**Rv 6:15**	*3175*
the **g** day of their wrath has come,	**Rv 6:17**	*3173*
looked, and behold, a **g** multitude which	**Rv 7:9**	*4183*
who come out of the **g** tribulation,	**Rv 7:14**	*3173*
and *something* like a **g** mountain	**Rv 8:8**	*3173*
and a **g** star fell from heaven,	**Rv 8:10**	*3173*
like the smoke of a **g** furnace;	**Rv 9:2**	*3173*
bound at the **g** river Euphrates."	**Rv 9:14**	*3173*
bodies *will lie* in the street of the **g** city	**Rv 11:8**	*3173*
and **g** fear fell upon those who	**Rv 11:11**	*3173*
hour there was a **g** earthquake,	**Rv 11:13**	*3173*
g power and have begun to reign.	**Rv 11:17**	*3173*
Your name, the small and the **g**,	**Rv 11:18**	*3173*
an earthquake and a **g** hailstorm.	**Rv 11:19**	*3173*
A **g** sign appeared in heaven:	**Rv 12:1**	*3173*
a **g** red dragon having seven heads	**Rv 12:3**	*3173*
And the **g** dragon was thrown down,	**Rv 12:9**	*3173*
come down to you, having **g** wrath,	**Rv 12:12**	*3173*
two wings of the **g** eagle were given	**Rv 12:14**	*3173*
and his throne and **g** authority.	**Rv 13:2**	*3173*
He performs **g** signs, so that	**Rv 13:13**	*3173*
causes all, the small and the **g**,	**Rv 13:16**	*3173*
"Fallen, fallen is Babylon the **g**,	**Rv 14:8**	*3173*
g wine press of the wrath of God.	**Rv 14:19**	*3173*
sign in heaven, **g** and marvelous,	**Rv 15:1**	*3173*
"**G** and marvelous are Your works, O	**Rv 15:3**	*3173*
out his bowl on the **g** river,	**Rv 16:12**	*3173*
for the war of the **g** day of God,	**Rv 16:14**	*3173*
and there was a **g** earthquake, such	**Rv 16:18**	*3173*
earth, so **g** an earthquake *was it,*	**Rv 16:18**	*3173*
The **g** city was split into	**Rv 16:19**	*3173*
Babylon the **g** was remembered	**Rv 16:19**	*3173*
the judgment of the **g** harlot who sits	**Rv 17:1**	*3173*
"BABYLON THE **G**, THE MOTHER	**Rv 17:5**	*3173*
woman whom you saw is the **g** city,	**Rv 17:18**	*3173*
from heaven, having **g** authority,	**Rv 18:1**	*3173*
"Fallen, fallen is Babylon the **g**!	**Rv 18:2**	*3173*
'Woe, woe, the **g** city, Babylon,	**Rv 18:10**	*3173*
'Woe, woe, the **g** city, she who was	**Rv 18:16**	*3173*
g wealth has been laid waste!'	**Rv 18:17**	*5118*
'What *city* is like the **g** city?'	**Rv 18:18**	*3173*
'Woe, woe, the **g** city, in which	**Rv 18:19**	*3173*
took up a stone like a **g** millstone	**Rv 18:21**	*3173*
"So will Babylon, the **g** city,	**Rv 18:21**	*3173*
were the **g** men of the earth,	**Rv 18:23**	*3175*
voice of a **g** multitude in heaven,	**Rv 19:1**	*4183*
for He has judged the **g** harlot who	**Rv 19:2**	*3173*
fear Him, the small and the **g**."	**Rv 19:5**	*3173*
the voice of a **g** multitude and like	**Rv 19:6**	*4183*
assemble for the **g** supper of God,	**Rv 19:17**	*3173*
men and slaves, and small and **g**."	**Rv 19:18**	*3173*
abyss and a **g** chain in his hand.	**Rv 20:1**	*3173*
Then I saw a **g** white throne and Him	**Rv 20:11**	*3173*
saw the dead, the **g** and the small,	**Rv 20:12**	*3173*
Spirit to a **g** and high mountain,	**Rv 21:10**	*3173*
It had a **g** and high wall, with	**Rv 21:12**	*3173*
its length is as **g** as the width;	**Rv 21:16**	*3745*

GREATER

the **g** light to govern the day,	**Gn 1:16**	1419
is no one **g** in this house than I,	**Gn 39:9**	1419
in the throne I will be **g** than you."	**Gn 41:40**	1431
brother shall be **g** than he,	**Gn 48:19**	1431
the LORD is **g** than all the gods;	**Ex 18:11**	1419
nation **g** and mightier than they."	**Nu 14:12**	1419
nations **g** and mightier than you,	**Dt 4:38**	1419
nations **g** and stronger than you,	**Dt 7:1**	7227a
'These nations are **g** than I;	**Dt 7:17**	7227a
nations **g** and mightier than you,	**Dt 9:1**	1419
nation mightier and **g** than they.'	**Dt 9:14**	7227a
nations **g** and mightier than you.	**Dt 11:23**	1419
and because it was **g** than Ai,	**Jos 10:2**	1419
David became **g** and greater,	**2Sa 5:10**	1980
David became greater and **g**,	**2Sa 5:10**	1419
hatred with which he hated her was **g**	**2Sa 13:15**	1419
this wrong in sending me away is **g**	**2Sa 13:16**	1419
and make his throne **g** than the	**1Ki 1:37**	1431
his throne **g** than your throne!'	**1Ki 1:47**	1431

So King Solomon became **g** than all **1Ki 10:23** 1431
David became **g** and greater, **1Ch 11:9** 1980
David became greater and **g**, **1Ch 11:9** 1419
g is our God than all the gods. **2Ch 2:5** 1419
So King Solomon became **g** than all **2Ch 9:22** 1431
So Jehoshaphat grew **g** and greater, **2Ch 17:12** 4605
So Jehoshaphat grew greater and **g**, **2Ch 17:12** 1432
one with us is **g** than the one with **2Ch 32:7** 7227a
man Mordecai became **g** and greater. **Es 9:4** 1980
man Mordecai became greater and **g**. **Es 9:4** 1419
in this, For God is **g** than man. **Jb 33:12** 7235a
Whose graven images *were* **g** than **Is 10:10**
people Is **g** than the sin of Sodom, **La 4:6** 1431
will see still **g** abominations." **Ezk 8:6** 1419
you will see still **g** abominations **Ezk 8:13** 1419
still **g** abominations than these." **Ezk 8:15** 1419
a **g** multitude than the former, **Da 11:13** 7227a
is their territory **g** than yours? **Am 6:2** 7227a
house will be **g** than the former,' **Hg 2:9** 1419
anyone **g** than John the Baptist! **Mt 11:11** *3173*
kingdom of heaven is **g** than he. **Mt 11:11** *3173*
something **g** than the temple is here. **Mt 12:6** *3173*
something **g** than Jonah is here. **Mt 12:41** *4183*
something **g** than Solomon is here. **Mt 12:42** *4183*
you will receive **g** condemnation. **Mt 23:14** *4053*
other commandment **g** than these." **Mk 12:31** *3173*
will receive **g** condemnation." **Mk 12:40** *4053*
there is no one **g** than John; **Lk 7:28** *3173*
the kingdom of God is **g** than he." **Lk 7:28** *3173*
something **g** than Solomon is here. **Lk 11:31** *4183*
something **g** than Jonah is here. **Lk 11:32** *4183*
suppose that these Galileans were **g** **Lk 13:2**
will receive **g** condemnation." **Lk 20:47** *4053*
who is **g**, the one who reclines *at* **Lk 22:27** *3173*
will see **g** things than these." **Jn 1:50** *3173*
are not **g** than our father Jacob, **Jn 4:12** *3173*
the Father will show Him **g** works **Jn 5:20** *3173*
I have is **g** than *the testimony of* John; **Jn 5:36** *3173*
are not **g** than our father Abraham, **Jn 8:53** *3173*
given *them* to Me, is **g** than all; **Jn 10:29** *3173*
a slave is not **g** than his master, **Jn 13:16** *3173*
sent **g** than the one who sent him. **Jn 13:16** *3173*
g *works* than these he will do; **Jn 14:12** *3173*
for the Father is **g** than I. **Jn 14:28** *3173*
"**G** love has no one than this, **Jn 15:13** *3173*
'A slave is not **g** than his master.' **Jn 15:20** *3173*
Me to you has *the* **g** sin." **Jn 19:11** *3173*
no **g** burden than these essentials: **Ac 15:28** *4183*
But earnestly desire the **g** gifts. **1Co 12:31** *3173*
and **g** is one who prophesies than **1Co 14:5** *3173*
for the **g** progress of the gospel, **Php 1:12** *3123*
toward one another grows *ever* **g**; **2Th 1:3** *4121*
since He could swear by no one **g**, **Heb 6:13** *3173*
swear by one **g** *than themselves,* **Heb 6:16** *3173*
the lesser is blessed by the **g**. **Heb 7:7** *2909*
one hand, existed in **g** numbers because **Heb 7:23** *4183*
the **g** and more perfect tabernacle, **Heb 9:11** *3173*
g riches than the treasures of Egypt; **Heb 11:26** *3173*
But He gives a **g** grace. **Jas 4:6** *3173*
whereas angels who are **g** in might **2Pe 2:11** *3173*
for God is **g** than our heart and **1Jn 3:20** *3173*
because **g** is He who is in you than **1Jn 4:4** *3173*
of men, the testimony of God is **g**; **1Jn 5:9** *3173*
I have no **g** joy than this, to hear **3Jn 1:4** *3173*
deeds of late are **g** than at first. **Rv 2:19** *4183*

GREATEST

was the **g** man among the Anakim. **Jos 14:15** 1419
a hundred and the **g** to a thousand. **1Ch 12:14** 1419
for until now the **g** part of them **1Ch 12:29** 4768
people, from the **g** to the least; **2Ch 34:30** 1419
Susa, from the **g** to the least, **Es 1:5** 1419
the **g** of all the men of the east. **Jb 1:3** 1419
least of them even to the **g** of them, **Jer 6:13** 1419
from the least even to the **g** **Jer 8:10** 1419
least of them to the **g** of them," **Jer 31:34** 1419
from the **g** to the least of them. **Jon 3:5** 1419
is **g** in the kingdom of heaven?" **Mt 18:1** *3173*
is the **g** in the kingdom of heaven. **Mt 18:4** *3173*
g among you shall be your servant. **Mt 23:11** *3173*
another which *of them was* the **g**. **Mk 9:34** *3173*
to which of them might be the **g**. **Lk 9:46** *3173*
one of them was regarded to be **g**. **Lk 22:24** *3173*
but the one who is the **g** among you **Lk 22:26** *3173*
and they all, from smallest to **g**, **Ac 8:10** *3173*
but the **g** of these is love. **1Co 13:13** *3173*
FROM THE LEAST TO THE **G** OF THEM. **Heb 8:11** *3173*

GREATLY

"I will **g** multiply Your pain in **Gn 3:16** 7235a
and increased **g** upon the earth, **Gn 7:18** 3966
"I will **g** multiply your **Gn 16:10** 7235a
and the men were **g** frightened. **Gn 20:8** 3966
The matter distressed Abraham **g** **Gn 21:11** 3966
indeed I will **g** bless you, and I **Gn 22:17** 1288
and I will **g** multiply your seed as **Gn 22:17** 7235a
The LORD has **g** blessed my master, **Gn 24:35** 3966
longed **g** for your father's house; **Gn 31:30** 3700
Jacob was **g** afraid and distressed; **Gn 32:7** 3966
were fruitful and increased **g**, **Ex 1:7** 8317
g esteemed in the land of Egypt, **Ex 11:3** 3966
anger of the LORD was kindled **g**, **Nu 11:10** 3966
of Israel, the people mourned **g**. **Nu 14:39** 3966
I said I would honor you **g**, **Nu 24:11** 3513
you and that you may multiply **g**, **Dt 6:3** 3966
nor shall he **g** increase silver and **Dt 17:17** 3966
we feared **g** for our lives because **Jos 9:24** 3966
that he feared **g**, because Gibeon **Jos 10:2** 3966
so that Israel was **g** distressed. **Jg 10:9** 3966
She, **g** distressed, prayed to **1Sa 1:10** 4751
all the men of Israel rejoiced **g**. **1Sa 11:15** 3966
g feared the LORD and Samuel. **1Sa 12:18** 3966
him; and Saul loved him **g** **1Sa 16:21** 3966
they were dismayed and **g** afraid. **1Sa 17:11** 3966
fled from him and were **g** afraid. **1Sa 17:24** 3966
Saul saw that he was prospering **g**, **1Sa 18:15** 3966
Saul's son, **g** delighted in David. **1Sa 19:1** 3966
and **g** feared Achish king of Gath. **1Sa 21:12** 3966
afraid and his heart trembled **g**. **1Sa 28:5** 3966
"I am **g** distressed; **1Sa 28:15** 3966
Moreover David was **g** distressed **1Sa 30:6** 3966
would not, for he was **g** afraid. **1Sa 31:4** 3966
for the men were **g** humiliated. **2Sa 10:5** 3966
anger burned **g** against the man, **2Sa 12:5** 3966
have sinned **g** in what I have done. **2Sa 24:10** 3966
he rejoiced **g** and said, **1Ki 5:7** 3966
(Now Obadiah feared the LORD **g**; **1Ki 18:3** 3966
But they feared **g** and said, **2Ki 10:4** 3966
their fathers' houses increased **g**. **1Ch 4:38** 7230
would not, for he was **g** afraid. **1Ch 10:4** 3966
is the LORD, and **g** to be praised; **1Ch 16:25** 3966
for the men were **g** humiliated. **1Ch 19:5** 3966
"I have sinned **g**, in that I have **1Ch 21:8** 3966
and King David also rejoiced **g**. **1Ch 29:9** 1419
was with him and exalted him **g**. **2Ch 1:1** 4605
city and strengthened them **g**. **2Ch 11:12**
7235a, 3966
humbled himself **g** before the God **2Ch 33:12** 3966
transgressed **g** in this matter. **Ezr 10:13** 7235a
Who rejoice **g**, *And* exult when **Jb 3:22**
413, 1524a
Yet your end will increase **g**. **Jb 8:7** 3966
And my soul is **g** dismayed; **Ps 6:3** 3966
will be ashamed and **g** dismayed; **Ps 6:10** 3966
salvation how **g** he will rejoice! **Ps 21:1** 3966
I am bent over and **g** bowed down; **Ps 38:6** 3966
is the LORD, and **g** to be praised, **Ps 48:1** 3966
I shall not be **g** shaken. **Ps 62:2** 7227a
You **g** enrich it; **Ps 65:9** 7227a
with wrath And **g** abhorred Israel; **Ps 78:59** 3966
A God **g** feared in the council of **Ps 89:7** 7227a
is the LORD and **g** to be praised; **Ps 96:4** 3966
blesses them and they multiply **g**, **Ps 107:38** 3966
g delights in His commandments. **Ps 112:1** 3966
"I am **g** afflicted." **Ps 116:10** 3966
For we are **g** filled with contempt. **Ps 123:3** 7227a
Our soul is **g** filled With the **Ps 123:4** 7227a
of the righteous will **g** rejoice, **Pr 23:24** 1524a
high and lifted up and **g** exalted. **Is 52:13** 3966
I will rejoice **g** in the LORD, My **Is 61:10** 7797
Your mother will be **g** ashamed, **Jer 50:12** 3966
Jerusalem sinned **g**, **La 1:8** 2399
My spirit is **g** troubled; **La 1:20** 2560a
of tears, My spirit is **g** troubled; **La 2:11** 2560a
and My sabbaths they **g** profaned. **Ezk 20:13** 3966
King Belshazzar was **g** alarmed, **Da 5:9** 7690
my thoughts were **g** alarming me and **Da 7:28** 7690
You are **g** despised. **Ob 1:2** 3966
Then the men feared the LORD **g**, **Jon 1:16** 1419
But it **g** displeased Jonah and he **Jon 4:1** 1419
Rejoice **g**, O daughter of Zion! **Zch 9:9** 3966
I suffered **g** in a dream because of **Mt 27:19** *4183*
you are **g** mistaken." **Mk 12:27** *4183*
and he was **g** perplexed, because it **Lk 9:7** *1280*
He rejoiced **g** in the Holy Spirit, **Lk 10:21** *21*
rejoices **g** because of the **Jn 3:29** *5479*
being **g** disturbed because they **Ac 4:2** *1278*
they were **g** perplexed about them **Ac 5:24** *1280*
to increase **g** in Jerusalem, **Ac 6:7** *4970*
Now while Peter was **g** perplexed in **Ac 10:17** *1280*
But Paul was **g** annoyed, and turned **Ac 16:18** *1278*
food before them, and rejoiced **g**, **Ac 16:34** *21*
he **g** helped those who had believed **Ac 18:27** *4183*
boy alive, and were **g** comforted. **Ac 20:12**
3756, 3357
I encouraged him **g** to come to you **1Co 16:12** *4183*
But I rejoiced in the Lord **g**, **Php 4:10** *3171*
because your faith is **g** enlarged, **2Th 1:3** *5232*
In this you **g** rejoice, even though **1Pe 1:6** *21*
you **g** rejoice with joy inexpressible **1Pe 1:8** *21*
Then I *began* to weep **g** **Rv 5:4** *4183*
When I saw her, I wondered **g**. **Rv 17:6**
2295, 3173

GREATNESS

"And in the **g** of Your excellence **Ex 15:7** 7230
By the **g** of Your arm they are **Ex 15:16** 1419
to the **g** of Your lovingkindness, **Nu 14:19** 1433
servant Your **g** and Your strong hand; **Dt 3:24** 1433
has shown us His glory and His **g**, **Dt 5:24** 1433
You have redeemed through Your **g**, **Dt 9:26** 1433
His **g**, His mighty hand and His **Dt 11:2** 1433
Ascribe **g** to our God! **Dt 32:3** 1433
You have done all this **g** to let **2Sa 7:21** 1420
You have wrought all this **g**, **1Ch 17:19** 1420
the **g** and the power and the glory **1Ch 29:11** 1420
the half of the **g** of your wisdom **2Ch 9:6** 4768
to the **g** of Your lovingkindness. **Ne 13:22** 7230
full account of the **g** of Mordecai to **Es 10:2** 1420
with me by the **g** of *His* power? **Jb 23:6** 7230
g of the ransom turn you aside. **Jb 36:18** 7230
According to the **g** of Your **Ps 51:1** 7230
Because of the **g** of Your power **Ps 66:3** 7230
in the **g** of Your lovingkindness, **Ps 69:13** 7230
to the **g** of Your compassion, **Ps 69:16** 7230
May You increase my **g** And **Ps 71:21** 1420
According to the **g** of Your power **Ps 79:11** 1433
to the **g** of His lovingkindness. **Ps 106:45** 7230
And His **g** is unsearchable. **Ps 145:3** 1420
And I will tell of Your **g**. **Ps 145:6** 1420
Him according to His excellent **g**. **Ps 150:2** 1433
And in the **g** of his folly he will **Pr 5:23** 7230
Because of the **g** of His might and **Is 40:26** 7230
Marching in the **g** of His strength? **Is 63:1** 7230
'Whom are you like in your **g**? **Ezk 31:2** 1433
'So it was beautiful in its **g**, **Ezk 31:7** 1433
are you thus equal in glory and **g**? **Ezk 31:18** 1433
and surpassing **g** was added to me. **Da 4:36** 7238
and the **g** of *all* the kingdoms **Da 7:27** 7238
were all amazed at the **g** of God. **Lk 9:43** *3168*
that the surpassing **g** of the power **2Co 4:7** *5236*
surpassing **g** of the revelations, **2Co 12:7** *5236*
is the surpassing **g** of His power **Eph 1:19** *3174*

GREAVES

He also *had* bronze **g** on his legs **1Sa 17:6** 4697

GREECE

goat *represents* the kingdom of **G**, **Da 8:21** 3120
the prince of **G** is about to come. **Da 10:20** 3120
empire against the realm of **G**. **Da 11:2** 3120
O Zion, against your sons, O **G**; **Zch 9:13** 3120
much exhortation, he came to **G**. **Ac 20:2** *1671*

GREED

will be caught by *their own* **g**. **Pr 11:6** 1942
guard against every form of **g**; **Lk 12:15** *4124*
unrighteousness, wickedness, **g**, **Ro 1:29** *4124*
or **g** must not even be named **Eph 5:3** *4124*
passion, evil desire, and **g**, **Col 3:5** *4124*
you know, nor with a pretext for **g** **1Th 2:5** *4124*
and in *their* **g** they will exploit **2Pe 2:3** *4124*
having a heart trained in **g**, **2Pe 2:14** *4124*

GREEDILY

people rushed **g** upon the spoil, **1Sa 14:32** 6213a

GREEDINESS

of every kind of impurity with **g**. **Eph 4:19** *4124*

GREEDY

who were among them had **g** desires; **Nu 11:4** 8378
buried the people who had been **g**. **Nu 11:34** 183
And the **g** man curses *and* spurns **Ps 10:3** 1214
And the dogs are **g**, **Is 56:11**
5315, 5794
of them, Everyone is **g** for gain, **Jer 6:13** 1214
greatest Everyone is **g** for gain; **Jer 8:10** 1214

GREEK

in Hebrew, Latin *and* in **G**. **Jn 19:20** *1676*
Tabitha (which translated *in* **G** **Ac 9:36**
believer, but his father was a **G**, **Ac 16:1** *1672*
all knew that his father was a **G**. **Ac 16:3** *1672*
of prominent **G** women and men. **Ac 17:12** *1674*
And he said, "Do you know **G**? **Ac 21:37** *1676*
the Jew first and also to the **G**. **Ro 1:16** *1672*
the Jew first and also of the **G**, **Ro 2:9** *1672*
the Jew first and also to the **G**. **Ro 2:10** *1672*
no distinction between Jew and **G**; **Ro 10:12** *1672*
was with me, though he was a **G**, **Ga 2:3** *1672*
There is neither Jew nor **G**, **Ga 3:28** *1672*
no *distinction between* **G** and Jew, **Col 3:11** *1672*
in the **G** he has the name Apollyon. **Rv 9:11** *1673*

GREEKS

to the **G** in order to remove them far **Jl 3:6** 3125
go to the Dispersion among the **G**, **Jn 7:35** *1672*
among the Greeks, and teach the **G**, **Jn 7:35** *1672*
Now there were some **G** among **Jn 12:20** *1672*
and *began* speaking to the **G** also, **Ac 11:20** *1672*
believed, both of Jews and of **G**. **Ac 14:1** *1672*
large number of the God-fearing **G** **Ac 17:4** *1672*
and trying to persuade Jews and **G**. **Ac 18:4** *1672*
word of the Lord, both Jews and **G**. **Ac 19:10** *1672*
known to all, both Jews and **G**, **Ac 19:17** *1672*
testifying to both Jews and **G** of **Ac 20:21** *1672*
he has even brought **G** into the temple **Ac 21:28** *1672*
both to **G** and to barbarians, **Ro 1:14** *1672*
both Jews and **G** are all under sin; **Ro 3:9** *1672*
signs and **G** search for wisdom; **1Co 1:22** *1672*
are the called, both Jews and **G**, **1Co 1:24** *1672*
or to **G** or to the church of God; **1Co 10:32** *1672*
into one body, whether Jews or **G**, **1Co 12:13** *1672*

GREEN

given every **g** plant for food"; **Gn 1:30** 3418
all to you, as *I gave* the **g** plant. **Gn 9:3** 3418
Thus nothing **g** was left on tree or **Ex 10:15** 3418
the hills and under every **g** tree. **Dt 12:2** 7488
the hills and under every **g** tree. **2Ki 16:4** 7488
high hill and under every **g** tree, **2Ki 17:10** 7488
of the field and as the **g** herb, **2Ki 19:26** 3419
the hills and under every **g** tree. **2Ch 28:4** 7488
it is still **g** *and* not cut down, **Jb 8:12** 3
And his palm branch will not be **g**. **Jb 15:32** 7487a
And searches after every **g** thing. **Jb 39:8** 3387
makes me lie down in **g** pastures; **Ps 23:2** 1877
grass And fade like the **g** herb. **Ps 37:2** 3418
I am like a **g** olive tree in the **Ps 52:8** 7488
the **g** and the burning alike. **Ps 58:9** 2416a
shall be full of sap and very **g**, **Ps 92:14** 7488
righteous will flourish like the **g** **Pr 11:28**
died out, There is no **g** thing. **Is 15:6** 3418
of the field and *as* the **g** herb, **Is 37:27** 3419
And under every **g** tree You have lain **Jer 2:20** 7488
high hill and under every **g** tree; **Jer 3:6** 7488
the strangers under every **g** tree, **Jer 3:13** 7488
"A **g** olive tree, beautiful in **Jer 11:16** 7488
By **g** trees on the high hills. **Jer 17:2** 7488
But its leaves will be **g**, **Jer 17:8** 7488
the mountains, under every **g** tree and **Ezk 6:13** 7488
the low tree, dry up the **g** tree and **Ezk 17:24** 3892
will consume every **g** tree in you, **Ezk 20:47** 3892
of the wilderness have turned **g**, **Jl 2:22** 1876
down by groups on the **g** grass. **Mk 6:39** *5515*

do these things when the tree is **g**, **Lk 23:31** *5200*
and all the **g** grass was burned up. **Rv 8:7** *5515*
of the earth, nor any **g** thing, **Rv 9:4** *5515*

GREENISH
if the mark is **g** or reddish in the **Lv 13:49** 3422
has **g** or reddish depressions and **Lv 14:37** 3422

GREET
and they will **g** you and give you **1Sa 10:4** 7592, 7965
went out to meet him *and* to **g** him. **1Sa 13:10** 1288
in order to **g** his brothers. **1Sa 17:22** 7592, 7965
visit Nabal and **g** him in my name; **1Sa 25:5** 7592, 7965
the wilderness to **g** our master, **1Sa 25:14** 1288
King David to **g** him and bless him, **2Sa 8:10** 7592, 7965
and we have come down to **g** the **2Ki 10:13** 7965
David to **g** him and to bless him, **1Ch 18:10** 7592, 7965
"If you **g** only your brothers, **Mt 5:47** *782*
and *began* running up to **g** Him. **Mk 9:15** *782*
and **g** no one on the way. **Lk 10:4** *782*
G Prisca and Aquila, my fellow **Ro 16:3** *782*
also **g** the church that is in **Ro 16:5**
G Epaenetus, my beloved, who is **Ro 16:5** *782*
G Mary, who has worked hard for **Ro 16:6** *782*
G Andronicus and Junias, my **Ro 16:7** *782*
G Ampliatus, my beloved in the **Ro 16:8** *782*
G Urbanus, our fellow worker in **Ro 16:9** *782*
G Apelles, the approved in Christ. **Ro 16:10** *782*
G those who are of the *household* **Ro 16:10** *782*
G Herodion, my kinsman. **Ro 16:11** *782*
G those of the *household* of **Ro 16:11** *782*
G Tryphaena and Tryphosa, workers **Ro 16:12** *782*
G Persis the beloved, who has **Ro 16:12** *782*
G Rufus, a choice man in the Lord, **Ro 16:13** *782*
G Asyncritus, Phlegon, Hermes, **Ro 16:14** *782*
G Philologus and Julia, Nereus and **Ro 16:15** *782*
G one another with a holy kiss. **Ro 16:16** *782*
All the churches of Christ **g** you. **Ro 16:16** *782*
this letter, **g** you in the Lord. **Ro 16:22** *782*
The churches of Asia **g** you. **1Co 16:19** *782*
Prisca **g** you heartily in the Lord, **1Co 16:19** *782*
All the brethren **g** you. **1Co 16:20** *782*
G one another with a holy kiss. **1Co 16:20** *782*
G one another with a holy kiss. **2Co 13:12** *782*
All the saints **g** you. **2Co 13:13** *782*
G every saint in Christ Jesus. **Php 4:21** *782*
brethren who are with me **g** you. **Php 4:21** *782*
All the saints **g** you, especially **Php 4:22** *782*
G the brethren who are in Laodicea **Col 4:15** *782*
G all the brethren with a holy **1Th 5:26** *782*
G Prisca and Aquila, and the **2Tm 4:19** *782*
All who are with me **g** you. **Ti 3:15** *782*
G those who love us in *the* faith. **Ti 3:15** *782*
G all of your leaders and all the **Heb 13:24** *782*
Those from Italy **g** you. **Heb 13:24** *782*
G one another with a kiss of love. **1Pe 5:14** *782*
children of your chosen sister **g** you. **2Jn 1:13** *782*
The friends **g** you. **3Jn 1:15** *782*
G the friends by name. **3Jn 1:15** *782*

GREETED
approached the people and **g** them. **1Sa 30:21** 7592, 7965
and he **g** him and said to him, **2Ki 10:15** 1288
behold, Jesus met them and **g** them. **Mt 28:9** *3004, 5463*
of Zacharias and **g** Elizabeth. **Lk 1:40** *782*
he went up and **g** the church, **Ac 18:22** *782*
After he had **g** them, **Ac 21:19** *782*

GREETING
enter the house, give it your **g**. **Mt 10:12** *782*
When Elizabeth heard Mary's **g**, **Lk 1:41** *783*
sound of your **g** reached my ears, **Lk 1:44** *783*
and after **g** the brethren, we **Ac 21:7** *782*
The **g** is in my own hand—Paul. **1Co 16:21** *783*
write this **g** with my own hand. **Col 4:18** *783*
write this **g** with my own hand, **2Th 3:17** *783*
house, and do not give him a **g**; **2Jn 1:10** *5463*
one who gives him a **g** participates **2Jn 1:11** *5463*

GREETINGS
respectful **g** in the market places, **Mt 23:7** *783*
respectful **g** in the market places, **Mk 12:38** *783*
And coming in, he said to her, "**G**, **Lk 1:28** *5463*
respectful **g** in the market places. **Lk 11:43** *783*
respectful **g** in the market places, **Lk 20:46** *783*
who are from the Gentiles, **g**. **Ac 15:23** *5463*
most excellent governor Felix, **g**. **Ac 23:26** *5463*
fellow prisoner, sends you his **g**; **Col 4:10** *782*
of Jesus Christ, sends you his **g**, **Col 4:12** *782*
physician, sends you his **g**, **Col 4:14** *782*
are dispersed abroad: **G**. **Jas 1:1** *5463*
together with you, sends you **g**, **1Pe 5:13** *782*

GREETS
Timothy my fellow worker **g** you, **Ro 16:21** *782*
me and to the whole church, **g** you. **Ro 16:23** *782*
Erastus, the city treasurer **g** you, **Ro 16:23** *782*
Eubulus **g** you, also Pudens and **2Tm 4:21** *782*
prisoner in Christ Jesus, **g** you, **Phm 1:23** *782*

GREW
cities, and what **g** on the ground. **Gn 19:25** 6780
The child **g** and was weaned, **Gn 21:8** 1431
God was with the lad, and he **g**; **Gn 21:20** 1431
When the boys **g** up, Esau became a **Gn 25:27** 1431
The child **g**, and she brought **Ex 2:10** 1431
but when the sun **g** hot, **Ex 16:21** 2552
the trumpet **g** louder and louder, **Ex 19:19** 1980
"But Jeshurun **g** fat and kicked **Dt 32:15** 8080
of the house of Joseph **g** strong, **Jg 1:35** 3513
and when his wife's sons **g** up, **Jg 11:2** 1431
g up and the LORD blessed him. **Jg 13:24** 1431
the boy Samuel **g** before the LORD. **1Sa 2:21** 1431
Thus Samuel **g** and the LORD was **1Sa 3:19** 1431
and David **g** steadily stronger, but **2Sa 3:1** 1980
of Saul **g** weaker continually. **2Sa 3:1** 1980
And it **g** up together with him and **2Sa 12:3** 1431
who **g** up with him and served him. **1Ki 12:8** 1431
who **g** up with him spoke to him, **1Ki 12:10** 1431
sky **g** black with clouds and wind, **1Ki 18:45** 6937
who **g** up with him and served him. **2Ch 10:8** 1431
who **g** up with him spoke to him, **2Ch 10:10** 1431
Jehoshaphat **g** greater and greater, **2Ch 17:12** 1980
they ate, were filled and **g** fat, **Ne 9:25** 8080
as it **g** dark at the gates of Jerusalem **Ne 13:19** 6751
he **g** up with me as with a father, **Jb 31:18** 1431
And my sorrow **g** worse. **Ps 39:2** 5916
For He **g** up before Him like a **Is 53:2** 5927
Then you **g** up, became tall and **Ezk 16:7** 7235a
on the beds where it **g**? **Ezk 17:10** 6780
sinews were on them, and flesh **g** and **Ezk 37:8** 5927
tree **g** large and became strong And **Da 4:11** 7236
which became large and **g** strong, **Da 4:20** 8631
Then the king's face **g** pale and **Da 5:6** 8133
alarmed, his face **g** *even* paler, **Da 5:9** 8133
alarming me and my face **g** pale, **Da 7:28** 8133
small horn which **g** exceedingly great **Da 8:9** 1431
It **g** up to the host of heaven **Da 8:10** 1431
a plant and it **g** up over Jonah to be **Jon 4:6** 5927
and as they **g** up and increased, **Mk 4:8** *305*
as soon as it **g** up, it withered **Lk 8:6** *5453*
and the thorns **g** up with it and **Lk 8:7** *4855*
fell into the good soil, and **g** up, **Lk 8:8** *5453*
and it **g** and became a tree, **Lk 13:19** *837*
unbelief but **g** strong in faith, **Ro 4:20** *1743*

GRIDDLE
a grain offering *made* on the **g**, **Lv 2:5** 4227
shall be prepared with oil on a **g**. **Lv 6:21** 4227
prepared in a pan or on a **g** shall **Lv 7:9** 4227

GRIEF
brought **g** to Isaac and Rebekah. **Gn 26:35** 4786, 7307
not cause **g** or a troubled heart **1Sa 25:31** 6330
"Oh that my **g** were actually weighed **Jb 6:2** 3708b
has also grown dim because of **g**, **Jb 17:7** 3708b
My eye has wasted away with **g**; **Ps 6:7** 3708a
My eye is wasted away from **g**, **Ps 31:9** 3708a
"It is my **g**, That the right hand **Ps 77:10** 2470a
My soul weeps because of **g**; **Ps 119:28** 8424
foolish son is a **g** to his mother. **Pr 10:1** 8424
pain, And the end of joy may be **g**. **Pr 14:13** 8424
foolish son is a **g** to his father And **Pr 17:25** 3708a
in much wisdom there is much **g**, **Ec 1:18** 3708a
So, remove **g** and anger from your **Ec 11:10** 3708a
of sorrows and acquainted with **g**; **Is 53:3** 2483
To crush Him, putting *Him* to **g**; **Is 53:10** 2470a
For the LORD has caused her **g** **La 1:5** 3013
For if He causes **g**, **La 3:32** 3013
when I did not cause him **g**, **Ezk 13:22** 3510
with breaking heart and bitter **g**, **Ezk 21:6** 4814
but your **g** will be turned into joy. **Jn 16:20** *3077*
"Therefore you too have **g** now; but **Jn 16:22** *3077*
and unceasing **g** in my heart. **Ro 9:2** *3601*
do this with joy and not with **g**, **Heb 13:17** *4727*

GRIEFS
Surely our **g** He Himself bore, And **Is 53:4** 2483
and pierced themselves with many **g**. **1Tm 6:10** *3601*

GRIEVE
fail *from weeping* and your soul **g**, **1Sa 2:33** 109
"How long will you **g** over Saul, **1Sa 16:1** 56
willingly Or **g** the sons of men. **La 3:33** 3013
Who will **g** for her?' **Na 3:7** 5110
"I will gather those who **g** about **Zph 3:18** 3013
you will **g**, but your grief will be **Jn 16:20** *3076*
Do not **g** the Holy Spirit of God, **Eph 4:30** *3076*
are asleep, so that you will not **g** **1Th 4:13** *3076*

GRIEVED
earth, and He was **g** in His heart. **Gn 6:6** 6087a
and the men were **g**, **Gn 34:7** 6087a
not be **g** or angry with yourselves, **Gn 45:5** 6087a
not be **g** when you give to him, **Dt 15:10** 7489a
for Samuel **g** over Saul. **1Sa 15:35** 56
Jonathan know this, or he will be **g**.' **1Sa 20:3** 6087a
for he was **g** over David because **1Sa 20:34** 6087a
"The king is **g** for his son." **2Sa 19:2** 6087a
Do not be **g**, for the joy of the **Ne 8:10** 6087a
for the day is holy; do not be **g**." **Ne 8:11** 6087a
Was not my soul **g** for the needy? **Jb 30:25** 5701
And **g** Him in the desert! **Ps 78:40** 6087a
hired laborers will be **g** in soul. **Is 19:10** 99
a wife forsaken and **g** in spirit, **Is 54:6** 6087a
rebelled And **g** His Holy Spirit; **Is 63:10** 6087a
not **g** over the ruin of Joseph. **Am 6:6** 2470a
Although he was **g**, **Mt 14:9** *3076*
And they were deeply **g**. **Mt 17:23** *3076*
they were deeply **g** and came and **Mt 18:31** *3076*
Being deeply **g**, **Mt 26:22** *3076*
and began to be **g** and distressed. **Mt 26:37** *3076*
"My soul is deeply **g**, **Mt 26:38** *4036*
g at their hardness of heart, **Mk 3:5** *4818*
be **g** and to say to Him one by one, **Mk 14:19** *3076*
is deeply **g** to the point of death; **Mk 14:34** *4036*
Peter was **g** because He said to him **Jn 21:17** *3076*

GRIEVING
"I have surely heard Ephraim **g**, **Jer 31:18** 5110
he went away **g**; for he was one who **Mt 19:22** *3076*
and he went away **g**, for he was one **Mk 10:22** *3076*
g especially over the word which **Ac 20:38** *3600*

GRIEVOUS
a **g** mourning for the Egyptians." **Gn 50:11** 3515
G punishment is for him who forsakes **Pr 15:10** 7451a
It is a **g** task *which* God has given **Ec 1:13** 7451a
done under the sun was **g** to me; **Ec 2:17** 7451a
days his task is painful and **g**; **Ec 2:23** 3708a
too is vanity and it is a **g** task. **Ec 4:8** 7451a
There is a **g** evil *which* I have **Ec 5:13** 2470a
This also is a **g** evil **Ec 5:16** 2470a
and has incurred **g** guilt, **Ezk 25:12** 816

GRIND
g *it* between two millstones or beat *it* **Nu 11:8** 2912
May my wife **g** for another, And let **Jb 31:10** 2912
"Take the millstones and **g** meal. **Is 47:2** 2912

GRINDER
and he was a **g** in the prison. **Jg 16:21** 2912

GRINDING
g it very small until it was as **Dt 9:21** 2912
the **g** ones stand idle because they **Ec 12:3** 2912
as the sound of the **g** mill is low, **Ec 12:4** 2913
And **g** the face of the poor?" **Is 3:15** 2912
Young men worked at the **g** mill, **La 5:13** 2911a
"Two women *will be* **g** at the mill; **Mt 24:41** *229*
be two women **g** at the same place; **Lk 17:35** *229*

GRINDS
foams *at the mouth,* and **g** his teeth and **Mk 9:18** *5149*

GRIP
It shall not fasten its **g** on me. **Ps 101:3** 1692

GRIPPED
g the inhabitants of Philistia. **Ex 15:14** 270
away to flee, And panic has **g** her; **Jer 49:24** 2388
Distress has **g** him, Agony like a **Jer 50:43** 2388
That agony has **g** you like a woman **Mi 4:9** 2388
and astonishment had **g** them; **Mk 16:8** *2192*
he saw *the angel,* and fear **g** him. **Lk 1:12** *1968*
Fear **g** them all, and they **Lk 7:16** *2983*
for they were **g** with great fear; **Lk 8:37** *4912*

GRIPS
leaders of Moab, trembling **g** them; **Ex 15:15** 270

GRITS
in the fire, **g** of new growth, **Lv 2:14** 1643
part of its **g** and its oil with all **Lv 2:16** 1643

GROAN
"From the city men **g**, **Jb 24:12** 5008
I **g** because of the agitation of my **Ps 38:8** 7580
And you **g** at your final end, When **Pr 5:11** 5098
when a wicked man rules, people **g**. **Pr 29:2** 584
like a woman in labor I will **g**, **Is 42:14** 6463
will **g** when pangs come upon you, **Jer 22:23** 2603a
will **g** throughout her land. **Jer 51:52** 602
All her people **g** seeking bread; **La 1:11** 584
"They have heard that I **g**; **La 1:21** 584
foreheads of the men who sigh and **g** **Ezk 9:4** 602
"As for you, son of man, **g** with **Ezk 21:6** 584
bitter grief, **g** in their sight. **Ezk 21:6** 584
they say to you, 'Why do you **g**?' **Ezk 21:7** 584
"**G** silently; make no mourning **Ezk 24:17** 602
and you will **g** to one another. **Ezk 24:23** 5098
of your fall when the wounded **g**, **Ezk 26:15** 602
g before him with the groanings **Ezk 30:24** 5008
How the beasts **g**! **Jl 1:18** 584
we ourselves **g** within ourselves, **Ro 8:23** *4727*
For indeed in this *house* we **g**, **2Co 5:2** *4727*
while we are in this tent, we **g**, **2Co 5:4** *4727*

GROANING
So God heard their **g**; **Ex 2:24** 5009
heard the **g** of the sons of Israel, **Ex 6:5** 5009
LORD was moved to pity by their **g** **Jg 2:18** 5009
g comes at the sight of my food, **Jb 3:24** 585
His hand is heavy despite my **g**. **Jb 23:2** 585
my words, O LORD, Consider my **g**. **Ps 5:1** 1901
because of the **g** of the needy, **Ps 12:5** 603
deliverance are the words of my **g**. **Ps 22:1** 7581
away Through my **g** all day long. **Ps 32:3** 7581
Let the **g** of the prisoner come **Ps 79:11** 603
Because of the loudness of my **g** **Ps 102:5** 585
To hear the **g** of the prisoner, **Ps 102:20** 603
end of all the **g** she has caused. **Is 21:2** 603
I am weary with my **g** and have **Jer 45:3** 603
Her priests are **g**, Her virgins are **La 1:4** 584
tears, with weeping and with **g**, **Mal 2:13** 603

GROANINGS
him with the **g** of a wounded man. **Ezk 30:24** 5009
for *us* with **g** too deep for words; **Ro 8:26** *4726*

GROANS
Even she herself **g** and turns away. **La 1:8** 584
For my **g** are many and my heart is **La 1:22** 585
IN EGYPT AND HAVE HEARD THEIR **G**, **Ac 7:34** *4726*
whole creation **g** and suffers the pains **Ro 8:22** *4959*

GROOM
the **g** and the voice of the bride. **Jer 16:9** 2860a

GROPE
you will **g** at noon, as the blind **Dt 28:29** 4959
And **g** at noon as in the night. **Jb 5:14** 4959
"They **g** in darkness with no **Jb 12:25** 4959
We **g** along the wall like blind **Is 59:10** 1659
We **g** like those who have no eyes; **Is 59:10** 1659
they might **g** for Him and find Him, **Ac 17:27** *5584*

GROPES
as the blind man **g** in darkness, **Dt 28:29** 4959

GROSS
these indulged in **g** immorality and **Jude 1:7** *1608*

GROSSNESS
Because of the **g** of your iniquity, **Hos 9:7** 7230
GROUND
creeps on the **g** after its kind; **Gn 1:25** 127
was no man to cultivate the **g**. **Gn 2:5** 127
water the whole surface of the **g**. **Gn 2:6** 127
God formed man of dust from the **g**, **Gn 2:7** 127
Out of the **g** the LORD God **Gn 2:9** 127
Out of the **g** the LORD God **Gn 2:19** 127
Cursed is the **g** because of you; **Gn 3:17** 127
eat bread, Till you return to the **g**, **Gn 3:19** 127
the **g** from which he was taken. **Gn 3:23** 127
but Cain was a tiller of the **g**. **Gn 4:2** 127
to the LORD of the fruit of the **g**. **Gn 4:3** 127
blood is crying to Me from the **g**. **Gn 4:10** 127
"Now you are cursed from the **g**, **Gn 4:11** 127
"When you cultivate the **g**, **Gn 4:12** 127
this day from the face of the **g**; **Gn 4:14** 127
the **g** which the LORD has cursed." **Gn 5:29** 127
of every creeping thing of the **g** **Gn 6:20** 127
everything that creeps on the **g**, **Gn 7:8** 127
the surface of the **g** was dried up. **Gn 8:13** 127
curse the **g** on account of man, **Gn 8:21** 127
everything that creeps on the **g**, **Gn 9:2** 127
bowed down *with his* face to the **g**. **Gn 19:1** 776
cities, and what grew on the **g**. **Gn 19:25** 127
himself to the **g** before the LORD. **Gn 24:52** 776
bowed down to the **g** seven times, **Gn 33:3** 776
down before you to the **g**?" **Gn 37:10** 776
wife, he wasted his seed on the **g** in **Gn 38:9** 776
to him with *their* faces to the **g**. **Gn 42:6** 776
and bowed to the **g** before him. **Gn 43:26** 776
man lowered his sack to the **g**, **Gn 44:11** 776
and they fell to the **g** before him. **Gn 44:14** 776
and bowed with his face to the **g**. **Gn 48:12** 776
you are standing is holy **g**." **Ex 3:5** 127
"Throw it on the **g**." **Ex 4:3** 776
So he threw it on the **g**, **Ex 4:3** 776
the Nile and pour it on the dry **g**; **Ex 4:9** 3004
will become blood on the dry **g**." **Ex 4:9** 3006
also the **g** on which they *dwell.* **Ex 8:21** 127
thing, fine as the frost on the **g**. **Ex 16:14** 776
it with fire, and **g** it to powder, **Ex 32:20** 2912
of finely **g** sweet incense, **Lv 16:12** 1851
by anything that creeps on the **g**, **Lv 20:25** 127
deep on the surface of the **g**. **Nu 11:31** 776
g opens its mouth and swallows them **Nu 16:30** 127
g that was under them split open; **Nu 16:31** 127
and he bowed all the way to the **g**. **Nu 22:31** 639
of anything that creeps on the **g**, **Dt 4:18** 127
your womb and the fruit of your **g**, **Dt 7:13** 127
g where there was no water; **Dt 8:15** 6774
the **g** will not yield its fruit; **Dt 11:17** 127
pour it out on the **g** like water. **Dt 12:16** 776
pour it out on the **g** like water. **Dt 12:24** 776
pour it out on the **g** like water. **Dt 15:23** 776
the way, in any tree or on the **g**, **Dt 22:6** 776
the first of all the produce of the **g** **Dt 26:2** 127
the produce of the **g** which You, **Dt 26:10** 127
the **g** which You have given us, **Dt 26:15** 127
and the produce of your **g** and the **Dt 28:4** 127
and in the produce of your **g**, **Dt 28:11** 127
body and the produce of your **g**, **Dt 28:18** 127
of your **g** and all your labors, **Dt 28:33** 127
trees and the produce of your **g**. **Dt 28:42** 127
the produce of your **g** until you **Dt 28:51** 127
to set the sole of her foot on the **g** **Dt 28:56** 776
and in the produce of your **g**, **Dt 30:9** 127
on dry **g** in the middle of the Jordan **Jos 3:17** 2724
while all Israel crossed on dry **g**, **Jos 3:17** 2724
feet were lifted up to the dry **g**, **Jos 4:18** 2724
crossed this Jordan on dry **g**.' **Jos 4:22** 3004
in the piece of **g** which Jacob had **Jos 24:32** 7704
and it went through into the **g**; **Jg 4:21** 776
only, and it is dry on all the **g**, **Jg 6:37** 776
let there be dew on all the **g**." **Jg 6:39** 776
fleece, and dew was on all the **g**. **Jg 6:40** 776
they fell on their faces to the **g**. **Jg 13:20** 776
felled to the **g** on that day 22,000 men **Jg 20:21** 776
and felled to the **g** again 18,000 men **Jg 20:25** 776
When the men of Israel gave **g** to **Jg 20:36** 4725
bowing to the **g** and said to him, **Ru 2:10** 776
the **g** before the ark of the LORD. **1Sa 5:3** 776
the **g** before the ark of the LORD. **1Sa 5:4** 776
and there was honey on the **g**. **1Sa 14:25** 6440, 7704
calves, and slew *them* on the **g**; **1Sa 14:32** 776
hair of his head shall fall to the **g**, **1Sa 14:45** 776
that he fell on his face to the **g**. **1Sa 17:49** 776
and fell on his face to the **g**, **1Sa 20:41** 776
David bowed with his face to the **g** **1Sa 24:8** 776
David and bowed herself to the **g**. **1Sa 25:23** 776
with her face to the **g** and said, **1Sa 25:41** 776
spear stuck in the **g** at his head; **1Sa 26:7** 776
spear to the **g** with one stroke, **1Sa 26:8** 776
do not let my blood fall to the **g** **1Sa 26:20** 776
his face to the **g** and did homage. **1Sa 28:14** 776
immediately fell full length upon the **g** **1Sa 28:20** 776
from the **g** and sat on the bed. **1Sa 28:23** 776
to the **g** and prostrated himself. **2Sa 1:2** 776
Why should I strike you to the **g**? **2Sa 2:22** 776
making them lie down on the **g**; **2Sa 8:2** 776
went and lay all night on the **g**. **2Sa 12:16** 776
order to raise him up from the **g**, **2Sa 12:17** 776
So David arose from the **g**, **2Sa 12:20** 776
tore his clothes and lay on the **g**; **2Sa 13:31** 776
she fell on her face to the **g** and **2Sa 14:4** 776
hair of your son shall fall to the **g**." **2Sa 14:11** 776
die and are like water spilled on the **g** **2Sa 14:14** 776
Joab fell on his face to the **g**, **2Sa 14:22** 776
his face to the **g** before the king, **2Sa 14:33** 776
on him as the dew falls on the **g**; **2Sa 17:12** 127
you not strike him there to the **g**? **2Sa 18:11** 776
the king with his face to the **g**. **2Sa 18:28** 776
out his inward parts on the **g**, **2Sa 20:10** 776
was a plot of **g** full of lentils, **2Sa 23:11** 7704
his face to the **g** before the king. **2Sa 24:20** 776
the king with his face to the **g**. **1Ki 1:23** 776
bowed with her face to the **g**, **1Ki 1:31** 776
of his hairs will fall to the **g**; **1Ki 1:52** 776
g between Succoth and Zarethan. **1Ki 7:46** 127
two of them crossed over on dry **g**. **2Ki 2:8** 2724
themselves to the **g** before him. **2Ki 2:15** 776
feet and bowed herself to the **g**, **2Ki 4:37** 776
to the king of Israel, "Strike the **g**," **2Ki 13:18** 776
brook Kidron, and **g** *it* to dust, **2Ki 23:6** 1854
its stones, **g** them to dust, **2Ki 23:15** 1854
was a plot of **g** full of barley; **1Ch 11:13** 7704
David with his face to the **g**. **1Ch 21:21** 776
g between Succoth and Zeredah. **2Ch 4:17** 127
pavement with their faces to the **g**, **2Ch 7:3** 776
his head with *his* face to the **g**, **2Ch 20:18** 776
they *were* corpses lying on the **g**, **2Ch 20:24** 776
images he broke in pieces and **g** to **2Ch 34:4** 1854
LORD with *their* faces to the **g**. **Ne 8:6** 776
the midst of the sea on dry **g**; **Ne 9:11** 3004
might bring the first fruits of our **g** **Ne 10:35** 127
the tithe of our **g** to the Levites, **Ne 10:37** 127
he fell to the **g** and worshiped. **Jb 1:20** 776
Then they sat down on the **g** with **Jb 2:13** 776
does trouble sprout from the **g**, **Jb 5:6** 127
its roots grow old in the **g** And **Jb 14:8** 776
grain will not bend down to the **g**. **Jb 15:29** 776
He pours out my gall on the **g**. **Jb 16:13** 776
noose for him is hidden in the **g**, **Jb 18:10** 776
they are gaunt Who gnaw the dry **g** **Jb 30:3**
and rage he races over the **g**, **Jb 39:24** 776
him trample my life down to the **g** **Ps 7:5** 776
eyes to cast *us* down to the **g**. **Ps 17:11** 776
burned Your sanctuary to the **g**; **Ps 74:7** 776
You cleared *the* **g** before it, **Ps 80:9**
Who became as dung for the **g**. **Ps 83:10** 127
And cast his throne to the **g**. **Ps 89:44** 776
You renew the face of the **g**. **Ps 104:30** 127
And ate up the fruit of their **g**. **Ps 105:35** 127
springs of water into a thirsty **g**; **Ps 107:33** 6774
He has crushed my life to the **g**; **Ps 143:3** 776
good Spirit lead me on level **g**. **Ps 143:10** 776
brings down the wicked to the **g**. **Ps 147:6** 776
is in the fallow **g** of the poor, **Pr 13:23** 5215b
into holes of the **g** Before the terror **Is 2:19** 6083
deserted she will sit on the **g**. **Is 3:26** 776
and it will become trampled **g**. **Is 5:5** 4823
her gods are shattered on the **g**." **Is 21:9** 776
down, Lay low *and* cast to the **g**, **Is 25:12** 776
it low, He lays it low to the **g**, **Is 26:5** 776
continually turn and harrow the **g**? **Is 28:24** 127
like that of a spirit from the **g**, **Is 29:4** 776
seed which you will sow in the **g**, **Is 30:23** 127
and bread *from* the yield of the **g**, **Is 30:23** 127
donkeys which work the **g** will eat **Is 30:24** 127
the thirsty **g** springs of water; **Is 35:7** 6774
let the rough **g** become a plain, **Is 40:4** 6121b
land And streams on the dry **g**; **Is 44:3** 3004
Sit on the **g** without a throne, O **Is 47:1** 776
even made your back like the **g** And **Is 51:23** 776
And like a root out of parched **g**; **Is 53:2** 776
"Break up your fallow **g**, **Jer 4:3** 5215b
field and on the fruit of the **g**; **Jer 7:20** 127
be as dung on the face of the **g**. **Jer 8:2** 127
Pick up your bundle from the **g**, **Jer 10:17** 776
They sit on the **g** in mourning, **Jer 14:2** 776
"Because the **g** is cracked, For **Jer 14:4** 127
will be as dung on the surface of the **g** **Jer 16:4** 127
which are upon the face of the **g**, **Jer 25:26** 127
be like dung on the face of the **g**. **Jer 25:33** 127
They did not stand *their* **g**. For **Jer 46:21**
glory And sit on the parched **g**, **Jer 48:18** 6772
He has brought *them* down to the **g**; **La 2:2** 776
Her gates have sunk into the **g**, **La 2:9** 776
the daughter of Zion Sit on the **g**, **La 2:10** 776
Have bowed their heads to the **g**. **La 2:10** 776
On the **g** in the streets Lie young **La 2:21** 776
up their wings to rise from the **g**, **Ezk 10:16** 776
and bring it down to the **g**, **Ezk 13:14** 776
It was cast down to the **g**; **Ezk 19:12** 776
it on the **g** To cover it with dust. **Ezk 24:7** 776
pillars will come down to the **g**. **Ezk 26:11** 776
they will sit on the **g**, **Ezk 26:16** 776
I cast you to the **g**; **Ezk 28:17** 776
grazing **g** will be on the mountain **Ezk 34:14** 5116a
will lie down on good grazing **g** **Ezk 34:14** 5116a
and every wall will fall to the **g**. **Ezk 38:20** 776
Gog a burial **g** there in Israel, **Ezk 39:11** 4725
left on the surface of the **g**, **Ezk 39:14** 776
and *from* the **g** to the windows **Ezk 41:16** 776
From the **g** to above the entrance **Ezk 41:20** 776
were set back from the **g** upward, **Ezk 42:6** 776
"From the base on the **g** to **Ezk 43:14** 776
the stump with its roots in the **g**, **Da 4:15** 772
the stump with its roots in the **g**, **Da 4:23** 772
find a **g** of accusation against Daniel **Da 6:4** 5931
they could find no **g** of accusation **Da 6:4** 5931
will not find any **g** of accusation **Da 6:5** 5931
and it was lifted up from the **g** **Da 7:4** 772
earth without touching the **g**; **Da 8:5** 776
him to the **g** and trampled on him, **Da 8:7** 776
and it will fling truth to the **g** **Da 8:12** 776
deep sleep with my face to the **g**; **Da 8:18** 776
on my face, with my face to the **g**. **Da 10:9** 776
the **g** and became speechless. **Da 10:15** 776
of the South will not stand *their* **g** **Da 11:15**
in the dust of the **g** will awake, **Da 12:2** 127
And the creeping things of the **g**. **Hos 2:18** 127
Break up your fallow **g**, **Hos 10:12** 5215b
grasps the bow will not stand *his* **g**, **Am 2:15**
a bird fall into a trap on the **g** **Am 3:5** 776
off And they will fall to the **g**. **Am 3:14** 776
not a kernel will fall to the **g**. **Am 9:9** 776
the oil, on what the **g** produces, **Hg 1:11** 127
I am a tiller of the **g**, **Zch 13:5** 127
not destroy the fruits of the **g**; **Mal 3:11** 127
and they fell to the **g** and worshiped **Mt 2:11**
not one of them will fall to the **g** **Mt 10:29** *1093*
people to sit down on the **g**; **Mt 15:35** *1093*
they fell face down to the **g** **Mt 17:6**
"So the slave fell *to the* **g** **Mt 18:26**
"So his fellow slave fell *to the* **g** **Mt 18:29**
dug *a hole* in the **g** and hid **Mt 25:18** *1093*
away and hid your talent in the **g**. **Mt 25:25** *1093*
"Other *seed* fell on the rocky **g** **Mk 4:5**
people to sit down on the **g**; **Mk 8:6** *1093*
it slams him *to the* **g** and he **Mk 9:18**
convulsion, and falling to the **g**, **Mk 9:20** *1093*
beyond *them,* and fell to the **g** and **Mk 14:35** *1093*
on the **g** without any foundation; **Lk 6:49** *1093*
the demon slammed him *to the* **g** **Lk 9:42**
Why does it even use up the **g**?' **Lk 13:7** *1093*
will level you to the **g** and your **Lk 19:44** *1474*
of blood, falling down upon the **g**. **Lk 22:44** *1093*
and bowed their faces to the **g**, **Lk 24:5** *1093*
near the parcel of **g** that Jacob **Jn 4:5** *5564*
with His finger wrote on the **g**. **Jn 8:6** *1093*
stooped down and wrote on the **g**. **Jn 8:8** *1093*
had said this, He spat on the **g**, **Jn 9:6** *5476*
they drew back and fell to the **g**. **Jn 18:6** *5476*
in it, not even a foot of **g**, **Ac 7:5** *968*
WHICH YOU ARE STANDING IS HOLY **G**. **Ac 7:33** *1093*
he fell to the **g** and heard a voice **Ac 9:4** *1093*
Saul got up from the **g**, **Ac 9:8** *1093*
lowered by four corners to the **g**, **Ac 10:11** *1093*
no **g** for *putting Him to* death, **Ac 13:28** *156*
I fell to the **g** and heard a voice **Ac 22:7** *1475*
when we had all fallen to the **g**, **Ac 26:14** *1093*
was no **g** for putting me to death. **Ac 28:18** *156*
For **g** that drinks the rain which **Heb 6:7** *1093*
and caves and holes in the **g**. **Heb 11:38** *1093*
GROUNDED
and our hope for you is firmly **g**, **2Co 1:7** *949*
you, being rooted and **g** in love, **Eph 3:17** *2311*
GROUNDS
And the shepherds' pasture **g** mourn, **Am 1:2** 4999
might have **g** for accusing Him. **Jn 8:6**
GROUP
"To the larger **g** you shall **Nu 26:54**
and to the smaller **g** you shall **Nu 26:54**
that you will meet a **g** of prophets **1Sa 10:5** 2256a
behold, a **g** of prophets met him; **1Sa 10:10** 2256a
beginning with the last **g** to **Mt 20:8**
he sent another **g** of slaves larger **Mt 21:36**
and a **g** of about four hundred men **Ac 5:36** *706*
But perceiving that one **g** were **Ac 23:6** *3313*
GROUPS
the larger and the smaller **g**." **Nu 26:56**
down by **g** on the green grass. **Mk 6:39** *4849*
They sat down in **g** of hundreds and of **Mk 6:40** *4237*
to eat in **g** of about fifty each." **Lk 9:14** *2828*
who made both **g** *into* one **Eph 2:14**
GROVE
your vineyard *and* your olive **g**. **Ex 23:11** 2132
GROVES
olive **g** which you did not plant.' **Jos 24:13** 2132
along with the vineyards *and* **g**. **Jg 15:5** 2132
your vineyards and your olive **g** and **1Sa 8:14** 2132
and to receive clothes and olive **g** and **2Ki 5:26** 2132
their vineyards, their olive **g** and **Ne 5:11** 2132
Hewn cisterns, vineyards, olive **g**, **Ne 9:25** 2132
GROW
the LORD God caused to **g** every tree **Gn 2:9** 6779
and thistles it shall **g** for you; **Gn 3:18** 6779
and continued to **g** richer until he **Gn 26:13** 1432
And may they **g** into a multitude in **Gn 48:16** 1711
locks of hair on his head **g** long. **Nu 6:5** 1431
beasts would **g** too numerous for you. **Dt 7:22** 7235a
g again after it was shaved off. **Jg 16:22** 6779
g dim *and* he could not see *well),* **1Sa 3:2**
at Jericho until your beards **g**, **2Sa 10:5** 6779
Will He not indeed make *it* **g**? **2Sa 23:5** 6779
at Jericho until your beards **g**, **1Ch 19:5** 6779
the papyrus **g** up without a marsh? **Jb 8:11** 1342
Can the rushes **g** without water? **Jb 8:11** 7685
its roots **g** old in the ground And **Jb 14:8** 2204
will **g** stronger and stronger. **Jb 17:9** 3254
Let briars **g** instead of wheat, And **Jb 31:40** 3318
they **g** up in the open field; **Jb 39:4** 7235a
My wounds **g** foul *and* fester Because **Ps 38:5** 887
g dim so that they cannot see, **Ps 69:23** 2821
He will **g** like a cedar in Lebanon. **Ps 92:12** 7685
the grass to **g** for the cattle, **Ps 104:14** 6779
makes grass to **g** on the mountains. **Ps 147:8** 6779
who look through windows **g** dim; **Ec 12:3** 2821
Though youths **g** weary and tired, **Is 40:30** 3286
a fir, and the rain makes it **g**. **Is 44:14** 1431
spirit would **g** faint before Me, **Is 57:16** 5848c
They **g**, they have even produced **Jer 12:2** 1980

so that your heart does not **g** faint, **Jer 51:46** 7401
'The waters made it **g**, **Ezk 31:4** 1431
on you, make flesh **g** back on you, **Ezk 37:6** 5927
shall not let their locks **g** long; **Ezk 44:20** 7971
g all *kinds of* trees for food. **Ezk 47:12** 5927
king of the South will **g** strong, **Da 11:5** 2388
thistle will **g** on their altars; **Hos 10:8** 5927
The sun and the moon **g** dark And **Jl 2:10** 6937
The sun and moon **g** dark And **Jl 3:15** 6937
and *which* you did not cause to **g**, **Jon 4:10** 1431
And nations **g** weary for nothing? **Hab 2:13** 3286
how the lilies of the field **g**; **Mt 6:28** *837*
to **g** together until the harvest; **Mt 13:30** *4885*
most people's love will **g** cold. **Mt 24:12** *5594*
And the child continued to **g** and **Lk 1:80** *837*
continued to **g** and become strong, **Lk 2:40** *837*
"Consider the lilies, how they **g**: **Lk 12:27** *837*
but when you **g** old, you will **Jn 21:18** *1095*
word of the Lord continued to **g** **Ac 12:24** *837*
will reap if we do not **g** weary. **Ga 6:9** *1590*
to **g** up in all *aspects* into Him who **Eph 4:15** *837*
do not **g** weary of doing good. **2Th 3:13** *1457b*
will not **g** weary and lose heart. **Heb 12:3** *2577*
you may **g** in respect to salvation, **1Pe 2:2** *837*
but **g** in the grace and knowledge **2Pe 3:18** *837*

GROWER
herdsman and a **g** of sycamore figs. **Am 7:14** 1103

GROWING
the boy Samuel was **g** in stature **1Sa 2:26** 1980, 1432
to irrigate a forest of **g** trees. **Ec 2:6** 6779
word of the Lord was **g** mightily **Ac 19:20** *837*
is **g** into a holy temple in the Lord, **Eph 2:21** *837*
and **g** old is ready to disappear. **Heb 8:13** *1095*

GROWL
And **g** if they are not satisfied. **Ps 59:15** 3885b
And it will **g** over it in that day **Is 5:30** 5098
All of us **g** like bears, And moan **Is 59:11** 1993
They will **g** like lions' cubs. **Jer 51:38** 5286
Does a young lion **g** from his den **Am 3:4** 5414, 6963

GROWLING
of a king is like the **g** of a lion; **Pr 20:2** 5099

GROWLS
It **g** as it seizes the prey And **Is 5:29** 5098
or the young lion **g** over his prey, **Is 31:4** 1897

GROWN
for she saw that Shelah had **g** up, **Gn 38:14** 1431
those days, when Moses had **g** up, **Ex 2:11** 1431
and no yellowish hair has **g** in it, **Lv 13:32** 1961
and black hair has **g** in it, **Lv 13:37** 6779
You are **g** fat, thick, and sleek **Dt 32:15** 8080
therefore wait until they were **g**? **Ru 1:13** 1431
"Behold, you have **g** old, **1Sa 8:5** 2204
When the child was **g**, **2Ki 4:18** 1431
is scorched before it is **g** up. **2Ki 19:26** 7054
guilt has **g** even to the heavens. **Ezr 9:6** 1431
has also **g** dim because of grief, **Jb 17:7** 3543a
And my flesh has **g** lean, **Ps 109:24** 3584
is scorched before it is **g** up. **Is 37:27** 7054
has **g** into a rod of wickedness. **Ezk 7:11** 6965
were formed and your hair had **g**. **Ezk 16:7** 6779
have become great and **g** strong, **Da 4:22** 8631
until his hair had **g** like eagles' **Da 4:33** 7236
And all their faces are **g** pale! **Na 2:10** 6908
but when it is full **g**, **Mt 13:32** *837*
at all, but rather had **g** worse **Mk 5:26** *2064*
By faith Moses, when he had **g** up, **Heb 11:24** *3173, 1096*
name's sake, and have not **g** weary. **Rv 2:3** *2872*

GROWN-UP
in their youth be as **g** plants, **Ps 144:12** 1431

GROWS
house until my son Shelah **g** up"; **Gn 38:11** 1431
and no grass **g** in it, **Dt 29:23** 5927
to the hyssop that **g** on the wall; **1Ki 4:33** 3318
eat this year what **g** of itself, **2Ki 19:29** 5599b
I sigh, then my spirit **g** faint. **Ps 77:3** 5848c
Which withers before it **g** up; **Ps 129:6** 8025
'Who is this that **g** like the dawn, **SS 6:10** 8259
eat this year what **g** of itself, **Is 37:30** 5599b
and the seed sprouts and **g** **Mk 4:27** *3373*
g up and becomes larger than all **Mk 4:32** *305*
the hope that as your faith **g**, **2Co 10:15** *837*
g with a growth which is from God. **Col 2:19** *837*
toward one another **g** *ever* greater; **2Th 1:3** *4121*

GROWTH
in the fire, grits of new **g**, **Lv 2:14** 3759
bread nor roasted grain nor new **g**. **Lv 23:14** 3759
You bless its **g**. **Ps 65:10** 6780
disappears, the new **g** is seen, **Pr 27:25** 1877
but God was causing the **g**. **1Co 3:6** *837*
but God who causes the **g**. **1Co 3:7** *837*
causes the **g** of the body for the **Eph 4:16** *838*
grows with a **g** which is from God. **Col 2:19** *838*

GRUB
And the **g** will eat them like wool. **Is 51:8** 5580

GRUDGE
So Esau bore a **g** against Jacob **Gn 27:41** 7852
"What if Joseph bears a **g** **Gn 50:15** 7852
nor bear any **g** against the sons of **Lv 19:18** 5201
in anger they bear a **g** against me. **Ps 55:3** 7852
Herodias had a **g** against him **Mk 6:19** *1758*

GRUDGINGLY
not **g** or under compulsion, **2Co 9:7** *1537, 3077*

GRUMBLE
are we, that you **g** against us?" **Ex 16:7** 3885b
which you **g** against Him. **Ex 16:8** 3885b
made all the congregation **g** against **Nu 14:36** 3885b
is he that you **g** against him?" **Nu 16:11** 3885b
and the scribes *began* to **g**, **Lk 15:2** *1234*
they saw it, they all *began* to **g**, **Lk 19:7** *1234*
"Do not **g** among yourselves. **Jn 6:43** *1111*
Nor **g**, as some of them did, and **1Co 10:10** *1111*

GRUMBLED
So the people **g** at Moses, saying, **Ex 15:24** 3885b
Israel **g** against Moses and Aaron **Ex 16:2** 3885b
and they **g** against Moses and said, **Ex 17:3** 3885b
Israel **g** against Moses and Aaron; **Nu 14:2** 3885b
and upward, who have **g** against Me. **Nu 14:29** 3885b
Israel **g** against Moses and Aaron, **Nu 16:41** 3885b
and you **g** in your tents and said, **Dt 1:27** 7279
g against the leaders. **Jos 9:18** 3885b
But **g** in their tents; **Ps 106:25** 7279
it, they **g** at the landowner, **Mt 20:11** *1111*
that His disciples **g** at this, **Jn 6:61** *1111*

GRUMBLERS
These are **g**, finding fault, **Jude 1:16** *1113*

GRUMBLING
congregation who are **g** against Me? **Nu 14:27** 3885b
Israel, who are **g** against you." **Nu 17:5** 3885b
scribes *began* **g** at His disciples, **Lk 5:30** *1111*
Jews were **g** about Him, **Jn 6:41** *1111*
was much **g** among the crowds **Jn 7:12** *1112*
all things without **g** or disputing; **Php 2:14** *1112*

GRUMBLINGS
He hears your **g** against the LORD; **Ex 16:7** 8519b
g which you grumble against Him. **Ex 16:8** 8519b
Your **g** are not against us but **Ex 16:8** 8519b
LORD, for He has heard your **g**.' " **Ex 16:9** 8519b
heard the **g** of the sons of Israel; **Ex 16:12** 8519b
the **g** of the sons of Israel, **Nu 17:5** 8519b
put an end to their **g** against Me, **Nu 17:10** 8519b

GUARANTEE
become the **g** of a better covenant. **Heb 7:22** *1450*

GUARANTEED
so that the promise will be **g** to all **Ro 4:16** *949*

GUARANTOR
Who is there that will be my **g**? **Jb 17:3** 8628, 3027
He who is **g** for a stranger will **Pr 11:15** 6148
But he who hates being a **g** is secure. **Pr 11:15** 8628
in sense pledges And becomes **g** in **Pr 17:18** 6161

GUARANTORS
Among those who become **g** for debts. **Pr 22:26** 6148

GUARD
to **g** the way to the tree of life. **Gn 3:24** 8104
authority, and let them **g** *it.* **Gn 41:35** 8104
I have said to you, be on your **g**; **Ex 23:13** 8104
send an angel before you to **g** you **Ex 23:20** 8104
"Be on your **g** before him and obey **Ex 23:21** 8104
the rear **g** for all the camps, **Nu 10:25** 622
and the rear **g** came after the ark, **Jos 6:9** 622
and the rear **g** came after the ark **Jos 6:13** 622
g on the west side of the city, **Jos 8:13** 6119
and assign men by it to **g** them, **Jos 10:18** 8104
please be on **g** in the morning, **1Sa 19:2** 8104
who is captain over your **g**, **1Sa 22:14** 4928
because you did not **g** your lord, **1Sa 26:16** 8104
and placed them under **g** and **2Sa 20:3** 1004, 4931
But Amasa was not on **g** against the **2Sa 20:10** 8104
David appointed him over his **g**. **2Sa 23:23** 4928
the care of the commanders of the **g** **1Ki 14:27** 7323
a man to me and said, '**G** this man; **1Ki 20:39** 8104
the **g** and to the royal officers, **2Ki 10:25** 7323
and the **g** and the royal officers **2Ki 10:25** 7323
of the Carites and of the **g**, **2Ki 11:4** 7323
noise of the **g** *and of* the people, **2Ki 11:13** 7323
Nebuzaradan the captain of the **g**, **2Ki 25:8** 2876
who *were with* the captain of the **g** **2Ki 25:10** 2876
Nebuzaradan the captain of the **g** **2Ki 25:11** 2876
But the captain of the **g** left some **2Ki 25:12** 2876
The captain of the **g** also took **2Ki 25:15** 2876
Then the captain of the **g** took **2Ki 25:18** 2876
Nebuzaradan the captain of the **g** **2Ki 25:20** 2876
David appointed him over his **g**. **1Ch 11:25** 4928
G corresponded to guard. **1Ch 26:16** 4929
Guard corresponded to **g**. **1Ch 26:16** 4929
g who guarded the door of the king's **2Ch 12:10** 7323
which is by the court of the **g**. **Ne 3:25** 4307
up a **g** against them day and night. **Ne 4:9** 4929
they may be a **g** for us by night and **Ne 4:22** 4929
the men of the **g** who followed me, **Ne 4:23** 4929
and while they are standing **g** **Ne 7:3**
they stopped at the Gate of the **G**. **Ne 12:39** 4307
That You set a **g** over me? **Jb 7:12** 4929
G my soul and deliver me; **Ps 25:20** 8104
"I will **g** my ways That I may not **Ps 39:1** 8104
will **g** my mouth as with a muzzle **Ps 39:1** 8104
you, To **g** you in all your ways. **Ps 91:11** 8104
The LORD will **g** your going out and **Ps 121:8** 8104
Set a **g**, O LORD, over my mouth; **Ps 141:3** 8108
Discretion will **g** you, **Pr 2:11** 8104
forsake her, and she will **g** you; **Pr 4:6** 8104
G her, for she is your life. **Pr 4:13** 5341
G your steps as you go to the **Ec 5:1** 8104
stationed every night at my **g** post. **Is 21:8** 4931
damage it, I **g** it night and day. **Is 27:3** 5341
God of Israel *will be* your rear **g**. **Is 52:12** 622
of the LORD will be your rear **g**. **Is 58:8** 622
be on **g** against his neighbor, **Jer 9:4** 8104
was shut up in the court of the **g**, **Jer 32:2** 4307
son came to me in the court of the **g** **Jer 32:8** 4307
sitting in the court of the **g**. **Jer 32:12** 4307
confined in the court of the **g**, **Jer 33:1** 4307
of the **g** whose name was Irijah, **Jer 37:13** 6488
Post a strong **g**, Station sentries, **Jer 51:12** 4929
who *were* with the captain of the **g** **Jer 52:14** 2876
Nebuzaradan the captain of the **g** **Jer 52:15** 2876
Nebuzaradan the captain of the **g** left **Jer 52:16** 2876
of the **g** also took away the bowls, **Jer 52:19** 2876
Then the captain of the **g** took **Jer 52:24** 2876
Nebuzaradan the captain of the **g** took **Jer 52:26** 2876
Nebuzaradan the captain of the **g** **Jer 52:30** 2876
about you, and be a **g** for them. **Ezk 38:7** 4929
great prince who stands **g** over **Da 12:1**
its rear **g** into the western sea. **Jl 2:20**
lies in your bosom **G** your lips. **Mi 7:5** 8104
I will stand on my **g** post And **Hab 2:1** 4931
with him keeping **g** over Jesus, **Mt 27:54** *5083*
Pilate said to them, "You have a **g**; **Mt 27:65** *2892*
along with the **g** they set a seal **Mt 27:66** *2892*
some of the **g** came into the city **Mt 28:11** *2892*
be on your **g**; for they will deliver **Mk 13:9** *991*
Him and lead Him away under **g**." **Mk 14:44** *806*
CONCERNING YOU TO **G** YOU,' **Lk 4:10** *1314*
and shackles and kept under **g**, **Lk 8:29** *5442*
g against every form of greed; **Lk 12:15** *5442*
"Be on your **g**! If your brother sins, **Lk 17:3** *4337*
"Be on **g**, so that your hearts will **Lk 21:34** *4337*
and the captain of the temple **g** **Ac 4:1**
when the captain of the temple **g** **Ac 5:24**
four squads of soldiers to **g** him, **Ac 12:4** *5442*
had passed the first and second **g**, **Ac 12:10** *5438*
the jailer to **g** them securely; **Ac 16:23** *5083*
"Be on **g** for yourselves and for **Ac 20:28** *4337*
praetorian **g** and to everyone else, **Php 1:13** *4232*
will **g** your hearts and your minds **Php 4:7** *5432*
g what has been entrusted to you, **1Tm 6:20** *5442*
He is able to **g** what I have entrusted **2Tm 1:12** *5442*
G, through the Holy Spirit who **2Tm 1:14** *5442*
Be on **g** against him yourself, for **2Tm 4:15** *5442*
beforehand, be on your **g** so **2Pe 3:17** *5442*
children, **g** yourselves from idols. **1Jn 5:21** *5442*

GUARDED
He **g** him as the pupil of His eye. **Dt 32:10** 5431
"Surely in vain I have **g** all that **1Sa 25:21** 8104
have you not **g** your lord the king? **1Sa 26:15** 8104
who **g** the doorway of the king's house **1Ki 14:27** 8104
him, so that he **g** himself there, **2Ki 6:10** 8104
the priests who **g** the threshold **2Ki 12:9** 8104
who **g** the door of the king's house. **2Ch 12:10** 8104
from those who **g** the door, **Es 2:21** 8104
and I **g** them and not one of them **Jn 17:12** *5442*

GUARDHOUSE
Jeremiah to the court of the **g** **Jer 37:21** 4307
remained in the court of the **g**. **Jer 37:21** 4307
which was in the court of the **g**; **Jer 38:6** 4307
stayed in the court of the **g**. **Jer 38:13** 4307
Jeremiah stayed in the court of the **g** **Jer 38:28** 4307
Jeremiah out of the court of the **g** **Jer 39:14** 4307
confined in the court of the **g**, **Jer 39:15** 4307

GUARDIAN
g of the temple of the great Artemis and **Ac 19:35** *3511*
the Shepherd and **G** of your souls. **1Pe 2:25** *1985*

GUARDIANS
to the **g** of *the children of* Ahab, **2Ki 10:1** 539
elders, and the **g** of *the children,* **2Ki 10:5** 539
"Kings will be your **g**, **Is 49:23** 539
but he is under **g** and managers **Ga 4:2** *2012*

GUARDING
G the paths of justice, And He **Pr 2:8** 5341
G against the terrors of **SS 3:8**
with the soldier who was **g** him. **Ac 28:16** *5442*
ethnarch under Aretas the king was **g** **2Co 11:32** *5432*

GUARDROOM
The **g** *was* one rod long and one **Ezk 40:7** 8372
from the roof of the one **g** to the **Ezk 40:13** 8372

GUARDROOMS
were five cubits between the **g**. **Ezk 40:7** 8372
The **g** of the gate toward the east **Ezk 40:10** 8372
in front of the **g** on each side; **Ezk 40:12** 8372
and the **g** *were* six cubits *square* **Ezk 40:12** 8372
windows *looking* toward the **g**, **Ezk 40:16** 8372
It had three **g** on each side; **Ezk 40:21** 8372
Its **g** also, its side pillars and **Ezk 40:29** 8372
Its **g** also, its side pillars and **Ezk 40:33** 8372
with its **g**, its side pillars and **Ezk 40:36** 8372

GUARDS
to the **g** who were attending him, **1Sa 22:17** 7323
that the **g** would carry them and **1Ki 14:28** 7323
third at the gate behind the **g**), **2Ki 11:6** 7323
The **g** stood each with his weapons **2Ki 11:11** 7323
Carites and the **g** and all the people **2Ki 11:19** 7323
gate of the **g** to the king's house. **2Ki 11:19** 7323
even the house of the tent, as **g**. **1Ch 9:23** 4931
the **g** came and carried them and **2Ch 12:11** 7323
appoint **g** from the inhabitants of **Ne 7:3** 4931
Unless the LORD **g** the city, The **Ps 127:1** 8104
g his mouth preserves his life; **Pr 13:3** 5341
Righteousness **g** the one whose way **Pr 13:6** 5341
He who **g** his mouth and his tongue, **Pr 21:23** 8104
tongue, **G** his soul from troubles. **Pr 21:23** 8104
g himself will be far from them. **Pr 22:5** 8104
The **g** shook for fear of him **Mt 28:4** *5083*
fully armed, **g** his own house, **Lk 11:21** *5442*
and the **g** standing at the doors; **Ac 5:23** *5441*
and **g** in front of the door were **Ac 12:6** *5441*

he examined the **g** and ordered that **Ac 12:19** *5441*

GUARDS'
bring them back into the **g** room. **1Ki 14:28** 7323
brought them back into the **g** room. **2Ch 12:11** 7323

GUARDSMEN
The **g** of the walls took away my **SS 5:7** 8104
g are like the swarming locust. **Na 3:17** 4502

GUDGODAH
From there they set out to **G**, **Dt 10:7** 1412
and from **G** to Jotbathah, a land of **Dt 10:7** 1412

GUEST
"Where is My **g** room in which I **Mk 14:14** *2646*
the **g** of a man who is a sinner." **Lk 19:7** *2647*
"Where is the **g** room in which I **Lk 22:11** *2646*

GUESTS
the **g** who *were* with him heard *it* **1Ki 1:41** 7121
the **g** of Adonijah were terrified; **1Ki 1:49** 7121
her **g** are in the depths of Sheol. **Pr 9:18** 7121
He has consecrated His **g**. **Zph 1:7** 7121
and because of his dinner **g**, **Mt 14:9** *4873*
hall was filled with dinner **g**. **Mt 22:10** *345*
came in to look over the dinner **g**, **Mt 22:11** *345*
pleased Herod and his dinner **g**; **Mk 6:22** *4873*
oaths and because of his dinner **g**, **Mk 6:26** *345*
speaking a parable to the invited **g** **Lk 14:7** *2564*

GUIDANCE
turning around by His **g**, **Jb 37:12** 8458
Where there is no **g** the people fall, **Pr 11:14** 8458
And make war by wise **g**. **Pr 20:18** 8458
For by wise **g** you will wage war, **Pr 24:6** 8458

GUIDE
by day, To **g** them on their way, **Ne 9:19** 5148
g the Bear with her satellites? **Jb 38:32** 5148
sake You will lead me and **g** me. **Ps 31:3** 5095
He will **g** us until death. **Ps 48:14** 5090a
And **g** the nations on the earth. **Ps 67:4** 5148
With Your counsel You will **g** me, **Ps 73:24** 5148
you walk about, they will **g** you; **Pr 6:22** 5148
integrity of the upright will **g** them, **Pr 11:3** 5148
righteous is a **g** to his neighbor, **Pr 12:26** 8446
Those who **g** you lead *you* astray And **Is 3:12** 833
For those who **g** this people are **Is 9:16** 833
they do not know I will **g** them. **Is 42:16** 1869
will **g** them to springs of water. **Is 49:10** 5095
There is none to **g** her among all **Is 51:18** 5095
the LORD will continually **g** you, **Is 58:11** 5148
To **g** our feet into the way of **Lk 1:79** *2720*
"A blind man cannot **g** a blind man, **Lk 6:39** *3594*
He will **g** you into all the truth; **Jn 16:13** *3594*
a **g** to those who arrested Jesus. **Ac 1:16** *3595*
you yourself are a **g** to the blind, **Ro 2:19** *3595*
and will **g** them to springs of the **Rv 7:17** *3594*

GUIDED
the LORD has **g** me in the way to **Gn 24:27** 5148
who had **g** me in the right way to **Gn 24:48** 5148
g *them* to Your holy habitation. **Ex 15:13** 5095
"The LORD alone **g** him, And there **Dt 32:12** 5148
others, and **g** them on every side. **2Ch 32:22** 5095
father, And from infancy I **g** her), **Jb 31:18** 5148
And **g** them in the wilderness like **Ps 78:52** 5090a
g them with his skillful hands. **Ps 78:72** 5148
He **g** them to their desired haven. **Ps 107:30** 5148
And those who are **g** by them are **Is 9:16** 833

GUIDEPOSTS
roadmarks, Place for yourself **g**; **Jer 31:21** 8564

GUIDES
He **g** me in the paths of **Ps 23:3** 5148
they are blind **g** of the blind. **Mt 15:14** *3595*
And if a blind man **g** a blind man, **Mt 15:14** *3594*
"Woe to you, blind **g**, **Mt 23:16** *3595*
"You blind **g**, who strain out a **Mt 23:24** *3595*
could I, unless someone **g** me?" **Ac 8:31** *3594*

GUIDING
while my mind was **g** *me* wisely, **Ec 2:3** 5090a

GUILE
his hatred covers itself with **g**, **Pr 26:26** 4860
your trust in oppression and **g**, **Is 30:12** 3868

GUILT
would have brought **g** upon us." **Gn 26:10** 817
that they do not incur **g** and die. **Ex 28:43** 5771
so as to bring **g** on the people, **Lv 4:3** 819
tell *it,* then he will bear his **g**. **Lv 5:1** 5771
'He shall also bring his **g** offering **Lv 5:6** 817
shall bring to the LORD his **g** offering **Lv 5:7** 817
bring his **g** offering to the LORD: **Lv 5:15** 817
the sanctuary, for a **g** offering. **Lv 5:15** 817
with the ram of the **g** offering, **Lv 5:16** 817
your valuation, for a **g** offering. **Lv 5:18** 817
'It is a **g** offering; **Lv 5:19** 817
day *he presents* his **g** offering. **Lv 6:5** 819
priest his **g** offering to the LORD, **Lv 6:6** 817
your valuation, for a **g** offering, **Lv 6:6** 817
he may have done to incur **g**." **Lv 6:7** 819
sin offering and the **g** offering. **Lv 6:17** 817
this is the law of the **g** offering; **Lv 7:1** 817
they are to slay the **g** offering, **Lv 7:2** 817
it is a **g** offering. **Lv 7:5** 817
'The **g** offering is like the sin **Lv 7:7** 817
and the sin offering and the **g** offering **Lv 7:37** 817
away the **g** of the congregation, **Lv 10:17** 5771
and bring it for a **g** offering, **Lv 14:12** 817
for the **g** offering, like the sin offering, **Lv 14:13** 817
of the blood of the **g** offering, **Lv 14:14** 817
on the blood of the **g** offering; **Lv 14:17** 817
take one male lamb for a **g** offering **Lv 14:21** 817
take the lamb of the **g** offering and **Lv 14:24** 817
the lamb of the **g** offering; **Lv 14:25** 817
some of the blood of the **g** offering **Lv 14:25** 817
of the blood of the **g** offering. **Lv 14:28** 817
body, then he shall bear his **g**." **Lv 17:16** 5771
'He shall bring his **g** offering **Lv 19:21** 817
meeting, a ram for a **g** offering. **Lv 19:21** 817
ram of the **g** offering before the LORD **Lv 19:22** 817
his sister's nakedness; he bears his **g**. **Lv 20:17** 5771
they will bear their **g**. **Lv 20:19** 5771
to bear punishment for **g** by eating **Lv 22:16** 819
the man will be free from **g**, **Nu 5:31** 5771
that woman shall bear her **g**.' " **Nu 5:31** 5771
lamb a year old for a **g** offering; **Nu 6:12** 817
day you shall bear your **g** a year, **Nu 14:34** 5771
his **g** *will be* on him.' " **Nu 15:31** 5771
shall bear the **g** in connection with **Nu 18:1** 5771
your sons with you shall bear the **g** **Nu 18:1** 5771
sin offering and every **g** offering, **Nu 18:9** 817
them, then he shall bear her **g**." **Nu 30:15** 5771
and do not place the **g** of innocent **Dt 21:8** 1818
"So you shall remove the **g** of **Dt 21:9** 1818
of stripes according to his **g**. **Dt 25:2** 7564
surely return to Him a **g** offering. **1Sa 6:3** 817
"What shall be the **g** offering **1Sa 6:4** 817
a **g** offering in a box by its side. **1Sa 6:8** 817
for a **g** offering to the LORD: **1Sa 6:17** 817
LORD's anointed and be without **g**?" **1Sa 26:9** 5352
me with a **g** concerning the woman. **2Sa 3:8** 5771
The money from the **g** offerings and **2Ki 12:16** 817
he be a cause of **g** to Israel?" **1Ch 21:3** 819
and Jerusalem for this their **g**. **2Ch 24:18** 819
to bring upon us **g** against the LORD **2Ch 28:13** 819
LORD adding to our sins and our **g**; **2Ch 28:13** 819
for our **g** is great so that *His* **2Ch 28:13** 819
had done, but Amon multiplied **g**. **2Ch 33:23** 819
g has grown even to the heavens. **Ezr 9:6** 819
this day we *have been* in great **g**, **Ezr 9:7** 819
our evil deeds and our great **g**, **Ezr 9:13** 819
we are before You in our **g**, **Ezr 9:15** 819
wives adding to the **g** of Israel. **Ezr 10:10** 819
That You should seek for my **g** And **Jb 10:6** 5771
And would not acquit me of my **g**. **Jb 10:14** 5771
"For your **g** teaches your mouth, **Jb 15:5** 5771
innocent and there is no **g** in me. **Jb 33:9** 5771
And You forgave the **g** of my sin. **Ps 32:5** 5771
For no **g** of *mine,* they run and set **Ps 59:4** 5771
A man who is laden with the **g** of **Pr 28:17**
render Himself *as* a **g** offering, **Is 53:10** 817
g Before the Holy One of Israel. **Jer 51:5** 817
was the **g** of your sister Sodom: **Ezk 16:49** 5771
and has incurred grievous **g**, **Ezk 25:12** 816
sin offering and the **g** offering. **Ezk 40:39** 817
sin offering and the **g** offering; **Ezk 42:13** 817
sin offering and the **g** offering; **Ezk 44:29** 817
g offering and the sin offering **Ezk 46:20** 817
their **g** and seek My face; **Hos 5:15** 816
Now they must bear their **g**. **Hos 10:2** 816
they are bound for their double **g**. **Hos 10:10** 5772a
who swear by the **g** of Samaria, **Am 8:14** 819
the measure *of the* **g** of your **Mt 23:32**
so that upon you may fall *the* **g** *of* **Mt 23:35**
"I find no **g** in this man." **Lk 23:4** *159a*
I have found no **g** in this man **Lk 23:14** *159a*
found in Him no **g** *demanding* death; **Lk 23:22** *159a*
"I find no **g** in Him. **Jn 18:38** *156*
know that I find no **g** in Him." **Jn 19:4** *156*
Him, for I find no **g** in Him." **Jn 19:6** *156*

GUILTLESS
the king and his throne are **g**." **2Sa 14:9** 5355a
Though I am **g**, He will declare me **Jb 9:20** 8535
I am **g**; I do not take notice of **Jb 9:21** 8535
'He destroys the **g** and the wicked.' **Jb 9:22** 8535

GUILTY
we are **g** concerning our brother, **Gn 42:21** 818
for I will not acquit the **g**. **Ex 23:7** 7563
yet He will by no means leave *the* **g** **Ex 34:7**
not to be done, and they become **g**; **Lv 4:13** 816
not to be done, and he becomes **g**, **Lv 4:22** 816
not to be done, and becomes **g**, **Lv 4:27** 816
he is unclean, then he will be **g**. **Lv 5:2** 816
he comes to know *it,* he will be **g**. **Lv 5:3** 816
it, he will be **g** in one of these. **Lv 5:4** 816
when he becomes **g** in one of these, **Lv 5:5** 816
he was unaware, still he is **g** and **Lv 5:17** 816
was certainly **g** before the LORD." **Lv 5:19** 816
be, when he sins and becomes **g**, **Lv 6:4** 816
the LORD, and that person is **g**, **Nu 5:6** 816
but He will by no means clear *the* **g**, **Nu 14:18**
he will not be **g** of blood **Nu 35:27**
of a murderer who is **g** of death, **Nu 35:31** 7563
them, *else* you would now be **g**.' " **Jg 21:22** 816
word the king is as one who is **g**, **2Sa 14:13** 818
"Let not my lord consider me **g**, **2Sa 19:19** 5771
they may not be **g** before the LORD, **2Ch 19:10** 816
shall do and you will not be **g**. **2Ch 19:10** 816
put away their wives, and being **g**, **Ezr 10:19** 818
guiltless, He will declare me **g**. **Jb 9:20** 6140
Your knowledge I am indeed not **g**, **Jb 10:7** 7561
Hold them **g**, O God; **Ps 5:10** 816
of him who goes on in his **g** deeds. **Ps 68:21** 817
is judged, let him come forth **g**, **Ps 109:7** 7563
The way of a **g** man is crooked, But **Pr 21:8** 2054
will curse you and you will be found **g**. **Pr 30:10** 816
those who live in it are held **g**. **Is 24:6** 816
All who ate of it became **g**; **Jer 2:3** 816
'We are not **g**, Inasmuch as they **Jer 50:7** 816
"You have become **g** by the blood **Ezk 22:4** 816
harlot, Do not let Judah become **g**; **Hos 4:15** 816
Samaria will be held **g**, **Hos 13:16** 816
LORD will by no means leave *the* **g** **Na 1:3**
But they will be held **g**, **Hab 1:11** 816
shall be **g** before the court; **Mt 5:22** *1777*
be **g** before the supreme court; **Mt 5:22** *1777*
shall be **g** *enough to go* into the **Mt 5:22** *1777*
but is **g** of an eternal sin" **Mk 3:29** *1777*
be **g** of the body and the blood **1Co 11:27** *1777*
one *point,* he has become **g** of all. **Jas 2:10** *1777*

GULL
sea **g** and the hawk in its kind, **Lv 11:16** 7828
the ostrich, the owl, the sea **g**, **Dt 14:15** 7828

GUM
aromatic **g** and balm and myrrh, **Gn 37:25** 5219
honey, aromatic **g** and myrrh, **Gn 43:11** 5219

GUNI
and **G** and Jezer and Shillem. **Gn 46:24** 1476
of **G**, the family of the Gunites; **Nu 26:48** 1476
the son of Abdiel, the son of **G**, **1Ch 5:15** 1476
sons of Naphtali *were* Jahziel, **G**, **1Ch 7:13** 1476

GUNITES
of Guni, the family of the **G**; **Nu 26:48** 1477

GUR
they shot him at the ascent of **G**, **2Ki 9:27** 1483

GUR-BAAL
the Arabians who lived in **G**, **2Ch 26:7** 1485

GUSHED
until the blood **g** out on them. **1Ki 18:28** 8210
the rock so that waters **g** out, **Ps 78:20** 2100
the rock and the water **g** forth. **Is 48:21** 2100
middle and all his intestines **g** out. **Ac 1:18** *1632b*

GUTTERS
in front of the flocks in the **g**, **Gn 30:38** 7298a
the sight of the flock in the **g**, **Gn 30:41** 7298a

H

HA
their heads, and saying, "**H**! **Mk 15:29** *3758*

HAAHASHTARI
Ahuzzam, Hepher, Temeni and **H**. **1Ch 4:6** 326

HABAIAH
the sons of **H**, the sons of Hakkoz, **Ezr 2:61** 2252

HABAKKUK
oracle which **H** the prophet saw. **Hab 1:1** 2265
A prayer of **H** the prophet, **Hab 3:1** 2265

HABAZZINIAH
the son of Jeremiah, son of **H**, **Jer 35:3** 2262

HABIT
was previously in the **h** of goring and **Ex 21:29** 5056
was previously in the **h** of goring, **Ex 21:36** 5056
together, as is the **h** of some, **Heb 10:25** *1485*

HABITATION
have guided *them* to Your holy **h**. **Ex 15:13** 5116a
'Look down from Your holy **h**, **Dt 26:15** 4583
and show me both it and His **h**. **2Sa 15:25** 5116a
Brimstone is scattered on his **h**. **Jb 18:15** 5116a
"He sinks a shaft far from **h**, **Jb 28:4** 1481a
O LORD, I love the **h** of Your house **Ps 26:8** 4583
consume So that they have no **h**. **Ps 49:14** 2073
the widows, Is God in His holy **h**. **Ps 68:5** 4583
Be to me a rock of **h** **Ps 71:3** 4583
Jacob And laid waste his **h**. **Ps 79:7** 5116a
He has desired it for His **h**. **Ps 132:13** 4186
people will live in a peaceful **h**, **Is 32:18** 5116a
see Jerusalem, an undisturbed **h**, **Is 33:20** 5116a
see from Your holy and glorious **h**; **Is 63:15** 2073
him And have laid waste his **h**. **Jer 10:25** 5116a
utter His voice from His holy **h**; **Jer 25:30** 4583
a **h** of shepherds who rest their **Jer 33:12** 5116a
who is the **h** of righteousness, **Jer 50:7** 5116a
He is aroused from His holy **h**." **Zch 2:13** 4583
and the boundaries of their **h**, **Ac 17:26** *2733a*

HABITATIONS
according to their **h** in the land **Gn 36:43** 4186
are full of the **h** of violence. **Ps 74:20** 4999
Or who will enter into our **h**?' **Jer 21:13** 4585
has not spared All the **h** of Jacob. **La 2:2** 4999
throughout all their **h** I will stretch **Ezk 6:14** 4186

HABITUALLY
and he **h** dressed in purple and **Lk 16:19**

HABOR
and settled them in Halah and **H**, **2Ki 17:6** 2249
put them in Halah and on the **H**, **2Ki 18:11** 2249
and brought them to Halah, **H**, **1Ch 5:26** 2249

HACALIAH
words of Nehemiah the son of **H**. **Ne 1:1** 2446
the governor, the son of **H**, **Ne 10:1** 2446

HACHILAH
at Horesh, on the hill of **H**, **1Sa 23:19** 2444
not David hiding on the hill of **H**, **1Sa 26:1** 2444
Saul camped in the hill of **H**, **1Sa 26:3** 2444

HACHMONI
son of **H** tutored the king's sons. **1Ch 27:32** 2453

HACHMONITE
Jashobeam, the son of a **H**, **1Ch 11:11** 2453

HAD
God saw all that He **h** made, **Gn 1:31**
His work which He **h** done, **Gn 2:2**
from all His work which He **h** done. **Gn 2:2**
work which God **h** created and made. **Gn 2:3**
plant of the field **h** yet sprouted, **Gn 2:5**

h not sent rain upon the earth,	**Gn 2:5**	
placed the man whom He **h** formed.	**Gn 2:8**	
rib which He **h** taken from the man,	**Gn 2:22**	
field which the LORD God **h** made.	**Gn 3:1**	
man **h** relations with his wife Eve,	**Gn 4:1**	3045
And the LORD **h** regard for Abel and	**Gn 4:4**	8159
for his offering He **h** no regard.	**Gn 4:5**	8159
Cain **h** relations with his wife	**Gn 4:17**	3045
h relations with his wife again;	**Gn 4:25**	3045
When Adam **h** lived one hundred and	**Gn 5:3**	
and he **h** *other* sons and daughters.	**Gn 5:4**	3205
and he **h** *other* sons and daughters.	**Gn 5:7**	3205
and he **h** *other* sons and daughters.	**Gn 5:10**	3205
and he **h** *other* sons and daughters.	**Gn 5:13**	3205
and he **h** *other* sons and daughters.	**Gn 5:16**	3205
and he **h** *other* sons and daughters.	**Gn 5:19**	3205
and he **h** *other* sons and daughters.	**Gn 5:22**	3205
and he **h** *other* sons and daughters.	**Gn 5:26**	3205
and he **h** *other* sons and daughters.	**Gn 5:30**	3205
that He **h** made man on the earth,	**Gn 6:6**	
all flesh **h** corrupted their way	**Gn 6:12**	
to all that God **h** commanded him,	**Gn 6:22**	
all that the LORD **h** commanded him.	**Gn 7:5**	
female, as God **h** commanded Noah.	**Gn 7:9**	
entered as God **h** commanded him	**Gn 7:16**	
window of the ark which he **h** made;	**Gn 8:6**	
his youngest son **h** done to him.	**Gn 9:24**	
which the sons of men **h** built.	**Gn 11:5**	
and he **h** *other* sons and daughters.	**Gn 11:11**	3205
and he **h** *other* sons and daughters.	**Gn 11:13**	3205
and he **h** *other* sons and daughters.	**Gn 11:15**	3205
and he **h** *other* sons and daughters.	**Gn 11:17**	3205
and he **h** *other* sons and daughters.	**Gn 11:19**	3205
and he **h** *other* sons and daughters.	**Gn 11:21**	3205
and he **h** *other* sons and daughters.	**Gn 11:23**	3205
and he **h** *other* sons and daughters.	**Gn 11:25**	3205
Sarai was barren; she **h** no child.	**Gn 11:30**	369
forth as the LORD **h** spoken to him;	**Gn 12:4**	
which they **h** accumulated,	**Gn 12:5**	
which they **h** acquired in Haran,	**Gn 12:5**	
to the LORD who **h** appeared to him.	**Gn 12:7**	
his tent **h** been at the beginning,	**Gn 13:3**	
which he **h** made there formerly;	**Gn 13:4**	
also **h** flocks and herds and tents.	**Gn 13:5**	1961
after Lot **h** separated from him,	**Gn 13:14**	
years they **h** served Chedorlaomer,	**Gn 14:4**	
his relative **h** been taken captive,	**Gn 14:14**	
It came about when the sun **h** set,	**Gn 15:17**	
wife **h** borne him no *children,*	**Gn 16:1**	
and she **h** an Egyptian maid whose	**Gn 16:1**	
After Abram **h** lived ten years	**Gn 16:3**	
when she saw that she **h** conceived,	**Gn 16:4**	
when she saw that she **h** conceived,	**Gn 16:5**	
same day, as God **h** said to him.	**Gn 17:23**	
and the calf which he **h** prepared,	**Gn 18:8**	
As soon as He **h** finished	**Gn 18:33**	
who have not **h** relations with man;	**Gn 19:8**	3045
When they **h** brought them outside,	**Gn 19:17**	
The sun **h** risen over the earth	**Gn 19:23**	
where he **h** stood before the LORD;	**Gn 19:27**	
Now Abimelech **h** not come near her;	**Gn 20:4**	
For the LORD **h** closed fast all the	**Gn 20:18**	
took note of Sarah as He **h** said,	**Gn 21:1**	
did for Sarah as He **h** promised.	**Gn 21:1**	
time of which God **h** spoken to him.	**Gn 21:2**	
days old, as God **h** commanded him.	**Gn 21:4**	
whom she **h** borne to Abraham,	**Gn 21:9**	
servants of Abimelech **h** seized.	**Gn 21:25**	
the place of which God **h** told him.	**Gn 22:3**	
the place of which God **h** told him;	**Gn 22:9**	
the silver which he **h** named in the	**Gn 23:16**	
h blessed Abraham in every way.	**Gn 24:1**	
who **h** charge of all that he owned,	**Gn 24:2**	4910
Before he **h** finished speaking,	**Gn 24:15**	
no man **h** had relations with her;	**Gn 24:16**	
no man had **h** relations with her;	**Gn 24:16**	3045
she **h** finished giving him a drink,	**Gn 24:19**	
to know whether the LORD **h** made	**Gn 24:21**	
the camels **h** finished drinking,	**Gn 24:22**	
Now Rebekah **h** a brother whose name	**Gn 24:29**	
I **h** finished speaking in my heart,	**Gn 24:45**	
who **h** guided me in the right way	**Gn 24:48**	
Now Isaac **h** come from going to	**Gn 24:62**	
all the things that he **h** done.	**Gn 24:66**	
gave all that he **h** to Isaac;	**Gn 25:5**	
because he **h** a taste for game,	**Gn 25:28**	
When Jacob **h** cooked stew, Esau	**Gn 25:29**	
famine that **h** occurred in the days of	**Gn 26:1**	
when he **h** been there a long time,	**Gn 26:8**	
for he **h** possessions of flocks and	**Gn 26:14**	1961
wells which his father's servants **h** dug	**Gn 26:15**	
the wells of water which **h** been dug	**Gn 26:18**	
for the Philistines **h** stopped them	**Gn 26:18**	
which his father **h** given them.	**Gn 26:18**	
about the well which they **h** dug,	**Gn 26:32**	
and the bread, which she **h** made,	**Gn 27:17**	
Isaac **h** finished blessing Jacob,	**Gn 27:30**	
and Jacob **h** hardly gone out from	**Gn 27:30**	
which his father **h** blessed him;	**Gn 27:41**	
Now Esau saw that Isaac **h** blessed	**Gn 28:6**	
and that Jacob **h** obeyed his father	**Gn 28:7**	
mother and **h** gone to Paddan-aram.	**Gn 28:7**	
besides the wives that he **h**,	**Gn 28:9**	
there, because the sun **h** set;	**Gn 28:11**	
He **h** a dream, and behold, a	**Gn 28:12**	2492b
and took the stone that he **h** put	**Gn 28:18**	
the name of the city **h** been Luz.	**Gn 28:19**	
Now Laban **h** two daughters;	**Gn 29:16**	
saw that she **h** stopped bearing,	**Gn 30:9**	
about when Rachel **h** borne Joseph,	**Gn 30:25**	
"For you **h** little before I came and	**Gn 30:30**	1961
He set the rods which he **h** peeled	**Gn 30:38**	
h large flocks and female and male	**Gn 30:43**	1961
his property which he **h** gathered,	**Gn 31:18**	
which he **h** gathered in Paddan-aram,	**Gn 31:18**	
Laban **h** gone to shear his flock,	**Gn 31:19**	
So he fled with all that he **h**;	**Gn 31:21**	
the third day that Jacob **h** fled,	**Gn 31:22**	
Now Jacob **h** pitched his tent in	**Gn 31:25**	
know that Rachel **h** stolen them.	**Gn 31:32**	
Rachel **h** taken the household idols	**Gn 31:34**	
fear of Isaac, **h** not been for me,	**Gn 31:42**	1961
Then he selected from what he **h**	**Gn 32:13**	935
And he sent across whatever he **h**.	**Gn 32:23**	
he **h** not prevailed against him,	**Gn 32:25**	
land where he **h** pitched his tent	**Gn 33:19**	
Leah, whom she **h** borne to Jacob,	**Gn 34:1**	
he **h** defiled Dinah his daughter;	**Gn 34:5**	
he **h** done a disgraceful thing in Israel	**Gn 34:7**	
he **h** defiled Dinah their sister.	**Gn 34:13**	
they **h** defiled their sister.	**Gn 34:27**	
all the foreign gods which they **h** and	**Gn 35:4**	3027
God **h** revealed Himself to him when	**Gn 35:7**	
place where He **h** spoken with him.	**Gn 35:13**	
place where He **h** spoken with him,	**Gn 35:14**	
place where God **h** spoken with him,	**Gn 35:15**	
Abraham and Isaac **h** sojourned.	**Gn 35:27**	
he **h** acquired in the land of Canaan,	**Gn 36:6**	
For their property **h** become too	**Gn 36:7**	
land where his father **h** sojourned,	**Gn 37:1**	
Then Joseph **h** a dream, and when he	**Gn 37:5**	2492b
to this dream which I have **h**;	**Gn 37:6**	2492b
Now he **h** still another dream, and	**Gn 37:9**	2492b
"Lo, I have **h** still another dream;	**Gn 37:9**	2492b
is this dream that you have **h**?	**Gn 37:10**	2492b
she saw that Shelah **h** grown up,	**Gn 38:14**	
and she **h** not been given to him as	**Gn 38:14**	
for she **h** covered her face.	**Gn 38:15**	
who **h** the scarlet *thread* on his hand;	**Gn 38:30**	
Joseph **h** been taken down to Egypt;	**Gn 39:1**	
who **h** taken him down there.	**Gn 39:1**	
he **h** left his garment in her hand and	**Gn 39:13**	
in her hand and **h** fled outside,	**Gn 39:13**	
both **h** a dream the same night,	**Gn 40:5**	2492b
"We have **h** a dream and there is	**Gn 40:8**	2492b
that he **h** interpreted favorably,	**Gn 40:16**	
as Joseph **h** interpreted to them.	**Gn 40:22**	
full years that Pharaoh **h** a dream,	**Gn 41:1**	2492b
We **h** a dream on the same night,	**Gn 41:11**	2492b
and when he **h** shaved himself and	**Gn 41:14**	
"I have **h** a dream, but no one can	**Gn 41:15**	2492b
such as I **h** never seen for	**Gn 41:19**	
"Yet when they **h** devoured them,	**Gn 41:21**	
that they **h** devoured them,	**Gn 41:21**	
He **h** him ride in his second	**Gn 41:43**	
seven years of plenty which **h** been in	**Gn 41:53**	
to come, just as Joseph **h** said,	**Gn 41:54**	
Joseph **h** recognized his brothers,	**Gn 42:8**	
the dreams which he **h** about them,	**Gn 42:9**	2492b
him all that **h** happened to them,	**Gn 42:29**	
they **h** finished eating the grain	**Gn 43:2**	
which they **h** brought from Egypt,	**Gn 43:2**	
you still **h** *another* brother?"	**Gn 43:6**	
"For if we **h** not delayed, surely	**Gn 43:10**	
I **h** your money."	**Gn 43:23**	935
they **h** heard that they were to eat	**Gn 43:25**	
And he did as Joseph **h** told *him.*	**Gn 44:2**	
They **h** *just* gone out of the city,	**Gn 44:4**	
that Joseph's brothers **h** come,	**Gn 45:16**	
Joseph that he **h** spoken to them,	**Gn 45:27**	
that Joseph **h** sent to carry him,	**Gn 45:27**	
Israel set out with all that he **h**,	**Gn 46:1**	
which Pharaoh **h** sent to carry him.	**Gn 46:5**	
which they **h** acquired in the land	**Gn 46:6**	
of Rameses, as Pharaoh **h** ordered.	**Gn 47:11**	
priests **h** an allotment from Pharaoh,	**Gn 47:22**	
did for him as he **h** charged them;	**Gn 50:12**	
which Abraham **h** bought along with	**Gn 50:13**	
After he **h** buried his father,	**Gn 50:14**	
and all who **h** gone up with him to	**Gn 50:14**	
king of Egypt **h** commanded them,	**Ex 1:17**	
And she **h** pity on him and said,	**Ex 2:6**	2550
those days, when Moses **h** grown up,	**Ex 2:11**	
of Midian **h** seven daughters;	**Ex 2:16**	
the LORD with which He **h** sent him,	**Ex 4:28**	
that He **h** commanded him *to do.*	**Ex 4:28**	
which the LORD **h** spoken to Moses.	**Ex 4:30**	
that He **h** seen their affliction,	**Ex 4:31**	
just as when you **h** straw."	**Ex 5:13**	1961
taskmasters **h** set over them,	**Ex 5:14**	
did just as the LORD **h** commanded;	**Ex 7:10**	
to them, as the LORD **h** said.	**Ex 7:13**	
did even as the LORD **h** commanded.	**Ex 7:20**	
to them, as the LORD **h** said.	**Ex 7:22**	
after the LORD **h** struck the Nile.	**Ex 7:25**	
which He **h** inflicted upon Pharaoh.	**Ex 8:12**	
to them, as the LORD **h** said.	**Ex 8:15**	
to them, as the LORD **h** said.	**Ex 8:19**	
as the LORD **h** spoken to Moses.	**Ex 9:12**	
if by now I **h** put forth My hand	**Ex 9:15**	
such as **h** not been in all the land	**Ex 9:24**	
the hail and the thunder **h** ceased,	**Ex 9:34**	
the LORD **h** spoken through Moses.	**Ex 9:35**	
h never been so *many* locusts,	**Ex 10:14**	
of the trees that the hail **h** left.	**Ex 10:15**	
Israel **h** light in their dwellings.	**Ex 10:23**	1961
LORD **h** commanded Moses and Aaron,	**Ex 12:28**	
Now the sons of Israel **h** done	**Ex 12:35**	
they **h** requested from the Egyptians	**Ex 12:35**	
and the LORD **h** given the people	**Ex 12:36**	
They baked the dough which they **h**	**Ex 12:39**	
For it **h** not become leavened,	**Ex 12:39**	
nor **h** they prepared any provisions	**Ex 12:39**	
LORD **h** commanded Moses and Aaron.	**Ex 12:50**	
when Pharaoh **h** let the people go,	**Ex 13:17**	
for he **h** made the sons of Israel	**Ex 13:19**	
was told that the people **h** fled,	**Ex 14:5**	
and his servants **h** a change of heart	**Ex 14:5**	2015
who **h** been going before the camp	**Ex 14:19**	
h gone into the sea after them;	**Ex 14:28**	
LORD **h** used against the Egyptians,	**Ex 14:31**	
"Would that we **h** died by the	**Ex 16:3**	
who **h** gathered much had no excess,	**Ex 16:18**	7235a
who had gathered much **h** no excess,	**Ex 16:18**	
who **h** gathered little had no lack;	**Ex 16:18**	4591
who had gathered little **h** no lack;	**Ex 16:18**	
until morning, as Moses **h** ordered,	**Ex 16:24**	
heard of all that God **h** done for	**Ex 18:1**	
h brought Israel out of Egypt.	**Ex 18:1**	
after he **h** sent her away,	**Ex 18:2**	
all that the LORD **h** done to Pharaoh	**Ex 18:8**	
h befallen them on the journey,	**Ex 18:8**	
and *how* the LORD **h** delivered them.	**Ex 18:8**	
which the LORD **h** done to Israel,	**Ex 18:9**	
and did all that he **h** said.	**Ex 18:24**	
h gone out of the land of Egypt,	**Ex 19:1**	
which the LORD **h** commanded him.	**Ex 19:7**	
When He **h** finished speaking	**Ex 31:18**	
h made and burned *it* with fire,	**Ex 32:20**	
Aaron **h** let them get out of control	**Ex 32:25**	
with the calf which Aaron **h** made.	**Ex 32:35**	
For the LORD **h** said to Moses,	**Ex 33:5**	
as the LORD **h** commanded him,	**Ex 34:4**	
h spoken to him on Mount Sinai.	**Ex 34:32**	
h finished speaking with them,	**Ex 34:33**	
Israel what he **h** been commanded,	**Ex 34:34**	
who **h** in his possession blue and	**Ex 35:23**	4672
who **h** in his possession acacia	**Ex 35:24**	4672
and brought what they **h** spun,	**Ex 35:25**	
which the LORD **h** commanded through	**Ex 35:29**	
in whom the LORD **h** put skill,	**Ex 36:2**	
which the sons of Israel **h** brought to	**Ex 36:3**	
the material they **h** was sufficient	**Ex 36:7**	1961
curtains **h** the same measurements.	**Ex 36:9**	
curtains **h** the same measurements.	**Ex 36:15**	
h *their* wings spread upward,	**Ex 37:9**	1961
that the LORD **h** commanded Moses.	**Ex 38:22**	
as the LORD **h** commanded Moses.	**Ex 39:1**	
as the LORD **h** commanded Moses.	**Ex 39:5**	
as the LORD **h** commanded Moses.	**Ex 39:7**	
as the LORD **h** commanded Moses.	**Ex 39:21**	
as the LORD **h** commanded Moses.	**Ex 39:26**	
as the LORD **h** commanded Moses.	**Ex 39:29**	
as the LORD **h** commanded Moses.	**Ex 39:31**	
that the LORD **h** commanded Moses;	**Ex 39:32**	
that the LORD **h** commanded Moses.	**Ex 39:42**	
work and behold, they **h** done it;	**Ex 39:43**	
just as the LORD **h** commanded,	**Ex 39:43**	
had commanded, this they **h** done.	**Ex 39:43**	
all that the LORD **h** commanded him,	**Ex 40:16**	
as the LORD **h** commanded Moses.	**Ex 40:19**	
as the LORD **h** commanded Moses.	**Ex 40:21**	
as the LORD **h** commanded Moses.	**Ex 40:23**	
as the LORD **h** commanded Moses.	**Ex 40:25**	
as the LORD **h** commanded Moses.	**Ex 40:27**	
as the LORD **h** commanded Moses.	**Ex 40:29**	
as the LORD **h** commanded Moses.	**Ex 40:32**	
because the cloud **h** settled on it,	**Ex 40:35**	
'These the LORD **h** commanded to be	**Lv 7:36**	
h Aaron and his sons come near and	**Lv 8:6**	
as the LORD **h** commanded Moses.	**Lv 8:9**	
Next Moses **h** Aaron's sons come	**Lv 8:13**	
as the LORD **h** commanded Moses.	**Lv 8:13**	
as the LORD **h** commanded Moses.	**Lv 8:17**	
he **h** cut the ram into its pieces,	**Lv 8:20**	
After he **h** washed the entrails and	**Lv 8:21**	
as the LORD **h** commanded Moses.	**Lv 8:21**	
He also **h** Aaron's sons come near;	**Lv 8:24**	
as the LORD **h** commanded Moses.	**Lv 8:29**	
LORD **h** commanded through Moses.	**Lv 8:36**	
So they took what Moses **h**	**Lv 9:5**	
as the LORD **h** commanded Moses.	**Lv 9:10**	
LORD, just as Moses **h** commanded.	**Lv 9:21**	
which He **h** not commanded them.	**Lv 10:1**	
of the camp, as Moses **h** said.	**Lv 10:5**	
and behold, it **h** been burned up	**Lv 10:16**	
blood **h** not been brought inside,	**Lv 10:18**	
if I **h** eaten a sin offering today,	**Lv 10:19**	
when they **h** approached the	**Lv 16:1**	
as the LORD **h** commanded Moses,	**Lv 16:34**	
him because she has **h** no husband;	**Lv 21:3**	1961
I **h** the sons of Israel live in booths	**Lv 23:43**	
they brought the one who **h** cursed	**Lv 24:23**	
as the LORD **h** commanded Moses.	**Lv 24:23**	
h come out of the land of Egypt,	**Nu 1:1**	
men who **h** been designated by name,	**Nu 1:17**	
as the LORD **h** commanded Moses.	**Nu 1:19**	
For the LORD **h** spoken to Moses,	**Nu 1:48**	
which the LORD **h** commanded Moses,	**Nu 1:54**	
as the LORD **h** commanded Moses.	**Nu 2:33**	
and they **h** no children.	**Nu 3:4**	1961
LORD, just as he **h** been commanded.	**Nu 3:16**	
and **h** the oversight of those who	**Nu 3:32**	
just as the LORD **h** commanded him;	**Nu 3:42**	
as the LORD **h** commanded Moses.	**Nu 3:51**	
as the LORD **h** commanded Moses.	**Nu 4:49**	
as the LORD **h** spoken to Moses,	**Nu 5:4**	

has **h** intercourse with you" Nu 5:20 5414
day that Moses **h** finished setting up Nu 7:1
as the LORD **h** commanded Moses. Nu 8:3
which the LORD **h** shown Moses, Nu 8:4
according to all that the LORD **h** Nu 8:20
just as the LORD **h** commanded Moses Nu 8:22
h come out of the land of Egypt, Nu 9:1
that the LORD **h** commanded Moses, Nu 9:5
were among them **h** greedy desires; Nu 11:4 183
two men **h** remained in the camp; Nu 11:26
among those who **h** been registered, Nu 11:26
but **h** not gone out to the tent), Nu 11:26
the people who **h** been greedy. Nu 11:34
Cushite woman whom he **h** married Nu 12:1
(for he **h** married a Cushite woman); Nu 12:1
When they **h** both come forward, Nu 12:5
h withdrawn from over the tent, Nu 12:10
her father **h** but spit in her face, Nu 12:14
they **h** gone up into the Negev, Nu 13:22
men who **h** gone up with him said, Nu 13:31
the land which they **h** spied out, Nu 13:32
we **h** died in the land of Egypt! Nu 14:2
that we **h** died in this wilderness! Nu 14:2
of those who **h** spied out the land, Nu 14:6
because he has **h** a different spirit Nu 14:24 1961
put him in custody because it **h** not Nu 15:34
as the LORD **h** commanded Moses. Nu 15:36
the men who were burned **h** offered, Nu 16:39
h spoken to him through Moses. Nu 16:40
when the congregation **h** assembled Nu 16:42
Aaron took *it* as Moses **h** spoken, Nu 16:47
plague **h** begun among the people. Nu 16:47
for the plague **h** been checked. Nu 16:50
house of Levi **h** sprouted and put forth Nu 17:8
just as the LORD **h** commanded him, Nu 17:11
"If only we **h** perished when our Nu 20:3
LORD, just as He **h** commanded him; Nu 20:9
did just as the LORD **h** commanded, Nu 20:27
After Moses **h** stripped Aaron Nu 20:28
saw that Aaron **h** died, Nu 20:29
who **h** fought against the former Nu 21:26
king of Moab and **h** taken all his land Nu 21:26
Israel **h** done to the Amorites. Nu 22:2
there **h** been a sword in my hand, Nu 22:29 1426
If she **h** not turned aside from me, Nu 22:33
Balak did just as Balaam **h** spoken, Nu 23:2
Balak did just as Balaam **h** said, Nu 23:30
messengers whom you **h** sent to me, Nu 24:12
the son of Hepher **h** no sons, Nu 26:33 1961
For the LORD **h** said of them, Nu 26:65
in his own sin, and he **h** no sons. Nu 27:3 1961
his family because he **h** no son? Nu 27:4 369
the LORD **h** spoken through Moses. Nu 27:23
that the LORD **h** commanded Moses. Nu 29:40
her father **h** forbidden her. Nu 30:5
as the LORD **h** commanded Moses, Nu 31:7
h come from service in the war. Nu 31:14
men of war who **h** gone to battle, Nu 31:21
as the LORD **h** commanded Moses. Nu 31:31
war **h** plundered was 675,000 sheep, Nu 31:32
who **h** not known man intimately, Nu 31:35
as the LORD **h** commanded Moses. Nu 31:41
from the men who **h** gone to war Nu 31:42
as the LORD **h** commanded Moses. Nu 31:47
The men of war **h** taken booty, Nu 31:53
Gad **h** an exceedingly large number Nu 32:1 1961
land which the LORD **h** given them Nu 32:9
generation of those who **h** done evil Nu 32:13
the LORD **h** struck down among them. Nu 33:4
The LORD **h** also executed judgments Nu 33:4
the people **h** no water to drink. Nu 33:14 1961
Israel **h** come from the land of Egypt Nu 33:38
as the LORD **h** commanded Moses, Nu 36:10
h commanded him *to give* to them, Dt 1:3
after he **h** defeated Sihon the king Dt 1:4
the LORD our God **h** commanded us; Dt 1:19
camp, as the LORD **h** sworn to them. Dt 2:14
all the men of war **h** finally perished Dt 2:16
of the cities which we **h** captured. Dt 2:35
the LORD our God **h** commanded us. Dt 2:37
that they **h** such a heart in them, Dt 5:29 1961
which He **h** sworn to our fathers.' Dt 6:23
which the LORD **h** made with you, Dt 9:9
the words which the LORD **h** spoken Dt 9:10
"And I saw that you **h** indeed Dt 9:16
You **h** made for yourselves a molten Dt 9:16
you **h** turned aside quickly from Dt 9:16
which the LORD **h** commanded you. Dt 9:16
all your sin which you **h** committed Dt 9:18
thing, the calf which you **h** made, Dt 9:21
LORD **h** said He would destroy you. Dt 9:25
into the land which He **h** promised Dt 9:28
Commandments which the LORD **h** Dt 10:4
tablets in the ark which I **h** made; Dt 10:5
he **h** not hated him previously. Dt 19:6
h intended to do to his brother. Dt 19:19
He **h** made with them at Horeb. Dt 29:1
which *they* **h** with them); Dt 29:17
whom He **h** not allotted to them. Dt 29:26
H I not feared the provocation by Dt 32:27
Unless their Rock **h** sold them Dt 32:30
And the LORD **h** given them up? Dt 32:30
When Moses **h** finished speaking all Dt 32:45
for Moses **h** laid his hands on him; Dt 34:9
did as the LORD **h** commanded Moses. Dt 34:9
But the woman **h** taken the two men Jos 2:4
But she **h** brought them up to the Jos 2:6
she **h** laid in order on the roof. Jos 2:6
who were pursuing them **h** gone out, Jos 2:7

Now the pursuers **h** sought *them* all Jos 2:22
the road, but **h** not found *them.* Jos 2:22
him all that **h** happened to them. Jos 2:23
h finished crossing the Jordan. Jos 3:17
h finished crossing the Jordan, Jos 4:1
the twelve men whom he **h** appointed Jos 4:4
LORD **h** commanded Joshua to speak Jos 4:10
all that Moses **h** commanded Joshua. Jos 4:10
the people **h** finished crossing, Jos 4:11
just as Moses **h** spoken to them; Jos 4:12
just as they **h** revered Moses all Jos 4:14
ark of the covenant of the LORD **h** Jos 4:18
they **h** taken from the Jordan, Jos 4:20
before you until you **h** crossed, Jos 4:23
your God **h** done to the Red Sea, Jos 4:23
up before us until we **h** crossed; Jos 4:23
heard how the LORD **h** dried up the Jos 5:1
of Israel until they **h** crossed, Jos 5:1
of Egypt **h** not been circumcised. Jos 5:5
to whom the LORD **h** sworn that He Jos 5:6
land which the LORD **h** sworn to their Jos 5:6
because they **h** not circumcised Jos 5:7
Now when they **h** finished Jos 5:8
the day after they **h** eaten some of Jos 5:12
sons of Israel no longer **h** manna, Jos 5:12 1961
Joshua **h** spoken to the people, Jos 6:8
So he **h** the ark of the LORD taken Jos 6:11
two men who **h** spied out the land, Jos 6:22
and her brothers and all she **h**; Jos 6:23
father's household and all she **h**, Jos 6:25
If only we **h** been willing to dwell Jos 7:7
they **h** stoned them with stones. Jos 7:25
who **h** not gone out after Israel, Jos 8:17
when he **h** stretched out his hand, Jos 8:19
and they **h** no place to flee this Jos 8:20 1961
for the people who **h** been fleeing Jos 8:20
the *men in* ambush **h** captured the city Jos 8:21
Now when Israel **h** finished Jos 8:24
until he **h** utterly destroyed all the Jos 8:26
LORD which He **h** commanded Joshua. Jos 8:27
h commanded the sons of Israel, Jos 8:31
no man **h** wielded an iron *tool;* Jos 8:31
law of Moses, which he **h** written, Jos 8:32
the LORD **h** given command at first Jos 8:33
word of all that Moses **h** commanded Jos 8:35
h done to Jericho and to Ai, Jos 9:3
was dry *and* **h** become crumbled. Jos 9:5
they **h** made a covenant with them, Jos 9:16
leaders of the congregation **h** sworn Jos 9:18
as the leaders **h** spoken to them. Jos 9:21
God **h** commanded His servant Moses Jos 9:24
heard that Joshua **h** captured Ai, Jos 10:1
Ai, and **h** utterly destroyed it Jos 10:1
he **h** done to Jericho and its king, Jos 10:1
so he **h** done to Ai and its king), Jos 10:1
Gibeon **h** made peace with Israel Jos 10:1
Now these five kings **h** fled and Jos 10:16
sons of Israel **h** finished slaying them Jos 10:20
h entered the fortified cities, Jos 10:20
men of war who **h** gone with him, Jos 10:24
where they **h** hidden themselves, Jos 10:27
he **h** done to the king of Jericho. Jos 10:28
he **h** done to the king of Jericho. Jos 10:30
to all that he **h** done to Libnah. Jos 10:32
until he **h** left him no survivor. Jos 10:33
to all that he **h** done to Lachish. Jos 10:35
to all that he **h** done to Eglon. Jos 10:37
Just as he **h** done to Hebron, so he Jos 10:39
as he **h** also done to Libnah and Jos 10:39
the God of Israel, **h** commanded. Jos 10:40
to them as the LORD **h** told him; Jos 11:9
servant of the LORD **h** commanded. Jos 11:12
until they **h** destroyed them. Jos 11:14
the LORD **h** commanded Moses Jos 11:15
that the LORD **h** commanded Moses. Jos 11:15
as the LORD **h** commanded Moses. Jos 11:20
that the LORD **h** spoken to Moses, Jos 11:23
Thus the land **h** rest from war. Jos 11:23 8252
as He **h** promised to them. Jos 13:33
For Moses **h** given the inheritance Jos 14:3
as the LORD **h** commanded Moses, Jos 14:5
Then the land **h** rest from war. Jos 14:15 8252
the son of Manasseh, **h** no sons, Jos 17:3 1961
Manasseh **h** Beth-shean and its Jos 17:11 1961
h not divided their inheritance. Jos 18:2
So they **h** as their inheritance Jos 19:2 1961
LORD **h** commanded through Moses. Jos 21:8
h its surrounding pasture lands; Jos 21:42 1961
all the land which He **h** sworn to give Jos 21:43
that He **h** sworn to their fathers, Jos 21:44
promises which the LORD **h** made to Jos 21:45
h given *a possession* in Bashan, Jos 22:7
possession which they **h** possessed, Jos 22:9
when the LORD **h** given rest to Jos 23:1
So he **h** to bless you, and I Jos 24:10 1288
a land on which you **h** not labored, Jos 24:13
and cities which you **h** not built, Jos 24:13
and **h** known all the deeds of the Jos 24:31
LORD which He **h** done for Israel. Jos 24:31
ground which Jacob **h** bought from Jos 24:32
because they **h** iron chariots. Jg 1:19
to Caleb, as Moses **h** promised; Jg 1:20
Joshua **h** dismissed the people, Jg 2:6
who **h** seen all the great work of Jg 2:7
LORD which He **h** done for Israel. Jg 2:7
work which He **h** done for Israel. Jg 2:10
who **h** brought them out of the land Jg 2:12
as the LORD **h** spoken and as the Jg 2:15
and as the LORD **h** sworn to them, Jg 2:15

way in which their fathers **h** walked Jg 2:17
all who **h** not experienced any of Jg 3:1
h not experienced it formerly). Jg 3:2
which He **h** commanded their fathers Jg 3:4
Then the land **h** rest forty years. Jg 3:11 8252
because they **h** done evil in the Jg 3:12
himself a sword which **h** two edges, Jg 3:16
he **h** finished presenting the tribute Jg 3:18
people who **h** carried the tribute. Jg 3:18
When he **h** gone out, his servants Jg 3:24
master **h** fallen to the floor dead. Jg 3:25
It came about when he **h** arrived, Jg 3:27
he **h** nine hundred iron chariots, Jg 4:3
Now Heber the Kenite **h** separated Jg 4:11
and **h** pitched his tent as far away Jg 4:11
Abinoam **h** gone up to Mount Tabor. Jg 4:12
until they **h** destroyed Jabin the Jg 4:24
For it was when Israel **h** sown, Jg 6:3
did as the LORD **h** spoken to him; Jg 6:27
on the altar which **h** been built. Jg 6:28
because he **h** torn down his altar. Jg 6:32
"Behold, I **h** a dream; Jg 7:13 2492b
when they **h** just posted the watch; Jg 7:19
as the men of Succoth **h** answered. Jg 8:8
if only you **h** let them live, Jg 8:19
(For they **h** gold earrings, because Jg 8:24
Now Gideon **h** seventy sons who were Jg 8:30 1961
descendants, for he **h** many wives. Jg 8:30 1961
who **h** delivered them from the Jg 8:34
the good that he **h** done to Israel. Jg 8:35
which he **h** done to his father in Jg 9:56
He **h** thirty sons who rode on Jg 10:4 1961
and they **h** thirty cities in the Jg 10:4
her he **h** no son or daughter. Jg 11:34 369
to the vow which he **h** made; Jg 11:39
and she **h** no relations with a man. Jg 11:39 3045
He **h** thirty sons, and thirty Jg 12:9 1961
He **h** forty sons and thirty Jg 12:14 1961
barren and **h** borne no Jg 13:2
"If the LORD **h** desired to kill Jg 13:23
though he **h** nothing in his hand; Jg 14:6 369
father or mother what he **h** done. Jg 14:6
he **h** scraped the honey out of the Jg 14:9
you **h** not plowed with my heifer, Jg 14:18
companion who **h** been his friend. Jg 14:20
When he **h** set fire to the torches, Jg 15:5
When he **h** finished speaking, Jg 15:17
fresh cords that **h** not been dried, Jg 16:8
Now she **h** *men* lying in wait in an Jg 16:9 3427
When Delilah saw that he **h** told Jg 16:18
h him shave off the seven locks of Jg 16:19
that the LORD **h** departed from him. Jg 16:20
he **h** judged Israel twenty years. Jg 16:31
And the man Micah **h** a shrine and Jg 17:5
inheritance **h** not been allotted to them Jg 18:1
and **h** no dealings with anyone. Jg 18:7 369
When they **h** gone some distance Jg 18:22
Then they took what Micah **h** made Jg 18:27
the priest who **h** belonged to him, Jg 18:27 1961
they **h** no dealings with anyone, Jg 18:28 369
graven image which he **h** made, Jg 18:31
of Israel **h** gone up to Mizpah.) Jg 20:3
place where they **h** arrayed themselves Jg 20:22
whom they **h** set against Gibeah, Jg 20:36
men of Israel **h** sworn in Mizpah, Jg 21:1
For they **h** taken a great oath Jg 21:5
no one **h** come to the camp from Jg 21:8
young virgins who **h** not known a man Jg 21:12
the women whom they **h** kept alive Jg 21:14
LORD **h** made a breach in the tribes Jg 21:15
For the sons of Israel **h** sworn, Jg 21:18
for she **h** heard in the land of Ru 1:6
LORD **h** visited His people in giving Ru 1:6
when they **h** come to Bethlehem, Ru 1:19
Naomi **h** a kinsman of her husband, Ru 2:1
and was satisfied and **h** some left. Ru 2:14 3498
she beat out what she **h** gleaned, Ru 2:17
saw what she **h** gleaned. Ru 2:18
gave Naomi what she **h** left after Ru 2:18 3498
with whom she **h** worked and said, Ru 2:19
her mother-in-law **h** commanded her. Ru 3:6
When Boaz **h** eaten and drunk and Ru 3:7
all that the man **h** done for her. Ru 3:16
He **h** two wives: 1Sa 1:2
and Peninnah **h** children, but 1Sa 1:2 1961
but Hannah **h** no children. 1Sa 1:2 369
but the LORD **h** closed her womb. 1Sa 1:5
the LORD **h** closed her womb. 1Sa 1:6
And Elkanah **h** relations with 1Sa 1:19 3045
time, after Hannah **h** conceived, 1Sa 1:20
Now when she **h** weaned him, she 1Sa 1:24
now his eyesight **h** begun to grow dim 1Sa 3:2
lamp of God **h** not yet gone out, 1Sa 3:3
nor **h** the word of the LORD yet 1Sa 3:7
of the LORD **h** come into the camp. 1Sa 4:6
and her husband **h** died, 1Sa 4:19
Dagon **h** fallen on his face to the 1Sa 5:3
Dagon **h** fallen on his face to the 1Sa 5:4
After they **h** brought it around, 1Sa 5:9
Now the ark of the LORD **h** been in 1Sa 6:1
He **h** severely dealt with them, 1Sa 6:6
they **h** looked into the ark of the LORD. 1Sa 6:19
LORD **h** struck the people with a great 1Sa 6:19
of Israel **h** gathered to Mizpah, 1Sa 7:7
The cities which the Philistines **h** taken 1Sa 7:14
people who **h** asked of him a king. 1Sa 8:10
Now after Samuel **h** heard all the 1Sa 8:21
He **h** a son whose name was Saul, 1Sa 9:2 1961
the LORD **h** revealed *this* to Samuel 1Sa 9:15

When he **h** finished prophesying, he **1Sa 10:13**
that the donkeys **h** been found." **1Sa 10:16**
kingdom which Samuel **h** mentioned. **1Sa 10:16**
men whose hearts God **h** touched **1Sa 10:26**
said to the messengers who **h** come, **1Sa 11:9**
Saul **h** smitten the garrison of the **1Sa 13:4**
and also that Israel **h** become **1Sa 13:4**
did not know that Jonathan **h** gone. **1Sa 14:3**
And when they **h** numbered, behold, **1Sa 14:17**
all the men of Israel who **h** hidden **1Sa 14:22**
heard that the Philistines **h** fled, **1Sa 14:22**
Saul **h** put the people under oath, **1Sa 14:24**
But Jonathan **h** not heard when his **1Sa 14:27**
if only the people **h** eaten freely **1Sa 14:30**
h taken the kingdom over Israel, **1Sa 14:47**
He **h** made Saul king over Israel. **1Sa 15:35**
He **h** a bronze helmet on his head, **1Sa 17:5**
He also **h** bronze greaves on **1Sa 17:6**
was Jesse, and he **h** eight sons. **1Sa 17:12**
h gone after Saul to the battle. **1Sa 17:13**
and went as Jesse **h** commanded him. **1Sa 17:20**
to walk, for he **h** not tested *them.* **1Sa 17:39**
in the shepherd's bag which he **h**, **1Sa 17:40**
he **h** finished speaking to Saul, **1Sa 18:1**
with him but **h** departed from Saul. **1Sa 18:12**
Before the days **h** expired **1Sa 18:26**
him all that Saul **h** done to him. **1Sa 19:18**
h decided to put David to death. **1Sa 20:33**
his father **h** dishonored him. **1Sa 20:34**
the arrow which Jonathan **h** shot, **1Sa 20:37**
were with him **h** been discovered. **1Sa 22:6**
Saul **h** killed the priests of the LORD. **1Sa 22:21**
Saul that David **h** come to Keilah, **1Sa 23:7**
that David **h** escaped from Keilah, **1Sa 23:13**
Saul **h** come out to seek his life **1Sa 23:15**
for you have **h** compassion on me. **1Sa 23:21** 2550
he **h** cut off the edge of Saul's *robe.* **1Sa 24:5**
LORD **h** given you today into my hand **1Sa 24:10**
you, but *my eye* **h** pity on you; **1Sa 24:10**
When David **h** finished speaking **1Sa 24:16**
and he **h** three thousand sheep and **1Sa 25:2**
Now David **h** said, **1Sa 25:21**
you **h** come quickly to meet me, **1Sa 25:34**
her hand what she **h** brought him and **1Sa 25:35**
when the wine **h** gone out of Nabal, **1Sa 25:37**
h also taken Ahinoam of Jezreel, **1Sa 25:43**
Saul **h** given Michal his daughter, **1Sa 25:44**
to the place where Saul **h** camped. **1Sa 26:5**
from the LORD **h** fallen on them. **1Sa 26:12**
Saul that David **h** fled to Gath, **1Sa 27:4**
and all Israel **h** lamented him and **1Sa 28:3**
And Saul **h** removed from the land **1Sa 28:3**
for he **h** eaten no food all day and **1Sa 28:20**
h a fattened calf in the house, **1Sa 28:24**
that the Amalekites **h** made a raid **1Sa 30:1**
and **h** overthrown Ziklag and burned **1Sa 30:1**
daughters **h** been taken captive. **1Sa 30:3**
two wives **h** been taken captive, **1Sa 30:5**
For he **h** not eaten bread or drunk **1Sa 30:12**
When he **h** brought him down, **1Sa 30:16**
spoil that they **h** taken from the land **1Sa 30:16**
all that the Amalekites **h** taken, **1Sa 30:18**
spoil or anything that they **h** taken **1Sa 30:19**
So David **h** captured all the sheep **1Sa 30:20**
who **h** also been left at the brook **1Sa 30:21**
saw that the men of Israel **h** fled **1Sa 31:7**
the Philistines **h** done to Saul, **1Sa 31:11**
when David **h** returned from the **2Sa 1:1**
could not live after he **h** fallen. **2Sa 1:10**
they **h** fallen by the sword. **2Sa 1:12**
h taken Ish-bosheth the son of **2Sa 2:8**
where Asahel **h** fallen and died, **2Sa 2:23**
"As God lives, if you **h** not spoken, **2Sa 2:27**
when he **h** gathered all the people **2Sa 2:30**
But the servants of David **h** struck **2Sa 2:31**
Now Saul **h** a concubine whose name **2Sa 3:7**
Now Abner **h** consultation with the **2Sa 3:17** 1961
in Hebron, for he **h** sent him away, **2Sa 3:22**
him away, and he **h** gone in peace. **2Sa 3:22**
he **h** put their brother Asahel to death **2Sa 3:30**
it **h** not been *the will* of the king to **2Sa 3:37**
heard that Abner **h** died in Hebron, **2Sa 4:1**
Saul's son **h** two men who were **2Sa 4:2**
son, **h** a son crippled in his feet. **2Sa 4:4**
the LORD **h** established him as king **2Sa 5:12**
and that He **h** exalted his kingdom **2Sa 5:12**
they **h** anointed David king over Israel **2Sa 5:17**
just as the LORD **h** commanded him, **2Sa 5:25**
ark of the LORD **h** gone six paces, **2Sa 6:13**
tent which David **h** pitched for it; **2Sa 6:17**
When David **h** finished offering **2Sa 6:18**
the daughter of Saul **h** no child **2Sa 6:23** 1961
and the LORD **h** given him rest on **2Sa 7:1**
David **h** defeated all the army of **2Sa 8:9**
because he **h** fought against **2Sa 8:10**
Hadadezer **h** been at war with Toi. **2Sa 8:10**
silver and gold that he **h** dedicated **2Sa 8:11**
the nations which he **h** subdued: **2Sa 8:11**
Now Ziba **h** fifteen sons and twenty **2Sa 9:10**
Mephibosheth **h** a young son **2Sa 9:12**
they **h** become odious to David, **2Sa 10:6**
they **h** been defeated by Israel, **2Sa 10:15**
and when she **h** purified herself **2Sa 11:4**
He **h** written in the letter, **2Sa 11:15**
all that Joab **h** sent him *to tell.* **2Sa 11:22**
But the thing that David **h** done **2Sa 11:27**
The rich man **h** a great many flocks **2Sa 12:2** 1961
the poor man **h** nothing except one **2Sa 12:3**
the wayfarer who **h** come to him; **2Sa 12:4**
for the man who **h** come to him." **2Sa 12:4**
this thing and **h** no compassion." **2Sa 12:6** 2550
and if *that* **h** *been* too little, **2Sa 12:8**
the son of David **h** a beautiful sister **2Sa 13:1**
But Amnon **h** a friend whose name **2Sa 13:3**
So Tamar took the cakes which she **h** **2Sa 13:10**
love with which he **h** loved her. **2Sa 13:15**
she **h** on a long-sleeved garment; **2Sa 13:18**
he **h** violated his sister Tamar. **2Sa 13:22**
h sheepshearers in Baal-hazor, **2Sa 13:23** 1961
just as Absalom **h** commanded. **2Sa 13:29**
Now Absalom **h** fled. **2Sa 13:34**
As soon as he **h** finished speaking, **2Sa 13:36**
Absalom **h** fled and gone to Geshur, **2Sa 13:38**
"Your maidservant **h** two sons, **2Sa 14:6**
any man **h** a suit to come to the king **2Sa 15:2** 1961
men who **h** come with him from Gath, **2Sa 15:18**
people **h** finished passing from the city **2Sa 15:24**
Now when David **h** passed a little **2Sa 16:1**
When Hushai **h** come to Absalom, **2Sa 17:6**
For the LORD **h** ordained to thwart **2Sa 17:14**
who **h** a well in his courtyard, **2Sa 17:18**
after they **h** departed that **2Sa 17:21**
who **h** not crossed the Jordan. **2Sa 17:22**
when David **h** come to Mahanaim, **2Sa 17:27**
said to the man who **h** told him, **2Sa 18:11**
if I **h** dealt treacherously against **2Sa 18:13**
Now Absalom in his lifetime **h** **2Sa 18:18**
Would I **h** died instead of you, O **2Sa 18:33**
Now Israel **h** fled, each to his **2Sa 19:8**
he **h** neither cared for his feet, **2Sa 19:24**
h come down from Rogelim; **2Sa 19:31**
and he **h** sustained the king while **2Sa 19:32**
"Why **h** our brothers the men of **2Sa 19:41**
whom he **h** left to keep the house, **2Sa 20:3**
set time which he **h** appointed him. **2Sa 20:5**
but Saul **h** sought to kill them in **2Sa 21:2**
whom she **h** borne to Saul, **2Sa 21:8**
whom she **h** borne to Adriel the son **2Sa 21:8**
the concubine of Saul, **h** done, **2Sa 21:11**
who **h** stolen them from the open **2Sa 21:12**
where the Philistines **h** hanged **2Sa 21:12**
bones of those who **h** been hanged. **2Sa 21:13**
man of *great* stature who **h** six fingers **2Sa 21:20**
he also **h** been born to the giant. **2Sa 21:20**
of the mighty men whom David **h**: **2Sa 23:8**
and the men of Israel **h** withdrawn. **2Sa 23:9**
David **h** a craving and said, **2Sa 23:15** 183
and **h** a name as well as the three. **2Sa 23:18**
Kabzeel, who **h** done mighty deeds, **2Sa 23:20**
Now the Egyptian **h** a spear in his **2Sa 23:21**
and **h** a name as well as the three **2Sa 23:22**
So when they **h** gone about through **2Sa 24:8**
after he **h** numbered the people. **2Sa 24:10**
Gad, just as the LORD **h** commanded. **2Sa 24:19**
His father **h** never crossed him **1Ki 1:6**
He **h** conferred with Joab the **1Ki 1:7**
h Solomon ride on King David's mule **1Ki 1:38**
then he **h** a throne set for the king's **1Ki 2:19**
which He **h** spoken concerning the **1Ki 2:27**
for Joab **h** followed Adonijah, **1Ki 2:28**
he **h** not followed Absalom. **1Ki 2:28**
h fled to the tent of the LORD, **1Ki 2:29**
h gone from Jerusalem to Gath, **1Ki 2:41**
Jerusalem to Gath, and **h** returned. **1Ki 2:41**
until he **h** finished building his **1Ki 3:1**
that Solomon **h** asked this thing. **1Ki 3:10**
was not my son, whom I **h** borne." **1Ki 3:21**
which the king **h** handed down, **1Ki 3:28**
Solomon **h** twelve deputies over **1Ki 4:7**
each man **h** to provide for a month **1Ki 4:7** 3557
For he **h** dominion over everything **1Ki 4:24** 7287a
and he **h** peace on all sides around **1Ki 4:24** 1961
Solomon **h** 40,000 stalls of **1Ki 4:26**
earth who **h** heard of his wisdom. **1Ki 4:34**
when he heard that they **h** anointed **1Ki 5:1**
h always been a friend of David. **1Ki 5:1** 1961
Now Solomon **h** 70,000 transporters, **1Ki 5:15** 1961
All the doorways and doorposts **h** **1Ki 7:5**
daughter, whom Solomon **h** married. **1Ki 7:8**
So the great court all around **h** **1Ki 7:12**
they **h** borders, even borders **1Ki 7:28**
each stand **h** four bronze wheels **1Ki 7:30**
and its four feet **h** supports; **1Ki 7:30**
all of them **h** one casting, one **1Ki 7:37**
When Solomon **h** finished praying this **1Ki 8:54**
goodness that the LORD **h** shown to **1Ki 8:66**
when Solomon **h** finished building **1Ki 9:1**
as He **h** appeared to him at Gibeon. **1Ki 9:2**
Solomon **h** built the two houses, **1Ki 9:10**
(Hiram king of Tyre **h** supplied **1Ki 9:11**
cities which Solomon **h** given him, **1Ki 9:12**
h gone up and captured Gezer and **1Ki 9:16**
and **h** given it *as* a dowry to his **1Ki 9:16**
storage cities which Solomon **h**, **1Ki 9:19** 1961
which *Solomon* **h** built for her, **1Ki 9:24**
the house that he **h** built, **1Ki 10:4**
I came and my eyes **h** seen it. **1Ki 10:7**
For the king **h** at sea the ships of **1Ki 10:22**
which God **h** put in his heart. **1Ki 10:24**
and he **h** 1,400 chariots and 12,000 **1Ki 10:26** 1961
LORD **h** said to the sons of Israel, **1Ki 11:2**
He **h** seven hundred wives, **1Ki 11:3** 1961
as the heart of David his father **h** **1Ki 11:4**
as David his father **h** *done.* **1Ki 11:6**
who **h** appeared to him twice, **1Ki 11:9**
and **h** commanded him concerning **1Ki 11:10**
observe what the LORD **h** commanded. **1Ki 11:10**
army **h** gone up to bury the slain, **1Ki 11:15**
and **h** struck down every male in **1Ki 11:15**
he **h** cut off every male in Edom), **1Ki 11:16**
who **h** fled from his lord Hadadezer **1Ki 11:23**
Now Ahijah **h** clothed himself with **1Ki 11:29**
for all Israel **h** come to Shechem **1Ki 12:1**
where he **h** fled from the presence **1Ki 12:2**
consulted with the elders who **h** served **1Ki 12:6** 1961
the elders which they **h** given him, **1Ki 12:8**
third day as the king **h** directed, **1Ki 12:12**
the elders which they **h** given him, **1Ki 12:13**
heard that Jeroboam **h** returned, **1Ki 12:20**
when Rehoboam **h** come to Jerusalem, **1Ki 12:21**
to the calves which he **h** made. **1Ki 12:32**
the high places which he **h** made. **1Ki 12:32**
the altar which he **h** made in Bethel **1Ki 12:33**
he **h** devised in his own heart; **1Ki 12:33**
h given by the word of the LORD. **1Ki 13:5**
of God **h** done that day in Bethel; **1Ki 13:11**
which he **h** spoken to the king, **1Ki 13:11**
Now his sons **h** seen the way which **1Ki 13:12**
of God who came from Judah **h** gone. **1Ki 13:12**
prophet who **h** brought him back; **1Ki 13:20**
It came about after he **h** eaten **1Ki 13:23**
eaten bread and after he **h** drunk, **1Ki 13:23**
prophet whom he **h** brought back. **1Ki 13:23**
Now when he **h** gone, a lion met him **1Ki 13:24**
the lion **h** not eaten the body nor **1Ki 13:28**
After he **h** buried him, **1Ki 13:31**
Now the LORD **h** said to Ahijah, **1Ki 14:5**
the city which the LORD **h** chosen **1Ki 14:21**
all that their fathers **h** done, **1Ki 14:22**
of gold which Solomon **h** made. **1Ki 14:26**
which he **h** committed before him; **1Ki 15:3**
and **h** not turned aside from **1Ki 15:5**
idols which his fathers **h** made. **1Ki 15:12**
because she **h** made a horrid image **1Ki 15:13**
timber with which Baasha **h** built. **1Ki 15:22**
alive, until he **h** destroyed them, **1Ki 15:29**
as though it **h** been a trivial **1Ki 16:31**
altar of the LORD which **h** been torn **1Ki 18:30**
whom the word of the LORD **h** come, **1Ki 18:31**
Jezebel all that Elijah **h** done, **1Ki 19:1**
and how he **h** killed all the **1Ki 19:1**
And as soon as he **h** departed from **1Ki 20:36**
whom I **h** devoted to destruction, **1Ki 20:42**
Naboth the Jezreelite **h** a vineyard **1Ki 21:1** 1961
the Jezreelite **h** spoken to him; **1Ki 21:4**
as Jezebel **h** sent *word* to them, **1Ki 21:11**
the letters which she **h** sent them. **1Ki 21:11**
Naboth **h** been stoned and was dead, **1Ki 21:15**
to all that the Amorites **h** done, **1Ki 21:26**
Now the king of Aram **h** commanded **1Ki 22:31**
to all that his father **h** done. **1Ki 22:53**
of the LORD which Elijah **h** spoken. **2Ki 1:17**
And because he **h** no son, Jehoram **2Ki 1:17** 1961
When they **h** crossed over, **2Ki 2:9**
when he also **h** struck the waters, **2Ki 2:14**
of Baal which his father **h** made. **2Ki 3:2**
h come up to fight against them. **2Ki 3:21**
And when he **h** called her, she **2Ki 4:12**
When he **h** called her, she stood in **2Ki 4:15**
year, as Elisha **h** said to her. **2Ki 4:17**
When he **h** taken him and brought **2Ki 4:20**
and they ate and **h** *some* left over, **2Ki 4:44**
the LORD **h** given victory to Aram. **2Ki 5:1**
the Arameans **h** gone out in bands and **2Ki 5:2**
and **h** taken captive a little girl **2Ki 5:2**
king of Israel **h** torn his clothes, **2Ki 5:8**
h the prophet told you *to do some* **2Ki 5:13**
which the man of God **h** told him; **2Ki 6:10**
of God **h** risen early and gone out, **2Ki 6:15**
When they **h** come into Samaria, **2Ki 6:20**
and when they **h** eaten and drunk he **2Ki 6:23**
h sackcloth beneath on his body. **2Ki 6:30**
For the Lord **h** caused the army of **2Ki 7:6**
h thrown away in their haste. **2Ki 7:15**
just as the man of God **h** said, **2Ki 7:17**
man of God **h** spoken to the king, **2Ki 7:18**
whose son he **h** restored to life, **2Ki 8:1**
relating to the king how he **h** restored **2Ki 8:5**
son he **h** restored to life appealed **2Ki 8:5**
just as the house of Ahab **h** done, **2Ki 8:18**
He **h** promised him to give a lamp **2Ki 8:19**
the Edomites who **h** surrounded him **2Ki 8:21**
like the house of Ahab **h** *done,* **2Ki 8:27**
h inflicted on him at Ramah when **2Ki 8:29**
but King Joram **h** returned to **2Ki 9:15**
the wounds which the Arameans **h** **2Ki 9:15**
of Judah **h** come down to see Joram. **2Ki 9:16**
Ahab **h** seventy sons in Samaria. **2Ki 10:1**
Now when he **h** departed from there, **2Ki 10:15**
Samaria, until he **h** destroyed him, **2Ki 10:17**
Now Jehu **h** stationed for himself **2Ki 10:24**
eighty men outside, and he **h** said, **2Ki 10:24**
as soon as he **h** finished offering **2Ki 10:25**
shields that **h** *been* King David's, **2Ki 11:10**
For they **h** put Athaliah to death **2Ki 11:20**
priests **h** not repaired the damages **2Ki 12:6**
who **h** the oversight of the house **2Ki 12:11**
kings of Judah, **h** dedicated, **2Ki 12:18**
for the king of Aram **h** destroyed **2Ki 13:7**
king of Aram **h** oppressed Israel **2Ki 13:22**
gracious to them and **h** compassion **2Ki 13:23** 7355
cities which he **h** taken in war from **2Ki 13:25** 7355
all that Joash his father **h** done. **2Ki 14:3** 7355
who **h** slain the king his father. **2Ki 14:5**
which **h** *belonged* to Judah, are **2Ki 14:28**
that his father Amaziah **h** done. **2Ki 15:3**
the LORD, as his fathers **h** done; **2Ki 15:9**

Context	Reference	Number
all that his father Uzziah **h** done.	**2Ki 15:34**	
as his father David **h** *done.*	**2Ki 16:2**	
nations whom the LORD **h** driven out	**2Ki 16:3**	
King Ahaz **h** sent from Damascus,	**2Ki 16:11**	
which they **h** built in the house,	**2Ki 16:18**	
who **h** sent messengers to So king	**2Ki 17:4**	
and **h** offered no tribute to the king of	**2Ki 17:4**	
as *he* **h** *done* year by year; so	**2Ki 17:4**	
the sons of Israel **h** sinned against	**2Ki 17:7**	
who **h** brought them up from the	**2Ki 17:7**	
and they **h** feared other gods	**2Ki 17:7**	
nations whom the LORD **h** driven out	**2Ki 17:8**	
of Israel which they **h** introduced.	**2Ki 17:8**	
nations *did* which the LORD **h** carried	**2Ki 17:11**	
which the LORD **h** said to them,	**2Ki 17:12**	
concerning which the LORD **h**	**2Ki 17:15**	
customs which Israel **h** introduced.	**2Ki 17:19**	
He **h** cast them out of His sight.	**2Ki 17:20**	
When He **h** torn Israel from the	**2Ki 17:21**	
So one of the priests whom they **h**	**2Ki 17:28**	
the people of Samaria **h** made,	**2Ki 17:29**	
h been carried away into exile.	**2Ki 17:33**	
all that his father David **h** done.	**2Ki 18:3**	
bronze serpent that Moses **h** made,	**2Ki 18:4**	
which the LORD **h** commanded Moses.	**2Ki 18:6**	
Hezekiah king of Judah **h** overlaid,	**2Ki 18:16**	
for he **h** heard that the king had	**2Ki 19:8**	
that the king **h** left Lachish.	**2Ki 19:8**	
h gone out of the middle court	**2Ki 20:4**	
h gone down on the stairway of Ahaz.	**2Ki 20:11**	
heard that Hezekiah **h** been sick.	**2Ki 20:12**	
Hezekiah his father **h** destroyed;	**2Ki 21:3**	
as Ahab king of Israel **h** done,	**2Ki 21:3**	
LORD, of which the LORD **h** said,	**2Ki 21:4**	
image of Asherah that he **h** made,	**2Ki 21:7**	
he **h** filled Jerusalem from one end to	**2Ki 21:16**	
as Manasseh his father **h** done.	**2Ki 21:20**	
the way that his father **h** walked,	**2Ki 21:21**	
father **h** served and worshiped them.	**2Ki 21:21**	
who **h** conspired against King Amon,	**2Ki 21:24**	
whom the kings of Judah **h** appointed	**2Ki 23:5**	
the priests **h** burned incense,	**2Ki 23:8**	
kings of Judah **h** given to the sun,	**2Ki 23:11**	
which the kings of Judah **h** made,	**2Ki 23:12**	
and the altars which Manasseh **h**	**2Ki 23:12**	
king of Israel **h** built for Ashtoreth	**2Ki 23:13**	
who made Israel sin, **h** made,	**2Ki 23:15**	
Israel **h** made provoking the LORD;	**2Ki 23:19**	
them just as he **h** done in Bethel.	**2Ki 23:19**	
Surely such a Passover **h** not been	**2Ki 23:22**	
which Manasseh **h** provoked Him.	**2Ki 23:26**	
to all that his fathers **h** done.	**2Ki 23:32**	
to all that his fathers **h** done.	**2Ki 23:37**	
which He **h** spoken through His	**2Ki 24:2**	
according to all that he **h** done,	**2Ki 24:3**	
for the king of Babylon **h** taken	**2Ki 24:7**	
to all that his father **h** done.	**2Ki 24:9**	
Solomon king of Israel **h** made in the	**2Ki 24:13**	
the LORD, just as the LORD **h** said	**2Ki 24:13**	
to all that Jehoiakim **h** done.	**2Ki 24:19**	
who **h** deserted to the king of Babylon	**2Ki 25:11**	
and the stands which Solomon **h**	**2Ki 25:16**	
king of Babylon **h** left,	**2Ki 25:22**	
h appointed Gedaliah *governor,*	**2Ki 25:23**	
h his meals in the king's presence	**2Ki 25:29**	398
Judah **h** five sons in all.	**1Ch 2:4**	
Hezron **h** sons by Azubah *his* wife,	**1Ch 2:18**	3205
who **h** twenty-three cities in the	**1Ch 2:22**	1961
Jerahmeel **h** another wife,	**1Ch 2:26**	1961
Now Sheshan **h** no sons, only	**1Ch 2:34**	1961
And Sheshan **h** an Egyptian servant	**1Ch 2:34**	
father of Kiriath-jearim **h** sons	**1Ch 2:52**	1961
the father of Tekoa, **h** two wives,	**1Ch 4:5**	1961
Now Shimei **h** sixteen sons and six	**1Ch 4:27**	
because their cattle **h** increased	**1Ch 5:9**	
whom God **h** destroyed before them.	**1Ch 5:25**	
until Solomon **h** built the house of	**1Ch 6:32**	
the servant of God **h** commanded.	**1Ch 6:49**	
Kohath **h** cities of their territory from	**1Ch 6:66**	1961
for they **h** many wives and sons.	**1Ch 7:4**	7235a
and Zelophehad **h** daughters.	**1Ch 7:15**	1961
misfortune **h** come upon his house.	**1Ch 7:23**	
Bela **h** sons: Addar, Gera, Abihud,	**1Ch 8:3**	1961
after he **h** sent away Hushim and	**1Ch 8:8**	
Azel **h** six sons, and these	**1Ch 8:38**	
and **h** many sons and grandsons,	**1Ch 8:40**	7235a
and their fathers **h** been over the	**1Ch 9:19**	
So they and their sons **h** charge of	**1Ch 9:23**	
Now some of them **h** charge of the	**1Ch 9:28**	
h the responsibility over the	**1Ch 9:31**	
Azel **h** six sons whose names	**1Ch 9:44**	
the valley saw that they **h** fled,	**1Ch 10:7**	
the Philistines **h** done to Saul,	**1Ch 10:11**	
Now David **h** said,	**1Ch 11:6**	
of the mighty men whom David **h**,	**1Ch 11:10**	
of the mighty men whom David **h**:	**1Ch 11:11**	
David **h** a craving and said,	**1Ch 11:17**	183
he **h** a name as well as the thirty.	**1Ch 11:20**	
and **h** a name as well as the three	**1Ch 11:24**	
part of them **h** kept their allegiance to	**1Ch 12:29**	
their kinsmen **h** prepared for them.	**1Ch 12:39**	
of Obed-edom with all that he **h**.	**1Ch 13:14**	
the LORD **h** established him as king	**1Ch 14:2**	
David **h** been anointed king over all	**1Ch 14:8**	
Now the Philistines **h** come and	**1Ch 14:9**	
did just as God **h** commanded him,	**1Ch 14:16**	
place which he **h** prepared for it.	**1Ch 15:3**	
poles thereon, as Moses **h** commanded	**1Ch 15:15**	
tent which David **h** pitched for it,	**1Ch 16:1**	
When David **h** finished offering the	**1Ch 16:2**	
heard that David **h** defeated all the	**1Ch 18:9**	
because he **h** fought against	**1Ch 18:10**	
Hadadezer and **h** defeated him;	**1Ch 18:10**	
Hadadezer **h** been at war with Tou.	**1Ch 18:10**	1961
and the gold which he **h** carried away	**1Ch 18:11**	
sons of Ammon saw that they **h** made	**1Ch 19:6**	
and the kings who **h** come were by	**1Ch 19:9**	
they **h** been defeated by Israel,	**1Ch 19:16**	
who **h** twenty-four fingers and toes,	**1Ch 20:6**	
when David saw that the LORD **h**	**1Ch 21:28**	
Moses **h** made in the wilderness,	**1Ch 21:29**	
I **h** intended to build a house to	**1Ch 22:7**	
and Eliezer **h** no other sons, but	**1Ch 23:17**	1961
Eleazar died and **h** no sons,	**1Ch 23:22**	1961
before their father and **h** no sons.	**1Ch 24:2**	1961
God of Israel **h** commanded him.	**1Ch 24:19**	
Eleazar, who **h** no sons.	**1Ch 24:28**	1961
Meshelemiah **h** sons:	**1Ch 26:2**	
Obed-edom **h** sons:	**1Ch 26:4**	
God **h** indeed blessed him.	**1Ch 26:5**	
Meshelemiah **h** sons and relatives,	**1Ch 26:9**	
one of the sons of Merari **h** sons:	**1Ch 26:10**	
h charge of the treasures of the	**1Ch 26:20**	
h charge of the treasures of the	**1Ch 26:22**	
Shelomoth and his relatives **h** charge	**1Ch 26:26**	
of the army, **h** dedicated.	**1Ch 26:26**	
And all that Samuel the seer **h**	**1Ch 26:28**	
everyone who **h** dedicated *anything,*	**1Ch 26:28**	
h charge of the affairs of Israel	**1Ch 26:30**	
son of Zabdiel **h** charge of the first	**1Ch 27:2**	
Dodai the Ahohite and his division **h**	**1Ch 27:4**	
thirty, and **h** charge of thirty;	**1Ch 27:6**	
because the LORD **h** said He would	**1Ch 27:23**	
of Zeruiah **h** begun to count *them,*	**1Ch 27:24**	
Now Azmaveth the son of Adiel **h**	**1Ch 27:25**	
And Jonathan the son of Uzziah **h**	**1Ch 27:25**	
Ezri the son of Chelub **h**	**1Ch 27:26**	
h charge of the vineyards;	**1Ch 27:27**	
and Zabdi the Shiphmite **h** charge	**1Ch 27:27**	
Baal-hanan the Gederite **h**	**1Ch 27:28**	
h charge of the stores of oil.	**1Ch 27:28**	
Shitrai the Sharonite **h** charge	**1Ch 27:29**	
and Shaphat the son of Adlai **h**	**1Ch 27:29**	
Ishmaelite **h** charge of the camels;	**1Ch 27:30**	
h charge of the donkeys.	**1Ch 27:30**	
Hagrite **h** charge of the flocks.	**1Ch 27:31**	
I **h** intended to build a permanent	**1Ch 28:2**	
I **h** made preparations to build *it.*	**1Ch 28:2**	
the plan of all that he **h** in mind,	**1Ch 28:12**	1961
they **h** offered so willingly,	**1Ch 29:9**	
majesty which **h** not been on any king	**1Ch 29:25**	1961
the LORD **h** made in the wilderness.	**2Ch 1:3**	
David **h** brought up the ark of God	**2Ch 1:4**	
to the place he **h** prepared for it,	**2Ch 1:4**	
for he **h** pitched a tent for it in	**2Ch 1:4**	
of Uri, the son of Hur, **h** made,	**2Ch 1:5**	
"Because you **h** this in mind, and	**2Ch 1:11**	1961
He **h** 1,400 chariots and 12,000	**2Ch 1:14**	1961
which his father David **h** taken;	**2Ch 2:17**	
h appeared to his father David,	**2Ch 3:1**	
the place that David **h** prepared on	**2Ch 3:1**	
that David his father **h** dedicated,	**2Ch 5:1**	
priests who were present **h** sanctified	**2Ch 5:11**	
Solomon **h** made a bronze platform,	**2Ch 6:13**	
and **h** set it in the midst of the	**2Ch 6:13**	
when Solomon **h** finished praying,	**2Ch 7:1**	
which King David **h** made for giving	**2Ch 7:6**	
bronze altar which Solomon **h** made	**2Ch 7:7**	
the goodness that the LORD **h** shown	**2Ch 7:10**	
completed all that he **h** planned	**2Ch 7:11**	
Solomon **h** built the house of the	**2Ch 8:1**	
cities which Huram **h** given to him,	**2Ch 8:2**	
cities which he **h** built in Hamath.	**2Ch 8:4**	
the storage cities that Solomon **h**,	**2Ch 8:6**	1961
sons of Israel **h** not destroyed,	**2Ch 8:8**	
house which he **h** built for her,	**2Ch 8:11**	
which he **h** built before the porch;	**2Ch 8:12**	
the man of God **h** so commanded.	**2Ch 8:14**	
She **h** a very large retinue, with	**2Ch 9:1**	
h seen the wisdom of Solomon,	**2Ch 9:3**	
the house which he **h** built,	**2Ch 9:3**	
I came and my eyes **h** seen it.	**2Ch 9:6**	
there **h** never been spice like that	**2Ch 9:9**	1961
what she **h** brought to the king.	**2Ch 9:12**	
For the king **h** ships which went to	**2Ch 9:21**	
which God **h** put in his heart.	**2Ch 9:23**	
Now Solomon **h** 4,000 stalls for	**2Ch 9:25**	1961
for all Israel **h** come to Shechem	**2Ch 10:1**	
he was in Egypt where he **h** fled from	**2Ch 10:2**	
consulted with the elders who **h** served	**2Ch 10:6**	1961
the elders which they **h** given him,	**2Ch 10:8**	
third day as the king **h** directed,	**2Ch 10:12**	
when Rehoboam **h** come to Jerusalem,	**2Ch 11:1**	
for Jeroboam and his sons **h**	**2Ch 11:14**	
for the calves which he **h** made.	**2Ch 11:15**	
For he **h** taken eighteen wives and	**2Ch 11:21**	
h been unfaithful to the LORD,	**2Ch 12:2**	
princes of Judah who **h** gathered at	**2Ch 12:5**	
shields which Solomon **h** made.	**2Ch 12:9**	
the city which the LORD **h** chosen	**2Ch 12:13**	
But Jeroboam **h** set an ambush to	**2Ch 13:13**	
because the LORD **h** given him rest.	**2Ch 14:6**	
h an army of 300,000 from Judah,	**2Ch 14:8**	1961
dread of the LORD **h** fallen on them;	**2Ch 14:14**	
cities which he **h** captured in the hill	**2Ch 15:8**	
from the spoil they **h** brought.	**2Ch 15:11**	
they **h** sworn with their whole heart	**2Ch 15:15**	
heart and **h** sought Him earnestly,	**2Ch 15:15**	
because she **h** made a horrid image	**2Ch 15:16**	
with which Baasha **h** been building,	**2Ch 16:6**	
tomb which he **h** cut out for himself	**2Ch 16:14**	
in the resting place which he **h** filled	**2Ch 16:14**	
which Asa his father **h** captured.	**2Ch 17:2**	
and he **h** great riches and honor.	**2Ch 17:5**	1961
He **h** large supplies in the	**2Ch 17:13**	1961
h great riches and honor;	**2Ch 18:1**	1961
Now the king of Aram **h** commanded	**2Ch 18:30**	
he **h** consulted with the people,	**2Ch 20:21**	
Seir, who **h** come against Judah;	**2Ch 20:22**	
and when they **h** finished with the	**2Ch 20:23**	
the ground, and no one **h** escaped.	**2Ch 20:24**	
for the LORD **h** made them to	**2Ch 20:27**	
LORD **h** fought against the enemies of	**2Ch 20:29**	
the people **h** not yet directed	**2Ch 20:33**	
He **h** brothers, the sons of	**2Ch 21:2**	
Now when Jehoram **h** taken over the	**2Ch 21:4**	
which He **h** made with David,	**2Ch 21:7**	
and since He **h** promised to give a	**2Ch 21:7**	
because he **h** forsaken the LORD God	**2Ch 21:10**	
camp **h** slain all the older *sons.*	**2Ch 22:1**	
they **h** inflicted on him at Ramah,	**2Ch 22:6**	
whom the LORD **h** anointed to cut	**2Ch 22:7**	
shields which **h** been King David'	**2Ch 23:9**	
whom David **h** assigned over the	**2Ch 23:18**	
For they **h** put Athaliah to death	**2Ch 23:21**	
sons of the wicked Athaliah **h** broken	**2Ch 24:7**	
the chest until they **h** finished.	**2Ch 24:10**	
When they **h** finished, they	**2Ch 24:14**	
because he **h** done well in Israel	**2Ch 24:16**	
his father Jehoiada **h** shown him,	**2Ch 24:22**	
because they **h** forsaken the	**2Ch 24:24**	
When they **h** departed from him	**2Ch 24:25**	
who **h** slain his father the king.	**2Ch 25:3**	
they **h** sought the gods of Edom.	**2Ch 25:20**	
that his father Amaziah **h** done.	**2Ch 26:4**	
h understanding through the vision	**2Ch 26:5**	
cisterns, for he **h** much livestock,	**2Ch 26:10**	1961
He also **h** plowmen	**2Ch 26:10**	
Uzziah **h** an army ready for battle,	**2Ch 26:11**	1961
because the LORD **h** smitten him.	**2Ch 26:20**	
all that his father Uzziah **h** done;	**2Ch 27:2**	
the LORD as David his father **h**	**2Ch 28:1**	
nations whom the LORD **h** driven out	**2Ch 28:3**	
because they **h** forsaken the LORD	**2Ch 28:6**	
h come and attacked Judah and	**2Ch 28:17**	
The Philistines also **h** invaded the	**2Ch 28:18**	
of Judah, and **h** taken Beth-shemesh,	**2Ch 28:18**	
for he **h** brought about a lack of	**2Ch 28:19**	
of Damascus which **h** defeated him,	**2Ch 28:23**	
all that his father David **h** done.	**2Ch 29:2**	
utensils which King Ahaz **h** discarded	**2Ch 29:19**	
priests **h** consecrated themselves.	**2Ch 29:34**	
God **h** prepared for the people,	**2Ch 29:36**	
assembly in Jerusalem **h** decided to	**2Ch 30:2**	
because the priests **h** not	**2Ch 30:3**	
nor **h** the people been gathered to	**2Ch 30:3**	
For they **h** not celebrated *it* in	**2Ch 30:5**	
who **h** not consecrated themselves;	**2Ch 30:17**	
h not purified themselves,	**2Ch 30:18**	
For Hezekiah king of Judah **h**	**2Ch 30:24**	
and the princes **h** contributed to	**2Ch 30:24**	
until they **h** destroyed them all.	**2Ch 31:1**	
we have **h** enough to eat with	**2Ch 31:10**	
saw that Sennacherib **h** come and	**2Ch 32:2**	
the wall that **h** been broken down and	**2Ch 32:5**	
h entered the temple of his god,	**2Ch 32:21**	
h immense riches and honor;	**2Ch 32:27**	1961
God **h** given him very great wealth.	**2Ch 32:29**	
that **h** happened in the land,	**2Ch 32:31**	
Hezekiah his father **h** broken down;	**2Ch 33:3**	
the LORD of which the LORD **h** said,	**2Ch 33:4**	
he **h** made in the house of God,	**2Ch 33:7**	
of which God **h** said to David and	**2Ch 33:7**	
all the altars which he **h** built on the	**2Ch 33:15**	
as Manasseh his father **h** done,	**2Ch 33:22**	
which his father Manasseh **h** made,	**2Ch 33:22**	
as his father Manasseh **h** done,	**2Ch 33:23**	
of those who **h** sacrificed to them.	**2Ch 34:4**	
h purged the land and the house,	**2Ch 34:8**	
h collected from Manasseh and	**2Ch 34:9**	
the workmen who **h** the oversight of	**2Ch 34:10**	6485
kings of Judah **h** let go to ruin.	**2Ch 34:11**	
the money which **h** been brought into	**2Ch 34:14**	
Hilkiah and *those* whom the king **h**	**2Ch 34:22**	
There **h** not been celebrated a	**2Ch 35:18**	
nor **h** any of the kings of Israel	**2Ch 35:18**	
Josiah **h** set the temple in order,	**2Ch 35:20**	
in the second chariot which he **h**,	**2Ch 35:24**	
Nebuchadnezzar who **h** made him	**2Ch 36:13**	
He **h** sanctified in Jerusalem.	**2Ch 36:14**	
because He **h** compassion on His	**2Ch 36:15**	2550
and **h** no compassion on young man	**2Ch 36:17**	2550
Those who **h** escaped from the	**2Ch 36:20**	
the land **h** enjoyed its sabbaths.	**2Ch 36:21**	
even everyone whose spirit God **h**	**Ezr 1:5**	
which Nebuchadnezzar **h** carried	**Ezr 1:7**	
h them brought out by the hand of	**Ezr 1:8**	
Babylon **h** carried away to Babylon,	**Ezr 2:1**	
they **h** 200 singing men and women.	**Ezr 2:65**	
of the LORD **h** not been laid.	**Ezr 3:6**	
they **h** from Cyrus king of Persia.	**Ezr 3:7**	
Now when the builders **h** laid the	**Ezr 3:10**	
men who **h** seen the first temple,	**Ezr 3:12**	
'But because our fathers **h**	**Ezr 5:12**	
Nebuchadnezzar **h** taken from the	**Ezr 5:14**	
whom he **h** appointed governor.	**Ezr 5:14**	
just as King Darius **h** sent.	**Ezr 6:13**	

h purified themselves together;	Ezr 6:20	
all those who **h** separated themselves	Ezr 6:21	
the LORD **h** caused them to rejoice,	Ezr 6:22	
and **h** turned the heart of the king	Ezr 6:22	
the LORD God of Israel **h** given;	Ezr 7:6	
For Ezra **h** set his heart to study	Ezr 7:10	
whom David and the princes **h** given	Ezr 8:20	
because we **h** said to the king,	Ezr 8:22	
Israel present *there* **h** offered.	Ezr 8:25	
The exiles who **h** come from the	Ezr 8:35	
these things **h** been completed,	Ezr 9:1	
the men who **h** married foreign wives	Ezr 10:17	
the sons of the priests who **h** married	Ezr 10:18	
All these **h** married foreign wives,	Ezr 10:44	
and some of them **h** wives *by whom*	Ezr 10:44	3426
had wives *by whom* they **h** children.	Ezr 10:44	7760
asked them concerning the Jews who **h**	Ne 1:2	
and **h** survived the captivity,	Ne 1:2	
I **h** not been sad in his presence.	Ne 2:1	
Now the king **h** sent with me	Ne 2:9	
someone **h** come to seek the welfare of	Ne 2:10	
where I **h** gone or what I had done;	Ne 2:16	
where I had gone or what I **h** done;	Ne 2:16	
nor **h** I as yet told the Jews, the	Ne 2:16	
of my God **h** been favorable to me and	Ne 2:18	
words which he **h** spoken to me.	Ne 2:18	
for the people **h** a mind to work.	Ne 4:6	1961
that God **h** frustrated their plan,	Ne 4:15	
Then I was very angry when I **h**	Ne 5:6	
enemies that I **h** rebuilt the wall,	Ne 6:1	
I **h** not set up the doors in the gates	Ne 6:1	
that surely God **h** not sent him,	Ne 6:12	
Tobiah and Sanballat **h** hired him.	Ne 6:12	
this work **h** been accomplished with	Ne 6:16	
and his son Jehohanan **h** married	Ne 6:18	
rebuilt and I **h** set up the doors,	Ne 7:1	
king of Babylon **h** carried away,	Ne 7:6	
h 245 male and female singers.	Ne 7:67	
which the LORD **h** given to Israel.	Ne 8:1	
which they **h** made for the purpose.	Ne 8:4	
which **h** been made known to them.	Ne 8:12	
LORD **h** commanded through Moses	Ne 8:14	
who **h** returned from the captivity	Ne 8:17	
The sons of Israel **h** indeed not	Ne 8:17	
which You **h** performed among them;	Ne 9:17	
land Which You **h** told their fathers	Ne 9:23	
killed Your prophets who **h** admonished	Ne 9:26	
"But as soon as they **h** rest,	Ne 9:28	5117
and all those who **h** separated	Ne 10:28	
who **h** knowledge and understanding,	Ne 10:28	3045
for the singers **h** built themselves	Ne 12:29	
Then I **h** the leaders of Judah come	Ne 12:31	
God **h** given them great joy,	Ne 12:43	
h prepared a large room for him,	Ne 13:5	
of Babylon I **h** gone to the king.	Ne 13:6	
that Eliashib **h** done for Tobiah,	Ne 13:7	
the Levites **h** not been given *them,*	Ne 13:10	
performed the service **h** gone away,	Ne 13:10	
Jews **h** married women from Ashdod,	Ne 13:23	
for so the king **h** given orders to	Es 1:8	
princes of Persia and Media who **h**	Es 1:14	
anger of King Ahasuerus **h** subsided	Es 2:1	
Vashti and what she **h** done and what	Es 2:1	
what **h** been decreed against her.	Es 2:1	
who **h** been taken into exile from	Es 2:6	
who **h** been exiled with Jeconiah king	Es 2:6	
the king of Babylon **h** exiled.	Es 2:6	
she **h** no father or mother.	Es 2:7	369
for Mordecai **h** instructed her that	Es 2:10	
who **h** taken her as his daughter,	Es 2:15	
Esther **h** not yet made known her	Es 2:20	
even as Mordecai **h** commanded her;	Es 2:20	
as she **h** done when under his care.	Es 2:20	
king **h** commanded concerning him.	Es 3:2	
when they **h** spoken daily to him	Es 3:4	
he **h** told them that he was a Jew.	Es 3:4	
for they **h** told him *who* the people	Es 3:6	
learned all that **h** been done,	Es 4:1	
king **h** appointed to attend her,	Es 4:5	
him all that **h** happened to him,	Es 4:7	
money that Haman **h** promised to pay	Es 4:7	
the edict which **h** been issued in Susa	Es 4:8	
just as Esther **h** commanded him.	Es 4:17	
banquet which Esther **h** prepared.	Es 5:5	
where the king **h** magnified him and	Es 5:11	
and how he **h** promoted him above	Es 5:11	
the banquet which she **h** prepared;	Es 5:12	
Haman, so he **h** the gallows made.	Es 5:14	
what Mordecai **h** reported concerning	Es 6:2	
that they **h** sought to lay hands on	Es 6:2	
Now Haman **h** just entered the outer	Es 6:4	
gallows which he **h** prepared for him	Es 6:4	
everything that **h** happened to him.	Es 6:13	
banquet which Esther **h** prepared.	Es 6:14	
if we **h** only been sold as slaves,	Es 7:4	
saw that harm **h** been determined	Es 7:7	
which he **h** prepared for Mordecai,	Es 7:10	
h disclosed what he was to her.	Es 8:1	
which he **h** taken away from Haman,	Es 8:2	
he **h** devised against the Jews.	Es 8:3	
hanged on the gallows because he **h**	Es 8:7	
of the Jews **h** fallen on them.	Es 8:17	
the dread of them **h** fallen on all	Es 9:2	
of Mordecai **h** fallen on them.	Es 9:3	
what they **h** started to do,	Es 9:23	
what Mordecai **h** written to them.	Es 9:23	
h schemed against the Jews to	Es 9:24	
to destroy them and **h** cast Pur,	Es 9:24	
he **h** devised against the Jews,	Es 9:25	
both what they **h** seen in this	Es 9:26	
and what **h** happened to them,	Es 9:26	
Esther **h** established for them,	Es 9:31	
and just as they **h** established for	Es 9:31	
days of feasting **h** completed their	Jb 1:5	
adversity that **h** come upon him,	Jb 2:11	
Or with princes who **h** gold,	Jb 3:15	
disappointed for they **h** trusted,	Jb 6:20	
I **h** died and no eye had seen me!	Jb 10:18	
I had died and no eye **h** seen me!	Jb 10:18	
have been as though I **h** not been,	Jb 10:19	
And the orphan who **h** no helper.	Jb 29:12	
Vigor **h** perished from them.	Jb 30:2	
Or that the needy **h** no covering,	Jb 31:19	369
I saw I **h** support in the gate,	Jb 31:21	
because my hand **h** secured *so* much;	Jb 31:25	
"Oh that I **h** one to hear me!	Jb 31:35	5414
because they **h** found no answer,	Jb 32:3	
answer, and yet **h** condemned Job.	Jb 32:3	
Now Elihu **h** waited to speak to Job	Jb 32:4	
h no regard for any of His ways;	Jb 34:27	7919a
I have, more than if I **h** sinned?'	Jb 35:3	
LORD **h** spoken these words to Job,	Jb 42:7	
increased all that Job **h** twofold.	Jb 42:10	
and all who **h** known him before came	Jb 42:11	
that the LORD **h** brought on him.	Jb 42:11	
beginning; and he **h** 14,000 sheep	Jb 42:12	1961
He **h** seven sons and three	Jb 42:13	1961
I would have despaired unless I **h**	Ps 27:13	
h forgotten the name of our God Or	Ps 44:20	
great fear *where* no fear **h** been;	Ps 53:5	
because God **h** rejected them.	Ps 53:5	
"Oh, that I **h** wings like a dove!	Ps 55:6	5414
who **h** sweet fellowship together	Ps 55:14	4985
My steps **h** almost slipped.	Ps 73:2	
If I **h** said, "I will speak thus,"	Ps 73:15	
seems as if one **h** lifted up *His* axe	Ps 74:5	
His miracles that He **h** shown them.	Ps 78:11	
they **h** satisfied their desire,	Ps 78:30	
which His right hand **h** gained.	Ps 78:54	
tent which He **h** pitched among men,	Ps 78:60	
His virgins **h** no wedding songs.	Ps 78:63	
For my soul has **h** enough troubles,	Ps 88:3	7646
If the LORD **h** not been my help, My	Ps 94:17	
Me, though they **h** seen My work.	Ps 95:9	
And Aaron, whom He **h** chosen.	Ps 105:26	
dread of them **h** fallen upon them.	Ps 105:38	
Who **h** done great things in Egypt,	Ps 106:21	
H not Moses His chosen one stood	Ps 106:23	
Because they **h** rebelled against	Ps 107:11	
If Your law **h** not been my delight,	Ps 119:92	
Too long has my soul **h** its dwelling	Ps 120:6	
"**H** it not been the LORD who was	Ps 124:1	
"**H** it not been the LORD who was	Ps 124:2	
While He **h** not yet made the earth	Pr 8:26	
slaves and I **h** homeborn slaves.	Ec 2:7	1961
my activities which my hands **h** done	Ec 2:11	
and the labor which I **h** exerted,	Ec 2:11	
for the work which **h** been done	Ec 2:17	
which I **h** labored under the sun,	Ec 2:18	
which I **h** labored under the sun.	Ec 2:20	
they **h** no one to comfort *them;*	Ec 4:1	369
but they **h** no one to comfort *them.*	Ec 4:1	369
and he **h** fathered a son,	Ec 5:14	
As he **h** come naked from his	Ec 5:15	
"Scarcely **h** I left them When	SS 3:4	
Until I **h** brought him to my	SS 3:4	
But my beloved **h** turned away *and*	SS 5:6	
my beloved had turned away *and* **h**	SS 5:6	
To see whether the vine **h** budded	SS 6:11	
Or the pomegranates **h** bloomed.	SS 6:11	
"Solomon **h** a vineyard at Baal-hamon;	SS 8:11	1961
hosts **H** left us a few survivors,	Is 1:9	
"I have **h** enough of burnt offerings	Is 1:11	7646
h a vineyard on a fertile hill.	Is 5:1	1961
coal in his hand, which he **h** taken	Is 6:6	
Though they **h** fled far away.	Is 22:3	
for he **h** heard that the king had	Is 37:8	
that the king **h** left Lachish.	Is 37:8	
stairway on which it **h** gone down.	Is 38:8	
own welfare I **h** great bitterness;	Is 38:17	4843
Now Isaiah **h** said,	Is 38:21	
Then Hezekiah **h** said,	Is 38:22	
he **h** been sick and had recovered.	Is 39:1	
he had been sick and **h** recovered.	Is 39:1	
By a way he **h** not been traversing	Is 41:3	
"If only you **h** paid attention to	Is 48:18	
For what **h** not been told them they	Is 52:15	
And what they **h** not heard they	Is 52:15	
Because He **h** done no violence,	Is 53:9	
favor I have **h** compassion on you.	Is 60:10	7355
Yet you **h** a harlot's forehead	Jer 3:3	1961
things, And you have **h** your way.	Jer 3:5	3201
I **h** sent her away and given her a	Jer 3:8	
the heavens, and they **h** no light.	Jer 4:23	369
the birds of the heavens **h** fled.	Jer 4:25	
When I **h** fed them to the full,	Jer 5:7	
of the abomination they **h** done	Jer 8:12	
Oh that I **h** in the desert A	Jer 9:2	5414
they **h** devised plots against me,	Jer 11:19	
as the LORD **h** commanded me.	Jer 13:5	
the place where I **h** hidden it;	Jer 13:7	
And you yourself **h** taught them	Jer 13:21	
where He **h** banished them.'	Jer 16:15	
which I **h** promised to bless it	Jer 18:10	
the kings of Judah **h** *ever* known,	Jer 19:4	
the LORD **h** sent him to prophesy;	Jer 19:14	
h Jeremiah the prophet beaten	Jer 20:2	
into a land that they **h** not known?	Jer 22:28	
countries where I **h** driven them.'	Jer 23:8	
"But if they **h** stood in My council	Jer 23:22	
'I **h** a dream, I had a dream!'	Jer 23:25	2492b
I **h** a dream!'	Jer 23:25	2492b
king of Babylon **h** carried away	Jer 24:1	
and **h** brought them to Babylon,	Jer 24:1	
One basket **h** very good figs, like	Jer 24:2	
the other basket **h** very bad figs	Jer 24:2	
the LORD **h** commanded *him* to speak	Jer 26:8	
He **h** pronounced against them?	Jer 26:19	
after Hananiah the prophet **h**	Jer 28:12	
people whom Nebuchadnezzar **h** taken	Jer 29:1	
smiths **h** departed from Jerusalem.)	Jer 29:2	
king of Judah **h** shut him up,	Jer 32:3	
"After I **h** given the deed of	Jer 32:16	
which I **h** not commanded them nor	Jer 32:35	
nor **h** it entered My mind that they	Jer 32:35	
after King Zedekiah **h** made a	Jer 34:8	
who **h** entered into the covenant	Jer 34:10	
servants whom they **h** set free,	Jer 34:11	
"Although recently you **h** turned	Jer 34:15	
and you **h** made a covenant before	Jer 34:15	
whom you **h** set free according to	Jer 34:16	
LORD which He **h** spoken to him	Jer 36:4	
h heard all the words of the LORD	Jer 36:11	
all the words that he **h** heard when	Jer 36:13	
When they **h** heard all the words,	Jer 36:16	
but they **h** deposited the scroll in	Jer 36:20	
h read three or four columns,	Jer 36:23	
after the king **h** burned the scroll	Jer 36:27	
and the words which Baruch **h** written	Jer 36:27	
of Judah **h** burned in the fire;	Jer 36:32	
king of Babylon **h** made king in the	Jer 37:1	
h not *yet* put him in the prison.	Jer 37:4	
army **h** set out from Egypt;	Jer 37:5	
who **h** been besieging Jerusalem	Jer 37:5	
if you **h** defeated the entire army	Jer 37:10	
when the army of the Chaldeans **h**	Jer 37:11	
which they **h** made into the prison.	Jer 37:15	
Jeremiah **h** come into the dungeon,	Jer 37:16	
h put Jeremiah into the cistern.	Jer 38:7	
Then King Zedekiah sent and **h**	Jer 38:14	
words which the king **h** commanded	Jer 38:27	
conversation **h** not been overheard.	Jer 38:27	
the deserters who **h** gone over to	Jer 39:9	
the poorest people who **h** nothing,	Jer 39:10	369
Now the word of the LORD **h** come to	Jer 39:15	
h released him from Ramah,	Jer 40:1	
he **h** taken him bound in chains among	Jer 40:1	
bodyguard **h** taken Jeremiah and said	Jer 40:2	
heard that the king of Babylon **h**	Jer 40:7	
he **h** put him in charge of the men,	Jer 40:7	
who **h** not been exiled to Babylon.	Jer 40:7	
heard that the king of Babylon **h**	Jer 40:11	
he **h** appointed over them Gedaliah	Jer 40:11	
the places to which they **h** been driven	Jer 40:12	
Babylon **h** appointed over the land.	Jer 41:2	
cistern where Ishmael **h** cast all the	Jer 41:9	
corpses of the men whom he **h** struck	Jer 41:9	
Asa **h** made on account of Baasha,	Jer 41:9	
captain of the bodyguard **h** put under	Jer 41:10	
the son of Nethaniah **h** done.	Jer 41:11	
So all the people whom Ishmael **h**	Jer 41:14	
the people whom he **h** recovered from	Jer 41:16	
after he **h** struck down Gedaliah	Jer 41:16	
he **h** brought back from Gibeon.	Jer 41:16	
the son of Nethaniah **h** struck down	Jer 41:18	
Babylon **h** appointed over the land.	Jer 41:18	
whom the LORD their God **h** sent,	Jer 43:1	
h finished telling all the people	Jer 43:1	
remnant of Judah who **h** returned	Jer 43:5	
to which they **h** been driven away,	Jer 43:5	
captain of the bodyguard **h** left with	Jer 43:6	
other gods whom they **h** not known,	Jer 44:3	
for *then* we **h** plenty of food and	Jer 44:17	
when he **h** written down these words	Jer 45:1	
destroy *only* until they **h** enough.	Jer 49:9	
like all that Jehoiakim **h** done.	Jer 52:2	
the deserters who **h** deserted to	Jer 52:15	
which King Solomon **h** made for the	Jer 52:20	
h his meals in the king's presence	Jer 52:33	398
were finished For our end **h** come.	La 4:18	
in their pits, Of whom we **h** said,	La 4:20	
they **h** human form.	Ezk 1:5	
them **h** four faces and four wings.	Ezk 1:6	
faces, *each* **h** the face of a man;	Ezk 1:10	
all four **h** the face of a lion on	Ezk 1:10	
all four **h** the face of an eagle.	Ezk 1:10	
each **h** two touching another *being,*	Ezk 1:11	
all four of them **h** the same form,	Ezk 1:16	
each one also **h** two wings covering	Ezk 1:23	
the cherub on which it **h** been,	Ezk 9:3	
four of them **h** the same likeness,	Ezk 10:10	
And each one **h** four faces.	Ezk 10:14	
Each one **h** four faces and each one	Ezk 10:21	
I **h** seen by the river Chebar.	Ezk 10:22	
"Though I **h** removed them far away	Ezk 11:16	
and though I **h** scattered them	Ezk 11:16	
countries where they **h** gone."	Ezk 11:16	
the vision that I **h** seen left me.	Ezk 11:24	
things that the LORD **h** shown me.	Ezk 11:25	
I did so, as I **h** been commanded.	Ezk 12:7	
were formed and your hair **h** grown.	Ezk 16:7	
of My silver, which I **h** given you,	Ezk 16:17	
daughters whom you **h** borne to Me and	Ezk 16:20	
she and her daughters **h** arrogance,	Ezk 16:49	1961
transgressions which he **h** committed	Ezk 18:28	
'And it **h** strong branches *fit* for	Ezk 19:11	1961
a land that I **h** selected for them,	Ezk 20:6	

before whose sight I **h** brought them	**Ezk 20:14**	
the land which I **h** given them,	**Ezk 20:15**	
in whose sight I **h** brought them out.	**Ezk 20:22**	
they **h** not observed My ordinances,	**Ezk 20:24**	
but **h** rejected My statutes and	**Ezk 20:24**	
and **h** profaned My sabbaths,	**Ezk 20:24**	
"When I **h** brought them into the	**Ezk 20:28**	
in her youth men **h** lain with her,	**Ezk 23:8**	
I saw that she **h** defiled herself;	**Ezk 23:13**	
when she **h** been defiled by them,	**Ezk 23:17**	
as I **h** become disgusted with her	**Ezk 23:18**	
"For when they **h** slaughtered	**Ezk 23:39**	
you **h** set My incense and My oil.	**Ezk 23:41**	
"You **h** the seal of perfection,	**Ezk 28:12**	
But he and his army **h** no wages	**Ezk 29:18**	1961
that he **h** performed against it."	**Ezk 29:18**	
But **h** he taken warning, he would	**Ezk 33:5**	
h been upon me in the evening,	**Ezk 33:22**	
"Because you have **h** everlasting	**Ezk 35:5**	1961
which they **h** shed on the land,	**Ezk 36:18**	
they **h** defiled it with their	**Ezk 36:18**	
But I **h** concern for My holy name	**Ezk 36:21**	
Israel **h** profaned among the nations	**Ezk 36:21**	
which **h** been a continual waste;	**Ezk 38:8**	
of them **h** the same measurement.	**Ezk 40:10**	
The side pillars also **h** the same	**Ezk 40:10**	
h three guardrooms on each side;	**Ezk 40:21**	
its porches **h** the same measurement	**Ezk 40:21**	1961
and its palm tree ornaments **h**	**Ezk 40:22**	
The inner court **h** a gate	**Ezk 40:23**	
The gate and its porches **h**	**Ezk 40:25**	
and it **h** palm tree ornaments on	**Ezk 40:26**	
court **h** a gate toward the south;	**Ezk 40:27**	
its porches **h** windows all around;	**Ezk 40:29**	
and its stairway **h** eight steps.	**Ezk 40:31**	
its porches **h** windows all around;	**Ezk 40:33**	
and its stairway **h** eight steps.	**Ezk 40:34**	
And the gate **h** windows all around;	**Ezk 40:36**	
and its stairway **h** eight steps.	**Ezk 40:37**	
h a raised platform all around;	**Ezk 41:8**	
and every cherub **h** two faces,	**Ezk 41:18**	
sanctuary each **h** a double door.	**Ezk 41:23**	
Each of the doors **h** two leaves,	**Ezk 41:24**	
were in three stories and **h** no pillars	**Ezk 42:6**	369
Now when he **h** finished measuring	**Ezk 42:15**	
it **h** a wall all around, the length	**Ezk 42:20**	
a sister who has not **h** a husband,	**Ezk 44:25**	1961
not ford, for the water **h** risen,	**Ezk 47:5**	
Now when I **h** returned, behold, on	**Ezk 47:7**	
and who **h** ability for serving in	**Da 1:4**	
officials **h** appointed over Daniel,	**Da 1:11**	
fatter than all the youths who **h** been	**Da 1:15**	
h specified for presenting them,	**Da 1:18**	
Nebuchadnezzar **h** dreams;	**Da 2:1**	2492b
I **h** a dream and my spirit is	**Da 2:3**	2492b
who **h** gone forth to slay the wise	**Da 2:14**	
whom the king **h** appointed to	**Da 2:24**	
Nebuchadnezzar the king **h** set up.	**Da 3:2**	
Nebuchadnezzar the king **h** set up;	**Da 3:3**	
that Nebuchadnezzar **h** set up.	**Da 3:3**	
Nebuchadnezzar the king **h** set up.	**Da 3:7**	
furnace **h** been made extremely hot,	**Da 3:22**	
fire **h** no effect on the bodies of these	**Da 3:27**	7981
nor the **h** smell of fire *even* come	**Da 3:27**	
until his hair **h** grown like	**Da 4:33**	
his father **h** taken out of the temple	**Da 5:2**	
h been taken out of the temple,	**Da 5:3**	
he *now* **h** authority as the third *ruler*	**Da 5:29**	1934
he **h** windows open toward Jerusalem);	**Da 6:10**	
as he **h** been doing previously.	**Da 6:10**	
he **h** come near the den to Daniel,	**Da 6:20**	
because he **h** trusted in his God.	**Da 6:23**	
who **h** maliciously accused Daniel,	**Da 6:24**	
and they **h** not reached the bottom	**Da 6:24**	
lion and **h** *the* wings of an eagle.	**Da 7:4**	
which **h** on its back four wings of	**Da 7:6**	
the beast also **h** four heads, and	**Da 7:6**	
and it **h** large iron teeth.	**Da 7:7**	
before it, and it **h** ten horns.	**Da 7:7**	
that horn which **h** eyes and a mouth	**Da 7:20**	
a ram which **h** two horns was	**Da 8:3**	
and the goat **h** a conspicuous horn	**Da 8:5**	
to the ram that **h** the two horns,	**Da 8:6**	
which I **h** seen standing in front	**Da 8:6**	
h no strength to withstand him.	**Da 8:7**	1961
When I, Daniel, **h** seen the vision,	**Da 8:15**	
words which He **h** spoken against us	**Da 9:12**	
I **h** seen in the vision previously,	**Da 9:21**	
and **h** an understanding of the vision.	**Da 10:1**	
h been mourning for three entire	**Da 10:2**	
h the appearance of lightning,	**Da 10:6**	
when he **h** spoken this word to me,	**Da 10:11**	
for I **h** been left there with the	**Da 10:13**	
When he **h** spoken to me	**Da 10:15**	
When she **h** weaned Lo-ruhamah, she	**Hos 1:8**	
her who **h** not obtained compassion,	**Hos 2:23**	
As *they* **h** their pasture, they	**Hos 13:6**	
when it **h** finished eating the	**Am 7:2**	
steal *only* until they **h** enough?	**Ob 1:5**	1767
become as if they **h** never existed.	**Ob 1:16**	
But Jonah **h** gone below into the	**Jon 1:5**	
the LORD, because he **h** told them.	**Jon 1:10**	
"For You **h** cast me into the	**Jon 2:3**	
the calamity which He **h** declared He	**Jon 3:10**	
"You **h** compassion on the plant	**Jon 4:10**	2347
falsehood **H** told lies *and said,*	**Mi 2:11**	
as the LORD their God **h** sent him.	**Hg 1:12**	
and they **h** wings like the wings of	**Zch 5:9**	
Now *the town of* Bethel **h** sent	**Zch 7:2**	
words which the LORD of hosts **h** sent	**Zch 7:12**	
I have **h** compassion on them;	**Zch 10:6**	7355
as though I **h** not rejected them,	**Zch 10:6**	
I **h** made with all the peoples.	**Zch 11:10**	
father of Solomon by Bathsheba who **h**	**Mt 1:6**	
Mary **h** been betrothed to Joseph,	**Mt 1:18**	
But when he **h** considered this,	**Mt 1:20**	
which they **h** seen in the east,	**Mt 2:9**	
Now when they **h** gone, behold,	**Mt 2:13**	
This was to fulfill what **h** been	**Mt 2:15**	
he **h** been tricked by the magi,	**Mt 2:16**	
he **h** determined from the magi.	**Mt 2:16**	
Then what **h** been spoken through	**Mt 2:17**	
h a garment of camel's hair and	**Mt 3:4**	*2192*
And after He **h** fasted forty days	**Mt 4:2**	
and **h** Him stand on the pinnacle	**Mt 4:5**	
John **h** been taken into custody,	**Mt 4:12**	
it **h** been founded on the rock.	**Mt 7:25**	
When Jesus **h** finished these words,	**Mt 7:28**	
including what **h** happened to	**Mt 8:33**	*3588*
who **h** given such authority to men.	**Mt 9:8**	
a woman who **h** been suffering from	**Mt 9:20**	
But when the crowd **h** been sent out,	**Mt 9:25**	
Jesus **h** finished giving instructions to	**Mt 11:1**	
For if the miracles **h** occurred in	**Mt 11:21**	
for if the miracles **h** occurred in	**Mt 11:23**	
if you **h** known what this means,	**Mt 12:7**	
because they **h** no depth of soil.	**Mt 13:5**	*2192*
"But when the sun **h** risen,	**Mt 13:6**	
and because they **h** no root,	**Mt 13:6**	*2192*
he went and sold all that he **h** and	**Mt 13:46**	*2192*
Jesus **h** finished these parables,	**Mt 13:53**	
For when Herod **h** John arrested, he	**Mt 14:3**	
For John **h** been saying to him,	**Mt 14:4**	
and **h** John beheaded in the prison.	**Mt 14:10**	
He **h** sent the crowds away,	**Mt 14:23**	
When they **h** crossed over, they	**Mt 14:34**	
h forgotten to bring *any* bread.	**Mt 16:5**	
He **h** spoken to them about John the	**Mt 17:13**	
"When he **h** begun to settle *them,*	**Mt 18:24**	
and children and all that he **h**,	**Mt 18:25**	*2192*
fellow slaves saw what **h** happened,	**Mt 18:31**	
to their lord all that **h** happened.	**Mt 18:31**	
have **h** mercy on your fellow slave,	**Mt 18:33**	*1653*
same way that I **h** mercy on you?'	**Mt 18:33**	*1653*
When Jesus **h** finished these words,	**Mt 19:1**	
"When he **h** agreed with the	**Mt 20:2**	
When they **h** approached	**Mt 21:1**	
Jerusalem and **h** come to Bethphage,	**Mt 21:1**	
did just as Jesus **h** instructed them,	**Mt 21:6**	
When He **h** entered Jerusalem,	**Mt 21:10**	
wonderful things that He **h** done,	**Mt 21:15**	
A man **h** two sons, and he came to	**Mt 21:28**	*2192*
who **h** been invited to the wedding	**Mt 22:3**	
For they all **h** *married* her."	**Mt 22:28**	*2192*
Jesus **h** silenced the Sadducees,	**Mt 22:34**	
'If we **h** been *living* in the days	**Mt 23:30**	
those days **h** been cut short,	**Mt 24:22**	
that if the head of the house **h**	**Mt 24:43**	
"Immediately the one who **h**	**Mt 25:16**	
"In the same manner the one who **h**	**Mt 25:17**	
"The one who **h** received the	**Mt 25:20**	
"Also the one who **h** *received*	**Mt 25:22**	
"And the one also who **h** received	**Mt 25:24**	
Jesus **h** finished all these words,	**Mt 26:1**	
did as Jesus **h** directed them;	**Mt 26:19**	
that man if he **h** not been born."	**Mt 26:24**	
He **h** taken a cup and given thanks,	**Mt 26:27**	
Those who **h** seized Jesus led	**Mt 26:57**	
When he **h** gone out to the gateway,	**Mt 26:71**	
the word which Jesus **h** said,	**Mt 26:75**	
when Judas, who **h** betrayed Him,	**Mt 27:3**	
Him, saw that He **h** been condemned,	**Mt 27:3**	
THE PRICE OF THE ONE WHOSE PRICE **H**	**Mt 27:9**	
of envy they **h** handed Him over.	**Mt 27:18**	
After they **h** mocked Him, they	**Mt 27:31**	
And when they **h** crucified Him,	**Mt 27:35**	
The robbers who **h** been	**Mt 27:44**	
who **h** fallen asleep were raised;	**Mt 27:52**	
who **h** followed Jesus from Galilee	**Mt 27:55**	
who himself **h** also become a	**Mt 27:57**	
which he **h** hewn out in the rock;	**Mt 27:60**	
a severe earthquake **h** occurred,	**Mt 28:2**	
chief priests all that **h** happened.	**Mt 28:11**	
And when they **h** assembled with the	**Mt 28:12**	
and did as they **h** been instructed;	**Mt 28:15**	
mountain which Jesus **h** designated.	**Mt 28:16**	
John **h** been taken into custody,	**Mk 1:14**	
came, after the sun **h** set,	**Mk 1:32**	
whole city **h** gathered at the door.	**Mk 1:33**	
When He **h** come back to	**Mk 2:1**	
and when they **h** dug an opening,	**Mk 2:4**	
for He **h** healed many, with the	**Mk 3:10**	
those who **h** afflictions pressed around	**Mk 3:10**	*2192*
up because it **h** no depth of soil.	**Mk 4:5**	*2192*
"And after the sun **h** risen	**Mk 4:6**	
and because it **h** no root, it	**Mk 4:6**	*2192*
he **h** his dwelling among the tombs.	**Mk 5:3**	*2192*
because he **h** often been bound with	**Mk 5:4**	
chains **h** been torn apart by him and	**Mk 5:4**	
For He **h** been saying to him,	**Mk 5:8**	
see what it was that **h** happened.	**Mk 5:14**	
the man who **h** been demon-possessed	**Mk 5:15**	
very man who **h** had the "legion";	**Mk 5:15**	
very man who had **h** the "legion";	**Mk 5:15**	*2192*
Those who **h** seen it described	**Mk 5:16**	
described to them how it **h** happened	**Mk 5:16**	
the man who **h** been demon-possessed	**Mk 5:18**	
you, and *how* He **h** mercy on you."	**Mk 5:19**	*1653*
great things Jesus **h** done for him;	**Mk 5:20**	
When Jesus **h** crossed over	**Mk 5:21**	
A woman who **h** had a hemorrhage	**Mk 5:25**	
h a hemorrhage for twelve years,	**Mk 5:25**	*1510*
and **h** endured much at the hands of	**Mk 5:26**	
and **h** spent all that she had and	**Mk 5:26**	
she **h** and was not helped at all,	**Mk 5:26**	*3844*
at all, but rather **h** grown worse	**Mk 5:26**	
proceeding from Him **h** gone forth,	**Mk 5:30**	
to see the woman who **h** done this.	**Mk 5:32**	
aware of what **h** happened to her,	**Mk 5:33**	
for His name **h** become well known;	**Mk 6:14**	
For Herod himself **h** sent and had	**Mk 6:17**	
For Herod himself had sent and **h**	**Mk 6:17**	
Philip, because he **h** married her.	**Mk 6:17**	
For John **h** been saying to Herod,	**Mk 6:18**	
Herodias **h** a grudge against	**Mk 6:19**	*1758*
and **h** him beheaded in the prison,	**Mk 6:27**	
all that they **h** done and taught.	**Mk 6:30**	
for they **h** not gained any insight	**Mk 6:52**	
When they **h** crossed over they	**Mk 6:53**	
when they **h** come from Jerusalem,	**Mk 7:1**	
and **h** seen that some of His	**Mk 7:2**	
When he **h** left the crowd *and*	**Mk 7:17**	
And when He **h** entered a house, He	**Mk 7:24**	
daughter **h** an unclean spirit	**Mk 7:25**	*2192*
and they **h** nothing to eat,	**Mk 8:1**	*2192*
They also **h** a few small fish;	**Mk 8:7**	*2192*
and after He **h** blessed them, He	**Mk 8:7**	
And they **h** forgotten to take bread,	**Mk 8:14**	
the fact that they **h** no bread.	**Mk 8:16**	*2192*
relate to anyone what they **h** seen,	**Mk 9:9**	
for on the way they **h** discussed	**Mk 9:34**	
neck, he **h** been cast into the sea.	**Mk 9:42**	
to them just as Jesus **h** told *them,*	**Mk 11:6**	
which they **h** cut from the fields.	**Mk 11:8**	
when they **h** left Bethany,	**Mk 11:12**	
"He **h** one more *to send,* a beloved	**Mk 12:6**	*2192*
For all seven **h** married her."	**Mk 12:23**	*2192*
that He **h** answered them well,	**Mk 12:28**	
that he **h** answered intelligently,	**Mk 12:34**	
she owned, all she **h** to live on."	**Mk 12:44**	
the Lord **h** shortened *those* days,	**Mk 13:20**	
found *it* just as He **h** told them;	**Mk 14:16**	
that man if he **h** not been born."	**Mk 14:21**	
And when He **h** taken a cup *and*	**Mk 14:23**	
Him **h** given them a signal,	**Mk 14:44**	
h followed Him at a distance,	**Mk 14:54**	
Jesus **h** made the remark to him,	**Mk 14:72**	
The man named Barabbas **h** been	**Mk 15:7**	
who **h** committed murder in the	**Mk 15:7**	
to do as he **h** been accustomed to do	**Mk 15:8**	
the chief priests **h** handed Him over	**Mk 15:10**	
After they **h** mocked Him, they	**Mk 15:20**	
When evening **h** already come,	**Mk 15:42**	
which **h** been hewn out in the rock;	**Mk 15:46**	
to the tomb when the sun **h** risen.	**Mk 16:2**	
that the stone **h** been rolled away,	**Mk 16:4**	
and astonishment **h** gripped them;	**Mk 16:8**	
[Now after He **h** risen early on the	**Mk 16:9**	
whom He **h** cast out seven demons.	**Mk 16:9**	
to those who **h** been with Him,	**Mk 16:10**	
was alive and **h** been seen by her,	**Mk 16:11**	
because they **h** not believed those	**Mk 16:14**	
who **h** seen Him after He had risen.	**Mk 16:14**	
who had seen Him after He **h** risen.	**Mk 16:14**	
the Lord Jesus **h** spoken to them,	**Mk 16:19**	
and he **h** a wife from the daughters	**Lk 1:5**	
But they **h** no child, because	**Lk 1:7**	*1510*
he **h** seen a vision in the temple;	**Lk 1:22**	
be a fulfillment of what **h** been spoken	**Lk 1:45**	
"For He has **h** regard for the	**Lk 1:48**	*1914*
Now the time **h** come for Elizabeth	**Lk 1:57**	
the Lord **h** displayed His great mercy	**Lk 1:58**	
the angels **h** gone away from them	**Lk 2:15**	
When they **h** seen this, they	**Lk 2:17**	
the statement which **h** been told them	**Lk 2:17**	
all that they **h** heard and seen,	**Lk 2:20**	
seen, just as **h** been told them.	**Lk 2:20**	
And when eight days **h** passed, before	**Lk 2:21**	
And it **h** been revealed to him by	**Lk 2:26**	
before he **h** seen the Lord's Christ.	**Lk 2:26**	
She was advanced in years and **h** lived	**Lk 2:36**	
When they **h** performed	**Lk 2:39**	
I **h** to be in My Father's *house?*"	**Lk 2:49**	*1163*
statement which He **h** made to them.	**Lk 2:50**	
wicked things which Herod **h** done,	**Lk 3:19**	
and when they **h** ended, He became	**Lk 4:2**	
h Him stand on the pinnacle of the	**Lk 4:9**	
devil **h** finished every temptation,	**Lk 4:13**	
where He **h** been brought up;	**Lk 4:16**	
on which their city **h** been built,	**Lk 4:29**	
And when the demon **h** thrown him	**Lk 4:35**	
all those who **h** any *who were* sick	**Lk 4:40**	*2192*
fishermen **h** gotten out of them and	**Lk 5:2**	
When He **h** finished speaking,	**Lk 5:4**	
When they **h** done this, they	**Lk 5:6**	
For amazement **h** seized him and all	**Lk 5:9**	
catch of fish which they **h** taken;	**Lk 5:9**	
h brought their boats to land,	**Lk 5:11**	
who **h** come from every village of	**Lk 5:17**	
picked up what he **h** been lying on,	**Lk 5:25**	
who **h** come to hear Him and to be	**Lk 6:18**	
it, because it **h** been well built.	**Lk 6:48**	
When He **h** completed all His	**Lk 7:1**	
When those who **h** been sent	**Lk 7:10**	
the messengers of John **h** left,	**Lk 7:24**	
who **h** invited Him saw this,	**Lk 7:39**	
A moneylender **h** two debtors:	**Lk 7:41**	*1510*

women who **h** been healed of evil	Lk 8:2	
from whom seven demons **h** gone out,	Lk 8:2	
away, because it **h** no moisture.	Lk 8:6	2192
and who **h** not put on any clothing	Lk 8:27	
For He **h** commanded the	Lk 8:29	
For it **h** seized him many times;	Lk 8:29	
for many demons **h** entered him.	Lk 8:30	
the herdsmen saw what **h** happened,	Lk 8:34	
went out to see what **h** happened;	Lk 8:35	
from whom the demons **h** gone out,	Lk 8:35	
Those who **h** seen it reported	Lk 8:36	
demon-possessed **h** been made well.	Lk 8:36	
man from whom the demons **h** gone	Lk 8:38	
great things Jesus **h** done for him.	Lk 8:39	
they **h** all been waiting for Him.	Lk 8:40	
for he **h** an only daughter, about	Lk 8:42	1510
h a hemorrhage for twelve years,	Lk 8:43	1722
that power **h** gone out of Me."	Lk 8:46	
saw that she **h** not escaped notice,	Lk 8:47	
the reason why she **h** touched Him,	Lk 8:47	
how she **h** been immediately healed.	Lk 8:47	
at Him, knowing that she **h** died.	Lk 8:53	
to tell no one what **h** happened	Lk 8:56	
that John **h** risen from the dead,	Lk 9:7	
by some that Elijah **h** appeared,	Lk 9:8	
the prophets of old **h** risen again.	Lk 9:8	
"I myself **h** John beheaded;	Lk 9:9	
to Him of all that they **h** done.	Lk 9:10	
those who **h** need of healing.	Lk 9:11	2192
did so, and **h** them all sit down.	Lk 9:15	
they **h** left over were picked up,	Lk 9:17	
h been overcome with sleep;	Lk 9:32	
And when the voice **h** spoken,	Lk 9:36	
of the things which they **h** seen.	Lk 9:36	
For if the miracles **h** been	Lk 10:13	
She **h** a sister called Mary,	Lk 10:39	1510
place, after He **h** finished,	Lk 11:1	
when the demon **h** gone out,	Lk 11:14	
his armor on which he **h** relied and	Lk 11:22	
Now when He **h** spoken, a Pharisee	Lk 11:37	
he was surprised that He **h** not	Lk 11:38	
thousands of people **h** gathered	Lk 12:1	
that if the head of the house **h**	Lk 12:39	
h mixed with their sacrifices	Lk 13:1	
"A man **h** a fig tree which	Lk 13:6	2192
h been planted in his vineyard;	Lk 13:6	
a woman who for eighteen years **h**	Lk 13:11	
h a sickness caused by a spirit;	Lk 13:11	2192
Jesus **h** healed on the Sabbath,	Lk 13:14	
He noticed how they **h** been picking	Lk 14:7	
say to the one who **h** invited Him,	Lk 14:12	
say to those who **h** been invited,	Lk 14:17	
found the coin which I **h** lost!'	Lk 15:9	
"A man **h** two sons	Lk 15:11	2192
"Now when he **h** spent everything,	Lk 15:14	
'But we **h** to celebrate and rejoice,	Lk 15:32	1163
rich man who **h** a manager,	Lk 16:1	2192
because he **h** acted shrewdly;	Lk 16:8	
you **h** faith like a mustard seed,	Lk 17:6	2192
when he saw that he **h** been healed,	Lk 17:15	
But when he **h** heard these things,	Lk 18:23	
to whom he **h** given the money,	Lk 19:15	
know what business they **h** done.	Lk 19:15	
After He **h** said these things,	Lk 19:28	
found it just as He **h** told them.	Lk 19:32	
the miracles which they **h** seen,	Lk 19:37	
"If you **h** known in this day, even	Lk 19:42	
For all seven **h** married her."	Lk 20:33	2192
in all that she **h** to live on."	Lk 21:4	2192
Passover *lamb* **h** to be sacrificed.	Lk 22:7	1163
everything just as He **h** told them;	Lk 22:13	
When the hour **h** come, He reclined	Lk 22:14	
He **h** taken a cup *and* given thanks,	Lk 22:17	
And when He **h** taken *some* bread	Lk 22:19	
took the cup after they **h** eaten,	Lk 22:20	
and elders who **h** come against Him,	Lk 22:52	
After they **h** kindled a fire in	Lk 22:55	
courtyard and **h** sat down together,	Lk 22:55	
After about an hour **h** passed,	Lk 22:59	
of the Lord, how He **h** told him,	Lk 22:61	
for he **h** wanted to see Him for a	Lk 23:8	1510
because he **h** been hearing about	Lk 23:8	
for before they **h** been enemies	Lk 23:12	
(He was one who **h** been thrown into	Lk 23:19	
who **h** been thrown into prison for	Lk 23:25	
the centurion saw what **h** happened,	Lk 23:47	
they observed what **h** happened,	Lk 23:48	
(he **h** not consented to their plan	Lk 23:51	
rock, where no one **h** ever lain.	Lk 23:53	
Now the women who **h** come with Him	Lk 23:55	
the spices which they **h** prepared.	Lk 24:1	
marveling at what **h** happened.	Lk 24:12	
these things which **h** taken place.	Lk 24:14	
h also seen a vision of angels who	Lk 24:23	
exactly as the women also **h** said;	Lk 24:24	
When He **h** reclined *at the table*	Lk 24:30	
And when He **h** said this, He	Lk 24:40	
h been sent from the Pharisees.	Jn 1:24	
the water which **h** become wine,	Jn 2:9	
who **h** drawn the water knew),	Jn 2:9	
and the word which Jesus **h** spoken.	Jn 2:22	
for John **h** not yet been thrown	Jn 3:24	
the Pharisees **h** heard that Jesus was	Jn 4:1	
And He **h** to pass through Samaria.	Jn 4:4	1163
For His disciples **h** gone away into	Jn 4:8	
for you have **h** five husbands, and	Jn 4:18	2192
He **h** been speaking with a woman,	Jn 4:27	
where He **h** made the water wine.	Jn 4:46	
When he heard that Jesus **h** come	Jn 4:47	2240
when He **h** come out of Judea into	Jn 4:54	
who **h** been ill for thirty-eight	Jn 5:5	
and knew that he **h** already been a	Jn 5:6	
for Jesus **h** slipped away while	Jn 5:13	
it was Jesus who **h** made him well.	Jn 5:15	
left over by those who **h** eaten.	Jn 6:13	
saw the sign which He **h** performed,	Jn 6:14	
It **h** already become dark, and	Jn 6:17	
and Jesus **h** not yet come to them.	Jn 6:17	
Then, when they **h** rowed about	Jn 6:19	
and that Jesus **h** not entered with	Jn 6:22	
His disciples **h** gone away alone.	Jn 6:22	
after the Lord **h** given thanks.	Jn 6:23	
brothers **h** gone up to the feast,	Jn 7:10	
because His hour **h** not yet come.	Jn 7:30	
because His hour **h** not yet come.	Jn 8:20	
that He **h** been speaking to them	Jn 8:27	
to those Jews who **h** believed Him,	Jn 8:31	
When He **h** said this, He spat on	Jn 9:6	
it of him, that he **h** been blind	Jn 9:18	
been blind and **h** received sight,	Jn 9:18	
very one who **h** received his sight,	Jn 9:18	
for the Jews **h** already agreed that	Jn 9:22	
called the man who **h** been blind,	Jn 9:24	
heard that they **h** put him out,	Jn 9:35	
which He **h** been saying to them.	Jn 10:6	
Now Jesus **h** spoken of his death,	Jn 11:13	
He found that he **h** already been in	Jn 11:17	
Jews **h** come to Martha and Mary,	Jn 11:19	
"Lord, if You **h** been here, my	Jn 11:21	
When she **h** said this, she went	Jn 11:28	
h not yet come into the village,	Jn 11:30	
"Lord, if You **h** been here, my	Jn 11:32	
When He **h** said these things,	Jn 11:43	
man who **h** died came forth, bound	Jn 11:44	
to Mary, and saw what He **h** done,	Jn 11:45	
the things which Jesus **h** done.	Jn 11:46	
Pharisees **h** given orders that if anyone	Jn 11:57	
whom Jesus **h** raised from the dead.	Jn 12:1	
thief, and as he **h** the money box,	Jn 12:6	2192
crowd who **h** come to the feast,	Jn 12:12	
they **h** done these things to Him.	Jn 12:16	
that He **h** performed this sign.	Jn 12:18	
were saying that it **h** thundered	Jn 12:29	
But though He **h** performed so many	Jn 12:37	
Jesus knowing that His hour **h** come	Jn 13:1	
knowing that the Father **h** given	Jn 13:3	
and that He **h** come forth from God	Jn 13:3	
So when He **h** washed their feet,	Jn 13:12	
When Jesus **h** said this, He became	Jn 13:21	
So when He **h** dipped the morsel, He	Jn 13:26	
for what purpose He **h** said this to	Jn 13:28	
because Judas **h** the money box,	Jn 13:29	2192
Therefore when he **h** gone out,	Jn 13:31	
"If you **h** known Me, you would	Jn 14:7	
I **h** not come and spoken to them,	Jn 15:22	
"If I **h** not done among them the	Jn 15:24	
with the glory which I **h** with You	Jn 17:5	2192
When Jesus **h** spoken these words,	Jn 18:1	
for Jesus **h** often met there with	Jn 18:2	
Now Caiaphas was the one who **h**	Jn 18:14	
When He **h** said this, one of	Jn 18:22	
And when he **h** said this, he went	Jn 18:38	
it **h** been given you from above;	Jn 19:11	
when they **h** crucified Jesus,	Jn 19:23	
h already been accomplished,	Jn 19:28	
h received the sour wine,	Jn 19:30	
who **h** first come to Him by night,	Jn 19:39	
in which no one **h** yet been laid.	Jn 19:41	
which **h** been on His head,	Jn 20:7	
who **h** first come to the tomb	Jn 20:8	
the body of Jesus **h** been lying.	Jn 20:12	
When she **h** said this, she turned	Jn 20:14	
He **h** said these things to her.	Jn 20:18	
And when He **h** said this, He showed	Jn 20:20	
And when He **h** said this, He	Jn 20:22	
So when they **h** finished breakfast,	Jn 21:15	
And when He **h** spoken this, He said	Jn 21:19	
the one who also **h** leaned back on	Jn 21:20	
after He **h** by the Holy Spirit	Ac 1:2	
to the apostles whom He **h** chosen.	Ac 1:2	
for what the Father **h** promised,	Ac 1:4	
So when they **h** come together,	Ac 1:6	
And after He **h** said these things,	Ac 1:9	
When they **h** entered *the city,*	Ac 1:13	
the Scripture **h** to be fulfilled,	Ac 1:16	1163
When the day of Pentecost **h** come,	Ac 2:1	
was a prophet and knew that GOD **H**	Ac 2:30	
those who **h** received his word were	Ac 2:41	
who **h** believed were together and	Ac 2:44	
and **h** all things in common;	Ac 2:44	2192
And a man who **h** been lame	Ac 3:2	
at what **h** happened to him.	Ac 3:10	
power or piety we **h** made him walk?	Ac 3:12	
when he **h** decided to release Him.	Ac 3:13	
who **h** heard the message believed;	Ac 4:4	
they **h** placed them in the center,	Ac 4:7	
man who **h** been healed	Ac 4:14	
they **h** nothing to say in reply.	Ac 4:14	2192
But when they **h** ordered them to leave	Ac 4:15	
And when they **h** summoned them,	Ac 4:18	
they **h** threatened them further,	Ac 4:21	
God for what **h** happened;	Ac 4:21	
of healing **h** been performed.	Ac 4:22	
When they **h** been released,	Ac 4:23	
and the elders **h** said to them.	Ac 4:23	
And when they **h** prayed, the place	Ac 4:31	
the place where they **h** gathered	Ac 4:31	
to each as any **h** need.	Ac 4:35	2192
in, not knowing what **h** happened.	Ac 5:7	
but when we **h** opened up, we found	Ac 5:23	
When they **h** brought them, they	Ac 5:27	
whom you **h** put to death by hanging	Ac 5:30	
rejoicing that they **h** been	Ac 5:41	
God **h** him move to this country in	Ac 7:4	
and *yet,* even when he **h** no child,	Ac 7:5	
tomb which Abraham **h** purchased	Ac 7:16	
which God **h** assured to Abraham,	Ac 7:17	
"And after he **h** been set	Ac 7:21	
"After forty years **h** passed,	Ac 7:30	
"Our fathers **h** the tabernacle of	Ac 7:44	1510
to the pattern which he **h** seen.	Ac 7:44	
They killed those who **h**	Ac 7:52	
they **h** driven him out of the city,	Ac 7:58	
those who **h** been scattered went	Ac 8:4	
of many who **h** unclean spirits,	Ac 8:7	2192
and many who **h** been paralyzed and	Ac 8:7	
he **h** for a long time astonished them	Ac 8:11	
h received the word of God,	Ac 8:14	
For He **h** not yet fallen upon any	Ac 8:16	
they **h** simply been baptized in the	Ac 8:16	
when they **h** solemnly testified and	Ac 8:25	
he **h** come to Jerusalem to worship,	Ac 8:27	
and *who* **h** come here for the	Ac 9:21	
When many days **h** elapsed,	Ac 9:23	
he **h** seen the Lord on the road,	Ac 9:27	
road, and that He **h** talked to him,	Ac 9:27	
and how at Damascus he **h** spoken	Ac 9:27	
who **h** been bedridden eight years,	Ac 9:33	
and when they **h** washed her body,	Ac 9:37	
of God who **h** *just* come in	Ac 10:3	
was speaking to him **h** left,	Ac 10:7	
he **h** explained everything to them,	Ac 10:8	
vision which he **h** seen might be,	Ac 10:17	
men who **h** been sent by Cornelius,	Ac 10:17	
and **h** called together his	Ac 10:24	
Holy Spirit **h** been poured out on	Ac 10:45	
also **h** received the word of God.	Ac 11:1	
and when I **h** fixed my gaze on it	Ac 11:6	
how he **h** seen the angel standing	Ac 11:13	
and when he **h** found him, he	Ac 11:26	
that any of the disciples **h** means,	Ac 11:29	2141
And he **h** James the brother of John	Ac 12:2	
When he **h** seized him, he put	Ac 12:4	
When they **h** passed the first	Ac 12:10	
and when they **h** opened *the door*	Ac 12:16	
Lord **h** led him out of the prison.	Ac 12:17	
When Herod **h** searched for him	Ac 12:19	
for him and **h** not found him,	Ac 12:19	
they **h** fulfilled their mission,	Ac 12:25	
and Manaen who **h** been brought up	Ac 13:1	
when they **h** fasted and prayed and	Ac 13:3	
they also **h** John as their helper.	Ac 13:5	2192
When they **h** gone through the	Ac 13:6	
when he saw what **h** happened	Ac 13:12	
When He **h** destroyed seven nations	Ac 13:19	
"After He **h** removed him, He	Ac 13:22	
after John **h** proclaimed before His	Ac 13:24	
"When they **h** carried out all	Ac 13:29	
after he **h** served the purpose of	Ac 13:36	
meeting of the synagogue **h** broken	Ac 13:43	
and as many as **h** been appointed to	Ac 13:48	
At Lystra a man was sitting who **h** no	Ac 14:8	
mother's womb, who **h** never walked.	Ac 14:8	
when he **h** fixed his gaze on him	Ac 14:9	
and **h** seen that he had faith to be	Ac 14:9	
that he **h** faith to be made well,	Ac 14:9	2192
crowds saw what Paul **h** done,	Ac 14:11	
After they **h** preached the	Ac 14:21	
city and **h** made many disciples,	Ac 14:21	
When they **h** appointed elders	Ac 14:23	
the Lord in whom they **h** believed.	Ac 14:23	
they **h** spoken the word in Perga,	Ac 14:25	
from which they **h** been commended	Ac 14:26	
the work that they **h** accomplished.	Ac 14:26	
When they **h** arrived and	Ac 14:27	
things that God **h** done with them	Ac 14:27	
how He **h** opened a door of faith to	Ac 14:27	
Paul and Barnabas **h** great dissension	Ac 15:2	1096
all that God **h** done with them.	Ac 15:4	
of the Pharisees who **h** believed stood	Ac 15:5	
After there **h** been much debate,	Ac 15:7	
what signs and wonders God **h** done	Ac 15:12	
After they **h** stopped speaking,	Ac 15:13	
When they **h** read it, they	Ac 15:31	
After they **h** spent time	Ac 15:33	
to those who **h** sent them out.	Ac 15:33	
who **h** deserted them in Pamphylia	Ac 15:38	
and **h** not gone with them to the work	Ac 15:38	
which **h** been decided upon by the	Ac 16:4	
When he **h** seen the vision,	Ac 16:10	
concluding that God **h** called us to	Ac 16:10	
to the women who **h** assembled.	Ac 16:13	
and her household **h** been baptized,	Ac 16:15	
and when they **h** brought them to	Ac 16:20	
When they **h** struck them	Ac 16:23	
that the prisoners **h** escaped.	Ac 16:27	
and when they **h** brought them out,	Ac 16:39	
Now when they **h** traveled through	Ac 17:1	
Christ **h** to suffer and rise again from	Ac 17:3	1163
And when they **h** received a pledge	Ac 17:9	
the word of God **h** been proclaimed	Ac 17:13	
because Claudius **h** commanded all	Ac 18:2	
In Cenchrea he **h** his hair cut, for	Ac 18:18	
When he **h** landed at Caesarea,	Ac 18:22	
This man **h** been instructed in the	Ac 18:25	
and when he **h** arrived, he greatly	Ac 18:27	
who **h** believed through grace,	Ac 18:27	

Paul **h** laid his hands upon them, **Ac 19:6**
name over those who **h** the evil spirits **Ac 19:13** *2192*
those who **h** believed kept coming, **Ac 19:18**
after he **h** passed through Macedonia **Ac 19:21**
what reason they **h** come together. **Ac 19:32**
since the Jews **h** put him forward; **Ac 19:33**
After the uproar **h** ceased, **Ac 20:1**
when he **h** exhorted them and taken **Ac 20:1**
When he **h** gone through those **Ac 20:2**
and **h** given them much exhortation, **Ac 20:2**
But these **h** gone on ahead and were **Ac 20:5**
When he **h** gone *back* up and **Ac 20:11**
and **h** broken the bread and eaten, **Ac 20:11**
for so he **h** arranged it, **Ac 20:13**
For Paul **h** decided to sail past **Ac 20:16**
And when they **h** come to him, he **Ac 20:18**
When he **h** said these things, **Ac 20:36**
over the word which he **h** spoken, **Ac 20:38**
we **h** parted from them and had set **Ac 21:1**
parted from them and **h** set sail, **Ac 21:1**
h finished the voyage from Tyre, **Ac 21:7**
this man **h** four virgin daughters **Ac 21:9** *1510*
When we **h** heard this, we as **Ac 21:12**
After he **h** greeted them, he **Ac 21:19**
which God **h** done among the Gentiles **Ac 21:19**
For they **h** previously seen **Ac 21:29**
h brought him into the temple. **Ac 21:29**
who he was and what he **h** done. **Ac 21:33**
When he **h** given him permission, **Ac 21:40**
because he **h** put him in chains. **Ac 22:29**
why he **h** been accused by the Jews, **Ac 22:30**
drink until they **h** killed Paul. **Ac 23:12**
When these **h** come to Caesarea **Ac 23:33**
When he **h** read it, he asked **Ac 23:34**
After *Paul* **h** been summoned, **Ac 24:2**
h nodded for him to speak, **Ac 24:10**
But after two years **h** passed, **Ac 24:27**
After he **h** spent not more than **Ac 25:6**
the Jews who **h** come down from **Ac 25:7**
h conferred with his council, **Ac 25:12**
Now when several days **h** elapsed, **Ac 25:13**
"So after they **h** assembled here, **Ac 25:17**
but they *simply* **h** some points of **Ac 25:19** *2192*
"But I found that he **h** committed **Ac 25:25**
I thought to myself that I **h** to do **Ac 26:9** *1163*
we **h** all fallen to the ground, **Ac 26:14**
and when they **h** gone aside, they **Ac 26:31**
if he **h** not appealed to Caesar." **Ac 26:32**
When we **h** sailed through the **Ac 27:5**
When we **h** sailed slowly for a **Ac 27:7**
difficulty **h** arrived off Cnidus, **Ac 27:7**
When considerable time **h** passed **Ac 27:9**
that they **h** attained their purpose, **Ac 27:13**
After they **h** hoisted it up, **Ac 27:17**
h gone a long time without food, **Ac 27:21**
and **h** let down the *ship's* boat **Ac 27:30**
When they **h** eaten enough, they **Ac 27:38**
h been brought safely through, **Ac 28:1**
for because of the rain that **h** set **Ac 28:2**
But when Paul **h** gathered a bundle **Ac 28:3**
But after they **h** waited a long **Ac 28:6**
waited a long time and **h** seen nothing **Ac 28:6**
to see him and after he **h** prayed, **Ac 28:8**
After this **h** happened, the **Ac 28:9**
people on the island who **h** diseases **Ac 28:9** *2192*
which **h** wintered at the island, **Ac 28:11**
and which **h** the Twin Brothers for **Ac 28:11** *3902*
though I **h** done nothing against **Ac 28:17**
"And when they **h** examined me, **Ac 28:18**
not that I **h** any accusation **Ac 28:19** *2192*
When they **h** set a day for Paul, **Ac 28:23**
Paul **h** spoken one *parting* word, **Ac 28:25**
[When he **h** spoken these words, **Ac 28:29**
which he **h** while uncircumcised, **Ro 4:11**
which he **h** while uncircumcised. **Ro 4:12**
to that which **h** been spoken, **Ro 4:18**
assured that what God **h** promised, **Ro 4:21**
even over those who **h** not sinned **Ro 5:14**
coveting if the Law **h** not said, **Ro 7:7**
she **h** conceived *twins* by one man, **Ro 9:10**
h not done anything good or bad, **Ro 9:11**
"UNLESS THE LORD OF SABAOTH **H** LEFT **Ro 9:29**
but as it is written, "THEY WHO **H** **Ro 15:21** *312*
and since I have **h** for many years **Ro 15:23** *2192*
for if they **h** understood it they **1Co 2:8**
boast as if you **h** not received it? **1Co 4:7**
wish that you **h** become kings **1Co 4:8**
so that the one who **h** done **1Co 5:2**
should be as though they **h** none; **1Co 7:29** *2192*
and when He **h** given thanks, He **1Co 11:24**
we **h** the sentence of death within **2Co 1:9** *2192*
I **h** no rest for my spirit, not **2Co 2:13** *2192*
For indeed what **h** glory, in this **2Co 3:10** *1392*
Macedonia our flesh **h** no rest, **2Co 7:5** *2192*
and *this,* not as we **h** expected, **2Co 8:5**
he **h** previously made a beginning, **2Co 8:6**
AND HE WHO *gathered* LITTLE **H** **2Co 8:15** *1641*
But when God, who **h** set me apart **Ga 1:15**
that I might be running, or **h** run, **Ga 2:2**
who **h** sneaked in to spy **Ga 2:4**
seeing that I **h** been entrusted **Ga 2:7**
just as Peter **h** *been* to **Ga 2:7**
the grace that **h** been given to me, **Ga 2:9**
to whom the promise **h** been made. **Ga 3:19**
For if a law **h** been given which **Ga 3:21**
is that sense of blessing you **h**? **Ga 4:15**
written that Abraham **h** two sons, **Ga 4:22** *2192*
He also **h** descended into the lower **Eph 4:9**
you **h** heard that he was sick. **Php 2:26**
of death, but God **h** mercy on him, **Php 2:27** *1653*
When He **h** disarmed the rulers and **Col 2:15**
kind of a reception we **h** with you, **1Th 1:9** *2192*
but after we **h** already suffered **1Th 2:2**
we **h** the boldness in our God to **1Th 2:2** *3955*
you **h** become very dear to us. **1Th 2:8**
He **h** made purification of sins, **Heb 1:3**
him who **h** the power of death, **Heb 2:14** *2192*
He **h** to be made like His brethren **Heb 2:17** *3784*
provoked *Him* when they **h** heard? **Heb 3:16**
have **h** good news preached to us, **Heb 4:2**
and those who formerly **h** good news **Heb 4:6**
For if Joshua **h** given them rest, **Heb 4:8**
the one who **h** the promises. **Heb 7:6** *2192*
first *covenant* **h** been faultless, **Heb 8:7**
first *covenant* **h** regulations of divine **Heb 9:1** *2192*
every commandment **h** been spoken **Heb 9:19**
have **h** consciousness of sins? **Heb 10:2** *2192*
Him faithful who **h** promised. **Heb 11:11**
And indeed if they **h** been thinking **Heb 11:15**
have **h** opportunity to return. **Heb 11:15** *2192*
and he who **h** received the promises **Heb 11:17**
faith Moses, when he **h** grown up, **Heb 11:24**
h been encircled for seven days. **Heb 11:30**
she **h** welcomed the spies in peace. **Heb 11:31**
because God **h** provided something **Heb 11:40**
we **h** earthly fathers to discipline **Heb 12:9** *2192*
you **h** NOT RECEIVED MERCY, but now **1Pe 2:10**
powers **h** been subjected to Him. **1Pe 3:22**
you have **h** from the beginning; **1Jn 2:7** *2192*
for if they **h** been of us, they **1Jn 2:19**
we have **h** from the beginning, **2Jn 1:5** *2192*
I **h** many things to write to you, **3Jn 1:13** *2192*
the first voice which I **h** heard, **Rv 4:1**
h a face like that of a man, **Rv 4:7** *2192*
When He **h** taken the book, the **Rv 5:8**
and he who sat on it **h** a bow; **Rv 6:2** *2192*
he who sat on it **h** a pair of scales **Rv 6:5** *2192*
he who sat on it **h** the name Death; **Rv 6:8**
the souls of those who **h** been slain **Rv 6:9**
testimony which they **h** maintained; **Rv 6:9**
to be killed even as they **h** been, **Rv 6:11**
And the seven angels who **h** the **Rv 8:6** *2192*
which were in the sea and **h** life, **Rv 8:9** *2192*
which **h** fallen to the earth; **Rv 9:1**
h hair like the hair of women, **Rv 9:8** *2192*
They **h** breastplates like **Rv 9:9** *2192*
the sixth angel who **h** the trumpet, **Rv 9:14** *2192*
who **h** been prepared for the hour **Rv 9:15**
the riders **h** breastplates *the color* **Rv 9:17** *2192*
and he **h** in his hand a little book **Rv 10:2** *2192*
and when he **h** cried out, the seven **Rv 10:3**
seven peals of thunder **h** spoken, **Rv 10:4**
and when I **h** eaten it, my stomach **Rv 10:10**
she **h** a place prepared by God, **Rv 12:6** *2192*
his heads as if it **h** been slain, **Rv 13:3**
and he **h** two horns like a lamb and **Rv 13:11** *2192*
beast who **h** the wound of the sword **Rv 13:14** *2192*
h been purchased from the earth. **Rv 14:3**
and he also **h** a sharp sickle. **Rv 14:17** *2192*
to him who **h** the sharp sickle, **Rv 14:18** *2192*
seven angels who **h** seven plagues, **Rv 15:1** *2192*
and those who **h** been **Rv 15:2**
and the seven angels who **h** the **Rv 15:6** *2192*
the people who **h** the mark of the beast **Rv 16:2** *2192*
such as there **h** not been since man **Rv 16:18**
Then one of the seven angels who **h** **Rv 17:1** *2192*
in which all who **h** ships at sea **Rv 18:19** *2192*
by which he deceived those who **h** **Rv 19:20**
souls of those who **h** been beheaded **Rv 20:4**
and those who **h** not worshiped the **Rv 20:4**
and **h** not received the mark on **Rv 20:4**
Then one of the seven angels who **h** **Rv 21:9** *2192*
It **h** a great and high wall, with **Rv 21:12** *2192*
city **h** twelve foundation stones, **Rv 21:14** *2192*
The one who spoke with me **h** a **Rv 21:15** *2192*

HADAD

H and Tema, Jetur, Naphish and **Gn 25:15** 2301
died, and **H** the son of Bedad, **Gn 36:35** 1908
Then **H** died, and Samlah of **Gn 36:36** 1908
to Solomon, **H** the Edomite; **1Ki 11:14** 1908
that **H** fled to Egypt, he and **1Ki 11:17** 1908
with him, while **H** *was* a young boy. **1Ki 11:17** 1908
Now **H** found great favor before **1Ki 11:19** 1908
But when **H** heard in Egypt that **1Ki 11:21** 1908
army was dead, **H** said to Pharaoh, **1Ki 11:21** 1908
along with the evil that **H** *did;* **1Ki 11:25** 1908
Mishma, Dumah, Massa, **H**, **1Ch 1:30** 2301
Husham died, **H** the son of Bedad, **1Ch 1:46** 1908
When **H** died, Samlah of Masrekah **1Ch 1:47** 1908
died, **H** became king in his place; **1Ch 1:50** 1908
H died. Now the chiefs of Edom were **1Ch 1:51** 1908

HADADEZER

Then David defeated **H**, **2Sa 8:3** 1909
of Damascus came to help **H**, **2Sa 8:5** 1909
were carried by the servants of **H** and **2Sa 8:7** 1909
and from Berothai, cities of **H**, **2Sa 8:8** 1909
had defeated all the army of **H**, **2Sa 8:9** 1909
fought against **H** and defeated him; **2Sa 8:10** 1909
for **H** had been at war with Toi. **2Sa 8:10** 1909
Amalek, and from the spoil of **H**, **2Sa 8:12** 1909
And **H** sent and brought out the **2Sa 10:16** 1909
the commander of the army of **H** **2Sa 10:16** 1909
When all the kings, servants of **H**, **2Sa 10:19** 1909
from his lord **H** king of Zobah. **1Ki 11:23** 1909
David also defeated **H** king of **1Ch 18:3** 1909
came to help **H** king of Zobah, **1Ch 18:5** 1909
were carried by the servants of **H** and **1Ch 18:7** 1909
Tibhath and from Cun, cities of **H**, **1Ch 18:8** 1909
all the army of **H** king of Zobah, **1Ch 18:9** 1909
against **H** and had defeated him; **1Ch 18:10** 1909
for **H** had been at war with Tou. **1Ch 18:10** 1909
of the army of **H** leading them. **1Ch 19:16** 1909
So when the servants of **H** saw that **1Ch 19:19** 1909

HADADRIMMON

of **H** in the plain of Megiddo. **Zch 12:11** 1910

HADAR

and **H** became king in his place; **Gn 36:39** 1924

HADASHAH

Zenan and **H** and Migdal-gad, **Jos 15:37** 2322a

HADASSAH

He was bringing up **H**, **Es 2:7** 1919

HADES

You will descend to **H**; **Mt 11:23** *86*
gates of **H** will not overpower it. **Mt 16:18** *86*
You will be brought down to **H**! **Lk 10:15** *86*
"In **H** he lifted up his eyes, **Lk 16:23** *86*
WILL NOT ABANDON MY SOUL TO **H**, **Ac 2:27** *86*
HE WAS NEITHER ABANDONED TO **H**, NOR **Ac 2:31** *86*
I have the keys of death and of **H**. **Rv 1:18** *86*
and **H** was following with him. **Rv 6:8** *86*
and death and **H** gave up the dead **Rv 20:13** *86*
Then death and **H** were thrown into **Rv 20:14** *86*

HADID

the sons of Lod, **H** and **Ezr 2:33** 2307
the sons of Lod, **H** and **Ne 7:37** 2307
H, Zeboim, Neballat, **Ne 11:34** 2307

HADLAI

of Shallum, and Amasa the son of **H** **2Ch 28:12** 2311

HADORAM

and **H** and Uzal and Diklah **Gn 10:27** 1913
H, Uzal, Diklah, **1Ch 1:21** 1913
he sent **H** his son to King David to **1Ch 18:10** 1913
And **H** *brought* all kinds of **1Ch 18:10**
Then King Rehoboam sent **H**, **2Ch 10:18** 1913

HADRACH

the LORD is against the land of **H**, **Zch 9:1** 2317

HAELEPH

and Zelah, **H** and the Jebusite **Jos 18:28** 507

HAGAB

the sons of **H**, the sons of **Ezr 2:46** 2285

HAGABA

the sons of Lebana, the sons of **H**, **Ne 7:48** 2286a

HAGABAH

sons of Lebanah, the sons of **H**, **Ezr 2:45** 2286b

HAGAR

an Egyptian maid whose name was **H**. **Gn 16:1** 1904
wife Sarai took **H** the Egyptian, **Gn 16:3** 1904
He went in to **H**, **Gn 16:4** 1904
"**H**, Sarai's maid, where have you **Gn 16:8** 1904
So **H** bore Abram a son; **Gn 16:15** 1904
the name of his son, whom **H** bore, **Gn 16:15** 1904
old when **H** bore Ishmael to him. **Gn 16:16** 1904
saw the son of **H** the Egyptian, **Gn 21:9** 1904
skin of water and gave *them* to **H**, **Gn 21:14** 1904
of God called to **H** from heaven and **Gn 21:17** 1904
"What is the matter with you, **H**? **Gn 21:17** 1904
Abraham's son, whom **H** the Egyptian, **Gn 25:12** 1904
who are to be slaves; she is **H**. **Ga 4:24** *28*
this **H** is Mount Sinai in Arabia and **Ga 4:25** *28*

HAGGAI

H the prophet and Zechariah the **Ezr 5:1** 2292b
the prophesying of **H** the prophet **Ezr 6:14** 2292b
came by the prophet **H** to Zerubbabel **Hg 1:1** 2292a
word of the LORD came by **H** **Hg 1:3** 2292a
and the words of **H** the prophet, **Hg 1:12** 2292a
Then **H**, the messenger of the LORD, **Hg 1:13** 2292a
the word of the LORD came by **H** **Hg 2:1** 2292a
the word of the LORD came to **H** **Hg 2:10** 2292a
Then **H** said, "If one who is unclean **Hg 2:13** 2292a
Then **H** said, **Hg 2:14** 2292a
of the LORD came a second time to **H** **Hg 2:20** 2292a

HAGGARD

see your faces looking more **h** than the **Da 1:10** 2196

HAGGEDOLIM

overseer was Zabdiel, the son of **H**. **Ne 11:14** 1896b

HAGGI

Ziphion and **H**, Shuni and Ezbon, **Gn 46:16** 2291
of **H**, the family of the Haggites; **Nu 26:15** 2291

HAGGIAH

Shimea his son, **H** his son, Asaiah **1Ch 6:30** 2293

HAGGITES

of Haggi, the family of the **H**; **Nu 26:15** 2291

HAGGITH

the fourth, Adonijah the son of **H**; **2Sa 3:4** 2294
the son of **H** exalted himself, **1Ki 1:5** 2294
the son of **H** has become king, **1Ki 1:11** 2294
Now Adonijah the son of **H** came to **1Ki 2:13** 2294
fourth *was* Adonijah the son of **H**; **1Ch 3:2** 2294

HAGRI

of Nathan, Mibhar the son of **H**, **1Ch 11:38** 1905

HAGRITE

the **H** had charge of the flocks. **1Ch 27:31** 1905

HAGRITES

of Saul they made war with the **H**, **1Ch 5:10** 1905
They made war against the **H**, **1Ch 5:19** 1905
and the **H** and all who *were* with **1Ch 5:20** 1905
the Ishmaelites, Moab and the **H**; **Ps 83:6** 1905

HAHIROTH

They journeyed from before **H** and **Nu 33:8** 6367

HAIL

I will send a very heavy **h**, **Ex 9:18** 1259

when the **h** comes down on them, Ex 9:19 1259
that **h** may fall on all the land of Ex 9:22 1259
and the LORD sent thunder and **h**, Ex 9:23 1259
rained **h** on the land of Egypt. Ex 9:23 1259
So there was **h**, and fire flashing Ex 9:24 1259
continually in the midst of the **h**, Ex 9:24 1259
The **h** struck all that was in Ex 9:25 1259
the **h** also struck every plant of Ex 9:25 1259
of Israel *were,* there was no **h**. Ex 9:26 1259
been enough of God's thunder and **h**; Ex 9:28 1259
and there will be **h** no longer, Ex 9:29 1259
and the thunder and the **h** ceased, Ex 9:33 1259
the **h** and the thunder had ceased, Ex 9:34 1259
what is left to you from the **h** Ex 10:5 1259
even all that the **h** has left." Ex 10:12 1259
of the trees that the **h** had left. Ex 10:15 1259
you seen the storehouses of the **h**, Jb 38:22 1259
He gave them **h** for rain, *And* Ps 105:32 1259
Fire and **h**, snow and clouds; Ps 148:8 1259
As a storm of **h**, a tempest of Is 28:2 1259
Then **h** will sweep away the refuge Is 28:17 1259
will **h** when the forest comes down, Is 32:19 1258
with blasting wind, mildew and **h**, Hg 2:17 1259
went to Jesus and said, "**H**, Rabbi!" Mt 26:49 *5463*
"**H**, King of the Jews!" Mt 27:29 *5463*
and they began to acclaim Him, "**H**, Mk 15:18 *5463*
"**H**, King of the Jews!" Jn 19:3 *5463*
and there came **h** and fire, Rv 8:7 *5464*
because of the plague of the **h**, Rv 16:21 *5464*

HAILED
the men of the garrison **h** Jonathan 1Sa 14:12 6030a

HAILSTONES
were more who died from the **h** than Jos 10:11 1259, 68
thick clouds, **H** and coals of fire. Ps 18:12 1259
His voice, **H** and coals of fire. Ps 18:13 1259
He destroyed their vines with **h** And Ps 78:47 1259
over their cattle also to the **h** And Ps 78:48 1259
In cloudburst, downpour and **h**. Is 30:30
rain will come, and you, O **h**, Ezk 13:11 1259, 68
rain and **h** to consume *it* in wrath. Ezk 13:13 417, 68
him, a torrential rain, with **h**, Ezk 38:22 417, 68
And huge **h**, about one hundred Rv 16:21 *5464*

HAILSTORM
and an earthquake and a great **h**. Rv 11:19 *5464*

HAIR
gray **h** down to Sheol in sorrow." Gn 42:38 7872
gray **h** down to Sheol in sorrow.' Gn 44:29 7872
your servants will bring the gray **h** of Gn 44:31 7872
fine linen, goat **h**, Ex 25:4
shall make curtains of goats' **h** Ex 26:7
fine linen, goats' **h**, Ex 35:6
and fine linen and goats' **h** Ex 35:23
with a skill spun the goats' **h**. Ex 35:26
Then he made curtains of goats' **h** Ex 36:14
and if the **h** in the infection has Lv 13:3 8181
the **h** on it has not turned white, Lv 13:4 8181
and it has turned the **h** white, Lv 13:10 8181
and the **h** on it has turned white, Lv 13:20 8181
And if the **h** in the bright spot Lv 13:25 8181
is no white **h** in the bright spot and Lv 13:26 8181
there is thin yellowish **h** in it, Lv 13:30 8181
and there is no black **h** in it, Lv 13:31 8181
no yellowish **h** has grown in it, Lv 13:32 8181
need not seek for the yellowish **h**; Lv 13:36 8181
and black **h** has grown in it, Lv 13:37 8181
if a man loses the **h** of his head, Lv 13:40 4803
the **h** of his head shall be uncovered Lv 13:45
clothes and shave off all his **h** and Lv 14:8 8181
that he shall shave off all his **h**: Lv 14:9 8181
and his eyebrows, even all his **h**. Lv 14:9 8181
before the LORD and let *the* **h** Nu 5:18
locks of **h** on his head grow long. Nu 6:5 8181
he defiles his dedicated head *of* **h**, Nu 6:9
then shave his dedicated head *of* **h** Nu 6:18
and take the dedicated **h** of his Nu 6:18 8181
after he has shaved his dedicated **h**. Nu 6:19
and all the work of goats' **h**, Nu 31:20
nursling with the man of gray **h**. Dt 32:25 7872
"If you weave the seven locks of my **h** Jg 16:13 7218
his **h** and weave them into the web]. Jg 16:14 7218
off the seven locks of his **h**. Jg 16:19 7218
the **h** of his head began to grow Jg 16:22 8181
sling a stone at a **h** and not miss. Jg 20:16 8185
not one **h** of his head shall 1Sa 14:45 8185
and put a quilt of goats' **h** at 1Sa 19:13
the bed with the quilt of goats' **h** 1Sa 19:16
not one **h** of your son shall fall 2Sa 14:11 8185
When he cut the **h** of his head 2Sa 14:26
he weighed the **h** of his head at 2Sa 14:26 8181
gray **h** go down to Sheol in peace. 1Ki 2:6 7872
gray **h** down to Sheol with blood." 1Ki 2:9 7872
the **h** from my head and my beard, Ezr 9:3 8181
of them and pulled out their **h**, Ne 13:25 4803
The **h** of my flesh bristled up. Jb 4:15 8185
honor of old men is their gray **h**. Pr 20:29 7872
Your **h** is like a flock of goats SS 4:1 8181
Your **h** is like a flock of goats SS 6:5 8181
Instead of well-set **h**, Is 3:24 4748
the head and the **h** of the legs; Is 7:20 8181
'Cut off your **h** and cast *it* away, Jer 7:29 5145
who clip the **h** on their temples; Jer 9:26
all who cut the corners *of their* **h**; Jer 25:23
who cut the corners *of their* **h**; Jer 49:32
for weighing and divide the **h**. Ezk 5:1
were formed and your **h** had grown. Ezk 16:7 8181
they shall only trim *the* **h** *of* Ezk 44:20
was the **h** of their head singed, Da 3:27 8177
until his **h** had grown like eagles' Da 4:33 8177
the **h** of His head like pure wool. Da 7:9 8177
yourself bald and cut off your **h**, Mi 1:16 1494
himself had a garment of camel's **h** Mt 3:4 *2359*
cannot make one **h** white or black. Mt 5:36 *2359*
John was clothed with camel's **h** Mk 1:6 *2359*
them with the **h** of her head, Lk 7:38 *2359*
tears and wiped them with her **h**. Lk 7:44 *2359*
not a **h** of your head will perish. Lk 21:18 *2359*
and wiped His feet with her **h**, Jn 11:2 *2359*
and wiped His feet with her **h**; Jn 12:3 *2359*
In Cenchrea he had his **h** cut, Ac 18:18 *2776*
for not a **h** from the head of any Ac 27:34 *2359*
let her also have her **h** cut off; 1Co 11:6 *2751*
her **h** cut off or her head shaved, 1Co 11:6 *2751*
you that if a man has long **h**, 1Co 11:14 *2863*
but if a woman has long **h**, 1Co 11:15 *2863*
For her **h** is given to her for a 1Co 11:15 *2864*
not with braided **h** and gold or 1Tm 2:9 *4117*
braiding the **h**, and wearing gold 1Pe 3:3 *1708*
His head and His **h** were white like Rv 1:14 *2359*
black as sackcloth *made* of **h**, Rv 6:12 *5155*
They had **h** like the hair of women, Rv 9:8 *2359*
They had hair like the **h** of women, Rv 9:8 *2359*

HAIRS
there are no white **h** in it and it Lv 13:21 8181
of his **h** will fall to the ground; 1Ki 1:52 8185
numerous than the **h** of my head, Ps 40:12 8185
are more than the **h** of my head; Ps 69:4 8185
Gray **h** also are sprinkled on him, Hos 7:9 7872
h of your head are all numbered. Mt 10:30 *2359*
h of your head are all numbered. Lk 12:7 *2359*

HAIRY
red, all over like a **h** garment; Gn 25:25 8181
is a **h** man and I am a smooth man. Gn 27:11 8163a
h like his brother Esau's hands; Gn 27:23 8163a
"*He was* a **h** man with a leather 2Ki 1:8 8181
The **h** crown of him who goes on in Ps 68:21 8181
The **h** goat also will cry to its Is 34:14 8163a
on a **h** robe in order to deceive; Zch 13:4 8181

HAKELDAMA
language that field was called **H**, Ac 1:19 *184*

HAKKATAN
son of **H** and 110 males with him; Ezr 8:12 6997

HAKKOZ
the seventh for **H**, the eighth for 1Ch 24:10 6976
sons of Habaiah, the sons of **H**, Ezr 2:61 6976
Uriah the son of **H** made repairs. Ne 3:4 6976
son of **H** repaired another section, Ne 3:21 6976
sons of Hobaiah, the sons of **H**, Ne 7:63 6976

HAKUPHA
the sons of Bakbuk, the sons of **H**, Ezr 2:51 2709
the sons of Bakbuk, the sons of **H**, Ne 7:53 2709

HALAH
and settled them in **H** and Habor, 2Ki 17:6 2477
put them in **H** and on the Habor, 2Ki 18:11 2477
Manasseh, and brought them to **H**, 1Ch 5:26 2477

HALAK
from Mount **H**, that rises toward Jos 11:17 2510
of Lebanon even as far as Mount **H**, Jos 12:7 2510

HALF
laid each **h** opposite the other; Gn 15:10 1335
Moses took **h** of the blood and Ex 24:6 2677
and the *other* **h** of the blood he Ex 24:6 2677
wood two and a **h** cubits long, Ex 25:10 2677
long, and one and a **h** cubits wide, Ex 25:10 2677
wide, and one and a **h** cubits high. Ex 25:10 2677
two and a **h** cubits long and one Ex 25:17 2677
long and one and a **h** cubits wide. Ex 25:17 2677
wide and one and a **h** cubits high. Ex 25:23 2677
the **h** curtain that is left over, Ex 26:12 2677
and one and a **h** cubits the width Ex 26:16 2677
h a shekel according to the shekel Ex 30:13 4276
h a shekel as a contribution to Ex 30:13 4276
not pay less than the **h** shekel, Ex 30:15 4276
of fragrant cinnamon **h** as much, Ex 30:23 4276
and one and a **h** cubits the width Ex 36:21 2677
its length was two and a **h** cubits, Ex 37:1 2677
and its width one and a **h** cubits, Ex 37:1 2677
and its height one and a **h** cubits; Ex 37:1 2677
gold, two and a **h** cubits long and Ex 37:6 2677
long and one and a **h** cubits wide. Ex 37:6 2677
wide and one and a **h** cubits high. Ex 37:10 2677
h a shekel according to the shekel Ex 38:26 4276
h of it in the morning and half of Lv 6:20 4276
and **h** of it in the evening. Lv 6:20 4276
whose flesh is **h** eaten away when Nu 12:12 2677
offerings shall be **h** a hin of wine Nu 28:14 2677
take it from their **h** and give it Nu 31:29 4276
"From the sons of Israel's **h**, Nu 31:30 4276
The **h**, the portion of those Nu 31:36 4275
As for the sons of Israel's **h**, Nu 31:42 4276
congregation's **h** was 337,500 sheep, Nu 31:43 4275
and from the sons of Israel's **h**, Nu 31:47 4276
give to the nine and a **h** tribes. Nu 34:13 2677
"The two and a **h** tribes have Nu 34:15 2677
and **h** the hill country of Gilead Dt 3:12 2677
H of them *stood* in front of Mount Jos 8:33 2677
and **h** of them in front of Mount Ebal Jos 8:33 2677
of the valley and **h** of Gilead, Jos 12:2 2677
the Maacathites, and **h** of Gilead, Jos 12:5 2677
h the land of the sons of Ammon, Jos 13:25 2677
also **h** of Gilead, with Ashtaroth Jos 13:31 2677
for **h** of the sons of Machir Jos 13:31 2677
but to the other **h** Joshua gave Jos 22:7 2677
h a furrow in an acre of land. 1Sa 14:14 2677
and shaved off **h** of their beards, 2Sa 10:4 2677
about us; even if **h** of us die, 2Sa 18:3 2677
h the people of Israel accompanied 2Sa 19:40 2677
and give **h** to the one and half to 1Ki 3:25 2677
to the one and **h** to the other 1Ki 3:25 2677
of a pedestal, a cubit and a **h**; 1Ki 7:31 2677
of a wheel *was* a cubit and a **h**. 1Ki 7:32 2677
a circular form **h** a cubit high, 1Ki 7:35 2677
And behold, the **h** was not told me. 1Ki 10:7 2677
"If you were to give me **h** your 1Ki 13:8 2677
commander of **h** his chariots, 1Ki 16:9 4276
h of the people followed Tibni the 1Ki 16:21 2677
the *other* **h** followed Omri. 1Ki 16:21 2677
Haroeh, **h** of the Manahathites, 1Ch 2:52 2677
and **h** of the Manahathites, 1Ch 2:54 2677
the half-tribe, the **h** of Manasseh, 1Ch 6:61 2677
the **h** of the greatness of your 2Ch 9:6 2677
of **h** the district of Jerusalem, Ne 3:9 2677
of **h** the district of Jerusalem, Ne 3:12 2677
of **h** the district of Beth-zur, Ne 3:16 2677
of **h** the district of Keilah, Ne 3:17 2677
other **h** of the district of Keilah. Ne 3:18 2677
joined together to **h** its *height,* Ne 4:6 2677
h of my servants carried on Ne 4:16 2677
while **h** of them held the spears, Ne 4:16 2677
So we carried on the work with **h** Ne 4:21 2677
Hoshaiah and **h** of the leaders of Ne 12:32 2677
with **h** of the people on the wall, Ne 12:38 2677
I and **h** of the officials with me; Ne 12:40 2677
h spoke in the language of Ashdod, Ne 13:24 2677
Even to **h** of the kingdom it shall Es 5:3 2677
Even to **h** of the kingdom it shall Es 5:6 2677
Even to **h** of the kingdom it shall Es 7:2 2677
will not live out **h** their days. Ps 55:23 2673
H of it he burns in the fire; Is 44:16 2677
over *this* **h** he eats meat as he Is 44:16 2677
"I have burned **h** of it in the Is 44:19 2677
did not commit **h** of your sins, Ezk 16:51 2677
hewn stone, a cubit and a **h** long, Ezk 40:42 2677
a half long, a cubit and a **h** wide and Ezk 40:42 2677
around it *shall be* **h** a cubit Ezk 43:17 2677
for a time, times, and **h** a time. Da 7:25 6387
for a time, times, and **h** *a time;* Da 12:7 2677
and a homer and a **h** of barley. Hos 3:2 3963
and **h** of the city exiled, Zch 14:2 2677
so that **h** of the mountain will Zch 14:4 2677
and the other **h** toward the south. Zch 14:4 2677
h of them toward the eastern sea Zch 14:8 2677
other **h** toward the western sea; Zch 14:8 2677
up to **h** of my kingdom." Mk 6:23 *2255*
and went away leaving him **h** dead. Lk 10:30 *2253*
h of my possessions I will give to Lk 19:8 *2255*
in heaven for about **h** an hour. Rv 8:1 *2256*
bodies for three and a **h** days, Rv 11:9 *2255*
But after the three and a **h** days Rv 11:11 *2255*
for a time and times and **h** a time, Rv 12:14 *2255*

HALF-SHEKEL
man took a gold ring weighing a **h** Gn 24:22 1235

HALF-TRIBE
to the **h** of Joseph's son Manasseh, Nu 32:33 2677, 7626
and the **h** of Manasseh have Nu 34:14 2677, 4294
Og, I gave to the **h** of Manasseh, Dt 3:13 2677, 7626
and the **h** of the Manassites. Dt 29:8 2677, 7626
Gadites and to the **h** of Manasseh, Jos 1:12 2677, 7626
h of Manasseh crossed over in battle Jos 4:12 2677, 7626
the **h** of Manasseh as a possession. Jos 12:6 2677, 7626
tribes and the **h** of Manasseh." Jos 13:7 2677, 7626
With the other **h**, the Reubenites Jos 13:8
inheritance to the **h** of Manasseh; Jos 13:29 2677, 7626
for the **h** of the sons of Manasseh Jos 13:29 2677, 4294
for the nine tribes and the **h**. Jos 14:2 2677, 4294
and the **h** beyond the Jordan; Jos 14:3 2677, 4294
Reuben and the **h** of Manasseh Jos 18:7 2677, 7626
of Dan and from the **h** of Manasseh. Jos 21:5 2677, 4294
from the **h** of Manasseh in Bashan. Jos 21:6 2677, 4294
From the **h** of Manasseh, Jos 21:25 4276, 4294
Levites, from the **h** of Manasseh, Jos 21:27 2677, 4294
the Gadites and the **h** of Manasseh, Jos 22:1 2677, 4294
Now to the one **h** of Manasseh Moses Jos 22:7 2677, 7626
and the **h** of Manasseh returned Jos 22:9 2677, 7626
and the **h** of Manasseh built an altar Jos 22:10 2677, 7626
the **h** of Manasseh have built an altar Jos 22:11 2677, 7626
of Gad and to the **h** of Manasseh, Jos 22:13 2677, 7626
of Gad and to the **h** of Manasseh, Jos 22:15 2677, 7626

and the **h** of Manasseh answered and **Jos 22:21** 2677, 7626
the Gadites and the **h** of Manasseh, **1Ch 5:18** 2677, 7626
h of Manasseh lived in the land; **1Ch 5:23** 2677, 7626
Gadites and the **h** of Manasseh, **1Ch 5:26** 2677, 7626
family of the tribe, from the **h**, **1Ch 6:61** 4276, 4294
and from the **h** of Manasseh: **1Ch 6:70** 4276, 4294
the family of the **h** of Manasseh: **1Ch 6:71** 2677, 4294
Of the **h** of Manasseh 18,000, **1Ch 12:31** 2677, 4294
Gadites and of the **h** of Manasseh, **1Ch 12:37** 2677, 7626
Gadites and the **h** of the Manassites **1Ch 26:32** 2677, 7626
for the **h** of Manasseh, Joel the **1Ch 27:20** 2677, 7626
for the **h** of Manasseh in Gilead, **1Ch 27:21** 2677

HALFWAY
the net will reach **h** up the altar. **Ex 27:5** 2677
under its ledge, reaching **h** up. **Ex 38:4** 2677

HALHUL
H, Beth-zur and Gedor, **Jos 15:58** 2478

HALI
and **H** and Beten and Achshaph, **Jos 19:25** 2482

HALL
and brought them into the **h** and **1Sa 9:22** 3957
Then he made the **h** of pillars; **1Ki 7:6** 197
He made the **h** of the throne **1Ki 7:7** 197
was to judge, the **h** of judgment, **1Ki 7:7** 197
the other court inward from the **h**, **1Ki 7:8** 197
like this **h** for Pharaoh's daughter, **1Ki 7:8** 197
has brought me to *his* banquet **h**, **SS 2:4** 1004
The queen entered the banquet **h** **Da 5:10** 1005
h was filled with dinner guests. **Mt 22:10** *3567*

HALLELUJAH
multitude in heaven, saying, "**H**! **Rv 19:1** *239*
And a second time they said, "**H**! **Rv 19:3** *239*
sits on the throne saying, "Amen. **H**!" **Rv 19:4** *239*
peals of thunder, saying, "**H**! **Rv 19:6** *239*

HALLOHESH
Next to him Shallum the son of **H**, **Ne 3:12** 3873
H, Pilha, Shobek, **Ne 10:24** 3873

HALLOWED
who is in heaven, **H** be Your name. **Mt 6:9** *37*
'Father, **h** be Your name. **Lk 11:2** *37*

HALT
Yet today he will **h** at Nob; **Is 10:32** 5975
and the bearers came to a **h**. **Lk 7:14** *2476*

HALTED
h and pursued Israel no longer, **2Sa 2:28** 5975

HAM
Noah became the father of Shem, **H**, **Gn 5:32** 2526
Shem, **H**, and Japheth. **Gn 6:10** 2526
Noah and Shem and **H** and Japheth, **Gn 7:13** 2526
ark were Shem and **H** and Japheth; **Gn 9:18** 2526
and **H** was the father of Canaan. **Gn 9:18** 2526
H, the father of Canaan, saw **Gn 9:22** 2526
of the generations of Shem, **H**, **Gn 10:1** 2526
The sons of **H** *were* Cush and **Gn 10:6** 2526
These are the sons of **H**, **Gn 10:20** 2526
and the Zuzim in **H** and the Emim in **Gn 14:5** 1990
Noah, Shem, **H** and Japheth. **1Ch 1:4** 2526
The sons of **H** *were* Cush, Mizraim, **1Ch 1:8** 2526
their virility in the tents of **H**. **Ps 78:51** 2526
Jacob sojourned in the land of **H**. **Ps 105:23** 2526
And miracles in the land of **H**. **Ps 105:27** 2526
Wonders in the land of **H** **Ps 106:22** 2526

HAMAN
events King Ahasuerus promoted **H**, **Es 3:1** 2001b
bowed down and paid homage to **H**; **Es 3:2** 2001b
that they told **H** to see whether **Es 3:4** 2001b
When **H** saw that Mordecai neither **Es 3:5** 2001b
to him, **H** was filled with rage. **Es 3:5** 2001b
therefore **H** sought to destroy all **Es 3:6** 2001b
was cast before **H** from day to day **Es 3:7** 2001b
Then **H** said to King Ahasuerus, **Es 3:8** 2001b
from his hand and gave it to **H**, **Es 3:10** 2001b
The king said to **H**, **Es 3:11** 2001b
and it was written just as **H** **Es 3:12** 2001b
the king and **H** sat down to drink, **Es 3:15** 2001b
money that **H** had promised to pay **Es 4:7** 2001b
may the king and **H** come this day **Es 5:4** 2001b
"Bring **H** quickly that we may do **Es 5:5** 2001b
So the king and **H** came to the **Es 5:5** 2001b
may the king and **H** come to the **Es 5:8** 2001b
Then **H** went out that day glad and **Es 5:9** 2001b
but when **H** saw Mordecai in the **Es 5:9** 2001b
H was filled with anger against **Es 5:9** 2001b
H controlled himself, however, **Es 5:10** 2001b
Then **H** recounted to them the glory **Es 5:11** 2001b
H also said, "Even Esther the queen **Es 5:12** 2001b
And the advice pleased **H**, **Es 5:14** 2001b
Now **H** had just entered the outer **Es 6:4** 2001b
H is standing in the court." **Es 6:5** 2001b
So **H** came in and the king said to **Es 6:6** 2001b
And **H** said to himself, **Es 6:6** 2001b
Then **H** said to the king, **Es 6:7** 2001b
Then the king said to **H**, **Es 6:10** 2001b
So **H** took the robe and the horse, **Es 6:11** 2001b
But **H** hurried home, mourning, with **Es 6:12** 2001b
H recounted to Zeresh his wife **Es 6:13** 2001b
and hastily brought **H** to the banquet **Es 6:14** 2001b
Now the king and **H** came to drink **Es 7:1** 2001b
and an enemy is this wicked **H**!" **Es 7:6** 2001b
Then **H** became terrified before the **Es 7:6** 2001b
but **H** stayed to beg for his life **Es 7:7** 2001b
H was falling on the couch where **Es 7:8** 2001b
which **H** made for Mordecai who **Es 7:9** 2001b
So they hanged **H** on the gallows **Es 7:10** 2001b
Ahasuerus gave the house of **H**, **Es 8:1** 2001b
which he had taken away from **H**, **Es 8:2** 2001b
set Mordecai over the house of **H**. **Es 8:2** 2001b
avert the evil *scheme* of **H** the Agagite **Es 8:3** 2001b
revoke the letters devised by **H**, **Es 8:5** 2001b
given the house of **H** to Esther, **Es 8:7** 2001b
sons of **H** the son of Hammedatha, **Es 9:10** 2001b
ten sons of **H** at the citadel **Es 9:12** 2001b
For **H** the son of Hammedatha, the **Es 9:24** 2001b

HAMAN'S
king's mouth, they covered **H** face. **Es 7:8** 2001b
at **H** house fifty cubits high, **Es 7:9** 2001b
and let **H** ten sons be hanged on **Es 9:13** 2001b
Susa, and **H** ten sons were hanged. **Es 9:14** 2001b

HAMATH
Now when Toi king of **H** heard that **2Sa 8:9** 2574
of **H** to the brook of Egypt, **1Ki 8:65** 2574
Israel from the entrance of **H** as far as **2Ki 14:25** 2574
for Israel, Damascus and **H**, **2Ki 14:28** 2574
Avva and from **H** and Sephar-vaim, **2Ki 17:24** 2574
Nergal, the men of **H** made Ashima, **2Ki 17:30** 2574
'Where are the gods of **H** and Arpad? **2Ki 18:34** 2574
'Where is the king of **H**, **2Ki 19:13** 2574
him at Riblah in the land of **H**, **2Ki 23:33** 2574
death at Riblah in the land of **H**. **2Ki 25:21** 2574
Egypt even to the entrance of **H**, **1Ch 13:5** 2574
king of Zobah *as far as* **H**, **1Ch 18:3** 2574
Now when Tou king of **H** heard that **1Ch 18:9** 2574
of **H** to the brook of Egypt. **2Ch 7:8** 2574
cities which he had built in **H** **2Ch 8:4** 2574
like Carchemish, Or **H** like Arpad, **Is 10:9** 2574
Pathros, Cush, Elam, Shinar, **H**, **Is 11:11** 2574
'Where are the gods of **H** and Arpad? **Is 36:19** 2574
'Where is the king of **H**, **Is 37:13** 2574
at Riblah in the land of **H**, **Jer 39:5** 2574
"**H** and Arpad are put to shame, **Jer 49:23** 2574
at Riblah in the land of **H**, **Jer 52:9** 2574
death at Riblah in the land of **H**. **Jer 52:27** 2574
H, Berothah, Sibraim, which is **Ezk 47:16** 2574
of Damascus and the border of **H**; **Ezk 47:16** 2574
the north is the border of **H**. **Ezk 47:17** 2574
toward the north beside **H**, **Ezk 48:1** 2574
And go from there to **H** the great, **Am 6:2** 2574
of **H** To the brook of the Arabah. **Am 6:14** 2574
And **H** also, which borders on it; **Zch 9:2** 2574

HAMATHITE
and the Zemarite and the **H**; **Gn 10:18** 2577

HAMATHITES
the Zemarites and the **H**. **1Ch 1:16** 2577

HAMATH-ZOBAH
Then Solomon went to **H** and captured **2Ch 8:3** 2578

HAMITES
who lived there formerly *were* **H**. **1Ch 4:40** 4480, 2526

HAMMATH
cities *were* Ziddim, Zer and **H**, **Jos 19:35** 2575a
are the Kenites who came from **H**, **1Ch 2:55** 2575b

HAMMEDATHA
Haman, the son of **H** the Agagite, **Es 3:1** 1992b
Haman, the son of **H** the Agagite, **Es 3:10** 1992b
Haman, the son of **H** the Agagite, **Es 8:5** 1992b
ten sons of Haman the son of **H**, **Es 9:10** 1992b
For Haman the son of **H**, the Agagite, **Es 9:24** 1992b

HAMMER
peg and seized a **h** in her hand, **Jg 4:21** 4717
her right hand for the workmen's **h**. **Jg 5:26** 1989
and there was neither **h** nor axe **1Ki 6:7** 4717
h their swords into plowshares and **Is 2:4** 3807
he who smooths *metal* with the **h** **Is 41:7** 6360
like a **h** which shatters a rock? **Jer 23:29** 6360
"How the **h** of the whole earth Has **Jer 50:23** 6360
Then they will **h** their swords into **Mi 4:3** 3807

HAMMERED
make them of **h** work at the two **Ex 25:18** 4749
shaft are to be made of **h** work; **Ex 25:31** 4749
one piece of **h** work of pure gold. **Ex 25:36** 4749
he made them of **h** work at the two **Ex 37:7** 4749
He made the lampstand of **h** work, **Ex 37:17** 4749
was a single **h** work of pure gold. **Ex 37:22** 4749
Then they **h** out gold sheets and **Ex 39:3** 7554
of the lampstand, **h** work of gold; **Nu 8:4** 4749
to its flowers it was **h** work; **Nu 8:4** 4749
of **h** work you shall make them; **Nu 10:2** 4749
let them be made into **h** sheets for **Nu 16:38** 7555
and they **h** them out as a plating **Nu 16:39** 7554

HAMMERS
They smash with hatchet and **h**. **Ps 74:6** 3597
the coals, fashioning it with **h** and **Is 44:12** 4717
with **h** So that it will not totter. **Jer 10:4** 4717

HAMMOLECHETH
His sister **H** bore Ishhod and **1Ch 7:18** 4447

HAMMON
Ebron and Rehob and **H** and Kanah, **Jos 19:28** 2540
lands, **H** with its pasture lands **1Ch 6:76** 2540

HAMMOTH-DOR
and **H** with its pasture lands and **Jos 21:32** 2576

HAMMUEL
The sons of Mishma *were* **H** his son, **1Ch 4:26** 2536a

HAMONAH
the name of *the* city will be **H**. **Ezk 39:16** 1997

HAMON-GOG
they will call *it* the valley of **H**. **Ezk 39:11** 1996
have buried it in the valley of **H**. **Ezk 39:15** 1996

HAMOR
from the hand of the sons of **H**, **Gn 33:19** 2544
Shechem the son of **H** the Hivite, **Gn 34:2** 2544
So Shechem spoke to his father **H**, **Gn 34:4** 2544
Then **H** the father of Shechem went **Gn 34:6** 2544
But **H** spoke with them, saying, **Gn 34:8** 2544
answered Shechem and his father **H** **Gn 34:13** 2544
reasonable to **H** and Shechem, **Gn 34:18** 2544
So **H** and his son Shechem came to **Gn 34:20** 2544
to **H** and to his son Shechem, **Gn 34:24** 2544
They killed **H** and his son **Gn 34:26** 2544
Jacob had bought from the sons of **H** **Jos 24:32** 2544
men of **H** the father of Shechem; **Jg 9:28** 2544
from the sons of **H** in Shechem. **Ac 7:16** *1697*

HAMOR'S
to Hamor and Shechem, **H** son. **Gn 34:18** 2544

HAMRAN
And the sons of Dishon *were* **H**, **1Ch 1:41** 2566

HAMSTRING
you shall **h** their horses and burn **Jos 11:6** 6136b

HAMSTRUNG
he **h** their horses and burned **Jos 11:9** 6136b
and David **h** the chariot horses, **2Sa 8:4** 6136b
David **h** all the chariot horses, **1Ch 18:4** 6136b

HAMUL
sons of Perez were Hezron and **H**. **Gn 46:12** 2538
of **H**, the family of the Hamulites. **Nu 26:21** 2538
sons of Perez *were* Hezron and **H**. **1Ch 2:5** 2538

HAMULITES
of Hamul, the family of the **H**. **Nu 26:21** 2539

HAMUTAL
and his mother's name was **H** the **2Ki 23:31** 2537
and his mother's name was **H** the **2Ki 24:18** 2537
and his mother's name was **H** the **Jer 52:1** 2537

HANAMEL
H the son of Shallum your uncle is **Jer 32:7** 2601
"Then **H** my uncle's son came to me **Jer 32:8** 2601
at Anathoth from **H** my uncle's son, **Jer 32:9** 2601
in the sight of **H** my uncle's **Jer 32:12** 2601

HANAN
Abdon, Zichri, **H**, **1Ch 8:23** 2605
Ishmael, Sheariah, Obadiah and **H**. **1Ch 8:38** 2605
and Sheariah and Obadiah and **H**. **1Ch 9:44** 2605
H the son of Maacah and Joshaphat **1Ch 11:43** 2605
sons of Shalmai, the sons of **H**, **Ezr 2:46** 2605
the sons of **H**, the sons of Giddel, **Ne 7:49** 2605
Kelita, Azariah, Jozabad, **H**, **Ne 8:7** 2605
Hodiah, Kelita, Pelaiah, **H**, **Ne 10:10** 2605
Pelatiah, **H**, Anaiah, **Ne 10:22** 2605
Ahiah, **H**, Anan, **Ne 10:26** 2605
to them was **H** the son of Zaccur, **Ne 13:13** 2605
the sons of **H** the son of Igdaliah, **Jer 35:4** 2605

HANANEL
of the Hundred *and* the Tower of **H**. **Ne 3:1** 2606
by the Fish Gate, the Tower of **H** and **Ne 12:39** 2606
the Tower of **H** to the Corner Gate. **Jer 31:38** 2606
of **H** to the king's wine presses. **Zch 14:10** 2606

HANANI
Jehu the son of **H** against Baasha, **1Ki 16:1** 2607
son of **H** also came against Baasha **1Ki 16:7** 2607
Shebuel and Jerimoth, Hananiah, **H**, **1Ch 25:4** 2607
to **H**, his sons and his relatives, **1Ch 25:25** 2607
At that time **H** the seer came to **2Ch 16:7** 2607
Jehu the son of **H** the seer **2Ch 19:2** 2607
the annals of Jehu the son of **H**, **2Ch 20:34** 2607
Immer *there were* **H** and Zebadiah; **Ezr 10:20** 2607
that **H**, one of my brothers, and **Ne 1:2** 2607
then I put **H** my brother, and **Ne 7:2** 2607
Maai, Nethanel, Judah *and* **H**, **Ne 12:36** 2607

HANANIAH
Zerubbabel *were* Meshullam and **H**, **1Ch 3:19** 2608a
of **H** *were* Pelatiah and Jeshaiah, **1Ch 3:21** 2608a
H, Elam, Anthothijah, **1Ch 8:24** 2608a
Uzziel, Shebuel and Jerimoth, **H**, **1Ch 25:4** 2608a
to **H**, his sons and his relatives, **1Ch 25:23** 2608a
under the direction of **H**, **2Ch 26:11** 2608a
Jehohanan, **H**, Zabbai *and* Athlai; **Ezr 10:28** 2608a
And next to him **H**, one of the **Ne 3:8** 2608a
After him **H** the son of Shelemiah, **Ne 3:30** 2608a
H the commander of the fortress, **Ne 7:2** 2608a
Hoshea, **H**, Hasshub, **Ne 10:23** 2608a
of Seraiah, Meraiah; of Jeremiah, **H** **Ne 12:12** 2608a
Elioenai, Zechariah and **H**, **Ne 12:41** 2608a
month, **H** the son of Azzur, **Jer 28:1** 2608a
Jeremiah spoke to the prophet **H** **Jer 28:5** 2608a
Then **H** the prophet took the yoke **Jer 28:10** 2608a
H spoke in the presence of all **Jer 28:11** 2608a
after **H** the prophet had broken the **Jer 28:12** 2608a
"Go and speak to **H**, saying, **Jer 28:13** 2608a
the prophet said to **H** the prophet, **Jer 28:15** 2608a
"Listen now, **H**, the LORD has not **Jer 28:15** 2608a
So **H** the prophet died in the same **Jer 28:17** 2608a
and Zedekiah the son of **H**, **Jer 36:12** 2608a
Shelemiah the son of **H** was there; **Jer 37:13** 2608a
the sons of Judah were Daniel, **H**, **Da 1:6** 2608a
name Belteshazzar, to **H** Shadrach, **Da 1:7** 2608a
had appointed over Daniel, **H**, **Da 1:11** 2608a
not one was found like Daniel, **H**, **Da 1:19** 2608a
house and informed his friends, **H**, **Da 2:17** 2608a

HAND
now, he might stretch out his **h**, **Gn 3:22** 3027

your brother's blood from your **h**.	Gn 4:11	3027
he put out his **h** and took her,	Gn 8:9	3027
sea, into your **h** they are given.	Gn 9:2	3027
your enemies into your **h**."	Gn 14:20	3027
His **h** *will be* against everyone,	Gn 16:12	3027
everyone's **h** *will be* against him;	Gn 16:12	3027
So the men seized his **h** and the	Gn 19:16	3027
seized his hand and the **h** of his	Gn 19:16	3027
up the lad, and hold him by the **h**,	Gn 21:18	3027
take these seven ewe lambs from my **h**	Gn 21:30	3027
in his **h** the fire and the knife.	Gn 22:6	3027
Abraham stretched out his **h** and	Gn 22:10	3027
out your **h** against the lad,	Gn 22:12	3027
place your **h** under my thigh,	Gn 24:2	3027
So the servant placed his **h** under	Gn 24:9	3027
things of his master's in his **h**;	Gn 24:10	3027
quickly lowered her jar to her **h**,	Gn 24:18	3027
turn to the right **h** or the left."	Gn 24:49	3225
his **h** holding on to Esau's heel,	Gn 25:26	3027
You required it of my **h**	Gn 31:39	3027
I pray, from the **h** of my brother,	Gn 32:11	3027
of my brother, from the **h** of Esau;	Gn 32:11	3027
them into the **h** of his servants,	Gn 32:16	3027
then take my present from my **h**,	Gn 33:10	3027
from the **h** of the sons of Hamor,	Gn 33:19	3027
your staff that is in your **h**."	Gn 38:18	3027
the pledge from the woman's **h**,	Gn 38:20	3027
was giving birth, one put out a **h**,	Gn 38:28	3027
tied a scarlet *thread* on his **h**,	Gn 38:28	3027
came about as he drew back his **h**,	Gn 38:29	3027
had the scarlet *thread* on his **h**;	Gn 38:30	3027
that he did to prosper in his **h**.	Gn 39:3	3027
his garment in her **h** and fled,	Gn 39:12	3027
he had left his garment in her **h** and	Gn 39:13	3027
"Now Pharaoh's cup was in my **h**;	Gn 40:11	3027
I put the cup into Pharaoh's **h**."	Gn 40:11	3709
you will put Pharaoh's cup into his **h**	Gn 40:13	3027
he put the cup into Pharaoh's **h**;	Gn 40:21	3709
off his signet ring from his **h** and	Gn 41:42	3027
his hand and put it on Joseph's **h**,	Gn 41:42	3027
no one shall raise his **h** or foot in all	Gn 41:44	3027
"Take double *the* money in your **h**,	Gn 43:12	3027
and take back in your **h** the money	Gn 43:12	3027
took double *the* money in their **h**,	Gn 43:15	3027
we have brought it back in our **h**.	Gn 43:21	3027
other money in our **h** to buy food;	Gn 43:22	3027
him the present which was in their **h**	Gn 43:26	3027
place now your **h** under my thigh	Gn 47:29	3027
his right **h** toward Israel's left,	Gn 48:13	3225
his left **h** toward Israel's right,	Gn 48:13	8040
Israel stretched out his right **h** and	Gn 48:14	3225
and his left **h** on Manasseh's head,	Gn 48:14	8040
laid his right **h** on Ephraim's head,	Gn 48:17	3027
and he grasped his father's **h** to	Gn 48:17	3027
Place your right **h** on his head."	Gn 48:18	3225
which I took from the **h** of the	Gn 48:22	3027
Your **h** shall be on the neck of	Gn 49:8	3027
us from the **h** of the shepherds,	Ex 2:19	3027
"So I will stretch out My **h** and	Ex 3:20	3027
"What is that in your **h**?"	Ex 4:2	3027
"Stretch out your **h** and grasp	Ex 4:4	3027
stretched out his **h** and caught it,	Ex 4:4	3027
and it became a staff in his **h**	Ex 4:4	3709
"Now put your **h** into your bosom."	Ex 4:6	3027
So he put his **h** into his bosom,	Ex 4:6	3027
his **h** was leprous like snow.	Ex 4:6	3027
your **h** into your bosom again.	Ex 4:7	3027
he put his **h** into his bosom again,	Ex 4:7	3027
shall take in your **h** this staff,	Ex 4:17	3027
took the staff of God in his **h**.	Ex 4:20	3027
a sword in their **h** to kill us."	Ex 5:21	3027
then I will lay My **h** on Egypt and	Ex 7:4	3027
when I stretch out My **h** on Egypt	Ex 7:5	3027
and you shall take in your **h** the	Ex 7:15	3027
with the staff that is in my **h**,	Ex 7:17	3027
your **h** over the waters of Egypt,	Ex 7:19	3027
'Stretch out your **h** with your	Ex 8:5	3027
his **h** over the waters of Egypt,	Ex 8:6	3027
out his **h** with his staff,	Ex 8:17	3027
the **h** of the LORD will come *with* a	Ex 9:3	3027
I had put forth My **h** and struck you	Ex 9:15	3027
"Stretch out your **h** toward the sky,	Ex 9:22	3027
"Stretch out your **h** over the land	Ex 10:12	3027
"Stretch out your **h** toward the sky,	Ex 10:21	3027
out his **h** toward the sky,	Ex 10:22	3027
feet, and your staff in your **h**;	Ex 12:11	3027
for by a powerful **h** the LORD	Ex 13:3	3027
serve as a sign to you on your **h**,	Ex 13:9	3027
for with a powerful **h** the LORD	Ex 13:9	3027
'With a powerful **h** the LORD	Ex 13:14	3027
shall serve as a sign on your **h** and	Ex 13:16	3027
for with a powerful **h** the LORD	Ex 13:16	3027
your **h** over the sea and divide it,	Ex 14:16	3027
stretched out his **h** over the sea;	Ex 14:21	3027
their right **h** and on their left.	Ex 14:22	3225
"Stretch out your **h** over the sea	Ex 14:26	3027
stretched out his **h** over the sea,	Ex 14:27	3027
their right **h** and on their left.	Ex 14:29	3225
day from the **h** of the Egyptians,	Ex 14:30	3027
"Your right **h**, O LORD, is majestic	Ex 15:6	3225
Your right **h**, O LORD, shatters the	Ex 15:6	3225
sword, my **h** will destroy them.'	Ex 15:9	3027
stretched out Your right **h**,	Ex 15:12	3225
sister, took the timbrel in her **h**,	Ex 15:20	3027
the LORD's **h** in the land of Egypt,	Ex 16:3	3027
and take in your **h** your staff with	Ex 17:5	3027
with the staff of God in my **h**."	Ex 17:9	3027
about when Moses held his **h** up,	Ex 17:11	3027
and when he let his **h** down,	Ex 17:11	3027
them from the **h** of the Egyptians.	Ex 18:9	3027
LORD who delivered you from the **h** of	Ex 18:10	3027
and from the **h** of Pharaoh,	Ex 18:10	3027
from under the **h** of the Egyptians.	Ex 18:10	3027
'No **h** shall touch him, but he	Ex 19:13	3027
but God let *him* fall into his **h**,	Ex 21:13	3027
with a rod and he dies at his **h**,	Ex 21:20	3027
eye, tooth for tooth, **h** for hand,	Ex 21:24	3027
eye, tooth for tooth, hand for **h**,	Ex 21:24	3027
do not join your **h** with a wicked	Ex 23:1	3027
of the land into your **h**,	Ex 23:31	3027
Yet He did not stretch out His **h**	Ex 24:11	3027
He took *this* from their **h**,	Ex 32:4	3027
great power and with a mighty **h**?	Ex 32:11	3027
tablets of the testimony in his **h**,	Ex 32:15	3027
with My **h** until I have passed by.	Ex 33:22	3709
'Then I will take My **h** away and	Ex 33:23	3709
took two stone tablets in his **h**.	Ex 34:4	3027
in Moses' **h** as he was coming down	Ex 34:29	3027
the Levites, by the **h** of Ithamar	Ex 38:21	3027
'He shall lay his **h** on the	Lv 1:4	3027
'He shall lay his **h** on the	Lv 3:2	3027
his **h** on the head of his offering and	Lv 3:8	3027
and he shall lay his **h** on its head	Lv 3:13	3027
lay his **h** on the head of the bull and	Lv 4:4	3027
h on the head of the male goat and	Lv 4:24	3027
'He shall lay his **h** on the	Lv 4:29	3027
'He shall lay his **h** on the	Lv 4:33	3027
and on the thumb of his right **h**	Lv 8:23	3027
and on the thumb of their right **h**	Lv 8:24	3027
and filled his **h** with some of it	Lv 9:17	3709
and on the thumb of his right **h** and	Lv 14:14	3027
and on the thumb of his right **h**,	Lv 14:17	3027
and on the thumb of his right **h** and	Lv 14:25	3027
and on the thumb of his right **h** and	Lv 14:28	3027
If, on the other **h**, the priest comes	Lv 14:48	
by the **h** of a man who *stands* in	Lv 16:21	3027
who has a broken foot or broken **h**,	Lv 21:19	3027
from the **h** of a foreigner for offering	Lv 22:25	3027
or buy from your friend's **h**,	Lv 25:14	3027
and in the **h** of the priest is to	Nu 5:18	3027
of jealousy from the woman's **h**,	Nu 5:25	3027
Then Moses lifted up his **h** and	Nu 20:11	3027
heavy force and with a strong **h**.	Nu 20:20	3027
deliver this people into my **h**,	Nu 21:2	3027
taken all his land out of his **h**,	Nu 21:26	3027
for I have given him into your **h**,	Nu 21:34	3027
fees for divination in their **h**;	Nu 22:7	3027
way with his drawn sword in his **h**,	Nu 22:23	3027
turn to the right **h** or the left.	Nu 22:26	3225
If there had been a sword in my **h**,	Nu 22:29	3027
way with his drawn sword in his **h**;	Nu 22:31	3027
and took a spear in his **h**,	Nu 25:7	3027
the Spirit, and lay your **h** on him;	Nu 27:18	3027
trumpets for the alarm in his **h**.	Nu 31:6	3027
him down with a stone in the **h**,	Nu 35:17	3027
him with a wooden object in the **h**,	Nu 35:18	3027
him down with his **h** in enmity,	Nu 35:21	3027
from the **h** of the blood avenger,	Nu 35:25	3027
h of the Amorites to destroy us.	Dt 1:27	3027
h of the LORD was against them,	Dt 2:15	3027
Heshbon, and his land into your **h**;	Dt 2:24	3027
order to deliver him into your **h**,	Dt 2:30	3027
people and his land into your **h**;	Dt 3:2	3027
with all his people into our **h**,	Dt 3:3	3027
took the land at that time from the **h**	Dt 3:8	3027
Your greatness and Your strong **h**;	Dt 3:24	3027
and by war and by a mighty **h** and	Dt 4:34	3027
h and by an outstretched arm;	Dt 5:15	3027
shall bind them as a sign on your **h**	Dt 6:8	3027
us from Egypt with a mighty **h**.	Dt 6:21	3027
brought you out by a mighty **h** and	Dt 7:8	3027
the **h** of Pharaoh king of Egypt.	Dt 7:8	3027
and the wonders and the mighty **h**	Dt 7:19	3027
will deliver their kings into your **h**	Dt 7:24	3027
of my **h** made me this wealth.'	Dt 8:17	3027
out of Egypt with a mighty **h**.	Dt 9:26	3027
with the two tablets in my **h**.	Dt 10:3	3027
God—His greatness, His mighty **h**	Dt 11:2	3027
bind them as a sign on your **h**,	Dt 11:18	3027
the contribution of your **h**,	Dt 12:6	3027
tithes and the contribution of your **h**,	Dt 12:11	3027
or the contribution of your **h**.	Dt 12:17	3027
your **h** shall be first against him	Dt 13:9	3027
the **h** of all the people.	Dt 13:9	3027
the ban shall cling to your **h**,	Dt 13:17	3027
and bind the money in your **h** and	Dt 14:25	3027
the work of your **h** which you do.	Dt 14:29	3027
but your **h** shall release whatever	Dt 15:3	3027
your **h** from your poor brother;	Dt 15:7	3027
shall freely open your **h** to him,	Dt 15:8	3027
open your **h** to your brother,	Dt 15:11	3027
of a freewill offering of your **h**,	Dt 16:10	3027
"The **h** of the witnesses shall be	Dt 17:7	3027
afterward the **h** of all the people.	Dt 17:7	3027
and his **h** swings the axe to cut	Dt 19:5	3027
the **h** of the avenger of blood,	Dt 19:12	3027
eye, tooth for tooth, **h** for hand,	Dt 19:21	3027
eye, tooth for tooth, hand for **h**,	Dt 19:21	3027
your God gives it into your **h**,	Dt 20:13	3027
"You shall not **h** over to his	Dt 23:15	5462
may pluck the heads with your **h**,	Dt 23:25	3027
and puts *it* in her **h** and sends her out	Dt 24:1	3027
and puts *it* in her **h** and sends her out	Dt 24:3	3027
to deliver her husband from the **h** of	Dt 25:11	3027
out her **h** and seizes his genitals,	Dt 25:11	3027
then you shall cut off her **h**;	Dt 25:12	3709
take the basket from your **h** and set it	Dt 26:4	3027
us out of Egypt with a mighty **h** and	Dt 26:8	3027
and in all that you put your **h** to,	Dt 28:8	3027
to bless all the work of your **h**;	Dt 28:12	3027
in all the work of your **h**,	Dt 30:9	3027
"Our **h** is triumphant, And the	Dt 32:27	3027
no one who can deliver from My **h**.	Dt 32:39	3027
'Indeed, I lift up My **h** to heaven,	Dt 32:40	3027
And My **h** takes hold on justice,	Dt 32:41	3027
At His right **h** there was flashing	Dt 33:2	3225
All Your holy ones are in Your **h**,	Dt 33:3	3027
our head if a **h** is *laid* on him.	Jos 2:19	3027
that the **h** of the LORD is mighty,	Jos 4:24	3027
him with his sword drawn in his **h**,	Jos 5:13	3027
I have given Jericho into your **h**,	Jos 6:2	3027
us into the **h** of the Amorites,	Jos 7:7	3027
given into your **h** the king of Ai,	Jos 8:1	3027
God will deliver it into your **h**.	Jos 8:7	3027
that is in your **h** toward Ai,	Jos 8:18	3027
for I will give it into your **h**."	Jos 8:18	3027
that was in his **h** toward the city.	Jos 8:18	3027
when he had stretched out his **h**,	Jos 8:19	3027
For Joshua did not withdraw his **h**	Jos 8:26	3027
Take provisions in your **h** for the	Jos 9:11	3027
has delivered them into your **h**."	Jos 10:19	3027
them into the **h** of Israel,	Jos 11:8	3027
deliver the manslayer into his **h**,	Jos 20:5	3027
and not die by the **h** of the	Jos 20:9	3027
all their enemies into their **h**.	Jos 21:44	3027
Israel from the **h** of the LORD."	Jos 22:31	3027
it to the right **h** or to the left,	Jos 23:6	3225
and I gave them into your **h**,	Jos 24:8	3027
and I delivered you from his **h**.	Jos 24:10	3027
Thus I gave them into your **h**.	Jos 24:11	3027
have given the land into his **h**."	Jg 1:2	3027
the **h** of the LORD was against them	Jg 2:15	3027
delivered them from the **h** of their	Jg 2:18	3027
give them into the **h** of Joshua.	Jg 2:23	3027
king of Mesopotamia into his **h**,	Jg 3:10	3027
Ehud stretched out his left **h**,	Jg 3:21	8040
that day under the **h** of Israel.	Jg 3:30	3027
the **h** of Jabin king of Canaan,	Jg 4:2	3027
I will give him into your **h**.' "	Jg 4:7	3027
peg and seized a hammer in her **h**,	Jg 4:21	3027
The **h** of the sons of Israel	Jg 4:24	3027
She reached out her **h** for the tent	Jg 5:26	3027
right **h** for the workmen's hammer.	Jg 5:26	3225
given us into the **h** of Midian."	Jg 6:13	3709
Israel from the **h** of Midian.	Jg 6:14	3709
staff that was in his **h** and touched the	Jg 6:21	3027
putting their **h** to their mouth,	Jg 7:6	3027
and all the camp into his **h**."	Jg 7:14	3027
Zebah and Zalmunna into my **h**,	Jg 8:7	3027
and Zalmunna already in your **h**,	Jg 8:15	3027
us from the **h** of Midian."	Jg 8:22	3027
you from the **h** of Midian;	Jg 9:17	3027
and Abimelech took an axe in his **h**	Jg 9:48	3027
his people into the **h** of Israel,	Jg 11:21	3027
give the sons of Ammon into my **h**,	Jg 11:30	3027
and the LORD gave them into his **h**.	Jg 11:32	3027
did not deliver me from their **h**.	Jg 12:2	3027
and the LORD gave them into my **h**.	Jg 12:3	3027
though he had nothing in his **h**;	Jg 14:6	3027
he threw the jawbone from his **h**;	Jg 15:17	3027
by the **h** of Your servant,	Jg 15:18	3027
to the boy who was holding his **h**,	Jg 16:26	3027
h and the other with his left.	Jg 16:29	3225
dedicate the silver from my **h** to the	Jg 17:3	3027
for God has given it into your **h**,	Jg 18:10	3027
put your **h** over your mouth and	Jg 18:19	3027
I will deliver them into your **h**."	Jg 20:28	3027
for the **h** of the LORD has gone	Ru 1:13	3027
buy the field from the **h** of Naomi,	Ru 4:5	3027
I have bought from the **h** of Naomi	Ru 4:9	3027
with a three-pronged fork in his **h**.	1Sa 2:13	3027
from the **h** of these mighty gods?	1Sa 4:8	3027
Now the **h** of the LORD was heavy on	1Sa 5:6	3027
for His **h** is severe on us and on	1Sa 5:7	3027
the **h** of the LORD was against the	1Sa 5:9	3027
the **h** of God was very heavy there.	1Sa 5:11	3027
His **h** is not removed from you."	1Sa 6:3	3027
He will ease His **h** from you,	1Sa 6:5	3027
it was not His **h** that struck us;	1Sa 6:9	3027
from the **h** of the Philistines."	1Sa 7:3	3027
from the **h** of the Philistines."	1Sa 7:8	3027
And the **h** of the LORD was against	1Sa 7:13	3027
from the **h** of the Philistines.	1Sa 7:14	3027
I have in my **h** a fourth of a	1Sa 9:8	3027
from the **h** of the Philistines.	1Sa 9:16	3027
you will accept from their **h**.	1Sa 10:4	3027
you from the **h** of the Egyptians and	1Sa 10:18	3027
of Israel by the **h** of messengers,	1Sa 11:7	3027
or from whose **h** have I taken a	1Sa 12:3	3027
taken anything from any man's **h**."	1Sa 12:4	3027
you have found nothing in my **h**."	1Sa 12:5	3027
He sold them into the **h** of Sisera,	1Sa 12:9	3027
and into the **h** of the Philistines	1Sa 12:9	3027
into the **h** of the king of Moab,	1Sa 12:9	3027
then the **h** of the LORD will be	1Sa 12:15	3027
"Withdraw your **h**."	1Sa 14:19	3027
but no man put his **h** to his mouth,	1Sa 14:26	3027
staff that *was* in his **h** and dipped it in	1Sa 14:27	3027
and put his **h** to his mouth,	1Sa 14:27	3027
give them into the **h** of Israel?"	1Sa 14:37	3027
end of the staff that was in my **h**.	1Sa 14:43	3027
he shall play *the harp* with his **h**,	1Sa 16:16	3027
the harp and play *it* with his **h**;	1Sa 16:23	3027
from the **h** of this Philistine."	1Sa 17:37	3027
He took his stick in his **h** and	1Sa 17:40	3027
pouch, and his sling was in his **h**;	1Sa 17:40	3027
And David put his **h** into his bag	1Sa 17:49	3027

Context	Reference	Number
there was no sword in David's **h**.	1Sa 17:50	3027
the Philistine's head in his **h**.	1Sa 17:57	3027
was playing *the harp* with his **h**,	1Sa 18:10	3027
and a spear *was* in Saul's **h**.	1Sa 18:10	3027
"My **h** shall not be against him,	1Sa 18:17	3027
but let the **h** of the Philistines	1Sa 18:17	3027
and that the **h** of the Philistines	1Sa 18:21	3027
fall by the **h** of the Philistines.	1Sa 18:25	3027
his **h** and struck the Philistine,	1Sa 19:5	3709
his house with his spear in his **h**,	1Sa 19:9	3027
was playing *the harp* with *his* **h**.	1Sa 19:9	3027
therefore, what do you have on **h**?	1Sa 21:3	3027
"There is no ordinary bread on **h**,	1Sa 21:4	3027
there not a spear or a sword on **h**?	1Sa 21:8	3027
height with his spear in his **h**,	1Sa 22:6	3027
because their **h** also is with David	1Sa 22:17	3027
the Philistines into your **h**."	1Sa 23:4	3027
came down *with* an ephod in his **h**.	1Sa 23:6	3027
"God has delivered him into my **h**,	1Sa 23:7	3027
of Keilah surrender me into his **h**?	1Sa 23:11	3027
and my men into the **h** of Saul?"	1Sa 23:12	3027
did not deliver him into his **h**.	1Sa 23:14	3027
because the **h** of Saul my father	1Sa 23:17	3027
surrender him into the king's **h**."	1Sa 23:20	3027
to give your enemy into your **h**,	1Sa 24:4	3027
to stretch out my **h** against him,	1Sa 24:6	3027
you today into my **h** in the cave,	1Sa 24:10	3027
stretch out my **h** against my lord,	1Sa 24:10	3027
see the edge of your robe in my **h**!	1Sa 24:11	3027
but my **h** shall not be against you.	1Sa 24:12	3027
but my **h** shall not be against you.	1Sa 24:13	3027
and deliver me from your **h**."	1Sa 24:15	3027
the LORD delivered me into your **h**	1Sa 24:18	3027
will be established in your **h**.	1Sa 24:20	3027
Please give whatever you find at **h** to	1Sa 25:8	3027
avenging yourself by your own **h**,	1Sa 25:26	3027
from avenging myself by my own **h**.	1Sa 25:33	3027
David received from her **h** what	1Sa 25:35	3027
my reproach from the **h** of Nabal and	1Sa 25:39	3027
delivered your enemy into your **h**;	1Sa 26:8	3027
for who can stretch out his **h**	1Sa 26:9	3027
my **h** against the LORD's anointed;	1Sa 26:11	3027
Or what evil is in my **h**?	1Sa 26:18	3027
delivered you into *my* **h** today,	1Sa 26:23	3027
my **h** against the LORD's anointed.	1Sa 26:23	3027
perish one day by the **h** of Saul.	1Sa 27:1	3027
and I will escape from his **h**."	1Sa 27:1	3027
has torn the kingdom out of your **h**	1Sa 28:17	3027
and I have taken my life in my **h** and	1Sa 28:21	3709
delivered into our **h** the band that	1Sa 30:23	3027
were not afraid to stretch out your **h**	2Sa 1:14	3027
my **h** shall be with you to bring	2Sa 3:12	3027
By the **h** of My servant David I	2Sa 3:18	3027
save My people Israel from the **h** of	2Sa 3:18	3027
the **h** of all their enemies.'	2Sa 3:18	3027
now require his blood from your **h** and	2Sa 4:11	3027
Will You give them into my **h**?"	2Sa 5:19	3027
the Philistines into your **h**."	2Sa 5:19	3027
from the **h** of the Philistines.	2Sa 8:1	3027
in the **h** of Abishai his brother,	2Sa 10:10	3027
and sent *it* by the **h** of Uriah.	2Sa 11:14	3027
delivered you from the **h** of Saul.	2Sa 12:7	3027
may see *it* and eat from her **h**.' "	2Sa 13:5	3027
that I may eat from her **h**."	2Sa 13:6	3027
that I may eat from your **h**."	2Sa 13:10	3027
her **h** on her head and went away,	2Sa 13:19	3027
'**H** over the one who struck his	2Sa 14:7	5414
deliver his maidservant from the **h** of	2Sa 14:16	3709
h of Joab with you in all this?"	2Sa 14:19	3027
he would put out his **h** and take	2Sa 15:5	3027
at his right **h** and at his left.	2Sa 16:6	3225
into the **h** of your son Absalom.	2Sa 16:8	3027
thousand *pieces of* silver in my **h**,	2Sa 18:12	3709
out my **h** against the king's son;	2Sa 18:12	3027
So he took three spears in his **h**	2Sa 18:14	3709
him from the **h** of his enemies."	2Sa 18:19	3027
freed you this day from the **h** of all	2Sa 18:31	3027
"The king delivered us from the **h**	2Sa 19:9	3709
us from the **h** of the Philistines,	2Sa 19:9	3709
with his right **h** to kiss him.	2Sa 20:9	3027
the sword which was in Joab's **h** so he	2Sa 20:10	3027
up his **h** against King David.	2Sa 20:21	3027
Only **h** him over, and I will depart	2Sa 20:21	5414
each **h** and six toes on each foot,	2Sa 21:20	3027
and they fell by the **h** of David	2Sa 21:22	3027
and by the **h** of his servants.	2Sa 21:22	3027
LORD delivered him from the **h** of all	2Sa 22:1	3709
enemies and from the **h** of Saul.	2Sa 22:1	3709
Because they cannot be taken in **h**;	2Sa 23:6	3027
struck the Philistines until his **h** was	2Sa 23:10	3027
the Egyptian *had* a spear in his **h**,	2Sa 23:21	3027
the spear from the Egyptian's **h** and	2Sa 23:21	3027
Let us now fall into the **h** of the	2Sa 24:14	3027
do not let me fall into the **h** of man	2Sa 24:14	3027
When the angel stretched out his **h**	2Sa 24:16	3027
Now relax your **h**!"	2Sa 24:16	3027
Please let Your **h** be against me and	2Sa 24:17	3027
and has fulfilled *it* with His **h**,	1Ki 8:15	3027
have fulfilled it with Your **h** as it is	1Ki 8:24	3027
Your great name and Your mighty **h**,	1Ki 8:42	3027
tear it out of the **h** of your son.	1Ki 11:12	3027
I will tear the kingdom out of the **h** of	1Ki 11:31	3027
the whole kingdom out of his **h**,	1Ki 11:34	3027
his son's **h** and give it to you,	1Ki 11:35	3027
Jeroboam stretched out his **h** from	1Ki 13:4	3027
But his **h** which he stretched out	1Ki 13:4	3027
that my **h** may be restored to me."	1Ki 13:6	3027
the king's **h** was restored to him,	1Ki 13:6	3027
them into the **h** of his servants.	1Ki 15:18	3027
me a piece of bread in your **h**."	1Ki 17:11	3027
your servant into the **h** of Ahab to	1Ki 18:9	3027
a cloud as small as a man's **h**	1Ki 18:44	3709
the **h** of the LORD was on Elijah,	1Ki 18:46	3027
will take in their **h** and carry away	1Ki 20:6	3027
deliver them into your **h** today,	1Ki 20:13	3027
this great multitude into your **h**,	1Ki 20:28	3027
you have let go out of *your* **h** the man	1Ki 20:42	3027
of the **h** of the king of Aram?"	1Ki 22:3	3027
give *it* into the **h** of the king."	1Ki 22:6	3027
give *it* into the **h** of the king."	1Ki 22:12	3027
give *it* into the **h** of the king."	1Ki 22:15	3027
to give them into the **h** of Moab."	2Ki 3:10	3027
to give them into the **h** of Moab."	2Ki 3:13	3027
the **h** of the LORD came upon him.	2Ki 3:15	3027
give the Moabites into your **h**.	2Ki 3:18	3027
loins and take my staff in your **h**,	2Ki 4:29	3027
and wave his **h** over the place and	2Ki 5:11	3027
and he leans on my **h** and I bow	2Ki 5:18	3027
he took them from their **h** and	2Ki 5:24	3027
So he put out his **h** and took it.	2Ki 6:7	3027
The royal officer on whose **h**	2Ki 7:2	3027
the royal officer on whose **h** he leaned	2Ki 7:17	3027
"Take a gift in your **h** and go	2Ki 8:8	3027
meet him and took a gift in his **h**,	2Ki 8:9	3027
from under the **h** of Judah,	2Ki 8:20	3027
take this flask of oil in your **h** and	2Ki 9:1	3027
of the LORD, at the **h** of Jezebel.	2Ki 9:7	3027
"If it is, give *me* your **h**."	2Ki 10:15	3027
And he gave him his **h**,	2Ki 10:15	3027
each with his weapons in his **h**;	2Ki 11:8	3027
each with his weapons in his **h**,	2Ki 11:11	3027
men into whose **h** they gave the money	2Ki 12:15	3027
into the **h** of Hazael king of Aram,	2Ki 13:3	3027
and into the **h** of Ben-hadad the	2Ki 13:3	3027
from under the **h** of the Arameans;	2Ki 13:5	3027
"Put your **h** on the bow."	2Ki 13:16	3027
And he put his **h** *on it,* then	2Ki 13:16	3027
took again from the **h** of Ben-hadad	2Ki 13:25	3027
from the **h** of Jehoahaz his father.	2Ki 13:25	3027
the kingdom was firmly in his **h**,	2Ki 14:5	3027
h of Jeroboam the son of Joash.	2Ki 14:27	3027
so that his **h** might be with him	2Ki 15:19	3027
me from the **h** of the king of Aram and	2Ki 16:7	3709
from the **h** of the king of Israel,	2Ki 16:7	3709
Egypt from under the **h** of Pharaoh,	2Ki 17:7	3027
them into the **h** of plunderers,	2Ki 17:20	3027
from the **h** of all your enemies."	2Ki 17:39	3027
will go into his **h** and pierce it.	2Ki 18:21	3709
be able to deliver you from my **h**;	2Ki 18:29	3027
the **h** of the king of Assyria."	2Ki 18:30	3027
from the **h** of the king of Assyria?	2Ki 18:33	3027
they delivered Samaria from my **h**?	2Ki 18:34	3027
delivered their land from my **h**,	2Ki 18:35	3027
deliver Jerusalem from my **h**?	2Ki 18:35	3027
the **h** of the king of Assyria."	2Ki 19:10	3027
h of the messengers and read it,	2Ki 19:14	3027
deliver us from his **h** that all the	2Ki 19:19	3027
from the **h** of the king of Assyria;	2Ki 20:6	3709
them into the **h** of their enemies,	2Ki 21:14	3027
deliver it into the **h** of the workmen	2Ki 22:5	3027
and have delivered it into the **h**	2Ki 22:9	3027
and that Your **h** might be with me,	1Ch 4:10	3027
the Hagrites, who fell by their **h**,	1Ch 5:10	3027
with them were given into their **h**;	1Ch 5:20	3027
Asaph stood at his right **h**,	1Ch 6:39	3225
On the left **h** *were* their kinsmen	1Ch 6:44	8040
Now in the Egyptian's **h** *was* a	1Ch 11:23	3027
the spear from the Egyptian's **h** and	1Ch 11:23	3027
using both the right **h** and the	1Ch 12:2	3231
put out his **h** to hold the ark,	1Ch 13:9	3027
he put out his **h** to the ark;	1Ch 13:10	3027
will You give them into my **h**?"	1Ch 14:10	3027
I will give them into your **h**."	1Ch 14:10	3027
broken through my enemies by my **h**,	1Ch 14:11	3027
from the **h** of the Philistines.	1Ch 18:1	3027
in the **h** of Abshai his brother;	1Ch 19:11	3027
six *fingers on each* **h** and six	1Ch 20:6	
and they fell by the **h** of David	1Ch 20:8	3027
and by the **h** of his servants.	1Ch 20:8	3027
me fall into the **h** of the LORD,	1Ch 21:13	3027
do not let me fall into the **h** of man."	1Ch 21:13	3027
now relax your **h**."	1Ch 21:15	3027
h stretched out over Jerusalem.	1Ch 21:16	3027
please let Your **h** be against me and	1Ch 21:17	3027
inhabitants of the land into my **h**,	1Ch 22:18	3027
in writing by His **h** upon me,	1Ch 28:19	3027
and in Your **h** is power and might;	1Ch 29:12	3027
it lies in Your **h** to make great	1Ch 29:12	3027
and from Your **h** we have given You.	1Ch 29:14	3027
Your holy name, it is from Your **h**,	1Ch 29:16	3027
and have fulfilled it with Your **h**,	2Ch 6:15	3027
h and Your outstretched arm,	2Ch 6:32	3027
Judah, God gave them into their **h**.	2Ch 13:16	3027
of Aram has escaped out of your **h**.	2Ch 16:7	3027
He delivered them into your **h**.	2Ch 16:8	3027
give *it* into the **h** of the king."	2Ch 18:5	3027
give *it* into the **h** of the king."	2Ch 18:11	3027
they will be given into your **h**."	2Ch 18:14	3027
Power and might are in Your **h** so	2Ch 20:6	3027
man with his weapons in his **h**;	2Ch 23:7	3027
each man with his weapon in his **h**,	2Ch 23:10	3027
their own people from your **h**?"	2Ch 25:15	3027
might deliver them into the **h** *of Joash*	2Ch 25:20	3027
with a censer in his **h** for burning	2Ch 26:19	3027
into the **h** of the king of Aram;	2Ch 28:5	3027
into the **h** of the king of Israel,	2Ch 28:5	3027
He has delivered them into your **h**,	2Ch 28:9	3027
the **h** of the king and his princes,	2Ch 30:6	3027
the **h** of the kings of Assyria.	2Ch 30:6	3709
The **h** of God was also on Judah to	2Ch 30:12	3027
from the **h** of the Levites.	2Ch 30:16	3027
the **h** of the king of Assyria"?	2Ch 32:11	3709
to deliver their land from my **h**?	2Ch 32:13	3027
deliver his people out of my **h**,	2Ch 32:14	3027
be able to deliver you from my **h**?	2Ch 32:14	3027
able to deliver his people from my **h**	2Ch 32:15	3027
hand or from the **h** of my fathers.	2Ch 32:15	3027
God deliver you from my **h**?'	2Ch 32:15	3027
delivered their people from my **h**,	2Ch 32:17	3027
deliver His people from my **h**."	2Ch 32:17	3027
Jerusalem from the **h** of Sennacherib	2Ch 32:22	3027
and from the **h** of all *others,*	2Ch 32:22	3027
the blood *received* from their **h**,	2Ch 35:11	3027
He gave *them* all into his **h**.	2Ch 36:17	3027
the **h** of Mithredath the treasurer,	Ezr 1:8	3027
He gave them into the **h** of	Ezr 5:12	3028
the **h** of the LORD his God *was* upon	Ezr 7:6	3027
good **h** of his God *was* upon him.	Ezr 7:9	3027
of your God which is in your **h**,	Ezr 7:14	3028
of your God which is in your **h**,	Ezr 7:25	3028
the **h** of the LORD my God upon me,	Ezr 7:28	3027
According to the good **h** of our	Ezr 8:18	3027
"The **h** of our God is favorably	Ezr 8:22	3027
and the **h** of our God was over us,	Ezr 8:31	3027
and He delivered us from the **h** of	Ezr 8:31	3709
into the **h** of Meremoth the son of	Ezr 8:33	3027
the **h** of the kings of the lands,	Ezr 9:7	3027
great power and by Your strong **h**.	Ne 1:10	3027
the good **h** of my God *was* on me.	Ne 2:8	3027
I told them how the **h** of my	Ne 2:18	3027
with one **h** doing the work and the	Ne 4:17	3027
time with an open letter in his **h**.	Ne 6:5	3027
and Maaseiah on his right **h**;	Ne 8:4	3225
and Meshullam on his left **h**.	Ne 8:4	8040
You gave them into their **h**,	Ne 9:24	3027
You delivered them into the **h** of	Ne 9:27	3027
from the **h** of their oppressors.	Ne 9:27	3027
them to the **h** of their enemies,	Ne 9:28	3027
the **h** of the peoples of the lands.	Ne 9:30	3027
from his **h** and gave it to Haman,	Es 3:10	3027
golden scepter which *was* in his **h**.	Es 5:2	3027
put forth Your **h** now and touch all	Jb 1:11	3027
do not put forth your **h** on him."	Jb 1:12	3027
"However, put forth Your **h** now	Jb 2:5	3027
the poor from the **h** of the mighty.	Jb 5:15	3027
would loose His **h** and cut me off!	Jb 6:9	3027
me from the **h** of the adversary,'	Jb 6:23	3027
me from the **h** of the tyrants'?	Jb 6:23	3027
is given into the **h** of the wicked;	Jb 9:24	3027
Who may lay his **h** upon us both.	Jb 9:33	3027
is no deliverance from Your **h**.	Jb 10:7	3027
And spread out your **h** to Him,	Jb 11:13	3709
If iniquity is in your **h**,	Jb 11:14	3027
the **h** of the LORD has done this,	Jb 12:9	3027
In whose **h** is the life of every	Jb 12:10	3027
Remove Your **h** from me, And let not	Jb 13:21	3709
that a day of darkness is at **h**.	Jb 15:23	3027
stretched out his **h** against God And	Jb 15:25	3027
For the **h** of God has struck me.	Jb 19:21	3027
The **h** of everyone who suffers will	Jb 20:22	3027
And put *your* **h** over *your* mouth.	Jb 21:5	3027
prosperity is not in their **h**;	Jb 21:16	3027
h is heavy despite my groaning.	Jb 23:2	3027
His **h** has pierced the fleeing serpent	Jb 26:13	3027
"He puts his **h** on the flint;	Jb 28:9	3027
And my bow is renewed in my **h**	Jb 29:20	3027
"On the right **h** their brood arises	Jb 30:12	3225
of Your **h** You persecute me.	Jb 30:21	3027
a heap of ruins stretch out *his* **h**,	Jb 30:24	3027
lifted up my **h** against the orphan,	Jb 31:21	3027
because my **h** had secured *so* much;	Jb 31:25	3027
my **h** threw a kiss from my mouth,	Jb 31:27	3027
mighty are taken away without a **h**.	Jb 34:20	3027
what does He receive from your **h**?	Jb 35:7	3027
"He seals the **h** of every man,	Jb 37:7	3027
I lay my **h** on my mouth.	Jb 40:4	3027
your own right **h** can save you.	Jb 40:14	3225
"Lay your **h** on him;	Jb 41:8	3709
O God, lift up Your **h**.	Ps 10:12	3027
vexation to take it into Your **h**.	Ps 10:14	3027
Because He is at my right **h**,	Ps 16:8	3225
h there are pleasures forever.	Ps 16:11	3225
those who take refuge at Your right **h**	Ps 17:7	3225
From men with Your **h**,	Ps 17:14	3027
And Your right **h** upholds me;	Ps 18:35	3225
saving strength of His right **h**.	Ps 20:6	3225
Your **h** will find out all your	Ps 21:8	3027
Your right **h** will find out those	Ps 21:8	3027
whose right **h** is full of bribes.	Ps 26:10	3225
Into Your **h** I commit my spirit;	Ps 31:5	3027
me over into the **h** of the enemy;	Ps 31:8	3027
My times are in Your **h**;	Ps 31:15	3027
me from the **h** of my enemies and	Ps 31:15	3027
and night Your **h** was heavy upon me;	Ps 32:4	3027
the **h** of the wicked drive me away.	Ps 36:11	3027
LORD is the One who holds his **h**.	Ps 37:24	3027
LORD will not leave him in his **h** Or	Ps 37:33	3027
And Your **h** has pressed down on me.	Ps 38:2	3027
of the opposition of Your **h** I	Ps 39:10	3027
own **h** drove out the nations;	Ps 44:2	3027
But Your right **h** and Your arm	Ps 44:3	3225
right **h** teach You awesome things.	Ps 45:4	3225

At Your right **h** stands the queen in **Ps 45:9** 3225
right **h** is full of righteousness. **Ps 48:10** 3225
delivered, Save with Your right **h**, **Ps 60:5** 3225
Your right **h** upholds me. **Ps 63:8** 3225
God, out of the **h** of the wicked, **Ps 71:4** 3027
have taken hold of my right **h**. **Ps 73:23** 3027
Why do You withdraw Your **h**, **Ps 74:11** 3027
Your hand, even Your right **h**? **Ps 74:11** 3225
For a cup is in the **h** of the LORD, **Ps 75:8** 3027
In the night my **h** was stretched **Ps 77:2** 3027
h of the Most High has changed." **Ps 77:10** 3225
By the **h** of Moses and Aaron. **Ps 77:20** 3027
which His right **h** had gained. **Ps 78:54** 3225
glory into the **h** of the adversary. **Ps 78:61** 3027
which Your right **h** has planted, **Ps 80:15** 3225
Let Your **h** be upon the man of Your **Ps 80:17** 3027
be upon the man of Your right **h**, **Ps 80:17** 3225
My **h** against their adversaries. **Ps 81:14** 3027
them out of the **h** of the wicked. **Ps 82:4** 3027
And they are cut off from Your **h**. **Ps 88:5** 3027
Your **h** is mighty, Your right hand is **Ps 89:13** 3027
is mighty, Your right **h** is exalted. **Ps 89:13** 3225
whom My **h** will be established **Ps 89:21** 3027
"I shall also set his **h** on the sea And **Ps 89:25** 3027
And his right **h** on the rivers. **Ps 89:25** 3225
the right **h** of his adversaries; **Ps 89:42** 3225
And ten thousand at your right **h**, **Ps 91:7** 3225
h are the depths of the earth, **Ps 95:4** 3027
pasture and the sheep of His **h**. **Ps 95:7** 3027
them from the **h** of the wicked. **Ps 97:10** 3027
His right **h** and His holy arm have **Ps 98:1** 3225
You open Your **h**, **Ps 104:28** 3027
the **h** of the one who hated *them*, **Ps 106:10** 3027
them from the **h** of the enemy. **Ps 106:10** 3027
them into the **h** of the nations, **Ps 106:41** 3027
from the **h** of the adversary **Ps 107:2** 3027
delivered, Save with Your right **h**, **Ps 108:6** 3225
an accuser stand at his right **h**. **Ps 109:6** 3225
let them know that this is Your **h**; **Ps 109:27** 3027
at the right **h** of the needy, **Ps 109:31** 3225
"Sit at My right **h** Until I make **Ps 110:1** 3225
The Lord is at Your right **h**; **Ps 110:5** 3225
h of the LORD does valiantly. **Ps 118:15** 3225
right **h** of the LORD is exalted; **Ps 118:16** 3225
The right **h** of the LORD **Ps 118:16** 3225
My life is continually in my **h**, **Ps 119:109** 3709
Let Your **h** be ready to help me, For **Ps 119:173** 3027
is your shade on your right **h**. **Ps 121:5** 3225
look to the **h** of their master, **Ps 123:2** 3027
a maid to the **h** of her mistress, **Ps 123:2** 3027
Like arrows in the **h** of a warrior, **Ps 127:4** 3027
the reaper does not fill his **h**, **Ps 129:7** 3709
strong **h** and an outstretched arm, **Ps 136:12** 3027
May my right **h** forget *her skill* **Ps 137:5** 3225
You will stretch forth Your **h** **Ps 138:7** 3027
And Your right **h** will save me. **Ps 138:7** 3225
before, And laid Your **h** upon me. **Ps 139:5** 3709
Even there Your **h** will lead me, And **Ps 139:10** 3027
Your right **h** will lay hold of me. **Ps 139:10** 3225
Stretch forth Your **h** from on high; **Ps 144:7** 3027
waters, Out of the **h** of aliens **Ps 144:7** 3027
h is a right hand of falsehood. **Ps 144:8** 3225
hand is a right **h** of falsehood. **Ps 144:8** 3225
deliver me out of the **h** of aliens, **Ps 144:11** 3027
h is a right hand of falsehood. **Ps 144:11** 3225
hand is a right **h** of falsehood. **Ps 144:11** 3225
You open Your **h** **Ps 145:16** 3027
And a two-edged sword in their **h**, **Ps 149:6** 3027
I stretched out my **h** and **Pr 1:24** 3027
Long life is in her right **h**; **Pr 3:16** 3225
her left **h** are riches and honor. **Pr 3:16** 8040
come into the **h** of your neighbor, **Pr 6:3** 3709
like a gazelle from *the hunter's* **h** **Pr 6:5** 3027
a bird from the **h** of the fowler. **Pr 6:5** 3027
he who works with a negligent **h**, **Pr 10:4** 3709
the **h** of the diligent makes rich. **Pr 10:4** 3027
of the foolish, ruin is at **h**. **Pr 10:14** 7138
The **h** of the diligent will rule, **Pr 12:24** 3027
But the slack **h** will be put to **Pr 12:24**
a price in the **h** of a fool to buy **Pr 17:16** 3027
sluggard buries his **h** in the dish, **Pr 19:24** 3027
of water in the **h** of the LORD; **Pr 21:1** 3027
a message by the **h** of a fool. **Pr 26:6** 3027
falls into the **h** of a drunkard, **Pr 26:9** 3027
sluggard buries his **h** in the dish; **Pr 26:15** 3027
And grasps oil with his right **h**. **Pr 27:16** 3225
evil, put your **h** on your mouth. **Pr 30:32** 3027
She extends her **h** to the poor, **Pr 31:20** 3027
that it is from the **h** of God. **Ec 2:24** 3027
One **h** full of rest is better than **Ec 4:6** 3709
labor that he can carry in his **h** **Ec 5:15** 3027
On the other **h**, there are evil men **Ec 8:14**
their deeds are in the **h** of God. **Ec 9:1** 3027
Whatever your **h** finds to do, **Ec 9:10** 3027
"Let his left **h** be under my head **SS 2:6** 8040
head And his right **h** embrace me." **SS 2:6** 3225
his **h** through the opening, **SS 5:4** 3027
"Let his left **h** be under my head And **SS 8:3** 8040
And his right **h** embrace me." **SS 8:3** 3225
"I will also turn My **h** against you, **Is 1:25** 3027
h mirrors, undergarments, turbans and **Is 3:23** 1549
And He has stretched out His **h** **Is 5:25** 3027
But His **h** is still stretched out. **Is 5:25** 3027
with a burning coal in his **h**, **Is 6:6** 3027
And His **h** is still stretched out. **Is 9:12** 3027
And His **h** is still stretched out. **Is 9:17** 3027
They slice off *what is* on the right **h** **Is 9:20** 3225
they eat *what is* on the left **h** but **Is 9:20** 8040
And His **h** is still stretched out. **Is 9:21** 3027
And His **h** is still stretched out. **Is 10:4** 3027
"As my **h** has reached to the **Is 10:10** 3027
my **h** and by my wisdom I did *this,* **Is 10:13** 3027
And my **h** reached to the riches of **Is 10:14** 3027
will put his **h** on the viper's den. **Is 11:8** 3027
His **h** The remnant of His people, **Is 11:11** 3027
And He will wave His **h** over the **Is 11:15** 3027
Wave the **h** that they may enter the **Is 13:2** 3027
h that is stretched out against all **Is 14:26** 3027
And as for His stretched-out **h**, **Is 14:27** 3027
into the **h** of a cruel master, **Is 19:4** 3027
of the **h** of the LORD of hosts, **Is 19:16** 3027
stretched His **h** out over the sea, **Is 23:11** 3027
For the **h** of the LORD will rest on **Is 25:10** 3027
Your **h** is lifted up *yet* they do not **Is 26:11** 3027
it down to the earth with *His* **h**. **Is 28:2** 3027
And as soon as it is in his **h**, **Is 28:4** 3709
the LORD will stretch out His **h**, **Is 31:3** 3027
And His **h** has divided it to them **Is 34:17** 3027
will go into his **h** and pierce it. **Is 36:6** 3709
the **h** of the king of Assyria." **Is 36:15** 3027
from the **h** of the king of Assyria? **Is 36:18** 3027
they delivered Samaria from my **h**? **Is 36:19** 3027
delivered their land from my **h**, **Is 36:20** 3027
deliver Jerusalem from my **h**?' " **Is 36:20** 3027
the **h** of the king of Assyria." **Is 37:10** 3027
h of the messengers and read it, **Is 37:14** 3027
deliver us from his **h** that all the **Is 37:20** 3027
from the **h** of the king of Assyria; **Is 38:6** 3709
LORD's **h** Double for all her sins." **Is 40:2** 3027
the waters in the hollow of His **h**, **Is 40:12** 8168
you with My righteous right **h**.' **Is 41:10** 3225
God, who upholds your right **h**, **Is 41:13** 3225
the **h** of the LORD has done this, **Is 41:20** 3027
you by the **h** and watch over you, **Is 42:6** 3027
none who can deliver out of My **h**; **Is 43:13** 3027
And another will write *on* his **h**, **Is 44:5** 3027
"Is there not a lie in my right **h**?" **Is 44:20** 3225
Whom I have taken by the right **h**, **Is 45:1** 3225
And gave them into your **h**. **Is 47:6** 3027
"Surely My **h** founded the earth, **Is 48:13** 3027
My right **h** spread out the heavens; **Is 48:13** 3225
of His **h** He has concealed Me; **Is 49:2** 3027
will lift up My **h** to the nations And **Is 49:22** 3027
Is My **h** so short that it cannot **Is 50:2** 3027
This you will have from My **h**: **Is 50:11** 3027
you with the shadow of My **h**, **Is 51:16** 3027
the LORD's **h** the cup of His anger; **Is 51:17** 3027
Nor is there one to take her by the **h** **Is 51:18** 3027
out of your **h** the cup of reeling, **Is 51:22** 3027
it into the **h** of your tormentors, **Is 51:23** 3027
of the LORD will prosper in His **h**. **Is 53:10** 3027
keeps his **h** from doing any evil." **Is 56:2** 3027
the LORD's **h** is not so short That **Is 59:1** 3027
of beauty in the **h** of the LORD, **Is 62:3** 3027
royal diadem in the **h** of your God. **Is 62:3** 3709
His right **h** and by His strong arm, **Is 62:8** 3225
arm to go at the right **h** of Moses, **Is 63:12** 3225
all of us are the work of Your **h**. **Is 64:8** 3027
"For My **h** made all these things, **Is 66:2** 3027
And the **h** of the LORD will be **Is 66:14** 3027
out His **h** and touched my mouth, **Jer 1:9** 3027
Pass your **h** again like a grape **Jer 6:9** 3027
For I will stretch out My **h** **Jer 6:12** 3027
that you will not die at our **h**" **Jer 11:21** 3027
My soul Into the **h** of her enemies. **Jer 12:7** 3709
My **h** against you and destroy you; **Jer 15:6** 3027
of Your **h** *upon me* I sat alone, **Jer 15:17** 3027
you from the **h** of the wicked, **Jer 15:21** 3027
spoiled in the **h** of the potter; **Jer 18:4** 3027
like the clay in the potter's **h**, **Jer 18:6** 3027
so are you in My **h**, O house of **Jer 18:6** 3027
h of those who seek their life; **Jer 19:7** 3027
to the **h** of the king of Babylon, **Jer 20:4** 3027
over to the **h** of their enemies, **Jer 20:5** 3027
needy one From the **h** of evildoers. **Jer 20:13** 3027
outstretched **h** and a mighty arm, **Jer 21:5** 3027
into the **h** of Nebuchadnezzar king **Jer 21:7** 3027
and into the **h** of their foes and **Jer 21:7** 3027
h of those who seek their lives; **Jer 21:7** 3027
into the **h** of the king of Babylon and **Jer 21:10** 3027
were a signet *ring* on My right **h**, **Jer 22:24** 3225
will give you over into the **h** of those **Jer 22:25** 3027
the **h** of those whom you dread, **Jer 22:25** 3027
even into the **h** of Nebuchadnezzar **Jer 22:25** 3027
and into the **h** of the Chaldeans. **Jer 22:25** 3027
of the wine of wrath from My **h** and **Jer 25:15** 3027
I took the cup from the LORD's **h** **Jer 25:17** 3027
take the cup from your **h** to drink, **Jer 25:28** 3027
But the **h** of Ahikam the son of **Jer 26:24** 3027
lands into the **h** of Nebuchadnezzar **Jer 27:6** 3027
I have destroyed it by his **h**. **Jer 27:8** 3027
h of Elasah the son of Shaphan, **Jer 29:3** 3027
I will deliver them into the **h** of **Jer 29:21** 3027
And redeemed him from the **h** of him **Jer 31:11** 3027
I took them by the **h** to bring them **Jer 31:32** 3027
into the **h** of the king of Babylon, **Jer 32:3** 3027
out of the **h** of the Chaldeans, **Jer 32:4** 3027
into the **h** of the king of Babylon, **Jer 32:4** 3027
h and with an outstretched arm and **Jer 32:21** 3027
and the city is given into the **h** **Jer 32:24** 3027
into the **h** of the Chaldeans.' **Jer 32:25** 3027
this city into the **h** of the Chaldeans **Jer 32:28** 3027
and into the **h** of Nebuchadnezzar **Jer 32:28** 3027
'It is given into the **h** of the **Jer 32:36** 3027
into the **h** of the Chaldeans." **Jer 32:43** 3027
into the **h** of the king of Babylon, **Jer 34:2** 3027
You will not escape from his **h**, **Jer 34:3** 3027
captured and delivered into his **h**; **Jer 34:3** 3027
I will give them into the **h** of **Jer 34:20** 3027
the **h** of those who seek their life. **Jer 34:20** 3027
give into the **h** of their enemies and **Jer 34:21** 3027
h of those who seek their life, **Jer 34:21** 3027
and into the **h** of the army of the **Jer 34:21** 3027
"Take in your **h** the scroll from **Jer 36:14** 3027
scroll in his **h** and went to them. **Jer 36:14** 3027
the **h** of the king of Babylon!" **Jer 37:17** 3027
city will certainly be given into the **h** **Jer 38:3** 3027
nor will I give you over to the **h** of **Jer 38:16** 3027
over to the **h** of the Chaldeans; **Jer 38:18** 3027
will not escape from their **h**.' **Jer 38:18** 3027
into their **h** and they will abuse me." **Jer 38:19** 3027
will not escape from their **h**, **Jer 38:23** 3027
by the **h** of the king of Babylon, **Jer 38:23** 3027
the **h** of the men whom you dread. **Jer 39:17** 3027
you and deliver you from his **h**. **Jer 42:11** 3027
over into the **h** of the Chaldeans, **Jer 43:3** 3027
of Egypt to the **h** of his enemies, **Jer 44:30** 3027
the **h** of those who seek his life, **Jer 44:30** 3027
Judah to the **h** of Nebuchadnezzar **Jer 44:30** 3027
even into the **h** of Nebuchadnezzar **Jer 46:26** 3027
and into the **h** of his officers. **Jer 46:26** 3027
a golden cup in the **h** of the LORD, **Jer 51:7** 3027
will stretch out My **h** against you, **Jer 51:25** 3027
fell into the **h** of the adversary And **La 1:7** 3027
h Over all her precious things, **La 1:10** 3027
By His **h** they are knit together. **La 1:14** 3027
His right **h** From before the enemy. **La 2:3** 3225
He has set His right **h** like an **La 2:4** 3225
He has delivered into the **h** of the **La 2:7** 3027
restrained His **h** from destroying, **La 2:8** 3027
His **h** Repeatedly all the day. **La 3:3** 3027
no one to deliver us from their **h**. **La 5:8** 3027
the **h** of the LORD came upon him.) **Ezk 1:3** 3027
behold, a **h** was extended to me; **Ezk 2:9** 3027
h of the LORD was strong on me. **Ezk 3:14** 3027
blood I will require at your **h**. **Ezk 3:18** 3027
blood I will require at your **h**. **Ezk 3:20** 3027
The **h** of the LORD was on me there, **Ezk 3:22** 3027
'Clap your **h**, stamp your foot and **Ezk 6:11** 3709
I will stretch out My **h** against them **Ezk 6:14** 3027
that the **h** of the Lord GOD fell on **Ezk 8:1** 3027
He stretched out the form of a **h** and **Ezk 8:3** 3027
each man with his censer in his **h** and **Ezk 8:11** 3027
his destroying weapon in his **h**." **Ezk 9:1** 3027
his shattering weapon in his **h**; **Ezk 9:2** 3027
the cherub stretched out his **h** from **Ezk 10:7** 3027
of a man's **h** under their wings. **Ezk 10:8** 3027
"So My **h** will be against the **Ezk 13:9** 3027
deliver My people out of your **h**. **Ezk 13:23** 3027
and I will stretch out My **h** **Ezk 14:9** 3027
and I stretch out My **h** against it, **Ezk 14:13** 3027
I have stretched out My **h** against **Ezk 16:27** 3027
if he keeps his **h** from iniquity **Ezk 18:8** 3027
he keeps his **h** from the poor, does **Ezk 18:17** 3027
"But I withdrew My **h** and acted **Ezk 20:22** 3027
"surely with a mighty **h** and with **Ezk 20:33** 3027
with a mighty **h** and with an **Ezk 20:34** 3027
give it into the **h** of the slayer. **Ezk 21:11** 3027
his right **h** came the divination, **Ezk 21:22** 3225
you will be seized with the **h**. **Ezk 21:24** 3709
give you into the **h** of brutal men, **Ezk 21:31** 3027
I smite My **h** at your dishonest **Ezk 22:13** 3709
gave her into the **h** of her lovers, **Ezk 23:9** 3027
into the **h** of the Assyrians, **Ezk 23:9** 3027
into the **h** of those whom you hate, **Ezk 23:28** 3027
into the **h** of those from whom you **Ezk 23:28** 3027
I will give her cup into your **h**.' **Ezk 23:31** 3027
stretched out My **h** against you **Ezk 25:7** 3027
"I will also stretch out My **h** **Ezk 25:13** 3027
Edom by the **h** of My people Israel. **Ezk 25:14** 3027
out My **h** against the Philistines, **Ezk 25:16** 3027
By the **h** of strangers, **Ezk 28:10** 3027
they took hold of you with the **h**, **Ezk 29:7** 3709
hordes of Egypt cease By the **h** of **Ezk 30:10** 3027
is in it, By the **h** of strangers; **Ezk 30:12** 3027
make the sword fall from his **h**. **Ezk 30:22** 3027
Babylon and put My sword in his **h**; **Ezk 30:24** 3027
when I put My sword into the **h** of **Ezk 30:25** 3027
the **h** of a despot of the nations; **Ezk 31:11** 3027
require from the watchman's **h** **Ezk 33:6** 3027
blood I will require from your **h**. **Ezk 33:8** 3027
Now the **h** of the LORD had been **Ezk 33:22** 3027
the **h** of those who enslaved them. **Ezk 34:27** 3027
will stretch out My **h** against you And **Ezk 35:3** 3027
The **h** of the LORD was upon me, and **Ezk 37:1** 3027
they may become one in your **h**. **Ezk 37:17** 3027
which is in the **h** of Ephraim, **Ezk 37:19** 3027
and they will be one in My **h**."' **Ezk 37:19** 3027
be in your **h** before their eyes. **Ezk 37:20** 3027
to turn your **h** against the waste **Ezk 38:12** 3027
strike your bow from your left **h** and **Ezk 39:3** 3027
your arrows from your right **h**. **Ezk 39:3** 3027
My **h** which I have laid on them. **Ezk 39:21** 3027
into the **h** of their adversaries, **Ezk 39:23** 3027
on that same day the **h** of the LORD **Ezk 40:1** 3027
flax and a measuring rod in his **h**; **Ezk 40:3** 3027
and in the man's **h** was a measuring **Ezk 40:5** 3027
the east with a line in his **h**, **Ezk 47:3** 3027
king of Judah into his **h**, **Da 1:2** 3027
He has given *them* into your **h** and **Da 2:38** 3028
He will deliver us out of your **h**, **Da 3:17** 3028
can ward off His **h** Or say to Him, **Da 4:35** 3028
Suddenly the fingers of a man's **h** **Da 5:5** 3028
of the **h** that did the writing. **Da 5:5** 3028
But the God in whose **h** are your **Da 5:23** 3028
"Then the **h** was sent from Him and **Da 5:24** 3028
be given into his **h** for a time, **Da 7:25** 3028

the land of Egypt with a mighty **h** Da 9:15 3027
a **h** touched me and set me Da 10:10 3027
be given into the **h** of the *former.* Da 11:11 3027
Land, with destruction in his **h**. Da 11:16 3027
will be rescued out of his **h**: Da 11:41 3027
out his **h** against *other* countries, Da 11:42 3027
as he raised his right **h** and his left Da 12:7 3225
one will rescue her out of My **h**. Hos 2:10 3027
stretched out his **h** with scoffers, Hos 7:5 3027
into the **h** of the sons of Judah, Jl 3:8 3027
leans his **h** against the wall And Am 5:19 3027
wall with a plumb line in His **h**. Am 7:7 3027
From there will My **h** take them; Am 9:2 3027
between their right and left **h**, Jon 4:11 8040
On the other **h** I am filled with Mi 3:8 199
you From the **h** of your enemies. Mi 4:10 3709
Your **h** will be lifted up against Mi 5:9 3027
cut off sorceries from your **h**, Mi 5:12 3027
will put *their* **h** on *their* mouth, Mi 7:16 3027
delivered from the **h** of calamity! Hab 2:9 3709
cup in the LORD's right **h** will come Hab 2:16 3225
He has rays *flashing* from His **h**, Hab 3:4 3027
"So I will stretch out My **h** Zph 1:4 3027
And He will stretch out His **h** Zph 2:13 3027
hiss *And* wave his **h** *in contempt.* Zph 2:15 3027
with a measuring line in his **h**. Zch 2:1 3027
I will wave My **h** over them so Zch 2:9 3027
at his right **h** to accuse him. Zch 3:1 3225
the plumb line in the **h** of Zerubbabel Zch 4:10 3027
his staff in his **h** because of age. Zch 8:4 3027
they will consume on the right **h** and Zch 12:6 3225
turn My **h** against the little ones. Zch 13:7 3027
they will seize one another's **h**, Zch 14:13 3027
and the **h** of one will be lifted Zch 14:13 3027
lifted against the **h** of another. Zch 14:13 3027
I receive that from your **h**?" Mal 1:13 3027
accepts *it with* favor from your **h**. Mal 2:13 3027
the kingdom of heaven is at **h**." Mt 3:2 *1448*
His winnowing fork is in His **h**, Mt 3:12 *5495*
"On the other **h**, it is written, Mt 4:7 *3825*
the kingdom of heaven is at **h**." Mt 4:17 *1448*
so that your opponent may not **h** you Mt 5:25 *3860*
If your right **h** makes you stumble, Mt 5:30 *5495*
do not let your left **h** know what Mt 6:3 *710*
know what your right **h** is doing Mt 6:3 *1188*
out His **h** and touched him, Mt 8:3 *5495*
He touched her **h**, Mt 8:15 *5495*
but come and lay Your **h** on her, Mt 9:18 *5495*
He entered and took her by the **h**, Mt 9:25 *5495*
'The kingdom of heaven is at **h**.' Mt 10:7 *1448*
"But beware of men, for they will **h** Mt 10:17 *3860*
"But when they **h** you over, do not Mt 10:19 *3860*
a man *was there* whose **h** was withered. Mt 12:10 *5495*
"Stretch out your **h**!" Mt 12:13 *5495*
out His **h** toward His disciples, Mt 12:49 *5495*
out His **h** and took hold of him, Mt 14:31 *5495*
"If your **h** or your foot Mt 18:8 *5495*
and will **h** Him over to the Gentiles Mt 20:19 *3860*
'Bind him **h** and foot, and throw him Mt 22:13 *5495*
"SIT AT MY RIGHT **H**, UNTIL I Mt 22:44 *1188*
"He who dipped his **h** with Me in Mt 26:23 *5495*
the hour is at **h** and the Son of Mt 26:45 *1448*
the one who betrays Me is at **h**!" Mt 26:46 *1448*
THE SON OF MAN SITTING AT THE RIGHT **H** Mt 26:64 *1188*
head, and a reed in His right **h**; Mt 27:29 *1188*
and the kingdom of God is at **h**; Mk 1:15 *1448*
her up, taking her by the **h**, Mk 1:31 *5495*
Jesus stretched out His **h** Mk 1:41 *5495*
a man was there whose **h** was withered. Mk 3:1 *5495*
to the man with the withered **h**, Mk 3:3 *5495*
"Stretch out your **h**." Mk 3:5 *5495*
it out, and his **h** was restored. Mk 3:5 *5495*
Taking the child by the **h**, Mk 5:41 *5495*
Him to lay His **h** on him. Mk 7:32 *5495*
Taking the blind man by the **h**, Mk 8:23 *5495*
took him by the **h** and raised him; Mk 9:27 *5495*
If your **h** causes you to stumble, Mk 9:43 *5495*
will condemn Him to death and will **h** Mk 10:33 *3860*
"SIT AT MY RIGHT **H**, UNTIL I Mk 12:36 *1188*
"When they arrest you and **h** you over, Mk 13:11 *3860*
the one who betrays Me is at **h**!" Mk 14:42 *1448*
THE SON OF MAN SITTING AT THE RIGHT **H** Mk 14:62 *1188*
sat down at the right **h** of God. Mk 16:19 *1188*
For the **h** of the Lord was Lk 1:66 *5495*
And FROM THE **H** OF ALL WHO HATE US; Lk 1:71 *5495*
from the **h** of our enemies, Lk 1:74 *5495*
"His winnowing fork is in His **h** Lk 3:17 *5495*
And He stretched out His **h** and Lk 5:13 *5495*
there whose right **h** was withered. Lk 6:6 *5495*
to the man with the withered **h**, Lk 6:8 *5495*
"Stretch out your **h**!" Lk 6:10 *5495*
and his **h** was restored. Lk 6:10 *5495*
nor, on the other **h**, Lk 6:43 *3825*
took her by the **h** and called, Lk 8:54 *5495*
h to the plow and looking back, Lk 9:62 *5495*
on his **h** and sandals on his feet; Lk 15:22 *5495*
"SIT AT MY RIGHT **H**, Lk 20:42 *1188*
the **h** of the one betraying Me is Lk 22:21 *5495*
OF MAN WILL BE SEATED AT THE RIGHT **H** Lk 22:69 *1188*
has given all things into His **h**. Jn 3:35 *5495*
and no man laid his **h** on Him, Jn 7:30 *5495*
"He who is a hired **h**, and not a Jn 10:12 *3411*
"*He flees* because he is a hired **h** Jn 10:13 *3411*
one will snatch them out of My **h**. Jn 10:28 *5495*
snatch *them* out of the Father's **h**. Jn 10:29 *5495*
bound **h** and foot with wrappings, Jn 11:44 *5495*
nails, and put my **h** into His side, Jn 20:25 *5495*
and reach here your **h** and Jn 20:27 *5495*
FOR HE IS AT MY RIGHT **H**, SO THAT I Ac 2:25 *1188*
exalted to the right **h** of God, Ac 2:33 *1188*
"SIT AT MY RIGHT **H**, Ac 2:34 *1188*
And seizing him by the right **h**, Ac 3:7 *5495*
to do whatever Your **h** and Your Ac 4:28 *5495*
You extend Your **h** to heal, Ac 4:30 *5495*
right **h** as a Prince and a Savior, Ac 5:31 *1188*
'WAS IT NOT MY **H** WHICH MADE ALL Ac 7:50 *5495*
standing at the right **h** of God; Ac 7:55 *1188*
standing at the right **h** of God." Ac 7:56 *1188*
and leading him by the **h**, Ac 9:8 *5496*
gave her his **h** and raised her up; Ac 9:41 *5495*
the **h** of the Lord was with them, Ac 11:21 *5495*
and rescued me from the **h** of Herod Ac 12:11 *5495*
motioning to them with his **h** to be Ac 12:17 *5495*
the **h** of the Lord is upon you, Ac 13:11 *5495*
those who would lead him by the **h**. Ac 13:11 *5497*
up, and motioning with his **h** Ac 13:16 *5495*
and having motioned with his **h**, Ac 19:33 *5495*
motioned to the people with his **h**; Ac 21:40 *5495*
I was led by the **h** by those who Ac 22:11 *5496*
him by the **h** and stepping aside, Ac 23:19 *5495*
me, no one can **h** me over to them. Ac 25:11 *5483*
custom of the Romans to **h** over any Ac 25:16 *5483*
Then Paul stretched out his **h** and Ac 26:1 *5495*
the heat and fastened itself on his **h**. Ac 28:3 *5495*
the creature hanging from his **h**, Ac 28:4 *5495*
for on the one **h** the judgment Ro 5:16 *3303a*
but on the other **h** the free gift Ro 5:16 *1161*
on the one **h** I myself with my mind Ro 7:25 *3303a*
who is at the right **h** of God, Ro 8:34 *1188*
"Because I am not a **h**, 1Co 12:15 *5495*
And the eye cannot say to the **h**, 1Co 12:21 *5495*
The greeting is in my own **h**—Paul. 1Co 16:21 *5495*
for the right **h** and the left, 2Co 6:7 *1188*
the right **h** of fellowship, Ga 2:9 *1188*
I am writing to you with my own **h**. Ga 6:11 *5495*
right **h** in the heavenly *places,* Eph 1:20 *1188*
is, seated at the right **h** of God. Col 3:1 *1188*
write this greeting with my own **h**. Col 4:18 *5495*
write this greeting with my own **h**, 2Th 3:17 *5495*
On the other **h**, discipline 1Tm 4:7 *1161*
am writing this with my own **h**, Phm 1:19 *5495*
right **h** of the Majesty on high, Heb 1:3 *1188*
"SIT AT MY RIGHT **H**, UNTIL I Heb 1:13 *1188*
on the one **h**, there is a setting aside Heb 7:18 *3303a*
on the other **h** there is a bringing in Heb 7:19 *1161*
The *former* priests, on the one **h**, Heb 7:23 *3303a*
but Jesus, on the other **h**, Heb 7:24 *1161*
who has taken His seat at the right **h** Heb 8:1 *1188*
THE DAY WHEN I TOOK THEM BY THE **H** Heb 8:9 *5495*
SAT DOWN AT THE RIGHT **H** OF GOD, Heb 10:12 *1188*
the right **h** of the throne of God. Heb 12:2 *1188*
who is at the right **h** of God, 1Pe 3:22 *1188*
under the mighty **h** of God, 1Pe 5:6 *5495*
On the other **h**, I am writing a new 1Jn 2:8 *3825*
His right **h** He held seven stars, Rv 1:16 *5495*
And He placed His right **h** on me, Rv 1:17 *1188*
stars which you saw in My right **h**, Rv 1:20 *1188*
the seven stars in His right **h**, Rv 2:1 *1188*
I saw in the right **h** of Him Rv 5:1 *1188*
h of Him who sat on the throne. Rv 5:7 *1188*
it had a pair of scales in his **h**. Rv 6:5 *5495*
up before God out of the angel's **h**. Rv 8:4 *5495*
h a little book which was open. Rv 10:2 *5495*
lifted up his right **h** to heaven, Rv 10:5 *5495*
the book which is open in the **h** of the Rv 10:8 *5495*
out of the angel's **h** and ate it, Rv 10:10 *5495*
be given a mark on their right **h** or Rv 13:16 *5495*
on his forehead or on his **h**, Rv 14:9 *5495*
head and a sharp sickle in His **h**. Rv 14:14 *5495*
having in her **h** a gold cup full of Rv 17:4 *5495*
abyss and a great chain in his **h**. Rv 20:1 *5495*
their forehead and on their **h**; Rv 20:4 *5495*

HANDBREADTH

for it a rim of a **h** around Ex 25:25 2948
a rim for it of a **h** all around, Ex 37:12 2948
It was a **h** thick, and its brim 1Ki 7:26 2947
It was a **h** thick, and its brim 2Ch 4:5 2947
each of which was a cubit and a **h**. Ezk 40:5 2948
The double hooks, one **h** in length, Ezk 40:43 2948
(the cubit being a cubit and a **h**): Ezk 43:13 2948

HANDBREADTHS

You have made my days *as* **h**, Ps 39:5 2947

HANDED

and Aaron's sons **h** the blood to Lv 9:12 4672
They **h** the burnt offering to Lv 9:13 4672
and Aaron's sons **h** the blood to Lv 9:18 4672
which the king had **h** down, 1Ki 3:28 8199
let the robe and the horse be **h** over Es 6:9 3027
been **h** over to Me by My Father; Mt 11:27 *3860*
h him over to the torturers until Mt 18:34 *3860*
and the Son of Man is *to be* **h** Mt 26:2 *3860*
because of envy they had **h** Him over. Mt 27:18 *3860*
he **h** Him over to be crucified. Mt 27:26 *3860*
tradition which you have **h** down; Mk 7:13 *3860*
aware that the chief priests had **h** Mk 15:10 *3860*
he **h** Him over to be crucified. Mk 15:15 *3860*
as they were **h** down to us Lk 1:2 *3860*
for it has been **h** over to me, and Lk 4:6 *3860*
book of the prophet Isaiah was **h** to Lk 4:17 *1929*
been **h** over to Me by My Father, Lk 10:22 *3860*
"For He will be **h** over to Lk 18:32 *3860*
so that I would not be **h** over Jn 18:36 *3860*
So he then **h** Him over to them to be Jn 19:16 *3860*
which Moses **h** down to us." Ac 6:14 *3860*
whom I have **h** over to Satan, so that 1Tm 1:20 *3860*
from the holy commandment **h** on to 2Pe 2:21 *3860*
faith which was once for all **h** down Jude 1:3 *3860*

HANDFUL

and shall take from it his **h** of Lv 2:2
4393, 7062
and the priest shall take his **h** of Lv 5:12
4393, 7062
lift up from it a **h** of the fine flour Lv 6:15 7062
and the priest shall take a **h** of Nu 5:26 7061
only a **h** of flour in the bowl and 1Ki 17:12
4393, 3709

HANDFULS

yourselves **h** of soot from a kiln, Ex 9:8
4393, 2651
and two **h** of finely ground sweet Lv 16:12
4393, 2651
dust of Samaria will suffice for **h** for 1Ki 20:10 8168
"For **h** of barley and Ezk 13:19 8168

HANDIWORK

For *its* maker trusts in his *own* **h** Hab 2:18 3336

HANDKERCHIEF

which I kept put away in a **h**; Lk 19:20 *4676*

HANDKERCHIEFS

so that **h** or aprons were even Ac 19:12 *4676*

HANDLE

iron *head* slips off the **h** and strikes Dt 19:5 6086
h also went in after the blade, Jg 3:22 5325
war, who could **h** shield and spear, 1Ch 12:8 6186a
go to war *and* **h** spear and shield. 2Ch 25:5 270
who **h** the law did not know Me; Jer 2:8 8610
and Put, that **h** the shield, Jer 46:9 8610
Lydians, that **h** *and* bend the bow. Jer 46:9 8610
"All who **h** the oar, The Ezk 27:29 8610
"Do not **h**, do not taste, do not Col 2:21 *681*

HANDLED

to be polished, that it may be **h**; Ezk 21:11 8610
there their virgin bosom was **h**. Ezk 23:3 6213b
and they **h** her virgin bosom and Ezk 23:8 6213b
when the Egyptians **h** your bosom Ezk 23:21 6213b

HANDLES

myrrh, On the **h** of the bolt. SS 5:5 3709

HANDLING

h the word of truth. 2Tm 2:15 *3718*

HANDMAID

And save the son of Your **h**. Ps 86:16 519
am Your servant, the son of Your **h**, Ps 116:16 519

HANDMAIDS

And her **h** are moaning like the Na 2:7 519

HANDMILL

"No one shall take a **h** or an Dt 24:6 7347

HANDS

our work and from the toil of our **h** Gn 5:29 3027
But the men reached out their **h** Gn 19:10 3027
wife and the **h** of his two daughters, Gn 19:16 3027
of my **h** I have done this." Gn 20:5 3709
the skins of the young goats on his **h** Gn 27:16 3027
but the **h** are the hands of Esau." Gn 27:22 3027
but the hands are the **h** of Esau." Gn 27:22 3027
because his **h** were hairy like his Gn 27:23 3027
hairy like his brother Esau's **h**; Gn 27:23 3027
affliction and the toil of my **h**, Gn 31:42 3709
him out of their **h** and said, Gn 37:21 3027
but do not lay **h** on him" Gn 37:22 3027
might rescue him out of their **h**, Gn 37:22 3027
and not lay our **h** on him, Gn 37:27 3027
on Manasseh's head, crossing his **h**, Gn 48:14 3027
the **h** of the Mighty One of Jacob Gn 49:24 3027
will spread out my **h** to the LORD; Ex 9:29 3709
and spread out his **h** to the LORD; Ex 9:33 3709
which Your **h** have established. Ex 15:17 3027
But Moses' **h** were heavy. Ex 17:12 3027
and Aaron and Hur supported his **h**, Ex 17:12 3027
Thus his **h** were steady until the Ex 17:12 3027
his **h** on his neighbor's property. Ex 22:8 3027
laid his **h** on his neighbor's property; Ex 22:11 3027
their **h** on the head of the bull. Ex 29:10 3027
their **h** on the head of the ram; Ex 29:15 3027
their **h** on the head of the ram. Ex 29:19 3027
and on the thumbs of their right **h** Ex 29:20 3027
shall put all these in the **h** of Aaron Ex 29:24 3709
of Aaron and in the **h** of his sons, Ex 29:24 3709
You shall take them from their **h**, Ex 29:25 3027
his sons shall wash their **h** and their Ex 30:19 3027
shall wash their **h** and their feet, Ex 30:21 3027
and he threw the tablets from his **h** Ex 32:19 3027
skilled women spun with their **h**, Ex 35:25 3027
washed their **h** and their feet. Ex 40:31 3027
congregation shall lay their **h** on the Lv 4:15 3027
'His own **h** are to bring offerings Lv 7:30 3027
Aaron and his sons laid their **h** on the Lv 8:14 3027
their **h** on the head of the ram. Lv 8:18 3027
their **h** on the head of the ram. Lv 8:22 3027
He then put all *these* on the **h** of Lv 8:27 3709
of Aaron and on the **h** of his sons and Lv 8:27 3709
Then Moses took them from their **h** Lv 8:28 3709
Then Aaron lifted up his **h** toward Lv 9:22 3027
without having rinsed his **h** in water Lv 15:11 3027
h on the head of the live goat, Lv 16:21 3027
heard him lay their **h** on his head; Lv 24:14 3027
shall remain in the **h** of its purchaser Lv 25:28 3027
shall be delivered into enemy **h**. Lv 26:25 3027
offering of memorial in her **h**, Nu 5:18 3709
and shall put *them* on the **h** of the Nu 6:19 3709
shall lay their **h** on the Levites. Nu 8:10 3027
their **h** on the heads of the bulls Nu 8:12 3027
and he struck his **h** together; Nu 24:10 3709
his **h** on him and commissioned him, Nu 27:23 3027
their **h** and brought it down to us; Dt 1:25 3027
serve gods, the work of man's **h**, Dt 4:28 3027

of the covenant were in my two **h**. **Dt 9:15** 3027
tablets and threw them from my **h** and **Dt 9:17** 3027
and in all the work of your **h**, **Dt 16:15** 3027
shall wash their **h** over the heifer **Dt 21:6** 3027
'Our **h** did not shed this blood, **Dt 21:7** 3027
God delivers them into your **h** and **Dt 21:10** 3027
you in all the work of your **h**. **Dt 24:19** 3027
work of the **h** of the craftsman, **Dt 27:15** 3027
anger with the work of your **h**." **Dt 31:29** 3027
With his **h** he contended for them, **Dt 33:7** 3027
And accept the work of his **h**; **Dt 33:11** 3027
for Moses had laid his **h** on him; **Dt 34:9** 3027
has given all the land into our **h**; **Jos 2:24** 3027
"Now behold, we are in your **h**; **Jos 9:25** 3027
from the **h** of the sons of Israel, **Jos 9:26** 3027
for I have given them into your **h**; **Jos 10:8** 3027
its king into the **h** of Israel, **Jos 10:30** 3027
gave Lachish into the **h** of Israel; **Jos 10:32** 3027
and the Perizzites into their **h**, **Jg 1:4** 3027
and He gave them into the **h** of **Jg 2:14** 3027
and He sold them into the **h** of **Jg 2:14** 3027
the **h** of those who plundered them. **Jg 2:16** 3027
so that He sold them into the **h** of **Jg 3:8** 3027
the Moabites into your **h**." **Jg 3:28** 3027
Sisera into the **h** of a woman." **Jg 4:9** 3027
LORD has given Sisera into your **h**; **Jg 4:14** 3027
into the **h** of Midian seven years. **Jg 6:1** 3027
'I delivered you from the **h** of **Jg 6:9** 3027
from the **h** of all your oppressors, **Jg 6:9** 3027
Me to give Midian into their **h**, **Jg 7:2** 3027
give the Midianites into your **h**; **Jg 7:7** 3027
and their trumpets into their **h**. **Jg 7:8** 3027
for I have given it into your **h**. **Jg 7:9** 3027
and afterward your **h** will be **Jg 7:11** 3027
the camp of Midian into your **h**." **Jg 7:15** 3027
into the **h** of all of them, **Jg 7:16** 3027
the pitchers that were in their **h**. **Jg 7:19** 3027
they held the torches in their left **h** **Jg 7:20** 3027
trumpets in their right **h** for blowing **Jg 7:20** 3027
Midian, Oreb and Zeeb into your **h**; **Jg 8:3** 3027
"Are the **h** of Zebah and Zalmunna **Jg 8:6** 3709
and Zalmunna already in your **h**, **Jg 8:6** 3027
'Are the **h** of Zebah and Zalmunna **Jg 8:15** 3709
delivered them from the **h** of all their **Jg 8:34** 3027
his **h** to kill his brothers. **Jg 9:24** 3027
into the **h** of the Philistines and **Jg 10:7** 3027
into the **h** of the sons of Ammon. **Jg 10:7** 3027
and I delivered you from their **h**. **Jg 10:12** 3027
I took my life in my **h** and crossed **Jg 12:3** 3709
the LORD gave them into the **h** of the **Jg 13:1** 3027
from the **h** of the Philistines." **Jg 13:5** 3027
and a grain offering from our **h**, **Jg 13:23** 3027
the honey into his **h** and went on, **Jg 14:9** 3709
into the **h** of the Philistines." **Jg 15:12** 3027
fast and give you into their **h**; **Jg 15:13** 3027
and his bonds dropped from his **h**. **Jg 15:14** 3027
into the **h** of the uncircumcised?" **Jg 15:18** 3027
and brought the money in their **h**. **Jg 16:18** 3027
Samson our enemy into our **h**." **Jg 16:23** 3027
has given our enemy into our **h**, **Jg 16:24** 3027
with her **h** on the threshold. **Jg 19:27** 3027
both the palms of his **h** *were* cut off **1Sa 5:4** 3027
us from the **h** of our enemies, **1Sa 12:10** 3027
the **h** of your enemies all around, **1Sa 12:11** 3027
sword nor spear was found in the **h** of **1Sa 13:22** 3027
LORD has given them into our **h**; **1Sa 14:10** 3027
given them into the **h** of Israel." **1Sa 14:12** 3027
climbed up on his **h** and feet, **1Sa 14:13** 3027
the **h** of those who plundered them. **1Sa 14:48** 3027
will deliver you up into my **h**, **1Sa 17:46** 3027
and He will give you into our **h**." **1Sa 17:47** 3027
it at the **h** of David's enemies." **1Sa 20:16** 3027
and acted insanely in their **h**, **1Sa 21:13** 3027
were not willing to put forth their **h** to **1Sa 22:17** 3027
is no evil or rebellion in my **h**, **1Sa 24:11** 3027
you into the **h** of the Philistines, **1Sa 28:19** 3027
into the **h** of the Philistines!" **1Sa 28:19** 3027
me into the **h** of my master, **1Sa 30:15** 3027
therefore, let your **h** be strong and **2Sa 2:7** 3027
delivered you into the **h** of David; **2Sa 3:8** 3027
"Your **h** were not bound, nor your **2Sa 3:34** 3027
them and cut off their **h** and feet and **2Sa 4:12** 3027
The **h** of all who are with you will **2Sa 16:21** 3027
h against my lord the king." **2Sa 18:28** 3027
them into the **h** of the Gibeonites, **2Sa 21:9** 3027
of my **h** He has recompensed me. **2Sa 22:21** 3027
"He trains my **h** for battle, So **2Sa 22:35** 3027
established in the **h** of Solomon. **1Ki 2:46** 3027
spread out his **h** toward heaven. **1Ki 8:22** 3709
spreading his **h** toward this house; **1Ki 8:38** 3709
with his **h** spread toward heaven. **1Ki 8:54** 3709
to anger with the work of his **h**, **1Ki 16:7** 3027
pour water on the **h** of Elijah." **2Ki 3:11** 3027
his eyes and his hands on his **h**, **2Ki 4:34** 3027
his eyes and his hands on his **h**, **2Ki 4:34** 3709
by not receiving from his **h** what he **2Ki 5:20** 3027
the feet and the palms of her **h**. **2Ki 9:35** 3027
the men whom I bring into your **h** **2Ki 10:24** 3027
and they clapped their **h** and said, **2Ki 11:12** 3709
the **h** of those who did the work, **2Ki 12:11** 3027
laid his **h** on the king's hands. **2Ki 13:16** 3027
laid his hands on the king's **h**. **2Ki 13:16** 3027
not gods but the work of men's **h**, **2Ki 19:18** 3027
the money delivered into their **h**, **2Ki 22:7** 3027
with all the work of their **h**, **2Ki 22:17** 3027
since there is no wrong in my **h**, **1Ch 12:17** 3709
and has fulfilled *it* with His **h**, **2Ch 6:4** 3027
of Israel and spread out his **h**. **2Ch 6:12** 3709
spread out his **h** toward heaven. **2Ch 6:13** 3709

spreading his **h** toward this house, **2Ch 6:29** 3709
repair work progressed in their **h**, **2Ch 24:13** 3027
a very great army into their **h**, **2Ch 24:24** 3027
and they laid their **h** on them. **2Ch 29:23** 3027
of the earth, the work of men's **h**. **2Ch 32:19** 3027
Then they gave *it* into the **h** of **2Ch 34:10** 3027
and have delivered it into the **h** **2Ch 34:17** 3027
with all the works of their **h**; **2Ch 34:25** 3027
care and is succeeding in their **h**. **Ezr 5:8** 3028
I weighed into their **h** 650 talents **Ezr 8:26** 3027
the **h** of the princes and the **Ezr 9:2** 3027
out my **h** to the LORD my God; **Ezr 9:5** 3709
they put their **h** to the good *work.* **Ne 2:18** 3027
But now, *O God,* strengthen my **h**. **Ne 6:9** 3027
while lifting up their **h**; **Ne 8:6** 3027
sought to lay **h** on King Ahasuerus. **Es 2:21** 3027
to lay **h** on Mordecai alone, **Es 3:6** 3027
talents of silver into the **h** of those **Es 3:9** 3027
sought to lay **h** on King Ahasuerus. **Es 6:2** 3027
out his **h** against the Jews. **Es 8:7** 3027
lay **h** on those who sought their harm **Es 9:2** 3027
not lay their **h** on the plunder. **Es 9:10** 3027
not lay their **h** on the plunder. **Es 9:15** 3027
not lay their **h** on the plunder. **Es 9:16** 3027
have blessed the work of his **h**, **Jb 1:10** 3027
And you have strengthened weak **h**. **Jb 4:3** 3027
their **h** cannot attain success. **Jb 5:12** 3027
He wounds, and His **h** *also* heal. **Jb 5:18** 3027
snow And cleanse my **h** with lye, **Jb 9:30** 3709
To reject the labor of Your **h**, **Jb 10:3** 3709
'Your **h** fashioned and made me **Jb 10:8** 3027
my teeth And put my life in my **h**? **Jb 13:14** 3709
will long for the work of Your **h**. **Jb 14:15** 3027
"God **h** me over to ruffians And **Jb 16:11** 5462
me into the **h** of the wicked. **Jb 16:11** 3027
there is no violence in my **h**, **Jb 16:17** 3709
And he who has clean **h** will grow **Jb 17:9** 3027
And his **h** give back his wealth. **Jb 20:10** 3027
through the cleanness of your **h**." **Jb 22:30** 3709
"*Men* will clap their **h** at him **Jb 27:23** 3709
And put *their* **h** on their mouths; **Jb 29:9** 3709
was the strength of their **h** to me? **Jb 30:2** 3027
Or if any spot has stuck to my **h** **Jb 31:7** 3709
they all are the work of His **h**? **Jb 34:19** 3027
He claps his **h** among us, And **Jb 34:37**
covers *His* **h** with the lightning, **Jb 36:32** 3709
If there is injustice in my **h**, **Ps 7:3** 3709
to rule over the works of Your **h**; **Ps 8:6** 3027
In the work of his own **h** the wicked **Ps 9:16** 3709
According to the cleanness of my **h** **Ps 18:20** 3027
the cleanness of my **h** in His eyes. **Ps 18:24** 3027
He trains my **h** for battle, So that **Ps 18:34** 3027
is declaring the work of His **h**. **Ps 19:1** 3027
They pierced my **h** and my feet. **Ps 22:16** 3027
who has clean **h** and a pure heart, **Ps 24:4** 3709
I shall wash my **h** in innocence, **Ps 26:6** 3709
In whose **h** is a wicked scheme, And **Ps 26:10** 3027
up my **h** toward Your holy sanctuary. **Ps 28:2** 3027
according to the deeds of their **h**; **Ps 28:4** 3027
the LORD Nor the deeds of His **h**, **Ps 28:5** 3027
extended our **h** to a strange god, **Ps 44:20** 3709
O clap your **h**, all peoples; **Ps 47:1** 3709
He has put forth his **h** against **Ps 55:20** 3027
weigh out the violence of your **h**. **Ps 58:2** 3027
I will lift up my **h** in Your name. **Ps 63:4** 3709
quickly stretch out her **h** to God. **Ps 68:31** 3027
And washed my **h** in innocence; **Ps 73:13** 3709
none of the warriors could use his **h**. **Ps 76:5** 3027
guided them with his skillful **h**. **Ps 78:72** 3709
His **h** were freed from the basket. **Ps 81:6** 3709
I have spread out my **h** to You. **Ps 88:9** 3709
confirm for us the work of our **h**; **Ps 90:17** 3027
Yes, confirm the work of our **h**. **Ps 90:17** 3027
They will bear you up in their **h**, **Ps 91:12** 3709
sing for joy at the works of Your **h**. **Ps 92:4** 3027
And His **h** formed the dry land. **Ps 95:5** 3027
Let the rivers clap their **h**, **Ps 98:8** 3709
the heavens are the work of Your **h**. **Ps 102:25** 3027
works of His **h** are truth and justice **Ps 111:7** 3027
and gold, The work of man's **h**. **Ps 115:4** 3027
They have **h**, but they cannot feel; **Ps 115:7** 3027
lift up my **h** to Your commandments, **Ps 119:48** 3709
Your **h** made me and fashioned me; **Ps 119:73** 3027
not put forth their **h** to do wrong. **Ps 125:3** 3027
shall eat of the fruit of your **h**, **Ps 128:2** 3709
Lift up your **h** to the sanctuary And **Ps 134:2** 3027
and gold, The work of man's **h**. **Ps 135:15** 3027
Do not forsake the works of Your **h**. **Ps 138:8** 3027
O LORD, from the **h** of the wicked; **Ps 140:4** 3027
lifting up of my **h** as the evening **Ps 141:2** 3709
I muse on the work of Your **h**. **Ps 143:5** 3027
I stretch out my **h** to You; **Ps 143:6** 3027
my rock, Who trains my **h** for war, **Ps 144:1** 3027
little folding of the **h** to rest" **Pr 6:10** 3027
And **h** that shed innocent blood, **Pr 6:17** 3027
the deeds of a man's **h** will return **Pr 12:14** 3027
tears it down with her own **h**. **Pr 14:1** 3027
death, For his **h** refuse to work; **Pr 21:25** 3027
little folding of the **h** to rest," **Pr 24:33** 3027
lizard you may grasp with the **h**, **Pr 30:28** 3027
And works with her **h** in delight. **Pr 31:13** 3709
She stretches out her **h** to the distaff **Pr 31:19** 3027
And her **h** grasp the spindle. **Pr 31:19** 3709
stretches out her **h** to the needy. **Pr 31:20** 3027
Give her the product of her **h**, **Pr 31:31** 3027
all my activities which my **h** had done **Ec 2:11** 3027
The fool folds his **h** and consumes **Ec 4:5** 3027
and destroy the work of your **h**? **Ec 5:6** 3027
and nets, whose **h** are chains. **Ec 7:26** 3027

And my **h** dripped with myrrh, And **SS 5:5** 3027
"His **h** are rods of gold Set with **SS 5:14** 3027
The work of the **h** of an artist. **SS 7:1** 3027
you spread out your **h** *in prayer,* **Is 1:15** 3709
Your **h** are covered with blood. **Is 1:15** 3027
They worship the work of their **h**, **Is 2:8** 3027
they consider the work of His **h**. **Is 5:12** 3027
in whose **h** is My indignation, **Is 10:5** 3027
Therefore all **h** will fall limp, **Is 13:7** 3027
for the altars, the work of his **h**, **Is 17:8** 3027
and Assyria the work of My **h**, **Is 19:25** 3027
And he will spread out his **h** in **Is 25:11** 3027
it As a swimmer spreads out *his* **h** **Is 25:11**
with the trickery of his **h**. **Is 25:11** 3027
his children, the work of My **h**, **Is 29:23** 3027
which your sinful **h** have made **Is 31:7** 3027
his **h** so that they hold no bribe; **Is 33:15** 3709
not gods but the work of men's **h**, **Is 37:19** 3027
you are making *say,* 'He has no **h**'? **Is 45:9** 3027
commit to Me the work of My **h**. **Is 45:11** 3027
out the heavens with My **h** **Is 45:12** 3027
inscribed you on the palms *of My* **h**; **Is 49:16**
of the field will clap *their* **h**. **Is 55:12** 3709
For your **h** are defiled with blood **Is 59:3** 3709
an act of violence is in their **h**. **Is 59:6** 3709
of My planting, The work of My **h**, **Is 60:21** 3027
"I have spread out My **h** all day **Is 65:2** 3027
wear out the work of their **h**. **Is 65:22** 3027
the works of their own **h**. **Jer 1:16** 3027
go out With your **h** on your head; **Jer 2:37** 3027
for breath, Stretching out her **h**, **Jer 4:31** 3709
heard the report of it; Our **h** are limp **Jer 6:24** 3027
The work of the **h** of a craftsman **Jer 10:3** 3027
and of the **h** of a goldsmith; **Jer 10:9** 3027
of war which are in your **h**, **Jer 21:4** 3027
strengthen the **h** of evildoers, **Jer 23:14** 3027
to anger with the work of your **h**, **Jer 25:6** 3027
work of your **h** to your own harm. **Jer 25:7** 3027
according to the work of their **h**. **Jer 25:14** 3027
as for me, behold, I am in your **h**; **Jer 26:14** 3027
he was not given into the **h** of the **Jer 26:24** 3027
every man *With* his **h** on his loins, **Jer 30:6** 3027
to anger by the work of their **h**," **Jer 32:30** 3027
the **h** of the one who numbers them,' **Jer 33:13** 3027
"Behold, he is in your **h**; **Jer 38:5** 3027
the chains which are on your **h**. **Jer 40:4** 3027
incense in their **h** to bring to the house **Jer 41:5** 3027
"Take *some* large stones in your **h** **Jer 43:9** 3027
to anger with the works of your **h**, **Jer 44:8** 3027
and fulfilled *it* with your **h**, **Jer 44:25** 3027
of the limpness of *their* **h**, **Jer 47:3** 3027
the **h** and sackcloth on the loins. **Jer 48:37** 3027
about them, And his **h** hang limp; **Jer 50:43** 3027
The Lord has given me into the **h** **La 1:14** 3027
Zion stretches out her **h**; **La 1:17** 3027
Clap their **h** *in derision* at you; **La 2:15** 3709
Lift up your **h** to Him For the life **La 2:19** 3709
heart and **h** Toward God in heaven; **La 3:41** 3709
According to the work of their **h**. **La 3:64** 3027
jars, The work of a potter's **h**! **La 4:2** 3027
And no **h** were turned toward her. **La 4:6** 3027
The **h** of compassionate women **La 4:10** 3027
Princes were hung by their **h**; **La 5:12** 3027
on their four sides *were* human **h**. **Ezk 1:8** 3027
'All **h** will hang limp and all **Ezk 7:17** 3027
'I will give it into the **h** of **Ezk 7:21** 3027
and the **h** of the people of the **Ezk 7:27** 3027
and fill your **h** with coals of fire **Ezk 10:2** 2651
the **h** of the one clothed in linen, **Ezk 10:7** 2651
whole body, their backs, their **h**, **Ezk 10:12** 3027
wings *was* the form of human **h**. **Ezk 10:21** 3027
deliver you into the **h** of strangers **Ezk 11:9** 3027
I dug through the wall with my **h**; **Ezk 12:7** 3027
and deliver My people from your **h**, **Ezk 13:21** 3027
no longer be in your **h** to be hunted **Ezk 13:21** 3027
put bracelets on your **h** and **Ezk 16:11** 3027
you into the **h** of your lovers, **Ezk 16:39** 3027
will melt, all **h** will be feeble, **Ezk 21:7** 3027
and clap *your* **h** together; **Ezk 21:14** 3709
"I will also clap My **h** together, **Ezk 21:17** 3709
endure, or can your **h** be strong in **Ezk 22:14** 3027
adultery, and blood is on their **h**. **Ezk 23:37** 3027
And they put bracelets on the **h** of **Ezk 23:42** 3027
and blood is on their **h**. **Ezk 23:45** 3027
"Because you have clapped your **h** **Ezk 25:6** 3027
In the **h** of those who wound you? **Ezk 28:9** 3027
You broke and tore all their **h**; **Ezk 29:7** 3802
the land into the **h** of evil men. **Ezk 30:12** 3027
a stone was cut out without **h**, **Da 2:34** 3028
cut out of the mountain without **h** **Da 2:45** 3028
who can deliver you out of my **h**?" **Da 3:15** 3028
me trembling on my **h** and knees. **Da 10:10** 3709, 3027
in whose **h** are false balances, **Hos 12:7** 3027
'Our god,' To the work of our **h**; **Hos 14:3** 3027
the violence which is in his **h**. **Jon 3:8** 3709
For it is in the power of their **h**. **Mi 2:1** 3027
bow down To the work of your **h**. **Mi 5:13** 3027
evil, both **h** do it well. **Mi 7:3** 3709
you Will clap *their* **h** over you, **Na 3:19** 3709
its voice, It lifted high its **h**. **Hab 3:10** 3027
Do not let your **h** fall limp. **Zph 3:16** 3027
and on all the labor of your **h**. **Hg 1:11** 3709
'and so is every work of their **h**; **Hg 2:14** 3027
work of your **h** with blasting wind, **Hg 2:17** 3027
"The **h** of Zerubbabel have laid **Zch 4:9** 3027
house, and his **h** will finish *it.* **Zch 4:9** 3027
'Let your **h** be strong, you who are **Zch 8:9** 3027
let your **h** be strong.' **Zch 8:13** 3027

and 'ON *their* **H** THEY WILL **Mt 4:6** *5495*
their **h** when they eat bread." **Mt 15:2** *5495*
to eat with unwashed **h** does not **Mt 15:20** *5495*
is going to suffer at their **h**." **Mt 17:12** *5259*
to be delivered into the **h** of men; **Mt 17:22** *5495*
than to have two **h** or two feet **Mt 18:8** *5495*
might lay His **h** on them and pray; **Mt 19:13** *5495*
After laying His **h** on them, **Mt 19:15** *5495*
betrayed into the **h** of sinners. **Mt 26:45** *5495*
laid **h** on Jesus and seized Him. **Mt 26:50** *5495*
he took water and washed his **h** in **Mt 27:24** *5495*
please come and lay Your **h** on her, **Mk 5:23** *5495*
much at the **h** of many physicians, **Mk 5:26** *5259*
as these performed by His **h**? **Mk 6:2** *5495*
He laid His **h** on a few sick people **Mk 6:5** *5495*
eating their bread with impure **h**, **Mk 7:2** *5495*
they carefully wash their **h**, **Mk 7:3** *5495*
eat their bread with impure **h**?" **Mk 7:5** *5495*
eyes and laying His **h** on him, **Mk 8:23** *5495*
again He laid His **h** on his eyes; **Mk 8:25** *5495*
to be delivered into the **h** of men, **Mk 9:31** *5495*
crippled, than, having your two **h**, **Mk 9:43** *5495*
them, laying His **h** on them. **Mk 10:16** *5495*
betrayed into the **h** of sinners. **Mk 14:41** *5495*
They laid **h** on Him and seized **Mk 14:46** *5495*
destroy this temple made with **h**, **Mk 14:58** *5499*
build another made without **h**.' **Mk 14:58** *886*
they will lay **h** on the sick, and **Mk 16:18** *5495*
and, 'ON *their* **H** THEY **Lk 4:11** *5495*
laying His **h** on each one of them, **Lk 4:40** *5495*
of grain, rubbing them in their **h**, **Lk 6:1** *5495*
be delivered into the **h** of men." **Lk 9:44** *5495*
who fell into the robbers' **h**?" **Lk 10:36**
And He laid His **h** on her; **Lk 13:13** *5495*
to lay **h** on Him that very hour, **Lk 20:19** *5495*
they will lay their **h** on you and **Lk 21:12** *5495*
temple, you did not lay **h** on Me **Lk 22:53** *5495*
INTO YOUR **H** I COMMIT MY SPIRIT." **Lk 23:46** *5495*
into the **h** of sinful men, **Lk 24:7** *5495*
"See My **h** and My feet, that it is **Lk 24:39** *5495*
showed them His **h** and His feet. **Lk 24:40** *5495*
lifted up His **h** and blessed them. **Lk 24:50** *5495*
Him, but no one laid **h** on Him. **Jn 7:44** *5495*
had given all things into His **h**, **Jn 13:3** *5495*
but also my **h** and my head." **Jn 13:9** *5495*
them both His **h** and His side. **Jn 20:20** *5495*
in His **h** the imprint of the nails, **Jn 20:25** *5495*
here with your finger, and see My **h**; **Jn 20:27** *5495*
old, you will stretch out your **h** **Jn 21:18** *5495*
nailed to a cross by the **h** of godless **Ac 2:23** *5495*
And they laid **h** on them and put **Ac 4:3** *5495*
At the **h** of the apostles many **Ac 5:12** *5495*
They laid **h** on the apostles **Ac 5:18** *5495*
they laid their **h** on them. **Ac 6:6** *5495*
rejoicing in the works of their **h**. **Ac 7:41** *5495*
dwell in *houses* made by *human* **h**; **Ac 7:48** *5499*
they *began* laying their **h** on them, **Ac 8:17** *5495*
the laying on of the apostles' **h**, **Ac 8:18** *5495*
everyone on whom I lay my **h** may **Ac 8:19** *5495*
come in and lay his **h** on him, **Ac 9:12** *5495*
after laying his **h** on him said, **Ac 9:17** *5495*
Herod the king laid **h** on some who **Ac 12:1** *5495*
And his chains fell off his **h**. **Ac 12:7** *5495*
prayed and laid their **h** on them, **Ac 13:3** *5495*
and wonders be done by their **h**. **Ac 14:3** *5495*
not dwell in temples made with **h**; **Ac 17:24** *5499*
nor is He served by human **h**, **Ac 17:25** *5495*
Paul had laid his **h** upon them, **Ac 19:6** *5495*
miracles by the **h** of Paul, **Ac 19:11** *5495*
gods made with **h** are no gods *at all* **Ac 19:26** *5495*
"You yourselves know that these **h** **Ac 20:34** *5495*
belt and bound his own feet and **h**, **Ac 21:11** *5495*
into the **h** of the Gentiles.' " **Ac 21:11** *5495*
the crowd and laid **h** on him, **Ac 21:27** *5495*
violence took him out of our **h**, **Ac 24:7** *5495*
tackle overboard with their own **h**. **Ac 27:19** *849b*
laid his **h** on him and healed him. **Ac 28:8** *5495*
into the **h** of the Romans. **Ac 28:17** *5495*
LONG I HAVE STRETCHED OUT MY **H** TO **Ro 10:21** *5495*
we toil, working with our own **h**; **1Co 4:12** *5495*
then *comes* the end, when He **h** **1Co 15:24** *3860*
from God, a house not made with **h**, **2Co 5:1** *886*
in the wall, and *so* escaped his **h**. **2Co 11:33** *5495*
performed in the flesh by human **h** **Eph 2:11** *5499*
performing with his own **h** what is **Eph 4:28** *5495*
a circumcision made without **h**, **Col 2:11** *886*
at the **h** of your own countrymen, **1Th 2:14** *5259*
own business and work with your **h**, **1Th 4:11** *5495*
place to pray, lifting up holy **h**, **1Tm 2:8** *5495*
laying on of **h** by the presbytery. **1Tm 4:14** *5495*
Do not lay **h** upon anyone **1Tm 5:22** *5495*
you through the laying on of my **h**. **2Tm 1:6** *5495*
THE HEAVENS ARE THE WORKS OF YOUR **H**; **Heb 1:10** *5495*
HIM OVER THE WORKS OF YOUR **H**; **Heb 2:7** *5495*
washings and laying on of **h**, **Heb 6:2** *5495*
tabernacle, not made with **h**, **Heb 9:11** *5499*
enter a holy place made with **h**, **Heb 9:24** *5499*
fall into the **h** of the living God. **Heb 10:31** *5495*
strengthen the **h** that are weak and **Heb 12:12** *5495*
Cleanse your **h**, you sinners; **Jas 4:8** *5495*
looked at and touched with our **h**, **1Jn 1:1** *5495*
and palm branches *were* in their **h**; **Rv 7:9** *5495*
repent of the works of their **h**, **Rv 9:20** *5495*

HANDSOME

Now Joseph was **h** in form and **Gn 39:6** 3303
name was Saul, a choice and **h** *man*, **1Sa 9:2** 2896a
and there was not a more **h** person **1Sa 9:2** 2896a
beautiful eyes and a **h** appearance. **1Sa 16:12** 2896a
prudent in speech, and a **h** man; **1Sa 16:18** 8389
and ruddy, with a **h** appearance. **1Sa 17:42** 3303
Israel was no one as **h** as Absalom, **2Sa 14:25** 3303
And he was also a very **h** man, **1Ki 1:6** 2896a, 8389
"How **h** you are, my beloved, *And* **SS 1:16** 3303

HANES

And their ambassadors arrive at **H**. **Is 30:4** 2609

HANG

from you and will **h** you on a tree, **Gn 40:19** 8518
"You shall **h** it on four **Ex 26:32** 5414
h up the veil under the clasps, **Ex 26:33** 5414
and **h** up the veil for the gateway of **Ex 40:8** 5414
to death, and you **h** him on a tree, **Dt 21:22** 8518
shall not **h** all night on the tree, **Dt 21:23** 3885a
life shall **h** in doubt before you; **Dt 28:66** 8511
and we will **h** them before the LORD **2Sa 21:6** 3363
And the king said, "**H** him on it." **Es 7:9** 8518
They **h** and swing to and fro far **Jb 28:4** 1809
they will **h** on him all the glory of **Is 22:24** 8518
about them, And his hands **h** limp; **Jer 50:43** 7503
'All hands will **h** limp and all **Ezk 7:17** 7503
from it on which to **h** any vessel? **Ezk 15:3** 8518

HANGED

but he **h** the chief baker, just as **Gn 40:22** 8518
me in my office, but he **h** him." **Gn 41:13** 8518
he who is **h** is accursed of God), **Dt 21:23** 8518
He **h** the king of Ai on a tree **Jos 8:29** 8518
and he **h** them on five trees; **Jos 10:26** 8518
and they **h** them in the mountain **2Sa 21:9** 3363
where the Philistines had **h** them **2Sa 21:12** 8518
the bones of those who had been **h**. **2Sa 21:13** 3363
so, they were both **h** on a gallows; **Es 2:23** 8518
the king to have Mordecai **h** on it; **Es 5:14** 8518
So they **h** Haman on the gallows **Es 7:10** 8518
and him they have **h** on the gallows **Es 8:7** 8518
ten sons be **h** on the gallows." **Es 9:13** 8518
Susa, and Haman's ten sons were **h**. **Es 9:14** 8518
sons should be **h** on the gallows. **Es 9:25** 8518
and he went away and **h** himself. **Mt 27:5** *519*
One of the criminals who were **h** *there* **Lk 23:39** *2910*

HANGING

left **h** between heaven and earth, **2Sa 18:9** 5414
I saw Absalom **h** in an oak." **2Sa 18:10** 8518
and oxen *were* wreaths of **h** work. **1Ki 7:29** 4174
speak to the king about **h** Mordecai **Es 6:4** 8518
the load **h** on it will be cut off, **Is 22:25**
the people were **h** on to every word **Lk 19:48** *1582*
put to death by **h** Him on a cross. **Ac 5:30** *2910*
Him to death by **h** Him on a cross. **Ac 10:39** *2910*
saw the creature **h** from his hand, **Ac 28:4** *2910*

HANGINGS

On the south side *there shall be* **h** for **Ex 27:9** 7050b
be **h** one hundred *cubits* long, **Ex 27:11** 7050b
the west side *shall be* **h** of fifty cubits **Ex 27:12** 7050b
"The **h** for the *one* side *of the gate* **Ex 27:14** 7050b
other side *shall be* **h** of fifteen cubits **Ex 27:15** 7050b
the **h** of the court, its pillars **Ex 35:17** 7050b
for the south side the **h** of the **Ex 38:9** 7050b
west side *there were* **h** of fifty cubits **Ex 38:12** 7050b
The **h** for the *one* side *of the gate were* **Ex 38:14** 7050b
court *were* **h** of fifteen cubits, **Ex 38:15** 7050b
All the **h** of the court all around **Ex 38:16** 7050b
to the **h** of the court. **Ex 38:18** 7050b
the **h** for the court, its pillars **Ex 39:40** 7050b
and the **h** of the court, and the **Nu 3:26** 7050b
and the **h** of the court, and the **Nu 4:26** 7050b
were weaving **h** for the Asherah. **2Ki 23:7** 1004
There were **h** *of* fine white **Es 1:6**

HANGS

space And **h** the earth on nothing. **Jb 26:7** 8518
Your tackle **h** slack; **Is 33:23** 5203
"CURSED IS EVERYONE WHO **H** ON A **Ga 3:13** *2910*

HANNAH

the name of one was **H** and the name **1Sa 1:2** 2584
children, but **H** had no children. **1Sa 1:2** 2584
but to **H** he would give a double **1Sa 1:5** 2584
a double portion, for he loved **H**, **1Sa 1:5** 2584
"**H**, why do you weep and why do **1Sa 1:8** 2584
Then **H** rose after eating and **1Sa 1:9** 2584
As for **H**, she was speaking in her **1Sa 1:13** 2584
But **H** replied, **1Sa 1:15** 2584
had relations with **H** his wife, **1Sa 1:19** 2584
due time, after **H** had conceived, **1Sa 1:20** 2584
But **H** did not go up, for she said **1Sa 1:22** 2584
Then **H** prayed and said, **1Sa 2:1** 2584
The LORD visited **H**; **1Sa 2:21** 2584

HANNATHON

around it on the north to **H**, **Jos 19:14** 2615

HANNIEL

a leader, **H** the son of Ephod. **Nu 34:23** 2592
The sons of Ulla *were* Arah, **H** **1Ch 7:39** 2592

HANOCH

Epher and **H** and Abida and Eldaah. **Gn 25:4** 2585
H and Pallu and Hezron and Carmi. **Gn 46:9** 2585
H and Pallu, Hezron and Carmi; **Ex 6:14** 2585
of **H**, the family of **Nu 26:5** 2585
of Midian were Ephah, Epher, **H**, **1Ch 1:33** 2585
of Israel *were* **H** and Pallu, **1Ch 5:3** 2585

HANOCHITES

of Hanoch, the family of the **H** **Nu 26:5** 2599

HANUN

and **H** his son became king in his **2Sa 10:1** 2586
kindness to **H** the son of Nahash, **2Sa 10:2** 2586
Ammonites said to **H** their lord, **2Sa 10:3** 2586
So **H** took David's servants and **2Sa 10:4** 2586
kindness to **H** the son of Nahash, **1Ch 19:2** 2586
land of the sons of Ammon to **H** to **1Ch 19:2** 2586
of the sons of Ammon said to **H**, **1Ch 19:3** 2586
So **H** took David's servants and **1Ch 19:4** 2586
H and the sons of Ammon sent 1,000 **1Ch 19:6** 2586
H and the inhabitants of Zanoah **Ne 3:13** 2586
and **H** the sixth son of Zalaph, **Ne 3:30** 2586

HAPHARAIM

and **H** and Shion and Anaharath, **Jos 19:19** 2663a

HAPPEN

your God caused *it* to **h** to me." **Gn 27:20** 7136a
to find out what would **h** to him. **Ex 2:4** 6213a
Moses said, "*This will* **h** when **Ex 16:8**
If you **h** to come upon a bird's nest **Dt 22:6** 7122
the pursuers will not **h** upon you, **Jos 2:16** 6293
tell you what will **h** to the boy. **1Ki 14:3** 1961
lovingkindness, He causes it to **h**. **Jb 37:13** 4672
If no one knows what will **h**, **Ec 8:7** 1961
who can tell him when it will **h**? **Ec 8:7** 1961
No man knows what will **h**, **Ec 10:14** 1961
Then it will **h** on that day that **Is 11:11** 1961
end of seventy years it will **h** to Tyre **Is 23:15** 1961
So it will **h** in that day, That the **Is 24:21** 1961
And it will **h** instantly, suddenly. **Is 29:5** 1961
should never come about nor **h**. **Ezk 16:16** 1961
Behold, it comes and it will **h**,' **Ezk 21:7** 1961
will **h** to your people in the latter days **Da 10:14** 7136a
see what would **h** in the city. **Jon 4:5** 1961
This shall never **h** to You." **Mt 16:22** *1510*
and cast into the sea,' it will **h**. **Mt 21:21** *1096*
when will these things **h**, and what **Mt 24:3** *1510*
that it must **h** this way?" **Mt 26:54** *1096*
them what was going to **h** to Him, **Mk 10:32** *4819*
that what he says is going to **h**, **Mk 11:23** *1096*
that it may not **h** in the winter. **Mk 13:18** *1096*
when therefore will these things **h**? **Lk 21:7** *1510*
Him saw what was going to **h**, **Lk 22:49** *1510*
tree is green, what will **h** when **Lk 23:31** *1096*
knowing what will **h** to me there, **Ac 20:22** *4876*
had seen nothing unusual **h** to him, **Ac 28:6** *1096*

HAPPENED

Now it **h** one day that he went into **Gn 39:11** 1961
Now it **h** at the end of two full **Gn 41:1** 1961
as he interpreted for us, so it **h**; **Gn 41:13** 1961
told him all that had **h** to them, **Gn 42:29** 7136a
When things like these **h** to me, **Lv 10:19** 7122
for *it* **h** to all the people **Nu 15:26**
to him all that had **h** to them. **Jos 2:23** 4672
us, why then has all this **h** to us? **Jg 6:13** 4672
And it **h** when *any of* the fugitives **Jg 12:5** 1961
It so **h** when they were in high **Jg 16:25** 1961
"Nothing like this has *ever* **h** or **Jg 19:30** 1961
and she **h** to come to the portion **Ru 2:3** 7136a, 4745
It **h** in the middle of the **Ru 3:8** 1961
It **h** year after year, as often **1Sa 1:7** 6213a
It **h** at that time as Eli was **1Sa 3:2** 1961
nothing like this has **h** before. **1Sa 4:7** 1961
it **h** to us by chance." **1Sa 6:9** 1961
Then it **h** when he turned his back **1Sa 10:9** 1961
"What has **h** to the son of Kish? **1Sa 10:11** 1961
and see how this sin has **h** today. **1Sa 14:38** 1961
Then it **h** when the Philistine rose **1Sa 17:48** 1961
It **h** as they were coming, when **1Sa 18:6** 1961
it **h** as often as they went out, **1Sa 18:30** 1961
Then it **h** when David and his men **1Sa 30:1** 1961
chance I **h** to be on Mount Gilboa, **2Sa 1:6** 7136a
it **h** that in her hurry to flee, **2Sa 4:4** 1961
Then it **h** *as* the ark of the LORD **2Sa 6:16** 1961
Now it **h** afterwards that the king **2Sa 10:1** 1961
Then it **h** in the spring, at the **2Sa 11:1** 1961
Then it **h** on the seventh day that **2Sa 12:18** 1961
to your servant's word, so it **h**." **2Sa 13:35** 1961
It **h** as David was coming to the **2Sa 15:32** 1961
h to meet the servants of David. **2Sa 18:9**
Now a worthless fellow **h** to be **2Sa 20:1** 7122
"It **h** on the third day after **1Ki 3:18** 1961
It **h** that when the priests came from **1Ki 8:10** 1961
Now it **h** in the fifth year of King **1Ki 14:25** 1961
Then it **h** as often as the king **1Ki 14:28** 1961
It **h** after a while that the **1Ki 17:7** 1961
Now it **h** *after* many days that **1Ki 18:1** 1961
It **h** in the morning about the **2Ki 3:20** 1961
It **h** when Elisha the man of **2Ki 5:8** 1961
It **h** just as the man of God had **2Ki 7:18** 1961
And so it **h** to him, for the people **2Ki 7:20** 1961
Then it **h** that night that the **2Ki 19:35** 1961
It **h** when the ark of the **1Ch 15:29** 1961
Then it **h** in the spring, at the **1Ch 20:1** 1961
Now it **h** at the turn of the year that **2Ch 24:23** 1961
the wonder that had **h** in the land, **2Ch 32:31** 1961
Now it **h** in the month Chislev, **Ne 1:1** 1961
told him all that had **h** to him, **Es 4:7** 7136a
everything that had **h** to him. **Es 6:13** 7136a
regard and what had **h** to them, **Es 9:26** 5060
as I have intended so it has **h**, **Is 14:24** 1961
horrible thing Has **h** in the land: **Jer 5:30** 1961
'Why have these things **h** to me?' **Jer 13:22** 7122
Now it **h** when the army of the **Jer 37:11** 1961
therefore this thing has **h** to you. **Jer 40:3** 1961
Now it **h** on the next day after the **Jer 41:4** 1961
who escapes *And* say, 'What has **h**?' **Jer 48:19** 1961
so it **h**," declares the Lord GOD. **Ezk 16:19** 1961
this **h** to Nebuchadnezzar the king. **Da 4:28** 4291
Has *anything like* this **h** in your **Jl 1:2** 1961
including what had **h** to the demoniacs. **Mt 8:33** *3588*
it **h** that as Jesus was reclining **Mt 9:10** *1096*
his fellow slaves saw what had **h**, **Mt 18:31** *1096*
to their lord all that had **h**. **Mt 18:31** *1096*
the chief priests all that had **h**. **Mt 28:11** *1096*

And it **h** that He was reclining *at* Mk 2:15 *1096*
And it **h** that He was passing through Mk 2:23 *1096*
to see what it was that had **h**. Mk 5:14 *1096*
had **h** to the demon-possessed man, Mk 5:16 *1096*
aware of what had **h** to her, Mk 5:33 *1096*
Now it **h** *that* while he was Lk 1:8 *1096*
"And how has it **h** to me, that Lk 1:43
And it **h** that on the eighth day they Lk 1:59 *1096*
and see this thing that has **h** Lk 2:15 *1096*
Now it **h** that while the crowd was Lk 5:1 *1096*
Now it **h** that He was passing through Lk 6:1 *1096*
When the herdsmen saw what had **h**, Lk 8:34 *1096*
people went out to see what had **h**; Lk 8:35 *1096*
them to tell no one what had **h**. Lk 8:56 *1096*
And it **h** that while He was praying Lk 9:18 *1096*
It **h** that while Jesus was praying in Lk 11:1 *1096*
It **h** that when He went into the house Lk 14:1 *1096*
just as it **h** in the days of Noah, Lk 17:26 *1096*
the same as **h** in the days of Lot: Lk 17:28 *1096*
when the centurion saw what had **h**, Lk 23:47 *1096*
when they observed what had **h**, Lk 23:48 *1096*
marveling at what had **h**. Lk 24:12 *1096*
which have **h** here in these days?" Lk 24:18 *1096*
third day since these things **h**. Lk 24:21 *1096*
what then has **h** that You are going Jn 14:22 *1096*
amazement at what had **h** to him. Ac 3:10 *4819*
all glorifying God for what had **h**; Ac 4:21 *1096*
came in, not knowing what had **h**. Ac 5:7 *1096*
OF EGYPT—WE DO NOT KNOW WHAT **H**.' Ac 7:40 *1096*
As he was traveling, it **h** that he Ac 9:3 *1096*
And it **h** at that time that she fell Ac 9:37 *1096*
This **h** three times, Ac 10:16 *1096*
"This **h** three times, and Ac 11:10 *1096*
believed when he saw what had **h** Ac 13:12 *1096*
It **h** that as we were going to Ac 16:16 *1096*
with those who **h** to be present. Ac 17:17 *3909*
It **h** that while Apollos was at Ac 19:1 *1096*
"But it **h** that as I was on my way, Ac 22:6 *1096*
"It **h** when I returned to Jerusalem Ac 22:17 *1096*
And so it **h** that they all were Ac 27:44 *1096*
And it **h** that the father of Publius Ac 28:8 *1096*
After this had **h**, Ac 28:9 *1096*
a partial hardening has **h** to Israel Ro 11:25 *1096*
these things **h** as examples for us, 1Co 10:6 *1096*
things **h** to them as an example, 1Co 10:11 *4819*
such as **h** to me at Antioch, 2Tm 3:11 *1096*
It has **h** to them according to the 2Pe 2:22 *4819*

HAPPENING
and the things that were **h**, Mt 27:54 *1096*
"How long has this been **h** to him?" Mk 9:21 *1096*
too, when you see these things **h**, Mk 13:29 *1096*
tetrarch heard of all that was **h**; Lk 9:7 *1096*
also, when you see these things **h**, Lk 21:31 *1096*
some strange thing were **h** to you; 1Pe 4:12 *4819*

HAPPENS
and it **h** that she finds no favor Dt 24:1 1961
and if it **h** that the king's wrath 2Sa 11:20 1961
"But whatever **h**, please let me 2Sa 18:22 1961
whatever **h**," *he said,* "I will run." 2Sa 18:23 1961
righteous men to whom it **h** according Ec 8:14 5060
there are evil men to whom it **h** Ec 8:14 5060
so that nothing worse **h** to you." Jn 5:14 *1096*
"Now I have told you before it **h**, Jn 14:29 *1096*
so that when it **h**, you may believe. Jn 14:29 *1096*

HAPPIER
she is **h** if she remains as she is; 1Co 7:40 *3107*

HAPPINESS
h to his wife whom he has taken. Dt 24:5 8055
Go *then,* eat your bread in **h** and Ec 9:7 8057
peace And brings good news of **h**, Is 52:7 2896b
I have forgotten **h**. La 3:17 2899b

HAPPIZZEZ
for Hezir, the eighteenth for **H**, 1Ch 24:15 6483b

HAPPY
Then Leah said, "**H** Gn 30:13 837
For women will call me **h**." Gn 30:13 833
rejoicing and **h** of heart because 2Ch 7:10 2896a
h is the man whom God reproves, Jb 5:17 835
be **h** and it will be well with you. Ps 128:2 835
And **h** are all who hold her fast. Pr 3:18 833
But **h** is he who is gracious to the Pr 14:21 835
But **h** is he who keeps the law. Pr 29:18 835
man should be **h** in his activities, Ec 3:22 8055
come later will not be **h** with him, Ec 4:16 8055
a face is sad a heart may be **h**. Ec 7:3 3190
In the day of prosperity be **h**, Ec 7:14 2896b
And made him very **h**. Jer 20:15 8055
was extremely **h** about the plant. Jon 4:6 8055
H is he who does not condemn Ro 14:22 *3107*

HARA
brought them to Halah, Habor, **H** and 1Ch 5:26 2024

HARADAH
Mount Shepher and camped at **H**. Nu 33:24 2732
They journeyed from **H** and Nu 33:25 2732

HARAN
the father of Abram, Nahor and **H**. Gn 11:26 2039
the father of Abram, Nahor and **H**; Gn 11:27 2039
and **H** became the father of Lot. Gn 11:27 2039
H died in the presence of his Gn 11:28 2039
was Milcah, the daughter of **H**, Gn 11:29 2039
his son, and Lot the son of **H**, Gn 11:31 2039
and they went as far as **H**, Gn 11:31 2771a
and Terah died in **H**. Gn 11:32 2771a
years old when he departed from **H**. Gn 12:4 2771a
which they had acquired in **H**, Gn 12:5 2771a
my voice, and arise, flee to **H**, Gn 27:43 2771a
from Beersheba and went toward **H**. Gn 28:10 2771a
And they said, "We are from **H**." Gn 29:4 2771a
even Gozan and **H** and Rezeph and 2Ki 19:12 2771a
Ephah, Caleb's concubine, bore **H**, 1Ch 2:46 2771b
and **H** became the father of Gazez. 1Ch 2:46 2771b
were Shelomoth and Haziel and **H**, 1Ch 23:9 2039
even Gozan and **H** and Rezeph and Is 37:12 2771a
"**H**, Canneh, Eden, the traders of Ezk 27:23 2771a
Mesopotamia, before he lived in **H**, Ac 7:2 *5488*
the Chaldeans and settled in **H**. Ac 7:4 *5488*

HARARITE
was Shammah the son of Agee a **H**. 2Sa 23:11 2043
Shammah the **H**, Ahiam the son of 2Sa 23:33 2043
Jonathan the son of Shagee the **H**, 1Ch 11:34 2043
Ahiam the son of Sacar the **H**, 1Ch 11:35 2043

HARASS
'Do not **h** Moab, nor provoke them Dt 2:9 6696b
do not **h** them nor provoke them, Dt 2:19 6696b
those who **h** Judah will be cut off; Is 11:13 6887c
And Judah will not **h** Ephraim. Is 11:13 6887c

HARASSED
him, And shot *at him* and **h** him; Gn 49:23 7852

HARBONA
he commanded Mehuman, Biztha, **H**, Es 1:10 2726

HARBONAH
Then **H**, one of the eunuchs who Es 7:9 2726

HARBOR
is destroyed, without house *or* **h**; Is 23:1 935
Because the **h** was not suitable Ac 27:12 *3040*
could reach Phoenix, a **h** of Crete, Ac 27:12 *3040*

HARD
So they pressed **h** against Lot and Gn 19:9 3966
And if they are driven **h** one day, Gn 33:13 1849
them to afflict them with **h** labor. Ex 1:11 5450
made their lives bitter with **h** labor Ex 1:14 7186
and looked on their **h** labors; Ex 2:11 5450
You been so **h** on Your servant? Nu 11:11 7489a
The case that is too **h** for you, Dt 1:17 7185
h to you when you set him free, Dt 15:18 7185
us, and imposed **h** labor on us. Dt 26:6 7186
her because she pressed him so **h**. Jg 14:17 6693
and it seemed **h** to Amnon to do 2Sa 13:2 6381
"Your father made our yoke **h**; 1Ki 12:4 7185
therefore lighten the **h** service of 1Ki 12:4 7186
"You have asked a **h** thing. 2Ki 2:10 7185
"Your father made our yoke **h**; 2Ch 10:4 7185
now therefore lighten the **h** 2Ch 10:4 7186
wept for the one whose life is **h**? Jb 30:25 7186
"Water becomes **h** like stone, And Jb 38:30 2244
"His heart is as **h** as a stone, Jb 41:24 3332
Even as **h** as a lower millstone. Jb 41:24 3332
h with Moses on their account; Ps 106:32 7489a
the way of the treacherous is **h**. Pr 13:15 386
And drive **h** all your workers. Is 58:3 5065
your face as **h** as their faces and Ezk 3:8 2389
forehead as **h** as their foreheads. Ezk 3:8 2389
his army labor **h** against Tyre; Ezk 29:18 1419
it is **h** for a rich man to enter Mt 19:23 *1423*
'Master, I knew you to be a **h** man, Mt 25:24 *4642*
"How **h** it will be for those who Mk 10:23 *1423*
how **h** it is to enter the kingdom Mk 10:24 *1422b*
h all night and caught nothing, Lk 5:5 *2872*
men down with burdens **h** to bear, Lk 11:46 *1419*
"How **h** it is for those who are Lk 18:24 *1423*
by working **h** in this manner you must Ac 20:35 *2872*
It is **h** for you to kick against Ac 26:14 *4642*
Mary, who has worked **h** for you. Ro 16:6 *4183*
who has worked **h** in the Lord. Ro 16:12 *4183*
work **h** at preaching and teaching. 1Tm 5:17 *2872*
to say, and *it is* **h** to explain, Heb 5:11 *1421*
are some things **h** to understand, 2Pe 3:16 *1425*

HARD-EARNED
your **h** goods *will go* to the house Pr 5:10 6089a

HARDEN
but I will **h** his heart so that he Ex 4:21 2388
"But I will **h** Pharaoh's heart Ex 7:3 7185
"Thus I will **h** Pharaoh's heart, Ex 14:4 2388
I will **h** the hearts of the Ex 14:17 2388
you, you shall not **h** your heart, Dt 15:7 553
was of the LORD to **h** their hearts, Jos 11:20 2388
"Why then do you **h** your hearts as 1Sa 6:6 3513
Do not **h** your hearts, as at Ps 95:8 7185
And **h** our heart from fearing You? Is 63:17 7188
DO NOT **H** YOUR HEARTS AS WHEN THEY Heb 3:8 *4645*
DO NOT **H** YOUR HEARTS, AS WHEN THEY Heb 3:15 *4645*
DO NOT **H** YOUR HEARTS." Heb 4:7 *4645*

HARDENED
Yet Pharaoh's heart was **h**, Ex 7:13 2388
and Pharaoh's heart was **h**, Ex 7:22 2388
he **h** his heart and did not listen Ex 8:15 3513
But Pharaoh's heart was **h**, Ex 8:19 2388
h his heart this time also, Ex 8:32 3513
But the heart of Pharaoh was **h**, Ex 9:7 3513
And the LORD **h** Pharaoh's heart, Ex 9:12 2388
he sinned again and **h** his heart Ex 9:34 3513
Pharaoh's heart was **h**, Ex 9:35 2388
for I have **h** his heart and the Ex 10:1 3513
But the LORD **h** Pharaoh's heart, Ex 10:20 2388
But the LORD **h** Pharaoh's heart, Ex 10:27 2388
yet the LORD **h** Pharaoh's heart, Ex 11:10 2388
The LORD **h** the heart of Pharaoh, Ex 14:8 2388
for the LORD your God **h** his spirit Dt 2:30 7185
and Pharaoh **h** their hearts? 1Sa 6:6 3513
But he stiffened his neck and **h** 2Ch 36:13 553
the loaves, but their heart was **h**. Mk 6:52 *4456*
Do you have a **h** heart? Mk 8:17 *4456*
"HE HAS BLINDED THEIR EYES AND HE **H** Jn 12:40 *4456*
were becoming **h** and disobedient, Ac 19:9 *4645*
obtained it, and the rest were **h**; Ro 11:7 *4456*
But their minds were **h**; 2Co 3:14 *4456*
be **h** by the deceitfulness of sin. Heb 3:13 *4645*

HARDENING
a partial **h** has happened to Israel Ro 11:25 *4457*

HARDENS
My skin **h** and runs. Jb 7:5 7280c
When the dust **h** into a mass And Jb 38:38 3332
But he who **h** his heart will fall Pr 28:14 7185
A man who **h** *his* neck after much Pr 29:1 7185
desires, and He **h** whom He desires. Ro 9:18 *4645*

HARDER
for it is **h** for me than for you, Ru 1:13 3966, 4843
A brother offended *is* **h** *to be won* Pr 18:19
have made their faces **h** than rock; Jer 5:3 2388
"Like emery **h** than flint I have Ezk 3:9 2389

HARDLY
and Jacob had **h** gone out from the Gn 27:30 389, 3318
h a step between me and death." 1Sa 20:3
will **h** die for a righteous man; Ro 5:7 *3433*

HARDNESS
You will give them **h** of heart, La 3:65 4044
"Because of your **h** of heart Moses Mt 19:8 *4641*
grieved at their **h** of heart, Mk 3:5 *4457*
"Because of your **h** of heart he Mk 10:5 *4641*
for their unbelief and **h** of heart, Mk 16:14 *4641*
because of the **h** of their heart; Eph 4:18 *4457*

HARD-PRESSED
(for the people were **h**), 1Sa 13:6 5065
men of Israel were **h** on that day, 1Sa 14:24 5065
through the land **h** and famished, Is 8:21 7185
But I am **h** from both *directions,* Php 1:23 *4912*

HARDSHIP
all the **h** that had befallen them Ex 18:8 8513
all the **h** that has befallen us; Nu 20:14 8513
Do not let all the **h** seem Ne 9:32 8513
me; **H** after hardship is with me Jb 10:17 2487
me; Hardship after **h** is with me. Jb 10:17 6635
have made Your people experience **h**; Ps 60:3 7186
me with bitterness and **h**. La 3:5 8513
I have been in labor and **h**, 2Co 11:27 *3449*
recall, brethren, our labor and **h**, 1Th 2:9 *3449*
but with labor and **h** we 2Th 3:8 *3449*
Suffer **h** with *me,* as a good soldier 2Tm 2:3 *4777*
for which I suffer **h** even to 2Tm 2:9 *2553*
be sober in all things, endure **h**, 2Tm 4:5 *2553*

HARDSHIPS
endurance, in afflictions, in **h**, 2Co 6:4 *318*

HARD-WORKING
The **h** farmer ought to be the first 2Tm 2:6 *2872*

HAREM
to the citadel of Susa, to the **h**, Es 2:3 1004, 802
maids to the best place in the **h**. Es 2:9 1004, 802
court of the **h** to learn how Esther was Es 2:11 1004, 802
from the **h** to the king's palace. Es 2:13 1004, 802
she would return to the second **h**, Es 2:14 1004, 802

HAREPH
and **H** the father of Beth-gader. 1Ch 2:51 2780

HARHAIAH
Next to him Uzziel the son of **H** of Ne 3:8 2744b

HARHAS
the son of Tikvah, the son of **H**, 2Ki 22:14 2745

HARHUR
sons of Hakupha, the sons of **H**, Ezr 2:51 2744a
sons of Hakupha, the sons of **H**, Ne 7:53 2744a

HARIM
the third for **H**, the fourth for 1Ch 24:8 2766
the sons of **H**, 320; Ezr 2:32 2766
the sons of **H**, 1,017. Ezr 2:39 2766
and of the sons of **H**: Ezr 10:21 2766
and *of* the sons of **H**: Ezr 10:31 2766
Malchijah the son of **H** and Hasshub Ne 3:11 2766
the sons of **H**, 320; Ne 7:35 2766
the sons of **H**, 1,017. Ne 7:42 2766
H, Meremoth, Obadiah, Ne 10:5 2766
Malluch, **H**, Baanah. Ne 10:27 2766
of **H**, Adna; of Meraioth, Helkai; Ne 12:15 2766

HARIPH
the sons of **H**, 112; Ne 7:24 2756
H, Anathoth, Nebai, Ne 10:19 2756

HARLOT
he treat our sister as a **h**?" Gn 34:31 2181
saw her, he thought she *was* a **h**, Gn 38:15 2181
Tamar has played the **h**, Gn 38:24 2181
they would play the **h** with their gods Ex 34:15 2181
play the **h** with their gods and Ex 34:16 2181
to play the **h** with their gods. Ex 34:16 2181
demons with which they play the **h**. Lv 17:7 2181
your daughter by making her a **h**, Lv 19:29 2181
those who play the **h** after him, Lv 20:5 2181
by playing the **h** after Molech. Lv 20:5 2181
to play the **h** after them, Lv 20:6 2181
after which you played the **h**, Nu 15:39 2181
the people began to play the **h** with Nu 25:1 2181
playing the **h** in her father's house; Dt 22:21 2181
"You shall not bring the hire of a **h** Dt 23:18 2181
this people will arise and play the **h** Dt 31:16 2181
house of a **h** whose name was Rahab, Jos 2:1 802, 2181
only Rahab the **h** and all who are Jos 6:17 2181
Rahab the **h** and her father's Jos 6:25 2181
for they played the **h** after other Jg 2:17 2181

Israel played the **h** with it there, **Jg 8:27** 2181
again played the **h** with the Baals, **Jg 8:33** 2181
but he was the son of a **h**. **Jg 11:1** 802, 2181
went to Gaza and saw a **h** there, **Jg 16:1** 802, 2181
his concubine played the **h** against **Jg 19:2** 2181
and played the **h** after the gods of **1Ch 5:25** 2181
play the **h** and led Judah astray. **2Ch 21:11** 2181
inhabitants of Jerusalem to play the **h** **2Ch 21:13** 2181
as the house of Ahab played the **h**, **2Ch 21:13** 2181
And played the **h** in their deeds. **Ps 106:39** 2181
For on account of a **h** *one is* **Pr 6:26** 2181
Dressed as a **h** and cunning of heart **Pr 7:10** 2181
For a **h** is a deep pit And an **Pr 23:27** 2181
the faithful city has become a **h**, **Is 1:21** 2181
to Tyre as *in* the song of the **h**: **Is 23:15** 2181
about the city, O forgotten **h**; **Is 23:16** 2181
and will play the **h** with all the **Is 23:17** 2181
tree You have lain down as a **h**. **Jer 2:20** 2181
But you are a **h** *with* many lovers; **Jer 3:1** 2181
green tree, and she was a **h** there. **Jer 3:6** 2181
but she went and was a **h** also. **Jer 3:8** 2181
played the **h** after their idols; **Ezk 6:9** 2181
played the **h** because of your fame, **Ezk 16:15** 2181
colors and played the **h** on them, **Ezk 16:16** 2181
you might play the **h** with them. **Ezk 16:17** 2181
played the **h** with the Egyptians, **Ezk 16:26** 2181
you played the **h** with the **Ezk 16:28** 2181
you played the **h** with them **Ezk 16:28** 2181
the actions of a bold-faced **h**. **Ezk 16:30** 2181
money, you were not like a **h**. **Ezk 16:31** 2181
that no one plays the **h** as you do, **Ezk 16:34** 2181
Therefore, O **h**, hear the word of **Ezk 16:35** 2181
will stop you from playing the **h**, **Ezk 16:41** 2181
play the **h** after their detestable **Ezk 20:30** 2181
and they played the **h** in Egypt. **Ezk 23:3** 2181
They played the **h** in their youth; **Ezk 23:3** 2181
Oholah played the **h** while she was **Ezk 23:5** 2181
played the **h** in the land of Egypt. **Ezk 23:19** 2181
played the **h** with the nations, **Ezk 23:30** 2181
to her as they would go in to a **h**. **Ezk 23:44** 2181
"For their mother has played the **h**; **Hos 2:5** 2181
You shall not play the **h**, **Hos 3:3** 2181
They will play the **h**, **Hos 4:10** 2181
And they have played the **h**, **Hos 4:12** 2181
your daughters play the **h** And **Hos 4:13** 2181
your daughters when they play the **h** **Hos 4:14** 2181
Though you, Israel, play the **h**, **Hos 4:15** 2181
gone, They play the **h** continually; **Hos 4:18** 2181
O Ephraim, you have played the **h**, **Hos 5:3** 2181
For you have played the **h**, **Hos 9:1** 2181
My people, Traded a boy for a **h** And **Jl 3:3** 2181
wife will become a **h** in the city, your **Am 7:17** 2181
earnings of a **h** they will return. **Mi 1:7** 2181
of the many harlotries of the **h**, **Na 3:4** 2181
By faith Rahab the **h** did not **Heb 11:31** 4204
Rahab the **h** also justified by works **Jas 2:25** 4204
great **h** who sits on many waters, **Rv 17:1** 4204
which you saw where the **h** sits, **Rv 17:15** 4204
these will hate the **h** and will **Rv 17:16** 4204
for He has judged the great **h** who **Rv 19:2** 4204

HARLOTRIES

so long as the **h** of your mother **2Ki 9:22** 2183
and you poured out your **h** on every **Ezk 16:15** 8457
Were your **h** so small a matter? **Ezk 16:20** 8457
Besides all your abominations and **h** **Ezk 16:22** 8457
from every direction for your **h**. **Ezk 16:33** 8457
from those women in your **h**, **Ezk 16:34** 8457
nakedness uncovered through your **h** **Ezk 16:36** 8457
"She bestowed her **h** on them, **Ezk 23:7** 8457
her **h** from *the time in* Egypt; **Ezk 23:8** 8457
and her **h** were more than the **Ezk 23:11** 8457
more than the **h** of her sister. **Ezk 23:11** 2183
"So she increased her **h**. **Ezk 23:14** 8457
her **h** and uncovered her nakedness; **Ezk 23:18** 8457
"Yet she multiplied her **h**, **Ezk 23:19** 8457
of your **h** will be uncovered, **Ezk 23:29** 2183
both your lewdness and your **h**. **Ezk 23:29** 8457
of your lewdness and your **h**.' **Ezk 23:35** 8457
of the many **h** of the harlot, **Na 3:4** 2183
Who sells nations by her **h** **Na 3:4** 2183

HARLOTRY

she is also with child by **h**." **Gn 38:24** 2183
that the land will not fall to **h** **Lv 19:29** 2181
take a woman who is profaned by **h**, **Lv 21:7** 2181
if she profanes herself by **h**, **Lv 21:9** 2181
or one who is profaned by **h**, **Lv 21:14** 2181
have polluted a land With your **h** **Jer 3:2** 2183
Because of the lightness of her **h**, **Jer 3:9** 2184
every passer-by to multiply your **h**. **Ezk 16:25** 8457
multiplied your **h** to make Me angry **Ezk 16:26** 8457
multiplied your **h** with the land of **Ezk 16:29** 8457
and defiled her with their **h**. **Ezk 23:17** 8457
your **h** *brought* from the land of Egypt **Ezk 23:27** 2184
by their **h** and by the corpses of **Ezk 43:7** 2184
"Now let them put away their **h** **Ezk 43:9** 2184
"Go, take to yourself a wife of **h** **Hos 1:2** 2183
harlotry and *have* children of **h**; **Hos 1:2** 2183
for the land commits flagrant **h**, **Hos 1:2** 2181
her put away her **h** from her face And **Hos 2:2** 2183
Because they are children of **h**. **Hos 2:4** 2183
H, wine and new wine take away **Hos 4:11** 2184
a spirit of **h** has led *them* astray, **Hos 4:12** 2183
For a spirit of **h** is within them, **Hos 5:4** 2183
Ephraim's **h** is there, Israel has **Hos 6:10** 2184

HARLOT'S

"Go into the **h** house and bring **Jos 6:22** 802, 2181
she will go back to her **h** wages and **Is 23:17** 868
Her gain and her **h** wages will **Is 23:18** 868
Yet you had a **h** forehead; **Jer 3:3** 802, 2181
And trooped to the **h** house. **Jer 5:7** 2181
collected *them* from a **h** earnings, **Mi 1:7** 2181

HARLOTS

Then two women who were **h** came to **1Ki 3:16** 2181
the **h** bathed themselves *there*), **1Ki 22:38** 2181
company with **h** wastes *his* wealth. **Pr 29:3** 2181
"Men give gifts to all **h**, **Ezk 16:33** 2181
the men themselves go apart with **h** **Hos 4:14** 2181
THE MOTHER OF **H** AND OF THE **Rv 17:5** 4204

HARLOTS'

You have loved **h** earnings on **Hos 9:1**

HARM

that you will do us no **h**, **Gn 26:29** 7463a
"It is in my power to do you **h**, **Gn 31:29** 7451b
pass by this heap to you for **h**, **Gn 31:52**
heap and this pillar to me, for **h**. **Gn 31:52** 7463a
am afraid that **h** may befall him." **Gn 42:4** 611
If **h** should befall him on the **Gn 42:38** 611
also from me, and **h** befalls him, **Gn 44:29** 611
You brought **h** to this people? **Ex 5:22** 7489a
he has done **h** to this people, **Ex 5:23** 7489a
mind about *doing* **h** to Your people. **Ex 32:12** 7463a
LORD changed His mind about the **h** **Ex 32:14** 7463a
nor **h** the edges of your beard. **Lv 19:27** 7843
have I done **h** to any of them." **Nu 16:15** 7489a
then He will turn and do you **h** and **Jos 24:20** 7489a
Philistines when I do them **h**." **Jg 15:3** 7463a
it please my father *to do* you **h**, **1Sa 20:13** 7463a
there is safety for you and no **h**, **1Sa 20:21** 1697
'Behold, David seeks to **h** you'? **1Sa 24:9** 7463a
for I will not **h** you again because **1Sa 26:21** 7489a
since he might do *himself* **h**!" **2Sa 12:18** 7463a
will do us more **h** than Absalom; **2Sa 20:6** 7489a
Then there was no **h** in the pot. **2Ki 4:41** 1697, 7451a
that You would keep *me* from **h** **1Ch 4:10** 7463a
ones, And do My prophets no **h**." **1Ch 16:22** 7489a
But they were planning to **h** me. **Ne 6:2** 7463a
h had been determined against him **Es 7:7** 7463a
hands on those who sought their **h**; **Es 9:2** 7463a
Who has defied Him without **h**? **Jb 9:4** 7999a
ones, And do My prophets no **h**." **Ps 105:15** 7489a
devise **h** against your neighbor, **Pr 3:29** 7463a
cause, If he has done you no **h**. **Pr 3:30** 7463a
But the cruel man does himself **h**. **Pr 11:17** 5916
No **h** befalls the righteous, But **Pr 12:21** 205
companion of fools will suffer **h**. **Pr 13:20** 7489a
or **h** in all My holy mountain," **Is 65:25** 7843
fear them, For they can do no **h**, **Jer 10:5** 7489a
city for **h** and not for good," **Jer 21:10** 7463a
hands, and I will do you no **h**.' **Jer 25:6** 7489a
work of your hands to your own **h**. **Jer 25:7** 7451b
this people but rather their **h**." **Jer 38:4** 7463a
you doing great **h** to yourselves, **Jer 44:7** 7463a
over them for **h** and not for good, **Jer 44:27** 7463a
surely stand against you for **h**.' **Jer 44:29** 7463a
the midst of the fire without **h**, **Da 3:25** 2257
'Just as I purposed to do **h** to you **Zch 8:14** 7489a
do good or to do **h** on the Sabbath, **Mk 3:4** 2554
of him without doing him any **h**. **Lk 4:35** 984
do good or to do **h** on the Sabbath, **Lk 6:9** 2554
how much **h** he did to Your saints at **Ac 9:13** 2556
"Do not **h** yourself, for we are all **Ac 16:28** 2556
will attack you in order to **h** you, **Ac 18:10** 2559
into the fire and suffered no **h**. **Ac 28:5** 2556
the coppersmith did me much **h**; **2Tm 4:14** 2556
Who is there to **h** you if you **1Pe 3:13** 2559
to **h** the earth and the sea, **Rv 7:2** 91
"Do not **h** the earth or the sea or **Rv 7:3** 91
and with them they do **h**. **Rv 9:19** 91
And if anyone wants to **h** them, **Rv 11:5** 91
if anyone wants to **h** them, **Rv 11:5** 91

HAR-MAGEDON

which in Hebrew is called **H**. **Rv 16:16** 717

HARMED

mouths and they have not **h** me, **Da 6:22** 2255

HARMFUL

eliminate **h** beasts from the land, **Lv 26:6** 7451a
not put on you any of the **h** diseases **Dt 7:15** 7451a
him, and do nothing **h** to him, **Jer 39:12** 7451b
eliminate **h** beasts from the land so **Ezk 34:25** 7451a
foolish and **h** desires which plunge **1Tm 6:9** 983

HARMING

who has restrained me from **h** you, **1Sa 25:34** 7489a

HARMON

her, And you will be cast to **H**," **Am 4:3** 2038

HARMONIOUS

To sum up, all of you be **h**, **1Pe 3:8** 3675

HARMONY

Or what **h** has Christ with Belial, **2Co 6:15** 4857
Syntyche to live in **h** in the Lord. **Php 4:2** 5426

HARNEPHER

The sons of Zophah *were* Suah, **H**, **1Ch 7:36** 2774

HARNESS

"**H** the horses, And mount the **Jer 46:4** 631
I will **h** Ephraim, Judah will plow, **Hos 10:11** 7392
H the chariot to the team of **Mi 1:13** 7573

HAROD

and camped beside the spring of **H**; **Jg 7:1** 2730b

HARODITE

Shammah the **H**, Elika the Harodite, **2Sa 23:25** 2733
Shammah the Harodite, Elika the **H**, **2Sa 23:25** 2733

HAROEH

H, half of the Manahathites, **1Ch 2:52** 7204

HARORITE

Shammoth the **H**, Helez the **1Ch 11:27** 2033

HAROSHETH-HAGOYIM

army was Sisera, who lived in **H**. **Jg 4:2** 2800, 1471
him, from **H** to the river Kishon. **Jg 4:13** 2800, 1471
chariots and the army as far as **H**, **Jg 4:16** 2800, 1471

HARP

down from the high place with **h**, **1Sa 10:5** 5035b
who is a skillful player on the **h**; **1Sa 16:16** 3658
that he shall play *the* **h** with his **1Sa 16:16**
David would take the **h** and play **1Sa 16:23** 3658
while David was playing *the* **h** **1Sa 18:10**
and David was playing *the* **h** with **1Sa 19:9**
their father Jeduthun with the **h**, **1Ch 25:3** 3658
"They sing to the timbrel and **h** **Jb 21:12** 3658
my **h** is turned to mourning, **Jb 30:31** 3658
to Him with a **h** of ten strings. **Ps 33:2** 5035b
I will express my riddle on the **h**. **Ps 49:4** 3658
Awake, **h** and lyre! I will awaken **Ps 57:8** 5035b
I will also praise You with a **h**, **Ps 71:22** 5035b
sweet sounding lyre with the **h**. **Ps 81:2** 5035b
ten-stringed lute and with the **h** **Ps 92:3** 5035b
Awake, **h** and lyre; **Ps 108:2** 5035b
Upon a **h** of ten strings I will **Ps 144:9** 5035b
Praise Him with **h** and lyre. **Ps 150:3** 5035b
are *accompanied* by lyre and **h**, **Is 5:12** 5035b
my heart intones like a **h** for Moab And **Is 16:11** 3658
Take *your* **h**, walk about the city, **Is 23:16** 3658
stops, The gaiety of the **h** ceases. **Is 24:8** 3658
improvise to the sound of the **h**, **Am 6:5** 5035b
things, either flute or **h**, **1Co 14:7** 2788
played on the flute or on the **h**? **1Co 14:7** 2789
the Lamb, each one holding a **h** **Rv 5:8** 2788

HARPISTS

sound of **h** playing on their harps. **Rv 14:2** 2790
"And the sound of **h** and musicians **Rv 18:22** 2790

HARPOONS

Can you fill his skin with **h**, **Jb 41:7** 7905

HARPS

of fir wood, and with lyres, **h**, **2Sa 6:5** 5035b
also lyres and **h** for the singers; **1Ki 10:12** 5035b
even with songs and with lyres, **h**, **1Ch 13:8** 5035b
with instruments of music, **h**, **1Ch 15:16** 5035b
Benaiah, with **h** *tuned* to alamoth; **1Ch 15:20** 5035b
cymbals, with **h** and lyres. **1Ch 15:28** 5035b
with musical instruments, **h**, **1Ch 16:5** 5035b
were to prophesy with lyres, **h** **1Ch 25:1** 5035b
LORD, with cymbals, **h** and lyres, **1Ch 25:6** 5035b
in fine linen, with cymbals, **h**, **2Ch 5:12** 5035b
and lyres and **h** for the singers; **2Ch 9:11** 5035b
They came to Jerusalem with **h**, **2Ch 20:28** 5035b
of the LORD with cymbals, with **h** and **2Ch 29:25** 5035b
the accompaniment of cymbals, **h** **Ne 12:27** 5035b
in the midst of it We hung our **h**. **Ps 137:2** 3658
'Your pomp *and* the music of your **h** **Is 14:11** 5035b
of your **h** will be heard no more. **Ezk 26:13** 3658
listen to the sound of your **h**. **Am 5:23** 5035b
of harpists playing on their **h**. **Rv 14:2** 2788
sea of glass, holding **h** of God. **Rv 15:2** 2788

HARROW

will he **h** the valleys after you? **Jb 39:10** 7702
continually turn and **h** the ground? **Is 28:24** 7702
plow, Jacob will **h** for himself. **Hos 10:11** 7702

HARRY

him, And **h** him at every step. **Jb 18:11** 6327a

HARSH

was **h** and evil in *his* dealings, **1Sa 25:3** 7186
I am sent to you *with* a **h** *message*. **1Ki 14:6** 7186
But a **h** word stirs up anger. **Pr 15:1** 6089a
and **h** service in which you have been **Is 14:3** 7186
A **h** vision has been shown to me; **Is 21:2** 7186
affliction And under **h** servitude; **La 1:3** 7230
and of all the **h** things which **Jude 1:15** 4642

HARSHA

the sons of Mehida, the sons of **H**, **Ezr 2:52** 2797
the sons of Mehida, the sons of **H**, **Ne 7:54** 2797

HARSHER

the words of the men of Judah were **h** **2Sa 19:43** 7185

HARSHLY

So Sarai treated her **h**, **Gn 16:6** 6031a
to them and spoke to them **h**. **Gn 42:7** 7186
lord of the land, spoke **h** with us, **Gn 42:30** 7186
treated us **h** and afflicted us, **Dt 26:6** 7489a
me if your father answers you **h**? **1Sa 20:10** 7186
The king answered the people **h**, **1Ki 12:13** 7186
The king answered them **h**, **2Ch 10:13** 7186
priests *began* to accuse Him **h**. **Mk 15:3** 4183
when you sin and are **h** treated, **1Pe 2:20** 2852

HARUM

families of Aharhel the son of **H**. **1Ch 4:8** 2037

HARUMAPH

Next to them Jedaiah the son of **H** **Ne 3:10** 2739

HARUPHITE

Shemariah, Shephatiah the **H**, **1Ch 12:5** 2741

HARUZ

the daughter of **H** of Jotbah. **2Ki 21:19** 2743

Context	Reference	Number
HARVEST		
the earth remains, Seedtime and **h**,	Gn 8:22	7105a
Now in the days of wheat **h** Reuben	Gn 30:14	7105a
"At the **h** you shall give a	Gn 47:24	8393
from your **h** and your vintage.	Ex 22:29	4395
observe the Feast of the **H** *of* the first	Ex 23:16	7105a
plowing time and **h** you shall rest.	Ex 34:21	7105a
the first fruits of the wheat **h**,	Ex 34:22	7105a
when you reap the **h** of your land,	Lv 19:9	7105a
gather the gleanings of your **h**.	Lv 19:9	7105a
to give to you and reap its **h**,	Lv 23:10	7105a
fruits of your **h** to the priest.	Lv 23:10	7105a
'When you reap the **h** of your land,	Lv 23:22	7105a
nor gather the gleaning of your **h**;	Lv 23:22	7105a
"When you reap your **h** in your	Dt 24:19	7105a
all its banks all the days of **h**),	Jos 3:15	7105a
a while, in the time of wheat **h**,	Jg 15:1	7105a
at the beginning of barley **h**.	Ru 1:22	7105a
they have finished all my **h**.'	Ru 2:21	7105a
barley **h** and the wheat harvest.	Ru 2:23	7105a
barley harvest and the wheat **h**.	Ru 2:23	7105a
their wheat **h** in the valley,	1Sa 6:13	7105a
to do his plowing and to reap his **h**	1Sa 8:12	7105a
"Is it not the wheat **h** today?	1Sa 12:17	7105a
put to death in the first days of **h**	2Sa 21:9	7105a
at the beginning of barley **h**.	2Sa 21:9	7105a
from the beginning of **h** until it	2Sa 21:10	7105a
came to David in the **h** time	2Sa 23:13	7105a
And those who sow trouble **h** it.	Jb 4:8	7114b
"His **h** the hungry devour And	Jb 5:5	7105a
"They **h** their fodder in the	Jb 24:6	7114b
And gather a fruitful **h**.	Ps 107:37	8393
gathers her provision in the **h**.	Pr 6:8	7105a
he who sleeps in **h** is a son who acts	Pr 10:5	7105a
begs during the **h** and has nothing.	Pr 20:4	7105a
Like the cold of snow in the time of **h**	Pr 25:13	7105a
snow in summer and like rain in **h**,	Pr 26:1	7105a
As with the gladness of **h**,	Is 9:3	7105a
fruits and your **h** has fallen away.	Is 16:9	7105a
But the **h** will *be* a heap In a day	Is 17:11	7105a
a cloud of dew in the heat of **h**."	Is 18:4	7105a
For before the **h**, as soon as the	Is 18:5	7105a
earth will spend **h** time on them.	Is 18:6	2778b
h of the River was her revenue;	Is 23:3	7105a
when the grape **h** is over.	Is 24:13	1210
to the LORD, The first of His **h**.	Jer 2:3	8393
will devour your **h** and your food;	Jer 5:17	7105a
us The appointed weeks of the **h**."	Jer 5:24	7105a
"**H** is past, summer is ended, And	Jer 8:20	7105a
But be ashamed of your **h** Because	Jer 12:13	8393
summer fruits and your grape **h**	Jer 48:32	1210
the sickle at the time of **h**;	Jer 50:16	7105a
the time of **h** will come for her."	Jer 51:33	7105a
I will take back My grain at **h**	Hos 2:9	
there is a **h** appointed for you,	Hos 6:11	7105a
the **h** of the field is destroyed.	Jl 1:11	7105a
in the sickle, for the **h** is ripe.	Jl 3:13	7105a
were still three months until **h**.	Am 4:7	7105a
"You have sown much, but **h** little;	Hg 1:6	935
"The **h** is plentiful, but the	Mt 9:37	*2326*
beseech the Lord of the **h** to send out	Mt 9:38	*2326*
to send out workers into His **h**."	Mt 9:38	*2326*
both to grow together until the **h**;	Mt 13:30	*2326*
in the time of the **h** I will say to	Mt 13:30	*2326*
and the **h** is the end of the age;	Mt 13:39	*2326*
"When the **h** time approached,	Mt 21:34	*2590*
sickle, because the **h** has come."	Mk 4:29	*2326*
"At the **h** time he sent a slave	Mk 12:2	
"The **h** is plentiful, but the	Lk 10:2	*2326*
beseech the Lord of the **h** to send out	Lk 10:2	*2326*
to send out laborers into His **h**.	Lk 10:2	*2326*
"At the **h** time he sent a slave	Lk 20:10	
months, and *then* comes the **h**'?	Jn 4:35	*2326*
fields, that they are white for **h**.	Jn 4:35	*2326*
increase the **h** of your righteousness	2Co 9:10	*1079b*
the **h** of the earth is ripe."	Rv 14:15	*2326*
HARVESTING		
will be neither plowing nor **h**.	Gn 45:6	7105a
and the outcry of those who did the **h**	Jas 5:4	*2325*
HARVEST'S		
'Your **h** aftergrowth you shall not	Lv 25:5	7105a
HARVESTS		
grain, As his arm **h** the ears,	Is 17:5	7114b
HAS		
tree which **h** fruit yielding seed;	Gn 1:29	
moves on the earth which **h** life,	Gn 1:30	
"Indeed, **h** God said,	Gn 3:1	
middle of the garden, God **h** said,	Gn 3:3	
the man **h** become like one of Us,	Gn 3:22	
And why **h** your countenance fallen?	Gn 4:6	
which **h** opened its mouth to	Gn 4:11	
"God **h** appointed me another	Gn 4:25	
ground which the LORD **h** cursed."	Gn 5:29	
end of all flesh **h** come before Me;	Gn 6:13	
Who **h** delivered your enemies into	Gn 14:20	
the LORD **h** prevented me from	Gn 16:2	
h given heed to your affliction.	Gn 16:11	
he **h** broken My covenant."	Gn 17:14	
what He **h** spoken about him."	Gn 18:19	
to its outcry, which **h** come to Me;	Gn 18:21	
because their outcry **h** become so	Gn 19:13	
LORD **h** sent us to destroy it."	Gn 19:13	
h found favor in your sight,	Gn 19:19	
"God **h** made laughter for me;	Gn 21:6	
for God **h** heard the voice of the	Gn 21:17	
do not know who **h** done this thing;	Gn 21:26	
Milcah also **h** borne children to	Gn 22:20	
who **h** not forsaken His	Gn 24:27	
the LORD **h** guided me in the way to	Gn 24:27	
LORD **h** greatly blessed my master,	Gn 24:35	
master, so that he **h** become rich;	Gn 24:35	
He **h** given him flocks and herds,	Gn 24:35	
he **h** given him all that he has.	Gn 24:36	
he has given him all that he **h**.	Gn 24:36	
h appointed for my master's son.'	Gn 24:44	
son, as the LORD **h** spoken."	Gn 24:51	
since the LORD **h** prospered my way.	Gn 24:56	
last the LORD **h** made room for us,	Gn 26:22	
that the LORD **h** been with you;	Gn 26:28	
a field which the LORD **h** blessed;	Gn 27:27	
and **h** taken away your blessing."	Gn 27:35	
h supplanted me these two times?	Gn 27:36	
now he **h** taken away my blessing."	Gn 27:36	
the LORD **h** seen my affliction;	Gn 29:32	
LORD **h** heard that I am unloved,	Gn 29:33	
He **h** therefore given me this	Gn 29:33	
who **h** withheld from you the fruit	Gn 30:2	
"God **h** vindicated me, and has	Gn 30:6	
and **h** indeed heard my voice and	Gn 30:6	
my voice and **h** given me a son."	Gn 30:6	
"God **h** given me my wages because	Gn 30:18	
"God **h** endowed me with a good gift;	Gn 30:20	
"God **h** taken away my reproach."	Gn 30:23	
h blessed me on your account."	Gn 30:27	
and it **h** increased to a multitude,	Gn 30:30	
h blessed you wherever I turned.	Gn 30:30	
"Jacob **h** taken away all that was	Gn 31:1	
he **h** made all this wealth."	Gn 31:1	
God of my father **h** been with me.	Gn 31:5	
"Yet your father **h** cheated me and	Gn 31:7	
"Thus God **h** taken away your	Gn 31:9	
that Laban **h** been doing to you.	Gn 31:12	
For he **h** sold us, and has also	Gn 31:15	
and **h** also entirely consumed our	Gn 31:15	
wealth which God **h** taken away from	Gn 31:16	
do whatever God **h** said to you."	Gn 31:16	
God **h** seen my affliction and the	Gn 31:42	
yet my life **h** been preserved."	Gn 32:30	
h graciously given your servant."	Gn 33:5	
gift which **h** been brought to you,	Gn 33:11	
God **h** dealt graciously with me and	Gn 33:11	
and **h** been with me wherever I have	Gn 35:3	
A wild beast **h** devoured him;	Gn 37:33	
h surely been torn to pieces!"	Gn 37:33	
"There **h** been no temple	Gn 38:21	
'There **h** been no temple prostitute	Gn 38:22	
Tamar **h** played the harlot,	Gn 38:24	
and he **h** put all that he owns in	Gn 39:8	
and he **h** withheld nothing from me	Gn 39:9	
he **h** brought in a Hebrew to us to	Gn 39:14	
God **h** told to Pharaoh what He is	Gn 41:25	
God **h** shown to Pharaoh what He is	Gn 41:28	
God **h** informed you of all this,	Gn 41:39	
"God **h** made me forget all my	Gn 41:51	
"God **h** made me fruitful in the	Gn 41:52	
this distress **h** come upon us."	Gn 42:21	
"My money **h** been returned, and	Gn 42:28	
is this that God **h** done to us?"	Gn 42:28	
the God of your father **h** given you	Gn 43:23	
God **h** found out the iniquity of	Gn 44:16	
possession the cup **h** been found."	Gn 44:16	
possession the cup **h** been found,	Gn 44:17	
"For the famine **h** *been* in	Gn 45:6	
and He **h** made me a father to	Gn 45:8	
"God **h** made me lord of all Egypt;	Gn 45:9	
your son Joseph **h** come to you,"	Gn 48:2	
sons, whom God **h** given me here."	Gn 48:9	
God **h** let me see your children as	Gn 48:11	
The God who **h** been my shepherd all	Gn 48:15	
who **h** redeemed me from all evil,	Gn 48:16	
the matter **h** become known."	Ex 2:14	
the sons of Israel **h** come to Me;	Ex 3:9	
of your fathers **h** sent me to you.'	Ex 3:13	
'I AM **h** sent me to you.' "	Ex 3:14	
God of Jacob, **h** sent me to you.'	Ex 3:15	
Isaac and Jacob, **h** appeared to me,	Ex 3:16	
what **h** been done to you in Egypt.	Ex 3:16	
God of the Hebrews, **h** met with us.	Ex 3:18	
LORD **h** not appeared to you.' "	Ex 4:1	
God of Jacob, **h** appeared to you."	Ex 4:5	
"Who **h** made man's mouth?	Ex 4:11	
God of the Hebrews **h** met with us.	Ex 5:3	
he **h** done harm to this people,	Ex 5:23	
such as **h** not been *seen* in Egypt	Ex 9:18	
for there **h** been enough of God's	Ex 9:28	
also eat the rest of what **h** escaped	Ex 10:5	
even all that the hail **h** left."	Ex 10:12	
such as there **h** not been	Ex 11:6	
will give you, as He **h** promised,	Ex 12:25	
the wilderness **h** shut them in.'	Ex 14:3	
rider He **h** hurled into the sea.	Ex 15:1	
And He **h** become my salvation;	Ex 15:2	
his army He **h** cast into the sea;	Ex 15:4	
Anguish **h** gripped the inhabitants	Ex 15:14	
rider He **h** hurled into the sea."	Ex 15:21	
LORD **h** brought you out of the land	Ex 16:6	
He **h** heard your grumblings.'	Ex 16:9	
which the LORD **h** given you to eat.	Ex 16:15	
"This is what the LORD **h** commanded,	Ex 16:16	
each of you **h** in his tent.' "	Ex 16:16	3947
the LORD **h** given you the sabbath;	Ex 16:29	
"This is what the LORD **h** commanded,	Ex 16:32	
"The LORD **h** sworn;	Ex 17:16	
the LORD **h** spoken we will do!"	Ex 19:8	
God **h** come in order to test you,	Ex 20:20	
and its owner **h** been warned,	Ex 21:29	
yet its owner **h** not confined it,	Ex 21:36	
"*But* if the sun **h** risen on him,	Ex 22:3	
that he **h** not laid hands on his	Ex 22:11	
for what **h** been torn to pieces.	Ex 22:13	
the LORD **h** spoken we will do!"	Ex 24:3	
that the LORD **h** spoken we will do,	Ex 24:7	
which the LORD **h** made with you in	Ex 24:8	
whoever **h** a legal matter, let him	Ex 24:14	
not know what **h** become of him."	Ex 32:1	
do not know what **h** become of him.'	Ex 32:23	
'Whoever **h** any gold, let them tear	Ex 32:24	
for every man **h** been against his son	Ex 32:29	
people **h** committed a great sin,	Ex 32:31	
"Whoever **h** sinned against Me, I	Ex 32:33	
the LORD **h** commanded *you* to do:	Ex 35:1	
thing which the LORD **h** commanded,	Ex 35:4	
all that the LORD **h** commanded:	Ex 35:10	
the LORD **h** called by name Bezalel	Ex 35:30	
"And He **h** filled him with the	Ex 35:31	
also **h** put in his heart to teach,	Ex 35:34	
"He **h** filled them with skill to	Ex 35:35	
person in whom the LORD **h** put skill	Ex 36:1	
all that the LORD **h** commanded."	Ex 36:1	
LORD **h** commanded not to be done,	Lv 4:2	
for the sin he **h** committed.	Lv 4:3	
LORD **h** commanded not to be done,	Lv 4:13	
God **h** commanded not to be done,	Lv 4:22	
if his sin which he **h** committed is	Lv 4:23	
LORD **h** commanded not to be done,	Lv 4:27	
his sin which he **h** committed	Lv 4:28	
for his sin which he **h** committed.	Lv 4:28	
to his sin which he **h** committed,	Lv 4:35	
he **h** seen or *otherwise* known,	Lv 5:1	
confess that in which he **h** sinned.	Lv 5:5	
for his sin which he **h** committed,	Lv 5:6	
for that in which he **h** sinned,	Lv 5:7	
for his sin which he **h** committed,	Lv 5:10	
for that which he **h** sinned,	Lv 5:11	
his sin which he **h** committed	Lv 5:13	
h sinned against the holy thing,	Lv 5:16	
LORD **h** commanded not to be done,	Lv 5:17	
he **h** extorted from his companion,	Lv 6:2	
or **h** found what was lost and lied	Lv 6:3	
offering which he **h** presented.	Lv 7:8	
the LORD **h** commanded to do."	Lv 8:5	
"The LORD **h** commanded to do as	Lv 8:34	
to do as **h** been done this day,	Lv 8:34	
the LORD **h** commanded you to do,	Lv 9:6	
just as the LORD **h** commanded."	Lv 9:7	
which the LORD **h** brought about.	Lv 10:6	
h spoken to them through Moses."	Lv 10:11	
just as the LORD **h** commanded."	Lv 10:15	
all fours, whatever **h** many feet,	Lv 11:42	
"When a man **h** on the skin of his	Lv 13:2	1961
hair in the infection **h** turned white	Lv 13:3	
when the priest **h** looked at him,	Lv 13:3	
the hair on it **h** not turned white,	Lv 13:4	
the priest shall isolate *him who* **h**	Lv 13:4	
eyes the infection **h** not changed	Lv 13:5	
infection **h** not spread on the	Lv 13:5	
and if the infection **h** faded and	Lv 13:6	
the mark **h** not spread on the skin,	Lv 13:6	
after he **h** shown himself to the	Lv 13:7	
if the scab **h** spread on the skin,	Lv 13:8	
and it **h** turned the hair white,	Lv 13:10	
covers all the skin of *him who* **h**	Lv 13:12	
leprosy **h** covered all his body,	Lv 13:13	
he shall pronounce clean *him who* **h**	Lv 13:13	
it **h** all turned white *and* he is	Lv 13:13	
the infection **h** turned to white,	Lv 13:17	
shall pronounce clean *him who* **h**	Lv 13:17	
the body **h** a boil on its skin and	Lv 13:18	1961
and the hair on it **h** turned white,	Lv 13:20	
it **h** broken out in the boil.	Lv 13:20	
in the bright spot **h** turned white and	Lv 13:25	
it **h** broken out in the burn.	Lv 13:25	
and **h** not spread in the skin,	Lv 13:28	
if a man or woman **h** an infection	Lv 13:29	1961
and if the scale **h** not spread and	Lv 13:32	
no yellowish hair **h** grown in it,	Lv 13:32	
scale **h** not spread in the skin and	Lv 13:34	
if the scale **h** spread in the skin,	Lv 13:36	
in his sight the scale **h** remained,	Lv 13:37	
and black hair **h** grown in it,	Lv 13:37	
grown in it, the scale **h** healed,	Lv 13:37	
a man or a woman **h** bright spots	Lv 13:38	1961
that **h** broken out on the skin;	Lv 13:39	
for the leper who **h** the infection,	Lv 13:45	
during which he **h** the infection;	Lv 13:46	
garment **h** a mark of leprosy in it,	Lv 13:47	1961
the mark **h** spread in the garment,	Lv 13:51	
mark **h** not spread in the garment,	Lv 13:53	
with the mark **h** been washed,	Lv 13:55	
mark **h** not changed its appearance,	Lv 13:55	
even though the mark **h** not spread,	Lv 13:55	
whether an eating away **h** produced	Lv 13:55	
and if the mark **h** faded after it	Lv 13:56	
has faded after it **h** been washed,	Lv 13:56	
h departed when you washed it,	Lv 13:58	
infection of leprosy **h** been healed	Lv 14:3	
a mark *of leprosy* **h** become visible	Lv 14:35	
the mark on the walls of the house **h**	Lv 14:37	
If the mark **h** indeed spread in the	Lv 14:39	
after he **h** torn out the stones and	Lv 14:43	
and after it **h** been replastered,	Lv 14:43	
mark **h** indeed spread in the house,	Lv 14:44	
the time that he **h** quarantined it,	Lv 14:46	
and the mark **h** not indeed spread	Lv 14:48	
the house **h** been replastered,	Lv 14:48	
because the mark **h** not reappeared.	Lv 14:48	

Context	Reference	Number
man **h** a discharge from his body,	Lv 15:2	1961
with the discharge **h** been sitting,	Lv 15:6	
'Now if a man **h** a seminal emission,	Lv 15:16	3318
'When a woman **h** a discharge, *if*	Lv 15:19	1961
'Now if a woman **h** a discharge of	Lv 15:25	2100
or if she **h** a discharge beyond	Lv 15:25	2100
the man who **h** a seminal emission	Lv 15:32	3318
and for the one who **h** a discharge,	Lv 15:33	
'This is what the LORD **h** commanded,	Lv 17:2	
and **h** not brought it to the	Lv 17:4	
He **h** shed blood and that man shall	Lv 17:4	
'For the land **h** become defiled,	Lv 18:25	
land **h** spewed out its inhabitants.	Lv 18:25	
and the land **h** become defiled);	Lv 18:27	
as it **h** spewed out the nation	Lv 18:28	
nation which **h** been before you.	Lv 18:28	
for he **h** profaned the holy thing	Lv 19:8	
but who **h** in no way been redeemed	Lv 19:20	
for his sin which he **h** committed,	Lv 19:22	
and the sin which he **h** committed	Lv 19:22	
because he **h** given some of his	Lv 20:3	
he **h** cursed his father or his	Lv 20:9	
he **h** uncovered his father's	Lv 20:11	
He **h** uncovered his sister's	Lv 20:17	
he **h** laid bare her flow,	Lv 20:18	
h exposed the flow of her blood;	Lv 20:18	
h made naked his blood relative;	Lv 20:19	
he **h** uncovered his uncle's nakedness	Lv 20:20	
he **h** uncovered his brother's	Lv 20:21	
who **h** separated you from the	Lv 20:24	
him because she **h** had no husband;	Lv 21:3	1961
the anointing oil **h** been poured and	Lv 21:10	
and who **h** been consecrated to wear	Lv 21:10	
who **h** a defect shall approach to offer	Lv 21:17	1961
one who **h** a defect shall approach:	Lv 21:18	
or he who **h** a disfigured *face*,	Lv 21:18	
h a broken foot or broken hand,	Lv 21:19	1961
or *one who* **h** a defect in his eye	Lv 21:20	
Aaron the priest who **h** a defect	Lv 21:21	
since he **h** a defect, he shall not	Lv 21:21	
the altar because he **h** a defect,	Lv 21:23	
LORD, while he **h** an uncleanness,	Lv 22:3	
is a leper or who **h** a discharge,	Lv 22:4	
or if a man **h** a seminal emission,	Lv 22:4	3318
he **h** bathed his body in water.	Lv 22:6	
and **h** no child and returns to her	Lv 22:13	369
'Whatever **h** a defect, you shall	Lv 22:20	
ox or a lamb which **h** an overgrown	Lv 22:23	
one who **h** cursed outside the camp,	Lv 24:14	
his neighbor, just as he **h** done,	Lv 24:19	
just as he **h** injured a man, so it	Lv 24:20	
he **h** to sell part of his property,	Lv 25:25	
buy back what his relative **h** sold.	Lv 25:25	
'Or in case a man **h** no kinsman,	Lv 25:26	1961
'But if he **h** not found sufficient	Lv 25:28	
then what he **h** sold shall remain	Lv 25:28	
right after he **h** been sold.	Lv 25:48	
h sold the field to another man,	Lv 27:20	
LORD a field which he **h** bought,	Lv 27:22	
to the LORD out of all that he **h**,	Lv 27:28	
his sins which he **h** committed,	Nu 5:7	
give *it* to him whom he **h** wronged.	Nu 5:7	
'But if the man **h** no relative to	Nu 5:8	369
and a man **h** intercourse with her	Nu 5:13	7901
although she **h** defiled herself,	Nu 5:13	
she **h** not been caught in the act,	Nu 5:13	
wife when she **h** defiled herself	Nu 5:14	
when she **h** not defiled herself,	Nu 5:14	
"If no man **h** lain with you and if	Nu 5:19	
h had intercourse with you"	Nu 5:20	5414
he **h** made her drink the water,	Nu 5:27	
if she **h** defiled herself and has	Nu 5:27	
if she has defiled herself and **h**	Nu 5:27	
'But if the woman **h** not defiled	Nu 5:28	
ram's shoulder *when it* **h** *been*	Nu 6:19	
he **h** shaved his dedicated	Nu 6:19	
for the LORD **h** promised good	Nu 10:29	
"**H** the LORD indeed spoken only	Nu 12:2	
H He not spoken through us as well?"	Nu 12:2	
Their protection **h** been removed	Nu 14:9	
because he **h** had a different spirit	Nu 14:24	5973
spirit and **h** followed Me fully,	Nu 14:24	
place which the LORD **h** promised."	Nu 14:40	
which the LORD **h** spoken to Moses,	Nu 15:22	
h commanded you through Moses,	Nu 15:23	
'Because he **h** despised the word of	Nu 15:31	
LORD and **h** broken His commandment,	Nu 15:31	
God of Israel **h** separated you from	Nu 16:9	
and that He **h** brought you near,	Nu 16:10	
h sent me to do all these deeds;	Nu 16:28	
men, *then* the LORD **h** not sent me.	Nu 16:29	
wrath **h** gone forth from the LORD,	Nu 16:46	
the LORD, the plague **h** begun!"	Nu 16:46	
law which the LORD **h** commanded,	Nu 19:2	
which a yoke **h** never been placed.	Nu 19:2	
the body of a man who **h** died,	Nu 19:13	
h no covering tied down on it,	Nu 19:15	369
touches one who **h** been slain with a	Nu 19:16	
a sword or who **h** died *naturally*,	Nu 19:16	
because he **h** defiled the sanctuary	Nu 19:20	
h not been sprinkled on him,	Nu 19:20	
"Thus your brother Israel **h** said,	Nu 20:14	
the hardship that **h** befallen us;	Nu 20:14	
He **h** given his sons as fugitives,	Nu 21:29	
king of Moab, **h** sent *word* to me,	Nu 22:10	
h refused to let me go with you."	Nu 22:13	
"From Aram Balak **h** brought me,	Nu 23:7	
I curse whom God **h** not cursed?	Nu 23:8	
whom the LORD **h** not denounced?	Nu 23:8	

Context	Reference	Number
"What **h** the LORD spoken?"	Nu 23:17	
H He said, and will He not do it?	Nu 23:19	
Or **h** He spoken, and will He not	Nu 23:19	
When He **h** blessed, then I cannot	Nu 23:20	
"He **h** not observed misfortune in	Nu 23:21	
Nor **h** He seen trouble in Israel;	Nu 23:21	
And to Israel, what God **h** done!	Nu 23:23	
LORD **h** held you back from honor."	Nu 24:11	
can live except God **h** ordained it?	Nu 24:23	
h turned away My wrath from the	Nu 25:11	
as the LORD **h** commanded Moses."	Nu 26:4	
'If a man dies and **h** no son,	Nu 27:8	369
'If he **h** no daughter, then you	Nu 27:9	369
'If he **h** no brothers, then you	Nu 27:10	369
'If his father **h** no brothers,	Nu 27:11	369
word which the LORD **h** commanded.	Nu 30:1	
by which she **h** bound herself,	Nu 30:4	
she **h** bound herself shall stand.	Nu 30:4	
she **h** bound herself shall stand;	Nu 30:5	
lips by which she **h** bound herself,	Nu 30:6	
she **h** bound herself shall stand.	Nu 30:7	
lips by which she **h** bound herself;	Nu 30:8	
by which she **h** bound herself,	Nu 30:9	
her husband **h** annulled them, and	Nu 30:12	
he **h** confirmed them, because he	Nu 30:14	
annuls them after he **h** heard them,	Nu 30:15	
woman who **h** known man intimately.	Nu 31:17	
whoever **h** killed any person and	Nu 31:19	
and whoever **h** touched any slain,	Nu 31:19	
which the LORD **h** commanded Moses:	Nu 31:21	
land which the LORD **h** given them?	Nu 32:7	
h possessed his inheritance.	Nu 32:18	
because our inheritance **h** fallen	Nu 32:19	
until He **h** driven His enemies out	Nu 32:21	
the LORD **h** said to your servants,	Nu 32:31	
which the LORD **h** commanded to give	Nu 34:13	
that the manslayer who **h** killed	Nu 35:11	
who **h** fled to his city of refuge,	Nu 35:32	
"This is what the LORD **h**	Nu 36:6	
LORD your God **h** multiplied you,	Dt 1:10	
you, just as He **h** promised you!	Dt 1:11	
God **h** placed the land before you;	Dt 1:21	
of your fathers, **h** spoken to you.	Dt 1:21	
He **h** brought us out of the land of	Dt 1:27	
the land on which he **h** set foot,	Dt 1:36	
he **h** followed the LORD fully.	Dt 1:36	
"For the LORD your God **h** blessed	Dt 2:7	
He **h** known your wanderings through	Dt 2:7	
the LORD your God **h** been with you;	Dt 2:7	
'The LORD your God **h** given you	Dt 3:18	
God **h** done to these two kings;	Dt 3:21	
h done in the case of Baal-peor,	Dt 4:3	
h destroyed them from among you.	Dt 4:3	
nation is there that **h** a god so near to	Dt 4:7	
great nation is there that **h** statutes	Dt 4:8	
the LORD your God **h** allotted to all	Dt 4:19	
"But the LORD **h** taken you and	Dt 4:20	
the LORD your God **h** commanded you.	Dt 4:23	
H *anything* been done like this	Dt 4:32	
or **h** *anything* been heard like it?	Dt 4:32	
"**H** *any* people heard the voice of	Dt 4:33	
"Or **h** a god tried to go to take	Dt 4:34	
the LORD your God **h** commanded you,	Dt 5:16	
the LORD our God **h** shown us His	Dt 5:24	
who **h** heard the voice of the	Dt 5:26	
the LORD your God **h** commanded you;	Dt 5:32	
the LORD your God **h** commanded you,	Dt 5:33	
God **h** commanded *me* to teach you,	Dt 6:1	
of your fathers, **h** promised you,	Dt 6:3	
statutes which He **h** commanded you.	Dt 6:17	
before you, as the LORD **h** spoken.	Dt 6:19	
the LORD your God **h** chosen you to	Dt 7:6	
your God **h** led you in the wilderness	Dt 8:2	
good land which He **h** given you.	Dt 8:10	
just as the LORD **h** spoken to you.	Dt 9:3	
God **h** driven them out before you,	Dt 9:4	
the LORD **h** brought me in to possess	Dt 9:4	
He **h** brought them out to slay them	Dt 9:28	
who **h** done these great and awesome	Dt 10:21	
and now the LORD your God **h** made	Dt 10:22	
set foot, as He **h** spoken to you.	Dt 11:25	
h given you to possess as long as	Dt 12:1	
the LORD your God **h** blessed you.	Dt 12:7	
since he **h** no portion or	Dt 12:12	369
your God which He **h** given you;	Dt 12:15	
your border as He **h** promised you,	Dt 12:20	
flock which the LORD **h** given you,	Dt 12:21	
because he **h** counseled rebellion	Dt 13:5	
he **h** sought to seduce you from the	Dt 13:10	
abomination **h** been done among you,	Dt 13:14	
as He **h** sworn to your fathers,	Dt 13:17	
and the LORD **h** chosen you to be a	Dt 14:2	
divides the hoof and **h** the hoof split	Dt 14:6	8156
h fins and scales you may eat,	Dt 14:9	
for he **h** no portion or inheritance	Dt 14:27	369
because he **h** no portion or	Dt 14:29	369
what he **h** loaned to his neighbor;	Dt 15:2	
remission **h** been proclaimed.	Dt 15:2	
bless you as He **h** promised you,	Dt 15:6	
the LORD your God **h** blessed you.	Dt 15:14	
for he **h** given you six years	Dt 15:18	
"But if it **h** any defect, *such as*	Dt 15:21	1961
your God which He **h** given you.	Dt 16:17	
which **h** a blemish *or* any defect,	Dt 17:1	1961
and **h** gone and served other gods	Dt 17:3	
thing **h** been done in Israel,	Dt 17:4	
woman who **h** done this evil deed to	Dt 17:5	
since the LORD **h** said to you,	Dt 17:16	
"For the LORD your God **h** chosen	Dt 18:5	

Context	Reference	Number
God **h** not allowed you *to do* so.	Dt 18:14	
word which the LORD **h** not spoken?'	Dt 18:21	
thing which the LORD **h** not spoken.	Dt 18:22	
h spoken it presumptuously;	Dt 18:22	
as He **h** sworn to your fathers,	Dt 19:8	
or any sin which he **h** committed;	Dt 19:15	
he **h** accused his brother falsely,	Dt 19:18	
'Who is the man that **h** built a new	Dt 20:5	
new house and **h** not dedicated it?	Dt 20:5	
'Who is the man that **h** planted	Dt 20:6	
and **h** not begun to use its fruit?	Dt 20:6	
to a woman and **h** not married her?	Dt 20:7	
the LORD your God **h** given you.	Dt 20:14	
the LORD your God **h** commanded you,	Dt 20:17	
it is not known who **h** struck him,	Dt 21:1	
which **h** not been worked and which	Dt 21:3	
and which **h** not pulled in a yoke;	Dt 21:3	
which **h** not been plowed or sown,	Dt 21:4	
for the LORD your God **h** chosen	Dt 21:5	
"If a man **h** two wives, the one	Dt 21:15	1961
he wills what he **h** to his sons,	Dt 21:16	1961
a double portion of all that he **h**,	Dt 21:17	4672
"If any man **h** a stubborn and	Dt 21:18	1961
"If a man **h** committed a sin	Dt 21:22	
he **h** lost and you have found.	Dt 22:3	
he **h** charged her with shameful	Dt 22:17	
she **h** committed an act of folly	Dt 22:21	
he **h** violated his neighbor's wife.	Dt 22:24	
wife because he **h** violated her;	Dt 22:29	
or **h** his male organ cut off shall	Dt 23:1	
a slave who **h** escaped from his master	Dt 23:15	
he **h** found some indecency in her,	Dt 24:1	
wife, since she **h** been defiled;	Dt 24:4	
to his wife whom he **h** taken.	Dt 24:5	
and one of them dies and **h** no son,	Dt 25:5	369
the LORD your God **h** given you rest	Dt 25:19	
and He **h** brought us to this place and	Dt 26:9	
place and **h** given us this land,	Dt 26:9	
h given you and your household.	Dt 26:11	
"The LORD **h** today declared	Dt 26:18	
above all nations which He **h** made,	Dt 26:19	
LORD your God, as He **h** spoken."	Dt 26:19	
he **h** uncovered his father's skirt.'	Dt 27:20	
He **h** consumed you from the land	Dt 28:21	
neck until He **h** destroyed you.	Dt 28:48	
the LORD your God **h** given you.	Dt 28:52	
the LORD your God **h** given you,	Dt 28:53	
eat, since he **h** nothing *else* left,	Dt 28:55	
h not given you a heart to know,	Dt 29:4	
sandal **h** not worn out on your foot.	Dt 29:5	
which the LORD **h** afflicted it,	Dt 29:22	
'Why **h** the LORD done thus to this	Dt 29:24	
the LORD your God **h** banished you,	Dt 30:1	
the LORD your God **h** scattered you.	Dt 30:3	
and go, and the LORD **h** said to me,	Dt 31:2	
of you, just as the LORD **h** spoken.	Dt 31:3	
land which the LORD **h** sworn to their	Dt 31:7	
He your Father who **h** bought you?	Dt 32:6	
He **h** made you and established you.	Dt 32:6	
the LORD **h** not done all this."	Dt 32:27	
h risen in Israel like Moses,	Dt 34:10	
the LORD **h** given you the land,	Jos 2:9	
the terror of you **h** fallen on us,	Jos 2:9	
"Surely the LORD **h** given all the	Jos 2:24	
h my lord to say to his servant?"	Jos 5:14	
For the LORD **h** given you the city.	Jos 6:16	
woman and all she **h** out of there,	Jos 6:22	
and she **h** lived in the midst of	Jos 6:25	
what can I say since Israel **h**	Jos 7:8	
"Israel **h** sinned, and they have	Jos 7:11	
LORD, the God of Israel, **h** said,	Jos 7:13	
because he **h** transgressed the	Jos 7:15	
and because he **h** committed a	Jos 7:15	
h been called the valley of Achor	Jos 7:26	
it is dry and **h** become crumbled.	Jos 9:12	
for it **h** made peace with Joshua	Jos 10:4	
h delivered them into your hand."	Jos 10:19	
the land on which your foot **h** trodden	Jos 14:9	
behold, the LORD **h** let me live,	Jos 14:10	
them out as the LORD **h** spoken."	Jos 14:12	
the LORD **h** thus far blessed?"	Jos 17:14	
God of your fathers, **h** given you?	Jos 18:3	
God **h** given rest to your brothers,	Jos 22:4	
"For the LORD **h** made the Jordan a	Jos 22:25	
your God **h** done to all these nations	Jos 23:3	
is He who **h** been fighting for you.	Jos 23:3	
"For the LORD **h** driven out great	Jos 23:9	
h stood before you to this day.	Jos 23:9	
the LORD your God **h** given you.	Jos 23:13	
God spoke concerning you **h** failed;	Jos 23:14	
for you, not one of them **h** failed.	Jos 23:14	
until He **h** destroyed you from off	Jos 23:15	
the LORD your God **h** given you.	Jos 23:15	
good land which He **h** given you.	Jos 23:16	
you after He **h** done good to you."	Jos 24:20	
for it **h** heard all the words of	Jos 24:27	
I have done, so God **h** repaid me."	Jg 1:7	
"Because this nation **h**	Jg 2:20	
and **h** not listened to My voice,	Jg 2:20	
for the LORD **h** given your enemies	Jg 3:28	
the God of Israel, **h** commanded,	Jg 4:6	
LORD **h** given Sisera into your hands;	Jg 4:14	
the LORD **h** gone out before you."	Jg 4:14	
then **h** all this happened to us?	Jg 6:13	
But now the LORD **h** abandoned us	Jg 6:13	
he **h** torn down the altar of Baal,	Jg 6:30	
he **h** cut down the Asherah which	Jg 6:30	
someone **h** torn down his altar."	Jg 6:31	
'My own power **h** delivered me.'	Jg 7:2	

God **h** given Midian and all the Jg 7:14
for the LORD **h** given the camp of Jg 7:15
"God **h** given the leaders of Jg 8:3
when the LORD **h** given Zebah and Jg 8:7
our God **h** driven out before us, Jg 11:24
h avenged you of your enemies, Jg 11:36
the *other* day **h** appeared to me." Jg 13:10
"Samson **h** come here," Jg 16:2
"A razor **h** never come on my head, Jg 16:17
for he **h** told me all *that is* in Jg 16:18
"Our god **h** given Samson our enemy Jg 16:23
"Our god **h** given our enemy into Jg 16:24
country, Who **h** slain many of us." Jg 16:24
"Thus and so **h** Micah done to me, Jg 18:4
done to me, and he **h** hired me and Jg 18:4
are going **h** the LORD's approval." Jg 18:6
for God **h** given it into your hand, Jg 18:10
now, the day **h** drawn to a close; Jg 19:9
this man **h** come into my house, Jg 19:23
"Nothing like this **h** *ever* happened Jg 19:30
that **h** taken place among you? Jg 20:12
h this come about in Israel, Jg 21:3
woman who **h** lain with a man." Jg 21:11
LORD **h** gone forth against me." Ru 1:13
your sister-in-law **h** gone back to Ru 1:15
h dealt very bitterly with me. Ru 1:20
the LORD **h** brought me back empty Ru 1:21
since the LORD **h** witnessed against Ru 1:21
and the Almighty **h** afflicted me?" Ru 1:21
Thus she came and **h** remained from Ru 2:7
she **h** been sitting in the house Ru 2:7
h been fully reported to me, Ru 2:11
who **h** not withdrawn his kindness Ru 2:20
he **h** finished eating and drinking. Ru 3:3
until he **h** settled it today." Ru 3:18
who **h** come back from the land of Ru 4:3
h to sell the piece of land which Ru 4:3
"Blessed is the LORD who **h** not Ru 4:14
sons, **h** given birth to him." Ru 4:15
"A son **h** been born to Naomi!" Ru 4:17
and the LORD **h** given me my 1Sa 1:27
who **h** many children languishes. 1Sa 2:5
"Why **h** the LORD defeated us today 1Sa 4:3
"God **h** come into the camp." 1Sa 4:7
nothing like this **h** happened before. 1Sa 4:7
"Israel **h** fled before the 1Sa 4:17
there **h** also been a great slaughter 1Sa 4:17
and the ark of God **h** been taken." 1Sa 4:17
glory **h** departed from Israel," 1Sa 4:21
"The glory **h** departed from 1Sa 4:22
which there **h** never been a yoke; 1Sa 6:7
then He **h** done us this great evil. 1Sa 6:9
"Thus far the LORD **h** helped us." 1Sa 7:12
for he **h** come into the city today, 1Sa 9:12
because their cry **h** come to Me." 1Sa 9:16
"Here is what **h** been reserved! 1Sa 9:24
because it **h** been kept for you 1Sa 9:24
"**H** not the LORD anointed you a 1Sa 10:1
your father **h** ceased to be 1Sa 10:2
h happened to the son of Kish? 1Sa 10:11
"**H** the man come here yet?" 1Sa 10:22
see him whom the LORD **h** chosen? 1Sa 10:24
for today the LORD **h** accomplished 1Sa 11:13
the LORD **h** set a king over you. 1Sa 12:13
because the LORD **h** been pleased to 1Sa 12:22
great things He **h** done for you. 1Sa 12:24
The LORD **h** sought out for Himself 1Sa 13:14
and the LORD **h** appointed him as 1Sa 13:14
LORD **h** given them into our hands; 1Sa 14:10
for the LORD **h** given them into the 1Sa 14:12
now and see who **h** gone from us." 1Sa 14:17
My father **h** troubled the land. 1Sa 14:29
Philistines **h** not been great." 1Sa 14:30
see how this sin **h** happened today. 1Sa 14:38
who **h** brought about this great 1Sa 14:45
he **h** worked with God this day." 1Sa 14:45
and utterly destroy all that he **h**, 1Sa 15:3
h turned back from following Me and 1Sa 15:11
h not carried out My commands." 1Sa 15:11
"**H** the LORD as much delight in 1Sa 15:22
He **h** also rejected you from 1Sa 15:23
and the LORD **h** rejected you from 1Sa 15:26
"The LORD **h** torn the kingdom of 1Sa 15:28
and **h** given it to your neighbor 1Sa 15:28
your sword **h** made women childless, 1Sa 15:33
LORD **h** not chosen this one 1Sa 16:8
LORD **h** not chosen this one 1Sa 16:9
"The LORD **h** not chosen these." 1Sa 16:10
he **h** found favor in my sight." 1Sa 16:22
h been a warrior from his youth." 1Sa 17:33
"Your servant **h** killed both the 1Sa 17:36
since he **h** taunted the armies of 1Sa 17:36
"Saul **h** slain his thousands, And 1Sa 18:7
since he **h** not sinned against you, 1Sa 19:4
enemy go, so that he **h** escaped?" 1Sa 19:17
he **h** said, 'Do not let Jonathan 1Sa 20:3
know that he **h** decided on evil. 1Sa 20:7
evil **h** been decided by my father to 1Sa 20:9
you as He **h** been with my father. 1Sa 20:13
go, for the LORD **h** sent you away. 1Sa 20:22
"Why **h** the son of Jesse not come 1Sa 20:27
family **h** a sacrifice in the city, 1Sa 20:29
brother **h** commanded me to attend. 1Sa 20:29
h not come to the king's table." 1Sa 20:29
What **h** he done?" 1Sa 20:32
h commissioned me with a matter and 1Sa 21:2
with a matter and **h** said to me, 1Sa 21:2
'Saul **h** slain his thousands, And 1Sa 21:11
son **h** stirred up my servant against me 1Sa 22:8
"God **h** delivered him into my 1Sa 23:7
Your servant **h** heard for certain 1Sa 23:10
down just as Your servant **h** heard? 1Sa 23:11
is, *and* who **h** seen him there; 1Sa 23:22
h the king of Israel come out? 1Sa 24:14
that this *man* **h** in the wilderness, 1Sa 25:21
he **h** returned me evil for good. 1Sa 25:21
since the LORD **h** restrained you 1Sa 25:26
gift which your maidservant **h** brought 1Sa 25:27
that He **h** spoken concerning you, 1Sa 25:30
who **h** restrained me from harming 1Sa 25:34
who **h** pleaded the cause of my 1Sa 25:39
and **h** kept back His servant from 1Sa 25:39
The LORD **h** also returned the 1Sa 25:39
"David **h** sent us to you to take 1Sa 25:40
"Today God **h** delivered your enemy 1Sa 26:8
LORD **h** stirred you up against me, 1Sa 26:19
for the king of Israel **h** come out 1Sa 26:20
therefore Ziklag **h** belonged to the 1Sa 27:6 1961
'So **h** David done and so *has been* 1Sa 27:11
'So has David done and so **h** *been* 1Sa 27:11
all the time he **h** lived in the country 1Sa 27:11
"He **h** surely made himself odious 1Sa 27:12
"Behold, you know what Saul **h** done, 1Sa 28:9
how he **h** cut off those who are 1Sa 28:9
and God **h** departed from me and 1Sa 28:15
since the LORD **h** departed from you 1Sa 28:16
you and **h** become your adversary? 1Sa 28:16
"The LORD **h** done accordingly 1Sa 28:17
for the LORD **h** torn the kingdom 1Sa 28:17
so the LORD **h** done this thing to 1Sa 28:18
your maidservant **h** obeyed you, 1Sa 28:21
who **h** been with me these days, 1Sa 29:3
'Saul **h** slain his thousands, And 1Sa 29:5
with what the LORD **h** given us, 1Sa 30:23
who **h** kept us and delivered into 1Sa 30:23
it **h** been from that day forward, 1Sa 30:25
for agony **h** seized me because my 2Sa 1:9
mouth **h** testified against you, 2Sa 1:16
h anointed me king over them." 2Sa 2:7
if as the LORD **h** sworn to David, 2Sa 3:9
For the LORD **h** spoken of David, 2Sa 3:18
the king, and he **h** sent him away, 2Sa 3:23
away, and he **h** gone in peace." 2Sa 3:23
of Joab one who **h** a discharge, 2Sa 3:29
man **h** fallen this day in Israel? 2Sa 3:38
thus the LORD **h** given my lord the 2Sa 4:8
who **h** redeemed my life from all 2Sa 4:9
"The LORD **h** broken through my 2Sa 5:20
"The LORD **h** blessed the house of 2Sa 6:12
therefore Your servant **h** found 2Sa 7:27
he **h** sent consolers to you? 2Sa 10:3
H David not sent his servants to 2Sa 10:3
who **h** done this deserves to die. 2Sa 12:5
LORD also **h** taken away your sin; 2Sa 12:13
"But now he **h** died; 2Sa 12:23
"**H** Amnon your brother been with 2Sa 13:20
now, your servant **h** sheepshearers; 2Sa 13:24
"Absalom **h** struck down all the 2Sa 13:30
of Absalom this **h** been determined 2Sa 13:32
who **h** been mourning for the dead 2Sa 14:2
the whole family **h** risen against 2Sa 14:7
that my lord the king **h** spoken. 2Sa 14:19
your servant Joab **h** done this thing. 2Sa 14:20
in that the king **h** performed the 2Sa 14:22
to mine, and he **h** barley there; 2Sa 14:30
then every man who **h** any suit or 2Sa 15:4 1961
"The LORD **h** returned upon you all 2Sa 16:8
and the LORD **h** given the kingdom 2Sa 16:8
and if the LORD **h** told him, 2Sa 16:10
curse, for the LORD **h** told him. 2Sa 16:11
whom he **h** left to keep the house; 2Sa 16:21
let us hear what he **h** to say." 2Sa 17:5
"Ahithophel **h** spoken thus. 2Sa 17:6
the advice that Ahithophel **h** given 2Sa 17:7
he **h** now hidden himself in one of 2Sa 17:9
'There **h** been a slaughter among 2Sa 17:9
Ahithophel **h** counseled against you. 2Sa 17:21
king news that the LORD **h** freed him 2Sa 18:19
who **h** delivered up the men who 2Sa 18:28
for the LORD **h** freed you this day 2Sa 18:31
than all the evil that **h** come upon you 2Sa 19:7
but now he **h** fled out of the land 2Sa 19:9
over us, **h** died in battle. 2Sa 19:10
of all Israel **h** come to the king, 2Sa 19:11
he **h** slandered your servant to my 2Sa 19:27
h come safely to his own house." 2Sa 19:30
or **h** anything been taken for us?" 2Sa 19:42
h lifted up his hand against King 2Sa 20:21
"The LORD **h** rewarded me according 2Sa 22:21
of my hands He **h** recompensed me. 2Sa 22:21
"Therefore the LORD **h** recompensed 2Sa 22:25
For He **h** made an everlasting 2Sa 23:5
"Why **h** my lord the king come to 2Sa 24:21
the son of Haggith **h** become king, 1Ki 1:11
Why then **h** Adonijah become king?' 1Ki 1:13
"He **h** sacrificed oxen and 1Ki 1:19
and **h** invited all the sons of the 1Ki 1:19
but he **h** not invited Solomon your 1Ki 1:19
"For he **h** gone down today and has 1Ki 1:25
and **h** sacrificed oxen and fatlings 1Ki 1:25
and **h** invited all the king's sons 1Ki 1:25
servant Solomon, he **h** not invited. 1Ki 1:26
"**H** this thing been done by my 1Ki 1:27
who **h** redeemed my life from all 1Ki 1:29
LORD **h** been with my lord the king, 1Ki 1:37
King David **h** made Solomon king. 1Ki 1:43
"The king **h** also sent with him 1Ki 1:44
Solomon **h** even taken his seat on 1Ki 1:46
"The king **h** also said thus, 1Ki 1:48
who **h** granted one to sit on my 1Ki 1:48
he **h** taken hold of the horns of 1Ki 1:51
the kingdom **h** turned about and 1Ki 2:15
if Adonijah **h** not spoken this word 1Ki 2:23
who **h** established me and set me on 1Ki 2:24
and who **h** made me a house as He 1Ki 2:24
"Thus the king **h** said, 1Ki 2:30
"Do as he **h** spoken and fall upon 1Ki 2:31
As my lord the king **h** said, 1Ki 2:38
so that there **h** been no one like 1Ki 3:12
God **h** given me rest on every side; 1Ki 5:4
who **h** given to David a wise son 1Ki 5:7
"The LORD **h** said that He would 1Ki 8:12
and **h** fulfilled *it* with His hand, 1Ki 8:15
"Now the LORD **h** fulfilled His 1Ki 8:20
who **h** given rest to His people 1Ki 8:56
not one word **h** failed of all His 1Ki 8:56
'Why **h** the LORD done thus to this 1Ki 9:8
therefore the LORD **h** brought all 1Ki 9:9
So Israel **h** been in rebellion 1Ki 12:19
this thing **h** come from Me. 1Ki 12:24
the sign which the LORD **h** spoken, 1Ki 13:3
the LORD **h** given him to the lion, 1Ki 13:26
which **h** torn him and killed him, 1Ki 13:26
for the LORD **h** spoken *it*." ' 1Ki 14:11
"Zimri **h** conspired and has also 1Ki 16:16
and **h** also struck down the king." 1Ki 16:16
h not sent to search for you; 1Ki 18:10
"**H** it not been told to my master 1Ki 18:13
mouth that **h** not kissed him." 1Ki 19:18
"Naboth **h** been stoned and is 1Ki 21:14
vineyard of Naboth where he **h** gone 1Ki 21:18
Of Jezebel also **h** the LORD spoken, 1Ki 21:23
Ahab **h** humbled himself before Me? 1Ki 21:29
he **h** humbled himself before Me, 1Ki 21:29
the LORD **h** put a deceiving spirit 1Ki 22:23
and the LORD **h** proclaimed disaster 1Ki 22:23
the LORD **h** not spoken by me." 1Ki 22:28
LORD **h** sent me as far as Bethel." 2Ki 2:2
the LORD **h** sent me to Jericho." 2Ki 2:4
LORD **h** sent me to the Jordan." 2Ki 2:6
perhaps the Spirit of the LORD **h** 2Ki 2:16
of Moab **h** rebelled against me. 2Ki 3:7
For the LORD **h** called these three 2Ki 3:10
for the LORD **h** called these three 2Ki 3:13
and the creditor **h** come to take my 2Ki 4:1
"Your maidservant **h** nothing in 2Ki 4:2 369
h no son and her husband is old." 2Ki 4:14 369
and the LORD **h** hidden it from me 2Ki 4:27
it from me and **h** not told me." 2Ki 4:27
"The lad **h** not awakened." 2Ki 4:31
my master **h** spared this Naaman the 2Ki 5:20
My master **h** sent me, saying, 2Ki 5:22
but she **h** hidden her son." 2Ki 6:29
h sent to take away my head? 2Ki 6:32
the king of Israel **h** hired against 2Ki 7:6
the LORD **h** called for a famine, 2Ki 8:1
great things that Elisha **h** done." 2Ki 8:4
"The man of God **h** come here." 2Ki 8:7
king of Aram **h** sent me to you, 2Ki 8:9
but the LORD **h** shown me that he 2Ki 8:10
"The LORD **h** shown me that you 2Ki 8:13
for the LORD **h** done what He spoke 2Ki 10:10
and your heart **h** become proud. 2Ki 14:10
so he **h** sent lions among them, and 2Ki 17:26
altars Hezekiah **h** taken away, 2Ki 18:22
and **h** said to Judah and to 2Ki 18:22
H my master sent me only to your 2Ki 18:27
'**H** any one of the gods of the 2Ki 18:33
his master the king of Assyria **h** sent 2Ki 19:4
which the LORD your God **h** heard. 2Ki 19:4
h come out to fight against you," 2Ki 19:9
which he **h** sent to reproach the 2Ki 19:16
the LORD **h** spoken against him: 2Ki 19:21
'She **h** despised you and mocked 2Ki 19:21
She **h** shaken *her* head behind you, 2Ki 19:21
arrogance **h** come up to My ears, 2Ki 19:28
do the thing that He **h** spoken: 2Ki 20:9
Judah **h** done these abominations, 2Ki 21:11
and **h** also made Judah sin with his 2Ki 21:11
the priest **h** given me a book." 2Ki 22:10
of this book that **h** been found, 2Ki 22:13
which the king of Judah **h** read. 2Ki 22:16
"God **h** broken through my enemies 1Ch 14:11
wonderful deeds which He **h** done, 1Ch 16:12
therefore Your servant **h** found 1Ch 17:25
h pleased You to bless the house 1Ch 17:27
that he **h** sent comforters to you? 1Ch 19:3
h sinned and done very wickedly, 1Ch 21:17
as He **h** spoken concerning you. 1Ch 22:11
And **h** He not given you rest on 1Ch 22:18
For He **h** given the inhabitants of 1Ch 22:18
Israel **h** given rest to His people, 1Ch 23:25
He **h** chosen Judah to be a leader; 1Ch 28:4
the LORD **h** given me many sons), 1Ch 28:5
He **h** chosen my son Solomon to sit 1Ch 28:5
for the LORD **h** chosen you to build 1Ch 28:10
Solomon, whom alone God **h** chosen, 1Ch 29:1
who were before you **h** possessed nor 2Ch 1:12
He **h** made you king over them." 2Ch 2:11
who **h** made heaven and earth, 2Ch 2:12
who **h** given King David a wise son, 2Ch 2:12
and wine, of which he **h** spoken. 2Ch 2:15
"The LORD **h** said that He would 2Ch 6:1
and **h** fulfilled *it* with His hands, 2Ch 6:4
"Now the LORD **h** fulfilled His 2Ch 6:10
who **h** kept with Your servant David, 2Ch 6:15
'Why **h** the LORD done thus to this 2Ch 7:21

therefore He **h** brought all this **2Ch 7:22**
the ark of the LORD **h** entered." **2Ch 8:11**
So Israel **h** been in rebellion **2Ch 10:19**
h given us rest on every side." **2Ch 14:7**
Aram **h** escaped out of your hand. **2Ch 16:7**
the LORD **h** put a deceiving spirit **2Ch 18:22**
for the LORD **h** proclaimed disaster **2Ch 18:22**
the LORD **h** not spoken by me." **2Ch 18:27**
the LORD **h** destroyed your works." **2Ch 20:37**
as the LORD **h** spoken concerning **2Ch 23:3**
"Thus God **h** said, **2Ch 24:20**
LORD, He **h** also forsaken you.' " **2Ch 24:20**
for God **h** power to help and to **2Ch 25:8** 3426
"The LORD **h** much more to give you **2Ch 25:9** 3426
that God **h** planned to destroy you, **2Ch 25:16**
heart **h** become proud in boasting. **2Ch 25:19**
the son of Amoz, **h** written. **2Ch 26:22**
h delivered them into your hand, **2Ch 28:9**
rage *which* **h** even reached heaven. **2Ch 28:9**
h made them an object of terror, **2Ch 29:8**
for the LORD **h** chosen you to stand **2Ch 29:11**
which He **h** consecrated forever, **2Ch 30:8**
for the LORD **h** blessed His people, **2Ch 31:10**
'**H** not the same Hezekiah taken **2Ch 32:12**
of the book which **h** been found; **2Ch 34:21**
and God **h** ordered me to hurry. **2Ch 35:21**
h given me all the kingdoms of the **2Ch 36:23**
and He **h** appointed me to build Him **2Ch 36:23**
h given me all the kingdoms of the **Ezr 1:2**
and He **h** appointed me to build Him **Ezr 1:2**
king of Persia **h** commanded us." **Ezr 4:3**
document which you sent to us **h** been **Ezr 4:18**
"A decree **h** been issued by **Ezr 4:19**
and a search **h** been made and it **Ezr 4:19**
it **h** been discovered that that city has **Ezr 4:19**
that city **h** risen up against the kings **Ezr 4:19**
now it **h** been under construction and **Ezr 5:16**
"May the God who **h** caused His **Ezr 6:12**
who **h** put *such a thing* as this in **Ezr 7:27**
and **h** extended lovingkindness to **Ezr 7:28**
the holy race **h** intermingled with **Ezr 9:2**
guilt **h** grown even to the heavens. **Ezr 9:6**
grace **h** been *shown* from the LORD **Ezr 9:8**
our God **h** not forsaken us, **Ezr 9:9**
but **h** extended lovingkindness to **Ezr 9:9**
"After all that **h** come upon **Ezr 9:13**
servant **h** found favor before you, **Ne 2:5**
to him who **h** nothing prepared; **Ne 8:10**
before You, Which **h** come upon us, **Ne 9:32**
just in all that **h** come upon us; **Ne 9:33**
"Queen Vashti **h** wronged not only **Es 1:16**
is not summoned, he **h** but one law, **Es 4:11**
"What honor or dignity **h** been **Es 6:3**
"Nothing **h** been done for him." **Es 6:3**
royal robe which the king **h** worn, **Es 6:8**
horse on which the king **h** ridden, **Es 6:8**
head a royal crown **h** been placed; **Es 6:8**
and his house and all that he **h**, **Jb 1:10**
hand now and touch all that he **h**; **Jb 1:11**
all that he **h** is in your power, **Jb 1:12**
gave and the LORD **h** taken away. **Jb 1:21**
all that a man **h** he will give for his **Jb 2:4**
hidden, And whom God **h** hedged in? **Jb 3:23**
"But now it **h** come to you, and **Jb 4:5**
"So the helpless **h** hope, And **Jb 5:16** 1961
Who **h** defied Him without harm? **Jb 9:4**
Your care **h** preserved my spirit. **Jb 10:12**
For sound wisdom **h** two sides. **Jb 11:6**
the hand of the LORD **h** done this, **Jb 12:9**
"Behold, my eye **h** seen all *this*, **Jb 13:1**
My ear **h** heard and understood it. **Jb 13:1**
Because he **h** stretched out his **Jb 15:25**
h covered his face with his fat And **Jb 15:27**
"He **h** lived in desolate **Jb 15:28**
if I hold back, what **h** left me? **Jb 16:6**
"But now He **h** exhausted me; **Jb 16:7**
me up, It **h** become a witness; **Jb 16:8**
h torn me and hunted me down, **Jb 16:9**
He **h** gnashed at me with His teeth; **Jb 16:9**
And He **h** grasped me by the neck **Jb 16:12**
He **h** also set me up as His target. **Jb 16:12**
"But He **h** made me a byword of the **Jb 17:6**
"My eye **h** also grown dim because **Jb 17:7**
And he who **h** clean hands will **Jb 17:9**
earth, And he **h** no name abroad. **Jb 18:17**
"He **h** no offspring or posterity **Jb 18:19**
Know then that God **h** wronged me And **Jb 19:6**
And **h** closed His net around me. **Jb 19:6**
"He **h** walled up my way so that I **Jb 19:8**
And He **h** put darkness on my paths. **Jb 19:8**
"He **h** stripped my honor from me And **Jb 19:9**
He **h** uprooted my hope like a tree. **Jb 19:10**
"He **h** also kindled His anger **Jb 19:11**
"He **h** removed my brothers far **Jb 19:13**
For the hand of God **h** struck me. **Jb 19:21**
"He returns what he **h** attained **Jb 20:18**
"For he **h** oppressed *and* forsaken **Jb 20:19**
He **h** seized a house which he has **Jb 20:19**
a house which he **h** not built. **Jb 20:19**
will repay him for what he **h** done? **Jb 21:31**
of the orphans **h** been crushed. **Jb 22:9**
abundance the fire **h** consumed.' **Jb 22:20**
When He **h** tried me, I shall come **Jb 23:10**
"My foot **h** held fast to His path; **Jb 23:11**
is God *who* **h** made my heart faint, **Jb 23:16**
the Almighty *who* **h** dismayed me, **Jb 23:16**
but no one **h** assurance of life. **Jb 24:22** 539
"If even the moon **h** no brightness **Jb 25:5** 166
Him, And Abaddon **h** no covering. **Jb 26:6** 369

"He **h** inscribed a circle on the **Jb 26:10**
h pierced the fleeing serpent. **Jb 26:13**
lives, who **h** taken away my right, **Jb 27:2**
who **h** embittered my soul, **Jb 27:2**
"He **h** built his house like the **Jb 27:18**
a hut *which* the watchman **h** made. **Jb 27:18**
Nor **h** the falcon's eye caught **Jb 28:7**
Nor **h** the *fierce* lion passed over **Jb 28:8**
"Because He **h** loosed His **Jb 30:11**
h passed away like a cloud. **Jb 30:15**
"He **h** cast me into the mire, And **Jb 30:19**
my foot **h** hastened after deceit, **Jb 31:5**
"If my step **h** turned from the **Jb 31:7**
if any spot **h** stuck to my hands, **Jb 31:7**
heart **h** been enticed by a woman, **Jb 31:9**
And the orphan **h** not shared it **Jb 31:17**
And if he **h** not been warmed with **Jb 31:20**
'Who can find one who **h** not been **Jb 31:31**
"The alien **h** not lodged outside, **Jb 31:32**
which my adversary **h** written, **Jb 31:35**
"For he **h** not arranged *his* words **Jb 32:14**
"The Spirit of God **h** made me, **Jb 33:4**
'He **h** redeemed my soul from going **Jb 33:28**
"For Job **h** said, **Jb 34:5**
But God **h** taken away my right; **Jb 34:5**
"For he **h** said, **Jb 34:9**
who **h** laid *on Him* the whole world? **Jb 34:13**
"For **h** anyone said to God, **Jb 34:31**
He **h** not visited *in* His anger, **Jb 35:15**
Nor **h** He acknowledged **Jb 35:15**
throne He **h** seated them forever, **Jb 36:7**
"Who **h** appointed Him His way, And **Jb 36:23**
Him His way, And who **h** said, **Jb 36:23**
wind **h** passed and cleared them. **Jb 37:21**
h cleft a channel for the flood, **Jb 38:25**
"**H** the rain a father? **Jb 38:28** 3426
who **h** begotten the drops of dew? **Jb 38:28**
"From whose womb **h** come the ice? **Jb 38:29**
of heaven, who **h** given it birth? **Jb 38:29**
"Who **h** put wisdom in the **Jb 38:36**
God **h** made her forget wisdom, **Jb 39:17**
And **h** not given her a share of **Jb 39:17**
"Who **h** given to Me that I should **Jb 41:11**
what is right as My servant Job **h**. **Jb 42:7**
is right, as My servant Job **h**." **Jb 42:8**
But know that the LORD **h** set apart **Ps 4:3**
My eye **h** wasted away with grief; **Ps 6:7**
It **h** become old because of all my **Ps 6:7**
h heard the voice of my weeping. **Ps 6:8**
The LORD **h** heard my supplication, **Ps 6:9**
a God who **h** indignation every day. **Ps 7:11**
He **h** bent His bow and made it **Ps 7:12**
He **h** also prepared for Himself **Ps 7:13**
h dug a pit and hollowed it out, **Ps 7:15**
And **h** fallen into the hole which **Ps 7:15**
The enemy **h** come to an end in **Ps 9:6**
very memory of them **h** perished. **Ps 9:6**
He **h** established His throne for **Ps 9:7**
hid, their own foot **h** been caught. **Ps 9:15**
The LORD **h** made Himself known; **Ps 9:16**
He **h** executed judgment. **Ps 9:16**
He says to himself, "God **h** **Ps 10:11**
He **h** hidden His face; **Ps 10:11**
Why **h** the wicked spurned God? **Ps 10:13**
He **h** said to himself, **Ps 10:13**
He **h** dealt bountifully with me. **Ps 13:6**
The fool **h** said in his heart, **Ps 14:1**
The LORD **h** looked down from heaven **Ps 14:2**
bless the LORD who **h** counseled me; **Ps 16:7**
The LORD **h** rewarded me according **Ps 18:20**
of my hands He **h** recompensed me. **Ps 18:20**
Therefore the LORD **h** recompensed **Ps 18:24**
Their line **h** gone out through all **Ps 19:4**
He **h** placed a tent for the sun, **Ps 19:4**
of evildoers **h** encompassed me; **Ps 22:16**
For He **h** not despised nor abhorred **Ps 22:24**
Nor **h** He hidden His face from **Ps 22:24**
be born, that He **h** performed *it*. **Ps 22:31**
For He **h** founded it upon the seas And **Ps 24:2**
h clean hands and a pure heart, **Ps 24:4**
Who **h** not lifted up his soul to **Ps 24:4**
And **h** not sworn deceitfully. **Ps 24:4**
Because He **h** heard the voice of my **Ps 28:6**
My strength **h** failed because of my **Ps 31:10**
And my body **h** wasted away. **Ps 31:10**
For He **h** made marvelous His **Ps 31:21**
The people whom He **h** chosen for **Ps 33:12**
He **h** ceased to be wise *and* to do **Ps 36:3**
And Your hand **h** pressed down on me. **Ps 38:2**
my eyes, even that **h** gone from me. **Ps 38:10**
man who **h** made the LORD his trust, **Ps 40:4**
And **h** not turned to the proud, **Ps 40:4**
And my heart **h** failed me. **Ps 40:12**
H lifted up his heel against me. **Ps 41:9**
my humiliation **h** overwhelmed me, **Ps 44:15**
All this **h** come upon us, but we **Ps 44:17**
Our heart **h** not turned back, And **Ps 44:18**
soul **h** sunk down into the dust; **Ps 44:25**
God **h** blessed You forever. **Ps 45:2**
h anointed You With the oil of **Ps 45:7**
Who **h** wrought desolations in the **Ps 46:8**
God **h** ascended with a shout, The **Ps 47:5**
H made Himself known as a **Ps 48:3**
One, God, the LORD, **h** spoken, **Ps 50:1**
of beauty, God **h** shone forth. **Ps 50:2**
The fool **h** said in his heart, **Ps 53:1**
God **h** looked down from heaven upon **Ps 53:2**
Every one of them **h** turned aside; **Ps 53:3**
h delivered me from all trouble, **Ps 54:7**

And my eye **h** looked **Ps 54:7**
And horror **h** overwhelmed me. **Ps 55:5**
who **h** exalted himself against me, **Ps 55:12**
He **h** put forth his hands against **Ps 55:20**
He **h** violated his covenant. **Ps 55:20**
O God, for man **h** trampled upon me; **Ps 56:1**
God **h** spoken in His holiness: **Ps 60:6**
Once God **h** spoken; **Ps 62:11**
And will consider what He **h** done. **Ps 64:9**
of what He **h** done for my soul. **Ps 66:16**
But certainly God **h** heard; **Ps 66:19**
He **h** given heed to the voice of my **Ps 66:19**
Who **h** not turned away my prayer **Ps 66:20**
The earth **h** yielded its produce; **Ps 67:6**
which God **h** desired for His abode? **Ps 68:16**
God **h** commanded your strength; **Ps 68:28**
He **h** scattered the peoples who **Ps 68:30**
Dishonor **h** covered my face. **Ps 69:7**
zeal for Your house **h** consumed me, **Ps 69:9**
Reproach **h** broken my heart and I **Ps 69:20**
"God **h** forsaken him; **Ps 71:11**
also, and him who **h** no helper. **Ps 72:12** 369
The enemy **h** damaged everything **Ps 74:3**
O LORD, that the enemy **h** reviled, **Ps 74:18**
foolish people **h** spurned Your name. **Ps 74:18**
H His lovingkindness ceased **Ps 77:8**
H *His* promise come to an end **Ps 77:8**
H God forgotten to be gracious, **Ps 77:9**
Or **h** He in anger withdrawn His **Ps 77:9**
hand of the Most High **h** changed." **Ps 77:10**
His wondrous works that He **h** done. **Ps 78:4**
earth which He **h** founded forever. **Ps 78:69**
Your servants which **h** been shed. **Ps 79:10**
which Your right hand **h** planted, **Ps 80:15**
Assyria also **h** joined with them; **Ps 83:8**
The bird also **h** found a house, And **Ps 84:3**
For my soul **h** had enough troubles, **Ps 88:3**
And my life **h** drawn near to Sheol. **Ps 88:3**
Your wrath **h** rested upon me, And **Ps 88:7**
My eye **h** wasted away because of **Ps 88:9**
burning anger **h** passed over me; **Ps 88:16**
He **h** become a reproach to his **Ps 89:41** 1961
"Because he **h** loved Me, therefore **Ps 91:14**
high, because he **h** known My name. **Ps 91:14**
A senseless man **h** no knowledge, **Ps 92:6** 3045
And my eye **h** looked *exultantly* **Ps 92:11**
The LORD **h** clothed and girded **Ps 93:1**
"My foot **h** slipped," **Ps 94:18**
But the LORD **h** been my stronghold, **Ps 94:22**
He **h** brought back their **Ps 94:23**
For He **h** done wonderful things, **Ps 98:1**
LORD **h** made known His salvation; **Ps 98:2**
He **h** revealed His righteousness in **Ps 98:2**
He **h** remembered His lovingkindness **Ps 98:3**
It is He who **h** made us, and not we **Ps 100:3**
No one who **h** a haughty look and an **Ps 101:5**
My heart **h** been smitten like grass **Ps 102:4**
like grass and **h** withered away, **Ps 102:4**
For the appointed time **h** come. **Ps 102:13**
For the LORD **h** built up Zion; **Ps 102:16**
He **h** appeared in His glory. **Ps 102:16**
He **h** regarded the prayer of the **Ps 102:17**
And **h** not despised their prayer. **Ps 102:17**
He **h** weakened my strength in the **Ps 102:23**
He **h** shortened my days. **Ps 102:23**
He **h** not dealt with us according **Ps 103:10**
So far **h** He removed our **Ps 103:12**
h compassion on *his* children, **Ps 103:13** 7355
So the LORD **h** compassion on those **Ps 103:13** 7355
When the wind **h** passed over it, it **Ps 103:16**
The LORD **h** established His throne **Ps 103:19**
His wonders which He **h** done, **Ps 105:5**
He **h** remembered His covenant **Ps 105:8**
Whom He **h** redeemed from the hand **Ps 107:2**
He **h** satisfied the thirsty soul, **Ps 107:9**
He **h** filled with what is good. **Ps 107:9**
He **h** shattered gates of bronze And **Ps 107:16**
God **h** spoken in His holiness: **Ps 108:7**
the creditor seize all that he **h**, **Ps 109:11**
And my flesh **h** grown lean, without **Ps 109:24**
The LORD **h** sworn and will not **Ps 110:4**
He **h** made His wonders to be **Ps 111:4**
He **h** given food to those who fear **Ps 111:5**
He **h** made known to His people the **Ps 111:6**
h sent redemption to His people; **Ps 111:9**
h ordained His covenant forever; **Ps 111:9**
He **h** given freely to the poor, **Ps 112:9**
The LORD **h** been mindful of us; **Ps 115:12**
He **h** given to the sons of men. **Ps 115:16**
He **h** inclined His ear to me, **Ps 116:2**
LORD **h** dealt bountifully with you. **Ps 116:7**
And He **h** become my salvation. **Ps 118:14**
h disciplined me severely, **Ps 118:18**
He **h** not given me over to death. **Ps 118:18**
H become the chief corner *stone*. **Ps 118:22**
is the day which the LORD **h** made; **Ps 118:24**
is God, and He **h** given us light; **Ps 118:27**
That Your word **h** revived me. **Ps 119:50**
Burning indignation **h** seized me **Ps 119:53**
This **h** become mine, That I observe **Ps 119:56**
My zeal **h** consumed me, Because my **Ps 119:139**
Too long **h** my soul had its **Ps 120:6**
Who **h** not given us to be torn by **Ps 124:6**
Our soul **h** escaped as a bird out **Ps 124:7**
h done great things for them." **Ps 126:2**
LORD **h** done great things for us; **Ps 126:3**
He **h** cut in two the cords of the **Ps 129:4**
The LORD **h** sworn to David A truth **Ps 132:11**
For the LORD **h** chosen Zion; **Ps 132:13**

h desired it for His habitation.	Ps 132:13	
LORD **h** chosen Jacob for Himself,	Ps 135:4	
And **h** rescued us from our	Ps 136:24	
the enemy **h** persecuted my soul;	Ps 143:3	
He **h** crushed my life to the ground;	Ps 143:3	
He **h** made me dwell in dark places,	Ps 143:3	
For He **h** strengthened the bars of	Ps 147:13	
He **h** blessed your sons within you.	Ps 147:13	
He **h** not dealt thus with any	Ps 147:20	
He **h** also established them forever	Ps 148:6	
He **h** made a decree which will not	Ps 148:6	
And He **h** lifted up a horn for His	Ps 148:14	
that **h** breath praise the LORD.	Ps 150:6	
cause, If he **h** done you no harm.	Pr 3:30	
home, He **h** gone on a long journey;	Pr 7:19	
h taken a bag of money with him,	Pr 7:20	
are the victims she **h** cast down,	Pr 7:26	
Wisdom **h** built her house, She has	Pr 9:1	
She **h** hewn out her seven pillars;	Pr 9:1	
She **h** prepared her food, she has	Pr 9:2	
her food, she **h** mixed her wine;	Pr 9:2	
She **h** also set her table;	Pr 9:2	
She **h** sent out her maidens, she	Pr 9:3	
He who conceals hatred **h** lying	Pr 10:18	
But the righteous **h** an	Pr 10:25	
lightly esteemed and **h** a servant Than	Pr 12:9	
A righteous man **h** regard for the	Pr 12:10	3045
to be rich, but **h** nothing;	Pr 13:7	369
to be poor, but **h** great wealth.	Pr 13:7	
The righteous **h** enough to satisfy	Pr 13:25	398
easy to one who **h** understanding.	Pr 14:6	995
to anger **h** great understanding,	Pr 14:29	
righteous **h** a refuge when he dies.	Pr 14:32	2620
heart of one who **h** understanding,	Pr 14:33	995
But a cheerful heart **h** a	Pr 15:15	
A man **h** joy in an apt answer, And	Pr 15:23	
The LORD **h** made everything for its	Pr 16:4	
fountain of life to one who **h** it,	Pr 16:22	1167
deeper into one who **h** understanding	Pr 17:10	995
to buy wisdom, When he **h** no sense?	Pr 17:16	369
h a crooked mind finds no good,	Pr 17:20	6141
And the father of a fool **h** no joy.	Pr 17:21	8055
of the one who **h** understanding,	Pr 17:24	995
restrains his words **h** knowledge,	Pr 17:27	3045
And he who **h** a cool spirit is a	Pr 17:27	
reprove one who **h** understanding	Pr 19:25	995
during the harvest and **h** nothing.	Pr 20:4	369
eye, The LORD **h** made both of them.	Pr 20:12	
Who **h** woe? Who has sorrow?	Pr 23:29	
Who **h** sorrow? Who has contentions?	Pr 23:29	
Who **h** contentions? Who has	Pr 23:29	
Who **h** complaining?	Pr 23:29	
Who **h** wounds without cause?	Pr 23:29	
Who **h** redness of eyes?	Pr 23:29	
do to him as he **h** done to me;	Pr 24:29	
who **h** no control over his spirit.	Pr 25:28	369
But the poor who **h** understanding	Pr 28:11	995
When a wise man **h** a controversy	Pr 29:9	8199
Who **h** ascended into heaven and	Pr 30:4	
Who **h** gathered the wind in His	Pr 30:4	
Who **h** wrapped the waters in His	Pr 30:4	
Who **h** established all the ends of	Pr 30:4	
The leech **h** two daughters,	Pr 30:15	
That which **h** been is that which will	Ec 1:9	
And that which **h** been done is that	Ec 1:9	
Already it **h** existed for ages	Ec 1:10	
all that **h** been done under heaven.	Ec 1:13	
task *which* God **h** given to the sons of	Ec 1:13	
and my mind **h** observed a wealth of	Ec 1:16	
except what **h** already been done?	Ec 2:12	
a man who **h** labored with wisdom,	Ec 2:21	
one who **h** not labored with them.	Ec 2:21	
He **h** given wisdom and knowledge	Ec 2:26	
while to the sinner He **h** given the	Ec 2:26	
I have seen the task which God **h**	Ec 3:10	
He **h** made everything appropriate	Ec 3:11	
He **h** also set eternity in their	Ec 3:11	
the work which God **h** done from	Ec 3:11	
for God **h** *so* worked that men	Ec 3:14	
That which is **h** been already and	Ec 3:15	
that which will be **h** already been,	Ec 3:15	
for God seeks what **h** passed by.	Ec 3:15	
"God **h** surely tested them in	Ec 3:18	
is the one who **h** never existed,	Ec 4:3	
who **h** never seen the evil activity	Ec 4:3	
For he **h** come out of prison to	Ec 4:14	
of his life which God **h** given him;	Ec 5:18	
God **h** given riches and wealth,	Ec 5:19	
He **h** also empowered him to eat	Ec 5:19	
a man to whom God **h** given riches	Ec 6:2	
yet God **h** not empowered him to eat	Ec 6:2	
exists **h** already been named,	Ec 6:10	
able to straighten what He **h** bent?	Ec 7:13	
God **h** made the one as well as the	Ec 7:14	
What **h** been is remote and	Ec 7:24	
No man **h** authority to restrain the	Ec 8:8	7989
every deed that **h** been done under	Ec 8:9	
wherein a man **h** exercised authority	Ec 8:9	
God **h** given him under the sun.	Ec 8:15	
which **h** been done on the earth	Ec 8:16	
which **h** been done under the sun.	Ec 8:17	
God **h** already approved your works.	Ec 9:7	
He **h** given to you under the sun;	Ec 9:9	
Wisdom **h** the advantage of giving	Ec 10:10	
conclusion, when all **h** been heard,	Ec 12:13	
h brought me into his chambers."	SS 1:4	
swarthy, For the sun **h** burned me.	SS 1:6	
"He **h** brought me to *his* banquet	SS 2:4	
h arrived for pruning *the vines,*	SS 2:12	
h been heard in our land.	SS 2:12	
'The fig tree **h** ripened its figs,	SS 2:13	
Each man **h** his sword at his side,	SS 3:8	
"King Solomon **h** made for himself	SS 3:9	
With which his mother **h** crowned him	SS 3:11	
one among them **h** lost her young.	SS 4:2	
"Where **h** your beloved gone, O	SS 6:1	
Where **h** your beloved turned, That	SS 6:1	
beloved **h** gone down to his garden,	SS 6:2	
one among them **h** lost her young.	SS 6:6	
Let us see whether the vine **h**	SS 7:12	
sister, And she **h** no breasts;	SS 8:8	369
the mouth of the LORD **h** spoken.	Is 1:20	
faithful city **h** become a harlot,	Is 1:21	
Your silver **h** become dross, Your	Is 1:22	
Or as a garden that **h** no water.	Is 1:30	369
Their land **h** also been filled with	Is 2:7	
Their land **h** also been filled with	Is 2:7	
h also been filled with idols;	Is 2:8	
So the *common* man **h** been humbled	Is 2:9	
man *of importance* **h** been abased,	Is 2:9	
For Jerusalem **h** stumbled and	Is 3:8	
has stumbled and Judah **h** fallen,	Is 3:8	
When the Lord **h** washed away the	Is 4:4	
In my ears the LORD of hosts **h**	Is 5:9	
Therefore Sheol **h** enlarged its	Is 5:14	
LORD **h** burned against His people,	Is 5:25	
And He **h** stretched out His hand	Is 5:25	
"Behold, this **h** touched your lips;	Is 6:7	
"The LORD **h** removed men far away,	Is 6:12	
h planned evil against you,	Is 7:5	
children whom the LORD **h** given me	Is 8:18	
"As my hand **h** reached to the	Is 10:10	
the Lord **h** completed all His work on	Is 10:12	
he **h** said, "By the power of my hand	Is 10:13	
He **h** come against Aiath, He has	Is 10:28	
Aiath, He **h** passed through Migron;	Is 10:28	
and Gibeah of Saul **h** fled away.	Is 10:29	
Madmenah **h** fled.	Is 10:31	
And He **h** become my salvation.	Is 12:2	
for He **h** done excellent things;	Is 12:5	
"How the oppressor **h** ceased,	Is 14:4	
has ceased, *And how* fury **h** ceased!	Is 14:4	
"The LORD **h** broken the staff of	Is 14:5	
The LORD of hosts **h** sworn saying,	Is 14:24	
I have intended so it **h** happened,	Is 14:24	
"For the LORD of hosts **h** planned,	Is 14:27	
That the LORD **h** founded Zion, And	Is 14:32	
For the cry of distress **h** gone	Is 15:8	
the extortioner **h** come to an end,	Is 16:4	
to an end, destruction **h** ceased,	Is 16:4	
and your harvest **h** fallen away.	Is 16:9	
For thus the LORD **h** told me,	Is 18:4	
wisest advisers **h** become stupid.	Is 19:11	
of hosts **H** purposed against Egypt.	Is 19:12	
The LORD **h** mixed within her a	Is 19:14	
whom the LORD of hosts **h** blessed,	Is 19:25	
"Even as My servant Isaiah **h** gone	Is 20:3	
A harsh vision **h** been shown to me;	Is 21:2	
of all the groaning she **h** caused.	Is 21:2	
The twilight I longed for **h** been	Is 21:4	
the LORD God of Israel **h** spoken."	Is 21:17	
of hosts **h** a day of panic,	Is 22:5	
cut off, for the LORD **h** spoken."	Is 22:25	
Who **h** planned this against Tyre,	Is 23:8	
The LORD of hosts **h** planned it,	Is 23:9	
He **h** stretched His hand out over	Is 23:11	
He **h** made the kingdoms tremble;	Is 23:11	
The LORD **h** given a command	Is 23:11	
He **h** said, "You shall exult no more,	Is 23:12	
for the LORD **h** spoken this word.	Is 24:3	
For the LORD **h** spoken.	Is 25:8	
"For He **h** brought low those who	Is 26:5	
striking of Him who **h** struck them,	Is 27:7	
has struck them, **h** He struck them?	Is 27:7	
With His fierce wind He **h** expelled	Is 27:8	
Lord **h** a strong and mighty	Is 28:2	
He **h** cast *it* down to the earth	Is 28:2	
Who **h** made *His* counsel wonderful	Is 28:29	
For the LORD **h** poured over you a	Is 29:10	
deep sleep, He **h** shut your eyes,	Is 29:10	
And He **h** covered your heads, the	Is 29:10	
"He **h** no understanding"?	Is 29:16	
"Rahab who **h** been exterminated."	Is 30:7	
the Holy One of Israel, **h** said,	Is 30:15	
Although the Lord **h** given you	Is 30:20	
which **h** been winnowed with shovel	Is 30:24	
heals the bruise He **h** inflicted.	Is 30:26	
For Topheth **h** long been ready,	Is 30:33	
it **h** been prepared for the king.	Is 30:33	
He **h** made it deep and large, A	Is 30:33	
the palace **h** been abandoned,	Is 32:14	
He **h** filled Zion with justice and	Is 33:5	
desolate, the traveler **h** ceased,	Is 33:8	
ceased, He **h** broken the covenant,	Is 33:8	
he **h** despised the cities,	Is 33:8	
cities, He **h** no regard for man.	Is 33:8	
Trembling **h** seized the godless.	Is 33:14	
He **h** utterly destroyed them, He	Is 34:2	
He **h** given them over to slaughter.	Is 34:2	
the LORD **h** a sacrifice in Bozrah And	Is 34:6	
For the LORD **h** a day of vengeance,	Is 34:8	
For His mouth **h** commanded, And His	Is 34:16	
And His Spirit **h** gathered them.	Is 34:16	
He **h** cast the lot for them,	Is 34:17	
hand **h** divided it to them by line.	Is 34:17	
altars Hezekiah **h** taken away and	Is 36:7	
and **h** said to Judah and to	Is 36:7	
"**H** my master sent me only to your	Is 36:12	
H any one of the gods of the	Is 36:18	
king of Assyria **h** sent to reproach the	Is 37:4	
which the LORD your God **h** heard.	Is 37:4	
h come out to fight against you,"	Is 37:9	
the LORD **h** spoken against him:	Is 37:22	
"She **h** despised you and mocked	Is 37:22	
She **h** shaken *her* head behind you,	Is 37:22	
arrogance **h** come up to My ears,	Is 37:29	
do this thing that He **h** spoken:	Is 38:7	
which **h** gone down with the sun on	Is 38:8	
For He **h** spoken to me, and He	Is 38:15	
to me, and He Himself **h** done it;	Is 38:15	
It is You who **h** kept my soul from	Is 38:17	
to her, that her warfare **h** ended,	Is 40:2	
That her iniquity **h** been removed,	Is 40:2	
That she **h** received of the LORD's	Is 40:2	
the mouth of the LORD **h** spoken."	Is 40:5	
Who **h** measured the waters in the	Is 40:12	
Who **h** directed the Spirit of the	Is 40:13	
as His counselor **h** informed Him?	Is 40:13	
H it not been declared to you from	Is 40:21	
Scarcely **h** their stock taken root	Is 40:24	
And see who **h** created these *stars,*	Is 40:26	
"Who **h** aroused one from the east	Is 41:2	
h performed and accomplished *it,*	Is 41:4	
the hand of the LORD **h** done this,	Is 41:20	
Holy One of Israel **h** created it.	Is 41:20	
one from the north, and he **h** come;	Is 41:25	
Who **h** declared *this* from the	Is 41:26	
Until He **h** established justice in	Is 42:4	
Who **h** fashioned a god or cast an	Is 44:10	
for He **h** smeared over their eyes	Is 44:18	
deceived heart **h** turned him aside.	Is 44:20	
O heavens, for the LORD **h** done *it!*	Is 44:23	
For the LORD **h** redeemed Jacob And	Is 44:23	
are making *say,* 'He **h** no hands'?	Is 45:9	369
Israel **h** been saved by the LORD	Is 45:17	
Who **h** announced this from of old?	Is 45:21	
Who **h** long since declared it?	Is 45:21	
The word **h** gone forth from My	Is 45:23	
Bel **h** bowed down, Nebo stoops over;	Is 46:1	
Each **h** wandered in his own way;	Is 47:15	
'My idol **h** done them, And my	Is 48:5	
long ago your ear **h** not been open,	Is 48:8	
Who among them **h** declared these	Is 48:14	
And now the Lord GOD **h** sent Me,	Is 48:16	
h redeemed His servant Jacob."	Is 48:20	
He **h** made My mouth like a	Is 49:2	
of His hand He **h** concealed Me;	Is 49:2	
He **h** also made Me a select arrow,	Is 49:2	
He **h** hidden Me in His quiver.	Is 49:2	
One of Israel who **h** chosen You."	Is 49:7	
For He who **h** compassion on them	Is 49:10	7355
the LORD **h** comforted His people And	Is 49:13	
"The LORD **h** forsaken me, And the	Is 49:14	
me, And the Lord **h** forgotten me."	Is 49:14	
'Who **h** begotten these for me,	Is 49:21	
And who **h** reared these?	Is 49:21	
The Lord GOD **h** given Me the tongue	Is 50:4	
The Lord GOD **h** opened My ear;	Is 50:5	
Who **h** a case against Me?	Is 50:8	
walks in darkness and **h** no light?	Is 50:10	369
near, My salvation **h** gone forth,	Is 51:5	
among all the sons she **h** borne,	Is 51:18	
by the hand among all the sons she **h**	Is 51:18	
the LORD **h** comforted His people,	Is 52:9	
people, He **h** redeemed Jerusalem.	Is 52:9	
The LORD **h** bared His holy arm In	Is 52:10	
Who **h** believed our message?	Is 53:1	
And to whom **h** the arm of the LORD	Is 53:1	
He **h** no *stately* form or majesty	Is 53:2	
Each of us **h** turned to his own way	Is 53:6	
But the LORD **h** caused the iniquity	Is 53:6	
"For the LORD **h** called you, Like	Is 54:6	
the LORD who **h** compassion on you.	Is 54:10	7355
For He **h** glorified you."	Is 55:5	
Let not the foreigner who **h** joined	Is 56:3	
nation that **h** done righteousness And	Is 58:2	
And **h** not forsaken the ordinance	Is 58:2	
the mouth of the LORD **h** spoken."	Is 58:14	
truth **h** stumbled in the street,	Is 59:14	
for your light **h** come, And the	Is 60:1	
glory of the LORD **h** risen upon you	Is 60:1	
Israel because He **h** glorified you.	Is 60:9	
Because the LORD **h** anointed me To	Is 61:1	
He **h** sent me to bind up the	Is 61:1	
offspring *whom* the LORD **h** blessed.	Is 61:9	
For He **h** clothed me with garments	Is 61:10	
He **h** wrapped me with a robe of	Is 61:10	
The LORD **h** sworn by His right hand	Is 62:8	
the LORD **h** proclaimed to the end	Is 62:11	
And My year of redemption **h** come.	Is 63:4	
to all that the LORD **h** granted us,	Is 63:7	
Which He **h** granted them according	Is 63:7	
Nor **h** the eye seen a God	Is 64:4	
Zion **h** become a wilderness,	Is 64:10	
You, **H** been burned *by* fire;	Is 64:11	
"Who **h** heard such a thing?	Is 66:8	
Who **h** seen such things?	Is 66:8	
there **h** been such *a thing* as this!	Jer 2:10	
"**H** a nation changed gods When	Jer 2:11	
Why **h** he become a prey?	Jer 2:14	
Your sword **h** devoured your	Jer 2:30	
For the LORD **h** rejected those in	Jer 2:37	
And there **h** been no spring rain.	Jer 3:3	
'After she **h** done all these	Jer 3:7	
"Faithless Israel **h** proved	Jer 3:11	
the shameful thing **h** consumed the	Jer 3:24	
"A lion **h** gone up from his	Jer 4:7	

a destroyer of nations **h** set out;	**Jer 4:7**	
He **h** gone out from his place To	**Jer 4:7**	
LORD **H** not turned back from us."	**Jer 4:8**	
Because she **h** rebelled against Me,'	**Jer 4:17**	
How it **h** touched your heart!"	**Jer 4:18**	
'Why **h** the LORD our God done all	**Jer 5:19**	
'But this people **h** a stubborn and	**Jer 5:23**	1961
thing **H** happened in the land:	**Jer 5:30**	
LORD **h** become a reproach to them;	**Jer 6:10**	
Anguish **h** seized us, Pain as of a	**Jer 6:24**	
the road, For the enemy **h** a sword,	**Jer 6:25**	
Because the LORD **h** rejected them.	**Jer 6:30**	
"**H** this house, which is called by	**Jer 7:11**	
truth **h** perished and has been cut	**Jer 7:28**	
h been cut off from their mouth.	**Jer 7:28**	
For the LORD **h** rejected and	**Jer 7:29**	
Why then **h** this people,	**Jer 8:5**	
the scribes **H** made *it* into a lie.	**Jer 8:8**	
Because the LORD our God **h** doomed	**Jer 8:14**	
mourn, dismay **h** taken hold of me.	**Jer 8:21**	
Why then **h** not the health of the	**Jer 8:22**	
the mouth of the LORD **h** spoken,	**Jer 9:12**	
For death **h** come up through our	**Jer 9:21**	
It **h** entered our palaces To cut	**Jer 9:21**	
He **h** stretched out the heavens.	**Jer 10:12**	
"A conspiracy **h** been found among	**Jer 11:9**	
"What right **h** My beloved in My	**Jer 11:15**	
When she **h** done many vile deeds?	**Jer 11:15**	
tumult He **h** kindled fire on it,	**Jer 11:16**	
h pronounced evil against you	**Jer 11:17**	
Why **h** the way of the wicked	**Jer 12:1**	
"My inheritance **h** become to Me	**Jer 12:8**	
She **h** roared against Me;	**Jer 12:8**	
"It **h** been made a desolation,	**Jer 12:11**	
whole land **h** been made desolate,	**Jer 12:11**	
be haughty, For the LORD **h** spoken.	**Jer 13:15**	
the flock of the LORD **h** been taken	**Jer 13:17**	
H come down from your head."	**Jer 13:18**	
Judah **h** been carried into exile,	**Jer 13:19**	
the cry of Jerusalem **h** ascended.	**Jer 14:2**	
there **h** been no rain on the land;	**Jer 14:4**	
the doe in the field **h** given birth	**Jer 14:5**	
like a traveler who **h** pitched his	**Jer 14:8**	
daughter of my people **h** been crushed	**Jer 14:17**	
For You are the one who **h** done all	**Jer 14:22**	
sun **h** set while it was yet day;	**Jer 15:9**	
She **h** been shamed and humiliated.	**Jer 15:9**	
a fire **h** been kindled in My anger,	**Jer 15:14**	
Why **h** my pain been perpetual And	**Jer 15:18**	
'For what reason **h** the LORD	**Jer 16:10**	
hatches eggs which it **h** not laid,	**Jer 17:11**	
H done a most appalling thing.	**Jer 18:13**	
the name the LORD **h** called you,	**Jer 20:3**	
the word of the LORD **h** resulted In	**Jer 20:8**	
For He **h** delivered the soul of the	**Jer 20:13**	
"A baby boy **h** been born to you!"	**Jer 20:15**	
the *person* who **h** been robbed	**Jer 21:12**	
deliver the one who **h** been robbed	**Jer 22:3**	
'Why **h** the LORD done thus to this	**Jer 22:8**	
This **h** been your practice from	**Jer 22:21**	
So that no one **h** turned back from	**Jer 23:14**	
Pollution **h** gone forth into all the land.	**Jer 23:15**	
'The LORD **h** said,	**Jer 23:17**	
"But who **h** stood in the council	**Jer 23:18**	
Who **h** given heed to His word and	**Jer 23:18**	
of the LORD **h** gone forth in wrath,	**Jer 23:19**	
not turn back Until He **h** performed	**Jer 23:20**	
who **h** a dream may relate *his* dream,	**Jer 23:28**	854
but let him who **h** My word speak My	**Jer 23:28**	854
'What **h** the LORD answered?'	**Jer 23:35**	
'What **h** the LORD spoken?'	**Jer 23:35**	
'What **h** the LORD answered you?'	**Jer 23:37**	
'What **h** the LORD spoken?'	**Jer 23:37**	
the word of the LORD **h** come to me,	**Jer 25:3**	
"And the LORD **h** sent to you all	**Jer 25:4**	
land which the LORD **h** given to you	**Jer 25:5**	
which Jeremiah **h** prophesied	**Jer 25:13**	
h come to the end of the earth,	**Jer 25:31**	
Because the LORD **h** a controversy	**Jer 25:31**	
He **h** given them to the sword,'	**Jer 25:31**	
"He **h** left His hiding place like	**Jer 25:38**	
For their land **h** become a horror	**Jer 25:38**	
For he **h** prophesied against this	**Jer 26:11**	
which He **h** pronounced against you.	**Jer 26:13**	
for truly the LORD **h** sent me to	**Jer 26:15**	
For he **h** spoken to us in the name	**Jer 26:16**	
'Thus the LORD of hosts **h** said,	**Jer 26:18**	
as the LORD **h** spoken to that	**Jer 27:13**	
one whom the LORD **h** truly sent."	**Jer 28:9**	
Hananiah, the LORD **h** not sent you,	**Jer 28:15**	
'The LORD **h** raised up prophets for	**Jer 29:15**	
"The LORD **h** made you priest	**Jer 29:26**	
"For he **h** sent to us in Babylon,	**Jer 29:28**	
Shemaiah **h** prophesied to you,	**Jer 29:31**	
he **h** made you trust in a lie,"	**Jer 29:31**	
"because he **h** preached rebellion	**Jer 29:32**	
Wrath **h** gone forth, A sweeping	**Jer 30:23**	
turn back Until He **h** performed	**Jer 30:24**	
and until He **h** accomplished The	**Jer 30:24**	
For the LORD **h** ransomed Jacob And	**Jer 31:11**	
For the LORD **h** created a new thing	**Jer 31:22**	
who **h** set signs and wonders in	**Jer 32:20**	
You have spoken **h** come to pass;	**Jer 32:24**	
"Indeed this city **h** been to Me	**Jer 32:31**	
LORD chose, He **h** rejected them'?	**Jer 33:24**	
who **h** been sold to you and has	**Jer 34:14**	
to you and **h** served you six years,	**Jer 34:14**	
which **h** gone away from you.	**Jer 34:21**	
people **h** not listened to Me.	**Jer 35:16**	
wrath that the LORD **h** pronounced	**Jer 36:7**	
Pharaoh's army which **h** come out	**Jer 37:7**	
word which the LORD **h** shown me:	**Jer 38:21**	
and the LORD **h** brought *it* on and	**Jer 40:3**	
this thing **h** happened to you.	**Jer 40:3**	
king of Babylon **h** appointed over	**Jer 40:5**	
the king of the sons of Ammon **h** sent	**Jer 40:14**	
The LORD **h** spoken to you, O	**Jer 42:19**	
whatever He **h** sent me to *tell* you.	**Jer 42:21**	
our God **h** not sent you to say,	**Jer 43:2**	
that **h** proceeded from our mouths,	**Jer 44:17**	
thus your land **h** become a ruin, an	**Jer 44:22**	
this calamity **h** befallen you,	**Jer 44:23**	
as *it* **h** this day."	**Jer 44:23**	
LORD **h** added sorrow to my pain;	**Jer 45:3**	
And He **h** said, "I will rise and cover	**Jer 46:8**	
warrior **h** stumbled over another,	**Jer 46:12**	
h devoured those around you.'	**Jer 46:14**	
the LORD **h** thrust them down.	**Jer 46:15**	
He **h** let the appointed time pass	**Jer 46:17**	
their calamity **h** come upon them,	**Jer 46:21**	
of Egypt **h** been put to shame,	**Jer 46:24**	
"Baldness **h** come upon Gaza;	**Jer 47:5**	
Ashkelon **h** been ruined.	**Jer 47:5**	
When the LORD **h** given it an order?	**Jer 47:7**	
There He **h** assigned it."	**Jer 47:7**	
to Nebo, for it **h** been destroyed;	**Jer 48:1**	
Kiriathaim **h** been put to shame, it	**Jer 48:1**	
put to shame, it **h** been captured;	**Jer 48:1**	
The lofty stronghold **h** been put to	**Jer 48:1**	
be destroyed, As the LORD **h** said.	**Jer 48:8**	
h been at ease since his youth;	**Jer 48:11**	
He **h** also been undisturbed, *like wine*	**Jer 48:11**	
And he **h** not been emptied	**Jer 48:11**	
vessel, Nor **h** he gone into exile.	**Jer 48:11**	
And his aroma **h** not changed.	**Jer 48:11**	
"Moab **h** been destroyed and men	**Jer 48:15**	
his calamity **h** swiftly hastened.	**Jer 48:16**	
'How **h** the mighty scepter been	**Jer 48:17**	
of Moab **h** come up against you,	**Jer 48:18**	
you, He **h** ruined your strongholds.	**Jer 48:18**	
'What **h** happened?'	**Jer 48:19**	
"Moab **h** been put to shame, for it	**Jer 48:20**	
to shame, for it **h** been shattered.	**Jer 48:20**	
Arnon That Moab **h** been destroyed.	**Jer 48:20**	
h also come upon the plain,	**Jer 48:21**	
"The horn of Moab **h** been cut off and	**Jer 48:25**	
for he **h** become arrogant toward	**Jer 48:26**	
harvest The destroyer **h** fallen.	**Jer 48:32**	
How Moab **h** turned his back	**Jer 48:39**	
"Kerioth **h** been captured And the	**Jer 48:41**	
Because he **h** become arrogant toward	**Jer 48:42**	
a fire **h** gone forth from Heshbon And	**Jer 48:45**	
And it **h** devoured the forehead of	**Jer 48:45**	
Or **h** he no heirs?	**Jer 49:1**	369
Why then **h** Malcam taken possession	**Jer 49:1**	
Heshbon, for Ai **h** been destroyed!	**Jer 49:3**	
H good counsel been lost to the	**Jer 49:7**	
H their wisdom decayed?	**Jer 49:7**	
His offspring **h** been destroyed	**Jer 49:10**	
of your heart **h** deceived you,	**Jer 49:16**	
which He **h** planned against Edom,	**Jer 49:20**	
His purposes which He **h** purposed	**Jer 49:20**	
The earth **h** quaked at the noise of	**Jer 49:21**	
of it **h** been heard at the Red Sea.	**Jer 49:21**	
"Damascus **h** become helpless;	**Jer 49:24**	
She **h** turned away to flee, And	**Jer 49:24**	
to flee, And panic **h** gripped her;	**Jer 49:24**	
of praise **h** not been deserted,	**Jer 49:25**	
king of Babylon **h** formed a plan	**Jer 49:30**	
"It **h** no gates or bars;	**Jer 49:31**	
'Babylon **h** been captured, Bel has	**Jer 50:2**	
captured, Bel **h** been put to shame,	**Jer 50:2**	
to shame, Marduk **h** been shattered;	**Jer 50:2**	
"For a nation **h** come up against	**Jer 50:3**	
For she **h** sinned against the LORD.	**Jer 50:14**	
She **h** given herself up, her	**Jer 50:15**	
As she **h** done *to others, so* do to	**Jer 50:15**	
this last one *who* **h** broken his bones	**Jer 50:17**	
"How the hammer of the whole earth **H**	**Jer 50:23**	
How Babylon **h** become An object of	**Jer 50:23**	
The LORD **h** opened His armory And	**Jer 50:25**	
h brought forth the weapons of His	**Jer 50:25**	
upon them, for their day **h** come,	**Jer 50:27**	
According to all that she **h** done,	**Jer 50:29**	
For she **h** become arrogant against	**Jer 50:29**	
"For your day **h** come, The time	**Jer 50:31**	
h heard the report about them,	**Jer 50:43**	
Distress **h** gripped him, Agony like	**Jer 50:43**	
He **h** planned against Babylon,	**Jer 50:45**	
and His purposes which He **h**	**Jer 50:45**	
"Babylon **h** been seized!"	**Jer 50:46**	
Judah **h** been forsaken By his God,	**Jer 51:5**	
Babylon **h** been a golden cup in the	**Jer 51:7**	
Babylon **h** fallen and been broken;	**Jer 51:8**	
For her judgment **h** reached to	**Jer 51:9**	
h brought about our vindication;	**Jer 51:10**	
The LORD **h** aroused the spirit of	**Jer 51:11**	
For the LORD **h** both purposed and	**Jer 51:12**	
in treasures, Your end **h** come,	**Jer 51:13**	
LORD of hosts **h** sworn by Himself:	**Jer 51:14**	
h been captured from end *to end;*	**Jer 51:31**	
h devoured me *and* crushed me,	**Jer 51:34**	
He **h** set me down *like* an empty	**Jer 51:34**	
He **h** swallowed me like a monster,	**Jer 51:34**	
He **h** filled his stomach with my	**Jer 51:34**	
He **h** washed me away.	**Jer 51:34**	
"How Sheshak **h** been captured, And	**Jer 51:41**	
How Babylon **h** become an object of	**Jer 51:41**	
"The sea **h** come up over Babylon;	**Jer 51:42**	
She **h** been engulfed with its	**Jer 51:42**	
I will make what he **h** swallowed	**Jer 51:44**	
the wall of Babylon **h** fallen down!	**Jer 51:44**	
Disgrace **h** covered our faces, For	**Jer 51:51**	
She **h** become like a widow Who was	**La 1:1**	
H become a forced laborer!	**La 1:1**	
She **h** none to comfort her Among	**La 1:2**	369
Judah **h** gone into exile under	**La 1:3**	
nations, *But* she **h** found no rest;	**La 1:3**	
For the LORD **h** caused her grief	**La 1:5**	
All her majesty **H** departed	**La 1:6**	
she **h** become an unclean thing.	**La 1:8**	
she **h** fallen astonishingly;	**La 1:9**	
She **h** no comforter.	**La 1:9**	369
the enemy **h** magnified himself!"	**La 1:9**	
The adversary **h** stretched out his	**La 1:10**	
For she **h** seen the nations enter	**La 1:10**	
He **h** spread a net for my feet;	**La 1:13**	
He **h** turned me back;	**La 1:13**	
He **h** made me desolate, Faint all	**La 1:13**	
He **h** made my strength fail.	**La 1:14**	
The Lord **h** given me into the hands	**La 1:14**	
"The Lord **h** rejected all my	**La 1:15**	
He **h** called an appointed time	**La 1:15**	
The Lord **h** trodden *as in* a wine	**La 1:15**	
Because the enemy **h** prevailed."	**La 1:16**	
The LORD **h** commanded concerning	**La 1:17**	
Jerusalem **h** become an unclean	**La 1:17**	
How the Lord **h** covered the	**La 2:1**	
He **h** cast from heaven to earth The	**La 2:1**	
And **h** not remembered His footstool	**La 2:1**	
The Lord **h** swallowed up;	**La 2:2**	
He **h** not spared All the	**La 2:2**	
In His wrath He **h** thrown down The	**La 2:2**	
He **h** brought *them* down to the	**La 2:2**	
He **h** profaned the kingdom and its	**La 2:2**	
In fierce anger He **h** cut off All	**La 2:3**	
He **h** drawn back His right hand	**La 2:3**	
And He **h** burned in Jacob like a	**La 2:3**	
He **h** bent His bow like an enemy;	**La 2:4**	
He **h** set His right hand like an	**La 2:4**	
He **h** poured out His wrath like fire.	**La 2:4**	
The Lord **h** become like an enemy.	**La 2:5**	
He **h** swallowed up Israel;	**La 2:5**	
He **h** swallowed up all its palaces,	**La 2:5**	
He **h** destroyed its strongholds And	**La 2:5**	
And He **h** violently treated His	**La 2:6**	
He **h** destroyed His appointed	**La 2:6**	
The LORD **h** caused to be forgotten	**La 2:6**	
And He **h** despised king and priest	**La 2:6**	
The Lord **h** rejected His altar, He	**La 2:7**	
He **h** abandoned His sanctuary;	**La 2:7**	
He **h** delivered into the hand of	**La 2:7**	
He **h** stretched out a line, He has	**La 2:8**	
He **h** not restrained His hand from	**La 2:8**	
And He **h** caused rampart and wall to	**La 2:8**	
He **h** destroyed and broken her bars.	**La 2:9**	
The LORD **h** done what He purposed;	**La 2:17**	
He **h** accomplished His word Which	**La 2:17**	
He **h** thrown down without sparing,	**La 2:17**	
And He **h** caused the enemy to	**La 2:17**	
He **h** exalted the might of your	**La 2:17**	
I am the man who **h** seen affliction	**La 3:1**	
He **h** driven me and made me walk In	**La 3:2**	
Surely against me He **h** turned His	**La 3:3**	
He **h** caused my flesh and my skin	**La 3:4**	
waste away, He **h** broken my bones.	**La 3:4**	
He **h** besieged and encompassed me	**La 3:5**	
In dark places He **h** made me dwell,	**La 3:6**	
He **h** walled me in so that I cannot	**La 3:7**	
He **h** made my chain heavy.	**La 3:7**	
He **h** blocked my ways with hewn	**La 3:9**	
He **h** made my paths crooked.	**La 3:9**	
He **h** turned aside my ways and torn	**La 3:11**	
He **h** made me desolate.	**La 3:11**	
He **h** filled me with bitterness, He	**La 3:15**	
He **h** made me drunk with wormwood.	**La 3:15**	
He **h** broken my teeth with gravel;	**La 3:16**	
He **h** made me cower in the dust.	**La 3:16**	
soul **h** been rejected from peace;	**La 3:17**	
"My strength **h** perished, And *so has*	**La 3:18**	
And *so* **h** my hope from the LORD."	**La 3:18**	
silent Since He **h** laid *it* on him.	**La 3:28**	
Unless the Lord **h** commanded *it?*	**La 3:37**	
How dark the gold **h** become,	**La 4:1**	
How the pure gold **h** changed!	**La 4:1**	
But the daughter of my people **h**	**La 4:3**	
withered, it **h** become like wood.	**La 4:8**	
The LORD **h** accomplished His wrath,	**La 4:11**	
He **h** poured out His fierce anger;	**La 4:11**	
And He **h** kindled a fire in Zion	**La 4:11**	
Which **h** consumed its foundations.	**La 4:11**	
of the LORD **h** scattered them,	**La 4:16**	
of your iniquity **h** been completed,	**La 4:22**	
O LORD, what **h** befallen us;	**La 5:1**	
h been turned over to strangers,	**La 5:2**	
skin **h** become as hot as an oven,	**La 5:10**	
The joy of our hearts **h** ceased;	**La 5:15**	
h been turned into mourning.	**La 5:15**	
The crown **h** fallen from our head;	**La 5:16**	
that a prophet **h** been among them.	**Ezk 2:5**	
his righteous deeds which he **h** done	**Ezk 3:20**	
nor **h** any unclean meat ever	**Ezk 4:14**	
'But she **h** rebelled against My	**Ezk 5:6**	
'An end is coming; the end **h** come!	**Ezk 7:6**	
It **h** awakened against you;	**Ezk 7:6**	
behold, it **h** come!	**Ezk 7:6**	
'Your doom **h** come to you, O	**Ezk 7:7**	

Context	Reference	Number
The time **h** come, the day is	**Ezk 7:7**	
Your doom **h** gone forth;	**Ezk 7:10**	
the rod **h** budded, arrogance has	**Ezk 7:10**	
has budded, arrogance **h** blossomed.	**Ezk 7:10**	
'Violence **h** grown into a rod of	**Ezk 7:11**	
'The time **h** come, the day has	**Ezk 7:12**	
time has come, the day **h** arrived.	**Ezk 7:12**	
for their iniquity **h** become an	**Ezk 7:19**	
the LORD **h** forsaken the land.'	**Ezk 8:12**	
'The LORD **h** forsaken the land, and	**Ezk 9:9**	
h been given us as a possession.'	**Ezk 11:15**	
of man, **h** not the house of Israel,	**Ezk 12:9**	
when the LORD **h** not sent them;	**Ezk 13:6**	
"Behold, when the wall **h** fallen,	**Ezk 13:12**	
"If it **h** been put into the fire	**Ezk 15:4**	
fire **h** consumed both of its ends and	**Ezk 15:4**	
its middle part **h** been charred,	**Ezk 15:4**	
h consumed it and it is charred,	**Ezk 15:5**	
which he **h** committed against Me.	**Ezk 17:20**	
He **h** committed all these	**Ezk 18:13**	
he **h** a son who has observed all	**Ezk 18:14**	3205
he has a son who **h** observed all	**Ezk 18:14**	
When the son **h** practiced justice	**Ezk 18:19**	
and **h** observed all My statutes and	**Ezk 18:19**	
all his sins which he **h** committed	**Ezk 18:21**	
transgressions which he **h** committed	**Ezk 18:22**	
which he **h** practiced,	**Ezk 18:22**	
his righteous deeds which he **h** done	**Ezk 18:24**	
his treachery which he **h** committed	**Ezk 18:24**	
and his sin which he **h** committed;	**Ezk 18:24**	
his iniquity which he **h** committed	**Ezk 18:26**	
his wickedness which he **h** committed	**Ezk 18:27**	
fire **h** gone out from *its* branch;	**Ezk 19:14**	
h consumed its shoots *and* fruit,	**Ezk 19:14**	
and **h** become a lamentation.	**Ezk 19:14**	
of Israel, whose day **h** come,	**Ezk 21:25**	
who are slain, whose day **h** come,	**Ezk 21:29**	
"One **h** committed abomination	**Ezk 22:11**	
and another **h** lewdly defiled his	**Ezk 22:11**	
in you **h** humbled his sister,	**Ezk 22:11**	
of Israel **h** become dross to Me;	**Ezk 22:18**	
GOD,' when the LORD **h** not spoken.	**Ezk 22:28**	
The king of Babylon **h** laid siege	**Ezk 24:2**	
whose rust **h** not gone out of it!	**Ezk 24:6**	
"She **h** wearied *Me* with toil, Yet	**Ezk 24:12**	
great rust **h** not gone from her;	**Ezk 24:12**	
to all that he **h** done you will do;	**Ezk 24:24**	
"Because Edom **h** acted against the	**Ezk 25:12**	
and **h** incurred grievous guilt,	**Ezk 25:12**	
Tyre **h** said concerning Jerusalem,	**Ezk 26:2**	
it **h** opened to me.	**Ezk 26:2**	
The east wind **h** broken you In the	**Ezk 27:26**	
It **h** consumed you, And I have	**Ezk 28:18**	
That **h** said, 'My Nile is mine, and	**Ezk 29:3**	
it **h** not been bound up for healing	**Ezk 30:21**	
and **h** set its top among the clouds,	**Ezk 31:10**	
which he **h** committed he will die.	**Ezk 33:13**	
back what he **h** taken by robbery,	**Ezk 33:15**	
his sins that he **h** committed	**Ezk 33:16**	
He **h** practiced justice and	**Ezk 33:16**	
"The city **h** been taken."	**Ezk 33:21**	
h been given as a possession.'	**Ezk 33:24**	
like a sensual song by one who **h** a	**Ezk 33:32**	
a prophet **h** been in their midst."	**Ezk 33:33**	
because My flock **h** become a prey,	**Ezk 34:8**	
My flock **h** even become food for	**Ezk 34:8**	
the enemy **h** spoken against you,	**Ezk 36:2**	
My great name which **h** been profaned	**Ezk 36:23**	
'This desolate land **h** become like	**Ezk 36:35**	
dried up and our hope **h** perished.	**Ezk 37:11**	
God of Israel **h** entered by it;	**Ezk 44:2**	
a sister who **h** not had a husband,	**Ezk 44:25**	
or beast that **h** died a natural death	**Ezk 44:31**	
death or **h** been torn to pieces.	**Ezk 44:31**	
who **h** appointed your food and your	**Da 1:10**	
no great king or ruler **h** *ever* asked	**Da 2:10**	
about which the king **h** inquired,	**Da 2:27**	
and He **h** made known to King	**Da 2:28**	
and He who reveals mysteries **h**	**Da 2:29**	
this mystery **h** not been revealed	**Da 2:30**	383
God of heaven **h** given the kingdom,	**Da 2:37**	
He **h** given *them* into your hand and	**Da 2:38**	
h caused you to rule over them all.	**Da 2:38**	
the great God **h** made known to the	**Da 2:45**	
Nebuchadnezzar the king **h** set up.	**Da 3:5**	
who **h** sent His angel and delivered	**Da 3:28**	
"It **h** seemed good to me to	**Da 4:2**	
the Most High God **h** done for me.	**Da 4:2**	
and your majesty **h** become great	**Da 4:22**	
h come upon my lord the king:	**Da 4:24**	
h been removed from you,	**Da 4:31**	
God **h** numbered your kingdom	**Da 5:26**	
your kingdom **h** been divided and	**Da 5:28**	
of the living God, **h** your God,	**Da 6:20**	
Who **h** *also* delivered Daniel from	**Da 6:27**	
Which **h** been told is true;	**Da 8:26**	
"Indeed all Israel **h** transgressed	**Da 9:11**	
the curse **h** been poured out on us,	**Da 9:11**	
Thus He **h** confirmed His words	**Da 9:12**	
there **h** not been done *anything* like	**Da 9:12**	
all this calamity **h** come on us;	**Da 9:13**	
the LORD **h** kept the calamity in	**Da 9:14**	
to all His deeds which He **h** done,	**Da 9:14**	
the vision anguish **h** come upon me,	**Da 10:16**	
nor **h** any breath been left in me."	**Da 10:17**	
"But as soon as he **h** arisen,	**Da 11:4**	
of kingship **h** not been conferred,	**Da 11:21**	
their mother **h** played the harlot;	**Hos 2:5**	
conceived them **h** acted shamefully.	**Hos 2:5**	
For the LORD **h** a case against the	**Hos 4:1**	
of harlotry **h** led *them* astray,	**Hos 4:12**	
harlot, Israel **h** defiled itself.	**Hos 5:3**	
Judah also **h** stumbled with them.	**Hos 5:5**	
He **h** withdrawn from them.	**Hos 5:6**	
For He **h** torn *us,* but He will heal	**Hos 6:1**	
He **h** wounded *us,* but He will	**Hos 6:1**	
is there, Israel **h** defiled itself	**Hos 6:10**	
h become a cake not turned.	**Hos 7:8**	
h become like a silly dove,	**Hos 7:11**	
Israel **h** rejected the good;	**Hos 8:3**	
He **h** rejected your calf, O	**Hos 8:5**	
The standing grain **h** no heads;	**Hos 8:7**	369
Ephraim **h** hired lovers.	**Hos 8:9**	
h multiplied altars for sin,	**Hos 8:11**	
LORD **h** taken no delight in them.	**Hos 8:13**	
For Israel **h** forgotten his Maker	**Hos 8:14**	
h multiplied fortified cities,	**Hos 8:14**	
since it **h** departed from it.	**Hos 10:5**	
LORD also **h** a dispute with Judah,	**Hos 12:2**	
h provoked to bitter anger;	**Hos 12:14**	
she **h** rebelled against her God.	**Hos 13:16**	
My anger **h** turned away from them.	**Hos 14:4**	
H *anything like* this happened in	**Jl 1:2**	
What the gnawing locust **h** left,	**Jl 1:4**	
left, the swarming locust **h** eaten;	**Jl 1:4**	
what the swarming locust **h** left,	**Jl 1:4**	
left, the creeping locust **h** eaten;	**Jl 1:4**	
what the creeping locust **h** left,	**Jl 1:4**	
the stripping locust **h** eaten.	**Jl 1:4**	
For a nation **h** invaded my land,	**Jl 1:6**	
And it **h** the fangs of a lioness.	**Jl 1:6**	
It **h** made my vine a waste And my	**Jl 1:7**	
It **h** stripped them bare and cast	**Jl 1:7**	
H not food been cut off before our	**Jl 1:16**	
For fire **h** devoured the pastures	**Jl 1:19**	
And the flame **h** burned up all the	**Jl 1:19**	
And fire **h** devoured the pastures	**Jl 1:20**	
h never been *anything* like it,	**Jl 2:2**	
up, For it **h** done great things."	**Jl 2:20**	
For the LORD **h** done great things.	**Jl 2:21**	
For the tree **h** borne its fruit,	**Jl 2:22**	
For He **h** given you the early rain	**Jl 2:23**	
He **h** poured down for you the rain,	**Jl 2:23**	
That the swarming locust **h** eaten,	**Jl 2:25**	
Who **h** dealt wondrously with you;	**Jl 2:26**	
who escape, As the LORD **h** said,	**Jl 2:32**	
nation," for the LORD **h** spoken.	**Jl 3:8**	
the LORD **h** spoken against you,	**Am 3:1**	
in the forest when he **h** no prey?	**Am 3:4**	369
unless he **h** captured *something?*	**Am 3:4**	
in a city **h** not the LORD done it?	**Am 3:6**	
A lion **h** roared! Who will not fear?	**Am 3:8**	
The Lord GOD **h** spoken!	**Am 3:8**	
Lord GOD **h** sworn by His holiness,	**Am 4:2**	
She **h** fallen, she will not rise	**Am 5:2**	
The Lord GOD **h** sworn by Himself,	**Am 6:8**	
the LORD God of hosts **h** declared:	**Am 6:8**	
"Amos **h** conspired against you in	**Am 7:10**	
end **h** come for My people Israel.	**Am 8:2**	
h sworn by the pride of Jacob,	**Am 8:7**	
And **h** founded His vaulted dome	**Am 9:6**	
And an envoy **h** been sent among the	**Ob 1:1**	
of your heart **h** deceived you,	**Ob 1:3**	
of Esau," For the LORD **h** spoken.	**Ob 1:18**	
wickedness **h** come up before Me."	**Jon 1:2**	
account this calamity **h** *struck*	**Jon 1:7**	
On whose account **h** this calamity	**Jon 1:8**	
on account of me this great storm **h**	**Jon 1:12**	
incurable, For it **h** come to Judah;	**Mi 1:9**	
h reached the gate of my people,	**Mi 1:9**	
Because a calamity **h** come down	**Mi 1:12**	
of the LORD of hosts **h** spoken.	**Mi 4:4**	
you, Or **h** your counselor perished,	**Mi 4:9**	
That agony **h** gripped you like a	**Mi 4:9**	
For He **h** gathered them like	**Mi 4:12**	
who is in labor **h** borne a child.	**Mi 5:3**	
LORD **h** a case against His people;	**Mi 6:2**	
He **h** told you, O man, what is good;	**Mi 6:8**	
Who **h** appointed its time?	**Mi 6:9**	
person **h** perished from the land,	**Mi 7:2**	
From you **h** gone forth One who	**Na 1:11**	
The LORD **h** issued a command	**Na 1:14**	
The one who scatters **h** come up	**Na 2:1**	
For on whom **h** not your evil passed	**Na 3:19**	
idol when its maker **h** carved it,	**Hab 2:18**	
He **h** rays *flashing* from His hand,	**Hab 3:4**	
He **h** made my feet like hinds' *feet,*	**Hab 3:19**	
the LORD **h** prepared a sacrifice,	**Zph 1:7**	
He **h** consecrated His guests.	**Zph 1:7**	
For He **h** laid bare the cedar work.	**Zph 2:14**	
How she **h** become a desolation, A	**Zph 2:15**	
The LORD **h** taken away	**Zph 3:15**	
He **h** cleared away your enemies.	**Zph 3:15**	
"The time **h** not come, *even* the	**Hg 1:2**	
of you the sky **h** withheld its dew and	**Hg 1:10**	
the earth **h** withheld its produce.	**Hg 1:10**	
olive tree, it **h** not borne *fruit.*	**Hg 2:19**	
so He **h** dealt with us.	**Zch 1:6**	
LORD **h** sent to patrol the earth."	**Zch 1:10**	
"After glory He **h** sent Me against	**Zch 2:8**	
that the LORD of hosts **h** sent Me.	**Zch 2:9**	
LORD of hosts **h** sent Me to you.	**Zch 2:11**	
who **h** chosen Jerusalem rebuke you!	**Zch 3:2**	
LORD of hosts **h** sent me to you.	**Zch 4:9**	
"For who **h** despised the day of	**Zch 4:10**	
LORD of hosts **h** sent me to you.	**Zch 6:15**	
"Thus **h** the LORD of hosts said,	**Zch 7:9**	
her expectation **h** been confounded.	**Zch 9:5**	
LORD of hosts **h** visited His flock,	**Zch 10:3**	
O cypress, for the cedar **h** fallen,	**Zch 11:2**	
impenetrable forest **h** come down.	**Zch 11:2**	
who **h** a male in his flock and	**Mal 1:14**	3426
H not one God created us?	**Mal 2:10**	
"Judah **h** dealt treacherously, and	**Mal 2:11**	
an abomination **h** been committed	**Mal 2:11**	
for Judah **h** profaned the sanctuary	**Mal 2:11**	
and **h** married the daughter of a	**Mal 2:11**	
Because the LORD **h** been a witness	**Mal 2:14**	
"But not one **h** done *so* who has a	**Mal 2:15**	
so who **h** a remnant of the Spirit.	**Mal 2:15**	
for the Child who **h** been conceived in	**Mt 1:20**	
who **h** been born King of the Jews?	**Mt 2:2**	
what **h** been written by the prophet	**Mt 2:5**	
if the salt **h** become tasteless,	**Mt 5:13**	
brother **h** something against you,	**Mt 5:23**	*2192*
with lust for her **h** already committed	**Mt 5:28**	
day **h** enough trouble of its own.	**Mt 6:34**	
Man **h** nowhere to lay His head."	**Mt 8:20**	*2192*
Son of Man **h** authority on earth to	**Mt 9:6**	*2192*
"My daughter **h** just died;	**Mt 9:18**	
your faith **h** made you well."	**Mt 9:22**	
for the girl **h** not died, but is	**Mt 9:24**	
"Nothing like this **h** ever been seen	**Mt 9:33**	
but it is the one who **h** endured to	**Mt 10:22**	
"He who **h** found his life will	**Mt 10:39**	
and he who **h** lost his life for My	**Mt 10:39**	
h not arisen *anyone* greater than John	**Mt 11:11**	
"He who **h** ears to hear, let him	**Mt 11:15**	*2192*
and they say, 'He **h** a demon!'	**Mt 11:18**	*2192*
"What man is there among you who **h** a	**Mt 12:11**	*2192*
kingdom of God **h** come upon you.	**Mt 12:28**	
"He who **h** ears, let him hear."	**Mt 13:9**	*2192*
"To you it **h** been granted to know	**Mt 13:11**	
but to them it **h** not been granted.	**Mt 13:11**	
"For whoever **h**, to him *more*	**Mt 13:12**	*2192*
what he **h** shall be taken away	**Mt 13:12**	*2192*
FOR THE HEART OF THIS PEOPLE **H**	**Mt 13:15**	
what **h** been sown in his heart.	**Mt 13:19**	
yet he **h** no *firm* root in himself,	**Mt 13:21**	*2192*
'An enemy **h** done this!'	**Mt 13:28**	
He who **h** ears, let him hear.	**Mt 13:43**	*2192*
he goes and sells all that he **h** and	**Mt 13:44**	*2192*
scribe who **h** become a disciple	**Mt 13:52**	
he **h** risen from the dead,	**Mt 14:2**	
help you **h** been given *to God,*"	**Mt 15:5**	
the Son of Man **h** risen from the dead.	**Mt 17:9**	
the Son of Man **h** come to save	**Mt 18:11**	
If any man **h** a hundred sheep, and	**Mt 18:12**	*1096*
and one of them **h** gone astray,	**Mt 18:12**	
therefore God **h** joined together,	**Mt 19:6**	
beginning it **h** not been this way.	**Mt 19:8**	
those to whom it **h** been given.	**Mt 19:11**	
"And everyone who **h** left houses	**Mt 19:29**	
it **h** been prepared by My Father."	**Mt 20:23**	
'The Lord **h** need of them,' and	**Mt 21:3**	*2192*
such as **h** not occurred since the	**Mt 24:21**	
branch **h** already become tender and	**Mt 24:32**	
to the one who **h** the ten talents.'	**Mt 25:28**	*2192*
to everyone who **h**, *more* shall be	**Mt 25:29**	*2192*
into the eternal fire which **h** been	**Mt 25:41**	
For she **h** done a good deed to Me.	**Mt 26:10**	
what this woman **h** done will also	**Mt 26:13**	
"But all this **h** taken place to	**Mt 26:56**	
He **h** blasphemed! What further need	**Mt 26:65**	
that field **h** been called the Field of	**Mt 27:8**	
"Why, what evil **h** He done?"	**Mt 27:23**	
'He **h** risen from the dead,' and	**Mt 27:64**	
for Jesus who **h** been crucified.	**Mt 28:5**	
"He is not here, for He **h** risen,	**Mt 28:6**	
that He **h** risen from the dead;	**Mt 28:7**	
"All authority **h** been given to Me	**Mt 28:18**	
Son of Man **h** authority on earth to	**Mk 2:10**	*2192*
"He **h** lost His senses."	**Mk 3:21**	
"If Satan **h** risen up against	**Mk 3:26**	
never **h** forgiveness, but is guilty of	**Mk 3:29**	*2192*
"He **h** an unclean spirit."	**Mk 3:30**	*2192*
"He who **h** ears to hear, let him	**Mk 4:9**	*2192*
"To you **h** been given the mystery	**Mk 4:11**	
word which **h** been sown in them.	**Mk 4:15**	
nor **h** *anything* been secret,	**Mk 4:22**	
"If anyone **h** ears to hear, let	**Mk 4:23**	*2192*
"For whoever **h**, to him *more*	**Mk 4:25**	*2192*
even what he **h** shall be taken away	**Mk 4:25**	*2192*
because the harvest **h** come."	**Mk 4:29**	
things the Lord **h** done for you,	**Mk 5:19**	
your faith **h** made you well;	**Mk 5:34**	
"Your daughter **h** died;	**Mk 5:35**	
The child **h** not died, but is	**Mk 5:39**	
the Baptist **h** risen from the dead,	**Mk 6:14**	
"John, whom I beheaded, **h** risen!"	**Mk 6:16**	
["If anyone **h** ears to hear, let him	**Mk 7:16**	*2192*
h gone out of your daughter."	**Mk 7:29**	
"He **h** done all things well;	**Mk 7:37**	
God after it **h** come with power.	**Mk 9:1**	
to you that Elijah **h** indeed come,	**Mk 9:13**	
h this been happening to him?"	**Mk 9:21**	
"It **h** often thrown him both	**Mk 9:22**	
and when He **h** been killed, He will	**Mk 9:31**	
therefore God **h** joined together,	**Mk 10:9**	
there is no one who **h** left house	**Mk 10:29**	
for whom it **h** been prepared."	**Mk 10:40**	
your faith **h** made you well."	**Mk 10:52**	
on which no one yet **h** ever sat;	**Mk 11:2**	
'The Lord **h** need of it';	**Mk 11:3**	*2192*
which You cursed **h** withered."	**Mk 11:21**	
tribulation such as **h** not occurred	**Mk 13:19**	
branch **h** already become tender and	**Mk 13:28**	

“Why **h** this perfume been wasted? **Mk 14:4**
She **h** done a good deed to Me. **Mk 14:6**
“She **h** done what she could; **Mk 14:8**
she **h** anointed My body beforehand **Mk 14:8**
what this woman **h** done will also **Mk 14:9**
hour **h** come; behold, the Son of Man **Mk 14:41**
but *this* **h** *taken place* to **Mk 14:49**
“Why, what evil **h** He done?” **Mk 15:14**
Nazarene, who **h** been crucified. **Mk 16:6**
He **h** risen; He is not here; **Mk 16:6**
“He who **h** believed and has been **Mk 16:16**
h been baptized shall be saved; **Mk 16:16**
but he who **h** disbelieved shall be **Mk 16:16**
for your petition **h** been heard, **Lk 1:13**
“This is the way the Lord **h** dealt **Lk 1:25**
even your relative Elizabeth **h** **Lk 1:36**
“And how **h** it *happened* to me, **Lk 1:43**
h rejoiced in God my Savior. **Lk 1:47**
“For He **h** had regard for the **Lk 1:48**
One **h** done great things for me; **Lk 1:49**
“He **h** done mighty deeds with His **Lk 1:51**
He **h** scattered *those who were* **Lk 1:51**
“He **h** brought down rulers from **Lk 1:52**
h exalted those who were humble. **Lk 1:52**
“He **h** filled the hungry with good **Lk 1:53**
“He **h** given help to Israel His **Lk 1:54**
For He **h** visited us and **Lk 1:68**
And **h** raised up a horn of **Lk 1:69**
h been born for you a Savior, **Lk 2:11**
and see this thing that **h** happened **Lk 2:15**
the Lord **h** made known to us.” **Lk 2:15**
“The man who **h** two tunics **Lk 3:11** *2192*
to share with him who **h** none; **Lk 3:11** *2192*
he who **h** food is to do likewise.” **Lk 3:11** *2192*
for it **h** been handed over to me, **Lk 4:6**
He **h** sent Me to proclaim release to **Lk 4:18**
“Today this Scripture **h** been **Lk 4:21**
the Son of Man **h** authority on earth **Lk 5:24** *2192*
after he **h** been fully trained, **Lk 6:40**
“But the one who **h** heard and has **Lk 6:49**
and **h** not acted *accordingly,* **Lk 6:49**
great prophet **h** arisen among us!” **Lk 7:16**
“God **h** visited His people!” **Lk 7:16**
“John the Baptist **h** sent us to You, **Lk 7:20**
“For John the Baptist **h** come **Lk 7:33**
and you say, ‘He **h** a demon!’ **Lk 7:33** *2192*
of Man **h** come eating and drinking, **Lk 7:34**
she **h** wet My feet with her tears and **Lk 7:44**
in, **h** not ceased to kiss My feet. **Lk 7:45**
“Your faith **h** saved you; **Lk 7:50**
“He who **h** ears to hear, let him **Lk 8:8** *2192*
“To you it **h** been granted to know **Lk 8:10**
for whoever **h**, to him *more* **Lk 8:18** *2192*
what he thinks he **h** shall be taken **Lk 8:18** *2192*
great things God **h** done for you.” **Lk 8:39**
your faith **h** made you well; **Lk 8:48**
“Your daughter **h** died; **Lk 8:49**
“Stop weeping, for she **h** not died, **Lk 8:52**
prophets of old **h** risen again.” **Lk 9:19**
Man **h** nowhere to lay His head.” **Lk 9:58** *2192*
of God **h** come near to you.’ **Lk 10:9**
the kingdom of God **h** come near.’ **Lk 10:11**
my sister **h** left me to do all **Lk 10:40**
for Mary **h** chosen the good part, **Lk 10:42**
“Suppose one of you **h** a friend, **Lk 11:5** *2192*
a friend of mine **h** come to me **Lk 11:6**
the door **h** already been shut and **Lk 11:7**
kingdom of God **h** come upon you. **Lk 11:20**
fear the One who, after He **h** killed **Lk 12:5**
h authority to cast into hell; **Lk 12:5** *2192*
not *even* when one **h** an abundance **Lk 12:15** *4052*
for your Father **h** chosen gladly to **Lk 12:32**
From everyone who **h** been given **Lk 12:48**
Satan **h** bound for eighteen long **Lk 13:16**
the one who **h** invited you comes, **Lk 14:10**
what you commanded **h** been done, **Lk 14:22**
see if he **h** enough to complete it? **Lk 14:28** *2192*
when he **h** laid a foundation and **Lk 14:29**
if even salt **h** become tasteless, **Lk 14:34**
He who **h** ears to hear, let him **Lk 14:35** *2192*
if he **h** a hundred sheep and has **Lk 15:4** *2192*
sheep and **h** lost one of them, **Lk 15:4**
“When he **h** found it, he lays **Lk 15:5**
if she **h** ten silver coins and **Lk 15:8** *2192*
“When she **h** found it, she **Lk 15:9**
dead and **h** come to life again; **Lk 15:24**
he was lost and **h** been found.’ **Lk 15:24**
‘Your brother **h** come, and your **Lk 15:27** *2240*
father **h** killed the fattened calf because **Lk 15:27**
because he **h** received him back **Lk 15:27**
who **h** devoured your wealth with **Lk 15:30**
brother of yours was dead and **h** **Lk 15:32**
and *was* lost and **h** been found.’ ” **Lk 15:32**
the gospel of the kingdom of God **h** **Lk 16:16**
when he **h** come in from the field, **Lk 17:7**
your faith **h** made you well.” **Lk 17:19**
there is no one who **h** left house **Lk 18:29**
your faith **h** made you well.” **Lk 18:42**
“He **h** gone to be the guest of a **Lk 19:7**
salvation **h** come to this house, **Lk 19:9**
“For the Son of Man **h** come to **Lk 19:10**
your mina **h** made ten minas more.’ **Lk 19:16**
mina, master, **h** made five minas.’ **Lk 19:18**
to the one who **h** the ten minas.’ **Lk 19:24** *2192*
‘Master, he **h** ten minas *already.*’ **Lk 19:25** *2192*
who **h**, more shall be given, **Lk 19:26** *2192*
on which no one yet **h** ever sat; **Lk 19:30**
The Lord **h** need of it.’ **Lk 19:31** *2192*
“The Lord **h** need of it.” **Lk 19:34** *2192*

is going as it **h** been determined; **Lk 22:22** *2192*
My Father **h** granted Me a kingdom, **Lk 22:29** *2192*
Satan **h** demanded *permission* to **Lk 22:31** *2192*
whoever **h** a money belt is to take **Lk 22:36** *2192*
and whoever **h** no sword is to sell **Lk 22:36** *2192*
refers to Me **h** *its* fulfillment.” **Lk 22:37** *2192*
“No, nor **h** Herod, for he sent Him **Lk 23:15**
death **h** been done by Him. **Lk 23:15**
“Why, what evil **h** this man done? **Lk 23:22**
this man **h** done nothing wrong.” **Lk 23:41**
“He is not here, but He **h** risen. **Lk 24:6**
“The Lord **h** really risen and has **Lk 24:34**
risen and **h** appeared to Simon.” **Lk 24:34**
into being that **h** come into being. **Jn 1:3**
after me **h** a higher rank than I, **Jn 1:15** *1096*
No one **h** seen God at any time; **Jn 1:18**
of the Father, He **h** explained **Jn 1:18**
a Man who **h** a higher rank than I, **Jn 1:30** *1096*
My hour **h** not yet come.” **Jn 2:4** *2240*
“No one **h** ascended into **Jn 3:13**
not believe **h** been judged already, **Jn 3:18**
because he **h** not believed in the **Jn 3:18**
that the Light **h** come into the world, **Jn 3:19**
it **h** been given him from heaven. **Jn 3:27**
who **h** the bride is the bridegroom; **Jn 3:29** *2192*
this joy of mine **h** been made full. **Jn 3:29**
“What He **h** seen and heard, of **Jn 3:32**
“He who **h** received His testimony **Jn 3:33**
testimony **h** set his seal to *this,* **Jn 3:33**
He whom God **h** sent speaks the **Jn 3:34**
and **h** given all things into His **Jn 3:35**
in the Son **h** eternal life; **Jn 3:36** *2192*
h no honor in his own country. **Jn 4:44** *2192*
h given all judgment to the Son, **Jn 5:22**
Him who sent Me, **h** eternal life, **Jn 5:24** *2192*
h passed out of death into life. **Jn 5:24**
as the Father **h** life in Himself, **Jn 5:26** *2192*
he **h** testified to the truth. **Jn 5:33**
Father **h** given Me to accomplish **Jn 5:36**
about Me, that the Father **h** sent Me. **Jn 5:36**
sent Me, He **h** testified of Me. **Jn 5:37**
“There is a lad here who **h** five **Jn 6:9** *2192*
God, **h** set His seal.” **Jn 6:27**
believe in Him whom He **h** sent.” **Jn 6:29**
it is not Moses who **h** given you **Jn 6:32**
that He **h** given Me I lose nothing, **Jn 6:39**
Everyone who **h** heard and learned **Jn 6:45**
that anyone **h** seen the Father, **Jn 6:46**
He **h** seen the Father. **Jn 6:46**
he who believes **h** eternal life. **Jn 6:47** *2192*
drinks My blood **h** eternal life, **Jn 6:54** *2192*
unless it **h** been granted him from **Jn 6:65**
My time **h** not yet fully come.” **Jn 7:8**
“How **h** this man become learned, **Jn 7:15**
Moses **h** given you circumcision **Jn 7:22**
signs than those which this man **h**, **Jn 7:31**
“**H** not the Scripture said that **Jn 7:42**
The officers answered, “Never **h** a **Jn 7:46**
or Pharisees **h** believed in Him, **Jn 7:48**
has believed in Him, **h** he? **Jn 7:48**
woman **h** been caught in adultery, **Jn 8:4**
in your law it **h** been written that **Jn 8:17**
He **h** not left Me alone, for I **Jn 8:29**
because My word **h** no place in you. **Jn 8:37** *5562*
a man who **h** told you the truth, **Jn 8:40**
know that God **h** spoken to Moses, **Jn 9:29**
“Since the beginning of time it **h** **Jn 9:32**
“No one **h** taken it away from Me, **Jn 10:18**
“He **h** a demon and is insane. **Jn 10:20** *2192*
“My Father, who **h** given *them* to **Jn 10:29**
“**H** it not been written in your **Jn 10:34**
friend Lazarus **h** fallen asleep; **Jn 11:11**
“Lord, if he **h** fallen asleep, he **Jn 11:12**
for he **h** been *dead* four days.” **Jn 11:39**
the world **h** gone after Him.” **Jn 12:19**
“The hour **h** come for the Son of **Jn 12:23**
Now My soul **h** become troubled; **Jn 12:27**
“An angel **h** spoken to Him.” **Jn 12:29**
“This voice **h** not come for My **Jn 12:30**
who **h** believed our report? And to **Jn 12:38**
And to whom **h** the arm of the Lord **Jn 12:38**
“He **h** blinded their eyes and He **Jn 12:40**
My sayings, **h** one who judges him; **Jn 12:48** *2192*
sent Me **h** given Me a **Jn 12:49**
just as the Father **h** told Me.” **Jn 12:50**
“He who **h** bathed needs only to **Jn 13:10**
‘He who eats My bread **h** lifted up **Jn 13:18**
who **h** seen Me has seen the Father; **Jn 14:9**
who has seen Me **h** seen the Father; **Jn 14:9**
“He who **h** My commandments and **Jn 14:21** *2192*
what then **h** happened that You are **Jn 14:22**
is coming, and he **h** nothing in Me; **Jn 14:30** *2192*
“Just as the Father **h** loved Me, **Jn 15:9**
“Greater love **h** no one than this, **Jn 15:13** *2192*
it **h** hated Me before *it hated* you. **Jn 15:18**
you, sorrow **h** filled your heart. **Jn 16:6**
ruler of this world **h** been judged. **Jn 16:11**
things that the Father **h** are Mine; **Jn 16:15** *2192*
woman is in labor she **h** pain, **Jn 16:21** *2192*
pain, because her hour **h** come; **Jn 16:21**
child **h** been born into the world. **Jn 16:21**
is coming, and **h** *already* come, **Jn 16:32**
“Father, the hour **h** come; **Jn 17:1**
and the world **h** hated them, **Jn 17:14**
the world **h** not known You, **Jn 17:25**
cup which the Father **h** given Me, **Jn 18:11**
Me to you **h** *the* greater sin.” **Jn 19:11** *2192*
And he who **h** seen has testified, **Jn 19:35**
And he who has seen **h** testified, **Jn 19:35**

as the Father **h** sent Me, I also **Jn 20:21**
h fixed by His own authority; **Ac 1:7**
the Holy Spirit **h** come upon you; **Ac 1:8**
who **h** been taken up from you into **Ac 1:11**
He **h** poured forth this which you **Ac 2:33**
God **h** made Him both Lord and **Ac 2:36**
h glorified His servant Jesus, **Ac 3:13**
it is the name of Jesus which **h** **Ac 3:16**
which *comes* through Him **h** given **Ac 3:16**
suffer, He **h** thus fulfilled. **Ac 3:18**
to how this man **h** been made well, **Ac 4:9**
that **h** been given among men by **Ac 4:12**
miracle **h** taken place through them **Ac 4:16**
why **h** Satan filled your heart to **Ac 5:3**
h given to those who obey Him.” **Ac 5:32**
and he **h** seen in a vision a man **Ac 9:12**
and here he **h** authority from the **Ac 9:14** *2192*
h sent me so that you may regain **Ac 9:17**
“What God **h** cleansed, no **Ac 10:15**
and *yet* God **h** shown me that I **Ac 10:28**
your prayer **h** been heard and your **Ac 10:31**
this is the One who **h** been appointed **Ac 10:42**
unclean **h** ever entered my mouth.’ **Ac 11:8**
‘What God **h** cleansed, no longer **Ac 11:9**
God **h** granted to the Gentiles also **Ac 11:18**
that the Lord **h** sent forth His angel **Ac 12:11**
God **h** brought to Israel a Savior, **Ac 13:23**
to us the message of this salvation **h** **Ac 13:26**
that God **h** fulfilled this **Ac 13:33**
to decay, He **h** spoken in this way: **Ac 13:34**
“For so the Lord **h** commanded us, **Ac 13:47**
“Simeon **h** related how God first **Ac 15:14**
the tabernacle of David which **h** **Ac 15:16**
Moses from ancient generations **h** in **Ac 15:21** *2192*
and Jason **h** welcomed them, and **Ac 17:7**
because He **h** fixed a day in which **Ac 17:31**
through a Man whom He **h** appointed, **Ac 17:31**
this Paul **h** persuaded and turned **Ac 19:26**
Holy Spirit **h** made you overseers, **Ac 20:28**
besides he **h** even brought Greeks **Ac 21:28**
and **h** defiled this holy place.” **Ac 21:28**
h been appointed for you to do.’ **Ac 22:10**
‘The God of our fathers **h** **Ac 22:14**
or an angel **h** spoken to him?” **Ac 23:9**
he **h** something to report to him.” **Ac 23:17** *2192*
he **h** something to tell you.” **Ac 23:18** *2192*
and **h** an opportunity to make his **Ac 25:16** *2192*
the investigation **h** taken place, **Ac 25:26**
this **h** not been done in a corner. **Ac 26:26**
God **h** granted you all those who **Ac 27:24**
he **h** been saved from the sea, **Ac 28:4**
h not allowed him to live.” **Ac 28:4**
For the heart of this people **h** **Ac 28:27**
God **h** been sent to the Gentiles; **Ac 28:28**
through what **h** been made, **Ro 1:20** *4161*
h become uncircumcision. **Ro 2:25**
Then what advantage **h** the Jew? **Ro 3:1**
of God **h** been manifested, **Ro 3:21**
of the one who **h** faith in Jesus. **Ro 3:26**
according to the flesh, **h** found? **Ro 4:1**
he **h** something to boast about, **Ro 4:2** *2192*
because the love of God **h** been **Ro 5:5**
he who **h** died is freed from sin. **Ro 6:7**
that the law **h** jurisdiction over a **Ro 7:1** *2961*
life in Christ Jesus **h** set you free from **Ro 8:2**
though the word of God **h** failed. **Ro 9:6**
who runs, but on God who **h** mercy. **Ro 9:16** *1653*
He **h** mercy on whom He desires, **Ro 9:18** *1653*
who **h** believed our report?” **Ro 10:16**
“Their voice **h** gone out into all **Ro 10:18**
God **h** not rejected His people, **Ro 11:1**
has not rejected His people, **h** He? **Ro 11:1**
God **h** not rejected His people whom **Ro 11:2**
there **h** also come to be at the **Ro 11:5**
is seeking, it **h** not obtained, **Ro 11:7**
by their transgression salvation **h** **Ro 11:11**
that a partial hardening **h** **Ro 11:25**
fullness of the Gentiles **h** come in **Ro 11:25**
For God **h** shut up all in **Ro 11:32**
For who **h** known the mind of **Ro 11:34**
Or who **h** first given to Him that it **Ro 11:35**
as God **h** allotted to each a **Ro 12:3**
h opposed the ordinance of God; **Ro 13:2**
his neighbor **h** fulfilled *the* law. **Ro 13:8**
One person **h** faith that he may eat **Ro 14:2** *4100*
who eats, for God **h** accepted him. **Ro 14:3**
For I say that Christ **h** become a **Ro 15:8**
Christ **h** accomplished through me, **Ro 15:18**
h also been a helper of many, **Ro 16:2**
Mary, who **h** worked hard for you. **Ro 16:6**
who **h** worked hard in the Lord. **Ro 16:12**
your obedience **h** reached to all; **Ro 16:19**
the mystery which **h** been kept secret **Ro 16:25**
h been made known to all the **Ro 16:26**
H Christ been divided? **1Co 1:13**
H not God made foolish the wisdom **1Co 1:20**
but God **h** chosen the foolish **1Co 1:27**
and God **h** chosen the weak things **1Co 1:27**
and the despised God **h** chosen, **1Co 1:28**
rulers of this age **h** understood; **1Co 2:8**
“Things which eye **h** not seen **1Co 2:9**
which eye has not seen and ear **h** not **1Co 2:9**
All that God **h** prepared for those who **1Co 2:9**
For who **h** known the mind of **1Co 2:16**
which he **h** built on it remains, **1Co 3:14**
God **h** exhibited us apostles last **1Co 4:9**
that someone **h** his father’s wife. **1Co 5:1** *2192*
him who **h** so committed this, **1Co 5:3**
Passover also **h** been sacrificed. **1Co 5:7**

he **h** a case against his neighbor, **1Co 6:1** *2192*
God **h** not only raised the Lord, **1Co 6:14**
each man **h** his own gift from God, **1Co 7:7** *2192*
h a wife who is an unbeliever, **1Co 7:12** *2192*
who **h** an unbelieving husband, **1Co 7:13** *2192*
but God **h** called us to peace. **1Co 7:15**
the Lord **h** assigned to each one, **1Co 7:17**
to each one, as God **h** called each, **1Co 7:17**
H anyone been called in **1Co 7:18**
marries, she **h** not sinned. **1Co 7:28**
the time **h** been shortened, **1Co 7:29**
but **h** authority over his own will, **1Co 7:37** *2192*
h decided this in his own heart, **1Co 7:37**
he **h** not yet known as he ought to **1Co 8:2**
No temptation **h** overtaken you but **1Co 10:13**
Every man who **h** *something* on his **1Co 11:4** *2192*
But every woman who **h** her head **1Co 11:5**
so also the man **h** *his birth* **1Co 11:12**
you that if a man **h** long hair, **1Co 11:14** *2863*
but if a woman **h** long hair, it is **1Co 11:15** *2863*
is one and *yet* **h** many members, **1Co 12:12** *2192*
But now God **h** placed the members, **1Co 12:18**
But God **h** *so* composed the body, **1Co 12:24**
And God **h** appointed in the church, **1Co 12:28**
you assemble, each one **h** a psalm, **1Co 14:26** *2192*
one has a psalm, **h** a teaching, **1Co 14:26** *2192*
has a teaching, **h** a revelation, **1Co 14:26** *2192*
has a revelation, **h** a tongue, **1Co 14:26** *2192*
has a tongue, **h** an interpretation. **1Co 14:26** *2192*
Or **h** it come to you only? **1Co 14:36**
He **h** been raised from the dead, **1Co 15:12**
not even Christ **h** been raised; **1Co 15:13**
and if Christ **h** not been raised, **1Co 15:14**
not even Christ **h** been raised; **1Co 15:16**
and if Christ **h** not been raised, **1Co 15:17**
h been raised from the dead, **1Co 15:20**
when He **h** abolished all rule and **1Co 15:24**
reign until He **h** put all His enemies **1Co 15:25**
For He **h** PUT ALL THINGS IN **1Co 15:27**
effective *service* **h** opened to me, **1Co 16:9**
will come when he **h** opportunity. **1Co 16:12**
But if any **h** caused sorrow, he has **2Co 2:5**
he **h** caused sorrow not to me, **2Co 2:5**
ministry of condemnation **h** glory, **2Co 3:9**
in this case **h** no glory because **2Co 3:10** *1392*
god of this world **h** blinded the minds **2Co 4:4**
the One who **h** shone in our hearts **2Co 4:6**
body, according to what he **h** done, **2Co 5:10**
and He **h** committed to us the word **2Co 5:19**
Our mouth **h** spoken freely to you, **2Co 6:11**
fellowship **h** light with darkness? **2Co 6:14**
what harmony **h** Christ with Belial, **2Co 6:15**
or what **h** a believer in common **2Co 6:15**
h the temple of God with idols? **2Co 6:16**
godly sorrow, **h** produced in you: **2Co 7:11**
h been refreshed by you all. **2Co 7:13**
the grace of God which **h** been given **2Co 8:1**
according to what *a person* **h**, **2Co 8:12** *2192*
h gone to you of his own accord. **2Co 8:17**
in *the things of* the gospel **h** **2Co 8:18**
but he **h** also been appointed by **2Co 8:19**
h been prepared since last year, **2Co 9:2**
zeal **h** stirred up most of them. **2Co 9:2**
as he **h** purposed in his heart, **2Co 9:7**
and not to boast in what **h** been **2Co 10:16**
And He **h** said to me, **2Co 12:9**
Galatians, who **h** bewitched you, **Ga 3:1**
yet when it **h** been ratified, **Ga 3:15**
but God **h** granted it to Abraham by **Ga 3:18**
h shut up everyone under sin, **Ga 3:22**
Therefore the Law **h** become our **Ga 3:24**
But now that faith **h** come, **Ga 3:25**
God **h** sent forth the Spirit of His **Ga 4:6**
OF THE DESOLATE THAN OF THE ONE WHO **H** **Ga 4:27** *2192*
of the cross **h** been abolished. **Ga 5:11**
the world **h** been crucified to me, **Ga 6:14**
who **h** blessed us with every **Eph 1:3**
as it **h** now been revealed to His **Eph 3:5**
for ages **h** been hidden in God who **Eph 3:9**
which in *the likeness of* God **h** **Eph 4:24**
to share with one who **h** need. **Eph 4:28** *2192*
God in Christ also **h** forgiven you. **Eph 4:32**
h an inheritance in the kingdom of **Eph 5:5** *2192*
in *the cause of* Christ **h** become **Php 1:13**
For to you it **h** been granted for **Php 1:29**
If anyone else **h** a mind to put **Php 3:4** *1380*
the exertion of the power that He **h** **Php 3:21** *1410*
which **h** come to you, just as in **Col 1:6**
even as *it* **h** *been doing* in you **Col 1:6**
who **h** qualified us to share in the **Col 1:12**
yet He **h** now reconciled you in His **Col 1:22**
the mystery which **h** been hidden **Col 1:26**
but **h** now been manifested to His **Col 1:26**
and He **h** taken it out of the way, **Col 2:14**
his stand on *visions* he **h** seen, **Col 2:18**
h a complaint against anyone; **Col 3:13** *2192*
of the wrong which he **h** done, **Col 3:25**
For I testify for him that he **h** a **Col 4:13** *2192*
the Lord **h** sounded forth from you, **1Th 1:8**
faith toward God **h** gone forth, **1Th 1:8**
h come upon them to the utmost. **1Th 2:16**
Timothy **h** come to us from you, **1Th 3:6**
and **h** brought us good news of your **1Th 3:6**
For God **h** not called us for the **1Th 4:7**
God **h** not destined us for wrath, **1Th 5:9**
that the day of the Lord **h** come. **2Th 2:2**
because God **h** chosen you from the **2Th 2:13**
who **h** loved us and given us **2Th 2:16**
our Lord, who **h** strengthened me, **1Tm 1:12**

which God **h** created to be **1Tm 4:3**
widow **h** children or grandchildren, **1Tm 5:4** *2192*
and who **h** been left alone, **1Tm 5:5**
alone, **h** fixed her hope on God **1Tm 5:5**
household, he **h** denied the faith and **1Tm 5:8**
and if she **h** brought up children, if **1Tm 5:10**
if she **h** shown hospitality to **1Tm 5:10**
if she **h** washed the saints' feet, **1Tm 5:10**
she **h** assisted those in distress, **1Tm 5:10**
and if she **h** devoted herself to **1Tm 5:10**
is a believer **h** *dependent* widows, **1Tm 5:16** *2192*
but he **h** a morbid interest in **1Tm 6:4** *3552*
whom no man **h** seen or can see. **1Tm 6:16**
what **h** been entrusted to you, **1Tm 6:20**
For God **h** not given us a spirit of **2Tm 1:7**
who **h** saved us and called us with **2Tm 1:9**
but now **h** been revealed by the **2Tm 1:10**
which **h** been entrusted to **2Tm 1:14**
h already taken place, **2Tm 2:18**
the time of my departure **h** come. **2Tm 4:6**
h deserted me and gone to **2Tm 4:10**
Crescens **h** *gone* to Galatia, **2Tm 4:10**
For the grace of God **h** appeared, **Ti 2:11**
if he **h** wronged you in any way or **Phm 1:18**
days **h** spoken to us in His Son, **Heb 1:2**
as He **h** inherited a more excellent **Heb 1:4**
H ANOINTED YOU WITH THE OIL OF **Heb 1:9**
of the angels **h** He ever said, **Heb 1:13**
But one **h** testified somewhere, **Heb 2:6**
I AND THE CHILDREN WHOM GOD **H** **Heb 2:13**
in that which He **h** suffered, **Heb 2:18**
For He **h** been counted worthy of **Heb 3:3**
builder of the house **h** more honor **Heb 3:3** *2192*
that rest, just as He **h** said, **Heb 4:3**
For He **h** said somewhere **Heb 4:4**
a time just as **h** been said before, **Heb 4:7**
For the one who **h** entered His rest **Heb 4:10**
one who has entered His rest **h** himself **Heb 4:10**
who **h** passed through the heavens, **Heb 4:14**
but One who **h** been tempted in all **Heb 4:15**
where Jesus **h** entered as a **Heb 6:20**
no one **h** officiated at the altar. **Heb 7:13**
who **h** become *such* not on the basis **Heb 7:16**
"THE LORD **H** SWORN AND WILL NOT **Heb 7:21**
Jesus **h** become the guarantee of a **Heb 7:22**
point in what **h** been said *is this:* **Heb 8:1**
who **h** taken His seat at the right **Heb 8:1**
But now He **h** obtained a more **Heb 8:6**
which **h** been enacted on better **Heb 8:6**
He **h** made the first obsolete. **Heb 8:13**
place **h** not yet been disclosed while **Heb 9:8**
so that, since a death **h** **Heb 9:15**
He **h** been manifested to put away sin **Heb 9:26**
since it **h** *only* a shadow of the **Heb 10:1** *2192*
For by one offering He **h** perfected **Heb 10:14**
Anyone who **h** set aside the Law of **Heb 10:28**
who **h** trampled under foot the Son of **Heb 10:29**
and **h** regarded as unclean the **Heb 10:29**
and **h** insulted the Spirit of grace? **Heb 10:29**
which **h** a great reward. **Heb 10:35** *2192*
MY SOUL **H** NO PLEASURE IN HIM. **Heb 10:38** *2106*
for the city which **h** foundations, **Heb 11:10** *2192*
for He **h** prepared a city for them. **Heb 11:16**
and **h** sat down at the right hand **Heb 12:2**
For consider Him who **h** endured **Heb 12:3**
earth then, but now He **h** promised, **Heb 12:26**
for He Himself **h** said, **Heb 13:5**
brother Timothy **h** been released, **Heb 13:23**
for once he **h** been approved, he **Jas 1:12**
which *the Lord* **h** promised to those **Jas 1:12**
Then when lust **h** conceived, it **Jas 1:15**
for *once* he **h** looked at himself **Jas 1:24**
he **h** immediately forgotten what **Jas 1:24**
point, he **h** become guilty of all **Jas 2:10**
to one who **h** shown no mercy; **Jas 2:13**
if someone says he **h** faith **Jas 2:14** *2192*
if someone says he has faith but he **h** **Jas 2:14** *2192*
Even so faith, if it **h** no works, **Jas 2:17** *2192*
h been tamed by the human race. **Jas 3:7**
which He **h** made to dwell in us"? **Jas 4:5**
and which **h** been withheld by you, **Jas 5:4**
h reached the ears of the Lord of **Jas 5:4**
up, and if he **h** committed sins, **Jas 5:15**
h caused us to be born again to a **1Pe 1:3**
but **h** appeared in these last times **1Pe 1:20**
to Him as to a living stone which **h** **1Pe 2:4**
Him who **h** called you out of darkness **1Pe 2:9**
Christ **h** suffered in the flesh, **1Pe 4:1**
because he who **h** suffered in the **1Pe 4:1**
in the flesh **h** ceased from sin, **1Pe 4:1**
For the gospel **h** for this purpose **1Pe 4:6**
one **h** received a *special* gift, **1Pe 4:10**
seeing that His divine power **h** **2Pe 1:3**
For by these He **h** granted to us **2Pe 1:4**
Jesus Christ **h** made clear to me. **2Pe 1:14**
black darkness **h** been reserved. **2Pe 2:17**
the last state **h** become worse for **2Pe 2:20**
It **h** happened to them according to **2Pe 2:22**
of God **h** truly been perfected. **1Jn 2:5**
the darkness **h** blinded his eyes. **1Jn 2:11**
Him who **h** been from the beginning. **1Jn 2:13**
Him who **h** been from the beginning. **1Jn 2:14**
the Son **h** the Father also. **1Jn 2:23** *2192*
lie, and just as it **h** taught you, **1Jn 2:27**
the Father **h** bestowed on us, **1Jn 3:1**
and it **h** not appeared as yet what **1Jn 3:2**
And everyone who **h** this hope **1Jn 3:3** *2192*
who sins **h** seen Him or knows Him. **1Jn 3:6**
devil **h** sinned from the beginning. **1Jn 3:8**

h eternal life abiding in him. **1Jn 3:15** *2192*
But whoever **h** the world's goods, **1Jn 3:17** *2192*
by the Spirit whom He **h** given us. **1Jn 3:24**
h come in the flesh is from God; **1Jn 4:2**
that God **h** sent His only begotten **1Jn 4:9**
No one **h** seen God at any time; **1Jn 4:12**
He **h** given us of His Spirit. **1Jn 4:13**
Father **h** sent the Son *to be* the Savior **1Jn 4:14**
the love which God **h** for us. **1Jn 4:16** *2192*
love his brother whom he **h** seen, **1Jn 4:20**
love God whom he **h** not seen. **1Jn 4:20**
the victory that **h** overcome the world **1Jn 5:4**
that He **h** testified concerning **1Jn 5:9**
of God **h** the testimony in himself; **1Jn 5:10** *2192*
not believe God **h** made Him a liar, **1Jn 5:10**
because he **h** not believed in the **1Jn 5:10**
God **h** given concerning His Son. **1Jn 5:10**
that God **h** given us eternal life, **1Jn 5:11**
He who **h** the Son has the life; **1Jn 5:12** *2192*
He who has the Son **h** the life; **1Jn 5:12** *2192*
know that the Son of God **h** come, **1Jn 5:20** *2240*
and **h** given us understanding so **1Jn 5:20**
he **h** both the Father and the Son. **2Jn 1:9** *2192*
one who does evil **h** not seen God. **3Jn 1:11**
Demetrius **h** received a **3Jn 1:12**
He **h** kept in eternal bonds under **Jude 1:6**
darkness **h** been reserved forever. **Jude 1:13**
and He **h** made us *to be* a kingdom, **Rv 1:6**
when it **h** been made to glow in a **Rv 1:15**
'He who **h** an ear, let him hear **Rv 2:7** *2192*
who was dead, and **h** come to life, **Rv 2:8**
'He who **h** an ear, let him hear **Rv 2:11** *2192*
The One who **h** the sharp two-edged **Rv 2:12** *2192*
'He who **h** an ear, let him hear **Rv 2:17** *2192*
who **h** eyes like a flame of fire, **Rv 2:18** *2192*
'He who **h** an ear, let him hear **Rv 2:29** *2192*
He who **h** the seven Spirits of God and **Rv 3:1** *2192*
'He who **h** an ear, let him hear **Rv 3:6** *2192*
is true, who **h** the key of David, **Rv 3:7** *2192*
'He who **h** an ear, let him hear **Rv 3:13** *2192*
'He who **h** an ear, let him hear **Rv 3:22** *2192*
h overcome so as to open the book **Rv 5:5**
great day of their wrath **h** come, **Rv 6:17**
the Greek he **h** the name Apollyon. **Rv 9:11** *2192*
it **h** been given to the nations; **Rv 11:2**
"The kingdom of the world **h** **Rv 11:15**
our brethren **h** been thrown down, **Rv 12:10**
the devil **h** come down to you, **Rv 12:12**
that he **h** *only* a short time." **Rv 12:12** *2192*
everyone whose name **h** not been **Rv 13:8**
life of the Lamb who **h** been slain. **Rv 13:8**
If anyone **h** an ear, let him hear. **Rv 13:9** *2192*
of the sword and **h** come to life. **Rv 13:14**
except the one who **h** the mark, **Rv 13:17** *2192*
Let him who **h** understanding **Rv 13:18** *2192*
the hour of His judgment **h** come; **Rv 14:7**
she who **h** made all the nations **Rv 14:8**
for the hour to reap **h** come, **Rv 14:15**
the one who **h** power over fire, **Rv 14:18** *2192*
h the power over these plagues **Rv 16:9** *2192*
which **h** the seven heads and the **Rv 17:7** *2192*
whose name **h** not been written in **Rv 17:8**
"Here is the mind which **h** wisdom. **Rv 17:9** *2192*
one is, the other **h** not yet come; **Rv 17:10**
"For God **h** put it in their hearts **Rv 17:17**
She **h** become a dwelling place **Rv 18:2**
God **h** remembered her iniquities. **Rv 18:5**
"Pay her back even as she **h** paid, **Rv 18:6**
in the cup which she **h** mixed, **Rv 18:6**
in one hour your judgment **h** come.' **Rv 18:10**
you long for **h** gone from you, **Rv 18:14**
great wealth **h** been laid waste!' **Rv 18:17**
one hour she **h** been laid waste!' **Rv 18:19**
because God **h** pronounced judgment **Rv 18:20**
for He **h** judged the great harlot **Rv 19:2**
and HE **H** AVENGED THE BLOOD OF HIS **Rv 19:2**
for the marriage of the Lamb **h** **Rv 19:7**
His bride **h** made herself ready." **Rv 19:7**
and He **h** a name written *on Him* **Rv 19:12** *2192*
on His thigh He **h** a name written, **Rv 19:16** *2192*
Blessed and holy is the one who **h** **Rv 20:6** *2192*
these the second death **h** no power, **Rv 20:6** *2192*
And the city **h** no need of the sun **Rv 21:23** *2192*
the glory of God **h** illumined it, **Rv 21:23**
man according to what he **h** done. **Rv 22:12** *2041*

HASADIAH
and Hashubah, Ohel, Berechiah, **H** and **1Ch 3:20** 2619

HASHABIAH
the son of **H**, the son of Amaziah, **1Ch 6:45** 2811
the son of Azrikam, the son of **H**, **1Ch 9:14** 2811
Zeri, Jeshaiah, Shimei, **H** **1Ch 25:3** 2811
the twelfth to **H**, his sons and his **1Ch 25:19** 2811
Hebronites, **H** and his relatives, **1Ch 26:30** 2811
for Levi, **H** the son of Kemuel; **1Ch 27:17** 2811
and **H** and Jeiel and Jozabad, **2Ch 35:9** 2811
and **H** and Jeshaiah of the sons of **Ezr 8:19** 2811
the leading priests, Sherebiah, **H**, **Ezr 8:24** 2811
Next to him **H**, the official of **Ne 3:17** 2811
Mica, Rehob, **H**, **Ne 10:11** 2811
the son of Azrikam, the son of **H**, **Ne 11:15** 2811
the son of Bani, the son of **H**, **Ne 11:22** 2811
of Hilkiah, **H**; of Jedaiah, Nethanel. **Ne 12:21** 2811
The heads of the Levites *were* **H**, **Ne 12:24** 2811

HASHABNAH
Rehum, **H**, Maaseiah, **Ne 10:25** 2812

HASHABNEIAH
Hattush the son of **H** made repairs. **Ne 3:10** 2813
Levites, Jeshua, Kadmiel, Bani, **H**, **Ne 9:5** 2813

HASHBADDANAH
Mishael, Malchijah, Hashum, **H**, Ne 8:4 2806
HASHEM
the sons of **H** the Gizonite, 1Ch 11:34 2044
HASHMONAH
from Mithkah and camped at **H**. Nu 33:29 2832
They journeyed from **H** and Nu 33:30 2832
HASHUBAH
and **H**, Ohel, Berechiah, Hasadiah and 1Ch 3:20 2807
HASHUM
the sons of **H**, 223; Ezr 2:19 2828
of the sons of **H**: Ezr 10:33 2828
the sons of **H**, 328; Ne 7:22 2828
Pedaiah, Mishael, Malchijah, **H**, Ne 8:4 2828
Hodiah, **H**, Bezai, Ne 10:18 2828
HASRAH
the son of Tokhath, the son of **H**, 2Ch 34:22 2641
HASSENAAH
the sons of **H** built the Fish Gate; Ne 3:3 5570
HASSENUAH
the son of Hodaviah, the son of **H**, 1Ch 9:7 5574
and Judah the son of **H** was second Ne 11:9 5574
HASSHUB
were Shemaiah the son of **H**, 1Ch 9:14 2815
Malchijah the son of Harim and **H** Ne 3:11 2815
After them Benjamin and **H** carried Ne 3:23 2815
Hoshea, Hananiah, **H**, Ne 10:23 2815
Shemaiah the son of **H**, Ne 11:15 2815
HASSOPHERETH
the sons of Sotai, the sons of **H**, Ezr 2:55 5618
HASTE
and you shall eat it in **h**—it is Ex 12:11 2649
to send them out of the land in **h**, Ex 12:33 4116
Moses made **h** to bow low toward Ex 34:8 4116
came out of the land of Egypt in **h**), Dt 16:3 2649
Go in **h**, or he will overtake us 2Sa 15:14 4116
King Rehoboam made **h** to mount his 1Ki 12:18 553
Arameans had thrown away in their **h**. 2Ki 7:15 2648
King Rehoboam made **h** to mount his 2Ch 10:18 553
they went in **h** to Jerusalem to Ezr 4:23 924
Make **h** to help me, O Lord, my Ps 38:22 2363a
Make **h**, O LORD, to help me. Ps 40:13 2363a
But he who makes **h** to be rich will Pr 28:20 213
But you will not go out in **h**, Nor Is 52:12 2649
"Let them make **h** and take up a Jer 9:18 4116
king was astounded and stood up in **h**; Da 3:24 927
and went in **h** to the lions' den. Da 6:19 927
and I saw Him saying to me, 'Make **h**, Ac 22:18 *4692*
HASTEN
the middle of the sky and did not **h** Jos 10:13 213
h to my assistance. Ps 22:19 2363a
"I would **h** to my place of refuge Ps 55:8 2363a
O God, **h** to deliver me; Ps 70:1
h to my help! Ps 70:1 2363a
But I am afflicted and needy; **H** to Ps 70:5 2363a
h to my help! Ps 71:12 2363a
O Lord, I call upon You; **h** to me! Ps 141:1 2363a
For their feet run to evil And they **h** Pr 1:16 4116
let Him **h** His work, that we may see Is 5:19 2363a
the tongue of the stammerers will **h** Is 32:4 4116
Their feet run to evil, And they **h** Is 59:7 4116
will **h** it in its time." Is 60:22 2363a
H and come, all you surrounding Jl 3:11 5789
HASTENED
and he himself also **h** to get out 2Ch 26:20 1765
The couriers, **h** and impelled by Es 8:14 926
And my foot has **h** after deceit, Jb 31:5 2363a
I **h** and did not delay To keep Your Ps 119:60 2363a
And his calamity has swiftly **h**. Jer 48:16 4116
HASTENING
And the impending things are **h** upon Dt 32:35 2363a
And **h** to its place it rises there Ec 1:5 7602a
looking for and **h** the coming of 2Pe 3:12 *4692*
HASTENS
As a bird **h** to the snare, So he does Pr 7:23 4116
A man with an evil eye **h** after wealth Pr 28:22 926
It **h** toward the goal and it will not Hab 2:3 6315
HASTILY
Then he **h** took the bandage away from 1Ki 20:41 4116
the king's eunuchs arrived and **h** Es 6:14 926
Do not go out **h** to argue *your case;* Pr 25:8 4118b
not lay hands upon anyone *too* **h** 1Tm 5:22 *5030*
HASTY
But everyone who is **h** *comes* Pr 21:5 213
Do you see a man who is **h** in his Pr 29:20 213
Do not be **h** in word or impulsive in Ec 5:2 4116
The mind of the **h** will discern Is 32:4 4116
HASUPHA
the sons of Ziha, the sons of **H** Ezr 2:43 2817
the sons of Ziha, the sons of **H** Ne 7:46 2817
HATCH
And it will **h** and gather Is 34:15 1234
They **h** adders' eggs and weave the Is 59:5 1234
HATCHES
that **h** eggs which it has not laid, Jer 17:11 1716
HATCHET
They smash with **h** and hammers. Ps 74:6 3781
HATE
The gate of those who **h** them." Gn 24:60 8130
you come to me, since you **h** me and Gn 26:27 8130
join themselves to those who **h** us, Ex 1:10 8130
truth, those who **h** dishonest gain; Ex 18:21 8130
generations of those who **h** Me, Ex 20:5 8130
'You shall not **h** your fellow Lv 19:17 8130
who **h** you will rule over you, Lv 26:17 8130
who **h** You flee before You." Nu 10:35 8130
generations of those who **h** Me, Dt 5:9 8130
those who **h** Him to their faces, Dt 7:10 8130
He will lay them on all who **h** you. Dt 7:15 8130
enemies and on those who **h** you, Dt 30:7 8130
And I will repay those who **h** Me. Dt 32:41 8130
against him, And those who **h** him, Dt 33:11 8130
and did not **h** him beforehand. Jos 20:5 8130
"Did you not **h** me and drive me Jg 11:7 8130
"You only **h** me, and you do not Jg 14:16 8130
by loving those who **h** you, 2Sa 19:6 8130
inquire of the LORD, but I **h** him, 1Ki 22:8 8130
or the life of those who **h** you, 2Ch 1:11 8130
inquire of the LORD, but I **h** him, 2Ch 18:7 8130
who **h** the LORD and so *bring* wrath 2Ch 19:2 8130
"Those who **h** you will be clothed Jb 8:22 8130
You **h** all who do iniquity. Ps 5:5 8130
my affliction from those who **h** me, Ps 9:13 8130
will find out those who **h** you. Ps 21:8 8130
And they **h** me with violent hatred. Ps 25:19 8130
I **h** the assembly of evildoers, And Ps 26:5 8130
I **h** those who regard vain idols, Ps 31:6 8130
And those who **h** the righteous will Ps 34:21 8130
Nor let those who **h** me without Ps 35:19 8130
are those who **h** me wrongfully. Ps 38:19 8130
All who **h** me whisper together Ps 41:7 8130
have put to shame those who **h** us. Ps 44:7 8130
And those who **h** us have taken Ps 44:10 8130
"For you **h** discipline, And you Ps 50:17 8130
those who **h** Him flee before Him. Ps 68:1 8130
Those who **h** me without a cause are Ps 69:4 8130
"Those who **h** the LORD would Ps 81:15 8130
h You have exalted themselves. Ps 83:2 8130
That those who **h** me may see *it* Ps 86:17 8130
him, And strike those who **h** him. Ps 89:23 8130
H evil, you who love the LORD, Who Ps 97:10 8130
I **h** the work of those who fall Ps 101:3 8130
turned their heart to **h** His people, Ps 105:25 8130
satisfaction on those who **h** me. Ps 118:7 8130
Therefore I **h** every false way. Ps 119:104 8130
I **h** those who are double-minded, Ps 119:113 8130
everything, I **h** every false way. Ps 119:128 8130
I **h** and despise falsehood, *But* I Ps 119:163 8130
dwelling With those who **h** peace. Ps 120:6 8130
May all who **h** Zion Be put to Ps 129:5 8130
Do I not **h** those who hate You, O Ps 139:21 8130
Do I not hate those who **h** You, Ps 139:21 8130
I **h** them with the utmost hatred; Ps 139:22 8130
scoffing And fools **h** knowledge? Pr 1:22 8130
"The fear of the LORD is to **h** evil; Pr 8:13 8130
way And the perverted mouth, I **h**. Pr 8:13 8130
All those who **h** me love death." Pr 8:36 8130
not reprove a scoffer, or he will **h** Pr 9:8 8130
the brothers of a poor man **h** him; Pr 19:7 8130
he will become weary of you and **h** you. Pr 25:17 8130
Men of bloodshed **h** the blameless, Pr 29:10 8130
A time to love and a time to **h**; Ec 3:8 8130
Indeed their love, their **h** and Ec 9:6 8135
"I **h** your new moon *festivals* and Is 1:14 8130
I **h** robbery in the burnt offering; Is 61:8 8130
"Your brothers who **h** you, Is 66:5 8130
Therefore I have come to **h** her. Jer 12:8 8130
this abominable thing which I **h**." Jer 44:4 8130
to the desire of those who **h** you, Ezk 16:27 8130
into the hand of those whom you **h**, Ezk 23:28 8130
dream applied to those who **h** you and Da 4:19 8131
Indeed, I came to **h** them there! Hos 9:15 8130
h him who reproves in the gate, Am 5:10 8130
H evil, love good, And establish Am 5:15 8130
"I **h**, I reject your festivals, Am 5:21 8130
"You who **h** good and love evil, Mi 3:2 8130
for all these are what I **h** Zch 8:17 8130
"For I **h** divorce," Mal 2:16 8130
YOUR NEIGHBOR and **h** your enemy.' Mt 5:43 *3404*
will **h** the one and love the other, Mt 6:24 *3404*
betray one another and **h** one another. Mt 24:10 *3404*
And FROM THE HAND OF ALL WHO **H** US; Lk 1:71 *3404*
"Blessed are you when men **h** you, Lk 6:22 *3404*
do good to those who **h** you, Lk 6:27 *3404*
and does not **h** his own father and Lk 14:26 *3404*
for either he will **h** the one and Lk 16:13 *3404*
"The world cannot **h** you, Jn 7:7 *3404*
but I am doing the very thing I **h**. Ro 7:15 *3404*
h the deeds of the Nicolaitans, Rv 2:6 *3404*
the Nicolaitans, which I also **h**. Rv 2:6 *3404*
these will **h** the harlot and will Rv 17:16 *3404*
HATED
and *so* they **h** him and could not Gn 37:4 8130
brothers, they **h** him even more. Gn 37:5 8130
So they **h** him even more for his Gn 37:8 8130
because He **h** them He has brought Dt 9:28 8135
since he had not **h** him previously. Dt 19:6 8130
thought that you **h** her intensely; Jg 15:2 8130
blind, who are **h** by David's soul, 2Sa 5:8 8130
h her with a very great hatred; 2Sa 13:15 8130
for the hatred with which he **h** her 2Sa 13:15 8130
for Absalom **h** Amnon because he had 2Sa 13:22 8130
strong enemy, From those who **h** me, 2Sa 22:18 8130
And I destroyed those who **h** me. 2Sa 22:41 8130
the mastery over those who **h** them. Es 9:1 8130
they pleased to those who **h** them. Es 9:5 8130
kill 75,000 of those who **h** them; Es 9:16 8130
enemy, And from those who **h** me, Ps 18:17 8130
And I destroyed those who **h** me. Ps 18:40 8130
righteousness and **h** wickedness Ps 45:7 8130
the hand of the one who **h** *them,* Ps 106:10 8130
those who **h** them ruled over them. Ps 106:41 8130
Because they **h** knowledge And did Pr 1:29 8130
"How I have **h** instruction! Pr 5:12 8130
And a man of evil devices is **h**. Pr 14:17 8130
poor is **h** even by his neighbor, Pr 14:20 8130
So I **h** life, for the work which Ec 2:17 8130
Thus I **h** all the fruit of my labor Ec 2:18 8130
you have been forsaken and **h** Is 60:15 8130
loved *and* all those whom you **h**. Ezk 16:37 8130
since you have not **h** bloodshed, Ezk 35:6 8130
but I have **h** Esau, and I have made Mal 1:3 8130
be **h** by all because of My name, Mt 10:22 *3404*
and you will be **h** by all nations Mt 24:9 *3404*
be **h** by all because of My name, Mk 13:13 *3404*
"But his citizens **h** him and Lk 19:14 *3404*
be **h** by all because of My name. Lk 21:17 *3404*
it has **h** Me before *it hated* you. Jn 15:18 *3404*
that it has hated Me before *it* **h** Jn 15:18
and **h** Me and My Father as well. Jn 15:24 *3404*
'THEY **H** ME WITHOUT A CAUSE.' Jn 15:25 *3404*
and the world has **h** them, Jn 17:14 *3404*
BUT ESAU I **H**." Ro 9:13 *3404*
for no one ever **h** his own flesh, Eph 5:29 *3404*
"YOU HAVE LOVED RIGHTEOUSNESS AND **H** Heb 1:9 *3404*
HATEFUL
our life in malice and envy, **h**, Ti 3:3 *4767*
of every unclean and **h** bird. Rv 18:2 *3404*
HATERS
slanderers, **h** of God, insolent, Ro 1:30 *2319*
self-control, brutal, **h** of good, 2Tm 3:3 *865*
HATES
you see the donkey of one who **h** you Ex 23:5 8130
'Because the LORD **h** us, Dt 1:27 8135
will not delay with him who **h** Him, Dt 7:10 8130
abominable act which the LORD **h** Dt 12:31 8130
pillar which the LORD your God **h**. Dt 16:22 8130
"But if there is a man who **h** his Dt 19:11 8130
"Shall one who **h** justice rule? Jb 34:17 8130
one who loves violence His soul **h**. Ps 11:5 8130
Nor is it one who **h** me who has Ps 55:12 8130
are six things which the LORD **h**, Pr 6:16 8130
But he who **h** being a guarantor Pr 11:15 8130
But he who **h** reproof is stupid. Pr 12:1 8130
A righteous man **h** falsehood, But a Pr 13:5 8130
He who withholds his rod **h** his son, Pr 13:24 8130
He who **h** reproof will die. Pr 15:10 8130
But he who **h** bribes will live. Pr 15:27 8130
who **h** disguises *it* with his lips, Pr 26:24 8130
A lying tongue **h** those it crushes, Pr 26:28 8130
But he who **h** unjust gain will Pr 28:16 8130
with a thief **h** his own life; Pr 29:24 8130
who does evil **h** the Light, Jn 3:20 *3404*
it **h** Me because I testify of it, Jn 7:7 *3404*
and he who **h** his life in this Jn 12:25 *3404*
"If the world **h** you, you know Jn 15:18 *3404*
world, because of this the world **h** you. Jn 15:19 *3404*
"He who **h** Me hates My Father also. Jn 15:23 *3404*
"He who hates Me **h** My Father also. Jn 15:23 *3404*
he is in the Light and *yet* **h** his brother 1Jn 2:9 *3404*
But the one who **h** his brother is 1Jn 2:11 *3404*
brethren, if the world **h** you. 1Jn 3:13 *3404*
who **h** his brother is a murderer; 1Jn 3:15 *3404*
"I love God," and **h** his brother, 1Jn 4:20 *3404*
HATHACH
Then Esther summoned **H** from Es 4:5 2047
So **H** went out to Mordecai to the city Es 4:6 2047
H came back and related Mordecai's Es 4:9 2047
Then Esther spoke to **H** and ordered Es 4:10 2047
HATHATH
And the sons of Othniel *were* **H** 1Ch 4:13 2867
HATING
not **h** him previously Dt 19:4 8130
you, and by **h** those who love you. 2Sa 19:6 8130
and envy, hateful, **h** one another. Ti 3:3 *3404*
h even the garment polluted by the Jude 1:23 *3404*
HATIPHA
the sons of Neziah, the sons of **H**. Ezr 2:54 2412
the sons of Neziah, the sons of **H**. Ne 7:56 2412
HATITA
the sons of Akkub, the sons of **H**, Ezr 2:42 2410
the sons of Akkub, the sons of **H**, Ne 7:45 2410
HATRED
'If he pushed him of **h**, Nu 35:20 8135
hated her with a very great **h**; 2Sa 13:15 8135
for the **h** with which he hated her 2Sa 13:15 8135
And they hate me with violent **h**. Ps 25:19 8135
of his iniquity *and the* **h** *of it.* Ps 36:2 8130
surrounded me with words of **h**, Ps 109:3 8135
evil for good And **h** for my love. Ps 109:5 8135
I hate them with the utmost **h**; Ps 139:22 8135
H stirs up strife, But love covers Pr 10:12 8135
He who conceals **h** *has* lying lips, Pr 10:18 8135
Than a fattened ox *served* with **h**. Pr 15:17 8135
his **h** covers itself with guile, Pr 26:26 8135
know whether *it will be* love or **h**; Ec 9:1 8135
'They will deal with you in **h**, Ezk 23:29 8135
because of your **h** against them; Ezk 35:11 8135
HATTIL
sons of Shephatiah, the sons of **H**, Ezr 2:57 2411
sons of Shephatiah, the sons of **H**, Ne 7:59 2411
HATTUSH
and the sons of Shemaiah: **H**, 1Ch 3:22 2407
of the sons of David, **H**; Ezr 8:2 2407
And next to him **H** the son of Ne 3:10 2407
H, Shebaniah, Malluch, Ne 10:4 2407
Amariah, Malluch, **H**, Ne 12:2 2407
HAUGHTILY
voice, And **h** lifted up your eyes? 2Ki 19:22 4791
voice And **h** lifted up your eyes? Is 37:23 4791
And you will not walk **h**, Mi 2:3 7317

HAUGHTINESS
in the **h** of his countenance, Ps 10:4 1363
spirit is better than **h** of spirit. Ec 7:8 1364
Assyria and the pomp of his **h**." Is 10:12 7312
And abase the **h** of the ruthless. Is 13:11 1346
Of his **h**, his pride, his arrogance Jer 48:29 7312
HAUGHTY
But Your eyes are on the **h** 2Sa 22:28 7311
But **h** eyes You abase. Ps 18:27 7311
No one who has a **h** look and an Ps 101:5 1364
heart is not proud, nor my eyes **h**; Ps 131:1 7311
But the **h** He knows from afar. Ps 138:6 1364
H eyes, a lying tongue, And hands Pr 6:17 7311
And a **h** spirit before stumbling. Pr 16:18 1363
destruction the heart of man is **h**, Pr 18:12 1361b
H eyes and a proud heart, The lamp Pr 21:4 7312
"Proud," "**H**," "Scoffer," are his names, Pr 21:24 3093
Listen and give heed, do not be **h**, Jer 13:15 1361b
"Thus they were **h** and committed Ezk 16:50 1361b
its heart is **h** in its loftiness, Ezk 31:10 7311
wine betrays the **h** man, Hab 2:5 3093
And you will never again be **h** Zph 3:11 1361b
do not be **h** in mind, but associate Ro 12:16 *5308*
HAUL
and then they were not able to **h** Jn 21:6 *1670*
HAUNT
and see his place where his **h** is, 1Sa 23:22 7272
It will also be a **h** of jackals Is 34:13 5116a
In the **h** of jackals, its resting Is 35:7 5116a
a heap of ruins, A **h** of jackals; Jer 9:11 4583
A desolation, a **h** of jackals. Jer 10:22 4583
Hazor will become a **h** of jackals, Jer 49:33 4583
heap *of ruins,* a **h** of jackals, Jer 51:37 4583
HAURAN
which is by the border of **H**. Ezk 47:16 2362
between **H**, Damascus, Gilead and Ezk 47:18 2362
HAVE
I **h** given you every plant yielding Gn 1:29
I **h** *given* every green plant for Gn 1:30
H you eaten from the tree of which Gn 3:11
"What is this you **h** done?" Gn 3:13
"Because you **h** done this, Cursed Gn 3:14
"Because you **h** listened to the Gn 3:17
and **h** eaten from the tree about Gn 3:17
"I **h** gotten a manchild with Gn 4:1
He said, "What **h** you done? Gn 4:10
You **h** driven me this day from the Gn 4:14
of those who dwell in tents and **h** Gn 4:20
I **h** killed a man for wounding me; Gn 4:23
will blot out man whom I **h** created Gn 6:7
I am sorry that I **h** made them." Gn 6:7
for you *alone* I **h** seen *to be* Gn 7:1
living thing that I **h** made." Gn 7:4
every living thing, as I **h** done. Gn 8:21
of the covenant which I **h** established Gn 9:17
and they all **h** the same language. Gn 11:6
"What is this you **h** done to me? Gn 12:18
"I **h** sworn to the LORD God Most Gn 14:22
'I **h** made Abram rich.' Gn 14:23
except what the young men **h** eaten, Gn 14:24
You **h** given no offspring to me, Gn 15:3
descendants I **h** given this land, Gn 15:18
where **h** you come from and where Gn 16:8
"**H** I even remained alive here Gn 16:13
For I **h** made you the father of a Gn 17:5
"As for Ishmael, I **h** heard you; Gn 17:20
now I **h** found favor in Your sight, Gn 18:3
you **h** visited your servant." Gn 18:5
"So do, as you **h** said." Gn 18:5
Sarah your wife will **h** a son." Gn 18:10
"After I **h** become old, shall I Gn 18:12
become old, shall I **h** pleasure, Gn 18:12 1961
year, and Sarah will **h** a son." Gn 18:14
"For I **h** chosen him, so Gn 18:19
and see if they **h** done entirely Gn 18:21
I **h** ventured to speak to the Lord, Gn 18:27
I **h** ventured to speak to the Lord; Gn 18:31
we may **h** relations with them." Gn 19:5 3045
I **h** two daughters who have not had Gn 19:8
who **h** not had relations with man; Gn 19:8
inasmuch as they **h** come under the Gn 19:8
"Whom else **h** you here? Gn 19:12
and whomever you **h** in the city, Gn 19:12
you **h** magnified your lovingkindness, Gn 19:19
you **h** shown me by saving my life; Gn 19:19
the town of which you **h** spoken. Gn 19:21
of the woman whom you **h** taken, Gn 20:3
of my hands I **h** done this." Gn 20:5
of your heart you **h** done this, Gn 20:6
"What **h** you done to us? Gn 20:9
And how **h** I sinned against you, Gn 20:9
that you **h** brought on me and on my Gn 20:9
You **h** done to me things that ought Gn 20:9
"What **h** you encountered, that you Gn 20:10
that you **h** done this thing?" Gn 20:10
I **h** given your brother a thousand Gn 20:16
"Who would **h** said to Abraham that Gn 21:7
Yet I **h** borne him a son in his old Gn 21:7
kindness that I **h** shown to you, Gn 21:23
land in which you **h** sojourned." Gn 21:23
which you **h** set by themselves?" Gn 21:29
since you **h** not withheld your son, Gn 22:12
"By Myself I **h** sworn, declares Gn 22:16
because you **h** done this thing and Gn 22:16
and **h** not withheld your son, Gn 22:16
because you **h** obeyed My voice." Gn 22:18
whom You **h** appointed for Your Gn 24:14
that You **h** shown lovingkindness to Gn 24:14
until they **h** finished drinking." Gn 24:19
h plenty of both straw and feed, Gn 24:25
since I **h** prepared the house, Gn 24:31
eat until I **h** told my business." Gn 24:33
'The LORD, before whom I **h** walked, Gn 24:40
"Please let me **h** a swallow of Gn 25:30 3938
"What is this you **h** done to us? Gn 26:10
easily **h** lain with your wife, Gn 26:10
would **h** brought guilt upon us." Gn 26:10
"Why **h** you come to me, since you Gn 26:27
me and **h** sent me away from you?" Gn 26:27
just as we **h** not touched you and Gn 26:29
h done to you nothing but good and Gn 26:29
and **h** sent you away in peace. Gn 26:29
"We **h** found water." Gn 26:32
I **h** done as you told me. Gn 27:19
is it that you **h** *it* so quickly, Gn 27:20 4672
"**H** you not reserved a blessing Gn 27:36
"Behold, I **h** made him your Gn 27:37
I **h** given to him as servants; Gn 27:37
and new wine I **h** sustained him. Gn 27:37
"Do you **h** only one blessing, my Gn 27:38
h done what I have promised you." Gn 28:15
have done what I **h** promised you." Gn 28:15
which I **h** set up as a pillar, Gn 28:22
"What is this you **h** done to me? Gn 29:25
Why then **h** you deceived me?" Gn 29:25
I **h** borne him three sons." Gn 29:34
her I too may **h** children." Gn 30:3 1129
I **h** wrestled with my sister, Gn 30:8
and I **h** indeed prevailed." Gn 30:8
for I **h** surely hired you with my Gn 30:16
because I **h** borne him six sons." Gn 30:20
children for whom I **h** served you, Gn 30:26
service which I **h** rendered you." Gn 30:26
I **h** divined that the LORD has Gn 30:27
"You yourself know how I **h** served Gn 30:29
how your cattle **h** fared with me. Gn 30:29
"You know that I **h** served Gn 31:6
for I **h** seen all that Laban has Gn 31:12
"Do we still **h** any portion or Gn 31:14
"What **h** you done by deceiving me Gn 31:26
so that I might **h** sent you away Gn 31:27
Now you **h** done foolishly. Gn 31:28
"Now you **h** indeed gone away Gn 31:30
sin that you **h** hotly pursued me? Gn 31:36
you **h** felt through all my goods, Gn 31:37
what **h** you found of all your Gn 31:37
"These twenty years I **h** *been* Gn 31:38
female goats **h** not miscarried, Gn 31:38
nor **h** I eaten the rams of your Gn 31:38
years I **h** been in your house; Gn 31:41
would **h** sent me away empty-handed. Gn 31:42
their children whom they **h** borne? Gn 31:43
which I **h** set between you and me. Gn 31:51
"I **h** sojourned with Laban, and Gn 32:4
I **h** oxen and donkeys *and* Gn 32:5 1961
and I **h** sent to tell my lord, that Gn 32:5
which You **h** shown to Your servant; Gn 32:10
and now I **h** become two companies. Gn 32:10
for you **h** striven with God and Gn 32:28
and with men and **h** prevailed." Gn 32:28
I **h** seen God face to face, yet Gn 32:30
all this company which I **h** met?" Gn 33:8
I **h** plenty, my brother; Gn 33:9 3426
let what you **h** be your own." Gn 33:9 1961
now I **h** found favor in your sight, Gn 33:10
and you **h** received me favorably. Gn 33:10
with me and because I **h** plenty." Gn 33:11 3426
"You **h** brought trouble on me by Gn 34:30
been with me wherever I **h** gone." Gn 35:3
fear, for now you **h** another son." Gn 35:17
to this dream which I **h** had; Gn 37:6
"Lo, I **h** had still another dream; Gn 37:9
"What is this dream that you **h** had? Gn 37:10
"They **h** moved from here; Gn 37:17
not **h** relations with her again. Gn 38:26 3045
breach you **h** made for yourself!" Gn 38:29
"We **h** had a dream and there is no Gn 40:8
and even here I **h** done nothing Gn 40:15
h put me into the dungeon." Gn 40:15
"I **h** had a dream, but no one can Gn 41:15
and I **h** heard it said about you, Gn 41:15
"It is as I **h** spoken to Pharaoh: Gn 41:28
"See, I **h** set you over all the Gn 41:41
I **h** heard that there is grain in Gn 42:2
"Where **h** you come from?" Gn 42:7
you **h** come to look at the Gn 42:9
your servants **h** come to buy food. Gn 42:10
but you **h** come to look at the Gn 42:12
"You **h** bereaved me of my children: Gn 42:36
H you *another* brother? Gn 43:7 3426
now we could **h** returned twice." Gn 43:10
we **h** brought it back in our hand. Gn 43:21
"We **h** also brought down other Gn 43:22
'Why **h** you repaid evil for good? Gn 44:4
h done wrong in doing this.' Gn 44:5
we **h** brought back to you from the Gn 44:8
"What is this deed that you **h** done? Gn 44:15
H you a father or a brother?' Gn 44:19 3426
'We **h** an old father and a little Gn 44:20 3426
and I **h** not seen him since. Gn 44:28
"**H** everyone go out from me." Gn 45:1
and your herds and all that you **h**. Gn 45:10
all that you **h** would be impoverished. Gn 45:11
in Egypt, and all that you **h** seen; Gn 45:13
me die, since I **h** seen your face, Gn 46:30
the land of Canaan, **h** come to me; Gn 46:31
they **h** been keepers of livestock; Gn 46:32
and they **h** brought their flocks Gn 46:32
their herds and all that they **h**.' Gn 46:32
'Your servants **h** been keepers of Gn 46:34
their herds and all that they **h**, Gn 47:1
h come out of the land of Canaan Gn 47:1
"We **h** come to sojourn in the Gn 47:4
and your brothers **h** come to you. Gn 47:5
"How many years **h** you lived?" Gn 47:8
few and unpleasant **h** been the years Gn 47:9
nor **h** they attained the years that Gn 47:9
I **h** today bought you and your land Gn 47:23
"You **h** saved our lives! Gn 47:25
that Pharaoh should **h** the fifth Gn 47:26
if I **h** found favor in your sight, Gn 47:29
"I will do as you **h** said." Gn 47:30
"But your offspring that **h** been Gn 48:6
you shall not **h** preeminence, Gn 49:4 3498
the prey, my son, you **h** gone up. Gn 49:9
"The blessings of your father **H** Gn 49:26
now I **h** found favor in your sight, Gn 50:4
"Why **h** you done this thing, and Ex 1:18
h you come *back* so soon today?" Ex 2:18
it that you **h** left the man behind? Ex 2:20
him to **h** something to eat." Ex 2:20
"I **h** been a sojourner in a Ex 2:22
"I **h** surely seen the affliction Ex 3:7
and **h** given heed to their cry Ex 3:7
"So I **h** come down to deliver them Ex 3:8
I **h** seen the oppression with which Ex 3:9
you that it is I who **h** sent you: Ex 3:12
when you **h** brought the people out Ex 3:12
Lord, I **h** never been eloquent, Ex 4:10
You **h** spoken to Your servant; Ex 4:10
which I **h** put in your power; Ex 4:21
but you **h** refused to let him go. Ex 4:23
h them cease from their labors!" Ex 5:5
"Why **h** you not completed your Ex 5:14
for you **h** made us odious in Ex 5:21
why **h** You brought harm to this Ex 5:22
You **h** not delivered Your people Ex 5:23
"Furthermore I **h** heard the Ex 6:5
and I **h** remembered My covenant. Ex 6:5
of Israel **h** not listened to me; Ex 6:12
you **h** not listened until now." Ex 7:16
h been cut off from the earth. Ex 9:15
reason I **h** allowed you to remain, Ex 9:16
your livestock and whatever you **h** Ex 9:19
"I **h** sinned this time; Ex 9:27
for I **h** hardened his heart and the Ex 10:1
nor your grandfathers **h** seen, Ex 10:6
"I **h** sinned against the LORD your Ex 10:16
"You must also let us **h** sacrifices Ex 10:25 5414,3027
day you shall **h** a holy assembly, Ex 12:16
worship the LORD, as you **h** said. Ex 12:31
and your herds, as you **h** said, Ex 12:32
they let them **h** their request. Ex 12:36
after you **h** circumcised him, Ex 12:44
"What is this we **h** done, that we Ex 14:5
that we **h** let Israel go Ex 14:5
that you **h** taken us away to die in the Ex 14:11
h you dealt with us in this way, Ex 14:11
For it would **h** been better for us Ex 14:12
Egyptians whom you **h** seen today Ex 14:13
"In Your lovingkindness You **h** led Ex 15:13
the people whom You **h** redeemed; Ex 15:13
In Your strength You **h** guided Ex 15:13
"The peoples **h** heard, they Ex 15:14
of Canaan **h** melted away. Ex 15:15
pass over whom You **h** purchased. Ex 15:16
You **h** made for Your dwelling, Ex 15:17
which Your hands **h** established. Ex 15:17
which I **h** put on the Egyptians; Ex 15:26
for you **h** brought us out into this Ex 16:3
"I **h** heard the grumblings of the Ex 16:12
h you brought us up from Egypt, Ex 17:3
the LORD will **h** war against Amalek Ex 17:16
"I **h** been a sojourner in a Ex 18:3
"When they **h** a dispute, it comes to Ex 18:16 1961
'You yourselves **h** seen what I did Ex 19:4
shall **h** no other gods before Me. Ex 20:3 1961
'You yourselves **h** seen that I have Ex 20:22
I **h** spoken to you from heaven. Ex 20:22
He does not **h** authority to sell Ex 21:8 4910
"If men **h** a quarrel and one Ex 21:18 7378
everything which I **h** said to you, Ex 23:13
into the place which I **h** prepared. Ex 23:20
h written for their instruction." Ex 24:12
shall **h** *their* wings spread upward, Ex 25:20 1961
shall **h** the same measurements. Ex 26:2
shall **h** the same measurements. Ex 26:8
you **h** been shown in the mountain. Ex 26:30
I **h** endowed with the spirit of wisdom, Ex 28:3
"It shall **h** two shoulder pieces Ex 28:7 1961
and they shall **h** the priesthood by Ex 29:9 1961
to all that I **h** commanded you; Ex 29:35
"See, I **h** called by name Bezalel, Ex 31:2
"I **h** filled him with the Ex 31:3
h appointed with him Oholiab, Ex 31:6
who are skillful I **h** put skill, Ex 31:6
make all that I **h** commanded you Ex 31:6
to all that I **h** commanded you." Ex 31:11
of Egypt, **h** corrupted Ex 32:7
"They **h** quickly turned aside from Ex 32:8
They **h** made for themselves Ex 32:8
a molten calf, and **h** worshiped it and Ex 32:8
it and **h** sacrificed to it Ex 32:8
I **h** seen this people, and Ex 32:9
Your people whom You **h** brought out Ex 32:11
and all this land of which I **h** spoken Ex 32:13

that you **h** brought *such* great sin	Ex 32:21	
h committed a great sin;	Ex 32:30	
and they **h** made a god of gold for	Ex 32:31	
Your book which You **h** written!"	Ex 32:32	
you and the people whom you **h**	Ex 33:1	
But You Yourself **h** not let me know	Ex 33:12	
Moreover, You **h** said,	Ex 33:12	
'I **h** known you by name, and you	Ex 33:12	
h also found favor in My sight.'	Ex 33:12	
if I **h** found favor in Your sight,	Ex 33:13	
that I **h** found favor in Your sight,	Ex 33:16	
this thing of which you **h** spoken;	Ex 33:17	
for you **h** found favor in My sight	Ex 33:17	
and I **h** known you by name."	Ex 33:17	
with My hand until I **h** passed by.	Ex 33:22	
now I **h** found favor in Your sight,	Ex 34:9	
will perform miracles which **h** not been	Ex 34:10	
I **h** made a covenant with you and	Ex 34:27	
day you shall **h** a holy *day,*	Ex 35:2	1961
as you **h** anointed their father,	Ex 40:15	
the sin which they **h** committed	Lv 4:14	
he may **h** done to incur guilt."	Lv 6:7	
I **h** given it as their share from	Lv 6:17	
atonement with it shall **h** it.	Lv 7:7	1961
that priest shall **h** for himself	Lv 7:8	1961
'For I **h** taken the breast of the	Lv 7:34	
and **h** given them to Aaron the	Lv 7:34	
die, for so I **h** been commanded."	Lv 8:35	
for thus I **h** been commanded.	Lv 10:13	
for they **h** been given as your due	Lv 10:14	
h eaten it in the sanctuary,	Lv 10:18	
would it **h** been good in the sight	Lv 10:19	
all that **h** fins and scales, those	Lv 11:9	
that does not **h** fins and scales	Lv 11:10	369
'Whatever in the water does not **h**	Lv 11:12	369
those which **h** above their feet	Lv 11:21	
animals dies which you **h** for food,	Lv 11:39	
"He shall **h** the house scraped	Lv 14:41	
h this as a permanent statute,	Lv 16:34	1961
and I **h** given it to you on the	Lv 17:11	
'You shall not **h** intercourse	Lv 18:20	5414
'Also you shall not **h** intercourse	Lv 18:23	5414
out before you **h** become defiled.	Lv 18:24	
therefore I **h** brought its	Lv 18:25	
(for the men of the land who **h**	Lv 18:27	
you **h** done all these abominations,	Lv 18:27	
which **h** been practiced before you,	Lv 18:30	
'You shall **h** just balances, just	Lv 19:36	1961
they **h** committed incest, their	Lv 20:12	
them **h** committed a detestable act;	Lv 20:13	
and therefore I **h** abhorred them.	Lv 20:23	
'Hence I **h** said to you,	Lv 20:24	
I **h** separated for you as unclean.	Lv 20:25	
and I **h** set you apart from the	Lv 20:26	
is in them, they **h** a defect,	Lv 22:25	
you shall **h** a holy convocation;	Lv 23:7	1961
until you **h** brought in the	Lv 23:14	
you are to **h** a holy convocation.	Lv 23:21	1961
of the month you shall **h** a rest,	Lv 23:24	1961
On the eighth day you shall **h** a	Lv 23:36	1961
when you **h** gathered in the crops	Lv 23:39	
shall **h** a sabbath to the LORD.	Lv 25:2	7673b
the land shall **h** a sabbath rest,	Lv 25:4	1961
land shall **h** a sabbatical year.	Lv 25:5	1961
you shall **h** the sabbath	Lv 25:6	1961
land shall **h** all its crops to eat.	Lv 25:7	1961
so that you **h** the time of the	Lv 25:8	1961
'You shall **h** the fiftieth year as	Lv 25:11	1961
which **h** no surrounding wall shall	Lv 25:31	369
they **h** redemption rights and	Lv 25:31	1961
the Levites **h** a permanent right of	Lv 25:32	1961
and female slaves whom you may **h**	Lv 25:44	1961
they will **h** produced in your land;	Lv 25:45	
then he shall **h** redemption right	Lv 25:48	1961
and you will **h** *no strength* to	Lv 26:37	1961
'No one who may **h** been set apart	Lv 27:29	
I **h** taken the Levites from among	Nu 3:12	
"When Aaron and his sons **h**	Nu 4:15	
and **h** her stand before the LORD,	Nu 5:16	
'The priest shall then **h** the woman	Nu 5:18	
The priest shall **h** her take an oath	Nu 5:19	
with you and if you **h** not gone astray	Nu 5:19	
if you, however, **h** gone astray,	Nu 5:20	
and if you **h** defiled yourself and	Nu 5:20	
(then the priest shall **h** the woman	Nu 5:21	
"You shall **h** the Levites	Nu 8:13	
I **h** taken them for Myself instead	Nu 8:16	
"But I **h** taken the Levites	Nu 8:18	
"I **h** given the Levites as a	Nu 8:19	
you shall **h** one statute, both for	Nu 9:14	1961
"Why **h** You been so hard on Your	Nu 11:11	
And why **h** I not found favor in Your	Nu 11:11	
that You **h** laid the burden of all	Nu 11:11	
if I **h** found favor in Your sight,	Nu 11:15	
h wept in the ears of the LORD,	Nu 11:18	
because you **h** rejected the LORD	Nu 11:20	
among you and **h** wept before Him,	Nu 11:20	
yet You **h** said,	Nu 11:21	
in which we **h** acted foolishly and	Nu 12:11	
and in which we **h** sinned.	Nu 12:11	
"The land through which we **h** gone,	Nu 13:32	
I **h** performed in their midst?	Nu 14:11	
They **h** heard that You, O LORD,	Nu 14:14	
who **h** heard of Your fame will say,	Nu 14:15	
be great, just as You **h** declared,	Nu 14:17	
You also **h** forgiven this people,	Nu 14:19	
"I **h** pardoned *them* according to	Nu 14:20	
who **h** seen My glory and My	Nu 14:22	
yet **h** put Me to the test these ten	Nu 14:22	
and **h** not listened to My voice,	Nu 14:22	
I **h** heard the complaints of the	Nu 14:27	
as you **h** spoken in My hearing,	Nu 14:28	
upward, who **h** grumbled against Me.	Nu 14:29	
the land which you **h** rejected.	Nu 14:31	
'I, the LORD, **h** spoken, surely	Nu 14:35	
we **h** indeed sinned, but we will go	Nu 14:40	
inasmuch as you **h** turned back from	Nu 14:43	
and they **h** brought their offering,	Nu 15:25	
'You shall **h** one law for him who	Nu 15:29	1961
"You **h** gone far enough, for all	Nu 16:3	
You **h** gone far enough, you sons of	Nu 16:7	
not enough that you **h** brought us	Nu 16:13	
to **h** us die in the wilderness,	Nu 16:13	
you **h** not brought us into a land	Nu 16:14	
nor **h** you given us an inheritance	Nu 16:14	
I **h** not taken a single donkey from	Nu 16:15	
h I done harm to any of them."	Nu 16:15	
these men **h** spurned the LORD."	Nu 16:30	
the censers of these men who **h** sinned	Nu 16:38	
"You are the ones who **h** caused	Nu 16:41	
I Myself **h** taken your fellow	Nu 18:6	
I Myself **h** given you charge of My	Nu 18:8	
I **h** given them to you as a	Nu 18:8	
I **h** given them to you and to your	Nu 18:11	
I **h** given to you and your sons and	Nu 18:19	
h no inheritance in their land nor	Nu 18:20	
I **h** given all the tithe in Israel	Nu 18:21	
they shall **h** no inheritance.	Nu 18:23	5157
I **h** given to the Levites for an	Nu 18:24	
I **h** said concerning them,	Nu 18:24	
'They shall **h** no inheritance among	Nu 18:24	5157
tithe which I **h** given you from them	Nu 18:26	
'When you **h** offered from it the	Nu 18:30	
when you **h** offered the best of it.	Nu 18:32	
h you brought the LORD's assembly	Nu 20:4	
"Why **h** you made us come up	Nu 20:5	
"Because you **h** not believed Me,	Nu 20:12	
the land which I **h** given them."	Nu 20:12	
I **h** given to the sons of Israel,	Nu 20:24	
"Why **h** you brought us up out of	Nu 21:5	
"We **h** sinned, because we have	Nu 21:7	
because we **h** spoken against the	Nu 21:7	
we **h** passed through your border."	Nu 21:22	
"But we **h** cast them down, Heshbon	Nu 21:30	
we **h** laid waste even to Nophah,	Nu 21:30	
for I **h** given him into your hand,	Nu 21:34	
"If the men **h** come to call you,	Nu 22:20	
"What **h** I done to you, that you	Nu 22:28	
h struck me these three times?"	Nu 22:28	
you **h** made a mockery of me!	Nu 22:29	
I would **h** killed you by now."	Nu 22:29	
your donkey on which you **h** ridden	Nu 22:30	
H I ever been accustomed to do so	Nu 22:30	
"Why **h** you struck your donkey	Nu 22:32	
I **h** come out as an adversary,	Nu 22:32	
I would surely **h** killed you just now	Nu 22:33	
"I **h** sinned, for I did not know	Nu 22:34	
"Behold, I **h** come now to you!	Nu 22:38	
"I **h** set up the seven altars, and	Nu 23:4	
and I **h** offered up a bull and a	Nu 23:4	
"What **h** you done to me?	Nu 23:11	
you **h** actually blessed them!"	Nu 23:11	
I **h** received *a command* to bless;	Nu 23:20	
you **h** persisted in blessing them	Nu 24:10	
"One from Jacob shall **h** dominion,	Nu 24:19	7287a
who **h** joined themselves to Baal	Nu 25:5	
for they **h** been hostile to you	Nu 25:18	
with which they **h** deceived you in	Nu 25:18	
I **h** given to the sons of Israel.	Nu 27:12	
"When you **h** seen it, you too	Nu 27:13	
like sheep which **h** no shepherd."	Nu 27:17	369
and **h** him stand before Eleazar the	Nu 27:19	
you shall **h** a holy convocation;	Nu 28:25	1961
you shall **h** a holy convocation;	Nu 28:26	1961
shall also **h** a holy convocation;	Nu 29:1	1961
you shall **h** a holy convocation,	Nu 29:7	1961
you shall **h** a holy convocation;	Nu 29:12	1961
day you shall **h** a solemn assembly;	Nu 29:35	1961
"**H** you spared all the women?	Nu 31:15	
who **h** not known man intimately,	Nu 31:18	
"Your servants **h** taken a census	Nu 31:49	
"So we **h** brought as an offering	Nu 31:50	
and your servants **h** livestock."	Nu 32:4	
"If we **h** found favor in your	Nu 32:5	
they **h** followed the LORD fully.'	Nu 32:12	
you **h** risen up in your fathers'	Nu 32:14	
we **h** brought them to their place,	Nu 32:17	
"For we will not **h** an inheritance	Nu 32:19	5157
you **h** sinned against the LORD,	Nu 32:23	
and do what you **h** promised."	Nu 32:24	
they shall **h** possessions among you	Nu 32:30	270
for I **h** given the land to you to	Nu 33:53	
border, you shall **h** the Great Sea,	Nu 34:6	1961
tribe of the sons of Reuben **h** received	Nu 34:14	
h received their possession.	Nu 34:14	
two and a half tribes **h** received	Nu 34:15	
because he should **h** remained in	Nu 35:28	
'You **h** stayed long enough at this	Dt 1:6	
I **h** placed the land before you;	Dt 1:8	
which you **h** said to do is good.'	Dt 1:14	
'You **h** come to the hill country of	Dt 1:20	
brethren **h** made our hearts melt,	Dt 1:28	
in all the way which you **h** walked until	Dt 1:31	
h no knowledge of good or evil,	Dt 1:39	3045
'We **h** sinned against the LORD;	Dt 1:41	
'You **h** circled this mountain long	Dt 2:3	
because I **h** given Mount Seir to Esau	Dt 2:5	
you in all that you **h** done;	Dt 2:7	
you **h** not lacked a thing." '	Dt 2:7	
because I **h** given Ar to the sons	Dt 2:9	
because I **h** given it to the sons	Dt 2:19	
I **h** given Sihon the Amorite, king	Dt 2:24	
I **h** begun to deliver Sihon and his	Dt 2:31	
for I **h** delivered him and all his	Dt 3:2	
(I know that you **h** much livestock)	Dt 3:19	
your cities which I **h** given you,	Dt 3:19	
possession which I **h** given you.'	Dt 3:20	
'Your eyes **h** seen all that the	Dt 3:21	
You **h** begun to show Your servant	Dt 3:24	
"Your eyes **h** seen what the LORD	Dt 4:3	
I **h** taught you statutes and	Dt 4:5	
the things which your eyes **h** seen and	Dt 4:9	
and **h** remained long in the land,	Dt 4:25	
all these things **h** come upon you,	Dt 4:30	
of the fire, as you **h** heard *it,*	Dt 4:33	
shall **h** no other gods before Me.	Dt 5:7	1961
and we **h** heard His voice from the	Dt 5:24	
we **h** seen today that God speaks	Dt 5:24	
as we **h**, and lived?	Dt 5:26	
I **h** heard the voice of the words	Dt 5:28	
people which they **h** spoken to you.	Dt 5:28	
They **h** done well in all that they	Dt 5:28	
well in all that they **h** spoken.	Dt 5:28	
of Egypt which you **h** known,	Dt 7:15	
you until you **h** destroyed them.	Dt 7:24	
you **h** eaten and are satisfied,	Dt 8:10	
you **h** eaten and are satisfied,	Dt 8:12	
and **h** built good houses and lived	Dt 8:12	
and all that you **h** multiplies,	Dt 8:13	
and of whom you **h** heard *it said,*	Dt 9:2	
you **h** been rebellious against the	Dt 9:7	
you that He would **h** destroyed you.	Dt 9:8	
out of Egypt **h** acted corruptly.	Dt 9:12	
They **h** quickly turned aside from	Dt 9:12	
they **h** made a molten image for	Dt 9:12	
'I **h** seen this people, and indeed,	Dt 9:13	
the land which I **h** given you,'	Dt 9:23	
"You **h** been rebellious against	Dt 9:24	
whom You **h** redeemed through Your	Dt 9:26	
whom You **h** brought out of Egypt	Dt 9:26	
whom You **h** brought out by Your	Dt 9:29	
Levi does not **h** a portion or	Dt 10:9	1961
for you which your eyes **h** seen.	Dt 10:21	
with your sons who **h** not known and	Dt 11:2	
h not seen the discipline of the LORD	Dt 11:2	
but your own eyes **h** seen all the	Dt 11:7	
other gods which you **h** not known.	Dt 11:28	
for you **h** not as yet come to the	Dt 12:9	
given you, as I **h** commanded you;	Dt 12:21	
your holy things which you may **h**	Dt 12:26	1961
hates they **h** done for their gods;	Dt 12:31	
(whom you **h** not known)	Dt 13:2	
you nor your fathers **h** known,	Dt 13:6	
some worthless men **h** gone out from	Dt 13:13	
h seduced the inhabitants of their city,	Dt 13:13	
(whom you **h** not known),	Dt 13:13	
and **h** compassion on you and make	Dt 13:17	7355
but anything that does not **h** fins	Dt 14:10	369
seven days after you **h** gathered in from	Dt 16:13	
host, which I **h** not commanded,	Dt 17:3	
is told you and you **h** heard of it,	Dt 17:4	
shall **h** no portion or inheritance	Dt 18:1	1961
"They shall **h** no inheritance	Dt 18:2	1961
They **h** spoken well.	Dt 18:17	
I **h** not commanded him to speak,	Dt 18:20	
mark, which the ancestors **h** set,	Dt 19:14	
both the men who **h** the dispute	Dt 19:17	
When the officers **h** finished speaking	Dt 20:9	
which they **h** done for their gods,	Dt 20:18	
Israel whom You **h** redeemed,	Dt 21:8	
and **h** a desire for her and would	Dt 21:11	2836a
her, because you **h** humbled her.	Dt 21:14	
and the unloved **h** borne him sons,	Dt 21:15	
which he has lost and you **h** found.	Dt 22:3	
of the seed which you **h** sown and	Dt 22:9	
"You shall also **h** a place outside	Dt 23:12	1961
shall **h** a spade among your tools,	Dt 23:13	1961
just as you **h** voluntarily vowed to	Dt 23:23	
your God, what you **h** promised.	Dt 23:23	
as I **h** commanded them, so you	Dt 24:8	
and **h** forgotten a sheaf in the field,	Dt 24:19	
h in your bag differing weights,	Dt 25:13	1961
"You shall not **h** in your house	Dt 25:14	1961
shall **h** a full and just weight;	Dt 25:15	1961
shall **h** a full and just measure,	Dt 25:15	1961
I **h** entered the land which the LORD	Dt 26:3	
I **h** brought the first of the	Dt 26:10	
which You, O LORD **h** given me.'	Dt 26:10	
"When you **h** finished paying all	Dt 26:12	
'I **h** removed the sacred *portion*	Dt 26:13	
and also **h** given it to the Levite	Dt 26:13	
which You **h** commanded me;	Dt 26:13	
I **h** not transgressed or forgotten	Dt 26:13	
'I **h** not eaten of it while	Dt 26:14	
nor **h** I removed any of it while I	Dt 26:14	
I **h** listened to the voice of the	Dt 26:14	
I **h** done according to all that	Dt 26:14	
to all that You **h** commanded me.	Dt 26:14	
the ground which You **h** given us,	Dt 26:15	
"You **h** today declared the LORD to	Dt 26:17	
This day you **h** become a people for	Dt 27:9	
deeds, because you **h** forsaken Me.	Dt 28:20	
and you will **h** none to save you.	Dt 28:31	369
you nor your fathers **h** known,	Dt 28:36	
"You shall **h** olive trees	Dt 28:40	1961
"You shall **h** sons and daughters	Dt 28:41	3205
will **h** no respect for the old,	Dt 28:50	5375

until they **h** caused you to perish. **Dt 28:51**
you or your fathers **h** not known. **Dt 28:64**
shall **h** no assurance of your life. **Dt 28:66** 539
"You **h** seen all that the LORD did **Dt 29:2**
trials which your eyes **h** seen, **Dt 29:3**
"I **h** led you forty years in **Dt 29:5**
clothes **h** not worn out on you, **Dt 29:5**
"You **h** not eaten bread, nor have **Dt 29:6**
nor **h** you drunk wine or strong **Dt 29:6**
you **h** seen their abominations and **Dt 29:17**
'I **h** peace though I walk in the **Dt 29:19** 1961
gods whom they **h** not known and **Dt 29:26**
of these things **h** come upon you, **Dt 30:1**
curse which I **h** set before you, **Dt 30:1**
and **h** compassion on you, **Dt 30:3** 7355
I **h** set before you today life and **Dt 30:15**
I **h** set before you life and death, **Dt 30:19**
which I **h** commanded you. **Dt 31:5**
Their children, who **h** not known, **Dt 31:13**
covenant which I **h** made with them. **Dt 31:16**
that these evils **h** come upon us?' **Dt 31:17**
and they **h** eaten and are satisfied **Dt 31:20**
and troubles **h** come upon them, **Dt 31:21**
before I **h** brought them into the **Dt 31:21**
you **h** been rebellious against the **Dt 31:27**
the way which I **h** commanded you; **Dt 31:29**
"They **h** acted corruptly toward **Dt 32:5**
To gods whom they **h** not known, **Dt 32:17**
'They **h** made Me jealous with *what* **Dt 32:21**
They **h** provoked Me to anger with **Dt 32:21**
'I would **h** said, **Dt 32:26**
will **h** compassion on His servants **Dt 32:36** 5162
I **h** wounded and it is I who heal **Dt 32:39**
I **h** let you see *it* with your eyes, **Dt 34:4**
foot treads, I **h** given it to you, **Jos 1:3**
Just as I **h** been with Moses, I **Jos 1:5**
you may **h** success wherever you go. **Jos 1:7** 7919a
and then you will **h** success. **Jos 1:8** 7919a
"**H** I not commanded you? **Jos 1:9**
you **h** commanded us we will do, **Jos 1:16**
men from the sons of Israel **h** come **Jos 2:2**
out the men who **h** come to you, **Jos 2:3**
to you, who **h** entered your house, **Jos 2:3**
for they **h** come to search out all **Jos 2:3**
the land **h** melted away before you. **Jos 2:9**
"For we **h** heard how the LORD **Jos 2:10**
since I **h** dealt kindly with you, **Jos 2:12**
to you which you **h** made us swear, **Jos 2:17**
oath which you **h** made us swear." **Jos 2:20**
h melted away before us." **Jos 2:24**
h not passed this way before." **Jos 3:4**
that just as I **h** been with Moses, **Jos 3:7**
"Today I **h** rolled away the **Jos 5:9**
I **h** given Jericho into your hand, **Jos 6:2**
of there, as you **h** sworn to her." **Jos 6:22**
it that you **h** fallen on your face? **Jos 7:10**
and they **h** also transgressed My **Jos 7:11**
And they **h** even taken some of the **Jos 7:11**
and **h** both stolen and deceived. **Jos 7:11**
they **h** also put *them* among their **Jos 7:11**
for they **h** become accursed. **Jos 7:12**
until you **h** removed the things under **Jos 7:13**
and tell me now what you **h** done. **Jos 7:19**
I **h** sinned against the LORD, **Jos 7:20**
"Why **h** you troubled us? **Jos 7:25**
I **h** given into your hand the king **Jos 8:1**
h drawn them away from the city, **Jos 8:6**
be when you **h** seized the city, **Jos 8:8**
See, I **h** commanded you." **Jos 8:8**
"We **h** come from a far country; **Jos 9:6**
"Your servants **h** come from a very **Jos 9:9**
for we **h** heard the report of Him **Jos 9:9**
"We **h** sworn to them by the LORD, **Jos 9:19**
"Why **h** you deceived us, saying, **Jos 9:22**
of you, and **h** done this thing. **Jos 9:24**
country **h** assembled against us. **Jos 10:6**
I **h** given them into your hands; **Jos 10:8**
'The five kings **h** been found **Jos 10:17**
inheritance as I **h** commanded you. **Jos 13:6**
because you **h** followed the LORD my **Jos 14:9**
since you **h** given me the land of **Jos 15:19**
"Why **h** you given me only one lot **Jos 17:14**
valley land **h** chariots of iron, **Jos 17:16**
numerous people and **h** great power; **Jos 17:17**
you shall not **h** one lot *only,* **Jos 17:17** 1961
even though they **h** chariots of **Jos 17:18**
Levites **h** no portion among you, **Jos 18:7** 369
half-tribe of Manasseh also **h** received **Jos 18:7**
"You **h** kept all that Moses the **Jos 22:2**
and **h** listened to my voice in all **Jos 22:2**
"You **h** not forsaken your brothers **Jos 22:3**
but **h** kept the charge of the **Jos 22:3**
half-tribe of Manasseh **h** built an altar **Jos 22:11**
unfaithful act which you **h** committed **Jos 22:16**
from which we **h** not cleansed **Jos 22:17**
"If we **h** built us an altar to **Jos 22:23**
we **h** done this out of concern, **Jos 22:24**
"What **h** you to do with the LORD, **Jos 22:24**
you **h** no portion in the LORD." **Jos 22:25** 369
"You **h** no portion in the LORD." ' **Jos 22:27** 369
because you **h** not committed this **Jos 22:31**
now you **h** delivered the sons of **Jos 22:31**
"And you **h** seen all that the LORD **Jos 23:3**
I **h** apportioned to you these **Jos 23:4**
all the nations which I **h** cut off, **Jos 23:4**
God, as you **h** done to this day. **Jos 23:8**
all **h** been fulfilled for you, not **Jos 23:14**
God spoke to you **h** come upon you, **Jos 23:15**
built, and you **h** lived in them; **Jos 24:13**
you **h** chosen for yourselves the LORD, **Jos 24:22**
h given the land into his hand." **Jg 1:2**
as I **h** done, so God has repaid me." **Jg 1:7**
since you **h** given me the land of **Jg 1:15**
so the Jebusites **h** lived with the **Jg 1:21**
which I **h** sworn to your fathers; **Jg 2:1**
But you **h** not obeyed Me; **Jg 2:2**
what is this you **h** done? **Jg 2:2**
"I **h** a secret message for you, O **Jg 3:19**
"I **h** a message from God for you." **Jg 3:20**
But you **h** not obeyed Me." **Jg 6:10**
H I not sent you?" **Jg 6:14**
now I **h** found favor in Your sight, **Jg 6:17**
For now I **h** seen the angel of the **Jg 6:22**
through me, as You **h** spoken, **Jg 6:36**
through me, as You **h** spoken." **Jg 6:37**
for I **h** given it into your hands. **Jg 7:9**
is this thing you **h** done to us, **Jg 8:1**
"What **h** I done now in comparison **Jg 8:2**
for you **h** delivered us from the **Jg 8:22**
if you **h** dealt in truth and **Jg 9:16**
and if you **h** dealt well with **Jg 9:16**
and **h** dealt with him as he **Jg 9:16**
but you **h** risen against my **Jg 9:18**
house today and **h** killed his sons, **Jg 9:18**
one stone, and **h** made Abimelech, **Jg 9:18**
if then you **h** dealt in truth and **Jg 9:19**
his relatives **h** come to Shechem; **Jg 9:31**
"What you **h** seen me do, hurry *and* **Jg 9:48**
"We **h** sinned against You, for **Jg 10:10**
we **h** forsaken our God and served **Jg 10:10**
"Yet you **h** forsaken Me and served **Jg 10:13**
to the gods which you **h** chosen; **Jg 10:14**
"We **h** sinned, do to us whatever **Jg 10:15**
"You shall not **h** an inheritance **Jg 11:2** 5157
So why **h** you come to me now when **Jg 11:7**
reason we **h** now returned to you, **Jg 11:8**
surely we will do as you **h** said." **Jg 11:10**
that you **h** come to me to fight **Jg 11:12**
h not sinned against you, **Jg 11:27**
You **h** brought me very low, and you **Jg 11:35**
for I **h** given my word to the LORD, **Jg 11:35**
you **h** given your word to the LORD; **Jg 11:36**
do to me as you **h** said, since the **Jg 11:36**
then **h** you come up to me this day to **Jg 12:3**
barren and **h** borne no *children,* **Jg 13:3**
the man of God whom You **h** sent **Jg 13:8**
surely die, for we **h** seen God." **Jg 13:22**
He would not **h** accepted a burnt **Jg 13:23**
would He **h** shown us all these things **Jg 13:23**
nor would He **h** let us hear **Jg 13:23**
H you invited us to impoverish us? **Jg 14:15**
you **h** propounded a riddle to the **Jg 14:16**
people, and **h** not told *it* to me." **Jg 14:16**
I **h** not told *it* to my father or **Jg 14:16**
would not **h** found out my riddle." **Jg 14:18**
"Why **h** you come up against us?" **Jg 15:10**
"We **h** come up to bind Samson in **Jg 15:10**
is this that you **h** done to us?" **Jg 15:11**
did to me, so I **h** done to them." **Jg 15:11**
"We **h** come down to bind you so **Jg 15:12**
I **h** killed a thousand men." **Jg 15:16**
"You **h** given this great **Jg 15:18**
fresh cords that **h** not been dried, **Jg 16:7**
h deceived me and told me lies; **Jg 16:10**
new ropes which **h** not been used, **Jg 16:11**
h deceived me and told me lies; **Jg 16:13**
You **h** deceived me these three **Jg 16:15**
three times and **h** not told me where **Jg 16:15**
for I **h** been a Nazirite to God **Jg 16:17**
seeing I **h** a Levite as priest." **Jg 17:13** 1961
And what do you **h** here?" **Jg 18:3**
me and I **h** become his priest." **Jg 18:4** 1961
for we **h** seen the land, and **Jg 18:9**
that you **h** assembled together?" **Jg 18:23**
"You **h** taken away my gods which I **Jg 18:24**
and the priest, and **h** gone away, **Jg 18:24**
away, and what do I **h** besides? **Jg 18:24**
we may **h** relations with him." **Jg 19:22** 3045
for they **h** committed a lewd and **Jg 20:6**
that they **h** committed in Israel." **Jg 20:10**
since we **h** sworn by the LORD not **Jg 21:7**
deal kindly with you as you **h** dealt **Ru 1:8**
H I yet sons in my womb, that they **Ru 1:11**
for I am too old to **h** a husband. **Ru 1:12** 1961
If I said I **h** hope, if I should **Ru 1:12** 3426
if I should even **h** a husband **Ru 1:12** 1961
I **h** commanded the servants not to **Ru 2:9**
"Why **h** I found favor in your **Ru 2:10**
"All that you **h** done for your **Ru 2:11**
wings you **h** come to seek refuge." **Ru 2:12**
"I **h** found favor in your sight, **Ru 2:13**
for you **h** comforted me and indeed **Ru 2:13**
h spoken kindly to your maidservant, **Ru 2:13**
h finished all my harvest.' **Ru 2:21**
You **h** shown your last kindness to **Ru 3:10**
you *may* **h** my right of redemption, **Ru 4:6**
I **h** bought from the hand of Naomi **Ru 4:9**
I **h** acquired Ruth the Moabitess, **Ru 4:10**
I **h** drunk neither wine nor strong **1Sa 1:15**
but I **h** poured out my soul before **1Sa 1:15**
for I **h** spoken until now out of my **1Sa 1:16**
that you **h** asked of Him." **1Sa 1:17**
I **h** asked him of the LORD." **1Sa 1:20**
Remain until you **h** weaned him; **1Sa 1:23**
"So I **h** also dedicated him to the **1Sa 1:28**
I **h** commanded *in My* dwelling, **1Sa 2:29**
I **h** spoken concerning his house, **1Sa 3:12**
"For I **h** told him that I am about **1Sa 3:13**
"Therefore I **h** sworn to the **1Sa 3:14**
as they **h** been slaves to you; **1Sa 4:9**
for you **h** given birth to a son." **1Sa 4:20**
"They **h** brought the ark of the **1Sa 5:10**
"The Philistines **h** brought back **1Sa 6:21**
"We **h** sinned against the LORD." **1Sa 7:6**
"Behold, you **h** grown old, and **1Sa 8:5**
you, for they **h** not rejected you, **1Sa 8:7**
but they **h** rejected Me from being **1Sa 8:7**
"Like all the deeds which they **h** **1Sa 8:8**
they **h** forsaken Me and served other **1Sa 8:8**
whom you **h** chosen for yourselves, **1Sa 8:18**
journey on which we **h** set out." **1Sa 9:6**
to the man of God. What do we **h**?" **1Sa 9:7** 854
I **h** in my hand a fourth of a **1Sa 9:8** 4672
for the people **h** a sacrifice on **1Sa 9:12**
For I **h** regarded My people, **1Sa 9:16**
on them, for they **h** been found. **1Sa 9:20**
I said I **h** invited the people." **1Sa 9:24**
you went to look for **h** been found. **1Sa 10:2**
as you **h** come there to the city, **1Sa 10:5**
"But you **h** today rejected your God, **1Sa 10:19**
you **h** said, 'No, but set a king over **1Sa 10:19**
hot, you will **h** deliverance.' " **1Sa 11:9** 1961
I **h** listened to your voice in all **1Sa 12:1**
and I **h** appointed a king over you **1Sa 12:1**
And I **h** walked before you from my **1Sa 12:2**
Whose ox **h** I taken, or whose **1Sa 12:3**
taken, or whose donkey **h** I taken, **1Sa 12:3**
I taken, or whom **h** I defrauded? **1Sa 12:3**
Whom **h** I oppressed, or from whose **1Sa 12:3**
or from whose hand **h** I taken a **1Sa 12:3**
"You **h** not defrauded us or **1Sa 12:4**
you **h** found nothing in my hand." **1Sa 12:5**
'We **h** sinned because we have **1Sa 12:10**
because we **h** forsaken the LORD **1Sa 12:10**
h served the Baals and the Ashtaroth; **1Sa 12:10**
is the king whom you **h** chosen, **1Sa 12:13**
have chosen, whom you **h** asked for, **1Sa 12:13**
wickedness is great which you **h** done **1Sa 12:17**
for we **h** added to all our sins **1Sa 12:19**
You **h** committed all this evil, yet **1Sa 12:20**
"What **h** you done?" **1Sa 13:11**
and I **h** not asked the favor of the **1Sa 13:12**
"You **h** acted foolishly; **1Sa 13:13**
you **h** not kept the commandment of **1Sa 13:13**
for now the LORD would **h** **1Sa 13:13**
because you **h** not kept what the **1Sa 13:14**
where they **h** hidden themselves." **1Sa 14:11**
h avenged myself on my enemies." **1Sa 14:24**
how my eyes **h** brightened because **1Sa 14:29**
"You **h** acted treacherously; **1Sa 14:33**
"Tell me what you **h** done." **1Sa 14:43**
"I regret that I **h** made Saul king, **1Sa 15:11**
I **h** carried out the command of the **1Sa 15:13**
"They **h** brought them from the **1Sa 15:15**
the rest we **h** utterly destroyed." **1Sa 15:15**
and **h** brought back Agag the king **1Sa 15:20**
and **h** utterly destroyed the **1Sa 15:20**
h rejected the word of the LORD, **1Sa 15:23**
Saul said to Samuel, "I **h** sinned; **1Sa 15:24**
I **h** indeed transgressed the **1Sa 15:24**
h rejected the word of the LORD, **1Sa 15:26**
"I **h** sinned; *but* please honor me now **1Sa 15:30**
since I **h** rejected him from being **1Sa 16:1**
for I **h** selected a king for Myself **1Sa 16:1**
h come to sacrifice to the LORD.' **1Sa 16:2**
I **h** come to sacrifice to the LORD. **1Sa 16:5**
stature, because I **h** rejected him; **1Sa 16:7**
h seen a son of Jesse the **1Sa 16:18**
"**H** you seen this man who is **1Sa 17:25**
"Why **h** you come down? **1Sa 17:28**
And with whom **h** you left those few **1Sa 17:28**
for you **h** come down in order to **1Sa 17:28**
"What **h** I done now? **1Sa 17:29**
these, for I **h** not tested *them.*" **1Sa 17:39**
of Israel, whom you **h** taunted. **1Sa 17:45**
"They **h** ascribed to David ten **1Sa 18:8**
to me they **h** ascribed thousands. **1Sa 18:8**
more can he **h** but the kingdom?" **1Sa 18:8**
should **h** been given to David, **1Sa 18:19**
and since his deeds **h** *been* very **1Sa 19:4**
"Why **h** you deceived me like this **1Sa 19:17**
said to Jonathan, "What **h** I done? **1Sa 20:1**
I **h** found favor in your sight, **1Sa 20:3**
for you **h** brought your servant **1Sa 20:8**
When I **h** sounded out my father **1Sa 20:12**
"When you **h** stayed for three **1Sa 20:19**
of which you and I **h** spoken, **1Sa 20:23**
if I **h** found favor in your sight, **1Sa 20:29**
inasmuch as we **h** sworn to each **1Sa 20:42**
with which I **h** commissioned you; **1Sa 21:2**
and I **h** directed the young men to **1Sa 21:2**
therefore, what do you **h** on hand? **1Sa 21:3** 3426
h kept themselves from women." **1Sa 21:4**
"Surely women **h** been kept from us **1Sa 21:5**
that you **h** brought this one to act **1Sa 21:15**
"For all of you **h** conspired **1Sa 22:8**
"Why **h** you and the son of Jesse **1Sa 22:13**
in that you **h** given him bread and **1Sa 22:13**
and **h** inquired of God for him, **1Sa 22:13**
I **h** brought about *the death* of **1Sa 22:22**
for you **h** had compassion on me. **1Sa 23:21**
the Philistines **h** made a raid on the **1Sa 23:27**
this day your eyes **h** seen that the **1Sa 24:10**
and I **h** not sinned against you, **1Sa 24:11**
for you **h** dealt well with me, **1Sa 24:17**
while I **h** dealt wickedly with you. **1Sa 24:17**
"You **h** declared today that **1Sa 24:18**

today that you **h** done good to me, 1Sa 24:18
what you **h** done to me this day. 1Sa 24:19
'**H** a long life, peace be to you, 1Sa 25:6
and peace be to all that you **h**. 1Sa 25:6
I **h** heard that you have shearers; 1Sa 25:7
I have heard that you **h** shearers; 1Sa 25:7
now your shepherds **h** been with us 1Sa 25:7
us and we **h** not insulted them, 1Sa 25:7
nor **h** they missed anything all the 1Sa 25:7
for we **h** come on a festive day. 1Sa 25:8
I **h** slaughtered for my shearers, 1Sa 25:11
"Surely in vain I **h** guarded all 1Sa 25:21
who **h** kept me this day from 1Sa 25:33
surely there would not **h** been left 1Sa 25:34
I **h** listened to you and granted 1Sa 25:35
Why then **h** you not guarded your 1Sa 26:15
thing that you **h** done is not good. 1Sa 26:16
For what **h** I done? 1Sa 26:18
for they **h** driven me out today 1Sa 26:19
h no attachment with the inheritance 1Sa 26:19
Then Saul said, "I **h** sinned. 1Sa 26:21
I **h** played the fool and have 1Sa 26:21
and **h** committed a serious error." 1Sa 26:21
now I **h** found favor in your sight, 1Sa 27:5
"Where **h** you made a raid today?" 1Sa 27:10
"Why **h** you deceived me? 1Sa 28:12
"Why **h** you disturbed me by 1Sa 28:15
therefore I **h** called you, that you 1Sa 28:15
and I **h** taken my life in my hand and 1Sa 28:21
I have taken my life in my hand and **h** 1Sa 28:21
that *you may* eat and **h** strength when 1Sa 28:22 1961
and I **h** found no fault in him from 1Sa 29:3
place where you **h** assigned him, 1Sa 29:4
you **h** *been* upright, and your 1Sa 29:6
for I **h** not found evil in you from 1Sa 29:6
"But what **h** I done? 1Sa 29:8
And what **h** you found in your 1Sa 29:8
of the Philistines **h** said, 1Sa 29:9
of your lord who **h** come with you, 1Sa 29:10
and as soon as you **h** arisen early 1Sa 29:10
early in the morning and **h** light, 1Sa 29:10
of the spoil that we **h** recovered, 1Sa 30:22
"I **h** escaped from the camp of 2Sa 1:3
"The people **h** fled from the 2Sa 1:4
the people **h** fallen and are dead; 2Sa 1:4
h brought them here to my lord." 2Sa 1:10
'I **h** killed the LORD's anointed.' " 2Sa 1:16
How **h** the mighty fallen! 2Sa 1:19
"How **h** the mighty fallen in the 2Sa 1:25
You **h** been very pleasant to me. 2Sa 1:26
"How **h** the mighty fallen, And the 2Sa 1:27
you **h** shown this kindness to Saul 2Sa 2:5
Saul your lord, and **h** buried him. 2Sa 2:5
because you **h** done this thing. 2Sa 2:6
would **h** gone away in the morning, 2Sa 2:27
"Why **h** you gone in to my father's 2Sa 3:7
and **h** not delivered you into the 2Sa 3:8
"What **h** you done? Behold, Abner 2Sa 3:24
why then **h** you sent him away and 2Sa 3:24
before the wicked, you **h** fallen." 2Sa 3:34
and **h** been aliens there until this 2Sa 4:3
when wicked men **h** killed a 2Sa 4:11
for then the LORD will **h** gone out 2Sa 5:24
the maids of whom you **h** spoken, 2Sa 6:22
"For I **h** not dwelt in a house 2Sa 7:6
I **h** been moving about in a tent, 2Sa 7:6
"Wherever I **h** gone with all the 2Sa 7:7
'Why **h** you not built Me a house of 2Sa 7:7
"I **h** been with you wherever 2Sa 7:9
been with you wherever you **h** gone 2Sa 7:9
h cut off all your enemies from before 2Sa 7:9
that You **h** brought me this far? 2Sa 7:18
for You **h** spoken also of the 2Sa 7:19
You **h** done all this greatness to 2Sa 7:21
all that we **h** heard with our ears. 2Sa 7:22
Your people whom You **h** redeemed 2Sa 7:23
"For You **h** established for 2Sa 7:24
You, O LORD, **h** become their God. 2Sa 7:24
the word that You **h** spoken 2Sa 7:25
forever, and do as You **h** spoken, 2Sa 7:25
God of Israel, **h** made a revelation 2Sa 7:27
and You **h** promised this good 2Sa 7:28
For You, O Lord GOD, **h** spoken; 2Sa 7:29
to Saul and to all his house I **h** given 2Sa 9:9
your master's grandson may **h** food; 2Sa 9:10 1961
"**H** you not come from a journey? 2Sa 11:10
"When you **h** finished telling all 2Sa 11:19
I would **h** added to you many more 2Sa 12:8
'Why **h** you despised the word of 2Sa 12:9
You **h** struck down Uriah the 2Sa 12:9
h taken his wife to be your wife, 2Sa 12:9
and **h** killed him with the sword of 2Sa 12:9
because you **h** despised Me and have 2Sa 12:10
h taken the wife of Uriah the Hittite 2Sa 12:10
"I **h** sinned against the LORD." 2Sa 12:13
because by this deed you **h** given 2Sa 12:14
is this thing that you **h** done? 2Sa 12:21
"I **h** fought against Rabbah, I 2Sa 12:27
I **h** even captured the city of 2Sa 12:27
"**H** everyone go out from me." 2Sa 13:9
the other that you **h** done to me!" 2Sa 13:16
h not I myself commanded you? 2Sa 13:28
they **h** put to death all the young men, 2Sa 13:32
"Behold, the king's sons **h** come; 2Sa 13:35
"Why then **h** you planned such a 2Sa 14:13
"Now the reason I **h** come to speak 2Sa 14:15
the people **h** made me afraid; 2Sa 14:15
I **h** found favor in your sight, 2Sa 14:22
"Why **h** your servants set my field 2Sa 14:31

"Why **h** I come from Geshur? 2Sa 14:32
vow which I **h** vowed to the LORD, 2Sa 15:7
'I **h** no delight in you,' behold, 2Sa 15:26 2654a
as I **h** been your father's servant 2Sa 15:34
"Why do you **h** these?" 2Sa 16:2
in whose place you **h** reigned; 2Sa 16:8
"What **h** I to do with you, O sons 2Sa 16:10
'Why **h** you done so?' " 2Sa 16:10
all the men of Israel **h** chosen, 2Sa 16:18
As I **h** served in your father's 2Sa 16:19
h made yourself odious to your father. 2Sa 16:21
and this is what I **h** counseled. 2Sa 17:15
h crossed the brook of water. 2Sa 17:20
And I would **h** given you ten 2Sa 18:11
yourself would **h** stood aloof." 2Sa 18:13
"I **h** no son to preserve my name." 2Sa 18:18 369
tell the king what you **h** seen." 2Sa 18:21
you will **h** no reward for going?" 2Sa 18:22 369
"Today you **h** covered with shame 2Sa 19:5
who today **h** saved your life and 2Sa 19:5
For you **h** shown today that princes 2Sa 19:6
servant knows that I **h** sinned; 2Sa 19:20
therefore behold, I **h** come today, 2Sa 19:20
"What **h** I to do with you, O sons 2Sa 19:22
What right do I **h** yet that I 2Sa 19:28 3426
I **h** decided, 'You and Ziba shall 2Sa 19:29
"How long **h** I yet to live, that I 2Sa 19:34
H we eaten at all at the king's 2Sa 19:42
"We **h** ten parts in the king, 2Sa 19:43
h more *claim* on David than you. 2Sa 19:43
"We **h** no portion in David, Nor do 2Sa 20:1 369
Nor do we **h** inheritance in the son 2Sa 20:1
"We **h** no *concern* of silver or 2Sa 21:4 369
"For I **h** kept the ways of the 2Sa 22:22
And **h** not acted wickedly against 2Sa 22:22
"You **h** also given me the shield 2Sa 22:36
me, And my feet **h** not slipped. 2Sa 22:37
"And I **h** devoured them and 2Sa 22:39
"For You **h** girded me with 2Sa 22:40
You **h** subdued under me those who 2Sa 22:40
"You **h** also made my enemies turn 2Sa 22:41
"You **h** also delivered me from 2Sa 22:44
You **h** kept me as head of the 2Sa 22:44
whom I **h** not known serve me. 2Sa 22:44
"I **h** sinned greatly in what I 2Sa 24:10
sinned greatly in what I **h** done. 2Sa 24:10
for I **h** acted very foolishly." 2Sa 24:10
"Behold, it is I who **h** sinned, 2Sa 24:17
and it is I who **h** done wrong; 2Sa 24:17
but these sheep, what **h** they done? 2Sa 24:17
"Why **h** you done so?" 1Ki 1:6
"**H** you not heard that Adonijah 1Ki 1:11
'**H** you not, my lord, O king, sworn 1Ki 1:13
"My lord the king, **h** you said, 1Ki 1:24
and you **h** not shown to your 1Ki 1:27
and **h** my son Solomon ride on my 1Ki 1:33
for I **h** appointed him to be ruler 1Ki 1:35
and they **h** made him ride on the 1Ki 1:44
h anointed him king in Gihon, 1Ki 1:45
h come up from there rejoicing, 1Ki 1:45
is the noise which you **h** heard. 1Ki 1:45
"I **h** something *to say* to you." 1Ki 2:14
The word which I **h** heard is good.' 1Ki 2:42
Why then **h** you not kept the oath 1Ki 2:43
command which I **h** laid on you?" 1Ki 2:43
"You **h** shown great lovingkindness 1Ki 3:6
and You **h** reserved for him this 1Ki 3:6
that You **h** given him a son to sit 1Ki 3:6
You **h** made Your servant king in 1Ki 3:7
of Your people which You **h** chosen, 1Ki 3:8
"Because you **h** asked this thing 1Ki 3:11
and **h** not asked for yourself long life, 1Ki 3:11
nor **h** asked riches for yourself, 1Ki 3:11
nor **h** you asked for the life of 1Ki 3:11
but **h** asked for yourself 1Ki 3:11
I **h** done according to your words. 1Ki 3:12
I **h** given you a wise and 1Ki 3:12
"I **h** also given you what you 1Ki 3:13
given you what you **h** not asked, 1Ki 3:13
"I **h** heard *the message* which you 1Ki 5:8
the message which you **h** sent me; 1Ki 5:8
and I will **h** them broken up there, 1Ki 5:9
"I **h** surely built You a lofty 1Ki 8:13
for I **h** risen in place of my 1Ki 8:20
and **h** built the house for the name 1Ki 8:20
'There I **h** set a place for the ark, 1Ki 8:21
who **h** kept with Your servant, my 1Ki 8:24
that which You **h** promised him; 1Ki 8:24
You **h** spoken with Your mouth and 1Ki 8:24
spoken with Your mouth and **h** fulfilled 1Ki 8:24
that which You **h** promised him, 1Ki 8:25
walk before Me as you **h** walked.' 1Ki 8:25
You **h** spoken to Your servant, 1Ki 8:26
less this house which I **h** built! 1Ki 8:27
Yet **h** regard to the prayer of 1Ki 8:28 6437
the place of which You **h** said, 1Ki 8:29
they **h** sinned against You, 1Ki 8:33
they **h** sinned against You, 1Ki 8:35
which You **h** given Your people for 1Ki 8:36
which You **h** given to our fathers. 1Ki 8:40
this house which I **h** built is called 1Ki 8:43
toward the city which You **h** chosen 1Ki 8:44
which I **h** built for Your name, 1Ki 8:44
where they **h** been taken captive, 1Ki 8:47
of those who **h** taken them captive, 1Ki 8:47
'We **h** sinned and have committed 1Ki 8:47
sinned and **h** committed iniquity, 1Ki 8:47
iniquity, we **h** acted wickedly'; 1Ki 8:47
enemies who **h** taken them captive, 1Ki 8:48

You **h** given to their fathers, 1Ki 8:48
the city which You **h** chosen, 1Ki 8:48
which I **h** built for Your name; 1Ki 8:48
forgive Your people who **h** sinned 1Ki 8:50
they **h** transgressed against You, 1Ki 8:50
those who **h** taken them captive, 1Ki 8:50
they may **h** compassion on them 1Ki 8:50 7355
You **h** brought forth from Egypt, 1Ki 8:51
"For You **h** separated them from 1Ki 8:53
with which I **h** made supplication 1Ki 8:59
"I **h** heard your prayer and your 1Ki 9:3
which you **h** made before Me; 1Ki 9:3
I **h** consecrated this house which 1Ki 9:3
you **h** built by putting My name there 1Ki 9:3
according to all that I **h** commanded 1Ki 9:4
My statutes which I **h** set before you 1Ki 9:6
the land which I **h** given them, 1Ki 9:7
which I **h** consecrated for My name, 1Ki 9:7
these cities which you **h** given me, 1Ki 9:13
almug trees **h** not come in 1Ki 10:12
nor **h** they been seen to this day. 1Ki 10:12
"Because you **h** done this, and you 1Ki 11:11
and you **h** not kept My covenant and 1Ki 11:11
statutes, which I **h** commanded you, 1Ki 11:11
of Jerusalem which I **h** chosen." 1Ki 11:13
"But what **h** you lacked with me, 1Ki 11:22
(but he will **h** one tribe, for the 1Ki 11:32 1961
the city which I **h** chosen from all 1Ki 11:32
because they **h** forsaken Me, and 1Ki 11:33
and **h** worshiped Ashtoreth the 1Ki 11:33
and they **h** not walked in My ways, 1Ki 11:33
that My servant David may **h** a lamp 1Ki 11:36 1961
the city where I **h** chosen for 1Ki 11:36
this people who **h** spoken to me, 1Ki 12:9
"What portion do we **h** in David? 1Ki 12:16
We **h** no inheritance in the son of 1Ki 12:16
'Because you **h** disobeyed the 1Ki 13:21
and **h** not observed the commandment 1Ki 13:21
but **h** returned and eaten bread and 1Ki 13:22
you **h** not been like My servant David, 1Ki 14:8
you also **h** done more evil than all 1Ki 14:9
and **h** gone and made for yourself 1Ki 14:9
and **h** cast Me behind your back 1Ki 14:9
because they **h** made their Asherim, 1Ki 14:15
I **h** sent you a present of silver 1Ki 15:19
and you **h** walked in the way of 1Ki 16:2
and **h** made My people Israel sin, 1Ki 16:2
and I **h** commanded the ravens to 1Ki 17:4
I **h** commanded a widow there to 1Ki 17:9
LORD your God lives, I **h** no bread, 1Ki 17:12 3426
go, do as you **h** said, but make me 1Ki 17:13
"What do I **h** to do with you, O 1Ki 17:18
You **h** come to me to bring my 1Ki 17:18
h You also brought calamity to 1Ki 17:20
h to kill some of the cattle." 1Ki 18:5
"What sin **h** I committed, that you 1Ki 18:9
h feared the LORD from my youth. 1Ki 18:12
"I **h** not troubled Israel, but you 1Ki 18:18
but you and your father's house **h**, 1Ki 18:18
because you **h** forsaken the 1Ki 18:18
and you **h** followed the Baals. 1Ki 18:18
and I **h** done all these things 1Ki 18:36
h turned their heart back again." 1Ki 18:37
"I **h** been very zealous for the 1Ki 19:10
of Israel **h** forsaken Your covenant, 1Ki 19:10
I **h** been very zealous for the 1Ki 19:14
of Israel **h** forsaken Your covenant, 1Ki 19:14
Damascus, and when you **h** arrived, 1Ki 19:15
all the knees that **h** not bowed to 1Ki 19:18
again, for what **h** I done to you?" 1Ki 19:20
I am yours, and all that I **h**." 1Ki 20:4
'**H** you seen all this great 1Ki 20:13
"Men **h** come out from Samaria." 1Ki 20:17
"If they **h** come out for peace, 1Ki 20:18
or if they **h** come out for war, 1Ki 20:18
observe and see what you **h** to do; 1Ki 20:22
like the army that you **h** lost, 1Ki 20:25
'Because the Arameans **h** said, 1Ki 20:28
we **h** heard that the kings of the 1Ki 20:31
"Because you **h** not listened to 1Ki 20:36
as soon as you **h** departed from me, 1Ki 20:36
you yourself **h** decided *it*." 1Ki 20:40
'Because you **h** let go out of *your* 1Ki 20:42
that I may **h** it for a vegetable 1Ki 21:2 1961
"**H** you murdered and also taken 1Ki 21:19
"**H** you found me, O my enemy?" 1Ki 21:20
"I **h** found *you*, because you have 1Ki 21:20
because you **h** sold yourself to do 1Ki 21:20
which you **h** provoked *Me* to anger, 1Ki 21:22
and *because* you **h** made Israel sin. 1Ki 21:22
Like sheep which **h** no shepherd. 1Ki 22:17 369
'These **h** no master. 1Ki 22:17
from the bed where you **h** gone up, 2Ki 1:4
"Why **h** you returned?" 2Ki 1:5
from the bed where you **h** gone up, 2Ki 1:6
'Because you **h** sent messengers to 2Ki 1:16
from the bed where you **h** gone up, 2Ki 1:16
"You **h** asked a hard thing. 2Ki 2:10
'I **h** purified these waters; 2Ki 2:21
h been purified to this day, 2Ki 2:22
"What do I **h** to do with you? 2Ki 3:13
kings **h** surely fought together, 2Ki 3:23
and they **h** slain one another. 2Ki 3:23
me, what do you **h** in the house?" 2Ki 4:2 3426
you **h** been careful for us with all 2Ki 4:13
eat and **h** *some* left over.' " 2Ki 4:43
I **h** sent Naaman my servant to you, 2Ki 5:6
"Why **h** you torn your clothes? 2Ki 5:8
thing, would you not **h** done *it*? 2Ki 5:13

the sons of the prophets **h** come to me 2Ki 5:22
"Where **h** you been, Gehazi?" 2Ki 5:25
Would you kill those you **h** taken 2Ki 6:22
what the Arameans **h** done to us. 2Ki 7:12
therefore they **h** gone from the 2Ki 7:12
of Israel who **h** already perished, 2Ki 7:13
he leaned to **h** charge of the gate; 2Ki 7:17 5921
h anointed you king over Israel." 2Ki 9:3
"I **h** a word for you, O captain." 2Ki 9:5
'I **h** anointed you king over the 2Ki 9:6
h anointed you king over Israel. 2Ki 9:12
"What **h** you to do with peace? 2Ki 9:18
"What **h** you to do with peace? 2Ki 9:19
'Surely I **h** seen yesterday the 2Ki 9:26
"They **h** brought the heads of the 2Ki 10:8
and we **h** come down to greet the 2Ki 10:13
I **h** a great sacrifice for Baal; 2Ki 10:19
"Because you **h** done well in 2Ki 10:30
and **h** done to the house of Ahab 2Ki 10:30
until you **h** destroyed *them*." 2Ki 13:17
should **h** struck five or six times, 2Ki 13:19
then you would **h** struck Aram until 2Ki 13:19
until you would **h** destroyed *it*. 2Ki 13:19
"You **h** indeed defeated Edom, and 2Ki 14:10
and **h** lived there to this day. 2Ki 16:6
"The nations whom you **h** carried 2Ki 17:26
covenant that I **h** made with you, 2Ki 17:38
I **h** done wrong. Withdraw from me 2Ki 18:14
is this confidence that you **h**? 2Ki 18:19 982
'*I* **h** counsel and strength for 2Ki 18:20
that you **h** rebelled against me? 2Ki 18:20
"**H** I now come up without the 2Ki 18:25
H they delivered Samaria from my 2Ki 18:34
h delivered their land from my hand, 2Ki 18:35
for children **h** come to birth and 2Ki 19:3
of the words that you **h** heard, 2Ki 19:6
king of Assyria **h** blasphemed Me. 2Ki 19:6
you **h** heard what the kings of 2Ki 19:11
Assyria **h** done to all the lands, 2Ki 19:11
You **h** made heaven and earth. 2Ki 19:15
the kings of Assyria **h** devastated 2Ki 19:17
h cast their gods into the fire, 2Ki 19:18
So they **h** destroyed them. 2Ki 19:18
'Because you **h** prayed to Me about 2Ki 19:20
king of Assyria, I **h** heard *you*. 2Ki 19:20
h you reproached and blasphemed? 2Ki 19:22
whom **h** you raised *your* voice, 2Ki 19:22
you **h** reproached the Lord, 2Ki 19:23
the Lord, And you **h** said, 2Ki 19:23
'**H** you not heard? Long ago I did it; 2Ki 19:25
Now I **h** brought it to pass, That 2Ki 19:25
how I **h** walked before You in 2Ki 20:3
and **h** done what is good in Your 2Ki 20:3
"I **h** heard your prayer, I have 2Ki 20:5
your prayer, I **h** seen your tears; 2Ki 20:5
from where **h** they come to you?" 2Ki 20:14
"They **h** come from a far country, 2Ki 20:14
"What **h** they seen in your house?" 2Ki 20:15
h seen all that is in my house; 2Ki 20:15
that I **h** not shown them." 2Ki 20:15
and all that your fathers **h** laid 2Ki 20:17
LORD which you **h** spoken is good." 2Ki 20:19
which I **h** chosen from all the 2Ki 21:7
to all that I **h** commanded them, 2Ki 21:8
they **h** done evil in My sight, 2Ki 21:15
h been provoking Me to anger since 2Ki 21:15
h gathered from the people. 2Ki 22:4
workmen who **h** the oversight of the 2Ki 22:5
"I **h** found the book of the law in 2Ki 22:8
"Your servants **h** emptied out the 2Ki 22:9
and **h** delivered it into the hand 2Ki 22:9
workmen who **h** the oversight of the 2Ki 22:9
because our fathers **h** not listened 2Ki 22:13
"Because they **h** forsaken Me and 2Ki 22:17
and **h** burned incense to other gods 2Ki 22:17
the words which you **h** heard, 2Ki 22:18
and you **h** torn your clothes and 2Ki 22:19
before Me, I truly **h** heard you," 2Ki 22:19
you **h** done against the altar of Bethel 2Ki 23:17
My sight, as I **h** removed Israel. 2Ki 23:27
this city which I **h** chosen, 2Ki 23:27
his brothers did not **h** many sons, 1Ch 4:27 369
and they **h** their genealogy. 1Ch 4:33
and **h** lived there to this day. 1Ch 4:43
for God will **h** gone out before you 1Ch 14:15
place that I **h** prepared for it. 1Ch 15:12
for I **h** not dwelt in a house since 1Ch 17:5
but I **h** gone from tent to tent and 1Ch 17:5
where I **h** walked with all Israel, 1Ch 17:6
h I spoken a word with any of the 1Ch 17:6
'Why **h** you not built for Me a 1Ch 17:6
"I **h** been with you wherever you 1Ch 17:8
been with you wherever you **h** gone, 1Ch 17:8
and **h** cut off all your enemies 1Ch 17:8
that You **h** brought me this far? 1Ch 17:16
but You **h** spoken of Your servant's 1Ch 17:17
and **h** regarded me according to the 1Ch 17:17
You **h** wrought all this greatness, 1Ch 17:19
all that we **h** heard with our ears. 1Ch 17:20
let the word that You **h** spoken 1Ch 17:23
forever, and do as You **h** spoken. 1Ch 17:23
h revealed to Your servant that 1Ch 17:25
and **h** promised this good thing to 1Ch 17:26
for You, O LORD, **h** blessed, 1Ch 17:27
H not his servants come to you to 1Ch 19:3
"I **h** sinned greatly, in that I 1Ch 21:8
in that I **h** done this thing. 1Ch 21:8
for I **h** done very foolishly." 1Ch 21:8
what **h** they done? O LORD my God, 1Ch 21:17
'You **h** shed much blood and have 1Ch 22:8
'You have shed much blood and **h** 1Ch 22:8
because you **h** shed *so* much blood 1Ch 22:8
with great pains I **h** prepared for 1Ch 22:14
timber and stone I **h** prepared, 1Ch 22:14
and Beriah did not **h** many sons, 1Ch 23:11
a man of war and **h** shed blood.' 1Ch 28:3
I **h** chosen him to be a son to Me, 1Ch 28:6
I **h** provided for the house of my 1Ch 29:2
treasure I **h** of gold and silver, 1Ch 29:3 3426
over and above all that I **h** 1Ch 29:3
and from Your hand we **h** given You. 1Ch 29:14
all this abundance that we **h** 1Ch 29:16
h willingly offered all these 1Ch 29:17
so now with joy I **h** seen Your 1Ch 29:17
for which I **h** made provision." 1Ch 29:19
"You **h** dealt with my father 2Ch 1:8
and **h** made me king in his place. 2Ch 1:8
for You **h** made me king over a 2Ch 1:9
h you even asked for long life, 2Ch 1:11
but you **h** asked for yourself 2Ch 1:11
over whom I **h** made you king, 2Ch 1:11
knowledge **h** been granted to you. 2Ch 1:12
whom I **h** in Judah and Jerusalem, 2Ch 2:7 5973
"I **h** built You a lofty house, 2Ch 6:2
but I **h** chosen Jerusalem that My 2Ch 6:6
and I **h** chosen David to be over My 2Ch 6:6
for I **h** risen in the place of my 2Ch 6:10
and **h** built the house for the name 2Ch 6:10
"There I **h** set the ark in 2Ch 6:11
that which You **h** promised him; 2Ch 6:15
You **h** spoken with Your mouth and 2Ch 6:15
and **h** fulfilled it with Your hand, 2Ch 6:15
that which You **h** promised him, 2Ch 6:16
My law as you **h** walked before Me.' 2Ch 6:16
h spoken to Your servant David. 2Ch 6:17
less this house which I **h** built. 2Ch 6:18
"Yet **h** regard to the prayer of 2Ch 6:19 6437
toward the place of which You **h** 2Ch 6:20
they **h** sinned against You, 2Ch 6:24
the land which You **h** given to them 2Ch 6:25
they **h** sinned against You, 2Ch 6:26
which You **h** given to Your people 2Ch 6:27
which You **h** given to our fathers. 2Ch 6:31
this house which I **h** built is called 2Ch 6:33
this city which You **h** chosen and 2Ch 6:34
which I **h** built for Your name, 2Ch 6:34
'We **h** sinned, we have committed 2Ch 6:37
sinned, we **h** committed iniquity and 2Ch 6:37
iniquity and **h** acted wickedly'; 2Ch 6:37
where they **h** been taken captive, 2Ch 6:38
You **h** given to their fathers and 2Ch 6:38
and the city which You **h** chosen, 2Ch 6:38
which I **h** built for Your name, 2Ch 6:38
people who **h** sinned against You. 2Ch 6:39
I **h** heard your prayer and have 2Ch 7:12
and **h** chosen this place for Myself 2Ch 7:12
"For now I **h** chosen and 2Ch 7:16
do according to all that I **h** commanded 2Ch 7:17
My commandments which I **h** set 2Ch 7:19
from My land which I **h** given you, 2Ch 7:20
this house which I **h** consecrated 2Ch 7:20
this people, who **h** spoken to me, 2Ch 10:9
"What portion do we **h** in David? 2Ch 10:16
We **h** no inheritance in the son of 2Ch 10:16
'You **h** forsaken Me, so I also 2Ch 12:5
h forsaken you to Shishak.' 2Ch 12:5
'They **h** humbled themselves *so* I 2Ch 12:7
"**H** you not driven out the priests 2Ch 13:9
God, and we **h** not forsaken Him; 2Ch 13:10
our God, but you **h** forsaken Him. 2Ch 13:11
we **h** sought the LORD our God; 2Ch 14:7
we **h** sought Him, and He has given 2Ch 14:7
and those who **h** no strength; 2Ch 14:11 369
h come against this multitude. 2Ch 14:11
I **h** sent you silver and gold; 2Ch 16:3
"Because you **h** relied on the king 2Ch 16:7
h not relied on the LORD your God, 2Ch 16:7
You **h** acted foolishly in this. 2Ch 16:9
now on you will surely **h** wars." 2Ch 16:9 3426
Like sheep which **h** no shepherd; 2Ch 18:16 369
'These **h** no master. 2Ch 18:16
for you **h** removed the Asheroth 2Ch 19:3
and you **h** set your heart 2Ch 19:3
will **h** no part in unrighteousness or 2Ch 19:7 369
"They **h** lived in it, and have built 2Ch 20:8
and **h** built You a sanctuary there 2Ch 20:8
You **h** given us as an inheritance. 2Ch 20:11
Therefore they **h** named that place 2Ch 20:26
h allied yourself with Ahaziah, 2Ch 20:37
'Because you **h** not walked in the 2Ch 21:12
but **h** walked in the way of the 2Ch 21:13
and **h** caused Judah and the 2Ch 21:13
you **h** also killed your brothers, 2Ch 21:13
"Why **h** you not required the 2Ch 24:6
Because you **h** forsaken the LORD, 2Ch 24:20
h given to the troops of Israel?" 2Ch 25:9
"Why **h** you sought the gods of the 2Ch 25:15
gods of the people who **h** not delivered 2Ch 25:15
"**H** we appointed you a royal 2Ch 25:16
you, because you **h** done this and 2Ch 25:16
h not listened to my counsel." 2Ch 25:16
'Behold, you **h** defeated Edom.' 2Ch 25:19
for you **h** been unfaithful and 2Ch 26:18
h no honor from the LORD God." 2Ch 26:18
and you **h** slain them in a rage 2Ch 28:9
do you not **h** transgressions 2Ch 28:10
"For our fathers **h** been 2Ch 29:6
h done evil in the sight of the LORD 2Ch 29:6
and **h** forsaken Him and turned 2Ch 29:6
LORD, and **h** turned *their* backs. 2Ch 29:6
"They **h** also shut the doors of 2Ch 29:7
and **h** not burned incense or 2Ch 29:7
our fathers **h** fallen by the sword, 2Ch 29:9
"We **h** cleansed the whole house of 2Ch 29:18
we **h** prepared and consecrated; 2Ch 29:19
"Now *that* you **h** consecrated 2Ch 29:31
we **h** had enough to eat with plenty 2Ch 31:10
what I and my fathers **h** done to all 2Ch 32:13
h not delivered their people from my 2Ch 32:17
which I **h** chosen from all the 2Ch 33:7
I **h** appointed for your fathers, 2Ch 33:8
to do all that I **h** commanded them 2Ch 33:8
"I **h** found the book of the law in 2Ch 34:15
"They **h** also emptied out the 2Ch 34:17
and **h** delivered it into the hands 2Ch 34:17
our fathers **h** not observed the word of 2Ch 34:21
in the book which they **h** read in the 2Ch 34:24
"Because they **h** forsaken Me and 2Ch 34:25
h burned incense to other gods, 2Ch 34:25
the words which you **h** heard, 2Ch 34:26
before Me, I truly **h** heard you, 2Ch 34:27
h to depart from their service, 2Ch 35:15 369
"What **h** we to do with each other, 2Ch 35:21
and we **h** been sacrificing to Him Ezr 4:2
"You **h** nothing in common with us Ezr 4:3
you **h** come to us at Jerusalem; Ezr 4:12
we **h** sent and informed the king, Ezr 4:14
and that they **h** incited revolt Ezr 4:15
you will **h** no possession in Ezr 4:16 383
revolt **h** been perpetrated in it, Ezr 4:19
kings **h** ruled over Jerusalem, Ezr 4:20
h gone to the province of Judah, Ezr 5:8
I, Darius, **h** issued *this* decree, Ezr 6:12
I **h** issued a decree that any of Ezr 7:13
h freely offered to the God of Israel, Ezr 7:15
you may **h** occasion to provide, Ezr 7:20 5308
the Levites **h** not separated themselves Ezr 9:1
"For they **h** taken some of their Ezr 9:2
and the rulers **h** been foremost in this Ezr 9:2
h risen above our heads and Ezr 9:6
fathers to this day we **h** *been* Ezr 9:7
our kings *and* our priests **h** been Ezr 9:7
we **h** forsaken Your commandments, Ezr 9:10
which You **h** commanded by Your Ezr 9:11
with their abominations which **h** Ezr 9:11
since You our God **h** requited Ezr 9:13
and **h** given us an escaped remnant Ezr 9:13
we **h** been left an escaped remnant, Ezr 9:15
"We **h** been unfaithful to our God and Ezr 10:2
and **h** married foreign women from Ezr 10:2
"You **h** been unfaithful and have Ezr 10:10
"You have been unfaithful and **h** Ezr 10:10
As you **h** said, so it is our duty Ezr 10:12
for we **h** transgressed greatly in Ezr 10:13
who **h** married foreign wives come at Ezr 10:14
which we **h** sinned against You; Ne 1:6
I and my father's house **h** sinned. Ne 1:6
"We **h** acted very corruptly Ne 1:7
and **h** not kept the commandments, Ne 1:7
though those of you who **h** been Ne 1:9
them to the place where I **h** chosen Ne 1:9
gates **h** been consumed by fire?" Ne 2:3
and build, but you **h** no portion, Ne 2:20 369
they **h** demoralized the builders. Ne 4:5
"We **h** borrowed money for the Ne 5:4
h redeemed our Jewish brothers Ne 5:8
neither I nor my kinsmen **h** eaten Ne 5:14
all that I **h** done for this people. Ne 5:19
"You **h** also appointed Ne 6:7
as you are saying **h** not been done, Ne 6:8
so that they might **h** an evil Ne 6:13 1961
You **h** made the heavens, The Ne 9:6
And You **h** fulfilled Your promise, Ne 9:8
For You **h** dealt faithfully, but Ne 9:33
but we **h** acted wickedly. Ne 9:33
and our fathers **h** not kept Your law Ne 9:34
with which You **h** admonished them. Ne 9:34
the kings Whom You **h** set over us Ne 9:37
my loyal deeds which I **h** performed Ne 13:14
and **h** compassion on me according Ne 13:22 2347
you **h** committed all this great evil by Ne 13:27
because they **h** defiled the Ne 13:29
who **h** heard of the queen's conduct Es 1:18
And I **h** not been summoned to come Es 4:11
whether you **h** not attained royalty Es 4:14
that I **h** prepared for him." Es 5:4
if I **h** found favor in the sight of Es 5:8
"**H** a gallows fifty cubits high Es 5:14
king to **h** Mordecai hanged on it; Es 5:14
robes and the horse as you **h** said, Es 6:10
anything of all that you **h** said." Es 6:10
before whom you **h** begun to fall, Es 6:13
"If I **h** found favor in your Es 7:3
for we **h** been sold, I and my Es 7:4
women, I would **h** remained silent, Es 7:4
pleases the king and if I **h** found favor Es 8:5
I **h** given the house of Haman to Es 8:7
and him they **h** hanged on the Es 8:7
"The Jews **h** killed and destroyed Es 9:12
What then **h** they done in the rest Es 9:12
"Perhaps my sons **h** sinned and Jb 1:5
"**H** you considered My servant Job? Jb 1:8
"**H** You not made a hedge about Jb 1:10
h blessed the work of his hands, Jb 1:10
h increased in the land. Jb 1:10
I alone **h** escaped to tell you." Jb 1:15
I alone **h** escaped to tell you." Jb 1:16

I alone **h** escaped to tell you." Jb 1:17
I alone **h** escaped to tell you." Jb 1:19
"Where **h** you come from?" Jb 2:2
"**H** you considered My servant Job? Jb 2:3
Let it wait for light but **h** none, Jb 3:9 369
would **h** lain down and been quiet; Jb 3:13
I would **h** slept then, I would have Jb 3:13
then, I would **h** been at rest, Jb 3:13
"Behold you **h** admonished many, Jb 4:3
And you **h** strengthened weak hands. Jb 4:3
h helped the tottering to stand, Jb 4:4
you **h** strengthened feeble knees. Jb 4:4
"According to what I **h** seen, Jb 4:8
"I **h** seen the foolish taking Jb 5:3
"Behold this; we **h** investigated Jb 5:27
Therefore my words **h** been rash. Jb 6:3
That I **h** not denied the words of Jb 6:10
h acted deceitfully like a wadi, Jb 6:15
"Indeed, you **h** now become such, Jb 6:21
"**H** I said, 'Give me *something*,' Jb 6:22
And show me how I **h** erred. Jb 6:24
"**H** I sinned? What have I done to Jb 7:20
What **h** I done to You, O watcher Jb 7:20
Why **h** You set me as Your target, Jb 7:20
I would **h** to implore the mercy of Jb 9:15
'**H** You eyes of flesh? Jb 10:4
now, that You **h** made me as clay; Jb 10:9
'You **h** granted me life and Jb 10:12
You **h** concealed in Your heart; Jb 10:13
Why then **h** You brought me out of Jb 10:18
I should **h** been as though I had not Jb 10:19
me that I may **h** a little cheer Jb 10:20 1082
"For you **h** said, Jb 11:4
As waters that **h** passed by, Jb 11:16
I **h** intelligence as well as you; Jb 12:3
"Behold now, I **h** prepared my case; Jb 13:18
his limits You **h** set so that he Jb 14:5
what I **h** seen I will also declare; Jb 15:17
What wise men **h** told, And have not Jb 15:18
And **h** not concealed from their Jb 15:18
"I **h** heard many such things; Jb 16:2
You **h** laid waste all my company. Jb 16:7
"You **h** shriveled me up, It Jb 16:8
h gaped at me with their mouth, Jb 16:10
They **h** slapped me on the cheek Jb 16:10
They **h** massed themselves against me. Jb 16:10
"I **h** sewed sackcloth over my Jb 16:15
"For You **h** kept their heart from Jb 17:4
"These ten times you **h** insulted me; Jb 19:3
"Even if I **h** truly erred, My Jb 19:4
"My relatives **h** failed, And my Jb 19:14
intimate friends **h** forgotten me. Jb 19:14
I **h** to implore him with my mouth. Jb 19:16
those I love **h** turned against me. Jb 19:19
And I **h** escaped *only* by the skin Jb 19:20
Those who **h** seen him will say, Jb 20:7
Then after I **h** spoken, you may Jb 21:3
"**H** you not asked wayfaring men, Jb 21:29
"For you **h** taken pledges of your Jb 22:6
you **h** given no water to drink, Jb 22:7
the hungry you **h** withheld bread. Jb 22:7
"You **h** sent widows away empty, Jb 22:9
path Which wicked men **h** trod, Jb 22:15
I **h** kept His way and not turned Jb 23:11
"I **h** not departed from the Jb 23:12
I **h** treasured the words of His Jb 23:12
h no covering against the cold. Jb 24:7 369
"Others **h** been with those who Jb 24:13
So does Sheol *those who* **h** sinned. Jb 24:19
How you **h** saved the arm without Jb 26:2
you **h** given to *one* without wisdom! Jb 26:3
insight you **h** abundantly provided! Jb 26:3
"To whom **h** you uttered words? Jb 26:4
"Behold, all of you **h** seen *it;* Jb 27:12
"The proud beasts **h** not trodden it, Jb 28:8
ears we **h** heard a report of it.' Jb 28:22
"And now I **h** become their taunt, Jb 30:9
I **h** even become a byword to them. Jb 30:9
h cast off the bridle before me. Jb 30:11
Days of affliction **h** seized me. Jb 30:16
I **h** become like dust and ashes. Jb 30:19
"You **h** become cruel to me; Jb 30:21
"**H** I not wept for the one whose Jb 30:25
"I **h** become a brother to jackals And Jb 30:29
"I **h** made a covenant with my eyes; Jb 31:1
"If I **h** walked with falsehood, Jb 31:5
Or I **h** lurked at my neighbor's Jb 31:9
"If I **h** despised the claim of my Jb 31:13
"If I **h** kept the poor from Jb 31:16
Or **h** caused the eyes of the widow Jb 31:16
Or **h** eaten my morsel alone, And Jb 31:17
If I **h** seen anyone perish for lack Jb 31:19
If his loins **h** not thanked me, And Jb 31:20
If I **h** lifted up my hand against Jb 31:21
"If I **h** put my confidence Jb 31:24
If I **h** gloated because my wealth Jb 31:25
If I **h** looked at the sun when it Jb 31:26
That too would **h** been an iniquity Jb 31:28
For I would **h** denied God above. Jb 31:28
"**H** I rejoiced at the extinction Jb 31:29
I **h** not allowed my mouth to sin By Jb 31:30
"**H** the men of my tent not said, Jb 31:31
For I **h** opened my doors to the Jb 31:32
"**H** I covered my transgressions Jb 31:33
I **h** eaten its fruit without money, Jb 31:39
Or **h** caused its owners to lose Jb 31:39
'We **h** found wisdom; Jb 32:13
Words **h** failed them. Jb 32:15
I too **h** been formed out of the clay. Jb 33:6
"Surely you **h** spoken in my Jb 33:8
I **h** heard the sound of *your* words: Jb 33:8
to the pit, I **h** found a ransom'; Jb 33:24
'I **h** sinned and perverted what is Jb 33:27
"*Then* if you **h** anything to say, Jb 33:32 3426
"But if *you* **h** understanding, Jb 34:16
'I **h** borne *chastisement;* Jb 34:31
If I **h** done iniquity, I will not do it Jb 34:32
terms, because you **h** rejected *it?* Jb 34:33
What profit will I **h**, Jb 35:3
"If you **h** sinned, what do you Jb 35:6
that they **h** magnified themselves. Jb 36:9
h preferred this to affliction. Jb 36:21
'You **h** done wrong'? Jb 36:23
His work, Of which men **h** sung. Jb 36:24
"All men **h** seen it; Jb 36:25
Tell *Me*, if you **h** understanding, Jb 38:4 3045
"**H** you ever in your life Jb 38:12
"**H** you entered into the springs Jb 38:16
"**H** the gates of death been Jb 38:17
Or **h** you seen the gates of deep Jb 38:17
"**H** you understood the expanse of Jb 38:18
"**H** you entered the storehouses of Jb 38:22
Or **h** you seen the storehouses of Jb 38:22
Which I **h** reserved for the time of Jb 38:23
"Will you **h** faith in him that he Jb 39:12 539
"Once I **h** spoken, and I will not Jb 40:5
"Or do you **h** an arm like God, And Jb 40:9
"Therefore I **h** declared that Jb 42:3
"I **h** heard of You by the hearing Jb 42:5
because you **h** not spoken of Me Jb 42:7
because you **h** not spoken of Me Jb 42:8
I **h** installed My King Upon Zion, Ps 2:6
My Son, Today I **h** begotten You. Ps 2:7
how my adversaries **h** increased! Ps 3:1
people Who **h** set themselves against Ps 3:6
For You **h** smitten all my enemies Ps 3:7
You **h** shattered the teeth of the Ps 3:7
You **h** relieved me in my distress; Ps 4:1
You **h** put gladness in my heart, Ps 4:7
my God, in You I **h** taken refuge; Ps 7:1
O LORD my God, if I **h** done this, Ps 7:3
If I **h** rewarded evil to my friend, Ps 7:4
Or **h** plundered him who without Ps 7:4
You **h** appointed judgment. Ps 7:6
Who **h** displayed Your splendor above Ps 8:1
babes You **h** established strength Ps 8:2
the stars, which You **h** ordained; Ps 8:3
Yet You **h** made him a little lower Ps 8:5
h put all things under his feet, Ps 8:6
You **h** maintained my just cause; Ps 9:4
You **h** sat on the throne judging Ps 9:4
You **h** rebuked the nations, Ps 9:5
You **h** destroyed the wicked; Ps 9:5
You **h** blotted out their name Ps 9:5
And You **h** uprooted the cities; Ps 9:6
h not forsaken those who seek You. Ps 9:10
The nations **h** sunk down in the pit Ps 9:15
down in the pit which they **h** made; Ps 9:15
in the plots which they **h** devised. Ps 10:2
You **h** seen *it*, for You have Ps 10:14
for You **h** beheld mischief and Ps 10:14
h been the helper of the orphan. Ps 10:14
Nations **h** perished from His land. Ps 10:16
You **h** heard the desire of the Ps 10:17
Who **h** said, "With our tongue we Ps 12:4
"I **h** overcome him," Ps 13:4
I **h** trusted in Your lovingkindness; Ps 13:5
they **h** committed abominable deeds; Ps 14:1
They **h** all turned aside, Ps 14:3
together they **h** become corrupt; Ps 14:3
I **h** no good besides You." Ps 16:2
those who **h** bartered for another Ps 16:4
The lines **h** fallen to me in Ps 16:6
I **h** set the LORD continually Ps 16:8
You **h** tried my heart; Ps 17:3
You **h** visited *me* by night; Ps 17:3
You **h** tested me and You find Ps 17:3
I **h** purposed that my mouth will Ps 17:3
by the word of Your lips I **h** kept Ps 17:4
My steps **h** held fast to Your paths. Ps 17:5
My feet **h** not slipped. Ps 17:5
I **h** called upon You, for You Ps 17:6
h closed their unfeeling Ps 17:10
They **h** now surrounded us in our Ps 17:11
For I **h** kept the ways of the LORD, Ps 18:21
And **h** not wickedly departed from Ps 18:21
You **h** also given me the shield of Ps 18:35
me, And my feet **h** not slipped. Ps 18:36
For You **h** girded me with strength Ps 18:39
You **h** subdued under me those who Ps 18:39
You **h** also made my enemies turn Ps 18:40
You **h** delivered me from the Ps 18:43
You **h** placed me as head of the Ps 18:43
whom I **h** not known serve me. Ps 18:43
They **h** bowed down and fallen, Ps 20:8
But we **h** risen and stood upright. Ps 20:8
You **h** given him his heart's Ps 21:2
And You **h** not withheld the Ps 21:2
my God, why **h** You forsaken me? Ps 22:1
And by night, but I **h** no rest. Ps 22:2
You **h** been my God from my Ps 22:10
Many bulls **h** surrounded me; Ps 22:12
of Bashan **h** encircled me. Ps 22:12
For dogs **h** surrounded me; Ps 22:16
You **h** anointed my head with oil; Ps 23:5
For they **h** been from of old. Ps 25:6
for I **h** walked in my integrity, Ps 26:1
And I **h** trusted in the LORD Ps 26:1
eyes, And I **h** walked in Your truth. Ps 26:3
One thing I **h** asked from the LORD, Ps 27:4
You **h** been my help; Ps 27:9
and my mother **h** forsaken me, Ps 27:10
witnesses **h** risen against me, Ps 27:12
I would **h** *despaired* unless I had Ps 27:13
O LORD, for You **h** lifted me up, Ps 30:1
And **h** not let my enemies rejoice Ps 30:1
You **h** brought up my soul from Ps 30:3
You **h** kept me alive, that I Ps 30:3
by Your favor You **h** made my Ps 30:7
You **h** turned for me my mourning Ps 30:11
You **h** loosed my sackcloth and Ps 30:11
In You, O LORD, I **h** taken refuge; Ps 31:1
which they **h** secretly laid for me, Ps 31:4
You **h** ransomed me, O LORD, God of Ps 31:5
Because You **h** seen my affliction; Ps 31:7
You **h** known the troubles of my Ps 31:7
And You **h** not given me over into Ps 31:8
h set my feet in a large Ps 31:8
I **h** become a reproach, Ps 31:11
For I **h** heard the slander of many, Ps 31:13
Which You **h** stored up for those Ps 31:19
Which You **h** wrought for those who Ps 31:19
the mule which **h** no understanding, Ps 32:9 369
According as we **h** hoped in You. Ps 33:22
"Aha, aha, our eyes **h** seen it!" Ps 35:21
You **h** seen it, O LORD, do not Ps 35:22
"We **h** swallowed him up!" Ps 35:25
the doers of iniquity **h** fallen; Ps 36:12
They **h** been thrust down and cannot Ps 36:12
The wicked **h** drawn the sword and Ps 37:14
of famine they will **h** abundance. Ps 37:19 7646
I **h** been young and now I am old Ps 37:25
Yet I **h** not seen the righteous Ps 37:25
I **h** seen a wicked, violent man Ps 37:35
man of peace will **h** a posterity. Ps 37:37
Your arrows **h** sunk deep into me, Ps 38:2
me **h** threatened destruction, Ps 38:12
h made my days *as* handbreadths, Ps 39:5
"I **h** become mute, I do not open Ps 39:9
Because it is You who **h** done *it*. Ps 39:9
are the wonders which You **h** done, Ps 40:5
meal offering You **h** not desired; Ps 40:6
My ears You **h** opened; Ps 40:6
sin offering You **h** not required. Ps 40:6
I **h** proclaimed glad tidings of Ps 40:9
I **h** not hidden Your righteousness Ps 40:10
I **h** spoken of Your faithfulness and Ps 40:10
I **h** not concealed Your Ps 40:10
beyond number **h** surrounded me; Ps 40:12
My iniquities **h** overtaken me, so Ps 40:12
for I **h** sinned against You." Ps 41:4
I **h** been my food day and night, Ps 42:3
h you become disturbed Ps 42:5
and Your waves **h** rolled over me. Ps 42:7
"Why **h** You forgotten me? Ps 42:9
And why **h** you become disturbed Ps 42:11
why **h** You rejected me? Ps 43:2
O God, we **h** heard with our ears, Ps 44:1
our ears, Our fathers **h** told us The Ps 44:1
But You **h** saved us from our Ps 44:7
And You **h** put to shame those who Ps 44:7
In God we **h** boasted all day long, Ps 44:8
Yet You **h** rejected *us* and brought Ps 44:9
those who hate us **h** taken spoil Ps 44:10
And **h** scattered us among the Ps 44:11
And **h** not profited by their sale. Ps 44:12
us, but we **h** not forgotten You, Ps 44:17
And we **h** not dealt falsely with Ps 44:17
steps **h** not deviated from Your way, Ps 44:18
Yet You **h** crushed us in a place Ps 44:19
You **h** loved righteousness and Ps 45:7
instruments **h** made You glad. Ps 45:8
princes of the people **h** assembled Ps 47:9
As we **h** heard, so have we seen In Ps 48:8
so **h** we seen In the city of the Ps 48:8
h thought on Your lovingkindness, Ps 48:9
They **h** called their lands after Ps 49:11
So that they **h** no habitation. Ps 49:14
Those who **h** made a covenant with Ps 50:5
"What right **h** you to tell of My Ps 50:16
"These things you **h** done and Ps 50:21
You, You only, I **h** sinned And Ps 51:4
bones which You **h** broken rejoice. Ps 51:8
forever, because You **h** done *it*, Ps 52:9
and **h** committed abominable Ps 53:1
together they **h** become corrupt; Ps 53:3
H the workers of wickedness no Ps 53:4 3045
bread And **h** not called upon God? Ps 53:4
For strangers **h** risen against me And Ps 54:3
And violent men **h** sought my life; Ps 54:3
They **h** not set God before them Ps 54:3
terrors of death **h** fallen upon me. Ps 55:4
For I **h** seen violence and strife Ps 55:9
h trampled upon me all day long, Ps 56:2
I praise, In God I **h** put my trust; Ps 56:4
As they **h** waited *to take* my life. Ps 56:6
You **h** taken account of my Ps 56:8
In God I **h** put my trust, I shall Ps 56:11
h delivered my soul from death, Ps 56:13
h prepared a net for my steps; Ps 57:6
themselves **h** fallen into the midst of it Ps 57:6
They **h** venom like the venom of a Ps 58:4
they **h** set an ambush for my life; Ps 59:3
For You **h** been my stronghold And Ps 59:16
O God, You **h** rejected us. Ps 60:1
You **h** broken us; Ps 60:1
You **h** been angry; Ps 60:1

You **h** made the land quake, You — Ps 60:2
land quake, You **h** split it open; — Ps 60:2
You **h** made Your people experience — Ps 60:3
You **h** given us wine to drink that — Ps 60:3
You **h** given a banner to those who — Ps 60:4
H not You Yourself, O God, — Ps 60:10
For You **h** been a refuge for me, A — Ps 61:3
For You **h** heard my vows, O God; — Ps 61:5
You **h** given *me* the inheritance of — Ps 61:5
They **h** counseled only to thrust — Ps 62:4
Twice I **h** heard this: — Ps 62:11
I **h** seen You in the sanctuary, — Ps 63:2
For You **h** been my help, And in — Ps 63:7
Who **h** sharpened their tongue like — Ps 64:3
You **h** crowned the year with Your — Ps 65:11
For You **h** tried us, O God; — Ps 66:10
You **h** refined us as silver is — Ps 66:10
You **h** ascended on high, You have — Ps 68:18
You **h** led captive *Your* captives; — Ps 68:18
You **h** received gifts among men, — Ps 68:18
The tongue of your dogs *may* **h** its — Ps 68:23
They **h** seen Your procession, O God, — Ps 68:24
O God, who **h** acted on our behalf. — Ps 68:28
the waters **h** threatened my life. — Ps 69:1
I **h** sunk in deep mire, and there — Ps 69:2
I **h** come into deep waters, and a — Ps 69:2
not steal, I then **h** to restore. — Ps 69:4
for Your sake I **h** borne reproach; — Ps 69:7
I **h** become estranged from my — Ps 69:8 — 1961
who reproach You **h** fallen on me. — Ps 69:9
For they **h** persecuted him whom — Ps 69:26
him whom You Yourself **h** smitten, — Ps 69:26
pain of those whom You **h** wounded. — Ps 69:26
The humble **h** seen *it and* are glad; — Ps 69:32
In You, O LORD, I **h** taken refuge; — Ps 71:1
h given commandment to save me, — Ps 71:3
I **h** been sustained from *my* birth; — Ps 71:6
I **h** become a marvel to many, — Ps 71:7
my enemies **h** spoken against me; — Ps 71:10
for my life **h** consulted together, — Ps 71:10
You **h** taught me from my youth, — Ps 71:17
You who **h** done great things; — Ps 71:19
who **h** shown me many troubles and — Ps 71:20
my soul, which You **h** redeemed. — Ps 71:23
He will **h** compassion on the poor — Ps 72:13 — 2347
They **h** set their mouth against the — Ps 73:9
ease, they **h** increased *in* wealth. — Ps 73:12
in vain I **h** kept my heart pure And — Ps 73:13
I **h** been stricken all day long And — Ps 73:14
I would **h** betrayed the generation — Ps 73:15
h taken hold of my right hand. — Ps 73:23
Whom **h** I in heaven *but You?* — Ps 73:25
You **h** destroyed all those who are — Ps 73:27
I **h** made the Lord GOD my refuge, — Ps 73:28
why **h** You rejected *us* forever? — Ps 74:1
which You **h** purchased of old, — Ps 74:2
Which You **h** redeemed to be the — Ps 74:2
Mount Zion, where You **h** dwelt. — Ps 74:2
Your adversaries **h** roared in the — Ps 74:4
They **h** set up their own standards — Ps 74:4
They **h** burned Your sanctuary to the — Ps 74:7
They **h** defiled the dwelling place — Ps 74:7
They **h** burned all the meeting — Ps 74:8
You **h** prepared the light and the — Ps 74:16
You **h** established all the — Ps 74:17
You **h** made summer and winter. — Ps 74:17
It is I who **h** firmly set its pillars — Ps 75:3
You **h** held my eyelids — Ps 77:4
I **h** considered the days of old, — Ps 77:5
You **h** made known Your strength — Ps 77:14
You **h** by Your power redeemed Your — Ps 77:15
Which we **h** heard and known, And — Ps 78:3
known, And our fathers **h** told us. — Ps 78:3
h invaded Your inheritance; — Ps 79:1
They **h** defiled Your holy temple; — Ps 79:1
They **h** laid Jerusalem in ruins. — Ps 79:1
They **h** given the dead bodies of — Ps 79:2
They **h** poured out their blood like — Ps 79:3
We **h** become a reproach to our — Ps 79:4 — 1961
For they **h** devoured Jacob And — Ps 79:7
with which they **h** reproached You, — Ps 79:12
You **h** fed them with the bread of — Ps 80:5
And You **h** made them to drink — Ps 80:5
Why **h** You broken down its hedges, — Ps 80:12
You **h** strengthened for Yourself. — Ps 80:15
hate You **h** exalted themselves. — Ps 83:2
They **h** said, "Come, and let us wipe — Ps 83:4
For they **h** conspired together with — Ps 83:5
They **h** become a help to the — Ps 83:8 — 1961
Lovingkindness and truth **h** met — Ps 85:10
Righteousness and peace **h** kissed — Ps 85:10
All nations whom You **h** made shall — Ps 86:9
And You **h** delivered my soul from — Ps 86:13
men **h** risen up against me, — Ps 86:14
of violent men **h** sought my life, — Ps 86:14
they **h** not set You before them. — Ps 86:14
h helped me and comforted me. — Ps 86:17
I **h** cried out by day and in the — Ps 88:1
I **h** become like a man without — Ps 88:4 — 1961
You **h** put me in the lowest pit, — Ps 88:6
And You **h** afflicted me with all — Ps 88:7
You **h** removed my acquaintances — Ps 88:8
You **h** made me an object of — Ps 88:8
I **h** called upon You every day, O — Ps 88:9
I **h** spread out my hands to You. — Ps 88:9
h cried out to You for help, — Ps 88:13
Your terrors **h** destroyed me. — Ps 88:16
They **h** surrounded me like water — Ps 88:17
They **h** encompassed me altogether. — Ps 88:17

You **h** removed lover and friend — Ps 88:18
For I **h** said, "Lovingkindness will be — Ps 89:2
"I **h** made a covenant with My — Ps 89:3
I **h** sworn to David My servant, — Ps 89:3
it contains, You **h** founded them. — Ps 89:11
the south, You **h** created them; — Ps 89:12
You **h** a strong arm; — Ps 89:13
"I **h** given help to one who is — Ps 89:19
I **h** exalted one chosen from the — Ps 89:19
"I **h** found David My servant; — Ps 89:20
With My holy oil I **h** anointed him, — Ps 89:20
"Once I **h** sworn by My holiness; — Ps 89:35
But You **h** cast off and rejected, — Ps 89:38
You **h** been full of wrath against — Ps 89:38
You **h** spurned the covenant of Your — Ps 89:39
You **h** profaned his crown in the — Ps 89:39
You **h** broken down all his walls; — Ps 89:40
You **h** brought his strongholds to — Ps 89:40
You **h** exalted the right hand of — Ps 89:42
You **h** made all his enemies rejoice. — Ps 89:42
h not made him stand in battle. — Ps 89:43
You **h** made his splendor to cease And — Ps 89:44
You **h** shortened the days of his — Ps 89:45
You **h** covered him with shame. — Ps 89:45
h created all the sons of men! — Ps 89:47
which Your enemies **h** reproached, — Ps 89:51
With which they **h** reproached the — Ps 89:51
You **h** been our dwelling place in — Ps 90:1
You **h** swept them away like a flood, — Ps 90:5
we **h** been consumed by Your anger — Ps 90:7
by Your wrath we **h** been dismayed. — Ps 90:7
You **h** placed our iniquities — Ps 90:8
our days **h** declined in Your fury; — Ps 90:9
We **h** finished our years like a — Ps 90:9
to the days You **h** afflicted us, — Ps 90:15
us, *And* the years we **h** seen evil. — Ps 90:15
For you **h** made the LORD, my — Ps 91:9
h made me glad by what You have — Ps 92:4
made me glad by what You **h** done, — Ps 92:4
But You **h** exalted my horn like — Ps 92:10
I **h** been anointed with fresh oil. — Ps 92:10
The floods **h** lifted up, O LORD, — Ps 93:3
floods **h** lifted up their voice, — Ps 93:3
They **h** said, — Ps 94:7
h dwelt in *the abode of* silence. — Ps 94:17
all the peoples **h** seen His glory. — Ps 97:6
And the daughters of Judah **h** — Ps 97:8
arm **h** gained the victory for Him. — Ps 98:1
h seen the salvation of our God. — Ps 98:3
You **h** established equity; — Ps 99:4
You **h** executed justice and — Ps 99:4
my days **h** been consumed in smoke, — Ps 102:3
h been scorched like a hearth. — Ps 102:3
I **h** become like an owl of the — Ps 102:6
I **h** become like a lonely bird on a — Ps 102:7
h reproached me all day long; — Ps 102:8
me **h** used my *name* as a curse. — Ps 102:8
For I **h** eaten ashes like bread And — Ps 102:9
h lifted me up and cast me away. — Ps 102:10
arise *and* **h** compassion on Zion; — Ps 102:13 — 7355
In wisdom You **h** made them all; — Ps 104:24
Leviathan, which You **h** formed — Ps 104:26
to my God while I **h** my being. — Ps 104:33
We **h** sinned like our fathers, We — Ps 106:6
fathers, We **h** committed iniquity, — Ps 106:6
iniquity, we **h** behaved wickedly. — Ps 106:6
They **h** seen the works of the LORD, — Ps 107:24
H not You Yourself, O God, — Ps 108:11
For they **h** opened the wicked and — Ps 109:2
They **h** spoken against me with a — Ps 109:2
They **h** also surrounded me with — Ps 109:3
they **h** repaid me evil for good And — Ps 109:5
also **h** become a reproach to them; — Ps 109:25
You, LORD, **h** done it. — Ps 109:27
A good understanding **h** all those — Ps 111:10
They **h** mouths, but they cannot — Ps 115:5
They **h** eyes, but they cannot see; — Ps 115:5
They **h** ears, but they cannot hear; — Ps 115:6
They **h** noses, but they cannot — Ps 115:6
They **h** hands, but they cannot feel; — Ps 115:7
They **h** feet, but they cannot walk; — Ps 115:7
You **h** rescued my soul from death, — Ps 116:8
handmaid, You **h** loosed my bonds. — Ps 116:16
to You, for You **h** answered me, — Ps 118:21
And You **h** become my salvation. — Ps 118:21
We **h** blessed you from the house of — Ps 118:26
You **h** ordained Your precepts, That — Ps 119:4
With all my heart I **h** sought You; — Ps 119:10
word I **h** treasured in my heart, — Ps 119:11
With my lips I **h** told of All the — Ps 119:13
I **h** rejoiced in the way of Your — Ps 119:14
I **h** told of my ways, and You have — Ps 119:26
my ways, and You **h** answered me; — Ps 119:26
I **h** chosen the faithful way; — Ps 119:30
I **h** placed Your ordinances *before me* — Ps 119:30
So I will **h** an answer for him who — Ps 119:42 — 6030a
In which You **h** made me hope. — Ps 119:49
I **h** remembered Your ordinances — Ps 119:52
I **h** promised to keep Your words. — Ps 119:57
of the wicked **h** encircled me, — Ps 119:61
me, *But* I **h** not forgotten Your law. — Ps 119:61
h dealt well with Your servant, — Ps 119:65
h forged a lie against me; — Ps 119:69
faithfulness You **h** afflicted me. — Ps 119:75
Though I **h** become like a wineskin — Ps 119:83
The arrogant **h** dug pits for me, — Ps 119:85
They **h** persecuted me with a lie; — Ps 119:86
would **h** perished in my affliction. — Ps 119:92
For by them You **h** revived me. — Ps 119:93

For I **h** sought Your precepts. — Ps 119:94
I **h** seen a limit to all perfection; — Ps 119:96
I **h** more insight than all my — Ps 119:99
Because I **h** observed Your precepts. — Ps 119:100
I **h** restrained my feet from every — Ps 119:101
I **h** not turned aside from Your — Ps 119:102
For You Yourself **h** taught me. — Ps 119:102
I **h** sworn and I will confirm it, — Ps 119:106
The wicked **h** laid a snare for me, — Ps 119:110
Yet I **h** not gone astray from Your — Ps 119:110
I **h** inherited Your testimonies — Ps 119:111
I **h** inclined my heart to perform — Ps 119:112
That I may **h** regard for Your — Ps 119:117 — 8159
You **h** rejected all those who — Ps 119:118
You **h** removed all the wicked of — Ps 119:119
I **h** done justice and righteousness; — Ps 119:121
to act, *For* they **h** broken Your law. — Ps 119:126
do not let any iniquity **h** dominion — Ps 119:133 — 7980
You **h** commanded Your testimonies — Ps 119:138
adversaries **h** forgotten Your words. — Ps 119:139
and anguish **h** come upon me, — Ps 119:143
I **h** known from Your testimonies That — Ps 119:152
That You **h** founded them forever. — Ps 119:152
who love Your law **h** great peace, — Ps 119:165
me, For I **h** chosen Your precepts — Ps 119:173
I **h** gone astray like a lost sheep; — Ps 119:176
they would **h** swallowed us alive, — Ps 124:3
the waters would **h** engulfed us, — Ps 124:4
would **h** swept over our soul; — Ps 124:4
would **h** swept over our soul." — Ps 124:5
snare is broken and we **h** escaped. — Ps 124:7
"Many times they **h** persecuted me — Ps 129:1
"Many times they **h** persecuted me — Ps 129:2
they **h** not prevailed against me. — Ps 129:2
of the depths I **h** cried to You, — Ps 130:1
I **h** composed and quieted my soul; — Ps 131:2
I will dwell, for I **h** desired it. — Ps 132:14
I **h** prepared a lamp for Mine — Ps 132:17
will **h** compassion on His servants. — Ps 135:14 — 5162
They **h** mouths, but they do not — Ps 135:16
They **h** eyes, but they do not see; — Ps 135:16
They **h** ears, but they do not hear, — Ps 135:17
with which you **h** repaid us. — Ps 137:8
For You **h** magnified Your word — Ps 138:2
h heard the words of Your mouth. — Ps 138:4
You **h** searched me and known *me.* — Ps 139:1
h enclosed me behind and before, — Ps 139:5
eyes **h** seen my unformed substance — Ps 139:16
They **h** become my enemies. — Ps 139:22
Who **h** purposed to trip up my feet. — Ps 140:4
The proud **h** hidden a trap for me, — Ps 140:5
They **h** spread a net by the — Ps 140:5
They **h** set snares for me — Ps 140:5
You **h** covered my head in the day — Ps 140:7
Our bones **h** been scattered at the — Ps 141:7
the trap which they **h** set for me, — Ps 141:9
walk They **h** hidden a trap for me. — Ps 142:3
like those who **h** long been dead. — Ps 143:3
to my God while I **h** my being. — Ps 146:2
ordinances, they **h** not known them. — Ps 147:20
us, We shall all **h** one purse," — Pr 1:14 — 1961
give *it,*" When you **h** it with you. — Pr 3:28 — 3426
I **h** directed you in the way of — Pr 4:11
I **h** led you in upright paths. — Pr 4:11
"How I **h** hated instruction! — Pr 5:12
"I **h** not listened to the — Pr 5:13
if you **h** become surety for your — Pr 6:1
H given a pledge for a stranger, — Pr 6:1
If you **h** been snared with the — Pr 6:2
H been caught with the words of — Pr 6:2
Since you **h** come into the hand of — Pr 6:3
Today I **h** paid my vows. — Pr 7:14
I **h** come out to meet you, — Pr 7:15
earnestly, and I **h** found you. — Pr 7:15
I **h** spread my couch with — Pr 7:16
I **h** sprinkled my bed With myrrh, — Pr 7:17
And drink of the wine I **h** mixed. — Pr 9:5
his land will **h** plenty of bread, — Pr 12:11 — 7646
But counselors of peace **h** joy. — Pr 12:20
will **h** his fill of his own ways, — Pr 14:14 — 7646
And his children will **h** refuge. — Pr 14:26 — 1961
you will only **h** to do it again. — Pr 19:19
I **h** cleansed my heart, I am pure — Pr 20:9
rich and the poor **h** a common bond, — Pr 22:2 — 6298
in the LORD, I **h** taught you today, — Pr 22:19
H I not written to you excellent — Pr 22:20
you **h** nothing with which to pay, — Pr 22:27 — 369
boundary Which your fathers **h** set. — Pr 22:28
vomit up the morsel you **h** eaten, — Pr 23:8
the prince, Whom your eyes **h** seen. — Pr 25:7
H you found honey? — Pr 25:16
you not **h** it in excess and vomit it. — Pr 25:16 — 7646
his land will **h** plenty of food, — Pr 28:19 — 7646
pursuits will **h** poverty in plenty. — Pr 28:19 — 7646
shuts his eyes will **h** many curses. — Pr 28:27
poor man and the oppressor **h** this — Pr 29:13 — 6298
not **h** the understanding of a man. — Pr 30:2
Neither **h** I learned wisdom, Nor do — Pr 30:3
I **h** the knowledge of the Holy One. — Pr 30:3 — 3045
"I **h** done no wrong." — Pr 30:20
The locusts **h** no king, Yet all of — Pr 30:27 — 369
If you **h** been foolish in exalting — Pr 30:32
yourself Or if you **h** plotted *evil,* — Pr 30:32
And he will **h** no lack of gain. — Pr 31:11 — 2637
"Many daughters **h** done nobly, But — Pr 31:29
What advantage does man **h** in all — Ec 1:3
h been king over Israel in — Ec 1:12
I **h** seen all the works which have — Ec 1:14
which **h** been done under the sun, — Ec 1:14

I **h** magnified and increased wisdom Ec 1:16
then **h** I been extremely wise?" Ec 2:15
Yet he will **h** control over all the Ec 2:19
for which I **h** labored by acting wisely Ec 2:19
This also I **h** seen that it is Ec 2:24
who can **h** enjoyment without Him? Ec 2:25 2363b
I **h** seen the task which God has Ec 3:10
I **h** seen under the sun *that* in the Ec 3:16
they all **h** the same breath and Ec 3:19
I **h** seen that nothing is Ec 3:22
I **h** seen that every labor and Ec 4:4
h a good return for their labor. Ec 4:9 3426
I **h** seen all the living under the Ec 4:15
evil *which* I **h** seen under the sun: Ec 5:13
I **h** seen to be good and fitting: Ec 5:18
There is an evil which I **h** seen Ec 6:1
does not even **h** a *proper* burial, Ec 6:3 1961
does the wise man **h** over the fool? Ec 6:8
advantage does the poor man **h**, Ec 6:8
I **h** seen everything during my Ec 7:15
For you also **h** realized that you Ec 7:22
h many times cursed others. Ec 7:22
"Behold, I **h** discovered this," Ec 7:27
am still seeking but **h** not found. Ec 7:28
I **h** found one man among a Ec 7:28
but I **h** not found a woman among Ec 7:28
"Behold, I **h** found only this, Ec 7:29
they **h** sought out many devices." Ec 7:29
All this I **h** seen and applied my Ec 8:9
then, I **h** seen the wicked buried, Ec 8:10
For I **h** taken all this to my heart Ec 9:1
nor **h** they any longer a reward, Ec 9:5 369
and their zeal **h** already perished, Ec 9:6
and they will no longer **h** a share Ec 9:6 369
which you **h** labored under the sun. Ec 9:9
is an evil I **h** seen under the sun, Ec 10:5
I **h** seen slaves *riding* on horses Ec 10:7
"I **h** no delight in them" Ec 12:1 369
"Your oils **h** a pleasing SS 1:3
But I **h** not taken care of my own SS 1:6
h *already* appeared in the land; SS 2:12
h given forth *their* fragrance. SS 2:13
'**H** you seen him whom my soul loves?' SS 3:3
h descended from Mount Gilead. SS 4:1
h come up from *their* washing, SS 4:2
"You **h** made my heart beat faster, SS 4:9
You **h** made my heart beat faster SS 4:9
I **h** come into my garden, my SS 5:1
I **h** gathered my myrrh along with SS 5:1
I **h** eaten my honeycomb and my SS 5:1
I **h** drunk my wine and my milk. SS 5:1
"I **h** taken off my dress, How can SS 5:3
I **h** washed my feet, How can I SS 5:3
from me, For they **h** confused me; SS 6:5
That **h** descended from Gilead. SS 6:5
h come up from *their* washing, SS 6:6
budded *And its* blossoms **h** opened, SS 7:12
the pomegranates **h** bloomed. SS 7:12
mandrakes **h** given forth fragrance; SS 7:13
old, Which I **h** saved up for you, SS 7:13
"We **h** a little sister, And she SS 8:8
"Sons I **h** reared and brought up, Is 1:2
But they **h** revolted against Me. Is 1:2
They **h** abandoned the LORD, They Is 1:4
They **h** despised the Holy One of Is 1:4
They **h** turned away from Him. Is 1:4
I **h** had enough of burnt Is 1:11
They **h** become a burden to Me; Is 1:14
of the oaks which you **h** desired, Is 1:29
at the gardens which you **h** chosen. Is 1:29
For You **h** abandoned Your people, Is 2:6
That which their fingers **h** made. Is 2:8
For the LORD of hosts will **h** a day Is 2:12
"You **h** a cloak, you shall be our Is 3:6
they **h** brought evil on themselves. Is 3:9
you who **h** devoured the vineyard; Is 3:14
vineyard that I **h** not done in it? Is 5:4
So that you **h** to live alone in the Is 5:8
For they **h** rejected the law of the Is 5:24
For my eyes **h** seen the King, the Is 6:5
Arameans **h** camped in Ephraim," Is 7:2
h no fear and do not be Is 7:4 3372a
such days as **h** never come since the Is 7:17
these people **h** rejected the gently Is 8:6
it is because they **h** no dawn. Is 8:20 369
"The bricks **h** fallen down, But we Is 9:10
The sycamores **h** been cut down, But Is 9:10
Nor does He **h** pity on their Is 9:17 7355
h done to Samaria and her idols?" Is 10:11
I did *this*, For I **h** understanding; Is 10:13 995
the house of Jacob who **h** escaped, Is 10:20
They **h** gone through the pass, Is 10:29
of Gebim **h** sought refuge. Is 10:31
I **h** commanded My consecrated ones, Is 13:3
I **h** even called My mighty Is 13:3
They will not even **h** compassion on Is 13:18 7355
LORD will **h** compassion on Jacob Is 14:1 7355
in which you **h** been enslaved, Is 14:3
'Even you **h** been made weak as we, Is 14:10
weak as we, You **h** become like us. Is 14:10
H been brought down to Sheol; Is 14:11
"How you **h** fallen from heaven, O Is 14:12
You **h** been cut down to the earth, Is 14:12
You who **h** weakened the nations! Is 14:12
"But you **h** been cast out of your Is 14:19
Because you **h** ruined your country, Is 14:20
country, You **h** slain your people. Is 14:20
as I **h** intended so it has happened, Is 14:24
as I **h** planned so it will stand, Is 14:24

They **h** gone up to the temple and Is 15:2
In their streets they **h** girded Is 15:3
the abundance *which* they **h** acquired Is 15:7
Oppressors **h** completely Is 16:4
We **h** heard of the pride of Moab, Is 16:6
the fields of Heshbon **h** withered, Is 16:8
The lords of the nations **h** Is 16:8
I **h** made the shouting to cease. Is 16:10
man will **h** regard for his Maker And Is 17:7 8159
will not **h** regard for the altars, Is 17:8 8159
to that which his fingers **h** made, Is 17:8
For you **h** forgotten the God of Is 17:10
h not remembered the rock of your Is 17:10
princes of Zoan **h** acted foolishly, Is 19:13
of her tribes **H** led Egypt astray. Is 19:13
They **h** led Egypt astray in all Is 19:14
I **h** made an end of all the Is 21:2
Pains **h** seized me like the pains Is 21:3
I **h** heard from the LORD of hosts, Is 21:10
For they **h** fled from the swords, Is 21:15
h all gone up to the housetops? Is 22:1
All your rulers **h** fled together, Is 22:3
h been captured without the bow; Is 22:3
'What right do you **h** here, Is 22:16
have here, And whom do you **h** here, Is 22:16
h hewn a tomb for yourself here, Is 22:16
"I **h** neither travailed nor given Is 23:4
I **h** neither brought up young men Is 23:4
For You **h** worked wonders, Plans Is 25:1
You **h** made a city into a heap, Is 25:2
For You **h** been a defense for the Is 25:4
we **h** waited that He might save us. Is 25:9
is the LORD for whom we **h** waited; Is 25:9
"We **h** a strong city; Is 26:1
we **h** an everlasting Rock. Is 26:4
We **h** waited for You eagerly; Is 26:8
Since You **h** also performed for us Is 26:12
masters besides You **h** ruled us; Is 26:13
You **h** punished and destroyed Is 26:14
And You **h** wiped out all Is 26:14
You **h** increased the nation, O Is 26:15
LORD, You **h** increased the nation, Is 26:15
You **h** extended all the borders of Is 26:15
"I **h** no wrath. Should someone give Is 27:4 369
of His slain, **h** they been slain? Is 27:7
will not **h** compassion on them. Is 27:11 7355
Because you **h** said, Is 28:15
"We **h** made a covenant with death, Is 28:15
And with Sheol we **h** made a pact. Is 28:15
For we **h** made falsehood our refuge Is 28:15
h concealed ourselves with deception." Is 28:15
For I **h** heard from the Lord GOD of Is 28:22
Therefore, I **h** called her Is 30:7
"Since you **h** rejected this word And Is 30:12
And **h** put your trust in oppression Is 30:12
and guile, and **h** relied on them, Is 30:12
on high to **h** compassion on you. Is 30:18 7355
You will **h** songs as in the night Is 30:29 1961
from whom you **h** deeply defected Is 31:6
which your sinful hands **h** made Is 31:7
watch-tower **h** become caves forever, Is 32:14
we **h** waited for You. Is 33:2
"You **h** conceived chaff, you will Is 33:11
are far away, hear what I **h** done; Is 33:13
whom I **h** devoted to destruction. Is 34:5
is this confidence that you **h**? Is 36:4 982
that you **h** rebelled against me? Is 36:5
"**H** I now come up without the Is 36:10
And when **h** they delivered Samaria Is 36:19
h delivered their land from my hand, Is 36:20
for children **h** come to birth, and Is 37:3
of the words that you **h** heard, Is 37:6
king of Assyria **h** blasphemed Me. Is 37:6
you **h** heard what the kings of Is 37:11
Assyria **h** done to all the lands, Is 37:11
of those nations which my fathers **h** Is 37:12
You **h** made heaven and earth. Is 37:16
the kings of Assyria **h** devastated Is 37:18
h cast their gods into the fire, Is 37:19
So they **h** destroyed them. Is 37:19
'Because you **h** prayed to Me about Is 37:21
h you reproached and blasphemed? Is 37:23
whom **h** you raised *your* voice Is 37:23
you **h** reproached the Lord, Is 37:24
the Lord, And you **h** said, Is 37:24
"**H** you not heard? Long ago I did it, Is 37:26
Now I **h** brought it to pass, That Is 37:26
how I **h** walked before You in Is 38:3
and **h** done what is good in Your Is 38:3
"I **h** heard your prayer, I have Is 38:5
your prayer, I **h** seen your tears; Is 38:5
For You **h** cast all my sins behind Is 38:17
from where **h** they come to you?" Is 39:3
h come to me from a far country, Is 39:3
"What **h** they seen in your house?" Is 39:4
h seen all that is in my house; Is 39:4
that I **h** not shown them." Is 39:4
and all that your fathers **h** laid Is 39:6
LORD which you **h** spoken is good." Is 39:8
Do you not know? **H** you not heard? Is 40:21
H you not understood from the Is 40:21
Scarcely **h** they been planted, Is 40:24
Scarcely **h** they been sown, Is 40:24
Do you not know? **H** you not heard? Is 40:28
coastlands **h** seen and are afraid; Is 41:5
They **h** drawn near and have come. Is 41:5
They have drawn near and **h** come. Is 41:5
My servant, Jacob whom I **h** chosen, Is 41:8
You whom I **h** taken from the ends Is 41:9

I **h** chosen you and not rejected Is 41:9
"Behold, I **h** made you a new, Is 41:15
"I **h** aroused one from the north, Is 41:25
I **h** put My Spirit upon Him; Is 42:1
I **h** called you in righteousness, Is 42:6
the former things **h** come to pass, Is 42:9
"I **h** kept silent for a long time, Is 42:14
I **h** kept still and restrained Is 42:14
You **h** seen many things, but you do Is 42:20
They **h** become a prey with none to Is 42:22
LORD, against whom we **h** sinned, Is 42:24
"Do not fear, for I **h** redeemed you; Is 43:1
I **h** called you by name; Is 43:1
I **h** given Egypt as your ransom, Is 43:3
And whom I **h** created for My glory, Is 43:7
for My glory, Whom I **h** formed, Is 43:7
even whom I **h** made." Is 43:7
blind, even though they **h** eyes, Is 43:8 3426
the deaf, even though they **h** ears. Is 43:8
All the nations **h** gathered Is 43:9
"And My servant whom I **h** chosen, Is 43:10
"It is I who **h** declared and saved Is 43:12
"For your sake I **h** sent to Is 43:14
They **h** been quenched Is 43:17
Because I **h** given waters in the Is 43:20
"Yet you **h** not called on Me, O Is 43:22
But you **h** become weary of Me, O Is 43:22
"You **h** not brought to Me the Is 43:23
Nor **h** you honored Me with your Is 43:23
I **h** not burdened you with Is 43:23
"You **h** bought Me not sweet cane Is 43:24
Nor **h** you filled Me with the Is 43:24
you **h** burdened Me with your sins, Is 43:24
You **h** wearied Me with your Is 43:24
h transgressed against Me. Is 43:27
And Israel, whom I **h** chosen: Is 44:1
And you Jeshurun whom I **h** chosen. Is 44:2
H I not long since announced *it* to Is 44:8
I am warm, I **h** seen the fire." Is 44:16
"I **h** burned half of it in the Is 44:19
also **h** baked bread over its coals. Is 44:19
I **h** formed you, you are My Is 44:21
"I **h** wiped out your transgressions Is 44:22
to Me, for I **h** redeemed you." Is 44:22
Whom I **h** taken by the right hand, Is 45:1
I **h** also called you by your name Is 45:4
I **h** given you a title of honor Is 45:4
honor Though you **h** not known Me. Is 45:4
you, though you **h** not known Me; Is 45:5
I, the LORD, **h** created it. Is 45:8
h aroused him in Is 45:13
h not spoken in secret, In Is 45:19
They **h** no knowledge, Who carry Is 45:20 3045
"I **h** sworn by Myself, The word Is 45:23
over, they **h** bowed down together; Is 46:2
But **h** themselves gone into Is 46:2
who **h** been borne by Me from birth Is 46:3
And **h** been carried from the womb; Is 46:3
I **h** done *it*, and I will carry *you;* Is 46:4
things which **h** not been done, Is 46:10
Truly I **h** spoken; Is 46:11
I **h** planned *it, surely* I will do Is 46:11
knowledge, they **h** deluded you; Is 47:10
For you **h** said in your heart, Is 47:10
you **h** labored from your youth; Is 47:12
they **h** become like stubble, Is 47:14
"So **h** those become to you with Is 47:15
to you with whom you **h** labored, Is 47:15
Who **h** trafficked with you from Is 47:15
my molten image **h** commanded them.' Is 48:5
"You **h** heard; look at all this. Is 48:6
things which you **h** not known. Is 48:6
before today you **h** not heard them, Is 48:7
"You **h** not heard, you have not Is 48:8
have not heard, you **h** not known. Is 48:8
And you **h** been called a rebel from Is 48:8
"Behold, I **h** refined you, but not Is 48:10
I **h** tested you in the furnace of Is 48:10
"I, even I, **h** spoken; Is 48:15
indeed I **h** called him, I have Is 48:15
have called him, I **h** brought him, Is 48:15
first I **h** not spoken in secret, Is 48:16
would **h** been like a river, Is 48:18
would **h** been like the sand, Is 48:19
"I **h** toiled in vain, I have spent Is 49:4
I **h** spent My strength for nothing Is 49:4
a favorable time I **h** answered You, Is 49:8
a day of salvation I **h** helped You; Is 49:8
h compassion on His afflicted. Is 49:13 7355
And **h** no compassion on the son of Is 49:15 7355
I **h** inscribed you on the palms Is 49:16
I **h** been bereaved of my children And Is 49:21
which I **h** sent your mother away? Is 50:1
Or **h** I no power to deliver? Is 50:2 369
I **h** set My face like flint, Is 50:7
among the brands you **h** set ablaze. Is 50:11
This you will **h** from My hand: Is 50:11 1961
h forgotten the LORD your Maker, Is 51:13
I **h** put My words in your mouth and Is 51:16
and **h** covered you with the shadow Is 51:16
You who **h** drunk from the LORD's Is 51:17
you **h** drained to the dregs. Is 51:17
These two things **h** befallen you; Is 51:19
Your sons **h** fainted, They lie Is 51:20
I **h** taken out of your hand the cup Is 51:22
tormentors, Who **h** said to you, Is 51:23
You **h** even made your back like the Is 51:23
"Now therefore, what do I **h** here," Is 52:5
h been taken away without cause?" Is 52:5

Context	Reference	No.
of us like sheep **h** gone astray,	Is 53:6	
one, you who **h** borne no *child;*	Is 54:1	
aloud, you who **h** not travailed;	Is 54:1	
I will **h** compassion on you,"	Is 54:8	7355
So I **h** sworn that I will not be	Is 54:9	
I Myself **h** created the smith who	Is 54:16	
I **h** created the destroyer to ruin.	Is 54:16	
And you who **h** no money come, buy	Is 55:1	369
I **h** made him a witness to the	Is 55:4	
And He will **h** compassion on him,	Is 55:7	7355
shepherds who **h** no understanding;	Is 56:11	3045
h all turned to their own way,	Is 56:11	
them you **h** poured out a drink offering,	Is 57:6	
You **h** made a grain offering.	Is 57:6	
mountain You **h** made your bed.	Is 57:7	
doorpost You **h** set up your sign;	Is 57:8	
from Me, you **h** uncovered yourself	Is 57:8	
And **h** gone up and made your bed	Is 57:8	
And you **h** made an agreement for	Is 57:8	
with them, You **h** loved their bed,	Is 57:8	
You **h** looked on *their* manhood.	Is 57:8	
"You **h** journeyed to the king	Is 57:9	
You **h** sent your envoys a great	Is 57:9	
the breath *of those whom* I **h** made.	Is 57:16	
"I **h** seen his ways, but I will	Is 57:18	
'Why **h** we fasted and You do not	Is 58:3	
Why **h** we humbled ourselves and	Is 58:3	
But your iniquities **h** made a	Is 59:2	
sins **h** hidden *His* face from you	Is 59:2	
Your lips **h** spoken falsehood, Your	Is 59:3	
They **h** made their paths crooked,	Is 59:8	
We grope like those who **h** no eyes;	Is 59:10	369
words which I **h** put in your mouth shall	Is 59:21	
favor I **h** had compassion on you.	Is 60:10	
"Whereas you **h** been forsaken and	Is 60:15	
you **h** the sun for light by day,	Is 60:19	1961
But you will **h** the LORD for an	Is 60:19	1961
For you will **h** the LORD for an	Is 60:20	1961
Instead of your shame *you will* **h** *a*	Is 61:7	
Jerusalem, I **h** appointed watchmen;	Is 62:6	
wine for which you **h** labored."	Is 62:8	
"I **h** trodden the wine trough	Is 63:3	
Our adversaries **h** trodden *it* down.	Is 63:18	
We **h** become *like* those over whom	Is 63:19	
over whom You **h** never ruled,	Is 63:19	
For from days of old they **h** not heard	Is 64:4	
For all of us **h** become like one	Is 64:6	
You **h** hidden Your face from us And	Is 64:7	
And **h** delivered us into the power	Is 64:7	
holy cities **h** become a wilderness,	Is 64:10	
precious things **h** become a ruin.	Is 64:11	
"I **h** spread out My hands all day	Is 65:2	
"Because they **h** burned incense on	Is 65:7	
As they **h** chosen their *own* ways,	Is 66:3	
you for My name's sake, **H** said,	Is 66:5	
that **h** neither heard My fame nor	Is 66:19	
men Who **h** transgressed against Me.	Is 66:24	
I **h** appointed you a prophet to the	Jer 1:5	
I **h** put My words in your mouth.	Jer 1:9	
I **h** appointed you this day over	Jer 1:10	
"You **h** seen well, for I am	Jer 1:12	
whereby they **h** forsaken Me and	Jer 1:16	
forsaken Me and **h** offered sacrifices to	Jer 1:16	
I **h** made you today as a fortified	Jer 1:18	
But My people **h** changed their	Jer 2:11	
My people **h** committed two evils:	Jer 2:13	
They **h** forsaken Me, The fountain	Jer 2:13	
"The young lions **h** roared at him,	Jer 2:15	
at him, They **h** roared loudly.	Jer 2:15	
And they **h** made his land a waste;	Jer 2:15	
His cities **h** been destroyed,	Jer 2:15	
H shaved the crown of your head.	Jer 2:16	
"**H** you not done this to yourself By	Jer 2:17	
tree You **h** lain down as a harlot.	Jer 2:20	
How then **h** you turned yourself	Jer 2:21	
I **h** not gone after the Baals'?	Jer 2:23	
Know what you **h** done!	Jer 2:23	
For I **h** loved strangers, And after	Jer 2:25	
they **h** turned *their* back to Me,	Jer 2:27	
h all transgressed against Me,"	Jer 2:29	
"In vain I **h** struck your sons;	Jer 2:30	
H I been a wilderness to Israel,	Jer 2:31	
Yet My people **h** forgotten Me Days	Jer 2:32	
women You **h** taught your ways.	Jer 2:33	
Because you say, 'I **h** not sinned.'	Jer 2:35	
Where **h** you not been violated?	Jer 3:2	
By the roads you **h** sat for them	Jer 3:2	
And you **h** polluted a land With	Jer 3:2	
the showers **h** been withheld,	Jer 3:3	
"**H** you not just now called to Me,	Jer 3:4	
you **h** spoken And have done evil	Jer 3:5	
spoken And **h** done evil things,	Jer 3:5	
things, And you **h** had your way."	Jer 3:5	
"**H** you seen what faithless Israel	Jer 3:6	
That you **h** transgressed against	Jer 3:13	
And **h** scattered your favors to the	Jer 3:13	
And you **h** not obeyed My voice,'	Jer 3:13	
you **h** dealt treacherously with Me,	Jer 3:20	
they **h** perverted their way,	Jer 3:21	
h forgotten the LORD their God.	Jer 3:21	
for we **h** sinned against the LORD	Jer 3:25	
And we **h** not obeyed the voice of	Jer 3:25	
Surely You **h** utterly deceived	Jer 4:10	
'You will **h** peace';	Jer 4:10	1961
H brought these things to you.	Jer 4:18	
be silent, Because you **h** heard,	Jer 4:19	
And **h** no understanding.	Jer 4:22	995
above be dark, Because I **h** spoken,	Jer 4:28	
I have spoken, I **h** purposed,	Jer 4:28	
You **h** smitten them, *But* they did	Jer 5:3	
You **h** consumed them, But they	Jer 5:3	
They **h** made their faces harder	Jer 5:3	
They **h** refused to repent.	Jer 5:3	
h broken the yoke *And* burst the	Jer 5:5	
Your sons **h** forsaken Me And sworn	Jer 5:7	
of Judah **H** dealt very treacherously	Jer 5:11	
h lied about the LORD And said,	Jer 5:12	
"Because you **h** spoken this word,	Jer 5:14	
'As you **h** forsaken Me and served	Jer 5:19	
and senseless people, Who **h** eyes but	Jer 5:21	
Who **h** ears but do not hear.	Jer 5:21	
For I **h** placed the sand as a	Jer 5:22	
They **h** turned aside and departed.	Jer 5:23	
iniquities **h** turned these away,	Jer 5:25	
sins **h** withheld good from you.	Jer 5:25	
they **h** become great and rich.	Jer 5:27	
They **h** no delight in it.	Jer 6:10	2654a
"They **h** healed the brokenness	Jer 6:14	
of the abomination they **h** done?	Jer 6:15	
they **h** not listened to My words,	Jer 6:19	
My law, they **h** rejected it also.	Jer 6:19	
They are cruel and **h** no mercy;	Jer 6:23	7355
We **h** heard the report of it;	Jer 6:24	
"I **h** made you an assayer *and* a	Jer 6:27	
other gods that you **h** not known,	Jer 7:9	
Behold, I, even I, **h** seen *it,*"	Jer 7:11	
you **h** done all these things,"	Jer 7:13	
as I **h** cast out all your brothers,	Jer 7:15	
I **h** sent you all My servants the	Jer 7:25	
"For the sons of Judah **h** done	Jer 7:30	
"they **h** set their detestable	Jer 7:30	
"They **h** built the high places	Jer 7:31	
of heaven, which they **h** loved and	Jer 8:2	
and which they **h** served,	Jer 8:2	
and which they **h** gone after and	Jer 8:2	
after and which they **h** sought,	Jer 8:2	
and which they **h** worshiped.	Jer 8:2	
places to which I **h** driven them,"	Jer 8:3	
"I **h** listened and heard, They	Jer 8:6	
They **h** spoken what is not right;	Jer 8:6	
Saying, 'What **h** I done?'	Jer 8:6	
Behold, they **h** rejected the word of	Jer 8:9	
And what kind of wisdom do they **h**?	Jer 8:9	
what I **h** given them will pass away	Jer 8:13	
For we **h** sinned against the LORD.	Jer 8:14	
"Why **h** they provoked Me with	Jer 8:19	
They **h** taught their tongue to	Jer 9:5	
of the sky and the beasts **h** fled	Jer 9:10	
"Because they **h** forsaken My law	Jer 9:13	
and **h** not obeyed My voice nor	Jer 9:13	
but **h** walked after the	Jer 9:14	
they nor their fathers **h** known;	Jer 9:16	
them until I **h** annihilated them."	Jer 9:16	
shame, For we **h** left the land,	Jer 9:19	
h cast down our dwellings.'	Jer 9:19	
My sons **h** gone from me and are	Jer 10:20	
For the shepherds **h** become stupid	Jer 10:21	
stupid And **h** not sought the LORD;	Jer 10:21	
Therefore they **h** not prospered,	Jer 10:21	
For they **h** devoured Jacob;	Jer 10:25	
h devoured him and consumed him	Jer 10:25	
And **h** laid waste his habitation.	Jer 10:25	
"They **h** turned back to the	Jer 11:10	
and they **h** gone after other gods	Jer 11:10	
house of Judah **h** broken My covenant	Jer 11:10	
h set up to the shameful thing,	Jer 11:13	
which they **h** done to provoke Me by	Jer 11:17	
to You **h** I committed my cause.	Jer 11:20	
You **h** planted them, they have	Jer 12:2	
them, they **h** also taken root;	Jer 12:2	
grow, they **h** even produced fruit.	Jer 12:2	
and birds **h** been snatched away,	Jer 12:4	
snatched away, Because *men* **h** said,	Jer 12:4	
"If you **h** run with footmen and	Jer 12:5	
footmen and they **h** tired you out,	Jer 12:5	
h dealt treacherously with you,	Jer 12:6	
Even they **h** cried aloud after you.	Jer 12:6	
"I **h** forsaken My house, I have	Jer 12:7	
I **h** abandoned My inheritance;	Jer 12:7	
I **h** given the beloved of My soul	Jer 12:7	
Therefore I **h** come to hate her.	Jer 12:8	
shepherds **h** ruined My vineyard,	Jer 12:10	
They **h** trampled down My field;	Jer 12:10	
They **h** made My pleasant field A	Jer 12:10	
the wilderness Destroyers **h** come,	Jer 12:12	
"They **h** sown wheat and have	Jer 12:13	
sown wheat and **h** reaped thorns,	Jer 12:13	
They **h** strained themselves to no	Jer 12:13	
I **h** endowed My people Israel,	Jer 12:14	
that after I **h** uprooted them,	Jer 12:15	
I will again **h** compassion on them;	Jer 12:15	7355
the waistband that you **h** bought,	Jer 13:4	
h gone after other gods to serve them	Jer 13:10	
pity nor be sorry nor **h** compassion	Jer 13:14	7355
of the Negev **h** been locked up,	Jer 13:19	
h these things happened to me	Jer 13:22	
Your skirts **h** been removed And	Jer 13:22	
And your heels **h** been exposed.	Jer 13:22	
"Because you **h** forgotten Me And	Jer 13:25	
"So I Myself **h** also stripped your	Jer 13:26	
field, I **h** seen your abominations.	Jer 13:27	
h sent their servants for water;	Jer 14:3	
They **h** come to the cisterns and	Jer 14:3	
They **h** returned with their vessels	Jer 14:3	
They **h** been put to shame and	Jer 14:3	
The farmers **h** been put to shame,	Jer 14:4	
shame, They **h** covered their heads.	Jer 14:4	
Truly our apostasies **h** been many,	Jer 14:7	
many, We **h** sinned against You.	Jer 14:7	
"Even so they **h** loved to wander;	Jer 14:10	
h not kept their feet in check.	Jer 14:10	
the sword nor will you **h** famine,	Jer 14:13	1961
I **h** neither sent them nor	Jer 14:14	
For both prophet and priest **H** gone	Jer 14:18	
H You completely rejected Judah?	Jer 14:19	
Or **h** You loathed Zion?	Jer 14:19	
Why **h** You stricken us so that we	Jer 14:19	
for we **h** sinned against You.	Jer 14:20	
"Indeed, who will **h** pity on you,	Jer 15:5	2550
"You who **h** forsaken Me,"	Jer 15:6	
that you **h** borne me *As* a man of	Jer 15:10	
I **h** not lent, nor have men	Jer 15:10	
lent, nor **h** men lent money to me,	Jer 15:10	
For I **h** been called by Your name, O	Jer 15:16	
not take a wife for yourself nor **h** sons	Jer 16:2	1961
for I **h** withdrawn My peace from	Jer 16:5	
our sin which we **h** committed	Jer 16:10	
your forefathers **h** forsaken Me,'	Jer 16:11	
'and **h** followed other gods and	Jer 16:11	
but Me they **h** forsaken and have	Jer 16:11	
forsaken and **h** not kept My law.	Jer 16:11	
'You too **h** done evil, *even* more	Jer 16:12	
the land which you **h** not known,	Jer 16:13	
because they **h** polluted My land,	Jer 16:18	
they **h** filled My inheritance with	Jer 16:18	
"Our fathers **h** inherited nothing	Jer 16:19	
For you **h** kindled a fire in My	Jer 17:4	
they **h** forsaken the fountain of	Jer 17:13	
I **h** not hurried away from *being* a	Jer 17:16	
Nor **h** I longed for the woeful day;	Jer 17:16	
I **h** spoken turns from its evil,	Jer 18:8	
'For My people **h** forgotten Me,	Jer 18:15	
they **h** stumbled from their ways,	Jer 18:15	
For they **h** dug a pit for me.	Jer 18:20	
For they **h** dug a pit to capture me	Jer 18:22	
"Because they **h** forsaken Me and	Jer 19:4	
and **h** made this an alien place	Jer 19:4	
h burned sacrifices in it to other gods	Jer 19:4	
and *because* they **h** filled this	Jer 19:4	
and **h** built the high places of	Jer 19:5	
that I **h** declared against it,	Jer 19:15	
because they **h** stiffened their	Jer 19:15	
whom you **h** falsely prophesied.'	Jer 20:6	
You **h** deceived me and I was	Jer 20:7	
You **h** overcome me and prevailed.	Jer 20:7	
I **h** become a laughingstock all day	Jer 20:7	
I **h** heard the whispering of many,	Jer 20:10	
ashamed, because they **h** failed,	Jer 20:11	
to You I **h** set forth my cause.	Jer 20:12	
my mother would **h** been my grave,	Jer 20:17	
my days **h** been spent in shame?	Jer 20:18	
nor **h** pity nor compassion." '	Jer 21:7	2550
he will **h** his own life as booty.	Jer 21:9	1961
"For I **h** set My face against this	Jer 21:10	
all your lovers **h** been crushed.	Jer 22:20	
That you **h** not obeyed My voice.	Jer 22:21	
Why **h** he and his descendants been	Jer 22:28	
"You **h** scattered My flock and	Jer 23:2	
away, and **h** not attended to them;	Jer 23:2	
the countries where I **h** driven them	Jer 23:3	
I **h** become like a drunken man,	Jer 23:9	
of the wilderness **h** dried up.	Jer 23:10	
I **h** found their wickedness,"	Jer 23:11	
I **h** seen a horrible thing:	Jer 23:14	
of them **h** become to Me like Sodom,	Jer 23:14	
"You will **h** peace" ';	Jer 23:17	1961
Then they would **h** announced My	Jer 23:22	
And would **h** turned them back from	Jer 23:22	
"I **h** heard what the prophets have	Jer 23:25	
"I have heard what the prophets **h**	Jer 23:25	
straw **h** *in common* with grain?"	Jer 23:28	
who **h** prophesied false dreams,"	Jer 23:32	
and you **h** perverted the words of	Jer 23:36	
I **h** also sent to you, saying,	Jer 23:38	
whom I **h** sent out of this place	Jer 24:5	
I **h** spoken to you again and again,	Jer 25:3	
and again, but you **h** not listened.	Jer 25:3	
but you **h** not listened nor	Jer 25:4	
"Yet you **h** not listened to Me,"	Jer 25:7	
'Because you **h** not obeyed My	Jer 25:8	
which I **h** pronounced against it,	Jer 25:13	
and your dispersions **h** come,	Jer 25:34	
who **h** come to worship *in* the	Jer 26:2	
all the words that I **h** commanded	Jer 26:2	
My law which I **h** set before you,	Jer 26:4	
whom I **h** been sending to you again	Jer 26:5	
and again, but you **h** not listened;	Jer 26:5	
"Why **h** you prophesied in the name	Jer 26:9	
as you **h** heard in your hearing."	Jer 26:11	
all the words that you **h** heard.	Jer 26:12	
"I **h** made the earth, the men and	Jer 27:5	
"Now I **h** given all these	Jer 27:6	
and I **h** given him also the wild	Jer 27:6	
I **h** destroyed it by his hand.	Jer 27:8	
for I **h** not sent them,"	Jer 27:15	
'I **h** broken the yoke of the king	Jer 28:2	
your words which you **h** prophesied	Jer 28:6	
"You **h** broken the yokes of wood,	Jer 28:13	
but you **h** made instead of them	Jer 28:13	
"I **h** put a yoke of iron on the	Jer 28:14	
And I **h** also given him the beasts	Jer 28:14	
and you **h** made this people trust	Jer 28:15	
because you **h** counseled rebellion	Jer 28:16	
to all the exiles whom I **h** sent	Jer 29:4	
where I **h** sent you into exile,	Jer 29:7	
its welfare you will **h** welfare.'	Jer 29:7	1961
I **h** not sent them,' declares the	Jer 29:9	

Context	Reference	No.
h been completed for Babylon,	**Jer 29:10**	
I know the plans that I **h** for you,'	**Jer 29:11**	2803
the places where I **h** driven you,'	**Jer 29:14**	
"Because you **h** said,	**Jer 29:15**	
the nations where I **h** driven them,	**Jer 29:18**	
they **h** not listened to My words,'	**Jer 29:19**	
whom I **h** sent away from Jerusalem	**Jer 29:20**	
they **h** acted foolishly in Israel,	**Jer 29:23**	
and **h** committed adultery with	**Jer 29:23**	
and **h** spoken words in My name	**Jer 29:23**	
'Because you **h** sent letters in	**Jer 29:25**	
why **h** you not rebuked Jeremiah of	**Jer 29:27**	
he will not **h** anyone living among	**Jer 29:32**	1961
which I **h** spoken to you in a book.	**Jer 30:2**	
'I **h** heard a sound of terror, Of	**Jer 30:5**	
And *why* **h** all faces turned pale?	**Jer 30:6**	
nations where I **h** scattered you,	**Jer 30:11**	
'All your lovers **h** forgotten you,	**Jer 30:14**	
For I **h** wounded you with the wound	**Jer 30:14**	
I **h** done these things to you.	**Jer 30:15**	
they **h** called you an outcast,	**Jer 30:17**	
tents of Jacob And **h** compassion on	**Jer 30:18**	7355
"I **h** loved you with an	**Jer 31:3**	
I **h** drawn you with lovingkindness.	**Jer 31:3**	
"I **h** surely heard Ephraim grieving,	**Jer 31:18**	
'You **h** chastised me, and I was	**Jer 31:18**	
often as I **h** spoken against him,	**Jer 31:20**	
I will surely **h** mercy on him,"	**Jer 31:20**	7355
I **h** watched over them to pluck up,	**Jer 31:28**	
'The fathers **h** eaten sour grapes,	**Jer 31:29**	
Israel For all that they **h** done,"	**Jer 31:37**	
for you **h** the right of redemption	**Jer 32:7**	
for you **h** the right of possession	**Jer 32:8**	
You **h** made the heavens and the	**Jer 32:17**	
You **h** made a name for Yourself,	**Jer 32:20**	
they **h** done nothing of all that	**Jer 32:23**	
therefore You **h** made all this	**Jer 32:23**	
h reached the city to take it;	**Jer 32:24**	
what You **h** spoken has come to	**Jer 32:24**	
'You **h** said to me, O Lord	**Jer 32:25**	
where *people* **h** offered incense to	**Jer 32:29**	
sons of Judah **h** been doing only evil	**Jer 32:30**	
for the sons of Israel **h** been only	**Jer 32:30**	
which they **h** done to provoke Me to	**Jer 32:32**	
"They **h** turned *their* back to Me	**Jer 32:33**	
which I **h** driven them in My anger,	**Jer 32:37**	
men whom I **h** slain in My anger	**Jer 33:5**	
and I **h** hidden My face from this	**Jer 33:5**	
by which they **h** sinned against Me,	**Jer 33:8**	
by which they **h** sinned against Me	**Jer 33:8**	
they **h** transgressed against Me.	**Jer 33:8**	
word which I **h** spoken concerning the	**Jer 33:14**	
h a son to reign on his throne,	**Jer 33:21**	1961
"**H** you not observed what this	**Jer 33:24**	
what this people **h** spoken,	**Jer 33:24**	
and earth I **h** not established,	**Jer 33:25**	
and will **h** mercy on them.'	**Jer 33:26**	7355
For I **h** spoken the word,"	**Jer 34:5**	
'You **h** not obeyed Me in	**Jer 34:17**	
who **h** transgressed My covenant,	**Jer 34:18**	
who **h** not fulfilled the words of	**Jer 34:18**	
"We **h** obeyed the voice of	**Jer 35:8**	
not **h** vineyard or field or seed.	**Jer 35:9**	1961
"We **h** only dwelt in tents, and	**Jer 35:10**	
only dwelt in tents, and **h** obeyed	**Jer 35:10**	
and **h** done according to all that	**Jer 35:10**	
So we **h** dwelt in Jerusalem."	**Jer 35:11**	
h obeyed their father's command.	**Jer 35:14**	
I **h** spoken to you again and again;	**Jer 35:14**	
yet you **h** not listened to Me.	**Jer 35:14**	
"Also I **h** sent to you all My	**Jer 35:15**	
dwell in the land which I **h** given to	**Jer 35:15**	
but you **h** not inclined your ear or	**Jer 35:15**	
Jonadab the son of Rechab **h** observed	**Jer 35:16**	
that I **h** pronounced against them;	**Jer 35:17**	
and I **h** called them but they did	**Jer 35:17**	
'Because you **h** obeyed the command	**Jer 35:18**	
I **h** spoken to you concerning Israel and	**Jer 36:2**	
the scroll which you **h** written at my	**Jer 36:6**	
h read to the people and come."	**Jer 36:14**	
"You **h** burned this scroll,	**Jer 36:29**	
'Why **h** you written on it that the	**Jer 36:29**	
"He shall **h** no one to sit on the	**Jer 36:30**	1961
the calamity that I **h** declared to them	**Jer 36:31**	
what *way* **h** I sinned against you,	**Jer 37:18**	
that you **h** put me in prison?	**Jer 37:18**	
will live and **h** his *own* life as booty	**Jer 38:2**	1961
these men **h** acted wickedly in all	**Jer 38:9**	
in all that they **h** done to Jeremiah	**Jer 38:9**	
whom they **h** cast into the cistern;	**Jer 38:9**	
who **h** gone over to the Chaldeans,	**Jer 38:19**	
all of the women who **h** been left	**Jer 38:22**	
H misled and overpowered you;	**Jer 38:22**	
officials hear that I **h** talked with you	**Jer 38:25**	
you will **h** your *own* life as booty,	**Jer 39:18**	1961
because you **h** trusted in Me,"	**Jer 39:18**	
cities that you **h** taken over."	**Jer 40:10**	
for we **h** stores of wheat, barley,	**Jer 41:8**	3426
prophet said to them, "I **h** heard *you.*	**Jer 42:4**	
that I **h** inflicted on you.	**Jer 42:10**	
so that he will **h** compassion on	**Jer 42:12**	7355
and they will **h** no survivors or	**Jer 42:17**	1961
"As My anger and wrath **h** been	**Jer 42:18**	
today I **h** testified against you.	**Jer 42:19**	
you **h** *only* deceived yourselves;	**Jer 42:20**	
So I **h** told you today, but you	**Jer 42:21**	
h not obeyed the LORD your God,	**Jer 42:21**	
over these stones that I **h** hidden;	**Jer 43:10**	
'You yourselves **h** seen all the	**Jer 44:2**	
calamity that I **h** brought on Jerusalem	**Jer 44:2**	
so they **h** become a ruin and a	**Jer 44:6**	1961
"**H** you forgotten the wickedness	**Jer 44:9**	
"But they **h** not become contrite	**Jer 44:10**	
nor **h** they feared nor walked in My	**Jer 44:10**	
which I **h** set before you and	**Jer 44:10**	
the remnant of Judah who **h** set their	**Jer 44:12**	
Egypt, as I **h** punished Jerusalem,	**Jer 44:13**	
remnant of Judah who **h** entered the	**Jer 44:14**	
"As for the message that you **h**	**Jer 44:16**	
we **h** lacked everything and have	**Jer 44:18**	
we have lacked everything and **h**	**Jer 44:18**	
which you **h** committed;	**Jer 44:22**	
"Because you **h** burned sacrifices	**Jer 44:23**	
burned sacrifices and **h** sinned against	**Jer 44:23**	
you **h** spoken with your mouths and	**Jer 44:25**	
perform our vows that we **h** vowed,	**Jer 44:25**	
I **h** sworn by My great name,'	**Jer 44:26**	
remnant of Judah who **h** gone to the	**Jer 44:28**	
groaning and **h** found no rest." '	**Jer 45:3**	
what I **h** built I am about to tear	**Jer 45:4**	
what I **h** planted I am about to	**Jer 45:4**	
"Why **h** I seen *it?* They are terrified,	**Jer 46:5**	
And **h** taken refuge in flight,	**Jer 46:5**	
They **h** stumbled and fallen.	**Jer 46:6**	
In vain **h** you multiplied remedies;	**Jer 46:11**	
The nations **h** heard of your shame,	**Jer 46:12**	
of them **h** fallen down together.	**Jer 46:12**	
"Why **h** your mighty ones become	**Jer 46:15**	
"They **h** repeatedly stumbled;	**Jer 46:16**	
they **h** fallen one against another.	**Jer 46:16**	
For even they too **h** turned back	**Jer 46:21**	
back *and* **h** fled away together;	**Jer 46:21**	
"They **h** cut down her forest,"	**Jer 46:23**	
the nations Where I **h** driven you,	**Jer 46:28**	
The fathers **h** not turned back for	**Jer 47:3**	
h devised calamity against her:	**Jer 48:2**	
h sounded out a cry *of distress.*	**Jer 48:4**	
They **h** heard the anguished cry of	**Jer 48:5**	
and men **h** gone up to his cities;	**Jer 48:15**	
His choicest young men **h** also gone	**Jer 48:15**	
"We **h** heard of the pride of	**Jer 48:29**	
boasts **h** accomplished nothing.	**Jer 48:30**	
And I **h** made the wine to cease	**Jer 48:33**	
Jahaz they **h** raised their voice,	**Jer 48:34**	
Therefore they **h** lost the	**Jer 48:36**	
for I **h** broken Moab like an	**Jer 48:38**	
How they **h** wailed!	**Jer 48:39**	
And the strongholds **h** been seized,	**Jer 48:41**	
The people of Chemosh **h** perished;	**Jer 48:46**	
sons **h** been taken away captive And	**Jer 48:46**	
"Does Israel **h** no sons?	**Jer 49:1**	369
"But I **h** stripped Esau bare, I	**Jer 49:10**	
I **h** uncovered his hiding places So	**Jer 49:10**	
"For I **h** sworn by Myself,"	**Jer 49:13**	
I **h** heard a message from the LORD,	**Jer 49:14**	
I **h** made you small among the	**Jer 49:15**	
shame, For they **h** heard bad news;	**Jer 49:23**	
Distress and pangs **h** taken hold of	**Jer 49:24**	
them Until I **h** consumed them.	**Jer 49:37**	
Her images **h** been put to shame,	**Jer 50:2**	
her idols **h** been shattered.'	**Jer 50:2**	
Both man and beast **h** wandered off,	**Jer 50:3**	
wandered off, they **h** gone away!	**Jer 50:3**	
"My people **h** become lost sheep;	**Jer 50:6**	
Their shepherds **h** led them astray.	**Jer 50:6**	
They **h** made them turn aside *on* the	**Jer 50:6**	
They **h** gone along from mountain to	**Jer 50:6**	
h forgotten their resting place.	**Jer 50:6**	
came upon them **h** devoured them;	**Jer 50:7**	
And their adversaries **h** said,	**Jer 50:7**	
Inasmuch as they **h** sinned against	**Jer 50:7**	
who plunder her will **h** enough,"	**Jer 50:10**	7646
herself up, her pillars **h** fallen,	**Jer 50:15**	
Her walls **h** been torn down.	**Jer 50:15**	
the lions **h** driven *them* away.	**Jer 50:17**	
to all that I **h** commanded you.	**Jer 50:21**	
You **h** been found and also seized	**Jer 50:24**	
you **h** engaged in conflict with the	**Jer 50:24**	
them captive **h** held them fast,	**Jer 50:33**	
They **h** refused to let them go.	**Jer 50:33**	
They are cruel and **h** no mercy.	**Jer 50:42**	7355
The nations **h** drunk of her wine;	**Jer 51:7**	
h done in Zion before your eyes,"	**Jer 51:24**	
men of Babylon **h** ceased fighting,	**Jer 51:30**	
The fords also **h** been seized, And	**Jer 51:32**	
h burned the marshes with fire,	**Jer 51:32**	
h become an object of horror,	**Jer 51:43**	
slain of all the earth **h** fallen.	**Jer 51:49**	
You who **h** escaped the sword,	**Jer 51:50**	
because we **h** heard reproach;	**Jer 51:51**	
For aliens **h** entered The holy	**Jer 51:51**	
these words which **h** been written	**Jer 51:60**	
h promised concerning this place	**Jer 51:62**	
All her friends **h** dealt treacherously	**La 1:2**	
They **h** become her enemies.	**La 1:2**	
All her pursuers **h** overtaken her	**La 1:3**	
adversaries **h** become her masters,	**La 1:5**	
Her little ones **h** gone away As	**La 1:5**	
Her princes **h** become like deer	**La 1:6**	
deer That **h** found no pasture;	**La 1:6**	
And they **h** fled without strength	**La 1:6**	
Because they **h** seen her nakedness;	**La 1:8**	
They **h** given their precious things	**La 1:11**	
They **h** come upon my neck;	**La 1:14**	
I **h** rebelled against His command;	**La 1:18**	
young men **H** gone into captivity.	**La 1:18**	
me, For I **h** been very rebellious.	**La 1:20**	
"They **h** heard that I groan;	**La 1:21**	
my enemies **h** heard of my calamity;	**La 1:21**	
They are glad that You **h** done	**La 1:21**	
the day which You **h** proclaimed,	**La 1:21**	
And deal with them as You **h** dealt	**La 1:22**	
They **h** made a noise in the house	**La 2:7**	
They **h** languished together.	**La 2:8**	
Her gates **h** sunk into the ground,	**La 2:9**	
They **h** thrown dust on their heads;	**La 2:10**	
They **h** girded themselves with	**La 2:10**	
The virgins of Jerusalem **H** bowed	**La 2:10**	
Your prophets **h** seen for you False	**La 2:14**	
And they **h** not exposed your	**La 2:14**	
But they **h** seen for you false and	**La 2:14**	
All your enemies **H** opened their	**La 2:16**	
"We **h** swallowed *her* up!	**La 2:16**	
We **h** reached *it,* we have seen	**La 2:16**	
we **h** seen *it.*"	**La 2:16**	
Let your eyes **h** no rest.	**La 2:18**	1826a
With whom **h** You dealt thus?	**La 2:20**	
young men **H** fallen by the sword.	**La 2:21**	
You **h** slain *them* in the day of	**La 2:21**	
Your anger, You **h** slaughtered,	**La 2:21**	
Like those who **h** long been dead.	**La 3:6**	
I **h** become a laughingstock to all	**La 3:14**	
I **h** forgotten happiness.	**La 3:17**	
to my mind, Therefore I **h** hope.	**La 3:21**	3176
"Therefore I **h** hope in Him."	**La 3:24**	3176
Then He will **h** compassion	**La 3:32**	7355
We **h** transgressed and rebelled,	**La 3:42**	
and rebelled, You **h** not pardoned.	**La 3:42**	
You **h** covered *Yourself* with anger	**La 3:43**	
You **h** slain *and* have not spared.	**La 3:43**	
You have slain *and* **h** not spared.	**La 3:43**	
You **h** covered Yourself with a	**La 3:44**	
You **h** *made us mere* offscouring	**La 3:45**	
All our enemies **h** opened their	**La 3:46**	
Panic and pitfall **h** befallen us,	**La 3:47**	
They **h** silenced me in the pit And	**La 3:53**	
pit And **h** placed a stone on me.	**La 3:53**	
You **h** heard my voice,	**La 3:56**	
O Lord, You **h** pleaded my soul's	**La 3:58**	
You **h** redeemed my life.	**La 3:58**	
O LORD, You **h** seen my oppression;	**La 3:59**	
You **h** seen all their vengeance,	**La 3:60**	
You **h** heard their reproach, O	**La 3:61**	
Who **h** shed in her midst The blood	**La 4:13**	
In our watching we **h** watched For a	**La 4:17**	
We **h** become orphans without a	**La 5:3**	
h to pay for our drinking water,	**La 5:4**	
We **h** submitted to Egypt	**La 5:6**	
we who **h** borne their iniquities.	**La 5:7**	
Woe to us, for we **h** sinned!	**La 5:16**	
Unless You **h** utterly rejected us	**La 5:22**	
people who **h** rebelled against Me;	**Ezk 2:3**	
they and their fathers **h** transgressed	**Ezk 2:3**	
But I **h** sent you to them who	**Ezk 3:6**	
I **h** made your face as hard as	**Ezk 3:8**	
than flint I **h** made your forehead.	**Ezk 3:9**	
I **h** appointed you a watchman to	**Ezk 3:17**	
"Yet if you **h** warned the wicked and	**Ezk 3:19**	
but you **h** delivered yourself.	**Ezk 3:19**	
since you **h** not warned him, he	**Ezk 3:20**	
if you **h** warned the righteous man	**Ezk 3:21**	
and you **h** delivered yourself."	**Ezk 3:21**	
"For I **h** assigned you a number of	**Ezk 4:5**	
"When you **h** completed these, you	**Ezk 4:6**	
I **h** assigned it to you for forty	**Ezk 4:6**	
until you **h** completed the days of	**Ezk 4:8**	
Behold, I **h** never been defiled;	**Ezk 4:14**	
until now I **h** never eaten what died	**Ezk 4:14**	
I **h** set her at the center of	**Ezk 5:5**	
for they **h** rejected My ordinances	**Ezk 5:6**	
and **h** not walked in My statutes.'	**Ezk 5:6**	
'Because you **h** more turmoil than	**Ezk 5:7**	
and **h** not walked in My statutes,	**Ezk 5:7**	
do among you what I **h** not done,	**Ezk 5:9**	
because you **h** defiled My sanctuary	**Ezk 5:11**	
My eye will **h** no pity	**Ezk 5:11**	2347
I, the LORD, **h** spoken in My zeal	**Ezk 5:13**	
when I **h** spent My wrath upon them.	**Ezk 5:13**	
I, the LORD, **h** spoken.	**Ezk 5:15**	
I, the LORD, **h** spoken.' "	**Ezk 5:17**	
for you will **h** those who escaped	**Ezk 6:8**	1961
how I **h** been hurt by their	**Ezk 6:9**	
the evils which they **h** committed,	**Ezk 6:9**	
I **h** not said in vain that I would	**Ezk 6:10**	
'For My eye will **h** no pity on you,	**Ezk 7:4**	2347
They **h** blown the trumpet and made	**Ezk 7:14**	
which they **h** committed here,	**Ezk 8:17**	
that they **h** filled the land with	**Ezk 8:17**	
My eye will **h** no pity nor will I	**Ezk 8:18**	2347
do not let your eye **h** pity and	**Ezk 9:5**	2347
My eye will **h** no pity nor will I	**Ezk 9:10**	2347
I **h** done just as You have	**Ezk 9:11**	
just as You **h** commanded me."	**Ezk 9:11**	
The cherubim appeared to **h** the	**Ezk 10:8**	
You **h** multiplied your slain in	**Ezk 11:6**	
"Your slain whom you **h** laid in	**Ezk 11:7**	
"You **h** feared a sword;	**Ezk 11:8**	
for you **h** not walked in My	**Ezk 11:12**	
nor **h** you executed My ordinances,	**Ezk 11:12**	
but **h** acted according to the	**Ezk 11:12**	
inhabitants of Jerusalem **h** said,	**Ezk 11:15**	
among which you **h** been scattered,	**Ezk 11:17**	
who **h** eyes to see but do not see,	**Ezk 12:2**	
for I **h** set you as a sign to the	**Ezk 12:6**	
As I **h** done, so it will be done to	**Ezk 12:11**	
what is this proverb you *people* **h**	**Ezk 12:22**	
own spirit and **h** seen nothing.	**Ezk 13:3**	

your prophets **h** been like foxes Ezk 13:4
You **h** not gone up into the breaches Ezk 13:5
it is not I who **h** spoken? Ezk 13:7
"Because you **h** spoken falsehood Ezk 13:8
They will **h** no place in the Ezk 13:9 1961
they **h** misled My people by saying, Ezk 13:10
those who **h** plastered it over with Ezk 13:15
you **h** profaned Me to My people to Ezk 13:19
but **h** encouraged the wicked not to Ezk 13:22
these men **h** set up their idols in Ezk 14:3
and **h** put right before their faces Ezk 14:3
who **h** prevailed upon that prophet, Ezk 14:9
calamity which I **h** brought against Ezk 14:22
which I **h** brought upon it. Ezk 14:22
will know that I **h** not done in vain Ezk 14:23
I **h** given to the fire for fuel, Ezk 15:6
so **h** I given up the inhabitants of Ezk 15:6
they **h** come out of the fire, Ezk 15:7
they **h** acted unfaithfully,' " Ezk 15:8
for you, to **h** compassion on you. Ezk 16:5 2550
I **h** stretched out My hand against Ezk 16:27
"Because you **h** not remembered the Ezk 16:43
but **h** enraged Me by all these things, Ezk 16:43
"Yet you **h** not merely walked in Ezk 16:47
her daughters **h** not done as Ezk 16:48
as you and your daughters **h** done. Ezk 16:48
for you **h** multiplied your Ezk 16:51
Thus you **h** made your sisters Ezk 16:51
which you **h** committed. Ezk 16:51
you **h** made judgment favorable for Ezk 16:52
feel ashamed for all that you **h** done Ezk 16:54
so now you **h** become the reproach Ezk 16:57
"You **h** borne *the penalty of* your Ezk 16:58
also do with you as you **h** done, Ezk 16:59
you who **h** despised the oath by Ezk 16:59
when I **h** forgiven you for all that Ezk 16:63
you for all that you **h** done," Ezk 16:63
know that I, the LORD, **h** spoken." Ezk 17:21
I **h** spoken, and I will perform *it*." Ezk 17:24
h a violent son who sheds blood and Ezk 18:10 3205
"Do I **h** any pleasure in the death Ezk 18:23 2654a
which you **h** committed and Ezk 18:31
"For I **h** no pleasure in the death Ezk 18:32 2654a
your fathers **h** blasphemed Me by Ezk 20:27
which you **h** defiled yourselves; Ezk 20:43
the evil things that you **h** done. Ezk 20:43
I **h** dealt with you for My name's sake Ezk 20:44
that I, the LORD, **h** kindled it; Ezk 20:48
I, the LORD, **h** drawn My sword Ezk 21:5
I **h** given the glittering sword. Ezk 21:15
I, the LORD, **h** spoken." Ezk 21:17
they **h** *sworn* solemn oaths. Ezk 21:23
'Because you **h** made your iniquity Ezk 21:24
you **h** come to remembrance, Ezk 21:24
for I, the LORD, **h** spoken.' " Ezk 21:32
"You **h** become guilty by the blood Ezk 22:4
by the blood which you **h** shed, Ezk 22:4
by your idols which you **h** made. Ezk 22:4
Thus you **h** brought your day near Ezk 22:4
day near and **h** come to your years Ezk 22:4
therefore I **h** made you a reproach Ezk 22:4
h been in you for the purpose of Ezk 22:6
"They **h** treated father and mother Ezk 22:7
they **h** oppressed in your midst; Ezk 22:7
the widow they **h** wronged in you. Ezk 22:7
"You **h** despised My holy things Ezk 22:8
"Slanderous men **h** been in you for Ezk 22:9
h eaten at the mountain *shrines*. Ezk 22:9
they **h** committed acts of lewdness. Ezk 22:9
"In you they **h** uncovered Ezk 22:10
in you they **h** humbled her who was Ezk 22:10
they **h** taken bribes to shed blood; Ezk 22:12
you **h** taken interest and profits, Ezk 22:12
and you **h** injured your neighbors Ezk 22:12
and you **h** forgotten Me," Ezk 22:12
dishonest gain which you **h** acquired Ezk 22:13
the LORD, **h** spoken and will act. Ezk 22:14
'Because all of you **h** become dross, Ezk 22:19
h poured out My wrath on you. Ezk 22:22
They **h** devoured lives; Ezk 22:25
they **h** taken treasure and precious Ezk 22:25
they **h** made many widows in the Ezk 22:25
"Her priests **h** done violence to Ezk 22:26
law and **h** profaned My holy things; Ezk 22:26
they **h** made no distinction between Ezk 22:26
and they **h** not taught the Ezk 22:26
h smeared whitewash for them, Ezk 22:28
people of the land **h** practiced Ezk 22:29
and they **h** wronged the poor and Ezk 22:29
and **h** oppressed the sojourner Ezk 22:29
"Thus I **h** poured out My Ezk 22:31
I **h** consumed them with the fire of Ezk 22:31
I **h** brought upon their heads," Ezk 22:31
you **h** played the harlot with the Ezk 23:30
because you **h** defiled yourself Ezk 23:30
'You **h** walked in the way of your Ezk 23:31
for I **h** spoken,' declares the Lord Ezk 23:34
'Because you **h** forgotten Me and Ezk 23:35
"For they **h** committed adultery, Ezk 23:37
Thus they **h** committed adultery Ezk 23:37
"Again, they **h** done this to Me: Ezk 23:38
they **h** defiled My sanctuary on the Ezk 23:38
day and **h** profaned My sabbaths. Ezk 23:38
they **h** even sent for men who come Ezk 23:40
not commit lewdness as you **h** done. Ezk 23:48
I **h** put her blood on the bare rock, Ezk 24:8
Because I *would* **h** cleansed you, Ezk 24:13
Until I **h** spent My wrath on you. Ezk 24:13
I, the LORD, **h** spoken; Ezk 24:14
daughters whom you **h** left behind Ezk 24:21
'You will do as I **h** done; Ezk 24:22
"Because you **h** clapped your hands Ezk 25:6
I **h** stretched out My hand against Ezk 25:7
the Philistines **h** acted in revenge Ezk 25:15
h taken vengeance with scorn of soul Ezk 25:15
midst of the sea, for I **h** spoken,' Ezk 26:5
more, for I the LORD **h** spoken," Ezk 26:14
'How you **h** perished, O inhabited Ezk 26:17
"O Tyre, you **h** said, Ezk 27:3
builders **h** perfected your beauty. Ezk 27:4
"They **h** made all *your* planks of Ezk 27:5
They **h** taken a cedar from Lebanon Ezk 27:5
from Bashan they **h** made your oars; Ezk 27:6
With ivory they **h** inlaid your deck Ezk 27:6
Your rowers **h** brought you Into Ezk 27:26
and all your company **H** fallen in Ezk 27:34
You **h** become terrified And you Ezk 27:36
heart is lifted up And you **h** said, Ezk 28:2
h acquired riches for yourself And Ezk 28:4
And **h** acquired gold and silver for Ezk 28:4
trade You **h** increased your riches And Ezk 28:5
'Because you **h** made your heart Ezk 28:6
of strangers, For I **h** spoken!' Ezk 28:10
Therefore I **h** cast you as profane Ezk 28:16
And I **h** destroyed you, O covering Ezk 28:16
Therefore I **h** brought fire from Ezk 28:18
And I **h** turned you to ashes on the Ezk 28:18
You **h** become terrified And you Ezk 28:19
is mine, and I myself **h** made *it*.' Ezk 29:3
I **h** given you for food to the Ezk 29:5
Because they **h** been *only* a staff Ezk 29:6
'The Nile is mine, and I **h** made *it*,' Ezk 29:9
"I **h** given him the land of Egypt Ezk 29:20
I the LORD **h** spoken." Ezk 30:12
will be breached And Memphis *will* **h** Ezk 30:16
I **h** broken the arm of Pharaoh king Ezk 30:21
its wickedness I **h** driven it away. Ezk 31:11
nations **h** cut it down and left it; Ezk 31:12
the valleys its branches **h** fallen and Ezk 31:12
and its boughs **h** been broken in Ezk 31:12
the peoples of the earth **h** gone down Ezk 31:12
h all been given over to death, Ezk 31:14
into lands which you **h** not known. Ezk 32:9
they **h** drawn her and all her Ezk 32:20
'They **h** gone down, they lie still, Ezk 32:21
"They **h** made a bed for her among Ezk 32:25
he would **h** delivered his life. Ezk 33:5
I **h** appointed you a watchman for Ezk 33:7
but you **h** delivered your life. Ezk 33:9
'Thus you **h** spoken, saying, Ezk 33:10
which they **h** committed." Ezk 33:29
who **h** been feeding themselves! Ezk 34:2
are sickly you **h** not strengthened, Ezk 34:4
the diseased you **h** not healed, Ezk 34:4
the broken you **h** not bound up, Ezk 34:4
scattered you **h** not brought back, Ezk 34:4
nor **h** you sought for the lost; Ezk 34:4
severity you **h** dominated them. Ezk 34:4
until you **h** scattered them abroad, Ezk 34:21
I the LORD **h** spoken. Ezk 34:24
when I **h** broken the bars of their Ezk 34:27
and **h** delivered them from the hand Ezk 34:27
"Because you **h** had everlasting Ezk 35:5
and **h** delivered the sons of Israel to Ezk 35:5
since you **h** not hated bloodshed, Ezk 35:6
"Because you **h** said, Ezk 35:10
h heard all your revilings which Ezk 35:12
revilings which you **h** spoken against Ezk 35:12
"And you **h** spoken arrogantly Ezk 35:13
h multiplied your words against Me; Ezk 35:13
your words against Me; I **h** heard Ezk 35:13
heights **h** become our possession,' Ezk 36:2
"For good reason they **h** made you Ezk 36:3
and you **h** been taken up in the Ezk 36:3
which **h** become a prey and a Ezk 36:4
in the fire of My jealousy I **h** spoken Ezk 36:5
I **h** spoken in My jealousy and in Ezk 36:6
you **h** endured the insults of the Ezk 36:6
'I **h** sworn that surely the nations Ezk 36:7
h bereaved your nation of children Ezk 36:13
yet they **h** come out of His land.' Ezk 36:20
which you **h** profaned among the Ezk 36:22
you **h** profaned in their midst. Ezk 36:23
h rebuilt the ruined places Ezk 36:36
LORD, **h** spoken and will do it." Ezk 36:36
when I **h** opened your graves and Ezk 37:13
the LORD, **h** spoken and done it," Ezk 37:14
the nations where they **h** gone, Ezk 37:21
places in which they **h** sinned, Ezk 37:23
and they will all **h** one shepherd; Ezk 37:24 1961
whose inhabitants **h** been gathered Ezk 38:8
who **h** acquired cattle and goods, Ezk 38:12
'**H** you come to capture spoil? Ezk 38:13
H you assembled your company to Ezk 38:13
for it is I who **h** spoken," Ezk 39:5
is the day of which I **h** spoken. Ezk 39:8
the buriers **h** buried it in the valley of Ezk 39:15
which I **h** sacrificed for you. Ezk 39:19
My judgment which I **h** executed and Ezk 39:21
My hand which I **h** laid on them. Ezk 39:21
and **h** mercy on the whole house of Ezk 39:25 7355
for I will **h** poured out My Spirit Ezk 39:29
for you **h** been brought here in Ezk 40:4
And they **h** defiled My holy name by Ezk 43:8
which they **h** committed. Ezk 43:8
So I **h** consumed them in My anger. Ezk 43:8
ashamed of all that they **h** done, Ezk 43:11
'When you **h** finished cleansing *it*, Ezk 43:23
When they **h** completed the days, Ezk 43:27
"And you **h** not kept charge of My Ezk 44:8
but you **h** set *foreigners* to keep Ezk 44:8
I **h** sworn against them," Ezk 44:12
which they **h** committed. Ezk 44:13
in which they **h** been ministering and Ezk 44:19
"The prince shall **h** *land* on Ezk 45:7
"You shall **h** just balances, a Ezk 45:10 1961
month, you shall **h** the Passover, Ezk 45:21 1961
"Son of man, **h** you seen *this?*" Ezk 47:6
Joseph *shall* **h** two portions. Ezk 47:13
of Zadok, who **h** kept My charge, Ezk 48:11
of the priests the Levites *shall* **h** Ezk 48:13
"The city shall **h** open spaces: Ezk 48:17 1961
inasmuch as you **h** seen that the Da 2:8
For you **h** agreed together to speak Da 2:9
You **h** given me wisdom and power; Da 2:23
Even now You **h** made known to me Da 2:23
For You **h** made known to us the Da 2:23
I **h** found a man among the exiles Da 2:25
the dream which I **h** seen and its Da 2:26
h in it the toughness of iron, Da 2:41 1934
since you **h** been able to reveal Da 2:47
h made a decree that every man who Da 3:10
certain Jews whom you **h** appointed Da 3:12
men, O king, **h** disregarded you; Da 3:12
golden image which you **h** set up." Da 3:12
the golden image that I **h** set up? Da 3:14
worship the image that I **h** made, Da 3:15
golden image that you **h** set up." Da 3:18
of my dream which I **h** seen, Da 4:9
I, King Nebuchadnezzar, **h** seen. Da 4:18
h become great and grown strong, Da 4:22
which I myself **h** built as a royal Da 4:30
'What **h** You done? Da 4:35
shall be clothed with purple and **h** Da 5:7
and **h** authority as third *ruler* in Da 5:7 7981
"Now I **h** heard about you that a Da 5:14
wisdom **h** been found in you. Da 5:14
I personally **h** heard about you, Da 5:16
and you will **h** authority as the Da 5:16 7981
h not humbled your heart, Da 5:22
but you **h** exalted yourself against Da 5:23
and they **h** brought the vessels of Da 5:23
h been drinking wine from them; Da 5:23
and you **h** praised the gods of Da 5:23
your ways, you **h** not glorified. Da 5:23
you **h** been weighed on the scales Da 5:27
the governors **h** consulted together Da 6:7
mouths and they **h** not harmed me, Da 6:22
O king, I **h** committed no crime." Da 6:22
transgressors **h** run *their course*, Da 8:23
we **h** sinned, committed iniquity, Da 9:5
we **h** not listened to Your servants Da 9:6
to which You **h** driven them, Da 9:7
they **h** committed against You. Da 9:7
because we **h** sinned against You. Da 9:8
for we **h** rebelled against Him; Da 9:9
nor **h** we obeyed the voice of the Da 9:10
God, for we **h** sinned against Him. Da 9:11
yet we **h** not sought the favor of Da 9:13
but we **h** not obeyed His voice. Da 9:14
who **h** brought Your people out of Da 9:15
and **h** made a name for Yourself, Da 9:15
we **h** sinned, we have been wicked. Da 9:15
have sinned, we **h** been wicked. Da 9:15
Jerusalem and Your people **h** *become* Da 9:16
I **h** now come forth to give you Da 9:22
issued, and I **h** come to tell *you*, Da 9:23
"Seventy weeks **h** been decreed for Da 9:24
will be cut off and **h** nothing, Da 9:26 369
for I **h** now been sent to you." Da 10:11
and I **h** come in response to your Da 10:12
"Now I **h** come to give you an Da 10:14
me, and I **h** retained no strength. Da 10:16
for you **h** strengthened me." Da 10:19
"Those who **h** insight among Da 11:33 7919a
of those who **h** insight will fall, Da 11:35 7919a
"Those who **h** insight will Da 12:3 7919a
who **h** insight will understand. Da 12:10 7919a
yourself a wife of harlotry and **h** Hos 1:2
for I will no longer **h** compassion Hos 1:6 7355
"But I will **h** compassion on the Hos 1:7 7355
h no compassion on her children, Hos 2:4 7355
wages Which my lovers **h** given me. Hos 2:12
I will also **h** compassion on her Hos 2:23 7355
the harlot, nor shall you **h** a man; Hos 3:3 1961
Because you **h** rejected knowledge, Hos 4:6
you **h** forgotten the law of your God, Hos 4:6
They will eat, but not **h** enough; Hos 4:10 7646
Because they **h** stopped giving heed Hos 4:10
And they **h** played the harlot, Hos 4:12
For you **h** been a snare at Mizpah And Hos 5:1
revolters **h** gone deep in depravity, Hos 5:2
Ephraim, you **h** played the harlot, Hos 5:3
They **h** dealt treacherously against Hos 5:7
h borne illegitimate children. Hos 5:7
The princes of Judah **h** become like Hos 5:10
Therefore I **h** hewn *them* in pieces Hos 6:5
I **h** slain them by the words of My Hos 6:5
they **h** transgressed the covenant; Hos 6:7
There they **h** dealt treacherously Hos 6:7
Surely they **h** committed crime. Hos 6:9
Israel I **h** seen a horrible thing; Hos 6:10
All their kings **h** fallen. Hos 7:7
Yet they **h** not returned to the Hos 7:10
their God, Nor **h** they sought Him, Hos 7:10
them, for they **h** strayed from Me! Hos 7:13
for they **h** rebelled against Me! Hos 7:13

they **h** transgressed My covenant And **Hos 8:1**
They **h** set up kings, but not by Me; **Hos 8:4**
They **h** appointed princes, but I **Hos 8:4**
they **h** made idols for themselves, **Hos 8:4**
For they **h** gone up to Assyria **Hos 8:9**
They **h** become altars of sinning **Hos 8:11**
For you **h** played the harlot, **Hos 9:1**
You **h** loved *harlots'* earnings on **Hos 9:1**
The days of punishment **h** come, **Hos 9:7**
The days of retribution **h** come; **Hos 9:7**
They **h** gone deep in depravity As **Hos 9:9**
Ephraim, as I **h** seen, Is planted **Hos 9:13**
they **h** not listened to Him; **Hos 9:17**
"We **h** no king, For we do not **Hos 10:3** 369
the days of Gibeah you **h** sinned, **Hos 10:9**
You **h** plowed wickedness, you have **Hos 10:13**
you **h** reaped injustice, **Hos 10:13**
You **h** eaten the fruit of lies. **Hos 10:13**
Because you **h** trusted in your way, **Hos 10:13**
"Surely I **h** become rich, I have **Hos 12:8**
rich, I **h** found wealth for myself; **Hos 12:8**
But I **h** *been* the LORD your **Hos 12:9**
I **h** also spoken to the prophets, **Hos 12:10**
Yet I **h** *been* the LORD your **Hos 13:4**
For you **h** stumbled because of your **Hos 14:1**
what more **h** I to do with idols? **Hos 14:8**
Their branches **h** become white. **Jl 1:7**
And will **h** pity on His people. **Jl 2:18** 2550
of the wilderness **h** turned green, **Jl 2:22**
and the vine **h** yielded in full. **Jl 2:22**
"You will **h** plenty to eat **Jl 2:26**
Whom they **h** scattered among the **Jl 3:2**
And they **h** divided up My land. **Jl 3:2**
h also cast lots for My people, **Jl 3:3**
you **h** taken My silver and My gold, **Jl 3:5**
the place where you **h** sold them, **Jl 3:7**
land they **h** shed innocent blood. **Jl 3:19**
their blood which I **h** not avenged, **Jl 3:21**
LORD And **h** not kept His statutes; **Am 2:4**
Their lies also **h** led them astray, **Am 2:4**
wine of those who **h** been fined. **Am 2:8**
"You only **h** I chosen among all **Am 3:2**
unless they **h** made an appointment? **Am 3:3**
Yet you **h** not returned to Me," **Am 4:6**
Yet you **h** not returned to Me," **Am 4:8**
Yet you **h** not returned to Me," **Am 4:9**
Yet you **h** not returned to Me," **Am 4:10**
Yet you **h** not returned to Me," **Am 4:11**
strong Will **h** a hundred left, **Am 5:3** 7604
Will **h** ten left to the house of Israel **Am 5:3** 7604
Though you **h** built houses of **Am 5:11**
You **h** planted pleasant vineyards, **Am 5:11**
be with you, Just as you **h** said! **Am 5:14**
h composed songs for themselves, **Am 6:5**
Yet they **h** not grieved over the **Am 6:6**
you **h** turned justice into poison And **Am 6:12**
"**H** we not by our *own* strength **Am 6:13**
not **h** a fugitive who will flee, **Am 9:1**
"**H** I not brought up Israel from **Am 9:7**
their land Which I **h** given them **Am 9:15**
We **h** heard a report from the LORD, **Ob 1:1**
As you **h** done, it will be done to **Ob 1:15**
h done as You have pleased." **Jon 1:14**
have done as You **h** pleased." **Jon 1:14**
'I **h** been expelled from Your sight. **Jon 2:4**
But You **h** brought up my life from **Jon 2:6**
That which I **h** vowed I will pay. **Jon 2:9**
you **h** good reason to be angry?" **Jon 4:4**
"Do you **h** good reason to be angry **Jon 4:9**
"I **h** good reason to be angry, **Jon 4:9**
I not **h** compassion on Nineveh, **Jon 4:11** 2347
you will **h** no one stretching a **Mi 2:5** 1961
"Recently My people **h** arisen as **Mi 2:8**
they **h** practiced evil deeds. **Mi 3:4**
When they **h** *something* to bite with **Mi 3:5**
Even those whom I **h** afflicted. **Mi 4:6**
"And now many nations **h** been **Mi 4:11**
They **h** laid siege against us; **Mi 5:1**
you will **h** fortune-tellers no more. **Mi 5:12** 1961
the nations which **h** not obeyed." **Mi 5:15**
"My people, what **h** I done to you, **Mi 6:3**
to you, And how **h** I wearied you? **Mi 6:3**
Do not **h** confidence in a friend. **Mi 7:5** 982
Because I **h** sinned against Him, **Mi 7:9**
He will again **h** compassion on us; **Mi 7:19** 7355
Though I **h** afflicted you, I will **Na 1:12**
devastators **h** devastated them **Na 2:2**
You **h** increased your traders more **Na 3:16**
O LORD, **h** appointed them to judge; **Hab 1:12**
O Rock, **h** established them to correct. **Hab 1:12**
Why **h** You made men like the fish **Hab 1:14**
"Because you **h** looted many **Hab 2:8**
"You **h** devised a shameful thing **Hab 2:10**
I **h** heard the report about You **Hab 3:2**
And those who **h** turned back from **Zph 1:6**
And those who **h** not sought the **Zph 1:6**
they **h** sinned against the LORD; **Zph 1:17**
Who **h** carried out His ordinances; **Zph 2:3**
"I **h** heard the taunting of Moab **Zph 2:8**
With which they **h** taunted My **Zph 2:8**
will **h** in return for their pride, **Zph 2:10**
because they **h** taunted and become **Zph 2:10**
priests **h** profaned the sanctuary. **Zph 3:4**
They **h** done violence to the law . **Zph 3:4**
"I **h** cut off nations; **Zph 3:6**
I **h** made their streets desolate, **Zph 3:6**
that I **h** appointed concerning her. **Zph 3:7**
which you **h** rebelled against Me; **Zph 3:11**
"You **h** sown much, but harvest **Hg 1:6**
ring, for I **h** chosen you,'" **Hg 2:23**
"We **h** patrolled the earth, and **Zch 1:11**
how long will You **h** no compassion **Zch 1:12** 7355
with which You **h** been indignant **Zch 1:12**
the horns which **h** scattered Judah, **Zch 1:19**
the horns which **h** scattered Judah so **Zch 1:21**
craftsmen **h** come to terrify them, **Zch 1:21**
the nations who **h** lifted up *their* horns **Zch 1:21**
"for I **h** dispersed you as the **Zch 2:6**
I **h** taken your iniquity away from **Zch 3:4**
and also **h** charge of My courts, **Zch 3:7** 8104
stone that I **h** set before Joshua; **Zch 3:9**
'The hands of Zerubbabel **h** laid **Zch 4:9**
h appeased My wrath in the land of **Zch 6:8**
where they **h** arrived from Babylon. **Zch 6:10**
as I **h** done these many years?" **Zch 7:3**
the nations whom they **h** not known. **Zch 7:14**
'and I **h** not relented, **Zch 8:14**
so I **h** again purposed in these **Zch 8:15**
h heard that God is with you. **Zch 8:23**
For now I **h** seen with My eyes. **Zch 9:8**
I **h** set your prisoners free from **Zch 9:11**
O prisoners who **h** the hope; **Zch 9:12**
I **h** had compassion on them; **Zch 10:6** 7355
together, For I **h** redeemed them; **Zch 10:8**
glorious *trees* **h** been destroyed; **Zch 11:2**
be the LORD, for I **h** become rich!' **Zch 11:5**
own shepherds **h** no pity on them. **Zch 11:5** 2550
"For I will no longer **h** pity on **Zch 11:6** 2550
look on Me whom they **h** pierced; **Zch 12:10**
for you **h** spoken falsely in the **Zch 13:3**
h gone to war against Jerusalem; **Zch 14:12**
"I **h** loved you," says the LORD. **Mal 1:2**
"How **h** You loved us?" **Mal 1:2**
"Yet I **h** loved Jacob; **Mal 1:2**
but I **h** hated Esau, and I have **Mal 1:3**
and I **h** made his mountains a **Mal 1:3**
"We **h** been beaten down, but we **Mal 1:4**
'How **h** we despised Your name?' **Mal 1:6**
'How **h** we defiled You?' **Mal 1:7**
indeed, I **h** cursed them *already*, **Mal 2:2**
I **h** sent this commandment to you, **Mal 2:4**
you **h** turned aside from the way; **Mal 2:8**
you **h** caused many to stumble by **Mal 2:8**
you **h** corrupted the covenant of **Mal 2:8**
"So I also **h** made you despised **Mal 2:9**
"Do we not all **h** one father? **Mal 2:10**
whom you **h** dealt treacherously, **Mal 2:14**
You **h** wearied the LORD with your **Mal 2:17**
"How **h** we wearied *Him?*" **Mal 2:17**
h turned aside from My statutes and **Mal 3:7**
My statutes and **h** not kept *them*. **Mal 3:7**
'How **h** we robbed You?' **Mal 3:8**
h been arrogant against Me," **Mal 3:13**
'What **h** we spoken against You?' **Mal 3:13**
"You **h** said, 'It is vain to serve God; **Mal 3:14**
is it that we **h** kept His charge, **Mal 3:14**
and that we **h** walked in mourning **Mal 3:14**
east and **h** come to worship Him." **Mt 2:2**
and when you **h** found *Him*, report **Mt 2:8**
'We **h** Abraham for our father'; **Mt 3:9** *2192*
"I **h** need to be baptized by You, **Mt 3:14** *2192*
those who **h** been persecuted for **Mt 5:10**
"You **h** heard that the ancients **Mt 5:21**
until you **h** paid up the last cent. **Mt 5:26**
"You **h** heard that it was said, **Mt 5:27**
you **h** heard that the ancients were **Mt 5:33**
"You **h** heard that it was said, **Mt 5:38**
shirt, let him **h** your coat also. **Mt 5:40** *863*
"You **h** heard that it was said, **Mt 5:43**
who love you, what reward do you **h**? **Mt 5:46** *2192*
otherwise you **h** no reward with **Mt 6:1** *2192*
you, they **h** their reward in full. **Mt 6:2** *568*
you, they **h** their reward in full. **Mt 6:5** *568*
as we also **h** forgiven our debtors. **Mt 6:12**
you, they **h** their reward in full. **Mt 6:16** *568*
I **h** not found such great faith **Mt 8:10**
done for you as you **h** believed." **Mt 8:13**
Jesus said to him, "The foxes **h** **Mt 8:20** *2192*
birds of the air **h** nests, **Mt 8:20**
"What business do we **h** with each other, **Mt 8:29**
H You come here to torment us **Mt 8:29**
"**H** mercy on us, Son of David!" **Mt 9:27** *1653*
If they **h** called the head of the **Mt 10:25**
and *the* POOR **H** THE GOSPEL **Mt 11:5**
they would **h** repented long ago in **Mt 11:21**
it would **h** remained to this day. **Mt 11:23**
that You **h** hidden these things from **Mt 11:25**
the wise and intelligent and **h** **Mt 11:25**
"All things **h** been handed over to **Mt 11:27**
"**H** you not read what David did **Mt 12:3**
"Or **h** you not read in the Law, **Mt 12:5**
not **h** condemned the innocent. **Mt 12:7**
"BEHOLD, MY SERVANT WHOM I **H** **Mt 12:18**
where they did not **h** much soil; **Mt 13:5** *2192*
and he will **h** an abundance; **Mt 13:12** *4052*
but whoever does not **h**, **Mt 13:12** *2192*
AND THEY **H** CLOSED THEIR EYES, **Mt 13:15**
How then does it **h** tares?' **Mt 13:27** *2192*
"**H** you understood all these **Mt 13:51**
is not lawful for you to **h** her." **Mt 14:4** *2192*
"We **h** here only five loaves and **Mt 14:17** *2192*
"Whatever I **h** that would help you **Mt 15:5** *1473*
"**H** mercy on me, Lord, Son of **Mt 15:22** *1653*
because they **h** remained with Me **Mt 15:32**
three days and **h** nothing to eat; **Mt 15:32** *2192*
"How many loaves do you **h**?" **Mt 15:34** *2192*
yourselves that you **h** no bread? **Mt 16:8** *2192*
whatever you bind on earth shall **h** **Mt 16:19**
whatever you loose on earth shall **h** **Mt 16:19**
"Lord, **h** mercy on my son, for he **Mt 17:15** *1653*
if you **h** faith the size of **Mt 17:20** *2192*
it would be better for him to **h** a **Mt 18:6**
than to **h** two hands or two feet **Mt 18:8** *2192*
than to **h** two eyes and be cast into **Mt 18:9** *2192*
ninety-nine which **h** not gone astray **Mt 18:13**
to you, you **h** won your brother. **Mt 18:15**
whatever you bind on earth shall **h** **Mt 18:18**
whatever you loose on earth shall **h** **Mt 18:18**
For where two or three **h** gathered **Mt 18:20**
he did not **h** *the means* to repay, **Mt 18:25** *2192*
H patience with me and I will **Mt 18:26** *3114*
H patience with me and I will **Mt 18:29** *3114*
'Should you not also **h** had mercy **Mt 18:33**
"**H** you not read that He who **Mt 19:4**
"All these things I **h** kept; **Mt 19:20**
you will **h** treasure in heaven; **Mt 19:21** *2192*
we **h** left everything and followed **Mt 19:27**
you, that you who **h** followed Me, **Mt 19:28**
Why **h** you been standing here idle **Mt 20:6**
last men **h** worked *only* one hour, **Mt 20:12**
and you **h** made them equal to us **Mt 20:12**
equal to us who **h** borne the burden **Mt 20:12**
"Lord, **h** mercy on us, Son of **Mt 20:30** *1653*
"Lord, Son of David, **h** mercy **Mt 20:31** *1653*
h you never read, **Mt 21:16**
OF INFANTS AND NURSING BABIES YOU **H** **Mt 21:16**
I say to you, if you **h** faith and **Mt 21:21** *2192*
Tell those who **h** been invited, **Mt 22:4**
"Behold, I **h** prepared my dinner; **Mt 22:4**
h you not read what was **Mt 22:31**
Pharisees **h** seated themselves **Mt 23:2**
and **h** neglected the weightier **Mt 23:23**
these are the things you should **h** done **Mt 23:23**
we would not **h** been partners with **Mt 23:30**
short, no life would **h** been saved; **Mt 24:22**
"Behold, I **h** told you in advance. **Mt 24:25**
he would **h** been on the alert and **Mt 24:43**
would not **h** allowed his house to be **Mt 24:43**
I **h** gained five more talents.' **Mt 25:20**
See, I **h** gained two more talents.' **Mt 25:22**
See, you **h** what is yours.' **Mt 25:25** *2192*
to **h** put my money in the bank, **Mt 25:27**
I would **h** received my *money* back **Mt 25:27**
and he will **h** an abundance; **Mt 25:29** *4052*
but from the one who does not **h**, **Mt 25:29** *2192*
even what he does **h** shall be taken **Mt 25:29** *2192*
this *perfume* might **h** been sold for **Mt 26:9**
you always **h** the poor with you; **Mt 26:11** *2192*
but you do not always **h** Me. **Mt 26:11** *2192*
It would **h** been good for that man **Mt 26:24**
"You **h** said *it* yourself." **Mt 26:25**
"But after I **h** been raised, I **Mt 26:32**
"Even if I **h** to die with You, I **Mt 26:35** *1163*
"Friend, *do* what you **h** come for." **Mt 26:50** *3918b*
"**H** you come out with swords and **Mt 26:55**
"You **h** said it *yourself;* **Mt 26:64**
further need do we **h** of witnesses? **Mt 26:65** *2192*
you **h** now heard the blasphemy; **Mt 26:65**
I **h** sinned by betraying innocent **Mt 27:4**
"**H** nothing to do with that **Mt 27:19**
WHY **H** YOU FORSAKEN ME?" **Mt 27:46**
Pilate said to them, "You **h** a guard; **Mt 27:65** *2192*
behold, I **h** told you." **Mt 28:7**
"What business do we **h** with each **Mk 1:24**
H You come to destroy us? **Mk 1:24**
h never seen anything like this." **Mk 2:12**
they **h** the bridegroom with them, **Mk 2:19** *2192*
"**H** you never read what David did **Mk 2:25**
and to **h** authority to cast out the **Mk 3:15** *2192*
where it did not **h** much soil; **Mk 4:5** *2192*
they **h** no *firm* root in themselves, **Mk 4:17** *2192*
are the ones who **h** heard the word, **Mk 4:18**
and whoever does not **h**, **Mk 4:25** *2192*
Do you still **h** no faith?" **Mk 4:40** *2192*
"What business do we **h** with each **Mk 5:7**
for you to **h** your brother's wife." **Mk 6:18** *2192*
they did not even **h** time to eat.) **Mk 6:31** *2119*
"How many loaves do you **h**? **Mk 6:38** *2192*
h received in order to observe, **Mk 7:4**
whatever I **h** that would help you is **Mk 7:11** *1473*
tradition which you **h** handed down; **Mk 7:13**
they **h** remained with Me now three **Mk 8:2**
three days and **h** nothing to eat **Mk 8:2** *2192*
of them **h** come from a great distance." **Mk 8:3** *1510*
"How many loaves do you **h**?" **Mk 8:5** *2192*
and did not **h** more than one loaf **Mk 8:14** *2192*
the fact that you **h** no bread? **Mk 8:17** *2192*
Do you **h** a hardened heart? **Mk 8:17** *2192*
H salt in yourselves, and be at **Mk 9:50** *2192*
I **h** kept all these things from my **Mk 10:20**
you will **h** treasure in heaven; **Mk 10:21** *2192*
we **h** left everything and followed **Mk 10:28**
Son of David, **h** mercy on me!" **Mk 10:47** *1653*
Son of David, **h** mercy on me!" **Mk 10:48** *1653*
But you **h** made it a ROBBERS' DEN." **Mk 11:17**
saying to them, "**H** faith in God. **Mk 11:22** *2192*
believe that you **h** received them, **Mk 11:24**
if you **h** anything against anyone, **Mk 11:25** *2192*
John to **h** been a real prophet. **Mk 11:32**
"**H** you not even read this **Mk 12:10**
h you not read in the book of **Mk 12:26**
You **h** truly stated that HE IS ONE, **Mk 12:32**
parents and **h** them put to death. **Mk 13:12**
days, no life would **h** been saved; **Mk 13:20**
I **h** told you everything in advance. **Mk 13:23**
this perfume might **h** been sold for **Mk 14:5**
you always **h** the poor with you, **Mk 14:7** *2192*

but you do not always **h** Me. **Mk 14:7** *2192*
It would **h** *been* good for that man **Mk 14:21**
"But after I **h** been raised, I **Mk 14:28**
"*Even* if I **h** to die with You, I **Mk 14:31**
"Sit here until I **h** prayed." **Mk 14:32**
"**H** you come out with swords and **Mk 14:48**
further need do we **h** of witnesses? **Mk 14:63** *2192*
"You **h** heard the blasphemy; **Mk 14:64**
WHY **H** YOU FORSAKEN ME?" **Mk 15:34**
accompany those who **h** believed: **Mk 16:17**
inasmuch as many **h** undertaken to **Lk 1:1**
the things you **h** been taught. **Lk 1:4**
"You will **h** joy and gladness, **Lk 1:14**
and I **h** been sent to speak to you and **Lk 1:19**
for you **h** found favor with God. **Lk 1:30**
and His kingdom will **h** no end." **Lk 1:33**
For my eyes **h** seen Your salvation, **Lk 2:30**
Which You **h** prepared in the presence **Lk 2:31**
why **h** You treated us this way? **Lk 2:48**
Your father and I **h** been anxiously **Lk 2:48**
'We **h** Abraham for our father,' for **Lk 3:8** *2192*
than what you **h** been ordered to." **Lk 3:13**
business do we **h** with each other, **Lk 4:34**
H You come to destroy us? **Lk 4:34**
'Your sins **h** been forgiven you,' **Lk 5:23**
h seen remarkable things today." **Lk 5:26**
"I **h** not come to call the **Lk 5:32**
"**H** you not even read what David **Lk 6:3**
h I found such great faith." **Lk 7:9**
to John what you **h** seen and heard: **Lk 7:22**
the POOR **H** THE GOSPEL PREACHED **Lk 7:22**
I **h** something to say to you." **Lk 7:40** *2192*
"You **h** judged correctly." **Lk 7:43**
which are many, **h** been forgiven, **Lk 7:47**
"Your sins **h** been forgiven." **Lk 7:48**
the road are those who **h** heard; **Lk 8:12**
and these **h** no *firm* root; **Lk 8:13** *2192*
these are the ones who **h** heard, **Lk 8:14**
these are the ones who **h** heard the **Lk 8:15**
and whoever does not **h**, **Lk 8:18** *2192*
"What business do we **h** with each **Lk 8:28**
do not *even* **h** two tunics apiece. **Lk 9:3** *2192*
"We **h** no more than five loaves **Lk 9:13**
"**H** them sit down *to eat* in groups **Lk 9:14**
"The foxes **h** holes and the birds **Lk 9:58** *2192*
holes and the birds of the air **h** **Lk 9:58**
they would **h** repented long ago, **Lk 10:13**
I **h** given you authority to tread **Lk 10:19**
that You **h** hidden these things from **Lk 10:21**
the wise and intelligent and **h** **Lk 10:21**
"All things **h** been handed over to **Lk 10:22**
"You **h** answered correctly **Lk 10:28**
I **h** nothing to set before him'; **Lk 11:6** *2192*
asked Him to **h** lunch with him; **Lk 11:37** *709*
the things you should **h** done without **Lk 11:42**
For you **h** taken away the key of **Lk 11:52**
whatever you **h** said in the dark **Lk 12:3**
and what you **h** whispered in the **Lk 12:3**
that **h** no more that they can do. **Lk 12:4** *2192*
I **h** no place to store my crops?' **Lk 12:17** *2192*
you **h** many goods laid up for many **Lk 12:19** *2192*
who will own what you **h** prepared?' **Lk 12:20**
they **h** no storeroom nor barn **Lk 12:24**
and **h** them recline *at the table,* **Lk 12:37**
he would not **h** allowed his house **Lk 12:39**
"I **h** come to cast fire upon the **Lk 12:49**
"But I **h** a baptism to undergo, **Lk 12:50** *2192*
you **h** paid the very last cent." **Lk 12:59**
for three years I **h** come looking **Lk 13:7**
should she not **h** been released **Lk 13:16**
and you would not **h** *it!* **Lk 13:34**
"Which one of you will **h** a son **Lk 14:5**
you may **h** been invited by him, **Lk 14:8**
then you will **h** honor in the sight **Lk 14:10**
do not **h** *the means* to repay you **Lk 14:14** *2192*
'I **h** bought a piece of land and I **Lk 14:18**
'I **h** bought five yoke of oxen, and **Lk 14:19**
'I **h** married a wife, and for that **Lk 14:20**
h found my sheep which was lost! **Lk 15:6**
for I **h** found the coin which I had **Lk 15:9**
"And he would **h** gladly filled his **Lk 15:16**
men **h** more than enough bread, **Lk 15:17** *4052*
"Father, I **h** sinned against **Lk 15:18**
I **h** sinned against heaven and in **Lk 15:21**
many years I **h** been serving you **Lk 15:29**
and I **h** never neglected a command **Lk 15:29**
yet you **h** never given me a young **Lk 15:29**
Son, you **h** always been with me, **Lk 15:31**
"Therefore if you **h** not been faithful **Lk 16:11**
"And if you **h** not been faithful **Lk 16:12**
'Father Abraham, **h** mercy on me, **Lk 16:24** *1653*
for I **h** five brothers **Lk 16:28** *2192*
'They **h** Moses and the Prophets; **Lk 16:29** *2192*
we **h** done *only* that which we ought **Lk 17:10**
that which we ought to **h** done.' **Lk 17:10**
"Jesus, Master, **h** mercy on us!" **Lk 17:13** *1653*
things I **h** kept from *my* youth." **Lk 18:21**
you shall **h** treasure in heaven; **Lk 18:22** *2192*
"Behold, we **h** left our own **Lk 18:28**
and after they **h** scourged Him, **Lk 18:33**
Son of David, **h** mercy on me!" **Lk 18:38** *1653*
"Son of David, **h** mercy on me!" **Lk 18:39** *1653*
I **h** defrauded anyone of anything, **Lk 19:8**
because you **h** been faithful in a **Lk 19:17**
h collected it with interest?' **Lk 19:23**
but from the one who does not **h**, **Lk 19:26** *2192*
even what he does **h** shall be taken **Lk 19:26** *2192*
they **h** been hidden from your eyes. **Lk 19:42**
but you **h** made it a ROBBERS' DEN." **Lk 19:46**
and inscription does it **h**?" **Lk 20:24** *2192*
"Teacher, You **h** spoken well." **Lk 20:39**
For they did not **h** courage to **Lk 20:40** *5111*
that you may **h** strength to escape **Lk 21:36** *2729*
When you **h** entered the city, **Lk 22:10**
I **h** earnestly desired to eat **Lk 22:15**
and those who **h** authority over **Lk 22:25** *1850*
who **h** stood by Me in My trials; **Lk 22:28**
but I **h** prayed for you, that your **Lk 22:32**
you, when once you **h** turned again, **Lk 22:32**
until you **h** denied three times that you **Lk 22:34**
"**H** you come out with swords and **Lk 22:52**
further need do we **h** of testimony? For **Lk 22:71** *2192*
For we **h** heard it ourselves from **Lk 22:71**
I **h** found no guilt in this man **Lk 23:14**
I **h** found in Him no guilt **Lk 23:22**
h happened here in these days?" **Lk 24:18**
in all that the prophets **h** spoken! **Lk 24:25**
for a spirit does not **h** flesh and **Lk 24:39** *2192*
and bones as you see that I **h**." **Lk 24:39** *2192*
"**H** you anything here to eat?" **Lk 24:41** *2192*
of His fullness we **h** all received, **Jn 1:16**
"I **h** seen the Spirit descending **Jn 1:32**
"I myself **h** seen, and have **Jn 1:34**
and **h** testified that this is **Jn 1:34**
"We **h** found the Messiah" **Jn 1:41**
"We **h** found Him of whom Moses in **Jn 1:45**
"They **h** no wine." **Jn 2:3** *2192*
what does that **h** to do with us? **Jn 2:4**
and when *the people* **h** drunk freely, **Jn 2:10**
h kept the good wine until now." **Jn 2:10**
You **h** come from God *as* a teacher; **Jn 3:2**
testify of what we **h** seen, **Jn 3:11**
will in Him **h** eternal life. **Jn 3:15** *2192*
not perish, but **h** eternal life. **Jn 3:16** *2192*
to whom you **h** testified, **Jn 3:26**
'I **h** been sent ahead of Him.' **Jn 3:28**
Jews **h** no dealings with Samaritans **Jn 4:9** *4798*
Me a drink,' you would **h** asked Him, **Jn 4:10**
would **h** given you living water." **Jn 4:10**
You **h** nothing to draw with and the **Jn 4:11** *2192*
"I **h** no husband." **Jn 4:17** *2192*
"You **h** correctly said, **Jn 4:17**
'I **h** no husband'; **Jn 4:17** *2192*
for you **h** had five husbands, and **Jn 4:18** *2192*
you now **h** is not your husband; **Jn 4:18** *2192*
this you **h** said truly." **Jn 4:18**
who told me all the things that I **h** **Jn 4:29**
I **h** food to eat that you do not **Jn 4:32** *2192*
that for which you **h** not labored; **Jn 4:38**
others **h** labored and you have **Jn 4:38**
you **h** entered into their labor." **Jn 4:38**
"He told me all the things that I **h** **Jn 4:39**
for we **h** heard for ourselves and **Jn 4:42**
I **h** no man to put me into the pool **Jn 5:7** *2192*
"Behold, you **h** become well; **Jn 5:14**
the Son also to **h** life in Himself; **Jn 5:26** *2192*
"You **h** sent to John, and he has **Jn 5:33**
I **h** is greater than *the testimony of* **Jn 5:36** *2192*
You **h** neither heard His voice at **Jn 5:37**
do not **h** His word abiding in you, **Jn 5:38** *2192*
that in them you **h** eternal life; **Jn 5:39** *2192*
come to Me so that you may **h** life. **Jn 5:40** *2192*
that you do not **h** the love of God **Jn 5:42** *2192*
I **h** come in My Father's name, **Jn 5:43**
in whom you **h** set your hope. **Jn 5:45**
"**H** the people sit down." **Jn 6:10** *4160*
I said to you that you **h** seen Me, **Jn 6:36**
"For I **h** come down from heaven, **Jn 6:38**
in Him will **h** eternal life, **Jn 6:40** *2192*
I **h** come down out of heaven' **Jn 6:42**
you **h** no life in yourselves. **Jn 6:53** *2192*
the words that I **h** spoken to you **Jn 6:63**
"For this reason I **h** said to you, **Jn 6:65**
You **h** words of eternal life. **Jn 6:68** *2192*
"We **h** believed and have come **Jn 6:69**
have believed and **h** come to know **Jn 6:69**
crowd answered, "You **h** a demon! **Jn 7:20** *2192*
and I **h** not come of Myself, but He **Jn 7:28**
"You **h** not also been led astray, **Jn 7:47**
not also been led astray, **h** you? **Jn 7:47**
might **h** grounds for accusing Him. **Jn 8:6** *2192*
but will **h** the Light of life." **Jn 8:12** *2192*
"What **h** I been saying to you *from* **Jn 8:25**
I **h** many things to speak and to **Jn 8:26** *2192*
and **h** never yet been enslaved to **Jn 8:33**
which I **h** seen with *My* Father; **Jn 8:38**
we **h** one Father: God." **Jn 8:41** *2192*
forth and **h** come from God, **Jn 8:42** *2240*
for I **h** not even come on My own **Jn 8:42**
are a Samaritan and **h** a demon?" **Jn 8:48** *2192*
"I do not **h** a demon; **Jn 8:49** *2192*
"Now we know that You **h** a demon. **Jn 8:52** *2192*
and you **h** not come to know Him, **Jn 8:55**
old, and **h** You seen Abraham?" **Jn 8:57**
"You **h** both seen Him, and He is **Jn 9:37**
were blind, you would **h** no sin; **Jn 9:41** *2192*
I came that they may **h** life, **Jn 10:10** *2192*
life, and **h** *it* abundantly. **Jn 10:10** *2192*
"I **h** other sheep, which are **Jn 10:16** *2192*
I **h** authority to lay it down, and **Jn 10:18** *2192*
I **h** authority to take it up again. **Jn 10:18** *2192*
here, my brother would not **h** died. **Jn 11:21**
I **h** believed that You are the **Jn 11:27**
my brother would not **h** died." **Jn 11:32**
"Where **h** you laid him?" **Jn 11:34**
h kept this man also from dying?" **Jn 11:37** *4160*
I thank You that You **h** heard Me. **Jn 11:41**
you always **h** the poor with you, **Jn 12:8** *2192*
you, but you do not always **h** Me." **Jn 12:8** *2192*
"I **h** both glorified it, and will **Jn 12:28**
"We **h** heard out of the Law that **Jn 12:34**
Walk while you **h** the Light, **Jn 12:35** *2192*
"While you **h** the Light, believe **Jn 12:36** *2192*
"I **h** come *as* Light into the **Jn 12:46**
wash you, you **h** no part with Me." **Jn 13:8** *2192*
"Do you know what I **h** done to you? **Jn 13:12**
I know the ones I **h** chosen **Jn 13:18**
we **h** need of for the feast"; **Jn 13:29** *2192*
another, even as I **h** loved you, **Jn 13:34**
if you **h** love for one another." **Jn 13:35** *2192*
were not so, I would **h** told you **Jn 14:2**
you would **h** known My Father also; **Jn 14:7**
on you know Him, and **h** seen Him." **Jn 14:7**
H I been so long with you, and **Jn 14:9**
and *yet* you **h** not come to know Me, **Jn 14:9**
"These things I **h** spoken to you while **Jn 14:25**
loved Me, you would **h** rejoiced **Jn 14:28**
"Now I **h** told you before it **Jn 14:29**
the word which I **h** spoken to you. **Jn 15:3**
has loved Me, I **h** also loved you; **Jn 15:9**
I **h** kept My Father's commandments **Jn 15:10**
"These things I **h** spoken to you so **Jn 15:11**
another, just as I **h** loved you. **Jn 15:12**
but I **h** called you friends, for **Jn 15:15**
for all things that I **h** heard from **Jn 15:15**
My Father I **h** made known to you. **Jn 15:15**
to them, they would not **h** sin, **Jn 15:22** *2192*
they **h** no excuse for their sin. **Jn 15:22** *2192*
else did, they would not **h** sin; **Jn 15:24** *2192*
but now they **h** both seen and hated **Jn 15:24**
"But *they* **h** *done this* to fulfill **Jn 15:25**
because you **h** been with Me from **Jn 15:27**
"These things I **h** spoken to you so **Jn 16:1**
they **h** not known the Father or **Jn 16:3**
these things I **h** spoken to you, **Jn 16:4**
I **h** said these things to you, **Jn 16:6**
I **h** many more things to say to **Jn 16:12** *2192*
"Therefore you too **h** grief now; **Jn 16:22** *2192*
h asked for nothing in My name; **Jn 16:24**
"These things I **h** spoken to you **Jn 16:25**
loves you, because you **h** loved Me **Jn 16:27**
and **h** believed that I came forth **Jn 16:27**
Father and **h** come into the world; **Jn 16:28**
and **h** no need for anyone to **Jn 16:30** *2192*
"These things I **h** spoken to you, **Jn 16:33**
you, so that in Me you may **h** peace. **Jn 16:33** *2192*
In the world you **h** tribulation, **Jn 16:33** *2192*
I **h** overcome the world." **Jn 16:33**
that to all whom You **h** given Him, **Jn 17:2**
and Jesus Christ whom You **h** sent. **Jn 17:3**
work which You **h** given Me to do. **Jn 17:4**
"I **h** manifested Your name to the men **Jn 17:6**
to Me, and they **h** kept Your word. **Jn 17:6**
"Now they **h** come to know that **Jn 17:7**
You **h** given Me is from You; **Jn 17:7**
You gave Me I **h** given to them; **Jn 17:8**
but of those whom You **h** given Me; **Jn 17:9**
and I **h** been glorified in them. **Jn 17:10**
the name which You **h** given Me, **Jn 17:11**
in Your name which You **h** given Me; **Jn 17:12**
that they may **h** My joy made full **Jn 17:13** *2192*
"I **h** given them Your word; **Jn 17:14**
I also **h** sent them into the world. **Jn 17:18**
The glory which You **h** given Me **Jn 17:22**
have given Me I **h** given to them, **Jn 17:22**
even as You **h** loved Me. **Jn 17:23**
they also, whom You **h** given Me, **Jn 17:24**
My glory which You **h** given Me **Jn 17:24**
known You, yet I **h** known You; **Jn 17:25**
h known that You sent Me; **Jn 17:25**
I **h** made Your name known to them, **Jn 17:26**
Of those whom You **h** given Me **Jn 18:9**
I **h** spoken openly to the world; **Jn 18:20**
who **h** heard what I spoke to them; **Jn 18:21**
"If I **h** spoken wrongly, testify **Jn 18:23**
not **h** delivered Him to you." **Jn 18:30**
what **h** You done? **Jn 18:35**
For this I **h** been born, and for **Jn 18:37**
for this I **h** come into the world, **Jn 18:37**
"But you **h** a custom that I **Jn 18:39**
"We **h** a law, and by that law He **Jn 19:7** *2192*
that I **h** authority to release You, **Jn 19:10** *2192*
I **h** authority to crucify You?" **Jn 19:10** *2192*
"You would **h** no authority over **Jn 19:11** *2192*
"We **h** no king but Caesar." **Jn 19:15** *2192*
"What I **h** written I have written." **Jn 19:22**
"What I have written I **h** written." **Jn 19:22**
"They **h** taken away the Lord out **Jn 20:2**
not know where they **h** laid Him." **Jn 20:2**
"Because they **h** taken away my **Jn 20:13**
not know where they **h** laid Him." **Jn 20:13**
"Sir, if you **h** carried Him away, **Jn 20:15**
tell me where you **h** laid Him, **Jn 20:15**
for I **h** not yet ascended to the **Jn 20:17**
"I **h** seen the Lord," **Jn 20:18**
their sins **h** been forgiven them; **Jn 20:23**
of any, they **h** been retained." **Jn 20:23**
"We **h** seen the Lord!" **Jn 20:25**
"Because you **h** seen Me, have you **Jn 20:29**
you have seen Me, **h** you believed? **Jn 20:29**
but these **h** been written so that you **Jn 20:31**
you may **h** life in His name. **Jn 20:31** *2192*
"Children, you do not **h** any fish, **Jn 21:5** *2192*
the fish which you **h** now caught." **Jn 21:10**
"Come *and* **h** breakfast." **Jn 21:12** *709*
h watched Him go into heaven." **Ac 1:11**
of the men who **h** accompanied us **Ac 1:21**

Context	Reference	No.
one of these two You **h** chosen	Ac 1:24	
'YOU **H** MADE KNOWN TO ME THE WAYS	Ac 2:28	
with all, as anyone might **h** need.	Ac 2:45	2192
but what I do **h** I give to you:	Ac 3:6	2192
all the prophets who **h** spoken,	Ac 3:24	
in what name, **h** you done this?"	Ac 4:7	
what we **h** seen and heard."	Ac 4:20	
Why is it that you **h** conceived	Ac 5:4	
You **h** not lied to men but to God	Ac 5:4	
"Why is it that you **h** agreed	Ac 5:9	
the feet of those who **h** buried	Ac 5:9	
you **h** filled Jerusalem with your	Ac 5:28	
"We **h** heard him speak blasphemous	Ac 6:11	
for we **h** heard him say that this	Ac 6:14	
'I **H** CERTAINLY SEEN THE OPPRESSION	Ac 7:34	
OF MY PEOPLE IN EGYPT AND **H** HEARD	Ac 7:34	
AND I **H** COME DOWN TO RESCUE THEM;	Ac 7:34	
and murderers you **h** now become;	Ac 7:52	
"You **h** no part or portion in this	Ac 8:21	
that nothing of what you **h** said may	Ac 8:24	
I **h** heard from many about this	Ac 9:13	
"Your prayers and alms **h** ascended	Ac 10:4	
for I **h** never eaten anything	Ac 10:14	
for I **h** sent them Myself."	Ac 10:20	
the reason for which you **h** come?"	Ac 10:21	
what reason you **h** sent for me."	Ac 10:29	
alms **h** been remembered before God.	Ac 10:31	
you **h** been kind enough to come.	Ac 10:33	
h been commanded by the Lord."	Ac 10:33	
who **h** received the Holy Spirit	Ac 10:47	
'Send to Joppa and **h** Simon,	Ac 11:13	
to what could **h** become of Peter.	Ac 12:18	
work to which I **h** called them."	Ac 13:2	
if you **h** any word of exhortation	Ac 13:15	
'I **H** FOUND DAVID the son of	Ac 13:22	
TODAY I **H** BEGOTTEN YOU.'	Ac 13:33	
'I **H** PLACED YOU AS A LIGHT FOR	Ac 13:47	
"The gods **h** become like men and	Ac 14:11	
like men and **h** come down to us."	Ac 14:11	
nor we **h** been able to bear?	Ac 15:10	
"Since we **h** heard that some of	Ac 15:24	
h disturbed you with *their* words	Ac 15:24	
men who **h** risked their lives for	Ac 15:26	
we **h** sent Judas and Silas,	Ac 15:27	
"If you **h** judged me to be	Ac 16:15	
magistrates **h** sent to release you.	Ac 16:36	
"They **h** beaten us in public	Ac 16:37	
and **h** thrown us into prison;	Ac 16:37	
"These men who **h** upset the world	Ac 17:6	
upset the world **h** come here also;	Ac 17:6	
some of your own poets **h** said,	Ac 17:28	
I **h** many people in this city."	Ac 18:10	
we **h** not even heard whether there	Ac 19:2	
"After I **h** been there, I must	Ac 19:21	
"For you **h** brought these men	Ac 19:37	
him **h** a complaint against any man,	Ac 19:38	2192
would not **h** to spend time in Asia;	Ac 20:16	
"I **h** coveted no one's silver or	Ac 20:33	
the Jews of those who **h** believed,	Ac 21:20	
and they **h** been told about you,	Ac 21:21	
certainly hear that you **h** come.	Ac 21:22	
We **h** four men who are under a vow;	Ac 21:23	
which they **h** been told about you,	Ac 21:24	
the Gentiles who **h** believed,	Ac 21:25	
men of what you **h** seen and heard.	Ac 22:15	
I **h** lived my life with a perfectly	Ac 23:1	
for as you **h** solemnly witnessed to	Ac 23:11	
"We **h** bound ourselves under a	Ac 23:14	
nothing until we **h** killed Paul.	Ac 23:14	
it that you **h** to report to me?"	Ac 23:19	2192
"The Jews **h** agreed to ask you to	Ac 23:20	
who **h** bound themselves under a curse	Ac 23:21	
Tell no one that you **h** notified me	Ac 23:22	
"Since we **h** through you attained	Ac 24:2	
For we **h** found this man a real pest	Ac 24:5	
you **h** been a judge to this nation,	Ac 24:10	
to **h** been present before you and	Ac 24:19	
they should **h** anything against me.	Ac 24:19	2192
in custody and *yet* **h** *some* freedom,	Ac 24:23	2192
might **h** him brought to Jerusalem	Ac 25:3	
"I **h** committed no offense either	Ac 25:8	
I **h** done no wrong to *the* Jews, as	Ac 25:10	
and **h** committed anything worthy of	Ac 25:11	
"You **h** appealed to Caesar, to	Ac 25:12	
"Yet I **h** nothing definite about	Ac 25:26	2192
Therefore I **h** brought him before	Ac 25:26	
place, I may **h** something to write.	Ac 25:26	2192
since they **h** known about me for a	Ac 26:5	
this purpose I **h** appeared to you,	Ac 26:16	
to the things which you **h** seen,	Ac 26:16	
who **h** been sanctified by faith in Me.'	Ac 26:18	
"This man might **h** been set free	Ac 26:32	
you ought to **h** followed my advice	Ac 27:21	
and not to **h** set sail from Crete and	Ac 27:21	
turn out exactly as I **h** been told.	Ac 27:25	
you **h** been constantly watching and	Ac 27:33	
"We **h** neither received letters	Ac 28:21	
nor **h** any of the brethren come	Ac 28:21	
AND THEY **H** CLOSED THEIR EYES;	Ac 28:27	
through whom we **h** received grace	Ro 1:5	
often I **h** planned to come to you	Ro 1:13	
(and **h** been prevented so far)	Ro 1:13	
nature, **h** been clearly seen,	Ro 1:20	
Therefore you **h** no excuse, everyone	Ro 2:1	1510
For all who **h** sinned without the	Ro 2:12	
and all who **h** sinned under the Law	Ro 2:12	
Gentiles who do not **h** the Law	Ro 2:14	2192
for we **h** already charged that both	Ro 3:9	
ALL **H** TURNED ASIDE, TOGETHER THEY	Ro 3:12	
TOGETHER THEY **H** BECOME USELESS;	Ro 3:12	
AND THE PATH OF PEACE THEY **H** NOT	Ro 3:17	
for all **h** sinned and fall short of	Ro 3:23	
ARE THOSE WHOSE LAWLESS DEEDS **H** BEEN	Ro 4:7	
AND WHOSE SINS **H** BEEN COVERED.	Ro 4:7	
"A FATHER OF MANY NATIONS **H** I	Ro 4:17	
we **h** peace with God through our	Ro 5:1	2192
we **h** obtained our introduction	Ro 5:2	
through whom we **h** now received the	Ro 5:11	
us who **h** been baptized into Christ	Ro 6:3	
h been baptized into His death?	Ro 6:3	
Therefore we **h** been buried with	Ro 6:4	
For if we **h** become united with	Ro 6:5	
Now if we **h** died with Christ, we	Ro 6:8	
we **h** been released from the Law,	Ro 7:6	
I would not **h** come to know sin	Ro 7:7	
for I would not **h** known about	Ro 7:7	
does not **h** the Spirit of Christ,	Ro 8:9	2192
For you **h** not received a spirit of	Ro 8:15	
but you **h** received a spirit of	Ro 8:15	
For in hope we **h** been saved, but	Ro 8:24	
that I **h** great sorrow and	Ro 9:2	
AND SARAH SHALL **H** A SON."	Ro 9:9	1510
For He says to Moses, "I WILL **H**	Ro 9:15	1653
"I WILL HAVE MERCY ON WHOM I **H**	Ro 9:15	1653
AND I WILL **H** COMPASSION ON WHOM	Ro 9:15	3627
WILL HAVE COMPASSION ON WHOM I **H**	Ro 9:15	3627
potter **h** a right over the clay,	Ro 9:21	2192
WE WOULD **H** BECOME LIKE SODOM,	Ro 9:29	
AND WOULD **H** RESEMBLED GOMORRAH."	Ro 9:29	
that they **h** a zeal for God,	Ro 10:2	2192
Him in whom they **h** not believed?	Ro 10:14	
in Him whom they **h** not heard?	Ro 10:14	
I say, surely they **h** never heard,	Ro 10:18	
they have never heard, **h** they?	Ro 10:18	
heard, have they? Indeed they **h**;	Ro 10:18	
"ALL THE DAY LONG I **H**	Ro 10:21	
"Lord, THEY **H** KILLED YOUR	Ro 11:3	
THEY **H** TORN DOWN YOUR ALTARS, AND	Ro 11:3	
"I **H** KEPT for Myself SEVEN	Ro 11:4	
for Myself SEVEN THOUSAND MEN WHO **H**	Ro 11:4	
but now **h** been shown mercy because	Ro 11:30	
these also now **h** been disobedient,	Ro 11:31	
think so as to **h** sound judgment,	Ro 12:3	4993
For just as we **h** many members in	Ro 12:4	2192
do not **h** the same function,	Ro 12:4	2192
Since we **h** gifts that differ	Ro 12:6	2192
and they who **h** opposed will	Ro 13:2	
want to **h** no fear of authority?	Ro 13:3	5399
you will **h** praise from the same;	Ro 13:3	2192
The faith which you **h**,	Ro 14:22	2192
h as your own conviction before	Ro 14:22	2192
of the Scriptures we might **h** hope.	Ro 15:4	2192
But I **h** written very boldly to you	Ro 15:15	
in Christ Jesus I **h** found reason for	Ro 15:17	2192
I **h** fully preached the gospel of Christ.	Ro 15:19	
AND THEY WHO **H** NOT HEARD SHALL	Ro 15:21	
I **h** often been prevented from	Ro 15:22	
and since I **h** had for many years a	Ro 15:23	
when I **h** first enjoyed your	Ro 15:24	
and Achaia **h** been pleased to make	Ro 15:26	
For if the Gentiles **h** shared in	Ro 15:27	
Therefore, when I **h** finished this,	Ro 15:28	
and **h** put my seal on this fruit of	Ro 15:28	
matter she may **h** need of you;	Ro 16:2	5535
to those who **h** been sanctified in	1Co 1:2	
I **h** been informed concerning you,	1Co 1:11	
not **h** crucified the Lord of glory;	1Co 2:8	
AND *which* **H** NOT ENTERED THE HEART	1Co 2:9	
Now we **h** received, not the spirit	1Co 2:12	
But we **h** the mind of Christ.	1Co 2:16	2192
I **h** figuratively applied to myself	1Co 4:6	
What do you **h** that you did not	1Co 4:7	2192
filled, you **h** already become rich,	1Co 4:8	
you **h** become kings without us;	1Co 4:8	
because we **h** become a spectacle to	1Co 4:9	
we **h** become as the scum of the	1Co 4:13	
to **h** countless tutors in Christ,	1Co 4:15	2192
yet *you would* not **h** many	1Co 4:15	
reason I **h** sent to you Timothy,	1Co 4:17	
Now some **h** become arrogant, as	1Co 4:18	
You **h** become arrogant and	1Co 5:2	
and **h** not mourned instead,	1Co 5:2	
h already judged him who has so	1Co 5:3	
I **h** *decided* to deliver such a one	1Co 5:5	
would **h** to go out of the world.	1Co 5:10	3784
For what **h** I to do with judging	1Co 5:12	
So if you **h** law courts dealing	1Co 6:4	2192
you **h** lawsuits with one another.	1Co 6:7	2192
is in you, whom you **h** from God,	1Co 6:19	2192
you **h** been bought with a price:	1Co 6:20	
each man is to **h** his own wife,	1Co 7:2	2192
each woman is to **h** her own husband.	1Co 7:2	2192
not **h** authority over her own body,	1Co 7:4	1850
not **h** authority over his own body,	1Co 7:4	1850
But if they do not **h** self-control,	1Co 7:9	1467
I **h** no command of the Lord,	1Co 7:25	2192
marry, you **h** not sinned;	1Co 7:28	
such will **h** trouble in this life,	1Co 7:28	2192
those who **h** wives should be as	1Co 7:29	2192
that I also **h** the Spirit of God.	1Co 7:40	2192
we know that we all **h** knowledge.	1Co 8:1	2192
not all men **h** this knowledge;	1Co 8:7	
someone sees you, who **h** knowledge,	1Co 8:10	2192
H I not seen Jesus our Lord?	1Co 9:1	
we not **h** a right to eat and drink?	1Co 9:4	2192
Do we not **h** a right to take along	1Co 9:5	2192
Or do only Barnabas and I not **h** a	1Co 9:6	2192
h their share from the altar?	1Co 9:13	4829
But I **h** used none of these things.	1Co 9:15	
than **h** any man make my boast an	1Co 9:15	
gospel, I **h** nothing to boast of,	1Co 9:16	
do this voluntarily, I **h** a reward;	1Co 9:17	2192
I **h** a stewardship entrusted to me.	1Co 9:17	
I **h** made myself a slave to all,	1Co 9:19	
I **h** become all things to all men,	1Co 9:22	
after I **h** preached to others,	1Co 9:27	
whom the ends of the ages **h** come.	1Co 10:11	
let her also **h** her hair cut off;	1Co 11:6	
for a woman to **h** her hair cut off	1Co 11:6	
ought not to **h** his head covered,	1Co 11:7	
the woman ought to **h** *a symbol*	1Co 11:10	2192
we **h** no other practice,	1Co 11:16	2192
nor **h** the churches of God.	1Co 11:16	
Do you not **h** houses in which to	1Co 11:22	2192
and shame those who **h** nothing?	1Co 11:22	2192
"I **h** no need of you";	1Co 12:21	2192
"I **h** no need of you."	1Co 12:21	2192
presentable members **h** no need *of it.*	1Co 12:24	2192
members may **h** the same care	1Co 12:25	3309
All do not **h** gifts of healings, do	1Co 12:30	2192
and of angels, but do not **h** love,	1Co 13:1	2192
I **h** become a noisy gong or a	1Co 13:1	
If I **h** *the gift of* prophecy,	1Co 13:2	2192
and if I **h** all faith, so as to	1Co 13:2	2192
mountains, but do not **h** love,	1Co 13:2	2192
to be burned, but do not **h** love,	1Co 13:3	2192
just as I also **h** been fully known.	1Co 13:12	
now, but some **h** fallen asleep;	1Co 15:6	
who **h** fallen asleep in Christ have	1Co 15:18	
asleep in Christ **h** perished.	1Co 15:18	
If we **h** hoped in Christ in this	1Co 15:19	
I **h** in Christ Jesus our Lord,	1Co 15:31	2192
for some **h** no knowledge of God.	1Co 15:34	2192
h borne the image of the earthy,	1Co 15:49	
will **h** put on the imperishable,	1Co 15:54	
mortal will **h** put on immortality,	1Co 15:54	
and that they **h** devoted themselves	1Co 16:15	
because they **h** supplied what was	1Co 16:17	
For they **h** refreshed my spirit	1Co 16:18	
us, He on whom we **h** set our hope.	2Co 1:10	
we **h** conducted ourselves in the	2Co 1:12	
I would not **h** sorrow from those who	2Co 2:3	2192
love which I **h** especially for you.	2Co 2:4	2192
for indeed what I **h** forgiven,	2Co 2:10	
if I **h** forgiven anything,	2Co 2:10	
we **h** through Christ toward God.	2Co 3:4	2192
since we **h** this ministry,	2Co 4:1	2192
but we **h** renounced the things	2Co 4:2	
But we **h** this treasure in earthen	2Co 4:7	2192
down, we **h** a building from God,	2Co 5:1	2192
also **h** as our ambition,	2Co 5:9	5389
that you will **h** *an answer* for those	2Co 5:12	2192
even though we **h** known Christ	2Co 5:16	
behold, new things **h** come.	2Co 5:17	
h righteousness and lawlessness,	2Co 6:14	
for I **h** said before that you are	2Co 7:3	
this reason we **h** been comforted.	2Co 7:13	
I **h** boasted to him about you,	2Co 7:14	
everything I **h** confidence in you.	2Co 7:16	2292
according to what he does not **h**.	2Co 8:12	2192
WHO *gathered* MUCH DID NOT **H**	2Co 8:15	4121
We **h** sent along with him the	2Co 8:18	
we **h** regard for what is honorable,	2Co 8:21	4306
We **h** sent with them our brother,	2Co 8:22	
whom we **h** often tested and found	2Co 8:22	
But I **h** sent the brethren,	2Co 9:3	
you may **h** an abundance for every	2Co 9:8	2192
Jesus whom we **h** not preached,	2Co 11:4	
spirit which you **h** not received,	2Co 11:4	
gospel which you **h** not accepted,	2Co 11:4	
in every way we **h** made	2Co 11:6	
that we **h** been weak *by comparison.*	2Co 11:21	
and a day I **h** spent in the deep.	2Co 11:25	
I **h** *been* on frequent journeys,	2Co 11:26	
I **h** *been* in labor and hardship,	2Co 11:27	
If I **h** to boast, I will boast of	2Co 11:30	1163
I **h** become foolish;	2Co 12:11	
I should **h** been commended by you,	2Co 12:11	
Certainly I **h** not taken advantage	2Co 12:17	
any of those whom I **h** sent to you,	2Co 12:17	
whom I have sent to you, **h** I?	2Co 12:17	
All this time you **h** been thinking	2Co 12:19	
that we **h** been speaking in Christ;	2Co 12:19	
those who **h** sinned in the past	2Co 12:21	
sensuality which they **h** practiced.	2Co 12:21	
I **h** previously said when present	2Co 13:2	
to those who **h** sinned in the past and	2Co 13:2	
what we **h** preached to you,	Ga 1:8	
As we **h** said before, so I say	Ga 1:9	
For I would **h** you know, brethren,	Ga 1:11	1107
For you **h** heard of my former	Ga 1:13	
which we **h** in Christ Jesus,	Ga 2:4	2192
we **h** believed in Christ Jesus,	Ga 2:16	
h also been found sinners,	Ga 2:17	
I rebuild what I **h** *once* destroyed,	Ga 2:18	
"I **h** been crucified with Christ;	Ga 2:20	
would indeed **h** been based on law.	Ga 3:21	
h clothed yourselves with Christ.	Ga 3:27	
now that you **h** come to know God,	Ga 4:9	
I **h** labored over you in vain.	Ga 4:11	
for I also **h** *become* as you *are.*	Ga 4:12	
You **h** done me no wrong;	Ga 4:12	
you would **h** plucked out your eyes	Ga 4:15	
So **h** I become your enemy by telling	Ga 4:16	
You **h** been severed from Christ,	Ga 5:4	
you **h** fallen from grace.	Ga 5:4	
I **h** confidence in you in the Lord	Ga 5:10	3982

I **h** forewarned you, that those who Ga 5:21
who belong to Christ Jesus **h** crucified Ga 5:24
and then he will **h** *reason for* Ga 6:4 2192
So then, while we **h** opportunity, Ga 6:10 2192
they desire to **h** you circumcised Ga 6:13
we **h** redemption through His blood, Eph 1:7 2192
also we **h** obtained an inheritance, Eph 1:11
(by grace you **h** been saved), Eph 2:5
you **h** been saved through faith; Eph 2:8
h been brought near by the blood of Eph 2:13
through Him we both **h** our access Eph 2:18 2192
if indeed you **h** heard of the Eph 3:2
in whom we **h** boldness and Eph 3:12 2192
with which you **h** been called, Eph 4:1
h given themselves over to Eph 4:19
if indeed you **h** heard Him and have Eph 4:21
Him and **h** been taught in Him, Eph 4:21
so that he will **h** *something* Eph 4:28 2192
I **h** sent him to you for this Eph 6:22
all, because I **h** you in my heart, Php 1:7 2192
that my circumstances **h** turned out Php 1:12
h far more courage to speak the Php 1:14 5111
H this attitude in yourselves Php 2:5 5426
just as you **h** always obeyed, Php 2:12
day of Christ I will **h** reason to glory Php 2:16
For I **h** no one *else* of kindred Php 2:20 2192
I would not **h** sorrow upon sorrow. Php 2:27 2192
Therefore I **h** sent him all the Php 2:28
h confidence even in the flesh. Php 3:4 2192
those things I **h** counted as loss Php 3:7
for whom I **h** suffered the loss of Php 3:8
Not that I **h** already obtained Php 3:12
it or **h** already become perfect, Php 3:12
as are perfect, **h** this attitude; Php 3:15 5426
you **h** a different attitude, Php 3:15 5426
standard to which we **h** attained. Php 3:16
to the pattern you **h** in us. Php 3:17 2192
women who **h** shared my struggle Php 4:3
The things you **h** learned and Php 4:9
you **h** revived your concern for me; Php 4:10
for I **h** learned to be content in Php 4:11
I **h** learned the secret of being filled Php 4:12
you **h** done well to share *with me* Php 4:14
I **h** received everything in full and Php 4:18 568
in full and **h** an abundance; Php 4:18 4052
from Epaphroditus what you **h** sent, Php 4:18
which you **h** for all the saints; Col 1:4 2192
we **h** not ceased to pray for you Col 1:9
in whom we **h** redemption, the Col 1:14 2192
all things **h** been created through Him Col 1:16
to **h** first place in everything. Col 1:18 4409
of the gospel that you **h** heard, Col 1:23
a struggle I **h** on your behalf and Col 2:1 2192
who **h** not personally seen my face, Col 2:1
Therefore as you **h** received Christ Col 2:6
in Him you **h** been made complete, Col 2:10
If you **h** died with Christ to the Col 2:20
These are matters which **h**, Col 2:23 2192
you **h** been raised up with Christ, Col 3:1
For you **h** died and your life is Col 3:3
and **h** put on the new self who is Col 3:10
as those who **h** been chosen of God, Col 3:12
that you too **h** a Master in heaven. Col 4:1 2192
which I **h** also been imprisoned; Col 4:3
For I **h** sent him to you for this Col 4:8
and they **h** proved to be an Col 4:11
h it also read in the church of Col 4:16 4160
which you **h** received in the Lord, Col 4:17
that we **h** no need to say anything. 1Th 1:8 2192
but just as we **h** been approved by 1Th 2:4
we might **h** asserted our authority. 1Th 2:6
that we **h** been destined for this. 1Th 3:3
the tempter might **h** tempted you, 1Th 3:5
you **h** no need for *anyone* to write 1Th 4:9 2192
as do the rest who **h** no hope. 1Th 4:13 2192
who **h** fallen asleep in Jesus. 1Th 4:14
precede those who **h** fallen asleep. 1Th 4:15
you **h** no need of anything to be 1Th 5:1 2192
and **h** charge over you in the Lord 1Th 5:12 4291b
h this letter read to all the brethren. 1Th 5:27
marveled at among all who **h** believed 2Th 1:10
for not all **h** faith. 2Th 3:2
We **h** confidence in the Lord 2Th 3:4 3982
we do not **h** the right *to this,* 2Th 3:9 2192
h turned aside to fruitless 1Tm 1:6
with which I **h** been entrusted. 1Tm 1:11
which some **h** rejected and suffered 1Tm 1:19
whom I **h** handed over to Satan, 1Tm 1:20
And he must **h** a good reputation 1Tm 3:7 2192
For those who **h** served well as 1Tm 3:13
which you **h** been following. 1Tm 4:6
But **h** nothing to do with worldly 1Tm 4:7 3868
because we **h** fixed our hope on the 1Tm 4:10
because they **h** set aside their 1Tm 5:12
for some **h** already turned aside to 1Tm 5:15
who **h** believers as their masters 1Tm 6:2 2192
For we **h** brought nothing into the 1Tm 6:7
If we **h** food and covering, 1Tm 6:8 2192
it **h** wandered away from the faith and 1Tm 6:10
which some **h** professed and thus 1Tm 6:21
for I know whom I **h** believed and I 2Tm 1:12
He is able to guard what I **h** entrusted 2Tm 1:12
words which you **h** heard from me, 2Tm 1:13
The things which you **h** heard 2Tm 2:2
men who **h** gone astray from the 2Tm 2:18
although they **h** denied its power; 2Tm 3:5
continue in the things you **h** learned 2Tm 3:14
from whom you **h** learned 2Tm 3:14
you **h** known the sacred writings 2Tm 3:15
wanting to **h** their ears tickled, 2Tm 4:3
I **h** fought the good fight, I have 2Tm 4:7
fight, I **h** finished the course, 2Tm 4:7
the course, I **h** kept the faith; 2Tm 4:7
to all who **h** loved His appearing. 2Tm 4:8
But Tychicus I **h** sent to Ephesus. 2Tm 4:12
which we **h** done in righteousness, Ti 3:5
so that those who **h** believed God Ti 3:8
for I **h** decided to spend the Ti 3:12
which you **h** toward the Lord Jesus and Phm 1:5 2192
For I **h** come to have much joy and Phm 1:7
For I have come to **h** much joy and Phm 1:7 2192
hearts of the saints **h** been refreshed Phm 1:7
though I **h** enough confidence in Phm 1:8 2192
I **h** begotten in my imprisonment, Phm 1:10
I **h** sent him back to you in Phm 1:12
you would **h** him back forever, Phm 1:15 568
TODAY I **H** BEGOTTEN YOU"? Heb 1:5
"YOU **H** LOVED RIGHTEOUSNESS Heb 1:9
attention to what we **h** heard, Heb 2:1
"YOU **H** MADE HIM FOR A LITTLE WHILE Heb 2:7
YOU **H** CROWNED HIM WITH GLORY Heb 2:7
AND **H** APPOINTED HIM OVER THE WORKS OF Heb 2:7
YOU **H** PUT ALL THINGS IN SUBJECTION Heb 2:8
we **h** become partakers of Christ, Heb 3:14
may seem to **h** come short of it. Heb 4:1
we **h** had good news preached to us, Heb 4:2
we who **h** believed enter that rest, Heb 4:3
He would not **h** spoken of another Heb 4:8
eyes of Him with whom we **h** to do. Heb 4:13 3056
we **h** a great high priest who has Heb 4:14 2192
For we do not **h** a high priest who Heb 4:15 2192
TODAY I **H** BEGOTTEN YOU Heb 5:5
Concerning him we **h** much to say, Heb 5:11
you **h** become dull of hearing. Heb 5:11
you **h** need again for someone to Heb 5:12 2192
and you **h** come to need milk and Heb 5:12
who because of practice **h** their Heb 5:14 2192
those who **h** once been enlightened Heb 6:4
and **h** tasted of the heavenly gift Heb 6:4
h been made partakers of the Holy Heb 6:4
and **h** tasted the good word of God Heb 6:5
and *then* **h** fallen away, it is Heb 6:6
which you **h** shown toward His name, Heb 6:10
we who **h** taken refuge Heb 6:18
would **h** strong encouragement Heb 6:18 2192
we **h** as an anchor of the soul, Heb 6:19 2192
h commandment in the Law to collect Heb 7:5 2192
us to **h** such a high priest, Heb 7:26
we **h** such a high priest, who has Heb 8:1 2192
priest also **h** something to offer. Heb 8:3 2192
there would **h** been no occasion Heb 8:7
these things **h** been so prepared, Heb 9:6
those who **h** been defiled sanctify Heb 9:13
those who **h** been called may Heb 9:15
He would **h** needed to suffer often Heb 9:26
they not **h** ceased to be offered, Heb 10:2
h had consciousness of sins? Heb 10:2 2192
"SACRIFICE AND OFFERING YOU **H** NOT Heb 10:5
BUT A BODY YOU **H** PREPARED FOR ME; Heb 10:5
AND *sacrifices* FOR SIN YOU **H** Heb 10:6
I **H** COME (IN THE SCROLL OF Heb 10:7 2240
AND *sacrifices* FOR SIN YOU **H** Heb 10:8
NOR **H** YOU TAKEN PLEASURE *in them* Heb 10:8
then He said, "BEHOLD, I **H** Heb 10:9 2240
By this will we **h** been sanctified Heb 10:10
we **h** confidence to enter the holy Heb 10:19 2192
and since *we* **h** a great priest Heb 10:21
knowing that you **h** for yourselves Heb 10:34 2192
For you **h** need of endurance, so Heb 10:36 2192
when you **h** done the will of God, Heb 10:36
but of those who **h** faith to the Heb 10:39
would **h** had opportunity to return. Heb 11:15
since we **h** so great a cloud of Heb 12:1 2192
You **h** not yet resisted to the Heb 12:4
and you **h** forgotten the Heb 12:5
of which all **h** become partakers, Heb 12:8
to those who **h** been trained by it, Heb 12:11
For you **h** not come to *a mountain* Heb 12:18
But you **h** come to Mount Zion and Heb 12:22
for by this some **h** entertained Heb 13:2
being content with what you **h**; Heb 13:5 3918b
We **h** an altar from which those Heb 13:10 2192
the tabernacle **h** no right to eat. Heb 13:10 2192
here we do not **h** a lasting city, Heb 13:14 2192
sure that we **h** a good conscience, Heb 13:18 2192
for I **h** written to you briefly. Heb 13:22
endurance **h** *its* perfect result, Jas 1:4 2192
h you not made distinctions among Jas 2:4
But you **h** dishonored the poor man. Jas 2:6
name by which you **h** been called? Jas 2:7
you **h** become a transgressor of the Jas 2:11
"You **h** faith and I have works; show Jas 2:18 2192
"You have faith and I **h** works; Jas 2:18 2192
who **h** been made in the likeness of Jas 3:9
But if you **h** bitter jealousy and Jas 3:14 2192
You lust and do not **h**; Jas 4:2 2192
do not **h** because you do not ask. Jas 4:2 2192
Your riches **h** rotted and your Jas 5:2
your garments **h** become moth-eaten. Jas 5:2
gold and your silver **h** rusted; Jas 5:3
you **h** stored up your treasure! Jas 5:3
You **h** lived luxuriously on the Jas 5:5
you **h** fattened your hearts in a Jas 5:5
You **h** condemned and put to death Jas 5:6
You **h** heard of the endurance of Jas 5:11
and **h** seen the outcome of the Lord's Jas 5:11
you **h** been distressed by various 1Pe 1:6
and though you **h** not seen Him, you 1Pe 1:8
which now **h** been announced to you 1Pe 1:12
h in obedience to the truth purified 1Pe 1:22
for you **h** been born again not of 1Pe 1:23
if you **h** tasted the kindness of 1Pe 2:3
but now you **h** RECEIVED MERCY. 1Pe 2:10
h been called for this purpose, 1Pe 2:21
but now you **h** returned to the 1Pe 2:25
and you **h** become her children if 1Pe 3:6
sufficient *for you* to **h** carried out the 1Pe 4:3
you **h** suffered for a little while, 1Pe 5:10
I **h** written to you briefly, 1Pe 5:12
To those who **h** received a faith of 2Pe 1:1
and **h** been established in the 2Pe 1:12
So we **h** the prophetic word 2Pe 1:19 2192
where they **h** no knowledge, 2Pe 2:12 50
the right way, they **h** gone astray, 2Pe 2:15
For if, after they **h** escaped the 2Pe 2:20
be better for them not to **h** known the 2Pe 2:21
the beginning, what we **h** heard, 1Jn 1:1
what we **h** seen with our eyes, 1Jn 1:1
what we **h** looked at and touched with 1Jn 1:1
and we **h** seen and testify and 1Jn 1:2
what we **h** seen and heard we 1Jn 1:3
you too may **h** fellowship with us; 1Jn 1:3 2192
This is the message we **h** heard 1Jn 1:5
If we say that we **h** fellowship 1Jn 1:6 2192
we **h** fellowship with one another, 1Jn 1:7 2192
If we say that we **h** no sin, 1Jn 1:8 2192
If we say that we **h** not sinned, 1Jn 1:10
we **h** an Advocate with the Father, 1Jn 2:1 2192
know that we **h** come to know Him, 1Jn 2:3
"I **h** come to know Him," 1Jn 2:4
you **h** had from the beginning; 1Jn 2:7
is the word which you **h** heard. 1Jn 2:7
because your sins **h** been forgiven you 1Jn 2:12
you **h** overcome the evil one. 1Jn 2:13
I **h** written to you, children, 1Jn 2:13
I **h** written to you, fathers, 1Jn 2:14
I **h** written to you, young men, 1Jn 2:14
and you **h** overcome the evil one. 1Jn 2:14
now many antichrists **h** appeared; 1Jn 2:18
us, they would **h** remained with us; 1Jn 2:19
But you **h** an anointing from the 1Jn 2:20 2192
I **h** not written to you because you 1Jn 2:21
the Son does not **h** the Father; 1Jn 2:23 2192
These things I **h** written to you 1Jn 2:26
and you **h** no need for anyone to 1Jn 2:27 2192
we may **h** confidence and not shrink 1Jn 2:28 2192
you **h** heard from the beginning, 1Jn 3:11
h passed out of death into life, 1Jn 3:14
us, we **h** confidence before God; 1Jn 3:21 2192
h gone out into the world. 1Jn 4:1
you **h** heard that it is coming, 1Jn 4:3
children, and **h** overcome them; 1Jn 4:4
We **h** seen and testify 1Jn 4:14
We **h** come to know and have 1Jn 4:16
h believed the love which God has 1Jn 4:16
that we may **h** confidence in the 1Jn 4:17 2192
this commandment we **h** from Him, 1Jn 4:21 2192
he who does not **h** the Son of God 1Jn 5:12 2192
Son of God does not **h** the life. 1Jn 5:12 2192
These things I **h** written to you 1Jn 5:13
may know that you **h** eternal life. 1Jn 5:13 2192
confidence which we **h** before Him, 1Jn 5:14 2192
we know that we **h** the requests 1Jn 5:15 2192
which we **h** asked from Him. 1Jn 5:15
just as we **h** received commandment 2Jn 1:4
which we **h** had from the beginning, 2Jn 1:5
as you **h** heard from the beginning, 2Jn 1:6
h gone out into the world, 2Jn 1:7
not lose what we **h** accomplished, 2Jn 1:8
of Christ, does not **h** God; 2Jn 1:9 2192
Though I **h** many things to write to 2Jn 1:12 2192
I **h** no greater joy than this, to 3Jn 1:4 2192
and they **h** testified to your love 3Jn 1:6
persons **h** crept in unnoticed, Jude 1:4
For they **h** gone the way of Cain, Jude 1:11
and for pay they **h** rushed headlong Jude 1:11
they **h** done in an ungodly way, Jude 1:15
sinners **h** spoken against Him." Jude 1:15
And **h** mercy on some, who are Jude 1:22 1653
and on some **h** mercy with fear, Jude 1:23 1653
and I **h** the keys of death and of Rv 1:18 2192
the things which you **h** seen, Rv 1:19
and you **h** perseverance and have Rv 2:3 2192
and **h** endured for My name's sake, Rv 2:3
name's sake, and **h** not grown weary. Rv 2:3
'But I **h** *this* against you, that Rv 2:4 2192
that you **h** left your first love. Rv 2:4
remember from where you **h** fallen, Rv 2:5
'Yet this you do **h**, that you hate Rv 2:6 2192
you will **h** tribulation for ten days. Rv 2:10 2192
'But I **h** a few things against you, Rv 2:14 2192
because you **h** there some who hold Rv 2:14 2192
'So you also **h** some who in the Rv 2:15 2192
'But I **h** *this* against you, that Rv 2:20 2192
who **h** not known the deep things of Rv 2:24
what you **h**, hold fast until I come. Rv 2:25 2192
as I also **h** received Rv 2:27
you **h** a name that you are alive, Rv 3:1 2192
for I **h** not found your deeds Rv 3:2
what you **h** received and heard; Rv 3:3
'But you **h** a few people in Sardis Rv 3:4 2192
who **h** not soiled their garments; Rv 3:4
I **h** put before you an open door Rv 3:8
because you **h** a little power, Rv 3:8 2192
little power, and **h** kept My word, Rv 3:8
My word, and **h** not denied My name. Rv 3:8
make them know that I **h** loved you. Rv 3:9

'Because you **h** kept the word of My Rv 3:10
hold fast what you **h**, Rv 3:11 *2192*
"I am rich, and **h** become wealthy, Rv 3:17
wealthy, and **h** need of nothing," Rv 3:17 *2192*
"You **h** made them *to be* a Rv 5:10
until we **h** sealed the bond-servants Rv 7:3
and where **h** they come from?" Rv 7:13
and they **h** washed their robes and Rv 7:14
scorpions of the earth **h** power. Rv 9:3 *2192*
men who do not **h** the seal of God Rv 9:4 *2192*
They **h** tails like scorpions, Rv 9:10 *2192*
They **h** as king over them, the Rv 9:11 *2192*
are like serpents and **h** heads, Rv 9:19 *2192*
seven peals of thunder **h** spoken and Rv 10:4
h the power to shut up the sky, Rv 11:6 *2192*
and they **h** power over the waters Rv 11:6 *2192*
they **h** finished their testimony, Rv 11:7
because You **h** taken Your great Rv 11:17
great power and **h** begun to reign. Rv 11:17
authority of His Christ **h** come, Rv 12:10
who **h** not been defiled with women, Rv 14:4
for they **h** kept themselves chaste. Rv 14:4
These **h** been purchased from among Rv 14:4
they **h** no rest day and night, Rv 14:11 *2192*
RIGHTEOUS ACTS **H** BEEN REVEALED." Rv 15:4
You **h** given them blood to drink. Rv 16:6
five **h** fallen, one is, the other Rv 17:10
who **h** not yet received a kingdom, Rv 17:12
"These **h** one purpose, and they Rv 17:13 *2192*
"For all the nations **h** drunk of Rv 18:3
kings of the earth **h** committed Rv 18:3
merchants of the earth **h** become Rv 18:3
sins **h** piled up as high as heaven, Rv 18:5
and splendid **h** passed away from you Rv 18:14
who **h** been slain on the earth." Rv 18:24
the first things **h** passed away." Rv 21:4
and they will not **h** need of the Rv 22:5 *2192*
h the right to the tree of life, Rv 22:14
h sent My angel to testify to you Rv 22:16

HAVEN
And he *shall be* a **h** for ships, Gn 49:13 2348
He guided them to their desired **h**. Ps 107:30 4231

HAVENS
to a place called Fair **H**, Ac 27:8 *2568*

HAVILAH
flows around the whole land of **H**, Gn 2:11 2341
The sons of Cush *were* Seba and **H** and Gn 10:7 2341
and Ophir and **H** and Jobab; Gn 10:29 2341
They settled from **H** to Shur Gn 25:18 2341
from **H** as you go to Shur, 1Sa 15:7 2341
The sons of Cush *were* Seba, **H**, 1Ch 1:9 2341
Ophir, **H** and Jobab; 1Ch 1:23 2341

HAVING
for the LORD for **h** brought them Ex 12:42
without **h** rinsed his hands in water Lv 15:11
maimed or **h** a running sore or eczema Lv 22:22
every leper and everyone **h** a discharge Nu 5:2
and for **h** the camps set out. Nu 10:2
down, yet **h** his eyes uncovered, Nu 24:4
down, yet **h** his eyes uncovered. Nu 24:16
year old, **h** them without defect. Nu 28:19 1961
year old, **h** them without defect; Nu 29:8 1961
slew his neighbor without **h** enmity Dt 4:42
of these kings **h** agreed to meet, Jos 11:5
both by **h** shed blood without cause 1Sa 25:31
and by my lord **h** avenged himself. 1Sa 25:31
h with him three thousand chosen 1Sa 26:2
h done wickedly more than all the 2Ki 21:11
being a great multitude and **h** 2Ch 13:8
h died in the forty-first year of 2Ch 16:13
They taught in Judah, **h** the book 2Ch 17:9
H sorrow in my heart all the day? Ps 13:2
Which, **h** no chief, Officer or Pr 6:7 369
And **h** my delight in the sons of Pr 8:31
h neither a son nor a brother, Ec 4:8 369
stood above Him, each **h** six wings: Is 6:2
They reel while **h** visions, They Is 28:7
h grain offerings and incense in Jer 41:5
h baked *it* in their sight over Ezk 4:12
iniquity of their **h** turned to Egypt. Ezk 29:16
walls and **h** no bars or gates, Ezk 38:11 369
h oversight at the gates of the Ezk 44:11
And **h** been warned *by God* in a Mt 2:12
teaching them as *one* **h** authority, Mt 7:29 *2192*
H been prompted by her mother, she Mt 14:8
and **h** gone up on the mountain, Mt 15:29
'IF A MAN DIES **H** NO CHILDREN, HIS Mt 22:24 *2192*
and **h** no children left his wife Mt 22:25 *2192*
but after **h** Jesus scourged, he Mt 27:26
teaching them as *one* **h** authority, Mk 1:22 *2192*
on the bed, the demon **h** left. Mk 7:30
"**H** EYES, DO YOU NOT SEE? Mk 8:18 *2192*
AND **H** EARS, DO YOU NOT HEAR? Mk 8:18 *2192*
crippled, than, **h** your two hands, Mk 9:43 *2192*
life lame, than, **h** your two feet, Mk 9:45 *2192*
God with one eye, than, **h** two eyes, Mk 9:47 *2192*
them, and after **h** Jesus scourged, Mk 15:15
h investigated everything Lk 1:3
h been baptized with the baptism Lk 7:29
not **h** been baptized by John. Lk 7:30
h a slave plowing or tending Lk 17:7 *2192*
Now **h** been questioned by the Lk 17:20
my money in the bank, and **h** come, Lk 19:23
IF A MAN'S BROTHER DIES, **h** a wife, Lk 20:28 *2192*
H arrested Him, they led Him *away* Lk 22:54
behold, **h** examined Him before you, Lk 23:14
H said this, He breathed His last. Lk 23:46
as **h** been wrought in God." Jn 3:21
h seen all the things that He did Jn 4:45
Hebrew Bethesda, **h** five porticoes. Jn 5:2 *2192*
and **h** given thanks, He distributed Jn 6:11
H said these things to them, He Jn 7:9
learned, **h** never been educated?" Jn 7:15
and **h** set her in the center Jn 8:3
h loved His own who were in the Jn 13:1
the devil **h** already put into the Jn 13:2
h accomplished the work which You Jn 17:4
then, **h** received the *Roman* cohort and Jn 18:3
Simon Peter then, **h** a sword, Jn 18:10 *2192*
there, **h** made a charcoal fire, Jn 18:18
Jesus came, the doors **h** been shut, Jn 20:26
h been exalted to the right hand of Ac 2:33
and **h** received from the Father the Ac 2:33
and **h** favor with all the people. Ac 2:47 *2192*
them as **h** been with Jesus. Ac 4:13
"And **h** received it in their turn, Ac 7:45
H said this, he fell asleep. Ac 7:60
h heard that Peter was there, Ac 9:38
h asked directions for Simon's Ac 10:17
h been sent to me from Caesarea. Ac 11:11
and **h** won over Blastus the king's Ac 12:20
Herod, **h** put on his royal apparel, Ac 12:21
and **h** won over the crowds, Ac 14:19
church, **h** prayed with fasting, Ac 14:23
good to us, **h** become of one mind, Ac 15:25
and **h** gathered the congregation Ac 15:30
h been forbidden by the Holy Ac 16:6
slave-girl **h** a spirit of divination Ac 16:16 *2192*
and he, **h** received such a command, Ac 16:24
h believed in God with his whole Ac 16:34
h determined *their* appointed Ac 17:26
"Therefore **h** overlooked the times Ac 17:30
h furnished proof to all men by Ac 17:31
h recently come from Italy with Ac 18:2
Paul, **h** remained many days longer, Ac 18:18
And **h** spent some time *there*, he Ac 18:23
And **h** sent into Macedonia two of Ac 19:22
and **h** motioned with his hand, Ac 19:33
and **h** found a ship crossing over Ac 21:2
h decided that they should abstain Ac 21:25
And he wrote a letter **h** this form: Ac 23:25 *2192*
h learned that he was a Roman. Ac 23:27
h a hope in God, which these men Ac 24:15 *2192*
in the temple, **h** been purified, Ac 24:18
h a more exact knowledge about the Ac 24:22 *3609a*
h arrived in the province, Ac 25:1
h received authority from the Ac 26:10
"So, **h** obtained help from the Ac 26:22
without eating, **h** taken nothing. Ac 27:33
H said this, he took bread and gave Ac 27:35
h a great dispute among themselves. Ac 28:29 *2192*
of the Law, these, not **h** the Law, Ro 2:14 *2192*
h in the Law the embodiment of Ro 2:20 *2192*
who though **h** the letter *of the Law* Ro 2:27
h been justified by faith, Ro 5:1
h now been justified by His blood, Ro 5:9
Son, much more, **h** been reconciled, Ro 5:10
h been raised from the dead, Ro 6:9
and **h** been freed from sin, you Ro 6:18
But now **h** been freed from sin and Ro 6:22
h died to that by which we were Ro 7:6
h the first fruits of the Spirit, Ro 8:23 *2192*
h confidence in you all that my 2Co 2:3 *3982*
Therefore **h** such a hope, we use 2Co 3:12 *2192*
But **h** the same spirit of faith, 2Co 4:13 *2192*
inasmuch as we, **h** put it on, will 2Co 5:3
controls us, **h** concluded this, 2Co 5:14
as **h** nothing yet possessing all 2Co 6:10 *2192*
Therefore, **h** these promises, 2Co 7:1 *2192*
h all sufficiency in everything, 2Co 9:8 *2192*
H begun by the Spirit, are you now Ga 3:3
h become a curse for us Ga 3:13
h been ordained through angels by Ga 3:19
h been predestined according to Eph 1:11
h also believed, you were sealed in Eph 1:13
h heard of the faith in the Lord Eph 1:15
h no hope and without God in the Eph 2:12 *2192*
by it **h** put to death the enmity. Eph 2:16
h been built on the foundation Eph 2:20
and they, **h** become callous, have Eph 4:19
h cleansed her by the washing of Eph 5:26
h no spot or wrinkle or any such Eph 5:27 *2192*
h done everything, to stand firm. Eph 6:13
Stand firm therefore, **H** GIRDED Eph 6:14
and **H** PUT ON THE BREASTPLATE OF Eph 6:14
h shod YOUR FEET WITH THE PREPARATION Eph 6:15
h been filled with the fruit of Php 1:11
h the desire to depart and be with Php 1:23 *2192*
not **h** a righteousness of my own Php 3:9 *2192*
myself as **h** laid hold of *it* yet; Php 3:13
of **h** abundance and suffering need. Php 4:12 *4052*
h received from Epaphroditus what Php 4:18
h made peace through the blood of Col 1:20
h been knit together in love, Col 2:2
h been firmly rooted *and now* being Col 2:7
h been buried with Him in baptism, Col 2:12
h forgiven us all our Col 2:13
h canceled out the certificate of Col 2:14
the way, **h** nailed it to the cross. Col 2:14
h triumphed over them through Him. Col 2:15
h received the word in much 1Th 1:6
H so fond an affection for you, 1Th 2:8 *3655b*
h been taken away from you 1Th 2:17
h put on the breastplate of faith 1Th 5:8
h been the wife of one man, 1Tm 5:9
h a reputation for good works; 1Tm 5:10 *3140*
of God stands, **h** this seal, 2Tm 2:19 *2192*
h been held captive by him to do 2Tm 2:26
Demas, **h** loved this present world, 2Tm 4:10
one wife, **h** children who believe, Ti 1:6 *2192*
h nothing bad to say about us. Ti 2:8 *2192*
H confidence in your obedience, I Phm 1:21 *3982*
h become as much better than the Heb 1:4
And **h** been made perfect, He became Heb 5:9
in **h** ministered and in still Heb 6:10
And so, **h** patiently waited, he Heb 6:15
h become a high priest forever Heb 6:20
h neither beginning of days nor Heb 7:3 *2192*
h a golden altar of incense and Heb 9:4 *2192*
h obtained eternal redemption. Heb 9:12
h been offered once to bear the Heb 9:28
worshipers, **h** once been cleansed, Heb 10:2
h offered one sacrifice for sins Heb 10:12
h our hearts sprinkled *clean* from Heb 10:22
but **h** seen them and having Heb 11:13
but having seen them and **h** welcomed Heb 11:13
and **h** confessed that they were Heb 11:13
h gained approval through their Heb 11:39
not **h** become a forgetful hearer Jas 1:25
h been put to death in the flesh, 1Pe 3:18
hand of God, **h** gone into heaven, 1Pe 3:22
h pursued a course of sensuality, 1Pe 4:3
h escaped the corruption that is 2Pe 1:4
h forgotten *his* purification from 2Pe 1:9
h made them an example to those 2Pe 2:6
h eyes full of adultery that 2Pe 2:14 *2192*
souls, **h** a heart trained in greed, 2Pe 2:14 *2192*
h followed the way of Balaam, 2Pe 2:15
of righteousness, than **h** known it, 2Pe 2:21
And **h** turned I saw seven golden Rv 1:12
each one of them **h** six wings, Rv 4:8 *2192*
h seven horns and seven eyes, Rv 5:6 *2192*
sun, **h** the seal of the living God; Rv 7:2 *2192*
h seven heads and ten horns, Rv 12:3 *2192*
come down to you, **h** great wrath, Rv 12:12 *2192*
sea, **h** ten horns and seven heads, Rv 13:1 *2192*
h His name and the name of His Rv 14:1 *2192*
h an eternal gospel to preach to Rv 14:6 *2192*
man, **h** a golden crown on His head and Rv 14:14 *2192*
h seven heads and ten horns. Rv 17:3 *2192*
h in her hand a gold cup full of Rv 17:4 *2192*
His purpose by **h** a common purpose, Rv 17:17 *4160*
from heaven, **h** great authority, Rv 18:1 *2192*
h the glory of God. Rv 21:11 *2192*

HAVVOTH-JAIR
took its towns, and called them **H**. Nu 32:41 2334
is, Bashan, after his own name, **H**, Dt 3:14 2334
that are called **H** to this day. Jg 10:4 2334

HAWK
sea gull and the **h** in its kind, Lv 11:16 5322b
gull, and the **h** in their kinds, Dt 14:15 5322b
understanding that the **h** soars, Jb 39:26 5322b

HAWKS
the **h** will be gathered there, Is 34:15 1772

HAY
silver, precious stones, wood, **h**, 1Co 3:12 *5528*

HAZAEL
you shall anoint **H** king over Aram; 1Ki 19:15 2371
who escapes from the sword of **H**, 1Ki 19:17 2371
The king said to **H**, 2Ki 8:8 2371
So **H** went to meet him and took a 2Ki 8:9 2371
H said, "Why does my lord weep?" 2Ki 8:12 2371
H said, "But what is your servant, 2Ki 8:13 2371
And **H** became king in his place. 2Ki 8:15 2371
H king of Aram at Ramoth-gilead, 2Ki 8:28 2371
he fought against **H** king of Aram. 2Ki 8:29 2371
against **H** king of Aram, 2Ki 9:14 2371
he fought with **H** king of Aram. 2Ki 9:15 2371
and **H** defeated them throughout the 2Ki 10:32 2371
Then **H** king of Aram went up and 2Ki 12:17 2371
and **H** set his face to go up to 2Ki 12:17 2371
and sent *them* to **H** king of Aram. 2Ki 12:18 2371
into the hand of **H** king of Aram, 2Ki 13:3 2371
the hand of Ben-hadad the son of **H**. 2Ki 13:3 2371
Now **H** king of Aram had oppressed 2Ki 13:22 2371
When **H** king of Aram died, 2Ki 13:24 2371
the hand of Ben-hadad the son of **H** 2Ki 13:25 2371
H king of Aram at Ramoth-gilead. 2Ch 22:5 2371
he fought against **H** king of Aram. 2Ch 22:6 2371
send fire upon the house of **H** And Am 1:4 2371

HAZAIAH
the son of Col-hozeh, the son of **H**, Ne 11:5 2382

HAZARADDAR
and it shall reach **H** and Nu 34:4 2692

HAZAR-ENAN
and its termination shall be at **H**. Nu 34:9 2704
draw a line from **H** to Shepham, Nu 34:10 2704
to **H** *at* the border of Damascus, Ezk 47:17 2703
as **H** *at* the border of Damascus, Ezk 48:1 2704

HAZAR-GADDAH
and **H** and Heshmon and Beth-pelet, Jos 15:27 2693

HAZARMAVETH
and Sheleph and **H** and Jerah Gn 10:26 2700
the father of Almodad, Sheleph, **H**, 1Ch 1:20 2700

HAZAR-SHUAL
H and Beersheba and Biziothiah, Jos 15:28 2705
and **H** and Balah and Ezem, Jos 19:3 2705
at Beersheba, Moladah and **H**, 1Ch 4:28 2705
and in **H**, in Beersheba and its Ne 11:27 2705

HAZAR-SUSAH
Ziklag and Beth-marcaboth and **H**, Jos 19:5 2701

HAZAR-SUSIM
Beth-marcaboth, **H**, Beth-biri and 1Ch 4:31 2702

HAZAZON-TAMAR
also the Amorites, who lived in **H**. **Gn 14:7** 2688
of Aram and behold, they are in **H** **2Ch 20:2** 2688

HAZER-HATTICON
H, which is by the border of **Ezk 47:16** 2694

HAZEROTH
the people set out for **H**, **Nu 11:35** 2698
Hazeroth, and they remained at **H**. **Nu 11:35** 2698
the people moved out from **H** and **Nu 12:16** 2698
Kibroth-hattaavah and camped at **H**. **Nu 33:17** 2698
They journeyed from **H** and **Nu 33:18** 2698
and Laban and **H** and Dizahab. **Dt 1:1** 2698

HAZIEL
of Shimei *were* Shelomoth and **H** **1Ch 23:9** 2381

HAZO
and Chesed and **H** and Pildash and **Gn 22:22** 2375

HAZOR
when Jabin king of **H** heard *of it,* **Jos 11:1** 2674
and captured **H** and struck its king **Jos 11:10** 2674
for **H** formerly was the head of all **Jos 11:10** 2674
And he burned **H** with fire. **Jos 11:11** 2674
on their mounds, except **H** alone, **Jos 11:13** 2674
the king of **H**, one; **Jos 12:19** 2674
and Kedesh and **H** and Ithnan, **Jos 15:23** 2674
and Kerioth-hezron (that is, **H**), **Jos 15:25** 2674
and Adamah and Ramah and **H**, **Jos 19:36** 2674
king of Canaan, who reigned in **H**; **Jg 4:2** 2674
peace between Jabin the king of **H** **Jg 4:17** 2674
Sisera, captain of the army of **H**, **1Sa 12:9** 2674
Millo, the wall of Jerusalem, **H**, **1Ki 9:15** 2674
and **H** and Gilead and Galilee, **2Ki 15:29** 2674
H, Ramah, Gittaim, **Ne 11:33** 2674
Kedar and the kingdoms of **H**, **Jer 49:28** 2674
the depths, O inhabitants of **H**," **Jer 49:30** 2674
"**H** will become a haunt of **Jer 49:33** 2674

HAZOR-HADATTAH
and **H** and Kerioth-hezron **Jos 15:25** 2675

HAZZELELPONI
the name of their sister *was* **H**. **1Ch 4:3** 6753

HEAD
He shall bruise you on the **h**, **Gn 3:15** 7218
put it under his **h**, and lay down **Gn 28:11** 4763
stone that he had put under his **h** **Gn 28:18** 4763
Pharaoh will lift up your **h** and restore **Gn 40:13** 7218
baskets of white bread on my **h**; **Gn 40:16** 7218
them out of the basket on my **h**." **Gn 40:17** 7218
Pharaoh will lift up your **h** from you **Gn 40:19** 7218
and he lifted up the **h** of the **Gn 40:20** 7218
the **h** of the chief baker among his **Gn 40:20** 7218
in worship at the **h** of the bed. **Gn 47:31** 7218
and laid it on the **h** of Ephraim, **Gn 48:14** 7218
and his left hand on Manasseh's **h**, **Gn 48:14** 7218
laid his right hand on Ephraim's **h**, **Gn 48:17** 7218
from Ephraim's **h** to Manasseh's head. **Gn 48:17** 7218
from Ephraim's head to Manasseh's **h**. **Gn 48:17** 7218
Place your right hand on his **h**." **Gn 48:18** 7218
May they be on the **h** of Joseph, **Gn 49:26** 7218
And on the crown of the **h** of the **Gn 49:26** 6936
both its **h** and its legs along with **Ex 12:9** 7218
you shall set the turban on his **h** and **Ex 29:6** 7218
pour it on his **h** and anoint him. **Ex 29:7** 7218
their hands on the **h** of the bull. **Ex 29:10** 7218
their hands on the **h** of the ram; **Ex 29:15** 7218
them with its pieces and its **h**. **Ex 29:17** 7218
their hands on the **h** of the ram. **Ex 29:19** 7218
a beka a **h** **Ex 38:26** 1538
on the **h** of the burnt offering, **Lv 1:4** 7218
shall arrange the pieces, the **h** and **Lv 1:8** 7218
pieces with its **h** and its suet, **Lv 1:12** 7218
to the altar, and wring off its **h** **Lv 1:15** 7218
lay his hand on the **h** of his offering **Lv 3:2** 7218
his hand on the **h** of his offering and **Lv 3:8** 7218
he shall lay his hand on its **h** and slay **Lv 3:13** 7218
lay his hand on the **h** of the bull and **Lv 4:4** 7218
bull and all its flesh with its **h** and its **Lv 4:11** 7218
the **h** of the bull before the LORD, **Lv 4:15** 7218
hand on the **h** of the male goat and **Lv 4:24** 7218
hand on the **h** of the sin offering and **Lv 4:29** 7218
hand on the **h** of the sin offering and **Lv 4:33** 7218
nip its **h** at the front of its neck, **Lv 5:8** 7218
also placed the turban on his **h**, **Lv 8:9** 7218
oil on Aaron's **h** and anointed him, **Lv 8:12** 7218
laid their hands on the **h** of the bull **Lv 8:14** 7218
their hands on the **h** of the ram. **Lv 8:18** 7218
Moses offered up the **h** and the **Lv 8:20** 7218
their hands on the **h** of the ram. **Lv 8:22** 7218
to him in pieces, with the **h**, **Lv 9:13** 7218
from his **h** even to his feet, **Lv 13:12** 7218
on the **h** or on the beard, **Lv 13:29** 7218
leprosy of the **h** or of the beard. **Lv 13:30** 7218
if a man loses the hair of his **h**, **Lv 13:40** 7218
"If his **h** becomes bald at the **Lv 13:41** 7218
the bald **h** or the bald forehead, **Lv 13:42** 7146
bald **h** or on his bald forehead. **Lv 13:42** 7146
bald **h** or on his bald forehead, **Lv 13:43** 7146
his infection is on his **h**. **Lv 13:44** 7218
hair of his **h** shall be uncovered, **Lv 13:45** 7218
he shall shave his **h** and his beard **Lv 14:9** 7218
the **h** of the one to be cleansed. **Lv 14:18** 7218
the **h** of the one to be cleansed, **Lv 14:29** 7218
hands on the **h** of the live goat, **Lv 16:21** 7218
and he shall lay them on the **h** of **Lv 16:21** 7218
on whose **h** the anointing oil has **Lv 21:10** 7218
garments, shall not uncover his **h** nor **Lv 21:10** 7218
him lay their hands on his **h**; **Lv 24:14** 7218
of names, every male, **h** by head **Nu 1:2** 1538
of names, every male, head by **h** **Nu 1:2** 1538
one **h** of his father's household. **Nu 1:4** 7218
years old and upward, **h** by head, **Nu 1:18** 1538
years old and upward, head by **h**, **Nu 1:18** 1538
to the number of names, **h** by head, **Nu 1:20** 1538
to the number of names, head by **h**, **Nu 1:20** 1538
to the number of names, **h** by head, **Nu 1:22** 1538
to the number of names, head by **h**, **Nu 1:22** 1538
take five shekels apiece, per **h**; **Nu 3:47** 1538
the hair of the woman's **h** go loose, **Nu 5:18** 7218
no razor shall pass over his **h**. **Nu 6:5** 7218
locks of hair on his **h** grow long. **Nu 6:5** 7218
his separation to God is on his **h**. **Nu 6:7** 7218
defiles his dedicated **h** *of hair,* **Nu 6:9** 7218
then he shall shave his **h** on the **Nu 6:9** 7218
day he shall consecrate his **h**, **Nu 6:11** 7218
then shave his dedicated **h** *of hair* **Nu 6:18** 7218
and take the dedicated hair of his **h** **Nu 6:18** 7218
for there is one rod for the **h** **Nu 17:3** 7218
who was **h** of the people of a **Nu 25:15** 7218
go across at the **h** of this people, **Dt 3:28** 6440
and the iron **h** slips off **Dt 19:5**
of armies at the **h** of the people. **Dt 20:9** 7218
shave her **h** and trim her nails. **Dt 21:12** 7218
make you the **h** and not the tail, **Dt 28:13** 7218
The heaven which is over your **h** **Dt 28:23** 7218
your foot to the crown of your **h**. **Dt 28:35** 6936
he shall be the **h**, and you will **Dt 28:44** 7218
Let it come to the **h** of Joseph, **Dt 33:16** 7218
And to the crown of the **h** of the **Dt 33:16** 6936
the arm, also the crown of the **h**. **Dt 33:20** 6936
his blood *shall be* on his own **h**, **Jos 2:19** 7218
his blood *shall be* on our **h** if **Jos 2:19** 7218
was the **h** of all these kingdoms. **Jos 11:10** 7218
was the **h** of his father's household **Jos 22:14** 7218
struck Sisera, she smashed his **h**; **Jg 5:26** 7218
upper millstone on Abimelech's **h**, **Jg 9:53** 7218
h over all the inhabitants of Gilead **Jg 10:18** 7218
become **h** over all the inhabitants of **Jg 11:8** 7218
up to me, will I become your **h**?" **Jg 11:9** 7218
made him **h** and chief over them; **Jg 11:11** 7218
no razor shall come upon his **h**, **Jg 13:5** 7218
"A razor has never come on my **h**, **Jg 16:17** 7218
the hair of his **h** began to grow **Jg 16:22** 7218
razor shall never come on his **h**." **1Sa 1:11** 7218
clothes torn and dust on his **h**. **1Sa 4:12** 7218
And the **h** of Dagon and both the **1Sa 5:4** 7218
the **h** of those who were invited, **1Sa 9:22** 7218
flask of oil, poured it on his **h**, **1Sa 10:1** 7218
hair of his **h** shall fall to the ground, **1Sa 14:45** 7218
the **h** of the tribes of Israel? **1Sa 15:17** 7218
He had a bronze helmet on his **h**, **1Sa 17:5** 7218
and the **h** of his spear *weighed* six **1Sa 17:7** 3852
and put a bronze helmet on his **h**, **1Sa 17:38** 7218
down and remove your **h** from you. **1Sa 17:46** 7218
him, and cut off his **h** with it. **1Sa 17:51** 7218
David took the Philistine's **h** and **1Sa 17:54** 7218
the Philistine's **h** in his hand. **1Sa 17:57** 7218
a quilt of goats' *hair* at its **h**, **1Sa 19:13** 4763
the quilt of goats' *hair* at its **h**. **1Sa 19:16** 4763
evildoing of Nabal on his own **h**. **1Sa 25:39** 7218
stuck in the ground at his **h**; **1Sa 26:7** 4763
please take the spear that is at his **h** **1Sa 26:11** 4763
jug of water from *beside* Saul's **h**, **1Sa 26:12** 4763
jug of water that was at his **h**." **1Sa 26:16** 4763
They cut off his **h** and **1Sa 31:9** 7218
clothes torn and dust on his **h**. **2Sa 1:2** 7218
I took the crown which *was* on his **h** **2Sa 1:10** 7218
"Your blood is on your **h**, **2Sa 1:16** 7218
them seized his opponent by the **h** and **2Sa 2:16** 7218
I a dog's **h** that belongs to Judah? **2Sa 3:8** 7218
"May it fall on the **h** of Joab and **2Sa 3:29** 7218
And they took his **h** and traveled **2Sa 4:7** 7218
they brought the **h** of Ish-bosheth **2Sa 4:8** 7218
"Behold, the **h** of Ish-bosheth the **2Sa 4:8** 7218
But they took the **h** of Ish-bosheth **2Sa 4:12** 7218
crown of their king from his **h**; **2Sa 12:30** 7218
and it was *placed* on David's **h**. **2Sa 12:30** 7218
Tamar put ashes on her **h** and **2Sa 13:19** 7218
her hand on her **h** and went away, **2Sa 13:19** 7218
his **h** there was no defect in him. **2Sa 14:25** 6936
When he cut the hair of his **h** **2Sa 14:26** 7218
he weighed the hair of his **h** at **2Sa 14:26** 7218
and his **h** was covered and he **2Sa 15:30** 7218
each covered his **h** and went up **2Sa 15:30** 7218
his coat torn and dust on his **h**. **2Sa 15:32** 7218
go over now and cut off his **h**." **2Sa 16:9** 7218
And his **h** caught fast in the oak, **2Sa 18:9** 7218
his **h** will be thrown to you over **2Sa 20:21** 7218
And they cut off the **h** of Sheba **2Sa 20:22** 7218
have kept me as **h** of the nations; **2Sa 22:44** 7218
return his blood on his own **h**, **1Ki 2:32** 7218
their blood return on the **h** of Joab **1Ki 2:33** 7218
the **h** of his descendants forever; **1Ki 2:33** 7218
blood shall be on your own **h**." **1Ki 2:37** 7218
return your evil on your own **h**. **1Ki 2:44** 7218
by bringing his way on his own **h** **1Ki 8:32** 7218
there was at his **h** a bread cake **1Ki 19:6** 4763
Naboth at the **h** of the people; **1Ki 21:9** 7218
Naboth at the **h** of the people. **1Ki 21:12** 7218
He said to his father, "My **h**, my **2Ki 4:19** 7218
my **h**." And he said to his servant, **2Ki 4:19** 7218
the axe **h** fell into the water; **2Ki 6:5** 1270
until a donkey's **h** was sold for **2Ki 6:25** 7218
if the **h** of Elisha the son of **2Ki 6:31** 7218
has sent to take away my **h**? **2Ki 6:32** 7218
oil and pour it on his **h** and say, **2Ki 9:3** 7218
he poured the oil on his **h** and said **2Ki 9:6** 7218
her eyes and adorned her **h** and **2Ki 9:30** 7218
She has shaken *her* **h** behind you, **2Ki 19:21** 7218
was **h** of their fathers' households. **1Ch 5:15** 7218
So they stripped him and took his **h** **1Ch 10:9** 7218
his **h** in the house of Dagon. **1Ch 10:10** 1538
crown of their king from his **h**, **1Ch 20:2** 7218
and it was placed on David's **h**. **1Ch 20:2** 7218
the **h** of fathers' *households* as well as **1Ch 24:31** 7218
You exalt Yourself as **h** over all **1Ch 29:11** 7218
by bringing his way on his own **h** and **2Ch 6:23** 7218
the son of Maacah as **h** and leader **2Ch 11:22** 7218
God is with us at *our* **h** and His **2Ch 13:12** 7218
Jehoshaphat bowed his **h** with **2Ch 20:18**
with Jehoshaphat at their **h**, **2Ch 20:27** 7218
of the men who were at their **h**. **Ezr 5:10** 7217
the hair from my **h** and my beard, **Ezr 9:3** 7218
he set the royal crown on her **h** **Es 2:17** 7218
on whose **h** a royal crown has been **Es 6:8** 7218
mourning, with *his* **h** covered. **Es 6:12** 7218
Jews, should return on his own **h** and **Es 9:25** 7218
tore his robe and shaved his **h**, **Jb 1:20** 7218
of his foot to the crown of his **h**. **Jb 2:7** 6936
I dare not lift up my **h**. **Jb 10:15** 7218
'Should *my* **h** be lifted up, **Jb 10:16**
you And shake my **h** at you. **Jb 16:4** 7218
And removed the crown from my **h**. **Jb 19:9** 7218
And his **h** touches the clouds, **Jb 20:6** 7218
When His lamp shone over my **h**, **Jb 29:3** 7218
Or his **h** with fishing spears? **Jb 41:7** 7218
glory, and the One who lifts my **h**. **Ps 3:3** 7218
will return upon his own **h**, **Ps 7:16** 7218
placed me as **h** of the nations; **Ps 18:43** 7218
set a crown of fine gold on his **h**. **Ps 21:3** 7218
with the lip, they wag the **h**, **Ps 22:7** 7218
You have anointed my **h** with oil; **Ps 23:5** 7218
And now my **h** will be lifted up **Ps 27:6** 7218
my iniquities are gone over my **h**; **Ps 38:4** 7218
numerous than the hairs of my **h**, **Ps 40:12** 7218
also is the helmet of My **h**; **Ps 60:7** 7218
All who see them will shake the **h**. **Ps 64:8**
will shatter the **h** of His enemies, **Ps 68:21** 7218
are more than the hairs of my **h**; **Ps 69:4** 7218
also is the helmet of My **h**; **Ps 108:8** 7218
they see me, they wag their **h**. **Ps 109:25** 7218
Therefore He will lift up *His* **h**. **Ps 110:7** 7218
like the precious oil upon the **h**, **Ps 133:2** 7218
covered my **h** in the day of battle. **Ps 140:7** 7218
the **h** of those who surround me, **Ps 140:9** 7218
It is oil upon the **h**; **Ps 141:5** 7218
Do not let my **h** refuse it, For **Ps 141:5** 7218
are a graceful wreath to your **h** And **Pr 1:9** 7218
At the **h** of the noisy *streets* she **Pr 1:21** 7218
on your **h** a garland of grace; **Pr 4:9** 7218
are on the **h** of the righteous, **Pr 10:6** 7218
blessing will be on the **h** of him **Pr 11:26** 7218
A gray **h** is a crown of glory; **Pr 16:31** 7872
will heap burning coals on his **h**, **Pr 25:22** 7218
The wise man's eyes are in his **h**, **Ec 2:14** 7218
let not oil be lacking on your **h**. **Ec 9:8** 7218
Let his left hand be under my **h** **SS 2:6** 7218
For my **h** is drenched with dew, My **SS 5:2** 7218
"His **h** is *like* gold, pure gold; **SS 5:11** 7218
"Your **h** crowns you like Carmel, **SS 7:5** 7218
flowing locks of your **h** are like **SS 7:5** 7218
"Let his left hand be under my **h** And **SS 8:3** 7218
The whole **h** is sick And the whole **Is 1:5** 7218
sole of the foot even to the **h** **Is 1:6** 7218
"For the **h** of Aram is Damascus **Is 7:8** 7218
and the **h** of Damascus is Rezin **Is 7:8** 7218
and the **h** of Ephraim is Samaria **Is 7:9** 7218
h of Samaria is the son of **Is 7:9** 7218
the **h** and the hair of the legs; **Is 7:20** 7218
cuts off **h** and tail from Israel, **Is 9:14** 7218
The **h** is the elder and honorable **Is 9:15** 7218
Everyone's **h** is bald *and* every **Is 15:2** 7218
for Egypt Which *its* **h** or tail, **Is 19:15** 7218
to wailing, To shaving the **h** and **Is 22:12** 7144
is at the **h** of the fertile valley **Is 28:1** 7218
is at the **h** of the fertile valley, **Is 28:4** 7218
She has shaken *her* **h** behind you, **Is 37:22** 7218
helpless at the **h** of every street, **Is 51:20** 7218
it for bowing one's **h** like a reed And **Is 58:5** 7218
a helmet of salvation on His **h**; **Is 59:17** 7218
Have shaved the crown of your **h**. **Jer 2:16** 6936
go out With your hands on your **h**; **Jer 2:37** 7218
Oh that my **h** were waters And my **Jer 9:1** 7218
crown Has come down from your **h**." **Jer 13:18** 4763
companions to be **h** over you? **Jer 13:21** 7218
himself or shave his **h** for them. **Jer 16:6** 7139
be astonished And shake his **h**. **Jer 18:16** 7218
swirl down on the **h** of the wicked. **Jer 23:19** 7218
will burst on the **h** of the wicked. **Jer 30:23** 7218
speak about him you shake *your* **h** *in* **Jer 48:27**
"For every **h** is bald and every **Jer 48:37** 7218
male goats at the **h** of the flock. **Jer 50:8** 6440
hunger At the **h** of every street." **La 2:19** 7218
Waters flowed over my **h**; **La 3:54** 7218
The crown has fallen from our **h**; **La 5:16** 7218
barber's razor on your **h** and beard. **Ezk 5:1** 7218
and caught me by a lock of my **h**; **Ezk 8:3** 7218
and a beautiful crown on your **h**. **Ezk 16:12** 7218
your conduct down on your own **h**," **Ezk 16:43** 7218
he broke, I will inflict on his **h**. **Ezk 17:19** 7218
his blood will be on his own **h**. **Ezk 18:13**
at the **h** of the way to the city. **Ezk 21:19** 7218
the way, at the **h** of the two ways, **Ezk 21:21** 7218
every **h** was made bald and every **Ezk 29:18** 7218
his blood will be on his *own* **h**. **Ezk 33:4** 7218
an opening at the **h** of the way, **Ezk 42:12** 7218
make me forfeit my **h** to the king." **Da 1:10** 7218
"The **h** of that statue *was made* of **Da 2:32** 7217

You are the **h** of gold. Da 2:38 7217
was the hair of their **h** singed, Da 3:27 7217
the hair of His **h** like pure wool. Da 7:9 7217
the ten horns that *were* on its **h** Da 7:20 7217
return your recompense on your **h**. Jl 3:4 7218
return your recompense on your **h**. Jl 3:7 7218
of the earth on the **h** of the helpless Am 2:7 7218
into exile at the **h** of the exiles, Am 6:7 7218
loins And baldness on every **h**. Am 8:10 7218
will return on your own **h**. Ob 1:15 7218
Weeds were wrapped around my **h**. Jon 2:5 7218
over Jonah to be a shade over his **h** Jon 4:6 7218
and the sun beat down on Jonah's **h** Jon 4:8 7218
them, And the LORD at their **h**." Mi 2:13 7218
pieces At the **h** of every street; Na 3:10 7218
struck the **h** of the house of the evil Hab 3:13 7218
own spears The **h** of his throngs. Hab 3:14 7218
so that no man lifts up his **h**; Zch 1:21 7218
put a clean turban on his **h**." Zch 3:5 7218
So they put a clean turban on his **h** Zch 3:5 7218
and set *it* on the **h** of Joshua the Zch 6:11 7218
shall you make an oath by your **h**, Mt 5:36 *2776*
you, when you fast, anoint your **h** and Mt 6:17 *2776*
of Man has nowhere to lay His **h**." Mt 8:20 *2776*
the **h** of the house Beelzebul, Mt 10:25 *3617*
hairs of your **h** are all numbered. Mt 10:30 *2776*
heaven is like a **h** of a household, Mt 13:52 *3617*
the **h** of John the Baptist." Mt 14:8 *2776*
And his **h** was brought on a platter Mt 14:11 *2776*
that if the **h** of the house had Mt 24:43 *3617*
she poured it on His **h** as He Mt 26:7 *2776*
of thorns, they put it on His **h**, Mt 27:29 *2776*
and *began* to beat Him on the **h**. Mt 27:30 *2776*
above His **h** they put up the Mt 27:37 *2776*
first the blade, then the **h**, Mk 4:28 *4719*
then the mature grain in the **h**. Mk 4:28 *4719*
"The **h** of John the Baptist." Mk 6:24 *2776*
the **h** of John the Baptist on a platter. Mk 6:25 *2776*
commanded *him* to bring *back* his **h**. Mk 6:27 *2776*
and brought his **h** on a platter, Mk 6:28 *2776*
and they wounded him in the **h**, Mk 12:4 *2775*
the vial and poured it over His **h**. Mk 14:3 *2776*
kept beating His **h** with a reed, Mk 15:19 *2776*
them with the hair of her **h**, Lk 7:38 *2776*
"You did not anoint My **h** with oil, Lk 7:46 *2776*
of Man has nowhere to lay His **h**." Lk 9:58 *2776*
hairs of your **h** are all numbered. Lk 12:7 *2776*
that if the **h** of the house had Lk 12:39 *3617*
"Once the **h** of the house gets up Lk 13:25 *3617*
Then the **h** of the household became Lk 14:21 *3617*
not a hair of your **h** will perish. Lk 21:18 *2776*
but also my hands and my **h**." Jn 13:9 *2776*
of thorns and put it on His **h**, Jn 19:2 *2776*
And He bowed His **h** and gave up Jn 19:30 *2776*
which had been on His **h**, Jn 20:7 *2776*
in white sitting, one at the **h** and Jn 20:12 *2776*
not a hair from the **h** of any of you Ac 27:34 *2776*
WILL HEAP BURNING COALS ON HIS **H**." Ro 12:20 *2776*
that Christ is the **h** of every man, 1Co 11:3 *2776*
and the man is the **h** of a woman, 1Co 11:3 *2776*
woman, and God is the **h** of Christ. 1Co 11:3 *2776*
something on his **h** while praying or 1Co 11:4 *2776*
or prophesying disgraces his **h**. 1Co 11:4 *2776*
her **h** uncovered while praying or 1Co 11:5 *2776*
or prophesying disgraces her **h** 1Co 11:5 *2776*
as the woman whose **h** is shaved. 1Co 11:5
if a woman does not cover her **h**, 1Co 11:6
her hair cut off or her **h** shaved, 1Co 11:6
head shaved, let her cover her **h**. 1Co 11:6
ought not to have his **h** covered, 1Co 11:7 *2776*
a symbol of authority on her **h**, 1Co 11:10 *2776*
a woman to pray to God *with her* **h** 1Co 11:13
or again the **h** to the feet, 1Co 12:21 *2776*
gave Him as **h** over all things to Eph 1:22 *2776*
aspects into Him who is the **h**, Eph 4:15 *2776*
the husband is the **h** of the wife, Eph 5:23 *2776*
Christ also is the **h** of the church, Eph 5:23 *2776*
He is also **h** of the body, the Col 1:18 *2776*
the **h** over all rule and authority; Col 2:10 *2776*
and not holding fast to the **h**, Col 2:19 *2776*
His **h** and His hair were white Rv 1:14 *2776*
and the rainbow was upon his **h**, Rv 10:1 *2776*
on her **h** a crown of twelve stars; Rv 12:1 *2776*
having a golden crown on His **h** and Rv 14:14 *2776*
and on His **h** *are* many diadems; Rv 19:12 *2776*

HEADBANDS
the beauty of *their* anklets, **h**, Is 3:18 7636

HEADDRESSES
h, ankle chains, sashes, perfume Is 3:20 6287b

HEADING
wind, they were **h** for the beach. Ac 27:40 *2722*

HEADLESS
arrows, let them be as **h** shafts. Ps 58:7 4448d

HEADLONG
"He rushes **h** at Him With his Jb 15:26 6677
falls, he will not be hurled **h**, Ps 37:24 2904
the LORD is about to hurl you **h**, Is 22:17 2925
each of you will be driven out **h**, Jer 49:5 6440
and falling **h**, he burst open in Ac 1:18 *4248*
rushed **h** into the error of Balaam, Jude 1:11 *1632b*

HEADS
the **h** of their fathers' households. Ex 6:14 7218
are the **h** of the fathers' Ex 6:25 7218
and made them **h** over the people, Ex 18:25 7218
h of grain roasted in the fire, Lv 2:14 24
your **h** nor tear your clothes, Lv 10:6 7218
off the side-growth of your **h** nor Lv 19:27 7218
not make any baldness on their **h**, Lv 21:5 7218
the **h** of divisions of Israel." Nu 1:16 7218
the **h** of their fathers' households, Nu 7:2 7218
their hands on the **h** of the bulls; Nu 8:12 7218
the **h** of the divisions of Israel, Nu 10:4 7218
who were **h** of the sons of Israel. Nu 13:3 7218
Then Moses spoke to the **h** of the Nu 30:1 7218
the **h** of the fathers' *households* of the Nu 31:26 7218
to the **h** of the fathers' Nu 32:28 7218
And the **h** of the fathers' Nu 36:1 7218
the **h** of the fathers' Nu 36:1 7218
I will appoint them as your **h**.' Dt 1:13 7218
"So I took the **h** of your tribes, Dt 1:15 7218
and appointed them **h** over you, Dt 1:15 7218
all the **h** of your tribes and your Dt 5:23 7218
may pluck the **h** with your hand, Dt 23:25 4425
the **h** of the people were gathered, Dt 33:5 7218
and they put dust on their **h**. Jos 7:6 7218
and the **h** of the households of the Jos 14:1 7218
the **h** of the households of the tribes Jos 19:51 7218
Then the **h** of households of the Jos 21:1 7218
the **h** of households of the tribes of the Jos 21:1 7218
the **h** of the families of Israel. Jos 22:21 7218
even the **h** of the families of Jos 22:30 7218
for their elders and their **h** and Jos 23:2 7218
for their **h** and their judges and their Jos 24:1 7218
and they brought the **h** of Oreb and Jg 7:25 7218
did not lift up their **h** anymore. Jg 8:28 7218
of the men of Shechem on their **h**, Jg 9:57 7218
it not *be* with the **h** of these men? 1Sa 29:4 7218
and all the **h** of the tribes, 1Ki 8:1 7218
on our loins and ropes on our **h**, 1Ki 20:31 7218
loins and *put* ropes on their **h**, 1Ki 20:32 7218
my voice, take the **h** of the men, 2Ki 10:6 7218
and put their **h** in baskets, 2Ki 10:7 7218
brought the **h** of the king's sons," 2Ki 10:8 7218
the **h** of their fathers' households, 1Ch 5:24 7218
h of their fathers' households. 1Ch 5:24 7218
h of their fathers' households. 1Ch 7:2 7218
They *were* **h** of fathers' households, 1Ch 7:7 7218
h of their fathers' households, 1Ch 7:9 7218
the **h** of their fathers' households, 1Ch 7:11 7218
of Asher, **h** of the fathers' houses, 1Ch 7:40 7218
men of valor, **h** of the princes. 1Ch 7:40 7218
these are the **h** of fathers' 1Ch 8:6 7218
his sons, **h** of fathers' *households.* 1Ch 8:10 7218
who were **h** of fathers' 1Ch 8:13 7218
were **h** of the fathers' 1Ch 8:28 7218
All these *were* **h** of fathers' 1Ch 9:9 7218
h of their fathers' households, 1Ch 9:13 7218
h of fathers' *households* of the 1Ch 9:33 7218
These were **h** of fathers' 1Ch 9:34 7218
Now these are the **h** of the mighty 1Ch 11:10 7218
"At *the cost of* our **h** he may 1Ch 12:19 7218
are the **h** of the fathers' 1Ch 15:12 7218
were the **h** of the fathers' 1Ch 23:9 7218
even the **h** of the fathers' *households* 1Ch 23:24 7218
were sixteen **h** of fathers' households 1Ch 24:4 7218
and the **h** of the fathers' 1Ch 24:6 7218
and the **h** of the fathers' 1Ch 24:31 7218
the **h** of the fathers' *households,* 1Ch 26:21 7218
the **h** of the fathers' *households,* 1Ch 26:26 7218
number, **h** of fathers' *households.* 1Ch 26:32 7218
the **h** of fathers' *households,* 1Ch 27:1 7218
the **h** of the fathers' *households.* 2Ch 1:2 7218
and all the **h** of the tribes, 2Ch 5:2 7218
of the **h** of the fathers' 2Ch 19:8 7218
and the **h** of the fathers' 2Ch 23:2 7218
number of the **h** of the households, 2Ch 26:12 7218
Then some of the **h** of the sons of 2Ch 28:12 7218
Then the **h** of fathers' Ezr 1:5 7218
of the **h** of fathers' *households,* Ezr 2:68 7218
and **h** of fathers' *households,* Ezr 3:12 7218
and the **h** of fathers' *households,* Ezr 4:2 7218
of the **h** of fathers' *households* of Israel Ezr 4:3 7218
are the **h** of their fathers' Ezr 8:1 7218
and the **h** of the fathers' Ezr 8:29 8269
iniquities have risen above our **h** and Ezr 9:6 7218
men *who were* **h** of fathers' *households* Ezr 10:16 7218
Return their reproach on their own **h** Ne 4:4 7218
Some from among the **h** of Ne 7:70 7218
Some of the **h** of fathers' *households* Ne 7:71 7218
the **h** of fathers' *households* of all Ne 8:13 7218
the **h** of the provinces who lived in Ne 11:3 7218
kinsmen, **h** of fathers' *households,* Ne 11:13 7218
These were the **h** of the priests Ne 12:7 7218
the **h** of fathers' *households* were: Ne 12:12 7218
the **h** of fathers' *households* were Ne 12:22 7218
Levi, the **h** of fathers' *households,* Ne 12:23 7218
h of the Levites *were* Hashabiah, Ne 12:24 7218
dust over their **h** toward the sky. Jb 2:12 7218
the **h** of grain they are cut off. Jb 24:24 7218
Lift up your **h**, O gates, And be Ps 24:7 7218
Lift up your **h**, O gates, And lift Ps 24:9 7218
made men ride over our **h**; Ps 66:12 7218
You broke the **h** of the sea Ps 74:13 7218
crushed the **h** of Leviathan; Ps 74:14 7218
h held high and seductive eyes, Is 3:16 1627
And He has covered your **h**, Is 29:10 7218
With everlasting joy upon their **h**. Is 35:10 7218
joy *will be* on their **h**. Is 51:11 7218
And they cover their **h**. Jer 14:3 7218
shame, They have covered their **h**. Jer 14:4 7218
They have thrown dust on their **h**; La 2:10 7218
Have bowed their **h** to the ground. La 2:10 7218
They hiss and shake their **h** At the La 2:15 7218
Now over the **h** of the living Ezk 1:22 7218
of crystal, spread out over their **h**. Ezk 1:22 7218
the expanse that was over their **h**; Ezk 1:25 7218
the expanse that was over their **h** Ezk 1:26 7218
and baldness on all their **h**. Ezk 7:18 7218
their conduct upon their **h**." Ezk 9:10 7218
that was over the **h** of the cherubim Ezk 10:1 7218
their conduct down on their **h**," Ezk 11:21 7218
and make veils for the **h** of Ezk 13:18 7218
way I have brought upon their **h**," Ezk 22:31 7218
with flowing turbans on their **h**, Ezk 23:15 7218
and beautiful crowns on their **h**. Ezk 23:42 7218
Your turbans will be on your **h** Ezk 24:23 7218
They will cast dust on their **h**, Ezk 27:30 7218
swords were laid under their **h**; Ezk 32:27 7218
"Linen turbans shall be on their **h** and Ezk 44:18 7218
"Also they shall not shave their **h**, Ezk 44:20 7218
only trim *the hair of* their **h**. Ezk 44:20 7218
the beast also had four **h**, Da 7:6 7217
The standing grain has no **h**; Hos 8:7 6780
break them on the **h** of them all! Am 9:1 7218
h of Jacob And rulers of the house Mi 3:1 7218
h of the house of Jacob And rulers Mi 3:9 7218
to pick the **h** *of grain* and eat. Mt 12:1 *4719*
abuse at Him, wagging their **h** Mt 27:39 *2776*
while picking the **h** *of grain.* Mk 2:23 *4719*
abuse at Him, wagging their **h**, Mk 15:29 *2776*
picking the **h** of grain, Lk 6:1 *4719*
straighten up and lift up your **h**, Lk 21:28 *2776*
"Your blood *be* on your own **h**! Ac 18:6 *2776*
that they may shave their **h**; Ac 21:24 *2776*
and golden crowns on their **h**. Rv 4:4 *2776*
and on their **h** appeared to be crowns Rv 9:7 *2776*
and the **h** of the horses are like Rv 9:17 *2776*
horses are like the **h** of lions; Rv 9:17 *2776*
are like serpents and have **h**, Rv 9:19 *2776*
having seven **h** and ten horns, Rv 12:3 *2776*
and on his **h** *were* seven diadems. Rv 12:3 *2776*
sea, having ten horns and seven **h**, Rv 13:1 *2776*
on his **h** *were* blasphemous names. Rv 13:1 *2776*
of his **h** as if it had been slain, Rv 13:3 *2776*
having seven **h** and ten horns. Rv 17:3 *2776*
has the seven **h** and the ten horns. Rv 17:7 *2776*
The seven **h** are seven mountains on Rv 17:9 *2776*
on their **h** and were crying out, Rv 18:19 *2776*

HEADWAITER
out now and take it to the **h**." Jn 2:8 *755*
When the **h** tasted the water Jn 2:9 *755*
the **h** called the bridegroom, Jn 2:9 *755*

HEAL
"O God, **h** her, I pray!" Nu 12:13 7495
I have wounded and it is I who **h** Dt 32:39 7495
behold, I will **h** you. 2Ki 20:5 7495
the sign that the LORD will **h** me, 2Ki 20:8 7495
their sin and will **h** their land. 2Ch 7:14 7495
He wounds, and His hands *also* **h**. Jb 5:18 7495
H me, O LORD, for my bones are Ps 6:2 7495
H my soul, for I have sinned Ps 41:4 7495
H its breaches, for it totters. Ps 60:2 7495
A time to kill and a time to **h**; Ec 3:3 7495
respond to them and will **h** them. Is 19:22 7495
seen his ways, but I will **h** him; Is 57:18 7495
"and I will **h** him." Is 57:19 7495
I will **h** your faithlessness." Jer 3:22 7495
"They **h** the brokenness of the Jer 8:11 7495
H me, O LORD, and I will be healed; Jer 17:14 7495
And I will **h** you of your wounds,' Jer 30:17 7495
and healing, and I will **h** them; Jer 33:6 7495
as vast as the sea; Who can **h** you? La 2:13 7495
But he is unable to **h** you, Hos 5:13 7495
He has torn *us,* but He will **h** us; Hos 6:1 7495
When I would **h** Israel, The Hos 7:1 7495
I will **h** their apostasy, I will Hos 14:4 7495
seek the scattered, **h** the broken, Zch 11:16 7495
"I will come and **h** him." Mt 8:7 *2323*
and to **h** every kind of disease and Mt 10:1 *2323*
"**H** *the* sick, raise *the* dead, Mt 10:8 *2323*
"Is it lawful to **h** on the Sabbath?" Mt 12:10 *2323*
AND I WOULD **H** THEM.' Mt 13:15 *2390*
if He would **h** him on the Sabbath, Mk 3:2 *2323*
'Physician, **h** yourself! Lk 4:23 *2323*
all the demons and to **h** diseases. Lk 9:1 *2323*
and **h** those in it who are sick, Lk 10:9 *2323*
"Is it lawful to **h** on the Lk 14:3 *2323*
Him to come down and **h** his son; Jn 4:47 *2390*
AND BE CONVERTED AND I **H** THEM." Jn 12:40 *2390*
You extend Your hand to **h**, Ac 4:30 *2392*
AND I WOULD **H** THEM."' Ac 28:27 *2390*

HEALED
and God **h** Abimelech and his wife Gn 20:17 7495
of him until he is completely **h**. Ex 21:19 7495
a boil on its skin and it is **h**, Lv 13:18 7495
has grown in it, the scale has **h**, Lv 13:37 7495
leprosy has been **h** in the leper, Lv 14:3 7495
itch, from which you cannot be **h**. Dt 28:27 7495
boils, from which you cannot be **h**, Dt 28:35 7495
in the camp until they were **h**. Jos 5:8 2421a
Then you will be **h** and it will 1Sa 6:3 7495
So King Joram returned to be **h** in 2Ki 8:29 7495
Joram had returned to Jezreel to be **h** 2Ki 9:15 7495
So he returned to be **h** in Jezreel 2Ch 22:6 7495
heard Hezekiah and **h** the people. 2Ch 30:20 7495
help, and You **h** me. Ps 30:2 7495
He sent His word and **h** them, Ps 107:20 7495
hearts, And return and be **h**." Is 6:10 7495
And by His scourging we are **h**. Is 53:5 7495
"They have **h** the brokenness Jer 6:14 7495
wound incurable, refusing to be **h**? Jer 15:18 7495
Heal me, O LORD, and I will be **h**; Jer 17:14 7495
Perhaps she may be **h**. Jer 51:8 7495
to Babylon, but she was not **h**; Jer 51:9 7495
the diseased you have not **h**, Ezk 34:4 7495

they did not know that I **h** them. **Hos 11:3** 7495
epileptics, paralytics; and He **h** them. **Mt 4:24** *2323*
word, and my servant will be **h**. **Mt 8:8** *2390*
the servant was **h** that *very* moment. **Mt 8:13** *2390*
a word, and **h** all who were ill **Mt 8:16** *2323*
followed Him, and He **h** them all, **Mt 12:15** *2323*
brought to Jesus, and He **h** him, **Mt 12:22** *2323*
for them and **h** their sick. **Mt 14:14** *2323*
And her daughter was **h** at once. **Mt 15:28** *2390*
laid them down at His feet; and He **h** **Mt 15:30** *2323*
followed Him, and He **h** them there. **Mt 19:2** *2323*
Him in the temple, and He **h** them. **Mt 21:14** *2323*
And He **h** many who were ill with **Mk 1:34** *2323*
for He had **h** many, with the result **Mk 3:10** *2323*
that she was **h** of her affliction. **Mk 5:29** *2390*
and be **h** of your affliction." **Mk 5:34** *5199*
on a few sick people and **h** them **Mk 6:5** *2323*
and to be **h** of their sicknesses. **Lk 5:15** *2323*
to see if He **h** on the Sabbath, **Lk 6:7** *2323*
and to be **h** of their diseases; **Lk 6:18** *2390*
word, and my servant will be **h**. **Lk 7:7** *2390*
women who had been **h** of evil spirits **Lk 8:2** *2323*
and could not be **h** by anyone, **Lk 8:43** *2323*
how she had been immediately **h**. **Lk 8:47** *2390*
the unclean spirit, and **h** the boy and **Lk 9:42** *2390*
Jesus had **h** on the Sabbath, **Lk 13:14** *2323*
come during them and get **h**, **Lk 13:14** *2323*
He took hold of him and **h** him, **Lk 14:4** *2390*
when he saw that he had been **h**, **Lk 17:15** *2390*
And He touched his ear and **h** him. **Lk 22:51** *2390*
who was **h** did not know who it was, **Jn 5:13** *2390*
who had been **h** standing with them, **Ac 4:14** *2323*
and they were all being **h**. **Ac 5:16** *2323*
been paralyzed and lame were **h**. **Ac 8:7** *2323*
laid his hands on him and **h** him. **Ac 28:8** *2390*
put out of joint, but rather be **h**. **Heb 12:13** *2390*
one another so that you may be **h**. **Jas 5:16** *2390*
for by His wounds you were **h**. **1Pe 2:24** *2390*
slain, and his fatal wound was **h**. **Rv 13:3** *2323*
beast, whose fatal wound was **h**. **Rv 13:12** *2323*

HEALER
for I, the LORD, am your **h**." **Ex 15:26** 7495
"I will not be *your* **h**, **Is 3:7** 2280

HEALING
It will be **h** to your body And **Pr 3:8** 7500
be broken and there will be no **h**. **Pr 6:15** 4832
the tongue of the wise brings **h**. **Pr 12:18** 4832
But a faithful envoy *brings* **h**. **Pr 13:17** 4832
to the soul and **h** to the bones. **Pr 16:24** 4832
will strike Egypt, striking but **h**; **Is 19:22** 7495
For a time of **h**, but behold, **Jer 8:15** 4832
My sorrow is beyond **h**, **Jer 8:18** 4010
us so that we are beyond **h**? **Jer 14:19** 4832
And for a time of **h**, **Jer 14:19** 4832
No **h** for *your* sore, No recovery **Jer 30:13** 7499
I will bring to it health and **h**, **Jer 33:6** 4832
There is no **h** for you. **Jer 46:11** 8585b
We applied **h** to Babylon, but she **Jer 51:9** 7495
for **h** or wrapped with a bandage, **Ezk 30:21** 7499
for food and their leaves for **h**." **Ezk 47:12** 8644
will rise with **h** in its wings; **Mal 4:2** 4832
and **h** every kind of disease and **Mt 4:23** *2323*
and **h** every kind of disease and **Mt 9:35** *2323*
oil many sick people and **h** them. **Mk 6:13** *2323*
each one of them, He was **h** them. **Lk 4:40** *2323*
was *present* for Him to perform **h**. **Lk 5:17** *2390*
coming from Him and **h** *them* all. **Lk 6:19** *2390*
kingdom of God and to perform **h**. **Lk 9:2** *2390*
the gospel and **h** everywhere. **Lk 9:6** *2323*
curing those who had need of **h**. **Lk 9:11** *2322*
miracle of **h** had been performed. **Ac 4:22** *2392*
and **h** all who were oppressed by **Ac 10:38** *2390*
gifts of **h** by the one Spirit, **1Co 12:9** *2386*
were for the **h** of the nations. **Rv 22:2** *2322*

HEALINGS
then miracles, then gifts of **h**, **1Co 12:28** *2386*
All do not have gifts of **h**, **1Co 12:30** *2386*

HEALS
Who **h** all your diseases; **Ps 103:3** 7495
He **h** the brokenhearted And binds **Ps 147:3** 7495
and **h** the bruise He has inflicted. **Is 30:26** 7495
"Aeneas, Jesus Christ **h** you; **Ac 9:34** *2390*

HEALTH
h in my bones because of my sin. **Ps 38:3** 7965
You restore him to **h**. **Ps 41:3** 3605, 4904
And **h** to all their body. **Pr 4:22** 4832
O restore me to **h** and let me live! **Is 38:16** 2492a
Why then has not the **h** of the **Jer 8:22** 724
'For I will restore you to **h** And I **Jer 30:17** 724
I will bring to it **h** and healing, **Jer 33:6** 724
they found the slave in good **h**. **Lk 7:10** *5198*
h in the presence of you all. **Ac 3:16** *3647*
stands here before you in good **h**. **Ac 4:10** *5199*
you may prosper and be in good **h**, **3Jn 1:2** *5198*

HEALTHY
The little ones who were born **h**? **La 2:20** 2949
who are **h** who need a physician, **Mt 9:12** *2480*
who are **h** who need a physician, **Mk 2:17** *2480*

HEAP
So they took stones and made a **h**, **Gn 31:46** 1530
heap, and they ate there by the **h**. **Gn 31:46** 1530
"This **h** is a witness between you **Gn 31:48** 1530
"Behold this **h** and behold the **Gn 31:51** 1530
"This **h** is a witness, and the **Gn 31:52** 1530
pass by this **h** to you for harm, **Gn 31:52** 1530
by this **h** and this pillar to me, **Gn 31:52** 1530
flowing waters stood up like a **h**; **Ex 15:8** 5067a
and your remains on the remains **Lv 26:30** 5414
'I will **h** misfortunes on them; **Dt 32:23** 5595
from above will stand in one **h**." **Jos 3:13** 5067a
above stood *and* rose up in one **h**, **Jos 3:16** 5067a
raised over him a great **h** of stones **Jos 7:26** 1530
burned Ai and made it a **h** forever, **Jos 8:28** 8510
and raised over it a great **h** of **Jos 8:29** 1530
down at the end of the **h** of grain **Ru 3:7** 6194
h To make them sit with nobles, **1Sa 2:8** 6083
over him a very great **h** of stones. **2Sa 18:17** 1530
house will become a **h** of ruins; **1Ki 9:8** 5945a
a refuse **h** on account of this. **Ezr 6:11** 5122
a **h** of ruins stretch out *his* hand, **Jb 30:24** 5856
waters of the sea together as a **h**; **Ps 33:7** 5067a
made the waters stand up like a **h**. **Ps 78:13** 5067a
lifts the needy from the ash **h**, **Ps 113:7** 6083
will **h** burning coals on his head, **Pr 25:22** 2846
Your belly is like a **h** of wheat **SS 7:2** 6194
But the harvest will *be* a **h** In a **Is 17:11** 5067a
You have made a city into a **h**, **Is 25:2** 1530
will make Jerusalem a **h** of ruins, **Jer 9:11** 1530
And it will become a desolate **h**, **Jer 49:2** 8510
"Babylon will become a **h** *of ruins*, **Jer 51:37** 1530
"**H** on the wood, kindle the fire, **Ezk 24:10** 7235a
houses will be made a rubbish **h**. **Da 2:5** 5122
houses reduced to a rubbish **h**, **Da 3:29** 5122
a **h** of ruins in the open country, **Mi 1:6** 5856
will become a **h** of ruins, **Mi 3:12** 5856
And **h** up rubble to capture it. **Hab 1:10** 6651
to a *grain* **h** of twenty *measures*, **Hg 2:16** 6194
FOR IN SO DOING YOU WILL H BURNING **Ro 12:20** *4987*

HEAPS
So they piled them in **h**, **Ex 8:14** 2563b
jawbone of a donkey, **H** upon heaps, **Jg 15:16** 2565
jawbone of a donkey, Heaps upon **h**, **Jg 15:16** 2565
"Put them in two **h** at the **2Ki 10:8** 6652
fortified cities into ruinous **h**. **2Ki 19:25** 1530
their God, and placed *them* in **h**. **2Ch 31:6** 6194
month they began to make the **h**, **2Ch 31:7** 6194
and the rulers came and saw the **h**, **2Ch 31:8** 6194
and the Levites concerning the **h**. **2Ch 31:9** 6194
fortified cities into ruinous **h**. **Is 37:26** 1530
up like **h** And utterly destroy her, **Jer 50:26** 6194
Yes, their altars are like the stone **h** **Hos 12:11** 1530

HEAR
nor did I **h** of it until today." **Gn 21:26** 8085
"**H** us, my lord, you are a mighty **Gn 23:6** 8085
my dead out of my sight, **h** me, **Gn 23:8** 8085
"No, my lord, **h** me; **Gn 23:11** 8085
h a dream you can interpret it." **Gn 41:15** 8085
"Gather together and **h**, **Gn 49:2** 8085
may **h** when I speak with you and **Ex 19:9** 8085
to Me, I will surely **h** his cry; **Ex 22:23** 8085
he cries out to Me, I will **h** *him*, **Ex 22:27** 8085
But the sound of singing I **h**." **Ex 32:18** 8085
He said, "**H** now My words: **Nu 12:6** 8085
"Then the Egyptians will **h** of it, **Nu 14:13** 8085
"**H** now, you sons of Levi, **Nu 16:8** 8085
"Arise, O Balak, and **h**; **Nu 23:18** 8085
'**H** *the cases* between your fellow **Dt 1:16** 8085
h the small and the great alike. **Dt 1:17** 8085
bring to me, and I will **h** it.' **Dt 1:17** 8085
when they **h** the report of you, **Dt 2:25** 8085
will **h** all these statutes and say, **Dt 4:6** 8085
that I may let them **h** My words so **Dt 4:10** 8085
see nor **h** nor eat nor smell. **Dt 4:28** 8085
you **h** His voice to discipline you; **Dt 4:36** 8085
"**H**, O Israel, the statutes and **Dt 5:1** 8085
if we **h** the voice of the LORD our **Dt 5:25** 8085
'Go near and **h** all that the LORD **Dt 5:27** 8085
to you, and we will **h** and do *it*.' **Dt 5:27** 8085
"**H**, O Israel! The LORD is our God, **Dt 6:4** 8085
"**H**, O Israel! You are crossing over **Dt 9:1** 8085
all Israel will **h** and be afraid, **Dt 13:11** 8085
"If you **h** in one of your cities, **Dt 13:12** 8085
the people will **h** and be afraid, **Dt 17:13** 8085
'Let me not **h** again the voice of **Dt 18:16** 8085
"The rest will **h** and be afraid, **Dt 19:20** 8085
H, O Israel, you are approaching **Dt 20:3** 8085
all Israel will **h** *of it* and fear. **Dt 21:21** 8085
nor eyes to see, nor ears to **h**. **Dt 29:4** 8085
to get it for us and make us **h** it, **Dt 30:12** 8085
to get it for us and make us **h** it, **Dt 30:13** 8085
so that they may **h** and learn **Dt 31:12** 8085
will **h** and learn to fear the LORD **Dt 31:13** 8085
the earth **h** the words of my mouth. **Dt 32:1** 8085
"**H**, O LORD, the voice of Judah, **Dt 33:7** 8085
and **h** the words of the LORD your **Jos 3:9** 8085
you **h** the sound of the trumpet, **Jos 6:5** 8085
of the land will **h** of it, **Jos 7:9** 8085
"**H**, O kings; give ear, O rulers! **Jg 5:3** 8085
To **h** the piping for the flocks? **Jg 5:16** 8085
and you will **h** what they say; **Jg 7:11** 8085
h *things* like this at this time." **Jg 13:23** 8085
your riddle, that we may **h** it." **Jg 14:13** 8085
that I **h** from all these people? **1Sa 2:23** 8085
I **h** the LORD's people circulating. **1Sa 2:24** 8085
"Let the Hebrews **h**." **1Sa 13:3** 8085
lowing of the oxen which I **h**?" **1Sa 15:14** 8085
"**H** now, O Benjamites! **1Sa 22:7** 8085
when you **h** the sound of marching **2Sa 5:24** 8085
'For the king will **h** and deliver **2Sa 14:16** 8085
as you **h** the sound of the trumpet, **2Sa 15:10** 8085
you **h** from the king's house, **2Sa 15:35** 8085
send me everything that you **h**." **2Sa 15:36** 8085
then all Israel will **h** that you **2Sa 16:21** 8085
and let us **h** what he has to say." **2Sa 17:5** 8085
Or can I **h** anymore the voice of **2Sa 19:35** 8085
H, hear! Please tell Joab, 'Come here **2Sa 20:16** 8085
h! Please tell Joab, 'Come here **2Sa 20:16** 8085
As soon as they **h**, they obey me. **2Sa 22:45** 241, 8085
to **h** the wisdom of Solomon, **1Ki 4:34** 8085
h in heaven Your dwelling place; **1Ki 8:30** 8085
in heaven Your dwelling place; **h** and **1Ki 8:30** 8085
then **h** in heaven and act and **1Ki 8:32** 8085
then **h** in heaven, and forgive **1Ki 8:34** 8085
then **h** in heaven and forgive **1Ki 8:36** 8085
then **h** in heaven Your dwelling **1Ki 8:39** 8085
(for they will **h** of Your great name **1Ki 8:42** 8085
h in heaven Your dwelling **1Ki 8:43** 8085
then **h** in heaven their prayer and **1Ki 8:45** 8085
then **h** their prayer and their **1Ki 8:49** 8085
you continually *and* **h** your wisdom. **1Ki 10:8** 8085
to **h** his wisdom which God had put **1Ki 10:24** 8085
"Therefore, **h** the word of the LORD. **1Ki 22:19** 8085
Arameans to **h** a sound of chariots **2Ki 7:6** 8085
"**H** the word of the great king, **2Ki 18:28** 8085
will **h** all the words of Rabshakeh, **2Ki 19:4** 8085
he will **h** a rumor and return to his **2Ki 19:7** 8085
"Incline Your ear, O LORD, and **h**; **2Ki 19:16** 8085
"**H** the word of the LORD. **2Ki 20:16** 8085
when you **h** the sound of marching **1Ch 14:15** 8085
h from Your dwelling place, **2Ch 6:21** 8085
h and forgive. **2Ch 6:21** 8085
then **h** from heaven and act **2Ch 6:23** 8085
then **h** from heaven and **2Ch 6:25** 8085
then **h** in heaven and forgive **2Ch 6:27** 8085
then **h** from heaven Your **2Ch 6:30** 8085
then **h** from heaven, from Your **2Ch 6:33** 8085
then **h** from heaven their **2Ch 6:35** 8085
then **h** from heaven, from Your **2Ch 6:39** 8085
ways, then I will **h** from heaven, **2Ch 7:14** 8085
you continually and **h** your wisdom. **2Ch 9:7** 8085
to **h** his wisdom which God had put **2Ch 9:23** 8085
"Therefore, **h** the word of the LORD. **2Ch 18:18** 8085
and You will **h** and deliver *us*.' **2Ch 20:9** 8085
Your eyes open to **h** the prayer of **Ne 1:6** 8085
H, O our God, how we are despised! **Ne 4:4** 8085
you **h** the sound of the trumpet, **Ne 4:20** 8085
"Do we then **h** about you that you **Ne 13:27** 8085
not **h** the voice of the taskmaster. **Jb 3:18** 8085
H it, and know for yourself." **Jb 5:27** 8085
"Please **h** my argument And listen **Jb 13:6** 8085
you **h** the secret counsel of God, **Jb 15:8** 8085
pray to Him, and He will **h** you; **Jb 22:27** 8085
And how faint a word we **h** of Him! **Jb 26:14** 8085
"Will God **h** his cry When **Jb 27:9** 8085
"Oh that I had one to **h** me! **Jb 31:35** 8085
now, Job, please **h** my speech, **Jb 33:1** 8085
"**H** my words, you wise men, And **Jb 34:2** 8085
if *you have* understanding, **h** this; **Jb 34:16** 8085
might **h** the cry of the afflicted **Jb 34:28** 8085
"If they **h** and serve *Him*, They **Jb 36:11** 8085
"But if they do not **h**, **Jb 36:12** 8085
of the driver he does not **h**. **Jb 39:7** 8085
'**H**, now, and I will speak; **Jb 42:4** 8085
Be gracious to me and **h** my prayer. **Ps 4:1** 8085
O LORD, You will **h** my voice; **Ps 5:3** 8085
H a just cause, O LORD, give heed **Ps 17:1** 8085
Your ear to me, **h** my speech. **Ps 17:6** 8085
As soon as they **h**, they obey me; **Ps 18:44** 8088, 241
H, O LORD, when I cry with my **Ps 27:7** 8085
H the voice of my supplications **Ps 28:2** 8085
"**H**, O LORD, and be gracious to me; **Ps 30:10** 8085
The humble will **h** it and rejoice. **Ps 34:2** 8085
But I, like a deaf man, do not **h**; **Ps 38:13** 8085
I am like a man who does not **h**, **Ps 38:14** 8085
"**H** my prayer, O LORD, and give **Ps 39:12** 8085
H this, all peoples; **Ps 49:1** 8085
"**H**, O My people, and I will speak; **Ps 50:7** 8085
Make me to **h** joy and gladness, Let **Ps 51:8** 8085
H my prayer, O God; **Ps 54:2** 8085
murmur, And He will **h** my voice. **Ps 55:17** 8085
God will **h** and answer them **Ps 55:19** 8085
does not **h** the voice of charmers, **Ps 58:5** 8085
H my cry, O God; Give heed to my **Ps 61:1** 8085
H my voice, O God, in my complaint; **Ps 64:1** 8085
O You who **h** prayer, To You **Ps 65:2** 8085
Come *and* **h**, all who fear God, And **Ps 66:16** 8085
in my heart, The Lord will not **h**; **Ps 66:18** 8085
rises to God, and He will **h** me. **Ps 77:1** 238
"**H**, O My people, and I will **Ps 81:8** 8085
O LORD God of hosts, **h** my prayer; **Ps 84:8** 8085
will **h** what God the LORD will say; **Ps 85:8** 8085
My ears **h** of the evildoers who **Ps 92:11** 8085
planted the ear, does He not **h**? **Ps 94:9** 8085
Today, if you would **h** His voice, **Ps 95:7** 8085
H my prayer, O LORD! **Ps 102:1** 8085
To **h** the groaning of the prisoner, **Ps 102:20** 8085
They have ears, but they cannot **h**; **Ps 115:6** 8085
H my voice according to Your **Ps 119:149** 8085
Lord, **h** my voice! **Ps 130:2** 8085
They have ears, but they do not **h**, **Ps 135:17** 238
of the rock, And they **h** my words, **Ps 141:6** 8085
H my prayer, O LORD, Give ear to **Ps 143:1** 8085
Let me **h** Your lovingkindness in the **Ps 143:8** 8085
h their cry and will save them. **Ps 145:19** 8085
will **h** and increase in learning, **Pr 1:5** 8085
H, my son, your father's **Pr 1:8** 8085
H, *O* sons, the instruction of a **Pr 4:1** 8085
H, my son, and accept my sayings **Pr 4:10** 8085
ear and **h** the words of the wise, **Pr 22:17** 8085
not **h** your servant cursing you. **Ec 7:21** 8085
your form, Let me **h** your voice; **SS 2:14** 8085

for your voice—Let me **h** it!"	**SS 8:13**	8085
Listen, O heavens, and **h**,	**Is 1:2**	238
H the word of the LORD, You rulers	**Is 1:10**	8085
their eyes, **H** with their ears,	**Is 6:10**	8085
a decision by what His ears **h**;	**Is 11:3**	4926
trumpet is blown, you will **h** *it.*	**Is 18:3**	8085
I am so bewildered I cannot **h**,	**Is 21:3**	8085
the ends of the earth we **h** songs,	**Is 24:16**	8085
Therefore, **h** the word of the LORD,	**Is 28:14**	8085
Give ear and **h** my voice, Listen	**Is 28:23**	8085
my voice, Listen and **h** my words.	**Is 28:23**	8085
the deaf will **h** words of a book,	**Is 29:18**	8085
Let us **h** no more about the Holy	**Is 30:11**	7673a
ears will **h** a word behind you,	**Is 30:21**	8085
ears of those who **h** will listen.	**Is 32:3**	8085
who are at ease, *And* **h** my voice;	**Is 32:9**	8085
are far away, **h** what I have done;	**Is 33:13**	8085
Draw near, O nations, to **h**;	**Is 34:1**	8085
the earth and all it contains **h**,	**Is 34:1**	8085
"**H** the words of the great king,	**Is 36:13**	8085
God will **h** the words of Rabshakeh,	**Is 37:4**	8085
he will **h** a rumor and return to his	**Is 37:7**	8085
"Incline Your ear, O LORD, and **h**;	**Is 37:17**	8085
"**H** the word of the LORD of hosts,	**Is 39:5**	8085
H, you deaf! And look, you blind,	**Is 42:18**	8085
justified, Or let them **h** and say,	**Is 43:9**	8085
"Now, then, **h** this, you sensual	**Is 47:8**	8085
"**H** this, O house of Jacob, who	**Is 48:1**	8085
Therefore, please **h** this,	**Is 51:21**	8085
His ear so dull That it cannot **h**.	**Is 59:1**	8085
from you so that He does not **h**.	**Is 59:2**	8085
I spoke, but you did not **h**.	**Is 65:12**	8085
they are still speaking, I will **h**.	**Is 65:24**	8085
H the word of the LORD, you who	**Is 66:5**	8085
H the word of the LORD, O house of	**Jer 2:4**	8085
And **h** the sound of the trumpet?	**Jer 4:21**	8085
'Now **h** this, O foolish	**Jer 5:21**	8085
Who have ears but do not **h**.	**Jer 5:21**	8085
and give warning That they may **h**?	**Jer 6:10**	8085
"Therefore **h**, O nations, And	**Jer 6:18**	8085
"**H**, O earth: behold, I am bringing	**Jer 6:19**	8085
'**H** the word of the LORD, all you	**Jer 7:2**	8085
and speaking, but you did not **h**,	**Jer 7:13**	8085
for I do not **h** you.	**Jer 7:16**	8085
Now **h** the word of the LORD, O you	**Jer 9:20**	8085
H the word which the LORD speaks	**Jer 10:1**	8085
"**H** the words of this covenant,	**Jer 11:2**	8085
'**H** the words of this covenant and	**Jer 11:6**	8085
who refused to **h** My words,	**Jer 11:10**	8085
'**H** the word of the LORD, O kings	**Jer 19:3**	8085
And let him **h** an outcry in the	**Jer 20:16**	8085
'**H** the word of the LORD,	**Jer 21:11**	8085
'**H** the word of the LORD, O king of	**Jer 22:2**	8085
land, **H** the word of the LORD!	**Jer 22:29**	8085
That he should see and **h** His word?	**Jer 23:18**	8085
nor inclined your ear to **h**,	**Jer 25:4**	8085
"**H** the sound of the cry of	**Jer 25:36**	
"Yet **h** now this word which I am	**Jer 28:7**	8085
therefore, **h** the word of the LORD,	**Jer 29:20**	8085
H the word of the LORD, O nations,	**Jer 31:10**	8085
which will **h** of all the good that	**Jer 33:9**	8085
"Yet **h** the word of the LORD, O	**Jer 34:4**	8085
house of Judah will **h** all the calamity	**Jer 36:3**	8085
"But if the officials **h** that I	**Jer 38:25**	8085
or **h** the sound of a trumpet or	**Jer 42:14**	8085
"**H** the word of the LORD, all	**Jer 44:24**	8085
h the word of the LORD,	**Jer 44:26**	8085
Therefore **h** the plan of the LORD	**Jer 49:20**	8085
Therefore **h** the plan of the LORD	**Jer 50:45**	8085
H now, all peoples, And behold my	**La 1:18**	8085
you **h** a word from My mouth,	**Ezk 3:17**	8085
let him **h**; and he who refuses, let	**Ezk 3:27**	8085
see, ears to **h** but do not hear;	**Ezk 12:2**	8085
see, ears to hear but do not **h**;	**Ezk 12:2**	8085
O harlot, **h** the word of the LORD.	**Ezk 16:35**	8085
H now, O house of Israel!	**Ezk 18:25**	8085
'**H** the word of the LORD:	**Ezk 20:47**	8085
'**H** the word of the Lord GOD!	**Ezk 25:3**	8085
will **h** a message from My mouth and	**Ezk 33:7**	8085
and **h** what the message is which	**Ezk 33:30**	8085
as My people and **h** your words,	**Ezk 33:31**	8085
for they **h** your words but they do	**Ezk 33:32**	8085
shepherds, **h** the word of the LORD:	**Ezk 34:7**	8085
shepherds, **h** the word of the LORD:	**Ezk 34:9**	8085
of Israel, **h** the word of the LORD.	**Ezk 36:1**	8085
h the word of the Lord GOD.	**Ezk 36:4**	8085
"I will not let you **h** insults	**Ezk 36:15**	8085
bones, **h** the word of the LORD.'	**Ezk 37:4**	8085
with your eyes, **h** with your ears,	**Ezk 40:4**	8085
and **h** with your ears all that I	**Ezk 44:5**	8085
you **h** the sound of the horn,	**Da 3:5**	8086
you **h** the sound of the horn,	**Da 3:15**	8086
which do not see, **h** or understand.	**Da 5:23**	8086
"O my God, incline Your ear and **h**!	**Da 9:18**	8085
"O Lord, **h**! O Lord, forgive!	**Da 9:19**	8085
H this, O priests!	**Hos 5:1**	8085
H this, O elders, And listen, all	**Jl 1:2**	8085
H this word which the LORD has	**Am 3:1**	8085
"**H** and testify against the house	**Am 3:13**	8085
H this word, you cows of Bashan	**Am 4:1**	8085
H this word which I take up for	**Am 5:1**	8085
"Now **h** the word of the LORD:	**Am 7:16**	8085
H this, you who trample the needy,	**Am 8:4**	8085
H, O peoples, all of you;	**Mi 1:2**	8085
"**H** now, heads of Jacob And rulers	**Mi 3:1**	8085
Now **h** this, heads of the house of	**Mi 3:9**	8085
H now what the LORD is saying,	**Mi 6:1**	8085
And let the hills **h** your voice.	**Mi 6:1**	8085
"**H**, O tribe. Who has appointed	**Mi 6:9**	8085

My God will **h** me.	**Mi 7:7**	8085
All who **h** about you Will clap	**Na 3:19**	8085
for help, And You will not **h**?	**Hab 1:2**	8085
they could not **h** the law and the words	**Zch 7:12**	8085
what you **h** *whispered* in *your* ear,	**Mt 10:27**	*191*
report to John what you **h** and see:	**Mt 11:4**	*191*
are cleansed and *the* deaf **h**,	**Mt 11:5**	*191*
"He who has ears to **h**,	**Mt 11:15**	*191*
who has ears to hear, let him **h**.	**Mt 11:15**	*191*
NOR WILL ANYONE **H** HIS VOICE IN	**Mt 12:19**	*191*
earth to **h** the wisdom of Solomon;	**Mt 12:42**	*191*
"He who has ears, let him **h**."	**Mt 13:9**	*191*
and while hearing they do not **h**,	**Mt 13:13**	*191*
WITH THEIR EARS THEY SCARCELY **H**,	**Mt 13:15**	*191*
THEIR EYES, **H** WITH THEIR EARS,	**Mt 13:15**	*191*
and your ears, because they **h**.	**Mt 13:16**	*191*
and to **h** what you hear, and did	**Mt 13:17**	*191*
and to hear what you **h**,	**Mt 13:17**	*191*
and did not **h** *it.*	**Mt 13:17**	*191*
"**H** then the parable of the sower.	**Mt 13:18**	*191*
He who has ears, let him **h**.	**Mt 13:43**	*191*
"**H** and understand.	**Mt 15:10**	*191*
h what these *children* are saying?"	**Mt 21:16**	*191*
"Do You not **h** how many things	**Mt 27:13**	*191*
"He who has ears to **h**,	**Mk 4:9**	*191*
who has ears to hear, let him **h**."	**Mk 4:9**	*191*
THEY MAY **H** AND NOT UNDERSTAND,	**Mk 4:12**	*191*
and when they **h**, immediately Satan	**Mk 4:15**	*191*
places, who, when they **h** the word,	**Mk 4:16**	*191*
and they **h** the word and accept it and	**Mk 4:20**	*191*
"If anyone has ears to **h**,	**Mk 4:23**	*191*
ears to hear, let him **h**."	**Mk 4:23**	*191*
as they were able to **h** it;	**Mk 4:33**	*191*
["If anyone has ears to **h**,	**Mk 7:16**	*191*
ears to hear, let him **h**."]	**Mk 7:16**	*191*
He makes even the deaf to **h** and	**Mk 7:37**	*191*
DO YOU NOT **H**? And do you not	**Mk 8:18**	*191*
'**H**, O ISRAEL! THE LORD OUR GOD IS	**Mk 12:29**	*191*
you **h** of wars and rumors of wars,	**Mk 13:7**	*191*
crowds were gathering to **h** *Him*	**Lk 5:15**	*191*
who had come to **h** Him and to be	**Lk 6:18**	*191*
"But I say to you who **h**,	**Lk 6:27**	*191*
are cleansed, and *the* deaf **h**,	**Lk 7:22**	*191*
"He who has ears to **h**,	**Lk 8:8**	*191*
who has ears to hear, let him **h**."	**Lk 8:8**	*191*
who, when they **h**, receive the word	**Lk 8:13**	*191*
who **h** the word of God and do it."	**Lk 8:21**	*191*
man about whom I **h** such things?"	**Lk 9:9**	*191*
to **h** the things which you hear,	**Lk 10:24**	*191*
to hear the things which you **h**,	**Lk 10:24**	*191*
and did not **h** *them.*"	**Lk 10:24**	*191*
are those who **h** the word of God and	**Lk 11:28**	*191*
earth to **h** the wisdom of Solomon;	**Lk 11:31**	*191*
He who has ears to **h**,	**Lk 14:35**	*191*
who has ears to hear, let him **h**."	**Lk 14:35**	*191*
'What is this I **h** about you?	**Lk 16:2**	*191*
let them **h** them.'	**Lk 16:29**	*191*
"**H** what the unrighteous judge	**Lk 18:6**	*191*
you **h** of wars and disturbances,	**Lk 21:9**	*191*
wishes and you **h** the sound of it,	**Jn 3:8**	*191*
h the voice of the Son of God,	**Jn 5:25**	*191*
and those who **h** will live.	**Jn 5:25**	*191*
in the tombs will **h** His voice,	**Jn 5:28**	*191*
As I **h**, I judge; and My judgment	**Jn 5:30**	*191*
is because you cannot **h** My word.	**Jn 8:43**	*191*
for this reason you do not **h** *them,*	**Jn 8:47**	*191*
why do you want to **h** *it* again?	**Jn 9:27**	*191*
know that God does not **h** sinners;	**Jn 9:31**	*191*
opens, and the sheep **h** his voice,	**Jn 10:3**	*191*
but the sheep did not **h** them.	**Jn 10:8**	*191*
also, and they will **h** My voice;	**Jn 10:16**	*191*
My sheep **h** My voice, and I know	**Jn 10:27**	*191*
"I knew that You always **h** Me;	**Jn 11:42**	*191*
the word which you **h** is not Mine,	**Jn 14:24**	*191*
we each **h** *them* in our own language	**Ac 2:8**	*191*
we **h** them in our *own* tongues	**Ac 2:11**	*191*
this which you both see and **h**.	**Ac 2:33**	*191*
"**H** me, brethren and fathers!	**Ac 7:2**	*191*
house and **h** a message from you."	**Ac 10:22**	*191*
are all here present before God to **h**	**Ac 10:33**	*191*
and sought to **h** the word of God.	**Ac 13:7**	*191*
assembled to **h** the word of the Lord.	**Ac 13:44**	*191*
the Gentiles would **h** the	**Ac 15:7**	*191*
h you again concerning this."	**Ac 17:32**	*191*
and **h** that not only in Ephesus,	**Ac 19:26**	*191*
certainly **h** that you have come.	**Ac 21:22**	*191*
h my defense which I now *offer* to	**Ac 22:1**	*191*
to **h** an utterance from His mouth.	**Ac 22:14**	*191*
would like to **h** the man myself."	**Ac 25:22**	*191*
"you shall **h** him."	**Ac 25:22**	*191*
but also all who **h** me this day,	**Ac 26:29**	*191*
to **h** from you what your views are;	**Ac 28:22**	*191*
AND WITH THEIR EARS THEY SCARCELY **H**,	**Ac 28:27**	*191*
AND **H** WITH THEIR EARS, AND	**Ac 28:27**	*191*
will they **h** without a preacher?	**Ro 10:14**	*191*
EYES TO SEE NOT AND EARS TO **H** NOT,	**Ro 11:8**	*191*
I **h** that divisions exist among you;	**1Co 11:18**	*191*
it will give grace to those who **h**.	**Eph 4:29**	*191*
I will **h** of you that you are	**Php 1:27**	*191*
saw in me, and now **h** *to be* in me.	**Php 1:30**	*191*
For we **h** that some among you are	**2Th 3:11**	*191*
yourself and for those who **h** you.	**1Tm 4:16**	*191*
and that all the Gentiles might **h**;	**2Tm 4:17**	*191*
because I **h** of your love and of	**Phm 1:5**	*191*
"TODAY IF YOU **H** HIS VOICE,	**Heb 3:7**	*191*
while it is said, "TODAY IF YOU **H**	**Heb 3:15**	*191*
"TODAY IF YOU **H** HIS VOICE, DO NOT	**Heb 4:7**	*191*
But everyone must be quick to **h**,	**Jas 1:19**	*191*
to **h** of my children walking in the	**3Jn 1:4**	*191*

who **h** the words of the prophecy,	**Rv 1:3**	*191*
let him **h** what the Spirit says to	**Rv 2:7**	*191*
let him **h** what the Spirit says to	**Rv 2:11**	*191*
let him **h** what the Spirit says to	**Rv 2:17**	*191*
let him **h** what the Spirit says to	**Rv 2:29**	*191*
let him **h** what the Spirit says to	**Rv 3:6**	*191*
let him **h** what the Spirit says to	**Rv 3:13**	*191*
let him **h** what the Spirit says to	**Rv 3:22**	*191*
can neither see nor **h** nor walk;	**Rv 9:20**	*191*
If anyone has an ear, let him **h**.	**Rv 13:9**	*191*

HEARD

They **h** the sound of the LORD	**Gn 3:8**	8085
"I **h** the sound of You in the	**Gn 3:10**	8085
When Abram **h** that his relative	**Gn 14:14**	8085
"As for Ishmael, I have **h** you;	**Gn 17:20**	8085
God **h** the lad crying;	**Gn 21:17**	8085
for God has **h** the voice of the lad	**Gn 21:17**	8085
and when he **h** the words of Rebekah	**Gn 24:30**	8085
Abraham's servant **h** their words,	**Gn 24:52**	8085
I **h** your father speak to your	**Gn 27:6**	8085
Esau **h** the words of his father,	**Gn 27:34**	8085
when Laban **h** the news of Jacob his	**Gn 29:13**	8085
the LORD has **h** that I am unloved,	**Gn 29:33**	8085
and has indeed **h** my voice and has	**Gn 30:6**	8085
Jacob **h** the words of Laban's sons,	**Gn 31:1**	8085
Now Jacob **h** that he had defiled	**Gn 34:5**	8085
in from the field when they **h** *it;*	**Gn 34:7**	8085
and Israel **h** *of it.*	**Gn 35:22**	8085
I **h** *them* say, 'Let us go to Dothan	**Gn 37:17**	8085
But Reuben **h** *this* and rescued him	**Gn 37:21**	8085
"When he **h** that I raised my voice	**Gn 39:15**	8085
master **h** the words of his wife,	**Gn 39:19**	8085
and I have **h** it said about you,	**Gn 41:15**	8085
h that there is grain in Egypt;	**Gn 42:2**	8085
for they had **h** that they were to	**Gn 43:25**	8085
so loudly that the Egyptians **h** *it,*	**Gn 45:2**	8085
the household of Pharaoh **h** *of it.*	**Gn 45:2**	8085
the news was **h** in Pharaoh's house	**Gn 45:16**	8085
When Pharaoh **h** of this matter, he	**Ex 2:15**	8085
So God **h** their groaning;	**Ex 2:24**	8085
and when they **h** that the LORD was	**Ex 4:31**	8085
I have **h** the groaning of	**Ex 6:5**	8085
"The peoples have **h**,	**Ex 15:14**	8085
for He has **h** your grumblings.'	**Ex 16:9**	8085
"I have **h** the grumblings of the	**Ex 16:12**	8085
h of all that God had done for	**Ex 18:1**	8085
nor let *them* be **h** from your mouth.	**Ex 23:13**	8085
and its tinkling shall be **h** when he	**Ex 28:35**	8085
Now when Joshua **h** the sound of the	**Ex 32:17**	8085
When the people **h** this sad word,	**Ex 33:4**	8085
When Moses **h** *that,* it seemed	**Lv 10:20**	8085
and let all who **h** him lay their	**Lv 24:14**	8085
he **h** the voice speaking to him	**Nu 7:89**	8085
and when the LORD **h** *it,*	**Nu 11:1**	8085
Now Moses **h** the people weeping	**Nu 11:10**	8085
And the LORD **h** it.	**Nu 12:2**	8085
They have **h** that You, O LORD, are	**Nu 14:14**	8085
who have **h** of Your fame will say,	**Nu 14:15**	8085
I have **h** the complaints of the	**Nu 14:27**	8085
When Moses **h** *this,* he fell on his	**Nu 16:4**	8085
He **h** our voice and sent an angel	**Nu 20:16**	8085
h that Israel was coming by the	**Nu 21:1**	8085
The LORD **h** the voice of Israel	**Nu 21:3**	8085
Balak **h** that Balaam was coming,	**Nu 22:36**	8085
and her husband **h** *it,* but said	**Nu 30:11**	8085
to her on the day he **h** them.	**Nu 30:14**	8085
annuls them after he has **h** them,	**Nu 30:15**	8085
h of the coming of the sons of	**Nu 33:40**	8085
LORD **h** the sound of your words,	**Dt 1:34**	8085
you **h** the sound of words, but you	**Dt 4:12**	8085
or has *anything* been **h** like it?	**Dt 4:32**	8085
"Has *any* people **h** the voice of	**Dt 4:33**	8085
of the fire, as you have **h** *it,*	**Dt 4:33**	8085
and you **h** His words from the midst	**Dt 4:36**	8085
when you **h** the voice from the	**Dt 5:23**	8085
and we have **h** His voice from the	**Dt 5:24**	8085
who has **h** the voice of the living	**Dt 5:26**	8085
"The LORD **h** the voice of your	**Dt 5:28**	8085
'I have **h** the voice of the words	**Dt 5:28**	8085
and of whom you have **h** *it said,*	**Dt 9:2**	8085
is told you and you have **h** of it,	**Dt 17:4**	8085
and the LORD **h** our voice and saw	**Dt 26:7**	8085
"For we have **h** how the LORD dried	**Jos 2:10**	8085
"When we **h** *it,* our hearts	**Jos 2:11**	8085
h how the LORD had dried up the	**Jos 5:1**	8085
not shout nor let your voice be **h** nor	**Jos 6:10**	8085
people **h** the sound of the trumpet,	**Jos 6:20**	8085
Hivite and the Jebusite, **h** of it,	**Jos 9:1**	8085
When the inhabitants of Gibeon **h**	**Jos 9:3**	8085
for we have **h** the report of Him	**Jos 9:9**	8085
they **h** that they were neighbors	**Jos 9:16**	8085
h that Joshua had captured Ai,	**Jos 10:1**	8085
when Jabin king of Hazor **h** *of it,*	**Jos 11:1**	8085
for you **h** on that day that Anakim	**Jos 14:12**	8085
And the sons of Israel **h** *it* said,	**Jos 22:11**	8085
When the sons of Israel **h** *of it,*	**Jos 22:12**	8085
h the words which the sons of	**Jos 22:30**	8085
for it has **h** all the words of the	**Jos 24:27**	8085
Gideon **h** the account of the dream	**Jg 7:15**	8085
ruler of the city **h** the words of Gaal	**Jg 9:30**	8085
of the tower of Shechem **h** *of it,*	**Jg 9:46**	8085
not let your voice be **h** among us,	**Jg 18:25**	8085
(Now the sons of Benjamin **h** that	**Jg 20:3**	8085
for she had **h** in the land of Moab	**Ru 1:6**	8085
moving, but her voice was not **h**.	**1Sa 1:13**	8085
and he **h** all that his sons were	**1Sa 2:22**	8085
Philistines **h** the noise of the shout	**1Sa 4:6**	8085
Eli **h** the noise of the outcry,	**1Sa 4:14**	8085
and when she **h** the news that the	**1Sa 4:19**	8085

Now when the Philistines **h** that	1Sa 7:7	8085
And when the sons of Israel **h** it,	1Sa 7:7	8085
had **h** all the words of the people,	1Sa 8:21	8085
mightily when he **h** these words,	1Sa 11:6	8085
Geba, and the Philistines **h** *of it.*	1Sa 13:3	8085
All Israel **h** the news that	1Sa 13:4	8085
h that the Philistines had fled,	1Sa 14:22	8085
But Jonathan had not **h** when his	1Sa 14:27	8085
h these words of the Philistine,	1Sa 17:11	8085
and David **h** *them.*	1Sa 17:23	8085
h when he spoke to the men;	1Sa 17:28	8085
words which David spoke were **h**,	1Sa 17:31	8085
all his father's household **h** *of it,*	1Sa 22:1	8085
Then Saul **h** that David and the men	1Sa 22:6	8085
Your servant has **h** for certain that	1Sa 23:10	8085
down just as Your servant has **h**?	1Sa 23:11	8085
And when Saul **h** *it,* he pursued	1Sa 23:25	8085
that David **h** in the wilderness	1Sa 25:4	8085
I have **h** that you have shearers;	1Sa 25:7	8085
When David **h** that Nabal was dead,	1Sa 25:39	8085
of Jabesh-gilead **h** what the Philistines	1Sa 31:11	8085
Afterward when David **h** it,	2Sa 3:28	8085
h that Abner had died in Hebron,	2Sa 4:1	8085
When the Philistines **h** that they	2Sa 5:17	8085
and when David **h** *of it,* he went	2Sa 5:17	8085
all that we have **h** with our ears.	2Sa 7:22	8085
Now when Toi king of Hamath **h** that	2Sa 8:9	8085
When David **h** *of it,* he sent Joab	2Sa 10:7	8085
Now when the wife of Uriah **h** that	2Sa 11:26	8085
King David **h** of all these matters,	2Sa 13:21	8085
And all the people **h** when the king	2Sa 18:5	8085
for the people **h** *it* said that day,	2Sa 19:2	8085
And from His temple He **h** my voice,	2Sa 22:7	8085
"Have you not **h** that Adonijah the	1Ki 1:11	8085
the guests who *were* with him **h** *it*	1Ki 1:41	8085
Joab **h** the sound of the trumpet,	1Ki 1:41	8085
is the noise which you have **h**.	1Ki 1:45	8085
'The word which I have **h** is good.'	1Ki 2:42	8085
When all Israel **h** of the judgment	1Ki 3:28	8085
the earth who had **h** of his wisdom.	1Ki 4:34	8085
when he **h** that they had anointed	1Ki 5:1	8085
When Hiram **h** the words of Solomon,	1Ki 5:7	8085
"I have **h** *the message* which you	1Ki 5:8	8085
nor any iron tool **h** in the house while	1Ki 6:7	8085
"I have **h** your prayer and your	1Ki 9:3	8085
queen of Sheba **h** about the fame	1Ki 10:1	8085
"It was a true report which I **h**	1Ki 10:6	8085
prosperity the report which I **h**.	1Ki 10:7	8085
But when Hadad **h** in Egypt that	1Ki 11:21	8085
Jeroboam the son of Nebat **h** *of it,*	1Ki 12:2	8085
h that Jeroboam had returned,	1Ki 12:20	8085
h the saying of the man of God,	1Ki 13:4	8085
him back from the way **h** *it,*	1Ki 13:26	8085
When Ahijah **h** the sound of her feet	1Ki 14:6	8085
When Baasha **h** *of it,*	1Ki 15:21	8085
people who were camped **h** it said,	1Ki 16:16	8085
The LORD **h** the voice of Elijah,	1Ki 17:22	8085
When Elijah **h** *it,*	1Ki 19:13	8085
When *Ben-hadad* **h** this message,	1Ki 20:12	8085
we have **h** that the kings of the	1Ki 20:31	8085
When Jezebel **h** that Naboth	1Ki 21:15	8085
When Ahab **h** that Naboth was dead,	1Ki 21:16	8085
about when Ahab **h** these words,	1Ki 21:27	8085
Now all the Moabites **h** that the	2Ki 3:21	8085
Elisha the man of God **h** that the king	2Ki 5:8	8085
the king **h** the words of the woman,	2Ki 6:30	8085
came to Jezreel, Jezebel **h** *of it,*	2Ki 9:30	8085
When Athaliah **h** the noise of the	2Ki 11:13	8085
And when King Hezekiah **h** *it,*	2Ki 19:1	8085
which the LORD your God has **h**.	2Ki 19:4	8085
of the words that you have **h**,	2Ki 19:6	8085
for he had **h** that the king had	2Ki 19:8	8085
When he **h** *them* say concerning	2Ki 19:9	8085
you have **h** what the kings of	2Ki 19:11	8085
king of Assyria, I have **h** *you.*	2Ki 19:20	8085
'Have you not **h**? Long ago I did it;	2Ki 19:25	8085
"I have **h** your prayer, I have	2Ki 20:5	8085
he **h** that Hezekiah had been sick.	2Ki 20:12	8085
the king **h** the words of the book	2Ki 22:11	8085
the words which you have **h**,	2Ki 22:18	8085
when you **h** what I spoke against this	2Ki 22:19	8085
before Me, I truly have **h** you,"	2Ki 22:19	8085
h that the king of Babylon had	2Ki 25:23	8085
When all Jabesh-gilead **h** all that	1Ch 10:11	8085
When the Philistines **h** that David	1Ch 14:8	8085
and David **h** of it and went out	1Ch 14:8	8085
all that we have **h** with our ears.	1Ch 17:20	8085
Now when Tou king of Hamath **h** that	1Ch 18:9	8085
When David **h** *of it,* he sent Joab	1Ch 19:8	8085
to make themselves **h** with one voice	2Ch 5:13	8085
"I have **h** your prayer and have	2Ch 7:12	8085
of Sheba **h** of the fame of Solomon,	2Ch 9:1	8085
"It was a true report which I **h**	2Ch 9:5	8085
You surpass the report that I **h**.	2Ch 9:6	8085
Jeroboam the son of Nebat **h** *of it*	2Ch 10:2	8085
Now when Asa **h** these words and the	2Ch 15:8	8085
When Baasha **h** *of it,*	2Ch 16:5	8085
when they **h** that the LORD had fought	2Ch 20:29	8085
When Athaliah **h** the noise of the	2Ch 23:12	8085
So the LORD **h** Hezekiah and healed	2Ch 30:20	8085
and their voice was **h** and their	2Ch 30:27	8085
entreaty and **h** his supplication,	2Ch 33:13	8085
the king **h** the words of the law	2Ch 34:19	8085
the words which you have **h**,	2Ch 34:26	8085
when you **h** His words against this	2Ch 34:27	8085
before Me, I truly have **h** you,"	2Ch 34:27	8085
and the sound was **h** far away.	Ezr 3:13	8085
enemies of Judah and Benjamin **h** that	Ezr 4:1	8085
When I **h** about this matter, I	Ezr 9:3	8085
When I **h** these words,	Ne 1:4	8085
the Ammonite official **h** *about it,*	Ne 2:10	8085
and Geshem the Arab **h** *it,*	Ne 2:19	8085
Sanballat **h** that we were rebuilding	Ne 4:1	8085
and the Ashdodites **h** that the	Ne 4:7	8085
enemies **h** that it was known to us,	Ne 4:15	8085
h their outcry and these words.	Ne 5:6	8085
When all our enemies **h** *of it,*	Ne 6:16	8085
when they **h** the words of the law.	Ne 8:9	8085
And **h** their cry by the Red Sea.	Ne 9:9	8085
You **h** from heaven, and according to	Ne 9:27	8085
You **h** from heaven, And many times	Ne 9:28	8085
joy of Jerusalem was **h** from afar.	Ne 12:43	8085
when they **h** the law,	Ne 13:3	8085
who have **h** of the queen's conduct	Es 1:18	8085
is **h** throughout all his kingdom,	Es 1:20	8085
decree of the king were **h** and many	Es 2:8	8085
three friends **h** of all this adversity	Jb 2:11	8085
was silence, then I **h** a voice:	Jb 4:16	8085
My ear has **h** and understood it.	Jb 13:1	8085
"I have **h** many such things;	Jb 16:2	8085
ears we have **h** a report of it.'	Jb 28:22	8085
"For when the ear **h**,	Jb 29:11	8085
I have **h** the sound of *your* words:	Jb 33:8	8085
lightnings when His voice is **h**.	Jb 37:4	8085
"I have **h** of You by the hearing	Jb 42:5	8085
LORD has **h** the voice of my weeping.	Ps 6:8	8085
The LORD has **h** my supplication,	Ps 6:9	8085
have **h** the desire of the humble;	Ps 10:17	8085
He **h** my voice out of His temple,	Ps 18:6	8085
Their voice is not **h**.	Ps 19:3	8085
he cried to Him for help, He **h**.	Ps 22:24	8085
h the voice of my supplication.	Ps 28:6	8085
For I have **h** the slander of many,	Ps 31:13	8085
Nevertheless You **h** the voice of my	Ps 31:22	8085
poor man cried, and the LORD **h** him	Ps 34:6	8085
He inclined to me and **h** my cry.	Ps 40:1	8085
O God, we have **h** with our ears,	Ps 44:1	8085
As we have **h**, so have we seen In	Ps 48:8	8085
For You have **h** my vows, O God;	Ps 61:5	8085
Twice I have **h** this:	Ps 62:11	8085
But certainly God has **h**;	Ps 66:19	8085
judgment to be **h** from heaven;	Ps 76:8	8085
Which we have **h** and known, And our	Ps 78:3	8085
the LORD **h** and was full of wrath;	Ps 78:21	8085
When God **h**, He was filled with	Ps 78:59	8085
I **h** a language that I did not know:	Ps 81:5	8085
Zion **h** *this* and was glad, And the	Ps 97:8	8085
distress When He **h** their cry;	Ps 106:44	8085
Behold, we **h** of it in Ephrathah,	Ps 132:6	8085
have **h** the words of Your mouth.	Ps 138:4	8085
The words of the wise **h** in quietness	Ec 9:17	8085
conclusion, when all has been **h**,	Ec 12:13	8085
turtledove has been **h** in our land.	SS 2:12	8085
Then I **h** the voice of the Lord,	Is 6:8	8085
voice is **h** all the way to Jahaz;	Is 15:4	8085
We have **h** of the pride of Moab, an	Is 16:6	8085
I have **h** from the LORD of hosts,	Is 21:10	8085
have **h** from the Lord GOD of hosts	Is 28:22	8085
His voice of authority to be **h**,	Is 30:30	8085
And when King Hezekiah **h**	Is 37:1	8085
which the LORD your God has **h**.	Is 37:4	8085
of the words that you have **h**,	Is 37:6	8085
for he had **h** that the king had	Is 37:8	8085
When he **h** *them* say concerning	Is 37:9	8085
and when he **h** *it* he sent	Is 37:9	8085
you have **h** what the kings of	Is 37:11	8085
"Have you not **h**? Long ago I did it,	Is 37:26	8085
"I have **h** your prayer, I have	Is 38:5	8085
for he **h** that he had been sick and	Is 39:1	8085
Do you not know? Have you not **h**?	Is 40:21	8085
Do you not know? Have you not **h**?	Is 40:28	8085
there was no one who **h** your words.	Is 41:26	8085
make His voice **h** in the street.	Is 42:2	8085
"You have **h**; look at all this.	Is 48:6	8085
before today you have not **h** them,	Is 48:7	8085
"You have not **h**, you have not	Is 48:8	8085
had not **h** they will understand.	Is 52:15	8085
to make your voice **h** on high.	Is 58:4	8085
will not be **h** again in your land,	Is 60:18	8085
have not **h** or perceived by ear,	Is 64:4	8085
no longer be **h** in her The voice of	Is 65:19	8085
"Who has **h** such a thing?	Is 66:8	8085
h My fame nor seen My glory.	Is 66:19	8085
A voice is **h** on the bare heights,	Jer 3:21	8085
be silent, Because you have **h**,	Jer 4:19	8085
I **h** a cry as of a woman in labor,	Jer 4:31	8085
and destruction are **h** in her;	Jer 6:7	8085
We have **h** the report of it;	Jer 6:24	8085
"I have listened and **h**,	Jer 8:6	8085
is **h** the snorting of his horses;	Jer 8:16	8085
the lowing of the cattle is not **h**;	Jer 9:10	8085
a voice of wailing is **h** from Zion,	Jer 9:19	8085
Who ever **h** the like of this?	Jer 18:13	8085
an outcry be **h** from their houses,	Jer 18:22	8085
h Jeremiah prophesying these	Jer 20:1	8085
I have **h** the whispering of many,	Jer 20:10	8085
"I have **h** what the prophets have	Jer 23:25	8085
people **h** Jeremiah speaking these words	Jer 26:7	8085
officials of Judah **h** these things,	Jer 26:10	8085
as you have **h** in your hearing."	Jer 26:11	8085
all the words that you have **h**.	Jer 26:12	8085
and all the officials **h** his words,	Jer 26:21	8085
but Uriah **h** *it,* and he was afraid	Jer 26:21	8085
'I have **h** a sound of terror, Of	Jer 30:5	8085
"A voice is **h** in Ramah,	Jer 31:15	8085
"I have surely **h** Ephraim	Jer 31:18	8085
there will be **h** in this place,	Jer 33:10	8085
had **h** all the words of the	Jer 36:11	8085
them all the words that he had **h** when	Jer 36:13	8085
When they had **h** all the words,	Jer 36:16	8085
all his servants who **h** all these words	Jer 36:24	8085
Jerusalem **h** the report about them,	Jer 37:5	8085
the son of Malchijah **h** the words that	Jer 38:1	8085
h that they had put Jeremiah into	Jer 38:7	8085
h that the king of Babylon had	Jer 40:7	8085
h that the king of Babylon had	Jer 40:11	8085
h of all the evil that Ishmael the son	Jer 41:11	8085
prophet said to them, "I have **h** *you.*	Jer 42:4	8085
The nations have **h** of your shame,	Jer 46:12	8085
They have **h** the anguished cry of	Jer 48:5	8085
"We have **h** of the pride of Moab	Jer 48:29	8085
trumpet blast of war to be **h** Against	Jer 49:2	8085
I have **h** a message from the LORD,	Jer 49:14	8085
of it has been **h** at the Red Sea.	Jer 49:21	8085
shame, For they have **h** bad news;	Jer 49:23	8085
has **h** the report about them,	Jer 50:43	8085
an outcry is **h** among the nations.	Jer 50:46	8085
not afraid at the report that *will be* **h**	Jer 51:46	8085
because we have **h** reproach;	Jer 51:51	8085
"They have **h** that I groan;	La 1:21	8085
my enemies have **h** of my calamity;	La 1:21	8085
You have **h** my voice,	La 3:56	8085
You have **h** their reproach, O	La 3:61	8085
I also **h** the sound of their wings	Ezk 1:24	8085
on my face and **h** a voice speaking.	Ezk 1:28	8085
and I **h** *Him* speaking to me.	Ezk 2:2	8085
and I **h** a great rumbling sound	Ezk 3:12	8085
And I **h** the sound of the wings of	Ezk 3:13	
was **h** as far as the outer court,	Ezk 10:5	8085
name of your sister Sodom was not **h**	Ezk 16:56	8052
'Then nations **h** about him;	Ezk 19:4	8085
So that his voice would be **h** no more	Ezk 19:9	8085
of your harps will be **h** no more.	Ezk 26:13	8085
And they will make their voice **h**	Ezk 27:30	8085
'He **h** the sound of the trumpet	Ezk 33:5	8085
have **h** all your revilings which	Ezk 35:12	8085
your words against Me; I have **h** *it.*"	Ezk 35:13	8085
Then I **h** one speaking to me from	Ezk 43:6	8085
peoples **h** the sound of the horn,	Da 3:7	8086
"Now I have **h** about you that a	Da 5:14	8086
"But I personally have **h** about you,	Da 5:16	8086
soon as the king **h** this statement,	Da 6:14	8086
Then I **h** a holy one speaking, and	Da 8:13	8085
And I **h** the voice of a man between	Da 8:16	8085
But I **h** the sound of his words;	Da 10:9	8085
as I **h** the sound of his words,	Da 10:9	8085
your God, your words were **h**,	Da 10:12	8085
I **h** the man dressed in linen,	Da 12:7	8085
me, I **h** but could not understand;	Da 12:8	8085
We have **h** a report from the	Ob 1:1	8085
You **h** my voice.	Jon 2:2	8085
voice of your messengers be **h**."	Na 2:13	8085
I have **h** the report about You	Hab 3:2	8085
I **h** and my inward parts trembled,	Hab 3:16	8085
"I have **h** the taunting of Moab	Zph 2:8	8085
we have **h** that God is with you.	Zch 8:23	8085
the LORD gave attention and **h** *it,*	Mal 3:16	8085
When Herod the king **h**	Mt 2:3	*191*
"A VOICE WAS **H** IN RAMAH, WEEPING	Mt 2:18	*191*
But when he **h** that Archelaus was	Mt 2:22	*191*
Now when Jesus **h** that John had been	Mt 4:12	*191*
h that the ancients were told,	Mt 5:21	*191*
"You have **h** that it was said,	Mt 5:27	*191*
h that the ancients were told,	Mt 5:33	*191*
"You have **h** that it was said,	Mt 5:38	*191*
"You have **h** that it was said,	Mt 5:43	*191*
will be **h** for their many words.	Mt 6:7	*1522*
Now when Jesus **h** *this,* He	Mt 8:10	*191*
But when Jesus **h** *this,* He said,	Mt 9:12	*191*
h of the works of Christ,	Mt 11:2	*191*
But when the Pharisees **h**	Mt 12:24	*191*
tetrarch **h** the news about Jesus,	Mt 14:1	*191*
Now when Jesus **h** *about John,*	Mt 14:13	*191*
and when the people **h** *of this,*	Mt 14:13	*191*
when they **h** this statement?"	Mt 15:12	*191*
When the disciples **h**	Mt 17:6	*191*
the young man **h** this statement,	Mt 19:22	*191*
When the disciples **h** *this,*	Mt 19:25	*191*
and the Pharisees **h** His parables,	Mt 21:45	*191*
When the crowds **h** *this,*	Mt 22:33	*191*
But when the Pharisees **h** that Jesus	Mt 22:34	*191*
you have now **h** the blasphemy;	Mt 26:65	*191*
standing there, when they **h** it,	Mt 27:47	*191*
it was **h** that He was at home.	Mk 2:1	*191*
a great number of people **h**	Mk 3:8	*191*
When His own people **h** *of this,*	Mk 3:21	*191*
are the ones who have **h** the word,	Mk 4:18	*191*
And King Herod **h** *of it,* for His	Mk 6:14	*191*
But when Herod **h** *of it,* he kept	Mk 6:16	*191*
And when he **h** him, he was very	Mk 6:20	*191*
When his disciples **h** *about this,*	Mk 6:29	*191*
sick, to the place they **h** He was.	Mk 6:55	*191*
When he **h** that it was Jesus	Mk 10:47	*191*
priests and the scribes **h**	Mk 11:18	*191*
scribes came and **h** them arguing,	Mk 12:28	*191*
They were glad when they **h** *this,*	Mk 14:11	*191*
"We **h** Him say, 'I will destroy this	Mk 14:58	*191*
"You have **h** the blasphemy;	Mk 14:64	*191*
When some of the bystanders **h** it,	Mk 15:35	*191*
When they **h** that He was alive and	Mk 16:11	*191*
for your petition has been **h**,	Lk 1:13	*1522*
When Elizabeth **h** Mary's greeting,	Lk 1:41	*191*
Her neighbors and her relatives **h**	Lk 1:58	*191*
All who **h** them kept them in mind,	Lk 1:66	*191*
And all who **h** it wondered at the	Lk 2:18	*191*
for all that they had **h** and seen,	Lk 2:20	*191*
And all who **h** Him were amazed at	Lk 2:47	*191*

we **h** was done at Capernaum, **Lk 4:23** *191*
with rage as they **h** these things; **Lk 4:28** *191*
"But the one who has **h** and **Lk 6:49** *191*
When he **h** about Jesus, he sent **Lk 7:3** *191*
Now when Jesus **h** this, He marveled **Lk 7:9** *191*
to John what you have seen and **h**: **Lk 7:22** *191*
and the tax collectors **h** *this,* **Lk 7:29** *191*
the road are those who have **h**; **Lk 8:12** *191*
these are the ones who have **h**, **Lk 8:14** *191*
who have **h** the word in an honest **Lk 8:15** *191*
But when Jesus **h** *this,* He answered **Lk 8:50** *191*
tetrarch **h** of all that was happening **Lk 9:7** *191*
the dark will be **h** in the light, **Lk 12:3** *191*
at the table with Him **h** this, **Lk 14:15** *191*
the house, he **h** music and dancing. **Lk 15:25** *191*
When Jesus **h** *this,* He said to **Lk 18:22** *191*
But when he had **h** these things, he **Lk 18:23** *191*
They who **h** it said, **Lk 18:26** *191*
When they **h** it, they said, **Lk 20:16** *191*
For we have **h** it ourselves from **Lk 22:71** *191*
When Pilate **h** it, he asked **Lk 23:6** *191*
The two disciples **h** him speak, **Jn 1:37** *191*
One of the two who **h** John **Jn 1:40** *191*
"What He has seen and **h** **Jn 3:32** *191*
that the Pharisees had **h** that Jesus **Jn 4:1** *191*
for we have **h** for ourselves and **Jn 4:42** *191*
When he **h** that Jesus had come out **Jn 4:47** *191*
neither **h** His voice at any time nor **Jn 5:37** *191*
has **h** and learned from the Father, **Jn 6:45** *191*
disciples, when they **h** *this* said, **Jn 6:60** *191*
The Pharisees **h** the crowd **Jn 7:32** *191*
when they **h** these words, **Jn 7:40** *191*
When they **h** it, they *began* to **Jn 8:9** *191*
and the things which I **h** from Him, **Jn 8:26** *191*
which you **h** from *your* father." **Jn 8:38** *191*
you the truth, which I **h** from God; **Jn 8:40** *191*
beginning of time it has never been **h** **Jn 9:32** *191*
Jesus **h** that they had put him out, **Jn 9:35** *191*
who were with Him **h** these things and **Jn 9:40** *191*
But when Jesus **h** *this,* He said, **Jn 11:4** *191*
when He **h** that he was sick, **Jn 11:6** *191*
when she **h** that Jesus was coming, **Jn 11:20** *191*
And when she **h** it, she got **Jn 11:29** *191*
I thank You that You have **h** Me. **Jn 11:41** *191*
when they **h** that Jesus was coming **Jn 12:12** *191*
because they **h** that He had **Jn 12:18** *191*
who stood by and **h** it **Jn 12:29** *191*
"We have **h** out of the Law that **Jn 12:34** *191*
"You **h** that I said to you, **Jn 14:28** *191*
for all things that I have **h** from **Jn 15:15** *191*
who have **h** what I spoke to them; **Jn 18:21** *191*
Pilate **h** this statement, **Jn 19:8** *191*
Pilate **h** these words, **Jn 19:13** *191*
Peter **h** that it was the Lord, **Jn 21:7** *191*
"you **h** of from Me; **Ac 1:4** *191*
Now when they **h** *this,* they were **Ac 2:37** *191*
who had **h** the message believed; **Ac 4:4** *191*
what we have seen and **h**." **Ac 4:20** *191*
And when they **h** *this,* they lifted **Ac 4:24** *191*
And as he **h** these words, Ananias **Ac 5:5** *191*
fear came over all who **h** of it. **Ac 5:5** *191*
over all who **h** of these things. **Ac 5:11** *191*
the chief priests **h** these words, **Ac 5:24** *191*
But when they **h** this, they were **Ac 5:33** *191*
"We have **h** him speak blasphemous **Ac 6:11** *191*
have **h** him say that this Nazarene, **Ac 6:14** *191*
Jacob **h** that there was grain in **Ac 7:12** *191*
OF MY PEOPLE IN EGYPT AND HAVE **H** **Ac 7:34** *191*
Now when they **h** this, they were **Ac 7:54** *191*
as they **h** and saw the signs which **Ac 8:6** *191*
apostles in Jerusalem **h** that Samaria **Ac 8:14** *191*
and **h** him reading Isaiah the **Ac 8:30** *191*
and **h** a voice saying to him, **Ac 9:4** *191*
I have **h** from many about this man, **Ac 9:13** *191*
having **h** that Peter was there, **Ac 9:38** *191*
your prayer has been **h** and your **Ac 10:31** *1522*
h that the Gentiles also had received **Ac 11:1** *191*
"I also **h** a voice saying to **Ac 11:7** *191*
When they **h** this, they quieted **Ac 11:18** *191*
When the Gentiles **h** this, **Ac 13:48** *191*
Barnabas and Paul **h** of it, **Ac 14:14** *191*
"Since we have **h** that some of our **Ac 15:24** *191*
when they **h** that they were Romans, **Ac 16:38** *191*
authorities who **h** these things. **Ac 17:8** *191*
h of the resurrection of the dead, **Ac 17:32** *191*
many of the Corinthians when they **h** **Ac 18:8** *191*
when Priscilla and Aquila **h** him, **Ac 18:26** *191*
we have not even **h** whether there **Ac 19:2** *191*
When they **h** this, they were **Ac 19:5** *191*
in Asia **h** the word of the Lord, **Ac 19:10** *191*
When they **h** *this* and were **Ac 19:28** *191*
When we had **h** this, we as well **Ac 21:12** *191*
h it they *began* glorifying God; **Ac 21:20** *191*
they **h** that he was addressing them **Ac 22:2** *191*
ground and **h** a voice saying to me, **Ac 22:7** *191*
men of what you have seen and **h**. **Ac 22:15** *191*
When the centurion **h** *this,* **Ac 22:26** *191*
of Paul's sister **h** of their ambush, **Ac 23:16** *191*
and **h** him *speak* about faith in **Ac 24:24** *191*
I **h** a voice saying to me in the **Ac 26:14** *191*
brethren, when they **h** about us, **Ac 28:15** *191*
in Him whom they have not **h**? **Ro 10:14** *191*
I say, surely they have never **h**, **Ro 10:18** *191*
AND THEY WHO HAVE NOT **H** SHALL **Ro 15:21** *191*
EYE HAS NOT SEEN AND EAR HAS NOT **H**, **1Co 2:9** *191*
and **h** inexpressible words, **2Co 12:4** *191*
For you have **h** of my former manner **Ga 1:13** *191*
having **h** of the faith in the Lord **Eph 1:15** *191*
h of the stewardship of God's grace **Eph 3:2** *191*
if indeed you have **h** Him and have **Eph 4:21** *191*
you had **h** that he was sick. **Php 2:26** *191*
and received and **h** and seen in me, **Php 4:9** *191*
since we **h** of your faith in Christ **Col 1:4** *191*
previously **h** in the word of truth, **Col 1:5** *4257*
the day you **h** *of it* and understood **Col 1:6** *191*
also, since the day we **h** *of it,* **Col 1:9** *191*
of the gospel that you have **h**, **Col 1:23** *191*
word of God which you **h** from us, **1Th 2:13** *191*
words which you have **h** from me, **2Tm 1:13** *191*
h from me in the presence of many **2Tm 2:2** *191*
attention to what we have **h**, **Heb 2:1** *191*
confirmed to us by those who **h**, **Heb 2:3** *191*
who provoked *Him* when they had **h**? **Heb 3:16** *191*
word they **h** did not profit them, **Heb 4:2** *189*
united by faith in those who **h**. **Heb 4:2** *191*
and He was **h** because of His piety. **Heb 5:7** *1522*
was such that those who **h** begged **Heb 12:19** *191*
You have **h** of the endurance of Job **Jas 5:11** *191*
and we ourselves **h** this utterance **2Pe 1:18** *191*
he saw and **h** *that* righteous man, **2Pe 2:8** *189*
the beginning, what we have **h**, **1Jn 1:1** *191*
and **h** we proclaim to you also, **1Jn 1:3** *191*
h from Him and announce to you, **1Jn 1:5** *191*
is the word which you have **h**. **1Jn 2:7** *191*
you **h** that antichrist is coming, **1Jn 2:18** *191*
which you **h** from the beginning. **1Jn 2:24** *191*
If what you **h** from the beginning **1Jn 2:24** *191*
you have **h** from the beginning, **1Jn 3:11** *191*
you have **h** that it is coming, **1Jn 4:3** *191*
as you have **h** from the beginning, **2Jn 1:6** *191*
and I **h** behind me a loud voice **Rv 1:10** *191*
what you have received and **h**; **Rv 3:3** *191*
and the first voice which I had **h**, **Rv 4:1** *191*
and I **h** the voice of many angels **Rv 5:11** *191*
all things in them, I **h** saying, **Rv 5:13** *191*
and I **h** one of the four living **Rv 6:1** *191*
I **h** the second living creature **Rv 6:3** *191*
I **h** the third living creature **Rv 6:5** *191*
And I **h** *something* like a voice in the **Rv 6:6** *191*
I **h** the voice of the fourth living **Rv 6:7** *191*
And I **h** the number of those who **Rv 7:4** *191*
I **h** an eagle flying in midheaven, **Rv 8:13** *191*
and I **h** a voice from the four **Rv 9:13** *191*
I **h** the number of them. **Rv 9:16** *191*
I **h** a voice from heaven saying, **Rv 10:4** *191*
the voice which I **h** from heaven, **Rv 10:8** *191*
I **h** again speaking with me, **Rv 10:8**
And they **h** a loud voice from **Rv 11:12** *191*
Then I **h** a loud voice in heaven, **Rv 12:10** *191*
And I **h** a voice from heaven, like **Rv 14:2** *191*
and the voice which I **h** *was* like **Rv 14:2** *191*
And I **h** a voice from heaven, **Rv 14:13** *191*
I **h** a loud voice from the temple, **Rv 16:1** *191*
And I **h** the angel of the waters **Rv 16:5** *191*
And I **h** the altar saying, **Rv 16:7** *191*
I **h** another voice from heaven, **Rv 18:4** *191*
will not be **h** in you any longer; **Rv 18:22** *191*
will not be **h** in you any longer; **Rv 18:22** *191*
will not be **h** in you any longer; **Rv 18:23** *191*
After these things I **h** something **Rv 19:1** *191*
Then I **h** *something* like the voice of **Rv 19:6** *191*
I **h** a loud voice from the throne, **Rv 21:3** *191*
one who **h** and saw these things. **Rv 22:8** *191*
And when I **h** and saw, I fell down **Rv 22:8** *191*

HEARER

is a **h** of the word and not a doer, **Jas 1:23** *202*
forgetful **h** but an effectual doer, **Jas 1:25** *202*

HEARERS

for *it is* not the **h** of the Law **Ro 2:13** *202*
and leads to the ruin of the **h**. **2Tm 2:14** *191*
merely **h** who delude themselves. **Jas 1:22** *202*

HEARING

told all these things in their **h**; **Gn 20:8** 241
in the **h** of the sons of Heth; **Gn 23:10** 241
the **h** of the people of the land, **Gn 23:13** 241
in the **h** of the sons of Heth, **Gn 23:16** 241
you may tell in the **h** of your son, **Ex 10:2** 241
"Speak now in the **h** of the people **Ex 11:2** 241
read *it* in the **h** of the people; **Ex 24:7** 241
of adversity in the **h** of the LORD; **Nu 11:1** 241
'just as you have spoken in My **h**, **Nu 14:28** 241
I am speaking today in your **h**, **Dt 5:1** 241
in front of all Israel in their **h**. **Dt 31:11** 241
I may speak these words in their **h** **Dt 31:28** 241
Then Moses spoke in the **h** of all **Dt 31:30** 241
this song in the **h** of the people, **Dt 32:44** 241
the **h** of the elders of that city; **Jos 20:4** 241
proclaim in the **h** of the people, **Jg 7:3** 241
h of all the leaders of Shechem, **Jg 9:2** 241
h of all the leaders of Shechem; **Jg 9:3** 241
which you uttered a curse in my **h**, **Jg 17:2** 241
he repeated them in the LORD's **h**. **1Sa 8:21** 241
words in the **h** of the people, **1Sa 11:4** 241
also spoke in the **h** of Benjamin; **2Sa 3:19** 241
Abner went to speak in the **h** of David **2Sa 3:19** 241
for in our **h** the king charged you **2Sa 18:12** 241
in the **h** of the people who are on **2Ki 18:26** 241
and he read in their **h** all the **2Ki 23:2** 241
the LORD, and in the **h** of our God, **1Ch 28:8** 241
and he read in their **h** all the **2Ch 34:30** 241
of Moses in the **h** of the people; **Ne 13:1** 241
"Surely you have spoken in my **h**, **Jb 33:8** 241
heard of You by the **h** of the ear; **Jb 42:5** 8088
The **h** ear and the seeing eye, The **Pr 20:12** 8085
Do not speak in the **h** of a fool, **Pr 23:9** 241
Nor is the ear filled with **h**. **Ec 1:8** 8085
his ears from **h** about bloodshed And **Is 33:15** 8085
in the **h** of the people who are on **Is 36:11** 241
as you have heard in your **h**." **Jer 26:11** 241
speak all these words in your **h**." **Jer 26:15** 241
which I am about to speak in your **h** **Jer 28:7** 241
and in the **h** of all the people! **Jer 28:7** 241
in my **h** with a loud voice saying, **Ezk 9:1** 241
But to the others He said in my **h**, **Ezk 9:5** 241
The wheels were called in my **h**, **Ezk 10:13** 241
for **h** the words of the LORD. **Am 8:11** 8085
and stopped their ears from **h**. **Zch 7:11** 8085
After **h** the king, they went their **Mt 2:9** *191*
see, and while **h** they do not hear, **Mt 13:13** *191*
'YOU WILL KEEP ON **H**, BUT WILL NOT **Mt 13:14** *191*
And **h** *this,* the ten became **Mt 20:24** *191*
road, **h** that Jesus was passing by, **Mt 20:30** *191*
And **h** *this,* they were amazed, and **Mt 22:22** *191*
be **h** of wars and rumors of wars. **Mt 24:6** *191*
And **h** *this,* Jesus said to them, **Mk 2:17** *191*
AND WHILE **H**, THEY MAY HEAR AND NOT **Mk 4:12** *191*
after **h** about Jesus, she came up in **Mk 5:27** *191*
But after **h** of Him, a woman whose **Mk 7:25** *191*
H *this,* the ten began to feel **Mk 10:41** *191*
has been fulfilled in your **h**." **Lk 4:21** *3775*
discourse in the **h** of the people, **Lk 7:1** *189*
AND **H** THEY MAY NOT UNDERSTAND. **Lk 8:10** *191*
Now **h** a crowd going by, he **Lk 18:36** *191*
because he had been **h** about Him **Lk 23:8** *191*
because each one of them was **h** them **Ac 2:6** *191*
Upon **h** *this,* they entered into **Ac 5:21** *191*
him stood speechless, **h** the voice but **Ac 9:7** *191*
h him continued to be amazed, **Ac 9:21** *191*
For they were **h** them speaking with **Ac 10:46** *191*
than telling or **h** something new.) **Ac 17:21** *191*
"I will give you a **h** after your **Ac 23:35** *1251*
us, by your kindness, a brief **h**. **Ac 24:4** *191*
'YOU WILL KEEP ON **H**, BUT WILL NOT **Ac 28:26** *191*
So faith *comes* from **h** **Ro 10:17** *189*
and **h** by the word of Christ. **Ro 10:17** *189*
were an eye, where would the **h** be? **1Co 12:17** *189*
If the whole were **h**, **1Co 12:17** *189*
but only, they kept **h** **Ga 1:23** *191*
of the Law, or by **h** with faith? **Ga 3:2** *189*
of the Law, or by **h** with faith? **Ga 3:5** *189*
since you have become dull of **h**. **Heb 5:11** *189*

HEARS

who **h** will laugh with me." **Gn 21:6** 8085
for He **h** your grumblings against **Ex 16:7** 8085
for the LORD **h** your grumblings **Ex 16:8** 8085
after he **h** a public adjuration **Lv 5:1** 8085
of him who **h** the words of God, **Nu 24:4** 8085
of him who **h** the words of God, **Nu 24:16** 8085
and her father **h** her vow and her **Nu 30:4** 8085
forbid her on the day he **h** *of it,* **Nu 30:5** 8085
and her husband **h** of it and says **Nu 30:7** 8085
nothing to her on the day he **h** *it,* **Nu 30:7** 8085
if on the day her husband **h** *of it,* **Nu 30:8** 8085
annuls them on the day he **h** *them,* **Nu 30:12** 8085
when he **h** the words of this curse, **Dt 29:19** 8085
of everyone who **h** it will tingle. **1Sa 3:11** 8085
When Saul **h** *of it,* he will kill me." **1Sa 16:2** 8085
that whoever **h** *it* will say, **2Sa 17:9** 8085
and Judah, that whoever **h** of it, **2Ki 21:12** 8085
to me, And a wise man who **h** me, **Jb 34:34** 8085
The LORD **h** when I call to Him. **Ps 4:3** 8085
The righteous cry, and the LORD **h** **Ps 34:17** 8085
in their lips, For, *they say,* "Who **h**?" **Ps 59:7** 8085
For the LORD **h** the needy And does **Ps 69:33** 8085
h My voice *and* my supplications. **Ps 116:1** 8085
wealth, But the poor **h** no rebuke. **Pr 13:8** 8085
He **h** the prayer of the righteous. **Pr 15:29** 8085
who gives an answer before he **h** **Pr 18:13** 8085
Or he who **h** *it* will reproach you, **Pr 25:10** 8085
He **h** the oath but tells nothing. **Pr 29:24** 8085
when He **h** it, He will answer you. **Is 30:19** 8085
Your ears are open, but none **h**. **Is 42:20** 8085
everyone that **h** of it will tingle. **Jer 19:3** 8085
He who **h**, let him hear; **Ezk 3:27** 8085
then he who **h** the sound of the **Ezk 33:4** 8085
made a decree that every man who **h** **Da 3:10** 8086
who **h** these words of Mine and **Mt 7:24** *191*
who **h** these words of Mine and **Mt 7:26** *191*
anyone **h** the word of the kingdom and **Mt 13:19** *191*
this is the man who **h** the word and **Mt 13:20** *191*
this is the man who **h** the word, **Mt 13:22** *191*
who **h** the word and understands it; **Mt 13:23** *191*
who comes to Me and **h** My words **Lk 6:47** *191*
bridegroom, who stands and **h** him, **Jn 3:29** *191*
I say to you, he who **h** My word, **Jn 5:24** *191*
unless it first **h** from him and **Jn 7:51** *191*
who is of God **h** the words of God; **Jn 8:47** *191*
and does His will, He **h** him. **Jn 9:31** *191*
"If anyone **h** My sayings and **Jn 12:47** *191*
but whatever He **h**, He will speak; **Jn 16:13** *191*
who is of the truth **h** My voice." **Jn 18:37** *191*
than he sees *in* me or **h** from me. **2Co 12:6** *191*
according to His will, He **h** us. **1Jn 5:14** *191*
that He **h** us *in* whatever we ask, **1Jn 5:15** *191*
h My voice and opens the door, **Rv 3:20** *191*
And let the one who **h** say, **Rv 22:17** *191*
I testify to everyone who **h** the **Rv 22:18** *191*

HEART

his **h** was only evil continually. **Gn 6:5** 3820
and He was grieved in His **h**. **Gn 6:6** 3820
intent of man's **h** is evil from his **Gn 8:21** 3820
and laughed, and said in his **h** **Gn 17:17** 3820
In the integrity of my **h** and the **Gn 20:5** 3824
in the integrity of your **h** you have **Gn 20:6** 3824
I had finished speaking in my **h**, **Gn 24:45** 3820

Context	Reference	Number
you, he will be glad in his **h**.	**Ex 4:14**	3820
but I will harden his **h** so that he	**Ex 4:21**	3820
"But I will harden Pharaoh's **h**	**Ex 7:3**	3820
Yet Pharaoh's **h** was hardened, and	**Ex 7:13**	3820
"Pharaoh's **h** is stubborn;	**Ex 7:14**	3820
and Pharaoh's **h** was hardened, and	**Ex 7:22**	3820
he hardened his **h** and did not listen	**Ex 8:15**	3820
But Pharaoh's **h** was hardened, and	**Ex 8:19**	3820
Pharaoh hardened his **h** this time	**Ex 8:32**	3820
But the **h** of Pharaoh was hardened,	**Ex 9:7**	3820
And the LORD hardened Pharaoh's **h**,	**Ex 9:12**	3820
sinned again and hardened his **h**	**Ex 9:34**	3820
Pharaoh's **h** was hardened, and	**Ex 9:35**	3820
for I have hardened his **h** and the	**Ex 10:1**	3820
heart and the **h** of his servants,	**Ex 10:1**	3820
But the LORD hardened Pharaoh's **h**	**Ex 10:20**	3820
But the LORD hardened Pharaoh's **h**	**Ex 10:27**	3820
yet the LORD hardened Pharaoh's **h**,	**Ex 11:10**	3820
"Thus I will harden Pharaoh's **h**,	**Ex 14:4**	3820
a change of **h** toward the people,	**Ex 14:5**	3824
LORD hardened the **h** of Pharaoh,	**Ex 14:8**	3820
congealed in the **h** of the sea.	**Ex 15:8**	3820
from every man whose **h** moves him	**Ex 25:2**	3820
breastpiece of judgment over his **h**	**Ex 28:29**	3820
and they shall be over Aaron's **h**	**Ex 28:30**	3820
his **h** before the LORD continually.	**Ex 28:30**	3820
whoever is of a willing **h**,	**Ex 35:5**	3820
Everyone whose **h** stirred him	**Ex 35:21**	3820
All the women whose **h** stirred	**Ex 35:26**	3820
whose **h** moved them to bring	**Ex 35:29**	3820
"He also has put in his **h** to teach,	**Ex 35:34**	3820
everyone whose **h** stirred him,	**Ex 36:2**	3820
your fellow countryman in your **h**;	**Lv 19:17**	3824
uncircumcised **h** becomes humbled	**Lv 26:41**	3824
not follow after your own **h** and	**Nu 15:39**	3824
spirit and made his **h** obstinate,	**Dt 2:30**	3824
they do not depart from your **h** all the	**Dt 4:9**	3824
fire to the *very* **h** of the heavens:	**Dt 4:11**	3820
you search for Him with all your **h**	**Dt 4:29**	3824
today, and take it to your **h**,	**Dt 4:39**	3824
'Oh that they had such a **h** in them,	**Dt 5:29**	3824
the LORD your God with all your **h**	**Dt 6:5**	3824
you today, shall be on your **h**.	**Dt 6:6**	3824
"If you should say in your **h**,	**Dt 7:17**	3824
you, to know what was in your **h**,	**Dt 8:2**	3824
"Thus you are to know in your **h**	**Dt 8:5**	3824
then your **h** will become proud and you	**Dt 8:14**	3824
"Otherwise, you may say in your **h**,	**Dt 8:17**	3824
"Do not say in your **h** when the	**Dt 9:4**	3824
or for the uprightness of your **h** that	**Dt 9:5**	3824
the LORD your God with all your **h**	**Dt 10:12**	3824
"So circumcise your **h**,	**Dt 10:16**	3824
serve Him with all your **h** and all	**Dt 11:13**	3824
these words of mine on your **h** and	**Dt 11:18**	3824
all your **h** and with all your soul.	**Dt 13:3**	3824
money for whatever your **h** desires:	**Dt 14:26**	5315
drink, or whatever your **h** desires;	**Dt 14:26**	5315
you, you shall not harden your **h**,	**Dt 15:7**	3824
there is no base thought in your **h**,	**Dt 15:9**	3824
and your **h** shall not be grieved	**Dt 15:10**	3824
or else his **h** will turn away;	**Dt 17:17**	3824
that his **h** may not be lifted up	**Dt 17:20**	3824
"You may say in your **h**,	**Dt 18:21**	3824
brothers' hearts melt like his **h**	**Dt 20:8**	3824
he is poor and sets his **h** on it;	**Dt 24:15**	5315
careful to do them with all your **h**	**Dt 26:16**	3824
and with bewilderment of **h**;	**Dt 28:28**	3824
your God with joy and a glad **h**,	**Dt 28:47**	3824
LORD will give you a trembling **h**,	**Dt 28:65**	3820
dread of your **h** which you dread,	**Dt 28:67**	3824
has not given you a **h** to know,	**Dt 29:4**	3820
whose **h** turns away today from the	**Dt 29:18**	3824
I walk in the stubbornness of my **h**	**Dt 29:19**	3820
obey Him with all your **h** and soul	**Dt 30:2**	3824
LORD your God will circumcise your **h**	**Dt 30:6**	3824
and the **h** of your descendants,	**Dt 30:6**	3824
the LORD your God with all your **h**	**Dt 30:6**	3824
your God with all your **h** and soul.	**Dt 30:10**	3824
you, in your mouth and in your **h**,	**Dt 30:14**	3824
"But if your **h** turns away and you	**Dt 30:17**	3824
"Take to your **h** all the words	**Dt 32:46**	3824
back to him as *it was* in my **h**.	**Jos 14:7**	3824
h of the people melt with fear;	**Jos 14:8**	3820
serve Him with all your **h** and with	**Jos 22:5**	3824
"My **h** *goes out* to the commanders	**Jg 5:9**	3820
There were great resolves of **h**.	**Jg 5:15**	3820
There were great searchings of **h**.	**Jg 5:16**	3820
you,' when your **h** is not with me?	**Jg 16:15**	3820
So he told her all *that was* in his **h**	**Jg 16:17**	3820
told her all *that was* in his **h**,	**Jg 16:18**	3820
told me all *that is* in his **h**."	**Jg 16:18**	3820
The priest's **h** was glad, and	**Jg 18:20**	3820
night, and let your **h** be merry."	**Jg 19:6**	3820
here that your **h** may be merry.	**Jg 19:9**	3820
and drunk and his **h** was merry,	**Ru 3:7**	3820
you not eat and why is your **h** sad?	**1Sa 1:8**	3824
Hannah, she was speaking in her **h**,	**1Sa 1:13**	3820
"My **h** exults in the LORD;	**1Sa 2:1**	3820
to what is in My **h** and in My soul;	**1Sa 2:35**	3824
because his **h** was trembling for	**1Sa 4:13**	3820
to the LORD with all your **h**,	**1Sa 7:3**	3824
leave Samuel, God changed his **h**;	**1Sa 10:9**	3820
serve the LORD with all your **h**.	**1Sa 12:20**	3824
Him in truth with all your **h**;	**1Sa 12:24**	3824
for Himself a man after His own **h**,	**1Sa 13:14**	3824
"Do all that is in your **h**;	**1Sa 14:7**	3824
but the LORD looks at the **h**."	**1Sa 16:7**	3824
and the wickedness of your **h**;	**1Sa 17:28**	3824
no man's **h** fail on account of him;	**1Sa 17:32**	3820
David took these words to **h** and	**1Sa 21:12**	3824
grief or a troubled **h** to my lord,	**1Sa 25:31**	3820
And Nabal's **h** was merry within him,	**1Sa 25:36**	3820
and his **h** died within him so that	**1Sa 25:37**	3820
afraid and his **h** trembled greatly.	**1Sa 28:5**	3820
and she despised him in her **h**.	**2Sa 6:16**	3820
and according to Your own **h**,	**2Sa 7:21**	3820
do not take this matter to **h**."	**2Sa 13:20**	3820
when Amnon's **h** is merry with wine,	**2Sa 13:28**	3820
the king take the report to **h**,	**2Sa 13:33**	3820
The **h** *of* King David longed to go	**2Sa 13:39**	
the king's **h** *was inclined* toward	**2Sa 14:1**	3820
h is like the heart of a lion,	**2Sa 17:10**	3820
heart is like the **h** of a lion,	**2Sa 17:10**	3820
of a lion, will completely lose **h**;	**2Sa 17:10**	4549
thrust them through the **h** of Absalom	**2Sa 18:14**	3820
that the king would take *it* to **h**.	**2Sa 19:19**	3820
"Foreigners lose **h**, And come	**2Sa 22:46**	5034b
Now David's **h** troubled him after	**2Sa 24:10**	3820
before Me in truth with all their **h**	**1Ki 2:4**	3824
which you acknowledge in your **h**,	**1Ki 2:44**	3824
and uprightness of **h** toward You;	**1Ki 3:6**	3824
give Your servant an understanding **h**	**1Ki 3:9**	3820
given you a wise and discerning **h**,	**1Ki 3:12**	3820
"Now it was in the **h** of my father	**1Ki 8:17**	3824
in your **h** to build a house for My	**1Ki 8:18**	3824
did well that it was in your **h**.	**1Ki 8:18**	3824
walk before You with all their **h**,	**1Ki 8:23**	3820
the affliction of his own **h**,	**1Ki 8:38**	3824
his ways, whose **h** You know,	**1Ki 8:39**	3824
they return to You with all their **h**	**1Ki 8:48**	3824
"Let your **h** therefore be wholly	**1Ki 8:61**	3824
went to their tents joyful and glad of **h**	**1Ki 8:66**	3820
My **h** will be there perpetually.	**1Ki 9:3**	3820
in integrity of **h** and uprightness,	**1Ki 9:4**	3824
him about all that was in her **h**.	**1Ki 10:2**	3824
wisdom which God had put in his **h**.	**1Ki 10:24**	3820
turn your **h** away after their gods.	**1Ki 11:2**	3824
and his wives turned his **h** away.	**1Ki 11:3**	3820
turned his **h** away after other gods;	**1Ki 11:4**	3824
and his **h** was not wholly devoted	**1Ki 11:4**	3824
h of David his father *had been*.	**1Ki 11:4**	3824
h was turned away from the LORD,	**1Ki 11:9**	3824
Jeroboam said in his **h**,	**1Ki 12:26**	3820
then the **h** of this people will	**1Ki 12:27**	3820
which he had devised in his own **h**;	**1Ki 12:33**	3820
who followed Me with all his **h**,	**1Ki 14:8**	3824
and his **h** was not wholly devoted	**1Ki 15:3**	3824
like the **h** of his father David.	**1Ki 15:3**	3824
nevertheless the **h** of Asa was	**1Ki 15:14**	3824
have turned their **h** back again."	**1Ki 18:37**	3820
bread, and let your **h** be joyful;	**1Ki 21:7**	3820
"Did not my **h** go *with you*, when	**2Ki 5:26**	3820
Now the **h** of the king of Aram was	**2Ki 6:11**	3820
and the arrow went through his **h** and	**2Ki 9:24**	3820
"Is your **h** right, as my heart is	**2Ki 10:15**	3824
as my **h** is with your heart?"	**2Ki 10:15**	3824
as my heart is with your **h**?"	**2Ki 10:15**	3824
according to all that *was* in My **h**,	**2Ki 10:30**	3824
the God of Israel, with all his **h**;	**2Ki 10:31**	3824
money which any man's **h** prompts	**2Ki 12:4**	3820
Edom, and your **h** has become proud.	**2Ki 14:10**	3820
You in truth and with a whole **h** and	**2Ki 20:3**	3824
because your **h** was tender and you	**2Ki 22:19**	3824
with all his **h** and all *his* soul,	**2Ki 23:3**	3820
who turned to the LORD with all his **h**	**2Ki 23:25**	3824
me, my **h** shall be united with you;	**1Ch 12:17**	3824
helped *David* with an undivided **h**.	**1Ch 12:33**	3820
came to Hebron with a perfect **h** to	**1Ch 12:38**	3824
and she despised him in her **h**.	**1Ch 15:29**	3820
Let the **h** of those who seek the	**1Ch 16:10**	3820
"Do all that is in your **h**,	**1Ch 17:2**	3824
and according to Your own **h**,	**1Ch 17:19**	3820
"Now set your **h** and your soul to	**1Ch 22:19**	3824
with a whole **h** and a willing mind;	**1Ch 28:9**	3820
to the LORD with a whole **h**,	**1Ch 29:9**	3820
You try the **h** and delight in	**1Ch 29:17**	3824
I, in the integrity of my **h**,	**1Ch 29:17**	3824
intentions of the **h** of Your people,	**1Ch 29:18**	3824
and direct their **h** to You;	**1Ch 29:18**	3824
give to my son Solomon a perfect **h**	**1Ch 29:19**	3824
in the **h** of my father David to build	**2Ch 6:7**	3824
in your **h** to build a house for My	**2Ch 6:8**	3824
did well that it was in your **h**.	**2Ch 6:8**	3824
walk before You with all their **h**;	**2Ch 6:14**	3820
whose **h** You know for You	**2Ch 6:30**	3824
they return to You with all their **h**	**2Ch 6:38**	3820
rejoicing and happy of **h** because	**2Ch 7:10**	3820
My **h** will be there perpetually.	**2Ch 7:16**	3820
him about all that was on her **h**.	**2Ch 9:1**	3824
wisdom which God had put in his **h**.	**2Ch 9:23**	3820
not set his **h** to seek the LORD.	**2Ch 12:14**	3820
fathers with all their **h** and soul;	**2Ch 15:12**	3824
they had sworn with their whole **h**	**2Ch 15:15**	3824
Asa's **h** was blameless all his days.	**2Ch 15:17**	3824
those whose **h** is completely His.	**2Ch 16:9**	3824
you have set your **h** to seek God."	**2Ch 19:3**	3824
sought the LORD with all his **h**."	**2Ch 22:9**	3824
the LORD, yet not with a whole **h**.	**2Ch 25:2**	3824
h has become proud in boasting.	**2Ch 25:19**	3820
his **h** was so proud that he acted	**2Ch 26:16**	3820
in my **h** to make a covenant with	**2Ch 29:10**	3824
was also on Judah to give them one **h**	**2Ch 30:12**	3820
who prepares his **h** to seek God,	**2Ch 30:19**	3824
did with all his **h** and prospered.	**2Ch 31:21**	3824
received, because his **h** was proud;	**2Ch 32:25**	3820
humbled the pride of his **h**,	**2Ch 32:26**	3820
might know all that was in his **h**.	**2Ch 32:31**	3824
"Because your **h** was tender and	**2Ch 34:27**	3824
all his **h** and with all his soul,	**2Ch 34:31**	3824
stiffened his neck and hardened his **h**	**2Ch 36:13**	3824
and had turned the **h** of the king	**Ezr 6:22**	3820
set his **h** to study the law of the	**Ezr 7:10**	3824
a thing as this in the king's **h**,	**Ezr 7:27**	3820
is nothing but sadness of **h**."	**Ne 2:2**	3820
God put it into my **h** to assemble	**Ne 7:5**	3820
found his **h** faithful before You,	**Ne 9:8**	3824
when the **h** of the king was merry	**Es 1:10**	3820
that day glad and pleased of **h**;	**Es 5:9**	3820
"Wise in **h** and mighty in	**Jb 9:4**	3824
You have concealed in Your **h**;	**Jb 10:13**	3824
"If you would direct your **h** right	**Jb 11:13**	3820
"Why does your **h** carry you away?	**Jb 15:12**	3820
kept their **h** from understanding,	**Jb 17:4**	3820
apart, *Even* the wishes of my **h**.	**Jb 17:11**	3824
My **h** faints within me!	**Jb 19:27**	3629
And establish His words in your **h**.	**Jb 22:22**	3824
"*It is* God *who* has made my **h** faint,	**Jb 23:16**	3820
My **h** does not reproach any of my	**Jb 27:6**	3824
I made the widow's **h** sing for joy.	**Jb 29:13**	3820
the way, Or my **h** followed my eyes,	**Jb 31:7**	3820
my **h** has been enticed by a woman,	**Jb 31:9**	3820
And my **h** became secretly enticed,	**Jb 31:27**	3820
are *from* the uprightness of my **h**,	**Jb 33:3**	3820
"But the godless in **h** lay up anger;	**Jb 36:13**	3820
"At this also my **h** trembles, And	**Jb 37:1**	3820
regard any who are wise of **h**."	**Jb 37:24**	3820
"His **h** is as hard as a stone,	**Jb 41:24**	3820
Meditate in your **h** upon your bed,	**Ps 4:4**	3824
You have put gladness in my **h**,	**Ps 4:7**	3820
God, Who saves the upright in **h**.	**Ps 7:10**	3820
thanks to the LORD with all my **h**;	**Ps 9:1**	3820
You will strengthen their **h**,	**Ps 10:17**	3820
in darkness at the upright in **h**.	**Ps 11:2**	3820
and with a double **h** they speak.	**Ps 12:2**	3820
Having sorrow in my **h** all the day?	**Ps 13:2**	3824
My **h** shall rejoice in Your	**Ps 13:5**	3820
The fool has said in his **h**,	**Ps 14:1**	3820
And speaks truth in his **h**.	**Ps 15:2**	3824
Therefore my **h** is glad and my	**Ps 16:9**	3820
You have tried my **h**;	**Ps 17:3**	3820
They have closed their unfeeling **h**,	**Ps 17:10**	
LORD are right, rejoicing the **h**;	**Ps 19:8**	3820
meditation of my **h** Be acceptable	**Ps 19:14**	3820
My **h** is like wax;	**Ps 22:14**	3820
Let your **h** live forever!	**Ps 22:26**	3824
who has clean hands and a pure **h**	**Ps 24:4**	3824
The troubles of my **h** are enlarged;	**Ps 25:17**	3824
Test my mind and my **h**.	**Ps 26:2**	3820
against me, My **h** will not fear;	**Ps 27:3**	3820
"Seek My face," my **h** said to You,	**Ps 27:8**	3820
and let your **h** take courage;	**Ps 27:14**	3820
My **h** trusts in Him, and I am	**Ps 28:7**	3820
Therefore my **h** exults, And with my	**Ps 28:7**	3820
and let your **h** take courage,	**Ps 31:24**	3824
joy, all you who are upright in **h**.	**Ps 32:11**	3820
The plans of His **h** from generation	**Ps 33:11**	3820
For our **h** rejoices in Him, Because	**Ps 33:21**	3820
Do not let them say in their **h**,	**Ps 35:25**	3820
to the ungodly within his **h**;	**Ps 36:1**	3820
righteousness to the upright in **h**.	**Ps 36:10**	3820
give you the desires of your **h**.	**Ps 37:4**	3820
sword will enter their own **h**,	**Ps 37:15**	3820
The law of his God is in his **h**;	**Ps 37:31**	3820
because of the agitation of my **h**.	**Ps 38:8**	3820
My **h** throbs, my strength fails me;	**Ps 38:10**	3820
My **h** was hot within me,	**Ps 39:3**	3820
Your Law is within my **h**."	**Ps 40:8**	4578
Your righteousness within my **h**;	**Ps 40:10**	3820
And my **h** has failed me.	**Ps 40:12**	3820
h gathers wickedness to itself;	**Ps 41:6**	3820
Our **h** has not turned back, And our	**Ps 44:18**	3820
For He knows the secrets of the **h**.	**Ps 44:21**	3820
My **h** overflows with a good theme;	**Ps 45:1**	3820
are in the **h** of the King's enemies.	**Ps 45:5**	3820
slip into the **h** of the sea;	**Ps 46:2**	3820
And the meditation of my **h** *will be*	**Ps 49:3**	3820
Create in me a clean **h**,	**Ps 51:10**	3820
A broken and a contrite **h**,	**Ps 51:17**	3820
The fool has said in his **h**,	**Ps 53:1**	3820
My **h** is in anguish within me, And	**Ps 55:4**	3820
than butter, But his **h** was war;	**Ps 55:21**	3820
My **h** is steadfast, O God, my heart	**Ps 57:7**	3820
O God, my **h** is steadfast;	**Ps 57:7**	3820
No, in **h** you work unrighteousness;	**Ps 58:2**	3820
call to You when my **h** is faint;	**Ps 61:2**	3820
Pour out your **h** before Him;	**Ps 62:8**	3824
do not set *your* **h** *upon them.*	**Ps 62:10**	3820
and the **h** of a man are deep.	**Ps 64:6**	3820
all the upright in **h** will glory.	**Ps 64:10**	3820
If I regard wickedness in my **h**,	**Ps 66:18**	3820
Reproach has broken my **h** and	**Ps 69:20**	3820
who seek God, let your **h** revive.	**Ps 69:32**	3824
To those who are pure in **h**!	**Ps 73:1**	3824
imaginations of *their* **h** run riot.	**Ps 73:7**	3824
in vain I have kept my **h** pure And	**Ps 73:13**	3824
When my **h** was embittered And I	**Ps 73:21**	3824
My flesh and my **h** may fail, But	**Ps 73:26**	3824
God is the strength of my **h** and my	**Ps 73:26**	3824
They said in their **h**,	**Ps 74:8**	3820
I will meditate with my **h**,	**Ps 77:6**	3824
that did not prepare its **h** And	**Ps 78:8**	3820
And in their **h** they put God to the	**Ps 78:18**	3824
h was not steadfast toward Him,	**Ps 78:37**	3820
to the integrity of his **h**,	**Ps 78:72**	3824
to the stubbornness of their **h**,	**Ps 81:12**	3820
My **h** and my flesh sing for joy to	**Ps 84:2**	3820
In whose **h** are the highways	**Ps 84:5**	3824

Unite my **h** to fear Your name. **Ps 86:11** 3824
O Lord my God, with all my **h**, **Ps 86:12** 3824
may present to You a **h** of wisdom. **Ps 90:12** 3824
the upright in **h** will follow it. **Ps 94:15** 3820
are a people who err in their **h**, **Ps 95:10** 3824
And gladness for the upright in **h**. **Ps 97:11** 3820
my house in the integrity of my **h**. **Ps 101:2** 3824
A perverse **h** shall depart from me; **Ps 101:4** 3824
and an arrogant **h** will I endure. **Ps 101:5** 3824
My **h** has been smitten like grass **Ps 102:4** 3820
And wine which makes man's **h** glad, **Ps 104:15** 3824
And food which sustains man's **h**. **Ps 104:15** 3824
Let the **h** of those who seek the **Ps 105:3** 3820
turned their **h** to hate His people, **Ps 105:25** 3820
He humbled their **h** with labor; **Ps 107:12** 3820
My **h** is steadfast, O God; **Ps 108:1** 3820
man, And the despondent in **h**, **Ps 109:16** 3824
And my **h** is wounded within me. **Ps 109:22** 3820
thanks to the LORD with all *my* **h**, **Ps 111:1** 3824
His **h** is steadfast, trusting in **Ps 112:7** 3820
His **h** is upheld, he will not fear, **Ps 112:8** 3820
Who seek Him with all *their* **h**. **Ps 119:2** 3820
to You with uprightness of **h**, **Ps 119:7** 3824
With all my **h** I have sought You; **Ps 119:10** 3820
Your word I have treasured in my **h**, **Ps 119:11** 3820
For You will enlarge my **h**. **Ps 119:32** 3820
law And keep it with all *my* **h**. **Ps 119:34** 3820
Incline my **h** to Your testimonies And **Ps 119:36** 3820
sought Your favor with all *my* **h**; **Ps 119:58** 3820
With all *my* **h** I will observe Your **Ps 119:69** 3820
Their **h** is covered with fat, *But* I **Ps 119:70** 3820
my **h** be blameless in Your statutes, **Ps 119:80** 3820
For they are the joy of my **h**. **Ps 119:111** 3820
I have inclined my **h** to perform **Ps 119:112** 3820
I cried with all my **h**; **Ps 119:145** 3820
my **h** stands in awe of Your words. **Ps 119:161** 3820
O Lord, my **h** is not proud, nor my **Ps 131:1** 3820
give You thanks with all my **h**; **Ps 138:1** 3820
Search me, O God, and know my **h**; **Ps 139:23** 3824
incline my **h** to any evil thing, **Ps 141:4** 3820
My **h** is appalled within me. **Ps 143:4** 3820
Incline your **h** to understanding; **Pr 2:2** 3820
For wisdom will enter your **h** And **Pr 2:10** 3820
let your **h** keep my commandments; **Pr 3:1** 3820
them on the tablet of your **h**. **Pr 3:3** 3820
Trust in the LORD with all your **h** And **Pr 3:5** 3820
"Let your **h** hold fast my words; **Pr 4:4** 3820
Keep them in the midst of your **h**. **Pr 4:21** 3824
over your **h** with all diligence, **Pr 4:23** 3820
And my **h** spurned reproof! **Pr 5:12** 3820
Who *with* perversity in his **h** continually **Pr 6:14** 3820
A **h** that devises wicked plans, **Pr 6:18** 3820
Bind them continually on your **h**; **Pr 6:21** 3820
not desire her beauty in your **h**, **Pr 6:25** 3824
them on the tablet of your **h**. **Pr 7:3** 3820
as a harlot and cunning of **h**. **Pr 7:10** 3820
Do not let your **h** turn aside to her **Pr 7:25** 3820
wise of **h** will receive commands, **Pr 10:8** 3820
h of the wicked is *worth* little. **Pr 10:20** 3820
The perverse in **h** are an **Pr 11:20** 3820
in the **h** of those who devise evil, **Pr 12:20** 3820
the **h** of fools proclaims folly. **Pr 12:23** 3820
in a man's **h** weighs it down, **Pr 12:25** 3820
Hope deferred makes the **h** sick, **Pr 13:12** 3820
The **h** knows its own bitterness, **Pr 14:10** 3820
in laughter the **h** may be in pain, **Pr 14:13** 3820
The backslider in **h** will have his **Pr 14:14** 3820
A tranquil **h** is life to the body, **Pr 14:30** 3820
Wisdom rests in the **h** of one who **Pr 14:33** 3820
A joyful **h** makes a cheerful face, **Pr 15:13** 3820
when the **h** is sad, the spirit is **Pr 15:13** 3820
cheerful **h** *has* a continual feast. **Pr 15:15** 3820
The **h** of the righteous ponders how **Pr 15:28** 3820
Bright eyes gladden the **h**; **Pr 15:30** 3820
The plans of the **h** belong to man, **Pr 16:1** 3820
Everyone who is proud in **h** is an **Pr 16:5** 3820
wise in **h** will be called understanding, **Pr 16:21** 3820
h of the wise instructs his mouth **Pr 16:23** 3820
A joyful **h** is good medicine, But a **Pr 17:22** 3820
the **h** of man is haughty, **Pr 18:12** 3820
And his **h** rages against the LORD. **Pr 19:3** 3820
Many plans are in a man's **h**, **Pr 19:21** 3820
plan in the **h** of a man is *like* deep **Pr 20:5** 3820
I have cleansed my **h**, **Pr 20:9** 3820
The king's **h** is *like* channels of **Pr 21:1** 3820
Haughty eyes and a proud **h**, **Pr 21:4** 3820
He who loves purity of **h** **Pr 22:11** 3820
is bound up in the **h** of a child; **Pr 22:15** 3820
But his **h** is not with you. **Pr 23:7** 3820
Apply your **h** to discipline And **Pr 23:12** 3820
My son, if your **h** is wise, My own **Pr 23:15** 3820
wise, My own **h** also will be glad; **Pr 23:15** 3820
Do not let your **h** envy sinners, **Pr 23:17** 3820
And direct your **h** in the way. **Pr 23:19** 3820
Give me your **h**, my son, And let **Pr 23:26** 3820
your **h** be glad when he stumbles; **Pr 24:17** 3820
So the **h** of kings is unsearchable. **Pr 25:3** 3820
who sings songs to a troubled **h**. **Pr 25:20** 3820
Are burning lips and a wicked **h**. **Pr 26:23** 3820
But he lays up deceit in his **h**. **Pr 26:24** 7130
are seven abominations in his **h**. **Pr 26:25** 3820
Oil and perfume make the **h** glad, **Pr 27:9** 3820
wise, my son, and make my **h** glad, **Pr 27:11** 3820
So the **h** of man *reflects* man. **Pr 27:19** 3820
he who hardens his **h** will fall into **Pr 28:14** 3820
who trusts in his own **h** is a fool, **Pr 28:26** 3820
h of her husband trusts in her, **Pr 31:11** 3820
withhold my **h** from any pleasure, **Ec 2:10** 3820
for my **h** was pleased because of **Ec 2:10** 3820

has also set eternity in their **h**, **Ec 3:11** 3820
with the gladness of his **h**. **Ec 5:20** 3820
man, And the living takes *it* to **h**. **Ec 7:2** 3820
a face is sad a **h** may be happy. **Ec 7:3** 3820
mad, And a bribe corrupts the **h**. **Ec 7:7** 3820
be eager in your **h** to be angry, **Ec 7:9** 7307
woman whose **h** is snares and nets, **Ec 7:26** 3820
for a wise **h** knows the proper time **Ec 8:5** 3820
When I gave my **h** to know wisdom **Ec 8:16** 3820
For I have taken all this to my **h** **Ec 9:1** 3820
drink your wine with a cheerful **h**; **Ec 9:7** 3820
A wise man's **h** *directs him* toward **Ec 10:2** 3820
foolish man's **h** *directs him* toward **Ec 10:2** 3820
and let your **h** be pleasant during **Ec 11:9** 3820
follow the impulses of your **h** and **Ec 11:9** 3820
remove grief and anger from your **h** **Ec 11:10** 3820
on the day of his gladness of **h**." **SS 3:11** 3820
"You have made my **h** beat faster, **SS 4:9** 3823a
You have made my **h** beat faster **SS 4:9** 3823a
"I was asleep but my **h** was awake. **SS 5:2** 3820
My **h** went out *to him* as he spoke. **SS 5:6** 5315
"Put me like a seal over your **h**, **SS 8:6** 3820
is sick And the whole **h** is faint. **Is 1:5** 3824
his **h** and the hearts of his people **Is 7:2** 3824
in pride and in arrogance of **h**: **Is 9:9** 3824
Nor does it plan so in its **h**, **Is 10:7** 3824
the arrogant **h** of the king of Assyria **Is 10:12** 3824
limp, And every man's **h** will melt. **Is 13:7** 3824
"But you said in your **h**, **Is 14:13** 3824
My **h** cries out for Moab; **Is 15:5** 3820
my **h** intones like a harp for Moab And **Is 16:11** 4578
And the **h** of the Egyptians will **Is 19:1** 3824
And gladness of **h** as when one **Is 30:29** 3824
his **h** inclines toward wickedness: **Is 32:6** 3820
Your **h** will meditate on terror: **Is 33:18** 3820
Say to those with anxious **h**, **Is 35:4** 3820
You in truth and with a whole **h**, **Is 38:3** 3820
a deceived **h** has turned him aside. **Is 44:20** 3820
securely, Who says in your **h**, **Is 47:8** 3824
For you have said in your **h**, **Is 47:10** 3820
"Then you will say in your **h**, **Is 49:21** 3824
A people in whose **h** is My law; **Is 51:7** 3820
and no man takes it to **h**; **Is 57:1** 3820
to revive the **h** of the contrite. **Is 57:15** 3820
turning away, in the way of his **h**. **Is 57:17** 3820
uttering from the **h** lying words. **Is 59:13** 3820
your **h** will thrill and rejoice; **Is 60:5** 3824
the day of vengeance was in My **h**, **Is 63:4** 3820
The stirrings of Your **h** and Your **Is 63:15** 4578
harden our **h** from fearing You? **Is 63:17** 3820
shout joyfully with a glad **h**, **Is 65:14** 3820
you will cry out with a heavy **h**, **Is 65:14** 3820
this, and your **h** will be glad, **Is 66:14** 3820
not return to Me with all her **h**, **Jer 3:10** 3820
give you shepherds after My own **h**, **Jer 3:15** 3820
the stubbornness of their evil **h**. **Jer 3:17** 3820
remove the foreskins of your **h**, **Jer 4:4** 3824
"that the **h** of the king and the **Jer 4:9** 3820
the **h** of the princes will fail; **Jer 4:9** 3820
Wash your **h** from evil, O **Jer 4:14** 3820
How it has touched your **h**!" **Jer 4:18** 3820
my soul! I am in anguish! Oh, my **h**! **Jer 4:19** 3820
My **h** is pounding in me; **Jer 4:19** 3820
has a stubborn and rebellious **h**; **Jer 5:23** 3820
'They do not say in their **h**, **Jer 5:24** 3824
the stubbornness of their evil **h**, **Jer 7:24** 3820
healing, My **h** is faint *within me!* **Jer 8:18** 3820
after the stubbornness of their **h** **Jer 9:14** 3820
Israel are uncircumcised of **h**." **Jer 9:26** 3820
in the stubbornness of his evil **h**. **Jer 11:8** 3820
Who tries the feelings and the **h**, **Jer 11:20** 3820
Because no man lays it to **h**. **Jer 12:11** 3820
"If you say in your **h**, **Jer 13:22** 3824
My **h** would not be with this people **Jer 15:1** 5315
me a joy and the delight of my **h**; **Jer 15:16** 3824
stubbornness of his own evil **h**, **Jer 16:12** 3820
upon the tablet of their **h** And **Jer 17:1** 3820
whose **h** turns away from the LORD. **Jer 17:5** 3820
"The **h** is more deceitful than all **Jer 17:9** 3820
I, the LORD, search the **h**, **Jer 17:10** 3820
the stubbornness of his evil **h** **Jer 18:12** 3820
Then in my **h** it becomes like a **Jer 20:9** 3820
Who see the mind and the **h**; **Jer 20:12** 3820
"But your eyes and your **h** Are **Jer 22:17** 3820
My **h** is broken within me, All my **Jer 23:9** 3820
in the stubbornness of his own **h**, **Jer 23:17** 3820
carried out the purposes of His **h**; **Jer 23:20** 3820
of the deception of their own **h**, **Jer 23:26** 3820
I will give them a **h** to know Me, **Jer 24:7** 3820
return to Me with their whole **h**. **Jer 24:7** 3820
you search for Me with all your **h**. **Jer 29:13** 3824
accomplished The intent of His **h**; **Jer 30:24** 3820
Therefore My **h** yearns for him; **Jer 31:20** 4578
and on their **h** I will write it; **Jer 31:33** 3820
will give them one **h** and one way, **Jer 32:39** 3820
all My **h** and with all My soul. **Jer 32:41** 3820
My **h** wails for Moab like flutes; **Jer 48:36** 3820
My **h** also wails like flutes for **Jer 48:36** 3820
be like the **h** of a woman in labor. **Jer 48:41** 3820
arrogance of your **h** has deceived **Jer 49:16** 3820
be like the **h** of a woman in labor. **Jer 49:22** 3820
so that your **h** does not grow faint, **Jer 51:46** 3824
My **h** is overturned within me, For **La 1:20** 3820
are many and my **h** is faint." **La 1:22** 3820
My **h** is poured out on the earth Because **La 2:11** 3516
Their **h** cried out to the Lord, **La 2:18** 3820
Pour out your **h** like water Before **La 2:19** 3820
We lift up our **h** and hands Toward **La 3:41** 3824
You will give them hardness of **h**, **La 3:65** 3820

Because of this our **h** is faint, **La 5:17** 3820
take into your **h** all My words **Ezk 3:10** 3824
"And I will give them one **h**, **Ezk 11:19** 3820
And I will take the **h** of stone **Ezk 11:19** 3820
flesh and give them a **h** of flesh, **Ezk 11:19** 3820
who sets up his idols in his **h**, **Ezk 14:4** 3820
Me, sets up his idols in his **h**, **Ezk 14:7** 3820
"How languishing is your **h**," **Ezk 16:30** 3826
a new **h** and a new spirit! **Ezk 18:31** 3820
for their **h** continually went after **Ezk 20:16** 3820
with breaking **h** and bitter grief, **Ezk 21:6** 4975
and every **h** will melt, all hands **Ezk 21:7** 3820
Can your **h** endure, or can your **Ezk 22:14** 3820
borders are in the **h** of the seas; **Ezk 27:4** 3820
glorious In the **h** of the seas. **Ezk 27:25** 3820
broken you In the **h** of the seas. **Ezk 27:26** 3820
Will fall into the **h** of the seas **Ezk 27:27** 3820
"Because your **h** is lifted up And **Ezk 28:2** 3820
of gods In the **h** of the seas'; **Ezk 28:2** 3820
make your **h** like the heart of God **Ezk 28:2** 3820
make your heart like the **h** of God **Ezk 28:2** 3820
And your **h** is lifted up because of **Ezk 28:5** 3824
made your **h** Like the heart of God, **Ezk 28:6** 3824
made your heart Like the **h** of God, **Ezk 28:6** 3820
are slain In the **h** of the seas. **Ezk 28:8** 3820
"Your **h** was lifted up because of **Ezk 28:17** 3820
its **h** is haughty in its loftiness, **Ezk 31:10** 3824
and their **h** goes after their gain. **Ezk 33:31** 3820
I will give you a new **h** and put a **Ezk 36:26** 3820
and I will remove the **h** of stone **Ezk 36:26** 3820
flesh and give you a **h** of flesh. **Ezk 36:26** 3820
foreigners, uncircumcised in **h** and **Ezk 44:7** 3820
No foreigner uncircumcised in **h** **Ezk 44:9** 3820
"But when his **h** was lifted up and **Da 5:20** 3825
h was made like *that of* beasts, **Da 5:21** 3825
have not humbled your **h**, **Da 5:22** 3825
he will magnify *himself* in his **h**, **Da 8:25** 3824
you set your **h** on understanding **Da 10:12** 3820
away, his **h** will be lifted up, **Da 11:12** 3824
but his **h** will be *set* against the **Da 11:28** 3824
they do not cry to Me from their **h** **Hos 7:14** 3820
Their **h** is faithless; **Hos 10:2** 3820
My **h** is turned over within Me, All **Hos 11:8** 3820
satisfied, their **h** became proud; **Hos 13:6** 3820
"Return to Me with all your **h**, **Jl 2:12** 3824
rend your **h** and not your garments. **Jl 2:13** 3824
of your **h** has deceived you, **Ob 1:3** 3820
dwelling place, Who say in your **h**, **Ob 1:3** 3820
the deep, Into the **h** of the seas, **Jon 2:3** 3824
securely, Who says in her **h**, **Zph 2:15** 3824
Rejoice and exult with all *your* **h**, **Zph 3:14** 3820
none of you devise evil in your **h** **Zch 8:17** 3824
h will be glad as if *from* wine; **Zch 10:7** 3820
Their **h** will rejoice in the LORD. **Zch 10:7** 3820
not take it to **h** to give honor to My **Mal 2:2** 3820
you are not taking *it* to **h**. **Mal 2:2** 3820
"Blessed are the pure in **h**, **Mt 5:8** *2588*
adultery with her in his **h**. **Mt 5:28** *2588*
is, there your **h** will be also. **Mt 6:21** *2588*
for I am gentle and humble in **h**, **Mt 11:29** *2588*
out of that which fills the **h**. **Mt 12:34** *2588*
nights in the **h** of the earth. **Mt 12:40** *2588*
FOR THE **H** OF THIS PEOPLE HAS BECOME **Mt 13:15** *2588*
AND UNDERSTAND WITH THEIR **H** **Mt 13:15** *2588*
away what has been sown in his **h**. **Mt 13:19** *2588*
BUT THEIR **H** IS FAR AWAY FROM ME. **Mt 15:8** *2588*
out of the mouth come from the **h**, **Mt 15:18** *2588*
out of the **h** come evil thoughts, **Mt 15:19** *2588*
forgive his brother from your **h**." **Mt 18:35** *2588*
"Because of your hardness of **h** Moses **Mt 19:8** *4641*
THE LORD YOUR GOD WITH ALL YOUR **H**, **Mt 22:37** *2588*
if that evil slave says in his **h**, **Mt 24:48** *2588*
grieved at their hardness of **h**, **Mk 3:5** *2588*
loaves, but their **h** was hardened. **Mk 6:52** *2588*
BUT THEIR **H** IS FAR AWAY FROM ME. **Mk 7:6** *2588*
because it does not go into his **h**, **Mk 7:19** *2588*
from within, out of the **h** of men, **Mk 7:21** *2588*
Do you have a hardened **h**? **Mk 8:17** *2588*
"Because of your hardness of **h** **Mk 10:5** *4641*
sea,' and does not doubt in his **h**, **Mk 11:23** *2588*
THE LORD YOUR GOD WITH ALL YOUR **H**, **Mk 12:30** *2588*
AND TO LOVE HIM WITH ALL THE **H** **Mk 12:33** *2588*
their unbelief and hardness of **h**, **Mk 16:14** *4641*
proud in the thoughts of their **h**. **Lk 1:51** *2588*
things, pondering them in her **h**. **Lk 2:19** *2588*
treasured all *these* things in her **h**. **Lk 2:51** *2588*
out of the good treasure of his **h** **Lk 6:45** *2588*
from that which fills his **h**. **Lk 6:45** *2588*
takes away the word from their **h**, **Lk 8:12** *2588*
the word in an honest and good **h**, **Lk 8:15** *2588*
they were thinking in their **h**, **Lk 9:47** *2588*
THE LORD YOUR GOD WITH ALL YOUR **H**, **Lk 10:27** *2588*
is, there your **h** will be also. **Lk 12:34** *2588*
"But if that slave says in his **h**, **Lk 12:45** *2588*
ought to pray and not to lose **h**, **Lk 18:1** *1457b*
"O foolish men and slow of **h** to **Lk 24:25** *2588*
THEIR EYES AND HE HARDENED THEIR **H**, **Jn 12:40** *2588*
THEIR EYES AND PERCEIVE WITH THEIR **H**, **Jn 12:40** *2588*
put into the **h** of Judas Iscariot, **Jn 13:2** *2588*
"Do not let your **h** be troubled; **Jn 14:1** *2588*
Do not let your **h** be troubled, nor **Jn 14:27** *2588*
to you, sorrow has filled your **h**. **Jn 16:6** *2588*
again, and your **h** will rejoice, **Jn 16:22** *2588*
'THEREFORE MY **H** WAS GLAD AND MY **Ac 2:26** *2588*
this, they were pierced to the **h**, **Ac 2:37** *2588*
with gladness and sincerity of **h**, **Ac 2:46** *2588*
believed were of one **h** and soul; **Ac 4:32** *2588*
why has Satan filled your **h** to lie **Ac 5:3** *2588*
conceived this deed in your **h**? **Ac 5:4** *2588*

stiff-necked and uncircumcised in **h** **Ac 7:51** 2588
your **h** is not right before God. **Ac 8:21** 2588
intention of your **h** may be forgiven **Ac 8:22** 2588
"If you believe with all your **h**, **Ac 8:37** 2588
encourage them all with resolute **h** **Ac 11:23** 2588
A MAN AFTER MY **H**, who will do **Ac 13:22** 2588
"And God, who knows the **h**, **Ac 15:8** 2589
and the Lord opened her **h** to **Ac 16:14** 2588
doing, weeping and breaking my **h**? **Ac 21:13** 2588
FOR THE **H** OF THIS PEOPLE HAS BECOME **Ac 28:27** 2588
AND UNDERSTAND WITH THEIR **H** **Ac 28:27** 2588
and their foolish **h** was darkened. **Ro 1:21** 2588
your stubbornness and unrepentant **h** **Ro 2:5** 2588
is that which is of the **h**, **Ro 2:29** 2588
you became obedient from the **h** to **Ro 6:17** 2588
and unceasing grief in my **h**. **Ro 9:2** 2588
"DO NOT SAY IN YOUR **H**, 'WHO **Ro 10:6** 2588
IN YOUR MOUTH AND IN YOUR **H**" **Ro 10:8** 2588
and believe in your **h** that God **Ro 10:9** 2588
for with the **h** a person believes, **Ro 10:10** 2588
AND *which* HAVE NOT ENTERED THE **H** **1Co 2:9** 2588
But he who stands firm in his **h**, **1Co 7:37** 2588
and has decided this in his own **h**, **1Co 7:37** 2588
secrets of his **h** are disclosed; **1Co 14:25** 2588
affliction and anguish of **h** I wrote to **2Co 2:4** 2588
is read, a veil lies over their **h**; **2Co 3:15** 2588
received mercy, we do not lose **h**, **2Co 4:1** 1457b
Therefore we do not lose **h**, **2Co 4:16** 1457b
pride in appearance and not in **h**. **2Co 5:12** 2588
Corinthians, our **h** is opened wide. **2Co 6:11** 2588
on your behalf in the **h** of Titus. **2Co 8:16** 2588
just as he has purposed in his **h**, **2Co 9:7** 2588
Let us not lose **h** in doing good, **Ga 6:9** 1457b
eyes of your **h** may be enlightened, **Eph 1:18** 2588
Therefore I ask you not to lose **h** **Eph 3:13** 1457b
because of the hardness of their **h**; **Eph 4:18** 2588
melody with your **h** to the Lord; **Eph 5:19** 2588
in the sincerity of your **h**, **Eph 6:5** 2588
doing the will of God from the **h**. **Eph 6:6** 5590
all, because I have you in my **h**, **Php 1:7** 2588
beloved, put on a **h** of compassion, **Col 3:12** 4698
that they will not lose **h**. **Col 3:21** 120b
men, but with sincerity of **h**, **Col 3:22** 2588
our instruction is love from a pure **h** **1Tm 1:5** 2588
call on the Lord from a pure **h**. **2Tm 2:22** 2588
that is, *sending* my very **h**, **Phm 1:12** 4698
refresh my **h** in Christ. **Phm 1:20** 4698
'THEY ALWAYS GO ASTRAY IN THEIR **H**, **Heb 3:10** 2588
one of you an evil, unbelieving **h** that **Heb 3:12** 2588
thoughts and intentions of the **h**. **Heb 4:12** 2588
I WILL PUT MY LAWS UPON THEIR **H**, **Heb 10:16** 2588
draw near with a sincere **h** in full **Heb 10:22** 2588
you will not grow weary and lose **h**. **Heb 12:3** 5590
the **h** to be strengthened by grace, **Heb 13:9** 2588
his tongue but deceives his *own* **h**, **Jas 1:26** 2588
and selfish ambition in your **h**, **Jas 3:14** 2588
love one another from the **h**, **1Pe 1:22** 2588
it be the hidden person of the **h**, **1Pe 3:4** 2588
having a **h** trained in greed, **2Pe 2:14** 2588
need and closes his **h** against him, **1Jn 3:17** 4698
and will assure our **h** before Him **1Jn 3:19** 2588
in whatever our **h** condemns us; **1Jn 3:20** 2588
for God is greater than our **h** and **1Jn 3:20** 2588
if our **h** does not condemn us, **1Jn 3:21** 2588
for she says in her **h**, **Rv 18:7** 2588

HEARTH
offering itself *shall remain* on the **h** **Lv 6:9** 4169
bones have been scorched like a **h**. **Ps 102:3** 4168
its pieces To take fire from a **h** Or **Is 30:14** 3344
The altar **h** *shall be* four cubits; **Ezk 43:15** 741
and from the altar **h** shall extend **Ezk 43:15** 741
"Now the altar **h** *shall be* twelve **Ezk 43:16** 741

HEARTILY
Prisca greet you **h** in the Lord, **1Co 16:19** 4183
Whatever you do, do your work **h**, **Col 3:23** 5590

HEART'S
the wicked boasts of his **h** desire, **Ps 10:3** 5315
May He grant you your **h** desire And **Ps 20:4** 3824
You have given him his **h** desire, **Ps 21:2** 3820
examine my **h** *attitude* toward You. **Jer 12:3** 3820
their eyes and their **h** delight, **Ezk 24:25** 5315
my **h** desire and my prayer to God **Ro 10:1** 2588

HEARTS
And their **h** sank, and they *turned* **Gn 42:28** 3820
I will harden the **h** of the **Ex 14:17** 3820
and in the **h** of all who are skillful **Ex 31:6** 3820
Then all whose **h** moved them, both **Ex 35:22** 3820
will also bring weakness into their **h** **Lv 26:36** 3824
Our brethren have made our **h** melt, **Dt 1:28** 3824
that your **h** are not deceived, **Dt 11:16** 3824
brothers' **h** melt like his heart.' **Dt 20:8** 3824
our **h** melted and no courage **Jos 2:11** 3824
had crossed, that their **h** melted, **Jos 5:1** 3824
so the **h** of the people melted and **Jos 7:5** 3824
was of the LORD to harden their **h**, **Jos 11:20** 3820
and you know in all your **h** and in **Jos 23:14** 3824
and incline your **h** to the LORD, **Jos 24:23** 3824
"Why then do you harden your **h** as **1Sa 6:6** 3824
and Pharaoh hardened their **h**? **1Sa 6:6** 3820
direct your **h** to the LORD and serve **1Sa 7:3** 3824
men whose **h** God had touched **1Sa 10:26** 3820
away the **h** of the men of Israel. **2Sa 15:6** 3820
"The **h** of the men of Israel are **2Sa 15:13** 3820
turned the **h** of all the men of Judah **2Sa 19:14** 3824
know the **h** of all the sons of men, **1Ki 8:39** 3824
He may incline our **h** to Himself, **1Ki 8:58** 3824
for the LORD searches all **h**, **1Ch 28:9** 3824
know the **h** of the sons of men, **2Ch 6:30** 3824
who set their **h** on seeking the LORD **2Ch 11:16** 3824
not yet directed their **h** to the God **2Ch 20:33** 3824
and cursed God in their **h**." **Jb 1:5** 3824
God tries the **h** and minds. **Ps 7:9** 3820
While evil is in their **h**. **Ps 28:3** 3824
He who fashions the **h** of them all, **Ps 33:15** 3820
Do not harden your **h**, **Ps 95:8** 3824
those who are upright in their **h**. **Ps 125:4** 3820
Who devise evil things in *their* **h**; **Ps 140:2** 3820
But in the **h** of fools it is made **Pr 14:33** 7310
But the **h** of fools are not so. **Pr 15:7** 3820
LORD, How much more the **h** of men! **Pr 15:11** 3820
for gold, But the LORD tests **h**. **Pr 17:3** 3820
eyes, But the LORD weighs the **h**. **Pr 21:2** 3820
not consider *it* who weighs the **h**? **Pr 24:12** 3820
therefore the **h** of the sons of men **Ec 8:11** 3820
the **h** of the sons of men are full **Ec 9:3** 3820
insanity is in their **h** throughout **Ec 9:3** 3824
the **h** of this people insensitive, **Is 6:10** 3820
ears, Understand with their **h**, **Is 6:10** 3824
his heart and the **h** of his people **Is 7:2** 3824
they remove their **h** far from Me, **Is 29:13** 3820
h so that they cannot comprehend. **Is 44:18** 3820
walk in the stubbornness of their **h** **Jer 13:10** 3820
anything in the **h** of the prophets **Jer 23:26** 3820
I will put the fear of Me in their **h** so **Jer 32:40** 3824
So the **h** of the mighty men of Moab **Jer 48:41** 3820
and the **h** of the mighty men of **Jer 49:22** 3820
The joy of our **h** has ceased; **La 5:15** 3820
have been hurt by their adulterous **h** **Ezk 6:9** 3820
whose **h** go after their detestable **Ezk 11:21** 3820
set up their idols in their **h** and **Ezk 14:3** 3820
to lay hold of the **h** of the house of **Ezk 14:5** 3820
that *their* **h** may melt, and many **Ezk 21:15** 3820
trouble the **h** of many peoples when **Ezk 32:9** 3820
"As for both kings, their **h** will be **Da 11:27** 3824
And they do not consider in their **h** **Hos 7:2** 3824
For their **h** are like an oven **Hos 7:6** 3820
H are melting and knees knocking! **Na 2:10** 3820
in spirit, Who say in their **h**, **Zph 1:12** 3824
do not devise evil in your **h** against **Zch 7:10** 3824
"They made their **h** *like* flint **Zch 7:12** 3820
of Judah will say in their **h**, **Zch 12:5** 3820
He will restore the **h** of the fathers **Mal 4:6** 3820
the **h** of the children to their fathers, **Mal 4:6** 3820
are you thinking evil in your **h**? **Mt 9:4** 2588
there and reasoning in their **h**, **Mk 2:6** 2588
about these things in your **h**? **Mk 2:8** 2588
TO TURN THE **H** OF THE FATHERS BACK **Lk 1:17** 2588
that thoughts from many **h** may be **Lk 2:35** 2588
wondering in their **h** about John, **Lk 3:15** 2588
"Why are you reasoning in your **h**? **Lk 5:22** 2588
of men, but God knows your **h**; **Lk 16:15** 2588
that your **h** will not be weighted **Lk 21:34** 2588
"Were not our **h** burning within us **Lk 24:32** 2588
and why do doubts arise in your **h**? **Lk 24:38** 2588
who know the **h** of all men, **Ac 1:24** 2589
in their **h** turned back to Egypt, **Ac 7:39** 2588
satisfying your **h** with food and **Ac 14:17** 2588
them, cleansing their **h** by faith. **Ac 15:9** 2588
the lusts of their **h** to impurity, **Ro 1:24** 2588
of the Law written in their **h**, **Ro 2:15** 2588
God has been poured out within our **h** **Ro 5:5** 2588
and He who searches the **h** knows **Ro 8:27** 2588
flattering speech they deceive the **h** **Ro 16:18** 2588
disclose the motives of *men's* **h**; **1Co 4:5** 2588
the Spirit in our **h** as a pledge. **2Co 1:22** 2588
are our letter, written in our **h**, **2Co 3:2** 2588
stone but on tablets of human **h**. **2Co 3:3** 2588
is the One who has shone in our **h** to **2Co 4:6** 2588
Make room for us *in your* **h**; **2Co 7:2**
that you are in our **h** to die together **2Co 7:3** 2588
the Spirit of His Son into our **h**, **Ga 4:6** 2588
may dwell in your **h** through faith; **Eph 3:17** 2588
and that he may comfort your **h**. **Eph 6:22** 2588
will guard your **h** and your minds **Php 4:7** 2588
that their **h** may be encouraged, **Col 2:2** 2588
peace of Christ rule in your **h** **Col 3:15** 2588
thankfulness in your **h** to God. **Col 3:16** 2588
and that he may encourage your **h**; **Col 4:8** 2588
men, but God who examines our **h**. **1Th 2:4** 2588
so that He may establish your **h** **1Th 3:13** 2588
strengthen your **h** in every good **2Th 2:17** 2588
direct your **h** into the love of God **2Th 3:5** 2588
because the **h** of the saints have **Phm 1:7** 4698
DO NOT HARDEN YOUR **H** AS WHEN THEY **Heb 3:8** 2588
DO NOT HARDEN YOUR **H**, AS WHEN THEY **Heb 3:15** 2588
DO NOT HARDEN YOUR **H**." **Heb 4:7** 2588
AND I WILL WRITE THEM ON THEIR **H**. **Heb 8:10** 2588
having our **h** sprinkled *clean* from **Heb 10:22** 2588
and purify your **h**, you **Jas 4:8** 2588
have fattened your **h** in a day of **Jas 5:5** 2588
strengthen your **h**, for the coming **Jas 5:8** 2588
sanctify Christ as Lord in your **h**, **1Pe 3:15** 2588
the morning star arises in your **h**. **2Pe 1:19** 2588
He who searches the minds and **h**; **Rv 2:23** 2588
"For God has put it in their **h** to **Rv 17:17** 2588

HEARTY
Saul was in **h** agreement with **Ac 8:1** 4909
but also give **h** approval to those **Ro 1:32** 4909

HEAT
and harvest, And cold and **h**, **Gn 8:22** 2527
the tent door in the **h** of the day. **Gn 18:1** 2527
by day the **h** consumed me and the **Gn 31:40** 2721a
manslayer in the **h** of his anger, **Dt 19:6** 2552
and with fiery **h** and with the sword **Dt 28:22** 2746
Ammonites until the **h** of the day. **1Sa 11:11** 2527
to the house of Ish-bosheth in the **h** **2Sa 4:5** 2527
and **h** consume the snow waters, **Jb 24:19** 2527
is nothing hidden from its **h**. **Ps 19:6** 2535
as with the fever **h** of summer. **Ps 32:4** 2725
to *give* shade from the **h** by day, **Is 4:6** 2721a
Like dazzling **h** in the sunshine, **Is 18:4** 2527
of dew in the **h** of harvest." **Is 18:4** 2527
the storm, a shade from the **h**; **Is 25:4** 2721a
Like **h** in drought, You subdue **Is 25:5** 2721a
Like **h** by the shadow of a cloud, **Is 25:5** 2721a
So He poured out on him the **h** of **Is 42:25** 2534
h or sun strike them down; **Is 49:10** 8273
of her **h** who can turn her away? **Jer 2:24** 8385a
will not fear when the **h** comes; **Jer 17:8** 2527
dead body shall be cast out to the **h** **Jer 36:30** 2721a
of the burning **h** of famine. **La 5:10** 2152
giving orders to **h** the furnace seven **Da 3:19** 228
became sick with the **h** of wine; **Hos 7:5** 2534
and the scorching **h** of the day.' **Mt 20:12** 2742
a viper came out because of the **h** and **Ac 28:3** 2329
will be destroyed with intense **h**, **2Pe 3:10** 2741a
elements will melt with intense **h**! **2Pe 3:12** 2741a
sun beat down on them, nor any **h**; **Rv 7:16** 2738
Men were scorched with fierce **h**; **Rv 16:9** 2738

HEATED
"When they become **h** up, **Jer 51:39** 2552
times more than it was usually **h**. **Da 3:19** 228
Like an oven **h** by the baker Who **Hos 7:4** 1197a

HEATEDLY
stood up and *began* to argue **h**, **Ac 23:9** 1264

HEAVE
and the thigh of the **h** offering which **Ex 29:27** 8641
of Israel, for it is a **h** offering; **Ex 29:28** 8641
and it shall be a **h** offering from **Ex 29:28** 8641
even their **h** offering to the LORD. **Ex 29:28** 8641

HEAVEN
God called the expanse **h**. **Gn 1:8** 8064
the LORD God made earth and **h**. **Gn 2:4** 8064
the breath of life, from under **h**; **Gn 6:17** 8064
tower whose top *will reach* into **h**, **Gn 11:4** 8064
High, Possessor of **h** and earth; **Gn 14:19** 8064
High, possessor of **h** and earth, **Gn 14:22** 8064
and fire from the LORD out of **h**, **Gn 19:24** 8064
of God called to Hagar from **h** and **Gn 21:17** 8064
of the LORD called to him from **h** and **Gn 22:11** 8064
to Abraham a second time from **h**, **Gn 22:15** 8064
the God of **h** and the God of earth, **Gn 24:3** 8064
"The LORD, the God of **h**, **Gn 24:7** 8064
descendants as the stars of **h**, **Gn 26:4** 8064
may God give you of the dew of **h**, **Gn 27:28** 8064
away from the dew of **h** from above. **Gn 27:39** 8064
earth with its top reaching to **h**; **Gn 28:12** 8064
God, and this is the gate of **h**." **Gn 28:17** 8064
you *With* blessings of **h** above, **Gn 49:25** 8064
I will rain bread from **h** for you; **Ex 16:4** 8064
memory of Amalek from under **h**." **Ex 17:14** 8064
or any likeness of what is in **h** **Ex 20:4** 8064
that I have spoken to you from **h**. **Ex 20:22** 8064
days the LORD made **h** and earth, **Ex 31:17** 8064
like the stars of **h** in number. **Dt 1:10** 8064
are large and fortified to **h**. **Dt 1:28** 8064
for what god is there in **h** or on **Dt 3:24** 8064
not to lift up your eyes to **h** **Dt 4:19** 8064
and the stars, all the host of **h**, **Dt 4:19** 8064
all the peoples under the whole **h**. **Dt 4:19** 8064
I call **h** and earth to witness **Dt 4:26** 8064
in **h** above and on the earth below; **Dt 4:39** 8064
or any likeness *of* what is in **h** **Dt 5:8** 8064
their name perish from under **h**; **Dt 7:24** 8064
you, great cities fortified to **h**, **Dt 9:1** 8064
blot out their name from under **h**; **Dt 9:14** 8064
to the LORD your God belong **h** **Dt 10:14** 8064
you as numerous as the stars of **h**. **Dt 10:22** 8064
drinks water from the rain of **h**, **Dt 11:11** 8064
the memory of Amalek from under **h**; **Dt 25:19** 8064
from Your holy habitation, from **h**, **Dt 26:15** 8064
"The **h** which is over your **Dt 28:23** 8064
from **h** it shall come down on you **Dt 28:24** 8064
as numerous as the stars of **h**, **Dt 28:62** 8064
blot out his name from under **h**. **Dt 29:20** 8064
It is not in **h**, that you should **Dt 30:12** 8064
'Who will go up to **h** for us to get **Dt 30:12** 8064
"I call **h** and earth to witness **Dt 30:19** 8064
'Indeed, I lift up My hand to **h**, **Dt 32:40** 8064
land, With the choice things of **h**, **Dt 33:13** 8064
in **h** above and on earth beneath. **Jos 2:11** 8064
the LORD threw large stones from **h** **Jos 10:11** 8064
"The stars fought from **h**, **Jg 5:20** 8064
went up from the altar toward **h**, **Jg 13:20** 8064
city was going up *in smoke* to **h**. **Jg 20:40** 8064
the cry of the city went up to **h**. **1Sa 5:12** 8064
left hanging between **h** and earth, **2Sa 18:9** 8064
The foundations of **h** were **2Sa 22:8** 8064
"The LORD thundered from **h**, **2Sa 22:14** 8064
and spread out his hands toward **h**. **1Ki 8:22** 8064
no God like You in **h** above or on **1Ki 8:23** 8064
h and the highest heaven cannot **1Ki 8:27** 8064
the highest **h** cannot contain You, **1Ki 8:27** 8064
hear in **h** Your dwelling place; **1Ki 8:30** 8064
then hear in **h** and act and **1Ki 8:32** 8064
then hear in **h**, **1Ki 8:34** 8064
then hear in **h** and forgive **1Ki 8:36** 8064
hear in **h** Your dwelling place, **1Ki 8:39** 8064
hear in **h** Your dwelling place, **1Ki 8:43** 8064
then hear in **h** their prayer and **1Ki 8:45** 8064
in **h** Your dwelling place, **1Ki 8:49** 8064
with his hands spread toward **h**. **1Ki 8:54** 8064
field the birds of **h** will eat." **1Ki 21:24** 8064
and all the host of **h** standing by **1Ki 22:19** 8064

let fire come down from **h** and	2Ki 1:10	8064
Then fire came down from **h** and	2Ki 1:10	8064
let fire come down from **h** and	2Ki 1:12	8064
the fire of God came down from **h**	2Ki 1:12	8064
"Behold fire came down from **h** and	2Ki 1:14	8064
up Elijah by a whirlwind to **h**,	2Ki 2:1	8064
went up by a whirlwind to **h**.	2Ki 2:11	8064
the LORD should make *windows* in **h**,	2Ki 7:2	8064
the LORD should make windows in **h**,	2Ki 7:19	8064
the name of Israel from under **h**,	2Ki 14:27	8064
all the host of **h** and served Baal.	2Ki 17:16	8064
You have made **h** and earth.	2Ki 19:15	8064
all the host of **h** and served them.	2Ki 21:3	8064
he built altars for all the host of **h** in	2Ki 21:5	8064
and for all the host of **h**;	2Ki 23:4	8064
and to all the host of **h**.	2Ki 23:5	8064
LORD standing between earth and **h**,	1Ch 21:16	8064
He answered him with fire from **h** on	1Ch 21:26	8064
multiply Israel as the stars of **h**.	1Ch 27:23	8064
who has made **h** and earth,	2Ch 2:12	8064
and spread out his hands toward **h**.	2Ch 6:13	8064
no god like You in **h** or on earth,	2Ch 6:14	8064
h and the highest heaven cannot	2Ch 6:18	8064
the highest **h** cannot contain You;	2Ch 6:18	8064
from Your dwelling place, from **h**;	2Ch 6:21	8064
then hear from **h** and act and	2Ch 6:23	8064
then hear from **h** and forgive	2Ch 6:25	8064
then hear in **h** and forgive	2Ch 6:27	8064
hear from **h** Your dwelling place,	2Ch 6:30	8064
then hear from **h**,	2Ch 6:33	8064
then hear from **h** their prayer	2Ch 6:35	8064
then hear from **h**, from Your	2Ch 6:39	8064
fire came down from **h** and consumed	2Ch 7:1	8064
ways, then I will hear from **h**,	2Ch 7:14	8064
and all the host of **h** standing on	2Ch 18:18	8064
a rage *which* has even reached **h**.	2Ch 28:9	8064
to His holy dwelling place, to **h**.	2Ch 30:27	8064
about this and cried out to **h**.	2Ch 32:20	8064
all the host of **h** and served them.	2Ch 33:3	8064
he built altars for all the host of **h** in	2Ch 33:5	8064
'The LORD, the God of **h**,	2Ch 36:23	8064
'The LORD, the God of **h**,	Ezr 1:2	8064
servants of the God of **h** and earth	Ezr 5:11	8065
provoked the God of **h** to wrath,	Ezr 5:12	8065
a burnt offering to the God of **h**,	Ezr 6:9	8065
acceptable sacrifices to the God of **h**	Ezr 6:10	8065
scribe of the law of the God of **h**,	Ezr 7:12	8065
scribe of the law of the God of **h**,	Ezr 7:21	8065
is commanded by the God of **h**,	Ezr 7:23	8065
for the house of the God of **h**,	Ezr 7:23	8065
and praying before the God of **h**.	Ne 1:4	8064
"I beseech You, O LORD God of **h**,	Ne 1:5	8064
So I prayed to the God of **h**.	Ne 2:4	8064
"The God of **h** will give us success;	Ne 2:20	8064
The **h** of heavens with all their	Ne 9:6	8064
And spoke with them from **h**;	Ne 9:13	8064
"You provided bread from **h**	Ne 9:15	8064
sons numerous as the stars of **h**,	Ne 9:23	8064
distress, You heard from **h**,	Ne 9:27	8064
to You, You heard from **h**,	Ne 9:28	8064
"The fire of God fell from **h** and	Jb 1:16	8064
now, behold, my witness is in **h**,	Jb 16:19	8064
"Is not God *in* the height of **h**?	Jb 22:12	8064
And He walks on the vault of **h**	Jb 22:14	8064
"The pillars of **h** tremble And	Jb 26:11	8064
the whole **h** He lets it loose,	Jb 37:3	8064
frost of **h**, who has given it birth?	Jb 38:29	8064
is under the whole **h** is Mine.	Jb 41:11	8064
the LORD's throne is in **h**;	Ps 11:4	8064
down from **h** upon the sons of men To	Ps 14:2	8064
will answer him from His holy **h** With	Ps 20:6	8064
The LORD looks from **h**;	Ps 33:13	8064
down from **h** upon the sons of men To	Ps 53:2	8064
He will send from **h** and save me;	Ps 57:3	8064
Let **h** and earth praise Him, The	Ps 69:34	8064
Whom have I in **h** *but You?*	Ps 73:25	8064
caused judgment to be heard from **h**;	Ps 76:8	8064
above And opened the doors of **h**;	Ps 78:23	8064
to eat And gave them food from **h**.	Ps 78:24	8064
Look down from **h** and see, and take	Ps 80:14	8064
righteousness looks down from **h**.	Ps 85:11	8064
And his throne as the days of **h**.	Ps 89:29	8064
h the LORD gazed upon the earth,	Ps 102:19	8064
Stretching out **h** like a *tent* curtain.	Ps 104:2	8064
them with the bread of **h**.	Ps 105:40	8064
that are in **h** and in the earth?	Ps 113:6	8064
of the LORD, Maker of **h** and earth.	Ps 115:15	8064
O LORD, Your word is settled in **h**.	Ps 119:89	8064
the LORD, Who made **h** and earth.	Ps 121:2	8064
of the LORD, Who made **h** and earth.	Ps 124:8	8064
Zion, He who made **h** and earth.	Ps 134:3	8064
He does, In **h** and in earth,	Ps 135:6	8064
Give thanks to the God of **h**,	Ps 136:26	8064
If I ascend to **h**, You are there;	Ps 139:8	8064
Who made **h** and earth, The sea and	Ps 146:6	8064
His glory is above earth and **h**.	Ps 148:13	8064
has ascended into **h** and descended?	Pr 30:4	8064
all that has been done under **h**.	Ec 1:13	8064
for the sons of men to do under **h**	Ec 2:3	8064
a time for every event under **h**	Ec 3:1	8064
is in **h** and you are on the earth;	Ec 5:2	8064
it deep as Sheol or high as **h**."	Is 7:11	4605
For the stars of **h** and their	Is 13:10	4605
"How you have fallen from **h**,	Is 14:12	4605
'I will ascend to **h**;	Is 14:13	4605
LORD will punish the host of **h**	Is 24:21	4791
all the host of **h** will wear away,	Is 34:4	8064
For My sword is satiated in **h**,	Is 34:5	8064
You have made **h** and earth.	Is 37:16	8064

and the snow come down from **h**,	Is 55:10	8064
Look down from **h** and see from Your	Is 63:15	8064
"**H** is My throne and the earth is	Is 66:1	8064
to make cakes for the queen of **h**;	Jer 7:18	8064
moon and to all the host of **h**,	Jer 8:2	8064
the host of **h** cannot be counted and	Jer 33:22	8064
and the fixed patterns of **h** and	Jer 33:25	8064
burning sacrifices to the queen of **h**	Jer 44:17	8064
burning sacrifices to the queen of **h**	Jer 44:18	8064
sacrifices to the queen of **h** and	Jer 44:19	8064
burn sacrifices to the queen of **h**	Jer 44:25	8064
winds From the four ends of **h**,	Jer 49:36	8064
For her judgment has reached to **h**	Jer 51:9	8064
"Then **h** and earth and all that is	Jer 51:48	8064
cast from **h** to earth The glory of	La 2:1	8064
heart and hands Toward God in **h**;	La 3:41	8064
LORD looks down And sees from **h**.	La 3:50	8064
lifted me up between earth and **h**	Ezk 8:3	8064
God of **h** concerning this mystery,	Da 2:18	8065
Then Daniel blessed the God of **h**;	Da 2:19	8065
a God in **h** who reveals mysteries,	Da 2:28	8065
God of **h** has given the kingdom,	Da 2:37	8065
God of **h** will set up a kingdom which	Da 2:44	8065
a holy one, descended from **h**.	Da 4:13	8065
him be drenched with the dew of **h**,	Da 4:15	8065
one, descending from **h** and saying,	Da 4:23	8065
him be drenched with the dew of **h**,	Da 4:23	8065
and be drenched with the dew of **h**;	Da 4:25	8065
recognize that *it is* **H** *that* rules.	Da 4:26	8065
king's mouth, a voice came from **h**,	Da 4:31	8065
was drenched with the dew of **h** until	Da 4:33	8065
raised my eyes toward **h** and	Da 4:34	8065
according to His will in the host of **h**	Da 4:35	8065
exalt and honor the King of **h**,	Da 4:37	8065
was drenched with the dew of **h** until	Da 5:21	8065
yourself against the Lord of **h**;	Da 5:23	8065
and wonders In **h** and on earth,	Da 6:27	8065
the four winds of **h** were stirring	Da 7:2	8065
with the clouds of **h** One like a	Da 7:13	8065
of *all* the kingdoms under the whole **h**	Da 7:27	8065
horns toward the four winds of **h**.	Da 8:8	8064
It grew up to the host of **h**	Da 8:10	8064
for under the whole **h** there has	Da 9:12	8064
brightness of the expanse of **h**,	Da 12:3	7549
right hand and his left toward **h**,	Da 12:7	8064
And though they ascend to **h**,	Am 9:2	8064
and I fear the LORD God of **h** who	Jon 1:9	8064
your traders more than the stars of **h**	Na 3:16	8064
on the housetops to the host of **h**,	Zph 1:5	8064
"These are the four spirits of **h**,	Zch 6:5	8064
not open for you the windows of **h** and	Mal 3:10	8064
for the kingdom of **h** is at hand."	Mt 3:2	3772
for the kingdom of **h** is at hand."	Mt 4:17	3772
for theirs is the kingdom of **h**.	Mt 5:3	3772
for theirs is the kingdom of **h**.	Mt 5:10	3772
for your reward in **h** is great;	Mt 5:12	3772
glorify your Father who is in **h**.	Mt 5:16	3772
you, until **h** and earth pass away,	Mt 5:18	3772
called least in the kingdom of **h**;	Mt 5:19	3772
called great in the kingdom of **h**.	Mt 5:19	3772
will not enter the kingdom of **h**.	Mt 5:20	3772
make no oath at all, either by **h**,	Mt 5:34	3772
sons of your Father who is in **h**;	Mt 5:45	3772
with your Father who is in **h**.	Mt 6:1	3772
'Our Father who is in **h**,	Mt 6:9	3772
be done, On earth as it is in **h**.	Mt 6:10	3772
up for yourselves treasures in **h**,	Mt 6:20	3772
will your Father who is in **h** give	Mt 7:11	3772
Lord,' will enter the kingdom of **h**,	Mt 7:21	3772
the will of My Father who is in **h**	Mt 7:21	3772
and Jacob in the kingdom of **h**;	Mt 8:11	3772
'The kingdom of **h** is at hand.'	Mt 10:7	3772
him before My Father who is in **h**.	Mt 10:32	3772
him before My Father who is in **h**.	Mt 10:33	3772
kingdom of **h** is greater than he.	Mt 11:11	3772
the kingdom of **h** suffers violence,	Mt 11:12	3772
will not be exalted to **h**,	Mt 11:23	3772
Father, Lord of **h** and earth,	Mt 11:25	3772
the will of My Father who is in **h**,	Mt 12:50	3772
the mysteries of the kingdom of **h**,	Mt 13:11	3772
"The kingdom of **h** may be compared	Mt 13:24	3772
kingdom of **h** is like a mustard seed,	Mt 13:31	3772
"The kingdom of **h** is like leaven,	Mt 13:33	3772
kingdom of **h** is like a treasure	Mt 13:44	3772
the kingdom of **h** is like a	Mt 13:45	3772
the kingdom of **h** is like a dragnet	Mt 13:47	3772
h is like a head of a household,	Mt 13:52	3772
looking up toward **h**, He blessed	Mt 14:19	3772
Him to show them a sign from **h**.	Mt 16:1	3772
to you, but My Father who is in **h**.	Mt 16:17	3772
you the keys of the kingdom of **h**;	Mt 16:19	3772
on earth shall have been bound in **h**,	Mt 16:19	3772
on earth shall have been loosed in **h**."	Mt 16:19	3772
is greatest in the kingdom of **h**?"	Mt 18:1	3772
will not enter the kingdom of **h**.	Mt 18:3	3772
the greatest in the kingdom of **h**.	Mt 18:4	3772
their angels in **h** continually see	Mt 18:10	3772
the face of My Father who is in **h**.	Mt 18:10	3772
not *the* will of your Father who is in **h**	Mt 18:14	3772
on earth shall have been bound in **h**;	Mt 18:18	3772
on earth shall have been loosed in **h**.	Mt 18:18	3772
for them by My Father who is in **h**.	Mt 18:19	3772
"For this reason the kingdom of **h**	Mt 18:23	3772
for the sake of the kingdom of **h**	Mt 19:12	3772
of **h** belongs to such as these."	Mt 19:14	3772
and you will have treasure in **h**;	Mt 19:21	3772
man to enter the kingdom of **h**	Mt 19:23	3772
kingdom of **h** is like a landowner	Mt 20:1	3772
what *source,* from **h** or from men?"	Mt 21:25	3772

"If we say, 'From **h**,' He will say to	Mt 21:25	3772
of **h** may be compared to a king who	Mt 22:2	3772
but are like angels in **h**.	Mt 22:30	3772
is your Father, He who is in **h**.	Mt 23:9	3770
off the kingdom of **h** from people;	Mt 23:13	3772
"And whoever swears by **h**,	Mt 23:22	3772
"**H** and earth will pass away, but	Mt 24:35	3772
knows, not even the angels of **h**,	Mt 24:36	3772
"Then the kingdom of **h** will be	Mt 25:1	3772
and COMING ON THE CLOUDS OF **H**."	Mt 26:64	3772
angel of the Lord descended from **h**	Mt 28:2	3772
given to Me in **h** and on earth.	Mt 28:18	3772
looking up toward **h**, He blessed	Mk 6:41	3772
looking up to **h** with a deep sigh,	Mk 7:34	3772
seeking from Him a sign from **h**,	Mk 8:11	3772
and you will have treasure in **h**;	Mk 10:21	3772
Father who is in **h** will also forgive	Mk 11:25	3772
will your Father who is in **h** forgive	Mk 11:26	3772
"Was the baptism of John from **h**,	Mk 11:30	3772
"If we say, 'From **h**,' He will say,	Mk 11:31	3772
but are like angels in **h**.	Mk 12:25	3772
AND THE STARS WILL BE FALLING from **h**,	Mk 13:25	3772
earth to the farthest end of **h**.	Mk 13:27	3772
"**H** and earth will pass away, but	Mk 13:31	3772
knows, not even the angels in **h**,	Mk 13:32	3772
and COMING WITH THE CLOUDS OF **H**."	Mk 14:62	3772
them, He was received up into **h** and	Mk 16:19	3772
had gone away from them into **h**	Lk 2:15	3772
He was praying, **h** was opened,	Lk 3:21	3772
a dove, and a voice came out of **h**,	Lk 3:22	3772
behold, your reward is great in **h**.	Lk 6:23	3772
looking up to **h**, He blessed them,	Lk 9:16	3772
command fire to come down from **h**	Lk 9:54	3772
will not be exalted to **h**,	Lk 10:15	3772
Satan fall from **h** like lightning.	Lk 10:18	3772
your names are recorded in **h**."	Lk 10:20	3772
O Father, Lord of **h** and earth,	Lk 10:21	3772
demanding of Him a sign from **h**.	Lk 11:16	3772
out, an unfailing treasure in **h**,	Lk 12:33	3772
in **h** over one sinner who repents than	Lk 15:7	3772
"Father, I have sinned against **h**,	Lk 15:18	3772
against **h** and in your sight;	Lk 15:21	3772
"But it is easier for **h** and earth	Lk 16:17	3772
from **h** and destroyed them all.	Lk 17:29	3772
to lift up his eyes to **h**,	Lk 18:13	3772
and you shall have treasure in **h**;	Lk 18:22	3772
in **h** and glory in the highest!"	Lk 19:38	3772
of John from **h** or from men?"	Lk 20:4	3772
"If we say, 'From **h**,' He will say,	Lk 20:5	3772
be terrors and great signs from **h**.	Lk 21:11	3772
"**H** and earth will pass away, but	Lk 21:33	3772
an angel from **h** appeared to Him,	Lk 22:43	3772
from them and was carried up into **h**.	Lk 24:51	3772
descending as a dove out of **h**,	Jn 1:32	3772
"No one has ascended into **h**,	Jn 3:13	3772
but He who descended from **h**:	Jn 3:13	3772
it has been given him from **h**.	Jn 3:27	3772
He who comes from **h** is above all.	Jn 3:31	3772
'HE GAVE THEM BREAD OUT OF **H** TO	Jn 6:31	3772
has given you the bread out of **h**,	Jn 6:32	3772
gives you the true bread out of **h**.	Jn 6:32	3772
is that which comes down out of **h**,	Jn 6:33	3772
"For I have come down from **h**,	Jn 6:38	3772
bread that came down out of **h**."	Jn 6:41	3772
'I have come down out of **h**'?"	Jn 6:42	3772
bread which comes down out of **h**,	Jn 6:50	3772
bread that came down out of **h**;	Jn 6:51	3772
bread which came down out of **h**;	Jn 6:58	3772
Then a voice came out of **h**:	Jn 12:28	3772
and lifting up His eyes to **h**,	Jn 17:1	3772
the day when He was taken up *to* **h**,	Ac 1:2	
has been taken up from you into **h**,	Ac 1:11	3772
you have watched Him go into **h**."	Ac 1:11	3772
from **h** a noise like a violent rushing	Ac 2:2	3772
men from every nation under **h**.	Ac 2:5	3772
was not David who ascended into **h**,	Ac 2:34	3772
whom **h** must receive until	Ac 3:21	3772
no other name under **h** that has	Ac 4:12	3772
it is You who MADE THE **H**	Ac 4:24	3772
them up to serve the host of **h**;	Ac 7:42	3772
'**H** IS MY THRONE, AND EARTH IS THE	Ac 7:49	3772
into **h** and saw the glory of God,	Ac 7:55	3772
a light from **h** flashed around him;	Ac 9:3	3772
from **h** answered a second time,	Ac 11:9	3772
WHO MADE THE **H** AND THE EARTH	Ac 14:15	3772
rains from **h** and fruitful seasons,	Ac 14:17	3771
since He is Lord of **h** and earth,	Ac 17:24	3772
the *image* which fell down from **h**?	Ac 19:35	1356
flashed from **h** all around me,	Ac 22:6	3772
I saw on the way a light from **h**,	Ac 26:13	3771
the wrath of God is revealed from **h**	Ro 1:18	3772
'WHO WILL ASCEND INTO **H**?'	Ro 10:6	3772
gods whether in **h** or on earth,	1Co 8:5	3772
the second man is from **h**.	1Co 15:47	3772
clothed with our dwelling from **h**,	2Co 5:2	3772
man was caught up to the third **h**.	2Co 12:2	3772
if we, or an angel from **h**,	Ga 1:8	3772
every family in **h** and on earth	Eph 3:15	3772
their Master and yours is in **h**,	Eph 6:9	3772
WILL BOW, of those who are in **h**	Php 2:10	2032
For our citizenship is in **h**,	Php 3:20	3772
of the hope laid up for you in **h**,	Col 1:5	3772
things on earth or things in **h**.	Col 1:20	3772
in all creation under **h**,	Col 1:23	3772
that you too have a Master in **h**.	Col 4:1	3772
and to wait for His Son from **h**,	1Th 1:10	3772
will descend from **h** with a shout,	1Th 4:16	3772
Lord Jesus will be revealed from **h**	2Th 1:7	3772
the true one, but into **h** itself,	Heb 9:24	3772

descendants AS THE STARS OF **H** IN Heb 11:12 *3772*
firstborn who are enrolled in **h**, Heb 12:23 *3772*
away from Him who *warns* from **h**. Heb 12:25 *3772*
BUT ALSO THE **H**." Heb 12:26 *3772*
not swear, either by **h** or by earth Jas 5:12 *3772*
fade away, reserved in **h** for you, 1Pe 1:4 *3772*
to you by the Holy Spirit sent from **h** 1Pe 1:12 *3772*
hand of God, having gone into **h**, 1Pe 3:22 *3772*
heard this utterance made from **h** 2Pe 1:18 *3772*
comes down out of **h** from My God, Rv 3:12 *3772*
behold, a door *standing* open in **h**, Rv 4:1 *3772*
a throne was standing in **h**, Rv 4:2 *3772*
And no one in **h** or on the earth Rv 5:3 *3772*
And every created thing which is in **h** Rv 5:13 *3772*
silence in **h** for about half an hour. Rv 8:1 *3772*
and a great star fell from **h**, Rv 8:10 *3772*
star from **h** which had fallen to Rv 9:1 *3772*
strong angel coming down out of **h**, Rv 10:1 *3772*
and I heard a voice from **h** saying, Rv 10:4 *3772*
lifted up his right hand to **h**, Rv 10:5 *3772*
WHO CREATED **H** AND THE THINGS IN IT, Rv 10:6 *3772*
the voice which I heard from **h**, Rv 10:8 *3772*
loud voice from **h** saying to them, Rv 11:12 *3772*
they went up into **h** in the cloud, Rv 11:12 *3772*
and gave glory to the God of **h**. Rv 11:13 *3772*
and there were loud voices in **h**, Rv 11:15 *3772*
temple of God which is in **h** was Rv 11:19 *3772*
A great sign appeared in **h**: Rv 12:1 *3772*
Then another sign appeared in **h**: Rv 12:3 *3772*
away a third of the stars of **h** and Rv 12:4 *3772*
And there was war in **h**, Rv 12:7 *3772*
a place found for them in **h**. Rv 12:8 *3772*
Then I heard a loud voice in **h**, Rv 12:10 *3772*
that is, those who dwell in **h**. Rv 13:6 *3772*
even makes fire come down out of **h** Rv 13:13 *3772*
And I heard a voice from **h**, Rv 14:2 *3772*
worship Him who made the **h** and Rv 14:7 *3772*
And I heard a voice from **h**, Rv 14:13 *3772*
out of the temple which is in **h**, Rv 14:17 *3772*
Then I saw another sign in **h**, Rv 15:1 *3772*
of testimony in **h** was opened, Rv 15:5 *3772*
and they blasphemed the God of **h** Rv 16:11 *3772*
each, came down from **h** upon men; Rv 16:21 *3772*
another angel coming down from **h**, Rv 18:1 *3772*
I heard another voice from **h**, Rv 18:4 *3772*
sins have piled up as high as **h**, Rv 18:5 *3772*
"Rejoice over her, O **h**, Rv 18:20 *3772*
voice of a great multitude in **h**, Rv 19:1 *3772*
And I saw **h** opened, Rv 19:11 *3772*
And the armies which are in **h**, Rv 19:14 *3772*
I saw an angel coming down from **h**, Rv 20:1 *3772*
down from **h** and devoured them. Rv 20:9 *3772*
presence earth and **h** fled away, Rv 20:11 *3772*
Then I saw a new **h** and a new earth; Rv 21:1 *3772*
for the first **h** and the first Rv 21:1 *3772*
coming down out of **h** from God, Rv 21:2 *3772*
coming down out of **h** from God, Rv 21:10 *3772*

HEAVENLY

or the moon or any of the **h** host, Dt 17:3 8064
the **h** host bows down before You. Ne 9:6 8064
they burned sacrifices to all the **h** host Jer 19:13 8064
as your **h** Father is perfect. Mt 5:48 *3770*
h Father will also forgive you. Mt 6:14 *3770*
and *yet* your **h** Father feeds them. Mt 6:26 *3770*
for your **h** Father knows that you Mt 6:32 *3770*
"Every plant which My **h** Father Mt 15:13 *3770*
"My **h** Father will also do the same Mt 18:35 *3770*
of the **h** host praising God and Lk 2:13 *3770*
how much more will *your* **h** Father Lk 11:13 *1537, 3772*
believe if I tell you **h** things? Jn 3:12 *2032*
prove disobedient to the **h** vision, Ac 26:19 *3770*
also **h** bodies and earthly bodies, 1Co 15:40 *2032*
but the glory of the **h** is one, 1Co 15:40 *2032*
and as is the **h**, so also are those 1Co 15:48 *2032*
so also are those who are **h**. 1Co 15:48 *2032*
also bear the image of the **h**. 1Co 15:49 *2032*
in the **h** *places* in Christ, Eph 1:3 *2032*
at His right hand in the **h** *places*, Eph 1:20 *2032*
us with Him in the **h** Eph 2:6 *2032*
the authorities in the **h** *places*. Eph 3:10 *2032*
of wickedness in the **h** *places*. Eph 6:12 *2032*
bring me safely to His **h** kingdom; 2Tm 4:18 *2032*
partakers of a **h** calling, Heb 3:1 *2032*
have tasted of the **h** gift and have Heb 6:4 *2032*
a copy and shadow of the **h** things, Heb 8:5 *2032*
but the **h** things themselves with Heb 9:23 *2032*
a better *country*, that is, a **h** one. Heb 11:16 *2032*
the living God, the **h** Jerusalem, Heb 12:22 *2032*

HEAVENS

God created the **h** and the earth. Gn 1:1 8064
the waters below the **h** be gathered Gn 1:9 8064
be lights in the expanse of the **h** Gn 1:14 8064
h to give light on the earth"; Gn 1:15 8064
the **h** to give light on the earth, Gn 1:17 8064
in the open expanse of the **h**." Gn 1:20 8064
h and the earth were completed, Gn 2:1 8064
This is the account of the **h** and Gn 2:4 8064
under the **h** were covered. Gn 7:19 8064
"Now look toward the **h**, Gn 15:5 8064
your seed as the stars of the **h** and Gn 22:17 8064
the LORD made the **h** and the earth, Ex 20:11 8064
descendants as the stars of the **h**, Ex 32:13 8064
peoples everywhere under the **h**, Dt 2:25 8064
fire to the *very* heart of the **h**: Dt 4:11 8064
one end of the **h** to the other. Dt 4:32 8064
"Out of the **h** He let you hear His Dt 4:36 8064
belong heaven and the highest **h**, Dt 10:14 8064
and He will shut up the **h** so that Dt 11:17 8064
as the **h** *remain* above the earth. Dt 11:21 8064
you His good storehouse, the **h**, Dt 28:12 8064
call the **h** and the earth to witness Dt 31:28 8064
"Give ear, O **h**, and let me speak; Dt 32:1 8064
Who rides the **h** to your help, Dt 33:26 8064
His **h** also drop down dew. Dt 33:28 8064
earth quaked, the **h** also dripped, Jg 5:4 8064
them He will thunder in the **h** 1Sa 2:10 8064
"He bowed the **h** also, and came 2Sa 22:10 8064
"When the **h** are shut up and there 1Ki 8:35 8064
field the birds of the **h** will eat; 1Ki 14:11 8064
the birds of the **h** will eat." 1Ki 16:4 8064
idols, But the LORD made the **h**. 1Ch 16:26 8064
Let the **h** be glad, and let the 1Ch 16:31 8064
that is in the **h** and the earth; 1Ch 29:11 8064
for the **h** and the highest heavens 2Ch 2:6 8064
the highest **h** cannot contain Him? 2Ch 2:6 8064
"When the **h** are shut up and there 2Ch 6:26 8064
If I shut up the **h** so that there is no 2Ch 7:13 8064
are You not God in the **h**? 2Ch 20:6 8064
our guilt has grown even to the **h**. Ezr 9:6 8064
in the most remote part of the **h**, Ne 1:9 8064
You have made the **h**, Ne 9:6 8064
heaven of **h** with all their host, Ne 9:6 8064
Who alone stretches out the **h** And Jb 9:8 8064
They are high as the **h**, Jb 11:8 8064
And the birds of the **h**, Jb 12:7 8064
Until the **h** are no longer, He will Jb 14:12 8064
the **h** are not pure in His sight; Jb 15:15 8064
his loftiness reaches the **h**, Jb 20:6 8064
"The **h** will reveal his iniquity, Jb 20:27 8064
"By His breath the **h** are cleared; Jb 26:13 8064
And sees everything under the **h**. Jb 28:24 8064
"Look at the **h** and see; Jb 35:5 8064
us wiser than the birds of the **h**? Jb 35:11 8064
you know the ordinances of the **h**, Jb 38:33 8064
Or tip the water jars of the **h**, Jb 38:37 8064
He who sits in the **h** laughs, Ps 2:4 8064
Your splendor above the **h** Ps 8:1 8064
When I consider Your **h**, Ps 8:3 8064
The birds of the **h** and Ps 8:8 8064
He bowed the **h** also, and came down Ps 18:9 8064
The LORD also thundered in the **h**, Ps 18:13 8064
The **h** are telling of the glory of Ps 19:1 8064
rising is from one end of the **h**, Ps 19:6 8064
word of the LORD the **h** were made, Ps 33:6 8064
O LORD, extends to the **h**, Ps 36:5 8064
He summons the **h** above, And the Ps 50:4 8064
the **h** declare His righteousness, Ps 50:6 8064
Be exalted above the **h**, Ps 57:5 8064
lovingkindness is great to the **h** And Ps 57:10 8064
Be exalted above the **h**, Ps 57:11 8064
The **h** also dropped *rain* at the Ps 68:8 8064
Him who rides upon the highest **h**, Ps 68:33 8064
O God, *reaches* to the **h**, Ps 71:19 4791
set their mouth against the **h**, Ps 73:9 8064
the east wind to blow in the **h** And Ps 78:26 8064
for food to the birds of the **h**, Ps 79:2 8064
In the **h** You will establish Your Ps 89:2 8064
The **h** will praise Your wonders, Ps 89:5 8064
The **h** are Yours, the earth also is Ps 89:11 8064
idols, But the LORD made the **h**. Ps 96:5 8064
Let the **h** be glad, and let the Ps 96:11 8064
The **h** declare His righteousness, Ps 97:6 8064
the **h** are the work of Your hands. Ps 102:25 8064
high as the **h** are above the earth, Ps 103:11 8064
established His throne in the **h**, Ps 103:19 8064
them the birds of the **h** dwell; Ps 104:12 8064
They rose up to the **h**, Ps 107:26 8064
is great above the **h**, Ps 108:4 8064
Be exalted, O God, above the **h**, Ps 108:5 8064
His glory is above the **h**. Ps 113:4 8064
But our God is in the **h**; Ps 115:3 8064
The **h** are the heavens of the Ps 115:16 8064
The heavens are the **h** of the LORD, Ps 115:16 8064
O You who are enthroned in the **h**! Ps 123:1 8064
To Him who made the **h** with skill, Ps 136:5 8064
Bow Your **h**, O LORD, and come down; Ps 144:5 8064
Who covers the **h** with clouds, Who Ps 147:8 8064
Praise the LORD from the **h**; Ps 148:1 8064
Praise Him, highest **h**, Ps 148:4 8064
the waters that are above the **h**! Ps 148:4 8064
He established the **h**. Pr 3:19 8064
"When He established the **h**, Pr 8:27 8064
an eagle that flies *toward* the **h**. Pr 23:5 8064
As the **h** for height and the earth Pr 25:3 8064
bird of the **h** will carry the sound and Ec 10:20 8064
Listen, O **h**, and hear, O earth; Is 1:2 8064
I will make the **h** tremble, Is 13:13 8064
And marked off the **h** by the span, Is 40:12 8064
stretches out the **h** like a curtain Is 40:22 8064
Who created the **h** and stretched Is 42:5 8064
Shout for joy, O **h**, Is 44:23 8064
Stretching out the **h** by Myself And Is 44:24 8064
"Drip down, O **h**, from above, And Is 45:8 8064
I stretched out the **h** with My hands Is 45:12 8064
says the LORD, who created the **h** Is 45:18 8064
My right hand spread out the **h**; Is 48:13 8064
Shout for joy, O **h**! Is 49:13 8064
"I clothe the **h** with blackness And Is 50:3 8064
Maker, Who stretched out the **h** Is 51:13 8064
to establish the **h**, to found the earth, Is 51:16 8064
the **h** are higher than the earth, Is 55:9 8064
would rend the **h** *and* come down, Is 64:1 8064
I create new **h** and a new earth; Is 65:17 8064
"For just as the new **h** and the Is 66:22 8064
"Be appalled, O **h**, at this, And Jer 2:12 8064
And to the **h**, and they had no Jer 4:23 8064
all the birds of the **h** had fled. Jer 4:25 8064
mourn And the **h** above be dark, Jer 4:28 8064
not be terrified by the signs of the **h** Jer 10:2 8064
"The gods that did not make the **h** Jer 10:11 8065
the earth and from under the **h**." Jer 10:11 8065
He has stretched out the **h**. Jer 10:12 8064
is a tumult of waters in the **h**, Jer 10:13 8064
Or can the **h** grant showers? Jer 14:22 8064
I not fill the **h** and the earth?" Jer 23:24 8064
"If the **h** above can be measured Jer 31:37 8064
You have made the **h** and the earth Jer 32:17 8064
He stretched out the **h**. Jer 51:15 8064
is a tumult of waters in the **h**, Jer 51:16 8064
Babylon should ascend to the **h**, Jer 51:53 8064
them From under the **h** of the LORD! La 3:66 8064
the **h** were opened and I saw Ezk 1:1 8064
birds of the **h** nested in its boughs, Ezk 31:6 8064
all the birds of the **h** will dwell, Ezk 31:13 8064
birds of the **h** to dwell on you, Ezk 32:4 8064
you, I will cover the **h** and Ezk 32:7 8064
All the shining lights in the **h** Ezk 32:8 8064
of the sea, the birds of the **h**, Ezk 38:20 8064
"I will respond to the **h**, Hos 2:21 8064
the earth quakes, The **h** tremble, Jl 2:10 8064
And the **h** and the earth tremble. Jl 3:16 8064
His upper chambers in the **h** And Am 9:6 8064
His splendor covers the **h**, Hab 3:3 8064
to shake the **h** and the earth, Hg 2:6 8064
to shake the **h** and the earth. Hg 2:21 8064
you as the four winds of the **h**," Zch 2:6 8064
ephah between the earth and the **h**. Zch 5:9 8064
and the **h** will give their dew; Zch 8:12 8064
the LORD who stretches out the **h**, Zch 12:1 8064
and behold, the **h** were opened, and Mt 3:16 *3772*
and behold, a voice out of the **h** Mt 3:17 *3772*
powers of the **h** will be shaken. Mt 24:29 *3772*
the water, He saw the **h** opening, Mk 1:10 *3772*
and a voice came out of the **h**: Mk 1:11 *3772*
that are in the **h** will be shaken. Mk 13:25 *3772*
powers of the **h** will be shaken. Lk 21:26 *3772*
you, you will see the **h** opened Jn 1:51 *3772*
I see the **h** opened up and the Son Ac 7:56 *3772*
made with hands, eternal in the **h**. 2Co 5:1 *3772*
the **h** and things on the earth. Eph 1:10 *3772*
who ascended far above all the **h**, Eph 4:10 *3772*
both in the **h** and on earth, Col 1:16 *3772*
THE **H** ARE THE WORKS OF YOUR HANDS; Heb 1:10 *3772*
who has passed through the **h**, Heb 4:14 *3772*
sinners and exalted above the **h**; Heb 7:26 *3772*
throne of the Majesty in the **h**, Heb 8:1 *3772*
the **h** to be cleansed with these, Heb 9:23 *3772*
by the word of God *the* **h** existed long 2Pe 3:5 *3772*
by His word the present **h** and earth 2Pe 3:7 *3772*
in which the **h** will pass away with 2Pe 3:10 *3772*
h will be destroyed by burning, 2Pe 3:12 *3772*
looking for new **h** and a new earth, 2Pe 3:13 *3772*
O **h** and you who dwell in them. Rv 12:12 *3772*

HEAVIER

"Let the labor be **h** on the men, Ex 5:9 3513
hand of the sons of Israel pressed **h** Jg 4:24 1980
h upon Jabin the king of Canaan, Jg 4:24 7186
be **h** than the sand of the seas; Jb 6:3 3513
provocation of a fool is **h** than both Pr 27:3 3515

HEAVILY

The battle went **h** against Saul, 1Sa 31:3 3513
should my pressure weigh **h** on you. Jb 33:7 3513
let us drink **h** of strong drink; Is 56:12 5433a

HEAVY

I will send a very **h** hail, Ex 9:18 3515
But Moses' hands were **h**. Ex 17:12 3515
for the task is too **h** for you; Ex 18:18 3515
out against him with a **h** force and Nu 20:20 3515
and he died, for he was old and **h**. 1Sa 4:18 3513
the hand of the LORD was **h** on the 1Sa 5:6 3513
the hand of God was very **h** there. 1Sa 5:11 3513
for it was **h** on him so he cut it), 2Sa 14:26 3515
and his **h** yoke which he put on us, 1Ki 12:4 3515
'Your father made our yoke **h**, 1Ki 12:10 3513
father loaded you with a **h** yoke, 1Ki 12:11 3515
"My father made your yoke **h**, 1Ki 12:14 3513
is the sound of the roar of a **h** 1Ki 18:41
so that the **h** shower does not 1Ki 18:44
wind, and there was a **h** shower. 1Ki 18:45 1419
The battle became **h** against Saul, 1Ch 10:3 3513
and his **h** yoke which he put on us, 2Ch 10:4 3515
'Your father made our yoke **h**, 2Ch 10:10 3513
father loaded you with a **h** yoke, 2Ch 10:11 3515
"My father made your yoke **h**, 2Ch 10:14 3513
inflicted him with **h** casualties. 2Ch 28:5 1419
of this matter and the **h** rain. Ezr 10:9
servitude was **h** on this people. Ne 5:18 3513
And made his thighs **h** with flesh. Jb 15:27 6371b
His hand is **h** despite my groaning. Jb 23:2 3513
and night Your hand was **h** upon me; Ps 32:4 3513
As a **h** burden they weigh too much Ps 38:4 3515
Do not be with **h** drinkers of wine, Pr 23:20 5433a
For the **h** drinker and the glutton Pr 23:21 5433a
A stone is **h** and the sand weighty, Pr 27:3 3514
though a man's trouble is **h** upon him. Ec 8:6 7227a
its transgression is **h** upon it, Is 24:20 3513
And your sins like a **h** mist. Is 44:22 6051
aged you made your yoke very **h**. Is 47:6 3513
you will cry out with a **h** heart, Is 65:14 3511
He has made my chain **h**. La 3:7 3513
because you impose **h** rent on the Am 5:11 1318
I will make Jerusalem a **h** stone for Zch 12:3 4614
better for him to have a **h** millstone Mt 18:6 *3684*
"They tie up **h** burdens and lay Mt 23:4 *926*

sleeping, for their eyes were **h**. Mt 26:43 *916*
with a **h** millstone hung around his Mk 9:42 *3684*
for their eyes were very **h**; Mk 14:40 *2599b*

HEAVY-LADEN
to Me, all who are weary and **h**, Mt 11:28 *5412*

HEBER
the sons of Beriah: **H** and Malchiel. Gn 46:17 2268
of **H**, the family of the Heberites; Nu 26:45 2268
Now **H** the Kenite had separated Jg 4:11 2268
of Jael the wife of **H** the Kenite, Jg 4:17 2268
and the house of **H** the Kenite. Jg 4:17 2268
is Jael, The wife of **H** the Kenite; Jg 5:24 2268
Gedor, and **H** the father of Soco, 1Ch 4:18 2268
of Beriah *were* **H** and Malchiel, 1Ch 7:31 2268
H became the father of Japhlet, 1Ch 7:32 2268
Zebadiah, Meshullam, Hizki, **H**, 1Ch 8:17 2268
the son of Peleg, the son of **H**, Lk 3:35 *1443*

HEBERITES
of Heber, the family of the **H**; Nu 26:45 2277

HEBER'S
But Jael, **H** wife, took a tent peg Jg 4:21 2268

HEBREW
came and told Abram the **H**. Gn 14:13 5680
brought in a **H** to us to make sport Gn 39:14 5680
"The **H** slave, whom you brought to Gn 39:17 5680
"Now a **H** youth *was* with us there, Gn 41:12 5680
of Egypt spoke to the **H** midwives, Ex 1:15 5680
helping the **H** women to give birth Ex 1:16 5680
H women are not as the Egyptian Ex 1:19 5680
a nurse for you from the **H** women Ex 2:7 5680
he saw an Egyptian beating a **H**, Ex 2:11 5680
"If you buy a **H** slave, he shall Ex 21:2 5680
"If your kinsman, a **H** man or woman, Dt 15:12 5680
a **H** man or a Hebrew woman; Jer 34:9 5680
a Hebrew man or a **H** woman; Jer 34:9 5680
you shall set free his **H** brother who Jer 34:14 5680
"I am a **H**, and I fear the LORD Jon 1:9 5680
which is called in **H** Bethesda, Jn 5:2 *1447*
called The Pavement, but in **H**, Jn 19:13 *1447*
which is called in **H**, Golgotha. Jn 19:17 *1447*
and it was written in **H**, Jn 19:20 *1447*
She turned and said to Him in **H**, Jn 20:16 *1447*
he spoke to them in the **H** dialect, Ac 21:40 *1446*
addressing them in the **H** dialect, Ac 22:2 *1446*
saying to me in the **H** dialect, Ac 26:14 *1446*
tribe of Benjamin, a **H** of Hebrews; Php 3:5 *1445*
his name in **H** is Abaddon, and in Rv 9:11 *1447*
which in **H** is called Har-Magedon. Rv 16:16 *1447*

HEBREWS
kidnapped from the land of the **H**, Gn 40:15 5680
could not eat bread with the **H**, Gn 43:32 5680
H were fighting with each other; Ex 2:13 5680
'The LORD, the God of the **H**, Ex 3:18 5680
"The God of the **H** has met with us. Ex 5:3 5680
'The LORD, the God of the **H**, Ex 7:16 5680
says the LORD, the God of the **H**, Ex 9:1 5680
says the LORD, the God of the **H**, Ex 9:13 5680
says the LORD, the God of the **H**, Ex 10:3 5680
great shout in the camp of the **H** 1Sa 4:6 5680
or you will become slaves to the **H**, 1Sa 4:9 5680
"Let the **H** hear." 1Sa 13:3 5680
Also *some of the* **H** crossed the 1Sa 13:7 5680
the **H** will make swords or spears." 1Sa 13:19 5680
H are coming out of the holes 1Sa 14:11 5680
the **H** *who* were with the Philistines 1Sa 14:21 5680
"What *are* these **H** *doing here?*" 1Sa 29:3 5680
Jews against the *native* **H**, Ac 6:1 *1445*
Are they **H**? So am I. Are they 2Co 11:22 *1445*
tribe of Benjamin, a Hebrew of **H**; Php 3:5 *1445*

HEBREWS'
"This is one of the **H** children." Ex 2:6 5680

HEBRON
the oaks of Mamre, which are in **H**, Gn 13:18 2275a
died in Kiriath-arba (that is, **H**) Gn 23:2 2275a
Machpelah facing Mamre (that is, **H**) Gn 23:19 2275a
Mamre of Kiriath-arba (that is, **H**), Gn 35:27 2275a
he sent him from the valley of **H**, Gn 37:14 2275a
Amram and Izhar and **H** and Uzziel; Ex 6:18 2275b
Amram and Izhar, **H** and Uzziel; Nu 3:19 2275b
they came to **H** where Ahiman, Nu 13:22 2275a
(Now **H** was built seven years Nu 13:22 2275a
sent *word* to Hoham king of **H** Jos 10:3 2275a
king of Jerusalem, the king of **H**, Jos 10:5 2275a
king of Jerusalem, the king of **H**, Jos 10:23 2275a
with him went up from Eglon to **H**, Jos 10:36 2275a
Just as he had done to **H**, Jos 10:39 2275a
from the hill country, from **H**, Jos 11:21 2275a
the king of **H**, one; Jos 12:10 2275a
and gave **H** to Caleb the son of Jos 14:13 2275a
H became the inheritance of Caleb Jos 14:14 2275a
of **H** was formerly Kiriath-arba; Jos 14:15 2275a
the father of Anak (that is, **H**). Jos 15:13 2275a
and Kiriath-arba (that is, **H**), Jos 15:54 2275a
and Kiriath-arba (that is, **H**) Jos 20:7 2275a
the father of Anak (that is, **H**), Jos 21:11 2275a
of Aaron the priest they gave **H**, Jos 21:13 2275a
the Canaanites who lived in **H** Jg 1:10 2275a
of **H** formerly *was* Kiriath-arba); Jg 1:10 2275a
Then they gave **H** to Caleb, as Jg 1:20 2275a
the mountain which is opposite **H**. Jg 16:3 2275a
and to those who were in **H**, 1Sa 30:31 2275a
shall I go up?" And He said, "To **H**." 2Sa 2:1 2275a
and they lived in the cities of **H**. 2Sa 2:3 2275a
David was king in **H** over the house 2Sa 2:11 2275a
night until the day dawned at **H**. 2Sa 2:32 2275a
Sons were born to David at **H**: 2Sa 3:2 2275a
These were born to David at **H**. 2Sa 3:5 2275a
to speak in the hearing of David in **H** 2Sa 3:19 2275a
men with him came to David at **H**. 2Sa 3:20 2275a
but Abner was not with David in **H**, 2Sa 3:22 2275a
So when Abner returned to **H**, 2Sa 3:27 2275a
Thus they buried Abner in **H**; 2Sa 3:32 2275a
heard that Abner had died in **H**, 2Sa 4:1 2275a
head of Ish-bosheth to David at **H** and 2Sa 4:8 2275a
hung them up beside the pool in **H**. 2Sa 4:12 2275a
it in the grave of Abner in **H**. 2Sa 4:12 2275a
came to David at **H** and said, 2Sa 5:1 2275a
of Israel came to the king at **H**, 2Sa 5:3 2275a
with them before the LORD at **H**; 2Sa 5:3 2275a
At **H** he reigned over Judah seven 2Sa 5:5 2275a
Jerusalem, after he came from **H** 2Sa 5:13 2275a
I have vowed to the LORD, in **H**. 2Sa 15:7 2275a
So he arose and went to **H**. 2Sa 15:9 2275a
'Absalom is king in **H**.'" 2Sa 15:10 2275a
seven years he reigned in **H** and 1Ki 2:11 2275a
son was Mareshah, the father of **H**. 1Ch 2:42 2275b
The sons of **H** *were* Korah and 1Ch 2:43 2275b
David who were born to him in **H**: 1Ch 3:1 2275a
Six were born to him in **H**, 1Ch 3:4 2275a
of Kohath *were* Amram, Izhar, **H** and 1Ch 6:2 2275b
of Kohath *were* Amram, Izhar, **H** and 1Ch 6:18 2275b
they gave **H** in the land of Judah and 1Ch 6:55 2275a
H, Libnah also with its pasture 1Ch 6:57 2275a
gathered to David at **H** and said, 1Ch 11:1 2275a
of Israel came to the king at **H**, 1Ch 11:3 2275a
with them in **H** before the LORD; 1Ch 11:3 2275a
for war, who came to David at **H**, 1Ch 12:23 2275a
came to **H** with a perfect heart to 1Ch 12:38 2275a
of the sons of **H**, Eliel the chief, 1Ch 15:9 2275b
Amram, Izhar, **H** and Uzziel. 1Ch 23:12 2275b
sons of **H** *were* Jeriah the first, 1Ch 23:19 2275b
The sons *of* **H**: Jeriah 1Ch 24:23
he reigned in **H** seven years and in 1Ch 29:27 2275a
Zorah, Aijalon and **H**, 2Ch 11:10 2275a

HEBRONITES
Izharites and the family of the **H** and Nu 3:27 2276
the Libnites, the family of the **H**, Nu 26:58 2276
Amramites, the Izharites, the **H** 1Ch 26:23 2276
As for the **H**, Hashabiah and his 1Ch 26:30 2276
As for the **H**, Jerijah the chief 1Ch 26:31 2276
these **H** were investigated according 1Ch 26:31 2276

HEDGE
"Have You not made a **h** about him Jb 1:10 7753
the lazy is as a **h** of thorns, Pr 15:19 4881
My vineyard: I will remove its **h** Is 5:5 4905a
I will **h** up her way with thorns, Hos 2:6 7753
The most upright like a thorn **h**. Mi 7:4 4534

HEDGED
is hidden, And whom God has **h** in? Jb 3:23 5480b

HEDGEHOG
make it a possession for the **h** and Is 14:23 7090
pelican and **h** will possess it, Is 34:11 7090
pelican and the **h** Will lodge in the Zph 2:14 7090

HEDGES
Why have You broken down its **h**, Ps 80:12 1447
into the highways and along the **h**, Lk 14:23 *5418*

HEED
of Lamech, Give **h** to my speech, Gn 4:23 238
has given **h** to your affliction. Gn 16:11 8085
God gave **h** to Leah, and she Gn 30:17 8085
gave **h** to her and opened her womb. Gn 30:22 8085
and have given **h** to their cry Ex 3:7 8085
They will pay **h** to what you say; Ex 3:18 8085
h the witness of the first sign, Ex 4:8 8085
these two signs or **h** what you say, Ex 4:9 8085
Take **h**, for evil is in your mind. Ex 10:10 7200
"If you will give earnest **h** to Ex 15:26 8085
"Only give **h** to yourself and keep Dt 4:9 8104
"So take diligent **h** to yourselves Jos 23:11 8104
And to **h** than the fat of rams. 1Sa 15:22 7181
if only your sons take **h** to their 1Ki 8:25 8104
your sons take **h** to their way, 2Ch 6:16 8104
H the sound of my cry for help, my Ps 5:2 7181
cause, O LORD, give **h** to my cry; Ps 17:1 7181
Give **h** to me and answer me; Ps 55:2 7181
Give **h** to my prayer. Ps 61:1 7181
given **h** to the voice of my prayer. Ps 66:19 7181
And give **h** to the voice of my Ps 86:6 7181
Nor does the God of Jacob pay **h**." Ps 94:7 995
Pay **h**, you senseless among the Ps 94:8 995
will give **h** to the blameless way. Ps 101:2 7919a
Let him give **h** to these things, Ps 107:43 8104
"Give **h** to my cry, For I am Ps 142:6 7181
"**H** instruction and be wise, And Pr 8:33 8085
will give **h** and listen hereafter? Is 42:23 7181
h the word of the LORD. Jer 2:31 7200
not **h** the words of this covenant Jer 11:3 8085
Listen and give **h**, do not be Jer 13:15 238
"Take **h** for yourselves, and do Jer 17:21 8104
give no **h** to any of his words." Jer 18:18 7181
Do give **h** to me, O LORD, And Jer 18:19 7181
necks so as not to **h** My words.' Jer 19:15 8085
given **h** to His word and listened? Jer 23:18 7181
so give **h** to the message and gain Da 9:23 995
have stopped giving **h** to the LORD. Hos 4:10 8104
Give **h**, O house of Israel! Hos 5:1 7181
did not listen or give **h** to Me," Zch 1:4 7181
Take **h** then to your spirit, and Mal 2:15 8104
"So take **h** to your spirit, that Mal 2:16 8104
not receive you, nor **h** your words, Mt 10:14 *191*
"But take **h**; behold, I have told you Mk 13:23 *991*
"Take **h**, keep on the alert; Mk 13:33 *991*
to you and give **h** to my words. Ac 2:14 *1801*
TO HIM YOU SHALL GIVE **H** to Ac 3:22 *191*
soul that does not **h** that prophet shall Ac 3:23 *191*
give **h** to you rather than to God, Ac 4:19 *191*
"Therefore take **h**, so that the Ac 13:40 *991*
did not all **h** the good news; Ro 10:16 *5219*
let him who thinks he stands take **h** 1Co 10:12 *991*
"Take **h** to the ministry which you Col 4:17 *991*
and **h** the things which are written Rv 1:3 *5083*
who **h** the words of this book. Rv 22:9 *5083*

HEEDED
despised and his words are not **h**. Ec 9:16 8085
She **h** no voice, She accepted no Zph 3:2 8085

HEEDLESSLY
But they went up **h** to the ridge of Nu 14:44 6075b

HEEDS
path of life who **h** instruction, Pr 10:17 8104
Blessed is he who **h** the words of Rv 22:7 *5083*

HEEL
you shall bruise him on the **h**." Gn 3:15 6119
his hand holding on to Esau's **h**, Gn 25:26 6119
"A snare seizes *him* by the **h**, Jb 18:9 6119
Has lifted up his **h** against me. Ps 41:9 6119
womb he took his brother by the **h**, Hos 12:3 6117
WHO EATS MY BREAD HAS LIFTED UP HIS **H** Jn 13:18 *4418*

HEELS
the path, That bites the horse's **h**, Gn 49:17 6119
But he will raid *at* their **h**. Gn 49:19 6119
the valley they rushed at his **h**; Jg 5:15 7272
And your **h** have been exposed. Jer 13:22 6119
Ethiopians *will follow* at his **h**. Da 11:43 4703

HEGAI
the harem, into the custody of **H**, Es 2:3 1896a
of Susa into the custody of **H**, Es 2:8 1896a
palace into the custody of **H**, Es 2:8 1896a
request anything except what **H**, Es 2:15 1896a

HEIFER
"Bring Me a three year old **h**, Gn 15:9 5697
red **h** in which is no defect Nu 19:2 6499
h shall be burned in his sight; Nu 19:5 6499
into the midst of the burning **h**. Nu 19:6 6499
shall gather up the ashes of the **h** and Nu 19:9 6499
one who gathers the ashes of the **h** Nu 19:10 6499
city, shall take a **h** of the herd, Dt 21:3 5697
shall bring the **h** down to a valley Dt 21:4 5697
over the **h** whose neck was broken Dt 21:6 5697
"If you had not plowed with my **h**, Jg 14:18 5697
"Take a **h** with you and say, 1Sa 16:2 5697
alive a **h** and a pair of sheep; Is 7:21 5697
"Egypt is a pretty **h**, Jer 46:20 5697
h And neigh like stallions, Jer 50:11 5697
Israel is stubborn Like a stubborn **h** Hos 4:16 6499
a trained **h** that loves to thresh, Hos 10:11 5697
goats and bulls and the ashes of a **h** Heb 9:13 *1151*

HEIFER'S
the **h** neck there in the valley. Dt 21:4 5697

HEIGHT
cubits, and its **h** thirty cubits. Gn 6:15 6967
and its **h** shall be three cubits. Ex 27:1 6967
and the **h** five cubits of fine Ex 27:18 6967
and its **h** *shall be* two cubits; Ex 30:2 6967
and its **h** one and a half cubits; Ex 37:1 6967
cubits and the **h** *was* five cubits, Ex 38:18 6967
or at the **h** of his stature, 1Sa 16:7 6967
whose **h** was six cubits and a span. 1Sa 17:4 1363
under the tamarisk tree on the **h** 1Sa 22:6 7413
Ben-abinadab, *in* all the **h** of Dor 1Ki 4:11 5299b
cubits and its **h** thirty cubits. 1Ki 6:2 6967
in width, and twenty cubits in **h**, 1Ki 6:20 6967
The **h** of the one cherub *was* ten 1Ki 6:26 6967
50 cubits and its **h** 30 cubits, 1Ki 7:2 6967
cubits was the **h** of one pillar, 1Ki 7:15 6967
the **h** of the one capital was five 1Ki 7:16 6967
the **h** of the other capital was five 1Ki 7:16 6967
form, and its **h** was five cubits, 1Ki 7:23 6967
cubits and its **h** three cubits. 1Ki 7:27 6967
And the **h** of a wheel *was* a cubit 1Ki 7:32 6967
The **h** of the one pillar was 2Ki 25:17 6967
the **h** of the capital was three 2Ki 25:17 6967
twenty cubits, and the **h** 120; 2Ch 3:4 1363
in width and ten cubits in **h**. 2Ch 4:1 6967
and its **h** *was* five cubits and its 2Ch 4:2 6967
its **h** being 60 cubits and its Ezr 6:3 7314
was joined together to half its **h**, Ne 4:6
"Is not God *in* the **h** of heaven? Jb 22:12 1363
He looked down from His holy **h**; Ps 102:19 4791
As the heavens for **h** and the earth Pr 25:3 7312
here, You who hew a tomb on the **h**, Is 22:16 4791
shout for joy on the **h** of Zion, Jer 31:12 4791
Who occupy the **h** of the hill. Jer 49:16 4791
the **h** of each pillar *was* eighteen Jer 52:21 6967
and the **h** of each capital was five Jer 52:22 6967
And its **h** was raised above the Ezk 19:11 6967
it was seen in its **h** with the mass Ezk 19:11 1363
Therefore its **h** was loftier than Ezk 31:5 6967
ones stand *erect* in their **h**. Ezk 31:14 6967
and the **h**, one rod. Ezk 40:5 6967
a full rod of six long cubits *in* **h**. Ezk 41:8
and this *shall be* the **h** of Ezk 43:13
the **h** of which *was* sixty cubits Da 3:1 7314
of the earth and its **h** *was* great. Da 4:10 7314
And its **h** reached to the sky, Da 4:11 7314
whose **h** reached to the sky and was Da 4:20 7314
Though his **h** *was* like the height Am 2:9 1363
Though his height *was* like the **h** Am 2:9 1363
nor **h**, nor depth, nor any other Ro 8:39 *5313*
and length and **h** and depth, Eph 3:18 *5311*
length and width and **h** are equal. Rv 21:16 *5311*

HEIGHTS
Moab, The dominant **h** of the Arnon. Nu 21:28 1181

and on the **h** of Dor on the west **Jos 11:2** 5299b
the king of Dor in the **h** of Dor, **Jos 12:23** 5299b
came up to the **h** of the mountains, **2Ki 19:23** 4791
Who establishes peace in His **h**. **Jb 25:2** 4791
He built His sanctuary like the **h**, **Ps 78:69** 7311
Praise Him in the **h**! **Ps 148:1** 4791
On top of the **h** beside the way, **Pr 8:2** 4791
the tops of the **h** of the city: **Pr 9:3** 4791
ascend above the **h** of the clouds; **Is 14:14** 1116
He will dwell on the **h**, **Is 33:16** 4791
came up to the **h** of the mountains, **Is 37:24** 4791
My eyes look wistfully to the **h**; **Is 38:14** 4791
"I will open rivers on the bare **h** And **Is 41:18** 8205
pasture *will be* on all bare **h**. **Is 49:9** 8205
you ride on the **h** of the earth; **Is 58:14** 1116
your eyes to the bare **h** and see; **Jer 3:2** 8205
A voice is heard on the bare **h**, **Jer 3:21** 8205
"A scorching wind from the bare **h** **Jer 4:11** 8205
up a lamentation on the bare **h**; **Jer 7:29** 8205
"On all the bare **h** in the **Jer 12:12** 8205
wild donkeys stand on the bare **h**; **Jer 14:6** 8205
be on the mountain **h** of Israel. **Ezk 34:14** 4791
The everlasting **h** have become our **Ezk 36:2** 1116

HEIR
and the **h** of my house is Eliezer **Gn 15:2** 1121, 4943
one born in my house is my **h**." **Gn 15:3** 3423
"This man will not be your **h**; **Gn 15:4** 3423
own body, he shall be your **h**." **Gn 15:4** 3423
not be an **h** with my son Isaac." **Gn 21:10** 3423
killed, and destroy the **h** also.' **2Sa 14:7** 3423
an **h** of My mountains from Judah; **Is 65:9** 3423
'This is the **h**; come, let us kill him **Mt 21:38** *2818*
'This is the **h**; come, let us kill him, **Mk 12:7** *2818*
'This is the **h**; let us kill him so that **Lk 20:14** *2818*
that he would be **h** of the world was **Ro 4:13** *2818*
say, as long as the **h** is a child, **Ga 4:1** *2818*
if a son, then an **h** through God. **Ga 4:7** *2818*
OF THE BONDWOMAN SHALL NOT BE AN **H** **Ga 4:30** *2816*
whom He appointed **h** of all things, **Heb 1:2** *2818*
became an **h** of the righteousness **Heb 11:7** *2818*
a fellow **h** of the grace of life, **1Pe 3:7** *4789*

HEIRS
Israel have no sons? Or has he no **h**? **Jer 49:1** 3423
if those who are of the Law are **h**, **Ro 4:14** *2818*
and if children, **h** also, **Ro 8:17** *2818*
h of God and fellow heirs **Ro 8:17** *2818*
of God and fellow **h** with Christ, **Ro 8:17** *4789*
descendants, **h** according to promise. **Ga 3:29** *2818*
that the Gentiles are fellow **h** and **Eph 3:6** *4789*
we would be made **h** according to *the* **Ti 3:7** *2818*
to show to the **h** of the promise **Heb 6:17** *2818*
fellow **h** of the same promise; **Heb 11:9** *4789*
world *to be* rich in faith and **h** **Jas 2:5** *2818*

HELAH
had two wives, **H** and Naarah. **1Ch 4:5** 2458
The sons of **H** *were* Zereth, **1Ch 4:7** 2458

HELAM
the River, and they came to **H**; **2Sa 10:16** 2431
crossed the Jordan, and came to **H**. **2Sa 10:17** 2431

HELBAH
of Ahlab, or of Achzib, or of **H**, **Jg 1:31** 2462

HELBON
of the wine of **H** and white wool. **Ezk 27:18** 2463

HELD
about when Moses **h** his hand up, **Ex 17:11** 7311
LORD has **h** you back from honor." **Nu 24:11** 4513
"But you who **h** fast to the LORD **Dt 4:4** 1695
they **h** the torches in their left **Jg 7:20** 2388
and trod *them,* and **h** a festival; **Jg 9:27** 6213a
So she **h** it, and he measured six **Ru 3:15** 270
city, and the man is **h** in honor; **1Sa 9:6** 3513
that the plague may be **h** back from **2Sa 24:21** 6113
the plague was **h** back from Israel. **2Sa 24:25** 6113
bronze, one basin **h** forty baths; **1Ki 7:38** 3557
Solomon **h** fast to these in love. **1Ki 11:2** 1692
day they **h** a solemn assembly, **2Ch 7:9** 6213a
So he **h** Judah and Benjamin. **2Ch 11:12** 1961
while half of them **h** the spears, **Ne 4:16** 2388
I **h** a great assembly against them. **Ne 5:7** 5414
linen **h** by cords of fine purple linen **Es 1:6** 270
Complete darkness is **h** in reserve **Jb 20:26** 2934
"My foot has **h** fast to His path; **Jb 23:11** 270
My steps have **h** fast to Your paths. **Ps 17:5** 8551
You have **h** my eyelids *open;* **Ps 77:4** 270
be **h** with the cords of his sin. **Pr 5:22** 8551
I **h** on to him and would not let **SS 3:4** 270
proud And walk with heads **h** **Is 3:16** 5186
those who live in it are **h** guilty. **Is 24:6** 816
them captive have **h** them fast, **Jer 50:33** 2388
be laughed at and **h** in derision; **Ezk 23:32**
over it and **h** back its rivers. **Ezk 31:15** 4513
Belshazzar the king **h** a great feast **Da 5:1** 5648
Samaria will be **h** guilty, For she **Hos 13:16** 816
But they will be **h** guilty, **Hab 1:11** 816
immediately **h** a consultation; **Mk 15:1** *4160*
for Him to be **h** in its power. **Ac 2:24** *2902*
the people **h** them in high esteem. **Ac 5:13** *3170*
Paul appealed to be **h** in custody **Ac 25:21** *5083*
were **h** in bondage under the elemental **Ga 4:3** *1402*
body, being fitted and **h** together by **Eph 4:16** *4822*
and **h** together by the joints and **Col 2:19** *4822*
h captive by him to do his will. **2Tm 2:26** *2221*
Marriage *is to be* **h** in honor **Heb 13:4**
His right hand He **h** seven stars, **Rv 1:16** *2192*

HELDAI
was **H** the Netophathite of Othniel; **1Ch 27:15** 2469
offering from the exiles, from **H**, **Zch 6:10** 2469

HELEB
H the son of Baanah the **2Sa 23:29** 2460

HELED
H the son of Baanah the **1Ch 11:30** 2466

HELEK
of **H**, the family of the Helekites; **Nu 26:30** 2507a
sons of Abiezer and for the sons of **H** **Jos 17:2** 2507a

HELEKITES
of Helek, the family of the **H**; **Nu 26:30** 2516

HELEM
sons of his brother **H** *were* Zophah, **1Ch 7:35** 1987
in the temple of the LORD to **H**, **Zch 6:14** 2494

HELEPH
Their border was from **H**, **Jos 19:33** 2501

HELEZ
H the Paltite, Ira the son of **2Sa 23:26** 2503
Azariah became the father of **H**, **1Ch 2:39** 2503
H became the father of Eleasah, **1Ch 2:39** 2503
the Harorite, **H** the Pelonite, **1Ch 11:27** 2503
the seventh month *was* **H** the Pelonite **1Ch 27:10** 2503

HELIOPOLIS
also shatter the obelisks of **H**, **Jer 43:13** 1053

HELKAI
of Harim, Adna; of Meraioth, **H**; **Ne 12:15** 2517

HELKATH
Their territory was **H** and Hali **Jos 19:25** 2520
H with its pasture lands and Rehob **Jos 21:31** 2520

HELKATH-HAZZURIM
Therefore that place was called **H**, **2Sa 2:16** 2521

HELL
enough to go into the fiery **h**. **Mt 5:22** *1067*
whole body to be thrown into **h**. **Mt 5:29** *1067*
for your whole body to go into **h**. **Mt 5:30** *1067*
destroy both soul and body in **h**. **Mt 10:28** *1067*
eyes and be cast into the fiery **h**. **Mt 18:9** *1067*
as much a son of **h** as yourselves. **Mt 23:15** *1067*
you escape the sentence of **h**? **Mt 23:33** *1067*
your two hands, to go into **h**, **Mk 9:43** *1067*
your two feet, to be cast into **h**, **Mk 9:45** *1067*
two eyes, to be cast into **h**, **Mk 9:47** *1067*
has authority to cast into **h**; **Lk 12:5** *1067*
our life, and is set on fire by **h**. **Jas 3:6** *1067*
but cast them into **h** and committed **2Pe 2:4** *5020*

HELLENISTIC
the **H** *Jews* against the *native* Hebrews, **Ac 6:1** *1675*
and arguing with the **H** **Ac 9:29** *1675*

HELMET
He had a bronze **h** on his head, **1Sa 17:5** 3553
and put a bronze **h** on his head, **1Sa 17:38** 6959
Ephraim also is the **h** of My head; **Ps 60:7** 4581
Ephraim also is the **h** of My head; **Ps 108:8** 4581
And a **h** of salvation on His head; **Is 59:17** 3553
with buckler and shield and **h** **Ezk 23:24** 6959
They hung shield and **h** in you; **Ezk 27:10** 3553
all of them *with* shield and **h**; **Ezk 38:5** 3553
And take THE **H** OF SALVATION, **Eph 6:17** *4030*
of faith and love, and as a **h**, **1Th 5:8** *4030*

HELMETS
all the army shields, spears, **h**, **2Ch 26:14** 3553
And take your stand with **h** *on!* **Jer 46:4** 3553

HELON
of Zebulun, Eliab the son of **H**; **Nu 1:9** 2497
Eliab the son of **H**, **Nu 2:7** 2497
day *it was* Eliab the son of **H**, **Nu 7:24** 2497
offering of Eliab the son of **H**. **Nu 7:29** 2497
and Eliab the son of **H** over the **Nu 10:16** 2497

HELP
"I have gotten a manchild with *the* **h** **Gn 4:1**
cry for **h** because of *their* bondage **Ex 2:23** 7775
"The God of my father was my **h**, **Ex 18:4** 5828
certainly **h** him to raise *them* up. **Dt 22:4** 6965
Let them rise up and **h** you, **Dt 32:38** 5826
be a **h** against his adversaries." **Dt 33:7** 5828
Who rides the heavens to your **h**, **Dt 33:26** 5828
LORD, Who is the shield of your **h** **Dt 33:29** 5828
warriors, and shall **h** them, **Jos 1:14** 5826
"Come up to me and **h** me, **Jos 10:4** 5826
us quickly and save us and **h** us, **Jos 10:6** 5826
of Gezer came up to **h** Lachish, **Jos 10:33** 5826
did not come to the **h** of the LORD, **Jg 5:23** 5833
To the **h** of the LORD against the **Jg 5:23** 5833
of Damascus came to **h** Hadadezer, **2Sa 8:5** 5826
for me, then you shall **h** me, **2Sa 10:11** 3444
you, then I will come to **h** you. **2Sa 10:11** 3467
Arameans feared to **h** the sons of **2Sa 10:19** 3467
herself and said, "**H**, O king." **2Sa 14:4** 3467
be ready to **h** us from the city." **2Sa 18:3** 5826
my cry for **h** *came* into His ears. **2Sa 22:7** 7775
And Your **h** makes me great. **2Sa 22:36** 6038
"**H**, my lord, O king!" **2Ki 6:26** 3467
"If the LORD does not **h** you, **2Ki 6:27** 3467
you, from where shall I **h** you? **2Ki 6:27** 3467
you come peacefully to me to **h** me, **1Ch 12:17** 5826
But they did not **h** them, **1Ch 12:19** 5826
by day *men* came to David to **h** him, **1Ch 12:22** 5826
came to **h** Hadadezer king of Zobah, **1Ch 18:5** 5826
for me, then you shall **h** me; **1Ch 19:12** 1961, 8668
strong for you, then I will **h** you. **1Ch 19:12** 3467
Arameans were not willing to **h** the **1Ch 19:19** 3467
all the leaders of Israel to **h** his son **1Ch 22:17** 5826
no one besides You to **h** *in the battle* **2Ch 14:11** 5826
so **h** us, O LORD our God, for we **2Ch 14:11** 5826
"Should you **h** the wicked and love **2Ch 19:2** 5826
together to seek **h** from the LORD; **2Ch 20:4**
power to **h** and to bring down." **2Ch 25:8** 5826
to **h** the king against the enemy. **2Ch 26:13** 5826
to the kings of Assyria for **h**. **2Ch 28:16** 5826
it did not **h** him. **2Ch 28:21** 5833
to them that they may **h** me." **2Ch 28:23** 5826
our God to **h** us and to fight **2Ch 32:8** 5826
with the **h** of our God. **Ne 6:16** 4480, 854
"Is it that my **h** is not within **Jb 6:13** 5833
I shout for **h**, but there is no **Jb 19:7** 7768
"What a **h** you are to the weak! **Jb 26:2** 5826
the poor who cried for **h**, **Jb 29:12** 7768
"I cry out to You for **h**, **Jb 30:20** 7768
disaster therefore cry out for **h**? **Jb 30:24** 7769
in the assembly *and* cry out for **h**. **Jb 30:28** 7768
They cry for **h** because of the arm **Jb 35:9** 7768
not cry for **h** when He binds them. **Jb 36:13** 7768
Heed the sound of my cry for **h**, **Ps 5:2** 7773
H, LORD, for the godly man ceases **Ps 12:1** 3467
LORD, And cried to my God for **h**; **Ps 18:6** 7768
my cry for **h** before Him came into **Ps 18:6** 7775
They cried for **h**, but there was **Ps 18:41** 7768
He send you **h** from the sanctuary And **Ps 20:2** 5828
For there is none to **h**. **Ps 22:11** 5826
O You my **h**, hasten to my **Ps 22:19** 360
But when he cried to Him for **h**, **Ps 22:24** 7768
You have been my **h**; **Ps 27:9** 5833
when I cry to You for **h**, **Ps 28:2** 7768
my God, I cried to You for **h**, **Ps 30:2** 7768
He is our **h** and our shield. **Ps 33:20** 5828
and shield And rise up for my **h**. **Ps 35:2** 5833
Make haste to **h** me, O Lord, my **Ps 38:22** 5833
Make haste, O LORD, to **h** me. **Ps 40:13** 5833
You are my **h** and my deliverer; **Ps 40:17** 5833
Him *For* the **h** of His presence. **Ps 42:5** 3444
Him, The **h** of my countenance and **Ps 42:11** 3444
Him, The **h** of my countenance and **Ps 43:5** 3444
Rise up, be our **h**, And redeem us **Ps 44:26** 5833
A very present **h** in trouble. **Ps 46:1** 5833
God will **h** her when morning dawns. **Ps 46:5** 5826
Arouse Yourself to **h** me, **Ps 59:4** 7122
O give us **h** against the adversary, **Ps 60:11** 5833
For You have been my **h**, **Ps 63:7** 5833
O LORD, hasten to my **h**! **Ps 70:1** 5833
You are my **h** and my deliverer; **Ps 70:5** 5828
O my God, hasten to my **h**! **Ps 71:12** 5833
the needy when he cries for **h**, **Ps 72:12** 7768
H us, O God of our salvation, for **Ps 79:9** 5826
become a **h** to the children of Lot. **Ps 83:8** 2220
have cried out to You for **h**, **Ps 88:13** 7768
have given **h** to one who is mighty; **Ps 89:19** 5828
If the LORD had not been my **h**, **Ps 94:17** 5833
And let my cry for **h** come to You. **Ps 102:1** 7775
stumbled and there was none to **h**. **Ps 107:12** 5826
give us **h** against the adversary, **Ps 108:12** 5833
H me, O LORD my God; **Ps 109:26** 5826
He is their **h** and their shield. **Ps 115:9** 5828
He is their **h** and their shield. **Ps 115:10** 5828
He is their **h** and their shield. **Ps 115:11** 5828
is for me among those who **h** me; **Ps 118:7** 5826
have persecuted me with a lie; **h** me! **Ps 119:86** 5826
I rise before dawn and cry for **h**; **Ps 119:147** 7768
Let Your hand be ready to **h** me, **Ps 119:173** 5826
And let Your ordinances **h** me. **Ps 119:175** 5826
From where shall my **h** come? **Ps 121:1** 5828
My **h** *comes* from the LORD, Who **Ps 121:2** 5828
Our **h** is in the name of the LORD, **Ps 124:8** 5828
is he whose **h** is the God of Jacob, **Ps 146:5** 5828
To whom will you flee for **h**? **Is 10:3** 5833
where we fled for **h** to be **Is 20:6** 5833
them, *Who are* not for **h** or profit, **Is 30:5** 5828
Egypt, whose **h** is vain and empty. **Is 30:7** 5826
those who go down to Egypt for **h** **Is 31:1** 5833
the **h** of the workers of iniquity. **Is 31:2** 5833
you, surely I will **h** you, **Is 41:10** 5826
'Do not fear, I will **h** you.' **Is 41:13** 5826
I will **h** you," declares the LORD, **Is 41:14** 5826
you from the womb, who will **h** you, **Is 44:2** 5826
looked, and there was no one to **h**, **Is 63:5** 5826
when I cry out and call for **h**, **La 3:8** 7768
for relief, From my cry for **h**." **La 3:56** 7775
Looking for **h** was useless; **La 4:17** 5833
she did not **h** the poor and needy. **Ezk 16:49** 2388, 3027
company will not **h** him in the war, **Ezk 17:17** 6213a
the chief princes, came to **h** me, **Da 10:13** 5826
they will be granted a little **h**, **Da 11:34** 5828
strongest of fortresses with *the* **h** **Da 11:39**
to his end, and no one will **h** him. **Da 11:45** 5826
are against Me, against your **h**. **Hos 13:9** 5828
cried for **h** from the depth of Sheol; **Jon 2:2** 7768
long, O LORD, will I call for **h**, **Hab 1:2** 7768
"Whatever I have that would **h** you **Mt 15:5** *5623*
before Him, saying, "Lord, **h** me!" **Mt 15:25** *997*
whatever I have that would **h** you is **Mk 7:11** *5623*
take pity on us and **h** us!" **Mk 9:22** *997*
said, "I do believe; **h** my unbelief." **Mk 9:24** *997*
has given **h** to Israel His servant, **Lk 1:54** *482*
and they asked Him to **h** her. **Lk 4:38** *4012*
boat for them to come and **h** them. **Lk 5:7** *4815*
Then tell her to **h** me." **Lk 10:40** *4878*
a deliverer with the **h** of the angel **Ac 7:35** *5495*
"Come over to Macedonia and **h** us." **Ac 16:9** *997*
you must **h** the weak and remember **Ac 20:35** *482*
So, having obtained **h** from God, **Ac 26:22** *1947*
and that you **h** her in whatever **Ro 16:2** *3936*
I ask you also to **h** these women **Php 4:3** *4815*
the fainthearted, **h** the weak, **1Th 5:14** *472*
Diligently **h** Zenas the lawyer and **Ti 3:13** *4311*

He does not give **h** to angels, **Heb 2:16** *1949*
h to the descendant of Abraham. **Heb 2:16** *1949*
find grace to **h** in time of need. **Heb 4:16** *996*

HELPED
but Moses stood up and **h** them and **Ex 2:17** 3467
"Thus far the LORD has **h** us." **1Sa 7:12** 5826
the LORD **h** David wherever he went. **2Sa 8:6** 3467
the LORD **h** David wherever he went. **2Sa 8:14** 3467
Abishai the son of Zeruiah **h** him, **2Sa 21:17** 5826
and following Adonijah they **h** him. **1Ki 1:7** 5826
the thirty-two kings who **h** him. **1Ki 20:16** 5826
They were **h** against them, and **1Ch 5:20** 5826
the mighty men who **h** *him* in war. **1Ch 12:1** 5826
They **h** David against the band **1Ch 12:21** 5826
h *David* with an undivided heart. **1Ch 12:33** 5737a
the LORD **h** David wherever he went. **1Ch 18:6** 3467
the LORD **h** David wherever he went. **1Ch 18:13** 3467
cried out, and the LORD **h** him, **2Ch 18:31** 5826
they **h** to destroy one another. **2Ch 20:23** 5826
God **h** him against the Philistines, **2Ch 26:7** 5826
marvelously **h** until he *was* strong. **2Ch 26:15** 5826
gods of the kings of Aram **h** them, **2Ch 28:23** 5826
their brothers the Levites **h** them **2Ch 29:34** 2388
outside the city, and they **h** him. **2Ch 32:3** 5826
have **h** the tottering to stand, **Jb 4:4**
heart trusts in Him, and I am **h**; **Ps 28:7** 5826
LORD, have **h** me and comforted me. **Ps 86:17** 5826
I was falling, But the LORD **h** me. **Ps 118:13** 5826
stumble And he who is **h** will fall, **Is 31:3** 5826
a day of salvation I have **h** You; **Is 49:8** 5826
the adversary And no one **h** her. **La 1:7** 5826
that she had and was not **h** at all, **Mk 5:26** *5623*
he greatly **h** those who had **Ac 18:27** *4820*
to be **h** on my way there by you, **Ro 15:24** *4311*
to be **h** on my journey to Judea. **2Co 1:16** *4311*
AND ON THE DAY OF SALVATION I **H** **2Co 6:2** *997*
But the earth **h** the woman, and the **Rv 12:16** *997*

HELPER
make him a **h** suitable for him." **Gn 2:18** 5828
not found a **h** suitable for him. **Gn 2:20** 5828
nor was there any **h** for Israel. **2Ki 14:26** 5826
help, And the orphan who had no **h**. **Jb 29:12** 5826
have been the **h** of the orphan. **Ps 10:14** 5826
O LORD, be my **h**." **Ps 30:10** 5826
Behold, God is my **h**; **Ps 54:4** 5826
also, and him who has no **h**. **Ps 72:12** 5826
and He will give you another **H**, **Jn 14:16** *3875*
"But the **H**, the Holy Spirit, whom **Jn 14:26** *3875*
"When the **H** comes, whom I will **Jn 15:26** *3875*
away, the **H** will not come to you; **Jn 16:7** *3875*
and they also had John as their **h**. **Ac 13:5** *5257*
herself has also been a **h** of many, **Ro 16:2** *4368*
"THE LORD IS MY **H**, I WILL NOT **Heb 13:6** *998*

HELPERS
Beneath Him crouch the **h** of Rahab. **Jb 9:13** 5826
him, his **h** and all his troops; **Ezk 12:14** 5828
in Egypt And all her **h** are broken. **Ezk 30:8** 5826
and his **h** from the midst of Sheol, **Ezk 32:21** 1368
Put and Lubim were among her **h**. **Na 3:9** 5833

HELPFUL
What **h** insight you have abundantly **Jb 26:3** 8454

HELPING
"When you are **h** the Hebrew women **Ex 1:16**
God was **h** the Levites who were **1Ch 15:26** 5826
in **h** us through your prayers, **2Co 1:11** *4943*

HELPLESS
donkey of one who hates you lying **h** **Ex 23:5**
and we are **h** because our fields **Ne 5:5**
369, 410, 3027
"So the **h** has hope, And **Jb 5:16** 1800b
blessed is he who considers the **h**; **Ps 41:1** 1800b
"Those who are most **h** will eat, **Is 14:30** 1800b
have been a defense for the **h**, **Is 25:4** 1800b
afflicted, the steps of the **h**." **Is 26:6** 1800b
Your sons have fainted, They lie **h** **Is 51:20**
"Damascus has become **h**; **Jer 49:24** 7503
dust of the earth on the head of the **h** **Am 2:7** 1800b
So as to buy the **h** for money And **Am 8:6** 1800b
For while we were still **h**, **Ro 5:6** *772*

HELPS
the God of your father who **h** you, **Gn 49:25** 5826
you, And peace to him who **h** you; **1Ch 12:18** 5826
Indeed, your God **h** you!" **1Ch 12:18** 5826
The LORD **h** them and delivers **Ps 37:40** 5826
And he who **h** will stumble And he **Is 31:3** 5826
Each one **h** his neighbor And says **Is 41:6** 5826
For the Lord GOD **h** Me, **Is 50:7** 5826
Behold, the Lord GOD **h** Me; **Is 50:9** 5826
the Spirit also **h** our weakness; **Ro 8:26** *4878*
then gifts of healings, **h**, **1Co 12:28** *484*
who **h** in the work and labors. **1Co 16:16** *4903*

HEM
"You shall make on its **h** **Ex 28:33** 7757
material, all around on its **h**, **Ex 28:33** 7757
all around on the **h** of the robe. **Ex 28:34** 7757
linen on the **h** of the robe. **Ex 39:24** 7757
all around on the **h** of the robe, **Ex 39:25** 7757
all around on the **h** of the robe for **Ex 39:26** 7757
you and **h** you in on every side, **Lk 19:43** *4912*

HEMAM
The sons of Lotan were Hori and **H** **Gn 36:22** 1950

HEMAN
men, than Ethan the Ezrahite, **H**, **1Ki 4:31** 1968
of Zerah *were* Zimri, Ethan, **H**, **1Ch 2:6** 1968
the Kohathites *were* **H** the singer, **1Ch 6:33** 1968
appointed **H** the son of Joel, **1Ch 15:17** 1968
So the singers, **H**, Asaph and **1Ch 15:19** 1968
With them *were* **H** and Jeduthun, **1Ch 16:41** 1968
And with them *were* **H** and Jeduthun **1Ch 16:42** 1968
of Asaph and of **H** and of Jeduthun, **1Ch 25:1** 1968
Of **H**, the sons of Heman: **1Ch 25:4** 1968
Of Heman, the sons of **H**: **1Ch 25:4** 1968
All these *were* the sons of **H** the **1Ch 25:5** 1968
sons and three daughters to **H**. **1Ch 25:5** 1968
Jeduthun and **H** *were* under the **1Ch 25:6** 1968
the Levitical singers, Asaph, **H**, **2Ch 5:12** 1968
and from the sons of **H**, **2Ch 29:14** 1968
to the command of David, Asaph, **H**, **2Ch 35:15** 1968

HEMAN'S
H brother Asaph stood at his **1Ch 6:39**

HEMDAN
H and Eshban and Ithran and Cheran. **Gn 36:26** 2533

HEMORRHAGE
from a **h** for twelve years, **Mt 9:20** *131*
who had had a **h** for twelve years, **Mk 5:25**
4511, 129
who had a **h** for twelve years, **Lk 8:43**
4511, 129
and immediately her **h** stopped. **Lk 8:44**
4511, 129

HEN
and **H** the son of Zephaniah. **Zch 6:14** 2581
the way a **h** gathers her chicks **Mt 23:37** *3733*
just as a **h** *gathers* her brood **Lk 13:34** *3733*

HENA
gods of Sepharvaim, **H** and Ivvah? **2Ki 18:34** 2012
and *of* **H** and Ivvah?' " **2Ki 19:13** 2012
and of **H** and Ivvah?' " **Is 37:13** 2012

HENADAD
the sons of Judah *and* the sons of **H** **Ezr 3:9** 2582
repairs *under* Bavvai the son of **H**, **Ne 3:18** 2582
son of **H** repaired another section, **Ne 3:24** 2582
Azaniah, Binnui of the sons of **H**, **Ne 10:9** 2582

HENCE
H God led the people around by the **Ex 13:18**
'**H** I have said to you, **Lv 20:24**
H his fame spread afar, for he was **2Ch 26:15**
h the afflicted of the flock. **Zch 11:7** 3651

HENNA
is to me a cluster of **h** blossoms **SS 1:14** 3724c
choice fruits, **h** with nard plants, **SS 4:13** 3724c

HEPHER
and *of* **H**, the family of the **Nu 26:32** 2660a
the son of **H** had no sons, **Nu 26:33** 2660a
of Zelophehad, the son of **H**, **Nu 27:1** 2660a
the king of **H**, one; **Jos 12:17** 2660b
of **H** and for the sons of Shemida; **Jos 17:2** 2660a
However, Zelophehad, the son of **H**, **Jos 17:3** 2660a
was his and all the land of **H**); **1Ki 4:10** 2660b
Naarah bore him Ahuzzam, **H**, **1Ch 4:6** 2660a
H the Mecherathite, Ahijah the **1Ch 11:36** 2660a

HEPHERITES
of Hepher, the family of the **H**. **Nu 26:32** 2662

HEPHZIBAH
and his mother's name was **H**. **2Ki 21:1** 2657

HERALD
Then the **h** loudly proclaimed: **Da 3:4** 3744

HERB
grass And as the showers on the **h**. **Dt 32:2** 6212a
of the field and as the green **h**, **2Ki 19:26** 1877
grass And fade like the green **h**. **Ps 37:2** 1877
of the field and *as* the green **h**, **Is 37:27** 1877
rue and every *kind of* garden **h**, **Lk 11:42** *3001*

HERBS
unleavened bread and bitter **h**. **Ex 12:8** 4844
unleavened bread and bitter **h**. **Nu 9:11** 4844
out into the field to gather **h**, **2Ki 4:39** 219b
And the **h** of the mountains are **Pr 27:25** 6212a
balsam, Banks of sweet-scented **h**; **SS 5:13** 4840

HERD
Abraham also ran to the **h**, **Gn 18:7** 1241
animals from the **h** or the flock. **Lv 1:2** 1241
is a burnt offering from the **h**, **Lv 1:3** 1241
he is going to offer out of the **h**, **Lv 3:1** 1241
bull of the **h** for a sin offering and **Lv 4:14** 1241
of the **h** or of the flock, **Lv 22:21** 1241
defect, and a bull of the **h** and **Lv 23:18** 1241
every tenth part of **h** or flock, **Lv 27:32** 1241
from the **h** or from the flock. **Nu 15:3** 1241
h and the young of your flock, **Dt 7:13** 504
the firstborn of your **h** and of your **Dt 12:6** 1241
the firstborn of your **h** or flock, **Dt 12:17** 1241
then you may slaughter of your **h** **Dt 12:21** 1241
of your **h** and your flock, **Dt 14:23** 1241
born of your **h** and of your flock; **Dt 15:19** 1241
work with the firstborn of your **h**, **Dt 15:19** 7794
your God from the flock and the **h**, **Dt 16:2** 1241
shall take a heifer of the **h**, **Dt 21:3** 1241
increase of your **h** and the young **Dt 28:4** 504
the increase of your **h** and the young **Dt 28:18** 504
it shall eat the offspring of your **h** and **Dt 28:51** 929
nor the increase of your **h** or the **Dt 28:51** 504
from his own flock or his own **h**, **2Sa 12:4** 1241
curds, sheep, and cheese of the **h**, **2Sa 17:29** 1241
The **h** of bulls with the calves of **Ps 68:30** 5712
the young of the flock and the **h**; **Jer 31:12** 1241
"As a shepherd cares for his **h** in **Ezk 34:12** 5739
Do not let man, beast, **h**, **Jon 3:7** 1241
a **h** of many swine feeding **Mt 8:30** *34*
send us into the **h** of swine." **Mt 8:31** *34*
the whole **h** rushed down the steep **Mt 8:32** *34*
Now there was a large **h** of swine **Mk 5:11** *34*
and the **h** rushed down the steep **Mk 5:13** *34*
Now there was a **h** of many swine **Lk 8:32** *34*
and the **h** rushed down the steep **Lk 8:33** *34*

HERDS
also had flocks and **h** and tents. **Gn 13:5** 1241
and He has given him flocks and **h**, **Gn 24:35** 1241
and **h** and a great household, **Gn 26:14** 1241
and he put his own **h** apart, **Gn 30:40** 5739
flocks and the **h** and the camels, **Gn 32:7** 1241
h which are nursing are a care to me. **Gn 33:13** 1241
and their **h** and their donkeys, **Gn 34:28** 1241
and your **h** and all that you have. **Gn 45:10** 1241
their **h** and all that they have.' **Gn 46:32** 1241
their **h** and all that they have, **Gn 47:1** 1241
flocks and the **h** and the donkeys; **Gn 47:17** 1241
and their **h** in the land of Goshen. **Gn 50:8** 1241
donkeys, on the camels, on the **h**, **Ex 9:3** 1241
our flocks and our **h** we shall go, **Ex 10:9** 1241
flocks and your **h** be detained. **Ex 10:24** 1241
"Take both your flocks and your **h**, **Ex 12:32** 1241
them, along with flocks and **h**, **Ex 12:38** 1241
flocks and the **h** may not graze in **Ex 34:3** 1241
and **h** be slaughtered for them, **Nu 11:22** 1241
their **h** and for all their beasts. **Nu 35:3** 7399
your **h** and your flocks multiply, **Dt 8:13** 1241
man had a great many flocks and **h**. **2Sa 12:2** 1241
flocks and **h** in abundance, **2Ch 32:29** 1241
and the firstborn of our **h** and **Ne 10:36** 1241
And their **h** to bolts of lightning. **Ps 78:48** 4735
And pay attention to your **h**; **Pr 27:23** 5739
Also I possessed flocks and **h** **Ec 2:7** 1241
of Achor a resting place for **h**, **Is 65:10** 1241
youth, their flocks and their **h**, **Jer 3:24** 1241
devour your flocks and your **h**; **Jer 5:17** 1241
go with their flocks and **h** To seek **Hos 5:6** 1241
The **h** of cattle wander aimlessly **Jl 1:18** 5739
All beasts which range in **h**; **Zph 2:14** 1471

HERDSMAN
a **h** and a grower of sycamore figs. **Am 7:14** 951

HERDSMEN
was strife between the **h** of Abram's **Gn 13:7** 7462a
and the **h** of Lot's livestock. **Gn 13:7** 7462a
between my **h** and your herdsmen, **Gn 13:8** 7462a
between my herdsmen and your **h**, **Gn 13:8** 7462a
the **h** of Gerar quarreled with the **Gn 26:20** 7462a
quarreled with the **h** of Isaac, **Gn 26:20** 7462a
The **h** ran away, and went to **Mt 8:33** *1006*
Their **h** ran away and reported **Mk 5:14** *1006*
When the **h** saw what had happened, **Lk 8:34** *1006*

HERE
and it flew **h** and there until the **Gn 8:7** 3318
Now then, **h** is your wife, take her **Gn 12:19** 2009
generation they will return **h**, **Gn 15:16** 2008
alive **h** after seeing Him?" **Gn 16:13** 1988
"Whom else have you **h**? **Gn 19:12** 6311
and your two daughters who are **h**, **Gn 19:15** 4672
swear to me **h** by God that you will **Gn 21:23** 2008
"Abraham!" And he said, "**H** I am." **Gn 22:1** 2009
"Stay **h** with the donkey, and I **Gn 22:5** 6311
"**H** I am, my son." **Gn 22:7** 2009
Abraham!" And he said, "**H** I am." **Gn 22:11** 2009
"**H** is Rebekah before you, take **Gn 24:51** 2009
And he said to him, "**H** I am." **Gn 27:1** 2009
And he said, "**H** I am. Who are you, **Gn 27:18** 2009
and **h** is Rachel his daughter coming **Gn 29:6** 2009
"**H** is my maid Bilhah, go in to **Gn 30:3** 2009
'Jacob,' and I said, '**H** I am.' **Gn 31:11** 2009
Set *it* **h** before my kinsmen and **Gn 31:37** 3541
"They have moved from **h**; **Gn 37:17** 2088
"**H** comes this dreamer! **Gn 37:19** 2009
"**H** now, let me come in to you"; **Gn 38:16** 3051
has been no temple prostitute **h**." **Gn 38:21** 2088
been no temple prostitute **h**.' **Gn 38:22** 2088
with me **h**, my master does not **Gn 39:8**
and even **h** I have done nothing **Gn 40:15** 6311
your youngest brother comes **h**! **Gn 42:15** 2008
yourselves, because you sold me **h**, **Gn 45:5** 2008
it was not you who sent me **h**, **Gn 45:8** 2008
and bring my father down **h**." **Gn 45:13** 2008
Jacob." And he said, "**H** I am." **Gn 46:2** 2009
h is seed for you, and you may **Gn 47:23**
sons, whom God has given me **h**." **Gn 48:9** 2088
shall carry my bones up from **h**." **Gn 50:25** 2088
Moses!" And he said, "**H** I am." **Ex 3:4** 2009
"Do not come near **h**; **Ex 3:5** 1988
that he will let you go from **h**. **Ex 11:1** 2088
drive you out from **h** completely. **Ex 11:1** 2088
carry my bones from **h** with you." **Ex 13:19** 2088
Wait **h** for us until we return to you. **Ex 24:14** 2088
"Depart, go up from **h**, **Ex 33:1** 2088
with us, do not lead us up from **h**. **Ex 33:15** 2088
"**H** we are; we have indeed sinned, **Nu 14:40** 2009
for us and our beasts to die **h**? **Nu 20:4** 8033
"Spend the night **h**, and I will **Nu 22:8** 6311
please, you also stay **h** tonight, **Nu 22:19** 2088
"Build seven altars for me **h**, **Nu 23:1** 2088
bulls and seven rams for me **h**." **Nu 23:1** 2088
Stand **h** beside your burnt offering while **Nu 23:15** 3541
"Build seven altars for me **h** and **Nu 23:29** 2088
bulls and seven rams for me **h**." **Nu 23:29** 2088
to war while you yourselves sit **h**? **Nu 32:6** 6311
"We will build **h** sheepfolds for **Nu 32:16** 6311
all those of us alive **h** today. **Dt 5:3** 6311
'But as for you, stand **h** by Me, **Dt 5:31** 6311
'Arise, go down from **h** quickly, **Dt 9:12** 2088
at all what we are doing **h** today, **Dt 12:8** 6311
who stand **h** with us today **Dt 29:15** 6311
those who are not with us **h** today **Dt 29:15** 6311
the sons of Israel have come **h** tonight **Jos 2:2** 2008

“Come **h**, and hear the words of **Jos 3:9** 2008
twelve stones from **h** out of the middle **Jos 4:3** 2088
and bring *the description* **h** to me. **Jos 18:6** 2008
cast lots for you **h** before the LORD **Jos 18:6** 6311
cast lots for you **h** before the LORD **Jos 18:8** 6311
They gave these cities which are **h** **Jos 21:9** 2008
'Is there anyone **h**?' **Jg 4:20** 6311
“Please do not depart from **h**, **Jg 6:18** 2088
“Samson has come **h**,” **Jg 16:2** 2008
“Who brought you **h**? **Jg 18:3** 1988
And what do you have **h**?” **Jg 18:3** 6311
spend the night **h** that your heart **Jg 19:9** 6311
“**H** is my virgin daughter and his **Jg 19:24** 2009
give your advice and counsel **h**.” **Jg 20:7** 1988
one, but stay **h** with my maids. **Ru 2:8** 3541
“Come **h**, that you may eat of the **Ru 2:14** 1988
“Turn aside, friend, sit down **h**.” **Ru 4:1** 6311
“Sit down **h**.” So they sat down. **Ru 4:2** 6311
it before those who are sitting **h**, **Ru 4:4**
the woman who stood **h** beside you, **1Sa 1:26** 2088
called Samuel; and he said, “**H** I am.” **1Sa 3:4** 2009
“**H** I am, for you called me.” **1Sa 3:5** 2009
“**H** I am, for you called me.” **1Sa 3:6** 2009
“**H** I am, for you called me.” **1Sa 3:8** 2009
my son.” And he said, “**H** I am.” **1Sa 3:16** 2009
and said to them, “Is the seer **h**?” **1Sa 9:11** 2088
“**H** is what has been reserved! **1Sa 9:24** 2009
“Has the man come **h** yet?” **1Sa 10:22** 1988
h is the king walking before you, **1Sa 12:2** 2009
“**H** I am; bear witness against me **1Sa 12:3** 2009
h is the king whom you have **1Sa 12:13** 2009
and **h** I am with you according to **1Sa 14:7** 2009
and they went **h** and *there.* **1Sa 14:16** 1988
“Bring the ark of God **h**.” **1Sa 14:18** 5066
sheep, and slaughter *it* **h** and eat; **1Sa 14:34** 2088
“Let us draw near to God **h**.” **1Sa 14:36** 1988
“Draw near **h**, all you chiefs of **1Sa 14:38** 1988
H I am, I must die!” **1Sa 14:43** 2009
not sit down until he comes **h**.” **1Sa 16:11** 6311
“**H** is my older daughter Merab; **1Sa 18:17** 2009
there is no other except it **h**.” **1Sa 21:9** 2088
“**H** I am, my lord.” **1Sa 22:12** 2009
“Behold, we are afraid **h** in Judah. **1Sa 23:3** 6311
“Bring the ephod **h**.” **1Sa 23:9** 5066
are these Hebrews *doing* **h**?” **1Sa 29:3**
called to me. And I said, '**H** I am.' **2Sa 1:7** 2009
have brought them **h** to my lord.” **2Sa 1:10** 2008
“You shall not come in **h**, **2Sa 5:6** 2008
“David cannot enter **h**.” **2Sa 5:6** 2008
“**H** is your servant!” **2Sa 9:6** 2009
“Stay **h** today also, and tomorrow **2Sa 11:12** 2088
'Come **h**, that I may send you to **2Sa 14:32** 2008
behold, **h** I am, let Him do to me **2Sa 15:26**
will not waste time **h** with you. **2Sa 18:14** 3651
“Turn aside and stand **h**.” **2Sa 18:30** 3541
h is your servant Chimham, **2Sa 19:37** 2009
days, and be present **h** yourself.” **2Sa 20:4** 6311
Come **h** that I may speak with you. **2Sa 20:16** 5704, 2008
“**H** is Nathan the prophet.” **1Ki 1:23** 2009
“No, for I will die **h**.” **1Ki 2:30** 6311
“Go away from **h** and turn **1Ki 17:3** 2088
'Behold, Elijah *is* **h**.' ” **1Ki 18:8**
'He is not **h**,' he made **1Ki 18:10**
“Behold, Elijah *is* **h**” ' **1Ki 18:11**
“Behold, Elijah *is* **h**” '; **1Ki 18:14**
“What are you doing **h**, **1Ki 19:9** 6311
“What are you doing **h**, **1Ki 19:13** 6311
your servant was busy **h** and there, **1Ki 20:40** 2008
not yet a prophet of the LORD **h** that **1Ki 22:7** 6311
“Stay **h** please, for the LORD has **2Ki 2:2** 6311
“Elisha, please stay **h**, **2Ki 2:4** 6311
“Please stay **h**, for the LORD has **2Ki 2:6** 6311
and they were divided **h** and there, **2Ki 2:8** 2008
they were divided **h** and there; **2Ki 2:14** 2008
there not a prophet of the LORD **h**, **2Ki 3:11** 6311
“Elisha the son of Shaphat is **h**, **2Ki 3:11** 6311
“Why do we sit **h** until we die? **2Ki 7:3** 6311
and if we sit **h**, we die also. **2Ki 7:4** 6311
“The man of God has come **h**.” **2Ki 8:7** 5704, 2008
“Search and see that there is **h** with **2Ki 10:23** 6311
“You shall not enter **h**.” **1Ch 11:5** 2008
Your people, who are present **h**, **1Ch 29:17** 6311
not yet a prophet of the LORD **h** **2Ch 18:6** 6311
must not bring the captives in **h**, **2Ch 28:13** 2008
of Assyria, who brought us up **h**.” **Ezr 4:2** 6311
Behold, **h** is my signature; **Jb 31:35**
h shall your proud waves stop'? **Jb 38:11** 6311
And say to you, '**H** we are'? **Jb 38:35** 2009
Your arrows flashed **h** and there. **Ps 77:17**
H I will dwell, for I have desired **Ps 132:14** 6311
is naive, let him turn in **h**!” **Pr 9:4** 2008
is naive, let him turn in **h**,” **Pr 9:16** 2008
that it be said to you, “Come up **h**,” **Pr 25:7** 2008
H is what I have seen to be good **Ec 5:18** 2009
Then I said, “**H** am I. Send me!” **Is 6:8** 2009
behold, **h** comes a troop of riders, **Is 21:9** 2088
'What right do you have **h**, **Is 22:16** 6311
have here, And whom do you have **h**, **Is 22:16** 6311
have hewn a tomb for yourself **h**, **Is 22:16** 6311
line on line, A little **h**, a little there.' ” **Is 28:10** 8033
“**H** is rest, give rest to the weary,” **Is 28:12** 2088
“**H** is repose,” but they would not **Is 28:12** 2088
line on line, A little **h**, a little there, **Is 28:13** 8033
the cities of Judah, “**H** is your God!” **Is 40:9** 2009
'Behold, **h** they are.' **Is 41:27** 2009
Make room for me that I may live **h**.' **Is 49:20**
“Now therefore, what do I have **h**,” **Is 52:5** 6311
the one who is speaking, '**H** I am.' ” **Is 52:6** 2009
“But come **h**, you sons of a **Is 57:3** 2008
will cry, and He will say, '**H** I am.' **Is 58:9** 2009
'**H** am I, here am I,' To a nation **Is 65:1** 2009
'Here am I, **h** am I,' To a nation **Is 65:1** 2009
company, they will return **h**. **Jer 31:8** 2008
How long will you go **h** and there, **Jer 31:22** 2559
Take thirty men from **h** under your **Jer 38:10** 2088
the house of Israel are committing **h**, **Ezk 8:6** 6311
that they are committing **h**.” **Ezk 8:9** 6311
which they have committed **h**, **Ezk 8:17** 6311
you have been brought **h** in order to **Ezk 40:4** 2008
the Most High God, and come **h**!” **Da 3:26** 5312
among these who are standing **h**. **Zch 3:7**
Have You come **h** to torment us **Mt 8:29** *5602*
greater than the temple is **h**. **Mt 12:6** *5602*
something greater than Jonah is **h**. **Mt 12:41** *5602*
greater than Solomon is **h**. **Mt 12:42** *5602*
“Give me **h** on a platter the head **Mt 14:8** *5602*
We have **h** only five loaves and two **Mt 14:17** *5602*
“Bring them **h** to Me.” **Mt 14:18** *5602*
some of those who are standing **h** who **Mt 16:28** *5602*
“Lord, it is good for us to be **h**; **Mt 17:4** *5602*
I will make three tabernacles **h**, **Mt 17:4** *5602*
Bring him **h** to Me.” **Mt 17:17** *5602*
'Move from **h** to there,' and it **Mt 17:20** *1759b*
Why have you been standing **h** idle **Mt 20:6** *5602*
how did you come in **h** without **Mt 22:12** *5602*
not one stone **h** will be left upon **Mt 24:2** *5602*
'Behold, **h** is the Christ,' or **Mt 24:23** *5602*
“Sit **h** while I go over there and **Mt 26:36** *847*
remain **h** and keep watch with Me.” **Mt 26:38** *5602*
“He is not **h**, for He has risen, **Mt 28:6** *5602*
Are not His sisters **h** with us?” **Mk 6:3** *5602*
whole country and began to carry **h** **Mk 6:55** *4063*
bread **h** in *this* desolate place **Mk 8:4** *5602*
some of those who are standing **h** who **Mk 9:1** *5602*
“Rabbi, it is good for us to be **h**; **Mk 9:5** *5602*
“Call him **h**.” So they called **Mk 10:49**
untie it and bring it **h**. **Mk 11:2**
he will send it back **h**.” **Mk 11:3** *5602*
'Behold, **h** is the Christ'; **Mk 13:21** *5602*
“Sit **h** until I have prayed.” **Mk 14:32** *5602*
remain **h** and keep watch.” **Mk 14:34** *5602*
He has risen; He is not **h**; **Mk 16:6** *5602*
h *is* the place where they laid **Mk 16:6**
God, throw Yourself down from **h**; **Lk 4:9** *1782*
do **h** in your hometown as well.' ” **Lk 4:23** *5602*
h we are in a desolate place.” **Lk 9:12** *5602*
there are some of those standing **h** **Lk 9:27** *847*
“Master, it is good for us to be **h**; **Lk 9:33** *5602*
Bring your son **h**.” **Lk 9:41** *5602*
greater than Solomon is **h**. **Lk 11:31** *5602*
something greater than Jonah is **h**. **Lk 11:32** *5602*
“Go away, leave **h**, **Lk 13:31** *1782*
bring in **h** the poor and crippled and **Lk 14:21** *5602*
but I am dying **h** with hunger! **Lk 15:17** *5602*
but now he is being comforted **h**, **Lk 16:25** *5602*
wish to come over from **h** to you **Lk 16:26** *1759b*
nor will they say, 'Look, **h** *it is!*' **Lk 17:21** *5602*
will say to you, 'Look there! Look **h** **Lk 17:23** *5602*
h is your mina, which I kept put **Lk 19:20** *2400*
bring them **h** and slay them in my **Lk 19:27** *5602*
untie it and bring it **h**. **Lk 19:30**
“Lord, look, **h** are two swords.” **Lk 22:38** *5602*
“He is not **h**, but He has risen. **Lk 24:6** *5602*
have happened **h** in these days?” **Lk 24:18** *1722, 846*
“Have you anything **h** to eat?” **Lk 24:41** *1759a*
nor come all the way **h** to draw.” **Jn 4:15** *1759a*
call your husband and come **h**.” **Jn 4:16** *1759a*
“There is a lad **h** who has five **Jn 6:9** *5602*
“Rabbi, when did You get **h**?” **Jn 6:25** *5602*
“Leave **h** and go into **Jn 7:3** *1782*
“My time is not yet **h**, but your **Jn 7:6** *3918b*
“Well, **h** is an amazing thing, **Jn 9:30** *1722, 3778*
“Lord, if You had been **h**, **Jn 11:21** *5602*
“The Teacher is **h** and is calling **Jn 11:28** *3918b*
“Lord, if You had been **h**, **Jn 11:32** *5602*
up, let us go from **h**. **Jn 14:31** *1782*
“Reach **h** with your finger, and see My **Jn 20:27** *5602*
and reach **h** your hand and put it **Jn 20:27**
by this *name* this man stands **h** **Ac 4:10** *3936*
“**H** I am, Lord.” **Ac 9:10** *2400*
and **h** he has authority from the **Ac 9:14** *5602*
and *who* had come **h** for the purpose **Ac 9:21** *5602*
we are all **h** present before God to **Ac 10:33** *3918b*
is also called Peter, brought **h**; **Ac 11:13** *3343*
not harm yourself, for we are all **h**!” **Ac 16:28** *1759a*
upset the world have come **h** also; **Ac 17:6** *1759a*
“For you have brought these men **h** **Ac 19:37**
“So after they had assembled **h**, **Ac 25:17** *1759a*
you gentlemen **h** present with us, **Ac 25:24** *4840*
to me, both at Jerusalem and **h**, **Ac 25:24** *1759a*
nor have any of the brethren come **h** **Ac 28:21** *3854*
H for this third time I am ready **2Co 12:14** *2400*
tossed **h** and there by waves and **Eph 4:14** *2831*
you about the whole situation **h**. **Col 4:9** *5602*
h we do not have a lasting city, **Heb 13:14** *5602*
“You sit **h** in a good place,” **Jas 2:3** *5602*
“Come up **h**, and I will show you **Rv 4:1** *5602*
heaven saying to them, “Come up **h**.” **Rv 11:12** *5602*
H is the perseverance and the **Rv 13:10** *5602*
H is wisdom. Let him who has **Rv 13:18** *5602*
H is the perseverance of the **Rv 14:12** *5602*
“Come **h**, I will show you the **Rv 17:1** *1204*
“**H** is the mind which has wisdom. **Rv 17:9** *5602*
“Come **h**, I will show you the **Rv 21:9** *1204*

HEREAFTER
Who will give heed and listen **h**? **Is 42:23** 268
h you will see THE SON OF MAN SITTING **Mt 26:64** *575, 737*
now, but you will understand **h**.” **Jn 13:7** *3326, 3778*

HEREDITARY
give them a **h** possession among **Nu 27:7** 5159

HERES
persisted in living in Mount **H**, **Jg 1:35** 2776
the battle by the ascent of **H**. **Jg 8:13** 2776

HERESH
H and Galal and Mattaniah the son **1Ch 9:15** 2792

HERESIES
secretly introduce destructive **h**, **2Pe 2:1** *139*

HERETH
and went into the forest of **H**. **1Sa 22:5** 2802

HERITAGE
the **h** decreed to him by God.” **Jb 20:29** 5159
h of the Almighty from on high? **Jb 31:2** 5159
Indeed, my **h** is beautiful to me. **Ps 16:6** 5159
people, O LORD, And afflict Your **h**. **Ps 94:5** 5159
giving them the **h** of the nations. **Ps 111:6** 5159
And He gave their land as a **h**, **Ps 135:12** 5159
A **h** to Israel His people. **Ps 135:12** 5159
And gave their land as a **h**, **Ps 136:21** 5159
Even a **h** to Israel His servant, **Ps 136:22** 5159
with My people, I profaned My **h** And **Is 47:6** 5159
the **h** of the servants of the LORD, **Is 54:17** 5159
with the **h** of Jacob your father, **Is 58:14** 5159
Your servants, the tribes of Your **h**. **Is 63:17** 5159
jubilant, O you who pillage My **h**, **Jer 50:11** 5159

HERITAGES
make *them* inherit the desolate **h**; **Is 49:8** 5159

HERMAS
H and the brethren with them. **Ro 16:14** *2057*

HERMES
Barnabas, Zeus, and Paul, **H**, **Ac 14:12** *2060*
Greet Asyncritus, Phlegon, **H**, **Ro 16:14** *2060*

HERMOGENES
me, among whom are Phygelus and **H**. **2Tm 1:15** *2061*

HERMON
the valley of Arnon to Mount **H** **Dt 3:8** 2768
(Sidonians call **H** Sirion, and the **Dt 3:9** 2768
as far as Mount Sion (that is, **H**), **Dt 4:48** 2768
foot of **H** in the land of Mizpeh. **Jos 11:3** 2768
of Lebanon at the foot of Mount **H**. **Jos 11:17** 2768
of the Arnon as far as Mount **H**, **Jos 12:1** 2768
H and Salecah and all Bashan, **Jos 12:5** 2768
Mount **H** as far as Lebo-hamath. **Jos 13:5** 2768
and Maacathites, and all Mount **H**, **Jos 13:11** 2768
and Mount **H** they were numerous. **1Ch 5:23** 2768
of the Jordan And the peaks of **H**, **Ps 42:6** 2769
and **H** shout for joy at Your name. **Ps 89:12** 2768
It is like the dew of **H** Coming **Ps 133:3** 2768
From the summit of Senir and **H**, **SS 4:8** 2768

HEROD
Judea in the days of **H** the king, **Mt 2:1** *2264*
When **H** the king heard *this,* he **Mt 2:3** *2264*
Then **H** secretly called the magi and **Mt 2:7** *2264*
God in a dream not to return to **H** **Mt 2:12** *2264*
for **H** is going to search for the **Mt 2:13** *2264*
remained there until the death of **H** **Mt 2:15** *2264*
Then when **H** saw that he had been **Mt 2:16** *2264*
But when **H** died, behold, an **Mt 2:19** *2264*
Judea in place of his father **H**, **Mt 2:22** *2264*
At that time **H** the tetrarch heard **Mt 14:1** *2264*
For when **H** had John arrested, he **Mt 14:3** *2264*
Although **H** wanted to put him to death, **Mt 14:5**
danced before *them* and pleased **H**, **Mt 14:6** *2264*
And King **H** heard *of it,* for His **Mk 6:14** *2264*
But when **H** heard *of it,* he kept **Mk 6:16** *2264*
For **H** himself had sent and had **Mk 6:17** *2264*
For John had been saying to **H**, **Mk 6:18** *2264*
for **H** was afraid of John, knowing **Mk 6:20** *2264*
H on his birthday gave a banquet **Mk 6:21** *2264*
pleased **H** and his dinner guests; **Mk 6:22** *2264*
of the Pharisees and the leaven of **H**.” **Mk 8:15** *2264*
In the days of **H**, king of Judea, **Lk 1:5** *2264*
and **H** was tetrarch of Galilee, **Lk 3:1** *2264*
But when **H** the tetrarch was **Lk 3:19** *2264*
wicked things which **H** had done, **Lk 3:19** *2264*
H also added this to them all: he **Lk 3:20**
Now **H** the tetrarch heard of all **Lk 9:7** *2264*
H said, “I myself had John beheaded; **Lk 9:9** *2264*
here, for **H** wants to kill You.” **Lk 13:31** *2264*
jurisdiction, he sent Him to **H** , **Lk 23:7** *2264*
Now **H** was very glad when he saw **Lk 23:8** *2264*
And **H** with his soldiers, after **Lk 23:11** *2264*
Now **H** and Pilate became friends **Lk 23:12** *2264*
“No, nor has **H**, for he sent Him **Lk 23:15** *2264*
anointed, both **H** and Pontius Pilate, **Ac 4:27** *2264*
H the king laid hands on some who **Ac 12:1** *2264*
H was about to bring him forward, **Ac 12:6** *2264*
and rescued me from the hand of **H** **Ac 12:11** *2264*
When **H** had searched for him **Ac 12:19** *2264*
On an appointed day **H** **Ac 12:21** *2264*
who had been brought up with **H** **Ac 13:1** *2264*

HERODIANS
to Him, along with the **H**, **Mt 22:16** *2265*
conspiring with the **H** against Him, **Mk 3:6** *2265*
they sent some of the Pharisees and **H** **Mk 12:13** *2265*

HERODIAS
and put him in prison because of **H**, **Mt 14:3** *2266*
the daughter of **H** danced before **Mt 14:6** *2266*
bound in prison on account of **H** **Mk 6:17** *2266*

Context	Reference	Number
H had a grudge against him and	Mk 6:19	*2266*
the daughter of **H** herself came in	Mk 6:22	*2266*
reprimanded by him because of **H**,	Lk 3:19	*2266*
HERODION		
Greet **H**, my kinsman.	Ro 16:11	*2267*
HEROD'S		
But when **H** birthday came, the	Mt 14:6	*2264*
the wife of Chuza, **H** steward,	Lk 8:3	*2264*
He belonged to **H** jurisdiction,	Lk 23:7	*2264*
him to be kept in **H** Praetorium.	Ac 23:35	*2264*
HEROES		
those who are **h** in drinking wine And	Is 5:22	1368
the fallen **h** of the uncircumcised,	Ezk 32:27	1368
though the terror of *these* **h** *was once*	Ezk 32:27	1368
HERON		
and the stork, the **h** in its kinds,	Lv 11:19	601
stork, and the **h** in their kinds,	Dt 14:18	601
HERS		
"Restore all that was **h** and all	2Ki 8:6	
cruelly, as if *they* were not **h**;	Jb 39:16	
HERSELF		
Sarah laughed to **h**,	Gn 18:12	7130
And she **h** said, 'He is my brother.'	Gn 20:5	1931
she took her veil and covered **h**.	Gn 24:65	
her widow's garments and covered **h**	Gn 38:14	
with a veil, and wrapped **h**,	Gn 38:14	
shall count off for **h** seven days;	Lv 15:28	
she shall take for **h** two turtledove	Lv 15:29	
if she profanes **h** by harlotry,	Lv 21:9	
although she has defiled **h**,	Nu 5:13	1931
his wife when she has defiled **h**,	Nu 5:14	
wife when she has not defiled **h**,	Nu 5:14	
if she has defiled **h** and has been	Nu 5:27	
has not defiled **h** and is clean,	Nu 5:28	
goes astray and defiles **h**,	Nu 5:29	
she pressed **h** to the wall and	Nu 22:25	
and binds **h** by an obligation in	Nu 30:3	
by which she has bound **h**,	Nu 30:4	5315
which she has bound **h** shall stand.	Nu 30:4	5315
which she has bound **h** shall stand.	Nu 30:5	5315
her lips by which she has bound **h**,	Nu 30:6	5315
which she has bound **h** shall stand.	Nu 30:7	5315
her lips by which she has bound **h**;	Nu 30:8	5315
by which she has bound **h**,	Nu 30:9	5315
bound **h** by an obligation with an	Nu 30:10	5315
by which she bound **h** shall stand.	Nu 30:11	5315
or concerning the obligation of **h** shall	Nu 30:12	5315
every binding oath to humble **h**,	Nu 30:13	5315
Indeed she repeats her words to **h**,	Jg 5:29	
David and bowed **h** to the ground.	1Sa 25:23	
purified **h** from her uncleanness,	2Sa 11:4	
ground and prostrated **h** and said,	2Sa 14:4	
and spread it for **h** on the rock,	2Sa 21:10	
and prostrated **h** before the king.	1Ki 1:16	
prostrated **h** before the king and	1Ki 1:31	
feet and bowed **h** to the ground,	2Ki 4:37	
"When she lifts **h** on high, She	Jb 39:18	
And the swallow a nest for **h**,	Ps 84:3	
She girds **h** with strength And	Pr 31:17	4975
She makes coverings for **h**;	Pr 31:22	
why should I be like one who veils **h**	SS 1:7	
And will find **h** a resting place.	Is 34:14	
a bride adorns **h** with her jewels.	Is 61:10	
"Faithless Israel has proved **h**	Jer 3:11	5315
She has given **h** up, her pillars	Jer 50:15	3027
afflicted, And she **h** is bitter.	La 1:4	1931
Even she **h** groans and turns away.	La 1:8	1931
all their idols she defiled **h**.	Ezk 23:7	
"I saw that she had defiled **h**;	Ezk 23:13	
adorn **h** with her earrings and	Hos 2:13	
For Tyre built **h** a fortress And	Zch 9:3	
for she was saying to **h**,	Mt 9:21	*1438*
the daughter of Herodias **h** came in	Mk 6:22	*846*
and if she **h** divorces her husband	Mk 10:12	*846*
she kept **h** in seclusion for five	Lk 1:24	*1438*
for she **h** has also been a helper	Ro 16:2	*846*
she who gives **h** to wanton	1Tm 5:6	*4684*
has devoted **h** to every good work.	1Tm 5:10	*1872*
Sarah **h** received ability to conceive	Heb 11:11	*846*
Jezebel, who calls **h** a prophetess,	Rv 2:20	*1438*
glorified **h** and lived sensuously,	Rv 18:7	*846*
and His bride has made **h** ready."	Rv 19:7	*1438*
to her to clothe **h** in fine linen,	Rv 19:8	
HESHBON		
the cities of the Amorites, in **H**,	Nu 21:25	2809
For **H** was the city of Sihon, king	Nu 21:26	2809
"Come to **H**! Let it be built!	Nu 21:27	2809
"For a fire went forth from **H**,	Nu 21:28	2809
down, **H** is ruined as far as Dibon,	Nu 21:30	2809
of the Amorites, who lived at **H**."	Nu 21:34	2809
"Ataroth, Dibon, Jazer, Nimrah, **H**,	Nu 32:3	2809
H and Elealeh and Kiriathaim,	Nu 32:37	2809
of the Amorites, who lived in **H**,	Dt 1:4	2809
Sihon the Amorite, king of **H**,	Dt 2:24	2809
king of **H** with words of peace,	Dt 2:26	2809
"But Sihon king of **H** was not	Dt 2:30	2809
of the Amorites, who lived at **H**.'	Dt 3:2	2809
as we did to Sihon king of **H**,	Dt 3:6	2809
of the Amorites who lived at **H**,	Dt 4:46	2809
Sihon the king of **H** and Og the	Dt 29:7	2809
to Sihon king of **H** and to Og king	Jos 9:10	2809
of the Amorites, who lived in **H**,	Jos 12:2	2809
as the border of Sihon king of **H**.	Jos 12:5	2809
of the Amorites, who reigned in **H**,	Jos 13:10	2809
H, and all its cities which are on	Jos 13:17	2809
of the Amorites who reigned in **H**,	Jos 13:21	2809
and from **H** as far as Ramath-mizpeh	Jos 13:26	2809
of the kingdom of Sihon king of **H**,	Jos 13:27	2809
H with its pasture lands, Jazer	Jos 21:39	2809
of the Amorites, the king of **H**,	Jg 11:19	2809
lived in **H** and its villages,	Jg 11:26	2809
H with its pasture lands and	1Ch 6:81	2809
the land of Sihon the king of **H** And	Ne 9:22	2809
in **H** By the gate of Bath-rabbim;	SS 7:4	2809
H and Elealeh also cry out, Their	Is 15:4	2809
For the fields of **H** have withered,	Is 16:8	2809
with my tears, O **H** and Elealeh;	Is 16:9	2809
In **H** they have devised calamity	Jer 48:2	2809
the outcry at **H** even to Elealeh,	Jer 48:34	2809
"In the shadow of **H** The fugitives	Jer 48:45	2809
For a fire has gone forth from **H** And	Jer 48:45	2809
"Wail, O **H**, for Ai has been	Jer 49:3	2809
HESHMON		
Hazar-gaddah and **H** and Beth-pelet,	Jos 15:27	2829
HESITATE		
"How long *will* you **h** between two	1Ki 18:21	6452b
HESITATED		
But he **h**. So the men seized his hand	Gn 19:16	4102
HESLI		
the son of Nahum, the son of **H**,	Lk 3:25	*2069*
HETH		
of Sidon, his firstborn, and **H**	Gn 10:15	2845
dead, and spoke to the sons of **H**,	Gn 23:3	2845
The sons of **H** answered Abraham,	Gn 23:5	2845
people of the land, the sons of **H**.	Gn 23:7	2845
was sitting among the sons of **H**;	Gn 23:10	2845
in the hearing of the sons of **H**;	Gn 23:10	2845
in the hearing of the sons of **H**,	Gn 23:16	2845
in the presence of the sons of **H**,	Gn 23:18	2845
a burial site by the sons of **H**.	Gn 23:20	2845
purchased from the sons of **H**;	Gn 25:10	2845
because of the daughters of **H**;	Gn 27:46	2845
a wife from the daughters of **H**,	Gn 27:46	2845
purchased from the sons of **H**."	Gn 49:32	2845
father of Sidon, his firstborn, **H**,	1Ch 1:13	2845
HETHLON		
the Great Sea *by* the way of **H**,	Ezk 47:15	2855
beside the way of **H** to Lebo-hamath,	Ezk 48:1	2855
HEW		
pillars, and **h** down their Asherim,	Dt 7:5	1438
and he set stonecutters to **h** out	1Ch 22:2	2672
You who **h** a tomb on the height,	Is 22:16	2672
To **h** for themselves cisterns,	Jer 2:13	2672
HEWED		
And Samuel **h** Agag to pieces before	1Sa 15:33	8158
wilderness and **h** many cisterns,	2Ch 26:10	2672
of it And also **h** out a wine vat in it;	Is 5:2	2672
HEWERS		
So they became **h** of wood and	Jos 9:21	2404
both **h** of wood and drawers of	Jos 9:23	2404
h of wood and drawers of water	Jos 9:27	2404
h *of stone* in the mountains,	1Ki 5:15	2672
HEWN		
and **h** cisterns which you did not	Dt 6:11	2672
and for buying timber and **h** stone	2Ki 12:12	4274
and **h** stone to repair the house.	2Ki 22:6	4274
H cisterns, vineyards, olive groves	Ne 9:25	2672
She has **h** out her seven pillars;	Pr 9:1	2672
have **h** a tomb for yourself here,	Is 22:16	2672
to the rock from which you were **h** And	Is 51:1	2672
has blocked my ways with **h** stone;	La 3:9	1496
there were four tables of **h** stone,	Ezk 40:42	1496
Therefore I have **h** *them* in pieces	Hos 6:5	2672
which he had **h** out in the rock;	Mt 27:60	*2998*
which had been **h** out in the rock;	Mk 15:46	*2998*
HEWS		
"He **h** out channels through the	Jb 28:10	1234
of the LORD **h** out flames of fire.	Ps 29:7	2672
HEZEKIAH		
his son **H** reigned in his place.	2Ki 16:20	2396
that **H** the son of Ahaz king of	2Ki 18:1	2396
in the fourth year of King **H**,	2Ki 18:9	2396
in the sixth year of **H**,	2Ki 18:10	2396
in the fourteenth year of King **H**,	2Ki 18:13	2396
Then **H** king of Judah sent to the	2Ki 18:14	2396
Assyria required of **H** king of Judah	2Ki 18:14	2396
H gave *him* all the silver	2Ki 18:15	2396
At that time **H** cut off *the gold*	2Ki 18:16	2396
H king of Judah had overlaid,	2Ki 18:16	2396
from Lachish to King **H** with a large	2Ki 18:17	2396
"Say now to **H**, 'Thus says the great	2Ki 18:19	2396
and whose altars **H** has taken away,	2Ki 18:22	2396
'Do not let **H** deceive you, for he	2Ki 18:29	2396
let **H** make you trust in the LORD,	2Ki 18:30	2396
'Do not listen to **H**,	2Ki 18:31	2396
But do not listen to **H** when	2Ki 18:32	2396
came to **H** with their clothes torn	2Ki 18:37	2396
And when King **H** heard *it*, he tore	2Ki 19:1	2396
"Thus says **H**, 'This day is a day of	2Ki 19:3	2396
servants of King **H** came to Isaiah.	2Ki 19:5	2396
sent messengers again to **H** saying,	2Ki 19:9	2396
you shall say to **H** king of Judah,	2Ki 19:10	2396
Then **H** took the letter from the	2Ki 19:14	2396
H prayed before the LORD and	2Ki 19:15	2396
the son of Amoz sent to **H** saying,	2Ki 19:20	2396
those days **H** became mortally ill.	2Ki 20:1	2396
And **H** wept bitterly.	2Ki 20:3	2396
say to **H** the leader of My people,	2Ki 20:5	2396
Now **H** said to Isaiah,	2Ki 20:8	2396
So **H** answered, "It is easy for the	2Ki 20:10	2396
sent letters and a present to **H**,	2Ki 20:12	2396
for he heard that **H** had been sick.	2Ki 20:12	2396
H listened to them, and showed	2Ki 20:13	2396
that **H** did not show them.	2Ki 20:13	2396
came to King **H** and said to him,	2Ki 20:14	2396
H said, "They have come from a far	2Ki 20:14	2396
So **H** answered, "They have seen all	2Ki 20:15	2396
Then Isaiah said to **H**,	2Ki 20:16	2396
Then **H** said to Isaiah,	2Ki 20:19	2396
the acts of **H** and all his might,	2Ki 20:20	2396
So **H** slept with his fathers, and	2Ki 20:21	2396
which **H** his father had destroyed;	2Ki 21:3	2396
Ahaz his son, **H** his son, Manasseh	1Ch 3:13	2396
in the days of **H** king of Judah,	1Ch 4:41	2396
H his son reigned in his place.	2Ch 28:27	2396
H became king *when he was*	2Ch 29:1	2396
they went in to King **H** and said,	2Ch 29:18	2396
Then King **H** arose early and	2Ch 29:20	2396
Then **H** gave the order to offer the	2Ch 29:27	2396
King **H** and the officials ordered	2Ch 29:30	2396
Then **H** said,	2Ch 29:31	2396
Then **H** and all the people rejoiced	2Ch 29:36	2396
Now **H** sent to all Israel and Judah	2Ch 30:1	2396
For **H** prayed for them, saying,	2Ch 30:18	2396
So the LORD heard **H** and healed	2Ch 30:20	2396
Then **H** spoke encouragingly to all	2Ch 30:22	2396
For **H** king of Judah had	2Ch 30:24	2396
And **H** appointed the divisions of	2Ch 31:2	2396
When **H** and the rulers came and	2Ch 31:8	2396
Then **H** questioned the priests and	2Ch 31:9	2396
Then **H** commanded *them* to prepare	2Ch 31:11	2396
by the appointment of King **H**,	2Ch 31:13	2396
Thus **H** did throughout all Judah;	2Ch 31:20	2396
H saw that Sennacherib had come and	2Ch 32:2	2396
on the words of **H** king of Judah.	2Ch 32:8	2396
against **H** king of Judah and	2Ch 32:9	2396
'Is not **H** misleading you to give	2Ch 32:11	2396
'Has not the same **H** taken away His	2Ch 32:12	2396
do not let **H** deceive you or	2Ch 32:15	2396
God and against His servant **H**.	2Ch 32:16	2396
so the God of **H** will not deliver	2Ch 32:17	2396
But King **H** and Isaiah the prophet,	2Ch 32:20	2396
So the LORD saved **H** and the	2Ch 32:22	2396
presents to **H** king of Judah,	2Ch 32:23	2396
those days **H** became mortally ill	2Ch 32:24	2396
But **H** gave no return for the	2Ch 32:25	2396
H humbled the pride of his heart,	2Ch 32:26	2396
not come on them in the days of **H**.	2Ch 32:26	2396
H had immense riches and honor;	2Ch 32:27	2396
It was **H** who stopped the upper	2Ch 32:30	2396
H prospered in all that he did.	2Ch 32:30	2396
of **H** and his deeds of devotion,	2Ch 32:32	2396
So **H** slept with his fathers, and	2Ch 32:33	2396
H his father had broken down;	2Ch 33:3	2396
the sons of Ater of **H**,	Ezr 2:16	2396
the sons of Ater, of **H**,	Ne 7:21	2396
Ater, **H**, Azzur,	Ne 10:17	2396
of Solomon which the men of **H**,	Pr 25:1	2396
of Uzziah, Jotham, Ahaz *and* **H**,	Is 1:1	2396
in the fourteenth year of King **H**,	Is 36:1	2396
to King **H** with a large army.	Is 36:2	2396
"Say now to **H**, 'Thus says the great	Is 36:4	2396
and whose altars **H** has taken away and	Is 36:7	2396
'Do not let **H** deceive you, for he	Is 36:14	2396
let **H** make you trust in the LORD,	Is 36:15	2396
'Do not listen to **H**,'	Is 36:16	2396
'*Beware* that **H** does not mislead	Is 36:18	2396
came to **H** with their clothes torn	Is 36:22	2396
And when King **H** heard *it*, he tore	Is 37:1	2396
"Thus says **H**, 'This day is a day of	Is 37:3	2396
servants of King **H** came to Isaiah.	Is 37:5	2396
heard *it* he sent messengers to **H**,	Is 37:9	2396
you shall say to **H** king of Judah,	Is 37:10	2396
Then **H** took the letter from the	Is 37:14	2396
H prayed to the LORD saying,	Is 37:15	2396
the son of Amoz sent *word* to **H**,	Is 37:21	2396
those days **H** became mortally ill.	Is 38:1	2396
H turned his face to the wall and	Is 38:2	2396
And **H** wept bitterly.	Is 38:3	2396
"Go and say to **H**,	Is 38:5	2396
A writing of **H** king of Judah after	Is 38:9	2396
Then **H** had said,	Is 38:22	2396
sent letters and a present to **H**,	Is 39:1	2396
H was pleased, and showed them	Is 39:2	2396
that **H** did not show them.	Is 39:2	2396
came to King **H** and said to him,	Is 39:3	2396
H said, "They have come to me from	Is 39:3	2396
H answered, "They have seen all that	Is 39:4	2396
Then Isaiah said to **H**,	Is 39:5	2396
Then **H** said to Isaiah,	Is 39:8	2396
because of Manasseh, the son of **H**,	Jer 15:4	2396
in the days of **H** king of Judah;	Jer 26:18	2396
"Did **H** king of Judah and all	Jer 26:19	2396
of Uzziah, Jotham, Ahaz *and* **H**,	Hos 1:1	2396
the days of Jotham, Ahaz *and* **H**,	Mi 1:1	2396
son of Amariah, son of **H**,	Zph 1:1	2396
and Ahaz the father of **H**.	Mt 1:9	*1478*
H was the father of Manasseh,	Mt 1:10	*1478*
HEZION		
son of Tabrimmon, the son of **H**,	1Ki 15:18	2383
HEZIR		
the seventeenth for **H**,	1Ch 24:15	2387
Magpiash, Meshullam, **H**,	Ne 10:20	2387
HEZRO		
H the Carmelite, Paarai the	2Sa 23:35	2695
H the Carmelite, Naarai the son of	1Ch 11:37	2695
HEZRON		
Hanoch and Pallu and **H** and Carmi.	Gn 46:9	2696
sons of Perez were **H** and Hamul.	Gn 46:12	2696
Hanoch and Pallu, **H** and Carmi;	Ex 6:14	2696
of **H**, the family of the Hezronites;	Nu 26:6	2696
of **H**, the family of the Hezronites;	Nu 26:21	2696

Kadesh-barnea and continued to **H**, **Jos 15:3** 2696
to Perez was born **H**, **Ru 4:18** 2696
and to **H** was born Ram, and to Ram, **Ru 4:19** 2696
sons of Perez *were* **H** and Hamul. **1Ch 2:5** 2696
Now the sons of **H**, who were born **1Ch 2:9** 2696
of **H** had sons by Azubah *his* wife, **1Ch 2:18** 2696
Afterward **H** went in to the **1Ch 2:21** 2696
the death of **H** in Caleb-ephrathah, **1Ch 2:24** 2696
of **H** *were* Ram the firstborn, **1Ch 2:25** 2696
The sons of Judah *were* Perez, **H**, **1Ch 4:1** 2696
Hanoch and Pallu, **H** and Carmi. **1Ch 5:3** 2696
Perez was the father of **H**, **Mt 1:3** *2074*
and **H** the father of Ram. **Mt 1:3** *2074*
the son of Ram, the son of **H**, **Lk 3:33** *2074*

HEZRONITES
of Hezron, the family of the **H**; **Nu 26:6** 2697
of Hezron, the family of the **H**; **Nu 26:21** 2697

HEZRON'S
in Caleb-ephrathah, Abijah, **H** wife, **1Ch 2:24** 2696

HID
and the man and his wife **h** **Gn 3:8** 2244
afraid because I was naked; so I **h** **Gn 3:10** 2244
and Jacob **h** them under the oak **Gn 35:4** 2934
she **h** him for three months. **Ex 2:2** 6845
Egyptian and **h** him in the sand. **Ex 2:12** 2934
Then Moses **h** his face, for he was **Ex 3:6** 5641
she **h** the messengers whom we sent. **Jos 6:17** 2244
for she **h** the messengers whom **Jos 6:25** 2244
was left, for he **h** himself. **Jg 9:5** 2244
everything and **h** nothing from him. **1Sa 3:18** 3582
the people **h** themselves in caves, **1Sa 13:6** 2244
h yourself on that eventful day, **1Sa 20:19** 5641
So David **h** in the field; **1Sa 20:24** 5641
and **h** them by fifties in a cave, **1Ki 18:4** 2244
that I **h** a hundred prophets of the **1Ki 18:13** 2244
and clothes, and went and **h** *them;* **2Ki 7:8** 2934
there *also,* and went and **h** *them.* **2Ki 7:8** 2934
So they **h** him from Athaliah, and **2Ki 11:2** 5641
who were with him **h** themselves. **1Ch 21:20** 2244
h him from Athaliah so that she **2Ch 22:11** 5641
young men saw me and **h** themselves, **Jb 29:8** 2244
In the net which they **h**, **Ps 9:15** 2934
You **h** Your face, I was dismayed. **Ps 30:7** 5641
cause they **h** their net for me; **Ps 35:7** 2934
the net which he **h** catch himself; **Ps 35:8** 2934
I **h** My face from you for a moment, **Is 54:8** 5641
I **h** *My face* and was angry, And he **Is 57:17** 5641
I went and **h** it by the Euphrates, **Jer 13:5** 2934
the prophet, but the LORD **h** them. **Jer 36:26** 5641
Me, and I **h** My face from them; **Ezk 39:23** 5641
and I **h** My face from them. **Ezk 39:24** 5641
and **h** in three pecks of flour **Mt 13:33** *1470*
field, which a man found and **h** **Mt 13:44** *2928*
ground and **h** his master's money. **Mt 25:18** *2928*
and **h** your talent in the ground. **Mt 25:25** *2928*
took and **h** in three pecks of flour **Lk 13:21** *2928*
but Jesus **h** Himself and went out **Jn 8:59** *2928*
away and **h** Himself from them. **Jn 12:36** *2928*
h themselves in the caves and **Rv 6:15** *2928*

HIDDAI
H of the brooks of Gaash, **2Sa 23:30** 1914

HIDDEN
and from Your face I will be **h**, **Gn 4:14** 5641
things, though it is **h** from him and **Lv 5:2** 5956
unclean, and it is **h** from him, **Lv 5:3** 5956
an oath, and it is **h** from him, **Lv 5:4** 5956
it is **h** from the eyes of her husband **Nu 5:13** 5956
And the **h** treasures of the sand." **Dt 33:19** 2934
had taken the two men and **h** them, **Jos 2:4** 6845
to the roof and **h** them in the stalks **Jos 2:6** 2934
five kings had fled and **h** themselves **Jos 10:16** 2244
The five kings have been found **h** in **Jos 10:17** 2244
cave where they had **h** themselves, **Jos 10:27** 2244
where they have **h** themselves." **1Sa 14:11** 2244
men of Israel who had **h** themselves **1Sa 14:22** 2244
by the **h** part of the mountain, **1Sa 25:20** 5643a
he has now **h** himself in one of the **2Sa 17:9** 2244
there is nothing **h** from the king), **2Sa 18:13** 3582
nothing was **h** from the king which **1Ki 10:3** 5956
and the LORD has **h** it from me and **2Ki 4:27** 5956
but she has **h** her son." **2Ki 6:29** 2244
So he was **h** with her in the house **2Ki 11:3** 2244
nothing was **h** from Solomon which **2Ch 9:2** 5956
He was **h** with them in the **2Ch 22:12** 2244
for it more than for **h** treasures, **Jb 3:21** 4301
given to a man whose way is **h**, **Jb 3:23** 5641
"You will be **h** from the scourge **Jb 5:21** 2244
noose for him is **h** in the ground, **Jb 18:10** 2934
what is **h** he brings out to the light. **Jb 28:11** 8587
is **h** from the eyes of all living And **Jb 28:21** 5956
Bind them in the **h** *place.* **Jb 40:13** 2934
He has **h** His face; **Ps 10:11** 5641
there is nothing **h** from its heat. **Ps 19:6** 5641
Acquit me of **h** *faults.* **Ps 19:12** 5641
has He **h** His face from him; **Ps 22:24** 5641
And my sighing is not **h** from You. **Ps 38:9** 5641
I have not **h** Your righteousness **Ps 40:10** 3680
And in the **h** part You will make **Ps 51:6** 5640
And my wrongs are not **h** from You. **Ps 69:5** 3582
My frame was not **h** from You, **Ps 139:15** 3582
The proud have **h** a trap for me, **Ps 140:5** 2934
I walk They have **h** a trap for me. **Ps 142:3** 2934
search for her as for **h** treasures; **Pr 2:4** 4301
judgment, everything which is **h**, **Ec 12:14** 5956
"My way is **h** from the LORD, And **Is 40:27** 5641
caves, Or are **h** away in prisons; **Is 42:22** 2244
And **h** wealth of secret places, **Is 45:3** 4301
Even **h** things which you have not **Is 48:6** 5341
He has **h** Me in His quiver. **Is 49:2** 5641
sins have **h** *His* face from you **Is 59:2** 5641
For You have **h** Your face from us And **Is 64:7** 5641
because they are **h** from My sight! **Is 65:16** 5641
from the place where I had **h** it; **Jer 13:7** 2934
they are not **h** from My face, nor **Jer 16:17** 5641
me And **h** snares for my feet. **Jer 18:22** 2934
and I have **h** My face from this **Jer 33:5** 5641
oil and honey **h** in the field." **Jer 41:8** 4301
over these stones that I have **h**; **Jer 43:10** 2934
reveals the profound and **h** things; **Da 2:22** 5642a
h treasures of gold and silver **Da 11:43** 4362
and Israel is not **h** from Me; **Hos 5:3** 3582
will be **h** from My sight. **Hos 13:14** 5641
And his **h** treasures searched out! **Ob 1:6** 4710
will become drunk, You will be **h**. **Na 3:11** 5956
Perhaps you will be **h** In the day **Zph 2:3** 5641
A city set on a hill cannot be **h**; **Mt 5:14** *2928*
or **h** that will not be known. **Mt 10:26** *2927*
that You have **h** these things from **Mt 11:25** *2928*
I WILL UTTER THINGS **H** SINCE **Mt 13:35** *2928*
is like a treasure **h** in the field, **Mt 13:44** *2928*
"For nothing is **h**, except to be **Mk 4:22** *2927*
nothing is **h** that will not become **Lk 8:17** *2927*
that You have **h** these things from **Lk 10:21** *613*
and **h** that will not be known. **Lk 12:2** *2927*
this statement was **h** from them, **Lk 18:34** *2928*
they have been **h** from your eyes. **Lk 19:42** *2928*
wisdom in a mystery, the **h** **1Co 2:7** *613*
to light the things **h** in the darkness **1Co 4:5** *2927*
the things **h** because of shame, **2Co 4:2** *2927*
which for ages has been **h** in God who **Eph 3:9** *613*
the mystery which has been **h** from **Col 1:26** *613*
in whom are **h** all the treasures of **Col 2:3** *614*
your life is **h** with Christ in God. **Col 3:3** *2928*
is no creature **h** from His sight, **Heb 4:13** *852*
was **h** for three months by his **Heb 11:23** *2928*
it be the **h** person of the heart, **1Pe 3:4** *2927*
who are **h** reefs in your love feasts **Jude 1:12** *4694*
I will give *some* of the **h** manna, **Rv 2:17** *2928*

HIDE
"Shall I **h** from Abraham what I am **Gn 18:17** 3680
"We will not **h** from my lord that **Gn 47:18** 3582
when she could **h** him no longer, **Ex 2:3** 6845
the bull and its **h** and its refuse, **Ex 29:14** 5785
'But the **h** of the bull and all its **Lv 4:11** 5785
the bull and its **h** and its flesh and **Lv 8:17** 5785
its **h** and its flesh and its blood, **Nu 19:5** 5785
those who are left and **h** themselves **Dt 7:20** 5641
them and **h** My face from them, **Dt 31:17** 5641
"But I will surely **h** My face in **Dt 31:18** 5641
'I will **h** My face from them, I **Dt 32:20** 5641
and **h** yourselves there for three **Jos 2:16** 2247
Do not **h** it from me." **Jos 7:19** 3582
Please do not **h** it from me. **1Sa 3:17** 3582
if you **h** anything from me of all **1Sa 3:17** 3582
in a secret place and **h** yourself. **1Sa 19:2** 2244
my father **h** this thing from me? **1Sa 20:2** 5641
that I may **h** myself in the field **1Sa 20:5** 5641
"Please do not **h** anything from me **2Sa 14:18** 3582
h yourself by the brook Cherith, **1Ki 17:3** 5641
an inner room to **h** yourself." **1Ki 22:25** 2247
camp to **h** themselves in the field, **2Ki 7:12** 2247
an inner room to **h** yourself." **2Ch 18:24** 2244
womb, Or **h** trouble from my eyes. **Jb 3:10** 5641
Then I will not **h** from Your face: **Jb 13:20** 5641
"Why do You **h** Your face And **Jb 13:24** 5641
that You would **h** me in Sheol, **Jb 14:13** 6845
made to **h** themselves altogether. **Jb 24:4** 2244
of iniquity may **h** themselves. **Jb 34:22** 5641
"**H** them in the dust together; **Jb 40:13** 2934
h *Yourself* in times of trouble? **Ps 10:1** 5956
long will You **h** Your face from me? **Ps 13:1** 5641
H me in the shadow of Your wings **Ps 17:8** 5641
place of His tent He will **h** me; **Ps 27:5** 5641
Do not **h** Your face from me, Do not **Ps 27:9** 5641
You **h** them in the secret **Ps 31:20** 5641
You, And my iniquity I did not **h**; **Ps 32:5** 3680
Why do You **h** Your face *And* **Ps 44:24** 5641
H Your face from my sins And blot **Ps 51:9** 5641
not **h** Yourself from my supplication. **Ps 55:1** 5956
Then I could **h** myself from him. **Ps 55:12** 5641
H me from the secret counsel of **Ps 64:2** 5641
not **h** Your face from Your servant, **Ps 69:17** 5641
Why do You **h** Your face from me? **Ps 88:14** 5641
Will You **h** Yourself forever? **Ps 89:46** 5641
Do not **h** Your face from me in the **Ps 102:2** 5641
You **h** Your face, they are **Ps 104:29** 5641
Do not **h** Your commandments from **Ps 119:19** 5641
Do not **h** Your face from me, Or I **Ps 143:7** 5641
the wicked rise, men **h** themselves. **Pr 28:12** 2664
the wicked rise, men **h** themselves; **Pr 28:28** 5641
prayer, I will **h** My eyes from you **Is 1:15** 5956
Enter the rock and **h** in the dust **Is 2:10** 2934
H the outcasts, do not betray the **Is 16:3** 5641
H for a little while Until **Is 26:20** 2247
h their plans from the LORD, **Is 29:15** 5641
Teacher will no longer **h** Himself, **Is 30:20** 3670
one from whom men **h** their face He **Is 53:3** 4564
to **h** yourself from your own flesh? **Is 58:7** 5956
go to the Euphrates and **h** it there **Jer 13:4** 2934
I commanded you to **h** there." **Jer 13:6** 2934
a man **h** himself in hiding places So **Jer 23:24** 5641
"Go, **h** yourself, you and **Jer 36:19** 5641
do not **h** anything from me." **Jer 38:14** 3582
do not **h** *it* from us and we will **Jer 38:25** 3582
and **h** them in the mortar in the brick **Jer 43:9** 2934
"Do not **h** Your ear from my **La 3:56** 5956
h their eyes from My sabbaths, **Ezk 22:26** 5956
h My face from them any longer, **Ezk 39:29** 5641
and they ran away to **h** themselves. **Da 10:7** 2244
they **h** on the summit of Carmel, **Am 9:3** 2244
He will **h** His face from them at **Mi 3:4** 5641
"Fall on us and **h** us from the **Rv 6:16** *2928*

HIDES
camp, and they shall burn their **h**, **Lv 16:27** 5785
hiding places where he **h** himself and **1Sa 23:23** 2244
And he **h** it under his tongue, **Jb 20:12** 3582
And when He **h** His face, who then **Jb 34:29** 5641
that **h** counsel without knowledge? **Jb 42:3** 5956
sees the evil and **h** himself, **Pr 22:3** 5641
man sees evil *and* **h** himself, **Pr 27:12** 5641
You are a God who **h** Himself, **Is 45:15** 5641

HIDING
you, Let them be your **h** place! **Dt 32:38** 5643b
he is **h** himself by the baggage. **1Sa 10:22** 2244
"Is David not **h** with us in the **1Sa 23:19** 5641
h places where he hides himself and **1Sa 23:23** 4224b
David **h** on the hill of Hachilah, **1Sa 26:1** 5641
him while he was **h** in Samaria; **2Ch 22:9** 2244
'Clouds are a **h** place for Him, so **Jb 22:14** 5643a
By **h** my iniquity in my bosom, **Jb 31:33** 2934
In the **h** places he kills the innocent **Ps 10:8** 4565
lurks in a **h** place as a lion in his **Ps 10:9** 4565
a young lion lurking in **h** places. **Ps 17:12** 4565
He made darkness His **h** place, **Ps 18:11** 5643a
You are my **h** place; **Ps 32:7** 5643a
you in the **h** place of thunder; **Ps 81:7** 5643a
You are my **h** place and my shield; **Ps 119:114** 5643a
LORD who is **h** His face from the **Is 8:17** 5641
Be a **h** place to them from the **Is 16:4** 5643a
a man hide himself in **h** places So **Jer 23:24** 4565
left His **h** place like the lion; **Jer 25:38** 5520
I have uncovered his **h** places So **Jer 49:10** 4565
And there is the **h** of His power. **Hab 3:4** 2253

HIEL
H the Bethelite built Jericho; **1Ki 16:34** 2419

HIERAPOLIS
those who are in Laodicea and **H**. **Col 4:13** *2404*

HIGGAION
the wicked is snared. **H** Selah. **Ps 9:16** 1902

HIGH
so that all the **h** mountains **Gn 7:19** 1364
now he was a priest of God Most **H**. **Gn 14:18** 5945b
"Blessed be Abram of God Most **H**, **Gn 14:19** 5945b
And blessed be God Most **H**, **Gn 14:20** 5945b
have sworn to the LORD God Most **H**, **Gn 14:22** 5945b
"Behold, it is still **h** day; **Gn 29:7** 1419
wide, and one and a half cubits **h**. **Ex 25:10** 6967
wide and one and a half cubits **h**. **Ex 25:23** 6967
wide and one and a half cubits **h**. **Ex 37:10** 6967
wide, square, and two cubits **h**; **Ex 37:25** 6967
wide, square, and three cubits **h**. **Ex 38:1** 6967
'I then will destroy your **h** places, **Lv 26:30** 1116
him up to the **h** places of Baal, **Nu 22:41** 1116
knows the knowledge of the Most **H**, **Nu 24:16** 5945b
and demolish all their **h** places; **Nu 33:52** 1116
live in it until the death of the **h** priest **Nu 35:25** 1419
until the death of the **h** priest. **Nu 35:28** 1419
But after the death of the **h** priest **Nu 35:28** 1419
was no city that was too **h** for us; **Dt 2:36** 7682
cities fortified with **h** walls, **Dt 3:5** 1364
on the **h** mountains and on the **Dt 12:2** 7311
He will set you **h** above all nations **Dt 26:19** 5945a
set you **h** above all the nations of **Dt 28:1** 5945a
until your **h** and fortified walls in **Dt 28:52** 1364
"When the Most **H** gave the nations **Dt 32:8** 5945b
ride on the **h** places of the earth, **Dt 32:13** 1116
will tread upon their **h** places." **Dt 33:29** 1116
one who is **h** priest in those days. **Jos 20:6** 1419
on the **h** places of the field. **Jg 5:18** 4791
when they were in **h** spirits, **Jg 16:25** 2895
a sacrifice on the **h** place today. **1Sa 9:12** 1116
he goes up to the **h** place to eat, **1Sa 9:13** 1116
them to go up to the **h** place. **1Sa 9:14** 1116
Go up before me to the **h** place, **1Sa 9:19** 1116
from the **h** place into the city, **1Sa 9:25** 1116
down from the **h** place with harp, **1Sa 10:5** 1116
he came to the **h** place. **1Sa 10:13** 1116
Israel, is slain on your **h** places! **2Sa 1:19** 1116
is slain on your **h** places. **2Sa 1:25** 1116
And the Most **H** uttered His voice. **2Sa 22:14** 5945b
"He sent from on **h**, He took me; **2Sa 22:17** 4791
feet, And sets me on my **h** places. **2Sa 22:34** 1116
man who was raised on **h** declares, **2Sa 23:1** 5920
still sacrificing on the **h** places, **1Ki 3:2** 1116
burned incense on the **h** places. **1Ki 3:3** 1116
for that was the great **h** place; **1Ki 3:4** 1116
whole house, each five cubits **h**; **1Ki 6:10** 6967
of olive wood, each ten cubits **h**. **1Ki 6:23** 6967
a circular form half a cubit **h**, **1Ki 7:35** 6967
Then Solomon built a **h** place for **1Ki 11:7** 1116
And he made houses on **h** places, **1Ki 12:31** 1116
priests of the **h** places which he had **1Ki 12:32** 1116
sacrifice the priests of the **h** places **1Ki 13:2** 1116
against all the houses of the **h** places **1Ki 13:32** 1116
he made priests of the **h** places from **1Ki 13:33** 1116
to be priests of the **h** places. **1Ki 13:33** 1116
they also built for themselves **h** places **1Ki 14:23** 1116
pillars and Asherim on every **h** hill **1Ki 14:23** 1364
the **h** places were not taken away; **1Ki 15:14** 1116
the **h** places were not taken away; **1Ki 22:43** 1116
and burnt incense on the **h** places. **1Ki 22:43** 1116
the **h** places were not taken away; **2Ki 12:3** 1166
burned incense on the **h** places. **2Ki 12:3** 1116
the king's scribe and the **h** priest **2Ki 12:10** 1419
the **h** places were not taken away; **2Ki 14:4** 1116

burned incense on the **h** places.	**2Ki 14:4**	1116
the **h** places were not taken away;	**2Ki 15:4**	1116
burned incense on the **h** places.	**2Ki 15:4**	1116
the **h** places were not taken away;	**2Ki 15:35**	1116
burned incense on the **h** places.	**2Ki 15:35**	1116
and burned incense on the **h** places	**2Ki 16:4**	1116
they built for themselves **h** places in	**2Ki 17:9**	1116
pillars and Asherim on every **h** hill	**2Ki 17:10**	1364
they burned incense on all the **h** places	**2Ki 17:11**	1116
put them in the houses of the **h** places	**2Ki 17:29**	1116
priests of the **h** places,	**2Ki 17:32**	1116
in the houses of the **h** places.	**2Ki 17:32**	1116
He removed the **h** places and broke	**2Ki 18:4**	1116
is it not He whose **h** places and	**2Ki 18:22**	1116
For he rebuilt the **h** places which	**2Ki 21:3**	1116
"Go up to Hilkiah the **h** priest	**2Ki 22:4**	1419
Then Hilkiah the **h** priest said to	**2Ki 22:8**	1419
king commanded Hilkiah the **h** priest	**2Ki 23:4**	1419
to burn incense in the **h** places	**2Ki 23:5**	1116
and defiled the **h** places where the	**2Ki 23:8**	1116
and he broke down the **h** places of	**2Ki 23:8**	1116
priests of the **h** places did not go up	**2Ki 23:9**	1116
The **h** places which *were* before	**2Ki 23:13**	1116
and the **h** place which Jeroboam	**2Ki 23:15**	1116
and the **h** place he broke down.	**2Ki 23:15**	1116
removed all the houses of the **h** places	**2Ki 23:19**	1116
All the priests of the **h** places who	**2Ki 23:20**	1116
the **h** place which *was* at Gibeon,	**1Ch 16:39**	1116
the standard of a man of **h** degree,	**1Ch 17:17**	4609b
h place at Gibeon at that time.	**1Ch 21:29**	1116
the **h** place which was at Gibeon,	**2Ch 1:3**	1116
the **h** place which was at Gibeon,	**2Ch 1:13**	1116
of the house, thirty-five cubits **h**,	**2Ch 3:15**	753
cubits wide and three cubits **h**	**2Ch 6:13**	6967
of his own for the **h** places,	**2Ch 11:15**	1116
the foreign altars and **h** places,	**2Ch 14:3**	1116
He also removed the **h** places and	**2Ch 14:5**	1116
But the **h** places were not removed	**2Ch 15:17**	1116
removed the **h** places and the Asherim	**2Ch 17:6**	1116
The **h** places, however, were not	**2Ch 20:33**	1116
he made **h** places in the mountains	**2Ch 21:11**	1116
burned incense on the **h** places,	**2Ch 28:4**	1116
every city of Judah he made **h** places	**2Ch 28:25**	1116
and pulled down the **h** places and	**2Ch 31:1**	1116
away His **h** places and His altars,	**2Ch 32:12**	1116
For he rebuilt the **h** places which	**2Ch 33:3**	1116
Ophel *with it* and made it very **h**.	**2Ch 33:14**	1361b
still sacrificed in the **h** places,	**2Ch 33:17**	1116
sites on which he built **h** places and	**2Ch 33:19**	1116
and Jerusalem of the **h** places,	**2Ch 34:3**	1116
altars that were **h** above them	**2Ch 34:4**	4605
They came to Hilkiah the **h** priest	**2Ch 34:9**	1419
Then Eliashib the **h** priest arose	**Ne 3:1**	1419
house of Eliashib the **h** priest.	**Ne 3:20**	1419
the son of Eliashib the **h** priest,	**Ne 13:28**	1419
"Have a gallows fifty cubits **h**	**Es 5:14**	1364
at Haman's house fifty cubits **h**,	**Es 7:9**	1364
He sets on **h** those who are lowly,	**Jb 5:11**	4791
"*They are* **h** as the heavens, what	**Jb 11:8**	1363
heaven, And my advocate is on **h**.	**Jb 16:19**	4791
In that He judges those on **h**?	**Jb 21:22**	7311
the distant stars, how **h** they are!	**Jb 22:12**	7311
of the Almighty from on **h**?	**Jb 31:2**	4791
"When she lifts herself on **h**	**Jb 39:18**	4791
up And makes his nest on **h**?	**Jb 39:27**	7311
"He looks on everything that is **h**;	**Jb 41:34**	1364
And over them return on **h**.	**Ps 7:7**	4791
to the name of the LORD Most **H**.	**Ps 7:17**	5945b
sing praise to Your name, O Most **H**.	**Ps 9:2**	5945b
Your judgments are on **h**,	**Ps 10:5**	4791
And the Most **H** uttered His voice,	**Ps 18:13**	5945b
He sent from on **h**, He took me;	**Ps 18:16**	4791
And sets me upon my **h** places.	**Ps 18:33**	1116
God of Jacob set you *securely* on **h**!	**Ps 20:1**	7682
the Most **H** he will not be shaken.	**Ps 21:7**	5945b
dwelling places of the Most **H**.	**Ps 46:4**	5945b
the LORD Most **H** is to be feared,	**Ps 47:2**	5945b
Both low and **h**, Rich and poor	**Ps 49:2**	1121, 376
And pay your vows to the Most **H**;	**Ps 50:14**	5945b
I will cry to God Most **H**,	**Ps 57:2**	5945b
Set me *securely* on **h** away from	**Ps 59:1**	7682
him down from his **h** position;	**Ps 62:4**	7613
You have ascended on **h**,	**Ps 68:18**	4791
O God, set me *securely* on **h**.	**Ps 69:29**	7682
They speak from on **h**.	**Ps 73:8**	4791
there knowledge with the Most **H**?"	**Ps 73:11**	5945b
Do not lift up your horn on **h**,	**Ps 75:5**	4791
hand of the Most **H** has changed."	**Ps 77:10**	5945b
against the Most **H** in the desert.	**Ps 78:17**	5945b
And the Most **H** God their Redeemer.	**Ps 78:35**	5945b
rebelled against the Most **H** God And	**Ps 78:56**	5945b
provoked Him with their **h** places And	**Ps 78:58**	1116
all of you are sons of the Most **H**.	**Ps 82:6**	5945b
Are the Most **H** over all the earth.	**Ps 83:18**	5945b
Most **H** Himself will establish her.	**Ps 87:5**	5945b
dwells in the shelter of the Most **H**	**Ps 91:1**	5945b
LORD, my refuge, *Even* the Most **H**,	**Ps 91:9**	5945b
I will set him *securely* on **h**,	**Ps 91:14**	7682
praises to Your name, O Most **H**;	**Ps 92:1**	5945b
You, O LORD, are on **h** forever.	**Ps 92:8**	4791
the sea, The LORD on **h** is mighty.	**Ps 93:4**	4791
LORD Most **H** over all the earth;	**Ps 97:9**	5945b
For as **h** as the heavens are above	**Ps 103:11**	1361b
The **h** mountains are for the wild	**Ps 104:18**	1364
spurned the counsel of the Most **H**.	**Ps 107:11**	5945b
But He sets the needy securely on **h**	**Ps 107:41**	7682
The LORD is **h** above all nations;	**Ps 113:4**	7311
our God, Who is enthroned on **h**,	**Ps 113:5**	1361b
It is *too* **h**, I cannot attain to it.	**Ps 139:6**	7682
Stretch forth Your hand from on **h**;	**Ps 144:7**	4791
Let the **h** praises of God *be* in	**Ps 149:6**	7318
seat by the **h** places of the city,	**Pr 9:14**	4791
like a **h** wall in his own imagination.	**Pr 18:11**	7682
men are afraid of a **h** place and of	**Ec 12:5**	1364
Against every **h** tower, Against	**Is 2:15**	1364
proud And walk with heads held **h**	**Is 3:16**	5186
it deep as Sheol or **h** as heaven."	**Is 7:11**	1361b
will make myself like the Most **H**.'	**Is 14:14**	5945b
even to the **h** places to weep.	**Is 15:2**	1116
your shadow like night at **h** noon;	**Is 16:3**	8432
wearies himself upon *his* **h** place	**Is 16:12**	1116
punish the host of heaven on **h**,	**Is 24:21**	4791
brought low those who dwell on **h**,	**Is 26:5**	4791
to fall, A bulge in a **h** wall,	**Is 30:13**	7682
He waits on **h** to have compassion	**Is 30:18**	7311
on every **h** hill there will be streams	**Is 30:25**	5375
is poured out upon us from on **h**,	**Is 32:15**	4791
is exalted, for He dwells on **h**;	**Is 33:5**	4791
is it not He whose **h** places and	**Is 36:7**	1116
Get yourself up on a **h** mountain,	**Is 40:9**	1364
Lift up your eyes on **h** And see who	**Is 40:26**	4791
He will be **h** and lifted up and	**Is 52:13**	7311
"Upon a **h** and lofty mountain You	**Is 57:7**	1364
For thus says the **h** and exalted	**Is 57:15**	7311
"I dwell *on a* **h** and holy place,	**Is 57:15**	4791
to make your voice heard on **h**.	**Is 58:4**	4791
For on every **h** hill And under	**Jer 2:20**	1364
She went up on every **h** hill and	**Jer 3:6**	1364
built the **h** places of Topheth,	**Jer 7:31**	1116
By green trees on the **h** hills.	**Jer 17:2**	1364
Your **h** places for sin throughout	**Jer 17:3**	1116
A glorious throne on **h** from the	**Jer 17:12**	4791
and have built the **h** places of Baal	**Jer 19:5**	1116
'The LORD will roar from on **h**	**Jer 25:30**	4791
as the **h** places of a forest." '	**Jer 26:18**	1116
"They built the **h** places of Baal	**Jer 32:35**	1116
one who offers *sacrifice* on the **h** place	**Jer 48:35**	1116
make your nest as **h** as an eagle's,	**Jer 49:16**	1361b
her **h** gates will be set on fire;	**Jer 51:58**	1364
From on **h** He sent fire into my	**La 1:13**	4791
In the presence of the Most **H**,	**La 3:35**	5945b
from the mouth of the Most **H**	**La 3:38**	5945b
which resembled a throne, **h** up,	**Ezk 1:26**	4480, 4605
and I will destroy your **h** places.	**Ezk 6:3**	1116
and the **h** places will be desolate,	**Ezk 6:6**	1116
their altars, on every **h** hill,	**Ezk 6:13**	7311
h places of various colors and	**Ezk 16:16**	1116
a **h** place in every square.	**Ezk 16:24**	7413
"You built yourself a **h** place at	**Ezk 16:25**	7413
made your **h** place in every square,	**Ezk 16:31**	7413
shrines, demolish your **h** places,	**Ezk 16:39**	7413
it on a **h** and lofty mountain.	**Ezk 17:22**	1364
"On the **h** mountain of Israel I	**Ezk 17:23**	4791
I bring down the **h** tree,	**Ezk 17:24**	1364
every **h** hill and every leafy tree,	**Ezk 20:28**	7311
is the **h** place to which you go?	**Ezk 20:29**	1116
on the **h** mountain of Israel,"	**Ezk 20:40**	4791
is low and abase that which is **h**.	**Ezk 21:26**	1364
and forest shade, And very **h**,	**Ezk 31:3**	6967
made it grow, the deep made it **h**.	**Ezk 31:4**	7311
"Because it is **h** in stature and	**Ezk 31:10**	1361b
the mountains and on every **h** hill;	**Ezk 34:6**	7311
and set me on a very **h** mountain,	**Ezk 40:2**	1364
the side pillars sixty cubits **h**;	**Ezk 40:14**	
and a half wide and one cubit **h**,	**Ezk 40:42**	1363
six cubits **h**; and the width of	**Ezk 41:3**	
altar *was* of wood, three cubits **h**	**Ezk 41:22**	1364
said to his **h** officials,	**Da 3:24**	1907
you servants of the Most **H** God,	**Da 3:26**	5943
king's **h** officials gathered around	**Da 3:27**	1907
the Most **H** God has done for me.	**Da 4:2**	5943
the Most **H** is ruler over the realm of	**Da 4:17**	5943
this is the decree of the Most **H**,	**Da 4:24**	5943
the Most **H** is ruler over the realm of	**Da 4:25**	5943
the Most **H** is ruler over the realm of	**Da 4:32**	5943
and I blessed the Most **H** and	**Da 4:34**	5943
Most **H** God granted sovereignty,	**Da 5:18**	5943
Most **H** God is ruler over the realm	**Da 5:21**	5943
the **h** officials and the governors	**Da 6:7**	1907
He will speak out against the Most **H**	**Da 7:25**	5943
"O Daniel, man of **h** esteem,	**Da 10:11**	2536b
"O man of **h** esteem, do not be	**Da 10:19**	2536b
Also the **h** places of Aven, the sin	**Hos 10:8**	1116
they call them to *the One* on **h**,	**Hos 11:7**	5920
on the **h** places of the earth,	**Am 4:13**	1116
"The **h** places of Isaac will be	**Am 7:9**	1116
"Though you build **h** like the eagle,	**Ob 1:4**	1361b
on the **h** places of the earth.	**Mi 1:3**	1116
What is the **h** place of Judah?	**Mi 1:5**	1116
will become **h** places of a forest.	**Mi 3:12**	1116
bow myself before the God on **h**?	**Mi 6:6**	4791
To put his nest on **h**, To be delivered	**Hab 2:9**	4791
its voice, It lifted **h** its hands.	**Hab 3:10**	7315
And makes me walk on my **h** places.	**Hab 3:19**	1116
cities And the **h** corner towers.	**Zph 1:16**	1364
of Jehozadak, the **h** priest,	**Hg 1:1**	1419
son of Jehozadak, the **h** priest,	**Hg 1:12**	1419
son of Jehozadak, the **h** priest	**Hg 1:14**	1419
son of Jehozadak, the **h** priest,	**Hg 2:2**	1419
son of Jehozadak, the **h** priest,	**Hg 2:4**	1419
he showed me Joshua the **h** priest	**Zch 3:1**	1419
'Now listen, Joshua the **h** priest,	**Zch 3:8**	1419
son of Jehozadak, the **h** priest.	**Zch 6:11**	1419
took Him to a very **h** mountain and	**Mt 4:8**	*5308*
up on a **h** mountain by themselves.	**Mt 17:1**	*5308*
in the court of the **h** priest,	**Mt 26:3**	*749*
might have been sold for a **h** price	**Mt 26:9**	*4183*
struck the slave of the **h** priest and	**Mt 26:51**	*749*
away to Caiaphas, the **h** priest,	**Mt 26:57**	*749*
as the courtyard of the **h** priest,	**Mt 26:58**	*749*
The **h** priest stood up and said	**Mt 26:62**	*749*
And the **h** priest said to Him,	**Mt 26:63**	*749*
Then the **h** priest tore his robes and	**Mt 26:65**	*749*
the time of Abiathar *the* **h** priest,	**Mk 2:26**	*749*
other, Jesus, Son of the Most **H** God?	**Mk 5:7**	*5310*
brought them up on a **h** mountain	**Mk 9:2**	*5308*
struck the slave of the **h** priest and	**Mk 14:47**	*749*
led Jesus away to the **h** priest;	**Mk 14:53**	*749*
the courtyard of the **h** priest;	**Mk 14:54**	*749*
The **h** priest stood up *and came*	**Mk 14:60**	*749*
the **h** priest was questioning Him,	**Mk 14:61**	*749*
his clothes, the **h** priest said,	**Mk 14:63**	*749*
servant-girls of the **h** priest came,	**Mk 14:66**	*749*
be called the Son of the Most **H**;	**Lk 1:32**	*5310*
and the power of the Most **H** will	**Lk 1:35**	*5310*
called the prophet of the Most **H**;	**Lk 1:76**	*5310*
Sunrise from on **h** will visit us,	**Lk 1:78**	*5311*
in the **h** priesthood of Annas and	**Lk 3:2**	*749*
was suffering from a **h** fever,	**Lk 4:38**	*3173*
you will be sons of the Most **H**;	**Lk 6:35**	*5310*
other, Jesus, Son of the Most **H** God?	**Lk 8:28**	*5310*
struck the slave of the **h** priest and cut	**Lk 22:50**	*749*
Him to the house of the **h** priest;	**Lk 22:54**	*749*
clothed with power from on **h**."	**Lk 24:49**	*5311*
who was **h** priest that year,	**Jn 11:49**	*749*
but being **h** priest that year, he	**Jn 11:51**	*749*
and struck the **h** priest's slave,	**Jn 18:10**	*749*
who was **h** priest that year.	**Jn 18:13**	*749*
was known to the **h** priest,	**Jn 18:15**	*749*
into the court of the **h** priest,	**Jn 18:15**	*749*
who was known to the **h** priest,	**Jn 18:16**	*749*
The **h** priest then questioned	**Jn 18:19**	*749*
the way You answer the **h** priest?"	**Jn 18:22**	*749*
bound to Caiaphas the **h** priest.	**Jn 18:24**	*749*
One of the slaves of the **h** priest,	**Jn 18:26**	*749*
(for that Sabbath was a **h** day),	**Jn 19:31**	*3173*
and Annas the **h** priest *was there,*	**Ac 4:6**	*749*
the people held them in **h** esteem.	**Ac 5:13**	*3170*
But the **h** priest rose up, along	**Ac 5:17**	*749*
Now when the **h** priest and his	**Ac 5:21**	*749*
The **h** priest questioned them,	**Ac 5:27**	*749*
The **h** priest said,	**Ac 7:1**	*749*
the Most **H** does not dwell in	**Ac 7:48**	*5310*
of the Lord, went to the **h** priest,	**Ac 9:1**	*749*
bond-servants of the Most **H** God,	**Ac 16:17**	*5310*
the **h** priest and all the Council of	**Ac 22:5**	*749*
The **h** priest Ananias commanded	**Ac 23:2**	*749*
"Do you revile God's **h** priest?"	**Ac 23:4**	*749*
brethren, that he was **h** priest;	**Ac 23:5**	*749*
the **h** priest Ananias came down	**Ac 24:1**	*749*
those who were of **h** reputation	**Ga 2:6**	*5100*
"WHEN HE ASCENDED ON **H**, HE LED	**Eph 4:8**	*5311*
and hold men like him in **h** regard;	**Php 2:29**	*1784*
obtain for themselves a **h** standing	**1Tm 3:13**	*2570*
right hand of the Majesty on **h**,	**Heb 1:3**	*5308*
become a merciful and faithful **h** priest	**Heb 2:17**	*749*
and **H** Priest of our confession;	**Heb 3:1**	*749*
since we have a great **h** priest	**Heb 4:14**	*749*
For we do not have a **h** priest who	**Heb 4:15**	*749*
For every **h** priest taken from	**Heb 5:1**	*749*
so as to become a **h** priest,	**Heb 5:5**	*749*
designated by God as a **h** priest	**Heb 5:10**	*749*
having become a **h** priest forever	**Heb 6:20**	*749*
Salem, priest of the Most **H** God,	**Heb 7:1**	*5310*
us to have such a **h** priest,	**Heb 7:26**	*749*
need daily, like those **h** priests,	**Heb 7:27**	*749*
men as **h** priests who are weak,	**Heb 7:28**	*749*
we have such a **h** priest, who has	**Heb 8:1**	*749*
For every **h** priest is appointed to	**Heb 8:3**	*749*
so it is necessary that this **h** *priest*	**Heb 8:3**	
second, only the **h** priest *enters*	**Heb 9:7**	*749*
Christ appeared *as* a **h** priest of the	**Heb 9:11**	*749*
as the **h** priest enters the holy	**Heb 9:25**	*749*
by the **h** priest *as an offering* for sin,	**Heb 13:11**	*749*
glory in his **h** position;	**Jas 1:9**	*5311*
sins have piled up as **h** as heaven,	**Rv 18:5**	*891*
Spirit to a great and **h** mountain,	**Rv 21:10**	*5308*
It had a great and **h** wall,	**Rv 21:12**	*5308*

HIGHER

water prevailed fifteen cubits **h**,	**Gn 7:20**	4605
And his king shall be **h** than Agag,	**Nu 24:7**	7311
shall rise above you **h** and higher,	**Dt 28:43**	4605
shall rise above you higher and **h**,	**Dt 28:43**	4605
the clouds—they are **h** than you.	**Jb 35:5**	1361b
Lead me to the rock that is **h** than I	**Ps 61:2**	7311
there are **h** officials over them.	**Ec 5:8**	1364
the heavens are **h** than the earth,	**Is 55:9**	1361b
So are My ways **h** than your ways	**Is 55:9**	1361b
the temple *increased* as it went **h**;	**Ezk 41:7**	4605
'Friend, move up **h**';	**Lk 14:10**	*511*
after me has a **h** rank than I,	**Jn 1:15**	*1715*
a Man who has a **h** rank than I,	**Jn 1:30**	*1715*

HIGHEST

who is the **h** among his brothers,	**Lv 21:10**	1419
belong heaven and the **h** heavens,	**Dt 10:14**	8064
down from the **h** part of the land,	**Jg 9:37**	2872
the **h** heaven cannot contain You,	**1Ki 8:27**	8064
the **h** heavens cannot contain Him?	**2Ch 2:6**	8064
the **h** heaven cannot contain You;	**2Ch 6:18**	8064
Him who rides upon the **h** heavens,	**Ps 68:33**	8064
The **h** of the kings of the earth.	**Ps 89:27**	5945a
Praise Him, **h** heavens, And the	**Ps 148:4**	8064
And I will go to its **h** peak,	**Is 37:24**	7093
the **h** by way of the second *story.*	**Ezk 41:7**	5945a

'But the saints of the **H** One will — Da 7:18 — 5946
favor of the saints of the **H** One, — Da 7:22 — 5946
wear down the saints of the **H** One, — Da 7:25 — 5946
people of the saints of the **H** One; — Da 7:27 — 5946
Hosanna in the **h**!" — Mt 21:9 — *5310*
Hosanna in the **h**!" — Mk 11:10 — *5310*
"Glory to God in the **h**, — Lk 2:14 — *5310*
in heaven and glory in the **h**!" — Lk 19:38 — *5310*

HIGHLY
to the LORD, for He is **h** exalted; — Ex 15:1 — 1342
to the LORD, for He is **h** exalted; — Ex 15:21 — 1342
So his name was **h** esteemed. — 1Sa 18:30 — 3966
was **h** valued in my sight this day, — 1Sa 26:24 — 1431
so may my life be **h** valued in the — 1Sa 26:24 — 1431
handsome as Absalom, so **h** praised; — 2Sa 14:25 — 3966
with his master, and **h** respected, — 2Ki 5:1
that his kingdom was **h** exalted, — 1Ch 14:2 — 4605
The LORD **h** exalted Solomon in — 1Ch 29:25 — 4605
earth belong to God; He is **h** exalted. — Ps 47:9 — 3966
is the LORD, and **h** to be praised, — Ps 145:3 — 3966
tell *you*, for you are **h** esteemed; — Da 9:23 — 2536b
slave, who was **h** regarded by him, — Lk 7:2 — *1784*
which is **h** esteemed among men — Lk 16:15 — *5308*
not to think more **h** of himself than he — Ro 12:3 — *5252*
reason also, God **h** exalted Him, — Php 2:9 — *5251*
that you esteem them very **h** in love — 1Th 5:13 — *5239a*

HIGH-PRIESTLY
and all who were of **h** descent. — Ac 4:6 — *748*

HIGHWAY
We will go along the king's **h**, — Nu 20:17 — 1870
"We will go up by the **h**, — Nu 20:19 — 4546
We will go by the king's **h** until — Nu 21:22 — 1870
land, I will travel only on the **h**; — Dt 2:27 — 1870
on the east side of the **h** that — Jg 21:19 — 4546
they went along the **h**, — 1Sa 6:12 — 4546
his blood in the middle of the **h**. — 2Sa 20:12 — 4546
he removed Amasa from the **h** into — 2Sa 20:12 — 4546
soon as he was removed from the **h**, — 2Sa 20:13 — 4546
is on the **h** of the fuller's field. — 2Ki 18:17 — 4546
Shallecheth, on the ascending **h**. — 1Ch 26:16 — 4546
on the west *there were* four at the **h** — 1Ch 26:18 — 4546
the path of the upright is a **h**. — Pr 15:19 — 5549
The **h** of the upright is to depart — Pr 16:17 — 4546
on the **h** to the fuller's field, — Is 7:3 — 4546
And there will be a **h** from Assyria — Is 11:16 — 4546
will be a **h** from Egypt to Assyria, — Is 19:23 — 4546
A **h** will be there, a roadway, — Is 35:8 — 4547
will be called the **H** of Holiness. — Is 35:8 — 1870
on the **h** of the fuller's field. — Is 36:2 — 4546
in the desert a **h** for our God. — Is 40:3 — 4546
Build up, build up the **h**, — Is 62:10 — 4546
To walk in bypaths, Not on a **h**, — Jer 18:15 — 1870, 5549
Direct your mind to the **h**, — Jer 31:21 — 4546

HIGHWAYS
days of Jael, the **h** were deserted, — Jg 5:6 — 734
as at other times, on the **h**, — Jg 20:31 — 4546
away from the city to the **h**." — Jg 20:32 — 4546
they caught 5,000 of them on the **h** — Jg 20:45 — 4546
In whose heart are the **h** *to Zion!* — Ps 84:5 — 4546
The **h** are desolate, the traveler — Is 33:8 — 4546
road, And My **h** will be raised up. — Is 49:11 — 4546
and destruction are in their **h**. — Is 59:7 — 4546
'Go therefore to the main **h**, — Mt 22:9 — *3598*
into the **h** and along the hedges, — Lk 14:23 — *3598*

HILEN
H with its pasture lands, Debir — 1Ch 6:58 — 2432

HILKIAH
to the king, Eliakim the son of **H**, — 2Ki 18:18 — 2518
Then Eliakim the son of **H**, — 2Ki 18:26 — 2518
Then Eliakim the son of **H**, — 2Ki 18:37 — 2518
"Go up to **H** the high priest that — 2Ki 22:4 — 2518
Then **H** the high priest said to — 2Ki 22:8 — 2518
And **H** gave the book to Shaphan who — 2Ki 22:8 — 2518
"**H** the priest has given me a book." — 2Ki 22:10 — 2518
the king commanded **H** the priest, — 2Ki 22:12 — 2518
So **H** the priest, Ahikam, Achbor, — 2Ki 22:14 — 2518
king commanded **H** the high priest — 2Ki 23:4 — 2518
in the book that **H** the priest found — 2Ki 23:24 — 2518
Shallum became the father of **H**, — 1Ch 6:13 — 2518
H became the father of Azariah, — 1Ch 6:13 — 2518
the son of Amaziah, the son of **H**, — 1Ch 6:45 — 2518
and Azariah the son of **H**, — 1Ch 9:11 — 2518
H the second, Tebaliah the third, — 1Ch 26:11 — 2518
They came to **H** the high priest — 2Ch 34:9 — 2518
H the priest found the book of the — 2Ch 34:14 — 2518
H responded and said to — 2Ch 34:15 — 2518
And **H** gave the book to Shaphan. — 2Ch 34:15 — 2518
"**H** the priest gave me a book." — 2Ch 34:18 — 2518
Then the king commanded **H**, — 2Ch 34:20 — 2518
So **H** and *those* whom the king had — 2Ch 34:22 — 2518
H and Zechariah and Jehiel, the — 2Ch 35:8 — 2518
Seraiah, son of Azariah, son of **H**, — Ezr 7:1 — 2518
Shema, Anaiah, Uriah, **H**, — Ne 8:4 — 2518
Seraiah the son of **H**, — Ne 11:11 — 2518
Sallu, Amok, **H** and Jedaiah. — Ne 12:7 — 2518
of **H**, Hashabiah; of Jedaiah, — Ne 12:21 — 2518
My servant Eliakim the son of **H** — Is 22:20 — 2518
Then Eliakim the son of **H**, — Is 36:3 — 2518
Then Eliakim the son of **H**, — Is 36:22 — 2518
words of Jeremiah the son of **H**, — Jer 1:1 — 2518
and Gemariah the son of **H**, — Jer 29:3 — 2518

HILL
Sephar, the **h** country of the east. — Gn 10:30 — 2022
survived fled to the **h** country. — Gn 14:10 — 2022
toward the **h** country of Gilead. — Gn 31:21 — 2022
him in the **h** country of Gilead. — Gn 31:23 — 2022
pitched his tent in the **h** country, — Gn 31:25 — 2022
camped in the **h** country of Gilead. — Gn 31:25 — 2022
lived in the **h** country of Seir; — Gn 36:8 — 2022
Edomites in the **h** country of Seir. — Gn 36:9 — 2022
will station myself on the top of the **h** — Ex 17:9 — 1389
Hur went up to the top of the **h**. — Ex 17:10 — 1389
then go up into the **h** country. — Nu 13:17 — 2022
are living in the **h** country, — Nu 13:29 — 2022
up to the ridge of the **h** country, — Nu 14:40 — 2022
to the ridge of the **h** country; — Nu 14:44 — 2022
lived in that **h** country came down, — Nu 14:45 — 2022
So he went to a bare **h**. — Nu 23:3 — 8205
to the **h** country of the Amorites, — Dt 1:7 — 2022
in the **h** country and in the — Dt 1:7 — 2022
to the **h** country of the Amorites, — Dt 1:19 — 2022
'You have come to the **h** country of — Dt 1:20 — 2022
and went up into the **h** country, — Dt 1:24 — 2022
easy to go up into the **h** country. — Dt 1:41 — 2022
and went up into the **h** country. — Dt 1:43 — 2022
h country came out against you — Dt 1:44 — 2022
and the cities of the **h** country, — Dt 2:37 — 2022
and half the **h** country of Gilead — Dt 3:12 — 2022
that good **h** country and Lebanon.' — Dt 3:25 — 2022
"Go to the **h** country, so that — Jos 2:16 — 2022
and came to the **h** country, — Jos 2:22 — 2022
came down from the **h** country — Jos 2:23 — 2022
in the **h** country and in the — Jos 9:1 — 2022
Amorites that live in the **h** country — Jos 10:6 — 2022
the **h** country and the Negev and — Jos 10:40 — 2022
of the north in the **h** country, — Jos 11:2 — 2022
and the Jebusite in the **h** country, — Jos 11:3 — 2022
the **h** country and all the Negev, — Jos 11:16 — 2022
the **h** country of Israel and its — Jos 11:16 — 2022
off the Anakim from the **h** country, — Jos 11:21 — 2022
from all the **h** country of Judah — Jos 11:21 — 2022
from all the **h** country of Israel. — Jos 11:21 — 2022
in the **h** country, in the lowland, — Jos 12:8 — 2022
All the inhabitants of the **h** country — Jos 13:6 — 2022
on the **h** of the valley, — Jos 13:19 — 2022
give me this **h** country about which — Jos 14:12 — 2022
In the **h** country: — Jos 15:48 — 2022
through the **h** country to Bethel. — Jos 16:1 — 2022
since the **h** country of Ephraim is — Jos 17:15 — 2022
h country is not enough for us, — Jos 17:16 — 2022
but the **h** country shall be yours. — Jos 17:18 — 2022
up through the **h** country westward, — Jos 18:12 — 2022
near the **h** which *lies* on the south — Jos 18:13 — 2022
from the **h** which *lies* before — Jos 18:14 — 2022
border went down to the edge of the **h** — Jos 18:16 — 2022
in the **h** country of Ephraim. — Jos 19:50 — 2022
Kedesh in Galilee in the **h** country of — Jos 20:7 — 2022
in the **h** country of Ephraim, — Jos 20:7 — 2022
Hebron) in the **h** country of Judah. — Jos 20:7 — 2022
in the **h** country of Judah, with — Jos 21:11 — 2022
in the **h** country of Ephraim, — Jos 21:21 — 2022
is in the **h** country of Ephraim, — Jos 24:30 — 2022
him in the **h** country of Ephraim. — Jos 24:33 — 2022
the Canaanites living in the **h** country — Jg 1:9 — 2022
took possession of the **h** country; — Jg 1:19 — 2022
sons of Dan into the **h** country, — Jg 1:34 — 2022
in the **h** country of Ephraim, — Jg 2:9 — 2022
in the **h** country of Ephraim; — Jg 3:27 — 2022
down with him from the **h** country, — Jg 3:27 — 2022
in the **h** country of Ephraim; — Jg 4:5 — 2022
by the **h** of Moreh in the valley. — Jg 7:1 — 1389
all the **h** country of Ephraim, — Jg 7:24 — 2022
in the **h** country of Ephraim. — Jg 10:1 — 2022
the **h** country of the Amalekites. — Jg 12:15 — 2022
a man of the **h** country of Ephraim — Jg 17:1 — 2022
he came to the **h** country of — Jg 17:8 — 2022
came to the **h** country of Ephraim, — Jg 18:2 — 2022
there to the **h** country of Ephraim — Jg 18:13 — 2022
part of the **h** country of Ephraim, — Jg 19:1 — 2022
was from the **h** country of Ephraim, — Jg 19:16 — 2022
part of the **h** country of Ephraim, — Jg 19:18 — 2022
from the **h** country of Ephraim, — 1Sa 1:1 — 2022
the house of Abinadab on the **h**, — 1Sa 7:1 — 1389
through the **h** country of Ephraim — 1Sa 9:4 — 2022
you will come to the **h** of God — 1Sa 10:5 — 1389
When they came to the **h** there, — 1Sa 10:10 — 1389
and in the **h** country of Bethel, — 1Sa 13:2 — 2022
hidden themselves in the **h** country — 1Sa 14:22 — 2022
and remained in the **h** country in — 1Sa 23:14 — 2022
at Horesh, on the **h** of Hachilah, — 1Sa 23:19 — 1389
David hiding on the **h** of Hachilah, — 1Sa 26:1 — 1389
Saul camped in the **h** of Hachilah, — 1Sa 26:3 — 1389
they came to the **h** of Ammah, which — 2Sa 2:24 — 1389
they stood on the top of a certain **h**. — 2Sa 2:25 — 1389
of Abinadab which was on the **h**; — 2Sa 6:3 — 1389
of Abinadab, which was on the **h**; — 2Sa 6:4 — 1389
man from the **h** country of Ephraim, — 2Sa 20:21 — 2022
in the **h** country of Ephraim; — 1Ki 4:8 — 2022
in the **h** country of Ephraim, — 1Ki 12:25 — 2022
pillars and Asherim on every high **h** — 1Ki 14:23 — 1389
He bought the **h** Samaria from — 1Ki 16:24 — 2022
and he built on the **h**, — 1Ki 16:24 — 2022
of Shemer, the owner of the **h**. — 1Ki 16:24 — 2022
was sitting on the top of the **h**. — 2Ki 1:9 — 2022
came to the man of God to the **h**, — 2Ki 4:27 — 2022
me from the **h** country of Ephraim. — 2Ki 5:22 — 2022
When he came to the **h**, — 2Ki 5:24 — 6076a
Asherim on every high **h** and under — 2Ki 17:10 — 1389
Shechem in the **h** country of — 1Ch 6:67 — 2022
is in the **h** country of Ephraim, — 2Ch 13:4 — 2022
in the **h** country of Ephraim. — 2Ch 15:8 — 2022
to the **h** country of Ephraim and — 2Ch 19:4 — 2022
vinedressers in the **h** country and the — 2Ch 26:10 — 2022
cities in the **h** country of Judah, — 2Ch 27:4 — 2022
Who may dwell on Your holy **h**? — Ps 15:1 — 2022
may ascend into the **h** of the LORD? — Ps 24:3 — 2022
Let them bring me to Your holy **h** And — Ps 43:3 — 2022
To this **h** country which His right — Ps 78:54 — 2022
God And worship at His holy **h** — Ps 99:9 — 2022
And to the **h** of frankincense. — SS 4:6 — 1389
had a vineyard on a fertile **h**. — Is 5:1 — 7161
of Zion, the **h** of Jerusalem. — Is 10:32 — 1389
Lift up a standard on the bare **h**, — Is 13:2 — 2022
top And as a signal on a **h** — Is 30:17 — 1389
on every high **h** there will be streams — Is 30:25 — 1389
war on Mount Zion and on its **h**." — Is 31:4 — 1389
H and watch-tower have become — Is 32:14 — 6076a
every mountain and **h** be made low; — Is 40:4 — 1389
For on every high **h** And under — Jer 2:20 — 1389
on every high **h** and under every — Jer 3:6 — 2022
from every mountain and every **h** and — Jer 16:16 — 1389
the lowland, from the **h** country and — Jer 17:26 — 2022
abode of righteousness, O holy **h**!' — Jer 31:23 — 2022
straight ahead to the **h** Gareb; — Jer 31:39 — 1389
in the cities of the **h** country, — Jer 32:44 — 2022
'In the cities of the **h** country, — Jer 33:13 — 2022
Who occupy the height of the **h**. — Jer 49:16 — 1389
have gone along from mountain to **h** — Jer 50:6 — 1389
h country of Ephraim and Gilead. — Jer 50:19 — 2022
their altars, on every high **h**, — Ezk 6:13 — 1389
every high **h** and every leafy tree, — Ezk 20:28 — 1389
the mountains and on every high **h**; — Ezk 34:6 — 1389
the places around My **h** a blessing. — Ezk 34:26 — 1389
flock, **H** of the daughter of Zion, — Mi 4:8 — 6076a
city set on a **h** cannot be hidden; — Mt 5:14 — *3735*
went in a hurry to the **h** country, — Lk 1:39 — *3714*
in all the **h** country of Judea. — Lk 1:65 — *3714*
AND EVERY MOUNTAIN AND **H** WILL BE — Lk 3:5 — *1015*
and led Him to the brow of the **h** — Lk 4:29 — *3735*

HILLEL
Now Abdon the son of **H** the — Jg 12:13 — 1985
Then Abdon the son of **H** the — Jg 12:15 — 1985

HILLS
utmost bound of the everlasting **h**; — Gn 49:26 — 1389
And I look at him from the **h**; — Nu 23:9 — 1389
flowing forth in valleys and **h**; — Dt 8:7 — 2022
out of whose **h** you can dig copper. — Dt 8:9 — 2022
it, a land of **h** and valleys, — Dt 11:11 — 2022
the **h** and under every green tree. — Dt 12:2 — 1389
things of the everlasting **h**, — Dt 33:15 — 1389
the **h** and under every green tree. — 2Ki 16:4 — 1389
and towers on the wooded **h**. — 2Ch 27:4
on the high places, on the **h** and — 2Ch 28:4 — 1389
"Go out to the **h**, and bring olive — Ne 8:15 — 2022
you brought forth before the **h**? — Jb 15:7 — 1389
Mine, The cattle on a thousand **h**. — Ps 50:10 — 2022
And the **h** gird themselves with — Ps 65:12 — 1389
And the **h**, in righteousness. — Ps 72:3 — 1389
skipped like rams, The **h**, like lambs — Ps 114:4 — 1389
you skip like rams? O **h**, like lambs? — Ps 114:6 — 1389
Mountains and all **h**; — Ps 148:9 — 1389
Before the **h** I was brought forth; — Pr 8:25 — 1389
the mountains, Leaping on the **h**! — SS 2:8 — 1389
And will be raised above the **h**; — Is 2:2 — 1389
all the **h** that are lifted up, — Is 2:14 — 1389
As for all the **h** which used to — Is 7:25 — 2022
And the **h** in a pair of scales? — Is 40:12 — 1389
And will make the **h** like chaff. — Is 41:15 — 1389
lay waste the mountains and **h** And — Is 42:15 — 1389
be removed and the **h** may shake, — Is 54:10 — 1389
The mountains and the **h** will break — Is 55:12 — 1389
And scorned Me on the **h**, — Is 65:7 — 1389
"Surely, the **h** are a deception, A — Jer 3:23 — 1389
And all the **h** moved to and fro. — Jer 4:24 — 1389
On the **h** in the field, — Jer 13:27 — 1389
By green trees on the high **h**. — Jer 17:2 — 1389
vineyards On the **h** of Samaria; — Jer 31:5 — 2022
the **h** of Ephraim call out, — Jer 31:6 — 2022
Lord GOD to the mountains, the **h**, — Ezk 6:3 — 1389
on your **h** and in your valleys and — Ezk 35:8 — 1389
to the mountains and to the **h**, — Ezk 36:4 — 1389
say to the mountains and to the **h**, — Ezk 36:6 — 1389
And burn incense on the **h**, — Hos 4:13 — 1389
And to the **h**, "Fall on us!" — Hos 10:8 — 1389
And the **h** will flow with milk, — Jl 3:18 — 1389
And all the **h** will be dissolved. — Am 9:13 — 1389
It will be raised above the **h**, — Mi 4:1 — 1389
And let the **h** hear your voice. — Mi 6:1 — 1389
of Him And the **h** dissolve; — Na 1:5 — 1389
The ancient **h** collapsed. — Hab 3:6 — 1389
And a loud crash from the **h**. — Zph 1:10 — 1389
AND TO THE **H**, 'COVER US.' — Lk 23:30 — *1015*

HILLSIDE
and Shimei went along on the **h** — 2Sa 16:13 — 6763, 2022

HIMSELF
Lamech took to **h** two wives: — Gn 4:19
and brought her into the ark to **h**. — Gn 8:9
and the LORD said to **H**, — Gn 8:21 — 3820
and uncovered **h** inside his tent. — Gn 9:21
Lot chose for **h** all the valley of the — Gn 13:11
them and bowed **h** to the earth, — Gn 18:2
"Did he not **h** say to me, — Gn 20:5 — 1931
"God will provide for **H** the lamb — Gn 22:8
bowed **h** to the ground before the — Gn 24:52
and Esau said to **h**, — Gn 27:41 — 3820
is consoling **h** concerning you — Gn 27:42
to take to **h** a wife from there, — Gn 28:6
days' journey between **h** and Jacob, — Gn 30:36
he **h** spent that night in the camp. — Gn 32:21 — 1931
But he **h** passed on ahead of them — Gn 33:3 — 1931
and built for **h** a house and made — Gn 33:17
there God had revealed **H** to him when — Gn 35:7

he did not concern **h** with anything **Gn 39:6**
my master does not concern **h** with **Gn 39:8**
shaved **h** and changed his clothes, **Gn 41:14**
but he disguised **h** to them and **Gn 42:7**
and he controlled **h** and said, **Gn 43:31**
So they served him by **h**, **Gn 43:32** 905
Then Joseph could not control **h** **Gn 45:1**
made **h** known to his brothers. **Gn 45:1**
the man Moses **h** was greatly **Ex 11:3**
master who designated her for **h**, **Ex 21:8**
"If he takes to **h** another woman, **Ex 21:10**
give a ransom for **h** to the LORD, **Ex 30:12** 5315
that priest shall have for **h** the **Lv 7:8**
the sin offering which was for **h**. **Lv 9:8**
after he has shown **h** to the priest **Lv 13:7**
then he shall shave **h**, **Lv 13:33**
he shall count off for **h** seven days **Lv 15:13**
he shall take for **h** two turtledoves or **Lv 15:14**
the sin offering which is for **h**, **Lv 16:6**
make atonement for **h** and for his **Lv 16:6**
the sin offering which is for **h** and **Lv 16:11**
make atonement for **h** and for his **Lv 16:11**
the sin offering which is for **h**. **Lv 16:11**
that he may make atonement for **h** **Lv 16:17**
make atonement for **h** and for the **Lv 16:24**
'No one shall defile **h** for a *dead* **Lv 21:1**
for her he may defile **h**. **Lv 21:3**
'He shall not defile **h** as a **Lv 21:4**
his people, and so profane **h**. **Lv 21:4**
nor defile **h** *even* for his father **Lv 21:11**
not humble **h** on this same day, **Lv 23:29**
means to get it back for **h**, **Lv 25:28**
to you that he sells **h** to you, **Lv 25:39**
sell **h** to a stranger who is sojourning **Lv 25:47**
if he prospers, he may redeem **h**. **Lv 25:49**
from the year when he sold **h** to him **Lv 25:50**
LORD established between **H** and the **Lv 26:46**
to dedicate **h** to the LORD, **Nu 6:2**
which he separated **h** to the LORD; **Nu 6:5**
'He shall not make **h** unclean for **Nu 6:7**
and will bring *him* near to **H**; **Nu 16:5**
choose, He will bring near to **H**. **Nu 16:5**
of Israel, to bring you near to **H**, **Nu 16:9**
'That one shall purify **h** from **Nu 19:12**
but if he does not purify **h** on the **Nu 19:12**
has died, and does not purify **h**, **Nu 19:13**
shall wash his clothes and bathe **h** **Nu 19:19**
not purify **h** from uncleanness, **Nu 19:20**
and He proved **H** holy among them. **Nu 20:13**
bind **h** with a binding obligation, **Nu 30:2** 5315
had taken booty, every man for **h**. **Nu 31:53**
'The blood avenger **h** shall put the **Nu 35:19** 1931
you will **H** fight on your behalf, **Dt 1:30** 1931
a god tried to go to take for **h** a nation **Dt 4:34**
shall not multiply horses for **h**, **Dt 17:16**
shall not multiply wives for **h**, **Dt 17:17**
increase silver and gold for **h**. **Dt 17:17**
he shall write for **h** a copy of **Dt 17:18**
he shall bathe **h** with water, **Dt 23:11**
go in to her and take her to **h** as wife **Dt 25:5**
you as a holy people to **H**, **Dt 28:9**
he provided the first *part* for **h**, **Dt 33:21**
So Joshua made **h** flint knives and **Jos 5:3**
on it, may the LORD **H** require it. **Jos 22:23** 1931
gathered to **h** the sons of Ammon **Jg 3:13**
Ehud made **h** a sword which had **Jg 3:16**
But he **h** turned back from the **Jg 3:19** 1931
relieving **h** in the cool room." **Jg 3:24**
had separated **h** from the Kenites, **Jg 4:11**
is a god, let him contend for **h**, **Jg 6:31**
Jerubbaal was left, for he hid **h**. **Jg 9:5**
rested, and braced **h** against them, **Jg 16:29**
who took a concubine for **h** from **Jg 19:1**
up the priest would take for **h**. **1Sa 2:14**
because the LORD revealed **H** to **1Sa 3:21**
take your sons and place *them* for **h** **1Sa 8:11**
"He will appoint for **h** **1Sa 8:12**
he is hiding **h** by the baggage." **1Sa 10:22** 1931
to make you a people for **H**. **1Sa 12:22**
chose for **h** 3,000 men of Israel, **1Sa 13:2**
LORD has sought out for **H** a man **1Sa 13:14**
how he set **h** against him on the **1Sa 15:2**
he set up a monument for **h**, **1Sa 15:12**
and chose for **h** five smooth stones **1Sa 17:40**
and Jonathan loved him as **h**. **1Sa 18:1** 5315
David because he loved him as **h**. **1Sa 18:3** 5315
Jonathan stripped **h** of the **1Sa 18:4**
that David behaved **h** more wisely **1Sa 18:30**
Then he **h** went to Ramah and came **1Sa 19:22** 1931
for he shut **h** in by entering a **1Sa 23:7**
hiding places where he hides **h** and **1Sa 23:23**
and Saul went in to relieve **h**. **1Sa 24:3**
to the ground and prostrated **h**. **1Sa 24:8**
and by my lord having avenged **h**. **1Sa 25:31**
Then David said to **h**, **1Sa 27:1** 3820
"He has surely made **h** odious **1Sa 27:12**
Saul disguised **h** by putting on other **1Sa 28:8**
man make **h** acceptable to his lord? **1Sa 29:4**
h in the LORD his God. **1Sa 30:6**
the places where David **h** and his men **1Sa 30:31** 1931
to the ground and prostrated **h**. **2Sa 1:2**
Abner was making **h** strong in the **2Sa 3:6**
king of Israel distinguished **h** today! **2Sa 6:20**
He uncovered **h** today in the eyes **2Sa 6:20**
ones shamelessly uncovers **h**!" **2Sa 6:20**
whom God went to redeem for **H** as a **2Sa 7:23**
a people and to make a name for **H**, **2Sa 7:23**
So David made a name *for* **h** when **2Sa 8:13**
fell on his face and prostrated **h**. **2Sa 9:6**

Again he prostrated **h** and said, **2Sa 9:8**
since he might do **h** harm!" **2Sa 12:18**
anointed **h**, and changed his **2Sa 12:20**
sister Tamar that he made **h** ill, **2Sa 13:2**
prostrated **h** and blessed the king; **2Sa 14:22**
prostrated **h** on his face to the ground **2Sa 14:33**
Absalom provided for **h** a chariot **2Sa 15:1**
near to prostrate **h** before him, **2Sa 15:5**
weary and he refreshed **h** there. **2Sa 16:14**
he has now hidden **h** in one of the **2Sa 17:9** 1931
house in order, and strangled **h**; **2Sa 17:23**
had taken and set up for **h** a pillar **2Sa 18:18**
and behold, a man running by **h**. **2Sa 18:24** 905
"If he is by **h** there is good news **2Sa 18:25** 905
another man running by **h**." **2Sa 18:26** 905
And he prostrated **h** before the **2Sa 18:28**
does not find for **h** fortified cities **2Sa 20:6**
the son of Haggith exalted **h**, **1Ki 1:5**
So he prepared for **h** chariots and **1Ki 1:5**
he prostrated **h** before the king **1Ki 1:23**
And the king bowed **h** on the bed. **1Ki 1:47**
prostrated **h** before King Solomon, **1Ki 1:53**
He may incline our hearts to **H**, **1Ki 8:58**
He gathered men to **h** and **1Ki 11:24**
had clothed **h** with a new cloak; **1Ki 11:29**
he could not draw it back to **h**. **1Ki 13:4**
the LORD will raise up for **H** a **1Ki 14:14**
he *was* at Tirzah drinking **h** drunk **1Ki 16:9**
he stretched **h** upon the child three **1Ki 17:21**
So Elijah went to show **h** to Ahab. **1Ki 18:2**
Ahab went one way by **h** and Obadiah **1Ki 18:6** 905
and Obadiah went another way by **h**. **1Ki 18:6** 905
But he **h** went a day's journey into **1Ki 19:4** 1931
requested for **h** that he might die, **1Ki 19:4** 5315
Ben-hadad was drinking **h** drunk **1Ki 20:16**
disguised **h** with a bandage over his **1Ki 20:38**
like Ahab who sold **h** to do evil **1Ki 21:25**
how Ahab has humbled **h** before Me? **1Ki 21:29**
he has humbled **h** before Me, **1Ki 21:29**
made horns of iron for **h** and said, **1Ki 22:11**
So the king of Israel disguised **h** **1Ki 22:30**
hands, and he stretched **h** on him; **2Ki 4:34**
went up and stretched **h** on him; **2Ki 4:35**
So he went down and dipped **h** **2Ki 5:14**
him, so that he guarded **h** there, **2Ki 6:10**
Jehu had stationed for **h** eighty men **2Ki 10:24**
covered **h** with sackcloth and **2Ki 19:1**
houses for **h** in the city of David; **1Ch 15:1**
went to redeem for **H** *as* a people, **1Ch 17:21**
and prostrated **h** before David with **1Ch 21:21**
consecrate **h** this day to the LORD? **1Ch 29:5**
son of David established **h** securely **2Ch 1:1**
LORD and a royal palace for **h**. **2Ch 2:1**
the LORD and a royal palace for **h**. **2Ch 2:12**
And when he humbled **h**, **2Ch 12:12**
strengthened **h** in Jerusalem and **2Ch 12:13**
Whoever comes to consecrate **h** with **2Ch 13:9** 3027
and took fourteen wives to **h**, **2Ch 13:21**
out for **h** in the city of David, **2Ch 16:14**
he allied **h** by marriage with Ahab. **2Ch 18:1**
made horns of iron for **h** and said, **2Ch 18:10**
So the king of Israel disguised **h**, **2Ch 18:29**
and the king of Israel propped **h** **2Ch 18:34**
king of Judah allied **h** with Ahaziah **2Ch 20:35**
So he allied **h** with him to make **2Ch 20:36**
of his father and made **h** secure, **2Ch 21:4**
year Jehoiada strengthened **h**, **2Ch 23:1**
covenant between **h** and all the people **2Ch 23:16**
Now Amaziah strengthened **h** and **2Ch 25:11**
and he **h** also hastened to get out **2Ch 26:20** 1931
made altars for **h** in every corner of **2Ch 28:24**
thought to break into them for **h**. **2Ch 32:1**
made for **h** treasuries for silver, **2Ch 32:27**
He made cities for **h** and **2Ch 32:29**
humbled **h** greatly before the God of **2Ch 33:12**
images, before he humbled **h**, **2Ch 33:19**
he did not humble **h** before the **2Ch 33:23**
disguised **h** in order to make war **2Ch 35:22**
he did not humble **h** before **2Ch 36:12**
prostrating **h** before the house of **Ezr 10:1**
and he **h** excluded from the assembly **Ezr 10:8** 1931
Haman controlled **h** **Es 5:10**
And Haman said to **h**, **Es 6:6** 3820
them to present **h** before the LORD. **Jb 2:1**
And he took a potsherd to scrape **h** **Jb 2:8**
Surely now He would rouse **H** for **Jb 8:6**
him, And he mourns only for **h**." **Jb 14:22** 5315
And fill **h** with the east wind? **Jb 15:2** 990
And conducts **h** arrogantly against **Jb 15:25**
trust in emptiness, deceiving **h**; **Jb 15:31**
stir up **h** against the godless. **Jb 17:8**
Or a wise man be useful to **h**? **Jb 22:2**
because he justified **h** before God. **Jb 32:2** 5315
to **H** His spirit and His breath, **Jb 34:14**
"When he raises **h** up, the mighty **Jb 41:25**
has set apart the godly man for **H**; **Ps 4:3**
prepared for **H** deadly weapons; **Ps 7:13**
The LORD has made **H** known; **Ps 9:16**
He says to **h**, "I will not be moved; **Ps 10:6** 3820
He says to **h**, "God has forgotten; **Ps 10:11** 3820
He has said to **h**, **Ps 10:13** 3820
The unfortunate commits **h** to You; **Ps 10:14**
let the net which he hid catch **h**; **Ps 35:8**
sets **h** on a path that is not good; **Ps 36:4**
violent man Spreading **h** like a **Ps 37:35**
Has made **H** known as a stronghold. **Ps 48:3**
while he lives he congratulates **h** **Ps 49:18** 5315
righteousness, For God **H** is judge. **Ps 50:6** 1931
me who has exalted **h** against me, **Ps 55:12**

The God of Israel **H** gives strength **Ps 68:35** 1931
Most High **H** will establish her. **Ps 87:5** 1931
and girded **H** with strength; **Ps 93:1**
Know that the LORD **H** is God; **Ps 100:3** 1931
For He **H** knows our frame; **Ps 103:14** 1931
fetters, He **h** was laid in irons; **Ps 105:18** 5315
But he clothed **h** with cursing as **Ps 109:18**
a garment with which he covers **h**, **Ps 109:19**
with which he constantly girds **h**. **Ps 109:19**
Who humbles **H** to behold *The things* **Ps 113:6**
upon **h** his crown shall shine." **Ps 132:18**
the LORD has chosen Jacob for **H**, **Ps 135:4**
To satisfy **h** when he is hungry; **Pr 6:30** 5315
He who would destroy **h** does it. **Pr 6:32** 5315
he who sins against me injures **h**; **Pr 8:36** 5315
a scoffer gets dishonor for **h**, **Pr 9:7**
a wicked man *gets* insults for **h**. **Pr 9:7**
The merciful man does **h** good, **Pr 11:17** 5315
But the cruel man does **h** harm. **Pr 11:17** 7607
he who waters will **h** be watered. **Pr 11:25** 1931
he who honors **h** and lacks bread. **Pr 12:9**
neglects discipline despises **h**, **Pr 15:32** 5315
separates **h** seeks *his own* desire, **Pr 18:1**
lad distinguishes **h** If his conduct is **Pr 20:11**
also cry **h** and not be answered. **Pr 21:13** 1931
prudent sees the evil and hides **h**, **Pr 22:3**
He who guards **h** will be far from **Pr 22:5** 5315
the poor to make more for **h** **Pr 22:16**
For as he thinks within **h**, **Pr 23:7** 5315
prudent man sees evil *and* hides **h**, **Pr 27:12**
way Will **h** fall into his own pit, **Pr 28:10** 1931
and tell **h** that his labor is good. **Ec 2:24** 5315
the grasshopper drags **h** along, **Ec 12:5**
"King Solomon has made for **h** a **SS 3:9**
will show **H** holy in righteousness. **Is 5:16**
the Lord **H** will give you a sign: **Is 7:14** 1931
come about when Moab presents **h**, **Is 16:12**
he wearies **h** upon *his* high place **Is 16:12**
LORD will make **H** known to Egypt, **Is 19:21**
LORD of hosts revealed **H** to me, **Is 22:14**
Teacher will no longer hide **H**, **Is 30:20**
covered **h** with sackcloth and **Is 37:1**
to me, and He **H** has done it; **Is 38:15** 1931
He seeks out for **h** a skillful **Is 40:20**
Surely he cuts cedars for **h**, **Is 44:14**
raises *it* for **h** among the trees of the **Is 44:14**
he takes one of them and warms **h**; **Is 44:15**
He also warms **h** and says, **Is 44:16**
And he cannot deliver **h**, **Is 44:20** 5315
Truly, You are a God who hides **H**, **Is 45:15**
Surely our griefs He **H** bore, **Is 53:4** 1931
render **H** *as* a guilt offering, **Is 53:10** 5315
Because He poured out **H** to death, **Is 53:12** 5315
Yet He **H** bore the sin of many, And **Is 53:12** 1931
who has joined **h** to the LORD say, **Is 56:3**
a day for a man to humble **h**? **Is 58:5** 5315
aside from evil makes **h** a prey. **Is 59:15**
wrapped **H** with zeal as a mantle. **Is 59:17**
bridegroom decks **h** with a garland, **Is 61:10**
He turned **H** to become their enemy, **Is 63:10**
to make for **H** an everlasting name, **Is 63:12**
arouses **h** to take hold of You; **Is 64:7**
LORD, that a man's way is not in **h**, **Jer 10:23** 376
gash **h** or shave his head for them. **Jer 16:6**
Can man make gods for **h**? **Jer 16:20**
even the king **h** and his servants **Jer 22:4** 1931
"Can a man hide **h** in hiding **Jer 23:24**
So he will wrap **h** with the land of **Jer 43:12** 5844a
shepherd wraps **h** with his garment, **Jer 43:12** 5844a
so as to avenge **H** on His foes; **Jer 46:10**
he will not be able to conceal **h**; **Jer 49:10**
The LORD of hosts has sworn by **H**: **Jer 51:14** 5315
For the enemy has magnified **h**!" **La 1:9**
in Israel who separates **h** from Me, **Ezk 14:7**
prophet to inquire of Me for **h**, **Ezk 14:7**
(though he **h** did not do any of **Ezk 18:11** 1931
of the righteous will be upon **h**, **Ezk 18:20**
of the wicked will be upon **h**. **Ezk 18:20**
his blood will be on **h**. **Ezk 33:5**
feed them **h** and be their shepherd. **Ezk 34:23** 1931
prince shall provide for **h** and all the **Ezk 45:22**
he would not defile **h** with the king's **Da 1:8**
that he might not defile **h**. **Da 1:8**
Daniel began distinguishing **h** among **Da 6:3**
he kept exerting **h** to rescue him. **Da 6:14**
serve will **H** deliver you." **Da 6:16** 1932
did as he pleased and magnified **h**. **Da 8:4**
Then the male goat magnified **h** **Da 8:8**
And he will magnify **h** in his **Da 8:25**
and magnify **h** above every god and **Da 11:36**
he will magnify **h** above *them* all. **Da 11:37**
Ephraim mixes **h** with the nations; **Hos 7:8** 1931
He produces fruit for **h**. **Hos 10:1**
plow, Jacob will harrow for **h**. **Hos 10:11**
He exalted **h** in Israel, But **Hos 13:1** 1931
The Lord GOD has sworn by **H**, **Am 6:8** 5315
covered **h** with sackcloth and sat **Jon 3:6**
There he made a shelter for **h** and **Jon 4:5**
He also gathers to **h** all nations **Hab 2:5**
And collects to **h** all peoples. **Hab 2:5**
And makes **h** rich with loans? **Hab 2:6**
John **h** had a garment of camel's **Mt 3:4** *846*
clothed **h** like one of these. **Mt 6:29**
"HE **H** TOOK OUR INFIRMITIES AND CARRIED **Mt 8:17** *846*
but Jesus **H** was asleep. **Mt 8:24** *846*
accept *it*, John **h** is Elijah **Mt 11:14** *846*
Satan, he is divided against **h**; **Mt 12:26** *1438*
yet he has no *firm* root in **h**, **Mt 13:21** *1438*
in a boat to a secluded place by **H**; **Mt 14:13** *2398*

up on the mountain by **H** to pray; Mt 14:23 *2398*
to come after Me, he must deny **h**, Mt 16:24 *1438*
saw no one except Jesus **H** alone. Mt 17:8 *846*
He called a child to **H** and set him Mt 18:2
then humbles **h** as this child, Mt 18:4 *1438*
prostrated **h** before him, Mt 18:26 *4352*
But Jesus called them to **H** and Mt 20:25
Whoever exalts **h** shall be humbled; Mt 23:12 *1438*
whoever humbles **h** shall be exalted. Mt 23:12 *1438*
and he went away and hanged **h**. Mt 27:5
He cannot save **H**. Mt 27:42 *1438*
who **h** had also become a disciple Mt 27:57 *846*
summoned those whom He **H** wanted, Mk 3:13 *846*
And He called them to **H** and began Mk 3:23
If Satan has risen up against **h** and Mk 3:26 *1438*
how, he **h** does not know. Mk 4:27 *846*
Jesus **H** was in the stern, asleep Mk 4:38 *846*
and gashing **h** with stones. Mk 5:5 *1438*
perceiving in **H** that the power Mk 5:30 *1438*
For Herod **h** had sent and had John Mk 6:17 *846*
while He **H** was sending the Mk 6:45 *846*
him aside from the crowd, by **h**, Mk 7:33 *2398*
to come after Me, he must deny **h**, Mk 8:34 *1438*
Calling them to **H**, Mk 10:42
AND TO LOVE ONE'S NEIGHBOR AS **H**, Mk 12:33 *1438*
"David **h** said in the Holy Spirit, Mk 12:36 *846*
"David **h** calls Him Mk 12:37 *846*
"And he **h** will show you a large Mk 14:15 *846*
and warming **h** at the fire. Mk 14:54
and seeing Peter warming **h**, Mk 14:67
He cannot save **H** Mk 15:31 *1438*
who **h** was waiting for the kingdom Mk 15:43 *846*
Jesus **H** *sent out through them from* Mk 16:20
Jesus **H** was about thirty years of Lk 3:23 *846*
But Jesus **H** would *often* slip away to Lk 5:16 *846*
for He **H** is kind to ungrateful and Lk 6:35 *846*
Him saw this, he said to **h**, Lk 7:39 *1438*
He withdrew by **H** to a city called Lk 9:10 *2398*
to come after Me, he must deny **h**, Lk 9:23 *1438*
world, and loses or forfeits **h**? Lk 9:25 *1438*
where He **H** was going to come. Lk 10:1 *846*
But wishing to justify **h**, Lk 10:29 *1438*
Satan also is divided against **h**, Lk 11:18 *1438*
"And he began reasoning to **h**, Lk 12:17 *1438*
man who stores up treasure for **h**, Lk 12:21 *848*
clothed **h** like one of these. Lk 12:27
you, that he will gird **h** *to serve,* Lk 12:37
who exalts **h** will be humbled, Lk 14:11 *1438*
who humbles **h** will be exalted." Lk 14:11 *1438*
hired **h** out to one of the citizens Lk 15:15
"The manager said to **h**, Lk 16:3 *1438*
but afterward he said to **h**, Lk 18:4 *1438*
stood and was praying this to **h** Lk 18:11 *1438*
who exalts **h** will be humbled, Lk 18:14 *1438*
who humbles **h** will be exalted." Lk 18:14 *1438*
to receive a kingdom for **h**, Lk 19:12 *1438*
David **h** says in the book of Psalms, Lk 20:42 *846*
and saying that He **H** is Christ, Lk 23:2 *1438*
who **h** also was in Jerusalem at Lk 23:7 *846*
He saved others; let Him save **H** if Lk 23:35 *1438*
discussing, Jesus **H** approached Lk 24:15 *846*
concerning **H** in all the Scriptures. Lk 24:27 *1438*
things, He **H** stood in their midst Lk 24:36 *846*
was not entrusting **H** to them, Jn 2:24 *846*
man, for He **H** knew what was in man. Jn 2:25 *846*
Jesus **H** was not baptizing, Jn 4:2 *846*
us the well, and drank of it **h** and Jn 4:12 *846*
For Jesus **H** testified that a Jn 4:44 *846*
and he **h** believed and his whole Jn 4:53 *846*
Father, making **H** equal with God. Jn 5:18 *1438*
you, the Son can do nothing of **H**, Jn 5:19 *1438*
Him all things that He **H** is doing; Jn 5:20 *846*
just as the Father has life in **H**, Jn 5:26 *1438*
to the Son also to have life in **H**; Jn 5:26 *1438*
for He **H** knew what He was Jn 6:6 *846*
again to the mountain by **H** alone. Jn 6:15 *846*
he **h** seeks to be *known* publicly. Jn 7:4 *846*
the feast, then He **H** also went up, Jn 7:10 *846*
speaks from **h** seeks his own glory; Jn 7:18 *1438*
"Surely He will not kill **H**, Jn 8:22 *1438*
but Jesus hid **H** and went out of Jn 8:59
is of age, he will speak for **h**." Jn 9:21 *1438*
He went away and hid **H** from them. Jn 12:36
but the Father **H** who sent Me has Jn 12:49 *846*
taking a towel, He girded **H**. Jn 13:4 *1438*
God will also glorify Him in **H**, Jn 13:32 *846*
for the Father **H** loves you, Jn 16:27 *846*
with them, standing and warming **h**. Jn 18:18
Peter was standing and warming **h**. Jn 18:25
made **H** out *to be* the Son of God." Jn 19:7 *1438*
everyone who makes **h** out *to be* a Jn 19:12 *1438*
Jesus manifested **H** again to the Jn 21:1 *1438*
and He manifested **H** in this way. Jn 21:1
and threw **h** into the sea. Jn 21:7 *1438*
these He also presented **H** alive after Ac 1:3 *1438*
into heaven, but he **h** says: Ac 2:34 *846*
Lord our God will call to **H**." Ac 2:39
kept back *some* of the price for **h**, Ac 5:2
made **h** known to his brothers, Ac 7:13
Even Simon **h** believed; Ac 8:13 *846*
Of **h** or of someone else?" Ac 8:34 *1438*
But Philip found **h** at Azotus, Ac 8:40
When Peter came to **h**, Ac 12:11 *1438*
did not leave **H** without witness, Ac 14:17 *848*
God first concerned **H** about taking Ac 15:14
his sword and was about to kill **h**, Ac 16:27 *1438*
since He **H** gives to all *people* life Ac 17:25 *846*
devoting **h** completely to the word, Ac 18:5
Now he **h** entered the synagogue and Ac 18:19 *846*
he **h** stayed in Asia for a while. Ac 19:22 *846*
it, intending **h** to go by land. Ac 20:13 *846*
of the Lord Jesus, that He **H** said, Ac 20:35 *846*
day, purifying **h** along with them, Ac 21:26
he **h** was about to leave shortly. Ac 25:4 *1438*
he **h** appealed to the Emperor, Ac 25:25 *846*
Paul was allowed to stay by **h**, Ac 28:16 *1438*
The Spirit **H** testifies with Ro 8:16 *846*
but the Spirit **H** intercedes for Ro 8:26 *846*
not to think more highly of **h** than Ro 12:3
For not one of us lives for **h**, Ro 14:7 *1438*
himself, and not one dies for **h**; Ro 14:7 *1438*
will give an account of **h** to God. Ro 14:12 *1438*
not condemn **h** in what he approves. Ro 14:22 *1438*
For even Christ did not please **H**; Ro 15:3 *1438*
yet he **h** is appraised by no one. 1Co 2:15 *846*
but he **h** will be saved, yet so as 1Co 3:15 *846*
Let no man deceive **h**. 1Co 3:18 *1438*
one who joins **h** to a prostitute is one 1Co 6:16
one who joins **h** to the Lord is one 1Co 6:17
But a man must examine **h**, 1Co 11:28 *1438*
eats and drinks judgment to **h** 1Co 11:29 *1438*
who speaks in a tongue edifies **h**; 1Co 14:4 *1438*
who will prepare **h** for battle? 1Co 14:8
and let him speak to **h** and to God. 1Co 14:28 *1438*
then the Son **H** also will be 1Co 15:28 *846*
reconciled us to **H** through Christ and 2Co 5:18 *1438*
Christ reconciling the world to **H**, 2Co 5:19 *1438*
appeal, but being **h** very earnest, 2Co 8:17 *830*
by us for the glory of the Lord **H**, 2Co 8:19 *846*
confident in **h** that he is Christ's, 2Co 10:7 *1438*
him consider this again within **h**, 2Co 10:7 *1438*
he who commends **h** that is approved, 2Co 10:18 *1438*
disguises **h** as an angel of light. 2Co 11:14
advantage of you, anyone exalts **h**, 2Co 11:20
who gave **H** for our sins so that He Ga 1:4 *1438*
he *began* to withdraw and hold **h** Ga 2:12 *1438*
who loved me and gave **H** up for me. Ga 2:20 *1438*
as Christ Jesus **H**. Ga 4:14
he deceives **h**. Ga 6:3 *1438*
reason for boasting in regard to **h** Ga 6:4 *1438*
as sons through Jesus Christ to **H**, Eph 1:5 *846*
For He **H** is our peace, who made Eph 2:14 *846*
that in **H** He might make the two Eph 2:15 *846*
Jesus **H** being the corner *stone,* Eph 2:20 *846*
He who descended is **H** also He who Eph 4:10 *846*
loved you and gave **H** up for us, Eph 5:2 *1438*
He **H** *being* the Savior of the body. Eph 5:23 *846*
the church and gave **H** up for her, Eph 5:25 *1438*
He might present to **H** the church Eph 5:27 *1438*
He who loves his own wife loves **h**; Eph 5:28 *1438*
love his own wife even as **h**, Eph 5:33 *1438*
but emptied **H**, taking the form of Php 2:7 *1438*
He humbled **H** by becoming obedient Php 2:8 *1438*
even to subject all things to **H**. Php 3:21 *846*
so that He **H** will come to have Col 1:18 *846*
Him to reconcile all things to **H**, Col 1:20 *846*
that is, Christ **H**, Col 2:2
Now may our God and Father **H** and 1Th 3:11 *846*
For the Lord **H** will descend from 1Th 4:16 *846*
the God of peace **H** sanctify you 1Th 5:23 *846*
who opposes and exalts **h** above 2Th 2:4
of God, displaying **h** as being God. 2Th 2:4 *1438*
Jesus Christ **H** and God our Father, 2Th 2:16 *846*
Now may the Lord of peace **H** 2Th 3:16 *846*
who gave **H** as a ransom for all, 1Tm 2:6 *1438*
conduct **h** in the household of God, 1Tm 3:15
soldier in active service entangles **h** in 2Tm 2:4
for He cannot deny **H**. 2Tm 2:13 *1438*
anyone cleanses **h** from these *things,* 2Tm 2:21 *1438*
who gave **H** for us to redeem Ti 2:14 *1438*
purify for **H** a people for His own Ti 2:14 *1438*
He **H** likewise also partook of the Heb 2:14 *846*
For since He **H** was tempted in that Heb 2:18 *846*
has **h** also rested from his works, Heb 4:10 *846*
he **h** also is beset with weakness; Heb 5:2 *846*
as for the people, so also for **h**. Heb 5:3 *1438*
And no one takes the honor to **h**, Heb 5:4 *1438*
H so as to become a high priest, Heb 5:5 *1438*
by no one greater, He swore by **H**, Heb 6:13 *1438*
once for all when He offered up **H**. Heb 7:27 *1438*
which he offers for **h** and for the Heb 9:7 *1438*
offered **H** without blemish to God, Heb 9:14 *1438*
it that He would offer **H** often, Heb 9:25 *1438*
away sin by the sacrifice of **H**. Heb 9:26 *846*
hostility by sinners against **H**, Heb 12:3 *1438*
for He **H** has said, Heb 13:5 *846*
and He **H** does not tempt anyone. Jas 1:13 *846*
he has looked at **h** and gone away, Jas 1:24 *1438*
anyone thinks **h** to be religious, Jas 1:26
the world makes **h** an enemy of God. Jas 4:4
but kept entrusting **H** to Him who 1Pe 2:23
and He **H** bore our sins in His body 1Pe 2:24 *846*
glory in Christ, will **H** perfect, 1Pe 5:10 *846*
the Light as He **H** is in the Light, 1Jn 1:7 *846*
and He **H** is the propitiation for 1Jn 2:2 *846*
ought **h** to walk in the same manner 1Jn 2:6 *846*
the promise which He **H** made to us: 1Jn 2:25 *846*
this hope *fixed* on Him purifies **h**, 1Jn 3:3 *1438*
Son of God has the testimony in **h**; 1Jn 5:10 *846*
he **h** does not receive the brethren, 3Jn 1:10 *846*
and is not, is **h** also an eighth Rv 17:11 *846*
Him which no one knows except **H**. Rv 19:12 *846*
and God **H** will be among them, Rv 21:3 *846*
who is holy, still keep **h** holy." Rv 22:11

HIN

one-fourth of a **h** of beaten oil, Ex 29:40 1969
and one-fourth of a **h** of wine for Ex 29:40 1969
sanctuary, and of olive oil a **h**. Ex 30:24 1969
a just ephah, and a just **h**; Lv 19:36 1969
drink offering, a fourth of a **h** of wine. Lv 23:13 1969
with one-fourth of a **h** of oil, Nu 15:4 1969
the drink offering, one-fourth of a **h**, Nu 15:5 1969
mixed with one-third of a **h** of oil; Nu 15:6 1969
shall offer one-third of a **h** of wine Nu 15:7 1969
mixed with one-half a **h** of oil; Nu 15:9 1969
as the drink offering one-half a **h** of wine Nu 15:10 1969
a fourth of a **h** of beaten oil. Nu 28:5 1969
be a fourth of a **h** for each lamb, Nu 28:7 1969
offerings shall be half a **h** of wine for Nu 28:14 1969
and a third of a **h** for the ram Nu 28:14 1969
and a fourth of a **h** for a lamb; Nu 28:14 1969
the sixth part of a **h** by measure; Ezk 4:11 1969
ram and a **h** of oil with an ephah Ezk 45:24 1969
and a **h** of oil with an ephah. Ezk 46:5 1969
and a **h** of oil with an ephah. Ezk 46:7 1969
and a **h** of oil with an ephah. Ezk 46:11 1969
and a third of a **h** of oil to Ezk 46:14 1969

HIND

As a loving **h** and a graceful doe, Pr 5:19 355

HINDER

'Let nothing, I beg you, **h** you from Nu 22:16 4513
And **h** meditation before God. Jb 15:4 1639
do not **h** them from coming to Me; Mt 19:14 *2967*
"Do not **h** him, for there is no Mk 9:39 *2967*
children to come to Me; do not **h** Mk 10:14 *2967*
But Jesus said to him, "Do not **h** *him;* Lk 9:50 *2967*
to come to Me, and do not **h** them, Lk 18:16 *2967*

HINDERED

you **h** those who were entering." Lk 11:52 *2967*
who **h** you from obeying the truth? Ga 5:7 *1465*
than once—and *yet* Satan **h** us. 1Th 2:18 *1465*
so that your prayers will not be **h**. 1Pe 3:7 *1465*

HINDERING

h us from speaking to the Gentiles 1Th 2:16 *2967*

HINDQUARTERS

and all their **h** turned inwards. 2Ch 4:4 268

HINDRANCE

no **h** to the gospel of Christ. 1Co 9:12 *1464*

HINDRANCES

those who cause dissensions and **h** Ro 16:17 *4625*

HINDS

gazelles or by the **h** of the field, SS 2:7 355
gazelles or by the **h** of the field, SS 3:5 355

HINDS'

"He makes my feet like **h** *feet,* 2Sa 22:34 355
He makes my feet like **h** *feet,* Ps 18:33 355
has made my feet like **h** *feet,* Hab 3:19 355

HINGES

and the **h** both for the doors of 1Ki 7:50 6596
As the door turns on its **h**, Pr 26:14 6735b

HINNOM

the valley of **H** to the west, Jos 15:8 2011
it went down to the valley of **H**, Jos 18:16 2011
is in the valley of the son of **H**, 2Ki 23:10 2011
as far as the valley of **H**. Ne 11:30 2011
is in the valley of the son of **H**, Jer 7:31 2011
or the valley of the son of **H**, Jer 7:32 2011

HIP

do not eat the sinew of the **h** Gn 32:32 5384
thigh in the sinew of the **h**. Gn 32:32 5384
be carried on the **h** and fondled on Is 66:12 6654
and his **h** joints went slack and Da 5:6 2783

HIPS

in the middle as far as their **h**, 2Sa 10:4 8351
in the middle as far as their **h**, 1Ch 19:4 4667
curves of your **h** are like jewels, SS 7:1 3409
loosen the sackcloth from your **h** and Is 20:2 4975

HIRAH

whose name was **H**. Gn 38:1 2437
he and his friend **H** the Adullamite. Gn 38:12 2437

HIRAM

Then **H** king of Tyre sent 2Sa 5:11 2438
Now **H** king of Tyre sent his 1Ki 5:1 2438
for **H** had always been a friend of 1Ki 5:1 2438
Then Solomon sent *word* to **H**, 1Ki 5:2 2438
When **H** heard the words of Solomon, 1Ki 5:7 2438
So **H** sent *word* to Solomon, saying, 1Ki 5:8 2438
So **H** gave Solomon as much as he 1Ki 5:10 2438
Solomon then gave **H** 20,000 kors of 1Ki 5:11 2438
Solomon would give **H** year by year. 1Ki 5:11 2438
was peace between **H** and Solomon, 1Ki 5:12 2438
sent and brought **H** from Tyre. 1Ki 7:13 2438
Now **H** made the basins and the 1Ki 7:40 2438
So **H** finished doing all the work 1Ki 7:40 2438
which **H** made for King Solomon 1Ki 7:45 2438
(**H** king of Tyre had supplied 1Ki 9:11 2438
then King Solomon gave **H** twenty 1Ki 9:11 2438
So **H** came out from Tyre to see the 1Ki 9:12 2438
And **H** sent to the king 120 talents 1Ki 9:14 2438
And **H** sent his servants with the 1Ki 9:27 2438
Also the ships of **H**, 1Ki 10:11 2438
of Tarshish with the ships of **H**; 1Ki 10:22 2438
Now **H** king of Tyre sent messengers 1Ch 14:1 2438

HIRAM'S

So Solomon's builders and **H** 1Ki 5:18 2438

HIRE

if it is hired, it came for its **h**. Ex 22:15 7939
shall not bring the **h** of a harlot or Dt 23:18 868
full **h** themselves out for bread, 1Sa 2:5 7936
to **h** for themselves chariots and 1Ch 19:6 7936
silver on the scale **H** a goldsmith, Is 46:6 7936
they **h** *allies* among the nations, Hos 8:10 8566
to **h** laborers for his vineyard. Mt 20:1 *3409*

HIRED
h you with my son's mandrakes." **Gn 30:16** 7936
a **h** servant shall not eat of it. **Ex 12:45** 7916
if it is **h**, it came for its hire. **Ex 22:15** 7916
The wages of a **h** man are not to **Lv 19:13** 7916
a **h** man shall not eat of the holy *gift.* **Lv 22:10** 7916
h man and your foreign resident, **Lv 25:6** 7916
'He shall be with you as a **h** man, **Lv 25:40** 7916
It is like the days of a **h** man *that* **Lv 25:50** 7916
'Like a man **h** year by year he **Lv 25:53** 7916
double the service of a **h** man; **Dt 15:18** 7916
and because they **h** against you **Dt 23:4** 7936
a **h** servant *who is* poor and needy, **Dt 24:14** 7916
Abimelech **h** worthless and reckless **Jg 9:4** 7936
Micah done to me, and he has **h** me **Jg 18:4** 7936
the sons of Ammon sent and **h** the **2Sa 10:6** 7936
the king of Israel has **h** against **2Ki 7:6** 7936
So they **h** for themselves 32,000 **1Ch 19:7** 7936
and they **h** masons and carpenters **2Ch 24:12** 7936
He **h** also 100,000 valiant warriors **2Ch 25:6** 7936
and **h** counselors against them to **Ezr 4:5** 5534b
Tobiah and Sanballat had **h** him. **Ne 6:12** 7936
He was **h** for this reason, that I **Ne 6:13** 7936
but **h** Balaam against them to curse **Ne 13:2** 7936
his days like the days of a **h** man? **Jb 7:1** 7916
And as a **h** man who eagerly waits **Jb 7:2** 7916
he fulfills his day like a **h** man. **Jb 14:6** 7916
h from regions beyond the **Is 7:20** 7917a
as a **h** man would count them, **Is 16:14** 7916
All the **h** laborers will be grieved **Is 19:10** 7938
a year, as a **h** man would count it, **Is 21:16** 7916
Ephraim has **h** lovers. **Hos 8:9** 8566
'Because no one **h** us.' **Mt 20:7** *3409*
"When those **h** about the eleventh **Mt 20:9**
"When those **h** first came, they **Mt 20:10**
in the boat with the **h** servants, **Mk 1:20** *3411*
"So he went and **h** himself out to one **Lk 15:15** *2853*
'How many of my father's **h** men **Lk 15:17** *3407*
make me as one of your **h** men." **Lk 15:19** *3407*
"He who is a **h** hand, and not a **Jn 10:12** *3411*
"*He flees* because he is a **h** hand **Jn 10:13** *3411*

HIRES
So is he who **h** a fool or who hires **Pr 26:10** 7936
a fool or who **h** those who pass by. **Pr 26:10** 7936

HISS
will be astonished and **h** and say, **1Ki 9:8** 8319
And will **h** him from his place. **Jb 27:23** 8319
h because of all its disasters. **Jer 19:8** 8319
and will **h** at all its wounds. **Jer 49:17** 8319
will **h** because of all her wounds. **Jer 50:13** 8319
They **h** and shake their heads At **La 2:15** 8319
They **h** and gnash *their* teeth. **La 2:16** 8319
among the peoples **h** at you; **Ezk 27:36** 8319
h *And* wave his hand *in contempt.* **Zph 2:15** 8319

HISSING
of terror, of horror, and of **h**, **2Ch 29:8** 8322
An object of perpetual **h**; **Jer 18:16** 8292
a desolation and an *object of* **h**; **Jer 19:8** 8322
and make them a horror and a **h**, **Jer 25:9** 8322
make them a ruin, a horror, a **h** and **Jer 25:18** 8322
be a curse and a horror and a **h**, **Jer 29:18** 8322
An object of horror and **h**, **Jer 51:37** 8322

HIT
Saul, and the archers **h** him; **1Sa 31:3** 4672
who is the one who **h** You?" **Mt 26:68** *3817*
who is the one who **h** You?" **Lk 22:64** *3817*

HITCH
and **h** the cows to the cart and **1Sa 6:7** 631

HITCHED
milch cows and **h** them to the cart, **1Sa 6:10** 631

HITS
"Whoever **h** you on the cheek, **Lk 6:29** *5180*
himself, anyone **h** you in the face. **2Co 11:20** *1194*

HITTITE
and the **H** and the Perizzite and **Gn 15:20** 2850
and Ephron the **H** answered Abraham **Gn 23:10** 2850
of Ephron the son of Zohar the **H**, **Gn 25:9** 2850
the daughter of Beeri the **H**, **Gn 26:34** 2850
the daughter of Elon the **H**; **Gn 26:34** 2850
Adah the daughter of Elon the **H**, **Gn 36:2** 2850
is in the field of Ephron the **H**, **Gn 49:29** 2850
Ephron the **H** for a burial site. **Gn 49:30** 2850
a burial site from Ephron the **H**. **Gn 50:13** 2850
the place of the Canaanite and the **H** **Ex 3:8** 2850
the land of the Canaanite and the **H** **Ex 3:17** 2850
the land of the Canaanite, the **H**, **Ex 13:5** 2850
the Canaanite, the Amorite, the **H**, **Ex 33:2** 2850
you, and the Canaanite, the **H**, **Ex 34:11** 2850
them, the **H** and the Amorite, **Dt 20:17** 2850
before you the Canaanite, the **H**, **Jos 3:10** 2850
Lebanon, the **H** and the Amorite, **Jos 9:1** 2850
and the Amorite and the **H** and the **Jos 11:3** 2850
the **H**, the Amorite and the **Jos 12:8** 2850
and the **H** and the Girgashite, **Jos 24:11** 2850
said to Ahimelech the **H** and to **1Sa 26:6** 2850
Eliam, the wife of Uriah the **H**?" **2Sa 11:3** 2850
"Send me Uriah the **H**." **2Sa 11:6** 2850
and Uriah the **H** also died. **2Sa 11:17** 2850
Uriah the **H** is dead also.' **2Sa 11:21** 2850
Uriah the **H** is also dead." **2Sa 11:24** 2850
down Uriah the **H** with the sword, **2Sa 12:9** 2850
of Uriah the **H** to be your wife.' **2Sa 12:10** 2850
Uriah the **H**; thirty-seven in all. **2Sa 23:39** 2850
Edomite, Sidonian, and **H** women, **1Ki 11:1** 2850
except in the case of Uriah the **H**. **1Ki 15:5** 2850
Uriah the **H**, Zabad the son of **1Ch 11:41** 2850
Of the **H** and the Amorite, **Ne 9:8** 2850
an Amorite and your mother a **H**. **Ezk 16:3** 2850
Your mother was a **H** and your **Ezk 16:45** 2850

HITTITES
the land of the Amorites, the **H**, **Ex 23:23** 2850
Canaanites, and the **H** before you. **Ex 23:28** 2850
and the **H** and the Jebusites and the **Nu 13:29** 2850
the **H** and the Girgashites and the **Dt 7:1** 2850
Euphrates, all the land of the **H**, **Jos 1:4** 2850
The man went into the land of the **H** **Jg 1:26** 2850
lived among the Canaanites, the **H**, **Jg 3:5** 2850
were left of the Amorites, the **H**, **1Ki 9:20** 2850
to all the kings of the **H** and to the **1Ki 10:29** 2850
hired against us the kings of the **H** **2Ki 7:6** 2850
all the kings of the **H** and the kings **2Ch 1:17** 2850
the people who were left of the **H**, **2Ch 8:7** 2850
those of the Canaanites, the **H**, **Ezr 9:1** 2850

HIVITE
and the **H** and the Arkite and the **Gn 10:17** 2340
Shechem the son of Hamor the **H**, **Gn 34:2** 2340
the granddaughter of Zibeon the **H**; **Gn 36:2** 2340
and the **H** and the Jebusite. **Ex 3:8** 2340
and the **H** and the Jebusite, **Ex 3:17** 2340
Amorite, the **H** and the Jebusite, **Ex 13:5** 2340
Perizzite, the **H** and the Jebusite. **Ex 33:2** 2340
Perizzite, the **H** and the Jebusite. **Ex 34:11** 2340
Perizzite, the **H** and the Jebusite, **Dt 20:17** 2340
the Canaanite, the Hittite, the **H**, **Jos 3:10** 2340
Perizzite, the **H** and the Jebusite, **Jos 9:1** 2340
and the **H** at the foot of Hermon in **Jos 11:3** 2340
Perizzite, the **H** and the Jebusite: **Jos 12:8** 2340
the **H** and the Jebusite. **Jos 24:11** 2340

HIVITES
the **H** and the Jebusites; **Ex 23:23** 2340
that they will drive out the **H**, **Ex 23:28** 2340
and the **H** and the Jebusites, **Dt 7:1** 2340
The men of Israel said to the **H**, **Jos 9:7** 2340
except the **H** living in Gibeon; **Jos 11:19** 2340
the **H** who lived in Mount Lebanon, **Jg 3:3** 2340
Amorites, the Perizzites, the **H**, **Jg 3:5** 2340
to all the cities of the **H** and of the **2Sa 24:7** 2340
the **H** and the Jebusites, **1Ki 9:20** 2340
the **H**, the Arkites, the Sinites, **1Ch 1:15** 2340
Amorites, the Perizzites, the **H** and **2Ch 8:7** 2340

HIZKI
Zebadiah, Meshullam, **H**, **1Ch 8:17** 2395

HIZKIAH
sons of Neariah *were* Elioenai, **H** and **1Ch 3:23** 2396

HO
"**H**! Every one who thirsts, come to **Is 55:1** 1945
"**H** there! Flee from the land of the **Zch 2:6** 1945
"**H**, Zion! Escape, you who are living **Zch 2:7** 1945

HOARD
"these who **h** up violence and **Am 3:10** 686

HOARDED
riches being **h** by their owner to his **Ec 5:13** 8104
it will not be stored up or **h**, **Is 23:18** 2630

HOBAB
Then Moses said to **H** the son of **Nu 10:29** 2246
from the sons of **H** the father-in-law **Jg 4:11** 2246

HOBAH
and pursued them as far as **H**, **Gn 14:15** 2327

HOBAIAH
the sons of **H**, the sons of Hakkoz, **Ne 7:63** 2252

HOD
Bezer, **H**, Shamma, Shilshah, **1Ch 7:37** 1936

HODAVIAH
The sons of Elioenai *were* **H**, **1Ch 3:24** 1939
Ishi, Eliel, Azriel, Jeremiah, **H** and **1Ch 5:24** 1938
son of Meshullam, the son of **H**, **1Ch 9:7** 1938
and Kadmiel, of the sons of **H**, **Ezr 2:40** 1938

HODESH
By **H** his wife he became the **1Ch 8:9** 2321

HODEVAH
of Kadmiel, of the sons of **H**, **Ne 7:43** 1937

HODIAH
The sons of the wife of **H**, **1Ch 4:19** 1941
Jamin, Akkub, Shabbethai, **H**, **Ne 8:7** 1941
Bani, Hashabneiah, Sherebiah, **H**, **Ne 9:5** 1941
also their brothers Shebaniah, **H**, **Ne 10:10** 1941
H, Bani, Beninu. **Ne 10:13** 1941
H, Hashum, Bezai, **Ne 10:18** 1941

HOE
his mattock, his axe, and his **h**. **1Sa 13:20** 4281
used to be cultivated with the **h**, **Is 7:25** 4576

HOED
It will not be pruned or **h**, **Is 5:6** 5737b

HOES
and the axes, and to fix the **h**. **1Sa 13:21** 1861a

HOGLAH
Zelophehad were Mahlah, Noah, **H**, **Nu 26:33** 2295
Noah and **H** and Milcah and Tirzah. **Nu 27:1** 2295
Mahlah, Tirzah, **H**, Milcah and **Nu 36:11** 2295
Mahlah and Noah, **H**, **Jos 17:3** 2295

HOHAM
sent *word* to **H** king of Hebron **Jos 10:3** 1944

HOISTED
After they had **h** it up, **Ac 27:17** *142*

HOISTING
and **h** the foresail to the wind, **Ac 27:40** *1869*

HOLD
up the lad, and **h** him by the hand, **Gn 21:18** 2388
you may **h** me responsible for him. **Gn 43:9** 1245, 3027
them go and continue to **h** them, **Ex 9:2** 2388
we must **h** a feast to the LORD." **Ex 10:9**
each **h** to the inheritance of the tribe **Nu 36:7** 1692
each **h** to his own inheritance." **Nu 36:9** 1692
"I took **h** of the two tablets **Dt 9:17** 8610
in all His ways and **h** fast to Him, **Dt 11:22** 1692
And My hand takes **h** on justice, **Dt 32:41** 270
h fast to Him and serve Him with all **Jos 22:5** 1692
he arose and took **h** of the doors of **Jg 16:3** 270
laid **h** of his concubine and cut her **Jg 19:29** 2388
"And I took **h** of my concubine and **Jg 20:6** 270
cloak that is on you and **h** it." **Ru 3:15** 270
David took **h** of his clothes and tore **2Sa 1:11** 2388
arise and **h** a contest before us." **2Sa 2:14** 7832
and take **h** of one of the young men **2Sa 2:21** 270
or who takes **h** of a distaff, **2Sa 3:29** 2388
the ark of God and took **h** of it, **2Sa 6:6** 270
he took **h** of her and said to her, **2Sa 13:11** 2388
and take **h** of him and kiss him. **2Sa 15:5** 2388
took **h** of the horns of the altar. **1Ki 1:50** 2388
taken **h** of the horns of the altar, **1Ki 1:51** 270
took **h** of the horns of the altar. **1Ki 2:28** 2388
it could **h** two thousand baths. **1Ki 7:26** 3557
was too small to **h** the burnt offering **1Ki 8:64** 3557
Ahijah took **h** of the new cloak **1Ki 11:30** 8610
enough to **h** two measures of seed. **1Ki 18:32** 1004
Then he took **h** of his own clothes **2Ki 2:12** 2388
hill, she caught **h** of his feet. **2Ki 4:27** 2388
and **h** the door shut against him. **2Ki 6:32** 3905
put out his hand to **h** the ark, **1Ch 13:9** 270
it could **h** 3,000 baths. **2Ch 4:5** 3557
could not **h** his own against them. **2Ch 13:7** 2388
go and **h** a feast in the house of **Jb 1:4** 6213a
you still **h** fast your integrity? **Jb 2:9** 2388
And if I **h** back, what has left me? **Jb 16:6** 2308
the righteous will **h** to his way, **Jb 17:9** 270
And horror takes **h** of my flesh. **Jb 21:6** 270
"I **h** fast my righteousness and **Jb 27:6** 2388
and justice take **h** *of you.* **Jb 36:17** 8551
take **h** of the ends of the earth, **Jb 38:13** 270
H them guilty, O God; **Ps 5:10** 816
bit and bridle to **h** them in check, **Ps 32:9** 1102
Take **h** of buckler and shield And **Ps 35:2** 2388
They **h** fast to themselves an evil **Ps 64:5** 2388
have taken **h** of my right hand. **Ps 73:23** 270
O LORD, will **h** me up. **Ps 94:18** 5582
Your right hand will lay **h** of me. **Ps 139:10** 270
life to those who take **h** of her, **Pr 3:18** 2388
And happy are all who **h** her fast. **Pr 3:18** 8551
"Let your heart **h** fast my words **Pr 4:4** 8551
Take **h** of instruction; **Pr 4:13** 2388
death, Her steps take **h** of Sheol. **Pr 5:5** 8551
for foreigners, **h** him in pledge. **Pr 20:16** 2254a
gives and does not **h** back. **Pr 21:26** 2820
Do not **h** back discipline from the **Pr 23:13** 4513
to slaughter, Oh **h** *them* back. **Pr 24:11** 2820
adulterous woman **h** him in pledge. **Pr 27:13** 2254a
and how to take **h** of folly, **Ec 2:3** 270
will take **h** of its fruit stalks.' **SS 7:8** 270
When a man lays **h** of his brother **Is 3:6** 8610
seven women will take **h** of one man **Is 4:1** 2388
and anguish will take **h** of *them;* **Is 13:8** 270
his hands so that they **h** no bribe **Is 33:15** 8551
h the base of its mast firmly, **Is 33:23** 2388
I will also **h** you by the hand and **Is 42:6** 2388
'Do not **h** *them* back.' **Is 43:6** 3607
the son of man who takes **h** of it; **Is 56:2** 2388
Me, And **h** fast My covenant, **Is 56:4** 2388
"Cry loudly, do not **h** back; **Is 58:1** 2820
arouses himself to take **h** of You; **Is 64:7** 2388
cisterns That can **h** no water. **Jer 2:13** 3557
They **h** fast to deceit, They refuse **Jer 8:5** 2388
I mourn, dismay has taken **h** of me. **Jer 8:21** 2388
Will not pangs take **h** of you Like **Jer 13:21** 270
Distress and pangs have taken **h** of **Jer 49:24** 270
in order to lay **h** of the hearts of **Ezk 14:5** 8610
they took **h** of you with the hand, **Ezk 29:7** 8610
it may be strong to **h** the sword. **Ezk 30:21** 8610
gone below into the **h** of the ship, **Jon 1:5** 3411
Take **h** of the brick mold! **Na 3:14** 2388
Sabbath, will he not take **h** of it and **Mt 12:11** *2902*
out His hand and took **h** of him, **Mt 14:31** *1949*
took **h** of His feet and worshiped **Mt 28:9** *2902*
you **h** to the tradition of men." **Mk 7:8** *2902*
and good heart, and **h** it fast, **Lk 8:15** *2722*
And He took **h** of him and healed **Lk 14:4** *1949*
do not **h** this sin against them!" **Ac 7:60** *2476*
But Barnabas took **h** of him and **Ac 9:27** *1949*
And they all took **h** of Sosthenes, **Ac 18:17** *1949*
and taking **h** of Paul they dragged **Ac 21:30** *1949*
came up and took **h** of him, **Ac 21:33** *1949*
and **h** firmly to the traditions, **1Co 11:2** *2722*
if you **h** fast the word which I **1Co 15:2** *2722*
to withdraw and **h** himself aloof, **Ga 2:12** *873*
and **h** men like him in high regard; **Php 2:29** *2192*
I may lay **h** of that for which also I **Php 3:12** *2638*
I was laid **h** of by Christ Jesus. **Php 3:12** *2638*
myself as having laid **h** of *it* yet; **Php 3:13** *2638*
and in Him all things **h** together. **Col 1:17** *4921*
h fast to that which is good; **1Th 5:21** *2722*
stand firm and **h** to the traditions **2Th 2:15** *2902*
take **h** of the eternal life to **1Tm 6:12** *1949*
take **h** of that which is life indeed. **1Tm 6:19** *1949*
if we **h** fast our confidence and **Heb 3:6** *2722*
if we **h** fast the beginning of our **Heb 3:14** *2722*
God, let us **h** fast our confession. **Heb 4:14** *2902*
take **h** of the hope set before us. **Heb 6:18** *2902*
Let us **h** fast the confession of **Heb 10:23** *2722*
do not **h** your faith in our **Jas 2:1** *2192*
and you **h** fast My name, and did **Rv 2:13** *2902*

some who **h** the teaching of Balaam, **Rv 2:14** 2902
h the teaching of the Nicolaitans. **Rv 2:15** 2902
who do not **h** this teaching, **Rv 2:24** 2192
you have, **h** fast until I come. **Rv 2:25** 2902
h fast what you have, **Rv 3:11** 2902
and **h** to the testimony of Jesus. **Rv 12:17** 2192
who **h** the testimony of Jesus; **Rv 19:10** 2192
And he laid **h** of the dragon, the **Rv 20:2** 2902

HOLDERS
as **h** for the poles to carry the table. **Ex 25:27** 1004
rings of gold *as* **h** for the bars; **Ex 26:29** 1004
they shall be **h** for poles with which **Ex 30:4** 1004
rings of gold *as* **h** for the bars, **Ex 36:34** 1004
the **h** for the poles to carry the **Ex 37:14** 1004
as **h** for poles with which to carry it. **Ex 37:27** 1004
bronze grating *as* **h** for the poles. **Ex 38:5** 1004

HOLDING
with his hand **h** on to Esau's heel, **Gn 25:26** 270
Egyptians are **h** them in bondage, **Ex 6:5** 5647
His voice, and by **h** fast to Him; **Dt 30:20** 1692
to the boy who was **h** his hand, **Jg 16:26** 2388
he was **h** a feast in his house, **1Sa 25:36**
the work and the other **h** a weapon. **Ne 4:17** 2388
half of them **h** spears from dawn until **Ne 4:21** 2388
I am weary with **h** *it* in. **Jer 6:11** 3557
And I am weary of **h** *it* in, **Jer 20:9** 3557
h a notorious prisoner, called Barabbas. **Mt 27:16** 2192
men who were **h** Jesus in custody **Lk 22:63** 4912
h fast the word of life, so that **Php 2:16** 1907
and not **h** fast to the head, from **Col 2:19** 2902
but **h** to the mystery of the faith **1Tm 3:9** 2192
h to a form of godliness, although **2Tm 3:5** 2192
h fast the faithful word which is **Ti 1:9** 472
was a golden jar **h** the manna, **Heb 9:4** 2192
each one **h** a harp and golden bowls **Rv 5:8** 2198
h back the four winds of the **Rv 7:1** 2902
at the altar, **h** a golden censer; **Rv 8:3** 2192
the sea of glass, **h** harps of God. **Rv 15:2** 2192
h the key of the abyss and a great **Rv 20:1** 2192

HOLDS
unless the king **h** out to him the **Es 4:11** 3447
And he still **h** fast his integrity, **Jb 2:3** 2388
He **h** fast to it, but it does not **Jb 8:15** 2388
is at ease **h** calamity in contempt, **Jb 12:5** 6248
let it go, But **h** it in his mouth, **Jb 20:13** 4513
LORD is the One who **h** his hand. **Ps 37:24** 5564
temper, But a wise man **h** it back. **Pr 29:11** 7623a
sabbath And **h** fast My covenant; **Is 56:6** 2388
Aven, And him who **h** the scepter, **Am 1:5** 8551
Ashdod, And him who **h** the scepter, **Am 1:8** 8551
since it **h** promise for the present **1Tm 4:8** 2192
h His priesthood permanently. **Heb 7:24** 2192
The One who **h** the seven stars in **Rv 2:1** 2902

HOLE
a chest and bored a **h** in its lid and **2Ki 12:9** 2356
fallen into the **h** which he made. **Ps 7:15** 7845
will play by the **h** of the cobra, **Is 11:8** 2352b
I looked, behold, a **h** in the wall. **Ezk 8:7** 2356
"Dig a **h** through the wall in **Ezk 12:5**
They will dig a **h** through the wall **Ezk 12:12**
and dug *a* **h** in the ground and hid **Mt 25:18**

HOLES
Hebrews are coming out of the **h** **1Sa 14:11** 2356
h of the earth and of the rocks. **Jb 30:6** 2356
And into **h** of the ground Before **Is 2:19** 4247
to put into a purse with **h**." **Hg 1:6** 5344a
"The foxes have **h** and the birds **Mt 8:20** 5454
"The foxes have **h** and the birds **Lk 9:58** 5454
and caves and **h** in the ground. **Heb 11:38** 3692

HOLIDAY
he also made a **h** for the provinces **Es 2:18** 2010
joy for the Jews, a feast and a **h**. **Es 8:17** 2896a, 3117
a **h** for rejoicing and feasting and **Es 9:19** 2896a, 3117
and from mourning into a **h** **Es 9:22** 2896a, 3117

HOLIER
near me, For I am **h** than you!' **Is 65:5** 6942

HOLIES
the holy place and the holy of **h**. **Ex 26:33** 6944
of the testimony in the holy of **h**. **Ex 26:34** 6944
he made the room of the holy of **h**: **2Ch 3:8** 6944
in the room of the holy of **h** and **2Ch 3:10** 6944
its inner doors for the holy of **h** and **2Ch 4:22** 6944
of the house, to the holy of **h**, **2Ch 5:7** 6944
which is called the Holy of **H**, **Heb 9:3** 40

HOLINESS
Who is like You, majestic in **h**, **Ex 15:11** 6944
themselves faithfully in **h**. **2Ch 31:18** 6944
God has spoken in His **h**: **Ps 60:6** 6944
is among them *as at* Sinai, in **h**. **Ps 68:17** 6944
"Once I have sworn by My **h**; **Ps 89:35** 6944
H befits Your house, O LORD, **Ps 93:5** 6944
God has spoken in His **h**: **Ps 108:7** 6944
will be called the Highway of **H**. **Is 35:8** 6944
And I will manifest My **h** in her. **Ezk 28:22** 6942
and will manifest My **h** in them in **Ezk 28:25** 6942
vindicate the **h** of My great name **Ezk 36:23** 6942
they will not transmit **h** to the people **Ezk 44:19** 6942
to transmit **h** to the people." **Ezk 46:20** 6942
The Lord GOD has sworn by His **h**, **Am 4:2** 6944
In **h** and righteousness before Him **Lk 1:75** 3742
according to the Spirit of **h**, **Ro 1:4** 42
that in **h** and godly sincerity, **2Co 1:12** 41
perfecting **h** in the fear of God. **2Co 7:1** 42
righteousness and **h** of the truth. **Eph 4:24** 3742

hearts without blame in **h** before our **1Th 3:13** 42
so that we may share His **h**. **Heb 12:10** 41

HOLLOW
"You shall make it **h** with planks; **Ex 27:8** 5014
He made it **h** with planks. **Ex 38:7** 5014
But God split the **h** place that is **Jg 15:19** 4388
out as from the **h** of a sling. **1Sa 25:29** 3709
the waters in the **h** of His hand, **Is 40:12** 8168
four fingers in thickness, *and* **h**. **Jer 52:21** 5014

HOLLOWED
He has dug a pit and **h** it out, **Ps 7:15** 2658

HOLON
and Goshen and **H** and Giloh; **Jos 15:51** 2473
and **H** with its pasture lands and **Jos 21:15** 2473
also come upon the plain, upon **H**, **Jer 48:21** 2473

HOLY
you are standing is **h** ground." **Ex 3:5** 6944
day you shall have a **h** assembly, **Ex 12:16** 6944
h assembly on the seventh day; **Ex 12:16** 6944
guided *them* to Your **h** habitation. **Ex 15:13** 6944
a **h** sabbath to the LORD. **Ex 16:23** 6944
of priests and a **h** nation.' **Ex 19:6** 6918
the sabbath day, to keep it **h**. **Ex 20:8** 6942
the sabbath day and made it **h**. **Ex 20:11** 6942
"You shall be **h** men to Me, **Ex 22:31** 6944
h place and the holy of holies. **Ex 26:33** 6944
holy place and the **h** of holies. **Ex 26:33** 6944
the testimony in the **h** of holies. **Ex 26:34** 6944
"You shall make **h** garments **Ex 28:2** 6944
and they shall make **h** garments for **Ex 28:4** 6944
heart when he enters the **h** place, **Ex 28:29** 6944
the **h** place before the LORD, **Ex 28:35** 6944
engravings of a seal, '**H** to the LORD.' **Ex 28:36** 6944
take away the iniquity of the **h** things **Ex 28:38** 6944
with regard to all their **h** gifts; **Ex 28:38** 6944
altar to minister in the **h** place, **Ex 28:43** 6944
and put the **h** crown on the turban. **Ex 29:6** 6944
"The **h** garments of Aaron **Ex 29:29** 6944
to minister in the **h** place. **Ex 29:30** 6944
and boil its flesh in a **h** place. **Ex 29:31** 6918
not eat *them,* because they are **h**. **Ex 29:33** 6944
not be eaten, because it is **h**. **Ex 29:34** 6944
then the altar shall be most **h**, **Ex 29:37** 6944
touches the altar shall be **h**. **Ex 29:37** 6942
It is most **h** to the LORD." **Ex 30:10** 6944
make of these a **h** anointing oil, **Ex 30:25** 6944
it shall be a **h** anointing oil. **Ex 30:25** 6944
them, that they may be most **h**; **Ex 30:29** 6944
whatever touches them shall be **h**. **Ex 30:29** 6942
'This shall be a **h** anointing oil **Ex 30:31** 6944
it is **h**, *and* it shall be holy to **Ex 30:32** 6944
and it shall be **h** to you. **Ex 30:32** 6944
a perfumer, salted, pure, *and* **h**. **Ex 30:35** 6944
it shall be most **h** to you. **Ex 30:36** 6944
it shall be **h** to you for the LORD. **Ex 30:37** 6944
h garments for Aaron the priest, **Ex 31:10** 6944
fragrant incense for the **h** place, **Ex 31:11** 6944
the sabbath, for it is **h** to you. **Ex 31:14** 6944
of complete rest, **h** to the LORD; **Ex 31:15** 6944
day you shall have a **h** *day,* **Ex 35:2** 6944
for ministering in the **h** place, **Ex 35:19** 6944
the **h** garments for Aaron the **Ex 35:19** 6944
service and for the **h** garments. **Ex 35:21** 6944
the **h** anointing oil and the pure, **Ex 37:29** 6944
for ministering in the **h** place as **Ex 39:1** 6944
the **h** garments which were for Aaron, **Ex 39:1** 6944
plate of the **h** crown of pure gold, **Ex 39:30** 6944
"**H** to the LORD." **Ex 39:30** 6944
garments for ministering in the **h** place **Ex 39:41** 6944
the **h** garments for Aaron the priest **Ex 39:41** 6944
and it shall be **h**. **Ex 40:9** 6944
and the altar shall be most **h**. **Ex 40:10** 6944
"You shall put the **h** garments **Ex 40:13** 6944
a thing most **h**, of the offerings **Lv 2:3** 6944
a thing most **h** of the offerings **Lv 2:10** 6944
against the LORD's **h** things, **Lv 5:15** 6944
he has sinned against the **h** thing, **Lv 5:16** 6944
as unleavened cakes in a **h** place; **Lv 6:16** 6918
it is most **h**, like the sin **Lv 6:17** 6944
slain before the LORD; it is most **h**. **Lv 6:25** 6944
It shall be eaten in a **h** place, **Lv 6:26** 6918
in a **h** place you shall wash what **Lv 6:27** 6918
the priests may eat of it; it is most **h**. **Lv 6:29** 6944
to make atonement in the **h** plac **Lv 6:30** 6944
law of the guilt offering; it is most **h**. **Lv 7:1** 6944
It shall be eaten in a **h** place; **Lv 7:6** 6918
be eaten in a holy place; it is most **h**. **Lv 7:6** 6944
the golden plate, the **h** crown, **Lv 8:9** 6944
near Me I will be treated as **h**, **Lv 10:3** 6942
between the **h** and the profane, **Lv 10:10** 6944
the altar, for it is most **h**. **Lv 10:12** 6944
eat it, moreover, in a **h** place, **Lv 10:13** 6918
the sin offering at the **h** place? **Lv 10:17** 6944
For it is most **h**, and He gave it **Lv 10:17** 6944
yourselves therefore, and be **h** **Lv 11:44** 6918
and be holy, for I am **h**. **Lv 11:44** 6918
thus you shall be **h**, for I am holy.' " **Lv 11:45** 6918
for I am **h**.' " **Lv 11:45** 6918
belongs to the priest; it is most **h**. **Lv 14:13** 6944
into the **h** place inside the veil, **Lv 16:2** 6944
shall enter the **h** place with this: **Lv 16:3** 6944
"He shall put on the **h** linen tunic, **Lv 16:4** 6944
(these are **h** garments). **Lv 16:4** 6944
make atonement for the **h** place, **Lv 16:16** 6944
to make atonement in the **h** place, **Lv 16:17** 6944
finishes atoning for the **h** place and **Lv 16:20** 6944
on when he went into the **h** place, **Lv 16:23** 6944
his body with water in a **h** place **Lv 16:24** 6918

to make atonement in the **h** place, **Lv 16:27** 6944
linen garments, the **h** garments, **Lv 16:32** 6944
atonement for the **h** sanctuary, **Lv 16:33** 6944
'You shall be **h**, for I the LORD **Lv 19:2** 6918
for I the LORD your God am **h**. **Lv 19:2** 6918
profaned the **h** thing of the LORD; **Lv 19:8** 6944
year all its fruit shall be **h**, **Lv 19:24** 6944
and to profane My **h** name. **Lv 20:3** 6944
yourselves therefore and be **h**, **Lv 20:7** 6944
'Thus you are to be **h** to Me, **Lv 20:26** 6918
for I the LORD am **h**; and I have **Lv 20:26** 6918
'They shall be **h** to their God and **Lv 21:6** 6918
so they shall be **h**. **Lv 21:6** 6944
for he is **h** to his God. **Lv 21:7** 6918
he shall be **h** to you; **Lv 21:8** 6918
LORD, who sanctifies you, am **h**. **Lv 21:8** 6918
of the most **h** and of the holy, **Lv 21:22** 6944
of the most holy and of the **h**, **Lv 21:22** 6944
the **h** *gifts* of the sons of Israel, **Lv 22:2** 6944
so as not to profane My **h** name; **Lv 22:2** 6944
the **h** *gifts* which the sons of Israel **Lv 22:3** 6944
eat of the **h** *gifts* until he is clean. **Lv 22:4** 6944
and shall not eat of the **h** **Lv 22:6** 6944
he shall eat of the **h** **Lv 22:7** 6944
however, is to eat the **h** *gift;* **Lv 22:10** 6944
man shall not eat of the **h** **Lv 22:10** 6944
man eats a **h** *gift* unintentionally, **Lv 22:14** 6944
give the **h** *gift* to the priest. **Lv 22:14** 6944
the **h** *gifts* of the sons of Israel **Lv 22:15** 6944
for guilt by eating their **h** *gifts;* **Lv 22:16** 6944
"You shall not profane My **h** name, **Lv 22:32** 6944
you shall proclaim as **h** convocations **Lv 23:2** 6944
of complete rest, a **h** convocation. **Lv 23:3** 6944
h convocations which you shall **Lv 23:4** 6944
you shall have a **h** convocation; **Lv 23:7** 6944
seventh day is a **h** convocation; **Lv 23:8** 6944
be **h** to the LORD for the priest. **Lv 23:20** 6944
you are to have a **h** convocation. **Lv 23:21** 6944
of trumpets, a **h** convocation. **Lv 23:24** 6944
shall be a **h** convocation for you, **Lv 23:27** 6944
the first day is a **h** convocation; **Lv 23:35** 6944
you shall have a **h** convocation **Lv 23:36** 6944
shall proclaim as **h** convocations, **Lv 23:37** 6944
they shall eat it in a **h** place; **Lv 24:9** 6918
for it is most **h** to him from the **Lv 24:9** 6944
it shall be **h** to you. **Lv 25:12** 6944
one gives to the LORD shall be **h**. **Lv 27:9** 6944
and its substitute shall become **h**. **Lv 27:10** 6944
his house as **h** to the LORD, **Lv 27:14** 6944
the field shall be **h** to the LORD, **Lv 27:21** 6944
your valuation as **h** to the LORD. **Lv 27:23** 6944
destruction is most **h** to the LORD. **Lv 27:28** 6944
it is **h** to the LORD. **Lv 27:30** 6944
tenth one shall be **h** to the LORD. **Lv 27:32** 6944
and its substitute shall become **h**. **Lv 27:33** 6944
concerning the most **h** things. **Nu 4:4** 6944
have finished covering the **h** **Nu 4:15** 6944
not touch the **h** *objects* and die. **Nu 4:15** 6944
they approach the most **h** *objects:* **Nu 4:19** 6944
the **h** *objects* even for a moment, **Nu 4:20** 6944
the **h** *gifts* of the sons of Israel, **Nu 5:9** 6944
every man's **h** *gifts* shall be his; **Nu 5:10** 6944
and the priest shall take **h** water **Nu 5:17** 6918
He shall be **h** until the days are **Nu 6:5** 6918
separation he is **h** to the LORD. **Nu 6:8** 6918
It is **h** for the priest, together **Nu 6:20** 6944
was the service of the **h** *objects, which* **Nu 7:9** 6944
set out, carrying the **h** *objects;* **Nu 10:21** 4720
and be **h** to your God. **Nu 15:40** 6918
for all the congregation are **h**, **Nu 16:3** 6918
show who is His, and who is **h**, **Nu 16:5** 6918
chooses *shall be* the one who is **h**. **Nu 16:7** 6918
of the blaze, for they are **h**; **Nu 16:37** 6942
before the LORD and they are **h**; **Nu 16:38** 6942
the **h** gifts of the sons of Israel I **Nu 18:8** 6944
be yours from the most **h** *gifts reserved* **Nu 18:9** 6944
most **h** for you and for your sons. **Nu 18:9** 6944
the most **h** *gifts* you shall eat it; **Nu 18:10** 6944
It shall be **h** to you. **Nu 18:10** 6944
you shall not redeem; they are **h**. **Nu 18:17** 6944
"All the offerings of the **h** *gifts,* **Nu 18:19** 6944
to treat Me as **h** in the sight of **Nu 20:12** 6942
He proved Himself **h** among them. **Nu 20:13** 6942
My command to treat Me as **h** before **Nu 27:14** 6942
in the **h** place you shall pour out **Nu 28:7** 6944
day *shall be* a **h** convocation; **Nu 28:18** 6944
you shall have a **h** convocation; **Nu 28:25** 6944
you shall have a **h** convocation; **Nu 28:26** 6944
shall also have a **h** convocation; **Nu 29:1** 6944
you shall have a **h** convocation, **Nu 29:7** 6944
you shall have a **h** convocation; **Nu 29:12** 6944
and the **h** vessels and the trumpets **Nu 31:6** 6944
who was anointed with the **h** oil. **Nu 35:25** 6944
the sabbath day to keep it **h**, **Dt 5:12** 6942
a **h** people to the LORD your God; **Dt 7:6** 6918
"Only your **h** things which you may **Dt 12:26** 6944
a **h** people to the LORD your God **Dt 14:2** 6918
a **h** people to the LORD your God. **Dt 14:21** 6918
therefore your camp must be **h**; **Dt 23:14** 6918
'Look down from Your **h** habitation, **Dt 26:15** 6944
you as a **h** people to Himself, **Dt 28:9** 6918
you did not treat Me as **h** in the midst **Dt 32:51** 6942
the midst of ten thousand **h** ones; **Dt 33:2** 6944
All Your **h** ones are in Your hand, **Dt 33:3** 6918
where you are standing is **h**." **Jos 5:15** 6944
bronze and iron are **h** to the LORD; **Jos 6:19** 6944
serve the LORD, for He is a **h** God. **Jos 24:19** 6918
"There is no one **h** like the LORD, **1Sa 2:2** 6918
stand before the LORD, this **h** God? **1Sa 6:20** 6918

vessels of the young men were **h**,	1Sa 21:5	6944
then today will their vessels *be* **h**?	1Sa 21:5	
even as the most **h** place.	1Ki 6:16	6944
the inner house, the most **h** place,	1Ki 7:50	6944
of meeting and all the **h** utensils,	1Ki 8:4	6944
of the house, to the most **h** place,	1Ki 8:6	6944
poles could be seen from the **h** place	1Ki 8:8	6944
the priests came from the **h** place,	1Ki 8:10	6944
this is a **h** man of God passing by	2Ki 4:9	6918
Against the **H** One of Israel!	2Ki 19:22	6918
all the work of the most **h** place,	1Ch 6:49	6944
Glory in His **h** name;	1Ch 16:10	6944
Worship the LORD in **h** array.	1Ch 16:29	6944
To give thanks to Your **h** name,	1Ch 16:35	6944
and the **h** vessels of God into the	1Ch 22:19	6944
apart to sanctify him as most **h**,	1Ch 23:13	6944
in the purifying of all **h** things,	1Ch 23:28	6944
and charge of the **h** place,	1Ch 23:32	6944
already provided for the **h** temple,	1Ch 29:3	6944
build You a house for Your **h** name,	1Ch 29:16	6944
made the room of the **h** of holies:	2Ch 3:8	6944
in the room of the **h** of holies	2Ch 3:10	6944
inner doors for the **h** of holies and	2Ch 4:22	6944
the **h** utensils which *were* in the tent;	2Ch 5:5	6944
of the house, to the **h** of holies,	2Ch 5:7	6944
came forth from the **h** place	2Ch 5:11	6944
because the places are **h** where the	2Ch 8:11	6944
those who praised *Him* in **h** attire,	2Ch 20:21	6944
they may enter, for they are **h**.	2Ch 23:6	6944
even used the **h** things of the house of	2Ch 24:7	6944
uncleanness out from the **h** place.	2Ch 29:5	6944
the **h** place to the God of Israel.	2Ch 29:7	6944
came to His **h** dwelling place,	2Ch 30:27	6944
the LORD and the most **h** things.	2Ch 31:14	6944
Israel *and* who were **h** to the LORD,	2Ch 35:3	6918
"Put the **h** ark in the house which	2Ch 35:3	6944
stand in the **h** place according to	2Ch 35:5	6944
they boiled the **h** things in pots,	2Ch 35:13	6944
should not eat from the most **h** things	Ezr 2:63	6944
"You are **h** to the LORD, and the	Ezr 8:28	6944
the LORD, and the utensils are **h**;	Ezr 8:28	6944
the **h** race has intermingled with	Ezr 9:2	6944
to give us a peg in His **h** place,	Ezr 9:8	6944
should not eat from the most **h** things	Ne 7:65	6944
day is **h** to the LORD your God;	Ne 8:9	6918
for this day is **h** to our Lord.	Ne 8:10	6918
"Be still, for the day is **h**;	Ne 8:11	6918
made known to them Your **h** sabbath,	Ne 9:14	6944
them on the sabbath or a **h** day;	Ne 10:31	6944
for the **h** things and for the sin	Ne 10:33	6944
to live in Jerusalem, the **h** city,	Ne 11:1	6944
Levites in the **h** city *were* 284.	Ne 11:18	6944
which of the **h** ones will you turn?	Jb 5:1	6918
not denied the words of the **H** One.	Jb 6:10	6918
He puts no trust in His **h** ones,	Jb 15:15	6918
King Upon Zion, My **h** mountain."	Ps 2:6	6944
He answered me from His **h** mountain	Ps 3:4	6944
At Your **h** temple I will bow in	Ps 5:7	6944
The LORD is in His **h** temple;	Ps 11:4	6944
Who may dwell on Your **h** hill?	Ps 15:1	6944
allow Your **H** One to undergo decay.	Ps 16:10	2623
will answer him from His **h** heaven With	Ps 20:6	6944
Yet You are **h**, O You who are	Ps 22:3	6918
And who may stand in His **h** place?	Ps 24:3	6944
my hands toward Your **h** sanctuary.	Ps 28:2	6944
Worship the LORD in **h** array.	Ps 29:2	6944
And give thanks to His **h** name.	Ps 30:4	6944
Because we trust in His **h** name.	Ps 33:21	6944
Let them bring me to Your **h** hill And	Ps 43:3	6944
The **h** dwelling places of the Most	Ps 46:4	6918
nations, God sits on His **h** throne.	Ps 47:8	6944
city of our God, His **h** mountain.	Ps 48:1	6944
do not take Your **H** Spirit from me.	Ps 51:11	6944
of Your house, Your **h** temple.	Ps 65:4	6918
Is God in His **h** habitation.	Ps 68:5	6944
the lyre, O **H** One of Israel.	Ps 71:22	6918
Your way, O God, is **h**;	Ps 77:13	6944
And pained the **H** One of Israel.	Ps 78:41	6918
So He brought them to His **h** land,	Ps 78:54	6944
They have defiled Your **h** temple;	Ps 79:1	6944
foundation is in the **h** mountains.	Ps 87:1	6944
in the assembly of the **h** ones.	Ps 89:5	6918
in the council of the **h** ones,	Ps 89:7	6918
our king to the **H** One of Israel.	Ps 89:18	6918
With My **h** oil I have anointed him,	Ps 89:20	6944
Worship the LORD in **h** attire;	Ps 96:9	6944
And give thanks to His **h** name.	Ps 97:12	6944
His right hand and His **h** arm have	Ps 98:1	6944
great and awesome name; **H** is He.	Ps 99:3	6918
worship at His footstool; **H** is He.	Ps 99:5	6918
God And worship at His **h** hill	Ps 99:9	6944
For **h** is the LORD our God.	Ps 99:9	6918
He looked down from His **h** height;	Ps 102:19	6944
is within me, *bless* His **h** name.	Ps 103:1	6944
Glory in His **h** name;	Ps 105:3	6944
He remembered His **h** word	Ps 105:42	6944
of Aaron, the **h** one of the LORD,	Ps 106:16	6918
To give thanks to Your **h** name And	Ps 106:47	6944
In **h** array, from the womb of the	Ps 110:3	6944
H and awesome is His name.	Ps 111:9	6918
will bow down toward Your **h** temple	Ps 138:2	6944
all flesh will bless His **h** name	Ps 145:21	6944
the knowledge of the **H** One is	Pr 9:10	6918
for a man to say rashly, "It is **h**!"	Pr 20:25	6944
I have the knowledge of the **H** One.	Pr 30:3	6918
to go in and out from the **h** place,	Ec 8:10	6918
have despised the **H** One of Israel,	Is 1:4	6918
remains in Jerusalem will be called **h**	Is 4:3	6918
And the **h** God will show Himself	Is 5:16	6918
show Himself **h** in righteousness.	Is 5:16	6942
let the purpose of the **H** One of Israel	Is 5:19	6918
the word of the **H** One of Israel.	Is 5:24	6918
"**H**, Holy, Holy, is the LORD	Is 6:3	6918
H, Holy, is the LORD of hosts,	Is 6:3	6918
H, is the LORD of hosts,	Is 6:3	6918
The **h** seed is its stump."	Is 6:13	6944
hosts whom you should regard as **h**.	Is 8:13	6942
a fire and his **H** One a flame,	Is 10:17	6918
on the LORD, the **H** One of Israel.	Is 10:20	6918
or destroy in all My **h** mountain,	Is 11:9	6944
your midst is the **H** One of Israel.	Is 12:6	6918
will look to the **H** One of Israel.	Is 17:7	6918
in the **h** mountain at Jerusalem.	Is 27:13	6944
rejoice in the **H** One of Israel.	Is 29:19	6918
will sanctify the **H** One of Jacob And	Is 29:23	6918
more about the **H** One of Israel."	Is 30:11	6918
thus says the **H** One of Israel,	Is 30:12	6918
the Lord GOD, the **H** One of Israel,	Is 30:15	6918
not look to the **H** One of Israel,	Is 31:1	6918
Against the **H** One of Israel!	Is 37:23	6918
would be *his* equal?" says the **H** One.	Is 40:25	6918
Redeemer is the **H** One of Israel.	Is 41:14	6918
will glory in the **H** One of Israel.	Is 41:16	6918
H One of Israel has created it.	Is 41:20	6918
your God, The **H** One of Israel,	Is 43:3	6918
Redeemer, the **H** One of Israel,	Is 43:14	6918
"I am the LORD, your **H** One,	Is 43:15	6918
the LORD, the **H** One of Israel,	Is 45:11	6918
is His name, The **H** One of Israel.	Is 47:4	6918
call themselves after the **h** city And	Is 48:2	6944
Redeemer, the **H** One of Israel	Is 48:17	6918
Redeemer of Israel *and* its **H** One,	Is 49:7	6918
the **H** One of Israel who has chosen	Is 49:7	6918
garments, O Jerusalem, the **h** city;	Is 52:1	6944
The LORD has bared His **h** arm In	Is 52:10	6944
Redeemer is the **H** One of Israel,	Is 54:5	6918
God, even the **H** One of Israel;	Is 55:5	6918
I will bring to My **h** mountain And	Is 56:7	6944
And will possess My **h** mountain."	Is 57:13	6944
lives forever, whose name is **H**,	Is 57:15	6918
"I dwell *on* a high and **h** place,	Is 57:15	6918
your *own* pleasure on My **h** day,	Is 58:13	6944
the **h** *day* of the LORD honorable,	Is 58:13	6918
And for the **H** One of Israel	Is 60:9	6918
The Zion of the **H** One of Israel.	Is 60:14	6918
"The **h** people, The redeemed of	Is 62:12	6944
rebelled And grieved His **H** Spirit;	Is 63:10	6944
His **H** Spirit in the midst of them,	Is 63:11	6944
Your **h** and glorious habitation;	Is 63:15	6944
Your **h** people possessed Your	Is 63:18	6944
Your **h** cities have become a	Is 64:10	6944
Our **h** and beautiful house, Where	Is 64:11	6944
LORD, Who forget My **h** mountain,	Is 65:11	6944
or harm in all My **h** mountain,"	Is 65:25	6944
to My **h** mountain Jerusalem,"	Is 66:20	6944
"Israel was **h** to the LORD, The	Jer 2:3	6944
work, but keep the sabbath day **h**,	Jer 17:22	6942
keep the sabbath day **h** by doing no	Jer 17:24	6942
keep the sabbath day **h** by not	Jer 17:27	6942
LORD And because of His **h** words.	Jer 23:9	6944
His voice from His **h** habitation;	Jer 25:30	6944
abode of righteousness, O **h** hill!'	Jer 31:23	6944
the east, shall be **h** to the LORD;	Jer 31:40	6944
LORD, Against the **H** One of Israel.	Jer 50:29	6918
guilt Before the **H** One of Israel.	Jer 51:5	6918
The **h** places of the LORD's house.	Jer 51:51	4720
their **h** places will be profaned.	Ezk 7:24	6942
and My **h** name you will profane no	Ezk 20:39	6944
"For on My **h** mountain, on the	Ezk 20:40	6944
gifts, with all your **h** things.	Ezk 20:40	6944
I will prove Myself **h** among you	Ezk 20:41	6942
"You have despised My **h** things	Ezk 22:8	6944
law and have profaned My **h** things;	Ezk 22:26	6944
between the **h** and the profane,	Ezk 22:26	6944
You were on the **h** mountain of God;	Ezk 28:14	6944
went, they profaned My **h** name,	Ezk 36:20	6944
"But I had concern for My **h** name,	Ezk 36:21	6944
about to act, but for My **h** name,	Ezk 36:22	6944
when I prove Myself **h** among you	Ezk 36:23	6942
"My **h** name I will make known	Ezk 39:7	6944
will not let My **h** name be profaned	Ezk 39:7	6944
am the LORD, the **H** One in Israel.	Ezk 39:7	6918
I will be jealous for My **h** name.	Ezk 39:25	6944
"This is the most **h** *place*."	Ezk 41:4	6944
they are the **h** chambers where the	Ezk 42:13	6944
LORD shall eat the most **h** things.	Ezk 42:13	6944
they shall lay the most **h** things,	Ezk 42:13	6944
for the place is **h**.	Ezk 42:13	6918
they minister, for they are **h**.	Ezk 42:14	6944
between the **h** and the profane.	Ezk 42:20	6944
will not again defile My **h** name,	Ezk 43:7	6944
And they have defiled My **h** name by	Ezk 43:8	6944
all around *shall be* most **h**.	Ezk 43:12	6944
charge of My **h** things yourselves,	Ezk 44:8	6944
come near to any of My **h** things,	Ezk 44:13	6944
to the things that are most **h**;	Ezk 44:13	6944
and lay them in the **h** chambers;	Ezk 44:19	6944
between the **h** and the profane,	Ezk 44:23	6944
the LORD, a **h** portion of the land;	Ezk 45:1	6944
It shall be **h** within all its boundary	Ezk 45:1	6944
there shall be for the **h** place a square	Ezk 45:2	6944
the sanctuary, the most **h** place.	Ezk 45:3	6944
be the **h** portion of the land;	Ezk 45:4	6944
and a **h** place for the sanctuary.	Ezk 45:4	4720
the allotment of the **h** portion;	Ezk 45:6	6944
land on either side of the **h** allotment	Ezk 45:7	6944
adjacent to the **h** allotment and	Ezk 45:7	6944
the **h** chambers for the priests,	Ezk 46:19	6944
h allotment shall be for these,	Ezk 48:10	6944
of the land, a most **h** place,	Ezk 48:12	6944
for it is **h** to the LORD.	Ezk 48:14	6944
the length alongside the **h** allotment	Ezk 48:18	6944
be alongside the **h** allotment.	Ezk 48:18	6944
shall set apart the **h** allotment,	Ezk 48:20	6944
of the **h** allotment and of the property	Ezk 48:21	6944
And the **h** allotment and the	Ezk 48:21	6944
in whom is a spirit of the **h** gods;	Da 4:8	6922
I know that a spirit of the **h** gods is in	Da 4:9	6922
an *angelic* watcher, a **h** one,	Da 4:13	6922
is a command of the **h** ones,	Da 4:17	6922
a spirit of the **h** gods is in you.'	Da 4:18	6922
saw an *angelic* watcher, a **h** one,	Da 4:23	6922
in whom is a spirit of the **h** gods;	Da 5:11	6922
Then I heard a **h** one speaking, and	Da 8:13	6918
and another **h** one said to that	Da 8:13	6918
so as to allow both the **h** place	Da 8:13	6944
the **h** place will be properly restored	Da 8:14	6944
mighty men and the **h** people.	Da 8:24	6918
city Jerusalem, Your **h** mountain;	Da 9:16	6944
of the **h** mountain of my God,	Da 9:20	6944
for your people and your **h** city,	Da 9:24	6944
and to anoint the most **h** *place*.	Da 9:24	6944
be *set* against the **h** covenant,	Da 11:28	6944
become enraged at the **h** covenant	Da 11:30	6944
those who forsake the **h** covenant.	Da 11:30	6944
seas and the beautiful **H** Mountain;	Da 11:45	6944
the power of the **h** people,	Da 12:7	6944
not man, the **H** One in your midst,	Hos 11:9	6918
against the **H** One who is faithful.	Hos 11:12	6918
sound an alarm on My **h** mountain!	Jl 2:1	6944
Dwelling in Zion, My **h** mountain.	Jl 3:17	6944
So Jerusalem will be **h**,	Jl 3:17	6944
In order to profane My **h** name.	Am 2:7	6944
as you drank on My **h** mountain,	Ob 1:16	6944
who escape, And it will be **h**.	Ob 1:17	6944
look again toward Your **h** temple.'	Jon 2:4	6944
came to You, Into Your **h** temple.	Jon 2:7	6944
you, The Lord from His **h** temple.	Mi 1:2	6944
their mouths They declare **h** war.	Mi 3:5	6942
O LORD, my God, my **H** One?	Hab 1:12	6918
"But the LORD is in His **h** temple.	Hab 2:20	6944
And the **H** One from Mount Paran.	Hab 3:3	6918
again be haughty On My **h** mountain.	Zph 3:11	6944
'If a man carries **h** meat in the	Hg 2:12	6944
other food, will it become **h**?'"	Hg 2:12	6942
as His portion in the **h** land,	Zch 2:12	6944
aroused from His **h** habitation."	Zch 2:13	6944
will be called the **H** Mountain.'	Zch 8:3	6944
come, *and* all the **h** ones with Him!	Zch 14:5	6918
"**H** TO THE LORD." And the cooking	Zch 14:20	6944
will be **h** to the LORD of hosts;	Zch 14:21	6944
to be with child by the **H** Spirit.	Mt 1:18	*40*
in her is of the **H** Spirit.	Mt 1:20	*40*
you with the **H** Spirit and fire.	Mt 3:11	*40*
devil took Him into the **h** city and	Mt 4:5	*40*
"Do not give what is **h** to dogs,	Mt 7:6	*40*
speaks against the **H** Spirit,	Mt 12:32	*40*
prophet, standing in the **h** place	Mt 24:15	*40*
they entered the **h** city and appeared	Mt 27:53	*40*
and the Son and the **H** Spirit,	Mt 28:19	*40*
baptize you with the **H** Spirit."	Mk 1:8	*40*
who You are—the **H** One of God!"	Mk 1:24	*40*
blasphemes against the **H** Spirit	Mk 3:29	*40*
that he was a righteous and **h** man,	Mk 6:20	*40*
of His Father with the **h** angels."	Mk 8:38	*40*
himself said in the **H** Spirit,	Mk 12:36	*40*
who speak, but *it is* the **H** Spirit.	Mk 13:11	*40*
will be filled with the **H** Spirit while	Lk 1:15	*40*
"The **H** Spirit will come upon you,	Lk 1:35	*40*
h Child shall be called the Son	Lk 1:35	*40*
was filled with the **H** Spirit.	Lk 1:41	*40*
And **h** is His name.	Lk 1:49	*40*
was filled with the **H** Spirit,	Lk 1:67	*40*
by the mouth of His **h** prophets	Lk 1:70	*40*
And to remember His **h** covenant,	Lk 1:72	*40*
THAT OPENS THE WOMB SHALL BE CALLED **H**	Lk 2:23	*40*
and the **H** Spirit was upon him.	Lk 2:25	*40*
been revealed to him by the **H** Spirit	Lk 2:26	*40*
you with the **H** Spirit and fire.	Lk 3:16	*40*
and the **H** Spirit descended upon	Lk 3:22	*40*
Jesus, full of the **H** Spirit,	Lk 4:1	*40*
who You are—the **H** One of God!"	Lk 4:34	*40*
of the Father and of the **h** angels.	Lk 9:26	*40*
rejoiced greatly in the **H** Spirit,	Lk 10:21	*40*
heavenly Father give the **H** Spirit	Lk 11:13	*40*
blasphemes against the **H** Spirit,	Lk 12:10	*40*
for the **H** Spirit will teach you in	Lk 12:12	*40*
One who baptizes in the **H** Spirit.'	Jn 1:33	*40*
that You are the **H** One of God."	Jn 6:69	*40*
"But the Helper, the **H** Spirit,	Jn 14:26	*40*
H Father, keep them in Your name,	Jn 17:11	*40*
"Receive the **H** Spirit.	Jn 20:22	*40*
after He had by the **H** Spirit given	Ac 1:2	*40*
will be baptized with the **H** Spirit	Ac 1:5	*40*
the **H** Spirit has come upon you;	Ac 1:8	*40*
which the **H** Spirit foretold by the	Ac 1:16	*40*
they were all filled with the **H** Spirit	Ac 2:4	*40*
ALLOW YOUR **H** ONE TO UNDERGO DECAY.	Ac 2:27	*3741*
the promise of the **H** Spirit,	Ac 2:33	*40*
receive the gift of the **H** Spirit.	Ac 2:38	*40*
disowned the **H** and Righteous One and	Ac 3:14	*40*
by the mouth of His **h** prophets	Ac 3:21	*40*
Peter, filled with the **H** Spirit,	Ac 4:8	*40*
who by the **H** Spirit, *through* the	Ac 4:25	*40*
against Your **h** servant Jesus,	Ac 4:27	*40*
the name of Your **h** servant Jesus."	Ac 4:30	*40*
were all filled with the **H** Spirit and	Ac 4:31	*40*

your heart to lie to the **H** Spirit and Ac 5:3 *40*
and *so is* the **H** Spirit, whom God Ac 5:32 *40*
full of faith and of the **H** Spirit, Ac 6:5 *40*
speaks against this **h** place and Ac 6:13 *40*
WHICH YOU ARE STANDING IS **H** ground. Ac 7:33 *40*
are always resisting the **H** Spirit; Ac 7:51 *40*
But being full of the **H** Spirit, Ac 7:55 *40*
they might receive the **H** Spirit. Ac 8:15 *40*
they were receiving the **H** Spirit. Ac 8:17 *40*
hands may receive the **H** Spirit." Ac 8:19 *40*
and be filled with the **H** Spirit." Ac 9:17 *40*
in the comfort of the **H** Spirit, Ac 9:31 *40*
was *divinely* directed by a **h** angel Ac 10:22 *40*
God anointed Him with the **H** Spirit Ac 10:38 *40*
the **H** Spirit fell upon all those Ac 10:44 *40*
because the gift of the **H** Spirit Ac 10:45 *40*
received the **H** Spirit just as we Ac 10:47 *40*
the **H** Spirit fell upon them just Ac 11:15 *40*
be baptized with the **H** Spirit.' Ac 11:16 *40*
full of the **H** Spirit and of faith. Ac 11:24 *40*
and fasting, the **H** Spirit said, Ac 13:2 *40*
being sent out by the **H** Spirit, Ac 13:4 *40*
as Paul, filled with the **H** Spirit, Ac 13:9 *40*
'I WILL GIVE YOU THE **H** *and* Ac 13:34 *3741*
YOUR **H** ONE TO UNDERGO DECAY.' Ac 13:35 *3741*
with joy and with the **H** Spirit. Ac 13:52 *40*
to them giving them the **H** Spirit, Ac 15:8 *40*
seemed good to the **H** Spirit and to Ac 15:28 *40*
forbidden by the **H** Spirit to speak Ac 16:6 *40*
Did you receive the **H** Spirit when Ac 19:2 *40*
whether there is a **H** Spirit." Ac 19:2 *40*
them, the **H** Spirit came on them, Ac 19:6 *40*
the **H** Spirit solemnly testifies to me Ac 20:23 *40*
H Spirit has made you overseers, Ac 20:28 *40*
"This is what the **H** Spirit says: Ac 21:11 *40*
and has defiled this **h** place." Ac 21:28 *40*
"The **H** Spirit rightly spoke Ac 28:25 *40*
His prophets in the **h** Scriptures, Ro 1:2 *40*
the **H** Spirit who was given to us. Ro 5:5 *40*
So then, the Law is **h**, Ro 7:12 *40*
is **h** and righteous and good. Ro 7:12 *40*
me in the **H** Spirit, Ro 9:1 *40*
If the first piece *of dough* is **h**, Ro 11:16 *40*
and if the root is **h**, Ro 11:16 *40*
bodies a living and **h** sacrifice, Ro 12:1 *40*
and peace and joy in the **H** Spirit. Ro 14:17 *40*
hope by the power of the **H** Spirit. Ro 15:13 *40*
sanctified by the **H** Spirit. Ro 15:16 *40*
Greet one another with a **h** kiss. Ro 16:16 *40*
him, for the temple of God is **h**, 1Co 3:17 *40*
body is a temple of the **H** Spirit 1Co 6:19 *40*
are unclean, but now they are **h**. 1Co 7:14 *40*
may be **h** both in body and spirit; 1Co 7:34 *40*
is Lord," except by the **H** Spirit. 1Co 12:3 *40*
Greet one another with a **h** kiss. 1Co 16:20 *40*
in kindness, in the **H** Spirit, 2Co 6:6 *40*
Greet one another with a **h** kiss. 2Co 13:12 *40*
the fellowship of the **H** Spirit, 2Co 13:14 *40*
be **h** and blameless before Him. Eph 1:4 *40*
Him with the **H** Spirit of promise, Eph 1:13 *40*
into a **h** temple in the Lord, Eph 2:21 *40*
now been revealed to His **h** apostles Eph 3:5 *40*
Do not grieve the **H** Spirit of God, Eph 4:30 *40*
she would be **h** and blameless. Eph 5:27 *40*
to present you before Him **h** and Col 1:22 *40*
been chosen of God, **h** and beloved, Col 3:12 *40*
also in power and in the **H** Spirit 1Th 1:5 *40*
with the joy of the **H** Spirit, 1Th 1:6 *40*
God who gives His **H** Spirit to you. 1Th 4:8 *40*
all the brethren with a **h** kiss. 1Th 5:26 *40*
place to pray, lifting up **h** hands, 1Tm 2:8 *3741*
and called us with a **h** calling, 2Tm 1:9 *40*
the **H** Spirit who dwells in us, 2Tm 1:14 *40*
and renewing by the **H** Spirit, Ti 3:5 *40*
miracles and by gifts of the **H** Spirit Heb 2:4 *40*
Therefore, **h** brethren, partakers Heb 3:1 *40*
just as the **H** Spirit says, Heb 3:7 *40*
made partakers of the **H** Spirit, Heb 6:4 *40*
have such a high priest, **h**, Heb 7:26 *3741*
this is called the **h** place. Heb 9:2 *40*
which is called the **H** of Holies, Heb 9:3 *40*
The **H** Spirit *is* signifying this, Heb 9:8 *40*
that the way into the **h** place has Heb 9:8 *40*
entered the **h** place once for all, Heb 9:12 *40*
enter a **h** place made with hands, Heb 9:24 *40*
the high priest enters the **h** place Heb 9:25 *40*
the **H** Spirit also testifies to us; Heb 10:15 *40*
confidence to enter the **h** place by Heb 10:19 *40*
blood is brought into the **h** place Heb 13:11 *40*
by the **H** Spirit sent from heaven 1Pe 1:12 *40*
but like the **H** One who called you, 1Pe 1:15 *40*
be **h** yourselves also in all 1Pe 1:15 *40*
"YOU SHALL BE **H**, FOR I AM 1Pe 1:16 *40*
FOR I AM **H**." 1Pe 1:16 *40*
house for a **h** priesthood, 1Pe 2:5 *40*
A **H** NATION, A PEOPLE FOR *God's* 1Pe 2:9 *40*
in former times the **h** women also, 1Pe 3:5 *40*
were with Him on the **h** mountain. 2Pe 1:18 *40*
men moved by the **H** Spirit spoke 2Pe 1:21 *40*
turn away from the **h** commandment 2Pe 2:21 *40*
spoken beforehand by the **h** prophets 2Pe 3:2 *40*
to be in **h** conduct and godliness, 2Pe 3:11 *40*
have an anointing from the **H** One, 1Jn 2:20 *40*
with many thousands of His **h** ones, Jude 1:14 *40*
up on your most **h** faith, Jude 1:20 *40*
praying in the **H** Spirit, Jude 1:20 *40*
He who is **h**, who is true, who has Rv 3:7 *40*
"**H**, HOLY, HOLY *is* THE LORD Rv 4:8 *40*
H, HOLY *is* THE LORD GOD, Rv 4:8 *40*
H *is* THE LORD GOD, THE ALMIGHTY, Rv 4:8 *40*
"How long, O Lord, **h** and true, Rv 6:10 *40*
they will tread under foot the **h** city Rv 11:2 *40*
in the presence of the **h** angels and in Rv 14:10 *40*
For You alone are **h**; Rv 15:4 *3741*
who are and who were, O **H** One, Rv 16:5 *3741*
Blessed and **h** is the one who has a Rv 20:6 *40*
And I saw the **h** city, new Rv 21:2 *40*
and showed me the **h** city, Rv 21:10 *40*
and the one who is **h**, Rv 22:11 *40*
still keep himself **h**." Rv 22:11 *37*
tree of life and from the **h** city, Rv 22:19 *40*

HOMAGE

command all my people shall do **h**; Gn 41:40 5401a
They bowed down in **h**. Gn 43:28 7812
his face to the ground and did **h**. 1Sa 28:14 7812
did **h** to the LORD and to the king. 1Ch 29:20 7812
bowed down and paid **h** to Haman; Es 3:2 7812
neither bowed down nor paid **h**. Es 3:2 7812
bowed down nor paid **h** to him, Es 3:5 7812
Do **h** to the Son, that He not Ps 2:12 5401a
At that time a gift of **h** will be Is 18:7 7862
on his face and did **h** to Daniel, Da 2:46 5457

HOMAM

The sons of Lotan *were* Hori and **H** 1Ch 1:39 1950

HOME

field to hunt for game to bring **h**, Gn 27:5
her until his master came **h**. Gn 39:16 1004
When Joseph came **h**, Gn 43:26 1004
in the field and is not brought **h**, Ex 9:19 1004
for there was no **h** where there was Ex 12:30 1004
whether born at **h** or born outside, Lv 18:9 1004
shall bring her **h** to your house, Dt 21:12 8432
shall bring it **h** to your house, Dt 22:2 8432
he shall be free at **h** one year and Dt 24:5 1004
half-tribe of Manasseh returned **h** Jos 22:9
people go, each man to his **h**." Jg 7:7 4725
was dead, each departed to his **h**. Jg 9:55 4725
journey so that you may go **h**." Jg 19:9 168
the man arose and went to his **h**. Jg 19:28 4725
into your **h** like Rachel and Leah, Ru 4:11 1004
Elkanah went to his **h** at Ramah. 1Sa 2:11 1004
And they went to their own **h**. 1Sa 2:20 4725
the cart and take their calves **h**, 1Sa 6:7 1004
and shut up their calves at **h**. 1Sa 6:10 1004
And Saul went to his **h**, 1Sa 24:22 1004
and arose and went to his **h**, 2Sa 17:23 1004
departed until the day he came **h** 2Sa 19:24
a month *and* two months at **h**. 1Ki 5:14 1004
"Come **h** with me and refresh 1Ki 13:7 1004
"Come **h** with me and eat bread." 1Ki 13:15 1004
Enjoy your glory and stay at **h**; 2Ki 14:10 1004
of Assyria departed and returned **h**, 2Ki 19:36
"How can I bring the ark of God **h** 1Ch 13:12
build a permanent **h** for the ark of the 1Ch 28:2 1004
came to him from Ephraim, to go **h**; 2Ch 25:10 4725
they returned **h** in fierce anger. 2Ch 25:10 4725
Now stay at **h**; for why should you 2Ch 25:19 1004
Mehetabel, who was confined at **h**, Ne 6:10
But Haman hurried **h**, Es 6:12 1004
"If I look for Sheol as my **h**, Jb 17:13 1004
may discern the paths to its **h**? Jb 38:20 1004
I gave the wilderness for a **h** And Jb 39:6 1004
God makes a **h** for the lonely; Ps 68:6 1004
she who remains at **h** will divide Ps 68:12 1004
stork, whose **h** is the fir trees Ps 104:17 1004
Her feet do not remain at **h**; Pr 7:11 1004
"For my husband is not at **h**, Pr 7:19 1004
At the full moon he will come **h**." Pr 7:20 1004
is a man who wanders from his **h**. Pr 27:8 4725
For man goes to his eternal **h** Ec 12:5 1004
not allow his prisoners to *go* **h**?' Is 14:17 1004
of Assyria departed and returned **h** Is 37:37
the son of Shaphan, to take him **h**. Jer 39:14 1004
Or goes **h**, leans his hand against Am 5:19 1004
So that he does not stay at **h**. Hab 2:5 5115b
when you bring *it* **h**, Hg 1:9 1004
servant is lying paralyzed at **h**, Mt 8:6 *3614*
When Jesus came into Peter's **h**, Mt 8:14 *3614*
pick up your bed and go **h**." Mt 9:6 *3624*
And he got up and went **h**. Mt 9:7 *3624*
at the **h** of Simon the leper, Mt 26:6 *3614*
it was heard that He was at **h**. Mk 2:1 *3624*
pick up your pallet and go **h**." Mk 2:11 *3624*
And He came **h**, and the crowd Mk 3:20 *3624*
"Go **h** to your people and report Mk 5:19 *3624*
And going back to her **h**, Mk 7:30 *3624*
And He sent him to his **h**, Mk 8:26 *3624*
at the **h** of Simon the leper, Mk 14:3 *3614*
were ended, he went back **h**. Lk 1:23 *3624*
and *then* returned to her **h**. Lk 1:56 *3624*
synagogue, and entered Simon's **h**. Lk 4:38 *3614*
pick up your stretcher and go **h**." Lk 5:24 *3624*
lying on, and went **h** glorifying Lk 5:25 *3624*
me to say good-bye to those at **h**." Lk 9:61 *3624*
Martha welcomed Him into her **h**. Lk 10:38 *3614*
"And when he comes **h**, Lk 15:6 *3624*
and he went away to his **h** Lk 24:12 *848*
[Everyone went to his **h**. Jn 7:53 *3624*
each to his own **h**, and to leave Jn 16:32
three months in his father's **h**. Ac 7:20 *3624*
ship, and they returned **h** again. Ac 21:6 *2398*
is hungry, let him eat at **h** 1Co 11:34 *3624*
them ask their own husbands at **h**; 1Co 14:35 *3624*
while we are at **h** in the body we are 2Co 5:6 *1736*
body and to be at **h** with the Lord. 2Co 5:8 *1736*
ambition, whether at **h** or absent, 2Co 5:9 *1736*
be sensible, pure, workers at **h**, Ti 2:5 *3626*

HOMEBORN

female slaves and I had **h** slaves. Ec 2:7 1121, 1004
Or is he a **h** servant? Jer 2:14 3211, 1004

HOMELESS

bring the **h** poor into the house; Is 58:7 4788
are roughly treated, and are **h**; 1Co 4:11 *790*

HOMELESSNESS

In the days of her affliction and **h** La 1:7 4788

HOMER

a **h** of barley seed at fifty Lv 27:16 2563c
And a **h** of seed will yield *but* an Is 5:10 *2563c*
bath will contain a tenth of a **h** Ezk 45:11 2563c
and the ephah a tenth of a **h**; Ezk 45:11 2563c
shall be according to the **h**. Ezk 45:11 2563c
of an ephah from a **h** of wheat; Ezk 45:13 2563c
of an ephah from a **h** of barley; Ezk 45:13 2563c
or a **h**, for ten baths are a homer); Ezk 45:14 2563c
a homer, for ten baths are a **h**); Ezk 45:14 2563c
and a **h** and a half of barley. Hos 3:2 2563c

HOMERS

who gathered least gathered ten **h**) Nu 11:32 2563c

HOMES

Egyptians, but spared our **h**.' " Ex 12:27 1004
"We will not return to our **h** Nu 32:18 1004
far from their ruined **h**. Ps 109:10 2723
"If I send them away hungry to their **h**, Mk 8:3 *3624*
will welcome me into their **h**.' Lk 16:4 *3624*
we have left our own **h** Lk 18:28
went away again to their own **h**. Jn 20:10 *848*

HOMESTEAD

A **h** forlorn and forsaken like the Is 27:10 5116a
'LET HIS **H** BE MADE DESOLATE, Ac 1:20 *1886*

HOMETOWN

city at the gateway of his **h** Dt 21:19 4725
He came to His **h** and *began* Mt 13:54 *3968*
is not without honor except in his **h** Mt 13:57 *3968*
out from there and came into His **h**; Mk 6:1 *3968*
is not without honor except in his **h** Mk 6:4 *3968*
do here in your **h** as well.' " Lk 4:23 *3968*
no prophet is welcome in his **h**. Lk 4:24 *3968*

HOMICIDE

between one kind of **h** or another, Dt 17:8 1818

HOMOSEXUALS

adulterers, nor effeminate, nor **h**, 1Co 6:9 *733a*
and immoral men and **h** and 1Tm 1:10 *733a*

HONEST

we are **h** men, your servants are Gn 42:11 3653a
if you are **h** men, let one of your Gn 42:19 3653a
'We are **h** men; we are not spies Gn 42:31 3653a
I will know that you are **h** men: Gn 42:33 3653a
that you are not spies, but **h** men. Gn 42:34 3653a
"How painful are **h** words! Jb 6:25 3476
the word in an **h** and good heart, Lk 8:15 *2570*

HONESTLY

righteously and no one pleads **h**. Is 59:4 530

HONESTY

"So my **h** will answer for me Gn 30:33 6666

HONEY

a little balm and a little **h**, Gn 43:11 1706
to a land flowing with milk and **h**, Ex 3:8 1706
land flowing with milk and **h**." ' Ex 3:17 1706
a land flowing with milk and **h**, Ex 13:5 1706
its taste was like wafers with **h**. Ex 16:31 1706
to a land flowing with milk and **h**; Ex 33:3 1706
offer up in smoke any leaven or any **h** Lv 2:11 1706
a land flowing with milk and **h**." Lv 20:24 1706
does flow with milk and **h**, Nu 13:27 1706
land which flows with milk and **h**. Nu 14:8 1706
out of a land flowing with milk and **h** Nu 16:13 1706
a land flowing with milk and **h**, Nu 16:14 1706
in a land flowing with milk and **h** Dt 6:3 1706
a land of olive oil and **h**; Dt 8:8 1706
a land flowing with milk and **h**. Dt 11:9 1706
a land flowing with milk and **h**. Dt 26:9 1706
a land flowing with milk and **h**. Dt 26:15 1706
a land flowing with milk and **h**, Dt 27:3 1706
the land flowing with milk and **h**, Dt 31:20 1706
He made him suck **h** from the rock, Dt 32:13 1706
a land flowing with milk and **h**. Jos 5:6 1706
a swarm of bees and **h** were in the Jg 14:8 1706
he scraped the **h** into his hands Jg 14:9
he had scraped the **h** out of the body Jg 14:9 1706
"What is sweeter than **h**? Jg 14:18 1706
and there was **h** on the ground. 1Sa 14:25 1706
behold, *there was* a flow of **h**; 1Sa 14:26 1706
I tasted a little of this **h**. 1Sa 14:29 1706
"I indeed tasted a little **h** with 1Sa 14:43 1706
h, curds, sheep, and cheese of the 2Sa 17:29 1706
you, *some* cakes and a jar of **h**, 1Ki 14:3 1706
a land of olive trees and **h**, 2Ki 18:32 1706
fruits of grain, new wine, oil, **h** 2Ch 31:5 1706
rivers flowing with **h** and curds. Jb 20:17 1706
Sweeter also than **h** and the Ps 19:10 1706
And with **h** from the rock I would Ps 81:16 1706
Yes, sweeter than **h** to my mouth! Ps 119:103 1706
the lips of an adulteress drip **h** And Pr 5:3 5317
My son, eat **h**, for it is good, Pr 24:13 1706
the **h** from the comb is sweet to Pr 24:13 5317
Have you found **h**? Pr 25:16 1706
It is not good to eat much **h**, Pr 25:27 1706
A sated man loathes **h**, Pr 27:7 5317
"Your lips, *my* bride, drip **h**; SS 4:11 5317
H and milk are under your tongue, SS 4:11 1706
have eaten my honeycomb and my **h**; SS 5:1 1706

"He will eat curds and **h** at the	Is 7:15	1706
the land will eat curds and **h**.	Is 7:22	1706
a land flowing with milk and **h**,	Jer 11:5	1706
a land flowing with milk and **h**.	Jer 32:22	1706
oil and **h** hidden in the field."	Jer 41:8	1706
and it was sweet as **h** in my mouth.	Ezk 3:3	1706
You ate fine flour, **h** and	Ezk 16:13	1706
oil and **h** with which I fed you,	Ezk 16:19	1706
for them, flowing with milk and **h**,	Ezk 20:6	1706
them, flowing with milk and **h**,	Ezk 20:15	1706
the wheat of Minnith, cakes, **h**,	Ezk 27:17	1706
his food was locusts and wild **h**.	Mt 3:4	3192
his diet was locusts and wild **h**.	Mk 1:6	3192
mouth it will be sweet as **h**."	Rv 10:9	3192
and in my mouth it was sweet as **h**;	Rv 10:10	3192

HONEYCOMB

his hand and dipped it in the **h**,	1Sa 14:27	3295, 1706
honey and the drippings of the **h**.	Ps 19:10	6688
Pleasant words are a **h**,	Pr 16:24	1706, 6688
I have eaten my **h** and my honey;	SS 5:1	3293b

HONOR

"The **h** is yours to tell me:	Ex 8:9	6286
"**H** your father and your mother,	Ex 20:12	3513
the grayheaded and **h** the aged,	Lv 19:32	1921
for I will indeed **h** you richly,	Nu 22:17	3513
Am I really unable to **h** you?"	Nu 22:37	3513
I said I would **h** you greatly, but	Nu 24:11	3513
LORD has held you back from **h**."	Nu 24:11	3519b
'**H** your father and your mother, as	Dt 5:16	3513
has made, for praise, fame, and **h**;	Dt 26:19	8597
the **h** shall not be yours on the	Jg 4:9	8597
come *to pass*, we may **h** you?"	Jg 13:17	3513
nobles, And inherit a seat of **h**;	1Sa 2:8	3519b
and **h** your sons above Me,	1Sa 2:29	3513
for those who **h** Me I will honor,	1Sa 2:30	3513
for those who honor Me I will **h**,	1Sa 2:30	3513
city, and the man is held in **h**;	1Sa 9:6	3513
but please **h** me now before the	1Sa 15:30	3513
have not asked, both riches and **h**,	1Ki 3:13	3519b
the **h** *bestowed* on Your servant?	1Ch 17:18	3519b
Both riches and **h** *come* from You,	1Ch 29:12	3519b
age, full of days, riches and **h**;	1Ch 29:28	3519b
not ask for riches, wealth or **h**,	2Ch 1:11	3519b
give you riches and wealth and **h**,	2Ch 1:12	3519b
and he had great riches and **h**.	2Ch 17:5	3519b
had great riches and **h**;	2Ch 18:1	3519b
have no **h** from the LORD God."	2Ch 26:18	3519b
Hezekiah had immense riches and **h**;	2Ch 32:27	3519b
will give **h** to their husbands,	Es 1:20	3366
"What **h** or dignity has been	Es 6:3	3366
man whom the king desires to **h**?"	Es 6:6	3366
king desire to **h** more than me?"	Es 6:6	3366
man whom the king desires to **h**,	Es 6:7	3366
the man whom the king desires to **h**	Es 6:9	3366
the man whom the king desires to **h**	Es 6:9	3366
man whom the king desires to **h**."	Es 6:11	3366
light and gladness and joy and **h**.	Es 8:16	3366
"His sons achieve **h**,	Jb 14:21	3513
"He has stripped my **h** from me And	Jb 19:9	3519b
me; They pursue my **h** as the wind,	Jb 30:15	5082
clothe yourself with **h** and majesty.	Jb 40:10	1935
long will my **h** become a reproach?	Ps 4:2	3519b
rescue you, and you will **h** Me."	Ps 50:15	3513
I will rescue him and **h** him.	Ps 91:15	3513
His horn will be exalted in **h**.	Ps 112:9	3519b
is an **h** for all His godly ones.	Ps 149:9	1926
H the LORD from your wealth And	Pr 3:9	3513
In her left hand are riches and **h**.	Pr 3:16	3519b
The wise will inherit **h**,	Pr 3:35	3519b
She will **h** you if you embrace her.	Pr 4:8	3513
"Riches and **h** are with me,	Pr 8:18	3519b
A gracious woman attains **h**,	Pr 11:16	3519b
And before **h** *comes* humility.	Pr 15:33	3519b
But humility *goes* before **h**.	Pr 18:12	3519b
from strife is an **h** for a man,	Pr 20:3	3519b
h of old men is their gray hair.	Pr 20:29	1926
Finds life, righteousness and **h**.	Pr 21:21	3519b
the LORD Are riches, **h** and life.	Pr 22:4	3519b
h in the presence of the king,	Pr 25:6	1921
So **h** is not fitting for a fool.	Pr 26:1	3519b
So is he who gives **h** to a fool.	Pr 26:8	3519b
But a humble spirit will obtain **h**.	Pr 29:23	3519b
has given riches and wealth and **h** so	Ec 6:2	3519b
is weightier than wisdom *and* **h**.	Ec 10:1	3519b
And **h** Me with their lip service,	Is 29:13	3513
And will name Israel's name with **h**.	Is 44:5	3655
I have given you a title of **h**	Is 45:4	3655
LORD honorable, And **h** it,	Is 58:13	3513
I will also **h** them and they will	Jer 30:19	3513
They did not **h** the priests, They	La 4:16	5375, 6440
me gifts and a reward and great **h**;	Da 2:6	3367
exalt and **h** the King of heaven,	Da 4:37	1922
on whom the **h** of kingship has not	Da 11:21	1935
he will **h** a god of fortresses,	Da 11:38	3513
he will **h** *him* with gold, silver,	Da 11:38	3513
he will give great **h** to those who	Da 11:39	3519b
be filled with disgrace rather than **h**.	Hab 2:16	3519b
and He who will bear the **h** and sit	Zch 6:13	1935
if I am a father, where is My **h**?	Mal 1:6	3519b
to heart to give **h** to My name,"	Mal 2:2	3519b
A prophet is not without **h** except	Mt 13:57	820
'**H** YOUR FATHER AND MOTHER,' and,	Mt 15:4	5091
not to **h** his father or his mother.'	Mt 15:6	5091
H YOUR FATHER AND MOTHER;	Mt 19:19	5091
love the place of **h** at banquets and	Mt 23:6	4411
A prophet is not without **h** except	Mk 6:4	820
'**H** YOUR FATHER AND YOUR MOTHER';	Mk 7:10	5091
H YOUR FATHER AND MOTHER.'"	Mk 10:19	5091
and places of **h** at banquets,	Mk 12:39	4411
out the places of **h** *at the table*	Lk 14:7	4411
feast, do not take the place of **h**,	Lk 14:8	4411
then you will have **h** in the sight	Lk 14:10	1391
H YOUR FATHER AND MOTHER.'"	Lk 18:20	5091
and places of **h** at banquets,	Lk 20:46	4411
has no **h** in his own country.	Jn 4:44	5092
so that all will **h** the Son	Jn 5:23	5091
Son even as they **h** the Father.	Jn 5:23	5091
He who does not **h** the Son does not	Jn 5:23	5091
not **h** the Father who sent Him.	Jn 5:23	5091
but I **h** My Father, and you	Jn 8:49	5091
serves Me, the Father will **h** him.	Jn 12:26	5091
God, they did not **h** Him as God or	Ro 1:21	1392
for glory and **h** and immortality,	Ro 2:7	5092
but glory and **h** and peace to every	Ro 2:10	5092
preference to one another in **h**;	Ro 12:10	5092
fear to whom fear; **h** to whom honor.	Ro 13:7	5092
fear to whom fear; honor to whom **h**.	Ro 13:7	5092
but we are without **h**.	1Co 4:10	820
these we bestow more abundant **h**,	1Co 12:23	5092
more abundant **h** to that	1Co 12:24	5092
H YOUR FATHER AND MOTHER	Eph 6:2	5091
vessel in sanctification and **h**,	1Th 4:4	5092
be **h** and glory forever and ever.	1Tm 1:17	5092
H widows who are widows indeed;	1Tm 5:3	5091
be considered worthy of double **h**,	1Tm 5:17	5092
their own masters as worthy of all **h**	1Tm 6:1	5092
To Him *be* **h** and eternal dominion!	1Tm 6:16	5092
some to **h** and some to dishonor.	2Tm 2:20	5092
things, he will be a vessel for **h**,	2Tm 2:21	5092
CROWNED HIM WITH GLORY AND **H**,	Heb 2:7	5092
of death crowned with glory and **h**,	Heb 2:9	5092
house has more **h** than the house.	Heb 3:3	5092
And no one takes the **h** to himself,	Heb 5:4	5092
Marriage *is to be held* in **h**	Heb 13:4	5093
glory and **h** at the revelation of Jesus	1Pe 1:7	5092
H all people, love the brotherhood,	1Pe 2:17	5091
brotherhood, fear God, **h** the king.	1Pe 2:17	5091
and show her **h** as a fellow heir	1Pe 3:7	5092
h and glory from God the Father,	2Pe 1:17	5092
living creatures give glory and **h** and	Rv 4:9	5092
to receive glory and **h** and power;	Rv 4:11	5092
and **h** and glory and blessing."	Rv 5:12	5092
blessing and **h** and glory and	Rv 5:13	5092
and **h** and power and might,	Rv 7:12	5092
and the **h** of the nations into it;	Rv 21:26	5092

HONORABLE

was more **h** than his brothers,	1Ch 4:9	3513
the great and **h** Osnappar deported	Ezr 4:10	3358
man, And the **h** man dwells in it.	Jb 22:8	5375, 6440
captain of fifty and the **h** man,	Is 3:3	5375, 6440
And the inferior against the **h**.	Is 3:5	3513
And their **h** men are famished,	Is 5:13	3519b
The head is the elder and **h** man,	Is 9:15	6440, 5375
the holy *day* of the LORD **h**,	Is 58:13	3513
They cast lots for her **h** men,	Na 3:10	3513
same lump one vessel for **h** use and	Ro 9:21	5092
of the body which we deem less **h**,	1Co 12:23	820
for we have regard for what is **h**,	2Co 8:21	2570
whatever is true, whatever is **h**,	Php 4:8	4586

HONORABLY

conduct ourselves **h** in all things.	Heb 13:18	2573

HONORED

and I will be **h** through Pharaoh	Ex 14:4	3513
and I will be **h** through Pharaoh	Ex 14:17	3513
LORD, when I am **h** through Pharaoh,	Ex 14:18	3513
all the people I will be **h**.'"	Lv 10:3	3513
to fear this **h** and awesome name,	Dt 28:58	3513
with which God and men are **h**,	Jg 9:9	3513
guard, and is **h** in your house?	1Sa 22:14	3513
He was most **h** of the thirty,	2Sa 23:19	3513
He was **h** among the thirty, but he	2Sa 23:23	3513
the second *rank* he was the most **h** and	1Ch 11:21	3513
Behold, he was **h** among the thirty,	1Ch 11:25	3513
the inhabitants of Jerusalem **h** him	2Ch 32:33	3519b
he who regards reproof will be **h**.	Pr 13:18	3513
cares for his master will be **h**.	Pr 27:18	3513
traders were the **h** of the earth?	Is 23:8	3513
To despise all the **h** of the earth.	Is 23:9	3513
Since you are **h** and I love you,	Is 43:4	3513
Nor have you **h** Me with your	Is 43:23	3513
I am **h** in the sight of the LORD,	Is 49:5	3513
All who **h** her despise her Because	La 1:8	3513
and **h** Him who lives forever;	Da 4:34	1922
that they may be **h** by men.	Mt 6:2	1392
h us with many marks of respect;	Ac 28:10	5091
if *one* member is **h**,	1Co 12:26	1392

HONORING

David is **h** your father because he	2Sa 10:3	3513
think that David is **h** your father,	1Ch 19:3	3513

HONORS

But who **h** those who fear the LORD;	Ps 15:4	3513
a sacrifice of thanksgiving **h** Me;	Ps 50:23	3513
he who **h** himself and lacks bread.	Pr 12:9	3513
is gracious to the needy **h** Him.	Pr 14:31	3513
"'A son **h** *his* father, and a	Mal 1:6	3513
'THIS PEOPLE **H** ME WITH THEIR LIPS,	Mt 15:8	5091
'THIS PEOPLE **H** ME WITH THEIR LIPS,	Mk 7:6	5091

HOOF

not a **h** shall be left behind, for	Ex 10:26	6541
'Whatever divides a **h**,	Lv 11:3	6541
or among those which divide the **h**:	Lv 11:4	6541
cud, it does not divide the **h**,	Lv 11:4	6541
cud, it does not divide the **h**,	Lv 11:5	6541
cud, it does not divide the **h**,	Lv 11:6	6541
pig, for though it divides the **h**,	Lv 11:7	6541
the hoof, thus making a split **h**,	Lv 11:7	6541
the animals which divide the **h**	Lv 11:26	6541
the hoof but do not make a split **h**,	Lv 11:26	
"Any animal that divides the **h**	Dt 14:6	6541
has the **h** split in two *and* chews the	Dt 14:6	8157
those that divide the **h** in two:	Dt 14:7	6541
the cud, they do not divide the **h**;	Dt 14:7	6541
"The pig, because it divides the **h** but	Dt 14:8	6541
their feet were like a calf's **h**,	Ezk 1:7	3709, 7272

HOOFBEATS

do the **h** of his chariots tarry?	Jg 5:28	6471

HOOFS

a hoof, thus making split **h**,	Lv 11:3	6541
horses' **h** beat From the dashing,	Jg 5:22	6119
Or a young bull with horns and **h**.	Ps 69:31	6536
h of its horses seem like flint and	Is 5:28	6541
the galloping **h** of his stallions,	Jer 47:3	6541
"With the **h** of his horses he will	Ezk 26:11	6541
And the **h** of beasts will not	Ezk 32:13	6541
And your **h** I will make bronze,	Mi 4:13	6541
fat *sheep* and tear off their **h**.	Zch 11:16	6541

HOOK

I will put My **h** in your nose,	2Ki 19:28	2397
Or pierce his jaw with a **h**?	Jb 41:2	2336
I will put My **h** in your nose	Is 37:29	2397
bring all of them up with a **h**,	Hab 1:15	2443
go to the sea and throw in a **h**,	Mt 17:27	44

HOOKS

gold, their **h** *also being of* gold,	Ex 26:32	2053
gold, their **h** *also being of* gold;	Ex 26:37	2053
the **h** of the pillars and their	Ex 27:10	2053
the **h** of the pillars and their	Ex 27:11	2053
silver bands *with* their **h** of silver	Ex 27:17	2053
covering, its **h** and its boards,	Ex 35:11	7165
with gold, with their **h** of gold;	Ex 36:36	2053
its five pillars with their **h**,	Ex 36:38	2053
the flesh **h** and the firepans;	Ex 38:3	4207b
the **h** of the pillars and their	Ex 38:10	2053
the **h** of the pillars and their	Ex 38:11	2053
the **h** of the pillars and their	Ex 38:12	2053
the **h** of the pillars and their	Ex 38:17	2053
their **h** *were* of silver, and the	Ex 38:19	2053
he made **h** for the pillars and	Ex 38:28	2053
and they captured Manasseh with **h**,	2Ch 33:11	2336
and their spears into pruning **h**.	Is 2:4	4211
him with **h** To the land of Egypt.	Ezk 19:4	2397
'They put him in a cage with **h**	Ezk 19:9	2397
"I will put **h** in your jaws	Ezk 29:4	2397
about and put **h** into your jaws,	Ezk 38:4	2397
The double **h**, one handbreadth	Ezk 40:43	8240b
And your pruning **h** into spears;	Jl 3:10	4211
will take you away with meat **h**,	Am 4:2	6793a
And the last of you with fish **h**.	Am 4:2	5518b
And their spears into pruning **h**;	Mi 4:3	4211

HOOPOE

the heron in its kinds, and the **h**,	Lv 11:19	1744
kinds, and the **h** and the bat.	Dt 14:18	1744

HOPE

If I said I have **h**,	Ru 1:12	8615b
like a shadow, and there is no **h**.	1Ch 29:15	4723a
is **h** for Israel in spite of this.	Ezr 10:2	4723a
the integrity of your ways your **h**?	Jb 4:6	8615b
"So the helpless has **h**,	Jb 5:16	8615b
And come to an end without **h**.	Jb 7:6	8615b
the **h** of the godless will perish,	Jb 8:13	8615b
would trust, because there is **h**;	Jb 11:18	8615b
h is to breathe their last."	Jb 11:20	8615b
Though He slay me, I will **h** in Him	Jb 13:15	3176
"For there is **h** for a tree, When	Jb 14:7	8615b
So You destroy man's **h**.	Jb 14:19	8615b
Where now is my **h**?	Jb 17:15	8615b
And who regards my **h**?	Jb 17:15	8615b
He has uprooted my **h** like a tree.	Jb 19:10	8615b
"For what is the **h** of the godless	Jb 27:8	8615b
Nor the **h** of the afflicted perish	Ps 9:18	8615b
All you who **h** in the LORD.	Ps 31:24	3176
A horse is a false **h** for victory;	Ps 33:17	8267
who **h** for His lovingkindness,	Ps 33:18	3176
For I **h** in You, O LORD;	Ps 38:15	3176
for what do I wait? My **h** is in You.	Ps 39:7	8431
H in God, for I shall again praise	Ps 42:5	3176
H in God, for I shall yet praise	Ps 42:11	3176
H in God, for I shall again praise	Ps 43:5	3176
God only, For my **h** is from Him.	Ps 62:5	8615b
And do not vainly **h** in robbery;	Ps 62:10	1891
For You are my **h**;	Ps 71:5	8615b
as for me, I will **h** continually,	Ps 71:14	3176
In which You have made me **h**.	Ps 119:49	3176
do not let me be ashamed of my **h**.	Ps 119:116	7664
I **h** for Your salvation, O LORD, And	Ps 119:166	7663b
does wait, And in His word do I **h**.	Ps 130:5	3176
O Israel, **h** in the LORD;	Ps 130:7	3176
h in the LORD From this time forth	Ps 131:3	3176
Whose **h** is in the LORD his God,	Ps 146:5	7664
h of the righteous is gladness,	Pr 10:28	8431
And the **h** of strong men perishes.	Pr 11:7	8431
H deferred makes the heart sick,	Pr 13:12	8431
your son while there is **h**,	Pr 19:18	8615b
And your **h** will not be cut off.	Pr 23:18	8615b
And your **h** will not be cut off.	Pr 24:14	8615b
is more **h** for a fool than for him.	Pr 26:12	8615b
is more **h** for a fool than for him.	Pr 29:20	8615b

with all the living, there is **h**; **Ec 9:4** 986
Cush their **h** and Egypt their boast. **Is 20:5** 4007
'Behold, such is our **h**, **Is 20:6** 4007
pit cannot **h** for Your faithfulness. **Is 38:18** 7663b
We **h** for light, but behold, **Is 59:9** 6960a
We **h** for justice, but there is **Is 59:11** 6960a
"O **H** of Israel, Its Savior in **Jer 14:8** 4723a
Therefore we **h** in You, For You **Jer 14:22** 6960a
O LORD, the **h** of Israel, All who **Jer 17:13** 4723a
to give you a future and a **h**. **Jer 29:11** 8615b
"There is **h** for your future," **Jer 31:17** 8615b
the LORD, the **h** of their fathers.' **Jer 50:7** 4723a
And *so has* my **h** from the LORD." **La 3:18** 8431
to my mind, Therefore I have **h**. **La 3:21** 3176
"Therefore I have **h** in Him." **La 3:24** 3176
in the dust, Perhaps there is **h**. **La 3:29** 8615b
yet they **h** for the fulfillment of **Ezk 13:6** 3176
she waited, *That* her **h** was lost, **Ezk 19:5** 8615b
dried up and our **h** has perished. **Ezk 37:11** 8615b
valley of Achor as a door of **h**. **Hos 2:15** 8615b
O prisoners who have the **h**; **Zch 9:12** 8615b
"AND IN HIS NAME THE GENTILES WILL **H**." **Mt 12:21** *1679*
in whom you have set your **h**. **Jn 5:45** *1679*
MY FLESH ALSO WILL LIVE IN **H**; **Ac 2:26** *1680*
that their **h** of profit was gone, **Ac 16:19** *1680*
on trial for the **h** and resurrection **Ac 23:6** *1680*
having a **h** in God, which these men **Ac 24:15** *1680*
the **h** of the promise made by God to **Ac 26:6** *1680*
our twelve tribes **h** to attain, **Ac 26:7** *1679*
And for this **h**, O King, I am being **Ac 26:7** *1680*
all **h** of our being saved was **Ac 27:20** *1680*
for the sake of the **h** of Israel." **Ac 28:20** *1680*
In **h** against hope he believed, so **Ro 4:18** *1680*
In hope against **h** he believed, so **Ro 4:18** *1680*
we exult in **h** of the glory of God. **Ro 5:2** *1680*
and proven character, **h**; **Ro 5:4** *1680*
and **h** does not disappoint, because **Ro 5:5** *1680*
of Him who subjected it, in **h** **Ro 8:20** *1680*
For in **h** we have been saved, but **Ro 8:24** *1680*
but **h** that is seen is not hope; **Ro 8:24** *1680*
but hope that is seen is not **h**; **Ro 8:24** *1680*
if we **h** for what we do not see, **Ro 8:25** *1679*
rejoicing in **h**, persevering in **Ro 12:12** *1680*
of the Scriptures we might have **h**. **Ro 15:4** *1680*
IN HIM SHALL THE GENTILES **H**." **Ro 15:12** *1679*
Now may the God of **h** fill you with **Ro 15:13** *1680*
that you will abound in **h** by the **Ro 15:13** *1680*
I **h** to see you in passing, **Ro 15:24** *1679*
the plowman ought to plow in **h**, **1Co 9:10** *1680*
thresh in **h** of sharing *the crops.* **1Co 9:10** *1680*
But now faith, **h**, **1Co 13:13** *1680*
for I **h** to remain with you for **1Co 16:7** *1679*
our **h** for you is firmly grounded, **2Co 1:7** *1680*
us, He on whom we have set our **h**. **2Co 1:10** *1679*
and I **h** you will understand until **2Co 1:13** *1679*
Therefore having such a **h**, **2Co 3:12** *1680*
and I **h** that we are made manifest **2Co 5:11** *1679*
the **h** that as your faith grows, **2Co 10:15** *1680*
for the **h** of righteousness. **Ga 5:5** *1680*
we who were the first to **h** in Christ **Eph 1:12** *4276*
know what is the **h** of His calling, **Eph 1:18** *1680*
having no **h** and without God in **Eph 2:12** *1680*
called in one **h** of your calling; **Eph 4:4** *1680*
to my earnest expectation and **h**, **Php 1:20** *1680*
But I **h** in the Lord Jesus to send **Php 2:19** *1679*
I **h** to send him immediately, **Php 2:23** *1679*
the **h** laid up for you in heaven, **Col 1:5** *1680*
h of the gospel that you have heard **Col 1:23** *1680*
is Christ in you, the **h** of glory. **Col 1:27** *1680*
steadfastness of **h** in our Lord Jesus **1Th 1:3** *1680*
h or joy or crown of exultation? **1Th 2:19** *1680*
as do the rest who have no **h**. **1Th 4:13** *1680*
as a helmet, the **h** of salvation. **1Th 5:8** *1680*
comfort and good **h** by grace, **2Th 2:16** *1680*
and of Christ Jesus, *who is* our **h**, **1Tm 1:1** *1680*
fixed our **h** on the living God, **1Tm 4:10** *1679*
left alone, has fixed her **h** on God **1Tm 5:5** *1679*
to fix their **h** on the uncertainty of **1Tm 6:17** *1679*
in the **h** of eternal life, which **Ti 1:2** *1680*
looking for the blessed **h** and the **Ti 2:13** *1680*
to *the* **h** of eternal life. **Ti 3:7** *1680*
for I **h** that through your prayers **Phm 1:22** *1679*
boast of our **h** firm until the end. **Heb 3:6** *1680*
full assurance of **h** until the end, **Heb 6:11** *1680*
hold of the **h** set before us. **Heb 6:18** *1680*
This **h** we have as an anchor of the **Heb 6:19**
a **h** both sure and steadfast **Heb 6:19**
is a bringing in of a better **h**, **Heb 7:19** *1680*
hold fast the confession of our **h** **Heb 10:23** *1680*
to be born again to a living **h** through **1Pe 1:3** *1680*
fix your **h** completely on the grace **1Pe 1:13** *1679*
that your faith and **h** are in God. **1Pe 1:21** *1680*
to give an account for the **h** that is **1Pe 3:15** *1680*
who has this **h** *fixed* on Him **1Jn 3:3** *1680*
but I **h** to come to you and speak **2Jn 1:12** *1679*
but I **h** to see you shortly, and we **3Jn 1:14** *1679*

HOPED
h to gain the mastery over them, **Es 9:1** 7663b
The travelers of Sheba **h** for them. **Jb 6:19** 6960a
According as we have **h** in You. **Ps 33:22** 3176
h in Christ in this life only, **1Co 15:19** *1679*
faith is the assurance of *things* **h** for, **Heb 11:1** *1679*
the holy women also, who **h** in God, **1Pe 3:5** *1679*

HOPEFULLY
Those who **h** wait for Me will not **Is 49:23** 6960a

HOPELESS
Yet you did not say, 'It is **h**.' **Is 57:10** 2976
But you said, 'It is **h**! **Jer 2:25** 2976
"But they will say, 'It's **h**! **Jer 18:12** 2976

HOPES
for who **h** for what he *already* **Ro 8:24** *1680*
believes all things, **h** all things, **1Co 13:7** *1679*

HOPHNI
H and Phinehas, were priests to the **1Sa 1:3** 2652
your two sons, **H** and Phinehas: **1Sa 2:34** 2652
two sons of Eli, **H** and Phinehas, **1Sa 4:4** 2652
two sons of Eli, **H** and Phinehas, **1Sa 4:11** 2652
two sons also, **H** and Phinehas, **1Sa 4:17** 2652

HOPHRA
to give over Pharaoh **H** king of Egypt **Jer 44:30** 6548

HOPING
And while you are **h** for light He **Jer 13:16** 6960a
h to see some sign performed by Him. **Lk 23:8** *1679*
"But we were **h** that it was He who **Lk 24:21** *1679*
he was **h** that money would be given **Ac 24:26** *1679*
you, **h** to come to you before long; **1Tm 3:14** *1679*

HOR
congregation, came to Mount **H**. **Nu 20:22** 2023
to Moses and Aaron at Mount **H** **Nu 20:23** 2023
and bring them up to Mount **H**; **Nu 20:25** 2023
and they went up to Mount **H** in the **Nu 20:27** 2023
Mount **H** by the way of the Red Sea, **Nu 21:4** 2023
Kadesh and camped at Mount **H**, **Nu 33:37** 2023
the priest went up to Mount **H** **Nu 33:38** 2023
years old when he died on Mount **H**. **Nu 33:39** 2023
Then they journeyed from Mount **H** and **Nu 33:41** 2023
from the Great Sea to Mount **H**. **Nu 34:7** 2023
from Mount **H** to the Lebo-hamath, **Nu 34:8** 2023
Aaron your brother died on Mount **H** **Dt 32:50** 2023

HORAM
Then **H** king of Gezer came up to **Jos 10:33** 2036

HORDE
"Now this **h** will lick up all that **Nu 22:4** 6951
of Assyria nor because of all the **h** **2Ch 32:7** 1995
against Babylon A **h** of great nations **Jer 50:9** 6951
will bury Gog there with all his **h**, **Ezk 39:11** 1995
Their **h** of faces *moves* forward. **Hab 1:9** 4041

HORDES
"I will also make the **h** of Egypt **Ezk 30:10** 1995
I will also cut off the **h** of Thebes. **Ezk 30:15** 1995
to Pharaoh king of Egypt and to his **h**, **Ezk 31:2** 1995
So is Pharaoh and all his **h**!"' **Ezk 31:18** 1995
the mighty ones I will cause your **h** **Ezk 32:12** 1995
And all its **h** will be destroyed. **Ezk 32:12** 1995
Over Egypt and over all her **h** they **Ezk 32:16** 1995
"Son of man, wail for the **h** of **Ezk 32:18** 1995
they have drawn her and all her **h** **Ezk 32:20** 1995
"Elam is there and all her **h** around **Ezk 32:24** 1995
her among the slain with all her **h**. **Ezk 32:25** 1995
"Meshech, Tubal and all their **h** are **Ezk 32:26** 1995
he will be comforted for all his **h** **Ezk 32:31** 1995
even Pharaoh and all his **h**," **Ezk 32:32** 1995
marshals are like **h** of grasshoppers **Na 3:17** 1462

HOREB
of the wilderness and came to **H**, **Ex 3:1** 2722
before you there on the rock at **H**; **Ex 17:6** 2722
ornaments, from Mount **H** *onward.* **Ex 33:6** 2722
It is eleven days' *journey* from **H** **Dt 1:2** 2722
"The LORD our God spoke to us at **H**, **Dt 1:6** 2722
"Then we set out from **H**, **Dt 1:19** 2722
before the LORD your God at **H**, **Dt 4:10** 2722
the LORD spoke to you at **H** from **Dt 4:15** 2722
God made a covenant with us at **H**. **Dt 5:2** 2722
"Even at **H** you provoked the LORD **Dt 9:8** 2722
asked of the LORD your God in **H** **Dt 18:16** 2722
which He had made with them at **H**. **Dt 29:1** 2722
stone which Moses put there at **H**, **1Ki 8:9** 2722
forty days and forty nights to **H**, **1Ki 19:8** 2722
which Moses put *there* at **H**, **2Ch 5:10** 2722
They made a calf in **H** And **Ps 106:19** 2722
commanded him in **H** for all Israel. **Mal 4:4** 2722

HOREM
H and Beth-anath and Beth-shemesh; **Jos 19:38** 2765

HORESH
in the wilderness of Ziph at **H**. **1Sa 23:15** 2793
son, arose and went to David at **H**, **1Sa 23:16** 2793
and David stayed at **H** while **1Sa 23:18** 2793
with us in the strongholds at **H**, **1Sa 23:19** 2793

HOR-HAGGIDGAD
from Bene-jaakan and camped at **H**. **Nu 33:32** 2735
They journeyed from **H** and **Nu 33:33** 2735

HORI
sons of Lotan were **H** and Hemam; **Gn 36:22** 2752
of Simeon, Shaphat the son of **H** **Nu 13:5** 2752
sons of Lotan *were* **H** and Homam; **1Ch 1:39** 2752

HORITE
These are the sons of Seir the **H**, **Gn 36:20** 2752

HORITES
and the **H** in their Mount Seir, as **Gn 14:6** 2752
the chiefs descended from the **H**, **Gn 36:21** 2752
the chiefs descended from the **H**: **Gn 36:29** 2752
the chiefs descended from the **H**, **Gn 36:30** 2752
The **H** formerly lived in Seir, but **Dt 2:12** 2752
destroyed the **H** from before them; **Dt 2:22** 2752

HORIZONS
a far country, From the farthest **h**, **Is 13:5** 8064

HORMAH
and beat them down as far as **H**. **Nu 14:45** 2767
name of the place was called **H**. **Nu 21:3** 2767
and crushed you from Seir to **H**. **Dt 1:44** 2767
the king of **H**, one; **Jos 12:14** 2767
and Eltolad and Chesil and **H**, **Jos 15:30** 2767
and Eltolad and Bethul and **H**, **Jos 19:4** 2767
the name of the city was called **H**. **Jg 1:17** 2767
and to those who were in **H**, **1Sa 30:30** 2767
Bethuel, **H**, Ziklag, **1Ch 4:30** 2767

HORN
the ram's **h** sounds a long blast, **Ex 19:13** 3104
'You shall then sound a ram's **h** **Lv 25:9** 7782
sound a **h** all through your land. **Lv 25:9** 7782
make a long blast with the ram's **h**, **Jos 6:5** 7161
My **h** is exalted in the LORD, My **1Sa 2:1** 7161
exalt the **h** of His anointed." **1Sa 2:10** 7161
Fill your **h** with oil and go; **1Sa 16:1** 7161
Then Samuel took the **h** of oil and **1Sa 16:13** 7161
shield and the **h** of my salvation, **2Sa 22:3** 7161
the priest then took the **h** of oil **1Ki 1:39** 7161
shouting, and with sound of the **h**, **1Ch 15:28** 7782
skin And thrust my **h** in the dust. **Jb 16:15** 7161
shield and the **h** of my salvation, **Ps 18:2** 7161
'Do not lift up the **h**; **Ps 75:4** 7161
Do not lift up your **h** on high, **Ps 75:5** 7161
And by Your favor our **h** is exalted. **Ps 89:17** 7161
in My name his **h** will be exalted. **Ps 89:24** 7161
You have exalted my **h** like *that of* **Ps 92:10** 7161
With trumpets and the sound of the **h** **Ps 98:6** 7782
His **h** will be exalted in honor. **Ps 112:9** 7161
the **h** of David to spring forth; **Ps 132:17** 7161
has lifted up a **h** for His people, **Ps 148:14** 7161
"The **h** of Moab has been cut off and **Jer 48:25** 7161
will make a **h** sprout for the house **Ezk 29:21** 7161
you hear the sound of the **h**, **Da 3:5** 7162
peoples heard the sound of the **h**, **Da 3:7** 7162
man who hears the sound of the **h**, **Da 3:10** 7162
you hear the sound of the **h**, **Da 3:15** 7162
another **h**, a little one, came up **Da 7:8** 7162
this **h** possessed eyes like the **Da 7:8** 7162
words which the **h** was speaking; **Da 7:11** 7162
were on its head and the other **h** **Da 7:20**
that **h** which had eyes and a mouth **Da 7:20** 7162
and that **h** was waging war with the **Da 7:21** 7162
a conspicuous **h** between his eyes. **Da 8:5** 7161
mighty, the large **h** was broken; **Da 8:8** 7161
small **h** which grew exceedingly great **Da 8:9** 7161
host will be given over *to the* **h** **Da 8:12**
the large **h** that is between his eyes **Da 8:21** 7161
"The broken **h** and the four **Da 8:22**
Blow the **h** in Gibeah, The trumpet **Hos 5:8** 7782
For your **h** I will make iron And **Mi 4:13** 7161
And has raised up a **h** of salvation **Lk 1:69** *2768*

HORNED
in the way, A **h** snake in the path, **Gn 49:17** 8207

HORNET
God will send the **h** against them, **Dt 7:20** 6880
'Then I sent the **h** before you and **Jos 24:12** 6880

HORNETS
"I will send **h** ahead of you so **Ex 23:28** 6880

HORNS
caught in the thicket by his **h**; **Gn 22:13** 7161
make its **h** on its four corners; **Ex 27:2** 7161
its **h** shall be of one piece **Ex 27:2** 7161
h of the altar with your finger; **Ex 29:12** 7161
h *shall be* of one piece with it. **Ex 30:2** 7161
its sides all around, and its **h**; **Ex 30:3** 7161
atonement on its **h** once a year; **Ex 30:10** 7161
its **h** were *of one piece* with it. **Ex 37:25** 7161
its sides all around, and its **h**; **Ex 37:26** 7161
He made its **h** on its four corners, **Ex 38:2** 7161
its **h** being *of one piece* with it, **Ex 38:2** 7161
blood on the **h** of the altar of fragrant **Lv 4:7** 7161
some of the blood on the **h** of the altar **Lv 4:18** 7161
and put it on the **h** of the altar **Lv 4:25** 7161
on the **h** of the altar of burnt offering; **Lv 4:30** 7161
on the **h** of the altar of burnt offering, **Lv 4:34** 7161
it around on the **h** of the altar, **Lv 8:15** 7161
put *some* on the **h** of the altar, **Lv 9:9** 7161
the **h** of the altar on all sides. **Lv 16:18** 7161
them like the **h** of the wild ox. **Nu 23:22** 8443
for him like the **h** of the wild ox. **Nu 24:8** 8443
h are the horns of the wild ox; **Dt 33:17** 7161
horns are the **h** of the wild ox; **Dt 33:17** 7161
trumpets of rams' **h** before the ark; **Jos 6:4** 3104
trumpets of rams' **h** before the ark **Jos 6:6** 3104
carrying the seven trumpets of rams' **h** **Jos 6:8** 3104
carrying the seven trumpets of rams' **h** **Jos 6:13** 3104
took hold of the **h** of the altar. **1Ki 1:50** 7161
taken hold of the **h** of the altar, **1Ki 1:51** 7161
took hold of the **h** of the altar. **1Ki 2:28** 7161
son of Chenaanah made **h** of iron **1Ki 22:11** 7161
with trumpets and with **h**. **2Ch 15:14** 7782
son of Chenaanah made **h** of iron **2Ch 18:10** 7161
From the **h** of the wild oxen **Ps 22:21** 7161
Or a young bull with **h** and hoofs. **Ps 69:31** 7161
h of the wicked He will cut off, **Ps 75:10** 7161
h of the righteous will be lifted up. **Ps 75:10** 7161
with cords to the **h** of the altar. **Ps 118:27** 7161
And on the **h** of their altars, **Jer 17:1** 7161
at all the weak with your **h** until **Ezk 34:21** 7161
shall extend upwards four **h**. **Ezk 43:15** 7161
blood and put it on its four **h** **Ezk 43:20** 7161
were before it, and it had ten **h**. **Da 7:7** 7162
"While I was contemplating the **h**, **Da 7:8** 7162
and three of the first **h** were **Da 7:8** 7162
the ten **h** that *were* on its head **Da 7:20** 7162
'As for the ten **h**, out of this **Da 7:24** 7162
a ram which had two **h** was standing **Da 8:3** 7161
Now the two **h** *were* long, but one **Da 8:3** 7161
up to the ram that had the two **h**, **Da 8:6** 7161
the ram and shattered his two **h**, **Da 8:7** 7161
there came up four conspicuous **h** **Da 8:8**
ram which you saw with the two **h** **Da 8:20** 7161
"The broken *horn* and the four **h** **Da 8:22**

h of the altar will be cut off Am 3:14 7161
and behold, *there were* four **h**. Zch 1:18 7161
the **h** which have scattered Judah, Zch 1:19 7161
the **h** which have scattered Judah so Zch 1:21 7161
to throw down the **h** of the nations Zch 1:21 7161
the nations who have lifted up *their* **h** Zch 1:21 7161
having seven **h** and seven eyes, Rv 5:6 *2768*
from the four **h** of the golden altar Rv 9:13 *2768*
having seven heads and ten **h**, Rv 12:3 *2768*
sea, having ten **h** and seven heads, Rv 13:1 *2768*
and on his **h** *were* ten diadems, Rv 13:1 *2768*
and he had two **h** like a lamb and Rv 13:11 *2768*
having seven heads and ten **h**. Rv 17:3 *2768*
has the seven heads and the ten **h**. Rv 17:7 *2768*
ten **h** which you saw are ten kings who Rv 17:12 *2768*
"And the ten **h** which you saw, and Rv 17:16 *2768*

HORONAIM
Surely on the road to **H** they raise Is 15:5 2773
"The sound of an outcry from **H**, Jer 48:3 2773
For at the descent of **H** They have Jer 48:5 2773
from Zoar even to **H** *and to* Jer 48:34 2773

HORONITE
When Sanballat the **H** and Ne 2:10 2772
But when Sanballat the **H** and Ne 2:19 2772
was a son-in-law of Sanballat the **H**, Ne 13:28 2772

HORRIBLE
appalling and **h** thing Has happened Jer 5:30 8186a
Jerusalem I have seen a **h** thing: Jer 23:14 8186a
of Israel I have seen a **h** thing; Hos 6:10 8186b

HORRIBLY
you, And their kings are **h** afraid; Ezk 27:35 8178a
and their kings will be **h** afraid Ezk 32:10 8178a

HORRID
had made a **h** image as an Asherah; 1Ki 15:13 4656
and Asa cut down her **h** image and 1Ki 15:13 4656
had made a **h** image as an Asherah, 2Ch 15:16 4656
and Asa cut down her **h** image, 2Ch 15:16 4656

HORRIFIED
everyone who passes by it will be **h** Jer 49:17 8074
who passes by Babylon will be **h** Jer 50:13 8074

HORROR
"You shall become a **h**, Dt 28:37 8047
them an object of terror, of **h**, 2Ch 29:8 8047
fathers, so that He made them a **h**, 2Ch 30:7 8047
in the east are seized with **h**. Jb 18:20 8178a
And **h** takes hold of my flesh. Jb 21:6 6427
And **h** has overwhelmed me. Ps 55:5 6427
My mind reels, **h** overwhelms me; Is 21:4 6427
I will make them an object of **h** Jer 15:4 2113
destroy them and make them a **h** Jer 25:9 8047
will be a desolation and a **h**, Jer 25:11 8047
princes, to make them a ruin, a **h**, Jer 25:18 8047
For their land has become a **h** Jer 25:38 8047
the earth, to be a curse and a **h** Jer 29:18 8047
become a curse, an object of **h**, Jer 42:18 8047
become a curse, an object of **h**, Jer 44:12 8047
ruin, an object of **h** and a curse, Jer 44:22 8047
Bozrah will become an object of **h**, Jer 49:13 8047
Edom will become an object of **h**; Jer 49:17 8047
will make her land an object of **h**, Jer 50:3 8047
An object of **h** among the nations! Jer 50:23 8047
An object of **h** and hissing, Jer 51:37 8047
an object of **h** among the nations! Jer 51:41 8047
cities have become an object of **h**, Jer 51:43 8047
drink water by measure and in **h**, Ezk 4:16 8078
a warning and an object of **h** to Ezk 5:15 4923
the prince will be clothed with **h**, Ezk 7:27 8077
and drink their water with **h**, Ezk 12:19 8078
The cup of **h** and desolation, Ezk 23:33 8047
while the transgression causes **h**, Da 8:13 8074

HORSE
The **h** and its rider He has hurled Ex 15:1 5483b
The **h** and his rider He has hurled Ex 15:21 5483b
of silver, and a **h** for 150; 1Ki 10:29 5483b
Aram escaped on a **h** with horsemen. 1Ki 20:20 5483b
that you have lost, **h** for horse, 1Ki 20:25 5483b
that you have lost, horse for **h**, 1Ki 20:25 5483b
of the **H** Gate of the king's house, 2Ch 23:15 5483b
Above the **H** Gate the priests Ne 3:28 5483b
h on which the king has ridden, Es 6:8 5483b
let the robe and the **h** be handed Es 6:9 5483b
Take quickly the robes and the **h** Es 6:10 5483b
So Haman took the robe and the **h**, Es 6:11 5483b
She laughs at the **h** and his rider. Jb 39:18 5483b
"Do you give the **h** *his* might? Jb 39:19 5483b
Do not be as the **h** or as the mule Ps 32:9 5483b
A **h** is a false hope for victory; Ps 33:17 5483b
and **h** were cast into a dead sleep. Ps 76:6 5483b
delight in the strength of the **h**; Ps 147:10 5483b
The **h** is prepared for the day of Pr 21:31 5483b
A whip is for the **h**, Pr 26:3 5483b
forth the chariot and the **h**, Is 43:17 5483b
Like the **h** in the wilderness, they Is 63:13 5483b
Like a **h** charging into the battle. Jer 8:6 5483b
to the corner of the **H** Gate toward Jer 31:40 5483b
you I shatter the **h** and his rider, Jer 51:21 5483b
he who rides the **h** save his life. Am 2:15 5483b
a man was riding on a red **h**, Zch 1:8 5483b
Ephraim And the **h** from Jerusalem; Zch 9:10 5483b
like His majestic **h** in battle. Zch 10:3 5483b
strike every **h** with bewilderment and Zch 12:4 5483b
I strike every **h** of the peoples with Zch 12:4 5483b
will be the plague on the **h**, Zch 14:15 5483b
I looked, and behold, a white **h**, Rv 6:2 *2462*
And another, a red **h**, Rv 6:4 *2462*
I looked, and behold, a black **h**; Rv 6:5 *2462*
I looked, and behold, an ashen **h**; Rv 6:8 *2462*
and behold, a white **h**, Rv 19:11 *2462*
against Him who sat on the **h** Rv 19:19 *2462*
mouth of Him who sat on the **h**, Rv 19:21 *2462*

HORSEBACK
lead him on **h** through the city Es 6:9 5483b
and led him *on* **h** through the city Es 6:11

HORSEFLY
a **h** is coming from the north Jer 46:20 7171

HORSEMAN
"Take a **h** and send him to meet 2Ki 9:17 7395
So a **h** went to meet him and said, 2Ki 9:18 7392, 5483b
Then he sent out a second **h**, 2Ki 9:19 7392, 5483b
At the sound of the **h** and bowman Jer 4:29 6571b

HORSEMEN
up with him both chariots and **h**; Gn 50:9 6571b
of Pharaoh, his **h** and his army, Ex 14:9 6571b
through his chariots and his **h**. Ex 14:17 6571b
through his chariots and his **h**." Ex 14:18 6571b
his chariots and his **h** went in Ex 14:23 6571b
over their chariots and their **h**." Ex 14:26 6571b
covered the chariots and the **h**, Ex 14:28 6571b
and his **h** went into the sea, Ex 15:19 6571b
your fathers with chariots and **h** Jos 24:6 6571b
in his chariots and among his **h** 1Sa 8:11 6571b
30,000 chariots and 6,000 **h**, 1Sa 13:5 6571b
and the **h** pursued him closely. 2Sa 1:6 6571b
David captured from him 1,700 **h** 2Sa 8:4 6571b
40,000 **h** and struck down Shobach 2Sa 10:18 6571b
he prepared for himself chariots and **h** 1Ki 1:5 6571b
for his chariots, and 12,000 **h**. 1Ki 4:26 6571b
chariots and the cities for his **h**, 1Ki 9:19 6571b
his chariot commanders, and his **h**. 1Ki 9:22 6571b
Solomon gathered chariots and **h**; 1Ki 10:26 6571b
had 1,400 chariots and 12,000 **h**, 1Ki 10:26 6571b
of Aram escaped on a horse with **h**. 1Ki 20:20 6571b
chariots of Israel and its **h**!" 2Ki 2:12 6571b
of the army not more than fifty **h** 2Ki 13:7 6571b
chariots of Israel and its **h**!" 2Ki 13:14 6571b
on Egypt for chariots and for **h**? 2Ki 18:24 6571b
7,000 **h** and 20,000 foot soldiers, 1Ch 18:4 6571b
chariots and **h** from Mesopotamia, 1Ch 19:6 6571b
Solomon amassed chariots and **h**. 2Ch 1:14 6571b
had 1,400 chariots and 12,000 **h**, 2Ch 1:14 6571b
his chariots and cities for his **h**, 2Ch 8:6 6571b
of his chariots and his **h**. 2Ch 8:9 6571b
horses and chariots and 12,000 **h**, 2Ch 9:25 6571b
with 1,200 chariots and 60,000 **h**. 2Ch 12:3 6571b
with very many chariots and **h**? 2Ch 16:8 6571b
to request from the king troops and **h** Ezr 8:22 6571b
me officers of the army and **h**. Ne 2:9 6571b
"When he sees riders, **h** in pairs, Is 21:7 6571b
a troop of riders, **h** in pairs." Is 21:9 6571b
the chariots, infantry *and* **h**; Is 22:6 6571b
And the **h** took up fixed positions Is 22:7 6571b
in **h** because they are very strong, Is 31:1 6571b
on Egypt for chariots and for **h**? Is 36:9 6571b
young men, **h** riding on horses. Ezk 23:6 6571b
dressed, **h** riding on horses, Ezk 23:12 6571b
and all your army, horses and **h**, Ezk 38:4 6571b
against him with chariots, with **h** and Da 11:40 6571b
sword, battle, horses or **h**." Hos 1:7 6571b
H charging, Swords flashing, Na 3:3 6571b
Their **h** come galloping, Their Hab 1:8 6571b
galloping, Their **h** come from afar; Hab 1:8 6571b
with seventy **h** and two hundred Ac 23:23 *2460*
leaving the **h** to go on with him, Ac 23:32 *2460*
The number of the armies of the **h** Rv 9:16 *2461*

HORSE'S
the path, That bites the **h** heels, Gn 49:17 5483b

HORSES
gave them food in exchange for the **h** Gn 47:17 5483b
which are in the field, on the **h**, Ex 9:3 5483b
all the **h** *and* chariots of Pharaoh, Ex 14:9 5483b
all Pharaoh's **h**, his chariots and his Ex 14:23 5483b
the **h** of Pharaoh with his chariots Ex 15:19 5483b
army, to its **h** and its chariots, Dt 11:4 5483b
shall not multiply **h** for himself, Dt 17:16 5483b
to return to Egypt to multiply **h**, Dt 17:16 5483b
and see **h** and chariots *and* people Dt 20:1 5483b
with very many **h** and chariots. Jos 11:4 5483b
you shall hamstring their **h** and Jos 11:6 5483b
he hamstrung their **h** and Jos 11:9 5483b
and David hamstrung the chariot **h**, 2Sa 8:4 7393
for himself a chariot and **h** 2Sa 15:1 5483b
stalls of **h** for his chariots, 1Ki 4:26 5483b
brought barley and straw for the **h** 1Ki 4:28 5483b
garments, weapons, spices, **h**, 1Ki 10:25 5483b
Solomon's import of **h** was from 1Ki 10:28 5483b
and keep the **h** and mules alive, 1Ki 18:5 5483b
with him, and **h** and chariots. 1Ki 20:1 5483b
out and struck the **h** and chariots, 1Ki 20:21 5483b
people, my **h** as your horses." 1Ki 22:4 5483b
people, my horses as your **h**." 1Ki 22:4 5483b
appeared a chariot of fire and **h** of fire 2Ki 2:11 5483b
people, my **h** as your horses. 2Ki 3:7 5483b
my horses as your **h**." 2Ki 3:7 5483b
came with his **h** and his chariots and 2Ki 5:9 5483b
He sent **h** and chariots and a 2Ki 6:14 5483b
an army with **h** and chariots was 2Ki 6:15 5483b
the mountain was full of **h** and 2Ki 6:17 5483b
of chariots and a sound of **h**, 2Ki 7:6 5483b
and their **h** and their donkeys, 2Ki 7:7 5483b
the **h** tied and the donkeys tied, 2Ki 7:10 5483b
take five of the **h** which remain, 2Ki 7:13 5483b
therefore two chariots with **h**, 2Ki 7:14 5483b
on the wall and on the **h**, 2Ki 9:33 5483b
as well as the chariots and **h** and 2Ki 10:2 5483b
Then they brought him on **h** and he 2Ki 14:20 5483b
I will give you two thousand **h**, 2Ki 18:23 5483b
He did away with the **h** which 2Ki 23:11 5483b
David hamstrung all the chariot **h**, 1Ch 18:4 7393
Solomon's **h** were imported from 2Ch 1:16 5483b
apiece and **h** for 150 apiece, 2Ch 1:17 5483b
garments, weapons, spices, **h** 2Ch 9:24 5483b
Now Solomon had 4,000 stalls for **h** 2Ch 9:25 5483b
bringing **h** for Solomon from Egypt 2Ch 9:28 5483b
Then they brought him on **h** and 2Ch 25:28 5483b
Their **h** were 736; Ezr 2:66 5483b
Their **h** were 736; Ne 7:68 5483b
and sent letters by couriers on **h**, Es 8:10 5483b
boast in chariots and some in **h**, Ps 20:7 5483b
I have seen slaves *riding* on **h** and Ec 10:7 5483b
land has also been filled with **h** And Is 2:7 5483b
hoofs of its **h** seem like flint and Is 5:28 5483b
and his **h** *eventually* damage *it*, Is 28:28 6571a
"No, for we will flee on **h**," Is 30:16 5483b
"And we will ride on swift **h**," Is 30:16
to Egypt for help *And* rely on **h**, Is 31:1 5483b
their **h** are flesh and not spirit; Is 31:3 5483b
I will give you two thousand **h**, Is 36:8 5483b
grain offering to the LORD, on **h**, Is 66:20 5483b
His **h** are swifter than eagles. Jer 4:13 5483b
"They were well-fed lusty **h**, Jer 5:8 5483b
like the sea, And they ride on **h**, Jer 6:23 5483b
is heard the snorting of his **h**; Jer 8:16 5483b
Then how can you compete with **h**? Jer 12:5 5483b
riding in chariots and on **h**, Jer 17:25 5483b
riding in chariots and on **h**, Jer 22:4 5483b
"Harness the **h**, And mount the Jer 46:4 5483b
Go up, you **h**, and drive madly, you Jer 46:9 5483b
A sword against their **h** and against Jer 50:37 5483b
like the sea; And they ride on **h**, Jer 50:42 5483b
Bring up the **h** like bristly locusts. Jer 51:27 5483b
might give him **h** and many troops. Ezk 17:15 5483b
young men, horsemen riding on **h**. Ezk 23:6 5483b
dressed, horsemen riding on **h**, Ezk 23:12 5483b
issue is *like* the issue of **h**. Ezk 23:20 5483b
renown, all of them riding on **h**. Ezk 23:23 5483b
of Babylon, king of kings, with **h**, Ezk 26:7 5483b
"Because of the multitude of his **h**, Ezk 26:10 5483b
"With the hoofs of his **h** he will Ezk 26:11 5483b
"Those from Beth-togarmah gave **h** Ezk 27:14 5483b
war **h** and mules for your wares. Ezk 27:14 6571a
and all your army, **h** and horsemen, Ezk 38:4 5483b
with you, all of them riding on **h**, Ezk 38:15 5483b
My table with **h** and charioteers, Ezk 39:20 5483b
them by bow, sword, battle, **h** or Hos 1:7 5483b
save us, We will not ride on **h**; Hos 14:3 5483b
is like the appearance of **h**; Jl 2:4 5483b
And like war **h**, so they run. Jl 2:4 6571a
sword along with your captured **h**, Am 4:10 5483b
Do **h** run on rocks? Am 6:12 5483b
the chariot to the team of **h**, Mi 1:13 7409
"That I will cut off your **h** from Mi 5:10 5483b
of the wheel, Galloping **h** And Na 3:2 5483b
"Their **h** are swifter than Hab 1:8 5483b
That You rode on Your **h**, Hab 3:8 5483b
trampled on the sea with Your **h**, Hab 3:15 5483b
h and their riders will go down, Hg 2:22 5483b
sorrel and white **h** behind him. Zch 1:8 5483b
With the first chariot *were* red **h**, Zch 6:2 5483b
with the second chariot black **h**, Zch 6:2 5483b
with the third chariot white **h**, Zch 6:3 5483b
fourth chariot strong dappled **h**. Zch 6:3 5483b
black **h** are going forth to the north Zch 6:6 5483b
riders on **h** will be put to shame. Zch 10:5 5483b
inscribed on the bells of the **h**, Zch 14:20 5483b
appearance of the locusts was like **h** Rv 9:7 *2462*
of many **h** rushing to battle. Rv 9:9 *2462*
I saw in the vision the **h** and those Rv 9:17 *2462*
the heads of the **h** are like the heads Rv 9:17 *2462*
the power of the **h** is in their mouths Rv 9:19 *2462*
and *cargoes* of **h** and chariots and Rv 18:13 *2462*
were following Him on white **h**. Rv 19:14 *2462*
the flesh of **h** and of those who sit on Rv 19:18 *2462*

HORSES'
"Then the **h** hoofs beat From Jg 5:22 5483b
arrived at the **h** entrance 2Ki 11:16 5483b
put the bits into the **h** mouths Jas 3:3 *2462*
up to the **h** bridles, for a Rv 14:20 *2462*

HOSAH
then the border turned to **H**, Jos 19:29 2621
of Jeduthun, and **H** as gatekeepers. 1Ch 16:38 2621
Also **H**, *one* of the sons of Merari 1Ch 26:10 2621
sons and relatives of **H** *were* 13. 1Ch 26:11 2621
Shuppim and **H** *it was* to the west, 1Ch 26:16 2621

HOSANNA
"**H** to the Son of David; Mt 21:9 *5614*
H in the highest!" Mt 21:9 *5614*
"**H** to the Son of David," Mt 21:15 *5614*
"**H**! BLESSED IS HE WHO COMES IN THE Mk 11:9 *5614*
H in the highest!" Mk 11:10 *5614*
"**H**! BLESSED IS HE WHO COMES IN THE Jn 12:13 *5614*

HOSEA
which came to **H** the son of Beeri, Hos 1:1 1954
the LORD first spoke through **H**, Hos 1:2 1954
through Hosea, the LORD said to **H**, Hos 1:2 1954
As He says also in **H**, Ro 9:25 *5617*

HOSHAIAH
H and half of the leaders of Judah Ne 12:32 1955
of Kareah, Jezaniah the son of **H**, Jer 42:1 1955
Azariah the son of **H**, Jer 43:2 1955

HOSHAMA
Pedaiah, Shenazzar, Jekamiah, **H** and 1Ch 3:18 1953

HOSHEA

of Ephraim, **H** the son of Nun;	**Nu 13:8**	1954
but Moses called **H** the son of Nun,	**Nu 13:16**	1954
And **H** the son of Elah made a	**2Ki 15:30**	1954
H the son of Elah became king over	**2Ki 17:1**	1954
and **H** became his servant and paid	**2Ki 17:3**	1954
of Assyria found conspiracy in **H**,	**2Ki 17:4**	1954
In the ninth year of **H**,	**2Ki 17:6**	1954
came about in the third year of **H**,	**2Ki 18:1**	1954
the seventh year of **H** son of Elah	**2Ki 18:9**	1954
ninth year of **H** king of Israel,	**2Ki 18:10**	1954
of Ephraim, **H** the son of Azaziah;	**1Ch 27:20**	1954
H, Hananiah, Hasshub,	**Ne 10:23**	1954

HOSPITABLE

prudent, respectable, **h**,	**1Tm 3:2**	*5382*
but **h**, loving what is good,	**Ti 1:8**	*5382*
Be **h** to one another without	**1Pe 4:9**	*5382*

HOSPITALITY

needs of the saints, practicing **h**.	**Ro 12:13**	*5381*
if she has shown **h** to strangers,	**1Tm 5:10**	*3580*
not neglect to show **h** to strangers,	**Heb 13:2**	*5381*

HOST

the stars, all the **h** of heaven,	**Dt 4:19**	6635
the moon or any of the heavenly **h**,	**Dt 17:3**	6635
as captain of the **h** of the LORD."	**Jos 5:14**	6635
The captain of the LORD's **h** said to	**Jos 5:15**	6635
and all the **h** of heaven standing	**1Ki 22:19**	6635
worshiped all the **h** of heaven and	**2Ki 17:16**	6635
worshiped all the **h** of heaven and	**2Ki 21:3**	6635
built altars for all the **h** of heaven	**2Ki 21:5**	6635
and for all the **h** of heaven;	**2Ki 23:4**	6635
and to all the **h** of heaven.	**2Ki 23:5**	6635
and all the **h** of heaven standing	**2Ch 18:18**	6635
worshiped all the **h** of heaven and	**2Ch 33:3**	6635
built altars for all the **h** of heaven	**2Ch 33:5**	6635
heaven of heavens with all their **h**,	**Ne 9:6**	6635
heavenly **h** bows down before You.	**Ne 9:6**	6635
Though a **h** encamp against me, My	**Ps 27:3**	4264
breath of His mouth all their **h**.	**Ps 33:6**	6635
the *good* tidings are a great **h**:	**Ps 68:11**	6635
LORD will punish the **h** of heaven on	**Is 24:21**	6635
the **h** of heaven will wear away,	**Is 34:4**	6635
who leads forth their **h** by number,	**Is 40:26**	6635
hands And I ordained all their **h**.	**Is 45:12**	6635
moon and to all the **h** of heaven,	**Jer 8:2**	6635
burned sacrifices to all the heavenly **h**	**Jer 19:13**	6635
the **h** of heaven cannot be counted and	**Jer 33:22**	6635
to His will in the **h** of heaven	**Da 4:35**	2429
It grew up to the **h** of heaven	**Da 8:10**	6635
caused some of the **h** and some of the	**Da 8:10**	6635
equal with the Commander of the **h**;	**Da 8:11**	6635
the **h** will be given over *to the horn*	**Da 8:12**	6635
place and the **h** to be trampled?"	**Da 8:13**	6635
exiles of this **h** of the sons of Israel,	**Ob 1:20**	2426
the housetops to the **h** of heaven,	**Zph 1:5**	6635
multitude of the heavenly **h** praising	**Lk 2:13**	*4756*
them up to serve the **h** of heaven;	**Ac 7:42**	*4756*
h to me and to the whole church,	**Ro 16:23**	*3581*
HE LED CAPTIVE A **H** OF CAPTIVES, AND	**Eph 4:8**	*161*

HOSTAGES

of the king's house, the **h** also,	**2Ki 14:14**	8594
of the king's house, the **h** also,	**2Ch 25:24**	8594

HOSTILE

"Be **h** to the Midianites and	**Nu 25:17**	6887c
been **h** to you with their tricks,	**Nu 25:18**	6887c
eye is **h** toward your poor brother,	**Dt 15:9**	7489a
shall be **h** toward his brother and	**Dt 28:54**	7489a
shall be **h** toward the husband she	**Dt 28:56**	7489a
and the Pharisees began to be very **h**	**Lk 11:53**	*1758*
many things **h** to the name of Jesus	**Ac 26:9**	*1727*
set on the flesh is **h** toward God;	**Ro 8:7**	*2189b*
formerly alienated and **h** in mind,	**Col 1:21**	*2190*
against us, which was **h** to us;	**Col 2:14**	*5227*
pleasing to God, but **h** to all men,	**1Th 2:15**	*1727*

HOSTILITY

you act with **h** against Me and are	**Lv 26:21**	7147
to Me, but act with **h** against Me,	**Lv 26:23**	7147
I will act with **h** against you;	**Lv 26:24**	7147
Me, but act with **h** against Me,	**Lv 26:27**	7147
act with wrathful **h** against you,	**Lv 26:28**	7147
in their acting with **h** against Me	**Lv 26:40**	7147
was acting with **h** against them,	**Lv 26:41**	7147
And *because* your **h** is *so* great.	**Hos 9:7**	4895
is *only* **h** in the house of his God.	**Hos 9:8**	4895
endured such **h** by sinners against	**Heb 12:3**	*485*
with the world is **h** toward God?	**Jas 4:4**	*2189b*

HOSTS

were completed, and all their **h**.	**Gn 2:1**	6635
of Egypt according to their **h**."	**Ex 6:26**	6635
hand on Egypt and bring out My **h**,	**Ex 7:4**	6635
your **h** out of the land of Egypt;	**Ex 12:17**	6635
all the **h** of the LORD went	**Ex 12:41**	6635
of the land of Egypt by their **h**.	**Ex 12:51**	6635
to the LORD of **h** in Shiloh.	**1Sa 1:3**	6635
"O LORD of **h**, if You will indeed	**1Sa 1:11**	6635
the covenant of the LORD of **h**	**1Sa 4:4**	6635
'Thus says the LORD of **h**,	**1Sa 15:2**	6635
you in the name of the LORD of **h**,	**1Sa 17:45**	6635
the LORD God of **h** was with him.	**2Sa 5:10**	6635
the very name of the LORD of **h** who	**2Sa 6:2**	6635
in the name of the LORD of **h**.	**2Sa 6:18**	6635
Thus says the LORD of **h**,	**2Sa 7:8**	6635
'The LORD of **h** is God over Israel';	**2Sa 7:26**	6635
"For You, O LORD of **h**,	**2Sa 7:27**	6635
"As the LORD of **h** lives, before	**1Ki 18:15**	6635
for the LORD, the God of **h**;	**1Ki 19:10**	6635
for the LORD, the God of **h**;	**1Ki 19:14**	6635
"As the LORD of **h** lives, before	**2Ki 3:14**	6635
for the LORD of **h** *was* with him.	**1Ch 11:9**	6635
Thus says the LORD of **h**,	**1Ch 17:7**	6635
LORD of **h** is the God of Israel,	**1Ch 17:24**	6635
The LORD of **h**, He is the King of	**Ps 24:10**	6635
The LORD of **h** is with us;	**Ps 46:7**	6635
The LORD of **h** is with us;	**Ps 46:11**	6635
seen In the city of the LORD of **h**,	**Ps 48:8**	6635
You, O LORD God of **h**,	**Ps 59:5**	6635
through me, O Lord GOD of **h**;	**Ps 69:6**	6635
O LORD God *of* **h**, How long will	**Ps 80:4**	6635
O God *of* **h**, restore us And cause	**Ps 80:7**	6635
O God *of* **h**, turn again now, we	**Ps 80:14**	6635
O LORD God of **h**, restore us;	**Ps 80:19**	6635
Your dwelling places, O LORD of **h**!	**Ps 84:1**	6635
Even Your altars, O LORD of **h**,	**Ps 84:3**	6635
O LORD God of **h**, hear my prayer;	**Ps 84:8**	6635
O LORD of **h**, How blessed is the	**Ps 84:12**	6635
O LORD God of **h**, who is like You,	**Ps 89:8**	6635
Bless the LORD, all you His **h**,	**Ps 103:21**	6635
Praise Him, all His **h**!	**Ps 148:2**	6635
the LORD of **h** Had left us a few	**Is 1:9**	6635
Therefore the Lord GOD of **h**,	**Is 1:24**	6635
For the LORD of **h** will have a day	**Is 2:12**	6635
the Lord GOD of **h** is going to	**Is 3:1**	6635
Declares the Lord GOD of **h**.	**Is 3:15**	6635
the vineyard of the LORD of **h** is the	**Is 5:7**	6635
my ears the LORD of **h** *has sworn*,	**Is 5:9**	6635
But the LORD of **h** will be exalted in	**Is 5:16**	6635
rejected the law of the LORD of **h** And	**Is 5:24**	6635
Holy, Holy, is the LORD of **h**,	**Is 6:3**	6635
seen the King, the LORD of **h**."	**Is 6:5**	6635
"It is the LORD of **h** whom you	**Is 8:13**	6635
in Israel from the LORD of **h**,	**Is 8:18**	6635
The zeal of the LORD of **h** will	**Is 9:7**	6635
Nor do they seek the LORD of **h**.	**Is 9:13**	6635
LORD of **h** the land is burned up,	**Is 9:19**	6635
Therefore the Lord, the GOD of **h**,	**Is 10:16**	6635
the Lord GOD of **h** will execute in	**Is 10:23**	6635
thus says the Lord GOD of **h**,	**Is 10:24**	6635
The LORD of **h** will arouse a	**Is 10:26**	6635
Behold, the Lord, the GOD of **h**,	**Is 10:33**	6635
The LORD of **h** is mustering the	**Is 13:4**	6635
At the fury of the LORD of **h**	**Is 13:13**	6635
them," declares the LORD of **h**,	**Is 14:22**	6635
declares the LORD of **h**.	**Is 14:23**	6635
The LORD of **h** has sworn saying,	**Is 14:24**	6635
"For the LORD of **h** has planned,	**Is 14:27**	6635
of Israel," Declares the LORD of **h**.	**Is 17:3**	6635
will be brought to the LORD of **h**	**Is 18:7**	6635
place of the name of the LORD of **h**,	**Is 18:7**	6635
them," declares the Lord GOD of **h**.	**Is 19:4**	6635
what the LORD of **h** Has purposed	**Is 19:12**	6635
of the hand of the LORD of **h**,	**Is 19:16**	6635
the purpose of the LORD of **h** which	**Is 19:17**	6635
allegiance to the LORD of **h**;	**Is 19:18**	6635
witness to the LORD of **h** in the land	**Is 19:20**	6635
whom the LORD of **h** has blessed,	**Is 19:25**	6635
I have heard from the LORD of **h**,	**Is 21:10**	6635
Lord GOD of **h** has a day of panic,	**Is 22:5**	6635
in that day the Lord GOD of **h**	**Is 22:12**	6635
LORD of **h** revealed Himself to me,	**Is 22:14**	6635
you die," says the Lord GOD of **h**.	**Is 22:14**	6635
Thus says the Lord GOD of **h**,	**Is 22:15**	6635
that day," declares the LORD of **h**,	**Is 22:25**	6635
The LORD of **h** has planned it,	**Is 23:9**	6635
For the LORD of **h** will reign on	**Is 24:23**	6635
The LORD of **h** will prepare a	**Is 25:6**	6635
LORD of **h** will become a beautiful	**Is 28:5**	6635
have heard from the Lord GOD of **h**	**Is 28:22**	6635
also comes from the LORD of **h**,	**Is 28:29**	6635
From the LORD of **h** you will be	**Is 29:6**	6635
So will the LORD of **h** come down to	**Is 31:4**	6635
LORD of **h** will protect Jerusalem.	**Is 31:5**	6635
All their **h** will also wither away	**Is 34:4**	6635
"O LORD of **h**, the God of Israel,	**Is 37:16**	6635
zeal of the LORD of **h** will perform	**Is 37:32**	6635
"Hear the word of the LORD of **h**,	**Is 39:5**	6635
And his Redeemer, the LORD of **h**:	**Is 44:6**	6635
or reward," says the LORD of **h**.	**Is 45:13**	6635
the LORD of **h** is His name,	**Is 47:4**	6635
The LORD of **h** is His name.	**Is 48:2**	6635
(the LORD of **h** is His name).	**Is 51:15**	6635
Whose name is the LORD of **h**;	**Is 54:5**	6635
you," declares the Lord GOD of **h**.	**Jer 2:19**	6635
thus says the LORD, the God of **h**,	**Jer 5:14**	6635
For thus says the LORD of **h**,	**Jer 6:6**	6635
Thus says the LORD of **h**,	**Jer 6:9**	6635
Thus says the LORD of **h**,	**Jer 7:3**	6635
Thus says the LORD of **h**,	**Jer 7:21**	6635
them," declares the LORD of **h**.	**Jer 8:3**	6635
Therefore thus says the LORD of **h**,	**Jer 9:7**	6635
therefore thus says the LORD of **h**,	**Jer 9:15**	6635
Thus says the LORD of **h**,	**Jer 9:17**	6635
The LORD of **h** is His name.	**Jer 10:16**	6635
The LORD of **h**, who planted	**Jer 11:17**	6635
But, O LORD of **h**, who judges	**Jer 11:20**	6635
thus says the LORD of **h**,	**Jer 11:22**	6635
by Your name, O LORD God of **h**.	**Jer 15:16**	6635
For thus says the LORD of **h**,	**Jer 16:9**	6635
thus says the LORD of **h**,	**Jer 19:3**	6635
'Thus says the LORD of **h**,	**Jer 19:11**	6635
"Thus says the LORD of **h**	**Jer 19:15**	6635
Yet, O LORD of **h**, You who	**Jer 20:12**	6635
LORD of **h** concerning the prophets,	**Jer 23:15**	6635
Thus says the LORD of **h**,	**Jer 23:16**	6635
of the living God, the LORD of **h**,	**Jer 23:36**	6635
"Therefore thus says the LORD of **h**,	**Jer 25:8**	6635
Thus says the LORD of **h**,	**Jer 25:27**	6635
'Thus says the LORD of **h**:	**Jer 25:28**	6635
earth," declares the LORD of **h**.'	**Jer 25:29**	6635
Thus says the LORD of **h**,	**Jer 25:32**	6635
Thus the LORD of **h** has said,	**Jer 26:18**	6635
'Thus says the LORD of **h**,	**Jer 27:4**	6635
them now entreat the LORD of **h** that	**Jer 27:18**	6635
thus says the LORD of **h** concerning	**Jer 27:19**	6635
"Yes, thus says the LORD of **h**,	**Jer 27:21**	6635
"Thus says the LORD of **h**,	**Jer 28:2**	6635
'For thus says the LORD of **h**,	**Jer 28:14**	6635
"Thus says the LORD of **h**,	**Jer 29:4**	6635
For thus says the LORD of **h**,	**Jer 29:8**	6635
thus says the LORD of **h**,	**Jer 29:17**	6635
"Thus says the LORD of **h**,	**Jer 29:21**	6635
"Thus says the LORD of **h**,	**Jer 29:25**	6635
that day,' declares the LORD of **h**,	**Jer 30:8**	6635
Thus says the LORD of **h**,	**Jer 31:23**	6635
The LORD of **h** is His name:	**Jer 31:35**	6635
Thus says the LORD of **h**,	**Jer 32:14**	6635
'For thus says the LORD of **h**,	**Jer 32:15**	6635
The LORD of **h** is His name;	**Jer 32:18**	6635
"Give thanks to the LORD of **h**,	**Jer 33:11**	6635
"Thus says the LORD of **h**,	**Jer 33:12**	6635
Thus says the LORD of **h**,	**Jer 35:13**	6635
thus says the LORD, the God of **h**,	**Jer 35:17**	6635
"Thus says the LORD of **h**,	**Jer 35:18**	6635
therefore thus says the LORD of **h**,	**Jer 35:19**	6635
"Thus says the LORD God of **h**,	**Jer 38:17**	6635
'Thus says the LORD of **h**,	**Jer 39:16**	6635
Thus says the LORD of **h**,	**Jer 42:15**	6635
For thus says the LORD of **h**,	**Jer 42:18**	6635
'Thus says the LORD of **h**,	**Jer 43:10**	6635
Thus says the LORD of **h**,	**Jer 44:2**	6635
then thus says the LORD God of **h**,	**Jer 44:7**	6635
"Therefore thus says the LORD of **h**,	**Jer 44:11**	6635
thus says the LORD of **h**,	**Jer 44:25**	6635
day belongs to the Lord GOD of **h**,	**Jer 46:10**	6635
a slaughter for the Lord GOD of **h**,	**Jer 46:10**	6635
King Whose name is the LORD of **h**,	**Jer 46:18**	6635
The LORD of **h**, the God of Israel,	**Jer 46:25**	6635
Thus says the LORD of **h**,	**Jer 48:1**	6635
King, whose name is the LORD of **h**.	**Jer 48:15**	6635
you," Declares the Lord GOD of **h**.	**Jer 49:5**	6635
Thus says the LORD of **h**,	**Jer 49:7**	6635
that day," declares the LORD of **h**.	**Jer 49:26**	6635
"Thus says the LORD of **h**,	**Jer 49:35**	6635
"Therefore thus says the LORD of **h**,	**Jer 50:18**	6635
it is a work of the Lord GOD of **h**	**Jer 50:25**	6635
one," Declares the Lord GOD of **h**.	**Jer 50:31**	6635
Thus says the LORD of **h**,	**Jer 50:33**	6635
strong, the LORD of **h** is His name;	**Jer 50:34**	6635
By his God, the LORD of **h**,	**Jer 51:5**	6635
LORD of **h** has sworn by Himself:	**Jer 51:14**	6635
The LORD of **h** is His name.	**Jer 51:19**	6635
For thus says the LORD of **h**,	**Jer 51:33**	6635
King, whose name is the LORD of **h**.	**Jer 51:57**	6635
Thus says the LORD of **h**,	**Jer 51:58**	6635
Even the LORD, the God of **h**,	**Hos 12:5**	6635
the Lord GOD, the God of **h**.	**Am 3:13**	6635
The LORD God of **h** is His name.	**Am 4:13**	6635
may the LORD God of **h** be with you,	**Am 5:14**	6635
the LORD God of **h** May be gracious	**Am 5:15**	6635
thus says the LORD God of **h**,	**Am 5:16**	6635
LORD, whose name is the God of **h**.	**Am 5:27**	6635
the LORD God of **h** has declared:	**Am 6:8**	6635
declares the LORD God of **h**,	**Am 6:14**	6635
The Lord GOD of **h**,	**Am 9:5**	6635
mouth of the LORD of **h** has spoken.	**Mi 4:4**	6635
you," declares the LORD of **h**.	**Na 2:13**	6635
you," declares the LORD of **h**;	**Na 3:5**	6635
Is it not indeed from the LORD of **h**	**Hab 2:13**	6635
as I live," declares the LORD of **h**,	**Zph 2:9**	6635
the people of the LORD of **h**.	**Zph 2:10**	6635
"Thus says the LORD of **h**,	**Hg 1:2**	6635
thus says the LORD of **h**,	**Hg 1:5**	6635
Thus says the LORD of **h**,	**Hg 1:7**	6635
declares the LORD of **h**,	**Hg 1:9**	6635
on the house of the LORD of **h**,	**Hg 1:14**	6635
I am with you,' declares the LORD of **h**.	**Hg 2:4**	6635
"For thus says the LORD of **h**,	**Hg 2:6**	6635
with glory,' says the LORD of **h**.	**Hg 2:7**	6635
is Mine,' declares the LORD of **h**.	**Hg 2:8**	6635
the former,' says the LORD of **h**,	**Hg 2:9**	6635
peace,' declares the LORD of **h**."	**Hg 2:9**	6635
"Thus says the LORD of **h**,	**Hg 2:11**	6635
that day,' declares the LORD of **h**,	**Hg 2:23**	6635
you,' " declares the LORD of **h**.	**Hg 2:23**	6635
'Thus says the LORD of **h**,	**Zch 1:3**	6635
"Return to Me," declares the LORD of **h**,	**Zch 1:3**	6635
says the LORD of **h**.	**Zch 1:3**	6635
'Thus says the LORD of **h**,	**Zch 1:4**	6635
'As the LORD of **h** purposed to do	**Zch 1:6**	6635
"O LORD of **h**, how long will You	**Zch 1:12**	6635
'Thus says the LORD of **h**,	**Zch 1:14**	6635
in it," declares the LORD of **h**,	**Zch 1:16**	6635
'Thus says the LORD of **h**,	**Zch 1:17**	6635
For thus says the LORD of **h**,	**Zch 2:8**	6635
that the LORD of **h** has sent Me.	**Zch 2:9**	6635
the LORD of **h** has sent Me to you.	**Zch 2:11**	6635
"Thus says the LORD of **h**,	**Zch 3:7**	6635
on it,' declares the LORD of **h**,	**Zch 3:9**	6635
that day,' declares the LORD of **h**,	**Zch 3:10**	6635
by My Spirit,' says the LORD of **h**.	**Zch 4:6**	6635
the LORD of **h** has sent me to you.	**Zch 4:9**	6635
go forth," declares the LORD of **h**,	**Zch 5:4**	6635
'Thus says the LORD of **h**,	**Zch 6:12**	6635
the LORD of **h** has sent me to you.	**Zch 6:15**	6635
to the house of the LORD of **h**,	**Zch 7:3**	6635
word of the LORD of **h** came to me	**Zch 7:4**	6635

“Thus has the LORD of **h** said,	**Zch 7:9**	6635
the LORD of **h** had sent by His Spirit	**Zch 7:12**	6635
wrath came from the LORD of **h**.	**Zch 7:12**	6635
not listen,” says the LORD of **h**;	**Zch 7:13**	6635
word of the LORD of **h** came,	**Zch 8:1**	6635
“Thus says the LORD of **h**,	**Zch 8:2**	6635
the mountain of the LORD of **h** *will be*	**Zch 8:3**	6635
“Thus says the LORD of **h**,	**Zch 8:4**	6635
“Thus says the LORD of **h**,	**Zch 8:6**	6635
declares the LORD of **h**.	**Zch 8:6**	6635
“Thus says the LORD of **h**,	**Zch 8:7**	6635
“Thus says the LORD of **h**,	**Zch 8:9**	6635
house of the LORD of **h** was laid,	**Zch 8:9**	6635
days,’ declares the LORD of **h**.	**Zch 8:11**	6635
“For thus says the LORD of **h**,	**Zch 8:14**	6635
Me to wrath,’ says the LORD of **h**,	**Zch 8:14**	6635
word of the LORD of **h** came to me	**Zch 8:18**	6635
“Thus says the LORD of **h**,	**Zch 8:19**	6635
“Thus says the LORD of **h**,	**Zch 8:20**	6635
LORD, and to seek the LORD of **h**;	**Zch 8:21**	6635
seek the LORD of **h** in Jerusalem	**Zch 8:22**	6635
“Thus says the LORD of **h**,	**Zch 8:23**	6635
The LORD of **h** will defend them.	**Zch 9:15**	6635
LORD of **h** has visited His flock,	**Zch 10:3**	6635
Jerusalem through the LORD of **h**,	**Zch 12:5**	6635
that day,” declares the LORD of **h**,	**Zch 13:2**	6635
Associate,” Declares the LORD of **h**.	**Zch 13:7**	6635
worship the King, the LORD of **h**,	**Zch 14:16**	6635
worship the King, the LORD of **h**,	**Zch 14:17**	6635
will be holy to the LORD of **h**;	**Zch 14:21**	6635
house of the LORD of **h** in that day.	**Zch 14:21**	6635
thus says the LORD of **h**,	**Mal 1:4**	6635
says the LORD of **h** to you, O	**Mal 1:6**	6635
says the LORD of **h**.	**Mal 1:8**	6635
says the LORD of **h**.	**Mal 1:9**	6635
with you,” says the LORD of **h**,	**Mal 1:10**	6635
the nations,” says the LORD of **h**.	**Mal 1:11**	6635
sniff at it,” says the LORD of **h**,	**Mal 1:13**	6635
a great King,” says the LORD of **h**,	**Mal 1:14**	6635
to My name,” says the LORD of **h**,	**Mal 2:2**	6635
with Levi,” says the LORD of **h**.	**Mal 2:4**	6635
is the messenger of the LORD of **h**.	**Mal 2:7**	6635
of Levi,” says the LORD of **h**.	**Mal 2:8**	6635
an offering to the LORD of **h**.	**Mal 2:12**	6635
with wrong,” says the LORD of **h**.	**Mal 2:16**	6635
He is coming,” says the LORD of **h**.	**Mal 3:1**	6635
not fear Me,” says the LORD of **h**.	**Mal 3:5**	6635
return to you,” says the LORD of **h**.	**Mal 3:7**	6635
now in this,” says the LORD of **h**,	**Mal 3:10**	6635
its grapes,” says the LORD of **h**.	**Mal 3:11**	6635
land,” says the LORD of **h**.	**Mal 3:12**	6635
in mourning before the LORD of **h**?	**Mal 3:14**	6635
will be Mine,” says the LORD of **h**,	**Mal 3:17**	6635
them ablaze,” says the LORD of **h**,	**Mal 4:1**	6635
am preparing,” says the LORD of **h**.	**Mal 4:3**	6635

HOT

the Anah who found the **h** springs	**Gn 36:24**	3222
went out from Pharaoh in **h** anger.	**Ex 11:8**	2750
but when the sun grew **h**,	**Ex 16:21**	2552
afraid of the anger and **h** displeasure	**Dt 9:19**	2534
by the time the sun is **h**,	**1Sa 11:9**	2552
in order to put **h** bread *in its*	**1Sa 21:6**	2527
a bread cake *baked on* **h** stones,	**1Ki 19:6**	7531a
be opened until the sun is **h**,	**Ne 7:3**	2552
When it is **h**, they vanish from their	**Jb 6:17**	2552
You whose garments are **h**,	**Jb 37:17**	2525
My heart was **h** within me,	**Ps 39:3**	2552
Or can a man walk on **h** coals And	**Pr 6:28**	
charcoal to **h** embers and wood to	**Pr 26:21**	1513
skin has become as **h** as an oven,	**La 5:10**	3648
on its coals So that it may be **h**	**Ezk 24:11**	2552
furnace had been made extremely **h**,	**Da 3:22**	228
All of them are **h** like an oven,	**Hos 7:7**	2552
‘It will be a **h** day,’ and it turns	**Lk 12:55**	2742
that you are neither cold nor **h**;	**Rv 3:15**	*2200*
I wish that you were cold or **h**.	**Rv 3:15**	*2200*
lukewarm, and neither **h** nor cold,	**Rv 3:16**	*2200*

HOTHAM

father of Japhlet, Shomer and **H**,	**1Ch 7:32**	2369
Jeiel the sons of **H** the Aroerite,	**1Ch 11:44**	2369

HOTHIR

Joshbekashah, Mallothi, **H**,	**1Ch 25:4**	1956b
for the twenty-first to **H**,	**1Ch 25:28**	1956b

HOTLY

sin that you have **h** pursued me?	**Gn 31:36**	1814
the wicked **h** pursue the afflicted;	**Ps 10:2**	1814

HOT-TEMPERED

A **h** man stirs up strife, But the	**Pr 15:18**	2534
Or go with a **h** man,	**Pr 22:24**	2534
a **h** man abounds in transgression.	**Pr 29:22**	2534

HOUR

being worried can add a *single* **h**	**Mt 6:27**	*4083*
in that **h** what you are to say.	**Mt 10:19**	*5610*
“This place is desolate and the **h** is	**Mt 14:15**	*5610*
“And he went out about the third **h**	**Mt 20:3**	*5610*
about the sixth and the ninth **h**,	**Mt 20:5**	*5610*
“And about the eleventh **h** he	**Mt 20:6**	
hired about the eleventh **h** came,	**Mt 20:9**	*5610*
last men have worked *only* one **h**,	**Mt 20:12**	*5610*
of that day and **h** no one knows,	**Mt 24:36**	*5610*
Son of Man is coming at an **h** when	**Mt 24:44**	*5610*
at an **h** which he does not know,	**Mt 24:50**	*5610*
you do not know the day nor the **h**.	**Mt 25:13**	*5610*
not keep watch with Me for one **h**?	**Mt 26:40**	*5610*
the **h** is at hand and the Son of	**Mt 26:45**	*5610*
Now from the sixth **h** darkness fell	**Mt 27:45**	*5610*
all the land until the ninth **h**.	**Mt 27:45**	*5610*
About the ninth **h** Jesus cried	**Mt 27:46**	*5610*
whatever is given you in that **h**;	**Mk 13:11**	*5610*
“But of that day or **h** no one knows,	**Mk 13:32**	*5610*
possible, the **h** might pass Him by.	**Mk 14:35**	*5610*
you not keep watch for one **h**?	**Mk 14:37**	*5610*
It is enough; the **h** has come;	**Mk 14:41**	*5610*
third **h** when they crucified Him.	**Mk 15:25**	*5610*
When the sixth **h** came,	**Mk 15:33**	*5610*
the whole land until the ninth **h**.	**Mk 15:33**	*5610*
At the ninth **h** Jesus cried out	**Mk 15:34**	*5610*
at the **h** of the incense offering.	**Lk 1:10**	*5610*
Spirit will teach you in that very **h**	**Lk 12:12**	*5610*
by worrying can add a *single* **h** to	**Lk 12:25**	*4083*
at what **h** the thief was coming,	**Lk 12:39**	*5610*
at an **h** that you do not expect.”	**Lk 12:40**	*5610*
him and at an **h** he does not know,	**Lk 12:46**	*5610*
and at the dinner **h** he sent his	**Lk 14:17**	*5610*
to lay hands on Him that very **h**,	**Lk 20:19**	*5610*
When the **h** had come,	**Lk 22:14**	*5610*
but this **h** and the power of	**Lk 22:53**	*5610*
After about an **h** had passed,	**Lk 22:59**	*5610*
It was now about the sixth **h**,	**Lk 23:44**	*5610*
the whole land until the ninth **h**,	**Lk 23:44**	*5610*
they got up that very **h** and returned	**Lk 24:33**	*5610*
day, for it was about the tenth **h**.	**Jn 1:39**	*5610*
My **h** has not yet come.”	**Jn 2:4**	*5610*
It was about the sixth **h**.	**Jn 4:6**	*5610*
an **h** is coming when neither in	**Jn 4:21**	*5610*
“But an **h** is coming, and now is,	**Jn 4:23**	*5610*
the **h** when he began to get better.	**Jn 4:52**	*5610*
at the seventh **h** the fever left him.”	**Jn 4:52**	*5610*
that **h** in which Jesus said to him,	**Jn 4:53**	*5610*
to you, an **h** is coming and now is,	**Jn 5:25**	*5610*
for an **h** is coming, in which all	**Jn 5:28**	*5610*
because His **h** had not yet come.	**Jn 7:30**	*5610*
because His **h** had not yet come.	**Jn 8:20**	*5610*
“The **h** has come for the Son of	**Jn 12:23**	*5610*
‘Father, save Me from this **h**’?	**Jn 12:27**	*5610*
for this purpose I came to this **h**.	**Jn 12:27**	*5610*
Jesus knowing that His **h** had come	**Jn 13:1**	*5610*
but an **h** is coming for everyone	**Jn 16:2**	*5610*
to you, so that when their **h** comes,	**Jn 16:4**	*5610*
pain, because her **h** has come;	**Jn 16:21**	*5610*
an **h** is coming when I will no	**Jn 16:25**	*5610*
“Behold, an **h** is coming, and has	**Jn 16:32**	*5610*
“Father, the **h** has come;	**Jn 17:1**	*5610*
it was about the sixth **h**.	**Jn 19:14**	*5610*
From that **h** the disciple took	**Jn 19:27**	*5610*
it is *only* the third **h** of the day;	**Ac 2:15**	*5610*
up to the temple at the ninth **h**,	**Ac 3:1**	
the ninth *hour*, the **h** of prayer.	**Ac 3:1**	*5610*
About the ninth **h** of the day he	**Ac 10:3**	*5610*
about the sixth **h** to pray.	**Ac 10:9**	*5610*
“Four days ago to this **h**,	**Ac 10:30**	*5610*
in my house during the ninth **h**;	**Ac 10:30**	*1729a*
took them that *very* **h** of the night	**Ac 16:33**	*5610*
ready by the third **h** of the night	**Ac 23:23**	*5610*
it is already the **h** for you to awaken	**Ro 13:11**	*5610*
To this present **h** we are both	**1Co 4:11**	*5610*
Why are we also in danger every **h**?	**1Co 15:30**	*5610*
subjection to them for even an **h**,	**Ga 2:5**	*5610*
Children, it is the last **h**;	**1Jn 2:18**	*5610*
we know that it is the last **h**.	**1Jn 2:18**	*5610*
not know at what **h** I will come	**Rv 3:3**	*5610*
keep you from the **h** of testing,	**Rv 3:10**	*5610*
that **h** which is about to come	**Rv 3:10**	
in heaven for about half an **h**.	**Rv 8:1**	*2256*
the **h** and day and month and year,	**Rv 9:15**	*5610*
in that **h** there was a great	**Rv 11:13**	*5610*
the **h** of His judgment has come;	**Rv 14:7**	*5610*
for the **h** to reap has come,	**Rv 14:15**	*5610*
as kings with the beast for one **h**.	**Rv 17:12**	*5610*
in one **h** your judgment has come.’	**Rv 18:10**	*5610*
for in one **h** such great wealth has	**Rv 18:17**	*5610*
in one **h** she has been laid waste!	**Rv 18:19**	*5610*

HOURS

“Are there not twelve **h** in the day?	**Jn 11:9**	*5610*
an interval of about three **h**,	**Ac 5:7**	*5610*
as they shouted for about two **h**,	**Ac 19:34**	*5610*

HOUSE

relatives And from your father’s **h**,	**Gn 12:1**	1004
woman was taken into Pharaoh’s **h**.	**Gn 12:15**	1004
LORD struck Pharaoh and his **h** with	**Gn 12:17**	1004
his trained men, born in his **h**,	**Gn 14:14**	1004
the heir of my **h** is Eliezer of	**Gn 15:2**	1004
me, one born in my **h** is my heir.”	**Gn 15:3**	1004
a *servant* who is born in the **h** or	**Gn 17:12**	1004
“A *servant* who is born in your **h**	**Gn 17:13**	1004
all *the servants* who were born in his **h**	**Gn 17:23**	1004
who were born in the **h** or bought	**Gn 17:27**	1004
turn aside into your servant’s **h**,	**Gn 19:2**	1004
aside to him and entered his **h**;	**Gn 19:3**	1004
men of Sodom, surrounded the **h**,	**Gn 19:4**	1004
brought Lot into the **h** with them,	**Gn 19:10**	1004
doorway of the **h** with blindness,	**Gn 19:11**	1004
me to wander from my father’s **h**,	**Gn 20:13**	1004
who took me from my father’s **h**	**Gn 24:7**	1004
for us to lodge in your father’s **h**?”	**Gn 24:23**	1004
to the **h** of my master’s brothers.”	**Gn 24:27**	1004
since I have prepared the **h**,	**Gn 24:31**	1004
So the man entered the **h**.	**Gn 24:32**	1004
but you shall go to my father’s **h** and	**Gn 24:38**	1004
relatives and from my father’s **h**;	**Gn 24:40**	1004
son, which were with her in the **h**,	**Gn 27:15**	1004
to the **h** of Bethuel your mother’s	**Gn 28:2**	1004
is none other than the **h** of God,	**Gn 28:17**	1004
return to my father’s **h** in safety,	**Gn 28:21**	1004
up as a pillar, will be God’s **h**,	**Gn 28:22**	1004
him and brought him to his **h**.	**Gn 29:13**	1004
or inheritance in our father’s **h**?	**Gn 31:14**	1004
longed greatly for your father’s **h**;	**Gn 31:30**	1004
years I have been in your **h**;	**Gn 31:41**	1004
and built for himself a **h** and	**Gn 33:17**	1004
and took Dinah from Shechem’s **h**,	**Gn 34:26**	1004
“Remain a widow in your father’s **h**	**Gn 38:11**	1004
went and lived in her father’s **h**.	**Gn 38:11**	1004
And he was in the **h** of his master,	**Gn 39:2**	1004
he made him overseer over his **h**,	**Gn 39:4**	1004
he made him overseer in his **h**	**Gn 39:5**	1004
the LORD blessed the Egyptian’s **h**	**Gn 39:5**	1004
owned, in the **h** and in the field.	**Gn 39:5**	1004
himself with anything in the **h**,	**Gn 39:8**	1004
no one greater in this **h** than I,	**Gn 39:9**	1004
he went into the **h** to do his work,	**Gn 39:11**	1004
in confinement in the **h** of the captain	**Gn 40:3**	1004
in confinement in his master’s **h**,	**Gn 40:7**	1004
Pharaoh and get me out of this **h**.	**Gn 40:14**	1004
in confinement in the **h** of the captain	**Gn 41:10**	1004
“You shall be over my **h**,	**Gn 41:40**	1004
them, he said to his **h** steward,	**Gn 43:16**	1004
“Bring the men into the **h**,	**Gn 43:16**	1004
and brought the men to Joseph’s **h**.	**Gn 43:17**	1004
they were brought to Joseph’s **h**;	**Gn 43:18**	1004
came near to Joseph’s **h** steward,	**Gn 43:19**	1004
to him at the entrance of the **h**,	**Gn 43:19**	1004
brought the men into Joseph’s **h**	**Gn 43:24**	1004
they brought into the **h** to him the	**Gn 43:26**	1004
Then he commanded his **h** steward,	**Gn 44:1**	1004
when Joseph said to his **h** steward,	**Gn 44:4**	1004
silver or gold from your lord’s **h**?	**Gn 44:8**	1004
his brothers came to Joseph’s **h**,	**Gn 44:14**	1004
the news was heard in Pharaoh’s **h**	**Gn 45:16**	1004
all the persons of the **h** of Jacob,	**Gn 46:27**	1004
brought the money into Pharaoh’s **h**.	**Gn 47:14**	1004
Now a man from the **h** of Levi went	**Ex 2:1**	1004
and the woman who lives in her **h**,	**Ex 3:22**	1004
Pharaoh turned and went into his **h**	**Ex 7:23**	1004
will come up and go into your **h**	**Ex 8:3**	1004
insects into the **h** of Pharaoh and the	**Ex 8:24**	1004
he and his neighbor nearest to his **h**	**Ex 12:4**	1004
the door of his **h** until morning.	**Ex 12:22**	1004
“It is to be eaten in a single **h**;	**Ex 12:46**	1004
any of the flesh outside of the **h**,	**Ex 12:46**	1004
from Egypt, from the **h** of slavery;	**Ex 13:3**	1004
of Egypt, from the **h** of slavery.	**Ex 13:14**	1004
The **h** of Israel named it manna,	**Ex 16:31**	1004
Thus you shall say to the **h** of Jacob	**Ex 19:3**	1004
of Egypt, out of the **h** of slavery.	**Ex 20:2**	1004
shall not covet your neighbor’s **h**;	**Ex 20:17**	1004
and it is stolen from the man’s **h**,	**Ex 22:7**	1004
then the owner of the **h** shall	**Ex 22:8**	1004
into the **h** of the LORD your God.	**Ex 23:19**	1004
into the **h** of the LORD your God.	**Ex 34:26**	1004
the sight of all the **h** of Israel.	**Ex 40:38**	1004
kinsmen, the whole **h** of Israel,	**Lv 10:6**	1004
and I put a mark of leprosy on a **h**	**Lv 14:34**	1004
then the one who owns the **h** shall	**Lv 14:35**	1004
become visible to me in the **h**.’	**Lv 14:35**	1004
empty the **h** before the priest goes in	**Lv 14:36**	1004
everything in the **h** need not become	**Lv 14:36**	1004
shall go in to look at the **h**.	**Lv 14:36**	1004
if the mark on the walls of the **h** has	**Lv 14:37**	1004
priest shall come out of the **h**,	**Lv 14:38**	1004
quarantine the **h** for seven days.	**Lv 14:38**	1004
spread in the walls of the **h**,	**Lv 14:39**	1004
the **h** scraped all around inside,	**Lv 14:41**	1004
other plaster and replaster the **h**.	**Lv 14:42**	1004
mark breaks out again in the **h** after	**Lv 14:43**	1004
out the stones and scraped the **h**,	**Lv 14:43**	1004
mark has indeed spread in the **h**,	**Lv 14:44**	1004
it is a malignant mark in the **h**;	**Lv 14:44**	1004
shall therefore tear down the **h**,	**Lv 14:45**	1004
and all the plaster of the **h**,	**Lv 14:45**	1004
whoever goes into the **h** during the	**Lv 14:46**	1004
whoever lies down in the **h** shall	**Lv 14:47**	1004
whoever eats in the **h** shall wash his	**Lv 14:47**	1004
mark has not indeed spread in the **h**	**Lv 14:48**	1004
after the **h** has been replastered,	**Lv 14:48**	1004
the priest shall pronounce the **h** clean	**Lv 14:48**	1004
“To cleanse the **h** then, he shall	**Lv 14:49**	1004
and sprinkle the **h** seven times.	**Lv 14:51**	1004
“He shall thus cleanse the **h** with	**Lv 14:52**	1004
he shall make atonement for the **h**,	**Lv 14:53**	1004
and for the leprous garment or **h**,	**Lv 14:55**	1004
“Any man from the **h** of Israel who	**Lv 17:3**	1004
‘Any man from the **h** of Israel,	**Lv 17:8**	1004
‘And any man from the **h** of Israel,	**Lv 17:10**	1004
those who are born in his **h** may eat	**Lv 22:11**	1004
to her father’s **h** as in her youth,	**Lv 22:13**	1004
‘Any man of the **h** of Israel or of	**Lv 22:18**	1004
a dwelling **h** in a walled city,	**Lv 25:29**	1004
then the **h** that is in the walled	**Lv 25:30**	1004
a **h** sale in the city of this possession	**Lv 25:33**	1004
if a man consecrates his **h** as holy	**Lv 27:14**	1004
it should *wish to* redeem his **h**,	**Lv 27:15**	1004
the rod of Aaron for the **h** of Levi	**Nu 17:8**	1004
all the **h** of Israel wept for Aaron	**Nu 20:29**	1004
me his **h** full of silver and gold,	**Nu 22:18**	1004
me his **h** full of silver and gold,	**Nu 24:13**	1004
in her father’s **h** in her youth,	**Nu 30:3**	1004
if she vowed in her husband’s **h**,	**Nu 30:10**	1004
is in her youth in her father’s **h**.	**Nu 30:16**	1004
of Egypt, out of the **h** of slavery.	**Dt 5:6**	1004
shall not desire your neighbor’s **h**,	**Dt 5:21**	1004
talk of them when you sit in your **h**	**Dt 6:7**	1004
them on the doorposts of your **h**	**Dt 6:9**	1004
of Egypt, out of the **h** of slavery.	**Dt 6:12**	1004
you from the **h** of slavery,	**Dt 7:8**	1004

bring an abomination into your **h**,	**Dt 7:26**	1004
of Egypt, out of the **h** of slavery.	**Dt 8:14**	1004
of them when you sit in your **h**	**Dt 11:19**	1004
them on the doorposts of your **h**	**Dt 11:20**	1004
you from the **h** of slavery,	**Dt 13:5**	1004
of Egypt, out of the **h** of slavery.	**Dt 13:10**	1004
the man that has built a new **h** and	**Dt 20:5**	1004
him depart and return to his **h**,	**Dt 20:5**	1004
him depart and return to his **h**,	**Dt 20:6**	1004
him depart and return to his **h**,	**Dt 20:7**	1004
him depart and return to his **h**,	**Dt 20:8**	1004
shall bring her home to your **h**,	**Dt 21:12**	1004
and shall remain in your **h**,	**Dt 21:13**	1004
you shall bring it home to your **h**,	**Dt 22:2**	1004
"When you build a new **h**,	**Dt 22:8**	1004
will not bring bloodguilt on your **h**	**Dt 22:8**	1004
to the doorway of her father's **h**,	**Dt 22:21**	1004
the harlot in her father's **h**;	**Dt 22:21**	1004
into the **h** of the LORD your God	**Dt 23:18**	1004
hand and sends her out from his **h**,	**Dt 24:1**	1004
and she leaves his **h** and goes and	**Dt 24:2**	1004
hand and sends her out of his **h**,	**Dt 24:3**	1004
not enter his **h** to take his pledge.	**Dt 24:10**	1004
does not build up his brother's **h**.'	**Dt 25:9**	1004
'The **h** of him whose sandal is	**Dt 25:10**	1004
have in your **h** differing measures,	**Dt 25:14**	1004
the sacred *portion* from *my* **h**,	**Dt 26:13**	1004
you shall build a **h**,	**Dt 28:30**	1004
So they went and came into the **h**	**Jos 2:1**	1004
to you, who have entered your **h**,	**Jos 2:3**	1004
for her **h** was on the city wall,	**Jos 2:15**	1004
into the **h** your father and your	**Jos 2:18**	1004
doors of your **h** into the street,	**Jos 2:19**	1004
anyone who is with you in the **h**,	**Jos 2:19**	1004
are with her in the **h** shall live,	**Jos 6:17**	1004
"Go into the harlot's **h** and bring	**Jos 6:22**	1004
the treasury of the **h** of the LORD.	**Jos 6:24**	1004
of water for the **h** of my God."	**Jos 9:23**	1004
Joshua spoke to the **h** of Joseph,	**Jos 17:17**	1004
and the **h** of Joseph shall stay in	**Jos 18:5**	1004
to his own city and to his own **h**,	**Jos 20:6**	1004
made to the **h** of Israel failed;	**Jos 21:45**	1004
but as for me and my **h**,	**Jos 24:15**	1004
of Egypt, from the **h** of bondage,	**Jos 24:17**	1004
Likewise the **h** of Joseph went up	**Jg 1:22**	1004
The **h** of Joseph spied out Bethel	**Jg 1:23**	1004
power of the **h** of Joseph grew strong	**Jg 1:35**	1004
and the **h** of Heber the Kenite.	**Jg 4:17**	1004
you out from the **h** of slavery.	**Jg 6:8**	1004
am the youngest in my father's **h**."	**Jg 6:15**	1004
Joash went and lived in his own **h**.	**Jg 8:29**	1004
silver from the **h** of Baal-berith	**Jg 9:4**	1004
went to his father's **h** at Ophrah and	**Jg 9:5**	1004
well with Jerubbaal and his **h**,	**Jg 9:16**	1004
you have risen against my father's **h**	**Jg 9:18**	1004
with Jerubbaal and his **h** this day,	**Jg 9:19**	1004
they went into the **h** of their god,	**Jg 9:27**	1004
Benjamin, and the **h** of Ephraim,	**Jg 10:9**	1004
an inheritance in our father's **h**,	**Jg 11:2**	1004
me and drive me from my father's **h**?	**Jg 11:7**	1004
out of the doors of my **h** to meet me	**Jg 11:31**	1004
Jephthah came to his **h** at Mizpah,	**Jg 11:34**	1004
We will burn your **h** down on you."	**Jg 12:1**	1004
you and your father's **h** with fire."	**Jg 14:15**	1004
and he went up to his father's **h**.	**Jg 14:19**	1004
the pillars on which the **h** rests,	**Jg 16:26**	1004
the **h** was full of men and women,	**Jg 16:27**	1004
pillars on which the **h** rested,	**Jg 16:29**	1004
h fell on the lords and all the people	**Jg 16:30**	1004
and they were in the **h** of Micah.	**Jg 17:4**	1004
of Ephraim to the **h** of Micah.	**Jg 17:8**	1004
and lived in the **h** of Micah.	**Jg 17:12**	1004
of Ephraim, to the **h** of Micah,	**Jg 18:2**	1004
they were near the **h** of Micah,	**Jg 18:3**	1004
and came to the **h** of Micah.	**Jg 18:13**	1004
came to the **h** of the young man,	**Jg 18:15**	1004
the Levite, to the **h** of Micah,	**Jg 18:15**	1004
these went into Micah's **h** and took	**Jg 18:18**	1004
be a priest to the **h** of one man,	**Jg 18:19**	1004
some distance from the **h** of Micah,	**Jg 18:22**	1004
who *were* in the houses near Micah's **h**	**Jg 18:22**	1004
he turned and went back to his **h**.	**Jg 18:26**	1004
that the **h** of God was at Shiloh.	**Jg 18:31**	1004
father's **h** in Bethlehem in Judah,	**Jg 19:2**	1004
brought him into her father's **h**,	**Jg 19:3**	1004
into *his* **h** to spend the night.	**Jg 19:15**	1004
But I am *now* going to my **h**,	**Jg 19:18**	1004
no man will take me into his **h**.	**Jg 19:18**	1004
So he took him into his **h** and gave	**Jg 19:21**	1004
fellows, surrounded the **h**,	**Jg 19:22**	1004
they spoke to the owner of the **h**,	**Jg 19:22**	1004
the man who came into your **h**	**Jg 19:22**	1004
Then the man, the owner of the **h**,	**Jg 19:23**	1004
since this man has come into my **h**,	**Jg 19:23**	1004
at the doorway of the man's **h**	**Jg 19:26**	1004
opened the doors of the **h** and went	**Jg 19:27**	1004
was lying at the doorway of the **h** with	**Jg 19:27**	1004
When he entered his **h**,	**Jg 19:29**	1004
surrounded the **h** at night because	**Jg 20:5**	1004
will any of us return to his **h**.	**Jg 20:8**	1004
each of you to her mother's **h**.	**Ru 1:8**	1004
each in the **h** of her husband."	**Ru 1:9**	1004
sitting in the **h** for a little while."	**Ru 2:7**	1004
both of whom built the **h** of Israel;	**Ru 4:11**	1004
"Moreover, may your **h** be like	**Ru 4:12**	1004
may your house be like the **h** of	**Ru 4:12**	1004
she went up to the **h** of the LORD,	**1Sa 1:7**	1004
returned again to their **h** in Ramah.	**1Sa 1:19**	1004
to the **h** of the LORD in Shiloh,	**1Sa 1:24**	1004
reveal Myself to the **h** of your father	**1Sa 2:27**	1004
in Egypt *in bondage* to Pharaoh's **h**?	**1Sa 2:27**	1004
did I *not* give to the **h** of your father	**1Sa 2:28**	1004
'I did indeed say that your **h** and	**1Sa 2:30**	1004
h of your father should walk before	**1Sa 2:30**	1004
the strength of your father's **h** so that	**1Sa 2:31**	1004
will not be an old man in your **h**.	**1Sa 2:31**	1004
man will not be in your **h** forever.	**1Sa 2:32**	1004
all the increase of your **h** will die in	**1Sa 2:33**	1004
I will build him an enduring **h**,	**1Sa 2:35**	1004
'Everyone who is left in your **h** will	**1Sa 2:36**	1004
I have spoken concerning his **h**,	**1Sa 3:12**	1004
I am about to judge his **h** forever	**1Sa 3:13**	1004
I have sworn to the **h** of Eli that the	**1Sa 3:14**	1004
iniquity of Eli's **h** shall not be atoned	**1Sa 3:14**	1004
the doors of the **h** of the LORD.	**1Sa 3:15**	1004
and brought it to the **h** of Dagon and	**1Sa 5:2**	1004
nor all who enter Dagon's **h** tread on	**1Sa 5:5**	1004
the **h** of Abinadab on the hill,	**1Sa 7:1**	1004
and all the **h** of Israel lamented	**1Sa 7:2**	1004
spoke to all the **h** of Israel,	**1Sa 7:3**	1004
was to Ramah, for his **h** *was* there,	**1Sa 7:17**	1004
tell me where the seer's **h** is."	**1Sa 9:18**	1004
people away, each one to his **h**.	**1Sa 10:25**	1004
Saul also went to his **h** at Gibeah;	**1Sa 10:26**	1004
up to his **h** at Gibeah of Saul.	**1Sa 15:34**	1004
make his father's **h** free in Israel."	**1Sa 17:25**	1004
let him return to his father's **h**.	**1Sa 18:2**	1004
he raved in the midst of the **h**,	**1Sa 18:10**	1004
sitting in his **h** with his spear in his	**1Sa 19:9**	1004
Saul sent messengers to David's **h**	**1Sa 19:11**	1004
lovingkindness from my **h** forever,	**1Sa 20:15**	1004
a *covenant* with the **h** of David,	**1Sa 20:16**	1004
Shall this one come into my **h**?"	**1Sa 21:15**	1004
guard, and is honored in your **h**?	**1Sa 22:14**	1004
while Jonathan went to his **h**.	**1Sa 23:18**	1004
and buried him at his **h** in Ramah.	**1Sa 25:1**	1004
be to you, and peace be to your **h**,	**1Sa 25:6**	1004
make for my lord an enduring **h**,	**1Sa 25:28**	1004
"Go up to your **h** in peace.	**1Sa 25:35**	1004
he was holding a feast in his **h**,	**1Sa 25:36**	1004
had a fattened calf in the **h**,	**1Sa 28:24**	1004
the good news to the **h** of their idols	**1Sa 31:9**	1004
of the LORD and the **h** of Israel,	**2Sa 1:12**	1004
David king over the **h** of Judah.	**2Sa 2:4**	1004
the **h** of Judah has anointed me king	**2Sa 2:7**	1004
The **h** of Judah, however, followed	**2Sa 2:10**	1004
king in Hebron over the **h** of Judah	**2Sa 2:11**	1004
long war between the **h** of Saul and	**2Sa 3:1**	1004
house of Saul and the **h** of David;	**2Sa 3:1**	1004
but the **h** of Saul grew weaker	**2Sa 3:1**	1004
war between the **h** of Saul and the	**2Sa 3:6**	1004
the house of Saul and the **h** of David	**2Sa 3:6**	1004
himself strong in the **h** of Saul.	**2Sa 3:6**	1004
I show kindness to the **h** of Saul	**2Sa 3:8**	1004
the kingdom from the **h** of Saul and	**2Sa 3:10**	1004
and to the whole **h** of Benjamin.	**2Sa 3:19**	1004
of Joab and on all his father's **h**;	**2Sa 3:29**	1004
may there not fail from the **h** of Joab	**2Sa 3:29**	1004
came to the **h** of Ish-bosheth	**2Sa 4:5**	1004
They came to the middle of the **h**	**2Sa 4:6**	1004
Now when they came into the **h**,	**2Sa 4:7**	1004
killed a righteous man in his own **h**	**2Sa 4:11**	1004
lame shall not come into the **h**."	**2Sa 5:8**	1004
and they built a **h** for David.	**2Sa 5:11**	1004
might bring it from the **h** of Abinadab	**2Sa 6:3**	1004
ark of God from the **h** of Abinadab,	**2Sa 6:4**	1004
David and all the **h** of Israel were	**2Sa 6:5**	1004
to the **h** of Obed-edom the Gittite.	**2Sa 6:10**	1004
remained in the **h** of Obed-edom	**2Sa 6:11**	1004
blessed the **h** of Obed-edom and all	**2Sa 6:12**	1004
ark of God from the **h** of Obed-edom	**2Sa 6:12**	1004
So David and all the **h** of Israel	**2Sa 6:15**	1004
the people departed each to his **h**.	**2Sa 6:19**	1004
your father and above all his **h**,	**2Sa 6:21**	1004
when the king lived in his **h**,	**2Sa 7:1**	1004
"See now, I dwell in a **h** of cedar,	**2Sa 7:2**	1004
should build Me a **h** to dwell in?	**2Sa 7:5**	1004
"For I have not dwelt in a **h**	**2Sa 7:6**	1004
not built Me a **h** of cedar?	**2Sa 7:7**	1004
the LORD will make a **h** for you.	**2Sa 7:11**	1004
"He shall build a **h** for My name,	**2Sa 7:13**	1004
"Your **h** and your kingdom	**2Sa 7:16**	1004
I, O Lord GOD, and what is my **h**,	**2Sa 7:18**	1004
spoken also of the **h** of Your servant	**2Sa 7:19**	1004
concerning Your servant and his **h**,	**2Sa 7:25**	1004
and may the **h** of Your servant David	**2Sa 7:26**	1004
'I will build you a **h**';	**2Sa 7:27**	1004
to bless the **h** of Your servant,	**2Sa 7:29**	1004
may the **h** of Your servant be blessed	**2Sa 7:29**	1004
yet anyone left of the **h** of Saul,	**2Sa 9:1**	1004
servant of the **h** of Saul whose name	**2Sa 9:2**	1004
not yet anyone of the **h** of Saul	**2Sa 9:3**	1004
he is in the **h** of Machir the son	**2Sa 9:4**	1004
the **h** of Machir the son of Ammiel,	**2Sa 9:5**	1004
that belonged to Saul and to all his **h**	**2Sa 9:9**	1004
And all who lived in the **h** of Ziba	**2Sa 9:12**	1004
around on the roof of the king's **h**,	**2Sa 11:2**	1004
she returned to her **h**.	**2Sa 11:4**	1004
"Go down to your **h**, and wash your	**2Sa 11:8**	1004
And Uriah went out of the king's **h**,	**2Sa 11:8**	1004
Uriah slept at the door of the king's **h**	**2Sa 11:9**	1004
and did not go down to his **h**.	**2Sa 11:9**	1004
"Uriah did not go down to his **h**,"	**2Sa 11:10**	1004
did you not go down to your **h**?	**2Sa 11:10**	1004
Shall I then go to my **h** to eat and	**2Sa 11:11**	1004
but he did not go down to his **h**.	**2Sa 11:13**	1004
David sent and brought her to his **h**	**2Sa 11:27**	1004
'I also gave you your master's **h**	**2Sa 12:8**	1004
I gave you the **h** of Israel and Judah	**2Sa 12:8**	1004
shall never depart from your **h**,	**2Sa 12:10**	1004
So Nathan went to his **h**.	**2Sa 12:15**	1004
he came into the **h** of the LORD and	**2Sa 12:20**	1004
Then he came to his own **h**,	**2Sa 12:20**	1004
David sent to the **h** for Tamar,	**2Sa 13:7**	1004
"Go now to your brother Amnon's **h**,	**2Sa 13:7**	1004
went to her brother Amnon's **h**,	**2Sa 13:8**	1004
in her brother Absalom's **h**.	**2Sa 13:20**	1004
"Go to your **h**, and I will give	**2Sa 14:8**	1004
iniquity is on me and my father's **h**,	**2Sa 14:9**	1004
"Let him turn to his own **h**,	**2Sa 14:24**	1004
So Absalom turned to his own **h** and	**2Sa 14:24**	1004
came to Absalom at his **h** and said	**2Sa 14:31**	1004
left ten concubines to keep the **h**.	**2Sa 15:16**	1004
and they stopped at the last **h**.	**2Sa 15:17**	1004
you hear from the king's **h**,	**2Sa 15:35**	1004
h of Israel will restore the kingdom	**2Sa 16:3**	1004
a man of the family of the **h** of Saul	**2Sa 16:5**	1004
the bloodshed of the **h** of Saul,	**2Sa 16:8**	1004
whom he has left to keep the **h**;	**2Sa 16:21**	1004
came to the **h** of a man in Bahurim,	**2Sa 17:18**	1004
to the woman at the **h** and said,	**2Sa 17:20**	1004
his city, and set his **h** in order,	**2Sa 17:23**	1004
Joab came into the **h** to the king	**2Sa 19:5**	1004
to bring the king back to his **h**,	**2Sa 19:11**	1004
come to the king, *even* to his **h**?	**2Sa 19:11**	1004
Ziba the servant of the **h** of Saul,	**2Sa 19:17**	1004
the first of all the **h** of Joseph	**2Sa 19:20**	1004
has come safely to his own **h**."	**2Sa 19:30**	1004
David came to his **h** at Jerusalem,	**2Sa 20:3**	1004
whom he had left to keep the **h**,	**2Sa 20:3**	1004
"It is for Saul and his bloody **h**,	**2Sa 21:1**	1004
silver or gold with Saul or his **h**,	**2Sa 21:4**	1004
"Truly is not my **h** so with God?	**2Sa 23:5**	1004
me and against my father's **h**."	**2Sa 24:17**	1004
Solomon said to him, "Go to your **h**."	**1Ki 1:53**	1004
has made me a **h** as He promised,	**1Ki 2:24**	1004
concerning the **h** of Eli in Shiloh.	**1Ki 2:27**	1004
from my father's **h** the blood which	**1Ki 2:31**	1004
and his **h** and his throne,	**1Ki 2:33**	1004
and he was buried at his own **h** in	**1Ki 2:34**	1004
"Build for yourself a **h** in Jerusalem	**1Ki 2:36**	1004
he had finished building his own **h**	**1Ki 3:1**	1004
and the **h** of the LORD and the wall	**1Ki 3:1**	1004
no **h** built for the name of the LORD	**1Ki 3:2**	1004
woman and I live in the same **h**;	**1Ki 3:17**	1004
to a child while she *was* in the **h**.	**1Ki 3:17**	1004
was no stranger with us in the **h**,	**1Ki 3:18**	1004
only the two of us in the **h**.	**1Ki 3:18**	1004
my father was unable to build a **h** for	**1Ki 5:3**	1004
build a **h** for the name of the LORD	**1Ki 5:5**	1004
he will build the **h** for My name.'	**1Ki 5:5**	1004
to lay the foundation of the **h** with	**1Ki 5:17**	1004
and the stones to build the **h**.	**1Ki 5:18**	1004
began to build the **h** of the LORD.	**1Ki 6:1**	1004
the **h** which King Solomon built for	**1Ki 6:2**	1004
porch in front of the nave of the **h**	**1Ki 6:3**	1004
corresponding to the width of the **h**,	**1Ki 6:3**	1004
the front of the **h** *was* ten cubits.	**1Ki 6:3**	1004
Also for the **h** he made windows	**1Ki 6:4**	1004
Against the wall of the **h** he	**1Ki 6:5**	1004
encompassing the walls of the **h**	**1Ki 6:5**	1004
he made offsets *in the wall* of the **h**	**1Ki 6:6**	1004
be inserted in the walls of the **h**.	**1Ki 6:6**	1004
h, while it was being built	**1Ki 6:7**	1004
axe nor any iron tool heard in the **h**	**1Ki 6:7**	1004
was on the right side of the **h**;	**1Ki 6:8**	1004
So he built the **h** and finished it;	**1Ki 6:9**	1004
and he covered the **h** with beams	**1Ki 6:9**	1004
the stories against the whole **h**,	**1Ki 6:10**	1004
were fastened to the **h** with timbers	**1Ki 6:10**	1004
this **h** which you are building,	**1Ki 6:12**	1004
Solomon built the **h** and finished it.	**1Ki 6:14**	1004
Then he built the walls of the **h**	**1Ki 6:15**	1004
from the floor of the **h** to the	**1Ki 6:15**	1004
he overlaid the floor of the **h** with	**1Ki 6:15**	1004
twenty cubits on the rear part of the **h**	**1Ki 6:16**	1004
The **h**, that is, the nave in	**1Ki 6:17**	1004
There was cedar on the **h** within,	**1Ki 6:18**	1004
an inner sanctuary within the **h**	**1Ki 6:19**	1004
inside of the **h** with pure gold.	**1Ki 6:21**	1004
He overlaid the whole **h** with gold,	**1Ki 6:22**	1004
until all the **h** was finished.	**1Ki 6:22**	1004
in the midst of the inner **h**,	**1Ki 6:27**	1004
each other in the center of the **h**.	**1Ki 6:27**	1004
Then he carved all the walls of the **h**	**1Ki 6:29**	1004
overlaid the floor of the **h** with gold,	**1Ki 6:30**	1004
the foundation of the **h** of the LORD	**1Ki 6:37**	1004
the **h** was finished throughout all	**1Ki 6:38**	1004
building his own **h** thirteen years,	**1Ki 7:1**	1004
years, and he finished all his **h**.	**1Ki 7:1**	1004
built the **h** of the forest of Lebanon;	**1Ki 7:2**	1004
His **h** where he was to live,	**1Ki 7:8**	1004
He also made a **h** like this hall	**1Ki 7:8**	1004
inner court of the **h** of the LORD,	**1Ki 7:12**	1004
the LORD, and the porch of the **h**.	**1Ki 7:12**	1004
five on the right side of the **h**	**1Ki 7:39**	1004
five on the left side of the **h**;	**1Ki 7:39**	1004
cast metal on the right side of the **h**	**1Ki 7:39**	1004
King Solomon *in* the **h** of the LORD:	**1Ki 7:40**	1004
in the **h** of the LORD *were* of polished	**1Ki 7:45**	1004
which *was in* the **h** of the LORD:	**1Ki 7:48**	1004
both for the doors of the inner **h**,	**1Ki 7:50**	1004
place, *and* for the doors of the **h**,	**1Ki 7:50**	1004
performed *in* the **h** of the LORD	**1Ki 7:51**	1004
treasuries of the **h** of the LORD.	**1Ki 7:51**	1004
into the inner sanctuary of the **h**,	**1Ki 8:6**	1004
cloud filled the **h** of the LORD,	**1Ki 8:10**	1004

the LORD filled the **h** of the LORD.	**1Ki 8:11**	1004
have surely built You a lofty **h**,	**1Ki 8:13**	1004
in which to build a **h** that My name	**1Ki 8:16**	1004
build a **h** for the name of the LORD,	**1Ki 8:17**	1004
heart to build a **h** for My name,	**1Ki 8:18**	1004
you shall not build the **h**,	**1Ki 8:19**	1004
he will build the **h** for My name	**1Ki 8:19**	1004
the **h** for the name of the LORD,	**1Ki 8:20**	1004
much less this **h** which I have built!	**1Ki 8:27**	1004
open toward this **h** night and day,	**1Ki 8:29**	1004
oath before Your altar in this **h**,	**1Ki 8:31**	1004
supplication to You in this **h**,	**1Ki 8:33**	1004
spreading his hands toward this **h**;	**1Ki 8:38**	1004
he comes and prays toward this **h**,	**1Ki 8:42**	1004
this **h** which I have built is called by	**1Ki 8:43**	1004
the **h** which I have built for Your name	**1Ki 8:44**	1004
and the **h** which I have built for	**1Ki 8:48**	1004
Israel dedicated the **h** of the LORD.	**1Ki 8:63**	1004
that *was* before the **h** of the LORD,	**1Ki 8:64**	1004
building the **h** of the LORD,	**1Ki 9:1**	1004
of the LORD, and the king's **h**,	**1Ki 9:1**	1004
I have consecrated this **h** which	**1Ki 9:3**	1004
and the **h** which I have consecrated	**1Ki 9:7**	1004
"And this **h** will become a heap	**1Ki 9:8**	1004
thus to this land and to this **h**?	**1Ki 9:8**	1004
the **h** of the LORD and the king's	**1Ki 9:10**	1004
house of the LORD and the king's **h**	**1Ki 9:10**	1004
levied to build the **h** of the LORD,	**1Ki 9:15**	1004
the house of the LORD, his own **h**,	**1Ki 9:15**	1004
from the city of David to her **h**	**1Ki 9:24**	1004
So he finished the **h**.	**1Ki 9:25**	1004
Solomon, the **h** that he had built,	**1Ki 10:4**	1004
he went up to the **h** of the LORD,	**1Ki 10:5**	1004
supports for the **h** of the LORD and	**1Ki 10:12**	1004
of the LORD and for the king's **h**,	**1Ki 10:12**	1004
in the **h** of the forest of Lebanon.	**1Ki 10:17**	1004
all the vessels of the **h** of the forest	**1Ki 10:21**	1004
who gave him a **h** and assigned him	**1Ki 11:18**	1004
Tahpenes weaned in Pharaoh's **h**;	**1Ki 11:20**	1004
Genubath was in Pharaoh's **h**	**1Ki 11:20**	1004
forced labor of the **h** of Joseph.	**1Ki 11:28**	1004
build you an enduring **h** as I built	**1Ki 11:38**	1004
Now look after your own **h**, David!	**1Ki 12:16**	1004
in rebellion against the **h** of David	**1Ki 12:19**	1004
of Judah followed the **h** of David.	**1Ki 12:20**	1004
he assembled all the **h** of Judah	**1Ki 12:21**	1004
to fight against the **h** of Israel	**1Ki 12:21**	1004
and to all the **h** of Judah and	**1Ki 12:23**	1004
return every man to his **h**,	**1Ki 12:24**	1004
will return to the **h** of David.	**1Ki 12:26**	1004
offer sacrifices in the **h** of the LORD	**1Ki 12:27**	1004
son shall be born to the **h** of David,	**1Ki 13:2**	1004
"If you were to give me half your **h**	**1Ki 13:8**	1004
'Bring him back with you to your **h**,	**1Ki 13:18**	1004
ate bread in his **h** and drank water.	**1Ki 13:19**	1004
became sin to the **h** of Jeroboam,	**1Ki 13:34**	1004
and came to the **h** of Ahijah.	**1Ki 14:4**	1004
kingdom away from the **h** of David	**1Ki 14:8**	1004
calamity on the **h** of Jeroboam,	**1Ki 14:10**	1004
clean sweep of the **h** of Jeroboam,	**1Ki 14:10**	1004
"Now you, arise, go to your **h**.	**1Ki 14:12**	1004
of Israel in the **h** of Jeroboam.	**1Ki 14:13**	1004
who will cut off the **h** of Jeroboam	**1Ki 14:14**	1004
entering the threshold of the **h**,	**1Ki 14:17**	1004
the treasures of the **h** of the LORD	**1Ki 14:26**	1004
and the treasures of the king's **h**,	**1Ki 14:26**	1004
the doorway of the king's **h**.	**1Ki 14:27**	1004
king entered the **h** of the LORD,	**1Ki 14:28**	1004
He brought into the **h** of the LORD	**1Ki 15:15**	1004
in the treasuries of the **h** of the LORD	**1Ki 15:18**	1004
and the treasuries of the king's **h**,	**1Ki 15:18**	1004
the son of Ahijah of the **h** of Issachar	**1Ki 15:27**	1004
I will consume Baasha and his **h**,	**1Ki 16:3**	1004
and I will make your **h** like the	**1Ki 16:3**	1004
your house like the **h** of Jeroboam	**1Ki 16:3**	1004
in being like the **h** of Jeroboam,	**1Ki 16:7**	1004
himself drunk in the **h** of Arza,	**1Ki 16:9**	1004
went into the citadel of the king's **h**	**1Ki 16:18**	1004
burned the king's **h** over him with	**1Ki 16:18**	1004
altar for Baal in the **h** of Baal which	**1Ki 16:32**	1004
the woman, the mistress of the **h**,	**1Ki 17:17**	1004
from the upper room into the **h**	**1Ki 17:23**	1004
but you and your father's **h** *have*,	**1Ki 18:18**	1004
and they will search your **h** and	**1Ki 20:6**	1004
kings of the **h** of Israel are merciful	**1Ki 20:31**	1004
king of Israel went to his **h** sullen	**1Ki 20:43**	1004
because it is close beside my **h**,	**1Ki 21:2**	1004
So Ahab came into his **h** sullen and	**1Ki 21:4**	1004
and I will make your **h** like the	**1Ki 21:22**	1004
your house like the **h** of Jeroboam	**1Ki 21:22**	1004
the **h** of Baasha the son of Ahijah,	**1Ki 21:22**	1004
but I will bring the evil upon his **h**	**1Ki 21:29**	1004
them return to his **h** in peace.' "	**1Ki 22:17**	1004
and the ivory **h** which he built and all	**1Ki 22:39**	1004
me, what do you have in the **h**?"	**2Ki 4:2**	1004
maidservant has nothing in the **h**	**2Ki 4:2**	1004
When Elisha came into the **h**,	**2Ki 4:32**	1004
walked in the **h** once back and forth	**2Ki 4:35**	1004
at the doorway of the **h** of Elisha.	**2Ki 5:9**	1004
master goes into the **h** of Rimmon	**2Ki 5:18**	1004
I bow myself in the **h** of Rimmon,	**2Ki 5:18**	1004
I bow myself in the **h** of Rimmon,	**2Ki 5:18**	1004
hand and deposited them in the **h**,	**2Ki 5:24**	1004
Now Elisha was sitting in his **h**,	**2Ki 6:32**	1004
to the king for her **h** and	**2Ki 8:3**	1004
appealed to the king for her **h** and	**2Ki 8:5**	1004
just as the **h** of Ahab had done,	**2Ki 8:18**	1004
in the way of the **h** of Ahab and	**2Ki 8:27**	1004
LORD, like the **h** of Ahab *had done*,	**2Ki 8:27**	1004
was a son-in-law of the **h** of Ahab.	**2Ki 8:27**	1004
He arose and went into the **h**,	**2Ki 9:6**	1004
strike the **h** of Ahab your master,	**2Ki 9:7**	1004
the whole **h** of Ahab shall perish,	**2Ki 9:8**	1004
'I will make the **h** of Ahab	**2Ki 9:9**	1004
h of Jeroboam the son of Nebat,	**2Ki 9:9**	1004
the **h** of Baasha the son of Ahijah.	**2Ki 9:9**	1004
fled by the way of the garden **h**.	**2Ki 9:27**	1004
and fight for your master's **h**."	**2Ki 10:3**	1004
spoke concerning the **h** of Ahab,	**2Ki 10:10**	1004
all who remained of the **h** of Ahab	**2Ki 10:11**	1004
when they went into the **h** of Baal,	**2Ki 10:21**	1004
the **h** of Baal was filled from one	**2Ki 10:21**	1004
Jehu went into the **h** of Baal	**2Ki 10:23**	1004
the inner room of the **h** of Baal.	**2Ki 10:25**	1004
sacred pillars of the **h** of Baal	**2Ki 10:26**	1004
Baal and broke down the **h** of Baal,	**2Ki 10:27**	1004
and have done to the **h** of Ahab	**2Ki 10:30**	1004
in the **h** of the LORD six years,	**2Ki 11:3**	1004
them to him in the **h** of the LORD.	**2Ki 11:4**	1004
under oath in the **h** of the LORD,	**2Ki 11:4**	1004
and keep watch over the king's **h**	**2Ki 11:5**	1004
keep watch over the **h** for defense.	**2Ki 11:6**	1004
keep watch over the **h** of the LORD	**2Ki 11:7**	1004
which *were* in the **h** of the LORD.	**2Ki 11:10**	1004
right side of the **h** to the left side of	**2Ki 11:11**	1004
house to the left side of the **h**,	**2Ki 11:11**	1004
house, by the altar and by the **h**,	**2Ki 11:11**	1004
the people in the **h** of the LORD.	**2Ki 11:13**	1004
to death in the **h** of the LORD."	**2Ki 11:15**	1004
horses' entrance of the king's **h**,	**2Ki 11:16**	1004
of the land went to the **h** of Baal,	**2Ki 11:18**	1004
officers over the **h** of the LORD.	**2Ki 11:18**	1004
king down from the **h** of the LORD,	**2Ki 11:19**	1004
gate of the guards to the king's **h**.	**2Ki 11:19**	1004
with the sword at the king's **h**.	**2Ki 11:20**	1004
is brought into the **h** of the LORD,	**2Ki 12:4**	1004
to bring into the **h** of the LORD,	**2Ki 12:4**	1004
they shall repair the damages of the **h**	**2Ki 12:5**	1004
not repaired the damages of the **h**.	**2Ki 12:6**	1004
not repair the damages of the **h**?	**2Ki 12:7**	1004
pay it for the damages of the **h**."	**2Ki 12:7**	1004
nor repair the damages of the **h**.	**2Ki 12:8**	1004
one comes into the **h** of the LORD;	**2Ki 12:9**	1004
brought into the **h** of the LORD.	**2Ki 12:9**	1004
was found in the **h** of the LORD.	**2Ki 12:10**	1004
oversight of the **h** of the LORD;	**2Ki 12:11**	1004
who worked on the **h** of the LORD;	**2Ki 12:11**	1004
the damages to the **h** of the LORD,	**2Ki 12:12**	1004
laid out for the **h** to repair it.	**2Ki 12:12**	1004
for the **h** of the LORD silver cups,	**2Ki 12:13**	1004
brought into the **h** of the LORD;	**2Ki 12:13**	1004
they repaired the **h** of the LORD.	**2Ki 12:14**	1004
brought into the **h** of the LORD;	**2Ki 12:16**	1004
the treasuries of the **h** of the LORD	**2Ki 12:18**	1004
of the LORD and of the king's **h**,	**2Ki 12:18**	1004
struck down Joash at the **h** of Millo	**2Ki 12:20**	1004
the sins of the **h** of Jeroboam,	**2Ki 13:6**	1004
were found in the **h** of the LORD,	**2Ki 14:14**	1004
in the treasuries of the king's **h**,	**2Ki 14:14**	1004
And he lived in a separate **h**,	**2Ki 15:5**	1004
in the castle of the king's **h** with	**2Ki 15:25**	1004
upper gate of the **h** of the LORD.	**2Ki 15:35**	1004
that was found in the **h** of the LORD	**2Ki 16:8**	1004
in the treasuries of the king's **h**,	**2Ki 16:8**	1004
brought from the front of the **h**,	**2Ki 16:14**	1004
his altar and the **h** of the LORD,	**2Ki 16:14**	1004
which they had built in the **h**,	**2Ki 16:18**	1004
he removed from the **h** of the LORD	**2Ki 16:18**	1004
torn Israel from the **h** of David,	**2Ki 17:21**	1004
was found in the **h** of the LORD,	**2Ki 18:15**	1004
in the treasuries of the king's **h**.	**2Ki 18:15**	1004
and entered the **h** of the LORD.	**2Ki 19:1**	1004
he went up to the **h** of the LORD	**2Ki 19:14**	1004
remnant of the **h** of Judah will again	**2Ki 19:30**	1004
in the **h** of Nisroch his god,	**2Ki 19:37**	1004
'Set your **h** in order, for you	**2Ki 20:1**	1004
shall go up to the **h** of the LORD.	**2Ki 20:5**	1004
the **h** of the LORD the third day?"	**2Ki 20:8**	1004
showed them all his treasure **h**,	**2Ki 20:13**	1004
the precious oil and the **h** of his armor	**2Ki 20:13**	1004
There was nothing in his **h** nor	**2Ki 20:13**	1004
"What have they seen in your **h**?"	**2Ki 20:15**	1004
have seen all that is in my **h**;	**2Ki 20:15**	1004
coming when all that is in your **h**,	**2Ki 20:17**	1004
built altars in the **h** of the LORD,	**2Ki 21:4**	1004
two courts of the **h** of the LORD.	**2Ki 21:5**	1004
in the **h** of which the LORD said to	**2Ki 21:7**	1004
"In this **h** and in Jerusalem,	**2Ki 21:7**	1004
and the plummet of the **h** of Ahab,	**2Ki 21:13**	1004
buried in the garden of his own **h**,	**2Ki 21:18**	1004
and killed the king in his own **h**.	**2Ki 21:23**	1004
to the **h** of the LORD saying,	**2Ki 22:3**	1004
money brought in to the **h** of the LORD	**2Ki 22:4**	1004
oversight of the **h** of the LORD,	**2Ki 22:5**	1004
who are in the **h** of the LORD to repair	**2Ki 22:5**	1004
to repair the damages of the **h**,	**2Ki 22:5**	1004
and hewn stone to repair the **h**.	**2Ki 22:6**	1004
of the law in the **h** of the LORD."	**2Ki 22:8**	1004
the money that was found in the **h**,	**2Ki 22:9**	1004
oversight of the **h** of the LORD."	**2Ki 22:9**	1004
king went up to the **h** of the LORD	**2Ki 23:2**	1004
was found in the **h** of the LORD.	**2Ki 23:2**	1004
the Asherah from the **h** of the LORD	**2Ki 23:6**	1004
which *were* in the **h** of the LORD,	**2Ki 23:7**	1004
the entrance of the **h** of the LORD,	**2Ki 23:11**	1004
two courts of the **h** of the LORD,	**2Ki 23:12**	1004
priest found in the **h** of the LORD.	**2Ki 23:24**	1004
treasures of the **h** of the LORD,	**2Ki 24:13**	1004
and the treasures of the king's **h**,	**2Ki 24:13**	1004
He burned the **h** of the LORD,	**2Ki 25:9**	1004
house of the LORD, the king's **h**,	**2Ki 25:9**	1004
every great **h** he burned with fire.	**2Ki 25:9**	1004
which were in the **h** of the LORD,	**2Ki 25:13**	1004
which were in the **h** of the LORD,	**2Ki 25:13**	1004
had made for the **h** of the LORD	**2Ki 25:16**	1004
the father of the **h** of Rechab.	**1Ch 2:55**	1004
of the **h** of the linen workers at	**1Ch 4:21**	1004
h which Solomon built in Jerusalem),	**1Ch 6:10**	1004
of song in the **h** of the LORD,	**1Ch 6:31**	1004
the **h** of the LORD in Jerusalem;	**1Ch 6:32**	1004
of the tabernacle of the **h** of God.	**1Ch 6:48**	1004
misfortune had come upon his **h**.	**1Ch 7:23**	1004
the chief officer of the **h** of God;	**1Ch 9:11**	1004
of the service of the **h** of God.	**1Ch 9:13**	1004
his relatives of his father's **h**,	**1Ch 9:19**	1004
of the gates of the **h** of the LORD,	**1Ch 9:23**	1004
the LORD, *even* the **h** of the tent,	**1Ch 9:23**	1004
the treasuries in the **h** of God.	**1Ch 9:26**	1004
the night around the **h** of God,	**1Ch 9:27**	1004
all *those* of his **h** died together.	**1Ch 10:6**	1004
put his armor in the **h** of their gods	**1Ch 10:10**	1004
his head in the **h** of Dagon.	**1Ch 10:10**	1004
Jehoiada was the leader of *the* **h** *of*	**1Ch 12:27**	
his father's **h** twenty-two captains.	**1Ch 12:28**	1004
their allegiance to the **h** of Saul.	**1Ch 12:29**	1004
a new cart from the **h** of Abinadab,	**1Ch 13:7**	1004
to the **h** of Obed-edom the Gittite.	**1Ch 13:13**	1004
of Obed-edom in his **h** three months;	**1Ch 13:14**	1004
carpenters, to build a **h** for him.	**1Ch 14:1**	1004
from the **h** of Obed-edom with joy.	**1Ch 15:25**	1004
the people departed each to his **h**,	**1Ch 16:43**	1004
about, when David dwelt in his **h**,	**1Ch 17:1**	1004
I am dwelling in a **h** of cedar,	**1Ch 17:1**	1004
not build a **h** for Me to dwell in;	**1Ch 17:4**	1004
for I have not dwelt in a **h** since	**1Ch 17:5**	1004
built for Me a **h** of cedar?	**1Ch 17:6**	1004
the LORD will build a **h** for you.	**1Ch 17:10**	1004
"He shall build for Me a **h**,	**1Ch 17:12**	1004
in My **h** and in My kingdom forever,	**1Ch 17:14**	1004
and what is my **h** that You have	**1Ch 17:16**	1004
have spoken of Your servant's **h**	**1Ch 17:17**	1004
Your servant and concerning his **h** be	**1Ch 17:23**	1004
and the **h** of David Your servant is	**1Ch 17:24**	1004
that You will build for him a **h**;	**1Ch 17:25**	1004
to bless the **h** of Your servant,	**1Ch 17:27**	1004
"This is the **h** of the LORD God,	**1Ch 22:1**	1004
out stones to build the **h** of God.	**1Ch 22:2**	1004
and the **h** that is to be built for	**1Ch 22:5**	1004
a **h** for the LORD God of Israel.	**1Ch 22:6**	1004
I had intended to build a **h** to the	**1Ch 22:7**	1004
shall not build a **h** to My name,	**1Ch 22:8**	1004
'He shall build a **h** for My name,	**1Ch 22:10**	1004
and build the **h** of the LORD your	**1Ch 22:11**	1004
I have prepared for the **h** of the LORD	**1Ch 22:14**	1004
the **h** that is to be built for the name	**1Ch 22:19**	1004
the work of the **h** of the LORD;	**1Ch 23:4**	1004
the service of the **h** of the LORD,	**1Ch 23:24**	1004
the service of the **h** of the LORD,	**1Ch 23:28**	1004
of the service of the **h** of God,	**1Ch 23:28**	1004
the service of the **h** of the LORD.	**1Ch 23:32**	1004
they came in to the **h** of the LORD	**1Ch 24:19**	1004
to sing in the **h** of the LORD,	**1Ch 25:6**	1004
for the service of the **h** of God.	**1Ch 25:6**	1004
ruled over the **h** of their father,	**1Ch 26:6**	1004
to minister in the **h** of the LORD.	**1Ch 26:12**	1004
of the treasures of the **h** of God and	**1Ch 26:20**	1004
treasures of the **h** of the LORD.	**1Ch 26:22**	1004
to repair the **h** of the LORD.	**1Ch 26:27**	1004
'You shall not build a **h** for My	**1Ch 28:3**	1004
me from all the **h** of my father	**1Ch 28:4**	1004
and in the **h** of Judah, my father's	**1Ch 28:4**	1004
the house of Judah, my father's **h**,	**1Ch 28:4**	1004
shall build My **h** and My courts;	**1Ch 28:6**	1004
to build a **h** for the sanctuary;	**1Ch 28:10**	1004
the courts of the **h** of the LORD,	**1Ch 28:12**	1004
the storehouses of the **h** of God and	**1Ch 28:12**	1004
the service of the **h** of the LORD	**1Ch 28:13**	1004
of service in the **h** of the LORD;	**1Ch 28:13**	1004
for the service of the **h** of the LORD	**1Ch 28:20**	1004
all the service of the **h** of God,	**1Ch 28:21**	1004
provided for the **h** of my God the gold	**1Ch 29:2**	1004
in my delight in the **h** of my God,	**1Ch 29:3**	1004
silver, I give to the **h** of my God,	**1Ch 29:3**	1004
for the service for the **h** of God	**1Ch 29:7**	1004
the treasury of the **h** of the LORD,	**1Ch 29:8**	1004
build You a **h** for Your holy name,	**1Ch 29:16**	1004
a **h** for the name of the LORD and	**2Ch 2:1**	1004
to build him a **h** to dwell in,	**2Ch 2:3**	1004
I am about to build a **h** for the	**2Ch 2:4**	1004
"The **h** which I am about to	**2Ch 2:5**	1004
who is able to build a **h** for Him,	**2Ch 2:6**	1004
that I should build a **h** for Him,	**2Ch 2:6**	1004
for the **h** which I am about to	**2Ch 2:9**	1004
who will build a **h** for the LORD	**2Ch 2:12**	1004
began to build the **h** of the LORD	**2Ch 3:1**	1004
laid for building the **h** of God.	**2Ch 3:3**	1004
The porch which was in front of the **h**	**2Ch 3:4**	
was as long as the width of the **h**,	**2Ch 3:4**	1004
the **h** with precious stones;	**2Ch 3:6**	1004
He also overlaid the **h** with gold	**2Ch 3:7**	1004
length across the width of the **h**	**2Ch 3:8**	1004
cubits, touched the wall of the **h**,	**2Ch 3:11**	1004
cubits, touched the wall of the **h**;	**2Ch 3:12**	1004
pillars for the front of the **h**,	**2Ch 3:15**	1004
the sea on the right side *of the* **h**	**2Ch 4:10**	
for King Solomon in the **h** of God:	**2Ch 4:11**	1004
Solomon for the **h** of the LORD.	**2Ch 4:16**	1004

things that *were* in the **h** of God:	2Ch 4:19	1004
and the entrance of the **h**,	2Ch 4:22	1004
of holies and doors of the **h**,	2Ch 4:22	1004
the **h** of the LORD was finished.	2Ch 5:1	1004
in the treasuries of the **h** of God.	2Ch 5:1	1004
into the inner sanctuary of the **h**,	2Ch 5:7	1004
then the **h**, the house of the LORD,	2Ch 5:13	1004
then the house, the **h** of the LORD,	2Ch 5:13	1004
of the LORD filled the **h** of God.	2Ch 5:14	1004
"I have built You a lofty **h**,	2Ch 6:2	1004
a **h** that My name might be there,	2Ch 6:5	1004
a **h** for the name of the LORD,	2Ch 6:7	1004
heart to build a **h** for My name,	2Ch 6:8	1004
you shall not build the **h**,	2Ch 6:9	1004
he shall build the **h** for My name.'	2Ch 6:9	1004
the **h** for the name of the LORD,	2Ch 6:10	1004
much less this **h** which I have built.	2Ch 6:18	1004
open toward this **h** day and night,	2Ch 6:20	1004
oath before Your altar in this **h**,	2Ch 6:22	1004
supplication before You in this **h**,	2Ch 6:24	1004
spreading his hands toward this **h**,	2Ch 6:29	1004
they come and pray toward this **h**,	2Ch 6:32	1004
this **h** which I have built is called by	2Ch 6:33	1004
and the **h** which I have built for	2Ch 6:34	1004
and toward the **h** which I have	2Ch 6:38	1004
glory of the LORD filled the **h**.	2Ch 7:1	1004
enter into the **h** of the LORD because	2Ch 7:2	1004
of the LORD filled the LORD's **h**.	2Ch 7:2	1004
the glory of the LORD upon the **h**,	2Ch 7:3	1004
the people dedicated the **h** of God.	2Ch 7:5	1004
that *was* before the **h** of the LORD,	2Ch 7:7	1004
Solomon finished the **h** of the LORD	2Ch 7:11	1004
on doing in the **h** of the LORD	2Ch 7:11	1004
for Myself as a **h** of sacrifice.	2Ch 7:12	1004
I have chosen and consecrated this **h**	2Ch 7:16	1004
this **h** which I have consecrated for	2Ch 7:20	1004
"As for this **h**, which was	2Ch 7:21	1004
thus to this land and to this **h**?	2Ch 7:21	1004
Solomon had built the **h** of the LORD	2Ch 8:1	1004
house of the LORD and his own **h**	2Ch 8:1	1004
the **h** which he had built for her,	2Ch 8:11	1004
in the **h** of David king of Israel,	2Ch 8:11	1004
foundation of the **h** of the LORD,	2Ch 8:16	1004
the **h** of the LORD was completed.	2Ch 8:16	1004
Solomon, the **h** which he had built,	2Ch 9:3	1004
he went up to the **h** of the LORD,	2Ch 9:4	1004
king made steps for the **h** of the LORD	2Ch 9:11	1004
in the **h** of the forest of Lebanon.	2Ch 9:16	1004
of the **h** of the forest of Lebanon	2Ch 9:20	1004
Now look after your own **h**,	2Ch 10:16	1004
in rebellion against the **h** of David	2Ch 10:19	1004
the **h** of Judah and Benjamin,	2Ch 11:1	1004
return every man to his **h**,	2Ch 11:4	1004
the treasures of the **h** of the LORD	2Ch 12:9	1004
guarded the door of the king's **h**.	2Ch 12:10	1004
king entered the **h** of the LORD,	2Ch 12:11	1004
He brought into the **h** of God	2Ch 15:18	1004
the treasuries of the **h** of the LORD	2Ch 16:2	1004
house of the LORD and the king's **h**,	2Ch 16:2	1004
them return to his **h** in peace.'	2Ch 18:16	1004
in safety to his **h** in Jerusalem.	2Ch 19:1	1004
the ruler of the **h** of Judah,	2Ch 19:11	1004
in the **h** of the LORD before the	2Ch 20:5	1004
before this **h** and before You	2Ch 20:9	1004
(for Your name is in this **h**)	2Ch 20:9	1004
and trumpets to the **h** of the LORD.	2Ch 20:28	1004
Israel, just as the **h** of Ahab did	2Ch 21:6	1004
not willing to destroy the **h** of David	2Ch 21:7	1004
the **h** of Ahab played the harlot,	2Ch 21:13	1004
the possessions found in the king's **h**	2Ch 21:17	1004
in the ways of the **h** of Ahab,	2Ch 22:3	1004
of the LORD like the **h** of Ahab,	2Ch 22:4	1004
anointed to cut off the **h** of Ahab.	2Ch 22:7	1004
judgment on the **h** of Ahab,	2Ch 22:8	1004
no one of the **h** of Ahaziah to retain	2Ch 22:9	1004
royal offspring of the **h** of Judah.	2Ch 22:10	1004
was hidden with them in the **h** of God	2Ch 22:12	1004
with the king in the **h** of God.	2Ch 23:3	1004
one third *shall be* at the king's **h**,	2Ch 23:5	1004
the courts of the **h** of the LORD.	2Ch 23:5	1004
let no one enter the **h** of the LORD	2Ch 23:6	1004
and whoever enters the **h**,	2Ch 23:7	1004
which were in the **h** of God.	2Ch 23:9	1004
right side of the **h** to the left side of	2Ch 23:10	1004
house to the left side of the **h**,	2Ch 23:10	1004
house, by the altar and by the **h**,	2Ch 23:10	1004
the **h** of the LORD to the people.	2Ch 23:12	1004
to death in the **h** of the LORD."	2Ch 23:14	1004
of the Horse Gate of the king's **h**,	2Ch 23:15	1004
the people went to the **h** of Baal and	2Ch 23:17	1004
offices of the **h** of the LORD under the	2Ch 23:18	1004
assigned over the **h** of the LORD,	2Ch 23:18	1004
gatekeepers of the **h** of the LORD,	2Ch 23:19	1004
king down from the **h** of the LORD,	2Ch 23:20	1004
the upper gate to the king's **h**.	2Ch 23:20	1004
to restore the **h** of the LORD.	2Ch 24:4	1004
repair the **h** of your God annually,	2Ch 24:5	1004
Athaliah had broken into the **h** of God	2Ch 24:7	1004
even used the holy things of the **h** of	2Ch 24:7	1004
by the gate of the **h** of the LORD.	2Ch 24:8	1004
the service of the **h** of the LORD;	2Ch 24:12	1004
to restore the **h** of the LORD,	2Ch 24:12	1004
to repair the **h** of the LORD.	2Ch 24:12	1004
and they restored the **h** of God	2Ch 24:13	1004
utensils for the **h** of the LORD,	2Ch 24:14	1004
burnt offerings in the **h** of the LORD	2Ch 24:14	1004
in Israel and to God and His **h**.	2Ch 24:16	1004
They abandoned the **h** of the LORD,	2Ch 24:18	1004
in the court of the **h** of the LORD.	2Ch 24:21	1004
the rebuilding of the **h** of God,	2Ch 24:27	1004
in the **h** of God with Obed-edom,	2Ch 25:24	1004
and the treasures of the king's **h**,	2Ch 25:24	1004
the priests in the **h** of the LORD,	2Ch 26:19	1004
and he lived in a separate **h**,	2Ch 26:21	1004
cut off from the **h** of the LORD.	2Ch 26:21	1004
Jotham his son *was* over the king's **h**	2Ch 26:21	1004
upper gate of the **h** of the LORD,	2Ch 27:3	1004
and Azrikam the ruler of the **h** and	2Ch 28:7	1004
a portion out of the **h** of the LORD	2Ch 28:21	1004
the utensils of the **h** of God,	2Ch 28:24	1004
of the **h** of God in pieces;	2Ch 28:24	1004
the doors of the **h** of the LORD	2Ch 28:24	1004
the doors of the **h** of the LORD	2Ch 29:3	1004
and consecrate the **h** of the LORD,	2Ch 29:5	1004
in to cleanse the **h** of the LORD,	2Ch 29:15	1004
the inner part of the **h** of the LORD	2Ch 29:16	1004
to the court of the **h** of the LORD.	2Ch 29:16	1004
they consecrated the **h** of the LORD	2Ch 29:17	1004
cleansed the whole **h** of the LORD,	2Ch 29:18	1004
and went up to the **h** of the LORD.	2Ch 29:20	1004
in the **h** of the LORD with cymbals,	2Ch 29:25	1004
offerings to the **h** of the LORD."	2Ch 29:31	1004
the service of the **h** of the LORD	2Ch 29:35	1004
should come to the **h** of the LORD	2Ch 30:1	1004
offerings to the **h** of the LORD.	2Ch 30:15	1004
the chief priest of the **h** of Zadok	2Ch 31:10	1004
be brought into the **h** of the LORD,	2Ch 31:10	1004
rooms in the **h** of the LORD,	2Ch 31:11	1004
the *chief* officer of the **h** of God.	2Ch 31:13	1004
entered the **h** of the LORD for his daily	2Ch 31:16	1004
began in the service of the **h** of God	2Ch 31:21	1004
He built altars in the **h** of the LORD	2Ch 33:4	1004
two courts of the **h** of the LORD.	2Ch 33:5	1004
which he had made in the **h** of God,	2Ch 33:7	1004
"In this **h** and in Jerusalem,	2Ch 33:7	1004
the idol from the **h** of the LORD,	2Ch 33:15	1004
the mountain of the **h** of the LORD	2Ch 33:15	1004
and they buried him in his own **h**.	2Ch 33:20	1004
and put him to death in his own **h**.	2Ch 33:24	1004
he had purged the land and the **h**	2Ch 34:8	1004
repair the **h** of the LORD his God.	2Ch 34:8	1004
was brought into the **h** of God,	2Ch 34:9	1004
oversight of the **h** of the LORD,	2Ch 34:10	1004
were working in the **h** of the LORD	2Ch 34:10	1004
it to restore and repair the **h**.	2Ch 34:10	1004
brought into the **h** of the LORD,	2Ch 34:14	1004
of the law in the **h** of the LORD."	2Ch 34:15	1004
was found in the **h** of the LORD,	2Ch 34:17	1004
king went up to the **h** of the LORD	2Ch 34:30	1004
was found in the **h** of the LORD.	2Ch 34:30	1004
the service of the **h** of the LORD.	2Ch 35:2	1004
"Put the holy ark in the **h** which	2Ch 35:3	1004
the officials of the **h** of God,	2Ch 35:8	1004
the **h** with which I am at war,	2Ch 35:21	1004
the articles of the **h** of the LORD	2Ch 36:7	1004
articles of the **h** of the LORD,	2Ch 36:10	1004
and they defiled the **h** of the LORD	2Ch 36:14	1004
sword in the **h** of their sanctuary,	2Ch 36:17	1004
All the articles of the **h** of God,	2Ch 36:18	1004
treasures of the **h** of the LORD,	2Ch 36:18	1004
Then they burned the **h** of God and	2Ch 36:19	1004
me to build Him a **h** in Jerusalem,	2Ch 36:23	1004
me to build Him a **h** in Jerusalem,	Ezr 1:2	1004
and rebuild the **h** of the LORD,	Ezr 1:3	1004
a freewill offering for the **h** of God	Ezr 1:4	1004
go up and rebuild the **h** of the LORD	Ezr 1:5	1004
the articles of the **h** of the LORD,	Ezr 1:7	1004
and put in the **h** of his gods;	Ezr 1:7	1004
of Jedaiah of the **h** of Jeshua,	Ezr 2:36	1004
they arrived at the **h** of the LORD	Ezr 2:68	1004
offered willingly for the **h** of God	Ezr 2:68	1004
coming to the **h** of God at Jerusalem	Ezr 3:8	1004
the work of the **h** of the LORD.	Ezr 3:8	1004
the foundation of the **h** of the LORD	Ezr 3:11	1004
the foundation of this **h** was laid	Ezr 3:12	1004
us in building a **h** to our God;	Ezr 4:3	1004
work on the **h** of God in Jerusalem	Ezr 4:24	1005
h of God which is in Jerusalem;	Ezr 5:2	1005
Judah, to the **h** of the great God,	Ezr 5:8	1005
a decree to rebuild this **h** of God.	Ezr 5:13	1005
and silver utensils of the **h** of God	Ezr 5:14	1005
and let the **h** of God be rebuilt in	Ezr 5:15	1005
laid the foundations of the **h** of God	Ezr 5:16	1005
conducted in the king's treasure **h**,	Ezr 5:17	1005
this **h** of God at Jerusalem;	Ezr 5:17	1005
the **h** of God at Jerusalem,	Ezr 6:3	1005
the gold and silver utensils of the **h**	Ezr 6:5	1005
shall put *them* in the **h** of God.'	Ezr 6:5	1005
this work on the **h** of God alone;	Ezr 6:7	1005
rebuild this **h** of God on its site.	Ezr 6:7	1005
the rebuilding of this **h** of God:	Ezr 6:8	1005
a timber shall be drawn from his **h**	Ezr 6:11	1005
and his **h** shall be made a refuse heap	Ezr 6:11	1005
this **h** of God in Jerusalem.	Ezr 6:12	1005
dedication of this **h** of God with joy.	Ezr 6:16	1005
them in the work of the **h** of God,	Ezr 6:22	1004
willingly for the **h** of their God	Ezr 7:16	1005
on the altar of the **h** of your God	Ezr 7:17	1005
the service of the **h** of your God,	Ezr 7:19	1005
the needs for the **h** of your God,	Ezr 7:20	1005
for the **h** of the God of heaven,	Ezr 7:23	1005
or servants of this **h** of God.	Ezr 7:24	1005
to adorn the **h** of the LORD which	Ezr 7:27	1004
to us for the **h** of our God.	Ezr 8:17	1004
the offering for the **h** of our God	Ezr 8:25	1004
chambers of the **h** of the LORD."	Ezr 8:29	1004
to Jerusalem to the **h** of our God.	Ezr 8:30	1004
were weighed out in the **h** of our God	Ezr 8:33	1004
the people and the **h** of God.	Ezr 8:36	1004
to raise up the **h** of our God,	Ezr 9:9	1004
himself before the **h** of God,	Ezr 10:1	1004
Ezra rose from before the **h** of God	Ezr 10:6	1004
open square *before* the **h** of God,	Ezr 10:9	1004
I and my father's **h** have sinned.	Ne 1:6	1004
for the **h** to which I will go."	Ne 2:8	1004
made repairs opposite his **h**.	Ne 3:10	1004
pool and the **h** of the mighty men.	Ne 3:16	1004
the **h** of Eliashib the high priest.	Ne 3:20	1004
from the doorway of Eliashib's **h**	Ne 3:21	1004
even as far as the end of his **h**.	Ne 3:21	1004
out repairs in front of their **h**.	Ne 3:23	1004
carried out repairs beside his **h**.	Ne 3:23	1004
from the **h** of Azariah as far as	Ne 3:24	1004
from the upper **h** of the king,	Ne 3:25	1004
repairs, each in front of his **h**.	Ne 3:28	1004
carried out repairs in front of his **h**.	Ne 3:29	1004
as far as the **h** of the temple servants	Ne 3:31	1004
were behind the whole **h** of Judah.	Ne 4:16	1004
God shake out every man from his **h**	Ne 5:13	1004
When I entered the **h** of Shemaiah	Ne 6:10	1004
us meet together in the **h** of God,	Ne 6:10	1004
and each in front of his own **h**."	Ne 7:3	1004
of Jedaiah of the **h** of Jeshua,	Ne 7:39	1004
and in the courts of the **h** of God,	Ne 8:16	1004
the service of the **h** of our God:	Ne 10:32	1004
all the work of the **h** of our God.	Ne 10:33	1004
bring it to the **h** of our God,	Ne 10:34	1004
to the **h** of the LORD annually,	Ne 10:35	1004
and bring to the **h** of our God the	Ne 10:36	1004
ministering in the **h** of our God.	Ne 10:36	1004
the chambers of the **h** of our God,	Ne 10:37	1004
of the tithes to the **h** of our God,	Ne 10:38	1004
will not neglect the **h** of our God.	Ne 10:39	1004
the leader of the **h** of God,	Ne 11:11	1004
the outside work of the **h** of God;	Ne 11:16	1004
for the service of the **h** of God.	Ne 11:22	1004
the wall above the **h** of David to the	Ne 12:37	1004
took their stand in the **h** of God.	Ne 12:40	1004
the chambers of the **h** of our God,	Ne 13:4	1004
him in the courts of the **h** of God.	Ne 13:7	1004
the utensils of the **h** of God with the	Ne 13:9	1004
"Why is the **h** of God forsaken?"	Ne 13:11	1004
the **h** of my God and its services.	Ne 13:14	1004
should be the master in his own **h**	Es 1:22	1004
and your father's **h** will perish.	Es 4:14	1004
himself, however, went to his **h** and	Es 5:10	1004
the queen with me in the **h**?"	Es 7:8	1004
the gallows standing at Haman's **h**	Es 7:9	1004
Ahasuerus gave the **h** of Haman,	Es 8:1	1004
set Mordecai over the **h** of Haman.	Es 8:2	1004
given the **h** of Haman to Esther,	Es 8:7	1004
Mordecai was great in the king's **h**,	Es 9:4	1004
in the **h** of each one on his day,	Jb 1:4	1004
made a hedge about him and his **h**	Jb 1:10	1004
wine in their oldest brother's **h**,	Jb 1:13	1004
wine in their oldest brother's **h**,	Jb 1:18	1004
struck the four corners of the **h**,	Jb 1:19	1004
"He will not return again to his **h**,	Jb 7:10	1004
"He trusts in his **h**,	Jb 8:15	1004
pile, He grasps a **h** of stones.	Jb 8:17	1004
"Those who live in my **h** and my	Jb 19:15	1004
has seized a **h** which he has not built.	Jb 20:19	1004
"The increase of his **h** will depart;	Jb 20:28	1004
'Where is the **h** of the nobleman,	Jb 21:28	1004
built his **h** like the spider's web,	Jb 27:18	1004
the **h** of meeting for all living.	Jb 30:23	1004
they ate bread with him in his **h**;	Jb 42:11	1004
lovingkindness I will enter Your **h**,	Ps 5:7	1004
dwell in the **h** of the LORD forever.	Ps 23:6	1004
I love the habitation of Your **h** And	Ps 26:8	1004
I may dwell in the **h** of the LORD all	Ps 27:4	1004
fill of the abundance of Your **h**;	Ps 36:8	1004
in procession to the **h** of God,	Ps 42:4	1004
your people and your father's **h**;	Ps 45:10	1004
the glory of his **h** is increased;	Ps 49:16	1004
take no young bull out of your **h** Nor	Ps 50:9	1004
green olive tree in the **h** of God;	Ps 52:8	1004
in the **h** of God in the throng.	Ps 55:14	1004
with the goodness of Your **h**,	Ps 65:4	1004
into Your **h** with burnt offerings;	Ps 66:13	1004
zeal for Your **h** has consumed me,	Ps 69:9	1004
The bird also has found a **h**,	Ps 84:3	1004
are those who dwell in Your **h**!	Ps 84:4	1004
the threshold of the **h** of my God Than	Ps 84:10	1004
Planted in the **h** of the LORD, They	Ps 92:13	1004
Holiness befits Your **h**,	Ps 93:5	1004
His faithfulness to the **h** of Israel;	Ps 98:3	1004
walk within my **h** in the integrity of	Ps 101:2	1004
shall not dwell within my **h**;	Ps 101:7	1004
He made him lord of his **h** And	Ps 105:21	1004
Wealth and riches are in his **h**,	Ps 112:3	1004
the barren woman abide in the **h**	Ps 113:9	1004
The **h** of Jacob from a people of	Ps 114:1	1004
O **h** of Aaron, trust in the LORD;	Ps 115:10	1004
He will bless the **h** of Israel;	Ps 115:12	1004
He will bless the **h** of Aaron.	Ps 115:12	1004
In the courts of the LORD's **h**,	Ps 116:19	1004
Oh let the **h** of Aaron say,	Ps 118:3	1004
you from the **h** of the LORD.	Ps 118:26	1004
songs In the **h** of my pilgrimage.	Ps 119:54	1004
"Let us go to the **h** of the LORD."	Ps 122:1	1004
The thrones of the **h** of David.	Ps 122:5	1004
For the sake of the **h** of the LORD	Ps 122:9	1004
Unless the LORD builds the **h**,	Ps 127:1	1004
a fruitful vine Within your **h**,	Ps 128:3	1004
"Surely I will not enter my **h**,	Ps 132:3	1004
by night in the **h** of the LORD!	Ps 134:1	1004

who stand in the **h** of the LORD, Ps 135:2 1004
In the courts of the **h** of our God! Ps 135:2 1004
O **h** of Israel, bless the LORD; Ps 135:19 1004
O **h** of Aaron, bless the LORD; Ps 135:19 1004
O **h** of Levi, bless the LORD; Ps 135:20 1004
For her **h** sinks down to death And Pr 2:18 1004
LORD is on the **h** of the wicked, Pr 3:33 1004
do not go near the door of her **h**, Pr 5:8 1004
goods *will go* to the **h** of an alien; Pr 5:10 1004
give all the substance of his **h**. Pr 6:31 1004
For at the window of my **h** I looked Pr 7:6 1004
And he takes the way to her **h**, Pr 7:8 1004
Her **h** is the way to Sheol, Pr 7:27 1004
Wisdom has built her **h**, Pr 9:1 1004
She sits at the doorway of her **h**, Pr 9:14 1004
He who troubles his own **h** will Pr 11:29 1004
the **h** of the righteous will stand. Pr 12:7 1004
The wise woman builds her **h**, Pr 14:1 1004
The **h** of the wicked will be Pr 14:11 1004
wealth is *in* the **h** of the righteous, Pr 15:6 1004
will tear down the **h** of the proud, Pr 15:25 1004
illicitly troubles his own **h**, Pr 15:27 1004
a **h** full of feasting with strife. Pr 17:1 1004
Evil will not depart from his **h**. Pr 17:13 1004
H and wealth are an inheritance Pr 19:14 1004
h shared with a contentious woman. Pr 21:9 1004
one considers the **h** of the wicked, Pr 21:12 1004
By wisdom a **h** is built, And by Pr 24:3 1004
Afterwards, then, build your **h**. Pr 24:27 1004
rarely be in your neighbor's **h**, Pr 25:17 1004
a **h** shared with a contentious woman. Pr 25:24 1004
not go to your brother's **h** in the day Pr 27:10 1004
steps as you go to the **h** of God and Ec 5:1 1004
better to go to a **h** of mourning Ec 7:2 1004
Than to go to a **h** of feasting, Ec 7:2 1004
the wise is in the **h** of mourning, Ec 7:4 1004
of fools is in the **h** of pleasure. Ec 7:4 1004
and through slackness the **h** leaks. Ec 10:18 1004
the watchmen of the **h** tremble, Ec 12:3 1004
I had brought him to my mother's **h**, SS 3:4 1004
bring you Into the **h** of my mother, SS 8:2 1004
all the riches of his **h** for love, SS 8:7 1004
The mountain of the **h** of the LORD Is 2:2 1004
To the **h** of the God of Jacob; Is 2:3 1004
Come, **h** of Jacob, and let us walk Is 2:5 1004
Your people, the **h** of Jacob, Is 2:6 1004
of his brother in his father's **h**, Is 3:6 1004
For in my **h** there is neither bread Is 3:7 1004
LORD of hosts is the **h** of Israel And Is 5:7 1004
Woe to those who add **h** to house Is 5:8 1004
Woe to those who add house to **h** Is 5:8 1004
it was reported to the **h** of David, Is 7:2 1004
"Listen now, O **h** of David! Is 7:13 1004
and on your father's **h** such days Is 7:17 1004
His face from the **h** of Jacob; Is 8:17 1004
the **h** of Jacob who have escaped, Is 10:20 1004
themselves to the **h** of Jacob. Is 14:1 1004
and the **h** of Israel will possess Is 14:2 1004
weapons of the **h** of the forest, Is 22:8 1004
be, You shame of your master's **h** Is 22:18 1004
Jerusalem and to the **h** of Judah. Is 22:21 1004
of the **h** of David on his shoulder, Is 22:22 1004
throne of glory to his father's **h**. Is 22:23 1004
all the glory of his father's **h**, Is 22:24 1004
is destroyed, without **h** *or* harbor; Is 23:1 1004
Every **h** is shut up so that none Is 24:10 1004
concerning the **h** of Jacob: Is 29:22 1004
arise against the **h** of evildoers And Is 31:2 1004
and entered the **h** of the LORD. Is 37:1 1004
he went up to the **h** of the LORD Is 37:14 1004
remnant of the **h** of Judah will again Is 37:31 1004
in the **h** of Nisroch his god, Is 37:38 1004
'Set your **h** in order, for you Is 38:1 1004
our life at the **h** of the LORD." Is 38:20 1004
go up to the **h** of the LORD?" Is 38:22 1004
showed them *all* his treasure **h**, Is 39:2 1004
There was nothing in his **h** nor Is 39:2 1004
"What have they seen in your **h**?" Is 39:4 1004
have seen all that is in my **h**; Is 39:4 1004
coming when all that is in your **h** and Is 39:6 1004
of man, so that it may sit in a **h**. Is 44:13 1004
"Listen to Me, O **h** of Jacob, And Is 46:3 1004
the remnant of the **h** of Israel, Is 46:3 1004
"Hear this, O **h** of Jacob, who are Is 48:1 1004
To them I will give in My **h** and Is 56:5 1004
them joyful in My **h** of prayer. Is 56:7 1004
For My **h** will be called a house of Is 56:7 1004
h of prayer for all the peoples." Is 56:7 1004
And to the **h** of Jacob their sins. Is 58:1 1004
the homeless poor into the **h**; Is 58:7 1004
And I shall glorify My glorious **h**. Is 60:7 1004
goodness toward the **h** of Israel, Is 63:7 1004
Our holy and beautiful **h**, Is 64:11 1004
is a **h** you could build for Me? Is 66:1 1004
clean vessel to the **h** of the LORD. Is 66:20 1004
word of the LORD, O **h** of Jacob, Jer 2:4 1004
the families of the **h** of Israel. Jer 2:4 1004
So the **h** of Israel is shamed; Jer 2:26 1004
"In those days the **h** of Judah Jer 3:18 1004
will walk with the **h** of Israel, Jer 3:18 1004
with Me, O **h** of Israel," Jer 3:20 1004
And trooped to the harlot's **h**. Jer 5:7 1004
h of Israel and the house of Judah Jer 5:11 1004
house of Israel and the **h** of Judah Jer 5:11 1004
you from afar, O **h** of Israel," Jer 5:15 1004
"Declare this in the **h** of Jacob Jer 5:20 1004
"Stand in the gate of the LORD's **h** Jer 7:2 1004
and stand before Me in this **h**, Jer 7:10 1004
this **h**, which is called by My name, Jer 7:11 1004
the **h** which is called by My name, Jer 7:14 1004
the **h** which is called by My name, Jer 7:30 1004
all the **h** of Israel are uncircumcised Jer 9:26 1004
LORD speaks to you, O **h** of Israel. Jer 10:1 1004
h of Israel and the house of Judah Jer 11:10 1004
house of Israel and the **h** of Judah Jer 11:10 1004
"What right has My beloved in My **h** Jer 11:15 1004
because of the evil of the **h** of Israel Jer 11:17 1004
of Israel and of the **h** of Judah, Jer 11:17 1004
I have forsaken My **h**, Jer 12:7 1004
will uproot the **h** of Judah from Jer 12:14 1004
"Do not enter a **h** of mourning, or Jer 16:5 1004
you shall not go into a **h** of feasting Jer 16:8 1004
thanksgiving to the **h** of the LORD. Jer 17:26 1004
and go down to the potter's **h**, Jer 18:2 1004
Then I went down to the potter's **h**, Jer 18:3 1004
"Can I not, O **h** of Israel, deal Jer 18:6 1004
are you in My hand, O **h** of Israel. Jer 18:6 1004
stood in the court of the LORD's **h** Jer 19:14 1004
officer in the **h** of the LORD, Jer 20:1 1004
which was by the **h** of the LORD. Jer 20:2 1004
all who live in your **h** will go into Jer 20:6 1004
O **h** of David, thus says the LORD: Jer 21:12 1004
to the **h** of the king of Judah, Jer 22:1 1004
will enter the gates of this **h**, Jer 22:4 1004
that this **h** will become a desolation. Jer 22:5 1004
the **h** of the king of Judah: Jer 22:6 1004
"Woe to him who builds his **h** Jer 22:13 1004
roomy **h** With spacious upper rooms, Jer 22:14 1004
Even in My **h** I have found their Jer 23:11 1004
'Stand in the court of the LORD's **h**, Jer 26:2 1004
come to worship *in* the LORD's **h** Jer 26:2 1004
I will make this **h** like Shiloh, Jer 26:6 1004
these words in the **h** of the LORD. Jer 26:7 1004
'This **h** will be like Shiloh and Jer 26:9 1004
Jeremiah in the **h** of the LORD. Jer 26:9 1004
they came up from the king's **h** to Jer 26:10 1004
king's house to the **h** of the LORD Jer 26:10 1004
of the New Gate of the LORD's **h**. Jer 26:10 1004
sent me to prophesy against this **h** Jer 26:12 1004
And the mountain of the **h** as the Jer 26:18 1004
the vessels of the LORD's **h** will Jer 27:16 1004
are left in the **h** of the LORD, Jer 27:18 1004
in the **h** of the king of Judah and Jer 27:18 1004
are left in the **h** of the LORD and Jer 27:21 1004
and in the **h** of the king of Judah and Jer 27:21 1004
spoke to me in the **h** of the LORD Jer 28:1 1004
all the vessels of the LORD's **h**, Jer 28:3 1004
standing in the **h** of the LORD, Jer 28:5 1004
back the vessels of the LORD's **h** Jer 28:6 1004
be the overseer in the **h** of the LORD Jer 29:26 1004
"when I will sow the **h** of Israel Jer 31:27 1004
the **h** of Judah with the seed of man Jer 31:27 1004
a new covenant with the **h** of Israel Jer 31:31 1004
of Israel and with the **h** of Judah, Jer 31:31 1004
I will make with the **h** of Israel Jer 31:33 1004
was in the **h** of the king of Judah, Jer 32:2 1004
the **h** which is called by My name, Jer 32:34 1004
offering into the **h** of the LORD. Jer 33:11 1004
have spoken concerning the **h** of Israel Jer 33:14 1004
house of Israel and the **h** of Judah. Jer 33:14 1004
on the throne of the **h** of Israel; Jer 33:17 1004
of Egypt, from the **h** of bondage, Jer 34:13 1004
the **h** which is called by My name. Jer 34:15 1004
"Go to the **h** of the Rechabites and Jer 35:2 1004
bring them into the **h** of the LORD, Jer 35:2 1004
and the whole **h** of the Rechabites, Jer 35:3 1004
them into the **h** of the LORD, Jer 35:4 1004
the men of the **h** of the Rechabites Jer 35:5 1004
'You shall not build a **h**, Jer 35:7 1004
said to the **h** of the Rechabites, Jer 35:18 1004
"Perhaps the **h** of Judah will hear Jer 36:3 1004
cannot go into the **h** of the LORD. Jer 36:5 1004
in the LORD's **h** on a fast day. Jer 36:6 1004
words of the LORD in the LORD's **h**. Jer 36:8 1004
of Jeremiah in the **h** of the LORD Jer 36:10 1004
of the New Gate of the LORD's **h**, Jer 36:10 1004
he went down to the king's **h**, Jer 36:12 1004
the king was sitting in the winter **h** Jer 36:22 1004
in the **h** of Jonathan the scribe, Jer 37:15 1004
to the **h** of Jonathan the scribe, Jer 37:20 1004
that is in the **h** of the LORD; Jer 38:14 1004
return to the **h** of Jonathan to die Jer 38:26 1004
to bring to the **h** of the LORD. Jer 41:5 1004
as the **h** of Israel was ashamed of Jer 48:13 1004
The holy places of the LORD's **h**. Jer 51:51 1004
He burned the **h** of the LORD, Jer 52:13 1004
house of the LORD, the king's **h** and Jer 52:13 1004
every large **h** he burned with fire. Jer 52:13 1004
which belonged to the **h** of the LORD Jer 52:17 1004
which were in the **h** of the LORD, Jer 52:17 1004
had made for the **h** of the LORD Jer 52:20 1004
In the **h** it is like death. La 1:20 1004
made a noise in the **h** of the LORD La 2:7 1004
for they are a rebellious **h** Ezk 2:5 1004
for they are a rebellious **h**. Ezk 2:6 1004
rebellious like that rebellious **h**. Ezk 2:8 1004
go, speak to the **h** of Israel." Ezk 3:1 1004
go to the **h** of Israel and speak Ezk 3:4 1004
language, *but* to the **h** of Israel, Ezk 3:5 1004
yet the **h** of Israel will not be Ezk 3:7 1004
Surely the whole **h** of Israel is Ezk 3:7 1004
though they are a rebellious **h**." Ezk 3:9 1004
you a watchman to the **h** of Israel; Ezk 3:17 1004
"Go, shut yourself up in your **h**. Ezk 3:24 1004
them, for they are a rebellious **h**. Ezk 3:26 1004
for they are a rebellious **h**. Ezk 3:27 1004
This is a sign to the **h** of Israel. Ezk 4:3 1004
iniquity of the **h** of Israel on it; Ezk 4:4 1004
the iniquity of the **h** of Israel. Ezk 4:5 1004
the iniquity of the **h** of Judah; Ezk 4:6 1004
spread to all the **h** of Israel. Ezk 5:4 1004
abominations of the **h** of Israel, Ezk 6:11 1004
as I was sitting in my **h** with the Ezk 8:1 1004
h of Israel are committing here, Ezk 8:6 1004
all the idols of the **h** of Israel, Ezk 8:10 1004
seventy elders of the **h** of Israel, Ezk 8:11 1004
see what the elders of the **h** of Israel Ezk 8:12 1004
entrance of the gate of the LORD's **h** Ezk 8:14 1004
the inner court of the LORD's **h**. Ezk 8:16 1004
too light a thing for the **h** of Judah to Ezk 8:17 1004
iniquity of the **h** of Israel and Judah Ezk 9:9 1004
of the east gate of the LORD's **h**, Ezk 10:19 1004
to the east gate of the LORD's **h** Ezk 11:1 1004
"So you think, **h** of Israel, for I Ezk 11:5 1004
exiles and the whole **h** of Israel, Ezk 11:15 1004
in the midst of the rebellious **h**, Ezk 12:2 1004
for they are a rebellious **h**. Ezk 12:2 1004
though they are a rebellious **h**. Ezk 12:3 1004
as a sign to the **h** of Israel." Ezk 12:6 1004
Son of man, has not the **h** of Israel, Ezk 12:9 1004
house of Israel, the rebellious **h**, Ezk 12:9 1004
the **h** of Israel who are in it."' Ezk 12:10 1004
divination within the **h** of Israel. Ezk 12:24 1004
for in your days, O rebellious **h**, Ezk 12:25 1004
behold, the **h** of Israel is saying, Ezk 12:27 1004
build the wall around the **h** of Israel Ezk 13:5 1004
the register of the **h** of Israel, Ezk 13:9 1004
"Any man of the **h** of Israel who Ezk 14:4 1004
lay hold of the hearts of the **h** of Israel Ezk 14:5 1004
"Therefore say to the **h** of Israel, Ezk 14:6 1004
"For anyone of the **h** of Israel or Ezk 14:7 1004
in order that the **h** of Israel may Ezk 14:11 1004
a parable to the **h** of Israel, Ezk 17:2 1004
"Say now to the rebellious **h**, Ezk 17:12 1004
to the idols of the **h** of Israel, Ezk 18:6 1004
to the idols of the **h** of Israel, Ezk 18:15 1004
Hear now, O **h** of Israel! Ezk 18:25 1004
"But the **h** of Israel says, Ezk 18:29 1004
My ways not right, O **h** of Israel? Ezk 18:29 1004
I will judge you, O **h** of Israel, Ezk 18:30 1004
why will you die, O **h** of Israel? Ezk 18:31 1004
to the descendants of the **h** of Jacob Ezk 20:5 1004
"But the **h** of Israel rebelled Ezk 20:13 1004
of man, speak to the **h** of Israel and Ezk 20:27 1004
"Therefore, say to the **h** of Israel, Ezk 20:30 1004
inquired of by you, O **h** of Israel? Ezk 20:31 1004
"As for you, O **h** of Israel," Ezk 20:39 1004
"there the whole **h** of Israel, all Ezk 20:40 1004
corrupt deeds, O **h** of Israel," Ezk 20:44 1004
the **h** of Israel has become dross Ezk 22:18 1004
and lo, thus they did within My **h**. Ezk 23:39 1004
a parable to the rebellious **h** and Ezk 24:3 1004
'Speak to the **h** of Israel, Ezk 24:21 1004
and against the **h** of Judah when Ezk 25:3 1004
the **h** of Judah is like all the Ezk 25:8 1004
has acted against the **h** of Judah by Ezk 25:12 1004
will be no more for the **h** of Israel Ezk 28:24 1004
"When I gather the **h** of Israel Ezk 28:25 1004
staff *made* of reed to the **h** of Israel. Ezk 29:6 1004
the confidence of the **h** of Israel, Ezk 29:16 1004
a horn sprout for the **h** of Israel, Ezk 29:21 1004
a watchman for the **h** of Israel; Ezk 33:7 1004
of man, say to the **h** of Israel, Ezk 33:10 1004
then will you die, O **h** of Israel?' Ezk 33:11 1004
O **h** of Israel, I will judge each Ezk 33:20 1004
and that they, the **h** of Israel, Ezk 34:30 1004
the inheritance of the **h** of Israel Ezk 35:15 1004
men on you, all the **h** of Israel, Ezk 36:10 1004
when the **h** of Israel was living in Ezk 36:17 1004
which the **h** of Israel had profaned Ezk 36:21 1004
"Therefore say to the **h** of Israel, Ezk 36:22 1004
not for your sake, O **h** of Israel, Ezk 36:22 1004
for your ways, O **h** of Israel!" Ezk 36:32 1004
let the **h** of Israel ask Me to do for Ezk 36:37 1004
bones are the whole **h** of Israel; Ezk 37:11 1004
Ephraim and all the **h** of Israel, Ezk 37:16 1004
the **h** of Israel will be burying them Ezk 39:12 1004
"And the **h** of Israel will know that Ezk 39:22 1004
the **h** of Israel went into exile for their Ezk 39:23 1004
mercy on the whole **h** of Israel; Ezk 39:25 1004
My Spirit on the **h** of Israel," Ezk 39:29 1004
Declare to the **h** of Israel all that Ezk 40:4 1004
installed in the **h** all around; Ezk 40:43 1004
around about the **h** on every side. Ezk 41:5 1004
h had a raised platform all around; Ezk 41:8 1004
the entrance, and to the inner **h**, Ezk 41:17 1004
carved on all the **h** all around. Ezk 41:19 1004
the side chambers of the **h** and the Ezk 41:26 1004
finished measuring the inner **h**, Ezk 42:15 1004
the glory of the LORD came into the **h** Ezk 43:4 1004
glory of the LORD filled the **h**. Ezk 43:5 1004
one speaking to me from the **h**, Ezk 43:6 1004
And the **h** of Israel will not again Ezk 43:7 1004
the temple to the **h** of Israel, Ezk 43:10 1004
known to them the design of the **h**, Ezk 43:11 1004
"This is the law of the **h**: Ezk 43:12 1004
Behold, this is the law of the **h**. Ezk 43:12 1004
in the appointed place of the **h**, Ezk 43:21 1004
north gate to the front of the **h**; Ezk 44:4 1004
the LORD filled the **h** of the LORD, Ezk 44:4 1004
all the statutes of the **h** of the LORD Ezk 44:5 1004
mark well the entrance of the **h**, Ezk 44:5 1004

ones, to the **h** of Israel,	**Ezk 44:6**	1004
your abominations, O **h** of Israel,	**Ezk 44:6**	1004
sanctuary to profane it, *even* My **h**,	**Ezk 44:7**	1004
oversight at the gates of the **h** and	**Ezk 44:11**	1004
house and ministering in the **h**;	**Ezk 44:11**	1004
of iniquity to the **h** of Israel,	**Ezk 44:12**	1004
them to keep charge of the **h**,	**Ezk 44:14**	1004
of the inner court and in the **h**.	**Ezk 44:17**	1004
the offspring of the **h** of Israel,	**Ezk 44:22**	1004
a blessing to rest on your **h**.	**Ezk 44:30**	1004
Levites, the ministers of the **h**,	**Ezk 45:5**	1004
be for the whole **h** of Israel.	**Ezk 45:6**	1004
the land to the **h** of Israel according to	**Ezk 45:8**	1004
feasts of the **h** of Israel;	**Ezk 45:17**	1004
atonement for the **h** of Israel."	**Ezk 45:17**	1004
put *it* on the door posts of the **h**,	**Ezk 45:19**	1004
shall make atonement for the **h**.	**Ezk 45:20**	1004
the ministers of the **h** shall boil the	**Ezk 46:24**	1004
me back to the door of the **h**;	**Ezk 47:1**	1004
from under the threshold of the **h**	**Ezk 47:1**	1004
the east, for the **h** faced east.	**Ezk 47:1**	1004
from the right side of the **h**,	**Ezk 47:1**	1004
the sanctuary of the **h** shall be in	**Ezk 48:21**	1004
of the vessels of the **h** of God;	**Da 1:2**	1004
of Shinar, to the **h** of his god,	**Da 1:2**	1004
Daniel went to his **h** and informed	**Da 2:17**	1005
was at ease in my **h** and flourishing	**Da 4:4**	1005
h of God which *was* in Jerusalem;	**Da 5:3**	1005
the vessels of His **h** before you,	**Da 5:23**	1005
was signed, he entered his **h**	**Da 6:10**	1005
and I will punish the **h** of Jehu	**Hos 1:4**	1004
to the kingdom of the **h** of Israel.	**Hos 1:4**	1004
compassion on the **h** of Israel,	**Hos 1:6**	1004
have compassion on the **h** of Judah	**Hos 1:7**	1004
Give heed, O **h** of Israel!	**Hos 5:1**	1004
Listen, O **h** of the king!	**Hos 5:1**	1004
like rottenness to the **h** of Judah.	**Hos 5:12**	1004
a young lion to the **h** of Judah.	**Hos 5:14**	1004
In the **h** of Israel I have seen a	**Hos 6:10**	1004
comes against the **h** of the LORD,	**Hos 8:1**	1004
will not enter the **h** of the LORD.	**Hos 9:4**	1004
hostility in the **h** of his God.	**Hos 9:8**	1004
deeds I will drive them out of My **h**!	**Hos 9:15**	1004
And the **h** of Israel with deceit;	**Hos 11:12**	1004
cut off From the **h** of the LORD.	**Jl 1:9**	1004
withheld from the **h** of your God.	**Jl 1:13**	1004
To the **h** of the LORD your God,	**Jl 1:14**	1004
and joy from the **h** of our God?	**Jl 1:16**	1004
go out from the **h** of the LORD To	**Jl 3:18**	1004
send fire upon the **h** of Hazael And	**Am 1:4**	1004
And in the **h** of their God they	**Am 2:8**	1004
testify against the **h** of Jacob,"	**Am 3:13**	1004
"I will also smite the winter **h**	**Am 3:15**	1004
house together with the summer **h**;	**Am 3:15**	1004
for you as a dirge, O **h** of Israel:	**Am 5:1**	1004
ten left to the **h** of Israel."	**Am 5:3**	1004
says the LORD to the **h** of Israel,	**Am 5:4**	1004
forth like a fire, O **h** of Joseph,	**Am 5:6**	1004
for forty years, O **h** of Israel?	**Am 5:25**	1004
To whom the **h** of Israel comes.	**Am 6:1**	1004
be, if ten men are left in one **h**,	**Am 6:9**	1004
to carry out *his* bones from the **h**,	**Am 6:10**	1004
is in the innermost part of the **h**	**Am 6:10**	1004
command that the great **h** be smashed	**Am 6:11**	1004
and the small **h** to fragments.	**Am 6:11**	1004
against you, O **h** of Israel,"	**Am 6:14**	1004
I will rise up against the **h** of Jeroboam	**Am 7:9**	1004
in the midst of the **h** of Israel;	**Am 7:10**	1004
you speak against the **h** of Isaac.	**Am 7:16**	1004
totally destroy the **h** of Jacob,"	**Am 9:8**	1004
And I will shake the **h** of Israel	**Am 9:9**	1004
And the **h** of Jacob will possess	**Ob 1:17**	1004
"Then the **h** of Jacob will be a fire	**Ob 1:18**	1004
fire And the **h** of Joseph a flame;	**Ob 1:18**	1004
the **h** of Esau *will be* as stubble.	**Ob 1:18**	1004
be no survivor of the **h** of Esau,"	**Ob 1:18**	1004
for the sins of the **h** of Israel.	**Mi 1:5**	1004
They rob a man and his **h**,	**Mi 2:2**	1004
"Is it being said, O **h** of Jacob:	**Mi 2:7**	1004
Each *one* from her pleasant **h**.	**Mi 2:9**	1004
And rulers of the **h** of Israel.	**Mi 3:1**	1004
heads of the **h** of Jacob And rulers	**Mi 3:9**	1004
And rulers of the **h** of Israel,	**Mi 3:9**	1004
mountain of the **h** of the LORD Will be	**Mi 4:1**	1004
And to the **h** of the God of Jacob,	**Mi 4:2**	1004
ransomed you from the **h** of slavery	**Mi 6:4**	1004
there yet a man in the wicked **h**,	**Mi 6:10**	1004
all the works of the **h** of Ahab are	**Mi 6:16**	1004
and image From the **h** of your gods.	**Na 1:14**	1004
him who gets evil gain for his **h**	**Hab 2:9**	1004
devised a shameful thing for your **h**	**Hab 2:10**	1004
struck the head of the **h** of the evil	**Hab 3:13**	1004
Who fill the **h** of their lord with	**Zph 1:9**	1004
For the remnant of the **h** of Judah,	**Zph 2:7**	1004
for the **h** of the LORD to be rebuilt.	**Hg 1:2**	1004
while this **h** *lies* desolate?"	**Hg 1:4**	1004
of My **h** which *lies* desolate,	**Hg 1:9**	1004
each of you runs to his own **h**.	**Hg 1:9**	1004
on the **h** of the LORD of hosts,	**Hg 1:14**	1004
and I will fill this **h** with glory,'	**Hg 2:7**	1004
latter glory of this **h** will be greater	**Hg 2:9**	1004
My **h** will be built in it,"	**Zch 1:16**	1004
then you will also govern My **h** and	**Zch 3:7**	1004
laid the foundation of this **h**,	**Zch 4:9**	1004
it will enter the **h** of the thief and	**Zch 5:4**	1004
the **h** of the one who swears falsely	**Zch 5:4**	1004
it will spend the night within that **h**	**Zch 5:4**	1004
and enter the **h** of Josiah the son of	**Zch 6:10**	1004
to the **h** of the LORD of hosts,	**Zch 7:3**	1004
the foundation of the **h** of the LORD	**Zch 8:9**	1004
O **h** of Judah and house of Israel,	**Zch 8:13**	1004
O house of Judah and **h** of Israel,	**Zch 8:13**	1004
Jerusalem and to the **h** of Judah.	**Zch 8:15**	1004
feasts for the **h** of Judah;	**Zch 8:19**	1004
I will camp around My **h** because	**Zch 9:8**	1004
visited His flock, the **h** of Judah,	**Zch 10:3**	1004
"I will strengthen the **h** of Judah,	**Zch 10:6**	1004
And I will save the **h** of Joseph,	**Zch 10:6**	1004
the potter in the **h** of the LORD.	**Zch 11:13**	1004
I will watch over the **h** of Judah,	**Zch 12:4**	1004
that the glory of the **h** of David and	**Zch 12:7**	1004
the **h** of David *will be* like God,	**Zch 12:8**	1004
I will pour out on the **h** of David	**Zch 12:10**	1004
family of the **h** of David by itself and	**Zch 12:12**	1004
family of the **h** of Nathan by itself and	**Zch 12:12**	1004
family of the **h** of Levi by itself and	**Zch 12:13**	1004
will be opened for the **h** of David	**Zch 13:1**	1004
wounded in the **h** of my friends.'	**Zch 13:6**	1004
cooking pots in the LORD's **h** will be	**Zch 14:20**	1004
be a Canaanite in the **h** of the LORD	**Zch 14:21**	1004
so that there may be food in My **h**,	**Mal 3:10**	1004
After coming into the **h** they saw	**Mt 2:11**	*3614*
light to all who are in the **h**.	**Mt 5:15**	*3614*
who built his **h** on the rock	**Mt 7:24**	*3614*
blew and slammed against that **h**;	**Mt 7:25**	*3614*
who built his **h** on the sand.	**Mt 7:26**	*3614*
blew and slammed against that **h**;	**Mt 7:27**	*3614*
reclining *at the table* in the **h**,	**Mt 9:10**	*3614*
Jesus came into the official's **h**,	**Mt 9:23**	*3614*
When He entered the **h**,	**Mt 9:28**	*3614*
the lost sheep of the **h** of Israel.	**Mt 10:6**	*3624*
and stay at his **h** until you leave	**Mt 10:11**	*2546*
"As you enter the **h**,	**Mt 10:12**	*3614*
"If the **h** is worthy, give it your	**Mt 10:13**	*3614*
you go out of that **h** or that city,	**Mt 10:14**	*3614*
the head of the **h** Beelzebul,	**Mt 10:25**	*3617*
how he entered the **h** of God,	**Mt 12:4**	*3624*
any city or **h** divided against itself	**Mt 12:25**	*3614*
anyone enter the strong man's **h**	**Mt 12:29**	*3614*
And then he will plunder his **h**.	**Mt 12:29**	*3614*
return to my **h** from which I came';	**Mt 12:44**	*3624*
That day Jesus went out of the **h**	**Mt 13:1**	*3614*
crowds and went into the **h**.	**Mt 13:36**	*3614*
lost sheep of the **h** of Israel."	**Mt 15:24**	*3624*
And when he came into the **h**,	**Mt 17:25**	*3614*
'MY **H** SHALL BE CALLED A HOUSE OF	**Mt 21:13**	*3624*
'MY HOUSE SHALL BE CALLED A **H** OF	**Mt 21:13**	*3624*
h is being left to you desolate!	**Mt 23:38**	*3624*
the things out that are in his **h**.	**Mt 24:17**	*3614*
that if the head of the **h** had	**Mt 24:43**	*3617*
allowed his **h** to be broken into.	**Mt 24:43**	*3614*
I *am to* keep the Passover at your **h**	**Mt 26:18**	
into the **h** of Simon and Andrew,	**Mk 1:29**	*3614*
left *the* **h**, and went away to a	**Mk 1:35**	
reclining *at the table* in his **h**,	**Mk 2:15**	*3614*
how he entered the **h** of God in the	**Mk 2:26**	*3624*
If a **h** is divided against itself,	**Mk 3:25**	*3614*
that **h** will not be able to stand.	**Mk 3:25**	*3614*
no one can enter the strong man's **h**	**Mk 3:27**	*3614*
and then he will plunder his **h**.	**Mk 3:27**	*3614*
they came from the **h** *of*	**Mk 5:35**	
the **h** of the synagogue official;	**Mk 5:38**	*3624*
"Wherever you enter a **h**,	**Mk 6:10**	*3614*
crowd *and* entered the **h**,	**Mk 7:17**	*3624*
And when He had entered a **h**,	**Mk 7:24**	*3614*
When He came into *the* **h**,	**Mk 9:28**	*3624*
and when He was in the **h**,	**Mk 9:33**	*3614*
In the **h** the disciples	**Mk 10:10**	*3614*
there is no one who has left **h** or	**Mk 10:29**	*3614*
'MY **H** SHALL BE CALLED A HOUSE OF	**Mk 11:17**	*3624*
'MY HOUSE SHALL BE CALLED A **H** OF	**Mk 11:17**	*3624*
in to get anything out of his **h**;	**Mk 13:15**	*3614*
who upon leaving his **h** and putting	**Mk 13:34**	*3614*
the master of the **h** is coming,	**Mk 13:35**	*3614*
enters, say to the owner of the **h**,	**Mk 14:14**	*3617*
reign over the **h** of Jacob forever,	**Lk 1:33**	*3624*
and entered the **h** of Zacharias and	**Lk 1:40**	*3624*
us In the **h** of David His servant	**Lk 1:69**	*3624*
was of the **h** and family of David,	**Lk 2:4**	*3624*
that I had to be in My Father's **h**?"	**Lk 2:49**	
a big reception for Him in his **h**;	**Lk 5:29**	*3614*
how he entered the **h** of God,	**Lk 6:4**	*3624*
he is like a man building a **h**,	**Lk 6:48**	*3614*
the torrent burst against that **h** and	**Lk 6:48**	*3614*
man who built a **h** on the ground	**Lk 6:49**	*3614*
the ruin of that **h** was great."	**Lk 6:49**	*3614*
He was not far from the **h**,	**Lk 7:6**	*3614*
had been sent returned to the **h**,	**Lk 7:10**	*3624*
and He entered the Pharisee's **h**	**Lk 7:36**	*3624*
at the table in the Pharisee's **h**,	**Lk 7:37**	*3614*
I entered your **h**;	**Lk 7:44**	*3614*
time, and was not living in a **h**,	**Lk 8:27**	*3614*
"Return to your **h** and describe	**Lk 8:39**	*3624*
to implore Him to come to his **h**;	**Lk 8:41**	*3624*
someone came from *the* **h** *of*	**Lk 8:49**	
When He came to the **h**,	**Lk 8:51**	*3614*
"Whatever **h** you enter, stay	**Lk 9:4**	*3614*
"Whatever **h** you enter, first	**Lk 10:5**	*3614*
'Peace *be* to this **h**.'	**Lk 10:5**	*3624*
Stay in that **h**, eating and drinking	**Lk 10:7**	*3614*
not keep moving from **h** to house.	**Lk 10:7**	*3614*
not keep moving from house to **h**.	**Lk 10:7**	*3614*
a **h** *divided* against itself falls.	**Lk 11:17**	*3624*
guards his own **h**, his possessions	**Lk 11:21**	*833*
return to my **h** from which I came.'	**Lk 11:24**	*3624*
the altar and the **h** *of God*	**Lk 11:51**	*3624*
that if the head of the **h** had	**Lk 12:39**	*3617*
allowed his **h** to be broken into.	**Lk 12:39**	*3624*
the head of the **h** gets up and shuts	**Lk 13:25**	*3617*
your **h** is left to you	**Lk 13:35**	*3624*
went into the **h** of one of the leaders	**Lk 14:1**	*3624*
come in, so that my **h** may be filled.	**Lk 14:23**	*3624*
sweep the **h** and search carefully until	**Lk 15:8**	*3614*
when he came and approached the **h**,	**Lk 15:25**	*3614*
that you send him to my father's **h**	**Lk 16:27**	*3624*
whose goods are in the **h** must not	**Lk 17:31**	*3614*
this man went to his **h**	**Lk 18:14**	*3624*
there is no one who has left **h** or	**Lk 18:29**	*3614*
for today I must stay at your **h**."	**Lk 19:5**	*3624*
salvation has come to this **h**,	**Lk 19:9**	*3624*
'AND MY **H** SHALL BE A HOUSE OF	**Lk 19:46**	*3624*
'AND MY HOUSE SHALL BE A **H** OF	**Lk 19:46**	*3624*
follow him into the **h** that he enters.	**Lk 22:10**	*3614*
shall say to the owner of the **h**,	**Lk 22:11**	*3614*
Him to the **h** of the high priest;	**Lk 22:54**	*3614*
stop making My Father's **h** a place	**Jn 2:16**	*3624*
"ZEAL FOR YOUR **H** WILL CONSUME ME."	**Jn 2:17**	*3624*
does not remain in the **h** forever;	**Jn 8:35**	*3614*
but Mary stayed at the **h**.	**Jn 11:20**	*3624*
Jews who were with her in the **h**,	**Jn 11:31**	*3614*
the **h** was filled with the fragrance	**Jn 12:3**	*3614*
In My Father's **h** are many dwelling	**Jn 14:2**	*3614*
filled the whole **h** where they were	**Ac 2:2**	*3624*
all the **h** of Israel know for certain	**Ac 2:36**	*3624*
breaking bread from **h** to house,	**Ac 2:46**	*3624*
breaking bread from house to **h**,	**Ac 2:46**	*3624*
prison **h** for them to be brought.	**Ac 5:21**	*1201*
"We found the prison **h** locked	**Ac 5:23**	*1201*
in the temple and from **h** to house,	**Ac 5:42**	*3624*
in the temple and from house to **h**,	**Ac 5:42**	*3624*
O **H** OF ISRAEL?	**Ac 7:42**	*3624*
was Solomon who built a **h** for Him.	**Ac 7:47**	*3624*
KIND OF **H** WILL YOU BUILD FOR ME?'	**Ac 7:49**	*3624*
church, entering **h** after house,	**Ac 8:3**	*3624*
church, entering house after **h**,	**Ac 8:3**	*3624*
and inquire at the **h** of Judas for	**Ac 9:11**	*3614*
departed and entered the **h**,	**Ac 9:17**	*3614*
Simon, whose **h** is by the sea."	**Ac 10:6**	*3614*
asked directions for Simon's **h**,	**Ac 10:17**	*3614*
to send for you *to come* to his **h** and	**Ac 10:22**	*3624*
I was praying in my **h** during the	**Ac 10:30**	*3624*
he is staying at the **h** of Simon	**Ac 10:32**	*3614*
three men appeared at the **h**	**Ac 11:11**	*3614*
me and we entered the man's **h**.	**Ac 11:12**	*3624*
seen the angel standing in his **h**,	**Ac 11:13**	*3624*
this, he went to the **h** of Mary,	**Ac 12:12**	*3614*
Lord, come into my **h** and stay."	**Ac 16:15**	*3624*
of the prison **h** were shaken;	**Ac 16:26**	*1201*
with all who were in his **h**.	**Ac 16:32**	*3614*
he brought them into his **h** and set	**Ac 16:34**	*3624*
out of the prison and entered *the* **h**	**Ac 16:40**	
and attacking the **h** of Jason,	**Ac 17:5**	*3614*
the **h** of a man named Titius	**Ac 18:7**	*3614*
whose **h** was next to the synagogue.	**Ac 18:7**	*3614*
they fled out of that **h** naked and	**Ac 19:16**	*3624*
you publicly and from **h** to house,	**Ac 20:20**	*3624*
you publicly and from house to **h**,	**Ac 20:20**	*3624*
the **h** of Philip the evangelist,	**Ac 21:8**	*3624*
the church that is in their **h**.	**Ro 16:5**	*3624*
the church that is in their **h**.	**1Co 16:19**	*3624*
earthly tent which is our **h** is torn	**2Co 5:1**	*3624*
from God, a **h** not made with hands,	**2Co 5:1**	*3624*
For indeed in this **h** we groan,	**2Co 5:2**	
and the church that is in her **h**.	**Col 4:15**	*3624*
as they go around from **h** to house;	**1Tm 5:13**	*3614*
as they go around from house to **h**;	**1Tm 5:13**	*3614*
married, bear children, keep **h**,	**1Tm 5:14**	*3616*
grant mercy to the **h** of Onesiphorus	**2Tm 1:16**	*3624*
in a large **h** there are not only gold	**2Tm 2:20**	*3614*
and to the church in your **h**:	**Phm 1:2**	*3624*
as Moses also was in all His **h**.	**Heb 3:2**	*3624*
the builder of the **h** has more honor	**Heb 3:3**	*3624*
house has more honor than the **h**.	**Heb 3:3**	*3624*
For every **h** is built by someone,	**Heb 3:4**	*3624*
Moses was faithful in all His **h** as a	**Heb 3:5**	*3624*
was faithful as a Son over His **h**	**Heb 3:6**	*3624*
Son over His house—whose **h** we are,	**Heb 3:6**	*3624*
WILL EFFECT A NEW COVENANT WITH THE **H**	**Heb 8:8**	*3624*
THE HOUSE OF ISRAEL AND WITH THE **H** OF	**Heb 8:8**	*3624*
COVENANT THAT I WILL MAKE WITH THE **H**	**Heb 8:10**	*3624*
a great priest over the **h** of God,	**Heb 10:21**	*3624*
spiritual **h** for a holy priesthood,	**1Pe 2:5**	*3624*
do not receive him into *your* **h**,	**2Jn 1:10**	*3614*

HOUSEHOLD

"Enter the ark, you and all your **h**	**Gn 7:1**	1004
male among the men of Abraham's **h**,	**Gn 17:23**	1004
All the men of his **h**,	**Gn 17:27**	1004
may command his children and his **h**	**Gn 18:19**	1004
the wombs of the **h** of Abimelech	**Gn 20:18**	1004
his servant, the oldest of his **h**,	**Gn 24:2**	1004
her mother's **h** about these things.	**Gn 24:28**	1004
of flocks and herds and a great **h**,	**Gn 26:14**	5657
I provide for my own **h** also?"	**Gn 30:30**	1004
Rachel stole the **h** idols that were	**Gn 31:19**	8655
Now Rachel had taken the **h** idols	**Gn 31:34**	8655
but did not find the **h** idols.	**Gn 31:35**	8655
you found of all your **h** goods?	**Gn 31:37**	1004
than all the **h** of his father.	**Gn 34:19**	1004
will be destroyed, I and my **h**."	**Gn 34:30**	1004
Jacob said to his **h** and to all who	**Gn 35:2**	1004
and his daughters and all his **h**	**Gn 36:6**	1004
none of the men of the **h** was there	**Gn 39:11**	1004
she called to the men of her **h** and	**Gn 39:14**	1004
my trouble and all my father's **h**."	**Gn 41:51**	1004
and the **h** of Pharaoh heard *of it.*	**Gn 45:2**	1004
lord of all his **h** and ruler over all the	**Gn 45:8**	1004
and you and your **h** and all that	**Gn 45:11**	1004

his brothers and to his father's **h**,	**Gn 46:31**	1004
'My brothers and my father's **h**,	**Gn 46:31**	1004
and all his father's **h** with food,	**Gn 47:12**	1004
Joseph spoke to the **h** of Pharaoh,	**Gn 50:4**	1004
the elders of his **h** and all the	**Gn 50:7**	1004
and all the **h** of Joseph and his	**Gn 50:8**	1004
his brothers and his father's **h**;	**Gn 50:8**	1004
in Egypt, he and his father's **h**,	**Gn 50:22**	1004
they came each one with his **h**:	**Ex 1:1**	1004
households, a lamb for each **h**.	**Ex 12:3**	1004
if the **h** is too small for a lamb,	**Ex 12:4**	1004
for himself and for his **h**.	**Lv 16:6**	1004
for himself and for his **h**,	**Lv 16:11**	1004
atonement for himself and for his **h**	**Lv 16:17**	1004
each one head of his father's **h**.	**Nu 1:4**	1004
each of whom was of his father's **h**.	**Nu 1:44**	1004
according to his father's **h**.	**Nu 2:34**	1004
Moses, He is faithful in all My **h**;	**Nu 12:7**	1004
them a rod for each father's **h**:	**Nu 17:2**	1004
father's **h** with you shall bear the guilt	**Nu 18:1**	1004
Everyone of your **h** who is clean	**Nu 18:11**	1004
everyone of your **h** who is clean	**Nu 18:13**	1004
son of Salu, a leader of a father's **h**	**Nu 25:14**	1004
head of the people of a father's **h** in	**Nu 25:15**	1004
Egypt, Pharaoh and all his **h**;	**Dt 6:22**	1004
God and rejoice, you and your **h**.	**Dt 14:26**	1004
because he loves you and your **h**,	**Dt 15:16**	1004
"You and your **h** shall eat it	**Dt 15:20**	1004
your God has given you and your **h**.	**Dt 26:11**	1004
deal kindly with my father's **h**,	**Jos 2:12**	1004
brothers and all your father's **h**,	**Jos 2:18**	1004
Rahab the harlot and her father's **h**	**Jos 6:25**	1004
and the **h** which the LORD takes	**Jos 7:14**	1004
He brought his **h** near man by man;	**Jos 7:18**	1004
one chief for each father's **h** from	**Jos 22:14**	1004
the head of his father's **h** among the	**Jos 22:14**	1004
he was too afraid of his father's **h** and	**Jg 6:27**	1004
a snare to Gideon and his **h**.	**Jg 8:27**	1004
kindness to the **h** of Jerubbaal	**Jg 8:35**	1004
clan of the **h** of his mother's father,	**Jg 9:1**	1004
and all his father's **h** came down,	**Jg 16:31**	1004
he made an ephod and **h** idols	**Jg 17:5**	8655
in these houses an ephod and **h** idols	**Jg 18:14**	8655
and **h** idols and the molten image,	**Jg 18:17**	8655
and **h** idols and the molten image,	**Jg 18:18**	8655
and **h** idols and the graven image and	**Jg 18:20**	8655
life, with the lives of your **h**."	**Jg 18:25**	1004
Elkanah went up with all his **h** to offer	**1Sa 1:21**	1004
you and for all your father's **h**?"	**1Sa 9:20**	1004
Michal took the **h** idol and laid	**1Sa 19:13**	8655
the **h** idol *was* on the bed with the	**1Sa 19:16**	8655
and all his father's **h** heard *of it,*	**1Sa 22:1**	1004
of Ahitub, and all his father's **h**,	**1Sa 22:11**	1004
or to any of the **h** of my father,	**1Sa 22:15**	1004
you and all your father's **h**!"	**1Sa 22:16**	1004
of every person in your father's **h**.	**1Sa 22:22**	1004
my name from my father's **h**."	**1Sa 24:21**	1004
our master and against all his **h**;	**1Sa 25:17**	1004
he and his men, each with his **h**,	**1Sa 27:3**	1004
were with him, each with his **h**;	**2Sa 2:3**	1004
blessed Obed-edom and all his **h**.	**2Sa 6:11**	1004
David returned to bless his **h**,	**2Sa 6:20**	1004
evil against you from your own **h**;	**2Sa 12:11**	1004
The elders of his **h** stood	**2Sa 12:17**	1004
went out and all his **h** with him.	**2Sa 15:16**	1004
are for the king's **h** to ride,	**2Sa 16:2**	1004
ford to bring over the king's **h**,	**2Sa 19:18**	1004
"For all my father's **h** was	**2Sa 19:28**	1004
and brought the king and his **h** and	**2Sa 19:41**	1004
and Ahishar was over the **h**;	**1Ki 4:6**	1004
provided for the king and his **h**;	**1Ki 4:7**	1004
desire by giving food to my **h**."	**1Ki 5:9**	1004
kors of wheat as food for his **h**,	**1Ki 5:11**	1004
struck down all the **h** of Jeroboam.	**1Ki 15:29**	1004
came against Baasha and his **h**,	**1Ki 16:7**	1004
who *was* over the **h** at Tirzah.	**1Ki 16:9**	1004
he killed all the **h** of Baasha;	**1Ki 16:11**	1004
destroyed all the **h** of Baasha,	**1Ki 16:12**	1004
he and her his **h** ate for *many* days.	**1Ki 17:15**	1004
called Obadiah who *was* over the **h**.	**1Ki 18:3**	1004
let us go and tell the king's **h**."	**2Ki 7:9**	1004
and told *it* within the king's **h**.	**2Ki 7:11**	1004
"Arise and go with your **h**,	**2Ki 8:1**	1004
and she went with her **h** and	**2Ki 8:2**	1004
And the one who *was* over the **h**,	**2Ki 10:5**	1004
Jotham the king's son was over the **h**,	**2Ki 15:5**	1004
son of Hilkiah, who was over the **h**,	**2Ki 18:18**	1004
son of Hilkiah, who was over the **h**,	**2Ki 18:37**	1004
he sent Eliakim who was over the **h**	**2Ki 19:2**	1004
and David returned to bless his **h**.	**1Ch 16:43**	1004
be against me and my father's **h**,	**1Ch 21:17**	1004
sons, so they became a father's **h**,	**1Ch 23:11**	1004
one father's **h** taken for Eleazar	**1Ch 24:6**	1004
by division of a father's **h**.	**2Ch 35:5**	1004
I threw all of Tobiah's **h** goods out	**Ne 13:8**	1004
given orders to each official of his **h**	**Es 1:8**	1004
does he care for his **h** after him,	**Jb 21:21**	1004
your food, For the food of your **h**,	**Pr 27:27**	1004
night And gives food to her **h**	**Pr 31:15**	1004
not afraid of the snow for her **h**,	**Pr 31:21**	1004
her **h** are clothed with scarlet.	**Pr 31:21**	1004
looks well to the ways of her **h**,	**Pr 31:27**	1004
who is in charge of the *royal* **h**,	**Is 22:15**	1004
son of Hilkiah, who was over the **h**,	**Is 36:3**	1004
son of Hilkiah, who was over the **h**,	**Is 36:22**	1004
he sent Eliakim who was over the **h**	**Is 37:2**	1004
brothers and the **h** of your father,	**Jer 12:6**	1004
so I made the whole **h** of Israel	**Jer 13:11**	1004
the whole **h** of Judah cling to Me,'	**Jer 13:11**	1004
say to the **h** of the king of Judah,	**Jer 21:11**	1004
the descendants of the **h** of Israel	**Jer 23:8**	1004
upon that man and his **h**.	**Jer 23:34**	1004
and you and your **h** will survive.	**Jer 38:17**	1004
arrows, he consults the **h** idols,	**Ezk 21:21**	8655
and without ephod or **h** idols.	**Hos 3:4**	8655
enemies are the men of his own **h**.	**Mi 7:6**	1004
malign the members of his **h**!	**Mt 10:25**	*3615*
ENEMIES WILL BE THE MEMBERS OF HIS **H**	**Mt 10:36**	*3615*
of heaven is like a head of a **h**,	**Mt 13:52**	*3617*
his hometown and in his *own* **h**."	**Mt 13:57**	*3614*
his master put in charge of his **h**	**Mt 24:45**	*3610a*
own relatives and in his *own* **h**."	**Mk 6:4**	*3614*
members in one **h** will be divided,	**Lk 12:52**	*3624*
the head of the **h** became angry and	**Lk 14:21**	*3617*
himself believed and his whole **h**.	**Jn 4:53**	*3614*
disciple took her into his own **h**.	**Jn 19:27**	
governor over Egypt and all his **h**.	**Ac 7:10**	*3624*
one who feared God with all his **h**,	**Ac 10:2**	*3624*
be saved, you and all your **h**.'	**Ac 11:14**	*3624*
she and her **h** had been baptized,	**Ac 16:15**	*3624*
will be saved, you and your **h**."	**Ac 16:31**	*3624*
he and all his **h**.	**Ac 16:33**	
believed in God with his whole **h**.	**Ac 16:34**	*3832*
believed in the Lord with all his **h**,	**Ac 18:8**	*3624*
Greet those who are of the **h** of	**Ro 16:10**	
Greet those of the **h** of Narcissus,	**Ro 16:11**	
baptize also the **h** of Stephanas;	**1Co 1:16**	*3624*
(you know the **h** of Stephanas,	**1Co 16:15**	*3614*
especially to those who are of the **h**	**Ga 6:10**	*3609b*
the saints, and are of God's **h**,	**Eph 2:19**	*3609b*
especially those of Caesar's **h**.	**Php 4:22**	*3614*
be one who manages his own **h** well,	**1Tm 3:4**	*3624*
not know how to manage his own **h**,	**1Tm 3:5**	*3624*
conduct himself in the **h** of God,	**1Tm 3:15**	*3624*
and especially for those of his **h**,	**1Tm 5:8**	*3609b*
Aquila, and the **h** of Onesiphorus.	**2Tm 4:19**	*3624*
an ark for the salvation of his **h**,	**Heb 11:7**	*3624*
to begin with the **h** of God;	**1Pe 4:17**	*3624*

HOUSEHOLDS

grain for the famine of your **h**,	**Gn 42:19**	1004
grain for the famine of your **h**,	**Gn 42:33**	1004
father and your **h** and come to me,	**Gn 45:18**	1004
for your food and for those of your **h**	**Gn 47:24**	1004
He established **h** for them.	**Ex 1:21**	1004
are the heads of their fathers' **h**.	**Ex 6:14**	1004
are the heads of the fathers' **h**	**Ex 6:25**	
according to their fathers' **h**,	**Ex 12:3**	1004
families, by their fathers' **h**,	**Nu 1:2**	1004
families, by their fathers' **h**,	**Nu 1:18**	1004
families, by their fathers' **h**,	**Nu 1:20**	1004
families, by their fathers' **h**,	**Nu 1:22**	1004
families, by their fathers' **h**,	**Nu 1:24**	1004
families, by their fathers' **h**,	**Nu 1:26**	1004
families, by their fathers' **h**,	**Nu 1:28**	1004
families, by their fathers' **h**,	**Nu 1:30**	1004
families, by their fathers' **h**,	**Nu 1:32**	1004
families, by their fathers' **h**,	**Nu 1:34**	1004
families, by their fathers' **h**,	**Nu 1:36**	1004
families, by their fathers' **h**,	**Nu 1:38**	1004
families, by their fathers' **h**,	**Nu 1:40**	1004
families, by their fathers' **h**,	**Nu 1:42**	1004
sons of Israel by their fathers' **h**,	**Nu 1:45**	1004
the banners of their fathers' **h**;	**Nu 2:2**	1004
of Israel by their fathers' **h**;	**Nu 2:32**	1004
sons of Levi by their fathers' **h**,	**Nu 3:15**	1004
according to their fathers' **h**.	**Nu 3:20**	1004
and the leader of the fathers' **h**	**Nu 3:24**	1004
and the leader of the fathers' **h**	**Nu 3:30**	1004
The leader of the fathers' **h**	**Nu 3:35**	1004
families, by their fathers' **h**,	**Nu 4:2**	1004
Gershon also, by their fathers' **h**,	**Nu 4:22**	1004
families, by their fathers' **h**;	**Nu 4:29**	1004
families and by their fathers' **h**,	**Nu 4:34**	1004
families and by their fathers' **h**,	**Nu 4:38**	1004
families, by their fathers' **h**,	**Nu 4:40**	1004
families, by their fathers' **h**,	**Nu 4:42**	1004
families and by their fathers' **h**,	**Nu 4:46**	1004
the heads of their fathers' **h**,	**Nu 7:2**	1004
swallowed them up, and their **h**,	**Nu 16:32**	1004
according to their fathers' **h**.	**Nu 17:2**	1004
head *of each* of their fathers' **h**.	**Nu 17:3**	1004
according to their fathers' **h**,	**Nu 17:6**	1004
eat it anywhere, you and your **h**,	**Nu 18:31**	1004
and upward, by their fathers' **h**,	**Nu 26:2**	1004
and the heads of the fathers' **h**	**Nu 31:26**	
and to the heads of the fathers' **h**	**Nu 32:28**	
according to their fathers' **h**,	**Nu 34:14**	1004
Gad according to their fathers' **h**,	**Nu 34:14**	1004
And the heads of the fathers' **h**	**Nu 36:1**	
the heads of the fathers' **h** of	**Nu 36:1**	
mouth and swallowed them, their **h**	**Dt 11:6**	1004
your **h** shall eat before the LORD	**Dt 12:7**	1004
LORD takes shall come near by **h**,	**Jos 7:14**	1004
the heads of the **h** of the tribes of	**Jos 14:1**	1
the heads of the **h** of the tribes of	**Jos 19:51**	1
Then the heads of **h** of the Levites	**Jos 21:1**	1
the heads of **h** of the tribes of the	**Jos 21:1**	1
the leaders of the fathers' **h** of	**1Ki 8:1**	
Their kinsmen of their fathers' **h**	**1Ch 5:13**	1004
was head of their fathers' **h**.	**1Ch 5:15**	1004
were the heads of their fathers' **h**,	**1Ch 5:24**	1004
men, heads of their fathers' **h**.	**1Ch 5:24**	1004
according to their fathers' **h**.	**1Ch 6:19**	
Samuel, heads of their fathers' **h**.	**1Ch 7:2**	1004
according to their fathers' **h** were	**1Ch 7:4**	1004
They *were* heads of fathers' **h**,	**1Ch 7:7**	1004
heads of their fathers' **h**,	**1Ch 7:9**	1004
to the heads of their fathers' **h**,	**1Ch 7:11**	1
these are the heads of fathers' **h**	**1Ch 8:6**	
heads of fathers' **h**.	**1Ch 8:10**	
who were heads of fathers' **h** of	**1Ch 8:13**	
These were heads of the fathers' **h**	**1Ch 8:28**	
these *were* heads of fathers' **h**	**1Ch 9:9**	
heads of their fathers' **h**,	**1Ch 9:13**	1004
heads of fathers' **h** of	**1Ch 9:33**	
These were heads of fathers' **h**	**1Ch 9:34**	
famous men in their fathers' **h**.	**1Ch 12:30**	1004
are the heads of the fathers' **h**	**1Ch 15:12**	
were the heads of the fathers' **h**	**1Ch 23:9**	
Levi according to their fathers' **h**,	**1Ch 23:24**	1004
even the heads of the fathers' **h**	**1Ch 23:24**	
sixteen heads of fathers' **h** of the	**1Ch 24:4**	1004
according to their fathers' **h**.	**1Ch 24:4**	1004
and the heads of the fathers' **h**	**1Ch 24:6**	
according to their fathers' **h**.	**1Ch 24:30**	1004
and the heads of the fathers' **h**	**1Ch 24:31**	
the head of fathers' **h**	**1Ch 24:31**	
according to their fathers' **h**,	**1Ch 26:13**	1004
were the heads of the fathers' **h**,	**1Ch 26:21**	
and the heads of the fathers' **h**	**1Ch 26:26**	
their genealogies and fathers' **h**,	**1Ch 26:31**	
2,700 in number, heads of fathers' **h**.	**1Ch 26:32**	
the heads of fathers' **h**,	**1Ch 27:1**	
Then the rulers of the fathers' **h**,	**1Ch 29:6**	
the heads of the fathers' **h**.	**2Ch 1:2**	
the leaders of the fathers' **h** of	**2Ch 5:2**	
according to their fathers' **h**:	**2Ch 17:14**	1004
of the heads of the fathers' **h**	**2Ch 19:8**	
and the heads of the fathers' **h**	**2Ch 23:2**	
them according to *their* fathers' **h**	**2Ch 25:5**	1004
number of the heads of the **h**,	**2Ch 26:12**	1
according to their fathers' **h**,	**2Ch 31:17**	1004
your fathers' **h** in your divisions,	**2Ch 35:4**	1004
the sections of the fathers' **h** of your	**2Ch 35:5**	1004
of the fathers' **h** of the lay people	**2Ch 35:12**	1004
Then the heads of fathers' **h** of	**Ezr 1:5**	
give evidence of their fathers' **h** and	**Ezr 2:59**	1004
Some of the heads of fathers' **h**,	**Ezr 2:68**	
Levites and heads of fathers' **h**,	**Ezr 3:12**	
and the heads of fathers' **h**,	**Ezr 4:2**	
rest of the heads of fathers' **h**	**Ezr 4:3**	
are the heads of their fathers' **h**	**Ezr 8:1**	
and the heads of the fathers' **h**	**Ezr 8:29**	
who were heads of fathers' **h**	**Ezr 10:16**	
for *each of* their father's **h**,	**Ezr 10:16**	1004
from among the heads of fathers' **h**	**Ne 7:70**	
Some of the heads of fathers' **h**	**Ne 7:71**	
second day the heads of fathers' **h**	**Ne 8:13**	
God, according to our fathers' **h**,	**Ne 10:34**	1004
heads of fathers' **h**, 242;	**Ne 11:13**	
the heads of fathers' **h** were:	**Ne 12:12**	
the heads of fathers' **h** were	**Ne 12:22**	
the heads of fathers' **h**, were	**Ne 12:23**	
of *their* children and their own **h**.	**1Tm 3:12**	*3624*
those who enter into **h** and captivate	**2Tm 3:6**	*3614*

HOUSES

wives, even all that *was* in the **h**.	**Gn 34:29**	1004
and into the **h** of your servants	**Ex 8:3**	1004
be destroyed from you and your **h**,	**Ex 8:9**	1004
frogs will depart from you and your **h**	**Ex 8:11**	1004
and the frogs died out of the **h**,	**Ex 8:13**	1004
on your people and into your **h**;	**Ex 8:21**	1004
and the **h** of the Egyptians will	**Ex 8:21**	1004
and the **h** of his servants and the land	**Ex 8:24**	1004
and his livestock flee into the **h**;	**Ex 9:20**	1004
Then your **h** shall be filled and	**Ex 10:6**	1004
and the **h** of all your servants and	**Ex 10:6**	1004
and the **h** of all the Egyptians,	**Ex 10:6**	1004
lintel of the **h** in which they eat it.	**Ex 12:7**	1004
for you on the **h** where you live;	**Ex 12:13**	1004
shall remove leaven from your **h**;	**Ex 12:15**	1004
be no leaven found in your **h**;	**Ex 12:19**	1004
to come in to your **h** to smite *you.*	**Ex 12:23**	1004
passed over the **h** of the sons of Israel	**Ex 12:27**	1004
'The **h** of the villages, however,	**Lv 25:31**	1004
redemption for the **h** of the cities	**Lv 25:32**	1004
for the **h** of the cities of the	**Lv 25:33**	1004
and **h** full of all good things	**Dt 6:11**	1004
built good **h** and lived *in them,*	**Dt 8:12**	1004
in their cities and in their **h**,	**Dt 19:1**	1004
out of our **h** on the day that we left	**Jos 9:12**	1004
there are in these **h** an ephod and	**Jg 18:14**	1004
the men who *were* in the **h** near	**Jg 18:22**	1004
which Solomon had built the two **h**,	**1Ki 9:10**	1004
And he made **h** on high places, and	**1Ki 12:31**	1004
against all the **h** of the high places	**1Ki 13:32**	1004
house and the **h** of your servants;	**1Ki 20:6**	1004
put them in the **h** of the high places	**2Ki 17:29**	1004
them in the **h** of the high places.	**2Ki 17:32**	1004
the **h** of the *male* cult prostitutes	**2Ki 23:7**	1004
removed all the **h** of the high places	**2Ki 23:19**	1004
house, and all the **h** of Jerusalem;	**2Ki 25:9**	1004
their fathers' **h** increased greatly.	**1Ch 4:38**	1004
of Asher, heads of the fathers' **h**,	**1Ch 7:40**	1004
according to their fathers' **h**.	**1Ch 9:9**	1004
Now *David* built **h** for himself in	**1Ch 15:1**	1004
make beams for the **h** which the kings	**2Ch 34:11**	1004
your wives and your **h**."	**Ne 4:14**	1004
and our **h** that we might get grain	**Ne 5:3**	1004
their olive groves and their **h**,	**Ne 5:11**	1004
were few and the **h** were not built.	**Ne 7:4**	1004
they could not show their fathers' **h**	**Ne 7:61**	1004
took possession of **h** full of every	**Ne 9:25**	1004
were filling their **h** *with* silver.	**Jb 3:15**	1004
more those who dwell in **h** of clay,	**Jb 4:19**	1004
cities, In **h** no one would inhabit,	**Jb 15:28**	1004
Their **h** are safe from fear,	**Jb 21:9**	1004

filled their **h** with good Jb 22:18 1004
"In the dark they dig into **h**, Jb 24:16 1004
is *that* their **h** are forever Ps 49:11 1004
We will fill our **h** with spoil; Pr 1:13 1004
they make their **h** in the rocks; Pr 30:26 1004
I built **h** for myself, I planted Ec 2:4 1004
"The beams of our **h** are cedars, SS 1:17 1004
plunder of the poor is in your **h**. Is 3:14 1004
many **h** shall become desolate, Is 5:9 1004
inhabitant, **H** are without people Is 6:11 1004
But to both the **h** of Israel, a Is 8:14 1004
Their **h** will be plundered And Is 13:16 1004
And their **h** will be full of owls; Is 13:21 1004
you counted the **h** of Jerusalem And Is 22:10 1004
tore down **h** to fortify the wall. Is 22:10 1004
Yea, for all the joyful **h** Is 32:13 1004
will build **h** and inhabit *them;* Is 65:21 1004
So their **h** are full of deceit; Jer 5:27 1004
"Their **h** shall be turned over Jer 6:12 1004
shall not bring a load out of your **h** Jer 17:22 1004
an outcry be heard from their **h**, Jer 18:22 1004
"The **h** of Jerusalem and the Jer 19:13 1004
h of the kings of Judah will be defiled Jer 19:13 1004
h on whose rooftops they burned Jer 19:13 1004
'Build **h** and live *in them;* Jer 29:5 1004
build **h** and live *in them* and plant Jer 29:28 1004
"**H** and fields and vineyards will Jer 32:15 1004
with the **h** where *people* have Jer 32:29 1004
concerning the **h** of this city, Jer 33:4 1004
the **h** of the kings of Judah which Jer 33:4 1004
to build ourselves **h** to dwell in; Jer 35:9 1004
palace and the **h** of the people, Jer 39:8 1004
house and all the **h** of Jerusalem; Jer 52:13 1004
to strangers, Our **h** to aliens. La 5:2 1004
and they will possess their **h**. Ezk 7:24 1004
'*The time* is not near to build **h**. Ezk 11:3 1004
They will burn your **h** with fire and Ezk 16:41 1004
and burn their **h** with fire. Ezk 23:47 1004
walls and destroy your pleasant **h**, Ezk 26:12 1004
and they will build **h**, Ezk 28:26 1004
and in the doorways of the **h**, Ezk 33:30 1004
and it shall be a place for their **h** Ezk 45:4 1004
h will be made a rubbish heap. Da 2:5 1005
their **h** reduced to a rubbish heap, Da 3:29 1005
And I will settle them in their **h**, Hos 11:11 1004
They climb into the **h**, Jl 2:9 1004
The **h** of ivory will also perish Am 3:15 1004
the great **h** will come to an end," Am 3:15 1004
have built **h** of well-hewn stone, Am 5:11 1004
The **h** of Achzib *will* become a Mi 1:14 1004
And **h**, and take *them* away. Mi 2:2 1004
plunder And their **h** desolate; Zph 1:13 1004
will build **h** but not inhabit *them,* Zph 1:13 1004
In the **h** of Ashkelon they will lie Zph 2:7 1004
to dwell in your paneled **h** while this Hg 1:4 1004
will be captured, the **h** plundered, Zch 14:2 1004
"And everyone who has left **h** or Mt 19:29 *3614*
because you devour widows' **h**, Mt 23:14 *3614*
h and brothers and sisters and Mk 10:30 *3614*
who devour widows' **h**, Mk 12:40 *3614*
who devour widows' **h**, Lk 20:47 *3614*
owners of land or **h** would sell them Ac 4:34 *3614*
the Most High does not dwell in **h** Ac 7:48
have **h** in which to eat and drink? 1Co 11:22 *3614*

HOUSETOP
become like a lonely bird on a **h**. Ps 102:7 1406
"Whoever is on the **h** must not go Mt 24:17 *1430*
who is on the **h** must not go down, Mk 13:15 *1430*
the one who is on the **h** Lk 17:31 *1430*
Peter went up on the **h** about the Ac 10:9 *1430*

HOUSETOPS
As grass on the **h** is scorched 2Ki 19:26 1406
Let them be like grass upon the **h**, Ps 129:6 1406
On their **h** and in their squares Is 15:3 1406
you have all gone up to the **h**? Is 22:1 1406
As grass on the **h** is scorched Is 37:27 1406
"On all the **h** of Moab and in its Jer 48:38 1406
on the **h** to the host of heaven, Zph 1:5 1406
in *your* ear, proclaim upon the **h**. Mt 10:27 *1430*
will be proclaimed upon the **h**. Lk 12:3 *1430*

HOVERED
glory of the God of Israel **h** over Ezk 10:19 4480, 4605
glory of the God of Israel **h** over Ezk 11:22 4480, 4605

HOVERS
its nest, That **h** over its young, Dt 32:11 7363b

HOW
"This is **h** you shall make it: Gn 6:15 834
h may I know that I will possess Gn 15:8 4100
And **h** have I sinned against you, Gn 20:9 4100
H then did you say, Gn 26:9 349
"**H** is it that you have *it* so Gn 27:20 4100
"**H** awesome is this place! Gn 28:17 4100
Then Leah said, "**H** fortunate!" Gn 30:11
"You yourself know **h** I have Gn 30:29 854, 834
and **h** your cattle have fared with me. Gn 30:29 854, 834
the LORD was with him and **h** Gn 39:3
H then could I do this great evil and Gn 39:9 349
H then could we steal silver or Gn 44:8 349
And **h** can we justify ourselves? Gn 44:16 4100
"For **h** shall I go up to my father Gn 44:34 349
"**H** many years have you lived?" Gn 47:8 4100
h then will Pharaoh listen to me, Ex 6:12 349
h then will Pharaoh listen to me?" Ex 6:30 349
h I made a mockery of the Ex 10:2 854, 834
and **h** I performed My signs among Ex 10:2 834
'**H** long will you refuse to humble Ex 10:3 4970
"**H** long will this man be a snare Ex 10:7 4970
that you may understand **h** the LORD Ex 11:7 834
"**H** long do you refuse to keep My Ex 16:28 575
h the LORD had brought Israel out Ex 18:1 3588
and **h** the LORD had delivered Ex 18:8
h I bore you on eagles' wings, Ex 19:4
"For **h** then can it be known that Ex 33:16 4100
to know **h** to perform all the work Ex 36:1
"**H** is the land in which they live, Nu 13:19 4100
And **h** are the cities in which they Nu 13:19 4100
"**H** is the land, is it fat or lean? Nu 13:20 4100
"**H** long will this people spurn Me? Nu 14:11 575
And **h** long will they not believe Nu 14:11 575
"**H** long *shall I bear* with this Nu 14:27 4970
"**H** shall I curse whom God has Nu 23:8 4100
And **h** can I denounce whom the Nu 23:8 4100
H fair are your tents, O Jacob, Nu 24:5 4100
H long will Asshur keep you Nu 24:22 4100
'**H** can I alone bear the load and Dt 1:12 351a
h the LORD your God carried you, Dt 1:31 834
h can I dispossess them?' Dt 7:17 351a
do not forget **h** you provoked the Dt 9:7 854, 834
H do these nations serve their Dt 12:30 351a
'**H** will we know the word which Dt 18:21 351a
h he met you along the way and Dt 25:18 834
h we lived in the land of Egypt, Dt 29:16 834
and **h** we came through the midst of Dt 29:16 834
h much more, then, after my death? Dt 31:27 637
"**H** could one chase a thousand, Dt 32:30 351a
"For we have heard **h** the LORD Jos 2:10 834
heard **h** the LORD had dried up the Jos 5:1 854, 834
h then shall we make a covenant Jos 9:7 349
"**H** long will you put off entering Jos 18:3 575
"O Lord, **h** shall I deliver Israel? Jg 6:15 4100
h we may overpower him that we may Jg 16:5 4100
h you may be bound to afflict you." Jg 16:6 4100
tell me **h** you may be bound." Jg 16:10 4100
tell me **h** you may be bound." Jg 16:13 4100
"**H** can you say, 'I love you,' Jg 16:15 349
So **h** can you say to me, Jg 18:24 4100, 2088
h did this wickedness take place?" Jg 20:3 351a
and **h** you left your father and Ru 2:11
"**H** did it go, my daughter?" Ru 3:16 4310
you know **h** the matter turns out; Ru 3:18 349
"**H** long will you make yourself 1Sa 1:14 4970
and **h** they lay with the women who 1Sa 2:22 854, 834
"**H** did things go, my son?" 1Sa 4:16 4100
h we shall send it to its place." 1Sa 6:2 4100
"**H** can this one deliver us?" 1Sa 10:27 4100
h my eyes have brightened because 1Sa 14:29 3588
"**H** much more, if only the people 1Sa 14:30 637
see **h** this sin has happened today. 1Sa 14:38 4100
h he set himself against him on 1Sa 15:2 834
"**H** long will you grieve over 1Sa 16:1 4970
But Samuel said, "**H** can I go? 1Sa 16:2 349
h much more then today will their 1Sa 21:5 637
H much more then if we go to 1Sa 23:3 637
h he has cut off those who are 1Sa 28:9 834
David said to him, "**H** did things go? 2Sa 1:4 4100
"**H** do you know that Saul and his 2Sa 1:5 349
"**H** is it you were not afraid to 2Sa 1:14 349
H have the mighty fallen! 2Sa 1:19 349
"**H** have the mighty fallen in the 2Sa 1:25 349
"**H** have the mighty fallen, And 2Sa 1:27 349
H then could I lift up my face to 2Sa 2:22 349
H long will you refrain from 2Sa 2:26 4970
"**H** much more, when wicked men 2Sa 4:11 637
"**H** can the ark of the LORD come 2Sa 6:9 349
"**H** the king of Israel distinguished 2Sa 6:20 4100
H then can we tell him that the 2Sa 12:18 349
h much more now this Benjamite? 2Sa 16:11 637
"**H** long have I yet to live, that 2Sa 19:34 4100
And **h** can I make atonement that 2Sa 21:3 4100
not know **h** to go out or come in. 1Ki 3:7
no one among us who knows **h** to cut 1Ki 5:6
h much less this house which I 1Ki 8:27 637
"**H** blessed are your men, how 1Ki 10:8
h blessed are these your servants 1Ki 10:8
"**H** do you counsel *me* to answer 1Ki 12:6 349
h he made war and how he reigned, 1Ki 14:19 834
how he made war and **h** he reigned, 1Ki 14:19 834
"**H** long *will* you hesitate between 1Ki 18:21 4970
and **h** he had killed all the 1Ki 19:1 834
see **h** this man is looking for trouble 1Ki 20:7 3588
"**H** is it that your spirit is so 1Ki 21:5 4100
"Do you see **h** Ahab has humbled 1Ki 21:29 3588
"**H** many times must I adjure you 1Ki 22:16 5704, 4100
"The LORD said to him, '**H**?' 1Ki 22:22 4100
"**H** did the Spirit of the LORD 1Ki 22:24 335, 2088
which he showed and **h** he warred, 1Ki 22:45 834
and see **h** he is seeking a quarrel 2Ki 5:7 3588
H much more *then,* when he says to 2Ki 5:13 637
"Do you see **h** this son of a 2Ki 6:32 3588
h he had restored to life the one 2Ki 8:5 834
h then can we stand?" 2Ki 10:4 349
h the king of Aram oppressed them. 2Ki 13:4 3588
h he fought with Amaziah king of 2Ki 14:15 834
h he fought and how he recovered 2Ki 14:28 834
and **h** he recovered for Israel, 2Ki 14:28 834
them **h** they should fear the LORD. 2Ki 17:28 349
"**H** then can you repulse one 2Ki 18:24 349
h I have walked before You in 2Ki 20:3 834
and **h** he made the pool and the 2Ki 20:20 834
"**H** can I bring the ark of God 1Ch 13:12 1963
who knows **h** to make engravings, 2Ch 2:7
know **h** to cut timber of Lebanon; 2Ch 2:8
who knows **h** to work in gold, 2Ch 2:14
and *who knows* **h** to make all kinds 2Ch 2:14
h much less this house which I 2Ch 6:18 637
"**H** blessed are your men, how 2Ch 9:7
h blessed are these your servants 2Ch 9:7
"**H** do you counsel *me* to answer 2Ch 10:6 349
"**H** many times must I adjure you 2Ch 18:15 5704, 4100
And the LORD said to him, '**H**?' 2Ch 18:20 4100
"**H** did the Spirit of the LORD 2Ch 18:23 335, 2088
see **h** they are rewarding us by 2Ch 20:11
H much less will your God deliver 2Ch 32:15 637
His prayer also and **h** *God* was 2Ch 33:19
H long will your journey be, and Ne 2:6 4970
I told them **h** the hand of my Ne 2:18 834
O our God, **h** we are despised! Ne 4:4 3588
h the LORD had commanded through Ne 8:14 834
h Esther was and how she fared. Es 2:11 7965
how Esther was and **h** she fared. Es 2:11 4100
and **h** he had promoted him above Es 5:11 834
"For **h** can I endure to see the Es 8:6 351c
and **h** can I endure to see the Es 8:6 351c
'**H** much more those who dwell in Jb 4:19 637
h happy is the man whom God Jb 5:17
And show me **h** I have erred. Jb 6:24 4100
"**H** painful are honest words! Jb 6:25 4100
"**H** long will you say these Jb 8:2 575
But **h** can a man be in the right Jb 9:2 4100
the mountains, they know not **h**, Jb 9:5
"**H** then can I answer Him, *And* Jb 9:14 637
"**H** many are my iniquities and Jb 13:23 4100
H much less one who is detestable Jb 15:16 637
"**H** long will you hunt for words? Jb 18:2 575
"**H** long will you torment me And Jb 19:2 575
'**H** shall we persecute him?' Jb 19:28 4100
"**H** often is the lamp of the Jb 21:17 4100
"**H** then will you vainly comfort Jb 21:34 349
distant stars, **h** high they are! Jb 22:12 3588
"**H** then can a man be just with Jb 25:4 4100
Or **h** can he be clean who is born Jb 25:4 4100
H much less man, *that* maggot, And Jb 25:6 637
"**H** you have saved the arm without Jb 26:2
And **h** faint a word we hear of Him! Jb 26:14 4100
H then could I gaze at a virgin? Jb 31:1 4100
"For I do not know **h** to flatter, Jb 32:22
"**H** much less when you say you do Jb 35:14 637
you know **h** God establishes them, Jb 37:15
H blessed is the man who does not Ps 1:1
H blessed are all who take refuge Ps 2:12
h my adversaries have increased! Ps 3:1 4100
h long will my honor become a Ps 4:2 4100
H *long* will you love what is Ps 4:2
But You, O LORD—**h** long? Ps 6:3 4970
H majestic is Your name in all the Ps 8:1 4100
H majestic is Your name in all the Ps 8:9 4100
H can you say to my soul, Ps 11:1 349
H long, O LORD? Will You forget Ps 13:1 575
H long will You hide Your face Ps 13:1 575
H long shall I take counsel in my Ps 13:2 575
H long will my enemy be exalted Ps 13:2 575
h greatly he will rejoice! Ps 21:1 4100
H great is Your goodness, Which Ps 31:19 4100
H blessed is he whose Ps 32:1
H blessed is the man to whom the Ps 32:2
H blessed is the man who takes Ps 34:8
Lord, **h** long will You look on? Ps 35:17 4100
H precious is Your lovingkindness, Ps 36:7 4100
Let me know **h** transient I am. Ps 39:4 4100
H blessed is the man who has made Ps 40:4
H blessed is he who considers the Ps 41:1
H long will you assail a man, That Ps 62:3 575
H blessed is the one whom You Ps 65:4
"**H** awesome are Your works! Ps 66:3 4100
They say, "**H** does God know? Ps 73:11 351a
H they are destroyed in a moment! Ps 73:19 349
any among us who knows **h** long. Ps 74:9 4100
H long, O God, will the adversary Ps 74:10 4970
Remember **h** the foolish man Ps 74:22
H often they rebelled against Him Ps 78:40 4100
H long, O LORD? Will You be angry Ps 79:5 4100
H long will You be angry with the Ps 80:4 4970
H long will you judge unjustly And Ps 82:2 4970
H lovely are Your dwelling places, Ps 84:1 4100
H blessed are those who dwell in Ps 84:4
H blessed is the man whose Ps 84:5
H blessed is the man who trusts in Ps 84:12
H blessed are the people who know Ps 89:15
H long, O LORD? Will You hide Ps 89:46 4100
H I bear in my bosom *the reproach* Ps 89:50
h long *will it be?* Ps 90:13 4970
H great are Your works, O LORD! Ps 92:5 4100
H long shall the wicked, O LORD, Ps 94:3 4970
H long shall the wicked exult? Ps 94:3 4970
O LORD, **h** many are Your works! Ps 104:24 4100
H blessed are those who keep Ps 106:3
H blessed is the man who fears the Ps 112:1
H blessed are those whose way is Ps 119:1
H blessed are those who observe Ps 119:2
H can a young man keep his way Ps 119:9 4100
H many are the days of Your servant? Ps 119:84 4100
O **h** I love Your law! Ps 119:97 4100
H sweet are Your words to my taste! Ps 119:103 4100
Consider **h** I love Your precepts; Ps 119:159 3588
H blessed is the man whose quiver Ps 127:5
H blessed is everyone who fears the Ps 128:1
H he swore to the LORD And vowed Ps 132:2 834

h good and how pleasant it is For	Ps 133:1	4100
how good and **h** pleasant it is For	Ps 133:1	4100
H can we sing the LORD's song In a	Ps 137:4	349
H blessed will be the one who	Ps 137:8	
H blessed will be the one who	Ps 137:9	
H precious also are Your thoughts	Ps 139:17	4100
H vast is the sum of them!	Ps 139:17	4100
H blessed are the people who are so	Ps 144:15	
H blessed are the people whose God is	Ps 144:15	
H blessed is he whose help is the	Ps 146:5	
"**H** long, O naive ones, will you	Pr 1:22	4970
H blessed is the man who finds	Pr 3:13	
"**H** I have hated instruction!	Pr 5:12	349
H long will you lie down, O	Pr 6:9	4970
H much more the wicked and the	Pr 11:31	637
H much more the hearts of men!	Pr 15:11	637
And **h** delightful is a timely word!	Pr 15:23	4100
the righteous ponders **h** to answer,	Pr 15:28	
H much better it is to get wisdom	Pr 16:16	4100
H much more do his friends abandon	Pr 19:7	637
H blessed are his sons after him.	Pr 20:7	
H then can man understand his way?	Pr 20:24	4100
H much more when he brings it with	Pr 21:27	637
H blessed is the man who fears	Pr 28:14	
oh **h** lofty are his eyes!	Pr 30:13	4100
I explored with my mind **h** to	Ec 2:3	
and **h** to take hold of folly,	Ec 2:3	
And **h** the wise man and the fool	Ec 2:16	349
warm, but **h** can one be warm *alone?*	Ec 4:11	349
foolish king who no longer knows **h**	Ec 4:13	
knowing **h** to walk before	Ec 6:8	
not *even* know **h** to go to a city.	Ec 10:15	
and **h** bones *are formed* in the womb	Ec 11:5	
"**H** beautiful you are, my darling,	SS 1:15	2009
my darling, **H** beautiful you are!	SS 1:15	2009
"**H** handsome you are, my beloved,	SS 1:16	2009
"**H** beautiful you are, my darling,	SS 4:1	2009
my darling, **H** beautiful you are!	SS 4:1	2009
"**H** beautiful is your love, my	SS 4:10	4100
H much better is your love than	SS 4:10	4100
my dress, **H** can I put it on *again?*	SS 5:3	351c
my feet, **H** can I dirty them *again?*	SS 5:3	351c
"**H** beautiful are your feet in sandals	SS 7:1	4100
"**H** beautiful and how delightful	SS 7:6	4100
and **h** delightful you are,	SS 7:6	4100
H the faithful city has become a	Is 1:21	351a
Then I said, "Lord, **h** long?"	Is 6:11	4970
before the boy knows **h** to cry out	Is 8:4	
"**H** the oppressor has ceased, *And how*	Is 14:4	349
And **h** fury has ceased!	Is 14:4	
"**H** you have fallen from heaven, O	Is 14:12	349
"**H** then will one answer the	Is 14:32	4100
H can you *men* say to Pharaoh,	Is 19:11	349
and we, **h** shall we escape?'	Is 20:6	349
"Watchman, **h** far gone is the night?	Is 21:11	4100
h far gone is the night?"	Is 21:11	4100
H blessed are all those who long	Is 30:18	
H blessed will you be, you who sow	Is 32:20	
"**H** then can you repulse one	Is 36:9	349
h I have walked before You in	Is 38:3	834
you will not know **h** to charm away;	Is 47:11	
For **h** can *My name* be profaned?	Is 48:11	349
That I may know **h** to sustain the	Is 50:4	
H shall I comfort you?	Is 51:19	4310
H lovely on the mountains Are the	Is 52:7	4100
"**H** blessed is the man who does	Is 56:2	
Behold, I do not know **h** to speak,	Jer 1:6	
H then have you turned yourself	Jer 2:21	349
"**H** can you say,	Jer 2:23	349
"**H** well you prepare your way To	Jer 2:33	4100
'**H** I would set you among My sons	Jer 3:19	349
H long will your wicked thoughts	Jer 4:14	4970
This is your evil. **H** bitter!	Jer 4:18	3588
H it has touched your heart!"	Jer 4:18	3588
H long must I see the standard And	Jer 4:21	4970
They did not even know **h** to blush.	Jer 6:15	
"**H** can you say,	Jer 8:8	351a
And they did not know **h** to blush;	Jer 8:12	
is heard from Zion, '**H** are we ruined!	Jer 9:19	349
H long is the land to mourn And	Jer 12:4	4970
h can you compete with horses?	Jer 12:5	349
H will you do in the thicket of	Jer 12:5	349
H long will you remain unclean?"	Jer 13:27	4970
Remember **h** I stood before You To	Jer 18:20	
"This is **h** I will treat this	Jer 19:12	3651
H you will groan when pangs come	Jer 22:23	4100
"**H** long? Is there *anything* in the	Jer 23:26	4970
"**H** long will you go here and	Jer 31:22	4970
h did you write all these words?	Jer 36:17	349
H long will you gash yourself?	Jer 47:5	4970
H long will you not be quiet?	Jer 47:6	575
"**H** can it be quiet, When the LORD	Jer 47:7	349
"**H** can you say,	Jer 48:14	349
'**H** has the mighty scepter been	Jer 48:17	351a
"**H** shattered it is!	Jer 48:39	349
"How shattered it is! **H** they	Jer 48:39	
H Moab has turned his back	Jer 48:39	349
"**H** boastful you are about the	Jer 49:4	4100
"**H** the city of praise has not	Jer 49:25	349
"**H** the hammer of the whole earth	Jer 50:23	349
H Babylon has become An object of	Jer 50:23	349
"**H** Sheshak has been captured, And	Jer 51:41	349
H Babylon has become an object of	Jer 51:41	349
H lonely sits the city That was	La 1:1	351a
H the Lord has covered the	La 2:1	351a
H shall I admonish you?	La 2:13	4100
H dark the gold has become,	La 4:1	351a
How dark the gold has become, **H**	La 4:1	
H they are regarded as earthen	La 4:2	351a

h I have been hurt by their	Ezk 6:9	834
"**H** much more when I send My four	Ezk 14:21	637
h is the wood of the vine	Ezk 15:2	4100
H much less, when the fire has	Ezk 15:5	637
"**H** languishing is your heart,"	Ezk 16:30	4100
'**H** you have perished, O inhabited	Ezk 26:17	349
h then can we survive?"'	Ezk 33:10	349
"**H** great are His signs And how	Da 4:3	4101
And **h** mighty are His wonders!	Da 4:3	4101
"**H** long will the vision *about* the	Da 8:13	4970
"For **h** can such a servant of my	Da 10:17	1963
"**H** long *will it be* until the end	Da 12:6	4970
"**H** blessed is he who keeps	Da 12:12	
H long will they be incapable of	Hos 8:5	4970
H can I give you up, O Ephraim?	Hos 11:8	349
H can I surrender you, O Israel?	Hos 11:8	
H can I make you like Admah?	Hos 11:8	349
H can I treat you like Zeboiim?	Hos 11:8	
H the beasts groan!	Jl 1:18	4100
not know **h** to do what is right,	Am 3:10	
H can Jacob stand, For he is small?"	Am 7:2	4310
H can Jacob stand, for he is small?"	Am 7:5	4310
O **h** you will be ruined!	Ob 1:5	349
"O **h** Esau will be ransacked, *And*	Ob 1:6	349
"**H** is it that you are sleeping?	Jon 1:6	4100
"**H** could you do this?"	Jon 1:10	4100
H He removes it from me!	Mi 2:4	349
to you, And **h** have I wearied you?	Mi 6:3	4100
H long, O LORD, will I call for help,	Hab 1:2	575
And **h** I may reply when I am	Hab 2:1	4100
For **h** long	Hab 2:6	4970
H she has become a desolation,	Zph 2:15	349
And **h** do you see it now?	Hg 2:3	4100
h long will You have no	Zch 1:12	4970
to see **h** wide it is and how long it	Zch 2:2	4100
how wide it is and **h** long it is."	Zch 2:2	4100
"**H** have You loved us?"	Mal 1:2	4100
'**H** have we despised Your name?	Mal 1:6	4100
'**H** have we defiled You?	Mal 1:7	4100
'My, **h** tiresome it is!'	Mal 1:13	4100
"**H** have we wearied *Him?*"	Mal 2:17	4100
'**H** shall we return?'	Mal 3:7	4100
'**H** have we robbed You?	Mal 3:8	4100
h can it be made salty *again?*	Mt 5:13	
		1722, 5101
darkness, **h** great is the darkness!	Mt 6:23	4214
h the lilies of the field grow;	Mt 6:28	4459
"Or **h** can you say to your	Mt 7:4	4459
know **h** to give good gifts to your	Mt 7:11	3609a
h much more will your Father who	Mt 7:11	4214
about **h** or what you are to say;	Mt 10:19	4459
h much more *will they malign*	Mt 10:25	4214
h he entered the house of God, and	Mt 12:4	4459
"**H** much more valuable then is a man	Mt 12:12	4214
as to **h** they might destroy Him.	Mt 12:14	3704
h then will his kingdom stand?	Mt 12:26	4459
"Or **h** can anyone enter the strong	Mt 12:29	4459
"You brood of vipers, **h** can you,	Mt 12:34	4459
H then does it have tares?	Mt 13:27	4159
"**H** many loaves do you have?"	Mt 15:34	4214
Do you know **h** to discern the	Mt 16:3	1097
h many baskets *full* you picked up?	Mt 16:9	4214
h many large baskets *full* you picked	Mt 16:10	4214
"**H** is it that you do not	Mt 16:11	4459
h long shall I be with you?	Mt 17:17	2193
H long shall I put up with you?	Mt 17:17	2193
h often shall my brother sin	Mt 18:21	4212
"**H** did the fig tree wither	Mt 21:20	4459
h did you come in here without	Mt 22:12	4459
plotted together **h** they might trap	Mt 22:15	3704
"Then **h** does David in the Spirit	Mt 22:43	4459
'Lord,' **h** is He his son?"	Mt 22:45	4459
h will you escape the sentence of	Mt 23:33	4459
H often I wanted to gather your	Mt 23:37	4212
"**H** then will the Scriptures be	Mt 26:54	4459
"Do You not hear **h** many things	Mt 27:13	4214
make it *as* secure as you know **h**."	Mt 27:65	3609a
h he entered the house of God in	Mk 2:26	4459
as to **h** they might destroy Him.	Mk 3:6	3704
"**H** can Satan cast out Satan?	Mk 3:23	4459
H will you understand all	Mk 4:13	4459
h, he himself does not know.	Mk 4:27	5613
"**H** shall we picture the kingdom	Mk 4:30	4459
described to them **h** it had happened	Mk 5:16	4459
and **h** He had mercy on you."	Mk 5:19	
"**H** many loaves do you have?	Mk 6:38	4214
"**H** many loaves do you have?"	Mk 8:5	4214
h many baskets full of broken	Mk 8:19	4214
h many large baskets full of	Mk 8:20	4214
And *yet* **h** is it written of the Son	Mk 9:12	4459
h long shall I be with you?	Mk 9:19	2193
H long shall I put up with you?	Mk 9:19	2193
"**H** long has this been happening	Mk 9:21	4214
"**H** hard it will be for those who	Mk 10:23	4459
h hard it is to enter the kingdom	Mk 10:24	4459
began seeking **h** to destroy Him;	Mk 11:18	4459
burning bush, **h** God spoke to him,	Mk 12:26	4459
"**H** *is it that* the scribes say	Mk 12:35	4459
h the people were putting money	Mk 12:41	4459
seeking **h** to seize Him by stealth and	Mk 14:1	4459
And he *began* seeking **h** to betray	Mk 14:11	4459
h does it seem to you?"	Mk 14:64	5101
And Peter remembered **h** Jesus had	Mk 14:72	5613
See **h** many charges they bring	Mk 15:4	4214
"**H** will I know this *for certain?*	Lk 1:18	
		2596, 5101
"**H** can this be, since I am a	Lk 1:34	4459
"And **h** has it *happened* to me,	Lk 1:43	4159

h he entered the house of God, and	Lk 6:4	5613
"Or **h** can you say to your	Lk 6:42	4459
"So take care **h** you listen;	Lk 8:18	4459
h the man who was demon-possessed	Lk 8:36	4459
and **h** she had been immediately	Lk 8:47	5613
h long shall I be with you and	Lk 9:41	2193
H does it read to you?"	Lk 10:26	4459
know **h** to give good gifts to your	Lk 11:13	3609a
h much more will *your* heavenly	Lk 11:13	4214
h will his kingdom stand?	Lk 11:18	4459
about **h** or what you are to speak	Lk 12:11	4459
h much more valuable you are than	Lk 12:24	4214
"Consider the lilies, **h** they grow:	Lk 12:27	4459
h much more *will He clothe* you?	Lk 12:28	4214
and **h** I wish it were already	Lk 12:49	5101
and **h** distressed I am until it is	Lk 12:50	4459
You know **h** to analyze the	Lk 12:56	3609a
H often I wanted to gather your	Lk 13:34	4212
He noticed **h** they had been picking	Lk 14:7	4459
'**H** many of my father's hired men	Lk 15:17	4214
'**H** much do you owe my master?'	Lk 16:5	4214
'And **h** much do you owe?'	Lk 16:7	4214
"**H** hard it is for those who are	Lk 18:24	4459
"**H** *is it that* they say the Christ	Lk 20:41	4459
'Lord,' and **h** is He his son?"	Lk 20:44	4459
h they might put Him to death;	Lk 22:2	4459
h he might betray Him to them.	Lk 22:4	4459
of the Lord, **h** He had told him,	Lk 22:61	5613
the tomb and **h** His body was laid.	Lk 23:55	5613
Remember **h** He spoke to you while	Lk 24:6	5613
and **h** the chief priests and our	Lk 24:20	3704
and **h** He was recognized by them	Lk 24:35	5613
"**H** do You know me?"	Jn 1:48	4159
"**H** can a man be born when he is	Jn 3:4	4459
"**H** can these things be?"	Jn 3:9	4459
h will you believe if I tell you	Jn 3:12	4459
"**H** is it that You, being a Jew,	Jn 4:9	4459
"**H** can you believe, when you	Jn 5:44	4459
h will you believe My words?"	Jn 5:47	4459
H does He now say,	Jn 6:42	4459
"**H** can this man give us *His* flesh	Jn 6:52	4459
"**H** has this man become learned,	Jn 7:15	4459
h is it that You say,	Jn 8:33	4459
"**H** then were your eyes opened?"	Jn 9:10	4459
him again **h** he received his sight.	Jn 9:15	4459
"**H** can a man who is a sinner	Jn 9:16	4459
Then **h** does he now see?"	Jn 9:19	4459
but **h** he now sees, we do not know;	Jn 9:21	4459
H did He open your eyes?"	Jn 9:26	4459
"**H** long will You keep us in	Jn 10:24	2193
"See **h** He loved him!"	Jn 11:36	4459
and **h** can You say,	Jn 12:34	4459
are going, **h** do we know the way?"	Jn 14:5	4459
h *can* you say, 'Show us	Jn 14:9	4459
"And **h** is it that we each hear	Ac 2:8	4459
to **h** this man has been made well,	Ac 4:9	5101
"Well, **h** could I, unless someone	Ac 8:31	4459
h much harm he did to Your saints	Ac 9:13	3745
for I will show him **h** much he must	Ac 9:16	3745
h he had seen the Lord on the road,	Ac 9:27	4459
and **h** at Damascus he had spoken	Ac 9:27	4459
"You yourselves know **h** unlawful	Ac 10:28	5613
h God anointed Him with the Holy	Ac 10:38	5613
and **h** He went about doing good	Ac 10:38	
"And he reported to us **h** he had	Ac 11:13	4459
of the Lord, **h** He used to say,	Ac 11:16	5613
he described to them **h** the Lord	Ac 12:17	4459
h He had opened a door of faith to	Ac 14:27	3754
"Simeon has related **h** God first	Ac 15:14	2531a
of the Lord, *and see* **h** they are."	Ac 15:36	4459
h I was with you the whole time,	Ac 20:18	4459
h I did not shrink from declaring	Ac 20:20	5613
h many thousands there are among	Ac 21:20	4214
h to investigate such matters,	Ac 25:20	2214
is my witness *as to* **h** unceasingly	Ro 1:9	5613
h will God judge the world?	Ro 3:6	4459
H then was it credited?	Ro 4:10	4459
H shall we who died to sin still	Ro 6:2	4459
not know **h** to pray as we should,	Ro 8:26	5101
h will He not also with Him freely	Ro 8:32	4459
H then will they call on Him in	Ro 10:14	4459
H will they believe in Him whom they	Ro 10:14	4459
And **h** will they hear without a	Ro 10:14	4459
H will they preach unless they are	Ro 10:15	4459
"**H** BEAUTIFUL ARE THE FEET OF THOSE	Ro 10:15	5613
h he pleads with God against	Ro 11:2	5613
h much more will their fulfillment	Ro 11:12	4214
h much more will these who are	Ro 11:24	4214
H unsearchable are His judgments	Ro 11:33	5613
be careful **h** he builds on it.	1Co 3:10	4459
H much more matters of this life?	1Co 6:3	3386
For **h** do you know, O wife, whether	1Co 7:16	5101
Or **h** do you know, O husband,	1Co 7:16	5101
Lord, **h** he may please the Lord;	1Co 7:32	4459
world, **h** he may please his wife,	1Co 7:33	4459
h she may please her husband.	1Co 7:34	4459
h will it be known what is played	1Co 14:7	4459
h will it be known what is spoken?	1Co 14:9	4459
h will the one who fills the place	1Co 14:16	4459
h do some among you say that there	1Co 15:12	4459
"**H** are the dead raised?	1Co 15:35	4459
h will the ministry of the Spirit	2Co 3:8	4459
h you received him with fear and	2Co 7:15	5613
And I know **h** such a man	2Co 12:3	3609a
h I used to persecute the church	Ga 1:13	3754
h *is it that* you compel the Gentiles	Ga 2:14	4459
h is it that you turn back again	Ga 4:9	4459
Therefore be careful **h** you walk,	Eph 5:15	4459
my circumstances, **h** I am doing,	Eph 6:21	5101

h I long for you all with the Php 1:8 *5613*
soon as I see **h** things *go* with me; Php 2:23 *872*
I know **h** to get along with humble Php 4:12 *3609a*
also know **h** to live in prosperity; Php 4:12 *3609a*
want you to know **h** great a struggle Col 2:1 *2245*
so that you will know **h** you should Col 4:6 *4459*
and **h** you turned to God from idols 1Th 1:9 *4459*
h working night and day so as not 1Th 2:9
h devoutly and uprightly and 1Th 2:10 *5613*
you know **h** we *were* exhorting and 1Th 2:11 *5613*
instruction as to **h** you ought to walk 1Th 4:1 *4459*
that each of you know **h** to possess 1Th 4:4 *3609a*
For you yourselves know **h** you 2Th 3:7 *4459*
h to manage his own household, 1Tm 3:5 *3609a*
h will he take care of the church 1Tm 3:5 *4459*
h one ought to conduct himself in 1Tm 3:15 *4459*
to me, but **h** much more to you, Phm 1:16 *4214*
h will we escape if we neglect so Heb 2:3 *4459*
Now observe **h** great this man was Heb 7:4 *4080*
h much more will the blood of Heb 9:14 *4214*
and let us consider **h** to stimulate Heb 10:24
H much severer punishment do you Heb 10:29 *4214*
h great a forest is set aflame by Jas 3:5 *2245*
then the Lord knows **h** to rescue 2Pe 2:9 *3609a*
See **h** great a love the Father has 1Jn 3:1 *4217*
h does the love of God abide in 1Jn 3:17 *4459*
is, **h** you are walking in truth. 3Jn 1:3 *2531a*
"**H** long, O Lord, holy and true, Rv 6:10 *2193*
And this is **h** I saw in the vision Rv 9:17 *3779*

HOWEVER

Sarah denied *it* **h**, saying, Gn 18:15
They said **h**, "No, but we shall spend Gn 19:2
h, previously the name of the city Gn 28:19 199
h, God did not allow him to hurt Gn 31:7
They did not know, **h**, Gn 42:23
Judah spoke to him, **h**, Gn 43:3
"You said to your servants, **h**, Gn 44:23
H, his younger brother shall be Gn 48:19 199
"If, **h**, a man acts presumptuously Ex 21:14
"If, **h**, he survives a day or two, Ex 21:21 389
"If, **h**, an ox was previously in Ex 21:29
"Moses alone, **h**, shall come near Ex 24:2
'Its entrails, **h**, and its legs he Lv 1:9
'The entrails, **h**, and the legs he Lv 1:13
The flesh and the skin, **h**, Lv 9:11
breast of the wave offering, **h**, Lv 10:14
sight the scale has remained, **h**, Lv 13:37
"If, **h**, the mark breaks out again Lv 14:43
"**H**, he shall let the live bird go Lv 14:53
'**H**, an earthenware vessel which Lv 15:12
h, be put to death, because she Lv 19:20
'If the people of the land, **h**, Lv 20:4
'No layman, **h**, is to eat the holy Lv 22:10
'The houses of the villages, **h**, Lv 25:31
You, **h**, I will scatter among the Lv 26:33
If, **h**, it is any unclean animal Lv 27:11
his field after the jubilee, **h**, Lv 27:18
H, a firstborn among animals, Lv 27:26 389
The Levites, **h**, were not numbered Nu 1:47
The Levites, **h**, were not numbered Nu 2:33
if you, **h**, have gone astray, Nu 5:20
"They may, **h**, assist their Nu 8:26
on a distant journey, he may, **h**, Nu 9:10
"When convening the assembly, **h**, Nu 10:7
Afterward, **h**, the people moved out Nu 12:16
'Your children, **h**, whom you said Nu 14:31
In the morning, **h**, they rose up Nu 14:40
It came about, **h**, when the Nu 16:42
Edom, **h**, said to him, Nu 20:18
The sons of Korah, **h**, Nu 26:11
"**H**, if she should marry while Nu 30:6
"**H**, if she vowed in her husband's Nu 30:10
"**H**, you may slaughter and eat Dt 12:15 7534
"**H**, there will be no poor among Dt 15:4 657
H, if it does not make peace Dt 20:12
"**H**, if you refrain from vowing, Dt 23:22
"**H**, there shall be between you Jos 3:4 389
H, Rahab the harlot and her Jos 6:25
H, Israel did not burn any cities Jos 11:13 7534
H, Zelophehad, the son of Hepher, Jos 17:3
'If, **h**, the land of your Jos 22:19 389
H, his father and mother did not Jg 14:4
H she wept before him seven days Jg 14:17
H, the hair of his head began to Jg 16:22
h, the name of the city formerly Jg 18:29 199
H, his master said to him, Jg 19:12
h, do not spend the night in the Jg 19:20 7534
h, there is a relative closer than Ru 3:12 1571
Her rival, **h**, would provoke her 1Sa 1:6
His sons, **h**, did not walk in his 1Sa 8:3
h, you shall solemnly warn them 1Sa 8:9 389
H, his servants together with the 1Sa 28:23
The house of Judah, **h**, 2Sa 2:10 389
H, he refused to turn aside; 2Sa 2:23
"**H**, because by this deed you have 2Sa 12:14 657
H, he would not listen to her; 2Sa 13:14
H the king said, 2Sa 14:24
h, you shall carry no news today 2Sa 18:20
"**H**, Absalom, whom we anointed 2Sa 19:10
H, here is your servant Chimham, 2Sa 19:37
h, he did not attain to the three. 2Sa 23:19
H, the king said to Araunah, 2Sa 24:24
h, the kingdom has turned about 1Ki 2:15
"**H**, I will not tear away all the 1Ki 11:13 7534
H, the high places were not taken 1Ki 22:43 389
h, the slingers went about *it* and 2Ki 3:25
H, the LORD was not willing to 2Ki 8:19
H, *as for* the sins of Jeroboam the 2Ki 10:29 7534
H, they did not listen, but 2Ki 17:14
H, they did not listen, but they 2Ki 17:40
H, the LORD did not turn from the 2Ki 23:26 389
h, he did not attain to the *first* 1Ch 11:21
H, David had brought up the ark of 2Ch 1:4 61
The high places, **h**, 2Ch 20:33 389
H, he did not put their children 2Ch 25:4
h he did not enter the temple of 2Ch 27:2 7534
H, Hezekiah humbled the pride of 2Ch 32:26
H, Josiah would not turn away from 2Ch 35:22
'**H**, in the first year of Cyrus Ezr 5:13 1297
"**H**, You bore with them for Ne 9:30
"**H**, You are just in all that has Ne 9:33
H, our God turned the curse into a Ne 13:2
After some time, **h**, Ne 13:6
Haman controlled himself, **h**, Es 5:10
"**H**, put forth Your hand now, and Jb 2:5 199
"**H** now, Job, please hear my Jb 33:1 199
They, **h**, were rebellious in their Ps 106:43
lives many years, **h** many they be, Ec 6:3
Afterwards, **h**, it will be Jer 46:26
"**H**, if you have warned the Ezk 3:21
"**H**, I will leave a remnant, for Ezk 6:8
h, for father, for mother, for Ezk 44:25
3588, 518
"**H**, there is a God in heaven who Da 2:28 1297
h, I will read the inscription to Da 5:17 1297
H, I will tell you what is Da 10:21 61
H, the men rowed *desperately* to Jon 1:13
"**H**, so that we do not offend them, Mt 17:27 *1161*
He, **h**, took her by the hand and Lk 8:54 *1161*
H, when the Son of Man comes, will Lk 18:8 *4133*
"**H**, we know where this man is Jn 7:27 *235*
h, the people held them in high Ac 5:13 *235*
"**H**, the Most High does not dwell Ac 7:48 *235*
H he shook the creature off into Ac 28:5
3303a, 3767
H, you are not in the flesh but in Ro 8:9 *1161*
H, they did not all heed the good Ro 10:16 *235*
a wisdom, **h**, not of this age nor 1Co 2:6 *1161*
H, each man has his own gift from 1Co 7:7 *235*
H not all men have this knowledge; 1Co 8:7 *235*
H, in the Lord, neither is woman 1Co 11:11 *4133*
to the mute idols, **h** you were led. 1Co 12:2
5613, 302
h, in the church I desire to speak 1Co 14:19 *235*
H, the spiritual is not first, but 1Co 15:46 *235*
H, the Law is not of faith; Ga 3:12 *1161*
H at that time, when you did not Ga 4:8 *235*
h, let us keep living by that same Php 3:16 *4133*
You, **h**, continue in the things you 2Tm 3:14 *1161*
If, **h**, you are fulfilling the Jas 2:8 *3305*

HOWL

at evening, they **h** like a dog, Ps 59:6 1993
at evening, they **h** like a dog, Ps 59:14 1993
Hyenas will **h** in their Is 13:22 6031b
"Those who rule over them **h**, Is 52:5 3213
Come now, you rich, weep and **h** for Jas 5:1 *3649*

HOWLING

in the **h** waste of a wilderness; Dt 32:10 3214

HOZAI

written in the records of the **H**. 2Ch 33:19 2335

HUBS

spokes, and their **h** *were* all cast. 1Ki 7:33 2840

HUG

And **h** the rock for want of a Jb 24:8 2263

HUGE

is being built with **h** stones, Ezr 5:8 1560
with three layers of **h** stones and Ezr 6:4 1560
Like the shade of a **h** rock in a Is 32:2 3515
And **h** hailstones, about one Rv 16:21 *3173*

HUKKOK

and proceeded from there to **H**; Jos 19:34 2712

HUKOK

H with its pasture lands and 1Ch 6:75 2352a

HUL

were Uz and **H** and Gether and Mash. Gn 10:23 2343
Arpachshad, Lud, Aram, Uz, **H**, 1Ch 1:17 2343

HULDAH

Asaiah went to **H** the prophetess, 2Ki 22:14 2468
had told went to **H** the prophetess, 2Ch 34:22 2468

HUMAN

'Or if he touches **h** uncleanness, Lv 5:3 120
unclean, whether **h** uncleanness, Lv 7:21 120
man takes the life of any **h** being, Lv 24:17 120
naturally, or a **h** bone or a grave, Nu 19:16 120
and of **h** beings, of the women who Nu 31:35 120
and the **h** beings were 16,000, from Nu 31:40 120
and the **h** beings were 16,000 Nu 31:46 120
and **h** bones shall be burned on you. 1Ki 13:2 120
filled their places with **h** bones. 2Ki 23:14 120
altars and burned **h** bones on them; 2Ki 23:20 120
who is laden with the guilt of **h** blood Pr 28:17 5315
their appearance: they had **h** form. Ezk 1:5 120
on their four sides *were* **h** hands. Ezk 1:8 120
it in their sight over **h** dung." Ezk 4:12 120
cow's dung in place of **h** dung over Ezk 4:15 120
wings *was* the form of **h** hands. Ezk 10:21 120
a **h** mind also was given to it. Da 7:4 606
will be broken without **h** agency. Da 8:25 3027
one who resembled a **h** being Da 10:16 120
Then *this* one with **h** appearance Da 10:18 120
Because of **h** bloodshed and violence Hab 2:8 120
Because of **h** bloodshed and Hab 2:17 120
in *houses* made by **h** hands; Ac 7:48
nor is He served by **h** hands, Ac 17:25 *442*
(I am speaking in **h** terms.) Ro 3:5 *444*
I am speaking in **h** terms because Ro 6:19 *442*
not in words taught by **h** wisdom, 1Co 2:13 *442*
by you, or by *any* **h** court; 1Co 4:3 *442*
things according to **h** judgment, 1Co 9:8 *444*
If from **h** motives I fought with 1Co 15:32 *444*
stone but on tablets of **h** hearts. 2Co 3:3 *4560*
I speak in terms of **h** relations: Ga 3:15 *444*
performed in the flesh by **h** hands Eph 2:11 *5499*
and has been tamed by the **h** race. Jas 3:7 *442*
Lord's sake to every **h** institution, 1Pe 2:13 *442*
was ever made by an act of **h** will, 2Pe 1:21 *444*
chariots and slaves and **h** lives. Rv 18:13 *444*
according to **h** measurements, Rv 21:17 *444*

HUMBLE

refuse to **h** yourself before Me? Ex 10:3 6031a
the month, you shall **h** your souls and Lv 16:29 6031a
you, that you may **h** your souls Lv 16:31 6031a
and you shall **h** your souls and Lv 23:27 6031a
not **h** himself on this same day, Lv 23:29 6031a
you, and you shall **h** your souls; Lv 23:32 6031a
(Now the man Moses was very **h**, Nu 12:3 6035
and you shall **h** yourselves Nu 29:7 6031a
every binding oath to **h** herself, Nu 30:13 6031a
forty years, that He might **h** you, Dt 8:2 6031a
that He might **h** you and that He Dt 8:16 6031a
this and will be **h** in my own eyes, 2Sa 6:22 8217
by My name **h** themselves and pray and 2Ch 7:14 3665
he did not **h** himself before the 2Ch 33:23 3665
he did not **h** himself before 2Ch 36:12 3665
that we might **h** ourselves before Ezr 8:21 6031a
And the **h** person He will save. Jb 22:29
7807, 5869
everyone who is proud, *and* **h** him, Jb 40:12 3665
have heard the desire of the **h**; Ps 10:17 6035
He leads the **h** in justice, And He Ps 25:9 6035
And He teaches the **h** His way. Ps 25:9 6035
The **h** will hear it and rejoice. Ps 34:2 6035
But the **h** will inherit the land And Ps 37:11 6035
The **h** have seen *it and* are glad Ps 69:32 6035
To save all the **h** of the earth. Ps 76:9 6035
of your neighbor, Go, **h** yourself, Pr 6:3 7511
But with the **h** is wisdom. Pr 11:2 6794a
be **h** in spirit with the lowly Pr 16:19 8217
But a **h** spirit will obtain honor. Pr 29:23 8217
while rich men sit in **h** places. Ec 10:6 8216
a day for a man to **h** himself? Is 58:5 6031a
who is **h** and contrite of spirit, Is 66:2 6041
to **h** those who walk in pride." Da 4:37 8214
Also turn aside the way of the **h**; Am 2:7 6035
to do away with the **h** of the land, Am 8:4 6041
All you **h** of the earth Who have Zph 2:3 6035
among you A **h** and lowly people, Zph 3:12 6041
and endowed with salvation, **H**, Zch 9:9 6041
for I am gentle and **h** in heart Mt 11:29 *5011*
for the **h** state of His bondslave; Lk 1:48 *5014*
And has exalted those who were **h**. Lk 1:52 *5011*
transform the body of our **h** state into Php 3:21 *5014*
how to get along with **h** means, Php 4:12 *5013*
But the brother of **h** circumstances Jas 1:9 *5011*
BUT GIVES GRACE TO THE **H**." Jas 4:6 *5011*
H yourselves in the presence of Jas 4:10 *5013*
kindhearted, and **h** in spirit; 1Pe 3:8 *5012b*
BUT GIVES GRACE TO THE **H**. 1Pe 5:5 *5011*
Therefore **h** yourselves under 1Pe 5:6 *5013*

HUMBLED

if their uncircumcised heart becomes **h** Lv 26:41 3665
He **h** you and let you be hungry, Dt 8:3 6031a
her, because you have **h** her. Dt 21:14 6031a
how Ahab has **h** himself before Me? 1Ki 21:29 3665
he has **h** himself before Me, 1Ki 21:29 3665
and you **h** yourself before the LORD 2Ki 22:19 3665
the king **h** themselves and said, 2Ch 12:6 3665
LORD saw that they **h** themselves, 2Ch 12:7 3665
"They have **h** themselves *so* I will 2Ch 12:7 3665
And when he **h** himself, the anger 2Ch 12:12 3665
For the LORD **h** Judah because of 2Ch 28:19 3665
and Zebulun **h** themselves and came 2Ch 30:11 3665
Hezekiah **h** the pride of his heart, 2Ch 32:26 3665
and **h** himself greatly before the God 2Ch 33:12 3665
images, before he **h** himself, 2Ch 33:19 3665
and you **h** yourself before God when 2Ch 34:27 3665
because you **h** yourself before Me, 2Ch 34:27 3665
I **h** my soul with fasting, Ps 35:13 6031a
He **h** their heart with labor; Ps 107:12 3665
So the *common* man has been **h** And Is 2:9 7817
the loftiness of man will be **h**, Is 2:11 7817
The pride of man will be **h** And Is 2:17 7817
So the *common* man will be **h** and Is 5:15 7817
Why have we **h** ourselves and You Is 58:3 6031a
they have **h** her who was unclean in Ezk 22:10 6031a
another in you has **h** his sister, Ezk 22:11 6031a
and whomever he wished he **h**. Da 5:19 8214
Belshazzar, have not **h** your heart, Da 5:22 8214
Whoever exalts himself shall be **h**; Mt 23:12 *5013*
who exalts himself will be **h**, Lk 14:11 *5013*
who exalts himself will be **h**, Lk 18:14 *5013*
He **h** Himself by becoming obedient Php 2:8 *5013*

HUMBLES

Who **h** Himself to behold *The things* Ps 113:6 8213
Whoever then **h** himself as this child, Mt 18:4 *5013*
whoever **h** himself shall be exalted. Mt 23:12 *5013*
he who **h** himself will be exalted." Lk 14:11 *5013*
who **h** himself will be exalted." Lk 18:14 *5013*

HUMBLING

and on **h** yourself before your God, Da 10:12 6031a
Or did I commit a sin in **h** myself 2Co 11:7 *5013*

HUMBLY

And to walk **h** with your God? Mi 6:8 6800

HUMILIATE
again my God may **h** me before you, 2Co 12:21 *5013*

HUMILIATED
them, for the men were greatly **h**. 2Sa 10:5 3637
as people who are **h** steal away 2Sa 19:3 3637
them, for the men were greatly **h**. 1Ch 19:5 3637
Let those be turned back and **h** Ps 35:4 3637
Let those be ashamed and **h** Ps 35:26 2659
Let those be ashamed and **h** Ps 40:14 3637
be ashamed and **h** Who seek my life; Ps 70:2 2659
for they are **h** who seek my hurt. Ps 71:24 2659
And let them be **h** and perish, Ps 83:17 2659
will be put to shame and even **h**, Is 45:16 3637
You will not be put to shame or **h** Is 45:17 3637
not feel **h**, for you will not Is 54:4 3637
They have been put to shame and **h**, Jer 14:3 3637
She has been shamed and **h**. Jer 15:9 2659
you will surely be ashamed and **h** Jer 22:22 3637
I was ashamed and also **h** Jer 31:19 3637
She who gave you birth will be **h**. Jer 50:12 2659
all His opponents were being **h**; Lk 13:17 *2617b*

HUMILIATES
When your neighbor **h** you? Pr 25:8 3637
of gluttons **h** his father. Pr 28:7 3637

HUMILIATING
no ruler **h** *them* for anything in the Jg 18:7 3637

HUMILIATION
offering I arose from my **h**, Ezr 9:5 8589
me And my **h** has overwhelmed me, Ps 44:15 1322, 6440
in the shadow of Egypt, your **h**. Is 30:3 3639
idols will go away together in **h**. Is 45:16 3639
cover My face from **h** and spitting. Is 50:6 3639
instead of **h** they will shout for joy Is 61:7 3639
our shame, and let our **h** cover us; Jer 3:25 3639
h which will not be forgotten." Jer 23:40 3640
in order that you may bear your **h** and Ezk 16:54 3639
mouth anymore because of your **h**, Ezk 16:63 3639
"IN **H** HIS JUDGMENT WAS TAKEN AWAY; Ac 8:33 *5014*
rich man *is to glory* in his **h**, Jas 1:10 *5014*

HUMILITY
wisdom, And before honor *comes* **h**. Pr 15:33 6038
haughty, But **h** *goes* before honor. Pr 18:12 6038
The reward of **h** *and* the fear of Pr 22:4 6038
Seek righteousness, seek **h**. Zph 2:3 6038
serving the Lord with all **h** and Ac 20:19 *5012a*
with all **h** and gentleness, with Eph 4:2 *5012a*
but with **h** of mind regard one another Php 2:3 *5012a*
heart of compassion, kindness, **h**, Col 3:12 *5012a*
in **h** receive the word implanted, Jas 1:21 *4240*
clothe yourselves with **h** toward one 1Pe 5:5 *5012a*

HUMPS
And their treasures on camels' **h**, Is 30:6 1707

HUMTAH
and **H** and Kiriath-arba Jos 15:54 2547

HUNCHBACK
or a **h** or a dwarf, or *one who has* Lv 21:20 1384

HUNDRED
had lived one **h** and thirty years, Gn 5:3 3967
father of Seth were eight **h** years, Gn 5:4 3967
were nine **h** and thirty years, Gn 5:5 3967
Seth lived one **h** and five years, Gn 5:6 3967
Then Seth lived eight **h** and seven Gn 5:7 3967
Seth were nine **h** and twelve years, Gn 5:8 3967
Then Enosh lived eight **h** Gn 5:10 3967
Enosh were nine **h** and five years, Gn 5:11 3967
Then Kenan lived eight **h** and forty Gn 5:13 3967
Kenan were nine **h** and ten years, Gn 5:14 3967
Then Mahalalel lived eight **h** and Gn 5:16 3967
were eight **h** and ninety-five years, Gn 5:17 3967
lived one **h** and sixty-two years, Gn 5:18 3967
Then Jared lived eight **h** years Gn 5:19 3967
were nine **h** and sixty-two years, Gn 5:20 3967
Enoch walked with God three **h** years Gn 5:22 3967
were three **h** and sixty-five years. Gn 5:23 3967
lived one **h** and eighty-seven years, Gn 5:25 3967
Then Methuselah lived seven **h** and Gn 5:26 3967
were nine **h** and sixty-nine years, Gn 5:27 3967
lived one **h** and eighty-two years, Gn 5:28 3967
Then Lamech lived five **h** and Gn 5:30 3967
seven **h** and seventy-seven years, Gn 5:31 3967
Noah was five **h** years old, Gn 5:32 3967
shall be one **h** and twenty years." Gn 6:3 3967
length of the ark three **h** cubits, Gn 6:15 3967
Now Noah was six **h** years old when Gn 7:6 3967
the earth one **h** and fifty days. Gn 7:24 3967
and at the end of one **h** and fifty Gn 8:3 3967
about in the six **h** and first year, Gn 8:13 3967
Noah lived three **h** and fifty Gn 9:28 3967
Noah were nine **h** and fifty years, Gn 9:29 3967
Shem was one **h** years old, and Gn 11:10 3967
and Shem lived five **h** years after Gn 11:11 3967
and Arpachshad lived four **h** and Gn 11:13 3967
and Shelah lived four **h** and three Gn 11:15 3967
and Eber lived four **h** and thirty Gn 11:17 3967
and Peleg lived two **h** and nine Gn 11:19 3967
and Reu lived two **h** and seven Gn 11:21 3967
and Serug lived two **h** years after Gn 11:23 3967
and Nahor lived one **h** and nineteen Gn 11:25 3967
Terah were two **h** and five years; Gn 11:32 3967
his house, three **h** and eighteen, Gn 14:14 3967
and oppressed four **h** years. Gn 15:13 3967
"Will a child be born to a man one **h** Gn 17:17 3967
Now Abraham was one **h** years old Gn 21:5 3967
lived one **h** and twenty-seven years; Gn 23:1 3967
a piece of land worth four **h** shekels Gn 23:15 3967
of Heth, four **h** shekels of silver, Gn 23:16 3967
one **h** and seventy-five years. Gn 25:7 3967
one **h** and thirty-seven years; Gn 25:17 3967
and four **h** men are with him." Gn 32:6 3967
two **h** female goats and twenty male Gn 32:14 3967
goats, two **h** ewes and twenty rams, Gn 32:14 3967
coming, and four **h** men with him. Gn 33:1 3967
father, for one **h** pieces of money. Gn 33:19 3967
Isaac were one **h** and eighty years. Gn 35:28 3967
he gave three **h** *pieces of* silver and Gn 45:22 3967
sojourning are one **h** and thirty; Gn 47:9 3967
was one **h** and forty-seven years. Gn 47:28 3967
Joseph lived one **h** and ten years. Gn 50:22 3967
at the age of one **h** and ten years; Gn 50:26 3967
was one **h** and thirty-seven years. Ex 6:16 3967
was one **h** and thirty-three years. Ex 6:18 3967
was one **h** and thirty-seven years. Ex 6:20 3967
about six **h** thousand men on foot, Ex 12:37 3967
Egypt was four **h** and thirty years. Ex 12:40 3967
end of four **h** and thirty years, Ex 12:41 3967
and he took six **h** select chariots, Ex 14:7 3967
one **h** cubits long for one side Ex 27:9 3967
be hangings one **h** *cubits* long, Ex 27:11 3967
the court *shall be* one **h** cubits, Ex 27:18 3967
of flowing myrrh five **h** *shekels*, Ex 30:23 3967
half as much, two **h** and fifty, Ex 30:23 3967
of fragrant cane two **h** and fifty, Ex 30:23 3967
and of cassia five **h**, Ex 30:24 3967
fine twisted linen, one **h** cubits; Ex 38:9 3967
side *there were* one **h** cubits; Ex 38:11 3967
The **h** talents of silver were Ex 38:27 3967
one **h** sockets for the hundred Ex 38:27 3967
hundred sockets for the **h** talents, Ex 38:27 3967
five of you will chase a **h**, Lv 26:8 3967
and a **h** of you will chase ten Lv 26:8 3967
was one **h** and thirty *shekels*, Nu 7:13 3967
was one **h** and thirty *shekels*, Nu 7:19 3967
was one **h** and thirty *shekels*, Nu 7:25 3967
was one **h** and thirty *shekels*, Nu 7:31 3967
was one **h** and thirty *shekels*, Nu 7:37 3967
was one **h** and thirty *shekels*, Nu 7:43 3967
was one **h** and thirty *shekels*, Nu 7:49 3967
was one **h** and thirty *shekels*, Nu 7:55 3967
was one **h** and thirty *shekels*, Nu 7:61 3967
was one **h** and thirty *shekels*, Nu 7:67 3967
was one **h** and thirty *shekels*, Nu 7:73 3967
was one **h** and thirty *shekels*, Nu 7:79 3967
each silver dish *weighing* one **h** Nu 7:85 3967
two **h** and fifty leaders of the Nu 16:2 3967
LORD, two **h** and fifty firepans; Nu 16:17 3967
consumed the two **h** and fifty men Nu 16:35 3967
one in five **h** of the persons and Nu 31:28 3967
Aaron was one **h** twenty-three Nu 33:39 3967
shall fine him a **h** *shekels* of silver Dt 22:19 3967
am a **h** and twenty years old today; Dt 31:2 3967
Although Moses was one **h** and Dt 34:7 3967
and two **h** shekels of silver and a bar Jos 7:21 3967
being one **h** and ten years old. Jos 24:29 3967
Shechem for one **h** pieces of money; Jos 24:32 3967
died at the age of one **h** and ten. Jg 2:8 3967
six **h** Philistines with an oxgoad; Jg 3:31 3967
for he had nine **h** iron chariots, Jg 4:3 3967
chariots, nine **h** iron chariots, Jg 4:13 3967
So Gideon and the **h** men who were Jg 7:19 3967
banks of the Arnon, three **h** years, Jg 11:26 3967
went and caught three **h** foxes, Jg 15:4 3967
you eleven **h** *pieces* of silver." Jg 16:5 3967
"The eleven **h** *pieces* of silver Jg 17:2 3967
returned the eleven **h** *pieces* of silver Jg 17:3 3967
mother took two **h** *pieces* of silver Jg 17:4 3967
six **h** men armed with weapons of Jg 18:11 3967
The six **h** men armed with their Jg 18:16 3967
six **h** men armed with weapons of Jg 18:17 3967
present with him, about six **h** men. 1Sa 13:15 3967
with him *were* about six **h** men, 1Sa 14:2 3967
weighed six **h** shekels of iron; 1Sa 17:7 3967
a **h** foreskins of the Philistines, 1Sa 18:25 3967
two **h** men among the Philistines. 1Sa 18:27 3967
were about four **h** men with him. 1Sa 22:2 3967
David and his men, about six **h**, 1Sa 23:13 3967
and about four **h** men went up 1Sa 25:13 3967
two **h** stayed with the baggage. 1Sa 25:13 3967
Abigail hurried and took two **h** 1Sa 25:18 3967
roasted grain and a **h** clusters of raisins 1Sa 25:18 3967
raisins and two **h** cakes of figs, 1Sa 25:18 3967
the six **h** men who were with him, 1Sa 27:2 3967
the six **h** men who were with him, 1Sa 30:9 3967
David pursued, he and four **h** men, 1Sa 30:10 3967
for two **h** who were too exhausted 1Sa 30:10 3967
except four **h** young men who rode 1Sa 30:17 3967
When David came to the two **h** men 1Sa 30:21 3967
that three **h** and sixty men died. 2Sa 2:31 3967
h foreskins of the Philistines." 2Sa 3:14 3967
Then two **h** men went with Absalom 2Sa 15:11 3967
six **h** men who had come with him 2Sa 15:18 3967
them *were* two **h** loaves of bread, 2Sa 16:1 3967
of bread, a **h** clusters of raisins, 2Sa 16:1 3967
of raisins, a **h** summer fruits, 2Sa 16:1 3967
three **h** *shekels* of bronze in weight, 2Sa 21:16 3967
eight **h** slain *by him* at one time; 2Sa 23:8 3967
against three **h** and killed *them*, 2Sa 23:18 3967
a **h** times as many as they are, 2Sa 24:3 3967
in Israel eight **h** thousand valiant 2Sa 24:9 3967
of Judah were five **h** thousand men. 2Sa 24:9 3967
oxen, a **h** sheep besides deer, 1Ki 4:23 3967
Now it came about in the four **h** 1Ki 6:1 3967
two **h** in rows around both capitals. 1Ki 7:20 3967
and the four **h** pomegranates for 1Ki 7:42 3967
Solomon's work, five **h** and fifty, 1Ki 9:23 3967
and took four **h** and twenty talents 1Ki 9:28 3967
a **h** and twenty talents of gold, 1Ki 10:10 3967
He had seven **h** wives, 1Ki 11:3 3967
and three **h** concubines, 1Ki 11:3 3967
Obadiah took a **h** prophets and 1Ki 18:4 3967
that I hid a **h** prophets of the LORD 1Ki 18:13 3967
together, about four **h** men, 1Ki 22:6 3967
will I set this before a **h** men?" 2Ki 4:43 3967
king of Judah three **h** talents of silver 2Ki 18:14 3967
a fine of one **h** talents of silver and 2Ki 23:33 3967
five **h** men went to Mount Seir, 1Ch 4:42 3967
three **h** whom he killed at one time. 1Ch 11:11 3967
against three **h** and killed them; 1Ch 11:20 3967
he who was least was equal to a **h** 1Ch 12:14 3967
do, their chiefs *were* two **h**; 1Ch 12:32 3967
a **h** times as many as they are! 1Ch 21:3 3967
and he made one **h** pomegranates and 2Ch 3:16 3967
And he made one **h** golden bowls. 2Ch 4:8 3967
and the four **h** pomegranates for 2Ch 4:13 3967
and with them one **h** and twenty 2Ch 5:12 3967
two **h** and fifty who ruled over the 2Ch 8:10 3967
four **h** and fifty talents of gold and 2Ch 8:18 3967
one **h** and twenty talents of gold and 2Ch 9:9 3967
using three **h** shekels of gold on 2Ch 9:16 3967
the prophets, four **h** men, 2Ch 18:5 3967
he was one **h** and thirty years old 2Ch 24:15 3967
for one **h** talents of silver. 2Ch 25:6 3967
what *shall we* do for the **h** talents 2Ch 25:9 3967
that year one **h** talents of silver, 2Ch 27:5 3967
a fine of one **h** talents of silver and 2Ch 36:3 3967
the wall to the Tower of the **H** Ne 3:1 3968
h and fifty Jews and officials, Ne 5:17 3967
Hananel and the Tower of the **H**, Ne 12:39 3968
killed and destroyed five **h** men, Es 9:6 3967
destroyed five **h** men and the ten sons Es 9:12 3967
and killed three **h** men in Susa, Es 9:15 3967
Than a **h** blows into a fool. Pr 17:10 3967
If a man fathers a **h** *children* and Ec 6:3 3967
a sinner does evil a **h** *times* and Ec 8:12 3967
And two **h** are for those who take SS 8:12 3967
the youth will die at the age of one **h** Is 65:20 3967
does not reach the age of one **h** Is 65:20 3967
all the pomegranates *numbered* a **h** Jer 52:23 3967
iniquity, three **h** and ninety days; Ezk 4:5 3967
side, three **h** and ninety days. Ezk 4:9 3967
a **h** cubits on the east and on the Ezk 40:19 3967
a **h** cubits from gate to gate. Ezk 40:23 3967
gate toward the south, a **h** cubits. Ezk 40:27 3967
a **h** cubits long and a hundred Ezk 40:47 3967
cubits long and a **h** cubits wide; Ezk 40:47 3967
the temple, a **h** cubits long; Ezk 41:13 3967
walls *were* also a **h** cubits long. Ezk 41:13 3967
the east *side totaled* a **h** cubits. Ezk 41:14 3967
gallery on each side, a **h** cubits; Ezk 41:15 3967
the length, *which was* a **h** cubits, Ezk 42:2 3967
wide, a way of one **h** cubits; Ezk 42:4
facing the temple *was* a **h** cubits. Ezk 42:8 3967
the measuring reed five **h** reeds by Ezk 42:16 3967
on the north side five **h** reeds Ezk 42:17 3967
south side he measured five **h** reeds Ezk 42:18 3967
west side *and* measured five **h** reeds Ezk 42:19 3967
the length five **h** and the width five Ezk 42:20 3967
five hundred and the width five **h**, Ezk 42:20 3967
place a square round about five **h** by Ezk 45:2 3967
five hundred by five **h** *cubits*, Ezk 45:2 3967
one sheep from *each* flock of two **h** Ezk 45:15 3967
strong Will have a **h** left, Am 5:3 3967
And the one which goes forth a **h** Am 5:3 3967
If any man has a **h** sheep, Mt 18:12 *1540*
slaves who owed him a **h** denarii; Mt 18:28 *1540*
spend two **h** denarii on bread and Mk 6:37 *1250*
he will receive a **h** times as much Mk 10:30 *1542*
sold for over three **h** denarii, Mk 14:5 *5145*
one owed five **h** denarii, and the Lk 7:41 *4001*
a crop a **h** times as great." Lk 8:8 *1542*
if he has a **h** sheep and has lost Lk 15:4 *1540*
'A **h** measures of oil.' Lk 16:6 *1540*
'A **h** measures of wheat.' Lk 16:7 *1540*
"Two **h** denarii worth of bread is Jn 6:7 *1250*
not sold for three **h** denarii and Jn 12:5 *5145*
aloes, about a **h** pounds *weight*. Jn 19:39 *1540*
land, but about one **h** yards away, Jn 21:8 *1250*
of large fish, a **h** and fifty-three; Jn 21:11 *1540*
gathering of about one **h** and twenty Ac 1:15 *1540*
four **h** men joined up with him. Ac 5:36 *5071*
BE ENSLAVED AND MISTREATED FOR FOUR **H** Ac 7:6 *5071*
took about four **h** and fifty years. Ac 13:19 *5071*
"Get two **h** soldiers ready by the Ac 23:23 *1250*
horsemen and two **h** spearmen." Ac 23:23 *1250*
were two **h** and seventy-six persons. Ac 27:37 *1250*
since he was about a **h** years old, Ro 4:19 *1541*
than five **h** brethren at one time, 1Co 15:6 *4001*
four **h** and thirty years later, Ga 3:17 *5071*
one **h** and forty-four thousand Rv 7:4 *1540*
of the horsemen was two **h** million; Rv 9:16 *1365a, 3461*
for twelve **h** and sixty days, Rv 11:3 *5507, 1250*
one thousand two **h** and sixty days. Rv 12:6 *1250*
his number is six **h** and sixty-six. Rv 13:18 *1812*
Him one **h** and forty-four thousand, Rv 14:1 *1540*
one **h** and forty-four thousand who Rv 14:3 *1540*
for a distance of two **h** miles. Rv 14:20
about one **h** pounds each, Rv 16:21 *5006*
with the rod, fifteen **h** miles; Rv 21:16

HUNDREDFOLD
and reaped in the same year a **h**. Gn 26:12 3967, 8180
and yielded a crop, some a **h**, Mt 13:8 *1540*
fruit and brings forth, some a **h**, Mt 13:23 *1540*

produced thirty, sixty, and a **h**." **Mk 4:8** *1540*
fruit, thirty, sixty, and a **h**." **Mk 4:20** *1540*

HUNDREDS
as leaders of thousands, of **h**, **Ex 18:21** 3967
leaders of thousands, of **h**, **Ex 18:25** 3967
thousands and the captains of **h**, **Nu 31:14** 3967
thousands and the captains of **h**, **Nu 31:48** 3967
thousands and the captains of **h**, **Nu 31:52** 3967
captains of thousands and of **h**, **Nu 31:54** 3967
leaders of thousands and of **h**, **Dt 1:15** 3967
of thousands and commanders of **h**? **1Sa 22:7** 3967
on by **h** and by thousands, **1Sa 29:2** 3967
of thousands and commanders of **h**. **2Sa 18:1** 3967
went out by **h** and thousands. **2Sa 18:4** 3967
sent and brought the captains of **h** of **2Ki 11:4** 3967
So the captains of **h** did according **2Ki 11:9** 3967
priest gave to the captains of **h** the **2Ki 11:10** 3967
commanded the captains of **h** who **2Ki 11:15** 3967
He took the captains of **h** and **2Ki 11:19** 3967
of the thousands and the **h**, **1Ch 13:1** 3967
the commanders of thousands and **h**, **1Ch 26:26** 3967
commanders of thousands and of **h**, **1Ch 27:1** 3967
and the commanders of **h**, **1Ch 28:1** 3967
commanders of thousands and of **h**, **1Ch 29:6** 3967
thousands and of **h** and to the judges **2Ch 1:2** 3967
himself, and took captains of **h**: **2Ch 23:1** 3967
gave to the captains of **h** the spears **2Ch 23:9** 3967
priest brought out the captains of **h** **2Ch 23:14** 3967
He took the captains of **h**, **2Ch 23:20** 3967
commanders of **h** throughout Judah **2Ch 25:5** 3967
in groups of **h** and of fifties. **Mk 6:40** *1540*

HUNDREDTH
In the six **h** year of Noah's life, **Gn 7:11** 3967
also the **h** *part* of the money and **Ne 5:11** 3967

HUNG
and **h** up the veil for the gateway **Ex 40:33** 5414
they **h** on the trees until evening. **Jos 10:26** 8518
and **h** them up beside the pool in **2Sa 4:12** 8518
consecrated it and **h** its doors. **Ne 3:1** 5975
h its doors with its bolts and bars. **Ne 3:3** 5975
laid its beams and **h** its doors with **Ne 3:6** 5975
They built it and **h** its doors with **Ne 3:13** 5975
He built it and **h** its doors with **Ne 3:14** 5975
and **h** its doors with its bolts and **Ne 3:15** 5975
in the midst of it We **h** our harps. **Ps 137:2** 8518
On which are **h** a thousand shields, **SS 4:4** 8518
Princes were **h** by their hands; **La 5:12** 8518
They **h** shield and helmet in you; **Ezk 27:10** 8518
h their shields on your walls **Ezk 27:11** 8518
millstone **h** around his neck, **Mt 18:6** *2910*
heavy millstone **h** around his neck, **Mk 9:42** *4029*
if a millstone were **h** around his neck **Lk 17:2** *4029*

HUNGER
kill this whole assembly with **h**." **Ex 16:3** 7458
LORD will send against you, in **h**, **Dt 28:48** 7458
those who were hungry cease *to* **h**. **1Sa 2:5**
over to die by **h** and by thirst, **2Ch 32:11** 7458
from heaven for them for their **h**, **Ne 9:15** 7458
young lions do lack and suffer **h**; **Ps 34:10** 7456
will not allow the righteous to **h**, **Pr 10:3** 7456
for him, For his **h** urges him *on*. **Pr 16:26** 6310
And an idle man will suffer **h**. **Pr 19:15** 7456
awakens, his **h** is not satisfied, **Is 29:8** 5315
"They will not **h** or thirst, **Is 49:10** 7456
sound of a trumpet or **h** for bread, **Jer 42:14** 7456
ones Who are faint because of **h** **La 2:19** 7458
the sword Than those slain with **h**; **La 4:9** 7458
h and thirst for righteousness, **Mt 5:6** *3983*
"Blessed *are* you who **h** now, **Lk 6:21** *3983*
bread, but I am dying here with **h**! **Lk 15:17** *3042*
he who comes to Me will not **h**, **Jn 6:35** *3983*
in labors, in sleeplessness, in **h**, **2Co 6:5** *3521*
sleepless nights, in **h** and thirst, **2Co 11:27** *3042*
"They will **h** no longer, nor **Rv 7:16** *3983*

HUNGRY
He humbled you and let you be **h**, **Dt 8:3** 7456
those who were **h** cease *to hunger*. **1Sa 2:5** 7457
"The people are **h** and weary and **2Sa 17:29** 7457
They know that we are **h**; **2Ki 7:12** 7457
"His harvest the **h** devour And **Jb 5:5** 7457
from the **h** you have withheld bread. **Jb 22:7** 7457
take away the sheaves from the **h**. **Jb 24:10** 7457
"If I were **h** I would not tell **Ps 50:12** 7456
They were **h** and thirsty; **Ps 107:5** 7457
And the **h** soul He has filled with **Ps 107:9** 7457
And there He makes the **h** to dwell, **Ps 107:36** 7457
Who gives food to the **h**. **Ps 146:7** 7457
To satisfy himself when he is **h**; **Pr 6:30** 7456
If your enemy is **h**, **Pr 25:21** 7457
turn out that when they are **h**, **Is 8:21** 7456
on the right hand but *still* are **h**, **Is 9:20** 7456
as when a **h** man dreams **Is 29:8** 7457
To keep the **h** person unsatisfied **Is 32:6** 7457
gets **h** and his strength fails; **Is 44:12** 7456
to divide your bread with the **h** And **Is 58:7** 7457
And if you give yourself to the **h** And **Is 58:10** 7457
will eat, but you will be **h**. **Is 65:13** 7456
but gives his bread to the **h** **Ezk 18:7** 7457
but he gives his bread to the **h** **Ezk 18:16** 7457
forty nights, He then became **h**. **Mt 4:2** *3983*
and His disciples became **h** and **Mt 12:1** *3983*
what David did when he became **h**, **Mt 12:3** *3983*
I do not want to send them away **h**, **Mt 15:32** *3523*
returning to the city, He became **h**. **Mt 21:18** *3983*
'For I was **h**, and you gave Me **Mt 25:35** *3983*
'Lord, when did we see You **h**, **Mt 25:37** *3983*
for I was **h**, and you gave Me **Mt 25:42** *3983*
'Lord, when did we see You **h**, **Mt 25:44** *3983*
he and his companions became **h**; **Mk 2:25** *3983*
I send them away **h** to their homes, **Mk 8:3** *3523*
left Bethany, He became **h** **Mk 11:12** *3983*
"HE HAS FILLED THE **H** WITH GOOD **Lk 1:53** *3983*
when they had ended, He became **h**. **Lk 4:2** *3983*
read what David did when he was **h**, **Lk 6:3** *3983*
well-fed now, for you shall be **h**. **Lk 6:25** *3983*
But he became **h** and was desiring **Ac 10:10** *4361*
"BUT IF YOUR ENEMY IS **H**, FEED HIM, **Ro 12:20** *3983*
hour we are both **h** and thirsty, **1Co 4:11** *3983*
and one is **h** and another is drunk. **1Co 11:21** *3983*
If anyone is **h**, let him eat at **1Co 11:34** *3983*
of being filled and going **h**, **Php 4:12** *3983*

HUNT
to the field and **h** game for me; **Gn 27:3** 6679
field to **h** for game to bring *home*, **Gn 27:5** 6679
up, You would **h** me like a lion; **Jb 10:16** 6679
"How long will you **h** for words? **Jb 18:2** 7760, 7078
"Can you **h** the prey for the lion, **Jb 38:39** 6679
evil **h** the violent man speedily." **Ps 140:11** 6679
they will **h** them from every mountain **Jer 16:16** 6679
of every stature to **h** down lives! **Ezk 13:18** 6679
you **h** down the lives of My people, **Ezk 13:18** 6679
your *magic* bands by which you **h** **Ezk 13:20** 6679
those lives whom you **h** as birds. **Ezk 13:20** 6679

HUNTED
that **h** game and brought *it* to me, **Gn 27:33** 6679
anger has torn me and **h** me down, **Jb 16:9** 7852
it will be that like a **h** gazelle, **Is 13:14** 5080
cause **H** me down like a bird; **La 3:52** 6679
They **h** our steps So that we could **La 4:18** 6679
longer be in your hands to be **h**; **Ezk 13:21** 4686a

HUNTER
He was a mighty **h** before the LORD; **Gn 10:9** 6718a
"Like Nimrod a mighty **h** before the **Gn 10:9** 6718a
grew up, Esau became a skillful **h**, **Gn 25:27** 376, 6718a

HUNTER'S
like a gazelle from *the* **h** hand **Pr 6:5**

HUNTERS
I will send for many **h**, **Jer 16:16** 6719a

HUNTING
his brother came in from his **h**. **Gn 27:30** 6718a
in **h** catches a beast or a bird **Lv 17:13** 6718a
They brought him in **h** nets So that **Ezk 19:9** 4685c

HUNTS
h a partridge in the mountains." **1Sa 26:20** 7291
an adulteress **h** for the precious life. **Pr 6:26** 6679
of them **h** the other with a net. **Mi 7:2** 6679

HUPHAM
of **H**, the family of the Huphamites. **Nu 26:39** 2349

HUPHAMITES
of Hupham, the family of the **H**. **Nu 26:39** 2350

HUPPAH
the thirteenth for **H**, **1Ch 24:13** 2647

HUPPIM
and Rosh, Muppim and **H** and Ard. **Gn 46:21** 2650
Shuppim and **H** *were* the sons of Ir; **1Ch 7:12** 2650
took a wife for **H** and Shuppim, **1Ch 7:15** 2650

HUR
and **H** went up to the top of the **Ex 17:10** 2354
Aaron and **H** supported his hands, **Ex 17:12** 2354
behold, Aaron and **H** are with you; **Ex 24:14** 2354
the son of Uri, the son of **H**, **Ex 31:2** 2354
the son of Uri, the son of **H**, **Ex 35:30** 2354
the son of Uri, the son of **H**, **Ex 38:22** 2354
and Rekem and Zur and **H** and Reba, **Nu 31:8** 2354
and Rekem and Zur and **H** and Reba, **Jos 13:21** 2354
married Ephrath, who bore him **H** **1Ch 2:19** 2354
H became the father of Uri, **1Ch 2:20** 2354
The sons of **H**, the firstborn of **1Ch 2:50** 2354
Hezron, Carmi, **H** and Shobal. **1Ch 4:1** 2354
These *were* the sons of **H**, **1Ch 4:4** 2354
the son of Uri, the son of **H**, **2Ch 1:5** 2354
to them Rephaiah the son of **H**, **Ne 3:9** 2354

HURAI
H of the brooks of Gaash, Abiel **1Ch 11:32** 2360b

HURAM
Gera, Shephuphan and **H**. **1Ch 8:5** 2361
sent *word* to **H** the king of Tyre, **2Ch 2:3** 2361
Then **H**, king of Tyre, answered in **2Ch 2:11** 2361
Then **H** continued, **2Ch 2:12** 2361
H also made the pails, the **2Ch 4:11** 2361
So **H** finished doing the work which **2Ch 4:11** 2361
cities which **H** had given to him, **2Ch 8:2** 2361
And **H** by his servants sent him **2Ch 8:18** 2361
The servants of **H** and the **2Ch 9:10** 2361
Tarshish with the servants of **H**; **2Ch 9:21** 2361

HURAM-ABI
H, a skilled man, **2Ch 2:13** 2361, 1
H made of polished bronze for King **2Ch 4:16** 2361, 1

HURI
the son of **H**, the son of Jaroah, **1Ch 5:14** 2359

HURL
it will **h** at him without sparing; **Jb 27:22** 7993
LORD is about to **h** you headlong, **Is 22:17** 2904
'So I will **h** you out of this land **Jer 16:13** 2904
"I will **h** you and your mother **Jer 22:26** 2904

HURLED
its rider He has **h** into the sea. **Ex 15:1** 7411a
his rider He has **h** into the sea." **Ex 15:21** 7411a
Saul **h** the spear for he thought, **1Sa 18:11** 2904
Then Saul **h** his spear at him to **1Sa 20:33** 2904
And their pursuers You **h** into **Ne 9:11** 7993
falls, he will not be **h** headlong, **Ps 37:24** 2904
he and his descendants been **h** out **Jer 22:28** 2904
So he **h** him to the ground and **Da 8:7** 7993
The LORD **h** a great wind on the **Jon 1:4** 2904

HURLING
passing by were **h** abuse at Him, **Mt 27:39** *987*
passing by were **h** abuse at Him, **Mk 15:29** *987*
hanged *there* was **h** abuse at Him, **Lk 23:39** *987*

HURRIED
Abraham **h** into the tent to Sarah, **Gn 18:6** 4116
and he **h** to prepare it. **Gn 18:7** 4116
Joseph **h** *out* for he was deeply **Gn 43:30** 4116
Then they **h**, each man lowered *his* **Gn 44:11** 4116
And the people **h** and crossed; **Jos 4:10** 4116
that the men of the city **h** and **Jos 8:14** 4116
the men in ambush **h** and rushed **Jg 20:37** 2363a
Then Abigail **h** and took two **1Sa 25:18** 4116
she **h** and dismounted from her **1Sa 25:23** 4116
h and came down with the men of **2Sa 19:16** 4116
Then they **h** and each man took his **2Ki 9:13** 4116
and they **h** him out of there, and **2Ch 26:20** 926
But Haman **h** home, mourning, with **Es 6:12** 1765
sound of Your thunder they **h** away. **Ps 104:7** 2648
I have not **h** away from *being* a **Jer 17:16** 213
And he **h** and came down and **Lk 19:6** *4692*

HURRIEDLY
and they **h** brought him out of the **Gn 41:14** 7323
Pharaoh **h** called for Moses and **Ex 10:16** 4116
Then the man came **h** and told Eli. **1Sa 4:14** 4116
An inheritance gained **h** at the **Pr 20:21** 926
Then Arioch **h** brought Daniel into **Da 2:25** 927

HURRIES
And he who **h** his footsteps errs. **Pr 19:2** 213

HURRY
"**H**, escape there, for I cannot do **Gn 19:22** 4116
"**H** and go up to my father, and **Gn 45:9** 4116
h and bring my father down here." **Gn 45:13** 4116
seen me do, **h** *and* do likewise." **Jg 9:48** 4116
H now, for he has come into the **1Sa 9:12** 4116
"**H**, be quick, do not stay!" **1Sa 20:38** 4120
"**H** and come, for the Philistines **1Sa 23:27** 4116
it happened that in her **h** to flee **2Sa 4:4** 2648
war, and God has ordered me to **h**. **2Ch 35:21** 926
"Do not be in a **h** to leave him. **Ec 8:3** 926
"**H**, my beloved, And be like a **SS 8:14** 1272
"Your builders **h**; Your destroyers and **Is 49:17** 4116
their march, They **h** to her wall **Na 2:5** 4116
Immediately she came in a **h** to **Mk 6:25** *4710*
this time Mary arose and went in a **h** **Lk 1:39** *4710*
So they came in a **h** and found their **Lk 2:16** *4692*
"Zaccheus, **h** and come down, for **Lk 19:5** *4692*

HURRYING
David was **h** to get away from Saul, **1Sa 23:26** 2648
for he was **h** to be in Jerusalem, **Ac 20:16** *4692*

HURT
God did not allow him to **h** me. **Gn 31:7** 7489a
and it dies or is **h** or is driven **Ex 22:10** 7665
He swears to his own **h** and **Ps 15:4** 7489a
dishonored Who delight in my **h**. **Ps 40:14** 7463a
Against me they devise my **h**, **Ps 41:7** 7463a
dishonored Who delight in my **h**. **Ps 70:2** 7463a
they are humiliated who seek my **h**. **Ps 71:24** 7463a
hoarded by their owner to his **h**. **Ec 5:13** 7463a
over *another* man to his **h**. **Ec 8:9** 7451b
quarries stones may be **h** by them, **Ec 10:9** 6087a
They will not **h** or destroy in all **Is 11:9** 7489a
been **h** by their adulterous hearts **Ezk 6:9** 7665
poison, it will not **h** them; **Mk 16:18** *984*
because of food your brother is **h**, **Ro 14:15** *3076*
not be **h** by the second death.' **Rv 2:11** *91*
not to **h** the grass of the earth, **Rv 9:4** *91*
power to **h** men for five months. **Rv 9:10** *91*

HURTFUL
see if there be any **h** way in me, **Ps 139:24** 6090a

HURTS
ox **h** another's so that it dies, **Ex 21:35** 5062

HUSBAND
she gave also to her **h** with her, **Gn 3:6** 376
your desire will be for your **h**, **Gn 3:16** 376
her to her **h** Abram as his wife. **Gn 16:3** 376
surely now my **h** will love me." **Gn 29:32** 376
my **h** will become attached to me, **Gn 29:34** 376
small matter for you to take my **h**? **Gn 30:15** 376
because I gave my maid to my **h**." **Gn 30:18** 376
now my **h** will dwell with me, **Gn 30:20** 376
if he is the **h** of a wife, then his **Ex 21:3** 1167
as the woman's **h** may demand of him, **Ex 21:22** 1167
to him because she has had no **h**; **Lv 21:3** 376
take a woman divorced from her **h**; **Lv 21:7** 376
it is hidden from the eyes of her **h** **Nu 5:13** 376
under *the authority of* your **h**, **Nu 5:19** 376
under *the authority of* your **h**, **Nu 5:20** 376
man other than your **h** has had **Nu 5:20** 376
and has been unfaithful to her **h**, **Nu 5:27** 376
under *the authority of* her **h**, **Nu 5:29** 376
and her **h** hears of it and says **Nu 30:7** 376
if on the day her **h** hears *of it*, **Nu 30:8** 376
and her **h** heard *it*, but said **Nu 30:11** 376
"But if her **h** indeed annuls them **Nu 30:12** 376
her **h** has annulled them, and the **Nu 30:12** 376
her **h** may confirm it or her **Nu 30:13** 376
confirm it or her **h** may annul it. **Nu 30:13** 376
"But if her **h** indeed says nothing **Nu 30:14** 376
her **h** and she shall be your wife. **Dt 21:13** 1166
and if the latter **h** turns against **Dt 24:3** 376
or if the latter **h** dies who took **Dt 24:3** 376
then her former **h** who sent her **Dt 24:4** 1167

deliver her **h** from the hand of the one **Dt 25:11** 376
shall be hostile toward the **h** she **Dt 28:56** 376
the woman came and told her **h**, **Jg 13:6** 376
but Manoah her **h** was not with her. **Jg 13:9** 376
woman ran quickly and told her **h**, **Jg 13:10** 376
"Entice your **h**, so that he will **Jg 14:15** 376
Then her **h** arose and *went* after **Jg 19:3** 376
h of the woman who was murdered, **Jg 20:4** 376
Then Elimelech, Naomi's **h**, **Ru 1:3** 376
bereft of her two children and her **h**. **Ru 1:5** 376
each in the house of her **h**." **Ru 1:9** 376
Go, for I am too old to have a **h**. **Ru 1:12** 376
have a **h** tonight and also bear sons, **Ru 1:12** 376
Now Naomi had a kinsman of her **h**, **Ru 2:1** 376
the death of your **h** has been fully **Ru 2:11** 376
Then Elkanah her **h** said to her, **1Sa 1:8** 376
not go up, for she said to her **h**, **1Sa 1:22** 376
Elkanah her **h** said to her, **1Sa 1:23** 376
when she would come up with her **h** **1Sa 2:19** 376
father-in-law and her **h** had died, **1Sa 4:19** 376
of her father-in-law and her **h**. **1Sa 4:21** 376
But she did not tell her **h** Nabal. **1Sa 25:19** 376
sent and took her from *her* **h**, **2Sa 3:15** 376
But her **h** went with her, weeping **2Sa 3:16** 376
heard that Uriah her **h** was dead, **2Sa 11:26** 376
was dead, she mourned for her **h**. **2Sa 11:26** 1167
I am a widow, for my **h** is dead. **2Sa 14:5** 376
so as to leave my **h** neither name **2Sa 14:7** 376
"Your servant my **h** is dead, and **2Ki 4:1** 376
She said to her **h**, **2Ki 4:9** 376
she has no son and her **h** is old." **2Ki 4:14** 376
Then she called to her **h** and said, **2Ki 4:22** 376
Is it well with your **h**? **2Ki 4:26** 376
"For my **h** is not at home, He has **Pr 7:19** 376
wife is the crown of her **h**, **Pr 12:4** 1167
unloved woman when she gets a **h**, **Pr 30:23** 1166
The heart of her **h** trusts in her, **Pr 31:11** 1167
Her **h** is known in the gates, When **Pr 31:23** 1167
Her **h** *also,* and he praises her, **Pr 31:28** 1167
"For your **h** is your Maker, Whose **Is 54:5** 1166
"If a **h** divorces his wife And **Jer 3:1** 376
both **h** and wife shall be taken, **Jer 6:11** 376
although I was a **h** to them," **Jer 31:32** 1166
takes strangers instead of her **h**! **Ezk 16:32** 376
who loathed her **h** and children. **Ezk 16:45** 376
for a sister who has not had a **h**, **Ezk 44:25** 376
not my wife, and I am not her **h**; **Hos 2:2** 376
'I will go back to my first **h**, **Hos 2:7** 376
a woman *who* is loved by *her* **h**, **Hos 3:1** 7453
father of Joseph the **h** of Mary, **Mt 1:16** *435*
And Joseph her **h**, being a **Mt 1:19** *435*
if she herself divorces her **h** and **Mk 10:12** *435*
had lived with *her* **h** seven years **Lk 2:36** *435*
one who is divorced from a **h** **Lk 16:18** *435*
"Go, call your **h** and come here." **Jn 4:16** *435*
"I have no **h**." Jesus said to her, **Jn 4:17** *435*
"You have correctly said, 'I have no **h**'; **Jn 4:17** *435*
whom you now have is not your **h**; **Jn 4:18** *435*
buried your **h** are at the door, **Ac 5:9** *435*
out and buried her beside her **h**. **Ac 5:10** *435*
woman is bound by law to her **h** **Ro 7:2** *435*
but if her **h** dies, she is released **Ro 7:2** *435*
from the law concerning the **h**. **Ro 7:2** *435*
So then, if while her **h** is living **Ro 7:3** *435*
but if her **h** dies, she is free **Ro 7:3** *435*
each woman is to have her own **h**. **1Co 7:2** *435*
h must fulfill his duty to his wife, **1Co 7:3** *435*
likewise also the wife to her **h**. **1Co 7:3** *435*
over her own body, but the **h** **1Co 7:4** *435*
the **h** does not have authority over **1Co 7:4** *435*
the wife should not leave her **h** **1Co 7:10** *435*
or else be reconciled to her **h**) **1Co 7:11** *435*
h should not divorce his wife. **1Co 7:11** *435*
a woman who has an unbelieving **h**, **1Co 7:13** *435*
her, she must not send her **h** away. **1Co 7:13** *435*
unbelieving **h** is sanctified through **1Co 7:14** *435*
through her believing **h**; **1Co 7:14** *80*
whether you will save your **h**? **1Co 7:16** *435*
Or how do you know, O **h**, **1Co 7:16** *435*
world, how she may please her **h**. **1Co 7:34** *435*
is bound as long as her **h** lives; **1Co 7:39** *435*
but if her **h** is dead, she is free **1Co 7:39** *435*
for I betrothed you to one **h**, **2Co 11:2** *435*
THAN OF THE ONE WHO HAS A **H**." **Ga 4:27** *435*
For the **h** is the head of the wife, **Eph 5:23** *435*
see to it that she respects her **h**. **Eph 5:33** *435*
above reproach, the **h** of one wife, **1Tm 3:2** *435*
above reproach, the **h** of one wife, **Ti 1:6** *435*
as a bride adorned for her **h**. **Rv 21:2** *435*

HUSBAND'S
if she vowed in her **h** house, **Nu 30:10** 376
Her **h** brother shall go in to her **Dt 25:5** 2993
the duty of a **h** brother to her. **Dt 25:5** 2992
'My **h** brother refuses to establish **Dt 25:7** 2993
the duty of a **h** brother to me.' **Dt 25:7** 2992

HUSBANDS
my womb, that they may be your **h**? **Ru 1:11** 376
to look with contempt on their **h** **Es 1:17** 1167
women will give honor to their **h**, **Es 1:20** 1167
sons and give your daughters to **h**, **Jer 29:6** 376
was it without our **h** that we made **Jer 44:19** 376
who loathed their **h** and children. **Ezk 16:45** 376
the needy, Who say to your **h**, **Am 4:1** 113
for you have had five **h**, **Jn 4:18** *435*
let them ask their own **h** at home; **1Co 14:35** *435*
Wives, *be subject* to your own **h**, **Eph 5:22** *435*
also the wives *ought to be* to their **h** **Eph 5:24** *435*
H, love your wives, just as Christ **Eph 5:25** *435*
So **h** ought also to love their own **Eph 5:28** *435*
Wives, be subject to your **h**, **Col 3:18** *435*
H, love your wives and do not be **Col 3:19** *435*
Deacons must be **h** of *only* one wife, **1Tm 3:12** *435*
the young women to love their **h**, **Ti 2:4** *5362*
being subject to their own **h**, **Ti 2:5** *435*
be submissive to your own **h** so **1Pe 3:1** *435*
being submissive to their own **h**; **1Pe 3:5** *435*
You **h** in the same way, live with **1Pe 3:7** *435*

HUSH
"**H**, be still." And the wind died down **Mk 4:39** *4623*
and when there was a great **h**, **Ac 21:40** *4602*

HUSHAH
Gedor, and Ezer the father of **H**. **1Ch 4:4** 2364

HUSHAI
H the Archite met him with his **2Sa 15:32** 2365
So **H**, David's friend, came into **2Sa 15:37** 2365
it came about when **H** the Archite, **2Sa 16:16** 2365
Absalom, that **H** said to Absalom, **2Sa 16:16** 2365
Absalom said to **H**, **2Sa 16:17** 2365
Then **H** said to Absalom, **2Sa 16:18** 2365
"Now call **H** the Archite also, and **2Sa 17:5** 2365
When **H** had come to Absalom, **2Sa 17:6** 2365
So **H** said to Absalom, **2Sa 17:7** 2365
Moreover, **H** said, **2Sa 17:8** 2365
The counsel of **H** the Archite is **2Sa 17:14** 2365
Then **H** said to Zadok and to **2Sa 17:15** 2365
Baana the son of **H**, **1Ki 4:16** 2365
and **H** the Archite *was* the king's **1Ch 27:33** 2365

HUSHAM
and **H** of the land of the Temanites **Gn 36:34** 2367
Then **H** died, and Hadad the son of **Gn 36:35** 2367
H of the land of the Temanites **1Ch 1:45** 2367
When **H** died, Hadad the son of **1Ch 1:46** 2367

HUSHATHITE
Sibbecai the **H** struck down Saph, **2Sa 21:18** 2843
the Anathothite, Mebunnai the **H**, **2Sa 23:27** 2843
Sibbecai the **H**, Ilai the Ahohite, **1Ch 11:29** 2843
then Sibbecai the **H** killed Sippai, **1Ch 20:4** 2843
Sibbecai the **H** of the Zerahites; **1Ch 27:11** 2843

HUSHED
The voice of the nobles was **h**, **Jb 29:10** 2244
that the waves of the sea were **h**. **Ps 107:29** 2814

HUSHIM
The sons of Dan: **H**. **Gn 46:23** 2366b
H *was* the son of Aher. **1Ch 7:12** 2366b
sent away **H** and Baara his wives. **1Ch 8:8** 2366a
By **H** he became the father of **1Ch 8:11** 2366a

HUT
a **h** *which* the watchman has made. **Jb 27:18** 5521
a watchman's **h** in a cucumber field, **Is 1:8** 4412

HYACINTH
of fire and of **h** and of brimstone; **Rv 9:17** *5191*

HYENAS
H will howl in their fortified towers **Is 13:22** 338

HYMENAEUS
Among these are **H** and Alexander, **1Tm 1:20** *5211*
Among them are **H** and Philetus, **2Tm 2:17** *5211*

HYMN
After singing a **h**, **Mt 26:30** *5214*
After singing a **h**, **Mk 14:26** *5214*

HYMNS
with **h** of thanksgiving and with **Ne 12:27** 8426
and **h** of thanksgiving to God. **Ne 12:46** 3034
and singing **h** of praise to God, **Ac 16:25** *5214*
psalms and **h** and spiritual songs, **Eph 5:19** *5215*
psalms *and* **h** *and* spiritual songs, **Col 3:16** *5215*

HYPOCRISY
and many will join with them in **h**. **Da 11:34** 2519
you are full of **h** and lawlessness. **Mt 23:28** *5272*
But He, knowing their **h**, **Mk 12:15** *5272*
of the Pharisees, which is **h**. **Lk 12:1** *5272*
Let love *be* without **h**. **Ro 12:9** *505*
rest of the Jews joined him in **h**, **Ga 2:13** *4942*
was carried away by their **h**. **Ga 2:13** *5272*
by means of the **h** of liars seared **1Tm 4:2** *5272*
fruits, unwavering, without **h**. **Jas 3:17** *505*
and **h** and envy and all slander, **1Pe 2:1** *5272*

HYPOCRITE
"You **h**, first take the log out of **Mt 7:5** *5273*
You **h**, first take the log out of **Lk 6:42** *5273*

HYPOCRITES
as the **h** do in the synagogues and **Mt 6:2** *5273*
pray, you are not to be like the **h**; **Mt 6:5** *5273*
put on a gloomy face as the **h** *do,* **Mt 6:16** *5273*
"You **h**, rightly did Isaiah **Mt 15:7** *5273*
"Why are you testing Me, you **h**? **Mt 22:18** *5273*
to you, scribes and Pharisees, **h**, **Mt 23:13** *5273*
to you, scribes and Pharisees, **h**, **Mt 23:14** *5273*
to you, scribes and Pharisees, **h**, **Mt 23:15** *5273*
to you, scribes and Pharisees, **h**! **Mt 23:23** *5273*
to you, scribes and Pharisees, **h**! **Mt 23:25** *5273*
to you, scribes and Pharisees, **h**! **Mt 23:27** *5273*
to you, scribes and Pharisees, **h**! **Mt 23:29** *5273*
and assign him a place with the **h**; **Mt 24:51** *5273*
did Isaiah prophesy of you **h**, **Mk 7:6** *5273*
"You **h**! You know how to analyze **Lk 12:56** *5273*
"You **h**, does not each of you on **Lk 13:15** *5273*

HYSSOP
"You shall take a bunch of **h** **Ex 12:22** 231
cedar wood and a scarlet string and **h** **Lv 14:4** 231
wood and the scarlet string and the **h**, **Lv 14:6** 231
wood and a scarlet string and **h**, **Lv 14:49** 231
and the **h** and the scarlet string, **Lv 14:51** 231
the **h** and with the scarlet string. **Lv 14:52** 231
wood and **h** and scarlet **Nu 19:6** 231
take **h** and dip *it* in the water, **Nu 19:18** 231
to the **h** that grows on the wall; **1Ki 4:33** 231
Purify me with **h**, and I shall be **Ps 51:7** 231
the sour wine upon *a branch of* **h** **Jn 19:29** *5301*
with water and scarlet wool and **h**, **Heb 9:19** *5301*

I

IBEX
the roebuck, the wild goat, the **i**, **Dt 14:5** 1788

IBHAR
I, Elishua, Nepheg, Japhia, **2Sa 5:15** 2984
and **I**, Elishama, Eliphelet, **1Ch 3:6** 2984
I, Elishua, Elpelet, **1Ch 14:5** 2984

IBLEAM
and its towns and **I** and its towns, **Jos 17:11** 2991
inhabitants of **I** and its villages, **Jg 1:27** 2991
the ascent of Gur, which is at **I**. **2Ki 9:27** 2991

IBNEIAH
and **I** the son of Jeroham, and Elah **1Ch 9:8** 2997

IBNIJAH
the son of Reuel, the son of **I**; **1Ch 9:8** 2998

IBRI
were Beno, Shoham, Zaccur and **I**. **1Ch 24:27** 5681

IBSAM
Uzzi, Rephaiah, Jeriel, Jahmai, **I** and **1Ch 7:2** 3005

IBZAN
Now **I** of Bethlehem judged Israel **Jg 12:8** 78
Then **I** died and was buried in **Jg 12:10** 78

ICE
Which are turbid because of **i** **Jb 6:16** 7140
"From the breath of God **i** is made, **Jb 37:10** 7140
"From whose womb has come the **i**? **Jb 38:29** 7140
He casts forth His **i** as fragments; **Ps 147:17** 7140

ICHABOD
And she called the boy **I**, **1Sa 4:21** 350

ICHABOD'S
the son of Ahitub, **I** brother, **1Sa 14:3** 350

ICONIUM
against them and went to **I**. **Ac 13:51** *2430*
In **I** they **Ac 14:1** *2430*
But Jews came from Antioch and **I**, **Ac 14:19** *2430*
to Lystra and to **I** and to Antioch, **Ac 14:21** *2430*
brethren who were in Lystra and **I**. **Ac 16:2** *2430*
me at Antioch, at **I** *and* at Lystra; **2Tm 3:11** *2430*

IDALAH
and Shimron and **I** and Bethlehem; **Jos 19:15** 3030

IDBASH
Jezreel, Ishma and **I**; **1Ch 4:3** 3031

IDDO
Ahinadab the son of **I**, **1Ki 4:14** 5714
Joah his son, **I** his son, Zerah his **1Ch 6:21** 5714
in Gilead, **I** the son of Zechariah; **1Ch 27:21** 3035
and in the visions of **I** the seer **2Ch 9:29** 3260
the prophet and of **I** the seer, **2Ch 12:15** 5714
in the treatise of the prophet **I**. **2Ch 13:22** 5714
and Zechariah the son of **I**, **Ezr 5:1** 5714
and Zechariah the son of **I**. **Ezr 6:14** 5714
I sent them to **I** the leading man **Ezr 8:17** 112a
what to say to **I** *and* his brothers, **Ezr 8:17** 112a
I, Ginnethoi, Abijah, **Ne 12:4** 5714
of **I**, Zechariah; of Ginnethon, **Ne 12:16** 5714
of Berechiah, the son of **I** saying, **Zch 1:1** 5714
son of Berechiah, the son of **I**, **Zch 1:7** 5714

IDEA
"That is a good **i**." **1Ki 18:24** 1697

IDENTIFIED
its blood is **i** with its life. **Lv 17:14**

IDIOT
"An **i** will become intelligent **Jb 11:12** 376, 5014

IDLE
"For it is not an **i** word for you; **Dt 32:47** 7386
And an **i** man will suffer hunger. **Pr 19:15** 7423b
and do not be **i** in the evening, **Ec 11:6** 5117, 3027
the grinding ones stand **i** because **Ec 12:3** 988
His **i** boasts are false. **Is 16:6** 907
His **i** boasts have accomplished **Jer 48:30** 907
saw others standing **i** in the market **Mt 20:3** *692*
Why have you been standing here **i** **Mt 20:6** *692*
this **i** babbler wish to say?" **Ac 17:18** *4691*
same time they also learn *to be* **i**, **1Tm 5:13** *692*
and not merely **i**, but also gossips **1Tm 5:13** *692*
judgment from long ago is not **i**, **2Pe 2:3** *691*

IDLENESS
And does not eat the bread of **i**. **Pr 31:27** 6104

IDOL
shall not make for yourself an **i**, **Ex 20:4** 6459
make an **i** in the form of anything, **Dt 4:25** 6459
shall not make for yourself an **i**, **Dt 5:8** 6459
who makes an **i** or a molten image, **Dt 27:15** 6459
Michal took the household **i** and **1Sa 19:13** 8655
the household **i** *was* on the bed **1Sa 19:16** 8655
the detestable **i** of the Ammonites. **1Ki 11:5** 8251
Chemosh the detestable **i** of Moab, **1Ki 11:7** 8251
detestable **i** of the sons of Ammon. **1Ki 11:7** 8251
image of the **i** which he had made **2Ch 33:7** 5566
the **i** from the house of the LORD, **2Ch 33:15** 5566
As for the **i**, a craftsman casts **Is 40:19** 6459
prepare an **i** that will not totter. **Is 40:20** 6459
a god or cast an **i** to no profit? **Is 44:10** 6459

Who carry about their wooden i And Is 45:20 6459
'My i has done them, And my graven Is 48:5 6090b
is like the one who blesses an i. Is 66:3 205
their i is wood! Jer 10:8
the seat of the i of jealousy, Ezk 8:3 5566
i of jealousy at the entrance. Ezk 8:5 5566
My people consult their wooden i, Hos 4:12
I will cut off i and image From Na 1:14 6459
What profit is the i when its maker Hab 2:18 6459
and brought a sacrifice to the i, Ac 7:41 1497
such thing as an i in the world, 1Co 8:4 1497
accustomed to the i until now, 1Co 8:7 1497
as if it were sacrificed to an i; 1Co 8:7 1494
or that an i is anything? 1Co 10:19 1497

IDOLATER

person, or covetous, or an i, 1Co 5:11 1496
or covetous man, who is an i, Eph 5:5 1496

IDOLATERS

covetous and swindlers, or with i, 1Co 5:10 1496
neither fornicators, nor i, 1Co 6:9 1496
Do not be i, as some of them 1Co 10:7 1496
and sorcerers and i and all liars, Rv 21:8 1496
and the murderers and the i, Rv 22:15 1496

IDOLATRIES

drinking parties and abominable i. 1Pe 4:3 1495

IDOLATROUS

He did away with the i priests 2Ki 23:5 3649
i priests will cry out over it, Hos 10:5 3649
And the names of the i priests Zph 1:4 3649

IDOLATRY

insubordination is as iniquity and i. 1Sa 15:23 8655
my beloved, flee from i. 1Co 10:14 1495
i, sorcery, enmities, strife, Ga 5:20 1495
and greed, which amounts to i. Col 3:5 1495

IDOL'S

knowledge, dining in an i temple, 1Co 8:10 1493

IDOLS

Rachel stole the household i that Gn 31:19 8655
Rachel had taken the household i Gn 31:34 8655
but did not find the household i. Gn 31:35 8655
'Do not turn to i or make for Lv 19:4 457
shall not make for yourselves i, Lv 26:1 457
remains on the remains of your i, Lv 26:30 1544
abominations and their i of wood, Dt 29:17 1544
provoked Me to anger with their i. Dt 32:21 1892
from the i which were at Gilgal, Jg 3:19 6456
he passed by the i and escaped to Jg 3:26 6456
he made an ephod and household i Jg 17:5 8655
household i and a graven image and Jg 18:14 8655
household i and the molten image, Jg 18:17 8655
household i and the molten image, Jg 18:18 8655
household i and the graven image and Jg 18:20 8655
good news to the house of their i 1Sa 31:9 6091
They abandoned their i there, 2Sa 5:21 6091
the i which his fathers had made. 1Ki 15:12 1544
God of Israel to anger with their i. 1Ki 16:13 1892
LORD God of Israel with their i. 1Ki 16:26 1892
very abominably in following i, 1Ki 21:26 1544
They served i, concerning 2Ki 17:12 1544
LORD, they also served their i; 2Ki 17:41 6456
also made Judah sin with his i; 2Ki 21:11 1544
and served the i that his father 2Ki 21:21 1544
and the i and all the abominations 2Ki 23:24 1544
news to their i and to the people. 1Ch 10:9 6091
all the gods of the peoples are i, 1Ch 16:26 457
removed the abominable i from all 2Ch 15:8 8251
and served the Asherim and the i; 2Ch 24:18 6091
I hate those who regard vain i, Ps 31:6 1892
all the gods of the peoples are i, Ps 96:5 457
images, Who boast themselves of i; Ps 97:7 457
And served their i, Ps 106:36 6091
sacrificed to the i of Canaan; Ps 106:38 6091
Their i are silver and gold, The Ps 115:4 6091
The i of the nations are but silver Ps 135:15 6091
land has also been filled with i; Is 2:8 457
But the i will completely vanish. Is 2:18 457
i of silver and their idols of gold, Is 2:20 457
idols of silver and their i of gold, Is 2:20 457
reached to the kingdoms of the i, Is 10:10 457
have done to Samaria and her i?" Is 10:11 457
The i of Egypt will tremble at His Is 19:1 457
to i and ghosts of the dead And Is 19:3 457
his silver i and his gold idols, Is 31:7 457
his silver idols and his gold i, Is 31:7 457
put to shame, Who trust in i, Is 42:17 6459
The manufacturers of i will go Is 45:16 6736
let your collection of i deliver Is 57:13
graven images, with foreign i?" Jer 8:19 1892
is put to shame by his i; Jer 10:14 6459
i of the nations who give rain? Jer 14:22 1892
carcasses of their detestable i and Jer 16:18 8251
shame, her i have been shattered.' Jer 50:2 1544
For it is a land of i, Jer 50:38 6456
And they are mad over fearsome i. Jer 50:38
is put to shame by his i, Jer 51:17 6459
I will punish the i of Babylon; Jer 51:47 6456
"When I will punish her i, Jer 51:52 6456
with all your detestable i and with all Ezk 5:11 8251
slain fall in front of your i. Ezk 6:4 1544
of Israel in front of their i; Ezk 6:5 1544
your i may be broken and brought Ezk 6:6 1544
played the harlot after their i; Ezk 6:9 1544
among their i around their altars, Ezk 6:13 1544
soothing aroma to all their i. Ezk 6:13 1544
all the i of the house of Israel, Ezk 8:10 1544
set up their i in their hearts and Ezk 14:3 1544
who sets up his i in his heart, Ezk 14:4 1544
in view of the multitude of his i, Ezk 14:4 1544
from Me through all their i." Ezk 14:5 1544
"Repent and turn away from your i and Ezk 14:6 1544
Me, sets up his i in his heart, Ezk 14:7 1544
sacrificed them to i to be devoured. Ezk 16:20
and offered them up to i by Ezk 16:21
and with all your detestable i, Ezk 16:36 1544
of your sons which you gave to i, Ezk 16:36
lift up his eyes to the i of the house Ezk 18:6 1544
but lifts up his eyes to the i Ezk 18:12 1544
lift up his eyes to the i of the house Ezk 18:15 1544
defile yourselves with the i of Egypt; Ezk 20:7 1544
did they forsake the i of Egypt. Ezk 20:8 1544
continually went after their i. Ezk 20:16 1544
or defile yourselves with their i. Ezk 20:18 1544
eyes were on the i of their fathers. Ezk 20:24 1544
with all your i to this day. Ezk 20:31 1544
"Go, serve everyone his i; Ezk 20:39 1544
with your gifts and with your i. Ezk 20:39 1544
he consults the household i, Ezk 21:21 8655
makes i, contrary to her interest, for Ezk 22:3 1544
defiled by your i which you have Ezk 22:4 1544
with all their i she defiled herself. Ezk 23:7 1544
defiled yourself with their i. Ezk 23:30 1544
committed adultery with their i and Ezk 23:37 1544
slaughtered their children for their i, Ezk 23:39 1544
the penalty of worshiping your i; Ezk 23:49 1544
"I will also destroy the i And Ezk 30:13 1544
eyes to your i as you shed blood. Ezk 33:25 1544
they had defiled it with their i. Ezk 36:18 1544
filthiness and from all your i. Ezk 36:25 1544
defile themselves with their i, Ezk 37:23 1544
went astray from Me after their i, Ezk 44:10 1544
ministered to them before their i Ezk 44:12 1544
and without ephod or household i. Hos 3:4 8655
Ephraim is joined to i; Hos 4:17 6091
they have made i for themselves, Hos 8:4 6091
Baals And burning incense to i. Hos 11:2 6456
I skillfully made from their silver, Hos 13:2 6091
what more have I to do with i? Hos 14:8 6091
"Those who regard vain i Forsake Jon 2:8 1892
All of her i will be smashed, All Mi 1:7 6456
When he fashions speechless i. Hab 2:18 457
cut off the names of the i from the Zch 13:2 6091
abstain from things contaminated by i Ac 15:20 1497
you abstain from things sacrificed to i Ac 15:29 1494
was observing the city full of i. Ac 17:16 2712
abstain from meat sacrificed to i Ac 21:25 1494
You who abhor i, do you rob Ro 2:22 1497
concerning things sacrificed to i, 1Co 8:1 1494
eating of things sacrificed to i, 1Co 8:4 1494
to eat things sacrificed to i? 1Co 8:10 1494
thing sacrificed to i is anything, 1Co 10:19 1494
"This is meat sacrificed to i," 1Co 10:28 2410b
you were led astray to the mute i, 1Co 12:2 1497
has the temple of God with i? 2Co 6:16 1497
and how you turned to God from i 1Th 1:9 1497
children, guard yourselves from i. 1Jn 5:21 1497
to eat things sacrificed to i and Rv 2:14 1494
and eat things sacrificed to i. Rv 2:20 1494
and the i of gold and of silver Rv 9:20 1497

IDUMEA

and from Jerusalem, and from I, Mk 3:8 2401

IEZER

of I, the family of the Iezerites; Nu 26:30 372

IEZERITES

of Iezer, the family of the I; Nu 26:30 373

IF

"I you do well, will not your Gn 4:7 518
And i you do not do well, sin is Gn 4:7 518
I Cain is avenged sevenfold, Then Gn 4:24 3588
to see i the water was abated from Gn 8:8
i to the left, then I will go to Gn 13:9 518
or i to the right, then I will go Gn 13:9 518
so that i anyone can number the Gn 13:16 518
i you are able to count them." Gn 15:5 518
i now I have found favor in Your Gn 18:3 518
and see i they have done entirely Gn 18:21
and i not, I will know." Gn 18:21 518
"I I find in Sodom fifty Gn 18:26 518
it i I find forty-five there." Gn 18:28 518
not do it i I find thirty there." Gn 18:30 518
But i you do not restore her, know Gn 20:7 518
"I it is your wish for me to bury Gn 23:8 518
"I you will only please listen to Gn 23:13 518
"But i the woman is not willing Gn 24:8 518
and i they do not give her to you, Gn 24:41 518
i now You will make my journey on Gn 24:42 518
"So now i you are going to deal Gn 24:49 518
and i not, let me know, that I may Gn 24:49 518
"I it is so, why then am I this Gn 25:22 518
i Jacob takes a wife from the Gn 27:46 518
"I God will be with me and will Gn 28:20 518
"I now it pleases you, stay with Gn 30:27 518
I you will do this one thing for Gn 30:31 518
i found with me, will be Gn 30:33
"I he spoke thus, Gn 31:8 518
and i he spoke thus, Gn 31:8 518
"I the God of my father, the God Gn 31:42 3884a
"I you mistreat my daughters, or Gn 31:50 518
or i you take wives besides my Gn 31:50 518
"I Esau comes to the one company Gn 32:8 518
i now I have found favor in your Gn 33:10 518
i they are driven hard one day, Gn 33:13
"I I find favor in your sight, Gn 34:11
i you will become like us, in that Gn 34:15 518
"But i you will not listen to us Gn 34:17 518
But i not, by the life of Pharaoh, Gn 42:16 518
i you are honest men, let one of Gn 42:19 518
to death i I do not bring him back Gn 42:37 518
I harm should befall him on the Gn 42:38
"I you send our brother with us, Gn 43:4 518
"But i you do not send him, we Gn 43:5 518
I I do not bring him back to you Gn 43:9 518
"For i we had not delayed, surely Gn 43:10 3884a
"I it must be so, then do this: Gn 43:11 518
i I am bereaved of my children, Gn 43:14 834
for i he should leave his father, Gn 44:22
I our youngest brother is with us, Gn 44:26 518
'I you take this one also from me, Gn 44:29
'I I do not bring him back to you, Gn 44:32 518
father i the lad is not with me Gn 44:34
and i you know any capable men Gn 47:6 518
i I have found favor in your Gn 47:29 518
"I now I have found favor in your Gn 50:4 518
"What i Joseph bears a grudge Gn 50:15
the birthstool, i it is a son, Ex 1:16 518
but i it is a daughter, then she Ex 1:16 518
"What i they will not believe me or Ex 4:1 2005
"I they will not believe you or heed Ex 4:8 518
i they will not believe even these Ex 4:9 518
and see i they are still alive." Ex 4:18
"But i you refuse to let them go, Ex 8:2 518
i you do not let My people go, Ex 8:21 518
I we sacrifice what is an Ex 8:26 2005
"For i you refuse to let them go and Ex 9:2 518
"For i by now I had put forth My Ex 9:15
'For i you refuse to let My people Ex 10:4 518
i ever I let you and your little Ex 10:10 834
'Now i the household is too small Ex 12:4 518
i a stranger sojourns with you, Ex 12:48 3588
lamb, but i you do not redeem it, Ex 13:13 518
"I you will give earnest heed to Ex 15:26 518
"I you do this thing and God so Ex 18:23 518
i you will indeed obey My voice Ex 19:5 518
'I you make an altar of stone for Me, Ex 20:25 518
for i you wield your tool on it, Ex 20:25
"I you buy a Hebrew slave, he Ex 21:2 3588
"I he comes alone, he shall go Ex 21:3 518
i he is the husband of a wife, Ex 21:3 518
"I his master gives him a wife, Ex 21:4 518
"But i the slave plainly says, Ex 21:5 518
"I a man sells his daughter as a Ex 21:7 3588
"I she is displeasing in the eyes Ex 21:8 518
"I he designates her for his son, Ex 21:9 518
"I he takes to himself another Ex 21:10 518
"I he will not do these three Ex 21:11 518
"But i he did not lie in wait for Ex 21:13 834
"I, however, a man acts Ex 21:14 3588
"I men have a quarrel and one Ex 21:18 3588
i he gets up and walks around Ex 21:19 518
"I a man strikes his male or Ex 21:20 3588
"I, however, he survives a day or Ex 21:21 518
"I men struggle with each other Ex 21:22 3588
"But i there is any further injury, Ex 21:23 518
"I a man strikes the eye of his male Ex 21:26 3588
"And i he knocks out a tooth of Ex 21:27 518
"I an ox gores a man or a woman to Ex 21:28 3588
"I, however, an ox was previously Ex 21:29 518
"I a ransom is demanded of him, Ex 21:30 518
"I the ox gores a male or female Ex 21:32 518
"I a man opens a pit, or digs a pit Ex 21:33 3588
"I one man's ox hurts another's so Ex 21:35 3588
"Or i it is known that the ox Ex 21:36
"I a man steals an ox or a sheep and Ex 22:1 3588
"I the thief is caught while Ex 22:2 518
"But i the sun has risen on him, Ex 22:3 518
i he owns nothing, then he shall Ex 22:3 518
"I what he stole is actually Ex 22:4 518
"I a man lets a field or vineyard Ex 22:5 3588
"I a fire breaks out and spreads Ex 22:6 3588
"I a man gives his neighbor money Ex 22:7 3588
i the thief is caught, he shall pay Ex 22:7 518
"I the thief is not caught, then Ex 22:8 518
"I a man gives his neighbor a Ex 22:10 3588
"But i it is actually stolen from Ex 22:12 518
"I it is all torn to pieces, let Ex 22:13 518
"I a man borrows anything from Ex 22:14 3588
"I its owner is with it, he shall Ex 22:15 518
i it is hired, it came for its Ex 22:15 518
"I a man seduces a virgin who is not Ex 22:16 3588
"I her father absolutely refuses Ex 22:17 518
"I you afflict him at all, and if Ex 22:23 518
all, and i he does cry out to Me, Ex 22:23 518
"I you lend money to My people, Ex 22:25 518
"I you ever take your neighbor's Ex 22:26 518
"I you meet your enemy's ox or Ex 23:4 3588
"I you see the donkey of one who Ex 23:5 3588
"But i you truly obey his Ex 23:22 518
for i you serve their gods, it Ex 23:33
"I any of the flesh of ordination or Ex 29:34 518
"But now, i You will, forgive Ex 32:32 518
i not, please blot me out from Your Ex 32:32 518
i I have found favor in Your sight, Ex 33:13 518
"I Your presence does not go with Ex 33:15 518
"I now I have found favor in Your Ex 34:9 518
and i you do not redeem it, then Ex 34:20 518
but i the cloud was not taken up, Ex 40:37 518
'I his offering is a burnt Lv 1:3 518
'But i his offering is from the Lv 1:10 518
'But i his offering to the LORD is Lv 1:14 518
'I your offering is a grain offering Lv 2:5 518
'Now i your offering is a grain Lv 2:7 518
'Also i you bring a grain offering Lv 2:14 518
'Now i his offering is a sacrifice Lv 3:1 518
i he is going to offer out of the Lv 3:1 518
'But i his offering for a Lv 3:6 518

'I he is going to offer a lamb for Lv 3:7 518
i his offering is a goat, Lv 3:12 518
'I a person sins unintentionally Lv 4:2 3588
i the anointed priest sins so as Lv 4:3 518
'Now i the whole congregation of Lv 4:13 518
i his sin which he has committed Lv 4:23 176
'Now i anyone of the common people Lv 4:27 518
i his sin which he has committed Lv 4:28 176
'But i he brings a lamb as his Lv 4:32 518
'Now i a person sins after he Lv 5:1 3588
known, i he does not tell *it,* Lv 5:1 518
'Or i a person touches any unclean Lv 5:2 834
'Or i he touches human Lv 5:3 3588
'Or i a person swears Lv 5:4 3588
'But i he cannot afford a lamb, Lv 5:7 518
'But i his means are insufficient Lv 5:11 518
"I a person acts unfaithfully and Lv 5:15 3588
"Now i a person sins and does any Lv 5:17 518
or i he has extorted from his Lv 6:2
and i it was boiled in a bronze Lv 6:28 518
'I he offers it by way of Lv 7:12 518
i the sacrifice of his offering is a Lv 7:16 518
'So i any of the flesh of the Lv 7:18 518
i I had eaten a sin offering Lv 10:19
'I a part of their carcass falls on Lv 11:37 3588
'Though i water is put on the Lv 11:38 3588
'Also i one of the animals dies Lv 11:39 3588
'But i she bears a female *child,* Lv 12:5 518
'But i she cannot afford a lamb, Lv 12:8 518
and i the hair in the infection Lv 13:3
"But i the bright spot is white Lv 13:4 518
and i in his eyes the infection Lv 13:5 2009
and i the infection has faded and Lv 13:6 2009
"But i the scab spreads farther Lv 13:7 518
and i the scab has spread on the Lv 13:8 2009
and i there is a white swelling in Lv 13:10 2009
"I the leprosy breaks out farther on Lv 13:12 518
i the leprosy has covered all his Lv 13:13
"Or i the raw flesh turns again Lv 13:16 3588
i the infection has turned to Lv 13:17
i it appears to be lower than Lv 13:20
"But i the priest looks at it, Lv 13:21 518
i it spreads farther on the skin, Lv 13:22 518
"But i the bright spot remains in Lv 13:23 518
i the body sustains in its skin a burn Lv 13:24 3588
And i the hair in the bright spot Lv 13:25 2009
"But i the priest looks at it, Lv 13:26 518
I it spreads farther in the skin, Lv 13:27 518
"But i the bright spot remains in Lv 13:28 518
"Now i a man or woman has an Lv 13:29 3588
and i it appears to be deeper than Lv 13:30 2009
i the priest looks at the infection of Lv 13:31 3588
and i the scale has not spread and Lv 13:32 2009
and i the scale has not spread in Lv 13:34 2009
"But i the scale spreads farther Lv 13:35 518
and i the scale has spread in the Lv 13:36 2009
I in his sight the scale has remained Lv 13:37 518
and i the bright spots on the skin Lv 13:39 2009
"Now i a man loses the hair of Lv 13:40 3588
"I his head becomes bald at Lv 13:41 518
"But i on the bald head or the Lv 13:42 3588
i the swelling of the infection is Lv 13:43 2009
i the mark is greenish or reddish Lv 13:49
i the mark has spread in the Lv 13:51 3588
"But i the priest shall look, and Lv 13:53 518
and i the mark has not changed its Lv 13:55 2009
"Then i the priest looks, Lv 13:56 518
and i the mark has faded after it Lv 13:56 2009
and i it appears again in the Lv 13:57 518
and i the infection of leprosy has Lv 14:3 2009
"But i he is poor and his means Lv 14:21 518
and i the mark on the walls of the Lv 14:37 2009
I the mark has indeed spread in Lv 14:39 2009
"I, however, the mark breaks out Lv 14:43 518
I he sees that the mark has indeed Lv 14:44 2009
"I, on the other hand, the priest Lv 14:48 518
'Or i the man with the discharge Lv 15:8 3588
i a man has a seminal emission, Lv 15:16 3588
'I a man lies with a woman *so that* Lv 15:18
'When a woman has a discharge, i Lv 15:19
'I a man actually lies with her so Lv 15:24 518
'Now i a woman has a discharge of Lv 15:25 3588
or i she has a discharge beyond Lv 15:25 3588
"But i he does not wash *them* or Lv 17:16 518
a man may live i he does them; Lv 18:5
'So i it is eaten at all on the Lv 19:7 518
i a man lies carnally with a woman Lv 19:20 3588
'I the people of the land, Lv 20:4 518
'I *there is* anyone who curses his Lv 20:9 3588
'I *there is* a man who commits Lv 20:10
'I *there is* a man who lies with Lv 20:11
'I *there is* a man who lies with Lv 20:12
'I *there is* a man who lies with a Lv 20:13
'I *there is* a man who marries a Lv 20:14
'I *there is* a man who lies with an Lv 20:15
'I *there is* a woman who approaches Lv 20:16
'I *there is* a man who takes his Lv 20:17
'I *there is* a man who lies with a Lv 20:18
'I *there is* a man who lies with Lv 20:20
'I *there is* a man who takes his Lv 20:21
i she profanes herself by harlotry, Lv 21:9 3588
'I any man among all your Lv 22:3
And i one touches anything made Lv 22:4
or i a man has a seminal emission, Lv 22:4
or i a man touches any teeming Lv 22:5
'But i a priest buys a slave as Lv 22:11 3588
'I a priest's daughter is married to Lv 22:12 3588
'But i a priest's daughter becomes Lv 22:13 3588
'But i a man eats a holy *gift* Lv 22:14 3588
"I there is any person who will Lv 23:29 3588
'I anyone curses his God, then he Lv 24:15 3588
'I a man takes the life of any human Lv 24:17 3588
'I a man injures his neighbor, just Lv 24:19 3588
'I you make a sale, moreover, to Lv 25:14 3588
i you say, "What are we going to eat Lv 25:20 3588
on the seventh year i we do not sow Lv 25:20 2005
'I a fellow countryman of yours Lv 25:25 3588
'But i he has not found sufficient Lv 25:28 518
i a man sells a dwelling house in Lv 25:29 3588
'But i it is not bought back for Lv 25:30 518
'I a countryman of yours becomes so Lv 25:39 3588
man, as i he were a sojourner; Lv 25:40
'Now i the means of a stranger or Lv 25:47 3588
or i he prospers, he may redeem Lv 25:49
'I there are still many years, he Lv 25:51 518
and i few years remain until the Lv 25:52 518
'Even i he is not redeemed by Lv 25:54 518
'I you walk in My statutes and Lv 26:3 518
'But i you do not obey Me and do Lv 26:14 518
i, instead, you reject My statutes, Lv 26:15 518
i your soul abhors My ordinances Lv 26:15 518
'I also after these things you do Lv 26:18 518
'I then, you act with hostility Lv 26:21 518
'And i by these things you are not Lv 26:23 518
i in spite of this you do not obey Lv 26:27 518
other as i *running* from the sword, Lv 26:37
'I they confess their iniquity and Lv 26:40
i their uncircumcised heart becomes Lv 26:41 227
'I your valuation is of the male Lv 27:3
'Or i it is a female, then your Lv 27:4 518
'I it be from five years even to Lv 27:5 518
'But i *they are* from a month even Lv 27:6 518
'I *they are* from sixty years old Lv 27:7 518
i it is a male, then your valuation Lv 27:7 518
'But i he is poorer than your Lv 27:8 518
'Now i it is an animal of the kind Lv 27:9 518
or i he does exchange animal for Lv 27:10 518
I, however, it is any unclean animal Lv 27:11 518
'But i he should ever *wish to* Lv 27:13 518
'Now i a man consecrates his house Lv 27:14 3588
'Yet i the one who consecrates it Lv 27:15 518
i a man consecrates to the LORD Lv 27:16 518
'I he consecrates his field as of Lv 27:17 518
'I he consecrates his field after Lv 27:18 518
'I the one who consecrates it should Lv 27:19 518
i he will not redeem the field, Lv 27:20 518
'Or i he consecrates to the LORD a Lv 27:22 518
i *it is* among the unclean animals, Lv 27:27 518
and i it is not redeemed, then it Lv 27:27 518
'I, therefore, a man wishes to Lv 27:31 518
or i he does exchange it, then Lv 27:33 518
'But i the man has no relative to Nu 5:8 518
'I any man's wife goes astray and Nu 5:12 3588
i a spirit of jealousy comes over Nu 5:14
or i a spirit of jealousy comes Nu 5:14
"I no man has lain with you and Nu 5:19 518
i you have not gone astray Nu 5:19 518
i you, however, have gone astray, Nu 5:20 3588
and i you have defiled yourself Nu 5:20 3588
i she has defiled herself and has Nu 5:27 518
'But i the woman has not defiled Nu 5:28 518
'But i a man dies very suddenly Nu 6:9 3588
'I any one of you or of your Nu 9:10 3588
'I an alien sojourns among you Nu 9:14 3588
I sometimes the cloud remained a Nu 9:20
I sometimes the cloud remained Nu 9:21
or i *it remained* in the daytime Nu 9:21
"Yet i *only* one is blown, then Nu 10:4 518
"So it will be, i you go with us, Nu 10:32 3588
"So i You are going to deal thus Nu 11:15 518
i I have found favor in Your sight, Nu 11:15 518
I there is a prophet among you, I, Nu 12:6 518
I her father had but spit in her face Nu 12:14
"I the LORD is pleased with us, Nu 14:8 518
"Now i You slay this people Nu 14:15
'I an alien sojourns with you, or Nu 15:14 3588
be, i it is done unintentionally, Nu 15:24 518
'Also i one person sins Nu 15:27 518
"I these men die the death of all Nu 16:29 518
or i they suffer the fate of all Nu 16:29
"But i the LORD brings about an Nu 16:30 518
but i he does not purify himself Nu 19:12 518
"I only we had perished when our Nu 20:3 3863
and i I and my livestock do drink Nu 20:19 518
"I You will indeed deliver this Nu 21:2 518
that i a serpent bit any man, Nu 21:9 518
"I the men have come to call you, Nu 22:20 518
I there had been a sword in my Nu 22:29 3863
I she had not turned aside from Nu 22:33 194
then, i it is displeasing to you, Nu 22:34 518
'I a man dies and has no son, then Nu 27:8 3588
'I he has no daughter, then you Nu 27:9 518
'I he has no brothers, then you Nu 27:10 518
'I his father has no brothers, then Nu 27:11 518
"I a man makes a vow to the LORD, Nu 30:2 3588
"Also i a woman makes a vow to Nu 30:3 3588
"But i her father should forbid Nu 30:5 518
i she should marry while under her Nu 30:6 518
"But i on the day her husband Nu 30:8 518
i she vowed in her husband's Nu 30:10 518
"But i her husband indeed annuls Nu 30:12 518
"But i her husband indeed says Nu 30:14 518
"But i he indeed annuls them Nu 30:15 518
"I we have found favor in your Nu 32:5 518
"For i you turn away from Nu 32:15 3588
"I you will do this, if you will Nu 32:20 518
i you will arm yourselves before Nu 32:20 518
"But i you will not do so, Nu 32:23 518
"I the sons of Gad and the sons Nu 32:29 518
but i they will not cross over Nu 32:30 518
'But i you do not drive out the Nu 33:55 518
'But i he struck him down with an Nu 35:16 518
'I he struck him down with a stone Nu 35:17 518
'Or i he struck *him* with a wooden Nu 35:18
'I he pushed him of hatred, Nu 35:20 518
or i he struck him down with his Nu 35:21
'But i he pushed him suddenly Nu 35:22 518
'But i the manslayer at any Nu 35:26 518
'I anyone kills a person, the Nu 35:30
"But i they marry one of the sons Nu 36:3
and you will find *Him* i you search Dt 4:29 3588
i we hear the voice of the LORD Dt 5:25 518
righteousness for us i we are careful Dt 6:25 3588
"I you should say in your heart, Dt 7:17 3588
"It shall come about i you Dt 8:19 518
i you listen obediently to my Dt 11:13 518
"For i you are careful to keep Dt 11:22 518
i you listen to the commandments Dt 11:27 834
i you do not listen to the Dt 11:28 518
"I the place which the LORD your Dt 12:21 3588
"I a prophet or a dreamer of Dt 13:1 3588
to find out i you love the LORD Dt 13:3
"I your brother, your mother's Dt 13:6 3588
"I you hear in one of your Dt 13:12 3588
I it is true *and* the matter Dt 13:14 2009
i you will listen to the voice of Dt 13:18 3588
"I the distance is so great for you Dt 14:24 3588
i only you listen obediently to Dt 15:5 518
"I there is a poor man with you, Dt 15:7 3588
"I your kinsman, a Hebrew man or Dt 15:12 3588
shall come about i he says to you, Dt 15:16 3588
"But i it has any defect, *such as* Dt 15:21 3588
"I there is found in your midst, Dt 17:2 3588
and i it is told you and you have Dt 17:4
i it is true and the thing certain Dt 17:4
"I any case is too difficult for Dt 17:8 3588
"Now i a Levite comes from any of Dt 18:6 3588
i the thing does not come about or Dt 18:22
"I the LORD your God enlarges Dt 19:8 518
i you carefully observe all this Dt 19:9 3588
"But i there is a man who hates Dt 19:11 3588
"I a malicious witness rises up Dt 19:16 3588
and i the witness is a false Dt 19:18 2009
"I it agrees to make peace with you Dt 20:11 518
i it does not make peace with you, Dt 20:12 518
"I a slain person is found lying Dt 21:1 3588
i you are not pleased with her, Dt 21:14 518
"I a man has two wives, the one Dt 21:15 3588
i the firstborn son belongs to Dt 21:15
"I any man has a stubborn and Dt 21:18 3588
"I a man has committed a sin worthy Dt 21:22 3588
"I your countryman is not near you, Dt 22:2 518
you, or i you do not know him, Dt 22:2
"I you happen to come upon a Dt 22:6 3588
your house i anyone falls from it. Dt 22:8 3588
"I any man takes a wife and goes Dt 22:13 3588
"But i this charge is true, that Dt 22:20 518
"I a man is found lying with a Dt 22:22 3588
"I there is a girl who is a virgin Dt 22:23 3588
"But i in the field the man finds Dt 22:25 518
"I a man finds a girl who is a virgin Dt 22:28 3588
"I there is among you any man who Dt 23:10 3588
i you refrain from vowing, Dt 23:22 3588
and i the latter husband turns Dt 24:3
or i the latter husband dies who Dt 24:3 3588
"I a man is caught kidnapping any Dt 24:7 3588
"I he is a poor man, you shall not Dt 24:12 518
"I there is a dispute between men Dt 25:1 3588
i the wicked man deserves to be Dt 25:2 518
"But i the man does not desire to Dt 25:7 518
And i he persists and says, Dt 25:8
"I *two* men, a man and his Dt 25:11 3588
i you diligently obey the Dt 28:1 518
i you obey the LORD your God: Dt 28:2 3588
i you keep the commandments Dt 28:9 3588
i you listen to the Dt 28:13 3588
i you do not obey the LORD your Dt 28:15 518
"I you are not careful to observe Dt 28:58 518
"I your outcasts are at the ends Dt 30:4 518
i you obey the LORD your God to Dt 30:10 3588
i you turn to the LORD your God Dt 30:10 3588
"But i your heart turns away and Dt 30:17 518
I I sharpen My flashing sword, And Dt 32:41 518
I you do not tell this business of Jos 2:14 518
our head i a hand is *laid* on him. Jos 2:19 518
"But i you tell this business of Jos 2:20 518
I only we had been willing to Jos 7:7 3863
"I you are a numerous people, go Jos 17:15 518
'Now i the avenger of blood Jos 20:5 3588
I you rebel against the LORD Jos 22:18
'I, however, the land of your Jos 22:19 518
I *it was* in rebellion, or if in an Jos 22:22 518
or i in an unfaithful act against Jos 22:22 518
"I we have built us an altar to Jos 22:23
or i to offer a burnt offering or Jos 22:23 518
or i to offer sacrifices of peace Jos 22:23 518
i they say *this* to us or to our Jos 22:28 3588
"For i you ever go back and cling Jos 23:12 518
"I it is disagreeable in your sight Jos 24:15 518
"I you forsake the LORD and serve Jos 24:20 3588
to find out i they would obey the Jg 3:4
"I you will go with me, then I Jg 4:8 518
but i you will not go with me, I Jg 4:8 518
i anyone comes and inquires of you Jg 4:20 518
"O my lord, i the LORD is with Jg 6:13
"I now I have found favor in Your Jg 6:17 518
I he is a god, let him contend for Jg 6:31 518

Context	Ref.	No.
“I You will deliver Israel	Jg 6:36	518
I there is dew on the fleece only,	Jg 6:37	518
“But i you are afraid to go down,	Jg 7:10	518
i only you had let them live,	Jg 8:19	3863
‘I in truth you are anointing me	Jg 9:15	518
but i not, may fire come out from	Jg 9:15	518
i you have dealt in truth and	Jg 9:16	518
and i you have dealt well with	Jg 9:16	518
i then you have dealt in truth and	Jg 9:19	518
“But i not, let fire come out	Jg 9:20	518
the shadow of the mountains as i	Jg 9:36	
“I you take me back to fight	Jg 11:9	518
“I You will indeed give the sons	Jg 11:30	518
an Ephraimite?” I he said, “No,”	Jg 12:5	
i you prepare a burnt offering,	Jg 13:16	518
“I the LORD had desired to kill	Jg 13:23	3863
i you will indeed tell it to me	Jg 14:12	518
“But i you are unable to tell me,	Jg 14:13	518
“I you had not plowed with my	Jg 14:18	3884a
“I they bind me with seven fresh	Jg 16:7	518
“I they bind me tightly with new	Jg 16:11	518
“I you weave the seven locks of	Jg 16:13	518
I I am shaved, then my strength	Jg 16:17	518
i the daughters of Shiloh come out	Jg 21:21	518
I I said I have hope, if I should	Ru 1:12	3588
i I should even have a husband	Ru 1:12	
i *anything but* death parts you and	Ru 1:17	3588
comes, i he will redeem you,	Ru 3:13	518
But i he does not wish to redeem	Ru 3:13	518
I you will redeem *it,* redeem *it;*	Ru 4:4	518
but i not, tell me that I may know;	Ru 4:4	518
i You will indeed look on the	1Sa 1:11	518
I the man said to him, “They must	1Sa 2:16	518
and i not, I will take it by force.”	1Sa 2:16	518
“I one man sins against another,	1Sa 2:25	518
but i a man sins against the LORD,	1Sa 2:25	518
i He calls you, that you shall say,	1Sa 3:9	518
i you hide anything from me of all	1Sa 3:17	518
“I you send away the ark of the	1Sa 6:3	518
i it goes up by the way of its own	1Sa 6:9	518
But i not, then we will know that	1Sa 6:9	518
“I you return to the LORD with	1Sa 7:3	518
i we go, what shall we bring the	1Sa 9:7	
i there is no one to deliver us,	1Sa 11:3	518
“I you will fear the LORD and	1Sa 12:14	518
“I you will not listen to the voice	1Sa 12:15	518
“But i you still do wickedly,	1Sa 12:25	518
“I they say to us,	1Sa 14:9	518
“But i they say,	1Sa 14:10	518
i only the people had eaten freely	1Sa 14:30	3863
“I he is able to fight with me	1Sa 17:9	518
but i I prevail against him and	1Sa 17:9	518
i I find out anything, then I	1Sa 19:3	
“I you do not save your life	1Sa 19:11	518
“I your father misses me at all,	1Sa 20:6	518
“I he says, ‘It is good,’ your servant	1Sa 20:7	518
but i he is very angry, know that	1Sa 20:7	518
But i there is iniquity in me, put	1Sa 20:8	518
For i I should indeed learn that	1Sa 20:9	518
i your father answers you harshly?”	1Sa 20:10	176, 4100
i there is good *feeling* toward David	1Sa 20:12	518
“I it please my father *to do* you	1Sa 20:13	3588
i I do not make it known to you	1Sa 20:13	518
“I I am still alive, will you not	1Sa 20:14	518
I I specifically say to the lad,	1Sa 20:21	518
“But i I say to the youth,	1Sa 20:22	518
i I have found favor in your	1Sa 20:29	518
i only the young men have kept	1Sa 21:4	518
i you would take it for yourself,	1Sa 21:9	518
i we go to Keilah against the ranks	1Sa 23:3	3588
i he is in the land, I will search	1Sa 23:23	518
“For i a man finds his enemy,	1Sa 24:19	3588
i by morning I leave *as much as*	1Sa 25:22	518
I the LORD has stirred you up	1Sa 26:19	518
but i it is men, cursed are they	1Sa 26:19	518
“I now I have found favor in your	1Sa 27:5	518
God lives, i you had not spoken,	2Sa 2:27	3588, 3884a
i as the LORD has sworn to David,	2Sa 3:9	3588
i I taste bread or anything else	2Sa 3:35	3588, 518
of the house as i to get wheat,	2Sa 4:6	
“I the Arameans are too strong	2Sa 10:11	518
but i the sons of Ammon are too	2Sa 10:11	518
and i it happens that the king’s	2Sa 11:20	518
and i *that had been* too little, I	2Sa 12:8	518
“I not, please let my brother	2Sa 13:26	
and i there is iniquity in me, let	2Sa 14:32	518
‘I the LORD shall indeed bring me	2Sa 15:8	518
I I find favor in the sight of the	2Sa 15:25	518
“But i He should say thus,	2Sa 15:26	518
“I you pass over with me, then	2Sa 15:33	518
“But i you return to the city,	2Sa 15:34	518
I he curses, and if the LORD has	2Sa 16:10	3588
and i the LORD has told him,	2Sa 16:10	3588
was as i one inquired of the word	2Sa 16:23	3512c
I not, you speak.”	2Sa 17:6	518
“I he withdraws into a city, then	2Sa 17:13	518
for i we indeed flee, they will	2Sa 18:3	518
about us; even i half of us die,	2Sa 18:3	518
“Even i I should receive a thousand	2Sa 18:12	3863
i I had dealt treacherously	2Sa 18:13	
“I he is by himself there is good	2Sa 18:25	518
i Absalom were alive and all of us	2Sa 19:6	3863
by the LORD, i you do not go out,	2Sa 19:7	3588
i you will not be commander of the	2Sa 19:13	518
“I he is a worthy man, not	1Ki 1:52	518
but i wickedness is found in him,	1Ki 1:52	518
‘I your sons are careful of their	1Ki 2:4	518
i Adonijah has not spoken this	1Ki 2:23	3588
“I you walk in My ways, keeping My	1Ki 3:14	518
i you will walk in My statutes and	1Ki 6:12	518
i only your sons take heed to	1Ki 8:25	518
“I a man sins against his	1Ki 8:31	834
i they turn to You again and	1Ki 8:33	
“I there is famine in the land,	1Ki 8:37	3588
the land, i there is pestilence,	1Ki 8:37	3588
i there is blight *or* mildew,	1Ki 8:37	3588
i their enemy besieges them in	1Ki 8:37	3588
i they take thought in the land	1Ki 8:47	
i they return to You with all	1Ki 8:48	
i you will walk before Me as your	1Ki 9:4	518
“But i you or your sons indeed	1Ki 9:6	518
that i you listen to all that I	1Ki 11:38	518
“I you will be a servant to this	1Ki 12:7	518
“I this people go up to offer	1Ki 12:27	518
“I you were to give me half your	1Ki 13:8	518
I the LORD is God, follow Him;	1Ki 18:21	518
but i Baal, follow him.”	1Ki 18:21	518
i I do not make your life as the	1Ki 19:2	3588
i the dust of Samaria will	1Ki 20:10	518
“I they have come out for peace,	1Ki 20:18	518
or i they have come out for war,	1Ki 20:18	518
i for any reason he is missing,	1Ki 20:39	518
i you like, I will give you the	1Ki 21:2	518
or else, i it pleases you, I will	1Ki 21:6	518
“I you indeed return safely the	1Ki 22:28	518
“I I am a man of God, let fire	2Ki 1:10	518
“I I am a man of God, let fire	2Ki 1:12	518
i you see me when I am taken from	2Ki 2:10	518
but i not, it shall not be *so.*”	2Ki 2:10	518
i you meet any man, do not salute	2Ki 4:29	3588
i anyone salutes you, do not answer	2Ki 4:29	3588
“I not, please let your servant	2Ki 5:17	518
“I the LORD does not help you,	2Ki 6:27	518
i the head of Elisha the son of	2Ki 6:31	518
i the LORD should make windows in	2Ki 7:2	
“I we say, ‘We will enter the city,’	2Ki 7:4	518
and i we sit here, we die also.	2Ki 7:4	518
I they spare us, we will live;	2Ki 7:4	518
and i they kill us, we will but	2Ki 7:4	518
i we wait until morning light,	2Ki 7:9	
i the LORD should make windows in	2Ki 7:19	
“I this is your mind, *then* let no	2Ki 9:15	518
“I you are on my side, and you	2Ki 10:6	518
“I it is, give *me* your hand.”	2Ki 10:15	
on which i a man leans, it will go	2Ki 18:21	
“But i you say to me,	2Ki 18:22	3588
i you are able on your part to set	2Ki 18:23	518
i there will be peace and truth	2Ki 20:19	518
i only they will observe to do	2Ki 21:8	518
“I you come peacefully to me to	1Ch 12:17	518
i to betray me to my adversaries,	1Ch 12:17	518
“I it seems good to you, and if	1Ch 13:2	518
and i it is from the LORD our God,	1Ch 13:2	
“I the Arameans are too strong	1Ch 19:12	518
but i the sons of Ammon are too	1Ch 19:12	518
i you are careful to observe the	1Ch 22:13	518
i he resolutely performs My	1Ch 28:7	518
I you seek Him, He will let you	1Ch 28:9	518
but i you forsake Him, He will	1Ch 28:9	518
i only your sons take heed to	2Ch 6:16	518
“I a man sins against his	2Ch 6:22	518
“I Your people Israel are defeated	2Ch 6:24	518
“I there is famine in the land,	2Ch 6:28	3588
the land, i there is pestilence,	2Ch 6:28	3588
i there is blight or mildew,	2Ch 6:28	3588
i there is locust or grasshopper,	2Ch 6:28	3588
i their enemies besiege them in the	2Ch 6:28	3588
i they take thought in the land	2Ch 6:37	
i they return to You with all	2Ch 6:38	
“I I shut up the heavens so that	2Ch 7:13	2005
or i I command the locust to	2Ch 7:13	2005
or i I send pestilence among My	2Ch 7:13	2005
i you walk before Me as your	2Ch 7:17	518
“But i you turn away and forsake	2Ch 7:19	518
“I you will be kind to this	2Ch 10:7	518
And i you seek Him, He will let	2Ch 15:2	518
but i you forsake Him, He will	2Ch 15:2	518
“I you indeed return safely, the	2Ch 18:27	518
“But i you do go, do *it,* be	2Ch 25:8	518
“For i you return to the LORD,	2Ch 30:9	518
from you i you return to Him.”	2Ch 30:9	518
i only they will observe to do all	2Ch 33:8	518
that i that city is rebuilt and	Ezr 4:13	2006
i that city is rebuilt and the	Ezr 4:16	2006
i it pleases the king, let a search	Ezr 5:17	2006
i it be that a decree was issued	Ezr 5:17	2006
‘I you are unfaithful I will scatter	Ne 1:8	
but i you return to Me and keep My	Ne 1:9	
“I it please the king, and if	Ne 2:5	518
and i your servant has found favor	Ne 2:5	518
“I it please the king, let	Ne 2:7	518
i a fox should jump on *it,* he would	Ne 4:3	518
i a man observes them he shall live.	Ne 9:29	
I you do so again, I will use	Ne 13:21	518
“I it pleases the king, let a	Es 1:19	518
“I it is pleasing to the king,	Es 3:9	518
“For i you remain silent at this	Es 4:14	518
and i I perish, I perish.”	Es 4:16	834
“I it pleases the king, may the	Es 5:4	518
I I have found favor in the sight	Es 5:8	518
and i it pleases the king to grant	Es 5:8	518
“I Mordecai, before whom you have	Es 6:13	518
“I I have found favor in your	Es 7:3	518
i it pleases the king, let my life be	Es 7:3	518
i we had only been sold as slaves,	Es 7:4	432
“I it pleases the king and if I	Es 8:5	518
i I have found favor before him	Es 8:5	518
“I it pleases the king, let	Es 9:13	518
“I one ventures a word with you,	Jb 4:2	
me, And *see* i I lie to your face.	Jb 6:28	518
“I I say, ‘My bed will comfort me,	Jb 7:13	3588
“I your sons sinned against Him,	Jb 8:4	518
“I you would seek God And implore	Jb 8:5	518
I you are pure and upright, Surely	Jb 8:6	518
“I he is removed from his place,	Jb 8:18	518
“I one wished to dispute with	Jb 9:3	518
“I I called and He answered me, I	Jb 9:16	518
“I *it is a matter* of power,	Jb 9:19	518
And i *it is a matter* of justice,	Jb 9:19	518
“I the scourge kills suddenly, He	Jb 9:23	518
I *it is* not *He,* then who is it?	Jb 9:24	518
“I I should wash myself with snow	Jb 9:30	518
I I sin, then You would take	Jb 10:14	518
‘I I am wicked, woe to me!	Jb 10:15	518
And i I am righteous, I dare not	Jb 10:15	
“I He passes by or shuts up, Or	Jb 11:10	518
“I you would direct your heart	Jb 11:13	518
I iniquity is in your hand, put it	Jb 11:14	518
I you secretly show partiality.	Jb 13:10	518
“I a man dies, will he live *again?*	Jb 14:14	518
I I were in your place. I could	Jb 16:4	3863
“I I speak, my pain is not	Jb 16:6	518
i I hold back, what has left me?	Jb 16:6	
“I I look for Sheol as my home, I	Jb 17:13	518
I I call to the pit,	Jb 17:14	
“Even i I have truly erred, My	Jb 19:4	
“I indeed you vaunt yourselves	Jb 19:5	518
“I you say, ‘How shall we persecute	Jb 19:28	3588
would we gain i we entreat Him?’	Jb 21:15	3588
the Almighty i you are righteous,	Jb 22:3	3588
i you make your ways perfect?	Jb 22:3	3588
“I you return to the Almighty,	Jb 22:23	518
I you remove unrighteousness far	Jb 22:23	
“Now i it is not so, who can	Jb 24:25	518
“I even the moon has no brightness	Jb 25:5	2005
“I I have walked with falsehood,	Jb 31:5	518
“I my step has turned from the	Jb 31:7	518
i any spot has stuck to my hands,	Jb 31:7	
“I my heart has been enticed by a	Jb 31:9	518
“I I have despised the claim of	Jb 31:13	518
“I I have kept the poor from	Jb 31:16	518
I I have seen anyone perish for	Jb 31:19	518
I his loins have not thanked me,	Jb 31:20	518
And i he has not been warmed with	Jb 31:20	
I I have lifted up my hand against	Jb 31:21	518
“I I have put my confidence *in*	Jb 31:24	518
I I have gloated because my wealth	Jb 31:25	518
I I have looked at the sun when it	Jb 31:26	518
“I my land cries out against me,	Jb 31:38	518
I I have eaten its fruit without	Jb 31:39	518
‘Refute me i you can;	Jb 33:5	518
“I there is an angel *as* mediator	Jb 33:23	518
“*Then* i you have anything to say,	Jb 33:32	518
“I not, listen to me;	Jb 33:33	518
“I He should determine to do so,	Jb 34:14	518
I He should gather to Himself His	Jb 34:14	
“But i *you have* understanding,	Jb 34:16	518
I I have done iniquity, I will not	Jb 34:32	518
I have, more than i I had sinned?’	Jb 35:3	
“I you have sinned, what do you	Jb 35:6	518
i your transgressions are many,	Jb 35:6	
“I you are righteous, what do you	Jb 35:7	518
“And i they are bound in fetters,	Jb 36:8	518
“I they hear and serve *Him,* They	Jb 36:11	518
“But i they do not hear, they	Jb 36:12	518
Tell *Me,* i you have understanding,	Jb 38:4	518
Tell *Me,* i you know all this.	Jb 38:18	518
cruelly, as i *they* were not hers;	Jb 39:16	
“I a river rages, he is not	Jb 40:23	2005
O LORD my God, i I have done this,	Ps 7:3	518
I there is injustice in my hands,	Ps 7:3	518
I I have rewarded evil to my	Ps 7:4	518
I a man does not repent, He will	Ps 7:12	518
I the foundations are destroyed,	Ps 11:3	3588
i there are any who understand,	Ps 14:2	
me, For i You are silent to me,	Ps 28:1	
my blood, i I go down to the pit?	Ps 30:9	
I I would declare and speak of	Ps 40:5	
I we had forgotten the name of our	Ps 44:20	518
“I I were hungry I would not	Ps 50:12	518
To see i there is anyone who	Ps 53:2	
growl i they are not satisfied.	Ps 59:15	518
I riches increase, do not set *your*	Ps 62:10	3588
I I regard wickedness in my heart,	Ps 66:18	518
I I had said, “I will speak thus,”	Ps 73:15	518
It seems as i one had lifted up	Ps 74:5	
Then the Lord awoke as i *from*	Ps 78:65	
Israel, i you would listen to Me!	Ps 81:8	518
“I his sons forsake My law And	Ps 89:30	518
I they violate My statutes And do	Ps 89:31	518
Or i due to strength, eighty years,	Ps 90:10	518
I the LORD had not been my help,	Ps 94:17	3884a
I I should say, “My foot has slipped,	Ps 94:18	518
Today, i you would hear His voice,	Ps 95:7	518
I Your law had not been my delight,	Ps 119:92	3884a
I You, LORD, should mark	Ps 130:3	518
“I your sons will keep My	Ps 132:12	518
I I forget you, O Jerusalem, May	Ps 137:5	518
my mouth I I do not remember you,	Ps 137:6	518
I I do not exalt Jerusalem Above	Ps 137:6	518
I I ascend to heaven, You are	Ps 139:8	518
I I make my bed in Sheol, behold,	Ps 139:8	
I I take the wings of the dawn, If	Ps 139:9	
I I dwell in the remotest part of	Ps 139:9	

Context	Reference	No.
I I say, "Surely the darkness will	Ps 139:11	
I I should count them, they would	Ps 139:18	
And see i there be any hurtful way	Ps 139:24	518
My son, i sinners entice you, Do	Pr 1:10	518
I they say, "Come with us, Let us lie	Pr 1:11	518
i you will receive my words	Pr 2:1	518
For i you cry for discernment,	Pr 2:3	518
I you seek her as silver And	Pr 2:4	518
cause, I he has done you no harm.	Pr 3:30	518
will honor you i you embrace her.	Pr 4:8	3588
And i you run, you will not	Pr 4:12	518
i you have become surety for your	Pr 6:1	518
I you have been snared with	Pr 6:2	
i he steals To satisfy himself when	Pr 6:30	3588
I you are wise, you are wise for	Pr 9:12	518
i you scoff, you alone will bear it.	Pr 9:12	
I the righteous will be rewarded	Pr 11:31	2005
the penalty, For i you rescue *him,*	Pr 19:19	518
I his conduct is pure and right.	Pr 20:11	518
i you keep them within you,	Pr 22:18	3588
I you have nothing with which to	Pr 22:27	518
I you are a man of *great* appetite.	Pr 23:2	518
My son, i your heart is wise, My	Pr 23:15	518
I you are slack in the day of	Pr 24:10	
I you say, "See, we did not know this,	Pr 24:12	3588
I you find *it,* then there will be	Pr 24:14	518
I your enemy is hungry, give him	Pr 25:21	518
And i he is thirsty, give him	Pr 25:21	518
I a ruler pays attention to	Pr 29:12	
I a king judges the poor with truth,	Pr 29:14	
I you have been foolish in	Pr 30:32	518
Or i you have plotted *evil,*	Pr 30:32	518
For i either of them falls, the	Ec 4:10	518
I two lie down together they keep	Ec 4:11	518
And i one can overpower him who is	Ec 4:12	518
I you see oppression of the poor	Ec 5:8	518
I a man fathers a hundred *children*	Ec 6:3	518
"Even i the *other* man lives a	Ec 6:6	432
I no one knows what will happen,	Ec 8:7	3588
I the ruler's temper rises against	Ec 10:4	518
I the axe is dull and he does not	Ec 10:10	518
I the serpent bites before being	Ec 10:11	518
I the clouds are full, they pour	Ec 11:3	518
i a man should live many years,	Ec 11:8	518
"I you yourself do not know, Most	SS 1:8	518
Jerusalem, I you find my beloved,	SS 5:8	518
I I found you outdoors, I would	SS 8:1	
I a man were to give all the	SS 8:7	518
"I she is a wall, We will build	SS 8:9	518
But i she is a door, We will	SS 8:9	518
"I you consent and obey, You will	Is 1:19	518
"But i you refuse and rebel, You	Is 1:20	518
And sin as i with cart ropes;	Is 5:18	
I one looks to the land, behold,	Is 5:30	
I you will not believe, you surely	Is 7:9	518
I they do not speak according to	Is 8:20	518
I you would inquire, inquire;	Is 21:12	518
on which i a man leans, it will go	Is 36:6	
"But i you say to me,	Is 36:7	3588
i you are able on your part to set	Is 36:8	518
Who, i I ask, can give an answer.	Is 41:28	
"I only you had paid attention to	Is 48:18	3863
I He would render Himself *as* a	Is 53:10	518
"I anyone fiercely assails *you* it	Is 54:15	2005
I you remove the yoke from your	Is 58:9	518
i you give yourself to the hungry And	Is 58:10	
"I because of the sabbath, you	Is 58:13	518
And see i there has been such *a*	Jer 2:10	2005
i they can save you In the time of	Jer 2:28	518
"I a husband divorces his wife And	Jer 3:1	2005
"I you will return, O Israel,"	Jer 4:1	518
And i you will put away your	Jer 4:1	518
squares, I you can find a man,	Jer 5:1	518
man, I there is one who does justice,	Jer 5:1	518
"For i you truly amend your ways	Jer 7:5	518
i you truly practice justice	Jer 7:5	518
i you do not oppress the alien,	Jer 7:6	
"I you have run with footmen and	Jer 12:5	3588
I you fall down in a land of	Jer 12:5	
i they will really learn the ways of	Jer 12:16	518
"But i they will not listen, then	Jer 12:17	518
But i you will not listen to it,	Jer 13:17	518
"I you say in your heart, 'Why	Jer 13:22	3588
'I I go out to the country,	Jer 14:18	518
Or i I enter the city, Behold,	Jer 14:18	518
"I you return, then I will	Jer 15:19	518
And i you extract the precious	Jer 15:19	518
i you listen attentively to Me,"	Jer 17:24	518
"But i you do not listen to Me to	Jer 17:27	518
i that nation against which I have	Jer 18:8	
i it does evil in My sight by not	Jer 18:10	
i I say, "I will not remember Him	Jer 20:9	
"For i you men will indeed	Jer 22:4	518
i you will not obey these words,	Jer 22:5	518
i they had stood in My council,	Jer 23:22	518
i you say, 'The oracle of the LORD!'	Jer 23:38	518
i they refuse to take the cup from	Jer 25:28	3588
"I you will not listen to Me, to	Jer 26:4	518
that i you put me to death,	Jer 26:15	518
"But i they are prophets, and if	Jer 27:18	518
and i the word of the LORD is with	Jer 27:18	518
and see I a male can give birth.	Jer 30:6	518
"I this fixed order departs From	Jer 31:36	518
"I the heavens above can be	Jer 31:37	518
"I you fight against the	Jer 32:5	3588
'I you can break My covenant for	Jer 33:20	518
'I My covenant *for* day and night	Jer 33:25	518
i you had defeated the entire army	Jer 37:10	518
"I I tell you, will you not	Jer 38:15	3588
Besides, i I give you advice, you	Jer 38:15	3588
'I you will indeed go out to the	Jer 38:17	518
'But i you will not go out to the	Jer 38:18	518
'But i you keep refusing to go	Jer 38:21	518
'But i the officials hear that I	Jer 38:25	3588
I you would prefer to come with me	Jer 40:4	518
but i you would prefer not to come	Jer 40:4	518
i we do not act in accordance with	Jer 42:5	518
'I you will indeed stay in this	Jer 42:10	518
'But i you are going to say,	Jer 42:13	518
'I you really set your mind to	Jer 42:15	518
"I grape gatherers came to you,	Jer 49:9	518
I thieves *came* by night, They	Jer 49:9	518
see i there is any pain like my pain	La 1:12	518
For i He causes grief, Then He	La 3:32	518
i one wheel were within another.	Ezk 1:16	3512c
"Yet i you have warned the wicked	Ezk 3:19	3588
i you have warned the righteous	Ezk 3:21	3588
as i one wheel were within another	Ezk 10:10	834
"But i the prophet is prevailed	Ezk 14:9	3588
i a country sins against Me by	Ezk 14:13	3588
"I I were to cause wild beasts to	Ezk 14:15	3863
"Or i I should bring a sword on	Ezk 14:17	
"Or i I should send a plague	Ezk 14:19	
"I it has been put into the fire	Ezk 15:4	2009
but, as i that were too little,	Ezk 16:47	
"But i a man is righteous and	Ezk 18:5	3588
i a man does not oppress anyone,	Ezk 18:7	
i he does not lend *money* on	Ezk 18:8	
i he keeps his hand from iniquity	Ezk 18:8	
i he walks in My statutes and My	Ezk 18:9	
"But i the wicked man turns from	Ezk 18:21	3588
by which, i a man observes them,	Ezk 20:11	518
by which, i a man observes them,	Ezk 20:13	518
i a man observes them, he will	Ezk 20:21	518
what i even the rod which despises	Ezk 21:13	518
'I I bring a sword upon a land,	Ezk 33:2	3588
'But i the watchman sees the sword	Ezk 33:6	3588
"But i you on your part warn a	Ezk 33:9	3588
i *a* wicked man restores a pledge,	Ezk 33:15	518
'I they are ashamed of all that they	Ezk 43:11	518
'I the prince gives a gift *out of*	Ezk 46:16	3588
"But i he gives a gift from his	Ezk 46:17	3588
i you do not make known to me the	Da 2:5	2006
"But i you declare the dream and	Da 2:6	2006
that i you do not make the dream	Da 2:9	2006
"Now i you are ready, at the	Da 3:15	2006
But i you do not worship, you	Da 3:15	2006
"I it be *so,* our God whom we	Da 3:17	2006
"But *even* i *He does* not, let it	Da 3:18	2006
i *only* the dream applied to those	Da 4:19	
Now i you are able to read the	Da 5:16	2006
But i you do recompense Me,	Jl 3:4	518
I a trumpet is blown in a city	Am 3:6	518
I a calamity occurs in a city has	Am 3:6	518
i ten men are left in one house,	Am 6:9	518
"I thieves came to you, If	Ob 1:5	518
I robbers by night	Ob 1:5	518
I grape gatherers came to you,	Ob 1:5	518
as i they had never existed.	Ob 1:16	
But i they do not speak out	Mi 2:6	
"I a man walking after wind and	Mi 2:11	3863
sheep, Which, i he passes through,	Mi 5:8	518
would not believe i you were told.	Hab 1:5	3588
'I a man carries holy meat in the	Hg 2:12	2005
"I one who is unclean from a	Hg 2:13	518
'I you will walk in My ways and	Zch 3:7	518
and i you will perform My service,	Zch 3:7	518
i you completely obey the LORD	Zch 6:15	518
'I it is too difficult in the	Zch 8:6	3588
heart will be glad as i *from* wine;	Zch 10:7	3644
"I it is good in your sight, give	Zch 11:12	518
but i not, never mind!"	Zch 11:12	518
And i anyone still prophesies,	Zch 13:3	3588
I the family of Egypt does not go up	Zch 14:18	518
Then i I am a father, where is My	Mal 1:6	518
And i I am a master, where is My	Mal 1:6	518
"I you do not listen, and if you	Mal 2:2	518
and i you do not take it to heart	Mal 2:2	518
"I I will not open for you the	Mal 3:10	518
"I You are the Son of God,	Mt 4:3	*1487*
"I You are the Son of God,	Mt 4:6	*1487*
i You fall down and worship me."	Mt 4:9	*1437*
i the salt has become tasteless,	Mt 5:13	*1437*
"Therefore i you are presenting your	Mt 5:23	*1437*
"I your right eye makes you stumble,	Mt 5:29	*1487*
"I your right hand makes you stumble,	Mt 5:30	*1487*
"I anyone wants to sue you and take	Mt 5:40	
"For i you love those who love	Mt 5:46	*1437*
"I you greet only your brothers,	Mt 5:47	*1437*
"For i you forgive others for their	Mt 6:14	*1437*
"But i you do not forgive others,	Mt 6:15	*1437*
i your eye is clear,	Mt 6:22	*1437*
"But i your eye is bad, your	Mt 6:23	*1437*
I then the light that is in	Mt 6:23	*1487*
"But i God so clothes the grass of	Mt 6:30	*1487*
"Or i he asks for a fish, he	Mt 7:10	*2532*
"I you then, being evil, know how	Mt 7:11	*1487*
"Lord, i You are willing, You can	Mt 8:2	*1437*
"I You *are going to* cast us out,	Mt 8:31	*1487*
"I I only touch His garment, I	Mt 9:21	*1437*
"I the house is worthy, give it	Mt 10:13	*1437*
But i it is not worthy, take back	Mt 10:13	*1437*
I they have called the head of the	Mt 10:25	*1487*
"And i you are willing to accept *it,*	Mt 11:14	*1487*
For i the miracles had occurred in	Mt 11:21	*1487*
for i the miracles had occurred in	Mt 11:23	*1487*
i you had known what this means,	Mt 12:7	*1487*
and i it falls into a pit on the	Mt 12:11	*1437*
"I Satan casts out Satan, he is	Mt 12:26	*1487*
"I I by Beelzebul cast out demons,	Mt 12:27	*1487*
"But i I cast out demons by the	Mt 12:28	*1487*
"Lord, i it is You, command me to	Mt 14:28	*1487*
And i a blind man guides a blind	Mt 15:14	*1437*
"I anyone wishes to come after	Mt 16:24	*1487*
i he gains the whole world and	Mt 16:26	*1437*
i You wish, I will make three	Mt 17:4	*1487*
i you have faith the size of a mustard	Mt 17:20	*1437*
"I your hand or your foot causes you	Mt 18:8	*1487*
"I your eye causes you to stumble,	Mt 18:9	*1487*
I any man has a hundred sheep, and	Mt 18:12	*1437*
"I it turns out that he finds it,	Mt 18:13	*1437*
"I your brother sins, go and show	Mt 18:15	*1437*
i he listens to you, you have won	Mt 18:15	*1437*
"But i he does not listen *to you,*	Mt 18:16	*1437*
"I he refuses to listen to them,	Mt 18:17	*1437*
and i he refuses to listen even to	Mt 18:17	*1437*
that i two of you agree on earth	Mt 18:19	*1437*
i each of you does not forgive his	Mt 18:35	*1437*
"I the relationship of the man	Mt 19:10	*1487*
but i you wish to enter into life,	Mt 19:17	*1487*
"I you wish to be complete, go	Mt 19:21	*1487*
"I anyone says anything to you, you	Mt 21:3	*1437*
i you have faith and do not doubt	Mt 21:21	*1437*
even i you say to this mountain,	Mt 21:21	*2579*
which i you tell Me, I will also tell	Mt 21:24	*1437*
"I we say, 'From heaven,' He will say	Mt 21:25	*1437*
"But i we say, 'From men,' we fear	Mt 21:26	*1437*
'I A MAN DIES HAVING NO CHILDREN,	Mt 22:24	*1437*
"I David then calls Him 'Lord,'	Mt 22:45	*1487*
'I we had been *living* in the days	Mt 23:30	*1487*
"Then i anyone says to you,	Mt 24:23	*1437*
to mislead, i possible, even the elect	Mt 24:24	*1487*
"So i they say to you, 'Behold,	Mt 24:26	*1437*
i the head of the house had known	Mt 24:43	*1487*
"But i that evil slave says in	Mt 24:48	*1437*
that man i he had not been born."	Mt 26:24	*1487*
"Even i I have to die with You, I	Mt 26:35	*2579*
Father, i it is possible, let this cup	Mt 26:39	*1487*
i this cannot pass away unless I	Mt 26:42	*1487*
I You are the Son of God, come	Mt 27:40	*1487*
now, I HE DELIGHTS IN HIM;	Mt 27:43	*1487*
"And i this should come to the	Mt 28:14	*1437*
"I You are willing, You can make	Mk 1:40	*1437*
I He would heal him on the Sabbath,	Mk 3:2	*1487*
"I a kingdom is divided against	Mk 3:24	*1437*
"I a house is divided against itself,	Mk 3:25	*1437*
"I Satan has risen up against	Mk 3:26	*1487*
"I anyone has ears to hear, let	Mk 4:23	*1487*
"I I just touch His garments, I	Mk 5:28	*1437*
"I a man says to *his* father or *his*	Mk 7:11	*1437*
the man which can defile him i it	Mk 7:15	
["I anyone has ears to hear, let	Mk 7:16	*1487*
"I I send them away hungry to their	Mk 8:3	*1437*
"I anyone wishes to come after	Mk 8:34	*1487*
But i You can do anything, take	Mk 9:22	*1487*
And Jesus said to him, "'I You can?'	Mk 9:23	*1487*
"I anyone wants to be first, he	Mk 9:35	*1487*
i, with a heavy millstone hung	Mk 9:42	*1487*
"I your hand causes you to stumble,	Mk 9:43	*1437*
"I your foot causes you to stumble,	Mk 9:45	*1437*
"I your eye causes you to stumble,	Mk 9:47	*1437*
but i the salt becomes unsalty,	Mk 9:50	*1437*
and i she herself divorces her	Mk 10:12	*1437*
"I anyone says to you, 'Why are	Mk 11:3	*1437*
i perhaps He would find anything	Mk 11:13	*1487*
i you have anything against anyone,	Mk 11:25	*1487*
"But i you do not forgive,	Mk 11:26	*1487*
"I we say, 'From heaven,' He will say	Mk 11:31	*1437*
I A MAN'S BROTHER DIES and leaves	Mk 12:19	*1437*
"And then i anyone says to you,	Mk 13:21	*1437*
to lead astray, i possible, the elect.	Mk 13:22	*1487*
that man i he had not been born."	Mk 14:21	*1487*
"*Even* i I have to die with You, I	Mk 14:31	*1437*
to pray that i it were possible,	Mk 14:35	*1487*
i He was dead by this time,	Mk 15:44	*1487*
i they drink any deadly *poison,*	Mk 16:18	*2579*
"I You are the Son of God, tell	Lk 4:3	*1487*
"Therefore i You worship before	Lk 4:7	*1437*
"I You are the Son of God, throw	Lk 4:9	*1487*
"Lord, i You are willing, You can	Lk 5:12	*1437*
to see i He healed on the Sabbath,	Lk 6:7	*1487*
"I you love those who love you,	Lk 6:32	*1487*
"I you do good to those who do good	Lk 6:33	*1437*
"I you lend to those from whom you	Lk 6:34	*1437*
"I this man were a prophet He	Lk 7:39	*1487*
"I anyone wishes to come after	Lk 9:23	*1487*
i he gains the whole world,	Lk 9:25	
"I a man of peace is there, your	Lk 10:6	*1437*
but i not, it will return to you.	Lk 10:6	*1487*
i the miracles had been performed	Lk 10:13	*1487*
"Or i he is asked for an egg,	Lk 11:12	
"I you then, being evil, know how	Lk 11:13	*1487*
"I Satan also is divided against	Lk 11:18	*1487*
i I by Beelzebul cast out demons,	Lk 11:19	*1487*
i I cast out demons by the finger of	Lk 11:20	*1487*
"I therefore your whole body is	Lk 11:36	*1487*
"I then you cannot do even a very	Lk 12:26	*1487*
i God so clothes the grass in the field	Lk 12:28	*1487*
i the head of the house had known	Lk 12:39	*1487*
i that slave says in his heart,	Lk 12:45	*1437*
and i it bears fruit next year,	Lk 13:9	*2579*
but i not, cut it down.'"	Lk 13:9	*1487*
"I anyone comes to Me, and does	Lk 14:26	*1487*
i he has enough to complete it?	Lk 14:28	*1487*
but i even salt has become tasteless	Lk 14:34	*1437*
i he has a hundred sheep and has	Lk 15:4	
i she has ten silver coins and	Lk 15:8	*1437*

"Therefore **i** you have not been	Lk 16:11	1487
"And **i** you have not been faithful	Lk 16:12	1487
but **i** someone goes to them from	Lk 16:30	1437
'**I** they do not listen to Moses and	Lk 16:31	1487
i someone rises from the dead.' "	Lk 16:31	1437
i a millstone were hung around his	Lk 17:2	1487
I your brother sins, rebuke him;	Lk 17:3	1437
and **i** he repents, forgive him.	Lk 17:3	1437
"And **i** he sins against you seven	Lk 17:4	1437
"**I** you had faith like a mustard	Lk 17:6	1487
and **i** I have defrauded anyone of	Lk 19:8	1487
"**I** anyone asks you, 'Why are you	Lk 19:31	1437
i these become silent, the stones will	Lk 19:40	1437
"**I** you had known in this day,	Lk 19:42	1487
I we say, 'From heaven,' He will say,	Lk 20:5	1437
"But **i** we say, 'From men,' all the	Lk 20:6	1437
I A MAN'S BROTHER DIES,	Lk 20:28	1437
"Father, **i** You are willing,	Lk 22:42	1487
"**I** You are the Christ, tell us."	Lk 22:67	1487
"**I** I tell you, you will not believe;	Lk 22:67	1437
and **i** I ask a question, you will	Lk 22:68	1437
"For **i** they do these things	Lk 23:31	1487
i this is the Christ of God,	Lk 23:35	1487
"**I** You are the King of the Jews,	Lk 23:37	1487
i you are not the Christ,	Jn 1:25	1487
"**I** I told you earthly things and	Jn 3:12	1487
i I tell you heavenly things?	Jn 3:12	1437
"**I** you knew the gift of God, and	Jn 4:10	1487
"**I** I *alone* testify about Myself,	Jn 5:31	1437
i another comes in his own	Jn 5:43	1437
"For **i** you believed Moses, you	Jn 5:46	1487
i you do not believe his writings	Jn 5:47	1487
i anyone eats of this bread, he	Jn 6:51	1437
i you see the Son of Man	Jn 6:62	1437
I You do these things, show	Jn 7:4	1487
but as **i**, in secret.	Jn 7:10	5613
"**I** anyone is willing to do His	Jn 7:17	1437
"**I** a man receives circumcision on	Jn 7:23	1487
"**I** anyone is thirsty, let him	Jn 7:37	1437
"Even **i** I testify about Myself, My	Jn 8:14	2579
i I do judge, My judgment is true;	Jn 8:16	1437
i you knew Me, you would know My	Jn 8:19	1487
"**I** you continue in My word, *then* you	Jn 8:31	1437
"So **i** the Son makes you free, you	Jn 8:36	1437
"**I** you are Abraham's children, do	Jn 8:39	1487
"**I** God were your Father, you	Jn 8:42	1487
I I speak truth, why do you not	Jn 8:46	1487
i anyone keeps My word he will	Jn 8:51	1437
'**I** anyone keeps My word, he will	Jn 8:52	1437
"**I** I glorify Myself, My glory is	Jn 8:54	1437
i I say that I do not know Him,	Jn 8:55	2579
that **i** anyone confessed Him	Jn 9:22	1437
but **i** anyone is God-fearing and	Jn 9:31	1437
"**I** this man were not from God, He	Jn 9:33	1487
"**I** you were blind, you would have	Jn 9:41	1487
i anyone enters through Me, he	Jn 10:9	1437
I You are the Christ, tell us	Jn 10:24	1487
"**I** he called them gods, to whom	Jn 10:35	1487
"**I** I do not do the works of My	Jn 10:37	1487
but **i** I do them, though you do not	Jn 10:38	1487
I anyone walks in the day, he does	Jn 11:9	1437
"But **i** anyone walks in the night,	Jn 11:10	1437
"Lord, **i** he has fallen asleep, he	Jn 11:12	1487
"Lord, **i** You had been here, my	Jn 11:21	1487
in Me will live even **i** he dies,	Jn 11:25	2579
"Lord, **i** You had been here, my	Jn 11:32	1487
i you believe, you will see the glory	Jn 11:40	1437
"**I** we let Him *go on* like this,	Jn 11:48	1437
that **i** anyone knew where He was,	Jn 11:57	1437
but **i** it dies, it bears much fruit.	Jn 12:24	1437
"**I** anyone serves Me, he must	Jn 12:26	1437
i anyone serves Me, the Father	Jn 12:26	1437
i I am lifted up from the earth,	Jn 12:32	1437
"**I** anyone hears My sayings and does	Jn 12:47	1437
"**I** I do not wash you, you have no	Jn 13:8	1437
"**I** I then, the Lord and the Teacher	Jn 13:14	1487
"**I** you know these things, you are	Jn 13:17	1487
you are blessed **i** you do them.	Jn 13:17	1437
i God is glorified in Him, God	Jn 13:32	1487
i you have love for one another."	Jn 13:35	1437
i it were not so, I would have	Jn 14:2	1487
"**I** I go and prepare a place for you,	Jn 14:3	1437
"**I** you had known Me, you would	Jn 14:7	1487
"**I** you ask Me anything in My name	Jn 14:14	1437
"**I** you love Me, you will keep My	Jn 14:15	1437
"**I** anyone loves Me, he will keep	Jn 14:23	1437
"**I** you loved Me, you would have	Jn 14:28	1487
"**I** anyone does not abide in Me,	Jn 15:6	1437
"**I** you abide in Me, and My words	Jn 15:7	1437
"**I** you keep My commandments, you	Jn 15:10	1437
i you do what I command you.	Jn 15:14	1437
"**I** the world hates you, you know	Jn 15:18	1487
"**I** you were of the world, the	Jn 15:19	1487
I they persecuted Me,	Jn 15:20	1487
i they kept My word, they will	Jn 15:20	1487
"**I** I had not come and spoken to	Jn 15:22	1487
"**I** I had not done among them the	Jn 15:24	1487
for **i** I do not go away, the Helper	Jn 16:7	1437
but **i** I go, I will send Him to you.	Jn 16:7	1437
i you ask the Father for	Jn 16:23	302
i you seek Me, let these	Jn 18:8	1487
"**I** I have spoken wrongly, testify	Jn 18:23	1487
but **i** rightly, why do you strike Me?	Jn 18:23	1487
"**I** this Man were not an evildoer,	Jn 18:30	1487
I My kingdom were of this world,	Jn 18:36	1487
"**I** you release this Man, you are	Jn 19:12	1437
"Sir, **i** you have carried Him	Jn 20:15	1487
"**I** you forgive the sins of any,	Jn 20:23	302
i you retain the *sins* of any, they	Jn 20:23	302
"**I** I want him to remain until I	Jn 21:22	1437
"**I** I want him to remain until I	Jn 21:23	1437
i they were written in detail,	Jn 21:25	1437
as **i** by our own power or piety we	Ac 3:12	5613
i we are on trial today for a	Ac 4:9	1487
for **i** this plan or action is	Ac 5:38	1437
but **i** it is of God, you will not	Ac 5:39	1487
i possible, the intention of your	Ac 8:22	1487
"**I** you believe with all your heart,	Ac 8:37	1487
so that **i** he found any belonging	Ac 9:2	1437
"Therefore **i** God gave to them	Ac 11:17	1487
i you have any word of exhortation	Ac 13:15	1487
i you keep yourselves free from	Ac 15:29	
"**I** you have judged me to be	Ac 16:15	1487
i perhaps they might grope for Him	Ac 17:27	1487
"**I** it were a matter of wrong or	Ac 18:14	1487
i there are questions about words	Ac 18:15	1487
return to you again **i** God wills,"	Ac 18:21	
i Demetrius and the craftsmen who	Ac 19:38	1487
i you want anything beyond this,	Ac 19:39	1487
to be in Jerusalem, **i** possible,	Ac 20:16	1487
i they should have anything	Ac 24:19	1487
and **i** there is anything wrong	Ac 25:5	1487
"**I**, then, I am a wrongdoer and	Ac 25:11	1487
but **i** none of those things is *true*	Ac 25:11	1487
i they are willing to testify,	Ac 26:5	1437
people **i** God does raise the dead?	Ac 26:8	1487
i he had not appealed to Caesar."	Ac 26:32	1487
i somehow they could reach	Ac 27:12	1487
the ship onto it **i** they could.	Ac 27:39	1487
i perhaps now at last by the will	Ro 1:10	1487
But **i** you bear the name "Jew"	Ro 2:17	1487
of value **i** you practice the Law;	Ro 2:25	1437
but **i** you are a transgressor of	Ro 2:25	1437
So **i** the uncircumcised man keeps	Ro 2:26	1437
uncircumcised, **i** he keeps the Law,	Ro 2:27	
I some did not believe, their	Ro 3:3	1487
But **i** our unrighteousness	Ro 3:5	1487
i through my lie the truth of God	Ro 3:7	1487
i Abraham was justified by works,	Ro 4:2	1487
i those who are of the Law are heirs	Ro 4:14	1487
For **i** while we were enemies we	Ro 5:10	1487
For **i** by the transgression of the	Ro 5:15	1487
For **i** by the transgression of the	Ro 5:17	1487
For **i** we have become united with	Ro 6:5	1487
Now **i** we have died with Christ, we	Ro 6:8	1487
i her husband dies, she is released	Ro 7:2	1437
i while her husband is living she is	Ro 7:3	1437
but **i** her husband dies, she is	Ro 7:3	1437
coveting **i** the Law had not said,	Ro 7:7	1487
But **i** I do the very thing I do not	Ro 7:16	1487
But **i** I am doing the very thing I	Ro 7:20	1487
i indeed the Spirit of God dwells	Ro 8:9	1512
i anyone does not have the Spirit of	Ro 8:9	1487
I Christ is in you, though the body	Ro 8:10	1487
i the Spirit of Him who raised Jesus	Ro 8:11	1487
for **i** you are living according to	Ro 8:13	1487
but **i** by the Spirit you are	Ro 8:13	1487
i children, heirs also, heirs of God	Ro 8:17	1487
i indeed we suffer with *Him* so	Ro 8:17	1512
But **i** we hope for what we do not	Ro 8:25	1487
I God *is* for us, who *is* against us?	Ro 8:31	1487
What **i** God, although willing to	Ro 9:22	1487
i you confess with your mouth Jesus	Ro 10:9	1437
But **i** it is by grace, it is no	Ro 11:6	1487
Now **i** their transgression is riches	Ro 11:12	1487
i somehow I might move to jealousy	Ro 11:14	1487
i their rejection is the reconciliation	Ro 11:15	1487
I the first piece *of dough* is	Ro 11:16	1487
and **i** the root is holy, the	Ro 11:16	1487
But **i** some of the branches were	Ro 11:17	1487
but **i** you are arrogant, *remember*	Ro 11:18	1487
for **i** God did not spare the	Ro 11:21	1487
i you continue in His kindness;	Ro 11:22	1437
i they do not continue in their	Ro 11:23	1437
For **i** you were cut off from what	Ro 11:24	1437
i prophecy, according to the	Ro 12:6	1535a
i service, in his serving;	Ro 12:7	1535a
I possible, so far as it depends	Ro 12:18	1487
I YOUR ENEMY IS HUNGRY, FEED	Ro 12:20	1437
I HE IS THIRSTY, GIVE HIM A DRINK	Ro 12:20	1437
But **i** you do what is evil, be	Ro 13:4	1437
i there is any other commandment,	Ro 13:9	1487
for **i** we live, we live for the Lord,	Ro 14:8	1437
or **i** we die, we die for the	Ro 14:8	1437
For **i** because of food your brother	Ro 14:15	1487
who doubts is condemned **i** he eats,	Ro 14:23	1437
For **i** the Gentiles have shared in	Ro 15:27	1487
for **i** they had understood it they	1Co 2:8	1487
Now **i** any man builds on the	1Co 3:12	1487
I any man's work which he has	1Co 3:14	1487
I any man's work is burned up, he	1Co 3:15	1487
I any man destroys the temple of	1Co 3:17	1487
I any man among you thinks that he	1Co 3:18	1487
And **i** you did receive it, why do	1Co 4:7	1487
as **i** you had not received it?	1Co 4:7	5613
i you were to have countless tutors	1Co 4:15	1437
to you soon, **i** the Lord wills,	1Co 4:19	1437
i he is an immoral person,	1Co 5:11	1437
I the world is judged by you, are	1Co 6:2	1487
So **i** you have law courts dealing with	1Co 6:4	1437
for them **i** they remain even as I.	1Co 7:8	1437
i they do not have self-control,	1Co 7:9	1487
(but **i** she does leave, she must	1Co 7:11	1437
that **i** any brother has a wife who	1Co 7:12	1487
Yet **i** the unbelieving one leaves,	1Co 7:15	1487
i you are able also to become free,	1Co 7:21	1487
But **i** you marry, you have	1Co 7:28	1437
and **i** a virgin marries, she	1Co 7:28	1437
But **i** any man thinks that he is	1Co 7:36	1487
i she is past her youth,	1Co 7:36	1437
i it must be so, let him do what he	1Co 7:36	
i her husband is dead, she is free to	1Co 7:39	1437
happier **i** she remains as she is;	1Co 7:40	1437
I anyone supposes that he knows	1Co 8:2	1487
but **i** anyone loves God, he is	1Co 8:3	1487
For even **i** there are so-called gods	1Co 8:5	1512
i it were sacrificed to an idol;	1Co 8:7	5613
neither the worse **i** we do not eat,	1Co 8:8	1437
eat, nor the better **i** we do eat.	1Co 8:8	1437
For **i** someone sees you, who have	1Co 8:10	1437
not his conscience, **i** he is weak,	1Co 8:10	
i food causes my brother to	1Co 8:13	1487
I to others I am not an apostle,	1Co 9:2	1487
I we sowed spiritual things in	1Co 9:11	1487
i we reap material things	1Co 9:11	1487
I others share the right over you,	1Co 9:12	1487
For **i** I preach the gospel, I have	1Co 9:16	1437
me **i** I do not preach the gospel.	1Co 9:16	1437
For **i** I do this voluntarily, I	1Co 9:17	1487
but **i** against my will, I have a	1Co 9:17	1487
I one of the unbelievers invites	1Co 10:27	1487
But **i** anyone says to you,	1Co 10:28	1437
I I partake with thankfulness, why	1Co 10:30	1487
i a woman does not cover her head	1Co 11:6	1487
i it is disgraceful for a woman	1Co 11:6	1487
you that **i** a man has long hair,	1Co 11:14	1437
but **i** a woman has long hair, it is	1Co 11:15	1437
i one is inclined to be contentious	1Co 11:16	1487
i he does not judge the body	1Co 11:29	
But **i** we judged ourselves rightly,	1Co 11:31	1487
I anyone is hungry, let him eat at	1Co 11:34	1487
I the foot says,	1Co 12:15	1437
And **i** the ear says,	1Co 12:16	1437
I the whole body were an eye,	1Co 12:17	1487
I the whole were hearing, where	1Co 12:17	1487
I they were all one member, where	1Co 12:19	1487
And **i** one member suffers, all the	1Co 12:26	1535a
i *one* member is honored, all the	1Co 12:26	1535a
I I speak with the tongues of men	1Co 13:1	1437
I I have *the gift of* prophecy,	1Co 13:2	1437
and **i** I have all faith, so as to	1Co 13:2	1437
And **i** I give all my possessions to	1Co 13:3	1437
i I surrender my body to be burned	1Co 13:3	1437
but **i** *there are gifts of* prophecy,	1Co 13:8	1535a
i *there are* tongues, they will	1Co 13:8	1535a
i *there is* knowledge, it will be	1Co 13:8	1535a
i I come to you speaking in tongues	1Co 14:6	1437
i they do not produce a distinction	1Co 14:7	1437
For **i** the bugle produces an indistinct	1Co 14:8	1437
I then I do not know the meaning	1Co 14:11	1437
For **i** I pray in a tongue, my	1Co 14:14	1437
i you bless in the spirit *only,*	1Co 14:16	1437
Therefore **i** the whole church	1Co 14:23	1437
But **i** all prophesy, and an	1Co 14:24	1437
I anyone speaks in a tongue, *it*	1Co 14:27	1535a
but **i** there is no interpreter, he	1Co 14:28	1437
But **i** a revelation is made to	1Co 14:30	1437
I they desire to learn anything, let	1Co 14:35	1487
I anyone thinks he is a prophet or	1Co 14:37	1487
But **i** anyone does not recognize	1Co 14:38	1487
i you hold fast the word which I	1Co 15:2	1487
Now **i** Christ is preached, that He	1Co 15:12	1487
But **i** there is no resurrection of	1Co 15:13	1487
and **i** Christ has not been raised,	1Co 15:14	1487
i in fact the dead are not raised.	1Co 15:15	1512
For **i** the dead are not raised, not	1Co 15:16	1487
and **i** Christ has not been raised,	1Co 15:17	1487
I we have hoped in Christ in this	1Co 15:19	1487
I the dead are not raised at all,	1Co 15:29	1487
I from human motives I fought with	1Co 15:32	1487
I the dead are not raised, LET US	1Co 15:32	1487
I there is a natural body, there	1Co 15:44	1487
and **i** it is fitting for me to go	1Co 16:4	1437
for some time, **i** the Lord permits.	1Co 16:7	1437
Now **i** Timothy comes, see that he	1Co 16:10	1437
I anyone does not love the Lord,	1Co 16:22	1487
But **i** we are afflicted, it is for	2Co 1:6	1535a
or **i** we are comforted, it is for	2Co 1:6	1535a
For **i** I cause you sorrow, who then	2Co 2:2	1487
But **i** any has caused sorrow, he	2Co 2:5	1487
i I have forgiven anything,	2Co 2:10	1487
But **i** the ministry of death, in	2Co 3:7	1487
For **i** the ministry of condemnation	2Co 3:9	1487
For **i** that which fades away *was*	2Co 3:11	1487
And even **i** our gospel is veiled,	2Co 4:3	1487
i the earthly tent which is our house	2Co 5:1	1437
For **i** we are beside ourselves, it	2Co 5:13	1535a
i we are of sound mind, it is for	2Co 5:13	1535a
Therefore **i** anyone is in Christ,	2Co 5:17	1487
For **i** in anything I have boasted	2Co 7:14	1487
For **i** the readiness is present, it	2Co 8:12	1487
otherwise **i** any Macedonians come	2Co 9:4	1437
who regard us as **i** we walked	2Co 10:2	5613
I anyone is confident in himself	2Co 10:7	1487
For even **i** I boast somewhat	2Co 10:8	1437
seem as **i** I would terrify you by my	2Co 10:9	302
as **i** we did not reach to you,	2Co 10:14	5613
For **i** one comes and preaches	2Co 11:4	1487
even **i** I am unskilled in speech,	2Co 11:6	1487
i his servants also disguise	2Co 11:15	1487
but **i** *you do,* receive me even as	2Co 11:16	1487
i anyone enslaves you,	2Co 11:20	1487
I speak as **i** insane	2Co 11:23	
I I have to boast, I will boast of	2Co 11:30	1487
For **i** I do wish to boast I will	2Co 12:6	1437
I I love you more, am I to be	2Co 12:15	1487
rest *as well,* that **i** I come again	2Co 13:2	1437

to see **i** you are in the faith; 2Co 13:5 *1487*
But even **i** we, or an angel from Ga 1:8 *1487*
i any man is preaching to you a Ga 1:9 *1487*
i I were still trying to please Ga 1:10 *1487*
"**I** you, being a Jew, live like Ga 2:14 *1487*
i, while seeking to be justified in Ga 2:17 *1487*
"For **i** I rebuild what I have *once* Ga 2:18 *1487*
for **i** righteousness *comes* through Ga 2:21 *1487*
i indeed it was in vain? Ga 3:4 *1487*
i the inheritance is based on law Ga 3:18 *1487*
For **i** a law had been given which Ga 3:21 *1487*
And **i** you belong to Christ, then Ga 3:29 *1487*
and **i** a son, then an heir through Ga 4:7 *1487*
i possible, you would have plucked Ga 4:15 *1487*
that **i** you receive circumcision, Ga 5:2 *1437*
i I still preach circumcision, Ga 5:11 *1487*
But **i** you bite and devour one Ga 5:15 *1487*
But **i** you are led by the Spirit, Ga 5:18 *1487*
I we live by the Spirit, let us Ga 5:25 *1487*
i anyone is caught in any trespass, Ga 6:1 *1437*
For **i** anyone thinks he is Ga 6:3 *1487*
will reap **i** we do not grow weary. Ga 6:9
i indeed you have heard of the Eph 3:2 *1487*
i indeed you have heard Him and Eph 4:21 *1487*
i *I am* to live *on* in the flesh, Php 1:22 *1487*
Therefore **i** there is any Php 2:1 *1487*
i there is any consolation of Php 2:1 *1487*
i there is any fellowship of the Php 2:1 *1487*
i any affection and compassion, Php 2:1 *1487*
But even **i** I am being poured out Php 2:17 *1487*
I anyone else has a mind to put Php 3:4 *1487*
and **i** in anything you have a Php 3:15 *1487*
i there is any excellence and if Php 4:8 *1487*
and **i** anything worthy of praise, Php 4:8 *1487*
i indeed you continue in the faith Col 1:23 *1487*
I you have died with Christ to the Col 2:20 *1487*
as **i** you were living in the world, Col 2:20 *5613*
Therefore **i** you have been raised up Col 3:1 *1487*
i he comes to you, welcome him); Col 4:10 *1437*
i you stand firm in the Lord. 1Th 3:8 *1437*
For **i** we believe that Jesus died 1Th 4:14 *1487*
message or a letter as **i** from us, 2Th 2:2 *5613*
i anyone is not willing to work, then he 2Th 3:10 *1487*
I anyone does not obey our 2Th 3:14 *1487*
is good, **i** one uses it lawfully, 1Tm 1:8 *1437*
i they continue in faith and love and 1Tm 2:15 *1437*
i any man aspires to the office of 1Tm 3:1 *1487*
(but **i** a man does not know how to 1Tm 3:5 *1487*
i they are beyond reproach. 1Tm 3:10
i it is received with gratitude; 1Tm 4:4
but **i** any widow has children or 1Tm 5:4 *1487*
But **i** anyone does not provide for 1Tm 5:8 *1487*
i she is not less than sixty years old, 1Tm 5:9
and **i** she has brought up children, 1Tm 5:10 *1487*
i she has shown hospitality to 1Tm 5:10 *1487*
i she has washed the saints' feet, 1Tm 5:10 *1487*
i she has assisted those in 1Tm 5:10 *1487*
and **i** she has devoted herself to 1Tm 5:10 *1487*
I any woman who is a believer has 1Tm 5:16 *1487*
I anyone advocates a different 1Tm 6:3 *1487*
I we have food and covering, with 1Tm 6:8
i anyone competes as an athlete, 2Tm 2:5 *1437*
For **i** we died with Him, we will 2Tm 2:11 *1487*
I we endure, we will also reign 2Tm 2:12 *1487*
I we deny Him, He also will deny 2Tm 2:12 *1487*
I we are faithless, He remains 2Tm 2:13 *1487*
i anyone cleanses himself from 2Tm 2:21 *1437*
i perhaps God may grant them 2Tm 2:25 *3379*
i any man is above reproach, Ti 1:6 *1487*
I then you regard me a partner, Phm 1:17 *1487*
i he has wronged you in any way or Phm 1:18 *1487*
i the word spoken through angels Heb 2:2 *1487*
i we neglect so great a salvation? Heb 2:3
i we hold fast our confidence and Heb 3:6 *1437*
"TODAY **I** YOU HEAR HIS VOICE Heb 3:7 *1437*
i we hold fast the beginning of Heb 3:14 *1437, 4007a*
"TODAY **I** YOU HEAR HIS VOICE, Do Heb 3:15 *1437*
Therefore, let us fear **i**, while a Heb 4:1 *3379*
"TODAY **I** YOU HEAR HIS VOICE, Do Heb 4:7 *1437*
For **i** Joshua had given them rest, Heb 4:8 *1437*
this we will do, **i** God permits. Heb 6:3 *1437, 4007a*
i it yields thorns and thistles, Heb 6:8
Now **i** perfection was through the Heb 7:11 *1487*
i another priest arises according Heb 7:15 *1487*
Now **i** He were on earth, He would Heb 8:4 *1487*
For **i** that first *covenant* had been Heb 8:7 *1487*
For **i** the blood of goats and bulls Heb 9:13 *1487*
For **i** we go on sinning willfully Heb 10:26
I HE SHRINKS BACK, MY SOUL HAS Heb 10:38 *1437*
i they had been thinking of that Heb 11:15 *1487*
time will fail me **i** I tell of Gideon, Heb 11:32
But **i** you are without discipline, Heb 12:8 *1487*
"**I** EVEN A BEAST TOUCHES THE Heb 12:20 *2579*
For **i** those did not escape when Heb 12:25 *1487*
with whom, **i** he comes soon, Heb 13:23 *1437*
But **i** any of you lacks wisdom, let Jas 1:5 *1487*
i anyone is a hearer of the word Jas 1:23 *1487*
I anyone thinks himself to be Jas 1:26 *1487*
For **i** a man comes into your Jas 2:2 *1437*
I, however, you are fulfilling the Jas 2:8 *1487*
But **i** you show partiality, you are Jas 2:9 *1487*
Now **i** you do not commit adultery, Jas 2:11 *1487*
i someone says he has faith Jas 2:14 *1437*
I a brother or sister is without Jas 2:15 *1437*
faith, **i** it has no works, is dead, Jas 2:17 *1437*
I anyone does not stumble in what Jas 3:2 *1487*
i we put the bits into the horses' Jas 3:3 *1487*
But **i** you have bitter jealousy and Jas 3:14 *1487*
But **i** you judge the law, you are Jas 4:11 *1487*
"**I** the Lord wills, we will live Jas 4:15 *1437*
up, and **i** he has committed sins, Jas 5:15 *2579*
i any among you strays from the Jas 5:19 *1437*
for a little while, **i** necessary, 1Pe 1:6 *1487*
I you address as Father the One who 1Pe 1:17 *1487*
i you have tasted the kindness of 1Pe 2:3 *1487*
i for the sake of conscience 1Pe 2:19 *1487*
i, when you sin and are harshly 1Pe 2:20 *1487*
But **i** when you do what is right 1Pe 2:20 *1487*
even **i** any *of them* are disobedient 1Pe 3:1 *1487*
i you do what is right without being 1Pe 3:6 *1487*
i you prove zealous for what is good 1Pe 3:13 *1437*
But even **i** you should suffer for 1Pe 3:14 *1487*
better, **i** God should will it so, 1Pe 3:17 *1487*
I you are reviled for the name of 1Pe 4:14 *1487*
i *anyone suffers* as a Christian, 1Pe 4:16 *1487*
and **i** *it begins* with us first, 1Pe 4:17 *1487*
AND **I** IT IS WITH DIFFICULTY THAT 1Pe 4:18 *1487*
For **i** these *qualities* are yours 2Pe 1:8
For **i** God did not spare angels 2Pe 2:4 *1487*
and **i** He condemned the cities of 2Pe 2:6
and **i** He rescued righteous Lot, 2Pe 2:7
For **i**, after they have escaped the 2Pe 2:20 *1487*
I we say that we have fellowship 1Jn 1:6 *1437*
but **i** we walk in the Light as He 1Jn 1:7 *1437*
I we say that we have no sin, we 1Jn 1:8 *1437*
I we confess our sins, He is 1Jn 1:9 *1437*
I we say that we have not sinned, 1Jn 1:10 *1437*
i anyone sins, we have an Advocate 1Jn 2:1 *1437*
Him, **i** we keep His commandments. 1Jn 2:3 *1437*
I anyone loves the world, the love 1Jn 2:15 *1437*
for **i** they had been of us, they 1Jn 2:19 *1487*
I what you heard from the 1Jn 2:24 *1437*
I you know that He is righteous, 1Jn 2:29 *1437*
brethren, **i** the world hates you. 1Jn 3:13 *1487*
i our heart does not condemn us, 1Jn 3:21 *1437*
Beloved, **i** God so loved us, we 1Jn 4:11 *1487*
i we love one another, God abides 1Jn 4:12 *1437*
I someone says, "I love God," 1Jn 4:20 *1437*
I we receive the testimony of men, 1Jn 5:9 *1487*
i we ask anything according to His 1Jn 5:14 *1437*
And **i** we know that He hears us *in* 1Jn 5:15 *1437*
I anyone sees his brother 1Jn 5:16 *1437*
I anyone comes to you and does not 2Jn 1:10 *1487*
i I come, I will call attention to his 3Jn 1:10 *1437*
Therefore **i** you do not wake up, I Rv 3:3 *1437*
i anyone hears My voice and opens Rv 3:20 *1437*
a Lamb standing, as **i** slain, Rv 5:6 *5613*
And **i** anyone wants to harm them, Rv 11:5 *1487*
so **i** anyone wants to harm Rv 11:5 *1487*
his heads as **i** it had been slain, Rv 13:3 *5613*
I anyone has an ear, let him hear. Rv 13:9 *1487*
I anyone *is destined* for captivity, Rv 13:10 *1487*
i anyone kills with the sword, Rv 13:10 *1487*
"**I** anyone worships the beast and Rv 14:9 *1487*
And **i** anyone's name was not found Rv 20:15 *1487*
i anyone adds to them, God will Rv 22:18 *1437*
i anyone takes away from the words Rv 22:19 *1437*

IGAL
of Issachar, **I** the son of Joseph; Nu 13:7 3008
I the son of Nathan of Zobah, Bani 2Sa 23:36 3008
sons of Shemaiah: Hattush, **I**, 1Ch 3:22 3008

IGDALIAH
of the sons of Hanan the son of **I**, Jer 35:4 3012

IGNORANCE
I know that you acted in **i**, Ac 3:17 *52*
Therefore what you worship in **i**, Ac 17:23 *50*
having overlooked the times of **i**, Ac 17:30 *52*
because of the **i** that is in them, Eph 4:18 *52*
sins of the people committed in **i**. Heb 9:7 *51*
lusts *which were yours* in your **i**, 1Pe 1:14 *52*
may silence the **i** of foolish men. 1Pe 2:15 *56*

IGNORANT
may teach anyone who is **i** *of them.* Ezr 7:25 3809, 3046
Then I was senseless and **i**; Ps 73:22 3808, 3045
for we are not **i** of his schemes. 2Co 2:11 *50*
refuse foolish and **i** speculations, 2Tm 2:23 *521*
gently with the **i** and misguided, Heb 5:2 *50*

IGNORANTLY
because I acted **i** in unbelief; 1Tm 1:13 *50*

IGNORED
law is **i** And justice is never upheld. Hab 1:4 6313

IGNORES
But he who **i** reproof goes astray. Pr 10:17 5800a

IIM
Baalah and **I** and Ezem, Jos 15:29 5864

IJON
cities of Israel, and conquered **I**, 1Ki 15:20 5859
king of Assyria came and captured **I** 2Ki 15:29 5859
of Israel, and they conquered **I**, 2Ch 16:4 5859

IKKESH
Ira the son of **I** the Tekoite, 2Sa 23:26 6142
Ira the son of **I** the Tekoite, 1Ch 11:28 6142
was Ira the son of **I** the Tekoite; 1Ch 27:9 6142

ILAI
the Hushathite, **I** the Ahohite, 1Ch 11:29 5866

ILL
i because of menstrual impurity, Lv 15:33 1739
Tamar that he made himself **i**, 2Sa 13:2 2470a
on your bed and pretend to be **i**; 2Sa 13:5 2470a
lay down and pretended to be **i**; 2Sa 13:6 2470a
was in Samaria, and became **i**. 2Ki 1:2 2470a
days Hezekiah became mortally **i**. 2Ki 20:1 2470a
days Hezekiah became mortally **i**; 2Ch 32:24 2470a
struck me, *but* I did not become **i**; Pr 23:35 2470a
days Hezekiah became mortally **i**. Is 38:1 2470a
That both good and **i** go forth? La 3:38 7463a
will mock you, you of **i** repute, Ezk 22:5 2931
brought to Him all who were **i**, Mt 4:24 *2192, 2560*
word, and healed all who were **i** Mt 8:16 *2192, 2560*
he is a lunatic and is very **i**; Mt 17:15 *2192, 2560*
began bringing to Him all who were **i** Mk 1:32 *2192, 2560*
who were **i** with various diseases, Mk 1:34 *2192, 2560*
A man was there who had been **i** for Jn 5:5 *769*

ILLEGITIMATE
"No one of **i** birth shall enter Dt 23:2 4464
For they have borne **i** children. Hos 5:7 2114a
you are **i** children and not sons. Heb 12:8 *3541*

ILL-GOTTEN
I gains do not profit, But Pr 10:2 7562

ILLICITLY
profits **i** troubles his own house, Pr 15:27 1215

ILLITERATE
will be given to the one who is **i**, Is 29:12 3808, 3045, 5612

ILLNESS
with the **i** of which he was to die, 2Ki 13:14 2483
In his **i**, You restore him to Ps 41:3 2483
Judah after his **i** and recovery: Is 38:9 2483
because of a bodily **i** that I preached Ga 4:13 *769*

ILL-TREATED
being destitute, afflicted, **i** Heb 11:37 *2558*
with them, *and* those who are **i**, Heb 13:3 *2558*

ILL-TREATMENT
endure **i** with the people of God than Heb 11:25 *4778*

ILLUMINATION
and in the days of your father, **i**, Da 5:11 5094b
i, insight and extraordinary wisdom Da 5:14 5094b

ILLUMINE
covering, And fire to **i** by night. Ps 105:39 215
because the Lord God will **i** them; Rv 22:5 *5461*

ILLUMINED
part in it, it will be wholly **i**, Lk 11:36 *5460*
the earth was **i** with his glory. Rv 18:1 *5461*
it, for the glory of God has **i** it, Rv 21:23 *5461*

ILLUMINES
And the LORD **i** my darkness. 2Sa 22:29 5050
The LORD my God **i** my darkness. Ps 18:28 5050
A man's wisdom **i** him and causes Ec 8:1 215
the lamp **i** you with its rays." Lk 11:36 *5461*

ILLUSIONS
to us pleasant words, Prophesy **i**. Is 30:10 4123

ILLYRICUM
Jerusalem and round about as far as **I** Ro 15:19 *2437*

IMAGE
"Let Us make man in Our **i**, Gn 1:26 6754
God created man in His own **i**, Gn 1:27 6754
in the **i** of God He created him; Gn 1:27 6754
own likeness, according to his **i**, Gn 5:3 6754
For in the **i** of God He made man. Gn 9:6 6754
shall you set up for yourselves an **i** Lv 26:1 6459
make a graven **i** for yourselves Dt 4:16 6459
make for yourselves a graven **i** Dt 4:23 6459
made a molten **i** for themselves.' Dt 9:12 4541a
who makes an idol or a molten **i**, Dt 27:15 4541a
a graven **i** and a molten image; Jg 17:3 6459
a graven image and a molten **i**; Jg 17:3 4541a
a graven **i** and a molten image, Jg 17:4 6459
a graven image and a molten **i**, Jg 17:4 4541a
and a graven **i** and a molten image? Jg 18:14 6459
and a graven image and a molten **i**? Jg 18:14 4541a
and took the graven **i** and the Jg 18:17 6459
household idols and the molten **i**, Jg 18:17 4541a
house and took the graven **i**, Jg 18:18 6459
household idols and the molten **i**, Jg 18:18 4541a
household idols and the graven **i** and Jg 18:20 6459
up for themselves the graven **i**; Jg 18:30 6459
Micah's graven **i** which he had made, Jg 18:31 6459
had made a horrid **i** as an Asherah; 1Ki 15:13 4656
and Asa cut down her horrid **i** and 1Ki 15:13 4656
he set the carved **i** of Asherah that 2Ki 21:7 6459
had made a horrid **i** as an Asherah, 2Ch 15:16 4656
and Asa cut down her horrid **i**, 2Ch 15:16 4656
he put the carved **i** of the idol which 2Ch 33:7 6459
Horeb And worshiped a molten **i**. Ps 106:19 4541a
the **i** of an ox that eats grass. Ps 106:20 8403
a graven **i** are all of them futile, Is 44:9 6459
he makes it a graven **i** and Is 44:15 6459
he makes into a god, his graven **i**. Is 44:17 6459
And my graven **i** and my molten Is 48:5 6459
my molten **i** have commanded them.' Is 48:5 5262b
made for her *sacrificial* cakes in her **i** Jer 44:19 6087b
the king made an **i** of gold, Da 3:1 6755
to come to the dedication of the **i** that Da 3:2 6755
the **i** that Nebuchadnezzar the king Da 3:3 6755
and they stood before the **i** that Da 3:3 6755
fall down and worship the golden **i** Da 3:5 6755
fell down *and* worshiped the golden **i** Da 3:7 6755
down and worship the golden **i**. Da 3:10 6755
golden **i** which you have set up." Da 3:12 6755
the golden **i** that you have set up? Da 3:14 6755
worship the **i** that I have made, Da 3:15 6755
golden **i** that you have set up." Da 3:18 6755
cut off idol and **I** From the house of Na 1:14 4541a

its maker has carved it, *Or* an i, Hab 2:18 4541a
an i formed by the art and thought Ac 17:29 5480
of the great Artemis and of the i Ac 19:35
an i in the form of corruptible man Ro 1:23 1504
conformed to the i of His Son, Ro 8:29 1504
he is the i and glory of God; 1Co 11:7 1504
we have borne the i of the earthy, 1Co 15:49 1504
also bear the i of the heavenly. 1Co 15:49 1504
the same i from glory to glory, 2Co 3:18 1504
of Christ, who is the i of God. 2Co 4:4 1504
He is the i of the invisible God, Col 1:15 1504
the i of the One who created him Col 3:10 1504
an i to the beast who had the wound Rv 13:14 1504
give breath to the i of the beast, Rv 13:15 1504
the i of the beast would even speak Rv 13:15 1504
the i of the beast to be killed. Rv 13:15 1504
worships the beast and his i, Rv 14:9 1504
who worship the beast and his i, Rv 14:11 1504
over the beast and his i Rv 15:2 1504
the beast and who worshiped his i. Rv 16:2 1504
and those who worshiped his i; Rv 19:20 1504
not worshiped the beast or his i, Rv 20:4 1504

IMAGES
and destroy all their molten i and Nu 33:52 4541a
and burn their graven i with fire. Dt 7:5 6456
"The graven i of their gods you Dt 7:25 6456
down the engraved i of their gods and Dt 12:3 6456
molten i to provoke Me to anger, 1Ki 14:9 4541a
altars and his i they broke in pieces 2Ki 11:18 6754
and made for themselves molten i, 2Ki 17:16 4541a
broke in pieces his altars and his i, 2Ch 23:17 6754
also made molten i for the Baals. 2Ch 28:2 4541a
the Asherim and the carved i, 2Ch 33:19 6456
Amon sacrificed to all the carved i 2Ch 33:22 6456
places, the Asherim, the carved i and 2Ch 34:3 6456
carved images and the molten i. 2Ch 34:3 4541a
also the Asherim, the carved i and 2Ch 34:4 6456
and the molten i he broke in pieces 2Ch 34:4 4541a
and the carved i into powder, 2Ch 34:7 6456
His jealousy with their graven i. Ps 78:58 6456
be ashamed who serve graven i, Ps 97:7 6459
Whose graven i *were* greater than Is 10:10 6456
Shall I not do to Jerusalem and her i Is 10:11 6091
all the i of her gods are shattered Is 21:9 6456
you will defile your graven i overlaid Is 30:22 6456
your molten i plated with gold. Is 30:22 4541a
molten i are wind and emptiness. Is 41:29 5262b
Nor My praise to graven i. Is 42:8 6456
in idols, Who say to molten i, Is 42:17 4541a
Their i are *consigned* to the Is 46:1 6091
provoked Me with their graven i, Jer 8:19 6456
For his molten i are deceitful, Jer 10:14 5262b
Her i have been put to shame, her Jer 50:2 6091
For his molten i are deceitful, Jer 51:17 5262b
made the i of their abominations Ezk 7:20 6754
man in the room of his carved i? Ezk 8:12 4906
and made for yourself male i that Ezk 16:17 6754
i of the Chaldeans portrayed with Ezk 23:14 6754
And make the i cease from Memphis. Ezk 30:13 457
their gods with their metal i *and* their Da 11:8 5257a
And make for themselves molten i, Hos 13:2 4541a
your king and Kiyyun, your i, Am 5:26 6754
all of her i I will make desolate, Mi 1:7 6091
"I will cut off your carved i And Mi 5:13 6456
THE I WHICH YOU MADE TO WORSHIP Ac 7:43 5179b

IMAGINATION
And like a high wall in his own i. Pr 18:11 4906
speak a vision of their own i, Jer 23:16 3820

IMAGINATIONS
The i of *their* heart run riot. Ps 73:7 4906

IMAGINE
"Do not i that you in the king's Es 4:13 1819

IMBIBE
Drink and i deeply, O lovers." SS 5:1 7937

IMITATE
not learn to i the detestable things Dt 18:9 6213a
of their conduct, i their faith. Heb 13:7 3401
Beloved, do not i what is evil, 3Jn 1:11 3401

IMITATORS
exhort you, be i of me. 1Co 4:16 3402
Be i of me, just as I also am of 1Co 11:1 3402
Therefore be i of God, as beloved Eph 5:1 3402
became i of us and of the Lord, 1Th 1:6 3402
became i of the churches of God in 1Th 2:14 3402
but i of those who through faith Heb 6:12 3402

IMLA
He is Micaiah, son of I." 2Ch 18:7 3229

IMLAH
He is Micaiah son of I." 1Ki 22:8 3229
"Bring quickly Micaiah son of I." 1Ki 22:9 3229

IMLA'S
"Bring quickly Micaiah, I son." 2Ch 18:8 3229

IMMANUEL
son, and she will call His name I. Is 7:14 6005
the breadth of your land, O I. Is 8:8 6005
AND THEY SHALL CALL HIS NAME I," Mt 1:23 1694

IMMATURE
the foolish, a teacher of the i, Ro 2:20 3516

IMMEDIATELY
Then Saul i fell full length upon 1Sa 28:20 4116
root, And I cursed his abode i. Jb 5:3 6597
i be cast into the midst of a furnace Da 3:6 8160
you will i be cast into the midst Da 3:15 8160
"I the word concerning Da 4:33 8160
Jesus came up i from the water; Mt 3:16 2117
I they left their nets and followed Mt 4:20 2112
I they left the boat and their father, Mt 4:22 2112
And i his leprosy was cleansed. Mt 8:3 2112
and i they sprang up, because they Mt 13:5 2112
word and i receives it with joy; Mt 13:20 2117
of the word, i he falls away. Mt 13:21 2117
I He made the disciples get into Mt 14:22 2112
But i Jesus spoke to them, saying, Mt 14:27 2117
I Jesus stretched out His hand Mt 14:31 2112
and i they regained their sight Mt 20:34 2112
and i you will find a donkey tied Mt 21:2 2117
them,' and i he will send them." Mt 21:3 2117
"But i after the tribulation of Mt 24:29 2112
"I the one who had received the Mt 25:16 2112
I Judas went to Jesus and said, Mt 26:49 2112
And i a rooster crowed. Mt 26:74 2117
I one of them ran, and taking a Mt 27:48 2112
I coming up out of the water, He saw Mk 1:10 2117
I the Spirit impelled Him *to go* Mk 1:12 2117
I they left their nets and followed Mk 1:18 2117
I He called them; and they left Mk 1:20 2117
and i on the Sabbath He entered Mk 1:21 2117
I the news about Him spread Mk 1:28 2117
And i after they came out of Mk 1:29 2117
and i they spoke to Jesus about her. Mk 1:30 2117
I the leprosy left him and he was Mk 1:42 2117
warned him and i sent him away, Mk 1:43 2117
I Jesus, aware in His spirit that Mk 2:8 2117
he got up and i picked up the pallet Mk 2:12 2117
went out and i *began* conspiring Mk 3:6 2117
and i it sprang up because it had Mk 4:5 2117
i Satan comes and takes away the Mk 4:15 2117
the word, i receive it with joy; Mk 4:16 2117
of the word, i they fall away. Mk 4:17 2117
permits, he i puts in the sickle, Mk 4:29 2117
i a man from the tombs with an Mk 5:2 2117
I the flow of her blood was dried up; Mk 5:29 2117
I Jesus, perceiving in Himself that Mk 5:30 2117
I the girl got up and *began* to walk, Mk 5:42 2117
i they were completely astounded Mk 5:42 2117
I she came in a hurry to the king Mk 6:25 2117
I the king sent an executioner Mk 6:27 2117
I Jesus made His disciples get into Mk 6:45 2117
But i He spoke with them and said Mk 6:50 2117
boat, i *the people* recognized Him, Mk 6:54 2117
i came and fell at His feet. Mk 7:25 2117
And i He entered the boat with His Mk 8:10 2117
I, when the entire crowd saw Him, Mk 9:15 2117
i the spirit threw him into a Mk 9:20 2117
I the boy's father cried out and Mk 9:24 2117
I he regained his sight and *began* Mk 10:52 2117
i as you enter it, you will find a colt Mk 11:2 2117
and i he will send it back here." Mk 11:3 2117
I while He was still speaking, Judas, Mk 14:43 2117
After coming, Judas i went to Him, Mk 14:45 2117
I a rooster crowed a second time. Mk 14:72 2117
Council, i held a consultation; Mk 15:1 2117
she i got up and waited on them. Lk 4:39 3916
And i the leprosy left him. Lk 5:13 2112
I he got up before them, and picked Lk 5:25
against it and i it collapsed, Lk 6:49 2117
and i her hemorrhage stopped. Lk 8:44 3916
and how she had been i healed. Lk 8:47 3916
spirit returned, and she got up i; Lk 8:55 3916
so that they may i open *the door* Lk 12:36 2112
i you say, 'A shower is coming,' Lk 12:54 2112
and i she was made erect again and Lk 13:13 3916
i pull him out on a Sabbath day?" Lk 14:5 2112
'Come i and sit down to eat'? Lk 17:7 2112
I he regained his sight and *began* Lk 18:43 3916
of God was going to appear i. Lk 19:11 3916
but the end *does* not *follow* i." Lk 21:9 2112
I, while he was still speaking, a Lk 22:60 3916
I the man became well, and picked up Jn 5:9 2112
and i the boat was at the land to Jn 6:21 2112
the morsel he went out i; Jn 13:30 2117
Himself, and will glorify Him i. Jn 13:32 2117
and i a rooster crowed. Jn 18:27 2112
and i blood and water came out. Jn 19:34 2117
and i his feet and his ankles were Ac 3:7 3916
And i she fell at his feet and Ac 5:10 3916
And i there fell from his eyes Ac 9:18 2112
and i he *began* to proclaim Jesus Ac 9:20 2112
I he got up. Ac 9:34 2112
and i the object was taken up into Ac 10:16 2117
"So I sent for you i, Ac 10:33 1824
and i the angel departed from him. Ac 12:10 2112
And i an angel of the Lord struck Ac 12:23 3916
And i a mist and a darkness fell Ac 13:11 3916
i we sought to go into Macedonia, Ac 16:10 2112
and i all the doors were opened and Ac 16:26 3916
wounds, and i he was baptized, Ac 16:33 3916
The brethren i sent Paul and Ac 17:10 2112
Then i the brethren sent Paul Ac 17:14 2112
and i the doors were shut. Ac 21:30 2112
to examine him i let go of him; Ac 22:29 2112
But on the night i following, Ac 23:11
I did not i consult with flesh and Ga 1:16 2112
Therefore I hope to send him i, Php 2:23 1824
he has i forgotten what kind of Jas 1:24 2112
I I was in the Spirit; Rv 4:2 2112

IMMENSE
an i army with very many chariots 2Ch 16:8 7230
Hezekiah had i riches and honor; 2Ch 32:27 3966

IMMER
son of Meshillemith, the son of I; 1Ch 9:12 564
for Bilgah, the sixteenth for I, 1Ch 24:14 564
the sons of I, 1,052; Ezr 2:37 564
Tel-harsha, Cherub, Addan *and* I, Ezr 2:59 564
Of the sons of I *there were* Ezr 10:20 564
After them Zadok the son of I Ne 3:29 564
the sons of I, 1,052; Ne 7:40 564
Tel-harsha, Cherub, Addon and I; Ne 7:61 564
son of Meshillemoth, the son of I, Ne 11:13 564
Pashhur the priest, the son of I, Jer 20:1 564

IMMIGRANTS
or of the i who stay in Israel Ezk 14:7 1616

IMMINENT
aside of my *earthly* dwelling is i, 2Pe 1:14 5031

IMMORAL
not to associate with i people; 1Co 5:9 4205
with the i people of this world, 1Co 5:10 4205
if he is an i person, 1Co 5:11 4205
i man sins against his own body. 1Co 6:18 4203
that no i or impure person or Eph 5:5 4205
and i men and homosexuals and 1Tm 1:10 4205
no i or godless person like Esau, Heb 12:16 4205
murderers and i persons and sorcerers Rv 21:8 4205
and the sorcerers and the i persons Rv 22:15 4205

IMMORALITIES
But because of i, each man 1Co 7:2 4202

IMMORALITY
a woman and her mother, it is i; Lv 20:14 2154
there will be no i in your midst. Lv 20:14 2154
divorces his wife, except for i, Mt 19:9 4202
that there is i among you, 1Co 5:1 4202
and i of such a kind as does not 1Co 5:1 4202
Yet the body is not for i, 1Co 6:13 4202
Flee i. Every *other* sin that a man 1Co 6:18 4202
not repented of the impurity, i and 2Co 12:21 4202
i, impurity, sensuality, Ga 5:19 4202
But i or any impurity or greed must not Eph 5:3 4202
of your earthly body as dead to i, Col 3:5 4202
that you abstain from sexual i; 1Th 4:3 4202
indulged in gross i and went after Jude 1:7 1608
to idols and to commit *acts of* i. Rv 2:14 4203
so that they commit *acts of* i and Rv 2:20 4203
does not want to repent of her i. Rv 2:21 4202
of their i nor of their thefts. Rv 9:21 4202
wine of the passion of her i." Rv 14:8 4202
of the earth committed *acts of* i, Rv 17:2 4203
drunk with the wine of her i." Rv 17:2 4202
of the unclean things of her i, Rv 17:4 4202
the wine of the passion of her i, Rv 18:3 4202
have committed *acts of* i with her, Rv 18:3 4203
who committed *acts of* i and lived Rv 18:9 4203
corrupting the earth with her i, Rv 19:2 4202

IMMORALLY
Nor let us act i, as some of them 1Co 10:8 4203

IMMORTAL
Now to the King eternal, i, 1Tm 1:17 862a

IMMORTALITY
seek for glory and honor and i, Ro 2:7 861
and this mortal must put on i, 1Co 15:53 110
this mortal will have put on i, 1Co 15:54 110
who alone possesses i and dwells 1Tm 6:16 110
brought life and i to light through 2Tm 1:10 861

IMMOVABLE
together, Firm on him and i. Jb 41:23 1077, 4131
prow stuck fast and remained i, Ac 27:41 761
beloved brethren, be steadfast, i, 1Co 15:58 277

IMMUNE
be i to this water of bitterness Nu 5:19 5352

IMNA
his brother Helem *were* Zophah, I, 1Ch 7:35 3234

IMNAH
I and Ishvah and Ishvi and Beriah Gn 46:17 3232
of I, the family of the Imnites; Nu 26:44 3232
The sons of Asher *were* I, 1Ch 7:30 3232
Kore the son of I the Levite, 2Ch 31:14 3232

IMNITES
of Imnah, the family of the I; Nu 26:44 3232

IMPALED
from his house and he shall be i on it Ezr 6:11 2211, 4223

IMPART
may i some spiritual gift to you, Ro 1:11 3330
given which was able to i life, Ga 3:21 2227
we were well-pleased to i to you 1Th 2:8 3330

IMPARTED
"When He i weight to the wind And Jb 28:25 6213a

IMPARTIALLY
One who i judges according to each 1Pe 1:17 678

IMPATIENT
became i because of the journey. Nu 21:4 7114a
word with you, will you become i? Jb 4:2 3811
it has come to you, and you are i; Jb 4:5 3811
And why should I not be i? Jb 21:4 7114a
'Is the Spirit of the LORD i? Mi 2:7 7114a
for my soul was i with them, Zch 11:8 7114a

IMPEDED
walk, your steps will not be i; Pr 4:12 6887a

IMPEDIMENT
the i of his tongue was removed, Mk 7:35 1199

IMPELLED
went out i by the king's command Es 3:15 1765
and i by the king's command, Es 8:14 1765
the Spirit i Him *to go* out into the Mk 1:12 1544a

IMPENDING
And the i things are hastening Dt 32:35 6264

IMPENETRABLE
For the i forest has come down. Zch 11:2 1219

IMPERISHABLE
from east to west the sacred and **i** Mk 16:20
a perishable wreath, but we an **i**. 1Co 9:25 *862a*
body, it is raised an **i** *body;* 1Co 15:42 *861*
does the perishable inherit the **i**. 1Co 15:50 *861*
and the dead will be raised **i**, 1Co 15:52 *862a*
this perishable must put on the **i**, 1Co 15:53 *861*
perishable will have put on the **i**, 1Co 15:54 *861*
to *obtain* an inheritance *which is* **i** 1Pe 1:4 *862a*
of seed which is perishable but **i**, 1Pe 1:23 *862a*
with the **i** quality of a gentle and 1Pe 3:4 *862a*

IMPETUOUS
That fierce and **i** people Who march Hab 1:6 4116

IMPLANTED
in humility receive the word **i**, Jas 1:21 *1721*

IMPLEMENTS
forger of all **i** of bronze and iron; Gn 4:22 2790a
Their swords are **i** of violence. Gn 49:5 3627
flesh with the **i** of the oxen, 1Ki 19:21 3627
Because they threshed Gilead with **i** Am 1:3

IMPLORE
son, I **i** you, give glory to the LORD, Jos 7:19 4994
her to go in to the king to **i** his favor Es 4:8 2603a
i the compassion of the Almighty Jb 8:5 2603a
have to **i** the mercy of my judge. Jb 9:15 2603a
I have to **i** him with my mouth. Jb 19:16 2603a
I **i** You by God, do not torment me!" Mk 5:7 *3726*
And he *began* to **i** Him earnestly Mk 5:10 *3870*
And they began to **i** Him to leave Mk 5:17 *3870*
and *began* to **i** Him to come to his Lk 8:41 *3870*
i you to walk in a manner worthy of Eph 4:1 *3870*

IMPLORED
and **i** him to avert the evil *scheme* Es 8:3 2603a
they **i** Him to leave their region. Mt 8:34 *3870*
and they **i** Him that they might just Mt 14:36 *3870*
And His disciples came and **i** Him, Mt 15:23 *2065*
The demons **i** Him, saying, Mk 5:12 *3870*
and **i** Him earnestly, saying, Mk 5:23 *3870*
and they **i** Him to lay His hand on him. Mk 7:32 *3870*
brought a blind man to Jesus and **i** Mk 8:22 *3870*
he fell on his face and **i** Him, Lk 5:12 *1189a*
they earnestly **i** Him, saying, "He Lk 7:4 *3870*
and *the demons* **i** Him to permit Lk 8:32 *3870*
Concerning this I **i** the Lord three 2Co 12:8 *3870*

IMPLORING
i Him, Mt 8:5 *3870*
who had been demon-possessed was **i** Mk 5:18 *3870*
and **i** Him that they might just touch Mk 6:56 *3870*
They were **i** Him not to command them Lk 8:31 *3870*
he went to Him and was **i** *Him* to Jn 4:47 *2065*
i him, "Do not delay in coming to Ac 9:38 *3870*
encouraging and **i** each one of you 1Th 2:11 *3143*

IMPORT
Also Solomon's **i** of horses was 1Ki 10:28 4161

IMPORTANCE
has been humbled And the man of *of* **i** Is 2:9
will be humbled and the man of **i** Is 5:15
delivered to you as of first **i** what I 1Co 15:3 *4413*

IMPORTANT
Which is more **i**, the gold or the Mt 23:17 *3173*
which is more **i**, the offering, or the Mt 23:19 *3173*
another as more **i** than yourselves; Php 2:3 *5242*

IMPORTED
A chariot was **i** from Egypt for 1Ki 10:29 5927, 3318
were **i** from Egypt and from Kue; 2Ch 1:16 4161
They **i** chariots from Egypt for 2Ch 1:17 5927, 3318
i fish and all kinds of merchandise, Ne 13:16 935

IMPORTUNE
yourself, and **i** your neighbor. Pr 6:3 7292

IMPOSE
previously, you shall **i** on them; Ex 5:8 7760
whatever you **i** on me I will bear." 2Ki 18:14 5414
that it is not allowed to **i** tax, Ezr 7:24 7412
because you **i** heavy rent on the Am 5:11 1318

IMPOSED
which they rigorously **i** on them. Ex 1:14 5647
us, and **i** hard labor on us. Dt 26:6 5414
and he **i** on the land a fine of one 2Ki 23:33 5414
and **i** on the land a fine of one 2Ch 36:3 6064
Who **i** her terror On all her Ezk 26:17 5414
regulations for the body **i** until a Heb 9:10 *1945*

IMPOSSIBLE
purpose to do will be **i** for them. Gn 11:6 1219
and nothing will be **i** to you. Mt 17:20 *101*
"With people this is **i**, Mt 19:26 *102*
"With people it is **i**, but not with God Mk 10:27 *102*
"For nothing will be **i** with God." Lk 1:37 *101*
"The things that are **i** with people are Lk 18:27 *102*
since it was **i** for Him to be held Ac 2:24 *3756, 1415*
it is **i** to renew them again to Heb 6:6 *102*
in which it is **i** for God to lie, Heb 6:18 *102*
For it is **i** for the blood of bulls Heb 10:4 *102*
without faith it is **i** to please *Him,* Heb 11:6 *102*

IMPOSTORS
But evil men and **i** will proceed 2Tm 3:13 *1114*

IMPOTENT
will be very small *and* **i**." Is 16:14 3808, 3524

IMPOVERISH
Have you invited us to **i** us? Jg 14:15 3423

IMPOVERISHED
and all that you have would be **i**." ' Gn 45:11 3423

He who is too **i** for *such* an offering Is 40:20 5532b
and he began to be **i**. Lk 15:14 *5302*

IMPRECATION
curse, an object of horror, an **i** and Jer 42:18 7045
of horror, an **i** and a reproach. Jer 44:12 7045

IMPREGNABLE
His refuge will be the **i** rock; Is 33:16 4679

IMPRESS
i these words of mine on your heart Dt 11:18 7760

IMPRESSED
wisdom under the sun, and it **i** me. Ec 9:13 1419

IMPRESSIVE
He killed an Egyptian, an **i** man. 2Sa 23:21 4758

IMPRINT
in His hands the **i** of the nails, Jn 20:25 *5179b*

IMPRISON
To **i** his princes at will, That he Ps 105:22 631
And do not **i** their survivors In Ob 1:14 5462
I used to **i** and beat those who Ac 22:19 *5439*

IMPRISONED
the *same* place where Joseph was **i**. Gn 40:3 631
Pharaoh Neco **i** him at Riblah 2Ki 23:33 631
And the surface of the deep is **i**. Jb 38:30 3920
Now when John, while **i**, heard of Mt 11:2 *1201*
man named Barabbas had been **i** Mk 15:7 *1210*
Jews a favor, Felix left Paul **i**. Ac 24:27 *1210*
for which I have also been **i**; Col 4:3 *1210*
but the word of God is not **i**. 2Tm 2:9 *1210*

IMPRISONMENT
confiscation of goods or for **i**." Ezr 7:26 613
accusation deserving death or **i**. Ac 23:29 *1199*
anything worthy of death or **i**." Ac 26:31 *1199*
since both in my **i** and in the Php 1:7 *1199*
so that my **i** in *the cause of* Christ Php 1:13 *1199*
in the Lord because of my **i**, Php 1:14 *1199*
to cause me distress in my **i**. Php 1:17 *1199*
Remember my **i**. Grace be with you. Col 4:18 *1199*
hardship even to **i** as a criminal; 2Tm 2:9 *1199*
whom I have begotten in my **i**, Phm 1:10 *1199*
to me in my **i** for the gospel; Phm 1:13 *1199*
yes, also chains and **i**. Heb 11:36 *5438*

IMPRISONMENTS
in beatings, in **i**, in tumults, in 2Co 6:5 *5438*
in far more labors, in far more **i**, 2Co 11:23 *5438*

IMPRISONS
He **i** a man, and there can be no Jb 12:14 5462

IMPROPER
i for a woman to speak in church. 1Co 14:35 *150*

IMPROVISE
Who **i** to the sound of the harp, Am 6:5 6527

IMPULSE
rushed at him with one **i**. Ac 7:57 *3661*

IMPULSES
And follow the **i** of your heart and Ec 11:9 1870
with sins, led on by various **i**, 2Tm 3:6 *1939*

IMPULSIVE
not be hasty in word or **i** in thought Ec 5:2 4116

IMPURE
all the days of her **i** discharge Lv 15:25 2932a
LORD because of her **i** discharge.' Lv 15:30 2932a
will scatter them as an **i** thing, Is 30:22 1739
eating their bread with **i** hands, Mk 7:2 *2839*
eat their bread with **i** hands?" Mk 7:5 *2839*
or **i** person or covetous man, Eph 5:5 *169*

IMPURITIES
because of the **i** of the sons of Israel Lv 16:16 2932a
with them in the midst of their **i**. Lv 16:16 2932a
from the **i** of the sons of Israel Lv 16:19 2932a

IMPURITY
in her menstrual **i** for seven days; Lv 15:19 5079
her menstrual **i** shall be unclean, Lv 15:20 5079
so that her menstrual **i** is on him, Lv 15:24 5079
at the period of her menstrual **i**, Lv 15:25 5079
as though in her menstrual **i**; Lv 15:25 5079
who is ill because of menstrual **i**, Lv 15:33 5079
nakedness during her menstrual **i**. Lv 18:19 2932a
keep it as water to remove **i**; Nu 19:9 5079
the water for **i** was not sprinkled on Nu 19:13 5079
i has not been sprinkled on him, Nu 19:20 5079
he who sprinkles the water for **i** Nu 19:21 5079
he who touches the water for **i** shall Nu 19:21 5079
be purified with water for **i**. Nu 31:23 5079
from the **i** of the nations of the land Ezr 6:21 2932a
from end to end *and* with their **i**. Ezr 9:11 2932a
was unclean in her menstrual **i**. Ezk 22:10 5079
uncleanness of a woman in her **i**. Ezk 36:17 5079
of Jerusalem, for sin and for **i**. Zch 13:1 5079
in the lusts of their hearts to **i**, Ro 1:24 *167*
as slaves to **i** and to lawlessness, Ro 6:19 *167*
not repented of the **i**, immorality 2Co 12:21 *167*
immorality, **i**, sensuality, Ga 5:19 *167*
the practice of every kind of **i** with Eph 4:19 *167*
immorality or any **i** or greed must not Eph 5:3 *167*
body as dead to immorality, **i**, Col 3:5 *167*
from error or **i** or by way of deceit; 1Th 2:3 *167*
called us for the purpose of **i**, 1Th 4:7 *167*

IMPUTE
Do not let the king **i** anything to 1Sa 22:15 7760
whom the LORD does not **i** iniquity, Ps 32:2 2803

IMPUTED
sin is not **i** when there is no law. Ro 5:13 *1677*

IMRAH
Harnepher, Shual, Beri and **I**, 1Ch 7:36 3236

IMRI
the son of Omri, the son of **I**, 1Ch 9:4 566
to them Zaccur the son of **I** built. Ne 3:2 566

INACCESSIBLE
Upon the rocky crag, an **i** place. Jb 39:28 4686b

INASMUCH
i as they have come under the Gn 19:8 3588, 5921, 3651
i as I did not give her to my son Gn 38:26 3588, 5921, 3651
i as you know where we should camp Nu 10:31 3588, 5921, 3651
i as you have turned back from Nu 14:43 3588, 5921, 3651
i as we have sworn to each other 1Sa 20:42 834
"**I** as I exalted you from the dust 1Ki 16:2 3282, 834
i as *in* the coming days all will Ec 2:16 7945
"**I** as these people have rejected Is 8:6 3282, 3588
i as he is discouraging the men of Jer 38:4 3588, 5921, 3651
I as they have sinned against the Jer 50:7 8478, 834
i as you have seen that the Da 2:8 3606, 6903, 1768
i as no great king or ruler has Da 2:10 3606, 6903, 1768
i as iron crushes and shatters all Da 2:40 3606, 6903, 1768
i as you saw the iron mixed with Da 2:41 3606, 6903, 1768
"**I** as you saw that a stone was Da 2:45 3606, 6903, 1768
i as there is no other god who is Da 3:29 3606, 6903, 1768
i as none of the wise men of my Da 4:18 3606, 6903, 1768
corruption, **i** as he was faithful, Da 6:4 3606, 6903, 1768
i as I was found innocent before Da 6:22 3606, 6903, 1768
I as many have undertaken to Lk 1:1 *1895*
I then as I am an apostle of Ro 11:13 *1909, 3745*
i as we, having put it on, will 2Co 5:3 *1489*
And **i** as *it was* not without an oath Heb 7:20 *2596, 3745*
i as it is appointed for men to die Heb 9:27 *2596, 3745*

INAUGURATED
covenant was not **i** without blood. Heb 9:18 *1457a*
new and living way which He **i** for Heb 10:20 *1457a*

INCAPABLE
long will they be **i** of innocence? Hos 8:5 3808, 3201

INCENSE
oil and for the fragrant **i**, Ex 25:6 7004
an altar as a place for burning **i**; Ex 30:1 7004
Aaron shall burn fragrant **i** on it; Ex 30:7 7004
at twilight, he shall burn **i**. Ex 30:8 6999
There shall be perpetual **i** before Ex 30:8 7004
not offer any strange **i** on this altar, Ex 30:9 7004
its utensils, and the altar of **i**, Ex 30:27 7004
"With it you shall make **i**, Ex 30:35 7004
"The **i** which you shall make, Ex 30:37 7004
its utensils, and the altar of **i**, Ex 31:8 7004
the fragrant **i** for the holy place, Ex 31:11 7004
oil, and for the fragrant **i**, Ex 35:8 7004
and the altar of **i** and its poles, Ex 35:15 7004
anointing oil and the fragrant **i**, Ex 35:15 7004
oil and for the fragrant **i**. Ex 35:28 7004
the altar of **i** of acacia wood: Ex 37:25 7004
the pure, fragrant **i** of spices, Ex 37:29 7004
anointing oil and the fragrant **i**, Ex 39:38 7004
set the gold altar of **i** before the ark Ex 40:5 7004
and he burned fragrant **i** on it, Ex 40:27 7004
put oil on it and lay **i** on it; Lv 2:15 3828
its oil with all its **i** as an offering by Lv 2:16 3828
the horns of the altar of fragrant **i** Lv 4:7 7004
put oil on it or place **i** on it, Lv 5:11 3828
i that is on the grain offering, Lv 6:15 3828
placed **i** on it and offered strange Lv 10:1 7004
handfuls of finely ground sweet **i**, Lv 16:12 7004
the **i** on the fire before the LORD, Lv 16:13 7004
that the cloud of **i** may cover the Lv 16:13 7004
and cut down your **i** altars, Lv 26:30 2553
oil for the light and the fragrant **i** Nu 4:16 7004
pan of ten *shekels,* full of **i**; Nu 7:14 7004
pan of ten *shekels,* full of **i**; Nu 7:20 7004
pan of ten *shekels,* full of **i**; Nu 7:26 7004
pan of ten *shekels,* full of **i**; Nu 7:32 7004
pan of ten *shekels,* full of **i**; Nu 7:38 7004
pan of ten *shekels,* full of **i**; Nu 7:44 7004
pan of ten *shekels,* full of **i**; Nu 7:50 7004
pan of ten *shekels,* full of **i**; Nu 7:56 7004
pan of ten *shekels,* full of **i**; Nu 7:62 7004
pan of ten *shekels,* full of **i**; Nu 7:68 7004
pan of ten *shekels,* full of **i**; Nu 7:74 7004
pan of ten *shekels,* full of **i**; Nu 7:80 7004
the twelve gold pans, full of **i**, Nu 7:86 7004
and lay **i** upon them in the Nu 16:7 7004
take his firepan and put **i** on it, Nu 16:17 7004
put fire on it, and laid **i** on it; Nu 16:18 7004
fifty men who were offering the **i**. Nu 16:35 7004
near to burn **i** before the LORD; Nu 16:40 7004
from the altar, and lay **i** *on it;* Nu 16:46 7004
put *on* the **i** and made atonement Nu 16:47 7004
They shall put **i** before You, And Dt 33:10 6988
to go up to My altar, to burn **i**, 1Sa 2:28 7004
and burned **i** on the high places. 1Ki 3:3 6999

burning **i** with them *on the altar* 1Ki 9:25 6999
burned **i** and sacrificed to their gods 1Ki 11:8 6999
went up to the altar to burn **i**. 1Ki 12:33 6999
standing by the altar to burn **i**. 1Ki 13:1 6999
the high places who burn **i** on you, 1Ki 13:2 6999
and burnt **i** on the high places. 1Ki 22:43 6999
and burned **i** on the high places. 2Ki 12:3 6999
and burned **i** on the high places. 2Ki 14:4 6999
and burned **i** on the high places. 2Ki 15:4 6999
and burned **i** on the high places. 2Ki 15:35 6999
burned **i** on the high places and on 2Ki 16:4 6999
they burned **i** on all the high places 2Ki 17:11 6999
the sons of Israel burned **i** to it; 2Ki 18:4 6999
and have burned **i** to other gods that 2Ki 22:17 6999
to burn **i** in the high places 2Ki 23:5 6999
also those who burned **i** to Baal, 2Ki 23:5 6999
where the priests had burned **i**, 2Ki 23:8 6999
offering and on the altar of **i**, 1Ch 6:49 7004
to burn **i** before the LORD, 1Ch 23:13 6999
for the altar of **i** refined gold by 1Ch 28:18 7004
to burn fragrant **i** before Him and 2Ch 2:4 7004
except to burn **i** before Him? 2Ch 2:6
burnt offerings and fragrant **i**, 2Ch 13:11 7004
i altars from all the cities of Judah 2Ch 14:5 2553
before them and burned **i** to them. 2Ch 25:14 6999
to burn **i** on the altar of incense. 2Ch 26:16 6999
to burn incense on the altar of **i**. 2Ch 26:16 7004
Uzziah, to burn **i** to the LORD, 2Ch 26:18 6999
who are consecrated to burn **i**. 2Ch 26:18 6999
censer in his hand for burning **i**, 2Ch 26:19 6999
the LORD, beside the altar of **i**. 2Ch 26:19 7004
burned **i** in the valley of 2Ch 28:3 6999
and burned **i** on the high places, 2Ch 28:4 6999
places to burn **i** to other gods, 2Ch 28:25 6999
and have not burned **i** or offered 2Ch 29:7 7004
to be His ministers and burn **i**." 2Ch 29:11 6999
they also removed all the **i** altars 2Ch 30:14 4729c
and on it you shall burn **i**"? 2Ch 32:12 6999
and the **i** altars that were high 2Ch 34:4 2553
and chopped down all the **i** altars 2Ch 34:7 2553
and have burned **i** to other gods, 2Ch 34:25 6999
be counted as **i** before You; Ps 141:2 7004
longer, **I** is an abomination to Me. Is 1:13 7004
Even the Asherim and **i** stands. Is 17:8 2553
and **i** altars will not stand. Is 27:9 2553
offerings, Nor wearied you with **i**. Is 43:23 3828
gardens and burning **i** on bricks; Is 65:3 6999
have burned **i** on the mountains And Is 65:7 6999
He who burns **i** is *like* the one who Is 66:3 3828
to the gods to whom they burn **i**, Jer 11:12 6999
thing, altars to burn **i** to Baal. Jer 11:13 6999
sacrifices, grain offerings and **i**, Jer 17:26 3828
They burn **i** to worthless gods And Jer 18:15 6999
where *people* have offered **i** to Baal Jer 32:29 6999
having grain offerings and **i** in Jer 41:5 3828
the one who burns **i** to his gods. Jer 48:35 6999
and your **i** altars will be smashed; Ezk 6:4 2553
your **i** altars may be cut down, Ezk 6:6 2553
of the cloud of **i** rising. Ezk 8:11 7004
My oil and My **i** before them. Ezk 16:18 7004
which you had set My **i** and My oil. Ezk 23:41 7004
to him an offering and fragrant **i**. Da 2:46 5208
mountains And burn **i** on the hills, Hos 4:13 6999
the Baals And burning **i** to idols. Hos 11:2 6999
And burn **i** to their fishing net; Hab 1:16 6999
i is going to be offered to My name Mal 1:11 4729b
the temple of the Lord and burn **i**. Lk 1:9 *2370*
at the hour of the **i** offering. Lk 1:10 *2368*
to the right of the altar of **i**. Lk 1:11 *2368*
having a golden altar of **i** and the Heb 9:4 *2369*
harp and golden bowls full of **i**, Rv 5:8 *2368*
and much **i** was given to him, so Rv 8:3 *2368*
And the smoke of the **i**, Rv 8:4 *2368*
and cinnamon and spice and **i** and Rv 18:13 *2368*

INCESSANTLY
"This man **i** speaks against this Ac 6:13 *3756, 3973*

INCEST
they have committed **i**, Lv 20:12 8397

INCIDENT
not gained any insight from the **i** Mk 6:52

INCITE
i Egyptians against Egyptians; Is 19:2 5526a
"They will **i** a crowd against you and Ezk 16:40 5927

INCITED
it **i** David against them to say, 2Sa 24:1 5496
because Jezebel his wife **i** him. 1Ki 21:25 5496
i revolt within it in past days; Ezr 4:15 5648
although you **i** Me against him to Jb 2:3 5496
But the Jews **i** the devout women of Ac 13:50 *3951*

INCITES
one who **i** the people to rebellion, Lk 23:14 *654*

INCITING
but Baruch the son of Neriah is **i** Jer 43:3 5496

INCLINATION
wherever the **i** of the pilot desires. Jas 3:4 *3730*

INCLINE
and **i** your hearts to the LORD, Jos 24:23 5186
He may **i** our hearts to Himself, 1Ki 8:58 5186
"**I** Your ear, O LORD, and hear; 2Ki 19:16 5186
heart, You will **i** Your ear Ps 10:17 7181
I Your ear to me, hear my speech. Ps 17:6 5186
I Your ear to me, rescue me Ps 31:2 5186
give attention and **i** your ear: Ps 45:10 5186
I will **i** my ear to a proverb; Ps 49:4 5186
I Your ear to me and save me. Ps 71:2 5186
I your ears to the words of my Ps 78:1 5186
I Your ear, O LORD, *and* answer me; Ps 86:1 5186
I Your ear to my cry! Ps 88:2 5186
I Your ear to me; Ps 102:2 5186
I my heart to Your testimonies And Ps 119:36 5186
not **i** my heart to any evil thing, Ps 141:4 5186
I your heart to understanding; Pr 2:2 5186
I your ear to my sayings. Pr 4:20 5186
I your ear to my understanding; Pr 5:1 5186
I your ear and hear the words of Pr 22:17 5186
"**I** Your ear, O LORD, and hear; Is 37:17 5186
"**I** your ear and come to Me. Is 55:3 5186
they did not obey or **i** their ear, Jer 7:24 5186
not listen to Me or **i** their ear, Jer 7:26 5186
they did not obey or **i** their ear, Jer 11:8 5186
did not listen or **i** their ears, Jer 17:23 5186
not obey Me or **i** their ear to Me. Jer 34:14 5186
'But they did not listen or **i** Jer 44:5 5186
"O my God, **i** Your ear and hear! Da 9:18 5186

INCLINED
they were **i** to follow Abimelech, Jg 9:3 5186
that the king's heart *was* **i** 2Sa 14:1
And He **i** to me and heard my cry. Ps 40:1 5186
Because He has **i** His ear to me, Ps 116:2 5186
I have **i** my heart to perform Your Ps 119:112 5186
Nor **i** my ear to my instructors! Pr 5:13 5186
listened nor **i** your ear to hear, Jer 25:4 5186
not **i** your ear or listened to Me. Jer 35:15 5186
But if one is **i** to be contentious, 1Co 11:16 *1380*

INCLINES
And his heart **i** toward wickedness: Is 32:6 6213a

INCLUDE
Whose trappings **i** bit and bridle Ps 32:9

INCLUDED
I also *were* Kattah Jos 19:15
territory was to Jezreel and **i** Jos 19:18
I also *were* Ummah, and Aphek Jos 19:30
number was not **i** in the account of 1Ch 27:24 5927
The genealogical enrollment **i** all 2Ch 31:18

INCLUDING
not **i** the wives of Jacob's sons, Gn 46:26 905
unclean, **i** any wooden article, Lv 11:32 4480
Beersheba, **i** the land of Gilead, Jg 20:1
i his sword and his bow and his 1Sa 18:4 5704
i goods, garments and valuable 2Ch 20:25
attack them, **i** children and women, Es 8:11 854
i all the people who were living Jer 44:15
all the people, **i** all the women, Jer 44:24
was like these, **i** pomegranates. Jer 52:22
i some of the royal family and of Da 1:3
Even **i** the vine, the fig tree, the Hg 2:19 5704
i what had happened to the demoniacs. Mt 8:33 *2532*
i both Cyrenians and Alexandrians, Ac 6:9
i the overseers and deacons: Php 1:1 *4862*

INCOME
The **i** of the wicked, punishment Pr 10:16 8393
trouble is in the **i** of the wicked. Pr 15:6 8393
Than great **i** with injustice. Pr 16:8 8393
he who loves abundance *with its* **i**. Ec 5:10 8393

INCORRUPTIBLE
exchanged the glory of the **i** God Ro 1:23 *862a*
Lord Jesus Christ with **i** *love.* Eph 6:24 *861*

INCREASE
that its yield may **i** for you; Lv 19:25 8393
the years you shall **i** its price, Lv 25:16 7235a
I will **i** the plague on you seven Lv 26:21 3254
you shall **i** their inheritance, Nu 26:54 7235a
i you a thousand-fold more than Dt 1:11 3254
the **i** of your herd and the young Dt 7:13 7698
compassion on you and make you **i**, Dt 13:17 7235a
i silver and gold for himself. Dt 17:17 7235a
and the **i** of the vineyard will Dt 22:9 8393
tithe of your **i** in the third year, Dt 26:12 8393
the **i** of your herd and the young Dt 28:4 7698
the **i** of your herd and the young Dt 28:18 7698
nor the **i** of your herd or the Dt 28:51 7698
"**I** your army and come out." Jg 9:29 7235a
all the **i** of your house will die in 1Sa 2:33 4768
should damage **i** to the detriment Ezr 4:22 7680
Yet your end will **i** greatly. Jb 8:7 7685
me And **i** Your anger toward me; Jb 10:17 7235a
"The **i** of his house will depart; Jb 20:28 2981
And would uproot all my **i**. Jb 31:12 8393
If riches **i**, do not set *your* heart Ps 62:10 5107
May You **i** my greatness And Ps 71:21 7235a
name **i** as long as the sun *shines;* Ps 72:17 5125
May the LORD give you **i**, Ps 115:14 3254
man will hear and **i** in learning, Pr 1:5 3254
man and he will **i** *his* learning. Pr 9:9 3254
when they perish, the righteous **i**. Pr 28:28 7235a
When the righteous **i**, Pr 29:2 7235a
When the wicked **i**, transgression Pr 29:16 7235a
When good things **i**, Ec 5:11 7235a
those who consume them **i**. Ec 5:11 7231
are many words which **i** futility. Ec 6:11 7235a
You shall **i** their gladness; Is 9:3 1431
i of *His* government or of peace, Is 9:7 4766
i their gladness in the LORD, Is 29:19 3254
lend *money* on interest or take **i**, Ezk 18:8 8636
money on interest and takes **i**; Ezk 18:13 8636
poor, does not take interest or **i**, Ezk 18:17 8636
and the earth will yield its **i**, Ezk 34:27 2981
and they will **i** and be fruitful; Ezk 36:11 7235a
I will **i** their men like a flock. Ezk 36:37 7235a
and forth, and knowledge will **i**." Da 12:4 7235a
will play the harlot, but not **i**, Hos 4:10 6555
said to the Lord, "**I** our faith!" Lk 17:5 *4369*
"He must **i**, but I must decrease. Jn 3:30 *837*
the disciples continued to **i** greatly Ac 6:7 *4129*
Holy Spirit, it continued to **i**. Ac 9:31 *4129*
in so that the transgression would **i**; Ro 5:20 *4121*
in sin so that grace may **i**? Ro 6:1 *4121*
i the harvest of your righteousness; 2Co 9:10 *837*
and may the Lord cause you to **i** 1Th 3:12 *4121*

INCREASED
the water **i** and lifted up the ark, Gn 7:17 7235a
and **i** greatly upon the earth, Gn 7:18 7235a
came and it has **i** to a multitude Gn 30:30 6555
of Israel were fruitful and **i** greatly, Ex 1:7 8317
the Philistines continued and **i**; 1Sa 14:19 7227a
people **i** continually with Absalom. 2Sa 15:12 7227a
their fathers' houses **i** greatly. 1Ch 4:38 *6555*
had **i** in the land of Gilead. 1Ch 5:9 7235a
possessions have **i** in the land. Jb 1:10 6555
And **i** years should teach wisdom. Jb 32:7 7230
LORD **i** all that Job had twofold. Jb 42:10 3254
O Lord, how my adversaries have **i**! Ps 3:1 7231
When the glory of his house is **i**; Ps 49:16 7235a
at ease, they have **i** *in* wealth. Ps 73:12 7685
I have magnified and **i** wisdom more Ec 1:16 3254
Then I became great and **i** more Ec 2:9 3254
You have **i** the nation, O LORD, Is 26:15 3254
O LORD, You have **i** the nation; Is 26:15 3254
king with oil And **i** your perfumes; Is 57:9 7235a
multiplied and **i** in the land," Jer 3:16 6509
"So she **i** her harlotries. Ezk 23:14 3254
your trade You have **i** your riches And Ezk 28:5 7235a
therefore the width of the temple **i** Ezk 41:7
You have **i** your traders more than Na 3:16 7235a
"Because lawlessness is **i**, Mt 24:12 *4129*
soil, and as they grew up and **i**, Mk 4:8 *837*
people **i** and multiplied in Egypt, Ac 7:17 *837*
but where sin **i**, grace abounded Ro 5:20 *4121*

INCREASES
who scatters, and *yet* **i** all the more, Pr 11:24 3254
the one who gathers by labor **i** *it.* Pr 13:11 7235a
sweetness of speech **i** persuasiveness Pr 16:21 3254
And **i** the faithless among men. Pr 23:28 3254
And a man of knowledge **i** power. Pr 24:5 553
He who **i** his wealth by interest Pr 28:8 7235a
wicked increase, transgression **i**; Pr 29:16 7235a
to *him who* lacks might He **i** power. Is 40:29 7235a
'Woe to him who **i** what is not his Hab 2:6 7235a
profit which **i** to your account. Php 4:17 *4121*

INCREASING
i knowledge *results in* increasing Ec 1:18 3254
knowledge *results in* **i** pain. Ec 1:18 3254
and become strong, **i** in wisdom; Lk 2:40 *4137*
Jesus kept **i** in wisdom and stature, Lk 2:52 *4298*
As the crowds were **i**, Lk 11:29 *1865*
the disciples were **i** *in number,* Ac 6:1 *4129*
But Saul kept **i** in strength and Ac 9:22 *1743*
faith, and were **i** in number daily. Ac 16:5 *4052*
is constantly bearing fruit and **i**, Col 1:6 *837*
and **i** in the knowledge of God; Col 1:10 *837*
qualities are yours and are **i**, 2Pe 1:8 *4121*

INCREASINGLY
the sea was becoming **i** stormy. Jon 1:11 1980

INCREDIBLE
"Why is it considered **i** among you Ac 26:8 *571*

INCUR
that they do not **i** guilt and die. Ex 28:43 5375
he may have done to **i** guilt." Lv 6:7 819
shall not **i** sin because of him. Lv 19:17 5375
we will **i** a stricter judgment. Jas 3:1 *2983*

INCURABLE
in his bowels with an **i** sickness. 2Ch 21:18 369, 4832
My wound is **i**, *though I am* without Jb 34:6 605
In a day of sickliness and **i** pain. Is 17:11 605
because of my injury! My wound is **i**. Jer 10:19 2470a
my wound **i**, refusing to be healed? Jer 15:18 605
'Your wound is **i** And your injury Jer 30:12 605
Your pain is **i**. Because your iniquity Jer 30:15 605
For her wound is **i**, Mi 1:9 605
your breakdown, Your wound is **i**. Na 3:19 2470a

INCURRED
and has **i** grievous guilt, Ezk 25:12 816
Crete and **i** this damage and loss. Ac 27:21 *2770*
the condemnation **i** by the devil. 1Tm 3:6

INCURRING
thus **i** condemnation, because they 1Tm 5:12 *2192*

INDEBTED
forgive everyone who is **i** to us. Lk 11:4 *3784*
to do so, and they are **i** to them. Ro 15:27 *3781*
they are **i** to minister to them Ro 15:27 *3784*

INDECENCY
he has found some **i** in her, Dt 24:1 6172

INDECENT
and He must not see anything **i** Dt 23:14 6172
men with men committing **i** acts and Ro 1:27 *808*

INDEED
"**I**, has God said, 'You shall not eat Gn 3:1 637, 3588
I I will give you a son by her. Gn 17:16 1571
'Shall I **i** bear *a child,* when I am Gn 18:13 637, 552
of Sodom and Gomorrah is **i** great, Gn 18:20 3588
"Will You **i** sweep away the Gn 18:23 637
will You **i** sweep *it* away and not Gn 18:24 637
i I will greatly bless you, and I Gn 22:17 3588
i he loved Rachel more than Leah, Gn 29:30 1571
and has **i** heard my voice and has Gn 30:6 1571
sister, *and* I have **i** prevailed." Gn 30:8 1571
"Now you have **i** gone away Gn 31:30 1980

we i came down the first time to	Gn 43:20	3381
which he i uses for divination?	Gn 44:5	5172
as I can i practice divination?"	Gn 44:15	5172
and i he is ruler over all the	Gn 45:26	3588
"I am i concerned about you and	Ex 3:16	6485
i a bridegroom of blood to me."	Ex 4:25	3588
"But, i, for this reason I have	Ex 9:16	199
i, it was proven when they dealt	Ex 18:11	3588
if you will i obey My voice and	Ex 19:5	8085
i, there is no white hair in the	Lv 13:26	2009
i, it appears to be no deeper than	Lv 13:31	2009
i the mark has not spread in the	Lv 13:53	2009
If the mark has i spread in the	Lv 14:39	2009
mark has i spread in the house,	Lv 14:44	2009
and the mark has not i spread in	Lv 14:48	2009
'I, your threshing will last for	Lv 26:5	
LORD i spoken only through Moses?	Nu 12:2	389
but i, as I live, all the earth	Nu 14:21	199
we have i sinned, but we will go	Nu 14:40	3588
"I, you have not brought us into	Nu 16:14	637
"If You will i deliver this	Nu 21:2	5414
for I will i honor you richly, and	Nu 22:17	3513
"But if her husband i annuls them	Nu 30:12	6565a
"But if her husband i says nothing	Nu 30:14	2790b
"But if he i annuls them after he	Nu 30:15	6565a
was i a place suitable for livestock	Nu 32:1	2009
we will i go up and fight, just as	Dt 1:41	
"I, ask now concerning the former	Dt 4:32	3588
and i, it is a stubborn people.	Dt 9:13	2009
"And I saw that you had i sinned	Dt 9:16	2009
"I their rock is not like our	Dt 32:31	3588
'I, I lift up My hand to heaven,	Dt 32:40	3588
i it is your life.	Dt 32:47	3588
"I, He loves the people;	Dt 33:3	637
I i come now *as* captain of the host	Jos 5:14	3588
I she repeats her words to	Jg 5:29	637
and i, he has cut down the Asherah	Jg 6:30	3588
for i, we have forsaken our God	Jg 10:10	3588
"If You will i give the sons of	Jg 11:30	5414
if you will i tell it to me within	Jg 14:12	5046
I, I have commanded the servants	Ru 2:9	3808
and i have spoken kindly to your	Ru 2:13	3588
if You will i look on the affliction	1Sa 1:11	7200
I, there is no one besides You,	1Sa 2:2	3588
'Did I *not* i reveal Myself to the	1Sa 2:27	1540
'I did i say that your house and	1Sa 2:30	559
I, I escaped from the battle line	1Sa 4:16	3588
"I i tasted a little honey with	1Sa 14:43	2938
I have i transgressed the command	1Sa 15:24	3588
For if I should i learn that evil	1Sa 20:9	3045
I, see the edge of your robe in my	1Sa 24:11	1571
I the LORD will give over the army	1Sa 28:19	1571
'I you did it secretly, but I will	2Sa 12:12	3588
I, it was your servant Joab who	2Sa 14:19	3588
'If the LORD shall i bring me back	2Sa 15:8	7725
for if we i flee, they will not	2Sa 18:3	5127
Will He not i make *it* grow?	2Sa 23:5	3588
I will i do so this day."	1Ki 1:30	3588
i, You have spoken with Your mouth	1Ki 8:24	
"But will God i dwell on the earth?	1Ki 8:27	552
i, teach them the good way in	1Ki 8:36	3588
i turn away from following Me,	1Ki 9:6	7725
"If you i return safely the LORD	1Ki 22:28	7725
"You have i defeated Edom, and	2Ki 14:10	5221
"Oh that You would bless me i and	1Ch 4:10	1288
I, your God helps you!"	1Ch 12:18	3588
There was joy i in Israel.	1Ch 12:40	3588
I, the world is firmly established,	1Ch 16:30	637
I, I am the one who has sinned and	1Ch 21:17	
God had i blessed him.	1Ch 26:5	3588
i everything that is in the heavens	1Ch 29:11	3588
and i my servants *will work* with	2Ch 2:8	2009
"*He* i is good for His lovingkindness	2Ch 5:13	3588
i You have spoken with Your mouth	2Ch 6:15	
But will God i dwell with mankind	2Ch 6:18	552
i, teach them the good way in	2Ch 6:27	3588
I, from now on you will surely	2Ch 16:9	3588
"If you i return safely, the LORD	2Ch 18:27	7725
I the army of the Arameans came	2Ch 24:24	3588
i, the hands of the princes and	Ezr 9:2	
The sons of Israel had i not done	Ne 8:17	3588
"I, forty years You provided	Ne 9:21	
"Behold i, the gallows standing	Es 7:9	1571
I, Mordecai was great in the	Es 9:4	3588
Shall we i accept good from God	Jb 2:10	1571
"I, you have now become such, You	Jb 6:21	3588
'Is it right for You i to oppress,	Jb 10:3	3588
Your knowledge I am i not guilty,	Jb 10:7	3588
"Then, i, you could lift up your	Jb 11:15	3588
"I, you do away with reverence And	Jb 15:4	637
"I, the light of the wicked goes	Jb 18:5	1571
"If i you vaunt yourselves	Jb 19:5	551
"I, what *good was* the strength of	Jb 30:2	1571
I, there was no one who refuted Job	Jb 32:12	2009
"I God speaks once, Or twice, *yet*	Jb 33:14	3588
"Then i, He enticed you from the	Jb 36:16	637
I, my heritage is beautiful to me.	Ps 16:6	637
I, my mind instructs me in the	Ps 16:7	637
I, none of those who wait for You	Ps 25:3	1571
death, I my feet from stumbling,	Ps 56:13	3808
Do you i speak righteousness, O	Ps 58:1	552
I, the LORD will give what is good,	Ps 85:12	1571
I, the world is firmly established	Ps 93:1	637
I, the world is firmly established	Ps 96:10	637
I, I forget to eat my bread	Ps 102:4	3588
Shall i come again with a shout of	Ps 126:6	935
I, may you see your children's	Ps 128:6	
I, *more than* the watchmen for	Ps 130:6	
I, they are a graceful wreath to	Pr 1:9	3588
I, it is useless to spread the	Pr 1:17	3588
i, they all have the same breath	Ec 3:19	
I, his eyes were not satisfied	Ec 4:8	1571
I, there is not a righteous man on	Ec 7:20	3588
I their love, their hate and	Ec 9:6	1571
I, if a man should live many years	Ec 11:8	3588
I, our couch is luxuriant!	SS 1:16	637
I, *while following* the way of Your	Is 26:8	637
I, my spirit within me seeks You	Is 26:9	637
I, fire will devour Your enemies.	Is 26:11	637
I, He will speak to this people	Is 28:11	3588
I, he does not continue to thresh it	Is 28:28	3588
I all who are intent on doing evil	Is 29:20	
I, they will sanctify the Holy One	Is 29:23	
I, it has been prepared for the king.	Is 30:33	1571
I, do good or evil, that we may	Is 41:23	637
I, let them consult together.	Is 45:21	637
They bow down, i they worship it.	Is 46:6	637
i I have called him, I have	Is 48:15	637
I, the LORD will comfort Zion;	Is 51:3	3588
I, far removed from Me, you have	Is 57:8	3588
King of the nations? I it is Your due!	Jer 10:7	3588
I I would discuss matters of justice	Jer 12:1	389
"I, who will have pity on you, O	Jer 15:5	3588
Will You i be to me like a	Jer 15:18	1961
you men will i perform this thing,	Jer 22:4	6213a
i, thus says the LORD	Jer 24:8	3588
I, there was also a man who	Jer 26:20	1571
I, as often as I have spoken	Jer 31:20	3588
"I the sons of Israel and the	Jer 32:30	3588
"I this city has been to Me *a*	Jer 32:31	3588
'I, the sons of Jonadab the son of	Jer 35:16	3588
'If you will i go out to the officers	Jer 38:17	3318
'If you will i stay in this land,	Jer 42:10	7725
I, they have fallen one against	Jer 46:16	1571
I Babylon is to fall *for* the slain	Jer 51:49	1571
lovingkindnesses i never cease,	La 3:22	3588
'I, the seller will not regain	Ezk 7:13	3588
I i will deal in wrath.	Ezk 8:18	1571
i break the covenant and escape?	Ezk 17:15	
"I, those who support Egypt will	Ezk 30:6	
"I all Israel has transgressed	Da 9:11	
will be a great dominion i.	Da 11:5	
woe to them i when I depart from	Hos 9:12	1571
I, I came to hate them there!	Hos 9:15	3588
I, its people will mourn for it,	Hos 10:5	3588
I He will roar And *His* sons will	Hos 11:10	3588
I, rejoicing dries up From the	Jl 1:12	3588
day of the LORD is i great and very	Jl 2:11	3588
"I, I will never forget any of	Am 8:7	518
I, all of it will rise up like the Nile	Am 8:8	
I, they will all cover *their* mouths	Mi 3:7	
"I, I brought you up from the	Mi 6:4	3588
I the earth is upheaved by His	Na 1:5	
I, you will become plunder for	Hab 2:7	
"Is it not i from the LORD of hosts	Hab 2:13	2009
complete end, I a terrifying one,	Zph 1:18	389
I, My decision is to gather nations,	Zph 3:8	3588
I, I will give you renown and	Zph 3:20	3588
I, the LORD who has chosen	Zch 3:2	
I they are men who are a symbol,	Zch 3:8	3588
I, their children will see *it* and	Zch 10:7	
and i, I have cursed them *already,*	Mal 2:2	1571
who i bears fruit and brings	Mt 13:23	*1211*
to you that Elijah has i come,	Mk 9:13	*2532*
"No i; but he shall be called John."	Lk 1:60	*3780*
"I the axe is already laid at	Lk 3:9	*2532*
"I, the very hairs of your head	Lk 12:7	*235, 2532*
"For i, the Son of Man is going	Lk 22:22	*3303a*
"And we i *are suffering* justly,	Lk 23:41	*3303a*
I, besides all this, it is the	Lk 24:21	*235*
Israelite i, in whom there is no deceit!"	Jn 1:47	*230*
is i the Savior of the world."	Jn 4:42	*230*
you free, you will be free i.	Jn 8:36	*3689*
they sending us away secretly? No i!	Ac 16:37	*1063*
I we are in danger of being accused	Ac 19:40	*2532*
For i circumcision is of value if	Ro 2:25	*3303a*
since i God who will justify the	Ro 3:30	*1512*
if i the Spirit of God dwells in	Ro 8:9	*1512*
if i we suffer with *Him* so	Ro 8:17	*1512*
never heard, have they? I they have;	Ro 10:18	*3304*
All things i are clean, but they	Ro 14:20	*3303a*
For i Jews ask for signs and	1Co 1:22	*2532*
I, even now you are not yet able,	1Co 3:2	*235*
and i, *I* wish that you had become	1Co 4:8	*1065*
as i there are many gods and many	1Co 8:5	*5618*
for i man was not created for the	1Co 11:9	*2532*
i, we had the sentence of death	2Co 1:9	*235*
for i what I have forgiven, if I	2Co 2:10	*2532*
For i what had glory, in this case	2Co 3:10	*2532*
For i in this *house* we groan,	2Co 5:2	*2532*
For i while we are in this tent,	2Co 5:4	*2532*
but i you are bearing with me.	2Co 11:1	*2532*
For i He was crucified because of	2Co 13:4	*2532*
unless i you fail the test?	2Co 13:5	
if i it was in vain?	Ga 3:4	*1065, 2532*
would i have been based on law.	Ga 3:21	*3689*
if i you have heard of the	Eph 3:2	*1065*
if i you have heard Him and have	Eph 4:21	*1065*
For i he was sick to the point of	Php 2:27	*2532*
I, true companion, I ask you also to	Php 4:3	*3483a*
i, you were concerned *before,* but	Php 4:10	*2532*
if i you continue in the faith	Col 1:23	*1065*
i you were called in one body;	Col 3:15	*2532*
For i when we were with you, we	1Th 3:4	*2532*
for i you do practice it toward	1Th 4:10	*2532*
for which i you are suffering.	2Th 1:5	*2532*
Honor widows who are widows i;	1Tm 5:3	*3689*
Now she who is a widow i and	1Tm 5:5	*3689*
may assist those who are widows i.	1Tm 5:16	*3689*
take hold of that which is life i.	1Tm 6:19	*3689*
I, all who desire to live godly in	2Tm 3:12	*2532*
I, did not all those who came out	Heb 3:16	*235*
For i we have had good news	Heb 4:2	*2532*
And those i of the sons of Levi	Heb 7:5	*3303a*
(for they i became priests without	Heb 7:21	*3303a*
And i if they had been thinking of	Heb 11:15	*3303a*
i our fellowship is with the Father,	1Jn 1:3	*2532*
INDEPENDENT		
Lord, neither is woman i of man,	1Co 11:11	*5565*
of man, nor is man i of woman.	1Co 11:11	*5565*
INDESCRIBABLE		
Thanks be to God for His i gift!	2Co 9:15	*411*
INDESTRUCTIBLE		
to the power of an i life.	Heb 7:16	*179*
INDIA		
the Ahasuerus who reigned from I	Es 1:1	1912
which *extended* from I to Ethiopia,	Es 8:9	1912
INDICATE		
saying this to i the kind of death by	Jn 12:33	*4591*
i by the Spirit that there would	Ac 11:28	*4591*
i also the charges against him."	Ac 25:27	*4591*
INDICATING		
Spirit of Christ within them was i	1Pe 1:11	*1213*
INDICATION		
plain i of God's righteous judgment	2Th 1:5	*1730*
INDICTED		
cause a person to be i by a word,	Is 29:21	2398
INDICTMENT		
And the i which my adversary has	Jb 31:35	5612
mountains, to the i of the LORD,	Mi 6:2	7379
INDIGNANT		
He will be i toward His enemies.	Is 66:14	2194
Will He be i to the end?'	Jer 3:5	8104
king became i and very furious and	Da 2:12	1149
have been i these seventy years?"	Zch 1:12	2194
people toward whom the LORD is i	Mal 1:4	2194
became i with the two brothers.	Mt 20:24	*23*
the Son of David," they became i	Mt 21:15	*23*
disciples were i when they saw *this,*	Mt 26:8	*23*
this, He was i and said to them,	Mk 10:14	*23*
the ten began to feel i with James	Mk 10:41	*23*
i because Jesus had healed on the	Lk 13:14	*23*
INDIGNANTLY		
were i *remarking* to one another,	Mk 14:4	*23*
INDIGNATION		
And a God who has i every day.	Ps 7:11	2194
in my flesh because of Your i;	Ps 38:3	2195
Pour out Your i on them, And may	Ps 69:24	2195
His burning anger, Fury and i	Ps 78:49	2195
cause Your i toward us to cease.	Ps 85:4	3708a
Because of Your i and Your wrath	Ps 102:10	2195
Burning i has seized me because of	Ps 119:53	2152
the staff in whose hands is My i,	Is 10:5	2195
My i *against you* will be spent and	Is 10:25	2195
The LORD and His instruments of i,	Is 13:5	2195
while Until i runs *its* course.	Is 26:20	2195
His lips are filled with i And	Is 30:27	2195
LORD's i is against all the nations,	Is 34:2	7110a
the nations cannot endure His i.	Jer 10:10	2195
For You filled me with i.	Jer 15:17	2195
in anger and wrath and great i.	Jer 21:5	7110a
in My wrath and in great i;	Jer 32:37	7110a
"Because of the i of the LORD she	Jer 50:13	7110a
forth the weapons of His i,	Jer 50:25	2195
and priest In the i of His anger.	La 2:6	2195
'I will pour out My i on you;	Ezk 21:31	2195
or rained on in the day of i.'	Ezk 22:24	2195
I have poured out My i on them;	Ezk 22:31	2195
at the final period of the i,	Da 8:19	2195
prosper until the i is finished,	Da 11:36	2195
I will bear the i of the LORD	Mi 7:9	2197
Who can stand before His i?	Na 1:6	2195
In i You marched through the	Hab 3:12	2195
To pour out on them My i,	Zph 3:8	2195
obey unrighteousness, wrath and i.	Ro 2:8	*2372*
vindication of yourselves, what i,	2Co 7:11	*24*
INDISTINCT		
if the bugle produces an i sound,	1Co 14:8	*82*
INDIVIDUAL		
the proper working of each i part,	Eph 4:16	*1520*
each i among you also is to love his	Eph 5:33	*1520*
INDIVIDUALLY		
and i members one of another.	Ro 12:5	*2596, 1520*
to each one i just as He wills.	1Co 12:11	*2398*
Christ's body, and i members of it.	1Co 12:27	*3313*
INDOLENCE		
Through i the rafters sag, and	Ec 10:18	6103
INDUCED		
and i him to go up against	2Ch 18:2	5496
Then they secretly i men to say,	Ac 6:11	*5260*
INDULGE		
and especially those who i the	2Pe 2:10	*4198*
INDULGED		
i in gross immorality and went after	Jude 1:7	*1608*
INDULGENCE		
are of no value against fleshly i.	Col 2:23	*4140*
INDULGING		
i the desires of the flesh and of	Eph 2:3	*4160*

INDUSTRIOUS
saw that the young man was **i**, 1Ki 11:28 4399, 6213a
INEFFECTIVE
along, and the caperberry is **i**. Ec 12:5 6565a
INEVITABLE
is **i** that stumbling blocks come; Mt 18:7 *318*
"It is **i** that stumbling blocks Lk 17:1 *418, 3361*
INEXPERIENCED
"My son Solomon is young and **i**, 1Ch 22:5 7390
young and **i** and the work is great; 1Ch 29:1 7390
INEXPRESSIBLE
into Paradise and heard **i** words, 2Co 12:4 *731*
greatly rejoice with joy **i** and full of 1Pe 1:8 *412*
INFANCY
father, And from **i** I guided her), Jb 31:18 517, 990
INFANT
as a nurse carries a nursing **i**, Nu 11:12 3243
both man and woman, child and **i**, 1Sa 15:3 3243
an **i** *who lives but a few* days, Is 65:20 5764
you man and woman, child and **i**, Jer 44:7 3243
The tongue of the **i** cleaves To the La 4:4 3243
for he is an **i**. Heb 5:13 *3516*
INFANTRY
With the chariots, **i** *and* horsemen; Is 22:6 120
INFANTS
men and women, children and **i**; 1Sa 22:19 3243
with their **i**, their wives and their 2Ch 20:13 2945
not be, As **i** that never saw light. Jb 3:16 5768
From the mouth of **i** and nursing Ps 8:2 5768
When little ones and **i** faint In La 2:11 3243
the children and the nursing **i**. Jl 2:16 3243, 7699a
and have revealed them to **i**. Mt 11:25 *3516*
'OUT OF THE MOUTH OF **I** AND Mt 21:16 *3516*
and have revealed them to **i**. Yes, Lk 10:21 *3516*
they would expose their **i** and they Ac 7:19 *1025*
as to **i** in Christ. 1Co 3:1 *3516*
yet in evil be **i**, but in your 1Co 14:20 *3515*
INFECTED
blow, With a sorely **i** wound. Jer 14:17 2470a
INFECTION
and it becomes an **i** of leprosy on Lv 13:2 5061
if the hair in the **i** has turned white Lv 13:3 5061
the **i** appears to be deeper than the Lv 13:3 5061
his body, it is an **i** of leprosy; Lv 13:3 5061
priest shall isolate *him who has* the **i** Lv 13:4 5061
in his eyes the **i** has not changed Lv 13:5 5061
the **i** has not spread on the skin, Lv 13:5 5061
and if the **i** has faded and the Lv 13:6 5061
"When the **i** of leprosy is on a Lv 13:9 5061
all the skin of *him who has* the **i** Lv 13:12 5061
pronounce clean *him who has* the **i**; Lv 13:13 5061
if the **i** has turned to white, Lv 13:17 5061
pronounce clean *him who has* the **i**; Lv 13:17 5061
it is the **i** of leprosy, it has Lv 13:20 5061
pronounce him unclean; it is an **i**. Lv 13:22 5061
it is an **i** of leprosy. Lv 13:25 5061
it is an **i** of leprosy. Lv 13:27 5061
an **i** on the head or on the beard, Lv 13:29 5061
the priest shall look at the **i**, Lv 13:30 5061
the priest looks at the **i** of the scale, Lv 13:31 5061
isolate *the person* with the scaly **i** Lv 13:31 5061
the priest shall look at the **i**, Lv 13:32 5061
there occurs a reddish-white **i**, Lv 13:42 5061
the swelling of the **i** is reddish-white Lv 13:43 5061
his **i** is on his head. Lv 13:44 5061
"As for the leper who has the **i**, Lv 13:45 5061
days during which he has the **i**; Lv 13:46 5061
if the **i** of leprosy has been healed Lv 14:3 5061
in whom there is an **i** of leprosy, Lv 14:32 5061
careful against an **i** of leprosy, Dt 24:8 5061
INFERIOR
I am not **i** to you. Jb 12:3 5307
I am not **i** to you. Jb 13:2 5307
And the **i** against the honorable. Is 3:5 7034
arise another kingdom **i** to you, Da 2:39 772
i to the most eminent apostles. 2Co 11:5 *5302*
was I **i** to the most eminent apostles, 2Co 12:11 *5302*
as **i** to the rest of the churches, 2Co 12:13 *2274*
INFINITE
His understanding is **i**. Ps 147:5 369, 4557
INFIRM
young man or virgin, old man or **i**; 2Ch 36:17 3486
INFIRMITIES
"HE HIMSELF TOOK OUR **I** AND Mt 8:17 *769*
INFLAME
the evening that wine may **i** them! Is 5:11 1814
Who **i** yourselves among the oaks, Is 57:5 2552
INFLAMMATION
with fever and with **i** and with fiery Dt 28:22 1816
INFLATED
i without cause by his fleshly mind Col 2:18 *5448*
INFLICT
your God will **i** all these curses on Dt 30:7 5414
would **i** this disaster on them." Ezk 6:10 6213a
he broke, I will **i** on his head. Ezk 17:19 5414
INFLICTED
frogs which He had **i** upon Pharaoh. Ex 8:12 7760
a man, so it shall be **i** on him. Lv 24:20 5414
he turned, he **i** punishment. 1Sa 14:47 7561
Arameans had **i** on him at Ramah when 2Ki 8:29 5221
wounds which the Arameans had **i** 2Ki 9:15 5221
wounds which they had **i** on him at 2Ch 22:6 5221
who **i** him with heavy casualties. 2Ch 28:5 5221
and heals the bruise He has **i**. Is 30:26 4347
the calamity that I have **i** on you. Jer 42:10 6213a
Which the LORD **i** on the day of His La 1:12 3013
is this punishment which *was* **i** 2Co 2:6
INFLICTS
"For He **i** pain, and gives relief; Jb 5:18 3510
God who **i** wrath is not unrighteous, Ro 3:5 *2018*
INFLUENCE
cause deceit to succeed by his **i**; Da 8:25 3027
God will send upon them a deluding **i** 2Th 2:11 *1753b*
INFLUENCES
Because they are filled *with* **i** Is 2:6
INFLUENTIAL
"let the **i** men among you go there Ac 25:5 *1415*
INFORM
Ask your father, and he will **i** you, Dt 32:7 5046
then you shall **i** your children, Jos 4:22 3045
"So I thought to **i** you, saying, Ru 4:4 241, 1540
word comes from you to **i** me." 2Sa 15:28 5046
"We **i** the king that if that city Ezr 4:16 3046
them their names so as to **i** you, Ezr 5:10 3046
"We also **i** you that it is not allowed Ezr 7:24 3046
he might show Esther and **i** her, Es 4:8 5046
They will **i** you about the whole Col 4:9 *1107*
INFORMATION
come to you with **i** for *your* ears? Ezk 24:26 2045
in the Lord, will bring you **i**. Col 4:7 *1107*
INFORMED
months later that Judah was **i**, Gn 38:24 5046
"Since God has **i** you of all this, Gn 41:39 3045
we have sent and **i** the king, Ezr 4:14 3046
and Esther **i** the king in Mordecai's Es 2:22 559
Or as His counselor has **i** Him? Is 40:13 3045
i Him of the way of understanding Is 40:14 3045
and **i** them of My ordinances, Ezk 20:11 3045
Arioch **i** Daniel about the matter. Da 2:15 3046
to his house and **i** his friends, Da 2:17 3046
I was **i** that there would be a plot Ac 23:30 *3377*
For I have been **i** concerning you, 1Co 1:11 *1213*
for the sake of the one who **i** *you,* 1Co 10:28 *3377*
i us of your love in the Spirit. Col 1:8 *1213*
INFORMS
"He who **i** against friends for a Jb 17:5 5046
and their *diviner's* wand **i** them; Hos 4:12 5046
INFREQUENT
in those days, visions were **i**. 1Sa 3:1 369, 6555
INGATHERING
also the Feast of the **I** at the end Ex 23:16 614
Feast of **I** at the turn of the year. Ex 34:22 614
INHABIT
cities, In houses no one would **i**, Jb 15:28 3427
will build houses and **i** *them;* Is 65:21 3427
will not build and another **i**, Is 65:22 3427
who **i** the coastlands in safety; Ezk 39:6 3427
those who **i** the cities of Israel will Ezk 39:9 3427
will build houses but not **i** *them,* Zph 1:13 3427
INHABITANT
cities are devastated *and* without **i**, Is 6:11 3427
and shout for joy, O **i** of Zion, Is 12:6 3427
Confront you, O **i** of the earth. Is 24:17 3427
O people in Zion, **i** in Jerusalem, Is 30:19 3427
have been destroyed, without **i**. Jer 2:15 3427
cities will be ruins Without **i**. Jer 4:7 3427
Judah a desolation, without **i**." Jer 9:11 3427
A land of salt without **i**. Jer 17:6 3427
will be desolate, without **i**'?" Jer 26:9 3427
and without **i** and without beast, Jer 33:10 3427
Judah a desolation without **i**.' " Jer 34:22 3427
horror and a curse, without an **i**, Jer 44:22 3427
And every **i** of the land will wail. Jer 47:2 3427
road and keep watch, O **i** of Aroer; Jer 48:19 3427
coming upon you, O **i** of Moab," Jer 48:43 3427
and there will be no **i** in it. Jer 50:3 3427
Babylon," The **i** of Zion will say; Jer 51:35 3427
has come to you, O **i** of the land. Ezk 7:7 3427
off the **i** from the valley of Aven, Am 1:5 3427
also cut off the **i** from Ashdod, Am 1:8 3427
Go on your way, **i** of Shaphir, in Mi 1:11 3427
The **i** of Zaanan does not escape. Mi 1:11 3427
For the **i** of Maroth Becomes weak Mi 1:12 3427
to the team of horses, O **i** of Lachish Mi 1:13 3427
takes possession, O **i** of Mareshah. Mi 1:15 3427
you So that there will be no **i**. Zph 2:5 3427
Without a man, without an **i**. Zph 3:6 3427
INHABITANTS
and all the **i** of the cities, Gn 19:25 3427
me odious among the **i** of the land, Gn 34:30 3427
the Horite, the **i** of the land: Gn 36:20 3427
Now when the **i** of the land, the Gn 50:11 3427
has gripped the **i** of Philistia. Ex 15:14 3427
the **i** of Canaan have melted away. Ex 15:15 3427
I will deliver the **i** of the land into Ex 23:31 3427
no covenant with the **i** of the land Ex 34:12 3427
a covenant with the **i** of the land Ex 34:15 3427
so the land has spewed out its **i**. Lv 18:25 3427
through the land to all its **i**. Lv 25:10 3427
out, is a land that devours its **i**; Nu 13:32 3427
tell *it* to the **i** of this land. Nu 14:14 3427
because of the **i** of the land. Nu 32:17 3427
shall drive out all the **i** of the land Nu 33:52 3427
do not drive out the **i** of the land Nu 33:55 3427
have seduced the **i** of their city, Dt 13:13 3427
shall surely strike the **i** of that city Dt 13:15 3427
the **i** of the land have melted away Jos 2:9 3427
hands; moreover, all the **i** of the land Jos 2:24 3427
the **i** of the land will hear of it, Jos 7:9 3427
had finished killing all the **i** of Ai Jos 8:24 3427
utterly destroyed all the **i** of Ai. Jos 8:26 3427
When the **i** of Gibeon heard what Jos 9:3 3427
the **i** of our country spoke to us, Jos 9:11 3427
destroy all the **i** of the land before Jos 9:24 3427
the **i** of Gibeon had made peace Jos 10:1 3427
"All the **i** of the hill country Jos 13:6 3427
from there against the **i** of Debir; Jos 15:15 3427
the Jebusites, the **i** of Jerusalem, Jos 15:63 3427
southward to the **i** of En-tappuah. Jos 17:7 3427
and the **i** of Dor and its towns, Jos 17:11 3427
and the **i** of En-dor and its towns, Jos 17:11 3427
the **i** of Taanach and its towns, Jos 17:11 3427
the **i** of Megiddo and its towns, Jos 17:11 3427
he went against the **i** of Debir Jg 1:11 3427
could not drive out the **i** of the valley Jg 1:19 3427
or the **i** of Dor and its villages, Jg 1:27 3427
the **i** of Ibleam and its villages, Jg 1:27 3427
the **i** of Megiddo and its villages; Jg 1:27 3427
did not drive out the **i** of Kitron, Jg 1:30 3427
of Kitron, or the **i** of Nahalol; Jg 1:30 3427
did not drive out the **i** of Acco, Jg 1:31 3427
of Acco, or the **i** of Sidon, Jg 1:31 3427
the Canaanites, the **i** of the land; Jg 1:32 3427
drive out the **i** of Beth-shemesh, Jg 1:33 3427
or the **i** of Beth-anath, Jg 1:33 3427
the Canaanites, the **i** of the land; Jg 1:33 3427
and the **i** of Beth-shemesh and Jg 1:33 3427
covenant with the **i** of this land; Jg 2:2 3427
'Utterly curse its **i**; Jg 5:23 3427
head over all the **i** of Gilead." Jg 10:18 3427
head over all the **i** of Gilead." Jg 11:8 3427
Amorites, the **i** of that country. Jg 11:21 3427
the **i** of Gibeah who were numbered, Jg 20:15 3427
the **i** of Jabesh-gilead was there. Jg 21:9 3427
strike the **i** of Jabesh-gilead with Jg 21:10 3427
found among the **i** of Jabesh-gilead Jg 21:12 3427
to the **i** of Kiriath-jearim, 1Sa 6:21 3427
David delivered the **i** of Keilah. 1Sa 23:5 3427
for they were the **i** of the land 1Sa 27:8 3427
Now when the **i** of Jabesh-gilead 1Sa 31:11 3427
the Jebusites, the **i** of the land, 2Sa 5:6 3427
their **i** were short of strength, 2Ki 19:26 3427
bring evil on this place and on its **i**, 2Ki 22:16 3427
against this place and against its **i** 2Ki 22:19 3427
all the **i** of Jerusalem with him, 2Ki 23:2 3427
and the **i** of Netaim and Gederah; 1Ch 4:23 3427
households of the **i** of Geba, 1Ch 8:6 3427
households of the **i** of Aijalon, 1Ch 8:13 3427
who put to flight the **i** of Gath; 1Ch 8:13 3427
the Jebusites, the **i** of the land, 1Ch 11:4 3427
The **i** of Jebus said to David, 1Ch 11:5 3427
given the **i** of the land into my hand, 1Ch 22:18 3427
afflicted all the **i** of the lands. 2Ch 15:5 3427
disputes among the **i** of Jerusalem. 2Ch 19:8 3427
drive out the **i** of this land 2Ch 20:7 3427
all Judah and the **i** of Jerusalem 2Ch 20:15 3427
i of Jerusalem fell down before the 2Ch 20:18 3427
to me, O Judah and **i** of Jerusalem, 2Ch 20:20 3427
rose up against the **i** of Mount Seir 2Ch 20:23 3427
had finished with the **i** of Seir, 2Ch 20:23 3427
and caused the **i** of Jerusalem to 2Ch 21:11 3427
the **i** of Jerusalem to play the harlot 2Ch 21:13 3427
the **i** of Jerusalem made Ahaziah, 2Ch 22:1 3427
saved Hezekiah and the **i** of Jerusalem 2Ch 32:22 3427
both he and the **i** of Jerusalem, 2Ch 32:26 3427
i of Jerusalem honored him at his 2Ch 32:33 3427
misled Judah and the **i** of Jerusalem 2Ch 33:9 3427
Benjamin and the **i** of Jerusalem. 2Ch 34:9 3427
evil on this place and on its **i**, 2Ch 34:24 3427
this place and against its **i**, 2Ch 34:27 3427
will bring on this place and on its **i**. 2Ch 34:28 3427
men of Judah, the **i** of Jerusalem, 2Ch 34:30 3427
So the **i** of Jerusalem did 2Ch 34:32 3427
present, and the **i** of Jerusalem. 2Ch 35:18 3427
the **i** of Judah and Jerusalem. Ezr 4:6 3427
Hanun and the **i** of Zanoah repaired Ne 3:13 3427
guards from the **i** of Jerusalem, Ne 7:3 3427
before them the **i** of the land, Ne 9:24 3427
Under the waters and their **i**. Jb 26:5 7931
Let all the **i** of the world stand Ps 33:8 3427
out On all the **i** of the earth, Ps 33:14 3427
Give ear, all **i** of the world, Ps 49:1 3427
Philistia with the **i** of Tyre; Ps 83:7 3427
O **i** of Jerusalem and men of Judah, Is 5:3 3427
and a trap for the **i** of Jerusalem. Is 8:14 3427
is, Ephraim and the **i** of Samaria, Is 9:9 3427
mighty man I brought down *their* **i**, Is 10:13 3427
The **i** of Gebim have sought refuge. Is 10:31 3427
All you **i** of the world and Is 18:3 3427
"So the **i** of this coastland will say Is 20:6 3427
thirsty, O **i** of the land of Tema, Is 21:14 3427
become a father to the **i** of Jerusalem Is 22:21 3427
Be silent, you **i** of the coastland, Is 23:2 3427
Wail, O **i** of the coastland. Is 23:6 3427
its surface and scatters its **i**. Is 24:1 3427
earth is also polluted by its **i**, Is 24:5 3427
the **i** of the earth are burned, Is 24:6 3427
The **i** of the world learn righteousness. Is 26:9 3427
Nor were **i** of the world born. Is 26:18 3427
To punish the **i** of the earth for their Is 26:21 3427
their **i** were short of strength, Is 37:27 3427
no more among the **i** of the world. Is 38:11 3427
And its **i** are like grasshoppers, Is 40:22 3427
Let the **i** of Sela sing aloud, Let Is 42:11 3427
you will be too cramped for the **i**, Is 49:19 3427

And its **i** will die in like manner;	**Is 51:6**	3427
forth on all the **i** of the land.	**Jer 1:14**	3427
Men of Judah and **i** of Jerusalem,	**Jer 4:4**	3427
hand Against the **i** of the land,"	**Jer 6:12**	3427
bones of the **i** of Jerusalem from	**Jer 8:1**	3427
its fullness, The city and its **i**.	**Jer 8:16**	3427
I am slinging out the **i** of the land	**Jer 10:18**	3427
Judah and to the **i** of Jerusalem;	**Jer 11:2**	3427
and among the **i** of Jerusalem.	**Jer 11:9**	3427
and the **i** of Jerusalem will go and cry	**Jer 11:12**	3427
I am about to fill all the **i** of this land	**Jer 13:13**	3427
prophets and all the **i** of Jerusalem	**Jer 13:13**	3427
all Judah and all **i** of Jerusalem	**Jer 17:20**	3427
of Judah and the **i** of Jerusalem	**Jer 17:25**	3427
against the **i** of Jerusalem saying,	**Jer 18:11**	3427
kings of Judah and **i** of Jerusalem:	**Jer 19:3**	3427
treat this place and its **i**,"	**Jer 19:12**	3427
strike down the **i** of this city,	**Jer 21:6**	3427
Sodom, And her **i** like Gomorrah.	**Jer 23:14**	3427
and to all the **i** of Jerusalem,	**Jer 25:2**	3427
this land and against its **i**	**Jer 25:9**	3427
against all the **i** of the earth,"	**Jer 25:29**	3427
Against all the **i** of the earth.	**Jer 25:30**	3427
and on this city and on its **i**;	**Jer 26:15**	3427
of Judah and the **i** of Jerusalem.	**Jer 32:32**	3427
of Judah and the **i** of Jerusalem,	**Jer 35:13**	3427
on Judah and on all the **i** of Jerusalem	**Jer 35:17**	3427
bring on them and the **i** of Jerusalem	**Jer 36:31**	3427
poured out on the **i** of Jerusalem,	**Jer 42:18**	3427
destroy the city and its **i**."	**Jer 46:8**	3427
be burned down *and* bereft of **i**.	**Jer 46:19**	3427
a desolation, Without **i** in them.	**Jer 48:9**	3427
among the crags, O **i** of Moab,	**Jer 48:28**	3427
dwell in the depths, O **i** of Dedan,	**Jer 49:8**	3427
purposed against the **i** of Teman:	**Jer 49:20**	3427
in the depths, O **i** of Hazor,"	**Jer 49:30**	3427
it, And against the **i** of Pekod.	**Jer 50:21**	3427
But turmoil to the **i** of Babylon.	**Jer 50:34**	3427
"And against the **i** of Babylon And	**Jer 50:35**	3427
And against the **i** of Leb-kamai	**Jer 51:1**	3427
spoke concerning the **i** of Babylon.	**Jer 51:12**	3427
all the **i** of Chaldea for all their evil	**Jer 51:24**	3427
of Babylon A desolation without **i**.	**Jer 51:29**	3427
blood be upon the **i** of Chaldea,"	**Jer 51:35**	3427
of horror and hissing, without **i**.	**Jer 51:37**	3427
Nor *did* any of the **i** of the world,	**La 4:12**	3427
whom the **i** of Jerusalem have said,	**Ezk 11:15**	3427
concerning the **i** of Jerusalem in the	**Ezk 12:19**	3427
I given up the **i** of Jerusalem;	**Ezk 15:6**	3427
mighty on the sea, She and her **i**,	**Ezk 26:17**	3427
imposed her terror On all her **i**!	**Ezk 26:17**	3427
"The **i** of Sidon and Arvad were	**Ezk 27:8**	3427
'All the **i** of the coastlands Are	**Ezk 27:35**	3427
"Then all the **i** of Egypt will know	**Ezk 29:6**	3427
whose **i** have been gathered from	**Ezk 38:8**	3427
All the **i** of the earth are accounted	**Da 4:35**	1753
heaven And *among* the **i** of earth;	**Da 4:35**	1753
men of Judah, the **i** of Jerusalem and	**Da 9:7**	3427
a case against the **i** of the land,	**Hos 4:1**	3427
The **i** of Samaria will fear For the	**Hos 10:5**	7934
And listen, all **i** of the land.	**Jl 1:2**	3427
the elders *And* all the **i** of the land	**Jl 1:14**	3427
Let all the **i** of the land tremble,	**Jl 2:1**	3427
And your **i** for derision,	**Mi 6:16**	3427
become desolate because of her **i**,	**Mi 7:13**	3427
The world and all the **i** in it.	**Na 1:5**	3427
land, To the town and all its **i**.	**Hab 2:8**	3427
land, To the town and all its **i**.	**Hab 2:17**	3427
against all the **i** of Jerusalem.	**Zph 1:4**	3427
"Wail, O **i** of the Mortar, For all	**Zph 1:11**	3427
one, Of all the **i** of the earth.	**Zph 1:18**	3427
Woe to the **i** of the seacoast, The	**Zph 2:5**	3427
come, even the **i** of many cities.	**Zch 8:20**	3427
'The **i** of one will go to	**Zch 8:21**	3427
have pity on the **i** of the land,"	**Zch 11:6**	3427
support for us are the **i** of Jerusalem	**Zch 12:5**	3427
while the **i** of Jerusalem again	**Zch 12:6**	3427
the glory of the **i** of Jerusalem will	**Zch 12:7**	3427
LORD will defend the **i** of Jerusalem	**Zch 12:8**	3427
David and on the **i** of Jerusalem,	**Zch 12:10**	3427
David and for the **i** of Jerusalem,	**Zch 13:1**	3427

INHABITED

until they came to an **i** land;	**Ex 16:35**	3427
And chased from the **i** world.	**Jb 18:18**	8398
it On the face of the **i** earth.	**Jb 37:12**	8398
did not find a way to an **i** city.	**Ps 107:4**	4186
straight way, To go to an **i** city.	**Ps 107:7**	4186
that they may establish an **i** city,	**Ps 107:36**	4186
It will never be **i** or lived in	**Is 13:20**	3427
says of Jerusalem, 'She shall be **i**!'	**Is 44:26**	3427
place, *But* formed it to be **i**),	**Is 45:18**	3427
you a desolation, A land not **i**."	**Jer 6:8**	3427
and this city will be **i** forever.	**Jer 17:25**	3427
Like cities which are not **i**.	**Jer 22:6**	3427
will be **i** as in the days of old,"	**Jer 46:26**	7931
of the LORD she will not be **i**,	**Jer 50:13**	3427
And it will never again be **i** Or	**Jer 50:39**	3427
The **i** cities will be laid waste	**Ezk 12:20**	3427
'How you have perished, O **i** one,	**Ezk 26:17**	3427
like the cities which are not **i**,	**Ezk 26:19**	3427
pit, so that you will not be **i**;	**Ezk 26:20**	3427
it will not be **i** for forty years.	**Ezk 29:11**	3427
in all the **i** places of the land.	**Ezk 34:13**	4186
and your cities will not be **i**.	**Ezk 35:9**	3427
and the cities will be **i** and	**Ezk 36:10**	3427
and I will cause you to be **i** as	**Ezk 36:11**	3427
I will cause the cities to be **i**,	**Ezk 36:33**	3427
ruined cities are fortified *and* **i**.'	**Ezk 36:35**	3427
the waste places which are *now* **i**,	**Ezk 38:12**	3427
But Judah will be **i** forever And	**Jl 3:20**	3427
'Jerusalem will be **i** without walls	**Zch 2:4**	3427
when Jerusalem was **i** and	**Zch 7:7**	3427
the Negev and the foothills were **i**?	**Zch 7:7**	3427
Gaza, And Ashkelon will not be **i**.	**Zch 9:5**	3427
a census be taken of all the **i** earth.	**Lk 2:1**	*3625*

INHABITING

and all those **i** the desert who	**Jer 9:26**	3427

INHABITS

The settlements where Kedar **i**.	**Is 42:11**	3427

INHERIT

and they shall **i** *it* forever.' "	**Ex 32:13**	5157
'You shall **i** the land by lot	**Nu 33:54**	5157
You shall **i** according to the tribes	**Nu 33:54**	5157
for he will cause Israel to **i** it.	**Dt 1:38**	5157
LORD your God is giving you to **i**,	**Dt 12:10**	5157
you will **i** in the land that the LORD	**Dt 19:14**	5157
nobles, And **i** a seat of honor;	**1Sa 2:8**	5157
to **i** the iniquities of my youth.	**Jb 13:26**	3423
his descendants will **i** the land.	**Ps 25:13**	3423
the LORD, they will **i** the land.	**Ps 37:9**	3423
But the humble will **i** the land And	**Ps 37:11**	3423
blessed by Him will **i** the land,	**Ps 37:22**	3423
The righteous will **i** the land And	**Ps 37:29**	3423
He will exalt you to **i** the land;	**Ps 37:34**	3423
descendants of His servants will **i** it	**Ps 69:36**	5157
The wise will **i** honor, But fools	**Pr 3:35**	5157
his own house will **i** wind,	**Pr 11:29**	5157
The naive **i** foolishness, But the sensible	**Pr 14:18**	5157
But the blameless will **i** good.	**Pr 28:10**	5157
make *them* **i** the desolate heritages;	**Is 49:8**	5157
refuge in Me will **i** the land	**Is 57:13**	5157
Even My chosen ones shall **i** it,	**Is 65:9**	3423
remainder of My nation will **i** them	**Zph 2:9**	5157
remnant of this people to **i** all these	**Zch 8:12**	5157
for they shall **i** the earth.	**Mt 5:5**	*2816*
as much, and will **i** eternal life.	**Mt 19:29**	*2816*
i the kingdom prepared for you	**Mt 25:34**	*2816*
what shall I do to **i** eternal life?"	**Mk 10:17**	*2816*
what shall I do to **i** eternal life?"	**Lk 10:25**	*2816*
what shall I do to **i** eternal life?"	**Lk 18:18**	*2816*
unrighteous will not **i** the kingdom	**1Co 6:9**	*2816*
nor swindlers, will **i** the kingdom	**1Co 6:10**	*2816*
blood cannot **i** the kingdom of God;	**1Co 15:50**	*2816*
the perishable **i** the imperishable.	**1Co 15:50**	*2816*
will not **i** the kingdom of God.	**Ga 5:21**	*2816*
of those who will **i** salvation?	**Heb 1:14**	*2816*
faith and patience **i** the promises.	**Heb 6:12**	*2816*
when he desired to **i** the blessing,	**Heb 12:17**	*2816*
that you might **i** a blessing.	**1Pe 3:9**	*2816*
"He who overcomes will **i** these	**Rv 21:7**	*2816*

INHERITANCE

portion or **i** in our father's house?	**Gn 31:14**	5159
names of their brothers in their **i**.	**Gn 48:6**	5159
them in the mountain of Your **i**,	**Ex 15:17**	5159
us an **i** of fields and vineyards.	**Nu 16:14**	5159
"You shall have no **i** in their land nor	**Nu 18:20**	5157
your **i** among the sons of Israel.	**Nu 18:20**	5159
all the tithe in Israel for an **i**,	**Nu 18:21**	5159
of Israel they shall have no **i**.	**Nu 18:23**	5159
given to the Levites for an **i**;	**Nu 18:24**	5159
no **i** among the sons of Israel.' "	**Nu 18:24**	5159
given you from them for your **i**,	**Nu 18:26**	5159
the land shall be divided for an **i**	**Nu 26:53**	5159
group you shall increase their **i**,	**Nu 26:54**	5159
group you shall diminish their **i**;	**Nu 26:54**	5159
each shall be given their **i**	**Nu 26:54**	5159
They shall receive their **i**	**Nu 26:55**	5157
their **i** shall be divided between	**Nu 26:56**	5159
no **i** was given to them among the	**Nu 26:62**	5159
transfer the **i** of their father to them	**Nu 27:7**	5159
transfer his **i** to his daughter.	**Nu 27:8**	5159
shall give his **i** to his brothers.	**Nu 27:9**	5159
give his **i** to his father's brothers.	**Nu 27:10**	5159
give his **i** to his nearest relative in	**Nu 27:11**	5159
of Israel has possessed his **i**.	**Nu 32:18**	5159
we will not have an **i** with them on	**Nu 32:19**	5157
because our **i** has fallen to us on	**Nu 32:19**	5159
possession of our **i** *shall remain* with	**Nu 32:32**	5159
the larger you shall give more **i**,	**Nu 33:54**	5159
the smaller you shall give less **i**.	**Nu 33:54**	5159
that shall fall to you as an **i**,	**Nu 34:2**	5159
apportion the land to you for **i**:	**Nu 34:17**	5157
tribe to apportion the land for **i**.	**Nu 34:18**	5157
LORD commanded to apportion the **i**	**Nu 34:29**	5157
from the **i** of their possession cities	**Nu 35:2**	5159
lot to the sons of Israel as an **i**,	**Nu 36:2**	5159
give the **i** of Zelophehad our brother	**Nu 36:2**	5159
their **i** will be withdrawn from the	**Nu 36:3**	5159
withdrawn from the **i** of our fathers	**Nu 36:3**	5159
and will be added to the **i** of the tribe	**Nu 36:3**	5159
be withdrawn from our allotted **i**.	**Nu 36:3**	5159
then their **i** will be added to the	**Nu 36:4**	5159
will be added to the **i** of the tribe	**Nu 36:4**	5159
so their **i** will be withdrawn from	**Nu 36:4**	5159
withdrawn from the **i** of the tribe	**Nu 36:4**	5159
"Thus no **i** of the sons of Israel	**Nu 36:7**	5159
the **i** of the tribe of his fathers.	**Nu 36:7**	5159
who comes into possession of an **i**	**Nu 36:8**	5159
may possess the **i** of his fathers.	**Nu 36:8**	5159
"Thus no **i** shall be transferred	**Nu 36:9**	5159
shall each hold to his own **i**."	**Nu 36:9**	5159
their **i** remained with the tribe of	**Nu 36:12**	5159
give them as an **i** the land which	**Dt 3:28**	5157
your God is giving you as an **i**.	**Dt 4:21**	5159
to give you their land for an **i**,	**Dt 4:38**	5159
destroy Your people, even Your **i**,	**Dt 9:26**	5159
they are Your people, even Your **i**,	**Dt 9:29**	5159
a portion or **i** with his brothers;	**Dt 10:9**	5159
the LORD is his **i**, just as the	**Dt 10:9**	5159
i which the LORD your God is giving	**Dt 12:9**	5159
he has no portion or **i** with you.	**Dt 12:12**	5159
he has no portion or **i** among you.	**Dt 14:27**	5159
he has no portion or **i** among you,	**Dt 14:29**	5159
is giving you as an **i** to possess,	**Dt 15:4**	5159
have no portion or **i** with Israel;	**Dt 18:1**	5159
have no **i** among their countrymen;	**Dt 18:2**	5159
the LORD is their **i**,	**Dt 18:2**	5159
LORD your God gives you as an **i**,	**Dt 19:10**	5159
in your **i** which you will inherit	**Dt 19:14**	5159
your God is giving you as an **i**,	**Dt 20:16**	5159
LORD your God gives you as an **i**.	**Dt 21:23**	5159
LORD your God gives you as an **i**.	**Dt 24:4**	5159
God gives you as an **i** to possess,	**Dt 25:19**	5159
LORD your God gives you as an **i**,	**Dt 26:1**	5159
gave it as an **i** to the Reubenites,	**Dt 29:8**	5159
you shall give it to them as an **i**.	**Dt 31:7**	5157
Most High gave the nations their **i**,	**Dt 32:8**	5157
Jacob is the allotment of His **i**.	**Dt 32:9**	5159
and Joshua gave it for an **i** to	**Jos 11:23**	5159
allot it to Israel for an **i** as I have	**Jos 13:6**	5159
apportion this land for an **i** to the	**Jos 13:7**	5159
Gadites received their **i** which Moses	**Jos 13:8**	5159
of Levi he did not give an **i**;	**Jos 13:14**	5159
the God of Israel, are their **i**,	**Jos 13:14**	5159
So Moses gave *an* **i** to the tribe	**Jos 13:15**	
was the **i** of the sons of Reuben	**Jos 13:23**	5159
Moses also gave *an* **i** to the tribe	**Jos 13:24**	
This is the **i** of the sons of Gad	**Jos 13:28**	5159
Moses also gave *an* **i** to	**Jos 13:29**	
for an **i** in the plains of Moab,	**Jos 13:32**	5157
of Levi, Moses did not give an **i**;	**Jos 13:33**	5159
the God of Israel, is their **i**,	**Jos 13:33**	5159
apportioned to them for an **i**,	**Jos 14:1**	5157
by the lot of their **i**,	**Jos 14:2**	5159
had given the **i** of the two tribes	**Jos 14:3**	5159
did not give an **i** to the Levites	**Jos 14:3**	5159
be an **i** to you and to your children	**Jos 14:9**	5159
the son of Jephunneh for an **i**.	**Jos 14:13**	5159
Hebron became the **i** of Caleb the	**Jos 14:14**	5159
i of the tribe of the sons of Judah	**Jos 15:20**	5159
and Ephraim, received their **i**.	**Jos 16:4**	5157
their **i** eastward was Ataroth-addar,	**Jos 16:5**	5159
i of the tribe of the sons of Ephraim	**Jos 16:8**	5159
of the **i** of the sons of Manasseh,	**Jos 16:9**	5159
give us an **i** among our brothers."	**Jos 17:4**	5159
an **i** among our father's brothers.	**Jos 17:4**	5159
received an **i** among his sons.	**Jos 17:6**	5159
one lot and one portion for an **i**,	**Jos 17:14**	5159
tribes who had not divided their **i**.	**Jos 18:2**	5159
description of it according to their **i**;	**Jos 18:4**	5159
priesthood of the LORD is their **i**.	**Jos 18:7**	5159
i eastward beyond the Jordan,	**Jos 18:7**	5159
was the **i** of the sons of Benjamin,	**Jos 18:20**	5159
i of the sons of Benjamin according	**Jos 18:28**	5159
i was in the midst of the inheritance	**Jos 19:1**	5159
midst of the **i** of the sons of Judah.	**Jos 19:1**	5159
So they had as their **i** Beersheba	**Jos 19:2**	5159
i of the tribe of the sons of Simeon	**Jos 19:8**	5159
The **i** of the sons of Simeon *was*	**Jos 19:9**	5157
so the sons of Simeon received *an* **i**	**Jos 19:9**	5159
in the midst of Judah's **i**.	**Jos 19:9**	5159
of their **i** was as far as Sarid.	**Jos 19:10**	5159
i of the sons of Zebulun according	**Jos 19:16**	5159
i of the tribe of the sons of Issachar	**Jos 19:23**	5159
i of the tribe of the sons of Asher	**Jos 19:31**	5159
i of the tribe of the sons of Naphtali	**Jos 19:39**	5159
territory of their **i** was Zorah and	**Jos 19:41**	5159
i of the tribe of the sons of Dan	**Jos 19:48**	5159
finished apportioning the land for **i**	**Jos 19:49**	5157
the sons of Israel gave an **i** in	**Jos 19:49**	5159
gave the Levites from their **i** these	**Jos 21:3**	5159
remain as an **i** for your tribes,	**Jos 23:4**	5159
the people, each to his **i**.	**Jos 24:28**	5159
buried him in the territory of his **i**	**Jos 24:30**	5159
they became the **i** of Joseph's sons.	**Jos 24:32**	5159
the sons of Israel went each to his **i**	**Jg 2:6**	5159
buried him in the territory of his **i**	**Jg 2:9**	5159
not have an **i** in our father's house,	**Jg 11:2**	5157
seeking an **i** for themselves to live in	**Jg 18:1**	5159
an **i** had not been allotted to them	**Jg 18:1**	5159
throughout the land of Israel's **i**;	**Jg 20:6**	5159
i for the survivors of Benjamin,	**Jg 21:17**	3425
they went and returned to their **i** and	**Jg 21:23**	5159
them went out from there to his **i**.	**Jg 21:24**	5159
name of the deceased on his **i**."	**Ru 4:5**	5159
because I would jeopardize my own **i**.	**Ru 4:6**	5159
the name of the deceased on his **i**,	**Ru 4:10**	5159
anointed you a ruler over His **i**?	**1Sa 10:1**	5159
attachment with the **i** of the LORD,	**1Sa 26:19**	5159
me and my son from the **i** of God.'	**2Sa 14:16**	5159
do we have **i** in the son of Jesse;	**2Sa 20:1**	5159
swallow up the **i** of the LORD?"	**2Sa 20:19**	5159
you may bless the **i** of the LORD?"	**2Sa 21:3**	5159
have given Your people for an **i**.	**1Ki 8:36**	5159
they are Your people and Your **i**	**1Ki 8:51**	5159
peoples of the earth as Your **i**,	**1Ki 8:53**	5159
We have no **i** in the son of Jesse;	**1Ki 12:16**	5159
give you the **i** of my fathers."	**1Ki 21:3**	5159
give you the **i** of my fathers."	**1Ki 21:4**	5159
I will abandon the remnant of My **i**	**2Ki 21:14**	5159
As the portion of your **i**."	**1Ch 16:18**	5159
have given to Your people for an **i**.	**2Ch 6:27**	5159
We have no **i** in the son of Jesse.	**2Ch 10:16**	5159
which You have given us as an **i**.	**2Ch 20:11**	3423
leave *it* as an **i** to your sons forever	**Ezr 9:12**	3423
of Judah, each on his own **i**.	**Ne 11:20**	5159

And the **i** *which* tyrants receive Jb 27:13 5159
gave them **i** among their brothers. Jb 42:15 5159
give the nations as Your **i**, Ps 2:8 5159
is the portion of my **i** and my cup; Ps 16:5 2506
Your people and bless Your **i**; Ps 28:9 5159
whom He has chosen for His own **i**. Ps 33:12 5159
And their **i** will be forever. Ps 37:18 5159
He chooses our **i** for us, The glory Ps 47:4 5159
the **i** of those who fear Your name. Ps 61:5 3425
You confirmed Your **i** Ps 68:9 5159
to be the tribe of Your **i**; Ps 74:2 5159
And apportioned them for an **i** by Ps 78:55 5159
was filled with wrath at His **i**. Ps 78:62 5159
His people, And Israel His **i**. Ps 78:71 5159
the nations have invaded Your **i**; Ps 79:1 5159
people, Nor will He forsake His **i**. Ps 94:14 5159
Canaan As the portion of your **i**," Ps 105:11 5159
That I may glory with Your **i**. Ps 106:5 5159
His people And He abhorred His **i**. Ps 106:40 5159
A good man leaves an **i** to his Pr 13:22 5157
share in the **i** among brothers. Pr 17:2 5159
and wealth are an **i** from fathers, Pr 19:14 5159
An **i** gained hurriedly at the Pr 20:21 5159
Wisdom along with an **i** is good And Ec 7:11 5159
Israel will possess them as an **i** Is 14:2 5157
of My hands, and Israel My **i**." Is 19:25 5159
And My **i** you made an abomination. Jer 2:7 5159
that I gave your fathers as an **i**. Jer 3:18 5157
most beautiful **i** of the nations!' Jer 3:19 5159
And Israel is the tribe of His **i**; Jer 10:16 5159
My house, I have abandoned My **i**; Jer 12:7 5159
"My **i** has become to Me Like a Jer 12:8 5159
"Is My **i** like a speckled bird of Jer 12:9 5159
wicked neighbors who strike at the **i** Jer 12:14 5159
bring them back, each one to his **i** Jer 12:15 5159
have filled My **i** with the carcasses Jer 16:18 5159
let go of your **i** That I gave you; Jer 17:4 5159
is He, And of the tribe of His **i**; Jer 51:19 5159
Our **i** has been turned over to La 5:2 5159
rejoiced over the **i** of the house of Ezk 35:15 5159
so that you will become their **i** Ezk 36:12 5159
be with regard to an **i** for them, Ezk 44:28 5159
for them, *that* I am their **i**; Ezk 44:28 5159
divide by lot the land for **i**, Ezk 45:1 5159
the prince gives a gift *out of* his **i** to Ezk 46:16 5159
it is their possession by **i**. Ezk 46:16 5159
gives a gift from his **i** to one of his Ezk 46:17 5159
His **i** *shall be* only his sons'; Ezk 46:17 5159
shall not take from the people's **i**, Ezk 46:18 5159
he shall give his sons **i** from his Ezk 46:18 5157
divide the land for an **i** among the Ezk 47:13 5157
"You shall divide it for an **i**, Ezk 47:14 5157
land shall fall to you as an **i**. Ezk 47:14 5159
shall divide it by lot for an **i** among Ezk 47:22 5159
they shall be allotted an **i** with Ezk 47:22 5159
there you shall give *him* his **i**," Ezk 47:23 5159
to the tribes of Israel for an **i**, Ezk 48:29 5159
do not make Your **i** a reproach, Jl 2:17 5159
On behalf of My people and My **i**, Jl 3:2 5159
and his house, A man and his **i**. Mi 2:2 5159
appointed his **i** for the jackals of the Mal 1:3 5159
let us kill him and seize his **i**.' Mt 21:38 *2817*
kill him, and the **i** will be ours!' Mk 12:7 *2817*
to divide the *family* **i** with me." Lk 12:13 *2817*
kill him so that the **i** will be ours.' Lk 20:14 *2817*
"But He gave him no **i** in it, Ac 7:5 *2817*
He distributed their land as an **i** Ac 13:19 *2624*
to build *you* up and to give *you* the **i** Ac 20:32 *2817*
receive forgiveness of sins and an **i** Ac 26:18 *2819*
For if the **i** is based on law, it Ga 3:18 *2817*
also we have obtained an **i**, Eph 1:11 *2820*
who is given as a pledge of our **i**, Eph 1:14 *2817*
the glory of His **i** in the saints, Eph 1:18 *2817*
has an **i** in the kingdom of Christ Eph 5:5 *2817*
share in the **i** of the saints in Light. Col 1:12 *2819*
will receive the reward of the **i**. Col 3:24 *2817*
the promise of the eternal **i**. Heb 9:15 *2817*
which he was to receive for an **i**; Heb 11:8 *2817*
obtain an **i** *which is* imperishable 1Pe 1:4 *2817*

INHERITANCES

These are the **i** which Eleazar the Jos 19:51 5159

INHERITED

the sons of Israel **i** in the land of Jos 14:1 5157
I have **i** Your testimonies forever, Ps 119:111 5157
fathers have **i** nothing but falsehood Jer 16:19 5157
as He has **i** a more excellent name Heb 1:4 *2816*
way of life **i** from your forefathers, 1Pe 1:18 *3970b*

INHERITS

to his possession which he **i**." Nu 35:8 5157

INIQUITIES

all the **i** of the sons of Israel and Lv 16:21 5771
all their **i** to a solitary land; Lv 16:22 5771
because of the **i** of their forefathers Lv 26:39 5771
our **i** have risen above our heads and Ezr 9:6 5771
guilt, and on account of our **i** we, Ezr 9:7 5771
requited *us* less than our **i** *deserve*, Ezr 9:13 5771
sins and the **i** of their fathers. Ne 9:2 5771
"How many are my **i** and sins? Jb 13:23 5771
me to inherit the **i** of my youth. Jb 13:26 5771
great, And your **i** without end? Jb 22:5 5771
For my **i** are gone over my head; Ps 38:4 5771
My **i** have overtaken me, so that I Ps 40:12 5771
my sins And blot out all my **i**. Ps 51:9 5771
I prevail against me; Ps 65:3 5771
i of *our* forefathers against us; Ps 79:8 5771
have placed our **i** before You, Ps 90:8 5771
Who pardons all your **i**, Ps 103:3 5771
rewarded us according to our **i**. Ps 103:10 5771
way, And because of their **i**, Ps 107:17 5771
If You, LORD, should mark **i**, Ps 130:3 5771
will redeem Israel From all his **i**. Ps 130:8 5771
His own **i** will capture the wicked, Pr 5:22 5771
You have wearied Me with your **i**. Is 43:24 5771
Behold, you were sold for your **i**, Is 50:1 5771
He was crushed for our **i**; Is 53:5 5771
the many, As He will bear their **i**. Is 53:11 5771
But your **i** have made a separation Is 59:2 5771
are with us, And we know our **i**: Is 59:12 5771
our **i**, like the wind, take us away. Is 64:6 5771
delivered us into the power of our **i**. Is 64:7 5771
their own **i** and the iniquities of Is 65:7 5771
the **i** of their fathers together," Is 65:7 5771
'Your **i** have turned these away, Jer 5:25 5771
back to the **i** of their ancestors Jer 11:10 5771
"Although our **i** testify against us, Jer 14:7 5771
and I will pardon all their **i** by Jer 33:8 5771
prophets *And* the **i** of her priests, La 4:13 5771
It is we who have borne their **i**. La 5:7 5771
but you will rot away in your **i** and Ezk 24:23 5771
"By the multitude of your **i**, Ezk 28:18 5771
for your **i** and your abominations. Ezk 36:31 5771
I cleanse you from all your **i**, Ezk 36:33 5771
they may be ashamed of their **i**; Ezk 43:10 5771
from your **i** by showing mercy to Da 4:27 5758
our sins and the **i** of our fathers, Da 9:16 5771
will punish you for all your **i**." Am 3:2 5771
He will tread our **i** under foot. Mi 7:19 5771
"FOR I WILL BE MERCIFUL TO THEIR **I**, Heb 8:12 *93*
and God has remembered her **i**. Rv 18:5 *92*

INIQUITY

i of the Amorite is not yet complete Gn 15:16 5771
found out the **i** of your servants; Gn 44:16 5771
visiting the **i** of the fathers on Ex 20:5 5771
take away the **i** of the holy things Ex 28:38 5771
who forgives **i**, transgression and sin Ex 34:7 5771
visiting the **i** of fathers on the Ex 34:7 5771
pardon our **i** and our sin, Ex 34:9 5771
eats of it will bear his *own* **i**. Lv 7:18 5771
who eats it will bear his **i**, Lv 19:8 5771
will rot away because of their **i** Lv 26:39 5771
'If they confess their **i** and the Lv 26:40 5771
and the **i** of their forefathers, Lv 26:40 5771
they then make amends for their **i**, Lv 26:41 5771
be making amends for their **i**, Lv 26:43 5771
of memorial, a reminder of **i**. Nu 5:15 5771
forgiving **i** and transgression; Nu 14:18 5771
visiting the **i** of the fathers on Nu 14:18 5771
the **i** of this people according to Nu 14:19 5771
and they shall bear their **i**; Nu 18:23 5771
visiting the **i** of the fathers on Dt 5:9 5771
on account of any **i** or any sin which Dt 19:15 5771
not the **i** of Peor enough for us, Jos 22:17 5771
did not perish alone in his **i**.' " Jos 22:20 5771
to judge his house forever for the **i** 1Sa 3:13 5771
i of Eli's house shall not be atoned for 1Sa 3:14 5771
insubordination is as **i** and idolatry. 1Sa 15:23 205
What is my **i**? And what is my sin 1Sa 20:1 5771
if there is **i** in me, put me to death 1Sa 20:8 5771
when he commits **i**, I will correct 2Sa 7:14 5753b
the **i** is on me and my father's 2Sa 14:9 5771
and if there is **i** in me, let him 2Sa 14:32 5771
Him, And I kept myself from my **i**. 2Sa 22:24 5771
take away the **i** of Your servant, 2Sa 24:10 5771
have sinned and have committed **i**, 1Ki 8:47 5753b
me to bring my **i** to remembrance and 1Ki 17:18 5771
take away the **i** of Your servant, 1Ch 21:8 5771
have sinned, we have committed **i** and 2Ch 6:37 5753b
Do not forgive their **i** and let not Ne 4:5 5771
those who plow **i** And those who sow Jb 4:8 205
transgression And take away my **i**? Jb 7:21 5771
that God forgets a part of your **i**. Jb 11:6 5771
He sees **i** without investigating. Jb 11:11 205
If **i** is in your hand, put it far Jb 11:14 205
a bag, And You wrap up my **i**. Jb 14:17 5771
Man, who drinks **i** like water! Jb 15:16 5767b
mischief and bring forth **i**, Jb 15:35 205
"The heavens will reveal his **i**, Jb 20:27 5771
God stores away a man's **i** for his Jb 21:19 205
And disaster to those who work **i**? Jb 31:3 205
be an **i** *punishable by* judges. Jb 31:11 5771
been an **i** *calling for* judgment, Jb 31:28 5771
Adam, By hiding my **i** in my bosom, Jb 31:33 5771
in company with the workers of **i**, Jb 34:8 205
workers of **i** may hide themselves. Jb 34:22 205
If I have done **i**, I will not do it Jb 34:32 5766
You hate all who do **i**. Ps 5:5 205
Depart from me, all you who do **i**, Ps 6:8 205
Him, And I kept myself from my **i**. Ps 18:23 5771
name's sake, O LORD, Pardon my **i**, Ps 25:11 5771
wicked And with those who work **i**, Ps 28:3 205
strength has failed because of my **i**, Ps 31:10 5771
whom the LORD does not impute **i**, Ps 32:2 5771
to You, And my **i** I did not hide; Ps 32:5 5771
the discovery of his **i** *and* the hatred Ps 36:2 5771
There the doers of **i** have fallen; Ps 36:12 205
For I confess my **i**; Ps 38:18 5771
You chasten a man for **i**; Ps 39:11 5771
the **i** of my foes surrounds me, Ps 49:5 5771
Wash me thoroughly from my **i** And Ps 51:2 5771
Behold, I was brought forth in **i**, Ps 51:5 5771
i and mischief are in her midst. Ps 55:10 205
Deliver me from those who do **i** And Ps 59:2 205
to any *who are* treacherous in **i**. Ps 59:5 205
From the tumult of those who do **i**, Ps 64:2 205
Add **i** to their iniquity, And may Ps 69:27 5771
Add iniquity to their **i**, And may Ps 69:27 5771
compassionate, forgave *their* **i** and Ps 78:38 5771
forgave the **i** of Your people; Ps 85:2 5771
the rod And their **i** with stripes. Ps 89:32 5771
And all who did **i** flourished, Ps 92:7 205
All who do **i** will be scattered. Ps 92:9 205
of the LORD all those who do **i**. Ps 101:8 205
our fathers, We have committed **i**, Ps 106:6 5753b
And *so* sank down in their **i**. Ps 106:43 5771
Let the **i** of his fathers be Ps 109:14 5771
not let any **i** have dominion over me. Ps 119:133 205
lead them away with the doers of **i**. Ps 125:5 205
of wickedness With men who do **i**; Ps 141:4 205
from the snares of those who do **i**. Ps 141:9 205
But ruin to the workers of **i**. Pr 10:29 205
and truth **i** is atoned for, Pr 16:6 5771
the mouth of the wicked spreads **i**. Pr 19:28 205
But is terror to the workers of **i**. Pr 21:15 205
He who sows **i** will reap vanity, Pr 22:8 5767b
People weighed down with **i**, Is 1:4 5771
I cannot endure **i** and the solemn Is 1:13 205
drag **i** with the cords of falsehood, Is 5:18 5771
and your **i** is taken away and your Is 6:7 5771
evil And the wicked for their **i**; Is 13:11 5771
Because of the **i** of their fathers. Is 14:21 5771
"Surely this **i** shall not be forgiven Is 22:14 5771
inhabitants of the earth for their **i**; Is 26:21 5771
this Jacob's **i** will be forgiven; Is 27:9 5771
Therefore this **i** will be to you Is 30:13 5771
the help of the workers of **i**. Is 31:2 205
there will be forgiven *their* **i**. Is 33:24 5771
That her **i** has been removed, Is 40:2 5771
caused the **i** of us all To fall on Him. Is 53:6 5771
"Because of the **i** of his unjust gain Is 57:17 5771
blood And your fingers with **i**; Is 59:3 5771
mischief and bring forth **i**. Is 59:4 205
Their works are works of **i**, Is 59:6 205
Their thoughts are thoughts of **i**, Is 59:7 205
LORD, Nor remember **i** forever; Is 64:9 5771
stain of your **i** is before Me," Jer 2:22 5771
'Only acknowledge your **i**, Jer 3:13 5771
weary themselves committing **i**. Jer 9:5 5753b
Because of the magnitude of your **i** Jer 13:22 5771
now He will remember their **i** and Jer 14:10 5771
O LORD, The **i** of our fathers, Jer 14:20 5771
what is our **i**, or what is our sin Jer 16:10 5771
is their **i** concealed from My eyes. Jer 16:17 5771
doubly repay their **i** and their sin, Jer 16:18 5771
Do not forgive their **i** Or blot out Jer 18:23 5771
'for their **i**, and the land of the Jer 25:12 5771
Because your **i** is great *And* your Jer 30:14 5771
Because your **i** is great *And* your Jer 30:15 5771
everyone will die for his own **i**; Jer 31:30 5771
"for I will forgive their **i**, Jer 31:34 5771
but repays the **i** of fathers into Jer 32:18 5771
I will cleanse them from all their **i** Jer 33:8 5771
forgive their **i** and their sin." Jer 36:3 5771
and his servants for their **i**, Jer 36:31 5771
will be made for the **i** of Israel, Jer 50:20 5771
And they have not exposed your **i** La 2:14 5771
the **i** of the daughter of my people La 4:6 5771
The punishment of your **i** has been La 4:22 5771
But He will punish your **i**, La 4:22 5771
wicked man shall die in his **i**, Ezk 3:18 5771
wicked way, he shall die in his **i**; Ezk 3:19 5771
his righteousness and commits **i**, Ezk 3:20 5766
lay the **i** of the house of Israel on it Ezk 4:4 5771
bear their **i** for the number of days Ezk 4:4 5771
corresponding to the years of their **i** Ezk 4:5 5771
bear the **i** of the house of Israel. Ezk 4:5 5771
bear the **i** of the house of Judah; Ezk 4:6 5771
another and waste away in their **i**. Ezk 4:17 5771
them maintain his life by his **i**. Ezk 7:13 5771
mourning, each over his own **i**. Ezk 7:16 5771
for their **i** has become an occasion Ezk 7:19 5771
i of the house of Israel and Judah Ezk 9:9 5771
these are the men who devise **i** and Ezk 11:2 205
the stumbling block of their **i**. Ezk 14:3 5771
face the stumbling block of his **i**, Ezk 14:4 5771
face the stumbling block of his **i**, Ezk 14:7 5771
bear *the punishment of* their **i**; Ezk 14:10 5771
as the **i** of the inquirer is, so Ezk 14:10 5771
so the **i** of the prophet will be, Ezk 14:10 5771
if he keeps his hand from **i** Ezk 18:8 5766
he will not die for his father's **i**, Ezk 18:17 5771
behold, he will die for his **i**. Ezk 18:18 5771
the punishment for the father's **i**?' Ezk 18:19 5771
the punishment for the father's **i**, Ezk 18:20 5771
the punishment for the son's **i**; Ezk 18:20 5771
from his righteousness, commits **i** and Ezk 18:24 5766
from his righteousness, commits **i** and Ezk 18:26 5766
for his **i** which he has committed Ezk 18:26 5766
i may not become a stumbling block Ezk 18:30 5771
But he brings **i** to remembrance, Ezk 21:23 5771
have made your **i** to be remembered, Ezk 21:24 5771
i of their having turned to Egypt. Ezk 29:16 5771
the punishment for their **i** rested on Ezk 32:27 5771
them, he is taken away in his **i**; Ezk 33:6 5771
wicked man shall die in his **i**, Ezk 33:8 5771
his way, he will die in his **i**, Ezk 33:9 5771
righteousness that he commits **i**, Ezk 33:13 5766
but in that same **i** of his which he Ezk 33:13 5766
ensure life without committing **i**, Ezk 33:15 5766
his righteousness and commits **i**, Ezk 33:18 5766
went into exile for their **i** because they Ezk 39:23 5771
bear the punishment for their **i**. Ezk 44:10 5771
stumbling block of **i** to the house of Ezk 44:12 5771
bear *the punishment for* their **i**. Ezk 44:12 5771
we have sinned, committed **i**, Da 9:5 5753b
by turning from our **i** and giving Da 9:13 5771
of sin, to make atonement for **i**, Da 9:24 5771

direct their desire toward their **i**. Hos 4:8 5771
and Ephraim stumble in their **i**; Hos 5:5 5771
The **i** of Ephraim is uncovered, Hos 7:1 5771
Now He will remember their **i**, Hos 8:13 5771
Because of the grossness of your **i**, Hos 9:7 5771
He will remember their **i**, Hos 9:9 5771
battle against the sons of **i** overtake Hos 10:9 5767b
find in me No **i**, which *would be* sin Hos 12:8 5771
Is there **i** *in* Gilead? Hos 12:11 205
The **i** of Ephraim is bound up; Hos 13:12 5771
have stumbled because of your **i**. Hos 14:1 5771
"Take away all **i** And receive *us* Hos 14:2 5771
Woe to those who scheme **i**, Mi 2:1 205
is a God like You, who pardons **i** Mi 7:18 5771
Why do You make me see **i**, Hab 1:3 205
I have taken your **i** away from you Zch 3:4 5771
I will remove the **i** of that land in Zch 3:9 5771
For the teraphim speak **i**, Zch 10:2 205
and he turned many back from **i**. Mal 2:6 5771
and in the bondage of **i**." Ac 8:23 *93*
is a fire, the *very* world of **i**; Jas 3:6 *93*

INITIATIVE

on your own **i** judge what is right? Lk 12:57 *575*
"I can do nothing on My own **I**. Jn 5:30 *1683*
He, and I do nothing on My own **i**, Jn 8:28 *1683*
I have not even come on My own **i**, Jn 8:42 *1683*
Me, but I lay it down on My own **i**. Jn 10:18 *1683*
he did not say this on his own **i**, Jn 11:51 *1438*
"For I did not speak on My own **i**, Jn 12:49 *1683*
to you I do not speak on My own **i**, Jn 14:10 *1683*
He will not speak on His own **i**, Jn 16:13 *1438*
"Are you saying this on your own **i**, Jn 18:34 *1438*

INJUNCTION

enforce an **i** that anyone who makes a Da 6:7 633
establish the **i** and sign the Da 6:8 633
signed the document, that is, the **i**. Da 6:9 633
before the king about the king's **i**, Da 6:12 633
"Did you not sign an **i** that any Da 6:12 633
or to the **i** which you signed, Da 6:13 633
that no **i** or statute which the king Da 6:15 633

INJURE

And those who seek to **i** me have Ps 38:12 7463a
and dishonor, who seek to **i** me. Ps 71:13 7463a
enemy, and nothing will **i** you. Lk 10:19 *91*
why do you **i** one another?' Ac 7:26 *91*

INJURED

and it is **i** or dies while its owner is Ex 22:14 7665
just as he has **i** a man, so it Lv 24:20 5414, 4140b
and you have **i** your neighbors for Ezk 22:12 1214
who lift it will be severely **i**. Zch 12:3 8295

INJURES

'If a man **i** his neighbor, just Lv 24:19 5414, 4140b
he who sins against me **i** himself; Pr 8:36 2554

INJURING

i his neighbor pushed him away, Ac 7:27 *91*

INJURY

yet there is no **i**, Ex 21:22 611
"But if there is *any further* **i**, Ex 21:23 611
not his enemy nor seeking his **i**, Nu 35:23 7463a
Woe is me, because of my **i**! Jer 10:19 7667
incurable And your **i** is serious. Jer 30:12 4347
'Why do you cry out over your **i**? Jer 30:15 7667
no **i** whatever was found on him, Da 6:23 2257

INJUSTICE

'You shall do no **i** in judgment; Lv 19:15 5766
God of faithfulness and without **i**, Dt 32:4 5766
"Desist now, let there be no **i**; Jb 6:29 5767b
"Is there **i** on my tongue? Jb 6:30 5767b
this, If there is **i** in my hands, Ps 7:3 5766
and have committed abominable **i**; Ps 53:1 5766
poor, But it is swept away by **i**. Pr 13:23 3808, 4941
Than great income with **i**. Pr 16:8 3808, 4941
What **i** did your fathers find in Me, Jer 2:5 5766
wickedness, you have reaped **i**, Hos 10:13 5767b
And Jerusalem with violent **i**. Mi 3:10 5767b
righteous within her; He will do no **i**. Zph 3:5 5767b
There is no **i** with God, is there? Ro 9:14 *93*

INJUSTICES

They devise **i**, *saying,* Ps 64:6 5767b

INK

I wrote them with **i** on the book." Jer 36:18 1773
not with **i** but with the Spirit of 2Co 3:3 *3189*
want to *do so* with paper and **i**; 2Jn 1:12 *3189*
write *them* to you with pen and **i**; 3Jn 1:13 *3189*

INLAID

of wood, onyx stones and **i** *stones,* 1Ch 29:2 4394
is carved ivory **I** with sapphires. SS 5:14 5968
With ivory they have **i** your deck Ezk 27:6 6213a

INMOST

And my **i** being will rejoice When Pr 23:16 3629

INN

was no room for them in the **i**. Lk 2:7 *2646*
beast, and brought him to an **i** and Lk 10:34 *3829*

INNER

is toward the **i** side of the ephod. Ex 28:26 1004
on its **i** edge which was next to Ex 39:19 1004
they entered the **i** chamber of the Jg 9:46 6877
and put *them* on the **i** chamber and Jg 9:49 6877
set the **i** chamber on fire over those Jg 9:49 6877
men lying in wait in an **i** room. Jg 16:9 2315
were lying in wait in the **i** room. Jg 16:12 2315
in the **i** recesses of the cave. 1Sa 24:3 3411
both the nave and the **i** sanctuary; 1Ki 6:5 1687
on the inside as an **i** sanctuary, 1Ki 6:16 1687
the nave in front of *the* **i** 1Ki 6:17
Then he prepared an **i** sanctuary 1Ki 6:19 1687
The **i** sanctuary *was* twenty 1Ki 6:20 1687
the front of the **i** sanctuary, 1Ki 6:21 1687
altar which was by the **i** sanctuary 1Ki 6:22 1687
Also in the **i** sanctuary he made 1Ki 6:23 1687
in the midst of the **i** house, 1Ki 6:27 6442
flowers, **i** and outer *sanctuaries.* 1Ki 6:29 6441
gold, **i** and outer *sanctuaries.* 1Ki 6:30 6441
For the entrance of the **i** sanctuary 1Ki 6:31 1687
He built the **i** court with 1Ki 6:36 6442
the **i** court of the house of the LORD, 1Ki 7:12 6442
left, in front of the **i** sanctuary, 1Ki 7:49 1687
both for the doors of the **i** house, 1Ki 7:50 6442
into the **i** sanctuary of the house, 1Ki 8:6 1687
holy place before the **i** sanctuary, 1Ki 8:8 1687
into the city into an **i** chamber. 1Ki 20:30 2315
an **i** room to hide yourself." 1Ki 22:25 2315
and bring him to an **i** room. 2Ki 9:2 2315
the **i** room of the house of Baal. 2Ki 10:25 5892b
its upper rooms, its **i** rooms and 1Ch 28:11 6442
He made chains in the **i** sanctuary 2Ch 3:16 1687
to burn in front of the **i** sanctuary 2Ch 4:20 1687
i doors for the holy of holies and 2Ch 4:22 6442
into the **i** sanctuary of the house, 2Ch 5:7 1687
seen in front of the **i** sanctuary, 2Ch 5:9 1687
an **i** room to hide yourself." 2Ch 18:24 2315
the **i** part of the house of the LORD 2Ch 29:16 6441
comes to the king to the **i** court Es 4:11 6442
in the **i** court of the king's palace Es 5:1 6442
Their **i** thought is *that* their Ps 49:11 7130
of the north gate of the **i** *court,* Ezk 8:3 6442
the **i** court of the LORD's house. Ezk 8:16 6442
and the cloud filled the **i** court. Ezk 10:3 6442
to the front of the **i** porch of the gate Ezk 40:15 6442
of the exterior of the **i** court, Ezk 40:19 6442
The **i** court had a gate Ezk 40:23 6442
The **i** court had a gate toward Ezk 40:27 6442
to the **i** court by the south gate; Ezk 40:28 6442
into the **i** court toward the east. Ezk 40:32 6442
From the outside to the **i** gate Ezk 40:44 6442
for the singers in the **i** court, Ezk 40:44 6442
he also *measured* the **i** nave and Ezk 41:15 6442
the entrance, and to the **i** house, Ezk 41:17 6442
which belonged to the **i** court, Ezk 42:3 6442
Before the chambers *was* an **i** walk Ezk 42:4 6442
finished measuring the **i** house, Ezk 42:15 6442
and brought me into the **i** court; Ezk 43:5 6442
enter at the gates of the **i** court, Ezk 44:17 6442
in the gates of the **i** court and in the Ezk 44:17 6442
wine when they enter the **i** court. Ezk 44:21 6442
into the **i** court to minister in Ezk 44:27 6442
posts of the gate of the **i** court. Ezk 45:19 6442
"The gate of the **i** court facing east Ezk 46:1 6442
you pray, go into your **i** room, Mt 6:6 *5009*
'Behold, He is in the **i** rooms,' Mt 24:26 *5009*
you have whispered in the **i** rooms Lk 12:3 *5009*
threw them into the **i** prison and Ac 16:24 *2082*
with the law of God in the **i** man, Ro 7:22 *2080*
yet our **i** man is being renewed day 2Co 4:16 *2080*
through His Spirit in the **i** man, Eph 3:16 *2080*

INNERMOST

"Who has put wisdom in the **i** being Or Jb 38:36 2910
You desire truth in the **i** being, Ps 51:6 2910
down into the **i** parts of the body. Pr 18:8 2315
all the **i** parts of his being. Pr 20:27 2315
And strokes *reach* the **i** parts. Pr 20:30 2315
down into the **i** parts of the body. Pr 26:22 2315
who is in the **i** part of the house, Am 6:10 3411
From his **i** being will flow rivers of Jn 7:38 *2836*

INNKEEPER

and gave them to the **i** and said, Lk 10:35 *3830*

INNOCENCE

i of my hands I have done this." Gn 20:5 5356
I shall wash my hands in **i**, Ps 26:6 5356
pure And washed my hands in **i**; Ps 73:13 5356
long will they be incapable of **i**? Hos 8:5 5356

INNOCENT

and *the rest of* you shall be **i**." Gn 44:10 5355a
not kill the **i** or the righteous, Ex 23:7 5355a
"So **i** blood will not be shed in Dt 19:10 5355a
purge the blood of the **i** from Israel, Dt 19:13 5355a
do not place the guilt of **i** blood in Dt 21:8 5355a
remove the guilt of **i** blood from Dt 21:9 5355a
bribe to strike down an **i** person.' Dt 27:25 5355a
then will you sin against **i** blood by 1Sa 19:5 5355a
"I and my kingdom are **i** before 2Sa 3:28 5355a
"You are **i**; behold, I conspired 2Ki 10:9 6662
Manasseh shed very much **i** blood 2Ki 21:16 5355a
for the **i** blood which he shed, 2Ki 24:4 5355a
he filled Jerusalem with **i** blood; 2Ki 24:4 5355a
now, who *ever* perished being **i**? Jb 4:7 5355a
He mocks the despair of the **i**. Jb 9:23 5355a
is pure, And I am **i** in your eyes.' Jb 11:4 1249
And the **i** will stir up himself Jb 17:8 5355a
and are glad, And the **i** mock them, Jb 22:19 5355a
"He will deliver one who is not **i**, Jb 22:30 5355a
And the **i** will divide the silver. Jb 27:17 5355a
I am **i** and there is no guilt in me. Jb 33:9 2643
In the hiding places he kills the **i**; Ps 10:8 5355a
he take a bribe against the **i**. Ps 15:5 5355a
And condemn the **i** to death. Ps 94:21 5355a
And shed **i** blood, The blood of Ps 106:38 5355a
Let us ambush the **i** without cause; Pr 1:11 5355a
And hands that shed **i** blood, Pr 6:17 5355a
And they hasten to shed **i** blood; Is 59:7 5355a
found The lifeblood of the **i** poor; Jer 2:34 5355a
Yet you said, 'I am **i**; Jer 2:35 5352
do not shed **i** blood in this place, Jer 7:6 5355a
place with the blood of the **i** Jer 19:4 5355a
do not shed **i** blood in this place. Jer 22:3 5355a
And on shedding **i** blood And on Jer 22:17 5355a
will bring **i** blood on yourselves, Jer 26:15 5355a
as I was found **i** before Him; Da 6:22 2136
whose land they have shed **i** blood. Jl 3:19 5355b
life and do not put **i** blood on us; Jon 1:14 5355b
as serpents and **i** as doves. Mt 10:16 *185*
break the Sabbath and are **i**? Mt 12:5 *338*
would not have condemned the **i**. Mt 12:7 *338*
I have sinned by betraying **i** blood Mt 27:4 *121*
"I am **i** of this Man's blood; Mt 27:24 *121*
"Certainly this man was **i**." Lk 23:47 *1342*
I am **i** of the blood of all men. Ac 20:26 *2513*
is good and **i** in what is evil. Ro 16:19 *185*
you demonstrated yourselves to be **i** 2Co 7:11 *53*
yourselves to be blameless and **i**, Php 2:15 *185*
have such a high priest, holy, **i**, Heb 7:26 *172*

INNOCENTLY

who were invited and went **i**, 2Sa 15:11 8537

INNS

the Market of Appius and Three **I** Ac 28:15 *4999*

INNUMERABLE

both they and their camels were **i**; Jg 6:5 369, 4557
AND **I** AS THE SAND WHICH IS BY THE Heb 11:12 *382*

INQUIRE

So she went to **i** of the LORD. Gn 25:22 1875
the people come to me to **i** of God. Ex 18:15 1875
who shall **i** for him by the Nu 27:21 7592
and **i** from one end of the heavens Dt 4:32
you do not **i** after their gods, Dt 12:30 1875
and search out and **i** thoroughly. Dt 13:14 7592
it, then you shall **i** thoroughly. Dt 17:4 1875
days, and you shall **i** *of them* Dt 17:9 1875
"**I** of God, please, that we may Jg 18:5 7592
when a man went to **i** of God, 1Sa 9:9 1875
"You **i** whose son the youth is." 1Sa 17:56 7592
begin to **i** of God for him today? 1Sa 22:15 7592
I may go to her and **i** of her." 1Sa 28:7 1875
the wife of Jeroboam is coming to **i** 1Ki 14:5 1875
i first for the word of the LORD." 1Ki 22:5 1875
LORD here that we may **i** of him?" 1Ki 22:7 1875
man by whom we may **i** of the LORD, 1Ki 22:8 1875
"Go, **i** of Baal-zebub, the god of 2Ki 1:2 1875
you are going to **i** of Baal-zebub, 2Ki 1:3 1875
you are sending to **i** of Baal-zebub, 2Ki 1:6 1875
sent messengers to **i** of Baal-zebub, 2Ki 1:16 1875
is no God in Israel to **i** of His word? 2Ki 1:16 1875
we may **i** of the LORD by him?" 2Ki 3:11 1875
of God, and **i** of the LORD by him, 2Ki 8:8 1875
bronze altar shall be for me to **i** *by* 2Ki 16:15 1239
i of the LORD for me and the 2Ki 22:13 1875
Judah who sent you to **i** of the LORD 2Ki 22:18 1875
and did not **i** of the LORD. 1Ch 10:14 1875
not go before it to **i** of God, 1Ch 21:30 1875
"Please **i** first for the word of 2Ch 18:4 1875
LORD here that we may **i** of him?" 2Ch 18:6 1875
man by whom we may **i** of the LORD, 2Ch 18:7 1875
who sent to him to **i** of the wonder 2Ch 32:31 1875
i of the LORD for me and for those 2Ch 34:21 1875
who sent you to **i** of the LORD, 2Ch 34:26 1875
to **i** concerning Judah and Jerusalem Ezr 7:14 1240
"Please **i** of past generations, Jb 8:8 7592
If you would **i**, inquire; Is 21:12 1158
If you would inquire, **i**; Is 21:12 1158
i of the LORD on our behalf, Jer 21:2 1875
who sent you to Me to **i** of Me: Jer 37:7 1875
comes to the prophet to **i** of Me Ezk 14:7 1875
of Israel came to **i** of the LORD, Ezk 20:1 1875
"Do you come to **i** of Me? Ezk 20:3 1875
you enter, **i** who is worthy in it, Mt 10:11 *1833*
he *began* to **i** what this was. Lk 18:36 *4441*
in the center, they *began to* **i**, Ac 4:7 *4441*
and **i** at the house of Judas for a Ac 9:11 *2212*
began to **i** of him privately, Ac 23:19 *4441*
as though they were going to **i** Ac 23:20 *4441*

INQUIRED

the sons of Israel **i** of the LORD, Jg 1:1 7592
when they searched about and **i**, Jg 6:29 1245
went up to Bethel, and **i** of God and Jg 20:18 7592
until evening, and **i** of the LORD, Jg 20:23 7592
The sons of Israel **i** of the LORD Jg 20:27 7592
they **i** further of the LORD, 1Sa 10:22 7592
Saul **i** of God, 1Sa 14:37 7592
"He **i** of the LORD for him, 1Sa 22:10 7592
a sword and have **i** of God for him, 1Sa 22:13 7592
So David **i** of the LORD, saying, 1Sa 23:2 7592
David **i** of the LORD once more. 1Sa 23:4 7592
When Saul **i** of the LORD, the LORD 1Sa 28:6 7592
David **i** of the LORD, saying, 1Sa 30:8 7592
that David **i** of the LORD, 2Sa 2:1 7592
Then David **i** of the LORD, saying, 2Sa 5:19 7592
When David **i** of the LORD, He 2Sa 5:23 7592
David sent and **i** about the woman. 2Sa 11:3 1875
therefore **i** of God for the child; 2Sa 12:16 1245
as if one **i** of the word of God; 2Sa 16:23 7592
David **i** of God, saying, 1Ch 14:10 7592
David **i** again of God, and God 1Ch 14:14 7592
"I will not be **i** of by you." Ezk 20:3 1875
And shall I be **i** of by you, O Ezk 20:31 1875
"I will not be **i** of by you. Ezk 20:31 1875
mystery about which the king has **i**, Da 2:27 7593
not sought the LORD or **i** of Him." Zph 1:6 1875
he **i** of them where the Messiah was to Mt 2:4 *4441*
So he **i** of them the hour when he Jn 4:52 *4441*

INQUIRER
as the iniquity of the **i** is, **Ezk 14:10** 1875
INQUIRES
be if anyone comes and **i** of you, **Jg 4:20** 7592
INQUIRIES
to you made careful searches and **i**, **1Pe 1:10** *1830*
INQUIRING
i what these things could be. **Lk 15:26** *4441*
INQUIRY
of a medium, making **i** *of it,* **1Ch 10:13** 1875
in pieces mighty men without **i**, **Jb 34:24** 2714
And after the vows to make **i**. **Pr 20:25** 1239
INSANE
"He has a demon and is **i**. **Jn 10:20** *3105*
I speak as if **i** **2Co 11:23** *3912*
INSANELY
them, and acted **i** in their hands, **1Sa 21:13** 1984b
INSANITY
and **i** is in their hearts **Ec 9:3** 1947
INSCRIBE
before them And **i** it on a scroll, **Is 30:8** 2710
you and **i** a city on it, Jerusalem. **Ezk 4:1** 2710
the vision And **i** *it* on tablets, **Hab 2:2** 874
INSCRIBED
i it like the engravings of a signet, **Ex 39:30** 3789
Oh that they were **i** in a book! **Jb 19:23** 2710
"He has **i** a circle on the surface **Jb 26:10** 2328
When He **i** a circle on the face of **Pr 8:27** 2710
i you on the palms *of My hands;* **Is 49:16** 2710
what is **i** in the writing of truth. **Da 10:21** 7559
In that day there will *be* **i** on **Zch 14:20**
INSCRIPTION
"Any man who can read this **i** and **Da 5:7** 3792
but they could not read the **i** or **Da 5:8** 3792
they might read this **i** and make its **Da 5:15** 3792
if you are able to read the **i** and make **Da 5:16** 3792
I will read the **i** to the king and **Da 5:17** 3792
Him and this **i** was written out. **Da 5:24** 3792
is the **i** that was written out: **Da 5:25** 3792
Behold, I will engrave an **i** on it,' **Zch 3:9** 6603
"Whose likeness and **i** is this?" **Mt 22:20** *1923*
"Whose likeness and **i** is this?" **Mk 12:16** *1923*
i of the charge against Him read, **Mk 15:26** *1923*
Whose likeness and **i** does it have?" **Lk 20:24** *1923*
Now there was also an **i** above Him, **Lk 23:38** *1923*
Pilate also wrote an **i** **Jn 19:19** *5102b*
many of the Jews read this **i**, **Jn 19:20** *5102b*
I also found an altar with this **i**, **Ac 17:23** *1924*
INSCRUTABLE
His understanding is **i**. **Is 40:28**
369, 2714
INSECTS
I will send swarms of **i** on you and **Ex 8:21**
will be full of swarms of **i**, **Ex 8:21**
that no swarms of **i** will be there, **Ex 8:22**
And there came great swarms of **i** **Ex 8:24**
because of the swarms of **i** in all the **Ex 8:24**
that the swarms of **i** may depart **Ex 8:29**
the swarms of **i** from Pharaoh, **Ex 8:31**
the winged **i** that walk on *all* fours **Lv 11:20** 8318
may eat among all the winged **i** **Lv 11:21** 8318
'But all other winged **i** which are **Lv 11:23** 8318
INSENSITIVE
the hearts of this people **i**, **Is 6:10** 8080
INSERT
pure blue, and shall **i** its poles. **Nu 4:6** 7760
skin, and they shall **i** its poles. **Nu 4:8** 7760
skin, and shall **i** its poles; **Nu 4:11** 7760
skin over it and **i** its poles. **Nu 4:14** 7760
INSERTED
poles shall be **i** into the rings, **Ex 27:7** 935
He **i** the poles into the rings **Ex 38:7** 935
and **i** its bars and erected its **Ex 40:18** 5414
be **i** in the walls of the house. **1Ki 6:6** 270
INSHORE
sailing along Crete, close **i**. **Ac 27:13**
INSIDE
cover it **i** and out with pitch. **Gn 6:14**
4480, 1004
and uncovered himself **i** his tent. **Gn 9:21** 8432
men of the household was there **i**. **Gn 39:11** 1004
i and out you shall overlay it, **Ex 25:11**
4480, 1004
it with pure gold **i** and out, **Ex 37:2**
4480, 1004
its blood had not been brought **i**, **Lv 10:18** 6441
the house scraped all around **i**, **Lv 14:41**
4480, 1004
into the holy place **i** the veil, **Lv 16:2**
4480, 1004
incense, and bring *it* **i** the veil. **Lv 16:12**
4480, 1004
and bring its blood **i** the veil and **Lv 16:15**
413, 4480, 1004
the altar and **i** the veil, **Nu 18:7**
4480, 1004
the sword will bereave, And **i** terror **Dt 32:25**
4480, 2315
are concealed in the earth **i** my tent **Jos 7:21** 8432
They took them from **i** the tent **Jos 7:23** 8432
them, with torches **i** the pitchers. **Jg 7:16** 8432
inner chamber on fire over those **i**, **Jg 9:49**
sleeping **i** the circle of the camp with **1Sa 26:7**
and set it in its place **i** the tent **2Sa 6:17** 8432
built the walls of the house on the **i** **1Ki 6:15**
4480, 1004
he overlaid *the walls* on the **i** with **1Ki 6:15**
4480, 1004
built *them* for it on the **i** as an inner **1Ki 6:16**
4480, 1004
Solomon overlaid the **i** of the house **1Ki 6:21**
4480, 6441
sawed with saws, **i** and outside; **1Ki 7:9**
4480, 1004
Its opening **i** the crown at the **1Ki 7:31**
4480, 1004
killed a lion **i** a pit on a snowy day. **1Ch 11:22** 8432
ark of God and placed it **i** the tent **1Ch 16:1** 8432
i he overlaid it with pure gold. **2Ch 3:4**
4480, 6441
as soon as they came **i** the city, **Jer 41:7** 8432
rush back and forth **i** the walls; **Jer 49:3**
there were windows all around **i**; **Ezk 40:16** 6441
Then he went **i** and measured each **Ezk 41:3** 6441
the wall all around **i** and outside, **Ezk 41:17** 6442
there is no breath at all **i** it. **Hab 2:19** 7130
is a woman sitting **i** the ephah." **Zch 5:7** 8432
but **i** they are full of robbery and **Mt 23:25** *2081*
the **i** of the cup and of the dish, **Mt 23:26** *1787*
but **i** they are full of dead men's **Mt 23:27** *2081*
from **i** he answers and says, **Lk 11:7** *2081*
but **i** of you, you are full of **Lk 11:39** *2081*
made the outside make the **i** also? **Lk 11:40** *2081*
days His disciples were again **i**, **Jn 20:26** *2080*
opened up, we found no one **i**." **Ac 5:23** *2080*
a book written **i** and on the back, **Rv 5:1** *2081*
INSIGHT
son Zechariah, a counselor with **i**, **1Ch 26:14** 7922
good **i** *in the things* of the LORD. **2Ch 30:22** 7922
a man of **i** of the sons of Mahli, **Ezr 8:18** 7922
gain **i** into the words of the law. **Ne 8:13** 7919a
What helpful **i** you have abundantly **Jb 26:3** 8454
I have more **i** than all my teachers, **Ps 119:99** 7919a
be praised according to his **i**, **Pr 12:8** 7922
And consider and gain **i** as well, **Is 41:20** 7919a
illumination, **i** and wisdom like the **Da 5:11** 7924
spirit, knowledge and **i**, **Da 5:12** 7924
in you, and that illumination, **i** and **Da 5:14** 7924
to give you **i** with understanding. **Da 9:22** 7919a
Those who have **i** among the people **Da 11:33** 7919a
Some of those who have **i** will fall, **Da 11:35** 7919a
Those who have **i** will shine brightly **Da 12:3** 7919a
those who have **i** will understand. **Da 12:10** 7919a
for they had not gained any **i** from **Mk 6:52** *4920*
In all wisdom and **i** **Eph 1:8** *5428*
my **i** into the mystery of Christ, **Eph 3:4** *4907*
INSIGNIFICANT
"And yet this was **i** in Your eyes, **2Sa 7:19** 6994
the hardship seem **i** before You, **Ne 9:32** 4591
"Though your beginning was **i**, **Jb 8:7** 4705
Or they become **i**, but he does not **Jb 14:21** 6819
are **i** on the surface of the water; **Jb 24:18** 7031
I am **i**; what can I reply to You? **Jb 40:4** 7043
them and they will not be **i**. **Jer 30:19** 6819
Cilicia, a citizen of no **i** city; **Ac 21:39** *767*
INSINUATIONS
Even mockery *and* **i** against him And **Hab 2:6** 2420
INSIST
passed, another man *began* to **i**, **Lk 22:59** *1340*
INSISTENT
But they were **i**, with loud voices **Lk 23:23** *1945*
INSISTENTLY
But *Peter* kept saying **i**, **Mk 14:31** *1600a*
INSISTING
But they kept on **i**, **Lk 23:5** *2001*
But she kept **i** that it was so. **Ac 12:15** *1340*
But Paul kept **i** that they should **Ac 15:38** *515*
INSOLENCE
I know your **i** and the wickedness **1Sa 17:28** 2087
Through **i** comes nothing but strife, **Pr 13:10** 2087
Because of the **i** of their tongue. **Hos 7:16** 2195
INSOLENT
Do not speak with **i** pride.' " **Ps 75:5** 6277
his names, Who acts with **i** pride. **Pr 21:24** 2087
A king will arise, **I** and skilled in **Da 8:23**
5794, 6440
slanderers, haters of God, **i**, **Ro 1:30** *5197*
INSPECTED
by the ravine and **i** the wall. **Ne 2:15** 7663a
INSPECTING
i the walls of Jerusalem which **Ne 2:13** 7663a
INSPECTION
on the seventh day and make an **i**. **Lv 14:39** 7200
shall come in and make an **i**. **Lv 14:44** 7200
priest comes in and makes an **i** and **Lv 14:48** 7200
in front of the **I** Gate and as far **Ne 3:31** 4663
INSPIRATION
who prophesy from their own **i**, **Ezk 13:2** 3820
are prophesying from their own **i**. **Ezk 13:17** 3820
INSPIRED
is a fool, The **i** man is demented, **Hos 9:7** 7307
and in the love we **i** in you, **2Co 8:7** *1537*
All Scripture is **i** by God and **2Tm 3:16** *2315*
INSTALLED
Me, I have **i** My King Upon Zion, **Ps 2:6** 5258b
were **i** in the house all around; **Ezk 40:43** 3559
INSTANCE
and every **i** where the king had **Es 5:11**
INSTANT
collapse comes suddenly in an **i**, **Is 30:13** 6621
devastated, My curtains in an **i**. **Jer 4:20** 7281
for in an **i** I will make him run **Jer 49:19** 7280a
for in an **i** I will make them run **Jer 50:44** 7280a
INSTANTLY
that I may consume them **i**." **Nu 16:21** 7281
that I may consume them **i**." **Nu 16:45** 7281
I he will be broken and there **Pr 6:15** 6621
And it will happen **i**, suddenly. **Is 29:5** 6621
INSTEAD
let your servant remain **i** of the lad **Gn 44:33** 8478
if, **i**, you reject My statutes, and **Lv 26:15**
of Israel **i** of every firstborn, **Nu 3:12** 8478
i of all the firstborn among the **Nu 3:41** 8478
i of all the firstborn among the **Nu 3:41** 8478
the Levites **i** of all the firstborn **Nu 3:45** 8478
i of every first issue of the womb, **Nu 8:16** 8478
the Levites **i** of every firstborn **Nu 8:18** 8478
I you rebelled against the command **Dt 1:43**
Please let her be yours **i**." **Jg 15:2** 8478
i, they ravished my concubine so **Jg 20:5**
return good to me **i** of his cursing **2Sa 16:12** 8478
Would I had died **i** of you, **2Sa 18:33** 8478
as king **i** of David his father; **1Ch 29:23** 8478
afflicted him **i** of strengthening him. **2Ch 28:20** 3808
and made her queen **i** of Vashti. **Es 2:17** 8478
Let briars grow **i** of wheat, And **Jb 31:40** 8478
And stinkweed **i** of barley." **Jb 31:40** 8478
I of it, a broad place with no **Jb 36:16** 8478
i of sweet perfume there will be **Is 3:24** 8478
I of a belt, a rope; **Is 3:24** 8478
I of well-set hair, a plucked-out **Is 3:24** 8478
I of fine clothes, a donning of **Is 3:24** 8478
And branding **i** of beauty. **Is 3:24** 8478
I, there is gaiety and gladness, **Is 22:13**
"**I** of the thorn bush the cypress **Is 55:13** 8478
i of the nettle the myrtle will come **Is 55:13** 8478
"**I** of bronze I will bring gold, **Is 60:17** 8478
And **i** of iron I will bring silver, **Is 60:17** 8478
And **i** of wood, bronze, And instead **Is 60:17** 8478
wood, bronze, And **i** of stones, iron. **Is 60:17** 8478
Giving them a garland **i** of ashes, **Is 61:3** 8478
The oil of gladness **i** of mourning, **Is 61:3** 8478
praise **i** of a spirit of fainting. **Is 61:3** 8478
I of your shame *you will have a* **Is 61:7** 8478
And **i** *of* humiliation they will **Is 61:7**
made **i** of them yokes of iron." **Jer 28:13** 8478
priest **i** of Jehoiada the priest, **Jer 29:26** 8478
takes strangers **i** of her husband! **Ezk 16:32** 8478
be cultivated **i** of being a desolation **Ezk 36:34** 8478
i he will honor a god of fortresses, **Da 11:38**
5921, 3653b
the LORD *be* darkness **i** of light, **Am 5:20** 3808
I, He will hide His face from them **Mi 3:4**
go **i** to the dealers and buy *some* **Mt 25:9** *3123*
to release Barabbas for them **i**. **Mk 15:11** *3123*
not give him a snake **i** of a fish, **Lk 11:11** *473*
arrogant and have not mourned **i**, **1Co 5:2** *3123*
darkness, but **i** even expose them; **Eph 5:11** *3123*
I, *you ought* to say, **Jas 4:15** *473*
insult, but giving a blessing **i**; **1Pe 3:9** *5121*
INSTIGATED
and **i** a persecution against Paul **Ac 13:50** *1892*
INSTILLED
who **i** their terror in the land of **Ezk 32:24** 5414
terror was **i** in the land of the living **Ezk 32:25** 5414
they **i** their terror in the land of the **Ezk 32:26** 5414
I i a terror of him in the **Ezk 32:32** 5414
INSTINCT
born as creatures of **i** to be captured **2Pe 2:12** *5446*
the things which they know by **i**, **Jude 1:10** *5447*
INSTINCTIVELY
Law do **i** the things of the Law, **Ro 2:14** *5449*
INSTITUTED
Jeroboam **i** a feast in the **1Ki 12:32** 6213a
he **i** a feast for the sons of Israel and **1Ki 12:33** 6213a
INSTITUTION
the Lord's sake to every human **i**, **1Pe 2:13** *2937*
INSTRUCT
i you in the good and right way. **1Sa 12:23** 3384
gave Your good Spirit to **i** them, **Ne 9:20** 7919a
"I will **i** you in the power of God; **Jb 27:11** 3384
And I will ask you, and you **i** Me! **Jb 38:3** 3045
I will ask you, and you **i** Me. **Jb 40:7** 3045
will ask You, and You **i** me.' **Jb 42:4** 3045
He will **i** him in the way he should **Ps 25:12** 3384
I will **i** you and teach you in the **Ps 32:8** 7919a
of my mother, who used to **i** me; **SS 8:2** 3925
bribe, Her priests **i** for a price And **Mi 3:11** 3384
THE LORD, THAT HE WILL **I** HIM? **1Co 2:16** *4822*
my mind so that I may **i** others also, **1Co 14:19** *2727*
you may **i** certain men not to teach **1Tm 1:3** *3853*
I those who are rich in this present **1Tm 6:17** *3853*
I *them* to do good, to be rich in **1Tm 6:18**
INSTRUCTED
the sons of Levi did as Moses **i**, **Ex 32:28** 1697
which Jehoiada the priest **i** him. **2Ki 12:2** 3384
for Mordecai had **i** her that she **Es 2:10** 6680
But when the wise is **i**, **Pr 21:11** 7919a
A slave will not be **i** by words *alone* **Pr 29:19** 3256
i me not to walk in the way of this **Is 8:11** 3256
And after I was **i**, I smote on *my* **Jer 31:19** 3045
went and did just as Jesus had **i** them, **Mt 21:6** *4929*
money and did as they had been **i**; **Mt 28:15** *1321*
and He **i** them that they should **Mk 6:8** *3853*
but He **i** them to tell no one what **Lk 8:56** *3853*
and **i** *them* not to tell this to **Lk 9:21** *3853*
had been **i** in the way of the Lord; **Ac 18:25** *2727*
essential, being **i** out of the Law, **Ro 2:18** *2727*
in your faith, just as you were **i**, **Col 2:7** *1321*

INSTRUCTING
Jesus sent out after **i** them: **Mt 10:5** *3853*
let the young man go, **i** him, **Ac 23:22** *3853*
also **i** his accusers to bring charges **Ac 23:30** *3853*
i us to deny ungodliness and **Ti 2:12** *3811*

INSTRUCTION
or not they will walk in My **i**. **Ex 16:4** 8451
I have written for their **i**." **Ex 24:12** 3384
he gave **i** in singing because he **1Ch 15:22** 3256
"Please receive **i** from His mouth And **Jb 22:22** 8451
ears of men, And seals their **i**, **Jb 33:16** 4148
"He opens their ear to **i**, **Jb 36:10** 4148
Listen, O my people, to my **i**; **Ps 78:1** 8451
To know wisdom and **i**, **Pr 1:2** 4148
To receive **i** in wise behavior, **Pr 1:3** 4148
Fools despise wisdom and **i**. **Pr 1:7** 4148
Hear, my son, your father's **i** And **Pr 1:8** 4148
Hear, *O* sons, the **i** of a father, **Pr 4:1** 4148
Do not abandon my **i**. **Pr 4:2** 8451
Take hold of **i**; do not let go. **Pr 4:13** 4148
"How I have hated **i**! **Pr 5:12** 4148
He will die for lack of **i**, **Pr 5:23** 4148
"Take my **i** and not silver, And **Pr 8:10** 4148
"Heed **i** and be wise, And do not **Pr 8:33** 4148
Give **i** to a wise man and he will **Pr 9:9**
on the path of life who heeds **i**, **Pr 10:17** 4148
fear of the LORD is the **i** for wisdom, **Pr 15:33** 4148
wisdom and **i** and understanding. **Pr 23:23** 4148
I looked, *and* received **i**. **Pr 24:32** 4148
no longer knows *how* to receive **i**. **Ec 4:13** 2094b
Give ear to the **i** of our God, You **Is 1:10** 8451
those who criticize will accept **i**. **Is 29:24** 3948
to listen To the **i** of the LORD; **Is 30:9** 8451
would not listen and receive **i**. **Jer 32:33** 4148
Will you not receive **i** by listening **Jer 35:13** 4148
He gave *me* **i** and talked with me **Da 9:22** 995
She accepted no **i**. **Zph 3:2** 4148
you will revere Me, Accept **i**.' **Zph 3:7** 4148
"True **i** was in his mouth and **Mal 2:6** 8451
men should seek **i** from his mouth; **Mal 2:7** 8451
caused many to stumble by the **i**; **Mal 2:8** 8451
are showing partiality in the **i**. **Mal 2:9** 8451
of our number to whom we gave no **i** **Ac 15:24** *1291*
times was written for our **i**, **Ro 15:4** *1319*
and they were written for our **i**, **1Co 10:11** *3559*
in giving this **i**, I do not praise you, **1Co 11:17** *3853*
the discipline and **i** of the Lord. **Eph 6:4** *3559*
that as you received from us **i** as **1Th 4:1**
you in the Lord and give you **i**, **1Th 5:12** *3560*
not obey our **i** in this letter, **2Th 3:14** *3056*
But the goal of our **i** is love from **1Tm 1:5** *3852*
A woman must quietly receive **i** with **1Tm 2:11** *3129*
exhort, with great patience and **i**. **2Tm 4:2** *1322*
of **i** about washings and laying on **Heb 6:2** *1322*

INSTRUCTIONS
to keep My commandments and My **i**? **Ex 16:28** 8451
because of the **i** in this letter, **Es 9:26** 1697
with **i** for their times of fasting and **Es 9:31** 1697
Jesus had finished giving **i** to His **Mt 11:1** *1299*
they promptly reported all these **i** *to* **Mk 16:20**
But to the married I give **i**, **1Co 7:10** *3853*
Mark (about whom you received **i**; **Col 4:10** *1785*

INSTRUCTORS
Nor inclined my ear to my **i**! **Pr 5:13** 3925

INSTRUCTS
Indeed, my mind **i** me in the night. **Ps 16:7** 3256
Therefore He **i** sinners in the way. **Ps 25:8** 3384
The heart of the wise **i** his mouth **Pr 16:23** 7919a
God **i** and teaches him properly. **Is 28:26** 3256

INSTRUMENT
voice and plays well on an **i**; **Ezk 33:32**
"Go, for he is a chosen **i** of Mine, **Ac 9:15** *4632*

INSTRUMENTS
with joy and with musical **i**. **1Sa 18:6** 7991b
the LORD with all kinds of **i** **2Sa 6:5**
set *them* under saws, sharp iron **i**, **2Sa 12:31** 2757
the singers, with **i** of music, **1Ch 15:16** 3627
and Jeiel, with musical **i**, **1Ch 16:5** 3627
and *with* **i** *for* the songs of God, **1Ch 16:42** 3627
and with sharp **i** and with axes. **1Ch 20:3** 2757
were praising the LORD with the **i** **1Ch 23:5** 3627
and cymbals and **i** of music, **2Ch 5:13** 3627
with the **i** of music to the LORD, **2Ch 7:6** 3627
musical **i** leading the praise. **2Ch 23:13** 3627
stood with the *musical* **i** of David, **2Ch 29:26** 3627
accompanied by the **i** of David, **2Ch 29:27** 3627
after day with loud **i** to the LORD. **2Ch 30:21** 3627
who were skillful with musical **i**. **2Ch 34:12** 3627
musical **i** of David the man of God. **Ne 12:36** 3627
stringed **i** have made You glad. **Ps 45:8** 4482a
Him with stringed **i** and pipe. **Ps 150:4** 4482a
The LORD and His **i** of indignation, **Is 13:5** 3627
we will play my songs on stringed **i** **Is 38:20**
on which they lay the **i** with which **Ezk 40:42** 3627
choir director, on my stringed **i**. **Hab 3:19** 5058
to sin *as* **i** of unrighteousness; **Ro 6:13** *3696*
as **i** of righteousness to God. **Ro 6:13** *3696*

INSUBORDINATION
And **i** is as iniquity and idolatry. **1Sa 15:23** 6484

INSUFFICIENT
his means are **i** for two turtledoves **Lv 5:11** 5381
he is poor and his means are **i**, **Lv 14:21** 5381

INSULT
the sheaves, and do not **i** her. **Ru 2:15** 3637
He also wrote letters to **i** the LORD **2Ch 32:17** 2778a
"Blessed are you when *people* **i** **Mt 5:11** *3679*
and **i** you, and scorn your name as **Lk 6:22** *3679*
when You say this, You **i** us too." **Lk 11:45** *5195*
evil for evil or **i** for insult, **1Pe 3:9** *3059*
evil for evil or insult for **i**, **1Pe 3:9** *3059*

INSULTED
with us and we have not **i** them, **1Sa 25:7** 3637
good to us, and we were not **i**, **1Sa 25:15** 3637
"These ten times you have **i** me; **Jb 19:3** 3637
and has **i** the Spirit of grace? **Heb 10:29** *1796*

INSULTING
been crucified with Him were also **i** **Mt 27:44** *3679*
were crucified with Him were also **i** **Mk 15:32** *3679*

INSULTS
I listened to the reproof which **i** me **Jb 20:3** 3639
a wicked man *gets* **i** for himself. **Pr 9:7** 4140b
will not endure the **i** of the nations **Ezk 34:29** 3639
endured the **i** of the nations.' **Ezk 36:6** 3639
will themselves endure their **i**. **Ezk 36:7** 3639
not let you hear **i** from the nations **Ezk 36:15** 3639
content with weaknesses, with **i**, **2Co 12:10** *5196*

INSURRECTION
who had committed murder in the **i**. **Mk 15:7** *4714b*
for an **i** made in the city, **Lk 23:19** *4714b*
into prison for **i** and murder, **Lk 23:25** *4714b*

INSURRECTIONISTS
had been imprisoned with the **i** who **Mk 15:7** *4714a*

INTACT
"Behold, while it is **i**, **Ezk 15:5** 8549

INTEGRITY
In the **i** of my heart and the **Gn 20:5** 8537
I know that in the **i** of your heart **Gn 20:6** 8537
if you have dealt in truth and **i** in **Jg 9:16** 8549
if then you have dealt in truth and **i** **Jg 9:19** 8549
in **i** of heart and uprightness, **1Ki 9:4** 8537
I, in the **i** of my heart, **1Ch 29:17** 3476
And he still holds fast his **i**, **Jb 2:3** 8538
"Do you still hold fast your **i**? **Jb 2:9** 8538
And the **i** of your ways your hope? **Jb 4:6** 8537
God will not reject *a man of* **i**, **Jb 8:20** 8535
I will not put away my **i** from me. **Jb 27:5** 8538
scales, And let God know my **i**. **Jb 31:6** 8538
and my **i** that is in me. **Ps 7:8** 8537
He who walks with **i**, **Ps 15:2** 8549
Let **i** and uprightness preserve me, **Ps 25:21** 8537
O LORD, for I have walked in my **i**, **Ps 26:1** 8537
as for me, I shall walk in my **i**; **Ps 26:11** 8537
me, You uphold me in my **i**, **Ps 41:12** 8537
according to the **i** of his heart, **Ps 78:72** 8537
my house in the **i** of my heart. **Ps 101:2** 8537
a shield to those who walk in **i**, **Pr 2:7** 8537
He who walks in **i** walks securely, **Pr 10:9** 8537
The **i** of the upright will guide **Pr 11:3** 8538
a poor man who walks in his **i** **Pr 19:1** 8537
A righteous man who walks in his **i** **Pr 20:7** 8537
is the poor who walks in his **i** Than **Pr 28:6** 8537
they abhor him who speaks *with* **i**. **Am 5:10** 8549

INTELLIGENCE
"But I have **i** as well as you; **Jb 12:3** 3824
"He deprives of **i** the chiefs of **Jb 12:24** 3820
showing **i** in every *branch of* wisdom **Da 1:4** 7919a
God gave them knowledge and **i** in **Da 1:17** 7919a
Sergius Paulus, a man of **i**. **Ac 13:7** *4908*

INTELLIGENT
the woman was **i** and beautiful in **1Sa 25:3** 2896a, 7922
"An idiot will become **i** When **Jb 11:12** 3823a
The mind of the **i** seeks knowledge, **Pr 15:14** 995
hidden these things from *the* wise and **i** **Mt 11:25** *4908*
hidden these things from *the* wise and **i** **Lk 10:21** *4908*

INTELLIGENTLY
Jesus saw that he had answered **i**, **Mk 12:34** *3562*

INTEND
I **i** to build a house for the name **1Ki 5:5** 559
you **i** to resist the kingdom of the **2Ch 13:8** 559
"Do you **i** to reprove *my* words, **Jb 6:26** 2803
Yet it does not so **i**, Nor does it **Is 10:7** 1819
who **i** to make My people forget My **Jer 23:27** 2803
and he will **i** to make alterations **Da 7:25** 5452
"Where does this man **i** to go that **Jn 7:35** *3195*
i to bring this man's blood upon us. **Ac 5:28** *1014*

INTENDED
as he had **i** to do to his brother. **Dt 19:19** 2161
They **i** to kill me; **Jg 20:5** 1819
new *sword*, and he **i** to kill David. **2Sa 21:16** 559
I had **i** to build a house to the **1Ch 22:7** 3824
I *had* **i** to build a permanent home **1Ch 28:2** 3824
for he **i** to make him king. **2Ch 11:22**
he **i** to make war on Jerusalem, **2Ch 32:2** 6440
Though they **i** evil against You **Ps 21:11** 5186
as I have **i** so it has happened, **Is 14:24** 1819
i for the priests who keep charge **Ezk 40:45**
and He **i** to pass by them. **Mk 6:48** *2309*
they were cut to the quick and **i** to **Ac 5:33** *1014*
I **i** at first to come to you, **2Co 1:15** *1014*
not vacillating when I **i** to do this, **2Co 1:17** *1014*

INTENDING
Are you **i** to kill me as you **Ex 2:14** 559
Himself knew what He was **i** to do. **Jn 6:6** *3195*
i to come and take Him by force to **Jn 6:15** *3195*
He is not **i** to go to the Dispersion **Jn 7:35** *3195*
who was **i** to betray Him, **Jn 12:4** *3195*
i after the Passover to bring him **Ac 12:4** *1014*
Alexander was **i** to make a defense **Ac 19:33** *2309*
to them, **i** to leave the next day, **Ac 20:7** *3195*
i from there to take Paul **Ac 20:13** *3195*
it, **i** himself to go by land. **Ac 20:13** *3195*
the pretense of **i** to lay out anchors **Ac 27:30** *3195*

INTENSE
led into sin without my **i** concern? **2Co 11:29** *4448*
will be destroyed with **i** heat, **2Pe 3:10** *2741a*
elements will melt with **i** heat! **2Pe 3:12** *2741a*

INTENSELY
thought that you hated her **i**; **Jg 15:2** 8130
But craved **i** in the wilderness, **Ps 106:14** 8378

INTENSIFY
I will also **i** the famine upon you **Ezk 5:16** 3254

INTENT
that every **i** of the thoughts of his heart **Gn 6:5** 3336
for the **i** of man's heart is evil **Gn 8:21** 3336
'With evil **i** He brought them out **Ex 32:12**
for I know their **i** which they are **Dt 31:21** 3336
because by the **i** of Absalom this **2Sa 13:32** 6310
understands every **i** of the thoughts. **1Ch 28:9** 3336
when he brings it with evil **i**! **Pr 21:27** 2154
all who are **i** on doing evil will be **Is 29:20** 8245
"But your eyes and your heart Are **i** **Jer 22:17**
accomplished The **i** of His heart; **Jer 30:24** 4209
their hearts will be **i** on evil, **Da 11:27**
in spirit, **i** on one purpose. **Php 2:2** *5426*

INTENTION
the **i** of your heart may be forgiven **Ac 8:22** *1963*
through, kept them from their **i**, **Ac 27:43** *1013*
according to the kind **i** of His will, **Eph 1:5** *2107*
according to His kind **i** which He **Eph 1:9** *2107*

INTENTIONS
the **i** of the heart of Your people, **1Ch 29:18** 3336, 4284
the thoughts and **i** of the heart. **Heb 4:12** *1771*

INTENTLY
and he looked **i** and was restored, **Mk 8:25** *1227*
firelight and looking **i** at him, **Lk 22:56** *816*
as they were gazing **i** into the sky **Ac 1:10** *816*
he gazed **i** into heaven and saw the **Ac 7:55** *816*
Paul, looking **i** at the Council, **Ac 23:1** *816*
could not look **i** at the face of Moses **2Co 3:7** *816*
Israel would not look **i** at the end **2Co 3:13** *816*
who looks **i** at the perfect law, **Jas 1:25** *3879*

INTERCEDE
i with the LORD, that He may **Nu 21:7** 6419
the LORD, who can **i** for him?" **1Sa 2:25** 6419
that there was no one to **i**; **Is 59:16** 6293
for them, and do not **i** with Me; **Jer 7:16** 6293

INTERCEDED
And Moses **i** for the people. **Nu 21:7** 6419
many, And **i** for the transgressors. **Is 53:12** 6293

INTERCEDES
but the Spirit Himself **i** for *us* **Ro 8:26** *5241*
because He **i** for the saints **Ro 8:27** *1793*
hand of God, who also **i** for us. **Ro 8:34** *1793*

INTERCESSION
He always lives to make **i** for them. **Heb 7:25** *1793*

INTERCOURSE
not have **i** with your neighbor's wife **Lv 18:20** 2233, 7903
not have **i** with any animal to be **Lv 18:23** 7903
and a man has **i** with her and it is **Nu 5:13** 2233, 7902
your husband has had **i** with you" **Nu 5:20** 7903

INTEREST
you shall not charge him **i**. **Ex 22:25** 5392
'Do not take usurious **i** from him, **Lv 25:36** 5392
not give him your silver at **i**, **Lv 25:37** 5392
not charge **i** to your countrymen: **Dt 23:19** 5391b
i on money, food, *or* anything that **Dt 23:19** 5392
anything that may be loaned at **i**. **Dt 23:19** 5391b
"You may charge **i** to a foreigner, **Dt 23:20** 5391b
countrymen you shall not charge **i**, **Dt 23:20** 5391b
in the king's **i** to let them remain. **Es 3:8** 7737a
does not put out his money at **i**, **Ps 15:5** 5392
increases his wealth by **i** and usury **Pr 28:8** 5392
if he does not lend *money* on **i** or **Ezk 18:8** 5392
he lends *money* on **i** and takes **Ezk 18:13** 5392
poor, does not take **i** or increase, **Ezk 18:17** 5392
contrary to her **i**, for **Ezk 22:3**
you have taken **i** and profits, and **Ezk 22:12** 5392
received my *money* back with **i**. **Mt 25:27** *5110*
I would have collected it with **i**?' **Lk 19:23** *5110*
morbid **i** in controversial questions **1Tm 6:4** *3552*

INTERESTS
not setting your mind on God's **i**, **Mt 16:23**
not setting your mind on God's **i**, **Mk 8:33**
and *his* **i** are divided. The woman **1Co 7:34**
look out for your own personal **i**, **Php 2:4**
but also for the **i** of others. **Php 2:4**
they all seek after their own **i**, **Php 2:21**

INTERFERING
Stop for your own sake from **i** *with* **2Ch 35:21**

INTERIOR
With its **i** lovingly fitted out By **SS 3:10** 8432

INTERMARRY
"**I** with us; give your daughters to **Gn 34:9** 2859
you shall not **i** with them; **Dt 7:3** 2859
remain among you, and **i** with them, **Jos 23:12** 2859
i with the peoples who commit these **Ezr 9:14** 2859

INTERMINGLED
the holy race has **i** with the peoples **Ezr 9:2** 6148

INTERNALLY
You were **i** filled with violence, **Ezk 28:16** 8432

INTERPOSED
Then Phinehas stood up and **i**, **Ps 106:30** 6419
of His purpose, **i** with an oath, **Heb 6:17** *3315*

INTERPRET
and there is no one to **i** it.” Gn 40:8 6622
one who could **i** them to Pharaoh. Gn 41:8 6622
had a dream, but no one can **i** it; Gn 41:15 6622
you hear a dream you can **i** it.” Gn 41:15 6622
to whom would He **i** the message? Is 28:9 995
All do not **i**, do they? 1Co 12:30 *1329*
in a tongue pray that he may **i**. 1Co 14:13 *1329*
and *each* in turn, and one must **i**; 1Co 14:27 *1329*

INTERPRETATION
and each dream with its *own* **i**. Gn 40:5 6623
“This is the **i** of it: Gn 40:12 6623
“This is its **i**: the three baskets are Gn 40:18 6623
according to the **i** of his *own* dream. Gn 41:11 6623
account of the dream and its **i**, Jg 7:15 7667
and who knows the **i** of a matter? Ec 8:1 6592
and we will declare the **i**.” Da 2:4 6591
known to me the dream and its **i**, Da 2:5 6591
you declare the dream and its **i**, Da 2:6 6591
declare to me the dream and its **i**.” Da 2:6 6591
and we will declare the **i**.” Da 2:7 6591
you can declare to me its **i**.” Da 2:9 6591
might declare the **i** to the king. Da 2:16 6591
will declare the **i** to the king.” Da 2:24 6591
make the **i** known to the king!” Da 2:25 6591
dream which I have seen and its **i**? Da 2:26 6591
of making the **i** known to the king, Da 2:30 6591
will tell its **i** before the king. Da 2:36 6591
true and its **i** is trustworthy.” Da 2:45 6591
known to me the **i** of the dream. Da 4:6 6591
could not make its **i** known to me. Da 4:7 6591
I have seen, along with its **i**. Da 4:9 6591
you, Belteshazzar, tell *me* its **i**, Da 4:18 6591
is able to make known to me the **i**; Da 4:18 6591
not let the dream or its **i** alarm you Da 4:19 6591
and its **i** to your adversaries! Da 4:19 6591
this is the **i**, O king, and this is Da 4:24 6591
read this inscription and explain its **i** Da 5:7 6591
or make known its **i** to the king. Da 5:8 6591
knowledge and insight, **i** of dreams, Da 5:12 6590
and he will declare the **i**.” Da 5:12 6591
and make its **i** known to me, Da 5:15 6591
not declare the **i** of the message. Da 5:15 6591
and make its **i** known to me, Da 5:16 6591
king and make the **i** known to him. Da 5:17 6591
“This is the **i** of the message: Da 5:26 6591
known to me the **i** of these things: Da 7:16 6591
and to another the **i** of tongues. 1Co 12:10 *2058*
has a tongue, has an **i**. 1Co 14:26 *2058*
is *a matter* of one’s own **i**, 2Pe 1:20 *1955*

INTERPRETATIONS
“Do not **i** belong to God? Gn 40:8 6623
able to give **i** and solve difficult Da 5:16 6590

INTERPRETED
baker saw that he had **i** favorably, Gn 40:16 6622
just as Joseph had **i** to them. Gn 40:22 6622
him, and he **i** our dreams for us. Gn 41:12 6622
he **i** according to his *own* dream. Gn 41:12 6622
just as he **i** for us, so it happened; Gn 41:13 6622

INTERPRETER
for there was an **i** between them. Gn 42:23 3917b
if there is no **i**, he must keep silent 1Co 14:28 *1328*

INTERPRETS
witchcraft, or one who **i** omens, Dt 18:10 5172
speaks in tongues, unless he **i**, 1Co 14:5 *1329*

INTERVAL
and after an **i** of some years he Da 11:13
7093, 6256
elapsed an **i** of about three hours, Ac 5:7 *1292*
Then after an **i** of fourteen years Ga 2:1

INTERWOVEN
Her clothing is **i** with gold. Ps 45:13 4865

INTESTINES
open in the middle and all his **i** Ac 1:18 *4698*

INTIMATE
my **i** friends have forgotten me. Jb 19:14 3045
But He is **i** with the upright. Pr 3:32 5475
call understanding *your* **i** friend; Pr 7:4 4129
a slanderer separates **i** friends. Pr 16:28 441a
a matter separates **i** friends. Pr 17:9 441a

INTIMATELY
every woman who has known man **i**. Nu 31:17
4904, 2145
girls who have not known man **i**, Nu 31:18
4904, 2145
the women who had not known man **i**, Nu 31:35
4904, 2145
are **i** acquainted with all my ways. Ps 139:3 5532a

INTIMIDATION
AND DO NOT FEAR THEIR **I**, 1Pe 3:14 *5401*

INTONES
my heart **i** like a harp for Moab And Is 16:11 1993

INTOXICATED
whoever is **i** by it is not wise. Pr 20:1 7686

INTOXICATING
hand of the LORD, **I** all the earth. Jer 51:7 7937

INTRIGUE
arise, Insolent and skilled in **i**. Da 8:23 2420
and seize the kingdom by **i**. Da 11:21 2519

INTRODUCE
secretly **i** destructive heresies, 2Pe 2:1 *3919*

INTRODUCED
kings of Israel which they had **i**. 2Ki 17:8 6213a
in the customs which Israel had **i**. 2Ki 17:19 6213a

INTRODUCTION
obtained our **i** by faith into this grace Ro 5:2 *4318*

INUNDATE
them out, and they **i** the earth. Jb 12:15 2015

INVADE
the Moabites would **i** the land 2Ki 13:20 935
whom You did not let Israel **i** 2Ch 20:10 935
the people to arise *who* will **i** us. Hab 3:16 1464

INVADED
the king of Assyria **i** the whole land 2Ki 17:5 5927
they came against Judah and **i** it, 2Ch 21:17 1234
Philistines also had **i** the cities of 2Ch 28:18 6584
king of Assyria came and **i** Judah 2Ch 32:1 935
nations have **i** Your inheritance; Ps 79:1 935
For a nation has **i** my land, Jl 1:6 5927

INVADES
When the Assyrian **i** our land, Mi 5:5 935

INVALIDATE
not **i** a covenant previously ratified Ga 3:17 *208*

INVALIDATED
And *by this* you **i** the word of God for Mt 15:6 *208*

INVALIDATING
i the word of God by your tradition Mk 7:13 *208*

INVENTED
made engines *of war* **i** by skillful men 2Ch 26:15 4284

INVENTING
you are **i** them in your own mind.” Ne 6:8 908

INVENTIVE
so as to perform in every **i** work. Ex 35:33 4284

INVENTORS
arrogant, boastful, **i** of evil, Ro 1:30 *2182*

INVENTS
‘Behold, He **i** pretexts against me; Jb 33:10 4672

INVESTIGATE
then you shall **i** and search out Dt 13:14 1875
“The judges shall **i** thoroughly, Dt 19:18 1875
and **i** and see how this sin has 1Sa 14:38 3045
and **i** and see his place where his 1Sa 23:22 3045
the tenth month to **i** the matter. Ezr 10:16 1875
I directed my mind to know, to **i** and Ec 7:25 8446
at a loss how to **i** such matters, Ac 25:20 *2214*

INVESTIGATED
these Hebronites were **i** according to 1Ch 26:31 1875
the plot was **i** and found *to be so,* Es 2:23 1245
“Behold this; we have **i** it, Jb 5:27 2713
I **i** the case which I did not know. Jb 29:16 2713
having **i** everything carefully from Lk 1:3 *3877*

INVESTIGATING
They finished **i** all the men who Ezr 10:17
And He sees iniquity without **i**. Jb 11:11 995

INVESTIGATION
his case by a more thorough **i**; Ac 23:15 *199*
that after the **i** has taken place, Ac 25:26 *351*

INVESTMENT
riches were lost through a bad **i** Ec 5:14 6045

INVISIBLE
His **i** attributes, His eternal power Ro 1:20 *517*
He is the image of the **i** God, Col 1:15 *517*
and on earth, visible and **i**, Col 1:16 *517*
to the King eternal, immortal, **i**, 1Tm 1:17 *517*

INVITE
I him to have something to eat.” Ex 2:20 7121
i you to eat of his sacrifice, Ex 34:15 7121
shall **i** Jesse to the sacrifice, 1Sa 16:3 7121
he did not **i** Nathan the prophet, 1Ki 1:10 7121
i their three sisters to eat and drink Jb 1:4 7121
i his neighbor to *sit* under *his* vine Zch 3:10 7121
there, **i** to the wedding feast.’ Mt 22:9 *2564*
see You a stranger, and **i** You in, Mt 25:38 *4863*
stranger, and you did not **i** Me in; Mt 25:43 *4863*
do not **i** your friends or your Lk 14:12 *5455*
otherwise they may also **i** you in return Lk 14:12 *479*
you give a reception, **i** *the* poor, Lk 14:13 *2564*
send to Joppa and **i** Simon, Ac 10:32 *3333*

INVITED
they **i** the people to the sacrifices of Nu 25:2 7121
Have you **i** us to impoverish us? Jg 14:15 7121
afterward those who are **i** will eat. 1Sa 9:13 7121
at the head of those who were **i**, 1Sa 9:22 7121
I said I have **i** the people.” 1Sa 9:24 7121
sons and **i** them to the sacrifice. 1Sa 16:5 7121
and Absalom **i** all the king’s sons. 2Sa 13:23 7121
who were **i** and went innocently, 2Sa 15:11 7121
and he **i** all his brothers, the 1Ki 1:9 7121
and has **i** all the sons of the king 1Ki 1:19 7121
he has not **i** Solomon your servant. 1Ki 1:19 7121
and has **i** all the king’s sons and 1Ki 1:25 7121
servant Solomon, he has not **i**. 1Ki 1:26 7121
also I am **i** by her with the king. Es 5:12 7121
had been **i** to the wedding feast, Mt 22:3 *2564*
‘Tell those who have been **i**, Mt 22:4 *2564*
those who were **i** were not worthy. Mt 22:8 *2564*
I was a stranger, and you **i** Me in; Mt 25:35 *4863*
Pharisee who had **i** Him saw this, Lk 7:39 *2564*
speaking a parable to the **i** guests Lk 14:7 *2564*
i by someone to a wedding feast, Lk 14:8 *2564*
than you may have been **i** by him, Lk 14:8 *2564*
and he who **i** you both will come Lk 14:9 *2564*
“But when you are **i**, Lk 14:10 *2564*
when the one who has **i** you comes, Lk 14:10 *2564*
to say to the one who had **i** Him, Lk 14:12 *2564*
a big dinner, and he **i** many; Lk 14:16 *2564*
to say to those who had been **i**, Lk 14:17 *2564*
none of those men who were **i** shall Lk 14:24 *2564*
and both Jesus and His disciples were **i** Jn 2:2 *2564*

“Then Joseph sent *word* and **i** Jacob Ac 7:14 *3333*
And he **i** Philip to come up and sit Ac 8:31 *3870*
i them in and gave them lodging. Ac 10:23 *1528*
and were **i** to stay with them for Ac 28:14 *3870*
who are **i** to the marriage supper of Rv 19:9 *2564*

INVITES
If one of the unbelievers **i** you and 1Co 10:27 *2564*

INVOKE
i My name on the sons of Israel, Nu 6:27 7760
the LORD And **i** the God of Israel, Is 48:1 2142

INVOKED
‘never shall My name be **i** again by Jer 44:26 2142

INVOLVE
Nor do I **i** myself in great matters, Ps 131:1 1980

INVOLVED
of Gershon in the tent of meeting **i** Nu 3:25
Now their duties **i** the ark, Nu 3:31
duties of the sons of Merari **i** Nu 3:36

INVOLVES
fear, because fear **i** punishment, 1Jn 4:18 *2192*

INWARD
all around from the Millo and **i**. 2Sa 5:9 1004
poured out his **i** parts on the ground 2Sa 20:10 4578
the other court **i** from the hall, 1Ki 7:8
4480, 1004
and all their rear parts *turned* **i**. 1Ki 7:25 1004
Even because of my **i** agitation. Jb 20:2
Their **i** part is destruction *itself.* Ps 5:9 7130
i thought and the heart of a man Ps 64:6 7130
For You formed my **i** parts; Ps 139:13 3629
And my **i** feelings for Kir-hareseth. Is 16:11 7130
quiver To enter into my **i** parts. La 3:13 3629
porch of the gate facing **i** *was* one Ezk 40:7 1004
the porch of the gate facing **i**, Ezk 40:8 1004
the porch of the gate was faced **i**. Ezk 40:9 1004
stood on their **i** side all around, Ezk 41:6 1004
I heard and my **i** parts trembled, Hab 3:16 990

INWARDLY
their mouth, But **i** they curse. Ps 62:4 7130
But **i** he sets an ambush for him. Jer 9:8 7130
but **i** are ravenous wolves. Mt 7:15 *2081*
but **i** you are full of hypocrisy Mt 23:28 *2081*
But he is a Jew who is one **i**; Ro 2:29 *2927*

INWARDS
all their hindquarters turned **i**. 2Ch 4:4 1004

IOB
Tola and Puvvah and **I** and Shimron. Gn 46:13 3102

IPHDEIAH
I and Penuel *were* the sons of 1Ch 8:25 3301

IPHTAH
and **I** and Ashnah and Nezib, Jos 15:43 3316

IPHTAHEL
and it ended at the valley of **I**. Jos 19:14 3317
and to the valley of **I** northward Jos 19:27 3317

IR
and Huppim *were* the sons of **I**; 1Ch 7:12 5893

IRA
and **I** the Jairite was also a 2Sa 20:26 5896
I the son of Ikkesh the Tekoite, 2Sa 23:26 5896
I the Ithrite, Gareb the Ithrite, 2Sa 23:38 5896
I the son of Ikkesh the Tekoite, 1Ch 11:28 5896
I the Ithrite, Gareb the Ithrite, 1Ch 11:40 5896
I the son of Ikkesh the Tekoite; 1Ch 27:9 5896

IRAD
Now to Enoch was born **I**, Gn 4:18 5897
I became the father of Mehujael, Gn 4:18 5897

IRAM
chief Magdiel, chief **I**. Gn 36:43 5902
chief Magdiel, chief **I**. 1Ch 1:54 5902

IRI
Uzzi, Uzziel, Jerimoth and **I**. 1Ch 7:7 5901

IRIJAH
of the guard whose name was **I**, Jer 37:13 3376
So **I** arrested Jeremiah and brought Jer 37:14 3376

IR-NAHASH
and Tehinnah the father of **I**. 1Ch 4:12 5904

IRON
of all implements of bronze and **i**; Gn 4:22 1270
I will also make your sky like **i** Lv 26:19 1270
and the silver, the bronze, the **i**, Nu 31:22 1270
struck him down with an **i** object, Nu 35:16 1270
his bedstead was an **i** bedstead; Dt 3:11 1270
brought you out of the **i** furnace, Dt 4:20 1270
a land whose stones are **i**, Dt 8:9 1270
the **i** *head* slips off the handle and Dt 19:5 1270
shall not wield an **i** *tool* on them. Dt 27:5 1270
the earth which is under you, **i**. Dt 28:23 1270
He will put an **i** yoke on your neck Dt 28:48 1270
“Your locks will be **i** and bronze, Dt 33:25 1270
articles of bronze and **i** are holy to Jos 6:19 1270
gold, and articles of bronze and **i**, Jos 6:24 1270
no man had wielded an **i** *tool;* Jos 8:31 1270
valley land have chariots of **i**, Jos 17:16 1270
though they have chariots of **i** *and* Jos 17:18 1270
with silver, gold, bronze, **i**, Jos 22:8 1270
because they had **i** chariots. Jg 1:19 1270
he had nine hundred **i** chariots, Jg 4:3 1270
chariots, nine hundred **i** chariots, Jg 4:13 1270
weighed six hundred shekels of **i**; 1Sa 17:7 1270
under saws, sharp **i** instruments, 2Sa 12:31 1270
iron instruments, and **i** axes, 2Sa 12:31 1270
Must be armed with **i** and the shaft 2Sa 23:7 1270
axe nor any **i** tool heard in the house 1Ki 6:7 1270
from the midst of the **i** furnace), 1Ki 8:51 1270
son of Chenaanah made horns of **i** 1Ki 22:11 1270

it in there, and made the **i** float. 2Ki 6:6 1270
David prepared large quantities of **i** 1Ch 22:3 1270
and bronze and **i** beyond weight, 1Ch 22:14 1270
silver and the bronze and the **i** there 1Ch 22:16 1270
the **i** for the *things of* iron, 1Ch 29:2 1270
the iron for the *things of* **i**, 1Ch 29:2 1270
brass, and 100,000 talents of **i**. 1Ch 29:7 1270
work in gold, silver, brass and **i**, 2Ch 2:7 1270
work in gold, silver, bronze, **i**, 2Ch 2:14 1270
son of Chenaanah made horns of **i** 2Ch 18:10 1270
and also workers in **i** and bronze 2Ch 24:12 1270
"That with an **i** stylus and lead Jb 19:24 1270
"He may flee from the **i** weapon, Jb 20:24 1270
"**I** is taken from the dust, And Jb 28:2 1270
His limbs are like bars of **i**. Jb 40:18 1270
"He regards **i** as straw, Bronze as Jb 41:27 1270
shall break them with a rod of **i**, Ps 2:9 1270
bronze And cut bars of **i** asunder. Ps 107:16 1270
their nobles with fetters of **i**, Ps 149:8 1270
I sharpens iron, So one man Pr 27:17 1270
Iron sharpens **i**, So one man Pr 27:17 1270
thickets of the forest with an **i** *axe,* Is 10:34 1270
man shapes **i** into a cutting tool and Is 44:12 1270
and cut through their **i** bars. Is 45:2 1270
And your neck is an **i** sinew And Is 48:4 1270
instead of **i** I will bring silver, Is 60:17 1270
bronze, And instead of stones, **i**. Is 60:17 1270
and as a pillar of **i** and as walls Jer 1:18 1270
They are bronze and **i**; Jer 6:28 1270
land of Egypt, from the **i** furnace, Jer 11:4 1270
"Can anyone smash **i**, Jer 15:12 1270
smash iron, **I** from the north, Jer 15:12 1270
is written down with an **i** stylus; Jer 17:1 1270
made instead of them yokes of **i**." Jer 28:13 1270
"I have put a yoke of **i** on the Jer 28:14 1270
in the stocks and in the **i** collar, Jer 29:26 6729
"Then get yourself an **i** plate and Ezk 4:3 1270
set it up as an **i** wall between you Ezk 4:3 1270
tin and **i** and lead in the furnace; Ezk 22:18 1270
they gather silver and bronze and **i** Ezk 22:20 1270
with silver, **i**, tin and lead Ezk 27:12 1270
wrought **i**, cassia and sweet cane Ezk 27:19 1270
its legs of **i**, its feet partly of Da 2:33 6523
its feet partly of **i** and partly of clay. Da 2:33 6523
statue on its feet of **i** and clay and Da 2:34 6523
"Then the **i**, the clay, the Da 2:35 6523
a fourth kingdom as strong as **i**; Da 2:40 6523
inasmuch as **i** crushes and shatters Da 2:40 6523
so, like **i** that breaks in pieces, Da 2:40 6523
of potter's clay and partly of **i**, Da 2:41 6523
have in it the toughness of **i**, Da 2:41 6523
saw the **i** mixed with common clay. Da 2:41 6523
partly of **i** and partly of pottery, Da 2:42 6523
saw the **i** mixed with common clay, Da 2:43 6523
i does not combine with pottery. Da 2:43 6523
hands and that it crushed the **i**, Da 2:45 6523
But with a band of **i** and bronze Da 4:15 6523
but with a band of **i** and bronze Da 4:23 6523
of gold and silver, of bronze, **i**, Da 5:4 6523
of silver and gold, of bronze, **i**, Da 5:23 6523
and it had large **i** teeth. Da 7:7 6523
with its teeth of **i** and its claws of Da 7:19 6523
Gilead with *implements* of sharp **i**. Am 1:3 1270
For your horn I will make **i** And Mi 4:13 1270
i gate that leads into the city, Ac 12:10 *4603*
conscience as with a branding **i**, 1Tm 4:2 *2741b*
SHALL RULE THEM WITH A ROD OF **I**, Rv 2:27 *4603*
breastplates like breastplates of **i**; Rv 9:9 *4603*
all the nations with a rod of **i**; Rv 12:5 *4603*
wood and bronze and **i** and marble, Rv 18:12 *4604*
He will rule them with a rod of **i**; Rv 19:15 *4603*

IRONS
fetters, He himself was laid in **i**; Ps 105:18 1270

IRPEEL
and Rekem and **I** and Taralah, Jos 18:27 3416

IRRECONCILABLE
unloving, **i**, malicious gossips, 2Tm 3:3 *786*

IRREVERENCE
God struck him down there for his **i** 2Sa 6:7 7944

IRREVOCABLE
gifts and the calling of God are **i**. Ro 11:29 *278*

IRRIGATE
to **i** a forest of growing trees. Ec 2:6 8248

IRRITATE
provoke her bitterly to **i** her, 1Sa 1:6 7481

IR-SHEMESH
was Zorah and Eshtaol and **I**, Jos 19:41 5905

IRU
Caleb the son of Jephunneh *were* **I**, 1Ch 4:15 5900

ISAAC
and you shall call his name **I**; Gn 17:19 3327
My covenant I will establish with **I**, Gn 17:21 3327
to him, whom Sarah bore to him, **I**. Gn 21:3 3327
Abraham circumcised his son **I** Gn 21:4 3327
when his son **I** was born to him. Gn 21:5 3327
on the day that **I** was weaned. Gn 21:8 3327
not be an heir with my son **I**." Gn 21:10 3327
for through **I** your descendants Gn 21:12 3327
your only son, whom you love, **I**, Gn 22:2 3327
young men with him and **I** his son; Gn 22:3 3327
offering and laid it on **I** his son, Gn 22:6 3327
I spoke to Abraham his father Gn 22:7 3327
the wood, and bound his son **I** and Gn 22:9 3327
and take a wife for my son **I**." Gn 24:4 3327
have appointed for Your servant **I**; Gn 24:14 3327
Now **I** had come from going to Gn 24:62 3327
I went out to meditate in the field Gn 24:63 3327
when she saw **I** she dismounted Gn 24:64 3327
The servant told **I** all the Gn 24:66 3327
Then **I** brought her into his mother Gn 24:67 3327
thus **I** was comforted after his Gn 24:67 3327
Abraham gave all that he had to **I**; Gn 25:5 3327
sent them away from his son **I** Gn 25:6 3327
his sons **I** and Ishmael buried him Gn 25:9 3327
that God blessed his son **I**; Gn 25:11 3327
and **I** lived by Beer-lahai-roi. Gn 25:11 3327
records of the generations of **I**, Gn 25:19 3327
Abraham became the father of **I**; Gn 25:19 3327
and **I** was forty years old when he Gn 25:20 3327
I prayed to the LORD on behalf Gn 25:21 3327
and **I** was sixty years old when she Gn 25:26 3327
Now **I** loved Esau, because he had a Gn 25:28 3327
So **I** went to Gerar, to Abimelech Gn 26:1 3327
So **I** lived in Gerar. Gn 26:6 3327
I was caressing his wife Rebekah. Gn 26:8 3327
Then Abimelech called **I** and said, Gn 26:9 3327
And **I** said to him, Gn 26:9 3327
Now **I** sowed in that land and Gn 26:12 3327
Then Abimelech said to **I**, Gn 26:16 3327
And **I** departed from there and Gn 26:17 3327
I dug again the wells of water Gn 26:18 3327
quarreled with the herdsmen of **I**, Gn 26:20 3327
I said to them, Gn 26:27 3327
then **I** sent them away and they Gn 26:31 3327
brought grief to **I** and Rebekah. Gn 26:35 3327
when **I** was old and his eyes were Gn 27:1 3327
I said, "Behold now, I am old Gn 27:2 3327
while **I** spoke to his son Esau. Gn 27:5 3327
I said to his son, Gn 27:20 3327
Then **I** said to Jacob, Gn 27:21 3327
Jacob came close to **I** his father, Gn 27:22 3327
Then his father **I** said to him, Gn 27:26 3327
as **I** had finished blessing Jacob, Gn 27:30 3327
from the presence of **I** his father, Gn 27:30 3327
I his father said to him, Gn 27:32 3327
Then **I** trembled violently, and Gn 27:33 3327
But **I** replied to Esau, Gn 27:37 3327
Then **I** his father answered and Gn 27:39 3327
Rebekah said to **I**, Gn 27:46 3327
So **I** called Jacob and blessed him Gn 28:1 3327
Then **I** sent Jacob away, and he Gn 28:5 3327
Esau saw that **I** had blessed Jacob Gn 28:6 3327
of Canaan displeased his father **I**; Gn 28:8 3327
father Abraham and the God of **I**; Gn 28:13 3327
land of Canaan to his father **I**. Gn 31:18 3327
God of Abraham, and the fear of **I**, Gn 31:42 3327
swore by the fear of his father **I**. Gn 31:53 3327
Abraham and God of my father **I**, Gn 32:9 3327
which I gave to Abraham and **I**, Gn 35:12 3327
Jacob came to his father **I** at Gn 35:27 3327
where Abraham and **I** had sojourned. Gn 35:27 3327
Now the days of **I** were one hundred Gn 35:28 3327
I breathed his last and died and Gn 35:29 3327
to the God of his father **I**. Gn 46:1 3327
my fathers Abraham and **I** walked, Gn 48:15 3327
names of my fathers Abraham and **I**; Gn 48:16 3327
buried **I** and his wife Rebekah, Gn 49:31 3327
oath to Abraham, to **I** and to Jacob Gn 50:24 3327
His covenant with Abraham, **I**, Ex 2:24 3327
the God of Abraham, the God of **I**, Ex 3:6 3327
the God of Abraham, the God of **I**, Ex 3:15 3327
the God of Abraham, **I** and Jacob, Ex 3:16 3327
the God of Abraham, the God of **I**, Ex 4:5 3327
and I appeared to Abraham, **I**, Ex 6:3 3327
I swore to give to Abraham, **I**, Ex 6:8 3327
"Remember Abraham, **I**, and Israel Ex 32:13 3327
of which I swore to Abraham, **I**, Ex 33:1 3327
remember also My covenant with **I**, Lv 26:42 3327
to Abraham, to **I** and to Jacob; Nu 32:11 3327
to your fathers, to Abraham, to **I**, Dt 1:8 3327
fathers, Abraham, **I** and Jacob, Dt 6:10 3327
fathers, to Abraham, **I** and Jacob. Dt 9:5 3327
Your servants, Abraham, **I**, Dt 9:27 3327
to your fathers, to Abraham, **I**, Dt 29:13 3327
to your fathers, to Abraham, **I**, Dt 30:20 3327
land which I swore to Abraham, **I**, Dt 34:4 3327
his descendants and gave him **I**. Jos 24:3 3327
'To **I** I gave Jacob and Esau, Jos 24:4 3327
the God of Abraham, **I** and Israel, 1Ki 18:36 3327
of His covenant with Abraham, **I**, 2Ki 13:23 3327
The sons of Abraham *were* **I** and 1Ch 1:28 3327
Abraham became the father of **I**. 1Ch 1:34 3327
sons of **I** *were* Esau and Israel. 1Ch 1:34 3327
with Abraham, And His oath to **I**. 1Ch 16:16 3327
"O LORD, the God of Abraham, **I** and 1Ch 29:18 3327
to the LORD God of Abraham, **I** and 2Ch 30:6 3327
with Abraham, And His oath to **I**. Ps 105:9 3327
the descendants of Abraham, **I** and Jer 33:26 3327
high places of **I** will be desolated Am 7:9 3327
you speak against the house of **I**.' Am 7:16 3327
Abraham was the father of **I**, Mt 1:2 *2464*
I the father of Jacob, and Jacob Mt 1:2 *2464*
at the table with Abraham, **I** Mt 8:11 *2464*
OF ABRAHAM, AND THE GOD OF **I**, Mt 22:32 *2464*
OF ABRAHAM, AND THE GOD OF **I**, Mk 12:26 *2464*
the son of Jacob, the son of **I**, Lk 3:34 *2464*
you see Abraham and **I** and Jacob Lk 13:28 *2464*
OF ABRAHAM, AND THE GOD OF **I**, Lk 20:37 *2464*
"The God of Abraham, **I** and Ac 3:13 *2464*
so *Abraham* became the father of **I**, Ac 7:8 *2464*
and **I** *became the father of* Jacob, Ac 7:8 *2464*
GOD OF ABRAHAM AND **I** AND JACOB.' Ac 7:32 *2464*
"THROUGH **I** YOUR DESCENDANTS Ro 9:7 *2464*
twins by one man, our father **I**; Ro 9:10 *2464*
you brethren, like **I**, are children of Ga 4:28 *2464*
dwelling in tents with **I** and Jacob, Heb 11:9 *2464*
when he was tested, offered up **I**, Heb 11:17 *2464*
"IN **I** YOUR DESCENDANTS SHALL BE Heb 11:18 *2464*
By faith **I** blessed Jacob and Esau, Heb 11:20 *2464*
he offered up **I** his son on the altar? Jas 2:21 *2464*

ISAAC'S
But when **I** servants dug in the Gn 26:19 3327
and there **I** servants dug a well. Gn 26:25 3327
that **I** servants came in and told Gn 26:32 3327

ISAIAH
to **I** the prophet the son of Amoz. 2Ki 19:2 3470b
of King Hezekiah came to **I**. 2Ki 19:5 3470b
I said to them, 2Ki 19:6 3470b
I the son of Amoz sent to Hezekiah 2Ki 19:20 3470b
And **I** the prophet the son of Amoz 2Ki 20:1 3470b
Before **I** had gone out of the middle 2Ki 20:4 3470b
Then **I** said, "Take a cake of figs." 2Ki 20:7 3470b
Now Hezekiah said to **I**, 2Ki 20:8 3470b
I said, "This shall be the sign to you 2Ki 20:9 3470b
I the prophet cried to the LORD, 2Ki 20:11 3470b
Then **I** the prophet came to King 2Ki 20:14 3470b
Then **I** said to Hezekiah, 2Ki 20:16 3470b
Then Hezekiah said to **I**, 2Ki 20:19 3470b
first to last, the prophet **I**, 2Ch 26:22 3470b
King Hezekiah and **I** the prophet, 2Ch 32:20 3470b
in the vision of **I** the prophet, 2Ch 32:32 3470b
The vision of **I** the son of Amoz Is 1:1 3470b
The word which **I** the son of Amoz Is 2:1 3470b
Then the LORD said to **I**, Is 7:3 3470b
which **I** the son of Amoz saw. Is 13:1 3470b
LORD spoke through **I** the son of Is 20:2 3470b
My servant **I** has gone naked and Is 20:3 3470b
with sackcloth, to **I** the prophet, Is 37:2 3470b
of King Hezekiah came to **I**. Is 37:5 3470b
I said to them, Is 37:6 3470b
Then **I** the son of Amoz sent *word* Is 37:21 3470b
And **I** the prophet the son of Amoz Is 38:1 3470b
the word of the LORD came to **I**, Is 38:4 3470b
I had said, "Let them take a cake of Is 38:21 3470b
Then **I** the prophet came to King Is 39:3 3470b
Then **I** said to Hezekiah, Is 39:5 3470b
Then Hezekiah said to **I**, Is 39:8 3470b
one referred to by **I** the prophet when Mt 3:3 *2268*
was spoken through **I** the prophet: Mt 4:14 *2268*
was spoken through **I** the prophet Mt 8:17 *2268*
was spoken through **I** the prophet: Mt 12:17 *2268*
prophecy of **I** is being fulfilled, Mt 13:14 *2268*
rightly did **I** prophesy of you: Mt 15:7 *2268*
As it is written in **I** the prophet: Mk 1:2 *2268*
did **I** prophesy of you hypocrites, Mk 7:6 *2268*
book of the words of **I** the prophet, Lk 3:4 *2268*
book of the prophet **I** was handed Lk 4:17 *2268*
THE LORD,' as **I** the prophet said." Jn 1:23 *2268*
fulfill the word of **I** the prophet Jn 12:38 *2268*
not believe, for **I** said again, Jn 12:39 *2268*
These things **I** said because he Jn 12:41 *2268*
and was reading the prophet **I**. Ac 8:28 *2268*
heard him reading **I** the prophet, Ac 8:30 *2268*
Holy Spirit rightly spoke through **I** Ac 28:25 *2268*
I cries out concerning Israel, Ro 9:27 *2268*
And just as **I** foretold, Ro 9:29 *2268*
I says, "LORD, WHO HAS BELIEVED Ro 10:16 *2268*
And **I** is very bold and says, Ro 10:20 *2268*
Again **I** says, Ro 15:12 *2268*

ISCAH
Haran, the father of Milcah and **I**. Gn 11:29 3252

ISCARIOT
Simon the Zealot, and Judas **I**, Mt 10:4 *2469*
one of the twelve, named Judas **I**, Mt 26:14 *2469*
and Judas **I**, who betrayed Him. Mk 3:19 *2469*
Judas **I**, who was one of the twelve, Mk 14:10 *2469*
the son of James, and Judas **I**, Lk 6:16 *2469*
into Judas who was called **I**, Lk 22:3 *2469*
He meant Judas *the son* of Simon **I**, Jn 6:71 *2469*
But Judas **I**, one of His disciples, Jn 12:4 *2469*
put into the heart of Judas **I**, Jn 13:2 *2469*
it to Judas, *the son* of Simon **I**. Jn 13:26 *2469*
Judas (not **I**) said to Him, "Lord, Jn 14:22 *2469*

ISHBAH
and **I** the father of Eshtemoa. 1Ch 4:17 3431

ISHBAK
Medan and Midian and **I** and Shuah. Gn 25:2 3435
Zimran, Jokshan, Medan, Midian, **I** 1Ch 1:32 3435

ISHBI-BENOB
Then **I**, who was among the 2Sa 21:16 3430

ISH-BOSHETH
army, had taken **I** the son of Saul and 2Sa 2:8 378
I, Saul's son, was forty years old 2Sa 2:10 378
the servants of **I** the son of Saul. 2Sa 2:12 378
Benjamin and **I** the son of Saul, 2Sa 2:15 378
and **I** said to Abner, 2Sa 3:7
was very angry over the words of **I** 2Sa 3:8 378
So David sent messengers to **I**, 2Sa 3:14 378
I sent and took her from *her* 2Sa 3:15 378
Now when **I**, Saul's son, heard that 2Sa 4:1
departed and came to the house of **I** 2Sa 4:5 378
they brought the head of **I** to David 2Sa 4:8 378
"Behold, the head of **I** the 2Sa 4:8 378
But they took the head of **I** and 2Sa 4:12 378

ISHHOD
Hammolecheth bore **I** and Abiezer 1Ch 7:18 379

ISHI
The son of Appaim *was* **I**. 1Ch 2:31 3469
And the son of **I** *was* Sheshan. 1Ch 2:31 3469
And the sons of **I** *were* Zoheth and 1Ch 4:20 3469
and Uzziel, the sons of **I**, 1Ch 4:42 3469
fathers' households, even Epher, **I**, 1Ch 5:24 3469
"That you will call Me **I** And will Hos 2:16 376

ISHMA
Jezreel, **I** and Idbash; **1Ch 4:3** 3457
ISHMAEL
And you shall call his name **I**, **Gn 16:11** 3458
of his son, whom Hagar bore, **I**. **Gn 16:15** 3458
old when Hagar bore **I** to him. **Gn 16:16** 3458
that **I** might live before You!" **Gn 17:18** 3458
"As for **I**, I have heard you; **Gn 17:20** 3458
Then Abraham took **I** his son, **Gn 17:23** 3458
And **I** his son was thirteen years **Gn 17:25** 3458
was circumcised, and **I** his son. **Gn 17:26** 3458
his sons Isaac and **I** buried him in **Gn 25:9** 3458
records of the generations of **I**, **Gn 25:12** 3458
are the names of the sons of **I**, **Gn 25:13** 3458
Nebaioth, the firstborn of **I**, **Gn 25:13** 3458
These are the sons of **I** and these **Gn 25:16** 3458
are the years of the life of **I**, **Gn 25:17** 3458
and Esau went to **I**, **Gn 28:9** 3458
had, Mahalath the daughter of **I**, **Gn 28:9** 3458
namely, **I** the son of Nethaniah, **2Ki 25:23** 3458
that **I** the son of Nethaniah, **2Ki 25:25** 3458
sons of Abraham *were* Isaac and **I**. **1Ch 1:28** 3458
the firstborn of **I** *was* Nebaioth, **1Ch 1:29** 3458
these *were* the sons of **I**. **1Ch 1:31** 3458
Azrikam, Bocheru, **I**, **1Ch 8:38** 3458
Bocheru and **I** and Sheariah and **1Ch 9:44** 3458
and Zebadiah the son of **I**, **2Ch 19:11** 3458
of Jeroham, **I** the son of Johanan, **2Ch 23:1** 3458
Elioenai, Maaseiah, **I**, **Ezr 10:22** 3458
along with **I** the son of Nethaniah, **Jer 40:8** 3458
has sent **I** the son of Nethaniah **Jer 40:14** 3458
and kill **I** the son of Nethaniah, **Jer 40:15** 3458
you are telling a lie about **I**." **Jer 40:16** 3458
month **I** the son of Nethaniah, **Jer 41:1** 3458
I the son of Nethaniah and the ten **Jer 41:2** 3458
I also struck down all the Jews **Jer 41:3** 3458
Then **I** the son of Nethaniah went **Jer 41:6** 3458
I the son of Nethaniah and the men **Jer 41:7** 3458
were found among them said to **I**, **Jer 41:8** 3458
where **I** had cast all the corpses of **Jer 41:9** 3458
I the son of Nethaniah filled it **Jer 41:9** 3458
Then **I** took captive all the remnant **Jer 41:10** 3458
thus **I** the son of Nethaniah took **Jer 41:10** 3458
I the son of Nethaniah had done. **Jer 41:11** 3458
to fight with **I** the son of Nethaniah **Jer 41:12** 3458
people who were with **I** saw Johanan **Jer 41:13** 3458
people whom **I** had taken captive **Jer 41:14** 3458
But **I** the son of Nethaniah escaped **Jer 41:15** 3458
whom he had recovered from **I** the **Jer 41:16** 3458
I the son of Nethaniah had struck **Jer 41:18** 3458
ISHMAELITE
father of Amasa was Jether the **I**. **1Ch 2:17** 3459
Obil the **I** had charge of the camels **1Ch 27:30** 3459
ISHMAELITES
a caravan of **I** was coming from **Gn 37:25** 3459
"Come and let us sell him to the **I** **Gn 37:27** 3459
sold him to the **I** for twenty *shekels* **Gn 37:28** 3459
bodyguard, bought him from the **I**, **Gn 39:1** 3459
earrings, because they were **I**.) **Jg 8:24** 3459
The tents of Edom and the **I**, **Ps 83:6** 3459
ISHMAEL'S
also Basemath, **I** daughter, the **Gn 36:3** 3458
ISHMAIAH
and **I** the Gibeonite, a mighty man **1Ch 12:4** 3460
for Zebulun, **I** the son of Obadiah; **1Ch 27:19** 3460
ISHMERAI
I, Izliah and Jobab *were* the sons **1Ch 8:18** 3461
ISHPAH
Michael, **I** and Joha *were* the sons **1Ch 8:16** 3472
ISHPAN
I, Eber, Eliel, **1Ch 8:22** 3473
ISHVAH
Imnah and **I** and Ishvi and Beriah **Gn 46:17** 3438
The sons of Asher *were* Imnah, **I**, **1Ch 7:30** 3438
ISHVI
Imnah and Ishvah and **I** and Beriah **Gn 46:17** 3440
of **I**, the family of the Ishvites; **Nu 26:44** 3440
Jonathan and **I** and Malchi-shua; **1Sa 14:49** 3440
were Imnah, Ishvah, **I** and Beriah, **1Ch 7:30** 3440
ISHVITES
of Ishvi, the family of the **I**; **Nu 26:44** 3441
ISLAND
the whole **i** as far as Paphos, **Ac 13:6** *3520*
shelter of a small **i** called Clauda, **Ac 27:16** *3519*
must run aground on a certain **i**." **Ac 27:26** *3520*
out that the **i** was called Malta. **Ac 28:1** *3520*
to the leading man of the **i**, **Ac 28:7** *3520*
the rest of the people on the **i** **Ac 28:9** *3520*
ship which had wintered at the **i**, **Ac 28:11** *3520*
Jesus, was on the **i** called Patmos **Rv 1:9** *3520*
every mountain and **i** were moved **Rv 6:14** *3520*
And every **i** fled away, and the **Rv 16:20** *3520*
ISLANDS
kings of Tarshish and of the **i** bring **Ps 72:10** 339
Let the many **i** be glad. **Ps 97:1** 339
Hamath, And from the **i** of the sea. **Is 11:11** 339
He lifts up the **i** like fine dust. **Is 40:15** 339
You **i**, and those who dwell on them. **Is 42:10** 339
Listen to Me, O **i**, And pay **Is 49:1** 339
ISMACHIAH
Jerimoth, Jozabad, Eliel, **I**, **2Ch 31:13** 3253
ISOLATE
then the priest shall **i** *him who* **Lv 13:4** 5462
shall **i** him for seven more days. **Lv 13:5** 5462
he shall not **i** him, for he is **Lv 13:11** 5462
priest shall **i** him for seven days; **Lv 13:21** 5462
priest shall **i** him for seven days; **Lv 13:26** 5462
then the priest shall **i** *the person* **Lv 13:31** 5462
and the priest shall **i** *the person* **Lv 13:33** 5462
ISOLATED
For the fortified city is **i**, **Is 27:10** 910
ISRAEL
shall no longer be Jacob, but **I**; **Gn 32:28** 3478
the sons of **I** do not eat the sinew of **Gn 32:32** 3478
he had done a disgraceful thing in **I** **Gn 34:7** 3478
Jacob, But **I** shall be your name." **Gn 35:10** 3478
Thus He called him **I**. **Gn 35:10** 3478
Then **I** journeyed on and pitched **Gn 35:21** 3478
while **I** was dwelling in that land, **Gn 35:22** 3478
and **I** heard *of it*. **Gn 35:22** 3478
king reigned over the sons of **I**. **Gn 36:31** 3478
Now **I** loved Joseph more than all **Gn 37:3** 3478
I said to Joseph, **Gn 37:13** 3478
So the sons of **I** came to buy grain **Gn 42:5** 3478
Then **I** said, "Why did you treat me **Gn 43:6** 3478
Judah said to his father **I**, **Gn 43:8** 3478
Then their father **I** said to them, **Gn 43:11** 3478
Then the sons of **I** did so; **Gn 45:21** 3478
I said, "It is enough; my son Joseph **Gn 45:28** 3478
So **I** set out with all that he had, **Gn 46:1** 3478
God spoke to **I** in visions of **Gn 46:2** 3478
sons of **I** carried their father Jacob **Gn 46:5** 3478
are the names of the sons of **I**, **Gn 46:8** 3478
up to Goshen to meet his father **I**; **Gn 46:29** 3478
Then **I** said to Joseph, **Gn 46:30** 3478
Now **I** lived in the land of Egypt, **Gn 47:27** 3478
the time for **I** to die drew near, **Gn 47:29** 3478
Then **I** bowed *in worship* at the **Gn 47:31** 3478
I collected his strength and sat **Gn 48:2** 3478
When **I** saw Joseph's sons, he said, **Gn 48:8** 3478
the eyes of **I** were *so* dim from age **Gn 48:10** 3478
I said to Joseph, **Gn 48:11** 3478
But **I** stretched out his right hand **Gn 48:14** 3478
"By you **I** will pronounce blessing, **Gn 48:20** 3478
Then **I** said to Joseph, **Gn 48:21** 3478
And listen to **I** your father. **Gn 49:2** 3478
in Jacob, And scatter them in **I**. **Gn 49:7** 3478
people, As one of the tribes of **I**. **Gn 49:16** 3478
is the Shepherd, the Stone of **I**), **Gn 49:24** 3478
these are the twelve tribes of **I**, **Gn 49:28** 3478
So the physicians embalmed **I**. **Gn 50:2** 3478
Joseph made the sons of **I** swear, **Gn 50:25** 3478
these are the names of the sons of **I** **Ex 1:1** 3478
But the sons of **I** were fruitful **Ex 1:7** 3478
the people of the sons of **I** are more **Ex 1:9** 3478
were in dread of the sons of **I**. **Ex 1:12** 3478
Egyptians compelled the sons of **I** **Ex 1:13** 3478
the sons of **I** sighed because of the **Ex 2:23** 3478
God saw the sons of **I**, **Ex 2:25** 3478
cry of the sons of **I** has come to Me **Ex 3:9** 3478
bring My people, the sons of **I**, **Ex 3:10** 3478
bring the sons of **I** out of Egypt?" **Ex 3:11** 3478
I am going to the sons of **I**, **Ex 3:13** 3478
you shall say to the sons of **I**, **Ex 3:14** 3478
you shall say to the sons of **I**, **Ex 3:15** 3478
gather the elders of **I** together and **Ex 3:16** 3478
and you with the elders of **I** will **Ex 3:18** 3478
"**I** is My son, My firstborn. **Ex 4:22** 3478
all the elders of the sons of **I**; **Ex 4:29** 3478
was concerned about the sons of **I** **Ex 4:31** 3478
"Thus says the LORD, the God of **I**, **Ex 5:1** 3478
should obey His voice to let **I** go? **Ex 5:2** 3478
besides, I will not let **I** go." **Ex 5:2** 3478
the foremen of the sons of **I**, **Ex 5:14** 3478
the foremen of the sons of **I** came **Ex 5:15** 3478
The foremen of the sons of **I** saw **Ex 5:19** 3478
heard the groaning of the sons of **I**, **Ex 6:5** 3478
"Say, therefore, to the sons of **I**, **Ex 6:6** 3478
Moses spoke thus to the sons of **I**, **Ex 6:9** 3478
let the sons of **I** go out of his land." **Ex 6:11** 3478
sons of **I** have not listened to me; **Ex 6:12** 3478
gave them a charge to the sons of **I** **Ex 6:13** 3478
bring the sons of **I** out of the land **Ex 6:13** 3478
"Bring out the sons of **I** from the **Ex 6:26** 3478
out the sons of **I** from Egypt; **Ex 6:27** 3478
let the sons of **I** go out of his land. **Ex 7:2** 3478
My hosts, My people the sons of **I**, **Ex 7:4** 3478
the sons of **I** from their midst." **Ex 7:5** 3478
between the livestock of **I** and the **Ex 9:4** 3478
all that belongs to the sons of **I**. **Ex 9:4** 3478
of the livestock of the sons of **I**, **Ex 9:6** 3478
not even one of the livestock of **I** **Ex 9:7** 3478
Goshen, where the sons of **I** *were*, **Ex 9:26** 3478
he did not let the sons of **I** go, **Ex 9:35** 3478
he did not let the sons of **I** go. **Ex 10:20** 3478
all the sons of **I** had light in their **Ex 10:23** 3478
against any of the sons of **I** a dog **Ex 11:7** 3478
distinction between Egypt and **I**.' **Ex 11:7** 3478
let the sons of **I** go out of his land. **Ex 11:10** 3478
"Speak to all the congregation of **I**, **Ex 12:3** 3478
assembly of the congregation of **I** **Ex 12:6** 3478
person shall be cut off from **I**. **Ex 12:15** 3478
cut off from the congregation of **I**, **Ex 12:19** 3478
Moses called for all the elders of **I** and **Ex 12:21** 3478
passed over the houses of the sons of **I** **Ex 12:27** 3478
the sons of **I** went and did *so*; **Ex 12:28** 3478
both you and the sons of **I**; **Ex 12:31** 3478
Now the sons of **I** had done **Ex 12:35** 3478
Now the sons of **I** journeyed from **Ex 12:37** 3478
the time that the sons of **I** lived in **Ex 12:40** 3478
to be observed by all the sons of **I** **Ex 12:42** 3478
congregation of **I** are to celebrate **Ex 12:47** 3478
Then all the sons of **I** did *so*; **Ex 12:50** 3478
the LORD brought the sons of **I** out of **Ex 12:51** 3478
of every womb among the sons of **I**, **Ex 13:2** 3478
sons of **I** went up in martial array **Ex 13:18** 3478
made the sons of **I** solemnly swear, **Ex 13:19** 3478
"Tell the sons of **I** to turn back **Ex 14:2** 3478
Pharaoh will say of the sons of **I**, **Ex 14:3** 3478
have let **I** go from serving us?" **Ex 14:5** 3478
he chased after the sons of **I** **Ex 14:8** 3478
sons of **I** were going out boldly. **Ex 14:8** 3478
drew near, the sons of **I** looked, **Ex 14:10** 3478
sons of **I** cried out to the LORD. **Ex 14:10** 3478
Tell the sons of **I** to go forward. **Ex 14:15** 3478
and the sons of **I** shall go through **Ex 14:16** 3478
been going before the camp of **I**, **Ex 14:19** 3478
camp of Egypt and the camp of **I**; **Ex 14:20** 3478
The sons of **I** went through the **Ex 14:22** 3478
"Let us flee from **I**, **Ex 14:25** 3478
the sons of **I** walked on dry land **Ex 14:29** 3478
Thus the LORD saved **I** that day **Ex 14:30** 3478
and **I** saw the Egyptians dead on **Ex 14:30** 3478
When **I** saw the great power **Ex 14:31** 3478
sons of **I** sang this song to the LORD, **Ex 15:1** 3478
the sons of **I** walked on dry land **Ex 15:19** 3478
Then Moses led **I** from the Red Sea, **Ex 15:22** 3478
all the congregation of the sons of **I** **Ex 16:1** 3478
whole congregation of the sons of **I** **Ex 16:2** 3478
The sons of **I** said to them, **Ex 16:3** 3478
Aaron said to all the sons of **I**, **Ex 16:6** 3478
the congregation of the sons of **I**, **Ex 16:9** 3478
congregation of the sons of **I**, **Ex 16:10** 3478
the grumblings of the sons of **I**; **Ex 16:12** 3478
When the sons of **I** saw *it*, **Ex 16:15** 3478
The sons of **I** did so, and *some* **Ex 16:17** 3478
The house of **I** named it manna, **Ex 16:31** 3478
sons of **I** ate the manna forty years **Ex 16:35** 3478
all the congregation of the sons of **I** **Ex 17:1** 3478
with you some of the elders of **I**; **Ex 17:5** 3478
did so in the sight of the elders of **I**. **Ex 17:6** 3478
of the quarrel of the sons of **I**, **Ex 17:7** 3478
and fought against **I** at Rephidim. **Ex 17:8** 3478
his hand up, that **I** prevailed, **Ex 17:11** 3478
for Moses and for **I** His people, **Ex 18:1** 3478
LORD had brought **I** out of Egypt. **Ex 18:1** 3478
which the LORD had done to **I**, **Ex 18:9** 3478
Aaron came with all the elders of **I** **Ex 18:12** 3478
Moses chose able men out of all **I** and **Ex 18:25** 3478
sons of **I** had gone out of the land of **Ex 19:1** 3478
I camped in front of the mountain. **Ex 19:2** 3478
of Jacob and tell the sons of **I**: **Ex 19:3** 3478
shall speak to the sons of **I**." **Ex 19:6** 3478
you shall say to the sons of **I**, **Ex 20:22** 3478
and seventy of the elders of **I**, **Ex 24:1** 3478
pillars for the twelve tribes of **I**. **Ex 24:4** 3478
sent young men of the sons of **I**, **Ex 24:5** 3478
and seventy of the elders of **I**, **Ex 24:9** 3478
and they saw the God of **I**; **Ex 24:10** 3478
the nobles of the sons of **I**; **Ex 24:11** 3478
And to the eyes of the sons of **I** **Ex 24:17** 3478
"Tell the sons of **I** to raise a **Ex 25:2** 3478
in commandment for the sons of **I**. **Ex 25:22** 3478
You shall charge the sons of **I**, **Ex 27:20** 3478
generations for the sons of **I**. **Ex 27:21** 3478
him, from among the sons of **I**, **Ex 28:1** 3478
them the names of the sons of **I**, **Ex 28:9** 3478
to the names of the sons of **I**; **Ex 28:11** 3478
stones of memorial for the sons of **I** **Ex 28:12** 3478
to the names of the sons of **I**: **Ex 28:21** 3478
carry the names of the sons of **I** **Ex 28:29** 3478
carry the judgment of the sons of **I** **Ex 28:30** 3478
which the sons of **I** consecrate, **Ex 28:38** 3478
forever from the sons of **I**, **Ex 29:28** 3478
be a heave offering from the sons of **I** **Ex 29:28** 3478
meet there with the sons of **I**, **Ex 29:43** 3478
I will dwell among the sons of **I** **Ex 29:45** 3478
you take a census of the sons of **I** **Ex 30:12** 3478
money from the sons of **I** and **Ex 30:16** 3478
memorial for the sons of **I** before **Ex 30:16** 3478
You shall speak to the sons of **I**, **Ex 30:31** 3478
for you, speak to the sons of **I**, **Ex 31:13** 3478
sons of **I** shall observe the sabbath, **Ex 31:16** 3478
sign between Me and the sons of **I** **Ex 31:17** 3478
"This is your god, O **I**, **Ex 32:4** 3478
'This is your god, O **I**, **Ex 32:8** 3478
"Remember Abraham, Isaac, and **I**, **Ex 32:13** 3478
and made the sons of **I** drink *it*. **Ex 32:20** 3478
"Thus says the LORD, the God of **I**, **Ex 32:27** 3478
"Say to the sons of **I**, **Ex 33:5** 3478
So the sons of **I** stripped **Ex 33:6** 3478
before the Lord GOD, the God of **I**. **Ex 34:23** 3478
a covenant with you and with **I**." **Ex 34:27** 3478
and all the sons of **I** saw Moses, **Ex 34:30** 3478
all the sons of **I** came near, **Ex 34:32** 3478
he came out and spoke to the sons of **I** **Ex 34:34** 3478
sons of **I** would see the face of **Ex 34:35** 3478
the congregation of the sons of **I**, **Ex 35:1** 3478
the congregation of the sons of **I**, **Ex 35:4** 3478
all the congregation of the sons of **I** **Ex 35:20** 3478
Then Moses said to the sons of **I**, **Ex 35:30** 3478
contributions which the sons of **I** had **Ex 36:3** 3478
to the names of the sons of **I**. **Ex 39:6** 3478
memorial stones for the sons of **I**, **Ex 39:7** 3478
to the names of the sons of **I**; **Ex 39:14** 3478
and the sons of **I** did according to **Ex 39:32** 3478
So the sons of **I** did all the work **Ex 39:42** 3478
the sons of **I** would set out; **Ex 40:36** 3478
the sight of all the house of **I**. **Ex 40:38** 3478
"Speak to the sons of **I** and say to **Lv 1:2** 3478
"Speak to the sons of **I**, **Lv 4:2** 3478
congregation of **I** commits error and **Lv 4:13** 3478
"Speak to the sons of **I**, **Lv 7:23** 3478

“Speak to the sons of I, Lv 7:29 3478
the contribution from the sons of I Lv 7:34 3478
due forever from the sons of I. Lv 7:34 3478
to be given them from the sons of I Lv 7:36 3478
commanded the sons of I to present Lv 7:38 3478
and his sons and the elders of I; Lv 9:1 3478
to the sons of I you shall speak, Lv 9:3 3478
kinsmen, the whole house of I, Lv 10:6 3478
and so as to teach the sons of I Lv 10:11 3478
peace offerings of the sons of I. Lv 10:14 3478
“Speak to the sons of I, Lv 11:2 3478
“Speak to the sons of I, Lv 12:2 3478
“Speak to the sons of I, Lv 15:2 3478
you shall keep the sons of I separated Lv 15:31 3478
from the congregation of the sons of I Lv 16:5 3478
the impurities of the sons of I and Lv 16:16 3478
and for all the assembly of I. Lv 16:17 3478
from the impurities of the sons of I Lv 16:19 3478
the iniquities of the sons of I and Lv 16:21 3478
to make atonement for the sons of I Lv 16:34 3478
sons and to all the sons of I Lv 17:2 3478
house of I who slaughters an ox or Lv 17:3 3478
sons of I may bring their sacrifices Lv 17:5 3478
‘Any man from the house of I, Lv 17:8 3478
‘And any man from the house of I, Lv 17:10 3478
“Therefore I said to the sons of I, Lv 17:12 3478
when any man from the sons of I, Lv 17:13 3478
Therefore I said to the sons of I, Lv 17:14 3478
“Speak to the sons of I and say to Lv 18:2 3478
all the congregation of the sons of I Lv 19:2 3478
shall also say to the sons of I: Lv 20:2 3478
‘Any man from the sons of I or Lv 20:2 3478
from the aliens sojourning in I who Lv 20:2 3478
his sons and to all the sons of I. Lv 21:24 3478
the holy *gifts* of the sons of I, Lv 22:2 3478
sons of I dedicate to the LORD, Lv 22:3 3478
the holy *gifts* of the sons of I which Lv 22:15 3478
his sons and to all the sons of I and Lv 22:18 3478
‘Any man of the house of I or of Lv 22:18 3478
aliens in I who presents his offering Lv 22:18 3478
be sanctified among the sons of I; Lv 22:32 3478
“Speak to the sons of I and Lv 23:2 3478
“Speak to the sons of I and Lv 23:10 3478
“Speak to the sons of I, Lv 23:24 3478
“Speak to the sons of I, Lv 23:34 3478
native-born in I shall live in booths Lv 23:42 3478
I had the sons of I live in booths Lv 23:43 3478
Moses declared to the sons of I the Lv 23:44 3478
“Command the sons of I that they Lv 24:2 3478
covenant for the sons of I. Lv 24:8 3478
went out among the sons of I; Lv 24:10 3478
woman’s son and a man of I struggled Lv 24:10 3481
You shall speak to the sons of I, Lv 24:15 3478
Then Moses spoke to the sons of I, Lv 24:23 3478
Thus the sons of I did, Lv 24:23 3478
“Speak to the sons of I and Lv 25:2 3478
possession among the sons of I. Lv 25:33 3478
to your countrymen, the sons of I, Lv 25:46 3478
‘For the sons of I are My servants; Lv 25:55 3478
between Himself and the sons of I Lv 26:46 3478
“Speak to the sons of I and Lv 27:2 3478
commanded Moses for the sons of I Lv 27:34 3478
the congregation of the sons of I, Nu 1:2 3478
is able to go out to war in I, Nu 1:3 3478
the heads of divisions of I.” Nu 1:16 3478
numbered, with the leaders of I, Nu 1:44 3478
the numbered men of the sons of I Nu 1:45 3478
was able to go out to war in I, Nu 1:45 3478
their census among the sons of I. Nu 1:49 3478
“The sons of I shall camp, Nu 1:52 3478
the congregation of the sons of I. Nu 1:53 3478
Thus the sons of I did; Nu 1:54 3478
“The sons of I shall camp, each Nu 2:2 3478
the numbered men of the sons of I Nu 2:32 3478
not numbered among the sons of I, Nu 2:33 3478
Thus the sons of I did; Nu 2:34 3478
with the duties of the sons of I, Nu 3:8 3478
to him from among the sons of I. Nu 3:9 3478
Levites from among the sons of I Nu 3:12 3478
of the womb among the sons of I. Nu 3:12 3478
to Myself all the firstborn in I, Nu 3:13 3478
the obligation of the sons of I; Nu 3:38 3478
firstborn male of the sons of I Nu 3:40 3478
the firstborn among the sons of I, Nu 3:41 3478
the cattle of the sons of I.” Nu 3:41 3478
the firstborn among the sons of I, Nu 3:42 3478
the firstborn among the sons of I Nu 3:45 3478
273 of the firstborn of the sons of I Nu 3:46 3478
from the firstborn of the sons of I Nu 3:50 3478
and the leaders of I numbered, Nu 4:46 3478
“Command the sons of I that they Nu 5:2 3478
The sons of I did so and sent Nu 5:4 3478
to Moses, thus the sons of I did. Nu 5:4 3478
“Speak to the sons of I, Nu 5:6 3478
the holy *gifts* of the sons of I, Nu 5:9 3478
“Speak to the sons of I and Nu 5:12 3478
“Speak to the sons of I and Nu 6:2 3478
you shall bless the sons of I. Nu 6:23 3478
invoke My name on the sons of I, Nu 6:27 3478
Then the leaders of I, Nu 7:2 3478
for the altar from the leaders of I Nu 7:84 3478
Levites from among the sons of I Nu 8:6 3478
congregation of the sons of I, Nu 8:9 3478
the sons of I shall lay their hands Nu 8:10 3478
wave offering from the sons of I, Nu 8:11 3478
Levites from among the sons of I, Nu 8:14 3478
to Me from among the sons of I. Nu 8:16 3478
firstborn of all the sons of I. Nu 8:16 3478
every firstborn among the sons of I Nu 8:17 3478

every firstborn among the sons of I Nu 8:18 3478
his sons from among the sons of I, Nu 8:19 3478
perform the service of the sons of I Nu 8:19 3478
on behalf of the sons of I, Nu 8:19 3478
be no plague among the sons of I Nu 8:19 3478
all the congregation of the sons of I Nu 8:20 3478
so the sons of I did to them. Nu 8:20 3478
the sons of I observe the Passover Nu 9:2 3478
sons of I to observe the Passover. Nu 9:4 3478
Moses, so the sons of I did. Nu 9:5 3478
time among the sons of I?” Nu 9:7 3478
“Speak to the sons of I, Nu 9:10 3478
the sons of I would then set out; Nu 9:17 3478
there the sons of I would camp. Nu 9:17 3478
LORD the sons of I would set out, Nu 9:18 3478
the sons of I would keep the Nu 9:19 3478
the sons of I remained camped and Nu 9:22 3478
the heads of the divisions of I. Nu 10:4 3478
and the sons of I set out on their Nu 10:12 3478
the order of march of the sons of I Nu 10:28 3478
has promised good concerning I.” Nu 10:29 3478
To the myriad thousands of I.” Nu 10:36 3478
the sons of I wept again and said, Nu 11:4 3478
seventy men from the elders of I, Nu 11:16 3478
camp, *both* he and the elders of I. Nu 11:30 3478
am going to give to the sons of I; Nu 13:2 3478
who were heads of the sons of I. Nu 13:3 3478
the sons of I cut down from there. Nu 13:24 3478
all the congregation of the sons of I Nu 13:26 3478
So they gave out to the sons of I Nu 13:32 3478
All the sons of I grumbled Nu 14:2 3478
the congregation of the sons of I. Nu 14:5 3478
the congregation of the sons of I, Nu 14:7 3478
of meeting to all the sons of I. Nu 14:10 3478
the complaints of the sons of I, Nu 14:27 3478
these words to all the sons of I, Nu 14:39 3478
“Speak to the sons of I and Nu 15:2 3478
“Speak to the sons of I and Nu 15:18 3478
the congregation of the sons of I, Nu 15:25 3478
all the congregation of the sons of I Nu 15:26 3478
him who is native among the sons of I Nu 15:29 3478
sons of I were in the wilderness, Nu 15:32 3478
“Speak to the sons of I, Nu 15:38 3478
with some of the sons of I, Nu 16:2 3478
the God of I has separated you from Nu 16:9 3478
the *rest of* the congregation of I, Nu 16:9 3478
the elders of I following him, Nu 16:25 3478
All I who *were* around them Nu 16:34 3478
be for a sign to the sons of I.” Nu 16:38 3478
as a reminder to the sons of I Nu 16:40 3478
the sons of I grumbled against Moses Nu 16:41 3478
“Speak to the sons of I, Nu 17:2 3478
the grumblings of the sons of I, Nu 17:5 3478
therefore spoke to the sons of I, Nu 17:6 3478
of the LORD to all the sons of I; Nu 17:9 3478
Then the sons of I spoke to Moses, Nu 17:12 3478
longer be wrath on the sons of I. Nu 18:5 3478
Levites from among the sons of I; Nu 18:6 3478
the holy gifts of the sons of I I Nu 18:8 3478
wave offerings of the sons of I; Nu 18:11 3478
devoted thing in I shall be yours. Nu 18:14 3478
the sons of I offer to the LORD, Nu 18:19 3478
inheritance among the sons of I. Nu 18:20 3478
I have given all the tithe in I for an Nu 18:21 3478
“The sons of I shall not come Nu 18:22 3478
and among the sons of I they shall Nu 18:23 3478
“For the tithe of the sons of I, Nu 18:24 3478
no inheritance among the sons of I Nu 18:24 3478
‘When you take from the sons of I Nu 18:26 3478
you receive from the sons of I; Nu 18:28 3478
the sacred gifts of the sons of I, Nu 18:32 3478
‘Speak to the sons of I that they Nu 19:2 3478
the sons of I shall keep it as water Nu 19:9 3478
a perpetual statute to the sons of I Nu 19:10 3478
person shall be cut off from I. Nu 19:13 3478
sons of I, the whole congregation, Nu 20:1 3478
in the sight of the sons of I, Nu 20:12 3478
sons of I contended with the LORD, Nu 20:13 3478
“Thus your brother I has said, Nu 20:14 3478
Again, the sons of I said to him, Nu 20:19 3478
Edom refused to allow I to pass Nu 20:21 3478
so I turned away from him. Nu 20:21 3478
sons of I, the whole congregation, Nu 20:22 3478
I have given to the sons of I, Nu 20:24 3478
all the house of I wept for Aaron Nu 20:29 3478
heard that I was coming by the way Nu 21:1 3478
Atharim, then he fought against I and Nu 21:1 3478
So I made a vow to the LORD and Nu 21:2 3478
The LORD heard the voice of I and Nu 21:3 3478
so that many people of I died. Nu 21:6 3478
sons of I moved out and camped in Nu 21:10 3478
Then I sang this song: Nu 21:17 3478
Then I sent messengers to Sihon, Nu 21:21 3478
Sihon would not permit I to pass Nu 21:23 3478
went out against I in the wilderness Nu 21:23 3478
to Jahaz and fought against I. Nu 21:23 3478
Then I struck him with the edge of Nu 21:24 3478
I took all these cities and Nu 21:25 3478
I lived in all the cities of the Amorites Nu 21:25 3478
I lived in the land of the Amorites. Nu 21:31 3478
Then the sons of I journeyed, Nu 22:1 3478
that I had done to the Amorites. Nu 22:2 3478
Moab was in dread of the sons of I. Nu 22:3 3478
for me, And come, denounce I!’ Nu 23:7 3478
Or number the fourth part of I? Nu 23:10 3478
Nor has He seen trouble in I; Nu 23:21 3478
is there any divination against I; Nu 23:23 3478
shall be said to Jacob And to I, Nu 23:23 3478
it pleased the LORD to bless I, Nu 24:1 3478

and saw I camping tribe by tribe; Nu 24:2 3478
O Jacob, Your dwellings, O I! Nu 24:5 3478
A scepter shall rise from I, Nu 24:17 3478
While I performs valiantly. Nu 24:18 3478
While I remained at Shittim, the Nu 25:1 3478
So I joined themselves to Baal of Nu 25:3 3478
and the LORD was angry against I. Nu 25:3 3478
the LORD may turn away from I.” Nu 25:4 3478
So Moses said to the judges of I, Nu 25:5 3478
one of the sons of I came and Nu 25:6 3478
the congregation of the sons of I, Nu 25:6 3478
went after the man of I into the tent Nu 25:8 3478
the man of I and the woman, Nu 25:8 3478
plague on the sons of I was checked Nu 25:8 3478
away My wrath from the sons of I in Nu 25:11 3478
did not destroy the sons of I in My Nu 25:11 3478
atonement for the sons of I.’ ” Nu 25:13 3478
the name of the slain man of I who Nu 25:14 3478
all the congregation of the sons of I Nu 26:2 3478
is able to go out to war in I.” Nu 26:2 3478
Now the sons of I who came out of Nu 26:4 3478
were numbered of the sons of I, Nu 26:51 3478
not numbered among the sons of I Nu 26:62 3478
given to them among the sons of I. Nu 26:62 3478
who numbered the sons of I in the Nu 26:63 3478
priest, who numbered the sons of I Nu 26:64 3478
you shall speak to the sons of I, Nu 27:8 3478
ordinance to the sons of I, Nu 27:11 3478
I have given to the sons of I. Nu 27:12 3478
all the congregation of the sons of I Nu 27:20 3478
he and the sons of I with him, Nu 27:21 3478
“Command the sons of I and say to Nu 28:2 3478
Moses spoke to the sons of I Nu 29:40 3478
heads of the tribes of the sons of I, Nu 30:1 3478
full vengeance for the sons of I on Nu 31:2 3478
from each tribe of all the tribes of I Nu 31:4 3478
furnished from the thousands of I, Nu 31:5 3478
sons of I captured the women of Nu 31:9 3478
the congregation of the sons of I, Nu 31:12 3478
these caused the sons of I, Nu 31:16 3478
memorial for the sons of I before Nu 31:54 3478
before the congregation of I, Nu 32:4 3478
discouraging the sons of I from Nu 32:7 3478
they discouraged the sons of I so Nu 32:9 3478
the LORD’s anger burned against I, Nu 32:13 3478
anger of the LORD against I. Nu 32:14 3478
ready *to go* before the sons of I, Nu 32:17 3478
until every one of the sons of I has Nu 32:18 3478
toward the LORD and toward I, Nu 32:22 3478
of the tribes of the sons of I. Nu 32:28 3478
are the journeys of the sons of I, Nu 33:1 3478
the sons of I started out boldly Nu 33:3 3478
sons of I journeyed from Rameses and Nu 33:5 3478
after the sons of I had come from the Nu 33:38 3478
of the coming of the sons of I. Nu 33:40 3478
“Speak to the sons of I and say to Nu 33:51 3478
“Command the sons of I and say to Nu 34:2 3478
So Moses commanded the sons of I, Nu 34:13 3478
the inheritance to the sons of I in Nu 34:29 3478
“Command the sons of I that they Nu 35:2 3478
the possession of the sons of I, Nu 35:8 3478
“Speak to the sons of I and say to Nu 35:10 3478
be for refuge for the sons of I, Nu 35:15 3478
in the midst of the sons of I.’ ” Nu 35:34 3478
households of the sons of I, Nu 36:1 3478
give the land by lot to the sons of I Nu 36:2 3478
the *other* tribes of the sons of I, Nu 36:3 3478
jubilee of the sons of I comes, Nu 36:4 3478
Moses commanded the sons of I Nu 36:5 3478
no inheritance of the sons of I shall be Nu 36:7 3478
for the sons of I shall each hold Nu 36:7 3478
of any tribe of the sons of I shall Nu 36:8 3478
the sons of I each may possess the Nu 36:8 3478
for the tribes of the sons of I Nu 36:9 3478
the LORD commanded to the sons of I Nu 36:13 3478
Moses spoke to all I across the Jordan Dt 1:1 3478
Moses spoke to the children of I, Dt 1:3 3478
he will cause I to inherit it. Dt 1:38 3478
as I did to the land of their possession Dt 2:12 3478
your brothers, the sons of I. Dt 3:18 3478
“Now, O I, listen to the statutes Dt 4:1 3478
Moses set before the sons of I; Dt 4:44 3478
Moses spoke to the sons of I, Dt 4:45 3478
Moses and the sons of I defeated Dt 4:46 3478
Then Moses summoned all I and Dt 5:1 3478
“Hear, O I, the statutes and the Dt 5:1 3478
“O I, you should listen and be Dt 6:3 3478
“Hear, O I! The LORD is our God, Dt 6:4 3478
O I! You are crossing over the Jordan Dt 9:1 3478
(Now the sons of I set out from Dt 10:6 3478
“Now, I, what does the LORD Dt 10:12 3478
that followed them, among all I Dt 11:6 3478
all I will hear and be afraid, Dt 13:11 3478
detestable thing has been done in I, Dt 17:4 3478
you shall purge the evil from I. Dt 17:12 3478
in his kingdom in the midst of I. Dt 17:20 3478
no portion or inheritance with I; Dt 18:1 3478
throughout I where he resides, Dt 18:6 3478
the blood of the innocent from I, Dt 19:13 3478
‘Hear, O I, you are approaching Dt 20:3 3478
‘Forgive Your people I whom You Dt 21:8 3478
in the midst of Your people I.’ Dt 21:8 3478
all I will hear *of it* and fear. Dt 21:21 3478
he publicly defamed a virgin of I. Dt 22:19 3478
committed an act of folly in I by Dt 22:21 3478
you shall purge the evil from I. Dt 22:22 3478
“None of the daughters of I shall be Dt 23:17 3478
nor shall any of the sons of I be a cult Dt 23:17 3478
his countrymen of the sons of I, Dt 24:7 3478

will not be blotted out from **I**.	**Dt 25:6**	3478
a name for his brother in **I**;	**Dt 25:7**	3478
"In **I** his name shall be	**Dt 25:10**	3478
heaven, and bless Your people **I**,	**Dt 26:15**	3478
elders of **I** charged the people,	**Dt 27:1**	3478
Levitical priests spoke to all **I**,	**Dt 27:9**	3478
"Be silent and listen, O **I**!	**Dt 27:9**	3478
say to all the men of **I** with a loud	**Dt 27:14**	3478
Moses to make with the sons of **I**	**Dt 29:1**	3478
Moses summoned all **I** and said to	**Dt 29:2**	3478
officers, *even* all the men of **I**,	**Dt 29:10**	3478
from all the tribes of **I**,	**Dt 29:21**	3478
and spoke these words to all **I**.	**Dt 31:1**	3478
said to him in the sight of all **I**,	**Dt 31:7**	3478
LORD, and to all the elders of **I**.	**Dt 31:9**	3478
when all **I** comes to appear before	**Dt 31:11**	3478
shall read this law in front of all **I**	**Dt 31:11**	3478
and teach it to the sons of **I**;	**Dt 31:19**	3478
witness for Me against the sons of **I**	**Dt 31:19**	3478
and taught it to the sons of **I**.	**Dt 31:22**	3478
you shall bring the sons of **I** into the	**Dt 31:23**	3478
the hearing of all the assembly of **I**	**Dt 31:30**	3478
to the number of the sons of **I**.	**Dt 32:8**	3478
speaking all these words to all **I**,	**Dt 32:45**	3478
which I am giving to the sons of **I**	**Dt 32:49**	3478
with Me in the midst of the sons of **I**	**Dt 32:51**	3478
in the midst of the sons of **I**.	**Dt 32:51**	3478
which I am giving the sons of **I**."	**Dt 32:52**	3478
man of God blessed the sons of **I**	**Dt 33:1**	3478
The tribes of **I** together.	**Dt 33:5**	3478
to Jacob, And Your law to **I**.	**Dt 33:10**	3478
LORD, And His ordinances with **I**."	**Dt 33:21**	3478
"So **I** dwells in security, The	**Dt 33:28**	3478
"Blessed are you, O **I**;	**Dt 33:29**	3478
So the sons of **I** wept for Moses in	**Dt 34:8**	3478
and the sons of **I** listened to him	**Dt 34:9**	3478
no prophet has risen in **I** like Moses	**Dt 34:10**	3478
performed in the sight of all **I**.	**Dt 34:12**	3478
giving to them, to the sons of **I**.	**Jos 1:2**	3478
men from the sons of **I** have come	**Jos 2:2**	3478
he and all the sons of **I** set out from	**Jos 3:1**	3478
exalt you in the sight of all **I**,	**Jos 3:7**	3478
Then Joshua said to the sons of **I**,	**Jos 3:9**	3478
twelve men from the tribes of **I**,	**Jos 3:12**	3478
while all **I** crossed on dry ground,	**Jos 3:17**	3478
had appointed from the sons of **I**,	**Jos 4:4**	3478
of the tribes of the sons of **I**.	**Jos 4:5**	3478
to the sons of **I** forever."	**Jos 4:7**	3478
Thus the sons of **I** did as	**Jos 4:8**	3478
of the tribes of the sons of **I**;	**Jos 4:8**	3478
battle array before the sons of **I**,	**Jos 4:12**	3478
Joshua in the sight of all **I**;	**Jos 4:14**	3478
He said to the sons of **I**,	**Jos 4:21**	3478
I crossed this Jordan on dry ground.	**Jos 4:22**	3478
sons of **I** until they had crossed,	**Jos 5:1**	3478
longer because of the sons of **I**.	**Jos 5:1**	3478
circumcise again the sons of **I**	**Jos 5:2**	3478
circumcised the sons of **I** at	**Jos 5:3**	3478
the sons of **I** walked forty years in	**Jos 5:6**	3478
the sons of **I** camped at Gilgal they	**Jos 5:10**	3478
the sons of **I** no longer had manna,	**Jos 5:12**	3478
shut because of the sons of **I**;	**Jos 6:1**	3478
and make the camp of **I** accursed	**Jos 6:18**	3478
placed them outside the camp of **I**.	**Jos 6:23**	3478
she has lived in the midst of **I**	**Jos 6:25**	3478
the sons of **I** acted unfaithfully in	**Jos 7:1**	3478
LORD burned against the sons of **I**.	**Jos 7:1**	3478
both he and the elders of **I**;	**Jos 7:6**	3478
I has turned *their* back before their	**Jos 7:8**	3478
"**I** has sinned, and they have also	**Jos 7:11**	3478
sons of **I** cannot stand before their	**Jos 7:12**	3478
for thus the LORD, the God of **I**,	**Jos 7:13**	3478
under the ban in your midst, O **I**.	**Jos 7:13**	3478
committed a disgraceful thing in **I**	**Jos 7:15**	3478
and brought **I** near by tribes,	**Jos 7:16**	3478
glory to the LORD, the God of **I**,	**Jos 7:19**	3478
against the LORD, the God of **I**,	**Jos 7:20**	3478
Joshua and to all the sons of **I**,	**Jos 7:23**	3478
Then Joshua and all **I** with him,	**Jos 7:24**	3478
And all **I** stoned them with stones;	**Jos 7:25**	3478
he went up with the elders of **I**	**Jos 8:10**	3478
and went out to meet **I** in battle,	**Jos 8:14**	3478
all **I** pretended to be beaten before	**Jos 8:15**	3478
who had not gone out after **I**,	**Jos 8:17**	3478
the city unguarded and pursued **I**.	**Jos 8:17**	3478
When Joshua and all **I** saw that the	**Jos 8:21**	3478
were *trapped* in the midst of **I**,	**Jos 8:22**	3478
when **I** had finished killing all the	**Jos 8:24**	3478
then all **I** returned to Ai and	**Jos 8:24**	3478
I took only the cattle and the	**Jos 8:27**	3478
altar to the LORD, the God of **I**,	**Jos 8:30**	3478
LORD had commanded the sons of **I**,	**Jos 8:31**	3478
in the presence of the sons of **I**.	**Jos 8:32**	3478
All **I** with their elders and	**Jos 8:33**	3478
at first to bless the people of **I**.	**Jos 8:33**	3478
not read before all the assembly of **I**	**Jos 8:35**	3478
to fight with Joshua and with **I**.	**Jos 9:2**	3478
said to him and to the men of **I**,	**Jos 9:6**	3478
The men of **I** said to the Hivites,	**Jos 9:7**	3478
So the men *of* **I** took some of	**Jos 9:14**	3478
Then the sons of **I** set out and	**Jos 9:17**	3478
The sons of **I** did not strike	**Jos 9:18**	3478
to them by the LORD the God of **I**.	**Jos 9:18**	3478
to them by the LORD, the God of **I**,	**Jos 9:19**	3478
from the hands of the sons of **I**,	**Jos 9:26**	3478
Gibeon had made peace with **I** and	**Jos 10:1**	3478
Joshua and with the sons of **I**."	**Jos 10:4**	3478
the LORD confounded them before **I**,	**Jos 10:10**	3478
As they fled from before **I**,	**Jos 10:11**	3478
sons of **I** killed with the sword.	**Jos 10:11**	3478
the Amorites before the sons of **I**,	**Jos 10:12**	3478
and he said in the sight of **I**,	**Jos 10:12**	3478
for the LORD fought for **I**.	**Jos 10:14**	3478
Then Joshua and all **I** with him	**Jos 10:15**	3478
Joshua and the sons of **I** had finished	**Jos 10:20**	3478
word against any of the sons of **I**.	**Jos 10:21**	3478
called for all the men of **I**,	**Jos 10:24**	3478
Then Joshua and all **I** with him	**Jos 10:29**	3478
with its king into the hands of **I**,	**Jos 10:30**	3478
And Joshua and all **I** with him	**Jos 10:31**	3478
gave Lachish into the hands of **I**;	**Jos 10:32**	3478
And Joshua and all **I** with him	**Jos 10:34**	3478
Joshua and all **I** with him went up	**Jos 10:36**	3478
Joshua and all **I** with him returned	**Jos 10:38**	3478
just as the LORD, the God of **I**,	**Jos 10:40**	3478
because the LORD, the God of **I**,	**Jos 10:42**	3478
the God of Israel, fought for **I**.	**Jos 10:42**	3478
Joshua and all **I** with him returned	**Jos 10:43**	3478
of Merom, to fight against **I**.	**Jos 11:5**	3478
deliver all of them slain before **I**;	**Jos 11:6**	3478
delivered them into the hand of **I**,	**Jos 11:8**	3478
I did not burn any cities that	**Jos 11:13**	3478
sons of **I** took as their plunder;	**Jos 11:14**	3478
hill country of **I** and its lowland	**Jos 11:16**	3478
which made peace with the sons of **I**	**Jos 11:19**	3478
to meet **I** in battle in order that	**Jos 11:20**	3478
from all the hill country of **I**.	**Jos 11:21**	3478
left in the land of the sons of **I**;	**Jos 11:22**	3478
Joshua gave it for an inheritance to **I**	**Jos 11:23**	3478
land whom the sons of **I** defeated,	**Jos 12:1**	3478
and the sons of **I** defeated them;	**Jos 12:6**	3478
Joshua and the sons of **I** defeated	**Jos 12:7**	3478
and Joshua gave it to the tribes of **I**	**Jos 12:7**	3478
out from before the sons of **I**;	**Jos 13:6**	3478
only allot it to **I** for an inheritance	**Jos 13:6**	3478
the sons of **I** did not dispossess the	**Jos 13:13**	3478
live among **I** until this day.	**Jos 13:13**	3478
by fire to the LORD, the God of **I**,	**Jos 13:14**	3478
The sons of **I** also killed Balaam	**Jos 13:22**	3478
the God of **I**, is their inheritance,	**Jos 13:33**	3478
territories which the sons of **I** inherited	**Jos 14:1**	3478
tribes of the sons of **I** apportioned	**Jos 14:1**	3478
sons of **I** did just as the LORD had	**Jos 14:5**	3478
when **I** walked in the wilderness;	**Jos 14:10**	3478
followed the LORD God of **I** fully.	**Jos 14:14**	3478
when the sons of **I** became strong,	**Jos 17:13**	3478
whole congregation of the sons of **I**	**Jos 18:1**	3478
There remained among the sons of **I**	**Jos 18:2**	3478
So Joshua said to the sons of **I**,	**Jos 18:3**	3478
divided the land to the sons of **I**	**Jos 18:10**	3478
the sons of **I** gave an inheritance	**Jos 19:49**	3478
the tribes of the sons of **I** distributed	**Jos 19:51**	3478
"Speak to the sons of **I**,	**Jos 20:2**	3478
appointed cities for all the sons of **I**	**Jos 20:9**	3478
of the tribes of the sons of **I**.	**Jos 21:1**	3478
So the sons of **I** gave the Levites	**Jos 21:3**	3478
sons of **I** gave by lot to the Levites	**Jos 21:8**	3478
of the possession of the sons of **I** were	**Jos 21:41**	3478
So the LORD gave **I** all the land	**Jos 21:43**	3478
LORD had made to the house of **I**	**Jos 21:45**	3478
departed from the sons of **I** at Shiloh	**Jos 22:9**	3478
And the sons of **I** heard *it* said,	**Jos 22:11**	3478
side *belonging to* the sons of **I**."	**Jos 22:11**	3478
When the sons of **I** heard *of it*,	**Jos 22:12**	3478
whole congregation of the sons of **I**	**Jos 22:12**	3478
sons of **I** sent to the sons of Reuben	**Jos 22:13**	3478
from each of the tribes of **I**;	**Jos 22:14**	3478
among the thousands of **I**.	**Jos 22:14**	3478
committed against the God of **I**,	**Jos 22:16**	3478
whole congregation of **I** tomorrow.	**Jos 22:18**	3478
fall on all the congregation of **I**?	**Jos 22:20**	3478
to the heads of the families of **I**.	**Jos 22:21**	3478
He knows, and may **I** itself know.	**Jos 22:22**	3478
to do with the LORD, the God of **I**?	**Jos 22:24**	3478
heads of the families of **I** who *were*	**Jos 22:30**	3478
you have delivered the sons of **I**	**Jos 22:31**	3478
land of Canaan, to the sons of **I**,	**Jos 22:32**	3478
The word pleased the sons of **I**,	**Jos 22:33**	3478
and the sons of **I** blessed God;	**Jos 22:33**	3478
when the LORD had given rest to **I**	**Jos 23:1**	3478
that Joshua called for all **I**,	**Jos 23:2**	3478
Joshua gathered all the tribes of **I**	**Jos 24:1**	3478
and called for the elders of **I** and	**Jos 24:1**	3478
"Thus says the LORD, the God of **I**,	**Jos 24:2**	3478
Moab, arose and fought against **I**,	**Jos 24:9**	3478
to the LORD, the God of **I**."	**Jos 24:23**	3478
I served the LORD all the days	**Jos 24:31**	3478
the LORD which He had done for **I**.	**Jos 24:31**	3478
sons of **I** brought up from Egypt,	**Jos 24:32**	3478
sons of **I** inquired of the LORD,	**Jg 1:1**	3478
came about when **I** became strong,	**Jg 1:28**	3478
these words to all the sons of **I**,	**Jg 2:4**	3478
the sons of **I** went each to his	**Jg 2:6**	3478
the LORD which He had done for **I**.	**Jg 2:7**	3478
the work which He had done for **I**.	**Jg 2:10**	3478
Then the sons of **I** did evil in the	**Jg 2:11**	3478
anger of the LORD burned against **I**	**Jg 2:14**	3478
anger of the LORD burned against **I**	**Jg 2:20**	3478
in order to test **I** by them,	**Jg 2:22**	3478
the LORD left, to test **I** by them	**Jg 3:1**	3478
the sons of **I** might be taught war,	**Jg 3:2**	3478
They were for testing **I**,	**Jg 3:4**	3478
The sons of **I** lived among the	**Jg 3:5**	3478
The sons of **I** did what was evil in	**Jg 3:7**	3478
of the LORD was kindled against **I**,	**Jg 3:8**	3478
sons of **I** served Cushan-rishathaim	**Jg 3:8**	3478
the sons of **I** cried to the LORD,	**Jg 3:9**	3478
deliverer for the sons of **I** to deliver	**Jg 3:9**	3478
came upon him, and he judged **I**.	**Jg 3:10**	3478
Now the sons of **I** again did evil	**Jg 3:12**	3478
Eglon the king of Moab against **I**,	**Jg 3:12**	3478
and he went and defeated **I**,	**Jg 3:13**	3478
The sons of **I** served Eglon the	**Jg 3:14**	3478
the sons of **I** cried to the LORD,	**Jg 3:15**	3478
And the sons of **I** sent tribute by	**Jg 3:15**	3478
and the sons of **I** went down with	**Jg 3:27**	3478
that day under the hand of **I**.	**Jg 3:30**	3478
and he also saved **I**.	**Jg 3:31**	3478
Then the sons of **I** again did evil	**Jg 4:1**	3478
The sons of **I** cried to the LORD;	**Jg 4:3**	3478
he oppressed the sons of **I** severely	**Jg 4:3**	3478
was judging **I** at that time.	**Jg 4:4**	3478
the sons of **I** came up to her for	**Jg 4:5**	3478
"Behold, the LORD, the God of **I**,	**Jg 4:6**	3478
of Canaan before the sons of **I**.	**Jg 4:23**	3478
The hand of the sons of **I** pressed	**Jg 4:24**	3478
"That the leaders led in **I**,	**Jg 5:2**	3478
praise to the LORD, the God of **I**.	**Jg 5:3**	3478
of the LORD, the God of **I**.	**Jg 5:5**	3478
peasantry ceased, they ceased in **I**,	**Jg 5:7**	3478
Until I arose, a mother in **I**.	**Jg 5:7**	3478
seen Among forty thousand in **I**.	**Jg 5:8**	3478
goes out to the commanders of **I**,	**Jg 5:9**	3478
deeds for His peasantry in **I**.	**Jg 5:11**	3478
the sons of **I** did what was evil in	**Jg 6:1**	3478
power of Midian prevailed against **I**.	**Jg 6:2**	3478
Because of Midian the sons of **I**	**Jg 6:2**	3478
For it was when **I** had sown, that	**Jg 6:3**	3478
leave no sustenance in **I** as well as	**Jg 6:4**	3478
So **I** was brought very low because	**Jg 6:6**	3478
the sons of **I** cried to the LORD.	**Jg 6:6**	3478
when the sons of **I** cried to the LORD	**Jg 6:7**	3478
sent a prophet to the sons of **I**,	**Jg 6:8**	3478
"Thus says the LORD, the God of **I**,	**Jg 6:8**	3478
deliver **I** from the hand of Midian.	**Jg 6:14**	3478
"O Lord, how shall I deliver **I**?	**Jg 6:15**	3478
"If You will deliver **I** through me,	**Jg 6:36**	3478
You will deliver **I** through me,	**Jg 6:37**	3478
hands, for **I** would become boastful,	**Jg 7:2**	3478
Gideon sent all the *other* men of **I**,	**Jg 7:8**	3478
the son of Joash, a man of **I**;	**Jg 7:14**	3478
He returned to the camp of **I** and	**Jg 7:15**	3478
The men of **I** were summoned	**Jg 7:23**	3478
Then the men of **I** said to Gideon,	**Jg 8:22**	3478
and all **I** played the harlot with	**Jg 8:27**	3478
was subdued before the sons of **I**,	**Jg 8:28**	3478
sons of **I** again played the harlot	**Jg 8:33**	3478
sons of **I** did not remember the	**Jg 8:34**	3478
the good that he had done to **I**.	**Jg 8:35**	3478
Abimelech ruled over **I** three years.	**Jg 9:22**	3478
men of **I** saw that Abimelech was	**Jg 9:55**	3478
man of Issachar, arose to save **I**;	**Jg 10:1**	3478
He judged **I** twenty-three years.	**Jg 10:2**	3478
and judged **I** twenty-two years.	**Jg 10:3**	3478
Then the sons of **I** again did evil	**Jg 10:6**	3478
anger of the LORD burned against **I**	**Jg 10:7**	3478
crushed the sons of **I** that year;	**Jg 10:8**	3478
they *afflicted* all the sons of **I** who	**Jg 10:8**	3478
so that **I** was greatly distressed.	**Jg 10:9**	3478
sons of **I** cried out to the LORD,	**Jg 10:10**	3478
The LORD said to the sons of **I**,	**Jg 10:11**	3478
The sons of **I** said to the LORD,	**Jg 10:15**	3478
bear the misery of **I** no longer.	**Jg 10:16**	3478
the sons of **I** gathered together and	**Jg 10:17**	3478
sons of Ammon fought against **I**.	**Jg 11:4**	3478
the sons of Ammon fought against **I**	**Jg 11:5**	3478
"Because **I** took away my land when	**Jg 11:13**	3478
'**I** did not take away the land of	**Jg 11:15**	3478
and **I** went through the wilderness	**Jg 11:16**	3478
then **I** sent messengers to the king	**Jg 11:17**	3478
So **I** remained at Kadesh.	**Jg 11:17**	3478
'And **I** sent messengers to Sihon	**Jg 11:19**	3478
of Heshbon, and **I** said to him,	**Jg 11:19**	3478
But Sihon did not trust **I** to pass	**Jg 11:20**	3478
in Jahaz and fought with **I**.	**Jg 11:20**	3478
The LORD, the God of **I**, gave Sihon	**Jg 11:21**	3478
all his people into the hand of **I**,	**Jg 11:21**	3478
so **I** possessed all the land of the	**Jg 11:21**	3478
God of **I**, drove out the Amorites	**Jg 11:23**	3478
Amorites from before His people **I**,	**Jg 11:23**	3478
Did he ever strive with **I**,	**Jg 11:25**	3478
'While **I** lived in Heshbon and its	**Jg 11:26**	3478
judge today between the sons of **I**	**Jg 11:27**	3478
were subdued before the sons of **I**.	**Jg 11:33**	3478
Thus it became a custom in **I**,	**Jg 11:39**	3478
that the daughters of **I** went	**Jg 11:40**	3478
Jephthah judged **I** six years.	**Jg 12:7**	3478
Ibzan of Bethlehem judged **I** after	**Jg 12:8**	3478
And he judged **I** seven years.	**Jg 12:9**	3478
Elon the Zebulunite judged **I** after	**Jg 12:11**	3478
and he judged **I** ten years.	**Jg 12:11**	3478
Hillel the Pirathonite judged **I** after	**Jg 12:13**	3478
and he judged **I** eight years.	**Jg 12:14**	3478
Now the sons of **I** again did evil	**Jg 13:1**	3478
and he shall begin to deliver **I**	**Jg 13:5**	3478
Philistines were ruling over **I**.	**Jg 14:4**	3478
So he judged **I** twenty years in the	**Jg 15:20**	3478
Thus he had judged **I** twenty years.	**Jg 16:31**	3478
those days there was no king in **I**;	**Jg 17:6**	3478
those days there was no king of **I**;	**Jg 18:1**	3478
possession among the tribes of **I**.	**Jg 18:1**	3478
to a tribe and a family in **I**?"	**Jg 18:19**	3478
their father who was born in **I**;	**Jg 18:29**	3478
days, when there was no king in **I**,	**Jg 19:1**	3478
who are not of the sons of **I**;	**Jg 19:12**	3478
her throughout the territory of **I**.	**Jg 19:29**	3478
the sons of **I** came up from the land	**Jg 19:30**	3478

sons of **I** from Dan to Beersheba,	**Jg 20:1**	3478
even of all the tribes of **I**,	**Jg 20:2**	3478
sons of **I** had gone up to Mizpah.)	**Jg 20:3**	3478
And the sons of **I** said,	**Jg 20:3**	3478
a lewd and disgraceful act in **I**.	**Jg 20:6**	3478
"Behold, all you sons of **I**,	**Jg 20:7**	3478
of 100 throughout the tribes of **I**,	**Jg 20:10**	3478
that they have committed in **I**."	**Jg 20:10**	3478
the men of **I** were gathered against	**Jg 20:11**	3478
Then the tribes of **I** sent men	**Jg 20:12**	3478
remove *this* wickedness from **I**."	**Jg 20:13**	3478
of their brothers, the sons of **I**.	**Jg 20:13**	3478
to battle against the sons of **I**.	**Jg 20:14**	3478
Then the men of **I** besides Benjamin	**Jg 20:17**	3478
Now the sons of **I** arose, went up	**Jg 20:18**	3478
So the sons of **I** arose in the	**Jg 20:19**	3478
The men of **I** went out to	**Jg 20:20**	3478
and the men of **I** arrayed for	**Jg 20:20**	3478
on that day 22,000 men of **I**.	**Jg 20:21**	3478
But the people, the men of **I**,	**Jg 20:22**	3478
The sons of **I** went up and wept	**Jg 20:23**	3478
Then the sons of **I** came against	**Jg 20:24**	3478
again 18,000 men of the sons of **I**;	**Jg 20:25**	3478
Then all the sons of **I** and all the	**Jg 20:26**	3478
sons of **I** inquired of the LORD	**Jg 20:27**	3478
So **I** set men in ambush around	**Jg 20:29**	3478
The sons of **I** went up against	**Jg 20:30**	3478
the field, about thirty men of **I**.	**Jg 20:31**	3478
But the sons of **I** said,	**Jg 20:32**	3478
Then all the men of **I** arose from	**Jg 20:33**	3478
and the men of **I** in ambush broke	**Jg 20:33**	3478
from all **I** came against Gibeah,	**Jg 20:34**	3478
the LORD struck Benjamin before **I**,	**Jg 20:35**	3478
so that the sons of **I** destroyed	**Jg 20:35**	3478
When the men of **I** gave ground to	**Jg 20:36**	3478
sign between the men of **I** and the	**Jg 20:38**	3478
the men of **I** turned in the battle,	**Jg 20:39**	3478
and kill about thirty men of **I**,	**Jg 20:39**	3478
Then the men of **I** turned, and the	**Jg 20:41**	3478
turned their backs before the men of **I**	**Jg 20:42**	3478
The men of **I** then turned back	**Jg 20:48**	3478
the men of **I** had sworn in Mizpah,	**Jg 21:1**	3478
"Why, O LORD, God of **I**,	**Jg 21:3**	3478
Israel, has this come about in **I**,	**Jg 21:3**	3478
should be *missing* today in **I**?"	**Jg 21:3**	3478
Then the sons of **I** said,	**Jg 21:5**	3478
Who is there among all the tribes of **I**	**Jg 21:5**	3478
And the sons of **I** were sorry for	**Jg 21:6**	3478
"One tribe is cut off from **I** today.	**Jg 21:6**	3478
"What one is there of the tribes of **I**	**Jg 21:8**	3478
made a breach in the tribes of **I**.	**Jg 21:15**	3478
will not be blotted out from **I**.	**Jg 21:17**	3478
For the sons of **I** had sworn,	**Jg 21:18**	3478
The sons of **I** departed from	**Jg 21:24**	3478
those days there was no king in **I**;	**Jg 21:25**	3478
full from the LORD, the God of **I**,	**Ru 2:12**	3478
was *the custom* in former times in **I**	**Ru 4:7**	3478
the *manner of* attestation in **I**.	**Ru 4:7**	3478
both of whom built the house of **I**;	**Ru 4:11**	3478
may his name become famous in **I**.	**Ru 4:14**	3478
and may the God of **I** grant your	**1Sa 1:17**	3478
that his sons were doing to all **I**,	**1Sa 2:22**	3478
choose them from all the tribes of **I**	**1Sa 2:28**	3478
fire *offerings* of the sons of **I**?	**1Sa 2:28**	3478
of every offering of My people **I**?'	**1Sa 2:29**	3478
the LORD God of **I** declares,	**1Sa 2:30**	3478
spite of all the good that I do for **I**;	**1Sa 2:32**	3478
I am about to do a thing in **I** at	**1Sa 3:11**	3478
All **I** from Dan even to Beersheba	**1Sa 3:20**	3478
the word of Samuel came to all **I**.	**1Sa 4:1**	3478
Now **I** went out to meet the	**1Sa 4:1**	3478
drew up in battle array to meet **I**.	**1Sa 4:2**	3478
I was defeated before the	**1Sa 4:2**	3478
the camp, the elders of **I** said,	**1Sa 4:3**	3478
all **I** shouted with a great shout,	**1Sa 4:5**	3478
fought and **I** was defeated,	**1Sa 4:10**	3478
fell of **I** thirty thousand foot soldiers	**1Sa 4:10**	3478
"**I** has fled before the Philistines	**1Sa 4:17**	3478
Thus he judged **I** forty years.	**1Sa 4:18**	3478
"The glory has departed from **I**,"	**1Sa 4:21**	3478
"The glory has departed from **I**,	**1Sa 4:22**	3478
ark of the God of **I** must not remain	**1Sa 5:7**	3478
do with the ark of the God of **I**?"	**1Sa 5:8**	3478
the ark of the God of **I** be brought	**1Sa 5:8**	3478
the ark of the God of **I** *around*.	**1Sa 5:8**	3478
ark of the God of **I** around to us,	**1Sa 5:10**	3478
"Send away the ark of the God of **I**,	**1Sa 5:11**	3478
send away the ark of the God of **I**,	**1Sa 6:3**	3478
shall give glory to the God of **I**;	**1Sa 6:5**	3478
house of **I** lamented after the LORD.	**1Sa 7:2**	3478
Samuel spoke to all the house of **I**,	**1Sa 7:3**	3478
So the sons of **I** removed the Baals	**1Sa 7:4**	3478
"Gather all **I** to Mizpah and I	**1Sa 7:5**	3478
judged the sons of **I** at Mizpah.	**1Sa 7:6**	3478
sons of **I** had gathered to Mizpah,	**1Sa 7:7**	3478
the Philistines went up against **I**.	**1Sa 7:7**	3478
And when the sons of **I** heard it,	**1Sa 7:7**	3478
Then the sons of **I** said to Samuel,	**1Sa 7:8**	3478
Samuel cried to the LORD for **I** and	**1Sa 7:9**	3478
drew near to battle against **I**.	**1Sa 7:10**	3478
so that they were routed before **I**.	**1Sa 7:10**	3478
The men of **I** went out of	**1Sa 7:11**	3478
anymore within the border of **I**.	**1Sa 7:13**	3478
the Philistines had taken from **I**	**1Sa 7:14**	3478
from Israel were restored to **I**,	**1Sa 7:14**	3478
and **I** delivered their territory	**1Sa 7:14**	3478
peace between **I** and the Amorites.	**1Sa 7:14**	3478
judged **I** all the days of his life.	**1Sa 7:15**	3478
he judged **I** in all these places.	**1Sa 7:16**	3478
was there, and there he judged **I**;	**1Sa 7:17**	3478
appointed his sons judges over **I**.	**1Sa 8:1**	3478
Then all the elders of **I** gathered	**1Sa 8:4**	3478
So Samuel said to the men of **I**,	**1Sa 8:22**	3478
than he among the sons of **I**;	**1Sa 9:2**	3478
(Formerly in **I**, when a man went to	**1Sa 9:9**	3478
him to be prince over My people **I**;	**1Sa 9:16**	3478
is all that is desirable in **I**?	**1Sa 9:20**	3478
the smallest of the tribes of **I**,	**1Sa 9:21**	3478
and he said to the sons of **I**,	**1Sa 10:18**	3478
"Thus says the LORD, the God of **I**,	**1Sa 10:18**	3478
'I brought **I** up from Egypt, and I	**1Sa 10:18**	3478
brought all the tribes of **I** near,	**1Sa 10:20**	3478
make it a reproach on all **I**."	**1Sa 11:2**	3478
throughout the territory of **I**.	**1Sa 11:3**	3478
them throughout the territory of **I**	**1Sa 11:7**	3478
and the sons of **I** were 300,000,	**1Sa 11:8**	3478
accomplished deliverance in **I**."	**1Sa 11:13**	3478
all the men of **I** rejoiced greatly.	**1Sa 11:15**	3478
Then Samuel said to all **I**,	**1Sa 12:1**	3478
he reigned *forty* two years over **I**.	**1Sa 13:1**	3478
chose for himself 3,000 men of **I**,	**1Sa 13:2**	3478
All **I** heard the news that Saul	**1Sa 13:4**	3478
and also that **I** had become odious	**1Sa 13:4**	3478
assembled to fight with **I**,	**1Sa 13:5**	3478
When the men of **I** saw that they	**1Sa 13:6**	3478
your kingdom over **I** forever.	**1Sa 13:13**	3478
be found in all the land of **I**,	**1Sa 13:19**	3478
I went down to the Philistines,	**1Sa 13:20**	3478
given them into the hands of **I**."	**1Sa 14:12**	3478
at that time with the sons of **I**.	**1Sa 14:18**	3478
When all the men of **I** who had	**1Sa 14:22**	3478
So the LORD delivered **I** that day,	**1Sa 14:23**	3478
the men of **I** were hard-pressed	**1Sa 14:24**	3478
give them into the hand of **I**?"	**1Sa 14:37**	3478
as the LORD lives, who delivers **I**,	**1Sa 14:39**	3478
Then he said to all **I**,	**1Sa 14:40**	3478
said to the LORD, the God of **I**,	**1Sa 14:41**	3478
about this great deliverance in **I**?	**1Sa 14:45**	3478
Saul had taken the kingdom over **I**,	**1Sa 14:47**	3478
and delivered **I** from the hands of	**1Sa 14:48**	3478
as king over His people, over **I**;	**1Sa 15:1**	3478
Amalek *for* what he did to **I**,	**1Sa 15:2**	3478
showed kindness to all the sons of **I**	**1Sa 15:6**	3478
made the head of the tribes of **I**?	**1Sa 15:17**	3478
the LORD anointed you king over **I**,	**1Sa 15:17**	3478
you from being king over **I**."	**1Sa 15:26**	3478
has torn the kingdom of **I** from you	**1Sa 15:28**	3478
Glory of **I** will not lie or change His	**1Sa 15:29**	3478
elders of my people and before **I**,	**1Sa 15:30**	3478
that He had made Saul king over **I**.	**1Sa 15:35**	3478
him from being king over **I**?	**1Sa 16:1**	3478
and the men of **I** were gathered and	**1Sa 17:2**	3478
I stood on the mountain on the other	**1Sa 17:3**	3478
and shouted to the ranks of **I** and	**1Sa 17:8**	3478
"I defy the ranks of **I** this day;	**1Sa 17:10**	3478
When Saul and all **I** heard these	**1Sa 17:11**	3478
men of **I** are in the valley of Elah,	**1Sa 17:19**	3478
I and the Philistines drew up	**1Sa 17:21**	3478
When all the men of **I** saw the man,	**1Sa 17:24**	3478
The men of **I** said,	**1Sa 17:25**	3478
Surely he is coming up to defy **I**.	**1Sa 17:25**	3478
his father's house free in **I**."	**1Sa 17:25**	3478
takes away the reproach from **I**?	**1Sa 17:26**	3478
hosts, the God of the armies of **I**,	**1Sa 17:45**	3478
may know that there is a God in **I**,	**1Sa 17:46**	3478
The men of **I** and Judah arose	**1Sa 17:52**	3478
The sons of **I** returned from	**1Sa 17:53**	3478
came out of all the cities of **I**,	**1Sa 18:6**	3478
But all **I** and Judah loved David,	**1Sa 18:16**	3478
my life *or* my father's family in **I**,	**1Sa 18:18**	3478
a great deliverance for all **I**;	**1Sa 19:5**	3478
"The LORD, the God of **I**,	**1Sa 20:12**	3478
"O LORD God of **I**, Your servant has	**1Sa 23:10**	3478
O LORD God of **I**, I pray, tell Your	**1Sa 23:11**	3478
you will be king over **I** and I will	**1Sa 23:17**	3478
thousand chosen men from all **I** and	**1Sa 24:2**	3478
whom has the king of **I** come out?	**1Sa 24:14**	3478
kingdom of **I** will be established in	**1Sa 24:20**	3478
and all **I** gathered together and	**1Sa 25:1**	3478
appoints you ruler over **I**,	**1Sa 25:30**	3478
"Blessed be the LORD God of **I**,	**1Sa 25:32**	3478
as the LORD God of **I** lives,	**1Sa 25:34**	3478
three thousand chosen men of **I**,	**1Sa 26:2**	3478
And who is like you in **I**?	**1Sa 26:15**	3478
for the king of **I** has come out to	**1Sa 26:20**	3478
anymore in all the territory of **I**,	**1Sa 27:1**	3478
himself odious among his people **I**;	**1Sa 27:12**	3478
camps for war, to fight against **I**.	**1Sa 28:1**	3478
and all **I** had lamented him and	**1Sa 28:3**	3478
and Saul gathered all **I** together	**1Sa 28:4**	3478
LORD will also give over **I** along with	**1Sa 28:19**	3478
the LORD will give over the army of **I**	**1Sa 28:19**	3478
the servant of Saul the king of **I**,	**1Sa 29:3**	3478
an ordinance for **I** to this day.	**1Sa 30:25**	3478
were fighting against **I**,	**1Sa 31:1**	3478
and the men of **I** fled from before	**1Sa 31:1**	3478
When the men of **I** who were on	**1Sa 31:7**	3478
saw that the men of **I** had fled and	**1Sa 31:7**	3478
have escaped from the camp of **I**."	**2Sa 1:3**	3478
of the LORD and the house of **I**,	**2Sa 1:12**	3478
"Your beauty, O **I**, is slain on	**2Sa 1:19**	3478
"O daughters of **I**, weep over	**2Sa 1:24**	3478
over Benjamin, even over all **I**.	**2Sa 2:9**	3478
old when he became king over **I**,	**2Sa 2:10**	3478
Abner and the men of **I** were beaten	**2Sa 2:17**	3478
halted and pursued **I** no longer,	**2Sa 2:28**	3478
establish the throne of David over **I**	**2Sa 3:10**	3478
you to bring all **I** over to you."	**2Sa 3:12**	3478
consultation with the elders of **I**,	**2Sa 3:17**	3478
will save My people **I** from the hand	**2Sa 3:18**	3478
all that seemed good to **I** and to the	**2Sa 3:19**	3478
and gather all **I** to my lord the	**2Sa 3:21**	3478
all the people and all **I** understood	**2Sa 3:37**	3478
man has fallen this day in **I**?	**2Sa 3:38**	3478
courage, and all **I** was disturbed.	**2Sa 4:1**	3478
Then all the tribes of **I** came to	**2Sa 5:1**	3478
were the one who led **I** out and in.	**2Sa 5:2**	3478
'You will shepherd My people **I**,	**2Sa 5:2**	3478
you will be a ruler over **I**.' "	**2Sa 5:2**	3478
all the elders of **I** came to the king	**2Sa 5:3**	3478
they anointed David king over **I**.	**2Sa 5:3**	3478
reigned thirty-three years over all **I**	**2Sa 5:5**	3478
established him as king over **I**,	**2Sa 5:12**	3478
for the sake of His people **I**.	**2Sa 5:12**	3478
had anointed David king over **I**,	**2Sa 5:17**	3478
gathered all the chosen men of **I**,	**2Sa 6:1**	3478
David and all the house of **I** were	**2Sa 6:5**	3478
So David and all the house of **I**	**2Sa 6:15**	3478
people, to all the multitude of **I**,	**2Sa 6:19**	3478
the king of **I** distinguished himself	**2Sa 6:20**	3478
the people of the LORD, over **I**;	**2Sa 6:21**	3478
up the sons of **I** from Egypt,	**2Sa 7:6**	3478
have gone with all the sons of **I**,	**2Sa 7:7**	3478
word with one of the tribes of **I**,	**2Sa 7:7**	3478
commanded to shepherd My people **I**,	**2Sa 7:7**	3478
to be ruler over My people **I**.	**2Sa 7:8**	3478
appoint a place for My people **I**	**2Sa 7:10**	3478
judges to be over My people **I**;	**2Sa 7:11**	3478
on the earth is like Your people **I**,	**2Sa 7:23**	3478
established for Yourself Your people **I**	**2Sa 7:24**	3478
'The LORD of hosts is God over **I**';	**2Sa 7:26**	3478
O LORD of hosts, the God of **I**,	**2Sa 7:27**	3478
So David reigned over all **I**;	**2Sa 8:15**	3478
from all the choice men of **I**,	**2Sa 10:9**	3478
that they had been defeated by **I**,	**2Sa 10:15**	3478
he gathered all **I** together and	**2Sa 10:17**	3478
But the Arameans fled before **I**,	**2Sa 10:18**	3478
saw that they were defeated by **I**,	**2Sa 10:19**	3478
made peace with **I** and served them.	**2Sa 10:19**	3478
his servants with him and all **I**,	**2Sa 11:1**	3478
"The ark and **I** and Judah are	**2Sa 11:11**	3478
Thus says the LORD God of **I**,	**2Sa 12:7**	3478
'It is I who anointed you king over **I**	**2Sa 12:7**	3478
gave you the house of **I** and Judah;	**2Sa 12:8**	3478
I will do this thing before all **I**,	**2Sa 12:12**	3478
for such a thing is not done in **I**;	**2Sa 13:12**	3478
be like one of the fools in **I**.	**2Sa 13:13**	3478
in all **I** was no one as handsome as	**2Sa 14:25**	3478
is from one of the tribes of **I**."	**2Sa 15:2**	3478
Absalom dealt with all **I** who came to	**2Sa 15:6**	3478
away the hearts of the men of **I**.	**2Sa 15:6**	3478
throughout all the tribes of **I**,	**2Sa 15:10**	3478
the men of **I** are with Absalom."	**2Sa 15:13**	3478
'Today the house of **I** will restore	**2Sa 16:3**	3478
and all the people, the men of **I**,	**2Sa 16:15**	3478
and all the men of **I** have chosen,	**2Sa 16:18**	3478
then all **I** will hear that you have	**2Sa 16:21**	3478
concubines in the sight of all **I**.	**2Sa 16:22**	3478
Absalom and all the elders of **I**.	**2Sa 17:4**	3478
for all **I** knows that your father	**2Sa 17:10**	3478
all **I** be surely gathered to you,	**2Sa 17:11**	3478
then all **I** shall bring ropes to	**2Sa 17:13**	3478
Absalom and all the men of **I** said,	**2Sa 17:14**	3478
Absalom and the elders of **I**,	**2Sa 17:15**	3478
he and all the men of **I** with him.	**2Sa 17:24**	3478
And **I** and Absalom camped in the	**2Sa 17:26**	3478
went out into the field against **I**,	**2Sa 18:6**	3478
The people of **I** were defeated	**2Sa 18:7**	3478
people returned from pursuing **I**,	**2Sa 18:16**	3478
And all **I** fled, each to his tent.	**2Sa 18:17**	3478
Now **I** had fled, each to his tent.	**2Sa 19:8**	3478
throughout all the tribes of **I**,	**2Sa 19:9**	3478
word of all **I** has come to the king,	**2Sa 19:11**	3478
man be put to death in **I** today?	**2Sa 19:22**	3478
that I am king over **I** today?"	**2Sa 19:22**	3478
people of **I** accompanied the king.	**2Sa 19:40**	3478
all the men of **I** came to the king	**2Sa 19:41**	3478
of Judah answered the men of **I**,	**2Sa 19:42**	3478
But the men of **I** answered the men	**2Sa 19:43**	3478
than the words of the men of **I**.	**2Sa 19:43**	3478
Every man to his tents, O **I**!"	**2Sa 20:1**	3478
men of **I** withdrew from following	**2Sa 20:2**	3478
he went through all the tribes of **I**	**2Sa 20:14**	3478
are peaceable *and* faithful in **I**.	**2Sa 20:19**	3478
destroy a city, even a mother in **I**.	**2Sa 20:19**	3478
Joab was over the whole army of **I**,	**2Sa 20:23**	3478
Gibeonites were not of the sons of **I**	**2Sa 21:2**	3478
sons of **I** made a covenant with	**2Sa 21:2**	3478
zeal for the sons of **I** and Judah).	**2Sa 21:2**	3478
us to put any man to death in **I**."	**2Sa 21:4**	3478
remaining within any border of **I**,	**2Sa 21:5**	3478
were at war again with **I**,	**2Sa 21:15**	3478
not extinguish the lamp of **I**."	**2Sa 21:17**	3478
When he defied **I**,	**2Sa 21:21**	3478
And the sweet psalmist of **I**,	**2Sa 23:1**	3478
"The God of **I** said, The Rock of	**2Sa 23:3**	3478
said, The Rock of **I** spoke to me,	**2Sa 23:3**	3478
and the men of **I** had withdrawn.	**2Sa 23:9**	3478
anger of the LORD burned against **I**,	**2Sa 24:1**	3478
"Go, number **I** and Judah."	**2Sa 24:1**	3478
now through all the tribes of **I**,	**2Sa 24:2**	3478
king to register the people of **I**.	**2Sa 24:4**	3478
and there were in **I** eight hundred	**2Sa 24:9**	3478
So the LORD sent a pestilence upon **I**	**2Sa 24:15**	3478
the plague was held back from **I**.	**2Sa 24:25**	3478
throughout all the territory of **I**,	**1Ki 1:3**	3478
the eyes of all **I** are on you,	**1Ki 1:20**	3478

to you by the LORD the God of **I**,	1Ki 1:30	3478
anoint him there as king over **I**,	1Ki 1:34	3478
to be ruler over **I** and Judah."	1Ki 1:35	3478
'Blessed be the LORD, the God of **I**,	1Ki 1:48	3478
lack a man on the throne of **I**.'	1Ki 2:4	3478
two commanders of the armies of **I**,	1Ki 2:5	3478
reigned over **I** *were* forty years:	1Ki 2:11	3478
that all **I** expected me to be king;	1Ki 2:15	3478
Ner, commander of the army of **I**,	1Ki 2:32	3478
When all **I** heard of the judgment	1Ki 3:28	3478
King Solomon was king over all **I**.	1Ki 4:1	3478
had twelve deputies over all **I**,	1Ki 4:7	3478
Judah and **I** *were* as numerous as	1Ki 4:20	3478
So Judah and **I** lived in safety,	1Ki 4:25	3478
levied forced laborers from all **I**;	1Ki 5:13	3478
the sons of **I** came out of the land	1Ki 6:1	3478
year of Solomon's reign over **I**,	1Ki 6:1	3478
I will dwell among the sons of **I**,	1Ki 6:13	3478
will not forsake My people **I**."	1Ki 6:13	3478
Solomon assembled the elders of **I**	1Ki 8:1	3478
households of the sons of **I**,	1Ki 8:1	3478
All the men of **I** assembled	1Ki 8:2	3478
Then all the elders of **I** came,	1Ki 8:3	3478
and all the congregation of **I**,	1Ki 8:5	3478
a covenant with the sons of **I**,	1Ki 8:9	3478
and blessed all the assembly of **I**,	1Ki 8:14	3478
the assembly of **I** was standing.	1Ki 8:14	3478
"Blessed be the LORD, the God of **I**,	1Ki 8:15	3478
I brought My people **I** from Egypt,	1Ki 8:16	3478
choose a city out of all the tribes of **I**	1Ki 8:16	3478
David to be over My people **I**.'	1Ki 8:16	3478
name of the LORD, the God of **I**.	1Ki 8:17	3478
David and sit on the throne of **I**,	1Ki 8:20	3478
name of the LORD, the God of **I**.	1Ki 8:20	3478
the presence of all the assembly of **I**	1Ki 8:22	3478
"O LORD, the God of **I**,	1Ki 8:23	3478
therefore, O LORD, the God of **I**,	1Ki 8:25	3478
a man to sit on the throne of **I**,	1Ki 8:25	3478
"Now therefore, O God of **I**,	1Ki 8:26	3478
Your servant and of Your people **I**,	1Ki 8:30	3478
Your people **I** are defeated before an	1Ki 8:33	3478
forgive the sin of Your people **I**,	1Ki 8:34	3478
Your servants and of Your people **I**,	1Ki 8:36	3478
by any man *or* by all Your people **I**,	1Ki 8:38	3478
who is not of Your people **I**,	1Ki 8:41	3478
to fear You, as *do* Your people **I**,	1Ki 8:43	3478
the supplication of Your people **I**,	1Ki 8:52	3478
blessed all the assembly of **I** with a	1Ki 8:55	3478
has given rest to His people **I**,	1Ki 8:56	3478
and the cause of His people **I**,	1Ki 8:59	3478
Now the king and all **I** with him	1Ki 8:62	3478
king and all the sons of **I** dedicated	1Ki 8:63	3478
at that time, and all **I** with him,	1Ki 8:65	3478
His servant and to **I** His people.	1Ki 8:66	3478
of your kingdom over **I** forever,	1Ki 9:5	3478
not lack a man on the throne of **I**.'	1Ki 9:5	3478
then I will cut off **I** from the	1Ki 9:7	3478
So **I** will become a proverb and a	1Ki 9:7	3478
who were not of the sons of **I**,	1Ki 9:20	3478
whom the sons of **I** were unable to	1Ki 9:21	3478
not make slaves of the sons of **I**;	1Ki 9:22	3478
you to set you on the throne of **I**;	1Ki 10:9	3478
because the LORD loved **I** forever,	1Ki 10:9	3478
LORD had said to the sons of **I**,	1Ki 11:2	3478
away from the LORD, the God of **I**,	1Ki 11:9	3478
and all **I** stayed there six months,	1Ki 11:16	3478
was an adversary to **I** all the days	1Ki 11:25	3478
abhorred **I** and reigned over Aram.	1Ki 11:25	3478
thus says the LORD, the God of **I**,	1Ki 11:31	3478
chosen from all the tribes of **I**),	1Ki 11:32	3478
and you shall be king over **I**.	1Ki 11:37	3478
David, and I will give **I** to you.	1Ki 11:38	3478
reigned in Jerusalem over all **I**	1Ki 11:42	3478
for all **I** had come to Shechem to	1Ki 12:1	3478
and all the assembly of **I** came and	1Ki 12:3	3478
When all **I** *saw* that the king did	1Ki 12:16	3478
To your tents, O **I**!	1Ki 12:16	3478
So **I** departed to their tents.	1Ki 12:16	3478
But as for the sons of **I** who lived	1Ki 12:17	3478
and all **I** stoned him to death.	1Ki 12:18	3478
So **I** has been in rebellion against	1Ki 12:19	3478
when all **I** heard that Jeroboam had	1Ki 12:20	3478
and made him king over all **I**.	1Ki 12:20	3478
to fight against the house of **I** to	1Ki 12:21	3478
your relatives the sons of **I**;	1Ki 12:24	3478
behold your gods, O **I**,	1Ki 12:28	3478
a feast for the sons of **I** and	1Ki 12:33	3478
'Thus says the LORD God of **I**,	1Ki 14:7	3478
made you leader over My people **I**,	1Ki 14:7	3478
person, both bond and free in **I**,	1Ki 14:10	3478
"All **I** shall mourn for him	1Ki 14:13	3478
God of **I** in the house of Jeroboam.	1Ki 14:13	3478
will raise up for Himself a king over **I**	1Ki 14:14	3478
"For the LORD will strike **I**,	1Ki 14:15	3478
and He will uproot **I** from this	1Ki 14:15	3478
"He will give up **I** on account	1Ki 14:16	3478
and with which he made **I** to sin."	1Ki 14:16	3478
All **I** buried him and mourned	1Ki 14:18	3478
the Chronicles of the Kings of **I**.	1Ki 14:19	3478
had chosen from all the tribes of **I**	1Ki 14:21	3478
dispossessed before the sons of **I**.	1Ki 14:24	3478
year of Jeroboam the king of **I**,	1Ki 15:9	3478
between Asa and Baasha king of **I**	1Ki 15:16	3478
Baasha king of **I** went up	1Ki 15:17	3478
your treaty with Baasha king of **I**	1Ki 15:19	3478
armies against the cities of **I**,	1Ki 15:20	3478
son of Jeroboam became king over **I**	1Ki 15:25	3478
and he reigned over **I** two years.	1Ki 15:25	3478
in his sin which he made **I** sin.	1Ki 15:26	3478
while Nadab and all **I** were laying	1Ki 15:27	3478
sinned, and which he made **I** sin,	1Ki 15:30	3478
the LORD God of **I** to anger.	1Ki 15:30	3478
the Chronicles of the Kings of **I**?	1Ki 15:31	3478
Baasha king of **I** all their days.	1Ki 15:32	3478
became king over all **I** at Tirzah,	1Ki 15:33	3478
in his sin which he made **I** sin.	1Ki 15:34	3478
made you leader over My people **I**,	1Ki 16:2	3478
and have made My people **I** sin,	1Ki 16:2	3478
the Chronicles of the Kings of **I**?	1Ki 16:5	3478
became king over **I** at Tirzah,	1Ki 16:8	3478
sinned and which they made **I** sin,	1Ki 16:13	3478
of **I** to anger with their idols.	1Ki 16:13	3478
the Chronicles of the Kings of **I**?	1Ki 16:14	3478
Therefore all **I** made Omri, the	1Ki 16:16	3478
king over **I** that day in the camp.	1Ki 16:16	3478
Then Omri and all **I** with him went	1Ki 16:17	3478
sin which he did, making **I** sin.	1Ki 16:19	3478
the Chronicles of the Kings of **I**?	1Ki 16:20	3478
of **I** were divided into two parts:	1Ki 16:21	3478
of Judah, Omri became king over **I**	1Ki 16:23	3478
in his sins which he made **I** sin,	1Ki 16:26	3478
LORD God of **I** with their idols.	1Ki 16:26	3478
the Chronicles of the Kings of **I**?	1Ki 16:27	3478
the son of Omri became king over **I**	1Ki 16:29	3478
over **I** in Samaria twenty-two years.	1Ki 16:29	3478
more to provoke the LORD God of **I**	1Ki 16:33	3478
kings of **I** who were before him.	1Ki 16:33	3478
"As the LORD, the God of **I** lives,	1Ki 17:1	3478
"For thus says the LORD God of **I**,	1Ki 17:14	3478
"Is this you, you troubler of **I**?"	1Ki 18:17	3478
"I have not troubled **I**,	1Ki 18:18	3478
to me all **I** at Mount Carmel,	1Ki 18:19	3478
a message among all the sons of **I** and	1Ki 18:20	3478
"**I** shall be your name."	1Ki 18:31	3478
the God of Abraham, Isaac and **I**,	1Ki 18:36	3478
be known that You are God in **I** and	1Ki 18:36	3478
of **I** have forsaken Your covenant,	1Ki 19:10	3478
of **I** have forsaken Your covenant,	1Ki 19:14	3478
you shall anoint king over **I**;	1Ki 19:16	3478
"Yet I will leave 7,000 in **I**,	1Ki 19:18	3478
to the city to Ahab king of **I** and	1Ki 20:2	3478
The king of **I** replied,	1Ki 20:4	3478
Then the king of **I** called all the	1Ki 20:7	3478
the king of **I** replied,	1Ki 20:11	3478
Ahab king of **I** and said,	1Ki 20:13	3478
people, *even* all the sons of **I**,	1Ki 20:15	3478
Arameans fled and **I** pursued them,	1Ki 20:20	3478
The king of **I** went out and	1Ki 20:21	3478
came near to the king of **I** and	1Ki 20:22	3478
up to Aphek to fight against **I**.	1Ki 20:26	3478
The sons of **I** were mustered	1Ki 20:27	3478
and the sons of **I** camped before	1Ki 20:27	3478
spoke to the king of **I** and said,	1Ki 20:28	3478
and the sons of **I** killed *of* the	1Ki 20:29	3478
kings of the house of **I** are merciful	1Ki 20:31	3478
and go out to the king of **I**;	1Ki 20:31	3478
came to the king of **I** and said,	1Ki 20:32	3478
And the king of **I** said to him,	1Ki 20:40	3478
and the king of **I** recognized him	1Ki 20:41	3478
So the king of **I** went to his house	1Ki 20:43	3478
"Do you now reign over **I**?	1Ki 21:7	3478
go down to meet Ahab king of **I**,	1Ki 21:18	3478
male, both bond and free in **I**;	1Ki 21:21	3478
and *because* you have made **I** sin.	1Ki 21:22	3478
cast out before the sons of **I**.	1Ki 21:26	3478
without war between Aram and **I**.	1Ki 22:1	3478
Judah came down to the king of **I**.	1Ki 22:2	3478
king of **I** said to his servants,	1Ki 22:3	3478
Jehoshaphat said to the king of **I**,	1Ki 22:4	3478
Jehoshaphat said to the king of **I**,	1Ki 22:5	3478
Then the king of **I** gathered the	1Ki 22:6	3478
The king of **I** said to Jehoshaphat,	1Ki 22:8	3478
Then the king of **I** called an officer	1Ki 22:9	3478
Now the king of **I** and Jehoshaphat	1Ki 22:10	3478
all **I** Scattered on the mountains,	1Ki 22:17	3478
the king of **I** said to Jehoshaphat,	1Ki 22:18	3478
Then the king of **I** said,	1Ki 22:26	3478
So the king of **I** and Jehoshaphat	1Ki 22:29	3478
The king of **I** said to Jehoshaphat,	1Ki 22:30	3478
So the king of **I** disguised himself	1Ki 22:30	3478
but with the king of **I** alone."	1Ki 22:31	3478
"Surely it is the king of **I**,"	1Ki 22:32	3478
saw that it was not the king of **I**,	1Ki 22:33	3478
struck the king of **I** in a joint of the	1Ki 22:34	3478
the Chronicles of the Kings of **I**?	1Ki 22:39	3478
the fourth year of Ahab king of **I**.	1Ki 22:41	3478
made peace with the king of **I**.	1Ki 22:44	3478
the son of Ahab became king over **I**	1Ki 22:51	3478
and he reigned two years over **I**.	1Ki 22:51	3478
son of Nebat, who caused **I** to sin.	1Ki 22:52	3478
provoked the LORD God of **I** to anger	1Ki 22:53	3478
Moab rebelled against **I** after the	2Ki 1:1	3478
'Is it because there is no God in **I** *that*	2Ki 1:3	3478
'Is it because there is no God in **I** *that*	2Ki 1:6	3478
no God in **I** to inquire of His word?	2Ki 1:16	3478
the Chronicles of the Kings of **I**?	2Ki 1:18	3478
chariots of **I** and its horsemen!"	2Ki 2:12	3478
the son of Ahab became king over **I**	2Ki 3:1	3478
son of Nebat, which he made **I** sin;	2Ki 3:3	3478
and used to pay the king of **I**	2Ki 3:4	3478
rebelled against the king of **I**.	2Ki 3:5	3478
at that time and mustered all **I**.	2Ki 3:6	3478
So the king of **I** went with the	2Ki 3:9	3478
Then the king of **I** said,	2Ki 3:10	3478
So the king of **I** and Jehoshaphat	2Ki 3:12	3478
Now Elisha said to the king of **I**,	2Ki 3:13	3478
And the king of **I** said to him,	2Ki 3:13	3478
when they came to the camp of **I**,	2Ki 3:24	3478
there came great wrath against **I**,	2Ki 3:27	3478
a little girl from the land of **I**;	2Ki 5:2	3478
girl who is from the land of **I**."	2Ki 5:4	3478
send a letter to the king of **I**."	2Ki 5:5	3478
the letter to the king of **I**,	2Ki 5:6	3478
the king of **I** read the letter,	2Ki 5:7	3478
king of **I** had torn his clothes,	2Ki 5:8	3478
that there is a prophet in **I**."	2Ki 5:8	3478
better than all the waters of **I**?	2Ki 5:12	3478
no God in all the earth, but in **I**;	2Ki 5:15	3478
king of Aram was warring against **I**;	2Ki 6:8	3478
sent *word* to the king of **I** saying,	2Ki 6:9	3478
The king of **I** sent to the	2Ki 6:10	3478
which of us is for the king of **I**?"	2Ki 6:11	3478
Elisha, the prophet who is in **I**,	2Ki 6:12	3478
tells the king of **I** the words that	2Ki 6:12	3478
the king of **I** when he saw them,	2Ki 6:21	3478
not come again into the land of **I**.	2Ki 6:23	3478
As the king of **I** was passing	2Ki 6:26	3478
the king of **I** has hired against us	2Ki 7:6	3478
multitude of **I** who are left in it;	2Ki 7:13	3478
multitude of **I** who have already	2Ki 7:13	3478
that you will do to the sons of **I**:	2Ki 8:12	3478
Joram the son of Ahab king of **I**,	2Ki 8:16	3478
in the way of the kings of **I**,	2Ki 8:18	3478
Joram the son of Ahab king of **I**,	2Ki 8:25	3478
granddaughter of Omri king of **I**.	2Ki 8:26	3478
have anointed you king over **I**."	2Ki 9:3	3478
"Thus says the LORD, the God of **I**,	2Ki 9:6	3478
people of the LORD, *even* over **I**.	2Ki 9:6	3478
person both bond and free in **I**.	2Ki 9:8	3478
anointed you king over **I**.	2Ki 9:12	3478
Now Joram with all **I** was defending	2Ki 9:14	3478
Joram king of **I** and Ahaziah	2Ki 9:21	3478
Then Jehu sent throughout **I** and	2Ki 10:21	3478
Jehu eradicated Baal out of **I**.	2Ki 10:28	3478
son of Nebat, which he made **I** sin,	2Ki 10:29	3478
shall sit on the throne of **I**."	2Ki 10:30	3478
the law of the LORD, the God of **I**,	2Ki 10:31	3478
of Jeroboam, which he made **I** sin.	2Ki 10:31	3478
began to cut off *portions* from **I**;	2Ki 10:32	3478
throughout the territory of **I**:	2Ki 10:32	3478
the Chronicles of the Kings of **I**?	2Ki 10:34	3478
Jehu reigned over **I** in Samaria	2Ki 10:36	3478
the son of Jehu became king over **I**	2Ki 13:1	3478
Nebat, with which he made **I** sin;	2Ki 13:2	3478
of the LORD was kindled against **I**,	2Ki 13:3	3478
for He saw the oppression of **I**,	2Ki 13:4	3478
The LORD gave **I** a deliverer,	2Ki 13:5	3478
and the sons of **I** lived in their	2Ki 13:5	3478
with which he made **I** sin,	2Ki 13:6	3478
the Chronicles of the Kings of **I**?	2Ki 13:8	3478
became king over **I** in Samaria,	2Ki 13:10	3478
Nebat, with which he made **I** sin,	2Ki 13:11	3478
the Chronicles of the Kings of **I**?	2Ki 13:12	3478
in Samaria with the kings of **I**.	2Ki 13:13	3478
Joash the king of **I** came down to	2Ki 13:14	3478
chariots of **I** and its horsemen!"	2Ki 13:14	3478
Then he said to the king of **I**,	2Ki 13:16	3478
And he said to the king of **I**,	2Ki 13:18	3478
king of Aram had oppressed **I** all	2Ki 13:22	3478
him and recovered the cities of **I**.	2Ki 13:25	3478
of Joash son of Joahaz king of **I**,	2Ki 14:1	3478
Jehoahaz son of Jehu, king of **I**,	2Ki 14:8	3478
Jehoash king of **I** sent to Amaziah	2Ki 14:9	3478
So Jehoash king of **I** went up;	2Ki 14:11	3478
Judah was defeated by **I**,	2Ki 14:12	3478
Then Jehoash king of **I** captured	2Ki 14:13	3478
the Chronicles of the Kings of **I**?	2Ki 14:15	3478
in Samaria with the kings of **I**;	2Ki 14:16	3478
Jehoash son of Jehoahaz king of **I**.	2Ki 14:17	3478
king of **I** became king in Samaria,	2Ki 14:23	3478
son of Nebat, which he made **I** sin.	2Ki 14:24	3478
He restored the border of **I** from	2Ki 14:25	3478
word of the LORD, the God of **I**,	2Ki 14:25	3478
the LORD saw the affliction of **I**,	2Ki 14:26	3478
nor was there any helper for **I**.	2Ki 14:26	3478
He would blot out the name of **I**	2Ki 14:27	3478
fought and how he recovered for **I**,	2Ki 14:28	3478
the Chronicles of the Kings of **I**?	2Ki 14:28	3478
fathers, even with the kings of **I**,	2Ki 14:29	3478
year of Jeroboam king of **I**,	2Ki 15:1	3478
became king over **I** in Samaria *for*	2Ki 15:8	3478
son of Nebat, which he made **I** sin.	2Ki 15:9	3478
the Chronicles of the Kings of **I**.	2Ki 15:11	3478
shall sit on the throne of **I**."	2Ki 15:12	3478
the Chronicles of the Kings of **I**.	2Ki 15:15	3478
son of Gadi became king over **I**	2Ki 15:17	3478
son of Nebat, which he made **I** sin.	2Ki 15:18	3478
Menahem exacted the money from **I**,	2Ki 15:20	3478
the Chronicles of the Kings of **I**?	2Ki 15:21	3478
became king over **I** in Samaria,	2Ki 15:23	3478
son of Nebat, which he made **I** sin.	2Ki 15:24	3478
the Chronicles of the Kings of **I**.	2Ki 15:26	3478
became king over **I** in Samaria,	2Ki 15:27	3478
son of Nebat, which he made **I** sin.	2Ki 15:28	3478
In the days of Pekah king of **I**,	2Ki 15:29	3478
the Chronicles of the Kings of **I**.	2Ki 15:31	3478
the son of Remaliah king of **I**,	2Ki 15:32	3478
walked in the way of the kings of **I**,	2Ki 16:3	3478
out from before the sons of **I**.	2Ki 16:3	3478
Pekah son of Remaliah, king of **I**,	2Ki 16:5	3478
from the hand of the king of **I**,	2Ki 16:7	3478
became king over **I** in Samaria,	2Ki 17:1	3478
kings of **I** who were before him.	2Ki 17:2	3478
carried **I** away into exile to Assyria,	2Ki 17:6	3478
because the sons of **I** had sinned	2Ki 17:7	3478
driven out before the sons of **I**,	2Ki 17:8	3478
in the customs of the kings of **I**	2Ki 17:8	3478

The sons of **I** did things secretly	**2Ki 17:9**	3478
Yet the LORD warned **I** and Judah	**2Ki 17:13**	3478
So the LORD was very angry with **I** and	**2Ki 17:18**	3478
customs which **I** had introduced.	**2Ki 17:19**	3478
LORD rejected all the descendants of **I**	**2Ki 17:20**	3478
torn **I** from the house of David,	**2Ki 17:21**	3478
Jeroboam drove **I** away from	**2Ki 17:21**	3478
The sons of **I** walked in all	**2Ki 17:22**	3478
the LORD removed **I** from His sight,	**2Ki 17:23**	3478
So **I** was carried away into exile	**2Ki 17:23**	3478
Samaria in place of the sons of **I**.	**2Ki 17:24**	3478
sons of Jacob, whom He named **I**;	**2Ki 17:34**	3478
Hoshea, the son of Elah king of **I**,	**2Ki 18:1**	3478
sons of **I** burned incense to it;	**2Ki 18:4**	3478
trusted in the LORD, the God of **I**;	**2Ki 18:5**	3478
of Hoshea son of Elah king of **I**,	**2Ki 18:9**	3478
ninth year of Hoshea king of **I**,	**2Ki 18:10**	3478
king of Assyria carried **I** away into	**2Ki 18:11**	3478
"O LORD, the God of **I**,	**2Ki 19:15**	3478
"Thus says the LORD, the God of **I**,	**2Ki 19:20**	3478
Against the Holy One of **I**!	**2Ki 19:22**	3478
dispossessed before the sons of **I**.	**2Ki 21:2**	3478
as Ahab king of **I** had done,	**2Ki 21:3**	3478
chosen from all the tribes of **I**,	**2Ki 21:7**	3478
I will not make the feet of **I** wander	**2Ki 21:8**	3478
destroyed before the sons of **I**.	**2Ki 21:9**	3478
thus says the LORD, the God of **I**,	**2Ki 21:12**	3478
"Thus says the LORD God of **I**,	**2Ki 22:15**	3478
'Thus says the LORD God of **I**,	**2Ki 22:18**	3478
Solomon the king of **I** had built for	**2Ki 23:13**	3478
the son of Nebat, who made **I** sin,	**2Ki 23:15**	3478
which the kings of **I** had made	**2Ki 23:19**	3478
days of the judges who judged **I**,	**2Ki 23:22**	3478
in all the days of the kings of **I** and	**2Ki 23:22**	3478
My sight, as I have removed **I**.	**2Ki 23:27**	3478
Solomon king of **I** had made in the	**2Ki 24:13**	3478
The sons of Isaac *were* Esau and **I**.	**1Ch 1:34**	3478
any king of the sons of **I** reigned.	**1Ch 1:43**	3478
These are the sons of **I**:	**1Ch 2:1**	3478
was Achar, the troubler of **I**,	**1Ch 2:7**	3478
Now Jabez called on the God of **I**,	**1Ch 4:10**	3478
sons of Reuben the firstborn of **I**	**1Ch 5:1**	3478
the sons of Joseph the son of **I**;	**1Ch 5:1**	3478
sons of Reuben the firstborn of **I**	**1Ch 5:3**	3478
in the days of Jeroboam king of **I**.	**1Ch 5:17**	3478
God of **I** stirred up the spirit of Pul,	**1Ch 5:26**	3478
the son of Levi, the son of **I**.	**1Ch 6:38**	3478
and to make atonement for **I**,	**1Ch 6:49**	3478
So the sons of **I** gave to the	**1Ch 6:64**	3478
the sons of Joseph the son of **I**.	**1Ch 7:29**	3478
all **I** was enrolled by genealogies;	**1Ch 9:1**	3478
in the Book of the Kings of **I**.	**1Ch 9:1**	3478
in their cities *were* **I**,	**1Ch 9:2**	3478
the Philistines fought against **I**;	**1Ch 10:1**	3478
men of **I** fled before the Philistines and	**1Ch 10:1**	3478
When all the men of **I** who were in	**1Ch 10:7**	3478
Then all **I** gathered to David at	**1Ch 11:1**	3478
one who led out and brought in **I**;	**1Ch 11:2**	3478
'You shall shepherd My people **I**,	**1Ch 11:2**	3478
be prince over My people **I**.' "	**1Ch 11:2**	3478
the elders of **I** came to the king at	**1Ch 11:3**	3478
they anointed David king over **I**,	**1Ch 11:3**	3478
David and all **I** went to Jerusalem	**1Ch 11:4**	3478
his kingdom, together with all **I**,	**1Ch 11:10**	3478
the word of the LORD concerning **I**.	**1Ch 11:10**	3478
knowledge of what **I** should do,	**1Ch 12:32**	3478
to make David king over all **I**;	**1Ch 12:38**	3478
and all the rest also of **I** were of	**1Ch 12:38**	3478
There was joy indeed in **I**.	**1Ch 12:40**	3478
said to all the assembly of **I**,	**1Ch 13:2**	3478
who remain in all the land of **I**,	**1Ch 13:2**	3478
So David assembled all **I** together,	**1Ch 13:5**	3478
David and all **I** went up to Baalah,	**1Ch 13:6**	3478
David and all **I** were celebrating	**1Ch 13:8**	3478
established him as king over **I**,	**1Ch 14:2**	3478
for the sake of His people **I**.	**1Ch 14:2**	3478
had been anointed king over all **I**,	**1Ch 14:8**	3478
assembled all **I** at Jerusalem to	**1Ch 15:3**	3478
up the ark of the LORD God of **I** to	**1Ch 15:12**	3478
up the ark of the LORD God of **I**.	**1Ch 15:14**	3478
with the elders of **I** and the	**1Ch 15:25**	3478
Thus all **I** brought up the ark of	**1Ch 15:28**	3478
He distributed to everyone of **I**,	**1Ch 16:3**	3478
and praise the LORD God of **I**:	**1Ch 16:4**	3478
O seed of **I** His servant, Sons of	**1Ch 16:13**	3478
To **I** as an everlasting covenant,	**1Ch 16:17**	3478
Blessed be the LORD, the God of **I**,	**1Ch 16:36**	3478
of the LORD, which He commanded **I**.	**1Ch 16:40**	3478
that I brought up **I** to this day,	**1Ch 17:5**	3478
where I have walked with all **I**,	**1Ch 17:6**	3478
word with any of the judges of **I**,	**1Ch 17:6**	3478
to be leader over My people **I**.	**1Ch 17:7**	3478
appoint a place for My people **I**,	**1Ch 17:9**	3478
judges *to be* over My people **I**.	**1Ch 17:10**	3478
in the earth is like Your people **I**,	**1Ch 17:21**	3478
"For Your people **I** You made	**1Ch 17:22**	3478
'The LORD of hosts is the God of **I**,	**1Ch 17:24**	3478
God of Israel, *even* a God to **I**;	**1Ch 17:24**	3478
So David reigned over all **I**;	**1Ch 18:14**	3478
selected from all the choice men of **I**	**1Ch 19:10**	3478
that they had been defeated by **I**,	**1Ch 19:16**	3478
he gathered all **I** together and	**1Ch 19:17**	3478
The Arameans fled before **I**,	**1Ch 19:18**	3478
saw that they were defeated by **I**,	**1Ch 19:19**	3478
When he taunted **I**,	**1Ch 20:7**	3478
Then Satan stood up against **I** and	**1Ch 21:1**	3478
and moved David to number **I**.	**1Ch 21:1**	3478
number **I** from Beersheba even to	**1Ch 21:2**	3478
he be a cause of guilt to **I**?"	**1Ch 21:3**	3478

and went throughout all **I**,	**1Ch 21:4**	3478
And all **I** were 1,100,000 men who	**1Ch 21:5**	3478
with this thing, so He struck **I**.	**1Ch 21:7**	3478
all the territory of **I**.'	**1Ch 21:12**	3478
the LORD sent a pestilence on **I**;	**1Ch 21:14**	3478
70,000 men of **I** fell.	**1Ch 21:14**	3478
altar of burnt offering for **I**."	**1Ch 22:1**	3478
who were in the land of **I**,	**1Ch 22:2**	3478
a house for the LORD God of **I**.	**1Ch 22:6**	3478
peace and quiet to **I** in his days.	**1Ch 22:9**	3478
of his kingdom over **I** forever.'	**1Ch 22:10**	3478
and give you charge over **I**,	**1Ch 22:12**	3478
LORD commanded Moses concerning **I**.	**1Ch 22:13**	3478
commanded all the leaders of **I** to	**1Ch 22:17**	3478
made his son Solomon king over **I**.	**1Ch 23:1**	3478
gathered together all the leaders of **I**	**1Ch 23:2**	3478
The LORD God of **I** has given rest	**1Ch 23:25**	3478
LORD God of **I** had commanded him.	**1Ch 24:19**	3478
assigned to outside duties for **I**,	**1Ch 26:29**	3478
had charge of the affairs of **I** west	**1Ch 26:30**	3478
the enumeration of the sons of **I**,	**1Ch 27:1**	3478
Now in charge of the tribes of **I**:	**1Ch 27:16**	3478
the princes of the tribes of **I**.	**1Ch 27:22**	3478
multiply **I** as the stars of heaven.	**1Ch 27:23**	3478
of this, wrath came upon **I**,	**1Ch 27:24**	3478
Jerusalem all the officials of **I**,	**1Ch 28:1**	3478
"Yet, the LORD, the God of **I**,	**1Ch 28:4**	3478
father to be king over **I** forever.	**1Ch 28:4**	3478
in me to make *me* king over all **I**.	**1Ch 28:4**	3478
of the kingdom of the LORD over **I**.	**1Ch 28:5**	3478
"So now, in the sight of all **I**,	**1Ch 28:8**	3478
the princes of the tribes of **I**,	**1Ch 29:6**	3478
You, O LORD God of **I** our father,	**1Ch 29:10**	3478
the God of Abraham, Isaac and **I**,	**1Ch 29:18**	3478
sacrifices in abundance for all **I**.	**1Ch 29:21**	3478
prospered, and all **I** obeyed him.	**1Ch 29:23**	3478
Solomon in the sight of all **I**,	**1Ch 29:25**	3478
been on any king before him in **I**.	**1Ch 29:25**	3478
son of Jesse reigned over all **I**.	**1Ch 29:26**	3478
he reigned over **I** *was* forty years;	**1Ch 29:27**	3478
which came on him, on **I**,	**1Ch 29:30**	3478
Solomon spoke to all **I**,	**2Ch 1:2**	3478
and to every leader in all **I**,	**2Ch 1:2**	3478
Jerusalem, and he reigned over **I**.	**2Ch 1:13**	3478
this *being required* forever in **I**.	**2Ch 2:4**	3478
"Blessed be the LORD, the God of **I**,	**2Ch 2:12**	3478
aliens who *were* in the land of **I**,	**2Ch 2:17**	3478
assembled to Jerusalem the elders of **I**	**2Ch 5:2**	3478
households of the sons of **I**,	**2Ch 5:2**	3478
All the men of **I** assembled	**2Ch 5:3**	3478
Then all the elders of **I** came,	**2Ch 5:4**	3478
Solomon and all the congregation of **I**	**2Ch 5:6**	3478
a covenant with the sons of **I**,	**2Ch 5:10**	3478
and blessed all the assembly of **I**,	**2Ch 6:3**	3478
the assembly of **I** was standing.	**2Ch 6:3**	3478
"Blessed be the LORD, the God of **I**,	**2Ch 6:4**	3478
choose a city out of all the tribes of **I**	**2Ch 6:5**	3478
man for a leader over My people **I**;	**2Ch 6:5**	3478
David to be over My people **I**.'	**2Ch 6:6**	3478
name of the LORD, the God of **I**.	**2Ch 6:7**	3478
David and sit on the throne of **I**,	**2Ch 6:10**	3478
name of the LORD, the God of **I**.	**2Ch 6:10**	3478
He made with the sons of **I**."	**2Ch 6:11**	3478
presence of all the assembly of **I**	**2Ch 6:12**	3478
presence of all the assembly of **I** and	**2Ch 6:13**	3478
"O LORD, the God of **I**,	**2Ch 6:14**	3478
therefore, O LORD, the God of **I**,	**2Ch 6:16**	3478
a man to sit on the throne of **I**,	**2Ch 6:16**	3478
therefore, O LORD, the God of **I**,	**2Ch 6:17**	3478
Your servant and of Your people **I** when	**2Ch 6:21**	3478
Your people **I** are defeated before an	**2Ch 6:24**	3478
forgive the sin of Your people **I**,	**2Ch 6:25**	3478
of Your servants and Your people **I**,	**2Ch 6:27**	3478
by any man or by all Your people **I**,	**2Ch 6:29**	3478
who is not from Your people **I**,	**2Ch 6:32**	3478
and fear You as *do* Your people **I**,	**2Ch 6:33**	3478
All the sons of **I**,	**2Ch 7:3**	3478
and all **I** was standing.	**2Ch 7:6**	3478
seven days, and all **I** with him,	**2Ch 7:8**	3478
to Solomon and to His people **I**.	**2Ch 7:10**	3478
not lack a man *to be* ruler in **I**.'	**2Ch 7:18**	3478
and settled the sons of **I** there.	**2Ch 8:2**	3478
the Jebusites, who were not of **I**,	**2Ch 8:7**	3478
the sons of **I** had not destroyed,	**2Ch 8:8**	3478
for his work from the sons of **I**;	**2Ch 8:9**	3478
in the house of David king of **I**,	**2Ch 8:11**	3478
your God loved **I** establishing them	**2Ch 9:8**	3478
years in Jerusalem over all **I**.	**2Ch 9:30**	3478
for all **I** had come to Shechem to	**2Ch 10:1**	3478
When Jeroboam and all **I** came,	**2Ch 10:3**	3478
When all **I** *saw* that the king	**2Ch 10:16**	3478
Every man to your tents, O **I**;	**2Ch 10:16**	3478
So all **I** departed to their tents.	**2Ch 10:16**	3478
But as for the sons of **I** who lived	**2Ch 10:17**	3478
the sons of **I** stoned him to death.	**2Ch 10:18**	3478
So **I** has been in rebellion against	**2Ch 10:19**	3478
to fight against **I** to restore the	**2Ch 11:1**	3478
to all **I** in Judah and Benjamin,	**2Ch 11:3**	3478
the Levites who were in all **I** stood	**2Ch 11:13**	3478
all the tribes of **I** who set their hearts	**2Ch 11:16**	3478
on seeking the LORD God of **I** followed	**2Ch 11:16**	3478
he and all **I** with him forsook the law	**2Ch 12:1**	3478
So the princes of **I** and the king	**2Ch 12:6**	3478
chosen from all the tribes of **I**,	**2Ch 12:13**	3478
"Listen to me, Jeroboam and all **I**:	**2Ch 13:4**	3478
the LORD God of **I** gave the rule over	**2Ch 13:5**	3478
gave the rule over **I** forever to David	**2Ch 13:5**	3478
O sons of **I**, do not fight against	**2Ch 13:12**	3478
so that **I** was in front of Judah	**2Ch 13:13**	3478

and all **I** before Abijah and Judah.	**2Ch 13:15**	3478
the sons of **I** fled before Judah,	**2Ch 13:16**	3478
chosen men of **I** fell slain.	**2Ch 13:17**	3478
sons of **I** were subdued at that time,	**2Ch 13:18**	3478
I was without the true God and	**2Ch 15:3**	3478
they turned to the LORD God of **I**,	**2Ch 15:4**	3478
for many defected to him from **I**	**2Ch 15:9**	3478
would not seek the LORD God of **I**	**2Ch 15:13**	3478
places were not removed from **I**;	**2Ch 15:17**	3478
king of **I** came up against Judah	**2Ch 16:1**	3478
your treaty with Baasha king of **I**	**2Ch 16:3**	3478
armies against the cities of **I**,	**2Ch 16:4**	3478
Book of the Kings of Judah and **I**.	**2Ch 16:11**	3478
and made his position over **I** firm.	**2Ch 17:1**	3478
and did not act as **I** did.	**2Ch 17:4**	3478
Ahab king of **I** said to	**2Ch 18:3**	3478
Jehoshaphat said to the king of **I**,	**2Ch 18:4**	3478
king of **I** assembled the prophets,	**2Ch 18:5**	3478
The king of **I** said to Jehoshaphat,	**2Ch 18:7**	3478
the king of **I** called an officer and	**2Ch 18:8**	3478
Now the king of **I** and Jehoshaphat	**2Ch 18:9**	3478
all **I** Scattered on the mountains,	**2Ch 18:16**	3478
the king of **I** said to Jehoshaphat,	**2Ch 18:17**	3478
'Who will entice Ahab king of **I** to	**2Ch 18:19**	3478
Then the king of **I** said,	**2Ch 18:25**	3478
So the king of **I** and Jehoshaphat	**2Ch 18:28**	3478
The king of **I** said to Jehoshaphat,	**2Ch 18:29**	3478
the king of **I** disguised himself,	**2Ch 18:29**	3478
but with the king of **I** alone."	**2Ch 18:30**	3478
"It is the king of **I**,"	**2Ch 18:31**	3478
saw that it was not the king of **I**,	**2Ch 18:32**	3478
struck the king of **I** in a joint of the	**2Ch 18:33**	3478
and the king of **I** propped himself	**2Ch 18:34**	3478
heads of the fathers' *households* of **I**,	**2Ch 19:8**	3478
of this land before Your people **I** and	**2Ch 20:7**	3478
whom You did not let **I** invade	**2Ch 20:10**	3478
up to praise the LORD God of **I**,	**2Ch 20:19**	3478
fought against the enemies of **I**.	**2Ch 20:29**	3478
in the Book of the Kings of **I**.	**2Ch 20:34**	3478
himself with Ahaziah king of **I**.	**2Ch 20:35**	3478
the sons of Jehoshaphat king of **I**.	**2Ch 21:2**	3478
and some of the rulers of **I** also.	**2Ch 21:4**	3478
in the way of the kings of **I**,	**2Ch 21:6**	3478
in the way of the kings of **I**,	**2Ch 21:13**	3478
Jehoram the son of Ahab king of **I**	**2Ch 22:5**	3478
of the fathers' *households* of **I**,	**2Ch 23:2**	3478
and collect money from all **I** to	**2Ch 24:5**	3478
on the congregation of **I** for the tent	**2Ch 24:6**	3478
by Moses the servant of God on **I**	**2Ch 24:9**	3478
he had done well in **I** and to God	**2Ch 24:16**	3478
also 100,000 valiant warriors out of **I**	**2Ch 25:6**	3478
not let the army of **I** go with you,	**2Ch 25:7**	3478
for the LORD is not with **I** *nor*	**2Ch 25:7**	3478
I have given to the troops of **I**?"	**2Ch 25:9**	3478
the son of Jehu, the king of **I**,	**2Ch 25:17**	3478
Joash the king of **I** sent to Amaziah	**2Ch 25:18**	3478
So Joash king of **I** went up,	**2Ch 25:21**	3478
Judah was defeated by **I**,	**2Ch 25:22**	3478
Then Joash king of **I** captured	**2Ch 25:23**	3478
Joash, son of Jehoahaz, king of **I**,	**2Ch 25:25**	3478
Book of the Kings of Judah and **I**?	**2Ch 25:26**	3478
Book of the Kings of **I** and Judah.	**2Ch 27:7**	3478
in the ways of the kings of **I**;	**2Ch 28:2**	3478
driven out before the sons of **I**.	**2Ch 28:3**	3478
into the hand of the king of **I**,	**2Ch 28:5**	3478
The sons of **I** carried away	**2Ch 28:8**	3478
His burning anger is against **I**."	**2Ch 28:13**	3478
Judah because of Ahaz king of **I**,	**2Ch 28:19**	3478
the downfall of him and all **I**.	**2Ch 28:23**	3478
Book of the Kings of Judah and **I**.	**2Ch 28:26**	3478
into the tombs of the kings of **I**;	**2Ch 28:27**	3478
in the holy place to the God of **I**.	**2Ch 29:7**	3478
a covenant with the LORD God of **I**,	**2Ch 29:10**	3478
their blood to atone for all **I**,	**2Ch 29:24**	3478
and the sin offering for all **I**.	**2Ch 29:24**	3478
instruments of David, king of **I**.	**2Ch 29:27**	3478
Now Hezekiah sent to all **I** and	**2Ch 30:1**	3478
the Passover to the LORD God of **I**.	**2Ch 30:1**	3478
a proclamation throughout all **I**	**2Ch 30:5**	3478
to the LORD God of **I** at Jerusalem.	**2Ch 30:5**	3478
couriers went throughout all **I** and	**2Ch 30:6**	3478
"O sons of **I**, return to the LORD	**2Ch 30:6**	3478
LORD God of Abraham, Isaac and **I**,	**2Ch 30:6**	3478
The sons of **I** present in	**2Ch 30:21**	3478
all the assembly that came from **I**,	**2Ch 30:25**	3478
who came from the land of **I** and	**2Ch 30:25**	3478
the son of David, king of **I**,	**2Ch 30:26**	3478
all **I** who were present went out to	**2Ch 31:1**	3478
the sons of **I** returned to their cities,	**2Ch 31:1**	3478
the sons of **I** provided in	**2Ch 31:5**	3478
The sons of **I** and Judah who	**2Ch 31:6**	3478
blessed the LORD and His people **I**.	**2Ch 31:8**	3478
to insult the LORD God of **I**,	**2Ch 32:17**	3478
Book of the Kings of Judah and **I**.	**2Ch 32:32**	3478
dispossessed before the sons of **I**.	**2Ch 33:2**	3478
chosen from all the tribes of **I**,	**2Ch 33:7**	3478
I will not again remove the foot of **I**	**2Ch 33:8**	3478
destroyed before the sons of **I**.	**2Ch 33:9**	3478
Judah to serve the LORD God of **I**.	**2Ch 33:16**	3478
in the name of the LORD God of **I**,	**2Ch 33:18**	3478
the records of the kings of **I**.	**2Ch 33:18**	3478
altars throughout the land of **I**.	**2Ch 34:7**	3478
and from all the remnant of **I**,	**2Ch 34:9**	3478
who are left in **I** and in Judah,	**2Ch 34:21**	3478
"Thus says the LORD, the God of **I**,	**2Ch 34:23**	3478
'Thus says the LORD God of **I**	**2Ch 34:26**	3478
lands belonging to the sons of **I**,	**2Ch 34:33**	3478
made all who were present in **I** to	**2Ch 34:33**	3478
to the Levites who taught all **I** *and*	**2Ch 35:3**	3478

Context	Reference	Number
the LORD of hosts, the God of **I**,	**Jer 42:15**	3478
the LORD of hosts, the God of **I**,	**Jer 42:18**	3478
the LORD of hosts, the God of **I**,	**Jer 43:10**	3478
the LORD of hosts, the God of **I**,	**Jer 44:2**	3478
LORD God of hosts, the God of **I**,	**Jer 44:7**	3478
the LORD of hosts, the God of **I**,	**Jer 44:11**	3478
the LORD of hosts, the God of **I**,	**Jer 44:25**	3478
says the LORD the God of **I** to you,	**Jer 45:2**	3478
The LORD of hosts, the God of **I**,	**Jer 46:25**	3478
do not fear, Nor be dismayed, O **I**!	**Jer 46:27**	3478
the LORD of hosts, the God of **I**,	**Jer 48:1**	3478
house of **I** was ashamed of Bethel,	**Jer 48:13**	3478
was not **I** a laughingstock to you?	**Jer 48:27**	3478
"Does **I** have no sons?	**Jer 49:1**	3478
Then **I** will take possession of his	**Jer 49:2**	3478
"the sons of **I** will come, *both*	**Jer 50:4**	3478
"**I** is a scattered flock, the	**Jer 50:17**	3478
the LORD of hosts, the God of **I**:	**Jer 50:18**	3478
will bring **I** back to his pasture	**Jer 50:19**	3478
be made for the iniquity of **I**,	**Jer 50:20**	3478
LORD, Against the Holy One of **I**.	**Jer 50:29**	3478
"The sons of **I** are oppressed, And	**Jer 50:33**	3478
For neither **I** nor Judah has been	**Jer 51:5**	3478
of guilt Before the Holy One of **I**.	**Jer 51:5**	3478
the LORD of hosts, the God of **I**:	**Jer 51:33**	3478
is to fall *for* the slain of **I**,	**Jer 51:49**	3478
heaven to earth The glory of **I**,	**La 2:1**	3478
has cut off All the strength of **I**;	**La 2:3**	3478
He has swallowed up **I**;	**La 2:5**	3478
I am sending you to the sons of **I**,	**Ezk 2:3**	3478
and go, speak to the house of **I**."	**Ezk 3:1**	3478
go to the house of **I** and speak	**Ezk 3:4**	3478
language, *but* to the house of **I**,	**Ezk 3:5**	3478
yet the house of **I** will not be	**Ezk 3:7**	3478
house of **I** is stubborn and obstinate	**Ezk 3:7**	3478
you a watchman to the house of **I**;	**Ezk 3:17**	3478
This is a sign to the house of **I**.	**Ezk 4:3**	3478
iniquity of the house of **I** on it;	**Ezk 4:4**	3478
the iniquity of the house of **I**.	**Ezk 4:5**	3478
"Thus will the sons of **I** eat	**Ezk 4:13**	3478
will spread to all the house of **I**.	**Ezk 5:4**	3478
face toward the mountains of **I**,	**Ezk 6:2**	3478
'Mountains of **I**, listen to the	**Ezk 6:3**	3478
lay the dead bodies of the sons of **I**	**Ezk 6:5**	3478
abominations of the house of **I**,	**Ezk 6:11**	3478
the Lord GOD to the land of **I**,	**Ezk 7:2**	3478
glory of the God of **I** *was* there,	**Ezk 8:4**	3478
house of **I** are committing here,	**Ezk 8:6**	3478
all the idols of the house of **I**,	**Ezk 8:10**	3478
seventy elders of the house of **I**,	**Ezk 8:11**	3478
the elders of the house of **I** are	**Ezk 8:12**	3478
Then the glory of the God of **I**	**Ezk 9:3**	3478
destroying the whole remnant of **I**	**Ezk 9:8**	3478
iniquity of the house of **I** and Judah	**Ezk 9:9**	3478
glory of the God of **I** hovered over	**Ezk 10:19**	3478
the God of **I** by the river Chebar;	**Ezk 10:20**	3478
"So you think, house of **I**,	**Ezk 11:5**	3478
judge you to the border of **I**;	**Ezk 11:10**	3478
judge you to the border of **I**.	**Ezk 11:11**	3478
remnant of **I** to a complete end?"	**Ezk 11:13**	3478
exiles and the whole house of **I**,	**Ezk 11:15**	3478
will give you the land of **I**." '	**Ezk 11:17**	3478
glory of the God of **I** hovered over	**Ezk 11:22**	3478
you as a sign to the house of **I**."	**Ezk 12:6**	3478
of man, has not the house of **I**,	**Ezk 12:9**	3478
the house of **I** who are in it."	**Ezk 12:10**	3478
of Jerusalem in the land of **I**,	**Ezk 12:19**	3478
have concerning the land of **I**,	**Ezk 12:22**	3478
longer use it as a proverb in **I**."	**Ezk 12:23**	3478
divination within the house of **I**.	**Ezk 12:24**	3478
behold, the house of **I** is saying,	**Ezk 12:27**	3478
the prophets of **I** who prophesy,	**Ezk 13:2**	3478
"O **I**, your prophets have been	**Ezk 13:4**	3478
build the wall around the house of **I**	**Ezk 13:5**	3478
in the register of the house of **I**,	**Ezk 13:9**	3478
nor will they enter the land of **I**,	**Ezk 13:9**	3478
the prophets of **I** who prophesy to	**Ezk 13:16**	3478
Then some elders of **I** came to me	**Ezk 14:1**	3478
"Any man of the house of **I** who	**Ezk 14:4**	3478
the hearts of the house of **I** who are	**Ezk 14:5**	3478
"Therefore say to the house of **I**,	**Ezk 14:6**	3478
"For anyone of the house of **I** or	**Ezk 14:7**	3478
the immigrants who stay in **I** who	**Ezk 14:7**	3478
him from among My people **I**.	**Ezk 14:9**	3478
in order that the house of **I** may	**Ezk 14:11**	3478
speak a parable to the house of **I**,	**Ezk 17:2**	3478
"On the high mountain of **I** I will	**Ezk 17:23**	3478
concerning the land of **I**,	**Ezk 18:2**	3478
to use this proverb in **I** anymore.	**Ezk 18:3**	3478
to the idols of the house of **I**,	**Ezk 18:6**	3478
to the idols of the house of **I**,	**Ezk 18:15**	3478
Hear now, O house of **I**!	**Ezk 18:25**	3478
"But the house of **I** says,	**Ezk 18:29**	3478
My ways not right, O house of **I**?	**Ezk 18:29**	3478
I will judge you, O house of **I**,	**Ezk 18:30**	3478
why will you die, O house of **I**?	**Ezk 18:31**	3478
lamentation for the princes of **I**	**Ezk 19:1**	3478
no more On the mountains of **I**.	**Ezk 19:9**	3478
certain of the elders of **I** came to	**Ezk 20:1**	3478
of man, speak to the elders of **I** and	**Ezk 20:3**	3478
"On the day when I chose **I** and	**Ezk 20:5**	3478
"But the house of **I** rebelled	**Ezk 20:13**	3478
of man, speak to the house of **I** and	**Ezk 20:27**	3478
"Therefore, say to the house of **I**,	**Ezk 20:30**	3478
inquired of by you, O house of **I**?	**Ezk 20:31**	3478
they will not enter the land of **I**.	**Ezk 20:38**	3478
"As for you, O house of **I**,"	**Ezk 20:39**	3478
on the high mountain of **I**,"	**Ezk 20:40**	3478
"there the whole house of **I**,	**Ezk 20:40**	3478
I bring you into the land of **I**,	**Ezk 20:42**	3478
corrupt deeds, O house of **I**,"	**Ezk 20:44**	3478
prophesy against the land of **I**;	**Ezk 21:2**	3478
and say to the land of **I**,	**Ezk 21:3**	3478
is against all the officials of **I**.	**Ezk 21:12**	3478
wicked one, the prince of **I**,	**Ezk 21:25**	3478
"Behold, the rulers of **I**,	**Ezk 22:6**	3478
house of **I** has become dross to Me;	**Ezk 22:18**	3478
'Speak to the house of **I**,	**Ezk 24:21**	3478
against the land of **I** when it was	**Ezk 25:3**	3478
your soul against the land of **I**,	**Ezk 25:6**	3478
Edom by the hand of My people **I**.	**Ezk 25:14**	3478
"Judah and the land of **I**,	**Ezk 27:17**	3478
no more for the house of **I** a prickling	**Ezk 28:24**	3478
"When I gather the house of **I**	**Ezk 28:25**	3478
made of reed to the house of **I**	**Ezk 29:6**	3478
the confidence of the house of **I**,	**Ezk 29:16**	3478
a horn sprout for the house of **I**,	**Ezk 29:21**	3478
you a watchman for the house of **I**;	**Ezk 33:7**	3478
son of man, say to the house of **I**,	**Ezk 33:10**	3478
then will you die, O house of **I**?'	**Ezk 33:11**	3478
O house of **I**, I will judge each of	**Ezk 33:20**	3478
in the land of **I** are saying,	**Ezk 33:24**	3478
mountains of **I** will be desolate so	**Ezk 33:28**	3478
prophesy against the shepherds of **I**	**Ezk 34:2**	3478
Woe, shepherds of **I** who have been	**Ezk 34:2**	3478
feed them on the mountains of **I**,	**Ezk 34:13**	3478
be on the mountain heights of **I**.	**Ezk 34:14**	3478
pasture on the mountains of **I**.	**Ezk 34:14**	3478
they, the house of **I**, are My people	**Ezk 34:30**	3478
delivered the sons of **I** to the power of	**Ezk 35:5**	3478
against the mountains of **I** saying,	**Ezk 35:12**	3478
the inheritance of the house of **I**	**Ezk 35:15**	3478
to the mountains of **I** and say,	**Ezk 36:1**	3478
'O mountains of **I**, hear the word	**Ezk 36:1**	3478
'Therefore, O mountains of **I**,	**Ezk 36:4**	3478
prophesy concerning the land of **I** and	**Ezk 36:6**	3478
'But you, O mountains of **I**,	**Ezk 36:8**	3478
bear your fruit for My people **I**;	**Ezk 36:8**	3478
men on you, all the house of **I**,	**Ezk 36:10**	3478
I will cause men—My people **I**	**Ezk 36:12**	3478
house of **I** was living in their own	**Ezk 36:17**	3478
which the house of **I** had profaned	**Ezk 36:21**	3478
"Therefore say to the house of **I**,	**Ezk 36:22**	3478
not for your sake, O house of **I**,	**Ezk 36:22**	3478
for your ways, O house of **I**!"	**Ezk 36:32**	3478
house of **I** ask Me to do for them:	**Ezk 36:37**	3478
bones are the whole house of **I**;	**Ezk 37:11**	3478
will bring you into the land of **I**.	**Ezk 37:12**	3478
'For Judah and for the sons of **I**,	**Ezk 37:16**	3478
all the house of **I**, his companions.'	**Ezk 37:16**	3478
and the tribes of **I**, his companions;	**Ezk 37:19**	3478
I will take the sons of **I** from	**Ezk 37:21**	3478
the land, on the mountains of **I**;	**Ezk 37:22**	3478
I am the LORD who sanctifies **I**,	**Ezk 37:28**	3478
to the mountains of **I** which had been	**Ezk 38:8**	3478
My people **I** are living securely,	**Ezk 38:14**	3478
you will come up against My people **I**	**Ezk 38:16**	3478
My servants the prophets of **I**,	**Ezk 38:17**	3478
Gog comes against the land of **I**,"	**Ezk 38:18**	3478
great earthquake in the land of **I**.	**Ezk 38:19**	3478
you against the mountains of **I**.	**Ezk 39:2**	3478
will fall on the mountains of **I**,	**Ezk 39:4**	3478
known in the midst of My people **I**;	**Ezk 39:7**	3478
I am the LORD, the Holy One in **I**.	**Ezk 39:7**	3478
those who inhabit the cities of **I** will	**Ezk 39:9**	3478
give Gog a burial ground there in **I**,	**Ezk 39:11**	3478
"For seven months the house of **I**	**Ezk 39:12**	3478
sacrifice on the mountains of **I**,	**Ezk 39:17**	3478
"And the house of **I** will know	**Ezk 39:22**	3478
the house of **I** went into exile for their	**Ezk 39:23**	3478
mercy on the whole house of **I**;	**Ezk 39:25**	3478
out My Spirit on the house of **I**,"	**Ezk 39:29**	3478
He brought me into the land of **I** and	**Ezk 40:2**	3478
Declare to the house of **I** all that	**Ezk 40:4**	3478
the glory of the God of **I** was	**Ezk 43:2**	3478
dwell among the sons of **I** forever.	**Ezk 43:7**	3478
And the house of **I** will not again	**Ezk 43:7**	3478
the temple to the house of **I**,	**Ezk 43:10**	3478
LORD God of **I** has entered by it;	**Ezk 44:2**	3478
ones, to the house of **I**,	**Ezk 44:6**	3478
your abominations, O house of **I**,	**Ezk 44:6**	3478
who are among the sons of **I**,	**Ezk 44:9**	3478
far from Me when **I** went astray,	**Ezk 44:10**	3478
of iniquity to the house of **I**,	**Ezk 44:12**	3478
the sons of **I** went astray from Me,	**Ezk 44:15**	3478
the offspring of the house of **I**,	**Ezk 44:22**	3478
you shall give them no possession in **I**	**Ezk 44:28**	3478
devoted thing in **I** shall be theirs.	**Ezk 44:29**	3478
shall be for the whole house of **I**.	**Ezk 45:6**	3478
be his land for a possession in **I**;	**Ezk 45:8**	3478
rest of the land to the house of **I**	**Ezk 45:8**	3478
"Enough, you princes of **I**;	**Ezk 45:9**	3478
from the watering places of **I**	**Ezk 45:15**	3478
this offering for the prince in **I**.	**Ezk 45:16**	3478
feasts of the house of **I**;	**Ezk 45:17**	3478
atonement for the house of **I**."	**Ezk 45:17**	3478
among the twelve tribes of **I**;	**Ezk 47:13**	3478
Gilead and the land of **I**,	**Ezk 47:18**	3478
according to the tribes of **I**.	**Ezk 47:21**	3478
native-born among the sons of **I**;	**Ezk 47:22**	3478
with you among the tribes of **I**.	**Ezk 47:22**	3478
when the sons of **I** went astray as	**Ezk 48:11**	3478
city, out of all the tribes of **I**,	**Ezk 48:19**	3478
shall divide by lot to the tribes of **I**	**Ezk 48:29**	3478
city, named for the tribes of **I**,	**Ezk 48:31**	3478
to bring in some of the sons of **I**,	**Da 1:3**	3478
inhabitants of Jerusalem and all **I**,	**Da 9:7**	3478
"Indeed all **I** has transgressed	**Da 9:11**	3478
my sin and the sin of my people **I**,	**Da 9:20**	3478
the son of Joash, king of **I**.	**Hos 1:1**	3478
to the kingdom of the house of **I**.	**Hos 1:4**	3478
I will break the bow of **I** in the	**Hos 1:5**	3478
have compassion on the house of **I**,	**Hos 1:6**	3478
Yet the number of the sons of **I**	**Hos 1:10**	3478
sons of **I** will be gathered together,	**Hos 1:11**	3478
as the LORD loves the sons of **I**,	**Hos 3:1**	3478
For the sons of **I** will remain for	**Hos 3:4**	3478
the sons of **I** will return and seek	**Hos 3:5**	3478
the word of the LORD, O sons of **I**,	**Hos 4:1**	3478
Though you, **I**, play the harlot, Do	**Hos 4:15**	3478
Since **I** is stubborn Like a	**Hos 4:16**	3478
Give heed, O house of **I**!	**Hos 5:1**	3478
and **I** is not hidden from Me;	**Hos 5:3**	3478
the harlot, **I** has defiled itself.	**Hos 5:3**	3478
pride of **I** testifies against him,	**Hos 5:5**	3478
And **I** and Ephraim stumble in their	**Hos 5:5**	3478
Among the tribes of **I** I declare	**Hos 5:9**	3478
In the house of **I** I have seen a	**Hos 6:10**	3478
is there, **I** has defiled itself.	**Hos 6:10**	3478
When I would heal **I**,	**Hos 7:1**	3478
pride of **I** testifies against him,	**Hos 7:10**	3478
"My God, we of **I** know You!"	**Hos 8:2**	3478
I has rejected the good;	**Hos 8:3**	3478
For from **I** is even this!	**Hos 8:6**	3478
I is swallowed up;	**Hos 8:8**	3478
For **I** has forgotten his Maker and	**Hos 8:14**	3478
Do not rejoice, O **I**,	**Hos 9:1**	3478
Let **I** know *this!* The prophet is a fool,	**Hos 9:7**	3478
I like grapes in the wilderness;	**Hos 9:10**	3478
I is a luxuriant vine;	**Hos 10:1**	3478
And **I** will be ashamed of its own	**Hos 10:6**	3478
high places of Aven, the sin of **I**,	**Hos 10:8**	3478
of Gibeah you have sinned, O **I**;	**Hos 10:9**	3478
king of **I** will be completely cut off.	**Hos 10:15**	3478
When **I** *was* a youth I loved him,	**Hos 11:1**	3478
How can I surrender you, O **I**?	**Hos 11:8**	3478
And the house of **I** with deceit;	**Hos 11:12**	3478
of Aram, And **I** worked for a wife,	**Hos 12:12**	3478
the LORD brought **I** from Egypt,	**Hos 12:13**	3478
He exalted himself in **I**,	**Hos 13:1**	3478
It is your destruction, O **I**,	**Hos 13:9**	3478
Return, O **I**, to the LORD your God,	**Hos 14:1**	3478
I will be like the dew to **I**;	**Hos 14:5**	3478
know that I am in the midst of **I**,	**Jl 2:27**	3478
My people and My inheritance, **I**,	**Jl 3:2**	3478
And a stronghold to the sons of **I**.	**Jl 3:16**	3478
concerning **I** in the days of Uzziah	**Am 1:1**	3478
Jeroboam son of Joash, king of **I**,	**Am 1:1**	3478
"For three transgressions of **I**	**Am 2:6**	3478
Is this not so, O sons of **I**?"	**Am 2:11**	3478
has spoken against you, sons of **I**,	**Am 3:1**	3478
So will the sons of **I** dwelling in	**Am 3:12**	3478
you love *to do*, you sons of **I**,"	**Am 4:5**	3478
thus I will do to you, O **I**;	**Am 4:12**	3478
Prepare to meet your God, O **I**."	**Am 4:12**	3478
for you as a dirge, O house of **I**:	**Am 5:1**	3478
The virgin **I**. She *lies* neglected on	**Am 5:2**	3478
have ten left to the house of **I**."	**Am 5:3**	3478
says the LORD to the house of **I**,	**Am 5:4**	3478
for forty years, O house of **I**?	**Am 5:25**	3478
To whom the house of **I** comes.	**Am 6:1**	3478
against you, O house of **I**,"	**Am 6:14**	3478
line In the midst of My people **I**.	**Am 7:8**	3478
the sanctuaries of **I** laid waste.	**Am 7:9**	3478
sent *word* to Jeroboam king of **I**,	**Am 7:10**	3478
in the midst of the house of **I**;	**Am 7:10**	3478
I will certainly go from its land into	**Am 7:11**	3478
'Go prophesy to My people **I**.'	**Am 7:15**	3478
'You shall not prophesy against **I**	**Am 7:16**	3478
I will certainly go from its land	**Am 7:17**	3478
"The end has come for My people **I**.	**Am 8:2**	3478
of Ethiopia to Me, O sons of **I**?"	**Am 9:7**	3478
Have I not brought up **I** from the	**Am 9:7**	3478
And I will shake the house of **I**	**Am 9:9**	3478
the captivity of My people **I**,	**Am 9:14**	3478
of this host of the sons of **I**,	**Ob 1:20**	3478
for the sins of the house of **I**.	**Mi 1:5**	3478
found The rebellious acts of **I**.	**Mi 1:13**	3478
a deception To the kings of **I**.	**Mi 1:14**	3478
The glory of **I** will enter Adullam.	**Mi 1:15**	3478
surely gather the remnant of **I**.	**Mi 2:12**	3478
And rulers of the house of **I**.	**Mi 3:1**	3478
rebellious act, Even to **I** his sin.	**Mi 3:8**	3478
And rulers of the house of **I**,	**Mi 3:9**	3478
smite the judge of **I** on the cheek.	**Mi 5:1**	3478
go forth for Me to be ruler in **I**.	**Mi 5:2**	3478
Will return to the sons of **I**.	**Mi 5:3**	3478
Even with **I** He will dispute.	**Mi 6:2**	3478
of Jacob Like the splendor of **I**,	**Na 2:2**	3478
the LORD of hosts, The God of **I**,	**Zph 2:9**	3478
"The remnant of **I** will do no	**Zph 3:13**	3478
Shout *in triumph*, O **I**!	**Zph 3:14**	3478
The King of **I**, the LORD, is in	**Zph 3:15**	3478
which have scattered Judah, **I** and	**Zch 1:19**	3478
O house of Judah and house of **I**,	**Zch 8:13**	3478
especially of all the tribes of **I**,	**Zch 9:1**	3478
brotherhood between Judah and **I**.	**Zch 11:14**	3478
the word of the LORD concerning **I**.	**Zch 12:1**	3478
oracle of the word of the LORD to **I**	**Mal 1:1**	3478
magnified beyond the border of **I**!"	**Mal 1:5**	3478
committed in **I** and in Jerusalem;	**Mal 2:11**	3478
says the LORD, the God of **I**,	**Mal 2:16**	3478
commanded him in Horeb for all **I**.	**Mal 4:4**	3478
WHO WILL SHEPHERD MY PEOPLE **I**.' "	**Mt 2:6**	*2474*
mother, and go into the land of **I**;	**Mt 2:20**	*2474*
and came into the land of **I**.	**Mt 2:21**	*2474*
such great faith with anyone in **I**.	**Mt 8:10**	*2474*

like this has ever been seen in **I**." **Mt 9:33** *2474*
the lost sheep of the house of **I**. **Mt 10:6** *2474*
going through the cities of **I** until **Mt 10:23** *2474*
lost sheep of the house of **I**." **Mt 15:24** *2474*
and they glorified the God of **I**. **Mt 15:31** *2474*
judging the twelve tribes of **I**. **Mt 19:28** *2474*
HAD BEEN SET by the sons of **I**; **Mt 27:9** *2474*
He is the King of **I**; **Mt 27:42** *2474*
'HEAR, O **I**! THE LORD OUR GOD IS ONE **Mk 12:29** *2474*
"Let *this* Christ, the King of **I**, **Mk 15:32** *2474*
turn many of the sons of **I** back to **Lk 1:16** *2474*
has given help to **I** His servant, **Lk 1:54** *2474*
"Blessed *be* the Lord God of **I**, **Lk 1:68** *2474*
day of his public appearance to **I**. **Lk 1:80** *2474*
looking for the consolation of **I**; **Lk 2:25** *2474*
And the glory of Your people **I**." **Lk 2:32** *2474*
the fall and rise of many in **I**, **Lk 2:34** *2474*
widows in **I** in the days of Elijah, **Lk 4:25** *2474*
"And there were many lepers in **I** **Lk 4:27** *2474*
not even in **I** have I found such **Lk 7:9** *2474*
judging the twelve tribes of **I**. **Lk 22:30** *2474*
was He who was going to redeem **I**. **Lk 24:21** *2474*
that He might be manifested to **I**, **Jn 1:31** *2474*
You are the King of **I**." **Jn 1:49** *2474*
"Are you the teacher of **I** and **Jn 3:10** *2474*
OF THE LORD, even the King of **I**." **Jn 12:13** *2474*
are restoring the kingdom to **I**?" **Ac 1:6** *2474*
"Men of **I**, listen to these words: **Ac 2:22** *2475a*
let all the house of **I** know for **Ac 2:36** *2274*
"Men of **I**, why are you amazed at **Ac 3:12** *2475a*
you and to all the people of **I**, **Ac 4:10** *2274*
the Gentiles and the peoples of **I**, **Ac 4:27** *2274*
all the Senate of the sons of **I**, **Ac 5:21** *2274*
Savior, to grant repentance to **I**, **Ac 5:31** *2274*
"Men of **I**, take care what you **Ac 5:35** *2475a*
visit his brethren, the sons of **I**. **Ac 7:23** *2274*
Moses who said to the sons of **I**, **Ac 7:37** *2274*
WILDERNESS, WAS IT, O HOUSE OF **I**? **Ac 7:42** *2274*
and kings and the sons of **I**; **Ac 9:15** *2274*
which He sent to the sons of **I**, **Ac 10:36** *2274*
"Men of **I**, and you who fear God, **Ac 13:16** *2475a*
God of this people **I** chose our **Ac 13:17** *2274*
God has brought to **I** a Savior, **Ac 13:23** *2274*
repentance to all the people of **I**. **Ac 13:24** *2274*
"Men of **I**, come to our aid! **Ac 21:28** *2475a*
for the sake of the hope of **I**." **Ac 28:20** *2274*
they are not all **I** who are *descended* **Ro 9:6** *2274*
Israel who are *descended* from **I**; **Ro 9:6** *2274*
Isaiah cries out concerning **I**, **Ro 9:27** *2474*
THE NUMBER OF THE SONS OF **I** BE **Ro 9:27** *2274*
I, pursuing a law of righteousness **Ro 9:31** *2474*
But I say, surely **I** did not know, **Ro 10:19** *2474*
But as for **I** He says, **Ro 10:21** *2474*
how he pleads with God against **I**? **Ro 11:2** *2474*
What **I** is seeking, it **Ro 11:7** *2474*
a partial hardening has happened to **I** **Ro 11:25** *2474*
and so all **I** will be saved; **Ro 11:26** *2474*
Look at the nation **I**; **1Co 10:18** *2474*
sons of **I** could not look intently at **2Co 3:7** *2474*
sons of **I** would not look intently at **2Co 3:13** *2474*
upon them, and upon the **I** of God. **Ga 6:16** *2474*
from the commonwealth of **I**, **Eph 2:12** *2474*
eighth day, of the nation of **I**, **Php 3:5** *2474*
COVENANT WITH THE HOUSE OF **I** **Heb 8:8** *2474*
I WILL MAKE WITH THE HOUSE OF **I** **Heb 8:10** *2474*
of the exodus of the sons of **I**, **Heb 11:22** *2474*
block before the sons of **I**, **Rv 2:14** *2474*
from every tribe of the sons of **I**: **Rv 7:4** *2474*
twelve tribes of the sons of **I**. **Rv 21:12** *2474*

ISRAELITE
Now the son of an **I** woman, **Lv 24:10** 3482
and the **I** woman's son and a man of **Lv 24:10** 3482
The son of the **I** woman **Lv 24:11** 3482
a man whose name was Ithra the **I**, **2Sa 17:25** 3481
an **I** indeed, in whom there is no deceit!" **Jn 1:47** *2475a*
For I too am an **I**, a descendant of **Ro 11:1** *2475a*

ISRAELITES
The **I**, all the men and women, **Ex 35:29** 3478, 1121
to all the **I** who came there. **1Sa 2:14** 3478
I who *were* with Saul and Jonathan. **1Sa 14:21** 3478
while the **I** were camping by the **1Sa 29:1** 3478
I arose and struck the Moabites, **2Ki 3:24** 3478
the **I**, the priests, the Levites, **Ne 11:3** 3478
who are **I**, to whom belongs the **Ro 9:4** *2475a*
Are they **I**? So am I. **2Co 11:22** *2475a*

ISRAEL'S
with his right hand toward **I** left, **Gn 48:13** 3478
with his left hand toward **I** right, **Gn 48:13** 3478
The sons of Reuben, **I** firstborn: **Ex 6:14** 3478
and to the Egyptians for **I** sake, **Ex 18:8** 3478
the sons of Reuben, **I** firstborn, **Nu 1:20** 3478
Reuben, **I** firstborn, the sons of **Nu 26:5** 3478
"From the sons of **I** half, **Nu 31:30** 3478
As for the sons of **I** half, **Nu 31:42** 3478
and from the sons of **I** half, **Nu 31:47** 3478
the land of **I** inheritance; **Jg 20:6** 3478
And one of the king of **I** servants **2Ki 3:11** 3478
And will name **I** name with honor. **Is 44:5** 3478
that I punish **I** transgressions, **Am 3:14** 3478

ISSACHAR
So she named him **I**. **Gn 30:18** 3485
Levi and Judah and **I** and Zebulun; **Gn 35:23** 3485
The sons of **I**: **Gn 46:13** 3485
"**I** is a strong donkey, Lying down **Gn 49:14** 3485
I, Zebulun and Benjamin; **Ex 1:3** 3485
of **I**, Nethanel the son of Zuar; **Nu 1:8** 3485
Of the sons of **I**, their **Nu 1:28** 3485
numbered men of the tribe of **I** **Nu 1:29** 3485
to him *shall be* the tribe of **I**, **Nu 2:5** 3485
and the leader of the sons of **I**: **Nu 2:5** 3485
the son of Zuar, leader of **I**, **Nu 7:18** 3485
the tribal army of the sons of **I**; **Nu 10:15** 3485
from the tribe of **I**, **Nu 13:7** 3485
sons of **I** according to their families **Nu 26:23** 3485
These are the families of **I** **Nu 26:25** 3485
Of the tribe of the sons of **I** a leader **Nu 34:26** 3485
Simeon, Levi, Judah, **I**, **Dt 27:12** 3485
going forth, And, **I**, in your tents. **Dt 33:18** 3485
on the north and to **I** on the east. **Jos 17:10** 3485
In **I** and in Asher, Manasseh **Jos 17:11** 3485
The fourth lot fell to **I**, **Jos 19:17** 3485
sons of **I** according to their families **Jos 19:17** 3485
sons of **I** according to their families **Jos 19:23** 3485
from the families of the tribe of **I** **Jos 21:6** 3485
From the tribe of **I**, **Jos 21:28** 3485
princes of **I** *were* with Deborah; **Jg 5:15** 3485
As *was* **I**, so *was* Barak; **Jg 5:15** 3485
Puah, the son of Dodo, a man of **I**, **Jg 10:1** 3485
the son of Paruah, in **I**; **1Ki 4:17** 3485
the son of Ahijah of the house of **I** **1Ki 15:27** 3485
Reuben, Simeon, Levi, Judah, **I**, **1Ch 2:1** 3485
were given from the tribe of **I** and **1Ch 6:62** 3485
and from the tribe of **I**: **1Ch 6:72** 3485
Now the sons of **I** *were* four: **1Ch 7:1** 3485
relatives among all the families of **I** **1Ch 7:5** 3485
Of the sons of **I**, **1Ch 12:32** 3485
far as **I** and Zebulun and Naphtali, **1Ch 12:40** 3485
Ammiel the sixth, **I** the seventh **1Ch 26:5** 3485
for **I**, Omri the son of Michael; **1Ch 27:18** 3485
and Manasseh, **I** and Zebulun, **2Ch 30:18** 3485
the east side to the west side, **I**, **Ezk 48:25** 3485
"Beside the border of **I**, **Ezk 48:26** 3485
the gate of **I**, one; **Ezk 48:33** 3485
from the tribe of **I** twelve thousand, **Rv 7:7** *2475b*

ISSHIAH
were Michael, Obadiah, Joel, **I**; **1Ch 7:3** 3449
Elkanah, **I**, Azarel, Joezer, **1Ch 12:6** 3449
Micah the first and **I** the second. **1Ch 23:20** 3449
the sons of Rehabiah, **I** the first. **1Ch 24:21** 3449
The brother of Micah, **I**; **1Ch 24:25** 3449
of the sons of **I**, Zechariah. **1Ch 24:25** 3449

ISSHIJAH
Eliezer, **I**, Malchijah, Shemaiah, **Ezr 10:31** 3449

ISSUE
the first **i** of the womb among the **Nu 3:12** 6363a
of every first **i** of the womb, **Nu 8:16** 6363b
first **i** of the womb of all flesh, **Nu 18:15** 6363a
of your sons who shall **i** from you, **2Ki 20:18** 3318
now **i** a decree to make these men **Ezr 4:21** 7761
I **i** a decree concerning what you **Ezr 6:8** 7761
i a decree to all the treasurers **Ezr 7:21** 7761
The first **i** of their virility in **Ps 78:51**
father's house, offspring and **i**, **Is 22:24** 6849
of your sons who will **i** from you, **Is 39:7** 3318
whose **i** is *like* the issue of horses. **Ezk 23:20** 2231
whose issue is *like* the **i** of horses. **Ezk 23:20** 2231
those who were circumcised took **i** **Ac 11:2** *1252*
and elders concerning this **i**. **Ac 15:2** *2213*

ISSUED
So Moses **i** a command, and a **Ex 36:6** 6680
"A decree has been **i** by me, **Ezr 4:19** 7761
rebuilt until a decree is **i** by me. **Ezr 4:21** 7761
"Who **i** you a decree to rebuild **Ezr 5:3** 7761
'Who **i** you a decree to rebuild **Ezr 5:9** 7761
King Cyrus **i** a decree to rebuild **Ezr 5:13** 7761
that a decree was **i** by King Cyrus **Ezr 5:17** 7761
Then King Darius **i** a decree, **Ezr 6:1** 7761
Cyrus, Cyrus the king **i** a decree: **Ezr 6:3** 7761
"And I **i** a decree that any man **Ezr 6:11** 7761
I, Darius, have **i** *this* decree, let **Ezr 6:12** 7761
I have **i** a decree that any of the **Ezr 7:13** 7761
let a royal edict be **i** by him and **Es 1:19** 3318
A copy of the edict to be **i** as law **Es 3:14** 5414
decree was **i** at the citadel in Susa; **Es 3:15** 5414
text of the edict which had been **i** **Es 4:8** 5414
A copy of the edict to be **i** as law **Es 8:13** 5414
and an edict was **i** in Susa, **Es 9:14** 5414
and **i** a proclamation concerning **Da 5:29** 3745
supplications the command was **i**, **Da 9:23** 3318
He **i** a proclamation and it said, **Jon 3:7** 2199
The LORD has **i** a command **Na 1:14** 6680

ISSUES
which **i** from between her legs and **Dt 28:57** 3318

ISSUING
i of a decree to restore and rebuild **Da 9:25** 4161

ITALIAN
of what was called the **I** cohort, **Ac 10:1** *2483*

ITALY
recently come from **I** with his wife **Ac 18:2** *2482*
decided that we would sail for **I**, **Ac 27:1** *2482*
an Alexandrian ship sailing for **I**, **Ac 27:6** *2482*
Those from **I** greet you. **Heb 13:24** *2482*

ITCH
and with the scab and with the **i**, **Dt 28:27** 2775b

ITEMS
man by name the **i** he is to carry. **Nu 4:32** 3627

ITHAI
I the son of Ribai of Gibeah of **1Ch 11:31** 863a

ITHAMAR
Nadab and Abihu, Eleazar and **I**. **Ex 6:23** 385
Nadab and Abihu, Eleazar and **I**, **Ex 28:1** 385
of the Levites, by the hand of **I** the **Ex 38:21** 385
and to his sons Eleazar and **I**, **Lv 10:6** 385
his surviving sons, Eleazar and **I**, **Lv 10:12** 385
surviving sons Eleazar and **I**, **Lv 10:16** 385
and Abihu, Eleazar and **I**. **Nu 3:2** 385
So Eleazar and **I** served as priests **Nu 3:4** 385
of **I** the son of Aaron the priest. **Nu 4:28** 385
I the son of Aaron the priest." **Nu 4:33** 385
of **I** the son of Aaron the priest. **Nu 7:8** 385
Nadab and Abihu, Eleazar and **I**. **Nu 26:60** 385
were Nadab, Abihu, Eleazar and **I**. **1Ch 6:3** 385
were Nadab, Abihu, Eleazar and **I**. **1Ch 24:1** 385
Eleazar and **I** served as priests. **1Ch 24:2** 385
and Ahimelech of the sons of **I**, **1Ch 24:3** 385
Eleazar than the descendants of **I**, **1Ch 24:4** 385
and eight of the descendants of **I** **1Ch 24:4** 385
Eleazar and the descendants of **I**. **1Ch 24:5** *385*
for Eleazar and one taken for **I**. **1Ch 24:6** 385
of the sons of **I**, Daniel; **Ezr 8:2** 385

ITHIEL
the son of Maaseiah, the son of **I**, **Ne 11:7** 384
The man declares to **I**, **Pr 30:1** 384
declares to Ithiel, to **I** and Ucal: **Pr 30:1** 384

ITHLAH
and Shaalabbin and Aijalon and **I**, **Jos 19:42** 3494

ITHMAH
sons of Elnaam, and **I** the Moabite, **1Ch 11:46** 3495

ITHNAN
and Kedesh and Hazor and **I**, **Jos 15:23** 3497

ITHRA
whose name was **I** the Israelite, **2Sa 17:25** 3501

ITHRAN
and Eshban and **I** and Cheran. **Gn 36:26** 3506
of Dishon *were* Hamran, Eshban, **I** and **1Ch 1:41** 3506
Bezer, Hod, Shamma, Shilshah, **I** and **1Ch 7:37** 3506

ITHREAM
and the sixth, **I**, by David's wife **2Sa 3:5** 3507
the sixth *was* **I**, by his wife Eglah. **1Ch 3:3** 3507

ITHRITE
Ira the **I**, Gareb the Ithrite, **2Sa 23:38** 3505
Ira the Ithrite, Gareb the **I**, **2Sa 23:38** 3505
Ira the **I**, Gareb the Ithrite, **1Ch 11:40** 3505
Ira the Ithrite, Gareb the **I**, **1Ch 11:40** 3505

ITHRITES
the **I**, the Puthites, the **1Ch 2:53** 3505

IT'S
"But they will say, '**I** hopeless! **Jer 18:12**

ITSELF
of his servants, every drove by **i**, **Gn 32:16** 905
the standing grain or the field **i** **Ex 22:6**
sapphire, as clear as the sky **i**. **Ex 24:10** 6106
the burnt offering **i** *shall remain* **Lv 6:9** 1931
"The goat shall bear on **i** all **Lv 16:22**
lioness, And as a lion it lifts **i**; **Nu 23:24**
not eat anything which dies *of* **i**. **Dt 14:21**
He knows, and may Israel **i** know. **Jos 22:22** 1931
supports *were* part of the stand **i**. **1Ki 7:34**
eat this year what grows of **i**, **2Ki 19:29**
land of utter gloom as darkness **i**, **Jb 10:22**
Their inward part is destruction **i**. **Ps 5:9**
His heart gathers wickedness to **i**; **Ps 41:6**
Sinai **i** *quaked* at the presence of **Ps 68:8** 2088
wealth certainly makes **i** wings Like **Pr 23:5**
his hatred covers **i** with guile, **Pr 26:26**
Is the axe to boast **i** over the **Is 10:15**
Is the saw to exalt **i** over the one **Is 10:15**
eat this year what grows of **i**, **Is 37:30**
I have never eaten what died of **i** **Ezk 4:14**
be in subjection, not exalting **i**, **Ezk 17:14**
it will never again lift **i** up above **Ezk 29:15**
into the wall of the temple **i** **Ezk 41:6**
but it will **i** endure forever. **Da 2:44** 1932
It even magnified **i** to be equal **Da 8:11**
the harlot, Israel has defiled **i**. **Hos 5:3**
is there, Israel has defiled **i**. **Hos 6:10**
The thing **i** will be carried to **Hos 10:6** 1571
Which dwells by **i** in the woodland, **Mi 7:14** 910
will mourn, every family by **i**; **Zch 12:12** 905
family of the house of David by **i** and **Zch 12:12** 905
family of the house of Nathan by **i** and **Zch 12:12** 905
family of the house of Levi by **i** and **Zch 12:13** 905
the family of the Shimeites by **i** and **Zch 12:13** 905
that remain, every family by **i** and **Zch 12:14** 905
for tomorrow will care for **i**. **Mt 6:34** *1438*
Any kingdom divided against **i** is **Mt 12:25** *1438*
any city or house divided against **i** **Mt 12:25** *1438*
other spirits more wicked than **i**, **Mt 12:45** *1438*
If a kingdom is divided against **i**, **Mk 3:24** *1438*
If a house is divided against **i**, **Mk 3:25** *1438*
"The soil produces crops by **i**; **Mk 4:28** *844*
Any kingdom divided against **i** **Lk 11:17** *1438*
a house *divided* against **i** falls. **Lk 11:17** *3624*
other spirits more evil than **i**, **Lk 11:26** *1438*
the branch cannot bear fruit of **i** unless **Jn 15:4** *1438*
but rolled up in a place by **i**. **Jn 20:7** *5565*
even the world **i** would not contain **Jn 21:25** *846*
city, which opened for them by **i**; **Ac 12:10** *844*
nor in the city **i** did they find **Ac 24:12**
because of the heat and fastened **i** on **Ac 28:3**
not subject **i** to the law of God, **Ro 8:7**
creation **i** also will be set free from **Ro 8:21** *846*
that nothing is unclean in **i**; **Ro 14:14** *1438*
the fire **i** will test the quality of each **1Co 3:13** *846*
Does not even nature **i** teach you **1Co 11:14** *846*
for the building up of **i** in love. **Eph 4:16** *1438*
Not that I seek the gift **i**, **Php 4:17**
sprinkled both the book **i** and all **Heb 9:19** *846*
into heaven **i**, now to appear in the **Heb 9:24** *846*
has no works, is dead, *being* by **i**. **Jas 2:17** *1438*
everyone, and from the truth **i**; **3Jn 1:12** *846*

ITTAI
the king said to **I** the Gittite, 2Sa 15:19 863a
But **I** answered the king and said, 2Sa 15:21 863a
Therefore David said to **I**, 2Sa 15:22 863a
So **I** the Gittite passed over with 2Sa 15:22 863a
the command of **I** the Gittite. 2Sa 18:2 863a
charged Joab and Abishai and **I**, 2Sa 18:5 863a
charged you and Abishai and **I**, 2Sa 18:12 863a
I the son of Ribai of Gibeah of 2Sa 23:29 863a
ITURAEA
the region of **I** and Trachonitis, Lk 3:1 *2484*
IVORY
the king made a great throne of **i** 1Ki 10:18 8127
silver, **I** and apes and peacocks. 1Ki 10:22 8143
and the **i** house which he built 1Ki 22:39 8127
the king made a great throne of **i** 2Ch 9:17 8127
silver, **I** and apes and peacocks. 2Ch 9:21 8143
Out of **i** palaces stringed Ps 45:8 8127
His abdomen is carved **i** Inlaid with SS 5:14 8127
"Your neck is like a tower of **i**, SS 7:4 8127
With **i** they have inlaid your deck Ezk 27:6 8127
i tusks and ebony they brought as Ezk 27:15 8127
The houses of **i** will also perish Am 3:15 8127
Those who recline on beds of **i** Am 6:4 8127
every article of **i** and every article Rv 18:12 *1661*
IVVAH
gods of Sepharvaim, Hena and **I**? 2Ki 18:34 5755
Sepharvaim, and *of* Hena and **I**?' " 2Ki 19:13 5755
Sepharvaim, *and of* Hena and **I**?' " Is 37:13 5755
IYE-ABARIM
from Oboth and camped at **I**, Nu 21:11 5863
from Oboth and camped at **I**, Nu 33:44 5863
IYIM
They journeyed from **I** and Nu 33:45 5864
IZHAR
Amram and **I** and Hebron and Uzziel; Ex 6:18 3324
The sons of **I**: Ex 6:21 3324
Amram and **I**, Hebron and Uzziel; Nu 3:19 3324
Now Korah the son of **I**, Nu 16:1 3324
Helah *were* Zereth, **I** and Ethnan. 1Ch 4:7 3328
The sons of Kohath *were* Amram, **I**, 1Ch 6:2 3324
The sons of Kohath *were* Amram, **I**, 1Ch 6:18 3324
the son of **I**, the son of Kohath, 1Ch 6:38 3324
Amram, **I**, Hebron and Uzziel. 1Ch 23:12 3324
son of **I** was Shelomith the chief. 1Ch 23:18 3324
IZHARITES
the Amramites and the family of the **I** Nu 3:27 3325
Of the **I**, Shelomoth; 1Ch 24:22 3325
As for the Amramites, the **I**, 1Ch 26:23 3325
As for the **I**, Chenaniah and his 1Ch 26:29 3325
IZLIAH
Ishmerai, **I** and Jobab *were* the 1Ch 8:18 3152a
IZRAHIAH
The son of Uzzi *was* **I**. 1Ch 7:3 3156
And the sons of **I** *were* Michael, 1Ch 7:3 3156
IZRAHITE
was the commander Shamhuth the **I**; 1Ch 27:8 3155
IZRI
the fourth to **I**, his sons and his 1Ch 25:11 3339
IZZIAH
sons of Parosh *there were* Ramiah, **I** Ezr 10:25 3150

J

JAAKAN
of Ezer *were* Bilhan, Zaavan and **J**. 1Ch 1:42 3292
JAAKOBAH
and Elioenai, **J**, Jeshohaiah, 1Ch 4:36 3291
JAALA
the sons of **J**, the sons of Darkon, Ne 7:58 3279
JAALAH
the sons of **J**, the sons of Darkon, Ezr 2:56 3279
JAAR
We found it in the field of **J**. Ps 132:6 3293a
JAARE-OREGIM
and Elhanan the son of **J** the 2Sa 21:19 3296
JAARESHIAH
J, Elijah and Zichri *were* the 1Ch 8:27 3298
JAASIEL
and Obed and **J** the Mezobaite. 1Ch 11:47 3300
for Benjamin, **J** the son of Abner; 1Ch 27:21 3300
JAASU
Mattaniah, Mattenai, **J**, Ezr 10:37 3299
JAAZANIAH
and **J** the son of the Maacathite, 2Ki 25:23 2970
Then I took **J** the son of Jeremiah, Jer 35:3 2970
with **J** the son of Shaphan standing Ezk 8:11 2970
and among them I saw **J** son of Ezk 11:1 2970
JAAZIAH
the sons of **J**, Beno. 1Ch 24:26 3269
by **J** *were* Beno, Shoham, Zaccur and 1Ch 24:27 3269
JAAZIEL
second rank, Zechariah, Ben, **J**, 1Ch 15:18 3268
JABAL
Adah gave birth to **J**; Gn 4:20 2989
JABBOK
and crossed the ford of the **J**. Gn 32:22 2999
his land from the Arnon to the **J**, Nu 21:24 2999
all along the river **J** and the Dt 2:37 2999
border and as far as the river **J**, Dt 3:16 2999
even as far as the brook **J**, Jos 12:2 2999
as far as the **J** and the Jordan; Jg 11:13 2999
from the Arnon as far as the **J**, Jg 11:22 2999
JABESH
all the men of **J** said to Nahash, 1Sa 11:1 3003
The elders of **J** said to him, 1Sa 11:3 3003
to him the words of the men of **J**. 1Sa 11:5 3003
went and told the men of **J**; 1Sa 11:9 3003
Then the men of **J** said, 1Sa 11:10 3003
of Beth-shan, and they came to **J** and 1Sa 31:12 3003
them under the tamarisk tree at **J**, 1Sa 31:13 3003
Then Shallum the son of **J** 2Ki 15:10 3003
Shallum son of **J** became king in 2Ki 15:13 3003
Shallum son of **J** in Samaria, 2Ki 15:14 3003
and brought them to **J**, and they buried 1Ch 10:12 3003
their bones under the oak in **J**, 1Ch 10:12 3003
JABESH-GILEAD
the camp from **J** to the assembly. Jg 21:8 3003, 1568
of the inhabitants of **J** was there. Jg 21:9 3003, 1568
strike the inhabitants of **J** with the Jg 21:10 3003, 1568
they found among the inhabitants of **J** Jg 21:12 3003, 1568
kept alive from the women of **J**; Jg 21:14 3003, 1568
Ammonite came up and besieged **J**; 1Sa 11:1 3003, 1568
you shall say to the men of **J**, 1Sa 11:9 3003, 1568
Now when the inhabitants of **J** 1Sa 31:11 3003, 1568
the men of **J** who buried Saul." 2Sa 2:4 3003, 1568
sent messengers to the men of **J**, 2Sa 2:5 3003, 1568
his son from the men of **J**, 2Sa 21:12 3003, 1568
When all **J** heard all that the 1Ch 10:11 3003, 1568
JABEZ
lived at **J** *were* the Tirathites, 1Ch 2:55 3258
J was more honorable than his 1Ch 4:9 3258
and his mother named him **J** saying, 1Ch 4:9 3258
Now **J** called on the God of Israel, 1Ch 4:10 3258
JABIN
when **J** king of Hazor heard *of it*, Jos 11:1 2985
into the hand of **J** king of Canaan, Jg 4:2 2985
for *there was* peace between **J** the Jg 4:17 2985
So God subdued on that day **J** the Jg 4:23 2985
heavier upon **J** the king of Canaan, Jg 4:24 2985
destroyed **J** the king of Canaan. Jg 4:24 2985
with Midian, As with Sisera *and* **J** at Ps 83:9 2985
JABIN'S
Sisera, the commander of **J** army, Jg 4:7 2985
JABNEEL
Mount Baalah and proceeded to **J**, Jos 15:11 2995
in Zaanannim and Adami-nekeb and **J**, Jos 19:33 2995
JABNEH
wall of **J** and the wall of Ashdod; 2Ch 26:6 2996
JACAN
Meshullam, Sheba, Jorai, **J**, 1Ch 5:13 3275
JACHIN
Jemuel and Jamin and Ohad and **J** Gn 46:10 3199
Jemuel and Jamin and Ohad and **J** Ex 6:15 3199
of **J**, the family of the Jachinites; Nu 26:12 3199
the right pillar and named it **J**, 1Ki 7:21 3199
were Jedaiah, Jehoiarib, **J**, 1Ch 9:10 3199
the twenty-first for **J**, 1Ch 24:17 3199
J and the one on the left Boaz. 2Ch 3:17 3199
Jedaiah the son of Joiarib, **J**, Ne 11:10 3199
JACHINITES
of Jachin, the family of the **J**; Nu 26:12 3200
JACINTH
and the third row a **j**, Ex 28:19 3958
and the third row, a **j**, Ex 39:12 3958
the eleventh, **j**; the twelfth, amethyst. Rv 21:20 *5192*
JACKALS
"I have become a brother to **j** And Jb 30:29 8565
have crushed us in a place of **j** And Ps 44:19 8565
And **j** in their luxurious palaces. Is 13:22 8565
It will also be a haunt of **j** *And* an Is 34:13 8565
In the haunt of **j**, its resting Is 35:7 8565
The **j** and the ostriches, Is 43:20 8565
a heap of ruins, A haunt of **j**; Jer 9:11 8565
Judah A desolation, a haunt of **j**. Jer 10:22 8565
They pant for air like **j**, Jer 14:6 8565
Hazor will become a haunt of **j**, Jer 49:33 8565
will live *there* along with the **j**; Jer 50:39 338
a heap *of ruins*, a haunt of **j**, Jer 51:37 8565
Even **j** offer the breast, They La 4:3 8565
I must make a lament like the **j** Mi 1:8 8565
for the **j** of the wilderness." Mal 1:3 8565
JACOB
heel, so his name was called **J**; Gn 25:26 3290
but **J** was a peaceful man, living Gn 25:27 3290
but Rebekah loved **J**. Gn 25:28 3290
When **J** had cooked stew, Esau Gn 25:29 3290
and Esau said to **J**, Gn 25:30 3290
J said, "First sell me your birthright." Gn 25:31 3290
And **J** said, "First swear to me" Gn 25:33 3290
him, and sold his birthright to **J**. Gn 25:33 3290
Then **J** gave Esau bread and lentil Gn 25:34 3290
Rebekah said to her son **J**, Gn 27:6 3290
J answered his mother Rebekah, Gn 27:11 3290
and put them on **J** her younger son. Gn 27:15 3290
which she had made, to her son **J**. Gn 27:17 3290
J said to his father, Gn 27:19 3290
Then Isaac said to **J**, Gn 27:21 3290
So **J** came close to Isaac his Gn 27:22 3290
"The voice is the voice of **J**, Gn 27:22 3290
as Isaac had finished blessing **J**, Gn 27:30 3290
and **J** had hardly gone out from the Gn 27:30 3290
"Is he not rightly named **J**, Gn 27:36 3290
So Esau bore a grudge against **J** Gn 27:41 3290
then I will kill my brother **J**." Gn 27:41 3290
sent and called her younger son **J**, Gn 27:42 3290
if **J** takes a wife from the Gn 27:46 3290
So Isaac called **J** and blessed him Gn 28:1 3290
Then Isaac sent **J** away, and he Gn 28:5 3290
Rebekah, the mother of **J** and Esau. Gn 28:5 3290
Esau saw that Isaac had blessed **J** Gn 28:6 3290
and that **J** had obeyed his father Gn 28:7 3290
Then **J** departed from Beersheba and Gn 28:10 3290
J awoke from his sleep and said, Gn 28:16 3290
So **J** rose early in the morning, Gn 28:18 3290
Then **J** made a vow, saying, Gn 28:20 3290
Then **J** went on his journey, and Gn 29:1 3290
J said to them, Gn 29:4 3290
When **J** saw Rachel the daughter of Gn 29:10 3290
mother's brother, **J** went up Gn 29:10 3290
Then **J** kissed Rachel, and lifted Gn 29:11 3290
J told Rachel that he was a Gn 29:12 3290
the news of **J** his sister's son, Gn 29:13 3290
Then Laban said to **J**, Gn 29:15 3290
Now **J** loved Rachel, so he said, Gn 29:18 3290
So **J** served seven years for Rachel Gn 29:20 3290
Then **J** said to Laban, Gn 29:21 3290
and **J** went in to her. Gn 29:23
J did so and completed her week, Gn 29:28 3290
So **J** went in to Rachel also, Gn 29:30
saw that she bore **J** no children, Gn 30:1 3290
and she said to **J**, Gn 30:1 3290
as a wife, and **J** went in to her. Gn 30:4 3290
Bilhah conceived and bore **J** a son. Gn 30:5 3290
again and bore **J** a second son. Gn 30:7 3290
and gave her to **J** as a wife. Gn 30:9 3290
Leah's maid Zilpah bore **J** a son. Gn 30:10 3290
maid Zilpah bore **J** a second son. Gn 30:12 3290
When **J** came in from the field in Gn 30:16 3290
conceived and bore **J** a fifth son. Gn 30:17 3290
again and bore a sixth son to **J**. Gn 30:19 3290
Joseph, that **J** said to Laban, Gn 30:25 3290
And **J** said, "You shall not give me Gn 30:31 3290
journey between himself and **J**, Gn 30:36 3290
and **J** fed the rest of Laban's flocks. Gn 30:36 3290
Then **J** took fresh rods of poplar Gn 30:37 3290
J separated the lambs, and Gn 30:40 3290
J would place the rods in the Gn 30:41 3290
Now **J** heard the words of Laban's Gn 31:1
"**J** has taken away all that was Gn 31:1 3290
J saw the attitude of Laban, Gn 31:2 3290
Then the LORD said to **J**, Gn 31:3 3290
So **J** sent and called Rachel and Gn 31:4 3290
of God said to me in the dream, '**J**,' Gn 31:11 3290
Then **J** arose and put his children Gn 31:17 3290
And **J** deceived Laban the Aramean by Gn 31:20 3290
on the third day that **J** had fled, Gn 31:22 3290
speak to **J** either good or bad." Gn 31:24 3290
Laban caught up with **J**. Gn 31:25 3290
Now **J** had pitched his tent in the Gn 31:25 3290
Then Laban said to **J**, Gn 31:26 3290
to speak either good or bad to **J**.' Gn 31:29 3290
Then **J** replied to Laban, Gn 31:31 3290
For **J** did not know that Rachel had Gn 31:32 3290
Then **J** became angry and contended Gn 31:36 3290
and **J** said to Laban, Gn 31:36 3290
Then Laban replied to **J**, Gn 31:43 3290
Then **J** took a stone and set it up Gn 31:45 3290
J said to his kinsmen, Gn 31:46 3290
but **J** called it Galeed. Gn 31:47 3290
Laban said to **J**, Gn 31:51 3290
So **J** swore by the fear of his Gn 31:53 3290
Then **J** offered a sacrifice on the Gn 31:54 3290
Now as **J** went on his way, the Gn 32:1 3290
J said when he saw them, Gn 32:2 3290
Then **J** sent messengers before him Gn 32:3 3290
'Thus says your servant **J**, Gn 32:4 3290
The messengers returned to **J**, Gn 32:6 3290
Then **J** was greatly afraid and Gn 32:7 3290
J said, "O God of my father Gn 32:9 3290
'*These* belong to your servant **J**; Gn 32:18 3290
servant **J** also is behind us.' " Gn 32:20 3290
Then **J** was left alone, and a man Gn 32:24 3290
And he said, "**J**." Gn 32:27 3290
"Your name shall no longer be **J**, Gn 32:28 3290
Then **J** asked him and said, Gn 32:29 3290
So **J** named the place Peniel, for Gn 32:30 3290
Then **J** lifted his eyes and looked, Gn 33:1 3290
J said, "No, please, if now I Gn 33:10 3290
J journeyed to Succoth, Gn 33:17 3290
Now **J** came safely to the city of Gn 33:18 3290
of Leah, whom she had borne to **J**, Gn 34:1 3290
to Dinah the daughter of **J**, Gn 34:3 3290
Now **J** heard that he had defiled Gn 34:5 3290
so **J** kept silent until they came Gn 34:5 3290
went out to **J** to speak with him. Gn 34:6 3290
Now the sons of **J** came in from the Gn 34:7 3290
Then **J** said to Simeon and Levi, Gn 34:30 3290
Then God said to **J**, Gn 35:1 3290
So **J** said to his household and to Gn 35:2 3290
So they gave to **J** all the foreign Gn 35:4 3290
and **J** hid them under the oak which Gn 35:4 3290
they did not pursue the sons of **J**. Gn 35:5 3290
So **J** came to Luz Gn 35:6 3290

Then God appeared to **J** again when Gn 35:9 3290
God said to him, "Your name is **J**; Gn 35:10 3290
You shall no longer be called **J**, Gn 35:10 3290
J set up a pillar in the place Gn 35:14 3290
So **J** named the place where God had Gn 35:15 3290
J set up a pillar over her Gn 35:20 3290
Now there were twelve sons of **J** Gn 35:22 3290
These are the sons of **J** who were Gn 35:26 3290
J came to his father Isaac at Gn 35:27 3290
his sons Esau and **J** buried him. Gn 35:29 3290
land away from his brother **J**. Gn 36:6 3290
Now **J** lived in the land where his Gn 37:1 3290
records of the generations of **J**. Gn 37:2 3290
So **J** tore his clothes, and put Gn 37:34 3290
Now **J** saw that there was grain in Gn 42:1 3290
in Egypt, and **J** said to his sons, Gn 42:1 3290
But **J** did not send Joseph's Gn 42:4 3290
father **J** in the land of Canaan, Gn 42:29 3290
Their father **J** said to them, Gn 42:36 3290
J said, "My son shall not go down Gn 42:38 3290
land of Canaan to their father **J**. Gn 45:25 3290
spirit of their father **J** revived. Gn 45:27 3290
in visions of the night and said, "**J**, Gn 46:2 3290
"Jacob, **J**." And he said, "Here I am." Gn 46:2 3290
Then **J** arose from Beersheba; Gn 46:5 3290
sons of Israel carried their father **J** Gn 46:5 3290
J and all his descendants with him: Gn 46:6 3290
sons of Israel, **J** and his sons, Gn 46:8 3290
whom she bore to **J** in Paddan-aram, Gn 46:15 3290
bore to **J** these sixteen persons. Gn 46:18 3290
of Rachel, who were born to **J**; Gn 46:22 3290
Rachel, and she bore these to **J**; Gn 46:25 3290
All the persons belonging to **J**, Gn 46:26 3290
all the persons of the house of **J**, Gn 46:27 3290
J and presented him to Pharaoh; Gn 47:7 3290
and **J** blessed Pharaoh. Gn 47:7 3290
Pharaoh said to **J**, Gn 47:8 3290
So **J** said to Pharaoh, Gn 47:9 3290
And **J** blessed Pharaoh, and went Gn 47:10 3290
J lived in the land of Egypt Gn 47:28 3290
When it was told to **J**, Gn 48:2 3290
Then **J** said to Joseph, Gn 48:3 3290
Then **J** summoned his sons and said, Gn 49:1 3290
together and hear, O sons of **J**; Gn 49:2 3290
I will disperse them in **J**, Gn 49:7 3290
the hands of the Mighty One of **J** Gn 49:24 3290
When **J** finished charging his sons, Gn 49:33 3290
to Abraham, to Isaac and to **J**." Gn 50:24 3290
Israel who came to Egypt with **J**; Ex 1:1 3290
loins of **J** were seventy in number, Ex 1:5 3290
with Abraham, Isaac, and **J**. Ex 2:24 3290
God of Isaac, and the God of **J**." Ex 3:6 3290
God of Isaac, and the God of **J**, Ex 3:15 3290
the God of Abraham, Isaac and **J**, Ex 3:16 3290
God of Isaac, and the God of **J**, Ex 4:5 3290
appeared to Abraham, Isaac, and **J**, Ex 6:3 3290
to give to Abraham, Isaac, and **J**, Ex 6:8 3290
you shall say to the house of **J** and Ex 19:3 3290
I swore to Abraham, Isaac, and **J**, Ex 33:1 3290
will remember My covenant with **J**, Lv 26:42 3290
'Come curse **J** for me, And come, Nu 23:7 3290
"Who can count the dust of **J**, Nu 23:10 3290
has not observed misfortune in **J**; Nu 23:21 3290
"For there is no omen against **J**, Nu 23:23 3290
shall be said to **J** And to Israel, Nu 23:23 3290
How fair are your tents, O **J**, Nu 24:5 3290
A star shall come forth from **J**, Nu 24:17 3290
"One from **J** shall have dominion, Nu 24:19 3290
to Abraham, to Isaac and to **J**; Nu 32:11 3290
to Abraham, to Isaac, and to **J**, Dt 1:8 3290
fathers, Abraham, Isaac and **J**, Dt 6:10 3290
fathers, to Abraham, Isaac and **J**. Dt 9:5 3290
servants, Abraham, Isaac, and **J**; Dt 9:27 3290
fathers, to Abraham, Isaac, and **J**. Dt 29:13 3290
fathers, to Abraham, Isaac, and **J**, Dt 30:20 3290
J is the allotment of His Dt 32:9 3290
possession for the assembly of **J**. Dt 33:4 3290
shall teach Your ordinances to **J**, Dt 33:10 3290
The fountain of **J** secluded, Dt 33:28 3290
I swore to Abraham, Isaac, and **J**, Dt 34:4 3290
'To Isaac I gave **J** and Esau, Jos 24:4 3290
but **J** and his sons went down to Jos 24:4 3290
in the piece of ground which **J** had Jos 24:32 3290
"When **J** went into Egypt and your 1Sa 12:8 3290
The anointed of the God of **J**, 2Sa 23:1 3290
of the tribes of the sons of **J**, 1Ki 18:31 3290
with Abraham, Isaac, and **J**, 2Ki 13:23 3290
the LORD commanded the sons of **J**, 2Ki 17:34 3290
of Israel His servant, Sons of **J**, 1Ch 16:13 3290
confirmed it to **J** for a statute, 1Ch 16:17 3290
captive people, **J** will rejoice, Ps 14:7 3290
God of **J** set you *securely* on high! Ps 20:1 3290
All you descendants of **J**, Ps 22:23 3290
Who seek Your face—*even* **J**. Ps 24:6 3290
Command victories for **J**. Ps 44:4 3290
The God of **J** is our stronghold. Ps 46:7 3290
The God of **J** is our stronghold. Ps 46:11 3290
The glory of **J** whom He loves. Ps 47:4 3290
His captive people, Let **J** rejoice, Ps 53:6 3290
men may know that God rules in **J** To Ps 59:13 3290
will sing praises to the God of **J**. Ps 75:9 3290
At Your rebuke, O God of **J**, Ps 76:6 3290
The sons of **J** and Joseph. Ps 77:15 3290
He established a testimony in **J** And Ps 78:5 3290
And a fire was kindled against **J** And Ps 78:21 3290
him To shepherd **J** His people, Ps 78:71 3290
For they have devoured **J** And Ps 79:7 3290
Shout joyfully to the God of **J**. Ps 81:1 3290
An ordinance of the God of **J**. Ps 81:4 3290

Give ear, O God of **J**! Ps 84:8 3290
restored the captivity of **J**. Ps 85:1 3290
the *other* dwelling places of **J**. Ps 87:2 3290
Nor does the God of **J** pay heed." Ps 94:7 3290
justice and righteousness in **J**. Ps 99:4 3290
Abraham, His servant, O sons of **J**, Ps 105:6 3290
confirmed it to **J** for a statute, Ps 105:10 3290
J sojourned in the land of Ham. Ps 105:23 3290
The house of **J** from a people of Ps 114:1 3290
the Lord, Before the God of **J**, Ps 114:7 3290
And vowed to the Mighty One of **J**, Ps 132:2 3290
place for the Mighty One of **J**." Ps 132:5 3290
the LORD has chosen **J** for Himself, Ps 135:4 3290
is he whose help is the God of **J**, Ps 146:5 3290
He declares His words to **J**, Ps 147:19 3290
To the house of the God of **J**; Is 2:3 3290
Come, house of **J**, and let us walk Is 2:5 3290
Your people, the house of **J**, Is 2:6 3290
His face from the house of **J**; Is 8:17 3290
Lord sends a message against **J**, Is 9:8 3290
the house of **J** who have escaped, Is 10:20 3290
will return, the remnant of **J**, Is 10:21 3290
LORD will have compassion on **J** and Is 14:1 3290
themselves to the house of **J**. Is 14:1 3290
day the glory of **J** will fade, Is 17:4 3290
the days to come **J** will take root, Is 27:6 3290
concerning the house of **J**: Is 29:22 3290
"**J** shall not now be ashamed, nor Is 29:22 3290
will sanctify the Holy One of **J** And Is 29:23 3290
Why do you say, O **J**, Is 40:27 3290
My servant, **J** whom I have chosen, Is 41:8 3290
"Do not fear, you worm **J**, Is 41:14 3290
arguments," The King of **J** says. Is 41:21 3290
Who gave **J** up for spoil, and Is 42:24 3290
says the LORD, your Creator, O **J**, Is 43:1 3290
you have not called on Me, O **J**; Is 43:22 3290
And I will consign **J** to the ban and Is 43:28 3290
"But now listen, O **J**, Is 44:1 3290
'Do not fear, O **J** My servant; Is 44:2 3290
one will call on the name of **J**; Is 44:5 3290
"Remember these things, O **J**, Is 44:21 3290
For the LORD has redeemed **J** And in Is 44:23 3290
"For the sake of **J** My servant, Is 45:4 3290
did not say to the offspring of **J**, Is 45:19 3290
"Listen to Me, O house of **J**, Is 46:3 3290
"Hear this, O house of **J**, Is 48:1 3290
"Listen to Me, O **J**, even Israel Is 48:12 3290
LORD has redeemed His servant **J**." Is 48:20 3290
Servant, To bring **J** back to Him, Is 49:5 3290
To raise up the tribes of **J** and Is 49:6 3290
Redeemer, the Mighty One of **J**." Is 49:26 3290
And to the house of **J** their sins. Is 58:1 3290
the heritage of **J** your father, Is 58:14 3290
turn from transgression in **J**," Is 59:20 3290
Redeemer, the Mighty One of **J**. Is 60:16 3290
will bring forth offspring from **J**, Is 65:9 3290
word of the LORD, O house of **J**, Jer 2:4 3290
"Declare this in the house of **J** Jer 5:20 3290
portion of **J** is not like these; Jer 10:16 3290
For they have devoured **J**; Jer 10:25 3290
'Fear not, O **J** My servant,' Jer 30:10 3290
And **J** will return and will be Jer 30:10 3290
restore the fortunes of the tents of **J** Jer 30:18 3290
"Sing aloud with gladness for **J**, Jer 31:7 3290
For the LORD has ransomed **J** And Jer 31:11 3290
I would reject the descendants of **J** Jer 33:26 3290
of Abraham, Isaac and **J**. Jer 33:26 3290
"But as for you, O **J** My servant, Jer 46:27 3290
And **J** will return and be Jer 46:27 3290
"O **J** My servant, do not fear," Jer 46:28 3290
portion of **J** is not like these; Jer 51:19 3290
LORD has commanded concerning **J** La 1:17 3290
spared All the habitations of **J**. La 2:2 3290
And He has burned in **J** like a La 2:3 3290
to the descendants of the house of **J** Ezk 20:5 3290
land which I gave to My servant **J**. Ezk 28:25 3290
land that I gave to **J** My servant, Ezk 37:25 3290
I will restore the fortunes of **J** Ezk 39:25 3290
plow, **J** will harrow for himself. Hos 10:11 3290
punish **J** according to his ways; Hos 12:2 3290
Now **J** fled to the land of Aram, Hos 12:12 3290
testify against the house of **J**," Am 3:13 3290
"I loathe the arrogance of **J**, Am 6:8 3290
How can **J** stand, For he is small?" Am 7:2 3290
How can **J** stand, For he is small?" Am 7:5 3290
LORD has sworn by the pride of **J**, Am 8:7 3290
totally destroy the house of **J**," Am 9:8 3290
of violence to your brother **J**, Ob 1:10 3290
And the house of **J** will possess Ob 1:17 3290
"Then the house of **J** will be a Ob 1:18 3290
All this is for the rebellion of **J** Mi 1:5 3290
What is the rebellion of **J**? Mi 1:5 3290
"Is it being said, O house of **J**: Mi 2:7 3290
surely assemble all of you, **J**, Mi 2:12 3290
heads of **J** And rulers of the house Mi 3:1 3290
known to **J** his rebellious act, Mi 3:8 3290
heads of the house of **J** And rulers Mi 3:9 3290
And to the house of the God of **J**, Mi 4:2 3290
Then the remnant of **J** Will be Mi 5:7 3290
The remnant of **J** Will be among Mi 5:8 3290
You will give truth to **J** *And* Mi 7:20 3290
LORD will restore the splendor of **J** Na 2:2 3290
"Yet I have loved **J**; Mal 1:2 3290
the LORD cut off from the tents of **J** Mal 2:12 3290
therefore you, O sons of **J**, Mal 3:6 3290
of Isaac, Isaac the father of **J**, Mt 1:2 *2384*
J the father of Judah and his brothers. Mt 1:2 *2384*
and Matthan the father of **J**. Mt 1:15 *2384*
J was the father of Joseph Mt 1:16 *2384*

with Abraham, Isaac and **J** Mt 8:11 *2384*
GOD OF ISAAC, AND THE GOD OF **J**'? Mt 22:32 *2384*
GOD OF ISAAC, and the God of **J**'? Mk 12:26 *2384*
reign over the house of **J** forever, Lk 1:33 *2384*
the son of **J**, the son of Isaac, Lk 3:34 *2384*
you see Abraham and Isaac and **J** Lk 13:28 *2384*
GOD OF ISAAC, AND THE GOD OF **J**. Lk 20:37 *2384*
that **J** gave to his son Joseph; Jn 4:5 *2384*
are not greater than our father **J**, Jn 4:12 *2384*
"The God of Abraham, Isaac and **J**, Ac 3:13 *2384*
and Isaac *became the father of* **J**, Ac 7:8 *2384*
and **J** *of* the twelve patriarchs. Ac 7:8 *2384*
"But when **J** heard that there was Ac 7:12 *2384*
"Then Joseph sent *word* and invited **J** Ac 7:14 *2384*
"And **J** went down to Egypt and Ac 7:15 *2384*
GOD OF ABRAHAM AND ISAAC AND **J**.' Ac 7:32 *2384*
a dwelling place for the God of **J**. Ac 7:46 *2384*
"**J** I LOVED, BUT ESAU I HATED." Ro 9:13 *2384*
WILL REMOVE UNGODLINESS FROM **J**." Ro 11:26 *2384*
in tents with Isaac and **J**, Heb 11:9 *2384*
By faith Isaac blessed **J** and Esau, Heb 11:20 *2384*
By faith **J**, as he was dying, Heb 11:21 *2384*

JACOB'S

J anger burned against Rachel, Gn 30:2 3290
were Laban's and the stronger **J**. Gn 30:42 3290
So Laban went into **J** tent and Gn 31:33 3290
so the socket of **J** thigh was Gn 32:25 3290
he touched the socket of **J** thigh Gn 32:32 3290
Israel by lying with **J** daughter, Gn 34:7 3290
But **J** sons answered Shechem and Gn 34:13 3290
he was delighted with **J** daughter. Gn 34:19 3290
were in pain, that two of **J** sons, Gn 34:25 3290
J sons came upon the slain and Gn 34:27 3290
Reuben, **J** firstborn, then Simeon Gn 35:23 3290
Reuben, **J** firstborn. Gn 46:8 3290
The sons of **J** wife Rachel: Gn 46:19 3290
not including the wives of **J** sons, Gn 46:26 3290
so the length of **J** life was one Gn 47:28 3290
this **J** iniquity will be forgiven; Is 27:9 3290
And it is the time of **J** distress, Jer 30:7 3290
"*Was* not Esau **J** brother?" Mal 1:2 3290
and **J** well was there. Jn 4:6 *2384*

JADA

sons of Onam were Shammai and **J**. 1Ch 2:28 3047
The sons of **J** the brother of 1Ch 2:32 3047

JADDAI

Mattithiah, Zabad, Zebina, **J**, Ezr 10:43 3035

JADDUA

Meshezabel, Zadok, **J**, Ne 10:21 3037
Jonathan became the father of **J**. Ne 12:11 3037
Joiada, and Johanan and **J**; Ne 12:22 3037

JADON

Gibeonite and **J** the Meronothite, Ne 3:7 3036

JAEL

fled away on foot to the tent of **J** Jg 4:17 3278
J went out to meet Sisera, and Jg 4:18 3278
But **J**, Heber's wife, took a tent Jg 4:21 3278
J came out to meet him and said to Jg 4:22 3278
son of Anath, In the days of **J**, Jg 5:6 3278
"Most blessed of women is **J**, Jg 5:24 3278

JAGUR

south were Kabzeel and Eder and **J**, Jos 15:21 3017

JAHATH

of Shobal became the father of **J**, 1Ch 4:2 3189
and **J** became the father of Ahumai 1Ch 4:2 3189
Libni his son, **J** his son, Zimmah 1Ch 6:20 3189
the son of **J**, the son of Gershom, 1Ch 6:43 3189
The sons of Shimei *were* **J**, 1Ch 23:10 3189
J was the first and Zizah the 1Ch 23:11 3189
of the sons of Shelomoth, **J**. 1Ch 24:22 3189
J and Obadiah, the Levites of the 2Ch 34:12 3189

JAHAZ

to **J** and fought against Israel. Nu 21:23 3096
out to meet us in battle at **J**. Dt 2:32 3096
and **J** and Kedemoth and Mephaath, Jos 13:18 3096
and **J** with its pasture lands, Jos 21:36 3096
all his people and camped in **J** and Jg 11:20 3096
voice is heard all the way to **J**; Is 15:4 3096
to **J** they have raised their voice, Jer 48:34 3096

JAHAZIEL

Then Jeremiah, **J**, Johanan, Jozabad 1Ch 12:4 3166
and Benaiah and **J** the priests *blew* 1Ch 16:6 3166
J the third and Jekameam the 1Ch 23:19 3166
Amariah the second, **J** the third, 1Ch 24:23 3166
came upon **J** the son of Zechariah, 2Ch 20:14 3166
son of **J** and 300 males with him; Ezr 8:5 3166

JAHDAI

The sons of **J** *were* Regem, 1Ch 2:47 3056

JAHDIEL

Azriel, Jeremiah, Hodaviah and **J**, 1Ch 5:24 3164b

JAHDO

son of Jeshishai, the son of **J**, 1Ch 5:14 3163

JAHLEEL

Sered and Elon and **J**. Gn 46:14 3177
of **J**, the family of the Nu 26:26 3177

JAHLEELITES

of Jahleel, the family of the **J**. Nu 26:26 3178

JAHMAI

were Uzzi, Rephaiah, Jeriel, **J**, 1Ch 7:2 3181

JAHZAH

lands, **J** with its pasture lands, 1Ch 6:78 3096
upon the plain, upon Holon, **J** and Jer 48:21 3096

JAHZEEL

J and Guni and Jezer and Shillem. Gn 46:24 3183
of **J**, the family of the Nu 26:48 3183

JAHZEELITES
of Jahzeel, the family of the J; Nu 26:48 3184
JAHZEIAH
and J the son of Tikvah opposed this, Ezr 10:15 3167
JAHZERAH
the son of Adiel, *the* son of J, 1Ch 9:12 3170
JAHZIEL
The sons of Naphtali *were* J, 1Ch 7:13 3185
JAIL
took him and put him into the j, Gn 39:20 1004, 5470
and he was there in the j. Gn 39:20 1004, 5470
the prisoners who were in the j; Gn 39:22 1004, 5470
of the bodyguard, in the j, Gn 40:3 1004, 5470
of Egypt, who were confined in j, Gn 40:5 1004, 5470
and they put him in j in the house Jer 37:15 1004, 612
put them in j until the next day, Ac 4:3 *5084*
and put them in a public j. Ac 5:18 *5084*
JAILER
favor in the sight of the chief j. Gn 39:21 1004, 5470
The chief j committed to Gn 39:22 1004, 5470
The chief j did not supervise Gn 39:23 1004, 5470
the j to guard them securely; Ac 16:23 *1200*
When the j awoke Ac 16:27 *1200*
j reported these words to Paul, Ac 16:36 *1200*
JAIR
J the son of Manasseh went and Nu 32:41 2971
J the son of Manasseh took all the Dt 3:14 2971
of Bashan, and all the towns of J, Jos 13:30 2971
After him, J the Gileadite arose Jg 10:3 2971
J died and was buried in Kamon. Jg 10:5 2971
the towns of J, the son of Manasseh, 1Ki 4:13 2971
Segub became the father of J, 1Ch 2:22 2971
took the towns of J from them, 1Ch 2:23 2971
and Elhanan the son of J killed 1Ch 20:5 3265
name was Mordecai, the son of J, Es 2:5 2971
JAIRITE
Ira the J was also a priest to David. 2Sa 20:26 2972
JAIRUS
officials named J came up, Mk 5:22 *2383*
there came a man named J, Lk 8:41 *2383*
JAKEH
The words of Agur the son of J, Pr 30:1 3348
JAKIM
J, Zichri, Zabdi, 1Ch 8:19 3356
for Eliashib, the twelfth for J, 1Ch 24:12 3356
JALAM
bore Jeush and J and Korah. Gn 36:5 3281
to Esau, Jeush and J and Korah. Gn 36:14 3281
chief Jeush, chief J, Gn 36:18 3281
were Eliphaz, Reuel, Jeush, J and 1Ch 1:35 3281
JALON
were Jether, Mered, Epher and J. 1Ch 4:17 3210
JAMBRES
as Jannes and J opposed Moses, 2Tm 3:8 *2387*
JAMBRES'S
just as Jannes' and J folly was 2Tm 3:9
JAMES
brothers, J the *son* of Zebedee, Mt 4:21 *2385*
and J the son of Zebedee, and John Mt 10:2 *2385*
J the son of Alphaeus, and Mt 10:3 *2385*
J and Joseph and Simon and Judas? Mt 13:55 *2385*
Peter and J and John his brother, Mt 17:1 *2385*
Mary the mother of J and Joseph, Mt 27:56 *2385*
He saw J the son of Zebedee, Mk 1:19 *2385*
Simon and Andrew, with J and John. Mk 1:29 *2385*
and J, the *son* of Zebedee, and Mk 3:17 *2385*
and John the brother of J Mk 3:17 *2385*
Thomas, and J the son of Alphaeus, Mk 3:18 *2385*
J and John the brother of James. Mk 5:37 *2385*
James and John the brother of J. Mk 5:37 *2385*
the son of Mary, and brother of J and Mk 6:3 *2385*
with Him Peter and J and John, Mk 9:2 *2385*
J and John, the two sons of Mk 10:35 *2385*
to feel indignant with J and John. Mk 10:41 *2385*
Peter and J and John and Andrew Mk 13:3 *2385*
with Him Peter and J and John, Mk 14:33 *2385*
mother of J the Less and Joses, Mk 15:40 *2385*
and Mary the *mother* of J, Mk 16:1 *2385*
and so also *were* J and John, sons of Lk 5:10 *2385*
Andrew his brother; and J and John; Lk 6:14 *2385*
J *the son* of Alphaeus, and Simon Lk 6:15 *2385*
Judas *the son* of J, Lk 6:16 *2385*
Him, except Peter and John and J, Lk 8:51 *2385*
took along Peter and John and J, Lk 9:28 *2385*
His disciples J and John saw *this,* Lk 9:54 *2385*
Joanna and Mary the *mother* of J; Lk 24:10 *2385*
Peter and John and J and Andrew, Ac 1:13 *2385*
Matthew, J *the son* of Alphaeus, Ac 1:13 *2385*
Zealot, and Judas *the son* of J. Ac 1:13 *2385*
And he had J the brother of John Ac 12:2 *2385*
things to J and the brethren." Ac 12:17 *2385*
had stopped speaking, J answered, Ac 15:13 *2385*
day Paul went in with us to J, Ac 21:18 *2385*
then He appeared to J, 1Co 15:7 *2385*
other of the apostles except J, Ga 1:19 *2385*
to me, J and Cephas and John, Ga 2:9 *2385*
the coming of certain men from J, Ga 2:12 *2385*
J, a bond-servant of God and of Jas 1:1 *2385*
of Jesus Christ, and brother of J, Jude 1:1 *2385*
JAMIN
Jemuel and J and Ohad and Jachin Gn 46:10 3226
Jemuel and J and Ohad and Jachin Ex 6:15 3226
of J, the family of the Jaminites; Nu 26:12 3226
of Jerahmeel, were Maaz, J and 1Ch 2:27 3226
sons of Simeon *were* Nemuel and J, 1Ch 4:24 3226
Also Jeshua, Bani, Sherebiah, J, Ne 8:7 3226
JAMINITES
of Jamin, the family of the J; Nu 26:12 3228
JAMLECH
J and Joshah the son of Amaziah, 1Ch 4:34 3230
JANAI
then J and Shaphat in Bashan. 1Ch 5:12 3285
JANNAI
the son of Melchi, the son of J, Lk 3:24 *2388*
JANNES
as J and Jambres opposed Moses, 2Tm 3:8 *2389*
JANNES'S
just as J and Jambres' folly was 2Tm 3:9
JANOAH
beyond it to the east of J. Jos 16:6 3239b
from J to Ataroth and to Naarah, Jos 16:7 3239b
J and Kedesh and Hazor and Gilead 2Ki 15:29 3239a
JANUM
and J and Beth-tappuah and Jos 15:53 3241
JAPHETH
the father of Shem, Ham, and J. Gn 5:32 3315
Shem, Ham, and J. Gn 6:10 3315
day Noah and Shem and Ham and J, Gn 7:13 3315
the ark were Shem and Ham and J; Gn 9:18 3315
But Shem and J took a garment and Gn 9:23 3315
"May God enlarge J, And let him Gn 9:27 3315
generations of Shem, Ham, and J, Gn 10:1 3315
The sons of J *were* Gomer and Magog Gn 10:2 3315
Eber, *and* the older brother of J, Gn 10:21 3315
Noah, Shem, Ham and J. 1Ch 1:4 3315
The sons of J *were* Gomer, Magog, 1Ch 1:5 3315
JAPHIA
to J king of Lachish and to Debir Jos 10:3 3309
proceeded to Daberath and up to J. Jos 19:12 3309
Ibhar, Elishua, Nepheg, J, 2Sa 5:15 3309
Nogah, Nepheg and J, 1Ch 3:7 3309
Nogah, Nepheg, J, 1Ch 14:6 3309
JAPHLET
Heber became the father of J, 1Ch 7:32 3310
The sons of J *were* Pasach, 1Ch 7:33 3310
These were the sons of J. 1Ch 7:33 3310
JAPHLETITES
to the territory of the J, Jos 16:3 3311
JAR
let down your j so that I may drink,' Gn 24:14 3537
out with her j on her shoulder. Gn 24:15 3537
to the spring and filled her j and Gn 24:16 3537
a little water from your j." Gn 24:17 3537
quickly lowered her j to her hand, Gn 24:18 3537
emptied her j into the trough, Gn 24:20 3537
a little water from your j"; Gn 24:43 3537
out with her j on her shoulder, Gn 24:45 3537
lowered her j from her *shoulder,* Gn 24:46 3537
"Take a j and put an omerful of Ex 16:33 6803
you, *some* cakes and a j of honey, 1Ki 14:3 1228
get me a little water in a j, 1Ki 17:10 3627
bowl and a little oil in the j; 1Ki 17:12 6835
nor shall the j of oil be empty, 1Ki 17:14 6835
nor did the j of oil become empty, 1Ki 17:16 6835
on hot stones, and a j of water. 1Ki 19:6 6835
"Bring me a new j, and put salt 2Ki 2:20 6746
in the house except a j of oil." 2Ki 4:2 610
the sea like a j of ointment. Jb 41:31 4841
like the smashing of a potter's j, Is 30:14 5035a
and buy a potter's earthenware j, Jer 19:1 1228
"Then you are to break the j in Jer 19:10 1228
Coniah a despised, shattered j? Jer 22:28 6089b
and put them in an earthenware j, Jer 32:14 3627
A j full of sour wine was standing Jn 19:29 *4632*
was a golden j holding the manna, Heb 9:4 *4713*
JARAH
Ahaz became the father of J, 1Ch 9:42 3294
J became the father of Alemeth, 1Ch 9:42 3294
JAREB
to Assyria And sent to King J. Hos 5:13 3377
to Assyria As tribute to King J; Hos 10:6 3377
JARED
years, and became the father of J. Gn 5:15 3382
after he became the father of J, Gn 5:16 3382
J lived one hundred and Gn 5:18 3382
Then J lived eight hundred years Gn 5:19 3382
So all the days of J were nine Gn 5:20 3382
Kenan, Mahalalel, J, 1Ch 1:2 3382
the son of Enoch, the son of J, Lk 3:37 *2391*
JARHA
Egyptian servant whose name was J. 1Ch 2:34 3398
to J his servant in marriage, 1Ch 2:35 3398
JARIB
Simeon *were* Nemuel and Jamin, J, 1Ch 4:24 3402
Ariel, Shemaiah, Elnathan, J, Ezr 8:16 3402
Maaseiah, Eliezer, J and Ezr 10:18 3402
JARMUTH
and to Piram king of J and to Japhia Jos 10:3 3412
the king of Hebron, the king of J, Jos 10:5 3412
the king of Hebron, the king of J, Jos 10:23 3412
the king of J, one; Jos 12:11 3412
J and Adullam, Socoh and Azekah, Jos 15:35 3412
J with its pasture lands, Jos 21:29 3412
in En-rimmon, in Zorah and in J, Ne 11:29 3412
JAROAH
the son of Huri, the son of J, 1Ch 5:14 3386
JARS
its pans and its j and its bowls with Ex 25:29 7184
its pans and its bowls and its j, Ex 37:16 7184
bowls and the j for the drink offering, Nu 4:7 7184
go to the water j and drink from Ru 2:9 3627
Or tip the water j of the heavens, Jb 38:37 5035a
vessels, from bowls to all the j. Is 22:24 3627, 5035a
his vessels and shatter his j. Jer 48:12 5035a
they are regarded as earthen j, La 4:2 5035a
JASHAR
it not written in the book of J? Jos 10:13 3477
it is written in the book of J. 2Sa 1:18 3477
JASHEN
the Shaalbonite, the sons of J, 2Sa 23:32 3464
JASHOBEAM
J, the son of a Hachmonite, the 1Ch 11:11 3434
Isshiah, Azarel, Joezer, J, 1Ch 12:6 3434
J the son of Zabdiel had charge of 1Ch 27:2 3434
JASHUB
of J, the family of the Jashubites; Nu 26:24 3437
Tola, Puah, J and Shimron. 1Ch 7:1 3437
Meshullam, Malluch and Adaiah, J, Ezr 10:29 3437
JASHUBI-LEHEM
Saraph, who ruled in Moab, and J. 1Ch 4:22 3433
JASHUBITES
of Jashub, the family of the J; Nu 26:24 3432
JASON
and attacking the house of J, Ac 17:5 *2394*
they *began* dragging J and some Ac 17:6 *2394*
and J has welcomed them, and they Ac 17:7 *2394*
a pledge from J and the others, Ac 17:9 *2394*
so do Lucius and J and Sosipater, Ro 16:21 *2394*
JASPER
row a beryl and an onyx and a j; Ex 28:20 3471
row, a beryl, an onyx, and a j. Ex 39:13 3471
The beryl, the onyx and the j; Ezk 28:13 3471
He who was sitting *was* like a j stone Rv 4:3 *2393*
as a stone of crystal-clear j. Rv 21:11 *2393*
The material of the wall was j; Rv 21:18 *2393*
The first foundation stone was j; Rv 21:19 *2393*
JATHNIEL
Zebadiah the third, J the fourth, 1Ch 26:2 3496
JATTIR
Shamir and J and Socoh, Jos 15:48 3492
and J with its pasture lands and Jos 21:14 3492
Negev, and to those who were in J, 1Sa 30:27 3492
also with its pasture lands, J, 1Ch 6:57 3492
JAVAN
Magog and Madai and J and Tubal Gn 10:2 3120
sons of J *were* Elishah and Tarshish Gn 10:4 3120
were Gomer, Magog, Madai, J, 1Ch 1:5 3120
The sons of J *were* Elishah, 1Ch 1:7 3120
"J, Tubal and Meshech, they were Ezk 27:13 3120
J paid for your wares from Uzal; Ezk 27:19 3120
JAVELIN
"Stretch out the j that is in Jos 8:18 3591
So Joshua stretched out the j that Jos 8:18 3591
he stretched out the j until he had Jos 8:26 3591
bronze j *slung* between his shoulders. 1Sa 17:6 3591
me with a sword, a spear, and a j, 1Sa 17:45 3591
him, The flashing spear and j. Jb 39:23 3591
Nor the spear, the dart or the j. Jb 41:26 8301b
laughs at the rattling of the j. Jb 41:29 3591
"They seize *their* bow and j; Jer 50:42 3591
JAW
Or pierce his j with a hook? Jb 41:2 3895
And his j teeth *like* knives, Pr 30:14 4973
JAWBONE
He found a fresh j of a donkey, Jg 15:15 3895
"With the j of a donkey, Heaps Jg 15:16 3895
With the j of a donkey I have Jg 15:16 3895
he threw the j from his hand; Jg 15:17 3895
JAWS
"I broke the j of the wicked And Jb 29:17 4973
And my tongue cleaves to my j; Ps 22:15 4455b
Keep me from the j of the trap Ps 141:9 3027
they devour Israel with gaping j. Is 9:12 6310
And to *put* in the j of the peoples Is 30:28 3895
"I will put hooks in your j Ezk 29:4 3895
about and put hooks into your j, Ezk 38:4 3895
who lifts the yoke from their j; Hos 11:4 3895
JAZER
border of the sons of Ammon *was* J. Nu 21:24 3270
Moses sent to spy out J, Nu 21:32 3270
land of J and the land of Gilead, Nu 32:1 3270
"Ataroth, Dibon, J, Nimrah, Nu 32:3 3270
Atroth-shophan and J and Jogbehah, Nu 32:35 3270
Their territory was J, Jos 13:25 3270
lands, J with its pasture lands; Jos 21:39 3270
the valley of Gad and toward J. 2Sa 24:5 3270
and J with its pasture lands. 1Ch 6:81 3270
found among them at J of Gilead) 1Ch 26:31 3270
clusters Which reached as far as J Is 16:8 3270
I will weep bitterly for J, Is 16:9 3270
More than the weeping for J I will Jer 48:32 3270
sea, They reached to the sea of J; Jer 48:32 3270
JAZIZ
J the Hagrite had charge of 1Ch 27:31 3151

JEALOUS
she became **j** of her sister; **Gn 30:1** 7065
His brothers were **j** of him, **Gn 37:11** 7065
I, the LORD your God, am a **j** God, **Ex 20:5** 7067
for the LORD, whose name is **J**, **Ex 34:14** 7067
whose name is Jealous, is a **j** God **Ex 34:14** 7067
he is **j** of his wife when she has defiled **Nu 5:14** 7065
he is **j** of his wife when she has not **Nu 5:14** 7065
a man and he is **j** of his wife, **Nu 5:30** 7065
"Are you **j** for my sake? **Nu 11:29** 7065
was **j** with My jealousy among them, **Nu 25:11** 7065
because he was **j** for his God and **Nu 25:13** 7065
God is a consuming fire, a **j** God. **Dt 4:24** 7067
I, the LORD your God, am a **j** God, **Dt 5:9** 7067
in the midst of you is a **j** God; **Dt 6:15** 7067
"They made Him **j** with strange *gods;* **Dt 32:16** 7065
made Me **j** with *what* is not God; **Dt 32:21** 7065
So I will make them **j** with *those* **Dt 32:21** 7065
for He is a holy God. He is a **j** God; **Jos 24:19** 7072
Ephraim will not be **j** of Judah, **Is 11:13** 7065
the garden of God, were **j** of it. **Ezk 31:9** 7065
and I will be **j** for My holy name. **Ezk 39:25** 7065
A **j** and avenging God is the LORD; **Na 1:2** 7072
j for Jerusalem and Zion. **Zch 1:14** 7065
'I am exceedingly **j** for Zion, **Zch 8:2** 7065
with great wrath I am **j** for her.' **Zch 8:2** 7065
The patriarchs became **j** of Joseph **Ac 7:9** *2206*
becoming **j** and taking along some **Ac 17:5** *2206*
J BY THAT WHICH IS NOT A NATION, **Ro 10:19** *3863*
to the Gentiles, to make them **j**. **Ro 11:11** *3863*
love is kind *and* is not **j**; **1Co 13:4** *2206*
j for you with a godly jealousy; **2Co 11:2** *2206*

JEALOUSLY
"He **j** desires the Spirit which He **Jas 4:5** *5355*

JEALOUSY
if a spirit of **j** comes over him **Nu 5:14** 7068
or if a spirit of **j** comes over him **Nu 5:14** 7068
for it is a grain offering of **j**, **Nu 5:15** 7068
which is the grain offering of **j**, **Nu 5:18** 7068
shall take the grain offering of **j** **Nu 5:25** 7068
'This is the law of **j**: **Nu 5:29** 7068
or when a spirit of **j** comes over a **Nu 5:30** 7068
was jealous with My **j** among them, **Nu 25:11** 7068
the sons of Israel in My **j**. **Nu 25:11** 7068
His **j** will burn against that man, **Dt 29:20** 7068
and they provoked Him to **j** more **1Ki 14:22** 7065
And **j** kills the simple. **Jb 5:2** 7068
aroused His **j** with their graven **Ps 78:58** 7065
Will Your **j** burn like fire? **Ps 79:5** 7068
For **j** enrages a man, And he will **Pr 6:34** 7068
flood, But who can stand before **j**? **Pr 27:4** 7068
as death, **J** is as severe as Sheol; **SS 8:6** 7068
Then the **j** of Ephraim will depart, **Is 11:13** 7068
where the seat of the idol of **j**, **Ezk 8:3** 7068
of jealousy, which provokes to **j**, **Ezk 8:3** 7065
this idol of **j** at the entrance. **Ezk 8:5** 7068
on you the blood of wrath and **j**. **Ezk 16:38** 7068
and My **j** will depart from you, **Ezk 16:42** 7068
'I will set My **j** against you, **Ezk 23:25** 7068
"Surely in the fire of My **j** I **Ezk 36:5** 7068
I have spoken in My **j** and in My **Ezk 36:6** 7068
be devoured In the fire of His **j**, **Zph 1:18** 7068
and they were filled with **j**. **Ac 5:17** *2205b*
crowds, they were filled with **j** and **Ac 13:45** *2205b*
if somehow I might move to **j** my **Ro 11:14** *3863*
sensuality, not in strife and **j**. **Ro 13:13** *2205b*
there is **j** and strife among you, **1Co 3:3** *2205b*
Or do we provoke the Lord to **j**? **1Co 10:22** *3863*
am jealous for you with a godly **j**; **2Co 11:2** *2205b*
perhaps *there will be* strife, **j**, **2Co 12:20** *2205b*
sorcery, enmities, strife, **j**, **Ga 5:20** *2205b*
But if you have bitter **j** and **Jas 3:14** *2205b*
where **j** and selfish ambition exist, **Jas 3:16** *2205b*

JEARIM
the slope of Mount **J** on the north **Jos 15:10** 3297

JEATHERAI
his son, Zerah his son, **J** his son. **1Ch 6:21** 2979

JEBERECHIAH
and Zechariah the son of **J**." **Is 8:2** 3000

JEBUS
and came to *a place* opposite **J** **Jg 19:10** 2982
When they *were* near **J**, **Jg 19:11** 2982
went to Jerusalem (that is, **J**); **1Ch 11:4** 2982
inhabitants of **J** said to David, **1Ch 11:5** 2982

JEBUSITE
and the **J** and the Amorite and the **Gn 10:16** 2983
and the Girgashite and the **J**." **Gn 15:21** 2983
and the Hivite and the **J**. **Ex 3:8** 2983
and the Hivite and the **J**, **Ex 3:17** 2983
the Amorite, the Hivite and the **J**, **Ex 13:5** 2983
Perizzite, the Hivite and the **J**. **Ex 33:2** 2983
Perizzite, the Hivite and the **J**. **Ex 34:11** 2983
Perizzite, the Hivite and the **J**, **Dt 20:17** 2983
the Amorite, and the **J**. **Jos 3:10** 2983
Perizzite, the Hivite and the **J**, **Jos 9:1** 2983
and the **J** in the hill country, **Jos 11:3** 2983
Perizzite, the Hivite and the **J**: **Jos 12:8** 2983
the slope of the **J** on the south **Jos 15:8** 2983
to the slope of the **J** southward, **Jos 18:16** 2983
and Zelah, Haeleph and the **J** **Jos 18:28** 2983
Girgashite, the Hivite and the **J**. **Jos 24:11** 2983
threshing floor of Araunah the **J**. **2Sa 24:16** 2983
floor of Araunah the **J**." **2Sa 24:18** 2983
"Whoever strikes down a **J** first **1Ch 11:6** 2983
threshing floor of Ornan the **J**. **1Ch 21:15** 2983
threshing floor of Ornan the **J**. **1Ch 21:18** 2983
threshing floor of Ornan the **J**, **1Ch 21:28** 2983
threshing floor of Ornan the **J**. **2Ch 3:1** 2983
Amorite, Of the Perizzite, the **J** and **Ne 9:8** 2983
clan in Judah, And Ekron like a **J**. **Zch 9:7** 2983

JEBUSITES
Canaanites, the Hivites and the **J**; **Ex 23:23** 2983
the **J** and the Amorites are living in **Nu 13:29** 2983
and the Hivites and the **J**, **Dt 7:1** 2983
Now as for the **J**, the inhabitants **Jos 15:63** 2983
so the **J** live with the sons of **Jos 15:63** 2983
out the **J** who lived in Jerusalem; **Jg 1:21** 2983
so the **J** have lived with the sons **Jg 1:21** 2983
the Hivites, and the **J**; **Jg 3:5** 2983
us turn aside into this city of the **J** **Jg 19:11** 2983
went to Jerusalem against the **J**, **2Sa 5:6** 2983
"Whoever would strike the **J**, **2Sa 5:8** 2983
Perizzites, the Hivites and the **J**, **1Ki 9:20** 2983
and the **J**, the Amorites, the **1Ch 1:14** 2983
and the **J**, the inhabitants of the **1Ch 11:4** 2983
the Hivites and the **J**, **2Ch 8:7** 2983
Hittites, the Perizzites, the **J**, **Ezr 9:1** 2983

JECHILIAH
mother's name was **J** of Jerusalem. **2Ch 26:3** 3203

JECOLIAH
mother's name was **J** of Jerusalem. **2Ki 15:2** 3203

JECONIAH
sons of Jehoiakim *were* **J** his son, **1Ch 3:16** 3204
The sons of **J**, the prisoner, **1Ch 3:17** 3204
been exiled with **J** king of Judah, **Es 2:6** 3204
captive **J** the son of Jehoiakim, **Jer 24:1** 3204
into exile **J** the son of Jehoiakim, **Jer 27:20** 3204
this place **J** the son of Jehoiakim, **Jer 28:4** 3204
after King **J** and the queen mother, **Jer 29:2** 3204
became the father of **J** and his brothers, **Mt 1:11** *2423*
J became the father of Shealtiel, **Mt 1:12** *2423*

JEDAIAH
the son of Allon, the son of **J**, **1Ch 4:37** 3042
From the priests *were* **J**, **1Ch 9:10** 3048
for Jehoiarib, the second for **J**, **1Ch 24:7** 3048
sons of **J** of the house of Jeshua, **Ezr 2:36** 3048
Next to them **J** the son of Harumaph **Ne 3:10** 3042
sons of **J** of the house of Jeshua, **Ne 7:39** 3048
J the son of Joiarib, Jachin, **Ne 11:10** 3048
Shemaiah and Joiarib, **J**, **Ne 12:6** 3048
Sallu, Amok, Hilkiah and **J**. **Ne 12:7** 3048
of Joiarib, Mattenai; of **J**, Uzzi; **Ne 12:19** 3048
Hilkiah, Hashabiah; of **J**, Nethanel. **Ne 12:21** 3048
from Heldai, Tobijah and **J**; **Zch 6:10** 3048
of the LORD to Helem, Tobijah, **J** and **Zch 6:14** 3048

JEDIAEL
Bela and Becher and **J**. **1Ch 7:6** 3043
The son of **J** *was* Bilhan. **1Ch 7:10** 3043
All these *were* sons of **J**, **1Ch 7:11** 3043
J the son of Shimri and Joha his **1Ch 11:45** 3043
Adnah, Jozabad, **J**, Michael, **1Ch 12:20** 3043
the firstborn, **J** the second, **1Ch 26:2** 3043

JEDIDAH
and his mother's name *was* **J** the **2Ki 22:1** 3040

JEDIDIAH
he named him **J** for the LORD's sake. **2Sa 12:25** 3041

JEDUTHUN
the son of Galal, the son of **J**, **1Ch 9:16** 3038
Obed-edom, also the son of **J**, **1Ch 16:38** 3038
With them *were* Heman and **J**, **1Ch 16:41** 3038
And with them *were* Heman and **J** **1Ch 16:42** 3038
and the sons of **J** for the gate. **1Ch 16:42** 3038
of Asaph and of Heman and of **J**, **1Ch 25:1** 3038
Of **J**, the sons of Jeduthun: **1Ch 25:3** 3038
Of Jeduthun, the sons of **J**: **1Ch 25:3** 3038
under the direction of their father **J** **1Ch 25:3** 3038
J and Heman *were* under the **1Ch 25:6** 3038
singers, Asaph, Heman, **J**, **2Ch 5:12** 3038
and from the sons of **J**, **2Ch 29:14** 3038
Heman, and **J** the king's seer; **2Ch 35:15** 3038
the son of Galal, the son of **J**. **Ne 11:17** 3038

JEGAR-SAHADUTHA
Now Laban called it **J**, **Gn 31:47** 3026

JEHALLELEL
sons of **J** *were* Ziph and Ziphah, **1Ch 4:16** 3094
of Abdi and Azariah the son of **J**; **2Ch 29:12** 3094

JEHDEIAH
of the sons of Shubael, **J**. **1Ch 24:20** 3165
and **J** the Meronothite had charge **1Ch 27:30** 3165

JEHEZKEL
Pethahiah, the twentieth for **J**, **1Ch 24:16** 3168

JEHIAH
Obed-edom and **J** also *were* **1Ch 15:24** 3174

JEHIEL
Ben, Jaaziel, Shemiramoth, **J**, **1Ch 15:18** 3171
Zechariah, Aziel, Shemiramoth, **J**, **1Ch 15:20** 3171
then Jeiel, Shemiramoth, **J**, **1Ch 16:5** 3171
J the first and Zetham and Joel, **1Ch 23:8** 3171
and **J** the son of Hachmoni tutored **1Ch 27:32** 3171
LORD, in care of **J** the Gershonite. **1Ch 29:8** 3171
Azariah, **J**, Zechariah, Azaryahu, **2Ch 21:2** 3171
the sons of Heman, **J** and Shimei; **2Ch 29:14** 3171
J, Azaziah, Nahath, Asahel, **2Ch 31:13** 3171
Hilkiah and Zechariah and **J**, **2Ch 35:8** 3171
son of **J** and 218 males with him; **Ezr 8:9** 3171
Shecaniah the son of **J**, **Ezr 10:2** 3171
Maaseiah, Elijah, Shemaiah, **J** and **Ezr 10:21** 3171
Mattaniah, Zechariah, **J**, **Ezr 10:26** 3171

JEHIELI
The sons of **J**, Zetham and Joel his **1Ch 26:22** 3172

JEHIELITES
belonging to Ladan, *namely,* the **J**, **1Ch 26:21** 3172

JEHIZKIAH
J the son of Shallum, **2Ch 28:12** 3169

JEHOADDAH
Ahaz became the father of **J**, **1Ch 8:36** 3085
J became the father of Alemeth, **1Ch 8:36** 3085

JEHOADDAN
mother's name was **J** of Jerusalem. **2Ch 25:1** 3086

JEHOADDIN
mother's name was **J** of Jerusalem. **2Ki 14:2** 3086

JEHOAHAZ
And **J** his son became king in his **2Ki 10:35** 3059
J the son of Jehu became king over **2Ki 13:1** 3059
Then **J** entreated the favor of the **2Ki 13:4** 3059
For he left to **J** of the army not **2Ki 13:7** 3059
Now the rest of the acts of **J**, **2Ki 13:8** 3059
And **J** slept with his fathers, and **2Ki 13:9** 3059
of Judah, Jehoash the son of **J** became **2Ki 13:10** 3059
Israel all the days of **J**. **2Ki 13:22** 3059
Then Jehoash the son of **J** took **2Ki 13:25** 3059
war from the hand of **J** his father. **2Ki 13:25** 3059
Jehoash, the son of **J** son of Jehu, **2Ki 14:8** 3059
Jehoash son of **J** king of Israel. **2Ki 14:17** 3059
took **J** the son of Josiah and anointed **2Ki 23:30** 3059
J was twenty-three years old when **2Ki 23:31** 3059
J away and brought *him* to Egypt, **2Ki 23:34** 3059
no son was left to him except **J**, **2Ch 21:17** 3059
the son of **J** the son of Jehu, **2Ch 25:17** 3059
the son of Joash the son of **J**, **2Ch 25:23** 3059
the death of Joash, son of **J**, **2Ch 25:25** 3059

JEHOASH
J was seven years old when he **2Ki 11:21** 3060
year of Jehu, **J** became king, **2Ki 12:1** 3060
J did right in the sight of **2Ki 12:2** 3060
Then **J** said to the priests, **2Ki 12:4** 3060
in the twenty-third year of King **J** **2Ki 12:6** 3060
Then King **J** called for Jehoiada **2Ki 12:7** 3060
J king of Judah took all the **2Ki 12:18** 3060
of Judah, **J** the son of Jehoahaz became **2Ki 13:10** 3060
Then **J** the son of Jehoahaz took **2Ki 13:25** 3060
Then Amaziah sent messengers to **J**, **2Ki 14:8** 3060
J king of Israel sent to **2Ki 14:9** 3060
So **J** king of Israel went up; **2Ki 14:11** 3060
Then **J** king of Israel captured **2Ki 14:13** 3060
the son of **J** the son of Ahaziah, **2Ki 14:13** 3060
rest of the acts of **J** which he did, **2Ki 14:15** 3060
So **J** slept with his fathers and **2Ki 14:16** 3060
lived fifteen years after the death of **J** **2Ki 14:17** 3060

JEHOHANAN
chamber of **J** the son of Eliashib. **Ezr 10:6** 3076
J, Hananiah, Zabbai *and* Athlai; **Ezr 10:28** 3076
and his son **J** had married the **Ne 6:18** 3076
of Ezra, Meshullam; of Amariah, **J**; **Ne 12:13** 3076
Shemaiah, Eleazar, Uzzi, **J**, **Ne 12:42** 3076

JEHOIACHIN
and **J** his son became king in his **2Ki 24:6** 3078
J was eighteen years old when he **2Ki 24:8** 3078
J the king of Judah went out **2Ki 24:12** 3078
led **J** away into exile to Babylon; **2Ki 24:15** 3078
of the exile of **J** king of Judah, **2Ki 25:27** 3078
J king of Judah from prison; **2Ki 25:27** 3078
J changed his prison clothes and **2Ki 25:29**
And **J** his son became king in his **2Ch 36:8** 3078
J was eight years old when he **2Ch 36:9** 3078
of the exile of **J** king of Judah, **Jer 52:31** 3078
showed favor to **J** king of Judah **Jer 52:31** 3078
So **J** changed his prison clothes, **Jer 52:33**

JEHOIACHIN'S
in the fifth year of King **J** exile, **Ezk 1:2** 3078

JEHOIADA
Benaiah the son of **J** was over **2Sa 8:18** 3077
and Benaiah the son of **J** was over **2Sa 20:23** 3077
Then Benaiah the son of **J**, **2Sa 23:20** 3077
things Benaiah the son of **J** did, **2Sa 23:22** 3077
the priest, Benaiah the son of **J**, **1Ki 1:8** 3077
son of **J** and your servant Solomon, **1Ki 1:26** 3077
and Benaiah the son of **J**." **1Ki 1:32** 3077
of **J** answered the king and said, **1Ki 1:36** 3077
the prophet, Benaiah the son of **J**, **1Ki 1:38** 3077
the prophet, Benaiah the son of **J**, **1Ki 1:44** 3077
Solomon sent Benaiah the son of **J**; **1Ki 2:25** 3077
Solomon sent Benaiah the son of **J**, **1Ki 2:29** 3077
Then Benaiah the son of **J** went up **1Ki 2:34** 3077
of **J** over the army in his place, **1Ki 2:35** 3077
commanded Benaiah the son of **J**, **1Ki 2:46** 3077
the son of **J** *was* over the army; **1Ki 4:4** 3077
Now in the seventh year **J** sent and **2Ki 11:4** 3077
all that **J** the priest commanded. **2Ki 11:9** 3077
sabbath, and came to **J** the priest. **2Ki 11:9** 3077
And **J** the priest commanded the **2Ki 11:15** 3077
Then **J** made a covenant between the **2Ki 11:17** 3077
which **J** the priest instructed him. **2Ki 12:2** 3077
Jehoash called for **J** the priest, **2Ki 12:7** 3077
But **J** the priest took a chest and **2Ki 12:9** 3077
Benaiah the son of **J**, **1Ch 11:22** 3077
things Benaiah the son of **J** did, **1Ch 11:24** 3077
Now **J** was the leader of *the house* **1Ch 12:27** 3077
and Benaiah the son of **J** *was* over **1Ch 18:17** 3077
Benaiah, the son of **J** the priest, **1Ch 27:5** 3077
J the son of Benaiah, and **1Ch 27:34** 3077
Jehoram, the wife of **J** the priest **2Ch 22:11** 3077
year **J** strengthened himself, **2Ch 23:1** 3077
And **J** said to them, **2Ch 23:3**
all that **J** the priest commanded. **2Ch 23:8** 3077
for **J** the priest did not dismiss **2Ch 23:8** 3077
Then **J** the priest gave to the **2Ch 23:9** 3077
And **J** and his sons anointed him **2Ch 23:11** 3077
J the priest brought out the **2Ch 23:14** 3077

Then **J** made a covenant between	**2Ch 23:16**	3077
J placed the offices of the house	**2Ch 23:18**	3077
LORD all the days of **J** the priest.	**2Ch 24:2**	3077
J took two wives for him, and	**2Ch 24:3**	3077
So the king summoned **J** the chief	**2Ch 24:6**	3077
The king and **J** gave it to	**2Ch 24:12**	3077
the money before the king and **J**;	**2Ch 24:14**	3077
continually all the days of **J**.	**2Ch 24:14**	3077
Now when **J** reached a ripe old age	**2Ch 24:15**	3077
But after the death of **J** the	**2Ch 24:17**	3077
Zechariah the son of **J** the priest;	**2Ch 24:20**	3077
which his father **J** had shown him,	**2Ch 24:22**	3077
blood of the son of **J** the priest,	**2Ch 24:25**	3077
priest instead of **J** the priest,	**Jer 29:26**	3077

JEHOIAKIM

father, and changed his name to **J**.	**2Ki 23:34**	3079
So **J** gave the silver and gold to	**2Ki 23:35**	3079
J was twenty-five years old when	**2Ki 23:36**	3079
and **J** became his servant *for* three	**2Ki 24:1**	3079
the acts of **J** and all that he did,	**2Ki 24:5**	3079
So **J** slept with his fathers, and	**2Ki 24:6**	3079
according to all that **J** had done.	**2Ki 24:19**	3079
firstborn, and the second *was* **J**,	**1Ch 3:15**	3079
sons of **J** *were* Jeconiah his son,	**1Ch 3:16**	3079
and changed his name to **J**.	**2Ch 36:4**	3079
J was twenty-five years old when	**2Ch 36:5**	3079
Now the rest of the acts of **J** and	**2Ch 36:8**	3079
It came also in the days of **J** the	**Jer 1:3**	3079
in regard to **J** the son of Josiah,	**Jer 22:18**	3079
"even though Coniah the son of **J**	**Jer 22:24**	3079
captive Jeconiah the son of **J**,	**Jer 24:1**	3079
year of **J** the son of Josiah,	**Jer 25:1**	3079
the reign of **J** the son of Josiah,	**Jer 26:1**	3079
When King **J** and all his mighty men	**Jer 26:21**	3079
Then King **J** sent men to Egypt:	**Jer 26:22**	3079
from Egypt and led him to King **J**,	**Jer 26:23**	3079
into exile Jeconiah the son of **J**,	**Jer 27:20**	3079
this place Jeconiah the son of **J**,	**Jer 28:4**	3079
the days of **J** the son of Josiah,	**Jer 35:1**	3079
fourth year of **J** the son of Josiah,	**Jer 36:1**	3079
fifth year of **J** the son of Josiah,	**Jer 36:9**	3079
which **J** the king of Judah burned.	**Jer 36:28**	3079
J king of Judah you shall say,	**Jer 36:29**	3079
LORD concerning **J** king of Judah,	**Jer 36:30**	3079
the book which **J** king of Judah had	**Jer 36:32**	3079
in place of Coniah the son of **J**.	**Jer 37:1**	3079
fourth year of **J** the son of Josiah,	**Jer 45:1**	3079
fourth year of **J** the son of Josiah,	**Jer 46:2**	3079
the LORD like all that **J** had done.	**Jer 52:2**	3079
of the reign of **J** king of Judah,	**Da 1:1**	3079
J king of Judah into his hand,	**Da 1:2**	3079

JEHOIARIB

From the priests *were* Jedaiah, **J**,	**1Ch 9:10**	3080
Now the first lot came out for **J**,	**1Ch 24:7**	3080

JEHONADAB

he met **J** the son of Rechab *coming*	**2Ki 10:15**	3082
And **J** answered, "It is." *Jehu said,*	**2Ki 10:15**	3082
of Baal with **J** the son of Rechab;	**2Ki 10:23**	3082

JEHONATHAN

Zebadiah, Asahel, Shemiramoth, **J**,	**2Ch 17:8**	3083
of Bilgah, Shammua; of Shemaiah, **J**;	**Ne 12:18**	3083

JEHORAM

and **J** his son became king in his	**1Ki 22:50**	3088
J became king in his place in the	**2Ki 1:17**	3088
year of **J** the son of Jehoshaphat,	**2Ki 1:17**	3088
Now **J** the son of Ahab became king	**2Ki 3:1**	3088
And King **J** went out of Samaria at	**2Ki 3:6**	3088
J the son of Jehoshaphat king of	**2Ki 8:16**	3088
of **J** king of Judah began to reign.	**2Ki 8:25**	3088
Then Ahaziah the son of **J** king of	**2Ki 8:29**	3088
Jehoshaphat and **J** and Ahaziah,	**2Ki 12:18**	3088
and with them Elishama and **J**,	**2Ch 17:8**	3088
and **J** his son became king in his	**2Ch 21:1**	3088
he gave the kingdom to **J** because	**2Ch 21:3**	3088
when **J** had taken over the kingdom	**2Ch 21:4**	3088
J *was* thirty-two years old when he	**2Ch 21:5**	3088
Then **J** crossed over with his	**2Ch 21:9**	3088
LORD stirred up against **J** the spirit	**2Ch 21:16**	3088
Ahaziah the son of **J** king of Judah	**2Ch 22:1**	3088
and went with **J** the son of Ahab	**2Ch 22:5**	3088
the son of **J** king of Judah,	**2Ch 22:6**	3088
see **J** the son of Ahab in Jezreel,	**2Ch 22:6**	3088
he went out with **J** against Jehu	**2Ch 22:7**	3088
the daughter of King **J**,	**2Ch 22:11**	3088

JEHOSHABEATH

But **J** the king's daughter took	**2Ch 22:11**	3090
So **J**, the daughter of King	**2Ch 22:11**	3090

JEHOSHAPHAT

and **J** the son of Ahilud *was*	**2Sa 8:16**	3092
and **J** the son of Ahilud was the	**2Sa 20:24**	3092
J the son of Ahilud *was* the	**1Ki 4:3**	3092
J the son of Paruah, in Issachar;	**1Ki 4:17**	3092
J his son reigned in his place.	**1Ki 15:24**	3092
year **J** the king of Judah came down	**1Ki 22:2**	3092
And he said to **J**,	**1Ki 22:4**	3092
And **J** said to the king of Israel,	**1Ki 22:4**	3092
J said to the king of Israel,	**1Ki 22:5**	3092
J said, "Is there not yet a prophet of	**1Ki 22:7**	3092
The king of Israel said to **J**,	**1Ki 22:8**	3092
But **J** said, "Let not the king say so.	**1Ki 22:8**	3092
king of Israel and **J** king of Judah	**1Ki 22:10**	3092
Then the king of Israel said to **J**,	**1Ki 22:18**	3092
king of Israel and **J** king of Judah	**1Ki 22:29**	3092
The king of Israel said to **J**,	**1Ki 22:30**	3092
captains of the chariots saw **J**,	**1Ki 22:32**	3092
against him, and **J** cried out.	**1Ki 22:32**	3092
Now **J** the son of Asa became king	**1Ki 22:41**	3092
J was thirty-five years old when	**1Ki 22:42**	3092
J also made peace with the king of	**1Ki 22:44**	3092
Now the rest of the acts of **J**,	**1Ki 22:45**	3092
J made ships of Tarshish to go to	**1Ki 22:48**	3092
Ahaziah the son of Ahab said to **J**,	**1Ki 22:49**	3092
But **J** was not willing.	**1Ki 22:49**	3092
And **J** slept with his fathers and	**1Ki 22:50**	3092
year of **J** king of Judah,	**1Ki 22:51**	3092
year of Jehoram the son of **J**,	**2Ki 1:17**	3092
year of **J** king of Judah,	**2Ki 3:1**	3092
sent *word* to **J** the king of Judah,	**2Ki 3:7**	3092
J said, "Is there not a prophet of	**2Ki 3:11**	3092
J said, "The word of the LORD is	**2Ki 3:12**	3092
So the king of Israel and **J** and	**2Ki 3:12**	3092
presence of **J** the king of Judah,	**2Ki 3:14**	3092
J being then the king of Judah,	**2Ki 8:16**	3092
Jehoram the son of **J** king of Judah	**2Ki 8:16**	3092
the son of **J** the son of Nimshi,	**2Ki 9:2**	3092
So Jehu the son of **J** the son of	**2Ki 9:14**	3092
that **J** and Jehoram and Ahaziah,	**2Ki 12:18**	3092
his son, Asa his son, **J** his son,	**1Ch 3:10**	3092
and **J** the son of Ahilud *was*	**1Ch 18:15**	3092
J his son then became king in his	**2Ch 17:1**	3092
The LORD was with **J** because he	**2Ch 17:3**	3092
all Judah brought tribute to **J**,	**2Ch 17:5**	3092
they did not make war against **J**.	**2Ch 17:10**	3092
gifts and silver as tribute to **J**;	**2Ch 17:11**	3092
So **J** grew greater and greater, and	**2Ch 17:12**	3092
Now **J** had great riches and honor;	**2Ch 18:1**	3092
of Israel said to **J** king of Judah,	**2Ch 18:3**	3092
J said to the king of Israel,	**2Ch 18:4**	3092
J said, "Is there not yet a prophet of	**2Ch 18:6**	3092
The king of Israel said to **J**,	**2Ch 18:7**	3092
J said, "Let not the king say so."	**2Ch 18:7**	3092
and **J** the king of Judah were sitting	**2Ch 18:9**	3092
Then the king of Israel said to **J**,	**2Ch 18:17**	3092
So the king of Israel and **J** king	**2Ch 18:28**	3092
The king of Israel said to **J**,	**2Ch 18:29**	3092
captains of the chariots saw **J**,	**2Ch 18:31**	3092
But **J** cried out, and the LORD	**2Ch 18:31**	3092
Then **J** the king of Judah returned	**2Ch 19:1**	3092
to meet him and said to King **J**,	**2Ch 19:2**	3092
So **J** lived in Jerusalem and went	**2Ch 19:4**	3092
In Jerusalem also **J** appointed	**2Ch 19:8**	3092
came to make war against **J**.	**2Ch 20:1**	3092
Then some came and reported to **J**,	**2Ch 20:2**	3092
J was afraid and turned his	**2Ch 20:3**	3092
Then **J** stood in the assembly of	**2Ch 20:5**	3092
of Jerusalem and King **J**:	**2Ch 20:15**	3092
J bowed his head with *his* face	**2Ch 20:18**	3092
they went out, **J** stood and said,	**2Ch 20:20**	3092
When **J** and his people came to	**2Ch 20:25**	3092
returned with **J** at their head,	**2Ch 20:27**	3092
So the kingdom of **J** was at peace,	**2Ch 20:30**	3092
Now **J** reigned over Judah.	**2Ch 20:31**	3092
Now the rest of the acts of **J**,	**2Ch 20:34**	3092
After this **J** king of Judah	**2Ch 20:35**	3092
prophesied against **J** saying,	**2Ch 20:37**	3092
Then **J** slept with his fathers and	**2Ch 21:1**	3092
He had brothers, the sons of **J**:	**2Ch 21:2**	3092
were the sons of **J** king of Israel.	**2Ch 21:2**	3092
have not walked in the ways of **J**	**2Ch 21:12**	3092
"He is the son of **J**,	**2Ch 22:9**	3092
them down to the valley of **J**.	**Jl 3:2**	3092
And come up to the valley of **J**,	**Jl 3:12**	3092
Asa was the father of **J**,	**Mt 1:8**	*2498*
J the father of Joram, and Joram	**Mt 1:8**	*2498*

JEHOSHEBA

But **J**, the daughter of King Joram,	**2Ki 11:2**	3089

JEHOZABAD

Shimeath and **J** the son of Shomer,	**2Ki 12:21**	3075
the firstborn, **J** the second,	**1Ch 26:4**	3075
and next to him **J**, and with him	**2Ch 17:18**	3075
and **J** the son of Shimrith the	**2Ch 24:26**	3075

JEHOZADAK

Seraiah became the father of **J**;	**1Ch 6:14**	3087
and **J** went *along* when the LORD	**1Ch 6:15**	3087
Judah, and to Joshua the son of **J**,	**Hg 1:1**	3087
and Joshua the son of **J**,	**Hg 1:12**	3087
the spirit of Joshua the son of **J**,	**Hg 1:14**	3087
Judah, and to Joshua the son of **J**,	**Hg 2:2**	3087
courage also, Joshua son of **J**,	**Hg 2:4**	3087
the head of Joshua the son of **J**,	**Zch 6:11**	3087

JEHU

the word of the LORD came to **J**	**1Ki 16:1**	3058
the prophet **J** the son of Hanani	**1Ki 16:7**	3058
Baasha through **J** the prophet,	**1Ki 16:12**	3058
and **J** the son of Nimshi you shall	**1Ki 19:16**	3058
of Hazael, **J** shall put to death,	**1Ki 19:17**	3058
who escapes from the sword of **J**,	**1Ki 19:17**	3058
search out **J** the son of Jehoshaphat	**2Ki 9:2**	3058
And **J** said, "For which *one* of us?"	**2Ki 9:5**	3058
Now **J** came out to the servants of	**2Ki 9:11**	3058
blew the trumpet, saying, "**J** is king!	**2Ki 9:13**	3058
So **J** the son of Jehoshaphat the	**2Ki 9:14**	3058
So **J** said, "If this is your mind, *then*	**2Ki 9:15**	3058
Then **J** rode in a chariot and went	**2Ki 9:16**	3058
saw the company of **J** as he came,	**2Ki 9:17**	3058
J said, "What have you to do with	**2Ki 9:18**	3058
J answered, "What have you to do	**2Ki 9:19**	3058
driving of **J** the son of Nimshi,	**2Ki 9:20**	3058
and they went out to meet **J** and	**2Ki 9:21**	3058
When Joram saw **J**,	**2Ki 9:22**	3058
"Is it peace, **J**?"	**2Ki 9:22**	3058
And **J** drew his bow with his full	**2Ki 9:24**	3058
Then **J** said to Bidkar his officer,	**2Ki 9:25**	3058
And **J** pursued him and said,	**2Ki 9:27**	3058
When **J** came to Jezreel, Jezebel	**2Ki 9:30**	3058
As **J** entered the gate, she	**2Ki 9:31**	3058
And **J** wrote letters and sent *them*	**2Ki 10:1**	3058
of *the children,* sent *word* to **J**,	**2Ki 10:5**	3058
So **J** killed all who remained of	**2Ki 10:11**	3058
J met the relatives of Ahaziah	**2Ki 10:13**	3058
J *said,* "If it is, give *me*	**2Ki 10:15**	
Then **J** gathered all the people and	**2Ki 10:18**	3058
J will serve him much.	**2Ki 10:18**	3058
But **J** did it in cunning, so	**2Ki 10:19**	3058
J said, "Sanctify a solemn assembly	**2Ki 10:20**	3058
Then **J** sent throughout Israel and	**2Ki 10:21**	3058
J went into the house of Baal	**2Ki 10:23**	3058
Now **J** had stationed for himself	**2Ki 10:24**	3058
that **J** said to the guard and to	**2Ki 10:25**	3058
J eradicated Baal out of Israel.	**2Ki 10:28**	3058
sin, from these **J** did not depart,	**2Ki 10:29**	3058
The LORD said to **J**,	**2Ki 10:30**	3058
But **J** was not careful to walk in	**2Ki 10:31**	3058
Now the rest of the acts of **J** and	**2Ki 10:34**	3058
And **J** slept with his fathers, and	**2Ki 10:35**	3058
Now the time which **J** reigned over	**2Ki 10:36**	3058
In the seventh year of **J**,	**2Ki 12:1**	3058
Jehoahaz the son of **J** became king	**2Ki 13:1**	3058
the son of Jehoahaz son of **J**,	**2Ki 14:8**	3058
of the LORD which He spoke to **J**,	**2Ki 15:12**	3058
and Obed became the father of **J**,	**1Ch 2:38**	3058
J became the father of Azariah,	**1Ch 2:38**	3058
Joel and **J** the son of Joshibiah,	**1Ch 4:35**	3058
and Beracah and **J** the Anathothite,	**1Ch 12:3**	3058
J the son of Hanani the seer	**2Ch 19:2**	3058
the annals of **J** the son of Hanani,	**2Ch 20:34**	3058
against **J** the son of Nimshi,	**2Ch 22:7**	3058
It came about when **J** was	**2Ch 22:8**	3058
they brought him to **J**,	**2Ch 22:9**	3058
the son of Jehoahaz the son of **J**,	**2Ch 25:17**	3058
I will punish the house of **J** for the	**Hos 1:4**	3058

JEHUBBAH

were Ahi and Rohgah, **J** and Aram.	**1Ch 7:34**	3160

JEHUCAL

sent **J** the son of Shelemiah,	**Jer 37:3**	3081

JEHUD

and **J** and Bene-berak and	**Jos 19:45**	3055

JEHUDI

sent **J** the son of Nethaniah,	**Jer 36:14**	3065
the king sent **J** to get the scroll,	**Jer 36:21**	3065
And **J** read it to the king as well	**Jer 36:21**	3065
When **J** had read three or four	**Jer 36:23**	3065

JEIEL

generations, *were* **J** the chief,	**1Ch 5:7**	3262
Now in Gibeon, **J**, the father of	**1Ch 8:29**	
J the father of Gibeon lived,	**1Ch 9:35**	3262
Shama and **J** the sons of Hotham the	**1Ch 11:44**	3262
Mikneiah, Obed-edom and **J**,	**1Ch 15:18**	3262
Eliphelehu, Mikneiah, Obed-edom, **J**	**1Ch 15:21**	3262
second to him Zechariah, *then* **J**,	**1Ch 16:5**	3262
Eliab, Benaiah, Obed-edom and **J**,	**1Ch 16:5**	3262
the son of Benaiah, the son of **J**,	**2Ch 20:14**	3262
prepared by **J** the scribe and	**2Ch 26:11**	3262
sons of Elizaphan, Shimri and **J**;	**2Ch 29:13**	3262
and Hashabiah and **J** and Jozabad,	**2Ch 35:9**	3262
Of the sons of Nebo *there were* **J**,	**Ezr 10:43**	3262

JEKABZEEL

towns, and in **J** and its villages,	**Ne 11:25**	6909

JEKAMEAM

the third and **J** the fourth.	**1Ch 23:19**	3360
Jahaziel the third, **J** the fourth.	**1Ch 24:23**	3360

JEKAMIAH

Shallum became the father of **J**,	**1Ch 2:41**	3359
J became the father of Elishama.	**1Ch 2:41**	3359
Malchiram, Pedaiah, Shenazzar, **J**,	**1Ch 3:18**	3359

JEKUTHIEL

Soco, and **J** the father of Zanoah.	**1Ch 4:18**	3354

JEMIMAH

He named the first **J**,	**Jb 42:14**	3224

JEMUEL

J and Jamin and Ohad and Jachin	**Gn 46:10**	3223
J and Jamin and Ohad and Jachin	**Ex 6:15**	3223

JEOPARDIZE

because I would **j** my own inheritance.	**Ru 4:6**	7843

JEOPARDY

the blood of the men who went in **j**	**2Sa 23:17**	

JEPHTHAH

Now **J** the Gileadite was a valiant	**Jg 11:1**	3316
And Gilead was the father of **J**.	**Jg 11:1**	3316
they drove **J** out and said to him,	**Jg 11:2**	3316
So **J** fled from his brothers and	**Jg 11:3**	3316
gathered themselves about **J**,	**Jg 11:3**	3316
to get **J** from the land of Tob;	**Jg 11:5**	3316
and they said to **J**,	**Jg 11:6**	3316
J said to the elders of Gilead,	**Jg 11:7**	3316
The elders of Gilead said to **J**,	**Jg 11:8**	3316
So **J** said to the elders of Gilead,	**Jg 11:9**	3316
The elders of Gilead said to **J**,	**Jg 11:10**	3316
Then **J** went with the elders of	**Jg 11:11**	3316
and **J** spoke all his words before	**Jg 11:11**	3316
Now **J** sent messengers to the king	**Jg 11:12**	3316
Ammon said to the messengers of **J**,	**Jg 11:13**	3316
But **J** sent messengers again to the	**Jg 11:14**	3316
says **J**, 'Israel did not take away the	**Jg 11:15**	3316
the message which **J** sent him.	**Jg 11:28**	3316
Spirit of the LORD came upon **J**,	**Jg 11:29**	3316
J made a vow to the LORD and	**Jg 11:30**	3316
So **J** crossed over to the sons of	**Jg 11:32**	3316
J came to his house at Mizpah,	**Jg 11:34**	3316
to commemorate the daughter of **J**	**Jg 11:40**	3316
crossed to Zaphon and said to **J**,	**Jg 12:1**	3316

J said to them, Jg 12:2 3316
Then J gathered all the men of Jg 12:4 3316
J judged Israel six years. Jg 12:7 3316
Then J the Gileadite died and was Jg 12:7 3316
and Bedan and J and Samuel, 1Sa 12:11 3316
tell of Gideon, Barak, Samson, J, Heb 11:32 *2422*

JEPHUNNEH
of Judah, Caleb the son of J; Nu 13:6 3312
son of Nun and Caleb the son of J, Nu 14:6 3312
except Caleb the son of J and Nu 14:30 3312
Caleb the son of J remained alive Nu 14:38 3312
them, except Caleb the son of J and Nu 26:65 3312
except Caleb the son of J the Nu 32:12 3312
of Judah, Caleb the son of J. Nu 34:19 3312
except Caleb the son of J; Dt 1:36 3312
Caleb the son of J the Kenizzite Jos 14:6 3312
the son of J for an inheritance. Jos 14:13 3312
inheritance of Caleb the son of J Jos 14:14 3312
Now he gave to Caleb the son of J Jos 15:13 3312
Caleb the son of J as his possession. Jos 21:12 3312
sons of Caleb the son of J *were* Iru, 1Ch 4:15 3312
they gave to Caleb the son of J. 1Ch 6:56 3312
The sons of Jether *were* J, 1Ch 7:38 3312

JERAH
Sheleph and Hazarmaveth and J Gn 10:26 3392
Almodad, Sheleph, Hazarmaveth, J, 1Ch 1:20 3392

JERAHMEEL
who were born to him *were* J, 1Ch 2:9 3396
Now the sons of J the firstborn 1Ch 2:25 3396
J had another wife, whose name 1Ch 2:26 3396
sons of Ram, the firstborn of J, 1Ch 2:27 3396
These were the sons of J. 1Ch 2:33 3396
sons of Caleb, the brother of J, 1Ch 2:42 3396
the sons of Kish, J. 1Ch 24:29 3396
king commanded J the king's son, Jer 36:26 3396

JERAHMEELITES
and against the Negev of the J 1Sa 27:10 3397
who were in the cities of the J, 1Sa 30:29 3397

JERED
wife bore J the father of Gedor, 1Ch 4:18 3382

JEREMAI
Mattattah, Zabad, Eliphelet, J, Ezr 10:33 3413

JEREMIAH
the daughter of J of Libnah. 2Ki 23:31 3414
the daughter of J of Libnah. 2Ki 24:18 3414
Epher, Ishi, Eliel, Azriel, J, 1Ch 5:24 3414
Then J, Jahaziel, Johanan, Jozabad 1Ch 12:4 3414
the fourth, J the fifth, 1Ch 12:10 3414
J the tenth, Machbannai the 1Ch 12:13 3414
J chanted a lament for Josiah. 2Ch 35:25 3414
he did not humble himself before J 2Ch 36:12 3414
word of the LORD by the mouth of J, 2Ch 36:21 3414
word of the LORD by the mouth of J 2Ch 36:22 3414
of the LORD by the mouth of J, Ezr 1:1 3414
Seraiah, Azariah, J, Ne 10:2 3414
Seraiah, J, Ezra, Ne 12:1 3414
of Seraiah, Meraiah; of J, Hananiah; Ne 12:12 3414
Judah, Benjamin, Shemaiah, J, Ne 12:34 3414
The words of J the son of Jer 1:1 3414
"What do you see, J?" Jer 1:11 3414
word that came to J from the LORD, Jer 7:1 3414
which came to J from the LORD, Jer 11:1 3414
came as the word of the LORD to J Jer 14:1 3414
came to J from the LORD saying, Jer 18:1 3414
and let us devise plans against J. Jer 18:18 3414
Then J came from Topheth, where Jer 19:14 3414
heard J prophesying these things, Jer 20:1 3414
Pashhur had J the prophet beaten and Jer 20:2 3414
released J from the stocks, Jer 20:3 3414
the stocks, J said to him, Jer 20:3 3414
The word which came to J from the Jer 21:1 3414
Then J said to them, Jer 21:3 3414
"What do you see, J?" Jer 24:3 3414
The word that came to J concerning Jer 25:1 3414
which J the prophet spoke to all Jer 25:2 3414
which J has prophesied against all Jer 25:13 3414
people heard J speaking these words Jer 26:7 3414
When J finished speaking all Jer 26:8 3414
all the people gathered about J Jer 26:9 3414
Then J spoke to all the officials Jer 26:12 3414
words similar to all those of J. Jer 26:20 3414
the son of Shaphan was with J, Jer 26:24 3414
this word came to J from the LORD, Jer 27:1 3414
Then the prophet J spoke to the Jer 28:5 3414
and the prophet J said, Jer 28:6 3414
took the yoke from the neck of J Jer 28:10 3414
Then the prophet J went his way. Jer 28:11 3414
The word of the LORD came to J Jer 28:12 3414
off the neck of the prophet J, Jer 28:12 3414
Then J the prophet said to Jer 28:15 3414
the letter which J the prophet sent Jer 29:1 3414
why have you not rebuked J of Jer 29:27 3414
read this letter to J the prophet. Jer 29:29 3414
came the word of the LORD to J, Jer 29:30 3414
which came to J from the LORD, Jer 30:1 3414
The word that came to J from the Jer 32:1 3414
and J the prophet was shut up in Jer 32:2 3414
J said, "The word of the LORD came Jer 32:6 3414
the word of the LORD came to J, Jer 32:26 3414
LORD came to J the second time, Jer 33:1 3414
The word of the LORD came to J, Jer 33:19 3414
the word of the LORD came to J, Jer 33:23 3414
which came to J from the LORD, Jer 34:1 3414
Then J the prophet spoke all these Jer 34:6 3414
which came to J from the LORD after Jer 34:8 3414
the word of the LORD came to J Jer 34:12 3414
The word which came to J from the Jer 35:1 3414
I took Jaazaniah the son of J, Jer 35:3 3414
the word of the LORD came to J, Jer 35:12 3414
Then J said to the house of the Jer 35:18 3414
this word came to J from the LORD, Jer 36:1 3414
Then J called Baruch the son of Jer 36:4 3414
on a scroll at the dictation of J Jer 36:4 3414
J commanded Baruch, saying, Jer 36:5 3414
that J the prophet commanded him, Jer 36:8 3414
read from the book the words of J Jer 36:10 3414
"Go, hide yourself, you and J, Jer 36:19 3414
the scribe and J the prophet, Jer 36:26 3414
the word of the LORD came to J Jer 36:27 3414
had written at the dictation of J, Jer 36:27 3414
Then J took another scroll and Jer 36:32 3414
he wrote on it at the dictation of J Jer 36:32 3414
He spoke through J the prophet. Jer 37:2 3414
the priest, to J the prophet, Jer 37:3 3414
Now J was *still* coming in and Jer 37:4 3414
the word of the LORD came to J Jer 37:6 3414
that J went out from Jerusalem to Jer 37:12 3414
and he arrested J the prophet, Jer 37:13 3414
J said, "A lie! I am not going over Jer 37:14 3414
So Irijah arrested J and brought Jer 37:14 3414
were angry at J and beat him, Jer 37:15 3414
For J had come into the dungeon, Jer 37:16 3414
and J stayed there many days. Jer 37:16 3414
J said, "There is!" Then he said, Jer 37:17 3414
Moreover J said to King Zedekiah, Jer 37:18 3414
and they committed J to the court Jer 37:21 3414
So J remained in the court of the Jer 37:21 3414
heard the words that J was speaking Jer 38:1 3414
Then they took J and cast him into Jer 38:6 3414
and they let J down with ropes. Jer 38:6 3414
only mud, and J sank into the mud. Jer 38:6 3414
they had put J into the cistern. Jer 38:7 3414
J the prophet whom they have cast Jer 38:9 3414
and bring up J the prophet from Jer 38:10 3414
by ropes into the cistern to J. Jer 38:11 3414
the Ethiopian said to J, Jer 38:12 3414
under the ropes"; and J did so. Jer 38:12 3414
So they pulled J up with the ropes Jer 38:13 3414
and J stayed in the court of the Jer 38:13 3414
Then King Zedekiah sent and had J Jer 38:14 3414
and the king said to J, Jer 38:14 3414
Then J said to Zedekiah, Jer 38:15 3414
swore to J in secret saying, Jer 38:16 3414
Then J said to Zedekiah, Jer 38:17 3414
Then King Zedekiah said to J, Jer 38:19 3414
J said, "They will not give you over. Jer 38:20 3414
Then Zedekiah said to J, Jer 38:24 3414
came to J and questioned him. Jer 38:27 3414
So J stayed in the court of the Jer 38:28 3414
king of Babylon gave orders about J Jer 39:11 3414
they even sent and took J out of Jer 39:14 3414
word of the LORD had come to J Jer 39:15 3414
The word which came to J from the Jer 40:1 3414
had taken J and said to him, Jer 40:2 3414
As J was still not going back, *he* Jer 40:5 3414
Then J went to Mizpah to Gedaliah Jer 40:6 3414
and said to J the prophet, Jer 42:2 3414
Then J the prophet said to them, Jer 42:4 3414
Then they said to J, Jer 42:5 3414
the word of the LORD came to J. Jer 42:7 3414
as soon as J, whom the LORD their Jer 43:1 3414
all the arrogant men said to J, Jer 43:2 3414
together with J the prophet and Jer 43:6 3414
the LORD came to J in Tahpanhes, Jer 43:8 3414
The word that came to J for all Jer 44:1 3414
the land of Egypt, responded to J, Jer 44:15 3414
Then J said to all the people, to Jer 44:20 3414
Then J said to all the people, Jer 44:24 3414
is the message which J the Jer 45:1 3414
came as the word of the LORD to J Jer 46:1 3414
message which the LORD spoke to J Jer 46:13 3414
came as the word of the LORD to J Jer 47:1 3414
to J the prophet concerning Elam, Jer 49:34 3414
Chaldeans, through J the prophet: Jer 50:1 3414
The message which J the prophet Jer 51:59 3414
So J wrote in a single scroll all Jer 51:60 3414
Then J said to Seraiah, Jer 51:61 3414
Thus far are the words of J. Jer 51:64 3414
the daughter of J of Libnah. Jer 52:1 3414
word of the LORD to J the prophet Da 9:2 3414
J the prophet was fulfilled: Mt 2:17 *2408*
but still others, J, Mt 16:14 *2408*
J the prophet was fulfilled: Mt 27:9 *2408*

JEREMIAH'S
words in a book at J dictation, Jer 45:1 3414

JEREMOTH
Joash, Eliezer, Elioenai, Omri, J, 1Ch 7:8 3406
and Ahio, Shashak and J. 1Ch 8:14 3406
Mahli, Eder and J. 1Ch 23:23 3406
for the fifteenth to J, 1Ch 25:22 3406
for Naphtali, J the son of Azriel; 1Ch 27:19 3406
Zechariah, Jehiel, Abdi, J and Ezr 10:26 3406
Elioenai, Eliashib, Mattaniah, J, Ezr 10:27 3406
and Adaiah, Jashub, Sheal *and* J; Ezr 10:29 3406

JERIAH
sons of Hebron *were* J the first, 1Ch 23:19 3404
J *the first,* Amariah the second, 1Ch 24:23 3404

JERIBAI
the Mahavite and J and Joshaviah, 1Ch 11:46 3403

JERICHO
Moab beyond the Jordan *opposite* J. Nu 22:1 3405
plains of Moab by the Jordan at J, Nu 26:3 3405
plains of Moab by the Jordan at J. Nu 26:63 3405
are by the Jordan *opposite* J. Nu 31:12 3405
of Moab by the Jordan *opposite* J. Nu 33:48 3405
of Moab by the Jordan *opposite* J, Nu 33:50 3405
across the Jordan opposite J, Nu 34:15 3405
of Moab by the Jordan *opposite* J, Nu 35:1 3405
of Moab by the Jordan *opposite* J. Nu 36:13 3405
is in the land of Moab opposite J, Dt 32:49 3405
of Pisgah, which is opposite J. Dt 34:1 3405
and the plain in the valley of J, Dt 34:3 3405
"Go, view the land, especially J." Jos 2:1 3405
It was told the king of J, Jos 2:2 3405
the king of J sent *word* to Rahab, Jos 2:3 3405
So the people crossed opposite J. Jos 3:16 3405
LORD to the desert plains of J. Jos 4:13 3405
Gilgal on the eastern edge of J. Jos 4:19 3405
month on the desert plains of J. Jos 5:10 3405
came about when Joshua was by J, Jos 5:13 3405
Now J was tightly shut because of Jos 6:1 3405
I have given J into your hand, Jos 6:2 3405
whom Joshua sent to spy out J. Jos 6:25 3405
rises up and builds this city J; Jos 6:26 3405
Now Joshua sent men from J to Ai, Jos 7:2 3405
just as you did to J and its king; Jos 8:2 3405
Joshua had done to J and to Ai, Jos 9:3 3405
as he had done to J and its king, Jos 10:1 3405
as he had done to the king of J. Jos 10:28 3405
as he had done to the king of J. Jos 10:30 3405
the king of J, one; Jos 12:9 3405
the Jordan at J to the east. Jos 13:32 3405
from the Jordan at J to the waters of Jos 16:1 3405
to the waters of J on the east into Jos 16:1 3405
going up from J through the hill Jos 16:1 3405
J and came out at the Jordan. Jos 16:7 3405
up to the side of J on the north, Jos 18:12 3405
according to their families were J Jos 18:21 3405
Beyond the Jordan east of J, Jos 20:8 3405
crossed the Jordan and came to J; Jos 24:11 3405
citizens of J fought against you, Jos 24:11 3405
"Stay at J until your beards 2Sa 10:5 3405
days Hiel the Bethelite built J; 1Ki 16:34 3405
for the LORD has sent me to J." 2Ki 2:4 3405
So they came to J. 2Ki 2:4 3405
sons of the prophets who *were* at J 2Ki 2:5 3405
were at J opposite *him* saw him, 2Ki 2:15 3405
to him while he was staying at J; 2Ki 2:18 3405
and overtook him in the plains of J 2Ki 25:5 3405
and beyond the Jordan at J, 1Ch 6:78 3405
"Stay at J until your beards 1Ch 19:5 3405
on donkeys, and brought them to J, 2Ch 28:15 3405
the men of J, 345; Ezr 2:34 3405
Next to him the men of J built, Ne 3:2 3405
the men of J, 345; Ne 7:36 3405
Zedekiah in the plains of J; Jer 39:5 3405
Zedekiah in the plains of J, Jer 52:8 3405
As they were leaving J, Mt 20:29 *2410a*
Then they came to J. Mk 10:46 *2410a*
And as He was leaving J Mk 10:46 *2410a*
going down from Jerusalem to J, Lk 10:30 *2410a*
As Jesus was approaching J, Lk 18:35 *2410a*
entered J and was passing through. Lk 19:1 *2410a*
By faith the walls of J fell down after Heb 11:30 *2410a*

JERIEL
of Tola *were* Uzzi, Rephaiah, J, 1Ch 7:2 3400

JERIJAH
for the Hebronites, J the chief 1Ch 26:31 3404

JERIMOTH
Ezbon, Uzzi, Uzziel, J and 1Ch 7:7 3406
Eluzai, J, Bealiah, Shemariah, 1Ch 12:5 3406
Mahli, Eder and J. 1Ch 24:30 3406
Mattaniah, Uzziel, Shebuel and J, 1Ch 25:4 3406
J the son of David *and of* Abihail 2Ch 11:18 3406
Azaziah, Nahath, Asahel, J, 2Ch 31:13 3406

JERIOTH
sons by Azubah *his* wife, and by J; 1Ch 2:18 3408

JEROBOAM
Then J the son of Nebat, an 1Ki 11:26 3379
the man J was a valiant warrior, 1Ki 11:28 3379
when J went out of Jerusalem, 1Ki 11:29 3379
He said to J, 1Ki 11:31 3379
therefore to put J to death; 1Ki 11:40 3379
but J arose and fled to Egypt to 1Ki 11:40 3379
J the son of Nebat heard *of it,* 1Ki 12:2 3379
and J and all the assembly of 1Ki 12:3 3379
Then J and all the people came to 1Ki 12:12 3379
Shilonite to J the son of Nebat. 1Ki 12:15 3379
Israel heard that J had returned, 1Ki 12:20 3379
Then J built Shechem in the hill 1Ki 12:25 3379
J said in his heart, 1Ki 12:26 3379
J instituted a feast in the 1Ki 12:32 3379
while J was standing by the altar 1Ki 13:1 3379
J stretched out his hand from 1Ki 13:4 3379
After this event J did not return 1Ki 13:33 3379
became sin to the house of J, 1Ki 13:34 3379
Abijah the son of J became sick. 1Ki 14:1 3379
J said to his wife, 1Ki 14:2 3379
know that you are the wife of J, 1Ki 14:2 3379
the wife of J is coming to inquire 1Ki 14:5 3379
"Come in, wife of J, 1Ki 14:6 3379
"Go, say to J, 'Thus says the LORD 1Ki 14:7 3379
calamity on the house of J, 1Ki 14:10 3379
cut off from J every male person, 1Ki 14:10 3379
a clean sweep of the house of J, 1Ki 14:10 3379
"Anyone belonging to J who dies 1Ki 14:11 3379
God of Israel in the house of J. 1Ki 14:13 3379
who will cut off the house of J 1Ki 14:14 3379
on account of the sins of J, 1Ki 14:16 3379
Now the rest of the acts of J, 1Ki 14:19 3379
The time that J reigned *was* 1Ki 14:20 3379
Rehoboam and J continually. 1Ki 14:30 3379
in the eighteenth year of King J, 1Ki 15:1 3379

and J all the days of his life. 1Ki 15:6 3379
was war between Abijam and J. 1Ki 15:7 3379
year of J the king of Israel, 1Ki 15:9 3379
Now Nadab the son of J became king 1Ki 15:25 3379
down all the household of J. 1Ki 15:29 3379
not leave to J any persons alive, 1Ki 15:29 3379
of the sins of J which he sinned, 1Ki 15:30 3379
and walked in the way of J and in 1Ki 15:34 3379
you have walked in the way of J 1Ki 16:2 3379
the house of J the son of Nebat. 1Ki 16:3 3379
in being like the house of J, 1Ki 16:7 3379
walking in the way of J, and in his 1Ki 16:19 3379
For he walked in all the way of J 1Ki 16:26 3379
in the sins of J the son of Nebat, 1Ki 16:31 3379
the house of J the son of Nebat, 1Ki 21:22 3379
in the way of J the son of Nebat, 1Ki 22:52 3379
to the sins of J the son of Nebat, 2Ki 3:3 3379
the house of J the son of Nebat, 2Ki 9:9 3379
the sins of J the son of Nebat, 2Ki 10:29 3379
did not depart from the sins of J, 2Ki 10:31 3379
the sins of J the son of Nebat, 2Ki 13:2 3379
from the sins of the house of J, 2Ki 13:6 3379
the sins of J the son of Nebat, 2Ki 13:11 3379
fathers, and J sat on his throne; 2Ki 13:13 3379
and J his son became king in his 2Ki 14:16 3379
J the son of Joash king of Israel 2Ki 14:23 3379
the sins of J the son of Nebat, 2Ki 14:24 3379
by the hand of J the son of Joash. 2Ki 14:27 3379
Now the rest of the acts of J and 2Ki 14:28 3379
And J slept with his fathers, even 2Ki 14:29 3379
year of J king of Israel, 2Ki 15:1 3379
Zechariah the son of J became king 2Ki 15:8 3379
the sins of J the son of Nebat, 2Ki 15:9 3379
the sins of J the son of Nebat, 2Ki 15:18 3379
from the sins of J son of Nebat, 2Ki 15:24 3379
from the sins of J son of Nebat, 2Ki 15:28 3379
they made J the son of Nebat king. 2Ki 17:21 3379
Then J drove Israel away from 2Ki 17:21 3379
in all the sins of J which he did; 2Ki 17:22 3379
place which J the son of Nebat, 2Ki 23:15 3379
in the days of J king of Israel. 1Ch 5:17 3379
concerning J the son of Nebat? 2Ch 9:29 3379
J the son of Nebat heard *of it* 2Ch 10:2 3379
J returned from Egypt. 2Ch 10:2 3379
When J and all Israel came, they 2Ch 10:3 3379
So J and all the people came to 2Ch 10:12 3379
Shilonite to J the son of Nebat. 2Ch 10:15 3379
and returned from going against J. 2Ch 11:4 3379
for J and his sons had excluded 2Ch 11:14 3379
wars between Rehoboam and J 2Ch 12:15 3379
In the eighteenth year of King J, 2Ch 13:1 3379
was war between Abijah and J. 2Ch 13:2 3379
while J drew up in battle 2Ch 13:3 3379
"Listen to me, J and all Israel: 2Ch 13:4 3379
"Yet J the son of Nebat, the 2Ch 13:6 3379
which J made for gods for you. 2Ch 13:8 3379
But J had set an ambush to come 2Ch 13:13 3379
then it was that God routed J and 2Ch 13:15 3379
Abijah pursued J and 2Ch 13:19 3379
J did not again recover 2Ch 13:20 3379
the days of J the son of Joash, Hos 1:1 3379
and in the days of J son of Joash, Am 1:1 3379
rise up against the house of J with Am 7:9 3379
priest of Bethel, sent *word* to J king Am 7:10 3379
'J will die by the sword and Am 7:11 3379

JEROBOAM'S
J wife did so, and arose and 1Ki 14:4 3379
for he alone of J *family* will 1Ki 14:13 3379
Then J wife arose and departed and 1Ki 14:17 3379

JEROHAM
his name was Elkanah the son of J, 1Sa 1:1 3395
Eliab his son, J his son, Elkanah 1Ch 6:27 3395
the son of Elkanah, the son of J, 1Ch 6:34 3395
and Zichri *were* the sons of J. 1Ch 8:27 3395
and Ibneiah the son of J, 1Ch 9:8 3395
and Adaiah the son of J, 1Ch 9:12 3395
Zebadiah, the sons of J of Gedor. 1Ch 12:7 3395
for Dan, Azarel the son of J. 1Ch 27:22 3395
Azariah the son of J, 2Ch 23:1 3395
and Adaiah the son of J, Ne 11:12 3395

JERUBBAAL
on that day he named him J, Jg 6:32 3378
Then J (that is, Gideon) and all the Jg 7:1 3378
Then J the son of Joash went and Jg 8:29 3378
kindness to the household of J Jg 8:35 3378
And Abimelech the son of J went to Jg 9:1 3378
seventy men, all the sons of J, Jg 9:2 3378
killed his brothers the sons of J, Jg 9:5 3378
Jotham the youngest son of J was Jg 9:5 3378
dealt well with J and his house, Jg 9:16 3378
with J and his house this day, Jg 9:19 3378
the seventy sons of J might come, Jg 9:24 3378
Is he not the son of J, Jg 9:28 3378
the son of J came upon them. Jg 9:57 3378
"Then the LORD sent J and Bedan 1Sa 12:11 3378

JERUBBESHETH
down Abimelech the son of J? 2Sa 11:21 3380

JERUEL
in front of the wilderness of J. 2Ch 20:16 3385b

JERUSALEM
Adoni-zedek king of J heard that Jos 10:1 3389
Adoni-zedek king of J sent Jos 10:3 3389
of the Amorites, the king of J, Jos 10:5 3389
the king of J, the king of Hebron, Jos 10:23 3389
the king of J, one; Jos 12:10 3389
Jebusite on the south (that is, J); Jos 15:8 3389
Jebusites, the inhabitants of J, Jos 15:63 3389
sons of Judah at J until this day. Jos 15:63 3389
and the Jebusite (that is, J), Jos 18:28 3389
So they brought him to J and he Jg 1:7 3389
the sons of Judah fought against J Jg 1:8 3389
out the Jebusites who lived in J; Jg 1:21 3389
sons of Benjamin in J to this day. Jg 1:21 3389
place opposite Jebus (that is, J). Jg 19:10 3389
head and brought it to J, 1Sa 17:54 3389
and in J he reigned thirty-three 2Sa 5:5 3389
went to J against the Jebusites, 2Sa 5:6 3389
more concubines and wives from J, 2Sa 5:13 3389
those who were born to him in J: 2Sa 5:14 3389
Hadadezer and brought them to J. 2Sa 8:7 3389
So Mephibosheth lived in J, 2Sa 9:13 3389
the sons of Ammon and came to J. 2Sa 10:14 3389
But David stayed at J. 2Sa 11:1 3389
So Uriah remained in J that day 2Sa 11:12 3389
and all the people returned *to* J. 2Sa 12:31 3389
Geshur and brought Absalom to J. 2Sa 14:23 3389
Absalom lived two full years in J, 2Sa 14:28 3389
shall indeed bring me back to J, 2Sa 15:8 3389
men went with Absalom from J, 2Sa 15:11 3389
servants who were with him at J, 2Sa 15:14 3389
returned the ark of God to J and 2Sa 15:29 3389
the city, and Absalom came into J. 2Sa 15:37 3389
"Behold, he is staying in J, 2Sa 16:3 3389
the men of Israel, entered J, 2Sa 16:15 3389
not find *them,* they returned to J. 2Sa 17:20 3389
my lord the king came out from J, 2Sa 19:19 3389
he came from J to meet the king, 2Sa 19:25 3389
I will sustain you in J with me." 2Sa 19:33 3389
I should go up with the king to J? 2Sa 19:34 3389
king, from the Jordan even to J. 2Sa 20:2 3389
Then David came to his house at J, 2Sa 20:3 3389
and they went out from J to pursue 2Sa 20:7 3389
also returned to the king at J. 2Sa 20:22 3389
they came to J at the end of nine 2Sa 24:8 3389
his hand toward J to destroy it, 2Sa 24:16 3389
thirty-three years he reigned in J. 1Ki 2:11 3389
Build for yourself a house in J and 1Ki 2:36 3389
So Shimei lived in J many days. 1Ki 2:38 3389
Shimei had gone from J to Gath, 1Ki 2:41 3389
of the LORD and the wall around J. 1Ki 3:1 3389
And he came to J and stood before 1Ki 3:15 3389
of Israel, to King Solomon in J, 1Ki 8:1 3389
house, the Millo, the wall of J, 1Ki 9:15 3389
it pleased Solomon to build in J, 1Ki 9:19 3389
to J with a very large retinue, 1Ki 10:2 3389
cities and with the king in J. 1Ki 10:26 3389
silver *as common* as stones in J, 1Ki 10:27 3389
the mountain which is east of J, 1Ki 11:7 3389
sake of J which I have chosen." 1Ki 11:13 3389
time, when Jeroboam went out of J, 1Ki 11:29 3389
David and for the sake of J, 1Ki 11:32 3389
have a lamp always before Me in J, 1Ki 11:36 3389
Solomon reigned in J over all Israel 1Ki 11:42 3389
to mount his chariot to flee to J. 1Ki 12:18 3389
Now when Rehoboam had come to J, 1Ki 12:21 3389
in the house of the LORD at J, 1Ki 12:27 3389
is too much for you to go up to J; 1Ki 12:28 3389
he reigned seventeen years in J, 1Ki 14:21 3389
king of Egypt came up against J. 1Ki 14:25 3389
He reigned three years in J; 1Ki 15:2 3389
LORD his God gave him a lamp in J, 1Ki 15:4 3389
son after him and to establish J; 1Ki 15:4 3389
He reigned forty-one years in J; 1Ki 15:10 3389
he reigned twenty-five years in J. 1Ki 22:42 3389
and he reigned eight years in J. 2Ki 8:17 3389
and he reigned one year in J. 2Ki 8:26 3389
carried him in a chariot to J and 2Ki 9:28 3389
and he reigned forty years in J; 2Ki 12:1 3389
Hazael set his face to go up to J. 2Ki 12:17 3389
Then he went away from J. 2Ki 12:18 3389
he reigned twenty-nine years in J. 2Ki 14:2 3389
mother's name was Jehoaddin of J. 2Ki 14:2 3389
and came to J and tore down the 2Ki 14:13 3389
tore down the wall of J from the 2Ki 14:13 3389
They conspired against him in J, 2Ki 14:19 3389
he was buried at J with his fathers 2Ki 14:20 3389
he reigned fifty-two years in J; 2Ki 15:2 3389
mother's name was Jecoliah of J. 2Ki 15:2 3389
and he reigned sixteen years in J; 2Ki 15:33 3389
and he reigned sixteen years in J; 2Ki 16:2 3389
Israel, came up to J to *wage* war; 2Ki 16:5 3389
he reigned twenty-nine years in J; 2Ki 18:2 3389
Hezekiah with a large army to J. 2Ki 18:17 3389
So they went up and came to J. 2Ki 18:17 3389
and has said to Judah and to J, 2Ki 18:22 3389
worship before this altar in J'? 2Ki 18:22 3389
should deliver J from my hand?' " 2Ki 18:35 3389
"J will not be given into the 2Ki 19:10 3389
behind you, The daughter of J! 2Ki 19:21 3389
out of J will go forth a remnant, 2Ki 19:31 3389
he reigned fifty-five years in J; 2Ki 21:1 3389
"In J I will put My name." 2Ki 21:4 3389
"In this house and in J, 2Ki 21:7 3389
such calamity on J and Judah, 2Ki 21:12 3389
'I will stretch over J the 2Ki 21:13 3389
I will wipe J as one wipes a dish, 2Ki 21:13 3389
filled J from one end to another; 2Ki 21:16 3389
and he reigned two years in J; 2Ki 21:19 3389
he reigned thirty-one years in J; 2Ki 22:1 3389
lived in J in the Second Quarter); 2Ki 22:14 3389
all the elders of Judah and of J. 2Ki 23:1 3389
all the inhabitants of J with him, 2Ki 23:2 3389
he burned them outside J in the 2Ki 23:4 3389
and in the surrounding area of J, 2Ki 23:5 3389
outside J to the brook Kidron, 2Ki 23:6 3389
up to the altar of the LORD in J, 2Ki 23:9 3389
high places which *were* before J, 2Ki 23:13 3389
then he returned to J. 2Ki 23:20 3389
was observed to the LORD in J. 2Ki 23:23 3389
in the land of Judah and in J, 2Ki 23:24 3389
And I will cast off J, 2Ki 23:27 3389
and brought him to J and buried 2Ki 23:30 3389
and he reigned three months in J; 2Ki 23:31 3389
that he might not reign in J; 2Ki 23:33 3389
and he reigned eleven years in J; 2Ki 23:36 3389
he filled J with innocent blood; 2Ki 24:4 3389
and he reigned three months in J; 2Ki 24:8 3389
the daughter of Elnathan of J. 2Ki 24:8 3389
king of Babylon went up to J, 2Ki 24:10 3389
Then he led away into exile all J 2Ki 24:14 3389
away into exile from J to Babylon. 2Ki 24:15 3389
and he reigned eleven years in J; 2Ki 24:18 3389
this came about in J and Judah until 2Ki 24:20 3389
he and all his army, against J, 2Ki 25:1 3389
of the king of Babylon, came to J. 2Ki 25:8 3389
house, and all the houses of J; 2Ki 25:9 3389
broke down the walls around J. 2Ki 25:10 3389
in J he reigned thirty-three years. 1Ch 3:4 3389
These were born to him in J: 1Ch 3:5 3389
house which Solomon built in J), 1Ch 6:10 3389
the LORD carried Judah and J away 1Ch 6:15 3389
built the house of the LORD in J; 1Ch 6:32 3389
chief men who lived in J. 1Ch 8:28 3389
also lived with their relatives in J 1Ch 8:32 3389
Ephraim and Manasseh lived in J: 1Ch 9:3 3389
chief men, who lived in J. 1Ch 9:34 3389
also lived with their relatives in J 1Ch 9:38 3389
David and all Israel went to J 1Ch 11:4 3389
Then David took more wives at J, 1Ch 14:3 3389
of the children born *to him* in J: 1Ch 14:4 3389
David assembled all Israel at J to 1Ch 15:3 3389
Hadadezer and brought them to J. 1Ch 18:7 3389
Then Joab came to J. 1Ch 19:15 3389
But David stayed at J. 1Ch 20:1 3389
and all the people returned *to* J. 1Ch 20:3 3389
all Israel, and came to J. 1Ch 21:4 3389
God sent an angel to J to destroy it 1Ch 21:15 3389
in his hand stretched out over J. 1Ch 21:16 3389
and He dwells in J forever. 1Ch 23:25 3389
at J all the officials of Israel, 1Ch 28:1 3389
years and in J thirty-three *years.* 1Ch 29:27 3389
he had pitched a tent for it in J. 2Ch 1:4 3389
from the tent of meeting, to J, 2Ch 1:13 3389
cities and with the king at J. 2Ch 1:14 3389
gold as plentiful in J as stones, 2Ch 1:15 3389
men whom I have in Judah and J, 2Ch 2:7 3389
that you may carry it up to J." 2Ch 2:16 3389
build the house of the LORD in J on 2Ch 3:1 3389
Solomon assembled to J the elders 2Ch 5:2 3389
J that My name might be there, 2Ch 6:6 3389
it pleased Solomon to build in J, 2Ch 8:6 3389
she came to J to test Solomon with 2Ch 9:1 3389
cities and with the king in J. 2Ch 9:25 3389
silver *as common* as stones in J, 2Ch 9:27 3389
forty years in J over all Israel. 2Ch 9:30 3389
to mount his chariot to flee to J. 2Ch 10:18 3389
Now when Rehoboam had come to J, 2Ch 11:1 3389
Rehoboam lived in J and built 2Ch 11:5 3389
property and came to Judah and J, 2Ch 11:14 3389
followed them to J, to sacrifice to 2Ch 11:16 3389
king of Egypt came up against J 2Ch 12:2 3389
of Judah and came as far as J. 2Ch 12:4 3389
gathered at J because of Shishak, 2Ch 12:5 3389
wrath shall not be poured out on J 2Ch 12:7 3389
king of Egypt came up against J, 2Ch 12:9 3389
strengthened himself in J and 2Ch 12:13 3389
he reigned seventeen years in J, 2Ch 12:13 3389
He reigned three years in J; 2Ch 13:2 3389
Then they returned to J. 2Ch 14:15 3389
So they assembled at J in the 2Ch 15:10 3389
and warriors, valiant men, in J. 2Ch 17:13 3389
in safety to his house in J. 2Ch 19:1 3389
So Jehoshaphat lived in J and went 2Ch 19:4 3389
In J also Jehoshaphat appointed 2Ch 19:8 3389
among the inhabitants of J. 2Ch 19:8 3389
in the assembly of Judah and J, 2Ch 20:5 3389
all Judah and the inhabitants of J 2Ch 20:15 3389
on your behalf, O Judah and J.' 2Ch 20:17 3389
the inhabitants of J fell down before 2Ch 20:18 3389
me, O Judah and inhabitants of J, 2Ch 20:20 3389
Every man of Judah and J 2Ch 20:27 3389
head, returning to J with joy, 2Ch 20:27 3389
They came to J with harps, 2Ch 20:28 3389
he reigned in J twenty-five years. 2Ch 20:31 3389
and he reigned eight years in J. 2Ch 21:5 3389
and caused the inhabitants of J to 2Ch 21:11 3389
inhabitants of J to play the harlot 2Ch 21:13 3389
and he reigned in J eight years; 2Ch 21:20 3389
the inhabitants of J made Ahaziah, 2Ch 22:1 3389
and he reigned one year in J. 2Ch 22:2 3389
of Israel, and they came to J. 2Ch 23:2 3389
and he reigned forty years in J; 2Ch 24:1 3389
and from J the levy *fixed by* Moses 2Ch 24:6 3389
made a proclamation in Judah and J 2Ch 24:9 3389
Judah and J for this their guilt. 2Ch 24:18 3389
and they came to Judah and J, 2Ch 24:23 3389
he reigned twenty-nine years in J. 2Ch 25:1 3389
mother's name was Jehoaddan of J. 2Ch 25:1 3389
brought him to J and tore 2Ch 25:23 3389
tore down the wall of J from 2Ch 25:23 3389
they conspired against him in J, 2Ch 25:27 3389
he reigned fifty-two years in J; 2Ch 26:3 3389
mother's name was Jechiliah of J. 2Ch 26:3 3389
Uzziah built towers in J at the 2Ch 26:9 3389
In J he made engines *of war* 2Ch 26:15 3389
and he reigned sixteen years in J. 2Ch 27:1 3389

and he reigned sixteen years in **J**.	**2Ch 27:8**	3389
and he reigned sixteen years in **J**;	**2Ch 28:1**	3389
and **J** for male and female slaves.	**2Ch 28:10**	3389
for himself in every corner of **J**.	**2Ch 28:24**	3389
they buried him in the city, in **J**,	**2Ch 28:27**	3389
he reigned twenty-nine years in **J**.	**2Ch 29:1**	3389
the LORD was against Judah and **J**,	**2Ch 29:8**	3389
come to the house of the LORD at **J**	**2Ch 30:1**	3389
all the assembly in **J** had decided to	**2Ch 30:2**	3389
had the people been gathered to **J**.	**2Ch 30:3**	3389
to the LORD God of Israel at **J**.	**2Ch 30:5**	3389
humbled themselves and came to **J**.	**2Ch 30:11**	3389
people were gathered at **J** to celebrate	**2Ch 30:13**	3389
the altars which *were* in **J**;	**2Ch 30:14**	3389
sons of Israel present in **J** celebrated	**2Ch 30:21**	3389
So there was great joy in **J**,	**2Ch 30:26**	3389
there was nothing like this in **J**	**2Ch 30:26**	3389
commanded the people who lived in **J**	**2Ch 31:4**	3389
that he intended to make war on **J**,	**2Ch 32:2**	3389
king of Assyria sent his servants to **J**	**2Ch 32:9**	3389
against all Judah who *were* at **J**,	**2Ch 32:9**	3389
are remaining in **J** under siege?	**2Ch 32:10**	3389
altars, and said to Judah and **J**,	**2Ch 32:12**	3389
people of **J** who were on the wall,	**2Ch 32:18**	3389
They spoke of the God of **J** as	**2Ch 32:19**	3389
Hezekiah and the inhabitants of **J**	**2Ch 32:22**	3389
were bringing gifts to the LORD at **J**	**2Ch 32:23**	3389
came on him and on Judah and **J**.	**2Ch 32:25**	3389
both he and the inhabitants of **J**,	**2Ch 32:26**	3389
inhabitants of **J** honored him at his	**2Ch 32:33**	3389
he reigned fifty-five years in **J**.	**2Ch 33:1**	3389
"My name shall be in **J** forever."	**2Ch 33:4**	3389
"In this house and in **J**,	**2Ch 33:7**	3389
the inhabitants of **J** to do more evil	**2Ch 33:9**	3389
him again to **J** to his kingdom.	**2Ch 33:13**	3389
of the house of the LORD and in **J**,	**2Ch 33:15**	3389
and he reigned two years in **J**.	**2Ch 33:21**	3389
he reigned thirty-one years in **J**.	**2Ch 34:1**	3389
Judah and **J** of the high places,	**2Ch 34:3**	3389
altars and purged Judah and **J**.	**2Ch 34:5**	3389
Then he returned to **J**.	**2Ch 34:7**	3389
Benjamin and the inhabitants of **J**.	**2Ch 34:9**	3389
lived in **J** in the Second Quarter);	**2Ch 34:22**	3389
all the elders of Judah and **J**.	**2Ch 34:29**	3389
of Judah, the inhabitants of **J**,	**2Ch 34:30**	3389
he made all who were present in **J**	**2Ch 34:32**	3389
So the inhabitants of **J** did	**2Ch 34:32**	3389
the Passover to the LORD in **J**,	**2Ch 35:1**	3389
present, and the inhabitants of **J**.	**2Ch 35:18**	3389
and brought him to **J** where he died	**2Ch 35:24**	3389
Judah and **J** mourned for Josiah.	**2Ch 35:24**	3389
king in place of his father in **J**.	**2Ch 36:1**	3389
and he reigned three months in **J**.	**2Ch 36:2**	3389
king of Egypt deposed him at **J**,	**2Ch 36:3**	3389
his brother king over Judah and **J**,	**2Ch 36:4**	3389
and he reigned eleven years in **J**;	**2Ch 36:5**	3389
three months and ten days in **J**,	**2Ch 36:9**	3389
Zedekiah king over Judah and **J**.	**2Ch 36:10**	3389
and he reigned eleven years in **J**.	**2Ch 36:11**	3389
LORD which He had sanctified in **J**.	**2Ch 36:14**	3389
and broke down the wall of **J**,	**2Ch 36:19**	3389
me to build Him a house in **J**,	**2Ch 36:23**	3389
me to build Him a house in **J**,	**Ezr 1:2**	3389
him go up to **J** which is in Judah and	**Ezr 1:3**	3389
He is the God who is in **J**.	**Ezr 1:3**	3389
house of God which is in **J**.' "	**Ezr 1:4**	3389
house of the LORD which is in **J**.	**Ezr 1:5**	3389
had carried away from **J** and put in	**Ezr 1:7**	3389
who went up from Babylon to **J**.	**Ezr 1:11**	3389
and returned to **J** and Judah,	**Ezr 2:1**	3389
house of the LORD which is in **J**,	**Ezr 2:68**	3389
gathered together as one man to **J**.	**Ezr 3:1**	3389
coming to the house of God at **J**	**Ezr 3:8**	3389
who came from the captivity to **J**,	**Ezr 3:8**	3389
the inhabitants of Judah and **J**.	**Ezr 4:6**	3389
the scribe wrote a letter against **J**	**Ezr 4:8**	3390
up from you have come to us at **J**;	**Ezr 4:12**	3390
mighty kings have ruled over **J**,	**Ezr 4:20**	3390
they went in haste to **J** to the	**Ezr 4:23**	3390
on the house of God in **J** ceased,	**Ezr 4:24**	3390
the Jews who were in Judah and **J** in	**Ezr 5:1**	3390
the house of God which is in **J**;	**Ezr 5:2**	3390
had taken from the temple in **J**,	**Ezr 5:14**	3390
deposit them in the temple in **J** and	**Ezr 5:15**	3390
of the house of God in **J**;	**Ezr 5:16**	3390
to rebuild this house of God at **J**;	**Ezr 5:17**	3390
'*Concerning* the house of God at **J**,	**Ezr 6:3**	3390
took from the temple in **J** and	**Ezr 6:5**	3390
their places in the temple in **J**;	**Ezr 6:5**	3390
oil, as the priests in **J** request,	**Ezr 6:9**	3390
to destroy this house of God in **J**.	**Ezr 6:12**	3390
for the service of God in **J**,	**Ezr 6:18**	3390
the temple servants went up to **J**	**Ezr 7:7**	3389
He came to **J** in the fifth month,	**Ezr 7:8**	3389
of the fifth month he came to **J**,	**Ezr 7:9**	3389
who are willing to go to **J**,	**Ezr 7:13**	3390
to inquire concerning Judah and **J**	**Ezr 7:14**	3390
of Israel, whose dwelling is in **J**,	**Ezr 7:15**	3390
house of their God which is in **J**;	**Ezr 7:16**	3390
house of your God which is in **J**.	**Ezr 7:17**	3390
deliver in full before the God of **J**.	**Ezr 7:19**	3390
house of the LORD which is in **J**,	**Ezr 7:27**	3389
fathers' *households* of Israel at **J**,	**Ezr 8:29**	3389
them to **J** to the house of our God.	**Ezr 8:30**	3389
of the first month to go to **J**;	**Ezr 8:31**	3389
Thus we came to **J** and remained	**Ezr 8:32**	3389
to give us a wall in Judah and **J**.	**Ezr 9:9**	3389
Judah and **J** to all the exiles,	**Ezr 10:7**	3389
that they should assemble at **J**,	**Ezr 10:7**	3389
at **J** within the three days.	**Ezr 10:9**	3389
the captivity, and about **J**.	**Ne 1:2**	3389
and the wall of **J** is broken down	**Ne 1:3**	3389
So I came to **J** and was there three	**Ne 2:11**	3389
putting into my mind to do for **J**	**Ne 2:12**	3389
inspecting the walls of **J** which	**Ne 2:13**	3389
that **J** is desolate and its gates	**Ne 2:17**	3389
let us rebuild the wall of **J** so	**Ne 2:17**	3389
right or memorial in **J**."	**Ne 2:20**	3389
restored **J** as far as the Broad Wall.	**Ne 3:8**	3389
the official of half the district of **J**,	**Ne 3:9**	3389
the official of half the district of **J**,	**Ne 3:12**	3389
repair of the walls of **J** went on,	**Ne 4:7**	3389
to come *and* fight against **J** and to	**Ne 4:8**	3389
his servant spend the night within **J**	**Ne 4:22**	3389
to proclaim in **J** concerning you,	**Ne 6:7**	3389
of the fortress, in charge of **J**,	**Ne 7:2**	3389
"Do not let the gates of **J** be	**Ne 7:3**	3389
guards from the inhabitants of **J**,	**Ne 7:3**	3389
and who returned to **J** and Judah,	**Ne 7:6**	3389
in all their cities and in **J**,	**Ne 8:15**	3389
leaders of the people lived in **J**,	**Ne 11:1**	3389
bring one out of ten to live in **J**,	**Ne 11:1**	3389
men who volunteered to live in **J**.	**Ne 11:2**	3389
of the provinces who lived in **J**,	**Ne 11:3**	3389
the sons of Benjamin lived in **J**.	**Ne 11:4**	3389
who lived in **J** were 468 able men.	**Ne 11:6**	3389
the overseer of the Levites in **J** was	**Ne 11:22**	3389
at the dedication of the wall of **J**	**Ne 12:27**	3389
to bring them to **J** so that they	**Ne 12:27**	3389
from the district around **J**,	**Ne 12:28**	3389
themselves villages around **J**.	**Ne 12:29**	3389
the joy of **J** was heard from afar.	**Ne 12:43**	3389
all this *time* I was not in **J**,	**Ne 13:6**	3389
and I came to **J** and learned about	**Ne 13:7**	3389
them into **J** on the sabbath day.	**Ne 13:15**	3389
Judah on the sabbath, even in **J**.	**Ne 13:16**	3389
the gates of **J** before the sabbath,	**Ne 13:19**	3389
spent the night outside **J**.	**Ne 13:20**	3389
had been taken into exile from **J**	**Es 2:6**	3389
Build the walls of **J**.	**Ps 51:18**	3389
Because of Your temple at **J** Kings	**Ps 68:29**	3389
They have laid **J** in ruins.	**Ps 79:1**	3389
blood like water round about **J**;	**Ps 79:3**	3389
LORD in Zion And His praise in **J**	**Ps 102:21**	3389
house, In the midst of you, O **J**.	**Ps 116:19**	3389
standing Within your gates, O **J**,	**Ps 122:2**	3389
J, that is built As a city that is	**Ps 122:3**	3389
Pray for the peace of **J**:	**Ps 122:6**	3389
As the mountains surround **J**,	**Ps 125:2**	3389
may you see the prosperity of **J**	**Ps 128:5**	3389
LORD from Zion, Who dwells in **J**.	**Ps 135:21**	3389
If I forget you, O **J**,	**Ps 137:5**	3389
If I do not exalt **J** Above my chief	**Ps 137:6**	3389
the sons of Edom The day of **J**,	**Ps 137:7**	3389
The LORD builds up **J**;	**Ps 147:2**	3389
Praise the LORD, O **J**!	**Ps 147:12**	3389
the son of David, king in **J**.	**Ec 1:1**	3389
have been king over Israel in **J**.	**Ec 1:12**	3389
all who were over **J** before me;	**Ec 1:16**	3389
than all who preceded me in **J**.	**Ec 2:7**	3389
than all who preceded me in **J**.	**Ec 2:9**	3389
but lovely, O daughters of **J**,	**SS 1:5**	3389
"I adjure you, O daughters of **J**,	**SS 2:7**	3389
"I adjure you, O daughters of **J**,	**SS 3:5**	3389
fitted out By the daughters of **J**.	**SS 3:10**	3389
"I adjure you, O daughters of **J**,	**SS 5:8**	3389
is my friend, O daughters of **J**."	**SS 5:16**	3389
my darling, As lovely as **J**,	**SS 6:4**	3389
you to swear, O daughters of **J**,	**SS 8:4**	3389
concerning Judah and **J**, which he	**Is 1:1**	3389
Amoz saw concerning Judah and **J**.	**Is 2:1**	3389
And the word of the LORD from **J**.	**Is 2:3**	3389
going to remove from **J** and Judah	**Is 3:1**	3389
For **J** has stumbled and Judah has	**Is 3:8**	3389
who is left in Zion and remains in **J**	**Is 4:3**	3389
who is recorded for life in **J**.	**Is 4:3**	3389
the bloodshed of **J** from her midst,	**Is 4:4**	3389
inhabitants of **J** and men of Judah,	**Is 5:3**	3389
up to **J** to *wage* war against it,	**Is 7:1**	3389
a trap for the inhabitants of **J**.	**Is 8:14**	3389
than those of **J** and Samaria,	**Is 10:10**	3389
Shall I not do to **J** and her images	**Is 10:11**	3389
His work on Mount Zion and on **J**,	**Is 10:12**	3389
daughter of Zion, the hill of **J**.	**Is 10:32**	3389
Then you counted the houses of **J** And	**Is 22:10**	3389
a father to the inhabitants of **J**	**Is 22:21**	3389
will reign on Mount Zion and in **J**,	**Is 24:23**	3389
LORD in the holy mountain at **J**.	**Is 27:13**	3389
Who rule this people who are in **J**,	**Is 28:14**	3389
O people in Zion, inhabitant in **J**,	**Is 30:19**	3389
the LORD of hosts will protect **J**.	**Is 31:5**	3389
in Zion and whose furnace is in **J**.	**Is 31:9**	3389
see **J**, an undisturbed habitation,	**Is 33:20**	3389
sent Rabshakeh from Lachish to **J**	**Is 36:2**	3389
and has said to Judah and to **J**,	**Is 36:7**	3389
would deliver **J** from my hand?' "	**Is 36:20**	3389
"**J** will not be given into the	**Is 37:10**	3389
behind you, The daughter of **J**!	**Is 37:22**	3389
out of **J** will go forth a remnant	**Is 37:32**	3389
"Speak kindly to **J**;	**Is 40:2**	3389
Lift up your voice mightily, O **J**,	**Is 40:9**	3389
And to **J**, 'I will give a messenger	**Is 41:27**	3389
It is I who says of **J**,	**Is 44:26**	3389
And he declares of **J**,	**Is 44:28**	3389
Arise, O **J**, You who have drunk	**Is 51:17**	3389
in your beautiful garments, O **J**,	**Is 52:1**	3389
the dust, rise up, O captive **J**;	**Is 52:2**	3389
together, You waste places of **J**;	**Is 52:9**	3389
His people, He has redeemed **J**.	**Is 52:9**	3389
On your walls, O **J**,	**Is 62:6**	3389
And makes **J** a praise in the earth.	**Is 62:7**	3389
a wilderness, **J** a desolation.	**Is 64:10**	3389
behold, I create **J** *for* rejoicing And	**Is 65:18**	3389
"I will also rejoice in **J** and	**Is 65:19**	3389
joyful with **J** and rejoice for her,	**Is 66:10**	3389
And you will be comforted in **J**."	**Is 66:13**	3389
camels, to My holy mountain **J**,"	**Is 66:20**	3389
the exile of **J** in the fifth month.	**Jer 1:3**	3389
at the entrance of the gates of **J**,	**Jer 1:15**	3389
"Go and proclaim in the ears of **J**,	**Jer 2:2**	3389
"At that time they will call **J**	**Jer 3:17**	3389
will be gathered to it, to **J**,	**Jer 3:17**	3389
LORD to the men of Judah and to **J**,	**Jer 4:3**	3389
Men of Judah and inhabitants of **J**,	**Jer 4:4**	3389
in Judah and proclaim in **J**,	**Jer 4:5**	3389
deceived this people and **J**,	**Jer 4:10**	3389
be said to this people and to **J**,	**Jer 4:11**	3389
Wash your heart from evil, O **J**,	**Jer 4:14**	3389
Proclaim over **J**,	**Jer 4:16**	3389
and fro through the streets of **J**,	**Jer 5:1**	3389
of Benjamin, From the midst of **J**!	**Jer 6:1**	3389
And cast up a siege against **J**.	**Jer 6:6**	3389
"Be warned, O **J**, Or I shall be	**Jer 6:8**	3389
of Judah and in the streets of **J**?	**Jer 7:17**	3389
from the streets of **J** the voice of joy	**Jer 7:34**	3389
bones of the inhabitants of **J** from	**Jer 8:1**	3389
"Why then has this people, **J**,	**Jer 8:5**	3389
"I will make **J** a heap of ruins,	**Jer 9:11**	3389
Judah and to the inhabitants of **J**;	**Jer 11:2**	3389
of Judah and in the streets of **J**,	**Jer 11:6**	3389
and among the inhabitants of **J**.	**Jer 11:9**	3389
the inhabitants of **J** will go and cry	**Jer 11:12**	3389
and as many as the streets of **J**	**Jer 11:13**	3389
of Judah and the great pride of **J**.	**Jer 13:9**	3389
prophets and all the inhabitants of **J**	**Jer 13:13**	3389
Woe to you, O **J**! How long will you	**Jer 13:27**	3389
And the cry of **J** has ascended.	**Jer 14:2**	3389
thrown out into the streets of **J**	**Jer 14:16**	3389
of Judah, for what he did in **J**.	**Jer 15:4**	3389
who will have pity on you, O **J**,	**Jer 15:5**	3389
as well as in all the gates of **J**;	**Jer 17:19**	3389
Judah and all inhabitants of **J**	**Jer 17:20**	3389
in through the gates of **J**.	**Jer 17:21**	3389
Judah and the inhabitants of **J**	**Jer 17:25**	3389
Judah and from the environs of **J**,	**Jer 17:26**	3389
the gates of **J** on the sabbath day,	**Jer 17:27**	3389
it will devour the palaces of **J**	**Jer 17:27**	3389
the inhabitants of **J** saying,	**Jer 18:11**	3389
of Judah and inhabitants of **J**:	**Jer 19:3**	3389
void the counsel of Judah and **J**	**Jer 19:7**	3389
"The houses of **J** and the	**Jer 19:13**	3389
thrown out beyond the gates of **J**.	**Jer 22:19**	3389
among the prophets of **J** I have	**Jer 23:14**	3389
For from the prophets of **J**	**Jer 23:15**	3389
the craftsmen and smiths from **J**	**Jer 24:1**	3389
remnant of **J** who remain in this	**Jer 24:8**	3389
and to all the inhabitants of **J**,	**Jer 25:2**	3389
J and the cities of Judah and its	**Jer 25:18**	3389
a field, And **J** will become ruins,	**Jer 26:18**	3389
to **J** to Zedekiah king of Judah.	**Jer 27:3**	3389
of the king of Judah and in **J**	**Jer 27:18**	3389
king of Judah, from **J** to Babylon,	**Jer 27:20**	3389
and all the nobles of Judah and **J**.	**Jer 27:20**	3389
of the king of Judah and in **J**,	**Jer 27:21**	3389
Jeremiah the prophet sent from **J** to	**Jer 29:1**	3389
into exile from **J** to Babylon.	**Jer 29:1**	3389
the princes of Judah and **J**,	**Jer 29:2**	3389
the smiths had departed from **J**.)	**Jer 29:2**	3389
sent into exile from **J** to Babylon,	**Jer 29:4**	3389
have sent away from **J** to Babylon.	**Jer 29:20**	3389
to all the people who are in **J**,	**Jer 29:25**	3389
king of Babylon was besieging **J**,	**Jer 32:2**	3389
Judah and the inhabitants of **J**.	**Jer 32:32**	3389
of Benjamin, in the environs of **J**,	**Jer 32:44**	3389
streets of **J** that are desolate,	**Jer 33:10**	3389
of Benjamin, in the environs of **J** and	**Jer 33:13**	3389
and **J** will dwell in safety;	**Jer 33:16**	3389
fighting against **J** and against all its	**Jer 34:1**	3389
to Zedekiah king of Judah in **J**	**Jer 34:6**	3389
Babylon was fighting against **J** and	**Jer 34:7**	3389
with all the people who were in **J**	**Jer 34:8**	3389
of Judah and the officials of **J**,	**Jer 34:19**	3389
'Come and let us go to **J** before	**Jer 35:11**	3389
So we have dwelt in **J**."	**Jer 35:11**	3389
of Judah and the inhabitants of **J**,	**Jer 35:13**	3389
and on all the inhabitants of **J** all	**Jer 35:17**	3389
all the people in **J** and all	**Jer 36:9**	3389
came from the cities of Judah to **J**	**Jer 36:9**	3389
the inhabitants of **J** and the men of	**Jer 36:31**	3389
who had been besieging **J**	**Jer 37:5**	3389
they lifted the *siege* from **J**.	**Jer 37:5**	3389
had lifted *the siege* from **J** because	**Jer 37:11**	3389
that Jeremiah went out from **J** to	**Jer 37:12**	3389
until the day that **J** was captured.	**Jer 38:28**	3389
when **J** was captured in the ninth	**Jer 39:1**	3389
came to **J** and laid siege to it;	**Jer 39:1**	3389
they broke down the walls of **J**.	**Jer 39:8**	3389
all the exiles of **J** and Judah who	**Jer 40:1**	3389
out on the inhabitants of **J**,	**Jer 42:18**	3389
calamity that I have brought on **J**	**Jer 44:2**	3389
of Judah and in the streets of **J**,	**Jer 44:6**	3389
of Judah and in the streets of **J**?	**Jer 44:9**	3389
of Egypt, as I have punished **J**,	**Jer 44:13**	3389
of Judah and in the streets of **J**;	**Jer 44:17**	3389
of Judah and in the streets of **J**,	**Jer 44:21**	3389
of Chaldea," **J** will say.	**Jer 51:35**	3389
afar, And let **J** come to your mind.	**Jer 51:50**	3389

and he reigned eleven years in **J**;	**Jer 52:1**	3389
this came about in **J** and Judah	**Jer 52:3**	3389
he and all his army, against **J**,	**Jer 52:4**	3389
of the king of Babylon, came to **J**.	**Jer 52:12**	3389
house and all the houses of **J**;	**Jer 52:13**	3389
broke down all the walls around **J**.	**Jer 52:14**	3389
Nebuchadnezzar 832 persons from **J**;	**Jer 52:29**	3389
J remembers all her precious things	**La 1:7**	3389
J sinned greatly, Therefore she	**La 1:8**	3389
J has become an unclean thing	**La 1:17**	3389
The virgins of **J** Have bowed their	**La 2:10**	3389
I compare you, O daughter of **J**?	**La 2:13**	3389
their heads At the daughter of **J**,	**La 2:15**	3389
enemy Could enter the gates of **J**.	**La 4:12**	3389
you and inscribe a city on it, **J**.	**Ezk 4:1**	3389
siege of **J** with your arm bared and	**Ezk 4:7**	3389
to break the staff of bread in **J**,	**Ezk 4:16**	3389
'This is **J**; I have set her at the center	**Ezk 5:5**	3389
me in the visions of God to **J**,	**Ezk 8:3**	3389
city, *even* through the midst of **J**,	**Ezk 9:4**	3389
by pouring out Your wrath on **J**?"	**Ezk 9:8**	3389
the inhabitants of **J** have said,	**Ezk 11:15**	3389
burden *concerns* the prince in **J** as	**Ezk 12:10**	3389
concerning the inhabitants of **J** in	**Ezk 12:19**	3389
of Israel who prophesy to **J**,	**Ezk 13:16**	3389
four severe judgments against **J**:	**Ezk 14:21**	3389
which I have brought against **J**	**Ezk 14:22**	3389
I given up the inhabitants of **J**;	**Ezk 15:6**	3389
make known to **J** her abominations	**Ezk 16:2**	3389
'Thus says the Lord GOD to **J**,	**Ezk 16:3**	3389
the king of Babylon came to **J**,	**Ezk 17:12**	3389
of man, set your face toward **J**,	**Ezk 21:2**	3389
and to Judah into fortified **J**.	**Ezk 21:20**	3389
right hand came the divination, '**J**,'	**Ezk 21:22**	3389
to gather you into the midst of **J**.	**Ezk 22:19**	3389
is Oholah and **J** is Oholibah.	**Ezk 23:4**	3389
has laid siege to **J** this very day.	**Ezk 24:2**	3389
Tyre has said concerning **J**,	**Ezk 26:2**	3389
the refugees from **J** came to me,	**Ezk 33:21**	3389
the flock at **J** during her appointed	**Ezk 36:38**	3389
Babylon came to **J** and besieged it.	**Da 1:1**	3389
out of the temple which *was* in **J**,	**Da 5:2**	3390
the house of God which *was* in **J**;	**Da 5:3**	3390
he had windows open toward **J**);	**Da 6:10**	3390
completion of the desolations of **J**,	**Da 9:2**	3389
of Judah, the inhabitants of **J** and	**Da 9:7**	3389
anything like what was done to **J**.	**Da 9:12**	3389
wrath turn away from Your city **J**,	**Da 9:16**	3389
J and Your people *have become* a	**Da 9:16**	3389
decree to restore and rebuild **J** until	**Da 9:25**	3389
For on Mount Zion and in **J** There	**Jl 2:32**	3389
restore the fortunes of Judah and **J**,	**Jl 3:1**	3389
and sold the sons of Judah and **J**	**Jl 3:6**	3389
Zion And utters His voice from **J**,	**Jl 3:16**	3389
So **J** will be holy, And strangers	**Jl 3:17**	3389
And **J** for all generations.	**Jl 3:20**	3389
And from **J** He utters His voice;	**Am 1:2**	3389
will consume the citadels of **J**."	**Am 2:5**	3389
entered his gate And cast lots for **J**	**Ob 1:11**	3389
And the exiles of **J** who are in	**Ob 1:20**	3389
he saw concerning Samaria and **J**.	**Mi 1:1**	3389
the high place of Judah? Is it not **J**?	**Mi 1:5**	3389
the gate of my people, *Even* to **J**.	**Mi 1:9**	3389
from the LORD To the gate of **J**.	**Mi 1:12**	3389
And **J** with violent injustice.	**Mi 3:10**	3389
J will become a heap of ruins,	**Mi 3:12**	3389
Even the word of the LORD from **J**.	**Mi 4:2**	3389
The kingdom of the daughter of **J**.	**Mi 4:8**	3389
against all the inhabitants of **J**.	**Zph 1:4**	3389
That I will search **J** with lamps,	**Zph 1:12**	3389
all *your* heart, O daughter of **J**!	**Zph 3:14**	3389
In that day it will be said to **J**:	**Zph 3:16**	3389
You have no compassion for **J**	**Zch 1:12**	3389
jealous for **J** and Zion.	**Zch 1:14**	3389
will return to **J** with compassion;	**Zch 1:16**	3389
line will be stretched over **J**."	**Zch 1:16**	3389
comfort Zion and again choose **J**	**Zch 1:17**	3389
scattered Judah, Israel and **J**."	**Zch 1:19**	3389
"To measure **J**, to see how wide it	**Zch 2:2**	3389
'**J** will be inhabited without	**Zch 2:4**	3389
land, and will again choose **J**.	**Zch 2:12**	3389
LORD who has chosen **J** rebuke you!	**Zch 3:2**	3389
when **J** was inhabited and	**Zch 7:7**	3389
and will dwell in the midst of **J**.	**Zch 8:3**	3389
J will be called the City of Truth,	**Zch 8:3**	3389
again sit in the streets of **J**,	**Zch 8:4**	3389
they will live in the midst of **J**;	**Zch 8:8**	3389
do good to **J** and to the house of	**Zch 8:15**	3389
come to seek the LORD of hosts in **J**	**Zch 8:22**	3389
Shout *in triumph,* O daughter of **J**!	**Zch 9:9**	3389
Ephraim And the horse from **J**;	**Zch 9:10**	3389
I am going to make **J** a cup that	**Zch 12:2**	3389
and when the siege is against **J**,	**Zch 12:2**	3389
I will make **J** a heavy stone for all	**Zch 12:3**	3389
inhabitants of **J** through the LORD	**Zch 12:5**	3389
while the inhabitants of **J** again	**Zch 12:6**	3389
dwell on their own sites in **J**.	**Zch 12:6**	3389
the glory of the inhabitants of **J** will	**Zch 12:7**	3389
will defend the inhabitants of **J**,	**Zch 12:8**	3389
the nations that come against **J**.	**Zch 12:9**	3389
David and on the inhabitants of **J**,	**Zch 12:10**	3389
there will be great mourning in **J**,	**Zch 12:11**	3389
and for the inhabitants of **J**,	**Zch 13:1**	3389
the nations against **J** to battle,	**Zch 14:2**	3389
is in front of **J** on the east;	**Zch 14:4**	3389
living waters will flow out of **J**,	**Zch 14:8**	3389
from Geba to Rimmon south of **J**;	**Zch 14:10**	3389
but **J** will rise and remain on its	**Zch 14:10**	3389
for **J** will dwell in security.	**Zch 14:11**	3389
who have gone to war against **J**;	**Zch 14:12**	3389
Judah also will fight at **J**;	**Zch 14:14**	3389
all the nations that went against **J**	**Zch 14:16**	3389
go up to **J** to worship the King,	**Zch 14:17**	3389
Every cooking pot in **J** and in	**Zch 14:21**	3389
been committed in Israel and in **J**;	**Mal 2:11**	3389
J will be pleasing to the LORD as	**Mal 3:4**	3389
magi from the east arrived in **J**,	**Mt 2:1**	*2414*
was troubled, and all **J** with him.	**Mt 2:3**	*2414*
Then **J** was going out to him, and	**Mt 3:5**	*2414*
from Galilee and *the* Decapolis and **J**	**Mt 4:25**	*2414*
or by **J**, for it is THE CITY OF THE	**Mt 5:35**	*2414*
and scribes came to Jesus from **J** and	**Mt 15:1**	*2414*
disciples that He must go to **J**,	**Mt 16:21**	*2414*
As Jesus was about to go up to **J**,	**Mt 20:17**	*2414*
"Behold, we are going up to **J**;	**Mt 20:18**	*2414*
When they had approached **J** and	**Mt 21:1**	*2414*
When He had entered **J**,	**Mt 21:10**	*2414*
"**J**, Jerusalem, who kills the	**Mt 23:37**	*2419*
"Jerusalem, **J**, who kills the	**Mt 23:37**	*2419*
to him, and all the people of **J**;	**Mk 1:5**	*2415*
and from **J**, and from Idumea, and	**Mk 3:8**	*2414*
The scribes who came down from **J**	**Mk 3:22**	*2414*
Him when they had come from **J**,	**Mk 7:1**	*2414*
were on the road going up to **J**,	**Mk 10:32**	*2414*
"Behold, we are going up to **J**,	**Mk 10:33**	*2414*
As they approached **J**,	**Mk 11:1**	*2414*
Jesus entered **J** *and came* into the	**Mk 11:11**	*2414*
Then they came to **J**.	**Mk 11:15**	*2414*
They came again to **J**.	**Mk 11:27**	*2414*
who came up with Him to **J**.	**Mk 15:41**	*2414*
to **J** to present Him to the Lord	**Lk 2:22**	*2414*
a man in **J** whose name was Simeon;	**Lk 2:25**	*2419*
looking for the redemption of **J**.	**Lk 2:38**	*2419*
Now His parents went to **J**	**Lk 2:41**	*2419*
the boy Jesus stayed behind in **J**.	**Lk 2:43**	*2419*
not find Him, they returned to **J** looking	**Lk 2:45**	*2419*
And he led Him to **J** and had Him	**Lk 4:9**	*2419*
of Galilee and Judea and *from* **J**;	**Lk 5:17**	*2419*
people from all Judea and **J**	**Lk 6:17**	*2419*
He was about to accomplish at **J**.	**Lk 9:31**	*2419*
was determined to go to **J**;	**Lk 9:51**	*2419*
traveling toward **J**.	**Lk 9:53**	*2419*
was going down from **J** to Jericho,	**Lk 10:30**	*2419*
than all the men who live in **J**?	**Lk 13:4**	*2419*
and proceeding on His way to **J**.	**Lk 13:22**	*2414*
prophet would perish outside of **J**.	**Lk 13:33**	*2419*
"O **J**, Jerusalem, *the city* that kills	**Lk 13:34**	*2419*
"O Jerusalem, **J**, *the city* that kills	**Lk 13:34**	*2419*
While He was on the way to **J**,	**Lk 17:11**	*2419*
"Behold, we are going up to **J**,	**Lk 18:31**	*2419*
a parable, because He was near **J**,	**Lk 19:11**	*2419*
going on ahead, going up to **J**.	**Lk 19:28**	*2414*
When He approached **J**, He saw	**Lk 19:41**	*2419*
you see **J** surrounded by armies,	**Lk 21:20**	*2419*
and **J** will be trampled under foot	**Lk 21:24**	*2419*
also was in **J** at that time.	**Lk 23:7**	*2414*
"Daughters of **J**, stop weeping for	**Lk 23:28**	*2419*
was about seven miles from **J**.	**Lk 24:13**	*2419*
"Are You the only one visiting **J**	**Lk 24:18**	*2419*
that very hour and returned to **J**,	**Lk 24:33**	*2419*
all the nations, beginning from **J**.	**Lk 24:47**	*2419*
returned to **J** with great joy,	**Lk 24:52**	*2419*
and Levites from **J** to ask him,	**Jn 1:19**	*2414*
near, and Jesus went up to **J**.	**Jn 2:13**	*2414*
when He was in **J** at the Passover,	**Jn 2:23**	*2414*
and you *people* say that in **J** is	**Jn 4:20**	*2414*
nor in **J** will you worship the	**Jn 4:21**	*2414*
that He did in **J** at the feast;	**Jn 4:45**	*2414*
the Jews, and Jesus went up to **J**.	**Jn 5:1**	*2414*
is in **J** by the sheep *gate* a pool,	**Jn 5:2**	*2414*
of the people of **J** were saying,	**Jn 7:25**	*2415*
of the Dedication took place at **J**;	**Jn 10:22**	*2414*
Now Bethany was near **J**,	**Jn 11:18**	*2414*
and many went up to **J** out of the	**Jn 11:55**	*2414*
heard that Jesus was coming to **J**,	**Jn 12:12**	*2414*
He commanded them not to leave **J**,	**Ac 1:4**	*2414*
shall be My witnesses both in **J**,	**Ac 1:8**	*2419*
to **J** from the mount called Olivet,	**Ac 1:12**	*2419*
called Olivet, which is near **J**,	**Ac 1:12**	*2419*
known to all who were living in **J**;	**Ac 1:19**	*2419*
Now there were Jews living in **J**,	**Ac 2:5**	*2419*
Judea and all you who live in **J**,	**Ac 2:14**	*2419*
scribes were gathered together in **J**;	**Ac 4:5**	*2419*
is apparent to all who live in **J**,	**Ac 4:16**	*2419*
from the cities in the vicinity of **J**	**Ac 5:16**	*2419*
have filled **J** with your teaching and	**Ac 5:28**	*2419*
to increase greatly in **J**,	**Ac 6:7**	*2419*
began against the church in **J**	**Ac 8:1**	*2419*
Now when the apostles in **J** heard	**Ac 8:14**	*2414*
the Lord, they started back to **J**,	**Ac 8:25**	*2414*
that descends from **J** to Gaza."	**Ac 8:26**	*2419*
and he had come to **J** to worship,	**Ac 8:27**	*2419*
he might bring them bound to **J**.	**Ac 9:2**	*2419*
harm he did to Your saints at **J**;	**Ac 9:13**	*2419*
"Is this not he who in **J** destroyed	**Ac 9:21**	*2419*
When he came to **J**,	**Ac 9:26**	*2419*
them, moving about freely in **J**,	**Ac 9:28**	*2419*
in the land of the Jews and in **J**.	**Ac 10:39**	*2419*
And when Peter came up to **J**,	**Ac 11:2**	*2419*
reached the ears of the church at **J**,	**Ac 11:22**	*2419*
came down from **J** to Antioch.	**Ac 11:27**	*2414*
Barnabas and Saul returned from **J**	**Ac 12:25**	*2419*
John left them and returned to **J**.	**Ac 13:13**	*2414*
"For those who live in **J**,	**Ac 13:27**	*2419*
up with Him from Galilee to **J**,	**Ac 13:31**	*2419*
others of them should go up to **J**	**Ac 15:2**	*2419*
When they arrived at **J**,	**Ac 15:4**	*2414*
apostles and elders who were in **J**,	**Ac 16:4**	*2414*
Paul purposed in the Spirit to go to **J**	**Ac 19:21**	*2414*
for he was hurrying to be in **J**,	**Ac 20:16**	*2414*
the Spirit, I am on my way to **J**,	**Ac 20:22**	*2419*
the Spirit not to set foot in **J**.	**Ac 21:4**	*2414*
'In this way the Jews at **J** will	**Ac 21:11**	*2419*
begging him not to go up to **J**.	**Ac 21:12**	*2419*
but even to die at **J** for the name	**Ac 21:13**	*2419*
and started on our way up to **J**.	**Ac 21:15**	*2414*
After we arrived in **J**,	**Ac 21:17**	*2414*
that all **J** was in confusion.	**Ac 21:31**	*2419*
to **J** as prisoners to be punished.	**Ac 22:5**	*2419*
I returned to **J** and was praying	**Ac 22:17**	*2419*
haste, and get out of **J** quickly,	**Ac 22:18**	*2419*
witnessed to My cause at **J**,	**Ac 23:11**	*2419*
ago I went up to **J** to worship.	**Ac 24:11**	*2419*
later went up to **J** from Caesarea.	**Ac 25:1**	*2414*
he might have him brought to **J**	**Ac 25:3**	*2419*
Jews who had come down from **J**	**Ac 25:7**	*2414*
"Are you willing to go up to **J**	**Ac 25:9**	*2414*
and when I was at **J**,	**Ac 25:15**	*2414*
whether he was willing to go to **J**	**Ac 25:20**	*2414*
to me, both at **J** and here,	**Ac 25:24**	*2414*
among my *own* nation and at **J**;	**Ac 26:4**	*2414*
"And this is just what I did in **J**;	**Ac 26:10**	*2414*
and *also* at **J** and *then* throughout	**Ac 26:20**	*2414*
I was delivered as a prisoner from **J**	**Ac 28:17**	*2414*
so that from **J** and round about as	**Ro 15:19**	*2419*
am going to **J** serving the saints.	**Ro 15:25**	*2419*
the poor among the saints in **J**.	**Ro 15:26**	*2419*
and *that* my service for **J** may	**Ro 15:31**	*2419*
letters to carry your gift to **J**;	**1Co 16:3**	*2419*
nor did I go up to **J** to those who	**Ga 1:17**	*2414*
three years later I went up to **J**	**Ga 1:18**	*2414*
went up again to **J** with Barnabas,	**Ga 2:1**	*2414*
and corresponds to the present **J**,	**Ga 4:25**	*2419*
But the **J** above is free;	**Ga 4:26**	*2419*
of the living God, the heavenly **J**,	**Heb 12:22**	*2419*
of the city of My God, the new **J**,	**Rv 3:12**	*2419*
And I saw the holy city, new **J**,	**Rv 21:2**	*2419*
and showed me the holy city, **J**,	**Rv 21:10**	*2419*
JERUSALEM'S		
And **J** splendor, her multitude, her	**Is 5:14**	
for **J** sake I will not keep quiet,	**Is 62:1**	3389
JERUSHA		
name *was* **J** the daughter of Zadok.	**2Ki 15:33**	3388
JERUSHAH		
name was **J** the daughter of Zadok.	**2Ch 27:1**	3388
JESHAIAH		
of Hananiah *were* Pelatiah and **J**,	**1Ch 3:21**	3470a
Gedaliah, Zeri, **J**, Shimei,	**1Ch 25:3**	3470b
the eighth to **J**, his sons and his	**1Ch 25:15**	3470b
were Rehabiah his son, **J** his son,	**1Ch 26:25**	3470b
J the son of Athaliah and 70 males	**Ezr 8:7**	3470a
and **J** of the sons of Merari,	**Ezr 8:19**	3470a
the son of Ithiel, the son of **J**;	**Ne 11:7**	3470a
JESHANAH		
its villages, **J** with its villages and	**2Ch 13:19**	3466
JESHARELAH		
the seventh to **J**, his sons and his	**1Ch 25:14**	3480
JESHEBEAB		
for Huppah, the fourteenth for **J**,	**1Ch 24:13**	3428
JESHER		
J, Shobab, and Ardon.	**1Ch 2:18**	3475
JESHIMON		
which is on the south of **J**?	**1Sa 23:19**	3452
in the Arabah to the south of **J**.	**1Sa 23:24**	3452
of Hachilah, *which is* before **J**?"	**1Sa 26:1**	3452
of Hachilah, which is before **J**,	**1Sa 26:3**	3452
JESHISHAI		
the son of Michael, the son of **J**,	**1Ch 5:14**	3454
JESHOHAIAH		
and Elioenai, Jaakobah, **J**,	**1Ch 4:36**	3439
JESHUA		
the ninth for **J**, the tenth for	**1Ch 24:11**	3091
authority *were* Eden, Miniamin, **J**,	**2Ch 31:15**	3091
These came with Zerubbabel, **J**,	**Ezr 2:2**	3091
of the sons of **J** *and* Joab,	**Ezr 2:6**	3091
sons of Jedaiah of the house of **J**,	**Ezr 2:36**	3091
the sons of **J** and Kadmiel, of the	**Ezr 2:40**	3091
Then **J** the son of Jozadak and his	**Ezr 3:2**	3091
J the son of Jozadak and the rest	**Ezr 3:8**	3091
Then **J** *with* his sons and brothers	**Ezr 3:9**	3091
But Zerubbabel and **J** and the rest	**Ezr 4:3**	3091
J the son of Jozadak arose and	**Ezr 5:2**	3443
the Levites, Jozabad the son of **J**	**Ezr 8:33**	3091
the sons of **J** the son of Jozadak,	**Ezr 10:18**	3091
Next to him Ezer the son of **J**,	**Ne 3:19**	3091
who came with Zerubbabel, **J**,	**Ne 7:7**	3091
of the sons of **J** and Joab,	**Ne 7:11**	3091
sons of Jedaiah of the house of **J**,	**Ne 7:39**	3091
the sons of **J**, of Kadmiel, of the	**Ne 7:43**	3091
Also **J**, Bani, Sherebiah, Jamin,	**Ne 8:7**	3091
on the Levites' platform stood **J**,	**Ne 9:4**	3091
Then the Levites, **J**,	**Ne 9:5**	3091
J the son of Azaniah, Binnui of	**Ne 10:9**	3091
and in **J**, in Moladah and	**Ne 11:26**	3091
the son of Shealtiel, and **J**:	**Ne 12:1**	3091
their kinsmen in the days of **J**.	**Ne 12:7**	3091
The Levites *were* **J**,	**Ne 12:8**	3091
J became the father of Joiakim,	**Ne 12:10**	3091
and **J** the son of Kadmiel,	**Ne 12:24**	3091
the days of Joiakim the son of **J**,	**Ne 12:26**	3091
JESHURUN		
"But **J** grew fat and kicked	**Dt 32:15**	3484
"And He was king in **J**,	**Dt 33:5**	3484
"There is none like the God of **J**,	**Dt 33:26**	3484

And you **J** whom I have chosen. Is 44:2 3484
JESIMIEL
Jeshohaiah, Asaiah, Adiel, **J**, 1Ch 4:36 3450
JESSE
He is the father of **J**, Ru 4:17 3448
and to Obed was born **J**, Ru 4:22 3448
was born Jesse, and to **J**, David. Ru 4:22 3448
send you to **J** the Bethlehemite, 1Sa 16:1 3448
shall invite **J** to the sacrifice, 1Sa 16:3 3448
also consecrated **J** and his sons and 1Sa 16:5 3448
Then **J** called Abinadab and made 1Sa 16:8 3448
Next **J** made Shammah pass by. 1Sa 16:9 3448
Thus **J** made seven of his sons pass 1Sa 16:10 3448
But Samuel said to **J**, 1Sa 16:10 3448
And Samuel said to **J**, 1Sa 16:11 3448
Then Samuel said to **J**, 1Sa 16:11 3448
I have seen a son of **J** the 1Sa 16:18 3448
So Saul sent messengers to **J** and 1Sa 16:19 3448
J took a donkey *loaded with* 1Sa 16:20 3448
Saul sent to **J**, 1Sa 16:22 3448
in Judah, whose name was **J**, 1Sa 17:12 3448
And **J** was old in the days of Saul, 1Sa 17:12 3448
The three older sons of **J** had 1Sa 17:13 3448
Then **J** said to David his son, 1Sa 17:17 3448
and went as **J** had commanded him. 1Sa 17:20 3448
your servant **J** the Bethlehemite." 1Sa 17:58 3448
the son of **J** not come to the meal, 1Sa 20:27 3448
you are choosing the son of **J** to 1Sa 20:30 3448
the son of **J** lives on the earth, 1Sa 20:31 3448
Will the son of **J** also give to all 1Sa 22:7 3448
a covenant with the son of **J**, 1Sa 22:8 3448
"I saw the son of **J** coming to Nob, 1Sa 22:9 3448
the son of **J** conspired against me, 1Sa 22:13 3448
And who is the son of **J**? 1Sa 25:10 3448
have inheritance in the son of **J**; 2Sa 20:1 3448
David the son of **J** declares, 2Sa 23:1 3448
no inheritance in the son of **J**; 1Ki 12:16 3448
and Obed became the father of **J**; 1Ch 2:12 3448
and **J** became the father of Eliab 1Ch 2:13 3448
the kingdom to David the son of **J**. 1Ch 10:14 3448
O David, And with you, O son of **J**! 1Ch 12:18 3448
son of **J** reigned over all Israel. 1Ch 29:26 3448
no inheritance in the son of **J**. 2Ch 10:16 3448
daughter of Eliab the son of **J**, 2Ch 11:18 3448
prayers of David the son of **J** are Ps 72:20 3448
will spring from the stem of **J**, Is 11:1 3448
will resort to the root of **J**, Is 11:10 3448
Obed by Ruth, and Obed the father of **J**. Mt 1:5 2421
J was the father of David the king. Mt 1:6 2421
the son of **J**, the son of Obed, the Lk 3:32 2421
'I HAVE FOUND DAVID the son of **J**, Ac 13:22 2421
"THERE SHALL COME THE ROOT OF **J**, Ro 15:12 2421
JEST
"Against whom do you **j**? Is 57:4 6026
JESTERS
Like godless **j** at a feast, They Ps 35:16 3934
JESTING
appeared to his sons-in-law to be **j**. Gn 19:14 6711
and silly talk, or coarse **j**, Eph 5:4 2160
JESUS
the genealogy of **J** the Messiah, Mt 1:1 2424
of Mary, by whom **J** was born, Mt 1:16 2424
birth of **J** Christ was as follows: Mt 1:18 2424
and you shall call His name **J**, Mt 1:21 2424
and he called His name **J**. Mt 1:25 2424
Now after **J** was born in Bethlehem Mt 2:1 2424
Then **J** arrived from Galilee at the Mt 3:13 2424
But **J** answering said to him, Mt 3:15 2424
J came up immediately from the Mt 3:16 2424
Then **J** was led up by the Spirit Mt 4:1 2424
J said to him, "On the other hand, Mt 4:7 2424
Then **J** said to him, Mt 4:10 2424
Now when **J** heard that John had been Mt 4:12
time **J** began to preach and say, Mt 4:17 2424
Now as **J** was walking by the Sea of Mt 4:18
J was going throughout all Galilee, Mt 4:23
When **J** saw the crowds, He went up on Mt 5:1
When **J** had finished these words, Mt 7:28 2424
When **J** came down from the mountain, Mt 8:1
J stretched out His hand and touched Mt 8:3
And **J** said to him, Mt 8:4 2424
And when **J** entered Capernaum, a Mt 8:5
J said to him, "I will come Mt 8:7
Now when **J** heard *this,* He Mt 8:10 2424
And **J** said to the centurion, Mt 8:13 2424
When **J** came into Peter's home, Mt 8:14 2424
Now when **J** saw a crowd around Him, Mt 8:18 2424
J said to him, Mt 8:20 2424
But **J** said to him, Mt 8:22 2424
but **J** Himself was asleep. Mt 8:24
the whole city came out to meet **J**; Mt 8:34 2424
Getting into a boat, **J** crossed over Mt 9:1
Seeing their faith, **J** said to Mt 9:2 2424
And **J** knowing their thoughts said, Mt 9:4 2424
As **J** went on from there, He Mt 9:9 2424
Then it happened that as **J** was Mt 9:10 2424
dining with **J** and His disciples. Mt 9:10 2424
But when **J** heard *this,* He said, Mt 9:12 2424
And **J** said to them, Mt 9:15 2424
J got up and *began* to follow him, Mt 9:19 2424
But **J** turning and seeing her said, Mt 9:22 2424
When **J** came into the Mt 9:23 2424
As **J** went on from there, two Mt 9:27 2424
up to Him, and **J** said to them, Mt 9:28 2424
And **J** sternly warned them: Mt 9:30 2424
J was going through all the Mt 9:35 2424
J summoned His twelve disciples Mt 10:1
These twelve **J** sent out after Mt 10:5 2424

J had finished giving instructions Mt 11:1 2424
J answered and said to them, Mt 11:4 2424
J began to speak to the crowds Mt 11:7 2424
At that time **J** said, Mt 11:25 2424
J went through the grainfields Mt 12:1 2424
And they questioned **J**, asking, "Is Mt 12:10
But **J**, aware of *this,* withdrew Mt 12:15 2424
was blind and mute was brought to **J**, Mt 12:22
And knowing their thoughts **J** said to Mt 12:25 2424
But **J** answered the one who was Mt 12:48
That day **J** went out of the house Mt 13:1 2424
J answered them, "To you it has Mt 13:11
J presented another parable to them, Mt 13:24
All these things **J** spoke to the Mt 13:34 2424
And **J** said to them, "Therefore Mt 13:52
J had finished these parables, Mt 13:53 2424
But **J** said to them, Mt 13:57 2424
tetrarch heard the news about **J**, Mt 14:1 2424
and they went and reported to **J**. Mt 14:12 2424
J heard *about John,* He withdrew Mt 14:13 2424
But **J** said to them, Mt 14:16 2424
But immediately **J** spoke to them, Mt 14:27 2424
on the water and came toward **J**. Mt 14:29 2424
J stretched out His hand and took Mt 14:31 2424
scribes came to **J** from Jerusalem and Mt 15:1 2424
After **J** called the crowd to Him, He Mt 15:10
J said, "Are you still lacking in Mt 15:16
J went away from there, and Mt 15:21 2424
Then **J** said to her, Mt 15:28 2424
J went along by the Sea of Mt 15:29 2424
And **J** called His disciples to Him, Mt 15:32 2424
And **J** said to them, Mt 15:34 2424
And sending away the crowds, **J** got Mt 15:39
and testing **J**, they asked Him to Mt 16:1
And **J** said to them, Mt 16:6 2424
But **J**, aware of this, said, Mt 16:8 2424
Now when **J** came into the district Mt 16:13 2424
And **J** said to him, Mt 16:17 2424
From that time **J** began to Mt 16:21 2424
Then **J** said to His disciples, Mt 16:24 2424
Six days later **J** took with Him Mt 17:1 2424
Peter said to **J**, Mt 17:4 2424
And **J** came to *them* and touched Mt 17:7 2424
saw no one except **J** Himself alone. Mt 17:8 2424
the mountain, **J** commanded them, Mt 17:9 2424
a man came up to **J**, falling on his Mt 17:14 2424
And **J** answered and said, Mt 17:17 2424
And **J** rebuked him, and the demon Mt 17:18 2424
came to **J** privately and said, Mt 17:19 2424
in Galilee, **J** said to them, Mt 17:22 2424
the house, **J** spoke to him first, Mt 17:25 2424
J said to him, "Then the Mt 17:26 2424
that time the disciples came to **J** and Mt 18:1 2424
J said to him, "I do not say to you, Mt 18:22 2424
When **J** had finished these words, Mt 19:1
Some Pharisees came to **J**, Mt 19:3
But **J** said, "Let the children alone, Mt 19:14 2424
J said, "YOU SHALL NOT COMMIT Mt 19:18 2424
J said to him, "If you wish to be Mt 19:21 2424
And **J** said to His disciples, Mt 19:23 2424
looking at *them* **J** said to them, Mt 19:26 2424
And **J** said to them, Mt 19:28 2424
As **J** was about to go up to Mt 20:17 2424
of the sons of Zebedee came to **J** with Mt 20:20 2424
But **J** answered, Mt 20:22 2424
But **J** called them to Himself and Mt 20:25 2424
hearing that **J** was passing by, Mt 20:30 2424
And **J** stopped and called them, and Mt 20:32 2424
compassion, **J** touched their eyes; Mt 20:34 2424
Olives, then **J** sent two disciples, Mt 21:1 2424
did just as **J** had instructed them, Mt 21:6 2424
"This is the prophet **J**, Mt 21:11 2424
And **J** entered the temple and drove Mt 21:12 2424
And **J** said to them, Mt 21:16 2424
And **J** answered and said to them, Mt 21:21 2424
J said to them, Mt 21:24 2424
And answering **J**, they said, Mt 21:27 2424
J said to them, "Truly I say to you Mt 21:31 2424
J said to them, "Did you never read Mt 21:42 2424
J spoke to them Mt 22:1 2424
But **J** perceived their malice, and Mt 22:18 2424
there is no resurrection) came to **J** Mt 22:23 2424
But **J** answered and said to them, Mt 22:29 2424
But when the Pharisees heard that **J** Mt 22:34 2424
together, **J** asked them a question: Mt 22:41 2424
Then **J** spoke to the crowds and Mt 23:1 2424
J came out from the temple and Mt 24:1 2424
And **J** answered and said to them, Mt 24:4 2424
J had finished all these words, Mt 26:1 2424
together to seize **J** by stealth and Mt 26:4 2424
Now when **J** was in Bethany, at the Mt 26:6 2424
But **J**, aware of this, said to Mt 26:10 2424
for a good opportunity to betray **J**. Mt 26:16
Bread the disciples came to **J** and Mt 26:17 2424
did as **J** had directed them; Mt 26:19 2424
Now when evening came, **J** was Mt 26:20
J said to him, "You have said *it* Mt 26:25
were eating, **J** took *some* bread, Mt 26:26 2424
Then **J** said to them, Mt 26:31 2424
J said to him, "Truly I say to you Mt 26:34 2424
Then **J** came with them to a place Mt 26:36 2424
Immediately Judas went to **J** and said, Mt 26:49 2424
And **J** said to him, Mt 26:50 2424
laid hands on **J** and seized Him. Mt 26:50 2424
one of those who were with **J** Mt 26:51 2424
Then **J** said to him, Mt 26:52 2424
time **J** said to the crowds, Mt 26:55 2424
seized **J** led Him away to Caiaphas, Mt 26:57 2424
obtain false testimony against **J**, Mt 26:59 2424

But **J** kept silent. Mt 26:63 2424
J said to him, "You have said it Mt 26:64 2424
You too were with **J** the Galilean. Mt 26:69 2424
"This man was with **J** of Nazareth." Mt 26:71 2424
the word which **J** had said, Mt 26:75 2424
conferred together against **J** to put Him Mt 27:1 2424
Now **J** stood before the governor, Mt 27:11 2424
And **J** said to him, Mt 27:11 2424
or **J** who is called Christ?" Mt 27:17 2424
Barabbas and to put **J** to death. Mt 27:20 2424
what shall I do with **J** who is called Mt 27:22 2424
but after having **J** scourged, Mt 27:26 2424
soldiers of the governor took **J** into Mt 27:27 2424
IS **J** THE KING OF THE JEWS." Mt 27:37 2424
J cried out with a loud voice, Mt 27:46 2424
And **J** cried out again with a loud Mt 27:50 2424
with him keeping guard over **J**, Mt 27:54 2424
who had followed **J** from Galilee while Mt 27:55 2424
had also become a disciple of **J**. Mt 27:57 2424
and asked for the body of **J**. Mt 27:58 2424
I know that you are looking for **J** Mt 28:5 2424
J met them and greeted them. Mt 28:9 2424
Then **J** said to them, Mt 28:10 2424
mountain which **J** had designated. Mt 28:16 2424
And **J** came up and spoke to them, Mt 28:18 2424
beginning of the gospel of **J** Christ, Mk 1:1 2424
J came from Nazareth in Galilee and Mk 1:9 2424
into custody, **J** came into Galilee, Mk 1:14 2424
And **J** said to them, Mk 1:17 2424
do we have with each other, **J** Mk 1:24 2424
And **J** rebuked him, saying, Mk 1:25 2424
and immediately they spoke to **J** about Mk 1:30
J got up, left *the house,* Mk 1:35
And a leper came to **J**, beseeching Mk 1:40
Moved with compassion, **J** stretched Mk 1:41
J could no longer publicly enter a Mk 1:45
And **J** seeing their faith said to Mk 2:5 2424
Immediately **J**, aware in His Mk 2:8 2424
dining with **J** and His disciples; Mk 2:15 2424
And hearing *this,* **J** said to them, Mk 2:17 2424
And **J** said to them, Mk 2:19 2424
J said to them, "The Sabbath was Mk 2:27
J withdrew to the sea with His Mk 3:7 2424
J Himself was in the stern, asleep Mk 4:38
Seeing **J** from a distance, he Mk 5:6
do we have with each other, **J**, Mk 5:7
J gave them permission. And coming Mk 5:13
They came to **J** and observed Mk 5:15 2424
great things **J** had done for him; Mk 5:20 2424
When **J** had crossed over again Mk 5:21 2424
after hearing about **J**, Mk 5:27 2424
Immediately **J**, perceiving in Mk 5:30 2424
But **J**, overhearing what was being Mk 5:36 2424
J went out from there and came into Mk 6:1
J said to them, Mk 6:4 2424
apostles gathered together with **J**; Mk 6:30 2424
When **J** went ashore, He saw a large Mk 6:34
Immediately **J** made His disciples get Mk 6:45
J got up and went away from there to Mk 7:24
J took him aside from the crowd, Mk 7:33
J called His disciples and said to Mk 8:1
And **J**, aware of this, said to Mk 8:17 2424
And they brought a blind man to **J** Mk 8:22
J went out, along with His Mk 8:27
And **J** was saying to them, "Truly I Mk 9:1
J took with Him Peter and James Mk 9:2 2424
and they were talking with **J**. Mk 9:4 2424
Peter said to **J**, Mk 9:5 2424
with them anymore, except **J** alone. Mk 9:8 2424
And **J** said to him, Mk 9:23 2424
When **J** saw that a crowd was Mk 9:25 2424
But **J** took him by the hand and Mk 9:27 2424
But **J** said, "Do not hinder him, for Mk 9:39 2424
Some Pharisees came up to **J**, Mk 10:2
But **J** said to them, Mk 10:5 2424
But when **J** saw this, He was Mk 10:14 2424
And **J** said to him, Mk 10:18 2424
at him, **J** felt a love for him and Mk 10:21 2424
And **J**, looking around, said to His Mk 10:23 2424
But **J** answered again and said to Mk 10:24 2424
Looking at them, **J** said, Mk 10:27 2424
J said, "Truly I say to you, there is Mk 10:29 2424
J was walking on ahead of them; Mk 10:32 2424
came up to **J**, saying, "Teacher, Mk 10:35
But **J** said to them, Mk 10:38 2424
And **J** said to them, Mk 10:39 2424
them to Himself, **J** said to them, Mk 10:42 2424
heard that it was **J** the Nazarene, Mk 10:47 2424
"**J**, Son of David, have mercy on Mk 10:47 2424
And **J** stopped and said, Mk 10:49 2424
he jumped up and came to **J**. Mk 10:50
And answering him, **J** said, Mk 10:51 2424
And **J** said to him, Mk 10:52 2424
to them just as **J** had told *them,* Mk 11:6 2424
brought the colt to **J** and put Mk 11:7 2424
J entered Jerusalem *and came* into Mk 11:11
And **J** answered saying to them, Mk 11:22 2424
And **J** said to them, Mk 11:29 2424
Answering **J**, they said, Mk 11:33 2424
And **J** said to them, Mk 11:33 2424
And **J** said to them, Mk 12:17 2424
there is no resurrection) came to **J**, Mk 12:18
J said to them, "Is this not the Mk 12:24 2424
J answered, "The foremost is, Mk 12:29 2424
When **J** saw that he had Mk 12:34 2424
And **J** *began* to say, as Mk 12:35 2424
And **J** said to him, Mk 13:2 2424
And **J** began to say to them, Mk 13:5 2424
J said, "Let her alone; why do you Mk 14:6 2424

at the table and eating, **J** said, **Mk 14:18** *2424*
And **J** said to them, **Mk 14:27** *2424*
And **J** said to him, **Mk 14:30** *2424*
And **J** said to them, **Mk 14:48** *2424*
led **J** away to the high priest; **Mk 14:53** *2424*
trying to obtain testimony against **J** **Mk 14:55** *2424*
and came forward and questioned **J**, **Mk 14:60** *2424*
J said, "I am; and you shall see **Mk 14:62** *2424*
"You also were with **J** the Nazarene." **Mk 14:67** *2424*
how **J** had made the remark to him, **Mk 14:72** *2424*
and binding **J**, they led Him away and **Mk 15:1** *2424*
But **J** made no further answer; **Mk 15:5** *2424*
them, and after having **J** scourged, **Mk 15:15** *2424*
J cried out with a loud voice, **Mk 15:34** *2424*
And **J** uttered a loud cry, and **Mk 15:37** *2424*
and asked for the body of **J**. **Mk 15:43** *2424*
are looking for **J** the Nazarene, **Mk 16:6** *2424*
the Lord **J** had spoken to them, **Mk 16:19** *2424*
J *Himself sent out through them from* **Mk 16:20**
a son, and you shall name Him **J**. **Lk 1:31** *2424*
His name was *then* called **J**, **Lk 2:21** *2424*
parents brought in the child **J**, **Lk 2:27** *2424*
boy **J** stayed behind in Jerusalem. **Lk 2:43** *2424*
And **J** kept increasing in wisdom **Lk 2:52** *2424*
J was also baptized, **Lk 3:21** *2424*
J Himself was about thirty years **Lk 3:23** *2424*
J, full of the Holy Spirit, **Lk 4:1** *2424*
And **J** answered him, **Lk 4:4** *2424*
J answered him, **Lk 4:8** *2424*
And **J** answered and said to him, **Lk 4:12** *2424*
And **J** returned to Galilee in the **Lk 4:14** *2424*
do we have with each other, **J** **Lk 4:34** *2424*
But **J** rebuked him, saying, **Lk 4:35** *2424*
When day came, **J** left and went to a **Lk 4:42**
And **J** said to Simon, **Lk 5:10** *2424*
and when he saw **J**, he fell on his **Lk 5:12** *2424*
But **J** Himself would *often* slip **Lk 5:16**
the middle *of the crowd,* in front of **J**. **Lk 5:19** *2424*
But **J**, aware of their reasonings, **Lk 5:22** *2424*
And **J** answered and said to them, **Lk 5:31** *2424*
And **J** said to them, **Lk 5:34** *2424*
And **J** answering them said, **Lk 6:3** *2424*
And **J** said to them, **Lk 6:9** *2424*
together what they might do to **J**. **Lk 6:11** *2424*
J came down with them and stood on a **Lk 6:17**
When he heard about **J**, **Lk 7:3** *2424*
When they came to **J**, **Lk 7:4** *2424*
J *started* on His way with them; **Lk 7:6** *2424*
Now when **J** heard this, He marveled **Lk 7:9** *2424*
And **J** gave him back to his mother. **Lk 7:15**
And **J** answered him, **Lk 7:40** *2424*
Now on one of *those* days **J** **Lk 8:22**
They came to **J** and woke Him up, **Lk 8:24**
Seeing **J**, he cried out and **Lk 8:28** *2424*
do we have with each other, **J**, **Lk 8:28** *2424*
And **J** asked him, **Lk 8:30** *2424*
and they came to **J**, **Lk 8:35** *2424*
sitting down at the feet of **J**, **Lk 8:35** *2424*
great things **J** had done for him. **Lk 8:39** *2424*
And as **J** returned, the people **Lk 8:40** *2424*
J said, "Who is the one who touched **Lk 8:45** *2424*
But **J** said, "Someone did touch Me, **Lk 8:46** *2424*
But when **J** heard *this,* He answered **Lk 8:50** *2424*
leaving Him, Peter said to **J**, **Lk 9:33** *2424*
had spoken, **J** was found alone. **Lk 9:36** *2424*
And **J** answered and said, **Lk 9:41** *2424*
But **J** rebuked the unclean spirit, **Lk 9:42** *2424*
But **J**, knowing what they were **Lk 9:47** *2424*
But **J** said to him, **Lk 9:50** *2424*
And **J** said to him, **Lk 9:58** *2424*
But **J** said to him, **Lk 9:62** *2424*
to justify himself, he said to **J**, **Lk 10:29** *2424*
J replied and said, **Lk 10:30** *2424*
Then **J** said to him, **Lk 10:37** *2424*
It happened that while **J** was praying **Lk 11:1**
While **J** was saying these things, one **Lk 11:27**
And **J** said to them, "Do you suppose **Lk 13:2**
When **J** saw her, He called her **Lk 13:12** *2424*
J had healed on the Sabbath, **Lk 13:14** *2424*
And **J** answered and spoke to the **Lk 14:3** *2424*
"**J**, Master, have mercy on us!" **Lk 17:13** *2424*
Then **J** answered and said, **Lk 17:17** *2424*
But **J** called for them, saying, **Lk 18:16** *2424*
And **J** said to him, **Lk 18:19** *2424*
When **J** heard *this,* He said to **Lk 18:22** *2424*
And **J** looked at him and said, **Lk 18:24** *2424*
As **J** was approaching Jericho, a **Lk 18:35**
that **J** of Nazareth was passing by. **Lk 18:37** *2424*
"**J**, Son of David, have mercy on **Lk 18:38** *2424*
And **J** stopped and commanded that **Lk 18:40** *2424*
And **J** said to him, **Lk 18:42** *2424*
Zaccheus was trying to see who **J** was, **Lk 19:3** *2424*
When **J** came to the place, He **Lk 19:5** *2424*
And **J** said to him, **Lk 19:9** *2424*
J went on to tell a parable, because **Lk 19:11**
They brought it to **J**, **Lk 19:35** *2424*
on the colt and put **J** *on it.* **Lk 19:35** *2424*
But **J** answered, "I tell you, if **Lk 19:40**
J entered the temple and began to **Lk 19:45**
J answered and said to them, "I **Lk 20:3**
And **J** said to them, **Lk 20:8** *2424*
But **J** looked at them and said, **Lk 20:17**
J said to them, **Lk 20:34** *2424*
And **J** sent Peter and John, saying, **Lk 22:8**
and he approached **J** to kiss Him. **Lk 22:47** *2424*
But **J** said to him, **Lk 22:48** *2424*
But **J** answered and said, **Lk 22:51** *2424*
Then **J** said to the chief priests **Lk 22:52** *2424*
men who were holding **J** in custody **Lk 22:63**

Herod was very glad when he saw **J**; **Lk 23:8** *2424*
Pilate, wanting to release **J**, **Lk 23:20** *2424*
but he delivered **J** to their will. **Lk 23:25** *2424*
him the cross to carry behind **J**. **Lk 23:26** *2424*
But **J** turning to them said, **Lk 23:28** *2424*
But **J** was saying, **Lk 23:34** *2424*
"**J**, remember me when You come in **Lk 23:42** *2424*
And **J**, crying out with a loud **Lk 23:46** *2424*
and asked for the body of **J**. **Lk 23:52** *2424*
not find the body of the Lord **J**. **Lk 24:3** *2424*
discussing, **J** Himself approached and **Lk 24:15** *2424*
"The things about **J** the Nazarene, **Lk 24:19** *2424*
were realized through **J** Christ. **Jn 1:17** *2424*
next day he saw **J** coming to him and **Jn 1:29** *2424*
and he looked at **J** as He walked, **Jn 1:36** *2424*
him speak, and they followed **J**. **Jn 1:37** *2424*
And **J** turned and saw them **Jn 1:38** *2424*
He brought him to **J**. **Jn 1:42** *2424*
J looked at him and said, **Jn 1:42** *2424*
And **J** said to him, **Jn 1:43** *2424*
the Prophets wrote—**J** of Nazareth, **Jn 1:45** *2424*
J saw Nathanael coming to Him, and **Jn 1:47** *2424*
J answered and said to him, **Jn 1:48** *2424*
J answered and said to him, **Jn 1:50** *2424*
and the mother of **J** was there; **Jn 2:1** *2424*
and both **J** and His disciples were **Jn 2:2** *2424*
out, the mother of **J** said to Him, **Jn 2:3** *2424*
And **J** said to her, **Jn 2:4** *2424*
J said to them, "Fill the waterpots **Jn 2:7** *2424*
This beginning of *His* signs **J** did in **Jn 2:11** *2424*
near, and **J** went up to Jerusalem. **Jn 2:13** *2424*
J answered them, **Jn 2:19** *2424*
and the word which **J** had spoken. **Jn 2:22** *2424*
But **J**, on His part, was not **Jn 2:24** *2424*
this man came to **J** by night and said **Jn 3:2**
J answered and said to him, **Jn 3:3** *2424*
J answered, "Truly, truly, I say **Jn 3:5** *2424*
J answered and said to him, **Jn 3:10** *2424*
After these things **J** and His **Jn 3:22** *2424*
J was making and baptizing more **Jn 4:1** *2424*
J Himself was not baptizing, **Jn 4:2** *2424*
J, being wearied from **Jn 4:6** *2424*
J said to her, "Give Me a drink." **Jn 4:7** *2424*
J answered and said to her, **Jn 4:10** *2424*
J answered and said to her, **Jn 4:13** *2424*
J said to her, "You have correctly said, **Jn 4:17** *2424*
J said to her, "Woman, believe Me, **Jn 4:21** *2424*
J said to her, "I who speak to you **Jn 4:26** *2424*
J said to them, "My food is to do **Jn 4:34** *2424*
So when the Samaritans came to **J**, **Jn 4:40**
For **J** Himself testified that a **Jn 4:44** *2424*
When he heard that **J** had come out **Jn 4:47** *2424*
J said to him, **Jn 4:48** *2424*
J said to him, "Go; **Jn 4:50** *2424*
the word that **J** spoke to him and **Jn 4:50** *2424*
that hour in which **J** said to him, **Jn 4:53** *2424*
a second sign that **J** performed when **Jn 4:54** *2424*
Jews, and **J** went up to Jerusalem. **Jn 5:1** *2424*
When **J** saw him lying *there,* and **Jn 5:6** *2424*
J said to him, "Get up, pick up your **Jn 5:8** *2424*
for **J** had slipped away while there **Jn 5:13** *2424*
J found him in the temple and **Jn 5:14** *2424*
it was **J** who had made him well. **Jn 5:15** *2424*
the Jews were persecuting **J**, **Jn 5:16** *2424*
J answered and was **Jn 5:19** *2424*
After these things **J** went away to **Jn 6:1** *2424*
Then **J** went up on the mountain, and **Jn 6:3** *2424*
J, lifting up His eyes **Jn 6:5** *2424*
J said, "Have the people sit down." **Jn 6:10** *2424*
J then took the loaves **Jn 6:11** *2424*
J, perceiving that they **Jn 6:15** *2424*
and **J** had not yet come to them. **Jn 6:17** *2424*
they saw **J** walking on the sea **Jn 6:19** *2424*
and that **J** had not entered with **Jn 6:22** *2424*
saw that **J** was not there, **Jn 6:24** *2424*
and came to Capernaum seeking **J**. **Jn 6:24** *2424*
J answered them and said, **Jn 6:26** *2424*
J answered and said to them, **Jn 6:29** *2424*
J then said to them, **Jn 6:32** *2424*
J said to them, "I am the bread of **Jn 6:35** *2424*
"Is not this **J**, the son of **Jn 6:42** *2424*
J answered and said to them, **Jn 6:43** *2424*
J said to them, **Jn 6:53** *2424*
But **J**, conscious that His **Jn 6:61** *2424*
For **J** knew from the beginning who **Jn 6:64** *2424*
J said to the twelve, **Jn 6:67** *2424*
J answered them, **Jn 6:70** *2424*
things **J** was walking in Galilee, **Jn 7:1** *2424*
J said to them, **Jn 7:6** *2424*
feast **J** went up into the temple, **Jn 7:14** *2424*
So **J** answered them and **Jn 7:16** *2424*
J answered them, **Jn 7:21** *2424*
J cried out in the **Jn 7:28** *2424*
J said, **Jn 7:33** *2424*
the feast, **J** stood and cried out, **Jn 7:37** *2424*
because **J** was not yet glorified. **Jn 7:39** *2424*
But **J** went to the Mount of Olives. **Jn 8:1** *2424*
But **J** stooped down and with His **Jn 8:6** *2424*
Straightening up, **J** said to her, **Jn 8:10** *2424*
J said, "I do not condemn you, **Jn 8:11** *2424*
Then **J** again spoke to them, **Jn 8:12** *2424*
J answered and said to them, **Jn 8:14** *2424*
J answered, "You know neither Me nor **Jn 8:19** *2424*
J said to them, "What have I been **Jn 8:25** *2424*
J said, **Jn 8:28** *2424*
J was saying to those **Jn 8:31** *2424*
J answered them, **Jn 8:34** *2424*
J said to them, "If you are **Jn 8:39** *2424*
J said to them, "If God were your **Jn 8:42** *2424*

J answered, "I do not have a demon **Jn 8:49** *2424*
J answered, "If I glorify Myself, **Jn 8:54** *2424*
J said to them, "Truly, truly, I say **Jn 8:58** *2424*
but **J** hid Himself and went out of **Jn 8:59** *2424*
J answered, "*It was* neither *that* this **Jn 9:3** *2424*
"The man who is called **J** made clay, **Jn 9:11** *2424*
on the day when **J** made the clay and **Jn 9:14** *2424*
J heard that they had put him out, **Jn 9:35** *2424*
J said to him, "You have both seen **Jn 9:37** *2424*
And **J** said, "For judgment I came **Jn 9:39** *2424*
J said to them, "If you were blind, **Jn 9:41** *2424*
figure of speech **J** spoke to them, **Jn 10:6** *2424*
J said to them again, **Jn 10:7** *2424*
and **J** was walking in the temple in **Jn 10:23** *2424*
J answered them, **Jn 10:25** *2424*
J answered them, **Jn 10:32** *2424*
J answered them, **Jn 10:34** *2424*
But when **J** heard *this,* He said, **Jn 11:4** *2424*
Now **J** loved Martha and her **Jn 11:5** *2424*
J answered, "Are there not twelve **Jn 11:9** *2424*
Now **J** had spoken of his death, but **Jn 11:13** *2424*
So **J** then said to them **Jn 11:14** *2424*
So when **J** came, He found that he **Jn 11:17** *2424*
when she heard that **J** was coming, **Jn 11:20** *2424*
Martha then said to **J**, **Jn 11:21** *2424*
J said to her, "Your brother will **Jn 11:23** *2424*
J said to her, "I am the resurrection **Jn 11:25** *2424*
Now **J** had not yet come into the **Jn 11:30** *2424*
when Mary came where **J** was, **Jn 11:32** *2424*
When **J** therefore saw her weeping, **Jn 11:33** *2424*
J wept. **Jn 11:35** *2424*
J, again being deeply **Jn 11:38** *2424*
J said, "Remove the stone." **Jn 11:39** *2424*
J said to her, "Did I not say to you that **Jn 11:40** *2424*
Then **J** raised His eyes, and said, **Jn 11:41** *2424*
J said to them, "Unbind him, and **Jn 11:44** *2424*
them the things which **J** had done. **Jn 11:46** *2424*
he prophesied that **J** was going to **Jn 11:51** *2424*
J no longer continued to **Jn 11:54** *2424*
So they were seeking for **J**, **Jn 11:56** *2424*
J, therefore, six days before the **Jn 12:1** *2424*
whom **J** had raised from the dead. **Jn 12:1** *2424*
nard, and anointed the feet of **J** and **Jn 12:3** *2424*
J said, **Jn 12:7** *2424*
away and were believing in **J**. **Jn 12:11** *2424*
that **J** was coming to Jerusalem, **Jn 12:12** *2424*
J, finding a young donkey, sat **Jn 12:14** *2424*
but when **J** was glorified, then **Jn 12:16** *2424*
"Sir, we wish to see **J**." **Jn 12:21** *2424*
and Philip came and told **J**. **Jn 12:22** *2424*
And **J** answered them, saying, **Jn 12:23** *2424*
J answered and said, **Jn 12:30** *2424*
J said to them, **Jn 12:35** *2424*
These things **J** spoke, and He **Jn 12:36** *2424*
And **J** cried out and said, **Jn 12:44** *2424*
J knowing that His hour had come **Jn 13:1** *2424*
J, knowing that the Father had **Jn 13:3**
J answered and said to him, **Jn 13:7** *2424*
J answered him, "If I do not wash **Jn 13:8** *2424*
J said to him, "He who has bathed **Jn 13:10** *2424*
When **J** had said this, He became **Jn 13:21** *2424*
of His disciples, whom **J** loved. **Jn 13:23** *2424*
J then answered, **Jn 13:26** *2424*
J said to him, **Jn 13:27** *2424*
box, that **J** was saying to him, **Jn 13:29** *2424*
when he had gone out, **J** said, **Jn 13:31** *2424*
J answered, "Where I go, you **Jn 13:36** *2424*
J answered, "Will you lay down your **Jn 13:38** *2424*
J said to him, "I am the way, and **Jn 14:6** *2424*
J said to him, "Have I been so long **Jn 14:9** *2424*
J answered and said to him, **Jn 14:23** *2424*
J knew that they wished to **Jn 16:19** *2424*
J answered them, **Jn 16:31** *2424*
J spoke these things; **Jn 17:1** *2424*
and **J** Christ whom You have sent. **Jn 17:3** *2424*
When **J** had spoken these words, He **Jn 18:1** *2424*
for **J** had often met there with His **Jn 18:2** *2424*
J, knowing all the **Jn 18:4** *2424*
"**J** the Nazarene." **Jn 18:5** *2424*
"**J** the Nazarene." **Jn 18:7** *2424*
J answered, "I told you that I am **Jn 18:8** *2424*
J said to Peter, **Jn 18:11** *2424*
Jews, arrested **J** and bound Him, **Jn 18:12** *2424*
Simon Peter was following **J**, **Jn 18:15** *2424*
and entered with **J** into the court **Jn 18:15** *2424*
questioned **J** about His disciples, **Jn 18:19** *2424*
J answered him, "I have spoken **Jn 18:20** *2424*
standing nearby struck **J**, **Jn 18:22** *2424*
J answered him, "If I have spoken **Jn 18:23** *2424*
Then they led **J** from Caiaphas **Jn 18:28** *2424*
to fulfill the word of **J** **Jn 18:32** *2424*
the Praetorium, and summoned **J** and **Jn 18:33** *2424*
J answered, "Are you saying this on **Jn 18:34** *2424*
J answered, "My kingdom is not of **Jn 18:36** *2424*
J answered, "You say *correctly* that I **Jn 18:37** *2424*
Pilate then took **J** **Jn 19:1** *2424*
J then came out, wearing the **Jn 19:5** *2424*
Praetorium again and said to **J**, **Jn 19:9** *2424*
But **J** gave him no answer. **Jn 19:9** *2424*
J answered, "You would have no **Jn 19:11** *2424*
these words, he brought **J** out, **Jn 19:13** *2424*
They took **J**, therefore, and He went **Jn 19:17** *2424*
on either side, and **J** in between. **Jn 19:18** *2424*
"**J** THE NAZARENE, THE KING **Jn 19:19** *2424*
the place where **J** was crucified was **Jn 19:20** *2424*
when they had crucified **J**, **Jn 19:23** *2424*
by the cross of **J** were His mother, **Jn 19:25** *2424*
When **J** then saw His mother, **Jn 19:26** *2424*
After this, **J**, knowing that all **Jn 19:28** *2424*

Therefore when **J** had received the **Jn 19:30** *2424*
but coming to **J**, when they saw **Jn 19:33** *2424*
Arimathea, being a disciple of **J**, **Jn 19:38** *2424*
he might take away the body of **J**; **Jn 19:38** *2424*
So they took the body of **J** and **Jn 19:40** *2424*
was nearby, they laid **J** there. **Jn 19:42** *2424*
the other disciple whom **J** loved, **Jn 20:2** *2424*
the body of **J** had been lying. **Jn 20:12** *2424*
and saw **J** standing *there,* **Jn 20:14** *2424*
and did not know that it was **J**. **Jn 20:14** *2424*
J said to her, "Woman, why are you **Jn 20:15** *2424*
J said to her, "Mary!" She turned **Jn 20:16** *2424*
J said to her, "Stop clinging to Me, **Jn 20:17** *2424*
J came and stood in their midst and **Jn 20:19** *2424*
J said to them again, **Jn 20:21** *2424*
was not with them when **J** came. **Jn 20:24** *2424*
J came, the doors having been **Jn 20:26** *2424*
J said to him, "Because you have **Jn 20:29** *2424*
Therefore many other signs **J** also **Jn 20:30** *2424*
may believe that **J** is the Christ, **Jn 20:31** *2424*
After these things **J** manifested **Jn 21:1** *2424*
breaking, **J** stood on the beach; **Jn 21:4** *2424*
did not know that it was **J**. **Jn 21:4** *2424*
J said to them, **Jn 21:5** *2424*
whom **J** loved said to Peter, **Jn 21:7** *2424*
J said to them, "Bring some of the **Jn 21:10** *2424*
J said to them, "Come *and* have **Jn 21:12** *2424*
J came and took the bread and **Jn 21:13** *2424*
This is now the third time that **J** **Jn 21:14** *2424*
breakfast, **J** said to Simon Peter, **Jn 21:15** *2424*
J said to him, "Tend My sheep. **Jn 21:17** *2424*
saw the disciple whom **J** loved **Jn 21:20** *2424*
Peter seeing him said to **J**, **Jn 21:21** *2424*
J said to him, "If I want him to **Jn 21:22** *2424*
yet **J** did not say to him that he **Jn 21:23** *2424*
many other things which **J** did, **Jn 21:25** *2424*
all that **J** began to do and teach, **Ac 1:1** *2424*
This **J**, who has been taken up from **Ac 1:11** *2424*
women, and Mary the mother of **J**, **Ac 1:14** *2424*
a guide to those who arrested **J**. **Ac 1:16** *2424*
Lord **J** went in and out among us **Ac 1:21** *2424*
J the Nazarene, a man attested to **Ac 2:22** *2424*
"This **J** God raised up again, to **Ac 2:32** *2424*
this **J** whom you crucified." **Ac 2:36** *2424*
be baptized in the name of **J** Christ **Ac 2:38** *2424*
the name of **J** Christ the Nazarene **Ac 3:6** *2424*
has glorified His servant **J**, **Ac 3:13** *2424*
it is the name of **J** which has **Ac 3:16**
and that He may send **J**, **Ac 3:20** *2424*
proclaiming in **J** the resurrection **Ac 4:2** *2424*
the name of **J** Christ the Nazarene, **Ac 4:10** *2424*
them as having been with **J**. **Ac 4:13** *2424*
or teach at all in the name of **J**. **Ac 4:18** *2424*
against Your holy servant **J**, **Ac 4:27** *2424*
the name of Your holy servant **J**." **Ac 4:30** *2424*
to the resurrection of the Lord **J**, **Ac 4:33** *2424*
God of our fathers raised up **J**, **Ac 5:30** *2424*
not to speak in the name of **J**, **Ac 5:40** *2424*
and preaching **J** *as* the Christ. **Ac 5:42** *2424*
him say that this Nazarene, **J**, **Ac 6:14** *2424*
and **J** standing at the right hand **Ac 7:55** *2424*
"Lord **J**, receive my spirit!" **Ac 7:59** *2424*
of God and the name of **J** Christ, **Ac 8:12** *2424*
baptized in the name of the Lord **J**. **Ac 8:16** *2424*
Scripture he preached **J** to him. **Ac 8:35** *2424*
J Christ is the Son of God." **Ac 8:37** *2424*
"I am **J** whom you are persecuting, **Ac 9:5** *2424*
the Lord **J**, who appeared to you **Ac 9:17** *2424*
to proclaim **J** in the synagogues, **Ac 9:20** *2424*
at Damascus by proving that this **J** **Ac 9:22** *2424*
out boldly in the name of **J**. **Ac 9:27** *2424*
"Aeneas, **J** Christ heals you; **Ac 9:34** *2424*
preaching peace through **J** Christ **Ac 10:36** *2424*
"*You know of* **J** of Nazareth, how **Ac 10:38** *2424*
baptized in the name of **J** Christ. **Ac 10:48** *2424*
believing in the Lord **J** Christ, **Ac 11:17** *2424*
Greeks also, preaching the Lord **J**. **Ac 11:20** *2424*
has brought to Israel a Savior, **J**, **Ac 13:23** *2424*
children in that He raised up **J**, **Ac 13:33** *2424*
through the grace of the Lord **J**, **Ac 15:11** *2424*
for the name of our Lord **J** Christ. **Ac 15:26** *2424*
Spirit of **J** did not permit them; **Ac 16:7** *2424*
"I command you in the name of **J** **Ac 16:18** *2424*
"Believe in the Lord **J**, **Ac 16:31** *2424*
"This **J** whom I am proclaiming to **Ac 17:3** *2424*
that there is another king, **J**." **Ac 17:7** *2424*
preaching **J** and the resurrection. **Ac 17:18** *2424*
to the Jews that **J** was the Christ. **Ac 18:5** *2424*
the things concerning **J**, **Ac 18:25** *2424*
Scriptures that **J** was the Christ. **Ac 18:28** *2424*
coming after him, that is, in **J**." **Ac 19:4** *2424*
baptized in the name of the Lord **J**. **Ac 19:5** *2424*
evil spirits the name of the Lord **J**, **Ac 19:13** *2424*
I adjure you by **J** whom Paul **Ac 19:13** *2424*
"I recognize **J**, and I know about **Ac 19:15** *2424*
the name of the Lord **J** was being **Ac 19:17** *2424*
and faith in our Lord **J** Christ. **Ac 20:21** *2424*
which I received from the Lord **J**, **Ac 20:24** *2424*
remember the words of the Lord **J**, **Ac 20:35** *2424*
for the name of the Lord **J**." **Ac 21:13** *2424*
'I am **J** the Nazarene, whom you are **Ac 22:8** *2424*
him *speak* about faith in Christ **J**. **Ac 24:24** *2424*
and about a dead man, **J**, **Ac 25:19** *2424*
to the name of **J** of Nazareth. **Ac 26:9** *2424*
'I am **J** whom you are persecuting. **Ac 26:15** *2424*
to persuade them concerning **J**, **Ac 28:23** *2424*
teaching concerning the Lord **J** **Ac 28:31** *2424*
Paul, a bond-servant of Christ **J**, **Ro 1:1** *2424*
of holiness, **J** Christ our Lord, **Ro 1:4** *2424*
also are the called of **J** Christ; **Ro 1:6** *2424*
our Father and the Lord **J** Christ. **Ro 1:7** *2424*
God through **J** Christ for you all, **Ro 1:8** *2424*
secrets of men through Christ **J**. **Ro 2:16** *2424*
through faith in **J** Christ for all those **Ro 3:22** *2424*
redemption which is in Christ **J**; **Ro 3:24** *2424*
of the one who has faith in **J**. **Ro 3:26** *2424*
raised **J** our Lord from the dead, **Ro 4:24** *2424*
God through our Lord **J** Christ, **Ro 5:1** *2424*
in God through our Lord **J** Christ, **Ro 5:11** *2424*
grace of the one Man, **J** Christ, **Ro 5:15** *2424*
in life through the One, **J** Christ. **Ro 5:17** *2424*
life through **J** Christ our Lord. **Ro 5:21** *2424*
have been baptized into Christ **J** **Ro 6:3** *2424*
sin, but alive to God in Christ **J**. **Ro 6:11** *2424*
eternal life in Christ **J** our Lord. **Ro 6:23** *2424*
to God through **J** Christ our Lord! **Ro 7:25** *2424*
for those who are in Christ **J**. **Ro 8:1** *2424*
law of the Spirit of life in Christ **J** **Ro 8:2** *2424*
if the Spirit of Him who raised **J** **Ro 8:11** *2424*
He who raised Christ **J** from the **Ro 8:11** *2424*
Christ **J** is He who died, yes, **Ro 8:34** *2424*
love of God, which is in Christ **J** **Ro 8:39** *2424*
confess with your mouth **J** *as* Lord, **Ro 10:9** *2424*
But put on the Lord **J** Christ, **Ro 13:14** *2424*
and am convinced in the Lord **J** **Ro 14:14** *2424*
one another according to Christ **J**, **Ro 15:5** *2424*
and Father of our Lord **J** Christ. **Ro 15:6** *2424*
minister of Christ **J** to the Gentiles, **Ro 15:16** *2424*
Therefore in Christ **J** I have found **Ro 15:17** *2424*
by our Lord **J** Christ and by the **Ro 15:30** *2424*
my fellow workers in Christ **J**, **Ro 16:3** *2424*
grace of our Lord **J** be with you. **Ro 16:20** *2424*
The grace of our Lord **J** Christ be **Ro 16:24** *2424*
and the preaching of **J** Christ, **Ro 16:25** *2424*
only wise God, through **J** Christ, **Ro 16:27** *2424*
called *as* an apostle of **J** Christ by **1Co 1:1** *2424*
have been sanctified in Christ **J**, **1Co 1:2** *2424*
the name of our Lord **J** Christ, **1Co 1:2** *2424*
our Father and the Lord **J** Christ. **1Co 1:3** *2424*
which was given you in Christ **J**, **1Co 1:4** *2424*
revelation of our Lord **J** Christ, **1Co 1:7** *2424*
in the day of our Lord **J** Christ. **1Co 1:8** *2424*
with His Son, **J** Christ our Lord. **1Co 1:9** *2424*
by the name of our Lord **J** Christ, **1Co 1:10** *2424*
by His doing you are in Christ **J**, **1Co 1:30** *2424*
nothing among you except **J** Christ, **1Co 2:2** *2424*
which is laid, which is **J** Christ. **1Co 3:11** *2424*
for in Christ **J** I became your **1Co 4:15** *2424*
In the name of our Lord **J**, **1Co 5:4** *2424*
with the power of our Lord **J**, **1Co 5:4** *2424*
be saved in the day of the Lord **J**. **1Co 5:5** *2424*
in the name of the Lord **J** Christ and **1Co 6:11** *2424*
and one Lord, **J** Christ, by whom **1Co 8:6** *2424*
Have I not seen **J** our Lord? **1Co 9:1** *2424*
that the Lord **J** in the night in **1Co 11:23** *2424*
"**J** is accursed"; and no one can say, **1Co 12:3** *2424*
"**J** is Lord," except by the Holy **1Co 12:3** *2424*
which I have in Christ **J** our Lord, **1Co 15:31** *2424*
victory through our Lord **J** Christ. **1Co 15:57** *2424*
grace of the Lord **J** be with you. **1Co 16:23** *2424*
love be with you all in Christ **J**. **1Co 16:24** *2424*
Paul, an apostle of Christ **J** by the **2Co 1:1** *2424*
our Father and the Lord **J** Christ. **2Co 1:2** *2424*
and Father of our Lord **J** Christ, **2Co 1:3** *2424*
ours, in the day of our Lord **J**. **2Co 1:14** *2424*
For the Son of God, Christ **J**, **2Co 1:19** *2424*
ourselves but Christ **J** as Lord, **2Co 4:5** *2424*
about in the body the dying of **J**, **2Co 4:10** *2424*
that the life of **J** also may be **2Co 4:10** *2424*
that the life of **J** also may be **2Co 4:11** *2424*
He who raised the Lord **J** will raise **2Co 4:14** *2424*
Lord Jesus will raise us also with **J** **2Co 4:14** *2424*
the grace of our Lord **J** Christ, **2Co 8:9** *2424*
one comes and preaches another **J** **2Co 11:4** *2424*
The God and Father of the Lord **J**, **2Co 11:31** *2424*
that **J** Christ is in you **2Co 13:5** *2424*
The grace of the Lord **J** Christ, **2Co 13:14** *2424*
of man, but through **J** Christ and **Ga 1:1** *2424*
our Father and the Lord **J** Christ, **Ga 1:3** *2424*
through a revelation of **J** Christ. **Ga 1:12** *2424*
liberty which we have in Christ **J**, **Ga 2:4** *2424*
Law but through faith in Christ **J**, **Ga 2:16** *2424*
even we have believed in Christ **J**, **Ga 2:16** *2424*
before whose eyes **J** Christ was **Ga 3:1** *2424*
in Christ **J** the blessing of Abraham **Ga 3:14** *2424*
the promise by faith in **J** Christ **Ga 3:22** *2424*
of God through faith in Christ **J**. **Ga 3:26** *2424*
for you are all one in Christ **J**. **Ga 3:28** *2424*
angel of God, as Christ **J** *Himself.* **Ga 4:14** *2424*
in Christ **J** neither circumcision nor **Ga 5:6** *2424*
Now those who belong to Christ **J** **Ga 5:24** *2424*
in the cross of our Lord **J** Christ, **Ga 6:14** *2424*
on my body the brand-marks of **J**. **Ga 6:17** *2424*
Lord **J** Christ be with your spirit, **Ga 6:18** *2424*
Paul, an apostle of Christ **J** by the **Eph 1:1** *2424*
and *who are* faithful in Christ **J**: **Eph 1:1** *2424*
our Father and the Lord **J** Christ. **Eph 1:2** *2424*
and Father of our Lord **J** Christ, **Eph 1:3** *2424*
adoption as sons through **J** Christ **Eph 1:5** *2424*
heard of the faith in the Lord **J** **Eph 1:15** *2424*
that the God of our Lord **J** Christ, **Eph 1:17** *2424*
the heavenly *places* in Christ **J**, **Eph 2:6** *2424*
in kindness toward us in Christ **J**. **Eph 2:7** *2424*
created in Christ **J** for good works, **Eph 2:10** *2424*
But now in Christ **J** you who **Eph 2:13** *2424*
Christ **J** Himself being the corner **Eph 2:20** *2424*
the prisoner of Christ **J** for the **Eph 3:1** *2424*
in Christ **J** through the gospel, **Eph 3:6** *2424*
carried out in Christ **J** our Lord, **Eph 3:11** *2424*
glory in the church and in Christ **J** **Eph 3:21** *2424*
in Him, just as truth is in **J**, **Eph 4:21** *2424*
name of our Lord **J** Christ to God, **Eph 5:20** *2424*
the Father and the Lord **J** Christ. **Eph 6:23** *2424*
all those who love our Lord **J** Christ **Eph 6:24** *2424*
Timothy, bond-servants of Christ **J**, **Php 1:1** *2424*
all the saints in Christ **J** who are in **Php 1:1** *2424*
our Father and the Lord **J** Christ. **Php 1:2** *2424*
it until the day of Christ **J**. **Php 1:6** *2424*
with the affection of Christ **J**. **Php 1:8** *2424*
which *comes* through **J** Christ, **Php 1:11** *2424*
provision of the Spirit of **J** Christ, **Php 1:19** *2424*
may abound in Christ **J** through my **Php 1:26** *2424*
which was also in Christ **J**, **Php 2:5** *2424*
name of **J** EVERY KNEE WILL BOW, **Php 2:10** *2424*
confess that **J** Christ is Lord, **Php 2:11** *2424*
But I hope in the Lord **J** to send **Php 2:19** *2424*
interests, not those of Christ **J**. **Php 2:21** *2424*
and glory in Christ **J** and put no **Php 3:3** *2424*
value of knowing Christ **J** my Lord, **Php 3:8** *2424*
I was laid hold of by Christ **J**. **Php 3:12** *2424*
upward call of God in Christ **J**. **Php 3:14** *2424*
for a Savior, the Lord **J** Christ; **Php 3:20** *2424*
hearts and your minds in Christ **J**. **Php 4:7** *2424*
His riches in glory in Christ **J**. **Php 4:19** *2424*
Greet every saint in Christ **J**. **Php 4:21** *2424*
The grace of the Lord **J** Christ be **Php 4:23** *2424*
an apostle of **J** Christ by the will of **Col 1:1** *2424*
the Father of our Lord **J** Christ, **Col 1:3** *2424*
we heard of your faith in Christ **J** **Col 1:4** *2424*
have received Christ **J** the Lord, **Col 2:6** *2424*
do all in the name of the Lord **J**, **Col 3:17** *2424*
and *also* **J** who is called Justus; **Col 4:11** *2424*
number, a bondslave of **J** Christ, **Col 4:12** *2424*
the Father and the Lord **J** Christ: **1Th 1:1** *2424*
steadfastness of hope in our Lord **J** **1Th 1:3** *2424*
raised from the dead, *that is* **J**, **1Th 1:10** *2424*
the churches of God in Christ **J** **1Th 2:14** *2424*
killed the Lord **J** and the prophets, **1Th 2:15** *2424*
in the presence of our Lord **J** at His **1Th 2:19** *2424*
J our Lord direct our way to you; **1Th 3:11** *2424*
at the coming of our Lord **J** with all **1Th 3:13** *2424*
and exhort you in the Lord **J**, **1Th 4:1** *2424*
by *the authority of* the Lord **J**. **1Th 4:2** *2424*
that **J** died and rose again, **1Th 4:14** *2424*
those who have fallen asleep in **J**. **1Th 4:14** *2424*
through our Lord **J** Christ, **1Th 5:9** *2424*
is God's will for you in Christ **J**. **1Th 5:18** *2424*
the coming of our Lord **J** Christ. **1Th 5:23** *2424*
The grace of our Lord **J** Christ be **1Th 5:28** *2424*
our Father and the Lord **J** Christ: **2Th 1:1** *2424*
the Father and the Lord **J** Christ. **2Th 1:2** *2424*
when the Lord **J** will be revealed **2Th 1:7** *2424*
not obey the gospel of our Lord **J**. **2Th 1:8** *2424*
name of our Lord **J** will be glorified **2Th 1:12** *2424*
of our God and *the* Lord **J** Christ. **2Th 1:12** *2424*
the coming of our Lord **J** Christ and **2Th 2:1** *2424*
the glory of our Lord **J** Christ. **2Th 2:14** *2424*
Now may our Lord **J** Christ Himself **2Th 2:16** *2424*
in the name of our Lord **J** Christ, **2Th 3:6** *2424*
exhort in the Lord **J** Christ to work **2Th 3:12** *2424*
The grace of our Lord **J** Christ be **2Th 3:18** *2424*
an apostle of Christ **J** according **1Tm 1:1** *2424*
God our Savior, and of Christ **J**, **1Tm 1:1** *2424*
the Father and Christ **J** our Lord. **1Tm 1:2** *2424*
I thank Christ **J** our Lord, who has **1Tm 1:12** *2424*
love which are *found* in Christ **J**. **1Tm 1:14** *2424*
that Christ **J** came into the world **1Tm 1:15** *2424*
J Christ might demonstrate His **1Tm 1:16** *2424*
God and men, *the* man Christ **J**, **1Tm 2:5** *2424*
in the faith that is in Christ **J**. **1Tm 3:13** *2424*
be a good servant of Christ **J**, **1Tm 4:6** *2424*
presence of God and of Christ **J** **1Tm 5:21** *2424*
words, those of our Lord **J** Christ, **1Tm 6:3** *2424*
and of Christ **J**, who testified the **1Tm 6:13** *2424*
appearing of our Lord **J** Christ, **1Tm 6:14** *2424*
Paul, an apostle of Christ **J** by the **2Tm 1:1** *2424*
the promise of life in Christ **J**, **2Tm 1:1** *2424*
the Father and Christ **J** our Lord. **2Tm 1:2** *2424*
which was granted us in Christ **J** **2Tm 1:9** *2424*
appearing of our Savior Christ **J**, **2Tm 1:10** *2424*
and love which are in Christ **J**. **2Tm 1:13** *2424*
in the grace that is in Christ **J**. **2Tm 2:1** *2424*
me, as a good soldier of Christ **J**. **2Tm 2:3** *2424*
Remember **J** Christ, risen from the **2Tm 2:8** *2424*
the salvation which is in Christ **J** **2Tm 2:10** *2424*
who desire to live godly in Christ **J** **2Tm 3:12** *2424*
faith which is in Christ **J**. **2Tm 3:15** *2424*
presence of God and of Christ **J**, **2Tm 4:1** *2424*
God and an apostle of **J** Christ, **Ti 1:1** *2424*
Father and Christ **J** our Savior. **Ti 1:4** *2424*
great God and Savior, Christ **J**, **Ti 2:13** *2424*
through **J** Christ our Savior, **Ti 3:6** *2424*
Paul, a prisoner of Christ **J**, **Phm 1:1** *2424*
our Father and the Lord **J** Christ. **Phm 1:3** *2424*
which you have toward the Lord **J** and **Phm 1:5** *2424*
now also a prisoner of Christ **J** **Phm 1:9** *2424*
my fellow prisoner in Christ **J**, **Phm 1:23** *2424*
The grace of the Lord **J** Christ be **Phm 1:25** *2424*
lower than the angels, *namely,* **J**, **Heb 2:9** *2424*
consider **J**, the Apostle and High **Heb 3:1** *2424*
the heavens, **J** the Son of God, **Heb 4:14** *2424*
where **J** has entered as a forerunner **Heb 6:20** *2424*
J has become the guarantee of a **Heb 7:22** *2424*
but **J**, on the other hand, because **Heb 7:24**
the body of **J** Christ once for all. **Heb 10:10** *2424*
the holy place by the blood of **J**, **Heb 10:19** *2424*
fixing our eyes on **J**, **Heb 12:2** *2424*

and to J, the mediator of a new Heb 12:24 2424
J Christ *is* the same yesterday and Heb 13:8 2424
Therefore J also, that He might Heb 13:12 2424
eternal covenant, *even* J our Lord, Heb 13:20 2424
in His sight, through J Christ, Heb 13:21 2424
of God and of the Lord J Christ, Jas 1:1 2424
faith in our glorious Lord J Christ Jas 2:1 2424
Peter, an apostle of J Christ, 1Pe 1:1 2424
to obey J Christ and be 1Pe 1:2 2424
and Father of our Lord J Christ, 1Pe 1:3 2424
through the resurrection of J Christ 1Pe 1:3 2424
at the revelation of J Christ; 1Pe 1:7 2424
you at the revelation of J Christ. 1Pe 1:13 2424
acceptable to God through J Christ. 1Pe 2:5 2424
the resurrection of J Christ, 1Pe 3:21 2424
may be glorified through J Christ, 1Pe 4:11 2424
and apostle of J Christ, 2Pe 1:1 2424
of our God and Savior, J Christ: 2Pe 1:1 2424
of God and of J our Lord; 2Pe 1:2 2424
knowledge of our Lord J Christ. 2Pe 1:8 2424
kingdom of our Lord and Savior J 2Pe 1:11 2424
Lord J Christ has made clear to me. 2Pe 1:14 2424
and coming of our Lord J Christ, 2Pe 1:16 2424
of the Lord and Savior J Christ, 2Pe 2:20 2424
of our Lord and Savior J Christ. 2Pe 3:18 2424
Father, and with His Son J Christ. 1Jn 1:3 2424
blood of J His Son cleanses us from 1Jn 1:7 2424
Father, J Christ the righteous; 1Jn 2:1 2424
who denies that J is the Christ? 1Jn 2:22 2424
in the name of His Son J Christ, 1Jn 3:23 2424
that J Christ has come in the flesh 1Jn 4:2 2424
every spirit that does not confess J 1Jn 4:3 2424
that J is the Son of God, 1Jn 4:15 2424
Whoever believes that J is the Christ 1Jn 5:1 2424
believes that J is the Son of God? 1Jn 5:5 2424
came by water and blood, J Christ; 1Jn 5:6 2424
who is true, in His Son J Christ. 1Jn 5:20 2424
God the Father and from J Christ, 2Jn 1:3 2424
J Christ *as* coming in the flesh. 2Jn 1:7 2424
Jude, a bond-servant of J Christ, Jude 1:1 2424
the Father, and kept for J Christ: Jude 1:1 2424
only Master and Lord, J Christ. Jude 1:4 2424
the apostles of our Lord J Christ, Jude 1:17 2424
our Lord J Christ to eternal life. Jude 1:21 2424
Savior, through J Christ our Lord, Jude 1:25 2424
The Revelation of J Christ, Rv 1:1 2424
and to the testimony of J Christ, Rv 1:2 2424
from J Christ, the faithful witness Rv 1:5 2424
and perseverance *which are* in J, Rv 1:9 2424
of God and the testimony of J. Rv 1:9 2424
and hold to the testimony of J. Rv 12:17 2424
of God and their faith in J. Rv 14:12 2424
the blood of the witnesses of J. Rv 17:6 2424
who hold the testimony of J; Rv 19:10 2424
the testimony of J is the spirit of Rv 19:10 2424
because of their testimony of J Rv 20:4 2424
"I, J, have sent My angel to Rv 22:16 2424
Amen. Come, Lord J. Rv 22:20 2424
grace of the Lord J be with all. Rv 22:21 2424

JESUS'
he fell down at J feet, saying, Lk 5:8 2424
and he fell at J feet, and *began* Lk 8:41 2424
not for J sake only, but that they Jn 12:9 2424
There was reclining on J bosom one Jn 13:23 2424
He, leaning back thus on J bosom, Jn 13:25 2424
as your bond-servants for J sake. 2Co 4:5 2424
delivered over to death for J sake, 2Co 4:11 2424

JETHER
So he said to J his firstborn, Jg 8:20 3500
of Ner, and to Amasa the son of J, 1Ki 2:5 3500
of Israel, and Amasa the son of J, 1Ki 2:32 3500
of Amasa was J the Ishmaelite. 1Ch 2:17 3500
of Shammai *were* J and Jonathan, 1Ch 2:32 3500
Jonathan, and J died without sons. 1Ch 2:32 3500
The sons of Ezrah *were* J, 1Ch 4:17 3500
The sons of J *were* Jephunneh, 1Ch 7:38 3500

JETHETH
chief Timna, chief Alvah, chief J, Gn 36:40 3509
chief Timna, chief Aliah, chief J, 1Ch 1:51 3509

JETHRO
the flock of J his father-in-law, Ex 3:1 3503
and returned to J his father-in-law and Ex 4:18 3500
And J said to Moses, Ex 4:18 3503
Now J, the priest of Midian, Ex 18:1 3503
J, Moses' father-in-law, took Ex 18:2 3503
Then J, Moses' father-in-law, came Ex 18:5 3503
"I, your father-in-law J, Ex 18:6 3503
J rejoiced over all the Ex 18:9 3503
J said, "Blessed be the LORD who Ex 18:10 3503
Then J, Moses' father-in-law, took Ex 18:12 3503

JETTISON
they began to j the cargo; Ac 27:18 1546

JETUR
Hadad and Tema, J, Naphish and Gn 25:15 3195
J, Naphish and Kedemah; 1Ch 1:31 3195
made war against the Hagrites, J, 1Ch 5:19 3195

JEUEL
Zerah *were* J and their relatives, 1Ch 9:6 3262
being their names, Eliphelet, J and Ezr 8:13 3262

JEUSH
bore J and Jalam and Korah. Gn 36:5 3266
to Esau, J and Jalam and Korah. Gn 36:14 3266
chief J, chief Jalam, chief Korah. Gn 36:18 3266
of Esau *were* Eliphaz, Reuel, J, 1Ch 1:35 3266
And the sons of Bilhan *were* J, 1Ch 7:10 3266
Ulam his firstborn, J the second and 1Ch 8:39 3266
of Shimei *were* Jahath, Zina, J and 1Ch 23:10 3266
but J and Beriah did not have many 1Ch 23:11 3266
J, Shemariah and Zaham. 2Ch 11:19 3266

JEUZ
J, Sachia, Mirmah. 1Ch 8:10 3263

JEW
Now there was at the citadel in Susa a J Es 2:5 3064
he had told them that he was a J. Es 3:4 3064
every time I see Mordecai the J Es 5:13 3064
and do so for Mordecai the J, Es 6:10 3064
Esther and to Mordecai the J, Es 8:7 3064
of Abihail, with Mordecai the J, Es 9:29 3064
just as Mordecai the J and Queen Es 9:31 3064
For Mordecai the J was second *only* Es 10:3 3064
should keep them, a J his brother, Jer 34:9 3064
grasp the garment of a J, Zch 8:23 3064
with a J about purification. Jn 3:25 2453
"How is it that You, being a J, Jn 4:9 2453
"I am not a J, am I? Jn 18:35 2453
unlawful it is for a man who is a J Ac 10:28 2453
he found a J named Aquila, Ac 18:2 2453
Now a J named Apollos, an Ac 18:24 2453
they recognized that he was a J, Ac 19:34 2453
"I am a J of Tarsus in Cilicia, a Ac 21:39 2453
"I am a J, born in Tarsus of Ac 22:3 2453
the J first and also to the Greek. Ro 1:16 2453
the J first and also of the Greek, Ro 2:9 2453
the J first and also to the Greek. Ro 2:10 2453
But if you bear the name "J" Ro 2:17 2453
is not a J who is one outwardly, Ro 2:28 2453
But he is a J who is one inwardly; Ro 2:29 2453
Then what advantage has the J? Ro 3:1 2453
distinction between J and Greek; Ro 10:12 2453
To the Jews I became as a J, 1Co 9:20 2453
you, being a J, live like the Gentiles Ga 2:14 2453
There is neither J nor Greek, Ga 3:28 2453
no *distinction between* Greek and J, Col 3:11 2453

JEWEL
through the J of *his* kingdom; Da 11:20 1925

JEWELER
"As a j engraves a signet, you Ex 28:11
2796, 68

JEWELRY
herself with her earrings and j, Hos 2:13 2484
the hair, and wearing gold j, 1Pe 3:3 5553

JEWELS
She is more precious than j; Pr 3:15 6443
"For wisdom is better than j; Pr 8:11 6443
is gold, and an abundance of j; Pr 20:15 6443
For her worth is far above j. Pr 31:10 6443
curves of your hips are like j, SS 7:1 2481
surely put on all of them as j and Is 49:18 5716
a bride adorns herself with her j. Is 61:10 3627
"You also took your beautiful j Ezk 16:17 3627
your clothing, take away your j, Ezk 16:39
3627, 8597
and take away your beautiful j. Ezk 23:26 3627

JEWESS
Drusilla, his wife who was a J, Ac 24:24 2453

JEWISH
His J wife bore Jered the 1Ch 4:18 3057
wives against their J brothers. Ne 5:1 3064
have redeemed our J brothers who Ne 5:8 3064
begun to fall, is of J origin, Es 6:13 3064
carried into exile 745 J people; Jer 52:30 3064
he sent some J elders asking Him Lk 7:3 2453
for the J custom of purification, Jn 2:6 2453
of the J day of preparation, Jn 19:42 2453
and gave many alms to the J Ac 10:2
the J people were expecting." Ac 12:11 2453
a J false prophet whose name was Ac 13:6 2453
of a J woman who was a believer, Ac 16:1 2453
But also some of the J exorcists, Ac 19:13 2453
of one Sceva, a J chief priest, Ac 19:14 2453
rescuing you from the J people Ac 26:17
to proclaim light both to the J Ac 26:23
not paying attention to J myths Ti 1:14 2451

JEWS
he died along with the J and the 2Ki 25:25 3064
that the J who came up from you Ezr 4:12 3062
went in haste to Jerusalem to the J Ezr 4:23 3062
prophesied to the J who were in Ezr 5:1 3062
God was on the elders of the J, Ezr 5:5 3062
let the governor of the J and the Ezr 6:7 3062
elders of the J rebuild this house of Ezr 6:7 3062
And the elders of the J were Ezr 6:14 3062
concerning the J who had escaped Ne 1:2 3064
nor had I as yet told the J, Ne 2:16 3064
and very angry and mocked the J. Ne 4:1 3064
"What are these feeble J doing? Ne 4:2 3064
When the J who lived near them Ne 4:12 3064
hundred and fifty J and officials, Ne 5:17 3064
and the J are planning to rebel; Ne 6:6 3064
J had married women from Ashdod, Ne 13:23 3064
Haman sought to destroy all the J, Es 3:6 3064
the Agagite, the enemy of the J. Es 3:10 3064
kill and to annihilate all the J, Es 3:13 3064
was great mourning among the J, Es 4:3 3064
for the destruction of the J. Es 4:7 3064
escape any more than all the J. Es 4:13 3064
and deliverance will arise for the J Es 4:14 3064
all the J who are found in Susa, Es 4:16 3064
of Haman, the enemy of the J, Es 8:1 3064
he had devised against the J. Es 8:3 3064
which he wrote to destroy the J Es 8:5 3064
out his hands against the J. Es 8:7 3064
you write to the J as you see fit, Es 8:8 3064
that Mordecai commanded to the J, Es 8:9 3064
as well as to the J according to Es 8:9 3064
In them the king granted the J who Es 8:11 3064
so that the J would be ready for Es 8:13 3064
For the J there was light and Es 8:16 3064
was gladness and joy for the J, Es 8:17 3064
the peoples of the land became J, Es 8:17 3054
dread of the J had fallen on them. Es 8:17 3064
the enemies of the J hoped to gain Es 9:1 3064
the J themselves gained the mastery Es 9:1 3064
The J assembled in their cities Es 9:2 3064
the king's business assisted the J, Es 9:3 3064
Thus the J struck all their Es 9:5 3064
J killed and destroyed five hundred Es 9:6 3064
"The J have killed and destroyed Es 9:12 3064
granted to the J who are in Susa Es 9:13 3064
The J who were in Susa Es 9:15 3064
Now the rest of the J who *were* in Es 9:16 3064
But the J who were in Susa Es 9:18 3064
the J of the rural areas, Es 9:19 3064
and he sent letters to all the J Es 9:20 3064
the J rid themselves of their enemies Es 9:22 3064
Thus the J undertook what they had Es 9:23 3064
the adversary of all the J, Es 9:24 3064
schemed against the J to destroy Es 9:24 3064
he had devised against the J, Es 9:25 3064
the J established and made a Es 9:27 3064
were not to fail from among the J, Es 9:28 3064
He sent letters to all the J, Es 9:30 3064
Ahasuerus, and great among the J Es 10:3 3064
before all the J who were sitting Jer 32:12 3064
"I dread the J who have gone over Jer 38:19 3064
Likewise, also all the J who were Jer 40:11 3064
Then all the J returned from all Jer 40:12 3064
so that all the J who are gathered Jer 40:15 3063
Ishmael also struck down all the J Jer 41:3 3064
in the sight of some *of the* J; Jer 43:9 3064
the J living in the land of Egypt, Jer 44:1 3064
in the seventh year 3,023 J; Jer 52:28 3064
and brought charges against the J. Da 3:8 3062
"There are certain J whom you Da 3:12 3062
who has been born King of the J? Mt 2:2 2453
"Are You the King of the J?" Mt 27:11 2453
"Hail, King of the J!" Mt 27:29 2453
JESUS THE KING OF THE J." Mt 27:37 2453
was widely spread among the J, Mt 28:15 2453
(For the Pharisees and all the J Mk 7:3 2453
"Are You the King of the J?" Mk 15:2 2453
release for you the King of the J?" Mk 15:9 2453
whom you call the King of the J?" Mk 15:12 2453
"Hail, King of the J!" Mk 15:18 2453
"THE KING OF THE J." Mk 15:26 2453
"Are You the King of the J?" Lk 23:3 2453
"If You are the King of the J, Lk 23:37 2453
"THIS IS THE KING OF THE J." Lk 23:38 2453
from Arimathea, a city of the J, Lk 23:51 2453
when the J sent to him priests and Jn 1:19 2453
The Passover of the J was near, Jn 2:13 2453
The J then said to Him, Jn 2:18 2453
The J then said, Jn 2:20 2453
named Nicodemus, a ruler of the J; Jn 3:1 2453
J have no dealings with Samaritans Jn 4:9 2453
know, for salvation is from the J. Jn 4:22 2453
things there was a feast of the J, Jn 5:1 2453
So the J were saying to the man Jn 5:10 2453
and told the J that it was Jesus Jn 5:15 2453
the J were persecuting Jesus, Jn 5:16 2453
J were seeking all the more to kill Jn 5:18 2453
the Passover, the feast of the J, Jn 6:4 2453
Therefore the J were grumbling Jn 6:41 2453
Then the J *began* to argue Jn 6:52 2453
the J were seeking to kill Him. Jn 7:1 2453
Now the feast of the J, Jn 7:2 2453
So the J were seeking Him Jn 7:11 2453
openly of Him for fear of the J. Jn 7:13 2453
The J then were astonished, Jn 7:15 2453
J then said to one another, Jn 7:35 2453
So the J were saying, Jn 8:22 2453
to those J who had believed Him, Jn 8:31 2453
The J answered and said to Him, Jn 8:48 2453
The J said to Him, Jn 8:52 2453
So the J said to Him, Jn 8:57 2453
The J then did not believe *it* Jn 9:18 2453
because they were afraid of the J; Jn 9:22 2453
for the J had already agreed that Jn 9:22 2453
A division occurred again among the J Jn 10:19 2453
J then gathered around Him, Jn 10:24 2453
The J picked up stones again to Jn 10:31 2453
The J answered Him, Jn 10:33 2453
the J were just now seeking to Jn 11:8 2453
the J had come to Martha and Mary, Jn 11:19 2453
Then the J who were with her in Jn 11:31 2453
and the J who came with her Jn 11:33 2453
So the J were saying, Jn 11:36 2453
Therefore many of the J Jn 11:45 2453
to walk publicly among the J, Jn 11:54 2453
the Passover of the J was near, Jn 11:55 2453
the J then learned that He was there; Jn 12:9 2453
him many of the J were going away and Jn 12:11 2453
and as I said to the J, Jn 13:33 2453
and the officers of the J, Jn 18:12 2453
advised the J that it was expedient Jn 18:14 2453
where all the J come together; Jn 18:20 2453
The J said to him, Jn 18:31 2453
"Are You the King of the J?" Jn 18:33 2453
not be handed over to the J; Jn 18:36 2453
this, he went out again to the J and Jn 18:38 2453
release for you the King of the J?" Jn 19:39 2453
"Hail, King of the J!" Jn 19:3 2453
The J answered him, Jn 19:7 2453

release Him, but the J cried out saying Jn 19:12 2453
And he said to the J, Jn 19:14 2453
THE KING OF THE J." Jn 19:19 2453
Therefore many of the J read Jn 19:20 2453
chief priests of the J were saying Jn 19:21 2453
'The King of the J'; Jn 19:21 2453
'I am King of the J.' " Jn 19:21 2453
Then the J, because it was Jn 19:31 2453
a secret *one* for fear of the J, Jn 19:38 2453
as is the burial custom of the J. Jn 19:40 2453
disciples were, for fear of the J, Jn 20:19 2453
there were J living in Jerusalem, Ac 2:5 2453
from Rome, both J and proselytes, Ac 2:10 2453
on the part of the Hellenistic J Ac 6:1 1675
and confounding the J who lived at Ac 9:22 2453
the J plotted together to do away Ac 9:23 2453
arguing with the Hellenistic J; Ac 9:29 1675
of by the entire nation of the J, Ac 10:22 2453
land of the J and in Jerusalem. Ac 10:39 2453
word to no one except to J alone. Ac 11:19 2453
When he saw that it pleased the J, Ac 12:3 2453
of God in the synagogues of the J; Ac 13:5 2453
many of the J and of the Ac 13:43 2453
But when the J saw the crowds, Ac 13:45 2453
But the J incited the devout women Ac 13:50 2453
the synagogue of the J together, Ac 14:1 2453
believed, both of J and of Greeks. Ac 14:1 2453
But the J who disbelieved stirred Ac 14:2 2453
and some sided with the J, Ac 14:4 2453
and the J with their rulers, Ac 14:5 2453
J came from Antioch and Iconium, Ac 14:19 2453
circumcised him because of the J Ac 16:3 2453
our city into confusion, being J, Ac 16:20 2453
there was a synagogue of the J. Ac 17:1 2453
But the J, becoming jealous and Ac 17:5 2453
went into the synagogue of the J. Ac 17:10 2453
But when the J of Thessalonica Ac 17:13 2453
the J and the God-fearing *Gentiles*, Ac 17:17 2453
commanded all the J to leave Rome. Ac 18:2 2453
trying to persuade J and Greeks. Ac 18:4 2453
testifying to the J that Jesus was the Ac 18:5 2453
the J with one accord rose up Ac 18:12 2453
his mouth, Gallio said to the J, Ac 18:14 2453
of wrong or of vicious crime, O J, Ac 18:14 2453
synagogue and reasoned with the J. Ac 18:19 2453
refuted the J in public, Ac 18:28 2453
of the Lord, both J and Greeks. Ac 19:10 2453
known to all, both J and Greeks, Ac 19:17 2453
since the J had put him forward; Ac 19:33 2453
was formed against him by the J Ac 20:3 2453
me through the plots of the J; Ac 20:19 2453
solemnly testifying to both J and Ac 20:21 2453
J at Jerusalem will bind the man Ac 21:11 2453
thousands there are among the J Ac 21:20 2453
that you are teaching all the J Ac 21:21 2453
were almost over, the J from Asia, Ac 21:27 2453
of by all the J who lived there, Ac 22:12 2453
why he had been accused by the J, Ac 22:30 2453
the J formed a conspiracy and Ac 23:12 2453
"The J have agreed to ask you to Ac 23:20 2453
When this man was arrested by the J Ac 23:27 2453
stirs up dissension among all the J Ac 24:5 2453
The J also joined in the attack, Ac 24:9 2453
there were some J from Asia Ac 24:18 2453
and wishing to do the J a favor, Ac 24:27 2453
J brought charges against Paul, Ac 25:2 2453
the J who had come down from Ac 25:7 2453
either against the Law of the J or Ac 25:8 2453
wishing to do the J a favor, Ac 25:9 2453
I have done no wrong to *the* J, Ac 25:10 2453
the elders of the J brought charges Ac 25:15 2453
people of the J appealed to me, Ac 25:24 2453
of which I am accused by the J, Ac 26:2 2453
customs and questions among *the* J; Ac 26:3 2453
all J know my manner of life from Ac 26:4 2453
O King, I am being accused by J. Ac 26:7 2453
"For this reason *some* J seized me Ac 26:21 2453
who were the leading men of the J, Ac 28:17 2453
"But when the J objected, I was Ac 28:19 2453
these words, the J departed, Ac 28:29 2453
J and Greeks are all under sin; Ro 3:9 2453
Or is God *the God* of J only? Ro 3:29 2453
called, not from among J only, Ro 9:24 2453
For indeed J ask for signs and 1Co 1:22 2453
crucified, to J a stumbling block and 1Co 1:23 2453
are the called, both J and Greeks, 1Co 1:24 2453
To the J I became as a Jew, 1Co 9:20 2453
as a Jew, so that I might win J; 1Co 9:20 2453
Give no offense either to J or to 1Co 10:32 2453
one body, whether J or Greeks, 1Co 12:13 2453
I received from the J thirty-nine 2Co 11:24 2453
rest of the J joined him in hypocrisy Ga 2:13 2453
the Gentiles and not like the J, Ga 2:14 2452
compel the Gentiles to live like J? Ga 2:14 2450
"We *are* J by nature and not Ga 2:15 2453
even as they *did* from the J, 1Th 2:14 2453
who say they are J and are not, Rv 2:9 2453
of Satan, who say that they are J and Rv 3:9 2453

JEWS'

the J enemy; but they did not lay Es 9:10 3064

JEZANIAH

and J the son of the Maacathite, Jer 40:8 3153
of Kareah, J the son of Hoshaiah, Jer 42:1 3153

JEZEBEL

that he married J the daughter of 1Ki 16:31 348
when J destroyed the prophets of 1Ki 18:4 348
J killed the prophets of the LORD, 1Ki 18:13 348
told J all that Elijah had done, 1Ki 19:1 348
Then J sent a messenger to Elijah, 1Ki 19:2 348
But J his wife came to him and 1Ki 21:5 348
J his wife said to him, 1Ki 21:7 348
did as J had sent *word* to them, 1Ki 21:11 348
Then they sent *word* to J, 1Ki 21:14 348
When J heard 1Ki 21:15 348
and was dead, J said to Ahab, 1Ki 21:15 348
"Of J also has the LORD spoken, 1Ki 21:23 348
'The dogs will eat J in the district 1Ki 21:23 348
because J his wife incited him. 1Ki 21:25 348
of the LORD, at the hand of J. 2Ki 9:7 348
The dogs shall eat J in the territory 2Ki 9:10 348
the harlotries of your mother J 2Ki 9:22 348
came to Jezreel, J heard *of it,* 2Ki 9:30 348
the dogs shall eat the flesh of J; 2Ki 9:36 348
the corpse of J will be as dung on 2Ki 9:37 348
"This is J." 2Ki 9:37 348
that you tolerate the woman J, Rv 2:20 2403

JEZEBEL'S

the Asherah, who eat at J table." 1Ki 18:19 348

JEZER

and Guni and J and Shillem. Gn 46:24 3337
of J, the family of the Jezerites; Nu 26:49 3337
of Naphtali *were* Jahziel, Guni, J, 1Ch 7:13 3337

JEZERITES

of Jezer, the family of the J; Nu 26:49 3340

JEZIEL

and J and Pelet, the sons of 1Ch 12:3 3149

JEZRAHIAH

singers sang, with J *their* leader, Ne 12:42 3156

JEZREEL

and J and Jokdeam and Zanoah, Jos 15:56 3157
who are in the valley of J." Jos 17:16 3157
Their territory was to J and Jos 19:18 3157
and camped in the valley of J. Jg 6:33 3157
David had also taken Ahinoam of J, 1Sa 25:43 3157
by the spring which is in J. 1Sa 29:1 3157
And the Philistines went up to J. 1Sa 29:11 3157
over the Ashurites, over J, 2Sa 2:9 3157
of Saul and Jonathan came from J, 2Sa 4:4 3157
which is beside Zarethan below J, 1Ki 4:12 3157
And Ahab rode and went to J. 1Ki 18:45 3157
up his loins and outran Ahab to J. 1Ki 18:46 3157
a vineyard which *was* in J beside the 1Ki 21:1 3157
eat Jezebel in the district of J.' 1Ki 21:23 3157
Joram returned to be healed in J 2Ki 8:29 3157
of Ahab in J because he was sick. 2Ki 8:29 3157
eat Jezebel in the territory of J, 2Ki 9:10 3157
but King Joram had returned to J 2Ki 9:15 3157
the city to go tell *it* in J." 2Ki 9:15 3157
rode in a chariot and went to J, 2Ki 9:16 3157
was standing on the tower in J and 2Ki 9:17 3157
When Jehu came to J, 2Ki 9:30 3157
'In the property of J the dogs 2Ki 9:36 3157
of the field in the property of J, 2Ki 9:37 3157
to Samaria, to the rulers of J, 2Ki 10:1 3157
come to me at J tomorrow about 2Ki 10:6 3157
and sent *them* to him at J. 2Ki 10:7 3157
of the house of Ahab in J, 2Ki 10:11 3157
J, Ishma and Idbash; 1Ch 4:3 3157
So he returned to be healed in J 2Ch 22:6 3157
see Jehoram the son of Ahab in J, 2Ch 22:6 3157
LORD said to him, "Name him J; Hos 1:4 3157
of Jehu for the bloodshed of J, Hos 1:4 3157
of Israel in the valley of J." Hos 1:5 3157
For great will be the day of J. Hos 1:11 3157
oil, And they will respond to J. Hos 2:22 3157

JEZREELITE

that Naboth the J had a vineyard 1Ki 21:1 3158
Naboth the J had spoken to him; 1Ki 21:4 3158
"Because I spoke to Naboth the J and 1Ki 21:6 3158
the vineyard of Naboth the J." 1Ki 21:7 3158
of the vineyard of Naboth, the J, 1Ki 21:15 3158
to the vineyard of Naboth the J, 1Ki 21:16 3158
in the property of Naboth the J. 2Ki 9:21 3158
of the field of Naboth the J, 2Ki 9:25 3158

JEZREELITESS

with his two wives, Ahinoam the J, 1Sa 27:3 3159
Ahinoam the J and Abigail the 1Sa 30:5 3159
Ahinoam the J and Abigail the 2Sa 2:2 3159
was Amnon, by Ahinoam the J; 2Sa 3:2 3159
was Amnon, by Ahinoam the J; 1Ch 3:1 3159

JIDLAPH

and Pildash and J and Bethuel." Gn 22:22 3044

JOAB

And J the son of Zeruiah and the 2Sa 2:13 3097
Then Abner said to J, 2Sa 2:14 3097
And J said, "Let them arise." 2Sa 2:14 3097
there, J and Abishai and Asahel; 2Sa 2:18 3097
up my face to your brother J?" 2Sa 2:22 3097
But J and Abishai pursued Abner, 2Sa 2:24 3097
Then Abner called to J and said, 2Sa 2:26 3097
J said, "As God lives, if you had not 2Sa 2:27 3097
So J blew the trumpet; 2Sa 2:28 3097
J returned from following Abner; 2Sa 2:30 3097
Then J and his men went all night 2Sa 2:32 3097
the servants of David and J came 2Sa 3:22 3097
When J and all the army that was 2Sa 3:23 3097
was with him arrived, they told J, 2Sa 3:23 3097
Then J came to the king and said, 2Sa 3:24 3097
When J came out from David, he 2Sa 3:26 3097
J took him aside into the middle 2Sa 3:27 3097
May it fall on the head of J and on 2Sa 3:29 3097
not fail from the house of J one 2Sa 3:29 3097
So J and Abishai his brother killed 2Sa 3:30 3097
Then David said to J and to all 2Sa 3:31 3097
J the son of Zeruiah *was* over 2Sa 8:16 3097
of it, he sent J and all the army, 2Sa 10:7 3097
Now when J saw that the battle was 2Sa 10:9 3097
So J and the people who were with 2Sa 10:13 3097
Then J returned from *fighting* 2Sa 10:14 3097
that David sent J and his servants 2Sa 11:1 3097
Then David sent to J, 2Sa 11:6 3097
So J sent Uriah to David. 2Sa 11:6 3097
asked concerning the welfare of J 2Sa 11:7 3097
and my lord J and the servants of 2Sa 11:11 3097
morning David wrote a letter to J 2Sa 11:14 3097
was as J kept watch on the city, 2Sa 11:16 3097
went out and fought against J, 2Sa 11:17 3097
Then J sent and reported to David 2Sa 11:18 3097
all that J had sent him *to tell.* 2Sa 11:22 3097
"Thus you shall say to J, 2Sa 11:25 3097
Now J fought against Rabbah of the 2Sa 12:26 3097
J sent messengers to David and 2Sa 12:27 3097
Now J the son of Zeruiah perceived 2Sa 14:1 3097
So J sent to Tekoa and brought a 2Sa 14:2 3097
So J put the words in her mouth. 2Sa 14:3 3097
hand of J with you in all this?" 2Sa 14:19 3097
your servant J who commanded me, 2Sa 14:19 3097
servant J has done this thing. 2Sa 14:20 3097
Then the king said to J, 2Sa 14:21 3097
J fell on his face to the ground, 2Sa 14:22 3097
J said, "Today your servant knows 2Sa 14:22 3097
So J arose and went to Geshur and 2Sa 14:23 3097
Then Absalom sent for J, 2Sa 14:29 3097
Then J arose, came to Absalom at 2Sa 14:31 3097
Absalom answered J, 2Sa 14:32 3097
J came to the king and told him, 2Sa 14:33 3097
Amasa over the army in place of J. 2Sa 17:25 3097
one third under the command of J, 2Sa 18:2 3097
charged J and Abishai and Ittai, 2Sa 18:5 3097
man saw *it,* he told J and said, 2Sa 18:10 3097
Then J said to the man who had 2Sa 18:11 3097
The man said to J, 2Sa 18:12 3097
J said, "I will not waste time here 2Sa 18:14 3097
Then J blew the trumpet, and the 2Sa 18:16 3097
for J restrained the people. 2Sa 18:16 3097
But J said to him, 2Sa 18:20 3097
Then J said to the Cushite, 2Sa 18:21 3097
So the Cushite bowed to J and ran. 2Sa 18:21 3097
son of Zadok said once more to J, 2Sa 18:22 3097
J said, "Why would you run, my 2Sa 18:22 3097
"When J sent the king's servant, 2Sa 18:29 3097
Then it was told J, 2Sa 19:1 3097
Then J came into the house to the 2Sa 19:5 3097
me continually in place of J.' " 2Sa 19:13 3097
Now J was dressed in his military 2Sa 20:8 3097
J said to Amasa, 2Sa 20:9 3097
And J took Amasa by the beard with 2Sa 20:9 3097
Then J and Abishai his brother 2Sa 20:10 3097
"Whoever favors J and whoever is 2Sa 20:11 3097
is for David, *let him* follow J." 2Sa 20:11 3097
all the men passed on after J to 2Sa 20:13 3097
and all the people who were with J 2Sa 20:15 3097
Please tell J, 'Come here that I may 2Sa 20:16 3097
and the woman said, "Are you J?" 2Sa 20:17 3097
J replied, 2Sa 20:20 3097
And the woman said to J, 2Sa 20:21 3097
son of Bichri and threw it to J. 2Sa 20:22 3097
J also returned to the king at 2Sa 20:22 3097
Now J was over the whole army of 2Sa 20:23 3097
Abishai, the brother of J, 2Sa 23:18 3097
brother of J was among the thirty; 2Sa 23:24 3097
armor bearers of J the son of 2Sa 23:37 3097
The king said to J the 2Sa 24:2 3097
But J said to the king, 2Sa 24:3 3097
the king's word prevailed against J 2Sa 24:4 3097
So J and the commanders of the 2Sa 24:4 3097
And J gave the number of the 2Sa 24:9 3097
He had conferred with J the 1Ki 1:7 3097
and J the commander of the army, 1Ki 1:19 3097
When J heard the sound of the 1Ki 1:41 3097
J the son of Zeruiah did to me, 1Ki 2:5 3097
and for J the son of Zeruiah!" 1Ki 2:22 3097
Now the news came to J, 1Ki 2:28 3097
Joab, for J had followed Adonijah, 1Ki 2:28 3097
And J fled to the tent of the LORD 1Ki 2:28 3097
told King Solomon that J had fled 1Ki 2:29 3097
"Thus spoke J, and thus he 1Ki 2:30 3097
blood which J shed without cause. 1Ki 2:31 3097
their blood return on the head of J 1Ki 2:33 3097
and J the commander of the army 1Ki 11:15 3097
(for J and all Israel stayed there 1Ki 11:16 3097
J the commander of the army was 1Ki 11:21 3097
sons of Zeruiah *were* Abshai, J and 1Ch 2:16 3097
Seraiah became the father of J the 1Ch 4:14 3097
J the son of Zeruiah went up 1Ch 11:6 3097
J repaired the rest of the city. 1Ch 11:8 3097
As for Abshai the brother of J, 1Ch 11:20 3097
were Asahel the brother of J, 1Ch 11:26 3097
the armor bearer of J the son of 1Ch 11:39 3097
J the son of Zeruiah *was* over 1Ch 18:15 3097
of it, he sent J and all the army, 1Ch 19:8 3097
Now when J saw that the battle was 1Ch 19:10 3097
So J and the people who were with 1Ch 19:14 3097
Then J came to Jerusalem. 1Ch 19:15 3097
that J led out the army and 1Ch 20:1 3097
And J struck Rabbah and overthrew 1Ch 20:1 3097
So David said to J and to the 1Ch 21:2 3097
J said, "May the LORD add to His 1Ch 21:3 3097
king's word prevailed against J. 1Ch 21:4 3097
J departed and went throughout all 1Ch 21:4 3097
J gave the number of the 1Ch 21:5 3097
king's command was abhorrent to J. 1Ch 21:6 3097
of Ner and J the son of Zeruiah, 1Ch 26:28 3097
month *was* Asahel the brother of J, 1Ch 27:7 3097

J the son of Zeruiah had begun to | **1Ch 27:24** | 3097
and **J** was the commander of the | **1Ch 27:34** | 3097
of the sons of Jeshua *and* **J**, | **Ezr 2:6** | 3097
of the sons of **J**, Obadiah the son | **Ezr 8:9** | 3097
of the sons of Jeshua and **J**, | **Ne 7:11** | 3097

JOAB'S
the son of Zeruiah, **J** brother, | **1Sa 26:6** | 3097
"See, **J** field is next to mine, | **2Sa 14:30** | 3097
sister of Zeruiah, **J** mother. | **2Sa 17:25** | 3097
the son of Zeruiah, **J** brother, | **2Sa 18:2** | 3097
men who carried **J** armor gathered | **2Sa 18:15** | 3097
So **J** men went out after him, along | **2Sa 20:7** | 3097
the sword which was in **J** hand | **2Sa 20:10** | 3097
stood by him one of **J** young men, | **2Sa 20:11** | 3097

JOAH
J the son of Asaph the recorder, | **2Ki 18:18** | 3098
son of Hilkiah, and Shebnah and **J**, | **2Ki 18:26** | 3098
the scribe and **J** the son of Asaph, | **2Ki 18:37** | 3098
J his son, Iddo his son, Zerah his | **1Ch 6:21** | 3098
Jehozabad the second, **J** the third, | **1Ch 26:4** | 3098
J the son of Zimmah and Eden the | **2Ch 29:12** | 3098
of Zimmah and Eden the son of **J**; | **2Ch 29:12** | 3098
and **J** the son of Joahaz the | **2Ch 34:8** | 3098
scribe, and **J** the son of Asaph, | **Is 36:3** | 3098
Shebna and **J** said to Rabshakeh, | **Is 36:11** | 3098
the scribe and **J** the son of Asaph, | **Is 36:22** | 3098

JOAHAZ
of Joash son of **J** king of Israel, | **2Ki 14:1** | 3099
Joah the son of **J** the recorder, | **2Ch 34:8** | 3099
the land took **J** the son of Josiah, | **2Ch 36:1** | 3059
J was twenty-three years old when | **2Ch 36:2** | 3099
But Neco took **J** his brother and | **2Ch 36:4** | 3099

JOANAN
the son of **J**, the son of Rhesa, | **Lk 3:27** | *2489a*

JOANNA
and **J** the wife of Chuza, Herod's | **Lk 8:3** | *2489b*
J and Mary the *mother* of James; | **Lk 24:10** | *2489b*

JOASH
which belonged to **J** the Abiezrite | **Jg 6:11** | 3060
the son of **J** did this thing." | **Jg 6:29** | 3060
the men of the city said to **J**, | **Jg 6:30** | 3060
But **J** said to all who stood | **Jg 6:31** | 3060
the sword of Gideon the son of **J**, | **Jg 7:14** | 3060
Then Gideon the son of **J** returned | **Jg 8:13** | 3060
Then Jerubbaal the son of **J** went | **Jg 8:29** | 3060
And Gideon the son of **J** died at a | **Jg 8:32** | 3060
in the tomb of his father **J**, | **Jg 8:32** | 3060
the city and to **J** the king's son; | **1Ki 22:26** | 3060
took **J** the son of Ahaziah and | **2Ki 11:2** | 3060
the acts of **J** and all that he did, | **2Ki 12:19** | 3060
and struck down **J** at the house of | **2Ki 12:20** | 3060
year of **J** the son of Ahaziah, | **2Ki 13:1** | 3060
and **J** his son became king in his | **2Ki 13:9** | 3060
year of **J** king of Judah, | **2Ki 13:10** | 3060
Now the rest of the acts of **J** and | **2Ki 13:12** | 3060
So **J** slept with his fathers, and | **2Ki 13:13** | 3060
and **J** was buried in Samaria with | **2Ki 13:13** | 3060
J the king of Israel came down to | **2Ki 13:14** | 3060
Three times **J** defeated him and | **2Ki 13:25** | 3060
the second year of **J** son of Joahaz | **2Ki 14:1** | 3060
Amaziah the son of **J** king of Judah | **2Ki 14:1** | 3060
to all that **J** his father had done. | **2Ki 14:3** | 3060
Amaziah the son of **J** king of | **2Ki 14:17** | 3060
the son of **J** king of Judah, | **2Ki 14:23** | 3060
Jeroboam the son of **J** king of | **2Ki 14:23** | 3060
the hand of Jeroboam the son of **J**. | **2Ki 14:27** | 3060
son, Ahaziah his son, **J** his son, | **1Ch 3:11** | 3060
and Jokim, the men of Cozeba, **J**, | **1Ch 4:22** | 3060
sons of Becher *were* Zemirah, **J**, | **1Ch 7:8** | 3135
The chief was Ahiezer, then **J**, | **1Ch 12:3** | 3060
and **J** had charge of the stores of | **1Ch 27:28** | 3135
the city and to **J** the king's son; | **2Ch 18:25** | 3060
took **J** the son of Ahaziah, | **2Ch 22:11** | 3060
J *was* seven years old when he | **2Ch 24:1** | 3060
J did what was right in the | **2Ch 24:2** | 3060
J decided to restore the house of the | **2Ch 24:4** | 3060
Thus **J** the king did not remember | **2Ch 24:22** | 3060
Thus they executed judgment on **J**. | **2Ch 24:24** | 3060
sent to **J** the son of Jehoahaz the son | **2Ch 25:17** | 3060
J the king of Israel sent to | **2Ch 25:18** | 3060
deliver them into the hand *of* **J** | **2Ch 25:20**
So **J** king of Israel went up, and | **2Ch 25:21** | 3060
Then **J** king of Israel captured | **2Ch 25:23** | 3060
the son of **J** the son of Jehoahaz, | **2Ch 25:23** | 3060
the son of **J** king of Judah, | **2Ch 25:25** | 3060
years after the death of **J**, | **2Ch 25:25** | 3060
the days of Jeroboam the son of **J**, | **Hos 1:1** | 3060
in the days of Jeroboam son of **J**, | **Am 1:1** | 3060

JOB
all the workmen from **j** to job; | **2Ch 34:13** | 5656
all the workmen from job to **j**; | **2Ch 34:13** | 5656
the land of Uz whose name was **J** | **Jb 1:1** | 347
J would send and consecrate | **Jb 1:5** | 347
J said, "Perhaps my sons have sinned | **Jb 1:5** | 347
Thus **J** did continually. | **Jb 1:5** | 347
"Have you considered My servant **J**? | **Jb 1:8** | 347
"Does **J** fear God for nothing? | **Jb 1:9** | 347
a messenger came to **J** and said, | **Jb 1:14** | 347
Then **J** arose and tore his robe and | **Jb 1:20** | 347
Through all this **J** did not sin nor | **Jb 1:22** | 347
"Have you considered My servant **J**? | **Jb 2:3** | 347
and smote **J** with sore boils from | **Jb 2:7** | 347
this **J** did not sin with his lips. | **Jb 2:10** | 347
Afterward **J** opened his mouth and | **Jb 3:1** | 347
And **J** said, | **Jb 3:2** | 347
Then **J** answered, | **Jb 6:1** | 347
Then **J** answered, | **Jb 9:1** | 347
Then **J** responded, | **Jb 12:1** | 347
Then **J** answered, | **Jb 16:1** | 347
Then **J** responded, | **Jb 19:1** | 347
Then **J** answered, | **Jb 21:1** | 347
Then **J** replied, | **Jb 23:1** | 347
Then **J** responded, | **Jb 26:1** | 347
Then **J** continued his discourse and | **Jb 27:1** | 347
And **J** again took up his discourse | **Jb 29:1** | 347
The words of **J** are ended. | **Jb 31:40** | 347
three men ceased answering **J**, | **Jb 32:1** | 347
against **J** his anger burned because | **Jb 32:2** | 347
answer, and yet had condemned **J**. | **Jb 32:3** | 347
Now Elihu had waited to speak to **J** | **Jb 32:4** | 347
there was no one who refuted **J**, | **Jb 32:12** | 347
"However now, **J**, please hear my | **Jb 33:1** | 347
"Pay attention, O **J**, | **Jb 33:31** | 347
"For **J** has said, | **Jb 34:5** | 347
"What man is like **J**, | **Jb 34:7** | 347
'**J** speaks without knowledge, And | **Jb 34:35** | 347
'**J** ought to be tried to the limit, | **Jb 34:36** | 347
So **J** opens his mouth emptily; | **Jb 35:16** | 347
"Listen to this, O **J**, | **Jb 37:14** | 347
answered **J** out of the whirlwind | **Jb 38:1** | 347
Then the LORD said to **J**, | **Jb 40:1** | 347
Then **J** answered the LORD and said, | **Jb 40:3** | 347
LORD answered **J** out of the storm and | **Jb 40:6** | 347
Then **J** answered the LORD and | **Jb 42:1** | 347
LORD had spoken these words to **J**, | **Jb 42:7** | 347
what is right as My servant **J** has. | **Jb 42:7** | 347
rams, and go to My servant **J**, | **Jb 42:8** | 347
My servant **J** will pray for you. | **Jb 42:8** | 347
is right, as My servant **J** has." | **Jb 42:8** | 347
and the LORD accepted **J**. | **Jb 42:9** | 347
The LORD restored the fortunes of **J** | **Jb 42:10** | 347
increased all that **J** had twofold. | **Jb 42:10** | 347
LORD blessed the latter *days* of **J** | **Jb 42:12** | 347
After this, **J** lived 140 years, | **Jb 42:16** | 347
And **J** died, an old man and full of | **Jb 42:17** | 347
Daniel and **J** were in its midst, | **Ezk 14:14** | 347
Daniel and **J** were in its midst, | **Ezk 14:20** | 347
have heard of the endurance of **J** | **Jas 5:11** | *2492a*

JOBAB
and Ophir and Havilah and **J**; | **Gn 10:29** | 3103
and **J** the son of Zerah of Bozrah | **Gn 36:33** | 3103
Then **J** died, and Husham of the | **Gn 36:34** | 3103
that he sent to **J** king of Madon | **Jos 11:1** | 3103
Ophir, Havilah and **J**; | **1Ch 1:23** | 3103
J the son of Zerah of Bozrah | **1Ch 1:44** | 3103
When **J** died, Husham of the land of | **1Ch 1:45** | 3103
wife he became the father of **J**, | **1Ch 8:9** | 3103
and **J** *were* the sons of Elpaal. | **1Ch 8:18** | 3103

JOB'S
Now when **J** three friends heard of | **Jb 2:11** | 347
were found so fair as **J** daughters; | **Jb 42:15** | 347

JOCHEBED
married his father's sister **J**, | **Ex 6:20** | 3115
The name of Amram's wife was **J**, | **Nu 26:59** | 3115

JODA
the son of Josech, the son of **J**, | **Lk 3:26** | *2493a*

JOED
son of Meshullam, the son of **J**, | **Ne 11:7** | 3133

JOEL
the name of his firstborn was **J**, | **1Sa 8:2** | 3100
J and Jehu the son of Joshibiah, | **1Ch 4:35** | 3100
sons of **J** *were* Shemaiah his son, | **1Ch 5:4** | 3100
the son of Shema, the son of **J**, | **1Ch 5:8** | 3100
J *was* the chief and Shapham the | **1Ch 5:12** | 3100
The sons of Samuel *were* **J** the | **1Ch 6:28** | 3100
Heman the singer, the son of **J**, | **1Ch 6:33** | 3100
the son of Elkanah, the son of **J**, | **1Ch 6:36** | 3100
Izrahiah *were* Michael, Obadiah, **J**, | **1Ch 7:3** | 3100
J the brother of Nathan, Mibhar | **1Ch 11:38** | 3100
the sons of Gershom, **J** the chief, | **1Ch 15:7** | 3100
the Levites, for Uriel, Asaiah, **J**, | **1Ch 15:11** | 3100
appointed Heman the son of **J**, | **1Ch 15:17** | 3100
Jehiel the first and Zetham and **J**, | **1Ch 23:8** | 3100
Jehieli, Zetham and **J** his brother, | **1Ch 26:22** | 3100
of Manasseh, **J** the son of Pedaiah; | **1Ch 27:20** | 3100
Amasai and **J** the son of Azariah, | **2Ch 29:12** | 3100
Zabad, Zebina, Jaddai, **J** | **Ezr 10:43** | 3100
J the son of Zichri was their | **Ne 11:9** | 3100
word of the LORD that came to **J**, | **Jl 1:1** | 3100
spoken of through the prophet **J**: | **Ac 2:16** | *2493b*

JOELAH
and **J** and Zebadiah, the sons of | **1Ch 12:7** | 3132

JOEZER
Elkanah, Isshiah, Azarel, **J**, | **1Ch 12:6** | 3134

JOGBEHAH
and Atroth-shophan and Jazer and **J**, | **Nu 32:35** | 3011
tents on the east of Nobah and **J**, | **Jg 8:11** | 3011

JOGLI
Dan a leader, Bukki the son of **J**. | **Nu 34:22** | 3020

JOHA
and **J** *were* the sons of Beriah. | **1Ch 8:16** | 3109
son of Shimri and **J** his brother, | **1Ch 11:45** | 3109

JOHANAN
and **J** the son of Kareah, | **2Ki 25:23** | 3076
of Josiah *were* **J** the firstborn, | **1Ch 3:15** | 3076
Eliashib, Pelaiah, Akkub, **J**, | **1Ch 3:24** | 3076
Azariah became the father of **J**, | **1Ch 6:9** | 3076
J became the father of Azariah | **1Ch 6:10** | 3076
Then Jeremiah, Jahaziel, **J**, | **1Ch 12:4** | 3076
J the eighth, Elzabad the ninth, | **1Ch 12:12** | 3076
Elam the fifth, **J** the sixth, | **1Ch 26:3** | 3076
next to him *was* **J** the commander, | **2Ch 17:15** | 3076
of Jeroham, Ishmael the son of **J**, | **2Ch 23:1** | 3076
Azariah the son of **J**, Berechiah the | **2Ch 28:12** | 3076
J the son of Hakkatan and 110 | **Ezr 8:12** | 3076
days of Eliashib, Joiada, and **J** and | **Ne 12:22** | 3076
the days of **J** the son of Eliashib. | **Ne 12:23** | 3076
and **J** and Jonathan the sons of | **Jer 40:8** | 3076
Now **J** the son of Kareah and all | **Jer 40:13** | 3076
Then **J** the son of Kareah spoke | **Jer 40:15** | 3076
said to **J** the son of Kareah, | **Jer 40:16** | 3076
But **J** the son of Kareah and all | **Jer 41:11** | 3076
people who were with Ishmael saw **J** | **Jer 41:13** | 3076
and went to **J** the son of Kareah. | **Jer 41:14** | 3076
the son of Nethaniah escaped from **J** | **Jer 41:15** | 3076
Then **J** the son of Kareah and all | **Jer 41:16** | 3076
the forces, **J** the son of Kareah, | **Jer 42:1** | 3076
he called for **J** the son of Kareah and | **Jer 42:8** | 3076
Hoshaiah, and **J** the son of Kareah, | **Jer 43:2** | 3076
So **J** the son of Kareah and all the | **Jer 43:4** | 3076
But **J** the son of Kareah and all | **Jer 43:5** | 3076

JOHN
in those days **J** the Baptist came, | **Mt 3:1** | *2491*
Now **J** himself had a garment of | **Mt 3:4** | *2491*
Galilee at the Jordan *coming* to **J**, | **Mt 3:13** | *2491*
But **J** tried to prevent Him, | **Mt 3:14** | *2491*
J had been taken into custody, | **Mt 4:12** | *2491*
son of Zebedee, and **J** his brother, | **Mt 4:21** | *2491*
the disciples of **J** came to Him, | **Mt 9:14** | *2491*
son of Zebedee, and **J** his brother; | **Mt 10:2** | *2491*
Now when **J**, while imprisoned, heard | **Mt 11:2** | *2491*
report to **J** what you hear and see: | **Mt 11:4** | *2491*
speak to the crowds about **J**, | **Mt 11:7** | *2491*
anyone greater than **J** the Baptist! | **Mt 11:11** | *2491*
From the days of **J** the Baptist until | **Mt 11:12** | *2491*
and the Law prophesied until **J**. | **Mt 11:13** | *2491*
J himself is Elijah who was to come. | **Mt 11:14**
"For **J** came neither eating nor | **Mt 11:18** | *2491*
"This is **J** the Baptist; | **Mt 14:2** | *2491*
For when Herod had **J** arrested, | **Mt 14:3** | *2491*
For **J** had been saying to him, | **Mt 14:4** | *2491*
because they regarded **J** as a prophet. | **Mt 14:5** | *4053*
the head of **J** the Baptist." | **Mt 14:8** | *2491*
and had **J** beheaded in the prison. | **Mt 14:10** | *2491*
Now when Jesus heard *about* **J**, He | **Mt 14:13**
"Some *say* **J** the Baptist; | **Mt 16:14** | *2491*
Peter and James and **J** his brother, | **Mt 17:1** | *2491*
to them about **J** the Baptist. | **Mt 17:13** | *2491*
baptism of **J** was from what *source*, | **Mt 21:25** | *2491*
they all regard **J** as a prophet." | **Mt 21:26** | *2491*
"For **J** came to you in the way of | **Mt 21:32** | *2491*
J the Baptist appeared in the | **Mk 1:4** | *2491*
J was clothed with camel's hair and | **Mk 1:6** | *2491*
was baptized by **J** in the Jordan. | **Mk 1:9** | *2491*
J had been taken into custody, | **Mk 1:14** | *2491*
son of Zebedee, and **J** his brother, | **Mk 1:19** | *2491*
and Andrew, with James and **J**. | **Mk 1:29** | *2491*
and **J** the brother of James | **Mk 3:17** | *2491*
James and **J** the brother of James. | **Mk 5:37** | *2491*
"**J** the Baptist has risen from the | **Mk 6:14** | *2491*
"**J**, whom I beheaded, has risen!" | **Mk 6:16** | *2491*
had **J** arrested and bound in prison | **Mk 6:17** | *2491*
For **J** had been saying to Herod, | **Mk 6:18** | *2491*
for Herod was afraid of **J**, | **Mk 6:20** | *2491*
"The head of **J** the Baptist." | **Mk 6:24** | *2491*
at once the head of **J** the Baptist | **Mk 6:25** | *2491*
J the Baptist; and others *say* Elijah; | **Mk 8:28** | *2491*
with Him Peter and James and **J**, | **Mk 9:2** | *2491*
J said to Him, "Teacher, we saw | **Mk 9:38** | *2491*
James and **J**, the two sons of | **Mk 10:35** | *2491*
feel indignant with James and **J**. | **Mk 10:41** | *2491*
"Was the baptism of **J** from heaven, | **Mk 11:30** | *2491*
considered **J** to have been a real | **Mk 11:32** | *2491*
Peter and James and **J** and Andrew | **Mk 13:3** | *2491*
with Him Peter and James and **J**, | **Mk 14:33** | *2491*
and you will give him the name **J**. | **Lk 1:13** | *2491*
but he shall be called **J**." | **Lk 1:60** | *2491*
wrote as follows, "His name is **J**." | **Lk 1:63** | *2491*
the word of God came to **J**, | **Lk 3:2** | *2491*
wondering in their hearts about **J**, | **Lk 3:15** | *2491*
J answered and said to them all, | **Lk 3:16** | *2491*
he locked **J** up in prison. | **Lk 3:20** | *2491*
and so also *were* James and **J**, | **Lk 5:10** | *2491*
disciples of **J** often fast and offer | **Lk 5:33** | *2491*
and James and **J**; and Philip and | **Lk 6:14** | *2491*
The disciples of **J** reported to | **Lk 7:18** | *2491*
J sent them to the Lord, | **Lk 7:19** | *2491*
"**J** the Baptist has sent us to | **Lk 7:20** | *2491*
report to **J** what you have seen and | **Lk 7:22** | *2491*
When the messengers of **J** had left, | **Lk 7:24** | *2491*
speak to the crowds about **J**, | **Lk 7:24** | *2491*
there is no one greater than **J**; | **Lk 7:28** | *2491*
baptized with the baptism of **J**. | **Lk 7:29** | *2491*
not having been baptized by **J**. | **Lk 7:30**
"For **J** the Baptist has come | **Lk 7:33** | *2491*
Him, except Peter and **J** and James, | **Lk 8:51** | *2491*
that **J** had risen from the dead, | **Lk 9:7** | *2491*
"I myself had **J** beheaded; | **Lk 9:9** | *2491*
"**J** the Baptist, and others *say* | **Lk 9:19** | *2491*
took along Peter and **J** and James, | **Lk 9:28** | *2491*
J answered and said, | **Lk 9:49** | *2491*
disciples James and **J** saw *this*, | **Lk 9:54** | *2491*
as **J** also taught his disciples." | **Lk 11:1** | *2491*
Prophets *were proclaimed* until **J**; | **Lk 16:16** | *2491*
Was the baptism of **J** from heaven | **Lk 20:4** | *2491*
convinced that **J** was a prophet." | **Lk 20:6** | *2491*
And Jesus sent Peter and **J**, | **Lk 22:8** | *2491*
sent from God, whose name was **J**. | **Jn 1:6** | *2491*
J testified about Him and cried | **Jn 1:15** | *2491*
This is the testimony of **J**, | **Jn 1:19** | *2491*
J answered them saying, | **Jn 1:26** | *2491*
the Jordan, where **J** was baptizing. | **Jn 1:28** | *2491*
J testified saying, | **Jn 1:32** | *2491*

Again the next day J was standing	Jn 1:35	2491
One of the two who heard J *speak*	Jn 1:40	2491
"You are Simon the son of J;	Jn 1:42	2491
J also was baptizing in Aenon	Jn 3:23	2491
for J had not yet been thrown into	Jn 3:24	2491
they came to J and said to him,	Jn 3:26	2491
J answered and said,	Jn 3:27	2491
baptizing more disciples than J	Jn 4:1	2491
"You have sent to J,	Jn 5:33	2491
I have is greater than *the testimony of* J;	Jn 5:36	2491
place where J was first baptizing,	Jn 10:40	2491
"While J performed no sign, yet	Jn 10:41	2491
everything J said about this man	Jn 10:41	2491
"Simon, *son* of J, do you love Me	Jn 21:15	2491
"Simon, *son* of J, do you love Me?"	Jn 21:16	2491
"Simon, *son* of J, do you love Me?"	Jn 21:17	2491
for J baptized with water, but you	Ac 1:5	2491
Peter and J and James and Andrew,	Ac 1:13	2491
beginning with the baptism of J until	Ac 1:22	2491
Now Peter and J were going up to	Ac 3:1	2491
and J about to go into the temple,	Ac 3:3	2491
But Peter, along with J,	Ac 3:4	2491
he was clinging to Peter and J,	Ac 3:11	2491
and Caiaphas and J and Alexander,	Ac 4:6	2491
the confidence of Peter and J and	Ac 4:13	2491
and J answered and said to them,	Ac 4:19	2491
God, they sent them Peter and J,	Ac 8:14	2491
the baptism which J proclaimed.	Ac 10:37	2491
'J baptized with water, but you	Ac 11:16	2491
he had James the brother of J put	Ac 12:2	2491
of J who was also called Mark,	Ac 12:12	2491
J, who was also called Mark.	Ac 12:25	2491
they also had J as their helper.	Ac 13:5	2491
but J left them and returned to	Ac 13:13	2491
after J had proclaimed before His	Ac 13:24	2491
while J was completing his course,	Ac 13:25	2491
Barnabas wanted to take J,	Ac 15:37	2491
only with the baptism of J;	Ac 18:25	2491
"J baptized with the baptism of	Ac 19:4	2491
to me, James and Cephas and J,	Ga 2:9	2491
by His angel to His bond-servant J,	Rv 1:1	2491
J to the seven churches that are	Rv 1:4	2491
I, J, your brother and fellow	Rv 1:9	2491
I, J, am the one who heard and	Rv 22:8	2491
JOHN'S		
J disciples and the Pharisees	Mk 2:18	2491
"Why do J disciples and the	Mk 2:18	2491
discussion on the part of J disciples	Jn 3:25	2491
"Into J baptism."	Ac 19:3	2491
JOIADA		
J the son of Paseah and	Ne 3:6	3077
Eliashib became the father of J,	Ne 12:10	3077
J became the father of Jonathan,	Ne 12:11	3077
in the days of Eliashib, J,	Ne 12:22	3077
Even one of the sons of J,	Ne 13:28	3077
JOIAKIM		
Jeshua became the father of J,	Ne 12:10	3079
J became the father of Eliashib,	Ne 12:10	3079
Now in the days of J, the priests,	Ne 12:12	3079
the days of J the son of Jeshua,	Ne 12:26	3079
JOIARIB		
men, and for J and Elnathan,	Ezr 8:16	3080
the son of Adaiah, the son of J,	Ne 11:5	3080
Jedaiah the son of J,	Ne 11:10	3080
Shemaiah and J, Jedaiah,	Ne 12:6	3080
of J, Mattenai; of Jedaiah, Uzzi;	Ne 12:19	3080
JOIN		
they will also j themselves to those	Ex 1:10	3254
do not j your hand with a wicked	Ex 23:1	7896
and j the curtains to one another	Ex 26:6	2266
j five curtains by themselves and	Ex 26:9	2266
the loops and j the tent together so	Ex 26:11	2266
of bronze to j the tent together so	Ex 36:18	2266
of the nations of the land to j	Ezr 6:21	
Do not j in an evil matter, for he	Ec 8:3	5975
to house *and* j field to field,	Is 5:8	7126
then strangers will j them and	Is 14:1	3867a
who j themselves to the LORD,	Is 56:6	3867a
they will come that they may j	Jer 50:5	3867a
"Then j them for yourself one to	Ezk 37:17	7126
will j with them in hypocrisy.	Da 11:34	3867a
"Many nations will j	Zch 2:11	3867a
"Go up and j this chariot."	Ac 8:29	2853
j in following my example,	Php 3:17	4831, 1096
but j with *me* in suffering for the	2Tm 1:8	4777
JOINED		
and be j to his wife; and they shall	Gn 2:24	1692
curtains shall be j to one another,	Ex 26:3	2266
shall be j to one another.	Ex 26:3	2266
shoulder pieces j to its two ends,	Ex 28:7	2266
to its two ends, that it may be j.	Ex 28:7	2266
close to the place where it is j,	Ex 28:27	4225
He j five curtains to one another	Ex 36:10	2266
five curtains he j to one another.	Ex 36:10	2266
and j the curtains to one another	Ex 36:13	2266
He j five curtains by themselves and	Ex 36:16	2266
it, close to the place where it j,	Ex 39:20	4225
may be j with you and serve you,	Nu 18:2	3867a
"They shall be j with you and	Nu 18:4	3867a
Israel j themselves to Baal of Peor,	Nu 25:3	6775
j themselves to Baal of Peor."	Nu 25:5	6775
the seventh day the battle was j,	1Ki 20:29	7126
was j together to half its *height*,	Ne 4:6	7194
"They are j one to another;	Jb 41:17	1692
folds of his flesh are j together,	Jb 41:23	1692
Assyria also has j with them;	Ps 83:8	3867a
j themselves also to Baal-peor,	Ps 106:28	6775
For whoever is j with all the living,	Ec 9:4	2266
who has j himself to the LORD say,	Is 56:3	3867a
Ephraim is j to idols;	Hos 4:17	2266
LEAVE HIS FATHER AND MOTHER AND BE J	Mt 19:5	2853
What therefore God has j together,	Mt 19:6	4801
"What therefore God has j together,	Mk 10:9	4801
four hundred men j up with him.	Ac 5:36	4346a
persuaded and j Paul and Silas,	Ac 17:4	4345
But some men j him and believed,	Ac 17:34	2853
The Jews also j in the attack,	Ac 24:9	4902a
living she is j to another man,	Ro 7:3	1096
though she is j to another man.	Ro 7:3	1096
that you might be j to another,	Ro 7:4	1096
rest of the Jews j him in hypocrisy,	Ga 2:13	4942
HIS FATHER AND MOTHER AND SHALL BE J	Eph 5:31	4347
JOINING		
are j with their kinsmen, their	Ne 10:29	2388
you also j in helping us through	2Co 1:11	4943
JOINS		
who j himself to a prostitute is one body	1Co 6:16	2853
the one who j himself to the Lord is	1Co 6:17	2853
JOINT		
of Israel in a j of the armor.	1Ki 22:34	1694
of Israel in a j of the armor.	2Ch 18:33	1694
And all my bones are out of j;	Ps 22:14	6504
by what every j supplies,	Eph 4:16	860
is lame may not be put out of j,	Heb 12:13	1624
JOINTED		
which have above their feet j legs	Lv 11:21	
JOINTS		
and his hip j went slack and his	Da 5:6	7001
held together by the j and ligaments	Col 2:19	860
and spirit, of both j and marrow,	Heb 4:12	719
JOKDEAM		
and Jezreel and J and Zanoah,	Jos 15:56	3347
JOKE		
"I am a j to my friends,	Jb 12:4	7814
The just *and* blameless *man* is a j.	Jb 12:4	7814
JOKIM		
and J, the men of Cozeba, Joash,	1Ch 4:22	3137
JOKING		
And says, "Was I not j?"	Pr 26:19	7832
JOKMEAM		
as far as the other side of J;	1Ki 4:12	3361
J with its pasture lands,	1Ch 6:68	3361
JOKNEAM		
the king of J in Carmel, one;	Jos 12:22	3362
to the brook that is before J.	Jos 19:11	3362
J with its pasture lands and	Jos 21:34	3362
JOKSHAN		
She bore to him Zimran and J	Gn 25:2	3370
J became the father of Sheba	Gn 25:3	3370
whom she bore, *were* Zimran, J,	1Ch 1:32	3370
sons of J *were* Sheba and Dedan.	1Ch 1:32	3370
JOKTAN		
and his brother's name *was* J.	Gn 10:25	3355
J became the father of Almodad	Gn 10:26	3355
all these were the sons of J.	Gn 10:29	3355
and his brother's name was J.	1Ch 1:19	3355
J became the father of Almodad,	1Ch 1:20	3355
all these *were* the sons of J.	1Ch 1:23	3355
JOKTHEEL		
and Dilean and Mizpeh and J,	Jos 15:38	3371
war, and named it J to this day.	2Ki 14:7	3371
JONADAB		
had a friend whose name was J,	2Sa 13:3	3082
and J was a very shrewd man.	2Sa 13:3	3082
J then said to him,	2Sa 13:5	3082
J, the son of Shimeah, David's	2Sa 13:32	3082
J said to the king,	2Sa 13:35	3082
wine, for J the son of Rechab,	Jer 35:6	3082
the voice of J the son of Rechab,	Jer 35:8	3082
that J our father commanded us.	Jer 35:10	3082
"The words of J the son of Rechab	Jer 35:14	3082
the sons of J the son of Rechab	Jer 35:16	3082
the command of J your father,	Jer 35:18	3082
"J the son of Rechab shall not	Jer 35:19	3082
JONAH		
His servant J the son of Amittai,	2Ki 14:25	3124
The word of the LORD came to J	Jon 1:1	3124
But J rose up to flee to Tarshish	Jon 1:3	3124
But J had gone below into the hold	Jon 1:5	3124
cast lots and the lot fell on J.	Jon 1:7	3124
So they picked up J,	Jon 1:15	3124
a great fish to swallow J,	Jon 1:17	3124
J was in the stomach of the fish	Jon 1:17	3124
Then J prayed to the LORD his God	Jon 2:1	3124
it vomited J up onto the dry land.	Jon 2:10	3124
the word of the LORD came to J	Jon 3:1	3124
So J arose and went to Nineveh	Jon 3:3	3124
Then J began to go through the	Jon 3:4	3124
But it greatly displeased J and	Jon 4:1	3124
Then J went out from the city and	Jon 4:5	3124
it grew up over J to be a shade over	Jon 4:6	3124
And J was extremely happy about	Jon 4:6	3124
Then God said to J,	Jon 4:9	3124
it but the sign of J the prophet;	Mt 12:39	2495
for just as J WAS THREE DAYS AND	Mt 12:40	2495
repented at the preaching of J;	Mt 12:41	2495
something greater than J is here.	Mt 12:41	2495
given it, except the sign of J."	Mt 16:4	2495
be given to it but the sign of J.	Lk 11:29	2495
"For just as J became a sign to	Lk 11:30	2495
repented at the preaching of J;	Lk 11:32	2495
something greater than J is here.	Lk 11:32	2495
JONAH'S		
and the sun beat down on J head so	Jon 4:8	3124
JONAM		
the son of Joseph, the son of J,	Lk 3:30	2494
JONATHAN		
and J, the son of Gershom, the son	Jg 18:30	3083
were with J at Gibeah of Benjamin.	1Sa 13:2	3083
J smote the garrison of the	1Sa 13:3	3083
Now Saul and his son J and the	1Sa 13:16	3083
people who *were* with Saul and J,	1Sa 13:22	3083
found with Saul and his son J.	1Sa 13:22	3083
Now the day came that J,	1Sa 14:1	3083
did not know that J had gone.	1Sa 14:3	3083
by which J sought to cross over to	1Sa 14:4	3083
Then J said to the young man who	1Sa 14:6	3083
J said, "Behold, we will cross over	1Sa 14:8	3083
So the men of the garrison hailed J	1Sa 14:12	3083
And J said to his armor bearer,	1Sa 14:12	3083
Then J climbed up on his hands and	1Sa 14:13	3083
and they fell before J,	1Sa 14:13	3083
which J and his armor bearer made	1Sa 14:14	3083
J and his armor bearer were not	1Sa 14:17	3083
who *were* with Saul and J.	1Sa 14:21	3083
But J had not heard when his	1Sa 14:27	3083
J said, "My father has troubled the	1Sa 14:29	3083
Israel, though it is in J my son,	1Sa 14:39	3083
I and J my son will be on the other	1Sa 14:40	3083
And J and Saul were taken, but the	1Sa 14:41	3083
lots between me and J my son."	1Sa 14:42	3083
And J was taken.	1Sa 14:42	3083
Then Saul said to J,	1Sa 14:43	3083
So J told him and said,	1Sa 14:43	3083
for you shall surely die, J."	1Sa 14:44	3083
"Must J die, who has brought	1Sa 14:45	3083
rescued J and he did not die.	1Sa 14:45	3083
were J and Ishvi and Malchi-shua;	1Sa 14:49	3083
the soul of J was knit to the soul of	1Sa 18:1	3083
David, and J loved him as himself.	1Sa 18:1	3083
Then J made a covenant with David	1Sa 18:3	3083
J stripped himself of the robe	1Sa 18:4	3083
Now Saul told J his son and all	1Sa 19:1	3083
But J, Saul's son, greatly delighted	1Sa 19:1	3083
So J told David saying,	1Sa 19:2	3083
Then J spoke well of David to Saul	1Sa 19:4	3083
Saul listened to the voice of J,	1Sa 19:6	3083
Then J called David, and Jonathan	1Sa 19:7	3083
and J told him all these words.	1Sa 19:7	3083
And J brought David to Saul, and	1Sa 19:7	3083
in Ramah, and came and said to J,	1Sa 20:1	3083
'Do not let J know this, or he	1Sa 20:3	3083
Then J said to David,	1Sa 20:4	3083
So David said to J,	1Sa 20:5	3083
J said, "Far be it from you!	1Sa 20:9	3083
Then David said to J,	1Sa 20:10	3083
J said to David,	1Sa 20:11	3083
Then J said to David,	1Sa 20:12	3083
the LORD do so to J and more also,	1Sa 20:13	3083
So J made a *covenant* with the	1Sa 20:16	3083
J made David vow again because	1Sa 20:17	3083
Then J said to him,	1Sa 20:18	3083
then J rose up and Abner sat down	1Sa 20:25	3083
so Saul said to J his son,	1Sa 20:27	3083
J then answered Saul,	1Sa 20:28	3083
Then Saul's anger burned against J	1Sa 20:30	3083
But J answered Saul his father and	1Sa 20:32	3083
so J knew that his father had	1Sa 20:33	3083
Then J arose from the table in	1Sa 20:34	3083
J went out into the field for the	1Sa 20:35	3083
of the arrow which J had shot,	1Sa 20:37	3083
had shot, J called after the lad and	1Sa 20:37	3083
And J called after the lad,	1Sa 20:38	3083
only J and David knew about the	1Sa 20:39	3083
Then J gave his weapons to his lad	1Sa 20:40	3083
J said to David,	1Sa 20:42	3083
while J went into the city.	1Sa 20:42	3083
And J, Saul's son, arose and went	1Sa 23:16	3083
Horesh while J went to his house.	1Sa 23:18	3083
and the Philistines killed J and	1Sa 31:2	3083
Saul and J his son are dead also."	2Sa 1:4	3083
Saul and his son J are dead?"	2Sa 1:5	3083
for Saul and his son J and for the	2Sa 1:12	3083
lament over Saul and J his son,	2Sa 1:17	3083
The bow of J did not turn back,	2Sa 1:22	3083
"Saul and J, beloved and pleasant	2Sa 1:23	3083
J is slain on your high places.	2Sa 1:25	3083
distressed for you, my brother J;	2Sa 1:26	3083
Now J, Saul's son, had a son	2Sa 4:4	3083
when the report of Saul and J came	2Sa 4:4	3083
son of J who is crippled in both feet	2Sa 9:3	3083
the son of J the son of Saul,	2Sa 9:6	3083
you for the sake of your father J,	2Sa 9:7	3083
Ahimaaz and J the son of Abiathar.	2Sa 15:27	3083
there, Ahimaaz, Zadok's son and J,	2Sa 15:36	3083
Now J and Ahimaaz were staying at	2Sa 17:17	3083
"Where are Ahimaaz and J?"	2Sa 17:20	3083
the son of J the son of Saul,	2Sa 21:7	3083
between David and Saul's son J.	2Sa 21:7	3083
the bones of Saul and the bones of J	2Sa 21:12	3083
the bones of J his son from there,	2Sa 21:13	3083
They buried the bones of Saul and J	2Sa 21:14	3083
Israel, J the son of Shimei,	2Sa 21:21	3083
the sons of Jashen, J,	2Sa 23:32	3083
J the son of Abiathar the priest	1Ki 1:42	3083
J replied to Adonijah,	1Ki 1:43	3083
of Shammai *were* Jether and J,	1Ch 2:32	3083
sons of J *were* Peleth and Zaza.	1Ch 2:33	3083
and Saul became the father of J,	1Ch 8:33	3083
The son of J *was* Merib-baal,	1Ch 8:34	3083

and Saul became the father of **J**, **1Ch 9:39** 3083
The son of **J** *was* Merib-baal; **1Ch 9:40** 3083
and the Philistines struck down **J**, **1Ch 10:2** 3083
J the son of Shagee the Hararite, **1Ch 11:34** 3083
Israel, **J** the son of Shimea, **1Ch 20:7** 3083
And **J** the son of Uzziah had charge **1Ch 27:25** 3083
Also **J**, David's uncle, *was* a **1Ch 27:32** 3083
son of **J** and 50 males with him; **Ezr 8:6** 3083
Only **J** the son of Asahel and **Ezr 10:15** 3083
and Joiada became the father of **J**, **Ne 12:11** 3083
and **J** became the father of Jaddua. **Ne 12:11** 3083
Malluchi, **J**; of Shebaniah, Joseph; **Ne 12:14** 3083
and Zechariah the son of **J**, **Ne 12:35** 3083
jail in the house of **J** the scribe, **Jer 37:15** 3083
to the house of **J** the scribe, **Jer 37:20** 3083
the house of **J** to die there.' " **Jer 38:26** 3083
Johanan and **J** the sons of Kareah, **Jer 40:8** 3083

JONATHAN'S
And **J** lad picked up the arrow and **1Sa 20:38** 3083
show him kindness for **J** sake?" **2Sa 9:1** 3083

JOPPA
with the territory over against **J**. **Jos 19:46** 3305
it to you on rafts by sea to **J**, **2Ch 2:16** 3305
wood from Lebanon to the sea at **J**, **Ezr 3:7** 3305
So he went down to **J**, **Jon 1:3** 3305
in **J** there was a disciple **Ac 9:36** *2445*
Since Lydda was near **J**, **Ac 9:38** *2445*
It became known all over **J**, **Ac 9:42** *2445*
Peter stayed many days in **J** with a **Ac 9:43** *2445*
"Now dispatch *some* men to **J** and **Ac 10:5** *2445*
to them, he sent them to **J**. **Ac 10:8** *2445*
brethren from **J** accompanied him. **Ac 10:23** *2445*
send to **J** and invite Simon, **Ac 10:32** *2445*
"I was in the city of **J** praying; **Ac 11:5** *2445*
'Send to **J** and have Simon, who is **Ac 11:13** *2445*

JORAH
the sons of **J**, 112; **Ezr 2:18** 3139

JORAI
were Michael, Meshullam, Sheba, **J**, **1Ch 5:13** 3140

JORAM
Toi sent **J** his son to King David **2Sa 8:10** 3141
And **J** brought with him articles **2Sa 8:10** 3141
the fifth year of **J** the son of Ahab **2Ki 8:16** 3141
Then **J** crossed over to Zair, and **2Ki 8:21** 3141
the acts of **J** and all that he did, **2Ki 8:23** 3141
So **J** slept with his fathers and **2Ki 8:24** 3141
twelfth year of **J** the son of Ahab **2Ki 8:25** 3141
he went with **J** the son of Ahab **2Ki 8:28** 3141
and the Arameans wounded **J**. **2Ki 8:28** 3141
So King **J** returned to be healed in **2Ki 8:29** 3141
king of Judah went down to see **J** **2Ki 8:29** 3141
son of Nimshi conspired against **J**. **2Ki 9:14** 3141
Now **J** with all Israel was **2Ki 9:14** 3141
but King **J** had returned to Jezreel **2Ki 9:15** 3088
to Jezreel, for **J** was lying there. **2Ki 9:16** 3141
of Judah had come down to see **J**. **2Ki 9:16** 3141
J said, "Take a horseman and send **2Ki 9:17** 3088
Then **J** said, "Get ready." And they **2Ki 9:21** 3088
J king of Israel and Ahaziah **2Ki 9:21** 3088
When **J** saw Jehu, **2Ki 9:22** 3088
So **J** reined about and fled and **2Ki 9:23** 3088
and shot **J** between his arms; **2Ki 9:24** 3088
Now in the eleventh year of **J**, **2Ki 9:29** 3141
Jehosheba, the daughter of King **J**, **2Ki 11:2** 3141
J his son, Ahaziah his son, Joash **1Ch 3:11** 3141
son, Jeshaiah his son, **J** his son, **1Ch 26:25** 3141
But the Arameans wounded **J**. **2Ch 22:5** 3141
from God, in that he went to **J**. **2Ch 22:7** 3141
Jehoshaphat the father of **J**, **Mt 1:8** *2496*
and **J** the father of Uzziah. **Mt 1:8** *2496*

JORDAN
and saw all the valley of the **J**, **Gn 13:10** 3383
himself all the valley of the **J**, **Gn 13:11** 3383
my staff *only* I crossed this **J**, **Gn 32:10** 3383
of Atad, which is beyond the **J**, **Gn 50:10** 3383
which is beyond the **J**. **Gn 50:11** 3383
sea and by the side of the **J**." **Nu 13:29** 3383
beyond the **J** *opposite* Jericho. **Nu 22:1** 3383
plains of Moab by the **J** at Jericho, **Nu 26:3** 3383
plains of Moab by the **J** at Jericho. **Nu 26:63** 3383
are by the **J** *opposite* Jericho. **Nu 31:12** 3383
do not take us across the **J**." **Nu 32:5** 3383
other side of the **J** and beyond, **Nu 32:19** 3383
side of the **J** toward the east." **Nu 32:19** 3383
you armed men cross over the **J** **Nu 32:21** 3383
will cross with you over the **J** **Nu 32:29** 3383
remain with us across the **J**." **Nu 32:32** 3383
of Moab by the **J** *opposite* Jericho. **Nu 33:48** 3383
They camped by the **J**, **Nu 33:49** 3383
of Moab by the **J** *opposite* Jericho, **Nu 33:50** 3383
'When you cross over the **J** into the **Nu 33:51** 3383
the border shall go down to the **J** **Nu 34:12** 3383
across the **J** opposite Jericho, **Nu 34:15** 3383
of Moab by the **J** *opposite* Jericho, **Nu 35:1** 3383
'When you cross the **J** into the land **Nu 35:10** 3383
shall give three cities across the **J** **Nu 35:14** 3383
of Moab by the **J** *opposite* Jericho. **Nu 36:13** 3383
across the **J** in the wilderness, **Dt 1:1** 3383
Across the **J** in the land of Moab, **Dt 1:5** 3383
until I cross over the **J** into the **Dt 2:29** 3383
Amorites who were beyond the **J**, **Dt 3:8** 3383
also, with the **J** as *a* border, **Dt 3:17** 3383
God will give them beyond the **J**. **Dt 3:20** 3383
fair land that is beyond the **J**, **Dt 3:25** 3383
you shall not cross over this **J**. **Dt 3:27** 3383
that I would not cross the **J**, **Dt 4:21** 3383
land, I shall not cross the **J**, **Dt 4:22** 3383
going over the **J** to possess it. **Dt 4:26** 3383
cities across the **J** to the east, **Dt 4:41** 3383
across the **J**, in the valley **Dt 4:46** 3383
who were across the **J** to the east, **Dt 4:47** 3383
Arabah across the **J** to the east, **Dt 4:49** 3383
You are crossing over the **J** today **Dt 9:1** 3383
"Are they not across the **J**, **Dt 11:30** 3383
"For you are about to cross the **J** **Dt 11:31** 3383
"When you cross the **J** and live in **Dt 12:10** 3383
you cross the **J** to the land **Dt 27:2** 3383
it shall be when you cross the **J**, **Dt 27:4** 3383
"When you cross the **J**, **Dt 27:12** 3383
land where you are crossing the **J** **Dt 30:18** 3383
'You shall not cross this **J**.' **Dt 31:2** 3383
about to cross the **J** to possess." **Dt 31:13** 3383
about to cross the **J** to possess." **Dt 32:47** 3383
now therefore arise, cross this **J**, **Jos 1:2** 3383
days you are to cross this **J**, **Jos 1:11** 3383
which Moses gave you beyond the **J**, **Jos 1:14** 3383
beyond the **J** toward the sunrise." **Jos 1:15** 3383
on the road to the **J** to the fords; **Jos 2:7** 3383
Amorites who were beyond the **J**, **Jos 2:10** 3383
from Shittim and came to the **J**, **Jos 3:1** 3383
the edge of the waters of the **J**, **Jos 3:8** 3383
shall stand *still* in the **J**.' " **Jos 3:8** 3383
over ahead of you into the **J**. **Jos 3:11** 3383
rest in the waters of the **J**, **Jos 3:13** 3383
waters of the **J** will be cut off, **Jos 3:13** 3383
set out from their tents to cross the **J** **Jos 3:14** 3383
carried the ark came into the **J**, **Jos 3:15** 3383
for the **J** overflows all its banks **Jos 3:15** 3383
on dry ground in the middle of the **J** **Jos 3:17** 3383
had finished crossing the **J**. **Jos 3:17** 3383
had finished crossing the **J**, **Jos 4:1** 3383
here out of the middle of the **J**, **Jos 4:3** 3383
your God into the middle of the **J**, **Jos 4:5** 3383
'Because the waters of the **J** were **Jos 4:7** 3383
when it crossed the **J**, **Jos 4:7** 3383
the waters of the **J** were cut off.' **Jos 4:7** 3383
stones from the middle of the **J**, **Jos 4:8** 3383
twelve stones in the middle of the **J** **Jos 4:9** 3383
were standing in the middle of the **J** **Jos 4:10** 3383
that they come up from the **J**." **Jos 4:16** 3383
"Come up from the **J**." **Jos 4:17** 3383
come up from the middle of the **J**, **Jos 4:18** 3383
the waters of the **J** returned to their **Jos 4:18** 3383
Now the people came up from the **J** **Jos 4:19** 3383
which they had taken from the **J**, **Jos 4:20** 3383
Israel crossed this **J** on dry ground **Jos 4:22** 3383
God dried up the waters of the **J** **Jos 4:23** 3383
who *were* beyond the **J** to the west, **Jos 5:1** 3383
dried up the waters of the **J** before **Jos 5:1** 3383
ever bring this people over the **J**, **Jos 7:7** 3383
willing to dwell beyond the **J**! **Jos 7:7** 3383
the kings who were beyond the **J**, **Jos 9:1** 3383
Amorites who were beyond the **J**, **Jos 9:10** 3383
land they possessed beyond the **J** **Jos 12:1** 3383
beyond the **J** toward the west, **Jos 12:7** 3383
them beyond the **J** to the east, **Jos 13:8** 3383
of the sons of Reuben was the **J**. **Jos 13:23** 3383
Heshbon, with the **J** as a border, **Jos 13:27** 3383
beyond the **J** to the east. **Jos 13:27** 3383
beyond the **J** at Jericho to the east. **Jos 13:32** 3383
and the half-tribe beyond the **J**; **Jos 14:3** 3383
Sea, as far as the mouth of the **J**. **Jos 15:5** 3383
of the sea at the mouth of the **J**. **Jos 15:5** 3383
the sons of Joseph went from the **J** **Jos 16:1** 3383
Jericho and came out at the **J**. **Jos 16:7** 3383
and Bashan, which is beyond the **J**, **Jos 17:5** 3383
inheritance eastward beyond the **J**, **Jos 18:7** 3383
on the north side was from the **J**, **Jos 18:12** 3383
Sea, at the south end of the **J**. **Jos 18:19** 3383
the **J** was its border on the east **Jos 18:20** 3383
and their border ended at the **J**; **Jos 19:22** 3383
and it ended at the **J**. **Jos 19:33** 3383
to Judah at the **J** toward the east. **Jos 19:34** 3383
Beyond the **J** east of Jericho, **Jos 20:8** 3383
of the LORD gave you beyond the **J**. **Jos 22:4** 3383
brothers westward beyond the **J**. **Jos 22:7** 3383
they came to the region of the **J** **Jos 22:10** 3383
built an altar there by the **J**, **Jos 22:10** 3383
of Canaan, in the region of the **J**, **Jos 22:11** 3383
the LORD has made the **J** a border **Jos 22:25** 3383
from the **J** even to the Great Sea **Jos 23:4** 3383
Amorites who lived beyond the **J**, **Jos 24:8** 3383
crossed the **J** and came to Jericho; **Jos 24:11** 3383
the fords of the **J** opposite Moab, **Jg 3:28** 3383
"Gilead remained across the **J**; **Jg 5:17** 3383
as far as Beth-barah and the **J**." **Jg 7:24** 3383
as far as Beth-barah and the **J**. **Jg 7:24** 3383
Zeeb to Gideon from across the **J**. **Jg 7:25** 3383
came to the **J** *and* crossed over, **Jg 8:4** 3383
sons of Israel who were beyond the **J** **Jg 10:8** 3383
The sons of Ammon crossed the **J** to **Jg 10:9** 3383
as far as the Jabbok and the **J**; **Jg 11:13** 3383
the wilderness as far as the **J**. **Jg 11:22** 3383
fords of the **J** opposite Ephraim. **Jg 12:5** 3383
slew him at the fords of the **J**. **Jg 12:6** 3383
some of the Hebrews crossed the **J** **1Sa 13:7** 3383
with those who were beyond the **J**, **1Sa 31:7** 3383
so they crossed the **J**, **2Sa 2:29** 3383
Israel together and crossed the **J**, **2Sa 10:17** 3383
with him arose and crossed the **J**; **2Sa 17:22** 3383
who had not crossed the **J**. **2Sa 17:22** 3383
And Absalom crossed the **J**, **2Sa 17:24** 3383
returned and came as far as the **J**. **2Sa 19:15** 3383
to bring the king across the **J**. **2Sa 19:15** 3383
rushed to the **J** before the king. **2Sa 19:17** 3383
as he was about to cross the **J**. **2Sa 19:18** 3383
and he went on to the **J** with the **2Sa 19:31** 3383
the king to escort him over the **J**. **2Sa 19:31** 3383
cross over the **J** with the king. **2Sa 19:36** 3383
All the people crossed over the **J** **2Sa 19:39** 3383
David's men with him over the **J**?" **2Sa 19:41** 3383
from the **J** even to Jerusalem. **2Sa 20:2** 3383
crossed the **J** and camped in Aroer, **2Sa 24:5** 3383
when he came down to me at the **J**, **1Ki 2:8** 3383
In the plain of the **J** the king cast **1Ki 7:46** 3383
Cherith, which is east of the **J**. **1Ki 17:3** 3383
Cherith, which is east of the **J**. **1Ki 17:5** 3383
the LORD has sent me to the **J**." **2Ki 2:6** 3383
the two of them stood by the **J**. **2Ki 2:7** 3383
and stood by the bank of the **J**. **2Ki 2:13** 3383
"Go and wash in the **J** seven times, **2Ki 5:10** 3383
dipped *himself* seven times in the **J**, **2Ki 5:14** 3383
"Please let us go to the **J** and **2Ki 6:2** 3383
and when they came to the **J**, **2Ki 6:4** 3383
They went after them to the **J**, **2Ki 7:15** 3383
from the **J** eastward, all the land **2Ki 10:33** 3383
and beyond the **J** at Jericho, on **1Ch 6:78** 3383
on the east side of the **J**, **1Ch 6:78** 3383
who crossed the **J** in the first month **1Ch 12:15** 3383
From the other side of the **J**, **1Ch 12:37** 3383
Israel together and crossed the **J**, **1Ch 19:17** 3383
affairs of Israel west of the **J**, **1Ch 26:30** 3383
On the plain of the **J** the king cast **2Ch 4:17** 3383
though the **J** rushes to his mouth. **Jb 40:23** 3383
You from the land of the **J** And **Ps 42:6** 3383
The **J** turned back. **Ps 114:3** 3383
O **J**, that you turn back? **Ps 114:5** 3383
the sea, on the other side of **J**, **Is 9:1** 3383
you do in the thicket of the **J**? **Jer 12:5** 3383
like a lion from the thickets of the **J** **Jer 49:19** 3383
like a lion from the thicket of the **J** **Jer 50:44** 3383
land of Israel, *shall be* the **J**; **Ezk 47:18** 3383
For the pride of the **J** is ruined. **Zch 11:3** 3383
and all the district around the **J**; **Mt 3:5** *2446*
baptized by him in the **J** River, **Mt 3:6** *2446*
Jesus arrived from Galilee at the **J** **Mt 3:13** *2446*
THE WAY OF THE SEA, BEYOND THE **J**, **Mt 4:15** *2446*
and Judea and *from* beyond the **J**. **Mt 4:25** *2446*
the region of Judea beyond the **J**; **Mt 19:1** *2446*
baptized by him in the **J** River, **Mk 1:5** *2446*
and was baptized by John in the **J**. **Mk 1:9** *2446*
and from Idumea, and beyond the **J**, **Mk 3:8** *2446*
region of Judea and beyond the **J**; **Mk 10:1** *2446*
all the district around the **J**, **Lk 3:3** *2446*
returned from the **J** and was led **Lk 4:1** *2446*
place in Bethany beyond the **J**, **Jn 1:28** *2446*
He who was with you beyond the **J**, **Jn 3:26** *2446*
He went away again beyond the **J** **Jn 10:40** *2446*

JORIM
the son of Eliezer, the son of **J**, **Lk 3:29** *2497*

JORKEAM
father of Raham, the father of **J**; **1Ch 2:44** 3421

JOSECH
the son of Semein, the son of **J**, **Lk 3:26** *2502a*

JOSEPH
She named him **J**, **Gn 30:24** 3130
about when Rachel had borne **J**, **Gn 30:25** 3130
next, and Rachel and **J** last. **Gn 33:2** 3130
afterward **J** came near with Rachel, **Gn 33:7** 3130
the sons of Rachel: **J** and Benjamin; **Gn 35:24** 3130
J, when seventeen years of age, **Gn 37:2** 3130
And **J** brought back a bad report **Gn 37:2** 3130
Israel loved **J** more than all his sons **Gn 37:3** 3130
Then **J** had a dream, and when he **Gn 37:5** 3130
Israel said to **J**, **Gn 37:13** 3130
So **J** went after his brothers and **Gn 37:17** 3130
when **J** reached his brothers, **Gn 37:23** 3130
that they stripped **J** of his tunic, **Gn 37:23** 3130
up and lifted **J** out of the pit, **Gn 37:28** 3130
Thus they brought **J** into Egypt. **Gn 37:28** 3130
and behold, **J** was not in the pit; **Gn 37:29** 3130
J has surely been torn to pieces!" **Gn 37:33** 3130
J had been taken down to Egypt; **Gn 39:1** 3130
The LORD was with **J**, **Gn 39:2** 3130
So **J** found favor in his sight and **Gn 39:4** 3130
Egyptian's house on account of **J**; **Gn 39:5** 3130
Now **J** was handsome in form and **Gn 39:6** 3130
wife looked with desire at **J**, **Gn 39:7** 3130
As she spoke to **J** day after day, **Gn 39:10** 3130
the LORD was with **J** and extended **Gn 39:21** 3130
same place where **J** was imprisoned. **Gn 40:3** 3130
bodyguard put **J** in charge of them, **Gn 40:4** 3130
When **J** came to them in the morning **Gn 40:6** 3130
Then **J** said to them, **Gn 40:8** 3130
cupbearer told his dream to **J**, **Gn 40:9** 3130
Then **J** said to him, **Gn 40:12** 3130
favorably, he said to **J**, **Gn 40:16** 3130
Then **J** answered and said, **Gn 40:18** 3130
just as **J** had interpreted to them. **Gn 40:22** 3130
cupbearer did not remember **J**, **Gn 40:23** 3130
Pharaoh sent and called for **J**, **Gn 41:14** 3130
Pharaoh said to **J**, **Gn 41:15** 3130
J then answered Pharaoh, saying, **Gn 41:16** 3130
So Pharaoh spoke to **J**, **Gn 41:17** 3130
Now **J** said to Pharaoh, **Gn 41:25** 3130
So Pharaoh said to **J**, **Gn 41:39** 3130
Pharaoh said to **J**, **Gn 41:41** 3130
Moreover, Pharaoh said to **J**, **Gn 41:44** 3130
Pharaoh named **J** Zaphenath-paneah; **Gn 41:45** 3130
And **J** went forth over the land of **Gn 41:45** 3130
Now **J** was thirty years old when he **Gn 41:46** 3130
And **J** went out from the presence **Gn 41:46** 3130
Thus **J** stored up grain in great **Gn 41:49** 3130
came, two sons were born to **J**, **Gn 41:50** 3130
J named the firstborn Manasseh, **Gn 41:51** 3130

began to come, just as J had said, Gn 41:54 3130
said to all the Egyptians, "Go to J; Gn 41:55 3130
then J opened all the storehouses, Gn 41:56 3130
came to Egypt to buy grain from J, Gn 41:57 3130
Then ten brothers of J went down Gn 42:3 3130
Now J was the ruler over the land; Gn 42:6 3130
When J saw his brothers he Gn 42:7 3130
But J had recognized his brothers, Gn 42:8 3130
J remembered the dreams which Gn 42:9 3130
J said to them, Gn 42:14 3130
J said to them on the third day, Gn 42:18 3130
know, however, that J understood, Gn 42:23 3130
Then J gave orders to fill their Gn 42:25 3130
J is no more, and Simeon is no Gn 42:36 3130
down to Egypt and stood before J. Gn 43:15 3130
When J saw Benjamin with them, he Gn 43:16 3130
So the man did as J said, Gn 43:17 3130
When J came home, they brought Gn 43:26 3130
J hurried *out* for he was Gn 43:30 3130
And he did as J had told *him.* Gn 44:2 3130
when J said to his house steward, Gn 44:4 3130
J said to them, Gn 44:15 3130
Then J could not control himself Gn 45:1 3130
J made himself known to his Gn 45:1 3130
Then J said to his brothers, Gn 45:3 3130
Joseph said to his brothers, "I am J! Gn 45:3 3130
Then J said to his brothers, Gn 45:4 3130
"I am your brother J, Gn 45:4 3130
'Thus says your son J, Gn 45:9 3130
Then Pharaoh said to J, Gn 45:17 3130
and J gave them wagons according Gn 45:21 3130
"J is still alive, and indeed he Gn 45:26 3130
they told him all the words of J Gn 45:27 3130
that J had sent to carry him, Gn 45:27 3130
my son J is still alive. Gn 45:28 3130
and J will close your eyes." Gn 46:4 3130
sons of Jacob's wife Rachel: J and Gn 46:19 3130
Now to J in the land of Egypt were Gn 46:20 3130
and the sons of J, who were born Gn 46:27 3130
Now he sent Judah before him to J, Gn 46:28 3130
J prepared his chariot and Gn 46:29 3130
Then Israel said to J, Gn 46:30 3130
J said to his brothers and to Gn 46:31 3130
Then J went in and told Pharaoh, Gn 47:1 3130
Then Pharaoh said to J, Gn 47:5 3130
Then J brought his father Jacob Gn 47:7 3130
So J settled his father and his Gn 47:11 3130
J provided his father and his Gn 47:12 3130
J gathered all the money that Gn 47:14 3130
and J brought the money into Gn 47:14 3130
the Egyptians came to J and said, Gn 47:15 3130
J said, "Give up your livestock, Gn 47:16 3130
they brought their livestock to J, Gn 47:17 3130
and J gave them food in exchange Gn 47:17 3130
So J bought all the land of Egypt Gn 47:20 3130
Then J said to the people, Gn 47:23 3130
J made it a statute concerning Gn 47:26 3130
called his son J and said to him, Gn 47:29 3130
these things that J was told, Gn 48:1 3130
your son J has come to you," Gn 48:2 3130
Then Jacob said to J, Gn 48:3 3130
J said to his father, Gn 48:9 3130
Then J brought them close to him, Gn 48:10 3130
Israel said to J, Gn 48:11 3130
Then J took them from his knees, Gn 48:12 3130
J took them both, Ephraim with Gn 48:13 3130
He blessed J, and said, Gn 48:15 3130
When J saw that his father laid Gn 48:17 3130
J said to his father, Gn 48:18 3130
Then Israel said to J, Gn 48:21 3130
"J is a fruitful bough, A Gn 49:22 3130
May they be on the head of J, Gn 49:26 3130
Then J fell on his father's face, Gn 50:1 3130
J commanded his servants the Gn 50:2 3130
J spoke to the household of Gn 50:4 3130
So J went up to bury his father, Gn 50:7 3130
and all the household of J and his Gn 50:8 3130
his father, J returned to Egypt, Gn 50:14 3130
"What if J bears a grudge Gn 50:15 3130
So they sent *a message* to J, Gn 50:16 3130
'Thus you shall say to J, Gn 50:17 3130
And J wept when they spoke to him. Gn 50:17 3130
But J said to them, Gn 50:19 3130
Now J stayed in Egypt, he and his Gn 50:22 3130
and J lived one hundred and ten Gn 50:22 3130
J saw the third generation of Gn 50:23 3130
J said to his brothers, Gn 50:24 3130
J made the sons of Israel swear, Gn 50:25 3130
So J died at the age of one Gn 50:26 3130
but J was *already* in Egypt. Ex 1:5 3130
J died, and all his brothers Ex 1:6 3130
over Egypt, who did not know J. Ex 1:8 3130
Moses took the bones of J with him Ex 13:19 3130
of the sons of J: Nu 1:10 3130
Of the sons of J, *namely,* of the Nu 1:32 3130
of Issachar, Igal the son of J; Nu 13:7 3130
from the tribe of J, Nu 13:11 3130
sons of J according to their families Nu 26:28 3130
sons of J according to their families Nu 26:37 3130
families of Manasseh the son of J, Nu 27:1 3130
"Of the sons of J: Nu 34:23 3130
of the families of the sons of J, Nu 36:1 3130
The tribe of the sons of J are right Nu 36:5 3130
the sons of Manasseh the son of J, Nu 36:12 3130
Simeon, Levi, Judah, Issachar, J, Dt 27:12 3130
Of J he said, Dt 33:13 3130
Let it come to the head of J, Dt 33:16 3130
For the sons of J were two tribes, Jos 14:4 3130
Then the lot for the sons of J Jos 16:1 3130
The sons of J, Manasseh and Jos 16:4 3130
for he was the firstborn of J. Jos 17:1 3130
son of J according to their families Jos 17:2 3130
the sons of J spoke to Joshua, Jos 17:14 3130
The sons of J said, Jos 17:16 3130
Joshua spoke to the house of J, Jos 17:17 3130
and the house of J shall stay in Jos 18:5 3130
sons of Judah and the sons of J. Jos 18:11 3130
Now they buried the bones of J, Jos 24:32 3130
house of J went up against Bethel, Jg 1:22 3130
The house of J spied out Bethel Jg 1:23 3130
power of the house of J grew strong Jg 1:35 3130
the first of all the house of J to 2Sa 19:20 3130
forced labor of the house of J. 1Ki 11:28 3130
Dan, J, Benjamin, Naphtali, Gad and 1Ch 2:2 3130
birthright was given to the sons of J 1Ch 5:1 3130
yet the birthright belonged to J), 1Ch 5:2 3130
the sons of J the son of Israel. 1Ch 7:29 3130
Zaccur, J, Nethaniah and 1Ch 25:2 3130
first lot came out for Asaph to J, 1Ch 25:9 3130
Shallum, Amariah *and* J. Ezr 10:42 3130
Malluchi, Jonathan; of Shebaniah, J Ne 12:14 3130
The sons of Jacob and J. Ps 77:15 3130
He also rejected the tent of J, Ps 78:67 3130
You who lead J like a flock; Ps 80:1 3130
it for a testimony in J When Ps 81:5 3130
He sent a man before them, J, Ps 105:17 3130
'For J, the stick of Ephraim and Ezk 37:16 3130
I will take the stick of J, Ezk 37:19 3130
J *shall have* two portions. Ezk 47:13 3130
the gate of J, one; Ezk 48:32 3130
forth like a fire, O house of J, Am 5:6 3130
be gracious to the remnant of J. Am 5:15 3130
not grieved over the ruin of J. Am 6:6 3130
a fire And the house of J a flame; Ob 1:18 3130
And I will save the house of J, Zch 10:6 3130
was the father of J the husband of Mary, Mt 1:16 *2501*
Mary had been betrothed to J, Mt 1:18 *2501*
And J her husband, being a Mt 1:19 *2501*
"J, son of David, do not be Mt 1:20 *2501*
And J awoke from his sleep and Mt 1:24 *2501*
the Lord appeared to J in a dream and Mt 2:13 *2501*
So J got up and took the Child Mt 2:14
appeared in a dream to J in Egypt, Mt 2:19 *2501*
So J got up, took the Child and His Mt 2:21
James and J and Simon and Judas? Mt 13:55 *2501*
Mary the mother of James and J, Mt 27:56 *2501*
rich man from Arimathea, named J, Mt 27:57 *2501*
And J took the body and wrapped it Mt 27:59 *2501*
J of Arimathea came, a prominent Mk 15:43 *2501*
he granted the body to J. Mk 15:45 *2501*
J bought a linen cloth, took Him Mk 15:46
engaged to a man whose name was J, Lk 1:27 *2501*
J also went up from Galilee, Lk 2:4 *2501*
and found their way to Mary and J, Lk 2:16 *2501*
being, as was supposed, the son of J, Lk 3:23 *2501*
the son of Jannai, the son of J, Lk 3:24 *2501*
the son of Judah, the son of J, Lk 3:30 *2501*
And a man named J, Lk 23:50 *2501*
Jesus of Nazareth, the son of J." Jn 1:45 *2501*
that Jacob gave to his son J; Jn 4:5 *2501*
"Is not this Jesus, the son of J, Jn 6:42 *2501*
After these things J of Arimathea, Jn 19:38 *2501*
two men, J called Barsabbas Ac 1:23 *2501*
Now J, a Levite of Cyprian birth, Ac 4:36 *2501*
The patriarchs became jealous of J Ac 7:9 *2501*
"On the second *visit* J made Ac 7:13 *2501*
"Then J sent *word* and invited Ac 7:14 *2501*
EGYPT WHO KNEW NOTHING ABOUT J. Ac 7:18 *2501*
blessed each of the sons of J, Heb 11:21 *2501*
By faith J, when he was dying, Heb 11:22 *2501*
the tribe of J twelve thousand, Rv 7:8 *2501*

JOSEPH'S

So they took J tunic, and Gn 37:31 3130
everything he owned in J charge; Gn 39:6 3130
So J master took him and put him Gn 39:20 3130
chief jailer committed to J charge all Gn 39:22 3130
supervise anything under J charge Gn 39:23
his hand and put it on J hand, Gn 41:42 3130
But Jacob did not send J brother Gn 42:4 3130
And J brothers came and bowed down Gn 42:6 3130
and brought the men to J house. Gn 43:17 3130
they were brought to J house; Gn 43:18 3130
they came near to J house steward, Gn 43:19 3130
man brought the men into J house Gn 43:24 3130
prepared the present for J coming Gn 43:25 3130
and his brothers came to J house, Gn 44:14 3130
house that J brothers had come, Gn 45:16 3130
When Israel saw J sons, he said, Gn 48:8 3130
When J brothers saw that their Gn 50:15 3130
of Manasseh, were born on J knees. Gn 50:23 3130
the half-tribe of J son Manasseh, Nu 32:33 3130
became the inheritance of J sons. Jos 24:32 3130
"Is this not J son?" Lk 4:22 *2501*
and J family was disclosed to Ac 7:13 *2501*

JOSES

Mary, and brother of James and J Mk 6:3 *2500*
mother of James the Less and J, Mk 15:40 *2500*
and Mary the *mother* of J were Mk 15:47 *2500*

JOSHAH

Jamlech and J the son of Amaziah, 1Ch 4:34 3144

JOSHAPHAT

son of Maacah and J the Mithnite, 1Ch 11:43 3092
Shebaniah, J, Nethanel, 1Ch 15:24 3092

JOSHAVIAH

the Mahavite and Jeribai and J, 1Ch 11:46 3145

JOSHBEKASHAH

Giddalti and Romamti-ezer, J, 1Ch 25:4 3436
for the seventeenth to J, 1Ch 25:24 3436

JOSHEB-BASSHEBETH

J a Tahchemonite, chief of the 2Sa 23:8 3429

JOSHIBIAH

and Joel and Jehu the son of J, 1Ch 4:35 3143

JOSHUA

So Moses said to J, Ex 17:9 3091
J did as Moses told him, and Ex 17:10 3091
So J overwhelmed Amalek and his Ex 17:13 3091
as a memorial and recite it to J, Ex 17:14 3091
So Moses arose with J his servant, Ex 24:13 3091
Now when J heard the sound of the Ex 32:17 3091
to the camp, his servant J, Ex 33:11 3091
Then J the son of Nun, the Nu 11:28 3091
called Hoshea the son of Nun, J. Nu 13:16 3091
J the son of Nun and Caleb the Nu 14:6 3091
of Jephunneh and J the son of Nun. Nu 14:30 3091
But J the son of Nun and Caleb the Nu 14:38 3091
Jephunneh and J the son of Nun. Nu 26:65 3091
"Take J the son of Nun, a man in Nu 27:18 3091
and he took J and set him before Nu 27:22 3091
Kenizzite and J the son of Nun, Nu 32:12 3091
priest, and to J the son of Nun, Nu 32:28 3091
the priest and J the son of Nun. Nu 34:17 3091
'J the son of Nun, who stands Dt 1:38 3091
"I commanded J at that time, Dt 3:21 3091
'But charge J and encourage him Dt 3:28 3091
J is the one who will cross ahead Dt 31:3 3091
Then Moses called to J and said to Dt 31:7 3091
call J, and present yourselves at Dt 31:14 3091
So Moses and J went and presented Dt 31:14 3091
He commissioned J the son of Nun, Dt 31:23 3091
people, he, with J the son of Nun. Dt 32:44 1954
Now J the son of Nun was filled Dt 34:9 3091
LORD spoke to J the son of Nun, Jos 1:1 3091
Then J commanded the officers of Jos 1:10 3091
the half-tribe of Manasseh, J said, Jos 1:12 3091
They answered J, Jos 1:16 3091
Then J the son of Nun sent two men Jos 2:1 3091
over and came to J the son of Nun, Jos 2:23 3091
They said to J, Jos 2:24 3091
Then J rose early in the morning; Jos 3:1 3091
Then J said to the people, Jos 3:5 3091
And J spoke to the priests, Jos 3:6 3091
Now the LORD said to J, Jos 3:7 3091
Then J said to the sons of Israel, Jos 3:9 3091
J said, "By this you shall know Jos 3:10 3091
Jordan, the LORD spoke to J, Jos 4:1 3091
So J called the twelve men whom he Jos 4:4 3091
and J said to them, Jos 4:5 3091
of Israel did as J commanded, Jos 4:8 3091
just as the LORD spoke to J, Jos 4:8 3091
Then J set up twelve stones in the Jos 4:9 3091
LORD had commanded J to speak Jos 4:10 3091
to all that Moses had commanded J. Jos 4:10 3091
the LORD exalted J in the sight of Jos 4:14 3091
Now the LORD said to J, Jos 4:15 3091
So J commanded the priests, Jos 4:17 3091
the Jordan, J set up at Gilgal. Jos 4:20 3091
At that time the LORD said to J, Jos 5:2 3091
So J made himself flint knives and Jos 5:3 3091
the reason why J circumcised them: Jos 5:4 3091
up in their place, J circumcised; Jos 5:7 3091
Then the LORD said to J, Jos 5:9 3091
came about when J was by Jericho, Jos 5:13 3091
and J went to him and said to him, Jos 5:13 3091
J fell on his face to the earth, Jos 5:14 3091
captain of the LORD's host said to J Jos 5:15 3091
And J did so. Jos 5:15 3091
The LORD said to J, Jos 6:2 3091
So J the son of Nun called the Jos 6:6 3091
when J had spoken to the people, Jos 6:8 3091
But J commanded the people, Jos 6:10 3091
Now J rose early in the morning, Jos 6:12 3091
trumpets, J said to the people, Jos 6:16 3091
J said to the two men who had Jos 6:22 3091
and all she had, J spared; Jos 6:25 3091
whom J sent to spy out Jericho. Jos 6:25 3091
Then J made them take an oath at Jos 6:26 3091
So the LORD was with J, Jos 6:27 3091
Now J sent men from Jericho to Ai, Jos 7:2 3091
returned to J and said to him, Jos 7:3 3091
Then J tore his clothes and fell Jos 7:6 3091
J said, "Alas, O Lord GOD, Jos 7:7 3091
So the LORD said to J, Jos 7:10 3091
So J arose early in the morning Jos 7:16 3091
Then J said to Achan, Jos 7:19 3091
So Achan answered J and said, Jos 7:20 3091
So J sent messengers, and they ran Jos 7:22 3091
brought them to J and to all the Jos 7:23 3091
Then J and all Israel with him, Jos 7:24 3091
J said, "Why have you troubled us? Jos 7:25 3091
Now the LORD said to J, Jos 8:1 3091
So J rose with all the people of Jos 8:3 3091
and J chose 30,000 men, valiant Jos 8:3 3091
So J sent them away, and they went Jos 8:9 3091
but J spent that night among the Jos 8:9 3091
Now J rose early in the morning Jos 8:10 3091
and J spent that night in the Jos 8:13 3091
J and all Israel pretended to Jos 8:15 3091
pursue them, and they pursued J and Jos 8:16 3091
Then the LORD said to J, Jos 8:18 3091
So J stretched out the javelin Jos 8:18 3091
When J and all Israel saw that the Jos 8:21 3091
king of Ai and brought him to J. Jos 8:23 3091
For J did not withdraw his hand Jos 8:26 3091
the LORD which He had commanded J. Jos 8:27 3091
So J burned Ai and made it a heap Jos 8:28 3091

and at sunset J gave command and Jos 8:29 3091
Then J built an altar to the LORD, Jos 8:30 3091
which J did not read before all the Jos 8:35 3091
to fight with J and with Israel. Jos 9:2 3091
J had done to Jericho and to Ai, Jos 9:3 3091
went to J to the camp at Gilgal and Jos 9:6 3091
But they said to J, Jos 9:8 3091
Then J said to them, Jos 9:8 3091
J made peace with them and Jos 9:15 3091
Then J called for them and spoke Jos 9:22 3091
So they answered J and said, Jos 9:24 3091
But J made them that day hewers of Jos 9:27 3091
heard that J had captured Ai, Jos 10:1 3091
it has made peace with J and with Jos 10:4 3091
the men of Gibeon sent *word* to J Jos 10:6 3091
So J went up from Gilgal, he and Jos 10:7 3091
The LORD said to J, Jos 10:8 3091
So J came upon them suddenly by Jos 10:9 3091
Then J spoke to the LORD in the Jos 10:12 3091
Then J and all Israel with him Jos 10:15 3091
It was told J, saying, Jos 10:17 3091
J said, "Roll large stones against Jos 10:18 3091
J and the sons of Israel had finished Jos 10:20 3091
people returned to the camp to J at Jos 10:21 3091
J said, "Open the mouth of the cave Jos 10:22 3091
they brought these kings out to J, Jos 10:24 3091
J called for all the men of Jos 10:24 3091
J then said to them, Jos 10:25 3091
So afterward J struck them and put Jos 10:26 3091
about at sunset that J gave Jos 10:27 3091
J captured Makkedah on that day, Jos 10:28 3091
Then J and all Israel with him Jos 10:29 3091
And J and all Israel with him Jos 10:31 3091
and J defeated him and his people Jos 10:33 3091
And J and all Israel with him Jos 10:34 3091
Then J and all Israel with him Jos 10:36 3091
Then J and all Israel with him Jos 10:38 3091
Thus J struck all the land, the Jos 10:40 3091
J struck them from Jos 10:41 3091
J captured all these kings and Jos 10:42 3091
So J and all Israel with him Jos 10:43 3091
Then the LORD said to J, Jos 11:6 3091
So J and all the people of war Jos 11:7 3091
J did to them as the LORD had Jos 11:9 3091
Then J turned back at that time, Jos 11:10 3091
J captured all the cities of Jos 11:12 3091
Hazor alone, *which* J burned. Jos 11:13 3091
his servant, so Moses commanded J, Jos 11:15 3091
commanded Joshua, and so J did; Jos 11:15 3091
Thus J took all that land: Jos 11:16 3091
J waged war a long time with all Jos 11:18 3091
Then J came at that time and cut Jos 11:21 3091
J utterly destroyed them with Jos 11:21 3091
So J took the whole land, Jos 11:23 3091
and J gave it for an inheritance Jos 11:23 3091
J and the sons of Israel defeated Jos 12:7 3091
and J gave it to the tribes of Jos 12:7 3091
Now J was old *and* advanced in Jos 13:1 3091
the priest, and J the son of Nun, Jos 14:1 3091
of Judah drew near to J in Gilgal, Jos 14:6 3091
So J blessed him and gave Hebron Jos 14:13 3091
to the command of the LORD to J, Jos 15:13 3091
before J the son of Nun and before Jos 17:4 3091
the sons of Joseph spoke to J, Jos 17:14 3091
J said to them, Jos 17:15 3091
J spoke to the house of Joseph, Jos 17:17 3091
So J said to the sons of Israel, Jos 18:3 3091
and J commanded those who went to Jos 18:8 3091
came to J to the camp at Shiloh. Jos 18:9 3091
And J cast lots for them in Shiloh Jos 18:10 3091
and there J divided the land to Jos 18:10 3091
their midst to J the son of Nun. Jos 19:49 3091
the priest, and J the son of Nun Jos 19:51 3091
Then the LORD spoke to J, Jos 20:1 3091
J the son of Nun, and the heads of Jos 21:1 3091
Then J summoned the Reubenites and Jos 22:1 3091
So J blessed them and sent them Jos 22:6 3091
to the other half J gave *a possession* Jos 22:7 3091
J sent them away to their tents, Jos 22:7 3091
on every side, and J was old, Jos 23:1 3091
that J called for all Israel, for Jos 23:2 3091
Then J gathered all the tribes of Jos 24:1 3091
J said to all the people, Jos 24:2 3091
Then J said to the people, Jos 24:19 3091
The people said to J, Jos 24:21 3091
J said to the people, Jos 24:22 3091
The people said to J, Jos 24:24 3091
So J made a covenant with the Jos 24:25 3091
And J wrote these words in the Jos 24:26 3091
J said to all the people, Jos 24:27 3091
Then J dismissed the people, each Jos 24:28 3091
things that J the son of Nun, Jos 24:29 3091
served the LORD all the days of J Jos 24:31 3091
days of the elders who survived J, Jos 24:31 3091
it came about after the death of J Jg 1:1 3091
When J had dismissed the people, Jg 2:6 3091
served the LORD all the days of J, Jg 2:7 3091
days of the elders who survived J, Jg 2:7 3091
Then J the son of Nun, the servant Jg 2:8 3091
nations which J left when he died, Jg 2:21 3091
not give them into the hand of J. Jg 2:23 3091
into the field of J the Beth-shemite 1Sa 6:14 3091
in the field of J the Beth-shemite. 1Sa 6:18 3091
He spoke by J the son of Nun. 1Ki 16:34 3091
at the entrance of the gate of J 2Ki 23:8 3091
Non his son and J his son. 1Ch 7:27 3091
from the days of J the son of Nun Ne 8:17 3091
and to J the son of Jehozadak, Hg 1:1 3091
and J the son of Jehozadak, Hg 1:12 3091
spirit of J the son of Jehozadak, Hg 1:14 3091
and to J the son of Jehozadak, Hg 2:2 3091
courage also, J son of Jehozadak, Hg 2:4 3091
he showed me J the high priest Zch 3:1 3091
J was clothed with filthy garments Zch 3:3 3091
angel of the LORD admonished J Zch 3:6 3091
'Now listen, J the high priest, Zch 3:8 3091
stone that I have set before J; Zch 3:9 3091
crown and set *it* on the head of J Zch 6:11 3091
the son of J, the son of Eliezer, Lk 3:29 *2424*
our fathers brought it in with J Ac 7:45 *2424*
For if J had given them rest, He Heb 4:8 *2424*

JOSIAH

to the house of David, J by name; 1Ki 13:2 2977
made J his son king in his place. 2Ki 21:24 2977
and J his son became king in his 2Ki 21:26 2977
J was eight years old when he 2Ki 22:1 2977
in the eighteenth year of King J 2Ki 22:3 2977
Now when J turned, he saw the 2Ki 23:16 2977
J also removed all the houses 2Ki 23:19 2977
in the eighteenth year of King J, 2Ki 23:23 2977
J removed the mediums and the 2Ki 23:24 2977
the acts of J and all that he did, 2Ki 23:28 2977
And King J went to meet him, and 2Ki 23:29 2977
took Jehoahaz the son of J and 2Ki 23:30 2977
Neco made Eliakim the son of J king 2Ki 23:34 2977
king in the place of J his father, 2Ki 23:34 2977
Amon his son, J his son. 1Ch 3:14 2977
The sons of J *were* Johanan 1Ch 3:15 2977
made J his son king in his place. 2Ch 33:25 2977
J *was* eight years old when he 2Ch 34:1 2977
J removed all the abominations 2Ch 34:33 2977
Then J celebrated the Passover to 2Ch 35:1 2977
J contributed to the lay people, 2Ch 35:7 2977
to the command of King J. 2Ch 35:16 2977
celebrated such a Passover as J did 2Ch 35:18 2977
J had set the temple in order, 2Ch 35:20 2977
and J went out to engage him. 2Ch 35:20 2977
J would not turn away from him, 2Ch 35:22 2977
The archers shot King J, 2Ch 35:23 2977
Judah and Jerusalem mourned for J. 2Ch 35:24 2977
Jeremiah chanted a lament for J. 2Ch 35:25 2977
female singers speak about J in their 2Ch 35:25 2977
Now the rest of the acts of J and 2Ch 35:26 2977
the land took Joahaz the son of J, 2Ch 36:1 2977
of the LORD came in the days of J the Jer 1:2 2977
days of Jehoiakim the son of J, Jer 1:3 2977
year of Zedekiah the son of J, Jer 1:3 2977
LORD said to me in the days of J Jer 3:6 2977
in regard to Shallum the son of J, Jer 22:11 2977
king in the place of J his father, Jer 22:11 2977
regard to Jehoiakim the son of J, Jer 22:18 2977
year of Jehoiakim the son of J, Jer 25:1 2977
year of J the son of Amon, Jer 25:3 2977
reign of Jehoiakim the son of J, Jer 26:1 2977
reign of Zedekiah the son of J, Jer 27:1 2977
days of Jehoiakim the son of J, Jer 35:1 2977
year of Jehoiakim the son of J, Jer 36:1 2977
spoke to you, from the days of J, Jer 36:2 2977
year of Jehoiakim the son of J, Jer 36:9 2977
Now Zedekiah the son of J whom Jer 37:1 2977
year of Jehoiakim the son of J, Jer 45:1 2977
year of Jehoiakim the son of J, Jer 46:2 2977
in the days of J son of Amon, Zph 1:1 2977
house of J the son of Zephaniah, Zch 6:10 2977
Amon, and Amon the father of J. Mt 1:10 *2502b*
J became the father of Jeconiah and Mt 1:11 *2502b*

JOSIAH'S

In the eighteenth year of J reign 2Ch 35:19 2977

JOSIPHIAH

son of J and 160 males with him; Ezr 8:10 3131

JOTBAH

the daughter of Haruz of J. 2Ki 21:19 3192

JOTBATHAH

Hor-haggidgad and camped at J. Nu 33:33 3193
They journeyed from J and Nu 33:34 3193
and from Gudgodah to J, Dt 10:7 3193

JOTHAM

But J the youngest son of Jerubbaal Jg 9:5 3147
Now when they told J, Jg 9:7 3147
Then J escaped and fled, and went Jg 9:21 3147
the curse of J the son of Jerubbaal Jg 9:57 3147
while J the king's son was over 2Ki 15:5 3147
and J his son became king in his 2Ki 15:7 3147
year of J the son of Uzziah. 2Ki 15:30 3147
J the son of Uzziah king of Judah 2Ki 15:32 3147
the acts of J and all that he did, 2Ki 15:36 3147
And J slept with his fathers, and 2Ki 15:38 3147
of Remaliah, Ahaz the son of J, 2Ki 16:1 3147
The sons of Jahdai *were* Regem, J, 1Ch 2:47 3147
son, Azariah his son, J his son, 1Ch 3:12 3147
in the days of J king of Judah 1Ch 5:17 3147
And J his son *was* over the king's 2Ch 26:21 3147
And J his son became king in his 2Ch 26:23 3147
J was twenty-five years old when 2Ch 27:1 3147
So J became mighty because he 2Ch 27:6 3147
Now the rest of the acts of J, 2Ch 27:7 3147
And J slept with his fathers, and 2Ch 27:9 3147
during the reigns of Uzziah, J, Is 1:1 3147
in the days of Ahaz, the son of J, Is 7:1 3147
during the days of Uzziah, J, Hos 1:1 3147
of Moresheth in the days of J, Mi 1:1 3147
Uzziah was the father of J, Mt 1:9 *2488*
Uzziah was the father of Jotham, J Mt 1:9 *2488*

JOURNEY

the LORD had made his j successful Gn 24:21 1870
you to make your j successful, Gn 24:40 1870
make my j on which I go successful Gn 24:42 1870
keep me on this j that I take, Gn 28:20 1870
Then Jacob went on his j, Gn 29:1 7272
three days' j between himself and Gn 30:36 1870
him *a distance of* seven days' j, Gn 31:23 1870
"Let us take our j and go, and I Gn 33:12 5265
to give them provisions for the j. Gn 42:25 1870
If harm should befall him on the j Gn 42:38 1870
gave them provisions for the j. Gn 45:21 1870
sustenance for his father on the j. Gn 45:23 1870
"Do not quarrel on the j." Gn 45:24 1870
in the land of Canaan on the j, Gn 48:7 1870
three days' j into the wilderness, Ex 3:18 1870
let us go a three days' j into the Ex 5:3 1870
"We must go a three days' j into Ex 8:27 1870
that had befallen them on the j, Ex 18:8 1870
dead person, or is on a distant j, Nu 9:10 1870
who is clean and is not on a j, Nu 9:13 1870
mount of the LORD three days' j, Nu 10:33 1870
about a day's j on this side and a Nu 11:31 1870
and a day's j on the other side, Nu 11:31 1870
became impatient because of the j. Nu 21:4 1870
went three days' j in the wilderness Nu 33:8 1870
It is eleven days' j from Horeb Dt 1:2 1870
'Turn and set your j, Dt 1:7 5265
proceed on your j ahead of the Dt 10:11 4550
provisions in your hand for the j, Jos 9:11 1870
out because of the very long j." Jos 9:13 1870
honor shall not be yours on the j Jg 4:9 1870
and as he made his j, Jg 17:8 1870
you may arise early for your j Jg 19:9 1870
perhaps he can tell us about our j 1Sa 9:6 1870
holy, though it was an ordinary j; 1Sa 21:5 1870
"Have you not come from a j? 2Sa 11:10 1870
or gone aside, or is on a j, 1Ki 18:27 1870
went a day's j into the wilderness, 1Ki 19:4 1870
the j is too great for you." 1Ki 19:7 1870
made a circuit of seven days' j, 2Ki 3:9 1870
to seek from Him a safe j for us, Ezr 8:21 1870
"How long will your j be, Ne 2:6 4109
at home, He has gone on a long j; Pr 7:19 1870
J down from the summit of Amana, SS 4:8 7788
or a bag for *your* j, Mt 10:10 *3598*
to vine-growers and went on a j. Mt 21:33 *589*
like a man *about* to go on a j, Mt 25:14 *589*
and he went on his j. Mt 25:15 *589*
should take nothing for *their* j, Mk 6:8 *3598*
As He was setting out on a j, Mk 10:17 *3598*
to vine-growers and went on a j. Mk 12:1 *589*
"*It is* like a man away on a j, Mk 13:34 *590*
in the caravan, and went a day's j; Lk 2:44 *3598*
"Take nothing for *your* j, Lk 9:3 *3598*
a Samaritan, who was on a j, Lk 10:33 *3593*
of mine has come to me from a j, Lk 11:6 *3598*
"Nevertheless I must j on today Lk 13:33 *4198*
went on a j into a distant country, Lk 15:13 *589*
and went on a j for a long time. Lk 20:9 *589*
being wearied from His j, Jn 4:6 *3597*
Jerusalem, a Sabbath day's j away. Ac 1:12 *3598*
we left and started on our j, Ac 21:5 *4311*
you to be helped on my j to Judea. 2Co 1:16 *4311*

JOURNEYED

It came about as they j east, Gn 11:2 5265
Abram j on, continuing toward Gn 12:9 5265
and Lot j eastward. Gn 13:11 5265
Now Abraham j from there toward Gn 20:1 5265
Jacob j to Succoth, Gn 33:17 5265
As they j, there was a great terror Gn 35:5 5265
Then they j from Bethel; Gn 35:16 5265
Then Israel j on and pitched his Gn 35:21 5265
Israel j from Rameses to Succoth, Ex 12:37 5265
congregation of the sons of Israel j Ex 17:1 5265
They j from Oboth and camped Nu 21:11 5265
From there they j and camped on Nu 21:13 5265
Then the sons of Israel j, Nu 22:1 5265
They j from Rameses in the Nu 33:3 5265
the sons of Israel j from Rameses and Nu 33:5 5265
They j from Succoth and Nu 33:6 5265
They j from Etham and turned Nu 33:7 5265
They j from before Hahiroth and Nu 33:8 5265
They j from Marah and came to Nu 33:9 5265
They j from Elim and camped Nu 33:10 5265
They j from the Red Sea and Nu 33:11 5265
They j from the wilderness of Sin Nu 33:12 5265
They j from Dophkah and Nu 33:13 5265
They j from Alush and camped Nu 33:14 5265
They j from Rephidim and Nu 33:15 5265
j from the wilderness of Sinai and Nu 33:16 5265
They j from Kibroth-hattaavah and Nu 33:17 5265
They j from Hazeroth and Nu 33:18 5265
They j from Rithmah and Nu 33:19 5265
They j from Rimmon-perez and Nu 33:20 5265
They j from Libnah and camped Nu 33:21 5265
They j from Rissah and camped Nu 33:22 5265
They j from Kehelathah and Nu 33:23 5265
They j from Mount Shepher and Nu 33:24 5265
They j from Haradah and Nu 33:25 5265
They j from Makheloth and Nu 33:26 5265
They j from Tahath and camped Nu 33:27 5265
They j from Terah and camped Nu 33:28 5265
They j from Mithkah and Nu 33:29 5265
They j from Hashmonah and Nu 33:30 5265
They j from Moseroth and Nu 33:31 5265
They j from Bene-jaakan and Nu 33:32 5265
They j from Hor-haggidgad and Nu 33:33 5265
They j from Jotbathah and Nu 33:34 5265
They j from Abronah and Nu 33:35 5265
They j from Ezion-geber and Nu 33:36 5265
They j from Kadesh and camped Nu 33:37 5265

Then they **j** from Mount Hor and Nu 33:41 5265
They **j** from Zalmonah and Nu 33:42 5265
They **j** from Punon and camped Nu 33:43 5265
They **j** from Oboth and camped Nu 33:44 5265
They **j** from Iyim and camped Nu 33:45 5265
They **j** from Dibon-gad and Nu 33:46 5265
They **j** from Almon-diblathaim and Nu 33:47 5265
j from the mountains of Abarim and Nu 33:48 5265
Then we **j** from the river Ahava on Ezr 8:31 5265
"You have **j** to the king with Is 57:9 7788

JOURNEYING

the covenant of the LORD **j** in front Nu 10:33 5265
the various cities were **j** to Him, Lk 8:4 *1975*
as I was **j** to Damascus with the Ac 26:12 *4198*
me and those who were **j** with me. Ac 26:13 *4198*

JOURNEYS

He went on his **j** from the Gn 13:3 4550
Throughout all their **j** Ex 40:36 4550
For throughout all their **j**, Ex 40:38 4550
the sons of Israel set out on their **j** Nu 10:12 4550
are the **j** of the sons of Israel, Nu 33:1 4550
starting places according to their **j** Nu 33:2 4550
and these are their **j** according to Nu 33:2 4550
I have been on frequent **j**, 2Co 11:26 *3597*

JOY

you away with **j** and with songs, Gn 31:27 8057
your God with **j** and a glad heart, Dt 28:47 8057
with **j** and with musical instruments. 1Sa 18:6 8057
flutes and rejoicing with great **j**, 1Ki 1:40 8057
There was **j** indeed in Israel. 1Ch 12:40 8057
cymbals, to raise sounds of **j**. 1Ch 15:16 8057
from the house of Obed-edom with **j**. 1Ch 15:25 8057
Strength and **j** are in His place. 1Ch 16:27 2304
the trees of the forest will sing for **j** 1Ch 16:33 7442
now with **j** I have seen Your people, 1Ch 29:17 8057
returning to Jerusalem with **j**, 2Ch 20:27 8057
So they sang praises with **j**, 2Ch 29:30 8057
Bread *for* seven days with great **j**, 2Ch 30:21 8057
celebrated the seven days with **j**. 2Ch 30:23 8057
So there was great **j** in Jerusalem, 2Ch 30:26 8057
while many shouted aloud for **j**, Ezr 3:12 8057
the sound of the shout of **j** Ezr 3:13 8057
of this house of God with **j**. Ezr 6:16 2305
Bread seven days with **j**, Ezr 6:22 8057
j of the LORD is your strength." Ne 8:10 2304
God had given them great **j**, Ne 12:43 8057
j of Jerusalem was heard from afar. Ne 12:43 8057
and gladness and **j** and honor. Es 8:16 8342
was gladness and **j** for the Jews, Es 8:17 8342
"Behold, this is the **j** of His way; Jb 8:19 4885
the **j** of the godless momentary? Jb 20:5 8057
made the widow's heart sing for **j**. Jb 29:13 7442
That he may see His face with **j**, Jb 33:26 8643
all the sons of God shouted for **j**? Jb 38:7 7321
be glad, Let them ever sing for **j**; Ps 5:11 7442
In Your presence is fullness of **j**; Ps 16:11 8057
will sing for **j** over your victory, Ps 20:5 7442
tent sacrifices with shouts of **j**; Ps 27:6 8643
a shout of **j** *comes* in the morning. Ps 30:5 7440
And shout for **j**, all you who are Ps 32:11 7442
Sing for **j** in the LORD, O you Ps 33:1 7442
Play skillfully with a shout of **j**. Ps 33:3 8643
Let them shout for **j** and rejoice, Ps 35:27 7442
the voice of **j** and thanksgiving, Ps 42:4 7440
of God, To God my exceeding **j**; Ps 43:4 8057
has anointed You With the oil of **j** Ps 45:7 8342
Shout to God with the voice of **j**. Ps 47:1 7440
the **j** of the whole earth, Ps 48:2 4885
Make me to hear **j** and gladness, Ps 51:8 8342
Restore to me the **j** of Your salvation Ps 51:12 8342
shadow of Your wings I sing for **j**. Ps 63:7 7442
dawn and the sunset shout for **j**. Ps 65:8 7442
They shout for **j**, yes, they sing. Ps 65:13 7321
nations be glad and sing for **j**; Ps 67:4 7442
My lips will shout for **j** when I sing Ps 71:23 7442
Sing for **j** to God our strength; Ps 81:1 7442
My heart and my flesh sing for **j** to Ps 84:2 7442
"All my springs *of* **j** are in Ps 87:7
Hermon shout for **j** at Your name. Ps 89:12 7442
That we may sing for **j** and be glad Ps 90:14 7442
I will sing for **j** at the works of Your Ps 92:4 7442
let us sing for **j** to the LORD, Ps 95:1 7442
the trees of the forest will sing for **j** Ps 96:12 7442
and sing for **j** and sing praises. Ps 98:4 7442
the mountains sing together for **j** Ps 98:8 7442
brought forth His people with **j**, Ps 105:43 8342
For they are the **j** of my heart. Ps 119:111 8342
come again with a shout of **j**, Ps 126:6 7440
And let Your godly ones sing for **j**. Ps 132:9 7442
godly ones will sing aloud for **j**. Ps 132:16 7442
exalt Jerusalem Above my chief **j**. Ps 137:6 8057
Let them sing for **j** on their beds. Ps 149:5 7442
But counselors of peace have **j**. Pr 12:20 8057
a stranger does not share its **j**. Pr 14:10 8057
And the end of **j** may be grief. Pr 14:13 8057
Folly is **j** to him who lacks sense, Pr 15:21 8057
A man has **j** in an apt answer, And Pr 15:23 8057
And the father of a fool has no **j**. Pr 17:21 8055
of justice is **j** for the righteous, Pr 21:15 8057
given wisdom and knowledge and **j**, Ec 2:26 8057
Cry aloud and shout for **j**, Is 12:6 7442
They break forth into shouts of **j**. Is 14:7 7440
Gladness and **j** are taken away Is 16:10 1524a
no cries of **j** or jubilant shouting, Is 16:10 7442
All **j** turns to gloom. Is 24:11 8057
their voices, they shout for **j**; Is 24:14 7442
the dust, awake and shout for **j**, Is 26:19 7442
with rejoicing and shout of **j**. Is 35:2 7442
of the mute will shout for **j**. Is 35:6 7442
everlasting **j** upon their heads. Is 35:10 8057
They will find gladness and **j**, Is 35:10 8057
Let them shout for **j** from the tops Is 42:11 6681
Shout for **j**, O heavens, for the Is 44:23 7442
Break forth into a shout of **j**, Is 44:23 7440
Shout for **j**, O heavens! Is 49:13 7442
J and gladness will be found in Is 51:3 8342
everlasting **j** *will be* on their heads. Is 51:11 8057
They will obtain gladness and **j**, Is 51:11 8057
"Shout for **j**, O barren one, you Is 54:1 7442
"For you will go out with **j** And Is 55:12 8057
hills will break forth into shouts of **j** Is 55:12 7440
A **j** from generation to generation. Is 60:15 4885
shout for **j** over their portion. Is 61:7 7442
Everlasting **j** will be theirs. Is 61:7 8057
that we may see your **j**.' Is 66:5 8057
voice of **j** and the voice of gladness, Jer 7:34 8342
Your words became for me a **j** and Jer 15:16 8342
I will take from them the voice of **j** Jer 25:10 8342
shout for **j** on the height of Zion, Jer 31:12 7442
I will turn their mourning into **j** And Jer 31:13 8342
and give them **j** for their sorrow. Jer 31:13 8055
'It will be to Me a name of **j**, Jer 33:9 8342
voice of **j** and the voice of gladness, Jer 33:11 8342
"So gladness and **j** are taken away Jer 48:33 1524a
shouting will not be shouts *of* **j**. Jer 48:33
been deserted, The town of My **j**! Jer 49:25 4885
Will shout for **j** over Babylon, Jer 51:48 7442
beauty, A **j** to all the earth'?" La 2:15 4885
The **j** of our hearts has ceased; La 5:15 4885
stronghold, the **j** of their pride, Ezk 24:25 4885
as a possession with wholehearted **j** Ezk 36:5 8057
and **j** from the house of our God? Jl 1:16 1524a
Shout for **j**, O daughter of Zion! Zph 3:14 7442
He will exult over you with **j**, Zph 3:17 8057
rejoice over you with shouts of **j**. Zph 3:17 7440
"Sing for **j** and be glad, O Zch 2:10 7442
of the tenth *months* will become **j**, Zch 8:19 8342
rejoiced exceedingly with great **j**. Mt 2:10 *5479*
immediately receives it with **j**; Mt 13:20 *5479*
and from **j** over it he goes and Mt 13:44 *5479*
enter into the **j** of your master.' Mt 25:21 *5479*
enter into the **j** of your master.' Mt 25:23 *5479*
the tomb quickly with fear and great **j** Mt 28:8 *5479*
immediately receive it with **j**; Mk 4:16 *5479*
"You will have **j** and gladness, Lk 1:14 *5479*
the baby leaped in my womb for **j**. Lk 1:44 *20*
I bring you good news of great **j** Lk 2:10 *5479*
"Be glad in that day and leap *for* **j**, Lk 6:23
hear, receive the word with **j**; Lk 8:13 *5479*
The seventy returned with **j**, Lk 10:17 *5479*
there will be *more* **j** in heaven Lk 15:7 *5479*
there is **j** in the presence of the Lk 15:10 *5479*
not believe *it* because of their **j** Lk 24:41 *5479*
returned to Jerusalem with great **j**, Lk 24:52 *5479*
this **j** of mine has been made full. Jn 3:29 *5479*
to you so that My **j** may be in you, Jn 15:11 *5479*
and *that* your **j** may be made full. Jn 15:11 *5479*
your grief will be turned into **j**. Jn 16:20 *5479*
the **j** that a child has been born Jn 16:21 *5479*
no one *will* take your **j** away from you. Jn 16:22 *5479*
that your **j** may be made full. Jn 16:24 *5479*
have My **j** made full in themselves. Jn 17:13 *5479*
because of her **j** she did not open Ac 12:14 *5479*
filled with **j** and with the Holy Ac 13:52 *5479*
bringing great **j** to all the brethren. Ac 15:3 *5479*
peace and **j** in the Holy Spirit. Ro 14:17 *5479*
with all **j** and peace in believing, Ro 15:13 *5479*
so that I may come to you in **j** by Ro 15:32 *5479*
are workers with you for your **j**; 2Co 1:24 *5479*
my **j** would be *the joy* of you all. 2Co 2:3 *5479*
you all that my joy would be *the* **j** 2Co 2:3
with **j** in all our affliction. 2Co 7:4 *5479*
even much more for the **j** of Titus, 2Co 7:13 *5479*
their abundance of **j** and their deep 2Co 8:2 *5479*
fruit of the Spirit is love, **j**, Ga 5:22 *5479*
always offering prayer with **j** in Php 1:4 *5479*
your progress and **j** in the faith, Php 1:25 *5479*
make my **j** complete by being of the Php 2:2 *5479*
and share my **j** with you all. Php 2:17 *4796*
same way and share your **j** with me. Php 2:18 *4796*
Receive him then in the Lord with all **j**, Php 2:29 *5479*
I long *to see*, my **j** and crown, Php 4:1 *5479*
with the **j** of the Holy Spirit, 1Th 1:6 *5479*
hope or **j** or crown of exultation? 1Th 2:19 *5479*
For you are our glory and **j**. 1Th 2:20 *5479*
in return for all the **j** with which we 1Th 3:9 *5479*
so that I may be filled with **j**. 2Tm 1:4 *5479*
I have come to have much **j** and Phm 1:7 *5479*
who for the **j** set before Him Heb 12:2 *5479*
do this with **j** and not with grief, Heb 13:17 *5479*
Consider it all **j**, my brethren, Jas 1:2 *5479*
mourning and your **j** to gloom. Jas 4:9 *5479*
greatly rejoice with **j** inexpressible 1Pe 1:8 *5479*
that our **j** may be made complete. 1Jn 1:4 *5479*
that your **j** may be made full. 2Jn 1:12 *5479*
I have no greater **j** than this, 3Jn 1:4 *5479*
His glory blameless with great **j**, Jude 1:24 *20*

JOYFUL

so that you will be altogether **j**. Dt 16:15 8056
Then they went to their tents **j** 1Ki 8:66 8056
bread, and let your heart be **j**; 1Ki 21:7 3190
Let no **j** shout enter it. Jb 3:7 7445
You make him **j** with gladness Ps 21:6 2302b
mouth offers praises with **j** lips. Ps 63:5 7445
the people who know the **j** sound! Ps 89:15 8643
Come before Him with **j** singing. Ps 100:2 7445
His chosen ones with a **j** shout. Ps 105:43 7440
tell of His works with **j** singing. Ps 107:22 7440
house *As* a **j** mother of children. Ps 113:9 8056
The sound of **j** shouting and Ps 118:15 7440
And our tongue with **j** shouting; Ps 126:2 7440
tears shall reap with **j** shouting. Ps 126:5 7440
there is **j** shouting. Pr 11:10 7440
A **j** heart makes a cheerful face, Pr 15:13 8056
A **j** heart is good medicine, But a Pr 17:22 8056
Yea, for all the **j** houses Is 32:13 4885
And come with **j** shouting to Zion, Is 35:10 7440
with the sound of **j** shouting, Is 48:20 7440
Break forth into **j** shouting, Is 49:13 7440
And come with **j** shouting to Zion, Is 51:11 7440
Break forth into **j** shouting and cry Is 54:1 7440
make them **j** in My house of prayer. Is 56:7 8055
"Be **j** with Jerusalem and rejoice Is 66:10 8055
tumult rather than **j** shouting on Ezk 7:7 1906
for the moment seems not to be **j**, Heb 12:11 *5479*

JOYFULLY

go **j** with the king to the banquet." Es 5:14 8056
will **j** sing of Your righteousness. Ps 51:14 7442
I shall **j** sing of Your lovingkindness Ps 59:16 7442
Shout **j** to God, all the earth; Ps 66:1 7321
Shout **j** to the God of Jacob. Ps 81:1 7321
Let us shout **j** to the rock of our Ps 95:1 7321
Let us shout **j** to Him with psalms. Ps 95:2 7321
Shout **j** to the LORD, all the earth; Ps 98:4 7321
the horn Shout **j** before the King, Ps 98:6 7321
Shout **j** to the LORD, all the earth. Ps 100:1 7321
shout **j** of Your righteousness. Ps 145:7 7442
Shout **j**, you lower parts of the Is 44:23 7321
voices, They shout **j** together; Is 52:8 7442
Break forth, shout **j** together, Is 52:9 7442
will shout **j** with a glad heart, Is 65:14 7442
the disciples began to praise God **j** Lk 19:37 *5463*
For I **j** concur with the law of God Ro 7:22 *4913*
accepted **j** the seizure of your Heb 10:34 *5479*

JOYOUSLY

"The ostriches' wings flap **j** With Jb 39:13 5965
Therefore you will **j** draw water Is 12:3 8342
j living in splendor every day. Lk 16:19 *2165*
of all steadfastness and patience; **j** Col 1:11 *5479*

JOZABAD

Johanan, **J** the Gederathite, 1Ch 12:4 3107
Adnah, **J**, Jediael, Michael, 1Ch 12:20 3107
Jozabad, Jediael, Michael, **J**, 1Ch 12:20 3107
Nahath, Asahel, Jerimoth, **J**, 2Ch 31:13 3107
and Hashabiah and Jeiel and **J**, 2Ch 35:9 3107
J the son of Jeshua and Noadiah Ezr 8:33 3107
Maaseiah, Ishmael, Nethanel, **J** and Ezr 10:22 3107
Of Levites *there were* **J**, Ezr 10:23 3107
Maaseiah, Kelita, Azariah, **J**, Ne 8:7 3107
and Shabbethai and **J**, Ne 11:16 3107

JOZACAR

For **J** the son of Shimeath and 2Ki 12:21 3108

JOZADAK

Jeshua the son of **J** and his brothers Ezr 3:2 3087
Jeshua the son of **J** and the rest of Ezr 3:8 3087
Jeshua the son of **J** arose and began Ezr 5:2 3136b
the sons of Jeshua the son of **J**, Ezr 10:18 3087
the son of Jeshua, the son of **J**, Ne 12:26 3087

JUBAL

His brother's name was **J**; Gn 4:21 3106

JUBILANT

of revelry and the **j** within her, Is 5:14 5938
be no cries of joy or **j** shouting, Is 16:10 7321
Is this your **j** *city,* Whose origin Is 23:7 5947
joyful houses *and for* the **j** city. Is 32:13 5947
you are glad, because you are **j**, Jer 50:11 5937
that they may become **j** And may Jer 51:39 5937

JUBILEE

It shall be a **j** for you, and each Lv 25:10 3104
have the fiftieth year as a **j**; Lv 25:11 3104
'For it is a **j**; it shall be holy to you. Lv 25:12 3104
'On this year of **j** each of you Lv 25:13 3104
the number of years after the **j**, Lv 25:15 3104
its purchaser until the year of **j**; Lv 25:28 3104
but at the **j** it shall revert, that Lv 25:28 3104
it does not revert in the **j**. Lv 25:30 3104
rights and revert in the **j**. Lv 25:31 3104
this possession reverts in the **j**, Lv 25:33 3104
with you until the year of **j**. Lv 25:40 3104
to him up to the year of **j**; Lv 25:50 3104
years remain until the year of **j**, Lv 25:52 3104
still go out in the year of **j**, Lv 25:54 3104
his field as of the year of **j**, Lv 27:17 3104
consecrates his field after the **j**, Lv 27:18 3104
that are left until the year of **j**; Lv 27:18 3104
and when it reverts in the **j**, Lv 27:21 3104
valuation up to the year of **j**; Lv 27:23 3104
'In the year of **j** the field shall Lv 27:24 3104
the **j** of the sons of Israel comes, Nu 36:4 3104

JUCAL

and **J** the son of Shelemiah, Jer 38:1 3081

JUDAH

Therefore she named him **J**. Gn 29:35 3063
and **J** and Issachar and Zebulun; Gn 35:23 3063
J said to his brothers, Gn 37:26 3063
that **J** departed from his brothers and Gn 38:1 3063
J saw there a daughter of a Gn 38:2 3063
Now **J** took a wife for Er his Gn 38:6 3063
Then **J** said to Onan, Gn 38:8 3063
Then **J** said to his daughter-in-law Gn 38:11 3063
Shua's daughter, the wife of **J**, died Gn 38:12 3063
J went up to his sheepshearers at Gn 38:12 3063
When **J** saw her, he thought she *was* Gn 38:15 3063
When **J** sent the young goat by his friend Gn 38:20 3063

So he returned to **J**, **Gn 38:22** 3063
Then **J** said, "Let her keep them, **Gn 38:23** 3063
months later that **J** was informed, **Gn 38:24** 3063
J said, "Bring her out and let her be **Gn 38:24** 3063
J recognized *them,* and said, **Gn 38:26** 3063
J spoke to him, however, saying, **Gn 43:3** 3063
J said to his father Israel, **Gn 43:8** 3063
When **J** and his brothers came to **Gn 44:14** 3063
So **J** said, "What can we say to my **Gn 44:16** 3063
Then **J** approached him, and said, **Gn 44:18** 3063
The sons of **J**: **Gn 46:12** 3063
he sent **J** before him to Joseph, **Gn 46:28** 3063
"**J**, your brothers shall praise **Gn 49:8** 3063
"**J** is a lion's whelp; **Gn 49:9** 3063
scepter shall not depart from **J**, **Gn 49:10** 3063
Reuben, Simeon, Levi and **J**; **Ex 1:2** 3063
the son of Hur, of the tribe of **J**. **Ex 31:2** 3063
the son of Hur, of the tribe of **J**. **Ex 35:30** 3063
the son of Hur, of the tribe of **J**, **Ex 38:22** 3063
of **J**, Nahshon the son of Amminadab; **Nu 1:7** 3063
Of the sons of **J**, their **Nu 1:26** 3063
numbered men of the tribe of **J** **Nu 1:27** 3063
of the standard of the camp of **J**, **Nu 2:3** 3063
and the leader of the sons of **J**: **Nu 2:3** 3063
the numbered men of the camp of **J**: **Nu 2:9** 3063
of Amminadab, of the tribe of **J**; **Nu 7:12** 3063
of the camp of the sons of **J**, **Nu 10:14** 3063
from the tribe of **J**, **Nu 13:6** 3063
The sons of **J** *were* Er and Onan, **Nu 26:19** 3063
The sons of **J** according to **Nu 26:20** 3063
These are the families of **J** **Nu 26:22** 3063
of the tribe of **J**, Caleb the son **Nu 34:19** 3063
Simeon, Levi, **J**, Issachar, Joseph, **Dt 27:12** 3063
And this regarding **J**; **Dt 33:7** 3063
"Hear, O LORD, the voice of **J**, **Dt 33:7** 3063
land of **J** as far as the western sea, **Dt 34:2** 3063
son of Zerah, from the tribe of **J**, **Jos 7:1** 3063
and the tribe of **J** was taken. **Jos 7:16** 3063
He brought the family of **J** near, **Jos 7:17** 3063
son of Zerah, from the tribe of **J**, **Jos 7:18** 3063
and from all the hill country of **J** **Jos 11:21** 3063
J drew near to Joshua in Gilgal, **Jos 14:6** 3063
the lot for the tribe of the sons of **J** **Jos 15:1** 3063
is the border around the sons of **J** **Jos 15:12** 3063
a portion among the sons of **J**, **Jos 15:13** 3063
the tribe of the sons of **J** according **Jos 15:20** 3063
of the tribe of the sons of **J** toward **Jos 15:21** 3063
sons of **J** could not drive them out **Jos 15:63** 3063
Jebusites live with the sons of **J** **Jos 15:63** 3063
J shall stay in its territory on **Jos 18:5** 3063
lay between the sons of **J** and the **Jos 18:11** 3063
a city of the sons of **J**. **Jos 18:14** 3063
the inheritance of the sons of **J**. **Jos 19:1** 3063
from the portion of the sons of **J**, **Jos 19:9** 3063
share of the sons of **J** was too large **Jos 19:9** 3063
J at the Jordan toward the east. **Jos 19:34** 3063
in the hill country of **J**. **Jos 20:7** 3063
cities by lot from the tribe of **J** **Jos 21:4** 3063
name from the tribe of the sons of **J** **Jos 21:9** 3063
in the hill country of **J**, **Jos 21:11** 3063
The LORD said, "**J** shall go up; **Jg 1:2** 3063
Then **J** said to Simeon his brother, **Jg 1:3** 3063
J went up, and the LORD gave **Jg 1:4** 3063
Then the sons of **J** fought against **Jg 1:8** 3063
Afterward the sons of **J** went **Jg 1:9** 3063
So **J** went against the Canaanites **Jg 1:10** 3063
city of palms with the sons of **J**, **Jg 1:16** 3063
wilderness of **J** which is in the south **Jg 1:16** 3063
J went with Simeon his brother, **Jg 1:17** 3063
And **J** took Gaza with its territory **Jg 1:18** 3063
Now the LORD was with **J**, **Jg 1:19** 3063
Jordan to fight also against **J**, **Jg 10:9** 3063
Philistines went up and camped in **J** **Jg 15:9** 3063
The men of **J** said, **Jg 15:10** 3063
Then 3,000 men of **J** went down to **Jg 15:11** 3063
a young man from Bethlehem in **J**, **Jg 17:7** 3063
in Judah, of the family of **J**, **Jg 17:7** 3063
the city, from Bethlehem in **J**, **Jg 17:8** 3063
"I am a Levite from Bethlehem in **J**, **Jg 17:9** 3063
and camped at Kiriath-jearim in **J**. **Jg 18:12** 3063
for himself from Bethlehem in **J**. **Jg 19:1** 3063
father's house in Bethlehem in **J**, **Jg 19:2** 3063
We are passing from Bethlehem in **J** **Jg 19:18** 3063
and I went to Bethlehem in **J**. **Jg 19:18** 3063
"**J** *shall go up* first." **Jg 20:18** 3063
certain man of Bethlehem in **J** went **Ru 1:1** 3063
Ephrathites of Bethlehem in **J**. **Ru 1:2** 3063
way to return to the land of **J**. **Ru 1:7** 3063
of Perez whom Tamar bore to **J**, **Ru 4:12** 3063
300,000, and the men of **J** 30,000. **1Sa 11:8** 3063
foot soldiers and 10,000 men of **J**. **1Sa 15:4** 3063
at Socoh which belongs to **J**, **1Sa 17:1** 3063
the Ephrathite of Bethlehem in **J**, **1Sa 17:12** 3063
The men of Israel and **J** arose **1Sa 17:52** 3063
But all Israel and **J** loved David, **1Sa 18:16** 3063
and go into the land of **J**." **1Sa 22:5** 3063
"Behold, we are afraid here in **J**. **1Sa 23:3** 3063
among all the thousands of **J**." **1Sa 23:23** 3063
has belonged to the kings of **J** **1Sa 27:6** 3063
"Against the Negev of **J** and **1Sa 27:10** 3063
and on that which belongs to **J**, **1Sa 30:14** 3063
and from the land of **J**. **1Sa 30:16** 3063
of the spoil to the elders of **J**, **1Sa 30:26** 3063
he told *them* to teach the sons of **J** **2Sa 1:18** 3063
go up to one of the cities of **J**?" **2Sa 2:1** 3063
Then the men of **J** came and there **2Sa 2:4** 3063
David king over the house of **J**. **2Sa 2:4** 3063
house of **J** has anointed me king **2Sa 2:7** 3063
The house of **J**, however, followed **2Sa 2:10** 3063
king in Hebron over the house of **J** **2Sa 2:11** 3063
Am I a dog's head that belongs to **J**? **2Sa 3:8** 3063
of David over Israel and over **J**, **2Sa 3:10** 3063
At Hebron he reigned over **J** seven **2Sa 5:5** 3063
years over all Israel and **J**. **2Sa 5:5** 3063
"The ark and Israel and **J** are **2Sa 11:11** 3063
you the house of Israel and **J**; **2Sa 12:8** 3063
"Speak to the elders of **J**, **2Sa 19:11** 3063
turned the hearts of all the men of **J** **2Sa 19:14** 3063
And **J** came to Gilgal in order to **2Sa 19:15** 3063
came down with the men of **J** to **2Sa 19:16** 3063
and all the people of **J** and also **2Sa 19:40** 3063
the men of **J** stolen you away, **2Sa 19:41** 3063
all the men of **J** answered the men **2Sa 19:42** 3063
answered the men of **J** and said, **2Sa 19:43** 3063
words of the men of **J** were harsher **2Sa 19:43** 3063
the men of **J** remained steadfast to **2Sa 20:2** 3063
Call out the men of **J** for me within **2Sa 20:4** 3063
went to call out *the men of* **J**, **2Sa 20:5** 3063
for the sons of Israel and **J**). **2Sa 21:2** 3063
"Go, number Israel and **J**." **2Sa 24:1** 3063
they went out to the south of **J**, **2Sa 24:7** 3063
and the men of **J** were five hundred **2Sa 24:9** 3063
king's sons, and all the men of **J**, **1Ki 1:9** 3063
to be ruler over Israel and **J**." **1Ki 1:35** 3063
commander of the army of **J**. **1Ki 2:32** 3063
J and Israel *were* as numerous as **1Ki 4:20** 3063
So **J** and Israel lived in safety, **1Ki 4:25** 3063
in the land *of* **J**, **1Ki 9:18** 3063
who lived in the cities of **J**, **1Ki 12:17** 3063
None but the tribe of **J** followed **1Ki 12:20** 3063
he assembled all the house of **J** and **1Ki 12:21** 3063
the son of Solomon, king of **J**, **1Ki 12:23** 3063
and to all the house of **J** and **1Ki 12:23** 3063
lord, *even* to Rehoboam king of **J**; **1Ki 12:27** 3063
return to Rehoboam king of **J**." **1Ki 12:27** 3063
like the feast which is in **J**, **1Ki 12:32** 3063
there came a man of God from **J** to **1Ki 13:1** 3063
of God who came from **J** had gone. **1Ki 13:12** 3063
the man of God who came from **J**?" **1Ki 13:14** 3063
to the man of God who came from **J**, **1Ki 13:21** 3063
the son of Solomon reigned in **J**. **1Ki 14:21** 3063
J did evil in the sight of the **1Ki 14:22** 3063
the Chronicles of the Kings of **J**? **1Ki 14:29** 3063
Nebat, Abijam became king over **J**. **1Ki 15:1** 3063
the Chronicles of the Kings of **J**? **1Ki 15:7** 3063
Asa began to reign as king of **J**. **1Ki 15:9** 3063
king of Israel went up against **J** **1Ki 15:17** 3063
out or coming in to Asa king of **J**. **1Ki 15:17** 3063
Asa made a proclamation to all **J** **1Ki 15:22** 3063
the Chronicles of the Kings of **J**? **1Ki 15:23** 3063
the second year of Asa king of **J**, **1Ki 15:25** 3063
the third year of Asa king of **J** and **1Ki 15:28** 3063
the third year of Asa king of **J**, **1Ki 15:33** 3063
twenty-sixth year of Asa king of **J**, **1Ki 16:8** 3063
year of Asa king of **J**, **1Ki 16:10** 3063
year of Asa king of **J**, **1Ki 16:15** 3063
thirty-first year of Asa king of **J**, **1Ki 16:23** 3063
year of Asa king of **J**, **1Ki 16:29** 3063
to Beersheba, which belongs to **J**, **1Ki 19:3** 3063
year Jehoshaphat the king of **J** **1Ki 22:2** 3063
and Jehoshaphat king of **J** were **1Ki 22:10** 3063
Jehoshaphat king of **J** went up **1Ki 22:29** 3063
the son of Asa became king over **J** **1Ki 22:41** 3063
the Chronicles of the Kings of **J**? **1Ki 22:45** 3063
year of Jehoshaphat king of **J**, **1Ki 22:51** 3063
the son of Jehoshaphat, king of **J**. **2Ki 1:17** 3063
year of Jehoshaphat king of **J**, **2Ki 3:1** 3063
word to Jehoshaphat the king of **J**, **2Ki 3:7** 3063
king of **J** and the king of Edom; **2Ki 3:9** 3063
of Jehoshaphat the king of **J**, **2Ki 3:14** 3063
being then the king of **J**, **2Ki 8:16** 3063
the son of Jehoshaphat king of **J** **2Ki 8:16** 3063
LORD was not willing to destroy **J**, **2Ki 8:19** 3063
revolted from under the hand of **J**, **2Ki 8:20** 3063
Edom revolted against **J** to this day. **2Ki 8:22** 3063
the Chronicles of the Kings of **J**? **2Ki 8:23** 3063
Jehoram king of **J** began to reign. **2Ki 8:25** 3063
son of Jehoram king of **J** went down **2Ki 8:29** 3063
Ahaziah king of **J** had come down **2Ki 9:16** 3063
and Ahaziah king of **J** went out, **2Ki 9:21** 3063
Ahaziah the king of **J** saw *this,* **2Ki 9:27** 3063
Ahab, Ahaziah became king over **J**. **2Ki 9:29** 3063
the relatives of Ahaziah king of **J** **2Ki 10:13** 3063
Jehoash king of **J** took all the **2Ki 12:18** 3063
Ahaziah, his fathers, kings of **J**, **2Ki 12:18** 3063
the Chronicles of the Kings of **J**? **2Ki 12:19** 3063
the son of Ahaziah, king of **J**, **2Ki 13:1** 3063
year of Joash king of **J**, **2Ki 13:10** 3063
fought against Amaziah king of **J**, **2Ki 13:12** 3063
son of Joash king of **J** became king. **2Ki 14:1** 3063
Israel sent to Amaziah king of **J**, **2Ki 14:9** 3063
would fall, and **J** with you?" **2Ki 14:10** 3063
and he and Amaziah king of **J** faced **2Ki 14:11** 3063
Beth-shemesh, which belongs to **J**. **2Ki 14:11** 3063
J was defeated by Israel, and **2Ki 14:12** 3063
Israel captured Amaziah king of **J**, **2Ki 14:13** 3063
he fought with Amaziah king of **J**, **2Ki 14:15** 3063
Amaziah the son of Joash king of **J** **2Ki 14:17** 3063
the Chronicles of the Kings of **J**? **2Ki 14:18** 3063
All the people of **J** took Azariah, **2Ki 14:21** 3063
built Elath and restored it to **J** after **2Ki 14:22** 3063
the son of Joash king of **J**, **2Ki 14:23** 3063
Hamath, *which had belonged* to **J**, **2Ki 14:28** 3063
of Amaziah king of **J** became king. **2Ki 15:1** 3063
the Chronicles of the Kings of **J**? **2Ki 15:6** 3063
year of Azariah king of **J**, **2Ki 15:8** 3063
year of Uzziah king of **J**, **2Ki 15:13** 3063
year of Azariah king of **J**, **2Ki 15:17** 3063
year of Azariah king of **J**, **2Ki 15:23** 3063
year of Azariah king of **J**, **2Ki 15:27** 3063
of Uzziah king of **J** became king. **2Ki 15:32** 3063
the Chronicles of the Kings of **J**? **2Ki 15:36** 3063
the son of Remaliah against **J**. **2Ki 15:37** 3063
Ahaz the son of Jotham, king of **J**, **2Ki 16:1** 3063
the Chronicles of the Kings of **J**? **2Ki 16:19** 3063
twelfth year of Ahaz king of **J**, **2Ki 17:1** 3063
Yet the LORD warned Israel and **J** **2Ki 17:13** 3063
was left except the tribe of **J**. **2Ki 17:18** 3063
Also **J** did not keep the **2Ki 17:19** 3063
son of Ahaz king of **J** became king. **2Ki 18:1** 3063
like him among all the kings of **J**, **2Ki 18:5** 3063
against all the fortified cities of **J** **2Ki 18:13** 3063
Then Hezekiah king of **J** sent to **2Ki 18:14** 3063
required of Hezekiah king of **J** three **2Ki 18:14** 3063
Hezekiah king of **J** had overlaid, **2Ki 18:16** 3063
has said to **J** and to Jerusalem, **2Ki 18:22** 3063
shall say to Hezekiah king of **J**, **2Ki 19:10** 3063
surviving remnant of the house of **J** **2Ki 19:30** 3063
the Chronicles of the Kings of **J**? **2Ki 20:20** 3063
Manasseh king of **J** has done these **2Ki 21:11** 3063
also made **J** sin with his idols; **2Ki 21:11** 3063
such calamity on Jerusalem and **J**, **2Ki 21:12** 3063
his sin with which he made **J** sin, **2Ki 21:16** 3063
the Chronicles of the Kings of **J**? **2Ki 21:17** 3063
the Chronicles of the Kings of **J**? **2Ki 21:25** 3063
for me and the people and all **J** **2Ki 22:13** 3063
book which the king of **J** has read. **2Ki 22:16** 3063
"But to the king of **J** who sent **2Ki 22:18** 3063
the elders of **J** and of Jerusalem. **2Ki 23:1** 3063
men of **J** and all the inhabitants of **2Ki 23:2** 3063
whom the kings of **J** had appointed **2Ki 23:5** 3063
in the high places in the cities of **J** **2Ki 23:5** 3063
the priests from the cities of **J**, **2Ki 23:8** 3063
kings of **J** had given to the sun, **2Ki 23:11** 3063
which the kings of **J** had made, **2Ki 23:12** 3063
the man of God who came from **J** **2Ki 23:17** 3063
of Israel and of the kings of **J**. **2Ki 23:22** 3063
in the land of **J** and in Jerusalem, **2Ki 23:24** 3063
which His anger burned against **J**, **2Ki 23:26** 3063
will remove **J** also from My sight, **2Ki 23:27** 3063
the Chronicles of the Kings of **J**? **2Ki 23:28** 3063
sent them against **J** to destroy it, **2Ki 24:2** 3063
of the LORD it came upon **J**, **2Ki 24:3** 3063
the Chronicles of the Kings of **J**? **2Ki 24:5** 3063
Jehoiachin the king of **J** went **2Ki 24:12** 3063
this came about in Jerusalem and **J** **2Ki 24:20** 3063
So **J** was led away into exile from **2Ki 25:21** 3063
who were left in the land of **J**, **2Ki 25:22** 3063
the exile of Jehoiachin king of **J**, **2Ki 25:27** 3063
Jehoiachin king of **J** from prison; **2Ki 25:27** 3063
Reuben, Simeon, Levi, **J**, **1Ch 2:1** 3063
The sons of **J** *were* Er, Onan and **1Ch 2:3** 3063
J had five sons in all. **1Ch 2:4** 3063
Nahshon, leader of the sons of **J**; **1Ch 2:10** 3063
The sons of **J** *were* Perez, Hezron, **1Ch 4:1** 3063
The sons of Shelah the son of **J** **1Ch 4:21** 3063
multiply like the sons of **J**. **1Ch 4:27** 3063
in the days of Hezekiah king of **J**, **1Ch 4:41** 3063
J prevailed over his brothers, **1Ch 5:2** 3063
in the days of Jotham king of **J** **1Ch 5:17** 3063
LORD carried **J** and Jerusalem away **1Ch 6:15** 3063
they gave Hebron in the land of **J** and **1Ch 6:55** 3063
from the tribe of the sons of **J**, **1Ch 6:65** 3063
And **J** was carried away into exile **1Ch 9:1** 3063
Some of the sons of **J**, **1Ch 9:3** 3063
the sons of Perez the son of **J**. **1Ch 9:4** 3063
sons of Benjamin and **J** came to the **1Ch 12:16** 3063
The sons of **J** who bore shield and **1Ch 12:24** 3063
Kiriath-jearim, which belongs to **J**, **1Ch 13:6** 3063
and **J** *was* 470,000 men who drew the **1Ch 21:5** 3063
for **J**, Elihu, *one* of David's brothers **1Ch 27:18** 3063
He has chosen **J** to be a leader; **1Ch 28:4** 3063
and in the house of **J**, **1Ch 28:4** 3063
whom I have in **J** and Jerusalem, **2Ch 2:7** 3063
was seen before in the land of **J**. **2Ch 9:11** 3063
who lived in the cities of **J**, **2Ch 10:17** 3063
the house of **J** and Benjamin, **2Ch 11:1** 3063
the son of Solomon, king of **J**, **2Ch 11:3** 3063
to all Israel in **J** and Benjamin, **2Ch 11:3** 3063
and built cities for defense in **J**. **2Ch 11:5** 3063
cities in **J** and in Benjamin. **2Ch 11:10** 3063
So he held **J** and Benjamin. **2Ch 11:12** 3063
and came to **J** and Jerusalem, **2Ch 11:14** 3063
They strengthened the kingdom of **J** **2Ch 11:17** 3063
through all the territories of **J** **2Ch 11:23** 3063
the fortified cities of **J** **2Ch 12:4** 3063
to Rehoboam and the princes of **J** **2Ch 12:5** 3063
also conditions were good in **J**. **2Ch 12:12** 3063
Abijah became king over **J**. **2Ch 13:1** 3063
so that *Israel* was in front of **J** and **2Ch 13:13** 3063
When **J** turned around, behold, they **2Ch 13:14** 3063
the men of **J** raised a war cry, **2Ch 13:15** 3063
the men of **J** raised the war cry, **2Ch 13:15** 3063
all Israel before Abijah and **J**. **2Ch 13:15** 3063
the sons of Israel fled before **J**, **2Ch 13:16** 3063
and the sons of **J** conquered **2Ch 13:18** 3063
and commanded **J** to seek the LORD **2Ch 14:4** 3063
altars from all the cities of **J**. **2Ch 14:5** 3063
He built fortified cities in **J**, **2Ch 14:6** 3063
For he said to **J**, **2Ch 14:7** 3063
Asa had an army of 300,000 from **J**, **2Ch 14:8** 3063
before Asa and before **J**, **2Ch 14:12** 3063
"Listen to me, Asa, and all **J** and **2Ch 15:2** 3063
idols from all the land of **J** and **2Ch 15:8** 3063
He gathered all **J** and Benjamin **2Ch 15:9** 3063
J rejoiced concerning the oath, **2Ch 15:15** 3063
king of Israel came up against **J** **2Ch 16:1** 3063

out or coming in to Asa king of **J**.	**2Ch 16:1**	3063
Then King Asa brought all **J**,	**2Ch 16:6**	3063
the seer came to Asa king of **J**	**2Ch 16:7**	3063
Book of the Kings of **J** and Israel.	**2Ch 16:11**	3063
in all the fortified cities of **J**,	**2Ch 17:2**	3063
set garrisons in the land of **J** and	**2Ch 17:2**	3063
and all **J** brought tribute to	**2Ch 17:5**	3063
places and the Asherim from **J**.	**2Ch 17:6**	3063
to teach in the cities of **J**;	**2Ch 17:7**	3063
They taught in **J**,	**2Ch 17:9**	3063
went throughout all the cities of **J**	**2Ch 17:9**	3063
of the lands which *were* around **J**,	**2Ch 17:10**	3063
fortresses and store cities in **J**.	**2Ch 17:12**	3063
large supplies in the cities of **J**,	**2Ch 17:13**	3063
of **J**, commanders of thousands,	**2Ch 17:14**	3063
fortified cities through all **J**.	**2Ch 17:19**	3063
said to Jehoshaphat king of **J**,	**2Ch 18:3**	3063
and Jehoshaphat the king of **J** were	**2Ch 18:9**	3063
and Jehoshaphat king of **J** went up	**2Ch 18:28**	3063
Then Jehoshaphat the king of **J**	**2Ch 19:1**	3063
in all the fortified cities of **J**,	**2Ch 19:5**	3063
the ruler of the house of **J**,	**2Ch 19:11**	3063
proclaimed a fast throughout all **J**.	**2Ch 20:3**	3063
So **J** gathered together to seek help	**2Ch 20:4**	3063
even came from all the cities of **J**	**2Ch 20:4**	3063
the assembly of **J** and Jerusalem,	**2Ch 20:5**	3063
J was standing before the LORD,	**2Ch 20:13**	3063
all **J** and the inhabitants of	**2Ch 20:15**	3063
your behalf, O **J** and Jerusalem.'	**2Ch 20:17**	3063
and all **J** and the inhabitants of	**2Ch 20:18**	3063
O **J** and inhabitants of Jerusalem,	**2Ch 20:20**	3063
Seir, who had come against **J**;	**2Ch 20:22**	3063
When **J** came to the lookout of the	**2Ch 20:24**	3063
Every man of **J** and Jerusalem	**2Ch 20:27**	3063
Now Jehoshaphat reigned over **J**.	**2Ch 20:31**	3063
Jehoshaphat king of **J** allied himself	**2Ch 20:35**	3063
with fortified cities in **J**,	**2Ch 21:3**	3063
revolted against the rule of **J** and	**2Ch 21:8**	3063
revolted against **J** to this day.	**2Ch 21:10**	3063
high places in the mountains of **J**,	**2Ch 21:11**	3063
play the harlot and led **J** astray.	**2Ch 21:11**	3063
and the ways of Asa king of **J**,	**2Ch 21:12**	3063
and have caused **J** and the	**2Ch 21:13**	3063
came against **J** and invaded it,	**2Ch 21:17**	3063
Jehoram king of **J** began to reign.	**2Ch 22:1**	3063
the son of Jehoram king of **J**,	**2Ch 22:6**	3063
he found the princes of **J** and the	**2Ch 22:8**	3063
royal offspring of the house of **J**.	**2Ch 22:10**	3063
They went throughout **J** and	**2Ch 23:2**	3063
Levites from all the cities of **J**,	**2Ch 23:2**	3063
So the Levites and all **J** did	**2Ch 23:8**	3063
"Go out to the cities of **J** and	**2Ch 24:5**	3063
Levites to bring in from **J** and from	**2Ch 24:6**	3063
They made a proclamation in **J**	**2Ch 24:9**	3063
officials of **J** came and bowed down	**2Ch 24:17**	3063
so wrath came upon **J** and Jerusalem	**2Ch 24:18**	3063
and they came to **J** and Jerusalem,	**2Ch 24:23**	3063
Amaziah assembled **J** and appointed	**2Ch 25:5**	3063
throughout **J** and Benjamin;	**2Ch 25:5**	3063
so their anger burned against **J**	**2Ch 25:10**	3063
The sons of **J** also captured 10,000	**2Ch 25:12**	3063
to battle, raided the cities of **J**,	**2Ch 25:13**	3063
Then Amaziah king of **J** took	**2Ch 25:17**	3063
Israel sent to Amaziah king of **J**,	**2Ch 25:18**	3063
you, would fall and **J** with you?"	**2Ch 25:19**	3063
and he and Amaziah king of **J** faced	**2Ch 25:21**	3063
Beth-shemesh, which belonged to **J**.	**2Ch 25:21**	3063
J was defeated by Israel, and	**2Ch 25:22**	3063
Israel captured Amaziah king of **J**,	**2Ch 25:23**	3063
the son of Joash king of **J**,	**2Ch 25:25**	3063
Book of the Kings of **J** and Israel?	**2Ch 25:26**	3063
with his fathers in the city of **J**.	**2Ch 25:28**	3063
all the people of **J** took Uzziah,	**2Ch 26:1**	3063
He built Eloth and restored it to **J**	**2Ch 26:2**	3063
cities in the hill country of **J**,	**2Ch 27:4**	3063
Book of the Kings of Israel and **J**.	**2Ch 27:7**	3063
son of Remaliah slew in **J** 120,000	**2Ch 28:6**	3063
of your fathers, was angry with **J**,	**2Ch 28:9**	3063
for yourselves the people of **J** and	**2Ch 28:10**	3063
Edomites had come and attacked **J** and	**2Ch 28:17**	3063
the lowland and of the Negev of **J**,	**2Ch 28:18**	3063
For the LORD humbled **J** because of	**2Ch 28:19**	3063
brought about a lack of restraint in **J**	**2Ch 28:19**	3063
In every city of **J** he made	**2Ch 28:25**	3063
Book of the Kings of **J** and Israel.	**2Ch 28:26**	3063
LORD was against **J** and Jerusalem,	**2Ch 29:8**	3063
the kingdom, the sanctuary, and **J**.	**2Ch 29:21**	3063
Hezekiah sent to all Israel and **J**	**2Ch 30:1**	3063
went throughout all Israel and **J**	**2Ch 30:6**	3063
The hand of God was also on **J** to	**2Ch 30:12**	3063
Hezekiah king of **J** had contributed	**2Ch 30:24**	3063
All the assembly of **J** rejoiced,	**2Ch 30:25**	3063
of Israel and those living in **J**.	**2Ch 30:25**	3063
went out to the cities of **J**,	**2Ch 31:1**	3063
throughout all **J** and Benjamin,	**2Ch 31:1**	3063
The sons of Israel and **J** who	**2Ch 31:6**	3063
who lived in the cities of **J** also	**2Ch 31:6**	3063
Hezekiah did throughout all **J**;	**2Ch 31:20**	3063
king of Assyria came and invaded **J**	**2Ch 32:1**	3063
the words of Hezekiah king of **J**.	**2Ch 32:8**	3063
against Hezekiah king of **J** and	**2Ch 32:9**	3063
all **J** who *were* at Jerusalem,	**2Ch 32:9**	3063
and said to **J** and Jerusalem,	**2Ch 32:12**	3063
a loud voice in the language of **J**	**2Ch 32:18**	3066
presents to Hezekiah king of **J**,	**2Ch 32:23**	3063
wrath came on him and on **J** and	**2Ch 32:25**	3063
Book of the Kings of **J** and Israel.	**2Ch 32:32**	3063
and all **J** and the inhabitants of	**2Ch 32:33**	3063
Thus Manasseh misled **J** and the	**2Ch 33:9**	3063
in all the fortified cities of **J**.	**2Ch 33:14**	3063
and he ordered **J** to serve the LORD	**2Ch 33:16**	3063
he began to purge **J** and Jerusalem	**2Ch 34:3**	3063
and purged **J** and Jerusalem.	**2Ch 34:5**	3063
and from all **J** and Benjamin and	**2Ch 34:9**	3063
the kings of **J** had let go to ruin.	**2Ch 34:11**	3063
who are left in Israel and in **J**,	**2Ch 34:21**	3063
in the presence of the king of **J**.	**2Ch 34:24**	3063
"But to the king of **J** who sent	**2Ch 34:26**	3063
all the elders of **J** and Jerusalem.	**2Ch 34:29**	3063
of the LORD and all the men of **J**,	**2Ch 34:30**	3063
all **J** and Israel who were present,	**2Ch 35:18**	3063
do with each other, O King of **J**?	**2Ch 35:21**	3063
All **J** and Jerusalem mourned	**2Ch 35:24**	3063
Book of the Kings of Israel and **J**.	**2Ch 35:27**	3063
Eliakim his brother king over **J** and	**2Ch 36:4**	3063
Book of the Kings of Israel and **J**.	**2Ch 36:8**	3063
his kinsman Zedekiah king over **J**	**2Ch 36:10**	3063
house in Jerusalem, which is in **J**.	**2Ch 36:23**	3063
house in Jerusalem, which is in **J**.	**Ezr 1:2**	3063
go up to Jerusalem which is in **J** and	**Ezr 1:3**	3063
the heads of fathers' *households* of **J**	**Ezr 1:5**	3063
to Sheshbazzar, the prince of **J**.	**Ezr 1:8**	3063
and returned to Jerusalem and **J**,	**Ezr 2:1**	3063
the sons of **J** *and* the sons of	**Ezr 3:9**	3063
Now when the enemies of **J** and	**Ezr 4:1**	3063
land discouraged the people of **J**,	**Ezr 4:4**	3063
inhabitants of **J** and Jerusalem.	**Ezr 4:6**	3063
Jews who were in **J** and Jerusalem in	**Ezr 5:1**	3061
we have gone to the province of **J**,	**Ezr 5:8**	3061
you are to do for these elders of **J**	**Ezr 6:8**	3062
counselors to inquire concerning **J**	**Ezr 7:14**	3061
give us a wall in **J** and Jerusalem.	**Ezr 9:9**	3063
made a proclamation throughout **J**	**Ezr 10:7**	3063
So all the men of **J** and Benjamin	**Ezr 10:9**	3063
Pethahiah, **J** and Eliezer.	**Ezr 10:23**	3063
and some men from **J** came;	**Ne 1:2**	3063
favor before you, send me to **J**,	**Ne 2:5**	3063
to pass through until I come to **J**,	**Ne 2:7**	3063
Thus in **J** it was said,	**Ne 4:10**	3063
were behind the whole house of **J**.	**Ne 4:16**	3063
their governor in the land of **J**,	**Ne 5:14**	3063
concerning you, 'A king is in **J**!'	**Ne 6:7**	3063
from the nobles of **J** to Tobiah,	**Ne 6:17**	3063
For many in **J** were bound by oath	**Ne 6:18**	3063
who returned to Jerusalem and **J**,	**Ne 7:6**	3063
but in the cities of **J** each lived	**Ne 11:3**	3063
Some of the sons of **J** and some	**Ne 11:4**	3063
From the sons of **J**:	**Ne 11:4**	3063
and **J** the son of Hassenuah was	**Ne 11:9**	3063
were in all the cities of **J**,	**Ne 11:20**	3063
of the sons of Zerah the son of **J**,	**Ne 11:24**	3063
some of the sons of **J** lived in	**Ne 11:25**	3063
divisions in **J** belonged to Benjamin.	**Ne 11:36**	3063
Binnui, Kadmiel, Sherebiah, **J**,	**Ne 12:8**	3063
I had the leaders of **J** come up on	**Ne 12:31**	3063
and half of the leaders of **J** followed	**Ne 12:32**	3063
J, Benjamin, Shemaiah, Jeremiah,	**Ne 12:34**	3063
Maai, Nethanel, **J** *and* Hanani,	**Ne 12:36**	3063
for **J** rejoiced over the priests	**Ne 12:44**	3063
All **J** then brought the tithe of	**Ne 13:12**	3063
In those days I saw in **J** some who	**Ne 13:15**	3063
to the sons of **J** on the sabbath,	**Ne 13:16**	3063
the nobles of **J** and said to them,	**Ne 13:17**	3063
able to speak the language of **J**,	**Ne 13:24**	3066
exiled with Jeconiah king of **J**,	**Es 2:6**	3063
Let the daughters of **J** rejoice Because	**Ps 48:11**	3063
helmet of My head; **J** is My scepter.	**Ps 60:7**	3063
The princes of **J** *in* their throng,	**Ps 68:27**	3063
Zion and build the cities of **J**,	**Ps 69:35**	3063
God is known in **J**;	**Ps 76:1**	3063
But chose the tribe of **J**,	**Ps 78:68**	3063
And the daughters of **J** have	**Ps 97:8**	3063
helmet of My head; **J** is My scepter.	**Ps 108:8**	3063
J became His sanctuary, Israel,	**Ps 114:2**	3063
the men of Hezekiah, king of **J**,	**Pr 25:1**	3063
concerning **J** and Jerusalem,	**Is 1:1**	3063
Ahaz *and* Hezekiah, kings of **J**.	**Is 1:1**	3063
saw concerning **J** and Jerusalem.	**Is 2:1**	3063
to remove from Jerusalem and **J**	**Is 3:1**	3063
has stumbled and **J** has fallen,	**Is 3:8**	3063
of Jerusalem and men of **J**,	**Is 5:3**	3063
the men of **J** His delightful plant.	**Is 5:7**	3063
the son of Uzziah, king of **J**,	**Is 7:1**	3063
go up against **J** and terrorize it,	**Is 7:6**	3063
day that Ephraim separated from **J**,	**Is 7:17**	3063
"Then it will sweep on into **J**,	**Is 8:8**	3063
And together they are against **J**.	**Is 9:21**	3063
And will gather the dispersed of **J**	**Is 11:12**	3063
who harass **J** will be cut off;	**Is 11:13**	3063
Ephraim will not be jealous of **J**,	**Is 11:13**	3063
And **J** will not harass Ephraim.	**Is 11:13**	3063
J will become a terror to Egypt;	**Is 19:17**	3063
And He removed the defense of **J**.	**Is 22:8**	3063
Jerusalem and to the house of **J**.	**Is 22:21**	3063
will be sung in the land of **J**:	**Is 26:1**	3063
cities of **J** and seized them.	**Is 36:1**	3063
has said to **J** and to Jerusalem,	**Is 36:7**	3063
shall say to Hezekiah king of **J**,	**Is 37:10**	3063
remnant of the house of **J** will again	**Is 37:31**	3063
A writing of Hezekiah king of **J** after	**Is 38:9**	3063
Say to the cities of **J**,	**Is 40:9**	3063
And of the cities of **J**,	**Is 44:26**	3063
came forth from the loins of **J**,	**Is 48:1**	3063
an heir of My mountains from **J**;	**Is 65:9**	3063
the son of Amon, king of **J**,	**Jer 1:2**	3063
the son of Josiah, king of **J**,	**Jer 1:3**	3063
the son of Josiah, king of **J**,	**Jer 1:3**	3063
and against all the cities of **J**.	**Jer 1:15**	3063
the whole land, to the kings of **J**,	**Jer 1:18**	3063
of your cities Are your gods, O **J**.	**Jer 2:28**	3063
her treacherous sister **J** saw it.	**Jer 3:7**	3063
treacherous sister **J** did not fear;	**Jer 3:8**	3063
J did not return to Me with all her	**Jer 3:10**	3063
more righteous than treacherous **J**.	**Jer 3:11**	3063
house of **J** will walk with the house	**Jer 3:18**	3063
to the men of **J** and to Jerusalem,	**Jer 4:3**	3063
Men of **J** and inhabitants of	**Jer 4:4**	3063
Declare in **J** and proclaim in	**Jer 4:5**	3063
voices against the cities of **J**.	**Jer 4:16**	3063
Israel and the house of **J** Have dealt	**Jer 5:11**	3063
of Jacob And proclaim it in **J**,	**Jer 5:20**	3063
word of the LORD, all you of **J**,	**Jer 7:2**	3063
what they are doing in the cities of **J**	**Jer 7:17**	3063
"For the sons of **J** have done that	**Jer 7:30**	3063
make to cease from the cities of **J**	**Jer 7:34**	3063
out the bones of the kings of **J** and	**Jer 8:1**	3063
make the cities of **J** a desolation,	**Jer 9:11**	3063
Egypt and **J**, and Edom and the	**Jer 9:26**	3063
make the cities of **J** A desolation,	**Jer 10:22**	3063
and speak to the men of **J** and to	**Jer 11:2**	3063
all these words in the cities of **J**	**Jer 11:6**	3063
has been found among the men of **J**	**Jer 11:9**	3063
house of **J** have broken My covenant	**Jer 11:10**	3063
"Then the cities of **J** and the	**Jer 11:12**	3063
are as many as your cities, O **J**;	**Jer 11:13**	3063
of Israel and of the house of **J**,	**Jer 11:17**	3063
will uproot the house of **J** from	**Jer 12:14**	3063
'Just so will I destroy the pride of **J**	**Jer 13:9**	3063
whole household of **J** cling to Me,'	**Jer 13:11**	3063
All **J** has been carried into exile,	**Jer 13:19**	3063
"**J** mourns And her gates languish	**Jer 14:2**	3063
Have You completely rejected **J**?	**Jer 14:19**	3063
son of Hezekiah, the king of **J**,	**Jer 15:4**	3063
The sin of **J** is written down with	**Jer 17:1**	3063
the kings of **J** come in and go out,	**Jer 17:19**	3063
the word of the LORD, kings of **J**,	**Jer 17:20**	3063
LORD, kings of Judah, and all **J** and	**Jer 17:20**	3063
and their princes, the men of **J** and	**Jer 17:25**	3063
will come in from the cities of **J**	**Jer 17:26**	3063
speak to the men of **J** and against	**Jer 18:11**	3063
O kings of **J** and inhabitants of	**Jer 19:3**	3063
nor the kings of **J** had *ever* known,	**Jer 19:4**	3063
I will make void the counsel of **J**	**Jer 19:7**	3063
the houses of the kings of **J** will be	**Jer 19:13**	3063
So I will give over all **J** to the	**Jer 20:4**	3063
treasures of the kings of **J** I will	**Jer 20:5**	3063
"I will give over Zedekiah king of **J**	**Jer 21:7**	3063
to the household of the king of **J**,	**Jer 21:11**	3063
to the house of the king of **J**,	**Jer 22:1**	3063
the word of the LORD, O king of **J**,	**Jer 22:2**	3063
the house of the king of **J**:	**Jer 22:6**	3063
the son of Josiah, king of **J**,	**Jer 22:11**	3063
the son of Josiah, king of **J**,	**Jer 22:18**	3063
the son of Jehoiakim king of **J**	**Jer 22:24**	3063
of David Or ruling again in **J**.' "	**Jer 22:30**	3063
"In His days **J** will be saved, And	**Jer 23:6**	3063
the son of Jehoiakim, king of **J**,	**Jer 24:1**	3063
and the officials of **J** with the	**Jer 24:1**	3063
regard as good the captives of **J**,	**Jer 24:5**	3063
so I will abandon Zedekiah king of **J**	**Jer 24:8**	3063
concerning all the people of **J**,	**Jer 25:1**	3063
the son of Josiah, king of **J**	**Jer 25:1**	3063
prophet spoke to all the people of **J**	**Jer 25:2**	3063
Josiah the son of Amon, king of **J**,	**Jer 25:3**	3063
Jerusalem and the cities of **J** and	**Jer 25:18**	3063
the son of Josiah, king of **J**,	**Jer 26:1**	3063
and speak to all the cities of **J** who	**Jer 26:2**	3063
officials of **J** heard these things,	**Jer 26:10**	3063
in the days of Hezekiah king of **J**;	**Jer 26:18**	3063
he spoke to all the people of **J**,	**Jer 26:18**	3063
"Did Hezekiah king of **J** and all	**Jer 26:19**	3063
Judah and all **J** put him to death?	**Jer 26:19**	3063
the son of Josiah, king of **J**,	**Jer 27:1**	3063
Jerusalem to Zedekiah king of **J**.	**Jer 27:3**	3063
all these to Zedekiah king of **J**,	**Jer 27:12**	3063
in the house of the king of **J** and	**Jer 27:18**	3063
the son of Jehoiakim, king of **J**,	**Jer 27:20**	3063
all the nobles of **J** and Jerusalem.	**Jer 27:20**	3063
and in the house of the king of **J** and	**Jer 27:21**	3063
the reign of Zedekiah king of **J**,	**Jer 28:1**	3063
the son of Jehoiakim, king of **J**,	**Jer 28:4**	3063
exiles of **J** who went to Babylon,'	**Jer 28:4**	3063
the princes of **J** and Jerusalem,	**Jer 29:2**	3063
whom Zedekiah king of **J** sent to	**Jer 29:3**	3063
exiles from **J** who are in Babylon,	**Jer 29:22**	3063
fortunes of My people Israel and **J**.'	**Jer 30:3**	3063
Israel and concerning **J**:	**Jer 30:4**	3063
speak this word in the land of **J**	**Jer 31:23**	3063
"**J** and all its cities will	**Jer 31:24**	3063
house of Israel and the house of **J**	**Jer 31:27**	3063
of Israel and with the house of **J**,	**Jer 31:31**	3063
tenth year of Zedekiah king of **J**,	**Jer 32:1**	3063
was in the house of the king of **J**,	**Jer 32:2**	3063
king of **J** had shut him up,	**Jer 32:3**	3063
and Zedekiah king of **J** will not	**Jer 32:4**	3063
sons of **J** have been doing only evil	**Jer 32:30**	3063
sons of Israel and the sons of **J** which	**Jer 32:32**	3063
their prophets, the men of **J** and	**Jer 32:32**	3063
abomination, to cause **J** to sin.	**Jer 32:35**	3063
of Jerusalem, in the cities of **J**,	**Jer 32:44**	3063
the houses of the kings of **J** which	**Jer 33:4**	3063
I will restore the fortunes of **J** and	**Jer 33:7**	3063
in the cities of **J** and in the	**Jer 33:10**	3063
Jerusalem and in the cities of **J**,	**Jer 33:13**	3063
of Israel and the house of **J**.	**Jer 33:14**	3063
'In those days **J** will be saved	**Jer 33:16**	3063
Go and speak to Zedekiah king of **J**	**Jer 34:2**	3063

of the LORD, O Zedekiah king of **J**!	Jer 34:4	3063
these words to Zedekiah king of **J**	Jer 34:6	3063
all the remaining cities of **J**,	Jer 34:7	3063
cities among the cities of **J**.	Jer 34:7	3063
the officials of **J** and	Jer 34:19	3063
'Zedekiah *king of* **J** and his	Jer 34:21	3063
make the cities of **J** a desolation	Jer 34:22	3063
the son of Josiah, king of **J**,	Jer 35:1	3063
'Go and say to the men of **J** and	Jer 35:13	3063
I am bringing on **J** and on all the	Jer 35:17	3063
the son of Josiah, king of **J**,	Jer 36:1	3063
Israel and concerning **J**,	Jer 36:2	3063
"Perhaps the house of **J** will hear	Jer 36:3	3063
read them to all *the people of* **J**	Jer 36:6	3063
the son of Josiah, king of **J**,	Jer 36:9	3063
people who came from the cities of **J**	Jer 36:9	3063
Jehoiakim the king of **J** burned.	Jer 36:28	3063
Jehoiakim king of **J** you shall say,	Jer 36:29	3063
concerning Jehoiakim king of **J**,	Jer 36:30	3063
and the men of **J** all the calamity	Jer 36:31	3063
king of **J** had burned in the fire;	Jer 36:32	3063
had made king in the land of **J**,	Jer 37:1	3063
you are to say to the king of **J**,	Jer 37:7	3063
left in the palace of the king of **J**	Jer 38:22	3063
ninth year of Zedekiah king of **J**,	Jer 39:1	3063
When Zedekiah the king of **J** and	Jer 39:4	3063
also slew all the nobles of **J**.	Jer 39:6	3063
left behind in the land of **J**,	Jer 39:10	3063
all the exiles of Jerusalem and **J** who	Jer 40:1	3063
appointed over the cities of **J**,	Jer 40:5	3063
Babylon had left a remnant for **J**	Jer 40:11	3063
away and came to the land of **J**,	Jer 40:12	3063
and the remnant of **J** would perish?"	Jer 40:15	3063
word of the LORD, O remnant of **J**.	Jer 42:15	3063
has spoken to you, O remnant of **J**,	Jer 42:19	3063
to stay in the land of **J**.	Jer 43:4	3063
forces took the entire remnant of **J**	Jer 43:5	3063
order to reside in the land of **J**	Jer 43:5	3063
Jerusalem and all the cities of **J**;	Jer 44:2	3063
burned in the cities of **J** and in the	Jer 44:6	3063
child and infant, from among **J**,	Jer 44:7	3063
the wickedness of the kings of **J**,	Jer 44:9	3063
they committed in the land of **J**	Jer 44:9	3063
for woe, even to cut off all **J**.	Jer 44:11	3063
I will take away the remnant of **J**	Jer 44:12	3063
survivors for the remnant of **J**	Jer 44:14	3063
then to return to the land of **J**,	Jer 44:14	3063
and our princes did in the cities of **J**	Jer 44:17	3063
that you burned in the cities of **J**	Jer 44:21	3063
all **J** who are in the land of Egypt,	Jer 44:24	3063
all **J** who are living in the land	Jer 44:26	3063
by the mouth of any man of **J**	Jer 44:26	3063
and all the men of **J** who are in	Jer 44:27	3063
to the land of **J** few in number.	Jer 44:28	3063
Then all the remnant of **J** who have	Jer 44:28	3063
I gave over Zedekiah king of **J** to	Jer 44:30	3063
the son of Josiah, king of **J**,	Jer 45:1	3063
the son of Josiah, king of **J**:	Jer 46:2	3063
the reign of Zedekiah king of **J**,	Jer 49:34	3063
they and the sons of **J** as well;	Jer 50:4	3063
and for the sins of **J**,	Jer 50:20	3063
And the sons of **J** as well;	Jer 50:33	3063
nor **J** has been forsaken By his God	Jer 51:5	3063
he went with Zedekiah the king of **J**	Jer 51:59	3063
this came about in Jerusalem and **J**	Jer 52:3	3063
all the princes of **J** in Riblah.	Jer 52:10	3063
So **J** was led away into exile from	Jer 52:27	3063
the exile of Jehoiachin king of **J**,	Jer 52:31	3063
favor to Jehoiachin king of **J** and	Jer 52:31	3063
J has gone into exile under	La 1:3	3063
press The virgin daughter of **J**.	La 1:15	3063
strongholds of the daughter of **J**;	La 2:2	3063
And multiplied in the daughter of **J**	La 2:5	3063
The virgins in the cities of **J**.	La 5:11	3063
bear the iniquity of the house of **J**;	Ezk 4:6	3063
the elders of **J** sitting before me,	Ezk 8:1	3063
too light a thing for the house of **J**	Ezk 8:17	3063
iniquity of the house of Israel and **J**	Ezk 9:9	3063
and to **J** into fortified Jerusalem.	Ezk 21:20	3063
against the house of **J** when they	Ezk 25:3	3063
the house of **J** is like all the nations	Ezk 25:8	3063
has acted against the house of **J**	Ezk 25:12	3063
"**J** and the land of Israel, they	Ezk 27:17	3063
'For **J** and for the sons of Israel,	Ezk 37:16	3063
them with it, with the stick of **J**,	Ezk 37:19	3063
the east side to the west side, **J**,	Ezk 48:7	3063
"And beside the border of **J**,	Ezk 48:8	3063
everything between the border of **J**	Ezk 48:22	3063
the gate of **J**, one;	Ezk 48:31	3063
the reign of Jehoiakim king of **J**,	Da 1:1	3063
Jehoiakim king of **J** into his hand,	Da 1:2	3063
from the sons of **J** were Daniel,	Da 1:6	3063
a man among the exiles from **J**	Da 2:25	3061
who is one of the exiles from **J**,	Da 5:13	3061
my father the king brought from **J**?	Da 5:13	3061
who is one of the exiles from **J**,	Da 6:13	3061
to the men of **J**, the inhabitants of	Da 9:7	3063
Ahaz *and* Hezekiah, kings of **J**,	Hos 1:1	3063
have compassion on the house of **J**	Hos 1:7	3063
And the sons of **J** and the sons of	Hos 1:11	3063
Do not let **J** become guilty;	Hos 4:15	3063
J also has stumbled with them.	Hos 5:5	3063
The princes of **J** have become like	Hos 5:10	3063
like rottenness to the house of **J**.	Hos 5:12	3063
saw his sickness, And **J** his wound,	Hos 5:13	3063
a young lion to the house of **J**.	Hos 5:14	3063
What shall I do with you, O **J**?	Hos 6:4	3063
Also, O **J**, there is a harvest	Hos 6:11	3063
And **J** has multiplied fortified	Hos 8:14	3063
will harness Ephraim, **J** will plow,	Hos 10:11	3063
J is also unruly against God, Even	Hos 11:12	3063
LORD also has a dispute with **J**,	Hos 12:2	3063
When I restore the fortunes of **J**	Jl 3:1	3063
and sold the sons of **J** and	Jl 3:6	3063
into the hand of the sons of **J**,	Jl 3:8	3063
brooks of **J** will flow with water;	Jl 3:18	3063
violence done to the sons of **J**,	Jl 3:19	3063
But **J** will be inhabited forever And	Jl 3:20	3063
in the days of Uzziah king of **J**,	Am 1:1	3063
"For three transgressions of **J**	Am 2:4	3063
"So I will send fire upon **J** And	Am 2:5	3063
seer, flee away to the land of **J** and	Am 7:12	3063
do not rejoice over the sons of **J**	Ob 1:12	3063
Ahaz *and* Hezekiah, kings of **J**,	Mi 1:1	3063
What is the high place of **J**?	Mi 1:5	3063
incurable, For it has come to **J**;	Mi 1:9	3063
little to be among the clans of **J**,	Mi 5:2	3063
Celebrate your feasts, O **J**;	Na 1:15	3063
of Josiah son of Amon, king of **J**:	Zph 1:1	3063
I will stretch out My hand against **J**	Zph 1:4	3063
For the remnant of the house of **J**,	Zph 2:7	3063
son of Shealtiel, governor of **J**,	Hg 1:1	3063
son of Shealtiel, governor of **J**,	Hg 1:14	3063
son of Shealtiel, governor of **J**,	Hg 2:2	3063
Zerubbabel governor of **J**,	Hg 2:21	3063
for Jerusalem and the cities of **J**,	Zch 1:12	3063
the horns which have scattered **J**,	Zch 1:19	3063
the horns which have scattered **J** so	Zch 1:21	3063
horns against the land of **J**	Zch 1:21	3063
"The LORD will possess **J** as	Zch 2:12	3063
O house of **J** and house of Israel,	Zch 8:13	3063
Jerusalem and to the house of **J**.	Zch 8:15	3063
feasts for the house of **J**;	Zch 8:19	3063
our God, And be like a clan in **J**,	Zch 9:7	3063
For I will bend **J** as My bow, I	Zch 9:13	3063
visited His flock, the house of **J**,	Zch 10:3	3063
I will strengthen the house of **J**,	Zch 10:6	3063
brotherhood between **J** and Israel.	Zch 11:14	3063
it will also be against **J**.	Zch 12:2	3063
I will watch over the house of **J**,	Zch 12:4	3063
clans of **J** will say in their hearts,	Zch 12:5	3063
will make the clans of **J** like a firepot	Zch 12:6	3063
LORD also will save the tents of **J**	Zch 12:7	3063
will not be magnified above **J**.	Zch 12:7	3063
in the days of Uzziah king of **J**.	Zch 14:5	3063
J also will fight at Jerusalem;	Zch 14:14	3063
cooking pot in Jerusalem and in **J**	Zch 14:21	3063
"**J** has dealt treacherously, and	Mal 2:11	3063
for **J** has profaned the sanctuary	Mal 2:11	3063
"Then the offering of **J** and	Mal 3:4	3063
Jacob the father of **J** and his brothers.	Mt 1:2	2455
J was the father of Perez and Zerah	Mt 1:3	2455
'AND YOU, BETHLEHEM, LAND OF **J**,	Mt 2:6	2455
LEAST AMONG THE LEADERS OF **J**;	Mt 2:6	2455
the hill country, to a city of **J**,	Lk 1:39	2455
the son of Simeon, the son of **J**,	Lk 3:30	2455
the son of Perez, the son of **J**,	Lk 3:33	2455
our Lord was descended from **J**,	Heb 7:14	2455
OF ISRAEL AND WITH THE HOUSE OF **J**;	Heb 8:8	2455
Lion that is from the tribe of **J**,	Rv 5:5	2455
the tribe of **J**,	Rv 7:5	2455

JUDAH'S

But Er, **J** firstborn, was evil in	Gn 38:7	3063
in the midst of **J** inheritance.	Jos 19:9	
And Er, **J** firstborn, was wicked	1Ch 2:3	3063

JUDAISM

of my former manner of life in **J**,	Ga 1:13	2454
and I was advancing in **J** beyond	Ga 1:14	2454

JUDAS

Simon the Zealot, and **J** Iscariot,	Mt 10:4	2455
James and Joseph and Simon and **J**?	Mt 13:55	2455
of the twelve, named **J** Iscariot,	Mt 26:14	2455
And **J**, who was betraying Him,	Mt 26:25	2455
J, one of the twelve, came up	Mt 26:47	2455
Immediately **J** went to Jesus and said,	Mt 26:49	
Then when **J**, who had betrayed Him,	Mt 27:3	2455
and **J** Iscariot, who betrayed	Mk 3:19	2455
of James and Joses and **J**	Mk 6:3	2455
Then **J** Iscariot, who was one of the	Mk 14:10	2455
while He was still speaking, **J**,	Mk 14:43	2455
After coming, **J** immediately went to	Mk 14:45	
J *the son* of James, and Judas	Lk 6:16	2455
the son of James, and **J** Iscariot,	Lk 6:16	2455
Satan entered into **J** who was called	Lk 22:3	2455
came, and the one called **J**,	Lk 22:47	2455
"**J**, are you betraying the Son of	Lk 22:48	2455
meant **J** *the son* of Simon Iscariot,	Jn 6:71	2455
But **J** Iscariot, one of His	Jn 12:4	2455
put into the heart of **J** Iscariot,	Jn 13:2	2455
morsel, He took and gave it to **J**,	Jn 13:26	2455
because **J** had the money box,	Jn 13:29	2455
J (not Iscariot) said to Him, "Lord,	Jn 14:22	2455
Now **J** also, who was betraying Him,	Jn 18:2	2455
J then, having received the *Roman*	Jn 18:3	2455
And **J** also, who was betraying Him,	Jn 18:5	2455
Zealot, and **J** *the son* of James.	Ac 1:13	2455
the mouth of David concerning **J**,	Ac 1:16	2455
J turned aside to go to his own place.	Ac 1:25	2455
"After this man, **J** of Galilee rose	Ac 5:37	2455
and inquire at the house of **J** for	Ac 9:11	2455
J called Barsabbas, and Silas,	Ac 15:22	2455
we have sent **J** and Silas,	Ac 15:27	2455
J and Silas, also being	Ac 15:32	2455

JUDE

J, a bond-servant of Jesus Christ,	Jude 1:1	2455

JUDEA

Jesus was born in Bethlehem of **J**	Mt 2:1	2453
"In Bethlehem of **J**; for this is what	Mt 2:5	2453
that Archelaus was reigning over **J**	Mt 2:22	2453
preaching in the wilderness of **J**,	Mt 3:1	2453
was going out to him, and all **J** and	Mt 3:5	2453
and **J** and *from* beyond the Jordan.	Mt 4:25	2453
the region of **J** beyond the Jordan;	Mt 19:1	2453
those who are in **J** must flee to the	Mt 24:16	2453
country of **J** was going out to him,	Mk 1:5	2453
and *also* from **J**,	Mk 3:7	2453
from there to the region of **J** and	Mk 10:1	2453
those who are in **J** must flee to the	Mk 13:14	2453
In the days of Herod, king of **J**,	Lk 1:5	2453
in all the hill country of **J**.	Lk 1:65	2453
from the city of Nazareth, to **J**,	Lk 2:4	2453
Pontius Pilate was governor of **J**,	Lk 3:1	2453
preaching in the synagogues of **J**.	Lk 4:44	2453
from every village of Galilee and **J**	Lk 5:17	2453
a great throng of people from all **J**	Lk 6:17	2453
Him went out all over **J** and	Lk 7:17	2453
those who are in **J** must flee to the	Lk 21:21	2453
the people, teaching all over **J**,	Lk 23:5	2453
disciples came into the land of **J**,	Jn 3:22	2453
He left **J** and went away again into	Jn 4:3	2453
had come out of **J** into Galilee,	Jn 4:47	2453
He had come out of **J** into Galilee.	Jn 4:54	2453
He was unwilling to walk in **J** because	Jn 7:1	2453
"Leave here and go into **J**,	Jn 7:3	2453
"Let us go to **J** again."	Jn 11:7	2453
and in all **J** and Samaria,	Ac 1:8	2453
residents of Mesopotamia, **J** and	Ac 2:9	2453
"Men of **J** and all you who live	Ac 2:14	2453
the regions of **J** and Samaria,	Ac 8:1	2453
So the church throughout all **J** and	Ac 9:31	2453
which took place throughout all **J**,	Ac 10:37	2453
the brethren who were throughout **J**	Ac 11:1	2453
of the brethren living in **J**.	Ac 11:29	2453
Then he went down from **J** to	Ac 12:19	2453
Some men came down from **J** and	Ac 15:1	2453
named Agabus came down from **J**.	Ac 21:10	2453
throughout all the region of **J**,	Ac 26:20	2453
letters from **J** concerning you,	Ac 28:21	2453
those who are disobedient in **J**,	Ro 15:31	2453
to be helped on my journey to **J**.	2Co 1:16	2453
by sight to the churches of **J** which	Ga 1:22	2453
God in Christ Jesus that are in **J**,	1Th 2:14	2453

JUDEAN

and do not speak with us in **J** in	2Ki 18:26	3066
and cried with a loud voice in **J**,	2Ki 18:28	3066
and do not speak with us in **J** in	Is 36:11	3066
and cried with a loud voice in **J** and	Is 36:13	3066

JUDEANS

cleared the **J** out of Elath entirely;	2Ki 16:6	3064

JUDGE

"But I will also **j** the nation	Gn 15:14	1777
the LORD **j** between you and me."	Gn 16:5	8199
J of all the earth deal justly?"	Gn 18:25	8199
and already he is acting like a **j**;	Gn 19:9	8199
of their father, **j** between us."	Gn 31:53	8199
"Dan shall **j** his people, As one	Gn 49:16	1777
made you a prince or a **j** over us?	Ex 2:14	8199
the LORD look upon you and **j** *you*,	Ex 5:21	8199
that Moses sat to **j** the people,	Ex 18:13	8199
Why do you alone sit *as* **j** and all	Ex 18:14	
and I **j** between a man and his	Ex 18:16	8199
them **j** the people at all times;	Ex 18:22	8199
dispute they themselves will **j**.	Ex 18:22	8199
dispute they themselves would **j**.	Ex 18:26	8199
you are to **j** your neighbor fairly.	Lv 19:15	8199
then the congregation shall **j**	Nu 35:24	8199
and **j** righteously between a man	Dt 1:16	8199
and they shall **j** the people with	Dt 16:18	8199
come to the Levitical priest or the **j**	Dt 17:9	8199
the LORD your God, nor to the **j**,	Dt 17:12	8199
the **j** shall then make him lie down	Dt 25:2	8199
our enemies themselves **j** this.	Dt 32:31	6414
the LORD was with the **j** and	Jg 2:18	8199
enemies all the days of the **j**;	Jg 2:18	8199
But it came about when the **j** died,	Jg 2:19	8199
may the LORD, the **J**,	Jg 11:27	8199
j today between the sons of Israel	Jg 11:27	8199
LORD will **j** the ends of the earth;	1Sa 2:10	1777
I am about to **j** his house forever	1Sa 3:13	8199
us to **j** us like all the nations."	1Sa 8:5	8199
"Give us a king to **j** us."	1Sa 8:6	8199
that our king may **j** us and go out	1Sa 8:20	8199
"May the LORD **j** between you and	1Sa 24:12	8199
The LORD therefore be **j** and decide	1Sa 24:15	1781
would appoint me **j** in the land,	2Sa 15:4	8199
an understanding heart to **j** Your people	1Ki 3:9	8199
to **j** this great people of Yours?"	1Ki 3:9	8199
of the throne where he was to **j**,	1Ki 7:7	8199
heaven and act and **j** Your servants,	1Ki 8:32	8199
For He is coming to **j** the earth.	1Ch 16:33	8199
heaven and act and **j** Your servants,	2Ch 6:23	8199
for you do not **j** for man but for	2Ch 19:6	8199
to **j** disputes among the inhabitants	2Ch 19:8	7378
"O our God, will You not **j** them?	2Ch 20:12	8199
judges that they may **j** all the people	Ezr 7:25	1934, 1778
have to implore the mercy of my **j**.	Jb 9:15	8199
He **j** through the thick darkness?	Jb 22:13	8199
be delivered forever from my **J**.	Jb 23:7	8199
God is a righteous **j**,	Ps 7:11	8199
will **j** the world in righteousness;	Ps 9:8	8199
J me, O LORD my God, according to	Ps 35:24	8199
And the earth, to **j** His people:	Ps 50:4	1777
For God Himself is **j**.	Ps 50:6	8199
And blameless when You **j**.	Ps 51:4	8199

Do you **j** uprightly, O sons of men? Ps 58:1 8199
j the peoples with uprightness And Ps 67:4 8199
fatherless and a **j** for the widows, Ps 68:5 1781
j Your people with righteousness And Ps 72:2 1777
time, It is I who **j** with equity. Ps 75:2 8199
But God is the **J**; Ps 75:7 8199
How long will you **j** unjustly And Ps 82:2 8199
Arise, O God, **j** the earth! Ps 82:8 8199
Rise up, O **J** of the earth, Ps 94:2 8199
will **j** the peoples with equity." Ps 96:10 1777
For He is coming to **j** the earth. Ps 96:13 8199
will **j** the world in righteousness And Ps 96:13 8199
for He is coming to **j** the earth; Ps 98:9 8199
j the world with righteousness And Ps 98:9 8199
him from those who **j** his soul. Ps 109:31 8199
He will **j** among the nations, He Ps 110:6 1777
For the LORD will **j** His people And Ps 135:14 1777
and nobles, All who **j** rightly. Pr 8:16 8199
Open your mouth, **j** righteously, Pr 31:9 8199
"God will **j** both the righteous Ec 3:17 8199
And He will **j** between the nations, Is 2:4 8199
warrior, The **j** and the prophet, Is 3:2 8199
And stands to **j** the people. Is 3:13 1777
J between Me and My vineyard. Is 5:3 8199
will not **j** by what His eyes see, Is 11:3 8199
righteousness He will **j** the poor, Is 11:4 8199
And a **j** will sit on it in Is 16:5 8199
For the LORD is our **j**, Is 33:22 8199
And My arms will **j** the peoples; Is 51:5 8199
have seen my oppression; **J** my case. La 3:59 8199
j you according to your ways and Ezk 7:3 8199
you; **j** you according to your ways Ezk 7:8 8199
by their judgments I will **j** them. Ezk 7:27 8199
j you to the border of Israel; Ezk 11:10 8199
j you to the border of Israel. Ezk 11:11 8199
"Thus I will **j** you like women Ezk 16:38 8199
"Therefore I will **j** you, Ezk 18:30 8199
"Will you **j** them, will you judge Ezk 20:4 8199
you judge them, will you **j** them, Ezk 20:4 8199
of your origin, I will **j** you. Ezk 21:30 8199
"And you, son of man, will you **j**, Ezk 22:2 8199
will you **j** the bloody city? Ezk 22:2 8199
and they will **j** you according to Ezk 23:24 8199
will you **j** Oholah and Oholibah? Ezk 23:36 8199
will **j** them with the judgment of Ezk 23:45 8199
to your deeds I will **j** you," Ezk 24:14 8199
I will **j** each of you according to Ezk 33:20 8199
j between one sheep and another, Ezk 34:17 8199
will **j** between the fat sheep and Ezk 34:20 8199
j between one sheep and another. Ezk 34:22 8199
known among them when I **j** you. Ezk 35:11 8199
they shall take their stand to **j**; Ezk 44:24 8199
j it according to My ordinances. Ezk 44:24 8199
to **j** All the surrounding nations. Jl 3:12 8199
also cut off the **j** from her midst And Am 2:3 8199
Zion To **j** the mountain of Esau, Ob 1:21 8199
And He will **j** between many peoples Mi 4:3 8199
they will smite the **j** of Israel on the Mi 5:1 8199
The prince asks, also the **j**, Mi 7:3 8199
O LORD, have appointed them to **j**; Hab 1:12 4941
j with truth and judgment for Zch 8:16 8199
may not hand you over to the **j**, Mt 5:25 *2923*
judge, and the **j** to the officer, Mt 5:25 *2923*
"Do not **j** so that you will not be Mt 7:1 *2919*
"For in the way you **j**, Mt 7:2 *2919*
"Do not **j**, and you will not be Lk 6:37 *2919*
who appointed Me a **j** or arbitrator Lk 12:14 *2923*
own initiative **j** what is right? Lk 12:57 *2919*
he may not drag you before the **j**, Lk 12:58 *2923*
and the **j** turn you over to the Lk 12:58 *2923*
was a **j** who did not fear God Lk 18:2 *2923*
"Hear what the unrighteous **j** said; Lk 18:6 *2923*
'By your own words I will **j** you, Lk 19:22 *2919*
Son into the world to **j** the world, Jn 3:17 *2919*
As I hear, I **j**; and My judgment is Jn 5:30 *2919*
"Do not **j** according to appearance, Jn 7:24 *2919*
but **j** with righteous judgment." Jn 7:24 *2919*
"Our Law does not **j** a man unless Jn 7:51 *2919*
You **j** according to the flesh; Jn 8:15 *2919*
"But even if I do **j**, Jn 8:16 *2919*
have many things to speak and to **j** Jn 8:26 *2919*
not keep them, I do not **j** him; Jn 12:47 *2919*
for I did not come to **j** the world, Jn 12:47 *2919*
the word I spoke is what will **j** him Jn 12:48 *2919*
and **j** Him according to your law." Jn 18:31 *2919*
rather than to God, you be the **j**; Ac 4:19 *2919*
BE IN BONDAGE I MYSELF WILL **J**,' Ac 7:7 *2919*
MADE YOU A RULER AND **J** OVER US? Ac 7:27 *1348*
'WHO MADE YOU A RULER AND A **J**?' Ac 7:35 *1348*
as **J** of the living and the dead. Ac 10:42 *2923*
and **j** yourselves unworthy of Ac 13:46 *2919*
a day in which He will **j** the world Ac 17:31 *2919*
to be a **j** of these matters." Ac 18:15 *2923*
to **j** him according to our own Law. Ac 24:6 *2919*
you have been a **j** to this nation, Ac 24:10 *2923*
for in that which you **j** another, Ro 2:1 *2919*
you who **j** practice the same things. Ro 2:1 *2919*
God will **j** the secrets of men Ro 2:16 *2919*
will he not **j** you who though Ro 2:27 *2919*
how will God **j** the world? Ro 3:6 *2919*
eat is not to **j** the one who eats, Ro 14:3 *2919*
you to **j** the servant of another? Ro 14:4 *2919*
why do you **j** your brother? Ro 14:10 *2919*
let us not **j** one another anymore, Ro 14:13 *2919*
Do you not **j** those who are within 1Co 5:12 *2919*
that the saints will **j** the world? 1Co 6:2 *2919*
not know that we will **j** angels? 1Co 6:3 *2919*
you **j** what I say. 1Co 10:15 *2919*
J for yourselves: 1Co 11:13 *2919*
if he does not **j** the body rightly. 1Co 11:29 *1252*
no one is to act as your **j** in regard Col 2:16 *2919*
is to **j** the living and the dead, 2Tm 4:1 *2919*
which the Lord, the righteous **J**, 2Tm 4:8 *2923*
and able to **j** the thoughts and Heb 4:12 *2924*
"THE LORD WILL **J** HIS PEOPLE." Heb 10:30 *2919*
heaven, and to God, the **J** of all, Heb 12:23 *2923*
and adulterers God will **j**. Heb 13:4 *2919*
but if you **j** the law, you are not Jas 4:11 *2919*
a doer of the law but a **j** *of it.* Jas 4:11 *2923*
There is *only* one Lawgiver and **J**, Jas 4:12 *2923*
who are you who **j** your neighbor? Jas 4:12 *2919*
J is standing right at the door. Jas 5:9 *2923*
ready to **j** the living and the dead. 1Pe 4:5 *2919*

JUDGED

They **j** the people at all times; Ex 18:26 8199
came upon him, and he **j** Israel. Jg 3:10 8199
He **j** Israel twenty-three years. Jg 10:2 8199
and **j** Israel twenty-two years. Jg 10:3 8199
Jephthah **j** Israel six years. Jg 12:7 8199
Ibzan of Bethlehem **j** Israel after Jg 12:8 8199
And he **j** Israel seven years. Jg 12:9 8199
the Zebulunite **j** Israel after him; Jg 12:11 8199
and he **j** Israel ten years. Jg 12:11 8199
Pirathonite **j** Israel after him. Jg 12:13 8199
and he **j** Israel eight years. Jg 12:14 8199
So he **j** Israel twenty years in the Jg 15:20 8199
Thus he had **j** Israel twenty years. Jg 16:31 8199
Thus he **j** Israel forty years. 1Sa 4:18 8199
And Samuel **j** the sons of Israel at 1Sa 7:6 8199
Now Samuel **j** Israel all the days 1Sa 7:15 8199
he **j** Israel in all these places. 1Sa 7:16 8199
was there, and there he **j** Israel; 1Sa 7:17 8199
days of the judges who **j** Israel, 2Ki 23:22 8199
Let the nations be **j** before You. Ps 9:19 8199
let him be condemned when he is **j**. Ps 37:33 8199
When he is **j**, let him come forth Ps 109:7 8199
adultery or shed blood are **j**; Ezk 16:38 4941
ways and their deeds I **j** them. Ezk 36:19 8199
"Do not judge so that you will not be **j**. Mt 7:1 *2919*
the way you judge, you will be **j**; Mt 7:2 *2919*
not judge, and you will not be **j**; Lk 6:37 *2919*
"You have **j** correctly." Lk 7:43 *2919*
"He who believes in Him is not **j**; Jn 3:18 *2919*
not believe has been **j** already, Jn 3:18 *2919*
ruler of this world has been **j**. Jn 16:11 *2919*
j me to be faithful to the Lord, Ac 16:15 *2919*
the Law will be **j** by the Law; Ro 2:12 *2919*
PREVAIL WHEN YOU ARE **J**." Ro 3:4 *2919*
I also still being **j** as a sinner? Ro 3:7 *2919*
j him who has so committed this, 1Co 5:3 *2919*
If the world is **j** by you, 1Co 6:2 *2919*
why is my freedom **j** by another's 1Co 10:29 *2919*
But if we **j** ourselves rightly, we 1Co 11:31 *1252*
rightly, we would not be **j**. 1Co 11:31 *2919*
But when we are **j**, we are 1Co 11:32 *2919*
that they all may be **j** who did not 2Th 2:12 *2919*
are to be **j** by *the* law of liberty. Jas 2:12 *2919*
that you yourselves may not be **j**; Jas 5:9 *2919*
they are **j** in the flesh as men, 1Pe 4:6 *2919*
time *came* for the dead to be **j**, Rv 11:18 *2919*
because You **j** these things; Rv 16:5 *2919*
for He has **j** the great harlot who Rv 19:2 *2919*
and the dead were **j** from the Rv 20:12 *2919*
and they were **j**, every one *of them* Rv 20:13 *2919*

JUDGES

and he shall pay as the **j** *decide.* Ex 21:22 6414
house shall appear before the **j**, Ex 22:8 430
parties shall come before the **j**; Ex 22:9 430
he whom the **j** condemn shall pay Ex 22:9 430
So Moses said to the **j** of Israel, Nu 25:5 8199
I charged your **j** at that time, Dt 1:16 8199
"You shall appoint for yourself **j** Dt 16:18 8199
before the priests and the **j** who Dt 19:17 8199
j shall investigate thoroughly, Dt 19:18 8199
then your elders and your **j** shall Dt 21:2 8199
and the **j** decide their case, Dt 25:1 8199
their **j** were standing on both sides Jos 8:33 8199
and their **j** and their officers, Jos 23:2 8199
and their **j** and their officers; Jos 24:1 8199
Then the LORD raised up **j** who Jg 2:16 8199
they did not listen to their **j**, Jg 2:17 8199
the LORD raised up **j** for them, Jg 2:18 8199
in the days when the **j** governed, Ru 1:1 8199
appointed his sons **j** over Israel. 1Sa 8:1 8199
j to be over My people Israel; 2Sa 7:11 8199
days of the **j** who judged Israel, 2Ki 23:22 8199
word with any of the **j** of Israel, 1Ch 17:6 8199
j *to be* over My people Israel. 1Ch 17:10 8199
and 6,000 *were* officers and **j**, 1Ch 23:4 8199
for Israel, as officers and **j**. 1Ch 26:29 8199
to the **j** and to every leader in all 2Ch 1:2 8199
He appointed **j** in the land in 2Ch 19:5 8199
He said to the **j**, 2Ch 19:6 8199
the **j** and the lesser governors, Ezr 4:9 1784a
appoint magistrates and **j** that Ezr 7:25 1782
the elders and **j** of each city, Ezr 10:14 8199
He covers the faces of its **j**. Jb 9:24 8199
barefoot And makes fools of **j**. Jb 12:17 8199
In that He **j** those on high? Jb 21:22 8199
be an iniquity *punishable by* **j**. Jb 31:11 6414
"For by these He **j** peoples; Jb 36:31 1777
Take warning, O **j** of the earth. Ps 2:10 8199
The LORD **j** the peoples; Ps 7:8 1777
there is a God who **j** on earth!" Ps 58:11 8199
He **j** in the midst of the rulers. Ps 82:1 8199
Their **j** are thrown down by the Ps 141:6 8199
Princes and all **j** of the earth; Ps 148:11 8199
If a king **j** the poor with truth, Pr 29:14 8199
restore your **j** as at the first, Is 1:26 8199
makes the **j** of the earth meaningless Is 40:23 8199
LORD of hosts, who **j** righteously, Jer 11:20 8199
counselors, the treasurers, the **j**, Da 3:2 1884
counselors, the treasurers, the **j**, Da 3:3 1884
And your **j** of whom you requested, Hos 13:10 8199
Her **j** are wolves at evening; Zph 3:3 8199
For this reason they will be your **j**. Mt 12:27 *2923*
So they will be your **j**. Lk 11:19 *2923*
"For not even the Father **j** anyone, Jn 5:22 *2919*
there is One who seeks and **j**. Jn 8:50 *2919*
My sayings, has one who **j** him; Jn 12:48 *2919*
He gave *them* **j** until Samuel the Ac 13:20 *2923*
But those who are outside, God **j**. 1Co 5:13 *2919*
do you appoint them as **j** who are 1Co 6:4
and become **j** with evil motives? Jas 2:4 *2923*
a brother or **j** his brother, Jas 4:11 *2919*
against the law and **j** the law; Jas 4:11 *2919*
j according to each one's work, 1Pe 1:17 *2919*
Himself to Him who **j** righteously; 1Pe 2:23 *2919*
the Lord God who **j** her is strong. Rv 18:8 *2919*
righteousness He **j** and wages war. Rv 19:11 *2919*

JUDGING

was **j** Israel at that time. Jg 4:4 8199
they were **j** in Beersheba. 1Sa 8:2 8199
j the people of the land. 2Ki 15:5 8199
house **j** the people of the land. 2Ch 26:21 8199
sat on the throne **j** righteously. Ps 9:4 8199
j the twelve tribes of Israel. Mt 19:28 *2919*
j the twelve tribes of Israel. Lk 22:30 *2919*
I am not **j** anyone. Jn 8:15 *2919*
have I to do with **j** outsiders? 1Co 5:12 *2919*
will You refrain from **j** and Rv 6:10 *2919*

JUDGMENT

so He rendered **j** last night." Gn 31:42 3198
You shall make a breastpiece of **j**, Ex 28:15 4941
in the breastpiece of **j** over his heart Ex 28:29 4941
put in the breastpiece of **j** the Urim Ex 28:30 4941
and Aaron shall carry the **j** of the Ex 28:30 4941
'You shall do no injustice in **j**; Lv 19:15 4941
'You shall do no wrong in **j**, Lv 19:35 4941
the **j** of the Urim before the LORD. Nu 27:21 4941
shall not show partiality in **j**; Dt 1:17 4941
not fear man, for the **j** is God's. Dt 1:17 4941
judge the people with righteous **j**. Dt 16:18 4941
before the congregation for **j**, Jos 20:6 4941
of Israel came up to her for **j**. Jg 4:5 4941
a suit to come to the king for **j**, 2Sa 15:2 4941
Israel who came to the king for **j**; 2Sa 15:6 4941
When all Israel heard of the **j** 1Ki 3:28 4941
he was to judge, the hall of **j**, 1Ki 7:7 4941
"So shall your **j** be; 1Ki 20:40 4941
who is with you when you render **j**. 2Ch 19:6 4941
for the **j** of the LORD and to judge 2Ch 19:8 4941
come upon us, the sword, *or* **j**, 2Ch 20:9 8196
executing **j** on the house of Ahab, 2Ch 22:8 8199
Thus they executed **j** on Joash. 2Ch 24:24 8201
j be executed upon him strictly, Ezr 7:26 1780
And bring him into **j** with Yourself. Jb 14:3 4941
So that you may know there is **j**." Jb 19:29 1779
That He enters into **j** against you? Jb 22:4 4941
been an iniquity *calling for* **j**, Jb 31:28 6416
That he should go before God in **j**. Jb 34:23 4941
you were full of **j** on the wicked; Jb 36:17 1779
J and justice take hold *of you.* Jb 36:17 1779
"Will you really annul My **j**? Jb 40:8 4941
wicked will not stand in the **j**, Ps 1:5 4941
You have appointed **j**. Ps 7:6 4941
has established His throne for **j**, Ps 9:7 4941
He will execute **j** for the peoples Ps 9:8 1777
He has executed **j**. Ps 9:16 4941
my **j** come forth from Your presence; Ps 17:2 4941
light And your **j** as the noonday. Ps 37:6 4941
caused **j** to be heard from heaven; Ps 76:8 1779
When God arose to **j**, Ps 76:9 4941
For **j** will again be righteous, Ps 94:15 4941
He will maintain his cause in **j**. Ps 112:5 4941
When will You execute **j** on those Ps 119:84 4941
For there thrones were set for **j**, Ps 122:5 4941
not enter into **j** with Your servant, Ps 143:2 4941
To execute on them the **j** written; Ps 149:9 4941
His mouth should not err in **j**. Pr 16:10 4941
thrust aside the righteous in **j**. Pr 18:5 4941
show partiality in **j** is not good. Pr 24:23 4941
God will bring you to **j** for all these Ec 11:9 4941
For God will bring every act to **j**, Ec 12:14 4941
The LORD enters into **j** with the Is 3:14 4941
by the spirit of **j** and the spirit of Is 4:4 4941
of hosts will be exalted in **j**, Is 5:16 4941
of justice for him who sits in **j**, Is 28:6 4941
They totter *when rendering* **j**. Is 28:7 6417
it shall descend for **j** upon Edom And Is 34:5 4941
Let us come together for **j**. Is 41:1 4941
and **j** He was taken away; Is 53:8 4941
accuses you in **j** you will condemn. Is 54:17 4941
For the LORD will execute **j** by Is 66:16 8199
I will enter into **j** with you Because Jer 2:35 8199
is entering into **j** with all flesh; Jer 25:31 8199
"**J** has also come upon the plain, Jer 48:21 4941
Thus far the **j** on Moab. Jer 48:47 4941
For her **j** has reached to heaven Jer 51:9 4941
made **j** favorable for your sisters. Ezk 16:52 6419
to Babylon and enter into **j** with him Ezk 17:20 8199
there I will enter into **j** with you Ezk 20:35 8199
"As I entered into **j** with your Ezk 20:36 8199
so I will enter into **j** with you," Ezk 20:36 8199
and I will commit the **j** to them, Ezk 23:24 4941

them with the **j** of adulteresses and Ezk 23:45 4941
the **j** of women who shed blood, Ezk 23:45 4941
I will feed them with **j**. Ezk 34:16 4941
I will enter into **j** with him; Ezk 38:22 8199
see My **j** which I have executed and Ezk 39:21 4941
and **j** was passed in favor of the Da 7:22 1780
'But the court will sit *for* **j**, Da 7:26
For the **j** applies to you, For you Hos 5:1 4941
is oppressed, crushed in **j**, Hos 5:11 4941
And **j** sprouts like poisonous weeds Hos 10:4 4941
Then I will enter into **j** with them Jl 3:2 8199
leaders pronounce **j** for a bribe, Mi 3:11 8199
and **j** for peace in your gates. Zch 8:16 4941
I will draw near to you for **j**; Mal 3:5 4941
and Gomorrah in the day of **j** than Mt 10:15 *2920*
Tyre and Sidon in *the* day of **j** than Mt 11:22 *2920*
the land of Sodom in *the* day of **j**, Mt 11:24 *2920*
accounting for it in the day of **j**. Mt 12:36 *2920*
up with this generation at the **j**, Mt 12:41 *2920*
rise up with this generation at the **j** Mt 12:42 *2920*
he was sitting on the **j** seat, Mt 27:19 *968*
for Tyre and Sidon in the **j** than Lk 10:14 *2920*
the men of this generation at the **j** Lk 11:31 *2920*
up with this generation at the **j** Lk 11:32 *2920*
"This is the **j**, that the Jn 3:19 *2920*
but He has given all **j** to the Son, Jn 5:22 *2920*
life, and does not come into **j**, Jn 5:24 *2920*
gave Him authority to execute **j**, Jn 5:27 *2920*
evil *deeds* to a resurrection of **j**. Jn 5:29 *2920*
and My **j** is just, because I do not Jn 5:30 *2920*
but judge with righteous **j**." Jn 7:24 *2920*
even if I do judge, My **j** is true; Jn 8:16 *2920*
"For **j** I came into this world, Jn 9:39 *2917*
"Now **j** is upon this world; Jn 12:31 *2920*
sin and righteousness and **j**; Jn 16:8 *2920*
and concerning **j**, because the Jn 16:11 *2920*
and sat down on the **j** seat at a Jn 19:13 *968*
HUMILIATION HIS J WAS TAKEN AWAY; Ac 8:33 *2920*
"Therefore it is my **j** that we do Ac 15:19 *2919*
and brought him before the **j** seat, Ac 18:12 *968*
drove them away from the **j** seat. Ac 18:16 *968*
him in front of the **j** seat. Ac 18:17 *968*
self-control and the **j** to come, Ac 24:25 *2917*
everyone of you who passes **j**, Ro 2:1 *2919*
And we know that the **j** of God Ro 2:2 *2917*
when you pass **j** on those who Ro 2:3 *2919*
that you will escape the **j** of God? Ro 2:3 *2917*
revelation of the righteous **j** of God, Ro 2:5 *1341*
the **j** *arose* from one *transgression* Ro 5:16 *2917*
to think so as to have sound **j**, Ro 12:3 *4993*
of passing **j** on his opinions. Ro 14:1 *1253*
stand before the **j** seat of God. Ro 14:10 *968*
the same mind and in the same **j**. 1Co 1:10 *1106*
go on passing **j** before the time, 1Co 4:5 *2919*
these things according to human **j**, 1Co 9:8 *444*
eats and drinks **j** to himself if 1Co 11:29 *2917*
you will not come together for **j**. 1Co 11:34 *2917*
speak, and let the others pass **j**. 1Co 14:29 *1252*
before the **j** seat of Christ, 2Co 5:10 *968*
disturbing you will bear his **j**, Ga 5:10 *2917*
plain indication of God's righteous **j** 2Th 1:5 *2920*
evident, going before them to **j**; 1Tm 5:24 *2920*
of the dead and eternal **j**. Heb 6:2 *2917*
die once and after this *comes* **j**, Heb 9:27 *2920*
terrifying expectation of **j** and Heb 10:27 *2920*
For **j** *will be* merciless to one who Jas 2:13 *2920*
mercy triumphs over **j**. Jas 2:13 *2920*
such we will incur a stricter **j**. Jas 3:1 *2917*
so that you may not fall under **j**. Jas 5:12 *2920*
be of sound **j** and sober *spirit* for 1Pe 4:7 *4993*
For *it is* time for **j** to begin with 1Pe 4:17 *2917*
their **j** from long ago is not idle, 2Pe 2:3 *2917*
pits of darkness, reserved for **j**; 2Pe 2:4 *2920*
under punishment for the day of **j**, 2Pe 2:9 *2920*
do not bring a reviling **j** against 2Pe 2:11 *2920*
kept for the day of **j** and 2Pe 3:7 *2920*
have confidence in the day of **j**; 1Jn 4:17 *2920*
for the **j** of the great day, Jude 1:6 *2920*
pronounce against him a railing **j**, Jude 1:9 *2920*
to execute **j** upon all, and to Jude 1:15 *2920*
the hour of His **j** has come; Rv 14:7 *2920*
I will show you the **j** of the Rv 17:1 *2917*
For in one hour your **j** has come.' Rv 18:10 *2920*
God has pronounced **j** for you Rv 18:20 *2917*
them, and **j** was given to them. Rv 20:4 *2917*

JUDGMENTS

outstretched arm and with great **j**. Ex 6:6 8201
from the land of Egypt by great **j**. Ex 7:4 8201
I will execute **j**—I am the LORD. Ex 12:12 8201
perform My **j** and keep My statutes, Lv 18:4 4941
shall keep My statutes and My **j**, Lv 18:5 4941
are to keep My statutes and My **j** and Lv 18:26 4941
My statutes and keep My **j**, Lv 25:18 4941
had also executed **j** on their gods. Nu 33:4 8201
listen to the statutes and the **j** Dt 4:1 4941
I have taught you statutes and **j** Dt 4:5 4941
has statutes and **j** as righteous as this Dt 4:8 4941
time to teach you statutes and **j**, Dt 4:14 4941
the **j** which you shall teach them, Dt 5:31 4941
the statutes and the **j** which the Dt 6:1 4941
and the statutes and the **j** *mean* Dt 6:20 4941
the **j** which I am commanding you Dt 7:11 4941
because you listen to these **j** and Dt 7:12 4941
do all the statutes and the **j** which I Dt 11:32 4941
"These are the statutes and the **j** Dt 12:1 4941
and His statutes, and His **j**, Dt 30:16 4941
marvels and the **j** from His mouth, 1Ch 16:12 4941
His **j** are in all the earth. 1Ch 16:14 4941
Your **j** are on high, out of his Ps 10:5 4941
The **j** of the LORD are true; Ps 19:9 4941
Your **j** are *like* a great deep. Ps 36:6 4941
Judah rejoice Because of Your **j**. Ps 48:11 4941
Give the king Your **j**, Ps 72:1 4941
My law And do not walk in My **j**, Ps 89:30 4941
have rejoiced Because of Your **j**, Ps 97:8 4941
And **j** for all who are oppressed. Ps 103:6 4941
and the **j** uttered by His mouth, Ps 105:5 4941
His **j** are in all the earth. Ps 105:7 4941
When I learn Your righteous **j**. Ps 119:7 4941
O LORD, that Your **j** are righteous, Ps 119:75 4941
of You, And I am afraid of Your **j**. Ps 119:120 4941
O LORD, And upright are Your **j**. Ps 119:137 4941
J are prepared for scoffers, And Pr 19:29 8201
while following the way of Your **j**, Is 26:8 4941
when the earth experiences Your **j** Is 26:9 4941
"I will pronounce My **j** on Jer 1:16 4941
also pronounce **j** against them. Jer 4:12 4941
and I will execute **j** among you in Ezk 5:8 4941
for I will execute **j** on you and Ezk 5:10 8201
I execute **j** against you in anger, Ezk 5:15 8201
and by their **j** I will judge them. Ezk 7:27 4941
and execute **j** against you. Ezk 11:9 8201
four severe **j** against Jerusalem: Ezk 14:21 8201
execute **j** on you in the sight of many Ezk 16:41 8201
women, and they executed **j** on her. Ezk 23:10 8196
"Thus I will execute **j** on Moab, Ezk 25:11 8201
the LORD when I execute **j** in her, Ezk 28:22 8201
when I execute **j** upon all who Ezk 28:26 8201
in Zoan And execute **j** on Thebes. Ezk 30:14 8201
"Thus I will execute **j** on Egypt, Ezk 30:19 8201
And the **j** on you are *like* the Hos 6:5 4941
has taken away *His* **j** against you, Zph 3:15 4941
His **j** and unfathomable His ways! Ro 11:33 *2917*
true and righteous are Your **j**." Rv 16:7 *2920*
HIS J ARE TRUE AND RIGHTEOUS; Rv 19:2 *2920*

JUDITH

he married **J** the daughter of Beeri Gn 26:34 3067

JUG

ephah of flour and a **j** of wine, 1Sa 1:24 5035a
and another carrying a **j** of wine; 1Sa 10:3 5035a
and a **j** of wine and a young goat, 1Sa 16:20 4997
is at his head and the **j** of water, 1Sa 26:11 6835
So David took the spear and the **j** 1Sa 26:12 6835
j of water that was at his head." 1Sa 26:16 6835
summer fruits, and a **j** of wine. 2Sa 16:1 5035a
j is to be filled with wine." Jer 13:12 5035a
j is to be filled with wine?' Jer 13:12 5035a

JUGS

and two **j** of wine and five sheep 1Sa 25:18 5035a

JUICE

shall he drink any grape **j** nor Nu 6:3 4952
from the **j** of my pomegranates. SS 8:2 6071

JULIA

Greet Philologus and **J**, Ro 16:15 *2456*

JULIUS

of the Augustan cohort named **J**. Ac 27:1 *2457*
and **J** treated Paul with Ac 27:3 *2457*

JUMP

legs with which to **j** on the earth. Lv 11:21 5425a
if a fox should **j** on *it*, he would Ne 4:3 5927
that those who could swim should **j** Ac 27:43 *641*

JUMPED

Throwing aside his cloak, he **j** up Mk 10:50 *376a*

JUNIAS

Greet Andronicus and **J**, Ro 16:7 *2458*

JUNIPER

came and sat down under a **j** tree; 1Ki 19:4 7574
lay down and slept under a **j** tree; 1Ki 19:5 7574
I will place the **j** in the desert Together Is 41:19 1265
Lebanon will come to you, The **j**, Is 60:13 1265
may be like a **j** in the wilderness. Jer 48:6 6176

JURISDICTION

that He belonged to Herod's **j**, Lk 23:7 *1849*
that the law has **j** over a person Ro 7:1 *2961*

JUSHAB-HESED

Ohel, Berechiah, Hasadiah and **J**, 1Ch 3:20 3142

JUST

j as we have not touched you and Gn 26:29 3512c
him **j** as he crossed over Penuel, Gn 32:31 3512c
j as Joseph had interpreted to Gn 40:22 3512c
And **j** as he interpreted for us, Gn 41:13 3512c
for they were **j** as ugly as before. Gn 41:21 3512c
to come, **j** as Joseph had said, Gn 41:54 3512c
They had **j** gone out of the city, Gn 44:4
amount, **j** as when you had straw." Ex 5:13 3512c
did **j** as the LORD had commanded; Ex 7:10 3512c
j as the LORD had spoken to Moses. Ex 9:12 3512c
j as the LORD had spoken through Ex 9:35 3512c
j as the LORD had commanded Moses Ex 12:28 3512c
they did **j** as the LORD had Ex 12:50 3512c
and subverts the cause of the **j**. Ex 23:8 6662
j so you shall construct *it*. Ex 25:9
j as a man speaks to his friend. Ex 33:11 3512c
j as the LORD had commanded Moses. Ex 39:1 3512c
j as the LORD had commanded Moses. Ex 39:5 3512c
j as the LORD had commanded Moses. Ex 39:7 3512c
j as the LORD had commanded Moses. Ex 39:21 3512c
j as the LORD had commanded Moses. Ex 39:26 3512c
j as the LORD had commanded Moses. Ex 39:29 3512c
j as the LORD had commanded Moses. Ex 39:31 3512c
j as the LORD had commanded, this Ex 39:43 3512c
j as the LORD had commanded Moses. Ex 40:19 3512c
j as the LORD had commanded Moses. Ex 40:21 3512c
j as the LORD had commanded Moses. Ex 40:23 3512c
j as the LORD had commanded Moses. Ex 40:25 3512c
j as the LORD had commanded Moses. Ex 40:27 3512c
j as the LORD had commanded Moses. Ex 40:29 3512c
j as the LORD had commanded Moses. Ex 40:32 3512c
(**j** as it is removed from the ox of Lv 4:10 3512c
j as he did with the bull of the sin Lv 4:20 3512c
j as the fat was removed from the Lv 4:31 3512c
j as the fat of the lamb is Lv 4:35 3512c
did **j** as the LORD commanded him. Lv 8:4 3512c
j as the LORD had commanded Moses. Lv 8:9 3512c
j as the LORD had commanded Moses. Lv 8:13 3512c
j as the LORD had commanded Moses. Lv 8:17 3512c
j as the LORD had commanded Moses. Lv 8:21 3512c
j as the LORD had commanded Moses. Lv 8:29 3512c
offering, **j** as I commanded, Lv 8:31 3512c
j as the LORD has commanded." Lv 9:7 3512c
j as the LORD had commanded Lv 9:10 3512c
LORD, **j** as Moses had commanded. Lv 9:21 3512c
j as the LORD has commanded." Lv 10:15 3512c
the sanctuary, **j** as I commanded." Lv 10:18 3512c
And **j** as the LORD had commanded Lv 16:34 3512c
'You shall have **j** balances, just Lv 19:36 6664
have just balances, **j** weights, Lv 19:36 6664
balances, just weights, a **j** ephah, Lv 19:36 6664
a just ephah, and a **j** hin; Lv 19:36 6664
his neighbor, **j** as he has done, Lv 24:19 3512c
j as he has injured a man, so it Lv 24:20 3512c
j as the LORD had commanded Moses. Lv 24:23 3512c
j as the LORD had commanded Moses. Nu 1:19 3512c
j as they camp, so they shall set Nu 2:17 3512c
j as the LORD had commanded Moses. Nu 2:33 3512c
LORD, **j** as he had been commanded. Nu 3:16 3512c
j as the LORD had commanded him; Nu 3:42 3512c
j as the LORD had commanded Moses. Nu 3:51 3512c
j as the LORD had commanded Moses. Nu 4:49 834
j as the LORD had spoken to Moses, Nu 5:4 3512c
j as the LORD had commanded Moses. Nu 8:3 3512c
j as the LORD had commanded Moses Nu 8:22 3512c
be great, **j** as You have declared, Nu 14:17 3512c
j as You also have forgiven this Nu 14:19 3512c
'**j** as you have spoken in My Nu 14:28 3512c
aroma to the LORD, **j** as you do so Nu 15:14 3512c
j as the LORD had commanded Moses. Nu 15:36 3512c
j as the LORD had spoken to him Nu 16:40 3512c
j as the LORD had commanded him, Nu 17:11 3512c
LORD, **j** as He had commanded him; Nu 20:9 3512c
did **j** as the LORD had commanded, Nu 20:27 3512c
surely have killed you **j** now, Nu 22:33
Balak did **j** as Balaam had spoken, Nu 23:2 3512c
Balak did **j** as Balaam had said, Nu 23:30 3512c
j as the LORD commanded Moses.' " Nu 27:11 3512c
did **j** as the LORD commanded him; Nu 27:22 3512c
j as the LORD had spoken through Nu 27:23 3512c
j as the LORD had commanded Moses, Nu 31:7 3512c
Eleazar the priest did **j** as the LORD Nu 31:31 3512c
j as the LORD had commanded Moses. Nu 31:41 3512c
j as the LORD had commanded Moses. Nu 31:47 3512c
will do **j** as my lord commands. Nu 32:25 3512c
to battle, **j** as my lord says." Nu 32:27 3512c
J as the LORD had commanded Moses, Nu 36:10 3512c
you, **j** as He has promised you! Dt 1:11 3512c
j as the LORD our God had Dt 1:19 3512c
j as He did for you in Egypt Dt 1:30
3605, 834
you, **j** as a man carries his son, Dt 1:31 3512c
j as the LORD our God commanded us.' Dt 1:41
3605, 834
j as Israel did to the land of Dt 2:12 3512c
j as He did for the sons of Esau, Dt 2:22 3512c
j as the sons of Esau who live in Dt 2:29 3512c
j as you did to Sihon king of the Dt 3:2 3512c
j as the LORD my God commanded Dt 4:5 3512c
j as the LORD your God has Dt 5:32 3512c
multiply greatly, **j** as the LORD, Dt 6:3 3512c
our God, **j** as He commanded us. Dt 6:25 3512c
j as a man disciplines his son. Dt 8:5 3512c
j as the LORD has spoken to you. Dt 9:3 3512c
j as the LORD your God spoke to Dt 10:9 3512c
"**J** as a gazelle or a deer is Dt 12:22
389, 3512c
j as He has sworn to your fathers, Dt 13:17 3512c
j as the LORD your God blesses you Dt 16:10 3512c
j as He has sworn to your fathers, Dt 19:8 3512c
j as he had intended to do to his Dt 19:19 3512c
for **j** as a man rises against his Dt 22:26 3512c
j as you have voluntarily vowed to Dt 23:23 3512c
shall have a full and **j** weight; Dt 25:15 6664
shall have a full and **j** measure, Dt 25:15 6664
j as He spoke to you and as He Dt 29:13 3512c
j as He rejoiced over your fathers; Dt 30:9 3512c
of you, **j** as the LORD has spoken. Dt 31:3 3512c
them **j** as He did to Sihon and Og, Dt 31:4 3512c
perfect, For all His ways are **j**; Dt 32:4 4941
it to you, **j** as I spoke to Moses. Jos 1:3 3512c
J as I have been with Moses, I Jos 1:5 3512c
"**J** as we obeyed Moses in all Jos 1:17
3605, 834
that **j** as I have been with Moses, Jos 3:7 3512c
j as the LORD spoke to Joshua, Jos 4:8 3512c
j as Moses had spoken to them; Jos 4:12 3512c
j as they had revered Moses all Jos 4:14 3512c
j as the LORD your God had done to Jos 4:23 3512c
j as you did to Jericho and its king; Jos 8:2 3512c
j as Moses the servant of the LORD Jos 8:31 3512c
j as Moses the servant of the LORD Jos 8:33 3512c
j as the leaders had spoken to Jos 9:21 3512c
(**j** as he had done to Jericho and its Jos 10:1 3512c
j as he had done to the king of Jos 10:28 3512c
j as he had done to the king of Jos 10:30 3512c
J as he had done to Hebron, so he Jos 10:39 3512c

all who breathed, **j** as the LORD,	Jos 10:40	3512c
j as Moses the servant of the LORD	Jos 11:12	3512c
J as the LORD had commanded Moses	Jos 11:15	3512c
j as the LORD had commanded Moses.	Jos 11:20	3512c
j as Moses the servant of the LORD	Jos 13:8	3512c
j as the LORD had commanded	Jos 14:5	3512c
has let me live, **j** as He spoke,	Jos 14:10	3512c
j as the LORD your God promised	Jos 23:5	3512c
for you, **j** as He promised you.	Jos 23:10	3512c
j as all the good words which the	Jos 23:15	3512c
when they had **j** posted the watch;	Jg 7:19	389
j as the men of Succoth had	Jg 8:8	3512c
please strengthen me **j** this time,	Jg 16:28	389
Was it not **j** a question?"	1Sa 17:29	
"Did I **j** begin to inquire of God	1Sa 22:15	
down **j** as Your servant has heard?	1Sa 23:11	3512c
j as one hunts a partridge in the	1Sa 26:20	3512c
j as everything the king did	2Sa 3:36	
j as the LORD had commanded him,	2Sa 5:25	3512c
j as his father showed kindness to	2Sa 10:2	3512c
Amnon **j** as Absalom had commanded.	2Sa 13:29	3512c
Gad, **j** as the LORD had commanded.	2Sa 24:19	3512c
to Solomon, **j** as He promised him;	1Ki 5:12	3512c
j as I promised to your father	1Ki 9:5	3512c
j as it was written in the letters	1Ki 21:11	3512c
j now two young men of the sons of	2Ki 5:22	2088
even the camp **j** as it was,	2Ki 7:7	3512c
and the tents **j** as they were."	2Ki 7:10	3512c
died **j** as the man of God had said,	2Ki 7:17	3512c
j as the man of God had spoken to	2Ki 7:18	
j as the house of Ahab had done,	2Ki 8:18	3512c
them **j** as he had done in Bethel.	2Ki 23:19	
		3605, 4639
the LORD, **j** as the LORD had said.	2Ki 24:13	3512c
did **j** as God had commanded him,	1Ch 14:16	3512c
j as He has spoken concerning you.	1Ch 22:11	3512c
j as the LORD God of Israel had	1Ch 24:19	3512c
j as their relatives the sons of Aaron	1Ch 24:31	5980
j as the house of Ahab did	2Ch 21:6	3512c
j as King Darius had sent.	Ezr 6:13	6903
them **j** ordinances and true laws,	Ne 9:13	3477
j in all that has come upon us;	Ne 9:33	6662
j as it grew dark at the gates of	Ne 13:19	3512c
j as Haman commanded to the	Es 3:12	
		3605, 834
did **j** as Esther had commanded him.	Es 4:17	
		3605, 834
Now Haman had **j** entered the outer	Es 6:4	
j as Mordecai the Jew and Queen	Es 9:31	3512c
and **j** as they had established for	Es 9:31	3512c
'Can mankind be **j** before God?	Jb 4:17	6663
The **j** *and* blameless *man* is a joke.	Jb 12:4	6662
"How then can a man be **j** with God?	Jb 25:4	6663
it, but the **j** will wear *it*	Jb 27:17	6662
You have maintained my **j** cause;	Ps 9:4	4941
Hear a **j** cause, O LORD, give heed	Ps 17:1	6664
You thought that I was **j** like you;	Ps 50:21	
J as a father has compassion on	Ps 103:13	
But a **j** weight is His delight.	Pr 11:1	8003
thoughts of the righteous are **j**,	Pr 12:5	4941
A **j** balance and scales belong to	Pr 16:11	4941
For wisdom is protection **j** *as*	Ec 7:12	
J as you do not know the path of	Ec 11:5	3512c
J as I have done to Samaria and her	Is 10:11	3512c
J as there was for Israel In the	Is 11:16	3512c
j as I have intended so it has	Is 14:24	3512c
and **j** as I have planned so it will	Is 14:24	3512c
Those **j** weaned from milk?	Is 28:9	
Those **j** taken from the breast?	Is 28:9	
Is it not yet **j** a little while	Is 29:17	
J as many were astonished at you,	Is 52:14	3512c
They ask Me *for* **j** decisions, They	Is 58:2	6664
'**J** as the sons of Israel bring	Is 66:20	3512c
"For **j** as the new heavens and the	Is 66:22	3512c
"Have you not **j** now called to Me,	Jer 3:4	
'**J** so will I destroy the pride of	Jer 13:9	3602
let them be **j** like this waistband which	Jer 13:10	
"**J** so will I break this people	Jer 19:11	3602
j as their fathers forgot My name	Jer 23:27	3512c
'**J** as I brought all this great	Jer 32:42	3512c
deal with him **j** as he tells you."	Jer 39:12	3512c
it on and done **j** as He promised.	Jer 40:3	3512c
to her, **j** as we ourselves,	Jer 44:17	3512c
j as I gave over Zedekiah king of	Jer 44:30	3512c
j as I punished the king of	Jer 50:18	3512c
'**J** so shall Babylon sink down and	Jer 51:64	3602
j as You have commanded me."	Ezk 9:11	3512c
'Is he not **j** speaking parables?' "	Ezk 20:49	
"You shall have **j** balances, a	Ezk 45:10	6664
have just balances, a **j** ephah and	Ezk 45:10	6664
a just ephah and a **j** bath.	Ezk 45:10	6664
His works are true and His ways **j**,	Da 4:37	1780
"**J** now the wise men *and* the	Da 5:15	
remains **j** now no strength in me,	Da 10:17	
"**J** as the shepherd snatches from	Am 3:12	3512c
be with you, **J** as you have said!	Am 5:14	3512c
"Because **j** as you drank on My	Ob 1:16	3512c
j as He called and they would not	Zch 7:13	3512c
j as you were a curse among the	Zch 8:13	3512c
'**J** as I purposed to do harm to you	Zch 8:14	3512c
is **j** and endowed with salvation,	Zch 9:9	6662
you will flee **j** as you fled before	Zch 14:5	3512c
j as you are not keeping My ways but	Mal 2:9	6310, 834
under my roof, but **j** say the word,	Mt 8:8	3441
"My daughter has **j** died;	Mt 9:18	737
for **j** as JONAH WAS THREE DAYS AND	Mt 12:40	5618
j as the tares are gathered up and	Mt 13:40	5618
j touch the fringe of His cloak;	Mt 14:36	3441
j as the Son of Man did not come	Mt 20:28	5618

did **j** as Jesus had instructed them,	Mt 21:6	2531a
"For **j** as the lightning comes	Mt 24:27	5618
will be **j** like the days of Noah.	Mt 24:37	5618
"For *it is* **j** like a man *about* to	Mt 25:14	5618
to go, **j** as it is written of Him;	Mt 26:24	2531a
for He has risen, **j** as He said.	Mt 28:6	2531a
J then there was a man in their	Mk 1:23	2117
with them in the boat, **j** as He was;	Mk 4:36	5613
"If I **j** touch His garments, I	Mk 5:28	2579
j touch the fringe of His cloak;	Mk 6:56	2579
j as it is written of him."	Mk 9:13	2531a
to them **j** as Jesus had told *them,*	Mk 11:6	2531a
found *it* **j** as He had told them;	Mk 14:16	2531a
to go **j** as it is written of Him;	Mk 14:21	2531a
see Him, **j** as He told you.' "	Mk 16:7	2531a
j as they were handed down to us	Lk 1:2	2531a
and seen, **j** as had been told them.	Lk 2:20	2531a
cleansing, **j** as Moses commanded,	Lk 5:14	2531a
j as your Father is merciful.	Lk 6:36	2531a
but **j** say the word, and my	Lk 7:7	
teach us to pray **j** as John also	Lk 11:1	2531a
"For **j** as Jonah became a sign to	Lk 11:30	2531a
are there **j** a few who are being	Lk 13:23	
J at that time some Pharisees	Lk 13:31	846
j as a hen *gathers* her brood	Lk 13:34	
		3739, 5158
"For **j** like the lightning, when it	Lk 17:24	5618
"And **j** as it happened in the days	Lk 17:26	2531a
"It will be **j** the same on the day	Lk 17:30	2596
found it **j** as He had told them.	Lk 19:32	2531a
everything **j** as He had told them;	Lk 22:13	2531a
and **j** as My Father has granted Me	Lk 22:29	2531a
j exactly as the women also had said	Lk 24:24	2531a
"For **j** as the Father raises the	Jn 5:21	5618
"For **j** as the Father has life in	Jn 5:26	5618
and My judgment is **j**,	Jn 5:30	1342
were **j** now seeking to stone You,	Jn 11:8	3568
j as the Father has told Me."	Jn 12:50	2531a
"**J** as the Father has loved Me, I	Jn 15:9	2531a
j as I have kept My Father's	Jn 15:10	2531a
another, **j** as I have loved you.	Jn 15:12	2531a
they may be one, **j** as We are one;	Jn 17:22	2531a
will come in **j** the same way as you	Ac 1:11	3779
midst, **j** as you yourselves know	Ac 2:22	2531a
j as your rulers did also.	Ac 3:17	5618
j as He who spoke to Moses	Ac 7:44	2531a
are doing **j** as your fathers did.	Ac 7:51	5613
a vision an angel of God who had **j**	Ac 10:3	
I too am **j** a man."	Ac 10:26	
the Holy Spirit **j** as we *did,*	Ac 10:47	5613
j as *He did* upon us at the	Ac 11:15	5618
temple was **j** outside the city,	Ac 14:13	4253
Spirit, **j** as He also did to us;	Ac 15:8	2531a
agree, **j** as it is written,	Ac 15:15	2531a
for God **j** as you all are today.	Ac 22:3	2531a
this is **j** what I did in Jerusalem;	Ac 26:10	2532
And **j** as they did not see fit to	Ro 1:28	2531a
of the Law *who* are **j** before God,	Ro 2:13	1342
OF YOU," **j** as it is written.	Ro 2:24	2531a
Their condemnation is **j**.	Ro 3:8	1738
that He would be **j** and the justifier	Ro 3:26	1342
j as David also speaks of the	Ro 4:6	2509
j as through one man sin entered	Ro 5:12	5618
For **j** as you presented your	Ro 6:19	5618
J as it is written,	Ro 8:36	2531a
J as it is written,	Ro 9:13	2509
And **j** as Isaiah foretold,	Ro 9:29	2531a
j as it is written,	Ro 9:33	2531a
J as it is written,	Ro 10:15	2509
j as it is written,	Ro 11:8	2509
j as it is written,	Ro 11:26	2531a
For **j** as you once were disobedient	Ro 11:30	5618
For **j** as we have many members in	Ro 12:4	2509
of those without strength and not **j**	Ro 15:1	
j as Christ also accepted us to	Ro 15:7	2531a
that, **j** as it is written,	1Co 1:31	2531a
but **j** as it is written,	1Co 2:9	2531a
j as I teach everywhere in every	1Co 4:17	2531a
j as you are *in fact* unleavened.	1Co 5:7	2531a
j as I also please all men in all	1Co 10:33	2531a
of me, **j** as I also am of Christ.	1Co 11:1	2531a
j as I delivered them to you.	1Co 11:2	2531a
one individually **j** as He wills.	1Co 12:11	2531a
in the body, **j** as He desired.	1Co 12:18	2531a
but then I will know fully **j** as I	1Co 13:12	2531a
j as the Law also says.	1Co 14:34	2531a
gives it a body **j** as He wished,	1Co 15:38	2531a
J as we have borne the image of	1Co 15:49	2531a
For I do not wish to see you now **j**	1Co 16:7	
For **j** as the sufferings of Christ	2Co 1:5	2531a
j as you also partially did	2Co 1:14	2531a
to glory, **j** as from the Lord,	2Co 3:18	2509
j as God said, "I WILL DWELL IN	2Co 6:16	2531a
But **j** as you abound in everything,	2Co 8:7	5618
that **j** as *there was* the readiness	2Co 8:11	2509
Each one *must do* **j** as he has	2Co 9:7	2531a
himself, that **j** as he is Christ's,	2Co 10:7	2531a
be regarded **j** as we are in the matter	2Co 11:12	2531a
I am **j** as bold myself.	2Co 11:21	2532
j as Peter *had been* to the	Ga 2:7	2531a
j as I have forewarned you,	Ga 5:21	2531a
j as He chose us in Him before the	Eph 1:4	2531a
j as also you were called in one	Eph 4:4	2531a
j as the Gentiles also walk,	Eph 4:17	2531a
in Him, **j** as truth is in Jesus,	Eph 4:21	2531a
j as God in Christ also has	Eph 4:32	2531a
love, **j** as Christ also loved you and	Eph 5:2	2531a
j as Christ also loved the church	Eph 5:25	2531a
j as Christ also *does* the church,	Eph 5:29	2531a

j as you have always obeyed,	Php 2:12	2531a
j as in all the world also it is	Col 1:6	2531a
j as you learned *it* from Epaphras,	Col 1:7	2531a
faith, **j** as you were instructed,	Col 2:7	2531a
j as the Lord forgave you, so also	Col 3:13	2531a
j as you know what kind of men we	1Th 1:5	2531a
but **j** as we have been approved by	1Th 2:4	2531a
j as you know how we *were*	1Th 2:11	2509
us **j** as we also long to see you,	1Th 3:6	2509
all people, **j** as we also *do* for you;	1Th 3:12	2509
(**j** as you actually do walk),	1Th 4:1	2531a
j as we also told you before and	1Th 4:6	2531a
your hands, **j** as we commanded you,	1Th 4:11	2531a
come **j** like a thief in the night.	1Th 5:2	5613
another, **j** as you also are doing.	1Th 5:11	2531a
it is *only* **j** for God to repay with	2Th 1:6	1342
j as *it did* also with you;	2Th 3:1	2531a
J as Jannes and Jambres opposed	2Tm 3:8	3739
j as Jannes's and Jambres's folly was	2Tm 3:9	2532
loving what is good, sensible, **j**,	Ti 1:8	1342
received a **j** penalty,	Heb 2:2	1738
by **j** so much as the builder of the	Heb 3:3	2596
j as the Holy Spirit says,	Heb 3:7	2531a
preached to us, **j** as they also;	Heb 4:2	2509
enter that rest, **j** as He has said,	Heb 4:3	2531a
a time **j** as has been said before,	Heb 4:7	2531a
j as He says also in another	Heb 5:6	2531a
j as Moses was warned *by God* when	Heb 8:5	2531a
For **j** as the body without *the*	Jas 2:26	5618
You are **j** a vapor that appears	Jas 4:14	
j as Sarah obeyed Abraham, calling	1Pe 3:6	5613
for all, *the* **j** for *the* unjust,	1Pe 3:18	1342
j as there will also be false	2Pe 2:1	5613
all continues **j** as it was from the	2Pe 3:4	3779
j as also our beloved brother	2Pe 3:15	2531a
and **j** as you heard that antichrist	1Jn 2:18	2531a
a lie, and **j** as it has taught you,	1Jn 2:27	2531a
we will see Him **j** as He is.	1Jn 3:2	2531a
purifies himself, **j** as He is pure.	1Jn 3:3	2531a
righteous, **j** as He is righteous;	1Jn 3:7	2531a
one another, **j** as He commanded us.	1Jn 3:23	2531a
j as we have received commandment	2Jn 1:4	2531a
j as you have heard from the	2Jn 1:6	2531a
health, **j** as your soul prospers.	3Jn 1:2	2531a
j as Sodom and Gomorrah	Jude 1:7	5613

JUSTICE

LORD by doing righteousness and **j**,	Gn 18:19	4941
a multitude in order to pervert **j**;	Ex 23:2	
"You shall not pervert the **j** *due*	Ex 23:6	4941
j for the orphan and the widow,	Dt 10:18	4941
"You shall not distort **j**;	Dt 16:19	4941
"**J**, *and only* justice, you shall	Dt 16:20	6664
"Justice, *and only* **j**,	Dt 16:20	6664
the **j** due an alien *or* an orphan,	Dt 24:17	4941
who distorts the **j** due an alien,	Dt 27:19	4941
And My hand takes hold on **j**,	Dt 32:41	4941
He executed the **j** of the LORD, And	Dt 33:21	6666
and took bribes and perverted **j**.	1Sa 8:3	4941
and David administered **j** and	2Sa 8:15	4941
to me and I would give him **j**."	2Sa 15:4	6663
discernment to understand **j**,	1Ki 3:11	4941
of God was in him to administer **j**.	1Ki 3:28	4941
king, to do **j** and righteousness."	1Ki 10:9	4941
and he administered **j** and	1Ch 18:14	4941
them, to do **j** and righteousness."	2Ch 9:8	4941
before all who knew law and **j**	Es 1:13	1779
"Does God pervert **j**? Or does the	Jb 8:3	4941
And if *it is a matter* of **j**,	Jb 9:19	4941
shout for help, but there is no **j**.	Jb 19:7	4941
My **j** was like a robe and a turban.	Jb 29:14	4941
wise, Nor may elders understand **j**.	Jb 32:9	4941
the Almighty will not pervert **j**.	Jb 34:12	4941
"Shall one who hates **j** rule?	Jb 34:17	4941
you think this is according to **j**?	Jb 35:2	4941
But gives **j** to the afflicted.	Jb 36:6	4941
Judgment and **j** take hold *of you.*	Jb 36:17	4941
He will not do violence to **j** and	Jb 37:23	4941
He leads the humble in **j**,	Ps 25:9	4941
He loves righteousness and **j**;	Ps 33:5	4941
For the LORD loves **j** And	Ps 37:28	4941
wisdom, And his tongue speaks **j**.	Ps 37:30	4941
And Your afflicted with **j**.	Ps 72:2	4941
Do **j** to the afflicted and	Ps 82:3	6663
Righteousness and **j** are the	Ps 89:14	4941
Righteousness and **j** are the	Ps 97:2	4941
The strength of the King loves **j**;	Ps 99:4	4941
have executed **j** and righteousness	Ps 99:4	4941
will sing of lovingkindness and **j**,	Ps 101:1	4941
How blessed are those who keep **j**,	Ps 106:3	4941
works of His hands are truth and **j**;	Ps 111:7	4941
I have done **j** and righteousness;	Ps 119:121	4941
the afflicted And **j** for the poor.	Ps 140:12	4941
Who executes **j** for the oppressed;	Ps 146:7	4941
Righteousness, **j** and equity;	Pr 1:3	4941
Guarding the paths of **j**,	Pr 2:8	4941
you will discern righteousness and **j**	Pr 2:9	4941
kings reign, And rulers decree **j**.	Pr 8:15	6664
In the midst of the paths of **j**,	Pr 8:20	4941
bosom To pervert the ways of **j**.	Pr 17:23	4941
witness makes a mockery of **j**,	Pr 19:28	4941
A king who sits on the throne of **j**	Pr 20:8	1779
To do righteousness and **j** Is	Pr 21:3	4941
Because they refuse to act with **j**.	Pr 21:7	4941
The exercise of **j** is joy for the	Pr 21:15	4941
Evil men do not understand **j**,	Pr 28:5	4941
gives stability to the land by **j**,	Pr 29:4	4941
But **j** for man *comes* from the LORD.	Pr 29:26	4941
in the place of **j** there is wickedness	Ec 3:16	4941
denial of **j** and righteousness in the	Ec 5:8	4941

Seek **j**, Reprove the ruthless, Is 1:17 4941
a harlot, She *who* was full of **j**! Is 1:21 4941
Zion will be redeemed with **j** And Is 1:27 4941
Thus He looked for **j**, Is 5:7 4941
to uphold it with **j** and righteousness Is 9:7 4941
So as to deprive the needy of **j** And Is 10:2 1779
he will seek **j** And be prompt in Is 16:5 4941
A spirit of **j** for him who sits in Is 28:6 4941
I will make **j** the measuring line And Is 28:17 4941
For the LORD is a God of **j**; Is 30:18 4941
j will dwell in the wilderness And Is 32:16 4941
filled Zion with **j** and righteousness. Is 33:5 4941
who taught Him in the path of **j** Is 40:14 4941
And the **j** due me escapes the Is 40:27 4941
will bring forth **j** to the nations. Is 42:1 4941
He will faithfully bring forth **j**. Is 42:3 4941
He has established **j** in the earth; Is 42:4 4941
the **j** *due* to Me is with the LORD, Is 49:4 4941
My **j** for a light of the peoples. Is 51:4 4941
"Preserve **j** and do Is 56:1 4941
And there is no **j** in their tracks; Is 59:8 4941
Therefore **j** is far from us, And Is 59:9 4941
We hope for **j**, but there is none, Is 59:11 4941
J is turned back, And righteousness Is 59:14 4941
in His sight that there was no **j**. Is 59:15 4941
For I, the LORD, love **j**, Is 61:8 4941
'As the LORD lives,' In truth, in **j** and Jer 4:2 4941
a man, If there is one who does **j**, Jer 5:1 4941
if you truly practice **j** between a Jer 7:5 4941
who exercises lovingkindness, **j** and Jer 9:24 4941
Correct me, O LORD, but with **j**; Jer 10:24 4941
discuss matters of **j** with You: Jer 12:1 4941
"Administer **j** every morning; Jer 21:12 4941
"Do **j** and righteousness, and Jer 22:3 4941
And his upper rooms without **j**, Jer 22:13 4941
drink And do **j** and righteousness? Jer 22:15 4941
j and righteousness in the land. Jer 23:5 4941
and He shall execute **j** and Jer 33:15 4941
To deprive a man of **j** In the La 3:35 4941
and practices **j** and righteousness, Ezk 18:5 4941
true **j** between man and man, Ezk 18:8 4941
has practiced **j** and righteousness and Ezk 18:19 4941
and practices **j** and righteousness, Ezk 18:21 4941
and practices **j** and righteousness, Ezk 18:27 4941
oppressed the sojourner without **j**. Ezk 22:29 4941
and practices **j** and righteousness, Ezk 33:14 4941
has practiced **j** and righteousness; Ezk 33:16 4941
and practices **j** and righteousness, Ezk 33:19 4941
and practice **j** and righteousness. Ezk 45:9 4941
to Me in righteousness and in **j**, Hos 2:19 4941
your God, Observe kindness and **j**, Hos 12:6 4941
For those who turn **j** into wormwood Am 5:7 4941
good, And establish **j** in the gate! Am 5:15 4941
"But let **j** roll down like waters Am 5:24 4941
Yet you have turned **j** into poison And Am 6:12 4941
Is it not for you to know **j**? Mi 3:1 4941
And with **j** and courage To make Mi 3:8 4941
Who abhor **j** And twist everything Mi 3:9 4941
LORD require of you But to do **j**, Mi 6:8 4941
my case and executes **j** for me. Mi 7:9 4941
is ignored And **j** is never upheld. Hab 1:4 4941
Therefore **j** comes out perverted. Hab 1:4 4941
Their **j** and authority originate Hab 1:7 4941
morning He brings His **j** to light; Zph 3:5 4941
'Dispense true **j** and practice Zch 7:9 4941
"Where is the God of **j**?" Mal 2:17 4941
SHALL PROCLAIM **J** TO THE GENTILES. Mt 12:18 *2920*
OUT, UNTIL HE LEADS **J** TO VICTORY. Mt 12:20 *2920*
j and mercy and faithfulness; Mt 23:23 *2920*
this, they acknowledged God's **j**, Lk 7:29 *1344*
disregard **j** and the love of God; Lk 11:42 *2920*
God bring about **j** for His elect who Lk 18:7 *1557*
bring about **j** for them quickly. Lk 18:8 *1557*
j has not allowed him to live." Ac 28:4 *1349*
to your slaves **j** and fairness, Col 4:1 *1342*

JUSTIFICATION
and was raised because of our **j**. Ro 4:25 *1347*
transgressions resulting in **j**. Ro 5:16 *1345*
resulted **j** of life to all men. Ro 5:18 *1347*

JUSTIFIED
because he **j** himself before God. Jb 32:2 6663
you condemn Me that you may be **j**? Jb 40:8 6663
You are **j** when You speak Ps 51:4 6663
witnesses that they may be **j**, Is 43:9 6663
the offspring of Israel Will be **j** and Is 45:25 6663
"For by your words you will be **j**, Mt 12:37 *1344*
this man went to his house **j** Lk 18:14 *1344*
the doers of the Law will be **j**. Ro 2:13 *1344*
YOU MAY BE **J** IN YOUR WORDS, Ro 3:4 *1344*
no flesh will be **j** in His sight; Ro 3:20 *1344*
being **j** as a gift by His grace Ro 3:24 *1344*
man is **j** by faith apart from works Ro 3:28 *1344*
For if Abraham was **j** by works, Ro 4:2 *1344*
Therefore, having been **j** by faith, Ro 5:1 *1344*
having now been **j** by His blood, Ro 5:9 *1344*
whom He called, He also **j**; Ro 8:30 *1344*
and these whom He **j**, He also Ro 8:30 *1344*
but you were **j** in the name of the 1Co 6:11 *1344*
man is not **j** by the works of the Law Ga 2:16 *1344*
we may be **j** by faith in Christ and Ga 2:16 *1344*
of the Law no flesh will be **j**. Ga 2:16 *1344*
while seeking to be **j** in Christ, Ga 2:17 *1344*
Now that no one is **j** by the Law Ga 3:11 *1344*
Christ, so that we may be **j** by faith. Ga 3:24 *1344*
who are seeking to be **j** by law; Ga 5:4 *1344*
that being **j** by His grace we would Ti 3:7 *1344*
not Abraham our father **j** by works when Jas 2:21 *1344*
You see that a man is **j** by works and Jas 2:24 *1344*
Rahab the harlot also **j** by works when Jas 2:25 *1344*

JUSTIFIER
that He would be just and the **j** of Ro 3:26 *1344*

JUSTIFIES
He who **j** the wicked and he who Pr 17:15 6663
believes in Him who **j** the ungodly, Ro 4:5 *1344*
God is the one who **j**; Ro 8:33 *1344*

JUSTIFY
And how can we **j** ourselves? Gn 44:16 6663
and they **j** the righteous and Dt 25:1 6663
Speak, for I desire to **j** you. Jb 33:32 6663
Who **j** the wicked for a bribe, And Is 5:23 6663
One, My Servant, will **j** the many, Is 53:11 6663
"Can I **j** wicked scales And a bag Mi 6:11 2135
But wishing to **j** himself, he said Lk 10:29 *1344*
"You are those who **j** yourselves Lk 16:15 *1344*
who will **j** the circumcised by faith Ro 3:30 *1344*
God would **j** the Gentiles by faith, Ga 3:8 *1344*

JUSTIFYING
and **j** the righteous by giving 1Ki 8:32 6663
and **j** the righteous by giving him 2Ch 6:23 6663

JUSTLY
Judge of all the earth deal **j**?" Gn 18:25 4941
one who withholds what is **j** due, Pr 11:24 3476
And princes will rule **j**. Is 32:1 4941
But I will chasten you **j** And Jer 30:11 4941
we indeed *are suffering* **j**, for we are Lk 23:41 *1346*

JUSTUS
Barsabbas (who was also called **J**), Ac 1:23 *2459*
of a man named Titius **J**, Ac 18:7 *2459*
and *also* Jesus who is called **J**; Col 4:11 *2459*

JUTTAH
Maon, Carmel and Ziph and **J**, Jos 15:55 3194
and **J** with its pasture lands Jos 21:16 3194

K

KAB
and a fourth of a **k** of dove's dung 2Ki 6:25 6894

KABZEEL
south were **K** and Eder and Jagur, Jos 15:21 6909
the son of a valiant man of **K**, 2Sa 23:20 6909
the son of a valiant man of **K**, 1Ch 11:22 6909

KADESH
and came to En-mishpat (that is, **K**), Gn 14:7 6946
behold, it is between **K** and Bered. Gn 16:14 6946
and settled between **K** and Shur; Gn 20:1 6946
in the wilderness of Paran, at **K**; Nu 13:26 6946
and the people stayed at **K**. Nu 20:1 6946
From **K** Moses then sent messengers Nu 20:14 6946
now behold, we are at **K**, Nu 20:16 6946
Now when they set out from **K**, Nu 20:22 6946
are the waters of Meribah of **K** in Nu 27:14 6946
the wilderness of Zin, that is, **K**. Nu 33:36 6946
They journeyed from **K** and Nu 33:37 6946
"So you remained in **K** many days, Dt 1:46 6946
to the Red Sea and came to **K**, Jg 11:16 6946
So Israel remained at **K**. Jg 11:17 6946
LORD shakes the wilderness of **K**. Ps 29:8 6946

KADESH-BARNEA
sent them from **K** to see the land. Nu 32:8 6947
shall be to the south of **K**; Nu 34:4 6947
by the way of Mount Seir to **K**. Dt 1:2 6947
and we came to **K**. Dt 1:19 6947
it took for us to come from **K** until Dt 2:14 6947
"When the LORD sent you from **K**, Dt 9:23 6947
them from **K** even as far as Gaza, Jos 10:41 6947
of God concerning you and me in **K**. Jos 14:6 6947
the LORD sent me from **K** to spy out Jos 14:7 6947
then went up by the south of **K** and Jos 15:3 6947

KADMIEL
the sons of Jeshua and **K**, Ezr 2:40 6934
stood united with **K** and his sons, Ezr 3:9 6934
the sons of *Jeshua*, of **K**, Ne 7:43 6934
platform stood Jeshua, Bani, **K**, Ne 9:4 6934
Then the Levites, Jeshua, **K**, Ne 9:5 6934
Binnui of the sons of Henadad, **K**; Ne 10:9 6934
Levites *were* Jeshua, Binnui, **K**, Ne 12:8 6934
and Jeshua the son of **K**, Ne 12:24 6934

KADMONITE
and the Kenizzite and the **K** Gn 15:19 6935

KAIN
"Nevertheless **K** will be consumed; Nu 24:22 7014a
K, Gibeah and Timnah; Jos 15:57 7014a

KALLAI
of Sallai, **K**; of Amok, Eber; Ne 12:20 7040

KAMON
And Jair died and was buried in **K**. Jg 10:5 7056

KANAH
westward to the brook of **K**, Jos 16:8 7071
went down to the brook of **K**, Jos 17:9 7071
Ebron and Rehob and Hammon and **K**, Jos 19:28 7071

KAREAH
and Johanan the son of **K**, 2Ki 25:23 7143
and Jonathan the sons of **K**, Jer 40:8 7143
Now Johanan the son of **K** and all Jer 40:13 7143
Then Johanan the son of **K** spoke Jer 40:15 7143
said to Johanan the son of **K**, Jer 40:16 7143
But Johanan the son of **K** and all Jer 41:11 7143
Ishmael saw Johanan the son of **K** Jer 41:13 7143
and went to Johanan the son of **K**. Jer 41:14 7143
Then Johanan the son of **K** and all Jer 41:16 7143
the forces, Johanan the son of **K**, Jer 42:1 7143
called for Johanan the son of **K** and Jer 42:8 7143
and Johanan the son of **K**, Jer 43:2 7143
So Johanan the son of **K** and all Jer 43:4 7143
But Johanan the son of **K** and all Jer 43:5 7143

KARKA
up to Addar and turned about to **K**. Jos 15:3 7173

KARKOR
Now Zebah and Zalmunna were in **K**, Jg 8:10 7174a

KARNAIM
strength taken **K** for ourselves?" Am 6:13 7163b

KARTAH
and **K** with its pasture lands. Jos 21:34 7177

KARTAN
and **K** with its pasture lands; Jos 21:32 7178

KATTAH
Included also *were* **K** and Nahalal Jos 19:15 7005

KEDAR
and **K** and Adbeel and Mibsam Gn 25:13 6938
of Ishmael *was* Nebaioth, then **K**, 1Ch 1:29 6938
For I dwell among the tents of **K**! Ps 120:5 6938
of Jerusalem, Like the tents of **K**, SS 1:5 6938
the splendor of **K** will terminate; Is 21:16 6938
the mighty men of the sons of **K**, Is 21:17 6938
The settlements where **K** inhabits. Is 42:11 6938
"All the flocks of **K** will be Is 60:7 6938
And send to **K** and observe closely And Jer 2:10 6938
K and the kingdoms of Hazor, Jer 49:28 6938
go up to **K** And devastate the men Jer 49:28 6938
"Arabia and all the princes of **K**, Ezk 27:21 6938

KEDEMAH
and Tema, Jetur, Naphish and **K**. Gn 25:15 6929
Jetur, Naphish and **K**; 1Ch 1:31 6929

KEDEMOTH
from the wilderness of **K** to Sihon Dt 2:26 6932
and Jahaz and **K** and Mephaath, Jos 13:18 6932
K with its pasture lands and Jos 21:37 6932
K with its pasture lands and 1Ch 6:79 6932

KEDESH
the king of **K**, one; Jos 12:22 6943
and **K** and Hazor and Ithnan, Jos 15:23 6943
and **K** and Edrei and En-hazor, Jos 19:37 6943
So they set apart **K** in Galilee in Jos 20:7 6943
Naphtali, *they gave* **K** in Galilee, Jos 21:32 6943
arose and went with Barak to **K**. Jg 4:9 6943
and Naphtali together to **K**, Jg 4:10 6943
oak in Zaanannim, which is near **K**. Jg 4:11 6943
K and Hazor and Gilead and Galilee 2Ki 15:29 6943
K with its pasture lands, Daberath 1Ch 6:72 6943
K in Galilee with its pasture 1Ch 6:76 6943

KEDESH-NAPHTALI
Barak the son of Abinoam from **K**, Jg 4:6 6943, 5321

KEENER
And **k** than wolves in the evening. Hab 1:8 2300

KEEP
of Eden to cultivate it and **k** it. Gn 2:15 8104
the ark, to **k** *them* alive with you; Gn 6:19 2421a
will come to you to **k** *them* alive. Gn 6:20 2421a
to **k** offspring alive on the face Gn 7:3 2421a
for you, you shall **k** My covenant, Gn 17:9 8104
is My covenant, which you shall **k**, Gn 17:10 8104
to **k** the way of the LORD by doing Gn 18:19 8104
and will **k** you wherever you go, Gn 28:15 8104
"If God will be with me and will **k** me Gn 28:20 8104
again pasture *and* **k** your flock: Gn 30:31 8104
"Let her **k** them, otherwise we will Gn 38:23 3947
"Only **k** me in mind when it goes Gn 40:14 2142
and to **k** you alive by a great Gn 45:7 2421a
daughter you are to **k** alive." Ex 1:22 2421a
servants, yet they **k** saying to us, Ex 5:16
'You shall **k** it until the Ex 12:6 1961, 4931
you shall **k** this ordinance at its Ex 13:10 8104
for you while you **k** silent." Ex 14:14 2790b
and **k** all His statutes, Ex 15:26 8104
"How long do you refuse to **k** My Ex 16:28 8104
obey My voice and **k** My covenant, Ex 19:5 8104
love Me and **k** My commandments. Ex 20:6 8104
the sabbath day, to **k** it holy. Ex 20:8 6942
money or goods to **k** *for him* Ex 22:7 8104
sheep, or any animal to **k** *for him,* Ex 22:10 8104
"**K** far from a false charge, and Ex 23:7 7368
Aaron and his sons shall **k** it in Ex 27:21 6186a
and **k** the charge of the LORD, Lv 8:35 8104
"Thus you shall **k** the sons of Lv 15:31 5144a
My judgments and **k** My statutes, Lv 18:4 8104
k My statutes and My judgments, Lv 18:5 8104
to **k** My statutes and My judgments Lv 18:26 8104
'Thus you are to **k** My charge, that Lv 18:30 8104
and you shall **k** My sabbaths; Lv 19:3 8104
'You are to **k** My statutes. Lv 19:19 8104
'You shall **k** My sabbaths and Lv 19:30 8104
k My statutes and practice them; Lv 20:8 8104
'You are therefore to **k** all My Lv 20:22 8104
'They shall therefore **k** My charge, Lv 22:9 8104
"So you shall **k** My commandments, Lv 22:31 8104
you shall **k** your sabbath." Lv 23:32 7673b
Aaron shall **k** it in order from Lv 24:3 6186a
"He shall **k** the lamps in order on Lv 24:4 6186a
My statutes and **k** My judgments, Lv 25:18 8104
'You shall **k** My sabbaths and Lv 26:2 8104
k My commandments so as to carry Lv 26:3 8104
So the Levites shall **k** charge of Nu 1:53 8104
"They shall also **k** all the Nu 3:8 8104
that they may **k** their priesthood, Nu 3:10 8104
The LORD bless you, and **k** you; Nu 6:24 8104

of meeting, to **k** an obligation, **Nu 8:26** 8104
the sons of Israel would **k** the **Nu 9:19** 8104
k it as water to remove impurity; **Nu 19:9** 4931
long will Asshur **k** you captive?" **Nu 24:22** 7617
to the Levites who **k** charge of the **Nu 31:30** 8104
that you may **k** the commandments of **Dt 4:2** 8104
"So **k** and do *them,* for that is **Dt 4:6** 8104
and **k** your soul diligently, **Dt 4:9** 8104
"So you shall **k** His statutes and **Dt 4:40** 8104
love Me and **k** My commandments. **Dt 5:10** 8104
the sabbath day to **k** it holy, **Dt 5:12** 6942
and **k** all My commandments always, **Dt 5:29** 8104
to **k** all His statutes and His **Dt 6:2** 8104
"You should diligently **k** the **Dt 6:17** 8104
love Him and **k** His commandments; **Dt 7:9** 8104
you shall **k** the commandment and **Dt 7:11** 8104
these judgments and **k** and do them, **Dt 7:12** 8104
that the LORD your God will **k** with **Dt 7:12** 8104
would **k** His commandments or not. **Dt 8:2** 8104
you shall **k** the commandments of **Dt 8:6** 8104
and to **k** the LORD's commandments **Dt 10:13** 8104
your God, and always **k** His charge, **Dt 11:1** 8104
"You shall therefore **k** every **Dt 11:8** 8104
"For if you are careful to **k** all **Dt 11:22** 8104
and you shall **k** His commandments, **Dt 13:4** 8104
you shall **k** yourself from **Dt 23:9** 8104
in His ways and **k** His statutes, **Dt 26:17** 8104
you should **k** all His commandments; **Dt 26:18** 8104
"**K** all the commandments which I **Dt 27:1** 8104
if you **k** the commandments of **Dt 28:9** 8104
"So **k** the words of this covenant **Dt 29:9** 8104
to **k** His commandments and His **Dt 30:10** 8104
k His commandments and His **Dt 30:16** 8104
only **k** yourselves from the things **Jos 6:18** 8104
k His commandments and hold fast **Jos 22:5** 8104
to **k** and do all that is written in **Jos 23:6** 8104
whether they will **k** the way of the **Jg 2:22** 8104
And he said, "**K** silence." And all **Jg 3:19** 2013
his son to **k** the ark of the LORD. **1Sa 7:1** 8104
and one full line to **k** alive. **2Sa 8:2** 2421a
But now **k** silent, my sister, he is **2Sa 13:20** 2790b
ten concubines to **k** the house. **2Sa 15:16** 8104
whom he has left to **k** the house; **2Sa 16:21** 8104
whom he had left to **k** the house, **2Sa 20:3** 8104
clothes, but he could not **k** warm. **1Ki 1:1** 2552
my lord the king may **k** warm." **1Ki 1:2** 2552
"**K** the charge of the LORD your **1Ki 2:3** 8104
in His ways, to **k** His statutes, **1Ki 2:3** 8104
k all My commandments by walking **1Ki 6:12** 8104
k with Your servant David my father **1Ki 8:25** 8104
to **k** His commandments and His **1Ki 8:58** 8104
and to **k** His commandments, **1Ki 8:61** 8104
k My statutes and My ordinances, **1Ki 9:4** 8104
and do not **k** My commandments **1Ki 9:6** 8104
and **k** the horses and mules alive, **1Ki 18:5** 2421a
and **k** watch over the king's house **2Ki 11:5** 8104
shall **k** watch over the house for **2Ki 11:6** 8104
shall also **k** watch over the house **2Ki 11:7** 8104
evil ways and **k** My commandments, **2Ki 17:13** 8104
Also Judah did not **k** the **2Ki 17:19** 8104
and to **k** His commandments and His **2Ki 23:3** 8104
that You would **k** *me* from harm that **1Ch 4:10** 6213a
of the LORD which he did not **k**; **1Ch 10:13** 8104
k the law of the LORD your God. **1Ch 22:12** 8104
k charge of the tent of meeting, **1Ch 23:32** 8104
heart to **k** Your commandments, **1Ch 29:19** 8104
Israel, **k** with Your servant David, **2Ch 6:16** 8104
k My statutes and My ordinances, **2Ch 7:17** 8104
for we **k** the charge of the LORD **2Ch 13:11** 8104
people **k** the charge of the LORD. **2Ch 23:6** 8104
and to **k** His commandments and His **2Ch 34:31** 8104
the River, **k** away from there. **Ezr 6:6** 7352
"Watch and **k** *them* until you weigh **Ezr 8:29** 8104
love Him and **k** His commandments, **Ne 1:5** 8104
and **k** My commandments and do them, **Ne 1:9** 8104
and to **k** and to observe all the **Ne 10:29** 8104
Men will **k** watch over *his* tomb. **Jb 21:32** 8245
"Will you **k** to the ancient path **Jb 22:15** 8104
his conduct, And **k** man from pride; **Jb 33:17** 3680
K silent, and let me speak. **Jb 33:31** 2790b
K silent, and I will teach you **Jb 33:33** 2790b
"He does not **k** the wicked alive, **Jb 36:6** 2421a
your riches **k** you from distress, **Jb 36:19** 6186a
k silence concerning his limbs, **Jb 41:12** 2790b
You, O LORD, will **k** them; **Ps 12:7** 8104
K me as the apple of the eye; **Ps 17:8** 8104
Also **k** back Your servant from **Ps 19:13** 2820
he who cannot **k** his soul alive. **Ps 22:29** 2421a
To those who **k** His covenant **Ps 25:10** 5341
You **k** them secretly in a **Ps 31:20** 6845
And to **k** them alive in famine. **Ps 33:19** 2421a
K your tongue from evil And your **Ps 34:13** 5341
seen it, O LORD, do not **k** silent; **Ps 35:22** 2790b
Wait for the LORD and **k** His way, **Ps 37:34** 8104
will protect him and **k** him alive, **Ps 41:2** 2421a
our God come and not **k** silence; **Ps 50:3** 2790b
His eyes **k** watch on the nations; **Ps 66:7** 6822
of God, But **k** His commandments, **Ps 78:7** 5341
did not **k** the covenant of God And **Ps 78:10** 8104
And did not **k** His testimonies, **Ps 78:56** 8104
I will **k** for him forever, **Ps 89:28** 8104
And do not **k** My commandments, **Ps 89:31** 8104
Nor will He **k** *His anger* forever. **Ps 103:9** 5201
To those who **k** His covenant And **Ps 103:18** 8104
So that they might **k** His statutes And **Ps 105:45** 8104
blessed are those who **k** justice, **Ps 106:3** 8104
That we should **k** *them* diligently. **Ps 119:4** 8104
be established To **k** Your statutes! **Ps 119:5** 8104
I shall **k** Your statutes; **Ps 119:8** 8104
can a young man **k** his way pure? **Ps 119:9** 2135
That I may live and **k** Your word. **Ps 119:17** 8104
law And **k** it with all *my* heart. **Ps 119:34** 8104
So I will **k** Your law continually, **Ps 119:44** 8104
name in the night, And **k** Your law. **Ps 119:55** 8104
I have promised to **k** Your words. **Ps 119:57** 8104
not delay To **k** Your commandments. **Ps 119:60** 8104
And of those who **k** Your precepts. **Ps 119:63** 8104
went astray, But now I **k** Your word. **Ps 119:67** 8104
may **k** the testimony of Your mouth. **Ps 119:88** 8104
evil way, That I may **k** Your word. **Ps 119:101** 8104
I will **k** Your righteous ordinances. **Ps 119:106** 8104
of man, That I may **k** Your precepts. **Ps 119:134** 8104
Because they do not **k** Your law. **Ps 119:136** 8104
me And I shall **k** Your testimonies. **Ps 119:146** 8104
Because they do not **k** Your word. **Ps 119:158** 8104
I **k** Your precepts and Your **Ps 119:168** 8104
He will **k** your soul. **Ps 121:7** 8104
"If your sons will **k** My covenant And **Ps 132:12** 8104
K me, O LORD, from the hands of **Ps 140:4** 8104
K watch over the door of my lips. **Ps 141:3** 5341
K me from the jaws of the trap **Ps 141:9** 8104
K your foot from their path, **Pr 1:15** 4513
k to the paths of the righteous. **Pr 2:20** 8104
let your heart **k** my commandments; **Pr 3:1** 5341
K sound wisdom and discretion, **Pr 3:21** 5341
k your foot from being caught. **Pr 3:26** 8104
K my commandments and live; **Pr 4:4** 8104
K them in the midst of your heart. **Pr 4:21** 8104
K your way far from her And do **Pr 5:8** 7368
To **k** you from the evil woman, From **Pr 6:24** 8104
My son, **k** my words And treasure **Pr 7:1** 8104
K my commandments and live, And my **Pr 7:2** 8104
they may **k** you from an adulteress, **Pr 7:5** 8104
blessed are they who **k** my ways. **Pr 8:32** 8104
he may **k** away from Sheol below. **Pr 15:24** 5493
pleasant if you **k** them within you, **Pr 22:18** 8104
who **k** the law strive with them. **Pr 28:4** 8104
K deception and lies far from me, **Pr 30:8** 7368
A time to **k** and a time to throw **Ec 3:6** 8104
two lie down together they **k** warm, **Ec 4:11** 2552
"**K** the command of the king **Ec 8:2** 8104
fear God and **k** His commandments, **Ec 12:13** 8104
'**K** on listening, but do not **Is 6:9** 8085
K on looking, but do not **Is 6:9** 7200
k alive a heifer and a pair of sheep; **Is 7:21** 2421a
mind You will **k** in perfect peace, **Is 26:3** 5341
the night when you **k** the festival, **Is 30:29** 6942
To **k** the hungry person unsatisfied **Is 32:6** 7385a
And I will **k** You and give You for **Is 49:8** 5341
"To the eunuchs who **k** My sabbaths, **Is 56:4** 8104
Zion's sake I will not **k** silent, **Is 62:1** 2814
sake I will not **k** quiet, **Is 62:1** 8252
night they will never **k** silent. **Is 62:6** 2814
Will You **k** silent and afflict us **Is 64:12** 2814
'**K** to yourself, do not come near **Is 65:5** 7126
before Me, I will not **k** silent, **Is 65:6** 2814
"**K** your feet from being unshod **Jer 2:25** 4513
k saying, 'There will be no sword **Jer 14:15**
"You **k** going backward. **Jer 15:6**
Look, they **k** saying to me, **Jer 17:15**
work, but **k** the sabbath day holy, **Jer 17:22** 6942
but to **k** the sabbath day holy by **Jer 17:24** 6942
to **k** the sabbath day holy by not **Jer 17:27** 6942
"They **k** saying to those who **Jer 23:17**
And **k** him as a shepherd keeps his **Jer 31:10** 8104
so that no one should **k** them, **Jer 34:9** 5647
k them any longer in bondage; **Jer 34:10** 5647
"But if you **k** refusing to go out, **Jer 38:21**
will not **k** back a word from you." **Jer 42:4** 4513
"Stand by the road and **k** watch, **Jer 48:19** 6822
behind, I will **k** *them* alive; **Jer 49:11** 2421a
My statutes and **k** My ordinances and **Ezk 11:20** 8104
to **k** others alive who should not live, **Ezk 13:19** 2421a
fathers or **k** their ordinances **Ezk 20:18** 8104
My statutes and **k** My ordinances **Ezk 20:19** 8104
My ordinances and **k** My statutes **Ezk 37:24** 8104
who **k** charge of the temple; **Ezk 40:45** 8104
priests who **k** charge of the altar. **Ezk 40:46** 8104
to **k** charge of My sanctuary." **Ezk 44:8** 8104
them to **k** charge of the house, **Ezk 44:14** 8104
to minister to Me and **k** My charge. **Ezk 44:16** 8104
They shall also **k** My laws and My **Ezk 44:24** 8104
"**K** your gifts for yourself or **Da 5:17**
But **k** the vision secret, For *it* **Da 8:26** 5640
love Him and **k** His commandments, **Da 9:4** 8104
and one of them will **k** on coming **Da 11:10** 935
Then he will answer, "**K** quiet. **Am 6:10** 2013
And I will **k** watch to see what He **Hab 2:1** 6822
'YOU WILL **K** ON HEARING, BUT WILL **Mt 13:14** *189*
YOU WILL **K** ON SEEING, BUT WILL **Mt 13:14** *991*
into life, **k** the commandments." **Mt 19:17** *5083*
I *am to* **k** the Passover at your **Mt 26:18** *4160*
remain here and **k** watch with Me." **Mt 26:38** *1127*
not **k** watch with Me for one hour? **Mt 26:40** *1127*
"**K** watching and praying that you **Mt 26:41** *1127*
began to **k** watch over Him there. **Mt 27:36** *5083*
over and **k** you out of trouble." **Mt 28:14** *4160*
God in order to **k** your tradition. **Mk 7:9** *5083*
"Take heed, **k** on the alert; **Mk 13:33** *69*
remain here and **k** watch." **Mk 14:34** *1127*
you not **k** watch for one hour? **Mk 14:37** *1127*
"**K** watching and praying that you **Mk 14:38** *1127*
k Him from going away from them. **Lk 4:42** *2722*
not **k** moving from house to house. **Lk 10:7**
drink, and do not **k** worrying. **Lk 12:29**
"Be dressed in readiness, and **k** **Lk 12:35**
seeks to **k** his life will lose it, **Lk 17:33** *4046*
"But **k** on the alert at all times, **Lk 21:36** *69*
but I do know Him and **k** His word. **Jn 8:55** *5083*
He does not **k** the Sabbath." **Jn 9:16** *5083*
long will You **k** us in suspense? **Jn 10:24** *142*
may **k** it for the day of My burial. **Jn 12:7** *5083*
world will **k** it to life eternal. **Jn 12:25** *5442*
My sayings and does not **k** them, **Jn 12:47** *5442*
Me, you will **k** My commandments. **Jn 14:15** *5083*
loves Me, he will **k** My word; **Jn 14:23** *5083*
not love Me does not **k** My words; **Jn 14:24** *5083*
"If you **k** My commandments, you **Jn 15:10** *5083*
My word, they will **k** yours also. **Jn 15:20** *5083*
Holy Father, **k** them in Your name, **Jn 17:11** *5083*
but to **k** them from the evil *one.* **Jn 17:15** *5083*
and to **k** back *some* of the price of **Ac 5:3** *3557*
by angels, and *yet* did not **k** it." **Ac 7:53** *5442*
if you **k** yourselves free from such **Ac 15:29** *1301*
to **k** calm and to do nothing rash. **Ac 19:36** *2687*
I urge you to **k** up your courage, **Ac 27:22** *2114*
"Therefore, **k** up your courage, **Ac 27:25** *2114*
"YOU WILL **K** ON HEARING, BUT WILL **Ac 28:26** *189*
AND YOU WILL **K** ON SEEING, BUT WILL **Ac 28:26** *991*
THEIR TONGUES THEY **K** DECEIVING," **Ro 3:13**
k your eye on those who cause **Ro 16:17** *4648*
to **k** his own virgin *daughter,* **1Co 7:37** *5083*
he must **k** silent in the church; **1Co 14:28** *4601*
is seated, the first one must **k** silent. **1Co 14:30** *4601*
to **k** silent in the churches; **1Co 14:34** *4601*
to **k** me from exalting myself, **2Co 12:7** *3361*
to **k** me from exalting myself! **2Co 12:7** *3361*
therefore **k** standing firm and do **Ga 5:1**
obligation to **k** the whole Law. **Ga 5:3** *4160*
do not even **k** the Law themselves, **Ga 6:13** *5442*
let us **k** living by that same **Php 3:16**
Let no one **k** defrauding you of **Col 2:18**
k seeking the things above, **Col 3:1**
as we night and day **k** praying most **1Th 3:10**
that you **k** away from every **2Th 3:6** *4724*
married, bear children, **k** house, **1Tm 5:14** *3616*
k yourself free from sin. **1Tm 5:22** *5083*
that you **k** the commandment without **1Tm 6:14** *5083*
whom I wished to **k** with me, **Phm 1:13** *2722*
for they **k** watch over your souls as **Heb 13:17** *69*
and to **k** oneself unstained by the **Jas 1:27** *5083*
for action, **k** sober *in spirit,* **1Pe 1:13** *3525*
K your behavior excellent among **1Pe 2:12** *2192*
MUST **K** HIS TONGUE FROM EVIL AND HIS **1Pe 3:10** *3973*
and **k** a good conscience so that in **1Pe 3:16** *2192*
k fervent in your love for one **1Pe 4:8** *2192*
of Christ, **k** on rejoicing, **1Pe 4:13**
and to **k** the unrighteous under **2Pe 2:9** *5083*
Him, if we **k** His commandments. **1Jn 2:3** *5083*
and does not **k** His commandments, **1Jn 2:4** *5083*
because we **k** His commandments and **1Jn 3:22** *5083*
God, that we **k** His commandments; **1Jn 5:3** *5083*
who did not **k** their own domain, **Jude 1:6** *5083*
k yourselves in the love of God, **Jude 1:21** *5083*
is able to **k** you from stumbling, **Jude 1:24** *5442*
and **k** *it,* and repent. **Rv 3:3** *5083*
k you from the hour of testing, **Rv 3:10** *5083*
who **k** the commandments of God and **Rv 12:17** *5083*
the saints who **k** the commandments **Rv 14:12** *5083*
is holy, still **k** himself holy." **Rv 22:11** *37*

KEEPER

And Abel was a **k** of flocks, but **Gn 4:2** 7462a
Am I my brother's **k**?" **Gn 4:9** 8104
and left the flock with a **k** and took **1Sa 17:20** 8104
in the care of the baggage **k**, **1Sa 17:22** 8104
son of Harhas, **k** of the wardrobe **2Ki 22:14** 8104
Levite, the **k** of the eastern *gate,* **2Ch 31:14** 7778
of Hasrah, the **k** of the wardrobe **2Ch 34:22** 8104
Asaph the **k** of the king's forest, **Ne 2:8** 8104
Shecaniah, the **k** of the East Gate, **Ne 3:29** 8104
The LORD is your **k**; **Ps 121:5** 8104
"I, the LORD, am its **k**; **Is 27:3** 5341

KEEPERS

for they have been **k** of livestock; **Gn 46:32** 376
servants have been **k** of livestock **Gn 46:34** 376
k of the thresholds of the tent; **1Ch 9:19** 8104
of the LORD, **k** of the entrance. **1Ch 9:19** 8104

KEEPING

by not **k** His commandments **Dt 8:11** 8104
k all His commandments which I am **Dt 13:18** 8104
by **k** His commandments and His **Dt 28:45** 8104
k My statutes and commandments, **1Ki 3:14** 8104
k covenant and *showing* **1Ki 8:23** 8104
of good news, but we are **k** silent; **2Ki 7:9** 2814
k covenant and *showing* **2Ch 6:14** 8104
and Akkub *were* gatekeepers **k** watch **Ne 12:25** 4929
In **k** them there is great reward. **Ps 19:11** 8104
a multitude **k** festival. **Ps 42:4** 2287
By **k** *it* according to Your word. **Ps 119:9** 8104
K away from strife is an honor for **Pr 20:3** 7674
itself, *but* **k** his covenant that **Ezk 17:14** 8104
just as you are not **k** My ways but **Mal 2:9** 8104
bear fruit in **k** with repentance; **Mt 3:8** *514*
were with him **k** guard over Jesus, **Mt 27:54** *5083*
and **k** watch over their flock by **Lk 2:8** *5442*
bear fruits in **k** with repentance, **Lk 3:8** *514*
I was **k** them in Your name which **Jn 17:12** *5083*
his hair cut, for he was **k** a vow. **Ac 18:18** *2192*
also walk orderly, **k** the Law. **Ac 21:24** *5442*
the **k** of the commandments of God. **1Co 7:19** *5084*
k alert in it with *an attitude of* **Col 4:2** *1127*
k faith and a good conscience, **1Tm 1:19** *2192*
k his children under control with **1Tm 3:4** *2192*

KEEPS

k lovingkindness for thousands, **Ex 34:7** 5341
who **k** His covenant and His **Dt 7:9** 8104

“He **k** the feet of His godly ones, **1Sa 2:9** 8104
who **k** covenant and lovingkindness, **Ne 9:32** 8104
He **k** back his soul from the pit, **Jb 33:18** 2820
When He **k** quiet, who then can **Jb 34:29** 8252
He **k** all his bones, **Ps 34:20** 8104
Who **k** us in life And does not **Ps 66:9** 7760
My soul **k** Your testimonies, And I **Ps 119:167** 8104
He who **k** you will not slumber. **Ps 121:3** 8104
He who **k** Israel Will neither **Ps 121:4** 8104
The watchman **k** awake in vain. **Ps 127:1** 8245
The LORD **k** all who love Him, **Ps 145:20** 8104
Who **k** faith forever; **Ps 146:6** 8104
a man of understanding **k** silent. **Pr 11:12** 2790b
of the LORD one **k** away from evil. **Pr 16:6** 5493
Even a fool, when he **k** silent, **Pr 17:28** 2790b
He who **k** understanding will find **Pr 19:8** 8104
He who **k** the commandment keeps his **Pr 19:16** 8104
keeps the commandment **k** his soul, **Pr 19:16** 8104
He not know *it* who **k** your soul? **Pr 24:12** 5341
who **k** the law is a discerning son, **Pr 28:7** 5341
But he who **k** company with harlots **Pr 29:3** 7462b
But happy is he who **k** the law. **Pr 29:18** 8104
because God **k** him occupied with **Ec 5:20** 6030b
He who **k** a *royal* command **Ec 8:5** 8104
One **k** calling to me from Seir, **Is 21:11**
Who **k** from profaning the sabbath, **Is 56:2** 8104
k his hand from doing any evil.” **Is 56:2** 8104
who **k** from profaning the sabbath And **Is 56:6** 8104
Who **k** for us The appointed weeks **Jer 5:24** 8104
“As a well **k** its waters fresh, So **Jer 6:7** 7174b
So she **k** fresh her wickedness. **Jer 6:7** 7174b
him as a shepherd **k** his flock.’ **Jer 31:10**
if he **k** his hand from iniquity **Ezk 18:8** 7725
he **k** his hand from the poor, does **Ezk 18:17** 7725
but **k** making his petition three **Da 6:13**
who **k** His covenant and **Da 9:4** 8104
“How blessed is he who **k** waiting **Da 12:12**
time the prudent person **k** silent, **Am 5:13** 1826a
but whoever **k** and teaches *them,* he **Mt 5:19** *4160*
because she **k** shouting at us.” **Mt 15:23**
if anyone **k** My word he will never **Jn 8:51** *5083*
‘If anyone **k** My word, he will **Jn 8:52** *5083*
has My commandments and **k** them is **Jn 14:21** *5083*
man **k** the requirements of the Law, **Ro 2:26** *5442*
uncircumcised, if he **k** the Law, **Ro 2:27** *5055*
For whoever **k** the whole law and **Jas 2:10** *5083*
but whoever **k** His word, in him the **1Jn 2:5** *5083*
The one who **k** His commandments **1Jn 3:24** *5083*
but He who was born of God **k** him **1Jn 5:18** *5083*
he who **k** My deeds until the end, **Rv 2:26** *5083*
stays awake and **k** his clothes, **Rv 16:15** *5083*

KEHELATHAH
from Rissah and camped in **K**. **Nu 33:22** 6954
They journeyed from **K** and **Nu 33:23** 6954

KEILAH
and **K** and Achzib and Mareshah; **Jos 15:44** 7084
are fighting against **K** and **1Sa 23:1** 7084
the Philistines and deliver **K**.” **1Sa 23:2** 7084
How much more then if we go to **K** **1Sa 23:3** 7084
“Arise, go down to **K**, **1Sa 23:4** 7084
So David and his men went to **K** and **1Sa 23:5** 7084
delivered the inhabitants of **K**. **1Sa 23:5** 7084
of Ahimelech fled to David at **K**, **1Sa 23:6** 7084
Saul that David had come to **K**, **1Sa 23:7** 7084
to **K** to besiege David and his men. **1Sa 23:8** 7084
Saul is seeking to come to **K** **1Sa 23:10** 7084
of **K** surrender me into his hand? **1Sa 23:11** 7084
“Will the men of **K** surrender me **1Sa 23:12** 7084
arose and departed from **K**, **1Sa 23:13** 7084
that David had escaped from **K**, **1Sa 23:13** 7084
were the fathers of **K** the Garmite **1Ch 4:19** 7084
of half the district of **K**, **Ne 3:17** 7084
other half of the district of **K**. **Ne 3:18** 7084

KELAIAH
Jozabad, Shimei, **K** (that is, Kelita), **Ezr 10:23** 7041

KELITA
Shimei, Kelaiah (that is, **K**), **Ezr 10:23** 7042
Shabbethai, Hodiah, Maaseiah, **K**, **Ne 8:7** 7042
brothers Shebaniah, Hodiah, **K**, **Ne 10:10** 7042

KEMUEL
brother and **K** the father of Aram **Gn 22:21** 7055
a leader, **K** the son of Shiphtan. **Nu 34:24** 7055
for Levi, Hashabiah the son of **K**; **1Ch 27:17** 7055

KENAN
years, and became the father of **K**. **Gn 5:9** 7018
after he became the father of **K**, **Gn 5:10** 7018
K lived seventy years, and **Gn 5:12** 7018
Then **K** lived eight hundred and **Gn 5:13** 7018
So all the days of **K** were nine **Gn 5:14** 7018
K, Mahalalel, Jared, **1Ch 1:2** 7018

KENATH
went and took **K** and its villages, **Nu 32:42** 7079
them, with **K** and its villages, **1Ch 2:23** 7079

KENAZ
Omar, Zepho and Gatam and **K**. **Gn 36:11** 7073
chief Omar, chief Zepho, chief **K**, **Gn 36:15** 7073
chief **K**, chief Teman, chief **Gn 36:42** 7073
Othniel the son of **K**, **Jos 15:17** 7073
Othniel the son of **K**, **Jg 1:13** 7073
them, Othniel the son of **K**, **Jg 3:9** 7073
And Othniel the son of **K** died. **Jg 3:11** 7073
were Teman, Omar, Zephi, Gatam, **K**, **1Ch 1:36** 7073
chief **K**, chief Teman, chief **1Ch 1:53** 7073
sons of **K** *were* Othniel and Seraiah. **1Ch 4:13** 7073
and the son of Elah *was* **K**. **1Ch 4:15** 7073

KENITE
the **K** and the Kenizzite and the **Gn 15:19** 7017
And he looked at the **K**, **Nu 24:21** 7017
The descendants of the **K**, **Jg 1:16** 7017
Now Heber the **K** had separated **Jg 4:11** 7017
of Jael the wife of Heber the **K**, **Jg 4:17** 7017
and the house of Heber the **K**. **Jg 4:17** 7017
is Jael, The wife of Heber the **K**; **Jg 5:24** 7017

KENITES
had separated himself from the **K**, **Jg 4:11** 7014a
Saul said to the **K**, **1Sa 15:6** 7017
So the **K** departed from among the **1Sa 15:6** 7017
and against the Negev of the **K**.” **1Sa 27:10** 7017
who were in the cities of the **K**, **1Sa 30:29** 7017
are the **K** who came from Hammath, **1Ch 2:55** 7017

KENIZZITE
and the **K** and the Kadmonite **Gn 15:19** 7074
Caleb the son of Jephunneh the **K** **Nu 32:12** 7074
Caleb the son of Jephunneh the **K** **Jos 14:6** 7074
Caleb the son of Jephunneh the **K** **Jos 14:14** 7074

KEPT
k you from sinning against Me; **Gn 20:6** 2820
Abraham obeyed Me and **k** My charge, **Gn 26:5** 8104
Jacob **k** silent until they came in. **Gn 34:5** 2790b
his father **k** the saying *in mind.* **Gn 37:11** 8104
put aside to be **k** until morning.” **Ex 16:23** 4931
be **k** throughout your generations, **Ex 16:32** 4931
k throughout your generations.” **Ex 16:33** 4931
it before the Testimony, to be **k**. **Ex 16:34** 4931
altar is to be **k** burning on it. **Lv 6:9**
altar shall be **k** burning on it. **Lv 6:12**
‘Fire shall be **k** burning **Lv 6:13**
So Aaron, therefore, **k** silent. **Lv 10:3** 1826a
they **k** the LORD’s charge, **Nu 9:23** 8104
be **k** as a sign against the rebels, **Nu 17:10** 4931
who **k** charge of the tabernacle of **Nu 31:47** 8104
the LORD loved you and **k** the oath **Dt 7:8** 8104
Your word, And **k** Your covenant. **Dt 33:9** 5341
“You have **k** all that Moses the **Jos 22:2** 8104
but have **k** the charge of the **Jos 22:3** 8104
And they **k** silent all night, **Jg 16:2** 2790b
the women whom they had **k** alive **Jg 21:14** 2421a
because it has been **k** for you **1Sa 9:24** 8104
him any present. But he **k** silent. **1Sa 10:27** 2790b
you have not **k** the commandment of **1Sa 13:13** 8104
not **k** what the LORD commanded **1Sa 13:14** 8104
have **k** themselves from women.” **1Sa 21:4** 8104
“Surely women have been **k** from us **1Sa 21:5** 6113
have **k** me this day from bloodshed and **1Sa 25:33** 3607
has **k** back His servant from evil. **1Sa 25:39** 2820
who has **k** us and delivered into **1Sa 30:23** 8104
was as Joab **k** watch on the city, **2Sa 11:16** 8104
mule that was under him **k** going. **2Sa 18:9**
Then they **k** crossing the ford to **2Sa 19:18**
“For I have **k** the ways of the LORD, **2Sa 22:22** 8104
And I **k** myself from my iniquity. **2Sa 22:24** 8104
have **k** me as head of the nations; **2Sa 22:44** 8104
you not **k** the oath of the LORD, **1Ki 2:43** 8104
who have **k** with Your servant, my **1Ki 8:24** 8104
not **k** My covenant and My statutes, **1Ki 11:11** 8104
who **k** My commandments and who **1Ki 14:8** 8104
Him, but **k** His commandments, **2Ki 18:6** 8104
part of them had **k** their allegiance **1Ch 12:29** 8104
who has **k** with Your servant David, **2Ch 6:15** 8104
it **k** sabbath until seventy years were **2Ch 36:21** 7673b
and have not **k** the commandments, **Ne 1:7** 8104
and our fathers have not **k** Your law **Ne 9:34** 6213a
who **k** watch at the gates, **Ne 11:19** 8104
“For You have **k** their heart from **Jb 17:4** 6845
k His way and not turned aside. **Jb 23:11** 8104
And **k** silent for my counsel. **Jb 29:21** 1826a
have **k** the poor from *their* desire, **Jb 31:16** 4513
And **k** silent and did not go out of **Jb 31:34** 1826a
k from the paths of the violent. **Ps 17:4** 8104
For I have **k** the ways of the LORD, **Ps 18:21** 8104
And I **k** myself from my iniquity. **Ps 18:23** 8104
You have **k** me alive, that I **Ps 30:3** 2421a
When I **k** silent *about my sin,* my **Ps 32:3** 2790b
my prayer **k** returning to my bosom. **Ps 35:13**
you have done and I **k** silence; **Ps 50:21** 2790b
in vain I have **k** my heart pure And **Ps 73:13** 2135
They **k** His testimonies And the **Ps 99:7** 8104
It is You who has **k** my soul from **Is 38:17** 2836a
“I have **k** silent for a long time, **Is 42:14** 2814
I have **k** still and restrained **Is 42:14** 2814
have not **k** their feet in check. **Jer 14:10** 2820
forsaken and have not **k** My law. **Jer 16:11** 8104
your father, **k** all his commands and **Jer 35:18** 8104
“And you have not **k** charge of My **Ezk 44:8** 8104
who **k** charge of My sanctuary when **Ezk 44:15** 8104
of Zadok, who have **k** My charge, **Ezk 48:11** 8104
and **k** giving them vegetables. **Da 1:16** 5414
visions in my mind **k** alarming me. **Da 4:5** 927
he **k** exerting himself to rescue him. **Da 6:14**
I **k** looking until its wings were **Da 7:4** 1934
“After this I **k** looking, and **Da 7:6** 1934
I **k** looking in the night visions, **Da 7:7** 1934
“I **k** looking Until thrones were **Da 7:9** 1934
“Then I **k** looking because of the **Da 7:11** 1934
I **k** looking until the beast was **Da 7:11** 1934
“I **k** looking in the night visions, **Da 7:13** 1934
visions in my mind **k** alarming me. **Da 7:15**
“I **k** looking, and that horn was **Da 7:21** 1934
but I **k** the matter to myself.” **Da 7:28** 5202
the LORD has **k** the calamity in **Da 9:14** 8245
They **k** sacrificing to the Baals **Hos 11:2**
a wife, And for a wife he **k** *sheep.* **Hos 12:12** 8104
Egypt, And by a prophet he was **k**. **Hos 12:13** 8104
LORD And have not **k** His statutes; **Am 2:4** 8104
My statutes and have not **k** *them.* **Mal 3:7** 8104
is it that we have **k** His charge, **Mal 3:14** 8104
but **k** her a virgin until she gave **Mt 1:25**
3756, 1097
“All these things I have **k**; **Mt 19:20** *5442*
k trying to obtain false testimony **Mt 26:59**
But Jesus **k** silent. **Mt 26:63** *4623*
But they **k** shouting all the more, **Mt 27:23**
But they **k** silent. **Mk 3:4** *4623*
Herod heard of *it,* he **k** saying, **Mk 6:16**
and holy man, and he **k** him safe. **Mk 6:20** *4933*
He **k** giving *them* to the disciples **Mk 6:41**
And she **k** asking Him to cast the **Mk 7:26**
But they **k** silent, for on the way **Mk 9:34** *4623*
I have **k** all these things from my **Mk 10:20** *5442*
but he **k** crying out all the more, **Mk 10:48**
But *Peter* **k** saying insistently, **Mk 14:31**
Council **k** trying to obtain testimony **Mk 14:55**
But He **k** silent and did not **Mk 14:61** *4623*
k beating His head with a reed, **Mk 15:19**
and he **k** making signs to them, and **Lk 1:22**
and she **k** herself in seclusion for **Lk 1:24** *4032*
and **k** pondering what kind of **Lk 1:29**
All who heard them **k** them in mind, **Lk 1:66** *5087*
And Jesus **k** increasing in wisdom **Lk 2:52**
So He **k** on preaching in the **Lk 4:44**
and **k** wiping them with the hair of **Lk 7:38**
and shackles and **k** under guard, **Lk 8:29** *5442*
And he **k** trying to see Him. **Lk 9:9**
and **k** giving *them* to the disciples **Lk 9:16**
And they **k** silent, and reported to **Lk 9:36** *4601*
But they **k** silent. **Lk 14:4** *2270*
city, and she **k** coming to him, **Lk 18:3**
things I have **k** from *my* youth.” **Lk 18:21** *5442*
but he **k** crying out all the more, **Lk 18:39**
I **k** put away in a handkerchief; **Lk 19:20** *2192*
But they **k** on insisting, saying, **Lk 23:5**
but they **k** on calling out, saying, **Lk 23:21**
have **k** the good wine until now.” **Jn 2:10** *5083*
He **k** saying, “I am the one.” **Jn 9:9**
have **k** this man also from dying?” **Jn 11:37** *4160*
I have **k** My Father’s commandments **Jn 15:10** *5083*
if they **k** My word, they will keep **Jn 15:20** *5083*
that you may be **k** from stumbling. **Jn 16:1** *3361*
to Me, and they have **k** Your word. **Jn 17:6** *5083*
who **k** the door said to Peter, **Jn 18:17** *2377*
testified and **k** on exhorting them, **Ac 2:40**
Everyone **k** feeling a sense of awe; **Ac 2:43**
and **k** back *some* of the price for **Ac 5:2** *3557*
they **k** right on teaching and **Ac 5:42**
3756, 3973
The word of God **k** on spreading; **Ac 6:7**
he **k** preaching the gospel to all the **Ac 8:40**
But Saul **k** increasing in strength **Ac 9:22**
So Peter was **k** in the prison, but **Ac 12:5** *5083*
she **k** insisting that it was so. **Ac 12:15**
They **k** saying, “It is his angel.” **Ac 12:15**
The people **k** crying out, **Ac 12:22**
his course, he **k** saying, **Ac 13:25**
the people **k** begging that these **Ac 13:42**
All the people **k** silent, **Ac 15:12** *4601*
But Paul **k** insisting that they **Ac 15:38**
Paul and us, she **k** crying out, **Ac 16:17**
they **k** begging them to leave the **Ac 16:39**
those who had believed **k** coming, **Ac 19:18**
and as Paul **k** on talking, he was **Ac 20:9**
we **k** sailing to Syria and landed **Ac 21:3**
and they **k** telling Paul through **Ac 21:4**
multitude of the people **k** following **Ac 21:36**
him to be **k** in Herod’s Praetorium. **Ac 23:35** *5442*
for him to be **k** in custody and *yet* **Ac 24:23** *5083*
that Paul was being **k** in custody at **Ac 25:4** *5083*
I ordered him to be **k** in custody **Ac 25:21** *5083*
I **k** pursuing them even to foreign **Ac 26:11**
but **k** declaring both to those of **Ac 26:20**
k them from their intention, **Ac 27:43** *2967*
“I HAVE **K** for Myself SEVEN **Ro 11:4** *2641*
been **k** secret for long ages past, **Ro 16:25** *4601*
and in everything I **k** myself from **2Co 11:9** *5083*
but only, they **k** hearing, **Ga 1:23**
were **k** in custody under the law, **Ga 3:23** *5432*
we **k** telling you in advance that **1Th 3:4**
but with labor and hardship we **k** **2Th 3:8**
the course, I have **k** the faith; **2Tm 4:7** *5083*
By faith he **k** the Passover and the **Heb 11:28** *4160*
but **k** entrusting *Himself* to Him **1Pe 2:23**
God **k** waiting in the days of Noah, **1Pe 3:20**
k for the day of judgment and **2Pe 3:7** *5083*
Father, and **k** for Jesus Christ: **Jude 1:1** *5083*
He has **k** in eternal bonds under **Jude 1:6** *5083*
who **k** teaching Balak to put a **Rv 2:14**
little power, and have **k** My word, **Rv 3:8** *5083*
k the word of My perseverance, **Rv 3:10** *5083*
four living creatures **k** saying, **Rv 5:14**
for they have **k** themselves chaste. **Rv 14:4**

KEREN-HAPPUCH
second Keziah, and the third **K**. **Jb 42:14** 7163a

KERIOTH
against **K**, Bozrah and all the **Jer 48:24** 7152
“**K** has been captured And the **Jer 48:41** 7152
it will consume the citadels of **K**; **Am 2:2** 7152

KERIOTH-HEZRON
and Hazor-hadattah and **K** **Jos 15:25**
7152, 2696

KERNEL
not a **k** will fall to the ground. **Am 9:9** 6872b

KEROS
the sons of **K**, the sons of Siaha, **Ezr 2:44** 7026
the sons of **K**, the sons of Sia, **Ne 7:47** 7026

KETTLE
thrust it into the pan, or **k**, 1Sa 2:14 1731
for the pot And as meat in a **k**." Mi 3:3 7037
KETTLES
the holy things in pots, in **k**, 2Ch 35:13 1731
KETURAH
another wife, whose name was **K**. Gn 25:1 6989
All these *were* the sons of **K**. Gn 25:4 6989
The sons of **K**, Abraham's 1Ch 1:32 6989
All these were the sons of **K**. 1Ch 1:33 6989
KEY
they took the **k** and opened them, Jg 3:25 4668
will set the **k** of the house of David Is 22:22 4668
taken away the **k** of knowledge; Lk 11:52 *2807*
is true, who has the **k** of David, Rv 3:7 *2807*
and the **k** of the bottomless pit Rv 9:1 *2807*
holding the **k** of the abyss and a Rv 20:1 *2807*
KEYS
the **k** of the kingdom of heaven; Mt 16:19 *2807*
have the **k** of death and of Hades. Rv 1:18 *2807*
KEZIAH
first Jemimah, and the second **K**, Jb 42:14 7103
KIBROTH-HATTAAVAH
name of that place was called **K**, Nu 11:34 6914
From **K** the people set out for Nu 11:35 6914
of Sinai and camped at **K**. Nu 33:16 6914
They journeyed from **K** and Nu 33:17 6914
at **K** you provoked the LORD to Dt 9:22 6914
KIBZAIM
and **K** with its pasture lands and Jos 21:22 6911
KICK
'Why do you **k** at My sacrifice and 1Sa 2:29 1163
for you to **k** against the goads.' Ac 26:14 *2979b*
KICKED
"But Jeshurun grew fat and **k** Dt 32:15 1163
KIDNAPPED
k from the land of the Hebrews, Gn 40:15 1589
KIDNAPPERS
and **k** and liars and perjurers, 1Tm 1:10 *405*
KIDNAPPING
"If a man is caught **k** any of his Dt 24:7 1589
KIDNAPS
"He who **k** a man, whether he Ex 21:16 1589
KIDNEYS
two **k** and the fat that is on them, Ex 29:13 3629
and the two **k** and the fat that is Ex 29:22 3629
k with the fat that is on them, Lv 3:4 3629
which he shall remove with the **k**. Lv 3:4 3629
k with the fat that is on them, Lv 3:10 3629
which he shall remove with the **k**. Lv 3:10 3629
k with the fat that is on them, Lv 3:15 3629
which he shall remove with the **k**. Lv 3:15 3629
k with the fat that is on them, Lv 4:9 3629
which he shall remove with the **k** Lv 4:9 3629
k with the fat that is on them, Lv 7:4 3629
liver he shall remove with the **k**. Lv 7:4 3629
and the two **k** and their fat; Lv 8:16 3629
the lobe of the liver and the two **k** Lv 8:25 3629
The fat and the **k** and the lobe of Lv 9:10 3629
the **k** and the lobe of the liver, Lv 9:19 3629
Without mercy He splits my **k** open; Jb 16:13 3629
With the fat of the **k** of rams. Is 34:6 3629
KIDRON
king also passed over the brook **K**, 2Sa 15:23 6939
go out and cross over the brook **K**, 1Ki 2:37 6939
and burned *it* at the brook **K**. 1Ki 15:13 6939
Jerusalem in the fields of the **K**, 2Ki 23:4 6939
outside Jerusalem to the brook **K**, 2Ki 23:6 6939
and burned it at the brook **K**, 2Ki 23:6 6939
threw their dust into the brook **K**. 2Ki 23:12 6939
it and burned *it* at the brook **K**. 2Ch 15:16 6939
it to carry out to the **K** valley. 2Ch 29:16 6939
and cast *them* into the brook **K**. 2Ch 30:14 6939
the fields as far as the brook **K**, Jer 31:40 6939
over the ravine of the **K**, Jn 18:1 *2748*
KILL
and whoever finds me will **k** me." Gn 4:14 2026
and they will **k** me, but they will Gn 12:12 2026
they will **k** me because of my wife. Gn 20:11 2026
might **k** me on account of Rebekah, Gn 26:7 2026
then I will **k** my brother Jacob." Gn 27:41 2026
you *by planning* to **k** you. Gn 27:42 2026
come and let us **k** him and throw Gn 37:20 2026
"What profit is it for us to **k** Gn 37:26 2026
Are you intending to **k** me as Ex 2:14 2026
this matter, he tried to **k** Moses. Ex 2:15 2026
Behold, I will **k** your son, your Ex 4:23 2026
a sword in their hand to **k** us." Ex 5:21 2026
of Israel is to **k** it at twilight. Ex 12:6 7819
to **k** this whole assembly with hunger Ex 16:3 4191
to **k** us and our children and our Ex 17:3 4191
neighbor, so as to **k** him craftily, Ex 21:14 2026
and I will **k** you with the sword, Ex 22:24 2026
not **k** the innocent or the righteous, Ex 23:7 2026
He brought them out to **k** them in Ex 32:12 2026
camp, and **k** every man his brother, Ex 32:27 2026
you shall also **k** the animal. Lv 20:15 2026
shall **k** the woman and the animal; Lv 20:16 2026
you shall not **k** *both* it and its Lv 22:28 7819
thus with me, please **k** me at once, Nu 11:15 2026
k every male among the little Nu 31:17 2026
and **k** every woman who has known Nu 31:17 2026
"But you shall surely **k** him; Dt 13:9 2026
Israel, and they did not **k** them. Jos 9:26 2026
them live, I would not **k** you." Jg 8:19 2026
Jether his firstborn, "Rise, **k** them Jg 8:20 2026
his hands to **k** his brothers. Jg 9:24 2026
"Draw your sword and **k** me, Jg 9:54 4191
"If the LORD had desired to **k** us, Jg 13:23 4191
to me that you will not **k** me." Jg 15:12 6293
yet surely we will not **k** you." Jg 15:13 4191
light, then we will **k** him." Jg 16:2 2026
They intended to **k** me; Jg 20:5 2026
strike and **k** some of the people as Jg 20:31 5221
and **k** about thirty men of Israel, Jg 20:39 5221, 2491
to us, to **k** us and our people." 1Sa 5:10 4191
it will not **k** us and our people." 1Sa 5:11 4191
Saul hears *of it*, he will **k** me." 1Sa 16:2 2026
is able to fight with me and **k** me, 1Sa 17:9 5221
I prevail against him and **k** him, 1Sa 17:9 5221
the cave, and some said to **k** you, 1Sa 24:10 2026
of your robe and did not **k** you, 1Sa 24:11 2026
hand and *yet* you did not **k** me. 1Sa 24:18 2026
you will not **k** me or deliver me into 1Sa 30:15 4191
'Please stand beside me and **k** me, 2Sa 1:9 4191
but Saul had sought to **k** them in 2Sa 21:2 5221
sword, and he intended to **k** David. 2Sa 21:16 5221
child, and by no means **k** him." 1Ki 3:26 4191
child, and by no means **k** him. 1Ki 3:27 4191
and they will **k** me and return to 1Ki 12:27 2026
have to **k** some of the cattle." 1Ki 18:5 3772
he cannot find you, he will **k** me, 1Ki 18:12 2026
he will then **k** me." 1Ki 18:14 2026
from me, a lion will **k** you." 1Ki 20:36 5221
"Am I God, to **k** and to make 2Ki 5:7 4191
"My father, shall I **k** them? 2Ki 6:21 5221
Shall I **k** them?" 2Ki 6:21 5221
"You shall not **k** *them.* 2Ki 6:22 5221
Would you **k** those you have taken 2Ki 6:22 5221
and if they **k** us, we will but die." 2Ki 7:4 4191
men you will **k** with the sword, 2Ki 8:12 2026
"Go in, **k** them; let none come out." 2Ki 10:25 5221
they **k** them because they do not 2Ki 17:26 4191
until we come among them, **k** them and Ne 4:11 2026
for they are coming to **k** you, Ne 6:10 2026
are coming to **k** you at night." Ne 6:10 2026
king's provinces to destroy, to **k** and Es 3:13 2026
their lives, to destroy, to **k** and Es 8:11 2026
and **k** 75,000 of those who hated Es 9:16 2026
the righteous And seeks to **k** him. Ps 37:32 4191
of the naive will **k** them, Pr 1:32 2026
A time to **k** and a time to heal; Ec 3:3 2026
And it will **k** off your survivors. Is 14:30 2026
And He will **k** the dragon who *lives* Is 27:1 2026
he did not **k** me before birth, Jer 20:17 4191
k Ishmael the son of Nethaniah, Jer 40:15 5221
Daniel and his friends to **k** *them.* Da 2:13 6992
Do not fear those who **k** the body Mt 10:28 *615*
but are unable to **k** the soul; Mt 10:28 *615*
and they will **k** Him, and He will Mt 17:23 *615*
come, let us **k** him and seize his Mt 21:38 *615*
of them you will **k** and crucify, Mt 23:34 *615*
to tribulation, and will **k** you, Mt 24:9 *615*
seize Jesus by stealth and **k** Him. Mt 26:4 *615*
the Sabbath, to save a life or to **k**?" Mk 3:4 *615*
hands of men, and they will **k** Him; Mk 9:31 *615*
Him, and scourge Him and **k** *Him,* Mk 10:34 *615*
come, let us **k** him, and the Mk 12:7 *615*
seize Him by stealth and **k** *Him;* Mk 14:1 *615*
k and *some* they will persecute, Lk 11:49 *615*
be afraid of those who **k** the body and Lk 12:4 *615*
here, for Herod wants to **k** You." Lk 13:31 *615*
and bring the fattened calf, **k** it, Lk 15:23 *2380*
scourged Him, they will **k** Him; Lk 18:33 *615*
let us **k** him so that the inheritance Lk 20:14 *615*
seeking all the more to **k** Him, Jn 5:18 *615*
the Jews were seeking to **k** Him. Jn 7:1 *615*
Why do you seek to **k** Me?" Jn 7:19 *615*
Who seeks to **k** You?" Jn 7:20 *615*
man whom they are seeking to **k**? Jn 7:25 *615*
"Surely He will not **k** Himself, Jn 8:22 *615*
yet you seek to **k** Me, because My Jn 8:37 *615*
as it is, you are seeking to **k** Me, Jn 8:40 *615*
thief comes only to steal and **k** Jn 10:10 *2380*
on they planned together to **k** Him. Jn 11:53 *615*
cut to the quick and intended to **k** Ac 5:33 *337*
'YOU DO NOT MEAN TO **K** ME AS YOU Ac 7:28 *337*
"Get up, Peter, **k** and eat!" Ac 10:13 *2380*
saying to me, 'Get up, Peter; **k** and eat.' Ac 11:7 *2380*
sword and was about to **k** himself, Ac 16:27 *337*
While they were seeking to **k** him, Ac 21:31 *615*
an ambush to **k** him on the way). Ac 25:3 *337*
plan was to **k** the prisoners, Ac 27:42 *615*
who **k** their fathers or mothers, 1Tm 1:9 *3970a, 3389*
k her children with pestilence, Rv 2:23 *615*
to **k** with sword and with famine Rv 6:8 *615*
were not permitted to **k** anyone, Rv 9:5 *615*
they would **k** a third of mankind. Rv 9:15 *615*
and overcome them and **k** them. Rv 11:7 *615*
KILLED
Abel his brother and **k** him. Gn 4:8 2026
I have **k** a man for wounding me; Gn 4:23 2026
in place of Abel, for Cain **k** him." Gn 4:25 2026
city unawares, and **k** every male. Gn 34:25 2026
They **k** Hamor and his son Gn 34:26 2026
kill me as you **k** the Egyptian?" Ex 2:14 2026
that the LORD **k** every firstborn Ex 13:15 2026
So they **k** him and his sons and all Nu 21:35 5221
hand, I would have **k** you by now." Nu 22:29 2026
would surely have **k** you just now, Nu 22:33 2026
Moses, and they **k** every male. Nu 31:7 2026
They **k** the kings of Midian Nu 31:8 2026
they also **k** Balaam the son of Beor Nu 31:8 2026
whoever has **k** any person and Nu 31:19 2026
that the manslayer who has **k** any Nu 35:11 5221
sons of Israel **k** with the sword. Jos 10:11 2026
also **k** Balaam the son of Beor, Jos 13:22 2026
they **k** Oreb at the rock of Oreb, Jg 7:25 2026
and they **k** Zeeb at the wine press Jg 7:25 2026
Penuel and **k** the men of the city. Jg 8:17 2026
were they whom you **k** at Tabor?" Jg 8:18 2026
arose and **k** Zebah and Zalmunna, Jg 8:21 2026
and **k** his brothers the sons of Jg 9:5 2026
house today and have **k** his sons, Jg 9:18 2026
their brother, who **k** them, Jg 9:24 2026
and **k** the people who *were* in it; Jg 9:45 2026
k thirty of them and took their spoil and Jg 14:19 5221
it and **k** a thousand men with it. Jg 15:15 5221
donkey I have **k** a thousand men." Jg 15:16 5221
So the dead whom he **k** at his death Jg 16:30 4191
than those whom he **k** in his life. Jg 16:30 4191
them at Gidom and **k** 2,000 of them. Jg 20:45 5221
the Philistines who **k** about four 1Sa 4:2 5221
beard and struck him and **k** him. 1Sa 17:35 4191
has **k** both the lion and the bear; 1Sa 17:36 5221
struck the Philistine and **k** him; 1Sa 17:50 4191
it out of its sheath and **k** him, 1Sa 17:51 4191
whom you **k** in the valley of Elah, 1Sa 21:9 5221
and he **k** that day eighty-five men 1Sa 22:18 4191
had **k** the priests of the LORD. 1Sa 22:21 2026
and the Philistines **k** Jonathan and 1Sa 31:2 5221
"So I stood beside him and **k** him, 2Sa 1:10 4191
'I have **k** the LORD's anointed.' " 2Sa 1:16 4191
So Joab and Abishai his brother **k** 2Sa 3:30 2026
him and **k** him and beheaded him. 2Sa 4:7 4191
I seized him and **k** him in Ziklag, 2Sa 4:10 2026
when wicked men have **k** a righteous 2Sa 4:11 2026
and they **k** them and cut off their 2Sa 4:12 2026
of Zobah, David **k** 22,000 Arameans. 2Sa 8:5 5221
and David **k** 700 charioteers of the 2Sa 10:18 2026
and have **k** him with the sword of 2Sa 12:9 2026
so one struck the other and **k** him. 2Sa 14:6 4191
the life of his brother whom he **k**, 2Sa 14:7 2026
and struck Absalom and **k** him. 2Sa 18:15 4191
struck the Philistine and **k** him. 2Sa 21:17 4191
k Goliath the Gittite, 2Sa 21:19 5221
against three hundred and **k** *them,* 2Sa 23:18 2491a
k the two *sons of* Ariel of Moab. 2Sa 23:20 5221
He also went down and **k** a lion in 2Sa 23:20 5221
He **k** an Egyptian, an 2Sa 23:21 5221
and **k** him with his own spear. 2Sa 23:21 2026
the son of Jether, whom he **k**; 1Ki 2:5 2026
than he and **k** them with the sword, 1Ki 2:32 2026
and **k** the Canaanites who lived in 1Ki 9:16 2026
lion met him on the way and **k** him, 1Ki 13:24 4191
which has torn him and **k** him, 1Ki 13:26 4191
So Baasha **k** him in the third year 1Ki 15:28 4191
he **k** all the household of Baasha; 1Ki 16:11 5221
Jezebel **k** the prophets of the LORD, 1Ki 18:13 2026
and how he had **k** all the prophets 1Ki 19:1 2026
and **k** Your prophets with the sword. 1Ki 19:10 2026
and **k** Your prophets with the sword. 1Ki 19:14 2026
They **k** each his man; 1Ki 20:20 5221
and **k** the Arameans with a great 1Ki 20:21 5221
and the sons of Israel **k** *of* the 1Ki 20:29 5221
him a lion found him and **k** him. 1Ki 20:36 5221
against my master and **k** him, 2Ki 10:9 2026
killed him, but who **k** all these? 2Ki 10:9 5221
So Jehu **k** all who remained of the 2Ki 10:11 5221
and **k** them at the pit of Beth-eked, 2Ki 10:14 7819
he **k** all who remained to Ahab in 2Ki 10:17 5221
And they **k** them with the edge of 2Ki 10:25 5221
and **k** Mattan the priest of Baal 2Ki 11:18 2026
that he **k** his servants who had 2Ki 14:5 5221
He **k** *of* Edom in the Valley of Salt 2Ki 14:7 5221
him to Lachish and **k** him there. 2Ki 14:19 4191
him before the people and **k** him, 2Ki 15:10 4191
and **k** him and became king in his 2Ki 15:14 4191
and he **k** him and became king in 2Ki 15:25 4191
among them which **k** some of them. 2Ki 17:25 2026
and Sharezer **k** him with the sword; 2Ki 19:37 5221
and **k** the king in his own house. 2Ki 21:23 4191
Then the people of the land **k** all 2Ki 21:24 5221
Neco saw him he **k** him at Megiddo. 2Ki 23:29 4191
Gath who were born in the land **k**, 1Ch 7:21 2026
Therefore He **k** him and turned the 1Ch 10:14 4191
hundred whom he **k** at one time. 1Ch 11:11 2491a
against three hundred and **k** them; 1Ch 11:20 2491a
He also went down and **k** a lion 1Ch 11:22 5221
He **k** an Egyptian, a man of 1Ch 11:23 5221
and **k** him with his own spear. 1Ch 11:23 2026
k 22,000 men of the Arameans. 1Ch 18:5 5221
and David **k** of the Arameans 7,000 1Ch 19:18 2026
Sibbecai the Hushathite **k** Sippai, 1Ch 20:4 5221
Elhanan the son of Jair **k** Lahmi 1Ch 20:5 5221
of Shimea, David's brother, **k** him. 1Ch 20:7 5221
he **k** all his brothers with the 2Ch 21:4 2026
and you have also **k** your brothers, 2Ch 21:13 2026
enters the house, let him be **k**. 2Ch 23:7 4191
and **k** Mattan the priest of Baal 2Ch 23:17 2026
that he **k** his servants who had 2Ch 25:3 2026
him to Lachish and **k** him there. 2Ch 25:27 4191
k him there with the sword. 2Ch 32:21 5307
But the people of the land **k** all 2Ch 33:25 5221
k Your prophets who had admonished Ne 9:26 2026
to be **k** and to be annihilated. Es 7:4 2026
in Susa the Jews **k** and Es 9:6 2026
those who were **k** at the citadel in Susa Es 9:11 2026
"The Jews have **k** and destroyed Es 9:12 2026
and **k** three hundred men in Susa, Es 9:15 2026
Your sake we are **k** all day long; Ps 44:22 2026
And **k** some of their stoutest ones, Ps 78:31 2026

Context	Reference	No.
When He **k** them, then they sought	Ps 78:34	2026
I will be **k** in the streets!"	Pr 22:13	7523
his sons **k** him with the sword;	Is 37:38	5221
whomever he wished he **k** and	Da 5:19	6992
cubs, **K** *enough* for his lionesses,	Na 2:12	2614
be **k**, and be raised up on the third	Mt 16:21	*615*
and beat one, and **k** another,	Mt 21:35	*615*
out of the vineyard and **k** him.	Mt 21:39	*615*
and mistreated them and **k** them.	Mt 22:6	*615*
be **k**, and after three days rise again.	Mk 8:31	*615*
and when He has been **k**,	Mk 9:31	*615*
sent another, and that one they **k**;	Mk 12:5	*615*
"They took him, and **k** him and	Mk 12:8	*615*
be **k** and be raised up on the third	Lk 9:22	*615*
it was your fathers *who* **k** them.	Lk 11:47	*615*
because it was they who **k** them,	Lk 11:48	*615*
who was **k** between the altar	Lk 11:51	*622*
fear the One who, after He has **k**	Lk 12:5	*615*
tower in Siloam fell and **k** them were	Lk 13:4	*615*
father has **k** the fattened calf because	Lk 15:27	*2380*
you **k** the fattened calf for him.'	Lk 15:30	*2380*
him out of the vineyard and **k** him.	Lk 20:15	*615*
But he was **k**, and all who followed	Ac 5:36	*337*
AS YOU **K** THE EGYPTIAN YESTERDAY,	Ac 7:28	*337*
They **k** those who had	Ac 7:52	*615*
nor drink until they had **k** Paul.	Ac 23:12	*615*
nothing until we have **k** Paul.	Ac 23:14	*615*
deceived me and through it **k** me.	Ro 7:11	*615*
"Lord, THEY HAVE **K** YOUR PROPHETS,	Ro 11:3	*615*
who both **k** the Lord Jesus and the	1Th 2:15	*615*
of instinct to be captured and **k**,	2Pe 2:12	*5356*
faithful one, who was **k** among you,	Rv 2:13	*615*
to be **k** even as they had been,	Rv 6:11	*615*
was **k** by these three plagues,	Rv 9:18	*615*
who were not **k** by these plagues,	Rv 9:20	*615*
them, he must be **k** in this way.	Rv 11:5	*615*
people were **k** in the earthquake,	Rv 11:13	*615*
with the sword he must be **k**.	Rv 13:10	*615*
the image of the beast to be **k**.	Rv 13:15	*615*
And the rest were **k** with the sword	Rv 19:21	*615*

KILLING

Context	Reference	No.
when Israel had finished **k** all the	Jos 8:24	2026
father in **k** his seventy brothers.	Jg 9:56	2026
David returned from **k** the Philistine,	1Sa 17:57	5221
David returned from **k** the Philistine,	1Sa 18:6	5221
small and great, without **k** anyone,	1Sa 30:2	4191
he returned from **k** 18,000 Arameans	2Sa 8:13	5221
with the sword, **k** and destroying;	Es 9:5	2027
K of cattle and slaughtering of	Is 22:13	2026
next day after the **k** of Gedaliah,	Jer 41:4	4191
beating some and **k** others.	Mk 12:5	*615*

KILLS

Context	Reference	No.
"Therefore whoever **k** Cain,	Gn 4:15	2026
it and it **k** a man or a woman,	Ex 21:29	4191
who **k** an animal shall make it good,	Lv 24:21	5221
who **k** a man shall be put to death.	Lv 24:21	5221
that anyone who **k** a person	Nu 35:15	5221
the blood avenger **k** the manslayer,	Nu 35:27	7523
'If anyone **k** a person, the	Nu 35:30	5221
he **k** his friend unintentionally,	Dt 19:4	5221
who **k** any person unintentionally,	Jos 20:3	5221
that whoever **k** any person	Jos 20:9	5221
"The LORD **k** and makes alive;	1Sa 2:6	4191
king will enrich the man who **k** him	1Sa 17:25	5221
for the man who **k** this Philistine and	1Sa 17:26	5221
be done for the man who **k** him."	1Sa 17:27	5221
man, And jealousy **k** the simple.	Jb 5:2	4191
"If the scourge **k** suddenly, He	Jb 9:23	4191
He **k** the poor and the needy, And	Jb 24:14	6991
hiding places he **k** the innocent;	Ps 10:8	2026
"*But* he who **k** an ox is *like* one	Is 66:3	7819
who **k** the prophets and stones	Mt 23:37	*615*
the city that **k** the prophets and	Lk 13:34	*615*
hour is coming for everyone who **k**	Jn 16:2	*615*
the letter **k**, but the Spirit gives life.	2Co 3:6	*615*
if anyone **k** with the sword, with	Rv 13:10	*615*

KILN

Context	Reference	No.
handfuls of soot from a **k**,	Ex 9:8	3536
So they took soot from a **k**,	Ex 9:10	3536

KIN

Context	Reference	No.
AS NEXT OF **K** SHALL MARRY HIS WIFE,	Mt 22:24	

KINAH

Context	Reference	No.
and **K** and Dimonah and Adadah,	Jos 15:22	7016

KIND

Context	Reference	No.
earth bearing fruit after their **k**	Gn 1:11	4327
yielding seed after their **k**,	Gn 1:12	4327
with seed in them, after their **k**;	Gn 1:12	4327
the waters swarmed after their **k**,	Gn 1:21	4327
and every winged bird after its **k**;	Gn 1:21	4327
living creatures after their **k**:	Gn 1:24	4327
beasts of the earth after their **k**";	Gn 1:24	4327
beasts of the earth after their **k**,	Gn 1:25	4327
and the cattle after their **k**,	Gn 1:25	4327
creeps on the ground after its **k**;	Gn 1:25	4327
you shall bring two of every **k**	Gn 6:19	
"Of the birds after their **k**,	Gn 6:20	4327
and of the animals after their **k**,	Gn 6:20	4327
thing of the ground after its **k**,	Gn 6:20	4327
two of every **k** will come to you	Gn 6:20	
they and every beast after its **k**,	Gn 7:14	4327
and all the cattle after their **k**,	Gn 7:14	4327
creeps on the earth after its **k**,	Gn 7:14	4327
kind, and every bird after its **k**,	Gn 7:14	4327
the kite and the falcon in its **k**,	Lv 11:14	4327
every raven in its **k**,	Lv 11:15	4327
sea gull and the hawk in its **k**,	Lv 11:16	4327
do no laborious work of any **k**.	Lv 23:35	
'Now if it is an animal of the **k**	Lv 27:9	
any unclean animal of the **k** which	Lv 27:11	
and every raven in its **k**,	Dt 14:14	4327
an Asherah of any **k** of tree beside	Dt 16:21	
one **k** of homicide or another,	Dt 17:8	
one **k** of lawsuit or another,	Dt 17:8	
one **k** of assault or another,	Dt 17:8	
"What **k** of men *were* they whom you	Jg 8:18	375
the **k** You show Yourself kind,	2Sa 22:26	2623
the kind You show Yourself **k**,	2Sa 22:26	2616a
"What **k** of man was he who came up	2Ki 1:7	4941
every **k** of good thing of Damascus,	2Ki 8:9	
are skillful in every **k** of work.	1Ch 22:15	
utensils for every **k** of service;	1Ch 28:14	5656
utensils for every **k** of service;	1Ch 28:14	5656
"If you will be **k** to this people	2Ch 10:7	2896a
them with every **k** of distress.	2Ch 15:6	
410 silver bowls of a second **k**	Ezr 1:10	
merchants of every **k** of merchandise	Ne 13:20	
the **k** You show Yourself kind;	Ps 18:25	2623
the kind You show Yourself **k**;	Ps 18:25	2616a
furnishing every **k** of produce,	Ps 144:13	2177
His ways And **k** in all His deeds.	Ps 145:17	2623
a **k** of *man* who curses his father And	Pr 30:11	1755
a **k** who is pure in his own eyes,	Pr 30:12	1755
There is a **k**	Pr 30:13	1755
There is a **k** of *man* whose teeth	Pr 30:14	1755
"What **k** of beloved is your beloved,	SS 5:9	
What **k** of beloved is your beloved,	SS 5:9	
goat also will cry to its **k**;	Is 34:14	7453
there, Every one with its **k**.	Is 34:15	7468
And what **k** of wisdom do they have?	Jer 8:9	
birds of every **k** will nest under it;	Ezk 17:23	3671
as food to every **k** of predatory bird	Ezk 39:4	3671
'Speak to every **k** of bird and to	Ezk 39:17	3671
first of all the first fruits of every **k**	Ezk 44:30	
and every contribution of every **k**,	Ezk 44:30	
from every **k** of desirable object.	Na 2:9	
and healing every **k** of disease and	Mt 4:23	*3956*
every **k** of sickness among the	Mt 4:23	*3956*
"What **k** of a man is this, that	Mt 8:27	*4217*
and healing every **k** of disease and	Mt 9:35	*3956*
disease and every **k** of sickness.	Mt 9:35	*3956*
and to heal every **k** of disease and	Mt 10:1	*3956*
disease and every **k** of sickness.	Mt 10:1	*3956*
and gathering *fish* of every **k**;	Mt 13:47	*1085*
"But this **k** does not go out	Mt 17:21	*1085*
"This **k** cannot come out by	Mk 9:29	*1085*
kept pondering what **k** of salutation	Lk 1:29	*4217*
is **k** to ungrateful and evil *men*.	Lk 6:35	*5543*
know what **k** of spirit you are of;	Lk 9:55	*4169*
tithe of mint and rue and every **k**	Lk 11:42	
shrewd in relation to their own **k**	Lk 16:8	*1074*
k of death by which He was to die.	Jn 12:33	*4169*
k of death He was about to die.	Jn 18:32	*4169*
k of death he would glorify God.	Jn 21:19	*4169*
WHAT **K** OF HOUSE WILL YOU BUILD FOR	Ac 7:49	*4169*
you have been **k** enough to come.	Ac 10:33	*2573*
By what **k** of law? Of works? No,	Ro 3:27	*4169*
produced in me coveting of every **k**;	Ro 7:8	*3956*
and immorality of such a **k** as does	1Co 5:1	*5108*
Love is patient, love is **k**	1Co 13:4	*5541*
and no **k** is without meaning.	1Co 14:10	
with what **k** of body do they come?"	1Co 15:35	*4169*
to the **k** intention of His will,	Eph 1:5	*2107*
according to His **k** intention which	Eph 1:9	*2107*
the practice of every **k** of impurity	Eph 4:19	*3956*
Be **k** to one another,	Eph 4:32	*5543*
just as you know what **k** of men we	1Th 1:5	*3634*
what **k** of a reception we had	1Th 1:9	*3697*
be quarrelsome, but be **k** to all,	2Tm 2:24	*2261*
pure, workers at home, **k**,	Ti 2:5	*18*
so that we would be a **k** of first	Jas 1:18	*5100*
forgotten what **k** of person he was.	Jas 1:24	*3697*
a faith of the same **k** as ours,	2Pe 1:1	*2472*
and every **k** *of* citron wood	Rv 18:12	
with every **k** of precious stone.	Rv 21:19	*3956*

KINDHEARTED

Context	Reference	No.
sympathetic, brotherly, **k**,	1Pe 3:8	*2155*

KINDLE

Context	Reference	No.
"You shall not **k** a fire in any of	Ex 35:3	1197a
is a contentious man to **k** strife.	Pr 26:21	2787
Behold, all you who **k** a fire,	Is 50:11	6919
wood, and the fathers **k** the fire,	Jer 7:18	1197a
I will **k** a fire in its gates	Jer 17:27	3341
"And I will **k** a fire in its	Jer 21:14	3341
I am about to **k** a fire in you,	Ezk 20:47	3341
"Heap on the wood, **k** the fire,	Ezk 24:10	1814
k a fire on the wall of Rabbah And	Am 1:14	3341
not uselessly **k** *fire on* My altar!	Mal 1:10	215
k afresh the gift of God which is in	2Tm 1:6	*329*

KINDLED

Context	Reference	No.
and My anger will be **k**,	Ex 22:24	2734
LORD heard *it,* His anger was **k**,	Nu 11:1	2734
anger of the LORD was **k** greatly,	Nu 11:10	2734
the anger of the LORD was **k** against	Nu 11:33	2734
your God will be **k** against you,	Dt 6:15	2734
anger of the LORD will be **k** against	Dt 7:4	2734
anger of the LORD will be **k** against	Dt 11:17	2734
My anger will be **k** against them	Dt 31:17	2734
For a fire is **k** in My anger, And	Dt 32:22	6919
the anger of the LORD was **k** against	Jg 3:8	2734
Coals were **k** by it.	2Sa 22:9	1197a
before Him Coals of fire were **k**.	2Sa 22:13	1197a
the anger of the LORD was **k** against	2Ki 13:3	2734
has also **k** His anger against me And	Jb 19:11	2734
"My wrath is **k** against you and	Jb 42:7	2734
way, For His wrath may soon be **k**.	Ps 2:12	1197a
Coals were **k** by it.	Ps 18:8	1197a
And a fire was **k** against Jacob And	Ps 78:21	8026b
the anger of the LORD was **k** against	Ps 106:40	2734
When their anger was **k** against us;	Ps 124:3	2734
will be **k** like a burning flame.	Is 10:16	3344
great tumult He has **k** fire on it,	Jer 11:16	3341
For a fire has been **k** in My anger,	Jer 15:14	6919
For you have **k** a fire in My anger	Jer 17:4	6919
And He has **k** a fire in Zion Which	La 4:11	3341
see that I, the LORD, have **k** it;	Ezk 20:48	1197a
Me, All My compassions are **k**.	Hos 11:8	3648
anger is **k** against the shepherds,	Zch 10:3	2734
and how I wish it were already **k**!	Lk 12:49	*381*
After they had **k** a fire in the	Lk 22:55	*4015a*
they **k** a fire and received us all.	Ac 28:2	*681*

KINDLES

Context	Reference	No.
"His breath **k** coals, And a flame	Jb 41:21	3857
As fire **k** the brushwood, *as* fire	Is 64:2	6919

KINDLY

Context	Reference	No.
deal **k** and truly with my master,	Gn 24:49	2617a
them and spoke **k** to them.	Gn 50:21	3820
since I have dealt **k** with you,	Jos 2:12	2617a
deal **k** with my father's household,	Jos 2:12	2617a
deal **k** and faithfully with you."	Jos 2:14	2617a
city and we will treat you **k**."	Jg 1:24	2617a
May the LORD deal **k** with you as	Ru 1:8	2617a
have spoken **k** to your maidservant,	Ru 2:13	3820
deal **k** with your servant,	1Sa 20:8	2617a
out and speak **k** to your servants,	2Sa 19:7	3820
and he spoke **k** to him and set his	2Ki 25:28	2899b
k with me for Your name's sake;	Ps 109:21	
"Speak **k** to Jerusalem;	Is 40:2	3820
Then he spoke **k** to him and set his	Jer 52:32	2899b
wilderness And speak **k** to her.	Hos 2:14	3820
Or would he receive you **k**?"	Mal 1:8	6440
will He receive any of you **k**?"	Mal 1:9	6440
and that you always think **k** of us,	1Th 3:6	*18*

KINDNESS

Context	Reference	No.
the **k** which you will show to me:	Gn 20:13	2617a
to the **k** that I have shown to you,	Gn 21:23	2617a
with Joseph and extended **k** to him,	Gn 39:21	2617a
a **k** by mentioning me to Pharaoh and	Gn 40:14	2617a
with me in **k** and faithfulness.	Gn 47:29	2617a
nor did they show **k** to the	Jg 8:35	2617a
LORD who has not withdrawn his **k**	Ru 2:20	2617a
You have shown your last **k** to be	Ru 3:10	2617a
for you showed **k** to all the sons	1Sa 15:6	2617a
shown this **k** to Saul your lord,	2Sa 2:5	2617a
Today I show **k** to the house of	2Sa 3:8	2617a
show him **k** for Jonathan's sake?"	2Sa 9:1	2617a
to whom I may show the **k** of God?"	2Sa 9:3	2617a
for I will surely show **k** to you	2Sa 9:7	2617a
show **k** to Hanun the son of Nahash,	2Sa 10:2	2617a
as his father showed **k** to me."	2Sa 10:2	2617a
"But show **k** to the sons of	1Ki 2:7	2617a
show **k** to Hanun the son of Nahash,	1Ch 19:2	2617a
his father showed **k** to me."	1Ch 19:2	2617a
the **k** which his father Jehoiada had	2Ch 24:22	2617a
and she found favor and **k** with him	Es 2:17	2617a
there should be **k** from his friend;	Jb 6:14	2617a
smite me in **k** and reprove me;	Ps 141:5	2617a
Do not let **k** and truth leave you;	Pr 3:3	2617a
But **k** and truth *will be to* those	Pr 14:22	2617a
What is desirable in a man is his **k**,	Pr 19:22	2617a
teaching of **k** is on her tongue.	Pr 31:26	2617a
Because there is no faithfulness or **k**	Hos 4:1	2617a
Reap in accordance with **k**;	Hos 10:12	2617a
your God, Observe **k** and justice,	Hos 12:6	2617a
you But to do justice, to love **k**,	Mi 6:8	2617a
and practice **k** and compassion each	Zch 7:9	2617a
with deeds of **k** and charity which	Ac 9:36	*18*
I beg you to grant us, by your **k**,	Ac 24:4	*1932*
natives showed us extraordinary **k**;	Ac 28:2	*5363*
think lightly of the riches of His **k**	Ro 2:4	*5544*
not knowing that the **k** of God	Ro 2:4	*5543*
then the **k** and severity of God;	Ro 11:22	*5544*
severity, but to you, God's **k**,	Ro 11:22	*5544*
if you continue in His **k**;	Ro 11:22	*5544*
in knowledge, in patience, in **k**,	2Co 6:6	*5544*
is love, joy, peace, patience, **k**,	Ga 5:22	*5544*
in **k** toward us in Christ Jesus.	Eph 2:7	*5544*
put on a heart of compassion, **k**,	Col 3:12	*5544*
But when the **k** of God our Savior	Ti 3:4	*5544*
you have tasted the **k** of the Lord.	1Pe 2:3	*5543*
in *your* godliness, brotherly **k**,	2Pe 1:7	*5360*
kindness, and in *your* brotherly **k**,	2Pe 1:7	*5360*

KINDNESSES

Context	Reference	No.
did not remember Your abundant **k**,	Ps 106:7	2617a

KINDRED

Context	Reference	No.
make known her people or her **k**,	Es 2:10	4138
made known her **k** or her people,	Es 2:20	4138
to see the destruction of my **k**?"	Es 8:6	4138
For I have no one *else* of **k** spirit	Php 2:20	*2473*

KINDS

Context	Reference	No.
in mortar and bricks and at all **k**	Ex 1:14	
and in all **k** *of* craftsmanship,	Ex 31:3	
that he may work in all **k** *of*	Ex 31:5	
and the stork, the heron in its **k**,	Lv 11:19	4327
the locust in its **k**,	Lv 11:22	4327
the devastating locust in its **k**,	Lv 11:22	4327
kinds, and the cricket in its **k**,	Lv 11:22	4327
and the grasshopper in its **k**.	Lv 11:22	4327
and the great lizard in its **k**,	Lv 11:29	4327
together two **k** of your cattle;	Lv 19:19	3610
sow your field with two **k** of seed,	Lv 19:19	3610
two **k** of material mixed together.	Lv 19:19	3610
and plant all **k** of trees for food,	Lv 19:23	
them, all **k** of wrought articles.	Nu 31:51	
falcon, and the kite in their **k**,	Dt 14:13	4327

sea gull, and the hawk in their **k**, **Dt 14:15** 4327
stork, and the heron in their **k**, **Dt 14:18** 4327
your vineyard with two **k** of seed, **Dt 22:9** 3610
who smote the Egyptians with all **k** **1Sa 4:8**
all **k** of *instruments made of* fir wood, **2Sa 6:5**
with all **k** of weapons of war **1Ch 12:33**
120,000 with all **k** of weapons **1Ch 12:37**
all **k** of articles of gold and silver **1Ch 18:10**
all the work for all **k** of service. **1Ch 28:21**
and all **k** of precious stones and **1Ch 29:2**
how to make all **k** of engravings **2Ch 2:14**
had filled with spices of various **k** **2Ch 16:14** 2177
and all **k** of valuable articles, **2Ch 32:27**
pens for all **k** of cattle and **2Ch 32:28** 929
grapes, figs and all **k** of loads, **Ne 13:15**
fish and all **k** of merchandise, **Ne 13:16**
in golden vessels of various **k**, **Es 1:7** 3627
Their soul abhorred all **k** of food, **Ps 107:18**
We will find all **k** of precious **Pr 1:13**
in them all **k** of fruit trees; **Ec 2:5**
fragrance of your oils Than all **k** **SS 4:10**
over them four **k** *of doom*," **Jer 15:3** 4940
because of the abundance of all **k** **Ezk 27:12**
because of the abundance of all **k** **Ezk 27:18**
your wares with the best of all **k** **Ezk 27:22**
and with all **k** of precious stones **Ezk 27:22**
fish will be according to their **k**, **Ezk 47:10** 4327
will grow all **k** *of* trees for food. **Ezk 47:12**
Daniel even understood all **k** *of* **Da 1:17**
bagpipe and all **k** of music, **Da 3:5** 2178
bagpipe and all **k** of music, **Da 3:7** 2178
and bagpipe and all **k** of music, **Da 3:10** 2178
and bagpipe and all **k** of music, **Da 3:15** 2178
all **k** of evil against you because **Mt 5:11** *3956*
and there were in it all **k** *of* **Ac 10:12**
to another *various* **k** of tongues, **1Co 12:10** *1085*
various **k** of tongues. **1Co 12:28** *1085*
many **k** of languages in the world, **1Co 14:10** *1085*
bearing twelve **k** *of* fruit, **Rv 22:2**

KING

the days of Amraphel **k** of Shinar, **Gn 14:1** 4428
of Shinar, Arioch **k** of Ellasar, **Gn 14:1** 4428
Ellasar, Chedorlaomer **k** of Elam, **Gn 14:1** 4428
of Elam, and Tidal **k** of Goiim, **Gn 14:1** 4428
made war with Bera **k** of Sodom, **Gn 14:2** 4428
and with Birsha **k** of Gomorrah, **Gn 14:2** 4428
of Gomorrah, Shinab **k** of Admah, **Gn 14:2** 4428
Admah, and Shemeber **k** of Zeboiim, **Gn 14:2** 4428
of Zeboiim, and the **k** of Bela **Gn 14:2** 4428
And the **k** of Sodom and the king of **Gn 14:8** 4428
of Sodom and the **k** of Gomorrah **Gn 14:8** 4428
and the **k** of Admah and the king of **Gn 14:8** 4428
k of Zeboiim and the king of Bela **Gn 14:8** 4428
king of Zeboiim and the **k** of Bela **Gn 14:8** 4428
against Chedorlaomer **k** of Elam and **Gn 14:9** 4428
king of Elam and Tidal **k** of Goiim **Gn 14:9** 4428
Amraphel **k** of Shinar and Arioch **Gn 14:9** 4428
Shinar and Arioch **k** of Ellasar **Gn 14:9** 4428
the **k** of Sodom went out to meet **Gn 14:17** 4428
And Melchizedek **k** of Salem brought **Gn 14:18** 4428
The **k** of Sodom said to Abram, **Gn 14:21** 4428
Abram said to the **k** of Sodom, **Gn 14:22** 4428
k of Gerar sent and took Sarah. **Gn 20:2** 4428
to Abimelech **k** of the Philistines. **Gn 26:1** 4428
Abimelech **k** of the Philistines **Gn 26:8** 4428
before any **k** reigned over the sons of **Gn 36:31** 4428
of Bozrah became **k** in his place. **Gn 36:33** 4427a
Temanites became **k** in his place. **Gn 36:34** 4427a
of Moab, became **k** in his place; **Gn 36:35** 4427a
of Masrekah became **k** in his place. **Gn 36:36** 4427a
River became **k** in his place. **Gn 36:37** 4427a
of Achbor became **k** in his place. **Gn 36:38** 4427a
and Hadar became **k** in his place; **Gn 36:39** 4427a
and the baker for the **k** of Egypt **Gn 40:1** 4428
their lord, the **k** of Egypt. **Gn 40:1** 4428
and the baker for the **k** of Egypt, **Gn 40:5** 4428
stood before Pharaoh, **k** of Egypt. **Gn 41:46** 4428
Now a new **k** arose over Egypt, who **Ex 1:8** 4428
Then the **k** of Egypt spoke to the **Ex 1:15** 4428
the **k** of Egypt had commanded them, **Ex 1:17** 4428
So the **k** of Egypt called for the **Ex 1:18** 4428
days that the **k** of Egypt died. **Ex 2:23** 4428
will come to the **k** of Egypt and **Ex 3:18** 4428
"But I know that the **k** of Egypt **Ex 3:19** 4428
But the **k** of Egypt said to them, **Ex 5:4** 4428
tell Pharaoh **k** of Egypt to let the **Ex 6:11** 4428
Israel and to Pharaoh **k** of Egypt, **Ex 6:13** 4428
spoke to Pharaoh **k** of Egypt about **Ex 6:27** 4428
speak to Pharaoh **k** of Egypt all **Ex 6:29** 4428
When the **k** of Egypt was told that **Ex 14:5** 4428
the heart of Pharaoh, **k** of Egypt, **Ex 14:8** 4428
sent messengers to the **k** of Edom: **Nu 20:14** 4428
When the Canaanite, the **k** of Arad, **Nu 21:1** 4428
to Sihon, **k** of the Amorites, **Nu 21:21** 4428
city of Sihon, **k** of the Amorites, **Nu 21:26** 4428
fought against the former **k** of Moab **Nu 21:26** 4428
into captivity, To an Amorite **k**, **Nu 21:29** 4428
and Og the **k** of Bashan went out **Nu 21:33** 4428
did to Sihon, **k** of the Amorites, **Nu 21:34** 4428
the son of Zippor was **k** of Moab **Nu 22:4** 4428
the son of Zippor, **k** of Moab, **Nu 22:10** 4428
Moab's **k** from the mountains of the **Nu 23:7** 4428
the shout of a **k** is among them. **Nu 23:21** 4428
his **k** shall be higher than Agag, **Nu 24:7** 4428
kingdom of Sihon, **k** of the Amorites **Nu 32:33** 4428
kingdom of Og, the **k** of Bashan, **Nu 32:33** 4428
the **k** of Arad who lived in the **Nu 33:40** 4428
Sihon the **k** of the Amorites, **Dt 1:4** 4428
Heshbon, and Og the **k** of Bashan, **Dt 1:4** 4428

Sihon the Amorite, **k** of Heshbon, **Dt 2:24** 4428
to Sihon **k** of Heshbon with words of **Dt 2:26** 4428
"But Sihon **k** of Heshbon was not **Dt 2:30** 4428
to Bashan, and Og, **k** of Bashan, **Dt 3:1** 4428
did to Sihon **k** of the Amorites, **Dt 3:2** 4428
delivered Og also, **k** of Bashan, **Dt 3:3** 4428
as we did to Sihon **k** of Heshbon, **Dt 3:6** 4428
(For only Og **k** of Bashan was left **Dt 3:11** 4428
the land of Sihon **k** of the Amorites **Dt 4:46** 4428
and the land of Og **k** of Bashan, **Dt 4:47** 4428
the hand of Pharaoh **k** of Egypt. **Dt 7:8** 4428
to Pharaoh the **k** of Egypt and to **Dt 11:3** 4428
'I will set a **k** over me like all **Dt 17:14** 4428
you shall surely set a **k** over you **Dt 17:15** 4428
shall set a **k** over yourselves; **Dt 17:15** 4428
LORD will bring you and your **k**, **Dt 28:36** 4428
Sihon the **k** of Heshbon and Og the **Dt 29:7** 4428
and Og the **k** of Bashan came out **Dt 29:7** 4428
"And He was **k** in Jeshurun, When **Dt 33:5** 4428
It was told the **k** of Jericho, **Jos 2:2** 4428
k of Jericho sent *word* to Rahab, **Jos 2:3** 4428
its **k** *and* the valiant warriors. **Jos 6:2** 4428
given into your hand the **k** of Ai, **Jos 8:1** 4428
"You shall do to Ai and its **k** **Jos 8:2** 4428
as you did to Jericho and its **k**; **Jos 8:2** 4428
about when the **k** of Ai saw *it*, **Jos 8:14** 4428
But they took alive the **k** of Ai **Jos 8:23** 4428
He hanged the **k** of Ai on a tree **Jos 8:29** 4428
to Sihon **k** of Heshbon and to Og **Jos 9:10** 4428
Og **k** of Bashan who was at Ashtaroth **Jos 9:10** 4428
Adoni-zedek **k** of Jerusalem heard **Jos 10:1** 4428
he had done to Jericho and its **k**, **Jos 10:1** 4428
so he had done to Ai and its **k**), **Jos 10:1** 4428
Adoni-zedek **k** of Jerusalem sent *word* **Jos 10:3** 4428
sent *word* to Hoham **k** of Hebron **Jos 10:3** 4428
to Piram **k** of Jarmuth and to Japhia **Jos 10:3** 4428
to Japhia **k** of Lachish and to Debir **Jos 10:3** 4428
Lachish and to Debir **k** of Eglon, **Jos 10:3** 4428
the Amorites, the **k** of Jerusalem, **Jos 10:5** 4428
of Jerusalem, the **k** of Hebron, **Jos 10:5** 4428
king of Hebron, the **k** of Jarmuth, **Jos 10:5** 4428
king of Jarmuth, the **k** of Lachish, **Jos 10:5** 4428
of Lachish, *and* the **k** of Eglon, **Jos 10:5** 4428
the **k** of Jerusalem, the king of **Jos 10:23** 4428
of Jerusalem, the **k** of Hebron, **Jos 10:23** 4428
king of Hebron, the **k** of Jarmuth, **Jos 10:23** 4428
king of Jarmuth, the **k** of Lachish, **Jos 10:23** 4428
of Lachish, *and* the **k** of Eglon. **Jos 10:23** 4428
its **k** with the edge of the sword; **Jos 10:28** 4428
Thus he did to the **k** of Makkedah **Jos 10:28** 4428
he had done to the **k** of Jericho. **Jos 10:28** 4428
The LORD gave it also with its **k** into **Jos 10:30** 4428
Thus he did to its **k** just as he **Jos 10:30** 4428
he had done to the **k** of Jericho. **Jos 10:30** 4428
Then Horam **k** of Gezer came up to **Jos 10:33** 4428
captured it and struck it and its **k** **Jos 10:37** 4428
it and its **k** and all its cities, **Jos 10:39** 4428
so he did to Debir and its **k**, **Jos 10:39** 4428
had also done to Libnah and its **k**. **Jos 10:39** 4428
when Jabin **k** of Hazor heard *of it*, **Jos 11:1** 4428
that he sent to Jobab **k** of Madon **Jos 11:1** 4428
Madon and to the **k** of Shimron **Jos 11:1** 4428
Shimron and to the **k** of Achshaph, **Jos 11:1** 4428
and struck its **k** with the sword; **Jos 11:10** 4428
Sihon **k** of the Amorites, who lived **Jos 12:2** 4428
the territory of Og **k** of Bashan, **Jos 12:4** 4428
the border of Sihon **k** of Heshbon. **Jos 12:5** 4428
the **k** of Jericho, one; **Jos 12:9** 4428
the **k** of Ai, which is beside **Jos 12:9** 4428
the **k** of Jerusalem, one; **Jos 12:10** 4428
the **k** of Hebron, one; **Jos 12:10** 4428
the **k** of Jarmuth, one; **Jos 12:11** 4428
the **k** of Lachish, one; **Jos 12:11** 4428
the **k** of Eglon, one; **Jos 12:12** 4428
the **k** of Gezer, one; **Jos 12:12** 4428
the **k** of Debir, one; **Jos 12:13** 4428
the **k** of Geder, one; **Jos 12:13** 4428
the **k** of Hormah, one; **Jos 12:14** 4428
the **k** of Arad, one; **Jos 12:14** 4428
the **k** of Libnah, one; **Jos 12:15** 4428
the **k** of Adullam, one; **Jos 12:15** 4428
the **k** of Makkedah, one; **Jos 12:16** 4428
the **k** of Bethel, one; **Jos 12:16** 4428
the **k** of Tappuah, one; **Jos 12:17** 4428
the **k** of Hepher, one; **Jos 12:17** 4428
the **k** of Aphek, one; **Jos 12:18** 4428
the **k** of Lasharon, one; **Jos 12:18** 4428
the **k** of Madon, one; **Jos 12:19** 4428
the **k** of Hazor, one; **Jos 12:19** 4428
the **k** of Shimron-meron, one; **Jos 12:20** 4428
the **k** of Achshaph, one; **Jos 12:20** 4428
the **k** of Taanach, one; **Jos 12:21** 4428
the **k** of Megiddo, one; **Jos 12:21** 4428
the **k** of Kedesh, one; **Jos 12:22** 4428
the **k** of Jokneam in Carmel, one; **Jos 12:22** 4428
k of Dor in the heights of Dor, **Jos 12:23** 4428
the **k** of Goiim in Gilgal, one; **Jos 12:23** 4428
the **k** of Tirzah, one: **Jos 12:24** 4428
cities of Sihon **k** of the Amorites, **Jos 13:10** 4428
kingdom of Sihon **k** of the Amorites **Jos 13:21** 4428
the kingdom of Sihon **k** of Heshbon, **Jos 13:27** 4428
all the kingdom of Og **k** of Bashan, **Jos 13:30** 4428
the son of Zippor, **k** of Moab, **Jos 24:9** 4428
Cushan-rishathaim **k** of Mesopotamia; **Jg 3:8** 4428
k of Mesopotamia into his hand, **Jg 3:10** 4428
strengthened Eglon the **k** of Moab **Jg 3:12** 4428
Israel served Eglon the **k** of Moab **Jg 3:14** 4428
by him to Eglon the **k** of Moab. **Jg 3:15** 4428
the tribute to Eglon **k** of Moab. **Jg 3:17** 4428

a secret message for you, O **k**." **Jg 3:19** 4428
the hand of Jabin **k** of Canaan, **Jg 4:2** 4428
peace between Jabin the **k** of Hazor **Jg 4:17** 4428
on that day Jabin the **k** of Canaan **Jg 4:23** 4428
upon Jabin the **k** of Canaan, **Jg 4:24** 4428
destroyed Jabin the **k** of Canaan. **Jg 4:24** 4428
one resembling the son of a **k**." **Jg 8:18** 4428
they went and made Abimelech **k**, **Jg 9:6** 4428
forth to anoint a **k** over them, **Jg 9:8** 4428
are anointing me as **k** over you, **Jg 9:15** 4428
integrity in making Abimelech **k**, **Jg 9:16** 4427a
k over the men of Shechem, **Jg 9:18** 4427a
to the **k** of the sons of Ammon, **Jg 11:12** 4428
The **k** of the sons of Ammon **Jg 11:13** 4428
to the **k** of the sons of Ammon, **Jg 11:14** 4428
sent messengers to the **k** of Edom, **Jg 11:17** 4428
the **k** of Edom would not listen. **Jg 11:17** 4428
they also sent to the **k** of Moab, **Jg 11:17** 4428
to Sihon **k** of the Amorites, **Jg 11:19** 4428
of the Amorites, the **k** of Heshbon, **Jg 11:19** 4428
the son of Zippor, **k** of Moab? **Jg 11:25** 4428
But the **k** of the sons of Ammon **Jg 11:28** 4428
days there was no **k** in Israel; **Jg 17:6** 4428
days there was no **k** of Israel; **Jg 18:1** 4428
when there was no **k** in Israel, **Jg 19:1** 4428
days there was no **k** in Israel; **Jg 21:25** 4428
He will give strength to His **k**, **1Sa 2:10** 4428
Now appoint a **k** for us to judge us **1Sa 8:5** 4428
"Give us a **k** to judge us." **1Sa 8:6** 4428
rejected Me from being **k** over them. **1Sa 8:7** 4427a
the **k** who will reign over them." **1Sa 8:9** 4428
people who had asked of him a **k**. **1Sa 8:10** 4428
of the **k** who will reign over you: **1Sa 8:11** 4428
cry out in that day because of your **k** **1Sa 8:18** 4428
but there shall be a **k** over us, **1Sa 8:19** 4428
that our **k** may judge us and go out **1Sa 8:20** 4428
voice and appoint them a **k**." **1Sa 8:22** 4428
'No, but set a **k** over us!' **1Sa 10:19** 4428
"*Long* live the **k**!" **1Sa 10:24** 4428
they made Saul **k** before the LORD **1Sa 11:15** 4427a
and I have appointed a **k** over you. **1Sa 12:1** 4428
here is the **k** walking before you, **1Sa 12:2** 4428
into the hand of the **k** of Moab, **1Sa 12:9** 4428
Nahash the **k** of the sons of Ammon **1Sa 12:12** 4428
'No, but a **k** shall reign over us,' **1Sa 12:12** 4428
the LORD your God *was* your **k**. **1Sa 12:12** 4428
is the **k** whom you have chosen, **1Sa 12:13** 4428
the LORD has set a **k** over you. **1Sa 12:13** 4428
then both you and also the **k** who **1Sa 12:14** 4428
by asking for yourselves a **k**." **1Sa 12:17** 4428
by asking for ourselves a **k**." **1Sa 12:19** 4428
and your **k** will be swept away." **1Sa 12:25** 4428
anoint you as **k** over His people, **1Sa 15:1** 4428
Agag the **k** of the Amalekites **1Sa 15:8** 4428
"I regret that I have made Saul **k**, **1Sa 15:11** 4428
LORD anointed you **k** over Israel, **1Sa 15:17** 4428
brought back Agag the **k** of Amalek, **1Sa 15:20** 4428
also rejected you from *being* **k**." **1Sa 15:23** 4428
LORD has rejected you from being **k** **1Sa 15:26** 4428
Agag, the **k** of the Amalekites." **1Sa 15:32** 4428
He had made Saul **k** over Israel. **1Sa 15:35** 4427a
him from being **k** over Israel? **1Sa 16:1** 4427a
for I have selected a **k** for Myself **1Sa 16:1** 4428
k will enrich the man who kills him **1Sa 17:25** 4428
"By your life, O **k**, I do not know." **1Sa 17:55** 4428
The **k** said, "You inquire whose son **1Sa 17:56** 4428
and dancing, to meet **K** Saul, **1Sa 18:6** 4428
'Behold, the **k** delights in you, **1Sa 18:22** 4428
'The **k** does not desire any dowry **1Sa 18:25** 4428
gave them in full number to the **k**, **1Sa 18:27** 4428
k sin against his servant David, **1Sa 19:4** 4428
to sit down to eat with the **k**. **1Sa 20:5** 4428
came, the **k** sat down to eat food. **1Sa 20:24** 4428
The **k** sat on his seat as usual, **1Sa 20:25** 4428
"The **k** has commissioned me with a **1Sa 21:2** 4428
and went to Achish **k** of Gath. **1Sa 21:10** 4428
Is this not David the **k** of the land? **1Sa 21:11** 4428
greatly feared Achish **k** of Gath. **1Sa 21:12** 4428
and he said to the **k** of Moab, **1Sa 22:3** 4428
he left them with the **k** of Moab; **1Sa 22:4** 4428
Then the **k** sent someone to summon **1Sa 22:11** 4428
and all of them came to the **k**. **1Sa 22:11** 4428
Ahimelech answered the **k** and said, **1Sa 22:14** 4428
Do not let the **k** impute anything **1Sa 22:15** 4428
the **k** said, "You shall surely die, **1Sa 22:16** 4428
And the **k** said to the guards who **1Sa 22:17** 4428
But the servants of the **k** were not **1Sa 22:17** 4428
Then the **k** said to Doeg, **1Sa 22:18** 4428
and you will be **k** over Israel and **1Sa 23:17** 4427a
"Now then, O **k**, come down **1Sa 23:20** 4428
after Saul, saying, "My lord the **k**!" **1Sa 24:8** 4428
whom has the **k** of Israel come out? **1Sa 24:14** 4428
I know that you will surely be **k**, **1Sa 24:20** 4427a
his house, like the feast of a **k**. **1Sa 25:36** 4428
"Who are you who calls to the **k**?" **1Sa 26:14** 4428
you not guarded your lord the **k**? **1Sa 26:15** 4428
came to destroy the **k** your lord. **1Sa 26:15** 4428
"It is my voice, my lord the **k**." **1Sa 26:17** 4428
please let my lord the **k** listen to **1Sa 26:19** 4428
for the **k** of Israel has come out **1Sa 26:20** 4428
"Behold the spear of the **k**! **1Sa 26:22** 4428
the son of Maoch, **k** of Gath. **1Sa 27:2** 4428
The **k** said to her, **1Sa 28:13** 4428
servant of Saul the **k** of Israel, **1Sa 29:3** 4428
the enemies of my lord the **k**?" **1Sa 29:8** 4428
David **k** over the house of Judah. **2Sa 2:4** 4428
has anointed me **k** over them." **2Sa 2:7** 4428
He made him **k** over Gilead, **2Sa 2:9** 4427a
old when he became **k** over Israel, **2Sa 2:10** 4427a

and he was **k** for two years.	**2Sa 2:10**	4427a
The time that David was **k** in	**2Sa 2:11**	4428
daughter of Talmai, **k** of Geshur;	**2Sa 3:3**	4428
for David to be **k** over you.	**2Sa 3:17**	4428
gather all Israel to my lord the **k**	**2Sa 3:21**	4428
and that you may be **k** over all	**2Sa 3:21**	4427a
the son of Ner came to the **k**,	**2Sa 3:23**	4428
Then Joab came to the **k** and said,	**2Sa 3:24**	4428
K David walked behind the bier.	**2Sa 3:31**	4428
and the **k** lifted up his voice and	**2Sa 3:32**	4428
The **k** chanted a *lament* for	**2Sa 3:33**	4428
everything the **k** did pleased all the	**2Sa 3:36**	4428
that it had not been *the will* of the **k**	**2Sa 3:37**	4428
Then the **k** said to his servants,	**2Sa 3:38**	4428
am weak today, though anointed **k**;	**2Sa 3:39**	4428
at Hebron and said to the **k**,	**2Sa 4:8**	4428
has given my lord the **k** vengeance	**2Sa 4:8**	4428
when Saul was **k** over us,	**2Sa 5:2**	4428
of Israel came to the **k** at Hebron,	**2Sa 5:3**	4428
and **K** David made a covenant with	**2Sa 5:3**	4428
they anointed David **k** over Israel.	**2Sa 5:3**	4428
thirty years old when he became **k**,	**2Sa 5:4**	4427a
Now the **k** and his men went to	**2Sa 5:6**	4428
Then Hiram **k** of Tyre sent	**2Sa 5:11**	4428
established him as **k** over Israel,	**2Sa 5:12**	4428
had anointed David **k** over Israel,	**2Sa 5:17**	4428
Now it was told **K** David, saying,	**2Sa 6:12**	4428
saw **K** David leaping and dancing	**2Sa 6:16**	4428
"How the **k** of Israel distinguished	**2Sa 6:20**	4428
when the **k** lived in his house,	**2Sa 7:1**	4428
the **k** said to Nathan the prophet,	**2Sa 7:2**	4428
Nathan said to the **k**,	**2Sa 7:3**	4428
Then David the **k** went in and sat	**2Sa 7:18**	4428
the son of Rehob **k** of Zobah,	**2Sa 8:3**	4428
to help Hadadezer, **k** of Zobah,	**2Sa 8:5**	4428
K David took a very large amount	**2Sa 8:8**	4428
Now when Toi **k** of Hamath heard	**2Sa 8:9**	4428
Toi sent Joram his son to **K** David	**2Sa 8:10**	4428
K David also dedicated these to	**2Sa 8:11**	4428
son of Rehob, **k** of Zobah.	**2Sa 8:12**	4428
and the **k** said to him,	**2Sa 9:2**	4428
The **k** said, "Is there not yet anyone	**2Sa 9:3**	4428
And Ziba said to the **k**,	**2Sa 9:3**	4428
So the **k** said to him,	**2Sa 9:4**	4428
And Ziba said to the **k**,	**2Sa 9:4**	4428
Then **K** David sent and brought him	**2Sa 9:5**	4428
the **k** called Saul's servant Ziba and	**2Sa 9:9**	4428
Then Ziba said to the **k**,	**2Sa 9:11**	4428
to all that my lord the **k** commands	**2Sa 9:11**	4428
that the **k** of the Ammonites died,	**2Sa 10:1**	4428
his son became **k** in his place.	**2Sa 10:1**	4427a
k said, "Stay at Jericho until your	**2Sa 10:5**	4428
the **k** of Maacah with 1,000 men,	**2Sa 10:6**	4428
from the **k** was sent out after him.	**2Sa 11:8**	4428
the events of the war to the **k**,	**2Sa 11:19**	4428
'It is I who anointed you **k** over	**2Sa 12:7**	4428
crown of their **k** from his head;	**2Sa 12:30**	4428
"O son of the **k**, why are you so	**2Sa 13:4**	4428
when the **k** came to see him, Amnon	**2Sa 13:6**	4428
to see him, Amnon said to the **k**,	**2Sa 13:6**	4428
therefore, please speak to the **k**,	**2Sa 13:13**	4428
the virgin daughters of the **k** dressed	**2Sa 13:18**	4428
Now when **K** David heard of all	**2Sa 13:21**	4428
Absalom came to the **k** and said,	**2Sa 13:24**	4428
please let the **k** and his servants	**2Sa 13:24**	4428
But the **k** said to Absalom,	**2Sa 13:25**	4428
And the **k** said to him,	**2Sa 13:26**	4428
Then the **k** arose, tore his clothes	**2Sa 13:31**	4428
the **k** take the report to heart,	**2Sa 13:33**	4428
Jonadab said to the **k**,	**2Sa 13:35**	4428
also the **k** and all his servants wept	**2Sa 13:36**	4428
son of Ammihud, the **k** of Geshur.	**2Sa 13:37**	4428
The heart of **K** David longed to	**2Sa 13:39**	4428
then go to the **k** and speak to him	**2Sa 14:3**	4428
the woman of Tekoa spoke to the **k**,	**2Sa 14:4**	4428
herself and said, "Help, O **k**."	**2Sa 14:4**	4428
The **k** said to her,	**2Sa 14:5**	4428
Then the **k** said to the woman,	**2Sa 14:8**	4428
The woman of Tekoa said to the **k**,	**2Sa 14:9**	4428
"O my lord, the **k**, the iniquity	**2Sa 14:9**	4428
k and his throne are guiltless."	**2Sa 14:9**	4428
the **k** said, "Whoever speaks to you,	**2Sa 14:10**	4428
the **k** remember the LORD your God,	**2Sa 14:11**	4428
speak a word to my lord the **k**."	**2Sa 14:12**	4428
the **k** is as one who is guilty,	**2Sa 14:13**	4428
in that the **k** does not bring back	**2Sa 14:13**	4428
to speak this word to my lord the **k**	**2Sa 14:15**	4428
'Let me now speak to the **k**,	**2Sa 14:15**	4428
perhaps the **k** will perform the	**2Sa 14:15**	4428
'For the **k** will hear and deliver	**2Sa 14:16**	4428
word of my lord the **k** be comforting,	**2Sa 14:17**	4428
the **k** to discern good and evil.	**2Sa 14:17**	4428
Then the **k** answered and said to	**2Sa 14:18**	4428
"Let my lord the **k** please speak."	**2Sa 14:18**	4428
k said, "Is the hand of Joab with you	**2Sa 14:19**	4428
"As your soul lives, my lord the **k**,	**2Sa 14:19**	4428
that my lord the **k** has spoken.	**2Sa 14:19**	4428
Then the **k** said to Joab,	**2Sa 14:21**	4428
himself and blessed the **k**;	**2Sa 14:22**	4428
in your sight, O my lord, the **k**,	**2Sa 14:22**	4428
in that the **k** has performed the	**2Sa 14:22**	4428
However the **k** said,	**2Sa 14:24**	4428
for Joab, to send him to the **k**,	**2Sa 14:29**	4428
that I may send you to the **k**,	**2Sa 14:32**	4428
Joab came to the **k** and told him,	**2Sa 14:33**	4428
Thus he came to the **k** and	**2Sa 14:33**	4428
face to the ground before the **k**,	**2Sa 14:33**	4428
king, and the **k** kissed Absalom.	**2Sa 14:33**	4428
to come to the **k** for judgment,	**2Sa 15:2**	4428
to you on the part of the **k**."	**2Sa 15:3**	4428
who came to the **k** for judgment;	**2Sa 15:6**	4428
years that Absalom said to the **k**,	**2Sa 15:7**	4428
The **k** said to him,	**2Sa 15:9**	4428
'Absalom is **k** in Hebron.' "	**2Sa 15:10**	4427a
the king's servants said to the **k**,	**2Sa 15:15**	4428
whatever my lord the **k** chooses."	**2Sa 15:15**	4428
So the **k** went out and all his	**2Sa 15:16**	4428
But the **k** left ten concubines to	**2Sa 15:16**	4428
The **k** went out and all the	**2Sa 15:17**	4428
from Gath, passed on before the **k**.	**2Sa 15:18**	4428
the **k** said to Ittai the Gittite,	**2Sa 15:19**	4428
Return and remain with the **k**,	**2Sa 15:19**	4428
But Ittai answered the **k** and said,	**2Sa 15:21**	4428
lives, and as my lord the **k** lives,	**2Sa 15:21**	4428
wherever my lord the **k** may be,	**2Sa 15:21**	4428
The **k** also passed over the brook	**2Sa 15:23**	4428
The **k** said to Zadok,	**2Sa 15:25**	4428
k said also to Zadok the priest,	**2Sa 15:27**	4428
'I will be your servant, O **k**;	**2Sa 15:34**	4428
The **k** said to Ziba,	**2Sa 16:2**	4428
Then the **k** said,	**2Sa 16:3**	4428
And Ziba said to the **k**,	**2Sa 16:3**	4428
So the **k** said to Ziba,	**2Sa 16:4**	4428
in your sight, O my lord, the **k**!"	**2Sa 16:4**	4428
When **K** David came to Bahurim,	**2Sa 16:5**	4428
at all the servants of **K** David;	**2Sa 16:6**	4428
the son of Zeruiah said to the **k**,	**2Sa 16:9**	4428
this dead dog curse my lord the **k**?	**2Sa 16:9**	4428
k said, "What have I to do with you,	**2Sa 16:10**	4428
The **k** and all the people who	**2Sa 16:14**	4428
said to Absalom, "*Long* live the **k**!	**2Sa 16:16**	4428
Long live the **k**!"	**2Sa 16:16**	4428
I will strike down the **k** alone,	**2Sa 17:2**	4428
else the **k** and all the people who	**2Sa 17:16**	4428
they would go and tell **K** David,	**2Sa 17:17**	4428
well and went and told **K** David;	**2Sa 17:21**	4428
And then the **k** said to the people,	**2Sa 18:2**	4428
Then the **k** said to them,	**2Sa 18:4**	4428
So the **k** stood beside the gate,	**2Sa 18:4**	4428
The **k** charged Joab and Abishai	**2Sa 18:5**	4428
the **k** charged all the commanders	**2Sa 18:5**	4428
for in our hearing the **k** charged	**2Sa 18:12**	4428
is nothing hidden from the **k**),	**2Sa 18:13**	4428
let me run and bring the **k** news that	**2Sa 18:19**	4428
tell the **k** what you have seen."	**2Sa 18:21**	4428
watchman called and told the **k**.	**2Sa 18:25**	4428
And the **k** said, "If he is by himself	**2Sa 18:25**	4428
the **k** said, "This one also is bringing	**2Sa 18:26**	4428
And the **k** said, "This is a good man	**2Sa 18:27**	4428
Ahimaaz called and said to the **k**,	**2Sa 18:28**	4428
he prostrated himself before the **k**	**2Sa 18:28**	4428
hands against my lord the **k**."	**2Sa 18:28**	4428
The **k** said, "Is it well with the young	**2Sa 18:29**	4428
Then the **k** said,	**2Sa 18:30**	4428
my lord the **k** receive good news,	**2Sa 18:31**	4428
Then the **k** said to the Cushite,	**2Sa 18:32**	4428
"Let the enemies of my lord the **k**,	**2Sa 18:32**	4428
The **k** was deeply moved and	**2Sa 18:33**	4428
the **k** is weeping and mourns for	**2Sa 19:1**	4428
"The **k** is grieved for his son."	**2Sa 19:2**	4428
The **k** covered his face and	**2Sa 19:4**	4428
Joab came into the house to the **k**	**2Sa 19:5**	4428
the **k** arose and sat in the gate.	**2Sa 19:8**	4428
the **k** is sitting in the gate,"	**2Sa 19:8**	4428
all the people came before the **k**.	**2Sa 19:8**	4428
"The **k** delivered us from the hand	**2Sa 19:9**	4428
about bringing the **k** back?"	**2Sa 19:10**	4428
Then **K** David sent to Zadok and	**2Sa 19:11**	4428
to bring the **k** back to his house,	**2Sa 19:11**	4428
of all Israel has come to the **k**,	**2Sa 19:11**	4428
be the last to bring back the **k**?'	**2Sa 19:12**	4428
so that they sent *word* to the **k**,	**2Sa 19:14**	4428
The **k** then returned and came as	**2Sa 19:15**	4428
in order to go to meet the **k**,	**2Sa 19:15**	4428
to bring the **k** across the Jordan.	**2Sa 19:15**	4428
the men of Judah to meet **K** David.	**2Sa 19:16**	4428
rushed to the Jordan before the **k**.	**2Sa 19:17**	4428
son of Gera fell down before the **k**	**2Sa 19:18**	4428
So he said to the **k**,	**2Sa 19:19**	4428
the **k** came out from Jerusalem,	**2Sa 19:19**	4428
the **k** would take *it* to heart.	**2Sa 19:19**	4428
go down to meet my lord the **k**."	**2Sa 19:20**	4428
that I am **k** over Israel today?"	**2Sa 19:22**	4428
The **k** said to Shimei,	**2Sa 19:23**	4428
Thus the **k** swore to him.	**2Sa 19:23**	4428
of Saul came down to meet the **k**;	**2Sa 19:24**	4428
from the day the **k** departed until	**2Sa 19:24**	4428
came from Jerusalem to meet the **k**,	**2Sa 19:25**	4428
the king, that the **k** said to him,	**2Sa 19:25**	4428
"O my lord, the **k**, my servant	**2Sa 19:26**	4428
may ride on it and go with the **k**,'	**2Sa 19:26**	4428
your servant to my lord the **k**;	**2Sa 19:27**	4428
the **k** is like the angel of God,	**2Sa 19:27**	4428
but dead men before my lord the **k**;	**2Sa 19:28**	4428
complain anymore to the **k**?"	**2Sa 19:28**	4428
So the **k** said to him,	**2Sa 19:29**	4428
Mephibosheth said to the **k**,	**2Sa 19:30**	4428
since my lord the **k** has come	**2Sa 19:30**	4428
he went on to the Jordan with the **k**	**2Sa 19:31**	4428
and he had sustained the **k** while he	**2Sa 19:32**	4428
The **k** said to Barzillai,	**2Sa 19:33**	4428
But Barzillai said to the **k**,	**2Sa 19:34**	4428
go up with the **k** to Jerusalem?	**2Sa 19:34**	4428
an added burden to my lord the **k**?	**2Sa 19:35**	4428
cross over the Jordan with the **k**.	**2Sa 19:36**	4428
Why should the **k** compensate me	**2Sa 19:36**	4428
him cross over with my lord the **k**,	**2Sa 19:37**	4428
The **k** answered,	**2Sa 19:38**	4428
the Jordan and the **k** crossed too.	**2Sa 19:39**	4428
The **k** then kissed Barzillai and	**2Sa 19:39**	4428
Now the **k** went on to Gilgal, and	**2Sa 19:40**	4428
people of Israel accompanied the **k**.	**2Sa 19:40**	4428
all the men of Israel came to the **k**	**2Sa 19:41**	4428
to the king and said to the **k**,	**2Sa 19:41**	4428
and brought the **k** and his	**2Sa 19:41**	4428
the **k** is a close relative to us.	**2Sa 19:42**	4428
"We have ten parts in the **k**,	**2Sa 19:43**	4428
first to bring back our **k**?"	**2Sa 19:43**	4428
remained steadfast to their **k**,	**2Sa 20:2**	4428
and the **k** took the ten women,	**2Sa 20:3**	4428
Then the **k** said to Amasa,	**2Sa 20:4**	4428
up his hand against **K** David.	**2Sa 20:21**	4428
returned to the **k** at Jerusalem.	**2Sa 20:22**	4428
So the **k** called the Gibeonites and	**2Sa 21:2**	4428
So they said to the **k**,	**2Sa 21:5**	4428
And the **k** said, "I will give *them*.	**2Sa 21:6**	4428
But the **k** spared Mephibosheth, the	**2Sa 21:7**	4428
So the **k** took the two sons of	**2Sa 21:8**	4428
they did all that the **k** commanded,	**2Sa 21:14**	4428
a tower of deliverance to His **k**,	**2Sa 22:51**	4428
The **k** said to Joab the	**2Sa 24:2**	4428
But Joab said to the **k**,	**2Sa 24:3**	4428
eyes of my lord the **k** *still* see;	**2Sa 24:3**	4428
the **k** delight in this thing?"	**2Sa 24:3**	4428
out from the presence of the **k** to	**2Sa 24:4**	4428
registration of the people to the **k**;	**2Sa 24:9**	4428
Araunah looked down and saw the **k**	**2Sa 24:20**	4428
face to the ground before the **k**.	**2Sa 24:20**	4428
lord the **k** come to his servant?"	**2Sa 24:21**	4428
"Let my lord the **k** take and offer	**2Sa 24:22**	4428
"Everything, O **k**, Araunah gives	**2Sa 24:23**	4428
O king, Araunah gives to the **k**."	**2Sa 24:23**	4428
And Araunah said to the **k**,	**2Sa 24:23**	4428
However, the **k** said to Araunah,	**2Sa 24:24**	4428
Now **K** David was old, advanced in	**1Ki 1:1**	4428
a young virgin for my lord the **k**,	**1Ki 1:2**	4428
attend the **k** and become his nurse;	**1Ki 1:2**	4428
my lord the **k** may keep warm."	**1Ki 1:2**	4428
and brought her to the **k**.	**1Ki 1:3**	4428
the **k** did not cohabit with her.	**1Ki 1:4**	4428
exalted himself, saying, "I will be **k**.	**1Ki 1:5**	4427a
the son of Haggith has become **k**,	**1Ki 1:11**	4427a
"Go at once to **K** David and say to	**1Ki 1:13**	4428
'Have you not, my lord, O **k**,	**1Ki 1:13**	4428
your son shall be **k** after me,	**1Ki 1:13**	4427a
Why then has Adonijah become **k**?'	**1Ki 1:13**	4427a
still there speaking with the **k**,	**1Ki 1:14**	4428
went in to the **k** in the bedroom.	**1Ki 1:15**	4428
Now the **k** was very old, and	**1Ki 1:15**	4428
was ministering to the **k**.	**1Ki 1:15**	4428
prostrated herself before the **k**.	**1Ki 1:16**	4428
And the **k** said, "What do you wish?	**1Ki 1:16**	4428
Solomon shall be **k** after me	**1Ki 1:17**	4427a
"Now, behold, Adonijah is **k**;	**1Ki 1:18**	4427a
and now, my lord the **k**,	**1Ki 1:18**	4428
sons of the **k** and Abiathar the priest	**1Ki 1:19**	4428
"As for you now, my lord the **k**,	**1Ki 1:20**	4428
throne of my lord the **k** after him.	**1Ki 1:20**	4428
the **k** sleeps with his fathers,	**1Ki 1:21**	4428
she was still speaking with the **k**,	**1Ki 1:22**	4428
They told the **k**,	**1Ki 1:23**	4428
And when he came in before the **k**,	**1Ki 1:23**	4428
the **k** with his face to the ground.	**1Ki 1:23**	4428
"My lord the **k**, have you said,	**1Ki 1:24**	4428
'Adonijah shall be **k** after me,	**1Ki 1:24**	4427a
'*Long* live **K** Adonijah!'	**1Ki 1:25**	4428
thing been done by my lord the **k**,	**1Ki 1:27**	4428
throne of my lord the **k** after him?"	**1Ki 1:27**	4428
Then **K** David said,	**1Ki 1:28**	4428
presence and stood before the **k**.	**1Ki 1:28**	4428
The **k** vowed and said,	**1Ki 1:29**	4428
son Solomon shall be **k** after me,	**1Ki 1:30**	4427a
herself before the **k** and said,	**1Ki 1:31**	4428
my lord **K** David live forever."	**1Ki 1:31**	4428
Then **K** David said,	**1Ki 1:32**	4428
The **k** said to them,	**1Ki 1:33**	4428
anoint him there as **k** over Israel,	**1Ki 1:34**	4428
'*Long* live **K** Solomon!'	**1Ki 1:34**	4428
on my throne and be **k** in my place;	**1Ki 1:35**	4427a
Jehoiada answered the **k** and said,	**1Ki 1:36**	4428
LORD, the God of my lord the **k**,	**1Ki 1:36**	4428
LORD has been with my lord the **k**,	**1Ki 1:37**	4428
the throne of my lord **K** David!"	**1Ki 1:37**	4428
had Solomon ride on **K** David's mule,	**1Ki 1:38**	4428
"*Long* live **K** Solomon!"	**1Ki 1:39**	4428
K David has made Solomon king.	**1Ki 1:43**	4428
King David has made Solomon **k**.	**1Ki 1:43**	4428
"The **k** has also sent with him	**1Ki 1:44**	4428
have anointed him **k** in Gihon,	**1Ki 1:45**	4428
came to bless our lord **K** David,	**1Ki 1:47**	4428
the **k** bowed himself on the bed.	**1Ki 1:47**	4428
"The **k** has also said thus,	**1Ki 1:48**	4428
Adonijah is afraid of **K** Solomon,	**1Ki 1:51**	4428
'Let **K** Solomon swear to me today	**1Ki 1:51**	4428
So **K** Solomon sent, and they	**1Ki 1:53**	4428
himself before **K** Solomon,	**1Ki 1:53**	4428
all Israel expected me to be **k**;	**1Ki 2:15**	4427a
"Please speak to Solomon the **k**,	**1Ki 2:17**	4428
I will speak to the **k** for you."	**1Ki 2:18**	4428
So Bathsheba went to **K** Solomon to	**1Ki 2:19**	4428
And the **k** arose to meet her, bowed	**1Ki 2:19**	4428
And the **k** said to her,	**1Ki 2:20**	4428

K Solomon answered and said to	1Ki 2:22	4428
Then **K** Solomon swore by the LORD,	1Ki 2:23	4428
So **K** Solomon sent Benaiah the son	1Ki 2:25	4428
to Abiathar the priest the **k** said,	1Ki 2:26	4428
It was told **K** Solomon that	1Ki 2:29	4428
"Thus the **k** has said,	1Ki 2:30	4428
Benaiah brought the **k** word again,	1Ki 2:30	4428
The **k** said to him,	1Ki 2:31	4428
The **k** appointed Benaiah the	1Ki 2:35	4428
and the **k** appointed Zadok the	1Ki 2:35	4428
Now the **k** sent and called for	1Ki 2:36	4428
Shimei then said to the **k**,	1Ki 2:38	4428
As my lord the **k** has said, so your	1Ki 2:38	4428
Achish son of Maacah, **k** of Gath.	1Ki 2:39	4428
So the **k** sent and called for	1Ki 2:42	4428
The **k** also said to Shimei,	1Ki 2:44	4428
"But **K** Solomon shall be blessed,	1Ki 2:45	4428
So the **k** commanded Benaiah the son	1Ki 2:46	4428
alliance with Pharaoh **k** of Egypt,	1Ki 3:1	4428
The **k** went to Gibeon to	1Ki 3:4	4428
k in place of my father David,	1Ki 3:7	4427a
who were harlots came to the **k**	1Ki 3:16	4428
Thus they spoke before the **k**.	1Ki 3:22	4428
Then the **k** said,	1Ki 3:23	4428
The **k** said, "Get me a sword."	1Ki 3:24	4428
they brought a sword before the **k**.	1Ki 3:24	4428
The **k** said, "Divide the living child	1Ki 3:25	4428
was the living one spoke to the **k**,	1Ki 3:26	4428
Then the **k** said,	1Ki 3:27	4428
which the **k** had handed down,	1Ki 3:28	4428
handed down, they feared the **k**,	1Ki 3:28	4428
Now **K** Solomon was king over all	1Ki 4:1	4428
Solomon was **k** over all Israel.	1Ki 4:1	4428
for the **k** and his household;	1Ki 4:7	4428
country of Sihon **k** of the Amorites	1Ki 4:19	4428
Amorites and of Og **k** of Bashan;	1Ki 4:19	4428
deputies provided for **K** Solomon	1Ki 4:27	4428
all who came to **K** Solomon's table,	1Ki 4:27	4428
Now Hiram **k** of Tyre sent his	1Ki 5:1	4428
him **k** in place of his father,	1Ki 5:1	4428
Now **K** Solomon levied forced	1Ki 5:13	4428
Then the **k** commanded, and they	1Ki 5:17	4428
K Solomon built for the LORD,	1Ki 6:2	4428
Now **K** Solomon sent and brought	1Ki 7:13	4428
So he came to **K** Solomon and	1Ki 7:14	4428
which he performed for **K** Solomon	1Ki 7:40	4428
which Hiram made for **K** Solomon	1Ki 7:45	4428
of the Jordan the **k** cast them,	1Ki 7:46	4428
Thus all the work that **K** Solomon	1Ki 7:51	4428
Israel, to **K** Solomon in Jerusalem,	1Ki 8:1	4428
to **K** Solomon at the feast,	1Ki 8:2	4428
And **K** Solomon and all the	1Ki 8:5	4428
Then the **k** faced about and blessed	1Ki 8:14	4428
Now the **k** and all Israel with him	1Ki 8:62	4428
So the **k** and all the sons of	1Ki 8:63	4428
On the same day the **k** consecrated	1Ki 8:64	4428
away and they blessed the **k**.	1Ki 8:66	4428
(Hiram **k** of Tyre had supplied	1Ki 9:11	4428
then **K** Solomon gave Hiram twenty	1Ki 9:11	4428
sent to the **k** 120 talents of gold.	1Ki 9:14	4428
forced labor which **K** Solomon levied	1Ki 9:15	4428
For Pharaoh **k** of Egypt had gone up	1Ki 9:16	4428
K Solomon also built a fleet of	1Ki 9:26	4428
and brought *it* to **K** Solomon.	1Ki 9:28	4428
nothing was hidden from the **k**	1Ki 10:3	4428
Then she said to the **k**,	1Ki 10:6	4428
forever, therefore He made you **k**,	1Ki 10:9	4428
She gave the **k** a hundred and	1Ki 10:10	4428
the queen of Sheba gave **K** Solomon.	1Ki 10:10	4428
The **k** made of the almug trees	1Ki 10:12	4428
K Solomon gave to the queen of	1Ki 10:13	4428
K Solomon made 200 large	1Ki 10:16	4428
and the **k** put them in the house of	1Ki 10:17	4428
the **k** made a great throne of ivory	1Ki 10:18	4428
All **K** Solomon's drinking vessels	1Ki 10:21	4428
For the **k** had at sea the ships of	1Ki 10:22	4428
So **K** Solomon became greater than	1Ki 10:23	4428
and with the **k** in Jerusalem.	1Ki 10:26	4428
The **k** made silver *as common* as	1Ki 10:27	4428
Now **K** Solomon loved many foreign	1Ki 11:1	4428
to Egypt, to Pharaoh **k** of Egypt,	1Ki 11:18	4428
his lord Hadadezer **k** of Zobah.	1Ki 11:23	4428
also rebelled against the **k**.	1Ki 11:26	4428
why he rebelled against the **k**:	1Ki 11:27	4428
and you shall be **k** over Israel.	1Ki 11:37	4428
to Egypt to Shishak **k** of Egypt,	1Ki 11:40	4428
had come to Shechem to make him **k**.	1Ki 12:1	4427a
from the presence of **K** Solomon).	1Ki 12:2	4428
K Rehoboam consulted with the	1Ki 12:6	4428
third day as the **k** had directed,	1Ki 12:12	4428
The **k** answered the people harshly,	1Ki 12:13	4428
k did not listen to the people;	1Ki 12:15	4428
that the **k** did not listen to them,	1Ki 12:16	4428
them, the people answered the **k**,	1Ki 12:16	4428
Then **K** Rehoboam sent Adoram, who	1Ki 12:18	4428
And **K** Rehoboam made haste to mount	1Ki 12:18	4428
and made him **k** over all Israel.	1Ki 12:20	4427a
the son of Solomon, **k** of Judah,	1Ki 12:23	4428
lord, *even* to Rehoboam **k** of Judah;	1Ki 12:27	4428
return to Rehoboam **k** of Judah."	1Ki 12:27	4428
So the **k** consulted, and made two	1Ki 12:28	4428
Now when the **k** heard	1Ki 13:4	4428
The **k** said to the	1Ki 13:6	4428
Then the **k** said to the man of God,	1Ki 13:7	4428
But the man of God said to the **k**,	1Ki 13:8	4428
which he had spoken to the **k**,	1Ki 13:11	4428
I would be **k** over this people.	1Ki 14:2	4428
raise up for Himself a **k** over Israel	1Ki 14:14	4428
years old when he became **k**,	1Ki 14:21	4427a
in the fifth year of **K** Rehoboam,	1Ki 14:25	4428
that Shishak the **k** of Egypt came	1Ki 14:25	4428
So **K** Rehoboam made shields of	1Ki 14:27	4428
k entered the house of the LORD,	1Ki 14:28	4428
his son became **k** in his place.	1Ki 14:31	4427a
the eighteenth year of **K** Jeroboam,	1Ki 15:1	4428
Nebat, Abijam became **k** over Judah.	1Ki 15:1	4427a
Asa his son became **k** in his place.	1Ki 15:8	4427a
year of Jeroboam the **k** of Israel,	1Ki 15:9	4428
Asa began to reign as **k** of Judah.	1Ki 15:9	4428
Baasha **k** of Israel all their days.	1Ki 15:16	4428
Baasha **k** of Israel went up	1Ki 15:17	4428
or coming in to Asa **k** of Judah.	1Ki 15:17	4428
And **K** Asa sent them to Ben-hadad	1Ki 15:18	4428
the son of Hezion, **k** of Aram,	1Ki 15:18	4428
break your treaty with Baasha **k** of	1Ki 15:19	4428
So Ben-hadad listened to **K** Asa and	1Ki 15:20	4428
Then **K** Asa made a proclamation to	1Ki 15:22	4428
And **K** Asa built with them Geba of	1Ki 15:22	4428
the son of Jeroboam became **k**	1Ki 15:25	4427a
the second year of Asa **k** of Judah,	1Ki 15:25	4428
the third year of Asa **k** of Judah and	1Ki 15:28	4428
came about as soon as he was **k**,	1Ki 15:29	4427a
Baasha **k** of Israel all their days.	1Ki 15:32	4428
the third year of Asa **k** of Judah,	1Ki 15:33	4428
Baasha the son of Ahijah became **k**	1Ki 15:33	4427a
his son became **k** in his place.	1Ki 16:6	4427a
year of Asa **k** of Judah,	1Ki 16:8	4428
Elah the son of Baasha became **k**	1Ki 16:8	4427a
year of Asa **k** of Judah,	1Ki 16:10	4428
Judah, and became **k** in his place.	1Ki 16:10	4427a
It came about when he became **k**,	1Ki 16:11	4427a
year of Asa **k** of Judah,	1Ki 16:15	4428
and has also struck down the **k**."	1Ki 16:16	4428
k over Israel that day in the camp.	1Ki 16:16	4427a
the son of Ginath, to make him **k**;	1Ki 16:21	4427a
And Tibni died and Omri became **k**.	1Ki 16:22	4427a
year of Asa **k** of Judah,	1Ki 16:23	4428
Judah, Omri became **k** over Israel	1Ki 16:23	4427a
his son became **k** in his place.	1Ki 16:28	4427a
Now Ahab the son of Omri became **k**	1Ki 16:29	4427a
year of Asa **k** of Judah,	1Ki 16:29	4428
of Ethbaal **k** of the Sidonians,	1Ki 16:31	4428
shall anoint Hazael **k** over Aram;	1Ki 19:15	4428
you shall anoint **k** over Israel;	1Ki 19:16	4428
k of Aram gathered all his army,	1Ki 20:1	4428
to the city to Ahab **k** of Israel and	1Ki 20:2	4428
The **k** of Israel replied,	1Ki 20:4	4428
to your word, my lord, O **k**;	1Ki 20:4	4428
Then the **k** of Israel called all	1Ki 20:7	4428
"Tell my lord the **k**,	1Ki 20:9	4428
the **k** of Israel replied,	1Ki 20:11	4428
Ahab **k** of Israel and said,	1Ki 20:13	4428
and Ben-hadad **k** of Aram escaped on	1Ki 20:20	4428
The **k** of Israel went out and	1Ki 20:21	4428
came near to the **k** of Israel and	1Ki 20:22	4428
the year the **k** of Aram	1Ki 20:22	4428
of the **k** of Aram said to him,	1Ki 20:23	4428
spoke to the **k** of Israel and said,	1Ki 20:28	4428
and go out to the **k** of Israel;	1Ki 20:31	4428
came to the **k** of Israel and said,	1Ki 20:32	4428
and waited for the **k** by the way,	1Ki 20:38	4428
As the **k** passed by, he cried	1Ki 20:39	4428
by, he cried to the **k** and said,	1Ki 20:39	4428
And the **k** of Israel said to him,	1Ki 20:40	4428
and the **k** of Israel recognized him	1Ki 20:41	4428
So the **k** of Israel went to his	1Ki 20:43	4428
the palace of Ahab **k** of Samaria.	1Ki 21:1	4428
'You cursed God and the **k**.'	1Ki 21:10	4428
"Naboth cursed God and the **k**."	1Ki 21:13	4428
go down to meet Ahab **k** of Israel,	1Ki 21:18	4428
year Jehoshaphat the **k** of Judah	1Ki 22:2	4428
came down to the **k** of Israel.	1Ki 22:2	4428
Now the **k** of Israel said to his	1Ki 22:3	4428
of the hand of the **k** of Aram?"	1Ki 22:3	4428
said to the **k** of Israel,	1Ki 22:4	4428
said to the **k** of Israel,	1Ki 22:5	4428
Then the **k** of Israel gathered the	1Ki 22:6	4428
give *it* into the hand of the **k**."	1Ki 22:6	4428
k of Israel said to Jehoshaphat,	1Ki 22:8	4428
"Let not the **k** say so."	1Ki 22:8	4428
Then the **k** of Israel called an	1Ki 22:9	4428
Now the **k** of Israel and	1Ki 22:10	4428
Israel and Jehoshaphat **k** of Judah	1Ki 22:10	4428
give *it* into the hand of the **k**."	1Ki 22:12	4428
are uniformly favorable to the **k**.	1Ki 22:13	4428
When he came to the **k**,	1Ki 22:15	4428
to the king, the **k** said to him,	1Ki 22:15	4428
give *it* into the hand of the **k**."	1Ki 22:15	4428
Then the **k** said to him,	1Ki 22:16	4428
k of Israel said to Jehoshaphat,	1Ki 22:18	4428
Then the **k** of Israel said,	1Ki 22:26	4428
'Thus says the **k**,	1Ki 22:27	4428
So the **k** of Israel and Jehoshaphat	1Ki 22:29	4428
Jehoshaphat **k** of Judah went up	1Ki 22:29	4428
k of Israel said to Jehoshaphat,	1Ki 22:30	4428
So the **k** of Israel disguised	1Ki 22:30	4428
Now the **k** of Aram had commanded	1Ki 22:31	4428
but with the **k** of Israel alone."	1Ki 22:31	4428
"Surely it is the **k** of Israel,"	1Ki 22:32	4428
that it was not the **k** of Israel,	1Ki 22:33	4428
struck the **k** of Israel in a joint of	1Ki 22:34	4428
and the **k** was propped up in his	1Ki 22:35	4428
So the **k** died and was brought to	1Ki 22:37	4428
and they buried the **k** in Samaria.	1Ki 22:37	4428
his son became **k** in his place.	1Ki 22:40	4427a
the son of Asa became **k** over Judah	1Ki 22:41	4427a
fourth year of Ahab **k** of Israel.	1Ki 22:41	4428
years old when he became **k**,	1Ki 22:42	4427a
made peace with the **k** of Israel.	1Ki 22:44	4428
Now there was no **k** in Edom;	1Ki 22:47	4428
no king in Edom; a deputy was **k**.	1Ki 22:47	4428
his son became **k** in his place.	1Ki 22:50	4427a
Ahaziah the son of Ahab became **k**	1Ki 22:51	4427a
year of Jehoshaphat **k** of Judah,	1Ki 22:51	4428
the **k** of Samaria and say to them,	2Ki 1:3	4428
'Go, return to the **k** who sent you	2Ki 1:6	4428
Then *the* **k** sent to him a captain	2Ki 1:9	
"O man of God, the **k** says,	2Ki 1:9	4428
"O man of God, thus says the **k**,	2Ki 1:11	4428
and went down with him to the **k**.	2Ki 1:15	4428
Jehoram became **k** in his place in	2Ki 1:17	4427a
son of Jehoshaphat, **k** of Judah.	2Ki 1:17	4428
Jehoram the son of Ahab became **k**	2Ki 3:1	4427a
year of Jehoshaphat **k** of Judah,	2Ki 3:1	4428
k of Moab was a sheep breeder,	2Ki 3:4	4428
and used to pay the **k** of Israel	2Ki 3:4	4428
the **k** of Moab rebelled against the	2Ki 3:5	4428
rebelled against the **k** of Israel.	2Ki 3:5	4428
And **K** Jehoram went out of Samaria	2Ki 3:6	4428
to Jehoshaphat the **k** of Judah,	2Ki 3:7	4428
"The **k** of Moab has rebelled	2Ki 3:7	4428
So the **k** of Israel went with the	2Ki 3:9	4428
k of Judah and the king of Edom;	2Ki 3:9	4428
king of Judah and the **k** of Edom;	2Ki 3:9	4428
Then the **k** of Israel said,	2Ki 3:10	4428
And one of the **k** of Israel's servants	2Ki 3:11	4428
So the **k** of Israel and Jehoshaphat	2Ki 3:12	4428
the **k** of Edom went down to him.	2Ki 3:12	4428
Elisha said to the **k** of Israel,	2Ki 3:13	4428
And the **k** of Israel said to him,	2Ki 3:13	4428
of Jehoshaphat the **k** of Judah,	2Ki 3:14	4428
When the **k** of Moab saw that the	2Ki 3:26	4428
to break through to the **k** of Edom;	2Ki 3:26	4428
Would you be spoken for to the **k**	2Ki 4:13	4428
of the army of the **k** of Aram,	2Ki 5:1	4428
Then the **k** of Aram said,	2Ki 5:5	4428
a letter to the **k** of Israel."	2Ki 5:5	4428
the letter to the **k** of Israel,	2Ki 5:6	4428
the **k** of Israel read the letter,	2Ki 5:7	4428
heard that the **k** of Israel had torn	2Ki 5:8	4428
that he sent *word* to the **k**,	2Ki 5:8	4428
Now the **k** of Aram was warring	2Ki 6:8	4428
word to the **k** of Israel saying,	2Ki 6:9	4428
The **k** of Israel sent to the	2Ki 6:10	4428
Now the heart of the **k** of Aram was	2Ki 6:11	4428
which of us is for the **k** of Israel?"	2Ki 6:11	4428
"No, my lord, O **k**;	2Ki 6:12	4428
tells the **k** of Israel the words	2Ki 6:12	4428
the **k** of Israel when he saw them,	2Ki 6:21	4428
that Ben-hadad **k** of Aram gathered	2Ki 6:24	4428
As the **k** of Israel was passing	2Ki 6:26	4428
"Help, my lord, O **k**!"	2Ki 6:26	4428
And the **k** said to her,	2Ki 6:28	4428
k heard the words of the woman,	2Ki 6:30	4428
And *the* **k** sent a man from his	2Ki 6:32	
on whose hand the **k** was leaning	2Ki 7:2	4428
the **k** of Israel has hired against	2Ki 7:6	4428
Then the **k** arose in the night and	2Ki 7:12	4428
and the **k** sent after the army of	2Ki 7:14	4428
returned and told the **k**.	2Ki 7:15	4428
Now the **k** appointed the royal	2Ki 7:17	4428
spoke when the **k** came down to him.	2Ki 7:17	4428
man of God had spoken to the **k**,	2Ki 7:18	4428
and she went out to appeal to the **k**	2Ki 8:3	4428
Now the **k** was talking with Gehazi,	2Ki 8:4	4428
As he was relating to the **k** how he	2Ki 8:5	4428
appealed to the **k** for her house	2Ki 8:5	4428
"My lord, O **k**, this is the woman	2Ki 8:5	4428
When the **k** asked the woman, she	2Ki 8:6	4428
So the **k** appointed for her a	2Ki 8:6	4428
Now Ben-hadad **k** of Aram was sick,	2Ki 8:7	4428
The **k** said to Hazael,	2Ki 8:8	4428
k of Aram has sent me to you,	2Ki 8:9	4428
me that you will be **k** over Aram."	2Ki 8:13	4428
And Hazael became **k** in his place.	2Ki 8:15	4427a
Joram the son of Ahab **k** of Israel,	2Ki 8:16	4428
being then the **k** of Judah,	2Ki 8:16	4428
k of Judah became king.	2Ki 8:16	4428
king of Judah became **k**.	2Ki 8:16	4427a
years old when he became **k**,	2Ki 8:17	4427a
and made a **k** over themselves.	2Ki 8:20	4427a
his son became **k** in his place.	2Ki 8:24	4427a
Joram the son of Ahab **k** of Israel,	2Ki 8:25	4428
Jehoram **k** of Judah began to reign.	2Ki 8:25	4428
years old when he became **k**,	2Ki 8:26	4427a
granddaughter of Omri **k** of Israel.	2Ki 8:26	4428
Hazael **k** of Aram at Ramoth-gilead,	2Ki 8:28	4428
So **K** Joram returned to be healed	2Ki 8:29	4428
fought against Hazael **k** of Aram.	2Ki 8:29	4428
the son of Jehoram **k** of Judah went	2Ki 8:29	4428
anointed you **k** over Israel."	2Ki 9:3	4428
you **k** over the people of the LORD,	2Ki 9:6	4428
"I have anointed you **k** over Israel."	2Ki 9:12	4428
blew the trumpet, saying, "Jehu is **k**!	2Ki 9:13	4427a
against Hazael **k** of Aram,	2Ki 9:14	4428
but **K** Joram had returned to	2Ki 9:15	4428
he fought with Hazael **k** of Aram.	2Ki 9:15	4428
Ahaziah **k** of Judah had come	2Ki 9:16	4428
"Thus says the **k**,	2Ki 9:18	4428
"Thus says the **k**,	2Ki 9:19	4428
Joram **k** of Israel and Ahaziah	2Ki 9:21	4428
and Ahaziah **k** of Judah went out,	2Ki 9:21	4428
Ahaziah the **k** of Judah saw *this*,	2Ki 9:27	4428
Ahab, Ahaziah became **k** over Judah.	2Ki 9:29	4427a
do, we will not make any man **k**;	2Ki 10:5	4427a
of Ahaziah **k** of Judah and said,	2Ki 10:13	4428
come down to greet the sons of the **k**	2Ki 10:13	4428

his son became **k** in his place. **2Ki 10:35** 4427a
the daughter of **K** Joram, **2Ki 11:2** 4428
the house of the LORD for the **k**. **2Ki 11:7** 4428
"Then you shall surround the **k**, **2Ki 11:8** 4428
And be with the **k** when he goes out **2Ki 11:8** 4428
shields that *had been* **K** David's, **2Ki 11:10** 4428
and by the house, around the **k**. **2Ki 11:11** 4428
they made him **k** and anointed him, **2Ki 11:12** 4427a
"*Long* live the **k**!" **2Ki 11:12** 4428
the **k** was standing by the pillar, **2Ki 11:14** 4428
and the trumpeters beside the **k**; **2Ki 11:14** 4428
the LORD and the **k** and the people, **2Ki 11:17** 4428
also between the **k** and the people. **2Ki 11:17** 4428
and they brought the **k** down from **2Ki 11:19** 4428
seven years old when he became **k**. **2Ki 11:21** 4427a
year of Jehu, Jehoash became **k**, **2Ki 12:1** 4427a
in the twenty-third year of **K** Jehoash **2Ki 12:6** 4428
Then **K** Jehoash called for Jehoiada **2Ki 12:7** 4428
Then Hazael **k** of Aram went up and **2Ki 12:17** 4428
Jehoash **k** of Judah took all **2Ki 12:18** 4428
and sent *them* to Hazael **k** of Aram. **2Ki 12:18** 4428
his son became **k** in his place. **2Ki 12:21** 4427a
the son of Ahaziah, **k** of Judah, **2Ki 13:1** 4428
became **k** over Israel at Samaria, **2Ki 13:1** 4427a
into the hand of Hazael **k** of Aram, **2Ki 13:3** 4428
how the **k** of Aram oppressed them. **2Ki 13:4** 4428
for the **k** of Aram had destroyed **2Ki 13:7** 4428
his son became **k** in his place. **2Ki 13:9** 4427a
year of Joash **k** of Judah, **2Ki 13:10** 4428
became **k** over Israel in Samaria, **2Ki 13:10** 4427a
fought against Amaziah **k** of Judah, **2Ki 13:12** 4428
Joash the **k** of Israel came down to **2Ki 13:14** 4428
Then he said to the **k** of Israel, **2Ki 13:16** 4428
And he said to the **k** of Israel, **2Ki 13:18** 4428
Now Hazael **k** of Aram had oppressed **2Ki 13:22** 4428
When Hazael **k** of Aram died, **2Ki 13:24** 4428
his son became **k** in his place. **2Ki 13:24** 4427a
Joash son of Joahaz **k** of Israel, **2Ki 14:1** 4428
the son of Joash **k** of Judah became **2Ki 14:1** 4428
of Joash king of Judah became **k**. **2Ki 14:1** 4427a
years old when he became **k**, **2Ki 14:2** 4427a
who had slain the **k** his father. **2Ki 14:5** 4428
Jehoahaz son of Jehu, **k** of Israel, **2Ki 14:8** 4428
Jehoash **k** of Israel sent to **2Ki 14:9** 4428
Israel sent to Amaziah **k** of Judah, **2Ki 14:9** 4428
So Jehoash **k** of Israel went up; **2Ki 14:11** 4428
and he and Amaziah **k** of Judah **2Ki 14:11** 4428
Then Jehoash **k** of Israel captured **2Ki 14:13** 4428
captured Amaziah **k** of Judah, **2Ki 14:13** 4428
he fought with Amaziah **k** of Judah, **2Ki 14:15** 4428
his son became **k** in his place. **2Ki 14:16** 4427a
the son of Joash **k** of Judah lived **2Ki 14:17** 4428
Jehoash son of Jehoahaz **k** of Israel. **2Ki 14:17** 4428
and made him **k** in the place of his **2Ki 14:21** 4427a
the **k** slept with his fathers. **2Ki 14:22** 4428
the son of Joash **k** of Judah, **2Ki 14:23** 4428
Jeroboam the son of Joash **k** of **2Ki 14:23** 4428
of Israel became **k** in Samaria, **2Ki 14:23** 4427a
his son became **k** in his place. **2Ki 14:29** 4427a
year of Jeroboam **k** of Israel, **2Ki 15:1** 4428
of Amaziah **k** of Judah became king. **2Ki 15:1** 4428
of Amaziah king of Judah became **k**. **2Ki 15:1** 4427a
years old when he became **k**, **2Ki 15:2** 4427a
The LORD struck the **k**, **2Ki 15:5** 4428
his son became **k** in his place. **2Ki 15:7** 4427a
year of Azariah **k** of Judah, **2Ki 15:8** 4428
the son of Jeroboam became **k** **2Ki 15:8** 4427a
Shallum son of Jabesh became **k** in **2Ki 15:13** 4427a
year of Uzziah **k** of Judah, **2Ki 15:13** 4428
him and became **k** in his place. **2Ki 15:14** 4427a
year of Azariah **k** of Judah, **2Ki 15:17** 4428
Menahem son of Gadi became **k** over **2Ki 15:17** 4427a
Pul, **k** of Assyria, came against **2Ki 15:19** 4428
of silver to pay the **k** of Assyria. **2Ki 15:20** 4428
So the **k** of Assyria returned and **2Ki 15:20** 4428
his son became **k** in his place. **2Ki 15:22** 4427a
year of Azariah **k** of Judah, **2Ki 15:23** 4428
became **k** over Israel in Samaria, **2Ki 15:23** 4427a
him and became **k** in his place. **2Ki 15:25** 4427a
year of Azariah **k** of Judah, **2Ki 15:27** 4428
became **k** over Israel in Samaria, **2Ki 15:27** 4427a
In the days of Pekah **k** of Israel, **2Ki 15:29** 4428
Tiglath-pileser **k** of Assyria came **2Ki 15:29** 4428
death and became **k** in his place, **2Ki 15:30** 4427a
the son of Remaliah **k** of Israel, **2Ki 15:32** 4428
son of Uzziah **k** of Judah became **2Ki 15:32** 4428
of Uzziah king of Judah became **k**. **2Ki 15:32** 4427a
years old when he became **k**, **2Ki 15:33** 4427a
began to send Rezin **k** of Aram **2Ki 15:37** 4428
his son became **k** in his place. **2Ki 15:38** 4427a
Ahaz the son of Jotham, **k** of Judah, **2Ki 16:1** 4428
Jotham, king of Judah, became **k**. **2Ki 16:1** 4427a
twenty years old when he became **k**, **2Ki 16:2** 4427a
Then Rezin **k** of Aram and Pekah son **2Ki 16:5** 4428
Pekah son of Remaliah, **k** of Israel, **2Ki 16:5** 4428
At that time Rezin **k** of Aram **2Ki 16:6** 4428
to Tiglath-pileser **k** of Assyria, **2Ki 16:7** 4428
me from the hand of the **k** of Aram and **2Ki 16:7** 4428
from the hand of the **k** of Israel, **2Ki 16:7** 4428
a present to the **k** of Assyria. **2Ki 16:8** 4428
the **k** of Assyria listened to him; **2Ki 16:9** 4428
and the **k** of Assyria went up **2Ki 16:9** 4428
Now **K** Ahaz went to Damascus to **2Ki 16:10** 4428
meet Tiglath-pileser **k** of Assyria, **2Ki 16:10** 4428
and **K** Ahaz sent to Urijah the **2Ki 16:10** 4428
K Ahaz had sent from Damascus, **2Ki 16:11** 4428
coming of **K** Ahaz from Damascus. **2Ki 16:11** 4428
When the **k** came from Damascus, **2Ki 16:12** 4428
Damascus, the **k** saw the altar; **2Ki 16:12** 4428
then the **k** approached the altar **2Ki 16:12** 4428
Then **K** Ahaz commanded Urijah the **2Ki 16:15** 4428
to all that **K** Ahaz commanded. **2Ki 16:16** 4428
Then **K** Ahaz cut off the borders of **2Ki 16:17** 4428
and the outer entry of the **k**, **2Ki 16:18** 4428
LORD because of the **k** of Assyria. **2Ki 16:18** 4428
twelfth year of Ahaz **k** of Judah, **2Ki 17:1** 4428
became **k** over Israel in Samaria, **2Ki 17:1** 4427a
Shalmaneser **k** of Assyria came up **2Ki 17:3** 4428
But the **k** of Assyria found **2Ki 17:4** 4428
sent messengers to So **k** of Egypt **2Ki 17:4** 4428
no tribute to the **k** of Assyria, **2Ki 17:4** 4428
so the **k** of Assyria shut him up **2Ki 17:4** 4428
Then the **k** of Assyria invaded the **2Ki 17:5** 4428
the **k** of Assyria captured Samaria **2Ki 17:6** 4428
the hand of Pharaoh, **k** of Egypt, **2Ki 17:7** 4428
made Jeroboam the son of Nebat **k**. **2Ki 17:21** 4427a
The **k** of Assyria brought *men* **2Ki 17:24** 4428
So they spoke to the **k** of Assyria, **2Ki 17:26** 4428
Then the **k** of Assyria commanded, **2Ki 17:27** 4428
the son of Elah **k** of Israel, **2Ki 18:1** 4428
of Ahaz **k** of Judah became king. **2Ki 18:1** 4428
of Ahaz king of Judah became **k**. **2Ki 18:1** 4427a
years old when he became **k**, **2Ki 18:2** 4427a
he rebelled against the **k** of Assyria **2Ki 18:7** 4428
in the fourth year of **K** Hezekiah, **2Ki 18:9** 4428
of Hoshea son of Elah **k** of Israel, **2Ki 18:9** 4428
Shalmaneser **k** of Assyria came **2Ki 18:9** 4428
ninth year of Hoshea **k** of Israel, **2Ki 18:10** 4428
Then the **k** of Assyria carried **2Ki 18:11** 4428
the fourteenth year of **K** Hezekiah, **2Ki 18:13** 4428
Sennacherib **k** of Assyria came up **2Ki 18:13** 4428
Then Hezekiah **k** of Judah sent to **2Ki 18:14** 4428
to the **k** of Assyria at Lachish, **2Ki 18:14** 4428
So the **k** of Assyria required of **2Ki 18:14** 4428
required of Hezekiah **k** of Judah **2Ki 18:14** 4428
Hezekiah **k** of Judah had overlaid, **2Ki 18:16** 4428
and gave it to the **k** of Assyria. **2Ki 18:16** 4428
Then the **k** of Assyria sent Tartan **2Ki 18:17** 4428
to **K** Hezekiah with a large army **2Ki 18:17** 4428
When they called to the **k**, **2Ki 18:18** 4428
'Thus says the great **k**, **2Ki 18:19** 4428
the great king, the **k** of Assyria, **2Ki 18:19** 4428
So is Pharaoh **k** of Egypt to all **2Ki 18:21** 4428
with my master the **k** of Assyria, **2Ki 18:23** 4428
"Hear the word of the great **k**, **2Ki 18:28** 4428
the great king, the **k** of Assyria. **2Ki 18:28** 4428
'Thus says the **k**, **2Ki 18:29** 4428
the hand of the **k** of Assyria." **2Ki 18:30** 4428
for thus says the **k** of Assyria, **2Ki 18:31** 4428
from the hand of the **k** of Assyria? **2Ki 18:33** 4428
And when **K** Hezekiah heard *it*, he **2Ki 19:1** 4428
whom his master the **k** of Assyria **2Ki 19:4** 4428
servants of **K** Hezekiah came to **2Ki 19:5** 4428
the servants of the **k** of Assyria **2Ki 19:6** 4428
Rabshakeh returned and found the **k** **2Ki 19:8** 4428
heard that the **k** had left Lachish. **2Ki 19:8** 4428
say concerning Tirhakah **k** of Cush, **2Ki 19:9** 4428
shall say to Hezekiah **k** of Judah, **2Ki 19:10** 4428
the hand of the **k** of Assyria." **2Ki 19:10** 4428
'Where is the **k** of Hamath, the **2Ki 19:13** 4428
king of Hamath, the **k** of Arpad, **2Ki 19:13** 4428
the **k** of the city of Sepharvaim, **2Ki 19:13** 4428
Me about Sennacherib **k** of Assyria, **2Ki 19:20** 4428
LORD concerning the **k** of Assyria, **2Ki 19:32** 4428
So Sennacherib **k** of Assyria **2Ki 19:36** 4428
his son became **k** in his place. **2Ki 19:37** 4427a
from the hand of the **k** of Assyria; **2Ki 20:6** 4428
a son of Baladan, **k** of Babylon, **2Ki 20:12** 4428
the prophet came to **K** Hezekiah **2Ki 20:14** 4428
palace of the **k** of Babylon.'" **2Ki 20:18** 4428
his son became **k** in his place. **2Ki 20:21** 4427a
twelve years old when he became **k**, **2Ki 21:1** 4427a
as Ahab **k** of Israel had done, **2Ki 21:3** 4428
"Because Manasseh **k** of Judah has **2Ki 21:11** 4428
his son became **k** in his place. **2Ki 21:18** 4427a
years old when he became **k**, **2Ki 21:19** 4427a
and killed the **k** in his own house. **2Ki 21:23** 4428
who had conspired against **K** Amon, **2Ki 21:24** 4428
Josiah his son **k** in his place. **2Ki 21:24** 4427a
his son became **k** in his place. **2Ki 21:26** 4427a
eight years old when he became **k**, **2Ki 22:1** 4427a
in the eighteenth year of **K** Josiah **2Ki 22:3** 4428
Josiah, the **k** sent Shaphan, **2Ki 22:3** 4428
Shaphan the scribe came to the **k** **2Ki 22:9** 4428
back word to the **k** and said, **2Ki 22:9** 4428
the scribe told the **k** saying, **2Ki 22:10** 4428
read it in the presence of the **k**. **2Ki 22:10** 4428
the **k** heard the words of the book **2Ki 22:11** 4428
k commanded Hilkiah the priest, **2Ki 22:12** 4428
which the **k** of Judah has read. **2Ki 22:16** 4428
"But to the **k** of Judah who sent **2Ki 22:18** 4428
they brought back word to the **k**. **2Ki 22:20** 4428
Then the **k** sent, and they gathered **2Ki 23:1** 4428
The **k** went up to the house of **2Ki 23:2** 4428
The **k** stood by the pillar and **2Ki 23:3** 4428
Then the **k** commanded Hilkiah the **2Ki 23:4** 4428
of the LORD, the **k** broke down; **2Ki 23:12** 4428
Solomon the **k** of Israel had built **2Ki 23:13** 4428
the sons of Ammon, the **k** defiled. **2Ki 23:13** 4428
Then the **k** commanded all the **2Ki 23:21** 4428
the eighteenth year of **K** Josiah, **2Ki 23:23** 4428
Before him there was no **k** like **2Ki 23:25** 4428
Pharaoh Neco **k** of Egypt went up **2Ki 23:29** 4428
Neco king of Egypt went up to the **k** **2Ki 23:29** 4428
And **K** Josiah went to meet him, and **2Ki 23:29** 4428
made him **k** in place of his father. **2Ki 23:30** 4427a
years old when he became **k**, **2Ki 23:31** 4427a
made Eliakim the son of Josiah **k** **2Ki 23:34** 4427a
years old when he became **k**, **2Ki 23:36** 4427a
k of Babylon came up, **2Ki 24:1** 4428
his son became **k** in his place. **2Ki 24:6** 4427a
The **k** of Egypt did not come **2Ki 24:7** 4428
for the **k** of Babylon had taken all **2Ki 24:7** 4428
all that belonged to the **k** of Egypt **2Ki 24:7** 4428
years old when he became **k**, **2Ki 24:8** 4427a
the servants of Nebuchadnezzar **k** of **2Ki 24:10** 4428
the **k** of Babylon came to the city, **2Ki 24:11** 4428
Jehoiachin the **k** of Judah went **2Ki 24:12** 4428
went out to the **k** of Babylon, **2Ki 24:12** 4428
So the **k** of Babylon took him **2Ki 24:12** 4428
which Solomon **k** of Israel had made **2Ki 24:13** 4428
and these the **k** of Babylon brought **2Ki 24:16** 4428
Then the **k** of Babylon made his **2Ki 24:17** 4428
uncle Mattaniah **k** in his place, **2Ki 24:17** 4427a
years old when he became **k**, **2Ki 24:18** 4427a
rebelled against the **k** of Babylon. **2Ki 24:20** 4428
Nebuchadnezzar **k** of Babylon came, **2Ki 25:1** 4428
the eleventh year of **K** Zedekiah. **2Ki 25:2** 4428
army of the Chaldeans pursued the **k** **2Ki 25:5** 4428
Then they captured the **k** and **2Ki 25:6** 4428
him to the **k** of Babylon at Riblah, **2Ki 25:6** 4428
year of **K** Nebuchadnezzar, **2Ki 25:8** 4428
King Nebuchadnezzar, **k** of Babylon, **2Ki 25:8** 4428
a servant of the **k** of Babylon, **2Ki 25:8** 4428
had deserted to the **k** of Babylon **2Ki 25:11** 4428
to the **k** of Babylon at Riblah. **2Ki 25:20** 4428
Then the **k** of Babylon struck them **2Ki 25:21** 4428
k of Babylon had left, **2Ki 25:22** 4428
heard that the **k** of Babylon had **2Ki 25:23** 4428
land and serve the **k** of Babylon, **2Ki 25:24** 4428
exile of Jehoiachin **k** of Judah, **2Ki 25:27** 4428
that Evil-merodach **k** of Babylon, **2Ki 25:27** 4428
in the year that he became **k**, **2Ki 25:27** 4427a
Jehoiachin **k** of Judah from prison; **2Ki 25:27** 4428
allowance was given him by the **k**, **2Ki 25:30** 4428
k of the sons of Israel reigned. **1Ch 1:43** 4428
of Bozrah became **k** in his place. **1Ch 1:44** 4427a
Temanites became **k** in his place. **1Ch 1:45** 4427a
of Moab, became **k** in his place; **1Ch 1:46** 4427a
of Masrekah became **k** in his place. **1Ch 1:47** 4427a
the River became **k** in his place. **1Ch 1:48** 4427a
of Achbor became **k** in his place. **1Ch 1:49** 4427a
died, Hadad became **k** in his place; **1Ch 1:50** 4427a
daughter of Talmai **k** of Geshur; **1Ch 3:2** 4428
they lived there with the **k** for his **1Ch 4:23** 4428
the days of Hezekiah **k** of Judah, **1Ch 4:41** 4428
whom Tilgath-pilneser **k** of Assyria **1Ch 5:6** 4428
in the days of Jotham **k** of Judah **1Ch 5:17** 4428
the days of Jeroboam **k** of Israel. **1Ch 5:17** 4428
the spirit of Pul, **k** of Assyria, **1Ch 5:26** 4428
of Tilgath-pilneser **k** of Assyria, **1Ch 5:26** 4428
times past, even when Saul was **k**, **1Ch 11:2** 4428
of Israel came to the **k** at Hebron, **1Ch 11:3** 4428
they anointed David **k** over Israel, **1Ch 11:3** 4428
with all Israel, to make him **k**, **1Ch 11:10** 4427a
by name to come and make David **k**. **1Ch 12:31** 4427a
to make David **k** over all Israel; **1Ch 12:38** 4427a
were of one mind to make David **k**. **1Ch 12:38** 4427a
Now Hiram **k** of Tyre sent **1Ch 14:1** 4428
established him as **k** over Israel, **1Ch 14:2** 4428
been anointed **k** over all Israel, **1Ch 14:8** 4428
saw **K** David leaping and celebrating **1Ch 15:29** 4428
Then David the **k** went in and sat **1Ch 17:16** 4428
also defeated Hadadezer **k** of Zobah **1Ch 18:3** 4428
came to help Hadadezer **k** of Zobah, **1Ch 18:5** 4428
Now when Tou **k** of Hamath heard **1Ch 18:9** 4428
the army of Hadadezer **k** of Zobah, **1Ch 18:9** 4428
sent Hadoram his son to **K** David to **1Ch 18:10** 4428
K David also dedicated these to **1Ch 18:11** 4428
the **k** of the sons of Ammon died, **1Ch 19:1** 4428
and his son became **k** in his place. **1Ch 19:1** 4427a
the **k** said, "Stay at Jericho until **1Ch 19:5** 4428
the **k** of Maacah and his people, **1Ch 19:7** 4428
David took the crown of their **k** **1Ch 20:2** 4428
But, my lord the **k**, **1Ch 21:3** 4428
k do what is good in his sight. **1Ch 21:23** 4428
But **K** David said to Ornan, **1Ch 21:24** 4428
his son Solomon **k** over Israel. **1Ch 23:1** 4427a
them in the presence of the **k**, **1Ch 24:6** 4428
in the presence of David the **k**, **1Ch 24:31** 4428
under the direction of the **k**. **1Ch 25:2** 4428
were under the direction of the **k**. **1Ch 25:6** 4428
which **K** David and the heads of the **1Ch 26:26** 4428
the LORD and the service of the **k**. **1Ch 26:30** 4428
And **K** David made them overseers of **1Ch 26:32** 4428
the affairs of God and of the **k**. **1Ch 26:32** 4428
and their officers who served the **k** **1Ch 27:1** 4428
of the chronicles of **K** David. **1Ch 27:24** 4428
which belonged to **K** David. **1Ch 27:31** 4428
Ahithophel *was* counselor to the **k**; **1Ch 27:33** 4428
the divisions that served the **k**, **1Ch 28:1** 4428
belonging to the **k** and his sons, **1Ch 28:1** 4428
Then **K** David rose to his feet and **1Ch 28:2** 4428
to be **k** over Israel forever. **1Ch 28:4** 4428
me to make *me* **k** over all Israel. **1Ch 28:4** 4427a
Then **K** David said to the entire **1Ch 29:1** 4428
and **K** David also rejoiced greatly. **1Ch 29:9** 4428
homage to the LORD and to the **k**. **1Ch 29:20** 4428
made Solomon the son of David **k** **1Ch 29:22** 4427a
as **k** instead of David his father; **1Ch 29:23** 4428
and also all the sons of **K** David **1Ch 29:24** 4428
pledged allegiance to **K** Solomon. **1Ch 29:24** 4428
on any **k** before him in Israel. **1Ch 29:25** 4428
Now the acts of **K** David, from **1Ch 29:29** 4428
and have made me **k** in his place. **2Ch 1:8** 4427a
for You have made me **k** over a **2Ch 1:9** 4427a
over whom I have made you **k**, **2Ch 1:11** 4427a

and with the **k** at Jerusalem. 2Ch 1:14 4428
The **k** made silver and gold as 2Ch 1:15 4428
sent *word* to Huram the **k** of Tyre, 2Ch 2:3 4428
Then Huram, **k** of Tyre, answered in 2Ch 2:11 4428
He has made you **k** over them." 2Ch 2:11 4428
who has given **K** David a wise son, 2Ch 2:12 4428
for **K** Solomon in the house of God: 2Ch 4:11 4428
of polished bronze for **K** Solomon 2Ch 4:16 4428
of the Jordan the **k** cast them in 2Ch 4:17 4428
themselves to the **k** at the feast, 2Ch 5:3 4428
And **K** Solomon and all the 2Ch 5:6 4428
Then the **k** faced about and blessed 2Ch 6:3 4428
Then the **k** and all the people 2Ch 7:4 4428
K Solomon offered a sacrifice 2Ch 7:5 4428
Thus the **k** and all the people 2Ch 7:5 4428
which **K** David had made for giving 2Ch 7:6 4428
the chief officers of **K** Solomon, 2Ch 8:10 4428
in the house of David **k** of Israel, 2Ch 8:11 4428
commandment of the **k** to the priests 2Ch 8:15 4428
and brought them to **K** Solomon. 2Ch 8:18 4428
Then she said to the **k**, 2Ch 9:5 4428
setting you on His throne as **k** for 2Ch 9:8 4428
therefore He made you **k** over them, 2Ch 9:8 4428
Then she gave the **k** one hundred 2Ch 9:9 4428
queen of Sheba gave to **K** Solomon. 2Ch 9:9 4428
From the algum trees the **k** made 2Ch 9:11 4428
K Solomon gave to the queen of 2Ch 9:12 4428
for what she had brought to the **k**. 2Ch 9:12 4428
K Solomon made 200 large 2Ch 9:15 4428
and the **k** put them in the house of 2Ch 9:16 4428
the **k** made a great throne of ivory 2Ch 9:17 4428
All **K** Solomon's drinking vessels 2Ch 9:20 4428
For the **k** had ships which went to 2Ch 9:21 4428
So **K** Solomon became greater than 2Ch 9:22 4428
and with the **k** in Jerusalem. 2Ch 9:25 4428
The **k** made silver *as common* as 2Ch 9:27 4428
had come to Shechem to make him **k**. 2Ch 10:1 4427a
from the presence of **K** Solomon), 2Ch 10:2 4428
Then **K** Rehoboam consulted with the 2Ch 10:6 4428
third day as the **k** had directed, 2Ch 10:12 4428
The **k** answered them harshly, 2Ch 10:13 4428
and **K** Rehoboam forsook the counsel 2Ch 10:13 4428
k did not listen to the people, 2Ch 10:15 4428
all Israel *saw* that the **k** did not listen 2Ch 10:16 4428
to them the people answered the **k**, 2Ch 10:16 4428
Then **K** Rehoboam sent Hadoram, who 2Ch 10:18 4428
And **K** Rehoboam made haste to mount 2Ch 10:18 4428
the son of Solomon, **k** of Judah, 2Ch 11:3 4428
for he *intended* to make him **k**. 2Ch 11:22 4427a
about in **K** Rehoboam's fifth year, 2Ch 12:2 4428
that Shishak **k** of Egypt came up 2Ch 12:2 4428
the **k** humbled themselves and said, 2Ch 12:6 4428
So Shishak **k** of Egypt came up 2Ch 12:9 4428
Then **K** Rehoboam made shields of 2Ch 12:10 4428
k entered the house of the LORD, 2Ch 12:11 4428
So **K** Rehoboam strengthened himself 2Ch 12:13 4428
son Abijah became **k** in his place. 2Ch 12:16 4427a
the eighteenth year of **K** Jeroboam, 2Ch 13:1 4428
Abijah became **k** over Judah. 2Ch 13:1 4427a
his son Asa became **k** in his place. 2Ch 14:1 4427a
Maacah, the mother of **K** Asa, 2Ch 15:16 4428
k of Israel came up against Judah 2Ch 16:1 4428
or coming in to Asa **k** of Judah. 2Ch 16:1 4428
sent them to Ben-hadad **k** of Aram, 2Ch 16:2 4428
break your treaty with Baasha **k** of 2Ch 16:3 4428
So Ben-hadad listened to **K** Asa and 2Ch 16:4 4428
Then **K** Asa brought all Judah, and 2Ch 16:6 4428
the seer came to Asa **k** of Judah 2Ch 16:7 4428
"Because you have relied on the **k** 2Ch 16:7 4428
army of the **k** of Aram has escaped 2Ch 16:7 4428
son then became **k** in his place, 2Ch 17:1 4427a
These are they who served the **k**, 2Ch 17:19 4428
apart from those whom the **k** put in 2Ch 17:19 4428
Ahab **k** of Israel said to 2Ch 18:3 4428
said to Jehoshaphat **k** of Judah, 2Ch 18:3 4428
said to the **k** of Israel, 2Ch 18:4 4428
Then the **k** of Israel assembled the 2Ch 18:5 4428
give *it* into the hand of the **k**." 2Ch 18:5 4428
k of Israel said to Jehoshaphat, 2Ch 18:7 4428
"Let not the **k** say so." 2Ch 18:7 4428
Then the **k** of Israel called an 2Ch 18:8 4428
Now the **k** of Israel and 2Ch 18:9 4428
Jehoshaphat the **k** of Judah were 2Ch 18:9 4428
give *it* into the hand of the **k**." 2Ch 18:11 4428
are uniformly favorable to the **k**. 2Ch 18:12 4428
When he came to the **k**, 2Ch 18:14 4428
to the king, the **k** said to him, 2Ch 18:14 4428
Then the **k** said to him, 2Ch 18:15 4428
k of Israel said to Jehoshaphat, 2Ch 18:17 4428
'Who will entice Ahab **k** of Israel 2Ch 18:19 4428
Then the **k** of Israel said, 2Ch 18:25 4428
'Thus says the **k**, 2Ch 18:26 4428
So the **k** of Israel and Jehoshaphat 2Ch 18:28 4428
Jehoshaphat **k** of Judah went up 2Ch 18:28 4428
k of Israel said to Jehoshaphat, 2Ch 18:29 4428
the **k** of Israel disguised himself, 2Ch 18:29 4428
Now the **k** of Aram had commanded 2Ch 18:30 4428
but with the **k** of Israel alone." 2Ch 18:30 4428
"It is the **k** of Israel," 2Ch 18:31 4428
that it was not the **k** of Israel, 2Ch 18:32 4428
struck the **k** of Israel in a joint of 2Ch 18:33 4428
and the **k** of Israel propped 2Ch 18:34 4428
Then Jehoshaphat the **k** of Judah 2Ch 19:1 4428
him and said to **K** Jehoshaphat, 2Ch 19:2 4428
in all that pertains to the **k**. 2Ch 19:11 4428
of Jerusalem and **K** Jehoshaphat: 2Ch 20:15 4428
years old when he became **k**, 2Ch 20:31 4427a
Jehoshaphat **k** of Judah allied 2Ch 20:35 4428
himself with Ahaziah **k** of Israel. 2Ch 20:35 4428

his son became **k** in his place. 2Ch 21:1 4427a
sons of Jehoshaphat **k** of Israel. 2Ch 21:2 4428
years old when he became **k**, 2Ch 21:5 4427a
and set up a **k** over themselves. 2Ch 21:8 4428
and the ways of Asa **k** of Judah, 2Ch 21:12 4428
years old when he became **k**, 2Ch 21:20 4427a
his youngest son, **k** in his place, 2Ch 22:1 4427a
Jehoram **k** of Judah began to reign. 2Ch 22:1 4428
years old when he became **k**, 2Ch 22:2 4427a
Jehoram the son of Ahab **k** of Israel 2Ch 22:5 4428
Hazael **k** of Aram at Ramoth-gilead. 2Ch 22:5 4428
fought against Hazael **k** of Aram. 2Ch 22:6 4428
the son of Jehoram **k** of Judah, 2Ch 22:6 4428
the daughter of **K** Jehoram, 2Ch 22:11 4428
with the **k** in the house of God. 2Ch 23:3 4428
The Levites will surround the **k**, 2Ch 23:7 4428
Thus be with the **k** when he comes 2Ch 23:7 4428
shields which had been **K** David's, 2Ch 23:9 4428
and by the house, around the **k**. 2Ch 23:10 4428
him the testimony and made him **k**. 2Ch 23:11 4427a
"*Long* live the **k**!" 2Ch 23:11 4428
people running and praising the **k**, 2Ch 23:12 4428
the **k** was standing by his pillar 2Ch 23:13 4428
the trumpeters *were* beside the **k**. 2Ch 23:13 4428
and all the people and the **k**, 2Ch 23:16 4428
and brought the **k** down from the 2Ch 23:20 4428
the **k** upon the royal throne. 2Ch 23:20 4428
seven years old when he became **k**, 2Ch 24:1 4427a
So the **k** summoned Jehoiada the 2Ch 24:6 4428
So the **k** commanded, and they made 2Ch 24:8 4428
The **k** and Jehoiada gave it to 2Ch 24:12 4428
money before the **k** and Jehoiada; 2Ch 24:14 4428
came and bowed down to the **k**, 2Ch 24:17 4428
king, and the **k** listened to them. 2Ch 24:17 4428
at the command of the **k** they stoned 2Ch 24:21 4428
Thus Joash the **k** did not remember 2Ch 24:22 4428
their spoil to the **k** of Damascus. 2Ch 24:23 4428
his son became **k** in his place. 2Ch 24:27 4427a
years old when he became **k**, 2Ch 25:1 4427a
who had slain his father the **k**. 2Ch 25:3 4428
"O **k**, do not let the army of 2Ch 25:7 4428
with him, the **k** said to him, 2Ch 25:16 4428
Then Amaziah **k** of Judah took 2Ch 25:17 4428
the son of Jehu, the **k** of Israel, 2Ch 25:17 4428
Joash the **k** of Israel sent to 2Ch 25:18 4428
Israel sent to Amaziah **k** of Judah, 2Ch 25:18 4428
So Joash **k** of Israel went up, and 2Ch 25:21 4428
and he and Amaziah **k** of Judah 2Ch 25:21 4428
Then Joash **k** of Israel captured 2Ch 25:23 4428
captured Amaziah **k** of Judah, 2Ch 25:23 4428
the son of Joash **k** of Judah, 2Ch 25:25 4428
son of Jehoahaz, **k** of Israel. 2Ch 25:25 4428
and made him **k** in the place of his 2Ch 26:1 4427a
the **k** slept with his fathers. 2Ch 26:2 4428
years old when he became **k**, 2Ch 26:3 4427a
to help the **k** against the enemy. 2Ch 26:13 4428
Uzziah the **k** and said to him, 2Ch 26:18 4428
K Uzziah was a leper to the 2Ch 26:21 4428
his son became **k** in his place. 2Ch 26:23 4427a
years old when he became **k**, 2Ch 27:1 4427a
He fought also with the **k** of the 2Ch 27:5 4428
years old when he became **k**, 2Ch 27:8 4427a
his son became **k** in his place. 2Ch 27:9 4427a
twenty years old when he became **k**, 2Ch 28:1 4427a
into the hand of the **k** of Aram; 2Ch 28:5 4428
into the hand of the **k** of Israel, 2Ch 28:5 4428
and Elkanah the second to the **k**. 2Ch 28:7 4428
At that time **K** Ahaz sent to the 2Ch 28:16 4428
Judah because of Ahaz **k** of Israel, 2Ch 28:19 4428
So Tilgath-pilneser **k** of Assyria 2Ch 28:20 4428
of the **k** and of the princes, 2Ch 28:21 4428
and gave *it* to the **k** of Assyria 2Ch 28:21 4428
K Ahaz became yet more unfaithful 2Ch 28:22 4428
Hezekiah became **k** *when he was* 2Ch 29:1 4427a
of the **k** by the words of the LORD. 2Ch 29:15 4428
went in to **K** Hezekiah and said, 2Ch 29:18 4428
all the utensils which **K** Ahaz had 2Ch 29:19 4428
Then **K** Hezekiah arose early and 2Ch 29:20 4428
before the **k** and the assembly, 2Ch 29:23 4428
for the **k** ordered the burnt 2Ch 29:24 4428
instruments of David, **k** of Israel. 2Ch 29:27 4428
the **k** and all who were present 2Ch 29:29 4428
K Hezekiah and the officials 2Ch 29:30 4428
For the **k** and his princes and all 2Ch 30:2 4428
thing was right in the sight of the **k** 2Ch 30:4 4428
the hand of the **k** and his princes, 2Ch 30:6 4428
according to the command of the **k**, 2Ch 30:6 4428
the **k** and the princes commanded 2Ch 30:12 4428
For Hezekiah **k** of Judah had 2Ch 30:24 4428
the son of David, **k** of Israel. 2Ch 30:26 4428
by the appointment of **K** Hezekiah, 2Ch 31:13 4428
Sennacherib **k** of Assyria came 2Ch 32:1 4428
because of the **k** of Assyria nor 2Ch 32:7 4428
the words of Hezekiah **k** of Judah. 2Ch 32:8 4428
Sennacherib **k** of Assyria sent his 2Ch 32:9 4428
against Hezekiah **k** of Judah and 2Ch 32:9 4428
says Sennacherib **k** of Assyria, 2Ch 32:10 4428
the hand of the **k** of Assyria"? 2Ch 32:11 4428
But **K** Hezekiah and Isaiah the 2Ch 32:20 4428
in the camp of the **k** of Assyria. 2Ch 32:21 4428
of Sennacherib the **k** of Assyria and 2Ch 32:22 4428
presents to Hezekiah **k** of Judah, 2Ch 32:23 4428
Manasseh became **k** in his place. 2Ch 32:33 4427a
twelve years old when he became **k**, 2Ch 33:1 4427a
of the **k** of Assyria against them, 2Ch 33:11 4428
his son became **k** in his place. 2Ch 33:20 4427a
years old when he became **k**, 2Ch 33:21 4427a
the conspirators against **K** Amon, 2Ch 33:25 4428
Josiah his son **k** in his place. 2Ch 33:25 4427a

eight years old when he became **k**, 2Ch 34:1 4427a
Shaphan brought the book to the **k** 2Ch 34:16 4428
reported further word to the **k**, 2Ch 34:16 4428
the scribe told the **k** saying, 2Ch 34:18 4428
from it in the presence of the **k**. 2Ch 34:18 4428
When the **k** heard 2Ch 34:19 4428
Then the **k** commanded Hilkiah, 2Ch 34:20 4428
and *those* whom the **k** had told 2Ch 34:22 4428
in the presence of the **k** of Judah. 2Ch 34:24 4428
"But to the **k** of Judah who sent 2Ch 34:26 4428
they brought back word to the **k**. 2Ch 34:28 4428
Then the **k** sent and gathered all 2Ch 34:29 4428
The **k** went up to the house of 2Ch 34:30 4428
Then the **k** stood in his place and 2Ch 34:31 4428
son of David **k** of Israel built; 2Ch 35:3 4428
the writing of David **k** of Israel 2Ch 35:4 4428
to the command of **K** Josiah. 2Ch 35:16 4428
Neco **k** of Egypt came up to make 2Ch 35:20 4428
do with each other, O **K** of Judah? 2Ch 35:21 4428
The archers shot **K** Josiah, 2Ch 35:23 4428
and the **k** said to his servants, 2Ch 35:23 4428
and made him **k** in place of his 2Ch 36:1 4427a
years old when he became **k**, 2Ch 36:2 4427a
Then the **k** of Egypt deposed him at 2Ch 36:3 4428
The **k** of Egypt made Eliakim 2Ch 36:4 4428
k over Judah and Jerusalem, 2Ch 36:4 4427a
years old when he became **k**, 2Ch 36:5 4427a
Nebuchadnezzar **k** of Babylon came 2Ch 36:6 4428
his son became **k** in his place. 2Ch 36:8 4427a
eight years old when he became **k**, 2Ch 36:9 4427a
K Nebuchadnezzar sent and brought 2Ch 36:10 4428
k over Judah and Jerusalem. 2Ch 36:10 4427a
years old when he became **k**, 2Ch 36:11 4427a
rebelled against **K** Nebuchadnezzar 2Ch 36:13 4428
against them the **k** of the Chaldeans 2Ch 36:17 4428
of the **k** and of his officers, 2Ch 36:18 4428
in the first year of Cyrus **k** of Persia 2Ch 36:22 4428
the spirit of Cyrus **k** of Persia, 2Ch 36:22 4428
"Thus says Cyrus **k** of Persia, 2Ch 36:23 4428
first year of Cyrus **k** of Persia, Ezr 1:1 4428
the spirit of Cyrus **k** of Persia, Ezr 1:1 4428
"Thus says Cyrus **k** of Persia, Ezr 1:2 4428
Also **K** Cyrus brought out the Ezr 1:7 4428
and Cyrus, **k** of Persia, had them Ezr 1:8 4428
the **k** of Babylon had carried away Ezr 2:1 4428
they had from Cyrus **k** of Persia. Ezr 3:7 4428
directions of **K** David of Israel. Ezr 3:10 4428
days of Esarhaddon **k** of Assyria, Ezr 4:2 4428
as **K** Cyrus, the king of Persia has Ezr 4:3 4428
k of Persia has commanded us." Ezr 4:3 4428
all the days of Cyrus **k** of Persia, Ezr 4:5 4428
the reign of Darius **k** of Persia. Ezr 4:5 4428
wrote to Artaxerxes **k** of Persia; Ezr 4:7 4428
against Jerusalem to **K** Artaxerxes, Ezr 4:8 4430
"To **K** Artaxerxes: Your servants, Ezr 4:11 4430
let it be known to the **k** that Ezr 4:12 4430
"Now let it be known to the **k**, Ezr 4:13 4430
we have sent and informed the **k**, Ezr 4:14 4430
"We inform the **k** that if that Ezr 4:16 4430
Then the **k** sent an answer to Rehum Ezr 4:17 4430
the copy of **K** Artaxerxes' document Ezr 4:23 4430
the reign of Darius **k** of Persia. Ezr 4:24 4430
the River, sent to Darius the **k**. Ezr 5:6 4430
"To Darius the **k**, all peace. Ezr 5:7 4430
"Let it be known to the **k** that Ezr 5:8 4430
k of Israel built and finished. Ezr 5:11 4430
of Nebuchadnezzar **k** of Babylon, Ezr 5:12 4430
first year of Cyrus **k** of Babylon, Ezr 5:13 4430
K Cyrus issued a decree to rebuild Ezr 5:13 4430
these **K** Cyrus took from the temple Ezr 5:14 4430
if it pleases the **k**, let a search Ezr 5:17 4430
a decree was issued by **K** Cyrus to Ezr 5:17 4430
and let the **k** send to us his Ezr 5:17 4430
Then **K** Darius issued a decree, and Ezr 6:1 4430
"In the first year of **K** Cyrus, Ezr 6:3 4430
Cyrus the **k** issued a decree: Ezr 6:3 4430
the life of the **k** and his sons. Ezr 6:10 4430
overthrow any **k** or people who Ezr 6:12 4430
just as **K** Darius had sent. Ezr 6:13 4430
and Artaxerxes **k** of Persia. Ezr 6:14 4430
year of the reign of **K** Darius. Ezr 6:15 4430
turned the heart of the **k** of Assyria Ezr 6:22 4428
reign of Artaxerxes **k** of Persia, Ezr 7:1 4428
and the **k** granted him all he Ezr 7:6 4428
the seventh year of **K** Artaxerxes. Ezr 7:7 4428
was in the seventh year of the **k**. Ezr 7:8 4428
decree which **K** Artaxerxes gave to Ezr 7:11 4428
"Artaxerxes, **k** of kings, to Ezra Ezr 7:12 4430
Forasmuch as you are sent by the **k** Ezr 7:14 4430
which the **k** and his counselors Ezr 7:15 4430
"I, even I, **K** Artaxerxes, Ezr 7:21 4430
the kingdom of the **k** and his sons. Ezr 7:23 4430
of your God and the law of the **k**, Ezr 7:26 4430
lovingkindness to me before the **k** Ezr 7:28 4428
in the reign of **K** Artaxerxes: Ezr 8:1 4428
ashamed to request from the **k** troops Ezr 8:22 4428
way, because we had said to the **k**, Ezr 8:22 4428
house of our God which the **k** and Ezr 8:25 4428
Now I was the cupbearer to the **k**. Ne 1:11 4428
twentieth year of **K** Artaxerxes, Ne 2:1 4428
up the wine and gave it to the **k**. Ne 2:1 4428
So the **k** said to me, Ne 2:2 4428
I said to the **k**, Ne 2:3 4428
"Let the **k** live forever. Ne 2:3 4428
Then the **k** said to me, Ne 2:4 4428
I said to the **k**, Ne 2:5 4428
"If it please the **k**, Ne 2:5 4428
Then the **k** said to me, the queen Ne 2:6 4428
So it pleased the **k** to send me, Ne 2:6 4428

And I said to the **k**, **Ne 2:7** 4428
"If it please the **k**, **Ne 2:7** 4428
And the **k** granted *them* to me **Ne 2:8** 4428
Now the **k** had sent with me **Ne 2:9** 4428
Are you rebelling against the **k**?" **Ne 2:19** 4428
from the upper house of the **k**, **Ne 3:25** 4428
thirty-second year of **K** Artaxerxes, **Ne 5:14** 4428
And you are to be their **k**, **Ne 6:6** 4428
'A **k** is in Judah!' **Ne 6:7** 4428
now it will be reported to the **k** **Ne 6:7** 4428
the **k** of Babylon had carried away, **Ne 7:6** 4428
land of Sihon the **k** of Heshbon And **Ne 9:22** 4428
the land of Og the **k** of Bashan. **Ne 9:22** 4428
was a commandment from the **k** **Ne 11:23** 4428
year of Artaxerxes **k** of Babylon **Ne 13:6** 4428
of Babylon I had gone to the **k**. **Ne 13:6** 4428
however, I asked leave from the **k**, **Ne 13:6** 4428
"Did not Solomon **k** of Israel sin **Ne 13:26** 4428
nations there was no **k** like him, **Ne 13:26** 4428
God made him **k** over all Israel; **Ne 13:26** 4428
in those days as **K** Ahasuerus sat **Es 1:2** 4428
the **k** gave a banquet lasting seven **Es 1:5** 4428
for so the **k** had given orders to **Es 1:8** 4428
which belonged to **K** Ahasuerus. **Es 1:9** 4428
heart of the **k** was merry with wine, **Es 1:10** 4428
in the presence of **K** Ahasuerus, **Es 1:10** 4428
to bring Queen Vashti before the **k** **Es 1:11** 4428
Then the **k** became very angry and **Es 1:12** 4428
Then the **k** said to the wise men **Es 1:13** 4428
custom of the **k** so *to speak* before all **Es 1:13** 4428
obey the command of **K** Ahasuerus **Es 1:15** 4428
presence of the **k** and the princes, **Es 1:16** 4428
Vashti has wronged not only the **k** **Es 1:16** 4428
all the provinces of **K** Ahasuerus. **Es 1:16** 4428
'**K** Ahasuerus commanded Queen **Es 1:17** 4428
"If it pleases the **k**, **Es 1:19** 4428
into the presence of **K** Ahasuerus, **Es 1:19** 4428
and let the **k** give her royal **Es 1:19** 4428
pleased the **k** and the princes, **Es 1:21** 4428
and the **k** did as Memucan proposed. **Es 1:21** 4428
anger of **K** Ahasuerus had subsided, **Es 2:1** 4428
young virgins be sought for the **k**. **Es 2:2** 4428
"Let the **k** appoint overseers **Es 2:3** 4428
the young lady who pleases the **k** **Es 2:4** 4428
And the matter pleased the **k**, **Es 2:4** 4428
exiled with Jeconiah **k** of Judah, **Es 2:6** 4428
the **k** of Babylon had exiled. **Es 2:6** 4428
and decree of the **k** were heard **Es 2:8** 4428
lady came to go in to **K** Ahasuerus, **Es 2:12** 4428
would go in to the **k** in this way: **Es 2:13** 4428
She would not again go in to the **k** **Es 2:14** 4428
unless the **k** delighted in her **Es 2:14** 4428
daughter, came to go in to the **k**, **Es 2:15** 4428
So Esther was taken to **K** Ahasuerus **Es 2:16** 4428
The **k** loved Esther more than **Es 2:17** 4428
Then the **k** gave a great banquet, **Es 2:18** 4428
to lay hands on **K** Ahasuerus. **Es 2:21** 4428
informed the **k** in Mordecai's name. **Es 2:22** 4428
events **K** Ahasuerus promoted Haman, **Es 3:1** 4428
k had commanded concerning him. **Es 3:2** 4428
the twelfth year of **K** Ahasuerus, **Es 3:7** 4428
Then Haman said to **K** Ahasuerus, **Es 3:8** 4428
"If it is pleasing to the **k**, **Es 3:9** 4428
Then the **k** took his signet ring **Es 3:10** 4428
The **k** said to Haman, **Es 3:11** 4428
written in the name of **K** Ahasuerus **Es 3:12** 4428
the **k** and Haman sat down to drink, **Es 3:15** 4428
command and decree of the **k** came, **Es 4:3** 4428
the **k** had appointed to attend her, **Es 4:5** 4428
to go in to the **k** to implore his favor **Es 4:8** 4428
man or woman who comes to the **k** **Es 4:11** 4428
unless the **k** holds out to him the **Es 4:11** 4428
to the **k** for these thirty days." **Es 4:11** 4428
And thus I will go in to the **k**, **Es 4:16** 4428
and the **k** was sitting on his royal **Es 5:1** 4428
When the **k** saw **Es 5:2** 4428
and the **k** extended to Esther the **Es 5:2** 4428
Then the **k** said to her, **Es 5:3** 4428
"If it pleases the **k**, **Es 5:4** 4428
may the **k** and Haman come this day **Es 5:4** 4428
Then the **k** said, **Es 5:5** 4428
So the **k** and Haman came to the **Es 5:5** 4428
the banquet, the **k** said to Esther, **Es 5:6** 4428
found favor in the sight of the **k**, **Es 5:8** 4428
and if it pleases the **k** to grant my **Es 5:8** 4428
may the **k** and Haman come to the **Es 5:8** 4428
I will do as the **k** says." **Es 5:8** 4428
where the **k** had magnified him and **Es 5:11** 4428
the princes and servants of the **k**. **Es 5:11** 4428
let no one but me come with the **k** **Es 5:12** 4428
I am invited by her with the **k**. **Es 5:12** 4428
ask the **k** to have Mordecai hanged **Es 5:14** 4428
then go joyfully with the **k** to the **Es 5:14** 4428
During that night the **k** could not **Es 6:1** 4428
and they were read before the **k**. **Es 6:1** 4428
to lay hands on **K** Ahasuerus. **Es 6:2** 4428
The **k** said, "What honor or dignity **Es 6:3** 4428
the **k** said, "Who is in the court?" **Es 6:4** 4428
to speak to the **k** about hanging **Es 6:4** 4428
And the **k** said, "Let him come in." **Es 6:5** 4428
came in and the **k** said to him, **Es 6:6** 4428
man whom the **k** desires to honor?" **Es 6:6** 4428
k desire to honor more than me?" **Es 6:6** 4428
Then Haman said to the **k**, **Es 6:7** 4428
man whom the **k** desires to honor, **Es 6:7** 4428
a royal robe which the **k** has worn, **Es 6:8** 4428
horse on which the **k** has ridden, **Es 6:8** 4428
man whom the **k** desires to honor **Es 6:9** 4428
man whom the **k** desires to honor **Es 6:9** 4428
Then the **k** said to Haman, **Es 6:10** 4428
man whom the **k** desires to honor." **Es 6:11** 4428
Now the **k** and Haman came to drink **Es 7:1** 4428
And the **k** said to Esther on the **Es 7:2** 4428
found favor in your sight, O **k**, **Es 7:3** 4428
O king, and if it pleases the **k**, **Es 7:3** 4428
with the annoyance to the **k**." **Es 7:4** 4428
K Ahasuerus asked Queen Esther, **Es 7:5** 4428
terrified before the **k** and queen. **Es 7:6** 4428
The **k** arose in his anger from **Es 7:7** 4428
determined against him by the **k**. **Es 7:7** 4428
Now when the **k** returned from the **Es 7:8** 4428
Then the **k** said, **Es 7:8** 4428
who *were* before the **k** said, **Es 7:9** 4428
spoke good on behalf of the **k**!" **Es 7:9** 4428
And the **k** said, "Hang him on it." **Es 7:9** 4428
On that day **K** Ahasuerus gave the **Es 8:1** 4428
and Mordecai came before the **k**, **Es 8:1** 4428
The **k** took off his signet ring **Es 8:2** 4428
Then Esther spoke again to the **k**, **Es 8:3** 4428
The **k** extended the golden **Es 8:4** 4428
arose and stood before the **k**. **Es 8:4** 4428
"If it pleases the **k** and if I **Es 8:5** 4428
and the matter *seems* proper to the **k** **Es 8:5** 4428
So **K** Ahasuerus said to Queen **Es 8:7** 4428
which is written in the name of the **k** **Es 8:8** 4428
wrote in the name of **K** Ahasuerus, **Es 8:10** 4428
In them the **k** granted the Jews who **Es 8:11** 4428
all the provinces of **K** Ahasuerus, **Es 8:12** 4428
went out from the presence of the **k** **Es 8:15** 4428
all the provinces of **K** Ahasuerus **Es 9:2** 4428
the citadel in Susa was reported to the **k**. **Es 9:11** 4428
The **k** said to Queen Esther, **Es 9:12** 4428
"If it pleases the **k**, **Es 9:13** 4428
So the **k** commanded that it should **Es 9:14** 4428
all the provinces of **K** Ahasuerus, **Es 9:20** 4428
Now **K** Ahasuerus laid a tribute on **Es 10:1** 4428
to which the **k** advanced him, **Es 10:2** 4428
Jew was second *only* to **K** Ahasuerus **Es 10:3** 4428
him like a **k** ready for the attack, **Jb 15:24** 4428
march him before the **k** of terrors. **Jb 18:14** 4428
And dwelt as a **k** among the troops, **Jb 29:25** 4428
Who says to a **k**, **Jb 34:18** 4428
is **k** over all the sons of pride." **Jb 41:34** 4428
I have installed My **K** Upon Zion, **Ps 2:6** 4428
my cry for help, my **K** and my God, **Ps 5:2** 4428
The LORD is **K** forever and ever; **Ps 10:16** 4428
gives great deliverance to His **k**, **Ps 18:50** 4428
K answer us in the day we call. **Ps 20:9** 4428
Your strength the **k** will be glad, **Ps 21:1** 4428
For the **k** trusts in the LORD, And **Ps 21:7** 4428
That the **K** of glory may come in! **Ps 24:7** 4428
Who is the **K** of glory? **Ps 24:8** 4428
That the **K** of glory may come in! **Ps 24:9** 4428
Who is this **K** of glory? **Ps 24:10** 4428
of hosts, He is the **K** of glory. **Ps 24:10** 4428
The LORD sat *as* **K** at **Ps 29:10** 4428
Yes, the LORD sits as **K** forever. **Ps 29:10** 4428
k is not saved by a mighty army; **Ps 33:16** 4428
You are my **K**, O God; **Ps 44:4** 4428
I address my verses to the **K**; **Ps 45:1** 4428
the **K** will desire your beauty. **Ps 45:11** 4428
led to the **K** in embroidered work; **Ps 45:14** 4428
A great **K** over all the earth. **Ps 47:2** 4428
Sing praises to our **K**, **Ps 47:6** 4428
For God is the **K** of all the earth; **Ps 47:7** 4428
north, The city of the great **K**. **Ps 48:2** 4428
But the **k** will rejoice in God; **Ps 63:11** 4428
The procession of my God, my **K**, **Ps 68:24** 4428
Give the **k** Your judgments, O God, **Ps 72:1** 4428
Yet God is my **k** from of old, Who **Ps 74:12** 4428
O LORD of hosts, My **K** and my God. **Ps 84:3** 4428
our **k** to the Holy One of Israel. **Ps 89:18** 4428
God And a great **K** above all gods, **Ps 95:3** 4428
horn Shout joyfully before the **K**, **Ps 98:6** 4428
strength of the **K** loves justice; **Ps 99:4** 4428
The **k** sent and released him, The **Ps 105:20** 4428
Sihon, **k** of the Amorites, And Og, **Ps 135:11** 4428
the Amorites, And Og, **k** of Bashan, **Ps 135:11** 4428
Sihon, **k** of the Amorites, For His **Ps 136:19** 4428
And Og, **k** of Bashan, For His **Ps 136:20** 4428
I will extol You, my God, O **K**, **Ps 145:1** 4428
sons of Zion rejoice in their **K**. **Ps 149:2** 4428
the son of David, **k** of Israel: **Pr 1:1** 4428
decision is in the lips of the **k**; **Pr 16:10** 4428
The fury of a **k** is *like* messengers of **Pr 16:14** 4428
The terror of a **k** is like the **Pr 20:2** 4428
A **k** who sits on the throne of **Pr 20:8** 4428
A wise **k** winnows the wicked, And **Pr 20:26** 4428
Loyalty and truth preserve the **k**, **Pr 20:28** 4428
is gracious, the **k** is his friend. **Pr 22:11** 4428
My son, fear the LORD and the **k**; **Pr 24:21** 4428
the men of Hezekiah, **k** of Judah, **Pr 25:1** 4428
away the wicked before the **k**, **Pr 25:5** 4428
honor in the presence of the **k**, **Pr 25:6** 4428
The **k** gives stability to the land **Pr 29:4** 4428
If a **k** judges the poor with truth, **Pr 29:14** 4428
Under a slave when he becomes **k**, **Pr 30:22** 4427a
The locusts have no **k**, **Pr 30:27** 4428
And a **k** *when his* army is with him. **Pr 30:31** 4428
The words of **K** Lemuel, the oracle **Pr 31:1** 4428
the son of David, **k** in Jerusalem. **Ec 1:1** 4428
been **k** over Israel in Jerusalem. **Ec 1:12** 4428
man *do* who will come after the **k** **Ec 2:12** 4428
is better than an old and foolish **k** **Ec 4:13** 4428
come out of prison to become **k**, **Ec 4:14** 4427a
a **k** who cultivates the field is an **Ec 5:9** 4428
"Keep the command of the **k** **Ec 8:2** 4428
word of the **k** is authoritative, **Ec 8:4** 4428
in it and a great **k** came to it, **Ec 9:14** 4428
whose **k** is a lad and whose princes **Ec 10:16** 4428
whose **k** is of nobility and whose **Ec 10:17** 4428
your bedchamber do not curse a **k**, **Ec 10:20** 4428
The **k** has brought me into his **SS 1:4** 4428
"While the **k** was at his table, My **SS 1:12** 4428
"**K** Solomon has made for himself a **SS 3:9** 4428
And gaze on **K** Solomon with the **SS 3:11** 4428
k is captivated by *your* tresses. **SS 7:5** 4428
In the year of **K** Uzziah's death I **Is 6:1** 4428
For my eyes have seen the **K**, **Is 6:5** 4428
the son of Uzziah, **k** of Judah, **Is 7:1** 4428
that Rezin the **k** of Aram and Pekah **Is 7:1** 4428
the son of Remaliah, **k** of Israel, **Is 7:1** 4428
Tabeel as **k** in the midst of it," **Is 7:6** 4428
from Judah, the **k** of Assyria." **Is 7:17** 4428
(*that is*, with the **k** of Assyria), **Is 7:20** 4428
away before the **k** of Assyria." **Is 8:4** 4428
k of Assyria and all his glory; **Is 8:7** 4428
will be enraged and curse their **k** **Is 8:21** 4428
the arrogant heart of the **k** of Assyria **Is 10:12** 4428
taunt against the **k** of Babylon, **Is 14:4** 4428
that **K** Ahaz died this oracle came: **Is 14:28** 4428
a mighty **k** will rule over them," **Is 19:4** 4428
when Sargon the **k** of Assyria sent **Is 20:1** 4428
so the **k** of Assyria will lead away **Is 20:4** 4428
delivered from the **k** of Assyria; **Is 20:6** 4428
years like the days of one **k**. **Is 23:15** 4428
it has been prepared for the **k**. **Is 30:33** 4428
a **k** will reign righteously And **Is 32:1** 4428
eyes will see the **K** in His beauty; **Is 33:17** 4428
our lawgiver, The LORD is our **k**; **Is 33:22** 4428
Whom they may proclaim **k** **Is 34:12** 4410
the fourteenth year of **K** Hezekiah, **Is 36:1** 4428
Sennacherib **k** of Assyria came up **Is 36:1** 4428
And the **k** of Assyria sent **Is 36:2** 4428
to **K** Hezekiah with a large army. **Is 36:2** 4428
'Thus says the great **k**, **Is 36:4** 4428
the great king, the **k** of Assyria, **Is 36:4** 4428
So is Pharaoh **k** of Egypt to all **Is 36:6** 4428
with my master the **k** of Assyria, **Is 36:8** 4428
"Hear the words of the great **k**, **Is 36:13** 4428
the great king, the **k** of Assyria. **Is 36:13** 4428
"Thus says the **k**, **Is 36:14** 4428
the hand of the **k** of Assyria." **Is 36:15** 4428
for thus says the **k** of Assyria, **Is 36:16** 4428
from the hand of the **k** of Assyria? **Is 36:18** 4428
And when **K** Hezekiah heard *it*, he **Is 37:1** 4428
whom his master the **k** of Assyria **Is 37:4** 4428
the servants of **K** Hezekiah came to **Is 37:5** 4428
k of Assyria have blasphemed Me. **Is 37:6** 4428
k of Assyria fighting against Libnah, **Is 37:8**
heard that the **k** had left Lachish. **Is 37:8**
say concerning Tirhakah **k** of Cush, **Is 37:9** 4428
shall say to Hezekiah **k** of Judah, **Is 37:10** 4428
the hand of the **k** of Assyria." **Is 37:10** 4428
'Where is the **k** of Hamath, the **Is 37:13** 4428
king of Hamath, the **k** of Arpad, **Is 37:13** 4428
the **k** of the city of Sepharvaim, **Is 37:13** 4428
Me about Sennacherib **k** of Assyria, **Is 37:21** 4428
LORD concerning the **k** of Assyria, **Is 37:33** 4428
So Sennacherib **k** of Assyria **Is 37:37** 4428
his son became **k** in his place. **Is 37:38** 4427a
from the hand of the **k** of Assyria; **Is 38:6** 4428
A writing of Hezekiah **k** of Judah after **Is 38:9** 4428
son of Baladan, **k** of Babylon, **Is 39:1** 4428
the prophet came to **K** Hezekiah **Is 39:3** 4428
palace of the **k** of Babylon.' " **Is 39:7** 4428
arguments," The **K** of Jacob says. **Is 41:21** 4428
The Creator of Israel, your **K**." **Is 43:15** 4428
the **K** of Israel And his Redeemer, **Is 44:6** 4428
"You have journeyed to the **k** **Is 57:9** 4428
the son of Amon, **k** of Judah, **Jer 1:2** 4428
the son of Josiah, **k** of Judah, **Jer 1:3** 4428
the son of Josiah, **k** of Judah, **Jer 1:3** 4428
to me in the days of Josiah the **k**, **Jer 3:6** 4428
"that the heart of the **k** and the **Jer 4:9** 4428
Is her **K** not within her?" **Jer 8:19** 4428
not fear You, O **K** of the nations? **Jer 10:7** 4428
living God and the everlasting **K**. **Jer 10:10** 4428
Say to the **k** and the queen mother, **Jer 13:18** 4428
son of Hezekiah, the **k** of Judah, **Jer 15:4** 4428
to the hand of the **k** of Babylon, **Jer 20:4** 4428
K Zedekiah sent to him Pashhur **Jer 21:1** 4428
for Nebuchadnezzar **k** of Babylon is **Jer 21:2** 4428
warring against the **k** of Babylon **Jer 21:4** 4428
will give over Zedekiah **k** of Judah **Jer 21:7** 4428
of Nebuchadnezzar **k** of Babylon, **Jer 21:7** 4428
into the hand of the **k** of Babylon and **Jer 21:10** 4428
the household of the **k** of Judah, **Jer 21:11** 4428
to the house of the **k** of Judah, **Jer 22:1** 4428
word of the LORD, O **k** of Judah, **Jer 22:2** 4428
even the **k** himself and his **Jer 22:4** 4428
the house of the **k** of Judah: **Jer 22:6** 4428
the son of Josiah, **k** of Judah, **Jer 22:11** 4428
who became **k** in the place of **Jer 22:11** 4427a
"Do you become a **k** because you **Jer 22:15** 4427a
the son of Josiah, **k** of Judah, **Jer 22:18** 4428
the son of Jehoiakim **k** of Judah **Jer 22:24** 4428
of Nebuchadnezzar **k** of Babylon and **Jer 22:25** 4428
And He will reign as **k** and act **Jer 23:5** 4428
After Nebuchadnezzar **k** of Babylon **Jer 24:1** 4428
the son of Jehoiakim, **k** of Judah, **Jer 24:1** 4428
I will abandon Zedekiah **k** of Judah **Jer 24:8** 4428
the son of Josiah, **k** of Judah **Jer 25:1** 4428
of Nebuchadnezzar **k** of Babylon), **Jer 25:1** 4428
the son of Amon, **k** of Judah, **Jer 25:3** 4428
to Nebuchadnezzar **k** of Babylon, **Jer 25:9** 4428
nations will serve the **k** of Babylon **Jer 25:11** 4428

the **k** of Babylon and that nation,'	**Jer 25:12**	4428
Pharaoh **k** of Egypt, his servants,	**Jer 25:19**	4428
and the **k** of Sheshach shall drink	**Jer 25:26**	4428
the son of Josiah, **k** of Judah,	**Jer 26:1**	4428
the days of Hezekiah **k** of Judah;	**Jer 26:18**	4428
"Did Hezekiah **k** of Judah and all	**Jer 26:19**	4428
When **K** Jehoiakim and all his	**Jer 26:21**	4428
the **k** sought to put him to death;	**Jer 26:21**	4428
K Jehoiakim sent men to Egypt:	**Jer 26:22**	4428
Egypt and led him to **K** Jehoiakim,	**Jer 26:23**	4428
the son of Josiah, **k** of Judah,	**Jer 27:1**	4428
and send word to the **k** of Edom,	**Jer 27:3**	4428
king of Edom, to the **k** of Moab,	**Jer 27:3**	4428
to the **k** of the sons of Ammon,	**Jer 27:3**	4428
sons of Ammon, to the **k** of Tyre and	**Jer 27:3**	4428
and to the **k** of Sidon by the	**Jer 27:3**	4428
Jerusalem to Zedekiah **k** of Judah.	**Jer 27:3**	4428
of Nebuchadnezzar **k** of Babylon,	**Jer 27:6**	4428
him, Nebuchadnezzar **k** of Babylon,	**Jer 27:8**	4428
the yoke of the **k** of Babylon,	**Jer 27:8**	4428
will not serve the **k** of Babylon.'	**Jer 27:9**	4428
of the **k** of Babylon and serve him,	**Jer 27:11**	4428
all these to Zedekiah **k** of Judah,	**Jer 27:12**	4428
the yoke of the **k** of Babylon and	**Jer 27:12**	4428
will not serve the **k** of Babylon?	**Jer 27:13**	4428
will not serve the **k** of Babylon,'	**Jer 27:14**	4428
serve the **k** of Babylon, and live!	**Jer 27:17**	4428
in the house of the **k** of Judah and	**Jer 27:18**	4428
which Nebuchadnezzar **k** of Babylon	**Jer 27:20**	4428
the son of Jehoiakim, **k** of Judah,	**Jer 27:20**	4428
in the house of the **k** of Judah and	**Jer 27:21**	4428
the reign of Zedekiah **k** of Judah,	**Jer 28:1**	4428
the yoke of the **k** of Babylon.	**Jer 28:2**	4428
which Nebuchadnezzar **k** of Babylon	**Jer 28:3**	4428
the son of Jehoiakim, **k** of Judah,	**Jer 28:4**	4428
the yoke of the **k** of Babylon.'"	**Jer 28:4**	4428
the yoke of Nebuchadnezzar **k** of	**Jer 28:11**	4428
serve Nebuchadnezzar **k** of Babylon;	**Jer 28:14**	4428
K Jeconiah and the queen mother,	**Jer 29:2**	4428
whom Zedekiah **k** of Judah sent to	**Jer 29:3**	4428
to Nebuchadnezzar **k** of Babylon,	**Jer 29:3**	4428
thus says the LORD concerning the **k**	**Jer 29:16**	4428
of Nebuchadnezzar **k** of Babylon,	**Jer 29:21**	4428
whom the **k** of Babylon roasted in	**Jer 29:22**	4428
LORD their God and David their **k**,	**Jer 30:9**	4428
tenth year of Zedekiah **k** of Judah,	**Jer 32:1**	4428
the army of the **k** of Babylon was	**Jer 32:2**	4428
in the house of the **k** of Judah,	**Jer 32:2**	4428
k of Judah had shut him up,	**Jer 32:3**	4428
into the hand of the **k** of Babylon,	**Jer 32:3**	4428
and Zedekiah **k** of Judah will not	**Jer 32:4**	4428
into the hand of the **k** of Babylon,	**Jer 32:4**	4428
of Nebuchadnezzar **k** of Babylon,	**Jer 32:28**	4428
hand of the **k** of Babylon by sword,	**Jer 32:36**	4428
k of Babylon and all his army,	**Jer 34:1**	4428
and speak to Zedekiah **k** of Judah	**Jer 34:2**	4428
into the hand of the **k** of Babylon,	**Jer 34:2**	4428
see the **k** of Babylon eye to eye,	**Jer 34:3**	4428
the LORD, O Zedekiah **k** of Judah!	**Jer 34:4**	4428
Zedekiah **k** of Judah in Jerusalem	**Jer 34:6**	4428
when the army of the **k** of Babylon	**Jer 34:7**	4428
after **K** Zedekiah had made a	**Jer 34:8**	4428
'Zedekiah **k** of Judah and his	**Jer 34:21**	4428
hand of the army of the **k** of Babylon	**Jer 34:21**	4428
the son of Josiah, **k** of Judah,	**Jer 35:1**	4428
when Nebuchadnezzar **k** of Babylon	**Jer 35:11**	4428
the son of Josiah, **k** of Judah,	**Jer 36:1**	4428
the son of Josiah, **k** of Judah,	**Jer 36:9**	4428
report all these words to the **k**."	**Jer 36:16**	4428
they went to the **k** in the court,	**Jer 36:20**	4428
reported all the words to the **k**.	**Jer 36:20**	4428
k sent Jehudi to get the scroll,	**Jer 36:21**	4428
And Jehudi read it to the **k** as	**Jer 36:21**	4428
officials who stood beside the **k**.	**Jer 36:21**	4428
Now the **k** was sitting in the	**Jer 36:22**	4428
k cut it with a scribe's knife	**Jer 36:23**	4428
Yet the **k** and all his servants who	**Jer 36:24**	4428
Gemariah pleaded with the **k** not to	**Jer 36:25**	4428
And the **k** commanded Jerahmeel the	**Jer 36:26**	4428
after the **k** had burned the scroll	**Jer 36:27**	4428
Jehoiakim the **k** of Judah burned.	**Jer 36:28**	4428
concerning Jehoiakim **k** of Judah	**Jer 36:29**	4428
the **k** of Babylon will certainly come	**Jer 36:29**	4428
concerning Jehoiakim **k** of Judah,	**Jer 36:30**	4428
Jehoiakim **k** of Judah had burned	**Jer 36:32**	4428
Nebuchadnezzar **k** of Babylon had	**Jer 37:1**	4428
had made **k** in the land of Judah,	**Jer 37:1**	4427a
reigned as **k** in place of Coniah	**Jer 37:1**	4428
Yet **K** Zedekiah sent Jehucal the	**Jer 37:3**	4428
you are to say to the **k** of Judah,	**Jer 37:7**	4428
Now **K** Zedekiah sent and took him	**Jer 37:17**	4428
the **k** secretly asked him and said,	**Jer 37:17**	4428
the hand of the **k** of Babylon!"	**Jer 37:17**	4428
Jeremiah said to **K** Zedekiah,	**Jer 37:18**	4428
'The **k** of Babylon will not come	**Jer 37:19**	4428
please listen, O my lord the **k**;	**Jer 37:20**	4428
Then **K** Zedekiah gave commandment,	**Jer 37:21**	4428
of the army of the **k** of Babylon and	**Jer 38:3**	4428
Then the officials said to the **k**,	**Jer 38:4**	4428
So **K** Zedekiah said,	**Jer 38:5**	4428
k can *do* nothing against you."	**Jer 38:5**	4428
Now the **k** was sitting in the Gate	**Jer 38:7**	4428
king's palace and spoke to the **k**,	**Jer 38:8**	4428
"My lord the **k**, these men have	**Jer 38:9**	4428
Then the **k** commanded Ebed-melech	**Jer 38:10**	4428
Then **K** Zedekiah sent and had	**Jer 38:14**	4428
and the **k** said to Jeremiah,	**Jer 38:14**	4428
But **K** Zedekiah swore to Jeremiah	**Jer 38:16**	4428
the officers of the **k** of Babylon,	**Jer 38:17**	4428
the officers of the **k** of Babylon,	**Jer 38:18**	4428
Then **K** Zedekiah said to Jeremiah,	**Jer 38:19**	4428
left in the palace of the **k** of Judah	**Jer 38:22**	4428
the officers of the **k** of Babylon;	**Jer 38:22**	4428
by the hand of the **k** of Babylon,	**Jer 38:23**	4428
us now what you said to the **k** and	**Jer 38:25**	4428
king and what the **k** said to you;	**Jer 38:25**	4428
my petition before the **k**,	**Jer 38:26**	4428
words which the **k** had commanded;	**Jer 38:27**	4428
ninth year of Zedekiah **k** of Judah,	**Jer 39:1**	4428
Nebuchadnezzar **k** of Babylon and	**Jer 39:1**	4428
all the officials of the **k** of Babylon	**Jer 39:3**	4428
the officials of the **k** of Babylon.	**Jer 39:3**	4428
When Zedekiah the **k** of Judah and	**Jer 39:4**	4428
up to Nebuchadnezzar **k** of Babylon	**Jer 39:5**	4428
Then the **k** of Babylon slew the	**Jer 39:6**	4428
the **k** of Babylon also slew all the	**Jer 39:6**	4428
Now Nebuchadnezzar **k** of Babylon	**Jer 39:11**	4428
officers of the **k** of Babylon;	**Jer 39:13**	4428
whom the **k** of Babylon has	**Jer 40:5**	4428
heard that the **k** of Babylon had	**Jer 40:7**	4428
land and serve the **k** of Babylon,	**Jer 40:9**	4428
heard that the **k** of Babylon had	**Jer 40:11**	4428
Baalis the **k** of the sons of Ammon	**Jer 40:14**	4428
of the chief officers of the **k**,	**Jer 41:1**	4428
the one whom the **k** of Babylon had	**Jer 41:2**	4428
it was the one that **K** Asa had made	**Jer 41:9**	4428
on account of Baasha, **k** of Israel;	**Jer 41:9**	4428
whom the **k** of Babylon had	**Jer 41:18**	4428
not be afraid of the **k** of Babylon,	**Jer 42:11**	4428
Nebuchadnezzar the **k** of Babylon,	**Jer 43:10**	4428
give over Pharaoh Hophra **k** of Egypt	**Jer 44:30**	4428
just as I gave over Zedekiah **k** of	**Jer 44:30**	4428
of Nebuchadnezzar **k** of Babylon,	**Jer 44:30**	4428
the son of Josiah, **k** of Judah,	**Jer 45:1**	4428
army of Pharaoh Neco **k** of Egypt,	**Jer 46:2**	4428
which Nebuchadnezzar **k** of Babylon	**Jer 46:2**	4428
the son of Josiah, **k** of Judah:	**Jer 46:2**	4428
of Nebuchadnezzar **k** of Babylon to	**Jer 46:13**	4428
k of Egypt *is but* a big noise;	**Jer 46:17**	4428
declares the **K** Whose name is the	**Jer 46:18**	4428
of Nebuchadnezzar **k** of Babylon	**Jer 46:26**	4428
to the slaughter," Declares the **K**,	**Jer 48:15**	4428
k of Babylon defeated.	**Jer 49:28**	4428
"For Nebuchadnezzar **k** of Babylon	**Jer 49:30**	4428
the reign of Zedekiah **k** of Judah,	**Jer 49:34**	4428
destroy out of it **k** and princes,'	**Jer 49:38**	4428
devoured him was the **k** of Assyria,	**Jer 50:17**	4428
is Nebuchadnezzar **k** of Babylon.	**Jer 50:17**	4428
the **k** of Babylon and his land,	**Jer 50:18**	4428
as I punished the **k** of Assyria.	**Jer 50:18**	4428
"The **k** of Babylon has heard the	**Jer 50:43**	4428
To tell the **k** of Babylon That his	**Jer 51:31**	4428
"Nebuchadnezzar **k** of Babylon has	**Jer 51:34**	4428
and not wake up," Declares the **K**,	**Jer 51:57**	4428
when he went with Zedekiah the **k**	**Jer 51:59**	4428
years old when he became **k**,	**Jer 52:1**	4427a
rebelled against the **k** of Babylon.	**Jer 52:3**	4428
Nebuchadnezzar **k** of Babylon came,	**Jer 52:4**	4428
the eleventh year of **K** Zedekiah.	**Jer 52:5**	4428
army of the Chaldeans pursued the **k**	**Jer 52:8**	4428
Then they captured the **k** and	**Jer 52:9**	4428
brought him up to the **k** of Babylon	**Jer 52:9**	4428
The **k** of Babylon slaughtered	**Jer 52:10**	4428
and the **k** of Babylon bound him	**Jer 52:11**	4428
year of **K** Nebuchadnezzar,	**Jer 52:12**	4428
King Nebuchadnezzar, **k** of Babylon,	**Jer 52:12**	4428
the service of the **k** of Babylon,	**Jer 52:12**	4428
had deserted to the **k** of Babylon and	**Jer 52:15**	4428
which **K** Solomon had made for the	**Jer 52:20**	4428
to the **k** of Babylon at Riblah.	**Jer 52:26**	4428
Then the **k** of Babylon struck them	**Jer 52:27**	4428
exile of Jehoiachin **k** of Judah,	**Jer 52:31**	4428
that Evil-merodach **k** of Babylon,	**Jer 52:31**	4428
showed favor to Jehoiachin **k** of	**Jer 52:31**	4428
was given him by the **k** of Babylon,	**Jer 52:34**	4428
And He has despised **k** and priest	**La 2:6**	4428
Her **k** and her princes are among	**La 2:9**	4428
fifth year of **K** Jehoiachin's exile,	**Ezk 1:2**	4428
'The **k** will mourn, the prince will	**Ezk 7:27**	4428
k of Babylon came to Jerusalem,	**Ezk 17:12**	4428
Jerusalem, took its **k** and princes and	**Ezk 17:12**	4428
the **k** who put him on the throne,	**Ezk 17:16**	4428
brought him to the **k** of Babylon;	**Ezk 19:9**	4428
poured out, I shall be **k** over you.	**Ezk 20:33**	4427a
sword of the **k** of Babylon to come;	**Ezk 21:19**	4428
"For the **k** of Babylon stands at	**Ezk 21:21**	4428
The **k** of Babylon has laid siege to	**Ezk 24:2**	4428
north Nebuchadnezzar **k** of Babylon,	**Ezk 26:7**	4428
king of Babylon, **k** of kings,	**Ezk 26:7**	4428
a lamentation over the **k** of Tyre and	**Ezk 28:12**	4428
face against Pharaoh **k** of Egypt	**Ezk 29:2**	4428
against you, Pharaoh **k** of Egypt,	**Ezk 29:3**	4428
Nebuchadnezzar **k** of Babylon made	**Ezk 29:18**	4428
to Nebuchadnezzar **k** of Babylon.	**Ezk 29:19**	4428
of Nebuchadnezzar **k** of Babylon.	**Ezk 30:10**	4428
the arm of Pharaoh **k** of Egypt;	**Ezk 30:21**	4428
I am against Pharaoh **k** of Egypt	**Ezk 30:22**	4428
the arms of the **k** of Babylon	**Ezk 30:24**	4428
the arms of the **k** of Babylon,	**Ezk 30:25**	4428
into the hand of the **k** of Babylon	**Ezk 30:25**	4428
of man, say to Pharaoh **k** of Egypt and	**Ezk 31:2**	4428
over Pharaoh **k** of Egypt and	**Ezk 32:2**	4428
"The sword of the **k** of Babylon	**Ezk 32:11**	4428
one **k** will be king for all of them;	**Ezk 37:22**	4428
one king will be **k** for all of them;	**Ezk 37:22**	4428
servant David will be **k** over them,	**Ezk 37:24**	4428
the reign of Jehoiakim **k** of Judah,	**Da 1:1**	4428
Nebuchadnezzar **k** of Babylon came	**Da 1:1**	4428
k of Judah into his hand,	**Da 1:2**	4428
Then the **k** ordered Ashpenaz, the	**Da 1:3**	4428
The **k** appointed for them a	**Da 1:5**	4428
"I am afraid of my lord the **k**,	**Da 1:10**	4428
me forfeit my head to the **k**."	**Da 1:10**	4428
the days which the **k** had specified	**Da 1:18**	4428
The **k** talked with them, and	**Da 1:19**	4428
about which the **k** consulted them,	**Da 1:20**	4428
the first year of Cyrus the **k**.	**Da 1:21**	4428
Then the **k** gave orders to call in	**Da 2:2**	4428
to tell the **k** his dreams.	**Da 2:2**	4428
came in and stood before the **k**.	**Da 2:2**	4428
The **k** said to them,	**Da 2:3**	4428
spoke to the **k** in Aramaic:	**Da 2:4**	4428
"O **k**, live forever!	**Da 2:4**	4430
The **k** replied to the	**Da 2:5**	4430
"Let the **k** tell the dream to his	**Da 2:7**	4430
The **k** replied,	**Da 2:8**	4430
Chaldeans answered the **k** and said,	**Da 2:10**	4430
declare the matter for the **k**,	**Da 2:10**	4430
inasmuch as no great **k** or ruler	**Da 2:10**	4430
which the **k** demands is difficult,	**Da 2:11**	4430
declare it to the **k** except gods,	**Da 2:11**	4430
the **k** became indignant and very	**Da 2:12**	4430
the decree from the **k** *so* urgent?"	**Da 2:15**	4430
went in and requested of the **k**	**Da 2:16**	4430
the interpretation to the **k**.	**Da 2:16**	4430
whom the **k** had appointed to	**Da 2:24**	4430
the interpretation to the **k**."	**Da 2:24**	4430
interpretation known to the **k**!"	**Da 2:25**	4430
The **k** said to Daniel,	**Da 2:26**	4430
answered before the **k** and said,	**Da 2:27**	4430
about which the **k** has inquired,	**Da 2:27**	4430
are able to declare *it* to the **k**.	**Da 2:27**	4430
made known to **K** Nebuchadnezzar	**Da 2:28**	4430
"As for you, O **k**, *while* on your	**Da 2:29**	4430
the interpretation known to the **k**,	**Da 2:30**	4430
"You, O **k**, were looking and	**Da 2:31**	4430
its interpretation before the **k**.	**Da 2:36**	4430
"You, O **k**, are the king of kings,	**Da 2:37**	4430
"You, O king, are the **k** of kings,	**Da 2:37**	4430
great God has made known to the **k**	**Da 2:45**	4430
Then **K** Nebuchadnezzar fell on his	**Da 2:46**	4430
The **k** answered Daniel and said,	**Da 2:47**	4430
Then the **k** promoted Daniel and	**Da 2:48**	4430
And Daniel made request of the **k**,	**Da 2:49**	4430
the **k** made an image of gold,	**Da 3:1**	4430
Then Nebuchadnezzar the **k** sent	**Da 3:2**	4430
Nebuchadnezzar the **k** had set up.	**Da 3:2**	4430
Nebuchadnezzar the **k** had set up;	**Da 3:3**	4430
Nebuchadnezzar the **k** has set up.	**Da 3:5**	4430
Nebuchadnezzar the **k** had set up.	**Da 3:7**	4430
and said to Nebuchadnezzar the **k**:	**Da 3:9**	4430
"O **k**, live forever!	**Da 3:9**	4430
"You, O **k**, have made a	**Da 3:10**	4430
These men, O **k**, have disregarded	**Da 3:12**	4430
men were brought before the **k**.	**Da 3:13**	4430
replied to the **k**,	**Da 3:16**	4430
deliver us out of your hand, O **k**.	**Da 3:17**	4430
not, let it be known to you, O **k**,	**Da 3:18**	4430
Then Nebuchadnezzar the **k** was	**Da 3:24**	4430
They replied to the **k**,	**Da 3:24**	4430
"Certainly, O **k**."	**Da 3:24**	4430
Then the **k** caused Shadrach,	**Da 3:30**	4430
the **k** to all the peoples,	**Da 4:1**	4430
dream *which* I, **K** Nebuchadnezzar,	**Da 4:18**	4430
The **k** responded and said,	**Da 4:19**	4430
it is you, O **k**; for you have become	**Da 4:22**	4430
that the **k** saw an *angelic* watcher,	**Da 4:23**	4430
this is the interpretation, O **k**,	**Da 4:24**	4430
which has come upon my lord the **k**:	**Da 4:24**	4430
'Therefore, O **k**, may my advice be	**Da 4:27**	4430
happened to Nebuchadnezzar the **k**.	**Da 4:28**	4430
"The **k** reflected and said,	**Da 4:30**	4430
'**K** Nebuchadnezzar, to you it is	**Da 4:31**	4430
exalt and honor the **K** of heaven,	**Da 4:37**	4430
Belshazzar the **k** held a great	**Da 5:1**	4430
so that the **k** and his nobles,	**Da 5:2**	4430
and the **k** and his nobles, his	**Da 5:3**	4430
and the **k** saw the back of the hand	**Da 5:5**	4430
The **k** called aloud to bring in the	**Da 5:7**	4430
The **k** spoke and said to the wise	**Da 5:7**	4430
known its interpretation to the **k**.	**Da 5:8**	4430
Then **K** Belshazzar was greatly	**Da 5:9**	4430
the words of the **k** and his nobles;	**Da 5:10**	4430
"O **k**, live forever!	**Da 5:10**	4430
And **K** Nebuchadnezzar, your father,	**Da 5:11**	4430
your father, your father the **k**,	**Da 5:11**	4430
whom the **k** named Belteshazzar.	**Da 5:12**	4430
was brought in before the **k**.	**Da 5:13**	4430
The **k** spoke and said to Daniel,	**Da 5:13**	4430
father the **k** brought from Judah?	**Da 5:13**	4430
answered and said before the **k**,	**Da 5:17**	4430
I will read the inscription to the **k**	**Da 5:17**	4430
"O **k**, the Most High God granted	**Da 5:18**	4430
the Chaldean **k** was slain.	**Da 5:30**	4430
that the **k** might not suffer loss.	**Da 6:2**	4430
and the **k** planned to appoint him	**Da 6:3**	4430
satraps came by agreement to the **k**	**Da 6:6**	4430
"**K** Darius, live forever!	**Da 6:6**	4430
that the **k** should establish a statute	**Da 6:7**	4430
any god or man besides you, O **k**,	**Da 6:7**	4430
"Now, O **k**, establish the	**Da 6:8**	4430
K Darius signed the document,	**Da 6:9**	4430
spoke before the **k** about the king's	**Da 6:12**	4430
any god or man besides you, O **k**,	**Da 6:12**	4430
The **k** replied,	**Da 6:12**	4430
answered and spoke before the **k**,	**Da 6:13**	4430
pays no attention to you, O **k**,	**Da 6:13**	4430

as the **k** heard this statement,	**Da 6:14**	4430
to the **k** and said to the king,	**Da 6:15**	4430
to the king and said to the **k**,	**Da 6:15**	4430
"Recognize, O **k**, that it is a law	**Da 6:15**	4430
or statute which the **k** establishes	**Da 6:15**	4430
Then the **k** gave orders, and Daniel	**Da 6:16**	4430
The **k** spoke and said to Daniel,	**Da 6:16**	4430
and the **k** sealed it with his own	**Da 6:17**	4430
Then the **k** went off to his palace	**Da 6:18**	4430
Then the **k** arose at dawn, at	**Da 6:19**	4430
The **k** spoke and said to Daniel,	**Da 6:20**	4430
Then Daniel spoke to the **k**,	**Da 6:21**	4430
"O **k**, live forever!	**Da 6:21**	4430
and also toward you, O **k**,	**Da 6:22**	4430
Then the **k** was very pleased and	**Da 6:23**	4430
The **k** then gave orders, and they	**Da 6:24**	4430
the **k** wrote to all the peoples,	**Da 6:25**	4430
In the first year of Belshazzar **k**	**Da 7:1**	4430
year of the reign of Belshazzar the **k**	**Da 8:1**	4428
between his eyes is the first **k**.	**Da 8:21**	4428
A **k** will arise, Insolent and	**Da 8:23**	4428
who was made **k** over the kingdom of	**Da 9:1**	4427a
the third year of Cyrus **k** of Persia	**Da 10:1**	4428
"And a mighty **k** will arise, and	**Da 11:3**	4428
k of the South will grow strong,	**Da 11:5**	4428
the daughter of the **k** of the South	**Da 11:6**	4428
come to the **k** of the North to carry	**Da 11:6**	4428
fortress of the **k** of the North,	**Da 11:7**	4428
the **k** of the North for *some* years.	**Da 11:8**	4428
the realm of the **k** of the South,	**Da 11:9**	4428
"The **k** of the South will be	**Da 11:11**	4428
and fight with the **k** of the North.	**Da 11:11**	4428
"For the **k** of the North will	**Da 11:13**	4428
up against the **k** of the South;	**Da 11:14**	4428
"Then the **k** of the North will	**Da 11:15**	4428
courage against the **k** of the South	**Da 11:25**	4428
so the **k** of the South will	**Da 11:25**	4428
"Then the **k** will do as he	**Da 11:36**	4428
At the end time the **k** of the South	**Da 11:40**	4428
and the **k** of the North will storm	**Da 11:40**	4428
the son of Joash, **k** of Israel.	**Hos 1:1**	4428
for many days without **k** or prince,	**Hos 3:4**	4428
LORD their God and David their **k**;	**Hos 3:5**	4428
Listen, O house of the **k**!	**Hos 5:1**	4428
to Assyria And sent to **K** Jareb.	**Hos 5:13**	4428
wickedness they make the **k** glad,	**Hos 7:3**	4428
On the day of our **k**,	**Hos 7:5**	4428
of the burden of the **k** of princes.	**Hos 8:10**	4428
"We have no **k**, For we do not	**Hos 10:3**	4428
As for the **k**, what can he do for	**Hos 10:3**	4428
to Assyria As tribute to **K** Jareb;	**Hos 10:6**	4428
will be cut off *with* her **k** Like	**Hos 10:7**	4428
At dawn the **k** of Israel will be	**Hos 10:15**	4428
But Assyria—he will be their **k** Because	**Hos 11:5**	4428
Where now is your **k** That he may	**Hos 13:10**	4428
"Give me a **k** and princes"?	**Hos 13:10**	4428
I gave you a **k** in My anger And	**Hos 13:11**	4428
in the days of Uzziah **k** of Judah,	**Am 1:1**	4428
Jeroboam son of Joash, **k** of Israel,	**Am 1:1**	4428
"Their **k** will go into exile, He	**Am 1:15**	4428
burned the bones of the **k** of Edom	**Am 2:1**	4428
along Sikkuth your **k** and Kiyyun,	**Am 5:26**	4428
word to Jeroboam **k** of Israel,	**Am 7:10**	4428
of the **k** and a royal residence."	**Am 7:13**	4428
the word reached the **k** of Nineveh,	**Jon 3:6**	4428
decree of the **k** and his nobles:	**Jon 3:7**	4428
So their **k** goes on before them,	**Mi 2:13**	4428
Is there no **k** among you, Or has	**Mi 4:9**	4428
remember now What Balak **k** of Moab	**Mi 6:5**	4428
are sleeping, O **k** of Assyria;	**Na 3:18**	4428
of Josiah son of Amon, **k** of Judah:	**Zph 1:1**	4428
The **K** of Israel, the LORD, is in	**Zph 3:15**	4428
the second year of Darius the **k**,	**Hg 1:1**	4428
the second year of Darius the **k**.	**Hg 1:15**	4428
In the fourth year of **K** Darius,	**Zch 7:1**	4428
the **k** will perish from Gaza,	**Zch 9:5**	4428
Behold, your **k** is coming to you;	**Zch 9:9**	4428
power and into the power of his **k**;	**Zch 11:6**	4428
in the days of Uzziah **k** of Judah.	**Zch 14:5**	4428
LORD will be **k** over all the earth;	**Zch 14:9**	4428
year to year to worship the **K**,	**Zch 14:16**	4428
up to Jerusalem to worship the **K**,	**Zch 14:17**	4428
to the Lord, for I am a great **K**,"	**Mal 1:14**	4428
Jesse was the father of David the **k**.	**Mt 1:6**	*935*
Judea in the days of Herod the **k**,	**Mt 2:1**	*935*
who has been born **K** of the Jews?	**Mt 2:2**	*935*
When Herod the **k** heard	**Mt 2:3**	*935*
After hearing the **k**,	**Mt 2:9**	*935*
for it is THE CITY OF THE GREAT **K**.	**Mt 5:35**	*935*
the **k** commanded *it* to be given	**Mt 14:9**	*935*
k who wished to settle accounts with	**Mt 18:23**	*935*
'BEHOLD YOUR **K** IS COMING TO YOU,	**Mt 21:5**	*935*
of heaven may be compared to a **k** who	**Mt 22:2**	*444, 935*
"But the **k** was enraged, and he sent	**Mt 22:7**	*935*
"But when the **k** came in to look	**Mt 22:11**	*935*
"Then the **k** said to the servants,	**Mt 22:13**	*935*
"Then the **K** will say to those on	**Mt 25:34**	*935*
The **K** will answer and say to them,	**Mt 25:40**	*935*
"Are You the **K** of the Jews?"	**Mt 27:11**	*935*
"Hail, **K** of the Jews!"	**Mt 27:29**	*935*
JESUS THE **K** OF THE JEWS."	**Mt 27:37**	*935*
He is the **K** of Israel;	**Mt 27:42**	*935*
And **K** Herod heard *of it*, for His	**Mk 6:14**	*935*
and the **k** said to the girl,	**Mk 6:22**	*935*
in a hurry to the **k** and asked,	**Mk 6:25**	*935*
And although the **k** was very sorry,	**Mk 6:26**	*935*
Immediately the **k** sent an	**Mk 6:27**	*935*
"Are You the **K** of the Jews?"	**Mk 15:2**	*935*
for you the **K** of the Jews?"	**Mk 15:9**	*935*
whom you call the **K** of the Jews?"	**Mk 15:12**	*935*
"Hail, **K** of the Jews!"	**Mk 15:18**	*935*
"THE **K** OF THE JEWS."	**Mk 15:26**	*935*
"Let *this* Christ, the **K** of Israel,	**Mk 15:32**	*935*
In the days of Herod, **k** of Judea,	**Lk 1:5**	*935*
"Or what **k**, when he sets out to	**Lk 14:31**	*935*
out to meet another **k** in battle,	**Lk 14:31**	*935*
"BLESSED IS THE **K** WHO COMES IN	**Lk 19:38**	*935*
that He Himself is Christ, a **K**."	**Lk 23:2**	*935*
"Are You the **K** of the Jews?"	**Lk 23:3**	*935*
"If You are the **K** of the Jews,	**Lk 23:37**	*935*
"THIS IS THE **K** OF THE JEWS."	**Lk 23:38**	*935*
You are the **K** of Israel."	**Jn 1:49**	*935*
take Him by force to make Him **k**,	**Jn 6:15**	*935*
THE LORD, even the **K** of Israel."	**Jn 12:13**	*935*
BEHOLD, YOUR **K** IS COMING, SEATED	**Jn 12:15**	*935*
"Are You the **K** of the Jews?"	**Jn 18:33**	*935*
"So You are a **k**?"	**Jn 18:37**	*935*
"You say *correctly* that I am a **k**.	**Jn 18:37**	*935*
for you the **K** of the Jews?"	**Jn 18:39**	*935*
"Hail, **K** of the Jews!"	**Jn 19:3**	*935*
who makes himself out *to be* a **k**	**Jn 19:12**	*935*
"Behold, your **K**!"	**Jn 19:14**	*935*
"Shall I crucify your **K**?"	**Jn 19:15**	*935*
"We have no **k** but Caesar."	**Jn 19:15**	*935*
THE **K** OF THE JEWS."	**Jn 19:19**	*935*
'The **K** of the Jews';	**Jn 19:21**	*935*
'I am **K** of the Jews.' "	**Jn 19:21**	*935*
the sight of Pharaoh, **k** of Egypt,	**Ac 7:10**	*935*
AROSE ANOTHER **K** OVER EGYPT	**Ac 7:18**	*935*
Now about that time Herod the **k**	**Ac 12:1**	*935*
"Then they asked for a **k**,	**Ac 13:21**	*935*
He raised up David to be their **k**,	**Ac 13:22**	*935*
saying that there is another **k**,	**Ac 17:7**	*935*
K Agrippa and Bernice arrived at	**Ac 25:13**	*935*
laid Paul's case before the **k**,	**Ac 25:14**	*935*
"**K** Agrippa, and all you gentlemen	**Ac 25:24**	*935*
especially before you, **K** Agrippa,	**Ac 25:26**	*935*
myself fortunate, **K** Agrippa,	**Ac 26:2**	*935*
And for this hope, O **K**,	**Ac 26:7**	*935*
at midday, O **K**, I saw on the way a	**Ac 26:13**	*935*
"So, **K** Agrippa, I did	**Ac 26:19**	*935*
the **k** knows about these matters,	**Ac 26:26**	*935*
"**K** Agrippa, do you believe the	**Ac 26:27**	*935*
The **k** stood up and the governor	**Ac 26:30**	*935*
the ethnarch under Aretas the **k** was	**2Co 11:32**	*935*
Now to the **K** eternal, immortal,	**1Tm 1:17**	*935*
the **K** of kings and Lord of lords,	**1Tm 6:15**	*935*
For this Melchizedek, **k** of Salem,	**Heb 7:1**	*935*
of his name, **k** of righteousness,	**Heb 7:2**	*935*
and then also **k** of Salem,	**Heb 7:2**	*935*
of Salem, which is **k** of peace.	**Heb 7:2**	*935*
not fearing the wrath of the **k**;	**Heb 11:27**	*935*
to a **k** as the one in authority,	**1Pe 2:13**	*935*
fear God, honor the **k**.	**1Pe 2:17**	*935*
They have as **k** over them, the	**Rv 9:11**	*935*
Your ways, **K** of the nations!	**Rv 15:3**	*935*
is Lord of lords and **K** of kings,	**Rv 17:14**	*935*
"**K** OF KINGS, AND LORD OF	**Rv 19:16**	*935*
KINGDOM		
The beginning of his **k** was	**Gn 10:10**	4467
on me and on my **k** a great sin?	**Gn 20:9**	4467
a **k** of priests and a holy nation.'	**Ex 19:6**	4467
Agag, And his **k** shall be exalted.	**Nu 24:7**	4438
son Manasseh, the **k** of Sihon,	**Nu 32:33**	4467
of the Amorites and the **k** of Og,	**Nu 32:33**	4467
of Argob, the **k** of Og in Bashan.	**Dt 3:4**	4467
cities of the **k** of Og in Bashan.	**Dt 3:10**	4467
and All Bashan, the **k** of Og,	**Dt 3:13**	4467
he sits on the throne of his **k**,	**Dt 17:18**	4467
his sons may continue long in his **k**	**Dt 17:20**	4467
all the **k** of Og in Bashan, who	**Jos 13:12**	4468
the **k** of Sihon king of the Amorites	**Jos 13:21**	4468
of the **k** of Sihon king of Heshbon,	**Jos 13:27**	4468
all the **k** of Og king of Bashan,	**Jos 13:30**	4468
cities of the **k** of Og in Bashan,	**Jos 13:31**	4468
the **k** which Samuel had mentioned.	**1Sa 10:16**	4410
people the ordinances of the **k**,	**1Sa 10:25**	4410
to Gilgal and renew the **k** there."	**1Sa 11:14**	4410
LORD would have established your **k**	**1Sa 13:13**	4467
"But now your **k** shall not endure.	**1Sa 13:14**	4467
Saul had taken the **k** over Israel,	**1Sa 14:47**	4410
The LORD has torn the **k** of Israel	**1Sa 15:28**	4468
what more can he have but the **k**?"	**1Sa 18:8**	4410
nor your **k** will be established.	**1Sa 20:31**	4438
and that the **k** of Israel will be	**1Sa 24:20**	4467
for the LORD has torn the **k** out of	**1Sa 28:17**	4467
to transfer the **k** from the house of	**2Sa 3:10**	4467
"I and my **k** are innocent before	**2Sa 3:28**	4467
and that He had exalted his **k** for	**2Sa 5:12**	4467
you, and I will establish his **k**.	**2Sa 7:12**	4467
establish the throne of his **k** forever.	**2Sa 7:13**	4467
"Your house and your **k** shall	**2Sa 7:16**	4467
will restore the **k** of my father to me.	**2Sa 16:3**	4468
and the LORD has given the **k** into	**2Sa 16:8**	4410
his seat on the throne of the **k**.	**1Ki 1:46**	4410
and his **k** was firmly established.	**1Ki 2:12**	4438
"You know that the **k** was mine and	**1Ki 2:15**	4410
the **k** has turned about and become	**1Ki 2:15**	4410
Ask for him also the **k**	**1Ki 2:22**	4410
Thus the **k** was established in the	**1Ki 2:46**	4467
of your **k** over Israel forever,	**1Ki 9:5**	4467
like *it* was made for any other **k**.	**1Ki 10:20**	4467
I will surely tear the **k** from you,	**1Ki 11:11**	4467
I will not tear away all the **k**,	**1Ki 11:13**	4467
I will tear the **k** out of the hand	**1Ki 11:31**	4467
take the whole **k** out of his hand,	**1Ki 11:34**	4467
but I will take the **k** from his	**1Ki 11:35**	4410
to restore the **k** to Rehoboam	**1Ki 12:21**	4410
"Now the **k** will return to the	**1Ki 12:26**	4467
and tore the **k** away from the house	**1Ki 14:8**	4467
there is no nation or **k** where my	**1Ki 18:10**	4467
he made the **k** or nation swear that	**1Ki 18:10**	4467
as the **k** was firmly in his hand,	**2Ki 14:5**	4467
strengthen the **k** under his rule.	**2Ki 15:19**	4467
the **k** to David the son of Jesse.	**1Ch 10:14**	4410
gave him strong support in his **k**,	**1Ch 11:10**	4438
to turn the **k** of Saul to him,	**1Ch 12:23**	4438
and that his **k** was highly exalted,	**1Ch 14:2**	4438
And from *one* **k** to another people,	**1Ch 16:20**	4467
and I will establish his **k**.	**1Ch 17:11**	4438
in My house and in My **k** forever,	**1Ch 17:14**	4438
of his **k** over Israel forever.'	**1Ch 22:10**	4438
of the **k** of the LORD over Israel.	**1Ch 28:5**	4438
I will establish his **k** forever if	**1Ch 28:7**	4438
himself securely over his **k**,	**2Ch 1:1**	4438
like *it* was made for any *other* **k**.	**2Ch 9:19**	4467
to restore the **k** to Rehoboam.	**2Ch 11:1**	4467
They strengthened the **k** of Judah	**2Ch 11:17**	4438
the **k** of Rehoboam was established	**2Ch 12:1**	4438
you intend to resist the **k** of the LORD	**2Ch 13:8**	4467
the **k** was undisturbed under him.	**2Ch 14:5**	4467
established the **k** in his control,	**2Ch 17:5**	4467
the **k** of Jehoshaphat was at peace,	**2Ch 20:30**	4438
but he gave the **k** to Jehoram	**2Ch 21:3**	4467
when Jehoram had taken over the **k**	**2Ch 21:4**	4467
to retain the power of the **k**.	**2Ch 22:9**	4467
as the **k** was firmly in his grasp,	**2Ch 25:3**	4467
for a sin offering for the **k**,	**2Ch 29:21**	4467
for no god of any nation or **k** was	**2Ch 32:15**	4467
him again to Jerusalem to his **k**.	**2Ch 33:13**	4438
until the rule of the **k** of Persia,	**2Ch 36:20**	4438
a proclamation throughout his **k**,	**2Ch 36:22**	4438
proclamation throughout all his **k**,	**Ezr 1:1**	4438
the Levites in my **k** who are willing	**Ezr 7:13**	4437
the **k** of the king and his sons.	**Ezr 7:23**	4437
"But they, in their own **k**,	**Ne 9:35**	4438
sat in the first place in the **k**	**Es 1:14**	4438
is heard throughout all his **k**,	**Es 1:20**	4438
overseers in all the provinces of his **k**	**Es 2:3**	4438
the whole **k** of Ahasuerus.	**Es 3:6**	4438
in all the provinces of your **k**;	**Es 3:8**	4438
Even to half of the **k** it shall be given	**Es 5:3**	4438
half of the **k** it shall be done."	**Es 5:6**	4438
half of the **k** it shall be done."	**Es 7:2**	4438
provinces of the **k** of Ahasuerus,	**Es 9:30**	4438
For the **k** is the LORD's And He	**Ps 22:28**	4410
is the scepter of Your **k**.	**Ps 45:6**	4438
From *one* **k** to another people.	**Ps 105:13**	4467
shall speak of the glory of Your **k** And	**Ps 145:11**	4438
the glory of the majesty of Your **k**.	**Ps 145:12**	4438
Your **k** is an everlasting kingdom,	**Ps 145:13**	4438
Your kingdom is an everlasting **k**,	**Ps 145:13**	4438
though he was born poor in his **k**.	**Ec 4:14**	4438
throne of David and over his **k**,	**Is 9:7**	4467
city *and* **k** against kingdom.	**Is 19:2**	4467
city *and* kingdom against **k**.	**Is 19:2**	4467
"For the nation and the **k** which	**Is 60:12**	4467
or concerning a **k** to uproot,	**Jer 18:7**	4467
a **k** to build up or to plant *it*;	**Jer 18:9**	4467
or the **k** which will not serve him,	**Jer 27:8**	4467
profaned the **k** and its princes.	**La 2:2**	4467
that the **k** might be in subjection,	**Ezk 17:14**	4467
and there they will be a lowly **k**.	**Ezk 29:14**	4467
the God of heaven has given the **k**,	**Da 2:37**	4437
arise another **k** inferior to you,	**Da 2:39**	4437
then another third **k** of bronze,	**Da 2:39**	4437
be a fourth **k** as strong as iron;	**Da 2:40**	4437
of iron, it will be a divided **k**;	**Da 2:41**	4437
so some of the **k** will be strong	**Da 2:42**	4437
a **k** which will never be destroyed,	**Da 2:44**	4437
and *that* **k** will not be left for	**Da 2:44**	4437
His **k** is an everlasting kingdom And	**Da 4:3**	4437
His kingdom is an everlasting **k** And	**Da 4:3**	4437
none of the wise men of my **k** is able	**Da 4:18**	4437
your **k** will be assured to you	**Da 4:26**	4437
And His **k** *endures* from generation	**Da 4:34**	4437
to me for the glory of my **k**,	**Da 4:36**	4437
as third *ruler* in the **k**."	**Da 5:7**	4437
"There is a man in your **k** in whom	**Da 5:11**	4437
as the third *ruler* in the **k**."	**Da 5:16**	4437
God has numbered your **k** and put	**Da 5:26**	4437
your **k** has been divided and given	**Da 5:28**	4437
as the third *ruler* in the **k**.	**Da 5:29**	4437
So Darius the Mede received the **k**	**Da 5:31**	4437
to appoint 120 satraps over the **k**,	**Da 6:1**	4437
be in charge of the whole **k**,	**Da 6:1**	4437
to appoint him over the entire **k**.	**Da 6:3**	4437
"All the commissioners of the **k**,	**Da 6:7**	4437
in all the dominion of my **k** men are	**Da 6:26**	4437
And His **k** is one which will not be	**Da 6:26**	4437
was given dominion, Glory and a **k**,	**Da 7:14**	4437
And His **k** is one Which will not be	**Da 7:14**	4437
will receive the **k** and possess the	**Da 7:18**	4437
kingdom and possess the **k** forever,	**Da 7:18**	4437
saints took possession of the **k**.	**Da 7:22**	4437
will be a fourth **k** on the earth,	**Da 7:23**	4437
of this **k** ten kings will arise;	**Da 7:24**	4437
His **k** *will be* an everlasting	**Da 7:27**	4437
kingdom *will be* an everlasting **k**,	**Da 7:27**	4437
goat *represents* the **k** of Greece,	**Da 8:21**	4428
king over the **k** of the Chaldeans	**Da 9:1**	4438
"But the prince of the **k** of Persia	**Da 10:13**	4438
his **k** will be broken up and	**Da 11:4**	4438
with the power of his whole **k**,	**Da 11:17**	4438
through the Jewel of *his* **k**;	**Da 11:20**	4438
and seize the **k** by intrigue.	**Da 11:21**	4438
to the **k** of the house of Israel.	**Hos 1:4**	4468

the Lord GOD are on the sinful **k**, **Am 9:8** 4467
Esau, And the **k** will be the LORD's. **Ob 1:21** 4410
k of the daughter of Jerusalem. **Mi 4:8** 4467
for the **k** of heaven is at hand." **Mt 3:2** *932*
for the **k** of heaven is at hand." **Mt 4:17** *932*
proclaiming the gospel of the **k**, **Mt 4:23** *932*
for theirs is the **k** of heaven. **Mt 5:3** *932*
for theirs is the **k** of heaven. **Mt 5:10** *932*
called least in the **k** of heaven; **Mt 5:19** *932*
called great in the **k** of heaven. **Mt 5:19** *932*
will not enter the **k** of heaven. **Mt 5:20** *932*
'Your **k** come. Your will be done, **Mt 6:10** *932*
For Yours is the **k** and **Mt 6:13** *932*
first His **k** and His righteousness, **Mt 6:33** *932*
Lord,' will enter the **k** of heaven, **Mt 7:21** *932*
and Jacob in the **k** of heaven; **Mt 8:11** *932*
but the sons of the **k** will be **Mt 8:12** *932*
proclaiming the gospel of the **k**, **Mt 9:35** *932*
'The **k** of heaven is at hand.' **Mt 10:7** *932*
k of heaven is greater than he. **Mt 11:11** *932*
the **k** of heaven suffers violence, **Mt 11:12** *932*
"Any **k** divided against itself is **Mt 12:25** *932*
how then will his **k** stand? **Mt 12:26** *932*
the **k** of God has come upon you. **Mt 12:28** *932*
the mysteries of the **k** of heaven, **Mt 13:11** *932*
anyone hears the word of the **k** and **Mt 13:19** *932*
"The **k** of heaven may be compared **Mt 13:24** *932*
"The **k** of heaven is like a **Mt 13:31** *932*
"The **k** of heaven is like leaven, **Mt 13:33** *932*
seed, these are the sons of the **k**; **Mt 13:38** *932*
out of His **k** all stumbling blocks, **Mt 13:41** *932*
THE SUN in the **k** of their Father. **Mt 13:43** *932*
"The **k** of heaven is like a **Mt 13:44** *932*
the **k** of heaven is like a merchant **Mt 13:45** *932*
the **k** of heaven is like a dragnet **Mt 13:47** *932*
become a disciple of the **k** of heaven **Mt 13:52** *932*
you the keys of the **k** of heaven; **Mt 16:19** *932*
the Son of Man coming in His **k**." **Mt 16:28** *932*
is greatest in the **k** of heaven?" **Mt 18:1** *932*
will not enter the **k** of heaven. **Mt 18:3** *932*
the greatest in the **k** of heaven. **Mt 18:4** *932*
"For this reason the **k** of heaven **Mt 18:23** *932*
for the sake of the **k** of heaven. **Mt 19:12** *932*
for the **k** of heaven belongs to **Mt 19:14** *932*
rich man to enter the **k** of heaven. **Mt 19:23** *932*
rich man to enter the **k** of God." **Mt 19:24** *932*
"For the **k** of heaven is like a **Mt 20:1** *932*
"Command that in Your **k** these two **Mt 20:21** *932*
get into the **k** of God before you. **Mt 21:31** *932*
the **k** of God will be taken away **Mt 21:43** *932*
"The **k** of heaven may be compared **Mt 22:2** *932*
shut off the **k** of heaven from people; **Mt 23:13** *932*
nation, and **k** against kingdom, **Mt 24:7** *932*
nation, and kingdom against **k**, **Mt 24:7** *932*
"This gospel of the **k** shall **Mt 24:14** *932*
"Then the **k** of heaven will be **Mt 25:1** *932*
inherit the **k** prepared for you **Mt 25:34** *932*
it new with you in My Father's **k**." **Mt 26:29** *932*
and the **k** of God is at hand; **Mk 1:15** *932*
If a **k** is divided against itself, **Mk 3:24** *932*
itself, that **k** cannot stand. **Mk 3:24** *932*
given the mystery of the **k** of God, **Mk 4:11** *932*
"The **k** of God is like a man who **Mk 4:26** *932*
"How shall we picture the **k** of God, **Mk 4:30** *932*
up to half of my **k**." **Mk 6:23** *932*
not taste death until they see the **k** **Mk 9:1** *932*
enter the **k** of God with one eye, **Mk 9:47** *932*
for the **k** of God belongs to such **Mk 10:14** *932*
does not receive the **k** of God like a **Mk 10:15** *932*
wealthy to enter the **k** of God!" **Mk 10:23** *932*
hard it is to enter the **k** of God! **Mk 10:24** *932*
rich man to enter the **k** of God." **Mk 10:25** *932*
the coming **k** of our father David; **Mk 11:10** *932*
are not far from the **k** of God." **Mk 12:34** *932*
nation, and **k** against kingdom; **Mk 13:8** *932*
nation, and kingdom against **k**; **Mk 13:8** *932*
I drink it new in the **k** of God." **Mk 14:25** *932*
was waiting for the **k** of God; **Mk 15:43** *932*
and His **k** will have no end." **Lk 1:33** *932*
"I must preach the **k** of God to **Lk 4:43** *932*
poor, for yours is the **k** of God. **Lk 6:20** *932*
yet he who is least in the **k** of God is **Lk 7:28** *932*
and preaching the **k** of God. **Lk 8:1** *932*
the mysteries of the **k** of God, **Lk 8:10** *932*
them out to proclaim the **k** of God and **Lk 9:2** *932*
speaking to them about the **k** of God **Lk 9:11** *932*
until they see the **k** of God." **Lk 9:27** *932*
proclaim everywhere the **k** of God." **Lk 9:60** *932*
back, is fit for the **k** of God." **Lk 9:62** *932*
k of God has come near to you.' **Lk 10:9** *932*
that the **k** of God has come near.' **Lk 10:11** *932*
hallowed be Your name. Your **k** come. **Lk 11:2** *932*
"Any **k** divided against itself is **Lk 11:17** *932*
himself, how will his **k** stand? **Lk 11:18** *932*
the **k** of God has come upon you. **Lk 11:20** *932*
"But seek His **k**, **Lk 12:31** *932*
chosen gladly to give you the **k**. **Lk 12:32** *932*
"What is the **k** of God like, and **Lk 13:18** *932*
what shall I compare the **k** of God? **Lk 13:20** *932*
all the prophets in the **k** of God, **Lk 13:28** *932*
at the table in the **k** of God. **Lk 13:29** *932*
will eat bread in the **k** of God!" **Lk 14:15** *932*
the **k** of God has been preached, **Lk 16:16** *932*
to when the **k** of God was coming, **Lk 17:20** *932*
"The **k** of God is not coming with **Lk 17:20** *932*
the **k** of God is in your midst." **Lk 17:21** *932*
for the **k** of God belongs to such **Lk 18:16** *932*
does not receive the **k** of God like a **Lk 18:17** *932*
are wealthy to enter the **k** of God! **Lk 18:24** *932*
rich man to enter the **k** of God." **Lk 18:25** *932*
for the sake of the **k** of God, **Lk 18:29** *932*
they supposed that the **k** of God **Lk 19:11** *932*
to receive a **k** for himself, **Lk 19:12** *932*
returned, after receiving the **k**, **Lk 19:15** *932*
nation and **k** against kingdom, **Lk 21:10** *932*
nation and kingdom against **k**, **Lk 21:10** *932*
that the **k** of God is near. **Lk 21:31** *932*
it is fulfilled in the **k** of God." **Lk 22:16** *932*
now on until the **k** of God comes." **Lk 22:18** *932*
as My Father has granted Me a **k**, **Lk 22:29** *932*
eat and drink at My table in My **k**, **Lk 22:30** *932*
me when You come in Your **k**!" **Lk 23:42** *932*
who was waiting for the **k** of God; **Lk 23:51** *932*
he cannot see the **k** of God." **Jn 3:3** *932*
he cannot enter into the **k** of God. **Jn 3:5** *932*
"My **k** is not of this world. **Jn 18:36** *932*
If My **k** were of this world, then **Jn 18:36** *932*
is, My **k** is not of this realm." **Jn 18:36** *932*
things concerning the **k** of God. **Ac 1:3** *932*
are restoring the **k** to Israel?" **Ac 1:6** *932*
the good news about the **k** of God **Ac 8:12** *932*
we must enter the **k** of God." **Ac 14:22** *932*
persuading *them* about the **k** of God. **Ac 19:8** *932*
whom I went about preaching the **k**, **Ac 20:25** *932*
testifying about the **k** of God and **Ac 28:23** *932*
preaching the **k** of God and **Ac 28:31** *932*
for the **k** of God is not eating and **Ro 14:17** *932*
For the **k** of God does not consist **1Co 4:20** *932*
will not inherit the **k** of God? **1Co 6:9** *932*
will inherit the **k** of God. **1Co 6:10** *932*
He hands over the **k** to the God **1Co 15:24** *932*
blood cannot inherit the **k** of God; **1Co 15:50** *932*
will not inherit the **k** of God. **Ga 5:21** *932*
in the **k** of Christ and God. **Eph 5:5** *932*
us to the **k** of His beloved Son, **Col 1:13** *932*
only fellow workers for the **k** of God **Col 4:11** *932*
you into His own **k** and glory. **1Th 2:12** *932*
considered worthy of the **k** of God, **2Th 1:5** *932*
and by His appearing and His **k**: **2Tm 4:1** *932*
bring me safely to His heavenly **k**; **2Tm 4:18** *932*
SCEPTER IS THE SCEPTER OF HIS **K**. **Heb 1:8** *932*
a **k** which cannot be shaken, **Heb 12:28** *932*
heirs of the **k** which He promised **Jas 2:5** *932*
the eternal **k** of our Lord and Savior **2Pe 1:11** *932*
And He has made us *to be* a **k**, **Rv 1:6** *932*
partaker in the tribulation and **k** **Rv 1:9** *932*
to be a **k** and priests to our God; **Rv 5:10** *932*
"The **k** of the world has become **Rv 11:15** *932*
of the world has become *the* **k** of **Rv 11:15**
and the **k** of our God and the **Rv 12:10** *932*
and his **k** became darkened; **Rv 16:10** *932*
who have not yet received a **k**, **Rv 17:12** *932*
by giving their **k** to the beast, **Rv 17:17** *932*

KINGDOMS

so the LORD shall do to all the **k** **Dt 3:21** 4467
terror to all the **k** of the earth. **Dt 28:25** 4467
was the head of all these **k**. **Jos 11:10** 4467
the **k** that were oppressing you.' **1Sa 10:18** 4467
Now Solomon ruled over all the **k** **1Ki 4:21** 4467
You alone, of all the **k** of the earth. **2Ki 19:15** 4467
k of the earth may know that You **2Ki 19:19** 4467
and on all the **k** of the lands. **1Ch 29:30** 4467
service of the **k** of the countries." **2Ch 12:8** 4467
dread of the LORD was on all the **k** **2Ch 17:10** 4467
ruler over all the **k** of the nations? **2Ch 20:6** 4467
the dread of God was on all the **k** **2Ch 20:29** 4467
given me all the **k** of the earth, **2Ch 36:23** 4467
given me all the **k** of the earth and **Ezr 1:2** 4467
also gave them **k** and peoples, **Ne 9:22** 4467
made an uproar, the **k** tottered; **Ps 46:6** 4467
Sing to God, O **k** of the earth, **Ps 68:32** 4467
And upon the **k** which do not call **Ps 79:6** 4467
are gathered together, And the **k**, **Ps 102:22** 4467
Bashan, And all the **k** of Canaan; **Ps 135:11** 4467
has reached to the **k** of the idols, **Is 10:10** 4467
A sound of the uproar of **k**, **Is 13:4** 4467
And Babylon, the beauty of **k**, **Is 13:19** 4467
the earth tremble, Who shook **k**, **Is 14:16** 4467
sea, He has made the **k** tremble; **Is 23:11** 4467
will play the harlot with all the **k** **Is 23:17** 4467
You alone, of all the **k** of the earth. **Is 37:16** 4467
k of the earth may know that You **Is 37:20** 4467
no longer be called The queen of **k**. **Is 47:5** 4467
over the nations and over the **k**, **Jer 1:10** 4467
families of the **k** of the north," **Jer 1:15** 4467
the nations And in all their **k**, **Jer 10:7** 4438
an object of horror among all the **k** **Jer 15:4** 4467
evil for all the **k** of the earth, **Jer 24:9** 4467
and all the **k** of the earth which **Jer 25:26** 4467
many lands and against great **k**, **Jer 28:8** 4467
terror to all the **k** of the earth, **Jer 29:18** 4467
with all the **k** of the earth that **Jer 34:1** 4467
terror to all the **k** of the earth. **Jer 34:17** 4467
Kedar and the **k** of Hazor, **Jer 49:28** 4467
nations, And with you I destroy **k**. **Jer 51:20** 4467
against her the **k** of Ararat, **Jer 51:27** 4467
"It will be the lowest of the **k**, **Ezk 29:15** 4467
no longer be divided into two **k**. **Ezk 37:22** 4467
and put an end to all these **k**, **Da 2:44** 4437
be different from all the *other* **k** and **Da 7:23** 4437
and the greatness of *all* the **k** **Da 7:27** 4437
represent four **k** *which* will arise **Da 8:22** 4438
Are they better than these **k**, **Am 6:2** 4467
And to the **k** your disgrace. **Na 3:5** 4467
to gather nations, To assemble **k**, **Zph 3:8** 4467
I will overthrow the thrones of **k** **Hg 2:22** 4467
the power of the **k** of the nations; **Hg 2:22** 4467
showed Him all the **k** of the world and **Mt 4:8** *932*
showed Him all the **k** of the world **Lk 4:5** *932*
who by faith conquered **k**, **Heb 11:33** *932*

KING'S

of Shaveh (that is, the **K** Valley). **Gn 14:17** 4428
the **k** prisoners were confined; **Gn 39:20** 4428
We will go along the **k** highway, **Nu 20:17** 4428
We will go by the **k** highway until **Nu 21:22** 4428
that I should be the **k** son-in-law?" **1Sa 18:18** 4428
become the **k** son-in-law.' " **1Sa 18:22** 4428
sight to become the **k** son-in-law, **1Sa 18:23** 4428
vengeance on the **k** enemies.' " **1Sa 18:25** 4428
David to become the **k** son-in-law. **1Sa 18:26** 4428
he might become the **k** son-in-law. **1Sa 18:27** 4428
he has not come to the **k** table." **1Sa 20:29** 4428
because the **k** matter was urgent." **1Sa 21:8** 4428
as David, even the **k** son-in-law, **1Sa 22:14** 4428
surrender him into the **k** hand." **1Sa 23:20** 4428
And now, see where the **k** spear is and **1Sa 26:16** 4428
David's table as one of the **k** sons. **2Sa 9:11** 4428
he ate at the **k** table regularly. **2Sa 9:13** 4428
around on the roof of the **k** house, **2Sa 11:2** 4428
And Uriah went out of the **k** house, **2Sa 11:8** 4428
Uriah slept at the door of the **k** house **2Sa 11:9** 4428
and if it happens that the **k** wrath **2Sa 11:20** 4428
some of the **k** servants are dead, **2Sa 11:24** 4428
Absalom invited all the **k** sons. **2Sa 13:23** 4428
and all the **k** sons go with him. **2Sa 13:27** 4428
Then all the **k** sons arose and each **2Sa 13:29** 4428
has struck down all the **k** sons, **2Sa 13:30** 4428
all the young men, the **k** sons, **2Sa 13:32** 4428
'all the **k** sons are dead,' for **2Sa 13:33** 4428
"Behold, the **k** sons have come; **2Sa 13:35** 4428
the **k** sons came and lifted their **2Sa 13:36** 4428
k heart *was inclined* toward Absalom. **2Sa 14:1** 4428
house and did not see the **k** face. **2Sa 14:24** 4428
at 200 shekels by the **k** weight. **2Sa 14:26** 4428
and did not see the **k** face. **2Sa 14:28** 4428
therefore, let me see the **k** face, **2Sa 14:32** 4428
the **k** servants said to the king, **2Sa 15:15** 4428
you hear from the **k** house, **2Sa 15:35** 4428
are for the **k** household to ride, **2Sa 16:2** 4428
put out my hand against the **k** son; **2Sa 18:12** 4428
a pillar which is in the **K** Valley, **2Sa 18:18** 4428
today because the **k** son is dead." **2Sa 18:20** 4428
"When Joab sent the **k** servant, **2Sa 18:29** 4428
to bring over the **k** household, **2Sa 19:18** 4428
we eaten at all at the **k** *expense*, **2Sa 19:42** 4428
the **k** word prevailed against Joab **2Sa 24:4** 4428
became the **k** nurse and served him, **1Ki 1:4** 4428
all his brothers, the **k** sons, **1Ki 1:9** 4428
the men of Judah, the **k** servants. **1Ki 1:9** 4428
and has invited all the **k** sons and **1Ki 1:25** 4428
And she came into the **k** presence **1Ki 1:28** 4428
And they came into the **k** presence. **1Ki 1:32** 4428
have made him ride on the **k** mule. **1Ki 1:44** 4428
the **k** servants came to bless our **1Ki 1:47** 4428
had a throne set for the **k** mother, **1Ki 2:19** 4428
a priest, *was* the **k** friend; **1Ki 4:5** 4428
of the LORD, and the **k** house, **1Ki 9:1** 4428
house of the LORD and the **k** house **1Ki 9:10** 4428
of the LORD and for the **k** house, **1Ki 10:12** 4428
and the **k** merchants procured *them* **1Ki 10:28** 4428
the **k** hand was restored to him, **1Ki 13:6** 4428
and the treasures of the **k** house, **1Ki 14:26** 4428
guarded the doorway of the **k** house. **1Ki 14:27** 4428
and the treasuries of the **k** house, **1Ki 15:18** 4428
went into the citadel of the **k** house **1Ki 16:18** 4428
the **k** house over him with fire, **1Ki 16:18** 4428
the city and to Joash the **k** son; **1Ki 22:26** 4428
us go and tell the **k** household." **2Ki 7:9** 4428
told *it* within the **k** household. **2Ki 7:11** 4428
her, for she is a **k** daughter." **2Ki 9:34** 4428
Now the **k** sons, seventy persons, **2Ki 10:6** 4428
them, they took the **k** sons **2Ki 10:7** 4428
brought the heads of the **k** sons," **2Ki 10:8** 4428
stole him from among the **k** sons **2Ki 11:2** 4428
LORD, and showed them the **k** son. **2Ki 11:4** 4428
and keep watch over the **k** house **2Ki 11:5** 4428
Then he brought the **k** son out and **2Ki 11:12** 4428
horses' entrance of the **k** house, **2Ki 11:16** 4428
gate of the guards to the **k** house. **2Ki 11:19** 4428
with the sword at the **k** house. **2Ki 11:20** 4428
the **k** scribe and the high priest **2Ki 12:10** 4428
of the LORD and of the **k** house, **2Ki 12:18** 4428
laid his hands on the **k** hands. **2Ki 13:16** 4428
in the treasuries of the **k** house, **2Ki 14:14** 4428
the **k** son was over the household, **2Ki 15:5** 4428
the **k** house with Argob and Arieh; **2Ki 15:25** 4428
in the treasuries of the **k** house, **2Ki 16:8** 4428
k burnt offering and his meal offering **2Ki 16:15** 4428
in the treasuries of the **k** house. **2Ki 18:15** 4428
a word, for the **k** commandment was, **2Ki 18:36** 4428
and Asaiah the **k** servant saying, **2Ki 22:12** 4428
and the treasures of the **k** house, **2Ki 24:13** 4428
also the **k** mother and the king's **2Ki 24:15** 4428
the king's mother and the **k** wives **2Ki 24:15** 4428
the two walls beside the **k** garden, **2Ki 25:4** 4428
house of the LORD, the **k** house, **2Ki 25:9** 4428
and five of the **k** advisers who **2Ki 25:19** 4428
had his meals in the **k** presence **2Ki 25:29** 4428
now at the **k** gate to the east). **1Ch 9:18** 4428
David *were* chiefs at the **k** side. **1Ch 18:17** 4428
the **k** word prevailed against Joab. **1Ch 21:4** 4428
k command was abhorrent to Joab. **1Ch 21:6** 4428
were the sons of Heman the **k** seer **1Ch 25:5** 4428
had charge of the **k** storehouses. **1Ch 27:25** 4428
of Hachmoni tutored the **k** sons. **1Ch 27:32** 4428
the Archite *was* the **k** friend. **1Ch 27:33** 4428
was the commander of the **k** army. **1Ch 27:34** 4428

the overseers over the **k** work,	**1Ch 29:6**	4428
the **k** traders procured them from	**2Ch 1:16**	4428
of the LORD and the **k** palace,	**2Ch 7:11**	4428
of the LORD and for the **k** palace,	**2Ch 9:11**	4428
and the treasures of the **k** palace.	**2Ch 12:9**	4428
guarded the door of the **k** house.	**2Ch 12:10**	4428
house of the LORD and the **k** house,	**2Ch 16:2**	4428
the city and to Joash the **k** son;	**2Ch 18:25**	4428
the possessions found in the **k** house	**2Ch 21:17**	4428
But Jehoshabeath the **k** daughter	**2Ch 22:11**	4428
stole him from among the **k** sons	**2Ch 22:11**	4428
"Behold, the **k** son shall reign,	**2Ch 23:3**	4428
one third *shall be* at the **k** house,	**2Ch 23:5**	4428
k son and put the crown on him,	**2Ch 23:11**	4428
of the Horse Gate of the **k** house,	**2Ch 23:15**	4428
the upper gate to the **k** house.	**2Ch 23:20**	4428
to the **k** officer by the Levites,	**2Ch 24:11**	4428
then the **k** scribe and the chief	**2Ch 24:11**	4428
and the treasures of the **k** house,	**2Ch 25:24**	4428
Hananiah, one of the **k** officers.	**2Ch 26:11**	4428
Jotham his son *was* over the **k** house	**2Ch 26:21**	4428
Ephraim, slew Maaseiah the **k** son and	**2Ch 28:7**	4428
of David and of Gad the **k** seer,	**2Ch 29:25**	4428
He also *appointed* the **k** portion of	**2Ch 31:3**	4428
scribe, and Asaiah the **k** servant,	**2Ch 34:20**	4428
these were from the **k** possessions.	**2Ch 35:7**	4428
according to the **k** command.	**2Ch 35:10**	4428
Heman, and Jeduthun the **k** seer;	**2Ch 35:15**	4428
for us to see the **k** dishonor,	**Ezr 4:14**	4430
conducted in the **k** treasure house,	**Ezr 5:17**	4430
a thing as this in the **k** heart,	**Ezr 7:27**	4428
before all the **k** mighty princes.	**Ezr 7:28**	4428
the **k** edicts to the king's satraps and	**Ezr 8:36**	4428
the king's edicts to the **k** satraps and	**Ezr 8:36**	4428
Asaph the keeper of the **k** forest,	**Ne 2:8**	4428
River and gave them the **k** letters.	**Ne 2:9**	4428
the Fountain Gate and the **K** Pool,	**Ne 2:14**	4428
and also about the **k** words which	**Ne 2:18**	4428
the Pool of Shelah at the **k** garden	**Ne 3:15**	4428
have borrowed money for the **k** tax	**Ne 5:4**	4428
was the **k** representative in all	**Ne 11:24**	4428
of the garden of the **k** palace.	**Es 1:5**	4428
according to the **k** bounty.	**Es 1:7**	4428
refused to come at the **k** command	**Es 1:12**	4428
who had access to the **k** presence	**Es 1:14**	4428
the same way to all the **k** princes,	**Es 1:18**	4428
"When the **k** edict which he	**Es 1:20**	4428
letters to all the **k** provinces,	**Es 1:22**	4428
Then the **k** attendants, who served	**Es 2:2**	4428
custody of Hegai, the **k** eunuch,	**Es 2:3**	4428
Esther was taken to the **k** palace	**Es 2:8**	4428
choice maids from the **k** palace and	**Es 2:9**	4428
from the harem to the **k** palace.	**Es 2:13**	4428
the **k** eunuch who was in charge of	**Es 2:14**	4428
the **k** eunuch who was in charge of	**Es 2:15**	4428
gifts according to the **k** bounty.	**Es 2:18**	4428
Mordecai was sitting at the **k** gate.	**Es 2:19**	4428
Mordecai was sitting at the **k** gate,	**Es 2:21**	4428
two of the **k** officials from those	**Es 2:21**	4428
the Chronicles in the **k** presence.	**Es 2:23**	4428
All the **k** servants who were at	**Es 3:2**	4428
who were at the **k** gate bowed down	**Es 3:2**	4428
Then the **k** servants who were at	**Es 3:3**	4428
at the **k** gate said to Mordecai,	**Es 3:3**	4428
you transgressing the **k** command?"	**Es 3:3**	4428
they do not observe the **k** laws,	**Es 3:8**	4428
it is not in the **k** interest to let them	**Es 3:8**	4428
those who carry on the **k** business,	**Es 3:9**	4428
to put into the **k** treasuries."	**Es 3:9**	4428
Then the **k** scribes were summoned	**Es 3:12**	4428
Haman commanded to the **k** satraps,	**Es 3:12**	4428
and sealed with the **k** signet ring.	**Es 3:12**	4428
to all the **k** provinces to destroy,	**Es 3:13**	4428
went out impelled by the **k** command	**Es 3:15**	4428
He went as far as the **k** gate,	**Es 4:2**	4428
the **k** gate clothed in sackcloth.	**Es 4:2**	4428
Hathach from the **k** eunuchs,	**Es 4:5**	4428
city square in front of the **k** gate.	**Es 4:6**	4428
promised to pay to the **k** treasuries	**Es 4:7**	4428
"All the **k** servants and the	**Es 4:11**	4428
the people of the **k** provinces know	**Es 4:11**	4428
you in the **k** palace can escape any	**Es 4:13**	4428
in the inner court of the **k** palace	**Es 5:1**	4428
palace in front of the **k** rooms,	**Es 5:1**	4428
Haman saw Mordecai in the **k** gate and	**Es 5:9**	4428
the Jew sitting at the **k** gate."	**Es 5:13**	4428
k eunuchs who were doorkeepers,	**Es 6:2**	4428
Then the **k** servants who attended	**Es 6:3**	4428
the outer court of the **k** palace	**Es 6:4**	4428
The **k** servants said to him,	**Es 6:5**	4428
to one of the **k** most noble princes	**Es 6:9**	4428
Jew, who is sitting at the **k** gate;	**Es 6:10**	4428
Mordecai returned to the **k** gate.	**Es 6:12**	4428
the **k** eunuchs arrived and hastily	**Es 6:14**	4428
the word went out of the **k** mouth,	**Es 7:8**	4428
and the **k** anger subsided.	**Es 7:10**	4428
who are in all the **k** provinces.	**Es 8:5**	4428
as you see fit, in the **k** name,	**Es 8:8**	4428
seal *it* with the **k** signet ring;	**Es 8:8**	4428
and sealed with the **k** signet ring	**Es 8:8**	4428
So the **k** scribes were called at	**Es 8:9**	4428
sealed it with the **k** signet ring,	**Es 8:10**	4428
and impelled by the **k** command,	**Es 8:14**	4428
wherever the **k** commandment and his	**Es 8:17**	4428
when the **k** command and edict	**Es 9:1**	4428
those who were doing the **k** business	**Es 9:3**	4428
Mordecai was great in the **k** house,	**Es 9:4**	4428
in the rest of the **k** provinces!	**Es 9:12**	4428
Jews who *were* in the **k** provinces	**Es 9:16**	4428
when it came to the **k** attention,	**Es 9:25**	4428
are in the heart of the **K** enemies.	**Ps 45:5**	4428
The **K** daughter is all glorious	**Ps 45:13**	4428
They will enter into the **K** palace.	**Ps 45:15**	4428
You will prolong the **k** life;	**Ps 61:6**	4428
Your righteousness to the **k** son.	**Ps 72:1**	4428
multitude of people is a **k** glory,	**Pr 14:28**	4428
The **k** favor is toward a servant	**Pr 14:35**	4428
In the light of a **k** face is life,	**Pr 16:15**	4428
The **k** wrath is like the roaring of	**Pr 19:12**	4428
The **k** heart is *like* channels of	**Pr 21:1**	4428
for the **k** commandment was,	**Is 36:21**	4428
they came up from the **k** house to	**Jer 26:10**	4428
he went down to the **k** house,	**Jer 36:12**	4428
commanded Jerahmeel the **k** son,	**Jer 36:26**	4428
cistern *of* Malchijah the **k** son,	**Jer 38:6**	4428
while he was in the **k** palace,	**Jer 38:7**	4428
k palace and spoke to the king,	**Jer 38:8**	4428
and went into the **k** palace to *a place*	**Jer 38:11**	4428
city at night by way of the **k** garden	**Jer 39:4**	4428
also burned with fire the **k** palace	**Jer 39:8**	4428
the **k** daughters and all the people	**Jer 41:10**	4428
the **k** daughters and every person	**Jer 43:6**	4428
walls which *was* by the **k** garden,	**Jer 52:7**	4428
house of the LORD, the **k** house and	**Jer 52:13**	4428
and seven of the **k** advisers who	**Jer 52:25**	4428
and had his meals in the **k** presence	**Jer 52:33**	4428
for serving in the **k** court;	**Da 1:4**	4428
a daily ration from the **k** choice food	**Da 1:5**	4428
to enter the **k** personal service.	**Da 1:5**	4428
defile himself with the **k** choice food	**Da 1:8**	4428
who are eating the **k** choice food;	**Da 1:13**	4428
had been eating the **k** choice food.	**Da 1:15**	4428
entered the **k** personal service.	**Da 1:19**	4428
the captain of the **k** bodyguard,	**Da 2:14**	4430
said to Arioch, the **k** commander,	**Da 2:15**	4430
made known to us the **k** matter."	**Da 2:23**	4430
Take me into the **k** presence,	**Da 2:24**	4430
brought Daniel into the **k** presence	**Da 2:25**	4430
while Daniel *was* at the **k** court.	**Da 2:49**	4430
because the **k** command *was* urgent	**Da 3:22**	4430
governors and the **k** high officials	**Da 3:27**	4430
in Him, violating the **k** command,	**Da 3:28**	4430
"While the word *was* in the **k** mouth,	**Da 4:31**	4430
plaster of the wall of the **k** palace,	**Da 5:5**	4430
Then the **k** face grew pale and his	**Da 5:6**	4430
Then all the **k** wise men came in,	**Da 5:8**	4430
the king about the **k** injunction,	**Da 6:12**	4430
and carried on the **k** business;	**Da 8:27**	4428
crop *was* after the **k** mowing.	**Am 7:1**	4428
punish the princes, the **k** sons And	**Zph 1:8**	4428
of Hananel to the **k** wine presses.	**Zch 14:10**	4428
over Blastus the **k** chamberlain,	**Ac 12:20**	*935*
country was fed by the **k** country.	**Ac 12:20**	*937*
were not afraid of the **k** edict.	**Heb 11:23**	*935*

KINGS

and the **k** that were with him,	**Gn 14:5**	4428
four **k** against five.	**Gn 14:9**	4428
the **k** of Sodom and Gomorrah fled,	**Gn 14:10**	4428
and the **k** who were with him,	**Gn 14:17**	4428
and **k** will come forth from you.	**Gn 17:6**	4428
k of peoples will come from her."	**Gn 17:16**	4428
And **k** shall come forth from you.	**Gn 35:11**	4428
Now these are the **k** who reigned in	**Gn 36:31**	4428
They killed the **k** of Midian	**Nu 31:8**	4428
and Reba, the five **k** of Midian;	**Nu 31:8**	4428
hand of the two **k** of the Amorites	**Dt 3:8**	4428
your God has done to these two **k**;	**Dt 3:21**	4428
Bashan, the two **k** of the Amorites,	**Dt 4:47**	4428
"He will deliver their **k** into	**Dt 7:24**	4428
Sihon and Og, the **k** of the Amorites,	**Dt 31:4**	4428
did to the two **k** of the Amorites	**Jos 2:10**	4428
all the **k** of the Amorites who *were*	**Jos 5:1**	4428
and all the **k** of the Canaanites	**Jos 5:1**	4428
the **k** who were beyond the Jordan,	**Jos 9:1**	4428
He did to the two **k** of the Amorites	**Jos 9:10**	4428
So the five **k** of the Amorites, the	**Jos 10:5**	4428
for all the **k** of the Amorites that	**Jos 10:6**	4428
Now these five **k** had fled and	**Jos 10:16**	4428
"The five **k** have been found	**Jos 10:17**	4428
five **k** out to me from the cave."	**Jos 10:22**	4428
five **k** out to him from the cave:	**Jos 10:23**	4428
brought these **k** out to Joshua,	**Jos 10:24**	4428
feet on the necks of these **k**."	**Jos 10:24**	4428
and the slopes and all their **k**.	**Jos 10:40**	4428
Joshua captured all these **k** and	**Jos 10:42**	4428
and to the **k** who were of the north	**Jos 11:2**	4428
of these **k** having agreed to meet,	**Jos 11:5**	4428
all the cities of these **k**,	**Jos 11:12**	4428
of these kings, and all their **k**,	**Jos 11:12**	4428
And he captured all their **k** and	**Jos 11:17**	4428
war a long time with all these **k**.	**Jos 11:18**	4428
Now these are the **k** of the land	**Jos 12:1**	4428
Now these are the **k** of the land	**Jos 12:7**	4428
in all, thirty-one **k**.	**Jos 12:24**	4428
drove out the two **k** of the Amorites	**Jos 24:12**	4428
"Seventy **k** with their thumbs and	**Jg 1:7**	4428
"Hear, O **k**; give ear, O rulers!	**Jg 5:3**	4428
"The **k** came *and* fought;	**Jg 5:19**	4428
Then fought the **k** of Canaan At	**Jg 5:19**	4428
and Zalmunna, the **k** of Midian."	**Jg 8:5**	4428
and captured the two **k** of Midian,	**Jg 8:12**	4428
which *were* on the **k** of Midian,	**Jg 8:26**	4428
of Ammon, Edom, the **k** of Zobah,	**1Sa 14:47**	4428
to the **k** of Judah to this day.	**1Sa 27:6**	4428
When all the **k**, servants of	**2Sa 10:19**	4428
the time when **k** go out *to battle*,	**2Sa 11:1**	4428
not be any among the **k** like you	**1Ki 3:13**	4428
over all the **k** west of the River;	**1Ki 4:24**	4428
from all the **k** of the earth who	**1Ki 4:34**	4428
the **k** of the Arabs and the governors	**1Ki 10:15**	4428
greater than all the **k** of the earth	**1Ki 10:23**	4428
to all the **k** of the Hittites and to the	**1Ki 10:29**	4428
and to the **k** of the Arameans.	**1Ki 10:29**	4428
the Chronicles of the **K** of Israel.	**1Ki 14:19**	4428
the Chronicles of the **K** of Judah?	**1Ki 14:29**	4428
the Chronicles of the **K** of Judah?	**1Ki 15:7**	4428
the Chronicles of the **K** of Judah?	**1Ki 15:23**	4428
the Chronicles of the **K** of Israel?	**1Ki 15:31**	4428
the Chronicles of the **K** of Israel?	**1Ki 16:5**	4428
the Chronicles of the **K** of Israel?	**1Ki 16:14**	4428
the Chronicles of the **K** of Israel?	**1Ki 16:20**	4428
the Chronicles of the **K** of Israel?	**1Ki 16:27**	4428
k of Israel who were before him.	**1Ki 16:33**	4428
there *were* thirty-two **k** with him,	**1Ki 20:1**	4428
the **k** in the temporary shelters,	**1Ki 20:12**	4428
the thirty-two **k** who helped him.	**1Ki 20:16**	4428
remove the **k**, each from his place,	**1Ki 20:24**	4428
k of the house of Israel are merciful	**1Ki 20:31**	4428
house of Israel are merciful **k**,	**1Ki 20:31**	4428
the Chronicles of the **K** of Israel?	**1Ki 22:39**	4428
the Chronicles of the **K** of Judah?	**1Ki 22:45**	4428
the Chronicles of the **K** of Israel?	**2Ki 1:18**	4428
the LORD has called these three **k**	**2Ki 3:10**	4428
for the LORD has called these three **k**	**2Ki 3:13**	4428
Moabites heard that the **k** had come	**2Ki 3:21**	4428
the **k** have surely fought together,	**2Ki 3:23**	4428
hired against us the **k** of the Hittites	**2Ki 7:6**	4428
and the **k** of the Egyptians,	**2Ki 7:6**	4428
in the way of the **k** of Israel,	**2Ki 8:18**	4428
the Chronicles of the **K** of Judah?	**2Ki 8:23**	4428
two **k** did not stand before him;	**2Ki 10:4**	4428
the Chronicles of the **K** of Israel?	**2Ki 10:34**	4428
And he sat on the throne of the **k**.	**2Ki 11:19**	4428
Ahaziah, his fathers, **k** of Judah,	**2Ki 12:18**	4428
the Chronicles of the **K** of Judah?	**2Ki 12:19**	4428
the Chronicles of the **K** of Israel?	**2Ki 13:8**	4428
the Chronicles of the **K** of Israel?	**2Ki 13:12**	4428
in Samaria with the **k** of Israel.	**2Ki 13:13**	4428
the Chronicles of the **K** of Israel?	**2Ki 14:15**	4428
in Samaria with the **k** of Israel;	**2Ki 14:16**	4428
the Chronicles of the **K** of Judah?	**2Ki 14:18**	4428
the Chronicles of the **K** of Israel?	**2Ki 14:28**	4428
even with the **k** of Israel,	**2Ki 14:29**	4428
the Chronicles of the **K** of Judah?	**2Ki 15:6**	4428
the Chronicles of the **K** of Israel.	**2Ki 15:11**	4428
the Chronicles of the **K** of Israel.	**2Ki 15:15**	4428
the Chronicles of the **K** of Israel?	**2Ki 15:21**	4428
the Chronicles of the **K** of Israel.	**2Ki 15:26**	4428
the Chronicles of the **K** of Israel.	**2Ki 15:31**	4428
the Chronicles of the **K** of Judah?	**2Ki 15:36**	4428
in the way of the **k** of Israel,	**2Ki 16:3**	4428
the Chronicles of the **K** of Judah?	**2Ki 16:19**	4428
k of Israel who were before him.	**2Ki 17:2**	4428
and *in the customs* of the **k** of Israel	**2Ki 17:8**	4428
like him among all the **k** of Judah,	**2Ki 18:5**	4428
what the **k** of Assyria have done	**2Ki 19:11**	4428
the **k** of Assyria have devastated	**2Ki 19:17**	4428
the Chronicles of the **K** of Judah?	**2Ki 20:20**	4428
the Chronicles of the **K** of Judah?	**2Ki 21:17**	4428
the Chronicles of the **K** of Judah?	**2Ki 21:25**	4428
whom the **k** of Judah had appointed	**2Ki 23:5**	4428
k of Judah had given to the sun,	**2Ki 23:11**	4428
which the **k** of Judah had made,	**2Ki 23:12**	4428
which the **k** of Israel had made	**2Ki 23:19**	4428
nor in all the days of the **k** of Israel	**2Ki 23:22**	4428
of Israel and of the **k** of Judah.	**2Ki 23:22**	4428
the Chronicles of the **K** of Judah?	**2Ki 23:28**	4428
the Chronicles of the **K** of Judah?	**2Ki 24:5**	4428
k who *were* with him in Babylon.	**2Ki 25:28**	4428
Now these are the **k** who reigned in	**1Ch 1:43**	4428
in the Book of the **K** of Israel.	**1Ch 9:1**	4428
And He reproved **k** for their sakes,	**1Ch 16:21**	4428
and the **k** who had come were by	**1Ch 19:9**	4428
the time when **k** go out *to battle*,	**1Ch 20:1**	4428
such as none of the **k** who were	**2Ch 1:12**	4428
to all the **k** of the Hittites and the	**2Ch 1:17**	4428
of the Hittites and the **k** of Aram.	**2Ch 1:17**	4428
and all the **k** of Arabia and the	**2Ch 9:14**	4428
greater than all the **k** of the earth	**2Ch 9:22**	4428
And all the **k** of the earth were	**2Ch 9:23**	4428
He was the ruler over all the **k**	**2Ch 9:26**	4428
Book of the **K** of Judah and Israel.	**2Ch 16:11**	4428
in the Book of the **K** of Israel.	**2Ch 20:34**	4428
in the way of the **k** of Israel,	**2Ch 21:6**	4428
in the way of the **k** of Israel,	**2Ch 21:13**	4428
but not in the tombs of the **k**.	**2Ch 21:20**	4428
in the city of David among the **k**,	**2Ch 24:16**	4428
bury him in the tombs of the **k**.	**2Ch 24:25**	4428
the treatise of the Book of the **K**.	**2Ch 24:27**	4428
Book of the **K** of Judah and Israel?	**2Ch 25:26**	4428
the grave which belonged to the **k**,	**2Ch 26:23**	4428
Book of the **K** of Israel and Judah.	**2Ch 27:7**	4428
in the ways of the **k** of Israel;	**2Ch 28:2**	4428
sent to the **k** of Assyria for help.	**2Ch 28:16**	4428
gods of the **k** of Aram helped them,	**2Ch 28:23**	4428
Book of the **K** of Judah and Israel.	**2Ch 28:26**	4428
into the tombs of the **k** of Israel;	**2Ch 28:27**	4428
from the hand of the **k** of Assyria.	**2Ch 30:6**	4428
"Why should the **k** of Assyria come	**2Ch 32:4**	4428
Book of the **K** of Judah and Israel.	**2Ch 32:32**	4428
the records of the **k** of Israel.	**2Ch 33:18**	4428
the **k** of Judah had let go to ruin.	**2Ch 34:11**	4428
nor had any of the **k** of Israel	**2Ch 35:18**	4428
Book of the **K** of Israel and Judah.	**2Ch 35:27**	4428
Book of the **K** of Israel and Judah.	**2Ch 36:8**	4428
will damage the revenue of the **k**.	**Ezr 4:13**	4430
and damaging to **k** and provinces,	**Ezr 4:15**	4430

that city has risen up against the **k** **Ezr 4:19** 4430
k have ruled over Jerusalem, **Ezr 4:20** 4430
to the detriment of the **k**?" **Ezr 4:22** 4430
"Artaxerxes, king of **k**, **Ezr 7:12** 4430
our **k** *and* our priests have been **Ezr 9:7** 4428
the hand of the **k** of the lands, **Ezr 9:7** 4428
in the sight of the **k** of Persia, **Ezr 9:9** 4428
into their hand, with their **k** and **Ne 9:24** 4428
Which has come upon us, our **k**, **Ne 9:32** 4428
From the days of the **k** of Assyria **Ne 9:32** 4428
"For our **k**, our leaders, our **Ne 9:34** 4428
Its abundant produce is for the **k** **Ne 9:37** 4428
of the **K** of Media and Persia? **Es 10:2** 4428
With **k** and *with* counselors of the **Jb 3:14** 4428
"He loosens the bond of **k** And **Jb 12:18** 4428
But with **k** on the throne He has **Jb 36:7** 4428
k of the earth take their stand And **Ps 2:2** 4428
therefore, O **k**, show discernment; **Ps 2:10** 4428
lo, the **k** assembled themselves, **Ps 48:4** 4428
"**K** of armies flee, they flee, And **Ps 68:12** 4428
Almighty scattered the **k** there, **Ps 68:14** 4428
K will bring gifts to You. **Ps 68:29** 4428
Let the **k** of Tarshish and of the **Ps 72:10** 4428
k of Sheba and Seba offer gifts. **Ps 72:10** 4428
And let all **k** bow down before him, **Ps 72:11** 4428
He is feared by the **k** of the earth. **Ps 76:12** 4428
The highest of the **k** of the earth. **Ps 89:27** 4428
all the **k** of the earth Your glory. **Ps 102:15** 4428
And He reproved **k** for their sakes: **Ps 105:14** 4428
Even in the chambers of their **k**. **Ps 105:30** 4428
shatter **k** in the day of His wrath. **Ps 110:5** 4428
speak of Your testimonies before **k** And **Ps 119:46** 4428
many nations And slew mighty **k**, **Ps 135:10** 4428
To Him who smote great **k**, **Ps 136:17** 4428
And slew mighty **k**, For His **Ps 136:18** 4428
All the **k** of the earth will give **Ps 138:4** 4428
Who gives salvation to **k**, **Ps 144:10** 4428
K of the earth and all peoples; **Ps 148:11** 4428
To bind their **k** with chains And **Ps 149:8** 4428
"By me **k** reign, And rulers decree **Pr 8:15** 4428
for **k** to commit wicked **Pr 16:12** 4428
Righteous lips are the delight of **k**, **Pr 16:13** 4428
He will stand before **k**; **Pr 22:29** 4428
glory of **k** is to search out a matter. **Pr 25:2** 4428
So the heart of **k** is unsearchable. **Pr 25:3** 4428
ways to that which destroys **k**. **Pr 31:3** 4428
It is not for **k**, O Lemuel, It is **Pr 31:4** 4428
It is not for **k** to drink wine, **Pr 31:4** 4428
the treasure of **k** and provinces. **Ec 2:8** 4428
Ahaz *and* Hezekiah, **k** of Judah. **Is 1:1** 4428
two **k** you dread will be forsaken. **Is 7:16** 4428
"Are not my princes all **k**? **Is 10:8** 4428
It raises all the **k** of the nations **Is 14:9** 4428
the **k** of the nations lie in glory, **Is 14:18** 4428
of the wise, a son of ancient **k**"? **Is 19:11** 4428
on high, And the **k** of the earth on **Is 24:21** 4428
what the **k** of Assyria have done to **Is 37:11** 4428
the **k** of Assyria have devastated **Is 37:18** 4428
nations before him And subdues **k**. **Is 41:2** 4428
him And to loose the loins of **k**; **Is 45:1** 4428
"**K** will see and arise, Princes **Is 49:7** 4428
"**K** will be your guardians, **Is 49:23** 4428
K will shut their mouths on **Is 52:15** 4428
And **k** to the brightness of your **Is 60:3** 4428
And their **k** will minister to you; **Is 60:10** 4428
With their **k** led in procession. **Is 60:11** 4428
And suck the breast of **k**; **Is 60:16** 4428
And all **k** your glory; **Is 62:2** 4428
the whole land, to the **k** of Judah, **Jer 1:18** 4428
They, their **k**, their princes And **Jer 2:26** 4428
out the bones of the **k** of Judah and **Jer 8:1** 4428
the **k** that sit for David on his throne **Jer 13:13** 4428
the **k** of Judah come in and go out, **Jer 17:19** 4428
the word of the LORD, **k** of Judah, **Jer 17:20** 4428
k and princes sitting on the throne **Jer 17:25** 4428
O **k** of Judah and inhabitants of **Jer 19:3** 4428
nor the **k** of Judah had *ever* known, **Jer 19:4** 4428
the houses of the **k** of Judah will be **Jer 19:13** 4428
all the treasures of the **k** of Judah **Jer 20:5** 4428
then **k** will enter the gates of **Jer 22:4** 4428
great **k** will make slaves of them, **Jer 25:14** 4428
Judah and its **k** *and* its princes, **Jer 25:18** 4428
all the **k** of the land of Uz, **Jer 25:20** 4428
all the **k** of the land of the **Jer 25:20** 4428
and all the **k** of Tyre, all the **Jer 25:22** 4428
kings of Tyre, all the **k** of Sidon and **Jer 25:22** 4428
and the **k** of the coastlands which **Jer 25:22** 4428
and all the **k** of Arabia and all **Jer 25:24** 4428
all the **k** of the foreign people who **Jer 25:24** 4428
and all the **k** of Zimri, all the **Jer 25:25** 4428
kings of Zimri, all the **k** of Elam and **Jer 25:25** 4428
of Elam and all the **k** of Media; **Jer 25:25** 4428
and all the **k** of the north, near **Jer 25:26** 4428
k will make him their servant. **Jer 27:7** 4428
their **k**, their leaders, their priests, **Jer 32:32** 4428
the houses of the **k** of Judah which **Jer 33:4** 4428
the former **k** who were before you, **Jer 34:5** 4428
the wickedness of the **k** of Judah, **Jer 44:9** 4428
our **k** and our princes did in the **Jer 44:17** 4428
your **k** and your princes, **Jer 44:21** 4428
along with her gods and her **k**, **Jer 46:25** 4428
And a great nation and many **k** Will **Jer 50:41** 4428
the spirit of the **k** of the Medes, **Jer 51:11** 4428
against her, The **k** of the Medes, **Jer 51:28** 4428
k who *were* with him in Babylon. **Jer 52:32** 4428
k of the earth did not believe, **La 4:12** 4428
king of Babylon, king of **k**, **Ezk 26:7** 4428
You enriched the **k** of earth. **Ezk 27:33** 4428
And their **k** are horribly afraid; **Ezk 27:35** 4428
I put you before **k**, **Ezk 28:17** 4428
and their **k** will be horribly afraid **Ezk 32:10** 4428
"There also is Edom, its **k** and **Ezk 32:29** 4428
name, neither they nor their **k**, **Ezk 43:7** 4428
corpses of their **k** when they die, **Ezk 43:7** 4428
corpses of their **k** far from Me; **Ezk 43:9** 4428
removes **k** and establishes kings; **Da 2:21** 4430
removes kings and establishes **k**; **Da 2:21** 4430
"You, O king, are the king of **k**, **Da 2:37** 4430
"In the days of those **k** the **Da 2:44** 4430
is a God of gods and a Lord of **k** **Da 2:47** 4430
k *who* will arise from the earth. **Da 7:17** 4430
of this kingdom ten **k** will arise; **Da 7:24** 4430
ones and will subdue three **k**. **Da 7:24** 4430
the **k** of Media and Persia. **Da 8:20** 4428
who spoke in Your name to our **k**, **Da 9:6** 4428
belongs to us, O Lord, to our **k**, **Da 9:8** 4428
left there with the **k** of Persia. **Da 10:13** 4428
k are going to arise in Persia. **Da 11:2** 4428
"As for both **k**, their hearts will **Da 11:27** 4428
Ahaz *and* Hezekiah, **k** of Judah, **Hos 1:1** 4428
All their **k** have fallen. **Hos 7:7** 4428
They have set up **k**, **Hos 8:4** 4427a
Ahaz *and* Hezekiah, **k** of Judah, **Mi 1:1** 4428
a deception To the **k** of Israel. **Mi 1:14** 4428
"They mock at **k** And rulers are a **Hab 1:10** 4428
governors and **k** for My sake, **Mt 10:18** *935*
From whom do the **k** of the earth **Mt 17:25** *935*
governors and **k** for My sake, **Mk 13:9** *935*
that many prophets and **k** wished to **Lk 10:24** *935*
bringing you before **k** and governors **Lk 21:12** *935*
"The **k** of the Gentiles lord it **Lk 22:25** *935*
K OF THE EARTH TOOK THEIR STAND, **Ac 4:26** *935*
and **k** and the sons of Israel; **Ac 9:15** *935*
you have become **k** without us; **1Co 4:8** *936*
indeed, *I* wish that you had become **k** **1Co 4:8** *936*
k and all who are in authority, **1Tm 2:2** *935*
the King of **k** and Lord of lords, **1Tm 6:15** *936*
returning from the slaughter of the **k** **Heb 7:1** *935*
the ruler of the **k** of the earth. **Rv 1:5** *935*
Then the **k** of the earth and the **Rv 6:15** *935*
and nations and tongues and **k**." **Rv 10:11** *935*
prepared for the **k** from the east. **Rv 16:12** *935*
out to the **k** of the whole world, **Rv 16:14** *935*
with whom the **k** of the earth **Rv 17:2** *935*
and they are seven **k**; **Rv 17:10** *935*
ten horns which you saw are ten **k** who **Rv 17:12** *935*
receive authority as **k** with the beast **Rv 17:12** *935*
He is Lord of lords and King of **k**, **Rv 17:14** *935*
reigns over the **k** of the earth." **Rv 17:18** *935*
and the **k** of the earth have **Rv 18:3** *935*
"And the **k** of the earth, who **Rv 18:9** *935*
"KING OF **K**, AND LORD OF **Rv 19:16** *935*
that you may eat the flesh of **k** **Rv 19:18** *935*
k of the earth and their armies **Rv 19:19** *935*
and the **k** of the earth will bring **Rv 21:24** *935*

KINGS'
K daughters are among Your noble **Ps 45:9** 4428
Yet it is in **k** palaces. **Pr 30:28** 4428
who wear soft *clothing* are in **k** **Mt 11:8** *935*

KINGSHIP
honor of **k** has not been conferred, **Da 11:21** 4438

KINSMAN
take the daughter of my master's **k** **Gn 24:48** 251
then his nearest **k** is to come and **Lv 25:25** 1350
'Or in case a man has no **k**, **Lv 25:26** 1350
"If your **k**, a Hebrew man or **Dt 15:12** 251
Now Naomi had a **k** of her husband, **Ru 2:1** 4129
"Now is not Boaz our **k**, **Ru 3:2** 4130
and he made his **k** Zedekiah king **2Ch 36:10** 251
Greet Herodion, my **k**. **Ro 16:11** *4773a*

KINSMEN
then he took his **k** with him and **Gn 31:23** 251
and Laban with his **k** camped in the **Gn 31:25** 251
in the presence of our **k** point out **Gn 31:32** 251
here before my **k** and your kinsmen, **Gn 31:37** 251
here before my kinsmen and your **k**, **Gn 31:37** 251
Jacob said to his **k**, **Gn 31:46** 251
and called his **k** to the meal; **Gn 31:54** 251
your **k**, the whole house of Israel, **Lv 10:6** 251
said to their **k**, **Jg 18:14** 251
His **k** by their families, in **1Ch 5:7** 251
Their **k** of their fathers' **1Ch 5:13** 251
were their **k** the sons of Merari: **1Ch 6:44** 251
Their **k** the Levites were **1Ch 6:48** 251
they were Saul's **k** from Benjamin. **1Ch 12:2** 251
Of the sons of Benjamin, Saul's **k**, **1Ch 12:29** 251
all their **k** *were* at their command. **1Ch 12:32** 251
for their **k** had prepared for them. **1Ch 12:39** 251
let us send everywhere to our **k** **1Ch 13:2** 251
Jeduthun, and their sons and **k**, **2Ch 5:12** 251
neither I nor my **k** have eaten the **Ne 5:14** 251
are joining with their **k**, **Ne 10:29** 251
and their **k** who performed the work **Ne 11:12** 251
his **k**, heads of fathers' *households*, **Ne 11:13** 251
the heads of the priests and their **k** **Ne 12:7** 251
and his **k**, Shemaiah, Azarel, **Ne 12:36** 251
task to distribute to their **k**. **Ne 13:13** 251
favor with his many **k**, **Es 10:3** 251
And my **k** stand afar off. **Ps 38:11** 7138
my **k** according to the flesh, **Ro 9:3** *4773a*
Greet Andronicus and Junias, my **k** and **Ro 16:7** *4773a*
and Jason and Sosipater, my **k**. **Ro 16:21** *4773a*

KIR
people of it away into exile to **K**, **2Ki 16:9** 7024b
Surely in a night **K** of Moab is **Is 15:1** 7024a
And **K** uncovered the shield. **Is 22:6** 7024b
of Aram will go exiled to **K**," **Am 1:5** 7024b
Caphtor and the Arameans from **K**? **Am 9:7** 7024b

KIR-HARESETH
in **K** *only* they left its stones; **2Ki 3:25** 7025
will moan for the raisin cakes of **K** **Is 16:7** 7025
And my inward feelings for **K**. **Is 16:11** 7025

KIR-HERES
I will moan for the men of **K**. **Jer 48:31** 7025
like flutes for the men of **K**. **Jer 48:36** 7025

KIRIATH
Gibeah, **K**; fourteen cities with their **Jos 18:28** 7157

KIRIATHAIM
built Heshbon and Elealeh and **K**, **Nu 32:37** 7156
and **K** and Sibmah and Zereth-shahar **Jos 13:19** 7156
and **K** with its pasture lands. **1Ch 6:76** 7156
K has been put to shame, it has **Jer 48:1** 7156
against **K**, Beth-gamul and **Jer 48:23** 7156
Beth-jeshimoth, Baal-meon and **K**, **Ezk 25:9** 7156

KIRIATH-ARBA
Sarah died in **K** **Gn 23:2** 7153
to his father Isaac at Mamre of **K** **Gn 35:27** 7153
the name of Hebron was formerly **K**; **Jos 14:15** 7153
of the LORD to Joshua, *namely*, **K**, **Jos 15:13** 7153
and Humtah and **K** **Jos 15:54** 7153
hill country of Ephraim, and **K** **Jos 20:7** 7153
Thus they gave them **K**, **Jos 21:11** 7153
name of Hebron formerly *was* **K**); **Jg 1:10** 7153
of Judah lived in **K** and its towns, **Ne 11:25** 7153

KIRIATH-ARIM
the sons of **K**, Chephirah and **Ezr 2:25** 7157

KIRIATH-BAAL
K (that is, Kiriath-jearim), **Jos 15:60** 7154
and it ended at **K** **Jos 18:14** 7154

KIRIATH-HUZOTH
with Balak, and they came to **K**. **Nu 22:39** 7155

KIRIATH-JEARIM
and Chephirah and Beeroth and **K**. **Jos 9:17** 7157
curved to Baalah (that is, **K**). **Jos 15:9** 7157
Kiriath-baal (that is, **K**), **Jos 15:60** 7157
ended at Kiriath-baal (that is, **K**), **Jos 18:14** 7157
south side *was* from the edge of **K**, **Jos 18:15** 7157
went up and camped at **K** in Judah. **Jg 18:12** 7157
behold, it is west of **K**. **Jg 18:12** 7157
to the inhabitants of **K**, **1Sa 6:21** 7157
And the men of **K** came and took the **1Sa 7:1** 7157
the day that the ark remained at **K** **1Sa 7:2** 7157
were Shobal the father of **K**, **1Ch 2:50** 7157
Shobal the father of **K** had sons: **1Ch 2:52** 7157
and the families of **K**: **1Ch 2:53** 7157
to bring the ark of God from **K**. **1Ch 13:5** 7157
went up to Baalah, *that is*, to **K**, **1Ch 13:6** 7157
brought up the ark of God from **K** **2Ch 1:4** 7157
the men of **K**, Chephirah and **Ne 7:29** 7157
Uriah the son of Shemaiah from **K**; **Jer 26:20** 7157

KIRIATH-SANNAH
and Dannah and **K** **Jos 15:49** 7158

KIRIATH-SEPHER
the name of Debir formerly was **K**. **Jos 15:15** 7158
one who attacks **K** and captures it, **Jos 15:16** 7158
the name of Debir formerly *was* **K**). **Jg 1:11** 7158
one who attacks **K** and captures it, **Jg 1:12** 7158

KISH
whose name was **K** the son of Abiel, **1Sa 9:1** 7027
Now the donkeys of **K**, **1Sa 9:3** 7027
So **K** said to his son Saul, **1Sa 9:3** 7027
"What has happened to the son of **K**? **1Sa 10:11** 7027
And Saul the son of **K** was taken; **1Sa 10:21** 7027
K *was* the father of Saul, and **1Sa 14:51** 7027
in the grave of **K** his father; **2Sa 21:14** 7027
son *was* Abdon, then Zur, **K**, **1Ch 8:30** 7027
Ner became the father of **K**, **1Ch 8:33** 7027
and **K** became the father of Saul, **1Ch 8:33** 7027
son *was* Abdon, then Zur, **K**, **1Ch 9:36** 7027
Ner became the father of **K**, **1Ch 9:39** 7027
and **K** became the father of Saul, **1Ch 9:39** 7027
because of Saul the son of **K**; **1Ch 12:1** 7027
sons of Mahli *were* Eleazar and **K**. **1Ch 23:21** 7027
so their brothers, the sons of **K**, **1Ch 23:22** 7027
By **K**: the sons of Kish, Jerahmeel. **1Ch 24:29** 7027
the sons of **K**, Jerahmeel. **1Ch 24:29** 7027
dedicated and Saul the son of **K**, **1Ch 26:28** 7027
K the son of Abdi and Azariah the **2Ch 29:12** 7027
the son of Shimei, the son of **K**, **Es 2:5** 7027
God gave them Saul the son of **K**, **Ac 13:21** *2797*

KISHI
Ethan the son of **K**, **1Ch 6:44** 7029

KISHION
and Rabbith and **K** and Ebez, **Jos 19:20** 7191
gave **K** with its pasture lands, **Jos 21:28** 7191

KISHON
his many *troops* to the river **K**, **Jg 4:7** 7028
Harosheth-hagoyim to the river **K**. **Jg 4:13** 7028
"The torrent of **K** swept them **Jg 5:21** 7028
ancient torrent, the torrent **K**. **Jg 5:21** 7028
brought them down to the brook **K**, **1Ki 18:40** 7028
and Jabin at the torrent of **K**, **Ps 83:9** 7028

KISS
"Please come close and **k** me, **Gn 27:26** 5401a
me to **k** my sons and my daughters? **Gn 31:28** 5401a
and take hold of him and **k** him. **2Sa 15:5** 5401a
with his right hand to **k** him. **2Sa 20:9** 5401a
let me **k** my father and my mother, **1Ki 19:20** 5401a
my hand threw a **k** from my mouth, **Jb 31:27** 5401a
"May he **k** me with the kisses of **SS 1:2** 5401a
found you outdoors, I would **k** you; **SS 8:1** 5401a
men who sacrifice **k** the calves!" **Hos 13:2** 5401a
"Whomever I **k**, He is the one; **Mt 26:48** *5368*

"Whomever I **k**, He is the one; Mk 14:44 5368
"You gave Me no **k**; Lk 7:45 5370
in, has not ceased to **k** My feet. Lk 7:45 2705
and he approached Jesus to **k** Him. Lk 22:47 5368
betraying the Son of Man with a **k**?" Lk 22:48 5370
Greet one another with a holy **k**. Ro 16:16 5370
Greet one another with a holy **k**. 1Co 16:20 5370
Greet one another with a holy **k**. 2Co 13:12 5370
Greet all the brethren with a holy **k**. 1Th 5:26 5370
Greet one another with a **k** of love. 1Pe 5:14 5370

KISSED
So he came close and **k** him; Gn 27:27 5401a
Then Jacob **k** Rachel, and lifted Gn 29:11 5401a
him, and embraced him and **k** him and Gn 29:13 5401a
and **k** his sons and his daughters Gn 31:55 5401a
and fell on his neck and **k** him, Gn 33:4 5401a
He **k** all his brothers and wept Gn 45:15 5401a
and he **k** them and embraced them. Gn 48:10 5401a
face, and wept over him and **k** him. Gn 50:1 5401a
the mountain of God and **k** him. Ex 4:27 5401a
and he bowed down and **k** him; Ex 18:7 5401a
Then she **k** them, and they lifted Ru 1:9 5401a
and Orpah **k** her mother-in-law, but Ru 1:14 5401a
it on his head, **k** him and said, 1Sa 10:1 5401a
k each other and wept together, 1Sa 20:41 5401a
the king, and the king **k** Absalom. 2Sa 14:33 5401a
king then **k** Barzillai and blessed 2Sa 19:39 5401a
every mouth that has not **k** him." 1Ki 19:18 5401a
Righteousness and peace have **k** each Ps 85:10 5401a
said, "Hail, Rabbi!" and **k** Him. Mt 26:49 2705
saying, "Rabbi!" and **k** Him. Mk 14:45 2705
ran and embraced him and **k** him. Lk 15:20 2705
Paul, and repeatedly **k** him, Ac 20:37 2705

KISSES
So she seizes him and **k** him And Pr 7:13 5401a
He **k** the lips Who gives a right Pr 24:26 5401a
deceitful are the **k** of an enemy. Pr 27:6 5390
kiss me with the **k** of his mouth! SS 1:2 5390

KISSING
hair of her head, and **k** His feet and Lk 7:38 2705

KITE
the **k** and the falcon in its kind, Lv 11:14 1676
and the red **k**, the falcon, and the Dt 14:13 1676
falcon, and the **k** in their kinds, Dt 14:13 1676

KITRON
drive out the inhabitants of **K**, Jg 1:30 7003

KITTIM
and Tarshish, **K** and Dodanim. Gn 10:4 3794
shall come from the coast of **K**, Nu 24:24 3794
Javan *were* Elishah, Tarshish, **K** and 1Ch 1:7 3794
cross to the coastlands of **K** and see, Jer 2:10 3794
ships of **K** will come against him; Da 11:30 3794

KIYYUN
along Sikkuth your king and **K**, Am 5:26 3594

KNEAD
measures of fine flour, **k** *it* Gn 18:6 3888
the women **k** dough to make cakes Jer 7:18 3888

KNEADED
and she took flour, **k** it and 1Sa 28:24 3888
And she took dough, **k** *it*, 2Sa 13:8 3888

KNEADING
your ovens and into your **k** bowls. Ex 8:3 4863
with their **k** bowls bound up in the Ex 12:34 4863
be your basket and your **k** bowl. Dt 28:5 4863
be your basket and your **k** bowl. Dt 28:17 4863
From the **k** of the dough until it is Hos 7:4 3888

KNEE
proclaimed before him, "Bow the **k**! Gn 41:43 86
back, That to Me every **k** will bow, Is 45:23 1290
HAVE NOT BOWED THE **K** TO BAAL." Ro 11:4 1119
THE LORD, EVERY **K** SHALL BOW TO ME, Ro 14:11 1119
name of Jesus EVERY **K** WILL BOW, Php 2:10 1119

KNEEL
He made the camels **k** down Gn 24:11 1288
And let others **k** down over her. Jb 31:10 3766
"They **k** down, they bring forth Jb 39:3 3766
us **k** before the LORD our Maker. Ps 95:6 1288

KNEELED
all the rest of the people **k** to drink Jg 7:6 3766, 1290
died, she **k** down and gave birth, 1Sa 4:19 3766

KNEELING
from **k** on his knees with his hands 1Ki 8:54 3766
and he continued **k** on his knees Da 6:10 1289
Him, and **k** and bowing before Him. Mk 15:19 1119, 5087
k down on the beach and praying, Ac 21:5 1119, 5087

KNEELS
well as everyone who **k** to drink." Jg 7:5 1290, 3766

KNEES
to her that she may bear on my **k**, Gn 30:3 1290
Then Joseph took them from his **k**, Gn 48:12 1290
Manasseh, were born on Joseph's **k**. Gn 50:23 1290
"The LORD will strike you on the **k** Dt 28:35 1290
She made him sleep on her **k**, Jg 16:19 1290
from kneeling on his **k** with his 1Ki 8:54 1290
and put his face between his **k**. 1Ki 18:42 1290
all the **k** that have not bowed to 1Ki 19:18 1290
bowed down on his **k** before Elijah, 2Ki 1:13 1290
knelt on his **k** in the presence 2Ch 6:13 1290
and I fell on my **k** and stretched Ezr 9:5 1290
"Why did the **k** receive me, And Jb 3:12 1290
you have strengthened feeble **k**. Jb 4:4 1290
My **k** are weak from fasting, Ps 109:24 1290
on the hip and fondled on the **k**. Is 66:12 1290
and all **k** will become *like* water. Ezk 7:17 1290
and all **k** will be weak as water. Ezk 21:7 1290
the water, water *reaching* the **k**. Ezk 47:4 1290
and his **k** began knocking together. Da 5:6 755a
on his **k** three times a day, Da 6:10 1291
me trembling on my hands and **k**. Da 10:10 1290
Hearts are melting and **k** knocking! Na 2:10 1290
Jesus, falling on his **k** before Him Mt 17:14 1120
and falling on his **k** before Him, Mk 1:40 1120
Then falling on his **k**, Ac 7:60 1119
I bow my **k** before the Father, Eph 3:14 1119
weak and the **k** that are feeble, Heb 12:12 1119

KNELT
k on his knees in the presence 2Ch 6:13 1288
they **k** down before Him and mocked Mt 27:29 1120
ran up to Him and **k** before Him, Mk 10:17 1120
and He **k** down and *began* to pray, Lk 22:41 1119, 5087
all out and **k** down and prayed, Ac 9:40 1119, 5087
k down and prayed with them all. Ac 20:36 1119, 5087

KNEW
and they **k** that they were naked; Gn 3:7 3045
So Noah **k** that the water was Gn 8:11 3045
he **k** what his youngest son had Gn 9:24 3045
Onan **k** that the offspring Gn 38:9 3045
the LORD from the day I **k** you. Dt 9:24 3045
whom the LORD **k** face to face, Dt 34:10 3045
Then Manoah **k** that he was the Jg 13:21 3045
for the iniquity which he **k**, 1Sa 3:13 3045
Israel from Dan even to Beersheba **k** 1Sa 3:20 3045
when all who **k** him previously saw 1Sa 10:11 3045
k that the LORD was with David, 1Sa 18:28 3045
so Jonathan **k** that his father had 1Sa 20:33 3045
only Jonathan and David **k** about 1Sa 20:39 3045
because they **k** that he was fleeing 1Sa 22:17 3045
"I **k** on that day, when Doeg the 1Sa 22:22 3045
Now David **k** that Saul was plotting 1Sa 23:9 3045
and he **k** that Saul was definitely 1Sa 26:4 3045
went away, but no one saw or **k** *it*, 1Sa 26:12 3045
And Saul **k** that it was Samuel, and 1Sa 28:14 3045
because I **k** that he could not live 2Sa 1:10 3045
where he **k** there *were* valiant men. 2Sa 11:16 3045
the fleet, sailors who **k** the sea, 1Ki 9:27 3045
ships and servants who **k** the sea; 2Ch 8:18 3045
Manasseh **k** that the LORD *was* God. 2Ch 33:13 3045
For You **k** that they acted arrogantly Ne 9:10 3045
before all who **k** law and justice Es 1:13 3045
"Because he **k** no quiet within him Jb 20:20 3045
that I **k** where I might find Him, Jb 23:3 3045
You **k** my path. In the way where I Ps 142:3 3045
'Behold, I **k** them.' Is 48:7 3045
Because I **k** that you would deal Is 48:8 3045
I formed you in the womb I **k** you, Jer 1:5 3045
made it known to me and I **k** it; Jer 11:18 3045
Then I **k** that this was the word of Jer 32:8 3045
Gedaliah, when no one **k** about *it*, Jer 41:4 3045
so I **k** that they *were* cherubim. Ezk 10:20 3045
heart, even though you **k** all this, Da 5:22 3046
k that the document was signed, Da 6:10 3046
For the men **k** that he was fleeing Jon 1:10 3045
for I **k** that You are a gracious Jon 4:2 3045
will declare to them, 'I never **k** you; Mt 7:23 1097
'Master, I **k** you to be a hard man, Mt 25:24 1097
you **k** that I reap where I did not Mt 25:26 3609a
For he **k** that because of envy they Mt 27:18 3609a
speak, because they **k** who He was. Mk 1:34 3609a
they **k** Him to be the Christ. Lk 4:41 3609a
But He **k** what they were thinking, Lk 6:8 3609a
But He **k** their thoughts and said Lk 11:17 3609a
that slave who **k** his master's will Lk 12:47 1097
who had drawn the water **k**), Jn 2:9 3609a
Himself to them, for He **k** all men, Jn 2:24 1097
for He Himself **k** what was in man. Jn 2:25 1097
Therefore when the Lord **k** that the Jn 4:1 1097
"If you **k** the gift of God, and Jn 4:10 3609a
So the father **k** that *it was* at Jn 4:53 1097
and **k** that He had already been a Jn 5:6 1097
k what He was intending to do. Jn 6:6 3609a
For Jesus **k** from the beginning who Jn 6:64 3609a
if you **k** Me, you would know My Jn 8:19 3609a
"I **k** that You always hear Me; Jn 11:42 3609a
that if anyone **k** where He was, Jn 11:57 1097
k the one who was betraying Him; Jn 13:11 3609a
one of those reclining *at the table* **k** Jn 13:28 1097
Jesus **k** that they wished to Jn 16:19 1097
was betraying Him, **k** the place, Jn 18:2 3609a
and **k** that GOD HAD SWORN TO HIM Ac 2:30 3609a
EGYPT WHO **K** NOTHING ABOUT JOSEPH. Ac 7:18 3609a
all **k** that his father was a Greek. Ac 16:3 3609a
For even though they **k** God, Ro 1:21 1097
He made Him who **k** no sin *to be* sin 2Co 5:21 1097

KNIFE
in his hand the fire and the **k**. Gn 22:6 3979
and took the **k** to slay his son. Gn 22:10 3979
he took a **k** and laid hold of his Jg 19:29 3979
And put a **k** to your throat If you Pr 23:2 7915
the king cut it with a scribe's **k** Jer 36:23 8593

KNIT
was **k** to the soul of David, 1Sa 18:1 7194
And **k** me together with bones and Jb 10:11 5526b
sinews of his thighs are **k** together. Jb 40:17 8276
By His hand they are **k** together. La 1:14 8276
having been **k** together in love, Col 2:2 4822

KNIVES
"Make for yourself flint **k** and Jos 5:2 2719
So Joshua made himself flint **k** and Jos 5:3 2719
swords And his jaw teeth *like* **k**, Pr 30:14 3979
will cut off the sprigs with pruning **k** Is 18:5 4211

KNOCK
k, and it will be opened to you. Mt 7:7 2925
k, and it will be opened to you. Lk 11:9 2925
stand outside and **k** on the door, Lk 13:25 2925
'Behold, I stand at the door and **k**; Rv 3:20 2925

KNOCKED
When he **k** at the door of the gate, Ac 12:13 2925

KNOCKING
My beloved was **k**: SS 5:2 1849
and his knees began **k** together. Da 5:6 5368
Hearts are melting and knees **k**! Na 2:10 6375
But Peter continued **k**; Ac 12:16 2925

KNOCKS
"And if he **k** out a tooth of his Ex 21:27 5307
to him who **k** it will be opened. Mt 7:8 2925
and to him who **k**, it will be Lk 11:10 2925
door to him when he comes and **k**. Lk 12:36 2925

KNOW
"I do not **k**. Am I my brother's Gn 4:9 3045
I **k** that you are a beautiful woman; Gn 12:11 3045
may I **k** that I will possess it?" Gn 15:8 3045
"**K** for certain that your Gn 15:13 3045
and if not, I will **k**." Gn 18:21 3045
and he did not **k** when she lay down Gn 19:33 3045
and he did not **k** when she lay down Gn 19:35 3045
I **k** that in the integrity of your Gn 20:6 3045
her, **k** that you shall surely die, Gn 20:7 3045
do not **k** who has done this thing; Gn 21:26 3045
for now I **k** that you fear God, Gn 22:12 3045
and by this I will **k** that You Gn 24:14 3045
to **k** whether the LORD had made his Gn 24:21 3045
and if not, let me **k**, Gn 24:49 5046
I do not **k** the day of my death. Gn 27:2 3045
this place, and I did not **k** it." Gn 28:16 3045
"Do you **k** Laban the son of Nahor?" Gn 29:5 3045
And they said, "We **k** *him*." Gn 29:5 3045
for you yourself **k** my service Gn 30:26 3045
"You yourself **k** how I have served Gn 30:29 3045
"You **k** that I have served Gn 31:6 3045
Jacob did not **k** that Rachel had Gn 31:32 3045
for he did not **k** that she was his Gn 38:16 3045
They did not **k**, however, that Gn 42:23 3045
I will **k** that you are honest men: Gn 42:33 3045
I may **k** that you are not spies, Gn 42:34 3045
we possibly **k** that he would say, Gn 43:7 3045
we do not **k** who put our money in Gn 43:22 3045
Do you not **k** that such a man as I Gn 44:15 3045
k that my wife bore me two sons; Gn 44:27 3045
you **k** any capable men among them, Gn 47:6 3045
'I **k**, my son, I know; Gn 48:19 3045
"I know, my son, I **k**; Gn 48:19 3045
over Egypt, who did not **k** Joseph. Ex 1:8 3045
"But I **k** that the king of Egypt Ex 3:19 3045
I **k** that he speaks fluently. Ex 4:14 3045
I do not **k** the LORD, and besides, Ex 5:2 3045
k that I am the LORD your God, Ex 6:7 3045
shall **k** that I am the LORD, Ex 7:5 3045
you shall **k** that I am the LORD: Ex 7:17 3045
that you may **k** that there is no Ex 8:10 3045
in order that you may **k** that I, Ex 8:22 3045
so that you may **k** that there is no Ex 9:14 3045
may **k** that the earth is the LORD's. Ex 9:29 3045
I **k** that you do not yet fear the Ex 9:30 3045
you may **k** that I am the LORD." Ex 10:2 3045
we ourselves do not **k** with what we Ex 10:26 3045
will **k** that I am the LORD." Ex 14:4 3045
will **k** that I am the LORD, Ex 14:18 3045
"At evening you will **k** that the Ex 16:6 3045
k that I am the LORD your God.'" Ex 16:12 3045
For they did not **k** what it was. Ex 16:15 3045
"Now I **k** that the LORD is greater Ex 18:11 3045
k the feelings of a stranger, Ex 23:9 3045
"They shall **k** that I am the Ex 29:46 3045
that you may **k** that I am the LORD Ex 31:13 3045
do not **k** what has become of him." Ex 32:1 3045
you **k** the people yourself, that Ex 32:22 3045
do not **k** what has become of him.' Ex 32:23 3045
I may **k** what I shall do with you.'" Ex 33:5 3045
You Yourself have not let me **k** Ex 33:12 3045
in Your sight, let me **k** Your ways that Ex 33:13 3045
know Your ways that I may **k** You, Ex 33:13 3045
that Moses did not **k** that the skin Ex 34:29 3045
to **k** how to perform all the work Ex 36:1 3045
him, and then he comes to **k** *it*, Lv 5:3 3045
him, and then he comes to **k** *it*, Lv 5:4 3045
unintentionally and did not **k** *it*, Lv 5:18 3045
so that your generations may **k** Lv 23:43 3045
inasmuch as you **k** where we should Nu 10:31 3045
whom you **k** to be the elders of the Nu 11:16 3045
and they will **k** the land which Nu 14:31 3045
and you will **k** My opposition. Nu 14:34 3045
"By this you shall **k** that the Nu 16:28 3045
'You **k** all the hardship that has Nu 20:14 3045
For I **k** that he whom you bless is Nu 22:6 3045
for I did not **k** that you were Nu 22:34 3045
(I **k** that you have much livestock) shall Dt 3:19 3045
that you might **k** that the LORD, Dt 4:35 3045
"**K** therefore today, and take it Dt 4:39 3045
"**K** therefore that the LORD your Dt 7:9 3045
you, to **k** what was in your heart, Dt 8:2 3045
with manna which you did not **k**, Dt 8:3 3045
not know, nor did your fathers **k**, Dt 8:3 3045
"Thus you are to **k** in your heart Dt 8:5 3045
which your fathers did not **k**, Dt 8:16 3045
whom you **k** and of whom you have Dt 9:2 3045

“**K** therefore today that it is the	**Dt 9:3**	3045
“**K**, then, *it is* not because of	**Dt 9:6**	3045
“**K** this day that I *am* not	**Dt 11:2**	3045
‘How will we **k** the word which the	**Dt 18:21**	3045
“Only the trees which you **k** are	**Dt 20:20**	3045
near you, or if you do not **k** him,	**Dt 22:2**	3045
“A people whom you do not **k** shall	**Dt 28:33**	3045
has not given you a heart to **k**,	**Dt 29:4**	3045
k that I am the LORD your God.	**Dt 29:6**	3045
(for you **k** how we lived in the	**Dt 29:16**	3045
for I **k** their intent which they	**Dt 31:21**	3045
“For I **k** your rebellion and your	**Dt 31:27**	3045
“For I **k** that after my death you	**Dt 31:29**	3045
I did not **k** where they were from.	**Jos 2:4**	3045
I do not **k** where the men went.	**Jos 2:5**	3045
“I **k** that the LORD has given you	**Jos 2:9**	3045
k the way by which you shall go,	**Jos 3:4**	3045
that they may **k** that just as I	**Jos 3:7**	3045
“By this you shall **k** that the	**Jos 3:10**	3045
peoples of the earth may **k** that the	**Jos 4:24**	3045
But he did not **k** that *there was* an	**Jos 8:14**	3045
“You **k** the word which the LORD	**Jos 14:6**	3045
He knows, and may Israel itself **k**.	**Jos 22:22**	3045
k that the LORD is in our midst,	**Jos 22:31**	3045
k with certainty that the LORD	**Jos 23:13**	3045
and you **k** in all your hearts and	**Jos 23:14**	3045
after them who did not **k** the LORD,	**Jg 2:10**	3045
then I will **k** that You will	**Jg 6:37**	3045
For Manoah did not **k** that he was	**Jg 13:16**	3045
did not **k** that it was of the LORD,	**Jg 14:4**	3045
“Do you not **k** that the	**Jg 15:11**	3045
But he did not **k** that the LORD had	**Jg 16:20**	3045
I **k** that the LORD will prosper me,	**Jg 17:13**	3045
that we may **k** whether our way on	**Jg 18:5**	3045
“Do you **k** that there are in these	**Jg 18:14**	3045
but Benjamin did not **k** that	**Jg 20:34**	3045
that you did not previously **k**.	**Ru 2:11**	3045
for all my people in the city **k**	**Ru 3:11**	3045
you **k** how the matter turns out;	**Ru 3:18**	3045
but if not, tell me that I may **k**;	**Ru 4:4**	3045
they did not **k** the LORD	**1Sa 2:12**	3045
Now Samuel did not yet **k** the LORD,	**1Sa 3:7**	3045
then we will **k** that it was not	**1Sa 6:9**	3045
Then you will **k** and see that your	**1Sa 12:17**	3045
did not **k** that Jonathan had gone.	**1Sa 14:3**	3045
I **k** your insolence and the	**1Sa 17:28**	3045
k that there is a God in Israel,	**1Sa 17:46**	3045
and that all this assembly may **k**	**1Sa 17:47**	3045
your life, O king, I do not **k**.”	**1Sa 17:55**	3045
‘Do not let Jonathan **k** this,	**1Sa 20:3**	3045
k that he has decided on evil.	**1Sa 20:7**	3045
Do I not **k** that you are choosing	**1Sa 20:30**	3045
‘Let no one **k** anything about the	**1Sa 21:2**	3045
I **k** what God will do for me.”	**1Sa 22:3**	3045
k and perceive that there is no	**1Sa 24:11**	3045
I **k** that you will surely be king,	**1Sa 24:20**	3045
to men whose origin I do not **k**?”	**1Sa 25:11**	3045
k and consider what you should do,	**1Sa 25:17**	3045
“**K** assuredly that you will go out	**1Sa 28:1**	3045
k what your servant can do.”	**1Sa 28:2**	3045
“Behold, you **k** what Saul has	**1Sa 28:9**	3045
“I **k** that you are pleasing in my	**1Sa 29:9**	3045
“How do you **k** that Saul and his	**2Sa 1:5**	3045
Do you not **k** that it will be	**2Sa 2:26**	3045
“You **k** Abner the son of Ner, that	**2Sa 3:25**	3045
but David did not **k** *it.*	**2Sa 3:26**	3045
“Do you not **k** that a prince and a	**2Sa 3:38**	3045
For You **k** Your servant, O Lord GOD!	**2Sa 7:20**	3045
greatness to let Your servant **k**.	**2Sa 7:21**	3045
Did you not **k** that they would	**2Sa 11:20**	3045
to **k** all that is in the earth.”	**2Sa 14:20**	3045
and they did not **k** anything.	**2Sa 15:11**	3045
“You **k** your father and his men,	**2Sa 17:8**	3045
but I did not **k** what *it was.*”	**2Sa 18:29**	3045
for I **k** this day that if Absalom	**2Sa 19:6**	3045
For do I not **k** that I am king over	**2Sa 19:22**	3045
may **k** the number of the people.”	**2Sa 24:2**	3045
and David our lord does not **k** *it?*	**1Ki 1:11**	3045
my lord the king, you do not **k** *it.*	**1Ki 1:18**	3045
“Now you also **k** what Joab the son	**1Ki 2:5**	3045
k what you ought to do to him,	**1Ki 2:9**	3045
“You **k** that the kingdom was mine	**1Ki 2:15**	3045
my father David did not **k** *it:*	**1Ki 2:32**	3045
you will **k** for certain that you	**1Ki 2:37**	3045
‘You will **k** for certain that on	**1Ki 2:42**	3045
“You **k** all the evil which you	**1Ki 2:44**	3045
do not **k** how to go out or come in.	**1Ki 3:7**	3045
“You **k** that David my father was	**1Ki 5:3**	3045
“You **k** that there is no one	**1Ki 5:6**	3045
all his ways, whose heart You **k**,	**1Ki 8:39**	3045
for You alone **k** the hearts	**1Ki 8:39**	3045
of the earth may **k** Your name,	**1Ki 8:43**	3045
and that they may **k** that this house	**1Ki 8:43**	3045
earth may **k** that the LORD is God;	**1Ki 8:60**	3045
they will not **k** that you are the wife	**1Ki 14:2**	3045
“Now I **k** that you are a man of	**1Ki 17:24**	3045
will carry you where I do not **k**;	**1Ki 18:12**	3045
that this people may **k** that You,	**1Ki 18:37**	3045
shall **k** that I am the LORD.’ ”	**1Ki 20:13**	3045
shall **k** that I am the LORD.’ ”	**1Ki 20:28**	3045
“Do you **k** that Ramoth-gilead	**1Ki 22:3**	3045
“Do you **k** that the LORD will take	**2Ki 2:3**	3045
And he said, “Yes, I **k**; be still.”	**2Ki 2:3**	3045
“Do you **k** that the LORD will take	**2Ki 2:5**	3045
he answered, “Yes, I **k**; be still.”	**2Ki 2:5**	3045
and you **k** that your servant feared	**2Ki 4:1**	3045
for they did not **k** *what they were.*	**2Ki 4:39**	3045
and he shall **k** that there is a	**2Ki 5:8**	3045
I **k** that there is no God in all	**2Ki 5:15**	3045
They **k** that we are hungry;	**2Ki 7:12**	3045
“Because I **k** the evil that you	**2Ki 8:12**	3045
“You **k** *very well* the man and his	**2Ki 9:11**	3045
“**K** then that there shall fall to	**2Ki 10:10**	3045
do not **k** the custom of the god of	**2Ki 17:26**	3045
they do not **k** the custom of the god	**2Ki 17:26**	3045
the earth may **k** that You alone,	**2Ki 19:19**	3045
‘But I **k** your sitting down, And	**2Ki 19:27**	3045
For You **k** Your servant.	**1Ch 17:18**	3045
word that I may **k** their number.”	**1Ch 21:2**	3045
Solomon, **k** the God of your father,	**1Ch 28:9**	3045
“Since I **k**, O my God, that You	**1Ch 29:17**	3045
for I **k** that your servants know	**2Ch 2:8**	3045
k how to cut timber of Lebanon;	**2Ch 2:8**	3045
whose heart You **k** for You alone	**2Ch 6:30**	3045
k the hearts of the sons of men,	**2Ch 6:30**	3045
of the earth may **k** Your name,	**2Ch 6:33**	3045
and that they may **k** that this house	**2Ch 6:33**	3045
“Do you not **k** that the LORD God	**2Ch 13:5**	3045
nor do we **k** what to do, but our	**2Ch 20:12**	3045
“I **k** that God has planned to	**2Ch 25:16**	3045
‘Do you not **k** what I and my	**2Ch 32:13**	3045
might **k** all that was in his heart.	**2Ch 32:31**	3045
those who **k** the laws of your God;	**Ezr 7:25**	3046
The officials did not **k** where	**Ne 2:16**	3045
“They will not **k** or see until we	**Ne 4:11**	3045
people of the king’s provinces **k** that	**Es 4:11**	3045
will **k** that your tent is secure,	**Jb 5:24**	3045
“You will **k** also that your	**Jb 5:25**	3045
Hear it, and **k** for yourself.”	**Jb 5:27**	3045
Nor will his place **k** him anymore.	**Jb 7:10**	5234
only of yesterday and **k** nothing,	**Jb 8:9**	3045
“In truth I **k** that this is so;	**Jb 9:2**	3045
the mountains, they **k** not *how,*	**Jb 9:5**	3045
I **k** that You will not acquit me.	**Jb 9:28**	3045
k why You contend with me.	**Jb 10:2**	3045
I **k** that this is within You:	**Jb 10:13**	3045
K then that God forgets a part of	**Jb 11:6**	3045
Deeper than Sheol, what can you **k**?	**Jb 11:8**	3045
does not **k** such things as these?	**Jb 12:3**	854
“Who among all these does not **k**	**Jb 12:9**	3045
“What you **k** I also know;	**Jb 13:2**	3045
“What you know I also **k**;	**Jb 13:2**	1847
I **k** that I will be vindicated.	**Jb 13:18**	3045
honor, but he does not **k** *it;*	**Jb 14:21**	3045
“What do you **k** that we do not know?	**Jb 15:9**	3045
“What do you know that we do not **k**?	**Jb 15:9**	3045
place of him who does not **k** God.”	**Jb 18:21**	3045
K then that God has wronged me And	**Jb 19:6**	3045
me, I **k** that my Redeemer lives,	**Jb 19:25**	3045
you may **k** there is judgment.”	**Jb 19:29**	3045
“Do you **k** this from of old, From	**Jb 20:4**	3045
God repay him so that he may **k** *it.*	**Jb 21:19**	3045
“Behold, I **k** your thoughts, And	**Jb 21:27**	3045
“You say, ‘What does God **k**?	**Jb 22:13**	3045
those who **k** Him not see His days?	**Jb 24:1**	3045
They do not want to **k** its ways Nor	**Jb 24:13**	5234
They do not **k** the light.	**Jb 24:16**	3045
“Man does not **k** its value, Nor is	**Jb 28:13**	3045
the case which I did not **k**.	**Jb 29:16**	3045
“For I **k** that You will bring me	**Jb 30:23**	3045
And let God **k** my integrity.	**Jb 31:6**	3045
“For I do not **k** how to flatter,	**Jb 32:22**	3045
men, And listen to me, you who **k**.	**Jb 34:2**	3045
us **k** among ourselves what is good.	**Jb 34:4**	3045
Therefore declare what you **k**.	**Jb 34:33**	3045
is exalted, and we do not **k** *Him;*	**Jb 36:26**	3045
man, That all men may **k** His work.	**Jb 37:7**	3045
“Do you **k** how God establishes	**Jb 37:15**	3045
“Do you **k** about the layers of the	**Jb 37:16**	3045
set its measurements? Since you **k**.	**Jb 38:5**	3045
caused the dawn to **k** its place,	**Jb 38:12**	3045
Tell *Me,* if you **k** all this.	**Jb 38:18**	3045
“You **k**, for you were born then,	**Jb 38:21**	3045
k the ordinances of the heavens,	**Jb 38:33**	3045
“Do you **k** the time the mountain	**Jb 39:1**	3045
do you **k** the time they give birth?	**Jb 39:2**	3045
“I **k** that You can do all	**Jb 42:2**	3045
for me, which I did not **k**.”	**Jb 42:3**	3045
But **k** that the LORD has set apart	**Ps 4:3**	3045
And those who **k** Your name will put	**Ps 9:10**	3045
nations **k** that they are but men.	**Ps 9:20**	3045
the workers of wickedness not **k**,	**Ps 14:4**	3045
Now I **k** that the LORD saves His	**Ps 20:6**	3045
Make me **k** Your ways, O LORD;	**Ps 25:4**	3045
He will make them **k** His covenant.	**Ps 25:14**	3045
ask me of things that I do not **k**.	**Ps 35:11**	3045
The smiters whom I did not **k**	**Ps 35:15**	3045
lovingkindness to those who **k** You,	**Ps 36:10**	3045
“LORD, make me to **k** my end And	**Ps 39:4**	3045
days; Let me **k** how transient I am.	**Ps 39:4**	3045
does not **k** who will gather them.	**Ps 39:6**	3045
restrain my lips, O LORD, You **k**.	**Ps 40:9**	3045
I **k** that You are pleased with me,	**Ps 41:11**	3045
striving and **k** that I am God;	**Ps 46:10**	3045
“I **k** every bird of the mountains,	**Ps 50:11**	3045
For I **k** my transgressions, And my	**Ps 51:3**	3045
part You will make me **k** wisdom.	**Ps 51:6**	3045
This I **k**, that God is for me.	**Ps 56:9**	3045
men may **k** that God rules in Jacob To	**Ps 59:13**	3045
You **k** my reproach and my	**Ps 69:19**	3045
For I do not **k** the sum *of them.*	**Ps 71:15**	3045
They say, “How does God **k**?	**Ps 73:11**	3045
the generation to come might **k**,	**Ps 78:6**	3045
the nations which do not **k** You,	**Ps 79:6**	3045
heard a language that I did not **k**:	**Ps 81:5**	3045
do not **k** nor do they understand;	**Ps 82:5**	3045
That they may **k** that You alone,	**Ps 83:18**	3045
and Babylon among those who **k** Me;	**Ps 87:4**	3045
the people who **k** the joyful sound!	**Ps 89:15**	3045
heart, And they do not **k** My ways.	**Ps 95:10**	3045
K that the LORD Himself is God;	**Ps 100:3**	3045
I will **k** no evil.	**Ps 101:4**	3045
let them **k** that this is Your hand;	**Ps 109:27**	3045
I **k**, O LORD, that Your judgments	**Ps 119:75**	3045
Even those who **k** Your testimonies.	**Ps 119:79**	3045
That I may **k** Your testimonies.	**Ps 119:125**	3045
For I **k** that the LORD is great And	**Ps 135:5**	3045
You **k** when I sit down and	**Ps 139:2**	3045
O LORD, You **k** it all.	**Ps 139:4**	3045
Search me, O God, and **k** my heart;	**Ps 139:23**	3045
Try me and **k** my anxious thoughts;	**Ps 139:23**	3045
I **k** that the LORD will maintain	**Ps 140:12**	3045
To **k** wisdom and instruction, To	**Pr 1:2**	3045
do not **k** over what they stumble.	**Pr 4:19**	3045
are unstable, she does not **k** *it.*	**Pr 5:6**	3045
So he does not **k** that it *will cost*	**Pr 7:23**	3045
not **k** that the dead are there,	**Pr 9:18**	3045
To make you **k** the certainty of the	**Pr 22:21**	3045
They beat me, *but* I did not **k** *it.*	**Pr 23:35**	3045
“See, we did not **k** this,”	**Pr 24:12**	3045
He not **k** *it* who keeps your soul?	**Pr 24:12**	3045
K *that* wisdom is thus for your	**Pr 24:14**	3045
not **k** what a day may bring forth.	**Pr 27:1**	3045
K well the condition of your	**Pr 27:23**	3045
And does not **k** that want will come	**Pr 28:22**	3045
or His son’s name? Surely you **k**!	**Pr 30:4**	3045
And I set my mind to **k** wisdom and	**Ec 1:17**	3045
wisdom and to **k** madness and folly;	**Ec 1:17**	3045
And yet I **k** that one fate befalls	**Ec 2:14**	3045
I **k** that there is nothing better	**Ec 3:12**	3045
I **k** that everything God does will	**Ec 3:14**	3045
they do not **k** they are doing evil.	**Ec 5:1**	3045
I directed my mind to **k**,	**Ec 7:25**	3045
and to **k** the evil of folly and the	**Ec 7:25**	3045
still I **k** that it will be well for	**Ec 8:12**	3045
When I gave my heart to **k** wisdom	**Ec 8:16**	3045
the wise man should say, “I **k**,”	**Ec 8:17**	3045
Man does not **k** whether *it will be*	**Ec 9:1**	3045
For the living **k** they will die;	**Ec 9:5**	3045
but the dead do not **k** anything,	**Ec 9:5**	3045
Moreover, man does not **k** his time:	**Ec 9:12**	3045
not *even* **k** how to go to a city.	**Ec 10:15**	3045
for you do not **k** what misfortune	**Ec 11:2**	3045
Just as you do not **k** the path of	**Ec 11:5**	3045
so you do not **k** the activity of	**Ec 11:5**	3045
for you do not **k** whether morning	**Ec 11:6**	3045
Yet **k** that God will bring you to	**Ec 11:9**	3045
“If you yourself do not **k**,	**SS 1:8**	3045
manger, *But* Israel does not **k**,	**Is 1:3**	3045
come to pass, that we may **k** *it!*”	**Is 5:19**	3045
“For before the boy will **k** *enough*	**Is 7:16**	3045
And all the people **k** *it,*	**Is 9:9**	3045
will **k** the LORD in that day.	**Is 19:21**	3045
who err in mind will **k** the truth,	**Is 29:24**	3045
all the kingdoms of the earth may **k**	**Is 37:20**	3045
“But I **k** your sitting down And	**Is 37:28**	3045
Do you not **k**? Have you not heard?	**Is 40:21**	3045
Do you not **k**? Have you not heard?	**Is 40:28**	3045
them and **k** their outcome	**Is 41:22**	3045
That we may **k** that you are gods;	**Is 41:23**	3045
the beginning, that we might **k**?	**Is 41:26**	3045
the blind by a way they do not **k**,	**Is 42:16**	3045
they do not **k** I will guide them.	**Is 42:16**	3045
that you may **k** and believe Me And	**Is 43:10**	3045
is there any *other* Rock? I **k** of none	**Is 44:8**	3045
own witnesses fail to see or **k**,	**Is 44:9**	3045
They do not **k**, nor do they	**Is 44:18**	3045
So that you may **k** that it is I,	**Is 45:3**	3045
That men may **k** from the rising to	**Is 45:6**	3045
Nor **k** loss of children.’	**Is 47:8**	3045
you will not **k** how to charm away;	**Is 47:11**	3045
not **k** Will come on you suddenly.	**Is 47:11**	3045
I **k** that you are obstinate,	**Is 48:4**	3045
And *you* will **k** that I am the LORD;	**Is 49:23**	3045
And all flesh will **k** that I,	**Is 49:26**	3045
That I may **k** how to sustain the	**Is 50:4**	3045
I **k** that I will not be ashamed.	**Is 50:7**	3045
to Me, you who **k** righteousness,	**Is 51:7**	3045
My people shall **k** My name;	**Is 52:6**	3045
will call a nation you do not **k**,	**Is 55:5**	3045
are blind, All of them **k** nothing.	**Is 56:10**	3045
by day and delight to **k** My ways,	**Is 58:2**	1847
They do not **k** the way of peace,	**Is 59:8**	3045
treads on them does not **k** peace.	**Is 59:8**	3045
with us, And we **k** our iniquities:	**Is 59:12**	3045
Then you will **k** that I, the LORD,	**Is 60:16**	3045
though Abraham does not **k** us And	**Is 63:16**	3045
“For I **k** their works and their	**Is 66:18**	
Behold, I do not **k** how to speak,	**Jer 1:6**	3045
who handle the law did not **k** Me;	**Jer 2:8**	3045
K therefore and see that it is	**Jer 2:19**	3045
K what you have done!	**Jer 2:23**	3045
people are foolish, They **k** Me not;	**Jer 4:22**	3045
But to do good they do not **k**.”	**Jer 4:22**	3045
For they do not **k** the way of the	**Jer 5:4**	3045
For they **k** the way of the LORD	**Jer 5:5**	3045
whose language you do not **k**,	**Jer 5:15**	3045
They did not even **k** how to blush.	**Jer 6:15**	3045
“Therefore hear, O nations, And **k**,	**Jer 6:18**	3045
you may **k** and assay their way.”	**Jer 6:27**	3045
My people do not **k** The ordinance	**Jer 8:7**	3045
And they did not **k** how to blush;	**Jer 8:12**	3045
to evil, And they do not **k** Me,”	**Jer 9:3**	3045
deceit they refuse to **k** Me,”	**Jer 9:6**	3045
I **k**, O LORD, that a man’s way is	**Jer 10:23**	3045
on the nations that do not **k** You And	**Jer 10:25**	3045
And I did not **k** that they had	**Jer 11:19**	3045

But You **k** me, O LORD;	**Jer 12:3**	3045
'Do we not very well **k** that every	**Jer 13:12**	3045
the land that they do not **k**.' "	**Jer 14:18**	3045
We **k** our wickedness, O LORD, The	**Jer 14:20**	3045
bring *it* Into a land you do not **k**;	**Jer 15:14**	3045
You who **k**, O LORD, Remember me,	**Jer 15:15**	3045
K that for Your sake I endure	**Jer 15:15**	3045
behold, I am going to make them **k**	**Jer 16:21**	3045
make them **k** My power and My might;	**Jer 16:21**	3045
k that My name is the LORD."	**Jer 16:21**	3045
In the land which you do not **k**;	**Jer 17:4**	3045
You Yourself **k** that the utterance of my	**Jer 17:16**	3045
k All their deadly designs against	**Jer 18:23**	3045
not that what it means to **k** Me?"	**Jer 22:16**	1847
I will give them a heart to **k** Me,	**Jer 24:7**	3045
"Only **k** for certain that if you	**Jer 26:15**	3045
I **k** the plans that I have for you,'	**Jer 29:11**	3045
'**K** the LORD,' for they will all	**Jer 31:34**	3045
the LORD,' for they will all **k** Me,	**Jer 31:34**	3045
things, which you do not **k**.'	**Jer 33:3**	3045
not let anyone **k** where you are."	**Jer 36:19**	3045
"Let no man **k** about these words	**Jer 38:24**	3045
Nethaniah, and not a man will **k**!	**Jer 40:15**	3045
will **k** whose word will stand,	**Jer 44:28**	3045
so that you may **k** that My words	**Jer 44:29**	3045
Even all of you who **k** his name;	**Jer 48:17**	3045
"I **k** his fury," declares the LORD,	**Jer 48:30**	3045
they will **k** that a prophet has been	**Ezk 2:5**	3045
then they will **k** that I, the LORD,	**Ezk 5:13**	3045
and you will **k** that I am the LORD.	**Ezk 6:7**	3045
they will **k** that I am the LORD;	**Ezk 6:10**	3045
you will **k** that I am the LORD,	**Ezk 6:13**	3045
will **k** that I am the LORD.	**Ezk 6:14**	3045
you will **k** that I am the LORD!'	**Ezk 7:4**	3045
then you will **k** that I, the LORD,	**Ezk 7:9**	3045
will **k** that I am the LORD.' "	**Ezk 7:27**	3045
of Israel, for I **k** your thoughts.	**Ezk 11:5**	3045
so you shall **k** that I am the LORD.	**Ezk 11:10**	3045
you will **k** that I am the LORD;	**Ezk 11:12**	3045
"So they will **k** that I am the	**Ezk 12:15**	3045
and may **k** that I am the LORD."	**Ezk 12:16**	3045
will **k** that I am the LORD.	**Ezk 12:20**	3045
you may **k** that I am the Lord GOD.	**Ezk 13:9**	3045
And you will **k** that I am the LORD.	**Ezk 13:14**	3045
and you will **k** that I am the LORD.	**Ezk 13:21**	3045
you will **k** that I am the LORD."	**Ezk 13:23**	3045
So you will **k** that I am the LORD.	**Ezk 14:8**	3045
for you will **k** that I have not	**Ezk 14:23**	3045
you will **k** that I am the LORD,	**Ezk 15:7**	3045
you shall **k** that I am the LORD,	**Ezk 16:62**	3045
you not **k** what these things *mean?*'	**Ezk 17:12**	3045
and you will **k** that I, the LORD,	**Ezk 17:21**	3045
field will **k** that I am the LORD;	**Ezk 17:24**	3045
Make them **k** the abominations of	**Ezk 20:4**	3045
that they might **k** that I am the	**Ezk 20:12**	3045
k that I am the LORD your God.'	**Ezk 20:20**	3045
might **k** that I am the LORD." '	**Ezk 20:26**	3045
you will **k** that I am the LORD.	**Ezk 20:38**	3045
"And you will **k** that I am the LORD,	**Ezk 20:42**	3045
"Then you will **k** that I am the LORD	**Ezk 20:44**	3045
"Thus all flesh will **k** that I,	**Ezk 21:5**	3045
her to **k** all her abominations.	**Ezk 22:2**	3045
will **k** that I am the LORD.	**Ezk 22:16**	3045
and you will **k** that I, the LORD,	**Ezk 22:22**	3045
will **k** that I am the Lord GOD.' "	**Ezk 23:49**	3045
will **k** that I am the Lord GOD.	**Ezk 24:24**	3045
will **k** that I am the LORD.' "	**Ezk 24:27**	3045
you will **k** that I am the LORD."	**Ezk 25:5**	3045
you will **k** that I am the LORD."	**Ezk 25:7**	3045
they will **k** that I am the LORD."	**Ezk 25:11**	3045
thus they will **k** My vengeance,"	**Ezk 25:14**	3045
and they will **k** that I am the LORD	**Ezk 25:17**	3045
will **k** that I am the LORD.' "	**Ezk 26:6**	3045
"All who **k** you among the peoples	**Ezk 28:19**	3045
they will **k** that I am the LORD when	**Ezk 28:22**	3045
they will **k** that I am the LORD.	**Ezk 28:23**	3045
will **k** that I am the Lord GOD."	**Ezk 28:24**	3045
k that I am the LORD their God.	**Ezk 28:26**	3045
Egypt will **k** that I am the LORD,	**Ezk 29:6**	3045
they will **k** that I am the LORD.	**Ezk 29:9**	3045
k that I am the Lord GOD.	**Ezk 29:16**	3045
they will **k** that I am the LORD."	**Ezk 29:21**	3045
they will **k** that I am the LORD,	**Ezk 30:8**	3045
will **k** that I am the LORD.	**Ezk 30:19**	3045
they will **k** that I am the LORD,	**Ezk 30:25**	3045
will **k** that I am the LORD.' "	**Ezk 30:26**	3045
they shall **k** that I am the LORD.	**Ezk 32:15**	3045
they will **k** that I am the LORD,	**Ezk 33:29**	3045
then they will **k** that a prophet has	**Ezk 33:33**	3045
they will **k** that I am the LORD,	**Ezk 34:27**	3045
"Then they will **k** that I, the	**Ezk 34:30**	3045
you will **k** that I am the LORD.	**Ezk 35:4**	3045
you will **k** that I am the LORD.	**Ezk 35:9**	3045
"Then you will **k** that I, the	**Ezk 35:12**	3045
will **k** that I am the LORD."	**Ezk 35:15**	3045
you will **k** that I am the LORD.	**Ezk 36:11**	3045
nations will **k** that I am the LORD,"	**Ezk 36:23**	3045
round about you will **k** that I,	**Ezk 36:36**	3045
will **k** that I am the LORD.	**Ezk 36:38**	3045
"O Lord GOD, You **k**."	**Ezk 37:3**	3045
you will **k** that I am the LORD.' "	**Ezk 37:6**	3045
you will **k** that I am the LORD,	**Ezk 37:13**	3045
Then you will **k** that I, the LORD,	**Ezk 37:14**	3045
"And the nations will **k** that I am	**Ezk 37:28**	3045
securely, will you not **k** *it?*	**Ezk 38:14**	3045
so that the nations may **k** Me	**Ezk 38:16**	3045
will **k** that I am the LORD."	**Ezk 38:23**	3045
they will **k** that I am the LORD.	**Ezk 39:6**	3045
nations will **k** that I am the LORD,	**Ezk 39:7**	3045
"And the house of Israel will **k**	**Ezk 39:22**	3045
"The nations will **k** that the	**Ezk 39:23**	3045
they will **k** that I am the LORD	**Ezk 39:28**	3045
"I **k** for certain that you are	**Da 2:8**	3046
that I may **k** that you can declare	**Da 2:9**	3046
since I **k** that a spirit of the	**Da 4:9**	3046
In order that the living may **k**	**Da 4:17**	3046
"Then I desired to **k** the exact	**Da 7:19**	3321
I am going to let you **k** what will	**Da 8:19**	3045
"So you are to **k** and discern *that*	**Da 9:25**	3045
but the people who **k** their God	**Da 11:32**	3045
a god whom his fathers did not **k**;	**Da 11:38**	3045
"For she does not **k** that it was I	**Hos 2:8**	3045
Then you will **k** the LORD.	**Hos 2:20**	3045
I **k** Ephraim, and Israel is not	**Hos 5:3**	3045
them, And they do not **k** the LORD.	**Hos 5:4**	3045
"So let us **k**, let us press on to	**Hos 6:3**	3045
let us press on to **k** the LORD.	**Hos 6:3**	3045
strength, Yet he does not **k** *it;*	**Hos 7:9**	3045
on him, Yet he does not **k** *it.*	**Hos 7:9**	3045
"My God, we of Israel **k** You!"	**Hos 8:2**	3045
princes, but I did not **k** *it.*	**Hos 8:4**	3045
Let Israel **k** *this!*	**Hos 9:7**	3045
they did not **k** that I healed them.	**Hos 11:3**	3045
were not to **k** any god except Me,	**Hos 13:4**	3045
is discerning, let him **k** them.	**Hos 14:9**	3045
"Thus you will **k** that I am in the	**Jl 2:27**	3045
k that I am the LORD your God,	**Jl 3:17**	3045
not **k** how to do what is right,"	**Am 3:10**	3045
For I **k** your transgressions are	**Am 5:12**	3045
for I **k** that on account of me this	**Jon 1:12**	3045
persons who do not **k** *the difference*	**Jon 4:11**	3045
Is it not for you to **k** justice?	**Mi 3:1**	3045
do not **k** the thoughts of the LORD,	**Mi 4:12**	3045
So that you might **k** the	**Mi 6:5**	3045
Then you will **k** that the LORD of	**Zch 2:9**	3045
and you will **k** that the LORD of	**Zch 2:11**	3045
"Do you not **k** what these are?"	**Zch 4:5**	3045
Then you will **k** that the LORD of	**Zch 4:9**	3045
"Do you not **k** what these are?"	**Zch 4:13**	3045
Then you will **k** that the LORD of	**Zch 6:15**	3045
"Then you will **k** that I have sent	**Mal 2:4**	3045
do not let your left hand **k** what	**Mt 6:3**	*1097*
k how to give good gifts to your	**Mt 7:11**	*3609a*
"You will **k** them by their fruits.	**Mt 7:16**	*1921*
you will **k** them by their fruits.	**Mt 7:20**	*1921*
"But so that you may **k** that	**Mt 9:6**	*3609a*
nor does anyone **k** the Father except	**Mt 11:27**	*1921*
"To you it has been granted to **k**	**Mt 13:11**	*1097*
"Do You **k** that the Pharisees were	**Mt 15:12**	*3609a*
Do you **k** how to discern the	**Mt 16:3**	*1097*
do not **k** what you are asking.	**Mt 20:22**	*3609a*
"You **k** that the rulers of the	**Mt 20:25**	*3609a*
they said, "We do not **k**."	**Mt 21:27**	*3609a*
we **k** that You are truthful and	**Mt 22:16**	*3609a*
leaves, you **k** that summer is near;	**Mt 24:32**	*1097*
k which day your Lord is coming.	**Mt 24:42**	*3609a*
at an hour which he does not **k**,	**Mt 24:50**	*1097*
I say to you, I do not **k** you.'	**Mt 25:12**	*3609a*
you do not **k** the day nor the hour.	**Mt 25:13**	*3609a*
"You **k** that after two days the	**Mt 26:2**	*3609a*
not **k** what you are talking about."	**Mt 26:70**	*3609a*
"I do not **k** the man."	**Mt 26:72**	*3609a*
"I do not **k** the man!"	**Mt 26:74**	*3609a*
make it *as* secure as you **k** how."	**Mt 27:65**	*3609a*
for I **k** that you are looking for	**Mt 28:5**	*3609a*
I **k** who You are—the Holy One of	**Mk 1:24**	*3609a*
"But so that you may **k** that	**Mk 2:10**	*3609a*
grows—how, he himself does not **k**.	**Mk 4:27**	*3609a*
that no one should **k** about this,	**Mk 5:43**	*1097*
He wanted no one to **k** *of it*	**Mk 7:24**	*1097*
For he did not **k** what to answer;	**Mk 9:6**	*3609a*
did not want anyone to **k** *about it.*	**Mk 9:30**	*1097*
"You **k** the commandments,	**Mk 10:19**	*3609a*
do not **k** what you are asking.	**Mk 10:38**	*3609a*
"You **k** that those who are	**Mk 10:42**	*3609a*
they said, "We do not **k**."	**Mk 11:33**	*3609a*
we **k** that You are truthful and	**Mk 12:14**	*3609a*
leaves, you **k** that summer is near.	**Mk 13:28**	*1097*
k when the *appointed* time will come.	**Mk 13:33**	*3609a*
you do not **k** when the master of the	**Mk 13:35**	*3609a*
they did not **k** what to answer Him.	**Mk 14:40**	*3609a*
"I neither **k** nor understand what	**Mk 14:68**	*3609a*
"I do not **k** this man you are	**Mk 14:71**	*3609a*
so that you may **k** the exact	**Lk 1:4**	*1921*
"How will I **k** this *for certain?*	**Lk 1:18**	*1097*
Did you not **k** that I had to be in	**Lk 2:49**	*3609a*
I **k** who You are—the Holy One of	**Lk 4:34**	*3609a*
"But, so that you may **k** that	**Lk 5:24**	*3609a*
He would **k** who and what sort of	**Lk 7:39**	*1097*
"To you it has been granted to **k**	**Lk 8:10**	*1097*
"You do not **k** what kind of spirit	**Lk 9:55**	*3609a*
k how to give good gifts to your	**Lk 11:13**	*3609a*
him and at an hour he does not **k**,	**Lk 12:46**	*1097*
but the one who did not **k** *it,*	**Lk 12:48**	*1097*
You **k** how to analyze the	**Lk 12:56**	*3609a*
'I do not **k** where you are from.'	**Lk 13:25**	*3609a*
I do not **k** where you are from;	**Lk 13:27**	*3609a*
'I **k** what I shall do, so that when	**Lk 16:4**	*1097*
"You **k** the commandments,	**Lk 18:20**	*3609a*
k what business they had done.	**Lk 19:15**	*1097*
you **k** that I am an exacting man,	**Lk 19:22**	*3609a*
they did not **k** where *it came* from.	**Lk 20:7**	*3609a*
we **k** that You speak and teach	**Lk 20:21**	*3609a*
you see it and **k** for yourselves	**Lk 21:30**	*1097*
denied three times that you **k** Me."	**Lk 22:34**	*3609a*
"Woman, I do not **k** Him."	**Lk 22:57**	*3609a*
not **k** what you are talking about."	**Lk 22:60**	*3609a*
do not **k** what they are doing."	**Lk 23:34**	*3609a*
Him, and the world did not **k** Him.	**Jn 1:10**	*1097*
you stands One whom you do not **k**.	**Jn 1:26**	*3609a*
"How do You **k** me?"	**Jn 1:48**	*1097*
and did not **k** where it came from	**Jn 2:9**	*3609a*
we **k** that You have come from God	**Jn 3:2**	*3609a*
but do not **k** where it comes from	**Jn 3:8**	*3609a*
to you, we speak of what we **k**	**Jn 3:11**	*3609a*
worship what you do not **k**;	**Jn 4:22**	*3609a*
we worship what we **k**,	**Jn 4:22**	*3609a*
"I **k** that Messiah is coming	**Jn 4:25**	*3609a*
to eat that you do not **k** about."	**Jn 4:32**	*3609a*
k that this One is indeed the Savior	**Jn 4:42**	*3609a*
was healed did not **k** who it was,	**Jn 5:13**	*3609a*
and I **k** that the testimony which	**Jn 5:32**	*3609a*
but I **k** you, that you do not have	**Jn 5:42**	*1097*
whose father and mother we **k**?	**Jn 6:42**	*3609a*
k that You are the Holy One of God	**Jn 6:69**	*1097*
will, he will **k** of the teaching,	**Jn 7:17**	*1097*
really **k** that this is the Christ,	**Jn 7:26**	*1097*
we **k** where this man is from;	**Jn 7:27**	*3609a*
k Me and know where I am from;	**Jn 7:28**	*3609a*
know Me and **k** where I am from;	**Jn 7:28**	*3609a*
Me is true, whom you do not **k**.	**Jn 7:28**	*3609a*
"I **k** Him, because I am from Him,	**Jn 7:29**	*3609a*
crowd which does not **k** the Law	**Jn 7:49**	*1097*
for I **k** where I came from and	**Jn 8:14**	*3609a*
you do not **k** where I come from or	**Jn 8:14**	*3609a*
"You **k** neither Me nor My Father;	**Jn 8:19**	*3609a*
Me, you would **k** My Father also."	**Jn 8:19**	*3609a*
Man, then you will **k** that I am *He,*	**Jn 8:28**	*1097*
and you will **k** the truth, and the	**Jn 8:32**	*1097*
"I **k** that you are Abraham's	**Jn 8:37**	*3609a*
"Now we **k** that You have a demon.	**Jn 8:52**	*1097*
and you have not come to **k** Him,	**Jn 8:55**	*1097*
not come to know Him, but I **k** Him;	**Jn 8:55**	*3609a*
and if I say that I do not **k** Him,	**Jn 8:55**	*3609a*
a liar like you, but I do **k** Him and	**Jn 8:55**	*3609a*
Where is He?" He said, "I do not **k**.	**Jn 9:12**	*3609a*
"We **k** that this is our son, and	**Jn 9:20**	*3609a*
but how he now sees, we do not **k**;	**Jn 9:21**	*3609a*
who opened his eyes, we do not **k**.	**Jn 9:21**	*3609a*
we **k** that this man is a sinner."	**Jn 9:24**	*3609a*
He is a sinner, I do not **k**;	**Jn 9:25**	*3609a*
one thing I do **k**, that though I	**Jn 9:25**	*3609a*
"We **k** that God has spoken to Moses,	**Jn 9:29**	*3609a*
we do not **k** where He is from."	**Jn 9:29**	*3609a*
you do not **k** where He is from,	**Jn 9:30**	*3609a*
We **k** that God does not hear sinners	**Jn 9:31**	*3609a*
him because they **k** his voice.	**Jn 10:4**	*3609a*
do not **k** the voice of strangers."	**Jn 10:5**	*3609a*
and I **k** My own and My own know	**Jn 10:14**	*1097*
I know My own and My own **k** Me,	**Jn 10:14**	*1097*
knows Me and I **k** the Father;	**Jn 10:15**	*1097*
sheep hear My voice, and I **k** them,	**Jn 10:27**	*1097*
that you may **k** and understand that	**Jn 10:38**	*1097*
I **k** that whatever You ask of God,	**Jn 11:22**	*3609a*
"I **k** that he will rise again in	**Jn 11:24**	*3609a*
"You **k** nothing at all,	**Jn 11:49**	*3609a*
darkness does not **k** where he goes.	**Jn 12:35**	*3609a*
"I **k** that His commandment is	**Jn 12:50**	*3609a*
"Do you **k** what I have done to you?	**Jn 13:12**	*1097*
"If you **k** these things, you are	**Jn 13:17**	*3609a*
I **k** the ones I have chosen;	**Jn 13:18**	*3609a*
at a loss *to* **k** of which one He	**Jn 13:22**	
will **k** that you are My disciples,	**Jn 13:35**	*1097*
you **k** the way where I am going."	**Jn 14:4**	*3609a*
we do not **k** where You are going,	**Jn 14:5**	*3609a*
are going, how do we **k** the way?"	**Jn 14:5**	*3609a*
from now on you **k** Him, and have	**Jn 14:7**	*1097*
and *yet* you have not come to **k** Me,	**Jn 14:9**	*1097*
it does not see Him or **k** Him,	**Jn 14:17**	*1097*
but you **k** Him because He abides	**Jn 14:17**	*1097*
will **k** that I am in My Father,	**Jn 14:20**	*1097*
may **k** that I love the Father,	**Jn 14:31**	*1097*
not **k** what his master is doing;	**Jn 15:15**	*3609a*
you **k** that it has hated Me before	**Jn 15:18**	*1097*
they do not **k** the One who sent Me.	**Jn 15:21**	*3609a*
not **k** what He is talking about."	**Jn 16:18**	*3609a*
"Now we **k** that You know all	**Jn 16:30**	*3609a*
"Now we know that You **k** all things,	**Jn 16:30**	*3609a*
life, that they may **k** You,	**Jn 17:3**	*1097*
"Now they have come to **k** that	**Jn 17:7**	*1097*
may **k** that You sent Me,	**Jn 17:23**	*1097*
they **k** what I said."	**Jn 18:21**	*3609a*
k that I find no guilt in Him."	**Jn 19:4**	*1097*
Do You not **k** that I have authority	**Jn 19:10**	*3609a*
not **k** where they have laid Him."	**Jn 20:2**	*3609a*
not **k** where they have laid Him."	**Jn 20:13**	*3609a*
and did not **k** that it was Jesus.	**Jn 20:14**	*3609a*
did not **k** that it was Jesus.	**Jn 21:4**	*3609a*
You **k** that I love You."	**Jn 21:15**	*3609a*
You **k** that I love You."	**Jn 21:16**	*3609a*
"Lord, You **k** all things;	**Jn 21:17**	*3609a*
You **k** that I love You."	**Jn 21:17**	*1097*
and we **k** that his testimony is true.	**Jn 21:24**	*3609a*
"It is not for you to **k** times or	**Ac 1:7**	*1097*
Lord, who **k** the hearts of all men,	**Ac 1:24**	*2589*
midst, just as you yourselves **k**	**Ac 2:22**	*3609a*
house of Israel **k** for certain that God	**Ac 2:36**	*1097*
this man whom you see and **k**;	**Ac 3:16**	*3609a*
I **k** that you acted in ignorance,	**Ac 3:17**	*3609a*
DO NOT **K** WHAT HAPPENED TO HIM.'	**Ac 7:40**	*3609a*
"You yourselves **k** how unlawful it	**Ac 10:28**	*1987*
you yourselves **k** the thing which	**Ac 10:37**	*3609a*
"*You* **k** *of* Jesus of Nazareth,	**Ac 10:38**	
and he did not **k** that what was	**Ac 12:9**	*3609a*
"Now I **k** for sure that the Lord	**Ac 12:11**	*3609a*
you **k** that in the early days God	**Ac 15:7**	*1987*
"May we **k** what this new teaching	**Ac 17:19**	*1097*

we want to **k** what these	Ac 17:20	*1097*
Jesus, and I **k** about Paul,	Ac 19:15	*1987*
you **k** that our prosperity depends	Ac 19:25	*1987*
and the majority did not **k** for	Ac 19:32	*3609a*
not **k** that the city of the Ephesians is	Ac 19:35	*1097*
"You yourselves **k**, from the first	Ac 20:18	*1987*
now, behold, I **k** that all of you,	Ac 20:25	*3609a*
"I **k** that after my departure	Ac 20:29	*3609a*
"You yourselves **k** that these	Ac 20:34	*1097*
and all will **k** that there is	Ac 21:24	*1097*
And he said, "Do you **k** Greek?	Ac 21:37	*1097*
has appointed you to **k** His will and	Ac 22:14	*1097*
wishing to **k** for certain why he	Ac 22:30	*1097*
the Jews, as you also very well **k**.	Ac 25:10	*1921*
all Jews **k** my manner of life from	Ac 26:4	*3609a*
I **k** that you do."	Ac 26:27	*3609a*
they **k** the ordinance of God,	Ro 1:32	*1921*
And we **k** that the judgment of God	Ro 2:2	*3609a*
and **k** *His* will and approve the	Ro 2:18	*1097*
we **k** that whatever the Law says,	Ro 3:19	*3609a*
Or do you not **k** that all of us who	Ro 6:3	*50*
Do you not **k** that when you present	Ro 6:16	*3609a*
Or do you not **k**, brethren	Ro 7:1	*50*
speaking to those who **k** the law),	Ro 7:1	*1097*
to **k** sin except through the Law;	Ro 7:7	*1097*
we **k** that the Law is spiritual,	Ro 7:14	*3609a*
For I **k** that nothing good dwells	Ro 7:18	*3609a*
For we **k** that the whole creation	Ro 8:22	*3609a*
do not **k** how to pray as we should,	Ro 8:26	*3609a*
And we **k** that God causes all	Ro 8:28	*3609a*
I say, surely Israel did not **k**,	Ro 10:19	*1097*
Or do you not **k** what the Scripture	Ro 11:2	*3609a*
I **k** and am convinced in the Lord	Ro 14:14	*3609a*
I **k** that when I come to you, I	Ro 15:29	*3609a*
not **k** whether I baptized any other.	1Co 1:16	*3609a*
its wisdom did not *come to* **k** God,	1Co 1:21	*1097*
For I determined to **k** nothing	1Co 2:2	*3609a*
that we may **k** the things freely	1Co 2:12	*3609a*
k that you are a temple of God and	1Co 3:16	*3609a*
Do you not **k** that a little leaven	1Co 5:6	*3609a*
Or do you not **k** that the saints	1Co 6:2	*3609a*
not **k** that we will judge angels?	1Co 6:3	*3609a*
Or do you not **k** that the	1Co 6:9	*3609a*
Do you not **k** that your bodies are	1Co 6:15	*3609a*
Or do you not **k** that the one who	1Co 6:16	*3609a*
Or do you not **k** that your body is	1Co 6:19	*3609a*
For how do you **k**, O wife, whether	1Co 7:16	*3609a*
Or how do you **k**, O husband,	1Co 7:16	*3609a*
we **k** that we all have knowledge.	1Co 8:1	*3609a*
not yet known as he ought to **k**;	1Co 8:2	*1097*
we **k** that there is no such thing	1Co 8:4	*3609a*
Do you not **k** that those who	1Co 9:13	*3609a*
Do you not **k** that those who run in	1Co 9:24	*3609a*
You **k** that when you were pagans,	1Co 12:2	*3609a*
and **k** all mysteries and all	1Co 13:2	*3609a*
For we **k** in part and we prophesy	1Co 13:9	*1097*
now I **k** in part, but then I will	1Co 13:12	*1097*
but then I will **k** fully just as I	1Co 13:12	*1921*
not **k** the meaning of the language,	1Co 14:11	*3609a*
he does not **k** what you are saying?	1Co 14:16	*3609a*
(you **k** the household of Stephanas,	1Co 16:15	*3609a*
but that you might **k** the love	2Co 2:4	*1097*
For we **k** that if the earthly tent	2Co 5:1	*3609a*
yet now we **k** *Him in this way* no longer.	2Co 5:16	*1097*
For you **k** the grace of our Lord	2Co 8:9	*1097*
for I **k** your readiness, of which I	2Co 9:2	*3609a*
I **k** a man in Christ who fourteen	2Co 12:2	*3609a*
whether in the body I do not **k**,	2Co 12:2	*3609a*
or out of the body I do not **k**,	2Co 12:2	*3609a*
And I **k** how such a man	2Co 12:3	*3609a*
or apart from the body I do not **k**,	2Co 12:3	*3609a*
For I would have you **k**,	Ga 1:11	*1107*
that time, when you did not **k** God,	Ga 4:8	*3609a*
now that you have come to **k** God,	Ga 4:9	*1097*
but you **k** that it was because of a	Ga 4:13	*3609a*
so that you will **k** what is the hope	Eph 1:18	*3609a*
and to **k** the love of Christ which	Eph 3:19	*1097*
For this you **k** with certainty,	Eph 5:5	*3609a*
also may **k** about my circumstances,	Eph 6:21	*3609a*
so that you may **k** about us,	Eph 6:22	*1097*
Now I want you to **k**,	Php 1:12	*1097*
for I **k** that this will turn out	Php 1:19	*3609a*
and I do not **k** which to choose.	Php 1:22	*1107*
I **k** that I will remain and	Php 1:25	*3609a*
But you **k** of his proven worth,	Php 2:22	*1097*
that I may **k** Him and the power of	Php 3:10	*1097*
I **k** how to get along with humble	Php 4:12	*3609a*
also **k** how to live in prosperity;	Php 4:12	*3609a*
You yourselves also **k**,	Php 4:15	*3609a*
For I want you to **k** how great a	Col 2:1	*3609a*
so that you will **k** how you should	Col 4:6	*3609a*
that you may **k** about our	Col 4:8	*1097*
just as you **k** what kind of men we	1Th 1:5	*3609a*
For you yourselves **k**,	1Th 2:1	*3609a*
mistreated in Philippi, as you **k**,	1Th 2:2	*3609a*
with flattering speech, as you **k**,	1Th 2:5	*3609a*
just as you **k** how we *were*	1Th 2:11	*3609a*
for you yourselves **k** that we have	1Th 3:3	*3609a*
and so it came to pass, as you **k**.	1Th 3:4	*3609a*
For you **k** what commandments we	1Th 4:2	*3609a*
that each of you **k** how to possess	1Th 4:4	*3609a*
the Gentiles who do not **k** God;	1Th 4:5	*3609a*
For you yourselves **k** full well	1Th 5:2	*3609a*
to those who do not **k** God and to	2Th 1:8	*3609a*
And you **k** what restrains him now,	2Th 2:6	*3609a*
For you yourselves **k** how you ought	2Th 3:7	*3609a*
But we **k** that the Law is good, if	1Tm 1:8	*3609a*
if a man does not **k** how to manage	1Tm 3:5	*3609a*
I write so that you will **k** how one	1Tm 3:15	*3609a*
those who believe and **k** the truth.	1Tm 4:3	*1921*
for I **k** whom I have believed and I	2Tm 1:12	*3609a*
and you **k** very well what services he	2Tm 1:18	*1097*
They profess to **k** God, but by	Ti 1:16	*3609a*
since I **k** that you will do even	Phm 1:21	*3609a*
AND THEY DID NOT **K** MY WAYS';	Heb 3:10	*1097*
'**K** THE LORD,' FOR ALL WILL KNOW	Heb 8:11	*1097*
FOR ALL WILL **K** ME,	Heb 8:11	*3609a*
For we **k** Him who said,	Heb 10:30	*3609a*
For you **k** that even afterwards,	Heb 12:17	*3609a*
This you **k**, my beloved brethren.	Jas 1:19	*3609a*
do you not **k** that friendship with	Jas 4:4	*3609a*
Yet you do not **k** what your life	Jas 4:14	*1987*
let him **k** that he who turns a	Jas 5:20	*1097*
seeking to **k** what person or time	1Pe 1:11	*2045*
even though you *already* **k** *them,*	2Pe 1:12	*3609a*
But **k** this first of all, that no	2Pe 1:20	*1097*
K this first of all, that in the	2Pe 3:3	*1097*
k that we have come to know Him,	1Jn 2:3	*1097*
know that we have come to **k** Him,	1Jn 2:3	*1097*
"I have come to **k** Him,"	1Jn 2:4	*1097*
By this we **k** that we are in Him:	1Jn 2:5	*1097*
and does not **k** where he is going	1Jn 2:11	*3609a*
because you **k** Him who has been	1Jn 2:13	*1097*
because you **k** the Father	1Jn 2:13	*1097*
because you **k** Him who has been	1Jn 2:14	*1097*
we **k** that it is the last hour.	1Jn 2:18	*1097*
from the Holy One, and you all **k**.	1Jn 2:20	*3609a*
because you do not **k** the truth,	1Jn 2:21	*3609a*
truth, but because you do **k** it,	1Jn 2:21	*3609a*
If you **k** that He is righteous, you	1Jn 2:29	*3609a*
you **k** that everyone also who	1Jn 2:29	*1097*
reason the world does not **k** us,	1Jn 3:1	*1097*
know us, because it did not **k** Him.	1Jn 3:1	*1097*
We **k** that when He appears, we	1Jn 3:2	*3609a*
You **k** that He appeared in	1Jn 3:5	*3609a*
We **k** that we have passed out of	1Jn 3:14	*3609a*
and you **k** that no murderer has	1Jn 3:15	*3609a*
We **k** love by this, that He laid	1Jn 3:16	*1097*
We will **k** by this that we are of	1Jn 3:19	*1097*
We **k** by this that He abides in us,	1Jn 3:24	*1097*
By this you **k** the Spirit of God:	1Jn 4:2	*1097*
By this we **k** the spirit of truth	1Jn 4:6	*1097*
who does not love does not **k** God,	1Jn 4:8	*1097*
By this we **k** that we abide in Him	1Jn 4:13	*1097*
We have come to **k** and have	1Jn 4:16	*1097*
By this we **k** that we love the	1Jn 5:2	*1097*
may **k** that you have eternal life.	1Jn 5:13	*3609a*
And if we **k** that He hears us *in*	1Jn 5:15	*3609a*
we **k** that we have the requests	1Jn 5:15	*3609a*
We **k** that no one who is born of	1Jn 5:18	*3609a*
We **k** that we are of God, and that	1Jn 5:19	*3609a*
we **k** that the Son of God has come,	1Jn 5:20	*3609a*
that we may **k** Him who is true	1Jn 5:20	*1097*
I, but also all who **k** the truth,	2Jn 1:1	*1097*
you **k** that our testimony is true.	3Jn 1:12	*3609a*
you **k** all things once for all,	Jude 1:5	*3609a*
things which they **k** by instinct,	Jude 1:10	*1987*
'I **k** your deeds and your toil and	Rv 2:2	*3609a*
'I **k** your tribulation and your	Rv 2:9	*3609a*
'I **k** where you dwell, where	Rv 2:13	*3609a*
'I **k** your deeds, and your love and	Rv 2:19	*3609a*
and all the churches will **k** that I	Rv 2:23	*1097*
'I **k** your deeds, that you have a	Rv 3:1	*3609a*
and you will not **k** at what hour I	Rv 3:3	*1097*
'I **k** your deeds. Behold, I have put	Rv 3:8	*3609a*
and *make them* **k** that I have loved you.	Rv 3:9	*1097*
'I **k** your deeds, that you are	Rv 3:15	*3609a*
and you do not **k** that you are	Rv 3:17	*3609a*
"My lord, you **k**."	Rv 7:14	*3609a*

KNOWING

be like God, **k** good and evil."	Gn 3:5	3045
like one of Us, **k** good and evil;	Gn 3:22	3045
each **k** the affliction of his own	1Ki 8:38	3045
each **k** his own affliction and his	2Ch 6:29	3045
k *how* to walk before the living?	Ec 6:8	3045
And Jesus **k** their thoughts said,	Mt 9:4	*3609a*
And **k** their thoughts Jesus said to	Mt 12:25	*3609a*
k that he was a righteous and holy	Mk 6:20	*3609a*
But He, **k** their hypocrisy, said to	Mk 12:15	*3609a*
at Him, **k** that she had died.	Lk 8:53	*3609a*
k what they were thinking in their	Lk 9:47	*3609a*
Jesus **k** that His hour had come	Jn 13:1	*3609a*
k that the Father had given all	Jn 13:3	*3609a*
k all the things that were coming	Jn 18:4	*3609a*
k that all things had already been	Jn 19:28	*3609a*
k that it was the Lord.	Jn 21:12	*3609a*
came in, not **k** what had happened.	Ac 5:7	*3609a*
k what will happen to me there,	Ac 20:22	*3609a*
"**K** that for many years you have	Ac 24:10	*1987*
not **k** that the kindness of God	Ro 2:4	*50*
k that tribulation brings about	Ro 5:3	*3609a*
k this, that our old self was	Ro 6:6	*1097*
k that Christ, having been raised	Ro 6:9	*3609a*
not **k** about God's righteousness and	Ro 10:3	*50*
Do this, **k** the time, that it	Ro 13:11	*3609a*
k that your toil is not *in* vain in	1Co 15:58	*3609a*
k that as you are sharers of our	2Co 1:7	*3609a*
k that He who raised the Lord	2Co 4:14	*3609a*
and **k** that while we are at home in	2Co 5:6	*3609a*
Therefore, **k** the fear of the Lord,	2Co 5:11	*3609a*
nevertheless **k** that a man is not	Ga 2:16	*3609a*
k that whatever good thing each	Eph 6:8	*3609a*
k that both their Master and yours	Eph 6:9	*3609a*
k that I am appointed for the	Php 1:16	*3609a*
value of **k** Christ Jesus my Lord,	Php 3:8	*1108*
k that from the Lord you will	Col 3:24	*3609a*
k that you too have a Master in	Col 4:1	*3609a*
k, brethren beloved by God,	1Th 1:4	*3609a*
k that they produce quarrels.	2Tm 2:23	*3609a*
k from whom you have learned *them,*	2Tm 3:14	*3609a*
k that such a man is perverted and	Ti 3:11	*3609a*
k that you have for yourselves a	Heb 10:34	*1097*
out, not **k** where he was going.	Heb 11:8	*1987*
entertained angels without **k** it.	Heb 13:2	*2990*
k that the testing of your faith	Jas 1:3	*1097*
k that as such we will incur a	Jas 3:1	*3609a*
k that you were not redeemed with	1Pe 1:18	*3609a*
k that the same experiences of	1Pe 5:9	*3609a*
k that the laying aside of my	2Pe 1:14	*3609a*
beloved, **k** this beforehand,	2Pe 3:17	*4267*
k that he has *only* a short time."	Rv 12:12	*3609a*

KNOWLEDGE

tree of the **k** of good and evil.	Gn 2:9	1847
but from the tree of the **k** of good	Gn 2:17	1847
in wisdom, in understanding, in **k**,	Ex 31:3	1847
and in **k** and in all craftsmanship;	Ex 35:31	1847
without the **k** of the congregation,	Nu 15:24	5869
And knows the **k** of the Most High,	Nu 24:16	1847
day have no **k** of good or evil,	Dt 1:39	3045
For the LORD is a God of **k**,	1Sa 2:3	1844
with **k** of what Israel should do,	1Ch 12:32	3045
"Give me now wisdom and **k**,	2Ch 1:10	4093
asked for yourself wisdom and **k** that	2Ch 1:11	4093
and **k** have been granted to you.	2Ch 1:12	4093
those who had **k** and understanding,	Ne 10:28	3045
to Your **k** I am indeed not guilty,	Jb 10:7	1847
a wise man answer with windy **k** And	Jb 15:2	1847
not even desire the **k** of Your ways.	Jb 21:14	1847
"Can anyone teach God **k**,	Jb 21:22	1847
And my lips speak **k** sincerely.	Jb 33:3	1847
'Job speaks without **k**,	Jb 34:35	1847
He multiplies words without **k**."	Jb 35:16	1847
"I will fetch my **k** from afar, And	Jb 36:3	1843
One who is perfect in **k** is with you.	Jb 36:4	1844
And they will die without **k**.	Jb 36:12	1847
The wonders of one perfect in **k**,	Jb 37:16	1843
counsel By words without **k**?	Jb 38:2	1847
that hides counsel without **k**?'	Jb 42:3	1847
And night to night reveals **k**.	Ps 19:2	1847
the workers of wickedness no **k**,	Ps 53:4	3045
is there **k** with the Most High?"	Ps 73:11	1844
A senseless man has no **k**,	Ps 92:6	3045
rebuke, *Even* He who teaches man **k**?	Ps 94:10	1847
Teach me good discernment and **k**,	Ps 119:66	1847
Such **k** is too wonderful for me;	Ps 139:6	1847
man, that You take **k** of him?	Ps 144:3	3045
To the youth **k** and discretion,	Pr 1:4	1847
of the LORD is the beginning of **k**;	Pr 1:7	1847
in scoffing And fools hate **k**?	Pr 1:22	1847
Because they hated **k** And	Pr 1:29	1847
LORD And discover the **k** of God.	Pr 2:5	1847
mouth *come* **k** and understanding.	Pr 2:6	1847
k will be pleasant to your soul;	Pr 2:10	1847
By His **k** the deeps were broken up And	Pr 3:20	1847
And your lips may reserve **k**.	Pr 5:2	1847
And right to those who find **k**.	Pr 8:9	1847
And **k** rather than choicest gold.	Pr 8:10	1847
And I find **k** *and* discretion.	Pr 8:12	1847
And the **k** of the Holy One is	Pr 9:10	1847
Wise men store up **k**,	Pr 10:14	1847
But through **k** the righteous will	Pr 11:9	1847
Whoever loves discipline loves **k**,	Pr 12:1	1847
A prudent man conceals **k**,	Pr 12:23	1847
Every prudent man acts with **k**,	Pr 13:16	1847
But **k** is easy to one who has	Pr 14:6	1847
you will not discern words of **k**.	Pr 14:7	1847
the sensible are crowned with **k**.	Pr 14:18	1847
of the wise makes **k** acceptable,	Pr 15:2	1847
The lips of the wise spread **k**,	Pr 15:7	1847
mind of the intelligent seeks **k**,	Pr 15:14	1847
He who restrains his words has **k**,	Pr 17:27	1847
mind of the prudent acquires **k**,	Pr 18:15	1847
And the ear of the wise seeks **k**.	Pr 18:15	1847
good for a person to be without **k**,	Pr 19:2	1847
understanding and he will gain **k**.	Pr 19:25	1847
will stray from the words of **k**.	Pr 19:27	1847
lips of **k** are a more precious thing.	Pr 20:15	1847
wise is instructed, he receives **k**.	Pr 21:11	1847
The eyes of the LORD preserve **k**,	Pr 22:12	1847
wise, And apply your mind to my **k**;	Pr 22:17	1847
things Of counsels and **k**,	Pr 22:20	1847
And your ears to words of **k**.	Pr 23:12	1847
And by **k** the rooms are filled With	Pr 24:4	1847
And a man of **k** increases power.	Pr 24:5	1847
by a man of understanding *and* **k**,	Pr 28:2	3045
do I have the **k** of the Holy One.	Pr 30:3	1847
a wealth of wisdom and **k**."	Ec 1:16	1847
k *results in* increasing pain.	Ec 1:18	1847
labored with wisdom, **k** and skill,	Ec 2:21	1847
He has given wisdom and **k** and joy,	Ec 2:26	1847
But the advantage of **k** is that	Ec 7:12	1847
there is no activity or planning or **k**	Ec 9:10	1847
Preacher also taught the people **k**;	Ec 12:9	1847
go into exile for their lack of **k**;	Is 5:13	1847
spirit of **k** and the fear of the LORD.	Is 11:2	1847
earth will be full of the **k** of the LORD	Is 11:9	1844
"To whom would He teach **k**,	Is 28:9	1844
of salvation, wisdom and **k**;	Is 33:6	1847
path of justice and taught Him **k** And	Is 40:14	1847
nor is there **k** or understanding to	Is 44:19	1847
turning their **k** into foolishness,	Is 44:25	1847
They have no **k**, Who carry about	Is 45:20	3045
sees me,' Your wisdom and your **k**,	Is 47:10	1847
By His **k** the Righteous One, My	Is 53:11	1847
feed you on **k** and understanding.	Jer 3:15	1844
Every man is stupid, devoid of **k**;	Jer 10:14	1847
mankind is stupid, devoid of **k**;	Jer 51:17	1847

understanding and discerning **k**, Da 1:4 4093
God gave them **k** and intelligence Da 1:17 4093
And **k** to men of understanding. Da 2:21 4486
spirit, **k** and insight, Da 5:12 4486
and forth, and **k** will increase." Da 12:4 1847
kindness Or **k** of God in the land. Hos 4:1 1847
people are destroyed for lack of **k**. Hos 4:6 1847
Because you have rejected **k**, Hos 4:6 1847
And in the **k** of God rather than Hos 6:6 1847
the **k** of the glory of the LORD, Hab 2:14 3045
the lips of a priest should preserve **k**, Mal 2:7 1847
give to His people *the* **k** of salvation Lk 1:77 *1108*
you have taken away the key of **k**; Lk 11:52 *1108*
himself, with his wife's full **k**, Ac 5:2 *4924a*
a more exact **k** about the Way, Ac 24:22 *3609a*
embodiment of **k** and of the truth, Ro 2:20 *1108*
through the Law *comes* the **k** of sin. Ro 3:20 *1922*
God, but not in accordance with **k**. Ro 10:2 *1922*
both of the wisdom and **k** of God! Ro 11:33 *1108*
of goodness, filled with all **k** and Ro 15:14 *1108*
in Him, in all speech and all **k**, 1Co 1:5 *1108*
idols, we know that we all have **k**. 1Co 8:1 *1108*
K makes arrogant, but love edifies. 1Co 8:1 *1108*
However not all men have this **k**; 1Co 8:7 *1108*
if someone sees you, who have **k**, 1Co 8:10 *1108*
through your **k** he who is 1Co 8:11 *1108*
of **k** according to the same Spirit; 1Co 12:8 *1108*
and know all mysteries and all **k**; 1Co 13:2 *1108*
if *there is* **k**, it will be done 1Co 13:8 *1108*
k or of prophecy or of teaching? 1Co 14:6 *1108*
for some have no **k** of God. 1Co 15:34 *56*
of the **k** of Him in every place. 2Co 2:14 *1108*
Light of the **k** of the glory of God 2Co 4:6 *1108*
in purity, in **k**, in patience, in 2Co 6:6 *1108*
in faith and utterance and **k** and 2Co 8:7 *1108*
raised up against the **k** of God, 2Co 10:5 *1108*
in speech, yet I am not *so* in **k**; 2Co 11:6 *1108*
and of revelation in the **k** of Him. Eph 1:17 *1922*
love of Christ which surpasses **k**, Eph 3:19 *1108*
and of the **k** of the Son of God, Eph 4:13 *1922*
in real **k** and all discernment, Php 1:9 *1922*
may be filled with the **k** of His will Col 1:9 *1922*
and increasing in the **k** of God; Col 1:10 *1922*
in a true **k** of God's mystery, Col 2:2 *1922*
all the treasures of wisdom and **k**. Col 2:3 *1108*
self who is being renewed to a true **k** Col 3:10 *1922*
and to come to the **k** of the truth. 1Tm 2:4 *1922*
of what is falsely called "**k**" 1Tm 6:20 *1108*
leading to the **k** of the truth, 2Tm 2:25 *1922*
to come to the **k** of the truth. 2Tm 3:7 *1922*
the **k** of the truth which is according Ti 1:1 *1922*
through the **k** of every good thing Phm 1:6 *1922*
receiving the **k** of the truth, Heb 10:26 *1922*
k of God and of Jesus our Lord; 2Pe 1:2 *1922*
through the true **k** of Him who 2Pe 1:3 *1922*
and in *your* moral excellence, **k**, 2Pe 1:5 *1108*
and in *your* **k**, self-control, and 2Pe 1:6 *1108*
true **k** of our Lord Jesus Christ. 2Pe 1:8 *1922*
reviling where they have no **k**, 2Pe 2:12 *50*
by the **k** of the Lord and Savior 2Pe 2:20 *1922*
but grow in the grace and **k** of our 2Pe 3:18 *1108*

KNOWN

made himself **k** to his brothers. Gn 45:1 3045
"Surely the matter has become **k**." Ex 2:14 3045
I did not make Myself **k** to them. Ex 6:3 3045
and make **k** the statutes of God and Ex 18:16 3045
and make **k** to them the way in Ex 18:20 3045
"Or *if* it is **k** that the ox was Ex 21:36 3045
'I have **k** you by name, and you Ex 33:12 3045
"For how then can it be **k** that I Ex 33:16 3045
sight and I have **k** you by name." Ex 33:17 3045
they have committed becomes **k**, Lv 4:14 3045
he has committed is made **k** to him, Lv 4:23 3045
he has committed is made **k** to him, Lv 4:28 3045
he has seen or *otherwise* **k**, Lv 5:1 3045
make Myself **k** to him in a vision. Nu 12:6 3045
woman who has **k** man intimately. Nu 31:17 3045
who have not **k** man intimately, Nu 31:18 3045
who had not **k** man intimately, Nu 31:35 3045
He has **k** your wanderings through Dt 2:7 3045
but make them **k** to your sons and Dt 4:9 3045
diseases of Egypt which you have **k**, Dt 7:15 3045
your sons who have not **k** Dt 11:2 3045
other gods which you have not **k**. Dt 11:28 3045
other gods (whom you have not **k**) Dt 13:2 3045
you nor your fathers have **k**, Dt 13:6 3045
other gods' (whom you have not **k**), Dt 13:13 3045
it is not **k** who has struck him, Dt 21:1 3045
you nor your fathers have **k**, Dt 28:36 3045
you or your fathers have not **k**. Dt 28:64 3045
gods whom they have not **k** and whom Dt 29:26 3045
Their children, who have not **k**, Dt 31:13 3045
God, To gods whom they have not **k**, Dt 32:17 3045
and had **k** all the deeds of the LORD Jos 24:31 3045
had not **k** a man by lying with him; Jg 21:12 3045
but do not make yourself **k** to the Ru 3:3 3045
"Let it not be **k** that the woman Ru 3:14 3045
it will be **k** to you why His hand is 1Sa 6:3 3045
send to you and make it **k** to you? 1Sa 20:12
1540, 241
if I do not make it **k** to you and 1Sa 20:13
1540, 241
make **k** to me what I should do." 1Sa 28:15 3045
on it, so that nothing was **k**. 2Sa 17:19 3045
people whom I have not **k** serve me. 2Sa 22:44 3045
and his fame was **k** in all 1Ki 4:31
be **k** that You are God in Israel and 1Ki 18:36 3045
k His deeds among the peoples. 1Ch 16:8 3045
to make **k** all these great things. 1Ch 17:19 3045

let it be **k** to the king that the Ezr 4:12 3046
"Now let it be **k** to the king, Ezr 4:13 3046
"Let it be **k** to the king that we Ezr 5:8 3046
enemies heard that it was **k** to us, Ne 4:15 3045
which had been made **k** to them. Ne 8:12 3045
made **k** to them Your holy sabbath, Ne 9:14 3045
queen's conduct will become **k** to all Es 1:17 3318
make **k** her people or her kindred, Es 2:10 5046
that she should not make *them* **k**. Es 2:10 5046
made **k** her kindred or her people, Es 2:20 5046
But the plot became **k** to Mordecai and Es 2:22 3045
k to me my rebellion and my sin. Jb 13:23 3045
and all who had **k** him before came Jb 42:11 3045
The LORD has made Himself **k**; Ps 9:16 3045
make **k** to me the path of life; Ps 16:11 3045
people whom I have not **k** serve me. Ps 18:43 3045
have **k** the troubles of my soul, Ps 31:7 3045
made Himself **k** as a stronghold. Ps 48:3 3045
Your way may be **k** on the earth, Ps 67:2 3045
God is **k** in Judah; Ps 76:1 3045
You have made **k** Your strength Ps 77:14 3045
And Your footprints may not be **k**. Ps 77:19 3045
Which we have heard and **k**, Ps 78:3 3045
Let there be **k** among the nations Ps 79:10 3045
wonders be made **k** in the darkness? Ps 88:12 3045
To all generations I will make **k** Ps 89:1 3045
on high, because he has **k** My name. Ps 91:14 3045
The LORD has made **k** His salvation; Ps 98:2 3045
He made **k** His ways to Moses, His Ps 103:7 3045
k His deeds among the peoples. Ps 105:1 3045
That He might make His power **k**. Ps 106:8 3045
He has made **k** to His people the Ps 111:6 5046
old I have **k** from Your testimonies That Ps 119:152 3045
You have searched me and **k** *me*. Ps 139:1 3045
To make **k** to the sons of men Your Ps 145:12 3045
ordinances, they have not **k** them. Ps 147:20 3045
I will make my words **k** to you. Pr 1:23 3045
A fool's anger is **k** at once, Pr 12:16 3045
the hearts of fools it is made **k**. Pr 14:33 3045
Her husband is **k** in the gates, Pr 31:23 3045
named, and it is **k** what man is; Ec 6:10 3045
creature will make the matter **k**. Ec 10:20 5046
k His deeds among the peoples; Is 12:4 3045
this be **k** throughout the earth. Is 12:5 3045
LORD will make Himself **k** to Egypt, Is 19:21 3045
God of Israel, I make **k** to you. Is 21:10 5046
of honor Though you have not **k** Me. Is 45:4 3045
you, though you have not **k** Me; Is 45:5 3045
things which you have not **k**. Is 48:6 3045
have not heard, you have not **k**. Is 48:8 3045
their offspring will be **k** among the Is 61:9 3045
Your name **k** to Your adversaries, Is 64:2 3045
will be made **k** to His servants, Is 66:14 3045
other gods that you have not **k**, Jer 7:9 3045
they nor their fathers have **k**; Jer 9:16 3045
made it **k** to me and I knew it; Jer 11:18 3045
the land which you have not **k**, Jer 16:13 3045
nor the kings of Judah had *ever* **k**, Jer 19:4 3045
into a land that they had not **k**? Jer 22:28 3045
then that prophet will be **k** *as* one Jer 28:9 3045
other gods whom they had not **k**, Jer 44:3 3045
k to Jerusalem her abominations Ezk 16:2 3045
made Myself **k** to them in the land Ezk 20:5 3045
in whose sight I made Myself **k** to Ezk 20:9 3045
into lands which you have not **k**. Ezk 32:9 3045
k among them when I judge you. Ezk 35:11 3045
"let it be **k** to you. Ezk 36:32 3045
k in the sight of many nations; Ezk 38:23 3045
"My holy name I will make **k** Ezk 39:7 3045
make **k** to them the design of the Ezk 43:11 3045
if you do not make **k** to me the Da 2:5 3046
you do not make the dream **k** to me, Da 2:9 3046
Even now You have made **k** to me Da 2:23 3046
made **k** to us the king's matter." Da 2:23 3046
interpretation **k** to the king!" Da 2:25 3046
"Are you able to make **k** to me the Da 2:26 3046
and He has made **k** to King Da 2:28 3046
k to you what will take place. Da 2:29 3046
the interpretation **k** to the king, Da 2:30 3046
the great God has made **k** to the Da 2:45 3046
He does not, let it be **k** to you, Da 3:18 3046
that they might make **k** to me the Da 4:6 3046
make its interpretation **k** to me. Da 4:7 3046
make **k** to me the interpretation; Da 4:18 3046
make **k** its interpretation to the king. Da 5:8 3046
make its interpretation **k** to me, Da 5:15 3046
make its interpretation **k** to me, Da 5:16 3046
make the interpretation **k** to him. Da 5:17 3046
So he told me and made **k** to me the Da 7:16 3046
freewill offerings, make them **k**. Am 4:5 8085
k to Jacob his rebellious act, Mi 3:8 5046
the place where they are is not **k**. Na 3:17 3045
the midst of the years make it **k**; Hab 3:2 3045
the nations whom they have not **k**. Zch 7:14 3045
unique day which is **k** to the LORD, Zch 14:7 3045
or hidden that will not be **k**. Mt 10:26 *1097*
"But if you had **k** what this Mt 12:7 *1097*
for the tree is **k** by its fruit. Mt 12:33 *1097*
if the head of the house had **k** at Mt 24:43 *3609a*
for His name had become well **k**; Mk 6:14 *5318*
which the Lord has made **k** to us." Lk 2:15 *1107*
they made **k** the statement which Lk 2:17 *1107*
each tree is **k** by its own fruit. Lk 6:44 *1097*
will not be **k** and come to light. Lk 8:17 *1097*
and hidden that will not be **k**. Lk 12:2 *1097*
if the head of the house had **k** at Lk 12:39 *3609a*
"If you had **k** in this day, even Lk 19:42 *1097*
when he himself seeks to be **k** Jn 7:4
"If you had **k** Me, you would have Jn 14:7 *1097*

you would have **k** My Father also; Jn 14:7 *3609a*
My Father I have made **k** to you. Jn 15:15 *1107*
they have not **k** the Father or Jn 16:3 *1097*
although the world has not **k** You, Jn 17:25 *1097*
not known You, yet I have **k** You; Jn 17:25 *1097*
have **k** that You sent Me; Jn 17:25 *1097*
I have made Your name **k** to them, Jn 17:26 *1107*
known to them, and will make it **k**, Jn 17:26 *1107*
disciple was **k** to the high priest, Jn 18:15 *1110*
who was **k** to the high priest, Jn 18:16 *1110*
And it became **k** to all who were Ac 1:19 *1110*
Jerusalem, let this be **k** to you and Ac 2:14 *1110*
MADE **K** TO ME THE WAYS OF LIFE; Ac 2:28 *1107*
let it be **k** to all of you and to Ac 4:10 *1110*
made himself **k** to his brothers, Ac 7:13 *1107*
but their plot became **k** to Saul. Ac 9:24 *1097*
It became **k** all over Joppa, Ac 9:42 *1110*
But Saul, who was also **k** *as* Paul, Ac 13:9
"Therefore let it be **k** to you, Ac 13:38 *1110*
MAKES THESE THINGS **K** FROM LONG AGO. Ac 15:18 *1110*
This became **k** to all, both Ac 19:17 *1110*
since they have **k** about me for a Ac 26:5 *4267*
it is **k** to us that it is spoken Ac 28:22 *1110*
"Therefore let it be **k** to you Ac 28:28 *1110*
because that which is **k** about God Ro 1:19 *1110*
PATH OF PEACE THEY HAVE NOT **K**." Ro 3:17 *1097*
for I would not have **k** about Ro 7:7 *3609a*
His wrath and to make His power **k**, Ro 9:22 *1107*
He did so to make **k** the riches of His Ro 9:23 *1107*
WHO HAS **K** THE MIND OF THE LORD, Ro 11:34 *1097*
been made **k** to all the nations, Ro 16:26 *1107*
WHO HAS **K** THE MIND OF THE LORD, 1Co 2:16 *1097*
has not yet **k** as he ought to know; 1Co 8:2 *1097*
anyone loves God, he is **k** by Him. 1Co 8:3 *1097*
Therefore I make **k** to you that 1Co 12:3 *1107*
just as I also have been fully **k**. 1Co 13:12 *1921*
how will it be **k** what is played on 1Co 14:7 *1097*
how will it be **k** what is spoken? 1Co 14:9 *1097*
Now I make **k** to you, brethren, the 1Co 15:1 *1107*
our hearts, **k** and read by all men; 2Co 3:2 *1097*
k Christ according to the flesh, 2Co 5:16 *1097*
made **k** to you in the sight of God. 2Co 7:12 *5319*
we *wish to* make **k** to you the grace 2Co 8:1 *1107*
God, or rather to be **k** by God, Ga 4:9 *1097*
k to us the mystery of His will, Eph 1:9 *1107*
was made **k** to me the mystery, Eph 3:3 *1107*
was not made **k** to the sons of men, Eph 3:5 *1107*
now be made **k** through the church Eph 3:10 *1107*
to make **k** with boldness the Eph 6:19 *1107*
will make everything **k** to you. Eph 6:21 *1107*
the cause of Christ has become well **k** Php 1:13 *5318*
gentle *spirit* be **k** to all men. Php 4:5 *1097*
your requests be made **k** to God. Php 4:6 *1107*
to whom God willed to make **k** what Col 1:27 *1107*
you have **k** the sacred writings 2Tm 3:15 *3609a*
when we made **k** to you the power 2Pe 1:16 *1107*
have **k** the way of righteousness, 2Pe 2:21 *1921*
righteousness, than having **k** it, 2Pe 2:21 *1921*
not **k** the deep things of Satan, Rv 2:24 *1097*

KNOWS

"For God **k** that in the day you Gn 3:5 3045
"My lord **k** that the children are Gn 33:13 3045
And **k** the knowledge of the Most Nu 24:16 3045
no man **k** his burial place to this Dt 34:6 3045
He **k**, and may Israel itself know. Jos 22:22 3045
"Your father **k** well that I have 1Sa 20:3 3045
for your servant **k** nothing at all 1Sa 22:15 3045
and Saul my father **k** that also." 1Sa 23:17 3045
'Who **k**, the LORD may be gracious 2Sa 12:22 3045
"Today your servant **k** that I have 2Sa 14:22 3045
for all Israel **k** that your father 2Sa 17:10 3045
your servant **k** that I have sinned; 2Sa 19:20 3045
no one among us who **k** how to cut 1Ki 5:6 3045
and who **k** how to make engravings, 2Ch 2:7 3045
father, who **k** how to work in gold, 2Ch 2:14 3045
and *who* **k** *how* to make all kinds 2Ch 2:14
And who **k** whether you have not Es 4:14 3045
"For He **k** false men, And He sees Jb 11:11 3045
He **k** that a day of darkness is at Jb 15:23 3045
"But He **k** the way I take; Jb 23:10 3045
"The path no bird of prey **k**, Jb 28:7 3045
And He **k** its place. Jb 28:23 3045
"Therefore He **k** their works, And Jb 34:25 5234
LORD **k** the way of the righteous, Ps 1:6 3045
LORD **k** the days of the blameless, Ps 37:18 3045
For He **k** the secrets of the heart. Ps 44:21 3045
O God, it is You who **k** my folly, Ps 69:5 3045
Nor is there any among us who **k** Ps 74:9 3045
The LORD **k** the thoughts of man, Ps 94:11 3045
For He Himself **k** our frame; Ps 103:14 3045
sun **k** the place of its setting. Ps 104:19 3045
But the haughty He **k** from afar. Ps 138:6 3045
works, And my soul **k** it very well. Ps 139:14 3045
She is naive and **k** nothing. Pr 9:13 3045
The heart **k** its own bitterness, Pr 14:10 3045
And who **k** the ruin *that comes* from Pr 24:22 3045
And who **k** whether he will be a Ec 2:19 3045
Who **k** that the breath of man Ec 3:21 3045
king who no longer **k** *how* to receive Ec 4:13 3045
the sun and it never **k** *anything;* Ec 6:5 3045
For who **k** what is good for a man Ec 6:12 3045
who **k** the interpretation of a matter? Ec 8:1 3045
a wise heart **k** the proper time and Ec 8:5 3045
If no one **k** what will happen, who Ec 8:7 3045
No man **k** what will happen, and who Ec 10:14 3045
"An ox **k** its owner, And a donkey Is 1:3 3045
He **k** *enough* to refuse evil and Is 7:15 3045
before the boy **k** how to cry out Is 8:4 3045
"Who sees us?" or "Who **k** us?" Is 29:15 3045

a nation which **k** you not will run Is 55:5 3045
stork in the sky **K** her seasons; Jer 8:7 3045
that he understands and **k** Me, Jer 9:24 3045
and I am He who **k** and am a Jer 29:23 3045
He **k** what is in the darkness, And Da 2:22 3046
Who **k** whether He will *not* turn and Jl 2:14 3045
"Who **k**, God may turn and relent and Jon 3:9 3045
He **k** those who take refuge in Him. Na 1:7 3045
But the unjust **k** no shame. Zph 3:5 3045
for your Father **k** what you need before Mt 6:8 *3609a*
for your heavenly Father **k** that Mt 6:32 *3609a*
"See that no one **k** *about this!*" Mt 9:30 *1097*
and no one **k** the Son except the Mt 11:27 *1921*
"But of that day and hour no one **k**, Mt 24:36 *3609a*
"But of that day or hour no one **k**, Mk 13:32 *3609a*
and no one **k** who the Son is except Lk 10:22 *1097*
your Father **k** that you need these Lk 12:30 *3609a*
of men, but God **k** your hearts; Lk 16:15 *1097*
come, no one **k** where He is from." Jn 7:27 *1097*
from him and **k** what he is doing, Jn 7:51 *1097*
Father **k** Me and I know the Father; Jn 10:15 *1097*
he **k** that he is telling the truth, Jn 19:35 *3609a*
"And God, who **k** the heart, testified Ac 15:8 *2589*
the king **k** about these matters, Ac 26:26 *1987*
and He who searches the hearts **k** Ro 8:27 *3609a*
For who among men **k** the *thoughts* 1Co 2:11 *3609a*
no one **k** except the Spirit of God. 1Co 2:11 *1097*
LORD **K** THE REASONINGS of the wise, 1Co 3:20 *1097*
supposes that he **k** anything, 1Co 8:2 *1097*
I do not love you? God **k** *I do!* 2Co 11:11 *3609a*
forever, **k** that I am not lying. 2Co 11:31 *3609a*
of the body I do not know, God **k** 2Co 12:2 *3609a*
the body I do not know, God **k** 2Co 12:3 *3609a*
"The Lord **k** those who are His," 2Tm 2:19 *1097*
one who **k** *the* right thing to do and Jas 4:17 *3609a*
then the Lord **k** how to rescue the 2Pe 2:9 *3609a*
who sins has seen Him or **k** Him. 1Jn 3:6 *1097*
than our heart and **k** all things. 1Jn 3:20 *1097*
he who **k** God listens to us; 1Jn 4:6 *1097*
loves is born of God and **k** God. 1Jn 4:7 *1097*
no one **k** but he who receives it.' Rv 2:17 *3609a*
Him which no one **k** except Himself. Rv 19:12 *3609a*

KOA
Chaldeans, Pekod and Shoa and **K**, Ezk 23:23 6970

KOHATH
Gershon, **K**, and Merari. Gn 46:11 6955
Gershon and **K** and Merari; Ex 6:16 6955
The sons of **K**: Ex 6:18 6955
Gershon and **K** and Merari. Nu 3:17 6955
the sons of **K** by their families: Nu 3:19 6955
Of **K** *was* the family of the Nu 3:27 6955
The families of the sons of **K** were Nu 3:29 6955
of **K** from among the sons of Levi, Nu 4:2 6955
the work of the descendants of **K** Nu 4:4 6955
of **K** shall come to carry *them,* Nu 4:15 6955
which the sons of **K** are to carry. Nu 4:15 6955
he did not give *any* to the sons of **K** Nu 7:9 6955
the son of Izhar, the son of **K**, Nu 16:1 6955
of **K**, the family of the Kohathites; Nu 26:57 6955
K became the father of Amram. Nu 26:58 6955
The rest of the sons of **K** Jos 21:5 6955
to the families of the sons of **K**, Jos 21:20 6955
even to the rest of the sons of **K**. Jos 21:20 6955
rest of the sons of **K** were ten. Jos 21:26 6955
Levi *were* Gershon, **K** and Merari. 1Ch 6:1 6955
The sons of **K** *were* Amram, 1Ch 6:2 6955
The sons of Levi *were* Gershom, **K** and 1Ch 6:16 6955
The sons of **K** *were* Amram, 1Ch 6:18 6955
sons of **K** *were* Amminadab his son, 1Ch 6:22 6955
the son of Izhar, the son of **K**, 1Ch 6:38 6955
the sons of **K** *were given* by lot, 1Ch 6:61 6955
families of the sons of **K** had cities 1Ch 6:66 6955
of the family of the sons of **K**. 1Ch 6:70 6955
of the sons of **K**, Uriel the chief, 1Ch 15:5 6955
Gershon, **K**, and Merari. 1Ch 23:6 6955
The sons of **K** were four: 1Ch 23:12 6955

KOHATHITE
fathers' households of the **K** families Nu 3:30 6956
numbered men of the **K** families, Nu 4:37 6956

KOHATHITES
these were the families of the **K**. Nu 3:27 6956
the families of the **K** be cut off from Nu 4:18 6956
sons of the **K** by their families and Nu 4:34 6956
Then the **K** set out, carrying the Nu 10:21 6956
of Kohath, the family of the **K**; Nu 26:57 6956
out for the families of the **K**. Jos 21:4 6956
one of the families of the **K**, Jos 21:10 6956
of the **K** *were* Heman the singer, 1Ch 6:33 6956
of Aaron of the families of the **K** 1Ch 6:54 6956
the **K** *were* over the showbread 1Ch 9:32 6956
from the sons of the **K** and of the 2Ch 20:19 6956
Azariah, from the sons of the **K**; 2Ch 29:12 6956
Meshullam of the sons of the **K**, 2Ch 34:12 6956

KOHATH'S
and the length of **K** life was one Ex 6:18 6955

KOLAIAH
the son of Pedaiah, the son of **K**, Ne 11:7 6964
concerning Ahab the son of **K** and Jer 29:21 6964

KOR
a tenth of a bath from *each* **k** Ezk 45:14 3734a

KORAH
bore Jeush and Jalam and **K**. Gn 36:5 7141
to Esau, Jeush and Jalam and **K**. Gn 36:14 7141
chief **K**, chief Gatam, chief Amalek. Gn 36:16 7141
chief Jeush, chief Jalam, chief **K**. Gn 36:18 7141
K and Nepheg and Zichri. Ex 6:21 7141
The sons of **K**: Ex 6:24 7141
Now **K** the son of Izhar, the son of Nu 16:1 7141
he spoke to **K** and all his company, Nu 16:5 7141
K and all your company, Nu 16:6 7141
Then Moses said to **K**, Nu 16:8 7141
K, and all your brothers, sons Nu 16:10 7141
Moses said to **K**, Nu 16:16 7141
Thus **K** assembled all the Nu 16:19 7141
from around the dwellings of **K**, Nu 16:24 7141
from around the dwellings of **K**, Nu 16:27 7141
and all the men who belonged to **K** with Nu 16:32 7141
that he will not become like **K** Nu 16:40 7141
those who died on account of **K**. Nu 16:49 7141
against Aaron in the company of **K**, Nu 26:9 7141
swallowed them up along with **K**, Nu 26:10 7141
The sons of **K**, however, did not Nu 26:11 7141
the LORD in the company of **K**; Nu 27:3 7141
Reuel, Jeush, Jalam and **K**. 1Ch 1:35 7141
The sons of Hebron *were* **K** and 1Ch 2:43 7141
were Amminadab his son, **K** his son, 1Ch 6:22 7141
the son of Ebiasaph, the son of **K**, 1Ch 6:37 7141
the son of Ebiasaph, the son of **K**, 1Ch 9:19 7141
the gatekeepers of the sons of **K** 1Ch 26:19 7145
perished in the rebellion of **K**. Jude 1:11 *2879*

KORAHITE
the firstborn of Shallum the **K**, 1Ch 9:31 7145

KORAHITES
these are the families of the **K**. Ex 6:24 7145
the Mushites, the family of the **K**. Nu 26:58 7145
of his father's house, the **K**, 1Ch 9:19 7145
Azarel, Joezer, Jashobeam, the **K**, 1Ch 12:6 7145
gatekeepers *there were* of the **K**, 1Ch 26:1 7145
and of the sons of the **K**, 2Ch 20:19 7145

KORE
Shallum the son of **K**, 1Ch 9:19 6981
Meshelemiah the son of **K**, 1Ch 26:1 6981
K the son of Imnah the Levite, 2Ch 31:14 6981

KORS
thirty **k** of fine flour and sixty kors 1Ki 4:22 3734a
of fine flour and sixty **k** of meal, 1Ki 4:22 3734a
then gave Hiram 20,000 **k** of wheat 1Ki 5:11 3734a
and twenty **k** of beaten oil; 1Ki 5:11 3734a
timber, 20,000 **k** of crushed wheat and 2Ch 2:10 3734a
wheat and 20,000 **k** of barley, 2Ch 2:10 3734a
ten thousand **k** of wheat and ten 2Ch 27:5 3734a
talents of silver, 100 **k** of wheat, Ezr 7:22 3734b

KOZ
K became the father of Anub 1Ch 4:8 6976

KUE
of horses was from Egypt and **K**, 1Ki 10:28 6961b
procured *them* from **K** for a price. 1Ki 10:28 6961b
imported from Egypt and from **K**; 2Ch 1:16 6961b
procured them from **K** for a price. 2Ch 1:16 6961b

KUM
He said to her, "Talitha **k**!" Mk 5:41 *2891*

KUSHAIAH
relatives, Ethan the son of **K**, 1Ch 15:17 6984

L

LAADAH
and **L** the father of Mareshah, 1Ch 4:21 3935

LABAN
had a brother whose name was **L**; Gn 24:29 3837a
and **L** ran outside to the man at Gn 24:29 3837a
Then **L** unloaded the camels, and he Gn 24:32 3837a
L and Bethuel replied, Gn 24:50 3837a
the sister of **L** the Aramean, Gn 25:20 3837a
flee to Haran, to my brother **L**! Gn 27:43 3837a
a wife from the daughters of **L** Gn 28:2 3837a
and he went to Paddan-aram to **L**, Gn 28:5 3837a
"Do you know **L** the son of Nahor?" Gn 29:5 3837a
daughter of **L** his mother's brother, Gn 29:10 3837a
sheep of **L** his mother's brother, Gn 29:10 3837a
flock of **L** his mother's brother. Gn 29:10 3837a
when **L** heard the news of Jacob his Gn 29:13 3837a
he related to **L** all these things. Gn 29:13 3837a
L said to him, Gn 29:14 3837a
Then **L** said to Jacob, Gn 29:15 3837a
Now **L** had two daughters; Gn 29:16 3837a
L said, "It is better that I give her Gn 29:19 3837a
Then Jacob said to **L**, Gn 29:21 3837a
L gathered all the men of the Gn 29:22 3837a
L also gave his maid Zilpah to his Gn 29:24 3837a
And he said to **L**, Gn 29:25 3837a
But **L** said, "It is not the practice Gn 29:26 3837a
L also gave his maid Bilhah to his Gn 29:29 3837a
he served with **L** for another seven Gn 29:30 3837a
Joseph, that Jacob said to **L**, Gn 30:25 3837a
But **L** said to him, Gn 30:27 3837a
L said, "Good, let it be according to Gn 30:34 3837a
all the black in the flock of **L**; Gn 30:40 3837a
Jacob saw the attitude of **L**, Gn 31:2 3837a
all that **L** has been doing to you. Gn 31:12 3837a
L had gone to shear his flock, Gn 31:19 3837a
And Jacob deceived **L** the Aramean by Gn 31:20 3837a
When it was told **L** on the third Gn 31:22 3837a
God came to **L** the Aramean in a Gn 31:24 3837a
L caught up with Jacob. Gn 31:25 3837a
and **L** with his kinsmen camped in Gn 31:25 3837a
Then **L** said to Jacob, Gn 31:26 3837a
Then Jacob replied to **L**, Gn 31:31 3837a
So **L** went into Jacob's tent and Gn 31:33 3837a
And **L** felt through all the tent but Gn 31:34 3837a
became angry and contended with **L**; Gn 31:36 3837a
and Jacob said to **L**, Gn 31:36 3837a
Then **L** replied to Jacob, Gn 31:43 3837a
Now **L** called it Jegar-sahadutha, Gn 31:47 3837a
L said, "This heap is a witness Gn 31:48 3837a
L said to Jacob, Gn 31:51 3837a
Early in the morning **L** arose, Gn 31:55 3837a
Then **L** departed and returned to Gn 31:55 3837a
"I have sojourned with **L**, Gn 32:4 3837a
whom **L** gave to his daughter Leah; Gn 46:18 3837a
L gave to his daughter Rachel, Gn 46:25 3837a
and **L** and Hazeroth and Dizahab. Dt 1:1 3837b

LABAN'S
Jacob fed the rest of **L** flocks. Gn 30:36 3837a
and did not put them with **L** flock. Gn 30:40 3837a
the feebler were **L** and the stronger Gn 30:42 3837a
Jacob heard the words of **L** sons, Gn 31:1 3837a

LABOR
birth and she suffered severe **l**. Gn 35:16 3205
When she was in severe **l** the Gn 35:17 3205
And became a slave at forced **l**. Gn 49:15 4522
them to afflict them with hard **l**. Ex 1:11 5450
sons of Israel to **l** rigorously; Ex 1:13 5647
made their lives bitter with hard **l** Ex 1:14 5656
at all *kinds* of **l** in the field, Ex 1:14 5656
"Let the **l** be heavier on the men, Ex 5:9 5656
none of your **l** will be reduced. Ex 5:11 5656
Six days you shall **l** and do all your Ex 20:9 5647
seventh day you shall cease *from* **l** Ex 23:12
on the seventh day He ceased *from* **l**, Ex 31:17
Six days you shall **l** and do all your Dt 5:13 5647
shall become your forced **l** and shall Dt 20:11 4522
us, and imposed hard **l** on us. Dt 26:6 5656
put the Canaanites to forced **l**, Jos 17:13 4522
put the Canaanites to forced **l**, Jg 1:28 4522
and became subject to forced **l**. Jg 1:30 4522
became forced **l** for them. Jg 1:33 4522
grew strong, they became forced **l**. Jg 1:35 4522
and Adoram was over the forced **l**, 2Sa 20:24 4522
over the men subject to forced **l**. 1Ki 4:6 4522
forced **l** which King Solomon levied 1Ki 9:15 4522
forced **l** of the house of Joseph. 1Ki 11:28 5447
Adoram, who was over the forced **l**, 1Ki 12:18 4522
who was over the forced **l**, 2Ch 10:18 4522
"Is not man forced to **l** on earth, Jb 7:1 6635
To reject the **l** of Your hands, Jb 10:3 3018
They get rid of their **l** pains. Jb 39:3 2256b
is great And leave your **l** to him? Jb 39:11 3018
Though her **l** be in vain, *she* is Jb 39:16 3018
product of their **l** to the locust. Ps 78:46 3018
their pride is *but* **l** and sorrow; Ps 90:10 5999
And vegetation for the **l** of man, Ps 104:14 5656
work And to his **l** until evening. Ps 104:23 5656
of *the fruit of* the peoples' **l**, Ps 105:44 5999
He humbled their heart with **l**; Ps 107:12 5999
plunder the product of his **l**. Ps 109:11 3018
They **l** in vain who build it; Ps 127:1 5998
hand will be put to forced **l**. Pr 12:24 4522
one who gathers by **l** increases *it*. Pr 13:11 3027
In all **l** there is profit, But mere Pr 14:23 6089a
heart was pleased because of all my **l** Ec 2:10 5999
this was my reward for all my **l**. Ec 2:10 5999
and the **l** which I had exerted, Ec 2:11 5999
Thus I hated all the fruit of my **l** for Ec 2:18 5999
have control over all the fruit of my **l** Ec 2:19 5999
despaired of all the fruit of my **l** Ec 2:20 5999
For what does a man get in all his **l** Ec 2:22 5999
tell himself that his **l** is good. Ec 2:24 5999
eats and drinks sees good in all his **l** Ec 3:13 5999
I have seen that every **l** and Ec 4:4 5999
better than two fists full of **l** and Ec 4:6 5999
yet there was no end to all his **l**. Ec 4:8 5999
have a good return for their **l**. Ec 4:9 5999
take nothing from the fruit of his **l** Ec 5:15 5999
drink and enjoy oneself in all one's **l** Ec 5:18 5999
his reward and rejoice in his **l**; Ec 5:19 5999
All a man's **l** is for his mouth and Ec 6:7 5999
your mother was in **l** with you, SS 8:5 2254a
she was in **l** *and* gave you birth. SS 8:5 2254a
will writhe like a woman in **l**, Is 13:8 3205
me like the pains of a woman in **l**. Is 21:3 3205
and cries out in her **l** pains, Is 26:17 2256b
We were pregnant, we writhed *in* **l**, Is 26:18
like a woman in **l** I will groan, Is 42:14 3205
"They will not **l** in vain, Or Is 65:23 3021
shameful thing has consumed the **l** Jer 3:24 3018
I heard a cry as of a woman in **l**, Jer 4:31 2342a
and she who is in **l** with child, Jer 31:8 3205
be like the heart of a woman in **l**. Jer 48:41 6887b
be like the heart of a woman in **l**. Jer 49:22 6887b
made his army **l** hard against Tyre; Ezk 29:18 5656
had no wages from Tyre for the **l** that Ezk 29:18 5656
for his **l** which he performed, Ezk 29:20 6468
"Writhe and **l** to give birth, Mi 4:10 1518
she who is in **l** has borne a child. Mi 5:3 3205
and on all the **l** of your hands." Hg 1:11 3018
you have entered into their **l**." Jn 4:38 *2873*
"Whenever a woman is in **l** she has Jn 16:21 *5088*
own reward according to his own **l**. 1Co 3:8 *2873*
I have been in **l** and hardship, 2Co 11:27 *2873*
with whom I am again in **l** until Ga 4:19 *5605*
AND SHOUT, YOU WHO ARE NOT IN **L**; Ga 4:27 *5605*
but rather he must **l**, Eph 4:28 *2872*
this *will mean* fruitful **l** for me; Php 1:22 *2041*
For this purpose also I **l**, Col 1:29 *2872*
your work of faith and **l** of love 1Th 1:3 *2873*
brethren, our **l** and hardship, 1Th 2:9 *2873*
you, and our **l** would be in vain. 1Th 3:5 *2873*
will come upon them suddenly like **l** 1Th 5:3 *5604*

those who diligently **l** among you, 1Th 5:12 *2872*
but with **l** and hardship we *kept* 2Th 3:8 *2873*
it is for this we **l** and strive, 1Tm 4:10 *2872*
she cried out, being in **l** and in pain Rv 12:2 *5605*

LABORED
you a land on which you had not **l**, Jos 24:13 3021
So the workmen **l**, and the repair 2Ch 24:13 6213a
for which I had **l** under the sun, Ec 2:18 6001b
fruit of my labor for which I have **l** Ec 2:19 5998
for which I had **l** under the sun. Ec 2:20 5998
is a man who has **l** with wisdom, Ec 2:21 5998
to one who has not **l** with them. Ec 2:21 5998
in which you have **l** under the sun. Ec 9:9 6001b
which you have **l** from your youth; Is 47:12 3021
to you with whom you have **l**, Is 47:15 3021
new wine for which you have **l**." Is 62:8 3021
Her breathing is **l**. Jer 15:9 5301
that for which you have not **l**; Jn 4:38 *2872*
others have **l** and you have Jn 4:38 *2872*
I **l** even more than all of them, 1Co 15:10 *2872*
perhaps I have **l** over you in vain. Ga 4:11 *2872*

LABORER
for us by night and a **l** by day." Ne 4:22 4399
provinces Has become a forced **l**! La 1:1 4522
for the **l** is worthy of his wages. Lk 10:7 *2040*
"The **l** is worthy of his wages." 1Tm 5:18 *2040*

LABORERS
day, and they became forced **l**. Jos 16:10 5647, 4522
levied forced **l** from all Israel; 1Ki 5:13 4522
the forced **l** numbered 30,000 men. 1Ki 5:13 4522
Adoniram *was* over the forced **l**. 1Ki 5:14 4522
from them Solomon levied forced **l**, 1Ki 9:21 5647, 4522
raised as forced **l** to this day. 2Ch 8:8 4522
hired **l** will be grieved in soul. Is 19:10 6213a
young men will become forced **l**. Is 31:8 4522
to hire **l** for his vineyard. Mt 20:1 *2040*
When he had agreed with the **l** Mt 20:2 *2040*
'Call the **l** and pay them their wages, Mt 20:8 *2040*
is plentiful, but the **l** are few; Lk 10:2 *2040*
to send out **l** into His harvest. Lk 10:2 *2040*
pay of the **l** who mowed your fields, Jas 5:4 *2040*

LABORING
"And for whom am I **l** and Ec 4:8 6001b
always **l** earnestly for you in his Col 4:12 *75*

LABORIOUS
you shall not do any **l** work. Lv 23:7 5656
you shall not do any **l** work.' " Lv 23:8 5656
You shall do no **l** work. Lv 23:21 5656
'You shall not do any **l** work, Lv 23:25 5656
shall do no **l** work of any kind. Lv 23:35 5656
You shall do no **l** work. Lv 23:36 5656
you shall do no **l** work. Nu 28:18 5656
you shall do no **l** work. Nu 28:25 5656
you shall do no **l** work. Nu 28:26 5656
you shall do no **l** work. Nu 29:1 5656
you shall do no **l** work, and you Nu 29:12 5656
you shall do no **l** work. Nu 29:35 5656

LABORIOUSLY
Even though man should seek **l**, Ec 8:17 5998

LABORS
all their **l** which they rigorously Ex 1:14 5656
and looked on their hard **l**; Ex 2:11 5450
Get *back* to your **l**!" Ex 5:4 5450
have them cease from their **l**!" Ex 5:5 5450
Harvest *of* the first fruits of your **l** Ex 23:16 4639
fruit of your **l** from the field. Ex 23:16 4639
of your ground and all your **l**, Dt 28:33 3018
To eat the bread of painful **l**; Ps 127:2 6089a
with which he **l** under the sun? Ec 2:22 6001b
In all my **l** they will find in me Hos 12:8 3018
who helps in the work and **l**. 1Co 16:16 *2872*
imprisonments, in tumults, in **l**, 2Co 6:5 *2873*
measure, *that is,* in other men's **l**, 2Co 10:15 *2873*
in far more **l**, in far more 2Co 11:23 *2873*
"so that they may rest from their **l**, Rv 14:13 *2873*

LACHISH
to Japhia king of **L** and to Debir Jos 10:3 3923
king of Jarmuth, the king of **L**, Jos 10:5 3923
king of Jarmuth, the king of **L**, Jos 10:23 3923
him passed on from Libnah to **L**, Jos 10:31 3923
gave **L** into the hands of Israel; Jos 10:32 3923
king of Gezer came up to help **L**, Jos 10:33 3923
him passed on from **L** to Eglon, Jos 10:34 3923
to all that he had done to **L**. Jos 10:35 3923
the king of **L**, one; Jos 12:11 3923
L and Bozkath and Eglon, Jos 15:39 3923
in Jerusalem, and he fled to **L**; 2Ki 14:19 3923
him to **L** and killed him there. 2Ki 14:19 3923
sent to the king of Assyria at **L**, 2Ki 18:14 3923
and Rab-saris and Rabshakeh from **L** 2Ki 18:17 3923
heard that the king had left **L**. 2Ki 19:8 3923
Adoraim, **L**, Azekah, 2Ch 11:9 3923
in Jerusalem, and he fled to **L**; 2Ch 25:27 3923
they sent after him to **L** and killed 2Ch 25:27 3923
while he *was* besieging **L** with all 2Ch 32:9 3923
their villages, **L** and its fields, Ne 11:30 3923
from **L** to Jerusalem to King Hezekiah Is 36:2 3923
heard that the king had left **L**. Is 37:8 3923
of Judah, *that is,* **L** and Azekah, Jer 34:7 3923
the team of horses, O inhabitant of **L** Mi 1:13 3923

LACK
who had gathered little had no **l**; Ex 16:18 2637
in which you will not **l** anything; Dt 8:9 2637
and in the **l** of all things; Dt 28:48 2640
secretly for **l** of anything *else,* Dt 28:57 2640
place where there is no **l** of anything Jg 18:10 4270
there is no **l** of anything." Jg 19:19 4270
"Do I **l** madmen, that you have 1Sa 21:15 2638
not **l** a man on the throne of Israel.' 1Ki 2:4 3772
'You shall not **l** a man to sit on 1Ki 8:25 3772
not **l** a man on the throne of Israel.' 1Ki 9:5 3772
'You shall not **l** a man to sit on 2Ch 6:16 3772
not **l** a man *to be* ruler in Israel.' 2Ch 7:18 3772
had brought about a **l** of restraint 2Ch 28:19 6544a
"The lion perishes for **l** of prey, Jb 4:11 1097
anyone perish for **l** of clothing, Jb 31:19 1097
young lions do **l** and suffer hunger; Ps 34:10 7326
He will die for **l** of instruction, Pr 5:23 369
fools die for **l** of understanding. Pr 10:21 2638
For **l** of wood the fire goes out, Pr 26:20 657
And he will have no **l** of gain. Pr 31:11 2637
exile for their **l** of knowledge; Is 5:13 1097
None will **l** its mate. Is 34:16 6485
Their fish stink for **l** of water And Is 50:2 369
'David shall never **l** a man to sit Jer 33:17 3772
shall never **l** a man before Me to offer Jer 33:18 3772
the son of Rechab shall not **l** a man Jer 35:19 3772
For **l** of the fruits of the field. La 4:9
scattered for **l** of a shepherd, Ezk 34:5 1097
of the field for **l** of a shepherd, Ezk 34:8 369
are destroyed for **l** of knowledge. Hos 4:6 369
And **l** of bread in all your places, Am 4:6 2640
"One thing you **l**: go and sell all you Mk 10:21 *5302*
"One thing you still **l**; Lk 18:22 *3007*
sandals, you did not **l** anything, Lk 22:35 *5302*
because of your **l** of self-control. 1Co 7:5 *192*
HE WHO *gathered* LITTLE HAD NO **L**." 2Co 8:15 *1641*

LACKED
you have not **l** a thing." Dt 2:7 2637
"But what have you **l** with me, 1Ki 11:22 2638
we have **l** everything and have met Jer 44:18 2637
honor to that *member* which **l**, 1Co 12:24 *5302*
before, but you **l** opportunity. Php 4:10 *170*

LACKING
the fifty righteous are **l** five, Gn 18:28 2637
covenant of your God shall not be **l** Lv 2:13 7673a
they are a nation **l** in counsel, Dt 32:28 6
they left nothing **l**. 1Ki 4:27 5737c
adultery with a woman is **l** sense; Pr 6:32 2638
the youths A young man **l** sense, Pr 7:7 2638
A man **l** in sense pledges And Pr 17:18 2638
the vineyard of the man **l** sense, Pr 24:30 2638
and what is **l** cannot be counted. Ec 1:15 2642
and let not oil be **l** on your head. Ec 9:8 2637
along the road, his sense is **l** Ec 10:3 2637
dungeon, nor will his bread be **l**. Is 51:14 2637
truth is **l**; And he who turns aside Is 59:15 5737c
you still **l** in understanding also? Mt 15:16 *801*
what am I still **l**?" Mt 19:20 *5302*
you so **l** in understanding also? Mk 7:18 *801*
so that you are not **l** in any gift, 1Co 1:7 *5302*
supplied what was **l** on your part. 1Co 16:17 *5303*
what is **l** in Christ's afflictions. Col 1:24 *5303*
complete what is **l** in your faith? 1Th 3:10 *5303*
way so that nothing is **l** for them. Ti 3:13 *3007*
and complete, **l** in nothing. Jas 1:4 *3007*

LACKS
for his need *in* whatever he **l**. Dt 15:8 2637
by the sword, or who **l** bread." 2Sa 3:29 2638
him who **l** understanding she says, Pr 9:4 2638
him who **l** understanding she says, Pr 9:16 2638
back of him who **l** understanding. Pr 10:13 2638
who despises his neighbor **l** sense, Pr 11:12 2638
beautiful woman who **l** discretion. Pr 11:22 5493
he who honors himself and **l** bread. Pr 12:9 2638
who pursues worthless *things* **l** sense. Pr 12:11 2638
Folly is joy to him who **l** sense, Pr 15:21 2638
a great oppressor **l** understanding, Pr 28:16 2638
his soul **l** nothing of all that he desires; Ec 6:2 2638
goblet Which never **l** mixed wine; SS 7:2 2637
who **l** might He increases power. Is 40:29 369
But if any of you **l** wisdom, Jas 1:5 *3007*
For he who **l** these *qualities* is 2Pe 1:9 *3361, 3918b*

LAD
because of the **l** and your maid; Gn 21:12 5288
God heard the **l** crying; Gn 21:17 5288
God has heard the voice of the **l** Gn 21:17 5288
"Arise, lift up the **l**, Gn 21:18 5288
water and gave the **l** a drink. Gn 21:19 5288
God was with the **l**, Gn 21:20 5288
and I and the **l** will go over Gn 22:5 5288
out your hand against the **l**, Gn 22:12 5288
"Send the **l** with me and we will Gn 43:8 5288
'The **l** cannot leave his father, Gn 44:22 5288
father, and the **l** is not with us, Gn 44:30 5288
he sees that the **l** is not *with us,* Gn 44:31 5288
surety for the **l** to my father, Gn 44:32 5288
your servant remain instead of the **l** Gn 44:33 5288
let the **l** go up with his brothers. Gn 44:33 5288
my father if the **l** is not with me Gn 44:34 5288
"And behold, I will send the **l**, 1Sa 20:21 5288
If I specifically say to the **l**, 1Sa 20:21 5288
and a little **l** *was* with him. 1Sa 20:35 5288
He said to his **l**, 1Sa 20:36 5288
As the **l** was running, he shot an 1Sa 20:36 5288
When the **l** reached the place of 1Sa 20:37 5288
shot, Jonathan called after the **l** and 1Sa 20:37 5288
And Jonathan called after the **l**, 1Sa 20:38 5288
And Jonathan's **l** picked up the 1Sa 20:38 5288
the **l** was not aware of anything; 1Sa 20:39 5288
weapons to his **l** and said to him, 1Sa 20:40 5288
When the **l** was gone, David rose 1Sa 20:41 5288
But a **l** did see them and told 2Sa 17:18 5288
The mother of the **l** said, 2Ki 4:30 5288
"The **l** has not awakened." 2Ki 4:31 5288
l was dead and laid on his bed. 2Ki 4:32 5288
and the **l** sneezed seven times and 2Ki 4:35 5288
times and the **l** opened his eyes. 2Ki 4:35 5288
deeds that a **l** distinguishes himself Pr 20:11 5288
yet wise **l** is better than an old Ec 4:13 3206
throng to the side of the second **l** Ec 4:15 3206
whose king is a **l** and whose Ec 10:16 5288
"There is a **l** here who has five Jn 6:9 *3808*

LADAN
L his son, Ammihud his son, 1Ch 7:26 3936
the Gershonites *were* **L** and Shimei. 1Ch 23:7 3936
The sons of **L** *were* Jehiel the 1Ch 23:8 3936
of the fathers' *households* of **L**. 1Ch 23:9 3936
The sons of **L**, the sons of the 1Ch 26:21 3936
of the Gershonites belonging to **L**, 1Ch 26:21 3936
belonging to **L** the Gershonite. 1Ch 26:21 3936

LADDER
a **l** was set on the earth with its Gn 28:12 5551

LADEN
A man who is **l** with the guilt of Pr 28:17 6231

LADIES
"This day the **l** of Persia and Es 1:18 8282
many young **l** were gathered to the Es 2:8 5291
daughters are among Your noble **l**; Ps 45:9

LAD'S
life is bound up in the **l** life, Gn 44:30
and lay my staff on the **l** face." 2Ki 4:29 5288
and laid the staff on the **l** face, 2Ki 4:31 5288

LADS
me from all evil, Bless the **l**; Gn 48:16 5288
young **l** came out from the city and 2Ki 2:23 5288
tore up forty-two **l** of their number. 2Ki 2:24 3206
I will make mere **l** their princes Is 3:4 5288

LADY
"Then let the young **l** who pleases Es 2:4 5291
Now the young **l** was beautiful of Es 2:7 5291
Now the young **l** pleased him and Es 2:9 5291
Now when the turn of each young **l** Es 2:12 5291
the young **l** would go in to the Es 2:13 5291
to the chosen **l** and her children, 2Jn 1:1 *2959*
Now I ask you, **l**, 2Jn 1:5 *2959*

LAEL
was Eliasaph the son of **L**. Nu 3:24 3815

LAGGING
not **l** behind in diligence, fervent Ro 12:11 *3636*

LAHAD
became the father of Ahumai and **L**. 1Ch 4:2 3855

LAHMAS
and Cabbon and **L** and Chitlish, Jos 15:40 3903

LAHMI
and Elhanan the son of Jair killed **L** 1Ch 20:5 3902

LAID
and **l** it upon both their shoulders Gn 9:23 7760
l each half opposite the other; Gn 15:10 5414
and **l** it on Isaac his son, Gn 22:6 7760
and **l** him on the altar, on top of Gn 22:9 7760
and **l** it on the head of Ephraim, Gn 48:14 7896
that his father **l** his right hand on Gn 48:17 7896
the land was **l** waste because of the Ex 8:24 7843
to determine whether he **l** his hands Ex 22:8 7971
that he has not **l** hands on his Ex 22:11 7971
the tabernacle and **l** its sockets, Ex 40:18 5414
Aaron and his sons **l** their hands on Lv 8:14 5564
Aaron and his sons **l** their hands on Lv 8:18 5564
Aaron and his sons **l** their hands on Lv 8:22 5564
nakedness, he has **l** bare her flow, Lv 20:18 6168
that You have **l** the burden of all Nu 11:11 7760
fire on it, and **l** incense on it; Nu 16:18 7760
we have **l** waste even to Nophah, Nu 21:30 8074
Then he **l** his hands on him and Nu 27:23 5564
'Is it not **l** up in store with Me, Dt 32:34 3647
for Moses had **l** his hands on him; Dt 34:9 5564
she had **l** in order on the roof. Jos 2:6 6186a
be on our head if a hand is **l** Jos 2:19
their blood might be **l** on Abimelech Jg 9:24 7760
it and **l** *it* on his shoulder. Jg 9:48 7760
l hold of his concubine and cut her Jg 19:29 2388
of barley and **l** *it* on her. Ru 3:15 7896
the child and **l** him in her lap, Ru 4:16 7896
idol and **l** *it* on the bed, 1Sa 19:13 7760
foundations of the world were **l** bare By 2Sa 22:16 1540
command which I have **l** on you?" 1Ki 2:43 6680
slept, and **l** him in her bosom, 1Ki 3:20 7901
and **l** her dead son in my bosom. 1Ki 3:20 7901
of the house of the LORD was **l**, 1Ki 6:37 3245
man of God and **l** it on the donkey and 1Ki 13:29 5117
He **l** his body in his own grave, 1Ki 13:30 5117
he **l** its foundations with the *loss* 1Ki 16:34 3245
living, and **l** him on his own bed. 1Ki 17:19 7901
ox in pieces and **l** *it* on the wood. 1Ki 18:33 7760
l him on the bed of the man of God, 2Ki 4:21 7901
and **l** the staff on the lad's face, 2Ki 4:31 7760
the lad was dead and **l** on his bed. 2Ki 4:32 7901
LORD **l** this oracle against him: 2Ki 9:25 5375
and for all that was **l** out for the 2Ki 12:12 3318
l his hands on the king's hands. 2Ki 13:16 7760
they took and **l** *it* on the boil, 2Ki 20:7 7760
that your fathers have **l** up in store 2Ki 20:17 686
the foundations which Solomon **l** 2Ch 3:3 3245
they **l** him in the resting place 2Ch 16:14 7901
and they **l** their hands on them. 2Ch 29:23 5564
temple of the LORD had not been **l**. Ezr 3:3 3245
the builders had **l** the foundation of Ezr 3:10 3245

of the house of the LORD was l. Ezr 3:11 3245
the foundation of this house was l Ezr 3:12 3245
therefore that city was l waste. Ezr 4:15 2718
beams are being l in the walls; Ezr 5:8 7761
l the foundations of the house of Ezr 5:16 3052
they l its beams and hung its Ne 3:3 7136b
l its beams and hung its doors with Ne 3:6 7136b
who were before me l burdens on Ne 5:15 3513
And l down for them commandments, Ne 9:14 6680
Now King Ahasuerus l a tribute on Es 10:1 7760
And l in the balances together Jb 6:2 5375
You have l waste all my company. Jb 16:7 8074
who has l *on Him* the whole world? Jb 34:13 7760
I l the foundation of the earth? Jb 38:4 3245
Or who l its cornerstone, Jb 38:6 3384
be l low even at the sight of him? Jb 41:9 2904
foundations of the world were l bare Ps 18:15 1540
which they have secretly l for me, Ps 31:4 2934
You brought us into the net; You l Ps 66:11 7760
They have l Jerusalem in ruins. Ps 79:1 7760
Jacob And l waste his habitation. Ps 79:7 8074
He himself was l in irons; Ps 105:18 935
The wicked have l a snare for me, Ps 119:110 5414
before, And l Your hand upon me. Ps 139:5 7896
'Since you were l low, no *tree* Is 14:8 7901
The earth will be completely l waste Is 24:3 1238b
the city will be utterly l low. Is 32:19 8213
that your fathers have l up in store Is 39:6 686
'Your foundation will be l.'" Is 44:28 3245
l the foundations of the earth, Is 51:13 3245
a dirge, Because they are l waste so Jer 9:10 5327c
ruined, l waste like a desert, Jer 9:12 5327c
And have l waste his habitation. Jer 10:25 8074
hatches eggs which it has not l, Jer 17:11 3205
to Jerusalem and l siege to it; Jer 39:1 6696a
silent Since He has l *it* on him. La 3:28 5190
"Your slain whom you have l in Ezk 11:7 7760
inhabited cities will be l waste and Ezk 12:20 2717b
so that its foundation is l bare; Ezk 13:14 1540
towers And l waste their cities; Ezk 19:7 2717b
The king of Babylon has l siege to Ezk 24:2 5564
filled, *now that* she is l waste,' Ezk 26:2 2717b
midst of cities that are l waste, Ezk 29:12 2717b
swords were l under their heads; Ezk 32:27 5414
l with those slain by the sword; Ezk 32:29 5414
'They are l desolate; Ezk 35:12 8074
My hand which I have l on them. Ezk 39:21 7760
and l over the mouth of the den; Da 6:17 7761
the sanctuaries of Israel l waste. Am 7:9 2717b
throne, l aside his robe from him, Jon 3:6 5674a
They have l siege against us; Mi 5:1 7760
For He has l bare the cedar work. Zph 2:14 6168
Their cities are l waste, Zph 3:6 6658b
l the foundation of this house, Zch 4:9 3245
house of the LORD of hosts was l, Zch 8:9 3245
The axe is already l at the root of Mt 3:10 *2749*
divided against itself is l waste; Mt 12:25 *2049*
and they l them down at His feet; Mt 15:30 *4496*
and l their coats on them; Mt 21:7 *2007*
l hands on Jesus and seized Him. Mt 26:50 *1911*
and l it in his own new tomb, Mt 27:60 *5087*
He l His hands on a few sick people Mk 6:5 *2007*
away his body and l it in a tomb. Mk 6:29 *5087*
He l His hands on his eyes; Mk 8:25 *2007*
They l hands on Him and Mk 14:46 *1911*
and l Him in a tomb which had been Mk 15:46 *2698*
looking on *to see* where He was l. Mk 15:47 *5087*
is the place where they l Him. Mk 16:6 *5087*
in cloths, and l Him in a manger, Lk 2:7 *347*
the axe is already l at the root of Lk 3:9 *2749*
and l a foundation on the rock; Lk 6:48 *5087*
divided against itself is l waste; Lk 11:17 *2049*
goods l up for many years *to come* Lk 12:19 *2749*
And He l His hands on her; Lk 13:13 *2007*
when he has l a foundation and Lk 14:29 *5087*
named Lazarus was l at his gate, Lk 16:20 *906*
and l Him in a tomb cut into the Lk 23:53 *5087*
the tomb and how His body was l. Lk 23:55 *5087*
and no man l his hand on Him, Jn 7:30 *1911*
Him, but no one l hands on Him. Jn 7:44 *1911*
"Where have you l him?" Jn 11:34 *5087*
supper, and l aside His garments; Jn 13:4 *5087*
in which no one had yet been l. Jn 19:41 *5087*
was nearby, they l Jesus there. Jn 19:42 *5087*
not know where they have l Him." Jn 20:2 *5087*
not know where they have l Him." Jn 20:13 *5087*
tell me where you have l Him, Jn 20:15 *5087*
saw a charcoal fire *already* l and Jn 21:9 *2749*
And they l hands on them and put Ac 4:3 *1911*
and l it at the apostles' feet. Ac 4:37 *5087*
it, he l it at the apostles' feet. Ac 5:2 *5087*
and l them on cots and pallets, Ac 5:15 *5087*
They l hands on the apostles Ac 5:18 *1911*
they l their hands on them. Ac 6:6 *2007*
and l in the tomb which Abraham Ac 7:16 *5087*
and the witnesses l aside their robes Ac 7:58 *659*
body, they l it in an upper room. Ac 9:37 *5087*
Herod the king l hands on some who Ac 12:1 *1911*
prayed and l their hands on them, Ac 13:3 *2007*
the cross and l Him in a tomb. Ac 13:29 *5087*
and was l among his fathers and Ac 13:36 *4369*
Paul had l his hands upon them, Ac 19:6 *2007*
the crowd and l hands on him, Ac 21:27 *1911*
Festus l Paul's case before the king, Ac 25:14 *394*
of sticks and l them on the fire, Ac 28:3 *2007*
he l his hands on him and healed Ac 28:8 *2007*
master builder I l a foundation, 1Co 3:10 *5087*
other than the one which is l, 1Co 3:11 *2749*
they were l low in the wilderness. 1Co 10:5 *2693*
I was l hold of by Christ Jesus. Php 3:12 *2638*
myself as having l hold of *it* yet; Php 3:13 *2638*
the hope l up for you in heaven, Col 1:5 *606*
since you l aside the old self Col 3:9 *554*
in the future there is l up for me 2Tm 4:8 *606*
IN THE BEGINNING L THE FOUNDATION OF Heb 1:10 *2311*
but all things are open and l bare Heb 4:13 *5136*
that He l down His life for us; 1Jn 3:16 *5087*
dead bodies to be l in a tomb. Rv 11:9 *5087*
great wealth has been l waste!' Rv 18:17 *2049*
in one hour she has been l waste!' Rv 18:19 *2049*
And he l hold of the dragon, the Rv 20:2 *2902*
The city is l out as a square, Rv 21:16 *2749*

LAIN

easily have l with your wife, Gn 26:10 7901
"If no man has l with you and if Nu 5:19 7901
woman who has l with a man." Jg 21:11 3045, 4904
would have l down and been quiet; Jb 3:13 7901
tree You have l down as a harlot. Jer 2:20 6808
in her youth men had l with her, Ezk 23:8 7901
into the hold of the ship, l down and Jon 1:5 7901
the rock, where no one had ever l. Lk 23:53 *2749*

LAIR

"Then the beast goes into its l And Jb 37:8 695
dens *And* lie in wait in their l? Jb 38:40 5521
a hiding place as a lion in his l; Ps 10:9 5520

LAIRS

And filled his l with prey And his Na 2:12 2356

LAISH

the five men departed and came to L Jg 18:7 3919a
who went to spy out the country of L Jg 18:14 3919a
belonged to him, and came to L, Jg 18:27 3919a
name of the city formerly was L. Jg 18:29 3919a
wife, to Palti the son of L, 1Sa 25:44 3919b
from Paltiel the son of L. 2Sa 3:15 3919b

LAISHAH

L *and* wretched Anathoth! Is 10:30 3919c

LAKE

standing by the l of Gennesaret; Lk 5:1 *3041*
boats lying at the edge of the l; Lk 5:2 *3041*
over to the other side of the l." Lk 8:22 *3041*
gale of wind descended on the l, Lk 8:23 *3041*
down the steep bank into the l and Lk 8:33 *3041*
were thrown alive into the l of fire Rv 19:20 *3041*
into the l of fire and brimstone, Rv 20:10 *3041*
were thrown into the l of fire. Rv 20:14 *3041*
the second death, the l of fire. Rv 20:14 *3041*
he was thrown into the l of fire. Rv 20:15 *3041*
their part *will be* in the l that Rv 21:8 *3041*

LAKKUM

and Jabneel, as far as L, Jos 19:33 3946

LAMA

"ELI, ELI, L SABACHTHANI?" Mt 27:46 *2982*
"ELOI, ELOI, L SABACHTHANI?" Mk 15:34 *2982*

LAMB

is the l for the burnt offering?" Gn 22:7 7716
the l for the burnt offering, Gn 22:8 7716
one to take a l for themselves, Ex 12:3 7716
a l for each household. Ex 12:3 7716
household is too small for a l, Ex 12:4 7716
eat, you are to divide the l. Ex 12:4 7716
'Your l shall be an unblemished Ex 12:5 7716
and slay the Passover l. Ex 12:21
donkey you shall redeem with a l, Ex 13:13 7716
"The one l you shall offer in the Ex 29:39 3532
l you shall offer at twilight; Ex 29:39 3532
of wine for a drink offering with one l. Ex 29:40 3532
l you shall offer at twilight, Ex 29:41 3532
"You shall redeem with a l Ex 34:20 7716
to offer a l for his offering, Lv 3:7 3775
'But if he brings a l as his Lv 4:32 3532
just as the fat of the l is Lv 4:35 3775
a l or a goat as a sin offering. Lv 5:6 3776
'But if he cannot afford a l, Lv 5:7 7716
sin offering, and a calf and a l, Lv 9:3 3532
year old l for a burnt offering and Lv 12:6 3532
'But if she cannot afford a l, Lv 12:8 7716
a yearling ewe l without defect, Lv 14:10 3535
the priest shall take the one male l Lv 14:12 3532
he shall slaughter the male l in the Lv 14:13 3532
then he is to take one male l for Lv 14:21 3532
take the l of the guilt offering and Lv 14:24 3532
slaughter the l of the guilt offering; Lv 14:25 3532
who slaughters an ox or a l Lv 17:3 3775
'In respect to an ox or a l which Lv 22:23 7716
you shall offer a male l one year Lv 23:12 3532
and shall bring a male l a year old Nu 6:12 3532
one male l a year old without Nu 6:14 3532
one ram, one male l one year old, Nu 7:15 3532
one ram, one male l one year old, Nu 7:21 3532
one ram, one male l one year old, Nu 7:27 3532
one ram, one male l one year old, Nu 7:33 3532
one ram, one male l one year old, Nu 7:39 3532
one ram, one male l one year old, Nu 7:45 3532
one ram, one male l one year old, Nu 7:51 3532
one ram, one male l one year old, Nu 7:57 3532
one ram, one male l one year old, Nu 7:63 3532
one ram, one male l one year old, Nu 7:69 3532
one ram, one male l one year old, Nu 7:75 3532
one ram, one male l one year old, Nu 7:81 3532
or for the sacrifice, for each l. Nu 15:5 3532
offer the one l in the morning and Nu 28:4 3532
the other l you shall offer at twilight Nu 28:4 3532
be a fourth of a hin for each l, Nu 28:7 3532
The other l you shall offer at twilight Nu 28:8 3532
for a grain offering for each l, Nu 28:13 3532
ram and a fourth of a hin for a l; Nu 28:14 3532
Samuel took a suckling l and 1Sa 7:9 2924
came and took a l from the flock, 1Sa 17:34 7716
had nothing except one little ewe l 2Sa 12:3 3535
he took the poor man's ewe l and 2Sa 12:4 3535
restitution for the l fourfold, 2Sa 12:6 3535
they slaughtered the Passover l Ezr 6:20
the wolf will dwell with the l, Is 11:6 3532
Send the *tribute* l to the ruler of the Is 16:1 3733c
Like a l that is led to slaughter, Is 53:7 7716
wolf and the l will graze together, Is 65:25 2924
He who sacrifices a l is *like* the Is 66:3 7716
a gentle l led to the slaughter; Jer 11:19 3532
And you shall provide a l a year old Ezk 46:13 3532
"Thus they shall provide the l, Ezk 46:15 3532
them Like a l in a large field? Hos 4:16 3532
when the Passover l was being Mk 14:12
Bread on which the Passover l had Lk 22:7
the L of God who takes away the Jn 1:29 *286*
"Behold, the L of God!" Jn 1:36 *286*
A L BEFORE ITS SHEARER IS SILENT, Ac 8:32 *286*
of a l unblemished and spotless, 1Pe 1:19 *286*
a L standing, as if slain, having Rv 5:6 *721b*
elders fell down before the L, Rv 5:8 *721b*
"Worthy is the L that was slain Rv 5:12 *721b*
sits on the throne, and to the L, Rv 5:13 *721b*
L broke one of the seven seals, Rv 6:1 *721b*
When the L broke the fourth seal, I Rv 6:7
When the L broke the fifth seal, I Rv 6:9
and from the wrath of the L; Rv 6:16 *721b*
the throne and before the L, Rv 7:9 *721b*
on the throne, and to the L." Rv 7:10 *721b*
them white in the blood of the L. Rv 7:14 *721b*
for the L in the center of the Rv 7:17 *721b*
When the L broke the seventh seal, Rv 8:1
him because of the blood of the L Rv 12:11 *721b*
in the book of life of the L who has Rv 13:8 *721b*
and he had two horns like a l and Rv 13:11 *721b*
the L *was* standing on Mount Zion, Rv 14:1 *721b*
who follow the L wherever He goes. Rv 14:4 *721b*
first fruits to God and to the L. Rv 14:4 *721b*
and in the presence of the L. Rv 14:10 *721b*
of God, and the song of the L, Rv 15:3 *721b*
"These will wage war against the L, Rv 17:14 *721b*
and the L will overcome them, Rv 17:14 *721b*
for the marriage of the L has come Rv 19:7 *721b*
the marriage supper of the L.'" Rv 19:9 *721b*
the bride, the wife of the L." Rv 21:9 *721b*
of the twelve apostles of the L. Rv 21:14 *721b*
Lord God the Almighty and the L Rv 21:22 *721b*
it, and its lamp *is* the L. Rv 21:23 *721b*
the throne of God and of the L, Rv 22:1 *721b*
the throne of God and of the L Rv 22:3 *721b*

LAMB'S

are written in the L book of life. Rv 21:27 *721b*

LAMBS

ewe l of the flock by themselves. Gn 21:28 3535
"What do these seven ewe l mean, Gn 21:29 3535
"You shall take these seven ewe l Gn 21:30 3535
and every black one among the l and Gn 30:32 3775
the goats and black among the l, Gn 30:33 3775
Jacob separated the l, Gn 30:40 3775
l according to your families, Ex 12:21 6629
two one year old l each day, Ex 29:38 3532
to take two male l without defect, Lv 14:10 3532
one year old male l without defect, Lv 23:18 3532
two male l one year old for a sacrifice Lv 23:19 3532
with two l before the LORD; Lv 23:20 3532
goats, five male l one year old. Nu 7:17 3532
goats, five male l one year old. Nu 7:23 3532
goats, five male l one year old. Nu 7:29 3532
goats, five male l one year old. Nu 7:35 3532
goats, five male l one year old. Nu 7:41 3532
goats, five male l one year old. Nu 7:47 3532
goats, five male l one year old. Nu 7:53 3532
goats, five male l one year old. Nu 7:59 3532
goats, five male l one year old. Nu 7:65 3532
goats, five male l one year old. Nu 7:71 3532
goats, five male l one year old. Nu 7:77 3532
goats, five male l one year old. Nu 7:83 3532
the male l one year old with their Nu 7:87 3532
60, the male l one year old 60. Nu 7:88 3532
ram, or for each of the male l, Nu 15:11 7716
two male l one year old without Nu 28:3 3532
two male l one year old without Nu 28:9 3532
seven male l one year old without Nu 28:11 3532
ram and seven male l one year old, Nu 28:19 3532
offer for each of the seven l; Nu 28:21 3532
ram, seven male l one year old; Nu 28:27 3532
a tenth for each of the seven l; Nu 28:29 3532
seven male l one year old without Nu 29:2 3532
one-tenth for each of the seven l. Nu 29:4 3532
ram, seven male l one year old, Nu 29:8 3532
a tenth for each of the seven l; Nu 29:10 3532
fourteen male l one year old, Nu 29:13 3532
tenth for each of the fourteen l; Nu 29:15 3532
fourteen male l one year old without Nu 29:17 3532
bulls, for the rams and for the l, Nu 29:18 3532
fourteen male l one year old without Nu 29:20 3532
bulls, for the rams and for the l, Nu 29:21 3532
fourteen male l one year old without Nu 29:23 3532
bulls, for the rams and for the l, Nu 29:24 3532
fourteen male l one year old without Nu 29:26 3532
bulls, for the rams and for the l, Nu 29:27 3532
fourteen male l one year old without Nu 29:29 3532
bulls, for the rams and for the l, Nu 29:30 3532
fourteen male l one year old without Nu 29:32 3532
bulls, for the rams and for the l, Nu 29:33 3532

seven male **l** one year old without **Nu 29:36** 3532
bull, for the ram and for the **l**, **Nu 29:37** 3532
milk of the flock, With fat of **l**, **Dt 32:14** 3733c
the oxen, the fatlings, the **l**, **1Sa 15:9** 3733c
to pay the king of Israel 100,000 **l** **2Ki 3:4** 3733c
bulls, 1,000 rams *and* 1,000 **l**, **1Ch 29:21** 3532
seven bulls, seven rams, seven **l** and **2Ch 29:21** 3532
they slaughtered the **l** also and **2Ch 29:22** 3532
was 70 bulls, 100 rams, and 200 **l**; **2Ch 29:32** 3532
they slaughtered the Passover **l** **2Ch 30:15**
the slaughter of the Passover **l** **2Ch 30:17**
present, flocks of **l** and young goats, **2Ch 35:7** 3532
and **l** for a burnt offering to the **Ezr 6:9** 563
of God 100 bulls, 200 rams, 400 **l**, **Ezr 6:17** 563
diligently buy bulls, rams and **l**, **Ezr 7:17** 563
for all Israel, 96 rams, 77 **l**, **Ezr 8:35** 3532
with suckling **l** He brought him To **Ps 78:71** 5763
like rams, The hills, like **l**. **Ps 114:4** 1121, 6629
you skip like rams? O hills, like **l**? **Ps 114:6** 1121, 6629
The **l** *will be* for your clothing, **Pr 27:26** 3532
pleasure in the blood of bulls, **l** or **Is 1:11** 3532
Then the **l** will graze as in their **Is 5:17** 3532
with the blood of **l** and goats, **Is 34:6** 3733c
In His arm He will gather the **l** And **Is 40:11** 2924
them down like **l** to the slaughter, **Jer 51:40** 3733c
they were your customers for **l**, **Ezk 27:21** 3733c
as *though they were* rams, **l**, **Ezk 39:18** 3733c
shall be six **l** without blemish and a **Ezk 46:4** 3532
the grain offering with the **l** as much **Ezk 46:5** 3532
blemish, also six **l** and a ram, **Ezk 46:6** 3532
with the **l** as much as he is able, **Ezk 46:7** 3532
and with the **l** as much as one is **Ezk 46:11** 3532
And eat **l** from the flock And **Am 6:4** 3733c
out as **l** in the midst of wolves. **Lk 10:3** *704*
He said to him, "Tend My **l**." **Jn 21:15** *721b*

LAME
a blind man, or a **l** man, **Lv 21:18** 6455
to flee, he fell and became **l**. **2Sa 4:4** 6452b
blind and **l** will turn you away"; **2Sa 5:6** 6455
let him reach the **l** and the blind, **2Sa 5:8** 6455
"The blind or the **l** shall not **2Sa 5:8** 6455
Now he was **l** in both feet. **2Sa 9:13** 6455
king,' because your servant is **l**. **2Sa 19:26** 6455
to the blind And feet to the **l**. **Jb 29:15** 6455
legs *which are* useless to the **l**, **Pr 26:7** 6455
The **l** will take the plunder. **Is 33:23** 6455
Then the **l** will leap like a deer, **Is 35:6** 6455
Among them the blind and the **l**, **Jer 31:8** 6455
"I will assemble the **l** And **Mi 4:6** 6760
"I will make the **l** a remnant And **Mi 4:7** 6760
save the **l** And gather the outcast, **Zph 3:19** 6760
when you present the **l** and sick, **Mal 1:8** 6455
by robbery and *what is* **l** or sick; **Mal 1:13** 6455
RECEIVE SIGHT and *the* **l** walk, **Mt 11:5** *5560*
with them *those who were* **l**, **Mt 15:30** *5560*
restored, and the **l** walking, **Mt 15:31** *5560*
you to enter life crippled or **l**, **Mt 18:8** *5560*
the **l** came to Him in the temple, **Mt 21:14** *5560*
is better for you to enter life **l**, **Mk 9:45** *5560*
BLIND RECEIVE SIGHT, *the* **l** walk, **Lk 7:22** *5560*
the poor, *the* crippled, *the* **l**, **Lk 14:13** *5560*
and crippled and blind and **l**.' **Lk 14:21** *5560*
of those who were sick, blind, **l**, **Jn 5:3** *5560*
And a man who had been **l** **Ac 3:2** *5560*
been paralyzed and **l** were healed. **Ac 8:7** *5560*
his feet, **l** from his mother's womb, **Ac 14:8** *5560*
limb which is **l** may not be put out **Heb 12:13** *5560*

LAMECH
Methushael became the father of **L**. **Gn 4:18** 3929
L took to himself two wives: **Gn 4:19** 3929
L said to his wives, **Gn 4:23** 3929
to my voice, You wives of **L**, **Gn 4:23** 3929
Then **L** seventy-sevenfold." **Gn 4:24** 3929
years, and became the father of **L**. **Gn 5:25** 3929
after he became the father of **L**, **Gn 5:26** 3929
L lived one hundred and **Gn 5:28** 3929
Then **L** lived five hundred and **Gn 5:30** 3929
So all the days of **L** were seven **Gn 5:31** 3929
Enoch, Methuselah, **L**, **1Ch 1:3** 3929
the son of Noah, the son of **L**, **Lk 3:36** *2984*

LAMED
And in their self-will they **l** oxen. **Gn 49:6** 6136b

LAMENESS
defect, *such as* **l** or blindness, **Dt 15:21** 6455

LAMENT
Then David chanted with this **l** **2Sa 1:17** 7015
on sackcloth and **l** before Abner." **2Sa 3:31** 5594
The king chanted a **l** for Abner **2Sa 3:33**
Jeremiah chanted a **l** for Josiah. **2Ch 35:25** 6969
And her gates will **l** and mourn, **Is 3:26** 578
And the fishermen will **l**, **Is 19:8** 578
put on sackcloth, **L** and wail; **Jer 4:8** 5594
or go to **l** or to console them; **Jer 16:5** 5594
"They will not **l** for him: **Jer 22:18** 5594
They will not **l** for him: **Jer 22:18** 5594
and they will **l** for you, **Jer 34:5** 5594
yourselves with sackcloth and **l**, **Jer 49:3** 5594
has caused rampart and wall to **l**; **La 2:8** 56
for you And **l** over you: **Ezk 27:32** 6969
yourselves *with sackcloth* And **l**, **Jl 1:13** 5594
Because of this I must **l** and wail, **Mi 1:8** 5594
I must make a **l** like the jackals **Mi 1:8** 4553
to you, that you will weep and **l**, **Jn 16:20** *2354*
will weep and **l** over her when they **Rv 18:9** *2875*

LAMENTATION
with a very great and sorrowful **l**; **Gn 50:10** 4553
for an only son, A **l** most bitter. **Jer 6:26** 4553
take up a **l** on the bare heights; **Jer 7:29** 7015
in Ramah, **L** *and* bitter weeping. **Jer 31:15** 5092
its streets there is **l** everywhere; **Jer 48:38** 4553
up a **l** for the princes of Israel **Ezk 19:1** 7015
This is a **l**, and has become a **Ezk 19:14** 7015
a lamentation, and has become a **l**. **Ezk 19:14** 7015
up a **l** over you and say to you, **Ezk 26:17** 7015
son of man, take up a **l** over Tyre; **Ezk 27:2** 7015
a **l** for you And lament over you: **Ezk 27:32** 7015
take up a **l** over the king of Tyre and **Ezk 28:12** 7015
up a **l** over Pharaoh king of Egypt and **Ezk 32:2** 7015
is a **l** and they shall chant it. **Ezk 32:16** 7015
And professional mourners to **l**. **Am 5:16** 5092
And all your songs into **l**; **Am 8:10** 7015
The **l** of Beth-ezel: **Mi 1:11** 4553
And utter a bitter **l** *and* say, **Mi 2:4** 5092
Stephen, and made loud **l** over him. **Ac 8:2** *2870*

LAMENTATIONS
Josiah in their **l** to this day. **2Ch 35:25** 7015
they are also written in the **L**. **2Ch 35:25** 7015
times of fasting and their **l**. **Es 9:31** 2201
and written on it were **l**, **Ezk 2:10** 7015
it went down to Sheol I caused **l**; **Ezk 31:15** 56

LAMENTED
they **l** there with a very great and **Gn 50:10** 5594
of the window she looked and **l**, **Jg 5:28** 2980
house of Israel **l** after the LORD. **1Sa 7:2** 5091
and all Israel had **l** him and **1Sa 28:3** 5594
they will not be **l** or buried; **Jer 16:4** 5594
not be buried, they will not be **l**, **Jer 16:6** 5594
They will not be **l**, **Jer 25:33** 5594

LAMENTING
will be *a city of* **l** and mourning; **Is 29:2** 8386
were all weeping and **l** for her; **Lk 8:52** *2875*
women who were mourning and **l** Him. **Lk 23:27** *2354*

LAMP
to make a **l** burn continually. **Ex 27:20** 5216
to make a **l** burn continually. **Lv 24:2** 5216
the **l** of God had not yet gone out, **1Sa 3:3** 5216
not extinguish the **l** of Israel." **2Sa 21:17** 5216
"For You are my **l**, O LORD; **2Sa 22:29** 5216
a **l** always before Me in Jerusalem, **1Ki 11:36** 5215a
his God gave him a **l** in Jerusalem, **1Ki 15:4** 5215a
to give a **l** to him through his sons **2Ki 8:19** 5215a
a **l** to him and his sons forever. **2Ch 21:7** 5215a
And his **l** goes out above him. **Jb 18:6** 5216
is the **l** of the wicked put out, **Jb 21:17** 5216
When His **l** shone over my head, *And* **Jb 29:3** 5216
For You light my **l**; **Ps 18:28** 5216
Your word is a **l** to my feet And a **Ps 119:105** 5216
prepared a **l** for Mine anointed. **Ps 132:17** 5216
For the commandment is a **l** and **Pr 6:23** 5216
But the **l** of the wicked goes out. **Pr 13:9** 5216
His **l** will go out in time of **Pr 20:20** 5216
spirit of man is the **l** of the LORD, **Pr 20:27** 5216
proud heart, The **l** of the wicked, **Pr 21:4** 5215a
l of the wicked will be put out. **Pr 24:20** 5216
Her **l** does not go out at night. **Pr 31:18** 5216
millstones and the light of the **l**. **Jer 25:10** 5216
nor does *anyone* light a **l** **Mt 5:15** *3088*
"The eye is the **l** of the body; **Mt 6:22** *3088*
"A **l** is not brought to be put **Mk 4:21** *3088*
no one after lighting a **l** covers it **Lk 8:16** *3088*
"No one, after lighting a **l**, **Lk 11:33** *3088*
"The eye is the **l** of your body; **Lk 11:34** *3088*
l illumines you with its rays." **Lk 11:36** *3088*
does not light a **l** and sweep the **Lk 15:8** *3088*
"He was the **l** that was burning **Jn 5:35** *3088*
as to a **l** shining in a dark place, **2Pe 1:19** *3088*
and the light of a **l** will not **Rv 18:23** *3088*
it, and its **l** *is* the Lamb. **Rv 21:23** *3088*
not have need of the light of a **l** **Rv 22:5** *3088*

LAMPS
shall make its **l** seven *in number;* **Ex 25:37** 5216
and they shall mount its **l** so as **Ex 25:37** 5216
every morning when he trims the **l**. **Ex 30:7** 5216
Aaron trims the **l** at twilight, **Ex 30:8** 5216
its **l** and the oil for the light; **Ex 35:14** 5216
He made its seven **l** with its **Ex 37:23** 5216
with its arrangement of **l** and all its **Ex 39:37** 5216
in the lampstand and mount its **l**. **Ex 40:4** 5216
He lighted the **l** before the LORD, **Ex 40:25** 5216
"He shall keep the **l** in order on **Lv 24:4** 5216
along with its **l** and its snuffers, **Nu 4:9** 5216
'When you mount the **l**, **Nu 8:2** 5216
the seven **l** will give light in the **Nu 8:2** 5216
l at the front of the lampstand, **Nu 8:3** 5216
flowers and the **l** and the tongs, **1Ki 7:49** 5216
lampstands and their golden **l**, **1Ch 28:15** 5216
weight of each lampstand and its **l** **1Ch 28:15** 5216
weight of each lampstand and its **l** **1Ch 28:15** 5216
with their **l** of pure gold, **2Ch 4:20** 5216
the flowers, the **l**, **2Ch 4:21** 5216
lampstand with its **l** is *ready* to light **2Ch 13:11** 5216
of the porch and put out the **l**, **2Ch 29:7** 5216
I will search Jerusalem with **l**, **Zph 1:12** 5216
and its seven **l** on it with seven **Zch 4:2** 5216
spouts belonging to each of the **l** **Zch 4:2** 5216
to ten virgins, who took their **l** and **Mt 25:1** *2985*
"For when the foolish took their **l**, **Mt 25:3** *2985*
oil in flasks along with their **l**. **Mt 25:4** *2985*
virgins rose and trimmed their **l**. **Mt 25:7** *2985*
oil, for our **l** are going out.' **Mt 25:8** *2985*
readiness, and *keep* your **l** lit. **Lk 12:35** *3088*
There were many **l** in the upper **Ac 20:8** *2985*
And *there were* seven **l** of fire **Rv 4:5** *2985*

LAMPSTAND
you shall make a **l** of pure gold. **Ex 25:31** 4501
The **l** *and* its base and its shaft **Ex 25:31** 4501
three branches of the **l** from its one **Ex 25:32** 4501
three branches of the **l** from its **Ex 25:32** 4501
six branches going out from the **l**; **Ex 25:33** 4501
and in the **l** four cups shaped like **Ex 25:34** 4501
six branches coming out of the **l**. **Ex 25:35** 4501
and the **l** opposite the table on **Ex 26:35** 4501
and the **l** and its utensils, **Ex 30:27** 4501
pure *gold* **l** with all its utensils, **Ex 31:8** 4501
the **l** also for the light and its **Ex 35:14** 4501
Then he made the **l** of pure gold. **Ex 37:17** 4501
He made the **l** of hammered work, **Ex 37:17** 4501
three branches of the **l** from the one **Ex 37:18** 4501
the **l** from the other side of it; **Ex 37:18** 4501
six branches going out of the **l**. **Ex 37:19** 4501
In the **l** *there were* four cups **Ex 37:20** 4501
six branches coming out of the **l**. **Ex 37:21**
the pure *gold* **l**, with its **Ex 39:37** 4501
you shall bring in the **l** and mount **Ex 40:4** 4501
the **l** in the tent of meeting, **Ex 40:24** 4501
on the pure *gold* **l** before the LORD **Lv 24:4** 4501
the ark, the table, the **l**, **Nu 3:31** 4501
and cover the **l** for the light, **Nu 4:9** 4501
light in the front of the **l**.' " **Nu 8:2** 4501
its lamps at the front of the **l**, **Nu 8:3** 4501
this was the workmanship of the **l**, **Nu 8:4** 4501
showed Moses, so he made the **l**. **Nu 8:4** 4501
and a table and a chair and a **l**; **2Ki 4:10** 4501
with the weight of each **l** and its **1Ch 28:15** 4501
with the weight of each **l** and its **1Ch 28:15** 4501
according to the use of each **l**; **1Ch 28:15** 4501
and the golden **l** with its lamps is **2Ch 13:11** 4501
and began writing opposite the **l** on **Da 5:5** 5043
a **l** all of gold with its bowl on **Zch 4:2** 4501
right of the **l** and on its left?" **Zch 4:11** 4501
a basket, but on the **l**, **Mt 5:15** *3087*
Is it not *brought* to be put on the **l**? **Mk 4:21** *3087*
but he puts it on a **l**, **Lk 8:16** *3087*
under a basket, but on the **l**, **Lk 11:33** *3087*
in which *were* the **l** and the table **Heb 9:2** *3087*
and will remove your **l** out of its **Rv 2:5** *3087*

LAMPSTANDS
and the **l**, five on the right side **1Ki 7:49** 4501
golden **l** and their golden lamps, **1Ch 28:15** 4501
weight of silver for the silver **l**, **1Ch 28:15** 4501
Then he made the ten golden **l** in **2Ch 4:7** 4501
l with their lamps of pure gold, **2Ch 4:20** 4501
the basins, the pots, the **l**, **Jer 52:19** 4501
turned I saw seven golden **l**; **Rv 1:12** *3087*
middle of the **l** *I saw* one like a son **Rv 1:13** *3087*
hand, and the seven golden **l**: **Rv 1:20** *3087*
seven **l** are the seven churches. **Rv 1:20** *3087*
walks among the seven golden **l**, **Rv 2:1** *3087*
the two **l** that stand before the Lord **Rv 11:4** *3087*

LANCES
to their custom with swords and **l** **1Ki 18:28** 7420

LAND
place, and let the dry **l** appear"; **Gn 1:9** 3004
God called the dry **l** earth, **Gn 1:10** 3004
around the whole **l** of Havilah, **Gn 2:11** 776
The gold of that **l** is good; **Gn 2:12** 776
flows around the whole **l** of Cush. **Gn 2:13** 776
LORD, and settled in the **l** of Nod, **Gn 4:16** 776
to multiply on the face of the **l**, **Gn 6:1** 127
created from the face of the **l**, **Gn 6:7** 127
blot out from the face of the **l** every **Gn 7:4** 127
of all that was on the dry **l**, **Gn 7:22** 2724
that was upon the face of the **l**, **Gn 7:23** 127
was abated from the face of the **l**; **Gn 8:8** 127
and Calneh, in the **l** of Shinar. **Gn 10:10** 776
From that **l** he went forth into **Gn 10:11** 776
they found a plain in the **l** of Shinar **Gn 11:2** 776
Terah in the **l** of his birth, **Gn 11:28** 776
in order to enter the **l** of Canaan; **Gn 11:31** 776
To the **l** which I will show you; **Gn 12:1** 776
they set out for the **l** of Canaan; **Gn 12:5** 776
thus they came to the **l** of Canaan. **Gn 12:5** 776
Abram passed through the **l** as far **Gn 12:6** 776
the Canaanite *was* then in the **l**. **Gn 12:6** 776
descendants I will give this **l**." **Gn 12:7** 776
Now there was a famine in the **l**; **Gn 12:10** 776
the famine was severe in the **l**. **Gn 12:10** 776
And the **l** could not sustain them **Gn 13:6** 776
were dwelling then in the **l**. **Gn 13:7** 776
"Is not the whole **l** before you? **Gn 13:9** 776
the **l** of Egypt as you go to Zoar. **Gn 13:10** 776
Abram settled in the **l** of Canaan, **Gn 13:12** 776
for all the **l** which you see, **Gn 13:15** 776
walk about the **l** through its **Gn 13:17** 776
give you this **l** to possess it." **Gn 15:7** 776
strangers in a **l** that is not theirs, **Gn 15:13** 776
descendants I have given this **l**, **Gn 15:18** 776
ten years in the **l** of Canaan, **Gn 16:3** 776
you, the **l** of your sojournings, **Gn 17:8** 776
sojournings, all the **l** of Canaan, **Gn 17:8** 776
toward all the **l** of the valley, **Gn 19:28** 776
the smoke of the **l** ascended like **Gn 19:28** 776
there toward the **l** of the Negev, **Gn 20:1** 776
"Behold, my **l** is before you; **Gn 20:15** 776
wife for him from the **l** of Egypt. **Gn 21:21** 776
l in which you have sojourned." **Gn 21:23** 776
to the **l** of the Philistines. **Gn 21:32** 776
sojourned in the **l** of the Philistines **Gn 21:34** 776
Isaac, and go to the **l** of Moriah, **Gn 22:2** 776
in the **l** of Canaan; **Gn 23:2** 776
and bowed to the people of the **l**, **Gn 23:7** 776

bowed before the people of the **l**.	Gn 23:12	776
hearing of the people of the **l**,	Gn 23:13	776
a piece of **l** worth four hundred	Gn 23:15	776
in the **l** of Canaan.	Gn 23:19	776
not willing to follow me to this **l**;	Gn 24:5	776
to the **l** from where you came?"	Gn 24:5	776
house and from the **l** of my birth,	Gn 24:7	776
descendants I will give this **l**,'	Gn 24:7	776
the Canaanites, in whose **l** I live;	Gn 24:37	776
eastward, to the **l** of the east.	Gn 25:6	776
Now there was a famine in the **l**,	Gn 26:1	776
the **l** of which I shall tell you.	Gn 26:2	776
"Sojourn in this **l** and I will be	Gn 26:3	776
Now Isaac sowed in that **l** and	Gn 26:12	776
we will be fruitful in the **l**."	Gn 26:22	776
from the daughters of the **l**,	Gn 27:46	776
possess the **l** of your sojournings,	Gn 28:4	776
the **l** on which you lie, I will	Gn 28:13	776
and will bring you back to this **l**;	Gn 28:15	127
to the **l** of the sons of the east.	Gn 29:1	776
"Return to the **l** of your fathers	Gn 31:3	776
now arise, leave this **l**,	Gn 31:13	776
return to the **l** of your birth.' "	Gn 31:13	776
go to the **l** of Canaan to his father	Gn 31:18	776
his brother Esau in the **l** of Seir,	Gn 32:3	776
which is in the **l** of Canaan,	Gn 33:18	776
He bought the piece of **l** where	Gn 33:19	2513a
to visit the daughters of the **l**.	Gn 34:1	776
the Hivite, the prince of the **l**,	Gn 34:2	776
the **l** shall be *open* before you;	Gn 34:10	776
live in the **l** and trade in it,	Gn 34:21	776
the **l** is large enough for them.	Gn 34:21	776
among the inhabitants of the **l**,	Gn 34:30	776
which is in the **l** of Canaan, he	Gn 35:6	776
"The **l** which I gave to	Gn 35:12	776
I will give the **l** to your descendants	Gn 35:12	776
Israel was dwelling in that **l**,	Gn 35:22	776
born to him in the **l** of Canaan.	Gn 36:5	776
had acquired in the **l** of Canaan,	Gn 36:6	776
went to *another* **l** away from his	Gn 36:6	776
and the **l** where they sojourned	Gn 36:7	776
from Eliphaz in the **l** of Edom;	Gn 36:16	776
from Reuel in the **l** of Edom;	Gn 36:17	776
Horite, the inhabitants of the **l**:	Gn 36:20	776
the sons of Seir in the **l** of Edom.	Gn 36:21	776
various chiefs in the **l** of Seir.	Gn 36:30	776
kings who reigned in the **l** of Edom	Gn 36:31	776
Husham of the **l** of the Temanites	Gn 36:34	776
in the **l** of their possession.	Gn 36:43	776
Now Jacob lived in the **l** where his	Gn 37:1	776
had sojourned, in the **l** of Canaan.	Gn 37:1	776
from the **l** of the Hebrews,	Gn 40:15	776
ugliness in all the **l** of Egypt;	Gn 41:19	776
are coming in all the **l** of Egypt;	Gn 41:29	776
be forgotten in the **l** of Egypt,	Gn 41:30	776
and the famine will ravage the **l**.	Gn 41:30	776
abundance will be unknown in the **l**	Gn 41:31	776
and set him over the **l** of Egypt.	Gn 41:33	776
overseers in charge of the **l**,	Gn 41:34	776
a fifth *of the produce* of the **l** of Egypt	Gn 41:34	776
the food become as a reserve for the **l**	Gn 41:36	776
will occur in the **l** of Egypt,	Gn 41:36	776
so that the **l** will not perish	Gn 41:36	776
set you over all the **l** of Egypt."	Gn 41:41	776
set him over all the **l** of Egypt.	Gn 41:43	776
or foot in all the **l** of Egypt."	Gn 41:44	776
went forth over the **l** of Egypt.	Gn 41:45	776
went through all the **l** of Egypt.	Gn 41:46	776
the **l** brought forth abundantly.	Gn 41:47	776
which occurred in the **l** of Egypt and	Gn 41:48	776
in the **l** of my affliction."	Gn 41:52	776
which had been in the **l** of Egypt	Gn 41:53	776
in all the **l** of Egypt there was bread.	Gn 41:54	776
all the **l** of Egypt was famished,	Gn 41:55	776
famine was severe in the **l** of Egypt.	Gn 41:56	776
famine was in the **l** of Canaan *also*.	Gn 42:5	776
Joseph was the ruler over the **l**;	Gn 42:6	776
sold to all the people of the **l**.	Gn 42:6	776
"From the **l** of Canaan, to buy	Gn 42:7	776
the undefended parts of our **l**."	Gn 42:9	776
the undefended parts of our **l**!"	Gn 42:12	776
of one man in the **l** of Canaan;	Gn 42:13	776
father Jacob in the **l** of Canaan,	Gn 42:29	776
"The man, the lord of the **l**,	Gn 42:30	776
father today in the **l** of Canaan.'	Gn 42:32	776
"The man, the lord of the **l**,	Gn 42:33	776
and you may trade in the **l**.' "	Gn 42:34	776
the famine was severe in the **l**.	Gn 43:1	776
products of the **l** in your bags,	Gn 43:11	776
back to you from the **l** of Canaan.	Gn 44:8	776
has been in the **l** these two years,	Gn 45:6	776
and ruler over all the **l** of Egypt.	Gn 45:8	776
You shall live in the **l** of Goshen,	Gn 45:10	776
beasts and go to the **l** of Canaan,	Gn 45:17	776
give you the best of the **l** of Egypt	Gn 45:18	776
you will eat the fat of the **l**.'	Gn 45:18	776
take wagons from the **l** of Egypt	Gn 45:19	776
best of all the **l** of Egypt is yours	Gn 45:20	776
and came to the **l** of Canaan to	Gn 45:25	776
ruler over all the **l** of Egypt."	Gn 45:26	776
had acquired in the **l** of Canaan,	Gn 46:6	776
and Onan died in the **l** of Canaan).	Gn 46:12	776
Now to Joseph in the **l** of Egypt	Gn 46:20	776
they came into the **l** of Goshen.	Gn 46:28	776
who *were* in the **l** of Canaan,	Gn 46:31	776
you may live in the **l** of Goshen;	Gn 46:34	776
have come out of the **l** of Canaan;	Gn 47:1	776
they are in the **l** of Goshen."	Gn 47:1	776
"We have come to sojourn in the **l**,	Gn 47:4	776
is severe in the **l** of Canaan.	Gn 47:4	776
live in the **l** of Goshen."	Gn 47:4	776
l of Egypt is at your disposal;	Gn 47:6	776
brothers in the best of the **l**,	Gn 47:6	776
let them live in the **l** of Goshen;	Gn 47:6	776
a possession in the **l** of Egypt,	Gn 47:11	776
of Egypt, in the best of the **l**,	Gn 47:11	776
of the land, in the **l** of Rameses,	Gn 47:11	776
there was no food in all the **l**,	Gn 47:13	776
so that the **l** of Egypt and the	Gn 47:13	776
the **l** of Canaan languished because of	Gn 47:13	776
that was found in the **l** of Egypt and	Gn 47:14	776
land of Egypt and in the **l** of Canaan	Gn 47:14	776
money was all spent in the **l** of Egypt	Gn 47:15	776
of Egypt and in the **l** of Canaan,	Gn 47:15	776
your eyes, both we and our **l**?	Gn 47:19	127
Buy us and our **l** for food, and we	Gn 47:19	127
our **l** will be slaves to Pharaoh.	Gn 47:19	127
that the **l** may not be desolate."	Gn 47:19	127
all the **l** of Egypt for Pharaoh,	Gn 47:20	127
Thus the **l** became Pharaoh's.	Gn 47:20	776
l of the priests he did not buy,	Gn 47:22	127
they did not sell their **l**.	Gn 47:22	127
bought you and your **l** for Pharaoh;	Gn 47:23	127
for you, and you may sow the **l**.	Gn 47:23	127
a statute concerning the **l** of Egypt	Gn 47:26	127
only the **l** of the priests did not	Gn 47:26	127
Israel lived in the **l** of Egypt,	Gn 47:27	776
in the **l** of Egypt seventeen years;	Gn 47:28	776
in the **l** of Canaan and blessed me,	Gn 48:3	776
and will give this **l** to your	Gn 48:4	776
were born to you in the **l** of Egypt	Gn 48:5	776
in the **l** of Canaan on the journey,	Gn 48:7	776
you back to the **l** of your fathers.	Gn 48:21	776
good And that the **l** was pleasant,	Gn 49:15	776
before Mamre, in the **l** of Canaan,	Gn 49:30	776
dug for myself in the **l** of Canaan,	Gn 50:5	776
all the elders of the **l** of Egypt,	Gn 50:7	776
their herds in the **l** of Goshen.	Gn 50:8	776
Now when the inhabitants of the **l**,	Gn 50:11	776
carried him to the **l** of Canaan and	Gn 50:13	776
and bring you up from this **l** to	Gn 50:24	776
bring you up from this land to the **l**	Gn 50:24	776
that the **l** was filled with them.	Ex 1:7	776
us and depart from the **l**."	Ex 1:10	776
and settled in the **l** of Midian,	Ex 2:15	776
been a sojourner in a foreign **l**."	Ex 2:22	776
bring them up from that **l** to a good	Ex 3:8	776
land to a good and spacious **l**,	Ex 3:8	776
a **l** flowing with milk and honey,	Ex 3:8	776
to the **l** of the Canaanite and the	Ex 3:17	776
l flowing with milk and honey."	Ex 3:17	776
and returned to the **l** of Egypt.	Ex 4:20	776
the people of the **l** are now many,	Ex 5:5	776
scattered through all the **l** of Egypt	Ex 5:12	776
will drive them out of his **l**."	Ex 6:1	776
to give them the **l** of Canaan,	Ex 6:4	776
the **l** in which they sojourned.	Ex 6:4	776
'I will bring you to the **l**	Ex 6:8	776
sons of Israel go out of his **l**."	Ex 6:11	776
of Israel out of the **l** of Egypt.	Ex 6:13	776
the sons of Israel from the **l** of Egypt	Ex 6:26	776
spoke to Moses in the **l** of Egypt,	Ex 6:28	776
sons of Israel go out of his **l**.	Ex 7:2	776
and My wonders in the **l** of Egypt.	Ex 7:3	776
the **l** of Egypt by great judgments.	Ex 7:4	776
throughout all the **l** of Egypt,	Ex 7:19	776
was through all the **l** of Egypt.	Ex 7:21	776
come up on the **l** of Egypt.' "	Ex 8:5	776
up and covered the **l** of Egypt.	Ex 8:6	776
frogs come up on the **l** of Egypt.	Ex 8:7	776
in heaps, and the **l** became foul.	Ex 8:14	776
through all the **l** of Egypt.' "	Ex 8:16	776
gnats through all the **l** of Egypt.	Ex 8:17	776
I will set apart the **l** of Goshen,	Ex 8:22	776
LORD, am in the midst of the **l**.	Ex 8:22	776
the **l** was laid waste because of the	Ex 8:24	776
of insects in all the **l** of Egypt.	Ex 8:24	776
to your God within the **l**."	Ex 8:25	776
will do this thing in the **l**."	Ex 9:5	776
fine dust over all the **l** of Egypt,	Ex 9:9	776
through all the **l** of Egypt."	Ex 9:9	776
may fall on all the **l** of Egypt,	Ex 9:22	776
throughout the **l** of Egypt."	Ex 9:22	776
rained hail on the **l** of Egypt.	Ex 9:23	776
as had not been in all the **l** of Egypt	Ex 9:24	776
field through all the **l** of Egypt,	Ex 9:25	776
Only in the **l** of Goshen, where the	Ex 9:26	776
shall cover the surface of the **l**,	Ex 10:5	776
no one will be able to see the **l**.	Ex 10:5	776
the **l** of Egypt for the locusts,	Ex 10:12	776
may come up on the **l** of Egypt and	Ex 10:12	776
and eat every plant of the **l**,	Ex 10:12	776
out his staff over the **l** of Egypt,	Ex 10:13	776
LORD directed an east wind on the **l**	Ex 10:13	776
locusts came up over all the **l** of Egypt	Ex 10:14	776
covered the surface of the whole **l**,	Ex 10:15	776
land, so that the **l** was darkened;	Ex 10:15	776
and they ate every plant of the **l**	Ex 10:15	776
field through all the **l** of Egypt.	Ex 10:15	776
be darkness over the **l** of Egypt,	Ex 10:21	776
all the **l** of Egypt for three days.	Ex 10:22	776
esteemed in the **l** of Egypt,	Ex 11:3	776
in the **l** of Egypt shall die,	Ex 11:5	776
a great cry in all the **l** of Egypt,	Ex 11:6	776
be multiplied in the **l** of Egypt."	Ex 11:9	776
sons of Israel go out of his **l**.	Ex 11:10	776
Moses and Aaron in the **l** of Egypt,	Ex 12:1	776
I will go through the **l** of Egypt on	Ex 12:12	776
the firstborn in the **l** of Egypt,	Ex 12:12	776
you when I strike the **l** of Egypt.	Ex 12:13	776
your hosts out of the **l** of Egypt;	Ex 12:17	776
is an alien or a native of the **l**.	Ex 12:19	776
l which the LORD will give you,	Ex 12:25	776
the firstborn in the **l** of Egypt,	Ex 12:29	776
send them out of the **l** in haste,	Ex 12:33	776
LORD went out from the **l** of Egypt.	Ex 12:41	776
them out from the **l** of Egypt;	Ex 12:42	776
shall be like a native of the **l**.	Ex 12:48	776
sons of Israel out of the **l** of Egypt	Ex 12:51	776
you to the **l** of the Canaanite,	Ex 13:5	776
a **l** flowing with milk and honey,	Ex 13:5	776
you to the **l** of the Canaanite,	Ex 13:11	776
every firstborn in the **l** of Egypt,	Ex 13:15	776
way of the **l** of the Philistines,	Ex 13:17	776
martial array from the **l** of Egypt.	Ex 13:18	776
are wandering aimlessly in the **l**;	Ex 14:3	776
the midst of the sea on dry **l**.	Ex 14:16	3004
and turned the sea into dry **l**,	Ex 14:21	2724
the midst of the sea on the dry **l**,	Ex 14:22	3004
the sons of Israel walked on dry **l**	Ex 14:29	3004
the sons of Israel walked on dry **l**	Ex 15:19	3004
departure from the **l** of Egypt.	Ex 16:1	776
the LORD's hand in the **l** of Egypt,	Ex 16:3	776
brought you out of the **l** of Egypt;	Ex 16:6	776
you out of the **l** of Egypt.' "	Ex 16:32	776
until they came to an inhabited **l**;	Ex 16:35	776
to the border of the **l** of Canaan.	Ex 16:35	776
been a sojourner in a foreign **l**."	Ex 18:3	776
he went his way into his own **l**.	Ex 18:27	776
had gone out of the **l** of Egypt,	Ex 19:1	776
brought you out of the **l** of Egypt,	Ex 20:2	776
your days may be prolonged in the **l**	Ex 20:12	127
were strangers in the **l** of Egypt.	Ex 22:21	776
were strangers in the **l** of Egypt.	Ex 23:9	776
"You shall sow your **l** for six	Ex 23:10	776
you and bring you in to *the* **l** *of*	Ex 23:23	
miscarrying or barren in your **l**;	Ex 23:26	776
the **l** may not become desolate and	Ex 23:29	776
and take possession of the **l**.	Ex 23:30	776
deliver the inhabitants of the **l** into	Ex 23:31	776
"They shall not live in your **l**,	Ex 23:33	776
them out of the **l** of Egypt,	Ex 29:46	776
brought us up from the **l** of Egypt,	Ex 32:1	776
you up from the **l** of Egypt."	Ex 32:4	776
brought up from the **l** of Egypt,	Ex 32:7	776
you up from the **l** of Egypt!' "	Ex 32:8	776
have brought out from the **l** of Egypt	Ex 32:11	776
and all this **l** of which I have	Ex 32:13	776
brought us up from the **l** of Egypt,	Ex 32:23	776
brought up from the **l** of Egypt,	Ex 33:1	776
the **l** of which I swore to Abraham,	Ex 33:1	776
a **l** flowing with milk and honey;	Ex 33:3	776
with the inhabitants of the **l** into	Ex 34:12	776
covenant with the inhabitants of the **l**	Ex 34:15	776
and no man shall covet your **l** when	Ex 34:24	776
you up from the **l** of Egypt to	Lv 11:45	776
"When you enter the **l** of Canaan,	Lv 14:34	776
house in the **l** of your possession,	Lv 14:34	776
their iniquities to a solitary **l**;	Lv 16:22	776
in the **l** of Egypt where you lived,	Lv 18:3	776
in the **l** of Canaan where I am	Lv 18:3	776
'For the **l** has become defiled,	Lv 18:25	776
so the **l** has spewed out its	Lv 18:25	776
(for the men of the **l** who have	Lv 18:27	776
and the **l** has become defiled);	Lv 18:27	776
that the **l** will not spew you out,	Lv 18:28	776
you reap the harvest of your **l**,	Lv 19:9	776
'When you enter the **l** and	Lv 19:23	776
the **l** will not fall to harlotry	Lv 19:29	776
and the **l** become full of lewdness.	Lv 19:29	776
resides with you in your **l**,	Lv 19:33	776
you were aliens in the **l** of Egypt;	Lv 19:34	776
you out from the **l** of Egypt.	Lv 19:36	776
the people of the **l** shall stone him	Lv 20:2	776
'If the people of the **l**,	Lv 20:4	776
so that the **l** to which I am	Lv 20:22	776
"You are to possess their **l**,	Lv 20:24	127
a **l** flowing with milk and honey."	Lv 20:24	776
the LORD, or sacrifice in your **l**,	Lv 22:24	776
you out from the **l** of Egypt;	Lv 22:33	776
'When you enter the **l** which I am	Lv 23:10	776
you reap the harvest of your **l**,	Lv 23:22	776
gathered in the crops of the **l**,	Lv 23:39	776
them out from the **l** of Egypt.	Lv 23:43	776
into the **l** which I shall give you,	Lv 25:2	776
then the **l** shall have a sabbath to	Lv 25:2	776
the **l** shall have a sabbath rest,	Lv 25:4	776
l shall have a sabbatical year.	Lv 25:5	776
products of the **l** for food;	Lv 25:6	776
and the animals that are in your **l**	Lv 25:7	776
sound a horn all through your **l**.	Lv 25:9	776
proclaim a release through the **l** to	Lv 25:10	776
you may live securely on the **l**.	Lv 25:18	776
'Then the **l** will yield its produce	Lv 25:19	776
'The **l**, moreover, shall not be sold	Lv 25:23	776
permanently, for the **l** is Mine;	Lv 25:23	776
provide for the redemption of the **l**.	Lv 25:24	776
brought you out of the **l** of Egypt	Lv 25:38	776
to give you the **l** of Canaan *and* to	Lv 25:38	776
I brought out from the **l** of Egypt;	Lv 25:42	776
they will have produced in your **l**;	Lv 25:45	776
I brought out from the **l** of Egypt.	Lv 25:55	776
stone in your **l** to bow down to it;	Lv 26:1	776
so that the **l** will yield its produce	Lv 26:4	776
full and live securely in your **l**.	Lv 26:5	776
'I shall also grant peace in the **l**,	Lv 26:6	776
eliminate harmful beasts from the **l**,	Lv 26:6	776

no sword will pass through your **l**.	Lv 26:6	776
brought you out of the **l** of Egypt	Lv 26:13	776
for your **l** will not yield its produce	Lv 26:20	776
the trees of the **l** will not yield their	Lv 26:20	776
'I will make the **l** desolate so	Lv 26:32	776
as your **l** becomes desolate and	Lv 26:33	776
'Then the **l** will enjoy its sabbaths	Lv 26:34	776
while you are in your enemies' **l**;	Lv 26:34	776
then the **l** will rest and enjoy its	Lv 26:34	776
your enemies' **l** will consume you.	Lv 26:38	776
them into the **l** of their enemies	Lv 26:41	776
well, and I will remember the **l**.	Lv 26:42	776
the **l** will be abandoned by them,	Lv 26:43	776
are in the **l** of their enemies,	Lv 26:44	776
I brought out of the **l** of Egypt	Lv 26:45	776
the possession of the **l** belongs.	Lv 27:24	776
'Thus all the tithe of the **l**,	Lv 27:30	776
tithe of the land, of the seed of the **l**	Lv 27:30	776
had come out of the **l** of Egypt,	Nu 1:1	776
the firstborn in the **l** of Egypt,	Nu 3:13	776
all the firstborn in the **l** of Egypt	Nu 8:17	776
had come out of the **l** of Egypt,	Nu 9:1	776
and for the native of the **l**.' "	Nu 9:14	776
"When you go to war in your **l**	Nu 10:9	776
go to my *own* **l** and relatives."	Nu 10:30	776
to the **l** which You swore to	Nu 11:12	127
they may spy out the **l** of Canaan,	Nu 13:2	776
whom Moses sent to spy out the **l**;	Nu 13:16	776
them to spy out the **l** of Canaan,	Nu 13:17	776
"See what the **l** is like,	Nu 13:18	776
How is the **l** in which they live,	Nu 13:19	776
"How is the **l**, is it fat or	Nu 13:20	776
get some of the fruit of the **l**."	Nu 13:20	776
So they went up and spied out the **l**	Nu 13:21	776
returned from spying out the **l**,	Nu 13:25	776
showed them the fruit of the **l**.	Nu 13:26	776
in to the **l** where you sent us;	Nu 13:27	776
people who live in the **l** are strong,	Nu 13:28	776
is living in the **l** of the Negev	Nu 13:29	776
a bad report of the **l** which they	Nu 13:32	776
"The **l** through which we have	Nu 13:32	776
a **l** that devours its inhabitants;	Nu 13:32	776
we had died in the **l** of Egypt!	Nu 14:2	776
the LORD bringing us into this **l**,	Nu 14:3	776
of those who had spied out the **l**,	Nu 14:6	776
"The **l** which we passed through to	Nu 14:7	776
spy out is an exceedingly good **l**.	Nu 14:7	776
then He will bring us into this **l** and	Nu 14:8	776
l which flows with milk and honey.	Nu 14:8	776
do not fear the people of the **l**,	Nu 14:9	776
it to the inhabitants of this **l**.	Nu 14:14	776
could not bring this people into the **l**	Nu 14:16	776
shall by no means see the **l** which	Nu 14:23	776
bring into the **l** which he entered,	Nu 14:24	776
'Surely you shall not come into the **l**	Nu 14:30	776
the **l** which you have rejected.	Nu 14:31	776
of days which you spied out the **l**,	Nu 14:34	776
whom Moses sent to spy out the **l**	Nu 14:36	776
out a bad report concerning the **l**,	Nu 14:36	776
out the very bad report of the **l**	Nu 14:37	776
men who went to spy out the **l**.	Nu 14:38	776
enter the **l** where you are to live,	Nu 15:2	776
you enter the **l** where I bring you,	Nu 15:18	776
when you eat of the food of the **l**,	Nu 15:19	776
brought you out from the **l** of Egypt	Nu 15:41	776
a **l** flowing with milk and honey	Nu 16:13	776
a **l** flowing with milk and honey,	Nu 16:14	776
fruits of all that is in their **l**,	Nu 18:13	776
have no inheritance in their **l** nor	Nu 18:20	776
the **l** which I have given them."	Nu 20:12	776
'Please let us pass through your **l**.	Nu 20:17	776
by the border of the **l** of Edom.	Nu 20:23	776
for he shall not enter the **l** which	Nu 20:24	776
Sea, to go around the **l** of Edom;	Nu 21:4	776
valley that is in the **l** of Moab,	Nu 21:20	7704
"Let me pass through your **l**.	Nu 21:22	776
and took possession of his **l** from	Nu 21:24	776
taken all his **l** out of his hand,	Nu 21:26	776
lived in the **l** of the Amorites.	Nu 21:31	776
and all his people and his **l**;	Nu 21:34	776
and they possessed his **l**.	Nu 21:35	776
the **l** of the sons of his people,	Nu 22:5	776
they cover the surface of the **l**,	Nu 22:5	776
them and drive them out of the **l**.	Nu 22:6	776
they cover the surface of the **l**;	Nu 22:11	776
"Go back to your **l**, for the LORD	Nu 22:13	776
came out of the **l** of Egypt *were:*	Nu 26:4	776
and Onan died in the **l** of Canaan.	Nu 26:19	776
"Among these the **l** shall be divided	Nu 26:53	776
"But the **l** shall be divided by lot.	Nu 26:55	776
and see the **l** which I have given	Nu 27:12	776
So when they saw the **l** of Jazer	Nu 32:1	776
land of Jazer and the **l** of Gilead,	Nu 32:1	776
the **l** which the LORD conquered	Nu 32:4	776
of Israel, is a **l** for livestock,	Nu 32:4	776
let this **l** be given to your	Nu 32:5	776
l which the LORD has given them?	Nu 32:7	776
from Kadesh-barnea to see the **l**.	Nu 32:8	776
valley of Eshcol and saw the **l**,	Nu 32:9	776
l which the LORD had given them.	Nu 32:9	776
the **l** which I swore to Abraham,	Nu 32:11	127
because of the inhabitants of the **l**.	Nu 32:17	776
the **l** is subdued before the LORD,	Nu 32:22	776
and this **l** shall be yours for a	Nu 32:22	776
the **l** is subdued before you,	Nu 32:29	776
the **l** of Gilead for a possession;	Nu 32:29	776
among you in the **l** of Canaan."	Nu 32:30	776
of the LORD into the **l** of Canaan,	Nu 32:32	776
the **l** with its cities with *their*	Nu 32:33	776
the cities of the surrounding **l**.	Nu 32:33	776
the **l** of Egypt by their armies,	Nu 33:1	776
Hor, at the edge of the **l** of Edom.	Nu 33:37	776
had come from the **l** of Egypt, on the	Nu 33:38	776
in the Negev in the **l** of Canaan,	Nu 33:40	776
the Jordan into the **l** of Canaan,	Nu 33:51	776
drive out all the inhabitants of the **l**	Nu 33:52	776
you shall take possession of the **l**	Nu 33:53	776
I have given the **l** to you to possess	Nu 33:53	776
'You shall inherit the **l** by	Nu 33:54	776
not drive out the inhabitants of the **l**	Nu 33:55	776
they will trouble you in the **l**	Nu 33:55	776
'When you enter the **l** of Canaan,	Nu 34:2	776
this is the **l** that shall fall to	Nu 34:2	776
even the **l** of Canaan according to	Nu 34:2	776
This shall be your **l** according to	Nu 34:12	776
"This is the **l** that you are to	Nu 34:13	776
who shall apportion the **l** to you for	Nu 34:17	776
apportion the **l** for inheritance.	Nu 34:18	776
sons of Israel in the **l** of Canaan.	Nu 34:29	776
the Jordan into the **l** of Canaan,	Nu 35:10	776
three cities in the **l** of Canaan;	Nu 35:14	776
return to the **l** of his possession.	Nu 35:28	776
that he may return to live in the **l**	Nu 35:32	776
pollute the **l** in which you are;	Nu 35:33	776
for blood pollutes the **l** and no	Nu 35:33	776
no expiation can be made for the **l**	Nu 35:33	776
defile the **l** in which you live,	Nu 35:34	776
give the **l** by lot to the sons of Israel	Nu 36:2	776
the Jordan in the **l** of Moab,	Dt 1:5	776
seacoast, the **l** of the Canaanites,	Dt 1:7	776
I have placed the **l** before you;	Dt 1:8	776
go in and possess the **l** which the	Dt 1:8	776
God has placed the **l** before you;	Dt 1:21	776
they may search out the **l** for us,	Dt 1:22	776
they took *some* of the fruit of the **l**	Dt 1:25	776
'It is a good **l** which the LORD our	Dt 1:25	776
has brought us out of the **l** of Egypt	Dt 1:27	776
shall see the good **l** which I swore	Dt 1:35	776
the **l** on which he has set foot,	Dt 1:36	776
will not give you any of their **l**,	Dt 2:5	776
any of their **l** as a possession,	Dt 2:9	776
Israel did to the **l** of their possession	Dt 2:12	776
any of the **l** of the sons of Ammon	Dt 2:19	776
regarded as the **l** of the Rephaim,	Dt 2:20	776
Heshbon, and his **l** into your hand;	Dt 2:24	776
'Let me pass through your **l**,	Dt 2:27	776
until I cross over the Jordan into the **l**	Dt 2:29	776
for us to pass through his **l**;	Dt 2:30	
Sihon and his **l** over to you.	Dt 2:31	776
that you may possess his **l**.'	Dt 2:31	776
to the **l** of the sons of Ammon,	Dt 2:37	776
people and his **l** into your hand;	Dt 3:2	776
'Thus we took the **l** at that time	Dt 3:8	776
took possession of this **l** at that time	Dt 3:12	776
it is called the **l** of Rephaim.	Dt 3:13	776
given you this **l** to possess it;	Dt 3:18	776
and they also possess the **l** which	Dt 3:20	776
fair **l** that is beyond the Jordan,	Dt 3:25	776
the **l** which you will see.'	Dt 3:28	776
go in and take possession of the **l**	Dt 4:1	776
that you should do thus in the **l**	Dt 4:5	776
you might perform them in the **l**	Dt 4:14	776
and that I would not enter the good **l**	Dt 4:21	776
"For I will die in this **l**,	Dt 4:22	776
take possession of this good **l**.	Dt 4:22	776
and have remained long in the **l**,	Dt 4:25	776
will surely perish quickly from the **l**	Dt 4:26	776
give you their **l** for an inheritance,	Dt 4:38	776
that you may live long on the **l** which	Dt 4:40	127
in the **l** of Sihon king of the	Dt 4:46	776
They took possession of his **l**	Dt 4:47	776
and the **l** of Og king of Bashan,	Dt 4:47	776
brought you out of the **l** of Egypt,	Dt 5:6	776
were a slave in the **l** of Egypt,	Dt 5:15	776
that it may go well with you on the **l**	Dt 5:16	127
l which I give them to possess.'	Dt 5:31	776
in the **l** which you will possess.	Dt 5:33	776
that you might do *them* in the **l**	Dt 6:1	776
a **l** flowing with milk and honey.	Dt 6:3	776
LORD your God brings you into the **l**	Dt 6:10	776
brought you from the **l** of Egypt,	Dt 6:12	776
you may go in and possess the good **l**	Dt 6:18	776
to give us the **l** which He had	Dt 6:23	776
your God brings you into the **l**	Dt 7:1	776
in the **l** which He swore to your	Dt 7:13	127
and go in and possess the **l** which	Dt 8:1	776
God is bringing you into a good **l**,	Dt 8:7	776
good land, a **l** of brooks of water,	Dt 8:7	776
a **l** of wheat and barley, of vines	Dt 8:8	776
a **l** of olive oil and honey;	Dt 8:8	776
a **l** where you will eat food	Dt 8:9	776
a **l** whose stones are iron, and out	Dt 8:9	776
the good **l** which He has given you.	Dt 8:10	776
you out from the **l** of Egypt,	Dt 8:14	776
brought me in to possess this **l**,'	Dt 9:4	776
you are going to possess their **l**,	Dt 9:5	776
giving you this good **l** to possess,	Dt 9:6	776
from the day that you left the **l**	Dt 9:7	776
the **l** which I have given you,'	Dt 9:23	776
'Otherwise the **l** from which You	Dt 9:28	776
was not able to bring them into the **l**	Dt 9:28	776
Jotbathah, a **l** of brooks of water.	Dt 10:7	776
that they may go in and possess the **l**	Dt 10:11	776
you were aliens in the **l** of Egypt.	Dt 10:19	776
king of Egypt and to all his **l**;	Dt 11:3	776
be strong and go in and possess the **l**	Dt 11:8	776
you may prolong *your* days on the **l**	Dt 11:9	127
a **l** flowing with milk and honey.	Dt 11:9	776
"For the **l**, into which you are	Dt 11:10	776
the **l** of Egypt from which you came,	Dt 11:10	776
"But the **l** into which you are	Dt 11:11	776
it, a **l** of hills and valleys,	Dt 11:11	776
a **l** for which the LORD your God	Dt 11:12	776
the rain for your **l** in its season,	Dt 11:14	776
l which the LORD is giving you.	Dt 11:17	776
your sons may be multiplied on the **l**	Dt 11:21	127
all the **l** on which you set foot,	Dt 11:25	776
LORD your God brings you into the **l**	Dt 11:29	776
in the **l** of the Canaanites who	Dt 11:30	776
to possess the **l** which the LORD your	Dt 11:31	776
observe in the **l** which the LORD,	Dt 12:1	776
you cross the Jordan and live in the **l**	Dt 12:10	776
as long as you live in your **l**.	Dt 12:19	127
them and dwell in their **l**,	Dt 12:29	776
who brought you from the **l** of Egypt	Dt 13:5	776
you out from the **l** of Egypt,	Dt 13:10	776
the LORD will surely bless you in the **l**	Dt 15:4	776
in any of your towns in your **l**	Dt 15:7	776
will never cease *to be* in the **l**;	Dt 15:11	776
to your needy and poor in your **l**.'	Dt 15:11	776
were a slave in the **l** of Egypt,	Dt 15:15	776
out of the **l** of Egypt in haste),	Dt 16:3	776
you came out of the **l** of Egypt.	Dt 16:3	776
that you may live and possess the **l**	Dt 16:20	776
"When you enter the **l** which the	Dt 17:14	776
"When you enter the **l** which the	Dt 18:9	776
l the LORD your God gives you,	Dt 19:1	776
yourself in the midst of your **l**,	Dt 19:2	776
parts the territory of your **l** which	Dt 19:3	776
and gives you all the **l** which He	Dt 19:8	776
l which the LORD your God gives you	Dt 19:10	776
l that the LORD your God gives you	Dt 19:14	776
you up from the **l** of Egypt,	Dt 20:1	776
l which the LORD your God gives you	Dt 21:1	127
so that you do not defile your **l**	Dt 21:23	127
you were an alien in his **l**.	Dt 23:7	776
you in all that you undertake in the **l**	Dt 23:20	776
you shall not bring sin on the **l** which	Dt 24:4	776
who is in your **l** in your towns.	Dt 24:14	776
were a slave in the **l** of Egypt;	Dt 24:22	776
your days may be prolonged in the **l**	Dt 25:15	127
in the **l** which the LORD your God	Dt 25:19	776
when you enter the **l** which the	Dt 26:1	776
l that the LORD your God gives you	Dt 26:2	776
I have entered the **l** which the LORD	Dt 26:3	776
place and has given us this **l**,	Dt 26:9	776
a **l** flowing with milk and honey.	Dt 26:9	776
a **l** flowing with milk and honey,	Dt 26:15	776
you cross the Jordan to the **l**	Dt 27:2	776
so that you may enter the **l**	Dt 27:3	776
a **l** flowing with milk and honey,	Dt 27:3	776
and He will bless you in the **l**	Dt 28:8	776
in the **l** which the LORD swore to	Dt 28:11	127
to give rain to your **l** in its	Dt 28:12	776
He has consumed you from the **l** where	Dt 28:21	127
rain of your **l** powder and dust;	Dt 28:24	776
come down throughout your **l**,	Dt 28:52	776
in all your towns throughout your **l**	Dt 28:52	776
and you will be torn from the **l**	Dt 28:63	127
sons of Israel in the **l** of Moab,	Dt 29:1	776
LORD did before your eyes in the **l** of	Dt 29:2	776
all his servants and all his **l**;	Dt 29:2	776
and we took their **l** and gave it as	Dt 29:8	776
how we lived in the **l** of Egypt,	Dt 29:16	776
in order to destroy the watered **l**	Dt 29:19	
who comes from a distant **l**,	Dt 29:22	776
when they see the plagues of the **l**	Dt 29:22	776
'All its **l** is brimstone and salt,	Dt 29:23	776
has the LORD done thus to this **l**?	Dt 29:24	776
them out of the **l** of Egypt.	Dt 29:25	776
of the LORD burned against that **l**,	Dt 29:27	776
the LORD uprooted them from their **l**	Dt 29:28	127
and cast them into another **l**,	Dt 29:28	776
l which your fathers possessed,	Dt 30:5	776
your God may bless you in the **l**	Dt 30:16	776
will not prolong *your* days in the **l**	Dt 30:18	127
that you may live in the **l** which	Dt 30:20	127
kings of the Amorites, and to their **l**	Dt 31:4	776
into the **l** which the LORD has sworn	Dt 31:7	776
as long as you live on the **l** which	Dt 31:13	127
with the strange gods of the **l**,	Dt 31:16	776
the **l** flowing with milk and honey,	Dt 31:20	127
them into the **l** which I swore."	Dt 31:21	776
into the **l** which I swore to them,	Dt 31:23	776
"He found him in a desert **l**,	Dt 32:10	776
atone for His **l** *and* His people."	Dt 32:43	127
will prolong your days in the **l**,	Dt 32:47	127
in the **l** of Moab opposite Jericho,	Dt 32:49	776
and look at the **l** of Canaan,	Dt 32:49	776
you shall see the **l** at a distance,	Dt 32:52	776
into the **l** which I am giving the	Dt 32:52	776
"Blessed of the LORD *be* his **l**,	Dt 33:13	776
In a **l** of grain and new wine;	Dt 33:28	776
And the LORD showed him all the **l**,	Dt 34:1	776
and the **l** of Ephraim and Manasseh,	Dt 34:2	776
and all the **l** of Judah as far as	Dt 34:2	776
is the **l** which I swore to Abraham,	Dt 34:4	776
died there in the **l** of Moab,	Dt 34:5	776
in the valley in the **l** of Moab,	Dt 34:6	776
in the **l** of Egypt against Pharaoh,	Dt 34:11	776
all his servants, and all his **l**,	Dt 34:11	776
the **l** which I am giving to them,	Jos 1:2	776
all the **l** of the Hittites,	Jos 1:4	776
give this people possession of the **l**	Jos 1:6	776
to go in to possess the **l** which	Jos 1:11	776
rest and will give you this **l**.'	Jos 1:13	776
and your cattle shall remain in the **l**	Jos 1:14	776

and they also possess the **l** which	**Jos 1:15**	776
you shall return to your own **l**,	**Jos 1:15**	776
"Go, view the **l**, especially	**Jos 2:1**	776
tonight to search out the **l**."	**Jos 2:2**	776
come to search out all the **l**."	**Jos 2:3**	776
that the LORD has given you the **l**,	**Jos 2:9**	776
the inhabitants of the **l** have melted	**Jos 2:9**	776
when the LORD gives us the **l** that we	**Jos 2:14**	776
unless, when we come into the **l**,	**Jos 2:18**	776
given all the **l** into our hands;	**Jos 2:24**	776
all the inhabitants of the **l**	**Jos 2:24**	776
that He would not let them see the **l**	**Jos 5:6**	776
a **l** flowing with milk and honey.	**Jos 5:6**	776
ate some of the produce of the **l**,	**Jos 5:11**	776
some of the produce of the **l**,	**Jos 5:12**	776
some of the yield of the **l** of Canaan	**Jos 5:12**	776
two men who had spied out the **l**,	**Jos 6:22**	776
and his fame was in all the **l**.	**Jos 6:27**	776
"Go up and spy out the **l**."	**Jos 7:2**	776
all the inhabitants of the **l** will hear	**Jos 7:9**	776
his people, his city, and his **l**.	**Jos 8:1**	776
you are living within our **l**;	**Jos 9:7**	7130
they were living within their **l**.	**Jos 9:16**	7130
when you are living within our **l**?	**Jos 9:22**	7130
Moses to give you all the **l**,	**Jos 9:24**	776
inhabitants of the **l** before you;	**Jos 9:24**	776
Israel and were within their **l**,	**Jos 10:1**	7130
Thus Joshua struck all the **l**,	**Jos 10:40**	776
foot of Hermon in the **l** of Mizpeh.	**Jos 11:3**	776
Thus Joshua took all that **l**:	**Jos 11:16**	776
the Negev, all that **l** of Goshen,	**Jos 11:16**	776
in the **l** of the sons of Israel;	**Jos 11:22**	776
So Joshua took the whole **l**,	**Jos 11:23**	776
Thus the **l** had rest from war.	**Jos 11:23**	776
Now these are the kings of the **l**	**Jos 12:1**	776
and whose **l** they possessed beyond	**Jos 12:1**	776
Now these are the kings of the **l**	**Jos 12:7**	776
very much of the **l** remains to be	**Jos 13:1**	776
"This is the **l** that remains:	**Jos 13:2**	776
south, all the **l** of the Canaanite,	**Jos 13:4**	776
and the **l** of the Gebalite, and all	**Jos 13:5**	776
apportion this **l** for an	**Jos 13:7**	776
of Sihon, who lived in the **l**.	**Jos 13:21**	776
half the **l** of the sons of Ammon,	**Jos 13:25**	776
inherited in the **l** of Canaan,	**Jos 14:1**	776
a portion to the Levites in the **l**,	**Jos 14:4**	776
Moses, and they divided the **l**.	**Jos 14:5**	776
Kadesh-barnea to spy out the **l**,	**Jos 14:7**	776
'Surely the **l** on which your foot	**Jos 14:9**	776
Then the **l** had rest from war.	**Jos 14:15**	776
have given me the **l** of the Negev,	**Jos 15:19**	776
the **l** of Gilead and Bashan,	**Jos 17:5**	776
And the **l** of Gilead belonged to	**Jos 17:6**	776
The **l** of Tappuah belonged to	**Jos 17:8**	776
persisted in living in that **l**.	**Jos 17:12**	776
in the **l** of the Perizzites and of the	**Jos 17:15**	776
Canaanites who live in the valley **l**	**Jos 17:16**	776
and the **l** was subdued before them.	**Jos 18:1**	776
entering to take possession of the **l**	**Jos 18:3**	776
may arise and walk through the **l**	**Jos 18:4**	776
describe the **l** in seven divisions,	**Jos 18:6**	776
those who went to describe the **l**,	**Jos 18:8**	776
"Go and walk through the **l** and	**Jos 18:8**	776
men went and passed through the **l**,	**Jos 18:9**	776
and there Joshua divided the **l** to	**Jos 18:10**	776
When they finished apportioning the **l**	**Jos 19:49**	776
So they finished dividing the **l**.	**Jos 19:51**	776
them at Shiloh in the **l** of Canaan,	**Jos 21:2**	776
So the LORD gave Israel all the **l**	**Jos 21:43**	776
to the **l** of your possession,	**Jos 22:4**	776
which is in the **l** of Canaan,	**Jos 22:9**	776
Canaan, to go to the **l** of Gilead,	**Jos 22:9**	776
to the **l** of their possession which	**Jos 22:9**	776
which is in the **l** of Canaan,	**Jos 22:10**	776
the frontier of the **l** of Canaan,	**Jos 22:11**	776
of Manasseh, into the **l** of Gilead,	**Jos 22:13**	776
of Manasseh, to the **l** of Gilead,	**Jos 22:15**	776
l of your possession is unclean,	**Jos 22:19**	776
l of the possession of the LORD,	**Jos 22:19**	776
sons of Gad, from the **l** of Gilead to	**Jos 22:32**	776
of Gilead to the **l** of Canaan,	**Jos 22:32**	776
to destroy the **l** in which the sons	**Jos 22:33**	776
and you will possess their **l**,	**Jos 23:5**	776
until you perish from off this good **l**	**Jos 23:13**	127
destroyed you from off this good **l**	**Jos 23:15**	127
good **l** which He has given you."	**Jos 23:16**	776
him through all the **l** of Canaan,	**Jos 24:3**	776
you into the **l** of the Amorites	**Jos 24:8**	776
and you took possession of their **l**	**Jos 24:8**	776
a **l** on which you had not labored,	**Jos 24:13**	776
in whose **l** you are living;	**Jos 24:15**	776
fathers up out of the **l** of Egypt,	**Jos 24:17**	776
the Amorites who lived in the **l**.	**Jos 24:18**	776
have given the **l** into his hand."	**Jg 1:2**	776
have given me the **l** of the Negev,	**Jg 1:15**	776
man went into the **l** of the Hittites	**Jg 1:26**	776
persisted in living in that **l**.	**Jg 1:27**	776
the inhabitants of the **l**;	**Jg 1:32**	776
the inhabitants of the **l**;	**Jg 1:33**	776
led you into the **l** which I have sworn	**Jg 2:1**	776
with the inhabitants of this **l**;	**Jg 2:2**	776
his inheritance to possess the **l**.	**Jg 2:6**	776
brought them out of the **l** of Egypt,	**Jg 2:12**	776
Then the **l** had rest forty years.	**Jg 3:11**	776
And the **l** was undisturbed for	**Jg 3:30**	776
And the **l** was undisturbed for	**Jg 5:31**	776
came into the **l** to devastate it.	**Jg 6:5**	776
before you and gave you their **l**,	**Jg 6:9**	776
the Amorites in whose **l** you live.	**Jg 6:10**	776

And the **l** was undisturbed for	**Jg 8:28**	776
from the highest part of the **l**,	**Jg 9:37**	776
had thirty cities in the **l** of Gilead	**Jg 10:4**	776
Gilead in the **l** of the Amorites.	**Jg 10:8**	776
and lived in the **l** of Tob;	**Jg 11:3**	776
to get Jephthah from the **l** of Tob;	**Jg 11:5**	776
to me to fight against my **l**?"	**Jg 11:12**	776
"Because Israel took away my **l**	**Jg 11:13**	776
did not take away the **l** of Moab nor	**Jg 11:15**	776
nor the **l** of the sons of Ammon.	**Jg 11:15**	776
let us pass through your **l**,"	**Jg 11:17**	776
l of Edom and the land of Moab,	**Jg 11:18**	776
land of Edom and the **l** of Moab,	**Jg 11:18**	776
to the east side of the **l** of Moab,	**Jg 11:18**	776
through your **l** to our place."	**Jg 11:19**	776
all the **l** of the Amorites,	**Jg 11:21**	776
at Aijalon in the **l** of Zebulun.	**Jg 12:12**	776
at Pirathon in the **l** of Ephraim,	**Jg 12:15**	776
to spy out the **l** and to search it;	**Jg 18:2**	776
"Go, search the **l**."	**Jg 18:2**	776
them for anything in the **l**,	**Jg 18:7**	776
for we have seen the **l**,	**Jg 18:9**	776
to go, to enter, to possess the **l**.	**Jg 18:9**	776
a secure people with a spacious **l**;	**Jg 18:10**	776
five men who went to spy out the **l**	**Jg 18:17**	776
the day of the captivity of the **l**.	**Jg 18:30**	776
from the **l** of Egypt to this day.	**Jg 19:30**	776
including the **l** of Gilead,	**Jg 20:1**	776
the **l** of Israel's inheritance;	**Jg 20:6**	7704
which is in the **l** of Canaan.	**Jg 21:12**	776
and go to the **l** of Benjamin.	**Jg 21:21**	776
that there was a famine in the **l**.	**Ru 1:1**	776
went to sojourn in the **l** of Moab	**Ru 1:1**	7704
Now they entered the **l** of Moab	**Ru 1:2**	7704
might return from the **l** of Moab,	**Ru 1:6**	7704
for she had heard in the **l** of Moab	**Ru 1:6**	7704
way to return to the **l** of Judah.	**Ru 1:7**	776
who returned from the **l** of Moab.	**Ru 1:22**	7704
with Naomi from the **l** of Moab.	**Ru 2:6**	7704
mother and the **l** of your birth,	**Ru 2:11**	776
has come back from the **l** of Moab,	**Ru 4:3**	7704
has to sell the piece of **l** which	**Ru 4:3**	7704
redemption and the exchange *of* **l**	**Ru 4:7**	
of your mice that ravage the **l**,	**1Sa 6:5**	776
from you, your gods, and your **l**.	**1Sa 6:5**	776
passed through the **l** of Shalishah,	**1Sa 9:4**	776
passed through the **l** of Shaalim,	**1Sa 9:4**	776
through the **l** of the Benjamites,	**1Sa 9:4**	776
When they came to the **l** of Zuph,	**1Sa 9:5**	776
you a man from the **l** of Benjamin,	**1Sa 9:16**	776
fathers up from the **l** of Egypt.	**1Sa 12:6**	776
blew the trumpet throughout the **l**,	**1Sa 13:3**	776
into the **l** of Gad and Gilead.	**1Sa 13:7**	776
toward Ophrah, to the **l** of Shual,	**1Sa 13:17**	776
be found in all the **l** of Israel,	**1Sa 13:19**	776
half a furrow in an acre of **l**.	**1Sa 14:14**	7704
All *the people of* the **l** entered the	**1Sa 14:25**	776
"My father has troubled the **l**.	**1Sa 14:29**	776
this not David the king of the **l**?	**1Sa 21:11**	776
and go into the **l** of Judah."	**1Sa 22:5**	776
if he is in the **l**,	**1Sa 23:23**	776
have made a raid on the **l**."	**1Sa 23:27**	776
escape into the **l** of the Philistines.	**1Sa 27:1**	776
they were the inhabitants of the **l**	**1Sa 27:8**	776
even as far as the **l** of Egypt.	**1Sa 27:8**	776
David attacked the **l** and did	**1Sa 27:9**	776
And Saul had removed from the **l**	**1Sa 28:3**	776
mediums and spiritists from the **l**.	**1Sa 28:9**	776
return to the **l** of the Philistines.	**1Sa 29:11**	776
they were spread over all the **l**,	**1Sa 30:16**	776
taken from the **l** of the Philistines	**1Sa 30:16**	776
and from the **l** of Judah.	**1Sa 30:16**	776
the **l** of the Philistines,	**1Sa 31:9**	776
in his place, saying, "Whose is the **l**?	**2Sa 3:12**	776
the inhabitants of the **l**,	**2Sa 5:6**	776
You and awesome things for Your **l**,	**2Sa 7:23**	776
the **l** of your grandfather Saul;	**2Sa 9:7**	7704
shall cultivate the **l** for him,	**2Sa 9:10**	127
came to the **l** of the Ammonites,	**2Sa 10:2**	776
would appoint me judge in the **l**,	**2Sa 15:4**	776
Absalom camped in the **l** of Gilead.	**2Sa 17:26**	776
fled out of the **l** from Absalom.	**2Sa 19:9**	776
and Ziba shall divide the **l**.' "	**2Sa 19:29**	7704
was moved by prayer for the **l**.	**2Sa 21:14**	776
and to the **l** of Tahtim-hodshi,	**2Sa 24:6**	776
gone about through the whole **l**,	**2Sa 24:8**	776
of famine come to you in your **l**?	**2Sa 24:13**	776
three days' pestilence in your **l**?	**2Sa 24:13**	776
was moved by prayer for the **l**,	**2Sa 24:25**	776
was his and all the **l** of Hepher);	**1Ki 4:10**	776
son of Uri, in the **l** of Gilead,	**1Ki 4:19**	776
the only deputy who *was* in the **l**.	**1Ki 4:19**	776
the River *to* the **l** of the Philistines	**1Ki 4:21**	776
Israel came out of the **l** of Egypt,	**1Ki 6:1**	776
they came out of the **l** of Egypt.	**1Ki 8:9**	776
brought them from the **l** of Egypt."	**1Ki 8:21**	776
and bring them back to the **l** which	**1Ki 8:34**	127
And send rain on Your **l**,	**1Ki 8:36**	776
"If there is famine in the **l**,	**1Ki 8:37**	776
besieges them in the **l** of their cities,	**1Ki 8:37**	776
all the days that they live in the **l**	**1Ki 8:40**	127
captive to the **l** of the enemy,	**1Ki 8:46**	776
if they take thought in the **l**	**1Ki 8:47**	776
the **l** of those who have taken them	**1Ki 8:47**	776
the **l** of their enemies who have taken	**1Ki 8:48**	776
and pray to You toward their **l**	**1Ki 8:48**	776
the **l** which I have given them,	**1Ki 9:7**	127
has the LORD done thus to this **l**	**1Ki 9:8**	776
fathers out of the **l** of Egypt,	**1Ki 9:9**	776

twenty cities in the **l** of Galilee.	**1Ki 9:11**	776
called the **l** of Cabul to this day.	**1Ki 9:13**	776
the wilderness, in the **l** *of Judah*,	**1Ki 9:18**	776
and in all the **l** under his rule.	**1Ki 9:19**	776
who were left after them in the **l**	**1Ki 9:21**	776
of the Red Sea, in the **l** of Edom.	**1Ki 9:26**	776
report which I heard in my own **l**	**1Ki 10:6**	776
she turned and went to her own **l**	**1Ki 10:13**	776
assigned him food and gave him **l**.	**1Ki 11:18**	776
brought you up from the **l** of Egypt	**1Ki 12:28**	776
He will uproot Israel from this good **l**	**1Ki 14:15**	127
male cult prostitutes in the **l**.	**1Ki 14:24**	776
male cult prostitutes from the **l** and	**1Ki 15:12**	776
besides all the **l** of Naphtali.	**1Ki 15:20**	776
there was no rain in the **l**.	**1Ki 17:7**	776
"Go through the **l** to all the	**1Ki 18:5**	776
divided the **l** between them to survey	**1Ki 18:6**	776
Israel called all the elders of the **l**	**1Ki 20:7**	776
Asa, he expelled from the **l**.	**1Ki 22:46**	776
is bad and the **l** is unfruitful."	**2Ki 2:19**	776
mar every good piece of **l** with stones	**2Ki 3:19**	2513a
and they went forward into the **l**,	**2Ki 3:24**	
a stone on every piece of good **l**	**2Ki 3:25**	2513a
him and returned to their own **l**.	**2Ki 3:27**	776
there was a famine in the **l**.	**2Ki 4:38**	776
little girl from the **l** of Israel;	**2Ki 5:2**	776
who is from the **l** of Israel."	**2Ki 5:4**	776
come again into the **l** of Israel.	**2Ki 6:23**	776
come on the **l** for seven years."	**2Ki 8:1**	776
sojourned in the **l** of the Philistines	**2Ki 8:2**	776
returned from the **l** of the Philistines	**2Ki 8:3**	776
she left the **l** even until now."	**2Ki 8:6**	776
eastward, all the **l** of Gilead,	**2Ki 10:33**	776
Athaliah was reigning over the **l**.	**2Ki 11:3**	776
all the people of the **l** rejoiced and	**2Ki 11:14**	776
All the people of the **l** went to the	**2Ki 11:18**	776
and all the people of the **l**;	**2Ki 11:19**	776
So all the people of the **l** rejoiced	**2Ki 11:20**	776
the Moabites would invade the **l**	**2Ki 13:20**	776
judging the people of the **l**.	**2Ki 15:5**	776
of Assyria, came against the **l**,	**2Ki 15:19**	776
and did not remain there in the **l**.	**2Ki 15:20**	776
Galilee, all the **l** of Naphtali;	**2Ki 15:29**	776
offering of all the people of the **l**	**2Ki 16:15**	776
king of Assyria invaded the whole **l**	**2Ki 17:5**	776
brought them up from the **l** of Egypt	**2Ki 17:7**	776
away into exile from their own **l** to	**2Ki 17:23**	127
the custom of the god of the **l**;	**2Ki 17:26**	776
the custom of the god of the **l**."	**2Ki 17:26**	776
the custom of the god of the **l**."	**2Ki 17:27**	776
who brought you up from the **l** of	**2Ki 17:36**	776
'Go up against this **l** and destroy it.'	**2Ki 18:25**	776
take you away to a **l** like your own	**2Ki 18:32**	776
away to a land like your own **l**,	**2Ki 18:32**	776
land, a **l** of grain and new wine,	**2Ki 18:32**	776
wine, a **l** of bread and vineyards,	**2Ki 18:32**	776
a **l** of olive trees and honey,	**2Ki 18:32**	776
the gods of the nations delivered his **l**	**2Ki 18:33**	776
delivered their **l** from my hand,	**2Ki 18:35**	776
a rumor and return to his own **l**.	**2Ki 19:7**	776
fall by the sword in his own **l**	**2Ki 19:7**	776
they escaped into the **l** of Ararat.	**2Ki 19:37**	776
the **l** which I gave their fathers,	**2Ki 21:8**	127
Then the people of the **l** killed	**2Ki 21:24**	776
and the people of the **l** made	**2Ki 21:24**	776
the **l** of Judah and in Jerusalem,	**2Ki 23:24**	776
Then the people of the **l** took	**2Ki 23:30**	776
him at Riblah in the **l** of Hamath,	**2Ki 23:33**	776
and he imposed on the **l** a fine of	**2Ki 23:33**	776
but he taxed the **l** in order to	**2Ki 23:35**	776
and gold from the people of the **l**,	**2Ki 23:35**	776
did not come out of his **l** again,	**2Ki 24:7**	776
the poorest people of the **l**.	**2Ki 24:14**	776
and the leading men of the **l**,	**2Ki 24:15**	776
no food for the people of the **l**.	**2Ki 25:3**	776
poorest of the **l** to be vinedressers	**2Ki 25:12**	776
who mustered the people of the **l**;	**2Ki 25:19**	776
sixty men of the people of the **l** who	**2Ki 25:19**	776
at Riblah in the **l** of Hamath.	**2Ki 25:21**	776
led away into exile from its **l**.	**2Ki 25:21**	127
who were left in the **l** of Judah,	**2Ki 25:22**	776
live in the **l** and serve the king of	**2Ki 25:24**	776
kings who reigned in the **l** of Edom	**1Ch 1:43**	776
Husham of the **l** of the Temanites	**1Ch 1:45**	776
cities in the **l** of Gilead.	**1Ch 2:22**	776
and the **l** was broad and quiet and	**1Ch 4:40**	776
had increased in the **l** of Gilead.	**1Ch 5:9**	776
all the **l** east of Gilead.	**1Ch 5:10**	6440
the **l** of Bashan as far as Salecah.	**1Ch 5:11**	776
of Manasseh lived in the **l**;	**1Ch 5:23**	776
the gods of the peoples of the **l**,	**1Ch 5:25**	776
gave Hebron in the **l** of Judah and	**1Ch 6:55**	776
who were born in the **l** killed,	**1Ch 7:21**	776
around the **l** of the Philistines to	**1Ch 10:9**	776
the inhabitants of the **l**,	**1Ch 11:4**	776
who remain in all the **l** of Israel,	**1Ch 13:2**	776
you I will give the **l** of Canaan,	**1Ch 16:18**	776
l of the sons of Ammon to Hanun to	**1Ch 19:2**	776
overthrow and to spy out the **l**?"	**1Ch 19:3**	776
ravaged the **l** of the sons of Ammon	**1Ch 20:1**	776
LORD, even pestilence in the **l**,	**1Ch 21:12**	776
who were in the **l** of Israel,	**1Ch 22:2**	776
inhabitants of the **l** into my hand,	**1Ch 22:18**	776
and the **l** is subdued before the	**1Ch 22:18**	776
that you may possess the good **l**	**1Ch 28:8**	776
who *were* in the **l** of Israel,	**2Ch 2:17**	776
My people from the **l** of Egypt,	**2Ch 6:5**	776
and bring them back to the **l** which	**2Ch 6:25**	127
And send rain on Your **l** which	**2Ch 6:27**	776

"If there is famine in the **l**, 2Ch 6:28 776
besiege them in the **l** of their cities, 2Ch 6:28 776
live in the **l** which You have given 2Ch 6:31 127
captive to a **l** far off or near, 2Ch 6:36 776
if they take thought in the **l** 2Ch 6:37 776
You in the **l** of their captivity, 2Ch 6:37 776
soul in the **l** of their captivity, 2Ch 6:38 776
and pray toward their **l** which You 2Ch 6:38 776
the locust to devour the **l**, 2Ch 7:13 776
their sin and will heal their **l**. 2Ch 7:14 776
from My **l** which I have given you, 2Ch 7:20 127
thus to this **l** and to this house?' 2Ch 7:21 776
brought them from the **l** of Egypt, 2Ch 7:22 776
and in all the **l** under his rule. 2Ch 8:6 776
who were left after them in the **l** 2Ch 8:8 776
on the seashore in the **l** of Edom. 2Ch 8:17 776
report which I heard in my own **l** 2Ch 9:5 776
was seen before in the **l** of Judah. 2Ch 9:11 776
went to her own **l** with her servants. 2Ch 9:12 776
even to the **l** of the Philistines, 2Ch 9:26 776
The **l** was undisturbed for ten 2Ch 14:1 776
since the **l** was undisturbed, 2Ch 14:6 776
The **l** is still ours because we 2Ch 14:7 776
idols from all the **l** of Judah and 2Ch 15:8 776
set garrisons in the **l** of Judah and 2Ch 17:2 776
removed the Asheroth from the **l** 2Ch 19:3 776
He appointed judges in the **l** 2Ch 19:5 776
drive out the inhabitants of this **l** 2Ch 20:7 776
they came out of the **l** of Egypt 2Ch 20:10 776
while Athaliah reigned over the **l**. 2Ch 22:12 776
all the people of the **l** rejoiced and 2Ch 23:13 776
and all the people of the **l**, 2Ch 23:20 776
So all of the people of the **l** rejoiced 2Ch 23:21 776
house judging the people of the **l**. 2Ch 26:21 776
and will return to this **l**. 2Ch 30:9 776
who came from the **l** of 2Ch 30:25 776
to deliver their **l** from my hand? 2Ch 32:13 776
he returned in shame to his own **l**. 2Ch 32:21 776
wonder that had happened in the **l**, 2Ch 32:31 776
remove the foot of Israel from the **l** 2Ch 33:8 127
But the people of the **l** killed all 2Ch 33:25 776
and the people of the **l** made 2Ch 33:25 776
altars throughout the **l** of Israel. 2Ch 34:7 776
he had purged the **l** and the house, 2Ch 34:8 776
Then the people of the **l** took Joahaz 2Ch 36:1 776
and imposed on the **l** a fine of one 2Ch 36:3 776
the **l** had enjoyed its sabbaths. 2Ch 36:21 776
Then the people of the **l** Ezr 4:4 776
the impurity of the nations of the **l** Ezr 6:21 776
'The **l** which you are entering to Ezr 9:11 776
are entering to possess is an unclean **l** Ezr 9:11 776
eat the good *things* of the **l** and leave Ezr 9:12 776
women from the peoples of the **l**; Ezr 10:2 776
yourselves from the peoples of the **l** Ezr 10:11 776
for plunder in a **l** of captivity. Ne 4:4 776
their governor in the **l** of Judah, Ne 5:14 776
we did not buy any **l**, Ne 5:16 7704
give *him* the **l** of the Canaanite, Ne 9:8 776
and all the people of his **l**; Ne 9:10 776
The **l** which You swore to give them. Ne 9:15 776
took possession of the **l** of Sihon Ne 9:22 776
the **l** of Og the king of Bashan. Ne 9:22 776
And You brought them into the **l** Ne 9:23 776
sons entered and possessed the **l**. Ne 9:24 776
them the inhabitants of the **l**, Ne 9:24 776
kings and the peoples of the **l**, Ne 9:24 776
fortified cities and a fertile **l**. Ne 9:25 127
With the broad and rich **l** which Ne 9:35 776
And as to the **l** which You gave Ne 9:36 776
our daughters to the peoples of the **l** Ne 10:30 776
As for the peoples of the **l** who Ne 10:31 776
the peoples of the **l** became Jews, Es 8:17 776
Ahasuerus laid a tribute on the **l** and Es 10:1 776
There was a man in the **l** of Uz whose Jb 1:1 776
have increased in the **l**. Jb 1:10 776
the **l** of darkness and deep shadow, Jb 10:21 776
The **l** of utter gloom as darkness Jb 10:22 776
To whom alone the **l** was given, Jb 15:19 776
The poor of the **l** are made to hide Jb 24:4 776
it found in the **l** of the living. Jb 28:13 776
They were scourged from the **l**. Jb 30:8 776
"If my **l** cries out against me, Jb 31:38 127
When the **l** is still because of the Jb 37:17 776
bring rain on a **l** without people, Jb 38:26 776
satisfy the waste and desolate **l** And Jb 38:27
the salt **l** for his dwelling place? Jb 39:6 4420
In all the **l** no women were Jb 42:15 776
Nations have perished from His **l**. Ps 10:16 776
descendants will inherit the **l**. Ps 25:13 776
the LORD In the **l** of the living. Ps 27:13 776
those who are quiet in the **l**. Ps 35:20 776
Dwell in the **l** and cultivate Ps 37:3 776
the LORD, they will inherit the **l**. Ps 37:9 776
But the humble will inherit the **l** And Ps 37:11 776
blessed by Him will inherit the **l**, Ps 37:22 776
The righteous will inherit the **l** And Ps 37:29 776
will exalt you to inherit the **l**; Ps 37:34 776
You from the **l** of the Jordan And Ps 42:6 776
sword they did not possess the **l**, Ps 44:3 776
you from the **l** of the living. Ps 52:5 776
You have made the **l** quake, Ps 60:2 776
dry and weary **l** where there is no Ps 63:1 776
He turned the sea into dry **l**; Ps 66:6 3004
rebellious dwell in a parched **l**. Ps 68:6 6707
meeting places of God in the **l**. Ps 74:8 776
For the dark places of the **l** are Ps 74:20 776
their fathers In the **l** of Egypt, Ps 78:12 776
So He brought them to His holy **l**, Ps 78:54 1366
took deep root and filled the **l**. Ps 80:9 776

he went throughout the **l** of Egypt. Ps 81:5 776
brought you up from the **l** of Egypt; Ps 81:10 776
You showed favor to Your **l**; Ps 85:1 776
That glory may dwell in our **l**. Ps 85:9 776
And our **l** will yield its produce. Ps 85:12 776
in the **l** of forgetfulness? Ps 88:12 776
And His hands formed the dry **l**. Ps 95:5 3006
be upon the faithful of the **l**, Ps 101:6 776
destroy all the wicked of the **l**, Ps 101:8 776
"To you I will give the **l** of Canaan Ps 105:11 776
He called for a famine upon the **l**; Ps 105:16 776
Jacob sojourned in the **l** of Ham. Ps 105:23 776
And miracles in the **l** of Ham. Ps 105:27 776
Their **l** swarmed with frogs *Even* in Ps 105:30 776
rain, *And* flaming fire in their **l**. Ps 105:32 776
ate up all vegetation in their **l**, Ps 105:35 776
down all the firstborn in their **l**, Ps 105:36 776
Wonders in the **l** of Ham *And* Ps 106:22 776
Then they despised the pleasant **l**; Ps 106:24 776
the **l** was polluted with the blood. Ps 106:38 776
A fruitful **l** into a salt waste, Ps 107:34 776
And a dry **l** into springs of water; Ps 107:35 776
the LORD In the **l** of the living. Ps 116:9 776
rest upon the **l** of the righteous, Ps 125:3 1486
And He gave their **l** as a heritage, Ps 135:12 776
And gave their **l** as a heritage, Ps 136:21 776
the LORD's song In a foreign **l**? Ps 137:4 127
My portion in the **l** of the living. Ps 142:5 776
longs for You, as a parched **l**. Ps 143:6 776
the upright will live in the **l** And Pr 2:21 776
wicked will be cut off from the **l** And Pr 2:22 776
wicked will not dwell in the **l**. Pr 10:30 776
He who tills his **l** will have plenty Pr 12:11 127
is better to live in a desert **l** Than Pr 21:19 776
So is good news from a distant **l**. Pr 25:25 776
By the transgression of a **l** many are Pr 28:2 776
He who tills his **l** will have plenty Pr 28:19 127
The king gives stability to the **l** by Pr 29:4 776
he sits among the elders of the **l**. Pr 31:23 776
field is an advantage to the **l**. Ec 5:9 776
walking like slaves on the **l**. Ec 10:7 776
Woe to you, O **l**, whose king is a Ec 10:16 776
Blessed are you, O **l**, Ec 10:17 776
have *already* appeared in the **l**; SS 2:12 776
has been heard in our **l**. SS 2:12 776
Your **l** is desolate, Your cities Is 1:7 776
You will eat the best of the **l**; Is 1:19 776
Their **l** has also been filled with Is 2:7 776
Their **l** has also been filled with Is 2:7 776
Their **l** has also been filled with Is 2:8 776
live alone in the midst of the **l**! Is 5:8 776
If one looks to the **l**, Is 5:30 776
And the **l** is utterly desolate, Is 6:11 127
are many in the midst of the **l**. Is 6:12 776
the **l** whose two kings you dread Is 7:16 127
bee that is in the **l** of Assyria. Is 7:18 776
everyone that is left within the **l** will Is 7:22 776
the **l** will be briars and thorns. Is 7:24 776
will fill the breadth of your **l**, Is 8:8 776
will pass through the **l** hard-pressed Is 8:21
He treated the **l** of Zebulun and the Is 9:1 776
the **l** of Naphtali with contempt, Is 9:1 776
Those who live in a dark **l**, Is 9:2 776
LORD of hosts the **l** is burned up, Is 9:19 776
in the midst of the whole **l**. Is 10:23 776
came up out of the **l** of Egypt. Is 11:16 776
To destroy the whole **l**. Is 13:5 776
anger, To make the **l** a desolation; Is 13:9 776
And each one flee to his own **l**. Is 13:14 776
and settle them in their own **l**, Is 14:1 127
an inheritance in the **l** of the LORD Is 14:2 127
to break Assyria in My **l**, Is 14:25 776
and upon the remnant of the **l**. Is 15:9 127
lamb to the ruler of the **l**, Is 16:1 776
completely *disappeared* from the **l**. Is 16:4 776
And the **l** will be a desolation. Is 17:9
oh **l** of whirring wings Which lies Is 18:1 776
nation Whose **l** the rivers divide. Is 18:2 776
Whose **l** the rivers divide Is 18:7 776
The **l** of Judah will become a Is 19:17 127
five cities in the **l** of Egypt will be Is 19:18 776
in the midst of the **l** of Egypt, Is 19:19 776
LORD of hosts in the **l** of Egypt; Is 19:20 776
wilderness, from a terrifying **l**. Is 21:1 776
O inhabitants of the **l** of Tema, Is 21:14 776
to them from the **l** of Cyprus. Is 23:1 776
Overflow your **l** like the Nile, O Is 23:10 776
Behold, the **l** of the Chaldeans Is 23:13 776
will be sung in the **l** of Judah: Is 26:1 776
unjustly in the **l** of uprightness, Is 26:10 776
extended all the borders of the **l**. Is 26:15 776
who were perishing in the **l** of Assyria Is 27:13 776
who were scattered in the **l** of Egypt Is 27:13 776
a **l** of distress and anguish, Is 30:6 776
of a huge rock in a parched **l**. Is 32:2 776
For the **l** of my people *in which* Is 32:13 127
The **l** mourns *and* pines away, Is 33:9 776
They will behold a far-distant **l**. Is 33:17 776
great slaughter in the **l** of Edom. Is 34:6 776
l will be soaked with blood, Is 34:7 776
its **l** will become burning pitch. Is 34:9 776
The scorched **l** will become a pool Is 35:7 8273
against this **l** to destroy it? Is 36:10 776
'Go up against this **l** and Is 36:10 776
I come and take you away to a **l** Is 36:17 776
away to a land like your own **l**, Is 36:17 776
land, a **l** of grain and new wine, Is 36:17 776
wine, a **l** of bread and vineyards. Is 36:17 776
the gods of the nations delivered his **l** Is 36:18 776

delivered their **l** from my hand, Is 36:20 776
a rumor and return to his own **l**. Is 37:7 776
by the sword in his own **l**. Is 37:7 776
they escaped into the **l** of Ararat. Is 37:38 776
The LORD in the **l** of the living; Is 38:11 776
And the dry **l** fountains of water. Is 41:18 776
pour out water on the thirsty **l** Is 44:3
spoken in secret, In some dark **l**; Is 45:19 776
of the people, To restore the **l**, Is 49:8 776
And these from the **l** of Sinim." Is 49:12 776
desolate places and your destroyed **l** Is 49:19 776
off out of the **l** of the living For Is 53:8 776
refuge in Me will inherit the **l** Is 57:13 776
will not be heard again in your **l**, Is 60:18 776
They will possess the **l** forever, Is 60:21 776
a double *portion* in their **l**, Is 61:7 776
to your **l** will it any longer be said, Is 62:4 776
your **l**, "Married"; For the LORD Is 62:4 776
And *to Him* your **l** will be married. Is 62:4 776
will be a pasture **l** for flocks, Is 65:10 5116a
Can a **l** be born in one day? Is 66:8 776
in Anathoth in the **l** of Benjamin, Jer 1:1 776
on all the inhabitants of the **l**. Jer 1:14 776
of bronze against the whole **l**, Jer 1:18 776
and to the people of the **l**. Jer 1:18 776
wilderness, Through a **l** not sown. Jer 2:2 776
us up out of the **l** of Egypt, Jer 2:6 776
a **l** of deserts and of pits, Jer 2:6 776
Through a **l** of drought and of deep Jer 2:6 776
Through a **l** that no one crossed Jer 2:6 776
I brought you into the fruitful **l** To Jer 2:7 776
But you came and defiled My **l**, Jer 2:7 776
And they have made his **l** a waste; Jer 2:15 776
Israel, Or a **l** of thick darkness? Jer 2:31 776
not that **l** be completely polluted? Jer 3:1 776
And you have polluted a **l** With Jer 3:2 776
she polluted the **l** and Jer 3:9 776
and increased in the **l**," Jer 3:16 776
they will come together from the **l** Jer 3:18 776
from the land of the north to the **l** Jer 3:18 776
sons And give you a pleasant **l**, Jer 3:19 776
"Blow the trumpet in the **l**; Jer 4:5 776
his place To make your **l** a waste. Jer 4:7 776
For the whole **l** is devastated; Jer 4:20 776
the fruitful **l** was a wilderness, Jer 4:26 3759
"The whole **l** shall be a desolation, Jer 4:27 776
and served foreign gods in your **l**, Jer 5:19 776
in a **l** that is not yours.' Jer 5:19 776
thing Has happened in the **l**: Jer 5:30 776
a desolation, A **l** not inhabited." Jer 6:8 776
the inhabitants of the **l**," Jer 6:12 776
the sweet cane from a distant **l**? Jer 6:20 776
people is coming from the north **l**, Jer 6:22 776
in the **l** that I gave to your Jer 7:7 776
brought them out of the **l** of Egypt, Jer 7:22 776
fathers came out of the **l** of Egypt Jer 7:25 776
for the **l** will become a ruin. Jer 7:34 776
his stallions The whole **l** quakes; Jer 8:16 776
and devour the **l** and its fullness, Jer 8:16 776
of my people from a distant **l**: Jer 8:19 776
and not truth prevail in the **l**; Jer 9:3 776
Why is the **l** ruined, laid waste Jer 9:12 776
shame, For we have left the **l**, Jer 9:19 776
slinging out the inhabitants of the **l** Jer 10:18 776
commotion out of the **l** of the north Jer 10:22 776
brought them out of the **l** of Egypt, Jer 11:4 776
a **l** flowing with milk and honey, Jer 11:5 776
them up from the **l** of Egypt, Jer 11:7 776
him off from the **l** of the living, Jer 11:19 776
How long is the **l** to mourn And the Jer 12:4 776
If you fall down in a **l** of peace, Jer 12:5 776
whole **l** has been made desolate, Jer 12:11 776
one end of the **l** even to the other; Jer 12:12 776
about to uproot them from their **l** Jer 12:14 127
inheritance and each one to his **l**. Jer 12:15 776
to fill all the inhabitants of this **l** Jer 13:13 776
there has been no rain on the **l**; Jer 14:4 776
Why are You like a stranger in the **l** Jer 14:8 776
will be no sword or famine in this **l**' Jer 14:15 776
the **l** that they do not know.' Jer 14:18 776
fork At the gates of the **l**; Jer 15:7 776
a man of contention to all the **l**! Jer 15:10 776
bring *it* Into a **l** you do not know; Jer 15:14 776
fathers who beget them in this **l**: Jer 16:3 776
men and small will die in this **l**; Jer 16:6 776
'So I will hurl you out of this **l** Jer 16:13 776
the **l** which you have not known, Jer 16:13 776
of Israel out of the **l** of Egypt,' Jer 16:14 776
sons of Israel from the **l** of the north Jer 16:15 776
I will restore them to their own **l** Jer 16:15 127
because they have polluted My **l**; Jer 16:18 776
In the **l** which you do not know; Jer 17:4 776
A **l** of salt without inhabitant. Jer 17:6 776
Jerusalem, from the **l** of Benjamin, Jer 17:26 776
flowing water *from* a foreign **l** Jer 18:14
To make their **l** a desolation, *An* Jer 18:16 776
never return Or see his native **l**. Jer 22:10 776
will die and not see this **l** again. Jer 22:12 776
"But as for the **l** to which they Jer 22:27 776
into a **l** that they had not known? Jer 22:28 776
"O **l**, land, land, Hear the word Jer 22:29 776
"O land, **l**, land, Hear the word Jer 22:29 776
"O land, land, **l**, Hear the word Jer 22:29 776
do justice and righteousness in the **l**. Jer 23:5 776
of Israel from the **l** of Egypt,' Jer 23:7 776
household of Israel from *the* north **l** Jer 23:8 776
For the **l** is full of adulterers; Jer 23:10 776
the **l** mourns because of the curse. Jer 23:10 776
has gone forth into all the **l**.' " Jer 23:15 776

place *into* the **l** of the Chaldeans.	**Jer 24:5**	776
I will bring them again to this **l**;	**Jer 24:6**	776
of Jerusalem who remain in this **l** and	**Jer 24:8**	776
ones who dwell in the **l** of Egypt.	**Jer 24:8**	776
until they are destroyed from the **l**	**Jer 24:10**	127
and dwell on the **l** which the LORD	**Jer 25:5**	127
will bring them against this **l** and	**Jer 25:9**	776
'This whole **l** will be a	**Jer 25:11**	776
and the **l** of the Chaldeans;	**Jer 25:12**	776
'I will bring upon that **l** all	**Jer 25:13**	776
all the kings of the **l** of Uz,	**Jer 25:20**	776
kings of the **l** of the Philistines	**Jer 25:20**	776
For their **l** has become a horror	**Jer 25:38**	776
Then some of the elders of the **l**	**Jer 26:17**	776
against this city and against this **l**	**Jer 26:20**	776
until the time of his own **l** comes;	**Jer 27:7**	776
to remove you far from your **l**;	**Jer 27:10**	127
him, I will let remain on its **l**,"	**Jer 27:11**	127
'I will also bring them back to the **l**	**Jer 30:3**	776
from the **l** of their captivity.	**Jer 30:10**	776
return from the **l** of the enemy.	**Jer 31:16**	776
speak this word in the **l** of Judah	**Jer 31:23**	776
bring them out of the **l** of Egypt,	**Jer 31:32**	776
which is in the **l** of Benjamin;	**Jer 32:8**	776
again be bought in this **l**."	**Jer 32:15**	776
and wonders in the **l** of Egypt,	**Jer 32:20**	776
Israel out of the **l** of Egypt with	**Jer 32:21**	776
and gave them this **l**,	**Jer 32:22**	776
a **l** flowing with milk and honey.	**Jer 32:22**	776
will faithfully plant them in this **l**	**Jer 32:41**	776
bought in this **l** of which you say,	**Jer 32:43**	776
in witnesses in the **l** of Benjamin,	**Jer 32:44**	776
I will restore the fortunes of the **l**	**Jer 33:11**	776
the Negev, in the **l** of Benjamin,	**Jer 33:13**	776
brought them out of the **l** of Egypt,	**Jer 34:13**	776
and all the people of the **l** who	**Jer 34:19**	776
days in the **l** where you sojourn.'	**Jer 35:7**	127
of Babylon came up against the **l**,	**Jer 35:11**	776
Then you will dwell in the **l**	**Jer 35:15**	127
certainly come and destroy this **l**,	**Jer 36:29**	776
had made king in the **l** of Judah,	**Jer 37:1**	776
nor the people of the **l** listened to the	**Jer 37:2**	776
to return to its own **l** of Egypt.	**Jer 37:7**	776
to go to the **l** of Benjamin in order to	**Jer 37:12**	776
against you or against this **l**'?	**Jer 37:19**	776
at Riblah in the **l** of Hamath,	**Jer 39:5**	776
left behind in the **l** of Judah,	**Jer 39:10**	776
Look, the whole **l** is before you;	**Jer 40:4**	776
the people who were left in the **l**.	**Jer 40:6**	776
son of Ahikam over the **l** and that he	**Jer 40:7**	776
those of the poorest of the **l** who	**Jer 40:7**	776
stay in the **l** and serve the king of	**Jer 40:9**	776
away and came to the **l** of Judah,	**Jer 40:12**	776
Babylon had appointed over the **l**.	**Jer 41:2**	776
Babylon had appointed over the **l**.	**Jer 41:18**	776
'If you will indeed stay in this **l**,	**Jer 42:10**	776
"We will not stay in this **l**,"	**Jer 42:13**	776
but we will go to the **l** of Egypt,	**Jer 42:14**	776
you there in the **l** of Egypt;	**Jer 42:16**	776
to stay in the **l** of Judah.	**Jer 43:4**	776
order to reside in the **l** of Judah	**Jer 43:5**	776
and they entered the **l** of Egypt	**Jer 43:7**	776
come and strike the **l** of Egypt;	**Jer 43:11**	776
will wrap himself with the **l** of Egypt	**Jer 43:12**	776
which is in the **l** of Egypt;	**Jer 43:13**	776
the Jews living in the **l** of Egypt,	**Jer 44:1**	776
Memphis, and the **l** of Pathros,	**Jer 44:1**	776
to other gods in the **l** of Egypt,	**Jer 44:8**	776
they committed in the **l** of Judah	**Jer 44:9**	776
mind on entering the **l** of Egypt	**Jer 44:12**	776
meet their end in the **l** of Egypt;	**Jer 44:12**	776
those who live in the **l** of Egypt,	**Jer 44:13**	776
who have entered the **l** of Egypt to	**Jer 44:14**	776
then to return to the **l** of Judah,	**Jer 44:14**	776
in Pathros in the **l** of Egypt,	**Jer 44:15**	776
princes, and the people of the **l**,	**Jer 44:21**	776
thus your **l** has become a ruin, an	**Jer 44:22**	776
Judah who are in the **l** of Egypt,	**Jer 44:24**	776
who are living in the **l** of Egypt,	**Jer 44:26**	776
of Judah in all the **l** of Egypt,	**Jer 44:26**	776
of Judah who are in the **l** of Egypt	**Jer 44:27**	776
will return out of the **l** of Egypt to	**Jer 44:28**	776
to the **l** of Judah few in number.	**Jer 44:28**	776
who have gone to the **l** of Egypt to	**Jer 44:28**	776
to uproot, that is, the whole **l**."	**Jer 45:4**	776
"I will rise and cover *that* **l**;	**Jer 46:8**	776
In the **l** of the north by the river	**Jer 46:10**	776
Babylon to smite the **l** of Egypt:	**Jer 46:13**	776
To our own people and our native **l**	**Jer 46:16**	776
from the **l** of their captivity;	**Jer 46:27**	776
overflow the **l** and all its fullness,	**Jer 47:2**	776
inhabitant of the **l** will wail.	**Jer 47:2**	776
all the cities of the **l** of Moab,	**Jer 48:24**	776
field, even from the **l** of Moab.	**Jer 48:33**	776
Babylon, the **l** of the Chaldeans,	**Jer 50:1**	776
make her **l** an object of horror,	**Jer 50:3**	776
go forth from the **l** of the Chaldeans	**Jer 50:8**	776
nations from the **l** of the north,	**Jer 50:9**	776
A wilderness, a parched **l** and	**Jer 50:12**	6723
they will each flee to his own **l**.	**Jer 50:16**	776
the king of Babylon and his **l**,	**Jer 50:18**	776
"Against the **l** of Merathaim, go	**Jer 50:21**	776
"The noise of battle is in the **l**,	**Jer 50:22**	776
hosts In the **l** of the Chaldeans.	**Jer 50:25**	776
refugees from the **l** of Babylon,	**Jer 50:28**	776
For it is a **l** of idols, And they	**Jer 50:38**	776
against the **l** of the Chaldeans:	**Jer 50:45**	776
her And may devastate her **l**;	**Jer 51:2**	776
slain in the **l** of the Chaldeans,	**Jer 51:4**	776
Although their **l** is full of guilt	**Jer 51:5**	776
Lift up a signal in the **l**,	**Jer 51:27**	776
And every **l** of their dominion.	**Jer 51:28**	776
So the **l** quakes and writhes, For	**Jer 51:29**	776
To make the **l** of Babylon A	**Jer 51:29**	776
horror, A parched **l** and a desert,	**Jer 51:43**	776
desert, A **l** in which no man lives And	**Jer 51:43**	776
the report that *will be* heard in the **l**	**Jer 51:46**	776
violence *will be* in the **l** With ruler	**Jer 51:46**	776
her whole **l** will be put to shame And	**Jer 51:47**	776
will groan throughout her **l**.	**Jer 51:52**	776
from the **l** of the Chaldeans!	**Jer 51:54**	776
no food for the people of the **l**.	**Jer 52:6**	776
at Riblah in the **l** of Hamath,	**Jer 52:9**	776
the poorest of the **l** to be vinedressers	**Jer 52:16**	776
who mustered the people of the **l**,	**Jer 52:25**	776
and sixty men of the people of the **l**	**Jer 52:25**	776
at Riblah in the **l** of Hamath.	**Jer 52:27**	776
led away into exile from its **l**.	**Jer 52:27**	127
feet All the prisoners of the **l**,	**La 3:34**	776
Edom, Who dwells in the **l** of Uz;	**La 4:21**	776
in the **l** of the Chaldeans by the	**Ezk 1:3**	776
make the **l** more desolate and waste	**Ezk 6:14**	776
the Lord GOD to the **l** of Israel,	**Ezk 7:2**	127
on the four corners of the **l**.	**Ezk 7:2**	776
to you, O inhabitant of the **l**.	**Ezk 7:7**	776
the **l** is full of bloody crimes and	**Ezk 7:23**	776
the people of the **l** will tremble.	**Ezk 7:27**	776
the LORD has forsaken the **l**.' "	**Ezk 8:12**	776
that they have filled the **l** with	**Ezk 8:17**	776
and the **l** is filled with blood and	**Ezk 9:9**	776
'The LORD has forsaken the **l**,	**Ezk 9:9**	776
this **l** has been given us as a	**Ezk 11:15**	776
give you the **l** of Israel."	**Ezk 11:17**	127
so that you cannot see the **l**,	**Ezk 12:6**	776
can not see the **l** with *his* eyes.	**Ezk 12:12**	776
Babylon in the **l** of the Chaldeans;	**Ezk 12:13**	776
"Then say to the people of the **l**,	**Ezk 12:19**	776
of Jerusalem in the **l** of Israel,	**Ezk 12:19**	127
because their **l** will be stripped	**Ezk 12:19**	776
and the **l** will be a desolation.	**Ezk 12:20**	776
have concerning the **l** of Israel,	**Ezk 12:22**	127
will they enter the **l** of Israel,	**Ezk 13:9**	127
wild beasts to pass through the **l** and	**Ezk 14:15**	776
'Thus I will make the **l** desolate,	**Ezk 15:8**	776
are from the **l** of the Canaanite,	**Ezk 16:3**	776
harlotry with the **l** of merchants,	**Ezk 16:29**	776
brought it to a **l** of merchants;	**Ezk 17:4**	776
also took some of the seed of the **l**	**Ezk 17:5**	776
took away the mighty of the **l**,	**Ezk 17:13**	776
proverb concerning the **l** of Israel	**Ezk 18:2**	127
him with hooks To the **l** of Egypt.	**Ezk 19:4**	776
And the **l** and its fullness were	**Ezk 19:7**	776
In a dry and thirsty **l**.	**Ezk 19:13**	776
known to them in the **l** of Egypt,	**Ezk 20:5**	776
bring them out from the **l** of Egypt	**Ezk 20:6**	776
a **l** that I had selected for them,	**Ezk 20:6**	776
in the midst of the **l** of Egypt.	**Ezk 20:8**	776
them out of the **l** of Egypt.	**Ezk 20:9**	776
I took them out of the **l** of Egypt	**Ezk 20:10**	776
into the **l** which I had given them,	**Ezk 20:15**	776
l which I swore to give to them,	**Ezk 20:28**	776
the wilderness of the **l** of Egypt,	**Ezk 20:36**	776
out of the **l** where they sojourn,	**Ezk 20:38**	776
will not enter the **l** of Israel.	**Ezk 20:38**	127
of them, will serve Me in the **l**;	**Ezk 20:40**	776
I bring you into the **l** of Israel,	**Ezk 20:42**	127
into the **l** which I swore to give	**Ezk 20:42**	776
against the forest **l** of the Negev,	**Ezk 20:46**	7704
prophesy against the **l** of Israel;	**Ezk 21:2**	127
and say to the **l** of Israel,	**Ezk 21:3**	127
both of them will go out of one **l**.	**Ezk 21:19**	776
created, in the **l** of your origin,	**Ezk 21:30**	776
will be in the midst of the **l**.	**Ezk 21:32**	776
'You are a **l** that is not cleansed	**Ezk 22:24**	776
'The people of the **l** have	**Ezk 22:29**	776
in the gap before Me for the **l**,	**Ezk 22:30**	776
in Chaldea, the **l** of their birth.	**Ezk 23:15**	776
the harlot in the **l** of Egypt.	**Ezk 23:19**	776
harlotry *brought* from the **l** of Egypt	**Ezk 23:27**	776
make lewdness cease from the **l**,	**Ezk 23:48**	776
and against the **l** of Israel when	**Ezk 25:3**	127
your soul against the **l** of Israel,	**Ezk 25:6**	127
its frontiers, the glory of the **l**,	**Ezk 25:9**	776
set glory in the **l** of the living.	**Ezk 26:20**	776
"Judah and the **l** of Israel, they	**Ezk 27:17**	776
They will stand on the **l**,	**Ezk 27:29**	776
then they will live in their **l**	**Ezk 28:25**	127
"The **l** of Egypt will become a	**Ezk 29:9**	776
and I will make the **l** of Egypt an	**Ezk 29:10**	776
"So I will make the **l** of Egypt a	**Ezk 29:12**	776
them return to the **l** of Pathros,	**Ezk 29:14**	776
Pathros, to the **l** of their origin,	**Ezk 29:14**	776
I will give the **l** of Egypt to	**Ezk 29:19**	776
"I have given him the **l** of Egypt	**Ezk 29:20**	776
and the people of the **l** that is in	**Ezk 30:5**	776
be brought in to destroy the **l**;	**Ezk 30:11**	776
And fill the **l** with the slain.	**Ezk 30:11**	776
sell the **l** into the hands of evil men.	**Ezk 30:12**	776
And I will make the **l** desolate And	**Ezk 30:12**	776
be a prince in the **l** of Egypt;	**Ezk 30:13**	776
I will put fear in the **l** of Egypt.	**Ezk 30:13**	776
it out against the **l** of Egypt.	**Ezk 30:25**	776
in all the ravines of the **l**.	**Ezk 31:12**	776
"I will leave you on the **l**;	**Ezk 32:4**	776
"I will also make the **l** drink the	**Ezk 32:6**	776
And will set darkness on your **l**,"	**Ezk 32:8**	776
make the **l** of Egypt a desolation,	**Ezk 32:15**	776
And the **l** is destitute of that	**Ezk 32:15**	776
terror in the **l** of the living.	**Ezk 32:23**	776
terror in the **l** of the living and	**Ezk 32:24**	776
instilled in the **l** of the living),	**Ezk 32:25**	776
terror in the **l** of the living.	**Ezk 32:26**	776
was once in the **l** of the living.	**Ezk 32:27**	776
of him in the **l** of the living,	**Ezk 32:32**	776
'If I bring a sword upon a **l**,	**Ezk 33:2**	776
and the people of the **l** take one	**Ezk 33:2**	776
sees the sword coming upon the **l** and	**Ezk 33:3**	776
these waste places in the **l** of Israel	**Ezk 33:24**	127
only one, yet he possessed the **l**;	**Ezk 33:24**	776
so to us who are many the **l** has	**Ezk 33:24**	776
Should you then possess the **l**?	**Ezk 33:25**	776
Should you then possess the **l**?" '	**Ezk 33:26**	776
make the **l** a desolation and a waste,	**Ezk 33:28**	776
when I make the **l** a desolation and	**Ezk 33:29**	776
and bring them to their own **l**;	**Ezk 34:13**	127
all the inhabited places of the **l**.	**Ezk 34:13**	776
eliminate harmful beasts from the **l** so	**Ezk 34:25**	776
they will be secure on their **l**.	**Ezk 34:27**	127
be victims of famine in the **l**,	**Ezk 34:29**	776
who appropriated My **l** for	**Ezk 36:5**	776
prophesy concerning the **l** of Israel and	**Ezk 36:6**	127
Israel was living in their own **l**,	**Ezk 36:17**	127
which they had shed on the **l**,	**Ezk 36:18**	776
yet they have come out of His **l**.'	**Ezk 36:20**	776
and bring you into your own **l**.	**Ezk 36:24**	127
"You will live in the **l** that	**Ezk 36:28**	776
"The desolate **l** will be	**Ezk 36:34**	776
'This desolate **l** has become like	**Ezk 36:35**	776
bring you into the **l** of Israel.	**Ezk 37:12**	127
I will place you on your own **l**.	**Ezk 37:14**	127
and bring them into their own **l**;	**Ezk 37:21**	127
make them one nation in the **l**,	**Ezk 37:22**	776
"They will live on the **l**	**Ezk 37:25**	776
face toward Gog of the **l** of Magog,	**Ezk 38:2**	776
will come into the **l** that is restored	**Ezk 38:8**	776
be like a cloud covering the **l**,	**Ezk 38:9**	776
the **l** of unwalled villages.	**Ezk 38:11**	776
like a cloud to cover the **l**.	**Ezk 38:16**	776
I will bring you against My **l**,	**Ezk 38:16**	776
comes against the **l** of Israel,"	**Ezk 38:18**	127
earthquake in the **l** of Israel.	**Ezk 38:19**	127
them in order to cleanse the **l**.	**Ezk 39:12**	776
people of the **l** will bury *them;*	**Ezk 39:13**	776
constantly pass through the **l**,	**Ezk 39:14**	776
"As those who pass through the **l**	**Ezk 39:15**	776
So they will cleanse the **l**."	**Ezk 39:16**	776
when they live securely on their *own* **l**	**Ezk 39:26**	127
them *again* to their own **l**;	**Ezk 39:28**	127
brought me into the **l** of Israel and	**Ezk 40:2**	776
divide by lot the **l** for inheritance,	**Ezk 45:1**	776
the LORD, a holy portion of the **l**;	**Ezk 45:1**	776
be the holy portion of the **l**;	**Ezk 45:4**	776
"The prince shall have **l** on	**Ezk 45:7**	
his **l** for a possession in Israel;	**Ezk 45:8**	776
but they shall give *the rest of* the **l** to	**Ezk 45:8**	776
"All the people of the **l** shall	**Ezk 45:16**	776
all the people of the **l** a bull for a	**Ezk 45:22**	776
"The people of the **l** shall also	**Ezk 46:3**	776
"But when the people of the **l** come	**Ezk 46:9**	776
divide the **l** for an inheritance among	**Ezk 47:13**	776
and this **l** shall fall to you as an	**Ezk 47:14**	776
shall be the boundary of the **l**:	**Ezk 47:15**	776
Gilead and the **l** of Israel,	**Ezk 47:18**	776
"So you shall divide this **l** among	**Ezk 47:21**	776
them from the allotment of the **l**,	**Ezk 48:12**	776
alienate this choice *portion* of **l**;	**Ezk 48:14**	776
"This is the **l** which you shall	**Ezk 48:29**	776
brought them to the **l** of Shinar,	**Da 1:2**	776
who were living in all the **l**:	**Da 6:25**	772
and toward the Beautiful **L**.	**Da 8:9**	
and all the people of the **l**.	**Da 9:6**	776
Your people out of the **l** of Egypt	**Da 9:15**	776
but will return to his *own* **l**.	**Da 11:9**	127
for a time in the Beautiful **L**,	**Da 11:16**	776
the fortresses of his own **l**,	**Da 11:19**	776
return to his **l** with much plunder;	**Da 11:28**	776
and *then* return to his *own* **l**.	**Da 11:28**	776
and will parcel out **l** for a price.	**Da 11:39**	127
will also enter the Beautiful **L**,	**Da 11:41**	776
the **l** of Egypt will not escape.	**Da 11:42**	776
the **l** commits flagrant harlotry,	**Hos 1:2**	776
And they will go up from the **l**,	**Hos 1:11**	776
Make her like desert **l** And	**Hos 2:3**	776
she came up from the **l** of Egypt.	**Hos 2:15**	776
the sword and war from the **l**,	**Hos 2:18**	776
will sow her for Myself in the **l**.	**Hos 2:23**	776
against the inhabitants of the **l**,	**Hos 4:1**	776
Or knowledge of God in the **l**.	**Hos 4:1**	776
Therefore the **l** mourns, And	**Hos 4:3**	776
will devour them with their **l**.	**Hos 5:7**	2506
their derision in the **l** of Egypt.	**Hos 7:16**	776
will not remain in the LORD's **l**,	**Hos 9:3**	776
The richer his **l**, The better he	**Hos 10:1**	776
will not return to the **l** of Egypt;	**Hos 11:5**	776
like doves from the **l** of Assyria;	**Hos 11:11**	776
your God since the **l** of Egypt;	**Hos 12:9**	776
Now Jacob fled to the **l** of Aram,	**Hos 12:12**	7704
your God Since the **l** of Egypt;	**Hos 13:4**	776
wilderness, In the **l** of drought.	**Hos 13:5**	776
listen, all inhabitants of the **l**.	**Jl 1:2**	776
For a nation has invaded my **l**,	**Jl 1:6**	776
The field is ruined, The **l** mourns;	**Jl 1:10**	127
elders *And* all the inhabitants of the **l**	**Jl 1:14**	776
the inhabitants of the **l** tremble,	**Jl 2:1**	776
The **l** is like the garden of Eden	**Jl 2:3**	776
LORD will be zealous for His **l** And	**Jl 2:18**	776
it into a parched and desolate **l**,	**Jl 2:20**	776

Do not fear, O **l**, rejoice and be Jl 2:21 127
And they have divided up My **l**. Jl 3:2 776
In whose **l** they have shed innocent Jl 3:19 776
you up from the **l** of Egypt, Am 2:10 776
possession of the **l** of the Amorite. Am 2:10 776
He brought up from the **l** of Egypt: Am 3:1 776
on the citadels in the **l** of Egypt and Am 3:9 776
enemy, even one surrounding the **l**, Am 3:11 776
She *lies* neglected on her **l**; Am 5:2 127
eating the vegetation of the **l**, Am 7:2 776
and began to consume the farm **l**. Am 7:4 2506
the **l** is unable to endure all his Am 7:10 776
go from its **l** into exile.' " Am 7:11 127
seer, flee away to the **l** of Judah and Am 7:12 776
your **l** will be parceled up by a Am 7:17 127
go from its **l** into exile.' " Am 7:17 127
do away with the humble of the **l**, Am 8:4 776
"Because of this will not the **l** quake Am 8:8 776
I will send a famine on the **l**, Am 8:11 776
touches the **l** so that it melts, Am 9:5 776
up Israel from the **l** of Egypt, Am 9:7 776
"I will also plant them on their **l**, Am 9:15 127
their **l** Which I have given them," Am 9:15 127
who made the sea and the dry **l**." Jon 1:9 3004
men rowed *desperately* to return to **l** Jon 1:13 3004
vomited Jonah up onto the dry **l**. Jon 2:10 3004
When the Assyrian invades our **l**, Mi 5:5 776
They will shepherd the **l** of Assyria Mi 5:6 776
The **l** of Nimrod at its entrances; Mi 5:6 776
the Assyrian When he attacks our **l** Mi 5:6 776
will also cut off the cities of your **l** Mi 5:11 776
brought you up from the **l** of Egypt Mi 6:4 776
person has perished from the **l**, Mi 7:2 776
you came out from the **l** of Egypt, Mi 7:15 776
will cut off your prey from the **l**, Na 2:13 776
The gates of your **l** are opened Na 3:13 776
and violence done to the **l**, Hab 2:8 776
and violence done to the **l**, Hab 2:17 776
The tent curtains of the **l** of Midian Hab 3:7 776
O Canaan, **l** of the Philistines; Zph 2:5 776
I called for a drought on the **l**, Hg 1:11 776
you people of the **l** take courage,' Hg 2:4 776
earth, the sea also and the dry **l**. Hg 2:6 2724
up *their* horns against the **l** of Judah Zch 1:21 776
Flee from the **l** of the north," Zch 2:6 776
as His portion in the holy **l**, Zch 2:12 127
the iniquity of that **l** in one day. Zch 3:9 776
over the face of the whole **l**; Zch 5:3 776
is their appearance in all the **l** Zch 5:6 776
temple for her in the **l** of Shinar; Zch 5:11 776
who are going to the **l** of the north Zch 6:8 776
My wrath in the **l** of the north." Zch 6:8 776
Say to all the people of the **l** and to Zch 7:5 776
the **l** is desolated behind them so Zch 7:14 776
made the pleasant **l** desolate." Zch 7:14 776
save My people from the **l** of the east Zch 8:7 776
east and from the **l** of the west; Zch 8:7 776
the **l** will yield its produce and Zch 8:12 776
LORD is against the **l** of Hadrach, Zch 9:1 776
of a crown, Sparkling in His **l**. Zch 9:16 127
them back from the **l** of Egypt And Zch 10:10 776
into the **l** of Gilead and Lebanon Until Zch 10:10 776
have pity on the inhabitants of the **l** Zch 11:6 776
and they will strike the **l**, Zch 11:6 776
going to raise up a shepherd in the **l** Zch 11:16 776
"The **l** will mourn, every Zch 12:12 776
the names of the idols from the **l**, Zch 13:2 776
and the unclean spirit from the **l**. Zch 13:2 776
It will come about in all the **l**," Zch 13:8 776
All the **l** will be changed into a Zch 14:10 776
for you shall be a delightful **l**," Mal 3:12 776
and smite the **l** with a curse." Mal 4:6 776
'AND YOU, BETHLEHEM, L OF JUDAH, Mt 2:6 *1093*
and go into the **l** of Israel; Mt 2:20 *1093*
and came into the **l** of Israel. Mt 2:21 *1093*
"THE L OF ZEBULUN AND THE LAND OF Mt 4:15 *1093*
OF ZEBULUN AND THE L OF NAPHTALI, Mt 4:15 *1093*
IN THE L AND SHADOW OF DEATH, Mt 4:16 *5561*
news spread throughout all that **l**. Mt 9:26 *1093*
news about Him throughout all that **l**. Mt 9:31 *1093*
be more tolerable for *the* **l** of Sodom Mt 10:15 *1093*
more tolerable for the **l** of Sodom in Mt 11:24 *1093*
a long distance from the **l**, Mt 14:24 *1093*
they came to **l** at Gennesaret. Mt 14:34 *1093*
you travel around on sea and **l** to Mt 23:15 *3584*
darkness fell upon all the **l** until Mt 27:45 *1093*
crowd was by the sea on the **l**. Mk 4:1 *1093*
sea, and He was alone on the **l**. Mk 6:47 *1093*
over they came to **l** at Gennesaret, Mk 6:53 *1093*
darkness fell over the whole **l** until Mk 15:33 *1093*
great famine came over all the **l**; Lk 4:25 *1093*
in the **l** of Sidon, to a woman Lk 4:26
put out a little way from the **l**. Lk 5:3 *1093*
they had brought their boats to **l**, Lk 5:11 *1093*
when He came out onto the **l**, Lk 8:27 *1093*
"The **l** of a rich man was Lk 12:16 *5561*
'I have bought a piece of **l** and I Lk 14:18 *68*
will be great distress upon the **l** and Lk 21:23 *1093*
darkness fell over the whole **l** until Lk 23:44 *1093*
disciples came into the **l** of Judea, Jn 3:22 *1093*
immediately the boat was at the **l** Jn 6:21 *1093*
for they were not far from the **l**, Jn 21:8 *1093*
So when they got out on the **l**, Jn 21:9 *1093*
went up and drew the net to **l**, Jn 21:11 *1093*
for all who were owners of **l** or Ac 4:34 *5564*
and who owned a tract of **l**, Ac 4:37 *68*
back *some* of the price of the **l**? Ac 5:3 *5564*
"Tell me whether you sold the **l** for Ac 5:8 *5564*
INTO THE L THAT I WILL SHOW YOU.' Ac 7:3 *1093*
left the **l** of the Chaldeans Ac 7:4 *1093*
WOULD BE ALIENS IN A FOREIGN L, Ac 7:6 *1093*
AN ALIEN IN THE L OF MIDIAN, Ac 7:29 *1093*
wonders and signs in the **l** of Egypt Ac 7:36 *1093*
WHO LED US OUT OF THE L OF EGYPT Ac 7:40 *1093*
He did both in the **l** of the Jews and Ac 10:39 *5561*
their stay in the **l** of Egypt, Ac 13:17 *1093*
seven nations in the **l** of Canaan, Ac 13:19 *1093*
He distributed their **l** as an Ac 13:19 *1093*
it, intending himself to go by **l**. Ac 20:13 *3978*
down from the **l** a violent wind, Ac 27:14
that they were approaching some **l**. Ac 27:27 *5561*
they could not recognize the **l**; Ac 27:39 *1093*
jump overboard first and get to **l**, Ac 27:43 *1093*
they all were brought safely to **l**. Ac 27:44 *1093*
LEAD THEM OUT OF THE L OF EGYPT; Heb 8:9 *1093*
as an alien in the **l** of promise, Heb 11:9 *1093*
as in a foreign **l**, dwelling in Heb 11:9
they were passing through dry **l**; Heb 11:29 *1093*
a people out of the **l** of Egypt, Jude 1:5 *1093*
on the sea and his left on the **l**; Rv 10:2 *1093*
saw standing on the sea and on the **l** Rv 10:5 *1093*
stands on the sea and on the **l**." Rv 10:8 *1093*

LANDED

When he had **l** at Caesarea, he Ac 18:22 *2718*
sailing to Syria and **l** at Tyre; Ac 21:3 *2718*
Pamphylia, we **l** at Myra in Lycia. Ac 27:5 *2718*

LANDINGS

seashore, And remained by its **l**. Jg 5:17 4664

LANDMARKS

"Some remove the **l**; Jb 24:2 1367

LANDOWNER

slaves of the **l** came and said to him Mt 13:27 *3617*
the kingdom of heaven is like a **l** Mt 20:1 *3617*
it, they grumbled at the **l**, Mt 20:11 *3617*
There was a **l** who PLANTED A Mt 21:33 *3617*

LANDS

were separated into their **l**, Gn 10:5 776
to their languages, by their **l**, Gn 10:20 776
to their languages, by their **l**, Gn 10:31 776
I will give all these **l**, Gn 26:3 776
give your descendants all these **l**; Gn 26:4 776
there was famine in all the **l**, Gn 41:54 776
lord except our bodies and our **l**. Gn 47:18 127
hearts in the **l** of their enemies. Lv 26:36 776
iniquity in the **l** of your enemies; Lv 26:39 776
pasture **l** around the cities. Nu 35:2 4054
and their pasture **l** shall be for Nu 35:3 4054
"The pasture **l** of the cities Nu 35:4 4054
as pasture **l** for the cities. Nu 35:5 4054
together with their pasture **l**. Nu 35:7 4054
kings and their **l** at one time, Jos 10:42 776
with their pasture **l** for their Jos 14:4 4054
their pasture **l** for our cattle." Jos 21:2 4054
these cities with their pasture **l**, Jos 21:3 4054
these cities with their pasture **l**, Jos 21:8 4054
with its surrounding pasture **l**. Jos 21:11 4054
the manslayer, with its pasture **l**, Jos 21:13 4054
and Libnah with its pasture **l**, Jos 21:13 4054
and Jattir with its pasture **l** and Jos 21:14 4054
and Eshtemoa with its pasture **l**, Jos 21:14 4054
and Holon with its pasture **l** and Jos 21:15 4054
and Debir with its pasture **l**, Jos 21:15 4054
and Ain with its pasture **l** and Jos 21:16 4054
and Juttah with its pasture **l** Jos 21:16 4054
Beth-shemesh with its pasture **l**; Jos 21:16 4054
Gibeon with its pasture **l**, Jos 21:17 4054
lands, Geba with its pasture **l**, Jos 21:17 4054
Anathoth with its pasture **l** and Jos 21:18 4054
and Almon with its pasture **l**; Jos 21:18 4054
cities with their pasture **l**. Jos 21:19 4054
the manslayer, with its pasture **l**, Jos 21:21 4054
and Gezer with its pasture **l**, Jos 21:21 4054
and Kibzaim with its pasture **l** and Jos 21:22 4054
and Beth-horon with its pasture **l**; Jos 21:22 4054
of Dan, Elteke with its pasture **l**, Jos 21:23 4054
Gibbethon with its pasture **l**, Jos 21:23 4054
Aijalon with its pasture **l**, Jos 21:24 4054
Gath-rimmon with its pasture **l**; Jos 21:24 4054
allotted Taanach with its pasture **l** Jos 21:25 4054
and Gath-rimmon with its pasture **l**; Jos 21:25 4054
All the cities with their pasture **l** Jos 21:26 4054
the manslayer, with its pasture **l**, Jos 21:27 4054
and Be-eshterah with its pasture **l**; Jos 21:27 4054
gave Kishion with its pasture **l**, Jos 21:28 4054
Daberath with its pasture **l**, Jos 21:28 4054
Jarmuth with its pasture **l**, Jos 21:29 4054
En-gannim with its pasture **l**; Jos 21:29 4054
gave Mishal with its pasture **l**, Jos 21:30 4054
lands, Abdon with its pasture **l**, Jos 21:30 4054
Helkath with its pasture **l** and Jos 21:31 4054
and Rehob with its pasture **l**; Jos 21:31 4054
with its pasture **l** and Hammoth-dor Jos 21:32 4054
and Hammoth-dor with its pasture **l** Jos 21:32 4054
and Kartan with its pasture **l**; Jos 21:32 4054
cities with their pasture **l**. Jos 21:33 4054
Jokneam with its pasture **l** and Jos 21:34 4054
and Kartah with its pasture **l**. Jos 21:34 4054
Dimnah with its pasture **l**, Jos 21:35 4054
lands, Nahalal with its pasture **l**; Jos 21:35 4054
they gave Bezer with its pasture **l** Jos 21:36 4054
and Jahaz with its pasture **l**, Jos 21:36 4054
Kedemoth with its pasture **l** and Jos 21:37 4054
and Mephaath with its pasture **l**; Jos 21:37 4054
with its pasture **l** and Mahanaim Jos 21:38 4054
and Mahanaim with its pasture **l**, Jos 21:38 4054
Heshbon with its pasture **l**, Jos 21:39 4054
lands, Jazer with its pasture **l**; Jos 21:39 4054
cities with their pasture **l**. Jos 21:41 4054
had its surrounding pasture **l**; Jos 21:42 4054
'Who among all the gods of the **l** 2Ki 18:35 776
of Assyria have done to all the **l**, 2Ki 19:11 776
devastated the nations and their **l** 2Ki 19:17 776
in all the pasture **l** of Sharon, 1Ch 5:16 4054
and its pasture **l** around it; 1Ch 6:55 4054
Libnah also with its pasture **l**, 1Ch 6:57 4054
Eshtemoa with its pasture **l**, 1Ch 6:57 4054
Hilen with its pasture **l**, 1Ch 6:58 4054
lands, Debir with its pasture **l**, 1Ch 6:58 4054
Ashan with its pasture **l** and 1Ch 6:59 4054
Beth-shemesh with its pasture **l**; 1Ch 6:59 4054
Geba with its pasture **l**, 1Ch 6:60 4054
Allemeth with its pasture **l**, 1Ch 6:60 4054
and Anathoth with its pasture **l**. 1Ch 6:60 4054
the cities with their pasture **l**. 1Ch 6:64 4054
of Ephraim with its pasture **l**, 1Ch 6:67 4054
Gezer also with its pasture **l**, 1Ch 6:67 4054
Jokmeam with its pasture **l**, 1Ch 6:68 4054
Beth-horon with its pasture **l**, 1Ch 6:68 4054
Aijalon with its pasture **l** and 1Ch 6:69 4054
and Gath-rimmon with its pasture **l**; 1Ch 6:69 4054
Aner with its pasture **l** and Bileam 1Ch 6:70 4054
and Bileam with its pasture **l**, 1Ch 6:70 4054
Golan in Bashan with its pasture **l** 1Ch 6:71 4054
and Ashtaroth with its pasture **l**; 1Ch 6:71 4054
Kedesh with its pasture **l**, 1Ch 6:72 4054
Daberath with its pasture **l** 1Ch 6:72 4054
and Ramoth with its pasture **l**, 1Ch 6:73 4054
Anem with its pasture **l**; 1Ch 6:73 4054
Mashal with its pasture **l**, 1Ch 6:74 4054
lands, Abdon with its pasture **l**, 1Ch 6:74 4054
Hukok with its pasture **l** and 1Ch 6:75 4054
and Rehob with its pasture **l**; 1Ch 6:75 4054
in Galilee with its pasture **l**, 1Ch 6:76 4054
lands, Hammon with its pasture **l** and 1Ch 6:76 4054
and Kiriathaim with its pasture **l**. 1Ch 6:76 4054
Rimmono with its pasture **l**, 1Ch 6:77 4054
lands, Tabor with its pasture **l**; 1Ch 6:77 4054
the wilderness with its pasture **l**, 1Ch 6:78 4054
lands, Jahzah with its pasture **l**, 1Ch 6:78 4054
Kedemoth with its pasture **l** and 1Ch 6:79 4054
and Mephaath with its pasture **l**; 1Ch 6:79 4054
in Gilead with its pasture **l**, 1Ch 6:80 4054
Mahanaim with its pasture **l**, 1Ch 6:80 4054
Heshbon with its pasture **l** and 1Ch 6:81 4054
and Jazer with its pasture **l**. 1Ch 6:81 4054
in their cities with pasture **l**, 1Ch 13:2 4054
of David went out into all the **l**; 1Ch 14:17 776
and glorious throughout all **l**. 1Ch 22:5 776
and on all the kingdoms of the **l**. 1Ch 29:30 776
For the Levites left their pasture **l** 2Ch 11:14 4054
like the peoples of *other* **l**? 2Ch 13:9 776
all the inhabitants of the **l**. 2Ch 15:5 776
was on all the kingdoms of the **l** 2Ch 17:10 776
God was on all the kingdoms of the **l** 2Ch 20:29 776
in the pasture **l** of their cities, 2Ch 31:19 7704
done to all the peoples of the **l**? 2Ch 32:13 776
Were the gods of the nations of the **l** 2Ch 32:13 776
gods of the nations of the **l** have not 2Ch 32:17 776
the **l** belonging to the sons of Israel, 2Ch 34:33 776
because of the peoples of the **l**; Ezr 3:3 776
from the peoples of the **l**, Ezr 9:1 776
with the peoples of the **l**; Ezr 9:2 776
the hand of the kings of the **l**, Ezr 9:7 776
uncleanness of the peoples of the **l**, Ezr 9:11 776
the hand of the peoples of the **l**. Ne 9:30 776
from the peoples of the **l** to the law Ne 10:28 776
They have called their **l** after their Ps 49:11 127
them also the **l** of the nations, Ps 105:44 776
And scatter them in the **l**. Ps 106:27 776
And gathered from the **l**, Ps 107:3 776
'Who among all the gods of these **l** Is 36:20 776
of Assyria have done to all the **l**, Is 37:11 776
all the countries and their **l**, Is 37:18 776
"Now I have given all these **l** Jer 27:6 776
prophesied against many **l** and Jer 28:8 776
I will gather them out of all the **l** Jer 32:37 776
of the nations, with **l** around her. Ezk 5:5 776
than the **l** which surround her; Ezk 5:6 776
which is the glory of all **l**. Ezk 20:6 776
which is the glory of all **l**, Ezk 20:15 776
and disperse them among the **l**, Ezk 20:23 776
nations, like the tribes of the **l**, Ezk 20:32 776
the **l** where you are scattered, Ezk 20:34 776
the **l** where you are scattered; Ezk 20:41 776
and a mocking to all the **l**. Ezk 22:4 776
will disperse you through the **l**, Ezk 22:15 776
and make you perish from the **l**; Ezk 25:7 776
pilots The pasture **l** will shake. Ezk 27:28 4054
in the midst of desolated **l**. Ezk 29:12 776
and disperse them among the **l**." Ezk 29:12 776
In the midst of the desolated **l**; Ezk 30:7 776
and disperse them among the **l**. Ezk 30:23 776
and disperse them among the **l**, Ezk 30:26 776
into **l** which you have not known. Ezk 32:9 776
and these two **l** will be mine, Ezk 35:10 776
were dispersed throughout the **l**. Ezk 36:19 776
gather you from all the **l** and Ezk 36:24 776
them from the **l** of their enemies, Ezk 39:27 776
the neighborhood of that place were **l** Ac 28:7 *5564*

LANES

'Go out at once into the streets and **l** Lk 14:21 *4505*

LANGUAGE

every one according to his **l**, Gn 10:5 3956
the same **l** and the same words. Gn 11:1 8193
and they all have the same **l**. Gn 11:6 8193

go down and there confuse their **l**, Gn 11:7 8193
confused the **l** of the whole earth; Gn 11:9 8193
whose **l** you shall not understand, Dt 28:49 3956
with a loud voice in the **l** of Judah 2Ch 32:18 3066
half spoke in the **l** of Ashdod, Ne 13:24 797
was able to speak the **l** of Judah, Ne 13:24 3066
but the **l** of his own people. Ne 13:24 3956
every people according to their **l**, Es 1:22 3956
speaks in the **l** of his own people. Es 1:22 3956
each people according to its **l**, Es 3:12 3956
every people according to their **l** as Es 8:9 3956
to their script and their **l**. Es 8:9 3956
you choose the **l** of the crafty. Jb 15:5 3956
I heard a **l** that I did not know: Ps 81:5 8193
Jacob from a people of strange **l**, Ps 114:1 3937
he who is perverted in his **l** falls Pr 17:20 3956
will be speaking the **l** of Canaan Is 19:18 8193
A nation whose **l** you do not know, Jer 5:15 3956
unintelligible speech or difficult **l**, Ezk 3:5 3956
unintelligible speech or difficult **l**, Ezk 3:6 3956
literature and **l** of the Chaldeans. Da 1:4 3956
nations and *men of every* **l**, Da 3:4 3961
nations and *men of every* **l** fell Da 3:7 3961
men of every **l** that live in all the Da 4:1 3961
and *men of every* **l** feared and Da 5:19 3961
and *men of every* **l** who were living Da 6:25 3961
men of every **l** Might serve Him. Da 7:14 3961
spoken to you in figurative **l**; Jn 16:25 *3942*
no longer speak to you in figurative **l**, Jn 16:25 *3942*
so that in their own **l** that field Ac 1:19 *1258*
hearing them speak in his own **l**. Ac 2:6 *1258*
we each hear *them* in our own **l** to Ac 2:8 *1258*
voice, saying in the Lycaonian **l**, Ac 14:11 *3072*
do not know the meaning of the **l**, 1Co 14:11 *5456*
arise envy, strife, abusive **l**, 1Tm 6:4 *988*

LANGUAGES
families, according to their **l**, Gn 10:20 3956
families, according to their **l**, Gn 10:31 3956
many kinds of **l** in the world, 1Co 14:10 *5456*

LANGUISH
eyes of his children also will **l**. Jb 17:5 3615
"Judah mourns And her gates **l** Jer 14:2 535
And they will never **l** again. Jer 31:12 1669

LANGUISHED
of Canaan **l** because of the famine. Gn 47:13 3856
They have **l** together. La 2:8 535

LANGUISHES
But she who has many children **l**. 1Sa 2:5 535
My soul **l** for Your salvation; Ps 119:81 3615
ones and refresh everyone who **l**." Jer 31:25 1669
And everyone who lives in it **l** Hos 4:3 535

LANGUISHING
"How **l** is your heart," Ezk 16:30 535

LANTERNS
with **l** and torches and weapons. Jn 18:3 *5322*

LAODICEA
and for those who are at **L**, Col 2:1 *2993*
those who are in **L** and Hierapolis. Col 4:13 *2993*
Greet the brethren who are in **L** Col 4:15 *2993*
my letter *that is coming* from **L**. Col 4:16 *2993*
and to Philadelphia and to **L**." Rv 1:11 *2993*
angel of the church in **L** write: Rv 3:14 *2993*

LAODICEANS
also read in the church of the **L**; Col 4:16 *2994*

LAP
shall **l** over the back of the Ex 26:12 5628
shall **l** over the sides of the Ex 26:13 5628
the child and laid him in her **l**, Ru 4:16 2436
he sat on her **l** until noon, 2Ki 4:20 1290
from it his **l** full of wild gourds, 2Ki 4:39 899b
The lot is cast into the **l**, Pr 16:33 2436
They will pour into your **l** Lk 6:38 *2859*

LAPIS
Their polishing *was like* **l** lazuli. La 4:7 5601
like **l** lazuli in appearance; Ezk 1:26 68, 5601
The **l** lazuli, the turquoise and Ezk 28:13 5601

LAPPED
Now the number of those who **l**, Jg 7:6 3952
deliver you with the 300 men who **l** Jg 7:7 3952

LAPPIDOTH
a prophetess, the wife of **L**, Jg 4:4 3941

LAPS
who **l** the water with his tongue as Jg 7:5 3952
water with his tongue as a dog **l**, Jg 7:5 3952

LAPSE
nor to those who **l** into falsehood. Ps 40:4 7750

LARGE
on the mouth of the well was **l**. Gn 29:2 1419
and had **l** flocks and female and Gn 30:43 7227a
the land is **l** enough for them. Gn 34:21 7342, 3027
a very **l** number of livestock. Ex 12:38 3515
cities are fortified *and* very **l**; Nu 13:28 1419
exceedingly **l** number of livestock. Nu 32:1 6099
cities are **l** and fortified to heaven. Dt 1:28 1419
weights, a **l** and a small. Dt 25:13 1419
measures, a **l** and a small. Dt 25:14 1419
set up for yourself **l** stones and Dt 27:2 1419
the LORD threw **l** stones from Jos 10:11 1419
"Roll **l** stones against the mouth Jos 10:18 1419
and put **l** stones over the mouth of Jos 10:27 1419
sons of Judah was too **l** for them; Jos 19:9 7227a
Jordan, a **l** altar in appearance. Jos 22:10 1419
and he took a **l** stone and set it Jos 24:26 1419
there where there *was* a **l** stone; 1Sa 6:14 1419
gold, and put them on the **l** stone; 1Sa 6:15 1419
The **l** stone on which they set the 1Sa 6:18 1419
far as the **l** well that is in Secu; 1Sa 19:22 1419
with a **l** area between them. 1Sa 26:13 7227a
took a very **l** amount of bronze. 2Sa 8:8 7235a
at the **l** stone which is in Gibeon, 2Sa 20:8 1419
of costly stones, *even* **l** stones, 1Ki 7:10 1419
Jerusalem with a very **l** retinue, 1Ki 10:2 3515
made 200 **l** shields of beaten gold, 1Ki 10:16 6793c
shekels of gold on each **l** shield. 1Ki 10:16 6793c
l enough to hold two measures of 1Ki 18:32 1004
borrow vessels at **l** for yourself 2Ki 4:3 2351
"Put on the **l** pot and boil stew 2Ki 4:38 1419
with a **l** army to Jerusalem. 2Ki 18:17 3515
took a very **l** amount of bronze, 1Ch 18:8 7227a
David prepared **l** quantities of iron 1Ch 22:3 7230
Tyrians brought **l** quantities of cedar 1Ch 22:4 7230
She had a very **l** retinue, with 2Ch 9:1 3515
and a **l** amount of gold and 2Ch 9:1 7230
made 200 **l** shields of beaten gold, 2Ch 9:15 6793c
of beaten gold on each **l** shield. 2Ch 9:15 6793c
bearing **l** shields and spears, 2Ch 14:8 6793c
l numbers of sheep and camels. 2Ch 14:15 7230
He had **l** supplies in the 2Ch 17:13 7227a
l and small shields which had been 2Ch 23:9 4043
second month, a very **l** assembly. 2Ch 30:13 7230
and a **l** number of priests 2Ch 30:24 7230
house of God, a very **l** assembly, Ezr 10:1 7227a
Now the city was **l** and spacious, Ne 7:4 7342, 3027
had prepared a **l** room for him, Ne 13:5 1419
with a **l** crown of gold and a Es 8:15 1419
have set my feet in a **l** place. Ps 31:8 4800
them to drink tears in **l** measure. Ps 80:5 7991a
me *and set me* in a **l** place. Ps 118:5 4800
constructed **l** siegeworks against it. Ec 9:14 1419
"Take for yourself a **l** tablet and Is 8:1 1419
He has made it deep and **l**, Is 30:33 7337
to King Hezekiah with a **l** army. Is 36:2 3515
"Take *some* **l** stones in your hands Jer 43:9 1419
standing by, *as* a **l** assembly, Jer 44:15 1419
every **l** house he burned with fire. Jer 52:13 1419
raise up a **l** shield against you. Ezk 26:8 6793c
that statue, which was **l** and of Da 2:31 7229
'The tree grew **l** and became Da 4:11 7236
which became **l** and grew strong, Da 4:20 7236
and it had **l** iron teeth. Da 7:7 7229
was mighty, the **l** horn was broken; Da 8:8 1419
and the **l** horn that is between his Da 8:21 1419
king of the South with a **l** army; Da 11:25 1419
an extremely **l** and mighty army for Da 11:25 1419
them Like a lamb in a **l** field? Hos 4:16 4800
these things their catch is **l**, Hab 1:16 8082a
east to west by a very **l** valley, Zch 14:4 1419
L crowds followed Him from Galilee Mt 4:25 *4183*
l crowds followed Him. Mt 8:1 *4183*
And **l** crowds gathered to Him, so He Mt 13:2 *4183*
When He went ashore, He saw a **l** Mt 14:14 *4183*
And **l** crowds came to Him, bringing Mt 15:30 *4183*
desolate place to satisfy such a **l** Mt 15:33 *4183*
pieces, seven **l** baskets full. Mt 15:37 *4711*
how many **l** baskets *full* you picked up? Mt 16:10 *4711*
and **l** crowds followed Him, and He Mt 19:2 *4183*
As they were leaving Jericho, a **l** Mt 20:29 *4183*
came up accompanied by a **l** crowd with Mt 26:47 *4183*
and he rolled a **l** stone against Mt 27:60 *3173*
a **l** sum of money to the soldiers, Mt 28:12 *2425*
And such a very **l** crowd gathered to Mk 4:1 *4183*
plants and forms **l** branches; Mk 4:32 *3173*
Now there was a **l** herd of swine Mk 5:11 *3173*
a **l** crowd gathered around Him; Mk 5:21 *4183*
And He went off with him; and a **l** Mk 5:24 *4183*
When Jesus went ashore, He saw a **l** Mk 6:34 *4183*
when there was again a **l** crowd Mk 8:1 *4183*
seven **l** baskets full of what was left Mk 8:8 *4711*
how many **l** baskets full of broken Mk 8:20 *4711*
they saw a **l** crowd around them, Mk 9:14 *4183*
Jericho with His disciples and a **l** Mk 10:46 *2425*
And the **l** crowd enjoyed listening to Mk 12:37 *4183*
people were putting in **l** sums. Mk 12:41 *4183*
a **l** upper room furnished *and* ready Mk 14:15 *3173*
away, although it was extremely **l**. Mk 16:4 *3173*
and **l** crowds were gathering to hear Lk 5:15 *4183*
and *there was* a **l** crowd of His Lk 6:17 *4183*
Him, accompanied by a **l** crowd. Lk 7:11 *4183*
When a **l** crowd was coming together, Lk 8:4 *4183*
a **l** crowd met Him. Lk 9:37 *4183*
Now **l** crowds were going along with Lk 14:25 *4183*
show you a **l**, furnished upper room Lk 22:12 *3173*
And following Him was a **l** crowd of Lk 23:27 *4183*
A **l** crowd followed Him, because they Jn 6:2 *4183*
up His eyes and seeing that a **l** crowd Jn 6:5 *4183*
The **l** crowd of the Jews then learned Jn 12:9 *4183*
On the next day the **l** crowd who had Jn 12:12 *4183*
the net to land, full of **l** fish, Jn 21:11 *3173*
wall, lowering him in a **l** basket. Ac 9:25 *4711*
and a **l** number who believed turned Ac 11:21 *4183*
and spoke in such a manner that a **l** Ac 14:1 *4183*
along with a **l** number of Ac 17:4 *4183*
citizenship with a **l** sum of money." Ac 22:28 *4183*
him at his lodging in **l** numbers; Ac 28:23 *4183*
See with what **l** letters I am Ga 6:11 *4080*
Now in a **l** house there are not 2Tm 2:20 *3173*

LARGER
"To the **l** *group* you shall Nu 26:54 7227a
the **l** and the smaller *groups*." Nu 26:56 7227a
to the **l** you shall give more Nu 33:54 7227a
you shall take more from the **l** and Nu 35:8 7227a
herds **l** than all who preceded me Ec 2:7 7235a
from the smaller ledge to the **l** ledge Ezk 43:14 1419
l in appearance than its associates Da 7:20 7229
it is **l** than the garden plants and Mt 13:32 *3173*
group of slaves **l** than the first; Mt 21:36 *4183*
becomes **l** than all the garden plants Mk 4:32 *3173*
down my barns and build **l** ones, Lk 12:18 *3173*

LASEA
near which was the city of **L**. Ac 27:8 *2996*

LASHA
Admah and Zeboiim, as far as **L**. Gn 10:19 3962

LASHARON
the king of **L**, one; Jos 12:18 8289

LASHES
his will, will receive many **l**, Lk 12:47 *1194*
from the Jews thirty-nine **l**. 2Co 11:24

LAST
I lay **l** night with my father; Gn 19:34 570
Abraham breathed his **l** and died in Gn 25:8 1478
and he breathed his **l** and died, Gn 25:17 1478
At **l** the LORD has made room for us Gn 26:22 3588, 6258
your father spoke to me **l** night, Gn 31:29 570
so He rendered judgment **l** night." Gn 31:42 570
next, and Rachel and Joseph **l**. Gn 33:2 314
Isaac breathed his **l** and died and Gn 35:29 1478
into the bed and breathed his **l**, Gn 49:33 1478
believe the witness of the **l** sign. Ex 4:8 314
your threshing will **l** for you until Lv 26:5 5381
grape gathering will **l** until sowing Lv 26:5 5381
set out **l** by their standards." Nu 2:31 314
You have shown your **l** kindness to Ru 3:10 314
the LORD said to me **l** night." 1Sa 15:16
and they stopped at the **l** house. 2Sa 15:17 4801
'Why are you the **l** to bring the 2Sa 19:11 314
be the **l** to bring back the king?' 2Sa 19:12 314
these are the **l** words of David. 2Sa 23:1 314
For by the **l** words of David the 1Ch 23:27 314
acts of King David, from first to **l**, 1Ch 29:29 314
acts of Solomon, from first to **l**, 2Ch 9:29 314
acts of Rehoboam, from first to **l**, 2Ch 12:15 314
the acts of Asa from first to **l**, 2Ch 16:11 314
acts of Jehoshaphat, first to **l**, 2Ch 20:34 314
acts of Amaziah, from first to **l**, 2Ch 25:26 314
of the acts of Uzziah, first to **l**, 2Ch 26:22 314
and all his ways, from first to **l**, 2Ch 28:26 314
and his acts, first to **l**, 2Ch 35:27 314
the sons of Adonikam, the **l** ones, Ezr 8:13 314
from the first day to the **l** day. Ne 8:18 314
hope is to breathe their **l**." Jb 11:20 4646
And at the **l** He will take His Jb 19:25 314
Weeping may **l** for the night, But a Ps 30:5 3885a
At the **l** it bites like a serpent And Pr 23:32 319
come about that In the **l** days The Is 2:2 319
you surely shall not **l**. Is 7:9 539
am the first, and with the **l**. Is 41:4 314
'I am the first and I am the **l**, Is 44:6 314
I am the first, I am also the **l**. Is 48:12 314
to his unjust gain, to the **l** one. Is 56:11 7097a
In the **l** days you will clearly Jer 23:20 319
that they may **l** a long time." Jer 32:14 5975
But it will come about in the **l** days Jer 49:39 319
and this **l** one *who* has broken his Jer 50:17 314
It shall come about in the **l** days Ezk 38:16 319
with the longer one coming up **l**. Da 8:3 314
but this **l** time it will not turn Da 11:29 314
and to His goodness in the **l** days. Hos 3:5 319
And the **l** of you with fish hooks. Am 4:2 319
And it will come about in the **l** days Mi 4:1 319
until you have paid up the **l** cent. Mt 5:26 *2078*
and the **l** state of that man Mt 12:45 *2078*
"But many *who are* first will be **l**; Mt 19:30 *2078*
and *the* **l**, first. Mt 19:30 *2078*
beginning with the **l** *group* to the Mt 20:8 *2078*
l men have worked *only* one hour, Mt 20:12 *2078*
I wish to give to this **l** man the same Mt 20:14 *2078*
"So the **l** shall be first, and the Mt 20:16 *2078*
shall be first, and the first **l**." Mt 20:16 *2078*
"**L** of all, the woman died. Mt 22:27 *5305*
for **l** night I suffered greatly in Mt 27:19 *4594*
and the **l** deception will be worse Mt 27:64 *2078*
to be first, he shall be **l** of all and Mk 9:35 *2078*
"But many *who are* first will be **l** Mk 10:31 *2078*
and the **l**, first." Mk 10:31 *2078*
he sent him **l** *of all* to them, Mk 12:6 *2078*
L of all the woman died also. Mk 12:22 *2078*
a loud cry, and breathed His **l**. Mk 15:37 *1606*
saw the way He breathed His **l**, Mk 15:39 *1606*
and the **l** state of that man Lk 11:26 *2078*
you have paid the very **l** cent." Lk 12:59 *2078*
some are **l** who will be first and Lk 13:30 *2078*
some are first who will be **l**." Lk 13:30 *2078*
you proceed to occupy the **l** place. Lk 14:9 *2078*
go and recline at the **l** place, Lk 14:10 *2078*
said this, He breathed His **l**. Lk 23:46 *1606*
but raise it up on the **l** day. Jn 6:39 *2078*
will raise him up on the **l** day." Jn 6:40 *2078*
I will raise him up on the **l** day. Jn 6:44 *2078*
I will raise him up on the **l** day. Jn 6:54 *2078*
Now on the **l** day, the great *day* of Jn 7:37 *2078*
the resurrection on the **l** day." Jn 11:24 *2078*
what will judge him at the **l** day. Jn 12:48 *2078*
'AND IT SHALL BE IN THE **L** DAYS,' Ac 2:17 *2078*
fell down and breathed his **l**; Ac 5:5 *1634*
at his feet and breathed her **l** Ac 5:10 *1634*
if perhaps now at **l** by the will of Ro 1:10 *4218*
exhibited us apostles **l** of all, 1Co 4:9 *2078*
and **l** of all, as to one 1Co 15:8 *2078*
The **l** enemy that will be abolished 1Co 15:26 *2078*
The **l** Adam *became* a life-giving 1Co 15:45 *2078*

of an eye, at the **l** trumpet; **1Co 15:52** *2078*
has been prepared since **l** year, **2Co 9:2** *4070*
that now at **l** you have revived **Php 4:10** *4218*
that in the **l** days difficult times **2Tm 3:1** *2078*
in these **l** days has spoken to us **Heb 1:2** *2078*
It is in the **l** days that you have **Jas 5:3** *2078*
to be revealed in the **l** time. **1Pe 1:5** *2078*
has appeared in these **l** times for **1Pe 1:20** *2078*
the **l** state has become worse for **2Pe 2:20** *2078*
that in the **l** days mockers will **2Pe 3:3** *2078*
Children, it is the **l** hour; **1Jn 2:18** *2078*
we know that it is the **l** hour. **1Jn 2:18** *2078*
In the **l** time there will be mockers, **Jude 1:18** *2078*
I am the first and the **l**, **Rv 1:17** *2078*
The first and the **l**, **Rv 2:8** *2078*
seven plagues, *which are* the **l**, **Rv 15:1** *2078*
bowls full of the seven **l** plagues came **Rv 21:9** *2078*
the Omega, the first and the **l**, **Rv 22:13** *2078*

LASTED
seven days while their feast **l**. **Jg 14:17** 1961

LASTING
even severe and **l** plagues, **Dt 28:59** 539
king gave a banquet **l** seven days **Es 1:5**
no **l** remembrance of the wise man **Ec 2:16** 5769
you **l** peace in this place.' " **Jer 14:13** 571
a better possession and a **l** one. **Heb 10:34** *3306*
For here we do not have a **l** city, **Heb 13:14** *3306*

LASTS
right of redemption **l** a full year. **Lv 25:29** 1961

LATE
not ruined, for they *ripen* **l**.) **Ex 9:32** 648
its season, the early and **l** rain, **Dt 11:14** 4456
you to rise up early, To retire **l**, **Ps 127:2** 309
to God, do not be **l** in paying it; **Ec 5:4** 309
Who stay up **l** in the evening that **Is 5:11** 309
is desolate and the hour is already **l**; **Mt 14:15** *3928*
When it was already quite **l**, **Mk 6:35**
5610, 4183
and it is already quite **l**; **Mk 6:35**
5610, 4183
twelve, since it was already **l**. **Mk 11:11** *3796*
it gets the early and **l** rains. **Jas 5:7** *3797*
your deeds of **l** are greater than at **Rv 2:19** *2078*

LATELY
not known, New *gods* who came **l**, **Dt 32:17** 7138

LATER
my honesty will answer for me **l**, **Gn 30:33**
4279, 3117
it was about three months **l** that **Gn 38:24**
so that when your children ask **l**, **Jos 4:6** 4279
When he returned **l** to take her, **Jg 14:8**
4480, 3117
About ten days **l**, **1Sa 25:38**
Some years **l** he went down to **2Ch 18:2** 7093
of the **l** things which will occur, **Ec 1:11** 314
Among those who will come **l** *still*. **Ec 1:11** 314
even the ones who will come **l** **Ec 4:16** 314
l on He shall make *it* glorious, **Is 9:1** 314
but **l** you will surely listen to **Ezk 20:39** 310
"Twelve months **l** he was walking **Da 4:29** 7118
Six days **l** Jesus took with Him **Mt 17:1** *3326*
"**L** the other virgins also came, **Mt 25:11** *5305*
But **l** on two came forward, **Mt 26:60** *5305*
A little **l** the bystanders came **Mt 26:73** *3326*
Six days **l**, Jesus took with **Mk 9:2** *3326*
He will rise three days **l**." **Mk 9:31** *3326*
three days **l** He will rise again." **Mk 10:34** *3326*
"And not many days **l**, **Lk 15:13** *3326*
A little **l**, another saw him **Lk 22:58** *3326*
but you will follow **l**." **Jn 13:36** *5305*
But some days **l** Felix arrived **Ac 24:24** *3326*
three days **l** went up to Jerusalem **Ac 25:1** *3326*
a day **l** a south wind sprang up, **Ac 28:13** *3326*
Then three years **l** I went up to **Ga 1:18** *3326*
four hundred and thirty years **l**, **Ga 3:17** *3326*
faith which was **l** to be revealed. **Ga 3:23** *3195*
in **l** times some will fall away from **1Tm 4:1** *5306*
things which were to be spoken **l**; **Heb 3:5**

LATIN
written in Hebrew, **L** *and* in Greek. **Jn 19:20** *4515*

LATRINE
Baal, and made it a **l** to this day. **2Ki 10:27** 4280

LATTER
have come upon you, in the **l** days you **Dt 4:30** 319
and if the **l** husband turns against **Dt 24:3** 314
or if the **l** husband dies who took **Dt 24:3** 314
will befall you in the **l** days, **Dt 31:29** 319
The LORD blessed the **l** *days* of Job **Jb 42:12** 319
"He will not see our **l** ending." **Jer 12:4** 319
In the **l** days you will understand **Jer 30:24** 319
fortunes of Moab In the **l** days," **Jer 48:47** 319
in the **l** years you will come into **Ezk 38:8** 319
will take place in the **l** days. **Da 2:28** 320
"In the **l** period of their rule, **Da 8:23** 319
to your people in the **l** days, **Da 10:14** 319
"Then the **l** will enter the realm **Da 11:9**
l will raise a great multitude, **Da 11:11**
The early and **l** rain as before. **Jl 2:23** 4456
'The **l** glory of this house will be **Hg 2:9** 314
will *the* **l** become unclean?" **Hg 2:13**
the **l** *do it* out of love, knowing **Php 1:16** *3303a*

LATTICE
mother of Sisera through the **l**, **Jg 5:28** 822
And Ahaziah fell through the **l** in **2Ki 1:2** 7639
house I looked out through my **l**, **Pr 7:6** 822
He is peering through the **l**. **SS 2:9** 2762

LATTICED
The thresholds, the **l** windows and **Ezk 41:16** 331
There were **l** windows and palm **Ezk 41:26** 331

LATTICES
And like the doves to their **l**? **Is 60:8** 699

LAUD
L Him, all peoples! **Ps 117:1** 7623b

LAUGH
"Why did Sarah **l**, saying, **Gn 18:13** 6711
"I did not **l**"; for she was afraid. **Gn 18:15** 6711
"No, but you did **l**." **Gn 18:15** 6711
everyone who hears will **l** with me." **Gn 21:6** 6711
"You will **l** at violence and **Jb 5:22** 7832
see and fear, And will **l** at him, **Ps 52:6** 7832
But You, O LORD, **l** at them; **Ps 59:8** 7832
our enemies **l** among themselves. **Ps 80:6** 3932
I will also **l** at your calamity; **Pr 1:26** 7832
A time to weep and a time to **l**; **Ec 3:4** 7832
They **l** at every fortress And heap **Hab 1:10** 7832
you who weep now, for you shall **l**. **Lk 6:21** *1070*
Woe *to you* who **l** now, for you **Lk 6:25** *1070*

LAUGHED
Abraham fell on his face and **l**, **Gn 17:17** 6711
Sarah **l** to herself, saying, **Gn 18:12** 6711
Zebulun, but they **l** them to scorn and **2Ch 30:10** 7832
will be **l** at and held in derision; **Ezk 23:32** 6712

LAUGHING
And rulers are a **l** matter to them. **Hab 1:10** 4890
And they *began* **l** at Him. **Mt 9:24** *2606*
They *began* **l** at Him. **Mk 5:40** *2606*
And they *began* **l** at Him, knowing **Lk 8:53** *2606*

LAUGHINGSTOCK
otherwise we will become a **l**. **Gn 38:23** 937
nations, A **l** among the peoples. **Ps 44:14**
4493, 7218
I have become a **l** all day long; **Jer 20:7** 7814
and he also will become a **l**. **Jer 48:26** 7814
"Now was not Israel a **l** to you? **Jer 48:27** 7814
So Moab will become a **l** and an **Jer 48:39** 7814
have become a **l** to all my people, **La 3:14** 7814

LAUGHS
She **l** at the horse and his rider. **Jb 39:18** 7832
"He **l** at fear and is not dismayed; **Jb 39:22** 7832
He **l** at the rattling of the **Jb 41:29** 7832
He who sits in the heavens **l**, **Ps 2:4** 7832
The Lord **l** at him, **Ps 37:13** 7832
The foolish man either rages or **l**, **Pr 29:9** 7832

LAUGHTER
"God has made **l** for me; **Gn 21:6** 6712
will yet fill your mouth with **l** And **Jb 8:21** 7814
Then our mouth was filled with **l** And **Ps 126:2** 7814
in **l** the heart may be in pain, **Pr 14:13** 7814
I said of **l**, "It is madness," **Ec 2:2** 7814
Sorrow is better than **l**, **Ec 7:3** 7814
a pot, So is the **l** of the fool; **Ec 7:6** 7814
let your **l** be turned into mourning and **Jas 4:9** *1071*

LAUNCH
Fierce men **l** an attack against me, **Ps 59:3** 1481b

LAUNCHED
So they **l** out. **Lk 8:22** *321*

LAUNDERER
as no **l** on earth can whiten them. **Mk 9:3** *1102*

LAVER
"You shall also make a **l** of bronze, **Ex 30:18** 3595
utensils, and the **l** and its stand. **Ex 30:28** 3595
utensils, and the **l** and its stand, **Ex 31:9** 3595
he made the **l** of bronze with its **Ex 38:8** 3595
its utensils, the **l** and its stand; **Ex 39:39** 3595
"You shall set the **l** between **Ex 40:7** 3595
shall anoint the **l** and its stand, **Ex 40:11** 3595
He placed the **l** between the **Ex 40:30** 3595
and removed the **l** from them; **2Ki 16:17** 3595

LAVISH
prepare a **l** banquet for all peoples **Is 25:6** 8081
"Those who **l** gold from the purse **Is 46:6** 2107

LAVISHED
oil, And **l** on her silver and gold, **Hos 2:8** 7235a
which He **l** on us. **Eph 1:8** *4052*

LAW
"The same **l** shall apply to the **Ex 12:49** 8451
that the **l** of the LORD may be in **Ex 13:9** 8451
give you the stone tablets with the **l** **Ex 24:12** 8451
is the **l** for the burnt offering: **Lv 6:9** 8451
is the **l** of the grain offering: **Lv 6:14** 8451
'This is the **l** of the sin offering: **Lv 6:25** 8451
is the **l** of the guilt offering; **Lv 7:1** 8451
offering, there is one **l** for them; **Lv 7:7** 8451
l of the sacrifice of peace offerings **Lv 7:11** 8451
is the **l** of the burnt offering, **Lv 7:37** 8451
is the **l** regarding the animal and **Lv 11:46** 8451
the **l** for her who bears *a child*, **Lv 12:7** 8451
This is the **l** for the mark of leprosy **Lv 13:59** 8451
"This shall be the **l** of the leper **Lv 14:2** 8451
"This is the **l** *for him* in whom **Lv 14:32** 8451
This is the **l** for any mark of leprosy **Lv 14:54** 8451
This is the **l** of leprosy. **Lv 14:57** 8451
l for the one with a discharge, **Lv 15:32** 8451
'This is the **l** of jealousy: **Nu 5:29** 8451
shall apply all this **l** to her. **Nu 5:30** 8451
'Now this is the **l** of the Nazirite **Nu 6:13** 8451
"This is the **l** of the Nazirite **Nu 6:21** 8451
to the **l** of his separation." **Nu 6:21** 8451
'There is to be one **l** and one **Nu 15:16** 8451
'You shall have one **l** for him who **Nu 15:29** 8451
l which the LORD has commanded, **Nu 19:2** 8451
the **l** when a man dies in a tent: **Nu 19:14** 8451
"This is the statute of the **l** **Nu 31:21** 8451
Moses undertook to expound this **l**, **Dt 1:5** 8451
as righteous as this whole **l** which I **Dt 4:8** 8451
Now this is the **l** which Moses set **Dt 4:44** 8451
terms of the **l** which they teach you, **Dt 17:11** 8451
write for himself a copy of this **l** on **Dt 17:18** 8451
observing all the words of this **l** and **Dt 17:19** 8451
on them all the words of this **l**, **Dt 27:3** 8451
all the words of this **l** very distinctly **Dt 27:8** 8451
does not confirm the words of this **l** **Dt 27:26** 8451
observe all the words of this **l** **Dt 28:58** 8451
not written in the book of this **l**, **Dt 28:61** 8451
are written in this book of the **l**. **Dt 29:21** 8451
observe all the words of this **l**. **Dt 29:29** 8451
are written in this book of the **l**, **Dt 30:10** 8451
Moses wrote this **l** and gave it to **Dt 31:9** 8451
you shall read this **l** in front of **Dt 31:11** 8451
observe all the words of this **l**. **Dt 31:12** 8451
finished writing the words of this **l** **Dt 31:24** 8451
"Take this book of the **l** and **Dt 31:26** 8451
even all the words of this **l**. **Dt 32:46** 8451
"Moses charged us with a **l**, **Dt 33:4** 8451
to Jacob, And Your **l** to Israel. **Dt 33:10** 8451
do according to all the **l** which Moses **Jos 1:7** 8451
"This book of the **l** shall not depart **Jos 1:8** 8451
in the book of the **l** of Moses, **Jos 8:31** 8451
stones a copy of the **l** of Moses, **Jos 8:32** 8451
he read all the words of the **l**, **Jos 8:34** 8451
is written in the book of the **l**. **Jos 8:34** 8451
observe the commandment and the **l** **Jos 22:5** 8451
in the book of the **l** of Moses, **Jos 23:6** 8451
words in the book of the **l** of God; **Jos 24:26** 8451
according to what is written in the **L** **1Ki 2:3** 8451
to walk in the **l** of the LORD, **2Ki 10:31** 8451
written in the book of the **L** of Moses, **2Ki 14:6** 8451
My statutes according to all the **l** **2Ki 17:13** 8451
or their ordinances or the **l**, **2Ki 17:34** 8451
and the **l** and the commandment which **2Ki 17:37** 8451
and according to all the **l** that My **2Ki 21:8** 8451
"I have found the book of the **l** in **2Ki 22:8** 8451
the words of the book of the **l**, **2Ki 22:11** 8451
he might confirm the words of the **l** **2Ki 23:24** 8451
according to all the **l** of Moses; **2Ki 23:25** 8451
is written in the **l** of the LORD, **1Ch 16:40** 8451
keep the **l** of the LORD your God. **1Ch 22:12** 8451
to walk in My **l** as you have walked **2Ch 6:16** 8451
him forsook the **l** of the LORD. **2Ch 12:1** 8451
observe the **l** and the commandment. **2Ch 14:4** 8451
a teaching priest and without **l**. **2Ch 15:3** 8451
having the book of the **l** of the LORD **2Ch 17:9** 8451
blood, between **l** and commandment, **2Ch 19:10** 8451
as it is written in the **l** of Moses **2Ch 23:18** 8451
in the **l** in the book of Moses, **2Ch 25:4** 8451
to the **l** of Moses the man of God; **2Ch 30:16** 8451
is written in the **l** of the LORD. **2Ch 31:3** 8451
themselves to the **l** of the LORD. **2Ch 31:4** 8451
of God in **l** and in commandment, **2Ch 31:21** 8451
them according to all the **l**, **2Ch 33:8** 8451
found the book of the **l** of the LORD **2Ch 34:14** 8451
"I have found the book of the **l** in **2Ch 34:15** 8451
the king heard the words of the **l** **2Ch 34:19** 8451
as written in the **l** of the LORD, **2Ch 35:26** 8451
it is written in the **l** of Moses, **Ezr 3:2** 8451
scribe skilled in the **l** of Moses, **Ezr 7:6** 8451
heart to study the **l** of the LORD and **Ezr 7:10** 8451
scribe of the **l** of the God of heaven, **Ezr 7:12** 1882
according to the **l** of your God **Ezr 7:14** 1882
scribe of the **l** of the God of heaven, **Ezr 7:21** 1882
will not observe the **l** of your God **Ezr 7:26** 1882
of your God and the **l** of the king, **Ezr 7:26** 1882
let it be done according to the **l**. **Ezr 10:3** 8451
to bring the book of the **l** of Moses **Ne 8:1** 8451
Ezra the priest brought the **l** before **Ne 8:2** 8451
attentive to the book of the **l**. **Ne 8:3** 8451
explained the **l** to the people **Ne 8:7** 8451
from the book, from the **l** of God, **Ne 8:8** 8451
they heard the words of the **l**. **Ne 8:9** 8451
insight into the words of the **l**. **Ne 8:13** 8451
They found written in the **l** **Ne 8:14** 8451
read from the book of the **l** of God **Ne 8:18** 8451
they read from the book of the **l** **Ne 9:3** 8451
commandments, statutes and **l**, **Ne 9:14** 8451
And cast Your **l** behind their backs **Ne 9:26** 8451
order to turn them back to Your **l**. **Ne 9:29** 8451
and our fathers have not kept Your **l** **Ne 9:34** 8451
of the lands to the **l** of God, **Ne 10:28** 8451
and an oath to walk in God's **l**, **Ne 10:29** 8451
our God, as it is written in the **l**; **Ne 10:34** 8451
flocks as it is written in the **l**, **Ne 10:36** 8451
the portions required by the **l** for **Ne 12:44** 8451
when they heard the **l**, **Ne 13:3** 8451
was *done* according to the **l**, **Es 1:8** 1881
before all who knew **l** and justice **Es 1:13** 1881
"According to **l**, what is to be **Es 1:15** 1881
A copy of the edict to be issued as **l** **Es 3:14** 1881
is not summoned, he has but one **l**, **Es 4:11** 1881
which is not according to the **l**; **Es 4:16** 1881
A copy of the edict to be issued as **l** **Es 8:13** 1881
his delight is in the **l** of the LORD, **Ps 1:2** 8451
in His **l** he meditates day and night. **Ps 1:2** 8451
The **l** of the LORD is perfect, **Ps 19:7** 8451
The **l** of his God is in his heart; **Ps 37:31** 8451
Your **L** is within my heart." **Ps 40:8** 8451
And appointed a **l** in Israel, **Ps 78:5** 8451
God And refused to walk in His **l**; **Ps 78:10** 8451
"If his sons forsake My **l** And **Ps 89:30** 8451
whom You teach out of Your **l**; **Ps 94:12** 8451
Who walk in the **l** of the LORD. **Ps 119:1** 8451
Wonderful things from Your **l**. **Ps 119:18** 8451

me, And graciously grant me Your **l**.	Ps 119:29	8451
that I may observe Your **l** And	Ps 119:34	8451
So I will keep Your **l** continually,	Ps 119:44	8451
I do not turn aside from Your **l**.	Ps 119:51	8451
of the wicked, Who forsake Your **l**.	Ps 119:53	8451
name in the night, And keep Your **l**.	Ps 119:55	8451
But I have not forgotten Your **l**.	Ps 119:61	8451
with fat, *But* I delight in Your **l**.	Ps 119:70	8451
The **l** of Your mouth is better to me	Ps 119:72	8451
may live, For Your **l** is my delight.	Ps 119:77	8451
who are not in accord with Your **l**.	Ps 119:85	8451
If Your **l** had not been my delight,	Ps 119:92	8451
O how I love Your **l**!	Ps 119:97	8451
hand, Yet I do not forget Your **l**.	Ps 119:109	8451
double-minded, But I love Your **l**.	Ps 119:113	8451
act, *For* they have broken Your **l**.	Ps 119:126	8451
Because they do not keep Your **l**.	Ps 119:136	8451
righteousness, And Your **l** is truth.	Ps 119:142	8451
They are far from Your **l**.	Ps 119:150	8451
me, For I do not forget Your **l**.	Ps 119:153	8451
falsehood, *But* I love Your **l**.	Ps 119:163	8451
who love Your **l** have great peace,	Ps 119:165	8451
O LORD, And Your **l** is my delight.	Ps 119:174	8451
Those who forsake the **l** praise the	Pr 28:4	8451
who keep the **l** strive with them.	Pr 28:4	8451
He who keeps the **l** is a discerning	Pr 28:7	8451
his ear from listening to the **l**,	Pr 28:9	8451
But happy is he who keeps the **l**.	Pr 29:18	8451
For the **l** will go forth from Zion And	Is 2:3	8451
the **l** of the LORD of hosts And	Is 5:24	8451
seal the **l** among my disciples.	Is 8:16	8451
To the **l** and to the testimony!	Is 8:20	8451
will wait expectantly for His **l**."	Is 42:4	8451
To make the **l** great and glorious.	Is 42:21	8451
And whose **l** they did not obey?	Is 42:24	8451
For a **l** will go forth from Me, And	Is 51:4	8451
A people in whose heart is My **l**;	Is 51:7	8451
who handle the **l** did not know Me;	Jer 2:8	8451
to My words, And as for My **l**,	Jer 6:19	8451
And the **l** of the LORD is with us'?	Jer 8:8	8451
My **l** which I set before them,	Jer 9:13	8451
forsaken and have not kept My **l**.	Jer 16:11	8451
Surely the **l** is not going to be	Jer 18:18	8451
not listen to Me, to walk in My **l** which	Jer 26:4	8451
"I will put My **l** within them and	Jer 31:33	8451
obey Your voice or walk in Your **l**;	Jer 32:23	8451
nor walked in My **l** or My statutes,	Jer 44:10	8451
of the LORD or walked in His **l**,	Jer 44:23	8451
The **l** is no more.	La 2:9	8451
but the **l** will be lost from the	Ezk 7:26	8451
priests have done violence to My **l**	Ezk 22:26	8451
"This is the **l** of the house:	Ezk 43:12	8451
this is the **l** of the house.	Ezk 43:12	8451
with regard to the **l** of his God."	Da 6:5	1882
the **l** of the Medes and Persians,	Da 6:8	1882
the **l** of the Medes and Persians,	Da 6:12	1882
that it is a **l** of the Medes and	Da 6:15	1882
alterations in times and in **l**;	Da 7:25	1882
all Israel has transgressed Your **l** and	Da 9:11	8451
the **l** of Moses the servant of God,	Da 9:11	8451
it is written in the **l** of Moses,	Da 9:13	8451
have forgotten the **l** of your God,	Hos 4:6	8451
And rebelled against My **l**.	Hos 8:1	8451
him ten thousand *precepts* of My **l**,	Hos 8:12	8451
they rejected the **l** of the LORD	Am 2:4	8451
For from Zion will go forth the **l**,	Mi 4:2	8451
the **l** is ignored And justice is	Hab 1:4	8451
They have done violence to the **l**.	Zph 3:4	8451
flint so that they could not hear the **l**	Zch 7:12	8451
the **l** of Moses My servant,	Mal 4:4	8451
to abolish the **L** or the Prophets;	Mt 5:17	3551
stroke shall pass from the **L**	Mt 5:18	3551
opponent at **l** while you are with him	Mt 5:25	476
this is the **L** and the Prophets.	Mt 7:12	3551
and the **L** prophesied until John.	Mt 11:13	3551
"Or have you not read in the **L**,	Mt 12:5	3551
the great commandment in the **L**?"	Mt 22:36	3551
the whole **L** and the Prophets."	Mt 22:40	3551
the weightier provisions of the **l**:	Mt 23:23	3551
to the **l** of Moses were completed,	Lk 2:22	3551
is written in the **L** of the Lord,	Lk 2:23	3551
was said in the **L** of the Lord,	Lk 2:24	3551
out for Him the custom of the **L**,	Lk 2:27	3551
according to the **L** of the Lord,	Lk 2:39	3551
teachers of the **l** sitting *there,*	Lk 5:17	3547
"What is written in the **L**?	Lk 10:26	3551
"The **L** and the Prophets *were*	Lk 16:16	3551
one stroke of a letter of the **L** to fail	Lk 16:17	3551
written about Me in the **L** of Moses	Lk 24:44	3551
For the **L** was given through Moses;	Jn 1:17	3551
found Him of whom Moses in the **L**	Jn 1:45	3551
"Did not Moses give you the **L**,	Jn 7:19	3551
yet none of you carries out the **L**?	Jn 7:19	3551
the **L** of Moses will not be broken,	Jn 7:23	3551
does not know the **L** is accursed."	Jn 7:49	3551
"Our **L** does not judge a man unless	Jn 7:51	3551
"Now in the **L** Moses commanded us	Jn 8:5	3551
in your **l** it has been written that	Jn 8:17	3551
"Has it not been written in your **L**,	Jn 10:34	3551
"We have heard out of the **L** that	Jn 12:34	3551
that is written in their **L**,	Jn 15:25	3551
judge Him according to your **l**."	Jn 18:31	3551
"We have a **l**, and by that law He	Jn 19:7	3551
and by that **l** He ought to die	Jn 19:7	3551
Gamaliel, a teacher of the **L**,	Ac 5:34	3547
this holy place and the **L**;	Ac 6:13	3551
the **l** as ordained by angels,	Ac 7:53	3551
After the reading of the **L** and	Ac 13:15	3551
be freed through the **L** of Moses.	Ac 13:39	3551

them to observe the **L** of Moses."	Ac 15:5	3551
worship God contrary to the **l**."	Ac 18:13	3551
words and names and your own **l**,	Ac 18:15	3551
they are all zealous for the **L**;	Ac 21:20	3551
also walk orderly, keeping the **L**.	Ac 21:24	3551
against our people and the **L**	Ac 21:28	3551
according to the **l** of our fathers,	Ac 22:3	3551
devout by the standard of the **L**,	Ac 22:12	3551
sit to try me according to the **L**,	Ac 23:3	3551
in violation of the **L** order me to be	Ac 23:3	3891
over questions about their **L**,	Ac 23:29	3551
judge him according to our own **L**.	Ac 24:6	3551
that is in accordance with the **L** and	Ac 24:14	3551
against the **L** of the Jews or against	Ac 25:8	3551
from both the **L** of Moses and from	Ac 28:23	3551
all who have sinned without the **L**	Ro 2:12	460
will also perish without the **L**,	Ro 2:12	460
all who have sinned under the **L**	Ro 2:12	3551
the Law will be judged by the **L**;	Ro 2:12	3551
it is not the hearers of the **L**	Ro 2:13	3551
doers of the **L** will be justified.	Ro 2:13	3551
Gentiles who do not have the **L**	Ro 2:14	3551
do instinctively the things of the **L**,	Ro 2:14	3551
the Law, these, not having the **L**,	Ro 2:14	3551
the Law, are a **l** to themselves,	Ro 2:14	3551
show the work of the **L** written in	Ro 2:15	3551
"Jew" and rely upon the **L**	Ro 2:17	3551
being instructed out of the **L**,	Ro 2:18	3551
having in the **L** the embodiment of	Ro 2:20	3551
You who boast in the **L**,	Ro 2:23	3551
Law, through your breaking the **L**,	Ro 2:23	3551
of value if you practice the **L**;	Ro 2:25	3551
you are a transgressor of the **L**,	Ro 2:25	3551
keeps the requirements of the **L**,	Ro 2:26	3551
uncircumcised, if he keeps the **L**,	Ro 2:27	3551
though having the letter *of the* **L**	Ro 2:27	
are a transgressor of the **L**?	Ro 2:27	3551
we know that whatever the **L** says,	Ro 3:19	3551
to those who are under the **L**,	Ro 3:19	3551
because by the works of the **L** no	Ro 3:20	3551
through the **L** *comes* the knowledge	Ro 3:20	3551
But now apart from the **L** *the*	Ro 3:21	3551
by the **L** and the Prophets,	Ro 3:21	3551
By what kind of **l**?	Ro 3:27	3551
No, but by a **l** of faith.	Ro 3:27	3551
faith apart from works of the **L**.	Ro 3:28	3551
then nullify the **L** through faith?	Ro 3:31	3551
the contrary, we establish the **L**.	Ro 3:31	3551
the world was not through the **L**,	Ro 4:13	3551
those who are of the **L** are heirs,	Ro 4:14	3551
for the **L** brings about wrath, but	Ro 4:15	3551
wrath, but where there is no **l**,	Ro 4:15	3551
only to those who are of the **L**,	Ro 4:16	3551
until the **L** sin was in the world,	Ro 5:13	3551
is not imputed when there is no **l**.	Ro 5:13	3551
The **L** came in so that the transgression	Ro 5:20	3551
over you, for you are not under **l** but	Ro 6:14	3551
are not under **l** but under grace?	Ro 6:15	3551
speaking to those who know the **l**),	Ro 7:1	3551
that the **l** has jurisdiction over a	Ro 7:1	3551
the married woman is bound by **l** to	Ro 7:2	3551
she is released from the **l** concerning	Ro 7:2	3551
dies, she is free from the **l**,	Ro 7:3	3551
you also were made to die to the **L**	Ro 7:4	3551
which were *aroused* by the **L**,	Ro 7:5	3551
we have been released from the **L**,	Ro 7:6	3551
Is the **L** sin? May it never be!	Ro 7:7	3551
to know sin except through the **L**;	Ro 7:7	3551
coveting if the **L** had not said,	Ro 7:7	3551
for apart from the **L** sin *is* dead.	Ro 7:8	3551
I was once alive apart from the **L**;	Ro 7:9	3551
So then, the **L** is holy, and the	Ro 7:12	3551
we know that the **L** is spiritual,	Ro 7:14	3551
want *to do,* I agree with the **L**,	Ro 7:16	3551
confessing that the **L** is good.	Ro 7:16	3551
the **l** of God in the inner man,	Ro 7:22	3551
l in the members of my body,	Ro 7:23	3551
war against the **l** of my mind and	Ro 7:23	3551
prisoner of the **l** of sin which	Ro 7:23	3551
my mind am serving the **l** of God,	Ro 7:25	3551
other, with my flesh the **l** of sin.	Ro 7:25	3551
For the **l** of the Spirit of life in	Ro 8:2	3551
from the **l** of sin and of death.	Ro 8:2	3551
For what the **L** could not do, weak	Ro 8:3	3551
the requirement of the **L** might be	Ro 8:4	3551
subject itself to the **l** of God,	Ro 8:7	3551
covenants and the giving of the **L**	Ro 9:4	3548
pursuing a **l** of righteousness,	Ro 9:31	3551
did not arrive at *that* **l**.	Ro 9:31	3551
For Christ is the end of the **l** for	Ro 10:4	3551
the righteousness which is based on **l**	Ro 10:5	3551
his neighbor has fulfilled *the* **l**.	Ro 13:8	3551
is the fulfillment of *the* **l**.	Ro 13:10	3551
to go to **l** before the unrighteous and	1Co 6:1	2919
constitute the smallest **l** courts?	1Co 6:2	2922
So if you have **l** courts dealing	1Co 6:4	2922
brother goes to **l** with brother,	1Co 6:6	2919
not the **L** also say these things?	1Co 9:8	3551
it is written in the **L** of Moses,	1Co 9:9	3551
to those who are under the **L**,	1Co 9:20	3551
under the Law, as under the **L** though	1Co 9:20	3551
not being myself under the **L**,	1Co 9:20	3551
win those who are under the **L**;	1Co 9:20	3551
to those who are without **l**,	1Co 9:21	459
who are without law, as without **l**,	1Co 9:21	459
not being without the **l** of God	1Co 9:21	459
of God but under the **l** of Christ,	1Co 9:21	1772
might win those who are without **l**.	1Co 9:21	459
In the **L** it is written,	1Co 14:21	3551

just as the **L** also says.	1Co 14:34	3551
and the power of sin is the **l**;	1Co 15:56	3551
is not justified by the works of the **L**	Ga 2:16	3551
and not by the works of the **L**;	Ga 2:16	3551
by the works of the **L** no flesh	Ga 2:16	3551
through the **L** I died to the Law,	Ga 2:19	3551
through the Law I died to the **L**,	Ga 2:19	3551
righteousness *comes* through the **L**,	Ga 2:21	3551
the Spirit by the works of the **L**,	Ga 3:2	3551
you, do it by the works of the **L**,	Ga 3:5	3551
as many as are of the works of the **L**	Ga 3:10	3551
WRITTEN IN THE BOOK OF THE **L**,	Ga 3:10	3551
no one is justified by the **L** before	Ga 3:11	3551
However, the **L** is not of faith;	Ga 3:12	3551
us from the curse of the **L**,	Ga 3:13	3551
the **L**, which came four hundred and	Ga 3:17	3551
if the inheritance is based on **l**,	Ga 3:18	3551
Why the **L** then? It was added	Ga 3:19	3551
Is the **L** then contrary to the	Ga 3:21	3551
For if a **l** had been given which	Ga 3:21	3551
would indeed have been based on **l**.	Ga 3:21	3551
were kept in custody under the **l**,	Ga 3:23	3551
the **L** has become our tutor *to lead us*	Ga 3:24	3551
born of a woman, born under the **L**,	Ga 4:4	3551
redeem those who were under the **L**,	Ga 4:5	3551
me, you who want to be under **l**,	Ga 4:21	3551
law, do you not listen to the **l**?	Ga 4:21	3551
obligation to keep the whole **L**.	Ga 5:3	3551
are seeking to be justified by **l**;	Ga 5:4	3551
whole **L** is fulfilled in one word,	Ga 5:14	3551
Spirit, you are not under the **L**.	Ga 5:18	3551
against such things there is no **l**.	Ga 5:23	3551
and thereby fulfill the **l** of Christ.	Ga 6:2	3551
do not even keep the **L** themselves,	Ga 6:13	3551
which is the **L** of commandments	Eph 2:15	3551
as to the **L**, a Pharisee;	Php 3:5	3551
righteousness which is in the **L**,	Php 3:6	3551
of my own derived from *the* **L**,	Php 3:9	3551
wanting to be teachers of the **L**,	1Tm 1:7	3547
But we know that the **L** is good,	1Tm 1:8	3551
realizing the fact that **l** is not	1Tm 1:9	3551
strife and disputes about the **L**,	Ti 3:9	3544
commandment in the **L** to collect	Heb 7:5	3551
of it the people received the **L**),	Heb 7:11	3549
takes place a change of **l** also.	Heb 7:12	3551
basis of a **l** of physical requirement,	Heb 7:16	3551
(for the **L** made nothing perfect),	Heb 7:19	3551
For the **L** appoints men as high	Heb 7:28	3551
the oath, which came after the **L**,	Heb 7:28	3551
the gifts according to the **L**;	Heb 8:4	3551
all the people according to the **L**,	Heb 9:19	3551
And according to the **L**,	Heb 9:22	3551
For the **L**, since it has *only* a	Heb 10:1	3551
are offered according to the **L**),	Heb 10:8	3551
who has set aside the **L** of Moses	Heb 10:28	3551
looks intently at the perfect **l**,	Jas 1:25	3551
the **l** of liberty, and abides by	Jas 1:25	
you are fulfilling the royal **l** according	Jas 2:8	3551
convicted by the **l** as transgressors.	Jas 2:9	3551
whoever keeps the whole **l** and yet	Jas 2:10	3551
become a transgressor of the **l**.	Jas 2:11	3551
to be judged by *the* **l** of liberty.	Jas 2:12	3551
his brother, speaks against the **l** and	Jas 4:11	3551
against the law and judges the **l**;	Jas 4:11	3551
but if you judge the **l**,	Jas 4:11	3551
law, you are not a doer of the **l** but	Jas 4:11	3551

LAWFUL

is not **l** to do on a Sabbath."	Mt 12:2	1832
which was not **l** for him to eat nor	Mt 12:4	1832
"Is it **l** to heal on the Sabbath?"	Mt 12:10	1832
is **l** to do good on the Sabbath."	Mt 12:12	1832
"It is not **l** for you to have her."	Mt 14:4	1832
"Is it **l** *for a man* to divorce his	Mt 19:3	1832
'Is it not **l** for me to do what I	Mt 20:15	1832
it **l** to give a poll-tax to Caesar,	Mt 22:17	1832
"It is not **l** to put them into the	Mt 27:6	1832
what is not **l** on the Sabbath?"	Mk 2:24	1832
which is not **l** for *anyone* to eat	Mk 2:26	1832
"Is it **l** to do	Mk 3:4	1832
"It is not **l** for you to have your	Mk 6:18	1832
was **l** for a man to divorce a wife.	Mk 10:2	1832
it **l** to pay a poll-tax to Caesar,	Mk 12:14	1832
do what is not **l** on the Sabbath?"	Lk 6:2	1832
bread which is not **l** for any to eat	Lk 6:4	1832
is it **l** to do good	Lk 6:9	1832
"Is it **l** to heal on the Sabbath,	Lk 14:3	1832
l for us to pay taxes to Caesar,	Lk 20:22	1832
proclaiming customs which it is not **l**	Ac 16:21	1832
be settled in the **l** assembly.	Ac 19:39	1772
"Is it **l** for you to scourge a man	Ac 22:25	1832
All things are **l** for me, but not	1Co 6:12	1832
All things are **l** for me, but I	1Co 6:12	1832
All things are **l**, but not all	1Co 10:23	1832
All things are **l**, but not all	1Co 10:23	1832

LAWFULLY

the Law is good, if one uses it **l**,	1Tm 1:8	3545

LAWGIVER

is our judge, The LORD is our **l**,	Is 33:22	2710
There is *only* one **L** and Judge,	Jas 4:12	3550

LAWLESS

WHOSE **L** DEEDS HAVE BEEN FORGIVEN,	Ro 4:7	458
Then that **l** one will be revealed	2Th 2:8	459
those who are **l** and rebellious,	1Tm 1:9	459
to redeem us from every **l** deed	Ti 2:14	458
L DEEDS I WILL REMEMBER NO MORE."	Heb 10:17	458
day after day by *their* **l** deeds),	2Pe 2:8	459

LAWLESSNESS

FROM ME, YOU WHO PRACTICE **L**.'	Mt 7:23	458

blocks, and those who commit l, Mt 13:41 458
you are full of hypocrisy and l. Mt 23:28 458
"Because l is increased, most Mt 24:12 458
as slaves to impurity and to l, Ro 6:19 458
resulting in *further* l, Ro 6:19 458
have righteousness and l, 2Co 6:14 458
and the man of l is revealed, 2Th 2:3 458
mystery of l is already at work; 2Th 2:7 458
LOVED RIGHTEOUSNESS AND HATED L; Heb 1:9 458
practices sin also practices l; 1Jn 3:4 458
practices lawlessness; and sin is l. 1Jn 3:4 458

LAWS
My statutes and My l." Gn 26:5 8451
the statutes of God and His l." Ex 18:16 8451
teach them the statutes and the l, Ex 18:20 8451
and l which the LORD established Lv 26:46 8451
those who know the l of your God; Ezr 7:25 1882
them just ordinances and true l, Ne 9:13 8451
let it be written in the l of Persia Es 1:19 1881
their l are different from *those* Es 3:8 1881
they do not observe the king's l, Es 3:8 1881
His statutes And observe His l, Ps 105:45 8451
for they transgressed l, Is 24:5 8451
all its statutes, and all its l. Ezk 43:11 8451
the LORD and concerning all its l; Ezk 44:5 8451
They shall also keep My l and My Ezk 44:24 8451
I WILL PUT MY L INTO THEIR MINDS, Heb 8:10 3551
I WILL PUT MY L UPON THEIR HEART, Heb 10:16 3551

LAWSUIT
between one kind of l or another, Dt 17:8 1779
To defraud a man in his l La 3:36 7379

LAWSUITS
that you have l with one another. 1Co 6:7 2917

LAWYER
One of them, a l, Mt 22:35 3544
a l stood up and put Him Lk 10:25 3544
Diligently help Zenas the l and Ti 3:13 3544

LAWYERS
But the Pharisees and the l rejected Lk 7:30 3544
One of the l said to Him in reply, Lk 11:45 3544
"Woe to you l as well! Lk 11:46 3544
"Woe to you l! For you have taken Lk 11:52 3544
and spoke to the l and Pharisees, Lk 14:3 3544

LAY
Before they l down, the men of the Gn 19:4 7901
went in and l with her father; Gn 19:33 7901
when she l down or when she arose. Gn 19:33 7901
I l last night with my father; Gn 19:34 7901
the younger arose and l with him; Gn 19:35 7901
when she l down or when she arose. Gn 19:35 7901
head, and l down in that place. Gn 28:11 7901
So he l with her that night. Gn 30:16 7901
took her and l with her by force. Gn 34:2 7901
that Reuben went and l with Bilhah Gn 35:22 7901
but do not l hands on him Gn 37:22 7971
and not l our hands on him, Gn 37:27 1961
then I will l My hand on Egypt and Ex 7:4 5414
and Aaron and his sons shall l Ex 29:10 5564
and Aaron and his sons shall l Ex 29:15 5564
and Aaron and his sons shall l Ex 29:19 5564
'He shall l his hand on the Lv 1:4 5564
put oil on it and l incense on it; Lv 2:15 7760
'He shall l his hand on the Lv 3:2 5564
and he shall l his hand on the Lv 3:8 5564
and he shall l his hand on its Lv 3:13 5564
and he shall l his hand on the Lv 4:4 5564
l their hands on the head of the bull Lv 4:15 5564
'He shall l his hand on the Lv 4:24 5564
'He shall l his hand on the Lv 4:29 5564
'He shall l his hand on the Lv 4:33 5564
l out the burnt offering on it, Lv 6:12 6186a
"Then Aaron shall l both of his Lv 16:21 5564
and he shall l them on the head of Lv 16:21 5414
him l their hands on his head; Lv 24:14 5564
will l waste your cities as well and Lv 26:31 5414
and they shall l a covering of Nu 4:6 5414
l their hands on the Levites. Nu 8:10 5564
"Now the Levites shall l their Nu 8:12 5564
and l incense upon them in the Nu 16:7 7760
the altar, and l incense *on it;* Nu 16:46 7760
the LORD, she l down under Balaam; Nu 22:27 7257
Spirit, and l your hand on him; Nu 27:18 5564
will l them on all who hate you. Dt 7:15 5414
your God will l the dread of you Dt 11:25 5414
die, the man who l with the woman, Dt 22:22 7901
then the man who l with her shall Dt 22:29 7901
Now before they l down, she came Jos 2:8 7901
and l them down in the lodging Jos 4:3 5117
he shall l its foundation, Jos 6:26 3245
the territory of their lot l between Jos 18:11 3318
her feet he bowed, he fell, he l; Jg 5:27 7901
offering and l it before You." Jg 6:18 5117
bread and l them on this rock, Jg 6:20 5117
down so that the tent l flat." Jg 7:13 5307
arose by night and l in wait against Jg 9:34 693
and l in wait in the field; Jg 9:43 693
l in wait for him all night at the Jg 16:2 693
Now Samson l until midnight, and Jg 16:3 7901
and uncovered his feet and l down. Ru 3:7 7901
So she l at his feet until morning Ru 3:14 7901
and how they l with the women who 1Sa 2:22 7901
So he went and l down. 1Sa 3:5 7901
went and l down in his place. 1Sa 3:9 7901
So Samuel l down until morning. 1Sa 3:15 7901
the slain Philistines l along the way 1Sa 17:52 5307
l down naked all that day and all 1Sa 19:24 5307
David saw the place where Saul l, 1Sa 26:5 7901
Saul l sleeping inside the circle 1Sa 26:7 7901
she came to him, he l with her; 2Sa 11:4 7901
and l all night on the ground. 2Sa 12:16 7901
and went in to her and l with her; 2Sa 12:24 7901
l down and pretended to be ill; 2Sa 13:6 7901
he violated her and l with her. 2Sa 13:14 7901
his clothes and l on the ground; 2Sa 13:31 7901
But Amasa l wallowing in *his* blood 2Sa 20:12 1556
in the night, because she l on it. 1Ki 3:19 7901
to l the foundation of the house 1Ki 5:17 3245
l my bones beside his bones. 1Ki 13:31 5117
other ox and l it on the wood, 1Ki 18:23 7760
He l down and slept under a 1Ki 19:5 7901
he ate and drank and l down again. 1Ki 19:6 7901
And he l down on his bed and 1Ki 21:4 7901
and he l in sackcloth and went 1Ki 21:27 7901
and l my staff on the lad's face." 2Ki 4:29 7760
And he went up and l on the child, 2Ki 4:34 7901
of your brethren the l people, 2Ch 35:5 1121
contributed to the l people, 2Ch 35:7 1121
fathers' households of the l people 2Ch 35:12 1121
them speedily to all the l people. 2Ch 35:13 1121
to l hands on King Ahasuerus. Es 2:21 7971
to l hands on Mordecai alone, Es 3:6 7971
and many l on sackcloth and ashes. Es 4:3 3331
to l hands on King Ahasuerus. Es 6:2 7971
to l hands on those who sought their Es 9:2 7971
not l their hands on the plunder. Es 9:10 7971
not l their hands on the plunder. Es 9:15 7971
not l their hands on the plunder. Es 9:16 7971
Who may l his hand upon us both. Jb 9:33 7896
"L down, now, a pledge for me Jb 17:3 7760
the godless in heart l up anger; Jb 36:13 7760
I l my hand on my mouth. Jb 40:4 7760
"L your hand on him; Jb 41:8 7760
I l down and slept; Ps 3:5 7901
And l my glory in the dust Ps 7:5 7931
You l me in the dust of death. Ps 22:15 8239
who seek my life l snares *for me;* Ps 38:12 5367
where she may l her young, Ps 84:3 7896
Your right hand will l hold of me. Ps 139:10 270
"I will l it waste; Is 5:6 7896
and their corpses l like refuse in Is 5:25 1961
Go up, Elam, l siege, Media; Is 21:2 6696a
But *the Lord* will l low his pride Is 25:11 8213
walls He will bring down, L low Is 25:12 8213
Which the LORD will l on him, Is 30:32 5117
make its nest and l *eggs* there, Is 34:15 4422
l waste the mountains and hills And Is 42:15 2717b
foundations I will l in sapphires. Is 54:11 3245
"Then l siege against it, build a Ezk 4:2 5414
and l the iniquity of the house of Ezk 4:4 7760
"I will also l the dead bodies Ezk 6:5 5414
in order to l hold of the hearts Ezk 14:5 8610
She l down among young lions, She Ezk 19:2 7257
I will l you *there* and melt you. Ezk 22:20 5117
And I will l it waste; Ezk 25:13 5414
"I will l My vengeance on Ezk 25:14 5414
I l My vengeance on them. Ezk 25:17 5414
l your flesh on the mountains And Ezk 32:5 5414
So they l down uncircumcised with Ezk 32:30 7901
"I will l waste your cities And Ezk 35:4 7760
on which they l the instruments Ezk 40:42 5117
they shall l the most holy things, Ezk 42:13 5117
and l them in the holy chambers; Ezk 44:19 5117
and *these* fantasies *as I* l on Da 4:5
the visions in my mind *as I* l Da 4:10
in the visions in my mind *as I* l Da 4:13
and visions in his mind *as he* l Da 7:1
And will l bare her foundations. Mi 1:6 1540
To l him open from thigh to neck Hab 3:13 6168
Man has nowhere to l His head." Mt 8:20 2827
but come and l Your hand on her, Mt 9:18 2007
l His hands on them and pray; Mt 19:13 2007
and l them on men's shoulders, Mt 23:4 2007
come and l Your hands on her, Mk 5:23 2007
Him to l His hand on him. Mk 7:32 2007
they will l hands on the sick, and Mk 16:18 2007
the baby as He l in the manger. Lk 2:16 2749
Man has nowhere to l His head." Lk 9:58 2827
take up what you did not l down and Lk 19:21 5087
taking up what I did not l down and Lk 19:22 5087
chief priests tried to l hands on Him Lk 20:19 1911
they will l their hands on you and Lk 21:12 1911
temple, you did not l hands on Me; Lk 22:53 1614
In these l a multitude of those Jn 5:3 2621
I l down My life for the sheep. Jn 10:15 5087
because I l down My life so that I Jn 10:17 5087
I l it down on My own initiative. Jn 10:18 5087
I have authority to l it down, Jn 10:18 5087
I will l down my life for You." Jn 13:37 5087
"Will you l down your life for Me? Jn 13:38 5087
l down his life for his friends. Jn 15:13 5087
and l them at the apostles' feet, Ac 4:35 5087
everyone on whom I l my hands Ac 8:19 2007
come in and l his hands on him, Ac 9:12 2007
to l upon you no greater burden than Ac 15:28 2007
to l out anchors from the bow, Ac 27:30 1614
I L IN ZION A STONE OF STUMBLING Ro 9:33 5087
Therefore let us l aside the deeds Ro 13:12 659
For no man can l a foundation 1Co 3:11 5087
of life, you l aside the old self, Eph 4:22 659
I press on so that I may l hold Php 3:12 2638
Do not l hands upon anyone *too* 1Tm 5:22 2007
us also l aside every encumbrance and Heb 12:1 659
"BEHOLD, I L IN ZION A CHOICE STONE, 1Pe 2:6 5087
and we ought to l down our lives 1Jn 3:16 5087

LAYER
was a l of dew around the camp. Ex 16:13 7902
When the l of dew evaporated, Ex 16:14 7902
huge stones and one l of timbers. Ezr 6:4 5073

LAYERS
with three l of huge stones and Ezr 6:4 5073
about the l of the thick clouds, Jb 37:16 4657

LAYING
Why are you then l a snare for my 1Sa 28:9 5367
Israel were l siege to Gibbethon. 1Ki 15:27 6696a
They talk of l snares secretly; Ps 64:5 2934
"Behold, I am l in Zion a stone, Is 28:16 3245
I am l stumbling blocks before Jer 6:21 5414
without l there their garments Ezk 42:14 5117
After l His hands on them, He Mt 19:15 2007
l the sick in the market places, Mk 6:56 5087
eyes and l His hands on him, Mk 8:23 2007
them, l His hands on them. Mk 10:16 5087
and l His hands on each one of Lk 4:40 2007
they *began* l their hands on them, Ac 8:17 2007
the l on of the apostles' hands, Ac 8:18 1936
and after l his hands on him said, Ac 9:17 2007
Therefore, l aside falsehood, Eph 4:25 659
l on of hands by the presbytery. 1Tm 4:14 1936
you through the l on of my hands. 2Tm 1:6 1936
not l again a foundation of Heb 6:1 2598
about washings and l on of hands, Heb 6:2 1936
the l aside of my *earthly* dwelling is 2Pe 1:14 595

LAYMAN
but a l shall not eat *them,* Ex 29:33 2114a
or whoever puts any of it on a l shall Ex 30:33 2114a
'No l, however, is to eat the holy Lv 22:10 2114a
daughter is married to a l, Lv 22:12 2114a
but no l shall eat of it. Lv 22:13 2114a
But the l who comes near shall be Nu 1:51 2114a
but the l who comes near shall be Nu 3:10 2114a
but the l coming near was to be Nu 3:38 2114a
no l who is not of the descendants of Nu 16:40 2114a

LAYS
He l up the deeps in storehouses. Ps 33:7 5414
destruction that l waste at noon. Ps 91:6 7703
He l the beams of His upper Ps 104:3 7136b
But he l up deceit in his heart. Pr 26:24 7896
When a man l hold of his brother Is 3:6 8610
the LORD l the earth waste, Is 24:1 1238b
He l it low, He lays it low to the Is 26:5 8213
it low, He l it low to the ground, Is 26:5 8213
Because no man l it to heart. Jer 12:11 7760
l the foundation of the earth, Zch 12:1 3245
it, he l it on his shoulders, Lk 15:5 2007
l down His life for the sheep. Jn 10:11 5087

LAZARUS
man named L was laid at his gate, Lk 16:20 2976
far away and L in his bosom. Lk 16:23 2976
have mercy on me, and send L so Lk 16:24 2976
things, and likewise L bad things; Lk 16:25 2976
man was sick, L of Bethany, Jn 11:1 2976
hair, whose brother L was sick. Jn 11:2 2976
Martha and her sister and L. Jn 11:5 2976
"Our friend L has fallen asleep; Jn 11:11 2976
said to them plainly, "L is dead, Jn 11:14 2976
"L, come forth." Jn 11:43 2976
came to Bethany where L was, Jn 12:1 2976
but L was one of those reclining Jn 12:2 2976
but that they might also see L, Jn 12:9 2976
put L to death also; Jn 12:10 2976
when He called L out of the tomb and Jn 12:17 2976

LAZINESS
L casts into a deep sleep, And an Pr 19:15 6103

LAZULI
Their polishing *was like* lapis l. La 4:7 5601
like lapis l in appearance; Ezk 1:26 68, 5601
The lapis l, the turquoise and Ezk 28:13 5601

LAZY
Because they are l, Ex 5:8 7503
"You are l, *very* lazy; Ex 5:17 7503
"You are lazy, *very* l; Ex 5:17 7503
the l one to those who send him. Pr 10:26 6102
A l man does not roast his prey, Pr 12:27 7423b
The way of the l is as a hedge of Pr 15:19 6102
'You wicked, l slave, you knew Mt 25:26 3636
liars, evil beasts, l gluttons." Ti 1:12 692

LEAD
God did not l them by the way Ex 13:17 5148
cloud by day to l them on the way, Ex 13:21 5148
sank like l in the mighty waters. Ex 15:10 5777
l the people where I told you. Ex 32:34 5148
with us, do not l us up from here. Ex 33:15 5927
will l them out and bring them in, Nu 27:17 3318
the iron, the tin and the l, Nu 31:22 5777
they may l *them* away and depart." 1Sa 30:22 5090a
to l with lyres tuned to the 1Ch 15:21 5329
l him on horseback through the city Es 6:9 7392
"That with an iron stylus and l Jb 19:24 5777
"Can you l forth a constellation Jb 38:32 3318
l me in Your righteousness because Ps 5:8 5148
L me in Your truth and teach me, Ps 25:5 1869
O LORD, And l me in a level path Ps 27:11 5148
sake You will l me and guide me. Ps 31:3 5148
l them in procession to the house of Ps 42:4 1718
and Your truth, let them l me; Ps 43:3 5148
Who will l me to Edom? Ps 60:9 5148
L me to the rock that is higher Ps 61:2 5148
who l Joseph like a flock; Ps 80:1 5090a
Who will l me to Edom? Ps 108:10 5148
The LORD will l them away with the Ps 125:5 1980
Even there Your hand will l me, Ps 139:10 5148
And l me in the everlasting way. Ps 139:24 5148
Let Your good Spirit l me on level Ps 143:10 5148
down to death And her tracks l to Pr 2:18

The plans of the diligent **l** Pr 21:5
"I would **l** you *and* bring you Into SS 8:2 5090a
Those who guide you **l** *you* astray And Is 3:12 8582
And a little boy will **l** them. Is 11:6 5090a
so the king of Assyria will **l** away Is 20:4 5090a
He will gently **l** the nursing *ewes.* Is 40:11 5095
"I will **l** the blind by a way Is 42:16 1980
compassion on them will **l** them And Is 49:10 5090a
I will **l** him and restore comfort Is 57:18 5148
The **l** is consumed by the fire; Jer 6:29 5777
And by supplication I will **l** them; Jer 31:9 2986
tin and iron and **l** in the furnace; Ezk 22:18 5777
silver and bronze and iron and **l** Ezk 22:20 5777
with silver, iron, tin and **l** Ezk 27:12 5777
flock and I will **l** them to rest," Ezk 34:15 7257
who **l** the many to righteousness, Da 12:3 6663
prophets who **l** my people astray; Mi 3:5 8582
behold, a **l** cover was lifted up); Zch 5:7 5777
cast the **l** weight on its opening. Zch 5:8 5777
'And do not **l** us into temptation, Mt 6:13 *1533*
to **l** astray, if possible, the elect. Mk 13:22 *635*
Him and **l** Him away under guard." Mk 14:44 *520*
And **l** us not into temptation.'" Lk 11:4 *1533*
and **l** him away to water *him?* Lk 13:15 *520*
"It will **l** to an opportunity for Lk 21:13 *576*
those who would **l** him by the hand. Ac 13:11 *5497*
"**L** this young man to the Ac 23:17 *520*
asked me to **l** this young man to you Ac 23:18 *71*
the Law has become our tutor *to* **l** Ga 3:24
your ambition to **l** a quiet life and 1Th 4:11 *2270*
so that we may **l** a tranquil 1Tm 2:2 *1236*
it will **l** to further ungodliness, 2Tm 2:16 *4298*
L THEM OUT OF THE LAND OF EGYPT; Heb 8:9 *1806*

LEADER
'When a **l** sins and unintentionally Lv 4:22 5387a
and the **l** of the sons of Judah: Nu 2:3 5387a
and the **l** of the sons of Issachar: Nu 2:5 5387a
and the **l** of the sons of Zebulun: Nu 2:7 5387a
and the **l** of the sons of Reuben: Nu 2:10 5387a
and the **l** of the sons of Simeon: Nu 2:12 5387a
Gad, and the **l** of the sons of Gad: Nu 2:14 5387a
and the **l** of the sons of Ephraim Nu 2:18 5387a
and the **l** of the sons of Manasseh: Nu 2:20 5387a
and the **l** of the sons of Benjamin: Nu 2:22 5387a
and the **l** of the sons of Dan: Nu 2:25 5387a
and the **l** of the sons of Asher: Nu 2:27 5387a
and the **l** of the sons of Naphtali: Nu 2:29 5387a
and the **l** of the fathers' households Nu 3:24 5387a
and the **l** of the fathers' households Nu 3:30 5387a
The **l** of the fathers' households Nu 3:35 5387a
their offering, one **l** each day, Nu 7:11 5387a
the son of Zuar, **l** of Issachar, Nu 7:18 5387a
Helon, **l** of the sons of Zebulun; Nu 7:24 5387a
Shedeur, **l** of the sons of Reuben; Nu 7:30 5387a
l of the children of Simeon; Nu 7:36 5387a
of Deuel, **l** of the sons of Gad; Nu 7:42 5387a
Ammihud, **l** of the sons of Ephraim; Nu 7:48 5387a
l of the sons of Manasseh; Nu 7:54 5387a
l of the sons of Benjamin; Nu 7:60 5387a
Ammishaddai, **l** of the sons of Dan; Nu 7:66 5387a
of Ochran, **l** of the sons of Asher; Nu 7:72 5387a
Enan, **l** of the sons of Naphtali; Nu 7:78 5387a
every one a **l** among them." Nu 13:2 5387a
appoint a **l** and return to Egypt." Nu 14:4 7218
for each **l** according to their Nu 17:6 5387a
a **l** of a father's household among Nu 25:14 5387a
the daughter of the **l** of Midian, Nu 25:18 5387a
You shall take one **l** of every tribe Nu 34:18 5387a
the tribe of the sons of Dan a **l**, Nu 34:22 5387a
tribe of the sons of Manasseh a **l**, Nu 34:23 5387a
tribe of the sons of Ephraim a **l**, Nu 34:24 5387a
tribe of the sons of Zebulun a **l**, Nu 34:25 5387a
tribe of the sons of Issachar a **l**, Nu 34:26 5387a
tribe of the sons of Asher a **l**, Nu 34:27 5387a
tribe of the sons of Naphtali a **l**, Nu 34:28 5387a
and became **l** of a marauding band, 1Ki 11:24 8269
made you **l** over My people Israel, 1Ki 14:7 5057
made you **l** over My people Israel, 1Ki 16:2 5057
to Hezekiah the **l** of My people, 2Ki 20:5 5057
Nahshon, **l** of the sons of Judah; 1Ch 2:10 5387a
brothers, and from him *came* the **l**, 1Ch 5:2 5057
he was **l** of the Reubenites. 1Ch 5:6 5387a
was the **l** of *the house of* Aaron, 1Ch 12:27 5057
the hundreds, even with every **l**. 1Ch 13:1 5057
and Chenaniah the **l** of the singing 1Ch 15:27 8269
to be **l** over My people Israel. 1Ch 17:7 5057
For He has chosen Judah to be a **l**; 1Ch 28:4 5057
and to every **l** in all Israel, 2Ch 1:2 5387a
man for a **l** over My people Israel; 2Ch 6:5 5057
as head and **l** among his brothers, 2Ch 11:22 5057
became stubborn and appointed a **l** Ne 9:17 7218
Ahitub, the **l** of the house of God, Ne 11:11 5057
who was the **l** in beginning the Ne 11:17 7218
sang, with Jezrahiah *their* **l**, Ne 12:42 6496
A **l** who is a great oppressor lacks Pr 28:16 5057
A **l** and commander for the peoples. Is 55:4 5057
'Their **l** shall be one of them, Jer 30:21 117
"Son of man, say to the **l** of Tyre, Ezk 28:2 5057
will appoint for themselves one **l**, Hos 1:11 7218
for One is your **L**, *that is,* Christ. Mt 23:10 *2519*
and the **l** like the servant. Lk 22:26 *2233*
Crispus, the **l** of the synagogue, Ac 18:8 *752*
Sosthenes, the **l** of the synagogue, Ac 18:17 *752*

LEADERS
The **l** of Moab, trembling grips Ex 15:15 352c
When all the **l** of the congregation Ex 16:22 5387a
over them *as* **l** of thousands, Ex 18:21 8269
over the people, **l** of thousands, Ex 18:25 8269
the **l** of their fathers' tribes; Nu 1:16 5387a
numbered, with the **l** of Israel, Nu 1:44 5387a
was the chief of the **l** of Levi, Nu 3:32 5387a
Aaron and the **l** of the congregation Nu 4:34 5387a
and the **l** of Israel numbered, Nu 4:46 5387a
Then the **l** of Israel, the heads of Nu 7:2 5387a
(they were the **l** of the tribes; Nu 7:2 5387a
a cart for *every* two of the **l** and an Nu 7:3 5387a
The **l** offered the dedication Nu 7:10 5387a
so the **l** offered their offering Nu 7:10 5387a
for the altar from the **l** of Israel Nu 7:84 5387a
if *only* one is blown, then the **l**, Nu 10:4 5387a
and fifty **l** of the congregation, Nu 16:2 5387a
from all their **l** according to Nu 17:2 5387a
all their **l** gave him a rod apiece, Nu 17:6 5387a
"The well, which the **l** sank, Nu 21:18 8269
the **l** of Moab stayed with Balaam. Nu 22:8 8269
the morning and said to Balak's **l**, Nu 22:13 8269
The **l** of Moab arose and went Nu 22:14 8269
Then Balak again sent **l**, Nu 22:15 8269
and went with the **l** of Moab. Nu 22:21 8269
went along with the **l** of Balak. Nu 22:35 8269
and the **l** who were with him. Nu 22:40 8269
he and all the **l** of Moab. Nu 23:6 8269
and the **l** of Moab with him. Nu 23:17 8269
"Take all the **l** of the people and Nu 25:4 7218
the **l** and all the congregation, Nu 27:2 5387a
all the **l** of the congregation went Nu 31:13 5387a
and to the **l** of the congregation, Nu 32:2 5387a
before Moses and before the **l**, Nu 36:1 5387a
heads over you, **l** of thousands and Dt 1:15 8269
the long-haired **l** of the enemy.' Dt 32:42 7218
he came *with* the **l** of the people; Dt 33:21 7218
and the **l** of the congregation Jos 9:15 5387a
the **l** of the congregation had sworn Jos 9:18 5387a
grumbled against the **l**. Jos 9:18 5387a
But all the **l** said to the whole Jos 9:19 5387a
The **l** said to them, Jos 9:21 5387a
just as the **l** had spoken to them. Jos 9:21 5387a
the son of Nun and before the **l**, Jos 17:4 5387a
and the **l** of the congregation, Jos 22:30 5387a
l returned from the sons of Reuben Jos 22:32 5387a
"That the **l** led in Israel, That Jg 5:2 6546
They captured the two **l** of Midian, Jg 7:25 8269
"God has given the **l** of Midian, Jg 8:3 8269
The **l** of Succoth said, Jg 8:6 8269
hearing of all the **l** of Shechem, Jg 9:2 1167
hearing of all the **l** of Shechem; Jg 9:3 1167
went out before the **l** of Shechem Jg 9:39 1167
all the **l** of the tower of Shechem Jg 9:46 1167
all the **l** of the tower of Shechem Jg 9:47 1167
and women with all the **l** of the city Jg 9:51 1167
The people, the **l** of Gilead, Jg 10:18 8269
the **l** of the fathers' *households* 1Ki 8:1 5387a
by name *were* **l** in their families; 1Ch 4:38 5387a
the sons of Ishi, as their **l**. 1Ch 4:42 7218
also commanded all the **l** of Israel 1Ch 22:17 8269
gathered together all the **l** of Israel 1Ch 23:2 8269
the **l** of the fathers' *households* 2Ch 5:2 5387a
counsel of the **l** and the elders, Ezr 10:8 8269
"Let our **l** represent the whole Ezr 10:14 8269
"For our kings, our **l**, Ne 9:34 8269
document *are the names of* our **l**, Ne 9:38 8269
The **l** of the people: Ne 10:14 7218
Now the **l** of the people lived in Ne 11:1 8269
from the **l** of the Levites, Ne 11:16 7218
and a firm regulation for the song **l** Ne 11:23 7891
Then I had the **l** of Judah come up Ne 12:31 8269
half of the **l** of Judah followed them Ne 12:32 8269
there were **l** of the singers, Ne 12:46 7218
the dead, all the **l** of the earth; Is 14:9 6260
they, their kings, their **l**, their priests Jer 32:32 8269
son of Benaiah, **l** of the people. Ezk 11:1 8269
Her **l** pronounce judgment for a Mi 3:11 7218
shepherds and eight **l** of men. Mi 5:5 5257b
MEANS LEAST AMONG THE **L** OF JUDAH; Mt 2:6 *2233*
"Do not be called **l**; Mt 23:10 *2519*
house of one of the **l** of the Pharisees Lk 14:1 *758*
Obey your **l** and submit *to them* Heb 13:17 *2233*
Greet all of your **l** and all the saints Heb 13:24 *2233*

LEADERSHIP
under the **l** of Moses and Aaron. Nu 33:1 3027

LEADING
of Abinadab, were **l** the new cart. 2Sa 6:3 5090a
and the **l** men of the land, 2Ki 24:15 193b
of the army of Hadadezer **l** them. 1Ch 19:16 6440
musical instruments **l** the praise. 2Ch 23:13 3045
and I gathered **l** men from Israel Ezr 7:28 7218
Zechariah and Meshullam, **l** men, Ezr 8:16 7218
I sent them to Iddo the **l** man Ezr 8:17 7218
set apart twelve of the **l** priests, Ezr 8:24 8269
weigh *them* before the **l** priests, Ezr 8:29 8269
Ezra rose and made the **l** priests, Ezr 10:5 8269
this people are **l** *them* astray; Is 9:16 8582
They are **l** you into futility; Jer 23:16 1891
and all the **l** officers of the king Jer 39:13 7227b
and the **l** men of Galilee; Mk 6:21 *4413*
priests and the scribes and the **l** men Lk 19:47 *4413*
and **l** him by the hand, they Ac 9:8 *5496*
and the **l** men of the city, Ac 13:50 *4413*
Silas, **l** men among the brethren, Ac 15:22 *2233*
which is a **l** city of the district Ac 16:12 *4413*
and a number of the **l** women. Ac 17:4 *4413*
And the chief priests and the **l** men Ac 25:2 *4413*
to the **l** man of the island, Ac 28:7 *4413*
who were the **l** men of the Jews, Ac 28:17 *4413*
spirit of slavery **l** to fear again, Ro 8:15 *1519*
l to obedience of faith; Ro 16:26
l to salvation, but the sorrow 2Co 7:10
you are **l** an undisciplined life, 2Th 3:11 *4043*
l to the knowledge of the truth, 2Tm 2:25 *1519*
his brother committing a sin not **l** 1Jn 5:16
life to those who commit sin not **l** 1Jn 5:16
There is a sin **l** to death; I do 1Jn 5:16
and there is a sin not **l** to death. 1Jn 5:17

LEADS
the nations, then **l** them away. Jb 12:23 5148
He **l** me beside quiet waters. Ps 23:2 5095
He **l** the humble in justice, And He Ps 25:9 1869
it **l** only to evildoing. Ps 37:8
He **l** out the prisoners into Ps 68:6 3318
way of the wicked **l** them astray. Pr 12:26 8582
But mere talk **l** only to poverty. Pr 14:23
The path of life **l** upward for Pr 15:24
l him in a way that is not good. Pr 16:29 1980
The fear of the LORD **l** to Pr 19:23
He who **l** the upright astray in an Pr 28:10 7686
the bridle which **l** to ruin. Is 30:28 8582
who **l** forth their host by number, Is 40:26 3318
l you in the way you should go. Is 48:17 1869
way is broad that **l** to destruction, Mt 7:13 *520*
the way is narrow that **l** to life, Mt 7:14 *520*
UNTIL HE **L** JUSTICE TO VICTORY. Mt 12:20 *1544b*
He **l** the people astray." Jn 7:12 *4105*
own sheep by name and **l** them out. Jn 10:3 *1806*
Gentiles also the repentance *that* **l** Ac 11:18
iron gate that **l** into the city, Ac 12:10 *5342*
kindness of God **l** you to repentance Ro 2:4 *71*
he who **l**, with diligence; Ro 12:8 *4291b*
l us in triumph in Christ, 2Co 2:14 *2358*
every brother who **l** an unruly life 2Th 3:6 *4043*
which is useless *and* **l** to 2Tm 2:14
the wisdom that **l** to salvation 2Tm 3:15 *1519*
and **l** My bond-servants astray so Rv 2:20 *4105*

LEAF
beak was a freshly picked olive **l**. Gn 8:11 5929
And the sound of a driven **l** will Lv 26:36 5929
You cause a driven **l** to tremble? Jb 13:25 5929
season And its **l** does not wither; Ps 1:3 5929
will flourish like the *green* **l**. Pr 11:28 5929
be like an oak whose **l** fades away Or Is 1:30 5929
away As a **l** withers from the vine, Is 34:4 5929
And all of us wither like a **l**, Is 64:6 5929
fig tree, And the **l** will wither; Jer 8:13 5929
at a distance a fig tree in **l**, Mk 11:13 *5444*

LEAFY
palm branches and boughs of **l** trees Lv 23:40 5687
and branches of *other* **l** trees, Ne 8:15 5687
green tree and under every **l** oak Ezk 6:13 5687
every high hill and every **l** tree, Ezk 20:28 5687
and others *spread* **l** branches which Mk 11:8 *4742a*

LEAGUE
in **l** with the stones of the field, Jb 5:23 1285
people of the land that is in **l** will Ezk 30:5 1285

LEAH
the name of the older was **L**, Gn 29:16 3812
evening he took his daughter **L**, Gn 29:23 3812
to his daughter **L** as a maid. Gn 29:24 3812
morning that, behold, it was **L**! Gn 29:25 3812
he loved Rachel more than **L**, Gn 29:30 3812
the LORD saw that **L** was unloved, Gn 29:31 3812
L conceived and bore a son and Gn 29:32 3812
When **L** saw that she had stopped Gn 30:9 3812
Then **L** said, "How fortunate! Gn 30:11 3812
Then **L** said, "Happy am I! Gn 30:13 3812
and brought them to his mother **L**. Gn 30:14 3812
Then Rachel said to **L**, Gn 30:14 3812
L went out to meet him and said, Gn 30:16 3812
God gave heed to **L**, Gn 30:17 3812
Then **L** said, "God has given me Gn 30:18 3812
L conceived again and bore a Gn 30:19 3812
Then **L** said, "God has endowed me Gn 30:20 3812
Jacob sent and called Rachel and **L** Gn 31:4 3812
and **L** said to him, Gn 31:14 3812
L and Rachel and the two maids. Gn 33:1 3812
and **L** and her children next, Gn 33:2 3812
L likewise came near with her Gn 33:7 3812
Now Dinah the daughter of **L**, Gn 34:1 3812
the sons of **L**: Reuben, Jacob's Gn 35:23 3812
These are the sons of **L**, Gn 46:15 3812
whom Laban gave to his daughter **L**; Gn 46:18 3812
Rebekah, and there I buried **L** Gn 49:31 3812
into your home like Rachel and **L**, Ru 4:11 3812

LEAH'S
And **L** eyes were weak, but Rachel Gn 29:17 3812
L maid Zilpah bore Jacob a son. Gn 30:10 3812
L maid Zilpah bore Jacob a Gn 30:12 3812
into Jacob's tent and into **L** tent Gn 31:33 3812
Then he went out of **L** tent and Gn 31:33 3812
and the sons of Zilpah, **L** maid: Gn 35:26 3812

LEAKS
and through slackness the house **l**. Ec 10:18 1811

LEAN
and the **l** and ugly cows ate up the Gn 41:20 7534
"The seven **l** and ugly cows Gn 41:27 7534
How is the land, is it fat or **l**? Nu 13:20 7330
that I may **l** against them." Jg 16:26 8172
And my flesh has grown **l**, Ps 109:24 3584
not **l** on your own understanding. Pr 3:5 8172
the fatness of his flesh will become **l** Is 17:4 7329
city And **l** on the God of Israel; Is 48:2 5564
the fat sheep and the **l** sheep. Ezk 34:20 7330
Yet they **l** on the LORD saying, Mi 3:11 8172

LEANED
the royal officer on whose hand he **l** 2Ki 7:17 8172

And when they l on you, You broke Ezk 29:7 8172
the one who also had l back on His Jn 21:20 377

LEANING
behold, Saul was l on his spear. 2Sa 1:6 8172
officer on whose hand the king was l 2Ki 7:2 8172
Like a l wall, like a tottering fence? Ps 62:3 5186
wilderness L on her beloved? SS 8:5 7514b
He, l back thus on Jesus' bosom, Jn 13:25 377
l on the top of his staff. Heb 11:21

LEANNESS
And my l rises up against me, It Jb 16:8 3585

LEANS
Ar, And l to the border of Moab." Nu 21:15 8172
and he l on my hand and I bow 2Ki 5:18 8172
on which if a man l, 2Ki 18:21 5564
on which if a man l, Is 36:6 5564
home, l his hand against the wall And Am 5:19 5564

LEAP
By my God I can l over a wall. 2Sa 22:30 1801
"Do you make him l like the locust? Jb 39:20 7493
Sparks of fire l forth. Jb 41:19 4422
And by my God I can l over a wall. Ps 18:29 1801
Then the lame will l like a deer, Is 35:6 1801
l on the tops of the mountains, Jl 2:5 7540
all who l on the *temple* threshold, Zph 1:9 1801
glad in that day and l *for joy,* Lk 6:23 *4640*
With a l he stood upright and Ac 3:8 *1814*

LEAPED
And they l about the altar which 1Ki 18:26 6452b
greeting, the baby l in her womb; Lk 1:41 *4640*
the baby l in my womb for joy. Lk 1:44 *4640*
And he l up and *began* to walk. Ac 14:10 *242*
l on them and subdued all of them Ac 19:16 *2177*

LEAPING
l and dancing before the LORD; 2Sa 6:16 6339
saw King David l and celebrating; 1Ch 15:29 7540
on the mountains, L on the hills! SS 2:8 7092
walking and l and praising God. Ac 3:8 *242*

LEAPS
whelp, That l forth from Bashan." Dt 33:22 2187
trembles, And l from its place. Jb 37:1 5425a
strength, And dismay l before him. Jb 41:22 1750

LEARN
hear My words so they may l to fear Dt 4:10 3925
that you may l them and observe Dt 5:1 3925
so that you may l to fear Dt 14:23 3925
he may l to fear the LORD his God, Dt 17:19 3925
you shall not l to imitate the Dt 18:9 3925
and l and fear the LORD your God, Dt 31:12 3925
and l to fear the LORD your God, Dt 31:13 3925
For if I should indeed l that evil 1Sa 20:9 3045
and l about all the hiding places 1Sa 23:23 3045
to l of your going out and coming in and 2Sa 3:25 3045
l *the difference between* My service 2Ch 12:8 3045
and l that that city is a Ezr 4:15 3046
l how Esther was and how she fared Es 2:11 3045
l what this *was* and why it *was.* Es 4:5 3045
"I would l the words *which* He Jb 23:5 3045
When I l Your righteous judgments. Ps 119:7 3925
That I may l Your statutes. Ps 119:71 3925
that I may l Your commandments. Ps 119:73 3925
Or you will l his ways And find Pr 22:25 502
L to do good; Seek justice, Reprove Is 1:17 3925
And never again will they l war. Is 2:4 3925
of the world l righteousness. Is 26:9 3925
He does not l righteousness; Is 26:10 3925
"Do not l the way of the nations, Jer 10:2 3925
really l the ways of My people, Jer 12:16 3925
let us cast lots so we may l on Jon 1:7 3045
"But go and l what this means: Mt 9:13 *3129*
My yoke upon you and l from Me, Mt 11:29 *3129*
l the parable from the fig tree: Mt 24:32 *3129*
l the parable from the fig tree: Mk 13:28 *3129*
l not to exceed what is written, 1Co 4:6 *3129*
all may l and all may be exhorted; 1Co 14:31 *3129*
If they desire to l anything, 1Co 14:35 *3129*
you did not l Christ in this way, Eph 4:20 *3129*
to l what is pleasing to the Lord. Eph 5:10 *1381a*
when I l of your condition. Php 2:19 *1097*
they must first l to practice piety 1Tm 5:4 *3129*
same time they also l *to be* idle, 1Tm 5:13 *3129*
Our people must also l to Ti 3:14 *3129*
and no one could l the song except Rv 14:3 *3129*

LEARNED
l in the words of the commandments Ezr 7:11 5613b
l about the evil that Eliashib had Ne 13:7 995
Mordecai l all that had been done, Es 4:1 3045
nations And l their practices, Ps 106:35 3925
Neither have I l wisdom, Nor do I Pr 30:3 3925
consists of tradition l *by rote,* Is 29:13 3925
a lion, And he l to tear *his* prey; Ezk 19:3 3925
young lion, He l to tear *his* prey; Ezk 19:6 3925
and when she l that He was Lk 7:37 *1921*
And when he l that He belonged to Lk 23:7 *1921*
has heard and l from the Father, Jn 6:45 *3129*
"How has this man become l, Jn 7:15 *3609a*
of the Jews then l that He was there; Jn 12:9 *1097*
But when the brethren l *of it,* Ac 9:30 *1921*
him, having l that he was a Roman. Ac 23:27 *3129*
he l that he was from Cilicia, Ac 23:34 *4441*
to the teaching which you l, Ro 16:17 *3129*
The things you have l and received Php 4:9 *3129*
for I have l to be content in Php 4:11 *3129*
I have l the secret of being filled Php 4:12 *3453*
just as you l *it* from Epaphras, Col 1:7 *3129*
continue in the things you have l 2Tm 3:14 *3129*
knowing from whom you have l *them,* 2Tm 3:14 *3129*
He l obedience from the things Heb 5:8 *3129*

LEARNING
man will hear and increase in l, Pr 1:5 3948
man and he will increase *his* l. Pr 9:9 3948
in all the l of the Egyptians, Ac 7:22 *4678*
Your great l is driving you mad." Ac 26:24 *1121*
always l and never able to come to 2Tm 3:7 *3129*

LEAST
he who gathered l gathered ten Nu 11:32 4591
my family is the l in Manasseh, Jg 6:15 1800b
my family the l of all the families 1Sa 9:21 6810
please let your servant at l be 2Ki 5:17
of the l of my master's servants, 2Ki 18:24 6996a
he who was l was equal to a 1Ch 12:14 6996a
from the greatest to the l; 2Ch 34:30 6996a
from the greatest to the l, Es 1:5 6996a
and issue, all the l of vessels, Is 22:24 6996a
of the l of my master's servants and Is 36:9 6996a
And the l one a mighty nation. Is 60:22 6810
"For from the l of them even to Jer 6:13 6996a
Because from the l even to the Jer 8:10 6996a
from the l of them to the greatest Jer 31:34 6996a
she will be the l of the nations, Jer 50:12 319
the greatest to the l of them. Jon 3:5 6996a
L AMONG THE LEADERS OF JUDAH; Mt 2:6 *1646*
of the l of these commandments, Mt 5:19 *1646*
called l in the kingdom of heaven; Mt 5:19 *1646*
Yet the one who is l in the kingdom Mt 11:11 *3398*
of Mine, *even* the l *of them,* Mt 25:40 *1646*
do it to one of the l of these, Mt 25:45 *1646*
yet he who is l in the kingdom of Lk 7:28 *3398*
for the one who is l among all of Lk 9:48 *3398*
at l his shadow might fall on any Ac 5:15 *2579*
not an apostle, at l I am to you; 1Co 9:2 *235, 1065*
For I am the l of the apostles, 1Co 15:9 *1646*
I consider myself not in the l inferior 2Co 11:5 *3367*
To me, the very l of all saints, Eph 3:8 *1646*
THE L TO THE GREATEST OF THEM. Heb 8:11 *3398*

LEATHER
whether in l or in any article Lv 13:48 5785
or in any article made of l, Lv 13:48 5785
in the garment or in the l, Lv 13:49 5785
the woof, or in any article of l, Lv 13:49 5785
warp or in the woof, or in the l, Lv 13:51 5785
purpose for which the l is used, Lv 13:51 5785
any article of l in which the mark Lv 13:52 5785
the woof, or in any article of l, Lv 13:53 5785
of the garment or out of the l, Lv 13:56 5785
the woof, or in any article of l, Lv 13:57 5785
or any article of l from which the Lv 13:58 5785
the woof, or in any article of l, Lv 13:59 5785
'As for any garment or any l on Lv 15:17 5785
every garment and every article of l Nu 31:20 5785
l girdle bound about his loins." 2Ki 1:8 5785
and a l belt around his waist; Mt 3:4 *1193*
wore a l belt around his waist, Mk 1:6 *1193*

LEAVE
shall l his father and his mother, Gn 2:24 5800a
for I will not l you until I have Gn 28:15 5800a
now arise, l this land, and return Gn 31:13 3318
"Please let me l with you some of Gn 33:15 3322
l one of your brothers with me and Gn 42:33 5117
'The lad cannot l his father, for Gn 44:22 5800a
for if he should l his father, Gn 44:22 5800a
l any of it over until morning, Ex 12:10 3498
'L us alone that we may serve the Ex 14:12 2308
man l any of it until morning." Ex 16:19 3498
for the LORD will not l him Ex 20:7 5352
and whatever they l the beast of Ex 23:11 3499a
no means l *the guilty* unpunished, Ex 34:7 5352
l any of it over until morning. Lv 7:15 5117
place, and shall l them there. Lv 16:23 5117
you shall l them for the needy and Lv 19:10 5800a
shall l none of it until morning; Lv 22:30 3498
you are to l them for the needy Lv 23:22 5800a
shall l none of it until morning, Nu 9:12 7604
"Please do not l us, inasmuch as Nu 10:31 5800a
"Why did we ever l Egypt?" Nu 11:20
3318, 4480
for the LORD will not l him Dt 5:11 5352
l alive anything that breathes. Dt 20:16 2421a
and l no sustenance in Israel as Jg 6:4 7604
'Shall I l my fatness with which Jg 9:9 2308
'Shall I l my sweetness and my Jg 9:11 2308
'Shall I l my new wine, which Jg 9:13 2308
then my strength will l me and I Jg 16:17
5493, 4480
"Do not urge me to l you *or* turn Ru 1:16 5800a
and l *it* that she may glean, Ru 2:16 5800a
he turned his back to l Samuel, 1Sa 10:9
1980, 4480, 5973
and let us not l a man of them." 1Sa 14:36 7604
'David earnestly asked l of me 1Sa 20:6
asked l of me *to go* to Bethlehem, 1Sa 20:28 7592
if by morning I l *as much as* one 1Sa 25:22 7604
did not l a man or a woman alive, 1Sa 27:9 2421a
did not l a man or a woman alive to 1Sa 27:11 2421a
so as to l my husband neither name 2Sa 14:7 7760
may He not l us or forsake us, 1Ki 8:57 5800a
l to Jeroboam any persons alive, 1Ki 15:29 7604
he did not l a single male, 1Ki 16:11 7604
"It will come about when I l 1Ki 18:12
1980, 4480
"Yet I will l 7,000 in Israel, 1Ki 19:18 7604
yourself live, I will not l you." 2Ki 2:2 5800a
yourself live, I will not l you." 2Ki 2:4 5800a
yourself live, I will not l you." 2Ki 2:6 5800a
yourself live, I will not l you." 2Ki 4:30 5800a
then let no one escape *or* l the city 2Ki 9:15
3318, 4480
"L this work on the house of God Ezr 6:7 7662
to l us an escaped remnant and to Ezr 9:8 7604
l *it* as an inheritance to your sons Ezr 9:12 3423
Please, let us l off this usury. Ne 5:10 5800a
I l it and come down to you?" Ne 6:3 7503
pillar of cloud did not l them by day Ne 9:19
5493, 4480, 5921
however, I asked l from the king, Ne 13:6
L me alone, for my days are *but* a Jb 7:16 2308
I will l off my *sad* countenance Jb 9:27 5800a
They l and do not return to them. Jb 39:4 3318
is great And l your labor to him? Jb 39:11 5800a
And l their abundance to their Ps 17:14 5117
LORD will not l him in his hand Or Ps 37:33 5800a
And l their wealth to others. Ps 49:10 5800a
Do not l me to my oppressors. Ps 119:121 5117
do not l me defenseless. Ps 141:8 6168
who l the paths of uprightness To Pr 2:13 5800a
not let kindness and truth l you; Pr 3:3 5800a
L the presence of a fool, Or you Pr 14:7 1980
for I must l it to the man who Ec 2:18 5117
"Do not be in a hurry to l him. Ec 8:3
1980, 4480
And where will you l your wealth? Is 10:3 5800a
And I will not l them undone." Is 42:16 5800a
"You will l your name for a Is 65:15 5117
That I might l my people And go Jer 9:2 5800a
by no means l you unpunished.' Jer 30:11 5352
by no means l you unpunished." Jer 46:28 5352
"L the cities and dwell among the Jer 48:28 5800a
you, Would they not l gleanings? Jer 49:9 7604
'L your orphans behind, I will Jer 49:11 5800a
those whom I l as a remnant.' Jer 50:20 7604
"However, I will l a remnant, Ezk 6:8 3498
and will l you naked and bare. Ezk 16:39 5117
and l you naked and bare. Ezk 23:29 5800a
'I will l you on the land; Ezk 32:4 5203
l none of them there any longer. Ezk 39:28 3498
"Yet l the stump with its roots Da 4:15 7662
yet l the stump with its roots in Da 4:23 7662
it was commanded to l the stump Da 4:26 7662
Lord will l his bloodguilt on him And Hos 12:14 5203
And l a blessing behind Him, Jl 2:14 7604
Would they not l *some* gleanings? Ob 1:5 7604
no means l *the guilty* unpunished. Na 1:3 5352
They l nothing for the morning. Zph 3:3 1633a
"But I will l among you A humble Zph 3:12 7604
l them neither root nor branch." Mal 4:1 5800a
l your offering there before the Mt 5:24 *863*
they implored Him to l their region. Mt 8:34 *3327*
He said, "L; for the girl has not Mt 9:24 *402*
and stay at his house until you l Mt 10:11 *1831*
does he not l the ninety-nine on Mt 18:12 *863*
MAN SHALL L HIS FATHER AND MOTHER Mt 19:5 *2641*
to My brethren to l for Galilee, Mt 28:10 *565*
And they began to implore Him to l Mk 5:17 *565*
stay there until you l town. Mk 6:10 *1831*
MAN SHALL L HIS FATHER AND MOTHER, Mk 10:7 *2641*
surrounding district asked Him to l Lk 8:37 *565*
there until you l that city. Lk 9:4 *1831*
and only with difficulty does it l Lk 9:39 *672*
l here, for Herod wants to kill You." Lk 13:31 *4198*
does not l the ninety-nine in the Lk 15:4 *2641*
l in you one stone upon another, Lk 19:44 *863*
are in the midst of the city must l, Lk 21:21 *1633*
"L here and go into Judea, so that Jn 7:3 *3327*
"I will not l you as orphans; Jn 14:18 *863*
"Peace I l with you; Jn 14:27 *863*
his own *home,* and to l Me alone; Jn 16:32 *863*
commanded them not to l Jerusalem, Ac 1:4 *5563*
But when they had ordered them to l Ac 4:15 *565*
and said to him, 'L YOUR COUNTRY Ac 7:3 *1831*
did not l Himself without witness, Ac 14:17 *863*
kept begging them to l the city. Ac 16:39 *565*
commanded all the Jews to l Rome. Ac 18:2 *5563*
took l of the brethren and put out Ac 18:18 *657*
but taking l of them and saying, Ac 18:21 *657*
them and taken his l of them, Ac 20:1 *782*
intending to l the next day, and he Ac 20:7 *1826*
he himself was about to l shortly. Ac 25:4 *1607*
but l room for the wrath *of God,* Ro 12:19 *1325*
the wife should not l her husband 1Co 7:10 *5563*
(but if she does l, she must remain 1Co 7:11 *5563*
unbelieving one leaves, let him l; 1Co 7:15 *5563*
but taking my l of them, I went on 2Co 2:13 *657*
the Lord three times that it might l 2Co 12:8 *868*
MAN SHALL L HIS FATHER AND MOTHER Eph 5:31 *2641*
"L out the court which is outside Rv 11:2 *1544b*

LEAVEN
shall remove l from your houses; Ex 12:15 7603
be no l found in your houses; Ex 12:19 7603
nor shall any l be seen among you Ex 13:7 7603
to the LORD, shall be made with l, Lv 2:11 2557
you shall not offer up in smoke any l Lv 2:11 7603
'It shall not be baked with l. Lv 6:17 2557
baked with l as first fruits to the Lv 23:17 2557
"For seven days no l shall be Dt 16:4 7603
"The kingdom of heaven is like l, Mt 13:33 *2219*
the l of the Pharisees and Sadducees Mt 16:6 *2219*
the l of the Pharisees and Sadducees Mt 16:11 *2219*
say to beware of the l of bread, Mt 16:12 *2219*
Beware of the l of the Pharisees Mk 8:15 *2219*
Pharisees and the l of Herod." Mk 8:15 *2219*
"Beware of the l of the Pharisees, Lk 12:1 *2219*
"It is like l, which a woman took Lk 13:21 *2219*
a little l leavens the whole lump 1Co 5:6 *2219*
Clean out the old l so 1Co 5:7 *2219*

the feast, not with old **l**, **1Co 5:8** *2219*
the **l** of malice and wickedness, **1Co 5:8** *2219*
A little **l** leavens the whole lump **Ga 5:9** *2219*

LEAVENED
for whoever eats anything **l** from **Ex 12:15** 2557
for whoever eats what is **l**, **Ex 12:19** 4263b
'You shall not eat anything **l**; **Ex 12:20** 4263b
took their dough before it was **l**, **Ex 12:34** 2556a
For it had not become **l**, **Ex 12:39** 2556a
And nothing **l** shall be eaten. **Ex 13:3** 2557
nothing **l** shall be seen among you, **Ex 13:7** 2557
of My sacrifice with **l** bread; **Ex 23:18** 2557
of My sacrifice with **l** bread, **Ex 34:25** 2557
offering with cakes of **l** bread. **Lv 7:13** 2557
"You shall not eat **l** bread with it; **Dt 16:3** 2557
of the dough until it is **l**. **Hos 7:4** 2556a
also from that which is **l**, **Am 4:5** 2557
of flour until it was all **l**." **Mt 13:33** *2220*
of flour until it was all **l**." **Lk 13:21** *2220*

LEAVENS
leaven **l** the whole lump *of dough?* **1Co 5:6** *2220*
leaven **l** the whole lump *of dough.* **Ga 5:9** *2220*

LEAVES
and they sewed fig **l** together and **Gn 3:7** 5929
when he enters and **l** the holy place **Ex 28:35** 3318
and she **l** his house and goes and **Dt 24:2** 3318
who also **l** you no grain, **Dt 28:51** 7604
the two **l** of the one door turned **1Ki 6:34** 6763
and the two **l** of the other door **1Ki 6:34** 7050b
That **l** the companion of her youth And **Pr 2:17** 5800a
A good man **l** an inheritance to his **Pr 13:22** 5157
a driving rain which **l** no food. **Pr 28:3** 369
But its **l** will be green, And it **Jer 17:8** 5929
that all its sprouting **l** wither? **Ezk 17:9** 2964
Each of the doors had two **l**, **Ezk 41:24** 1817
had two leaves, two swinging **l**; **Ezk 41:24** 1817
two **l** for one door and two leaves **Ezk 41:24**
one door and two **l** for the other. **Ezk 41:24** 1817
Their **l** will not wither and their **Ezk 47:12** 5929
food and their **l** for healing." **Ezk 47:12** 5929
shepherd Who **l** the flock! **Zch 11:17** 5800a
found nothing on it except **l** only; **Mt 21:19** *5444*
tender and puts forth its **l**, **Mt 24:32** *5444*
to it, He found nothing but **l**, **Mk 11:13** *5444*
BROTHER DIES and **l** behind a wife **Mk 12:19** *2641*
behind a wife AND **L** NO CHILD, **Mk 12:19** *863*
tender and puts forth its **l**, **Mk 13:28** *5444*
mauling him *as it* **l**. **Lk 9:39** *672*
as soon as they put forth **l**, you **Lk 21:30**
the wolf coming, and **l** the sheep and **Jn 10:12** *863*
Yet if the unbelieving one **l**, **1Co 7:15** *5563*
and the **l** of the tree were for the **Rv 22:2** *5444*

LEAVING
shall refrain from **l** it to him, **Ex 23:5** 5800a
l yourselves without remnant, **Jer 44:7** 3498
and **l** Nazareth, He came and **Mt 4:13** *2641*
As they were **l** Jericho, a large **Mt 20:29** *1607*
and **l** Him, they went away. **Mt 22:22** *863*
L the crowd, they took Him along **Mk 4:36** *863*
L them, He again embarked and went **Mk 8:13** *863*
And as He was **l** Jericho with His **Mk 10:46** *1607*
a wife, and died **l** no children. **Mk 12:20** *863*
and died **l** behind no children; **Mk 12:21** *2641*
who upon **l** his house and putting **Mk 13:34** *863*
And as these were **l** Him, Peter said **Lk 9:33** *1316*
him, and went away **l** him half dead. **Lk 10:30** *863*
way all seven died, **l** no children. **Lk 20:31** *2641*
I am **l** the world again and going **Jn 16:28** *863*
sight of Cyprus, **l** it on the left, **Ac 21:3** *2641*
l the horsemen to go on with him, **Ac 23:32** *1439*
they *began* **l** after Paul had spoken **Ac 28:25** *630*
Therefore **l** the elementary teaching **Heb 6:1** *863*
l you an example for you to follow **1Pe 2:21** *5277*

LEBANA
the sons of **L**, the sons of Hagaba, **Ne 7:48** 3838

LEBANAH
the sons of **L**, the sons of **Ezr 2:45** 3838

LEBANON
the land of the Canaanites, and **L**, **Dt 1:7** 3844
that good hill country and **L**.' **Dt 3:25** 3844
will be from the wilderness to **L**, **Dt 11:24** 3844
"From the wilderness and this **L**, **Jos 1:4** 3844
coast of the Great Sea toward **L**, **Jos 9:1** 3844
as far as Baal-gad in the valley of **L** **Jos 11:17** 3844
from Baal-gad in the valley of **L** **Jos 12:7** 3844
of the Gebalite, and all of **L**, **Jos 13:5** 3844
from **L** as far as Misrephoth-maim, **Jos 13:6** 3844
the Hivites who lived in Mount **L**, **Jg 3:3** 3844
and consume the cedars of **L**.' **Jg 9:15** 3844
from the cedar that is in **L** even **1Ki 4:33** 3844
they cut for me cedars from **L**, **1Ki 5:6** 3844
bring *them* down from **L** to the sea; **1Ki 5:9** 3844
He sent them to **L**, **1Ki 5:14** 3844
they were in **L** a month *and* two **1Ki 5:14** 3844
the house of the forest of **L**; **1Ki 7:2** 3844
to build in Jerusalem, in **L**, **1Ki 9:19** 3844
in the house of the forest of **L**. **1Ki 10:17** 3844
the forest of **L** *were* of pure gold. **1Ki 10:21** 3844
"The thorn bush which was in **L** **2Ki 14:9** 3844
sent to the cedar which was in **L**, **2Ki 14:9** 3844
by a wild beast that was in **L**, **2Ki 14:9** 3844
To the remotest parts of **L**; **2Ki 19:23** 3844
cypress and algum timber from **L**, **2Ch 2:8** 3844
know how to cut timber of **L**; **2Ch 2:8** 3844
whatever timber you need from **L** and **2Ch 2:16** 3844
to build in Jerusalem, in **L**, **2Ch 8:6** 3844
in the house of the forest of **L**. **2Ch 9:16** 3844
the forest of **L** *were* of pure gold; **2Ch 9:20** 3844
"The thorn bush which was in **L** **2Ch 25:18** 3844
sent to the cedar which was in **L**, **2Ch 25:18** 3844
by a wild beast that was in **L** and **2Ch 25:18** 3844
wood from **L** to the sea at Joppa, **Ezr 3:7** 3844
breaks in pieces the cedars of **L**. **Ps 29:5** 3844
He makes **L** skip like a calf, **Ps 29:6** 3844
will wave like *the cedars of* **L**; **Ps 72:16** 3844
He will grow like a cedar in **L**. **Ps 92:12** 3844
The cedars of **L** which He planted, **Ps 104:16** 3844
sedan chair From the timber of **L**. **SS 3:9** 3844
"*Come* with me from **L**, **SS 4:8** 3844
May you come with me from **L**. **SS 4:8** 3844
is like the fragrance of **L**. **SS 4:11** 3844
And streams *flowing* from **L**." **SS 4:15** 3844
His appearance is like **L** Choice **SS 5:15** 3844
Your nose is like the tower of **L**, **SS 7:4** 3844
all the cedars of **L** that are lofty **Is 2:13** 3844
And **L** will fall by the Mighty One. **Is 10:34** 3844
over you, *and* the cedars of **L**, **Is 14:8** 3844
L will be turned into a fertile field, **Is 29:17** 3844
away, **L** is shamed *and* withers; **Is 33:9** 3844
glory of **L** will be given to it, **Is 35:2** 3844
To the remotest parts of **L**; **Is 37:24** 3844
Even **L** is not enough to burn, Nor **Is 40:16** 3844
"The glory of **L** will come to you, **Is 60:13** 3844
'Does the snow of **L** forsake the **Jer 18:14** 3844
to Me, *Like* the summit of **L**; **Jer 22:6** 3844
"Go up to **L** and cry out, And lift **Jer 22:20** 3844
"You who dwell in **L**, **Jer 22:23** 3844
came to **L** and took away the top of **Ezk 17:3** 3844
They have taken a cedar from **L** to **Ezk 27:5** 3844
Assyria *was* a cedar in **L** With **Ezk 31:3** 3844
up, and I made **L** mourn for it, **Ezk 31:15** 3844
Eden, the choicest and best of **L**, **Ezk 31:16** 3844
take root like *the cedars of* **L**. **Hos 14:5** 3844
fragrance like *the cedars of* **L**. **Hos 14:6** 3844
renown *will be* like the wine of **L**. **Hos 14:7** 3844
The blossoms of **L** wither. **Na 1:4** 3844
"For the violence done to **L** will **Hab 2:17** 3844
into the land of Gilead and **L** Until **Zch 10:10** 3844
Open your doors, O **L**, **Zch 11:1** 3844

LEBAOTH
and **L** and Shilhim and Ain and **Jos 15:32** 3822

LEB-KAMAI
And against the inhabitants of **L** **Jer 51:1** 3846b

LEBO-HAMATH
of Zin as far as Rehob, at **L**. **Nu 13:21** 935
a line from Mount Hor to the **L**, **Nu 34:8** 935
below Mount Hermon as far as **L**. **Jos 13:5** 935
from Mount Baal-hermon as far as **L**. **Jg 3:3** 935
border to a point opposite **L**. **Ezk 47:20** 935
beside the way of Hethlon to **L**, **Ezk 48:1** 935

LEBONAH
and on the south side of **L**." **Jg 21:19** 3829

LECAH
son of Judah *were* Er the father of **L** **1Ch 4:21** 3922

LED
captive, he **l** out his trained men, **Gn 14:14** 7385a
and he **l** the flock to the west **Ex 3:1** 5090a
Hence God **l** the people around by **Ex 13:18** 5437
"In Your lovingkindness You have **l** **Ex 15:13** 5148
Moses **l** Israel from the Red Sea, **Ex 15:22** 5265
your God has **l** you in the wilderness **Dt 8:2** 1980
"He **l** you through the great and **Dt 8:15** 1980
"I have **l** you forty years in **Dt 29:5** 1980
and **l** him through all the land of **Jos 24:3** 1980
out of Egypt and **l** you into the land **Jg 2:1** 935
"That the leaders **l** in Israel, **Jg 5:2** 6544b
and he **l** away their livestock and **1Sa 23:5** 5090a
the one who **l** Israel out and in. **2Sa 5:2** 3318
of the army of Hadadezer **l** them. **2Sa 10:16** 6440
Then he **l** away into exile all **2Ki 24:14** 1540
So he **l** Jehoiachin away into exile **2Ki 24:15** 1540
he **l** away into exile from **2Ki 24:15** 1980
So Judah was **l** away into exile from **2Ki 25:21** 1540
who **l** out and brought in Israel; **1Ch 11:2** 3318
that Joab **l** out the army and **1Ch 20:1** 5090a
the harlot and **l** Judah astray. **2Ch 21:11** 5080
himself and **l** his people forth, **2Ch 25:11** 5090a
l all their feeble ones on **2Ch 28:15** 5095
before those who **l** them captive and **2Ch 30:9** 7617
"And with a pillar of cloud You **l** **Ne 9:12** 5148
and **l** him *on horseback* through the **Es 6:11** 7392
be **l** forth at the day of fury. **Jb 21:30** 2986
She will be **l** to the King in **Ps 45:14** 2986
They will be **l** forth with gladness **Ps 45:15** 2986
You have **l** captive *Your* captives; **Ps 68:18** 7617
You **l** Your people like a flock By **Ps 77:20** 5148
He **l** them with the cloud by day And **Ps 78:14** 5148
But He **l** forth His own people like **Ps 78:52** 5265
He **l** them safely, so that they **Ps 78:53** 5148
And He **l** them through the deeps, **Ps 106:9** 1980
He **l** them also by a straight way, **Ps 107:7** 1869
To Him who **l** His people through **Ps 136:16** 1980
I have **l** you in upright paths. **Pr 4:11** 1869
of her tribes Have **l** Egypt astray. **Is 19:13** 8582
They have **l** Egypt astray in all **Is 19:14** 8582
He **l** them through the deserts. **Is 48:21** 1980
a lamb that is **l** to slaughter, **Is 53:7** 2986
joy And be **l** forth with peace; **Is 55:12** 2986
With their kings **l** in procession. **Is 60:11** 5090a
Who **l** them through the depths? **Is 63:13** 1980
So You **l** Your people, To make for **Is 63:14** 5090a
Who **l** us through the wilderness, **Jer 2:6** 1980
God When He **l** you in the way? **Jer 2:17** 1980
a gentle lamb **l** to the slaughter; **Jer 11:19** 2986
place where they **l** him captive, **Jer 22:12** 1540
who brought up and **l** back the **Jer 23:8** 935
and **l** My people Israel astray. **Jer 23:13** 8582
and **l** My people astray by their **Jer 23:32** 8582
Egypt and **l** him to King Jehoiakim, **Jer 26:23** 935
shepherds have **l** them astray. **Jer 50:6** 8582
So Judah was **l** away into exile from **Jer 52:27** 1540
Then he **l** me toward the south, and **Ezk 40:24** 1980
Then he **l** me to the gate, the gate **Ezk 43:1** 1980
l me across to the four corners of **Ezk 46:21** 5674a
and **l** me around on the outside **Ezk 47:2** 5437
and he **l** me through the water, **Ezk 47:3** 5674a
and **l** me through the water, **Ezk 47:4** 5674a
and **l** me through *the water,* **Ezk 47:4** 5674a
spirit of harlotry has **l** *them* astray, **Hos 4:12** 8582
I **l** them with cords of a man, with **Hos 11:4** 4900
lies also have **l** them astray, **Am 2:4** 8582
And I **l** you in the wilderness **Am 2:10** 1980
Then Jesus was **l** up by the Spirit **Mt 4:1** *321*
and **l** them up on a high mountain by **Mt 17:1** *399*
Those who had seized Jesus **l** Him **Mt 26:57** *520*
they bound Him, and **l** Him away and **Mt 27:2** *520*
and **l** Him away to crucify Him. **Mt 27:31** *520*
l Jesus away to the high priest; **Mk 14:53** *520*
binding Jesus, they **l** Him away and **Mk 15:1** *667*
And they **l** Him out to crucify Him. **Mk 15:20** *1806*
l around by the Spirit in the wilderness **Lk 4:1** *71*
And he **l** Him up and showed Him all **Lk 4:5** *321*
And he **l** Him to Jerusalem and had **Lk 4:9** *71*
and **l** Him to the brow of the hill **Lk 4:29** *71*
Those who **l** the way were **Lk 18:39** *4254*
be **l** captive into all the nations; **Lk 21:24** *163*
arrested Him, they **l** Him *away* **Lk 22:54** *71*
and they **l** Him away to their **Lk 22:66** *520*
When they **l** Him away, they **Lk 23:26** *520*
were being **l** away to be put to **Lk 23:32** *71*
He **l** them out as far as Bethany, **Lk 24:50** *1806*
"You have not also been **l** astray, **Jn 7:47** *4105*
and **l** Him to Annas first; **Jn 18:13** *71*
Then they **l** Jesus from **Jn 18:28** *71*
"This man **l** them out, performing **Ac 7:36** *1806*
FOR THIS MOSES WHO **L** US OUT OF THE **Ac 7:40** *1806*
"HE WAS **L** AS A SHEEP TO SLAUGHTER; **Ac 8:32** *71*
Lord had **l** him out of the prison. **Ac 12:17** *1806*
that they be **l** away *to execution.* **Ac 12:19** *520*
arm He **l** them out from it. **Ac 13:17** *1806*
a revolt and **l** the four thousand men **Ac 21:38** *1806*
I was **l** by the hand by those who **Ac 22:11** *5496*
l him to the commander and said, **Ac 23:18** *71*
are being **l** by the Spirit of God, **Ro 8:14** *71*
were **l** astray to the mute idols, **1Co 12:2** *520*
mute idols, however you were **l**. **1Co 12:2** *71*
your minds will be **l** astray from **2Co 11:3** *5351*
Who is **l** into sin without my **2Co 11:29** *4624*
But if you are **l** by the Spirit, **Ga 5:18** *71*
HE **L** CAPTIVE A HOST OF CAPTIVES, **Eph 4:8** *162*
sins, **l** on by various impulses, **2Tm 3:6** *71*
all those who came out of Egypt **l** **Heb 3:16**
Remember those who **l** you, **Heb 13:7** *2233*
and **l** a life of wanton pleasure; **Jas 5:5** *4684*

LEDGE
beneath, under the **l** of the altar, **Ex 27:5** 3749
network beneath, under its **l**, **Ex 38:4** 3749
the lower **l** *shall be* two cubits and **Ezk 43:14** 5835
and from the smaller **l** to the **Ezk 43:14** 5835
the larger **l** *shall be* four cubits and **Ezk 43:14** 5835
"The **l** *shall be* fourteen **Ezk 43:17** 5835
and on the four corners of the **l** and **Ezk 43:20** 5835
corners of the **l** of the altar and **Ezk 45:19** 5835

LEDGES
ravines, on the **l** of the cliffs, **Is 7:19** 5357

LEECH
The **l** has two daughters, **Pr 30:15** 5936

LEEKS
l and the onions and the garlic, **Nu 11:5** 2682

LEFT
and only Noah was **l**, **Gn 7:23** 7604
if *to* the **l**, then I will go to the **Gn 13:9** 8040
right, then I will go to the **l**." **Gn 13:9** 8041
she **l** the boy under one of the **Gn 21:15** 7993
turn to the right hand or the **l**." **Gn 24:49** 8040
company which is **l** will escape." **Gn 32:8** 7604
Then Jacob was **l** alone, and a man **Gn 32:24** 3498
So he **l** everything he owned in **Gn 39:6** 5800a
And he **l** his garment in her hand **Gn 39:12** 5800a
he had **l** his garment in her hand and **Gn 39:13** 5800a
he **l** his garment beside me **Gn 39:15** 5800a
So she **l** his garment beside her **Gn 39:16** 5117
he **l** his garment beside me **Gn 39:18** 5800a
is dead, and he alone is **l**. **Gn 42:38** 7604
so he alone is **l** of his mother, **Gn 44:20** 3498
There is nothing **l** for my lord **Gn 47:18** 7604
his right hand toward Israel's **l**, **Gn 48:13** 8040
his **l** hand toward Israel's right, **Gn 48:13** 8040
and his **l** hand on Manasseh's head, **Gn 48:14** 8040
they **l** only their little ones and **Gn 50:8** 5800a
it that you have **l** the man behind? **Ex 2:20** 5800a
When they **l** Pharaoh's presence, **Ex 5:20** 3318
they may be **l** only in the Nile?" **Ex 8:9** 7604
they will be **l** only in the Nile." **Ex 8:11** 7604
l his servants and his livestock in the **Ex 9:21** 5800a
what is **l** to you from the hail **Ex 10:5** 7604
even all that the hail has **l**." **Ex 10:12** 7604
of the trees that the hail had **l**. **Ex 10:15** 3498
Thus nothing green was **l** on tree **Ex 10:15** 3498
not one locust was **l** in all the **Ex 10:19** 7604
not a hoof shall be **l** behind, **Ex 10:26** 7604
whatever is **l** of it until morning, **Ex 12:10** 3498
their right hand and on their **l**. **Ex 14:22** 8040

their right hand and on their **l**. Ex 14:29 8040
some **l** part of it until morning, Ex 16:20 3498
and all that is **l** over put aside Ex 16:23 5736
part that is **l** over in the curtains of Ex 26:12 5736
the half curtain that is **l** over, Ex 26:12 5736
of what is **l** over in the length of Ex 26:13 5736
to be **l** over until morning. Ex 34:25 3885a
'What is **l** of it Aaron and his Lv 6:16 3498
day what is **l** of it may be eaten; Lv 7:16 3498
but what is **l** over from the flesh Lv 7:17 3498
Take the grain offering that is **l** over Lv 10:12 3498
oil, and pour *it* into his **l** palm; Lv 14:15 8042
the oil that is in his **l** palm, Lv 14:16 8042
some of the oil into his **l** palm; Lv 14:26 8042
some of the oil that is in his **l** palm Lv 14:27 8042
'As for those of you who may be **l**, Lv 26:36 7604
'So those of you who may be **l** will Lv 26:39 7604
proportionate to the years that are **l** Lv 27:18 3498
of the LORD nor Moses **l** the camp. Nu 14:44 4185
not turning to the right or **l**, Nu 20:17 8040
until there was no remnant **l** him; Nu 21:35 7604
turn to the right hand or the **l**. Nu 22:26 8040
And not a man was **l** of them, Nu 26:65 3498
aside to the right or to the **l**. Dt 2:27 8040
We **l** no survivor. Dt 2:34 7604
them until no survivor was **l**. Dt 3:3 7604
For only Og king of Bashan was **l** Dt 3:11 7604
and you will be **l** few in number Dt 4:27 7604
aside to the right or to the **l**. Dt 5:32 8040
until those who are **l** and hide Dt 7:20 7604
from the day that you **l** the land Dt 9:7 3318
to you, to the right or the **l**. Dt 17:11 8040
to the right or the **l**, Dt 17:20 8040
today, to the right or to the **l**, Dt 28:14 8040
eat, since he has nothing *else* **l**, Dt 28:55 7604
"Then you shall be **l** few in number, Dt 28:62 7604
from it to the right or to the **l**, Jos 1:7 8040
So not a man was **l** in Ai or Bethel Jos 8:17 7604
and they **l** the city unguarded and Jos 8:17 5800a
they slew them until no one was **l** Jos 8:22 7604
the day that we **l** to come to you; Jos 9:12 3318
He **l** no survivor. Jos 10:28 7604
He **l** no survivor in it. Jos 10:30 7604
until he had **l** him no survivor. Jos 10:33 7604
He **l** no survivor, according to all Jos 10:37 7604
He **l** no survivor. Jos 10:39 7604
He **l** no survivor, but he utterly Jos 10:40 7604
until no survivor was **l** to them. Jos 11:8 7604
there was no one **l** who breathed. Jos 11:11 3498
They **l** no one who breathed. Jos 11:14 7604
he **l** nothing undone of all that Jos 11:15 5493
There were no Anakim **l** in the land Jos 11:22 3498
he alone was **l** of the Jos 13:12 7604
it to the right hand or to the **l**, Jos 23:6 8040
which Joshua **l** when he died, Jg 2:21 5800a
are the nations which the LORD **l**, Jg 3:1 5117
And all who attended him **l** him. Jg 3:19 3318
Ehud stretched out his **l** hand, Jg 3:21 8040
not even one was **l**. Jg 4:16 7604
held the torches in their **l** hands Jg 7:20 8040
all who were **l** of the entire army Jg 8:10 3498
youngest son of Jerubbaal was **l**, Jg 9:5 3498
and she **l** with her companions, and Jg 11:38 1980
him, and his strength **l** him. Jg 16:19 5493
hand and the other with his **l**. Jg 16:29 8040
do for wives for those who are **l**, Jg 21:7 3498
do for wives for those who are **l**, Jg 21:16 3498
and she was **l** with her two sons. Ru 1:3 7604
and how you **l** your father and your Ru 2:11 5800a
and was satisfied and had some **l**. Ru 2:14 3498
she had **l** after she was satisfied. Ru 2:18 3498
the LORD who has not **l** you without Ru 4:14 7673a
'Everyone who is **l** in your house will 1Sa 2:36 3498
the trunk of Dagon was **l** to him. 1Sa 5:4 7604
aside to the right or to the **l**. 1Sa 6:12 8040
no two of them were **l** together. 1Sa 11:11 7604
l the flock with a keeper and took 1Sa 17:20 5203
Then David **l** his baggage in the 1Sa 17:22 5203
And with whom have you **l** those few 1Sa 17:28 5203
he **l** them with the king of Moab; 1Sa 22:4 5148
And Saul arose, **l** the cave, and 1Sa 24:7 4480
would not have been **l** to Nabal 1Sa 25:34 3498
where those **l** behind remained. 1Sa 30:9 3498
and my master **l** me behind when I 1Sa 30:13 5800a
also been **l** at the brook Besor, 1Sa 30:21 3427
did not turn to the right or to the **l** 2Sa 2:19 8040
"Turn to your right or to your **l**, 2Sa 2:21 8040
yet anyone **l** of the house of Saul, 2Sa 9:1 3498
sons, and not one of them is **l**." 2Sa 13:30 3498
extinguish my coal which is **l**, 2Sa 14:7 7604
one can turn to the right or to the **l** 2Sa 14:19 8041
But the king **l** ten concubines to 2Sa 15:16 5800a
at his right hand and at his **l**. 2Sa 16:6 8040
whom he has **l** to keep the house; 2Sa 16:21 5117
with him, not even one will be **l**. 2Sa 17:12 3498
so he was **l** hanging between heaven 2Sa 18:9 5414
whom he had **l** to keep the house, 2Sa 20:3 5117
they **l** nothing lacking. 1Ki 4:27 5737c
he set up the **l** pillar and named it 1Ki 7:21 8042
five on the **l** side of the house; 1Ki 7:39 8040
Solomon **l** all the utensils *unweighed,* 1Ki 7:47 5117
the right side and five on the **l**, 1Ki 7:49 8040
people who were **l** of the Amorites, 1Ki 9:20 3498
their descendants who were **l** after 1Ki 9:21 3498
the silver and the gold which were **l** 1Ki 15:18 3498
that there was no breath **l** in him. 1Ki 17:17 3498
I alone am **l** a prophet of the LORD, 1Ki 18:22 3498
to Judah, and **l** his servant there. 1Ki 19:3 5117
And I alone am **l**; 1Ki 19:10 3498
And I alone am **l**; 1Ki 19:14 3498
He **l** the oxen and ran after 1Ki 19:20 5800a
fell on 27,000 men who were **l**. 1Ki 20:30 3498
by Him on His right and on His **l**. 1Ki 22:19 8040
only they **l** its stones; 2Ki 3:25 7604
eat and have *some* **l** over.' " 2Ki 4:43 3498
and they ate and had *some* **l** over, 2Ki 4:44 3498
and **l** their tents and their horses 2Ki 7:7 5800a
remain, which are **l** in the city. 2Ki 7:13 7604
of Israel who are **l** in it; 2Ki 7:13 7604
she **l** the land even until now." 2Ki 8:6 5800a
until he **l** him without a survivor. 2Ki 10:11 7604
and he **l** none of them. 2Ki 10:14 7604
was not a man **l** who did not come. 2Ki 10:21 7604
house to the **l** side of the house, 2Ki 11:11 8042
For he **l** to Jehoahaz of the army 2Ki 13:7 7604
was **l** except the tribe of Judah. 2Ki 17:18 7604
for the remnant that is **l**.' " 2Ki 19:4 4672
heard that the king had **l** Lachish. 2Ki 19:8 5265
nothing shall be **l**,' 2Ki 20:17 3498
aside to the right or to the **l**. 2Ki 22:2 8040
were on one's **l** at the city gate. 2Ki 23:8 8040
So they **l** his bones undisturbed 2Ki 23:18 4422
the rest of the people who were **l** 2Ki 25:11 7604
But the captain of the guard **l** 2Ki 25:12 7604
who were **l** in the land of Judah, 2Ki 25:22 7604
king of Babylon had **l**, 2Ki 25:22 7604
On the **l** hand *were* their 1Ch 6:44 8040
using both the right hand and the **l** 1Ch 12:2 8041
So he **l** Asaph and his relatives 1Ch 16:37 5800a
He **l** Zadok the priest and his 1Ch 16:39
the right and the other on the **l**, 2Ch 3:17 8040
Jachin and the one on the **l** Boaz. 2Ch 3:17 8042
the right side and five on the **l** to 2Ch 4:6 8040
the right side and five on the **l**, 2Ch 4:7 8040
the right side and five on the **l**. 2Ch 4:8 8040
people who were **l** of the Hittites, 2Ch 8:7 3498
from their descendants who were **l** 2Ch 8:8 3498
For the Levites **l** their pasture 2Ch 11:14 5800a
on His right and on His **l**. 2Ch 18:18 8040
son was **l** to him except Jehoahaz, 2Ch 21:17 7604
house to the **l** side of the house, 2Ch 23:10 8042
him (for they **l** him very sick), 2Ch 24:25 5800a
So the armed men **l** the captives 2Ch 28:14 5800a
those of you who escaped *and* are **l** 2Ch 30:6 7604
enough to eat with plenty **l** over, 2Ch 31:10 3498
this great quantity is **l** over." 2Ch 31:10 3498
God **l** him *alone only* to test him, 2Ch 32:31 5800a
aside to the right or to the **l**. 2Ch 34:2 8040
who are **l** in Israel and in Judah, 2Ch 34:21 7604
we have been **l** an escaped remnant, Ezr 9:15 7604
and Meshullam on his **l** hand. Ne 8:4 8040
second choir proceeded to the **l**, Ne 12:38 4136
And if I hold back, what has **l** me? Jb 16:6 1980
When He acts on the **l**, Jb 23:9 8040
Not one of them was **l**. Ps 106:11 3498
In her **l** hand are riches and honor. Pr 3:16 8040
turn to the right nor to the **l**; Pr 4:27 8040
heart *directs him* toward the **l**. Ec 10:2 8040
"Let his **l** hand be under my head SS 2:6 8040
"Scarcely had I **l** them When I SS 3:4 5674a
"Let his **l** hand be under my head And SS 8:3 8040
daughter of Zion is **l** like a shelter Is 1:8 3498
of hosts Had **l** us a few survivors, Is 1:9 3498
come about that he who is **l** in Zion Is 4:3 7604
for everyone that is **l** within the Is 7:22 3498
And they eat *what is* on the **l** hand Is 9:20 8040
remnant of His people who will be **l** Is 11:16 7604
Yet gleanings will be **l** in it like Is 17:6 7604
They will be **l** together for Is 18:6 5800a
are burned, and few men are **l**. Is 24:6 7604
Desolation is **l** in the city And Is 24:12 7604
you are **l** as a flag on a mountain Is 30:17 3498
you turn to the right or to the **l**. Is 30:21 8041
for the remnant that is **l**.' " Is 37:4 4672
heard that the king had **l** Lachish. Is 37:8 5265
nothing will be **l**,' Is 39:6 3498
Behold, I was **l** alone; Is 49:21 7604
abroad to the right and to the **l**. Is 54:3 8040
shame, For we have **l** the land, Jer 9:19 5800a
a remnant will not be **l** to them, Jer 11:23 1961
"He has **l** His hiding place like Jer 25:38 5800a
are **l** in the house of the LORD, Jer 27:18 3498
vessels that are **l** in this city, Jer 27:19 3498
are **l** in the house of the LORD and Jer 27:21 3498
only wounded men **l** among them, Jer 37:10 7604
the men of war who are **l** in this city Jer 38:4 7604
all of the women who have been **l** Jer 38:22 7604
the people who were **l** in the city, Jer 39:9 7604
l behind in the land of Judah, Jer 39:10 7604
the people who were **l** in the land. Jer 40:6 7604
king of Babylon had **l** a remnant for Jer 40:11 5414
the people who were **l** in Mizpah, Jer 41:10 7604
we are **l** *but* a few out of many, Jer 42:2 7604
the captain of the bodyguard had **l** Jer 43:6 5117
and Sidon Every ally that is **l**; Jer 47:4 8300
her, Let nothing be **l** to her. Jer 50:26 7611
the people who were **l** in the city, Jer 52:15 7604
l some of the poorest of the land Jer 52:16 7604
and the face of a bull on the **l**, Ezk 1:10 8040
for you, lie down on your **l** side and Ezk 4:4 8042
striking *the people* and I *alone* was **l**, Ezk 9:8 7604
the vision that I had seen **l** me. Ezk 11:24 5927
survivors will be **l** in it who will be Ezk 14:22 3498
go to the **l**, wherever your edge is Ezk 21:16 8041
daughters whom you have **l** behind Ezk 24:21 5800a
nations have cut it down and **l** it; Ezk 31:12 5203
gone down from its shade and **l** it. Ezk 31:12 5203
"Then the nations that are **l** Ezk 36:36 7604
strike your bow from your **l** hand and Ezk 39:3 8040
l on the surface of the ground, Ezk 39:14 3498
they will be **l** for salt. Ezk 47:11 5414
was troubled and his sleep **l** him. Da 2:1 1961
will not be **l** for another people; Da 2:44 7662
So I was **l** alone and saw this Da 10:8 7604
yet no strength was **l** in me, Da 10:8 7604
for I had been **l** there with the Da 10:13 3498
nor has any breath been **l** in me." Da 10:17 7604
hand and his **l** toward heaven, Da 12:7 8040
bereave them until not a man is **l**. Hos 9:12
What the gnawing locust has **l**, Jl 1:4 3499a
what the swarming locust has **l**, Jl 1:4 3499a
what the creeping locust has **l**, Jl 1:4 3499a
strong Will have a hundred **l**, Am 5:3 7604
ten **l** to the house of Israel." Am 5:3 7604
be, if ten men are **l** in one house, Am 6:9 3498
between their right and **l** hand, Jon 4:11 8040
'Who is **l** among you who saw this Hg 2:3 7604
and the other on its **l** side." Zch 4:3 8040
of the lampstand and on its **l**?" Zch 4:11 8040
let those who are **l** eat one another's Zch 11:9 7604
on the right hand and on the **l** Zch 12:6 8040
But the third will be **l** in it. Zch 13:8 3498
that any who are **l** of all the nations Zch 14:16 3498
the magi **l** for their own country by Mt 2:12 *402*
and **l** for Egypt. Mt 2:14 *402*
he **l** for the regions of Galilee, Mt 2:22 *402*
Then the devil **l** Him; Mt 4:11 *863*
Immediately they **l** their nets Mt 4:20 *863*
l the boat and their father, Mt 4:22 *863*
do not let your **l** hand know what Mt 6:3 *710*
her hand, and the fever **l** her; Mt 8:15 *863*
Then He **l** the crowds and went Mt 13:36 *863*
They picked up what was **l** over Mt 14:20 *4052*
and they picked up what was **l** over Mt 15:37 *4052*
And He **l** them and went away. Mt 16:4 *2641*
l everything and followed You; Mt 19:27 *863*
"And everyone who has **l** houses or Mt 19:29 *863*
on Your right and one on Your **l**." Mt 20:21 *2176*
to sit on My right and on *My* **l**, Mt 20:23 *2176*
And He **l** them and went out of the Mt 21:17 *2641*
l his wife to his brother; Mt 22:25 *863*
house is being **l** to you desolate! Mt 23:38 *863*
not one stone here will be **l** upon Mt 24:2 *863*
will be taken and one will be **l**. Mt 24:40 *863*
will be taken and one will be **l**. Mt 24:41 *863*
His right, and the goats on the **l**. Mt 25:33 *2176*
will also say to those on His **l**, Mt 25:41 *2176*
And He **l** them again, and went away Mt 26:44 *863*
all the disciples **l** Him and fled. Mt 26:56 *863*
one on the right and one on the **l**. Mt 27:38 *2176*
And they **l** the tomb quickly with fear Mt 28:8 *565*
l their nets and followed Him. Mk 1:18 *863*
and they **l** their father Zebedee in Mk 1:20 *863*
by the hand, and the fever **l** her, Mk 1:31 *863*
l *the house,* and went away to a Mk 1:35 *565*
leprosy **l** him and he was cleansed. Mk 1:42 *565*
After bidding them farewell, He **l** Mk 6:46 *565*
When he had **l** the crowd *and* Mk 7:17 *575*
the demon having **l**. Mk 7:30 *1831*
large baskets full of what was **l** over Mk 8:8 *4051*
l everything and followed You." Mk 10:28 *863*
there is no one who has **l** house or Mk 10:29 *863*
Your right and one on *Your* **l**. Mk 10:37 *710*
"But to sit on My right or on *My* **l**, Mk 10:40 *2176*
He **l** for Bethany with the twelve, Mk 11:11 *1831*
On the next day, when they had **l** Mk 11:12 *1831*
And *so* they **l** Him and went away. Mk 12:12 *863*
and *so* all seven **l** no children. Mk 12:22 *863*
Not one stone will be **l** upon Mk 13:2 *863*
And they all **l** Him and fled. Mk 14:50 *863*
one on His right and one on His **l**. Mk 15:27 *2176*
She never **l** the temple, Lk 2:37 *868*
he **l** Him until an opportune time. Lk 4:13 *868*
Then He got up and **l** Lk 4:38
rebuked the fever, and it **l** her; Lk 4:39 *863*
When day came, Jesus **l** and went to a Lk 4:42 *1831*
l everything and followed Him. Lk 5:11 *863*
And immediately the leprosy **l** him. Lk 5:13 *565*
And he **l** everything behind, and Lk 5:28 *2641*
When the messengers of John had **l**, Lk 7:24 *565*
broken pieces which they had **l** over Lk 9:17 *4052*
do You not care that my sister has **l** Lk 10:40 *2641*
When He **l** there, the scribes Lk 11:53 *1831*
your house is **l** to you *desolate;* Lk 13:35 *863*
be taken and the other will be **l**. Lk 17:34 *863*
be taken and the other will be **l**. Lk 17:35 *863*
taken and the other will be **l**." Lk 17:36 *863*
"Behold, we have **l** our own *homes* Lk 18:28 *863*
there is no one who has **l** house or Lk 18:29 *863*
will not be **l** one stone upon another Lk 21:6 *863*
And they **l** and found *everything* Lk 22:13 *565*
the right and the other on the **l**. Lk 23:33 *710*
He **l** Judea and went away again Jn 4:3 *863*
So the woman **l** her waterpot, and Jn 4:28 *863*
seventh hour the fever **l** him." Jn 4:52 *863*
l over by those who had eaten. Jn 6:13 *4052*
older ones, and He was **l** alone, Jn 8:9 *2641*
He has not **l** Me alone, for I Jn 8:29 *863*
"Then he **l** the land of the Chaldeans Ac 7:4 *1831*
angel who was speaking to him had **l**, Ac 10:7 *565*
he **l** for Tarsus to look for Saul; Ac 11:25 *1831*
Then he **l** and went to another place. Ac 12:17 *1831*
but John **l** them and returned to Ac 13:13 *672*
But Paul chose Silas and **l**, being Ac 15:40 *1831*
as possible, they **l**. Ac 17:15 *1826*
he **l** Athens and went to Corinth. Ac 18:1 *5563*
Then he **l** there and went to the house Ac 18:7 *3327*

to Ephesus, and he l them there.	Ac 18:19	2641
he l and passed successively	Ac 18:23	1831
and the diseases l them and the	Ac 19:12	525
he l to go to Macedonia.	Ac 20:1	1831
daybreak, and then l.	Ac 20:11	1831
of Cyprus, leaving it on the l,	Ac 21:3	2176
When our days there were ended, we l	Ac 21:5	1831
On the next day we l and came to	Ac 21:8	1831
a favor, Felix l Paul imprisoned.	Ac 24:27	2641
man who was l as a prisoner by Felix;	Ac 25:14	2641
they l them in the sea while at	Ac 27:40	1439
SABAOTH HAD L TO US A POSTERITY,	Ro 9:29	1459
YOUR ALTARS, AND I ALONE AM L,	Ro 11:3	5275b
for the right hand and the l,	2Co 6:7	710
after I l Macedonia, no church	Php 4:15	1831
to be l behind at Athens alone,	1Th 3:1	2641
and who has been l alone, has fixed	1Tm 5:5	3443
which I l at Troas with Carpus,	2Tm 4:13	620
but Trophimus I l sick at Miletus.	2Tm 4:20	620
For this reason I l you in Crete,	Ti 1:5	620
He l nothing that is not subject	Heb 2:8	863
By faith he l Egypt, not fearing	Heb 11:27	2641
that you have l your first love.	Rv 2:4	863
on the sea and his l on the land;	Rv 10:2	2176
LEFT-HANDED		
of Gera, the Benjamite, a l man.	Jg 3:15	334, 3225, 3027
people 700 choice men were l;	Jg 20:16	334, 3225, 3027
LEFTOVER		
"Gather up the l fragments so	Jn 6:12	4052
LEG		
Then the cook took up the l with	1Sa 9:24	7785
off the skirt, Uncover the l,	Is 47:2	7785
LEGACY		
then he gives his l to one who has	Ec 2:21	2506
LEGAL		
whoever has a l matter, let him	Ex 24:14	
me l protection from my opponent.'	Lk 18:3	1556
me, I will give her l protection,	Lk 18:5	1556
LEGION		
"My name is L; for we are many."	Mk 5:9	3003
very man who had had the "l";	Mk 5:15	3003
And he said, "L";	Lk 8:30	3003
LEGIONS		
more than twelve l of angels?	Mt 26:53	3003
LEGS		
and its l along with its entrails.	Ex 12:9	3767
and wash its entrails and its l,	Ex 29:17	3767
its l he shall wash with water.	Lv 1:9	3767
the l he shall wash with water.	Lv 1:13	3767
all its flesh with its head and its l	Lv 4:11	3767
the entrails and the l with water,	Lv 8:21	3767
washed the entrails and the l,	Lv 9:14	3767
which have above their feet jointed l	Lv 11:21	3767
the knees and l with sore boils,	Dt 28:35	7785
which issues from between her l	Dt 28:57	7272
He also *had* bronze greaves on his l	1Sa 17:6	7272
take pleasure in the l of a man.	Ps 147:10	7785
l *which* are useless to the lame,	Pr 26:7	7785
"His l are pillars of alabaster	SS 5:15	7785
the head and the hair of the l;	Is 7:20	7272
Their l were straight and	Ezk 1:7	7272
and you spread your l to every	Ezk 16:25	7272
its l of iron, its feet partly of	Da 2:33	8243
couple of l or a piece of an ear,	Am 3:12	3767
that their l might be broken,	Jn 19:31	4628
and broke the l of the first man and	Jn 19:32	4628
dead, they did not break His l.	Jn 19:33	4628
LEHAB		
of the people of Lud, Anam, L,	1Ch 1:11	3853
LEHABIM		
and Anamim and L and Naphtuhim	Gn 10:13	3853
LEHI		
in Judah, and spread out in L.	Jg 15:9	3896
When he came to L, the Philistines	Jg 15:14	3896
split the hollow place that is in L	Jg 15:19	3896
which is in L to this day.	Jg 15:19	3896
LEISURE		
and I will proceed at my l,	Gn 33:14	328
LEISURELY		
days, so will your l walk be.	Dt 33:25	1679
LEMUEL		
The words of King L,	Pr 31:1	3927
It is not for kings, O L,	Pr 31:4	3927
LEND		
"If you l money to My people, to	Ex 22:25	3867b
and you will l to many nations,	Dt 15:6	5670
and shall generously l him	Dt 15:8	5670
and you shall l to many nations,	Dt 28:12	3867b
"He shall l to you, but you will	Dt 28:44	3867b
you, but you will not l to him;	Dt 28:44	3867b
if he does not l *money* on interest	Ezk 18:8	5414
"If you l to those from whom	Lk 6:34	1155
Even sinners l to sinners in	Lk 6:34	1155
and l, expecting nothing in return;	Lk 6:35	1155
'Friend, l me three loaves;	Lk 11:5	5531
LENDER		
seller, the l like the borrower,	Is 24:2	3867b
LENDER'S		
the borrower *becomes* the l slave.	Pr 22:7	3867b
LENDING		
are l them money and grain.	Ne 5:10	5383
LENDS		
All day long he is gracious and l,	Ps 37:26	3867b
the man who is gracious and l;	Ps 112:5	3867b
to a poor man l to the LORD,	Pr 19:17	3867b
he l *money* on interest and takes	Ezk 18:13	5414
LENGTH		
the l of the ark three hundred	Gn 6:15	753
land through its l and breadth;	Gn 13:17	753
so the l of Jacob's life was one	Gn 47:28	3117
and the l of Levi's life was one	Ex 6:16	8141
and the l of Kohath's life was one	Ex 6:18	8141
and the l of Amram's life was one	Ex 6:20	8141
"The l of each curtain shall be	Ex 26:2	753
"The l of each curtain *shall be*	Ex 26:8	753
the l of the curtains of the tent,	Ex 26:13	753
shall be the l of each board and	Ex 26:16	753
"Likewise for the north side in l	Ex 27:11	753
"The l of the court *shall be* one	Ex 27:18	753
a span in l and a span in width.	Ex 28:16	753
"Its l *shall be* a cubit, and its	Ex 30:2	753
The l of each curtain was	Ex 36:9	753
The l of each curtain *was* thirty	Ex 36:15	753
cubits *was* the l of each board	Ex 36:21	753
its l was two and a half cubits,	Ex 37:1	753
And the l *was* twenty cubits and	Ex 38:18	753
Its l was nine cubits and its	Dt 3:11	753
your life and the l of your days,	Dt 30:20	753
which had two edges, a cubit in l,	Jg 3:16	753
Then Saul immediately fell full l	1Sa 28:20	6967
its l *was* sixty cubits and its	1Ki 6:2	753
the house *was* twenty cubits in l,	1Ki 6:3	753
sanctuary *was* twenty cubits in l,	1Ki 6:20	753
its l was 100 cubits and its width	1Ki 7:2	753
its l was 50 cubits and its width	1Ki 7:6	753
the l of each stand was four	1Ki 7:27	753
The l in cubits, according to the	2Ch 3:3	753
its l across the width of the	2Ch 3:8	753
twenty cubits in l and twenty	2Ch 4:1	753
him, L of days forever and ever.	Ps 21:4	753
man who desires life And loves l *of*	Ps 34:12	
For l of days and years of life And	Pr 3:2	753
tired out by the l of your road,	Is 57:10	7230
in the l of its branches;	Ezk 31:7	753
ten cubits, and the l of the gate,	Ezk 40:11	753
to the l of the gates.	Ezk 40:18	753
he measured its l and its width.	Ezk 40:20	753
Its l *was* fifty cubits and the	Ezk 40:21	753
the l *was* fifty cubits and the	Ezk 40:25	753
the l *was* fifty cubits and the	Ezk 40:36	753
hooks, one handbreadth in l,	Ezk 40:43	
The l of the porch *was* twenty	Ezk 40:49	753
And he measured the l of the nave,	Ezk 41:2	753
He measured its l,	Ezk 41:4	753
and its l *was* ninety cubits.	Ezk 41:12	753
He measured the l of the building	Ezk 41:15	753
cubits high and its l two cubits;	Ezk 41:22	753
Along the l, *which was* a hundred	Ezk 42:2	753
chambers, its l *was* fifty cubits.	Ezk 42:7	753
For the l of the chambers which	Ezk 42:8	753
the l *of those* facing the temple	Ezk 42:8	
to their l so was their width,	Ezk 42:11	753
the l five hundred and the width	Ezk 42:20	753
the l shall be the length of	Ezk 45:1	753
shall be the l of 25,000 *cubits,*	Ezk 45:1	753
measure a l of 25,000 *cubits*	Ezk 45:3	753
"*An area* 25,000 *cubits* in l	Ezk 45:5	753
and in l comparable to one of the	Ezk 45:7	753
and in l like one of the portions,	Ezk 48:8	753
LORD *shall be* 25,000 *cubits* in l and	Ezk 48:9	753
25,000 *cubits in* l, toward the west	Ezk 48:10	
and toward the south 25,000 in l;	Ezk 48:10	753
shall have 25,000 *cubits* in l and	Ezk 48:13	753
The whole l *shall be* 25,000 *cubits*	Ezk 48:13	753
cubits in width and 25,000 in l.	Ezk 48:15	5921, 6440
"The remainder of the l	Ezk 48:18	753
its l is twenty cubits and its	Zch 5:2	753
And he questioned Him at some l;	Lk 23:9	3056, 2425
and l and height and depth,	Eph 3:18	3372
its l is as great as the width;	Rv 21:16	3372
its l and width and height are	Rv 21:16	3372
LENGTHEN		
hundred *times* and may l his *life,*	Ec 8:12	748
will not l his days like a shadow,	Ec 8:13	748
L your cords And strengthen your	Is 54:2	748
For the shadows of the evening l!	Jer 6:4	5186
l the tassels *of their garments.*	Mt 23:5	3170
LENGTHENED		
My days are like a l shadow,	Ps 102:11	5186
They l their furrows."	Ps 129:3	748
LENGTHENS		
passing like a shadow when it l;	Ps 109:23	5186
LENGTHY		
the brethren with a l message.	Ac 15:32	4183
LENT		
I have not l, nor have men	Jer 15:10	5383
lent, nor have men l money to me,	Jer 15:10	5383
LENTIL		
Jacob gave Esau bread and l stew;	Gn 25:34	5742
LENTILS		
flour, parched *grain,* beans, l,	2Sa 17:28	5742
was a plot of ground full of l,	2Sa 23:11	5742
you, take wheat, barley, beans, l,	Ezk 4:9	5742
LEOPARD		
the l will lie down with the young goat,	Is 11:6	5246
A l is watching their cities.	Jer 5:6	5246
his skin Or the l his spots?	Jer 13:23	5246
and behold, another one, like a l,	Da 7:6	5245
Like a l I will lie in wait by the	Hos 13:7	5246
beast which I saw was like a l,	Rv 13:2	3917
LEOPARDS		
of lions, From the mountains of l.	SS 4:8	5246
"Their horses are swifter than l	Hab 1:8	5246
LEPER		
for the l who has the infection,	Lv 13:45	6879
the law of the l in the day of his	Lv 14:2	6879
leprosy has been healed in the l,	Lv 14:3	6879
who is a l or who has a discharge,	Lv 22:4	6879
send away from the camp every l	Nu 5:2	6879
has a discharge, or who is a l,	2Sa 3:29	6879
a valiant warrior, *but he was* a l.	2Ki 5:1	6879
over the place and cure the l.'	2Ki 5:11	6879
his presence a l *as white* as snow.	2Ki 5:27	6879
was a l to the day of his death.	2Ki 15:5	6879
was a l to the day of his death;	2Ch 26:21	6879
in a separate house, being a l,	2Ch 26:21	6879
the kings, for they said, "He is a l."	2Ch 26:23	6879
And a l came to Him and	Mt 8:2	3015
at the home of Simon the l,	Mt 26:6	3015
And a l came to Jesus, beseeching	Mk 1:40	3015
at the home of Simon the l,	Mk 14:3	3015
LEPERS		
When these l came to the outskirts	2Ki 7:8	6879
raise *the* dead, cleanse *the* l,	Mt 10:8	3015
the l are cleansed and the deaf	Mt 11:5	3015
"And there were many l in Israel	Lk 4:27	3015
the lame walk, *the* l are cleansed,	Lk 7:22	3015
LEPROSY		
an infection of l on the skin of his	Lv 13:2	6883
his body, it is an infection of l;	Lv 13:3	6883
shall pronounce him unclean; it is l.	Lv 13:8	6883
the infection of l is on a man,	Lv 13:9	6883
chronic l on the skin of his body,	Lv 13:11	6883
"If the l breaks out farther	Lv 13:12	6883
and the l covers all the skin of	Lv 13:12	6883
if the l has covered all his body,	Lv 13:13	6883
the raw flesh is unclean, it is l.	Lv 13:15	6883
it is the infection of l,	Lv 13:20	6883
be deeper than the skin, it is l;	Lv 13:25	6883
it is an infection of l.	Lv 13:25	6883
it is an infection of l.	Lv 13:27	6883
is l of the head or of the beard.	Lv 13:30	6883
it is l breaking out on his bald	Lv 13:42	6883
like the appearance of l in the skin	Lv 13:43	6883
a garment has a mark of l in it,	Lv 13:47	6883
law for the mark of l in a garment	Lv 13:59	6883
the infection of l has been healed in	Lv 14:3	6883
who is to be cleansed from the l and	Lv 14:7	6883
whom there is an infection of l,	Lv 14:32	6883
and I put a mark of l on a house	Lv 14:34	6883
'*Something* like a mark *of* l	Lv 14:35	
This is the law for any mark of l	Lv 14:54	6883
This is the law of l.	Lv 14:57	6883
careful against an infection of l,	Dt 24:8	6883
Then he would cure him of his l."	2Ki 5:3	6883
that you may cure him of his l."	2Ki 5:6	6883
word to me to cure a man of his l?	2Ki 5:7	6883
the l of Naaman shall cling to	2Ki 5:27	6883
the l broke out on his forehead	2Ch 26:19	6883
immediately his l was cleansed.	Mt 8:3	3014
l left him and he was cleansed.	Mk 1:42	3014
behold, *there was* a man covered with l;	Lk 5:12	3014
And immediately the l left him.	Lk 5:13	3014
LEPROUS		
behold, his hand was l like snow.	Ex 4:6	6879
he is a l man, he is unclean.	Lv 13:44	6879
it is a l mark and shall be shown	Lv 13:49	6883
used, the mark is a l malignancy,	Lv 13:51	6883
occurs, for it is a l malignancy;	Lv 13:52	6883
and for the l garment or house,	Lv 14:55	6883
the tent, behold, Miriam *was* l,	Nu 12:10	6879
toward Miriam, behold, she *was* l.	Nu 12:10	6879
Now there were four l men at the	2Ki 7:3	6879
behold, he *was* l on his forehead;	2Ch 26:20	6879
ten l men who stood at a distance	Lk 17:12	3015
LESHEM		
and fought with L and captured it.	Jos 19:47	3959
and they called L Dan after the	Jos 19:47	3959
LESS		
not pay l than the half shekel,	Ex 30:15	4591
you shall give l inheritance.	Nu 33:54	4591
you shall take l from the smaller;	Nu 35:8	4591
"This is nothing l than the sword	Jg 7:14	1115, 518
how much l this house which I have	1Ki 8:27	637
how much l this house which I have	2Ch 6:18	637
How much l will your God deliver	2Ch 32:15	637
us l than our iniquities *deserve,*	Ezr 9:13	4295
How much l one who is detestable	Jb 15:16	637
How much l man, *that* maggot, And	Jb 25:6	637
"How much l when you say you do	Jb 35:14	637
Much l are lying lips to a prince.	Pr 17:7	637
Much l for a slave to rule over	Pr 19:10	637
as l than nothing and meaningless.	Is 40:17	657
How much l, when the fire has	Ezk 15:5	637
mother of James the L and Joses,	Mk 15:40	3398
any the l *a part* of the body.	1Co 12:15	3756
any the l *a part* of the body.	1Co 12:16	3756
body which we deem l honorable,	1Co 12:23	820
and our l presentable members become	1Co 12:23	820
more, am I to be loved l?	2Co 12:15	2269b
I may be l concerned *about you.*	Php 2:28	253
she is not l than sixty years old,	1Tm 5:9	1640
much l *will we escape* who turn	Heb 12:25	3123

LESSEN		
Thus I will **l** from upon Myself	Nu 17:5	7918
of my lips could **l** *your pain.*	Jb 16:5	2820
LESSENED		
"If I speak, my pain is not **l**,	Jb 16:6	2820
LESSER		
the **l** light to govern the night;	Gn 1:16	6996b
the judges and the **l** governors,	Ezr 4:9	671b
the **l** is blessed by the greater.	Heb 7:7	*1640*
LET		
"**L** there be light";	Gn 1:3	
"**L** there be an expanse in the	Gn 1:6	
and **l** it separate the waters from	Gn 1:6	
"**L** the waters below the heavens	Gn 1:9	
and **l** the dry land appear";	Gn 1:9	
"**L** the earth sprout vegetation,	Gn 1:11	
"**L** there be lights in the expanse	Gn 1:14	
night, and **l** them be for signs and	Gn 1:14	
and **l** them be for lights in the	Gn 1:15	
"**L** the waters teem with swarms of	Gn 1:20	
and **l** birds fly above the earth in	Gn 1:20	
l birds multiply on the earth."	Gn 1:22	
"**L** the earth bring forth living	Gn 1:24	
"**L** Us make man in Our image,	Gn 1:26	
and **l** them rule over the fish of	Gn 1:26	
And **l** Canaan be his servant.	Gn 9:26	
And **l** him dwell in the tents of	Gn 9:27	
And **l** Canaan be his servant."	Gn 9:27	
l us make bricks and burn *them*	Gn 11:3	
l us build for ourselves a city,	Gn 11:4	
l us make for ourselves a name,	Gn 11:4	
l Us go down and there confuse	Gn 11:7	
kill me, but they will **l** you live.	Gn 12:12	
"Please **l** there be no strife	Gn 13:8	
l them take their share."	Gn 14:24	
"Please **l** a little water be	Gn 18:4	
please **l** me bring them out to you,	Gn 19:8	
Please, **l** me escape there	Gn 19:20	
l us make our father drink wine,	Gn 19:32	
drink wine, and **l** us lie with him that	Gn 19:32	
l us make him drink wine tonight	Gn 19:34	
I did not **l** you touch her.	Gn 20:6	5414
"Do not **l** me see the boy die."	Gn 21:16	
for the full price **l** him give it	Gn 23:9	
'Please **l** down your jar so that I	Gn 24:14	5186
"Please **l** me drink a little water	Gn 24:17	
"Please **l** me drink a little water	Gn 24:43	
l her be the woman whom the LORD	Gn 24:44	
'Please **l** me drink.'	Gn 24:45	
and if not, **l** me know, that I may	Gn 24:49	
and **l** her be the wife of your	Gn 24:51	
"**L** the girl stay with us *a few*	Gn 24:55	
"Please **l** me have a swallow of	Gn 25:30	
'**L** there now be an oath between	Gn 26:28	
and **l** us make a covenant with you,	Gn 26:28	
"**L** my father arise and eat of	Gn 27:31	
have served you, and **l** me depart;	Gn 30:26	
l me pass through your entire	Gn 30:32	
l it be according to your word."	Gn 30:34	
"**L** not my lord be angry that I	Gn 31:35	
So now come, **l** us make a covenant	Gn 31:44	
and **l** it be a witness between you	Gn 31:44	
"**L** me go, for the dawn is	Gn 32:26	7971
will not **l** you go unless you bless me	Gn 32:26	7971
l what you have be your own."	Gn 33:9	
"**L** us take our journey and go,	Gn 33:12	
"Please **l** my lord pass on before	Gn 33:14	
"Please **l** me leave with you some	Gn 33:15	
L me find favor in the sight of my	Gn 33:15	
therefore **l** them live in the land	Gn 34:21	
L us take their daughters in	Gn 34:21	
Only **l** us consent to them, and	Gn 34:23	
l us arise and go up to Bethel,	Gn 35:3	
'**L** us go to Dothan.' "	Gn 37:17	
come and **l** us kill him and throw	Gn 37:20	
Then **l** us see what will become of	Gn 37:20	
"**L** us not take his life."	Gn 37:21	
"Come and **l** us sell him to the	Gn 37:27	
"Here now, **l** me come in to you";	Gn 38:16	
"**L** her keep them, otherwise we	Gn 38:23	
her out and **l** her be burned!"	Gn 38:24	
"Now **l** Pharaoh look for a man	Gn 41:33	
"**L** Pharaoh take action to appoint	Gn 41:34	
and **l** him exact a fifth *of the*	Gn 41:34	
"Then **l** them gather all the food	Gn 41:35	
authority, and **l** them guard *it.*	Gn 41:35	
"**L** the food become as a reserve for	Gn 41:36	
l one of your brothers be confined	Gn 42:19	
then **l** me bear the blame before	Gn 43:9	
servants it is found, **l** him die,	Gn 44:9	
"Now **l** it also be according to	Gn 44:10	
then **l** me bear the blame before my	Gn 44:32	
please **l** your servant remain	Gn 44:33	
and **l** the lad go up with his	Gn 44:33	
"Now **l** me die, since I have seen	Gn 46:30	
please **l** your servants live in the	Gn 47:4	
l them live in the land of Goshen;	Gn 47:6	
L us find favor in the sight of my	Gn 47:25	
l me see your children as well."	Gn 48:11	
"**L** my soul not enter into their	Gn 49:6	
L not my glory be united with	Gn 49:6	
"Naphtali is a doe **l** loose,	Gn 49:21	7971
l me go up and bury my father;	Gn 50:5	
"Come, **l** us deal wisely with	Ex 1:10	
them, but **l** the boys live.	Ex 1:17	
this thing, and **l** the boys live?"	Ex 1:18	
l us go a three days' journey into	Ex 3:18	
and after that he will **l** you go.	Ex 3:20	
"Please, **l** me go, that I may	Ex 4:18	
that he will not **l** the people go.	Ex 4:21	7971
'**L** My son go that he may serve	Ex 4:23	7971
but you have refused to **l** him go.	Ex 4:23	7971
So He **l** him alone.	Ex 4:26	7503
'**L** My people go that they may	Ex 5:1	7971
obey His voice to **l** Israel go?	Ex 5:2	7971
besides, I will not **l** Israel go."	Ex 5:2	7971
l us go a three days' journey into	Ex 5:3	
l them go and gather straw for	Ex 5:7	
'**L** us go and sacrifice to our God.'	Ex 5:8	
"**L** the labor be heavier on the	Ex 5:9	
and **l** them work at it so that they	Ex 5:9	
'**L** us go *and* sacrifice to the LORD.'	Ex 5:17	
compulsion he will **l** them go,	Ex 6:1	7971
to **l** the sons of Israel go out of his	Ex 6:11	7971
that he **l** the sons of Israel go out of	Ex 7:2	7971
he refuses to **l** the people go.	Ex 7:14	7971
"**L** My people go, that they may	Ex 7:16	7971
"**L** My people go, that they may	Ex 8:1	7971
"But if you refuse to **l** *them* go,	Ex 8:2	7971
and I will **l** the people go, that	Ex 8:8	7971
"**L** My people go, that they may	Ex 8:20	7971
if you do not **l** My people go,	Ex 8:21	7971
"I will **l** you go, that you may	Ex 8:28	7971
only do not **l** Pharaoh deal	Ex 8:29	
and he did not **l** the people go.	Ex 8:32	7971
"**L** My people go, that they may	Ex 9:1	7971
"For if you refuse to **l** *them* go and	Ex 9:2	7971
and he did not **l** the people go.	Ex 9:7	7971
and **l** Moses throw it toward the	Ex 9:8	
"**L** My people go, that they may	Ex 9:13	7971
and I will **l** you go, and you shall	Ex 9:28	7971
did not **l** the sons of Israel go,	Ex 9:35	7971
L My people go, that they may	Ex 10:3	7971
if you refuse to **l** My people go,	Ex 10:4	7971
L the men go, that they may serve	Ex 10:7	7971
I **l** you and your little ones go!	Ex 10:10	7971
did not **l** the sons of Israel go.	Ex 10:20	7971
only **l** your flocks and your herds	Ex 10:24	
"You must also **l** us have	Ex 10:25	5414
he was not willing to **l** them go.	Ex 10:27	7971
that he will **l** you go from here.	Ex 11:1	7971
and he did not **l** the sons of	Ex 11:10	7971
they **l** them have their request.	Ex 12:36	
l all his males be circumcised,	Ex 12:48	
l him come near to celebrate it;	Ex 12:48	
when Pharaoh had **l** the people go,	Ex 13:17	7971
l Israel go from serving us?"	Ex 14:5	7971
"**L** us flee from Israel, for the	Ex 14:25	
"**L** no man leave any of it until	Ex 16:19	
l no man go out of his place on	Ex 16:29	
'**L** an omerful of it be kept	Ex 16:32	
and when he **l** his hand down,	Ex 17:11	
"**L** them judge the people at all	Ex 18:22	
and **l** it be that every major	Ex 18:22	
and **l** them wash their garments;	Ex 19:10	
and **l** them be ready for the third	Ex 19:11	
"Also **l** the priests who come	Ex 19:22	
but do not **l** the priests and the	Ex 19:24	
but **l** not God speak to us, or we	Ex 20:19	
then he shall **l** her be redeemed.	Ex 21:8	
but God **l** *him* fall into his hand,	Ex 21:13	579
he shall **l** him go free on account	Ex 21:26	
he shall **l** him go free on account	Ex 21:27	
l him bring it as evidence;	Ex 22:13	
shall **l** it rest and lie fallow,	Ex 23:11	8058
l *them* be heard from your mouth.	Ex 23:13	
matter, **l** him approach them."	Ex 24:14	
"**L** them construct a sanctuary for Me,	Ex 25:8	
"Now then **l** Me alone, that My	Ex 32:10	5117
not **l** the anger of my lord burn;	Ex 32:22	
has any gold, **l** them tear it off.'	Ex 32:24	
Aaron had **l** them get out of control	Ex 32:25	
But You Yourself have not **l** me	Ex 33:12	
l me know Your ways that I may	Ex 33:13	
nor **l** any man be seen anywhere on	Ex 34:3	
l the Lord go along in our midst,	Ex 34:9	
l him bring it as the LORD's	Ex 35:5	
'**L** every skillful man among you come,	Ex 35:10	
"**L** no man or woman any	Ex 36:6	
then **l** him offer to the LORD a	Lv 4:3	
and shall **l** the live bird go free	Lv 14:7	
he shall **l** the live bird go free	Lv 14:53	
and **l** all who heard him lay their	Lv 24:14	
then **l** all the congregation stone	Lv 24:14	
'I will **l** loose among you the	Lv 26:22	7971
"Do not **l** the tribe of the	Nu 4:18	
l *the hair of* the woman's head go	Nu 5:18	6544a
he shall **l** the locks of hair on	Nu 6:5	
"**L** them present their offering,	Nu 7:11	
and **l** them use a razor over their	Nu 8:7	
"Then **l** them take a bull with its	Nu 8:8	
l the sons of Israel observe the	Nu 9:2	
And **l** Your enemies be scattered,	Nu 10:35	
And **l** those who hate You flee	Nu 10:35	
do not **l** me see my wretchedness."	Nu 11:15	
and **l** them take their stand there	Nu 11:16	
and **l** *them* fall beside the camp,	Nu 11:31	
"Oh, do not **l** her be like one	Nu 12:12	
L her be shut up for seven days	Nu 12:14	
"**L** us appoint a leader and return	Nu 14:4	
l the power of the Lord be great,	Nu 14:17	
l them be made into hammered	Nu 16:38	
l the congregation and their beasts	Nu 20:8	
l us pass through your land.	Nu 20:17	
L me only pass through on my feet,	Nu 20:19	
"**L** me pass through your land.	Nu 21:22	
"Come to Heshbon! **L** it be built!	Nu 21:27	
So **l** the city of Sihon be	Nu 21:27	
has refused to **l** me go with you."	Nu 22:13	5414
'**L** nothing, I beg you, hinder you	Nu 22:16	
you just now, and **l** her live."	Nu 22:33	
L me die the death of the upright,	Nu 23:10	
And **l** my end be like his!"	Nu 23:10	
l this land be given to your	Nu 32:5	
those whom you **l** remain of them	Nu 33:55	3498
'**L** them marry whom they wish;	Nu 36:6	
'**L** us send men before us, that	Dt 1:22	
'**L** me pass through your land, I	Dt 2:27	
only **l** me pass through on foot,	Dt 2:28	
'**L** me, I pray, cross over and see	Dt 3:25	
that I may **l** them hear My words so	Dt 4:10	
"Out of the heavens He **l** you hear	Dt 4:36	
earth He **l** you see His great fire,	Dt 4:36	
humbled you and **l** you be hungry,	Dt 8:3	
'**L** Me alone, that I may destroy	Dt 9:14	7503
'**L** us go after other gods	Dt 13:2	
and **l** us serve them,'	Dt 13:2	
'**L** us go and serve other gods'	Dt 13:6	
'**L** us go and serve other gods'	Dt 13:13	
'**L** me not hear again the voice of	Dt 18:16	
l me not see this great fire	Dt 18:16	
L him depart and return to his	Dt 20:5	
L him depart and return to his	Dt 20:6	
L him depart and return to his	Dt 20:7	
L him depart and return to his	Dt 20:8	
l her go wherever she wishes;	Dt 21:14	7971
shall certainly **l** the mother go,	Dt 22:7	7971
ear, O heavens, and **l** me speak;	Dt 32:1	
And **l** the earth hear the words of	Dt 32:1	
"**L** my teaching drop as the rain,	Dt 32:2	
L them rise up and help you, Let	Dt 32:38	
you, **L** them be your hiding place!	Dt 32:38	
Of Levi he said, "**L** Your	Dt 33:8	
L it come to the head of Joseph,	Dt 33:16	
have **l** you see *it* with your eyes,	Dt 34:4	
Then she **l** them down by a rope	Jos 2:15	3381
through which you **l** us down,	Jos 2:18	3381
"**L** this be a sign among you, so	Jos 4:6	
He would not **l** them see the land	Jos 5:6	
and **l** seven priests carry seven	Jos 6:6	
and **l** the armed men go on before	Jos 6:7	
shout nor **l** your voice be heard nor	Jos 6:10	
nor **l** a word proceed out of your	Jos 6:10	
"Do not **l** all the people go up;	Jos 7:3	
with them, to **l** them live;	Jos 9:15	
will do to them, even **l** them live,	Jos 9:20	
leaders said to them, "**L** them live."	Jos 9:21	
help me, and **l** us attack Gibeon,	Jos 10:4	
behold, the LORD has **l** me live,	Jos 14:10	
'**L** us build an altar, not for	Jos 22:26	
but they **l** the man and all his	Jg 1:25	7971
"Thus **l** all Your enemies perish,	Jg 5:31	
But **l** those who love Him be like	Jg 5:31	
a god, **l** him contend for himself,	Jg 6:31	
"**L** Baal contend against him,"	Jg 6:32	
"Do not **l** Your anger burn	Jg 6:39	
please **l** me make a test once more	Jg 6:39	
l it now be dry only on the	Jg 6:39	
and **l** there be dew on all the	Jg 6:39	
l him return and depart from Mount	Jg 7:3	
so **l** all the *other* people go, each	Jg 7:7	
if only you had **l** them live,	Jg 8:19	
and **l** him also rejoice in you.	Jg 9:19	
l fire come out from Abimelech and	Jg 9:20	
and **l** fire come out from the men	Jg 9:20	
l them deliver you in the time of	Jg 10:14	
l us pass through your land,"	Jg 11:17	
"Please **l** us pass through your	Jg 11:19	
"**L** this thing be done for me;	Jg 11:37	
l me alone two months, that I may	Jg 11:37	7503
"**L** me cross over,"	Jg 12:5	
please **l** the man of God whom You	Jg 13:8	
"**L** the woman pay attention to all	Jg 13:13	
l her observe all that I commanded."	Jg 13:14	
"Please **l** us detain you so that	Jg 13:15	
nor would He have **l** us hear *things*	Jg 13:23	
"**L** me now propound a riddle to	Jg 14:12	
her father did not **l** him enter.	Jg 15:1	5414
Please **l** her be yours instead."	Jg 15:2	
"**L** *us wait* until the morning	Jg 16:2	
"**L** me feel the pillars on which	Jg 16:26	
"**L** me die with the Philistines!"	Jg 16:30	
and **l** us go up against them;	Jg 18:9	
l your voice be heard among us,	Jg 18:25	
and **l** your heart be merry."	Jg 19:6	
and **l** us turn aside into this city	Jg 19:11	
"Come and **l** us approach one of	Jg 19:13	
Only **l** me *take care of* all your	Jg 19:20	
Please **l** me bring them out that	Jg 19:24	
then **l** her go at the approach of	Jg 19:25	7971
"Get up and **l** us go,"	Jg 19:28	
"**L** us flee that we may draw them	Jg 20:32	
"Please **l** me go to the field and	Ru 2:2	
'Please **l** me glean and gather	Ru 2:7	
"**L** your eyes be on the field	Ru 2:9	
"**L** her glean even among the	Ru 2:15	
l him redeem you.	Ru 3:13	
"**L** it not be known that the woman	Ru 3:14	
"**L** your maidservant find favor in	1Sa 1:18	
Do not **l** arrogance come out of	1Sa 2:3	
l Him do what seems good to Him."	1Sa 3:18	
him and **l** none of his words fail.	1Sa 3:19	
L us take to ourselves from Shiloh	1Sa 4:3	
"**L** the ark of the God of Israel	1Sa 5:11	
and **l** it return to its own place,	1Sa 5:11	
"Come, and **l** us return, or else my	1Sa 9:5	

Now **l** us go there, perhaps he can **1Sa 9:6**
"Come, and **l** us go to the seer"; **1Sa 9:9**
"Well said; come, **l** us go." **1Sa 9:10**
in the morning I will **l** you go, **1Sa 9:19** 7971
"**L** us alone for seven days, that **1Sa 11:3** 7503
"Come and **l** us go to Gilgal and **1Sa 11:14**
"**L** the Hebrews hear." **1Sa 13:3**
"Come and **l** us cross over to the **1Sa 14:1**
"Come and **l** us cross over to the **1Sa 14:6**
"**L** us go down after the **1Sa 14:36**
l us not leave a man of them." **1Sa 14:36**
"**L** us draw near to God here." **1Sa 14:36**
and **l** me tell you what the LORD **1Sa 15:16**
"**L** our lord now command your **1Sa 16:16**
L them seek a man who is a **1Sa 16:16**
"**L** David now stand before me, **1Sa 16:22**
and **l** him come down to me. **1Sa 17:8**
"**L** no man's heart fail on account **1Sa 17:32**
not **l** him return to his father's house. **1Sa 18:2** 5414
but **l** the hand of the Philistines **1Sa 18:17**
"Do not **l** the king sin against **1Sa 19:4**
So Michal **l** David down through a **1Sa 19:12** 3381
me like this and **l** my enemy go, **1Sa 19:17** 7971
"He said to me, '**L** me go! **1Sa 19:17** 7971
'Do not **l** Jonathan know this, or **1Sa 20:3**
But **l** me go, that I may hide **1Sa 20:5** 7971
and **l** us go out into the field." **1Sa 20:11**
'Please **l** me go, since our family **1Sa 20:29** 7971
please **l** me get away that I may **1Sa 20:29**
'**L** no one know anything about the **1Sa 21:2**
and **l** his saliva run down into his **1Sa 21:13**
"Please **l** my father and my mother **1Sa 22:3**
Do not **l** the king impute anything **1Sa 22:15**
will he **l** him go away safely? **1Sa 24:19**
Therefore **l** *my* young men find **1Sa 25:8**
l your maidservant speak to you, **1Sa 25:24**
"Please do not **l** my lord pay **1Sa 25:25**
own hand, now then **l** your enemies and **1Sa 25:26**
"Now **l** this gift which your **1Sa 25:27**
please **l** me strike him with the **1Sa 26:8**
the jug of water, and **l** us go." **1Sa 26:11**
please **l** my lord the king listen **1Sa 26:19**
me, **l** Him accept an offering; **1Sa 26:19**
do not **l** my blood fall to the **1Sa 26:20**
Now **l** one of the young men come **1Sa 26:22**
l them give me a place in one of **1Sa 27:5**
and **l** me set a piece of bread **1Sa 28:22**
l him go down to battle with us, **1Sa 29:4**
L not dew or rain be on you, **2Sa 1:21**
therefore, **l** your hands be strong and **2Sa 2:7**
"Now **l** the young men arise and **2Sa 2:14**
And Joab said, "**L** them arise." **2Sa 2:14**
"**L** me arise and go and gather **2Sa 3:21**
l him reach the lame and the **2Sa 5:8**
greatness to **l** Your servant know. **2Sa 7:21**
and **l** us show ourselves courageous **2Sa 10:12**
and tomorrow I will **l** you go." **2Sa 11:12** 7971
'Do not **l** this thing displease **2Sa 11:25**
'Please **l** my sister Tamar come and **2Sa 13:5**
and **l** her prepare the food in my **2Sa 13:5**
"Please **l** my sister Tamar come **2Sa 13:6**
please **l** the king and his servants **2Sa 13:24**
l my brother Amnon go with us." **2Sa 13:26**
he **l** Amnon and all the king's sons **2Sa 13:27** 7971
"Do not **l** my lord suppose they **2Sa 13:32**
do not **l** my lord the king take the **2Sa 13:33**
"Please **l** the king remember the **2Sa 14:11**
"Please **l** your maidservant speak **2Sa 14:12**
'**L** me now speak to the king, **2Sa 14:15**
'Please **l** the word of my lord the **2Sa 14:17**
"**L** my lord the king please speak." **2Sa 14:18**
"**L** him turn to his own house, and **2Sa 14:24**
and **l** him not see my face." **2Sa 14:24**
l me see the king's face, **2Sa 14:32**
in me, **l** him put me to death." **2Sa 14:32**
"Please **l** me go and pay my vow **2Sa 15:7**
"Arise and **l** us flee, for **2Sa 15:14**
l Him do to me as seems good to **2Sa 15:26**
l me find favor in your sight, O **2Sa 16:4**
L me go over now and cut off his **2Sa 16:9**
L him alone and let him curse, **2Sa 16:11** 5117
Let him alone and **l** him curse, **2Sa 16:11**
"Please **l** me choose 12,000 men **2Sa 17:1**
l us hear what he has to say." **2Sa 17:5**
"Please **l** me run and bring the **2Sa 18:19**
l me also run after the Cushite." **2Sa 18:22**
"**L** my lord the king receive good **2Sa 18:31**
"**L** the enemies of my lord the **2Sa 18:32**
"**L** not my lord consider me **2Sa 19:19**
"**L** him even take it all, since my **2Sa 19:30**
"Please **l** your servant return, **2Sa 19:37**
l him cross over with my lord the **2Sa 19:37**
l *him* follow Joab." **2Sa 20:11**
l seven men from his sons be given **2Sa 21:6**
L us now fall into the hand of the **2Sa 24:14**
l me fall into the hand of man." **2Sa 24:14**
Please **l** Your hand be against me **2Sa 24:17**
"**L** my lord the king take and **2Sa 24:22**
"**L** them seek a young virgin for **1Ki 1:2**
and **l** her attend the king and **1Ki 1:2**
and **l** her lie in your bosom, that **1Ki 1:2**
please **l** me give you counsel and **1Ki 1:12**
"**L** Zadok the priest and Nathan **1Ki 1:34**
'**L** King Solomon swear to me today **1Ki 1:51**
and do not **l** his gray hair go down **1Ki 2:6**
and **l** them be among those who eat **1Ki 2:7**
do not **l** him go unpunished, **1Ki 2:9**
"**L** Abishag the Shunammite be **1Ki 2:21**
O God of Israel, **l** Your word, **1Ki 8:26**

"**L** your heart therefore be wholly **1Ki 8:61**
you must surely **l** me go." **1Ki 11:22** 7971
"**L** *there be* a treaty between you **1Ki 15:19**
l this child's life return to him." **1Ki 17:21**
"Now **l** them give us two oxen; **1Ki 18:23**
and **l** them choose one ox for **1Ki 18:23**
today **l** it be known that You are **1Ki 18:36**
do not **l** one of them escape." **1Ki 18:40**
"Please **l** me kiss my father and **1Ki 19:20**
'**L** not him who girds on *his armor* **1Ki 20:11**
but rather **l** us fight against them **1Ki 20:23**
please **l** us put sackcloth on our **1Ki 20:31**
'Please **l** me live.' " **1Ki 20:32**
l you go with this covenant." **1Ki 20:34** 7971
a covenant with him and **l** him go. **1Ki 20:34** 7971
'Because you have **l** go out of *your* **1Ki 20:42** 7971
bread, and **l** your heart be joyful; **1Ki 21:7**
and **l** them testify against him, **1Ki 21:10**
"**L** not the king say so." **1Ki 22:8**
Please **l** your word be like the **1Ki 22:13**
L each of them return to his house **1Ki 22:17**
"**L** my servants go with your **1Ki 22:49**
l fire come down from heaven and **2Ki 1:10**
l fire come down from heaven and **2Ki 1:12**
please **l** my life and the lives of **2Ki 1:13**
but now **l** my life be precious in **2Ki 1:14**
l a double portion of your spirit **2Ki 2:9**
please **l** them go and search for **2Ki 2:16**
l us make a little walled upper **2Ki 4:10**
and **l** us set a bed for him there, **2Ki 4:10**
"**L** her alone, for her soul is **2Ki 4:27** 7503
Now **l** him come to me, and he shall **2Ki 5:8**
please **l** your servant at least be **2Ki 5:17**
"Please **l** us go to the Jordan and **2Ki 6:2**
and **l** us make a place there for **2Ki 6:2**
and **l** us go over to the camp of **2Ki 7:4**
l us go and tell the king's **2Ki 7:9**
l some *men* take five of the horses **2Ki 7:13**
perished, so **l** us send and see." **2Ki 7:13**
then **l** no one escape *or* leave the **2Ki 9:15**
him to meet them and **l** him say, **2Ki 9:17**
l no one be missing, for I have a **2Ki 10:19**
l none come out." **2Ki 10:25**
"**L** her not be put to death in the **2Ki 11:15**
l the priests take it for **2Ki 12:5**
"Come, **l** us face each other." **2Ki 14:8**
and **l** him go and live there; **2Ki 17:27**
and **l** him teach them the custom of **2Ki 17:27**
'Do not **l** Hezekiah deceive you, **2Ki 18:29**
nor **l** Hezekiah make you trust in **2Ki 18:30**
'Do not **l** your God in whom you **2Ki 19:10**
but **l** the shadow turn backward ten **2Ki 20:10**
"**L** them deliver it into the hand of **2Ki 22:5**
and **l** them give it to the workmen **2Ki 22:5**
"**L** him alone; let no one disturb his **2Ki 23:18** 5117
l no one disturb his bones." **2Ki 23:18**
l us send everywhere to our **1Ch 13:2**
and **l** us bring back the ark of our **1Ch 13:3**
L the heart of those who seek the **1Ch 16:10**
L the heavens be glad, and let the **1Ch 16:31**
be glad, and **l** the earth rejoice; **1Ch 16:31**
And **l** them say among the nations, **1Ch 16:31**
L the sea roar, and all it **1Ch 16:32**
L the field exult, and all that is **1Ch 16:32**
l the word that You have spoken **1Ch 17:23**
"**L** Your name be established **1Ch 17:24**
and **l** us show ourselves courageous **1Ch 19:13**
please **l** me fall into the hand of **1Ch 21:13**
l me fall into the hand of man." **1Ch 21:13**
please **l** Your hand be against me **1Ch 21:17**
and **l** my lord the king do what is **1Ch 21:23**
seek Him, He will **l** you find Him; **1Ch 28:9**
l my lord send to his servants **2Ch 2:15**
l Your word be confirmed which You **2Ch 6:17**
I pray, **l** Your eyes be open **2Ch 6:40**
l Your priests, O LORD God, be **2Ch 6:41**
and **l** Your godly ones rejoice in **2Ch 6:41**
"**L** us build these cities and **2Ch 14:7**
l not man prevail against You." **2Ch 14:11**
seek Him, He will **l** you find Him; **2Ch 15:2**
Him, and He **l** them find Him. **2Ch 15:4**
earnestly, and He **l** them find Him. **2Ch 15:15**
"**L** *there be* a treaty between you **2Ch 16:3**
"**L** not the king say so." **2Ch 18:7**
So please **l** your word be like one **2Ch 18:12**
L each of them return to his house **2Ch 18:16**
"Now then **l** the fear of the LORD **2Ch 19:7**
You did not **l** Israel invade when **2Ch 20:10** 5414
"But **l** no one enter the house of **2Ch 23:6**
And **l** all the people keep the **2Ch 23:6**
enters the house, **l** him be killed. **2Ch 23:7**
"**L** her not be put to death in the **2Ch 23:14**
do not **l** the army of Israel go **2Ch 25:7**
"Come, **l** us face each other." **2Ch 25:17**
do not **l** Hezekiah deceive you or **2Ch 32:15**
kings of Judah had **l** go to ruin. **2Ch 34:11**
be with him, and **l** him go up!' " **2Ch 36:23**
L him go up to Jerusalem which is **Ezr 1:3**
l the men of that place support **Ezr 1:4**
"**L** us build with you, for we, **Ezr 4:2**
l it be known to the king that **Ezr 4:12**
"Now **l** it be known to the king, **Ezr 4:13**
"**L** it be known to the king that **Ezr 5:8**
and **l** the house of God be rebuilt **Ezr 5:15**
l a search be conducted in the king's **Ezr 5:17**
and **l** the king send to us his **Ezr 5:17**
of God at Jerusalem, **l** the temple, **Ezr 6:3**
and **l** its foundations be retained, **Ezr 6:3**
And **l** the cost be paid from the **Ezr 6:4**

'Also **l** the gold and silver **Ezr 6:5**
l the governor of the Jews and the **Ezr 6:7**
l *it* be carried out with all **Ezr 6:12**
l it be done with zeal for the **Ezr 7:23**
l judgment be executed upon him **Ezr 7:26**
"So now **l** us make a covenant with **Ezr 10:3**
and **l** it be done according to the **Ezr 10:3**
"**L** our leaders represent the **Ezr 10:14**
and **l** all those in our cities who have **Ezr 10:14**
l Your ear now be attentive and **Ne 1:6**
"**L** the king live forever. **Ne 2:3**
l letters be given me for the **Ne 2:7**
l us rebuild the wall of Jerusalem **Ne 2:17**
"**L** us arise and build." **Ne 2:18**
l not their sin be blotted out before **Ne 4:5**
"**L** each man with his servant **Ne 4:22**
therefore **l** us get grain that we **Ne 5:2**
Please, **l** us leave off this usury. **Ne 5:10**
l us meet together at Chephirim in **Ne 6:2**
now, **l** us take counsel together." **Ne 6:7**
"**L** us meet together in the house **Ne 6:10**
and **l** us close the doors of the **Ne 6:10**
"Do not **l** the gates of Jerusalem **Ne 7:3**
l them shut and bolt the doors. **Ne 7:3**
Do not **l** all the hardship seem **Ne 9:32**
l a royal edict be issued by him **Es 1:19**
l it be written in the laws of Persia and **Es 1:19**
and **l** the king give her royal **Es 1:19**
"**L** beautiful young virgins be **Es 2:2**
"**L** the king appoint overseers in all **Es 2:3**
l their cosmetics be given *them.* **Es 2:3**
"Then **l** the young lady who **Es 2:4**
king's interest to **l** them remain. **Es 3:8**
l it be decreed that they be **Es 3:9**
l no one but me come with the king **Es 5:12**
the king said, "**L** him come in." **Es 6:5**
l them bring a royal robe which **Es 6:8**
and **l** the robe and the horse be **Es 6:9**
and **l** them array the man **Es 6:9**
l my life be given me as my **Es 7:3**
l it be written to revoke the **Es 8:5**
l tomorrow also be granted to the **Es 9:13**
and **l** Haman's ten sons be hanged **Es 9:13**
"**L** the day perish on which I was **Jb 3:3**
L not God above care for it, Nor **Jb 3:4**
"**L** darkness and black gloom claim **Jb 3:5**
L a cloud settle on it; **Jb 3:5**
L the blackness of the day terrify **Jb 3:5**
that night, **l** darkness seize it; **Jb 3:6**
L it not rejoice among the days of **Jb 3:6**
L it not come into the number of **Jb 3:6**
"Behold, **l** that night be barren; **Jb 3:7**
L no joyful shout enter it. **Jb 3:7**
"**L** those curse it who curse the **Jb 3:8**
"**L** the stars of its twilight be **Jb 3:9**
L it wait for light but have none, **Jb 3:9**
l it not see the breaking dawn; **Jb 3:9**
now, **l** there be no injustice; **Jb 6:29**
Nor **l** me alone until I swallow my **Jb 7:19** 7503
"**L** Him remove His rod from me, **Jb 9:34**
And **l** not dread of Him terrify me. **Jb 9:34**
L me know why You contend **Jb 10:2**
"Would He not **l** my few days alone? **Jb 10:20** 2308
And do not **l** wickedness dwell in **Jb 11:14**
the beasts, and **l** them teach you; **Jb 12:7**
the heavens, and **l** them tell you. **Jb 12:7**
to the earth, and **l** it teach you; **Jb 12:8**
And **l** the fish of the sea declare **Jb 12:8**
Then **l** come on me what may. **Jb 13:13**
l my declaration *fill* your ears. **Jb 13:17**
And **l** not the dread of You **Jb 13:21**
Or **l** me speak, then reply to me. **Jb 13:22**
"**L** him not trust in emptiness, **Jb 15:31**
And **l** there be no *resting* place **Jb 16:18**
desires it and will not **l** it go, **Jb 20:13** 5800a
l this be your *way of* consolation. **Jb 21:2**
L God repay him so that he may **Jb 21:19**
"**L** his own eyes see his decay, **Jb 21:20**
And **l** him drink of the wrath of **Jb 21:20**
and will not **l** it go. **Jb 27:6** 7503
L Him weigh me with accurate **Jb 31:6**
And **l** God know my integrity. **Jb 31:6**
L me sow and another eat, And let **Jb 31:8**
eat, And **l** my crops be uprooted. **Jb 31:8**
And **l** others kneel down over her. **Jb 31:10**
L my shoulder fall from the **Jb 31:22**
L the Almighty answer me! **Jb 31:35**
L briars grow instead of wheat, **Jb 31:40**
"**L** me speak that I may get relief; **Jb 32:20**
L me open my lips and answer. **Jb 32:20**
"**L** me now be partial to no one, **Jb 32:21**
"Behold, **l** me tell you, you are **Jb 33:12**
Then **l** him be gracious to him, and **Jb 33:24**
L his flesh become fresher than in **Jb 33:25**
L him return to the days of his **Jb 33:25**
Keep silent, and **l** me speak. **Jb 33:31**
"**L** us choose for ourselves what **Jb 34:4**
L us know among ourselves what is **Jb 34:4**
And do not **l** the greatness of the **Jb 36:18**
L him who reproves God answer it." **Jb 40:2**
L his maker bring near his sword. **Jb 40:19**
"**L** us tear their fetters apart And **Ps 2:3**
By their own devices **l** them fall! **Ps 5:10**
But **l** all who take refuge in You **Ps 5:11**
be glad, **L** them ever sing for joy; **Ps 5:11**
L the enemy pursue my soul and **Ps 7:5**
And **l** him trample my life down to **Ps 7:5**
L the assembly of the peoples **Ps 7:7**
O **l** the evil of the wicked come to **Ps 7:9**

O LORD, do not **l** man prevail;	Ps 9:19	
L the nations be judged before	Ps 9:19	
L the nations know that they are	Ps 9:20	
L them be caught in the plots	Ps 10:2	
L my judgment come forth from Your	Ps 17:2	
L Your eyes look with equity.	Ps 17:2	
L them not rule over me;	Ps 19:13	
L the words of my mouth and the	Ps 19:14	
l Him deliver him;	Ps 22:8	
L Him rescue him, because He	Ps 22:8	
L your heart live forever!	Ps 22:26	
I trust, Do not **l** me be ashamed;	Ps 25:2	
Do not **l** my enemies exult over me.	Ps 25:2	
Do not **l** me be ashamed, for I take	Ps 25:20	
L integrity and uprightness	Ps 25:21	
and **l** your heart take courage;	Ps 27:14	
not **l** my enemies rejoice over me.	Ps 30:1	
L me never be ashamed;	Ps 31:1	
L me not be put to shame, O LORD,	Ps 31:17	
L the wicked be put to shame, let	Ps 31:17	
shame, **l** them be silent in Sheol.	Ps 31:17	
L the lying lips be mute, Which	Ps 31:18	
and **l** your heart take courage,	Ps 31:24	
l everyone who is godly pray to	Ps 32:6	
L all the earth fear the LORD;	Ps 33:8	
L all the inhabitants of the world	Ps 33:8	
L Your lovingkindness, O LORD, be	Ps 33:22	
And **l** us exalt His name together.	Ps 34:3	
L those be ashamed and dishonored	Ps 35:4	
L those be turned back and	Ps 35:4	
L them be like chaff before the	Ps 35:5	
L their way be dark and slippery,	Ps 35:6	
L destruction come upon him	Ps 35:8	
And **l** the net which he hid catch	Ps 35:8	
that very destruction **l** him fall.	Ps 35:8	
Do not **l** those who are wrongfully	Ps 35:19	
Nor **l** those who hate me	Ps 35:19	
And do not **l** them rejoice over me.	Ps 35:24	
Do not **l** them say in their heart,	Ps 35:25	
Do not **l** them say,	Ps 35:25	
L those be ashamed and humiliated	Ps 35:26	
L those be clothed with shame and	Ps 35:26	
L them shout for joy and rejoice,	Ps 35:27	
And **l** them say continually,	Ps 35:27	
L not the foot of pride come upon	Ps 36:11	
And **l** not the hand of the wicked	Ps 36:11	
Or **l** him be condemned when he is	Ps 37:33	
L me know how transient I am.	Ps 39:4	
L those be ashamed and humiliated	Ps 40:14	
L those be turned back and	Ps 40:14	
L those be appalled because of	Ps 40:15	
L all who seek You rejoice and be	Ps 40:16	
L those who love Your salvation say	Ps 40:16	
L the Lord be mindful of me.	Ps 40:17	
and Your truth, **l** them lead me;	Ps 43:3	
L them bring me to Your holy hill And	Ps 43:3	
L Your right hand teach You	Ps 45:4	
L Mount Zion be glad, Let the	Ps 48:11	
L the daughters of Judah rejoice	Ps 48:11	
"You **l** your mouth loose in evil And	Ps 50:19	7971
L the bones which You have broken	Ps 51:8	
captive people, **L** Jacob rejoice,	Ps 53:6	
Jacob rejoice, **l** Israel be glad.	Ps 53:6	
L death come deceitfully upon them;	Ps 55:15	
L them go down alive to Sheol, For	Ps 55:15	
L Your glory *be* above all	Ps 57:5	
L Your glory *be* above all	Ps 57:11	
L them flow away like water that	Ps 58:7	
l them be as headless shafts.	Ps 58:7	
L *them be* as a snail which melts	Ps 58:8	
God will **l** me look *triumphantly*	Ps 59:10	
L them even be caught in their	Ps 59:12	
L me dwell in Your tent forever;	Ps 61:4	
L me take refuge in the shelter of	Ps 61:4	
There **l** us rejoice in Him!	Ps 66:6	
L not the rebellious exalt	Ps 66:7	
L the peoples praise You, O God;	Ps 67:3	
L all the peoples praise You.	Ps 67:3	
L the nations be glad and sing for	Ps 67:4	
L the peoples praise You, O God;	Ps 67:5	
L all the peoples praise You.	Ps 67:5	
L God arise, let His enemies be	Ps 68:1	
arise, **l** His enemies be scattered,	Ps 68:1	
And **l** those who hate Him flee	Ps 68:1	
So **l** the wicked perish before God.	Ps 68:2	
But **l** the righteous be glad;	Ps 68:3	
l them exult before God;	Ps 68:3	
Yes, **l** them rejoice with gladness.	Ps 68:3	
the mire and do not **l** me sink;	Ps 69:14	
who seek God, **l** your heart revive.	Ps 69:32	
L heaven and earth praise Him, The	Ps 69:34	
L those be ashamed and humiliated	Ps 70:2	
L those be turned back and	Ps 70:2	
L those be turned back because of	Ps 70:3	
L all who seek You rejoice and be	Ps 70:4	
And **l** those who love Your salvation	Ps 70:4	
"**L** God be magnified."	Ps 70:4	
L me never be ashamed.	Ps 71:1	
L those who are adversaries of my	Ps 71:13	
L them be covered with reproach	Ps 71:13	
L the mountains bring peace to the	Ps 72:3	
L them fear You while the sun	Ps 72:5	
L the nomads of the desert bow	Ps 72:9	
L the kings of Tarshish and of the	Ps 72:10	
l all kings bow down before him,	Ps 72:11	
l them pray for him continually;	Ps 72:15	
L them bless him all day long.	Ps 72:15	
And **l** *men* bless themselves by him;	Ps 72:17	
L all nations call him blessed.	Ps 72:17	
"**L** us completely subdue them."	Ps 74:8	
L not the oppressed return	Ps 74:21	
L the afflicted and needy praise	Ps 74:21	
L all who are around Him bring	Ps 76:11	
Then He **l** *them* fall in the midst	Ps 78:28	
L Your compassion come quickly to	Ps 79:8	
L there be known among the nations	Ps 79:10	
L the groaning of the prisoner	Ps 79:11	
L Your hand be upon the man of Your	Ps 80:17	
"**L** there be no strange god among	Ps 81:9	
l us wipe them out as a nation,	Ps 83:4	
"**L** us possess for ourselves The	Ps 83:12	
L them be ashamed and dismayed	Ps 83:17	
l them be humiliated and perish,	Ps 83:17	
But **l** them not turn back to folly.	Ps 85:8	
L my prayer come before You;	Ps 88:2	
L Your work appear to Your servants	Ps 90:16	
L the favor of the Lord our God be	Ps 90:17	
And **l** him see My salvation."	Ps 91:16	
l us sing for joy to the LORD,	Ps 95:1	
L us shout joyfully to the rock of	Ps 95:1	
L us come before His presence with	Ps 95:2	
L us shout joyfully to Him with	Ps 95:2	
Come, **l** us worship and bow down,	Ps 95:6	
L us kneel before the LORD our	Ps 95:6	
L the heavens be glad, and let the	Ps 96:11	
be glad, and **l** the earth rejoice;	Ps 96:11	
L the sea roar, and all it	Ps 96:11	
L the field exult, and all that is	Ps 96:12	
l the earth rejoice;	Ps 97:1	
L the many islands be glad.	Ps 97:1	
L all those be ashamed who serve	Ps 97:7	
L the sea roar and all it	Ps 98:7	
L the rivers clap their hands,	Ps 98:8	
L the mountains sing together for	Ps 98:8	
reigns, **l** the peoples tremble;	Ps 99:1	
the cherubim, **l** the earth shake!	Ps 99:1	
L them praise Your great and	Ps 99:3	
l my cry for help come to You.	Ps 102:1	
L the glory of the LORD endure	Ps 104:31	
L the LORD be glad in His works;	Ps 104:31	
L my meditation be pleasing to Him;	Ps 104:34	
L sinners be consumed from the	Ps 104:35	
And **l** the wicked be no more.	Ps 104:35	
L the heart of those who seek the	Ps 105:3	
And **l** all the people say, "Amen."	Ps 106:48	
L the redeemed of the LORD say *so,*	Ps 107:2	
L them give thanks to the LORD for	Ps 107:8	
L them give thanks to the LORD for	Ps 107:15	
L them give thanks to the LORD for	Ps 107:21	
L them also offer sacrifices of	Ps 107:22	
L them give thanks to the LORD for	Ps 107:31	
L them extol Him also in the	Ps 107:32	
does not **l** their cattle decrease.	Ps 107:38	
L him give heed to these things,	Ps 107:43	
And **l** an accuser stand at his	Ps 109:6	
judged, **l** him come forth guilty,	Ps 109:7	
And **l** his prayer become sin.	Ps 109:7	
L his days be few;	Ps 109:8	
L another take his office.	Ps 109:8	
L his children be fatherless And	Ps 109:9	
L his children wander about and	Ps 109:10	
And **l** them seek *sustenance* far	Ps 109:10	
L the creditor seize all that he	Ps 109:11	
And **l** strangers plunder the	Ps 109:11	
L there be none to extend	Ps 109:12	
L his posterity be cut off;	Ps 109:13	
l their name be blotted out.	Ps 109:13	
L the iniquity of his fathers be	Ps 109:14	
And do not **l** the sin of his mother	Ps 109:14	
L them be before the LORD	Ps 109:15	
L it be to him as a garment with	Ps 109:19	
L this be the reward of my	Ps 109:20	
And **l** them know that this is Your	Ps 109:27	
L them curse, but You bless;	Ps 109:28	
L my accusers be clothed with	Ps 109:29	
And **l** them cover themselves with	Ps 109:29	
Oh **l** Israel say,	Ps 118:2	
Oh **l** the house of Aaron say,	Ps 118:3	
Oh **l** those who fear the LORD say,	Ps 118:4	
L us rejoice and be glad in it.	Ps 118:24	
Do not **l** me wander from Your	Ps 119:10	
do not **l** me be ashamed of my hope.	Ps 119:116	
Do not **l** the arrogant oppress me.	Ps 119:122	
And do not **l** any iniquity have	Ps 119:133	
L my cry come before You, O LORD;	Ps 119:169	
L my supplication come before You;	Ps 119:170	
L my lips utter praise, For You	Ps 119:171	
L my tongue sing of Your word, For	Ps 119:172	
L Your hand be ready to help me,	Ps 119:173	
L my soul live that it may praise	Ps 119:175	
And **l** Your ordinances help me.	Ps 119:175	
"**L** us go to the house of the LORD."	Ps 122:1	
was on our side," **L** Israel now say,	Ps 124:1	
my youth up," **L** Israel now say,	Ps 129:1	
L them be like grass upon the	Ps 129:6	
L Your ears be attentive To the	Ps 130:2	
L us go into His dwelling place;	Ps 132:7	
L us worship at His footstool.	Ps 132:7	
L Your priests be clothed with	Ps 132:9	
And **l** Your godly ones sing for joy.	Ps 132:9	
not **l** me eat of their delicacies.	Ps 141:4	
L the righteous smite me in	Ps 141:5	
Do not **l** my head refuse it, For	Ps 141:5	
L the wicked fall into their own	Ps 141:10	
L me hear Your lovingkindness in	Ps 143:8	
L Your good Spirit lead me on level	Ps 143:10	
L our sons in their youth be as	Ps 144:12	
L our garners be full, furnishing	Ps 144:13	
L our cattle bear Without mishap	Ps 144:14	
L *there be* no outcry in our	Ps 144:14	
L them praise the name of the	Ps 148:5	
L them praise the name of the	Ps 148:13	
L Israel be glad in his Maker;	Ps 149:2	
L the sons of Zion rejoice in	Ps 149:2	
L them praise His name with	Ps 149:3	
L them sing praises to Him with	Ps 149:3	
L the godly ones exult in glory;	Ps 149:5	
L them sing for joy on their beds.	Ps 149:5	
L the high praises of God *be*	Ps 149:6	
L everything that has breath	Ps 150:6	
L us lie in wait for blood,	Pr 1:11	
L us ambush the innocent	Pr 1:11	
L us swallow them alive like	Pr 1:12	
But **l** your heart keep my	Pr 3:1	
Do not **l** kindness and truth leave	Pr 3:3	
l them not vanish from your sight;	Pr 3:21	
"**L** your heart hold fast my words;	Pr 4:4	
hold of instruction; do not **l** go.	Pr 4:13	7503
not **l** them depart from your sight;	Pr 4:21	
L your eyes look directly ahead And	Pr 4:25	
And **l** your gaze be fixed straight	Pr 4:25	
L them be yours alone And not for	Pr 5:17	
L your fountain be blessed, And	Pr 5:18	
L her breasts satisfy you at all	Pr 5:19	
Nor **l** her capture you with her	Pr 6:25	
l us drink our fill of love until	Pr 7:18	
L us delight ourselves with	Pr 7:18	
Do not **l** your heart turn aside to	Pr 7:25	
is naive, **l** him turn in here!"	Pr 9:4	
is naive, **l** him turn in here,"	Pr 9:16	
L a man meet a bear robbed of her	Pr 17:12	
Do not **l** your heart envy sinners,	Pr 23:17	
L your father and your mother be	Pr 23:25	
And **l** her rejoice who gave birth	Pr 23:25	
l your eyes delight in my ways.	Pr 23:26	
And do not **l** your heart be glad	Pr 24:17	
L your foot rarely be in your	Pr 25:17	
L another praise you, and not your	Pr 27:2	
l no one support him.	Pr 28:17	
L him drink and forget his	Pr 31:7	
And **l** her works praise her in the	Pr 31:31	
therefore **l** your words be few.	Ec 5:2	
Do not **l** your speech cause you to	Ec 5:6	5414
and also not **l** go of the other;	Ec 7:18	
		5117, 3027
L your clothes be white all the	Ec 9:8	
and **l** not oil be lacking on your	Ec 9:8	
years, **l** him rejoice in them all,	Ec 11:8	
and **l** him remember the days of	Ec 11:8	
and **l** your heart be pleasant	Ec 11:9	
after you *and* **l** us run *together!*	SS 1:4	
"**L** his left hand be under my head	SS 2:6	
steep pathway, **L** me see your form,	SS 2:14	
your form, **L** me hear your voice;	SS 2:14	
on to him and would not **l** him go Until	SS 3:4	7503
L its spices be wafted abroad.	SS 4:16	
l us go out into the country,	SS 7:11	
L us spend the night in the	SS 7:11	
"**L** us rise early *and go* to the	SS 7:12	
L us see whether the vine has	SS 7:12	
"**L** his left hand be under my	SS 8:3	
for your voice—**L** me hear it!"	SS 8:13	
now, and **l** us reason together,"	Is 1:18	
l us go up to the mountain of the	Is 2:3	
l us walk in the light of the LORD.	Is 2:5	
only **l** us be called by your name;	Is 4:1	
L me sing now for my well-beloved	Is 5:1	
"So now **l** Me tell you what I am	Is 5:5	
"**L** Him make speed, let Him hasten	Is 5:19	
make speed, **l** Him hasten His work,	Is 5:19	
And **l** the purpose of the Holy One	Is 5:19	
"**L** us go up against Judah and	Is 7:6	
L this be known throughout the	Is 12:5	
"**L** the outcasts of Moab stay with	Is 16:4	
Please **l** them tell you, And let	Is 19:12	
And **l** them understand what the	Is 19:12	
l him report what he sees.	Is 21:6	
camels, **L** him pay close attention,	Is 21:7	
away from me, **L** me weep bitterly,	Is 22:4	
"**L** us eat and drink, for tomorrow	Is 22:13	
L us rejoice and be glad in His	Is 25:9	
"Or **l** him rely on My protection,	Is 27:5	
L him make peace with Me,	Is 27:5	
Me, **L** him make peace with Me."	Is 27:5	
L us hear no more about the Holy	Is 30:11	
Who **l** out freely the ox and the	Is 32:20	7971
L the earth and all it contains	Is 34:1	
'Do not **l** Hezekiah deceive you,	Is 36:14	
nor **l** Hezekiah make you trust in	Is 36:15	
'Do not **l** your God in whom you	Is 37:10	
me to health and **l** me live!	Is 38:16	
"**L** them take a cake of figs and	Is 38:21	
"**L** every valley be lifted up, And	Is 40:4	
l the rough ground become a plain,	Is 40:4	
l the peoples gain new strength;	Is 41:1	
L them come forward, then let them	Is 41:1	
come forward, then **l** them speak;	Is 41:1	
L us come together for judgment.	Is 41:1	
L them bring forth and declare to	Is 41:22	
L the wilderness and its cities	Is 42:11	
L the inhabitants of Sela sing	Is 42:11	
L them shout for joy from the tops	Is 42:11	
L them give glory to the LORD And	Is 42:12	
L them present their witnesses	Is 43:9	
justified, Or **l** them hear and say,	Is 43:9	
l us argue our case together;	Is 43:26	
L him proclaim and declare it;	Is 44:7	

l him recount it to Me in order, Is 44:7
And l them declare to them the Is 44:7
L them all assemble themselves, Is 44:11
themselves, l them stand up, Is 44:11
let them stand up, l them tremble, Is 44:11
l them together be put to shame. Is 44:11
And l the clouds pour down Is 45:8
L the earth open up and salvation Is 45:8
and will l My exiles go free, Is 45:13 7971
Indeed, l them consult together. Is 45:21
L now the astrologers, Those who Is 47:13
L us stand up to each other; Is 50:8
L him draw near to Me. Is 50:8
L him trust in the name of the Is 50:10
L the wicked forsake his way And Is 55:7
And l him return to the LORD, And Is 55:7
L not the foreigner who has joined Is 56:3
Nor l the eunuch say, Is 56:3
"l us get wine, and let us drink Is 56:12
and l us drink heavily of strong Is 56:12
l your collection *of idols* deliver Is 57:13
And to l the oppressed go free And Is 58:6 7971
'L the LORD be glorified, that we Is 66:5
L them arise, if they can save you Jer 2:28
"L us lie down in our shame, and Jer 3:25
and l our humiliation cover us; Jer 3:25
and l us go Into the fortified Jer 4:5
"L us now fear the LORD our God, Jer 5:24
Arise, and l us attack at noon. Jer 6:4
and l us attack by night And Jer 6:5
I will l you dwell in this place. Jer 7:3
I will l you dwell in this place, Jer 7:7
and l us go into the fortified Jer 8:14
cities And l us perish there, Jer 8:14
"L everyone be on guard against Jer 9:4
"L them make haste and take up a Jer 9:18
And l your ear receive the word of Jer 9:20
"L not a wise man boast of his Jer 9:23
and l not the mighty man boast of Jer 9:23
l not a rich man boast of his Jer 9:23
l him who boasts boast of this, Jer 9:24
"L us destroy the tree with its Jer 11:19
And l us cut him off from the land Jer 11:19
L me see Your vengeance on them, Jer 11:20
l them be just like this Jer 13:10
'L my eyes flow down with tears Jer 14:17
and day, And l them not cease; Jer 14:17
from My presence and l them go! Jer 15:1
l go of your inheritance That I Jer 17:4 8058
word of the LORD? L it come now!" Jer 17:15
L those who persecute me be put to Jer 17:18
for me, l me not be put to shame; Jer 17:18
L them be dismayed, but let me not Jer 17:18
but l me not be dismayed. Jer 17:18
"Come and l us devise plans Jer 18:18
Come on and l us strike at him Jer 18:18
and l us give no heed to any of Jer 18:18
And l their wives become childless Jer 18:21
L their men also be smitten to Jer 18:21
yes, l us denounce him!" Jer 20:10
L me see Your vengeance on them; Jer 20:12
L the day not be blessed when my Jer 20:14
But l that man be like the cities Jer 20:16
And l him hear an outcry in the Jer 20:16
but l him who has My word speak My Jer 23:28
I will l remain on its land," Jer 27:11
l them now entreat the LORD of Jer 27:18
'Do not l your prophets who are in Jer 29:8
'Arise, and l us go up *to* Zion, To Jer 31:6
'Come and l us go to Jerusalem Jer 35:11
not l anyone know where you are." Jer 36:19
l my petition come before you and Jer 37:20
"Now l this man be put to death, Jer 38:4
they l Jeremiah down with ropes. Jer 38:6 7971
l them down by ropes into the cistern Jer 38:11 7971
"L no man know about these words Jer 38:24
a ration and a gift and l him go. Jer 40:5 7971
"L me go and kill Ishmael the son Jer 40:15
l our petition come before you, Jer 42:2
L not the swift man flee, Nor the Jer 46:6
And l us go back To our own people Jer 46:16
has l the appointed time pass by!' Jer 46:17
'Come and l us cut her off from Jer 48:2
And l your widows trust in Me." Jer 49:11
her, L nothing be left to her. Jer 50:26
L them go down to the slaughter! Jer 50:27
every side, L there be no escape. Jer 50:29
They have refused to l them go. Jer 50:33 7971
"L not him who bends his bow bend Jer 51:3
Nor l him rise up in his Jer 51:3
l us each go to his own country, Jer 51:9
Come and l us recount in Zion The Jer 51:10
And l Jerusalem come to your mind. Jer 51:50
"L all their wickedness come La 1:22
L *your* tears run down like a river La 2:18
L your eyes have no rest. La 2:18
L him sit alone and be silent La 3:28
L him put his mouth in the dust, La 3:29
L him give his cheek to the smiter, La 3:30
L him be filled with reproach. La 3:30
L us examine and probe our ways, La 3:40
ways, And l us return to the LORD. La 3:40
He who hears, l him hear; Ezk 3:27
and he who refuses, l him refuse; Ezk 3:27
L not the buyer rejoice nor the Ezk 7:12
do not l your eye have pity and Ezk 9:5
and I will l them go, even those Ezk 13:20 7971
'L the sword pass through the Ezk 14:17
and l the sword be doubled the Ezk 21:14
spices, And l the bones be burned. Ezk 24:10
L her rust *be* in the fire! Ezk 24:12
"I will not l you hear Ezk 36:15
"l it be known to you. Ezk 36:32
I will l the house of Israel ask Me Ezk 36:37
and I will not l My holy name be Ezk 39:7
"Now l them put away their Ezk 43:9
and l them measure the plan. Ezk 43:10
shall not l their locks grow long; Ezk 44:20
and l us be given some vegetables Da 1:12
"Then l our appearance be Da 1:13
"L the king tell the dream to his Da 2:7
"L the name of God be blessed Da 2:20
He does not, l it be known to you, Da 3:18
L the beasts flee from under it And Da 4:14
And l him be drenched with the dew Da 4:15
And l him share with the beasts in Da 4:15
"L his mind be changed from *that* Da 4:16
And l a beast's mind be given to Da 4:16
And l seven periods of time pass Da 4:16
do not l the dream or its Da 4:19
and l him be drenched with the dew Da 4:23
and l him share with the beasts of Da 4:23
Do not l your thoughts alarm you Da 5:10
L Daniel now be summoned and he Da 5:12
I am going to l you know what will Da 8:19
l now Your anger and Your wrath Da 9:16
l Your face shine on Your desolate Da 9:17
And l her put away her harlotry Hos 2:2
Yet l no one find fault, and let Hos 4:4
fault, and l none offer reproof; Hos 4:4
Do not l Judah become guilty; Hos 4:15
is joined to idols; L him alone. Hos 4:17 5117
"Come, l us return to the LORD. Hos 6:1
"So l us know, let us press on to Hos 6:3
l us press on to know the LORD. Hos 6:3
L Israel know *this!* Hos 9:7
"L the men who sacrifice kiss the Hos 13:2
Whoever is wise, l him understand Hos 14:9
Whoever is discerning, l him know them. Hos 14:9
Tell your sons about it, And l Jl 1:3
L all the inhabitants of the land Jl 2:1
L the bridegroom come out of his Jl 2:16
L the priests, the LORD's ministers, Jl 2:17
and the altar, And l them say, Jl 2:17
L all the soldiers draw near, let Jl 3:9
draw near, l them come up! Jl 3:9
L the weak say, "I am a mighty Jl 3:10
L the nations be aroused And come Jl 3:12
"But l justice roll down like Am 5:24
l us go against her for battle" Ob 1:1
l us cast lots so we may learn on Jon 1:7
do not l us perish on account of Jon 1:14
Do not l man, beast, herd, or Jon 3:7
Do not l them eat or drink water. Jon 3:7
and l men call on God earnestly Jon 3:8
And l the Lord GOD be a witness Mi 1:2
"Come and l us go up to the Mi 4:2
'L her be polluted, And let our Mi 4:11
And l our eyes gloat over Zion.' Mi 4:11
And l the hills hear your voice. Mi 6:1
L them feed in Bashan and Gilead Mi 7:14
L all the earth be silent before Him. Hab 2:20
Do not l your hands fall limp. Zph 3:16
"L them put a clean turban on his Zch 3:5
'L your hands be strong, you who Zch 8:9
l your hands be strong.' Zch 8:13
'Also l none of you devise evil in Zch 8:17
"L us go at once to entreat the Zch 8:21
"L us go with you, for we have Zch 8:23
What is to die, l it die, and what Zch 11:9
annihilated, l it be annihilated; Zch 11:9
and l those who are left eat one Zch 11:9
and l no one deal treacherously Mal 2:15
"L your light shine before men in Mt 5:16
L HIM GIVE HER A CERTIFICATE OF Mt 5:31
"But l your statement be, 'Yes, yes' Mt 5:37
shirt, l him have your coat also. Mt 5:40 863
do not l your left hand know what Mt 6:3
'L me take the speck out of your Mt 7:4 863
who has ears to hear, l him hear. Mt 11:15
"He who has ears, l him hear." Mt 13:9
He who has ears, l him hear. Mt 13:43
L them alone; they are blind guides Mt 15:14 863
l him be to you as a Gentile and a Mt 18:17
together, l no man separate." Mt 19:6
to accept *this,* l him accept *it.*" Mt 19:12
"L the children alone, and do not Mt 19:14 863
come, l us kill him and seize his Mt 21:38
(l the reader understand), Mt 24:15
possible, l this cup pass from Me; Mt 26:39
"Get up, l us be going; Mt 26:46
l Him now come down from the Mt 27:42
L GOD RESCUE *Him* now, IF HE Mt 27:43
"L us see whether Elijah will Mt 27:49 863
"L us go somewhere else to the Mk 1:38
they l down the pallet on which Mk 2:4 5465
has ears to hear, l him hear." Mk 4:9
has ears to hear, l him hear." Mk 4:23
"L us go over to the other side." Mk 4:35
And He did not l him, but He said Mk 5:19 863
has ears to hear, l him hear." Mk 7:16
"L the children be satisfied Mk 7:27 863
l us make three tabernacles, Mk 9:5
together, l no man separate." Mk 10:9
come, l us kill him, and the Mk 12:7
(l the reader understand), Mk 13:14
But Jesus said, "L her alone; Mk 14:6 863
"Get up, l us be going; Mk 14:42
"L *this* Christ, the King of Israel, Mk 15:32
"L us see whether Elijah will Mk 15:36 863
"L us go straight to Bethlehem Lk 2:15
"L us alone! What business do we Lk 4:34 1436
l down your nets for a catch." Lk 5:4 5465
as You say *and* l down the nets." Lk 5:5 5465
l him down through the tiles with Lk 5:19 2524
l me take out the speck that is in Lk 6:42 863
has ears to hear, l him hear." Lk 8:8
"L us go over to the other side Lk 8:22
l us make three tabernacles: Lk 9:33
"L these words sink into your Lk 9:44
'L it alone, sir, for this year Lk 13:8 863
has ears to hear, l him hear." Lk 14:35
it, and l us eat and celebrate; Lk 15:23
l them hear them.' Lk 16:29
l us kill him so that the inheritance Lk 20:14
l Him save Himself if this is the Lk 23:35
l him come to Me and drink. Jn 7:37
l him *be the* first to throw a Jn 8:7
"L us go to Judea again." Jn 11:7
but l us go to him." Jn 11:15
"L us also go, so that we may die Jn 11:16
"Unbind him, and l him go." Jn 11:44 863
"If we l Him *go on* like this, all Jn 11:48 863
"L her alone, so that she Jn 12:7 863
"Do not l your heart be troubled; Jn 14:1
Do not l your heart be troubled, nor Jn 14:27
be troubled, nor l it be fearful. Jn 14:27
up, l us go from here. Jn 14:31
seek Me, l these go their way," Jn 18:8 863
"L us not tear it, but cast lots Jn 19:24
'L HIS HOMESTEAD BE MADE DESOLATE, Ac 1:20
AND L NO ONE DWELL IN IT'; Ac 1:20
'L ANOTHER MAN TAKE HIS OFFICE.' Ac 1:20
Jerusalem, l this be known to you and Ac 2:14
l all the house of Israel know for Ac 2:36
l it be known to all of you and Ac 4:10
l us warn them to speak no longer to Ac 4:17
them further, they l them go Ac 4:21 630
from these men and l them alone, Ac 5:38 863
and l him down through *an opening* Ac 9:25 2524
"Therefore l it be known to you, Ac 13:38
"L us return and visit the Ac 15:36
But l them come themselves and Ac 16:37
the disciples would not l him. Ac 19:30 1439
l them bring charges against one Ac 19:38
him immediately l go of him; Ac 22:29 868
the commander l the young man go, Ac 23:22 630
"Or else l these men themselves tell Ac 24:20
"l the influential men among you Ac 25:5
the man, l them prosecute him." Ac 25:5
and l ourselves be driven along. Ac 27:15
they l down the sea anchor and Ac 27:17 5465
way l themselves be driven along. Ac 27:17
and had l down the *ship's* boat Ac 27:30 5465
ship's boat and l it fall away. Ac 27:32 1439
"Therefore l it be known to you that Ac 28:28
Rather, l God be found true, Ro 3:4
"L us do evil that good may come"? Ro 3:8
Therefore do not l sin reign in Ro 6:12
"L THEIR TABLE BECOME A SNARE AND Ro 11:9
"L THEIR EYES BE DARKENED TO SEE Ro 11:10
L love *be* without hypocrisy. Ro 12:9
Therefore l us lay aside the deeds of Ro 13:12
L us behave properly as in the Ro 13:13
l us not judge one another anymore, Ro 14:13
Therefore do not l what is for you Ro 14:16
L ALL THE PEOPLES PRAISE HIM." Ro 15:11
"L HIM WHO BOASTS, BOAST IN THE 1Co 1:31
L no man deceive himself. 1Co 3:18
So then l no one boast in men. 1Co 3:21
L a man regard us in this manner, 1Co 4:1
Therefore l us celebrate the feast, 1Co 5:8
have self-control, l them marry; 1Co 7:9
one leaves, l him leave; 1Co 7:15
each, in this manner l him walk. 1Co 7:17
be so, l him do what he wishes, 1Co 7:36
he does not sin; l her marry. 1Co 7:36
Nor l us act immorally, as some of 1Co 10:8
Nor l us try the Lord, as some of 1Co 10:9
l him who thinks he stands take 1Co 10:12
L no one seek his own *good,* but 1Co 10:24
l her also have her hair cut off; 1Co 11:6
head shaved, l her cover her head. 1Co 11:6
is hungry, l him eat at home, 1Co 11:34
Therefore l one who speaks in a 1Co 14:13
L all things be done for 1Co 14:26
and l him speak to himself and to 1Co 14:28
L two or three prophets speak, 1Co 14:29
and l the others pass judgment. 1Co 14:29
l them ask their own husbands at 1Co 14:35
l him recognize that the things 1Co 14:37
not raised, L US EAT AND DRINK, 1Co 15:32
So l no one despise him. But send 1Co 16:11
L all that you do be done in love. 1Co 16:14
l us cleanse ourselves from all 2Co 7:1
l him consider this again within 2Co 10:7
L such a person consider this, 2Co 10:11
I say, l no one think me foolish; 2Co 11:16
and I was l down in a basket 2Co 11:33 5465
l us also walk by the Spirit. Ga 5:25
L us not become boastful, Ga 5:26
L us not lose heart in doing good, Ga 6:9
l us do good to all people, Ga 6:10
on l no one cause trouble for me, Ga 6:17
do not l the sun go down on your Eph 4:26
L no unwholesome word proceed from Eph 4:29
L all bitterness and wrath and Eph 4:31

L no one deceive you with empty Eph 5:6
L us therefore, as many as are Php 3:15
l us keep living by that same Php 3:16
L your gentle *spirit* be known Php 4:5
l your requests be made known to Php 4:6
L no one keep defrauding you of Col 2:18
L the peace of Christ rule in your Col 3:15
L the word of Christ richly dwell Col 3:16
L your speech always be with Col 4:6
then **l** us not sleep as others do, 1Th 5:6
do, but **l** us be alert and sober. 1Th 5:6
we are of *the* day, **l** us be sober, 1Th 5:8
L no one in any way deceive you, 2Th 2:3
then **l** them serve as deacons if 1Tm 3:10
L no one look down on your 1Tm 4:12
L no one disregard you. Ti 2:15
l me benefit from you in the Lord; Phm 1:20
"AND **L** ALL THE ANGELS OF GOD Heb 1:6
Therefore, **l** us fear if, while a Heb 4:1
Therefore **l** us be diligent to enter Heb 4:11
l us hold fast our confession. Heb 4:14
Therefore **l** us draw near with Heb 4:16
Christ, **l** us press on to maturity, Heb 6:1
l us draw near with a sincere heart Heb 10:22
L us hold fast the confession of Heb 10:23
and **l** us consider how to stimulate Heb 10:24
l us also lay aside every Heb 12:1
and **l** us run with endurance the Heb 12:1
be shaken, **l** us show gratitude, Heb 12:28
L love of the brethren continue. Heb 13:1
l us go out to Him outside the Heb 13:13
l us continually offer up a Heb 13:15
L them do this with joy and not Heb 13:17
And **l** endurance have *its* perfect Jas 1:4
lacks wisdom, **l** him ask of God, Jas 1:5
L no one say when he is tempted, Jas 1:13
L not many *of you* become teachers, Jas 3:1
L him show by his good behavior Jas 3:13
l your laughter be turned into Jas 4:9
l him know that he who turns a Jas 5:20
but **l** *it be* the hidden person of 1Pe 3:4
But do not **l** this one *fact* escape 2Pe 3:8
l that abide in you which you 1Jn 2:24
l us not love with word or with 1Jn 3:18
Beloved, **l** us love one another, 1Jn 4:7
l him hear what the Spirit says to Rv 2:7
l him hear what the Spirit says to Rv 2:11
l him hear what the Spirit says to Rv 2:17
l him hear what the Spirit says to Rv 2:29
l him hear what the Spirit says to Rv 3:6
l him hear what the Spirit says to Rv 3:13
l him hear what the Spirit says to Rv 3:22
If anyone has an ear, **l** him hear. Rv 13:9
L him who has understanding Rv 13:18
"**L** us rejoice and be glad and Rv 19:7
"**L** the one who does wrong, still Rv 22:11
and **l** the one who is righteous, still Rv 22:11
And **l** the one who hears say, Rv 22:17
And **l** the one who is thirsty come; Rv 22:17
l the one who wishes take the Rv 22:17

LETS
When he **l** you go, he will surely Ex 11:1 7971
"If a man **l** a field or vineyard Ex 22:5
l his animal loose so that it grazes Ex 22:5 7971
the whole heaven He **l** it loose, Jb 37:3 8281

LETTER
morning David wrote a **l** to Joab 2Sa 11:14 5612
He had written in the **l**, 2Sa 11:15 5612
send a **l** to the king of Israel." 2Ki 5:5 5612
brought the **l** to the king of Israel, 2Ki 5:6 5612
"And now as this **l** comes to you, 2Ki 5:6 5612
the king of Israel read the **l**, 2Ki 5:7 5612
"Now, when this **l** comes to you, 2Ki 10:2 5612
he wrote a **l** to them a second time 2Ki 10:6 5612
When the **l** came to them, 2Ki 10:7 5612
Then Hezekiah took the **l** from the 2Ki 19:14 5612
answered in a **l** sent to Solomon: 2Ch 2:11 3791
Then a **l** came to him from Elijah 2Ch 21:12 4385
and the text of the **l** was written Ezr 4:7 5406
scribe wrote a **l** against Jerusalem Ezr 4:8 104
copy of the **l** which they sent to him Ezr 4:11 104
the copy of the **l** which Tattenai, Ezr 5:6 104
and a **l** to Asaph the keeper of the Ne 2:8 107
time with an open **l** in his hand. Ne 6:5 107
he commanded by **l** that his wicked Es 9:25 5612
of the instructions in this **l**, Es 9:26 107
confirm this second **l** about Purim. Es 9:29 107
Then Hezekiah took the **l** from the Is 37:14 5612
Now these are the words of the **l** Jer 29:1 5612
The **l** *was sent* by the hand of Jer 29:3
Zephaniah the priest read this **l** to Jer 29:29 5612
not the smallest **l** or stroke shall Mt 5:18 *2503*
one stroke of a **l** of the Law to fail. Lk 16:17 *2762*
and they sent this **l** by them, Ac 15:23 *1125*
together, they delivered the **l**. Ac 15:30 *1992*
And he wrote a **l** having this form: Ac 23:25 *1992*
delivered the **l** to the governor, Ac 23:33 *1992*
who though having the **l** *of the Law* Ro 2:27 *1121*
by the Spirit, not by the **l**; Ro 2:29 *1121*
and not in oldness of the **l**. Ro 7:6 *1121*
I, Tertius, who write this **l**, Ro 16:22 *1992*
I wrote you in my **l** not to 1Co 5:9 *1992*
You are our **l**, written in our 2Co 3:2 *1992*
that you are a **l** of Christ, 2Co 3:3 *1992*
of a new covenant, not of the **l** but 2Co 3:6 *1121*
for the **l** kills, but the Spirit 2Co 3:6 *1121*
I caused you sorrow by my **l**, 2Co 7:8 *1992*
see that that **l** caused you sorrow, 2Co 7:8 *1992*
When this **l** is read among you, Col 4:16 *1992*
my **l** *that is coming* from Laodicea. Col 4:16
this **l** read to all the brethren. 1Th 5:27 *1992*
or a message or a **l** as if from us, 2Th 2:2 *1992*
by word *of mouth* or by **l** from us. 2Th 2:15 *1992*
obey our instruction in this **l**, 2Th 3:14 *1992*
a distinguishing mark in every **l**; 2Th 3:17 *1992*
the second **l** I am writing to you 2Pe 3:1 *1992*

LETTERS
So she wrote **l** in Ahab's name and 1Ki 21:8 5612
and sent **l** to the elders and to 1Ki 21:8 5612
Now she wrote in the **l**, 1Ki 21:9 5612
in the **l** which she had sent them. 1Ki 21:11 5612
And Jehu wrote **l** and sent *them* to 2Ki 10:1 5612
sent **l** and a present to Hezekiah, 2Ki 20:12 5612
l also to Ephraim and Manasseh, 2Ch 30:1 107
with the **l** from the hand of the king 2Ch 30:6 107
He also wrote **l** to insult the LORD 2Ch 32:17 5612
let **l** be given me for the Ne 2:7 107
River and gave them the king's **l**. Ne 2:9 107
Also in those days many **l** went Ne 6:17 107
and Tobiah's **l** came to them. Ne 6:17
Then Tobiah sent **l** to frighten me. Ne 6:19 107
sent **l** to all the king's provinces, Es 1:22 5612
L were sent by couriers to all Es 3:13 5612
to revoke the **l** devised by Haman, Es 8:5 5612
and sent **l** by couriers on horses, Es 8:10 5612
and he sent **l** to all the Jews who Es 9:20 5612
He sent **l** to all the Jews, to Es 9:30 5612
and write on it in ordinary **l**: Is 8:1 2747
sent **l** and a present to Hezekiah, Is 39:1 5612
'Because you have sent **l** in your Jer 29:25 5612
and asked for **l** from him to the Ac 9:2 *1992*
I also received **l** to the brethren, Ac 22:5 *1992*
"We have neither received **l** from Ac 28:21 *1121*
I will send them with **l** to carry 1Co 16:3 *1992*
l of commendation to you or from 2Co 3:1 *1992*
of death, in **l** engraved on stones, 2Co 3:7 *1121*
as if I would terrify you by my **l**. 2Co 10:9 *1992*
"His **l** are weighty and strong, 2Co 10:10 *1992*
we are in word by **l** when absent, 2Co 10:11 *1992*
See with what large **l** I am writing Ga 6:11 *1121*
as also in all *his* **l**, 2Pe 3:16 *1992*

LETTING
not **l** the people go to sacrifice Ex 8:29 7971
My people by not **l** them go. Ex 9:17 7971
Pharaoh was stubborn about **l** us go, Ex 13:15 7971
of strife is *like* **l** out water, Pr 17:14 6362

LETUSHIM
were Asshurim and **L** and Leummim. Gn 25:3 3912

LEUMMIM
were Asshurim and Letushim and **L**. Gn 25:3 3817

LEVEL
My foot stands on a **l** place; Ps 26:12 4334
O LORD, And lead me in a **l** path Ps 27:11 4334
good Spirit lead me on **l** ground. Ps 143:10 4334
make the path of the righteous **l**. Is 26:7 6424
line And righteousness the **l**; Is 28:17 4949
Does he not **l** its surface And sow Is 28:25 7737a
with them and stood on a **l** place; Lk 6:17 *3977*
and they will **l** you to the ground and Lk 19:44 *1474*

LEVELED
He **l** a path for His anger; Ps 78:50 6424

LEVI
Therefore he was named **L**. Gn 29:34 3878
two of Jacob's sons, Simeon and **L**, Gn 34:25 3878
Then Jacob said to Simeon and **L**, Gn 34:30 3878
then Simeon and **L** and Judah and Gn 35:23 3878
The sons of **L**: Gn 46:11 3878
"Simeon and **L** are brothers; Gn 49:5 3878
Reuben, Simeon, **L** and Judah; Ex 1:2 3878
Now a man from the house of **L** went Ex 2:1 3878
went and married a daughter of **L**. Ex 2:1 3878
These are the names of the sons of **L** Ex 6:16 3878
all the sons of **L** gathered together Ex 32:26 3878
sons of **L** did as Moses instructed, Ex 32:28 3878
tribe of **L** you shall not number, Nu 1:49 3878
"Bring the tribe of **L** near and Nu 3:6 3878
"Number the sons of **L** by their Nu 3:15 3878
are the sons of **L** by their names: Nu 3:17 3878
was the chief of the leaders of **L**, Nu 3:32 3878
Kohath from among the sons of **L**, Nu 4:2 3878
the son of Kohath, the son of **L**, Nu 16:1 3878
gone far enough, you sons of **L**!" Nu 16:7 3878
"Hear now, you sons of **L**, Nu 16:8 3878
and all your brothers, sons of **L**, Nu 16:10 3878
write Aaron's name on the rod of **L**; Nu 17:3 3878
the rod of Aaron for the house of **L** Nu 17:8 3878
your brothers, the tribe of **L**, Nu 18:2 3878
"To the sons of **L**, Nu 18:21 3878
These are the families of **L**: Nu 26:58 3878
was Jochebed, the daughter of **L**, Nu 26:59 3878
Levi, who was born to **L** in Egypt; Nu 26:59 3878
the LORD set apart the tribe of **L** Dt 10:8 3878
L does not have a portion or Dt 10:9 3878
priests, the whole tribe of **L**, Dt 18:1 3878
"Then the priests, the sons of **L**, Dt 21:5 3878
Simeon, **L**, Judah, Issachar, Dt 27:12 3878
the sons of **L** who carried the ark Dt 31:9 3878
Of **L** he said, Dt 33:8 3878
Only to the tribe of **L** he did not Jos 13:14 3878
But to the tribe of **L**, Jos 13:33 3878
the Kohathites, of the sons of **L**, Jos 21:10 3878
who were not of the sons of **L**. 1Ki 12:31 3878
Reuben, Simeon, **L**, Judah, 1Ch 2:1 3878
The sons of **L** *were* Gershon, Kohath 1Ch 6:1 3878
The sons of **L** *were* Gershom, 1Ch 6:16 3878
the son of Kohath, the son of **L**, 1Ch 6:38 3878
the son of Gershom, the son of **L**. 1Ch 6:43 3878
the son of Merari, the son of **L**. 1Ch 6:47 3878
for the camp of the sons of **L**. 1Ch 9:18 3878
Of the sons of **L** 4,600. 1Ch 12:26 3878
number **L** and Benjamin among them, 1Ch 21:6 3878
according to the sons of **L**: 1Ch 23:6 3878
were named among the tribe of **L**. 1Ch 23:14 3878
These were the sons of **L** according 1Ch 23:24 3878
David the sons of **L** *were* numbered 1Ch 23:27 3878
Now for the rest of the sons of **L**: 1Ch 24:20 3878
for **L**, Hashabiah the son of Kemuel; 1Ch 27:17 3878
the sons of Mahli, the son of **L**, Ezr 8:18 3878
sons of **L** shall bring the contribution Ne 10:39 3878
The sons of **L**, the heads of Ne 12:23 3878
O house of **L**, bless the LORD; Ps 135:20 3878
who from the sons of **L** come near Ezk 40:46 3878
the gate of **L**, one. Ezk 48:31 3878
family of the house of **L** by itself and Zch 12:13 3878
My covenant may continue with **L**," Mal 2:4 3878
corrupted the covenant of **L**," Mal 2:8 3878
and He will purify the sons of **L** Mal 3:3 3878
He saw **L** the *son* of Alphaeus Mk 2:14 *3017*
the son of Matthat, the son of **L**, Lk 3:24 *3017*
the son of Matthat, the son of **L**, Lk 3:29 *3017*
a tax collector named **L** sitting Lk 5:27 *3017*
And **L** gave a big reception for Him Lk 5:29 *3017*
And those indeed of the sons of **L** Heb 7:5 *3017*
to speak, through Abraham even **L**, Heb 7:9 *3017*
the tribe of **L** twelve thousand, Rv 7:7 *3017*

LEVIATHAN
day, Who are prepared to rouse **L**. Jb 3:8 3882
you draw out **L** with a fishhook? Jb 41:1 3882
You crushed the heads of **L**; Ps 74:14 3882
There the ships move along, *And* **L**, Ps 104:26 3882
will punish **L** the fleeing serpent, Is 27:1 3882
sword, Even **L** the twisted serpent; Is 27:1 3882

LEVIED
Now King Solomon **l** forced laborers 1Ki 5:13 5927
forced labor which King Solomon **l** 1Ki 9:15 5927
them Solomon **l** forced laborers, 1Ki 9:21 5927

LEVIES
brought in their **l** and dropped *them* 2Ch 24:10

LEVI'S
and the length of **L** life was one Ex 6:16 3878

LEVITE
not your brother Aaron the **L**? Ex 4:14 3881
the **L** who is within your gates, Dt 12:12 3881
the **L** who is within your gates; Dt 12:18 3881
careful that you do not forsake the **L** Dt 12:19 3881
"Also you shall not neglect the **L** Dt 14:27 3881
"The **L**, because he has no Dt 14:29 3881
and the **L** who is in your town, Dt 16:11 3881
servants and the **L** and the stranger Dt 16:14 3881
"Now if a **L** comes from any of Dt 18:6 3881
and you and the **L** and the alien Dt 26:11 3881
then you shall give it to the **L**, Dt 26:12 3881
given it to the **L** and the alien, Dt 26:13 3881
the family of Judah, who was a **L**; Jg 17:7 3881
"I am a **L** from Bethlehem in Jg 17:9 3881
So the **L** went *in*. Jg 17:10 3881
The **L** agreed to live with the man Jg 17:11 3881
So Micah consecrated the **L**, Jg 17:12 3881
me, seeing I have a **L** as priest." Jg 17:13 3881
the voice of the young man, the **L**; Jg 18:3 3881
the house of the young man, the **L**, Jg 18:15 3881
that there was a certain **L** staying Jg 19:1 3881
So the **L**, the husband of the woman Jg 20:4 3881
the **L** of the sons of Asaph; 2Ch 20:14 3881
and Conaniah the **L** *was* the officer 2Ch 31:12 3881
Kore the son of Imnah the **L**, 2Ch 31:14 3881
Shabbethai the **L** supporting them. Ezr 10:15 3881
"Likewise a **L** also, when he Lk 10:32 *3019*
Now Joseph, a **L** of Cyprian birth, Ac 4:36 *3019*

LEVITES
These are the families of the **L** Ex 6:19 3881
the **L** according to their families. Ex 6:25 3881
Moses, for the service of the **L**, Ex 38:21 3881
'As for cities of the **L**, Lv 25:32 3881
the **L** have a permanent right of Lv 25:32 3881
belongs to the **L** may be redeemed Lv 25:33 3881
cities of the **L** are their possession Lv 25:33 3881
The **L**, however, were not numbered Nu 1:47 3881
"But you shall appoint the **L** over Nu 1:50 3881
set out, the **L** shall take it down; Nu 1:51 3881
encamps, the **L** shall set it up. Nu 1:51 3881
"But the **L** shall camp around the Nu 1:53 3881
So the **L** shall keep charge of the Nu 1:53 3881
shall set out *with* the camp of the **L** Nu 2:17 3881
The **L**, however, were not numbered Nu 2:33 3881
give the **L** to Aaron and to his sons; Nu 3:9 3881
I have taken the **L** from among the Nu 3:12 3881
So the **L** shall be Mine. Nu 3:12 3881
These are the families of the **L** Nu 3:20 3881
All the numbered men of the **L**, Nu 3:39 3881
"You shall take the **L** for Me, Nu 3:41 3881
and the cattle of the **L** instead of Nu 3:41 3881
"Take the **L** instead of all the Nu 3:45 3881
of Israel and the cattle of the **L**. Nu 3:45 3881
And the **L** shall be Mine; Nu 3:45 3881
who are in excess beyond the **L**, Nu 3:46 3881
beyond those ransomed by the **L**; Nu 3:49 3881
be cut off from among the **L**. Nu 4:18 3881
All the numbered men of the **L**, Nu 4:46 3881
and you shall give them to the **L**, Nu 7:5 3881
the oxen and gave them to the **L**. Nu 7:6 3881
"Take the **L** from among the sons Nu 8:6 3881
shall present the **L** before the tent Nu 8:9 3881

and present the L before the LORD; Nu 8:10 3881
shall lay their hands on the L. Nu 8:10 3881
"Aaron then shall present the L Nu 8:11 3881
"Now the L shall lay their hands Nu 8:12 3881
LORD, to make atonement for the L. Nu 8:12 3881
"You shall have the L stand Nu 8:13 3881
separate the L from among the sons Nu 8:14 3881
Israel, and the L shall be Mine. Nu 8:14 3881
"Then after that the L may go in Nu 8:15 3881
"But I have taken the L instead Nu 8:18 3881
"I have given the L as a gift Nu 8:19 3881
of the sons of Israel to the L; Nu 8:20 3881
commanded Moses concerning the L, Nu 8:20 3881
The L, too, purified themselves Nu 8:21 3881
Then after that the L went in to Nu 8:22 3881
commanded Moses concerning the L, Nu 8:22 3881
"This is what *applies* to the L: Nu 8:24 3881
Thus you shall deal with the L Nu 8:26 3881
I Myself have taken your fellow L Nu 18:6 3881
"Only the L shall perform the Nu 18:23 3881
given to the L for an inheritance; Nu 18:24 3881
speak to the L and say to them, Nu 18:26 3881
the rest shall be reckoned to the L Nu 18:30 3881
those who were numbered of the L Nu 26:57 3881
and give them to the L who keep Nu 31:30 3881
animals, and gave them to the L, Nu 31:47 3881
give to the L from the inheritance Nu 35:2 3881
and you shall give to the L Nu 35:2 3881
cities which you shall give to the L Nu 35:4 3881
cities which you shall give to the L Nu 35:6 3881
the L *shall be* forty-eight cities, Nu 35:7 3881
shall give some of his cities to the L Nu 35:8 3881
like all his fellow L who stand Dt 18:7 3881
"The L shall then answer and say Dt 27:14 3881
that Moses commanded the L who Dt 31:25 3881
inheritance to the L among them. Jos 14:3 3881
a portion to the L in the land, Jos 14:4 3881
the L have no portion among you, Jos 18:7 3881
the heads of households of the L Jos 21:1 3881
So the sons of Israel gave the L Jos 21:3 3881
the priest, who were of the L, Jos 21:4 3881
gave by lot to the L these cities Jos 21:8 3881
of the sons of Kohath, the L, Jos 21:20 3881
one of the families of the L, Jos 21:27 3881
sons of Merari, the rest of the L, Jos 21:34 3881
the rest of the families of the L; Jos 21:40 3881
All the cities of the L in the Jos 21:41 3881
The L took down the ark of the 1Sa 6:15 3881
and all the L with him carrying 2Sa 15:24 3881
priests and the L brought them up. 1Ki 8:4 3881
And these are the families of the L 1Ch 6:19 3881
Their kinsmen the L were 1Ch 6:48 3881
sons of Israel gave to the L the cities 1Ch 6:64 3881
To the rest of *the* L, the sons 1Ch 6:77 3881
the L and the temple servants. 1Ch 9:2 3881
Of the L *were* Shemaiah the son 1Ch 9:14 3881
four chief gatekeepers who *were* L, 1Ch 9:26 3881
Mattithiah, one of the L, 1Ch 9:31 3881
heads of fathers' *households* of the L 1Ch 9:33 3881
heads of fathers' *households* of the L 1Ch 9:34 3881
also to the priests and L who are 1Ch 13:2 3881
to carry the ark of God but the L; 1Ch 15:2 3881
the sons of Aaron and the L: 1Ch 15:4 3881
the priests, and for the L, 1Ch 15:11 3881
the fathers' *households* of the L; 1Ch 15:12 3881
So the priests and the L 1Ch 15:14 3881
The sons of the L carried the 1Ch 15:15 3881
David spoke to the chiefs of the L 1Ch 15:16 3881
So the L appointed Heman the son 1Ch 15:17 3881
Chenaniah, chief of the L, 1Ch 15:22 3881
God was helping the L who were 1Ch 15:26 3881
the L who were carrying the ark, 1Ch 15:27 3881
He appointed some of the L *as* 1Ch 16:4 3881
Israel with the priests and the L. 1Ch 23:2 3881
The L were numbered from 1Ch 23:3 3881
the L will no longer need to carry 1Ch 23:26 3881
Nethanel the scribe, from the L, 1Ch 24:6 3881
of the priests and of the L; 1Ch 24:6 3881
These *were* the sons of the L 1Ch 24:30 3881
households of the priests and of the L 1Ch 24:31 3881
On the east there were six L, 1Ch 26:17 3881
The L, their relatives, had 1Ch 26:20 3881
the divisions of the priests and the L 1Ch 28:13 3881
the divisions of the priests and the L 1Ch 28:21 3881
came, and the L took up the ark. 2Ch 5:4 3881
stood at their posts, and the L 2Ch 7:6 3881
and the L for their duties of 2Ch 8:14 3881
to the priests and L in any manner 2Ch 8:15 3881
the priests and the L who were in 2Ch 11:13 3881
For the L left their pasture lands 2Ch 11:14 3881
LORD, the sons of Aaron and the L, 2Ch 13:9 3881
and the L attend to their work. 2Ch 13:10 3881
and with them the L, 2Ch 17:8 3881
Tobijah and Tobadonijah, the L; 2Ch 17:8 3881
some of the L and priests, 2Ch 19:8 3881
L shall be officers before you. 2Ch 19:11 3881
The L, from the sons of the 2Ch 20:19 3881
L from all the cities of Judah, 2Ch 23:2 3881
and L who come in on the sabbath, 2Ch 23:4 3881
the priests and the ministering L; 2Ch 23:6 3881
"The L will surround the 2Ch 23:7 3881
So the L and all Judah did 2Ch 23:8 3881
He gathered the priests and L and 2Ch 24:5 3881
But the L did not act quickly. 2Ch 24:5 3881
"Why have you not required the L 2Ch 24:6 3881
in to the king's officer by the L, 2Ch 24:11 3881
brought in the priests and the L and 2Ch 29:4 3881
"Listen to me, O L. 2Ch 29:5 3881
Then the L arose: 2Ch 29:12 3881

Then the L received *it* to carry 2Ch 29:16 3881
He then stationed the L in the 2Ch 29:25 3881
The L stood with the *musical* 2Ch 29:26 3881
officials ordered the L to sing praises 2Ch 29:30 3881
therefore their brothers the L 2Ch 29:34 3881
For the L were more conscientious 2Ch 29:34 3881
And the priests and L were ashamed 2Ch 30:15 3881
received from the hand of the L. 2Ch 30:16 3881
the L *were* over the slaughter of 2Ch 30:17 3881
and the L and the priests praised 2Ch 30:21 3881
spoke encouragingly to all the L 2Ch 30:22 3881
with the priests and the L and 2Ch 30:25 3881
and the L by their divisions, 2Ch 31:2 3881
both the priests and the L, 2Ch 31:2 3881
due to the priests and the L, 2Ch 31:4 3881
questioned the priests and the L 2Ch 31:9 3881
and the L from twenty years old 2Ch 31:17 3881
enrolled among the L. 2Ch 31:19 3881
the house of God, which the L, 2Ch 34:9 3881
the L of the sons of Merari, 2Ch 34:12 3881
sons of the Kohathites, and the L, 2Ch 34:12 3881
and *some* of the L *were* scribes and 2Ch 34:13 3881
of Jerusalem, the priests, the L and 2Ch 34:30 3881
He also said to the L who taught 2Ch 35:3 3881
according to the L, by division of a 2Ch 35:5 3881
people, the priests and the L. 2Ch 35:8 3881
Jozabad, the officers of the L, 2Ch 35:9 3881
contributed to the L for the 2Ch 35:9 3881
the L by their divisions according 2Ch 35:10 3881
their hand, the L skinned *them.* 2Ch 35:11 3881
therefore the L prepared for 2Ch 35:14 3881
because the L their brethren 2Ch 35:15 3881
did with the priests, the L, 2Ch 35:18 3881
and the priests and the L arose, Ezr 1:5 3881
L: the sons of Jeshua and Kadmiel, Ezr 2:40 3881
Now the priests and the L, Ezr 2:70 3881
brothers the priests and the L, Ezr 3:8 3881
began *the work* and appointed the L Ezr 3:8 3881
their sons and brothers the L, Ezr 3:9 3881
L, the sons of Asaph, with cymbals, Ezr 3:10 3881
Yet many of the priests and L and Ezr 3:12 3881
of Israel, the priests, the L and Ezr 6:16 3879
the L in their orders for the service Ezr 6:18 3879
For the priests and the L had Ezr 6:20 3881
and some of the priests, the L, Ezr 7:7 3881
the L in my kingdom who are willing Ezr 7:13 3879
or toll *on* any of the priests, L, Ezr 7:24 3879
I did not find any L there. Ezr 8:15 1121, 3881
given for the service of the L, Ezr 8:20 3881
before the leading priests, the L and Ezr 8:29 3881
So the priests and the L accepted Ezr 8:30 3881
and with them *were* the L, Ezr 8:33 3881
the L have not separated themselves Ezr 9:1 3881
made the leading priests, the L and Ezr 10:5 3881
Of L *there were* Jozabad, Ezr 10:23 3881
After him the L carried out Ne 3:17 3881
singers and the L were appointed, Ne 7:1 3881
L: the sons of Jeshua, of Kadmiel, Ne 7:43 3881
Now the priests, the L, Ne 7:73 3881
Hanan, Pelaiah, the L, Ne 8:7 3881
and the L who taught the people Ne 8:9 3881
So the L calmed all the people, Ne 8:11 3881
and the L were gathered to Ezra Ne 8:13 3881
Then the L, Jeshua, Kadmiel, Bani, Ne 9:5 3881
leaders, our L *and* our priests." Ne 9:38 3881
the L: Jeshua the son of Azaniah, Ne 10:9 3881
of the people, the priests, the L, Ne 10:28 3881
of wood *among* the priests, the L and Ne 10:34 3881
the tithe of our ground to the L, Ne 10:37 3881
for the L are they who receive the Ne 10:37 3881
shall be with the L when the Ne 10:38 3881
Levites when the L receive tithes, Ne 10:38 3881
and the L shall bring up the tenth Ne 10:38 3881
Israelites, the priests, the L, Ne 11:3 3881
Now from the L: Shemaiah the son Ne 11:15 3881
from the leaders of the L, Ne 11:16 3881
the L in the holy city *were* 284. Ne 11:18 3881
of the priests *and* of the L, Ne 11:20 3881
Now the overseer of the L in Ne 11:22 3881
From the L, *some* divisions in Ne 11:36 3881
the L who came up with Zerubbabel Ne 12:1 3881
The L *were* Jeshua, Binnui, Ne 12:8 3881
As for the L, the heads of Ne 12:22 3881
The heads of the L *were* Hashabiah, Ne 12:24 3881
they sought out the L from all their Ne 12:27 3881
and the L purified themselves; Ne 12:30 3881
by the law for the priests and L; Ne 12:44 3881
over the priests and L who served. Ne 12:44 3881
the consecrated *portion* for the L, Ne 12:47 3881
and the L set apart the Ne 12:47 3881
wine and oil prescribed for the L, Ne 13:5 3881
portions of the L had not been given Ne 13:10 3881
so that the L and the singers who Ne 13:10 3881
the scribe, and Pedaiah of the L, Ne 13:13 3881
And I commanded the L that they Ne 13:22 3881
of the priesthood and the L. Ne 13:29 3881
duties for the priests and the L, Ne 13:30 3881
of them for priests *and* for L," Is 66:21 3881
and the L who minister to Me.'" Jer 33:22 3881
"But the L who went far from Me when Ezk 44:10 3881
in width shall be for the L, Ezk 45:5 3881
went astray as the L went astray. Ezk 48:11 3881
place, by the border of the L. Ezk 48:12 3881
L *shall have* 25,000 *cubits* in length Ezk 48:13 3881
Exclusive of the property of the L Ezk 48:22 3881
the Jews sent to him priests and L Jn 1:19 *3019*

LEVITES'

Now on the L platform stood Jeshua, Ne 9:4 3881

LEVITICAL

"So you shall come to the L priest Dt 17:9 3881
in the presence of the L priests. Dt 17:18 3881
"The L priests, the whole tribe Dt 18:1 3881
the L priests teach you; Dt 24:8 3881
the L priests spoke to all Israel, Dt 27:9 3881
with the L priests carrying it, Jos 3:3 3881
the L priests who carried the ark Jos 8:33 3881
the L priests brought them up. 2Ch 5:5 3881
and all the L singers, Asaph, 2Ch 5:12 3881
the authority of the L priests, 2Ch 23:18 3881
Then the L priests arose and 2Ch 30:27 3881
and the L priests shall never lack Jer 33:18 3881
throne, and with the L priests, Jer 33:21 3881
'You shall give to the L priests Ezk 43:19 3881
"But the L priests, the sons of Ezk 44:15 3881
was through the L priesthood Heb 7:11 *3020*

LEVY

"L a tax for the LORD from Nu 31:28 7311
the LORD'S l of the sheep was 675; Nu 31:37 4371
from which the LORD'S l was 72; Nu 31:38 4371
from which the LORD'S l was 61; Nu 31:39 4371
whom the LORD'S l was 32 persons. Nu 31:40 4371
Moses gave the l *which was* the Nu 31:41 4371
the l *fixed by* Moses the servant of 2Ch 24:6 4864
l *fixed by* Moses the servant of God 2Ch 24:9 4864

LEWD

a l and disgraceful act in Israel. Jg 20:6 2154
who are ashamed of your l conduct. Ezk 16:27 2154
and to Oholibah, the l women. Ezk 23:44 2154

LEWDLY

has l defiled his daughter-in-law. Ezk 22:11 2154

LEWDNESS

they are blood relatives. It is l. Lv 18:17 2154
and the land become full of l. Lv 19:29 2154
The l of your prostitution On the Jer 13:27 2154
"Because your l was poured out Ezk 16:36 5179a
"so that you will not commit this l Ezk 16:43 2154
penalty of your l and abominations," Ezk 16:58 2154
they have committed acts of l. Ezk 22:9 2154
longed for the l of your youth, Ezk 23:21 2154
'Thus I will make your l and your Ezk 23:27 2154
both your l and your harlotries. Ezk 23:29 2154
bear now the *punishment* of your l Ezk 23:35 2154
will make l cease from the land, Ezk 23:48 2154
and not commit l as you have done. Ezk 23:48 2154
Your l will be requited upon you, Ezk 23:49 2154
"In your filthiness is l. Ezk 24:13 2154
I will uncover her l In the sight of Hos 2:10 5040

LIABLE

murder shall be l to the court.' Mt 5:21 *1777*

LIAR

is not so, who can prove me a l, Jb 24:25 3576
A l pays attention to a Pr 17:4 8267
better to be a poor man than a l. Pr 19:22 376, 3577
you, and you will be proved a l. Pr 30:6 3576
for he is a l and the father of Jn 8:44 *5583*
know Him, I will be a l like you, Jn 8:55 *5583*
though every man *be found* a l, Ro 3:4 *5583*
have not sinned, we make Him a l and 1Jn 1:10 *5583*
not keep His commandments, is a l, 1Jn 2:4 *5583*
Who is the l but the one who 1Jn 2:22 *5583*
and hates his brother, he is a l; 1Jn 4:20 *5583*
not believe God has made Him a l, 1Jn 5:10 *5583*

LIARS

I said in my alarm, "All men are l." Ps 116:11 3576
kidnappers and l and perjurers, 1Tm 1:10 *5583*
by means of the hypocrisy of l 1Tm 4:2 *5573*
"Cretans are always l, Ti 1:12 *5583*
sorcerers and idolaters and all l, Rv 21:8 *5571*

LIBATIONS

the l for the burnt offerings. 2Ch 29:35 5262a

LIBERALITY

he who gives, with l; Ro 12:8 *572*
overflowed in the wealth of their l. 2Co 8:2 *572*
enriched in everything for all l, 2Co 9:11 *572*
and for the l of your contribution 2Co 9:13 *572*

LIBERALLY

"You shall furnish him l from Dt 15:14 6059

LIBERTY

And I will walk at l, Ps 119:45 7342
To proclaim l to captives And Is 61:1 1865
shall be his until the year of l; Ezk 46:17 1865
But take care that this l of yours 1Co 8:9 *1849*
Spirit of the Lord is, *there* is l. 2Co 3:17 *1657*
who had sneaked in to spy out our l Ga 2:4 *1657*
at the perfect law, the *law* of l, Jas 1:25 *1657*
are to be judged by *the* law of l. Jas 2:12 *1657*

LIBNAH

from Rimmon-perez and camped at L. Nu 33:20 3841
They journeyed from L and Nu 33:21 3841
him passed on from Makkedah to L, Jos 10:29 3841
to Libnah, and fought against L. Jos 10:29 3841
him passed on from L to Lachish, Jos 10:31 3841
to all that he had done to L. Jos 10:32 3841
had also done to L and its king. Jos 10:39 3841
the king of L, one; Jos 12:15 3841
L and Ether and Ashan, Jos 15:42 3841
and L with its pasture lands, Jos 21:13 3841
Then L revolted at the same time. 2Ki 8:22 3841
of Assyria fighting against L, 2Ki 19:8 3841
the daughter of Jeremiah of L. 2Ki 23:31 3841
the daughter of Jeremiah of L. 2Ki 24:18 3841
L also with its pasture lands, 1Ch 6:57 3841
Then L revolted at the same time 2Ch 21:10 3841
of Assyria fighting against L, Is 37:8 3841

the daughter of Jeremiah of **L**. Jer 52:1 3841

LIBNI

L and Shimei, according to their Ex 6:17 3845
sons of Gershon by their families: **L** Nu 3:18 3845
The sons of Gershom: **L** and Shimei. 1Ch 6:17 3845
L his son, Jahath his son, Zimmah 1Ch 6:20 3845
of Merari *were* Mahli, **L** his son, 1Ch 6:29 3845

LIBNITES

Of Gershon *was* the family of the **L** Nu 3:21 3846a
the family of the **L**, Nu 26:58 3846a

LIBYA

"Ethiopia, Put, Lud, all Arabia, **L** Ezk 30:5 3864
the districts of **L** around Cyrene, Ac 2:10 *3033*

LIBYANS

and **L** and Ethiopians *will follow* Da 11:43 3864

LICENTIOUSNESS

who turn the grace of our God into **l** Jude 1:4 *766*

LICK

horde will **l** up all that is around us, Nu 22:4 3897
the dogs will **l** up your blood, 1Ki 21:19 3952
And his enemies **l** the dust. Ps 72:9 3897
And **l** the dust of your feet; Is 49:23 3897
will **l** the dust like a serpent, Mi 7:17 3897

LICKED

and **l** up the water that was in the 1Ki 18:38 3897
the dogs **l** up the blood of Naboth 1Ki 21:19 3952
and the dogs **l** up his blood 1Ki 22:38 3952

LICKING

dogs were coming and **l** his sores. Lk 16:21 *1952b*

LICKS

ox **l** up the grass of the field." Nu 22:4 3897

LID

a chest and bored a hole in its **l** and 2Ki 12:9 1817

LIE

drink wine, and let us **l** with him that Gn 19:32 7901
then you go in and **l** with him, Gn 19:34 7901
the land on which you **l**, Gn 28:13 7901
"Therefore he may **l** with you Gn 30:15 7901
Joseph, and she said, "**L** with me." Gn 39:7 7901
not listen to her to **l** beside her Gn 39:10 7901
by his garment, saying, "**L** with me! Gn 39:12 7901
he came in to me to **l** with me, Gn 39:14 7901
but when I **l** down with my fathers, Gn 47:30 7901
if he did not **l** in wait *for him,* Ex 21:13 6658a
shall let it rest and **l** fallow, Ex 23:11 5203
'You shall not **l** with a male as Lv 18:22 7901
falsely, nor **l** to one another. Lv 19:11 8266
male as those who **l** with a woman, Lv 20:13 4904
so that you may **l** down with no one Lv 26:6 7901
so that your roads **l** deserted. Lv 26:22 8074
your corpses **l** in the wilderness. Nu 14:33 8552
God is not a man, that He should **l**, Nu 23:19 3576
It will not **l** down until it Nu 23:24 7901
you **l** down and when you rise up. Dt 6:7 7901
you **l** down and when you rise up. Dt 11:19 7901
judge shall then make him **l** down Dt 25:2 5307
about to **l** down with your fathers; Dt 31:16 7901
you, and **l** in wait in the field. Jg 9:32 693
"Go and **l** in wait in the Jg 21:20 693
and uncover his feet and **l** down; Ru 3:4 7901
he went to **l** down at the end of Ru 3:7 7901
L down until morning." Ru 3:13 7901
"I did not call, **l** down again." 1Sa 3:5 7901
not call, my son, **l** down again." 1Sa 3:6 7901
"Go **l** down, and it shall be if He 1Sa 3:9 7901
Also the Glory of Israel will not **l** or 1Sa 15:29 8266
servant against me to **l** in ambush, 1Sa 22:8 693
and you **l** down with your fathers, 2Sa 7:12 7901
making them **l** down on the ground; 2Sa 8:2 7901
to drink and to **l** with my wife? 2Sa 11:11 7901
he went out to **l** on his bed 2Sa 11:13 7901
of his cup and **l** in his bosom, 2Sa 12:3 7901
and he will **l** with your wives in 2Sa 12:11 7901
"**L** down on your bed and pretend 2Sa 13:5 7901
"Come, **l** with me, my sister." 2Sa 13:11 7901
and let her **l** in your bosom, that 1Ki 1:2 7901
do not **l** to your maidservant." 2Ki 4:16 3576
"It is a **l**, tell us now." 2Ki 9:12 8267
me, And *see* if I **l** to your face. Jb 6:28 3576
"When I **l** down I say, Jb 7:4 7901
For now I will **l** down in the dust; Jb 7:21 7901
"You would **l** down and none would Jb 11:19 7257
"Together they **l** down in the Jb 21:26 7901
Should I **l** concerning my right? Jb 34:6 3576
dens *And* **l** in wait in *their* lair? Jb 38:40 695
I will both **l** down and sleep, Ps 4:8 7901
makes me **l** down in green pastures; Ps 23:2 7257
I must **l** among those who breathe Ps 57:4 7901
vanity and men of rank are a **l**; Ps 62:9 3577
you **l** down among the sheepfolds, Ps 68:13 7901
Like the slain who **l** in the grave, Ps 88:5 7901
I will not **l** to David. Ps 89:35 3576
I **l** awake, I have become like a Ps 102:7 8245
And **l** down in their dens. Ps 104:22 7257
have forged a **l** against me; Ps 119:69 8267
for they subvert me with a **l**; Ps 119:78 8267
They have persecuted me with a **l**; Ps 119:86 8267
enter my house, Nor **l** on my bed; Ps 132:3 5927
Let us **l** in wait for blood, Pr 1:11 693
l in wait for their own blood; Pr 1:18 693
When you **l** down, you will not be Pr 3:24 7901
When you **l** down, your sleep will Pr 3:24 7901
How long will you **l** down, Pr 6:9 7901
The words of the wicked **l** in wait Pr 12:6 693
A trustworthy witness will not **l**, Pr 14:5 3576
Sheol and Abaddon **l** *open* before Pr 15:11
Do not **l** in wait, O wicked man, Pr 24:15 693
if two **l** down together they keep Ec 4:11 7901
do you make *it* **l** down at noon? SS 1:7 7257
leopard will **l** down with the young goat, Is 11:6 7257
Their young will **l** down together, Is 11:7 7257
make *their flocks* **l** down there. Is 13:20 7257
creatures will **l** down there, Is 13:21 7257
kings of the nations **l** in glory, Is 14:18 7901
the needy will **l** down in security; Is 14:30 7257
will be for flocks to **l** down in, Is 17:2 7257
You who **l** in the dust, awake and Is 26:19 7931
l down and feed on its branches. Is 27:10 7257
They will **l** down together *and* not Is 43:17 7901
"Is there not a **l** in my right hand?" Is 44:20 8267
You will **l** down in torment. Is 50:11 7901
They **l** *helpless* at the head of Is 51:20 7901
'**L** down that we may walk over *you.*' Is 51:23 7812
"Let us **l** down in our shame, and Jer 3:25 7901
the scribes Has made *it* into a **l**. Jer 8:8 8267
"For they prophesy a **l** to you in Jer 27:10 8267
for they prophesy a **l** to you; Jer 27:14 8267
they are prophesying a **l** to you. Jer 27:16 8267
made this people trust in a **l**. Jer 28:15 8267
he has made you trust in a **l**," Jer 29:31 8267
But Jeremiah said, "A **l**! I am not Jer 37:14 8267
are telling a **l** about Ishmael." Jer 40:16 8267
"You are telling a **l**! Jer 43:2 8267
in the streets **L** young and old; La 2:21 7901
for you, **l** down on your left side and Ezk 4:4 7901
number of days that you **l** on it. Ezk 4:4 7901
you shall **l** down a second time, Ezk 4:6 7901
the days that you **l** on your side, Ezk 4:9 7901
spoken falsehood and seen a **l**, Ezk 13:8 3577
you will **l** in the midst of the Ezk 31:18 7901
'They have gone down, they **l** still, Ezk 32:21 7901
"Nor do they **l** beside the fallen Ezk 32:27 7901
l with those slain by the sword. Ezk 32:28 7901
will **l** with the uncircumcised and Ezk 32:29 7901
yet he will be made to **l** down Ezk 32:32 7901
l down on good grazing ground Ezk 34:14 7257
will make them **l** down in safety. Hos 2:18 7901
I will **l** in wait by the wayside. Hos 13:7 7789
of them **l** in wait for bloodshed; Mi 7:2 693
they will **l** down at evening; Zph 2:7 7257
Flocks will **l** down in her midst, Zph 2:14 7257
For they will feed and **l** down Zph 3:13 7257
Whenever he speaks a **l**, Jn 8:44 *5579*
heart to **l** to the Holy Spirit and Ac 5:3 *5574*
exchanged the truth of God for a **l**, Ro 1:25 *5579*
But if through my **l** the truth of Ro 3:7 *5582*
Do not **l** to one another, since you Col 3:9 *5574*
life, which God, who cannot **l**, Ti 1:2 *893*
it is impossible for God to **l**, Heb 6:18 *5574*
and *so* **l** against the truth. Jas 3:14 *5574*
we **l** and do not practice the truth; 1Jn 1:6 *5574*
and because no **l** is of the truth. 1Jn 2:21 *5579*
and is true and is not a **l**, 1Jn 2:27 *5579*
they are Jews and are not, but **l** Rv 3:9 *5574*
And their dead bodies *will* **l** in Rv 11:8
And no **l** was found in their mouth; Rv 14:5 *5579*

LIED

and **l** about it and sworn falsely, Lv 6:3 3584
and drink water.' " *But* he **l** to him. 1Ki 13:18 3584
And **l** to Him with their tongue. Ps 78:36 3576
worried and fearful When you **l**, Is 57:11 3576
have **l** about the LORD And said, Jer 5:12 3584
You have not **l** to men but to God." Ac 5:4 *5574*

LIES

He couches, he **l** down as a lion, Gn 49:9 7257
Blessings of the deep that **l** beneath, Gn 49:25 7257
is not engaged, and **l** with her, Ex 22:16 7901
"Whoever **l** with an animal shall Ex 22:19 7901
whoever **l** down in the house shall Lv 14:47 7901
the person with the discharge **l** Lv 15:4 7901
'If a man **l** with a woman *so that* Lv 15:18 7901
'Everything also on which she **l** Lv 15:20 7901
'If a man actually **l** with her so Lv 15:24 7901
bed on which he **l** shall be unclean. Lv 15:24 7901
'Any bed on which she **l** all the Lv 15:26 7901
a man who **l** with an unclean woman. Lv 15:33 7901
a male as one **l** with a female; Lv 18:22 7901
'Now if a man **l** carnally with a Lv 19:20 7901
a man who **l** with his father's wife, Lv 20:11 7901
man who **l** with his daughter-in-law, Lv 20:12 7901
'If *there is* a man who **l** with a Lv 20:13 7901
is a man who **l** with an animal, Lv 20:15
5414, 7903
'If *there is* a man who **l** with a Lv 20:18 7901
'If *there is* a man who **l** with his Lv 20:20 7901
"He couches, he **l** down as a lion, Nu 24:9 7901
who hates his neighbor and **l** in wait Dt 19:11 693
her in the city and **l** with her, Dt 22:23 7901
the man forces her and **l** with her, Dt 22:25 7901
the man who **l** with her shall die. Dt 22:25 7901
and seizes her and **l** with her and Dt 22:28 7901
is he who **l** with his father's wife, Dt 27:20 7901
is he who **l** with any animal.' Dt 27:21 7901
is he who **l** with his sister, Dt 27:22 7901
is he who **l** with his mother-in-law.' Dt 27:23 7901
He **l** down as a lion, And tears the Dt 33:20 7931
near the hill which **l** on Jos 18:13
from the hill which **l** before Jos 18:14
and see where his great strength **l** Jg 16:5
have deceived me and told me **l**; Jg 16:10 3577
have deceived me and told me **l**; Jg 16:13 3577
"It shall be when he **l** down, Ru 3:4 7901
shall notice the place where he **l**, Ru 3:4 7901
it **l** in Your hand to make great and 1Ch 29:12
l desolate and its gates have been Ne 2:3
"But you smear with **l**; Jb 13:4 8267
"But man dies and **l** prostrate. Jb 14:10 2522
So man **l** down and does not rise. Jb 14:12 7901
it **l** down with him in the dust. Jb 20:11 7901
"He **l** down rich, but never again; Jb 27:19 7901
And dew **l** all night on my branch. Jb 29:19 3885a
"Under the lotus plants he **l** down, Jb 40:21 7901
when he **l** down, he will not rise up Ps 41:8 7901
who speak **l** go astray from birth. Ps 58:3 3577
of curses and **l** which they utter. Ps 59:12 3585
those who speak **l** will be stopped. Ps 63:11 8267
A false witness *who* utters **l**, Pr 6:19 3577
lie, But a false witness utters **l**. Pr 14:5 3577
he who utters **l** is treacherous. Pr 14:25 3577
he who tells **l** will not escape. Pr 19:5 3577
And he who tells **l** will perish. Pr 19:9 3577
one who **l** down in the Pr 23:34 7901
who **l** down on the top of a mast. Pr 23:34 7901
Keep deception and **l** far from me, Pr 30:8 3577
the tree falls, there it **l**. Ec 11:3 1961
l all night between my breasts. SS 1:13 3885a
Which **l** beyond the rivers of Cush, Is 18:1
will sweep away the refuge of **l** Is 28:17 3577
trust in confusion and speak **l**; Is 59:4 7723
L and not truth prevail in the Jer 9:3 8267
taught their tongue to speak **l**; Jer 9:5 8267
of Mount Zion which **l** desolate, La 5:18 8074
My people who listen to **l**. Ezk 13:19 3577
visions, while they divine **l** for you Ezk 21:29 3577
visions and divining **l** for them, Ezk 22:28 3577
that **l** in the midst of his rivers, Ezk 29:3 7257
and they will speak **l** *to each* Da 11:27 3577
And the princes with their **l**. Hos 7:3 3585
them, but they speak **l** against Me. Hos 7:13 3577
You have eaten the fruit of **l**. Hos 10:13 3585
Ephraim surrounds Me with **l** And Hos 11:12 3585
He multiplies **l** and violence. Hos 12:1 3577
Their **l** also have led them astray, Am 2:4 3577
She **l** neglected on her land; Am 5:2
and falsehood Had told **l** *and said,* Mi 2:11 3576
violence, Her residents speak **l**, Mi 6:12 8267
From her who **l** in your bosom Mi 7:5 7901
completely full of **l** *and* pillage; Na 3:1 3585
will do no wrong And tell no **l**, Zph 3:13 3577
paneled houses while this house **l** Hg 1:4
"Because of My house which **l** Hg 1:9
he is a liar and the father of **l**. Jn 8:44 *846*
read, a veil **l** over their heart; 2Co 3:15 *2749*
forgetting what **l** behind Php 3:13
and reaching forward to what **l** Php 3:13
world **l** in *the power of* the evil one. 1Jn 5:19 *2749*

LIEUTENANT

Jerubbaal, and *is* Zebul *not* his **l**? Jg 9:28 6496

LIFE

moves on the earth which has **l**, Gn 1:30
5315, 2421b
into his nostrils the breath of **l**; Gn 2:7 2425b
the tree of **l** also in the midst of Gn 2:9 2425b
you will eat All the days of your **l**; Gn 3:14 2425b
eat of it All the days of your **l**. Gn 3:17 2425b
and take also from the tree of **l**, Gn 3:22 2425b
to guard the way to the tree of **l**. Gn 3:24 2425b
flesh in which is the breath of **l**, Gn 6:17 2425b
the six hundredth year of Noah's **l**, Gn 7:11 2425b
in which was the breath of **l**. Gn 7:15 2425b
was the breath of the spirit of **l**, Gn 7:22 2425b
shall not eat flesh with its **l**, Gn 9:4 5315
I will require the **l** of man. Gn 9:5 5315
"Escape for your **l**! Gn 19:17 5315
you have shown me by saving my **l**; Gn 19:19 5315
that my **l** may be saved." Gn 19:20 5315
were the years of the **l** of Sarah. Gn 23:1 2425b
years of Abraham's **l** that he lived, Gn 25:7 2425b
an old man and satisfied *with* **l**; Gn 25:8
are the years of the **l** of Ishmael, Gn 25:17 2425b
what good will my **l** be to me?" Gn 27:46 2425b
yet my **l** has been preserved." Gn 32:30 5315
"Let us not take his **l**." Gn 37:21 5315
the LORD, so the LORD took his **l**. Gn 38:7 4191
so He took his **l** also. Gn 38:10 4191
by the **l** of Pharaoh, you shall not Gn 42:15 2416a
But if not, by the **l** of Pharaoh, Gn 42:16 2416a
l is bound up in the lad's life, Gn 44:30 5315
life is bound up in the lad's **l**, Gn 44:30 5315
sent me before you to preserve **l**. Gn 45:5 4241
have been the years of my **l**, Gn 47:9 2425b
so the length of Jacob's **l** was one Gn 47:28 2425b
my shepherd all my **l** to this day, Gn 48:15 5750
all the men who were seeking your **l** Ex 4:19 5315
and the length of Levi's **l** was one Ex 6:16 2425b
and the length of Kohath's **l** was Ex 6:18 2425b
and the length of Amram's **l** was Ex 6:20 2425b
appoint *as a penalty* **l** for life, Ex 21:23 5315
appoint *as a penalty* life for **l**, Ex 21:23 5315
give for the redemption of his **l** Ex 21:30 5315
all the teeming **l** of the water, Lv 11:10 8318
For the **l** of the flesh Lv 17:11 5315
blood by reason of the **l** that makes Lv 17:11 5315
"For *as for the* **l** of all flesh, Lv 17:14 5315
blood is *identified* with its **l**. Lv 17:14 5315
the **l** of all flesh is its blood; Lv 17:14 5315
against the **l** of your neighbor; Lv 19:16 1818
takes the **l** of any human being, Lv 24:17 5315
one who takes the **l** of an animal Lv 24:18 5315
shall make it good, **l** for life. Lv 24:18 5315
shall make it good, life for **l**. Lv 24:18 5315
ridden all your **l** to this day? Nu 22:30 5750
ransom for the **l** of a murderer Nu 35:31 5315

your heart all the days of your l; Dt 4:9 2425b
you, all the days of your l, Dt 6:2 2425b
the blood, for the blood is the l, Dt 12:23 5315
not eat the l with the flesh. Dt 12:23 5315
teeming l with wings are unclean Dt 14:19 8318
may remember all the days of your l Dt 16:3 2425b
read it all the days of his l, Dt 17:19 2425b
the way is long, and take his l, Dt 19:6 5315
l for life, eye for eye, tooth for Dt 19:21 5315
life for l, eye for eye, tooth for Dt 19:21 5315
he would be taking a l in pledge. Dt 24:6 5315
"So your l shall hang in doubt Dt 28:66 2425b
shall have no assurance of your l. Dt 28:66 2425b
before you today l and prosperity, Dt 30:15 2425b
I have set before you l and death, Dt 30:19 2425b
choose l in order that you may live, Dt 30:19 2425b
your l and the length of your days, Dt 30:20 2425b
is I who put to death and give l. Dt 32:39 2421a
indeed it is your l. Dt 32:47 2425b
before you all the days of your l. Jos 1:5 2425b
"Our l for yours if you do not Jos 2:14 5315
Moses all the days of his l. Jos 4:14 2425b
father fought for you and risked his l Jg 9:17 5315
I took my l in my hands and Jg 12:3 5315
boy's mode of l and his vocation?" Jg 13:12 4941
those whom he killed in his l. Jg 16:30 2425b
fall upon you and you will lose your l, Jg 18:25 5315
May he also be to you a restorer of l Ru 4:15 5315
to the LORD all the days of his l, 1Sa 1:11 2425b
house will die in the prime of l. 1Sa 2:33 582
Israel all the days of his l. 1Sa 7:15 2425b
"By your l, O king, I do not know." 1Sa 17:55 5315
and what is my l *or* my father's 1Sa 18:18 2416a
"For he took his l in his hand 1Sa 19:5 5315
"If you do not save your l tonight, 1Sa 19:11 5315
father, that he is seeking my l?" 1Sa 20:1 5315
loved him as he loved his own l. 1Sa 20:17 5315
he who seeks my l seeks your life, 1Sa 22:23 5315
he who seeks my life seeks your l, 1Sa 22:23 5315
Saul had come out to seek his l 1Sa 23:15 5315
lying in wait for my l to take it. 1Sa 24:11 5315
'Have a long l, peace be to you, 1Sa 25:6 2416a
to pursue you and to seek your l, 1Sa 25:29 5315
then the l of my lord shall be 1Sa 25:29 5315
my l was precious in your sight 1Sa 26:21 5315
as your l was highly valued in my 1Sa 26:24 5315
so may my l be highly valued in 1Sa 26:24 5315
make you my bodyguard for l." 1Sa 28:2 3605, 3117
are you then laying a snare for my l 1Sa 28:9 5315
and I have taken my l in my hand and 1Sa 28:21 5315
because my l still lingers in me.' 2Sa 1:9 5315
beloved and pleasant in their l, 2Sa 1:23 2425b
your enemy, who sought your l; 2Sa 4:8 5315
redeemed my l from all distress, 2Sa 4:9 5315
your l and the life of your soul, 2Sa 11:11 2416a
your life and the l of your soul, 2Sa 11:11 2416a
him to death for the l of his brother 2Sa 14:7 5315
Yet God does not take away l, 2Sa 14:14 5315
be, whether for death or for l, 2Sa 15:21 2425b
who came out from me seeks my l; 2Sa 16:11 5315
dealt treacherously against his l 2Sa 18:13 5315
who today have saved your l and 2Sa 19:5 5315
save your l and the life of your son 1Ki 1:12 5315
and the l of your son Solomon. 1Ki 1:12 5315
redeemed my l from all distress, 1Ki 1:29 5315
this word against his own l. 1Ki 2:23 5315
not asked for yourself long l, 1Ki 3:11 3117
asked for the l of your enemies, 1Ki 3:11 5315
Solomon all the days of his l. 1Ki 4:21 2425b
him ruler all the days of his l, 1Ki 11:34 2425b
him all the days of his l, 1Ki 15:5 2425b
Jeroboam all the days of his l. 1Ki 15:6 2425b
let this child's l return to him." 1Ki 17:21 5315
and the l of the child returned to 1Ki 17:22 5315
if I do not make your l as the 1Ki 19:2 5315
make your life as the l of one of 1Ki 19:2 5315
for his l and came to Beersheba, 1Ki 19:3 5315
now, O LORD, take my l, 1Ki 19:4 5315
and they seek my l, 1Ki 19:10 5315
and they seek my l, 1Ki 19:14 5315
perhaps he will save your l." 1Ki 20:31 5315
then your l shall be for his life, 1Ki 20:39 5315
then your life shall be for his l, 1Ki 20:39 5315
your l shall go for his life, 1Ki 20:42 5315
your life shall go for his l, 1Ki 20:42 5315
please let my l and the lives of 2Ki 1:13 5315
my l be precious in your sight." 2Ki 1:14 5315
as it was, and fled for their l. 2Ki 7:7 5315
whose son he had restored to l, 2Ki 8:1 2421a
how he had restored to l the one 2Ki 8:5 2421a
whose son he had restored to l appealed 2Ki 8:5 2421a
son, whom Elisha restored to l." 2Ki 8:5 2421a
shall give up his l in exchange." 2Ki 10:24 5315
will add fifteen years to your l, 2Ki 20:6 3117
regularly all the days of his l; 2Ki 25:29 2425b
each day, all the days of his l. 2Ki 25:30 2425b
or the l of those who hate you, 2Ch 1:11 5315
have you even asked for long l, 2Ch 1:11 3117
pray for the l of the king and his Ezr 6:10 2417
go into the temple to save his l? Ne 6:11 2421a
You give l to all of them Ne 9:6 2421a
my l be given me as my petition, Es 7:3 5315
beg for his l from Queen Esther, Es 7:7 5315
a man has he will give for his l. Jb 2:4 5315
in your power, only spare his l." Jb 2:6 5315
And l to the bitter of soul, Jb 3:20 2425b
"Remember that my l is *but* breath; Jb 7:7 2425b
take notice of myself; I despise my l. Jb 9:21 2425b

"I loathe my own l; Jb 10:1 2425b
granted me l and lovingkindness; Jb 10:12 2425b
"Your l would be brighter Jb 11:17 2465
is the l of every living thing, Jb 12:10 5315
men, *With* long l is understanding. Jb 12:12 3117
teeth And put my l in my hands? Jb 13:14 5315
but no one has assurance of l. Jb 24:22 2425b
For as long as l is in me, And the Jb 27:3 5397
cut off, When God requires his l? Jb 27:8 5315
wept for the one whose l is hard? Jb 30:25 3117
By asking for his l in a curse. Jb 31:30 5315
breath of the Almighty gives me l. Jb 33:4 2421a
l from passing over into Sheol. Jb 33:18 2421b
So that his l loathes bread, And Jb 33:20 2421b
his l to those who bring death. Jb 33:22 2421b
And my l shall see the light.' Jb 33:28 2421b
enlightened with the light of l. Jb 33:30 2425b
And their l *perishes* among the Jb 36:14 2421b
Have you ever in your l commanded Jb 38:12 4480, 3117
trample my l down to the ground And Ps 7:5 2425b
make known to me the path of l; Ps 16:11 2425b
world, whose portion is in *this* l, Ps 17:14 2425b
He asked l of You, You gave Ps 21:4 2425b
My only l from the power of Ps 22:20
follow me all the days of my l, Ps 23:6 2425b
Nor my l with men of bloodshed, Ps 26:9 2425b
The LORD is the defense of my l; Ps 27:1 2425b
of the LORD all the days of my l, Ps 27:4 2425b
For my l is spent with sorrow And Ps 31:10 2425b
They schemed to take away my l. Ps 31:13 5315
Who is the man who desires l And Ps 34:12 2425b
and dishonored who seek my l; Ps 35:4 5315
My only l from the lions. Ps 35:17
with You is the fountain of l; Ps 36:9 2425b
who seek my l lay snares *for me;* Ps 38:12 5315
Who seek my l to destroy it; Ps 40:14 5315
A prayer to the God of my l. Ps 42:8 2425b
And violent men have sought my l; Ps 54:3 5315
As they have waited *to take* my l. Ps 56:6 5315
they have set an ambush for my l; Ps 59:3 5315
You will prolong the king's l; Ps 61:6 3117
lovingkindness is better than l, Ps 63:3 2425b
But those who seek my l to Ps 63:9 5315
Preserve my l from dread of the Ps 64:1 2425b
Who keeps us in l And does not Ps 66:9 2425b
the waters have threatened my l. Ps 69:1 5315
be blotted out of the book of l And Ps 69:28 2416a
and humiliated Who seek my l; Ps 70:2 5315
those who watch for my l have Ps 71:10 5315
He will rescue their l from Ps 72:14 5315
Do not forget the l of Your afflicted Ps 74:19 2421b
gave over their l to the plague, Ps 78:50 2421b
of violent men have sought my l, Ps 86:14 5315
And my l has drawn near to Sheol. Ps 88:3 2425b
Remember what my span of l is; Ps 89:47 2465
As for the days of our l, Ps 90:10 8141
"With a long l I will satisfy Ps 91:16 3117
against the l of the righteous And Ps 94:21 5315
Who redeems your l from the pit, Ps 103:4 2425b
LORD, I beseech You, save my l!" Ps 116:4 5315
My l is continually in my hand, Ps 119:109 5315
Jerusalem all the days of your l. Ps 128:5 2425b
commanded the blessing—l forever. Ps 133:3 2425b
He has crushed my l to the ground; Ps 143:3 2421b
away the l of its possessors. Pr 1:19 5315
Nor do they reach the paths of l. Pr 2:19 2425b
For length of days and years of l And Pr 3:2 2425b
Long l is in her right hand; Pr 3:16 3117
She is a tree of l to those who take Pr 3:18 2425b
So they will be l to your soul And Pr 3:22 2425b
the years of your l will be many. Pr 4:10 2425b
Guard her, for she is your l. Pr 4:13 2425b
they are l to those who find them And Pr 4:22 2425b
For from it *flow* the springs of l. Pr 4:23 2425b
She does not ponder the path of l; Pr 5:6 2425b
for discipline are the way of l Pr 6:23 2425b
hunts for the precious l. Pr 6:26 5315
know that it *will cost him* his l. Pr 7:23 5315
"For he who finds me finds l And Pr 8:35 2425b
years of l will be added to you. Pr 9:11 2425b
the righteous is a fountain of l, Pr 10:11 2425b
The wages of the righteous is l, Pr 10:16 2425b
path of l who heeds instruction, Pr 10:17 2425b
The fear of the LORD prolongs l, Pr 10:27 3117
in righteousness *will attain* to l, Pr 11:19 2425b
fruit of the righteous is a tree of l, Pr 11:30 2425b
has regard for the l of his animal, Pr 12:10 5315
In the way of righteousness is l, Pr 12:28 2425b
guards his mouth preserves his l; Pr 13:3 5315
ransom of a man's l is his wealth, Pr 13:8 5315
desire fulfilled is a tree of l. Pr 13:12 2425b
of the wise is a fountain of l, Pr 13:14 2425b
fear of the LORD is a fountain of l, Pr 14:27 2425b
A tranquil heart is l to the body, Pr 14:30 2425b
A soothing tongue is a tree of l, Pr 15:4 2425b
path of l *leads* upward for the wise That Pr 15:24 2425b
In the light of a king's face is l, Pr 16:15 2425b
watches his way preserves his l. Pr 16:17 5315
Understanding is a fountain of l to Pr 16:22 2425b
Death and l are in the power of Pr 18:21 2425b
The fear of the LORD *leads* to l, Pr 19:23 2425b
him to anger forfeits his own l. Pr 20:2 5315
righteousness and loyalty Finds l, Pr 21:21 2425b
the LORD Are riches, honor and l. Pr 22:4 2425b
take the l of those who rob them. Pr 22:23 5315
upright are concerned for his l. Pr 29:10 5315
partner with a thief hates his own l; Pr 29:24 5315
And wine to him whose l is bitter. Pr 31:6 5315

not evil All the days of her l. Pr 31:12 2425b
So I hated l, for the work which Ec 2:17 2425b
Throughout his l *he* also eats in Ec 5:17 3117
during the few years of his l which Ec 5:18 2425b
often consider the years of his l, Ec 5:20 2425b
the few years of his futile l? Ec 6:12 2425b
is a wicked man who prolongs *his* l Ec 7:15
times and may lengthen his l, Ec 8:12
days of his l which God has given Ec 8:15 2425b
Enjoy l with the woman whom you Ec 9:9 2425b
love all the days of your fleeting l Ec 9:9 2425b
for this is your reward in l and Ec 9:9 2425b
enjoyment, and wine makes l merry, Ec 10:19 2425b
and the prime of l are fleeting. Ec 11:10 7839
whose breath *of* l is in his Is 2:22
is recorded for l in Jerusalem. Is 4:3 2425b
will add fifteen years to your l. Is 38:5 3117
"In the middle of my l I am to Is 38:10 3117
As a weaver I rolled up my l. Is 38:12 2425b
all these is the l of my spirit; Is 38:16 2425b
our l at the house of the LORD." Is 38:20 2425b
peoples in exchange for your l. Is 43:4 5315
They seek your l. Jer 4:30 5315
death will be chosen rather than l Jer 8:3 2425b
men of Anathoth, who seek your l, Jer 11:21 5315
hand of those who seek their l; Jer 19:7 5315
their l will distress them." Jer 19:9 5315
the way of l and the way of death. Jer 21:8 2425b
he will have his own l as booty. Jer 21:9 5315
of those who are seeking your l, Jer 22:25 5315
to risk his l to approach Me?' Jer 30:21 3820
And their l will be like a Jer 31:12 5315
hand of those who seek their l. Jer 34:20 5315
hand of those who seek their l, Jer 34:21 5315
own l as booty and stay alive.' Jer 38:2 5315
lives, who made this l for us, Jer 38:16 5315
men who are seeking your l." Jer 38:16 5315
you will have your *own* l as booty, Jer 39:18 5315
son of Nethaniah to take your l?" Jer 40:14 5315
Why should he take your l, Jer 40:15 5315
the hand of those who seek his l, Jer 44:30 5315
enemy and was seeking his l.'" Jer 44:30 5315
'but I will give your l to you as Jer 45:5 5315
And each of you save his l! Jer 51:6 5315
regularly all the days of his l. Jer 52:33 2425b
a daily portion all the days of his l Jer 52:34 2425b
As their l is poured out On their La 2:12 5315
For the l of your little ones Who are La 2:19 5315
You have redeemed my l. La 3:58 2425b
maintain his l by his iniquity. Ezk 7:13 2421b
his wicked way *and* preserve his l, Ezk 13:22 2421a
righteousness, he will save his l. Ezk 18:27 5315
moment, every man for his own l, Ezk 32:10 5315
he would have delivered his l. Ezk 33:5 5315
but you have delivered your l. Ezk 33:9 5315
walks by the statutes which ensure l Ezk 33:15 2425b
enter you that you may come to l. Ezk 37:5 2421a
slain, that they come to l. Ezk 37:9 2421a
into them, and they came to l and Ezk 37:10 2421a
you and you will come to l, Ezk 37:14 2421a
but an extension of l was granted Da 7:12 2417
awake, these to everlasting l, Da 12:2 2425b
Nor the mighty man save his l. Am 2:14 5315
he who rides the horse save his l. Am 2:15 5315
us perish on account of this man's l Jon 1:14 5315
have brought up my l from the pit, Jon 2:6 2425b
O LORD, please take my l from me, Jon 4:3 5315
death is better to me than l." Jon 4:3 2425b
"Death is better to me than l." Jon 4:8 2425b
with him was *one of* l and peace, Mal 2:5 2425b
sought the Child's l are dead." Mt 2:20 *5590*
you, do not be worried about your l, Mt 6:25 *5590*
Is not l more than food, and the Mt 6:25 *5590*
can add a *single* hour to his l? Mt 6:27 *2244*
the way is narrow that leads to l, Mt 7:14 *2222*
who has found his l will lose it, Mt 10:39 *5590*
he who has lost his l for My sake Mt 10:39 *5590*
whoever wishes to save his l will Mt 16:25 *5590*
whoever loses his l for My sake Mt 16:25 *5590*
you to enter l crippled or lame, Mt 18:8 *2222*
for you to enter l with one eye, Mt 18:9 *2222*
do that I may obtain eternal l?" Mt 19:16 *2222*
but if you wish to enter into l, Mt 19:17 *2222*
much, and will inherit eternal l. Mt 19:29 *2222*
to give His l a ransom for many." Mt 20:28 *5590*
short, no l would have been saved; Mt 24:22 *4561*
the righteous into eternal l." Mt 25:46 *2222*
the Sabbath, to save a l or to kill?" Mk 3:4 *5590*
to save his l will lose it Mk 8:35 *5590*
but whoever loses his l for My Mk 8:35 *5590*
for you to enter l crippled, Mk 9:43 *2222*
is better for you to enter l lame, Mk 9:45 *2222*
shall I do to inherit eternal l?" Mk 10:17 *2222*
and in the age to come, eternal l. Mk 10:30 *2222*
to give His l a ransom for many." Mk 10:45 *5590*
days, no l would have been saved; Mk 13:20 *4561*
the Sabbath, to save a l or to destroy Lk 6:9 *5590*
come and save the l of his slave. Lk 7:3 *1295*
riches and pleasures of *this* l, Lk 8:14 *979*
whoever wishes to save his l will Lk 9:24 *5590*
whoever loses his l for My sake, Lk 9:24 *5590*
shall I do to inherit eternal l?" Lk 10:25 *2222*
does his l consist of his possessions." Lk 12:15 *2222*
you, do not worry about *your* l, Lk 12:22 *5590*
"For l is more than food, and the Lk 12:23 *5590*
sisters, yes, and even his own l, Lk 14:26 *5590*
was dead and has come to l again; Lk 15:24 *326*
during your l you received your Lk 16:25 *2222*
"Whoever seeks to keep his l will Lk 17:33 *5590*

and whoever loses *his* **l** will Lk 17:33
shall I do to inherit eternal **l**?" Lk 18:18 *2222*
in the age to come, eternal **l**." Lk 18:30 *2222*
drunkenness and the worries of **l**, Lk 21:34 *982*
In Him was **l**, and the life was the Jn 1:4 *2222*
and the **l** was the Light of men. Jn 1:4 *2222*
will in Him have eternal **l**. Jn 3:15 *2222*
not perish, but have eternal **l**. Jn 3:16 *2222*
believes in the Son has eternal **l**; Jn 3:36 *2222*
not obey the Son will not see **l**, Jn 3:36 *2222*
water springing up to eternal **l**." Jn 4:14 *2222*
is gathering fruit for **l** eternal; Jn 4:36 *2222*
raises the dead and gives them **l**, Jn 5:21 *2227*
also gives **l** to whom He wishes. Jn 5:21 *2227*
Him who sent Me, has eternal **l**, Jn 5:24 *2222*
has passed out of death into **l**. Jn 5:24 *2222*
as the Father has **l** in Himself, Jn 5:26 *2222*
the Son also to have **l** in Himself; Jn 5:26 *2222*
good *deeds* to a resurrection of **l**, Jn 5:29 *2222*
that in them you have eternal **l**; Jn 5:39 *2222*
come to Me so that you may have **l**. Jn 5:40 *2222*
food which endures to eternal **l**, Jn 6:27 *2222*
and gives **l** to the world." Jn 6:33 *2222*
"I am the bread of **l**; Jn 6:35 *2222*
in Him will have eternal **l**, Jn 6:40 *2222*
he who believes has eternal **l**. Jn 6:47 *2222*
"I am the bread of **l**. Jn 6:48 *2222*
I will give for the **l** of the world Jn 6:51 *2222*
you have no **l** in yourselves. Jn 6:53 *2222*
and drinks My blood has eternal **l**, Jn 6:54 *2222*
"It is the Spirit who gives **l**; Jn 6:63 *2227*
to you are spirit and are **l**. Jn 6:63 *2222*
You have words of eternal **l**. Jn 6:68 *2222*
but will have the Light of **l**." Jn 8:12 *2222*
I came that they may have **l**, Jn 10:10 *2222*
lays down His **l** for the sheep. Jn 10:11 *5590*
and I lay down My **l** for the sheep. Jn 10:15 *5590*
I lay down My **l** so that I may take it Jn 10:17 *5590*
and I give eternal **l** to them, Jn 10:28 *2222*
"I am the resurrection and the **l**; Jn 11:25 *2222*
"He who loves his **l** loses it, Jn 12:25 *5590*
and he who hates his **l** in this Jn 12:25 *5590*
world will keep it to **l** eternal. Jn 12:25 *2222*
that His commandment is eternal **l**; Jn 12:50 *2222*
I will lay down my **l** for You." Jn 13:37 *5590*
"Will you lay down your **l** for Me? Jn 13:38 *5590*
the way, and the truth, and the **l**; Jn 14:6 *2222*
lay down his **l** for his friends. Jn 15:13 *5590*
given Him, He may give eternal **l**. Jn 17:2 *2222*
"This is eternal **l**, Jn 17:3 *2222*
you may have **l** in His name. Jn 20:31 *2222*
MADE KNOWN TO ME THE WAYS OF **L**; Ac 2:28 *2222*
but put to death the Prince of **l**, Ac 3:15 *2222*
the whole message of this **L**." Ac 5:20 *2222*
HIS **L** IS REMOVED FROM THE EARTH." Ac 8:33 *2222*
the repentance *that leads* to **l**." Ac 11:18 *2222*
yourselves unworthy of eternal **l**, Ac 13:46 *2222*
appointed to eternal **l** believed. Ac 13:48 *2222*
He Himself gives to all *people* **l** and Ac 17:25 *2222*
troubled, for his **l** is in him." Ac 20:10 *5590*
"But I do not consider my **l** of Ac 20:24 *5590*
I have lived my **l** with a perfectly Ac 23:1 *4176*
my manner of **l** from my youth up, Ac 26:4 *981*
will be no loss of **l** among you, Ac 27:22 *5590*
honor and immortality, eternal **l**; Ro 2:7 *2222*
who gives **l** to the dead and calls Ro 4:17 *2227*
we shall be saved by His **l**. Ro 5:10 *2222*
will reign in **l** through the One, Ro 5:17 *2222*
justification of **l** to all men. Ro 5:18 *2222*
through righteousness to eternal **l** Ro 5:21 *2222*
we too might walk in newness of **l**. Ro 6:4 *2222*
but the **l** that He lives, He lives Ro 6:10 *2198*
and the outcome, eternal **l**. Ro 6:22 *2222*
the free gift of God is eternal **l** in Ro 6:23 *2222*
which was to result in **l**, Ro 7:10 *2222*
For the law of the Spirit of **l** in Ro 8:2 *2222*
mind set on the Spirit is **l** and peace, Ro 8:6 *2222*
Jesus from the dead will also give **l** Ro 8:11 *2227*
that neither death, nor **l**, Ro 8:38 *2222*
LEFT, AND THEY ARE SEEKING MY **L**." Ro 11:3 *5590*
acceptance be but **l** from the dead? Ro 11:15 *2222*
for my **l** risked their own necks, Ro 16:4 *5590*
Cephas or the world or **l** or death 1Co 3:22 *2222*
How much more matters of this **l**? 1Co 6:3 *982*
dealing with matters of this **l**, 1Co 6:4 *982*
such will have trouble in this **l**, 1Co 7:28 *4561*
hoped in Christ in this **l** only, 1Co 15:19 *2222*
does not come to **l** unless it dies; 1Co 15:36 *2227*
so that we despaired even of **l**; 2Co 1:8 *2198*
the other an aroma from **l** to life. 2Co 2:16 *2222*
the other an aroma from life to **l**. 2Co 2:16 *2222*
kills, but the Spirit gives **l**. 2Co 3:6 *2227*
that the **l** of Jesus also may be 2Co 4:10 *2222*
that the **l** of Jesus also may be 2Co 4:11 *2222*
death works in us, but **l** in you. 2Co 4:12 *2222*
mortal will be swallowed up by **l**. 2Co 5:4 *2222*
my former manner of **l** in Judaism, Ga 1:13 *391*
and the **l** which I now live in Ga 2:20
given which was able to impart **l**, Ga 3:21 *2227*
from the Spirit reap eternal **l**. Ga 6:8 *2222*
excluded from the **l** of God because Eph 4:18 *2222*
to your former manner of **l**, Eph 4:22 *391*
my body, whether by **l** or by death. Php 1:20 *2222*
holding fast the word of **l**, Php 2:16 *2222*
risking his **l** to complete what was Php 2:30 *5590*
whose names are in the book of **l**. Php 4:3 *2222*
l is hidden with Christ in God. Col 3:3 *2222*
When Christ, who is our **l**, Col 3:4 *2222*
your ambition to lead a quiet **l** 1Th 4:11 *2270*
every brother who leads an unruly **l** 2Th 3:6 *4043*
are leading an undisciplined **l**, 2Th 3:11 *4043*
believe in Him for eternal **l**. 1Tm 1:16 *2222*
we may lead a tranquil and quiet **l** 1Tm 2:2 *979*
it holds promise for the present **l** 1Tm 4:8 *2222*
present life and *also* for the **l** 1Tm 4:8
take hold of the eternal **l** to which 1Tm 6:12 *2222*
of God, who gives **l** to all things, 1Tm 6:13 *2225*
hold of that which is **l** indeed. 1Tm 6:19 *2222*
the promise of **l** in Christ Jesus, 2Tm 1:1 *2222*
and brought **l** and immortality to 2Tm 1:10 *2222*
in the affairs of everyday **l**, 2Tm 2:4 *979*
in the hope of eternal **l**, Ti 1:2 *2222*
spending our **l** in malice and envy, Ti 3:3 *1236*
to *the* hope of eternal **l**. Ti 3:7 *2222*
beginning of days nor end of **l**, Heb 7:3 *2222*
the power of an indestructible **l**. Heb 7:16 *2222*
even beyond the proper time of **l**, Heb 11:11 *2244*
he will receive the crown of **l** which Jas 1:12 *2222*
sets on fire the course of *our* **l**, Jas 3:6 *1078*
what your **l** will be like tomorrow. Jas 4:14 *2222*
and led a **l** of wanton pleasure; Jas 5:5 *4684*
from your futile way of **l** inherited 1Pe 1:18 *391*
a fellow heir of the grace of **l**, 1Pe 3:7 *2222*
WHO DESIRES **L**, TO LOVE AND SEE GOOD, 1Pe 3:10 *2222*
pertaining to **l** and godliness, 2Pe 1:3 *2222*
hands, concerning the Word of **L** 1Jn 1:1 *2222*
and the **l** was manifested, and we 1Jn 1:2 *2222*
and proclaim to you the eternal **l**, 1Jn 1:2 *2222*
eyes and the boastful pride of **l**, 1Jn 2:16 *979*
He Himself made to us: eternal **l**. 1Jn 2:25 *2222*
have passed out of death into **l**, 1Jn 3:14 *2222*
has eternal **l** abiding in him. 1Jn 3:15 *2222*
that He laid down His **l** for us; 1Jn 3:16 *5590*
that God has given us eternal **l**, 1Jn 5:11 *2222*
life, and this **l** is in His Son. 1Jn 5:11 *2222*
He who has the Son has the **l**; 1Jn 5:12 *2222*
does not have the **l**. 1Jn 5:12 *2222*
may know that you have eternal **l**. 1Jn 5:13 *2222*
shall ask and *God* will for him give **l** 1Jn 5:16 *2222*
is the true God and eternal **l**. 1Jn 5:20 *2222*
Lord Jesus Christ to eternal **l**. Jude 1:21 *2222*
grant to eat of the tree of **l** which Rv 2:7 *2222*
who was dead, and has come to **l**, Rv 2:8 *2198*
I will give you the crown of **l**. Rv 2:10 *2222*
erase his name from the book of **l**, Rv 3:5 *2222*
them to springs of the water of **l**; Rv 7:17 *2222*
which were in the sea and had **l**, Rv 8:9 *5590*
the breath of **l** from God came into Rv 11:11 *2222*
not love their **l** even when faced Rv 12:11 *5590*
in the book of **l** of the Lamb who has Rv 13:8 *2222*
of the sword and has come to **l**. Rv 13:14 *2198*
has not been written in the book of **l** Rv 17:8 *2222*
and they came to **l** and reigned Rv 20:4 *2198*
rest of the dead did not come to **l** Rv 20:5 *2198*
opened, which is *the book* of **l**; Rv 20:12 *2222*
found written in the book of **l**, Rv 20:15 *2222*
from the spring of the water of **l** Rv 21:6 *2222*
written in the Lamb's book of **l**. Rv 21:27 *2222*
me a river of the water of **l**, Rv 22:1 *2222*
of the river was the tree of **l**, Rv 22:2 *2222*
have the right to the tree of **l**, Rv 22:14 *2222*
take the water of **l** without cost. Rv 22:17 *2222*
tree of **l** and from the holy city, Rv 22:19 *2222*

LIFEBLOOD

"Surely I will require your **l**; Gn 9:5 1818, 5315
l is sprinkled on My garments, Is 63:3 5332
poured out their **l** on the earth." Is 63:6 5332
found The **l** of the innocent poor; Jer 2:34 1818, 5315

LIFE-BREATH

hand are your **l** and your ways, Da 5:23 5396

LIFE-GIVING

He whose ear listens to the **l** reproof Pr 15:31 2425b
The last Adam *became* a **l** spirit. 1Co 15:45 *2227*

LIFELESS

Yet *even* **l** things, either flute or 1Co 14:7 *895*

LIFE'S

add a *single* hour to his **l** span? Lk 12:25 *2244*

LIFETIME

in the **l** of their father Aaron. Nu 3:4 6440
Now Absalom in his **l** had taken and 2Sa 18:18 2425b
Throughout his **l** they did not turn 2Ch 34:33 3605, 3117
a moment, His favor is for a **l**; Ps 30:5 2425b
And my **l** as nothing in Your sight; Ps 39:5 2465
rejoice and to do good in one's **l**; Ec 3:12 2425b
is good for a man during *his* **l**, Ec 6:12 2425b
during my **l** of futility; Ec 7:15 3117
For as the **l** of a tree, *so will be* Is 65:22 3117

LIFT

"Now **l** up your eyes and look from Gn 13:14 5375
"Arise, **l** up the lad, and hold Gn 21:18 5375
'**L** up now your eyes and see *that* Gn 31:12 5375
Pharaoh will **l** up your head and Gn 40:13 5375
Pharaoh will **l** up your head from you Gn 40:19 5375
l up your staff and stretch out Ex 14:16 7311
'Then one *of them* shall **l** up from Lv 6:15 7311
LORD **l** up His countenance on you, Nu 6:26 5375
l up an offering to the LORD. Nu 15:19 7311
shall **l** up a cake as an offering; Nu 15:20 7311
floor, so you shall **l** it up. Nu 15:20 7311
l up your eyes to the west and north Dt 3:27 5375
not to **l** up your eyes to heaven Dt 4:19 5375
'Indeed, I **l** up My hand to heaven, Dt 32:40 5375
did not **l** up their heads anymore. Jg 8:28 5375
How then could I **l** up my face to 2Sa 2:22 5375
You even **l** me above those 2Sa 22:49 7311
to **l** up my face to You, Ezr 9:6 7311
I dare not **l** up my head. Jb 10:15 5375
you could **l** up your face without Jb 11:15 5375
And **l** up your face to God. Jb 22:26 5375
"You **l** me up to the wind Jb 30:22 5375
you **l** up your voice to the clouds, Jb 38:34 7311
L up the light of Your countenance Ps 4:6 5375
L up Yourself against the rage of Ps 7:6 5375
l me up from the gates of death, Ps 9:13 7311
O God, **l** up Your hand. Ps 10:12 5375
Surely You **l** me above those Ps 18:48 7311
L up your heads, O gates, And be Ps 24:7 5375
L up your heads, O gates, And lift Ps 24:9 5375
And **l** *them* up, O ancient doors, Ps 24:9 5375
To You, O LORD, I **l** up my soul. Ps 25:1 5375
He will **l** me up on a rock. Ps 27:5 7311
When I **l** up my hands toward Your Ps 28:2 5375
I will **l** up my hands in Your name. Ps 63:4 5375
L up *a song* for Him who rides Ps 68:4 5549
'Do not **l** up the horn; Ps 75:4 7311
Do not **l** up your horn on high, Do Ps 75:5 7311
to You, O Lord, I **l** up my soul. Ps 86:4 5375
floods **l** up their pounding waves. Ps 93:3 5375
They **l** up *their* voices among the Ps 104:12 5414
Therefore He will **l** up *His* head. Ps 110:7 7311
I shall **l** up the cup of salvation And Ps 116:13 5375
And I shall **l** up my hands to Your Ps 119:48 5375
l up my eyes to the mountains; Ps 121:1 5375
To You I **l** up my eyes, O You who Ps 123:1 5375
L up your hands to the sanctuary And Ps 134:2 5375
For to You I **l** up my soul. Ps 143:8 5375
L your voice for understanding; Pr 2:3 5414
And understanding **l** up her voice? Pr 8:1 5414
the one will **l** up his companion. Ec 4:10 6965
there is not another to **l** him up. Ec 4:10 6965
Nation will not **l** up sword against Is 2:4 5375
He will also **l** up a standard to Is 5:26 5375
a club wielding those who **l** it, Is 10:15 7311
l it up the way *He did* in Egypt. Is 10:26 5375
l up a standard for the nations And Is 11:12 5375
L up a standard on the bare hill, Is 13:2 5375
news, **L** up your voice mightily, Is 40:9 7311
L *it* up, do not fear. Is 40:9 7311
L up your eyes on high And see who Is 40:26 5375
and its cities **l** up *their voices,* Is 42:11 5375
"They **l** it upon the shoulder Is 46:7 5375
"**L** up your eyes and look around; Is 49:18 5375
will **l** up My hand to the nations And Is 49:22 5375
"**L** up your eyes to the sky, Then Is 51:6 5375
Your watchmen **l** up *their* voices, Is 52:8 5375
"**L** up your eyes round about and Is 60:4 5375
l up a standard over the peoples. Is 62:10 7311
"**L** up your eyes to the bare Jer 3:2 5375
"**L** up a standard toward Zion! Jer 4:6 5375
And **l** their voices against the Jer 4:16 5414
not **l** up cry or prayer for them, Jer 7:16 5375
nor **l** up a cry or prayer for them; Jer 11:14 5375
"**L** up your eyes and see Those Jer 13:20 5375
And **l** up your voice in Bashan; Jer 22:20 5414
Proclaim it and **l** up a standard. Jer 50:2 5375
L up a signal against the walls of Jer 51:12 5375
L up a signal in the land, Blow a Jer 51:27 5375
L up your hands to Him For the La 2:19 5375
We **l** up our heart and hands Toward La 3:41 5375
or **l** up his eyes to the idols of the Ezk 18:6 5375
or **l** up his eyes to the idols of the Ezk 18:15 5375
to **l** up the voice with a battle Ezk 21:22 7311
so that you will not **l** up your Ezk 23:27 5375
l itself up above the nations. Ezk 29:15 5375
And they shall **l** you up in My net. Ezk 32:3 5927
l up your eyes to your idols as Ezk 33:25 5375
also **l** themselves up in order to fulfill Da 11:14 5375
will **l** him up to carry out *his* Am 6:10 5375
Nation will not **l** up sword against Mi 4:3 5375
l up your skirts over your face, Na 3:5 1540
"**L** up now your eyes and see what Zch 5:5 5375
who **l** it will be severely injured. Zch 12:3 6006
not take hold of it and **l** it out? Mt 12:11 *1453*
unwilling to **l** up his eyes to heaven, Lk 18:13 *1869*
straighten up and **l** up your heads, Lk 21:28 *1869*
I say to you, **l** up your eyes and Jn 4:35 *1869*
"When you **l** up the Son of Man, Jn 8:28 *5312*

LIFTED

will not *your countenance* be **l** up? Gn 4:7 7613
water increased and **l** up the ark, Gn 7:17 5375
Lot **l** up his eyes and saw all Gn 13:10 5375
When he **l** up his eyes and looked, Gn 18:2 5375
him, and **l** up her voice and wept. Gn 21:16 5375
and he **l** up his eyes and looked, Gn 24:63 5375
Rebekah **l** up her eyes, and Gn 24:64 5375
So Esau **l** his voice and wept. Gn 27:38 5375
Rachel, and **l** his voice and wept. Gn 29:11 5375
I **l** up my eyes and saw in a dream, Gn 31:10 5375
Then Jacob **l** his eyes and looked, Gn 33:1 5375
He **l** his eyes and saw the Gn 33:5 5375
up and **l** Joseph out of the pit, Gn 37:28 5927
and he **l** up the head of the chief Gn 40:20 5375
As he **l** his eyes and saw his Gn 43:29 5375
And he **l** up the staff and struck Ex 7:20 7311
Then Aaron **l** up his hands toward Lv 9:22 5375
cloud was **l** from over the tent, Nu 9:17 5927
the cloud was **l** in the morning, Nu 9:21 5927
night, whenever the cloud was **l**, Nu 9:21 5927
but when it was **l**, they did set Nu 9:22 5927
the cloud was **l** from over the Nu 10:11 5927
all the congregation **l** up their voices Nu 14:1 5375
Then Moses **l** up his hand and Nu 20:11 7311

And Balaam l up his eyes and saw Nu 24:2 5375
that his heart may not be l up Dt 17:20 7311
feet were l up to the dry ground, Jos 4:18 5423
that he l up his eyes and looked, Jos 5:13 5375
people l up their voices and wept. Jg 2:4 5375
and l his voice and called out. Jg 9:7 5375
and l it and laid *it* on his Jg 9:48 5375
And he l up his eyes and saw the Jg 19:17 5375
and l up their voices and wept Jg 21:2 5375
they l up their voices and wept. Ru 1:9 5375
And they l up their voices and Ru 1:14 5375
people l up their voices and wept. 1Sa 11:4 5375
Then Saul l up his voice and wept. 1Sa 24:16 5375
l their voices and wept until there was 1Sa 30:4 5375
and the king l up his voice and 2Sa 3:32 5375
came and l their voices and wept; 2Sa 13:36 5375
who l their hands against my lord the 2Sa 18:28 5375
has l up his hand against King 2Sa 20:21 5375
Then he l up his face to the 2Ki 9:32 5375
And haughtily l up your eyes? 2Ki 19:22 5375
he l up his spear against three 1Ch 11:11 5782
Then David l up his eyes and saw 1Ch 21:16 5375
and when they l up their voice 2Ch 5:13 7311
l up their eyes at a distance and Jb 2:12 5375
those who mourn are l to safety. Jb 5:11 7682
'Should *my head* be l up, Jb 10:16 1342
l up my hand against the orphan, Jb 31:21 5130
not l up his soul to falsehood And Ps 24:4 5375
And be l up, O ancient doors, Ps 24:7 5375
now my head will be l up above my Ps 27:6 7311
O LORD, for You have l me up, Ps 30:1 1802a
Has l up his heel against me. Ps 41:9 1431
It seems as if one had l up *His* axe Ps 74:5 935
horns of the righteous will be l up. Ps 75:10 7311
The floods have l up, O LORD, The Ps 93:3 5375
The floods have l up their voice, Ps 93:3 5375
have l me up and cast me away. Ps 102:10 5375
Which l up the waves of the sea. Ps 107:25 7311
He has l up a horn for His people, Ps 148:14 7311
And against everyone who is l up, Is 2:12 5375
Lebanon that are lofty and l up, Is 2:13 5375
all the hills that are l up, Is 2:14 5375
Your hand is l up *yet* they do not see Is 26:11 7311
be exalted, now I will be l up. Is 33:10 5375
And haughtily l up your eyes? Is 37:23 5375
"Let every valley be l up, Is 40:4 5375
prosper, He will be high and l up and Is 52:13 5375
And He l them and carried them all Is 63:9 5190
they l the *siege* from Jerusalem. Jer 37:5 5927
army of the Chaldeans had l *the siege* Jer 37:11 5927
and l him out of the cistern, Jer 38:13 5927
Then the Spirit l me up, and I Ezk 3:12 5375
Spirit l me up and took me away; Ezk 3:14 5375
and the Spirit l me up between Ezk 8:3 5375
also when the cherubim l up their Ezk 10:16 5375
they l their wings and rose up Ezk 10:19 5375
the Spirit l me up and brought me Ezk 11:1 5375
Then the cherubim l up their wings Ezk 11:22 5375
And the Spirit l me up and brought Ezk 11:24 5375
"Because your heart is l up And you Ezk 28:2 1361b
your heart is l up because of your Ezk 28:5 1361b
Your heart was l up because of your Ezk 28:17 1361b
And the Spirit l me up and brought Ezk 43:5 5375
"But when his heart was l up and Da 5:20 7313
and it was l up from the ground Da 7:4 5191
Then I l my eyes and looked, and Da 8:3 5375
I l my eyes and looked, and Da 10:5 5375
away, his heart will be l up, Da 11:12 7311
Your hand will be l up against your Mi 5:9 7311
its voice, It l high its hands. Hab 3:10 5375
Then I l up my eyes and looked, Zch 1:18 5375
nations who have l up *their* horns Zch 1:21 5375
Then I l up my eyes and looked, Zch 2:1 5375
I l up my eyes again and looked, Zch 5:1 5375
behold, a lead cover was l up); Zch 5:7 5375
Then I l up my eyes and looked, Zch 5:9 5375
and they l up the ephah between Zch 5:9 5375
I l up my eyes again and looked, Zch 6:1 5375
the hand of one will be l against the Zch 14:13 5927
"In Hades he l up his eyes, Lk 16:23 *1869*
He l up His hands and blessed them Lk 24:50 *1869*
"As Moses l up the serpent in Jn 3:14 *5312*
so must the Son of Man be l up; Jn 3:14 *5312*
I, if I am l up from the earth, Jn 12:32 *5312*
'The Son of Man must be l up'? Jn 12:34 *5312*
HAS L UP HIS HEEL AGAINST ME.' Jn 13:18 *1869*
He was l up while they were looking Ac 1:9 *1869*
they l their voices to God with Ac 4:24 *142*
l up his right hand to heaven, Rv 10:5 *142*

LIFTING

"The thigh offered by l up and Lv 10:15 8641
and the thigh offered by l up; Nu 6:20 8641
while l up their hands; Ne 8:6 4607
The l up of my hands as the Ps 141:2 4864
like a rod l *him who* is not wood. Is 10:15 7311
At the l up of Yourself nations Is 33:3 7427
And l up their eyes, they saw no Mt 17:8 *1869*
Therefore Jesus, l up His eyes and Jn 6:5 *1869*
and l up His eyes to heaven, He Jn 17:1 *1869*
place to pray, l up holy hands, 1Tm 2:8 *1869*

LIFTS

And as a lion it l itself; Nu 23:24 5375
He l the needy from the ash heap 1Sa 2:8 7311
"When she l herself on high, She Jb 39:18 4754
glory, and the One who l my head. Ps 3:3 7311
And l the needy from the ash heap, Ps 113:7 7311
She l her voice in the square; Pr 1:20 5414
and l up his staff against you, Is 10:24 5375

l up the islands like fine dust. Is 40:15 5190
but l up his eyes to the idols Ezk 18:12 5375
who l the yoke from their jaws; Hos 11:4 7311
so that no man l up his head; Zch 1:21 5375

LIGAMENTS

held together by the joints and l, Col 2:19 *4886*

LIGHT

"Let there be l"; Gn 1:3 216
"Let there be light"; and there was l. Gn 1:3 216
God saw that the l was good; Gn 1:4 216
separated the l from the darkness. Gn 1:4 216
God called the l day, Gn 1:5 216
heavens to give l on the earth"; Gn 1:15 215
the greater l to govern the day, Gn 1:16 3974
the lesser l to govern the night; Gn 1:16 3974
heavens to give l on the earth, Gn 1:17 215
separate the l from the darkness; Gn 1:18 216
As soon as it was l, Gn 44:3 215
Israel had l in their dwellings. Ex 10:23 216
pillar of fire by night to give them l, Ex 13:21 215
darkness, yet it gave l at night. Ex 14:20 215
mount its lamps so as to shed l on Ex 25:37 215
oil of beaten olives for the l, Ex 27:20 3974
the lampstand also for the l and Ex 35:14 3974
its lamps and the oil for the l; Ex 35:14 3974
and the spice and the oil for the l Ex 35:28 3974
utensils, and the oil for the l; Ex 39:37 3974
oil from beaten olives for the l, Lv 24:2 3974
and cover the lampstand for the l, Nu 4:9 3974
Aaron the priest is the oil for the l Nu 4:16 3974
the seven lamps will give l in the Nu 8:2 215
"*Let us wait* until the morning l, Jg 16:2 216
among them until the morning l, 1Sa 14:36 216
left to Nabal until the morning l 1Sa 25:34 216
at all until the morning l. 1Sa 25:36 216
early in the morning and have l, 1Sa 29:10 215
Is as the l of the morning *when* 2Sa 23:4 216
if we wait until morning l, 2Ki 7:9 216
lamps is *ready* to l every evening; 2Ch 13:11 1197a
fire by night To l for them the way Ne 9:12 215
to l for them the way in which Ne 9:19 215
For the Jews there was l and Es 8:16 219a
care for it, Nor l shine on it. Jb 3:4 5105
Let it wait for l but have none, Jb 3:9 216
be, As infants that never saw l. Jb 3:16 216
"Why is l given to him who Jb 3:20 216
"*Why is* l *given* to a man whose Jb 3:23
brings the deep darkness into l. Jb 12:22 216
"They grope in darkness with no l, Jb 12:25 216
saying, 'The l is near,' Jb 17:12 216
the l of the wicked goes out, Jb 18:5 216
the flame of his fire gives no l. Jb 18:5 5050
"The l in his tent is darkened, Jb 18:6 216
"He is driven from l into darkness, Jb 18:18 216
And l will shine on your ways. Jb 22:28 216
those who rebel against the l; Jb 24:13 216
They do not know the l. Jb 24:16 216
And upon whom does His l not rise? Jb 25:3 216
At the boundary of l and darkness. Jb 26:10 216
is hidden he brings out to the l. Jb 28:11 216
by His l I walked through darkness; Jb 29:3 216
And the l of my face they did not Jb 29:24 216
When I waited for l, Jb 30:26 216
pit, And my life shall see the l.' Jb 33:28 216
be enlightened with the l of life. Jb 33:30 216
l which is bright in the skies; Jb 37:21 216
the wicked their l is withheld, Jb 38:15 216
is the way to the dwelling of l? Jb 38:19 216
is the way that the l is divided, Jb 38:24 216
"His sneezes flash forth l, Jb 41:18 216
the l of Your countenance upon us, Ps 4:6 216
For You l my lamp; Ps 18:28 215
The LORD is my l and my salvation; Ps 27:1 216
In Your l we see light. Ps 36:9 216
In Your light we see l. Ps 36:9 216
forth your righteousness as the l And Ps 37:6 216
And the l of my eyes, even that Ps 38:10 216
O send out Your l and Your truth, Ps 43:3 216
arm and the l of Your presence, Ps 44:3 216
They will never see the l. Ps 49:19 216
before God In the l of the living. Ps 56:13 216
have prepared the l and the sun. Ps 74:16 3974
all the night with a l of fire. Ps 78:14 216
walk in the l of Your countenance. Ps 89:15 216
sins in the l of Your presence. Ps 90:8 3974
L is sown *like seed* for the Ps 97:11 216
Yourself with l as with a cloak, Ps 104:2 216
L arises in the darkness for the Ps 112:4 216
is God, and He has given us l; Ps 118:27 215
to my feet And a l to my path. Ps 119:105 216
unfolding of Your words gives l; Ps 119:130 215
the l around me will be night," Ps 139:11 216
Darkness and l are alike *to You.* Ps 139:12 219a
Praise Him, all stars of l! Ps 148:3 216
righteous is like the l of dawn, Pr 4:18 216
is a lamp and the teaching is l; Pr 6:23 216
The l of the righteous rejoices, Pr 13:9 216
In the l of a king's face is life, Pr 16:15 216
LORD gives l to the eyes of both. Pr 29:13 215
excels folly as l excels darkness. Ec 2:13 216
The l is pleasant, and *it is* good Ec 11:7 216
before the sun and the l, Ec 12:2 216
let us walk in the l of the LORD. Is 2:5 216
Who substitute darkness for l and Is 5:20 216
for light and l for darkness; Is 5:20 216
the l is darkened by its clouds. Is 5:30 216
in darkness Will see a great l; Is 9:2 216
land, The l will shine on them. Is 9:2 216

And the l of Israel will become a Is 10:17 216
Will not flash forth their l; Is 13:10 216
And the moon will not shed its l. Is 13:10 216
The l of the moon will be as Is 30:26 216
moon will be as the l of the sun, Is 30:26 216
and the l of the sun will be seven Is 30:26 216
like the l of seven days, Is 30:26 216
the people, As a l to the nations, Is 42:6 216
I will make darkness into l before Is 42:16 216
forming l and creating darkness, Is 45:7 216
I will also make You a l of the Is 49:6 216
walks in darkness and has no l? Is 50:10 5051
Walk in the l of your fire And Is 50:11 217
My justice for a l of the peoples. Is 51:4 216
l will break out like the dawn, Is 58:8 216
Then your l will rise in darkness And Is 58:10 216
We hope for l, but behold, Is 59:9 216
for your l has come, And the glory Is 60:1 216
"Nations will come to your l, Is 60:3 216
you have the sun for l by day, Is 60:19 216
will the moon give you l; Is 60:19 215
the LORD for an everlasting l, Is 60:19 216
the LORD for an everlasting l, Is 60:20 216
to the heavens, and they had no l. Jer 4:23 216
And while you are hoping for l He Jer 13:16 216
millstones and the l of the lamp. Jer 25:10 216
Who gives the sun for l by day And Jer 31:35 216
moon and the stars for l by night, Jer 31:35 216
me walk In darkness and not in l. La 3:2 216
and a bright l around it, Ezk 1:4 5051
Is it too l a thing for the house Ezk 8:17 7043
And the moon will not give its l. Ezk 32:7 216
And the l dwells with Him. Da 2:22 5094a
are *like* the l that goes forth. Hos 6:5 216
It *will be* darkness and not l; Am 5:18 216
the LORD *be* darkness instead of l, Am 5:20 216
darkness, the LORD is a l for me. Mi 7:8 216
He will bring me out to the l, Mi 7:9 216
away at the l of Your arrows, Hab 3:11 216
He brings His justice to l; Zph 3:5 216
that day there will be no l; Zch 14:6 216
at evening time there will be l. Zch 14:7 216
SITTING IN DARKNESS SAW A GREAT L, Mt 4:16 *5457*
UPON THEM A L DAWNED." Mt 4:16 *5457*
"You are the l of the world. Mt 5:14 *5457*
nor does *anyone* l a lamp and put it Mt 5:15 *2545*
gives l to all who are in the house. Mt 5:15 *2989*
"Let your l shine before men in Mt 5:16 *5457*
your whole body will be full of l. Mt 6:22 *5460*
the l that is in you is darkness, Mt 6:23 *5457*
in the darkness, speak in the l; Mt 10:27 *5457*
yoke is easy and My burden is l." Mt 11:30 *1645*
His garments became as white as l. Mt 17:2 *5457*
AND THE MOON WILL NOT GIVE ITS L, Mt 24:29 *5338*
but that it would come to l. Mk 4:22 *5318*
AND THE MOON WILL NOT GIVE ITS L, Mk 13:24 *5338*
A L OF REVELATION TO THE GENTILES, Lk 2:32 *5457*
those who come in may see the l. Lk 8:16 *5457*
will not be known and come to l. Lk 8:17 *5318*
those who enter may see the l. Lk 11:33 *5338*
your whole body also is full of l; Lk 11:34 *5460*
the l in you is not darkness. Lk 11:35 *5457*
your whole body is full of l, Lk 11:36 *5460*
the dark will be heard in the l, Lk 12:3 *5457*
does not l a lamp and sweep the Lk 15:8 *681*
their own kind than the sons of l. Lk 16:8 *5457*
and the life was the L of men. Jn 1:4 *5457*
The L shines in the darkness, Jn 1:5 *5457*
to testify about the L, so that all Jn 1:7 *5457*
He was not the L, but *he came* to Jn 1:8 *5457*
he came to testify about the L. Jn 1:8 *5457*
There was the true L which, coming Jn 1:9 *5457*
"This is the judgment, that the L Jn 3:19 *5457*
loved the darkness rather than the L, Jn 3:19 *5457*
everyone who does evil hates the L, Jn 3:20 *5457*
and does not come to the L for fear Jn 3:20 *5457*
practices the truth comes to the L, Jn 3:21 *5457*
to rejoice for a while in his l. Jn 5:35 *5457*
"I am the L of the world; he who Jn 8:12 *5457*
but will have the L of life." Jn 8:12 *5457*
I am the L of the world." Jn 9:5 *5457*
he sees the l of this world. Jn 11:9 *5457*
because the l is not in him." Jn 11:10 *5457*
"For a little while longer the L is Jn 12:35 *5457*
Walk while you have the L, so that Jn 12:35 *5457*
"While you have the L, believe in Jn 12:36 *5457*
believe in the L, so that you may Jn 12:36 *5457*
so that you may become sons of L." Jn 12:36 *5457*
"I have come *as* L into the world, Jn 12:46 *5457*
and suddenly a l from heaven Ac 9:3 *5457*
and a l shone in the cell; Ac 12:7 *5457*
YOU AS A L FOR THE GENTILES, Ac 13:47 *5457*
a very bright l suddenly flashed Ac 22:6 *5457*
who were with me saw the l, Ac 22:9 *5457*
of the brightness of that l, Ac 22:11 *5457*
I saw on the way a l from heaven, Ac 26:13 *5457*
that they may turn from darkness to l Ac 26:18 *5457*
He would be the first to proclaim l Ac 26:23 *5457*
a l to those who are in darkness, Ro 2:19 *5457*
and put on the armor of l. Ro 13:12 *5457*
bring to l the things hidden in the 1Co 4:5 *5461*
l of the gospel of the glory of Christ, 2Co 4:4 *5462*
"L shall shine out of darkness," 2Co 4:6 *5457*
has shone in our hearts to give the L 2Co 4:6 *5462*
l affliction is producing for us 2Co 4:17 *1645*
what fellowship has l with darkness 2Co 6:14 *5457*
disguises himself as an angel of l. 2Co 11:14 *5457*
and to bring to l what is the Eph 3:9 *5461*
but now you are L in the Lord; walk Eph 5:8 *5457*

in the Lord; walk as children of L Eph 5:8 5457
(for the fruit of the L *consists* Eph 5:9 5457
when they are exposed by the l, Eph 5:13 5457
that becomes visible is l. Eph 5:13 5457
in the inheritance of the saints in L. Col 1:12 5457
are all sons of l and sons of day. 1Th 5:5 5457
and dwells in unapproachable l, 1Tm 6:16 5457
brought life and immortality to l 2Tm 1:10 5461
of darkness into His marvelous l; 1Pe 2:9 5457
that God is L, and in Him there is 1Jn 1:5 5457
but if we walk in the L as He Himself 1Jn 1:7 5457
the Light as He Himself is in the L, 1Jn 1:7 5457
is passing away and the true L is 1Jn 2:8 5457
The one who says he is in the L and 1Jn 2:9 5457
who loves his brother abides in the L 1Jn 2:10 5457
and the l of a lamp will not shine Rv 18:23 5457
The nations will walk by its l, Rv 21:24 5457
not have need of the l of a lamp nor Rv 22:5 5457
of a lamp nor the l of the sun, Rv 22:5 5457

LIGHTED

He l the lamps before the LORD, Ex 40:25 5927

LIGHTEN

therefore l the hard service of 1Ki 12:4 7043
'L the yoke which your father put 1Ki 12:9 7043
now therefore l the hard service 2Ch 10:4 7043
'L the yoke which your father put 2Ch 10:9 7043
into the sea to l *it for them.* Jon 1:5 7043
they *began* to l the ship by Ac 27:38 2893

LIGHTER

heavy, now you make it l for us!' 1Ki 12:10 7043
heavy, but you make it l for us.' 2Ch 10:10 7043
They are together l than breath. Ps 62:9

LIGHTING

oil for l, spices for the Ex 25:6 3974
and oil for l, and spices for the Ex 35:8 3974
of God descending as a dove *and* l Mt 3:16 2064
"Now no one after l a lamp covers Lk 8:16 681
"No one, after l a lamp, puts it Lk 11:33 681

LIGHTLY

who despise Me will be l esteemed. 1Sa 2:30 7043
I am a poor man and l esteemed?" 1Sa 18:23 7034
"I will be more l esteemed 2Sa 6:22 7043
Better is he who is l esteemed and Pr 12:9 7034
have treated father and mother l Ezk 22:7 7043
Or do you think l of the riches of Ro 2:4 2706
DO NOT REGARD L THE DISCIPLINE OF Heb 12:5 3643a

LIGHTNESS

Because of the l of her harlotry, Jer 3:9 7032b

LIGHTNING

that there were thunder and l Ex 19:16 1300
perceived the thunder and the l Ex 20:18 3940
there was flashing l for them. Dt 33:2 799
out arrows, and scattered them, L, 2Sa 22:15 1300
He spreads His l about Him, Jb 36:30 216
"He covers *His* hands with the l, Jb 36:32 216
His l to the ends of the earth. Jb 37:3 216
He disperses the cloud of His l. Jb 37:11 216
makes the l of His cloud to shine? Jb 37:15 216
them, And l flashes in abundance, Ps 18:14 1300
And their herds to bolts of l. Ps 78:48 7565
Flash forth l and scatter them; Ps 144:6 1300
He makes l for the rain, And Jer 10:13 1300
He makes l for the rain And Jer 51:16 1300
and l was flashing from the fire. Ezk 1:13 1300
ran to and fro like bolts of l. Ezk 1:14 965
Polished to flash like l!' Ezk 21:10 1300
It is made *for striking* like l, Ezk 21:15 1300
to consume, that it may be like l Ezk 21:28 1300
his face had the appearance of l, Da 10:6 1300
dash to and fro like l flashes. Na 2:4 1300
His arrow will go forth like l; Zch 9:14 1300
just as the l comes from the east and Mt 24:27 796
And his appearance was like l, Mt 28:3 796
Satan fall from heaven like l. Lk 10:18 796
"For just like the l, when it Lk 17:24 796
from the throne come flashes of l Rv 4:5 796
flashes of l and an earthquake. Rv 8:5 796
and there were flashes of l and Rv 11:19 796
And there were flashes of l and Rv 16:18 796

LIGHTNINGS

He does not restrain the l when His Jb 37:4
"Can you send forth l that they Jb 38:35 1300
The l lit up the world; Ps 77:18 1300
His l lit up the world; Ps 97:4 1300
Who makes l for the rain, Ps 135:7 1300

LIGHTS

"Let there be l in the expanse of Gn 1:14 3974
and let them be for l in the Gn 1:15 3974
God made the two great l, Gn 1:16 3974
To Him who made *the* great l, Ps 136:7 216
"All the shining l in the heavens Ezk 32:8 216
he called for l and rushed in, Ac 16:29 5457
whom you appear as l in the world, Php 2:15 5458
coming down from the Father of l, Jas 1:17 5457

LIKE

be opened, and you will be l God, Gn 3:5
the man has become l one of Us, Gn 3:22
"L Nimrod a mighty hunter before Gn 10:9
l the garden of the LORD, Gn 13:10
l the land of Egypt as you go to Gn 13:10
and do to them whatever you l; Gn 19:8 2896a, 5869
already he is acting l a judge; Gn 19:9
ascended l the smoke of a furnace. Gn 19:28
red, all over l a hairy garment; Gn 25:25
hairy l his brother Esau's hands; Gn 27:23
the smell of my son Is l the smell Gn 27:27

the daughters of Heth, l these, Gn 27:46
also be l the dust of the earth, Gn 28:14
daughters l captives of the sword? Gn 31:26
if you will become l us, Gn 34:15 3644
he too may die l his brothers." Gn 38:11
"Can we find a man l this, Gn 41:38
abundance l the sand of the sea, Gn 41:49
you l Ephraim and Manasseh!' " Gn 48:20
his hand was leprous l snow. Ex 4:6
restored l *the rest of* his flesh. Ex 4:7
is no one l the LORD our God. Ex 8:10
is no one l Me in all the earth. Ex 9:14 3644
shall be l a native of the land. Ex 12:48
and the waters *were* l a wall to Ex 14:22
and the waters *were* l a wall to Ex 14:29
down into the depths l a stone. Ex 15:5 3644
flowing waters stood up l a heap; Ex 15:8 3644
sank l lead in the mighty waters. Ex 15:10
"Who is l You among the gods, O Ex 15:11 3644
Who is l You, majestic in Ex 15:11 3644
and it was l coriander seed, Ex 16:31
its taste was l wafers with honey. Ex 16:31
ascended l the smoke of a furnace, Ex 19:18
l a consuming fire on the mountain Ex 24:17
shall be shaped l almond *blossoms* Ex 25:33 8246
cups shaped l almond *blossoms* Ex 25:33 8246
cups shaped l almond *blossoms,* Ex 25:34 8246
on it, shall be l its workmanship, Ex 28:8
l the work of the ephod you shall Ex 28:15
they shall be l the engravings of Ex 28:21
l the opening of a coat of mail, Ex 28:32
on it, l the engravings of a seal, Ex 28:36
body, nor shall you make *any* l it in Ex 30:32 3644
'Whoever shall mix *any* l it or Ex 30:33 3644
"Whoever shall make *any* l it, Ex 30:38 3644
stone tablets l the former ones, Ex 34:1
stone tablets l the former ones, Ex 34:4
cups shaped l almond *blossoms,* Ex 37:19 8246
cups shaped l almond *blossoms,* Ex 37:19 8246
cups shaped l almond *blossoms,* Ex 37:20 8246
was on it was l its workmanship, Ex 39:5
filigree *settings;* they were engraved l Ex 39:6
l the workmanship of the ephod: Ex 39:8
on the breastpiece chains l cords, Ex 39:15
it l the engravings of a signet, Ex 39:30
priest's, l the grain offering.' " Lv 5:13
l the sin offering and the guilt Lv 6:17
offering is l the sin offering, Lv 7:7
offered it for sin, l the first. Lv 9:15
things l these happened to me, Lv 10:19
l the appearance of leprosy in the Lv 13:43
offering, l the sin offering, Lv 14:13
'*Something* l a mark *of leprosy* has Lv 14:35
to her l her bed at menstruation; Lv 15:26
l her uncleanness at that time. Lv 15:26
him, l a stranger or a sojourner, Lv 25:35
It is l the days of a hired man Lv 25:50
'L a man hired year by year he Lv 25:53
I will also make your sky l iron Lv 26:19
like iron and your earth l bronze. Lv 26:19
to the LORD, l a field set apart; Lv 27:21
it was l the appearance of fire over Nu 9:15
l those who complain of adversity Nu 11:1
the manna was l coriander seed, Nu 11:7
its appearance l that of bdellium. Nu 11:7
"Oh, do not let her be l one dead, Nu 12:12
"See what the land is l, Nu 13:18
are *they* l *open* camps or with Nu 13:19
l grasshoppers in our own sight, Nu 13:33
that he will not become l Korah Nu 16:40
l the breast of a wave offering and Nu 18:18
offering and l the right thigh. Nu 18:18
And let my end be l his!" Nu 23:10 3644
them l the horns of the wild ox. Nu 23:22
a people rises l a lioness, Nu 23:24
"L valleys that stretch out, Like Nu 24:6
out, L gardens beside the river, Nu 24:6
river, L aloes planted by the LORD, Nu 24:6
LORD, L cedars beside the waters. Nu 24:6
him l the horns of the wild ox. Nu 24:8
l sheep which have no shepherd." Nu 27:17
you are this day l the stars of Dt 1:10
L the Anakim, they are also Dt 2:11
been done l this great thing, Dt 4:32
or has *anything* been heard l it? Dt 4:32 3644
and l it come under the ban; Dt 7:26 3644
"L the nations that the LORD Dt 8:20
of stone l the former ones, Dt 10:1
of stone l the former ones, Dt 10:3
the tablets, l the former writing, Dt 10:4
and forty nights l the first time, Dt 10:10
is not l the land of Egypt from Dt 11:10
your foot l a vegetable garden. Dt 11:10
shall not act l this toward the LORD Dt 12:4 3651
pour it out on the ground l water. Dt 12:16
pour it out on the ground l water. Dt 12:24
pour it out on the ground l water. Dt 15:23
a king over me l all the nations who Dt 17:14
l all his fellow Levites who stand Dt 18:7
you a prophet l me from among you, Dt 18:15 3644
from among their countrymen l you, Dt 18:18 3644
brothers' hearts melt l his heart.' Dt 20:8
l the overthrow of Sodom and Dt 29:23
"L an eagle that stirs up its Dt 32:11
their rock is not l our Rock, Dt 32:31
is none l the God of Jeshurun, Dt 33:26
Who is l you, a people saved by Dt 33:29 3644
has risen in Israel l Moses, Dt 34:10
city, l one of the royal cities, Jos 10:2

day l that before it or after it, Jos 10:14
l the rising of the sun in its might Jg 5:31
come in l locusts for number, Jg 6:5
"They were l you, each one Jg 8:18 3644
l the appearance of the angel of God, Jg 13:6
hear *things* l this at this time." Jg 13:23
"Since you act l this, I will Jg 15:7
weak and be l any *other* man." Jg 16:7
weak and be l any *other* man." Jg 16:11
ropes from his arms l a thread. Jg 16:12
weak and be l any other man." Jg 16:13
weak and be l any *other* man." Jg 16:17
became to him l one of his sons. Jg 17:11
"Nothing l this has *ever* happened Jg 19:30
not l one of your maidservants." Ru 2:13
into your home l Rachel and Leah, Ru 4:11
your house be l the house of Perez Ru 4:12
"There is no one holy l the LORD, 1Sa 2:2
Nor is there any rock l our God. 1Sa 2:2
nothing l this has happened before. 1Sa 4:7
to judge us l all the nations." 1Sa 8:5
"L all the deeds which they have 1Sa 8:8
we also may be l all the nations, 1Sa 8:20
one l him among all the people." 1Sa 10:24 3644
and people l the sand which is on 1Sa 13:5
of his spear was l a weaver's beam, 1Sa 17:7
Philistine will be l one of them, 1Sa 17:36
"Why have you deceived me l this 1Sa 19:17 3602
"There is none l it; 1Sa 21:9 3644
his house, l the feast of a king. 1Sa 25:36
And who is l you in Israel? 1Sa 26:15 3644
in my sight, l an angel of God; 1Sa 29:9
me l the breakthrough of waters." 2Sa 5:20
l the names of the great men who 2Sa 7:9
for there is none l You, 2Sa 7:22 3644
the earth is l Your people Israel, 2Sa 7:23
should regard a dead dog l me?" 2Sa 9:8 3644
And was l a daughter to him. 2Sa 12:3
to you many more things l these! 2Sa 12:8
be l one of the fools in Israel. 2Sa 13:13
but be l a woman who has been 2Sa 14:2
will surely die and are l water spilled 2Sa 14:14
l the wisdom of the angel of God, 2Sa 14:20
l a bear robbed of her cubs in the 2Sa 17:8
heart is l the heart of a lion, 2Sa 17:10
first one is l the running of Ahimaaz 2Sa 18:27
the king is l the angel of God, 2Sa 19:27
whose spear was l a weaver's beam. 2Sa 21:19
"He makes my feet l hinds' *feet,* 2Sa 22:34
them will be thrust away l thorns, 2Sa 23:6
has been no one l you before you, 1Ki 3:12 3644
shall one l you arise after you. 1Ki 3:12 3644
the kings l you all your days. 1Ki 3:13 3644
l the sand that is on the seashore. 1Ki 4:29
to cut timber l the Sidonians." 1Ki 5:6
He also made a house l this hall 1Ki 7:8
brim was made l the brim of a cup, 1Ki 7:26
round l the design of a pedestal, 1Ki 7:31
l the workmanship of a chariot wheel 1Ki 7:33
He made the ten stands l this: 1Ki 7:37
there is no God l You in heaven 1Ki 8:23 3644
nothing l *it* was made for any 1Ki 10:20 3651
l the feast which is in Judah, 1Ki 12:32
"I also am a prophet l you, 1Ki 13:18 3644
have not been l My servant David, 1Ki 14:8
l the heart of his father David. 1Ki 15:3
of the LORD, l David his father. 1Ki 15:11
your house l the house of Jeroboam 1Ki 16:3
in being l the house of Jeroboam, 1Ki 16:7
boast l him who takes *it* off.' " 1Ki 20:11
l the army that you have lost, 1Ki 20:25
them l two little flocks of goats, 1Ki 20:27
if you l, I will give you the 1Ki 21:2 2896a, 5869
your house l the house of Jeroboam 1Ki 21:22
and l the house of Baasha the son 1Ki 21:22
Surely there was no one l Ahab who 1Ki 21:25
word be l the word of one of them, 1Ki 22:13
L sheep which have no shepherd. 1Ki 22:17
not l his father and his mother; 2Ki 3:2
l the flesh of a little child and 2Ki 5:14
l all the multitude of Israel who are 2Ki 7:13
l all the multitude of Israel who 2Ki 7:13
l the house of Ahab *had done,* 2Ki 8:27
l the house of Jeroboam the son of 2Ki 9:9
and l the house of Baasha the son 2Ki 9:9
the driving is l the driving of Jehu 2Ki 9:20
made them l the dust at threshing. 2Ki 13:7
LORD, yet not l David his father; 2Ki 14:3
stiffened their neck l their fathers, 2Ki 17:14
commanded them not to do l them. 2Ki 17:15
was none l him among all the kings 2Ki 18:5 3644
away to a land l your own land, 2Ki 18:32
king l him who turned to the LORD 2Ki 23:25 3644
nor did any l him arise after him. 2Ki 23:25 3644
pillar was l these with network. 2Ki 25:17
multiply l the sons of Judah. 1Ch 4:27 5704
hand *was* a spear l a weaver's beam, 1Ch 11:23
faces were l the faces of lions, 1Ch 12:8
a great army l the army of God. 1Ch 12:22
l the breakthrough of waters." 1Ch 14:11
a name l the name of the great ones 1Ch 17:8
"O LORD, there is none l You, 1Ch 17:20 3644
the earth is l Your people Israel, 1Ch 17:21
whose spear *was* l a weaver's beam. 1Ch 20:5
were given duties l their relatives 1Ch 26:12 5980
days on the earth are l a shadow, 1Ch 29:15
Now figures l oxen *were* under it 2Ch 4:3 1823
brim was made l the brim of a cup, 2Ch 4:5

l a lily blossom; it could hold	2Ch 4:5	
no god l You in heaven or on earth	2Ch 6:14	3644
there had never been spice l that	2Ch 9:9	
and none l that was seen before in	2Ch 9:11	
nothing l *it* was made for any	2Ch 9:19	3651
l the peoples of *other* lands?	2Ch 13:9	
So please let your word be l one	2Ch 18:12	
L sheep which have no shepherd;	2Ch 18:16	
him l the fire for his fathers.	2Ch 21:19	
of the LORD l the house of Ahab,	2Ch 22:4	
"Do not be l your fathers and	2Ch 30:7	
stiffen your neck l your fathers,	2Ch 30:8	
because there was nothing l this	2Ch 30:26	
deceive you or mislead you l this,	2Ch 32:15	
not been celebrated a Passover l it in	2Ch 35:18	3644
us build with you, for we, l you,	Ezr 4:2	
is l the flesh of our brothers,	Ne 5:5	
our children l their children.	Ne 5:5	
"Should a man l me flee?	Ne 6:11	3644
L a stone into raging waters.	Ne 9:11	3644
nations there was no king l him,	Ne 13:26	3644
is no one l him on the earth,	Jb 1:8	3644
is no one l him on the earth,	Jb 2:3	3644
"Or l a miscarriage which is	Jb 3:16	
And my cries pour out l water.	Jb 3:24	
L the stacking of grain in its	Jb 5:26	
They are l loathsome food to me.	Jb 6:7	
have acted deceitfully l a wadi,	Jb 6:15	3644
L the torrents of wadis which	Jb 6:15	
days l the days of a hired man?	Jb 7:1	
"They slip by l reed boats, Like	Jb 9:26	5973
L an eagle that swoops on its prey.	Jb 9:26	
But I am not l that in myself.	Jb 9:35	3651
'Did You not pour me out l milk And	Jb 10:10	
like milk And curdle me l cheese;	Jb 10:10	
up, You would hunt me l a lion;	Jb 10:16	
Darkness would be l the morning.	Jb 11:17	
them stagger l a drunken man.	Jb 12:25	
I am decaying l a rotten thing,	Jb 13:28	
L a garment that is moth-eaten.	Jb 13:28	
"L a flower he comes forth and	Jb 14:2	
He also flees l a shadow and does	Jb 14:2	
he fulfills his day l a hired man.	Jb 14:6	
And put forth sprigs l a plant.	Jb 14:9	3644
Man, who drinks iniquity l water!	Jb 15:16	
him l a king ready for the attack,	Jb 15:24	
off his unripe grape l the vine,	Jb 15:33	
off his flower l the olive tree.	Jb 15:33	
"I too could speak l you,	Jb 16:4	
He runs at me l a warrior.	Jb 16:14	
He has uprooted my hope l a tree.	Jb 19:10	
He perishes forever l his refuse;	Jb 20:7	
"He flies away l a dream, and	Jb 20:8	
Even l a vision of the night he is	Jb 20:8	
their little ones l the flock,	Jb 21:11	
And l chaff which the storm	Jb 21:18	
will be broken l a tree.	Jb 24:20	
low and l everything gathered up;	Jb 24:24	
Even l the heads of grain they are	Jb 24:24	
"Though he piles up silver l dust And	Jb 27:16	
built his house l the spider's web,	Jb 27:18	
"Terrors overtake him l a flood;	Jb 27:20	
justice was l a robe and a turban.	Jb 29:14	
has passed away l a cloud.	Jb 30:15	
I have become l dust and ashes.	Jb 30:19	4911a
covered my transgressions l Adam,	Jb 31:33	
would bind it to myself l a crown.	Jb 31:36	
L a prince I would approach Him.	Jb 31:37	3644
my belly is l unvented wine,	Jb 32:19	
L new wineskins it is about to	Jb 32:19	
"Behold, I belong to God l you;	Jb 33:6	
"What man is l Job, Who drinks up	Jb 34:7	
Who drinks up derision l water,	Jb 34:7	
l the wicked In a public place,	Jb 34:26	8478
Because he answers l wicked men.	Jb 34:36	
is for a man l yourself,	Jb 35:8	3644
Who is a teacher l Him?	Jb 36:22	3644
"Now gird up your loins l a man,	Jb 38:3	
is changed l clay *under* the seal;	Jb 38:14	
And they stand forth l a garment.	Jb 38:14	3644
"Water becomes hard l stone,	Jb 38:30	
"Do you make him leap l the locust?	Jb 39:20	
"Now gird up your loins l a man;	Jb 40:7	
"Or do you have an arm l God,	Jb 40:9	
you thunder with a voice l His?	Jb 40:9	3644
He eats grass l an ox.	Jb 40:15	
"He bends his tail l a cedar;	Jb 40:17	3644
His limbs are l bars of iron.	Jb 40:18	
are l the eyelids of the morning.	Jb 41:18	
"His underparts are l sharp	Jb 41:30	
He spreads out l a threshing	Jb 41:30	
"He makes the depths boil l a pot;	Jb 41:31	
makes the sea l a jar of ointment.	Jb 41:31	
"Nothing on earth is l him,	Jb 41:33	4915b
l a tree *firmly* planted by streams of	Ps 1:3	
But they are l chaff which the	Ps 1:4	
shatter them l earthenware.' "	Ps 2:9	
Or he will tear my soul l a lion,	Ps 7:2	
is l a lion that is eager to tear,	Ps 17:12	1825
He makes my feet l hinds' *feet*,	Ps 18:33	
I am poured out l water, And all	Ps 22:14	
My heart is l wax;	Ps 22:14	
strength is dried up l a potsherd,	Ps 22:15	
l those who go down to the pit.	Ps 28:1	4911a
He makes Lebanon skip l a calf,	Ps 29:6	3644
And Sirion l a young wild ox.	Ps 29:6	3644
of mind; I am l a broken vessel.	Ps 31:12	
them be l chaff before the wind,	Ps 35:5	
"LORD, who is l You, Who	Ps 35:10	3644
L godless jesters at a feast, They	Ps 35:16	
is l the mountains of God;	Ps 36:6	
Your judgments are l a great deep.	Ps 36:6	
will wither quickly l the grass And	Ps 37:2	
grass And fade l the green herb.	Ps 37:2	
be l the glory of the pastures,	Ps 37:20	
l smoke they vanish away.	Ps 37:20	
Spreading himself l a luxuriant tree	Ps 37:35	
But I, l a deaf man, do not hear;	Ps 38:13	
And *I am* l a mute man who does not	Ps 38:13	
I am l a man who does not hear,	Ps 38:14	
A sojourner l all my fathers.	Ps 39:12	
He is l the beasts that perish.	Ps 49:12	4911a
Is l the beasts that perish.	Ps 49:20	4911a
You thought that I was just l you;	Ps 50:21	3644
destruction, L a sharp razor,	Ps 52:2	
I am l a green olive tree in the	Ps 52:8	
"Oh, that I had wings l a dove!	Ps 55:6	
venom l the venom of a serpent;	Ps 58:4	1823
L a deaf cobra that stops up its	Ps 58:4	3644
flow away l water that runs off;	Ps 58:7	3644
L the miscarriages of a woman	Ps 58:8	
at evening, they howl l a dog,	Ps 59:6	
at evening, they howl l a dog,	Ps 59:14	
him, all of you, L a leaning wall,	Ps 62:3	
leaning wall, l a tottering fence?	Ps 62:3	
sharpened their tongue l a sword.	Ps 64:3	
You are l the wings of a dove	Ps 68:13	
O God, who is l You?	Ps 71:19	3644
down l rain upon the mown grass,	Ps 72:6	
L showers that water the earth.	Ps 72:6	
will wave l *the cedars of* Lebanon;	Ps 72:16	
l vegetation of the earth.	Ps 72:16	
Nor are they plagued l mankind.	Ps 73:5	5973
L a dream when one awakes, O Lord,	Ps 73:20	
I was l a beast before You.	Ps 73:22	
What god is great l our God?	Ps 77:13	
led Your people l a flock	Ps 77:20	
And not be l their fathers, A	Ps 78:8	
made the waters stand up l a heap.	Ps 78:13	3644
abundant drink l the ocean depths.	Ps 78:15	
waters to run down l rivers.	Ps 78:16	
rained meat upon them l the dust,	Ps 78:27	
fowl l the sand of the seas,	Ps 78:27	
led forth His own people l sheep And	Ps 78:52	
them in the wilderness l a flock;	Ps 78:52	
treacherously l their fathers;	Ps 78:57	
turned aside l a treacherous bow.	Ps 78:57	
L a warrior overcome by wine.	Ps 78:65	
built His sanctuary l the heights,	Ps 78:69	3644
L the earth which He has founded	Ps 78:69	
l water round about Jerusalem;	Ps 79:3	
Will Your jealousy burn l fire?	Ps 79:5	3644
who lead Joseph l a flock;	Ps 80:1	
"Nevertheless you will die l men And	Ps 82:7	
fall l *any* one of the princes."	Ps 82:7	
Make their nobles l Oreb and Zeeb And	Ps 83:11	
princes l Zebah and Zalmunna,	Ps 83:11	
make them l the whirling dust,	Ps 83:13	
L chaff before the wind.	Ps 83:13	
L fire that burns the forest And	Ps 83:14	
And l a flame that sets the	Ps 83:14	
is no one l You among the gods,	Ps 86:8	3644
Nor are there any works l Yours.	Ps 86:8	
become l a man without strength,	Ps 88:4	
L the slain who lie in the grave,	Ps 88:5	3644
me l water all day long;	Ps 88:17	
sons of the mighty is l the LORD,	Ps 89:6	1819
LORD God of hosts, who is l You,	Ps 89:8	3644
crushed Rahab l one who is slain;	Ps 89:10	
be established forever l the moon,	Ps 89:37	
Will Your wrath burn l fire?	Ps 89:46	3644
Are l yesterday when it passes by,	Ps 90:4	
have swept them away l a flood,	Ps 90:5	2229
are l grass which sprouts anew.	Ps 90:5	
have finished our years l a sigh.	Ps 90:9	3644
the wicked sprouted up l grass And	Ps 92:7	3644
my horn l *that of* the wild ox;	Ps 92:10	
man will flourish l the palm tree,	Ps 92:12	
He will grow l a cedar in Lebanon.	Ps 92:12	
The mountains melted l wax at the	Ps 97:5	
Light is sown l *seed* for	Ps 97:11	
have been scorched l a hearth.	Ps 102:3	
My heart has been smitten l grass	Ps 102:4	
l an owl of the waste places.	Ps 102:6	
l a lonely bird on a housetop.	Ps 102:7	
For I have eaten ashes l bread And	Ps 102:9	
My days are l a lengthened shadow,	Ps 102:11	
And I wither away l grass.	Ps 102:11	
of them will wear out l a garment;	Ps 102:26	
L clothing You will change them and	Ps 102:26	
your youth is renewed l the eagle.	Ps 103:5	
As for man, his days are l grass;	Ps 103:15	
out heaven l a *tent* curtain.	Ps 104:2	
It ran in the dry places l a	Ps 105:41	
We have sinned l our fathers, We	Ps 106:6	5973
and staggered l a drunken man,	Ps 107:27	
And makes *his* families l a flock.	Ps 107:41	
it entered into his body l water And	Ps 109:18	
water And l oil into his bones.	Ps 109:18	
l a shadow when it lengthens;	Ps 109:23	
I am shaken off l the locust.	Ps 109:23	
Who is l the LORD our God, Who is	Ps 113:5	
The mountains skipped l rams,	Ps 114:4	
like rams, The hills, l lambs.	Ps 114:4	
O mountains, that you skip l rams?	Ps 114:6	
O hills, l lambs?	Ps 114:6	
who make them will become l them,	Ps 115:8	3644
They surrounded me l bees;	Ps 118:12	
become l a wineskin in the smoke,	Ps 119:83	
all the wicked of the earth l	Ps 119:119	
I have gone astray l a lost sheep;	Ps 119:176	
Zion, We were l those who dream.	Ps 126:1	
L arrows in the hand of a warrior,	Ps 127:4	
wife shall be l a fruitful vine Within	Ps 128:3	
Your children l olive plants	Ps 128:3	
be l grass upon the housetops,	Ps 129:6	
L a weaned child *rests* against his	Ps 131:2	
is l a weaned child within me.	Ps 131:2	
It is l the precious oil upon the	Ps 133:2	
It is l the dew of Hermon Coming	Ps 133:3	
who make them will be l them,	*Ps 135:18*	3644
l those who have long been dead.	Ps 143:3	
l those who go down to the pit.	Ps 143:7	4911a
Man is l a mere breath;	Ps 144:4	1819
His days are l a passing shadow.	Ps 144:4	
He gives snow l wool;	Ps 147:16	
He scatters the frost l ashes.	Ps 147:16	
Let us swallow them alive l Sheol,	Pr 1:12	
When your dread comes l a storm And	Pr 1:27	
calamity comes l a whirlwind,	Pr 1:27	
righteous is l the light of dawn,	Pr 4:18	
way of the wicked is l darkness;	Pr 4:19	
Deliver yourself l a gazelle from	Pr 6:5	
And l a bird from the hand of the	Pr 6:5	
poverty will come in l a vagabond And	Pr 6:11	
And your need l an armed man.	Pr 6:11	
wickedness is l sport to a fool,	Pr 10:23	
L vinegar to the teeth and smoke	Pr 10:26	
will flourish l the *green* leaf.	Pr 11:28	
But she who shames *him* is l	Pr 12:4	
rashly l the thrusts of a sword,	Pr 12:18	
The fury of a king is l	Pr 16:14	
is l a cloud with the spring rain.	Pr 16:15	
While his words are l scorching fire.	Pr 16:27	
The beginning of strife is l	Pr 17:14	
a whisperer are l dainty morsels,	Pr 18:8	
And l a high wall in his own	Pr 18:11	
are l the bars of a citadel.	Pr 18:19	
wrath is l the roaring of a lion,	Pr 19:12	
his favor is l dew on the grass.	Pr 19:12	
king is l the growling of a lion;	Pr 20:2	
A plan in the heart of a man is l	Pr 20:5	
The king's heart is l channels of	Pr 21:1	
L an eagle that flies *toward* the	Pr 23:5	
At the last it bites l a serpent And	Pr 23:32	
a serpent And stings l a viper.	Pr 23:32	
l one who lies down in the middle	Pr 23:34	
Or l one who lies down on the top	Pr 23:34	
And your want l an armed man.	Pr 24:34	
L apples of gold in settings of	Pr 25:11	
L an earring of gold and an	Pr 25:12	
L the cold of snow in the time of	Pr 25:13	
L clouds and wind without rain Is	Pr 25:14	
L a club and a sword and a sharp	Pr 25:18	
L a bad tooth and an unsteady	Pr 25:19	
L one who takes off a garment on	Pr 25:20	
or l vinegar on soda, Is he who	Pr 25:20	
L cold water to a weary soul, So	Pr 25:25	
L a trampled spring and a	Pr 25:26	
L a city that is broken into	Pr 25:28	
L snow in summer and like rain in	Pr 26:1	
in summer and l rain in harvest,	Pr 26:1	
L a sparrow in *its* flitting, like	Pr 26:2	
l a swallow in *its* flying,	Pr 26:2	
his folly, Or you will also be l him.	Pr 26:4	7737a
L the legs *which* are useless	Pr 26:7	
L one who binds a stone in a	Pr 26:8	
L a thorn *which* falls into	Pr 26:9	
L an archer who wounds everyone,	Pr 26:10	
L a dog that returns to its vomit	Pr 26:11	
L one who takes a dog by the ears	Pr 26:17	
L a madman who throws Firebrands,	Pr 26:18	
L charcoal to hot embers and wood	Pr 26:21	
a whisperer are l dainty morsels,	Pr 26:22	
L an earthen vessel overlaid with	Pr 26:23	
L a bird that wanders from her	Pr 27:8	
man who oppresses the lowly Is l	Pr 28:3	
L a roaring lion and a rushing	Pr 28:15	
a kind of *man* whose teeth are l	Pr 30:14	
like swords And his jaw teeth l	Pr 30:14	
She is l merchant ships;	Pr 31:14	
He will spend them l a shadow.	Ec 6:12	
Who is l the wise man and who	Ec 8:1	
not lengthen his days l a shadow,	Ec 8:13	
l fish caught in a treacherous	Ec 9:12	
l an error which goes forth from	Ec 10:5	
walking l slaves on the land.	Ec 10:7	
The words of wise men are l goads,	Ec 12:11	
are l well-driven nails;	Ec 12:11	
Your name is l purified oil;	SS 1:3	
Jerusalem, L the tents of Kedar,	SS 1:5	
Kedar, L the curtains of Solomon.	SS 1:5	
should I be l one who veils herself	SS 1:7	
you are l My mare among the	SS 1:9	1819
Your eyes are l doves."	SS 1:15	
"L a lily among the thorns, So is	SS 2:2	
"L an apple tree among the trees	SS 2:3	
is l a gazelle or a young stag.	SS 2:9	1819
and be l a gazelle Or a young stag	SS 2:17	1819
the wilderness L columns of smoke,	SS 3:6	
Your eyes are l doves behind your	SS 4:1	
Your hair is l a flock of goats	SS 4:1	
are l a flock of *newly* shorn ewes	SS 4:2	
"Your lips are l a scarlet thread,	SS 4:3	
are l a slice of a pomegranate	SS 4:3	
"Your neck is l the tower of David	SS 4:4	
"Your two breasts are l two fawns,	SS 4:5	

is l the fragrance of Lebanon. SS 4:11
"His head is l gold, pure gold; SS 5:11
His locks are l clusters of dates SS 5:11
"His eyes are l doves Beside SS 5:12
"His cheeks are l a bed of balsam, SS 5:13
His appearance is l Lebanon Choice SS 5:15
Your hair is l a flock of goats SS 6:5
"Your teeth are l a flock of ewes SS 6:6
are l a slice of a pomegranate SS 6:7
'Who is this that grows l the dawn, SS 6:10 3644
curves of your hips are l jewels, SS 7:1 3644
"Your navel is l a round goblet SS 7:2
Your belly is l a heap of wheat SS 7:2
"Your two breasts are l two fawns, SS 7:3
"Your neck is l a tower of ivory, SS 7:4
Your eyes l the pools in Heshbon SS 7:4
nose is l the tower of Lebanon, SS 7:4
"Your head crowns you l Carmel, SS 7:5
of your head are l purple threads; SS 7:5
"Your stature is l a palm tree, SS 7:7 1819
And your breasts are l its SS 7:7
breasts be l clusters of the vine, SS 7:8
fragrance of your breath l apples, SS 7:8
And your mouth l the best wine!" SS 7:9
"Oh that you were l a brother to SS 8:1
"Put me l a seal over your heart, SS 8:6
your heart, L a seal on your arm. SS 8:6
and my breasts were l towers; SS 8:10
And be l a gazelle or a young stag SS 8:14 1819
is left l a shelter in a vineyard, Is 1:8
L a watchman's hut in a cucumber field, Is 1:8
cucumber field, l a besieged city. Is 1:8
survivors, We would be l Sodom, Is 1:9
Sodom, We would be l Gomorrah. Is 1:9 1819
Though they are red l crimson, Is 1:18
like crimson, They will be l wool. Is 1:18
be l an oak whose leaf fades away Or Is 1:30
are soothsayers l the Philistines, Is 2:6
they display their sin l Sodom; Is 3:9
So their root will become l rot Is 5:24
and their corpses lay l refuse in Is 5:25
hoofs of its horses seem l flint and Is 5:28
its chariot wheels l a whirlwind. Is 5:28
Its roaring is l a lioness, and it Is 5:29
and it roars l young lions; Is 5:29
that day l the roaring of the sea. Is 5:30
L a terebinth or an oak Whose Is 6:13
For wickedness burns l a fire; Is 9:18
people are l fuel for the fire; Is 9:19
them down l mud in the streets. Is 10:6
"Is not Calno l Carchemish, Or Is 10:9
Carchemish, Or Hamath l Arpad, Is 10:9
like Arpad, Or Samaria l Damascus? Is 10:9
And l a mighty man I brought down Is 10:13
riches of the peoples l a nest, Is 10:14
That would be l a club wielding Is 10:15
Or l a rod lifting him who is not Is 10:15
will be kindled l a burning flame. Is 10:16
may be l the sand of the sea, Is 10:22
l the slaughter of Midian at the rock Is 10:26
the lion will eat straw l the ox. Is 11:7
mountains, L that of many people! Is 13:4 1823
will writhe l a woman in labor, Is 13:8
will be that l a hunted gazelle, Is 13:14
Or l sheep with none to gather Is 13:14
weak as we, You have become l us. Is 14:10 4911a
will make myself l the Most High.' Is 14:14 1819
Who made the world l a wilderness Is 14:17
of your tomb L a rejected branch, Is 14:19
of the pit L a trampled corpse. Is 14:19
l fleeing birds or scattered Is 16:2
your shadow l night at high noon; Is 16:3
heart intones l a harp for Moab And Is 16:11
be l the glory of the sons of Israel," Is 17:3
It will be even l the reaper Is 17:5
Or it will be l one gleaning ears Is 17:5
it l the shaking of an olive tree, Is 17:6
l forsaken places in the forest, Is 17:9
Or l branches which they abandoned Is 17:9
roar l the roaring of the seas, Is 17:12
l the rumbling of mighty waters! Is 17:12
on l the rumbling of many waters, Is 17:13
And be chased l chaff in the Is 17:13
Or l whirling dust before a gale. Is 17:13
L dazzling heat in the sunshine, Is 18:4
L a cloud of dew in the heat of Is 18:4
the Egyptians will become l women, Is 19:16
l the pains of a woman in labor. Is 21:3
And roll you tightly l a ball, Is 22:18
"I will drive him l a peg in a Is 22:23
Overflow your land l the Nile, Is 23:10
years l the days of one king. Is 23:15
the people will be l the priest, Is 24:2
priest, the servant l his master, Is 24:2
master, the maid l her mistress, Is 24:2
mistress, the buyer l the seller, Is 24:2
seller, the lender l the borrower, Is 24:2
the creditor l the debtor. Is 24:2
reels to and fro l a drunkard And Is 24:20
And it totters l a shack, Is 24:20
They will be gathered together L Is 24:22
Is l a rain storm against a wall. Is 25:4
L heat in drought, You subdue Is 25:5
L heat by the shadow of a cloud, Is 25:5
L the striking of Him who has Is 27:7
Or l the slaughter of His slain, Is 27:7
stones l pulverized chalk stones; Is 27:9
forlorn and forsaken l the desert; Is 27:10
L a storm of mighty overflowing Is 28:2
Will be l the first-ripe fig prior Is 28:4
And she will be l an Ariel to me. Is 29:2
be l that of a spirit from the ground, Is 29:4
enemies will become l fine dust, Is 29:5
ones l the chaff which blows away; Is 29:5
distress her, will be l a dream, Is 29:7
you l the words of a sealed book, Is 29:11
to you L a breach about to fall, Is 30:13
is l the smashing of a potter's jar, Is 30:14
l the light of seven days, Is 30:26
His tongue is l a consuming fire; Is 30:27
is l an overflowing torrent, Is 30:28
LORD, l a torrent of brimstone, Is 30:33
L flying birds so the LORD of Is 31:5
will be l a refuge from the wind And Is 32:2
L streams of water in a dry Is 32:2
L the shade of a huge rock in a Is 32:2
Sharon is l a desert plain, And Is 33:9
breath will consume you l a fire. Is 33:11
L cut thorns which are burned in Is 33:12
sky will be rolled up l a scroll; Is 34:4
rejoice and blossom; L the crocus Is 35:1
Then the lame will leap l a deer, Is 35:6
away to a land l your own land, Is 36:17
"L a shepherd's tent my dwelling Is 38:12
L a lion—so He breaks all my Is 38:13
"L a swallow, like a crane, so I Is 38:14
"Like a swallow, l a crane, so Is 38:14
a crane, so I twitter; I moan l a dove; Is 38:14
is l the flower of the field. Is 40:6
L a shepherd He will tend His Is 40:11
are l a drop from a bucket, Is 40:15
lifts up the islands l fine dust. Is 40:15
inhabitants are l grasshoppers, Is 40:22
stretches out the heavens l a curtain Is 40:22
them out l a tent to dwell in. Is 40:22
storm carries them away l stubble. Is 40:24
will mount up with wings l eagles, Is 40:31
makes them l dust with his sword, Is 41:2
And will make the hills l chaff. Is 41:15
LORD will go forth l a warrior, Is 42:13
arouse His zeal l a man of war. Is 42:13
l a woman in labor I will groan, Is 42:14
and extinguished l a wick): Is 43:17
L poplars by streams of water.' Is 44:4
'Who is l Me? Let him proclaim Is 44:7 3644
and makes it l the form of a man, Is 44:13
of a man, l the beauty of man, Is 44:13
transgressions l a thick cloud And Is 44:22
And your sins l a heavy mist. Is 44:22
am God, and there is no one l Me, Is 46:9 3644
they have become l stubble, Is 47:14
would have been l a river, Is 48:18
l the waves of the sea. Is 48:18
would have been l the sand, Is 48:19
And your offspring l its grains; Is 48:19
has made My mouth l a sharp sword, Is 49:2
I have set My face l flint, Is 50:7
will all wear out l a garment; Is 50:9
wilderness He will make l Eden, Is 51:3
desert l the garden of the LORD; Is 51:3
For the sky will vanish l smoke, Is 51:6
earth will wear out l a garment And Is 51:6
inhabitants will die in l manner; Is 51:6 3644
moth will eat them l a garment, Is 51:8
And the grub will eat them l wool. Is 51:8
son of man who is made l grass, Is 51:12
street, L an antelope in a net, Is 51:20
even made your back l the ground And Is 51:23
And l the street for those who Is 51:23
up before Him l a tender shoot, Is 53:2
l a root out of parched ground; Is 53:2
And l one from whom men hide their Is 53:3
of us l sheep have gone astray, Is 53:6
L a lamb that is led to slaughter, Is 53:7
And l a sheep that is silent Is 53:7
L a wife forsaken and grieved in Is 54:6
Even l a wife of one's youth when Is 54:6
this is l the days of Noah to Me, Is 54:9
And tomorrow will be l today, Is 56:12
the wicked are l the tossing sea, Is 57:20
Raise your voice l a trumpet, Is 58:1
You do not fast l you do today to Is 58:4
it a fast l this which I choose, Is 58:5
it for bowing one's head l a reed And Is 58:5
light will break out l the dawn, Is 58:8
your gloom will become l midday. Is 58:10
you will be l a watered garden, Is 58:11
And l a spring of water whose Is 58:11
grope along the wall l blind men, Is 59:10
We grope l those who have no eyes; Is 59:10
are vigorous we are l dead men. Is 59:10
All of us growl l bears, And moan Is 59:11
bears, And moan sadly l doves; Is 59:11
on righteousness l a breastplate, Is 59:17
He will come l a rushing stream Which Is 59:19
"Who are these who fly l a cloud And Is 60:8
And l the doves to their lattices? Is 60:8
goes forth l brightness, Is 62:1
l a torch that is burning. Is 62:1
And Your garments l the one who Is 63:2
L the horse in the wilderness, Is 63:13
We have become l those over whom Is 63:19
L those who were not called by Is 63:19
have become l one who is unclean, Is 64:6
deeds are l a filthy garment; Is 64:6
And all of us wither l a leaf, Is 64:6
And our iniquities, l the wind, Is 64:6
the lion will eat straw l the ox; Is 65:25
"But he who kills an ox is l Is 66:3
He who sacrifices a lamb is l Is 66:3
He who offers a grain offering is l Is 66:3
He who burns incense is l the one Is 66:3
I extend peace to her l a river, Is 66:12
nations l an overflowing stream; Is 66:12
will flourish l the new grass; Is 66:14
And His chariots l the whirlwind, Is 66:15
your prophets L a destroying lion. Jer 2:30
for them L an Arab in the desert, Jer 3:2
Or else My wrath will go forth l fire Jer 4:4
"Behold, he goes up l clouds, Jer 4:13
And his chariots l the whirlwind; Jer 4:13
'L watchmen of a field they are Jer 4:17
"Their quiver is l an open grave, Jer 5:16
watch l fowlers lying in wait; Jer 5:26
'L a cage full of birds, So their Jer 5:27
your hand again l a grape gatherer Jer 6:9
Their voice roars l the sea, Jer 6:23
L a horse charging into the battle. Jer 8:6
"They bend their tongue l their Jer 9:3
ruined, laid waste l a desert, Jer 9:12
fall l dung on the open field, Jer 9:22
And l the sheaf after the reaper, Jer 9:22
"L a scarecrow in a cucumber Jer 10:5
There is none l You, O LORD; Jer 10:6 3644
kingdoms, There is none l You. Jer 10:7 3644
portion of Jacob is not l these; Jer 10:16
But I was l a gentle lamb led to Jer 11:19
Drag them off l sheep for the Jer 12:3
to Me L a lion in the forest; Jer 12:8
l a speckled bird of prey to Me? Jer 12:9
let them be just l this waistband which Jer 13:10
of you L a woman in childbirth? Jer 13:21 3644
I will scatter them l drifting straw Jer 13:24
They pant for air l jackals, Jer 14:6
Why are You l a stranger in the Jer 14:8
l a traveler who has pitched his tent Jer 14:8
"Why are You l a man dismayed, Jer 14:9
L a mighty man who cannot save? Jer 14:9
indeed be to me l a deceptive stream Jer 15:18 3644
"For he will be l a bush in the Jer 17:6
be l a tree planted by the water, Jer 17:8
l the clay in the potter's hand, Jer 18:6
Who ever heard the l of this? Jer 18:13
'L an east wind I will scatter Jer 18:17
"so as to make this city l Topheth. Jer 19:12
be defiled l the place Topheth, Jer 19:13
l a burning fire Shut up in my bones; Jer 20:9
is with me l a dread champion; Jer 20:11
But let that man be l the cities Jer 20:16
My wrath may not go forth l fire Jer 21:12
"You are l Gilead to Me, Like Jer 22:6
L the summit of Lebanon; Jer 22:6
I will make you l a wilderness, Jer 22:6
L cities which are not inhabited. Jer 22:6
you, Pain l a woman in childbirth! Jer 22:23
I have become l a drunken man, Jer 23:9
Even l a man overcome with wine, Jer 23:9
will be l slippery paths to them, Jer 23:12
of them have become to Me l Sodom, Jer 23:14
And her inhabitants l Gomorrah. Jer 23:14
"Is not My word l fire?" Jer 23:29
"and l a hammer which shatters a Jer 23:29
very good figs, l first-ripe figs, Jer 24:2
'L these good figs, so I will Jer 24:5
'But l the bad figs which cannot Jer 24:8
l those who tread the grapes, Jer 25:30
they will be l dung on the face Jer 25:33
you will fall l a choice vessel. Jer 25:34
left His hiding place l the lion; Jer 25:38
I will make this house l Shiloh, Jer 26:6
'This house will be l Shiloh and Jer 26:9
I spoke words l all these to Jer 27:12
I will make them l split-open figs Jer 29:17
make you l Zedekiah and like Ahab, Jer 29:22
make you like Zedekiah and l Ahab, Jer 29:22
day is great, There is none l it; Jer 30:7 3644
life will be l a watered garden, Jer 31:12
chastised, L an untrained calf; Jer 31:18
not l the covenant which I made Jer 31:32
Who is this that rises l the Nile, Jer 46:7
L the rivers whose waters surge Jer 46:7
Egypt rises l the Nile, Even like Jer 46:8
Even l the rivers whose waters Jer 46:8
up l Tabor among the mountains, Jer 46:18
mountains, Or l Carmel by the sea. Jer 46:18
her midst Are l fattened calves, Jer 46:21
"Its sound moves along l a serpent; Jer 46:22
For they move on l an army And Jer 46:22
be l a juniper in the wilderness. Jer 48:6
l wine on its dregs, And he has Jer 48:11
And be l a dove that nests Beyond Jer 48:28
My heart wails for Moab l flutes; Jer 48:36
My heart also wails l flutes for Jer 48:36
Moab l an undesirable vessel," Jer 48:38
one will fly swiftly l an eagle And Jer 48:40
l the heart of a woman in labor. Jer 48:41
"L the overthrow of Sodom and Jer 49:18
one will come up l a lion from the Jer 49:19
For who is l Me, and who will Jer 49:19 3644
mount up and swoop l an eagle and Jer 49:22
l the heart of a woman in labor. Jer 49:22
of her L a woman in childbirth. Jer 49:24
Be also l male goats at the head Jer 50:8
arrows will be l an expert warrior Jer 50:9
you skip about l a threshing heifer Jer 50:11
heifer And neigh l stallions, Jer 50:11
Pile her up l heaps And utterly Jer 50:26 3644

Their voice roars **l** the sea; **Jer 50:42**
Marshalled **l** a man for the battle **Jer 50:42**
Agony **l** a woman in childbirth. **Jer 50:43**
one will come up **l** a lion from the **Jer 50:44**
For who is **l** Me, and who will **Jer 50:44** 3644
you with a population **l** locusts, **Jer 51:14**
portion of Jacob is not **l** these; **Jer 51:19**
up the horses **l** bristly locusts. **Jer 51:27**
They are becoming **l** women; **Jer 51:30**
of Babylon is **l** a threshing floor **Jer 51:33**
He has set me down **l** an empty **Jer 51:34**
He has swallowed me **l** a monster, **Jer 51:34**
will roar together **l** young lions, **Jer 51:38**
They will growl **l** lions' cubs. **Jer 51:38**
down **l** lambs to the slaughter, **Jer 51:40**
L rams together with male goats. **Jer 51:40**
waves will roar **l** many waters; **Jer 51:55**
l all that Jehoiakim had done. **Jer 52:2**
And the second pillar was **l** these, **Jer 52:22**
She has become **l** a widow Who was **La 1:1**
Her princes have become **l** deer **La 1:6**
see if there is any pain **l** my pain **La 1:12**
In the house it is **l** death. **La 1:20**
That they may become **l** me. **La 1:21** 3644
has burned in Jacob **l** a flaming fire **La 2:3**
He has bent His bow **l** an enemy; **La 2:4**
set His right hand **l** an adversary **La 2:4**
has poured out His wrath **l** fire. **La 2:4**
The Lord has become **l** an enemy. **La 2:5**
His tabernacle **l** a garden *booth;* **La 2:6**
As they faint **l** a wounded man In **La 2:12**
run down **l** a river day and night; **La 2:18**
Pour out your heart **l** water Before **La 2:19**
L those who have long been dead. **La 3:6**
is to me **l** a bear lying in wait, **La 3:10**
L a lion in secret places. **La 3:10**
cause Hunted me down **l** a bird; **La 3:52**
L ostriches in the wilderness. **La 4:3**
polishing *was* **l** lapis lazuli. **La 4:7**
is withered, it has become **l** wood. **La 4:8**
father, Our mothers are **l** widows. **La 5:3**
its midst something **l** glowing metal **Ezk 1:4**
their feet were **l** a calf's hoof, **Ezk 1:7**
they gleamed **l** burnished bronze. **Ezk 1:7**
looked **l** burning coals of fire, **Ezk 1:13**
l torches darting back and forth **Ezk 1:13** 4758
to and fro **l** bolts of lightning. **Ezk 1:14** 4758
workmanship *was* **l** sparkling beryl, **Ezk 1:16**
there was something **l** an expanse, **Ezk 1:22** 1823
l the awesome gleam of crystal, **Ezk 1:22**
l the sound of abundant waters as **Ezk 1:24**
went, **l** the voice of the Almighty, **Ezk 1:24**
l the sound of an army camp; **Ezk 1:24**
l lapis lazuli in appearance; **Ezk 1:26**
upward something **l** glowing metal **Ezk 1:27**
l fire all around within it, **Ezk 1:27**
downward I saw something **l** fire; **Ezk 1:27**
l that rebellious house. **Ezk 2:8**
"**L** emery harder than flint I have **Ezk 3:9**
l the glory which I saw by the **Ezk 3:23**
and the **l** of which I will never do **Ezk 5:9** 3644
mountains **l** doves of the valleys, **Ezk 7:16**
and all knees will become **l** water. **Ezk 7:17**
l the appearance of glowing metal. **Ezk 8:2**
l the appearance which I saw in **Ezk 8:4**
something **l** a sapphire stone, **Ezk 10:1**
l the voice of God Almighty when **Ezk 10:5**
l the gleam of a Tarshish stone. **Ezk 10:9**
baggage **l** the baggage of an exile. **Ezk 12:7**
have been **l** foxes among ruins. **Ezk 13:4**
numerous **l** plants of the field. **Ezk 16:7**
money, you were not **l** a harlot. **Ezk 16:31**
l women who commit adultery or **Ezk 16:38**
'**L** mother, like daughter.' **Ezk 16:44**
'Like mother, **l** daughter.' **Ezk 16:44**
he set it **l** a willow. **Ezk 17:5**
was **l** a vine in your vineyard, **Ezk 19:10**
'We will be **l** the nations, like **Ezk 20:32**
l the tribes of the lands, **Ezk 20:32**
Polished to flash **l** lightning!' **Ezk 21:10**
is made *for striking* **l** lightning, **Ezk 21:15**
it will be to them **l** a false divination **Ezk 21:23**
that it may be **l** lightning **Ezk 21:28**
l a roaring lion tearing the prey. **Ezk 22:25**
her are **l** wolves tearing the prey, **Ezk 22:27**
all of them looking **l** officers, **Ezk 23:15**
l the Babylonians *in* Chaldea, **Ezk 23:15** 1823
whose flesh is **l** the flesh of **Ezk 23:20**
of donkeys and whose issue is **l** **Ezk 23:20**
of Judah is **l** all the nations,' **Ezk 25:8**
l the cities which are not **Ezk 26:19**
earth, **l** the ancient waste places, **Ezk 26:20**
'Who is **l** Tyre, Like her who is **Ezk 27:32**
L her who is silent in the midst **Ezk 27:32**
your heart **l** the heart of God **Ezk 28:2**
your heart **L** the heart of God, **Ezk 28:6**
'Whom are you **l** in your greatness? **Ezk 31:2** 1819
you are **l** the monster in the seas; **Ezk 32:2**
cause their rivers to run **l** oil," **Ezk 32:14**
you are to them **l** a sensual song **Ezk 33:32**
l the uncleanness of a woman in her **Ezk 36:17**
has become **l** the garden of Eden; **Ezk 36:35**
will increase their men **l** a flock. **Ezk 36:37**
"**L** the flock for sacrifices, like **Ezk 36:38**
l the flock at Jerusalem during **Ezk 36:38**
go up, you will come **l** a storm; **Ezk 38:9**
be **l** a cloud covering the land, **Ezk 38:9**
l a cloud to cover the land. **Ezk 38:16**
there was a structure **l** a city. **Ezk 40:2**
was **l** the appearance of bronze, **Ezk 40:3**
all around **l** those other windows; **Ezk 40:25**
doorpost was **l** that of the other. **Ezk 41:21**
trees **l** those carved on the walls; **Ezk 41:25**
l the pillars of the courts; **Ezk 42:6**
l the appearance of the chambers **Ezk 42:11**
l the sound of many waters; **Ezk 43:2**
it was **l** the appearance of the vision **Ezk 43:3**
l the vision which I saw when He **Ezk 43:3**
And the visions *were* **l** the vision **Ezk 43:3**
feast, he shall provide **l** this, **Ezk 45:25**
l the fish of the Great Sea, **Ezk 47:10**
in length **l** one of the portions, **Ezk 48:8**
all not one was found **l** Daniel, **Da 1:19**
anything **l** this of any magician, **Da 2:10**
and became **l** chaff from the summer **Da 2:35**
so, **l** iron that breaks in pieces, **Da 2:40**
fourth is **l** a son of *the* gods!" **Da 3:25** 1821
you be given grass to eat **l** cattle **Da 4:25**
be given grass to eat **l** cattle, **Da 4:32**
and began eating grass **l** cattle, **Da 4:33**
his hair had grown **l** eagles' *feathers* **Da 4:33**
and his nails **l** birds' *claws.* **Da 4:33**
wisdom **l** the wisdom of the gods **Da 5:11**
heart was made **l** *that of* beasts, **Da 5:21** 5974, 7739a
was given grass to eat **l** cattle, **Da 5:21**
"The first *was* **l** a lion and had **Da 7:4**
made to stand on two feet **l** a man; **Da 7:4**
behold, another one, **l** a leopard, **Da 7:6**
eyes **l** the eyes of a man and **Da 7:8**
His vesture *was* **l** white snow And **Da 7:9**
the hair of His head **l** pure wool. **Da 7:9**
One **l** a Son of Man was coming, **Da 7:13**
me was one who looked **l** a man. **Da 8:15**
l what was done to Jerusalem. **Da 9:12**
His body also *was* **l** beryl, **Da 10:6**
his eyes were **l** flaming torches, **Da 10:6**
l the gleam of polished bronze, **Da 10:6**
his words **l** the sound of a tumult. **Da 10:6**
l the brightness of the expanse of **Da 12:3**
l the stars forever and ever. **Da 12:3**
Will be **l** the sand of the sea, **Hos 1:10**
will also make her **l** a wilderness, **Hos 2:3**
Make her **l** desert land And **Hos 2:3**
l those who contend with the priest. **Hos 4:4**
And it will be, **l** people, like priest; **Hos 4:9**
it will be, like people, **l** priest; **Hos 4:9**
is stubborn **L** a stubborn heifer, **Hos 4:16**
them **L** a lamb in a large field? **Hos 4:16**
l those who move a boundary; **Hos 5:10**
I will pour out My wrath **l** water. **Hos 5:10**
I am **l** a moth to Ephraim And **Hos 5:12**
And **l** rottenness to the house of **Hos 5:12**
For I *will be* **l** a lion to Ephraim And **Hos 5:14**
And **l** a young lion to the house of **Hos 5:14**
And He will come to us **l** the rain, **Hos 6:3**
L the spring rain watering the **Hos 6:3**
your loyalty is **l** a morning cloud And **Hos 6:4**
l the dew which goes away early. **Hos 6:4**
And the judgments on you are **l** **Hos 6:5**
But **l** Adam they have transgressed **Hos 6:7**
L an oven heated by the baker Who **Hos 7:4** 3644
For their hearts are **l** an oven *As* **Hos 7:6**
morning it burns **l** a flaming fire. **Hos 7:6**
All of them are hot **l** an oven, **Hos 7:7**
Ephraim has become **l** a silly dove, **Hos 7:11**
them down **l** the birds of the sky. **Hos 7:12**
They are **l** a deceitful bow; **Hos 7:16**
L an eagle *the enemy comes* against **Hos 8:1**
L a vessel in which no one delights. **Hos 8:8**
L a wild donkey all alone; **Hos 8:9**
with exultation **l** the nations! **Hos 9:1**
bread will be **l** mourners' bread; **Hos 9:4**
Israel **l** grapes in the wilderness; **Hos 9:10**
their glory will fly away **l** a bird **Hos 9:11**
in a pleasant meadow **l** Tyre; **Hos 9:13**
judgment sprouts **l** poisonous weeds **Hos 10:4**
L a stick on the surface of the **Hos 10:7**
How can I make you **l** Admah? **Hos 11:8**
How can I treat you **l** Zeboiim? **Hos 11:8**
the LORD, He will roar **l** a lion; **Hos 11:10**
come trembling **l** birds from Egypt And **Hos 11:11**
And **l** doves from the land of **Hos 11:11**
their altars are **l** the stone heaps **Hos 12:11**
they will be **l** the morning cloud And **Hos 13:3**
And **l** dew which soon disappears, **Hos 13:3**
L chaff which is blown away from **Hos 13:3**
floor And **l** smoke from a chimney. **Hos 13:3**
So I will be **l** a lion to them; **Hos 13:7** 3644
L a leopard I will lie in wait by **Hos 13:7**
them **l** a bear robbed of her cubs, **Hos 13:8**
will also devour them **l** a lioness, **Hos 13:8**
I will be **l** the dew to Israel; **Hos 14:5**
He will blossom **l** the lily, And he **Hos 14:5**
take root **l** *the cedars of* Lebanon. **Hos 14:5**
beauty will be **l** the olive tree And **Hos 14:6**
fragrance **l** *the cedars of* Lebanon. **Hos 14:6**
And they will blossom **l** the vine. **Hos 14:7**
will be **l** the wine of Lebanon. **Hos 14:7**
I am **l** a luxuriant cypress; **Hos 14:8**
Has *anything* **l** this happened in **Jl 1:2**
Wail **l** a virgin girded with **Jl 1:8**
has never been *anything* **l** it, **Jl 2:2** 3644
The land is **l** the garden of Eden **Jl 2:3**
is **l** the appearance of horses; **Jl 2:4**
And **l** war horses, so they run. **Jl 2:4**
L the crackling of a flame of fire **Jl 2:5**
L a mighty people arranged for **Jl 2:5**
They run **l** mighty men, **Jl 2:7**
They climb the wall **l** soldiers; **Jl 2:7**
through the windows **l** a thief. **Jl 2:9**
his height *was* **l** the height of cedars **Am 2:9**
And you were **l** a firebrand **Am 4:11**
Or He will break forth **l** a fire, **Am 5:6**
"But let justice roll down **l** waters **Am 5:24**
l an ever-flowing stream. **Am 5:24**
And **l** David have composed songs **Am 6:5**
all of it will rise up **l** the Nile, **Am 8:8**
And subside **l** the Nile of Egypt. **Am 8:8**
l *a time of* mourning for an only son **Am 8:10**
end of it will be **l** a bitter day. **Am 8:10**
And all of it rises up **l** the Nile **Am 9:5**
And subsides **l** the Nile of Egypt; **Am 9:5**
"Though you build high **l** the eagle, **Ob 1:4**
be split, **L** wax before the fire, **Mi 1:4**
L water poured down a steep place. **Mi 1:4**
I must make a lament **l** the jackals **Mi 1:8**
And a mourning **l** the ostriches. **Mi 1:8**
Extend your baldness **l** the eagle, **Mi 1:16**
them together **l** sheep in the fold; **Mi 2:12**
L a flock in the midst of its **Mi 2:12**
you **l** a woman in childbirth? **Mi 4:9**
of Zion, **L** a woman in childbirth; **Mi 4:10**
For He has gathered them **l** sheaves **Mi 4:12**
many peoples **L** dew from the LORD, **Mi 5:7**
L showers on vegetation Which do **Mi 5:7**
Among many peoples **L** a lion among **Mi 5:8**
L a young lion among flocks of **Mi 5:8**
For I am **L** the fruit pickers, **Mi 7:1**
l the grape gatherers. There is not **Mi 7:1**
The best of them is **l** a briar, **Mi 7:4**
The most upright **l** a thorn hedge. **Mi 7:4**
down **L** mire of the streets. **Mi 7:10**
will lick the dust **l** a serpent, **Mi 7:17**
serpent, **L** reptiles of the earth. **Mi 7:17**
Who is a God **l** You, who pardons **Mi 7:18** 3644
His wrath is poured out **l** fire And **Na 1:6**
L tangled thorns, And like those **Na 1:10** 5704
And **l** those who are drunken with **Na 1:10**
of Jacob **L** the splendor of Israel, **Na 2:2**
Their appearance is **l** torches, **Na 2:4**
to and fro **l** lightning flashes. **Na 2:4**
are moaning **l** the sound of doves, **Na 2:7**
Nineveh *was* **l** a pool of water **Na 2:8**
yourself **l** the creeping locust, **Na 3:15**
yourself **l** the swarming locust. **Na 3:15**
are **l** the swarming locust. **Na 3:17**
are **l** hordes of grasshoppers Settling **Na 3:17**
They fly **l** an eagle swooping *down* **Hab 1:8**
They collect captives **l** sand. **Hab 1:9**
"Then they will sweep through **l** **Hab 1:11**
made men **l** the fish of the sea, **Hab 1:14**
L creeping things without a ruler **Hab 1:14**
He enlarges his appetite **l** Sheol, **Hab 2:5**
like Sheol, And he is **l** death, **Hab 2:5**
His radiance is **l** the sunlight; **Hab 3:4**
l those Who devour the oppressed **Hab 3:14** 3644
He has made my feet **l** hinds' *feet,* **Hab 3:19**
that they will walk **l** the blind, **Zph 1:17**
blood will be poured out **l** dust And **Zph 1:17**
like dust And their flesh **l** dung. **Zph 1:17**
The day passes **l** the chaff **Zph 2:2**
"Surely Moab will be **l** Sodom And **Zph 2:9**
And the sons of Ammon **l** Gomorrah **Zph 2:9**
Parched **l** the wilderness. **Zph 2:13**
to you **l** nothing in comparison? **Hg 2:3**
I will make you **l** a signet *ring,* **Hg 2:23**
"Do not be **l** your fathers, to **Zch 1:4**
had wings **l** the wings of a stork, **Zch 5:9**
"They made their hearts **l** flint **Zch 7:12**
And piled up silver **l** dust, **Zch 9:3**
gold **l** the mire of the streets. **Zch 9:3**
our God, And be **l** a clan in Judah, **Zch 9:7**
in Judah, And Ekron **l** a Jebusite. **Zch 9:7**
will make you **l** a warrior's sword. **Zch 9:13**
arrow will go forth **l** lightning; **Zch 9:14**
be filled **l** a *sacrificial* basin, **Zch 9:15**
l the corners of the altar. **Zch 9:15**
the people wander **l** sheep, **Zch 10:2** 3644
l His majestic horse in battle. **Zch 10:3**
Ephraim will be **l** a mighty man, **Zch 10:7**
make the clans of Judah **l** a firepot **Zch 12:6**
them in that day will be **l** David, **Zch 12:8**
the house of David *will be* **l** God, **Zch 12:8**
l the angel of the LORD before **Zch 12:8**
l the bitter weeping over a **Zch 12:10**
l the mourning of Hadadrimmon in **Zch 12:11**
So also **l** this plague will be the **Zch 14:15**
be **l** the bowls before the altar. **Zch 14:20**
For He is **l** a refiner's fire and **Mal 3:2**
refiner's fire and **l** fullers' soap. **Mal 3:2**
and refine them **l** gold and silver, **Mal 3:3**
is coming, burning **l** a furnace; **Mal 4:1**
about **l** calves from the stall. **Mal 4:2**
"When you pray, you are not to be **l** **Mt 6:5** *5613*
"So do not be **l** them; **Mt 6:8** *3666*
clothed himself **l** one of these. **Mt 6:29** *5613*
them, will be **l** a foolish man who **Mt 7:26** *3666*
"Nothing **l** this has ever been seen **Mt 9:33** *3779*
l sheep without a shepherd. **Mt 9:36** *5616*
for the disciple that he become **l** his **Mt 10:25** *5613*
and the slave **l** his master. If they **Mt 10:25** *5613*
It is **l** children sitting in the **Mt 11:16** *3664*
restored to normal, **l** the other. **Mt 12:13** *5613*
of heaven is **l** a mustard seed, **Mt 13:31** *3664*
"The kingdom of heaven is **l** leaven, **Mt 13:33** *3664*
is **l** a treasure hidden in the field, **Mt 13:44** *3664*

is **l** a merchant seeking fine pearls Mt 13:45 *3664*
is **l** a dragnet cast into the sea, Mt 13:47 *3664*
heaven is **l** a head of a household, Mt 13:52 *3664*
and His face shone **l** the sun, Mt 17:2 *5613*
converted and become **l** children, Mt 18:3 *5613*
the man with his wife is **l** this, Mt 19:10 *3779*
kingdom of heaven is **l** a landowner Mt 20:1 *3664*
it will scatter him **l** dust." Mt 21:44 *3039*
but are **l** angels in heaven. Mt 22:30 *5613*
"The second is **l** it, Mt 22:39 *3664*
For you are **l** whitewashed tombs Mt 23:27 *3945*
will be just **l** the days of Noah. Mt 24:37 *5618*
l a man *about* to go on a journey, Mt 25:14 *5618*
his appearance was **l** lightning, Mt 28:3 *5613*
of him and became **l** dead men. Mt 28:4 *5613*
l a dove descending upon Him; Mk 1:10 *5613*
have never seen anything **l** this." Mk 2:12 *3779*
"The kingdom of God is **l** a man Mk 4:26 *3779, 5613*
"*It is* **l** a mustard seed, which, Mk 4:31 *5613*
l one of the prophets *of old*." Mk 6:15 *5613*
were **l** sheep without a shepherd; Mk 6:34 *5613*
men, for I see *them* **l** trees, Mk 8:24 *5613*
the boy became so much **l** a corpse Mk 9:26 *5616*
"Whoever receives one child **l** this Mk 9:37 *5108*
receive the kingdom of God **l** a child Mk 10:15 *5613*
but are **l** angels in heaven. Mk 12:25 *5613*
l to walk around in long robes, Mk 12:38 *2309*
and **l** respectful greetings in Mk 12:38
"*It is* **l** a man away on a Mk 13:34 *5613*
upon Him in bodily form **l** a dove, Lk 3:22 *5613*
trained, will be **l** his teacher. Lk 6:40 *5613*
I will show you whom he is **l**: Lk 6:47 *3664*
he is **l** a man building a house, Lk 6:48 *3664*
is **l** a man who built a house on Lk 6:49 *3664*
generation, and what are they **l**? Lk 7:31 *3664*
"They are **l** children who sit in Lk 7:32 *3664*
fall from heaven **l** lightning. Lk 10:18 *5613*
For you are **l** concealed tombs, and Lk 11:44 *5613*
clothed himself **l** one of these. Lk 12:27 *5613*
"Be **l** men who are waiting for Lk 12:36 *3664*
"What is the kingdom of God **l**, Lk 13:18 *3664*
"It is **l** a mustard seed, which a Lk 13:19 *3664*
"It is **l** leaven, which a woman Lk 13:21 *3664*
"If you had faith **l** a mustard seed, Lk 17:6 *5613*
"For just **l** the lightning, when it Lk 17:24 *5618*
You that I am not **l** other people: Lk 18:11 *5618*
or even **l** this tax collector. Lk 18:11 *5613*
receive the kingdom of God **l** a child Lk 18:17 *5613*
it will scatter him **l** dust." Lk 20:18 *3039*
anymore, because they are **l** angels, Lk 20:36 *2465*
l to walk around in long robes, Lk 20:46 *2309*
not come on you suddenly **l** a trap; Lk 21:34 *5613*
the greatest among you must become **l** Lk 22:26 *5613*
and the leader **l** the servant. Lk 22:26 *5613*
permission to sift you **l** wheat; Lk 22:31 *5613*
His sweat became **l** drops of blood, Lk 22:44 *5616*
the Son also does in **l** manner. Jn 5:19 *3668*
know Him, I will be a liar **l** you, Jn 8:55 *3664*
"No, but he is **l** him." Jn 9:9 *3664*
"If we let Him *go on* **l** this, Jn 11:48 *3779*
a noise **l** a violent rushing wind, Ac 2:2 *5618*
A PROPHET **L** ME FROM YOUR BRETHREN; Ac 3:22 *5613*
his face **l** the face of an angel. Ac 6:15 *5616*
PROPHET **L** ME FROM YOUR BRETHREN.' Ac 7:37 *5613*
from his eyes something **l** scales, Ac 9:18 *5613*
l a great sheet coming down, Ac 10:11 *5613*
object coming down **l** a great sheet Ac 11:5 *5613*
"The gods have become **l** men and Ac 14:11 *3666*
is **l** gold or silver or stone, Ac 17:29 *3664*
would **l** to hear the man myself." Ac 25:22 *1014*
gift is not **l** the transgression. Ro 5:15 *5613*
The gift is not **l** *that which came* Ro 5:16 *5613*
practicing what I *would* **l** *to do*, Ro 7:15 *2309*
"Why did you make me **l** this," Ro 9:20 *3779*
THE NUMBER OF THE SONS OF ISRAEL BE **L** Ro 9:27 *5613*
WE WOULD HAVE BECOME **L** SODOM, Ro 9:29 *5613*
are you not walking **l** mere men? 1Co 3:3 *2596*
l a wise master builder I laid a 1Co 3:10 *5613*
I used to speak **l** a child, think 1Co 13:11 *5613*
think **l** a child, reason like a child; 1Co 13:11 *5613*
reason **l** a child; when I became a 1Co 13:11 *5613*
firm in the faith, act **l** men, 1Co 16:13 *407*
For we are not **l** many, peddling 2Co 2:17 *5613*
and *are* not **l** Moses, *who* 2Co 3:13 *2509*
Now in a **l** exchange 2Co 6:13 *846*
live **l** the Gentiles and not like Ga 2:14 *1483*
the Gentiles and not **l** the Jews, Ga 2:14 *2452*
the Gentiles to live **l** Jews? Ga 2:14 *2450*
And you brethren, **l** Isaac, Ga 4:28 *2596*
carousing, and things **l** these, Ga 5:21 *3664*
l a child *serving* his father. Php 2:22 *5613*
and hold men **l** him in high regard; Php 2:29 *5108*
l the Gentiles who do not know God; 1Th 4:5 *2509*
come just **l** a thief in the night. 1Th 5:2 *5613*
upon them suddenly **l** labor pains 1Th 5:3 *5618*
day would overtake you **l** a thief; 1Th 5:4 *5613*
at all, but acting **l** busybodies. 2Th 3:11 *4020*
their talk will spread **l** gangrene. 2Tm 2:17 *5613*
AND THEY ALL WILL BECOME OLD **L** A Heb 1:11 *5613*
AND **L** A MANTLE YOU WILL ROLL THEM Heb 1:12 *5613*
L A GARMENT THEY WILL ALSO BE CHANGED. Heb 1:12 *5613*
made **l** His brethren in all things, Heb 2:17 *3666*
life, but made **l** the Son of God, Heb 7:3 *871*
need daily, **l** those high priests, Heb 7:27 *5618*
NOT **L** THE COVENANT WHICH I MADE Heb 8:9 *2596*
immoral or godless person **l** Esau, Heb 12:16 *5613*
is **l** the surf of the sea, driven and Jas 1:6 *1858a*
because **l** flowering grass he will Jas 1:10 *5613*
he is **l** a man who looks at his Jas 1:23 *1858a*
what your life will be **l** tomorrow. Jas 4:14
will consume your flesh **l** fire. Jas 5:3 *5613*
was a man with a nature **l** ours, Jas 5:17 *3663*
but **l** the Holy One who called you, 1Pe 1:15 *2596*
perishable things **l** silver or gold 1Pe 1:18
"ALL FLESH IS **L** GRASS, AND ALL 1Pe 1:24 *5613*
ITS GLORY **L** THE FLOWER OF GRASS. 1Pe 1:24 *5613*
l newborn babies, long for the pure 1Pe 2:2 *5613*
were continually straying **l** sheep, 1Pe 2:25 *5613*
prowls around **l** a roaring lion, 1Pe 5:8 *5613*
But these, **l** unreasoning animals, 2Pe 2:12 *5613*
that with the Lord one day is **l** a 2Pe 3:8 *5613*
and a thousand years **l** one day. 2Pe 3:8 *5613*
of the Lord will come **l** a thief, 2Pe 3:10 *5613*
He appears, we will be **l** Him, 1Jn 3:2 *3664*
instinct, **l** unreasoning animals, Jude 1:10 *5613*
casting up their own shame **l** foam; Jude 1:13 *1890*
voice **l** *the sound* of a trumpet, Rv 1:10 *5613*
I saw one **l** a son of man, Rv 1:13 *3664*
His hair were white **l** white wool, Rv 1:14 *5613*
white like white wool, **l** snow; Rv 1:14 *5613*
His eyes were **l** a flame of fire. Rv 1:14 *5613*
His feet *were* **l** burnished bronze, Rv 1:15 *3664*
was **l** the sound of many waters. Rv 1:15 *5613*
and His face was **l** the sun shining Rv 1:16 *5613*
When I saw Him, I fell at His feet **l** Rv 1:17 *5613*
who has eyes **l** a flame of fire, Rv 2:18 *5613*
His feet are **l** burnished bronze, Rv 2:18 *3664*
wake up, I will come **l** a thief, Rv 3:3 *5613*
l *the sound* of a trumpet speaking Rv 4:1 *5613*
was **l** a jasper stone and a sardius in Rv 4:3 *3664*
l an emerald in appearance. Rv 4:3 *3664*
the throne *there was something* **l** Rv 4:6 *5613*
l crystal; and in the center Rv 4:6 *3664*
The first creature *was* **l** a lion, Rv 4:7 *3664*
and the second creature **l** a calf, Rv 4:7 *3664*
had a face **l** that of a man, Rv 4:7 *5613*
creature *was* **l** a flying eagle. Rv 4:7 *3664*
And I heard *something* **l** a voice Rv 6:6 *5613*
and the whole moon became **l** blood; Rv 6:12 *5613*
l a scroll when it is rolled up, Rv 6:14 *5613*
and *something* **l** a great mountain Rv 8:8 *5613*
from heaven, burning **l** a torch, Rv 8:10 *5613*
l the smoke of a great furnace; Rv 9:2 *5613*
was **l** the torment of a scorpion Rv 9:5 *5613*
was **l** horses prepared for battle; Rv 9:7 *3664*
heads appeared to be crowns **l** gold, Rv 9:7 *3664*
faces were **l** the faces of men. Rv 9:7 *5613*
They had hair **l** the hair of women, Rv 9:8 *5613*
teeth were **l** *the teeth* of lions. Rv 9:8 *5613*
l breastplates of iron; Rv 9:9 *5613*
wings was **l** the sound of chariots, Rv 9:9 *5613*
They have tails **l** scorpions, Rv 9:10 *3664*
horses are **l** the heads of lions; Rv 9:17 *5613*
for their tails are **l** serpents and Rv 9:19 *3664*
head, and his face was **l** the sun, Rv 10:1 *5613*
and his feet **l** pillars of fire; Rv 10:1 *5613*
me a measuring rod **l** a staff; Rv 11:1 *3664*
the serpent poured water **l** a river Rv 12:15 *5613*
beast which I saw was **l** a leopard, Rv 13:2 *3664*
and his feet were **l** *those* of a Rv 13:2 *3664*
his mouth **l** the mouth of a lion. Rv 13:2 *5613*
"Who is **l** the beast, and who is Rv 13:4 *3664*
and he had two horns **l** a lamb and Rv 13:11 *3664*
l the sound of many waters and Rv 14:2 *5613*
and **l** the sound of loud thunder, Rv 14:2 *5613*
was **l** *the sound* of harpists playing Rv 14:2 *5613*
the cloud *was* one **l** a son of man, Rv 14:14 *3664*
And I saw something **l** a sea of glass Rv 15:2 *5613*
became blood **l** *that* of a dead man; Rv 16:3 *5613*
three unclean spirits **l** frogs; Rv 16:13 *5613*
("Behold, I am coming **l** a thief. Rv 16:15 *5618*
'What *city* is **l** the great city?' Rv 18:18 *3664*
took up a stone **l** a great millstone Rv 18:21 *5613*
these things I heard something **l** a Rv 19:1 *5613*
Then I heard *something* **l** Rv 19:6 *5613*
the voice of a great multitude and **l** Rv 19:6 *5613*
like the sound of many waters and **l** Rv 19:6 *5613*
is **l** the sand of the seashore. Rv 20:8 *5613*
was **l** a very costly stone, Rv 21:11 *3664*
city was pure gold, **l** clear glass. Rv 21:18 *3664*
pure gold, **l** transparent glass. Rv 21:21 *5613*

LIKE-MINDED

made complete, be comforted, be **l**, 2Co 13:11 *846*

LIKEN

To whom then will you **l** God? Is 40:18 1819
"To whom then will you **l** Me That Is 40:25 1819
"To whom would you **l** Me And Is 46:5 1819
To what shall I **l** you as I comfort La 2:13 7737a

LIKENESS

in Our image, according to Our **l**; Gn 1:26 1823
man, He made him in the **l** of God. Gn 5:1 1823
the father of *a son* in his own **l**, Gn 5:3 1823
or any **l** of what is in heaven Ex 20:4 8544
figure, the **l** of male or female, Dt 4:16 8403
the **l** of any animal that is on the Dt 4:17 8403
the **l** of any winged bird that Dt 4:17 8403
the **l** of anything that creeps on Dt 4:18 8403
the **l** of any fish that is in the Dt 4:18 8403
or any **l** *of* what is in heaven Dt 5:8 8544
satisfied with Your **l** when I awake. Ps 17:15 8544
what **l** will you compare with Him? Is 40:18 1823
of the **l** of the glory of the LORD. Ezk 1:28 1823
a **l** as the appearance of a man; Ezk 8:2 1823
all four of them had the same **l**, Ezk 10:10 1823
As for the **l** of their faces, they Ezk 10:22 1823
"Whose **l** and inscription is this?" Mt 22:20 *1504*
"Whose **l** and inscription is this?" Mk 12:16 *1504*
Whose **l** and inscription does it have Lk 20:24 *1504*
in the **l** of the offense of Adam, Ro 5:14 *3667*
with *Him* in the **l** of His death, Ro 6:5 *3667*
certainly we shall also be *in the* **l** Ro 6:5 *3667*
His own Son in the **l** of sinful flesh Ro 8:3 *3667*
which in *the* **l** *of* God has been Eph 4:24
and being made in the **l** of men. Php 2:7 *3667*
according to the **l** of Melchizedek, Heb 7:15 *3665*
have been made in the **l** of God; Jas 3:9 *3669*

LIKENESSES

"So you shall make **l** of your tumors 1Sa 6:5 6754
l of your mice that ravage the land, 1Sa 6:5 6754
mice and the **l** of their tumors. 1Sa 6:11 6754

LIKEWISE

Leah **l** came near with her children, Gn 33:7 1571
and **l** you shall make *them* on the Ex 26:4 3651
"**L** for the north side in length Ex 27:11 3651
he did **l** on the edge of the Ex 36:11 3651
'**L**, every grain offering that is Lv 7:9
'**L**, the shaphan, for though it Lv 11:5
"**L**, whoever lies down in the Lv 14:47
'**L**, whomever the one with the Lv 15:11
'**L**, whoever touches them shall be Lv 15:27
'**L**, if a man sells a dwelling Lv 25:29
the priest shall **l** offer its grain Nu 6:17
their gods, that I also may do **l**?' Dt 12:30 3651
shall do **l** to your maidservant. Dt 15:17 3651
and you shall do **l** with anything Dt 22:3 3651
L the house of Joseph went up Jg 1:22
"Look at me and do **l**. Jg 7:17 3651
have seen me do, hurry *and* do **l**." Jg 9:48 3644
their idols; their children **l** and their 2Ki 17:41 1571
he **l** fell on his sword and died. 1Ch 10:5 1571
praise the LORD, and **l** at evening, 1Ch 23:30 3651
"And **l** I, my brothers and my Ne 5:10 1571
L we cast lots for the supply of Ne 10:34
l have many times cursed others. Ec 7:22 1571
L, also all the Jews who were in Jer 40:11
and observing does not do **l**. Ezk 18:14 2004
all around, and **l** for the porches. Ezk 40:16 3651
are at full *strength* and **l** many, Na 1:12 3651
behind no children; and the third **l**; Mk 12:21 *5615*
he who has food is to do **l**." Lk 3:11 *3668*
"**L** a Levite also, when he came to Lk 10:32 *3668*
you repent, you will all **l** perish. Lk 13:3 *3668*
repent, you will all **l** perish." Lk 13:5 *5615*
things, and **l** Lazarus bad things; Lk 16:25 *3668*
and **l** the one who is in Lk 17:31 *3668*
to take it along, **l** also a bag, Lk 22:36 *3668*
l also of the fish as much as they Jn 6:11 *3668*
gave *it* to them, and the fish **l**. Jn 21:13 *3668*
"And **l**, all the prophets who have Ac 3:24 *2532*
l also the wife to her husband. 1Co 7:3 *3668*
and **l** also the husband does not 1Co 7:4 *3668*
l he who was called while free, is 1Co 7:22 *3668*
L, *I want* women to adorn 1Tm 2:9 *5615*
Deacons **l** *must be* men of dignity, 1Tm 3:8 *5615*
Women *must* **l** *be* dignified, not 1Tm 3:11 *5615*
L also, deeds that are good are 1Tm 5:25 *5615*
Older women **l** are to be reverent Ti 2:3 *5615*
L urge the young men to be Ti 2:6 *5615*
He Himself **l** also partook of the Heb 2:14 *3898*
You younger men, **l**, be subject to 1Pe 5:5 *3668*

LIKHI

Ahian and Shechem and **L** and Aniam. 1Ch 7:19 3949

LILIES

He pastures *his flock* among the **l**. SS 2:16 7799
a gazelle Which feed among the **l**. SS 4:5 7799
His lips are **l** Dripping with SS 5:13 7799
flock in the gardens And gather **l**. SS 6:2 7799
pastures *his flock* among the **l**." SS 6:3 7799
heap of wheat Fenced about with **l**. SS 7:2 7799
how the **l** of the field grow; Mt 6:28 *2918*
"Consider the **l**, how they grow: Lk 12:27 *2918*

LILY

in the porch were of **l** design, 1Ki 7:19 7799
top of the pillars was **l** design. 1Ki 7:22 7799
the brim of a cup, *as* a **l** blossom; 1Ki 7:26 7799
brim of a cup, *like* a **l** blossom;" 2Ch 4:5 7799
of Sharon, The **l** of the valleys." SS 2:1 7799
"Like a **l** among the thorns, So is SS 2:2 7799
He will blossom like the **l**, Hos 14:5 7799

LIMB

disfigured *face*, or any deformed **l**, Lv 21:18
her in twelve pieces, **l** by limb, Jg 19:29
her in twelve pieces, limb by **l**, Jg 19:29 6106
you will be torn **l** from limb and Da 2:5 1917
you will be torn limb from **l** and Da 2:5
Abed-nego shall be torn **l** from limb Da 3:29 1917
Abed-nego shall be torn limb from **l** Da 3:29
so that *the* **l** which is lame may Heb 12:13

LIMBS

firstborn of death devours his **l**. Jb 18:13 905
His **l** are like bars of iron. Jb 40:18 1634
not keep silence concerning his **l**, Jb 41:12 905
When its **l** are dry, they are Is 27:11 7105b

LIME

stones and coat them with **l** Dt 27:2 7875
and you shall coat them with **l**. Dt 27:4 7875
The peoples will be burned to **l**, Is 33:12 7875
bones of the king of Edom to **l**. Am 2:1 7875

LIMIT

and the iron there is no **l**. 1Ch 22:16 4557
set a **l** for the soles of my feet, Jb 13:27 2707
set a **l** for me and remember me! Jb 14:13 2706
of God, And **l** wisdom to yourself? Jb 15:8 1639

“Is there *no* **l** to windy words? **Jb 16:3** 7093
And to the farthest **l** he searches **Jb 28:3** 8503
When He set a **l** for the rain And **Jb 28:26** 2706
‘Job ought to be tried to the **l**, **Jb 34:36** 5331
I have seen a **l** to all perfection; **Ps 119:96** 7093
For there is no **l** to the treasure **Na 2:9** 7097b

LIMITED
means are **l** for his cleansing.” **Lv 14:32** 5381
“Is the LORD’s power **l**? **Nu 11:23** 7114a
we are living is too **l** for us. **2Ki 6:1** 6862a
of distress, Your strength is **l**. **Pr 24:10** 6862a

LIMITS
discover the **l** of the Almighty? **Jb 11:7** 8503
And his **l** You have set so that he **Jb 14:5** 2706
might, And Egypt too, without **l**. **Na 3:9** 7097b

LIMP
Therefore all hands will fall **l**, **Is 13:7** 7503
Our hands are **l**. Anguish has seized **Jer 6:24** 7503
about them, And his hands hang **l**; **Jer 50:43** 7503
‘All hands will hang **l** and **Ezk 7:17** 7503
Do not let your hands fall **l**. **Zph 3:16** 7503

LIMPING
Penuel, and he was **l** on his thigh. **Gn 32:31** 6760

LIMPNESS
Because of the **l** of *their* hands, **Jer 47:3** 7510

LINE
you shall draw your *border* **l** from **Nu 34:7** 8376
‘You shall draw a **l** from Mount Hor **Nu 34:8** 8376
a **l** from Hazar-enan to Shepham, **Nu 34:10** 1366
ran from the battle **l** and came to **1Sa 4:12** 4634
one who came from the battle **l**. **1Sa 4:16** 4634
escaped from the battle **l** today.” **1Sa 4:16** 4634
and ran to the battle **l** and **1Sa 17:22** 4634
ran quickly toward the battle **l** to **1Sa 17:48** 4634
and measured them with the **l**, **2Sa 8:2** 2256a
and one full **l** to keep alive. **2Sa 8:2** 2256a
“Place Uriah in the front **l** of **2Sa 11:15** 6440
and a **l** of twelve cubits measured **1Ki 7:15** 2339
he was of the royal **l** in Edom. **1Ki 11:14** 2233
over Jerusalem the **l** of Samaria **2Ki 21:13** 6957b
Or who stretched the **l** on it? **Jb 38:5** 6957b
Their **l** has gone out through all **Ps 19:4** 6957b
cast a **l** into the Nile will mourn, **Is 19:8** 2443
order, order on order, **L** on line, **Is 28:10** 6957b
order, order on order, Line on **l**, **Is 28:10** 6957b
on order, Line on line, **l** on line, **Is 28:10** 6957b
on order, Line on line, line on **l**, **Is 28:10** 6957b
order, order on order, **L** on line, **Is 28:13** 6957b
order, order on order, Line on **l**, **Is 28:13** 6957b
on order, Line on line, **l** on line, **Is 28:13** 6957b
on order, Line on line, line on **l**, **Is 28:13** 6957b
will make justice the measuring **l** And **Is 28:17** 6957b
will stretch over it the **l** of desolation **Is 34:11** 6957b
And the plumb **l** of emptiness. **Is 34:11** 68
hand has divided it to them by **l**. **Is 34:17** 6957b
wood, he extends a measuring **l**; **Is 44:13** 6957b
“The measuring **l** will go out **Jer 31:39** 6957b
“**L** up the shield and buckler, And **Jer 46:3** 6186a
He has stretched out a **l**, **La 2:8** 6957b
with a **l** of flax and a measuring **Ezk 40:3** 6616
the east with a **l** in his hand, **Ezk 47:3** 6957b
one of the descendants of her **l** will **Da 11:7** 8328
And they each march in **l**, **Jl 2:7** 1870
wall with a plumb **l** in His hand. **Am 7:7** 594
And I said, “A plumb **l**.” **Am 7:8** 594
“Behold I am about to put a plumb **l** **Am 7:8** 594
be parceled up by a *measuring* **l** and **Am 7:17** 2256a
have no one stretching a measuring **l** **Mi 2:5** 2256a
“and a measuring **l** will be **Zch 1:16** 6957b
with a measuring **l** in his hand. **Zch 2:1** 2256a
be glad when they see the plumb **l** **Zch 4:10** 68, 913

LINEN
clothed him in garments of fine **l** and **Gn 41:42** 8336
and scarlet *material,* fine **l**, **Ex 25:4** 8336
with ten curtains of fine twisted **l** **Ex 26:1** 8336
material and fine twisted **l**; **Ex 26:31** 8336
material and fine twisted **l**, **Ex 26:36** 8336
fine twisted **l** one hundred cubits **Ex 27:9** 8336
material and fine twisted **l**, **Ex 27:16** 8336
five cubits of fine twisted **l**, **Ex 27:18** 8336
scarlet *material* and the fine **l**. **Ex 28:5** 8336
material and fine twisted **l**, **Ex 28:6** 8336
material and fine twisted **l**. **Ex 28:8** 8336
fine twisted **l** you shall make it. **Ex 28:15** 8336
tunic of checkered work of fine **l**, **Ex 28:39** 8336
and shall make a turban of fine **l**, **Ex 28:39** 8336
You shall make for them **l** breeches **Ex 28:42** 906
and scarlet *material,* fine **l**, **Ex 35:6** 8336
purple and scarlet *material* and fine **l** **Ex 35:23** 8336
scarlet *material* and *in* fine **l**. **Ex 35:25** 8336
scarlet *material,* and in fine **l**, **Ex 35:35** 8336
of fine twisted **l** and blue and **Ex 36:8** 8336
material, and fine twisted **l**; **Ex 36:35** 8336
material, and fine twisted **l**, **Ex 36:37** 8336
the court were of fine twisted **l**, **Ex 38:9** 8336
all around *were* of fine twisted **l**. **Ex 38:16** 8336
material and fine twisted **l**. **Ex 38:18** 8336
in scarlet *material,* and fine **l**. **Ex 38:23** 8336
material, and fine twisted **l**. **Ex 39:2** 8336
scarlet *material,* and the fine **l**, **Ex 39:3** 8336
material, and fine twisted **l**, **Ex 39:5** 8336
material and fine twisted **l**. **Ex 39:8** 8336
scarlet *material and* twisted **l** **Ex 39:24**
woven **l** for Aaron and his sons, **Ex 39:27** 8336
and the turban of fine **l**, **Ex 39:28** 8336
and the decorated caps of fine **l**, **Ex 39:28** 8336
and the **l** breeches of fine twisted **Ex 39:28** 906
linen breeches of fine twisted **l**, **Ex 39:28** 8336
and the sash of fine twisted **l**, **Ex 39:29** 8336
priest is to put on his **l** robe, **Lv 6:10** 906
is a wool garment or a **l** garment, **Lv 13:47** 6593
in warp or woof, of **l** or of wool, **Lv 13:48** 6593
warp or the woof, in wool or in **l**, **Lv 13:52** 6593
leprosy in a garment of wool or **l**, **Lv 13:59** 6593
“He shall put on the holy **l** tunic, **Lv 16:4** 906
and the **l** undergarments shall be **Lv 16:4** 906
shall be girded with the **l** sash and **Lv 16:4** 906
and attired with the **l** turban **Lv 16:4** 906
and take off the **l** garments which **Lv 16:23** 906
shall thus put on the **l** garments, **Lv 16:32** 906
mixed of wool and **l** together. **Dt 22:11** 6593
then I will give you thirty **l** wraps **Jg 14:12** 5466
you shall give me thirty **l** wraps **Jg 14:13** 5466
LORD, *as* a boy wearing a **l** ephod. **1Sa 2:18** 906
men who wore the **l** ephod. **1Sa 22:18** 906
and David was wearing a **l** ephod. **2Sa 6:14** 906
of the **l** workers at Beth-ashbea; **1Ch 4:21** 948
was clothed with a robe of fine **l** **1Ch 15:27** 948
David also wore an ephod of **l**. **1Ch 15:27** 906
violet, **l** and crimson fabrics, **2Ch 2:14** 948
purple, crimson and fine **l**, **2Ch 3:14** 948
and kinsmen, clothed in fine **l**, **2Ch 5:12** 948
hangings of fine white and violet **l** **Es 1:6** 3768
linen held by cords of fine purple **l** **Es 1:6** 948
a garment of fine **l** and purple; **Es 8:15** 948
Her clothing is fine **l** and purple. **Pr 31:22** 8336
makes **l** garments and sells *them,* **Pr 31:24** 5466
the manufacturers of **l** made from **Is 19:9** 6593
“Go and buy yourself a **l** waistband and **Jer 13:1** 6593
man clothed in **l** with a writing case **Ezk 9:2** 906
He called to the man clothed in **l** **Ezk 9:3** 906
the man clothed in **l** at whose **Ezk 9:11** 906
to the man clothed in **l** and said, **Ezk 10:2** 906
He commanded the man clothed in **l**, **Ezk 10:6** 906
the hands of the one clothed in **l**, **Ezk 10:7** 906
fine **l** and covered you with silk. **Ezk 16:10** 8336
and your dress was of fine **l**, **Ezk 16:13** 8336
“Your sail was of fine embroidered **l** **Ezk 27:7** 8336
purple, embroidered work, fine **l**, **Ezk 27:16** 948
shall be clothed with **l** garments; **Ezk 44:17** 6593
“**L** turbans shall be on their **Ezk 44:18** 6593
and **l** undergarments shall be on **Ezk 44:18** 6593
was a certain man dressed in **l**, **Da 10:5** 906
one said to the man dressed in **l**, **Da 12:6** 906
I heard the man dressed in **l**, **Da 12:7** 906
and wrapped it in a clean **l** cloth, **Mt 27:59** *4616*
but a **l** sheet over *his* naked *body* **Mk 14:51** *4616*
But he pulled free of the **l** sheet **Mk 14:52** *4616*
Joseph bought a **l** cloth, **Mk 15:46** *4616*
down, wrapped Him in the **l** cloth and **Mk 15:46** *4616*
dressed in purple and fine **l**, **Lk 16:19** *1040*
down and wrapped it in a **l** cloth, **Lk 23:53** *4616*
in, he saw the **l** wrappings only; **Lk 24:12** *3608*
it in **l** wrappings with the spices, **Jn 19:40** *3608*
saw the **l** wrappings lying *there* **Jn 20:5** *3608*
the **l** wrappings lying *there,* **Jn 20:6** *3608*
not lying with the **l** wrappings, **Jn 20:7** *3608*
out of the temple, clothed in **l**, **Rv 15:6** *3043*
precious stones and pearls and fine **l** **Rv 18:12** *1039*
in fine **l** and purple and scarlet, **Rv 18:16** *1039*
her to clothe herself in fine **l**, **Rv 19:8** *1039*
for the fine **l** is the righteous **Rv 19:8** *1039*
are in heaven, clothed in fine **l**, **Rv 19:14** *1039*

LINENS
With colored **l** of Egypt. **Pr 7:16** 330a

LINES
and he measured two **l** to put to **2Sa 8:2** 2256a
The **l** have fallen to me in **Ps 16:6** 2256a
up *their* battle **l** against her; **Jer 50:9** 6186a
“Draw up your battle **l** against **Jer 50:14** 6186a

LINGER
Those who **l** long over wine, Those **Pr 23:30** 309

LINGERED
Even when the cloud **l** over the **Nu 9:19** 748
the cloud **l** over the tabernacle, **Nu 9:22** 748

LINGERS
me because my life still **l** in me.’ **2Sa 1:9**

LINTEL
doorposts and on the **l** of the houses **Ex 12:7** 4947
to the **l** and the two doorposts; **Ex 12:22** 4947
on the **l** and on the two doorposts, **Ex 12:23** 4947
the **l** *and* five-sided doorposts. **1Ki 6:31** 352b

LINUS
also Pudens and **L** and Claudia and **2Tm 4:21** *3044*

LION
He couches, he lies down as a **l**, **Gn 49:9** 743b
as a **l**, who dares rouse him up? **Gn 49:9** 3833b
And as a **l** it lifts itself; **Nu 23:24** 738
“He couches, he lies down as a **l**, **Nu 24:9** 738
And as a **l**, who dares rouse him? **Nu 24:9** 3833b
He lies down as a **l**, **Dt 33:20** 3833b
a young **l** *came* roaring toward him. **Jg 14:5** 738
to look at the carcass of the **l**; **Jg 14:8** 743b
honey were in the body of the **l**. **Jg 14:8** 743b
honey out of the body of the **l**. **Jg 14:9** 743b
And what is stronger than a **l**?” **Jg 14:18** 738
When a **l** or a bear came and took a **1Sa 17:34** 738
killed both the **l** and the bear; **1Sa 17:36** 738
delivered me from the paw of the **l** **1Sa 17:37** 738
heart is like the heart of a **l**, **2Sa 17:10** 743b
He also went down and killed a **l** **2Sa 23:20** 743b
a **l** met him on the way and killed **1Ki 13:24** 743b
the **l** also was standing beside the **1Ki 13:24** 743b
the **l** standing beside the body; **1Ki 13:25** 743b
the LORD has given him to the **l**, **1Ki 13:26** 743b
the **l** standing beside the body; **1Ki 13:28** 743b
the **l** had not eaten the body nor **1Ki 13:28** 743b
from me, a **l** will kill you.” **1Ki 20:36** 743b
departed from him a **l** found him and **1Ki 20:36** 743b
killed a **l** inside a pit on a snowy **1Ch 11:22** 738
“The roaring of the **l** and the **Jb 4:10** 743b
and the voice of the *fierce* **l**, **Jb 4:10** 7826
“The **l** perishes for lack of prey, **Jb 4:11** 3918
up, You would hunt me like a **l**; **Jb 10:16** 7826
has the *fierce* **l** passed over it. **Jb 28:8** 7826
“Can you hunt the prey for the **l**, **Jb 38:39** 3833b
Or he will tear my soul like a **l**, **Ps 7:2** 743b
a hiding place as a **l** in his lair; **Ps 10:9** 743b
is like a **l** that is eager to tear, **Ps 17:12** 743b
young **l** lurking in hiding places. **Ps 17:12** 3715
me, As a ravening and a roaring **l**. **Ps 22:13** 743b
will tread upon the **l** and cobra, **Ps 91:13** 7826
The young **l** and the serpent you **Ps 91:13** 3715
wrath is like the roaring of a **l**, **Pr 19:12** 3715
king is like the growling of a **l**; **Pr 20:2** 3715
“There is a **l** outside; **Pr 22:13** 738
“There is a **l** in the road! **Pr 26:13** 7826
A **l** is in the open square!” **Pr 26:13** 738
But the righteous are bold as a **l**. **Pr 28:1** 3715
Like a roaring **l** and a rushing **Pr 28:15** 738
The **l** *which* is mighty among beasts **Pr 30:30** 3918
live dog is better than a dead **l**. **Ec 9:4** 743b
young **l** and the fatling together; **Is 11:6** 3715
the **l** will eat straw like the ox. **Is 11:7** 743b
A **l** upon the fugitives of Moab and **Is 15:9** 743b
From where *come* lioness and **l**, **Is 30:6** 3918
“As the **l** or the young lion **Is 31:4** 743b
the young **l** growls over his prey, **Is 31:4** 3715
No **l** will be there, Nor will any **Is 35:9** 743b
Like a **l**—so He breaks all my bones, **Is 38:13** 738
the **l** will eat straw like the ox; **Is 65:25** 743b
your prophets Like a destroying **l**. **Jer 2:30** 743b
“A **l** has gone up from his **Jer 4:7** 743b
Therefore a **l** from the forest **Jer 5:6** 743b
to Me Like a **l** in the forest; **Jer 12:8** 743b
left His hiding place like the **l**; **Jer 25:38** 3715
one will come up like a **l** from the **Jer 49:19** 743b
one will come up like a **l** from the **Jer 50:44** 743b
wait, *Like* a **l** in secret places. **La 3:10** 743b
all four had the face of a **l** on **Ezk 1:10** 743b
a man, the third the face of a **l**, **Ezk 10:14** 743b
up one of her cubs, He became a **l**, **Ezk 19:3** 3715
her cubs And made him a young **l**. **Ezk 19:5** 3715
He became a young **l**, **Ezk 19:6** 3715
like a roaring **l** tearing the prey. **Ezk 22:25** 738
to a young **l** of the nations, **Ezk 32:2** 3715
“The first *was* like a **l** and had *the* **Da 7:4** 744
For I *will be* like a **l** to Ephraim And **Hos 5:14** 7826
a young **l** to the house of Judah. **Hos 5:14** 3715
the LORD, He will roar like a **l**; **Hos 11:10** 743b
So I will be like a **l** to them; **Hos 13:7** 7826
Its teeth are the teeth of a **l**, **Jl 1:6** 743b
Does a **l** roar in the forest when **Am 3:4** 743b
Does a young **l** growl from his den **Am 3:4** 3715
A **l** has roared! Who will not fear? **Am 3:8** 743b
As when a man flees from a **l** And **Am 5:19** 738
Like a **l** among the beasts of the **Mi 5:8** 743b
a young **l** among flocks of sheep, **Mi 5:8** 3715
of the young lions, Where the **l**, **Na 2:11** 743b
The **l** tore enough for his cubs, **Na 2:12** 743b
prowls around like a roaring **l**, **1Pe 5:8** *3023*
The first creature *was* like a **l**, **Rv 4:7** *3023*
the **L** that is from the tribe of **Rv 5:5** *3023*
a loud voice, as when a **l** roars; **Rv 10:3** *3023*
his mouth like the mouth of a **l**. **Rv 13:2** *3023*

LIONESS
“Behold, a people rises like a **l**, **Nu 23:24** 3833b
the whelps of the **l** are scattered. **Jb 4:11** 3833b
Its roaring is like a **l**, **Is 5:29** 3833b
From where *come* **l** and lion, **Is 30:6** 3833b
was your mother? A **l** among lions! **Ezk 19:2** 3833b
I will also devour them like a **l**, **Hos 13:8** 3833b
lion, And it has the fangs of a **l**. **Jl 1:6** 3833b
young lions, Where the lion, **l** and **Na 2:11** 3833b

LIONESSES
his cubs, Killed *enough* for his **l**, **Na 2:12** 3833b

LION’S
“Judah is a **l** whelp; **Gn 49:9** 743b
“Dan is a **l** whelp, That leaps **Dt 33:22** 743b
Save me from the **l** mouth; **Ps 22:21** 743b
and a young **l** face toward the palm **Ezk 41:19** 3715
shepherd snatches from the **l** mouth **Am 3:12** 738
lion, lioness and **l** cub prowled, **Na 2:11** 743b
was rescued out of the **l** mouth. **2Tm 4:17** *3023*

LIONS
eagles, They were stronger than **l**. **2Sa 1:23** 738
were between the frames *were* **l**, **1Ki 7:29** 738
and beneath the **l** and oxen *were* **1Ki 7:29** 738
cherubim, **l** and palm trees, **1Ki 7:36** 738
two **l** standing beside the arms. **1Ki 10:19** 738
Twelve **l** were standing there **1Ki 10:20** 738
therefore the LORD sent **l** among **2Ki 17:25** 738
so he has sent **l** among them, and **2Ki 17:26** 738
faces were like the faces of **l**, **1Ch 12:8** 743b
two **l** standing beside the arms. **2Ch 9:18** 738
Twelve **l** were standing there **2Ch 9:19** 738
teeth of the young **l** are broken. **Jb 4:10** 3715
the appetite of the young **l**, **Jb 38:39** 3715
young **l** do lack and suffer hunger; **Ps 34:10** 3715
ravages, My only *life* from the **l**. **Ps 35:17** 3715
My soul is among **l**; **Ps 57:4** 3833a
out the fangs of the young **l**, **Ps 58:6** 3715

The young **l** roar after their prey And Ps 104:21 3715
and Hermon, From the dens of **l**, SS 4:8 738
and it roars like young **l**; Is 5:29 3715
"The young **l** have roared at him, Jer 2:15 3715
the **l** have driven *them* away. Jer 50:17 738
will roar together like young **l**, Jer 51:38 3715
A lioness among **l**! Ezk 19:2 738
She lay down among young **l**, Ezk 19:2 3715
'And he walked about among the **l**; Ezk 19:6 738
able to deliver you from the **l**?" Da 6:20 744
before the **l** overpowered them and Da 6:24 744
Daniel from the power of the **l**." Da 6:27 744
Where is the den of the **l** And the Na 2:11 743b
the feeding place of the young **l**, Na 2:11 3715
a sword will devour your young **l**; Na 2:13 3715
princes within her are roaring **l**, Zph 3:3 738
promises, shut the mouths of **l**, Heb 11:33 *3023*
teeth were like *the teeth* of **l**. Rv 9:8 *3023*
horses are like the heads of **l**; Rv 9:17 *3023*

LIONS'
They will growl like **l** cubs. Jer 51:38 738
shall be cast into the **l** den. Da 6:7 744
is to be cast into the **l** den?" Da 6:12 744
in and cast into the **l** den. Da 6:16 744
and went in haste to the **l** den. Da 6:19 744
sent His angel and shut the **l** mouths Da 6:22 744
and their wives into the **l** den; Da 6:24 744
is a sound of the young **l** roar, Zch 11:3 3715

LIP
They separate with the **l**, Ps 22:7 8193
And honor Me with their **l** service, Is 29:13 8193

LIPS
swears thoughtlessly with his **l** Lv 5:4 8193
vows or the rash statement of her **l** Nu 30:6 8193
under and the rash statement of her **l** Nu 30:8 8193
then whatever proceeds out of her **l** Nu 30:12 8193
perform what goes out from your **l**, Dt 23:23 8193
put it on their **l**, so that Dt 31:19 6310
from the **l** of their descendants); Dt 31:21 6310
her heart, only her **l** were moving, 1Sa 1:13 8193
nose, And My bridle in your **l**, 2Ki 19:28 8193
this Job did not sin with his **l**. Jb 2:10 8193
And your **l** with shouting. Jb 8:21 8193
speak, And open His **l** against you, Jb 11:5 8193
listen to the contentions of my **l**. Jb 13:6 8193
your own **l** testify against you. Jb 15:6 8193
the solace of my **l** could lessen *your* Jb 16:5 8193
from the command of His **l**; Jb 23:12 8193
My **l** certainly will not speak Jb 27:4 8193
Let me open my **l** and answer. Jb 32:20 8193
my **l** speak knowledge sincerely. Jb 33:3 8193
With flattering **l** and with a Ps 12:2 8193
the LORD cut off all flattering **l**, Ps 12:3 8193
Our **l** are our own; Ps 12:4 8193
I take their names upon my **l**. Ps 16:4 8193
which is not from deceitful **l**. Ps 17:1 8193
by the word of Your **l** I have kept Ps 17:4 8193
have not withheld the request of his **l**. Ps 21:2 8193
Let the lying **l** be mute, Which Ps 31:18 8193
And your **l** from speaking deceit. Ps 34:13 8193
Behold, I will not restrain my **l**, Ps 40:9 8193
Grace is poured upon Your **l**; Ps 45:2 8193
O Lord, open my **l**, That my mouth Ps 51:15 8193
Swords are in their **l**, Ps 59:7 8193
mouth *and* the words of their **l**, Ps 59:12 8193
than life, My **l** will praise You. Ps 63:3 8193
offers praises with joyful **l**. Ps 63:5 8193
Which my **l** uttered And my mouth Ps 66:14 8193
My **l** will shout for joy when I Ps 71:23 8193
I alter the utterance of My **l**. Ps 89:34 8193
He spoke rashly with his **l**. Ps 106:33 8193
With my **l** I have told of All the Ps 119:13 8193
Let my **l** utter praise, For You Ps 119:171 8193
my soul, O LORD, from lying **l**, Ps 120:2 8193
Poison of a viper is under their **l** Ps 140:3 8193
mischief of their **l** cover them. Ps 140:9 8193
Keep watch over the door of my **l**. Ps 141:3 8193
And your **l** may reserve knowledge. Pr 5:2 8193
the **l** of an adulteress drip honey And Pr 5:3 8193
With her flattering **l** she seduces him Pr 7:21 8193
opening of my **l** *will reveal* right Pr 8:6 8193
is an abomination to my **l**. Pr 8:7 8193
On the **l** of the discerning, wisdom Pr 10:13 8193
who conceals hatred *has* lying **l**, Pr 10:18 8193
he who restrains his **l** is wise. Pr 10:19 8193
The **l** of the righteous feed many, Pr 10:21 8193
The **l** of the righteous bring forth Pr 10:32 8193
by the transgression of his **l**, Pr 12:13 8193
Truthful **l** will be established forever Pr 12:19 8193
Lying **l** are an abomination to the Pr 12:22 8193
one who opens wide his **l** comes to Pr 13:3 8193
But the **l** of the wise will Pr 14:3 8193
l of the wise spread knowledge, Pr 15:7 8193
decision is in the **l** of the king; Pr 16:10 8193
Righteous **l** are the delight of kings, Pr 16:13 8193
And adds persuasiveness to his **l**. Pr 16:23 8193
He who compresses his **l** brings evil Pr 16:30 8193
An evildoer listens to wicked **l**; Pr 17:4 8193
Much less are lying **l** to a prince. Pr 17:7 8193
When he closes his **l**, Pr 17:28 8193
A fool's **l** bring strife, And his Pr 18:6 8193
his **l** are the snare of his soul. Pr 18:7 8193
with the product of his **l**. Pr 18:20 8193
But the **l** of knowledge are a more Pr 20:15 8193
That they may be ready on your **l**. Pr 22:18 8193
When your **l** speak what is right. Pr 23:16 8193
And their **l** talk of trouble. Pr 24:2 8193
He kisses the **l** Who gives a right Pr 24:26 8193
And do not deceive with your **l**. Pr 24:28 8193
Are burning **l** and a wicked heart. Pr 26:23 8193
who hates disguises *it* with his **l**, Pr 26:24 8193
A stranger, and not your own **l**. Pr 27:2 8193
while the **l** of a fool consume him; Ec 10:12 8193
"Your **l** are like a scarlet SS 4:3 8193
"Your **l**, *my* bride, drip honey; SS 4:11 8193
His **l** are lilies Dripping with SS 5:13 8193
Flowing gently *through* the **l** of SS 7:9 8193
Because I am a man of unclean **l**, Is 6:5 8193
live among a people of unclean **l**; Is 6:5 8193
"Behold, this has touched your **l**; Is 6:7 8193
with the breath of His **l** He will slay Is 11:4 8193
stammering **l** and a foreign tongue, Is 28:11 8193
His **l** are filled with indignation And Is 30:27 8193
nose And My bridle in your **l**, Is 37:29 8193
Creating the praise of the **l**. Is 57:19 8193
Your **l** have spoken falsehood, Your Is 59:3 8193
You are near to their **l** But far Jer 12:2 6310
the utterance of my **l** Was in Your Jer 17:16 8193
The **l** of my assailants and their La 3:62 8193
from your **l** in your day of pride, Ezk 16:56 6310
a human being was touching my **l**; Da 10:16 8193
Put the trumpet to your **l**! Hos 8:1 2441
we may present the fruit of our **l**. Hos 14:2 8193
lies in your bosom Guard your **l**. Mi 7:5 6310
At the sound my **l** quivered. Hab 3:16 8193
give to the peoples purified **l**, Zph 3:9 8193
was not found on his **l**; Mal 2:6 8193
"For the **l** of a priest should Mal 2:7 8193
PEOPLE HONORS ME WITH THEIR **L**, Mt 15:8 *5491*
PEOPLE HONORS ME WITH THEIR **L**, Mk 7:6 *5491*
which were falling from His **l**; Lk 4:22 *4750*
POISON OF ASPS IS UNDER THEIR **L**"; Ro 3:13 *5491*
BY THE **L** OF STRANGERS I WILL SPEAK 1Co 14:21 *5491*
the fruit of **l** that give thanks to His Heb 13:15 *5491*
AND HIS **L** FROM SPEAKING DECEIT. 1Pe 3:10 *5491*

LIQUID
and any **l** which may be drunk in Lv 11:34 4945b
And my fingers with **l** myrrh, SS 5:5 5674a
are lilies Dripping with **l** myrrh. SS 5:13 5674a

LIQUOR
Their **l** gone, They play the harlot Hos 4:18 5435
out to you concerning wine and **l**,' Mi 2:11 7941
and he will drink no wine or **l**, Lk 1:15 *4608*

LIST
and make a **l** of their names. Nu 3:40 4557
constitute the **l** of the mighty men 1Ch 11:11 4557
who were in the genealogical **l**; Ezr 8:3 3187
A widow is to be put on the **l** only 1Tm 5:9 *2639*
to put younger widows *on the* **l**, 1Tm 5:11

LISTEN
"Adah and Zillah, **L** to my voice, Gn 4:23 8085
Sarah tells you, **l** to her, Gn 21:12 8085
"If you will only please **l** to me; Gn 23:13 8085
"My lord, **l** to me; Gn 23:15 8085
my son, **l** to me as I command you. Gn 27:8 8085
not **l** to us to be circumcised, Gn 34:17 8085
"Please **l** to this dream which I Gn 37:6 8085
not **l** to her to lie beside her Gn 39:10 8085
with us, yet we would not **l**; Gn 42:21 8085
and you would not **l**? Gn 42:22 8085
And **l** to Israel your father. Gn 49:2 8085
believe me or **l** to what I say? Ex 4:1 8085
but they did not **l** to Moses on Ex 6:9 8085
how then will Pharaoh **l** to me, Ex 6:12 8085
how then will Pharaoh **l** to me?" Ex 6:30 8085
"When Pharaoh does not **l** to you, Ex 7:4 8085
and he did not **l** to them, Ex 7:13 8085
and he did not **l** to them, Ex 7:22 8085
his heart and did not **l** to them, Ex 8:15 8085
and he did not **l** to them, Ex 8:19 8085
heart, and he did not **l** to them, Ex 9:12 8085
"Pharaoh will not **l** to you, Ex 11:9 8085
But they did not **l** to Moses, Ex 16:20 8085
Now **l** to me: I will give you counsel Ex 18:19 8085
to us yourself and we will **l**; Ex 20:19 8085
and I will **l** to what the LORD will Nu 9:8 8085
"**L** now, you rebels; Nu 20:10 8085
spoke to you, but you would not **l**. Dt 1:43 8085
the LORD did not **l** to your voice nor Dt 1:45 8085
account, and would not **l** to me; Dt 3:26 8085
l to the statutes and the Dt 4:1 8085
LORD your God and **l** to His voice. Dt 4:30 8085
should **l** and be careful to do *it*, Dt 6:3 8085
because you **l** to these judgments Dt 7:12 8085
because you would not **l** to the Dt 8:20 8085
if you **l** obediently to my Dt 11:13 8085
if you **l** to the commandments of Dt 11:27 8085
if you do not **l** to the Dt 11:28 8085
"Be careful to **l** to all these Dt 12:28 8085
you shall not **l** to the words of Dt 13:3 8085
His commandments, **l** to His voice, Dt 13:4 8085
not yield to him or **l** to him; Dt 13:8 8085
if you will **l** to the voice of the Dt 13:18 8085
if only you **l** obediently to the Dt 15:5 8085
l to those who practice witchcraft Dt 18:14 8085
countrymen, you shall **l** to him. Dt 18:15 8085
that whoever will not **l** to My words Dt 18:19 8085
him, he will not even **l** to them, Dt 21:18 8085
was not willing to **l** to Balaam, Dt 23:5 8085
ordinances, and **l** to His voice. Dt 26:17 8085
"Be silent and **l**, O Israel! Dt 27:9 8085
if you **l** to the commandments Dt 28:13 8085
not **l** to the voice of the LORD, Jos 5:6 8085
I was not willing to **l** to Balaam. Jos 24:10 8085
they did not **l** to their judges, Jg 2:17 8085
"**L** to me, O men of Shechem, that Jg 9:7 8085
of Shechem, that God may **l** to you. Jg 9:7 8085
but the king of Edom would not **l**. Jg 11:17 8085
But the men would not **l** to him. Jg 19:25 8085
But the sons of Benjamin would not **l** Jg 20:13 8085
"**L** carefully, my daughter. Ru 2:8 8085
l to the voice of their father, 1Sa 2:25 8085
"**L** to the voice of the people in 1Sa 8:7 8085
"Now then, **l** to their voice; 1Sa 8:9 8085
to **l** to the voice of Samuel, 1Sa 8:19 8085
"**L** to their voice and appoint 1Sa 8:22 8085
and **l** to His voice and not rebel 1Sa 12:14 8085
not **l** to the voice of the LORD, 1Sa 12:15 8085
l to the words of the LORD. 1Sa 15:1 8085
"**L** now, son of Ahitub." 1Sa 22:12 8085
"Why do you **l** to the words of 1Sa 24:9 8085
and **l** to the words of your 1Sa 25:24 8085
l to the words of his servant. 1Sa 26:19 8085
please **l** to the voice of your 1Sa 28:22 8085
who will **l** to you in this matter? 1Sa 30:24 8085
him and he did not **l** to our voice. 2Sa 12:18 8085
However, he would not **l** to her; 2Sa 13:14 8085
Yet he would not **l** to her. 2Sa 13:16 8085
"**L** to the words of your 2Sa 20:17 8085
to **l** to the cry and to the prayer 1Ki 8:28 8085
to **l** to the prayer which Your 1Ki 8:29 8085
"**L** to the supplication of Your 1Ki 8:30 8085
to **l** to them whenever they call to 1Ki 8:52 8085
that if you **l** to all that I 1Ki 11:38 8085
the king did not **l** to the people; 1Ki 12:15 8085
that the king did not **l** to them, 1Ki 12:16 8085
"Do not **l** or consent." 1Ki 20:8 8085
"**L**, all you people." 1Ki 22:28 8085
"**L** to the word of the LORD; 2Ki 7:1 8085
side, and you will **l** to my voice, 2Ki 10:6 8085
But Amaziah would not **l**. 2Ki 14:11 8085
However, they did not **l**, 2Ki 17:14 8085
However, they did not **l**, 2Ki 17:40 8085
they would neither **l** nor 2Ki 18:12 8085
'Do not **l** to Hezekiah, for thus 2Ki 18:31 8085
But do not **l** to Hezekiah when he 2Ki 18:32 8085
and **l** to the words of Sennacherib, 2Ki 19:16 8085
But they did not **l**, 2Ki 21:9 8085
"**L** to me, my brethren and my 1Ch 28:2 8085
to **l** to the cry and to the prayer 2Ch 6:19 8085
to **l** to the prayer which Your 2Ch 6:20 8085
"**L** to the supplications of Your 2Ch 6:21 8085
the king did not **l** to the people, 2Ch 10:15 8085
all Israel *saw* that the king did not **l** 2Ch 10:16 8085
"**L** to me, Jeroboam and all Israel: 2Ch 13:4 8085
"**L** to me, Asa, and all Judah and 2Ch 15:2 8085
"**L**, all you people." 2Ch 18:27 8085
"**L**, all Judah and the inhabitants 2Ch 20:15 7181
"**L** to me, O Judah and inhabitants 2Ch 20:20 8085
against them, they would not **l**. 2Ch 24:19 238
But Amaziah would not **l**, 2Ch 25:20 8085
l to me and return the captives 2Ch 28:11 8085
"**L** to me, O Levites. 2Ch 29:5 8085
nor did he **l** to the words of Neco 2Ch 35:22 8085
who *could* **l** with understanding, Ne 8:2 8085
would not **l** to Your commandments. Ne 9:16 8085
"They refused to **l**, Ne 9:17 8085
did not **l** to Your commandments Ne 9:29 8085
their neck, and would not **l**. Ne 9:29 8085
to him and he would not **l** to them, Es 3:4 8085
l to the contentions of my lips. Jb 13:6 7181
"**L** carefully to my speech, And Jb 13:17 8085
"I will tell you, **l** to me; Jb 15:17 8085
"**L** carefully to my speech, And Jb 21:2 8085
'**L** to me, I too will tell what I Jb 32:10 8085
my speech, And **l** to all my words. Jb 33:1 238
"Pay attention, O Job, **l** to me; Jb 33:31 8085
l to me; Keep silent, and I will teach Jb 33:33 8085
words, you wise men, And **l** to me, Jb 34:2 238
"Therefore, **l** to me, you men of Jb 34:10 8085
L to the sound of my words. Jb 34:16 238
God will not **l** to an empty *cry*, Jb 35:13 8085
"**L** closely to the thunder of His Jb 37:2 8085
"**L** to this, O Job, Stand and Jb 37:14 238
Come, you children, **l** to me; Ps 34:11 8085
L, O daughter, give attention and Ps 45:10 8085
L, O my people, to my instruction; Ps 78:1 238
O Israel, if you would **l** to Me! Ps 81:8 8085
My people did not **l** to My voice, Ps 81:11 8085
"Oh that My people would **l** to Me, Ps 81:13 8085
not **l** to the voice of the LORD. Ps 106:25 8085
Now then, *my* sons, **l** to me And Pr 5:7 8085
Now therefore, *my* sons, **l** to me, Pr 7:24 8085
"**L**, for I will speak noble Pr 8:6 8085
"Now therefore, *O* sons, **l** to me, Pr 8:32 8085
a scoffer does not **l** to rebuke. Pr 13:1 8085
L to counsel and accept Pr 19:20 8085
L, my son, and be wise, And direct Pr 23:19 8085
L to your father who begot you, Pr 23:22 8085
and draw near to **l** rather than to Ec 5:1 8085
It is better to **l** to the rebuke of Ec 7:5 8085
for one to **l** to the song of fools. Ec 7:5 8085
"**L**! My beloved! Behold, he is SS 2:8 6963
L, O heavens, and hear, O earth; Is 1:2 8085
multiply prayers, I will not **l**. Is 1:15 8085
"**L** now, O house of David! Is 7:13 8085
is repose," but they would not **l**. Is 28:12 8085
my voice, **L** and hear my words. Is 28:23 7181
Sons who refuse to **l** To the Is 30:9 8085
the ears of those who hear will **l**. Is 32:3 7181
and **l**, O peoples! Is 34:1 7181
'Do not **l** to Hezekiah,' for thus Is 36:16 8085
and **l** to all the words of Is 37:17 8085
"Coastlands, **l** to Me in silence, Is 41:1
will give heed and **l** hereafter? Is 42:23 8085

"But now **l**, O Jacob, My servant, Is 44:1 8085
"**L** to Me, O house of Jacob, And Is 46:3 8085
"**L** to Me, you stubborn-minded, Is 46:12 8085
"**L** to Me, O Jacob, even Israel Is 48:12 8085
"Assemble, all of you, and **l**! Is 48:14 8085
"Come near to Me, **l** to this: Is 48:16 8085
L to Me, O islands, And pay Is 49:1 8085
awakens My ear to **l** as a disciple. Is 50:4 8085
"**L** to me, you who pursue Is 51:1 8085
"**L** to Me, you who know Is 51:7 8085
L! Your watchmen lift up *their* voices Is 52:8 6963
L carefully to Me, and eat what is Is 55:2 8085
L, that you may live; Is 55:3 8085
I spoke, but they did not **l**. Is 66:4 8085
are closed And they cannot **l**. Jer 6:10 7181
'**L** to the sound of the trumpet!' Jer 6:17 7181
But they said, 'We will not **l**.' Jer 6:17 7181
not **l** to Me or incline their ear, Jer 7:26 8085
them, but they will not **l** to you; Jer 7:27 8085
Behold, **l**! The cry of the daughter Jer 8:19 6963
'**L** to My voice, and do according Jer 11:4 8085
saying, "**L** to My voice." Jer 11:7 8085
to Me, yet I will not **l** to them. Jer 11:11 8085
for I will not **l** when they call to Jer 11:14 8085
"But if they will not **l**, Jer 12:17 8085
who refuse to **l** to My words, Jer 13:10 8085
but they did not **l**.' Jer 13:11 8085
L and give heed, do not be Jer 13:15 8085
But if you will not **l** to it, Jer 13:17 8085
I am not going to **l** to their cry; Jer 14:12 8085
'**L** to the word of the LORD, kings Jer 17:20 8085
did not **l** or incline their ears, Jer 17:23 8085
order not to **l** or take correction. Jer 17:23 8085
if you **l** attentively to Me," Jer 17:24 8085
"But if you do not **l** to Me to Jer 17:27 8085
And **l** to what my opponents are Jer 18:19 8085
But you said, 'I will not **l**!' Jer 22:21 8085
"Do not **l** to the words of the Jer 23:16 8085
'Perhaps they will **l** and everyone Jer 26:3 8085
"If you will not **l** to Me, to walk Jer 26:4 8085
to **l** to the words of My servants Jer 26:5 8085
you, do not **l** to your prophets, Jer 27:9 8085
"So do not **l** to the words of the Jer 27:14 8085
Do not **l** to the words of your Jer 27:16 8085
"Do not **l** to them; Jer 27:17 8085
"**L** now, Hananiah, the LORD has Jer 28:15 8085
and do not **l** to the dreams which Jer 29:8 8085
pray to Me, and I will **l** to you. Jer 29:12 8085
but you did not **l**,' declares the Jer 29:19 8085
not **l** and receive instruction. Jer 32:33 8085
spoke to them but they did not **l**, Jer 35:17 8085
scroll, he would not **l** to them. Jer 36:25 8085
but they did not **l**. Jer 36:31 8085
yet he would not **l** to him. Jer 37:14 8085
"But now, please **l**, O my lord the Jer 37:20 8085
advice, you will not **l** to me." Jer 38:15 8085
LORD and did not **l** to His voice, Jer 40:3 8085
we will **l** to the voice of the LORD Jer 42:6 8085
when we **l** to the voice of the LORD Jer 42:6 8085
so as not to **l** to the voice of the Jer 42:13 8085
case **l** to the word of the LORD, Jer 42:15 8085
'But they did not **l** or incline Jer 44:5 8085
we are not going to **l** to you! Jer 44:16 8085
whether they **l** or not Ezk 2:5 8085
to them whether they **l** or not, Ezk 2:7 8085
l to what I am speaking to you; Ezk 2:8 8085
you to them who should **l** to you; Ezk 3:6 8085
will not be willing to **l** to you, Ezk 3:7 8085
they are not willing to **l** to Me. Ezk 3:7 8085
will speak to you and **l** closely. Ezk 3:10 8085
tell them, whether they **l** or not, Ezk 3:11 8085
l to the word of the Lord GOD! Ezk 6:3 8085
yet I will not **l** to them." Ezk 8:18 8085
'**L** to the word of the LORD!' Ezk 13:2 8085
to My people who **l** to lies. Ezk 13:19 8085
and were not willing to **l** to Me; Ezk 20:8 8085
later you will surely **l** to Me, Ezk 20:39 8085
l to the prayer of Your servant and Da 9:17 8085
O Lord, **l** and take action! Da 9:19 7181
L to the word of the LORD, O sons Hos 4:1 8085
L, O house of the king! Hos 5:1 238
And **l**, all inhabitants of the land. Jl 1:2 238
even **l** to the sound of your harps. Am 5:23 8085
L, O earth and all it contains, Mi 1:2 7181
"**L**, you mountains, to the Mi 6:2 8085
L, the day of the LORD! Zph 1:14 6963
did not **l** or give heed to Me," Zch 1:4 8085
'Now **l**, Joshua the high priest, Zch 3:8 8085
as He called and they would not **l**, Zch 7:13 8085
they called and I would not **l**," Zch 7:13 8085
"If you do not **l**, and if you do Mal 2:2 8085
I am well-pleased; **l** to Him!" Mt 17:5 *191*
"But if he does not **l** *to you,* Mt 18:16 *191*
"If he refuses to **l** to them, Mt 18:17 *3878*
refuses to **l** even to the church, Mt 18:17 *3878*
"**L** to another parable. Mt 21:33 *191*
"**L** *to this!* Behold, the sower went Mk 4:3 *191*
"Take care what you **l** to. Mk 4:24 *191*
does not receive you or **l** to you, Mk 6:11 *191*
"**L** to Me, all of you, and Mk 7:14 *191*
is My beloved Son, **l** to Him!" Mk 9:7 *191*
"So take care how you **l**; Lk 8:18 *191*
My Chosen One; **l** to Him!" Lk 9:35 *191*
were coming near Him to **l** to Him. Lk 15:1 *191*
not **l** to Moses and the Prophets, Lk 16:31 *191*
to Him in the temple to **l** to Him. Lk 21:38 *191*
who can **l** to it?" Jn 6:60 *191*
you already and you did not **l**; Jn 9:27 *191*
Why do you **l** to Him?" Jn 10:20 *191*
"Men of Israel, **l** to these words: Ac 2:22 *191*
Israel, and you who fear God, **l**: Ac 13:16 *191*
"Brethren, **l** to me. Ac 15:13 *191*
"So do not **l** to them, for more Ac 23:21 *3982*
I beg you to **l** to me patiently. Ac 26:3 *191*
they will also **l**." Ac 28:28 *191*
EVEN SO THEY WILL NOT **L** TO ME," 1Co 14:21 *1522*
law, do you not **l** to the law? Ga 4:21 *191*
L, my beloved brethren: Jas 2:5 *191*
is not from God does not **l** to us. 1Jn 4:6 *191*

LISTENED

have **l** to the voice of your wife, Gn 3:17 8085
And Abram **l** to the voice of Sarai. Gn 16:2 8085
Abraham **l** to Ephron; Gn 23:16 8085
l to Hamor and to his son Shechem, Gn 34:24 8085
And his brothers **l** *to him.* Gn 37:27 8085
sons of Israel have not **l** to me; Ex 6:12 8085
you have not **l** until now." Ex 7:16 8085
So Moses **l** to his father-in-law and Ex 18:24 8085
times and have not **l** to My voice, Nu 14:22 8085
the LORD **l** to me that time also. Dt 9:19 8085
believed Him nor **l** to His voice. Dt 9:23 8085
the LORD **l** to me that time also; Dt 10:10 8085
I have **l** to the voice of the LORD Dt 26:14 8085
and the sons of Israel **l** to him Dt 34:9 8085
the LORD **l** to the voice of a man; Jos 10:14 8085
and have **l** to my voice in all that Jos 22:2 8085
and has not **l** to My voice, Jg 2:20 8085
God **l** to the voice of Manoah; Jg 13:9 8085
I have **l** to your voice in all that 1Sa 12:1 8085
the people and **l** to their voice. 1Sa 15:24 8085
Saul **l** to the voice of Jonathan, 1Sa 19:6 8085
I have **l** to you and granted your 1Sa 25:35 8085
and have **l** to your words which you 1Sa 28:21 8085
woman urged him, and he **l** to them. 1Sa 28:23 8085
So they **l** to the word of the LORD, 1Ki 12:24 8085
So Ben-hadad **l** to King Asa and 1Ki 15:20 8085
he **l** to their voice and did so. 1Ki 20:25 8085
not **l** to the voice of the LORD, 1Ki 20:36 8085
the LORD, and the LORD **l** to him; 2Ki 13:4 8085
So the king of Assyria **l** to him; 2Ki 16:9 8085
Hezekiah **l** to them, and showed 2Ki 20:13 8085
not **l** to the words of this book, 2Ki 22:13 8085
So they **l** to the words of the LORD 2Ch 11:4 8085
So Ben-hadad **l** to King Asa and 2Ch 16:4 8085
the king, and the king **l** to them. 2Ch 24:17 8085
and have not **l** to my counsel." 2Ch 25:16 8085
matter, and He **l** to our entreaty. Ezr 8:23 6279
"I **l** to the reproof which insults Jb 20:3 8085
"To me they **l** and waited, And Jb 29:21 8085
words, I **l** to your reasonings, Jb 32:11 238
not **l** to the voice of my teachers, Pr 5:13 8085
they have not **l** to My words, Jer 6:19 7181
"I have **l** and heard, They have Jer 8:6 7181
has given heed to His word and **l**? Jer 23:18 8085
and again, but you have not **l**. Jer 25:3 8085
l nor inclined your ear to hear, Jer 25:4 8085
"Yet you have not **l** to Me," Jer 25:7 8085
and again, but you have not **l**; Jer 26:5 8085
they have not **l** to My words,' Jer 29:19 8085
yet you have not **l** to Me. Jer 35:14 8085
not inclined your ear or **l** to Me. Jer 35:15 8085
this people has not **l** to Me. Jer 35:16 8085
l to the words of the LORD which Jer 37:2 8085
So he **l** to them in this matter and Da 1:14 8085
l to Your servants the prophets, Da 9:6 8085
Because they have not **l** to Him; Hos 9:17 8085
l to him up to this statement, Ac 22:22 *191*
"AT THE ACCEPTABLE TIME I **L** TO YOU, 2Co 6:2 *1873*

LISTENERS

and the many **l** were astonished, Mk 6:2 *191*

LISTENING

And Sarah was **l** at the tent door, Gn 18:10 8085
Rebekah was **l** while Isaac Gn 27:5 8085
who acts presumptuously by not **l** to Dt 17:12 8085
LORD, for Your servant is **l**.' " 1Sa 3:9 8085
"Speak, for Your servant is **l**." 1Sa 3:10 8085
And he answered, "I am **l**." 2Sa 20:17 8085
believe that He was **l** to my voice. Jb 9:16 238
Cease **l**, my son, to discipline, Pr 19:27 8085
Is a wise reprover to a **l** ear. Pr 25:12 8085
away his ear from **l** to the law, Pr 28:9 8085
My companions are **l** for your SS 8:13 7181
'Keep on **l**, but do not perceive; Is 6:9 8085
own evil heart, without **l** to Me. Jer 16:12 8085
instruction by **l** to My words?" Jer 35:13 8085
you who are **l** in these days to Zch 8:9 8085
but he used to enjoy **l** to him. Mk 6:20 *191*
And His disciples were **l**. Mk 11:14 *191*
the large crowd enjoyed **l** to Him. Mk 12:37 *191*
of the teachers, both **l** to them and Lk 2:46 *191*
Him and **l** to the word of God, Lk 5:1 *191*
l to His word. Lk 10:39 *191*
money, were **l** to all these things and Lk 16:14 *191*
While they were **l** to these things, Lk 19:11 *191*
And while all the people were **l**, Lk 20:45 *191*
those who were **l** to the message. Ac 10:44 *191*
man was **l** to Paul as he spoke, Ac 14:9 *191*
and they were **l** to Barnabas and Ac 15:12 *191*
a worshiper of God, was **l**; Ac 16:14 *191*
and the prisoners were **l** to them; Ac 16:25 *1874*
after **l** to the message of truth, Eph 1:13 *191*

LISTENS

but no man **l** to you on the part of 2Sa 15:3 8085
who **l** to me shall live securely And Pr 1:33 8085
"Blessed is the man who **l** to me, Pr 8:34 8085
a wise man is he who **l** to counsel. Pr 12:15 8085
He whose ear **l** to the life-giving Pr 15:31 8085
But he who **l** to reproof acquires Pr 15:32 8085
An evildoer **l** to wicked lips; A Pr 17:4 7181
But the man who **l** *to the truth* Pr 21:28 8085
if he **l** to you, you have won your Mt 18:15 *191*
one who **l** to you listens to Me, Lk 10:16 *191*
one who listens to you **l** to Me, Lk 10:16 *191*
world, and the world **l** to them. 1Jn 4:5 *191*
he who knows God **l** to us; 1Jn 4:6 *191*

LIT

The lightnings **l** up the world; Ps 77:18 215
His lightnings **l** up the world; Ps 97:4 215
and *keep* your lamps **l**. Lk 12:35 *2545*

LITERAL

that He was speaking of **l** sleep. Jn 11:13 *2838*

LITERATE

they give it to the one who is **l**, Is 29:11 3045, 5612

LITERATURE

l and language of the Chaldeans. Da 1:4 5612
in every *branch of* **l** and wisdom; Da 1:17 5612

LITTERS

on horses, in chariots, in **l**, Is 66:20 6632a

LITTLE

"Please let a **l** water be brought Gn 18:4 4592
drink a **l** water from your jar." Gn 24:17 4592
drink a **l** water from your jar", Gn 24:43 4592
"For you had **l** before I came and Gn 30:30 4592
all their **l** ones and their wives, Gn 34:29 2945
"Go back, buy us a **l** food." Gn 43:2 4592
we as well as you and our **l** ones. Gn 43:8 2945
a **l** balm and a little honey, Gn 43:11 4592
a little balm and a **l** honey, Gn 43:11 4592
and a **l** child of *his* old age. Gn 44:20 6996a
'Go back, buy us a **l** food.' Gn 44:25 4592
your **l** ones and for your wives, Gn 45:19 2945
and their **l** ones and their wives in Gn 46:5 2945
food, according to their **l** ones. Gn 47:12 2945
and as food for your **l** ones." Gn 47:24 2945
they left only their **l** ones and Gn 50:8 2945
provide for you and your **l** ones." Gn 50:21 2945
ever I let you and your **l** ones go! Ex 10:10 2945
your **l** ones may go with you." Ex 10:24 2945
and *some* gathered much and *some* **l**. Ex 16:17 4591
he who had gathered **l** had no lack; Ex 16:18 4591
A **l** more and they will stone me." Ex 17:4 4592
them out before you **l** by little, Ex 23:30 4592
them out before you little by **l**, Ex 23:30 4592
and the **l** owl and the cormorant Lv 11:17 3563b
our **l** ones will become plunder; Nu 14:3 2945
and their sons and their **l** ones. Nu 16:27 2945
women of Midian and their **l** ones; Nu 31:9 2945
kill every male among the **l** ones, Nu 31:17 2945
and cities for our **l** ones; Nu 32:16 2945
while our **l** ones live in the Nu 32:17 2945
yourselves cities for your **l** ones, Nu 32:24 2945
"Our **l** ones, our wives, our Nu 32:26 2945
your **l** ones who you said would Dt 1:39 2945
even *as* **l** *as* a footstep because I Dt 2:5
your **l** ones and your livestock Dt 3:19 2945
nations before you **l** by little; Dt 7:22 4592
nations before you little by **l**; Dt 7:22 4592
the **l** owl, the great owl, the Dt 14:16 3563b
field but you will gather in **l**, Dt 28:38 4592
your **l** ones, your wives, and the Dt 29:11 2945
"Your wives, your **l** ones, Jos 1:14 2945
with the women and the **l** ones and Jos 8:35 2945
"Please give me a **l** water to drink, Jg 4:19 4592
and put the **l** ones and the Jg 18:21 2945
with the women and the **l** ones. Jg 21:10 2945
in the house for a **l** while." Ru 2:7 4592
his mother would make him a **l** robe 1Sa 2:19 6996b
I tasted a **l** of this honey. 1Sa 14:29 4592
"I indeed tasted a **l** honey with 1Sa 14:43 4592
you were **l** in your own eyes, 1Sa 15:17 6996b
David, and a **l** lad *was* with him. 1Sa 20:35 6996b
had nothing except one **l** ewe lamb 2Sa 12:3 6996a
and if *that had been* too **l**, 2Sa 12:8 4592
all the **l** ones who *were* with him. 2Sa 15:22 2945
had passed a **l** beyond the summit, 2Sa 16:1 4592
David, yet I am but a **l** child; 1Ki 3:7 6996b
'My **l** finger is thicker than my 1Ki 12:10 6995
"Please get me a **l** water in a 1Ki 17:10 4592
the bowl and a **l** oil in the jar; 1Ki 17:12 4592
me a **l** bread cake from it first and 1Ki 17:13 6996a
In a **l** while the sky grew black 1Ki 18:45 5704, 3541
them like two **l** flocks of goats, 1Ki 20:27 2835
us make a **l** walled upper chamber 2Ki 4:10 6996a
a **l** girl from the land of Israel; 2Ki 5:2 6996a
like the flesh of a **l** child and 2Ki 5:14 6996b
l ones you will dash in pieces, 2Ki 8:12 5768
"Ahab served Baal a **l**; 2Ki 10:18 4592
'My **l** finger is thicker than my 2Ch 10:10 6995
included all their **l** children, 2Ch 31:18 2945
a safe journey for us, our **l** ones, Ezr 8:21 2945
us a **l** reviving in our bondage. Ezr 9:8 4592
from me that I may have a **l** cheer Jb 10:20 4592
forth their **l** ones like the flock, Jb 21:11 5759
"They are exalted a **l** while, Jb 24:24 4592
"Wait for me a **l**, and I will show Jb 36:2 2191
have made him a **l** lower than God, Ps 8:5 4592
Yet a **l** while and the wicked man Ps 37:10 4592
Better is the **l** of the righteous Ps 37:16 4592
your **l** ones Against the rock. Ps 137:9 5768
"A **l** sleep, a little slumber, A Pr 6:10 4592
"A little sleep, a **l** slumber, Pr 6:10 4592
A **l** folding of the hands to Pr 6:10 4592
heart of the wicked is *worth* **l**. Pr 10:20 4592

is a **l** with the fear of the LORD Than **Pr 15:16** 4592
Better is a **l** with righteousness **Pr 16:8** 4592
"A **l** sleep, a little slumber, A **Pr 24:33** 4592
"A little sleep, a **l** slumber, **Pr 24:33** 4592
A **l** folding of the hands to **Pr 24:33** 4592
whether he eats **l** or much; **Ec 5:12** 4592
so a **l** foolishness is weightier **Ec 10:1** 4592
The **l** foxes that are ruining the **SS 2:15** 6996a
"We have a **l** sister, And she has **SS 8:8** 6996a
"For in a very **l** while My **Is 10:25** 4592
And a **l** boy will lead them. **Is 11:6** 6996b
Their **l** ones also will be dashed **Is 13:16** 5768
Hide for a **l** while Until **Is 26:20** 4592
on line, line on line, A **l** here, **Is 28:10** 2191
A little here, a **l** there.' " **Is 28:10** 2191
on line, line on line, A **l** here, **Is 28:13** 2191
line, A little here, a **l** there," **Is 28:13** 2191
Is it not yet just a **l** while **Is 29:17** 4592
Your sanctuary for a **l** while, **Is 63:18** 4705
Her **l** ones have sounded out a cry **Jer 48:4** 6810
off, *even* the **l** ones of the flock; **Jer 49:20** 6810
off, *even* the **l** ones of the flock; **Jer 50:45** 6810
Yet in a **l** while the time of **Jer 51:33** 4592
Her **l** ones have gone away As **La 1:5** 5768
When **l** ones and infants faint In **La 2:11** 5768
For the life of your **l** ones Who are **La 2:19** 5768
The **l** ones who were born healthy? **La 2:20** 5768
The **l** ones ask for bread, *But* no **La 4:4** 5768
young men, maidens, **l** children, **Ezk 9:6** 2945
I was a sanctuary for them a **l** while **Ezk 11:16** 4592
but, as if that were too **l**, **Ezk 16:47** 4592
behold, another horn, a **l** one, **Da 7:8** 2192
they will be granted a **l** help, **Da 11:34** 4592
for yet a **l** while, and I will **Hos 1:4** 4592
l ones will be dashed in pieces, **Hos 13:16** 5768
Too **l** to be among the clans of **Mi 5:2** 6810
"You have sown much, but harvest **l**; **Hg 1:6** 4592
much, but behold, *it comes* to **l**; **Hg 1:9** 4592
'Once more in a **l** while, I am **Hg 2:6** 4592
for while I was only a **l** angry, **Zch 1:15** 4592
turn My hand against the **l** ones. **Zch 13:7** 6819
clothe you? You of **l** faith! **Mt 6:30** *3640b*
you afraid, you men of **l** faith?" **Mt 8:26** *3640b*
disciple gives to one of these **l** ones **Mt 10:42** *3398*
"You of **l** faith, why did you **Mt 14:31** *3640b*
"You men of **l** faith, why do you **Mt 16:8** *3640b*
whoever causes one of these **l** ones **Mt 18:6** *3398*
not despise one of these **l** ones, **Mt 18:10** *3398*
that one of these **l** ones perish. **Mt 18:14** *3398*
And He went a **l** beyond *them*, and **Mt 26:39** *3398*
A **l** later the bystanders came **Mt 26:73** *3398*
Going on a **l** farther, He saw **Mk 1:19** *3641*
"My **l** daughter is at the point of **Mk 5:23** *2365*
"**L** girl, I say to you, get up!"). **Mk 5:41** *2877*
a woman whose **l** daughter had an **Mk 7:25** *2365*
Whoever causes one of these **l** ones **Mk 9:42** *3398*
And He went a **l** beyond *them*, and **Mk 14:35** *3398*
And after a **l** while the bystanders **Mk 14:70** *3398*
to put out a **l** way from the land. **Lk 5:3** *3641*
but he who is forgiven **l**, **Lk 7:47** *3641*
who is forgiven little, loves **l**." **Lk 7:47** *3641*
you cannot do even a very **l** thing, **Lk 12:26** *1646*
He clothe you? You men of **l** faith! **Lk 12:28** *3640b*
"Do not be afraid, **l** flock, **Lk 12:32** *3398*
"He who is faithful in a very **l** thing **Lk 16:10** *1646*
who is unrighteous in a very **l** thing **Lk 16:10** *1646*
one of these **l** ones to stumble. **Lk 17:2** *3398*
been faithful in a very **l** thing, **Lk 19:17** *1646*
A **l** later, another saw him and **Lk 22:58** *1024*
for everyone to receive a **l**." **Jn 6:7** *1024*
a **l** while longer I am with you, **Jn 7:33** *3398*
"For a **l** while longer the Light **Jn 12:35** *3398*
"**L** children, I am with you a **Jn 13:33** *5040*
I am with you a **l** while longer. **Jn 13:33** *3398*
"After a **l** while the world will **Jn 14:19** *3398*
"A **l** while, and you will no **Jn 16:16** *3398*
and again a **l** while, and you will **Jn 16:16** *3398*
'A **l** while, and you will not **Jn 16:17** *3398*
and again a **l** while, and you will **Jn 16:17** *3398*
is this that He says, 'A **l** while'? **Jn 16:18** *3398*
'A **l** while, and you will not **Jn 16:19** *3398*
see Me, and again a **l** while, **Jn 16:19** *3398*
disciples came in the **l** boat, **Jn 21:8** *4142*
no **l** business to the craftsmen; **Ac 19:24** *3641*
and a **l** farther on they took **Ac 27:28** *1024*
a **l** leaven leavens the whole lump **1Co 5:6** *3398*
HE WHO *gathered* **L** HAD NO LACK." **2Co 8:15** *3641*
bear with me in a **l** foolishness; **2Co 11:1** *3398*
that I also may boast a **l**. **2Co 11:16** *3398*
A **l** leaven leavens the whole lump **Ga 5:9** *3398*
discipline is only of **l** profit, **1Tm 4:8** *3641*
but use a **l** wine for the sake of **1Tm 5:23** *3641*
YOU HAVE MADE HIM FOR A **L** WHILE **Heb 2:7** *1024*
who was made for a **l** while **Heb 2:9** *1024*
FOR YET IN A VERY **L** WHILE, **Heb 10:37** *3398*
a vapor that appears for a **l** while **Jas 4:14** *3641*
even though now for a **l** while, **1Pe 1:6** *3641*
you have suffered for a **l** while, **1Pe 5:10** *3641*
My **l** children, I am writing these **1Jn 2:1** *5040*
I am writing to you, **l** children, **1Jn 2:12** *5040*
Now, **l** children, abide in Him, **1Jn 2:28** *5040*
L children, make sure no one deceives **1Jn 3:7** *5040*
L children, let us not love with **1Jn 3:18** *5040*
You are from God, **l** children, **1Jn 4:4** *5040*
L children, guard yourselves from **1Jn 5:21** *5040*
shut, because you have a **l** power, **Rv 3:8** *3398*
should rest for a **l** while longer, **Rv 6:11** *3398*
his hand a **l** book which was open. **Rv 10:2** *974*
telling him to give me the **l** book. **Rv 10:9** *974*
I took the **l** book out of the **Rv 10:10** *974*
comes, he must remain a **l** while. **Rv 17:10** *3641*

LITTLENESS

"Because of the **l** of your faith; **Mt 17:20** *3640a*

LIVE

of life, and eat, and **l** forever" **Gn 3:22** 2421a
kill me, but they will let you **l**. **Gn 12:12** 2421a
that I may **l** on account of you." **Gn 12:13** 2421a
And he will **l** to the east of all **Gn 16:12** 7931
Ishmael might **l** before You!" **Gn 17:18** 2421a
will pray for you and you will **l**. **Gn 20:7** 2421a
of the Canaanites, among whom I **l**, **Gn 24:3** 3427
the Canaanites, in whose land I **l**; **Gn 24:37** 3427
"By your sword you shall **l**, **Gn 27:40** 2421a
you find your gods shall not **l**; **Gn 31:32** 2421a
"Thus you shall **l** with us, and **Gn 34:10** 3427
l and trade in it and acquire **Gn 34:10** 3427
and we will **l** with you and become **Gn 34:16** 3427
l in the land and trade in it, **Gn 34:21** 3427
men consent to us to **l** with us, **Gn 34:22** 3427
them, and they will **l** with us." **Gn 34:23** 3427
go up to Bethel and **l** there **Gn 35:1** 3427
too great for them to **l** together, **Gn 36:7** 3427
so that we may **l** and not die." **Gn 42:2** 2421a
"Do this and **l**, for I fear God: **Gn 42:18** 2421a
and go, that we may **l** and not die, **Gn 43:8** 2421a
You shall **l** in the land of Goshen, **Gn 45:10** 3427
you may **l** in the land of Goshen; **Gn 46:34** 3427
l in the land of Goshen." **Gn 47:4** 3427
let them **l** in the land of Goshen; **Gn 47:6** 3427
seed, that we may **l** and not die, **Gn 47:19** 2421a
And may my name **l** on in them, And **Gn 48:16** 7121
is a daughter, then she shall **l**." **Ex 1:16** 2421a
them, but let the boys **l**. **Ex 1:17** 2421a
this thing, and let the boys **l**?" **Ex 1:18** 2421a
for you on the houses where you **l**; **Ex 12:13**
beast or man, he shall not **l**.' **Ex 19:13** 2421a
then they shall sell the **l** ox and **Ex 21:35** 2416a
shall not allow a sorceress to **l**. **Ex 22:18** 2421a
"They shall not **l** in your land, **Ex 23:33** 3427
for no man can see Me and **l**!" **Ex 33:20** 2421a
all the people among whom you **l** **Ex 34:10**
He shall **l** alone; **Lv 13:46** 3427
give orders to take two **l** clean birds **Lv 14:4** 2416a
"*As for* the **l** bird, he shall take **Lv 14:6** 2416a
and shall dip them and the **l** bird **Lv 14:6** 2416a
and shall let the **l** bird go free **Lv 14:7** 2416a
scarlet string, with the **l** bird, **Lv 14:51** 2416a
along with the **l** bird and with the **Lv 14:52** 2416a
he shall let the **l** bird go free **Lv 14:53** 2416a
altar, he shall offer the **l** goat. **Lv 16:20** 2416a
hands on the head of the **l** goat, **Lv 16:21** 2416a
to **l** in accord with them; **Lv 18:4** 1980
which a man may **l** if he does them; **Lv 18:5** 2421a
to which I am bringing you to **l** **Lv 20:22** 3427
shall **l** in booths for seven days; **Lv 23:42** 3427
in Israel shall **l** in booths, **Lv 23:42** 3427
I had the sons of Israel **l** in booths **Lv 23:43** 3427
those who **l** as aliens with you. **Lv 25:6** 1481a
you may **l** securely on the land. **Lv 25:18** 3427
your fill and **l** securely on it. **Lv 25:19** 3427
sojourner, that he may **l** with you. **Lv 25:35** 2421a
your countryman may **l** with you. **Lv 25:36** 2421a
sons of the sojourners who **l** as aliens **Lv 25:45** 1481a
full and **l** securely in your land. **Lv 26:5** 3427
that they may **l** and not die when **Nu 4:19** 2421a
who **l** in it are strong *or* weak, **Nu 13:18** 3427
How is the land in which they **l**, **Nu 13:19** 3427
are the cities in which they **l**, **Nu 13:19** 3427
people who **l** in the land are strong, **Nu 13:28** 3427
but indeed, as I **l**, **Nu 14:21** 2416a
the Canaanites **l** in the valleys; **Nu 14:25** 3427
'As I **l**,' says the LORD, **Nu 14:28** 2416a
enter the land where you are to **l**, **Nu 15:2** 4186
when he looks at it, he will **l**." **Nu 21:8** 2421a
you just now, and let her **l**." **Nu 22:33** 2421a
who can **l** except God has ordained **Nu 24:23** 2421a
while our little ones **l** in the **Nu 32:17** 3427
of the land and **l** in it, **Nu 33:53** 3427
you in the land in which you **l**. **Nu 33:55** 3427
their possession cities to **l** in; **Nu 35:2** 3427
cities shall be theirs to **l** in; **Nu 35:3** 3427
and he shall **l** in it until the **Nu 35:25** 3427
that he may return to **l** in the **Nu 35:32** 3427
defile the land in which you **l**, **Nu 35:34** 3427
the sons of Esau who **l** in Seir; **Dt 2:4** 3427
the sons of Esau, who **l** in Seir, **Dt 2:8** 3427
the sons of Esau, who **l** in Seir, **Dt 2:22** 3427
as the sons of Esau who **l** in Seir **Dt 2:29** 3427
Moabites who **l** in Ar did for me, **Dt 2:29** 3427
so that you may **l** and go in **Dt 4:1** 2421a
all the days they **l** on the earth, **Dt 4:10** 2416a
You shall not **l** long on it, but **Dt 4:26** 748
and that you may **l** long on the **Dt 4:40** 748
to one of these cities he might **l**: **Dt 4:42** 2421a
commanded you, that you may **l** **Dt 5:33** 2421a
do, that you may **l** and multiply, **Dt 8:1** 2421a
man does not **l** by bread alone, **Dt 8:3** 2421a
Canaanites who **l** in the Arabah, **Dt 11:30** 3427
you shall possess it and **l** in it, **Dt 11:31** 3427
as long as you **l** on the earth. **Dt 12:1** 2416a
l in the land which the LORD your **Dt 12:10** 3427
you so that you **l** in security, **Dt 12:10** 3427
as long as you **l** in your land. **Dt 12:19** 3117
your God is giving you to **l** in, **Dt 13:12** 3427
that you may **l** and possess the **Dt 16:20** 2421a
and you possess it and **l** in it, **Dt 17:14** 3427
who may flee there and **l**: **Dt 19:4** 2421a
flee to one of these cities and **l**; **Dt 19:5** 2421a
"He shall **l** with you in your **Dt 23:16** 3427
"When brothers **l** together and one **Dt 25:5** 3427
and you possess it and **l** in it, **Dt 26:1** 3427
house, but you will not **l** in it; **Dt 28:30** 3427
soul, so that you may **l**. **Dt 30:6** 2425b
that you may **l** and multiply, **Dt 30:16** 2421a
life in order that you may **l**, **Dt 30:19** 2421a
that you may **l** in the land which **Dt 30:20** 3427
as long as you **l** on the land which **Dt 31:13** 2416a
heaven, And say, as I **l** forever, **Dt 32:40** 2416a
"May Reuben **l** and not die, Nor **Dt 33:6** 2421a
are with her in the house shall **l**, **Jos 6:17** 2421a
covenant with them, to let them **l**; **Jos 9:15** 2421a
will do to them, even let them **l**, **Jos 9:20** 2421a
leaders said to them, "Let them **l**." **Jos 9:21** 2421a
Amorites that **l** in the hill country **Jos 10:6** 3427
l among Israel until this day. **Jos 13:13** 3427
the land, except cities to **l** in, **Jos 14:4** 3427
Now behold, the LORD has let me **l**, **Jos 14:10** 2421a
so the Jebusites **l** with the sons **Jos 15:63** 3427
so the Canaanites **l** in the midst **Jos 16:10** 3427
Canaanites who **l** in the valley land **Jos 17:16** 3427
Moses to give us cities to **l** in, **Jos 21:2** 3427
the Amorites in whose land you **l**. **Jg 6:10** 3427
lives, if only you had let them **l**, **Jg 8:19** 2421a
Levite agreed to **l** with the man, **Jg 17:11** 3427
for themselves to **l** in, **Jg 18:1** 3427
"*Long* **l** the king!" **1Sa 10:24** 2421a
the country, that I may **l** there; **1Sa 27:5** 3427
l in the royal city with you?" **1Sa 27:5** 3427
could not **l** after he had fallen. **2Sa 1:10** 2421a
that they may **l** in their own place **2Sa 7:10** 7931
to me, that the child may **l**.' **2Sa 12:22** 2416a
said to Absalom, "*Long* **l** the king! **2Sa 16:16** 2421a
Long **l** the king!" **2Sa 16:16** 2421a
"How long have I yet to **l**, **2Sa 19:34** 2425b
'*Long* **l** King Adonijah!' **1Ki 1:25** 2421a
my lord King David **l** forever." **1Ki 1:31** 2421a
'*Long* **l** King Solomon!' **1Ki 1:34** 2421a
"*Long* **l** King Solomon!" **1Ki 1:39** 2421a
a house in Jerusalem and **l** there, **1Ki 2:36** 3427
woman and I **l** in the same house; **1Ki 3:17** 3427
His house where he was to **l**, **1Ki 7:8** 3427
all the days that they **l** in the land **1Ki 8:40** 2416a
'Please let me **l**.' " **1Ki 20:32** 2421a
LORD lives and as you yourself **l**, **2Ki 2:2** 2416a
LORD lives, and as you yourself **l**, **2Ki 2:4** 2416a
LORD lives, and as you yourself **l**, **2Ki 2:6** 2416a
and your sons can **l** on the rest." **2Ki 4:7** 2421a
"I **l** among my own people." **2Ki 4:13** 3427
LORD lives and as you yourself **l**, **2Ki 4:30** 2416a
for ourselves where we may **l**." **2Ki 6:2** 3427
If they spare us, we will **l**; **2Ki 7:4** 2421a
whoever is missing shall not **l**." **2Ki 10:19** 2421a
"*Long* **l** the king!" **2Ki 11:12** 2421a
exile and let him go and **l** there; **2Ki 17:27** 3427
that you may **l** and not die." **2Ki 18:32** 2421a
for you shall die and not **l**.' " **2Ki 20:1** 2421a
l in the land and serve the king **2Ki 25:24** 3427
l in the land which You have given **2Ch 6:31** 2416a
brethren who **l** in their cities, **2Ch 19:10** 3427
"*Long* **l** the king!" **2Ch 23:11** 2421a
at whatever place he may **l**, **Ezr 1:4** 1481a
their colleagues who **l** in Samaria **Ezr 4:17** 3488
"Let the king **l** forever. **Ne 2:3** 2421a
get grain that we may eat and **l**." **Ne 5:2** 2421a
the sons of Israel should **l** in booths **Ne 8:14** 3427
if a man observes them he shall **l**. **Ne 9:29** 2421a
one out of ten to **l** in Jerusalem, **Ne 11:1** 3427
who volunteered to **l** in Jerusalem. **Ne 11:2** 3427
golden scepter so that he may **l**. **Es 4:11** 2421a
areas, who **l** in the rural towns, **Es 9:19** 3427
I will not **l** forever. **Jb 7:16** 2421a
"If a man dies, will he **l** *again?* **Jb 14:14** 2421a
"Those who **l** in my house and my **Jb 19:15** 1481a
"Why do the wicked *still* **l**, **Jb 21:7** 2421a
Let your heart **l** forever! **Ps 22:26** 2421a
That he should **l** on eternally, **Ps 49:9** 2421a
will not **l** out half their days. **Ps 55:23** 2673
I will bless You as long as I **l**; **Ps 63:4** 2425b
So may he **l**, and may the gold of **Ps 72:15** 2421a
What man can **l** and not see death? **Ps 89:48** 2421a
sing to the LORD as long as I **l**; **Ps 104:33** 2425b
call *upon Him* as long as I **l**. **Ps 116:2** 3117
I will not die, but **l**, **Ps 118:17** 2421a
That I may **l** and keep Your word. **Ps 119:17** 2421a
come to me that I may **l**, **Ps 119:77** 2421a
to Your word, that I may **l**; **Ps 119:116** 2421a
me understanding that I may **l**. **Ps 119:144** 2421a
my soul **l** that it may praise You, **Ps 119:175** 2421a
I will praise the LORD while I **l**; **Ps 146:2** 2425b
listens to me shall **l** securely And **Pr 1:33** 7931
the upright will **l** in the land And **Pr 2:21** 7931
Keep my commandments and **l**; **Pr 4:4** 2421a
Keep my commandments and **l**, **Pr 7:2** 2421a
"Forsake *your* folly and **l**, **Pr 9:6** 2421a
But he who hates bribes will **l**. **Pr 15:27** 2421a
better to **l** in a corner of a roof Than **Pr 21:9** 3427
is better to **l** in a desert land Than **Pr 21:19** 3427
But **l** in the fear of the LORD **Pr 23:17**
It is better to **l** in a corner of **Pr 25:24** 3427
surely a **l** dog is better than a **Ec 9:4** 2416a
if a man should **l** many years, **Ec 11:8** 2421a
So that you have to **l** alone in the **Is 5:8** 3427
And I **l** among a people of unclean **Is 6:5** 3427
Those who **l** in a dark land, The **Is 9:2** 3427
owls; Ostriches also will **l** there, **Is 13:21** 7931
those who **l** in it are held guilty. **Is 24:6** 3427

The dead will not **l**,	**Is 26:14**	2421a
Your dead will **l**;	**Is 26:19**	2421a
will **l** in a peaceful habitation,	**Is 32:18**	3427
us can **l** with the consuming fire?	**Is 33:14**	1481a
us can **l** with continual burning?"	**Is 33:14**	1481a
for you shall die and not **l**.' "	**Is 38:1**	2421a
"O Lord, by *these* things *men* **l**,	**Is 38:16**	2421a
me to health and let me **l**!	**Is 38:16**	2421a
As I **l**," declares the LORD, "You	**Is 49:18**	2416a
room for me that I may **l** *here*.'	**Is 49:20**	3427
Listen, that you may **l**;	**Is 55:3**	2421a
man who does not **l** out his days;	**Is 65:20**	4390
But will **l** in stony wastes in the	**Jer 17:6**	7931
and all who **l** in your house will	**Jer 20:6**	3427
who are besieging you will **l**,	**Jer 21:9**	2421a
"As I **l**," declares the LORD, "even	**Jer 22:24**	2416a
they will **l** on their own soil."	**Jer 23:8**	3427
serve him and his people, and **l**!	**Jer 27:12**	2421a
serve the king of Babylon, and **l**!	**Jer 27:17**	2421a
'Build houses and **l** *in them;*	**Jer 29:5**	3427
build houses and **l** *in them* and	**Jer 29:28**	3427
that you may **l** many days in the	**Jer 35:7**	2421a
will **l** and have his *own* life as booty	**Jer 38:2**	2421a
king of Babylon, then you will **l**,	**Jer 38:17**	2421a
go well with you and you may **l**.	**Jer 38:20**	2421a
and **l** in your cities that you have	**Jer 40:10**	3427
those who **l** in the land of Egypt,	**Jer 44:13**	3427
they are longing to return and **l**;	**Jer 44:14**	3427
"As I **l**," declares the King	**Jer 46:18**	2416a
The city and those who **l** in it;	**Jer 47:2**	3427
"Mourn for him, all you who **l**	**Jer 48:17**	3427
who **l** in the clefts of the rock,	**Jer 49:16**	7931
"no one will **l** there, nor will a	**Jer 49:18**	3427
No one will **l** there, Nor will a	**Jer 49:33**	3427
the desert creatures will **l** *there*	**Jer 50:39**	3427
The ostriches also will **l** in it,	**Jer 50:39**	3427
"No man will **l** there, Nor will	**Jer 50:40**	3427
We shall **l** among the nations."	**La 4:20**	2421a
from his wicked way that he may **l**,	**Ezk 3:18**	2421a
he shall surely **l** because he took	**Ezk 3:21**	2421a
'So as I **l**,' declares the Lord	**Ezk 5:11**	2416a
he sold as long as they *both* **l**;	**Ezk 7:13**	2421b, 2425b
you **l** in the midst of the	**Ezk 12:2**	3427
the violence of all who **l** in it.	**Ezk 12:19**	3427
others alive who should not **l**,	**Ezk 13:19**	2421a
men were in its midst, as I **l**,"	**Ezk 14:16**	2416a
men were in its midst, as I **l**,"	**Ezk 14:18**	2416a
Job were in its midst, as I **l**,"	**Ezk 14:20**	2416a
while you were in your blood, '**L**!'	**Ezk 16:6**	2421a
while you were in your blood, '**L**!'	**Ezk 16:6**	2421a
"As I **l**," declares the Lord GOD,	**Ezk 16:48**	2416a
'As I **l**,' declares the Lord GOD,	**Ezk 17:16**	2416a
"As I **l**, surely My oath which he	**Ezk 17:19**	2416a
"As I **l**," declares the Lord GOD,	**Ezk 18:3**	2416a
is righteous *and* will surely **l**,"	**Ezk 18:9**	2421a
will he **l**? He will not live! He has	**Ezk 18:13**	2421a
He will not **l**! He has committed	**Ezk 18:13**	2421a
iniquity, he will surely **l**.	**Ezk 18:17**	2421a
and done them, he shall surely **l**.	**Ezk 18:19**	2421a
righteousness, he shall surely **l**;	**Ezk 18:21**	2421a
which he has practiced, he will **l**.	**Ezk 18:22**	2421a
should turn from his ways and **l**?	**Ezk 18:23**	2421a
that a wicked man does, will he **l**?	**Ezk 18:24**	2421a
had committed, he shall surely **l**;	**Ezk 18:28**	2421a
"Therefore, repent and **l**."	**Ezk 18:32**	2421a
"As I **l**," declares the Lord GOD,	**Ezk 20:3**	2416a
if a man observes them, he will **l**.	**Ezk 20:11**	2421a
if a man observes them, he will **l**;	**Ezk 20:13**	2421a
if a man observes them, he will **l**;	**Ezk 20:21**	2421a
by which they could not **l**;	**Ezk 20:25**	2421a
As I **l**," declares the Lord GOD,	**Ezk 20:31**	2416a
"As I **l**," declares the Lord GOD,	**Ezk 20:33**	2416a
then they will **l** in their land	**Ezk 28:25**	3427
"They will **l** in it securely;	**Ezk 28:26**	3427
plant vineyards and **l** securely	**Ezk 28:26**	3427
I smite all those who **l** in it,	**Ezk 32:15**	3427
'As I **l**!' declares the Lord GOD,	**Ezk 33:11**	2416a
wicked turn from his way and **l**.	**Ezk 33:11**	2421a
not be able to **l** by his righteousness	**Ezk 33:12**	2421a
to the righteous he will surely **l**,	**Ezk 33:13**	2421a
iniquity, he shall surely **l**;	**Ezk 33:15**	2421a
he shall surely **l**.	**Ezk 33:16**	2421a
righteousness, he will **l** by them.	**Ezk 33:19**	2421a
they who **l** in these waste places	**Ezk 33:24**	3427
"As I **l**, surely those who are in	**Ezk 33:27**	2416a
"As I **l**," declares the Lord GOD,	**Ezk 34:8**	2416a
so that they may **l** securely in the	**Ezk 34:25**	3427
but they will **l** securely, and no	**Ezk 34:28**	3427
therefore as I **l**,"	**Ezk 35:6**	2416a
therefore as I **l**,"	**Ezk 35:11**	2416a
"You will **l** in the land that	**Ezk 36:28**	3427
"Son of man, can these bones **l**?"	**Ezk 37:3**	2421a
"They will **l** on the land	**Ezk 37:25**	3427
and they will **l** on it, they, and	**Ezk 37:25**	3427
who are at rest, that **l** securely,	**Ezk 38:11**	3427
who **l** at the center of the world.'	**Ezk 38:12**	3427
when they **l** securely on their *own*	**Ezk 39:26**	3427
where the river goes, will **l**.	**Ezk 47:9**	2421a
so everything will **l** where the river	**Ezk 47:9**	2421a
"O king, **l** forever!	**Da 2:4**	2418
"O king, **l** forever!	**Da 3:9**	2418
language that **l** in all the earth:	**Da 4:1**	1753
"O king, **l** forever!	**Da 5:10**	2418
"King Darius, **l** forever!	**Da 6:6**	2418
"O king, **l** forever!	**Da 6:21**	2418
day, That we may **l** before Him.	**Hos 6:2**	2421a
I will make you **l** in tents again,	**Hos 12:9**	3427
Those who **l** in his shadow Will	**Hos 14:7**	3427
"Seek Me that you may **l**.	**Am 5:4**	2421a
"Seek the LORD that you may **l**,	**Am 5:6**	2421a
stone, Yet you will not **l** in them;	**Am 5:11**	3427
good and not evil, that you may **l**;	**Am 5:14**	2421a
the ruined cities and **l** *in them;*	**Am 9:14**	3427
who **l** in the clefts of the rock,	**Ob 1:3**	7931
the righteous will **l** by his faith.	**Hab 2:4**	2421a
"Therefore, as I **l**,"	**Zph 2:9**	2416a
the prophets, do they **l** forever?	**Zch 1:5**	2421a
will **l** in the midst of Jerusalem;	**Zch 8:8**	7931
children will **l** and come back.	**Zch 10:9**	2421a
'You shall not **l**, for you have	**Zch 13:3**	2421a
People will **l** in it, and there	**Zch 14:11**	3427
'MAN SHALL NOT **L** ON BREAD ALONE,	**Mt 4:4**	*2198*
hand on her, and she will **l**."	**Mt 9:18**	*2198*
and they go in and **l** there;	**Mt 12:45**	*2730*
that she will get well and **l**."	**Mk 5:23**	*2198*
she owned, all she had to **l** on."	**Mk 12:44**	*979*
SHALL NOT **L** ON BREAD ALONE.' "	**Lk 4:4**	*2198*
splendidly clothed and **l** in luxury	**Lk 7:25**	*5225*
DO THIS AND YOU WILL **L**."	**Lk 10:28**	*2198*
and they go in and **l** there;	**Lk 11:26**	*2730*
all the men who **l** in Jerusalem?	**Lk 13:4**	*2730*
yours was dead and *has begun* to **l**,	**Lk 15:32**	*2198*
for all **l** to Him."	**Lk 20:38**	*2198*
put in all that she had to **l** on."	**Lk 21:4**	*979*
and those who hear will **l**.	**Jn 5:25**	*2198*
of this bread, he will **l** forever;	**Jn 6:51**	*2198*
Me, and I **l** because of the Father,	**Jn 6:57**	*2198*
Me, he also will **l** because of Me.	**Jn 6:57**	*2198*
eats this bread will **l** forever."	**Jn 6:58**	*2198*
in Me will **l** even if he dies,	**Jn 11:25**	*2198*
because I **l**, you will live also.	**Jn 14:19**	*2198*
because I live, you will **l** also.	**Jn 14:19**	*2198*
and all you who **l** in Jerusalem,	**Ac 2:14**	*2730*
MY FLESH ALSO WILL **L** IN HOPE;	**Ac 2:26**	*2681*
to all who **l** in Jerusalem,	**Ac 4:16**	*2730*
"For those who **l** in Jerusalem,	**Ac 13:27**	*2730*
to **l** on all the face of the earth,	**Ac 17:26**	*2730*
in Him we **l** and move and exist,	**Ac 17:28**	*2198*
he should not be allowed to **l**!"	**Ac 22:22**	*2198*
that he ought not to **l** any longer.	**Ac 25:24**	*2198*
has not allowed him to **l**."	**Ac 28:4**	*2198*
RIGHTEOUS *man* SHALL **L** BY FAITH."	**Ro 1:17**	*2198*
we who died to sin still **l** in it?	**Ro 6:2**	*2198*
that we shall also **l** with Him,	**Ro 6:8**	*4800*
to **l** according to the flesh	**Ro 8:12**	*2198*
the deeds of the body, you will **l**.	**Ro 8:13**	*2198*
law shall **l** by that righteousness.	**Ro 10:5**	*2198*
for if we **l**, we live for the Lord,	**Ro 14:8**	*2198*
for if we live, we **l** for the Lord,	**Ro 14:8**	*2198*
therefore whether we **l** or die,	**Ro 14:8**	*2198*
"As I **L**, SAYS THE LORD, EVERY	**Ro 14:11**	*2198*
and she consents to **l** with him,	**1Co 7:12**	*3611*
and he consents to **l** with her,	**1Co 7:13**	*3611*
For we who **l** are constantly being	**2Co 4:11**	*2198*
that they who **l** might no longer	**2Co 5:15**	*2198*
might no longer **l** for themselves,	**2Co 5:15**	*2198*
as dying yet behold, we **l**;	**2Co 6:9**	*2198*
to die together and to **l** together.	**2Co 7:3**	*4800*
yet we will **l** with Him because of	**2Co 13:4**	*2198*
be like-minded, **l** in peace;	**2Co 13:11**	*1514*
l like the Gentiles and not like	**Ga 2:14**	*2198*
the Gentiles to **l** like Jews?	**Ga 2:14**	*2450*
to the Law, so that I might **l** to God.	**Ga 2:19**	*2198*
and it is no longer I who **l**,	**Ga 2:20**	*2198*
and the *life* which I now **l** in the	**Ga 2:20**	*2198*
I **l** by faith in the Son of God,	**Ga 2:20**	*2198*
RIGHTEOUS MAN SHALL **L** BY FAITH."	**Ga 3:11**	*2198*
PRACTICES THEM SHALL **L** BY THEM."	**Ga 3:12**	*2198*
If we **l** by the Spirit, let us also	**Ga 5:25**	*2198*
THAT YOU MAY **L** LONG ON THE EARTH.	**Eph 6:3**	*3118*
For to me, to **l** is Christ and to	**Php 1:21**	*2198*
But if *I am* to **l** *on* in the flesh,	**Php 1:22**	*2198*
to **l** in harmony in the Lord.	**Php 4:2**	*5426*
also know how to **l** in prosperity;	**Php 4:12**	*4052*
for now we *really* **l**,	**1Th 3:8**	*2198*
we will **l** together with Him.	**1Th 5:10**	*2198*
L in peace with one another.	**1Th 5:13**	*1514*
Him, we will also **l** with Him;	**2Tm 2:11**	*4800*
all who desire to **l** godly in Christ	**2Tm 3:12**	*2198*
worldly desires and to **l** sensibly,	**Ti 2:12**	*2198*
MY RIGHTEOUS ONE SHALL **L** BY FAITH;	**Heb 10:38**	*2198*
to the Father of spirits, and **l**?	**Heb 12:9**	*2198*
"If the Lord wills, we will **l** and	**Jas 4:15**	*2198*
die to sin and **l** to righteousness;	**1Pe 2:24**	*2198*
l with *your wives* in an	**1Pe 3:7**	*4924b*
so as to **l** the rest of the time in	**1Pe 4:2**	*980*
they may **l** in the spirit according	**1Pe 4:6**	*2198*
who would **l** ungodly	**2Pe 2:6**	*764*
from the ones who **l** in error,	**2Pe 2:18**	*390*
so that we might **l** through Him.	**1Jn 4:9**	*2198*
to those who **l** on the earth,	**Rv 14:6**	*2521*

LIVED

When Adam had **l** one hundred and	**Gn 5:3**	2421a
So all the days that Adam **l** were	**Gn 5:5**	2421a
Seth **l** one hundred and five years,	**Gn 5:6**	2421a
Then Seth **l** eight hundred and	**Gn 5:7**	2421a
Enosh **l** ninety years, and	**Gn 5:9**	2421a
Then Enosh **l** eight hundred and	**Gn 5:10**	2421a
Kenan **l** seventy years, and	**Gn 5:12**	2421a
Then Kenan **l** eight hundred and	**Gn 5:13**	2421a
Mahalalel **l** sixty-five years,	**Gn 5:15**	2421a
Then Mahalalel **l** eight hundred and	**Gn 5:16**	2421a
Jared **l** one hundred and	**Gn 5:18**	2421a
Then Jared **l** eight hundred years	**Gn 5:19**	2421a
Enoch **l** sixty-five years, and	**Gn 5:21**	2421a
Methuselah **l** one hundred and	**Gn 5:25**	2421a
Then Methuselah **l** seven hundred	**Gn 5:26**	2421a
Lamech **l** one hundred and	**Gn 5:28**	2421a
Then Lamech **l** five hundred and	**Gn 5:30**	2421a
Noah **l** three hundred and fifty	**Gn 9:28**	2421a
and Shem **l** five hundred years	**Gn 11:11**	2421a
Arpachshad **l** thirty-five	**Gn 11:12**	2421a
and Arpachshad **l** four hundred and	**Gn 11:13**	2421a
Shelah **l** thirty years, and	**Gn 11:14**	2421a
and Shelah **l** four hundred and	**Gn 11:15**	2421a
Eber **l** thirty-four years, and	**Gn 11:16**	2421a
and Eber **l** four hundred and thirty	**Gn 11:17**	2421a
Peleg **l** thirty years, and	**Gn 11:18**	2421a
and Peleg **l** two hundred and nine	**Gn 11:19**	2421a
Reu **l** thirty-two years, and	**Gn 11:20**	2421a
and Reu **l** two hundred and seven	**Gn 11:21**	2421a
Serug **l** thirty years, and	**Gn 11:22**	2421a
and Serug **l** two hundred years	**Gn 11:23**	2421a
Nahor **l** twenty-nine years, and	**Gn 11:24**	2421a
and Nahor **l** one hundred and	**Gn 11:25**	2421a
Terah **l** seventy years, and	**Gn 11:26**	2421a
Amorites, who **l** in Hazazon-tamar.	**Gn 14:7**	3427
After Abram had **l** ten years in	**Gn 16:3**	3427
the cities in which Lot **l**.	**Gn 19:29**	3427
and he **l** in the wilderness and	**Gn 21:20**	3427
He **l** in the wilderness of Paran	**Gn 21:21**	3427
and Abraham **l** at Beersheba.	**Gn 22:19**	3427
Now Sarah **l** one hundred and	**Gn 23:1**	2425b, 1961
years of Abraham's life that he **l**,	**Gn 25:7**	2421a
and Isaac **l** by Beer-lahai-roi.	**Gn 25:11**	3427
So Isaac **l** in Gerar.	**Gn 26:6**	3427
l in the hill country of Seir;	**Gn 36:8**	3427
Now Jacob **l** in the land where his	**Gn 37:1**	3427
went and **l** in her father's house.	**Gn 38:11**	3427
"How many years have you **l**?"	**Gn 47:8**	2425b
attained the years that my fathers **l**	**Gn 47:9**	2425b
and they **l** off the allotment which	**Gn 47:22**	398
Now Israel **l** in the land of Egypt,	**Gn 47:27**	3427
Jacob **l** in the land of Egypt	**Gn 47:28**	2421a
Joseph **l** one hundred and ten years.	**Gn 50:22**	2421a
the sons of Israel **l** in Egypt was	**Ex 12:40**	3427
in the land of Egypt where you **l**,	**Lv 18:3**	3427
Canaanites who **l** in that hill country	**Nu 14:45**	3427
king of Arad, who **l** in the Negev,	**Nu 21:1**	3427
to the bronze serpent, he **l**.	**Nu 21:9**	2421a
and Israel **l** in all the cities of the	**Nu 21:25**	3427
l in the land of the Amorites.	**Nu 21:31**	3427
the Amorites, who **l** at Heshbon."	**Nu 21:34**	3427
l and all their camps with fire.	**Nu 31:10**	4186
son of Manasseh, and he **l** in it.	**Nu 32:40**	3427
the king of Arad who **l** in the	**Nu 33:40**	3427
of the Amorites, who **l** in Heshbon,	**Dt 1:4**	3427
who **l** in Ashtaroth and Edrei.	**Dt 1:4**	3427
"The Amorites who **l** in that	**Dt 1:44**	3427
(The Emim **l** there formerly, a	**Dt 2:10**	3427
The Horites formerly **l** in Seir,	**Dt 2:12**	3427
for Rephaim formerly **l** in it,	**Dt 2:20**	3427
who **l** in villages as far as Gaza,	**Dt 2:23**	3427
them and **l** in their place.)	**Dt 2:23**	3427
the Amorites, who **l** at Heshbon.'	**Dt 3:2**	3427
of the Amorites who **l** at Heshbon,	**Dt 4:46**	3427
of the fire, as we *have*, and **l**?	**Dt 5:26**	2421a
built good houses and **l** *in them,*	**Dt 8:12**	3427
how we **l** in the land of Egypt,	**Dt 29:16**	3427
and she has **l** in the midst of	**Jos 6:25**	3427
of the Amorites, who **l** in Heshbon,	**Jos 12:2**	3427
who **l** at Ashtaroth and at Edrei,	**Jos 12:4**	3427
of Sihon, who **l** in the land.	**Jos 13:21**	3427
out the Canaanites who **l** in Gezer,	**Jos 16:10**	3427
and they possessed it and **l** in it.	**Jos 21:43**	3427
your fathers **l** beyond the River,	**Jos 24:2**	3427
And you **l** in the wilderness for a	**Jos 24:7**	3427
Amorites who **l** beyond the Jordan,	**Jos 24:8**	3427
not built, and you have **l** in them;	**Jos 24:13**	3427
the Amorites who **l** in the land.	**Jos 24:18**	3427
the Canaanites who **l** in Hebron	**Jg 1:10**	3427
they went and **l** with the people.	**Jg 1:16**	3427
the Jebusites who **l** in Jerusalem;	**Jg 1:21**	3427
so the Jebusites have **l** with the	**Jg 1:21**	3427
Canaanites **l** in Gezer among them.	**Jg 1:29**	3427
so the Canaanites **l** among them and	**Jg 1:30**	3427
Asherites **l** among the Canaanites,	**Jg 1:32**	3427
but **l** among the Canaanites,	**Jg 1:33**	3427
Hivites who **l** in Mount Lebanon,	**Jg 3:3**	3427
of Israel **l** among the Canaanites,	**Jg 3:5**	3427
Sisera, who **l** in Harosheth-hagoyim.	**Jg 4:2**	3427
those who **l** in tents on the east of	**Jg 8:11**	7931
Joash went and **l** in his own house.	**Jg 8:29**	3427
and he **l** in Shamir in the hill	**Jg 10:1**	3427
brothers and **l** in the land of Tob;	**Jg 11:3**	3427
l in Heshbon and its villages,	**Jg 11:26**	3427
l in the cleft of the rock of Etam.	**Jg 15:8**	3427
and **l** in the house of Micah.	**Jg 17:12**	1961
they rebuilt the city and **l** in it.	**Jg 18:28**	3427
rebuilt the cities and **l** in them.	**Jg 21:23**	3427
And they **l** there about ten years.	**Ru 1:4**	3427
And she **l** with her mother-in-law.	**Ru 2:23**	3427
around, so that you **l** in security.	**1Sa 12:11**	3427
And David **l** with Achish at Gath,	**1Sa 27:3**	3427
days that David **l** in the country of	**1Sa 27:7**	3427
l in the country of the Philistines.' "	**1Sa 27:11**	3427
Philistines came and **l** in them.	**1Sa 31:7**	3427
they **l** in the cities of Hebron.	**2Sa 2:3**	3427
So David **l** in the stronghold and	**2Sa 5:9**	3427
when the king **l** in his house,	**2Sa 7:1**	3427
And all who **l** in the house of Ziba	**2Sa 9:12**	4186
So Mephibosheth **l** in Jerusalem,	**2Sa 9:13**	3427
l two full years in Jerusalem,	**2Sa 14:28**	3427
Shimei **l** in Jerusalem many days.	**1Ki 2:38**	3427
So Judah and Israel **l** in safety,	**1Ki 4:25**	3427

the Canaanites who **l** in the city, **1Ki 9:16** 3427
who **l** in the cities of Judah, **1Ki 12:17** 3427
country of Ephraim, and **l** there. **1Ki 12:25** 3427
the city where the old prophet **l**. **1Ki 13:25** 3427
king of Aram, who **l** in Damascus, **1Ki 15:18** 3427
went and **l** by the brook Cherith, **1Ki 17:5** 3427
and the nobles who **l** in his city, **1Ki 21:11** 3427
l in their tents as formerly. **2Ki 13:5** 3427
king of Judah **l** fifteen years after **2Ki 14:17** 2421a
And he **l** in a separate house, **2Ki 15:5** 3427
and have **l** there to this day. **2Ki 16:6** 3427
Samaria and **l** in its cities. **2Ki 17:24** 3427
from Samaria came and **l** at Bethel, **2Ki 17:28** 3427
in their cities in which they **l**. **2Ki 17:29** 3427
returned *home*, and **l** at Nineveh. **2Ki 19:36** 3427
she **l** in Jerusalem in the Second **2Ki 22:14** 3427
families of scribes who **l** at Jabez **1Ch 2:55** 3427
they **l** there with the king for his **1Ch 4:23** 3427
They **l** at Beersheba, Moladah and **1Ch 4:28** 3427
who **l** there formerly *were* Hamites. **1Ch 4:40** 3427
to this day, and **l** in their place, **1Ch 4:41** 3427
and have **l** there to this day. **1Ch 4:43** 3427
the son of Joel, who **l** in Aroer, **1Ch 5:8** 3427
Now the sons of Gad **l** opposite **1Ch 5:11** 3427
They **l** in Gilead, in Bashan **1Ch 5:16** 3427
half-tribe of Manasseh **l** in the land; **1Ch 5:23** 3427
In these **l** the sons of Joseph the **1Ch 7:29** 3427
chief men who **l** in Jerusalem. **1Ch 8:28** 3427
Jeiel, the father of Gibeon **l**, **1Ch 8:29** 3427
And they also **l** with their relatives **1Ch 8:32** 3427
the first who **l** in their possessions **1Ch 9:2** 3427
and Manasseh **l** in Jerusalem: **1Ch 9:3** 3427
who **l** in the villages of the **1Ch 9:16** 3427
who **l** in the chambers *of* **1Ch 9:33**
chief men, who **l** in Jerusalem. **1Ch 9:34** 3427
Jeiel the father of Gibeon **l**, **1Ch 9:35** 3427
And they also **l** with their relatives **1Ch 9:38** 3427
Philistines came and **l** in them. **1Ch 10:7** 3427
who **l** in the cities of Judah, **2Ch 10:17** 3427
Rehoboam **l** in Jerusalem and built **2Ch 11:5** 3427
king of Aram, who **l** in Damascus, **2Ch 16:2** 3427
So Jehoshaphat **l** in Jerusalem and **2Ch 19:4** 3427
"They have **l** in it, and have built **2Ch 20:8** 3427
l fifteen years after the death of **2Ch 25:25** 2421a
the Arabians who **l** in Gur-baal, **2Ch 26:7** 3427
and he **l** in a separate house, **2Ch 26:21** 3427
he commanded the people who **l** in **2Ch 31:4** 3427
who **l** in the cities of Judah also **2Ch 31:6** 3427
she **l** in Jerusalem in the Second **2Ch 34:22** 3427
temple servants **l** in their cities, **Ezr 2:70** 3427
the Jews who **l** near them came and **Ne 4:12** 3427
and all Israel, **l** in their cities. **Ne 7:73** 3427
made booths and **l** in them. **Ne 8:17** 3427
of the people **l** in Jerusalem, **Ne 11:1** 3427
the provinces who **l** in Jerusalem, **Ne 11:3** 3427
l on his own property in their cities **Ne 11:3** 3427
sons of Benjamin **l** in Jerusalem. **Ne 11:4** 3427
All the sons of Perez who **l** in **Ne 11:6** 3427
l in Kiriath-arba and its towns, **Ne 11:25** 3427
The sons of Benjamin also **l** from **Ne 11:31** 3427
"He has **l** in desolate cities, **Jb 15:28** 7931
After this, Job **l** 140 years, **Jb 42:16** 2421a
It will never be inhabited or **l** in **Is 13:20** 7931
returned *home* and **l** at Nineveh. **Is 37:37** 3427
Then I came to the exiles who **l** **Ezk 3:15** 3427
of the nations among whom they **l**, **Ezk 20:9**
great nations **l** under its shade. **Ezk 31:6** 3427
those who were its strength **l** under **Ezk 31:17** 3427
servant, in which your fathers **l**; **Ezk 37:25** 3427
and came and **l** in a city called **Mt 2:23** *2730*
and he **l** in the deserts until the **Lk 1:80** *1510*
and had **l** with *her* husband seven **Lk 2:36** *2198*
Mesopotamia, before he **l** in Haran, **Ac 7:2** *2730*
and confounding the Jews who **l** at **Ac 9:22** *2730*
also to the saints who **l** at Lydda. **Ac 9:32** *2730*
who **l** at Lydda and Sharon saw him, **Ac 9:35** *2730*
so that all who **l** in Asia heard **Ac 19:10** *2730*
Jews and Greeks, who **l** in Ephesus; **Ac 19:17** *2730*
of by all the Jews who **l** there, **Ac 22:12** *2730*
I have **l** my life with a perfectly **Ac 23:1** *4176*
that I **l** *as* a Pharisee according **Ac 26:5** *2198*
this end Christ died and **l** again, **Ro 14:9** *2198*
l in the lusts of our flesh, **Eph 2:3** *390*
By faith he **l** as an alien in the **Heb 11:9** *3939*
You have **l** luxuriously on the **Jas 5:5** *5171*
herself and **l** sensuously, **Rv 18:7** *4763*
and **l** sensuously with her, **Rv 18:9** *4763*

LIVER

entrails and the lobe of the **l**, **Ex 29:13** 3516
entrails and the lobe of the **l**, **Ex 29:22** 3516
the loins, and the lobe of the **l**, **Lv 3:4** 3516
the loins, and the lobe of the **l**, **Lv 3:10** 3516
the loins, and the lobe of the **l**, **Lv 3:15** 3516
the loins, and the lobe of the **l**, **Lv 4:9** 3516
and the lobe on the **l** he shall **Lv 7:4** 3516
entrails and the lobe of the **l**, **Lv 8:16** 3516
and the lobe of the **l** and the two **Lv 8:25** 3516
lobe of the **l** of the sin offering, **Lv 9:10** 3516
the kidneys and the lobe of the **l**, **Lv 9:19** 3516
an arrow pierces through his **l**; **Pr 7:23** 3516
idols, he looks at the **l**. **Ezk 21:21** 3516

LIVES

"You have saved our **l**! **Gn 47:25** 2421a
and they made their **l** bitter with **Ex 1:14** 2425b
and the woman who **l** in her house, **Ex 3:22** 1481a
sinned at the cost of their **l**, **Nu 16:38** 5315
God speaks with man, yet he **l**. **Dt 5:24** 2421a
but man **l** by everything that **Dt 8:3** 2421a
and deliver our **l** from death." **Jos 2:13** 5315
greatly for our **l** because of you, **Jos 9:24** 5315
despised their **l** *even* to death, **Jg 5:18** 5315
As the LORD **l**, if only you had let **Jg 8:19** 2416a
with the **l** of your household." **Jg 18:25** 5315
I will redeem you, as the LORD **l**. **Ru 3:13** 2416a
As your soul **l**, my lord, I am the **1Sa 1:26** 2416a
as long as he **l** he is dedicated to **1Sa 1:28** 1961
"For as the LORD **l**, who delivers **1Sa 14:39** 2416a
As the LORD **l**, not one **1Sa 14:45** 2416a
"As the LORD **l**, he shall not be **1Sa 19:6** 2416a
as the LORD **l** and as your soul lives **1Sa 20:3** 2416a
the LORD lives and as your soul **l**, **1Sa 20:3** 2416a
you and no harm, as the LORD **l**. **1Sa 20:21** 2416a
the son of Jesse **l** on the earth, **1Sa 20:31** 2421a
therefore, my lord, as the LORD **l**, **1Sa 25:26** 2416a
LORD lives, and as your soul **l**, **1Sa 25:26** 2416a
but the **l** of your enemies He will **1Sa 25:29** 5315
as the LORD God of Israel **l**, **1Sa 25:34** 2416a
"As the LORD **l**, surely the LORD **1Sa 26:10** 2416a
As the LORD **l**, *all* of you must **1Sa 26:16** 2416a
"As the LORD **l**, no **1Sa 28:10** 2416a
"*As* the LORD **l**, you *have been* **1Sa 29:6** 2416a
"As God **l**, if you had not spoken, **2Sa 2:27** 2416a
"As the LORD **l**, who has redeemed **2Sa 4:9** 2416a
"As the LORD **l**, surely the man **2Sa 12:5** 2416a
"As the LORD **l**, not one hair of **2Sa 14:11** 2416a
"As your soul **l**, my lord the **2Sa 14:19** 2416a
"As the LORD **l**, and as my lord **2Sa 15:21** 2416a
lives, and as my lord the king **l**, **2Sa 15:21** 2416a
the **l** of your sons and daughters, **2Sa 19:5** 5315
daughters, the **l** of your wives, **2Sa 19:5** 5315
and the **l** of your concubines, **2Sa 19:5** 5315
"The LORD **l**, and blessed be my **2Sa 22:47** 2416a
who went in *jeopardy* of their **l**?" **2Sa 23:17** 5315
"As the LORD **l**, who has redeemed **1Ki 1:29** 2416a
"Now therefore, as the LORD **l**, **1Ki 2:24** 2416a
"As the LORD, the God of Israel **l**, **1Ki 17:1** 2416a
"As the LORD your God **l**, **1Ki 17:12** 2416a
"As the LORD your God **l**, **1Ki 18:10** 2416a
"As the LORD of hosts **l**, **1Ki 18:15** 2416a
"As the LORD **l**, what the LORD **1Ki 22:14** 2416a
the **l** of these fifty servants of yours **2Ki 1:13** 5315
"As the LORD **l** and as you yourself **2Ki 2:2** 2416a
"As the LORD **l**, and as you **2Ki 2:4** 2416a
"As the LORD **l**, and as you **2Ki 2:6** 2416a
"As the LORD of hosts **l**, **2Ki 3:14** 2416a
"As the LORD **l** and as you yourself **2Ki 4:30** 2416a
"As the LORD **l**, before whom I **2Ki 5:16** 2416a
As the LORD **l**, I will run after **2Ki 5:20** 2416a
who went at the risk of their **l**? **1Ch 11:19** 5315
risk of their **l** they brought it." **1Ch 11:19** 5315
"As the LORD **l**, what my God says, **2Ch 18:13** 2416a
to assemble and to defend their **l**, **Es 8:11** 5315
to defend their **l** and rid **Es 9:16** 5315
for me, I know that my Redeemer **l**, **Jb 19:25** 2416a
"As God **l**, who has taken away my **Jb 27:2** 2416a
caused its owners to lose their **l**, **Jb 31:39** 5315
The LORD **l**, and blessed be my rock; **Ps 18:46** 2416a
Though while he **l** he congratulates **Ps 49:18** 2425b
the **l** of the needy he will save. **Ps 72:13** 5315
They ambush their own **l**. **Pr 1:18** 5315
While he **l** securely beside you. **Pr 3:29** 3427
A truthful witness saves **l**, **Pr 14:25** 5315
heaven the few years of their **l**. **Ec 2:3** 2425b
hundred *children* and **l** many years, **Ec 6:3** 2421a
"Even if the *other* man **l** a **Ec 6:6** 2421a
preserves the **l** of its possessors. **Ec 7:12** 2421a
their hearts throughout their **l**. **Ec 9:3** 2425b
And He will kill the dragon who **l** **Is 27:1**
and exalted One Who **l** forever, **Is 57:15** 7931
will there be in it an infant *who* **l** **Is 65:20**
'As the LORD **l**,' In truth, in **Jer 4:2** 2416a
'As the LORD **l**,' Surely they swear **Jer 5:2** 2416a
'As the LORD **l**,' even as they **Jer 12:16** 2416a
'As the LORD **l**, who brought up the **Jer 16:14** 2416a
'As the LORD **l**, who brought up the **Jer 16:15** 2416a
hand of those who seek their **l**; **Jer 21:7** 5315
'As the LORD **l**, who brought up the **Jer 23:7** 2416a
'As the LORD **l**, who brought up and **Jer 23:8** 2416a
"As the LORD **l**, who made this **Jer 38:16** 2416a
are in ruins and no one **l** in them, **Jer 44:2** 3427
"As the Lord GOD **l**." **Jer 44:26** 2416a
of those who are seeking their **l**, **Jer 46:26** 5315
"Flee, save your **l**, That you may **Jer 48:6** 5315
is at ease, Which **l** securely," **Jer 49:31** 3427
And before those who seek their **l**; **Jer 49:37** 5315
desert, A land in which no man **l** And **Jer 51:43** 3427
To restore their **l** themselves. **La 1:11** 5315
get our bread at the risk of our **l** **La 5:9** 5315
of every stature to hunt down **l**! **Ezk 13:18** 5315
you hunt down the **l** of My people, **Ezk 13:18** 5315
preserve the **l** *of others* for yourselves **Ezk 13:18** 5315
which you hunt **l** there as birds and **Ezk 13:20** 5315
those **l** whom you hunt as birds. **Ezk 13:20** 5315
who **l** north of you with her **Ezk 16:46** 3427
sister, who **l** south of you, **Ezk 16:46** 3427
siege walls to cut off many **l**. **Ezk 17:17** 5315
They have devoured **l**; **Ezk 22:25** 5315
by shedding blood *and* destroying **l** **Ezk 22:27** 5315
with the **l** of men and vessels of **Ezk 27:13** 5315
and honored Him who **l** forever; **Da 4:34** 2417
and swore by Him who **l** forever **Da 12:7** 2416a
And everyone who **l** in it **Hos 4:3** 3427
take the oath: "As the LORD **l**!" **Hos 4:15** 2416a
'As your god **l**, O Dan,' And, **Am 8:14** 2416a
'As the way of Beersheba **l**,' **Am 8:14** 2416a
did not come to destroy men's **l**, **Lk 9:56** *5590*
endurance you will gain your **l**. **Lk 21:19** *5590*
"Go; your son **l**." **Jn 4:50** *2198*
Jesus said to him, "Your son **l**"; **Jn 4:53** *2198*
and everyone who **l** and believes in **Jn 11:26** *2198*
men who have risked their **l** for **Ac 15:26** *5590*
and the ship, but also of our **l**." **Ac 27:10** *5590*
but the life that He **l**, **Ro 6:10** *2198*
life that He lives, He **l** to God. **Ro 6:10** *2198*
over a person as long as he **l**? **Ro 7:1** *2198*
For not one of us **l** for himself, **Ro 14:7** *2198*
is bound as long as her husband **l**; **1Co 7:39** *2198*
He **l** because of the power of God. **2Co 13:4** *2198*
I who live, but Christ **l** in me; **Ga 2:20** *2198*
gospel of God but also our own **l**, **1Th 2:8** *5590*
pleasure is dead even while she **l**. **1Tm 5:6** *2198*
subject to slavery all their **l**. **Heb 2:15** *2198*
whom it is witnessed that he **l** on. **Heb 7:8** *2198*
l to make intercession for them. **Heb 7:25** *2198*
force while the one who made it **l**. **Heb 9:17** *2198*
to those who would live ungodly **l** **2Pe 2:6**
the one who does the will of God **l** **1Jn 2:17** *3306*
lay down our **l** for the brethren. **1Jn 3:16** *5590*
to Him who **l** forever and ever, **Rv 4:9** *2198*
Him who **l** forever and ever, **Rv 4:10** *2198*
by Him who **l** forever and ever, **Rv 10:6** *2198*
of God, who **l** forever and ever. **Rv 15:7** *2198*
chariots and slaves and human **l**. **Rv 18:13** *5590*

LIVESTOCK

who dwell in tents and *have* **l**. **Gn 4:20** 4735
Now Abram was very rich in **l**, **Gn 13:2** 4735
between the herdsmen of Abram's **l** **Gn 13:7** 4735
and the herdsmen of Lot's **l**. **Gn 13:7** 4735
not time for the **l** to be gathered. **Gn 29:7** 4735
God has taken away your father's **l** **Gn 31:9** 4735
and he drove away all his **l** and **Gn 31:18** 4735
his acquired **l** which he had **Gn 31:18** 4735
house and made booths for his **l** **Gn 33:17** 4735
sons were with his **l** in the field, **Gn 34:5** 4735
"Will not their **l** and their **Gn 34:23** 4735
and his **l** and all his cattle and **Gn 36:6** 4735
sustain them because of their **l**. **Gn 36:7** 4735
took their **l** and their property, **Gn 46:6** 4735
for they have been keepers of **l**; **Gn 46:32** 4735
servants have been keepers of **l** **Gn 46:34** 4735
then put them in charge of my **l**." **Gn 47:6** 4735
"Give up your **l**, and I will give **Gn 47:16** 4735
I will give you *food* for your **l**, **Gn 47:16** 4735
So they brought their **l** to Joseph, **Gn 47:17** 4735
with food in exchange for all their **l** **Gn 47:17** 4735
a very severe pestilence on your **l** **Ex 9:3** 4735
a distinction between the **l** of Israel **Ex 9:4** 4735
of Israel and the **l** of Egypt, **Ex 9:4** 4735
and all the **l** of Egypt died; **Ex 9:6** 4735
of the **l** of the sons of Israel, **Ex 9:6** 4735
even one of the **l** of Israel dead. **Ex 9:7** 4735
bring your **l** and whatever you have **Ex 9:19** 4735
and his **l** flee into the houses; **Ex 9:20** 4735
servants and his **l** in the field. **Ex 9:21** 4735
"Therefore, our **l** too shall go **Ex 10:26** 4735
herds, a very large number of **l**. **Ex 12:38** 4735
children and our **l** with thirst?" **Ex 17:3** 4735
to Me, and all your male **l**, **Ex 34:19** 4735
my **l** do drink any of your water, **Nu 20:19** 4735
an exceedingly large number of **l**. **Nu 32:1** 4735
was indeed a place suitable for **l**, **Nu 32:1** 4735
of Israel, is a land for **l**, **Nu 32:4** 4735
and your servants have **l**." **Nu 32:4** 4735
will build here sheepfolds for our **l** **Nu 32:16** 4735
our **l** and all our cattle shall **Nu 32:26** 4735
and your little ones and your **l** **Dt 3:19** 4735
(I know that you have much **l**) shall **Dt 3:19** 4735
their **l** and for their property. **Jos 14:4** 4735
great riches and with very much **l**, **Jos 22:8** 4735
up with their **l** and their tents, **Jg 6:5** 4735
put the little ones and the **l** and the **Jg 18:21** 4735
and he led away their **l** and struck **1Sa 23:5** 4735
people drove ahead of the *other* **l**, **1Sa 30:20** 4735
they came down to take their **l**. **1Ch 7:21** 4735
property and **l** belonging to the king **1Ch 28:1** 4735
struck down those who owned **l**, **2Ch 14:15** 4735
many cisterns, for he had much **l**, **2Ch 26:10** 4735
l will graze in a roomy pasture. **Is 30:23** 4735
my oxen and my fattened **l** are *all* **Mt 22:4** *4619b*

LIVING

teem with swarms of **l** creatures, **Gn 1:20** 2416a
and every **l** creature that moves, **Gn 1:21** 2416a
l creatures after their kind: **Gn 1:24** 2416a
l thing that moves on the earth." **Gn 1:28** 2416a
and man became a **l** being. **Gn 2:7** 2416a
the man called a **l** creature, **Gn 2:19** 2416a
she was the mother of all *the* **l**. **Gn 3:20** 2416a
"And of every **l** thing of all **Gn 6:19** 2416a
every **l** thing that I have made." **Gn 7:4** 3351
Thus He blotted out every **l** thing **Gn 7:23** 3351
"Bring out with you every **l** thing **Gn 8:17** 2421b
never again destroy every **l** thing, **Gn 8:21** 2416a
every **l** creature that is with you, **Gn 9:10** 2416a
every **l** creature that is with you, **Gn 9:12** 2416a
and every **l** creature of all flesh; **Gn 9:15** 2416a
between God and every **l** creature of **Gn 9:16** 2416a
departed, for he was **l** in Sodom. **Gn 14:12** 3427
Now he was **l** by the oaks of Mamre **Gn 14:13** 7931
for he was **l** in the Negev. **Gn 24:62** 3427
gave gifts while he was still **l**, **Gn 25:6** 2416a
was a peaceful man, **l** in tents. **Gn 25:27** 3427
"I am tired of **l** because of the **Gn 27:46** 2425b
of Goshen, where My people are **l**, **Ex 8:22** 5975
and among all the **l** creatures that **Lv 11:10** 2416a
and every **l** thing that moves in **Lv 11:46** 2416a

sabbaths, while you were l on it. Lv 26:35 3427
"Amalek is l in the land of the Nu 13:29 3427
are l in the hill country, Nu 13:29 3427
and the Canaanites are l by the Nu 13:29 3427
stand between the dead and the l, Nu 16:48 2416a
land, and they are l opposite me. Nu 22:5 3427
has heard the voice of the l God Dt 5:26 2416a
every l thing that followed them, Dt 11:6 3351
so that she was l on the wall. Jos 2:15 3427
know that the l God is among you, Jos 3:10 2416a
strangers who were l among them. Jos 8:35 1980
"Perhaps you are l within our land; Jos 9:7 3427
they were l within their land. Jos 9:16 3427
when you are l within our land? Jos 9:22 3427
except the Hivites l in Gibeon; Jos 11:19 3427
persisted in l in that land. Jos 17:12 3427
Reuben and the sons of Gad were l. Jos 22:33 3427
Amorites in whose land you are l; Jos 24:15 3427
fight against the Canaanites l in the Jg 1:9 3427
the Canaanites l in Zephath, Jg 1:17 3427
persisted in l in that land. Jg 1:27 3427
Canaanites who were l in Gezer; Jg 1:29 3427
persisted in l in Mount Heres, Jg 1:35 3427
who were l in it l in security, Jg 18:7 3427
to the l and to the dead." Ru 2:20 2416a
taunt the armies of the l God?" 1Sa 17:26 2416a
taunted the armies of the l God." 1Sa 17:36 2416a
be bound in the bundle of the l with 1Sa 25:29 2416a
while I was l at Geshur in Aram, 2Sa 15:8 3427
day of their death, l as widows. 2Sa 20:3 2424
For the l one is my son, and the 1Ki 3:22 2416a
son, and the l one is my son." 1Ki 3:22 2416a
'This is my son who is l, 1Ki 3:23 2416a
one, and my son is the l one.' " 1Ki 3:23 2416a
"Divide the l child in two, and 1Ki 3:25 2416a
woman whose child *was* the l one 1Ki 3:26 2416a
"Oh, my lord, give her the l child, 1Ki 3:26 2416a
"Give the first woman the l child, 1Ki 3:27 2416a
of it, he was l in Egypt 1Ki 12:2 3427
an old prophet was l in Bethel; 1Ki 13:11 3427
to the upper room where he was l, 1Ki 17:19 3427
were l with Naboth in his city. 1Ki 21:8 3427
we are l is too limited for us. 2Ki 6:1 3427
At the beginning of their l there, 2Ki 17:25 3427
has sent to reproach the l God, 2Ki 19:4 2416a
he has sent to reproach the l God. 2Ki 19:16 2416a
of Israel and those l in Judah. 2Ch 30:25 3427
The temple servants l in Ophel Ne 3:26 3427
temple servants were l in Ophel, Ne 11:21 3427
Also men of Tyre were l there *who* Ne 13:16 3427
hand is the life of every l thing, Jb 12:10 2416a
is it found in the land of the l. Jb 28:13 2416a
is hidden from the eyes of all l And Jb 28:21 2416a
to the house of meeting for all l. Jb 30:23 2416a
of the LORD In the land of the l. Ps 27:13 2416a
thirsts for God, for the l God; Ps 42:2 2416a
uproot you from the land of the l. Ps 52:5 2416a
before God In the light of the l. Ps 56:13 2416a
flesh sing for joy to the l God. Ps 84:2 2416a
the LORD In the land of the l. Ps 116:9 2416a
My portion in the land of the l. Ps 142:5 2416a
Your sight no man l is righteous. Ps 143:2 2416a
the desire of every l thing. Ps 145:16 2416a
than the l who are still living. Ec 4:2 2416a
than the living who are still l. Ec 4:2 2416a
I have seen all the l under the sun Ec 4:15 2416a
knowing *how* to walk before the l? Ec 6:8 2416a
man, And the l takes *it* to heart. Ec 7:2 2416a
For whoever is joined with all the l, Ec 9:4 2416a
For the l know they will die; Ec 9:5 2416a
the dead on behalf of the l? Is 8:19 2416a
has sent to reproach the l God, Is 37:4 2416a
sent *them* to reproach the l God. Is 37:17 2416a
The LORD in the land of the l; Is 38:11 2416a
is the l who give thanks to You, Is 38:19 2416a
cut off out of the land of the l For Is 53:8 2416a
Me, The fountain of l waters, Jer 2:13 2416a
l God and the everlasting King. Jer 10:10 2416a
him off from the land of the l, Jer 11:19 2416a
forsaken the fountain of l water, Jer 17:13 2416a
perverted the words of the l God, Jer 23:36 2416a
have anyone l among this people, Jer 29:32 3427
the Jews l in the land of Egypt, Jer 44:1 3427
Egypt, those who were l in Migdol, Jer 44:1 3427
all the people who were l in Pathros Jer 44:15 3427
who are l in the land of Egypt, Jer 44:26 3427
Why should *any* l mortal, or *any* La 3:39 2416a
figures resembling four l beings. Ezk 1:5 2421b
In the midst of the l beings there Ezk 1:13 2421b
back and forth among the l beings. Ezk 1:13 2421b
And the l beings ran to and fro Ezk 1:14 2421b
Now as I looked at the l beings, Ezk 1:15 2421b
on the earth beside the l beings, Ezk 1:15 2421b
Whenever the l beings moved, Ezk 1:19 2421b
the l beings rose from the earth, Ezk 1:19 2421b
for the spirit of the l beings *was* in Ezk 1:20 2421b
for the spirit of the l beings *was* in Ezk 1:21 2421b
Now over the heads of the l beings Ezk 1:22 2421b
the l beings touching one another and Ezk 3:13 2421b
seven days where they were l, Ezk 3:15 3427
They are the l beings that I saw Ezk 10:15 2421b
for the spirit of the l beings *was* in Ezk 10:17 2421b
These are the l beings that I saw Ezk 10:20 2421b
set glory in the land of the l. Ezk 26:20 2416a
terror in the land of the l. Ezk 32:23 2416a
their terror in the land of the l and Ezk 32:24 2416a
instilled in the land of the l), Ezk 32:25 2416a
their terror in the land of the l. Ezk 32:26 2416a
was once in the land of the l. Ezk 32:27 2416a
of him in the land of the l, Ezk 32:32 2416a
the house of Israel was l in their Ezk 36:17 3427
nations, and they are l securely, Ezk 38:8 3427
all of them l without walls and Ezk 38:11 3427
My people Israel are l securely, Ezk 38:14 3427
that every l creature which swarms Ezk 47:9 5315
me more than *in* any *other* l man, Da 2:30 2417
And all l creatures fed themselves Da 4:12 1321
In order that the l may know That Da 4:17 2417
"Daniel, servant of the l God, Da 6:20 2417
who were l in all the land: Da 6:25 1753
is the l God and enduring forever, Da 6:26 2417
"*You are* the sons of the l God." Hos 1:10 2416a
l with the daughter of Babylon." Zch 2:7 3427
l waters will flow out of Jerusalem, Zch 14:8 2416a
Christ, the Son of the l God." Mt 16:16 *2198*
God of the dead but of the l." Mt 22:32 *2198*
and say, 'If we had been l in Mt 23:30
"I adjure You by the l God, Mt 26:63 *2198*
the God of the dead, but of the l; Mk 12:27 *2198*
came on all those l around them; Lk 1:65 *4039*
time, and was not l in a house, Lk 8:27 *3306*
squandered his estate with loose l. Lk 15:13 *2198*
joyously l in splendor every day. Lk 16:19 *2165*
the God of the dead but of the l; Lk 20:38 *2198*
you seek the l One among the dead? Lk 24:5 *2198*
He would have given you l water." Jn 4:10 *2198*
then do You get that l water? Jn 4:11 *2198*
him, saying that his son was l. Jn 4:51 *2198*
"I am the l bread that came down Jn 6:51 *2198*
"As the l Father sent Me, and I Jn 6:57 *2198*
will flow rivers of l water.' " Jn 7:38 *2198*
to all who were l in Jerusalem; Ac 1:19 *2730*
there were Jews l in Jerusalem, Ac 2:5 *2730*
country in which you are now l. Ac 7:4 *2730*
l oracles to pass on to you. Ac 7:38 *2198*
as Judge of the l and the dead. Ac 10:42 *2198*
relief of the brethren l in Judea. Ac 11:29 *2730*
from these vain things to a l God, Ac 14:15 *2198*
law to her husband while he is l; Ro 7:2 *2198*
then, if while her husband is l Ro 7:3 *2198*
you are l according to the flesh, Ro 8:13 *2198*
BE CALLED SONS OF THE L GOD." Ro 9:26 *2198*
bodies a l and holy sacrifice, Ro 12:1 *2198*
both of the dead and of the l. Ro 14:9 *2198*
to get their l from the gospel. 1Co 9:14 *2198*
MAN, Adam, BECAME A L SOUL." 1Co 15:45 *2198*
but with the Spirit of the l God, 2Co 3:3 *2198*
we are the temple of the l God; 2Co 6:16 *2198*
let us keep l by that same Php 3:16 *4748*
as if you were l in the world, Col 2:20 *2198*
walked, when you were l in them. Col 3:7 *2198*
idols to serve a l and true God, 1Th 1:9 *2198*
which is the church of the l God, 1Tm 3:15 *2198*
have fixed our hope on the l God, 1Tm 4:10 *2198*
is to judge the l and the dead, 2Tm 4:1 *2198*
that falls away from the l God. Heb 3:12 *2198*
For the word of God is l and active Heb 4:12 *2198*
dead works to serve the l God? Heb 9:14 *2198*
by a new and l way which He Heb 10:20 *2198*
fall into the hands of the l God. Heb 10:31 *2198*
Zion and to the city of the l God, Heb 12:22 *2198*
be born again to a l hope through 1Pe 1:3 *2198*
the l and enduring word of God. 1Pe 1:23 *2198*
And coming to Him as to a l stone 1Pe 2:4 *2198*
you also, as l stones, are being 1Pe 2:5 *2198*
ready to judge the l and the dead. 1Pe 4:5 *2198*
righteous man, while l among them, 2Pe 2:8 *1460*
and the l One; and Rv 1:18 *2198*
four l creatures full of eyes in Rv 4:6 *2226*
And the four l creatures, each one Rv 4:8 *2226*
And when the l creatures give Rv 4:9 *2226*
throne (with the four l creatures) Rv 5:6 *2226*
the four l creatures and the Rv 5:8 *2226*
the l creatures and the elders; Rv 5:11 *2226*
the four l creatures kept saying, Rv 5:14 *2226*
I heard one of the four l creatures Rv 6:1 *2226*
the second l creature saying, Rv 6:3 *2226*
heard the third l creature saying, Rv 6:5 *2226*
of the four l creatures saying, Rv 6:6 *2226*
of the fourth l creature saying, Rv 6:7 *2226*
sun, having the seal of the l God; Rv 7:2 *2198*
elders and the four l creatures; Rv 7:11 *2226*
four l creatures and the elders; Rv 14:3 *2226*
Then one of the four l creatures Rv 15:7 *2226*
and every l thing in the sea died. Rv 16:3 *2222*
many as make their l by the sea, Rv 18:17 *2038b*
elders and the four l creatures fell Rv 19:4 *2226*

LIZARD
and the great l in its kinds, Lv 11:29 6632b
and the crocodile, and the l, Lv 11:30 3911
l you may grasp with the hands, Pr 30:28 8079

LO
l, my sheaf rose up and also stood Gn 37:7 2009
"L, I have had still another Gn 37:9 2009
And l, from the Nile there came up Gn 41:2 2009
"L, seven other cows came up after Gn 41:19 2009
and l, seven ears, withered, thin, Gn 41:23 2009
L, the day is coming to an end; Jg 19:9 2009
"L, God will not reject *a man of* Jb 8:20 2005
passed away, and l, he was no more Ps 37:36 2009
For, l, the kings assembled Ps 48:4 2009
"L, for *my own* welfare I had Is 38:17 2009
And l, these *will come* from the Is 49:12 2009
"L, your salvation comes; Is 62:11 2009
and l, the waistband was ruined, Jer 13:7 2009
and l, a scroll *was* in it. Ezk 2:9 2009
and l, thus they did within My Ezk 23:39 2009
messenger was sent; and l, they came Ezk 23:40 2009
and l, *they were* very dry. Ezk 37:2 2009
and l, I am with you always, even Mt 28:20 *2400*
"L, now You are speaking plainly and Jn 16:29 *2396*

LOAD
l your beasts and go to the land Gn 45:17 2943
you lying *helpless* under its l, Ex 23:5 4853a
of them to his work and to his l; Nu 4:19 4853a
'How can I alone bear the l and Dt 1:12 2960
be given two mules' l of earth; 2Ki 5:17 4853a
took *their* l with one hand doing the Ne 4:17 6006
that no l would enter on the sabbath Ne 13:19 4853a
l hanging on it will be cut off, Is 22:25 4853a
A l for the weary *beast.* Is 46:1 4853a
and do not carry any l on the Jer 17:21 4853a
"You shall not bring a l out Jer 17:22 4853a
"to bring no l in through the Jer 17:24 4853a
sabbath day holy by not carrying a l Jer 17:27 4853a
"L *the baggage* on *your* shoulder Ezk 12:6 5375
will l *his baggage* on *his* shoulder in Ezk 12:12 5375
For each one will bear his own l. Ga 6:5 *5413*

LOADED
So they l their donkeys with their Gn 42:26 5375
and when each man l his donkey, Gn 44:13 6006
l with the best things of Egypt, Gn 45:23 5375
and ten female donkeys l with Gn 45:23 5375
Jesse took a donkey l *with* bread 1Sa 16:20
of figs, and l *them* on donkeys. 1Sa 25:18 7760
my father l you with a heavy yoke, 1Ki 12:11 6006
my father l you with a heavy yoke, 2Ch 10:11 6006

LOADING
of grain and l *them* on donkeys, Ne 13:15 6006

LOADS
all their l and in all their work, Nu 4:27 4853a
to them as a duty all their l. Nu 4:27 4853a
"Now this is the duty of their l, Nu 4:31 4853a
of Damascus, forty camels' l; 2Ki 8:9 4853a
assigned 70,000 men to carry l and 2Ch 2:2 5449
70,000 of them to carry l and 2Ch 2:18 5449
grapes, figs and all kinds of l, Ne 13:15 4853a
moisture He l the thick cloud; Jb 37:11 2959
And youths stumbled under l of La 5:13

LOAF
a l of barley bread was tumbling Jg 7:13 6742
a piece of silver or a l of bread and 1Sa 2:36 3603
to everyone a l of bread and a 1Ch 16:3 3603
one is reduced to a l of bread, Pr 6:26 3603
gave him a l of bread daily from Jer 37:21 3603
his son asks for a l, Mt 7:9 *740*
did not have more than one l in the Mk 8:14 *740*

LO-AMMI
"Name him L, for you are not My Hos 1:9 3818

LOAN
your neighbor a l of any sort, Dt 24:10 4859
man to whom you make the l shall Dt 24:11 5383

LOANED
what he has l to his neighbor; Dt 15:2 5383
that may be l at interest. Dt 23:19 5391b

LOANS
And makes himself rich with l?' Hab 2:6 5671

LOATHE
and we l this miserable food." Nu 21:5 6973
"I l my own life; I will give full Jb 10:1 6962a
behold the treacherous and I l *them,* Ps 119:158 6962a
And do I not l those who rise up Ps 139:21 6962a
of the LORD Or l His reproof, Pr 3:11 6973
and they will l themselves in Ezk 6:9 6962a
and you will l yourselves in your Ezk 20:43 6962a
and you will l yourselves in your Ezk 36:31 6962a
"I l the arrogance of Jacob, And Am 6:8 8374
you did not despise or l, Ga 4:14 *1609*

LOATHED
forty years I l *that* generation, Ps 95:10 6962a
Or have You l Zion? Jer 14:19 1602
who l her husband and children. Ezk 16:45 1602
who l their husbands and children. Ezk 16:45 1602

LOATHES
So that his life l bread, Jb 33:20 2092
A sated man l honey, But to a Pr 27:7 947

LOATHING
made me an object of l to them; Ps 88:8 8441

LOATHSOME
for that is l to the Egyptians. Gn 43:32 8441
shepherd is l to the Egyptians." Gn 46:34 8441
nostrils and becomes l to you; Nu 11:20 2214
They are like l food to me. Jb 6:7 1741
And I am l to my own brothers. Jb 19:17 2603b
and it became a l and malignant Rv 16:2 *2556*

LOAVES
in from your dwelling places two l Lv 23:17
"Please give l of bread to the Jg 8:5 3603
another carrying three l of bread, 1Sa 10:3 3603
will greet you and give you two l 1Sa 10:4
roasted grain and these ten l and 1Sa 17:17 3899
Give me five l of bread, or 1Sa 21:3
hurried and took two hundred l of 1Sa 25:18
them *were* two hundred l of bread, 2Sa 16:1
"Take ten l with you, *some* 1Ki 14:3 3899
twenty l of barley and fresh ears 2Ki 4:42 3899
here only five l and two fish." Mt 14:17 *740*
took the five l and the two fish, Mt 14:19 *740*
breaking the l He gave them to the Mt 14:19 *740*
"Where would we get so many l in Mt 15:33 *740*
"How many l do you have?" Mt 15:34 *740*
He took the seven l and the fish; Mt 15:36 *740*
the five l of the five thousand, Mt 16:9 *740*

the seven **l** of the four thousand, Mt 16:10 *740*
"How many **l** do you have? Mk 6:38 *740*
took the five **l** and the two fish, Mk 6:41 *740*
He blessed *the food* and broke the **l** Mk 6:41 *740*
five thousand men who ate the **l**. Mk 6:44 *740*
from the *incident of* the **l**, Mk 6:52 *740*
"How many **l** do you have?" Mk 8:5 *740*
and taking the seven **l**, Mk 8:6 *740*
the five **l** for the five thousand, Mk 8:19 *740*
no more than five **l** and two fish, Lk 9:13 *740*
took the five **l** and the two fish, Lk 9:16 *740*
'Friend, lend me three **l**; Lk 11:5 *740*
has five barley **l** and two fish, Jn 6:9 *740*
Jesus then took the **l** Jn 6:11 *740*
fragments from the five barley **l** which Jn 6:13 *740*
but because you ate of the **l** and Jn 6:26 *740*

LOBE
entrails and the **l** of the liver, Ex 29:13 3508
put *it* on the **l** of Aaron's right ear Ex 29:20 8571
entrails and the **l** of the liver, Ex 29:22 3508
the loins, and the **l** of the liver, Lv 3:4 3508
the loins, and the **l** of the liver, Lv 3:10 3508
the loins, and the **l** of the liver, Lv 3:15 3508
the loins, and the **l** of the liver, Lv 4:9 3508
and the **l** on the liver he shall Lv 7:4 3508
entrails and the **l** of the liver, Lv 8:16 3508
it on the **l** of Aaron's right ear, Lv 8:23 8571
blood on the **l** of their right ear, Lv 8:24 8571
and the **l** of the liver and the two Lv 8:25 3508
the **l** of the liver of the sin offering Lv 9:10 3508
kidneys and the **l** of the liver, Lv 9:19 3508
shall put *it* on the **l** of the right ear Lv 14:14 8571
put some on the right ear **l** of the Lv 14:17 8571
put *it* on the **l** of the right ear of Lv 14:25 8571
on the **l** of the right ear of the one Lv 14:28 8571

LOBES
on the **l** of his sons' right ears and Ex 29:20 8571

LOCAL
we as well as the **l** residents Ac 21:12 *1786*

LOCALITIES
to their families *and* their **l**, Gn 36:40 4725

LOCALITY
every **l** in the surrounding district. Lk 4:37 *5117*

LOCATED
but they could not be **l**; Ezr 2:62 4672
but it could not be **l**; Ne 7:64 4672
provokes to jealousy, was **l**. Ezk 8:3

LOCK
and **l** the door behind her." 2Sa 13:17 5274a
and caught me by a **l** of my head; Ezk 8:3 6734
not only did I **l** up many of the Ac 26:10 *2623*

LOCKED
chamber behind him, and **l** *them*. Jg 3:23 5274a
doors of the roof chamber were **l**; Jg 3:24 5274a
her out and **l** the door behind her. 2Sa 13:18 5274a
"A garden **l** is my sister, *my* SS 4:12 5274a
sister, *my* bride, A rock garden **l**, SS 4:12 5274a
of the Negev have been **l** up, Jer 13:19 5462
all: he **l** John up in prison. Lk 3:20 *2623*
"We found the prison house **l** Ac 5:23 *2808*

LOCKS
l of hair on his head grow long. Nu 6:5 6545
"Your **l** will be iron and bronze, Dt 33:25 4515
If you weave the seven **l** of my hair Jg 16:13 4253
Delilah took the seven **l** of his hair Jg 16:14 4253
shave off the seven **l** of his hair. Jg 16:19 4253
My **l** with the damp of the night.' SS 5:2 6977
His **l** are *like* clusters of dates SS 5:11 6977
And the flowing **l** of your head are SS 7:5 1803a
shall not let their **l** grow long; Ezk 44:20 6545

LOCUST
not one **l** was left in all the Ex 10:19 697
the **l** in its kinds, and the Lv 11:22 697
the devastating **l** in its kinds, Lv 11:22 5556
for the **l** will consume it. Dt 28:38 697
or mildew, **l** *or* grasshopper, 1Ki 8:37 697
if there is **l** or grasshopper, 2Ch 6:28 697
command the **l** to devour the land, 2Ch 7:13 2284
"Do you make him leap like the **l**? Jb 39:20 697
product of their labor to the **l**. Ps 78:46 697
I am shaken off like the **l**. Ps 109:23 697
What the gnawing **l** has left, Jl 1:4 1501
left, the swarming **l** has eaten; Jl 1:4 697
And what the swarming **l** has left, Jl 1:4 697
left, the creeping **l** has eaten; Jl 1:4 3218
And what the creeping **l** has left, Jl 1:4 3218
left, the stripping **l** has eaten. Jl 1:4 2625
That the swarming **l** has eaten, Jl 2:25 697
locust has eaten, The creeping **l**, Jl 2:25 3218
creeping locust, the stripping **l** and Jl 2:25 2625
locust and the gnawing **l**, Jl 2:25 1501
It will consume you as the **l** *does*. Na 3:15 3218
yourself like the creeping **l**, Na 3:15 3218
yourself like the swarming **l**. Na 3:15 697
creeping **l** strips and flies away. Na 3:16 3218
guardsmen are like the swarming **l**. Na 3:17 697

LOCUSTS
will bring **l** into your territory. Ex 10:4 697
over the land of Egypt for the **l**, Ex 10:12 697
the east wind brought the **l**. Ex 10:13 697
The **l** came up over all the Ex 10:14 697
There had never been so *many* **l**, Ex 10:14 697
west wind which took up the **l** and Ex 10:19 697
would come in like **l** for number, Jg 6:5 697
in the valley as numerous as **l**; Jg 7:12 697
He spoke, and **l** came, And young Ps 105:34 697
and locusts came, And young **l**, Ps 105:34 3218
The **l** have no king, Yet all of Pr 30:27 697
As **l** rushing about men rush about Is 33:4 1361a
they are *now* more numerous than **l** Jer 46:23 697
fill you with a population like **l**, Jer 51:14 3218
up the horses like bristly **l**. Jer 51:27 3218
and his food was **l** and wild honey. Mt 3:4 *200*
and his diet was **l** and wild honey. Mk 1:6 *200*
smoke came **l** upon the earth Rv 9:3 *200*
The appearance of the **l** was Rv 9:7 *200*

LOCUST-SWARM
He was forming a **l** when the spring Am 7:1 1373b

LOD
and Shemed, who built Ono and **L**, 1Ch 8:12 3850a
the sons of **L**, Hadid and Ono, 725; Ezr 2:33 3850a
the sons of **L**, Hadid and Ono, 721; Ne 7:37 3850a
L and Ono, the valley of craftsmen. Ne 11:35 3850a

LO-DEBAR
Machir the son of Ammiel in **L**." 2Sa 9:4 3810
Machir the son of Ammiel, from **L**. 2Sa 9:5 3810
Machir the son of Ammiel from **L**, 2Sa 17:27 3810

LODEBAR
You who rejoice in **L**, And say, Am 6:13 3810

LODGE
us to **l** in your father's house?" Gn 24:23 3885a
and feed, and room to **l** in." Gn 24:25 3885a
where you will **l** tonight.' " Jos 4:3 3885a
in order to enter *and* **l** in Gibeah. Jg 19:15 3885a
and where you **l**, I will lodge. Ru 1:16 3885a
go, and where you lodge, I will **l**. Ru 1:16 3885a
I would **l** in the wilderness. Ps 55:7 3885a
your wicked thoughts **L** within you? Jer 4:14 3885a
Will **l** in the tops of her pillars; Zph 2:14 3885a
standing with whom we were to **l**. Ac 21:16 *3579*

LODGED
whose name was Rahab, and **l** there. Jos 2:1 7901
they **l** there before they crossed. Jos 3:1 3885a
the house of Micah, and **l** there. Jg 18:2 3885a
So they ate and drank and **l** there. Jg 19:4 3885a
came there to a cave and **l** there; 1Ki 19:9 3885a
"The alien has not **l** outside, Jb 31:32 3885a
Righteousness once **l** in her, Is 1:21 3885a
branches the birds of the sky **l** Da 4:21 7932

LODGES
truly erred, My error **l** with me. Jb 19:4 3885a
"On the cliff he dwells and **l**, Jb 39:28 3885a
"In his neck **l** strength, And Jb 41:22 3885a

LODGING
his donkey fodder at the **l** place, Gn 42:27 4411
about when we came to the **l** place, Gn 43:21 4411
Now it came about at the **l** place Ex 4:24 4411
and lay them down in the **l** place Jos 4:3 4411
over with them to the **l** place and Jos 4:8 4411
I entered its farthest **l** place, 2Ki 19:23 4411
"Geba will be our **l** place." Is 10:29 4411
in the desert A wayfarers' **l** place; Jer 9:2 4411
find **l** and get something to eat; Lk 9:12 *2647*
invited them in and gave them **l**. Ac 10:23 *3579*
to him at his **l** in large numbers; Ac 28:23 *3578*
the same time also prepare me a **l**, Phm 1:22 *3578*

LOFTIER
was **l** than all the trees of the field Ezk 31:5 1361b

LOFTINESS
"Though his **l** reaches the heavens, Jb 20:6 7863
And the **l** of man will be humbled, Is 2:11 7312
And the **l** of men will be abased; Is 2:17 7312
and its heart is haughty in its **l**, Ezk 31:10 1363
In the **l** of your dwelling place, Ob 1:3 4791

LOFTY
have surely built You a **l** house, 1Ki 8:13 2073
"I have built You a **l** house, 2Ch 6:2 2073
how **l** are his eyes! And his eyelids Pr 30:13 7311
everyone who is proud and **l** And Is 2:12 7311
Lebanon that are **l** and lifted up, Is 2:13 7311
Against all the **l** mountains, Is 2:14 7311
on a throne, **l** and exalted, Is 6:1 7311
those who are **l** will be abased. Is 10:33 1364
On every **l** mountain and on Is 30:25 1364
"Upon a high and **l** mountain You Is 57:7 5375
The **l** stronghold has been put to Jer 48:1 4869
should fortify her **l** stronghold, Jer 51:53 4791
rims they were **l** and awesome, Ezk 1:18 1363
a sprig from the **l** top of the cedar Ezk 17:22 7311
plant *it* on a high and **l** mountain. Ezk 17:22 8519a
every **l** thing raised up against the 2Co 10:5 *5313*

LOG
grain offering, and one **l** of oil; Lv 14:10 3849
guilt offering, with the **l** of oil, Lv 14:12 3849
also take some of the **l** of oil, Lv 14:15 3849
a grain offering, and a **l** of oil, Lv 14:21 3849
guilt offering and the **l** of oil, Lv 14:24 3849
the **l** that is in your own eye? Mt 7:3 *1385*
behold, the **l** is in your own eye? Mt 7:4 *1385*
take the **l** out of your own eye, Mt 7:5 *1385*
the **l** that is in your own eye? Lk 6:41 *1385*
see the **l** that is in your own eye? Lk 6:42 *1385*
take the **l** out of your own eye, Lk 6:42 *1385*

LOGS
timbers of cedar **l** beyond number, 1Ch 22:4
he who splits **l** may be endangered Ec 10:9 6086

LOIN
and made themselves **l** coverings. Gn 3:7 2290b

LOINS
and put sackcloth on his **l** and Gn 37:34 4975
who came from the **l** of Jacob Ex 1:5 3409
with your **l** girded, your sandals Ex 12:11 4975
from the **l** even to the thighs. Ex 28:42 4975
is on them, which is on the **l**, Lv 3:4 3689
is on them, which is on the **l**, Lv 3:10 3689
is on them, which is on the **l**, Lv 3:15 3689
is on them, which is on the **l**, Lv 4:9 3689
is on them, which is on the **l**, Lv 7:4 3689
Shatter the **l** of those who rise up Dt 33:11 4975
is thicker than my father's **l**! 1Ki 12:10 4975
he girded up his **l** and outran Ahab 1Ki 18:46 4975
please let us put sackcloth on our **l** 1Ki 20:31 4975
So they girded sackcloth on their **l** 1Ki 20:32 4975
girdle bound about his **l**." 2Ki 1:8 4975
"Gird up your **l** and take my staff 2Ki 4:29 4975
"Gird up your **l**, and take this 2Ki 9:1 4975
is thicker than my father's **l**! 2Ch 10:10 4975
And binds their **l** with a girdle. Jb 12:18 4975
If his **l** have not thanked me, And Jb 31:20 2504
"Now gird up your **l** like a man, Jb 38:3 2504
"Now gird up your **l** like a man; Jb 40:7 2504
"Behold now, his strength in his **l** And Jb 40:16 4975
For my **l** are filled with burning, Ps 38:7 3689
an oppressive burden upon our **l**. Ps 66:11 4975
make their **l** shake continually. Ps 69:23 4975
will be the belt about His **l**, Is 11:5 2504
reason my **l** are full of anguish; Is 21:3 4975
him And to loose the **l** of kings; Is 45:1 4975
came forth from the **l** of Judah, Is 48:1 4325
"Now, gird up your **l** and Jer 1:17 4975
every man *With* his hands on his **l**, Jer 30:6 2504
the hands and sackcloth on the **l**. Jer 48:37 4975
from the appearance of His **l** and Ezk 1:27 4975
and from the appearance of His **l** Ezk 1:27 4975
from His **l** and downward *there was* Ezk 8:2 4975
and from His **l** and upward the Ezk 8:2 4975
with a writing case at his **l**. Ezk 9:2 4975
at whose **l** was the writing case. Ezk 9:3 4975
at whose **l** was the writing case Ezk 9:11 4975
girded with belts on their **l**, Ezk 23:15 4975
and made all their **l** quake." Ezk 29:7 4975
undergarments shall be on their **l**; Ezk 44:18 4975
the water, water *reaching* the **l**. Ezk 47:4 4975
will bring sackcloth on everyone's **l** Am 8:10 4975
HAVING GIRDED YOUR L WITH TRUTH, Eph 6:14 *3751*
for he was still in the **l** of his father Heb 7:10 *3751*

LOIS
first dwelt in your grandmother **L** and 2Tm 1:5 *3090*

LONE
Seeing a **l** fig tree by the road, Mt 21:19 *1520*

LONELY
to me, For I am **l** and afflicted. Ps 25:16 3173
God makes a home for the **l**; Ps 68:6 3173
like a **l** bird on a housetop. Ps 102:7 909
How **l** sits the city That was full La 1:1 910

LONG
when he had been there a **l** time, Gn 26:8 748
and wept on his neck a **l** time. Gn 46:29 5750
'How **l** will you refuse to humble Ex 10:3 5704, 4970
"How **l** will this man be a snare Ex 10:7 5704, 4970
"How **l** do you refuse to keep My Ex 16:28 5704
the ram's horn sounds a **l** blast, Ex 19:13 4900
wood two and a half cubits **l**, Ex 25:10 753
two and a half cubits **l** and one Ex 25:17 753
two cubits **l** and one cubit wide Ex 25:23 753
five cubits **l** and five cubits wide; Ex 27:1 753
one hundred cubits **l** for one side; Ex 27:9 753
be hangings one hundred *cubits* **l**, Ex 27:11 753
gold, two and a half cubits **l** and Ex 37:6 753
two cubits **l** and a cubit wide and Ex 37:10 753
a cubit **l** and a cubit wide, Ex 37:25 753
of acacia wood, five cubits **l**, Ex 38:1 753
a span **l** and a span wide when Ex 39:9 753
locks of hair on his head grow **l**. Nu 6:5 1431
as **l** as the cloud settled over the Nu 9:18 3605, 3117
"How **l** will this people spurn Me? Nu 14:11 5704
how **l** will they not believe in Me, Nu 14:11 5704
"How **l** *shall I bear* with this Nu 14:27 5704, 4970
and we stayed in Egypt a **l** time, Nu 20:15 7227a
How **l** will Asshur keep you captive Nu 24:22 5704
stayed **l** enough at this mountain. Dt 1:6 7227a
circled this mountain **l** enough. Dt 2:3 7227a
and have remained **l** in the land, Dt 4:25 3462
You shall not live **l** on it, Dt 4:26 748, 3117
and that you may live **l** on the Dt 4:40 748, 3117
as **l** as the heavens *remain* above Dt 11:21 3117
as **l** as you live on the earth. Dt 12:1 3605, 3117
as **l** as you live in your land. Dt 12:19 3605, 3117
he and his sons may continue **l** in Dt 17:20 748, 3117
him, because the way is **l**, Dt 19:6 7235a
"When you besiege a city a **l** time, Dt 20:19 7227a
as **l** as you live on the land which Dt 31:13 3605, 3117
make a **l** blast with the ram's horn, Jos 6:5 4900
because of the very **l** journey." Jos 9:13 7231
war a **l** time with all these kings. Jos 11:18 7227a
"How **l** will you put off entering Jos 18:3 5704
in the wilderness for a **l** time. Jos 24:7 7227a
How **l** will you make yourself drunk 1Sa 1:14 5704, 4970
as **l** as he lives he is dedicated 1Sa 1:28 3605, 3117

Kiriath-jearim, the time was l, 1Sa 7:2 7235a
and said, "L live the king!" 1Sa 10:24
"How l will you grieve over Saul, 1Sa 16:1 5704
"For as l as the son of Jesse lives 1Sa 20:31
3605, 3117
'Have a l life, peace be to you, 1Sa 25:6
as l as we went about with them, 1Sa 25:15
3605, 3117
How l will you refrain from 2Sa 2:26
5704, 4970
Now there was a l war between the 2Sa 3:1 752
"L live the king! *Long* live 2Sa 16:16
L live the king!" 2Sa 16:16
"How l have I yet to live, that I 2Sa 19:34 4100
'L live King Adonijah!' 1Ki 1:25
'L live King Solomon!' 1Ki 1:34
"L live King Solomon!" 1Ki 1:39
not asked for yourself l life, 1Ki 3:11 7227a
the inner sanctuary, was forty cubits l. 1Ki 6:17
But the poles were so l that the 1Ki 8:8 748
"How l *will* you hesitate between 1Ki 18:21
5704, 4970
so l as the harlotries of your 2Ki 9:22 5704
"L live the king!" 2Ki 11:12
'Have you not heard? L ago I did it; 2Ki 19:25 7350
have you even asked for l life, 2Ch 1:11 7227a
as l as the width of the house, 2Ch 3:4 753
The poles were so l that the 2Ch 5:9 748
a bronze platform, five cubits l, 2Ch 6:13 753
to walk in Your ways as l as they 2Ch 6:31
3605, 3117
"L live the king!" 2Ch 23:11
and as l as he sought the LORD, 2Ch 26:5 3117
"How l will your journey be, and Ne 2:6
5704, 4970
Who l for death, but there is Jb 3:21 2442
"How l will you say these things, Jb 8:2 5704
men, *With* l life is understanding. Jb 12:12 753
You will l for the work of Your Jb 14:15 3700
"How l will you hunt for words? Jb 18:2 5704
"How l will you torment me And Jb 19:2 5704
For as l as life is in me, And the Jb 27:3
3605, 5750
"Do not l for the night, When Jb 36:20 7602a
how l will my honor become a Ps 4:2 5704
How l will you love what is Ps 4:2
But You, O LORD—how l? Ps 6:3
5704, 4970
How l, O LORD? Will You forget Ps 13:1 5704
How l will You hide Your face from Ps 13:1 5704
How l shall I take counsel in my Ps 13:2 5704
How l will my enemy be exalted Ps 13:2 5704
Through my groaning all day l. Ps 32:3
Lord, how l will You look on? Ps 35:17 4100
And Your praise all day l. Ps 35:28
All day l he is gracious and lends, Ps 37:26
I go mourning all day l. Ps 38:6
they devise treachery all day l. Ps 38:12
While *they* say to me all day l, Ps 42:3
While they say to me all day l, Ps 42:10
In God we have boasted all day l, Ps 44:8
All day l my dishonor is before me And Ps 44:15
Your sake we are killed all day l; Ps 44:22
of God *endures* all day l. Ps 52:1
all day l he oppresses me. Ps 56:1
have trampled upon me all day l, Ps 56:2
All day l they distort my words; Ps 56:5
How l will you assail a man, That Ps 62:3 5704
I will bless You as l as I live; Ps 63:4
And with Your glory all day l. Ps 71:8
And of Your salvation all day l; Ps 71:15
utter Your righteousness all day l; Ps 71:24
sun *endures,* And as l as the moon, Ps 72:5 6440
Let them bless him all day l. Ps 72:15
increase as l as the sun *shines;* Ps 72:17 6440
I have been stricken all day l And Ps 73:14
any among us who knows how l. Ps 74:9 5704
How l, O God, will the adversary Ps 74:10
5704, 4970
man reproaches You all day l. Ps 74:22
days of old, The years of l ago. Ps 77:5 5769
How l, O LORD? Will You be angry Ps 79:5 5704
How l will You be angry with the Ps 80:4
5704, 4970
How l will you judge unjustly And Ps 82:2
5704, 4970
Lord, For to You I cry all day l. Ps 86:3
me like water all day l; Ps 88:17
How l, O LORD? Will You hide Ps 89:46 5704
how l *will it be?* Ps 90:13
5704, 4970
"With a l life I will satisfy Ps 91:16 753
How l shall the wicked, O LORD, Ps 94:3
5704, 4970
How l shall the wicked exult? Ps 94:3
5704, 4970
have reproached me all day l; Ps 102:8
sing to the LORD as l as I live; Ps 104:33
call *upon Him* as l as I live. Ps 116:2 3117
Behold, I l for Your precepts; Ps 119:40 8373
I l for Your salvation, O LORD, And Ps 119:174 8373
Too l has my soul had its dwelling Ps 120:6 7227a
like those who have l been dead. Ps 143:3 5769
"How l, O naive ones, will you Pr 1:22
5704, 4970
L life is in her right hand; Pr 3:16 753
How l will you lie down, O Pr 6:9 5704
home, He has gone on a l journey; Pr 7:19
7350, 4970
All day l he is craving, While the Pr 21:26
Those who linger l over wine, Pr 23:30
Then I said, "Lord, how l?" Is 6:11
5704, 4970
Him who planned it l ago. Is 22:11 7350
wonders, Plans *formed* l ago, Is 25:1 7350
are all those who l for Him. Is 30:18 2442
For Topheth has l been ready, Is 30:33 865a
L ago I did it, From ancient times Is 37:26 7350
"I have kept silent for a l time, Is 42:14 5769
Have I not l since announced *it* to Is 44:8 3975b
Who has l since declared it? Is 45:21 3975b
"Remember the former things l past, Is 46:9 5769
"I declared the former things l ago Is 48:3 3975b
I declared *them* to you l ago, Is 48:5 3975b
are created now and not l ago; Is 48:7 3975b
Even from l ago your ear has not Is 48:8 3975b
of old, the generations of l ago. Is 51:9 5769
you fear continually all day l Is 51:13
continually blasphemed all day l. Is 52:5
Was I not silent even for a l time Is 57:11 5769
We continued in them a l time; Is 64:5 5769
have spread out My hands all day l Is 65:2
"For l ago I broke your yoke *And* Jer 2:20 5769
How l will your wicked thoughts Jer 4:14
5704, 4970
How l must I see the standard And Jer 4:21
5704, 4970
How l is the land to mourn And the Jer 12:4
5704, 4970
How l will you remain unclean?" Jer 13:27
310, 4970, 5750
become a laughingstock all day l; Jer 20:7
reproach and derision all day l. Jer 20:8
"How l? Is there *anything* in the Jer 23:26
5704, 4970
'*The exile* will be l; Jer 29:28 752
"How l will you go here and Jer 31:22
5704, 4970
that they may last a l time." Jer 32:14 7227a
How l will you gash yourself? Jer 47:5 5704
LORD, How l will you not be quiet? Jer 47:6 5704
made me desolate, Faint all day l. La 1:13
Like those who have l been dead. La 3:6 5769
Are against me all day l. La 3:62
Why do You forsake us so l? La 5:20
753, 3117
he sold as l as they *both* live; Ezk 7:13 5750
The days are l and every vision fails Ezk 12:22 748
l pinions and a full plumage of Ezk 17:3 750
became many and its branches l Ezk 31:5 748
was one rod l and one rod wide; Ezk 40:7 753
fifty cubits l and twenty-five cubits Ezk 40:29 753
twenty-five cubits l and five cubits Ezk 40:30 753
fifty cubits l and twenty-five cubits Ezk 40:33 753
hewn stone, a cubit and a half l, Ezk 40:42 753
a hundred cubits l and a hundred Ezk 40:47 753
rod of six l cubits *in height.* Ezk 41:8 679
the temple, a hundred cubits l; Ezk 41:13 753
were also a hundred cubits l. Ezk 41:13 753
be twelve *cubits* l by twelve wide, Ezk 43:16 753
fourteen *cubits* l by fourteen wide Ezk 43:17 753
shall not let their locks grow l; Ezk 44:20 7971
cubits wide and 25,000 *cubits* l, Ezk 45:6 753
forty *cubits* l and thirty wide; Ezk 46:22 753
Now the two horns *were* l, Da 8:3 1364
"How l will the vision *about* the Da 8:13
5704, 4970
"How l *will it be* until the end Da 12:6
5704, 4970
How l will they be incapable of Hos 8:5 5704
His goings forth are from l ago, Mi 5:2 6924a
How l, O LORD, will I call for Hab 1:2 5704
For how l Hab 2:6
5704, 4970
how l will You have no compassion Zch 1:12
5704, 4970
how wide it is and how l it is." Zch 2:2 753
as l as the bridegroom is with them, Mt 9:15 *3745*
they would have repented l ago in Mt 11:21 *3819*
But the boat was already a l distance Mt 14:24 *4183*
how l shall I be with you? Mt 17:17
2193, 4219
How l shall I put up with you? Mt 17:17
2193, 4219
standing here idle all day l?' Mt 20:6
for a pretense you make l prayers; Mt 23:14 *3117*
master is not coming for a l time,' Mt 24:48 *5549*
'Now after a l time the master of Mt 25:19 *4183*
So l as they have the bridegroom Mk 2:19 *5550*
how l shall I be with you? Mk 9:19
2193, 4219
How l shall I put up with you? Mk 9:19
2193, 4219
"How l has this been happening to Mk 9:21 *5550*
like to walk around in l robes, Mk 12:38 *4749*
appearance's sake offer l prayers; Mk 12:40 *3117*
put on any clothing for a l time, Lk 8:27 *2425*
how l shall I be with you and Lk 9:41
2193, 4219
they would have repented l ago, Lk 10:13 *3819*
master will be a l time in coming,' Lk 12:45 *5549*
has bound for eighteen l years, Lk 13:16 *2400*
while he was still a l way off, Lk 15:20 *3112*
you will l to see one of the days of Lk 17:22 *1937*
and will He delay l over them? Lk 18:7 *3114*
went on a journey for a l time. Lk 20:9 *2425*
like to walk around in l robes, Lk 20:46 *4749*
appearance's sake offer l prayers. Lk 20:47 *3117*
wanted to see Him for a l time, Lk 23:8 *2425*
been a l time *in that condition,* Jn 5:6 *4183*
who sent Me as l as it is day; Jn 9:4 *2193*
How l will You keep us in suspense Jn 10:24
2193, 4219
"Have I been so l with you, and Jn 14:9
5118, 5550
he had for a l time astonished them Ac 8:11 *2425*
Therefore they spent a l time Ac 14:3 *2425*
spent a l time with the disciples. Ac 14:28
3756, 3641
WHO MAKES THESE THINGS KNOWN FROM L Ac 15:18 *165*
he talked with them a l while until Ac 20:11 *2425*
a disciple of l standing with whom Ac 21:16 *744*
about me for a l time, Ac 26:5 *509*
that whether in a short or l time, Ac 26:29 *3173*
But before very l there rushed Ac 27:14 *4183*
had gone a l time without food, Ac 27:21 *4183*
But after they had waited a l time Ac 28:6 *4183*
For I l to see you so that I Ro 1:11 *1971*
over a person as l as he lives? Ro 7:1 *5550*
ARE BEING PUT TO DEATH ALL DAY L; Ro 8:36
"ALL THE DAY L I HAVE STRETCHED Ro 10:21
been kept secret for l ages past, Ro 16:25 *5550*
bound as l as her husband lives; 1Co 7:39 *5550*
you that if a man has l hair, 1Co 11:14 *2863*
but if a woman has l hair, 1Co 11:15 *2863*
say, as l as the heir is a child, Ga 4:1 *5550*
THAT YOU MAY LIVE L ON THE EARTH. Eph 6:3 *3118*
how I l for you all with the Php 1:8 *1971*
beloved brethren whom I l *to see,* Php 4:1 *1973*
us just as we also l to see you, 1Th 3:6
hoping to come to you before l; 1Tm 3:14 *5035*
cannot lie, promised l ages ago, Ti 1:2 *5550*
after He spoke l ago to the Heb 1:1 *3819*
day, as l as it is *still* called Heb 3:13 *891*
through David after so l a time Heb 4:7 *5118*
into which angels l to look. 1Pe 1:12 *1937*
l for the pure milk of the word, 1Pe 2:2 *1971*
as l as you practice these things, 2Pe 1:10
as l as I am in this *earthly* 2Pe 1:13 *3745*
judgment from l ago is not idle, 2Pe 2:3 *1597*
the heavens existed l ago and *the* 2Pe 3:5 *1597*
those who were l beforehand marked Jude 1:4 *3819*
"How l, O Lord, holy and true, Rv 6:10
2193, 4219
they will l to die, and death Rv 9:6 *1937*
fruit you l for has gone from you, Rv 18:14 *1939*

LONGED

you l greatly for your father's house; Gn 31:30 3700
King David l to go out to Absalom; 2Sa 13:39 3615
My soul l and even yearned for the Ps 84:2 3700
For I l for Your commandments. Ps 119:131 2968
The twilight I l for has been Is 21:4 2837
Nor have I l for the woeful day; Jer 17:16 183
"Thus you l for the lewdness of Ezk 23:21 6485

LONGER

no l yield its strength to you; Gn 4:12 3254
"No l shall your name be called Gn 17:5 5750
"Your name shall no l be Jacob, Gn 32:28 5750
You shall no l be called Jacob, Gn 35:10 5750
and one is no l alive." Gn 42:13 369
one is no l alive, and the youngest Gn 42:32 369
But when she could hide him no l, Ex 2:3 5750
"You are no l to give the people Ex 5:7 3254
you go, and you shall stay no l." Ex 9:28 3254
and there will be hail no l, Ex 9:29 5750
and rain no l poured on the earth. Ex 9:33
"Let no man or woman any l Ex 36:6 5750
"They shall no l sacrifice Lv 17:7 5750
man, it may no l be redeemed; Lv 27:20 5750
that there will no l be wrath on Nu 18:5 5750
voice of the LORD our God any l, Dt 5:25 5750
and stiffen your neck no l. Dt 10:16 5750
I am no l able to come and go, and Dt 31:2 5750
in any man any l because of you; Jos 2:11 5750
there was no spirit in them any l because Jos 5:1 5750
the sons of Israel no l had manna, Jos 5:12 5750
no l stand before their enemies. Jg 2:14 5750
I also will no l drive out before Jg 2:21 3254
therefore I will no l deliver you. Jg 10:13 3254
bear the misery of Israel no l. Jg 10:16 7114a
ate, and her face was no l *sad.* 1Sa 1:18 5750
Gath, so he no l searched for him. 1Sa 27:4
3254, 5750
and God has departed from me and no l 1Sa 28:15 5750
halted and pursued Israel no l, 2Sa 2:28 5750
he could no l answer Abner a word, 2Sa 3:11 5750
but he delayed l than the set time 2Sa 20:5
death or unfruitfulness any l.' " 2Ki 2:21 5750
for your servant will no l offer 2Ki 5:17 5750
I wait for the LORD any l?" 2Ki 6:33 5750
the Levites will no l need to 1Ch 23:26
a burden on *your* shoulders no l. 2Ch 35:3
that we will no l be a reproach." Ne 2:17 5750
that Vashti may no l come into Es 1:19
him who sees me will behold me no l; Jb 7:8
the tent of the wicked will be no l." Jb 8:22
"Its measure is l than the earth And Jb 11:9 752
Until the heavens are no l, He will Jb 14:12 1115
"The eye which saw him sees him no l, Jb 20:9
And his place no l beholds him. Jb 20:9 5750
worm feeds sweetly till he is no l Jb 24:20 5750
and it is no l. Jb 27:19 369
"They are dismayed, they no l Jb 32:15 5750
Because they stop *and* no l answer? Jb 32:16 5750
man who is of the earth will no l Ps 10:18
3254, 5750

There is no **l** any prophet, Nor is **Ps 74:9** 5750
its place acknowledges it no **l**. **Ps 103:16** 5750
king who no **l** knows *how* to receive **Ec 4:13** 5750
nor have they any **l** a reward, **Ec 9:5** 5750
and they will no **l** have a share in **Ec 9:6** 5750
your worthless offerings no **l**, **Is 1:13** 3254
so that it is no **l** a people), **Is 7:8**
And will no **l** cover her slain. **Is 26:21** 5750
it, He does not thresh it **l**. **Is 28:28**
in Jerusalem, you will weep no **l**. **Is 30:19** 1058
Teacher will no **l** hide Himself, **Is 30:20** 5750
No **l** will the fool be called noble, **Is 32:5** 5750
You will no **l** see a fierce people, **Is 33:19**
you shall no **l** be called tender and **Is 47:1** 3254
For you will no **l** be called The queen **Is 47:5** 3254
and the unclean Will no **l** come into **Is 52:1**
3254, 5750
"No **l** will you have the sun for **Is 60:19** 5750
"Your sun will no **l** set, Nor will **Is 60:20** 5750
It will no **l** be said to you, **Is 62:4** 5750
your land will it any **l** be said, **Is 62:4** 5750
And there will no **l** be heard in **Is 65:19** 5750
"No **l** will there be in it an **Is 65:20** 5750
We will no **l** come to You'? **Jer 2:31** 5750
"they will no **l** say, 'The ark of **Jer 3:16** 5750
"when it will no **l** be called **Jer 7:32** 5750
"when it will no **l** be said, **Jer 16:14** 5750
"when this place will no **l** be **Jer 19:6** 5750
and they will not be afraid any **l**, **Jer 23:4** 5750
"when they will no **l** say, **Jer 23:7** 5750
"For you will no **l** remember the **Jer 23:36** 5750
will no **l** make them their slaves. **Jer 30:8** 5750
no **l** are they as a nation in their **Jer 33:24** 5750
should keep them any **l** in bondage; **Jer 34:10** 5750
LORD was no **l** able to endure *it,* **Jer 44:22** 5750
"There is praise for Moab no **l**; **Jer 48:2** 5750
"Is there no **l** any wisdom in Teman? **Jer 49:7** 5750
nations will no **l** stream to him. **Jer 51:44** 5750
He will exile you no **l**. **La 4:22** 3254
no **l** use it as a proverb in Israel." **Ezk 12:23** 5750
"For there will no **l** be any false **Ezk 12:24** 5750
It will no **l** be delayed, for in **Ezk 12:25** 5750
of My words will be delayed any **l**. **Ezk 12:28** 5750
no **l** be in your hands to be hunted; **Ezk 13:21** 5750
you women will no **l** see false **Ezk 13:23** 5750
Israel may no **l** stray from Me and **Ezk 14:11** 5750
no **l** defile themselves with all their **Ezk 14:11** 5750
will also no **l** pay your lovers. **Ezk 16:41** 5750
My holy name you will profane no **l** **Ezk 20:39** 5750
this *will* no **l** *be* the same. **Ezk 21:26**
you will speak and be mute no **l**. **Ezk 24:27** 5750
And there will no **l** be a prince in **Ezk 30:13** 5750
opened and I was no **l** speechless. **Ezk 33:22** 5750
and they will no **l** be a prey; **Ezk 34:22** 5750
no **l** be a prey to the nations, **Ezk 34:28** 5750
you will no **l** devour men and **Ezk 36:14** 5750
and no **l** bereave your nation of **Ezk 36:14** 5750
disgrace from the peoples any **l**, **Ezk 36:15** 5750
your nation to stumble any **l**," **Ezk 36:15** 5750
and they will no **l** be two nations and **Ezk 37:22** 5750
no **l** be divided into two kingdoms. **Ezk 37:22** 5750
"They will no **l** defile **Ezk 37:23** 5750
leave none of them there any **l**. **Ezk 39:28** 5750
not hide My face from them any **l**, **Ezk 39:29** 5750
shall no **l** oppress My people, **Ezk 45:8** 5750
but one *was* **l** than the other, **Da 8:3** 1364
with the **l** one coming up last. **Da 8:3** 1364
for I will no **l** have compassion on **Hos 1:6**
3254, 5750
Ishi And will no **l** call Me Baali. **Hos 2:16** 5750
I will spare them no **l**. **Am 7:8**
3254, 5750
"But no **l** prophesy at Bethel, for **Am 7:13**
3254, 5750
I will spare them no **l**. **Am 8:2**
3254, 5750
So that you will no **l** bow down To **Mi 5:13** 5750
you, I will afflict you no **l**. **Na 1:12** 5750
name will no **l** be perpetuated. **Na 1:14** 5750
and no **l** will the voice of your **Na 2:13** 5750
"For I will no **l** have pity on **Zch 11:6** 5750
and they will no **l** be remembered; **Zch 13:2** 5750
and there will no **l** be a curse, for **Zch 14:11** 5750
And there will no **l** be a Canaanite **Zch 14:21** 5750
because He no **l** regards the **Mal 2:13** 5750
It is no **l** good for anything, except **Mt 5:13** *2089*
"So they are no **l** two, **Mt 19:6** *3765*
"No **l** shall there ever be *any* **Mt 21:19** *3371*
could no **l** publicly enter a city, **Mk 1:45** *3371*
so that there was no **l** room, **Mk 2:2** *3371*
"Do not be afraid *any* **l**, **Mk 5:36**
you no **l** permit him to do anything **Mk 7:12** *3765*
so they are no **l** two, **Mk 10:8** *3765*
"Do not be afraid *any* **l**; only **Lk 8:50**
no **l** worthy to be called your son; **Lk 15:19** *3765*
no **l** worthy to be called your son.' **Lk 15:21** *3765*
for you can no **l** be manager.' **Lk 16:2** *2089*
question Him any **l** about anything. **Lk 20:40** *3765*
"It is no **l** because of what you **Jn 4:42** *3765*
a little while **l** I am with you, **Jn 7:33** *2089*
He then stayed two days **l** in **Jn 11:6**
Jesus no **l** continued to **Jn 11:54** *3765*
little while **l** the Light is among you. **Jn 12:35** *2089*
I am with you a little while **l**. **Jn 13:33** *2089*
a little while the world will no **l** **Jn 14:19** *3765*
"No **l** do I call you slaves, for **Jn 15:15** *3765*
Father and you no **l** see Me; **Jn 16:10** *3765*
and you will no **l** see Me; **Jn 16:16** *3765*
she no **l** remembers the anguish **Jn 16:21** *3765*
an hour is coming when I will no **l** **Jn 16:25** *3765*
"I am no **l** in the world; and *yet* **Jn 17:11** *3765*
let us warn them to speak no **l** to any **Ac 4:17** *3371*
and the eunuch no **l** saw him, but **Ac 8:39** *3765*
no **l** consider unholy." **Ac 10:15**
cleansed, no **l** consider unholy.' **Ac 11:9**
no **l** to return to decay, He has **Ac 13:34** *3371*
"Do not be afraid *any* **l**, but go **Ac 18:9**
Paul, having remained many days **l**, **Ac 18:18** *2089*
asked him to stay for a **l** time, **Ac 18:20** *4183*
will no **l** see my face. **Ac 20:25** *3765*
that he ought not to live any **l**. **Ac 25:24** *3371*
see fit to acknowledge God any **l**, **Ro 1:28**
we would no **l** be slaves to sin; **Ro 6:6** *3371*
death no **l** is master over Him. **Ro 6:9** *3765*
now, no **l** am I the one doing it, **Ro 7:17** *3765*
want, I am no **l** the one doing it, **Ro 7:20** *3765*
it is no **l** on the basis of works, **Ro 11:6** *3765*
otherwise grace is no **l** grace. **Ro 11:6** *3765*
no **l** walking according to love. **Ro 14:15** *3765*
might no **l** live for themselves, **2Co 5:15** *3371*
we know *Him in this way* no **l**. **2Co 5:16** *3765*
and it is no **l** I who live, but **Ga 2:20** *3765*
it is no **l** based on a promise; **Ga 3:18** *3765*
come, we are no **l** under a tutor. **Ga 3:25** *3765*
Therefore you are no **l** a slave, **Ga 4:7** *3765*
you are no **l** strangers and aliens, **Eph 2:19** *3765*
we are no **l** to be children, **Eph 4:14** *3371*
that you walk no **l** just as the **Eph 4:17** *3371*
He who steals must steal no **l**; **Eph 4:28** *3371*
when we could endure *it* no **l**, **1Th 3:1** *3371*
when I could endure *it* no **l**, **1Th 3:5** *3371*
No **l** drink water *exclusively,* but **1Tm 5:23** *3371*
no **l** as a slave, but more than a **Phm 1:16** *3765*
would no **l** have had consciousness **Heb 10:2** *2089*
is no **l** *any* offering for sin. **Heb 10:18** *3765*
no **l** remains a sacrifice for sins, **Heb 10:26** *3765*
flesh no **l** for the lusts of men, **1Pe 4:2** *3371*
should rest for a little while **l**, **Rv 6:11** *2089*
"They will hunger no **l**, nor thirst **Rv 7:16** *2089*
that there will be delay no **l**, **Rv 10:6** *3765*
and there was no **l** a place found **Rv 12:8** *2089*
you and *men* will no **l** find them. **Rv 18:14** *3765*
and will not be found any **l**. **Rv 18:21** *2089*
will not be heard in you any **l**; **Rv 18:22** *2089*
craft will be found in you any **l**; **Rv 18:22** *2089*
will not be heard in you any **l**; **Rv 18:22** *2089*
lamp will not shine in you any **l**; **Rv 18:23** *2089*
will not be heard in you any **l**; **Rv 18:23** *2089*
not deceive the nations any **l**, **Rv 20:3** *2089*
away, and there is no **l** *any* sea. **Rv 21:1** *2089*
and there will no **l** be *any* death; **Rv 21:4** *2089*
there will no **l** be *any* mourning, **Rv 21:4** *2089*
There will no **l** be any curse; **Rv 22:3** *2089*
And there will no **l** be *any* night; **Rv 22:5** *2089*

LONG-HAIRED
From the **l** leaders of the enemy.' **Dt 32:42** 6546

LONGING
And that God would grant my **l**! **Jb 6:8** 8615b
My soul is crushed with **l** After **Ps 119:20** 8375
My eyes fail *with* **l** for Your word, **Ps 119:82**
My eyes fail *with* **l** for Your **Ps 119:123**
they are **l** to return and live; **Jer 44:14**
5375, 5315
who are **l** for the day of the LORD, **Am 5:18** 183
and **l** to be fed with the *crumbs* **Lk 16:21** *1937*
For the anxious **l** of the creation **Ro 8:19** *603*
for many years a **l** to come to you **Ro 15:23** *1974*
l to be clothed with our dwelling **2Co 5:2** *1971*
you, as he reported to us your **l**, **2Co 7:7** *1972*
indignation, what fear, what **l**, **2Co 7:11** *1972*
because he was **l** for you all and **Php 2:26** *1971*
l to see us just as we also long **1Th 3:6** *1971*
and some by **l** for it have wandered **1Tm 6:10** *3713*
l to see you, even as I recall **2Tm 1:4** *1971*

LONGS
son Shechem **l** for your daughter; **Gn 34:8** 2836a
in the safety for which he **l**." **Ps 12:5** 6315
My soul **l** for You, as a parched **Ps 143:6**
At night my soul **l** for You, **Is 26:9** 183
the LORD **l** to be gracious to you, **Is 30:18** 2442

LONG-SLEEVED
Now she had on a **l** garment; **2Sa 13:18** 6446
her **l** garment which *was* on her; **2Sa 13:19** 6446

LOOK
the cloud, then I will **l** upon it, **Gn 9:16** 7200
l from the place where you are, **Gn 13:14** 7200
"Now **l** toward the heavens, and **Gn 15:5** 5027
Do not **l** behind you, and do not **Gn 19:17** 5027
l for a man discerning and wise, **Gn 41:33** 7200
you have come to **l** at the **Gn 42:9** 7200
but you have come to **l** at the **Gn 42:12** 7200
saw that he turned aside to **l**, **Ex 3:4** 7200
for he was afraid to **l** at God. **Ex 3:6** 5027
"**L**, the people of the land are **Ex 5:5** 2005
the LORD **l** upon you and judge *you,* **Ex 5:21** 7200
"The priest shall **l** at the **Lv 13:3** 7200
shall **l** at him on the seventh day, **Lv 13:5** 7200
"The priest shall **l** at him **Lv 13:6** 7200
"The priest shall **l**, **Lv 13:8** 7200
"The priest shall then **l**, **Lv 13:10** 7200
then the priest shall **l**, **Lv 13:13** 7200
priest shall **l** at the raw flesh, **Lv 13:15** 7200
and the priest shall **l** at him, **Lv 13:17** 7200
and the priest shall **l**, **Lv 13:20** 7200
then the priest shall **l** at it. **Lv 13:25** 7200
shall **l** at him on the seventh day. **Lv 13:27** 7200
priest shall **l** at the infection, **Lv 13:30** 7200
priest shall **l** at the infection, **Lv 13:32** 7200
the priest shall **l** at the scale, **Lv 13:34** 7200
then the priest shall **l** at him, **Lv 13:36** 7200
then the priest shall **l**, **Lv 13:39** 7200
"Then the priest shall **l** at him; **Lv 13:43** 7200
the priest shall **l** at the mark and **Lv 13:50** 7200
"He shall then **l** at the mark on **Lv 13:51** 7200
"But if the priest shall **l**, **Lv 13:53** 7200
washed, the priest shall again **l**, **Lv 13:55** 7200
Thus the priest shall **l**, **Lv 14:3** 7200
priest goes in to **l** at the mark, **Lv 14:36** 7200
shall go in to **l** at the house. **Lv 14:36** 7200
"So he shall **l** at the mark, and **Lv 14:37** 7200
nothing at all to **l** at except this **Nu 11:6** 5869
tassel for you to **l** at and remember **Nu 15:39** 7200
And I **l** at him from the hills; **Nu 23:9** 7789
through the valley of Arnon. **L**! **Dt 2:24** 7200
do not **l** at the stubbornness of **Dt 9:27** 6437
'**L** down from Your holy habitation, **Dt 26:15** 8259
while your eyes **l** on and **Dt 28:32** 7200
and **l** at the land of Canaan, **Dt 32:49** 7200
"**L** at me and do likewise. **Jg 7:17** 7200
"**L**, people are coming down from **Jg 9:36** 2009
to **l** at the carcass of the lion; **Jg 14:8** 7200
if You will indeed **l** on the **1Sa 1:11** 7200
you went to **l** for have been found. **1Sa 10:2** 1245
"To **l** for the donkeys. **1Sa 10:14** 1245
"Do not **l** at his appearance or at **1Sa 16:7** 5027
and **l** into the welfare of your **1Sa 17:18** 6485
"So **l**, and learn about all the **1Sa 23:23** 7200
"Perhaps the LORD will **l** on my **2Sa 16:12** 7200
L, the oxen for the burnt **2Sa 24:22** 7200
to Achish to **l** for his servants. **1Ki 2:40** 1245
Now **l** after your own house, David!" **1Ki 12:16** 7200
"Go up now, **l** toward the sea." **1Ki 18:43** 5027
I would not **l** at you nor see you. **2Ki 3:14** 5027
L, when the messenger comes, shut **2Ki 6:32** 7200
may the God of our fathers **l** on *it* **1Ch 12:17** 7200
Now **l** after your own house, David." **2Ch 10:16** 7200
causing them to **l** with contempt on **Es 1:17** 5869
"Now please **l** at me, And *see* **Jb 6:28** 6437
And to **l** favorably on the schemes **Jb 10:3** 3313
would **l** around and rest securely. **Jb 11:18** 2658
"If I **l** for Sheol as my home, I **Jb 17:13** 6960a
"He does not **l** at the streams, **Jb 20:17** 7200
"**L** at me, and be astonished, And **Jb 21:5** 6437
L also at the distant stars, how **Jb 22:12** 7200
"**L** at the heavens and see; **Jb 35:5** 5027
And **l** on everyone who is proud, **Jb 40:11** 7200
"**L** on everyone who is proud, *and* **Jb 40:12** 7200
Let Your eyes **l** with equity. **Ps 17:2** 2372
They **l**, they stare at me; **Ps 22:17** 5027
L upon my affliction and my **Ps 25:18** 7200
L upon my enemies, for they are **Ps 25:19** 7200
Lord, how long will You **l** on? **Ps 35:17** 7200
will **l** carefully for his place and **Ps 37:10** 995
me **l** *triumphantly* upon my foes. **Ps 59:10** 7200
Why do you **l** with envy, O **Ps 68:16** 7520
L down from heaven and see, and **Ps 80:14** 5027
And **l** upon the face of Your **Ps 84:9** 5027
You will only **l** on with your eyes And **Ps 91:8** 5027
No one who has a haughty **l** and an **Ps 101:5** 5869
Therefore I will **l** *with* **Ps 118:7** 7200
I **l** upon all Your commandments. **Ps 119:6** 5027
L upon my affliction and rescue **Ps 119:153** 7200
Behold, as the eyes of servants **l** **Ps 123:2**
So our eyes **l** to the LORD our **Ps 123:2**
L to the right and see; **Ps 142:4** 5027
The eyes of all **l** to You, And **Ps 145:15** 7663b
Let your eyes **l** directly ahead And **Pr 4:25** 5027
not **l** on the wine when it is red, **Pr 23:31** 7200
to their owners except to **l** on? **Ec 5:11**
7212, 5869
who **l** through windows grow dim; **Ec 12:3** 7200
The proud **l** of man will be abased And **Is 2:11** 5869
I will even **l** eagerly for Him. **Is 8:17** 6960a
Then they will **l** to the earth, and **Is 8:22** 5027
They will **l** at one another in **Is 13:8** 8539
will **l** to the Holy One of Israel. **Is 17:7** 7200
Nor will he **l** to that which his **Is 17:8** 7200
"I will **l** from My dwelling place **Is 18:4** 5027
not **l** to the Holy One of Israel, **Is 31:1** 8159
L upon Zion, the city of our **Is 33:20** 2372
I will **l** on man no more among the **Is 38:11** 5027
eyes **l** wistfully to the heights; **Is 38:14** 1809
Do not anxiously **l** about you, **Is 41:10** 8159
l about us and fear together. **Is 41:23** 8159
"But when I **l**, there is no one, **Is 41:28** 7200
And **l**, you blind, that you may see. **Is 42:18** 5027
"You have heard; **l** at all this. **Is 48:6** 2372
"Lift up your eyes and **l** around; **Is 49:18** 7200
L to the rock from which you were **Is 51:1** 5027
"**L** to Abraham your father And to **Is 51:2** 5027
sky, Then **l** to the earth beneath; **Is 51:6** 5027
majesty That we should **l** upon Him, **Is 53:2** 7200
L down from heaven and see from **Is 63:15** 5027
Behold, **l** now, all of us are Your **Is 64:9** 5027
"But to this one I will **l**, **Is 66:2** 5027
"Then they will go forth and **l** **Is 66:24** 7200
L at your way in the valley! **Jer 2:23** 7200
'I will not **l** upon you in anger. **Jer 3:12** 5307
streets of Jerusalem, And **l** now and **Jer 5:1** 7200
do not Your eyes **l** for truth? **Jer 5:3**
"**L**, the prophets are telling **Jer 14:13** 2009
L, they keep saying to me, **Jer 17:15** 2009
and while your eyes **l** on, **Jer 20:4** 7200
womb To **l** on trouble and sorrow, **Jer 20:18** 7200
"Take him and **l** after him, and do **Jer 39:12**
5869, 7760

along, and I will **l** after you; **Jer 40:4** 7760, 5869
L, the whole land is before you; **Jer 40:4** 7200
"See, O LORD, and **l**, **La 1:11** 5027
L and see if there is any pain **La 1:12** 5027
See, O LORD, and **l**! **La 2:20** 5027
L on their sitting and their **La 3:63** 5027
L, and see our reproach! **La 5:1** 5027
He said, "**L**! **Da 3:25** 1888
is I who answer and **l** after you. **Hos 14:8** 7789
And I will not *even* **l** at the peace **Am 5:22** 5027
Go over to Calneh and **l**, **Am 6:2** 7200
l again toward Your holy temple.' **Jon 2:4** 5027
My eyes will **l** on her; **Mi 7:10** 7200
And cause *me* to **l** on wickedness? **Hab 1:3** 5027
"**L** among the nations! **Hab 1:5** 7200
not **l** on wickedness *with favor.* **Hab 1:13** 5027
Why do You **l** with favor On **Hab 1:13** 5027
So as to **l** on their nakedness! **Hab 2:15** 5027
"*You* **l** for much, but behold, *it* **Hg 1:9** 6437
l on Me whom they have pierced; **Zch 12:10** 5027
"**L** at the birds of the air, that **Mt 6:26** *1689*
"Why do you **l** at the speck **Mt 7:3** *991*
or shall we **l** for someone else?" **Mt 11:3** *4328*
"**L**, Your disciples do what is not **Mt 12:2** *2400*
in to **l** over the dinner guests, **Mt 22:11** *2300*
other Mary came to **l** at the grave. **Mt 28:1** *2334*
"**L**, why are they doing what is not **Mk 2:24** *2396*
Go **l**!" And when they found out, **Mk 6:38** *3708*
l, the fig tree which You cursed has **Mk 11:21** *2396*
Bring Me a denarius to **l** at." **Mk 12:15** *3708*
"Why do you **l** at the speck **Lk 6:41** *991*
or do we **l** for someone else?" **Lk 7:19** *4328*
or do we **l** for someone else?' " **Lk 7:20** *4328*
"Teacher, I beg You to **l** at my son, **Lk 9:38** *1914*
and I need to go out and **l** at it; **Lk 14:18** *3708*
and said to his father, '**L**! **Lk 15:29** *2400*
'**L**, here *it is!*' **Lk 17:21** *2400*
"They will say to you, '**L** there! **Lk 17:23** *2400*
L here!' Do not go away, and do **Lk 17:23** *2400*
"Lord, **l**, here are two swords." **Lk 22:38** *2400*
up your eyes and **l** on the fields, **Jn 4:35** *2300*
"**L**, He is speaking publicly, **Jn 7:26** *2396*
l, the world has gone after Him." **Jn 12:19** *2396*
L ON HIM WHOM THEY PIERCED." **Jn 19:37** *3708*
gaze on him and said, "**L** at us!" **Ac 3:4** *991*
he approached to **l** *more* closely, **Ac 7:31** *2657*
fear and would not venture to **l**. **Ac 7:32** *2657*
and the eunuch said, "**L**! **Ac 8:36** *2400*
he left for Tarsus to **l** for Saul; **Ac 11:25** *327*
together to **l** into this matter. **Ac 15:6** *3708*
own law, **l** after it yourselves; **Ac 18:15** *3708*
L at the nation Israel; **1Co 10:18** *991*
sons of Israel could not **l** intently at **2Co 3:7** *816*
sons of Israel would not **l** intently at **2Co 3:13** *816*
while we **l** not at the things which **2Co 4:18** *4648*
do not *merely* **l** out for your own **Php 2:4** *4648*
one **l** down on your youthfulness, **1Tm 4:12** *2706*
L at the ships also, though they are **Jas 3:4** *2400*
into which angels long to **l**. **1Pe 1:12** *3879*
since you **l** for these things, **2Pe 3:14** *4328*
to open the book or to **l** into it. **Rv 5:3** *991*
to open the book or to **l** into it; **Rv 5:4** *991*
nations *will* **l** at their dead bodies **Rv 11:9** *991*

LOOKED

God **l** on the earth, and **Gn 6:12** 7200
the covering of the ark, and **l**, **Gn 8:13** 7200
When he lifted up his eyes and **l**, **Gn 18:2** 7200
there, and **l** down toward Sodom; **Gn 18:16** 8259
his wife, from behind him, **l** *back,* **Gn 19:26** 5027
and he **l** down toward Sodom and **Gn 19:28** 8259
Abraham raised his eyes and **l**, **Gn 22:13** 7200
and he lifted up his eyes and **l**, **Gn 24:63** 7200
l out through a window, **Gn 26:8** 8259
He **l**, and saw a well in the **Gn 29:2** 7200
Then Jacob lifted his eyes and **l**, **Gn 33:1** 7200
as they raised their eyes and **l**, **Gn 37:25** 7200
wife **l** with desire at Joseph, **Gn 39:7** 5375, 5869
and the men **l** at one another in **Gn 43:33** 8539
and **l** on their hard labors; **Ex 2:11** 7200
So he **l** this way and that, and **Ex 2:12** 6437
and he **l**, and behold, the bush was **Ex 3:2** 7200
drew near, the sons of Israel **l**, **Ex 14:10** 5375, 5869
the LORD **l** down on the army **Ex 14:24** 8259
that they **l** toward the wilderness, **Ex 16:10** 6437
when the priest has **l** at him, **Lv 13:3** 7200
and they **l**, and each man took his **Nu 17:9** 7200
when he **l** to the bronze serpent, **Nu 21:9** 5027
And he **l** at Amalek and took up his **Nu 24:20** 7200
And he **l** at the Kenite, and took **Nu 24:21** 7200
that he lifted up his eyes and **l**, **Jos 5:13** 7200
the men of Ai turned back and **l**, **Jos 8:20** 7200
gone out, his servants came and **l**, **Jg 3:24** 7200
of the window she **l** and lamented, **Jg 5:28** 8259
The LORD **l** at him and said, **Jg 6:14** 6437
when he **l** and saw the people **Jg 9:43** 7200
while Manoah and his wife **l** on. **Jg 13:19** 7200
and she **l** good to Samson. **Jg 14:7** 3474, 5869
of smoke, Benjamin **l** behind them; **Jg 20:40** 6437
had **l** into the ark of the LORD. **1Sa 6:19** 7200
but when they **l** for him, he could **1Sa 10:21** 1245
watchmen in Gibeah of Benjamin **l**, **1Sa 14:16** 7200
he **l** at Eliab and thought, **1Sa 16:6** 7200
the Philistine **l** and saw David, **1Sa 17:42** 5027
Saul **l** at David with suspicion **1Sa 18:9** 5870b
And when Saul **l** behind him, David **1Sa 24:8** 5027
"When he **l** behind him, he saw **2Sa 1:7** 6437
Then Abner **l** behind him and said, **2Sa 2:20** 6437
daughter of Saul **l** out of the window **2Sa 6:16** 8259
watchman raised his eyes and **l**, **2Sa 13:34** 7200
wall, and raised his eyes and **l**, **2Sa 18:24** 7200
"They **l**, but there was none to **2Sa 22:42** 8159
Araunah **l** down and saw the **2Sa 24:20** 8259
but when I **l** at him carefully in **1Ki 3:21** 995
So he went up and **l** and said, **1Ki 18:43** 5027
Then he **l** and behold, there was at **1Ki 19:6** 5027
When he **l** behind him and saw them, **2Ki 2:24** 6437
the people **l**, and behold, he had **2Ki 6:30** 7200
her head and **l** out the window. **2Ki 9:30** 8259
or three officials **l** down at him. **2Ki 9:32** 8259
She **l** and behold, the king was **2Ki 11:14** 7200
daughter of Saul **l** out of the window **1Ch 15:29** 8259
to Ornan, Ornan **l** and saw David, **1Ch 21:21** 5027
they **l** toward the multitude, **2Ch 20:24** 6437
She **l**, and behold, the king **2Ch 23:13** 7200
and all the priests **l** at him, **2Ch 26:20** 6437
"The caravans of Tema **l**, **Jb 6:19** 5027
I have **l** at the sun when it shone Or **Jb 31:26** 7200
The LORD has **l** down from heaven **Ps 14:2** 8259
They **l** to Him and were radiant, **Ps 34:5** 5027
God has **l** down from heaven upon **Ps 53:2** 8259
And my eye has **l** *with satisfaction* **Ps 54:7** 7200
And I **l** for sympathy, but there **Ps 69:20** 6960a
eye has **l** *exultantly* upon my foes, **Ps 92:11** 5027
He **l** down from His holy height; **Ps 102:19** 8259
He **l** upon their distress When **Ps 106:44** 7200
The sea **l** and fled; **Ps 114:3** 7200
house I **l** out through my lattice, **Pr 7:6** 8259
I **l**, *and* received instruction. **Pr 24:32** 7200
Then I **l** again at all the acts of **Ec 4:1** 7200
I **l** again at vanity under the sun. **Ec 4:7** 7200
Thus He **l** for justice, but behold, **Is 5:7** 6960a
bed, You have **l** on *their* manhood. **Is 57:8** 2372
"I **l**, and there was no one to **Is 63:5** 5027
I **l** on the earth, and behold, *it* **Jer 4:23** 7200
I **l** on the mountains, and behold, **Jer 4:24** 7200
I **l**, and behold, there was no man, **Jer 4:25** 7200
I **l**, and behold, the fruitful land **Jer 4:26** 7200
At this I awoke and **l**, **Jer 31:26** 7200
As I **l**, behold, a storm wind **Ezk 1:4** 7200
that **l** like burning coals of fire, **Ezk 1:13** 4758
Now as I **l** at the living beings, **Ezk 1:15** 7200
glowing metal that **l** like fire all **Ezk 1:27** 4758
Then I **l**, and behold, a hand was **Ezk 2:9** 7200
Then I **l**, and behold, a likeness **Ezk 8:2** 7200
of the court, and when I **l**, **Ezk 8:7** 7200
So I entered and **l**, **Ezk 8:10** 7200
Then I **l**, and behold, in the **Ezk 10:1** 7200
Then I **l**, and behold, four wheels **Ezk 10:9** 7200
"No eye **l** with pity on you to do **Ezk 16:5** 2347
And I **l**, and behold, sinews were **Ezk 37:8** 7200
and I **l**, and behold, the glory of **Ezk 44:4** 7200
and they **l** for Daniel and his **Da 2:13** 1156
I **l** in the vision, **Da 8:2** 7200
and I **l** in the vision and I **Da 8:2** 7200
Then I lifted my eyes and **l**, **Da 8:3** 7200
me was one who **l** like a man. **Da 8:15** 4758
I lifted my eyes and **l**, **Da 10:5** 7200
Then I, Daniel, **l** and behold, two **Da 12:5** 7200
He **l** and startled the nations. **Hab 3:6** 7200
Then I lifted up my eyes and **l**, **Zch 1:18** 7200
Then I lifted up my eyes and **l**, **Zch 2:1** 7200
I lifted up my eyes again and **l**, **Zch 5:1** 7200
Then I lifted up my eyes and **l**, **Zch 5:9** 7200
I lifted up my eyes again and **l**, **Zch 6:1** 7200
And He **l** around to see the woman **Mk 5:32** *4017*
And he **l** up and said, **Mk 8:24** *308*
he **l** intently and was restored, **Mk 8:25** *1227*
All at once they **l** around and **Mk 9:8** *4017*
warming himself, she **l** at him and **Mk 14:67** *1689*
days when He **l** *with favor* upon *me,* **Lk 1:25** *1896*
And Jesus **l** at him and said, **Lk 18:24** *3708*
place, He **l** up and said to him, **Lk 19:5** *308*
But Jesus **l** at them and said, **Lk 20:17** *1689*
And He **l** up and saw the rich **Lk 21:1** *308*
The Lord turned and **l** at Peter. **Lk 22:61** *1689*
and he **l** at Jesus as He walked, **Jn 1:36** *1689*
Jesus **l** at him and said, **Jn 1:42** *1689*
she stooped and **l** into the tomb; **Jn 20:11** *3879*
he **l** ahead and spoke of the **Ac 2:31** *4275a*
at that very time I **l** up at him. **Ac 22:13** *308*
he has **l** at himself and gone away, **Jas 1:24** *2657*
what we have **l** at and touched with **1Jn 1:1** *2300*
After these things I **l**, **Rv 4:1** *3708*
Then I **l**, and I heard the voice of **Rv 5:11** *3708*
I **l**, and behold, a white **Rv 6:2** *3708*
I **l**, and behold, a black horse; **Rv 6:5** *3708*
I **l**, and behold, an ashen **Rv 6:8** *3708*
I **l** when He broke the sixth seal, **Rv 6:12** *3708*
After these things I **l**, **Rv 7:9** *3708*
Then I **l**, and I heard an eagle **Rv 8:13** *3708*
Then I **l**, and behold, the Lamb *was* **Rv 14:1** *3708*
Then I **l**, and behold, a white **Rv 14:14** *3708*
After these things I **l**, **Rv 15:5** *3708*

LOOKING

"What are you **l** for?" **Gn 37:15** 1245
"I am **l** for my brothers; **Gn 37:16** 1245
is driven away while no one is **l**, **Ex 22:10** 7200
men and women were on the roof **l** **Jg 16:27** 7200
see how this man is **l** for trouble; **1Ki 20:7** 1245
away my eyes from **l** at vanity, **Ps 119:37** 7200
wall, He is **l** through the windows, **SS 2:9** 7688
Keep on **l**, but do not understand.' **Is 6:9** 7200
shuts his eyes from **l** upon evil; **Is 33:15** 7200
Yet our eyes failed, **L** for help **La 4:17**
all of them **l** like officers, **Ezk 23:15** 4758
There were shuttered windows **l** **Ezk 40:16**
he see your faces **l** more haggard **Da 1:10** 2196
"You, O king, were **l** and behold, **Da 2:31** 2370
"You continued **l** until a stone **Da 2:34** 2370
I was **l**, and behold, *there was* a **Da 4:10** 2370
'I was **l** in the visions in my mind **Da 4:13** 2370
"I was **l** in my vision by night, **Da 7:2** 2370
l until its wings were plucked, **Da 7:4** 2370
"After this I kept **l**, **Da 7:6** 2370
I kept **l** in the night visions, **Da 7:7** 2370
kept **l** Until thrones were set up, **Da 7:9** 2370
"Then I kept **l** because of the **Da 7:11** 2370
kept **l** until the beast was slain, **Da 7:11** 2370
"I kept **l** in the night visions, **Da 7:13** 2370
"I kept **l**, and that horn was **Da 7:21** 2370
and while I was **l** **Da 8:2** 7200
two fish, and **l** up toward heaven, **Mt 14:19** *308*
l at *them* Jesus said to them, **Mt 19:26** *1689*
From then on he *began* **l** for a **Mt 26:16** *2212*
were there **l** on from a distance, **Mt 27:55** *2334*
for I know that you are **l** for Jesus **Mt 28:5** *2212*
"Everyone is **l** for You." **Mk 1:37** *2212*
After **l** around at them with anger, **Mk 3:5** *4017*
brothers are outside **l** for You." **Mk 3:32** *2212*
L about at those who were sitting **Mk 3:34** *4017*
two fish, and **l** up toward heaven, **Mk 6:41** *308*
l up to heaven with a deep sigh, **Mk 7:34** *308*
L at him, Jesus felt a love for him **Mk 10:21** *1689*
And Jesus, **l** around, said to His **Mk 10:23** *4017*
L at them, Jesus said, **Mk 10:27** *1689*
and after **l** around at everything, He **Mk 11:11** *4017*
some women **l** on from a distance, **Mk 15:40** *2334*
l on *to see* where He was laid. **Mk 15:47** *2334*
L up, they saw that the stone had **Mk 16:4** *308*
you are **l** for Jesus the Nazarene, **Mk 16:6** *2212*
l for the consolation of Israel; **Lk 2:25** *4327*
those who were **l** for the redemption **Lk 2:38** *4327*
and they *began* **l** for Him among **Lk 2:44** *327*
returned to Jerusalem **l** for Him. **Lk 2:45** *327*
I have been anxiously **l** for You." **Lk 2:48** *2212*
"Why is it that you were **l** for Me? **Lk 2:49** *2212*
After **l** around at them all, He **Lk 6:10** *4017*
the two fish, and **l** up to heaven, **Lk 9:16** *308*
his hand to the plow and **l** back, **Lk 9:62** *991*
and he came **l** for fruit on it and **Lk 13:6** *2212*
for three years I have come **l** for **Lk 13:7** *2212*
these things which you are **l** at, **Lk 21:6** *2334*
firelight and **l** intently at him, **Lk 22:56** *816*
And the people stood by, **l** on. **Lk 23:35** *2334*
stooping and **l** in, he saw the **Lk 24:12** *3879*
And they stood still, **l** sad. **Lk 24:17** *4659*
disciples *began* **l** at one another, **Jn 13:22** *991*
and stooping and **l** in, **Jn 20:5** *3879*
lifted up while they were **l** on, **Ac 1:9** *991*
why do you stand **l** into the sky? **Ac 1:11** *991*
"Behold, three men are **l** for you. **Ac 10:19** *2212*
I am the one you are **l** for; **Ac 10:21** *2212*
After **l** up the disciples, we **Ac 21:4** *429*
Paul, **l** intently at the Council, **Ac 23:1** *816*
You are **l** at things as they are **2Co 10:7** *991*
each one **l** to yourself, so that you **Ga 6:1** *4648*
l for the blessed hope and the **Ti 2:13** *4327*
for he was **l** for the city which **Heb 11:10** *1551*
for he was **l** to the reward. **Heb 11:26** *578*
l for and hastening the coming of **2Pe 3:12** *4328*
l for new heavens and a new earth, **2Pe 3:13** *4328*

LOOKOUT

came to the **l** of the wilderness, **2Ch 20:24** 4707
"Go, station the **l**, let him **Is 21:6** 6822
Then the **l** called, **Is 21:8** 4707

LOOKS

"But if the priest **l** at it, **Lv 13:21** 7200
"But if the priest **l** at it, **Lv 13:26** 7200
l at the infection of the scale, **Lv 13:31** 7200
"Then if the priest **l**, and if **Lv 13:56** 7200
who is bitten, when he **l** at it, **Nu 21:8** 7200
until your countryman **l** for it; **Dt 22:2** 1875
for me, for she **l** good to me." **Jg 14:3** 3474, 5869
man **l** at the outward appearance, **1Sa 16:7** 7200
but the LORD **l** at the heart." **1Sa 16:7** 7200
"For He **l** to the ends of the earth And **Jb 28:24** 5027
"He **l** on everything that is high; **Jb 41:34** 7200
The LORD **l** from heaven; **Ps 33:13** 5027
From His dwelling place He **l** out **Ps 33:14** 7688
righteousness **l** down from heaven. **Ps 85:11** 8259
He **l** at the earth, and it trembles; **Ps 104:32** 5027
Until he **l** *with satisfaction* on **Ps 112:8** 7200
She **l** for wool and flax And works **Pr 31:13** 1875
She **l** well to the ways of her **Pr 31:27** 6822
who **l** at the clouds will not reap. **Ec 11:4** 7200
If one **l** to the land, behold, **Is 5:30** 5027
For evil **l** down from the north, **Jer 6:1** 8259
LORD **l** down And sees from heaven. **La 3:50** 8259
idols, he **l** at the liver. **Ezk 21:21** 7200
that everyone who **l** at a woman with **Mt 5:28** *991*
a man who **l** at his natural face **Jas 1:23** *2657*
who **l** intently at the perfect law, **Jas 1:25** *3879*

LOOM

out the pin of the **l** and the web. **Jg 16:14** 708
He cuts me off from the **l**; **Is 38:12** 1803a

LOOMS

"Surely one shall come *who* **l** *up* **Jer 46:18**

LOOPS

"You shall make **l** of blue on **Ex 26:4** 3884b
make fifty **l** in the one curtain, **Ex 26:5** 3884b
and you shall make fifty **l** on the **Ex 26:5** 3884b

l shall be opposite each other. Ex 26:5 3884b
"You shall make fifty **l** on Ex 26:10 3884b
and fifty **l** on the edge of the Ex 26:10 3884b
you shall put the clasps into the **l** Ex 26:11 3884b
He made **l** of blue on the edge Ex 36:11 3884b
He made fifty **l** in the one curtain Ex 36:12 3884b
fifty **l** on the edge of the curtain Ex 36:12 3884b
the **l** were opposite each other. Ex 36:12 3884b
he made fifty **l** on the edge of the Ex 36:17 3884b
and he made fifty **l** on the edge of Ex 36:17 3884b

LOOSE

"Naphtali is a doe let **l**, Gn 49:21 7971
and lets his animal **l** so that it grazes Ex 22:5 7971
will not come **l** from the ephod. Ex 28:28 2118
would not come **l** from the ephod, Ex 39:21 2118
I will let **l** among you the beasts of Lv 26:22 7971
the hair of the woman's head go **l**, Nu 5:18 6544a
would **l** His hand and cut me off! Jb 6:9 5425b
the whole heaven He lets it **l**, Jb 37:3 8281
Pleiades, Or **l** the cords of Orion? Jb 38:31 6605a
"You let your mouth **l** in evil And Ps 50:19 7971
And its **l** earth into brimstone, Is 34:9 6083
him And to **l** the loins of kings; Is 45:1 6605a
L yourself from the chains around Is 52:2 6605a
and whatever you **l** on earth Mt 16:19 *3089*
and whatever you **l** on earth shall Mt 18:18 *3089*
squandered his estate with **l** living. Lk 15:13 *811*

LOOSED

"Because He has **l** His bowstring Jb 30:11 6605a
l the bonds of the swift donkey, Jb 39:5 6605a
You have **l** my sackcloth and Ps 30:11 6605a
handmaid, You have **l** my bonds. Ps 116:16 6605a
I see four men **l** *and* walking *about* Da 3:25 8271
on earth shall have been **l** in heaven." Mt 16:19 *3089*
on earth shall have been **l** in heaven. Mt 18:18 *3089*
mouth was opened and his tongue **l**, Lk 1:64

LOOSEN

l the sackcloth from your hips and Is 20:2 6605a
To **l** the bonds of wickedness, Is 58:6 6605a

LOOSENING

were **l** the ropes of the rudders; Ac 27:40 *447*

LOOSENS

"He **l** the bond of kings And Jb 12:18 6605a
And **l** the belt of the strong. Jb 12:21 7503

LOOT

And do not **l** their wealth In the Ob 1:13 7971
remainder of the peoples will **l** you Hab 2:8 7997b

LOOTED

upon the slain and **l** the city, Gn 34:27 962
they captured and **l** all their wealth Gn 34:29 962
you And your citadels will be **l**." Am 3:11 962
"Because you have **l** many nations, Hab 2:8 7997b

LOP

will **l** off the boughs with a Is 10:33 5586

LORD

the **L** God made earth and heaven. Gn 2:4 3068
for the **L** God had not sent rain Gn 2:5 3068
Then the **L** God formed man of dust Gn 2:7 3068
The **L** God planted a garden Gn 2:8 3068
the **L** God caused to grow every tree Gn 2:9 3068
Then the **L** God took the man and Gn 2:15 3068
The **L** God commanded the man, Gn 2:16 3068
Then the **L** God said, Gn 2:18 3068
the **L** God formed every beast of the Gn 2:19 3068
So the **L** God caused a deep sleep Gn 2:21 3068
The **L** God fashioned into a Gn 2:22 3068
field which the **L** God had made. Gn 3:1 3068
They heard the sound of the **L** Gn 3:8 3068
from the presence of the **L** God Gn 3:8 3068
Then the **L** God called to the man, Gn 3:9 3068
Then the **L** God said to the woman, Gn 3:13 3068
The **L** God said to the serpent, Gn 3:14 3068
The **L** God made garments of Gn 3:21 3068
Then the **L** God said, Gn 3:22 3068
therefore the **L** God sent him out Gn 3:23 3068
manchild with *the help of* the **L**." Gn 4:1 3068
Cain brought an offering to the **L** Gn 4:3 3068
And the **L** had regard for Abel and Gn 4:4 3068
Then the **L** said to Cain, Gn 4:6 3068
Then the **L** said to Cain, Gn 4:9 3068
Cain said to the **L**, Gn 4:13 3068
So the **L** said to him, Gn 4:15 3068
the **L** appointed a sign for Cain, Gn 4:15 3068
out from the presence of the **L**, Gn 4:16 3068
to call upon the name of the **L**. Gn 4:26 3068
ground which the **L** has cursed." Gn 5:29 3068
Then the **L** said, Gn 6:3 3068
Then the **L** saw that the wickedness Gn 6:5 3068
The **L** was sorry that He had Gn 6:6 3068
The **L** said, "I will blot out man Gn 6:7 3068
found favor in the eyes of the **L**. Gn 6:8 3068
Then the **L** said to Noah, Gn 7:1 3068
all that the **L** had commanded him. Gn 7:5 3068
and the **L** closed *it* behind him. Gn 7:16 3068
Then Noah built an altar to the **L**, Gn 8:20 3068
The **L** smelled the soothing aroma; Gn 8:21 3068
and the **L** said to Himself, Gn 8:21 3068
"Blessed be the **L**, The God of Gn 9:26 3068
was a mighty hunter before the **L**; Gn 10:9 3068
a mighty hunter before the **L**." Gn 10:9 3068
The **L** came down to see the Gn 11:5 3068
The **L** said, "Behold, they are Gn 11:6 3068
So the **L** scattered them abroad Gn 11:8 3068
because there the **L** confused the Gn 11:9 3068
and from there the **L** scattered Gn 11:9 3068
Now the **L** said to Abram, Gn 12:1 3068
forth as the **L** had spoken to him; Gn 12:4 3068
The **L** appeared to Abram and said, Gn 12:7 3068
So he built an altar there to the **L** Gn 12:7 3068
there he built an altar to the **L** and Gn 12:8 3068
and called upon the name of the **L**. Gn 12:8 3068
But the **L** struck Pharaoh and his Gn 12:17 3068
Abram called on the name of the **L**. Gn 13:4 3068
before the **L** destroyed Sodom and Gn 13:10 3068
like the garden of the **L**, Gn 13:10 3068
and sinners against the **L**. Gn 13:13 3068
The **L** said to Abram, after Lot Gn 13:14 3068
there he built an altar to the **L**. Gn 13:18 3068
have sworn to the **L** God Most High, Gn 14:22 3068
the word of the **L** came to Abram Gn 15:1 3068
"O **L** GOD, what will You give me, Gn 15:2 136
the word of the **L** came to him, Gn 15:4 3068
Then he believed in the **L**; Gn 15:6 3068
"I am the **L** who brought you out Gn 15:7 3068
"O **L** GOD, how may I know that I Gn 15:8 136
the **L** made a covenant with Abram, Gn 15:18 3068
the **L** has prevented me from Gn 16:2 3068
the **L** judge between you and me." Gn 16:5 3068
Now the angel of the **L** found her Gn 16:7 3068
the angel of the **L** said to her, Gn 16:9 3068
the angel of the **L** said to her, Gn 16:10 3068
angel of the **L** said to her further, Gn 16:11 3068
Because the **L** has given heed to Gn 16:11 3068
Then she called the name of the **L** Gn 16:13 3068
the **L** appeared to Abram and said Gn 17:1 3068
Now the **L** appeared to him by the Gn 18:1 3068
"My **L**, if now I have found favor Gn 18:3 113
pleasure, my **l** being old also?" Gn 18:12 113
And the **L** said to Abraham, Gn 18:13 3068
anything too difficult for the **L**? Gn 18:14 3068
The **L** said, "Shall I hide from Gn 18:17 3068
keep the way of the **L** by doing Gn 18:19 3068
so that the **L** may bring upon Gn 18:19 3068
L said, "The outcry of Sodom and Gn 18:20 3068
was still standing before the **L**. Gn 18:22 3068
So the **L** said, "If I find in Sodom Gn 18:26 3068
I have ventured to speak to the **L**, Gn 18:27 136
"Oh may the **L** not be angry, and I Gn 18:30 136
I have ventured to speak to the **L**; Gn 18:31 136
"Oh may the **L** not be angry, and I Gn 18:32 136
to Abraham the **L** departed, Gn 18:33 3068
has become so great before the **L** Gn 19:13 3068
the **L** has sent us to destroy it." Gn 19:13 3068
for the **L** will destroy the city." Gn 19:14 3068
compassion of the **L** *was* upon him; Gn 19:16 3068
Then the **L** rained on Sodom and Gn 19:24 3068
and fire from the **L** out of heaven, Gn 19:24 3068
where he had stood before the **L**; Gn 19:27 3068
"**L**, will You slay a nation, even Gn 20:4 136
For the **L** had closed fast all the Gn 20:18 3068
Then the **L** took note of Sarah as Gn 21:1 3068
and the **L** did for Sarah as He had Gn 21:1 3068
he called on the name of the **L**, Gn 21:33 3068
the **L** called to him from heaven and Gn 22:11 3068
of that place The **L** Will Provide, Gn 22:14 3068
In the mount of the **L** it will be Gn 22:14 3068
Then the angel of the **L** called to Gn 22:15 3068
I have sworn, declares the **L**, Gn 22:16 3068
"Hear us, my **l**, you are a mighty Gn 23:6 113
"No, my **l**, hear me; Gn 23:11 113
"My **l**, listen to me; Gn 23:15 113
and the **L** had blessed Abraham in Gn 24:1 3068
I will make you swear by the **L**, Gn 24:3 3068
"The **L**, the God of heaven, who Gn 24:7 3068
"O **L**, the God of my master Gn 24:12 3068
She said, "Drink, my **l**"; Gn 24:18 113
to know whether the **L** had made his Gn 24:21 3068
man bowed low and worshiped the **L**. Gn 24:26 3068
"Blessed be the **L**, the God of my Gn 24:27 3068
the **L** has guided me in the way to Gn 24:27 3068
"Come in, blessed of the **L**! Gn 24:31 3068
L has greatly blessed my master, Gn 24:35 3068
'The **L**, before whom I have walked, Gn 24:40 3068
'O **L**, the God of my master Gn 24:42 3068
woman whom the **L** has appointed Gn 24:44 3068
I bowed low and worshiped the **L**, Gn 24:48 3068
the LORD, and blessed the **L**, Gn 24:48 3068
"The matter comes from the **L**; Gn 24:50 3068
son, as the **L** has spoken." Gn 24:51 3068
to the ground before the **L**. Gn 24:52 3068
since the **L** has prospered my way. Gn 24:56 3068
Isaac prayed to the **L** on behalf of Gn 25:21 3068
and the **L** answered him and Rebekah Gn 25:21 3068
So she went to inquire of the **L**. Gn 25:22 3068
The **L** said to her, Gn 25:23 3068
The **L** appeared to him and said, Gn 26:2 3068
And the **L** blessed him, Gn 26:12 3068
last the **L** has made room for us, Gn 26:22 3068
The **L** appeared to him the same Gn 26:24 3068
and called upon the name of the **L**, Gn 26:25 3068
that the **L** has been with you; Gn 26:28 3068
are now the blessed of the **L**.' " Gn 26:29 3068
bless you in the presence of the **L** Gn 27:7 3068
"Because the **L** your God caused *it* Gn 27:20 3068
a field which the **L** has blessed; Gn 27:27 3068
the **L** stood above it and said, Gn 28:13 3068
"I am the **L**, the God of your Gn 28:13 3068
"Surely the **L** is in this place, Gn 28:16 3068
safety, then the **L** will be my God. Gn 28:21 3068
the **L** saw that Leah was unloved, Gn 29:31 3068
the **L** has seen my affliction; Gn 29:32 3068
the **L** has heard that I am unloved, Gn 29:33 3068
"This time I will praise the **L**." Gn 29:35 3068
"May the **L** give me another son." Gn 30:24 3068
that the **L** has blessed me on your Gn 30:27 3068
and the **L** has blessed you wherever Gn 30:30 3068
Then the **L** said to Jacob, Gn 31:3 3068
"Let not my **l** be angry that I Gn 31:35 113
"May the **L** watch between you and Gn 31:49 3068
"Thus you shall say to my **l** Esau: Gn 32:4 113
and I have sent to tell my **l**, Gn 32:5 113
and God of my father Isaac, O **L**, Gn 32:9 3068
it is a present sent to my **l** Esau. Gn 32:18 113
find favor in the sight of my **l**." Gn 33:8 113
"My **l** knows that the children are Gn 33:13 113
my **l** pass on before his servant, Gn 33:14 113
until I come to my **l** at Seir." Gn 33:14 113
find favor in the sight of my **l**." Gn 33:15 113
was evil in the sight of the **L**, Gn 38:7 3068
the LORD, so the **L** took his life. Gn 38:7 3068
displeasing in the sight of the **L**; Gn 38:10 3068
The **L** was with Joseph, so he Gn 39:2 3068
master saw that the **L** was with him Gn 39:3 3068
L caused all that he did to prosper Gn 39:3 3068
the **L** blessed the Egyptian's house Gn 39:5 3068
But the **L** was with Joseph and Gn 39:21 3068
charge because the **L** was with him; Gn 39:23 3068
he did, the **L** made to prosper. Gn 39:23 3068
king of Egypt offended their **l**, Gn 40:1 113
"No, my **l**, but your servants have Gn 42:10 113
"The man, the **l** of the land, Gn 42:30 113
'The man, the **l** of the land, Gn 42:33 113
"Oh, my **l**, we indeed came down Gn 43:20 113
the one from which my **l** drinks and Gn 44:5 113
my **l** speak such words as these? Gn 44:7 113
"What can we say to my **l**? Gn 44:16 113
"Oh my **l**, may your servant please Gn 44:18 113
"My **l** asked his servants, saying, Gn 44:19 113
"We said to my **l**, Gn 44:20 113
"But we said to my **l**, Gn 44:22 113
we told him the words of my **l**. Gn 44:24 113
of the lad a slave to my **l**, Gn 44:33 113
Pharaoh and **l** of all his household Gn 45:8 113
'God has made me **l** of all Egypt; Gn 45:9 113
We will not hide from my **l** that our Gn 47:18 113
There is nothing left for my **l** Gn 47:18 113
find favor in the sight of my **l**, Gn 47:25 113
"For Your salvation I wait, O **L**. Gn 49:18 3068
The angel of the **L** appeared to Ex 3:2 3068
When the **L** saw that he turned Ex 3:4 3068
The **L** said, "I have surely seen the Ex 3:7 3068
'The **L**, the God of your fathers, Ex 3:15 3068
'The **L**, the God of your fathers, Ex 3:16 3068
'The **L**, the God of the Hebrews, Ex 3:18 3068
may sacrifice to the **L** our God.' Ex 3:18 3068
'The **L** has not appeared to you.' " Ex 4:1 3068
The **L** said to him, Ex 4:2 3068
But the **L** said to Moses, Ex 4:4 3068
"that they may believe that the **L**, Ex 4:5 3068
The **L** furthermore said to him, Ex 4:6 3068
Then Moses said to the **L**, Ex 4:10 3068
"Please, **L**, I have never been Ex 4:10 136
The **L** said to him, Ex 4:11 3068
Is it not I, the **L**? Ex 4:11 3068
"Please, **L**, now send *the message* Ex 4:13 136
the anger of the **L** burned against Ex 4:14 3068
Now the **L** said to Moses in Midian, Ex 4:19 3068
The **L** said to Moses, Ex 4:21 3068
'Thus says the **L**, Ex 4:22 3068
L met him and sought to put him to Ex 4:24 3068
Now the **L** said to Aaron, Ex 4:27 3068
told Aaron all the words of the **L** Ex 4:28 3068
which the **L** had spoken to Moses. Ex 4:30 3068
and when they heard that the **L** was Ex 4:31 3068
"Thus says the **L**, the God of Ex 5:1 3068
"Who is the **L** that I should obey Ex 5:2 3068
I do not know the **L**, Ex 5:2 3068
we may sacrifice to the **L** our God, Ex 5:3 3068
'Let us go *and* sacrifice to the **L**.' Ex 5:17 3068
the **L** look upon you and judge *you*, Ex 5:21 3068
Moses returned to the **L** and said, Ex 5:22 3068
"O **L**, why have You brought harm Ex 5:22 136
Then the **L** said to Moses, Ex 6:1 3068
Moses and said to him, "I am the **L**; Ex 6:2 3068
God Almighty, but *by* My name, **L**, Ex 6:3 3068
'I am the **L**, and I will bring you Ex 6:6 3068
know that I am the **L** your God, Ex 6:7 3068
to you *for* a possession; I am the **L**. Ex 6:8 3068
Now the **L** spoke to Moses, saying, Ex 6:10 3068
But Moses spoke before the **L**, Ex 6:12 3068
the **L** spoke to Moses and to Aaron, Ex 6:13 3068
and Moses to whom the **L** said, Ex 6:26 3068
the day when the **L** spoke to Moses Ex 6:28 3068
that the **L** spoke to Moses, saying, Ex 6:29 3068
spoke to Moses, saying, "I am the **L**; Ex 6:29 3068
But Moses said before the **L**, Ex 6:30 3068
Then the **L** said to Moses, Ex 7:1 3068
shall know that I am the **L**, Ex 7:5 3068
as the **L** commanded them, thus they Ex 7:6 3068
the **L** spoke to Moses and Aaron, Ex 7:8 3068
did just as the **L** had commanded; Ex 7:10 3068
listen to them, as the **L** had said. Ex 7:13 3068
Then the **L** said to Moses, Ex 7:14 3068
'The **L**, the God of the Hebrews, Ex 7:16 3068
'Thus says the **L**, Ex 7:17 3068
you shall know that I am the **L**: Ex 7:17 3068
Then the **L** said to Moses, Ex 7:19 3068
did even as the **L** had commanded. Ex 7:20 3068
listen to them, as the **L** had said. Ex 7:22 3068
after the **L** had struck the Nile. Ex 7:25 3068
Then the **L** said to Moses, Ex 8:1 3068
'Thus says the **L**, Ex 8:1 3068
Then the **L** said to Moses, Ex 8:5 3068
"Entreat the **L** that He remove the Ex 8:8 3068
they may sacrifice to the **L**." Ex 8:8 3068

is no one like the **L** our God.	Ex 8:10	3068
and Moses cried to the **L**	Ex 8:12	3068
The **L** did according to the	Ex 8:13	3068
listen to them, as the **L** had said.	Ex 8:15	3068
Then the **L** said to Moses,	Ex 8:16	3068
listen to them, as the **L** had said.	Ex 8:19	3068
Now the **L** said to Moses,	Ex 8:20	3068
'Thus says the **L**,	Ex 8:20	3068
I, the **L**, am in the midst of the land	Ex 8:22	3068
Then the **L** did so.	Ex 8:24	3068
for we will sacrifice to the **L**	Ex 8:26	3068
sacrifice to the **L** our God as He	Ex 8:27	3068
may sacrifice to the **L** your God	Ex 8:28	3068
I shall make supplication to the **L**	Ex 8:29	3068
people go to sacrifice to the **L**."	Ex 8:29	3068
and made supplication to the **L**.	Ex 8:30	3068
The **L** did as Moses asked, and	Ex 8:31	3068
Then the **L** said to Moses,	Ex 9:1	3068
'Thus says the **L**, the God of the	Ex 9:1	3068
the hand of the **L** will come *with* a	Ex 9:3	3068
"But the **L** will make a	Ex 9:4	3068
The **L** set a definite time,	Ex 9:5	3068
"Tomorrow the **L** will do this	Ex 9:5	3068
L did this thing on the next	Ex 9:6	3068
the **L** said to Moses and Aaron,	Ex 9:8	3068
And the **L** hardened Pharaoh's heart	Ex 9:12	3068
just as the **L** had spoken to Moses.	Ex 9:12	3068
Then the **L** said to Moses,	Ex 9:13	3068
'Thus says the **L**, the God of the	Ex 9:13	3068
Pharaoh who feared the word of the **L**	Ex 9:20	3068
paid no regard to the word of the **L**	Ex 9:21	3068
Now the **L** said to Moses,	Ex 9:22	3068
and the **L** sent thunder and hail,	Ex 9:23	3068
And the **L** rained hail on the land	Ex 9:23	3068
the **L** is the righteous one, and I	Ex 9:27	3068
"Make supplication to the **L**,	Ex 9:28	3068
will spread out my hands to the **L**;	Ex 9:29	3068
you do not yet fear the **L** God."	Ex 9:30	3068
and spread out his hands to the **L**;	Ex 9:33	3068
as the **L** had spoken through Moses.	Ex 9:35	3068
Then the **L** said to Moses,	Ex 10:1	3068
you may know that I am the **L**."	Ex 10:2	3068
"Thus says the **L**, the God of the	Ex 10:3	3068
they may serve the **L** their God.	Ex 10:7	3068
"Go, serve the **L** your God!	Ex 10:8	3068
we must hold a feast to the **L**."	Ex 10:9	3068
"Thus may the **L** be with you, if	Ex 10:10	3068
men *among you*, and serve the **L**,	Ex 10:11	3068
Then the **L** said to Moses,	Ex 10:12	3068
and the **L** directed an east wind on	Ex 10:13	3068
have sinned against the **L** your God	Ex 10:16	3068
supplication to the **L** your God,	Ex 10:17	3068
and made supplication to the **L**.	Ex 10:18	3068
So the **L** shifted *the wind* to a	Ex 10:19	3068
But the **L** hardened Pharaoh's heart	Ex 10:20	3068
Then the **L** said to Moses,	Ex 10:21	3068
to Moses, and said, "Go, serve the **L**;	Ex 10:24	3068
sacrifice *them* to the **L** our God.	Ex 10:25	3068
of them to serve the **L** our God.	Ex 10:26	3068
with what we shall serve the **L**."	Ex 10:26	3068
But the **L** hardened Pharaoh's heart	Ex 10:27	3068
Now the **L** said to Moses,	Ex 11:1	3068
The **L** gave the people favor in	Ex 11:3	3068
"Thus says the **L**,	Ex 11:4	3068
L makes a distinction between Egypt	Ex 11:7	3068
Then the **L** said to Moses,	Ex 11:9	3068
yet the **L** hardened Pharaoh's heart,	Ex 11:10	3068
Now the **L** said to Moses and Aaron	Ex 12:1	3068
will execute judgments—I am the **L**.	Ex 12:12	3068
celebrate it *as* a feast to the **L**;	Ex 12:14	3068
"For the **L** will pass through to	Ex 12:23	3068
the **L** will pass over the door and	Ex 12:23	3068
land which the **L** will give you,	Ex 12:25	3068
'It is a Passover sacrifice to the **L**	Ex 12:27	3068
L had commanded Moses and Aaron,	Ex 12:28	3068
L struck all the firstborn in the land	Ex 12:29	3068
and go, worship the **L**,	Ex 12:31	3068
and the **L** had given the people	Ex 12:36	3068
all the hosts of the **L** went	Ex 12:41	3068
It is a night to be observed for the **L**	Ex 12:42	3068
this night is for the **L**,	Ex 12:42	3068
The **L** said to Moses and Aaron,	Ex 12:43	3068
celebrates the Passover to the **L**,	Ex 12:48	3068
L had commanded Moses and Aaron.	Ex 12:50	3068
the **L** brought the sons of Israel out	Ex 12:51	3068
Then the **L** spoke to Moses, saying,	Ex 13:1	3068
the **L** brought you out from this	Ex 13:3	3068
when the **L** brings you to the land	Ex 13:5	3068
there shall be a feast to the **L**.	Ex 13:6	3068
'It is because of what the **L** did	Ex 13:8	3068
law of the **L** may be in your mouth;	Ex 13:9	3068
the **L** brought you out of Egypt.	Ex 13:9	3068
when the **L** brings you to the land of	Ex 13:11	3068
you shall devote to the **L** the	Ex 13:12	3068
the males belong to the **L**.	Ex 13:12	3068
the **L** brought us out of Egypt,	Ex 13:14	3068
that the **L** killed every firstborn	Ex 13:15	3068
I sacrifice to the **L** the males,	Ex 13:15	3068
the **L** brought us out of Egypt."	Ex 13:16	3068
The **L** was going before them in	Ex 13:21	3068
Now the **L** spoke to Moses, saying,	Ex 14:1	3068
will know that I am the **L**."	Ex 14:4	3068
L hardened the heart of Pharaoh,	Ex 14:8	3068
sons of Israel cried out to the **L**.	Ex 14:10	3068
see the salvation of the **L** which He	Ex 14:13	3068
"The **L** will fight for you while	Ex 14:14	3068
Then the **L** said to Moses,	Ex 14:15	3068
will know that I am the **L**,	Ex 14:18	3068
and the **L** swept the sea *back* by a	Ex 14:21	3068

the **L** looked down on the army	Ex 14:24	3068
for the **L** is fighting for them	Ex 14:25	3068
Then the **L** said to Moses,	Ex 14:26	3068
then the **L** overthrew the Egyptians	Ex 14:27	3068
Thus the **L** saved Israel that day	Ex 14:30	3068
the great power which the **L** had used	Ex 14:31	3068
the people feared the **L**,	Ex 14:31	3068
they believed in the **L** and in His	Ex 14:31	3068
of Israel sang this song to the **L**,	Ex 15:1	3068
"I will sing to the **L**,	Ex 15:1	3068
"The **L** is my strength and song,	Ex 15:2	3050
"The **L** is a warrior;	Ex 15:3	3068
The **L** is His name.	Ex 15:3	3068
"Your right hand, O **L**,	Ex 15:6	3068
in power, Your right hand, O **L**,	Ex 15:6	3068
is like You among the gods, O **L**?	Ex 15:11	3068
Until Your people pass over, O **L**,	Ex 15:16	3068
Your inheritance, The place, O **L**,	Ex 15:17	3068
Your dwelling, The sanctuary, O **L**,	Ex 15:17	136
L shall reign forever and ever."	Ex 15:18	3068
and the **L** brought back the waters	Ex 15:19	3068
"Sing to the **L**, for He is highly	Ex 15:21	3068
Then he cried out to the **L**,	Ex 15:25	3068
and the **L** showed him a tree;	Ex 15:25	3068
to the voice of the **L** your God,	Ex 15:26	3068
for I, the **L**, am your healer."	Ex 15:26	3068
Then the **L** said to Moses,	Ex 16:4	3068
the **L** has brought you out of the land	Ex 16:6	3068
you will see the glory of the **L**,	Ex 16:7	3068
your grumblings against the **L**;	Ex 16:7	3068
when the **L** gives you meat to eat in	Ex 16:8	3068
for the **L** hears your grumblings	Ex 16:8	3068
against us but against the **L**."	Ex 16:8	3068
'Come near before the **L**,	Ex 16:9	3068
glory of the **L** appeared in the cloud.	Ex 16:10	3068
And the **L** spoke to Moses, saying,	Ex 16:11	3068
know that I am the **L** your God.' "	Ex 16:12	3068
which the **L** has given you to eat.	Ex 16:15	3068
"This is what the **L** has commanded,	Ex 16:16	3068
"This is what the **L** meant:	Ex 16:23	3068
a holy sabbath to the **L**.	Ex 16:23	3068
for today is a sabbath to the **L**;	Ex 16:25	3068
Then the **L** said to Moses,	Ex 16:28	3068
the **L** has given you the sabbath;	Ex 16:29	3068
"This is what the **L** has commanded,	Ex 16:32	3068
in it, and place it before the **L**	Ex 16:33	3068
As the **L** commanded Moses, so Aaron	Ex 16:34	3068
according to the command of the **L**,	Ex 17:1	3068
Why do you test the **L**?"	Ex 17:2	3068
So Moses cried out to the **L**,	Ex 17:4	3068
Then the **L** said to Moses,	Ex 17:5	3068
and because they tested the **L**,	Ex 17:7	3068
"Is the **L** among us, or not?"	Ex 17:7	3068
Then the **L** said to Moses,	Ex 17:14	3068
and named it The **L** is My Banner;	Ex 17:15	3068
and he said, "The **L** has sworn;	Ex 17:16	3050
the **L** will have war against Amalek	Ex 17:16	3068
how the **L** had brought Israel out	Ex 18:1	3068
all that the **L** had done to Pharaoh	Ex 18:8	3068
and *how* the **L** had delivered them.	Ex 18:8	3068
which the **L** had done to Israel,	Ex 18:9	3068
"Blessed be the **L** who delivered	Ex 18:10	3068
L is greater than all the gods;	Ex 18:11	3068
and the **L** called to him from the	Ex 19:3	3068
which the **L** had commanded him.	Ex 19:7	3068
the **L** has spoken we will do!"	Ex 19:8	3068
the words of the people to the **L**.	Ex 19:8	3068
The **L** said to Moses,	Ex 19:9	3068
the words of the people to the **L**.	Ex 19:9	3068
The **L** also said to Moses,	Ex 19:10	3068
the third day the **L** will come down	Ex 19:11	3068
the **L** descended upon it in fire;	Ex 19:18	3068
The **L** came down on Mount Sinai,	Ex 19:20	3068
and the **L** called Moses to the top	Ex 19:20	3068
Then the **L** spoke to Moses,	Ex 19:21	3068
break through to the **L** to gaze,	Ex 19:21	3068
the priests who come near to the **L**	Ex 19:22	3068
the **L** will break out against them."	Ex 19:22	3068
Moses said to the **L**,	Ex 19:23	3068
Then the **L** said to him,	Ex 19:24	3068
break through to come up to the **L**,	Ex 19:24	3068
"I am the **L** your God, who brought	Ex 20:2	3068
for I, the **L** your God, am a	Ex 20:5	3068
name of the **L** your God in vain,	Ex 20:7	3068
for the **L** will not leave him	Ex 20:7	3068
is a sabbath of the **L** your God;	Ex 20:10	3068
"For in six days the **L** made the	Ex 20:11	3068
therefore the **L** blessed the	Ex 20:11	3068
which the **L** your God gives you.	Ex 20:12	3068
Then the **L** said to Moses,	Ex 20:22	3068
an oath before the **L** shall be made	Ex 22:11	3068
god, other than to the **L** alone,	Ex 22:20	3068
shall appear before the **L** GOD.	Ex 23:17	3068
into the house of the **L** your God.	Ex 23:19	3068
you shall serve the **L** your God,	Ex 23:25	3068
"Come up to the **L**, you and Aaron,	Ex 24:1	3068
however, shall come near to the **L**,	Ex 24:2	3068
all the words of the **L** and all the	Ex 24:3	3068
the words which the **L** has spoken	Ex 24:3	3068
wrote down all the words of the **L**.	Ex 24:4	3068
bulls as peace offerings to the **L**.	Ex 24:5	3068
that the **L** has spoken we will do,	Ex 24:7	3068
which the **L** has made with you in	Ex 24:8	3068
Now the **L** said to Moses,	Ex 24:12	3068
The glory of the **L** rested on Mount	Ex 24:16	3068
the appearance of the glory of the **L**	Ex 24:17	3068
Then the **L** spoke to Moses, saying,	Ex 25:1	3068
evening to morning before the **L**;	Ex 27:21	3068
shall bear their names before the **L**	Ex 28:12	3068

memorial before the **L** continually.	Ex 28:29	3068
when he goes in before the **L**;	Ex 28:30	3068
heart before the **L** continually.	Ex 28:30	3068
the holy place before the **L**	Ex 28:35	3068
engravings of a seal, 'Holy to the **L**.'	Ex 28:36	3068
they may be accepted before the **L**.	Ex 28:38	3068
shall slaughter the bull before the **L**	Ex 29:11	3068
it is a burnt offering to the **L**:	Ex 29:18	3068
an offering by fire to the **L**.	Ex 29:18	3068
bread which is *set* before the **L**;	Ex 29:23	3068
as a wave offering before the **L**.	Ex 29:24	3068
for a soothing aroma before the **L**;	Ex 29:25	3068
is an offering by fire to the **L**.	Ex 29:25	3068
as a wave offering before the **L**;	Ex 29:26	3068
their heave offering to the **L**.	Ex 29:28	3068
an offering by fire to the **L**.	Ex 29:41	3068
the tent of meeting before the **L**,	Ex 29:42	3068
shall know that I am the **L** their God	Ex 29:46	3068
I am the **L** their God.	Ex 29:46	3068
be perpetual incense before the **L**	Ex 30:8	3068
It is most holy to the **L**."	Ex 30:10	3068
The **L** also spoke to Moses, saying,	Ex 30:11	3068
a ransom for himself to the **L**,	Ex 30:12	3068
shekel as a contribution to the **L**.	Ex 30:13	3068
give the contribution to the **L**.	Ex 30:14	3068
you give the contribution to the **L** to	Ex 30:15	3068
the sons of Israel before the **L**,	Ex 30:16	3068
The **L** spoke to Moses, saying,	Ex 30:17	3068
smoke a fire *sacrifice* to the **L**.	Ex 30:20	3068
Moreover, the **L** spoke to Moses,	Ex 30:22	3068
Then the **L** said to Moses,	Ex 30:34	3068
it shall be holy to you for the **L**.	Ex 30:37	3068
Now the **L** spoke to Moses, saying,	Ex 31:1	3068
The **L** spoke to Moses, saying,	Ex 31:12	3068
I am the **L** who sanctifies you.	Ex 31:13	3068
of complete rest, holy to the **L**;	Ex 31:15	3068
in six days the **L** made heaven and	Ex 31:17	3068
shall be a feast to the **L**."	Ex 32:5	3068
Then the **L** spoke to Moses,	Ex 32:7	3068
The **L** said to Moses,	Ex 32:9	3068
Moses entreated the **L** his God,	Ex 32:11	3068
"O **L**, why does Your anger burn	Ex 32:11	3068
So the **L** changed His mind about	Ex 32:14	3068
"Do not let the anger of my **l** burn;	Ex 32:22	113
"Whoever is for the **L**,	Ex 32:26	3068
"Thus says the **L**, the God of	Ex 32:27	3068
"Dedicate yourselves today to the **L**	Ex 32:29	3068
and now I am going up to the **L**,	Ex 32:30	3068
Then Moses returned to the **L**,	Ex 32:31	3068
The **L** said to Moses,	Ex 32:33	3068
Then the **L** smote the people,	Ex 32:35	3068
Then the **L** spoke to Moses,	Ex 33:1	3068
For the **L** had said to Moses,	Ex 33:5	3068
And everyone who sought the **L**	Ex 33:7	3068
and the **L** would speak with Moses.	Ex 33:9	3068
Thus the **L** used to speak to Moses	Ex 33:11	3068
Then Moses said to the **L**,	Ex 33:12	3068
The **L** said to Moses,	Ex 33:17	3068
proclaim the name of the **L** before	Ex 33:19	3068
Then the **L** said,	Ex 33:21	3068
Now the **L** said to Moses,	Ex 34:1	3068
Sinai, as the **L** had commanded him,	Ex 34:4	3068
The **L** descended in the cloud	Ex 34:5	3068
he called upon the name of the **L**.	Ex 34:5	3068
Then the **L** passed by in front of	Ex 34:6	3068
"The **L**, the LORD God,	Ex 34:6	3068
"The LORD, the **L** God,	Ex 34:6	3068
found favor in Your sight, O **L**,	Ex 34:9	136
let the **L** go along in our midst,	Ex 34:9	136
will see the working of the **L**,	Ex 34:10	3068
for the **L**, whose name is	Ex 34:14	3068
are to appear before the **L** GOD,	Ex 34:23	113
to appear before the **L** your God.	Ex 34:24	3068
into the house of the **L** your God.	Ex 34:26	3068
Then the **L** said to Moses,	Ex 34:27	3068
he was there with the **L** forty days	Ex 34:28	3068
do everything that the **L** had spoken	Ex 34:32	3068
Moses went in before the **L** to speak	Ex 34:34	3068
the **L** has commanded *you* to do:	Ex 35:1	3068
sabbath of complete rest to the **L**;	Ex 35:2	3068
thing which the **L** has commanded,	Ex 35:4	3068
among you a contribution to the **L**;	Ex 35:5	3068
make all that the **L** has commanded:	Ex 35:10	3068
an offering of gold to the **L**.	Ex 35:22	3068
which the **L** had commanded through	Ex 35:29	3068
a freewill offering to the **L**.	Ex 35:29	3068
the **L** has called by name Bezalel	Ex 35:30	3068
person in whom the **L** has put skill	Ex 36:1	3068
all that the **L** has commanded."	Ex 36:1	3068
in whom the **L** had put skill,	Ex 36:2	3068
the **L** commanded *us* to perform."	Ex 36:5	3068
that the **L** had commanded Moses.	Ex 38:22	3068
just as the **L** had commanded Moses.	Ex 39:1	3068
just as the **L** had commanded Moses.	Ex 39:5	3068
just as the **L** had commanded Moses.	Ex 39:7	3068
just as the **L** had commanded Moses.	Ex 39:21	3068
just as the **L** had commanded Moses.	Ex 39:26	3068
just as the **L** had commanded Moses.	Ex 39:29	3068
"Holy to the **L**."	Ex 39:30	3068
just as the **L** had commanded Moses.	Ex 39:31	3068
that the **L** had commanded Moses;	Ex 39:32	3068
that the **L** had commanded Moses.	Ex 39:42	3068
just as the **L** had commanded, this	Ex 39:43	3068
Then the **L** spoke to Moses, saying,	Ex 40:1	3068
all that the **L** had commanded him,	Ex 40:16	3068
just as the **L** had commanded Moses.	Ex 40:19	3068
just as the **L** had commanded Moses.	Ex 40:21	3068
bread in order on it before the **L**,	Ex 40:23	3068
just as the **L** had commanded Moses.	Ex 40:23	3068

Context	Reference	Number
He lighted the lamps before the **L**,	**Ex 40:25**	3068
just as the **L** had commanded Moses.	**Ex 40:25**	3068
just as the **L** had commanded Moses.	**Ex 40:27**	3068
just as the **L** had commanded Moses.	**Ex 40:29**	3068
just as the **L** had commanded Moses.	**Ex 40:32**	3068
glory of the **L** filled the tabernacle.	**Ex 40:34**	3068
glory of the **L** filled the tabernacle.	**Ex 40:35**	3068
the cloud of the **L** was on the	**Ex 40:38**	3068
Then the **L** called to Moses and	**Lv 1:1**	3068
you brings an offering to the **L**,	**Lv 1:2**	3068
he may be accepted before the **L**.	**Lv 1:3**	3068
slay the young bull before the **L**;	**Lv 1:5**	3068
fire of a soothing aroma to the **L**.	**Lv 1:9**	3068
the altar northward before the **L**,	**Lv 1:11**	3068
fire of a soothing aroma to the **L**.	**Lv 1:13**	3068
if his offering to the **L** is a burnt	**Lv 1:14**	3068
fire of a soothing aroma to the **L**.	**Lv 1:17**	3068
offering as an offering to the **L**,	**Lv 2:1**	3068
fire of a soothing aroma to the **L**.	**Lv 2:2**	3068
of the offerings to the **L** by fire.	**Lv 2:3**	3068
is made of these things to the **L**,	**Lv 2:8**	3068
fire of a soothing aroma to the **L**.	**Lv 2:9**	3068
of the offerings to the **L** by fire.	**Lv 2:10**	3068
which you bring to the **L**,	**Lv 2:11**	3068
as an offering by fire to the **L**.	**Lv 2:11**	3068
you shall bring them to the **L**,	**Lv 2:12**	3068
of early ripened things to the **L**,	**Lv 2:14**	3068
as an offering by fire to the **L**.	**Lv 2:16**	3068
it without defect before the **L**.	**Lv 3:1**	3068
an offering by fire to the **L**,	**Lv 3:3**	3068
fire of a soothing aroma to the **L**.	**Lv 3:5**	3068
sacrifice of peace offerings to the **L**	**Lv 3:6**	3068
he shall offer it before the **L**,	**Lv 3:7**	3068
as an offering by fire to the **L**,	**Lv 3:9**	3068
an offering by fire to the **L**.	**Lv 3:11**	3068
he shall offer it before the **L**,	**Lv 3:12**	3068
as an offering by fire to the **L**,	**Lv 3:14**	3068
Then the **L** spoke to Moses, saying,	**Lv 4:1**	3068
L has commanded not to be done,	**Lv 4:2**	3068
then let him offer to the **L** a bull	**Lv 4:3**	3068
the tent of meeting before the **L**,	**Lv 4:4**	3068
and slay the bull before the **L**.	**Lv 4:4**	3068
blood seven times before the **L**,	**Lv 4:6**	3068
incense which is before the **L** in the	**Lv 4:7**	3068
L has commanded not to be done,	**Lv 4:13**	3068
the head of the bull before the **L**,	**Lv 4:15**	3068
bull shall be slain before the **L**.	**Lv 4:15**	3068
it seven times before the **L**,	**Lv 4:17**	3068
the **L** in the tent of meeting;	**Lv 4:18**	3068
which the **L** his God has commanded	**Lv 4:22**	3068
the burnt offering before the **L**;	**Lv 4:24**	3068
L has commanded not to be done,	**Lv 4:27**	3068
for a soothing aroma to the **L**.	**Lv 4:31**	3068
on the offerings by fire to the **L**.	**Lv 4:35**	3068
also bring his guilt offering to the **L**	**Lv 5:6**	3068
then he shall bring to the **L** his	**Lv 5:7**	3068
the offerings of the **L** by fire:	**Lv 5:12**	3068
Then the **L** spoke to Moses, saying,	**Lv 5:14**	3068
bring his guilt offering to the **L**:	**Lv 5:15**	3068
L has commanded not to be done,	**Lv 5:17**	3068
certainly guilty before the **L**."	**Lv 5:19**	3068
Then the **L** spoke to Moses, saying,	**Lv 6:1**	3068
acts unfaithfully against the **L**,	**Lv 6:2**	3068
his guilt offering to the **L**,	**Lv 6:6**	3068
atonement for him before the **L**,	**Lv 6:7**	3068
Then the **L** spoke to Moses, saying,	**Lv 6:8**	3068
shall present it before the **L** in front	**Lv 6:14**	3068
as its memorial offering to the **L**.	**Lv 6:15**	3068
the offerings by fire to the **L**.	**Lv 6:18**	3068
Then the **L** spoke to Moses, saying,	**Lv 6:19**	3068
and his sons are to present to the **L**	**Lv 6:20**	3068
as a soothing aroma to the **L**.	**Lv 6:21**	3068
offered up in smoke to the **L**.	**Lv 6:22**	3068
Then the **L** spoke to Moses, saying,	**Lv 6:24**	3068
shall be slain before the **L**;	**Lv 6:25**	3068
as an offering by fire to the **L**;	**Lv 7:5**	3068
which shall be presented to the **L**.	**Lv 7:11**	3068
as a contribution to the **L**;	**Lv 7:14**	3068
offerings which belong to the **L**,	**Lv 7:20**	3068
offerings which belong to the **L**,	**Lv 7:21**	3068
Then the **L** spoke to Moses, saying,	**Lv 7:22**	3068
by fire is offered to the **L**,	**Lv 7:25**	3068
Then the **L** spoke to Moses, saying,	**Lv 7:28**	3068
sacrifice of his peace offerings to the **L**	**Lv 7:29**	3068
shall bring his offering to the **L** from	**Lv 7:29**	3068
bring offerings by fire to the **L**.	**Lv 7:30**	3068
as a wave offering before the **L**.	**Lv 7:30**	3068
the offerings by fire to the **L**,	**Lv 7:35**	3068
them to serve as priests to the **L**.	**Lv 7:35**	3068
'These the **L** had commanded to be	**Lv 7:36**	3068
which the **L** commanded Moses at	**Lv 7:38**	3068
to present their offerings to the **L** in	**Lv 7:38**	3068
Then the **L** spoke to Moses, saying,	**Lv 8:1**	3068
did just as the **L** commanded him.	**Lv 8:4**	3068
which the **L** has commanded to do."	**Lv 8:5**	3068
just as the **L** had commanded Moses.	**Lv 8:9**	3068
just as the **L** had commanded Moses.	**Lv 8:13**	3068
just as the **L** had commanded Moses.	**Lv 8:17**	3068
was an offering by fire to the **L**,	**Lv 8:21**	3068
just as the **L** had commanded Moses.	**Lv 8:21**	3068
bread that was before the **L**,	**Lv 8:26**	3068
as a wave offering before the **L**.	**Lv 8:27**	3068
was an offering by fire to the **L**.	**Lv 8:28**	3068
for a wave offering before the **L**;	**Lv 8:29**	3068
just as the **L** had commanded Moses.	**Lv 8:29**	3068
"The **L** has commanded to do as has	**Lv 8:34**	3068
and keep the charge of the **L**,	**Lv 8:35**	3068
the **L** had commanded through Moses.	**Lv 8:36**	3068
and offer *them* before the **L**.	**Lv 9:2**	3068

Context	Reference	Number
to sacrifice before the **L**,	**Lv 9:4**	3068
the **L** will appear to you.' "	**Lv 9:4**	3068
came near and stood before the **L**.	**Lv 9:5**	3068
the **L** has commanded you to do,	**Lv 9:6**	3068
of the **L** may appear to you."	**Lv 9:6**	3068
just as the **L** has commanded."	**Lv 9:7**	3068
just as the **L** had commanded Moses.	**Lv 9:10**	3068
as a wave offering before the **L**,	**Lv 9:21**	3068
the glory of the **L** appeared to all	**Lv 9:23**	3068
Then fire came out from before the **L**	**Lv 9:24**	3068
offered strange fire before the **L**,	**Lv 10:1**	3068
came out from the presence of the **L**	**Lv 10:2**	3068
them, and they died before the **L**.	**Lv 10:2**	3068
"It is what the **L** spoke, saying,	**Lv 10:3**	3068
which the **L** has brought about.	**Lv 10:6**	3068
The **L** then spoke to Aaron, saying,	**Lv 10:8**	3068
statutes which the **L** has spoken to	**Lv 10:11**	3068
as a wave offering before the **L**;	**Lv 10:15**	3068
just as the **L** has commanded."	**Lv 10:15**	3068
atonement for them before the **L**.	**Lv 10:17**	3068
their burnt offering before the **L**.	**Lv 10:19**	3068
been good in the sight of the **L**?"	**Lv 10:19**	3068
The **L** spoke again to Moses and to	**Lv 11:1**	3068
'For I am the **L** your God.	**Lv 11:44**	3068
'For I am the **L** who brought you	**Lv 11:45**	3068
Then the **L** spoke to Moses, saying,	**Lv 12:1**	3068
the **L** and make atonement for her,	**Lv 12:7**	3068
L spoke to Moses and to Aaron,	**Lv 13:1**	3068
Then the **L** spoke to Moses, saying,	**Lv 14:1**	3068
before the **L** at the doorway of the	**Lv 14:11**	3068
as a wave offering before the **L**.	**Lv 14:12**	3068
the oil seven times before the **L**.	**Lv 14:16**	3068
on his behalf before the **L**.	**Lv 14:18**	3068
the tent of meeting, before the **L**.	**Lv 14:23**	3068
for a wave offering before the **L**.	**Lv 14:24**	3068
palm seven times before the **L**.	**Lv 14:27**	3068
on his behalf before the **L**.	**Lv 14:29**	3068
atonement before the **L** on behalf of	**Lv 14:31**	3068
The **L** further spoke to Moses and	**Lv 14:33**	3068
The **L** also spoke to Moses and to	**Lv 15:1**	3068
and come before the **L** to the	**Lv 15:14**	3068
on his behalf before the **L** because	**Lv 15:15**	3068
atonement on her behalf before the **L**	**Lv 15:30**	3068
Now the **L** spoke to Moses after the	**Lv 16:1**	3068
approached the presence of the **L**	**Lv 16:1**	3068
The **L** said to Moses:	**Lv 16:2**	3068
goats and present them before the **L**	**Lv 16:7**	3068
one lot for the **L** and the other	**Lv 16:8**	3068
on which the lot for the **L** fell,	**Lv 16:9**	3068
be presented alive before the **L**,	**Lv 16:10**	3068
from upon the altar before the **L** and	**Lv 16:12**	3068
incense on the fire before the **L**,	**Lv 16:13**	3068
to the altar that is before the **L** and	**Lv 16:18**	3068
from all your sins before the **L**.	**Lv 16:30**	3068
just as the **L** had commanded Moses,	**Lv 16:34**	3068
Then the **L** spoke to Moses, saying,	**Lv 17:1**	3068
'This is what the **L** has commanded,	**Lv 17:2**	3068
to present *it* as an offering to the **L**	**Lv 17:4**	3068
before the tabernacle of the **L**,	**Lv 17:4**	3068
they may bring them in to the **L**,	**Lv 17:5**	3068
of peace offerings to the **L**.	**Lv 17:5**	3068
the blood on the altar of the **L** at the	**Lv 17:6**	3068
as a soothing aroma to the **L**.	**Lv 17:6**	3068
of meeting to offer it to the **L**,	**Lv 17:9**	3068
Then the **L** spoke to Moses, saying,	**Lv 18:1**	3068
'I am the **L** your God.	**Lv 18:2**	3068
I am the **L** your God.	**Lv 18:4**	3068
may live if he does them; I am the **L**.	**Lv 18:5**	3068
to uncover nakedness; I am the **L**.	**Lv 18:6**	3068
the name of your God; I am the **L**.	**Lv 18:21**	3068
I am the **L** your God.' "	**Lv 18:30**	3068
Then the **L** spoke to Moses, saying:	**Lv 19:1**	3068
for I the **L** your God am holy.	**Lv 19:2**	3068
I am the **L** your God.	**Lv 19:3**	3068
I am the **L** your God.	**Lv 19:4**	3068
sacrifice of peace offerings to the **L**,	**Lv 19:5**	3068
profaned the holy thing of the **L**;	**Lv 19:8**	3068
I am the **L** your God.	**Lv 19:10**	3068
the name of your God; I am the **L**.	**Lv 19:12**	3068
shall revere your God; I am the **L**.	**Lv 19:14**	3068
the life of your neighbor; I am the **L**.	**Lv 19:16**	3068
neighbor as yourself; I am the **L**.	**Lv 19:18**	3068
shall bring his guilt offering to the **L**	**Lv 19:21**	3068
guilt offering before the **L** for his sin	**Lv 19:22**	3068
an offering of praise to the **L**.	**Lv 19:24**	3068
I am the **L** your God.	**Lv 19:25**	3068
marks on yourselves: I am the **L**.	**Lv 19:28**	3068
revere My sanctuary; I am the **L**.	**Lv 19:30**	3068
I am the **L** your God.	**Lv 19:31**	3068
revere your God; I am the **L**.	**Lv 19:32**	3068
I am the **L** your God.	**Lv 19:34**	3068
I am the **L** your God, who brought	**Lv 19:36**	3068
ordinances and do them; I am the **L**.' "	**Lv 19:37**	3068
Then the **L** spoke to Moses, saying,	**Lv 20:1**	3068
be holy, for I am the **L** your God.	**Lv 20:7**	3068
I am the **L** who sanctifies you.	**Lv 20:8**	3068
I am the **L** your God, who has	**Lv 20:24**	3068
holy to Me, for I the **L** am holy;	**Lv 20:26**	3068
Then the **L** said to Moses,	**Lv 21:1**	3068
the offerings by fire to the **L**,	**Lv 21:6**	3068
I the **L**, who sanctifies you, am holy	**Lv 21:8**	3068
oil of his God is on him; I am the **L**.	**Lv 21:12**	3068
I am the **L** who sanctifies him.' "	**Lv 21:15**	3068
Then the **L** spoke to Moses, saying,	**Lv 21:16**	3068
am the **L** who sanctifies them.' "	**Lv 21:23**	3068
Then the **L** spoke to Moses, saying,	**Lv 22:1**	3068
My holy name; I am the **L**.	**Lv 22:2**	3068
sons of Israel dedicate to the **L**,	**Lv 22:3**	3068
cut off from before Me; I am the **L**.	**Lv 22:3**	3068

Context	Reference	Number
becoming unclean by it; I am the **L**.	**Lv 22:8**	3068
I am the **L** who sanctifies them.	**Lv 22:9**	3068
Israel which they offer to the **L**,	**Lv 22:15**	3068
am the **L** who sanctifies them.' "	**Lv 22:16**	3068
Then the **L** spoke to Moses, saying,	**Lv 22:17**	3068
to the **L** for a burnt offering	**Lv 22:18**	3068
to the **L** to fulfill a special vow or	**Lv 22:21**	3068
you shall not offer to the **L**,	**Lv 22:22**	3068
by fire on the altar to the **L**.	**Lv 22:22**	3068
cut, you shall not offer to the **L**,	**Lv 22:24**	3068
Then the **L** spoke to Moses, saying,	**Lv 22:26**	3068
of an offering by fire to the **L**.	**Lv 22:27**	3068
of thanksgiving to the **L**,	**Lv 22:29**	3068
none of it until morning; I am the **L**.	**Lv 22:30**	3068
and do them; I am the **L**.	**Lv 22:31**	3068
I am the **L** who sanctifies you,	**Lv 22:32**	3068
to be your God; I am the **L**."	**Lv 22:33**	3068
The **L** spoke again to Moses,	**Lv 23:1**	3068
it is a sabbath to the **L** in all your	**Lv 23:3**	3068
are the appointed times of the **L**,	**Lv 23:4**	3068
Feast of Unleavened Bread to the **L**;	**Lv 23:6**	3068
an offering by fire to the **L**.	**Lv 23:8**	3068
Then the **L** spoke to Moses, saying,	**Lv 23:9**	3068
He shall wave the sheaf before the **L**	**Lv 23:11**	3068
for a burnt offering to the **L**.	**Lv 23:12**	3068
an offering by fire to the **L** *for* a	**Lv 23:13**	3068
a new grain offering to the **L**.	**Lv 23:16**	3068
leaven as first fruits to the **L**.	**Lv 23:17**	3068
to be a burnt offering to the **L**,	**Lv 23:18**	3068
fire of a soothing aroma to the **L**	**Lv 23:18**	3068
with two lambs before the **L**;	**Lv 23:20**	3068
be holy to the **L** for the priest.	**Lv 23:20**	3068
I am the **L** your God.' "	**Lv 23:22**	3068
Again the **L** spoke to Moses,	**Lv 23:23**	3068
an offering by fire to the **L**.' "	**Lv 23:25**	3068
The **L** spoke to Moses, saying,	**Lv 23:26**	3068
an offering by fire to the **L**.	**Lv 23:27**	3068
your behalf before the **L** your God.	**Lv 23:28**	3068
Again the **L** spoke to Moses,	**Lv 23:33**	3068
of Booths for seven days to the **L**.	**Lv 23:34**	3068
an offering by fire to the **L**.	**Lv 23:36**	3068
an offering by fire to the **L**;	**Lv 23:36**	3068
are the appointed times of the **L**	**Lv 23:37**	3068
to present offerings by fire to the **L**	**Lv 23:37**	3068
those of the sabbaths of the **L**,	**Lv 23:38**	3068
which you give to the **L**.	**Lv 23:38**	3068
you shall celebrate the feast of the **L**	**Lv 23:39**	3068
you shall rejoice before the **L** your	**Lv 23:40**	3068
thus celebrate it *as* a feast to the **L**	**Lv 23:41**	3068
I am the **L** your God.' "	**Lv 23:43**	3068
the appointed times of the **L**.	**Lv 23:44**	3068
Then the **L** spoke to Moses, saying,	**Lv 24:1**	3068
morning before the **L** continually;	**Lv 24:3**	3068
before the **L** continually.	**Lv 24:4**	3068
the pure *gold* table before the **L**.	**Lv 24:6**	3068
even an offering by fire to the **L**.	**Lv 24:7**	3068
in order before the **L** continually;	**Lv 24:8**	3068
the command of the **L** might be made	**Lv 24:12**	3068
Then the **L** spoke to Moses, saying,	**Lv 24:13**	3068
who blasphemes the name of the **L**	**Lv 24:16**	3068
for I am the **L** your God.' "	**Lv 24:22**	3068
just as the **L** had commanded Moses.	**Lv 24:23**	3068
The **L** then spoke to Moses at Mount	**Lv 25:1**	3068
shall have a sabbath to the **L**.	**Lv 25:2**	3068
sabbath rest, a sabbath to the **L**;	**Lv 25:4**	3068
for I am the **L** your God.	**Lv 25:17**	3068
'I am the **L** your God, who brought	**Lv 25:38**	3068
I am the **L** your God.	**Lv 25:55**	3068
for I am the **L** your God.	**Lv 26:1**	3068
reverence My sanctuary; I am the **L**.	**Lv 26:2**	3068
'I am the **L** your God, who brought	**Lv 26:13**	3068
for I am the **L** their God.	**Lv 26:44**	3068
I might be their God. I am the **L**.	**Lv 26:45**	3068
and laws which the **L** established	**Lv 26:46**	3068
Again, the **L** spoke to Moses,	**Lv 27:1**	3068
of persons belonging to the **L**.	**Lv 27:2**	3068
present as an offering to the **L**,	**Lv 27:9**	3068
one gives to the **L** shall be holy.	**Lv 27:9**	3068
present as an offering to the **L**,	**Lv 27:11**	3068
his house as holy to the **L**,	**Lv 27:14**	3068
if a man consecrates to the **L** part	**Lv 27:16**	3068
the field shall be holy to the **L**,	**Lv 27:21**	3068
if he consecrates to the **L** a field	**Lv 27:22**	3068
your valuation as holy to the **L**.	**Lv 27:23**	3068
as a firstborn belongs to the **L**,	**Lv 27:26**	3068
which a man sets apart to the **L**	**Lv 27:28**	3068
destruction is most holy to the **L**.	**Lv 27:28**	3068
it is holy to the **L**.	**Lv 27:30**	3068
tenth one shall be holy to the **L**.	**Lv 27:32**	3068
are the commandments which the **L**	**Lv 27:34**	3068
Then the **L** spoke to Moses in the	**Nu 1:1**	3068
just as the **L** had commanded Moses.	**Nu 1:19**	3068
For the **L** had spoken to Moses,	**Nu 1:48**	3068
which the **L** had commanded Moses,	**Nu 1:54**	3068
the **L** spoke to Moses and to Aaron,	**Nu 2:1**	3068
just as the **L** had commanded Moses.	**Nu 2:33**	3068
to all that the **L** commanded Moses,	**Nu 2:34**	3068
L spoke with Moses on Mount Sinai.	**Nu 3:1**	3068
Nadab and Abihu died before the **L**	**Nu 3:4**	3068
offered strange fire before the **L**	**Nu 3:4**	3068
Then the **L** spoke to Moses, saying,	**Nu 3:5**	3068
Again the **L** spoke to Moses,	**Nu 3:11**	3068
They shall be Mine; I am the **L**."	**Nu 3:13**	3068
Then the **L** spoke to Moses in the	**Nu 3:14**	3068
according to the word of the **L**,	**Nu 3:16**	3068
at the command of the **L** by their	**Nu 3:39**	3068
Then the **L** said to Moses,	**Nu 3:40**	3068
the Levites for Me, I am the **L**,	**Nu 3:41**	3068
just as the **L** had commanded him;	**Nu 3:42**	3068

Then the **L** spoke to Moses, saying, **Nu 3:44** 3068
Levites shall be Mine; I am the **L**. **Nu 3:45** 3068
his sons, at the command of the **L**, **Nu 3:51** 3068
just as the **L** had commanded Moses. **Nu 3:51** 3068
the **L** spoke to Moses and to Aaron, **Nu 4:1** 3068
the **L** spoke to Moses and to Aaron, **Nu 4:17** 3068
Then the **L** spoke to Moses, saying, **Nu 4:21** 3068
the commandment of the **L** through **Nu 4:37** 3068
to the commandment of the **L**. **Nu 4:41** 3068
the commandment of the **L** through **Nu 4:45** 3068
the commandment of the **L** through **Nu 4:49** 3068
just as the **L** had commanded Moses. **Nu 4:49** 3068
Then the **L** spoke to Moses, saying, **Nu 5:1** 3068
just as the **L** had spoken to Moses, **Nu 5:4** 3068
Then the **L** spoke to Moses, saying, **Nu 5:5** 3068
acting unfaithfully against the **L**, **Nu 5:6** 3068
must go to the **L** for the priest, **Nu 5:8** 3068
Then the **L** spoke to Moses, saying, **Nu 5:11** 3068
and have her stand before the **L**, **Nu 5:16** 3068
have the woman stand before the **L** **Nu 5:18** 3068
"the **L** make you a curse and an **Nu 5:21** 3068
wave the grain offering before the **L** **Nu 5:25** 3068
make the woman stand before the **L**, **Nu 5:30** 3068
Again the **L** spoke to Moses, **Nu 6:1** 3068
to dedicate himself to the **L**, **Nu 6:2** 3068
he separated himself to the **L**; **Nu 6:5** 3068
'All the days of his separation to the **L** **Nu 6:6** 3068
separation he is holy to the **L**. **Nu 6:8** 3068
shall dedicate to the **L** his days as a **Nu 6:12** 3068
present his offering to the **L**: **Nu 6:14** 3068
priest shall present *them* before the **L** **Nu 6:16** 3068
of peace offerings to the **L**, **Nu 6:17** 3068
for a wave offering before the **L**. **Nu 6:20** 3068
who vows his offering to the **L** **Nu 6:21** 3068
Then the **L** spoke to Moses, saying, **Nu 6:22** 3068
The **L** bless you, and keep you; **Nu 6:24** 3068
The **L** make His face shine on you, **Nu 6:25** 3068
The **L** lift up His countenance on **Nu 6:26** 3068
their offering before the **L**, **Nu 7:3** 3068
Then the **L** spoke to Moses, saying, **Nu 7:4** 3068
Then the **L** said to Moses, **Nu 7:11** 3068
Then the **L** spoke to Moses, saying, **Nu 8:1** 3068
just as the **L** had commanded Moses. **Nu 8:3** 3068
which the **L** had shown Moses, **Nu 8:4** 3068
Again the **L** spoke to Moses, **Nu 8:5** 3068
present the Levites before the **L**; **Nu 8:10** 3068
shall present the Levites before the **L** **Nu 8:11** 3068
to perform the service of the **L**. **Nu 8:11** 3068
for a burnt offering to the **L**, **Nu 8:12** 3068
them as a wave offering to the **L**. **Nu 8:13** 3068
according to all that the **L** had **Nu 8:20** 3068
as a wave offering before the **L**. **Nu 8:21** 3068
just as the **L** had commanded Moses **Nu 8:22** 3068
Now the **L** spoke to Moses, saying, **Nu 8:23** 3068
Thus the **L** spoke to Moses in the **Nu 9:1** 3068
that the **L** had commanded Moses, **Nu 9:5** 3068
offering of the **L** at its appointed time **Nu 9:7** 3068
L will command concerning you." **Nu 9:8** 3068
Then the **L** spoke to Moses, saying, **Nu 9:9** 3068
observe the Passover to the **L**. **Nu 9:10** 3068
did not present the offering of the **L** **Nu 9:13** 3068
observes the Passover to the **L**, **Nu 9:14** 3068
At the command of the **L** the sons **Nu 9:18** 3068
command of the **L** they would camp; **Nu 9:18** 3068
according to the command of the **L** **Nu 9:20** 3068
the command of the **L** they set out. **Nu 9:20** 3068
the command of the **L** they camped, **Nu 9:23** 3068
the command of the **L** they set out; **Nu 9:23** 3068
command of the **L** through Moses. **Nu 9:23** 3068
The **L** spoke further to Moses, **Nu 10:1** 3068
remembered before the **L** your God, **Nu 10:9** 3068
I am the **L** your God." **Nu 10:10** 3068
the commandment of the **L** through **Nu 10:13** 3068
to the place of which the **L** said, **Nu 10:29** 3068
for the **L** has promised good **Nu 10:29** 3068
whatever good the **L** does for us, **Nu 10:32** 3068
set out from the mount of the **L** **Nu 10:33** 3068
with the ark of the covenant of the **L** **Nu 10:33** 3068
The cloud of the **L** was over them by **Nu 10:34** 3068
that Moses said, "Rise up, O **L**! **Nu 10:35** 3068
he said, "Return, O **L**, **Nu 10:36** 3068
adversity in the hearing of the **L**; **Nu 11:1** 3068
and when the **L** heard *it,* His anger **Nu 11:1** 3068
and the fire of the **L** burned among **Nu 11:1** 3068
Moses, and Moses prayed to the **L** **Nu 11:2** 3068
fire of the **L** burned among them. **Nu 11:3** 3068
anger of the **L** was kindled greatly, **Nu 11:10** 3068
So Moses said to the **L**, **Nu 11:11** 3068
The **L** therefore said to Moses, **Nu 11:16** 3068
have wept in the ears of the **L**, **Nu 11:18** 3068
Therefore the **L** will give you meat **Nu 11:18** 3068
because you have rejected the **L** **Nu 11:20** 3068
The **L** said to Moses, **Nu 11:23** 3068
the people the words of the **L**. **Nu 11:24** 3068
Then the **L** came down in the cloud **Nu 11:25** 3068
"Moses, my **l**, restrain them." **Nu 11:28** 113
that the **L** would put His Spirit **Nu 11:29** 3068
went forth a wind from the **L** **Nu 11:31** 3068
the anger of the **L** was kindled **Nu 11:33** 3068
and the **L** struck the people with a **Nu 11:33** 3068
"Has the **L** indeed spoken only **Nu 12:2** 3068
And the **L** heard it. **Nu 12:2** 3068
Suddenly the **L** said to Moses **Nu 12:4** 3068
Then the **L** came down in a pillar **Nu 12:5** 3068
I, the **L**, shall make Myself known **Nu 12:6** 3068
And he beholds the form of the **L**. **Nu 12:8** 3068
So the anger of the **L** burned **Nu 12:9** 3068
"Oh, my **l**, I beg you, do not **Nu 12:11** 113
Moses cried out to the **L**, **Nu 12:13** 3068

But the **L** said to Moses, **Nu 12:14** 3068
Then the **L** spoke to Moses saying, **Nu 13:1** 3068
of Paran at the command of the **L**, **Nu 13:3** 3068
the **L** bringing us into this land, **Nu 14:3** 3068
"If the **L** is pleased with us, **Nu 14:8** 3068
"Only do not rebel against the **L**; **Nu 14:9** 3068
from them, and the **L** is with us; **Nu 14:9** 3068
Then the glory of the **L** appeared **Nu 14:10** 3068
The **L** said to Moses, **Nu 14:11** 3068
But Moses said to the **L**, **Nu 14:13** 3068
They have heard that You, O **L**, **Nu 14:14** 3068
for You, O **L**, are seen eye to eye, **Nu 14:14** 3068
'Because the **L** could not bring **Nu 14:16** 3068
let the power of the **L** be great, **Nu 14:17** 136
'The **L** is slow to anger and **Nu 14:18** 3068
the **L** said, "I have pardoned *them* **Nu 14:20** 3068
be filled with the glory of the **L**. **Nu 14:21** 3068
The **L** spoke to Moses and Aaron, **Nu 14:26** 3068
'As I live,' says the **L**, **Nu 14:28** 3068
'I, the **L**, have spoken, surely **Nu 14:35** 3068
died by a plague before the **L**. **Nu 14:37** 3068
place which the **L** has promised." **Nu 14:40** 3068
the commandment of the **L**, **Nu 14:41** 3068
for the **L** is not among you. **Nu 14:42** 3068
turned back from following the **L**. **Nu 14:43** 3068
And the **L** will not be with you." **Nu 14:43** 3068
the ark of the covenant of the **L** **Nu 14:44** 3068
Now the **L** spoke to Moses, saying, **Nu 15:1** 3068
make an offering by fire to the **L**, **Nu 15:3** 3068
to make a soothing aroma to the **L**, **Nu 15:3** 3068
shall present to the **L** a grain offering **Nu 15:4** 3068
wine as a soothing aroma to the **L**. **Nu 15:7** 3068
or for peace offerings to the **L**, **Nu 15:8** 3068
as a soothing aroma to the **L**. **Nu 15:10** 3068
as a soothing aroma to the **L**. **Nu 15:13** 3068
as a soothing aroma to the **L**, **Nu 15:14** 3068
shall the alien be before the **L**. **Nu 15:15** 3068
Then the **L** spoke to Moses, saying, **Nu 15:17** 3068
lift up an offering to the **L**. **Nu 15:19** 3068
give to the **L** an offering throughout **Nu 15:21** 3068
which the **L** has spoken to Moses, **Nu 15:22** 3068
even all that the **L** has commanded **Nu 15:23** 3068
from the day when the **L** gave **Nu 15:23** 3068
as a soothing aroma to the **L**, **Nu 15:24** 3068
an offering by fire to the **L**, **Nu 15:25** 3068
their sin offering before the **L**, **Nu 15:25** 3068
shall make atonement before the **L** **Nu 15:28** 3068
that one is blaspheming the **L**; **Nu 15:30** 3068
he has despised the word of the **L** **Nu 15:31** 3068
Then the **L** said to Moses, **Nu 15:35** 3068
just as the **L** had commanded Moses. **Nu 15:36** 3068
The **L** also spoke to Moses, saying, **Nu 15:37** 3068
all the commandments of the **L**, **Nu 15:39** 3068
"I am the **L** your God who brought **Nu 15:41** 3068
I am the **L** your God." **Nu 15:41** 3068
them, and the **L** is in their midst; **Nu 16:3** 3068
above the assembly of the **L**?" **Nu 16:3** 3068
the **L** will show who is His, **Nu 16:5** 3068
in the presence of the **L** tomorrow; **Nu 16:7** 3068
and the man whom the **L** chooses **Nu 16:7** 3068
of the tabernacle of the **L**, **Nu 16:9** 3068
gathered together against the **L**; **Nu 16:11** 3068
but you would also **l** it over us? **Nu 16:13** 8323
very angry and said to the **L**, **Nu 16:15** 3068
be present before the **L** tomorrow, **Nu 16:16** 3068
you bring his censer before the **L**, **Nu 16:17** 3068
And the glory of the **L** appeared to **Nu 16:19** 3068
the **L** spoke to Moses and Aaron, **Nu 16:20** 3068
Then the **L** spoke to Moses, saying, **Nu 16:23** 3068
L has sent me to do all these deeds; **Nu 16:28** 3068
men, *then* the **L** has not sent me. **Nu 16:29** 3068
"But if the **L** brings about an **Nu 16:30** 3068
these men have spurned the **L**." **Nu 16:30** 3068
Fire also came forth from the **L** **Nu 16:35** 3068
Then the **L** spoke to Moses, saying, **Nu 16:36** 3068
they did present them before the **L** **Nu 16:38** 3068
near to burn incense before the **L**; **Nu 16:40** 3068
as the **L** had spoken to him through **Nu 16:40** 3068
and the glory of the **L** appeared. **Nu 16:42** 3068
and the **L** spoke to Moses, saying, **Nu 16:44** 3068
wrath has gone forth from the **L**, **Nu 16:46** 3068
Then the **L** spoke to Moses, saying, **Nu 17:1** 3068
deposited the rods before the **L** in **Nu 17:7** 3068
the rods from the presence of the **L** **Nu 17:9** 3068
But the **L** said to Moses, **Nu 17:10** 3068
just as the **L** had commanded him, **Nu 17:11** 3068
near to the tabernacle of the **L**, **Nu 17:13** 3068
So the **L** said to Aaron, **Nu 18:1** 3068
a gift to you, dedicated to the **L**, **Nu 18:6** 3068
Then the **L** spoke to Aaron, **Nu 18:8** 3068
of those which they give to the **L**, **Nu 18:12** 3068
land, which they bring to the **L**, **Nu 18:13** 3068
animal, which they offer to the **L**, **Nu 18:15** 3068
for a soothing aroma to the **L**. **Nu 18:17** 3068
the sons of Israel offer to the **L**, **Nu 18:19** 3068
covenant of salt before the **L** to you **Nu 18:19** 3068
Then the **L** said to Aaron, **Nu 18:20** 3068
offer as an offering to the **L**, **Nu 18:24** 3068
Then the **L** spoke to Moses, saying, **Nu 18:25** 3068
an offering from it to the **L**, **Nu 18:26** 3068
also present an offering to the **L** **Nu 18:28** 3068
every offering due to the **L**, **Nu 18:29** 3068
the **L** spoke to Moses and Aaron, **Nu 19:1** 3068
the law which the **L** has commanded, **Nu 19:2** 3068
defiles the tabernacle of the **L**; **Nu 19:13** 3068
defiled the sanctuary of the **L**; **Nu 19:20** 3068
brothers perished before the **L**! **Nu 20:3** 3068
glory of the **L** appeared to them; **Nu 20:6** 3068
and the **L** spoke to Moses, saying, **Nu 20:7** 3068

took the rod from before the **L**, **Nu 20:9** 3068
But the **L** said to Moses and Aaron, **Nu 20:12** 3068
of Israel contended with the **L**, **Nu 20:13** 3068
'But when we cried out to the **L**, **Nu 20:16** 3068
Then the **L** spoke to Moses and **Nu 20:23** 3068
did just as the **L** had commanded, **Nu 20:27** 3068
So Israel made a vow to the **L** **Nu 21:2** 3068
The **L** heard the voice of Israel **Nu 21:3** 3068
The **L** sent fiery serpents **Nu 21:6** 3068
have spoken against the **L** and you; **Nu 21:7** 3068
intercede with the **L**, **Nu 21:7** 3068
Then the **L** said to Moses, **Nu 21:8** 3068
in the Book of the Wars of the **L**, **Nu 21:14** 3068
well where the **L** said to Moses, **Nu 21:16** 3068
But the **L** said to Moses, **Nu 21:34** 3068
to you as the **L** may speak to me." **Nu 22:8** 3068
for the **L** has refused to let me go **Nu 22:13** 3068
to the command of the **L** my God. **Nu 22:18** 3068
else the **L** will speak to me." **Nu 22:19** 3068
and the angel of the **L** took his **Nu 22:22** 3068
the donkey saw the angel of the **L** **Nu 22:23** 3068
Then the angel of the **L** stood in a **Nu 22:24** 3068
the donkey saw the angel of the **L**, **Nu 22:25** 3068
The angel of the **L** went further, **Nu 22:26** 3068
the donkey saw the angel of the **L**, **Nu 22:27** 3068
And the **L** opened the mouth of the **Nu 22:28** 3068
the **L** opened the eyes of Balaam, **Nu 22:31** 3068
and he saw the angel of the **L** **Nu 22:31** 3068
The angel of the **L** said to him, **Nu 22:32** 3068
Balaam said to the angel of the **L**, **Nu 22:34** 3068
the angel of the **L** said to Balaam, **Nu 22:35** 3068
perhaps the **L** will come to meet me **Nu 23:3** 3068
Then the **L** put a word in Balaam's **Nu 23:5** 3068
whom the **L** has not denounced? **Nu 23:8** 3068
what the **L** puts in my mouth?" **Nu 23:12** 3068
offering while I myself meet *the* **L** **Nu 23:15** 3068
Then the **L** met Balaam and put a **Nu 23:16** 3068
"What has the **L** spoken?" **Nu 23:17** 3068
The **L** his God is with him, And the **Nu 23:21** 3068
'Whatever the **L** speaks, that I **Nu 23:26** 3068
it pleased the **L** to bless Israel, **Nu 24:1** 3068
Like aloes planted by the **L**, **Nu 24:6** 3068
L has held you back from honor." **Nu 24:11** 3068
contrary to the command of the **L**, **Nu 24:13** 3068
What the **L** speaks, that I will **Nu 24:13** 3068
the **L** was angry against Israel. **Nu 25:3** 3068
The **L** said to Moses, **Nu 25:4** 3068
in broad daylight before the **L**, **Nu 25:4** 3068
fierce anger of the **L** may turn away **Nu 25:4** 3068
Then the **L** spoke to Moses, saying, **Nu 25:10** 3068
Then the **L** spoke to Moses, saying, **Nu 25:16** 3068
that the **L** spoke to Moses and to **Nu 26:1** 3068
as the **L** has commanded Moses." **Nu 26:4** 3068
when they contended against the **L**, **Nu 26:9** 3068
Then the **L** spoke to Moses, saying, **Nu 26:52** 3068
offered strange fire before the **L**. **Nu 26:61** 3068
For the **L** had said of them, **Nu 26:65** 3068
themselves together against the **L** **Nu 27:3** 3068
brought their case before the **L**. **Nu 27:5** 3068
Then the **L** spoke to Moses, saying, **Nu 27:6** 3068
just as the **L** commanded Moses.' " **Nu 27:11** 3068
Then the **L** said to Moses, **Nu 27:12** 3068
Then Moses spoke to the **L**, **Nu 27:15** 3068
"May the **L**, the God of the spirits **Nu 27:16** 3068
that the congregation of the **L** will **Nu 27:17** 3068
So the **L** said to Moses, **Nu 27:18** 3068
judgment of the Urim before the **L**. **Nu 27:21** 3068
did just as the **L** commanded him; **Nu 27:22** 3068
as the **L** had spoken through Moses. **Nu 27:23** 3068
Then the **L** spoke to Moses, saying, **Nu 28:1** 3068
which you shall offer to the **L**: **Nu 28:3** 3068
an offering by fire to the **L**. **Nu 28:6** 3068
drink offering of strong drink to the **L**. **Nu 28:7** 3068
fire, a soothing aroma to the **L**. **Nu 28:8** 3068
present a burnt offering to the **L**: **Nu 28:11** 3068
an offering by fire to the **L**. **Nu 28:13** 3068
goat for a sin offering to the **L**; **Nu 28:15** 3068
fire, a burnt offering to the **L**: **Nu 28:19** 3068
of a soothing aroma to the **L**; **Nu 28:24** 3068
present a new grain offering to the **L** **Nu 28:26** 3068
for a soothing aroma to the **L**: **Nu 28:27** 3068
as a soothing aroma to the **L**: **Nu 29:2** 3068
an offering by fire to the **L**. **Nu 29:6** 3068
present a burnt offering to the **L** *as* **Nu 29:8** 3068
you shall observe a feast to the **L** **Nu 29:12** 3068
fire as a soothing aroma to the **L**: **Nu 29:13** 3068
as a soothing aroma to the **L**: **Nu 29:36** 3068
'You shall present these to the **L** at **Nu 29:39** 3068
that the **L** had commanded Moses. **Nu 29:40** 3068
word which the **L** has commanded. **Nu 30:1** 3068
"If a man makes a vow to the **L**, **Nu 30:2** 3068
if a woman makes a vow to the **L**, **Nu 30:3** 3068
and the **L** will forgive her because **Nu 30:5** 3068
and the **L** will forgive her. **Nu 30:8** 3068
them, and the **L** will forgive her. **Nu 30:12** 3068
which the **L** commanded Moses, **Nu 30:16** 3068
Then the **L** spoke to Moses, saying, **Nu 31:1** 3068
just as the **L** had commanded Moses, **Nu 31:7** 3068
trespass against the **L** in the matter **Nu 31:16** 3068
among the congregation of the **L**. **Nu 31:16** 3068
which the **L** has commanded Moses: **Nu 31:21** 3068
Then the **L** spoke to Moses, saying, **Nu 31:25** 3068
"Levy a tax for the **L** from **Nu 31:28** 3068
priest, as an offering to the **L**. **Nu 31:29** 3068
of the tabernacle of the **L**." **Nu 31:30** 3068
just as the **L** had commanded Moses. **Nu 31:31** 3068
just as the **L** had commanded Moses. **Nu 31:41** 3068
charge of the tabernacle of the **L**, **Nu 31:47** 3068
just as the **L** had commanded Moses. **Nu 31:47** 3068

brought as an offering to the **L**	**Nu 31:50**	3068
for ourselves before the **L**."	**Nu 31:50**	3068
which they offered up to the **L**,	**Nu 31:52**	3068
the sons of Israel before the **L**.	**Nu 31:54**	3068
the land which the **L** conquered	**Nu 32:4**	3068
land which the **L** has given them?	**Nu 32:7**	3068
land which the **L** had given them.	**Nu 32:9**	3068
they have followed the **L** fully.'	**Nu 32:12**	3068
had done evil in the sight of the **L**	**Nu 32:13**	3068
anger of the **L** against Israel.	**Nu 32:14**	3068
you will arm yourselves before the **L**	**Nu 32:20**	3068
cross over the Jordan before the **L**	**Nu 32:21**	3068
the land is subdued before the **L**,	**Nu 32:22**	3068
toward the **L** and toward Israel,	**Nu 32:22**	3068
for a possession before the **L**.	**Nu 32:22**	3068
you have sinned against the **L**,	**Nu 32:23**	3068
will do just as my **l** commands.	**Nu 32:25**	113
the presence of the **L** to battle,	**Nu 32:27**	3068
to battle, just as my **l** says."	**Nu 32:27**	113
Jordan in the presence of the **L**,	**Nu 32:29**	3068
the **L** has said to your servants,	**Nu 32:31**	3068
armed in the presence of the **L**	**Nu 32:32**	3068
journeys by the command of the **L**,	**Nu 33:2**	3068
the **L** had struck down among them.	**Nu 33:4**	3068
The **L** had also executed judgments	**Nu 33:4**	3068
Mount Hor at the command of the **L**,	**Nu 33:38**	3068
Then the **L** spoke to Moses in the	**Nu 33:50**	3068
Then the **L** spoke to Moses, saying,	**Nu 34:1**	3068
which the **L** has commanded to give	**Nu 34:13**	3068
Then the **L** spoke to Moses, saying,	**Nu 34:16**	3068
the **L** commanded to apportion the	**Nu 34:29**	3068
Now the **L** spoke to Moses in the	**Nu 35:1**	3068
Then the **L** spoke to Moses, saying,	**Nu 35:9**	3068
for I the **L** am dwelling in the	**Nu 35:34**	3068
"The **L** commanded my lord to give	**Nu 36:2**	3068
"The LORD commanded my **l** to give	**Nu 36:2**	113
and my **l** was commanded by the LORD	**Nu 36:2**	113
my lord was commanded by the **L** to	**Nu 36:2**	3068
according to the word of the **L**,	**Nu 36:5**	3068
"This is what the **L** has commanded	**Nu 36:6**	3068
Just as the **L** had commanded Moses,	**Nu 36:10**	3068
ordinances which the **L** commanded	**Nu 36:13**	3068
according to all that the **L** had	**Dt 1:3**	3068
L our God spoke to us at Horeb,	**Dt 1:6**	3068
L swore to give to your fathers,	**Dt 1:8**	3068
'The **L** your God has multiplied	**Dt 1:10**	3068
'May the **L**, the God of your fathers	**Dt 1:11**	3068
as the **L** our God had commanded us;	**Dt 1:19**	3068
the **L** our God is about to give us.	**Dt 1:20**	3068
the **L** your God has placed the land	**Dt 1:21**	3068
go up, take possession, as the **L**,	**Dt 1:21**	3068
L our God is about to give us.'	**Dt 1:25**	3068
the command of the **L** your God;	**Dt 1:26**	3068
'Because the **L** hates us, He has	**Dt 1:27**	3068
'The **L** your God who goes before	**Dt 1:30**	3068
how the **L** your God carried you,	**Dt 1:31**	3068
you did not trust the **L** your God,	**Dt 1:32**	3068
L heard the sound of your words,	**Dt 1:34**	3068
he has followed the **L** fully.'	**Dt 1:36**	3068
"The **L** was angry with me also on	**Dt 1:37**	3068
'We have sinned against the **L**;	**Dt 1:41**	3068
as the **L** our God commanded us.'	**Dt 1:41**	3068
"And the **L** said to me,	**Dt 1:42**	3068
against the command of the **L**,	**Dt 1:43**	3068
returned and wept before the **L**;	**Dt 1:45**	3068
L did not listen to your voice nor	**Dt 1:45**	3068
the Red Sea, as the **L** spoke to me,	**Dt 2:1**	3068
"And the **L** spoke to me, saying,	**Dt 2:2**	3068
"For the **L** your God has blessed	**Dt 2:7**	3068
the **L** your God has been with you;	**Dt 2:7**	3068
"Then the **L** said to me,	**Dt 2:9**	3068
which the **L** gave to them.)	**Dt 2:12**	3068
camp, as the **L** had sworn to them.	**Dt 2:14**	3068
hand of the **L** was against them,	**Dt 2:15**	3068
that the **L** spoke to me, saying,	**Dt 2:17**	3068
the **L** destroyed them before them.	**Dt 2:21**	3068
the **L** our God is giving to us.'	**Dt 2:29**	3068
for the **L** your God hardened his	**Dt 2:30**	3068
"The **L** said to me,	**Dt 2:31**	3068
"The **L** our God delivered him	**Dt 2:33**	3068
the **L** our God delivered all over	**Dt 2:36**	3068
the **L** our God had commanded us.	**Dt 2:37**	3068
"But the **L** said to me,	**Dt 3:2**	3068
the **L** our God delivered Og also,	**Dt 3:3**	3068
'The **L** your God has given you this	**Dt 3:18**	3068
until the **L** gives rest to your	**Dt 3:20**	3068
which the **L** your God will give them	**Dt 3:20**	3068
'Your eyes have seen all that the **L**	**Dt 3:21**	3068
so the **L** shall do to all the	**Dt 3:21**	3068
for the **L** your God is the one	**Dt 3:22**	3068
pleaded with the **L** at that time,	**Dt 3:23**	3068
'O **L** GOD, You have begun to show	**Dt 3:24**	136
"But the **L** was angry with me on	**Dt 3:26**	3068
and the **L** said to me,	**Dt 3:26**	3068
the **L**, the God of your fathers, is	**Dt 4:1**	3068
L your God which I command you.	**Dt 4:2**	3068
"Your eyes have seen what the **L**	**Dt 4:3**	3068
the **L** your God has destroyed them	**Dt 4:3**	3068
who held fast to the **L** your God	**Dt 4:4**	3068
just as the **L** my God commanded me,	**Dt 4:5**	3068
has a god so near to it as is the **L** our	**Dt 4:7**	3068
before the **L** your God at Horeb,	**Dt 4:10**	3068
at Horeb, when the **L** said to me,	**Dt 4:10**	3068
"Then the **L** spoke to you from the	**Dt 4:12**	3068
"The **L** commanded me at that	**Dt 4:14**	3068
the day the **L** spoke to you at Horeb	**Dt 4:15**	3068
those which the **L** your God has	**Dt 4:19**	3068
"But the **L** has taken you and	**Dt 4:20**	3068
"Now the **L** was angry with me on	**Dt 4:21**	3068
not enter the good land which the **L**	**Dt 4:21**	3068
the covenant of the **L** your God which	**Dt 4:23**	3068
the **L** your God has commanded you.	**Dt 4:23**	3068
L your God is a consuming fire,	**Dt 4:24**	3068
that which is evil in the sight of the **L**	**Dt 4:25**	3068
"The **L** will scatter you among	**Dt 4:27**	3068
where the **L** drives you.	**Dt 4:27**	3068
you will seek the **L** your God,	**Dt 4:29**	3068
you will return to the **L** your God	**Dt 4:30**	3068
"For the **L** your God is a	**Dt 4:31**	3068
as the **L** your God did for you in	**Dt 4:34**	3068
that you might know that the **L**,	**Dt 4:35**	3068
take it to your heart, that the **L**,	**Dt 4:39**	3068
live long on the land which the **L**	**Dt 4:40**	3068
"The **L** our God made a covenant	**Dt 5:2**	3068
"The **L** did not make this covenant	**Dt 5:3**	3068
"The **L** spoke to you face to face	**Dt 5:4**	3068
was standing between the **L** and you	**Dt 5:5**	3068
declare to you the word of the **L**;	**Dt 5:5**	3068
'I am the **L** your God who brought	**Dt 5:6**	3068
for I, the **L** your God, am a	**Dt 5:9**	3068
name of the **L** your God in vain,	**Dt 5:11**	3068
for the **L** will not leave him	**Dt 5:11**	3068
as the **L** your God commanded you.	**Dt 5:12**	3068
is a sabbath of the **L** your God;	**Dt 5:14**	3068
and the **L** your God brought you out	**Dt 5:15**	3068
therefore the **L** your God commanded	**Dt 5:15**	3068
the **L** your God has commanded you,	**Dt 5:16**	3068
which the **L** your God gives you.	**Dt 5:16**	3068
"These words the **L** spoke to all	**Dt 5:22**	3068
the **L** our God has shown us His	**Dt 5:24**	3068
voice of the **L** our God any longer,	**Dt 5:25**	3068
hear all that the **L** our God says;	**Dt 5:27**	3068
the **L** our God speaks to you,	**Dt 5:27**	3068
"The **L** heard the voice of	**Dt 5:28**	3068
spoke to me, and the **L** said to me,	**Dt 5:28**	3068
the **L** your God has commanded you;	**Dt 5:32**	3068
the **L** your God has commanded you,	**Dt 5:33**	3068
judgments which the **L** your God has	**Dt 6:1**	3068
might fear the **L** your God,	**Dt 6:2**	3068
multiply greatly, just as the **L**,	**Dt 6:3**	3068
The **L** is our God, the LORD is one!	**Dt 6:4**	3068
The LORD is our God, the **L** is one!	**Dt 6:4**	3068
"You shall love the **L** your	**Dt 6:5**	3068
when the **L** your God brings you into	**Dt 6:10**	3068
do not forget the **L** who brought	**Dt 6:12**	3068
shall fear *only* the **L** your God;	**Dt 6:13**	3068
for the **L** your God in the midst of	**Dt 6:15**	3068
otherwise the anger of the **L** your	**Dt 6:15**	3068
put the **L** your God to the test,	**Dt 6:16**	3068
commandments of the **L** your God,	**Dt 6:17**	3068
and good in the sight of the **L**,	**Dt 6:18**	3068
the **L** swore to *give* your fathers,	**Dt 6:18**	3068
before you, as the **L** has spoken.	**Dt 6:19**	3068
which the **L** our God commanded you	**Dt 6:20**	3068
and the **L** brought us from Egypt	**Dt 6:21**	3068
the **L** showed great and distressing	**Dt 6:22**	3068
"So the **L** commanded us to observe	**Dt 6:24**	3068
to fear the **L** our God for our good	**Dt 6:24**	3068
commandment before the **L** our God,	**Dt 6:25**	3068
"When the **L** your God brings	**Dt 7:1**	3068
and when the **L** your God delivers	**Dt 7:2**	3068
the **L** will be kindled against you and	**Dt 7:4**	3068
a holy people to the **L** your God;	**Dt 7:6**	3068
the **L** your God has chosen you to	**Dt 7:6**	3068
"The **L** did not set His love on	**Dt 7:7**	3068
but because the **L** loved you and	**Dt 7:8**	3068
the **L** brought you out by a mighty	**Dt 7:8**	3068
therefore that the **L** your God,	**Dt 7:9**	3068
that the **L** your God will keep with	**Dt 7:12**	3068
"The **L** will remove from you	**Dt 7:15**	3068
L your God will deliver to you;	**Dt 7:16**	3068
what the **L** your God did to Pharaoh	**Dt 7:18**	3068
the **L** your God brought you out.	**Dt 7:19**	3068
So shall the **L** your God do to all	**Dt 7:19**	3068
the **L** your God will send the	**Dt 7:20**	3068
the **L** your God is in your midst,	**Dt 7:21**	3068
"The **L** your God will clear	**Dt 7:22**	3068
"But the **L** your God will deliver	**Dt 7:23**	3068
an abomination to the **L** your God.	**Dt 7:25**	3068
the land which the **L** swore *to*	**Dt 8:1**	3068
way which the **L** your God has led	**Dt 8:2**	3068
out of the mouth of the **L**.	**Dt 8:3**	3068
the **L** your God was disciplining you	**Dt 8:5**	3068
commandments of the **L** your God,	**Dt 8:6**	3068
"For the **L** your God is bringing	**Dt 8:7**	3068
you shall bless the **L** your God for	**Dt 8:10**	3068
"Beware that you do not forget the **L**	**Dt 8:11**	3068
and you will forget the **L** your God who	**Dt 8:14**	3068
you shall remember the **L** your God,	**Dt 8:18**	3068
if you ever forget the **L** your God and	**Dt 8:19**	3068
the **L** makes to perish before you,	**Dt 8:20**	3068
to the voice of the **L** your God.	**Dt 8:20**	3068
it is the **L** your God who is crossing	**Dt 9:3**	3068
just as the **L** has spoken to you.	**Dt 9:3**	3068
the **L** your God has driven them out	**Dt 9:4**	3068
'Because of my righteousness the **L**	**Dt 9:4**	3068
the **L** is dispossessing them before	**Dt 9:4**	3068
the **L** your God is driving them out	**Dt 9:5**	3068
which the **L** swore to your fathers,	**Dt 9:5**	3068
that the **L** your God is giving you this	**Dt 9:6**	3068
how you provoked the **L** your God to	**Dt 9:7**	3068
been rebellious against the **L**.	**Dt 9:7**	3068
Horeb you provoked the **L** to wrath,	**Dt 9:8**	3068
and the **L** was so angry with you	**Dt 9:8**	3068
which the **L** had made with you,	**Dt 9:9**	3068
"The **L** gave me the two	**Dt 9:10**	3068
all the words which the **L** had spoken	**Dt 9:10**	3068
the **L** gave me the two tablets of stone	**Dt 9:11**	3068
"Then the **L** said to me,	**Dt 9:12**	3068
"The **L** spoke further to me,	**Dt 9:13**	3068
sinned against the **L** your God.	**Dt 9:16**	3068
way which the **L** had commanded you.	**Dt 9:16**	3068
"I fell down before the **L**,	**Dt 9:18**	3068
of the **L** to provoke Him to anger.	**Dt 9:18**	3068
and hot displeasure with which the **L**	**Dt 9:19**	3068
L listened to me at that time also.	**Dt 9:19**	3068
"The **L** was angry enough with	**Dt 9:20**	3068
you provoked the **L** to wrath.	**Dt 9:22**	3068
the **L** sent you from Kadesh-barnea,	**Dt 9:23**	3068
the command of the **L** your God;	**Dt 9:23**	3068
have been rebellious against the **L**	**Dt 9:24**	3068
I fell down before the **L** the forty	**Dt 9:25**	3068
L had said He would destroy you.	**Dt 9:25**	3068
"I prayed to the **L**	**Dt 9:26**	3068
'O **L** GOD, do not destroy Your	**Dt 9:26**	136
"Because the **L** was not able to	**Dt 9:28**	3068
"At that time the **L** said to me,	**Dt 10:1**	3068
the Ten Commandments which the **L**	**Dt 10:4**	3068
and the **L** gave them to me.	**Dt 10:4**	3068
they are, as the **L** commanded me."	**Dt 10:5**	3068
At that time the **L** set apart the	**Dt 10:8**	3068
the ark of the covenant of the **L**,	**Dt 10:8**	3068
to stand before the **L** to serve Him	**Dt 10:8**	3068
the **L** is his inheritance, just as	**Dt 10:9**	3068
as the **L** your God spoke to him.)	**Dt 10:9**	3068
L listened to me that time also;	**Dt 10:10**	3068
the **L** was not willing to destroy	**Dt 10:10**	3068
"Then the **L** said to me,	**Dt 10:11**	3068
the **L** your God require from you,	**Dt 10:12**	3068
you, but to fear the **L** your God,	**Dt 10:12**	3068
and to serve the **L** your God with	**Dt 10:12**	3068
to the **L** your God belong heaven	**Dt 10:14**	3068
"Yet on your fathers did the **L**	**Dt 10:15**	3068
"For the **L** your God is the God of	**Dt 10:17**	3068
God of gods and the **L** of lords,	**Dt 10:17**	136
"You shall fear the **L** your God;	**Dt 10:20**	3068
and now the **L** your God has made	**Dt 10:22**	3068
therefore love the **L** your God,	**Dt 11:1**	3068
the discipline of the **L** your God	**Dt 11:2**	3068
the **L** completely destroyed them;	**Dt 11:4**	3068
great work of the **L** which He did.	**Dt 11:7**	3068
days on the land which the **L** swore	**Dt 11:9**	3068
for which the **L** your God cares;	**Dt 11:12**	3068
eyes of the **L** your God are always	**Dt 11:12**	3068
to love the **L** your God and to	**Dt 11:13**	3068
the anger of the **L** will be kindled	**Dt 11:17**	3068
land which the **L** is giving you.	**Dt 11:17**	3068
be multiplied on the land which the **L**	**Dt 11:21**	3068
to do, to love the **L** your God,	**Dt 11:22**	3068
then the **L** will drive out all	**Dt 11:23**	3068
the **L** your God will lay the dread	**Dt 11:25**	3068
commandments of the **L** your God,	**Dt 11:27**	3068
commandments of the **L** your God,	**Dt 11:28**	3068
when the **L** your God brings you	**Dt 11:29**	3068
the **L** your God is giving you,	**Dt 11:31**	3068
observe in the land which the **L**,	**Dt 12:1**	3068
like this toward the **L** your God.	**Dt 12:4**	3068
"But you shall seek *the* **L** at	**Dt 12:5**	
at the place which the **L** your God	**Dt 12:5**	3068
shall eat before the **L** your God,	**Dt 12:7**	3068
the **L** your God has blessed you.	**Dt 12:7**	3068
the **L** your God is giving you.	**Dt 12:9**	3068
land which the **L** your God is giving	**Dt 12:10**	3068
that the place in which the **L** your	**Dt 12:11**	3068
which you will vow to the **L**.	**Dt 12:11**	3068
rejoice before the **L** your God,	**Dt 12:12**	3068
L chooses in one of your tribes,	**Dt 12:14**	3068
according to the blessing of the **L**	**Dt 12:15**	3068
"But you shall eat them before the **L**	**Dt 12:18**	3068
which the **L** your God will choose,	**Dt 12:18**	3068
and you shall rejoice before the **L**	**Dt 12:18**	3068
"When the **L** your God extends your	**Dt 12:20**	3068
"If the place which the **L** your	**Dt 12:21**	3068
flock which the **L** has given you,	**Dt 12:21**	3068
is right in the sight of the **L**.	**Dt 12:25**	3068
to the place which the **L** chooses.	**Dt 12:26**	3068
on the altar of the **L** your God;	**Dt 12:27**	3068
on the altar of the **L** your God,	**Dt 12:27**	3068
in the sight of the **L** your God.	**Dt 12:28**	3068
"When the **L** your God cuts off	**Dt 12:29**	3068
behave thus toward the **L** your God,	**Dt 12:31**	3068
for every abominable act which the **L**	**Dt 12:31**	3068
for the **L** your God is testing you	**Dt 13:3**	3068
to find out if you love the **L** your	**Dt 13:3**	3068
the **L** your God and fear Him;	**Dt 13:4**	3068
has counseled rebellion against the **L**	**Dt 13:5**	3068
from the way in which the **L** your	**Dt 13:5**	3068
has sought to seduce you from the **L**	**Dt 13:10**	3068
which the **L** your God is giving you	**Dt 13:12**	3068
burnt offering to the **L** your God;	**Dt 13:16**	3068
in order that the **L** may turn from	**Dt 13:17**	3068
to the voice of the **L** your God,	**Dt 13:18**	3068
in the sight of the **L** your God.	**Dt 13:18**	3068
are the sons of the **L** your God;	**Dt 14:1**	3068
a holy people to the **L** your God,	**Dt 14:2**	3068
and the **L** has chosen you to be a	**Dt 14:2**	3068
a holy people to the **L** your God.	**Dt 14:21**	3068
in the presence of the **L** your God,	**Dt 14:23**	3068
to fear the **L** your God always.	**Dt 14:23**	3068
since the place where the **L** your	**Dt 14:24**	3068
when the **L** your God blesses you,	**Dt 14:24**	3068
which the **L** your God chooses.	**Dt 14:25**	3068
shall eat in the presence of the **L**	**Dt 14:26**	3068
in order that the **L** your God may	**Dt 14:29**	3068
since the **L** will surely bless you	**Dt 15:4**	3068
land which the **L** your God is giving	**Dt 15:4**	3068
to the voice of the **L** your God,	**Dt 15:5**	3068

"For the **L** your God will bless	Dt 15:6	3068
the **L** your God is giving you,	Dt 15:7	3068
he may cry to the **L** against you,	Dt 15:9	3068
the **L** your God will bless you in all	Dt 15:10	3068
as the **L** your God has blessed you.	Dt 15:14	3068
and the **L** your God redeemed you;	Dt 15:15	3068
so the **L** your God will bless you	Dt 15:18	3068
"You shall consecrate to the **L**	Dt 15:19	3068
shall eat it every year before the **L**	Dt 15:20	3068
in the place which the **L** chooses.	Dt 15:20	3068
sacrifice it to the **L** your God.	Dt 15:21	3068
the Passover to the **L** your God,	Dt 16:1	3068
the **L** your God brought you out of	Dt 16:1	3068
shall sacrifice the Passover to the **L**	Dt 16:2	3068
L chooses to establish His name.	Dt 16:2	3068
the **L** your God is giving you;	Dt 16:5	3068
but at the place where the **L** your	Dt 16:6	3068
which the **L** your God chooses.	Dt 16:7	3068
solemn assembly to the **L** your God;	Dt 16:8	3068
celebrate the Feast of Weeks to the **L**	Dt 16:10	3068
as the **L** your God blesses you;	Dt 16:10	3068
rejoice before the **L** your God,	Dt 16:11	3068
in the place where the **L** your God	Dt 16:11	3068
you shall celebrate a feast to the **L**	Dt 16:15	3068
in the place which the **L** chooses,	Dt 16:15	3068
because the **L** your God will bless	Dt 16:15	3068
your males shall appear before the **L**	Dt 16:16	3068
appear before the **L** empty-handed.	Dt 16:16	3068
according to the blessing of the **L**	Dt 16:17	3068
the **L** your God is giving you,	Dt 16:18	3068
the **L** your God is giving you.	Dt 16:20	3068
the altar of the **L** your God,	Dt 16:21	3068
pillar which the **L** your God hates.	Dt 16:22	3068
"You shall not sacrifice to the **L**	Dt 17:1	3068
detestable thing to the **L** your God.	Dt 17:1	3068
the **L** your God is giving you,	Dt 17:2	3068
in the sight of the **L** your God,	Dt 17:2	3068
which the **L** your God chooses.	Dt 17:8	3068
that place which the **L** chooses;	Dt 17:10	3068
there to serve the **L** your God,	Dt 17:12	3068
which the **L** your God gives you,	Dt 17:14	3068
you whom the **L** your God chooses,	Dt 17:15	3068
since the **L** has said to you,	Dt 17:16	3068
may learn to fear the **L** his God,	Dt 17:19	3068
the **L** is their inheritance, as He	Dt 18:2	3068
"For the **L** your God has chosen	Dt 18:5	3068
in the name of the **L** forever.	Dt 18:5	3068
to the place which the **L** chooses,	Dt 18:6	3068
in the name of the **L** his God,	Dt 18:7	3068
who stand there before the **L**.	Dt 18:7	3068
which the **L** your God gives you,	Dt 18:9	3068
things is detestable to the **L**;	Dt 18:12	3068
the **L** your God will drive them out	Dt 18:12	3068
blameless before the **L** your God.	Dt 18:13	3068
the **L** your God has not allowed you	Dt 18:14	3068
"The **L** your God will raise up for	Dt 18:15	3068
asked of the **L** your God in Horeb	Dt 18:16	3068
again the voice of the **L** my God,	Dt 18:16	3068
"The **L** said to me,	Dt 18:17	3068
word which the **L** has not spoken?'	Dt 18:21	3068
speaks in the name of the **L**,	Dt 18:22	3068
thing which the **L** has not spoken.	Dt 18:22	3068
L your God cuts off the nations,	Dt 19:1	3068
land the **L** your God gives you,	Dt 19:1	3068
L your God gives you to possess.	Dt 19:2	3068
which the **L** your God will give you	Dt 19:3	3068
"If the **L** your God enlarges	Dt 19:8	3068
you today, to love the **L** your God,	Dt 19:9	3068
in the midst of your land which the **L**	Dt 19:10	3068
L your God gives you to possess.	Dt 19:14	3068
dispute shall stand before the **L**,	Dt 19:17	3068
for the **L** your God, who brought	Dt 20:1	3068
for the **L** your God is the one who	Dt 20:4	3068
"When the **L** your God gives it	Dt 20:13	3068
the **L** your God has given you.	Dt 20:14	3068
that the **L** your God is giving you as	Dt 20:16	3068
the **L** your God has commanded you,	Dt 20:17	3068
would sin against the **L** your God.	Dt 20:18	3068
L your God gives you to possess,	Dt 21:1	3068
for the **L** your God has chosen them	Dt 21:5	3068
and to bless in the name of the **L**;	Dt 21:5	3068
whom You have redeemed, O **L**,	Dt 21:8	3068
is right in the eyes of the **L**.	Dt 21:9	3068
and the **L** your God delivers them	Dt 21:10	3068
do not defile your land which the **L**	Dt 21:23	3068
an abomination to the **L** your God.	Dt 22:5	3068
shall enter the assembly of the **L**.	Dt 23:1	3068
shall enter the assembly of the **L**;	Dt 23:2	3068
shall enter the assembly of the **L**.	Dt 23:2	3068
shall enter the assembly of the **L**;	Dt 23:3	3068
ever enter the assembly of the **L**,	Dt 23:3	3068
the **L** your God was not willing to	Dt 23:5	3068
but the **L** your God turned the	Dt 23:5	3068
because the **L** your God loves you.	Dt 23:5	3068
may enter the assembly of the **L**.	Dt 23:8	3068
"Since the **L** your God walks in	Dt 23:14	3068
into the house of the **L** your God	Dt 23:18	3068
an abomination to the **L** your God.	Dt 23:18	3068
so that the **L** your God may bless	Dt 23:20	3068
you make a vow to the **L** your God,	Dt 23:21	3068
and the **L** your God will surely	Dt 23:21	3068
vowed to the **L** your God,	Dt 23:23	3068
is an abomination before the **L**,	Dt 24:4	3068
land which the **L** your God gives	Dt 24:4	3068
"Remember what the **L** your God did	Dt 24:9	3068
for you before the **L** your God.	Dt 24:13	3068
he will not cry against you to the **L**	Dt 24:15	3068
and that the **L** your God redeemed	Dt 24:18	3068
in order that the **L** your God may	Dt 24:19	3068

which the **L** your God gives you.	Dt 25:15	3068
an abomination to the **L** your God.	Dt 25:16	3068
L your God has given you rest from	Dt 25:19	3068
in the land which the **L** your God	Dt 25:19	3068
when you enter the land which the **L**	Dt 26:1	3068
that the **L** your God gives you,	Dt 26:2	3068
go to the place where the **L** your God	Dt 26:2	3068
'I declare this day to the **L** my	Dt 26:3	3068
entered the land which the **L** swore	Dt 26:3	3068
the altar of the **L** your God.	Dt 26:4	3068
and say before the **L** your God,	Dt 26:5	3068
'Then we cried to the **L**,	Dt 26:7	3068
and the **L** heard our voice and saw	Dt 26:7	3068
and the **L** brought us out of Egypt	Dt 26:8	3068
which You, O **L** have given me.'	Dt 26:10	3068
set it down before the **L** your God,	Dt 26:10	3068
and worship before the **L** your God;	Dt 26:10	3068
rejoice in all the good which the **L**	Dt 26:11	3068
shall say before the **L** your God,	Dt 26:13	3068
to the voice of the **L** my God;	Dt 26:14	3068
"This day the **L** your God commands	Dt 26:16	3068
declared the **L** to be your God,	Dt 26:17	3068
"The **L** has today declared you	Dt 26:18	3068
people to the **L** your God,	Dt 26:19	3068
which the **L** your God gives you,	Dt 27:2	3068
which the **L** your God gives you,	Dt 27:3	3068
as the **L**, the God of your fathers	Dt 27:3	3068
there an altar to the **L** your God,	Dt 27:5	3068
build the altar of the **L** your God	Dt 27:6	3068
burnt offerings to the **L** your God;	Dt 27:6	3068
rejoice before the **L** your God.	Dt 27:7	3068
a people for the **L** your God.	Dt 27:9	3068
therefore obey the **L** your God,	Dt 27:10	3068
image, an abomination to the **L**,	Dt 27:15	3068
diligently obey the **L** your God,	Dt 28:1	3068
the **L** your God will set you high	Dt 28:1	3068
if you obey the **L** your God:	Dt 28:2	3068
"The **L** shall cause your enemies	Dt 28:7	3068
"The **L** will command the blessing	Dt 28:8	3068
which the **L** your God gives you.	Dt 28:8	3068
"The **L** will establish you as a	Dt 28:9	3068
commandments of the **L** your God and	Dt 28:9	3068
are called by the name of the **L**,	Dt 28:10	3068
"The **L** will make you abound	Dt 28:11	3068
in the land which the **L** swore to	Dt 28:11	3068
"The **L** will open for you His good	Dt 28:12	3068
"The **L** will make you the	Dt 28:13	3068
commandments of the **L** your God,	Dt 28:13	3068
you do not obey the **L** your God,	Dt 28:15	3068
"The **L** will send upon you curses,	Dt 28:20	3068
"The **L** will make the pestilence	Dt 28:21	3068
"The **L** will smite you with	Dt 28:22	3068
"The **L** will make the rain of your	Dt 28:24	3068
"The **L** shall cause you to be	Dt 28:25	3068
"The **L** will smite you with the	Dt 28:27	3068
"The **L** will smite you with	Dt 28:28	3068
"The **L** will strike you on the	Dt 28:35	3068
L will bring you and your king,	Dt 28:36	3068
people where the **L** drives you.	Dt 28:37	3068
because you would not obey the **L**	Dt 28:45	3068
"Because you did not serve the **L**	Dt 28:47	3068
whom the **L** will send against you,	Dt 28:48	3068
"The **L** will bring a nation	Dt 28:49	3068
the **L** your God has given you.	Dt 28:52	3068
whom the **L** your God has given you,	Dt 28:53	3068
and awesome name, the **L** your God,	Dt 28:58	3068
then the **L** will bring	Dt 28:59	3068
the **L** will bring on you until you	Dt 28:61	3068
you did not obey the **L** your God.	Dt 28:62	3068
L delighted over you to prosper you	Dt 28:63	3068
so the **L** will delight over you to	Dt 28:63	3068
the **L** will scatter you among all	Dt 28:64	3068
but there the **L** will give you a	Dt 28:65	3068
"The **L** will bring you back to	Dt 28:68	3068
covenant which the **L** commanded	Dt 29:1	3068
"You have seen all that the **L** did	Dt 29:2	3068
"Yet to this day the **L** has not	Dt 29:4	3068
know that I am the **L** your God.	Dt 29:6	3068
all of you, before the **L** your God:	Dt 29:10	3068
the covenant with the **L** your God,	Dt 29:12	3068
and into His oath which the **L** your	Dt 29:12	3068
with us today in the presence of the **L**	Dt 29:15	3068
away today from the **L** our God,	Dt 29:18	3068
"The **L** shall never be willing to	Dt 29:20	3068
but rather the anger of the **L** and	Dt 29:20	3068
and the **L** will blot out his name	Dt 29:20	3068
"Then the **L** will single him out	Dt 29:21	3068
with which the **L** has afflicted it,	Dt 29:22	3068
which the **L** overthrew in His anger	Dt 29:23	3068
has the **L** done thus to this land?	Dt 29:24	3068
forsook the covenant of the **L**,	Dt 29:25	3068
the anger of the **L** burned against	Dt 29:27	3068
and the **L** uprooted them from their	Dt 29:28	3068
things belong to the **L** our God,	Dt 29:29	3068
the **L** your God has banished you,	Dt 30:1	3068
and you return to the **L** your God	Dt 30:2	3068
then the **L** your God will restore	Dt 30:3	3068
the **L** your God has scattered you.	Dt 30:3	3068
the **L** your God will gather you,	Dt 30:4	3068
"The **L** your God will bring	Dt 30:5	3068
"Moreover the **L** your God will	Dt 30:6	3068
to love the **L** your God with all	Dt 30:6	3068
"The **L** your God will inflict	Dt 30:7	3068
"And you shall again obey the **L**,	Dt 30:8	3068
"Then the **L** your God will prosper	Dt 30:9	3068
for the **L** will again rejoice over	Dt 30:9	3068
if you obey the **L** your God to keep	Dt 30:10	3068
if you turn to the **L** your God with	Dt 30:10	3068
you today to love the **L** your God,	Dt 30:16	3068

and that the **L** your God may bless	Dt 30:16	3068
by loving the **L** your God, by	Dt 30:20	3068
which the **L** swore to your fathers,	Dt 30:20	3068
and go, and the **L** has said to me,	Dt 31:2	3068
"It is the **L** your God who will	Dt 31:3	3068
of you, just as the **L** has spoken.	Dt 31:3	3068
"The **L** will do to them just	Dt 31:4	3068
"The **L** will deliver them up	Dt 31:5	3068
for the **L** your God is the one who	Dt 31:6	3068
into the land which the **L** has sworn	Dt 31:7	3068
"The **L** is the one who goes	Dt 31:8	3068
the ark of the covenant of the **L**,	Dt 31:9	3068
Israel comes to appear before the **L**	Dt 31:11	3068
and learn and fear the **L** your God,	Dt 31:12	3068
and learn to fear the **L** your God,	Dt 31:13	3068
Then the **L** said to Moses,	Dt 31:14	3068
The **L** appeared in the tent in	Dt 31:15	3068
The **L** said to Moses,	Dt 31:16	3068
the ark of the covenant of the **L**,	Dt 31:25	3068
of the covenant of the **L** your God,	Dt 31:26	3068
been rebellious against the **L**;	Dt 31:27	3068
is evil in the sight of the **L**,	Dt 31:29	3068
"For I proclaim the name of the **L**;	Dt 32:3	3068
"Do you thus repay the **L**,	Dt 32:6	3068
"The **L** alone guided him, And	Dt 32:12	3068
"The **L** saw *this*, and spurned	Dt 32:19	3068
the **L** has not done all this."	Dt 32:27	3068
them, And the **L** had given them up?	Dt 32:30	3068
the **L** will vindicate His people,	Dt 32:36	3068
The **L** spoke to Moses that very	Dt 32:48	3068
"The **L** came from Sinai, And	Dt 33:2	3068
"Hear, O **L**, the voice of Judah,	Dt 33:7	3068
"O **L**, bless his substance, And	Dt 33:11	3068
beloved of the **L** dwell in security	Dt 33:12	3068
"Blessed of the **L** *be* his land,	Dt 33:13	3068
He executed the justice of the **L**,	Dt 33:21	3068
And full of the blessing of the **L**,	Dt 33:23	3068
like you, a people saved by the **L**,	Dt 33:29	3068
And the **L** showed him all the land,	Dt 34:1	3068
Then the **L** said to him,	Dt 34:4	3068
So Moses the servant of the **L** died	Dt 34:5	3068
according to the word of the **L**.	Dt 34:5	3068
did as the **L** had commanded Moses.	Dt 34:9	3068
whom the **L** knew face to face,	Dt 34:10	3068
signs and wonders which the **L** sent	Dt 34:11	3068
death of Moses the servant of the **L**	Jos 1:1	3068
L spoke to Joshua the son of Nun,	Jos 1:1	3068
for the **L** your God is with you	Jos 1:9	3068
the **L** your God is giving you,	Jos 1:11	3068
servant of the **L** commanded you,	Jos 1:13	3068
'The **L** your God gives you rest and	Jos 1:13	3068
the **L** gives your brothers rest,	Jos 1:15	3068
the **L** your God is giving them.	Jos 1:15	3068
that which Moses the servant of the **L**	Jos 1:15	3068
may the **L** your God be with you as	Jos 1:17	3068
that the **L** has given you the land,	Jos 2:9	3068
heard how the **L** dried up the water	Jos 2:10	3068
for the **L** your God, He is God in	Jos 2:11	3068
please swear to me by the **L**,	Jos 2:12	3068
when the **L** gives us the land that we	Jos 2:14	3068
"Surely the **L** has given all the	Jos 2:24	3068
see the ark of the covenant of the **L**	Jos 3:3	3068
the **L** will do wonders among you."	Jos 3:5	3068
Now the **L** said to Joshua,	Jos 3:7	3068
the words of the **L** your God."	Jos 3:9	3068
the ark of the covenant of the **L**	Jos 3:11	136
who carry the ark of the **L**,	Jos 3:13	3068
the LORD, the **L** of all the earth,	Jos 3:13	136
ark of the covenant of the **L** stood	Jos 3:17	3068
the **L** spoke to Joshua,	Jos 4:1	3068
"Cross again to the ark of the **L**	Jos 4:5	3068
the ark of the covenant of the **L**;	Jos 4:7	3068
just as the **L** spoke to Joshua,	Jos 4:8	3068
L had commanded Joshua to speak to	Jos 4:10	3068
the ark of the **L** and the	Jos 4:11	3068
crossed for battle before the **L** to	Jos 4:13	3068
On that day the **L** exalted Joshua	Jos 4:14	3068
Now the **L** said to Joshua,	Jos 4:15	3068
the ark of the covenant of the **L** had	Jos 4:18	3068
"For the **L** your God dried up the	Jos 4:23	3068
just as the **L** your God had done to	Jos 4:23	3068
that the hand of the **L** is mighty,	Jos 4:24	3068
may fear the **L** your God forever."	Jos 4:24	3068
heard how the **L** had dried up the	Jos 5:1	3068
At that time the **L** said to Joshua,	Jos 5:2	3068
not listen to the voice of the **L**,	Jos 5:6	3068
to whom the **L** had sworn that He	Jos 5:6	3068
not let them see the land which the **L**	Jos 5:6	3068
Then the **L** said to Joshua,	Jos 5:9	3068
as captain of the host of the **L**."	Jos 5:14	3068
has my **l** to say to his servant?"	Jos 5:14	136
The **L** said to Joshua,	Jos 6:2	3068
horns before the ark of the **L**."	Jos 6:6	3068
go on before the ark of the **L**."	Jos 6:7	3068
trumpets of rams' horns before the **L**	Jos 6:8	3068
covenant of the **L** followed them.	Jos 6:8	3068
had the ark of the **L** taken around	Jos 6:11	3068
priests took up the ark of the **L**.	Jos 6:12	3068
ark of the **L** went on continually,	Jos 6:13	3068
guard came after the ark of the **L**,	Jos 6:13	3068
For the **L** has given you the city.	Jos 6:16	3068
that is in it belongs to the **L**;	Jos 6:17	3068
bronze and iron are holy to the **L**;	Jos 6:19	3068
go into the treasury of the **L**."	Jos 6:19	3068
treasury of the house of the **L**.	Jos 6:24	3068
"Cursed before the **L** is the man	Jos 6:26	3068
So the **L** was with Joshua, and his	Jos 6:27	3068
therefore the anger of the **L**	Jos 7:1	3068
ark of the **L** until the evening,	Jos 7:6	3068

"Alas, O **L** God, why did You	**Jos 7:7**	136
"O **L**, what can I say since Israel	**Jos 7:8**	136
So the **L** said to Joshua,	**Jos 7:10**	3068
for thus the **L**, the God of Israel,	**Jos 7:13**	3068
tribe which the **L** takes *by lot* shall	**Jos 7:14**	3068
and the family which the **L** takes	**Jos 7:14**	3068
and the household which the **L**	**Jos 7:14**	3068
the covenant of the **L**,	**Jos 7:15**	3068
implore you, give glory to the **L**,	**Jos 7:19**	3068
I have sinned against the **L**,	**Jos 7:20**	3068
they poured them out before the **L**.	**Jos 7:23**	3068
The **L** will trouble you this day."	**Jos 7:25**	3068
and the **L** turned from the	**Jos 7:26**	3068
Now the **L** said to Joshua,	**Jos 8:1**	3068
for the **L** your God will deliver it	**Jos 8:7**	3068
it according to the word of the **L**.	**Jos 8:8**	3068
Then the **L** said to Joshua,	**Jos 8:18**	3068
according to the word of the **L**	**Jos 8:27**	3068
Joshua built an altar to the **L**,	**Jos 8:30**	3068
just as Moses the servant of the **L**	**Jos 8:31**	3068
burnt offerings on it to the **L**,	**Jos 8:31**	3068
the ark of the covenant of the **L**,	**Jos 8:33**	3068
just as Moses the servant of the **L**	**Jos 8:33**	3068
of the fame of the **L** your God;	**Jos 9:9**	3068
not ask for the counsel of the **L**.	**Jos 9:14**	3068
them by the **L** the God of Israel.	**Jos 9:18**	3068
"We have sworn to them by the **L**,	**Jos 9:19**	3068
the **L** your God had commanded His	**Jos 9:24**	3068
and for the altar of the **L**,	**Jos 9:27**	3068
The **L** said to Joshua,	**Jos 10:8**	3068
L confounded them before Israel,	**Jos 10:10**	3068
the **L** threw large stones from	**Jos 10:11**	3068
Then Joshua spoke to the **L** in the	**Jos 10:12**	3068
the **L** delivered up the Amorites	**Jos 10:12**	3068
when the **L** listened to the voice	**Jos 10:14**	3068
for the **L** fought for Israel.	**Jos 10:14**	3068
for the **L** your God has delivered	**Jos 10:19**	3068
for thus the **L** will do to all your	**Jos 10:25**	3068
The **L** gave it also with its	**Jos 10:30**	3068
The **L** gave Lachish into the	**Jos 10:32**	3068
all who breathed, just as the **L**,	**Jos 10:40**	3068
the **L**, the God of Israel, fought for	**Jos 10:42**	3068
Then the **L** said to Joshua,	**Jos 11:6**	3068
The **L** delivered them into the	**Jos 11:8**	3068
did to them as the **L** had told him;	**Jos 11:9**	3068
servant of the **L** had commanded.	**Jos 11:12**	3068
Just as the **L** had commanded Moses	**Jos 11:15**	3068
that the **L** had commanded Moses.	**Jos 11:15**	3068
of the **L** to harden their hearts,	**Jos 11:20**	3068
just as the **L** had commanded Moses.	**Jos 11:20**	3068
that the **L** had spoken to Moses,	**Jos 11:23**	3068
Moses the servant of the **L** and the	**Jos 12:6**	3068
and Moses the servant of the **L**	**Jos 12:6**	3068
in years when the **L** said to him,	**Jos 13:1**	3068
the servant of the **L** gave to them;	**Jos 13:8**	3068
the offerings by fire to the **L**,	**Jos 13:14**	3068
the **L**, the God of Israel, is their	**Jos 13:33**	3068
as the **L** commanded through Moses,	**Jos 14:2**	3068
just as the **L** had commanded Moses,	**Jos 14:5**	3068
"You know the word which the **L**	**Jos 14:6**	3068
Moses the servant of the **L** sent me	**Jos 14:7**	3068
but I followed the **L** my God fully.	**Jos 14:8**	3068
have followed the **L** my God fully.'	**Jos 14:9**	3068
Now behold, the **L** has let me live,	**Jos 14:10**	3068
the **L** spoke this word to Moses,	**Jos 14:10**	3068
which the **L** spoke on that day,	**Jos 14:12**	3068
perhaps the **L** will be with me, and	**Jos 14:12**	3068
them out as the **L** has spoken."	**Jos 14:12**	3068
followed the **L** God of Israel fully.	**Jos 14:14**	3068
to the command of the **L** to Joshua,	**Jos 15:13**	3068
"The **L** commanded Moses to give us	**Jos 17:4**	3068
according to the command of the **L**	**Jos 17:4**	3068
whom the **L** has thus far blessed?"	**Jos 17:14**	3068
of the land which the **L**,	**Jos 18:3**	3068
for you here before the **L** our God.	**Jos 18:6**	3068
of the **L** is their inheritance.	**Jos 18:7**	3068
the servant of the **L** gave them."	**Jos 18:7**	3068
you here before the **L** in Shiloh."	**Jos 18:8**	3068
for them in Shiloh before the **L**,	**Jos 18:10**	3068
with the command of the **L** they gave	**Jos 19:50**	3068
by lot in Shiloh before the **L**	**Jos 19:51**	3068
Then the **L** spoke to Joshua,	**Jos 20:1**	3068
"The **L** commanded through Moses to	**Jos 21:2**	3068
according to the command of the **L**,	**Jos 21:3**	3068
the **L** had commanded through Moses.	**Jos 21:8**	3068
So the **L** gave Israel all the land	**Jos 21:43**	3068
L gave them rest on every side,	**Jos 21:44**	3068
the **L** gave all their enemies into	**Jos 21:44**	3068
good promises which the **L** had made	**Jos 21:45**	3068
servant of the **L** commanded you,	**Jos 22:2**	3068
the commandment of the **L** your God.	**Jos 22:3**	3068
"And now the **L** your God has given	**Jos 22:4**	3068
Moses the servant of the **L** gave you	**Jos 22:4**	3068
servant of the **L** commanded you,	**Jos 22:5**	3068
to love the **L** your God and walk in	**Jos 22:5**	3068
command of the **L** through Moses.	**Jos 22:9**	3068
the whole congregation of the **L**,	**Jos 22:16**	3068
from following the **L** this day,	**Jos 22:16**	3068
to rebel against the **L** this day?	**Jos 22:16**	3068
came on the congregation of the **L**,	**Jos 22:17**	3068
this day from following the **L**?	**Jos 22:18**	3068
If you rebel against the **L** today,	**Jos 22:18**	3068
land of the possession of the **L**,	**Jos 22:19**	3068
Only do not rebel against the **L**,	**Jos 22:19**	3068
the altar of the **L** our God.	**Jos 22:19**	3068
"The Mighty One, God, the **L**,	**Jos 22:22**	3068
Lord, the Mighty One, God, the **L**!	**Jos 22:22**	3068
if in an unfaithful act against the **L**,	**Jos 22:22**	3068
to turn away from following the **L**,	**Jos 22:23**	3068
it, may the **L** Himself require it.	**Jos 22:23**	3068
"What have you to do with the **L**,	**Jos 22:24**	3068
"For the **L** has made the Jordan a	**Jos 22:25**	3068
you have no portion in the **L**."	**Jos 22:25**	3068
make our sons stop fearing the **L**.'	**Jos 22:25**	3068
we are to perform the service of the **L**	**Jos 22:27**	3068
"You have no portion in the **L**."	**Jos 22:27**	3068
"See the copy of the altar of the **L**	**Jos 22:28**	3068
that we should rebel against the **L**	**Jos 22:29**	3068
from following the **L** this day,	**Jos 22:29**	3068
besides the altar of the **L** our God	**Jos 22:29**	3068
know that the **L** is in our midst,	**Jos 22:31**	3068
this unfaithful act against the **L**;	**Jos 22:31**	3068
Israel from the hand of the **L**."	**Jos 22:31**	3068
between us that the **L** is God."	**Jos 22:34**	3068
when the **L** had given rest to	**Jos 23:1**	3068
"And you have seen all that the **L**	**Jos 23:3**	3068
for the **L** your God is He who has	**Jos 23:3**	3068
"The **L** your God, He will	**Jos 23:5**	3068
as the **L** your God promised you.	**Jos 23:5**	3068
are to cling to the **L** your God,	**Jos 23:8**	3068
"For the **L** has driven out great	**Jos 23:9**	3068
for the **L** your God is He who	**Jos 23:10**	3068
yourselves to love the **L** your God.	**Jos 23:11**	3068
know with certainty that the **L**	**Jos 23:13**	3068
the **L** your God has given you.	**Jos 23:13**	3068
words which the **L** your God spoke	**Jos 23:14**	3068
words which the **L** your God spoke to	**Jos 23:15**	3068
so the **L** will bring upon you all	**Jos 23:15**	3068
the **L** your God has given you.	**Jos 23:15**	3068
the covenant of the **L** your God,	**Jos 23:16**	3068
the anger of the **L** will burn against	**Jos 23:16**	3068
"Thus says the **L**, the God of	**Jos 24:2**	3068
'But when they cried out to the **L**,	**Jos 24:7**	3068
fear the **L** and serve Him in	**Jos 24:14**	3068
and in Egypt, and serve the **L**.	**Jos 24:14**	3068
in your sight to serve the **L**,	**Jos 24:15**	3068
my house, we will serve the **L**."	**Jos 24:15**	3068
forsake the **L** to serve other gods;	**Jos 24:16**	3068
for the **L** our God is He who	**Jos 24:17**	3068
"The **L** drove out from before	**Jos 24:18**	3068
We also will serve the **L**,	**Jos 24:18**	3068
will not be able to serve the **L**,	**Jos 24:19**	3068
you forsake the **L** and serve foreign	**Jos 24:20**	3068
"No, but we will serve the **L**."	**Jos 24:21**	3068
have chosen for yourselves the **L**,	**Jos 24:22**	3068
and incline your hearts to the **L**,	**Jos 24:23**	3068
"We will serve the **L** our God and	**Jos 24:24**	3068
was by the sanctuary of the **L**.	**Jos 24:26**	3068
it has heard all the words of the **L**	**Jos 24:27**	3068
son of Nun, the servant of the **L**,	**Jos 24:29**	3068
Israel served the **L** all the	**Jos 24:31**	3068
had known all the deeds of the **L**	**Jos 24:31**	3068
sons of Israel inquired of the **L**,	**Jg 1:1**	3068
The **L** said, "Judah shall go up;	**Jg 1:2**	3068
and the **L** gave the Canaanites and	**Jg 1:4**	3068
Now the **L** was with Judah, and they	**Jg 1:19**	3068
Bethel, and the **L** was with them.	**Jg 1:22**	3068
L came up from Gilgal to Bochim.	**Jg 2:1**	3068
the angel of the **L** spoke these words	**Jg 2:4**	3068
there they sacrificed to the **L**.	**Jg 2:5**	3068
The people served the **L** all the days	**Jg 2:7**	3068
had seen all the great work of the **L**	**Jg 2:7**	3068
son of Nun, the servant of the **L**,	**Jg 2:8**	3068
after them who did not know the **L**,	**Jg 2:10**	3068
did evil in the sight of the **L**	**Jg 2:11**	3068
and they forsook the **L**,	**Jg 2:12**	3068
thus they provoked the **L** to anger.	**Jg 2:12**	3068
So they forsook the **L** and served	**Jg 2:13**	3068
The anger of the **L**	**Jg 2:14**	3068
the hand of the **L** was against them	**Jg 2:15**	3068
as the **L** had spoken and as the	**Jg 2:15**	3068
and as the **L** had sworn to them,	**Jg 2:15**	3068
Then the **L** raised up judges who	**Jg 2:16**	3068
obeying the commandments of the **L**;	**Jg 2:17**	3068
the **L** raised up judges for them,	**Jg 2:18**	3068
the **L** was with the judge and	**Jg 2:18**	3068
for the **L** was moved to pity by	**Jg 2:18**	3068
the anger of the **L** burned against	**Jg 2:20**	3068
keep the way of the **L** to walk in it	**Jg 2:22**	3068
So the **L** allowed those nations to	**Jg 2:23**	3068
are the nations which the **L** left,	**Jg 3:1**	3068
obey the commandments of the **L**,	**Jg 3:4**	3068
was evil in the sight of the **L**,	**Jg 3:7**	3068
Lord, and forgot the **L** their God and	**Jg 3:7**	3068
the anger of the **L** was kindled	**Jg 3:8**	3068
the sons of Israel cried to the **L**,	**Jg 3:9**	3068
the **L** raised up a deliverer for	**Jg 3:9**	3068
The Spirit of the **L** came upon him,	**Jg 3:10**	3068
the **L** gave Cushan-rishathaim king	**Jg 3:10**	3068
did evil in the sight of the **L**.	**Jg 3:12**	3068
So the **L** strengthened Eglon the	**Jg 3:12**	3068
done evil in the sight of the **L**.	**Jg 3:12**	3068
the sons of Israel cried to the **L**,	**Jg 3:15**	3068
the **L** raised up a deliverer for	**Jg 3:15**	3068
for the **L** has given your enemies	**Jg 3:28**	3068
did evil in the sight of the **L**,	**Jg 4:1**	3068
And the **L** sold them into the hand	**Jg 4:2**	3068
The sons of Israel cried to the **L**;	**Jg 4:3**	3068
"Behold, the **L**, the God of	**Jg 4:6**	3068
for the **L** will sell Sisera into	**Jg 4:9**	3068
L has given Sisera into your hands;	**Jg 4:14**	3068
the **L** has gone out before you."	**Jg 4:14**	3068
The **L** routed Sisera and all	**Jg 4:15**	3068
people volunteered, Bless the **L**!	**Jg 5:2**	3068
to the **L**, I will sing, I will sing praise	**Jg 5:3**	3068
sing, I will sing praise to the **L**,	**Jg 5:3**	3068
"**L**, when You went out from	**Jg 5:4**	3068
quaked at the presence of the **L**,	**Jg 5:5**	3068
Sinai, at the presence of the **L**,	**Jg 5:5**	3068
among the people; Bless the **L**!	**Jg 5:9**	3068
the righteous deeds of the **L**,	**Jg 5:11**	3068
the people of the **L** went down to	**Jg 5:11**	3068
people of the **L** came down to me	**Jg 5:13**	3068
Meroz,' said the angel of the **L**,	**Jg 5:23**	3068
did not come to the help of the **L**,	**Jg 5:23**	3068
help of the **L** against the warriors.'	**Jg 5:23**	3068
let all Your enemies perish, O **L**;	**Jg 5:31**	3068
was evil in the sight of the **L**;	**Jg 6:1**	3068
and the **L** gave them into the hands	**Jg 6:1**	3068
the sons of Israel cried to the **L**.	**Jg 6:6**	3068
the sons of Israel cried to the **L**	**Jg 6:7**	3068
that the **L** sent a prophet to the	**Jg 6:8**	3068
"Thus says the **L**, the God of	**Jg 6:8**	3068
"I am the **L** your God;	**Jg 6:10**	3068
Then the angel of the **L** came and	**Jg 6:11**	3068
The angel of the **L** appeared to	**Jg 6:12**	3068
"The **L** is with you, O valiant	**Jg 6:12**	3068
"O my **l**, if the Lord is with us,	**Jg 6:13**	113
"O my lord, if the **L** is with us,	**Jg 6:13**	3068
'Did not the **L** bring us up from	**Jg 6:13**	3068
But now the **L** has abandoned us and	**Jg 6:13**	3068
The **L** looked at him and said,	**Jg 6:14**	3068
"O **L**, how shall I deliver Israel?	**Jg 6:15**	136
But the **L** said to him,	**Jg 6:16**	3068
Then the angel of the **L** put out	**Jg 6:21**	3068
the angel of the **L** vanished from his	**Jg 6:21**	3068
that he was the angel of the **L**,	**Jg 6:22**	3068
Alas, O **L** God! For now I have seen	**Jg 6:22**	136
the angel of the **L** face to face."	**Jg 6:22**	3068
The **L** said to him,	**Jg 6:23**	3068
Gideon built an altar there to the **L**	**Jg 6:24**	3068
Lord and named it The **L** is Peace.	**Jg 6:24**	3068
the **L** said to him,	**Jg 6:25**	3068
and build an altar to the **L** your	**Jg 6:26**	3068
did as the **L** had spoken to him;	**Jg 6:27**	3068
Spirit of the **L** came upon Gideon;	**Jg 6:34**	3068
The **L** said to Gideon,	**Jg 7:2**	3068
Then the **L** said to Gideon,	**Jg 7:4**	3068
And the **L** said to Gideon,	**Jg 7:5**	3068
The **L** said to Gideon,	**Jg 7:7**	3068
came about that the **L** said to him,	**Jg 7:9**	3068
for the **L** has given the camp of	**Jg 7:15**	3068
'For the **L** and for Gideon.' "	**Jg 7:18**	3068
sword for the **L** and for Gideon!"	**Jg 7:20**	3068
the **L** set the sword of one against	**Jg 7:22**	3068
when the **L** has given Zebah and	**Jg 8:7**	3068
As the **L** lives, if only you had	**Jg 8:19**	3068
the **L** shall rule over you."	**Jg 8:23**	3068
did not remember the **L** their God,	**Jg 8:34**	3068
did evil in the sight of the **L**,	**Jg 10:6**	3068
the **L** and did not serve Him.	**Jg 10:6**	3068
of the **L** burned against Israel,	**Jg 10:7**	3068
sons of Israel cried out to the **L**,	**Jg 10:10**	3068
The **L** said to the sons of Israel,	**Jg 10:11**	3068
The sons of Israel said to the **L**,	**Jg 10:15**	3068
from among them and served the **L**;	**Jg 10:16**	3068
and the **L** gives them up to me,	**Jg 11:9**	3068
"The **L** is witness between us;	**Jg 11:10**	3068
his words before the **L** at Mizpah.	**Jg 11:11**	3068
'The **L**, the God of Israel,	**Jg 11:21**	3068
'Since now the **L**, the God of	**Jg 11:23**	3068
So whatever the **L** our God has	**Jg 11:24**	3068
may the **L**, the Judge, judge today	**Jg 11:27**	3068
Spirit of the **L** came upon Jephthah,	**Jg 11:29**	3068
made a vow to the **L** and said,	**Jg 11:30**	3068
and the **L** gave them into his hand.	**Jg 11:32**	3068
for I have given my word to the **L**,	**Jg 11:35**	3068
you have given your word to the **L**;	**Jg 11:36**	3068
since the **L** has avenged you of	**Jg 11:36**	3068
and the **L** gave them into my hand.	**Jg 12:3**	3068
did evil in the sight of the **L**,	**Jg 13:1**	3068
so that the **L** gave them into the	**Jg 13:1**	3068
of the **L** appeared to the woman and	**Jg 13:3**	3068
Manoah entreated the **L** and said,	**Jg 13:8**	3068
"O **L**, please let the man of God	**Jg 13:8**	136
the angel of the **L** said to Manoah,	**Jg 13:13**	3068
Manoah said to the angel of the **L**,	**Jg 13:15**	3068
The angel of the **L** said to Manoah,	**Jg 13:16**	3068
then offer it to the **L**."	**Jg 13:16**	3068
that he was the angel of the **L**.	**Jg 13:16**	3068
Manoah said to the angel of the **L**,	**Jg 13:17**	3068
the angel of the **L** said to him,	**Jg 13:18**	3068
offered it on the rock to the **L**,	**Jg 13:19**	3068
that the angel of the **L** ascended	**Jg 13:20**	3068
the angel of the **L** did not appear	**Jg 13:21**	3068
that he was the angel of the **L**.	**Jg 13:21**	3068
"If the **L** had desired to kill us,	**Jg 13:23**	3068
grew up and the **L** blessed him.	**Jg 13:24**	3068
And the Spirit of the **L** began to	**Jg 13:25**	3068
did not know that it was of the **L**,	**Jg 14:4**	3068
The Spirit of the **L** came upon him	**Jg 14:6**	3068
the Spirit of the **L** came upon him	**Jg 14:19**	3068
And the Spirit of the **L** came upon	**Jg 15:14**	3068
and he called to the **L** and said,	**Jg 15:18**	3068
that the **L** had departed from him.	**Jg 16:20**	3068
Samson called to the **L** and said,	**Jg 16:28**	3068
"O **L** God, please remember me and	**Jg 16:28**	136
"Blessed be my son by the **L**."	**Jg 17:2**	3068
silver from my hand to the **L** for my	**Jg 17:3**	3068
I know that the **L** will prosper me,	**Jg 17:13**	3068
as one man to the **L** at Mizpah.	**Jg 20:1**	3068
Then the **L** said,	**Jg 20:18**	3068

wept before the **L** until evening,	**Jg 20:23**	3068
evening, and inquired of the **L**,	**Jg 20:23**	3068
And the **L** said, "Go up against him	**Jg 20:23**	3068
they remained there before the **L**	**Jg 20:26**	3068
and peace offerings before the **L**.	**Jg 20:26**	3068
sons of Israel inquired of the **L**	**Jg 20:27**	3068
the **L** said, "Go up, for tomorrow I	**Jg 20:28**	3068
L struck Benjamin before Israel,	**Jg 20:35**	3068
"Why, O **L**, God of Israel, has	**Jg 21:3**	3068
up in the assembly to the **L**?"	**Jg 21:5**	3068
not come up to the **L** at Mizpah,	**Jg 21:5**	3068
since we have sworn by the **L** not	**Jg 21:7**	3068
not come up to the **L** at Mizpah?"	**Jg 21:8**	3068
L had made a breach in the tribes of	**Jg 21:15**	3068
the **L** from year to year in Shiloh,	**Jg 21:19**	3068
heard in the land of Moab that the **L**	**Ru 1:6**	3068
May the **L** deal kindly with you as	**Ru 1:8**	3068
L grant that you may find rest,	**Ru 1:9**	3068
the **L** has gone forth against me."	**Ru 1:13**	3068
Thus may the **L** do to me, and	**Ru 1:17**	3068
the **L** has brought me back empty.	**Ru 1:21**	3068
since the **L** has witnessed against	**Ru 1:21**	3068
"May the **L** be with you."	**Ru 2:4**	3068
"May the **L** bless you."	**Ru 2:4**	3068
"May the **L** reward your work, and	**Ru 2:12**	3068
and your wages be full from the **L**,	**Ru 2:12**	3068
found favor in your sight, my **l**,	**Ru 2:13**	113
"May he be blessed of the **L** who	**Ru 2:20**	3068
"May you be blessed of the **L**,	**Ru 3:10**	3068
I will redeem you, as the **L** lives.	**Ru 3:13**	3068
May the **L** make the woman who is	**Ru 4:11**	3068
offspring which the **L** will give you	**Ru 4:12**	3068
And the **L** enabled her to conceive,	**Ru 4:13**	3068
"Blessed is the **L** who has not	**Ru 4:14**	3068
sacrifice to the **L** of hosts in Shiloh.	**1Sa 1:3**	3068
were priests to the **L** there.	**1Sa 1:3**	3068
but the **L** had closed her womb.	**1Sa 1:5**	3068
because the **L** had closed her womb.	**1Sa 1:6**	3068
she went up to the house of the **L**,	**1Sa 1:7**	3068
doorpost of the temple of the **L**.	**1Sa 1:9**	3068
prayed to the **L** and wept bitterly.	**1Sa 1:10**	3068
"O **L** of hosts, if You will	**1Sa 1:11**	3068
give him to the **L** all the days of his	**1Sa 1:11**	3068
continued praying before the **L**,	**1Sa 1:12**	3068
"No, my **l**, I am a woman oppressed	**1Sa 1:15**	113
poured out my soul before the **L**.	**1Sa 1:15**	3068
and worshiped before the **L**,	**1Sa 1:19**	3068
wife, and the **L** remembered her.	**1Sa 1:19**	3068
I have asked him of the **L**."	**1Sa 1:20**	3068
to offer to the **L** the yearly sacrifice	**1Sa 1:21**	3068
the **L** and stay there forever."	**1Sa 1:22**	3068
only may the **L** confirm His word."	**1Sa 1:23**	3068
to the house of the **L** in Shiloh,	**1Sa 1:24**	3068
"Oh, my **l**! As your soul lives,	**1Sa 1:26**	113
As your soul lives, my **l**,	**1Sa 1:26**	113
here beside you, praying to the **L**.	**1Sa 1:26**	3068
and the **L** has given me my petition	**1Sa 1:27**	3068
have also dedicated him to the **L**;	**1Sa 1:28**	3068
lives he is dedicated to the **L**."	**1Sa 1:28**	3068
And he worshiped the **L** there.	**1Sa 1:28**	3068
"My heart exults in the **L**;	**1Sa 2:1**	3068
My horn is exalted in the **L**,	**1Sa 2:1**	3068
"There is no one holy like the **L**,	**1Sa 2:2**	3068
For the **L** is a God of knowledge,	**1Sa 2:3**	3068
"The **L** kills and makes alive;	**1Sa 2:6**	3068
"The **L** makes poor and rich;	**1Sa 2:7**	3068
"Those who contend with the **L** will	**1Sa 2:10**	3068
The **L** will judge the ends of the	**1Sa 2:10**	3068
boy ministered to the **L** before Eli	**1Sa 2:11**	3068
they did not know the **L**	**1Sa 2:12**	3068
men was very great before the **L**,	**1Sa 2:17**	3068
despised the offering of the **L**.	**1Sa 2:17**	3068
was ministering before the **L**,	**1Sa 2:18**	3068
"May the **L** give you children from	**1Sa 2:20**	3068
the one she dedicated to the **L**."	**1Sa 2:20**	3068
The **L** visited Hannah;	**1Sa 2:21**	3068
the boy Samuel grew before the **L**.	**1Sa 2:21**	3068
but if a man sins against the **L**,	**1Sa 2:25**	3068
L desired to put them to death.	**1Sa 2:25**	3068
both with the **L** and with men.	**1Sa 2:26**	3068
"Thus says the **L**,	**1Sa 2:27**	3068
the **L** God of Israel declares,	**1Sa 2:30**	3068
but now the **L** declares,	**1Sa 2:30**	3068
ministering to the **L** before Eli.	**1Sa 3:1**	3068
word from the **L** was rare in those	**1Sa 3:1**	3068
lying down in the temple of the **L**	**1Sa 3:3**	3068
that the **L** called Samuel;	**1Sa 3:4**	3068
The **L** called yet again,	**1Sa 3:6**	3068
Now Samuel did not yet know the **L**,	**1Sa 3:7**	3068
nor had the word of the **L** yet been	**1Sa 3:7**	3068
So the **L** called Samuel again for	**1Sa 3:8**	3068
that the **L** was calling the boy.	**1Sa 3:8**	3068
'Speak, **L**, for Your servant is	**1Sa 3:9**	3068
Then the **L** came and stood and	**1Sa 3:10**	3068
The **L** said to Samuel,	**1Sa 3:11**	3068
the doors of the house of the **L**.	**1Sa 3:15**	3068
And he said, "It is the **L**;	**1Sa 3:18**	3068
Thus Samuel grew and the **L** was	**1Sa 3:19**	3068
confirmed as a prophet of the **L**.	**1Sa 3:20**	3068
the **L** appeared again at Shiloh,	**1Sa 3:21**	3068
because the **L** revealed Himself to	**1Sa 3:21**	3068
at Shiloh by the word of the **L**.	**1Sa 3:21**	3068
"Why has the **L** defeated us today	**1Sa 4:3**	3068
the ark of the covenant of the **L**,	**1Sa 4:3**	3068
ark of the covenant of the **L** of hosts	**1Sa 4:4**	3068
ark of the covenant of the **L** came	**1Sa 4:5**	3068
the ark of the **L** had come into the	**1Sa 4:6**	3068
ground before the ark of the **L**.	**1Sa 5:3**	3068
ground before the ark of the **L**.	**1Sa 5:4**	3068
the hand of the **L** was heavy on the	**1Sa 5:6**	3068
the hand of the **L** was against the	**1Sa 5:9**	3068
Now the ark of the **L** had been in	**1Sa 6:1**	3068
shall we do with the ark of the **L**?	**1Sa 6:2**	3068
Take the ark of the **L** and place it on	**1Sa 6:8**	3068
put the ark of the **L** on the cart,	**1Sa 6:11**	3068
cows as a burnt offering to the **L**.	**1Sa 6:14**	3068
Levites took down the ark of the **L**	**1Sa 6:15**	3068
sacrifices that day to the **L**.	**1Sa 6:15**	3068
for a guilt offering to the **L**:	**1Sa 6:17**	3068
on which they set the ark of the **L**	**1Sa 6:18**	3068
had looked into the ark of the **L**.	**1Sa 6:19**	3068
mourned because the **L** had struck	**1Sa 6:19**	3068
"Who is able to stand before the **L**,	**1Sa 6:20**	3068
brought back the ark of the **L**;	**1Sa 6:21**	3068
came and took the ark of the **L**	**1Sa 7:1**	3068
his son to keep the ark of the **L**.	**1Sa 7:1**	3068
of Israel lamented after the **L**	**1Sa 7:2**	3068
to the **L** with all your heart,	**1Sa 7:3**	3068
to the **L** and serve Him alone;	**1Sa 7:3**	3068
Ashtaroth and served the **L** alone.	**1Sa 7:4**	3068
I will pray to the **L** for you."	**1Sa 7:5**	3068
and poured it out before the **L**,	**1Sa 7:6**	3068
"We have sinned against the **L**."	**1Sa 7:6**	3068
to cry to the **L** our God for us,	**1Sa 7:8**	3068
a whole burnt offering to the **L**;	**1Sa 7:9**	3068
and Samuel cried to the **L** for	**1Sa 7:9**	3068
for Israel and the **L** answered him.	**1Sa 7:9**	3068
But the **L** thundered with a great	**1Sa 7:10**	3068
"Thus far the **L** has helped us."	**1Sa 7:12**	3068
And the hand of the **L** was against	**1Sa 7:13**	3068
he built there an altar to the **L**.	**1Sa 7:17**	3068
And Samuel prayed to the **L**.	**1Sa 8:6**	3068
The **L** said to Samuel,	**1Sa 8:7**	3068
Samuel spoke all the words of the **L**	**1Sa 8:10**	3068
but the **L** will not answer you in	**1Sa 8:18**	3068
The **L** said to Samuel,	**1Sa 8:22**	3068
the **L** had revealed *this* to Samuel	**1Sa 9:15**	3068
saw Saul, the **L** said to him,	**1Sa 9:17**	3068
"Has not the **L** anointed you a	**1Sa 10:1**	3068
the **L** will come upon you mightily,	**1Sa 10:6**	3068
together to the **L** at Mizpah;	**1Sa 10:17**	3068
"Thus says the **L**, the God of	**1Sa 10:18**	3068
present yourselves before the **L** by	**1Sa 10:19**	3068
they inquired further of the **L**,	**1Sa 10:22**	3068
So the **L** said, "Behold, he is hiding	**1Sa 10:22**	3068
you see him whom the **L** has chosen?	**1Sa 10:24**	3068
book and placed *it* before the **L**.	**1Sa 10:25**	3068
dread of the **L** fell on the people,	**1Sa 11:7**	3068
for today the **L** has accomplished	**1Sa 11:13**	3068
Saul king before the **L** in Gilgal.	**1Sa 11:15**	3068
of peace offerings before the **L**;	**1Sa 11:15**	3068
me before the **L** and His anointed.	**1Sa 12:3**	3068
"The **L** is witness against you,	**1Sa 12:5**	3068
"It is the **L** who appointed Moses	**1Sa 12:6**	3068
I may plead with you before the **L**	**1Sa 12:7**	3068
righteous acts of the **L** which He did	**1Sa 12:7**	3068
your fathers cried out to the **L**,	**1Sa 12:8**	3068
then the **L** sent Moses and Aaron	**1Sa 12:8**	3068
"But they forgot the **L** their God,	**1Sa 12:9**	3068
They cried out to the **L** and said,	**1Sa 12:10**	3068
have forsaken the **L** and have served	**1Sa 12:10**	3068
"Then the **L** sent Jerubbaal and	**1Sa 12:11**	3068
the **L** your God *was* your king.	**1Sa 12:12**	3068
the **L** has set a king over you.	**1Sa 12:13**	3068
you will fear the **L** and serve Him,	**1Sa 12:14**	3068
against the command of the **L**,	**1Sa 12:14**	3068
you will follow the **L** your God.	**1Sa 12:14**	3068
not listen to the voice of the **L**,	**1Sa 12:15**	3068
against the command of the **L**,	**1Sa 12:15**	3068
hand of the **L** will be against you,	**1Sa 12:15**	3068
the **L** will do before your eyes.	**1Sa 12:16**	3068
I will call to the **L**,	**1Sa 12:17**	3068
you have done in the sight of the **L**	**1Sa 12:17**	3068
So Samuel called to the **L**,	**1Sa 12:18**	3068
the **L** sent thunder and rain	**1Sa 12:18**	3068
greatly feared the **L** and Samuel.	**1Sa 12:18**	3068
your servants to the **L** your God,	**1Sa 12:19**	3068
turn aside from following the **L**,	**1Sa 12:20**	3068
serve the **L** with all your heart.	**1Sa 12:20**	3068
"For the **L** will not abandon His	**1Sa 12:22**	3068
because the **L** has been pleased to	**1Sa 12:22**	3068
sin against the **L** by ceasing to pray	**1Sa 12:23**	3068
"Only fear the **L** and serve Him in	**1Sa 12:24**	3068
not asked the favor of the **L**.'	**1Sa 13:12**	3068
the commandment of the **L** your God,	**1Sa 13:13**	3068
for now the **L** would have	**1Sa 13:13**	3068
The **L** has sought out for Himself a	**1Sa 13:14**	3068
and the **L** has appointed him as	**1Sa 13:14**	3068
kept what the **L** commanded you."	**1Sa 13:14**	3068
the priest of the **L** at Shiloh,	**1Sa 14:3**	3068
perhaps the **L** will work for us,	**1Sa 14:6**	3068
for the **L** is not restrained to	**1Sa 14:6**	3068
L has given them into our hands;	**1Sa 14:10**	3068
for the **L** has given them into the	**1Sa 14:12**	3068
the **L** delivered Israel that day,	**1Sa 14:23**	3068
the people are sinning against the **L**	**1Sa 14:33**	3068
do not sin against the **L** by eating	**1Sa 14:34**	3068
And Saul built an altar to the **L**;	**1Sa 14:35**	3068
altar that he built to the **L**.	**1Sa 14:35**	3068
"For as the **L** lives, who delivers	**1Sa 14:39**	3068
Therefore, Saul said to the **L**,	**1Sa 14:41**	3068
As the **L** lives, not one hair	**1Sa 14:45**	3068
"The **L** sent me to anoint you as	**1Sa 15:1**	3068
listen to the words of the **L**.	**1Sa 15:1**	3068
"Thus says the **L** of hosts,	**1Sa 15:2**	3068
the word of the **L** came to Samuel,	**1Sa 15:10**	3068
and cried out to the **L** all night.	**1Sa 15:11**	3068
"Blessed are you of the **L**!	**1Sa 15:13**	3068
out the command of the **L**."	**1Sa 15:13**	3068
to sacrifice to the **L** your God;	**1Sa 15:15**	3068
the **L** said to me last night."	**1Sa 15:16**	3068
L anointed you king over Israel,	**1Sa 15:17**	3068
and the **L** sent you on a mission,	**1Sa 15:18**	3068
you not obey the voice of the **L**,	**1Sa 15:19**	3068
was evil in the sight of the **L**?"	**1Sa 15:19**	3068
"I did obey the voice of the **L**,	**1Sa 15:20**	3068
mission on which the **L** sent me,	**1Sa 15:20**	3068
sacrifice to the **L** your God at Gilgal	**1Sa 15:21**	3068
"Has the **L** as much delight in	**1Sa 15:22**	3068
As in obeying the voice of the **L**?	**1Sa 15:22**	3068
have rejected the word of the **L**,	**1Sa 15:23**	3068
command of the **L** and your words,	**1Sa 15:24**	3068
me, that I may worship the **L**."	**1Sa 15:25**	3068
have rejected the word of the **L**,	**1Sa 15:26**	3068
and the **L** has rejected you from	**1Sa 15:26**	3068
"The **L** has torn the kingdom of	**1Sa 15:28**	3068
I may worship the **L** your God."	**1Sa 15:30**	3068
Saul, and Saul worshiped the **L**.	**1Sa 15:31**	3068
hewed Agag to pieces before the **L**	**1Sa 15:33**	3068
And the **L** regretted that He had	**1Sa 15:35**	3068
Now the **L** said to Samuel,	**1Sa 16:1**	3068
the **L** said, "Take a heifer with you and	**1Sa 16:2**	3068
have come to sacrifice to the **L**.'	**1Sa 16:2**	3068
So Samuel did what the **L** said,	**1Sa 16:4**	3068
I have come to sacrifice to the **L**.	**1Sa 16:5**	3068
But the **L** said to Samuel,	**1Sa 16:7**	3068
but the **L** looks at the heart."	**1Sa 16:7**	3068
"The **L** has not chosen this one either."	**1Sa 16:8**	3068
"The **L** has not chosen this one either."	**1Sa 16:9**	3068
"The **L** has not chosen these."	**1Sa 16:10**	3068
And the **L** said, "Arise, anoint him;	**1Sa 16:12**	3068
and the Spirit of the **L** came	**1Sa 16:13**	3068
Spirit of the **L** departed from Saul,	**1Sa 16:14**	3068
spirit from the **L** terrorized him.	**1Sa 16:14**	3068
"Let our **l** now command your	**1Sa 16:16**	113
and the **L** is with him."	**1Sa 16:18**	3068
"The **L** who delivered me from the	**1Sa 17:37**	3068
"Go, and may the **L** be with you."	**1Sa 17:37**	3068
you in the name of the **L** of hosts,	**1Sa 17:45**	3068
"This day the **L** will deliver you	**1Sa 17:46**	3068
that the **L** does not deliver by sword	**1Sa 17:47**	3068
for the **L** was with him but had	**1Sa 18:12**	3068
his ways for the **L** *was* with him.	**1Sa 18:14**	3068
knew that the **L** was with David,	**1Sa 18:28**	3068
and the **L** brought about a great	**1Sa 19:5**	3068
"As the **L** lives, he shall not be	**1Sa 19:6**	3068
was an evil spirit from the **L** on Saul	**1Sa 19:9**	3068
L lives and as your soul lives,	**1Sa 20:3**	3068
into a covenant of the **L** with you.	**1Sa 20:8**	3068
"The **L**, the God of Israel, *be*	**1Sa 20:12**	3068
may the **L** do so to Jonathan and	**1Sa 20:13**	3068
And may the **L** be with you as He	**1Sa 20:13**	3068
me the lovingkindness of the **L**,	**1Sa 20:14**	3068
not even when the **L** cuts off every	**1Sa 20:15**	3068
"May the **L** require *it* at the	**1Sa 20:16**	3068
you and no harm, as the **L** lives.	**1Sa 20:21**	3068
go, for the **L** has sent you away.	**1Sa 20:22**	3068
L is between you and me forever."	**1Sa 20:23**	3068
each other in the name of the **L**,	**1Sa 20:42**	3068
'The **L** will be between me and you,	**1Sa 20:42**	3068
was removed from before the **L**,	**1Sa 21:6**	3068
that day, detained before the **L**;	**1Sa 21:7**	3068
"He inquired of the **L** for him,	**1Sa 22:10**	3068
"Here I am, my **l**."	**1Sa 22:12**	113
put the priests of the **L** to death,	**1Sa 22:17**	3068
to attack the priests of the **L**.	**1Sa 22:17**	3068
had killed the priests of the **L**.	**1Sa 22:21**	3068
So David inquired of the **L**,	**1Sa 23:2**	3068
And the **L** said to David,	**1Sa 23:2**	3068
David inquired of the **L** once more.	**1Sa 23:4**	3068
And the **L** answered him and said,	**1Sa 23:4**	3068
"O **L** God of Israel, Your servant	**1Sa 23:10**	3068
O **L** God of Israel, I pray, tell	**1Sa 23:11**	3068
And the **L** said, "He will come down	**1Sa 23:11**	3068
the **L** said, "They will surrender you	**1Sa 23:12**	3068
them made a covenant before the **L**;	**1Sa 23:18**	3068
"May you be blessed of the **L**,	**1Sa 23:21**	3068
day of which the **L** said to you,	**1Sa 24:4**	3068
"Far be it from me because of the **L**	**1Sa 24:6**	3068
I should do this thing to my **l**,	**1Sa 24:6**	113
after Saul, saying, "My **l** the king!"	**1Sa 24:8**	113
L had given you today into my hand	**1Sa 24:10**	3068
stretch out my hand against my **l**,	**1Sa 24:10**	113
the **L** judge between you and me,	**1Sa 24:12**	3068
and may the **L** avenge me on you;	**1Sa 24:12**	3068
"The **L** therefore be judge and	**1Sa 24:15**	3068
that the **L** delivered me into your	**1Sa 24:18**	3068
May the **L** therefore reward you	**1Sa 24:19**	3068
"So now swear to me by the **L** that	**1Sa 24:21**	3068
"On me alone, my **l**, be the blame.	**1Sa 25:24**	113
"Please do not let my **l** pay attention	**1Sa 25:25**	113
young men of my **l** whom you sent.	**1Sa 25:25**	113
"Now therefore, my **l**,	**1Sa 25:26**	113
my lord, as the **L** lives,	**1Sa 25:26**	3068
since the **L** has restrained you	**1Sa 25:26**	3068
those who seek evil against my **l**,	**1Sa 25:26**	113
your maidservant has brought to my **l**	**1Sa 25:27**	113
the young men who accompany my **l**.	**1Sa 25:27**	113
for the **L** will certainly make for	**1Sa 25:28**	3068
make for my **l** an enduring house,	**1Sa 25:28**	113
because my **l** is fighting the	**1Sa 25:28**	113
is fighting the battles of the **L**,	**1Sa 25:28**	3068
then the life of my **l** shall be	**1Sa 25:29**	113
of the living with the **L** your God;	**1Sa 25:29**	3068
"And when the **L** does for my lord	**1Sa 25:30**	3068
"And when the LORD does for my **l**	**1Sa 25:30**	3068
grief or a troubled heart to my **l**,	**1Sa 25:31**	113

by my l having avenged himself.	1Sa 25:31	113
When the L deals well with my	1Sa 25:31	3068
the LORD deals well with my l,	1Sa 25:31	113
"Blessed be the L God of Israel,	1Sa 25:32	3068
as the L God of Israel lives,	1Sa 25:34	3068
the L struck Nabal	1Sa 25:38	3068
"Blessed be the L, who has	1Sa 25:39	3068
The L has also returned the	1Sa 25:39	3068
"As the L lives, surely the LORD	1Sa 26:10	3068
surely the L will strike him,	1Sa 26:10	3068
"The L forbid that I should	1Sa 26:11	3068
a sound sleep from the L had fallen	1Sa 26:12	3068
you not guarded your l the king?	1Sa 26:15	113
came to destroy the king your l.	1Sa 26:15	113
As the L lives, *all* of you must	1Sa 26:16	3068
because you did not guard your l,	1Sa 26:16	113
"It is my voice, my l the king."	1Sa 26:17	113
then is my l pursuing his servant?	1Sa 26:18	113
please let my l the king listen to	1Sa 26:19	113
L has stirred you up against me,	1Sa 26:19	3068
men, cursed are they before the L,	1Sa 26:19	3068
with the inheritance of the L,	1Sa 26:19	3068
away from the presence of the L;	1Sa 26:20	3068
"The L will repay each man	1Sa 26:23	3068
for the L delivered you into *my*	1Sa 26:23	3068
valued in the sight of the L,	1Sa 26:24	3068
When Saul inquired of the L,	1Sa 28:6	3068
LORD, the L did not answer him,	1Sa 28:6	3068
Saul vowed to her by the L,	1Sa 28:10	3068
"As the L lives, no	1Sa 28:10	3068
since the L has departed from you	1Sa 28:16	3068
"The L has done accordingly	1Sa 28:17	3068
for the L has torn the kingdom out	1Sa 28:17	3068
"As you did not obey the L and	1Sa 28:18	3068
so the L has done this thing to	1Sa 28:18	3068
"Moreover the L will also give	1Sa 28:19	3068
Indeed the L will give over the	1Sa 28:19	3068
make himself acceptable to his l?	1Sa 29:4	113
"*As* the L lives, you *have been*	1Sa 29:6	3068
the enemies of my l the king?"	1Sa 29:8	113
servants of your l who have come	1Sa 29:10	113
himself in the L his God.	1Sa 30:6	3068
David inquired of the L,	1Sa 30:8	3068
with what the L has given us,	1Sa 30:23	3068
the spoil of the enemies of the L:	1Sa 30:26	3068
have brought them here to my l."	2Sa 1:10	113
for the people of the L and the	2Sa 1:12	3068
that David inquired of the L,	2Sa 2:1	3068
And the L said to him,	2Sa 2:1	3068
"May you be blessed of the L	2Sa 2:5	3068
this kindness to Saul your l,	2Sa 2:5	113
"Now may the L show	2Sa 2:6	3068
for Saul your l is dead, and also	2Sa 2:7	113
if as the L has sworn to David,	2Sa 3:9	3068
For the L has spoken of David,	2Sa 3:18	3068
and gather all Israel to my l the	2Sa 3:21	113
are innocent before the L forever of	2Sa 3:28	3068
May the L repay the evildoer	2Sa 3:39	3068
thus the L has given my lord the	2Sa 4:8	3068
thus the LORD has given my l the	2Sa 4:8	113
"As the L lives, who has redeemed	2Sa 4:9	3068
And the L said to you,	2Sa 5:2	3068
with them before the L at Hebron;	2Sa 5:3	3068
the L God of hosts was with him.	2Sa 5:10	3068
And David realized that the L had	2Sa 5:12	3068
Then David inquired of the L,	2Sa 5:19	3068
And the L said to David,	2Sa 5:19	3068
"The L has broken through my	2Sa 5:20	3068
When David inquired of the L,	2Sa 5:23	3068
for then the L will have gone out	2Sa 5:24	3068
just as the L had commanded him,	2Sa 5:25	3068
the very name of the L of hosts	2Sa 6:2	3068
Israel were celebrating before the L	2Sa 6:5	3068
of the L burned against Uzzah,	2Sa 6:7	3068
was afraid of the L that day;	2Sa 6:9	3068
can the ark of the L come to me?"	2Sa 6:9	3068
unwilling to move the ark of the L	2Sa 6:10	3068
Thus the ark of the L remained in	2Sa 6:11	3068
and the L blessed Obed-edom and	2Sa 6:11	3068
"The L has blessed the house of	2Sa 6:12	3068
ark of the L had gone six paces,	2Sa 6:13	3068
before the L with all *his* might,	2Sa 6:14	3068
were bringing up the ark of the L	2Sa 6:15	3068
the ark of the L came into the city of	2Sa 6:16	3068
leaping and dancing before the L;	2Sa 6:16	3068
So they brought in the ark of the L	2Sa 6:17	3068
and peace offerings before the L.	2Sa 6:17	3068
in the name of the L of hosts.	2Sa 6:18	3068
"*It was* before the L,	2Sa 6:21	3068
me ruler over the people of the L,	2Sa 6:21	3068
I will celebrate before the L.	2Sa 6:21	3068
and the L had given him rest on	2Sa 7:1	3068
mind, for the L is with you."	2Sa 7:3	3068
the word of the L came to Nathan,	2Sa 7:4	3068
'Thus says the L,	2Sa 7:5	3068
'Thus says the L of hosts,	2Sa 7:8	3068
The L also declares to you that	2Sa 7:11	3068
the L will make a house for you.	2Sa 7:11	3068
king went in and sat before the L,	2Sa 7:18	3068
"Who am I, O L GOD, and what is	2Sa 7:18	136
in Your eyes, O L GOD,	2Sa 7:19	136
is the custom of man, O L GOD.	2Sa 7:19	136
You know Your servant, O L GOD!	2Sa 7:20	136
reason You are great, O L GOD;	2Sa 7:22	136
You, O L, have become their God.	2Sa 7:24	3068
"Now therefore, O L God,	2Sa 7:25	3068
L of hosts is God over Israel';	2Sa 7:26	3068
"For You, O L of hosts, the God	2Sa 7:27	3068
"Now, O L GOD, You are God,	2Sa 7:28	136

For You, O L GOD, have spoken;	2Sa 7:29	136
L helped David wherever he went.	2Sa 8:6	3068
also dedicated these to the L,	2Sa 8:11	3068
L helped David wherever he went.	2Sa 8:14	3068
all that my l the king commands his	2Sa 9:11	113
Ammonites said to Hanun their l,	2Sa 10:3	113
L do what is good in His sight."	2Sa 10:12	3068
with all the servants of his l,	2Sa 11:9	113
and my l Joab and the servants of	2Sa 11:11	113
the servants of my l are camping in	2Sa 11:11	113
was evil in the sight of the L.	2Sa 11:27	3068
Then the L sent Nathan to David.	2Sa 12:1	3068
"As the L lives, surely the man	2Sa 12:5	3068
Thus says the L God of Israel,	2Sa 12:7	3068
have you despised the word of the L	2Sa 12:9	3068
"Thus says the L,	2Sa 12:11	3068
"I have sinned against the L."	2Sa 12:13	3068
L also has taken away your sin;	2Sa 12:13	3068
the enemies of the L to blaspheme,	2Sa 12:14	3068
Then the L struck the child that	2Sa 12:15	3068
he came into the house of the L and	2Sa 12:20	3068
the L may be gracious to me,	2Sa 12:22	3068
Now the L loved him	2Sa 12:24	3068
"Do not let my l suppose they	2Sa 13:32	113
do not let my l the king take the	2Sa 13:33	113
"O my l, the king, the iniquity	2Sa 14:9	113
the king remember the L your God,	2Sa 14:11	3068
"As the L lives, not one hair of	2Sa 14:11	3068
speak a word to my l the king."	2Sa 14:12	113
to speak this word to my l the king	2Sa 14:15	113
let the word of my l the king be	2Sa 14:17	113
so is my l the king to discern	2Sa 14:17	113
the L your God be with you.' "	2Sa 14:17	3068
"Let my l the king please speak."	2Sa 14:18	113
"As your soul lives, my l the king,	2Sa 14:19	113
that my l the king has spoken.	2Sa 14:19	113
But my l is wise, like the wisdom	2Sa 14:20	113
found favor in your sight, O my l,	2Sa 14:22	113
vow which I have vowed to the L,	2Sa 15:7	3068
'If the L shall indeed bring me	2Sa 15:8	3068
then I will serve the L.' "	2Sa 15:8	3068
whatever my l the king chooses."	2Sa 15:15	113
"As the L lives, and as my lord	2Sa 15:21	3068
lives, and as my l the king lives,	2Sa 15:21	113
wherever my l the king may be,	2Sa 15:21	113
find favor in the sight of the L,	2Sa 15:25	3068
"O L, I pray, make the counsel of	2Sa 15:31	3068
find favor in your sight, O my l,	2Sa 16:4	113
"The L has returned upon you all	2Sa 16:8	3068
and the L has given the kingdom	2Sa 16:8	3068
this dead dog curse my l the king?	2Sa 16:9	113
curses, and if the L has told him,	2Sa 16:10	3068
him curse, for the L has told him.	2Sa 16:11	3068
"Perhaps the L will look on my	2Sa 16:12	3068
For whom the L, this people, and	2Sa 16:18	3068
For the L had ordained to thwart	2Sa 17:14	3068
so that the L might bring	2Sa 17:14	3068
bring the king news that the L has	2Sa 18:19	3068
"Blessed is the L your God, who	2Sa 18:28	3068
hands against my l the king."	2Sa 18:28	113
my l the king receive good news,	2Sa 18:31	113
for the L has freed you this day	2Sa 18:31	3068
"Let the enemies of my l the king,	2Sa 18:32	113
servants, for I swear by the L,	2Sa 19:7	3068
"Let not my l consider me guilty,	2Sa 19:19	113
on the day when my l the king came	2Sa 19:19	113
go down to meet my l the king."	2Sa 19:20	113
"O my l, the king, my servant	2Sa 19:26	113
your servant to my l the king;	2Sa 19:27	113
but my l the king is like the	2Sa 19:27	113
but dead men before my l the king;	2Sa 19:28	113
since my l the king has come	2Sa 19:30	113
an added burden to my l the king?	2Sa 19:35	113
him cross over with my l the king,	2Sa 19:37	113
up the inheritance of the L?"	2Sa 20:19	3068
sought the presence of the L.	2Sa 21:1	3068
And the L said, "It is for Saul and	2Sa 21:1	3068
bless the inheritance of the L?"	2Sa 21:3	3068
before the L in Gibeah of Saul,	2Sa 21:6	3068
of Saul, the chosen of the L."	2Sa 21:6	3068
the oath of the L which was between	2Sa 21:7	3068
them in the mountain before the L,	2Sa 21:9	3068
spoke the words of this song to the L	2Sa 22:1	3068
in the day that the L delivered him	2Sa 22:1	3068
"The L is my rock and my fortress	2Sa 22:2	3068
"I call upon the L, who is worthy	2Sa 22:4	3068
my distress I called upon the L,	2Sa 22:7	3068
"The L thundered from heaven, And	2Sa 22:14	3068
laid bare By the rebuke of the L,	2Sa 22:16	3068
But the L was my support.	2Sa 22:19	3068
"The L has rewarded me according	2Sa 22:21	3068
"For I have kept the ways of the L,	2Sa 22:22	3068
"Therefore the L has recompensed	2Sa 22:25	3068
"For You are my lamp, O L;	2Sa 22:29	3068
And the L illumines my darkness.	2Sa 22:29	3068
The word of the L is tested;	2Sa 22:31	3068
"For who is God, besides the L?	2Sa 22:32	3068
Even to the L, but He did not	2Sa 22:42	3068
"The L lives, and blessed be my	2Sa 22:47	3068
I will give thanks to You, O L,	2Sa 22:50	3068
"The Spirit of the L spoke by me,	2Sa 23:2	3068
and the L brought about a great	2Sa 23:10	3068
L brought about a great victory.	2Sa 23:12	3068
it, but poured it out to the L;	2Sa 23:16	3068
"Be it far from me, O L,	2Sa 23:17	3068
the anger of the L burned against	2Sa 24:1	3068
"Now may the L your God add to	2Sa 24:3	3068
eyes of my l the king *still* see;	2Sa 24:3	113
but why does my l the king delight	2Sa 24:3	113

So David said to the L,	2Sa 24:10	3068
But now, O L, please take away the	2Sa 24:10	3068
word of the L came to the prophet	2Sa 24:11	3068
'Thus the L says,	2Sa 24:12	3068
us now fall into the hand of the L	2Sa 24:14	3068
So the L sent a pestilence upon	2Sa 24:15	3068
the L relented from the calamity and	2Sa 24:16	3068
And the angel of the L was by the	2Sa 24:16	3068
Then David spoke to the L when he	2Sa 24:17	3068
erect an altar to the L on the	2Sa 24:18	3068
Gad, just as the L had commanded.	2Sa 24:19	3068
l the king come to his servant?"	2Sa 24:21	113
order to build an altar to the L,	2Sa 24:21	3068
"Let my l the king take and offer	2Sa 24:22	113
"May the L your God accept you."	2Sa 24:23	3068
not offer burnt offerings to the L	2Sa 24:24	3068
built there an altar to the L	2Sa 24:25	3068
Thus the L was moved by prayer	2Sa 24:25	3068
a young virgin for my l the king,	1Ki 1:2	113
my l the king may keep warm."	1Ki 1:2	113
and David our l does not know *it?*	1Ki 1:11	113
'Have you not, my l,	1Ki 1:13	113
"My l, you swore to your	1Ki 1:17	113
maidservant by the L your God,	1Ki 1:17	3068
and now, my l the king, you do not	1Ki 1:18	113
"As for you now, my l the king,	1Ki 1:20	113
throne of my l the king after him.	1Ki 1:20	113
as soon as my l the king sleeps	1Ki 1:21	113
"My l the king, have you said,	1Ki 1:24	113
thing been done by my l the king,	1Ki 1:27	113
sit on the throne of my l the king	1Ki 1:27	113
"As the L lives, who has redeemed	1Ki 1:29	3068
to you by the L the God of Israel,	1Ki 1:30	3068
my l King David live forever."	1Ki 1:31	113
with you the servants of your l,	1Ki 1:33	113
Thus may the L, the God of my lord	1Ki 1:36	3068
LORD, the God of my l the king,	1Ki 1:36	113
"As the L has been with my lord	1Ki 1:37	3068
LORD has been with my l the king,	1Ki 1:37	113
the throne of my l King David!"	1Ki 1:37	113
Our l King David has made Solomon	1Ki 1:43	113
came to bless our l King David,	1Ki 1:47	113
'Blessed be the L, the God of	1Ki 1:48	3068
Keep the charge of the L your God,	1Ki 2:3	3068
so that the L may carry out His	1Ki 2:4	3068
Jordan, I swore to him by the L,	1Ki 2:8	3068
for it was his from the L.	1Ki 2:15	3068
Then King Solomon swore by the L,	1Ki 2:23	3068
"Now therefore, as the L lives,	1Ki 2:24	3068
you carried the ark of the L GOD	1Ki 2:26	136
from being priest to the L,	1Ki 2:27	3068
to fulfill the word of the L,	1Ki 2:27	3068
And Joab fled to the tent of the L	1Ki 2:28	3068
had fled to the tent of the L,	1Ki 2:29	3068
Benaiah came to the tent of the L	1Ki 2:30	3068
"The L will return his blood	1Ki 2:32	3068
be peace from the L forever."	1Ki 2:33	3068
As my l the king has said, so your	1Ki 2:38	113
"Did I not make you swear by the L	1Ki 2:42	3068
you not kept the oath of the L,	1Ki 2:43	3068
therefore the L shall return your	1Ki 2:44	3068
be established before the L forever."	1Ki 2:45	3068
own house and the house of the L	1Ki 3:1	3068
name of the L until those days.	1Ki 3:2	3068
Now Solomon loved the L,	1Ki 3:3	3068
In Gibeon the L appeared to	1Ki 3:5	3068
"Now, O L my God, You have	1Ki 3:7	3068
It was pleasing in the sight of the L	1Ki 3:10	136
the ark of the covenant of the L	1Ki 3:15	136
"Oh, my l, this woman and I live	1Ki 3:17	113
"Oh, my l, give her the living	1Ki 3:26	113
build a house for the name of the L	1Ki 5:3	3068
until the L put them under the	1Ki 5:3	3068
"But now the L my God has given	1Ki 5:4	3068
for the name of the L my God,	1Ki 5:5	3068
as the L spoke to David my father,	1Ki 5:5	3068
"Blessed be the L today, who has	1Ki 5:7	3068
The L gave wisdom to Solomon,	1Ki 5:12	3068
began to build the house of the L.	1Ki 6:1	3068
King Solomon built for the L,	1Ki 6:2	3068
the word of the L came to Solomon	1Ki 6:11	3068
the ark of the covenant of the L.	1Ki 6:19	3068
foundation of the house of the L	1Ki 6:37	3068
inner court of the house of the L,	1Ki 7:12	3068
Solomon *in* the house of the L:	1Ki 7:40	3068
King Solomon *in* the house of the L	1Ki 7:45	3068
which *was in* the house of the L:	1Ki 7:48	3068
the house of the L was finished.	1Ki 7:51	3068
treasuries of the house of the L.	1Ki 7:51	3068
the ark of the covenant of the L	1Ki 8:1	3068
They brought up the ark of the L	1Ki 8:4	3068
the ark of the covenant of the L	1Ki 8:6	3068
where the L made a covenant with	1Ki 8:9	3068
cloud filled the house of the L,	1Ki 8:10	3068
the glory of the L filled the house	1Ki 8:11	3068
LORD filled the house of the L.	1Ki 8:11	3068
"The L has said that He would	1Ki 8:12	3068
"Blessed be the L, the God of	1Ki 8:15	3068
a house for the name of the L,	1Ki 8:17	3068
"But the L said to my father	1Ki 8:18	3068
"Now the L has fulfilled His word	1Ki 8:20	3068
of Israel, as the L promised,	1Ki 8:20	3068
the house for the name of the L,	1Ki 8:20	3068
in which is the covenant of the L,	1Ki 8:21	3068
stood before the altar of the L in the	1Ki 8:22	3068
"O L, the God of Israel, there is	1Ki 8:23	3068
"Now therefore, O L,	1Ki 8:25	3068
to his supplication, O L my God,	1Ki 8:28	3068
and they pray to the L toward the	1Ki 8:44	3068

forth from Egypt, O **L** God."	1Ki 8:53	136
prayer and supplication to the **L**,	1Ki 8:54	3068
from before the altar of the **L**,	1Ki 8:54	3068
"Blessed be the **L**, who has given	1Ki 8:56	3068
"May the **L** our God be with us, as	1Ki 8:57	3068
made supplication before the **L**,	1Ki 8:59	3068
be near to the **L** our God day and	1Ki 8:59	3068
earth may know that the **L** is God;	1Ki 8:60	3068
wholly devoted to the **L** our God,	1Ki 8:61	3068
offered sacrifice before the **L**.	1Ki 8:62	3068
which he offered to the **L**,	1Ki 8:63	3068
dedicated the house of the **L**.	1Ki 8:63	3068
was before the house of the **L**,	1Ki 8:64	3068
the bronze altar that *was* before the **L**	1Ki 8:64	3068
of Egypt, before the **L** our God,	1Ki 8:65	3068
that the **L** had shown to David His	1Ki 8:66	3068
building the house of the **L**,	1Ki 9:1	3068
that the **L** appeared to Solomon a	1Ki 9:2	3068
The **L** said to him,	1Ki 9:3	3068
'Why has the **L** done thus to this	1Ki 9:8	3068
they forsook the **L** their God,	1Ki 9:9	3068
therefore the **L** has brought all	1Ki 9:9	3068
the house of the **L** and the king's	1Ki 9:10	3068
to build the house of the **L**,	1Ki 9:15	3068
the altar which he built to the **L**,	1Ki 9:25	3068
the altar which *was* before the **L**.	1Ki 9:25	3068
concerning the name of the **L**,	1Ki 10:1	3068
he went up to the house of the **L**,	1Ki 10:5	3068
"Blessed be the **L** your God who	1Ki 10:9	3068
the **L** loved Israel forever,	1Ki 10:9	3068
supports for the house of the **L**	1Ki 10:12	3068
the **L** had said to the sons of Israel,	1Ki 11:2	3068
wholly devoted to the **L** his God,	1Ki 11:4	3068
was evil in the sight of the **L**,	1Ki 11:6	3068
and did not follow the **L** fully,	1Ki 11:6	3068
Now the **L** was angry with Solomon	1Ki 11:9	3068
heart was turned away from the **L**,	1Ki 11:9	3068
observe what the **L** had commanded.	1Ki 11:10	3068
So the **L** said to Solomon,	1Ki 11:11	3068
Then the **L** raised up an adversary	1Ki 11:14	3068
his **l** Hadadezer king of Zobah.	1Ki 11:23	113
for thus says the **L**,	1Ki 11:31	3068
was a turn *of events* from the **L**,	1Ki 12:15	3068
which the **L** spoke through Ahijah	1Ki 12:15	3068
'Thus says the **L**,	1Ki 12:24	3068
listened to the word of the **L**,	1Ki 12:24	3068
according to the word of the **L**.	1Ki 12:24	3068
the house of the **L** at Jerusalem,	1Ki 12:27	3068
people will return to their **l**,	1Ki 12:27	113
to Bethel by the word of the **L**,	1Ki 13:1	3068
the altar by the word of the **L**,	1Ki 13:2	3068
"O altar, altar, thus says the **L**,	1Ki 13:2	3068
the sign which the **L** has spoken,	1Ki 13:3	3068
had given by the word of the **L**.	1Ki 13:5	3068
"Please entreat the **L** your God,	1Ki 13:6	3068
So the man of God entreated the **L**,	1Ki 13:6	3068
commanded me by the word of the **L**,	1Ki 13:9	3068
came to me by the word of the **L**,	1Ki 13:17	3068
spoke to me by the word of the **L**,	1Ki 13:18	3068
that the word of the **L** came to the	1Ki 13:20	3068
'Thus says the **L**,	1Ki 13:21	3068
disobeyed the command of the **L**,	1Ki 13:21	3068
the **L** your God commanded you,	1Ki 13:21	3068
disobeyed the command of the **L**;	1Ki 13:26	3068
the **L** has given him to the lion,	1Ki 13:26	3068
word of the **L** which He spoke to	1Ki 13:26	3068
which he cried by the word of the **L**	1Ki 13:32	3068
Now the **L** had said to Ahijah,	1Ki 14:5	3068
'Thus says the **L** God of Israel,	1Ki 14:7	3068
for the **L** has spoken *it*."	1Ki 14:11	3068
good was found toward the **L** God	1Ki 14:13	3068
the **L** will raise up for Himself a	1Ki 14:14	3068
"For the **L** will strike Israel, as	1Ki 14:15	3068
Asherim, provoking the **L** to anger.	1Ki 14:15	3068
according to the word of the **L**	1Ki 14:18	3068
the city which the **L** had chosen	1Ki 14:21	3068
did evil in the sight of the **L**,	1Ki 14:22	3068
the nations which the **L** dispossessed	1Ki 14:24	3068
the treasures of the house of the **L**	1Ki 14:26	3068
king entered the house of the **L**,	1Ki 14:28	3068
wholly devoted to the **L** his God,	1Ki 15:3	3068
But for David's sake the **L** his God	1Ki 15:4	3068
was right in the sight of the **L**,	1Ki 15:5	3068
was right in the sight of the **L**,	1Ki 15:11	3068
devoted to the **L** all his days.	1Ki 15:14	3068
He brought into the house of the **L**	1Ki 15:15	3068
the treasuries of the house of the **L**	1Ki 15:18	3068
He did evil in the sight of the **L**,	1Ki 15:26	3068
according to the word of the **L**,	1Ki 15:29	3068
the **L** God of Israel to anger.	1Ki 15:30	3068
He did evil in the sight of the **L**,	1Ki 15:34	3068
Now the word of the **L** came to Jehu	1Ki 16:1	3068
the word of the **L** through the	1Ki 16:7	3068
he did in the sight of the **L**,	1Ki 16:7	3068
according to the word of the **L**,	1Ki 16:12	3068
provoking the **L** God of Israel to	1Ki 16:13	3068
doing evil in the sight of the **L**,	1Ki 16:19	3068
did evil in the sight of the **L**,	1Ki 16:25	3068
provoking the **L** God of Israel with	1Ki 16:26	3068
of Omri did evil in the sight of the **L**	1Ki 16:30	3068
Ahab did more to provoke the **L** God	1Ki 16:33	3068
according to the word of the **L**,	1Ki 16:34	3068
"As the **L**, the God of Israel lives,	1Ki 17:1	3068
The word of the **L** came to him,	1Ki 17:2	3068
according to the word of the **L**,	1Ki 17:5	3068
the word of the **L** came to him,	1Ki 17:8	3068
"As the **L** your God lives, I have	1Ki 17:12	3068
"For thus says the **L** God of Israel,	1Ki 17:14	3068
until the day that the **L** sends	1Ki 17:14	3068
word of the **L** which He spoke	1Ki 17:16	3068
He called to the **L** and said,	1Ki 17:20	3068
"O **L** my God, have You also	1Ki 17:20	3068
three times, and called to the **L**	1Ki 17:21	3068
"O **L** my God, I pray You, let	1Ki 17:21	3068
The **L** heard the voice of Elijah,	1Ki 17:22	3068
word of the **L** in your mouth is truth	1Ki 17:24	3068
that the word of the **L** came to	1Ki 18:1	3068
(Now Obadiah feared the **L** greatly;	1Ki 18:3	3068
destroyed the prophets of the **L**,	1Ki 18:4	3068
"As the **L** your God lives, there	1Ki 18:10	3068
that the Spirit of the **L** will carry you	1Ki 18:12	3068
have feared the **L** from my youth.	1Ki 18:12	3068
killed the prophets of the **L**,	1Ki 18:13	3068
I hid a hundred prophets of the **L**	1Ki 18:13	3068
"As the **L** of hosts lives, before	1Ki 18:15	3068
the commandments of the **L** and	1Ki 18:18	3068
If the **L** is God, follow Him;	1Ki 18:21	3068
alone am left a prophet of the **L**,	1Ki 18:22	3068
I will call on the name of the **L**,	1Ki 18:24	3068
he repaired the altar of the **L** which	1Ki 18:30	3068
whom the word of the **L** had come,	1Ki 18:31	3068
an altar in the name of the **L**,	1Ki 18:32	3068
"O **L**, the God of Abraham, Isaac	1Ki 18:36	3068
"Answer me, O **L**, answer me, that	1Ki 18:37	3068
people may know that You, O **L**,	1Ki 18:37	3068
Then the fire of the **L** fell and	1Ki 18:38	3068
"The **L**, He is God;	1Ki 18:39	3068
the **L**, He is God."	1Ki 18:39	3068
the hand of the **L** was on Elijah,	1Ki 18:46	3068
now, O **L**, take my life, for I am	1Ki 19:4	3068
The angel of the **L** came again	1Ki 19:7	3068
the word of the **L** *came* to him,	1Ki 19:9	3068
have been very zealous for the **L**,	1Ki 19:10	3068
on the mountain before the **L**."	1Ki 19:11	3068
And behold, the **L** was passing by!	1Ki 19:11	3068
in pieces the rocks before the **L**;	1Ki 19:11	3068
but the **L** *was* not in the wind.	1Ki 19:11	3068
the **L** *was* not in the earthquake.	1Ki 19:11	3068
but the **L** *was* not in the fire;	1Ki 19:12	3068
have been very zealous for the **L**,	1Ki 19:14	3068
The **L** said to him,	1Ki 19:15	3068
is according to your word, my **l**,	1Ki 20:4	113
"Tell my **l** the king,	1Ki 20:9	113
"Thus says the **L**,	1Ki 20:13	3068
shall know that I am the **L**.' "	1Ki 20:13	3068
"Thus says the **L**,	1Ki 20:14	3068
"Thus says the **L**,	1Ki 20:28	3068
"The **L** is a god of *the* mountains,	1Ki 20:28	3068
shall know that I am the **L**.' "	1Ki 20:28	3068
to another by the word of the **L**,	1Ki 20:35	3068
listened to the voice of the **L**,	1Ki 20:36	3068
"Thus says the **L**,	1Ki 20:42	3068
"The **L** forbid me that I should	1Ki 21:3	3068
the **L** came to Elijah the Tishbite,	1Ki 21:17	3068
'Thus says the **L**,	1Ki 21:19	3068
'Thus says the **L**,	1Ki 21:19	3068
to do evil in the sight of the **L**.	1Ki 21:20	3068
Of Jezebel also has the **L** spoken,	1Ki 21:23	3068
to do evil in the sight of the **L**,	1Ki 21:25	3068
whom the **L** cast out before the	1Ki 21:26	3068
the **L** came to Elijah the Tishbite,	1Ki 21:28	3068
first for the word of the **L**."	1Ki 22:5	3068
for the **L** will give *it* into the	1Ki 22:6	136
not yet a prophet of the **L** here that	1Ki 22:7	3068
by whom we may inquire of the **L**,	1Ki 22:8	3068
'Thus says the **L**,	1Ki 22:11	3068
for the **L** will give *it* into the	1Ki 22:12	3068
"As the **L** lives, what the Lord	1Ki 22:14	3068
Lord lives, what the **L** says to me,	1Ki 22:14	3068
and the **L** will give *it* into the	1Ki 22:15	3068
the truth in the name of the **L**?"	1Ki 22:16	3068
the **L** said, 'These have no master.	1Ki 22:17	3068
"Therefore, hear the word of the **L**.	1Ki 22:19	3068
I saw the **L** sitting on His throne,	1Ki 22:19	3068
"The **L** said,	1Ki 22:20	3068
and stood before the **L** and said,	1Ki 22:21	3068
'The **L** said to him,	1Ki 22:22	3068
the **L** has put a deceiving spirit	1Ki 22:23	3068
and the **L** has proclaimed disaster	1Ki 22:23	3068
L pass from me to speak to you?"	1Ki 22:24	3068
the **L** has not spoken by me."	1Ki 22:28	3068
the word of the **L** which He spoke.	1Ki 22:38	3068
doing right in the sight of the **L**.	1Ki 22:43	3068
He did evil in the sight of the **L**	1Ki 22:52	3068
and provoked the **L** God of Israel to	1Ki 22:53	3068
the **L** said to Elijah the Tishbite,	2Ki 1:3	3068
"Now therefore thus says the **L**,	2Ki 1:4	3068
'Thus says the **L**,	2Ki 1:6	3068
The angel of the **L** said to Elijah,	2Ki 1:15	3068
"Thus says the **L**,	2Ki 1:16	3068
the word of the **L** which Elijah had	2Ki 1:17	3068
the **L** was about to take up Elijah	2Ki 2:1	3068
L has sent me as far as Bethel."	2Ki 2:2	3068
"As the **L** lives and as you	2Ki 2:2	3068
"Do you know that the **L** will take	2Ki 2:3	3068
the **L** has sent me to Jericho."	2Ki 2:4	3068
"As the **L** lives, and as you	2Ki 2:4	3068
"Do you know that the **L** will take	2Ki 2:5	3068
the **L** has sent me to the Jordan."	2Ki 2:6	3068
"As the **L** lives, and as you	2Ki 2:6	3068
"Where is the **L**, the God of	2Ki 2:14	3068
perhaps the Spirit of the **L** has	2Ki 2:16	3068
city is pleasant, as my **l** sees;	2Ki 2:19	113
'Thus says the **L**,	2Ki 2:21	3068
cursed them in the name of the **L**.	2Ki 2:24	3068
He did evil in the sight of the **L**,	2Ki 3:2	3068
For the **L** has called these three	2Ki 3:10	3068
there not a prophet of the **L** here,	2Ki 3:11	3068
we may inquire of the **L** by him?"	2Ki 3:11	3068
"The word of the **L** is with him."	2Ki 3:12	3068
for the **L** has called these three	2Ki 3:13	3068
"As the **L** of hosts lives, before	2Ki 3:14	3068
the hand of the **L** came upon him.	2Ki 3:15	3068
"Thus says the **L**,	2Ki 3:16	3068
"For thus says the **L**,	2Ki 3:17	3068
thing in the sight of the **L**;	2Ki 3:18	3068
that your servant feared the **L**;	2Ki 4:1	3068
"No, my **l**, O man of God, do not	2Ki 4:16	113
and the **L** has hidden it from me	2Ki 4:27	3068
"Did I ask for a son from my **l**?	2Ki 4:28	113
"As the **L** lives and as you	2Ki 4:30	3068
them both and prayed to the **L**.	2Ki 4:33	3068
they may eat, for thus says the **L**,	2Ki 4:43	3068
according to the word of the **L**.	2Ki 4:44	3068
the **L** had given victory to Aram.	2Ki 5:1	3068
call on the name of the **L** his God,	2Ki 5:11	3068
"As the **L** lives, before whom I	2Ki 5:16	3068
to other gods, but to the **L**.	2Ki 5:17	3068
may the **L** pardon your servant:	2Ki 5:18	3068
the **L** pardon your servant in this	2Ki 5:18	3068
As the **L** lives, I will run after	2Ki 5:20	3068
"No, my **l**, O king;	2Ki 6:12	113
"O **L**, I pray, open his eyes that	2Ki 6:17	3068
the **L** opened the servant's eyes and	2Ki 6:17	3068
Elisha prayed to the **L** and said,	2Ki 6:18	3068
"O **L**, open the eyes of these *men*,	2Ki 6:20	3068
So the **L** opened their eyes and	2Ki 6:20	3068
"Help, my **l**, O king!"	2Ki 6:26	113
"If the **L** does not help you, from	2Ki 6:27	3068
"Behold, this evil is from the **L**;	2Ki 6:33	3068
I wait for the **L** any longer?"	2Ki 6:33	3068
"Listen to the word of the **L**;	2Ki 7:1	3068
thus says the **L**,	2Ki 7:1	3068
L should make windows in heaven,	2Ki 7:2	3068
For the **L** had caused the army of	2Ki 7:6	136
according to the word of the **L**.	2Ki 7:16	3068
L should make windows in heaven,	2Ki 7:19	3068
for the **L** has called for a famine,	2Ki 8:1	3068
"My **l**, O king, this is the woman	2Ki 8:5	113
God, and inquire of the **L** by him,	2Ki 8:8	3068
but the **L** has shown me that he	2Ki 8:10	3068
"Why does my **l** weep?"	2Ki 8:12	113
"The **L** has shown me that you will	2Ki 8:13	3068
he did evil in the sight of the **L**.	2Ki 8:18	3068
the **L** was not willing to destroy	2Ki 8:19	3068
did evil in the sight of the **L**,	2Ki 8:27	3068
'Thus says the **L**,	2Ki 9:3	3068
'Thus says the **L**, the God of	2Ki 9:6	3068
you king over the people of the **L**,	2Ki 9:6	3068
blood of all the servants of the **L**,	2Ki 9:7	3068
'Thus says the **L**,	2Ki 9:12	3068
L laid this oracle against him:	2Ki 9:25	3068
the blood of his sons,' says the **L**,	2Ki 9:26	3068
you in this property,' says the **L**.	2Ki 9:26	3068
according to the word of the **L**."	2Ki 9:26	3068
"This is the word of the **L**,	2Ki 9:36	3068
nothing of the word of the **L**,	2Ki 10:10	3068
which the **L** spoke concerning the	2Ki 10:10	3068
for the **L** has done what He spoke	2Ki 10:10	3068
me and see my zeal for the **L**."	2Ki 10:16	3068
according to the word of the **L**	2Ki 10:17	3068
you none of the servants of the **L**,	2Ki 10:23	3068
The **L** said to Jehu,	2Ki 10:30	3068
to walk in the law of the **L**,	2Ki 10:31	3068
In those days the **L** began to cut	2Ki 10:32	3068
in the house of the **L** six years,	2Ki 11:3	3068
them to him in the house of the **L**,	2Ki 11:4	3068
under oath in the house of the **L**,	2Ki 11:4	3068
keep watch over the house of the **L**	2Ki 11:7	3068
which *were* in the house of the **L**.	2Ki 11:10	3068
the people in the house of the **L**.	2Ki 11:13	3068
to death in the house of the **L**."	2Ki 11:15	3068
the **L** and the king and the people,	2Ki 11:17	3068
officers over the house of the **L**.	2Ki 11:18	3068
king down from the house of the **L**,	2Ki 11:19	3068
Jehoash did right in the sight of the **L**	2Ki 12:2	3068
brought into the house of the **L**,	2Ki 12:4	3068
to bring into the house of the **L**,	2Ki 12:4	3068
one comes into the house of the **L**;	2Ki 12:9	3068
brought into the house of the **L**.	2Ki 12:9	3068
was found in the house of the **L**.	2Ki 12:10	3068
oversight of the house of the **L**;	2Ki 12:11	3068
who worked on the house of the **L**;	2Ki 12:11	3068
the damages to the house of the **L**,	2Ki 12:12	3068
not made for the house of the **L**	2Ki 12:13	3068
brought into the house of the **L**;	2Ki 12:13	3068
they repaired the house of the **L**.	2Ki 12:14	3068
brought into the house of the **L**;	2Ki 12:16	3068
the treasuries of the house of the **L**	2Ki 12:18	3068
He did evil in the sight of the **L**,	2Ki 13:2	3068
anger of the **L** was kindled against	2Ki 13:3	3068
entreated the favor of the **L**,	2Ki 13:4	3068
Lord, and the **L** listened to him;	2Ki 13:4	3068
The **L** gave Israel a deliverer,	2Ki 13:5	3068
He did evil in the sight of the **L**;	2Ki 13:11	3068
But the **L** was gracious to them and	2Ki 13:23	3068
did right in the sight of the **L**,	2Ki 14:3	3068
Law of Moses, as the **L** commanded,	2Ki 14:6	3068
were found in the house of the **L**,	2Ki 14:14	3068
He did evil in the sight of the **L**;	2Ki 14:24	3068
according to the word of the **L**,	2Ki 14:25	3068
L saw the affliction of Israel,	2Ki 14:26	3068
The **L** did not say that He	2Ki 14:27	3068
did right in the sight of the **L**,	2Ki 15:3	3068
The **L** struck the king, so that	2Ki 15:5	3068
He did evil in the sight of the **L**,	2Ki 15:9	3068
word of the **L** which He spoke to	2Ki 15:12	3068

He did evil in the sight of the **L**;	**2Ki 15:18**	3068
He did evil in the sight of the **L**;	**2Ki 15:24**	3068
He did evil in the sight of the **L**;	**2Ki 15:28**	3068
was right in the sight of the **L**;	**2Ki 15:34**	3068
upper gate of the house of the **L**.	**2Ki 15:35**	3068
In those days the **L** began to send	**2Ki 15:37**	3068
in the sight of the **L** his God,	**2Ki 16:2**	3068
nations whom the **L** had driven out	**2Ki 16:3**	3068
that was found in the house of the **L**	**2Ki 16:8**	3068
altar, which *was* before the **L**,	**2Ki 16:14**	3068
his altar and the house of the **L**,	**2Ki 16:14**	3068
he removed from the house of the **L**	**2Ki 16:18**	3068
He did evil in the sight of the **L**,	**2Ki 17:2**	3068
sinned against the **L** their God,	**2Ki 17:7**	3068
nations whom the **L** had driven out	**2Ki 17:8**	3068
right against the **L** their God.	**2Ki 17:9**	3068
the **L** had carried away to exile	**2Ki 17:11**	3068
did evil things provoking the **L**.	**2Ki 17:11**	3068
which the **L** had said to them,	**2Ki 17:12**	3068
Yet the **L** warned Israel and Judah	**2Ki 17:13**	3068
not believe in the **L** their God.	**2Ki 17:14**	3068
concerning which the **L** had	**2Ki 17:15**	3068
all the commandments of the **L**	**2Ki 17:16**	3068
to do evil in the sight of the **L**,	**2Ki 17:17**	3068
the **L** was very angry with Israel and	**2Ki 17:18**	3068
commandments of the **L** their God,	**2Ki 17:19**	3068
The **L** rejected all the	**2Ki 17:20**	3068
Israel away from following the **L**	**2Ki 17:21**	3068
L removed Israel from His sight,	**2Ki 17:23**	3068
they did not fear the **L**;	**2Ki 17:25**	3068
therefore the **L** sent lions among	**2Ki 17:25**	3068
them how they should fear the **L**.	**2Ki 17:28**	3068
They also feared the **L** and	**2Ki 17:32**	3068
They feared the **L** and served their	**2Ki 17:33**	3068
they do not fear the **L**,	**2Ki 17:34**	3068
the **L** commanded the sons of Jacob,	**2Ki 17:34**	3068
with whom the **L** made a covenant	**2Ki 17:35**	3068
"But the **L**, who brought you up	**2Ki 17:36**	3068
"But the **L** your God you shall fear;	**2Ki 17:39**	3068
while these nations feared the **L**,	**2Ki 17:41**	3068
did right in the sight of the **L**,	**2Ki 18:3**	3068
He trusted in the **L**,	**2Ki 18:5**	3068
For he clung to the **L**;	**2Ki 18:6**	3068
which the **L** had commanded Moses.	**2Ki 18:6**	3068
And the **L** was with him;	**2Ki 18:7**	3068
obey the voice of the **L** their God,	**2Ki 18:12**	3068
the servant of the **L** commanded;	**2Ki 18:12**	3068
was found in the house of the **L**,	**2Ki 18:15**	3068
the doors of the temple of the **L**,	**2Ki 18:16**	3068
'We trust in the **L** our God,' is it	**2Ki 18:22**	3068
The **L** said to me,	**2Ki 18:25**	3068
Hezekiah make you trust in the **L**,	**2Ki 18:30**	3068
"The **L** will surely deliver us,	**2Ki 18:30**	3068
"The **L** will deliver us."	**2Ki 18:32**	3068
that the **L** should deliver	**2Ki 18:35**	3068
and entered the house of the **L**.	**2Ki 19:1**	3068
'Perhaps the **L** your God will hear	**2Ki 19:4**	3068
which the **L** your God has heard.	**2Ki 19:4**	3068
'Thus says the **L**,	**2Ki 19:6**	3068
he went up to the house of the **L**	**2Ki 19:14**	3068
and spread it out before the **L**.	**2Ki 19:14**	3068
prayed before the **L** and said,	**2Ki 19:15**	3068
"O **L**, the God of Israel, who are	**2Ki 19:15**	3068
"Incline Your ear, O **L**,	**2Ki 19:16**	3068
open Your eyes, O **L**,	**2Ki 19:16**	3068
"Truly, O **L**, the kings of Assyria	**2Ki 19:17**	3068
"Now, O **L** our God, I pray,	**2Ki 19:19**	3068
know that You alone, O **L**, are God	**2Ki 19:19**	3068
"Thus says the **L**, the God of	**2Ki 19:20**	3068
that the **L** has spoken against him:	**2Ki 19:21**	3068
you have reproached the **L**,	**2Ki 19:23**	136
zeal of the **L** will perform this.	**2Ki 19:31**	3068
'Therefore thus says the **L**	**2Ki 19:32**	3068
come to this city," ' declares the **L**.	**2Ki 19:33**	3068
that the angel of the **L** went out and	**2Ki 19:35**	3068
"Thus says the **L**,	**2Ki 20:1**	3068
to the wall and prayed to the **L**,	**2Ki 20:2**	3068
"Remember now, O **L**, I beseech	**2Ki 20:3**	3068
the word of the **L** came to him,	**2Ki 20:4**	3068
'Thus says the **L**, the God of your	**2Ki 20:5**	3068
shall go up to the house of the **L**.	**2Ki 20:5**	3068
the sign that the **L** will heal me,	**2Ki 20:8**	3068
house of the **L** the third day?"	**2Ki 20:8**	3068
be the sign to you from the **L**,	**2Ki 20:9**	3068
that the **L** will do the thing that	**2Ki 20:9**	3068
Isaiah the prophet cried to the **L**,	**2Ki 20:11**	3068
"Hear the word of the **L**.	**2Ki 20:16**	3068
nothing shall be left,' says the **L**.	**2Ki 20:17**	3068
"The word of the **L** which you have	**2Ki 20:19**	3068
He did evil in the sight of the **L**,	**2Ki 21:2**	3068
the nations whom the **L** dispossessed	**2Ki 21:2**	3068
altars in the house of the **L**,	**2Ki 21:4**	3068
the LORD, of which the **L** had said,	**2Ki 21:4**	3068
two courts of the house of the **L**.	**2Ki 21:5**	3068
did much evil in the sight of the **L**	**2Ki 21:6**	3068
in the house of which the **L** said	**2Ki 21:7**	3068
the nations whom the **L** destroyed	**2Ki 21:9**	3068
Now the **L** spoke through His	**2Ki 21:10**	3068
therefore thus says the **L**,	**2Ki 21:12**	3068
doing evil in the sight of the **L**.	**2Ki 21:16**	3068
He did evil in the sight of the **L**,	**2Ki 21:20**	3068
So he forsook the **L**,	**2Ki 21:22**	3068
did not walk in the way of the **L**.	**2Ki 21:22**	3068
He did right in the sight of the **L**	**2Ki 22:2**	3068
to the house of the **L** saying,	**2Ki 22:3**	3068
brought in to the house of the **L**	**2Ki 22:4**	3068
oversight of the house of the **L**,	**2Ki 22:5**	3068
are in the house of the **L** to repair	**2Ki 22:5**	3068
the law in the house of the **L**."	**2Ki 22:8**	3068

oversight of the house of the **L**."	**2Ki 22:9**	3068
inquire of the **L** for me and the	**2Ki 22:13**	3068
for great is the wrath of the **L**	**2Ki 22:13**	3068
"Thus says the **L** God of Israel,	**2Ki 22:15**	3068
thus says the **L**,	**2Ki 22:16**	3068
who sent you to inquire of the **L**	**2Ki 22:18**	3068
'Thus says the **L** God of Israel,	**2Ki 22:18**	3068
you humbled yourself before the **L**	**2Ki 22:19**	3068
have heard you," declares the **L**.	**2Ki 22:19**	3068
king went up to the house of the **L**	**2Ki 23:2**	3068
was found in the house of the **L**.	**2Ki 23:2**	3068
and made a covenant before the **L**,	**2Ki 23:3**	3068
the LORD, to walk after the **L**,	**2Ki 23:3**	3068
to bring out of the temple of the **L**	**2Ki 23:4**	3068
the Asherah from the house of the **L**	**2Ki 23:6**	3068
which *were* in the house of the **L**,	**2Ki 23:7**	3068
the altar of the **L** in Jerusalem,	**2Ki 23:9**	3068
entrance of the house of the **L**,	**2Ki 23:11**	3068
two courts of the house of the **L**,	**2Ki 23:12**	3068
word of the **L** which the man of God	**2Ki 23:16**	3068
Israel had made provoking the **L**;	**2Ki 23:19**	3068
"Celebrate the Passover to the **L**	**2Ki 23:21**	3068
observed to the **L** in Jerusalem.	**2Ki 23:23**	3068
found in the house of the **L**.	**2Ki 23:24**	3068
no king like him who turned to the **L**	**2Ki 23:25**	3068
the **L** did not turn from the	**2Ki 23:26**	3068
The **L** said, "I will remove Judah	**2Ki 23:27**	3068
He did evil in the sight of the **L**,	**2Ki 23:32**	3068
He did evil in the sight of the **L**,	**2Ki 23:37**	3068
The **L** sent against him bands	**2Ki 24:2**	3068
according to the word of the **L**	**2Ki 24:2**	3068
at the command of the **L** it came	**2Ki 24:3**	3068
and the **L** would not forgive.	**2Ki 24:4**	3068
He did evil in the sight of the **L**,	**2Ki 24:9**	3068
treasures of the house of the **L**,	**2Ki 24:13**	3068
had made in the temple of the **L**,	**2Ki 24:13**	3068
the LORD, just as the **L** had said.	**2Ki 24:13**	3068
He did evil in the sight of the **L**,	**2Ki 24:19**	3068
For through the anger of the **L**	**2Ki 24:20**	3068
He burned the house of the **L**,	**2Ki 25:9**	3068
which were in the house of the **L**,	**2Ki 25:13**	3068
which were in the house of the **L**,	**2Ki 25:13**	3068
had made for the house of the **L**	**2Ki 25:16**	3068
was wicked in the sight of the **L**,	**1Ch 2:3**	3068
Jehozadak went *along* when the **L**	**1Ch 6:15**	3068
of song in the house of the **L**	**1Ch 6:31**	3068
the house of the **L** in Jerusalem;	**1Ch 6:32**	3068
had been over the camp of the **L**,	**1Ch 9:19**	3068
and the **L** was with him.	**1Ch 9:20**	3068
the gates of the house of the **L**,	**1Ch 9:23**	3068
which he committed against the **L**,	**1Ch 10:13**	3068
the word of the **L** which he did not	**1Ch 10:13**	3068
and did not inquire of the **L**.	**1Ch 10:14**	3068
and the **L** your God said to you,	**1Ch 11:2**	3068
with them in Hebron before the **L**;	**1Ch 11:3**	3068
the word of the **L** through Samuel.	**1Ch 11:3**	3068
for the **L** of hosts *was* with him.	**1Ch 11:9**	3068
word of the **L** concerning Israel.	**1Ch 11:10**	3068
L saved them by a great victory.	**1Ch 11:14**	3068
it, but poured it out to the **L**;	**1Ch 11:18**	3068
according to the word of the **L**.	**1Ch 12:23**	3068
and if it is from the **L** our God,	**1Ch 13:2**	3068
the **L** who is enthroned *above* the	**1Ch 13:6**	3068
anger of the **L** burned against Uzza	**1Ch 13:10**	3068
and the **L** blessed the family of	**1Ch 13:14**	3068
And David realized that the **L** had	**1Ch 14:2**	3068
Then the **L** said to him,	**1Ch 14:10**	3068
and the **L** brought the fear of him	**1Ch 14:17**	3068
for the **L** chose them to carry the	**1Ch 15:2**	3068
up the ark of the **L** to its place which	**1Ch 15:3**	3068
up the ark of the **L** God of Israel to	**1Ch 15:12**	3068
the **L** our God made an outburst on	**1Ch 15:13**	3068
up the ark of the **L** God of Israel.	**1Ch 15:14**	3068
according to the word of the **L**.	**1Ch 15:15**	3068
the ark of the covenant of the **L**	**1Ch 15:25**	3068
the ark of the covenant of the **L**,	**1Ch 15:26**	3068
covenant of the **L** with shouting,	**1Ch 15:28**	3068
the ark of the covenant of the **L**	**1Ch 15:29**	3068
the people in the name of the **L**.	**1Ch 16:2**	3068
ministers before the ark of the **L**,	**1Ch 16:4**	3068
and praise the **L** God of Israel:	**1Ch 16:4**	3068
relatives to give thanks to the **L**.	**1Ch 16:7**	3068
Oh give thanks to the **L**,	**1Ch 16:8**	3068
of those who seek the **L** be glad.	**1Ch 16:10**	3068
Seek the **L** and His strength;	**1Ch 16:11**	3068
He is the **L** our God;	**1Ch 16:14**	3068
Sing to the **L**, all the earth;	**1Ch 16:23**	3068
For great is the **L**,	**1Ch 16:25**	3068
idols, But the **L** made the heavens.	**1Ch 16:26**	3068
Ascribe to the **L**, O families of	**1Ch 16:28**	3068
Ascribe to the **L** glory and strength.	**1Ch 16:28**	3068
to the **L** the glory due His name;	**1Ch 16:29**	3068
Worship the **L** in holy array.	**1Ch 16:29**	3068
among the nations, "The **L** reigns."	**1Ch 16:31**	3068
will sing for joy before the **L**;	**1Ch 16:33**	3068
O give thanks to the **L**,	**1Ch 16:34**	3068
Blessed be the **L**, the God of	**1Ch 16:36**	3068
"Amen," and praised the **L**.	**1Ch 16:36**	3068
the ark of the covenant of the **L**	**1Ch 16:37**	3068
priests before the tabernacle of the **L**	**1Ch 16:39**	3068
to offer burnt offerings to the **L**	**1Ch 16:40**	3068
is written in the law of the **L**,	**1Ch 16:40**	3068
by name, to give thanks to the **L**,	**1Ch 16:41**	3068
the ark of the covenant of the **L** is	**1Ch 17:1**	3068
'Thus says the **L**,	**1Ch 17:4**	3068
'Thus says the **L** of hosts,	**1Ch 17:7**	3068
the **L** will build a house for you.	**1Ch 17:10**	3068
in and sat before the **L** and said,	**1Ch 17:16**	3068
"Who am I, O **L** God, and what is	**1Ch 17:16**	3068

of a man of high degree, O **L** God.	**1Ch 17:17**	3068
"O **L**, for Your servant's sake, and	**1Ch 17:19**	3068
"O **L**, there is none like You,	**1Ch 17:20**	3068
You, O **L**, became their God.	**1Ch 17:22**	3068
"Now, O **L**, let the word that	**1Ch 17:23**	3068
L of hosts is the God of Israel,	**1Ch 17:24**	3068
"Now, O **L**, You are God, and	**1Ch 17:26**	3068
for You, O **L**, have blessed, and	**1Ch 17:27**	3068
L helped David wherever he went.	**1Ch 18:6**	3068
David also dedicated these to the **L**	**1Ch 18:11**	3068
L helped David wherever he went.	**1Ch 18:13**	3068
L do what is good in His sight."	**1Ch 19:13**	3068
"May the **L** add to His people a	**1Ch 21:3**	3068
But, my **l** the king, are they not	**1Ch 21:3**	113
Why does my **l** seek this thing?	**1Ch 21:3**	113
The **L** spoke to Gad, David's	**1Ch 21:9**	3068
'Thus says the **L**,	**1Ch 21:10**	3068
'Thus says the **L**,	**1Ch 21:11**	3068
three days of the sword of the **L**,	**1Ch 21:12**	3068
and the angel of the **L** destroying	**1Ch 21:12**	3068
me fall into the hand of the **L**,	**1Ch 21:13**	3068
the **L** sent a pestilence on Israel;	**1Ch 21:14**	3068
the **L** saw and was sorry over the	**1Ch 21:15**	3068
And the angel of the **L** was	**1Ch 21:15**	3068
and saw the angel of the **L** standing	**1Ch 21:16**	3068
O **L** my God, please let Your hand be	**1Ch 21:17**	3068
L commanded Gad to say to David,	**1Ch 21:18**	3068
go up and build an altar to the **L** on	**1Ch 21:18**	3068
he spoke in the name of the **L**.	**1Ch 21:19**	3068
may build on it an altar to the **L**;	**1Ch 21:22**	3068
and let my **l** the king do what is	**1Ch 21:23**	113
not take what is yours for the **L**,	**1Ch 21:24**	3068
built an altar to the **L** there and	**1Ch 21:26**	3068
And he called to the **L** and He	**1Ch 21:26**	3068
The **L** commanded the angel, and	**1Ch 21:27**	3068
when David saw that the **L** had	**1Ch 21:28**	3068
For the tabernacle of the **L**,	**1Ch 21:29**	3068
the sword of the angel of the **L**.	**1Ch 21:30**	3068
"This is the house of the **L** God,	**1Ch 22:1**	3068
the house that is to be built for the **L**	**1Ch 22:5**	3068
a house for the **L** God of Israel.	**1Ch 22:6**	3068
house to the name of the **L** my God.	**1Ch 22:7**	3068
"But the word of the **L** came to me,	**1Ch 22:8**	3068
the **L** be with you that you may be	**1Ch 22:11**	3068
and build the house of the **L** your	**1Ch 22:11**	3068
"Only the **L** give you discretion	**1Ch 22:12**	3068
keep the law of the **L** your God.	**1Ch 22:12**	3068
which the **L** commanded Moses	**1Ch 22:13**	3068
have prepared for the house of the **L**	**1Ch 22:14**	3068
work, and may the **L** be with you."	**1Ch 22:16**	3068
"Is not the **L** your God with you?	**1Ch 22:18**	3068
the **L** and before His people.	**1Ch 22:18**	3068
your soul to seek the **L** your God;	**1Ch 22:19**	3068
build the sanctuary of the **L** God,	**1Ch 22:19**	3068
the ark of the covenant of the **L**	**1Ch 22:19**	3068
be built for the name of the **L**."	**1Ch 22:19**	3068
the work of the house of the **L**;	**1Ch 23:4**	3068
and 4,000 *were* praising the **L** with	**1Ch 23:5**	3068
to burn incense before the **L**,	**1Ch 23:13**	3068
the service of the house of the **L**,	**1Ch 23:24**	3068
"The **L** God of Israel has given	**1Ch 23:25**	3068
the service of the house of the **L**,	**1Ch 23:28**	3068
to thank and to praise the **L**,	**1Ch 23:30**	3068
all burnt offerings to the **L**,	**1Ch 23:31**	3068
them, continually before the **L**.	**1Ch 23:31**	3068
the service of the house of the **L**.	**1Ch 23:32**	3068
they came in to the house of the **L**	**1Ch 24:19**	3068
just as the **L** God of Israel had	**1Ch 24:19**	3068
giving thanks and praising the **L**.	**1Ch 25:3**	3068
to sing in the house of the **L**,	**1Ch 25:6**	3068
were trained in singing to the **L**,	**1Ch 25:7**	3068
to minister in the house of the **L**.	**1Ch 26:12**	3068
treasures of the house of the **L**.	**1Ch 26:22**	3068
to repair the house of the **L**.	**1Ch 26:27**	3068
for all the work of the **L** and the	**1Ch 26:30**	3068
because the **L** had said He would	**1Ch 27:23**	3068
for the ark of the covenant of the **L**	**1Ch 28:2**	3068
"Yet, the **L**, the God of Israel,	**1Ch 28:4**	3068
(for the **L** has given me many sons),	**1Ch 28:5**	3068
the kingdom of the **L** over Israel.	**1Ch 28:5**	3068
all Israel, the assembly of the **L**,	**1Ch 28:8**	3068
after all the commandments of the **L**	**1Ch 28:8**	3068
for the **L** searches all hearts, and	**1Ch 28:9**	3068
for the **L** has chosen you to build	**1Ch 28:10**	3068
the courts of the house of the **L**,	**1Ch 28:12**	3068
of the service of the house of the **L**	**1Ch 28:13**	3068
of service in the house of the **L**;	**1Ch 28:13**	3068
the ark of the covenant of the **L**.	**1Ch 28:18**	3068
"the **L** made me understand in	**1Ch 28:19**	3068
for the **L** God, my God, is with you	**1Ch 28:20**	3068
of the house of the **L** is finished.	**1Ch 28:20**	3068
is not for man, but for the **L** God.	**1Ch 29:1**	3068
himself this day to the **L**?"	**1Ch 29:5**	3068
treasury of the house of the **L**,	**1Ch 29:8**	3068
they made their offering to the **L**	**1Ch 29:9**	3068
So David blessed the **L** in the	**1Ch 29:10**	3068
O **L** God of Israel our father,	**1Ch 29:10**	3068
"Yours, O **L**, is the greatness and	**1Ch 29:11**	3068
Yours is the dominion, O **L**,	**1Ch 29:11**	3068
"O **L** our God, all this abundance	**1Ch 29:16**	3068
"O **L**, the God of Abraham, Isaac and	**1Ch 29:18**	3068
"Now bless the **L** your God."	**1Ch 29:20**	3068
all the assembly blessed the **L**,	**1Ch 29:20**	3068
homage to the **L** and to the king.	**1Ch 29:20**	3068
made sacrifices to the **L** and offered	**1Ch 29:21**	3068
offered burnt offerings to the **L**,	**1Ch 29:21**	3068
before the **L** with great gladness.	**1Ch 29:22**	3068
for the **L** and Zadok as priest.	**1Ch 29:22**	3068
Solomon sat on the throne of the **L**	**1Ch 29:23**	3068

The **L** highly exalted Solomon	1Ch 29:25	3068
and the **L** his God *was* with him and	2Ch 1:1	3068
the **L** had made in the wilderness.	2Ch 1:3	3068
before the tabernacle of the **L**.	2Ch 1:5	3068
Solomon went up there before the **L**	2Ch 1:6	3068
"Now, O **L** God, Your promise to my	2Ch 1:9	3068
a house for the name of the **L**	2Ch 2:1	3068
for the name of the **L** my God,	2Ch 2:4	3068
appointed feasts of the **L** our God,	2Ch 2:4	3068
"Because the **L** loves His people,	2Ch 2:11	3068
"Blessed be the **L**, the God of	2Ch 2:12	3068
who will build a house for the **L**	2Ch 2:12	3068
those of my **l** David your father.	2Ch 2:14	113
let my **l** send to his servants	2Ch 2:15	113
L in Jerusalem on Mount Moriah,	2Ch 3:1	3068
where *the* **L** had appeared to his	2Ch 3:1	
Solomon for the house of the **L**.	2Ch 4:16	3068
the house of the **L** was finished.	2Ch 5:1	3068
the ark of the covenant of the **L**	2Ch 5:2	3068
the ark of the covenant of the **L**	2Ch 5:7	3068
where the **L** made a covenant with	2Ch 5:10	3068
to praise and to glorify the **L**,	2Ch 5:13	3068
when they praised the **L** *saying,*	2Ch 5:13	3068
the house, the house of the **L**,	2Ch 5:13	3068
the glory of the **L** filled the house	2Ch 5:14	3068
"The **L** has said that He would	2Ch 6:1	3068
"Blessed be the **L**, the God of	2Ch 6:4	3068
a house for the name of the **L**,	2Ch 6:7	3068
"But the **L** said to my father	2Ch 6:8	3068
"Now the **L** has fulfilled His word	2Ch 6:10	3068
of Israel, as the **L** promised,	2Ch 6:10	3068
the house for the name of the **L**,	2Ch 6:10	3068
in which is the covenant of the **L**,	2Ch 6:11	3068
he stood before the altar of the **L**	2Ch 6:12	3068
"O **L**, the God of Israel, there is	2Ch 6:14	3068
"Now therefore, O **L**,	2Ch 6:16	3068
"Now therefore, O **L**,	2Ch 6:17	3068
to his supplication, O **L** my God,	2Ch 6:19	3068
"Now therefore arise, O **L** God,	2Ch 6:41	3068
let Your priests, O **L** God,	2Ch 6:41	3068
"O **L** God, do not turn away the	2Ch 6:42	3068
glory of the **L** filled the house.	2Ch 7:1	3068
not enter into the house of the **L** because	2Ch 7:2	3068
the glory of the **L** filled the LORD's	2Ch 7:2	3068
the glory of the **L** upon the house,	2Ch 7:3	3068
and gave praise to the **L**,	2Ch 7:3	3068
offered sacrifice before the **L**.	2Ch 7:4	3068
the instruments of music to the **L**,	2Ch 7:6	3068
had made for giving praise to the **L**	2Ch 7:6	3068
was before the house of the **L**,	2Ch 7:7	3068
because of the goodness that the **L**	2Ch 7:10	3068
Solomon finished the house of the **L**	2Ch 7:11	3068
house of the **L** and in his palace.	2Ch 7:11	3068
Then the **L** appeared to Solomon at	2Ch 7:12	3068
'Why has the **L** done thus to this	2Ch 7:21	3068
'Because they forsook the **L**,	2Ch 7:22	3068
house of the **L** and his own house	2Ch 8:1	3068
the ark of the **L** has entered."	2Ch 8:11	3068
offered burnt offerings to the **L** on	2Ch 8:12	3068
altar of the **L** which he had built	2Ch 8:12	3068
foundation of the house of the **L**,	2Ch 8:16	3068
the house of the **L** was completed.	2Ch 8:16	3068
he went up to the house of the **L**,	2Ch 9:4	3068
L your God who delighted in you,	2Ch 9:8	3068
throne as king for the **L** your God;	2Ch 9:8	3068
made steps for the house of the **L**	2Ch 9:11	3068
the **L** might establish His word,	2Ch 10:15	3068
But the word of the **L** came to	2Ch 11:2	3068
'Thus says the **L**,	2Ch 11:4	3068
they listened to the words of the **L**	2Ch 11:4	3068
from serving as priests to the **L**.	2Ch 11:14	3068
on seeking the **L** God of Israel followed	2Ch 11:16	3068
to the **L** God of their fathers.	2Ch 11:16	3068
with him forsook the law of the **L**.	2Ch 12:1	3068
they had been unfaithful to the **L**,	2Ch 12:2	3068
"Thus says the **L**,	2Ch 12:5	3068
"The **L** is righteous."	2Ch 12:6	3068
When the **L** saw that they	2Ch 12:7	3068
word of the **L** came to Shemaiah,	2Ch 12:7	3068
the treasures of the house of the **L**	2Ch 12:9	3068
king entered the house of the **L**,	2Ch 12:11	3068
the anger of the **L** turned away from	2Ch 12:12	3068
the city which the **L** had chosen	2Ch 12:13	3068
not set his heart to seek the **L**.	2Ch 12:14	3068
the **L** God of Israel gave the rule	2Ch 13:5	3068
to resist the kingdom of the **L**	2Ch 13:8	3068
driven out the priests of the **L**,	2Ch 13:9	3068
"But as for us, the **L** is our God,	2Ch 13:10	3068
ministering to the **L** as priests,	2Ch 13:10	3068
to the **L** burnt offerings and fragrant	2Ch 13:11	3068
keep the charge of the **L** our God,	2Ch 13:11	3068
against the **L** God of your fathers,	2Ch 13:12	3068
so they cried to the **L**,	2Ch 13:14	3068
because they trusted in the **L**,	2Ch 13:18	3068
and the **L** struck him and he died.	2Ch 13:20	3068
in the sight of the **L** his God,	2Ch 14:2	3068
and commanded Judah to seek the **L**	2Ch 14:4	3068
because the **L** had given him rest.	2Ch 14:6	3068
we have sought the **L** our God;	2Ch 14:7	3068
Then Asa called to the **L** his God and	2Ch 14:11	3068
"**L**, there is no one besides You	2Ch 14:11	3068
so help us, O **L** our God, for we	2Ch 14:11	3068
O **L**, You are our God;	2Ch 14:11	3068
So the **L** routed the Ethiopians	2Ch 14:12	3068
they were shattered before the **L**	2Ch 14:13	3068
dread of the **L** had fallen on them;	2Ch 14:14	3068
the **L** is with you when you are	2Ch 15:2	3068
turned to the **L** God of Israel,	2Ch 15:4	3068
He then restored the altar of the **L**	2Ch 15:8	3068
in front of the porch of the **L**.	2Ch 15:8	3068
that the **L** his God was with him.	2Ch 15:9	3068
They sacrificed to the **L** that	2Ch 15:11	3068
to seek the **L** God of their fathers	2Ch 15:12	3068
and whoever would not seek the **L**	2Ch 15:13	3068
oath to the **L** with a loud voice,	2Ch 15:14	3068
L gave them rest on every side.	2Ch 15:15	3068
the treasures of the house of the **L**	2Ch 16:2	3068
have not relied on the **L** your God,	2Ch 16:7	3068
Yet because you relied on the **L**,	2Ch 16:8	3068
"For the eyes of the **L** move to	2Ch 16:9	3068
his disease he did not seek the **L**,	2Ch 16:12	3068
The **L** was with Jehoshaphat	2Ch 17:3	3068
So the **L** established the kingdom	2Ch 17:5	3068
took great pride in the ways of the **L**	2Ch 17:6	3068
having the book of the law of the **L**	2Ch 17:9	3068
Now the dread of the **L** was on all	2Ch 17:10	3068
Zichri, who volunteered for the **L**,	2Ch 17:16	3068
first for the word of the **L**."	2Ch 18:4	3068
there not yet a prophet of the **L** here	2Ch 18:6	3068
by whom we may inquire of the **L**,	2Ch 18:7	3068
"Thus says the **L**,	2Ch 18:10	3068
for the **L** will give *it* into the	2Ch 18:11	3068
"As the **L** lives, what my God	2Ch 18:13	3068
the truth in the name of the **L**?"	2Ch 18:15	3068
the **L** said, 'These have no master.	2Ch 18:16	3068
"Therefore, hear the word of the **L**.	2Ch 18:18	3068
I saw the **L** sitting on His throne,	2Ch 18:18	3068
"The **L** said,	2Ch 18:19	3068
and stood before the **L** and said,	2Ch 18:20	3068
And the **L** said to him,	2Ch 18:20	3068
the **L** has put a deceiving spirit	2Ch 18:22	3068
for the **L** has proclaimed disaster	2Ch 18:22	3068
L pass from me to speak to you?"	2Ch 18:23	3068
the **L** has not spoken by me."	2Ch 18:27	3068
cried out, and the **L** helped him,	2Ch 18:31	3068
and love those who hate the **L**	2Ch 19:2	3068
wrath on yourself from the **L**?	2Ch 19:2	3068
and brought them back to the **L**,	2Ch 19:4	3068
do not judge for man but for the **L**	2Ch 19:6	3068
let the fear of the **L** be upon you;	2Ch 19:7	3068
for the **L** our God will have no	2Ch 19:7	3068
for the judgment of the **L** and to	2Ch 19:8	3068
you shall do in the fear of the **L**,	2Ch 19:9	3068
may not be guilty before the **L**,	2Ch 19:10	3068
in all that pertains to the **L**,	2Ch 19:11	3068
and the **L** be with the upright."	2Ch 19:11	3068
his attention to seek the **L**,	2Ch 20:3	3068
together to seek help from the **L**;	2Ch 20:4	3068
the cities of Judah to seek the **L**.	2Ch 20:4	3068
of the **L** before the new court,	2Ch 20:5	3068
"O **L**, the God of our fathers, are	2Ch 20:6	3068
Judah was standing before the **L**,	2Ch 20:13	3068
Spirit of the **L** came upon Jahaziel	2Ch 20:14	3068
thus says the **L** to you,	2Ch 20:15	3068
salvation of the **L** on your behalf,	2Ch 20:17	3068
them, for the **L** is with you."	2Ch 20:17	3068
Jerusalem fell down before the **L**,	2Ch 20:18	3068
before the LORD, worshiping the **L**.	2Ch 20:18	3068
up to praise the **L** God of Israel,	2Ch 20:19	3068
put your trust in the **L** your God and	2Ch 20:20	3068
appointed those who sang to the **L**	2Ch 20:21	3068
"Give thanks to the **L**,	2Ch 20:21	3068
the **L** set ambushes against the	2Ch 20:22	3068
for there they blessed the **L**.	2Ch 20:26	3068
for the **L** had made them to rejoice	2Ch 20:27	3068
trumpets to the house of the **L**.	2Ch 20:28	3068
the **L** had fought against the enemies	2Ch 20:29	3068
doing right in the sight of the **L**.	2Ch 20:32	3068
the **L** has destroyed your works."	2Ch 20:37	3068
he did evil in the sight of the **L**.	2Ch 21:6	3068
Yet the **L** was not willing to	2Ch 21:7	3068
forsaken the **L** God of his fathers.	2Ch 21:10	3068
the **L** God of your father David,	2Ch 21:12	3068
the **L** is going to strike your	2Ch 21:14	3068
Then the **L** stirred up against	2Ch 21:16	3068
So after all this the **L** smote him	2Ch 21:18	3068
He did evil in the sight of the **L**	2Ch 22:4	3068
whom the **L** had anointed to cut off	2Ch 22:7	3068
sought the **L** with all his heart."	2Ch 22:9	3068
as the **L** has spoken concerning the	2Ch 23:3	3068
the courts of the house of the **L**.	2Ch 23:5	3068
let no one enter the house of the **L**	2Ch 23:6	3068
people keep the charge of the **L**.	2Ch 23:6	3068
she came into the house of the **L** to	2Ch 23:12	3068
put to death in the house of the **L**."	2Ch 23:14	3068
the offices of the house of the **L**	2Ch 23:18	3068
assigned over the house of the **L**,	2Ch 23:18	3068
the burnt offerings of the **L**,	2Ch 23:18	3068
gatekeepers of the house of the **L**,	2Ch 23:19	3068
king down from the house of the **L**,	2Ch 23:20	3068
what was right in the sight of the **L**	2Ch 24:2	3068
to restore the house of the **L**.	2Ch 24:4	3068
fixed by Moses the servant of the **L**	2Ch 24:6	3068
the house of the **L** for the Baals.	2Ch 24:7	3068
by the gate of the house of the **L**.	2Ch 24:8	3068
to bring to the **L** the levy *fixed by*	2Ch 24:9	3068
the service of the house of the **L**;	2Ch 24:12	3068
to restore the house of the **L**,	2Ch 24:12	3068
to repair the house of the **L**.	2Ch 24:12	3068
utensils for the house of the **L**,	2Ch 24:14	3068
burnt offerings in the house of the **L**	2Ch 24:14	3068
They abandoned the house of the **L**,	2Ch 24:18	3068
them to bring them back to the **L**;	2Ch 24:19	3068
the commandments of the **L** and	2Ch 24:20	3068
Because you have forsaken the **L**,	2Ch 24:20	3068
the court of the house of the **L**.	2Ch 24:21	3068
"May the **L** see and avenge!"	2Ch 24:22	3068
yet the **L** delivered a very great	2Ch 24:24	3068
because they had forsaken the **L**,	2Ch 24:24	3068
did right in the sight of the **L**,	2Ch 25:2	3068
of Moses, which the **L** commanded,	2Ch 25:4	3068
for the **L** is not with Israel *nor*	2Ch 25:7	3068
"The **L** has much more to give you	2Ch 25:9	3068
the anger of the **L** burned against	2Ch 25:15	3068
turned away from following the **L**	2Ch 25:27	3068
He did right in the sight of the **L**	2Ch 26:4	3068
and as long as he sought the **L**,	2Ch 26:5	3068
was unfaithful to the **L** his God,	2Ch 26:16	3068
for he entered the temple of the **L** to	2Ch 26:16	3068
with him eighty priests of the **L**,	2Ch 26:17	3068
Uzziah, to burn incense to the **L**,	2Ch 26:18	3068
have no honor from the **L** God."	2Ch 26:18	
the priests in the house of the **L**,	2Ch 26:19	3068
out because the **L** had smitten him.	2Ch 26:20	3068
cut off from the house of the **L**.	2Ch 26:21	3068
did right in the sight of the **L**,	2Ch 27:2	3068
did not enter the temple of the **L**.	2Ch 27:2	3068
upper gate of the house of the **L**,	2Ch 27:3	3068
his ways before the **L** his God.	2Ch 27:6	3068
did not do right in the sight of the **L**	2Ch 28:1	3068
nations whom the **L** had driven out	2Ch 28:3	3068
the **L** his God delivered him into	2Ch 28:5	3068
the **L** God of their fathers.	2Ch 28:6	3068
But a prophet of the **L** was there,	2Ch 28:9	3068
the **L**, the God of your fathers, was	2Ch 28:9	3068
your own against the **L** your God?	2Ch 28:10	3068
anger of the **L** is against you."	2Ch 28:11	3068
to bring upon us guilt against the **L**	2Ch 28:13	3068
For the **L** humbled Judah because of	2Ch 28:19	3068
and was very unfaithful to the **L**.	2Ch 28:19	3068
a portion out of the house of the **L**	2Ch 28:21	3068
yet more unfaithful to the **L**.	2Ch 28:22	3068
the doors of the house of the **L**	2Ch 28:24	3068
to other gods, and provoked the **L**,	2Ch 28:25	3068
did right in the sight of the **L**,	2Ch 29:2	3068
the doors of the house of the **L** and	2Ch 29:3	3068
and consecrate the house of the **L**,	2Ch 29:5	3068
in the sight of the **L** our God,	2Ch 29:6	3068
from the dwelling place of the **L**,	2Ch 29:6	3068
"Therefore the wrath of the **L** was	2Ch 29:8	3068
covenant with the **L** God of Israel,	2Ch 29:10	3068
for the **L** has chosen you to stand	2Ch 29:11	3068
in to cleanse the house of the **L**,	2Ch 29:15	3068
of the king by the words of the **L**.	2Ch 29:15	3068
the house of the **L** to cleanse *it,*	2Ch 29:16	3068
they found in the temple of the **L**	2Ch 29:16	3068
the court of the house of the **L**.	2Ch 29:16	3068
they entered the porch of the **L**.	2Ch 29:17	3068
they consecrated the house of the **L**	2Ch 29:17	3068
cleansed the whole house of the **L**,	2Ch 29:18	3068
are before the altar of the **L**."	2Ch 29:19	3068
and went up to the house of the **L**.	2Ch 29:20	3068
offer *them* on the altar of the **L**.	2Ch 29:21	3068
the Levites in the house of the **L**	2Ch 29:25	3068
the command was from the **L**	2Ch 29:25	3068
the song to the **L** also began with	2Ch 29:27	3068
the Levites to sing praises to the **L**	2Ch 29:30	3068
consecrated yourselves to the **L**,	2Ch 29:31	3068
offerings to the house of the **L**."	2Ch 29:31	3068
for a burnt offering to the **L**.	2Ch 29:32	3068
service of the house of the **L** was	2Ch 29:35	3068
to the house of the **L** at Jerusalem	2Ch 30:1	3068
Passover to the **L** God of Israel.	2Ch 30:1	3068
Passover to the **L** God of Israel	2Ch 30:5	3068
return to the **L** God of Abraham,	2Ch 30:6	3068
to the **L** God of their fathers,	2Ch 30:7	3068
but yield to the **L** and enter His	2Ch 30:8	3068
forever, and serve the **L** your God,	2Ch 30:8	3068
"For if you return to the **L**,	2Ch 30:9	3068
For the **L** your God is gracious and	2Ch 30:9	3068
commanded by the word of the **L**.	2Ch 30:12	3068
offerings to the house of the **L**.	2Ch 30:15	3068
order to consecrate *them* to the **L**.	2Ch 30:17	3068
"May the good **L** pardon	2Ch 30:18	3068
God, the **L** God of his fathers,	2Ch 30:19	3068
So the **L** heard Hezekiah and healed	2Ch 30:20	3068
Levites and the priests praised the **L**	2Ch 30:21	3068
with loud instruments to the **L**.	2Ch 30:21	3068
insight *in the things* of the **L**.	2Ch 30:22	3068
to the **L** God of their fathers.	2Ch 30:22	3068
in the gates of the camp of the **L**.	2Ch 31:2	3068
it is written in the law of the **L**.	2Ch 31:3	3068
themselves to the law of the **L**.	2Ch 31:4	3068
consecrated to the **L** their God,	2Ch 31:6	3068
they blessed the **L** and His people	2Ch 31:8	3068
brought into the house of the **L**,	2Ch 31:10	3068
for the **L** has blessed His people,	2Ch 31:10	3068
rooms in the house of the **L**,	2Ch 31:11	3068
the contributions for the **L** and	2Ch 31:14	3068
who entered the house of the **L** for	2Ch 31:16	3068
and true before the **L** his God.	2Ch 31:20	3068
but with us is the **L** our God to	2Ch 32:8	3068
"The **L** our God will deliver us	2Ch 32:11	3068
servants spoke further against the **L**	2Ch 32:16	3068
to insult the **L** God of Israel,	2Ch 32:17	3068
And the **L** sent an angel who	2Ch 32:21	3068
So the **L** saved Hezekiah and the	2Ch 32:22	3068
bringing gifts to the **L** at Jerusalem	2Ch 32:23	3068
and he prayed to the **L**,	2Ch 32:24	3068
and the **L** spoke to him and gave	2Ch 32:24	
so that the wrath of the **L** did not	2Ch 32:26	3068
He did evil in the sight of the **L**	2Ch 33:2	3068
the nations whom the **L** dispossessed	2Ch 33:2	3068
He built altars in the house of the **L**	2Ch 33:4	3068
the LORD of which the **L** had said,	2Ch 33:4	3068
two courts of the house of the **L**.	2Ch 33:5	3068
much evil in the sight of the **L**,	2Ch 33:6	3068

the nations whom the **L** destroyed	**2Ch 33:9**	3068
The **L** spoke to Manasseh and	**2Ch 33:10**	3068
Therefore the **L** brought the	**2Ch 33:11**	3068
he entreated the **L** his God and	**2Ch 33:12**	3068
Manasseh knew that the **L** *was* God.	**2Ch 33:13**	3068
the idol from the house of the **L**,	**2Ch 33:15**	3068
the mountain of the house of the **L**	**2Ch 33:15**	3068
He set up the altar of the **L**	**2Ch 33:16**	3068
to serve the **L** God of Israel.	**2Ch 33:16**	3068
although only to the **L** their God.	**2Ch 33:17**	3068
the name of the **L** God of Israel,	**2Ch 33:18**	3068
He did evil in the sight of the **L**	**2Ch 33:22**	3068
did not humble himself before the **L**	**2Ch 33:23**	3068
did right in the sight of the **L**,	**2Ch 34:2**	3068
repair the house of the **L** his God.	**2Ch 34:8**	3068
oversight of the house of the **L**,	**2Ch 34:10**	3068
working in the house of the **L** used it	**2Ch 34:10**	3068
brought into the house of the **L**,	**2Ch 34:14**	3068
found the book of the law of the **L**	**2Ch 34:14**	3068
of the law in the house of the **L**."	**2Ch 34:15**	3068
was found in the house of the **L**,	**2Ch 34:17**	3068
"Go, inquire of the **L** for me	**2Ch 34:21**	3068
for great is the wrath of the **L**	**2Ch 34:21**	3068
not observed the word of the **L**,	**2Ch 34:21**	3068
"Thus says the **L**, the God of	**2Ch 34:23**	3068
thus says the **L**,	**2Ch 34:24**	3068
who sent you to inquire of the **L**,	**2Ch 34:26**	3068
'Thus says the **L** God of Israel	**2Ch 34:26**	3068
have heard you," declares the **L**.	**2Ch 34:27**	3068
king went up to the house of the **L**	**2Ch 34:30**	3068
was found in the house of the **L**.	**2Ch 34:30**	3068
and made a covenant before the **L**	**2Ch 34:31**	3068
the LORD to walk after the **L**,	**2Ch 34:31**	3068
Israel to serve the **L** their God.	**2Ch 34:33**	3068
the **L** God of their fathers.	**2Ch 34:33**	3068
Passover to the **L** in Jerusalem,	**2Ch 35:1**	3068
the service of the house of the **L**.	**2Ch 35:2**	3068
Israel *and* who were holy to the **L**,	**2Ch 35:3**	3068
Now serve the **L** your God and His	**2Ch 35:3**	3068
to the word of the **L** by Moses."	**2Ch 35:6**	3068
lay people to present to the **L**,	**2Ch 35:12**	3068
So all the service of the **L** was	**2Ch 35:16**	3068
burnt offerings on the altar of the **L**	**2Ch 35:16**	3068
as written in the law of the **L**,	**2Ch 35:26**	3068
in the sight of the **L** his God.	**2Ch 36:5**	3068
of the articles of the house of the **L**	**2Ch 36:7**	3068
he did evil in the sight of the **L**.	**2Ch 36:9**	3068
articles of the house of the **L**,	**2Ch 36:10**	3068
evil in the sight of the **L** his God;	**2Ch 36:12**	3068
the prophet who spoke for the **L**.	**2Ch 36:12**	3068
turning to the **L** God of Israel.	**2Ch 36:13**	3068
and they defiled the house of the **L**	**2Ch 36:14**	3068
The **L**, the God of their	**2Ch 36:15**	3068
of the **L** arose against His people,	**2Ch 36:16**	3068
treasures of the house of the **L**,	**2Ch 36:18**	3068
to fulfill the word of the **L** by the	**2Ch 36:21**	3068
in order to fulfill the word of the **L**	**2Ch 36:22**	3068
the **L** stirred up the spirit of Cyrus	**2Ch 36:22**	3068
'The **L**, the God of heaven, has	**2Ch 36:23**	3068
may the **L** his God be with him,	**2Ch 36:23**	3068
in order to fulfill the word of the **L**	**Ezr 1:1**	3068
the **L** stirred up the spirit of	**Ezr 1:1**	3068
'The **L**, the God of heaven, has	**Ezr 1:2**	3068
and rebuild the house of the **L**,	**Ezr 1:3**	3068
and rebuild the house of the **L**,	**Ezr 1:5**	3068
articles of the house of the **L**,	**Ezr 1:7**	3068
they arrived at the house of the **L**	**Ezr 2:68**	3068
burnt offerings on it to the **L**,	**Ezr 3:3**	3068
for all the fixed festivals of the **L**	**Ezr 3:5**	3068
a freewill offering to the **L**.	**Ezr 3:5**	3068
to offer burnt offerings to the **L**,	**Ezr 3:6**	3068
foundation of the temple of the **L**	**Ezr 3:6**	3068
the work of the house of the **L**.	**Ezr 3:8**	3068
foundation of the temple of the **L**,	**Ezr 3:10**	3068
to praise the **L** according to the	**Ezr 3:10**	3068
and giving thanks to the **L**,	**Ezr 3:11**	3068
great shout when they praised the **L**	**Ezr 3:11**	3068
foundation of the house of the **L**	**Ezr 3:11**	3068
a temple to the **L** God of Israel,	**Ezr 4:1**	3068
build to the **L** God of Israel,	**Ezr 4:3**	3068
them, to seek the **L** God of Israel,	**Ezr 6:21**	3068
the **L** had caused them to rejoice,	**Ezr 6:22**	3068
the **L** God of Israel had given;	**Ezr 7:6**	3068
the hand of the **L** his God *was* upon	**Ezr 7:6**	3068
heart to study the law of the **L**	**Ezr 7:10**	3068
the commandments of the **L** and	**Ezr 7:11**	3068
Blessed be the **L**, the God of our	**Ezr 7:27**	3068
to adorn the house of the **L** which	**Ezr 7:27**	3068
the hand of the **L** my God upon me,	**Ezr 7:28**	3068
"You are holy to the **L**,	**Ezr 8:28**	3068
to the **L** God of your fathers.	**Ezr 8:28**	3068
chambers of the house of the **L**."	**Ezr 8:29**	3068
all as a burnt offering to the **L**.	**Ezr 8:35**	3068
out my hands to the **L** my God;	**Ezr 9:5**	3068
has been *shown* from the **L** our God,	**Ezr 9:8**	3068
"O **L** God of Israel, You are	**Ezr 9:15**	3068
according to the counsel of my **l**	**Ezr 10:3**	136
to the **L** God of your fathers and	**Ezr 10:11**	3068
"I beseech You, O **L** God of heaven,	**Ne 1:5**	3068
"O **L**, I beseech You, may Your	**Ne 1:11**	136
the **L** who is great and awesome,	**Ne 4:14**	136
And they praised the **L**.	**Ne 5:13**	3068
which the **L** had given to Israel.	**Ne 8:1**	3068
Ezra blessed the **L** the great God.	**Ne 8:6**	3068
they bowed low and worshiped the **L**	**Ne 8:6**	3068
day is holy to the **L** your God;	**Ne 8:9**	3068
for this day is holy to our **L**.	**Ne 8:10**	136
joy of the **L** is your strength."	**Ne 8:10**	3068
L had commanded through Moses	**Ne 8:14**	3068
from the book of the law of the **L**	**Ne 9:3**	3068
and worshiped the **L** their God.	**Ne 9:3**	3068
a loud voice to the **L** their God.	**Ne 9:4**	3068
bless the **L** your God forever and	**Ne 9:5**	3068
"You alone are the **L**.	**Ne 9:6**	3068
"You are the **L** God, Who chose	**Ne 9:7**	3068
all the commandments of GOD our **L**,	**Ne 10:29**	136
to burn on the altar of the **L** our	**Ne 10:34**	3068
to the house of the **L** annually,	**Ne 10:35**	3068
present themselves before the **L**,	**Jb 1:6**	3068
The **L** said to Satan,	**Jb 1:7**	3068
Satan answered the **L** and said,	**Jb 1:7**	3068
The **L** said to Satan,	**Jb 1:8**	3068
Then Satan answered the **L**,	**Jb 1:9**	3068
Then the **L** said to Satan,	**Jb 1:12**	3068
from the presence of the **L**.	**Jb 1:12**	3068
The **L** gave and the LORD has taken	**Jb 1:21**	3068
gave and the **L** has taken away.	**Jb 1:21**	3068
Blessed be the name of the **L**."	**Jb 1:21**	3068
present themselves before the **L**,	**Jb 2:1**	3068
to present himself before the **L**.	**Jb 2:1**	3068
The **L** said to Satan,	**Jb 2:2**	3068
Satan answered the **L** and said,	**Jb 2:2**	3068
The **L** said to Satan,	**Jb 2:3**	3068
Satan answered the **L** and said,	**Jb 2:4**	3068
So the **L** said to Satan,	**Jb 2:6**	3068
out from the presence of the **L**	**Jb 2:7**	3068
the hand of the **L** has done this,	**Jb 12:9**	3068
'Behold, the fear of the **L**,	**Jb 28:28**	136
Then the **L** answered Job out of the	**Jb 38:1**	3068
Then the **L** said to Job,	**Jb 40:1**	3068
Then Job answered the **L** and said,	**Jb 40:3**	3068
L answered Job out of the storm and	**Jb 40:6**	3068
Then Job answered the **L** and	**Jb 42:1**	3068
L had spoken these words to Job,	**Jb 42:7**	3068
L said to Eliphaz the Temanite,	**Jb 42:7**	3068
went and did as the **L** told them;	**Jb 42:9**	3068
and the **L** accepted Job.	**Jb 42:9**	3068
The **L** restored the fortunes of Job	**Jb 42:10**	3068
and the **L** increased all that Job	**Jb 42:10**	3068
that the **L** had brought on him.	**Jb 42:11**	3068
The **L** blessed the latter *days*	**Jb 42:12**	3068
delight is in the law of the **L**,	**Ps 1:2**	3068
For the **L** knows the way of the	**Ps 1:6**	3068
Against the **L** and against His	**Ps 2:2**	3068
laughs, The **L** scoffs at them.	**Ps 2:4**	136
tell of the decree of the **L**:	**Ps 2:7**	3068
Worship the **L** with reverence And	**Ps 2:11**	3068
O **L**, how my adversaries have	**Ps 3:1**	3068
But You, O **L**, are a shield about	**Ps 3:3**	3068
was crying to the **L** with my voice,	**Ps 3:4**	3068
I awoke, for the **L** sustains me.	**Ps 3:5**	3068
Arise, O **L**; save me, O my God!	**Ps 3:7**	3068
Salvation belongs to the **L**;	**Ps 3:8**	3068
But know that the **L** has set apart	**Ps 4:3**	3068
The **L** hears when I call to Him.	**Ps 4:3**	3068
righteousness, And trust in the **L**.	**Ps 4:5**	3068
of Your countenance upon us, O **L**!	**Ps 4:6**	3068
You alone, O **L**, make me to	**Ps 4:8**	3068
Give ear to my words, O **L**,	**Ps 5:1**	3068
In the morning, O **L**, You will hear	**Ps 5:3**	3068
The **L** abhors the man of bloodshed	**Ps 5:6**	3068
O **L**, lead me in Your righteousness	**Ps 5:8**	3068
blesses the righteous man, O **L**,	**Ps 5:12**	3068
O **L**, do not rebuke me in Your	**Ps 6:1**	3068
Be gracious to me, O **L**,	**Ps 6:2**	3068
Heal me, O **L**, for my bones are	**Ps 6:2**	3068
is greatly dismayed; But You, O **L**	**Ps 6:3**	3068
Return, O **L**, rescue my soul;	**Ps 6:4**	3068
For the **L** has heard the voice of	**Ps 6:8**	3068
The **L** has heard my supplication,	**Ps 6:9**	3068
The **L** receives my prayer.	**Ps 6:9**	3068
O **L** my God, in You I have taken	**Ps 7:1**	3068
O **L** my God, if I have done this,	**Ps 7:3**	3068
Arise, O **L**, in Your anger;	**Ps 7:6**	3068
The **L** judges the peoples;	**Ps 7:8**	3068
Vindicate me, O **L**, according to my	**Ps 7:8**	3068
I will give thanks to the **L**	**Ps 7:17**	3068
to the name of the **L** Most High.	**Ps 7:17**	3068
O **L**, our Lord, How majestic is	**Ps 8:1**	3068
O LORD, our **L**, How majestic is	**Ps 8:1**	136
O **L**, our Lord, How majestic is Your	**Ps 8:9**	3068
O LORD, our **L**, How majestic is Your	**Ps 8:9**	136
thanks to the **L** with all my heart;	**Ps 9:1**	3068
But the **L** abides forever;	**Ps 9:7**	3068
The **L** also will be a stronghold	**Ps 9:9**	3068
For You, O **L**, have not forsaken	**Ps 9:10**	3068
Sing praises to the **L**,	**Ps 9:11**	3068
Be gracious to me, O **L**;	**Ps 9:13**	3068
The **L** has made Himself known;	**Ps 9:16**	3068
Arise, O **L**, do not let man prevail;	**Ps 9:19**	3068
Put them in fear, O **L**;	**Ps 9:20**	3068
Why do You stand afar off, O **L**?	**Ps 10:1**	3068
man curses *and* spurns the **L**.	**Ps 10:3**	3068
Arise, O **L**; O God, lift up Your hand.	**Ps 10:12**	3068
The **L** is King forever and ever;	**Ps 10:16**	3068
O **L**, You have heard the desire of	**Ps 10:17**	3068
In the **L** I take refuge;	**Ps 11:1**	3068
The **L** is in His holy temple;	**Ps 11:4**	3068
The **L** tests the righteous and the	**Ps 11:5**	3068
For the **L** is righteous,	**Ps 11:7**	3068
Help, **L**, for the godly man ceases	**Ps 12:1**	3068
the **L** cut off all flattering lips,	**Ps 12:3**	3068
who is **l** over us?"	**Ps 12:4**	113
Now I will arise," says the **L**;	**Ps 12:5**	3068
The words of the **L** are pure words;	**Ps 12:6**	3068
You, O **L**, will keep them;	**Ps 12:7**	3068
How long, O **L**? Will You forget	**Ps 13:1**	3068
Consider *and* answer me, O **L**	**Ps 13:3**	3068
I will sing to the **L**,	**Ps 13:6**	3068
The **L** has looked down from heaven	**Ps 14:2**	3068
bread, *And* do not call upon the **L**?	**Ps 14:4**	3068
But the **L** is his refuge.	**Ps 14:6**	3068
the **L** restores His captive people,	**Ps 14:7**	3068
O **L**, who may abide in Your tent?	**Ps 15:1**	3068
who honors those who fear the **L**;	**Ps 15:4**	3068
I said to the **L**,	**Ps 16:2**	3068
I said to the LORD, "You are my **L**	**Ps 16:2**	136
The **L** is the portion of my	**Ps 16:5**	3068
bless the **L** who has counseled me;	**Ps 16:7**	3068
set the **L** continually before me;	**Ps 16:8**	3068
Hear a just cause, O **L**,	**Ps 17:1**	3068
Arise, O **L**, confront him, bring	**Ps 17:13**	3068
From men with Your hand, O **L**,	**Ps 17:14**	3068
"I love You, O **L**, my strength."	**Ps 18:1**	3068
The **L** is my rock and my fortress	**Ps 18:2**	3068
I call upon the **L**, who is worthy	**Ps 18:3**	3068
my distress I called upon the **L**,	**Ps 18:6**	3068
L also thundered in the heavens,	**Ps 18:13**	3068
were laid bare At Your rebuke, O **L**,	**Ps 18:15**	3068
calamity, But the **L** was my stay.	**Ps 18:18**	3068
The **L** has rewarded me according to	**Ps 18:20**	3068
For I have kept the ways of the **L**,	**Ps 18:21**	3068
Therefore the **L** has recompensed me	**Ps 18:24**	3068
L my God illumines my darkness.	**Ps 18:28**	3068
The word of the **L** is tried;	**Ps 18:30**	3068
For who is God, but the **L**?	**Ps 18:31**	3068
was none to save, *Even* to the **L**,	**Ps 18:41**	3068
The **L** lives, and blessed be my	**Ps 18:46**	3068
to You among the nations, O **L**,	**Ps 18:49**	3068
The law of the **L** is perfect,	**Ps 19:7**	3068
The testimony of the **L** is sure,	**Ps 19:7**	3068
The precepts of the **L** are right,	**Ps 19:8**	3068
The commandment of the **L** is pure,	**Ps 19:8**	3068
The fear of the **L** is clean,	**Ps 19:9**	3068
The judgments of the **L** are true;	**Ps 19:9**	3068
Be acceptable in Your sight, O **L**,	**Ps 19:14**	3068
May the **L** answer you in the day of	**Ps 20:1**	3068
the **L** fulfill all your petitions.	**Ps 20:5**	3068
that the **L** saves His anointed;	**Ps 20:6**	3068
will boast in the name of the **L**,	**Ps 20:7**	3068
Save, O **L**; May the King answer us	**Ps 20:9**	3068
O **L**, in Your strength the king will	**Ps 21:1**	3068
For the king trusts in the **L**,	**Ps 21:7**	3068
The **L** will swallow them up in His	**Ps 21:9**	3068
Be exalted, O **L**,	**Ps 21:13**	3068
"Commit *yourself* to the **L**;	**Ps 22:8**	3068
But You, O **L**, be not far off;	**Ps 22:19**	3068
You who fear the **L**,	**Ps 22:23**	3068
who seek Him will praise the **L**.	**Ps 22:26**	3068
will remember and turn to the **L**,	**Ps 22:27**	3068
It will be told of the **L** to the *coming*	**Ps 22:30**	136
The **L** is my shepherd, I shall not	**Ps 23:1**	3068
dwell in the house of the **L** forever.	**Ps 23:6**	3068
may ascend into the hill of the **L**?	**Ps 24:3**	3068
shall receive a blessing from the **L**	**Ps 24:5**	3068
The **L** strong and mighty, The LORD	**Ps 24:8**	3068
mighty, The **L** mighty in battle.	**Ps 24:8**	3068
The **L** of hosts, He is the King of	**Ps 24:10**	3068
To You, O **L**, I lift up my soul.	**Ps 25:1**	3068
Make me know Your ways, O **L**;	**Ps 25:4**	3068
Remember, O **L**, Your compassion and	**Ps 25:6**	3068
me, For Your goodness' sake, O **L**.	**Ps 25:7**	3068
Good and upright is the **L**;	**Ps 25:8**	3068
All the paths of the **L** are	**Ps 25:10**	3068
For Your name's sake, O **L**,	**Ps 25:11**	3068
Who is the man who fears the **L**?	**Ps 25:12**	3068
The secret of the **L** is for those who	**Ps 25:14**	3068
eyes are continually toward the **L**,	**Ps 25:15**	3068
Vindicate me, O **L**, for I have	**Ps 26:1**	3068
trusted in the **L** without wavering.	**Ps 26:1**	3068
Examine me, O **L**, and try me;	**Ps 26:2**	3068
I will go about Your altar, O **L**,	**Ps 26:6**	3068
O **L**, I love the habitation of Your	**Ps 26:8**	3068
congregations I shall bless the **L**.	**Ps 26:12**	3068
L is my light and my salvation;	**Ps 27:1**	3068
The **L** is the defense of my life;	**Ps 27:1**	3068
One thing I have asked from the **L**,	**Ps 27:4**	3068
I may dwell in the house of the **L**	**Ps 27:4**	3068
To behold the beauty of the **L**	**Ps 27:4**	3068
yes, I will sing praises to the **L**.	**Ps 27:6**	3068
Hear, O **L**, when I cry with my	**Ps 27:7**	3068
"Your face, O **L**, I shall seek."	**Ps 27:8**	3068
me, But the **L** will take me up.	**Ps 27:10**	3068
Teach me Your way, O **L**,	**Ps 27:11**	3068
the **L** In the land of the living.	**Ps 27:13**	3068
Wait for the **L**; Be strong and	**Ps 27:14**	3068
Yes, wait for the **L**.	**Ps 27:14**	3068
To You, O **L**, I call;	**Ps 28:1**	3068
do not regard the works of the **L**	**Ps 28:5**	3068
Blessed be the **L**, Because He has	**Ps 28:6**	3068
L is my strength and my shield;	**Ps 28:7**	3068
The **L** is their strength, And He is	**Ps 28:8**	3068
Ascribe to the **L**, O sons of the	**Ps 29:1**	3068
Ascribe to the **L** glory and strength.	**Ps 29:1**	3068
the **L** the glory due to His name;	**Ps 29:2**	3068
Worship the **L** in holy array.	**Ps 29:2**	3068
voice of the **L** is upon the waters;	**Ps 29:3**	3068
The **L** is over many waters.	**Ps 29:3**	3068
The voice of the **L** is powerful,	**Ps 29:4**	3068
The voice of the **L** is majestic.	**Ps 29:4**	3068
voice of the **L** breaks the cedars;	**Ps 29:5**	3068
the **L** breaks in pieces the cedars	**Ps 29:5**	3068
The voice of the **L** hews out flames	**Ps 29:7**	3068
voice of the **L** shakes the wilderness	**Ps 29:8**	3068
The **L** shakes the wilderness of	**Ps 29:8**	3068
of the **L** makes the deer to calve And	**Ps 29:9**	3068
The **L** sat *as King* at the flood;	**Ps 29:10**	3068

Yes, the **L** sits as King forever. **Ps 29:10** 3068
The **L** will give strength to His **Ps 29:11** 3068
The **L** will bless His people with **Ps 29:11** 3068
I will extol You, O **L**, **Ps 30:1** 3068
O **L** my God, I cried to You for **Ps 30:2** 3068
O **L**, You have brought up my soul **Ps 30:3** 3068
Sing praise to the **L**, **Ps 30:4** 3068
O **L**, by Your favor You have made **Ps 30:7** 3068
To You, O **L**, I called, And to the **Ps 30:8** 3068
And to the **L** I made supplication: **Ps 30:8** 3068
"Hear, O **L**, and be gracious to me; **Ps 30:10** 3068
O **L**, be my helper." **Ps 30:10** 3068
O **L** my God, I will give thanks to **Ps 30:12** 3068
In You, O **L**, I have taken refuge; **Ps 31:1** 3068
You have ransomed me, O **L**, **Ps 31:5** 3068
But I trust in the **L**. **Ps 31:6** 3068
Be gracious to me, O **L**, **Ps 31:9** 3068
as for me, I trust in You, O **L**, **Ps 31:14** 3068
Let me not be put to shame, O **L**, **Ps 31:17** 3068
Blessed be the **L**, For He has made **Ps 31:21** 3068
O love the **L**, all you His godly **Ps 31:23** 3068
The **L** preserves the faithful And **Ps 31:23** 3068
All you who hope in the **L**. **Ps 31:24** 3068
the **L** does not impute iniquity, **Ps 32:2** 3068
confess my transgressions to the **L**"; **Ps 32:5** 3068
But he who trusts in the **L**, **Ps 32:10** 3068
Be glad in the **L** and rejoice, **Ps 32:11** 3068
Sing for joy in the **L**, **Ps 33:1** 3068
Give thanks to the **L** with the lyre; **Ps 33:2** 3068
For the word of the **L** is upright, **Ps 33:4** 3068
of the lovingkindness of the **L**. **Ps 33:5** 3068
By the word of the **L** the heavens **Ps 33:6** 3068
Let all the earth fear the **L**; **Ps 33:8** 3068
The **L** nullifies the counsel of the **Ps 33:10** 3068
counsel of the **L** stands forever, **Ps 33:11** 3068
is the nation whose God is the **L**, **Ps 33:12** 3068
The **L** looks from heaven; **Ps 33:13** 3068
eye of the **L** is on those who fear **Ps 33:18** 3068
Our soul waits for the **L**; **Ps 33:20** 3068
Let Your lovingkindness, O **L**, **Ps 33:22** 3068
I will bless the **L** at all times; **Ps 34:1** 3068
soul will make its boast in the **L**; **Ps 34:2** 3068
O magnify the **L** with me, And let **Ps 34:3** 3068
I sought the **L**, and He answered **Ps 34:4** 3068
man cried, and the **L** heard him **Ps 34:6** 3068
The angel of the **L** encamps around **Ps 34:7** 3068
taste and see that the **L** is good; **Ps 34:8** 3068
O fear the **L**, you His saints; **Ps 34:9** 3068
But they who seek the **L** shall not **Ps 34:10** 3068
will teach you the fear of the **L**. **Ps 34:11** 3068
The eyes of the **L** are toward the **Ps 34:15** 3068
face of the **L** is against evildoers, **Ps 34:16** 3068
The righteous cry, and the **L** hears **Ps 34:17** 3068
L is near to the brokenhearted And **Ps 34:18** 3068
L delivers him out of them all. **Ps 34:19** 3068
The **L** redeems the soul of His **Ps 34:22** 3068
Contend, O **L**, with those who **Ps 35:1** 3068
angel of the **L** driving *them* on. **Ps 35:5** 3068
the angel of the **L** pursuing them. **Ps 35:6** 3068
my soul shall rejoice in the **L**; **Ps 35:9** 3068
"**L**, who is like You, Who **Ps 35:10** 3068
L, how long will You look on? **Ps 35:17** 136
You have seen it, O **L**, **Ps 35:22** 3068
O **L**, do not be far from me. **Ps 35:22** 136
And to my cause, my God and my **L**. **Ps 35:23** 136
Judge me, O **L** my God, according to **Ps 35:24** 3068
"The **L** be magnified, Who delights **Ps 35:27** 3068
Your lovingkindness, O **L**, **Ps 36:5** 3068
O **L**, You preserve man and beast. **Ps 36:6** 3068
Trust in the **L** and do good; **Ps 37:3** 3068
Delight yourself in the **L**; **Ps 37:4** 3068
Commit your way to the **L**, **Ps 37:5** 3068
Rest in the **L** and wait patiently for **Ps 37:7** 3068
off, But those who wait for the **L**, **Ps 37:9** 3068
The **L** laughs at him, **Ps 37:13** 136
But the **L** sustains the righteous. **Ps 37:17** 3068
The **L** knows the days of the **Ps 37:18** 3068
And the enemies of the **L** will be **Ps 37:20** 3068
of a man are established by the **L**, **Ps 37:23** 3068
L is the One who holds his hand. **Ps 37:24** 3068
For the **L** loves justice And does **Ps 37:28** 3068
The **L** will not leave him in his **Ps 37:33** 3068
Wait for the **L** and keep His way, **Ps 37:34** 3068
of the righteous is from the **L**; **Ps 37:39** 3068
The **L** helps them and delivers **Ps 37:40** 3068
O **L**, rebuke me not in Your wrath, **Ps 38:1** 3068
L, all my desire is before You; **Ps 38:9** 136
For I hope in You, O **L**; **Ps 38:15** 3068
You will answer, O **L** my God. **Ps 38:15** 136
Do not forsake me, O **L**; **Ps 38:21** 3068
Make haste to help me, O **L**, **Ps 38:22** 136
"**L**, make me to know my end And **Ps 39:4** 3068
"And now, **L**, for what do I wait? **Ps 39:7** 136
"Hear my prayer, O **L**, **Ps 39:12** 3068
I waited patiently for the **L**; **Ps 40:1** 3068
and fear And will trust in the **L**. **Ps 40:3** 3068
man who has made the **L** his trust, **Ps 40:4** 3068
Many, O **L** my God, are the wonders **Ps 40:5** 3068
I will not restrain my lips, O **L**, **Ps 40:9** 3068
You, O **L**, will not withhold Your **Ps 40:11** 3068
Be pleased, O **L**, to deliver me; **Ps 40:13** 3068
Make haste, O **L**, to help me. **Ps 40:13** 3068
"The **L** be magnified!" **Ps 40:16** 3068
needy, Let the **L** be mindful of me. **Ps 40:17** 136
The **L** will deliver him in a day of **Ps 41:1** 3068
The **L** will protect him and keep **Ps 41:2** 3068
The **L** will sustain him upon his **Ps 41:3** 3068
"O **L**, be gracious to me; **Ps 41:4** 3068
But You, O **L**, be gracious to me and **Ps 41:10** 3068
Blessed be the **L**, the God of **Ps 41:13** 3068
The **L** will command His **Ps 42:8** 3068
Yourself, why do You sleep, O **L**? **Ps 44:23** 136
Because He is your **L**, **Ps 45:11** 136
The **L** of hosts is with us; **Ps 46:7** 3068
Come, behold the works of the **L**, **Ps 46:8** 3068
The **L** of hosts is with us; **Ps 46:11** 3068
the **L** Most High is to be feared, **Ps 47:2** 3068
The **L**, with the sound of a trumpet. **Ps 47:5** 3068
Great is the **L**, and greatly to be **Ps 48:1** 3068
In the city of the **L** of hosts, **Ps 48:8** 3068
The Mighty One, God, the **L**, **Ps 50:1** 3068
O **L**, open my lips, That my mouth **Ps 51:15** 136
The **L** is the sustainer of my soul. **Ps 54:4** 136
will give thanks to Your name, O **L**, **Ps 54:6** 3068
Confuse, O **L**, divide their **Ps 55:9** 136
upon God, And the **L** will save me. **Ps 55:16** 3068
Cast your burden upon the **L** **Ps 55:22** 3068
In the **L**, *whose* word I praise, **Ps 56:10** 3068
I will give thanks to You, O **L**, **Ps 57:9** 136
the fangs of the young lions, O **L**. **Ps 58:6** 3068
transgression nor for my sin, O **L**, **Ps 59:3** 3068
You, O **L** God of hosts, the **Ps 59:5** 3068
But You, O **L**, laugh at them; **Ps 59:8** 3068
power, and bring them down, O **L**, **Ps 59:11** 136
And lovingkindness is Yours, O **L**, **Ps 62:12** 136
man will be glad in the **L** **Ps 64:10** 3068
in my heart, The **L** will not hear; **Ps 66:18** 136
the deserts, Whose name is the **L**, **Ps 68:4** 3050
The **L** gives the command; **Ps 68:11** 136
the **L** will dwell *there* forever. **Ps 68:16** 3068
The **L** is among them *as at* Sinai, **Ps 68:17** 136
that the **L** God may dwell *there*. **Ps 68:18** 3050
Blessed be the **L**, who daily bears **Ps 68:19** 136
to GOD the **L** belong escapes from **Ps 68:20** 136
The **L** said, "I will bring *them* back **Ps 68:22** 136
in the congregations, *Even* the **L**, **Ps 68:26** 3068
Sing praises to the **L**, **Ps 68:32** 136
through me, O **L** GOD of hosts; **Ps 69:6** 136
for me, my prayer is to You, O **L**, **Ps 69:13** 3068
Answer me, O **L**, for Your **Ps 69:16** 3068
And it will please the **L** better **Ps 69:31** 3068
For the **L** hears the needy And **Ps 69:33** 3068
O **L**, hasten to my help! **Ps 70:1** 3068
O **L**, do not delay. **Ps 70:5** 3068
In You, O **L**, I have taken refuge; **Ps 71:1** 3068
O **L** GOD, *You are* my confidence **Ps 71:5** 136
the mighty deeds of the **L** GOD; **Ps 71:16** 136
Blessed be the **L** God, the God of **Ps 72:18** 3068
Like a dream when one awakes, O **L**, **Ps 73:20** 136
I have made the **L** GOD my refuge, **Ps 73:28** 136
Remember this, O **L**, **Ps 74:18** 3068
For a cup is in the hand of the **L**, **Ps 75:8** 3068
Make vows to the **L** your God and **Ps 76:11** 3068
day of my trouble I sought the **L**; **Ps 77:2** 136
Will the **L** reject forever? **Ps 77:7** 136
shall remember the deeds of the **L**; **Ps 77:11** 3050
to come the praises of the **L**, **Ps 78:4** 3068
the **L** heard and was full of wrath; **Ps 78:21** 3068
Then the **L** awoke as *if from* sleep, **Ps 78:65** 136
How long, O **L**? Will You be angry **Ps 79:5** 3068
they have reproached You, O **L**. **Ps 79:12** 136
O **L** God *of* hosts, How long will **Ps 80:4** 3068
O **L** God of hosts, restore us; **Ps 80:19** 3068
"I, the **L**, am your God, Who **Ps 81:10** 3068
"Those who hate the **L** would **Ps 81:15** 3068
That they may seek Your name, O **L**. **Ps 83:16** 3068
You alone, whose name is the **L**, **Ps 83:18** 3068
Your dwelling places, O **L** of hosts! **Ps 84:1** 3068
yearned for the courts of the **L**; **Ps 84:2** 3068
Even Your altars, O **L** of hosts, **Ps 84:3** 3068
O **L** God of hosts, hear my prayer; **Ps 84:8** 3068
For the **L** God is a sun and shield; **Ps 84:11** 3068
The **L** gives grace and glory; **Ps 84:11** 3068
O **L** of hosts, How blessed is the **Ps 84:12** 3068
O **L**, You showed favor to Your **Ps 85:1** 3068
Show us Your lovingkindness, O **L**, **Ps 85:7** 3068
will hear what God the **L** will say; **Ps 85:8** 3068
the **L** will give what is good, **Ps 85:12** 3068
Incline Your ear, O **L**, **Ps 86:1** 3068
Be gracious to me, O **L**, **Ps 86:3** 136
For to You, O **L**, I lift up my soul. **Ps 86:4** 136
For You, **L**, are good, and ready **Ps 86:5** 136
Give ear, O **L**, to my prayer; **Ps 86:6** 3068
one like You among the gods, O **L**, **Ps 86:8** 136
come and worship before You, O **L**, **Ps 86:9** 136
Teach me Your way, O **L**; **Ps 86:11** 3068
give thanks to You, O **L** my God, **Ps 86:12** 136
But You, O **L**, are a God merciful **Ps 86:15** 136
Because You, O **L**, have helped me **Ps 86:17** 3068
The **L** loves the gates of Zion More **Ps 87:2** 3068
The **L** will count when He **Ps 87:6** 3068
O **L**, the God of my salvation, I **Ps 88:1** 3068
called upon You every day, O **L**; **Ps 88:9** 3068
But I, O **L**, have cried out to You **Ps 88:13** 3068
O **L**, why do You reject my soul? **Ps 88:14** 3068
sing of the lovingkindness of the **L** **Ps 89:1** 3068
will praise Your wonders, O **L**; **Ps 89:5** 3068
the skies is comparable to the **L**? **Ps 89:6** 3068
sons of the mighty is like the **L**, **Ps 89:6** 3068
O **L** God of hosts, who is like **Ps 89:8** 3068
who is like You, O mighty **L**? **Ps 89:8** 3050
O **L**, they walk in the light of Your **Ps 89:15** 3068
For our shield belongs to the **L**, **Ps 89:18** 3068
How long, O **L**? Will You hide **Ps 89:46** 3068
Your former lovingkindnesses, O **L**, **Ps 89:49** 136
Remember, O **L**, the reproach of Your **Ps 89:50** 136
enemies have reproached, O **L**, **Ps 89:51** 3068
Blessed be the **L** forever! **Ps 89:52** 3068
L, You have been our dwelling **Ps 90:1** 136
Do return, O **L**; how long *will it be?* **Ps 90:13** 3068
favor of the **L** our God be upon us; **Ps 90:17** 136
I will say to the **L**, **Ps 91:2** 3068
you have made the **L**, my refuge, **Ps 91:9** 3068
is good to give thanks to the **L** **Ps 92:1** 3068
For You, O **L**, have made me glad **Ps 92:4** 3068
How great are Your works, O **L**! **Ps 92:5** 3068
But You, O **L**, are on high forever. **Ps 92:8** 3068
For, behold, Your enemies, O **L**, **Ps 92:9** 3068
Planted in the house of the **L**, **Ps 92:13** 3068
To declare that the **L** is upright; **Ps 92:15** 3068
The **L** reigns, He is clothed with **Ps 93:1** 3068
The **L** has clothed and girded **Ps 93:1** 3068
The floods have lifted up, O **L**, **Ps 93:3** 3068
the sea, The **L** on high is mighty. **Ps 93:4** 3068
Holiness befits Your house, O **L**, **Ps 93:5** 3068
O **L**, God of vengeance, **Ps 94:1** 3068
How long shall the wicked, O **L**, **Ps 94:3** 3068
They crush Your people, O **L**, **Ps 94:5** 3068
"The **L** does not see, Nor does the **Ps 94:7** 3050
The **L** knows the thoughts of man, **Ps 94:11** 3068
man whom You chasten, O **L**, **Ps 94:12** 3050
the **L** will not abandon His people, **Ps 94:14** 3068
If the **L** had not been my help, My **Ps 94:17** 3068
slipped," Your lovingkindness, O **L**, **Ps 94:18** 3068
But the **L** has been my stronghold, **Ps 94:22** 3068
The **L** our God will destroy them. **Ps 94:23** 3068
let us sing for joy to the **L**, **Ps 95:1** 3068
For the **L** is a great God And a **Ps 95:3** 3068
us kneel before the **L** our Maker. **Ps 95:6** 3068
Sing to the **L** a new song; **Ps 96:1** 3068
Sing to the **L**, all the earth. **Ps 96:1** 3068
Sing to the **L**, bless His name; **Ps 96:2** 3068
For great is the **L** **Ps 96:4** 3068
idols, But the **L** made the heavens. **Ps 96:5** 3068
Ascribe to the **L**, O families of **Ps 96:7** 3068
Ascribe to the **L** glory and strength. **Ps 96:7** 3068
to the **L** the glory of His name; **Ps 96:8** 3068
Worship the **L** in holy attire; **Ps 96:9** 3068
among the nations, "The **L** reigns; **Ps 96:10** 3068
Before the **L**, for He is coming, **Ps 96:13** 3068
The **L** reigns, let the earth rejoice; **Ps 97:1** 3068
like wax at the presence of the **L**, **Ps 97:5** 3068
presence of the **L** of the whole earth **Ps 97:5** 136
Because of Your judgments, O **L**. **Ps 97:8** 3068
L Most High over all the earth; **Ps 97:9** 3068
Hate evil, you who love the **L**, **Ps 97:10** 3068
Be glad in the **L**, you righteous **Ps 97:12** 3068
O sing to the **L** a new song, For He **Ps 98:1** 3068
L has made known His salvation; **Ps 98:2** 3068
Shout joyfully to the **L**, **Ps 98:4** 3068
praises to the **L** with the lyre, **Ps 98:5** 3068
joyfully before the King, the **L**. **Ps 98:6** 3068
Before the **L**, for He is coming **Ps 98:9** 3068
The **L** reigns, let the peoples **Ps 99:1** 3068
The **L** is great in Zion, And He is **Ps 99:2** 3068
Exalt the **L** our God And worship **Ps 99:5** 3068
They called upon the **L** **Ps 99:6** 3068
O **L** our God, You answered **Ps 99:8** 3068
Exalt the **L** our God And worship **Ps 99:9** 3068
For holy is the **L** our God. **Ps 99:9** 3068
Shout joyfully to the **L**, **Ps 100:1** 3068
Serve the **L** with gladness; **Ps 100:2** 3068
Know that the **L** Himself is God; **Ps 100:3** 3068
For the **L** is good; **Ps 100:5** 3068
To You, O **L**, I will sing praises. **Ps 101:1** 3068
as to cut off from the city of the **L** **Ps 101:8** 3068
Hear my prayer, O **L**! **Ps 102:1** 3068
But You, O **L**, abide forever **Ps 102:12** 3068
will fear the name of the **L** **Ps 102:15** 3068
For the **L** has built up Zion; **Ps 102:16** 3068
to be created may praise the **L**. **Ps 102:18** 3050
heaven the **L** gazed upon the earth, **Ps 102:19** 3068
tell of the name of the **L** in Zion And **Ps 102:21** 3068
And the kingdoms, to serve the **L**. **Ps 102:22** 3068
Bless the **L**, O my soul, **Ps 103:1** 3068
Bless the **L**, O my soul, And forget **Ps 103:2** 3068
The **L** performs righteous deeds And **Ps 103:6** 3068
L is compassionate and gracious, **Ps 103:8** 3068
So the **L** has compassion on those **Ps 103:13** 3068
But the lovingkindness of the **L** is **Ps 103:17** 3068
The **L** has established His throne **Ps 103:19** 3068
Bless the **L**, you His angels, **Ps 103:20** 3068
Bless the **L**, all you His hosts, **Ps 103:21** 3068
Bless the **L**, all you works of His, **Ps 103:22** 3068
Bless the **L**, O my soul! **Ps 103:22** 3068
Bless the **L**, O my soul! **Ps 104:1** 3068
O **L** my God, You are very great; **Ps 104:1** 3068
trees of the **L** drink their fill, **Ps 104:16** 3068
O **L**, how many are Your works! **Ps 104:24** 3068
the glory of the **L** endure forever; **Ps 104:31** 3068
Let the **L** be glad in His works; **Ps 104:31** 3068
sing to the **L** as long as I live; **Ps 104:33** 3068
for me, I shall be glad in the **L**. **Ps 104:34** 3068
Bless the **L**, O my soul. **Ps 104:35** 3068
O my soul. Praise the **L**! **Ps 104:35** 3050
Oh give thanks to the **L**, **Ps 105:1** 3068
of those who seek the **L** be glad. **Ps 105:3** 3068
Seek the **L** and His strength; **Ps 105:4** 3068
He is the **L** our God; **Ps 105:7** 3068
The word of the **L** tested him. **Ps 105:19** 3068
He made him **l** of his house And **Ps 105:21** 113
observe His laws, Praise the **L**! **Ps 105:45** 3050
Praise the **L**! Oh give thanks to the **Ps 106:1** 3050
Oh give thanks to the **L**, **Ps 106:1** 3068
of the mighty deeds of the **L**, **Ps 106:2** 3068
Remember me, O **L**, in *Your* favor **Ps 106:4** 3068
of Aaron, the holy one of the **L**, **Ps 106:16** 3068

not listen to the voice of the **L**.	**Ps 106:25**	3068
peoples, As the **L** commanded them,	**Ps 106:34**	3068
anger of the **L** was kindled against	**Ps 106:40**	3068
Save us, O **L** our God, And gather	**Ps 106:47**	3068
Blessed be the **L**, the God of	**Ps 106:48**	3068
"Amen." Praise the **L**!	**Ps 106:48**	3050
Oh give thanks to the **L**,	**Ps 107:1**	3068
Let the redeemed of the **L** say *so,*	**Ps 107:2**	3068
cried out to the **L** in their trouble;	**Ps 107:6**	3068
Let them give thanks to the **L** for	**Ps 107:8**	3068
cried out to the **L** in their trouble;	**Ps 107:13**	3068
Let them give thanks to the **L** for	**Ps 107:15**	3068
cried out to the **L** in their trouble;	**Ps 107:19**	3068
Let them give thanks to the **L** for	**Ps 107:21**	3068
They have seen the works of the **L**,	**Ps 107:24**	3068
cried to the **L** in their trouble,	**Ps 107:28**	3068
Let them give thanks to the **L** for	**Ps 107:31**	3068
the lovingkindnesses of the **L**.	**Ps 107:43**	3068
I will give thanks to You, O **L**,	**Ps 108:3**	3068
be remembered before the **L**,	**Ps 109:14**	3068
them be before the **L** continually,	**Ps 109:15**	3068
reward of my accusers from the **L**,	**Ps 109:20**	3068
But You, O GOD, the **L**,	**Ps 109:21**	136
Help me, O **L** my God;	**Ps 109:26**	3068
You, **L**, have done it.	**Ps 109:27**	3068
give thanks abundantly to the **L**;	**Ps 109:30**	3068
The **L** says to my Lord:	**Ps 110:1**	3068
The LORD says to my **L**:	**Ps 110:1**	136
The **L** will stretch forth Your	**Ps 110:2**	3068
The **L** has sworn and will not	**Ps 110:4**	3068
The **L** is at Your right hand;	**Ps 110:5**	136
Praise the **L**! I will give thanks	**Ps 111:1**	3050
thanks to the **L** with all *my* heart,	**Ps 111:1**	3068
Great are the works of the **L**;	**Ps 111:2**	3068
L is gracious and compassionate.	**Ps 111:4**	3068
the **L** is the beginning of wisdom;	**Ps 111:10**	3068
Praise the **L**! How blessed is the	**Ps 112:1**	3050
is the man who fears the **L**,	**Ps 112:1**	3068
is steadfast, trusting in the **L**.	**Ps 112:7**	3068
Praise the **L**! Praise, O servants of	**Ps 113:1**	3050
Praise, O servants of the **L**,	**Ps 113:1**	3068
Praise the name of the **L**.	**Ps 113:1**	3068
Blessed be the name of the **L** From	**Ps 113:2**	3068
name of the **L** is to be praised.	**Ps 113:3**	3068
The **L** is high above all nations;	**Ps 113:4**	3068
Who is like the **L** our God, Who is	**Ps 113:5**	3068
mother of children. Praise the **L**!	**Ps 113:9**	3050
Tremble, O earth, before the **L**,	**Ps 114:7**	136
Not to us, O **L**, not to us, But to	**Ps 115:1**	3068
O Israel, trust in the **L**;	**Ps 115:9**	3068
O house of Aaron, trust in the **L**;	**Ps 115:10**	3068
You who fear the **L**,	**Ps 115:11**	3068
who fear the LORD, trust in the **L**;	**Ps 115:11**	3068
The **L** has been mindful of us;	**Ps 115:12**	3068
will bless those who fear the **L**,	**Ps 115:13**	3068
May the **L** give you increase, You	**Ps 115:14**	3068
May you be blessed of the **L**,	**Ps 115:15**	3068
heavens are the heavens of the **L**,	**Ps 115:16**	3068
The dead do not praise the **L**,	**Ps 115:17**	3050
we will bless the **L** From this time	**Ps 115:18**	3050
time forth and forever. Praise the **L**!	**Ps 115:18**	3050
I love the **L**, because He hears My	**Ps 116:1**	3068
I called upon the name of the **L**:	**Ps 116:4**	3068
"O **L**, I beseech You, save my	**Ps 116:4**	3068
Gracious is the **L**, and righteous;	**Ps 116:5**	3068
The **L** preserves the simple;	**Ps 116:6**	3068
For the **L** has dealt bountifully	**Ps 116:7**	3068
I shall walk before the **L** In the land	**Ps 116:9**	3068
What shall I render to the **L** For	**Ps 116:12**	3068
And call upon the name of the **L**.	**Ps 116:13**	3068
I shall pay my vows to the **L**,	**Ps 116:14**	3068
Precious in the sight of the **L** Is	**Ps 116:15**	3068
O **L**, surely I am Your servant, I am	**Ps 116:16**	3068
And call upon the name of the **L**.	**Ps 116:17**	3068
I shall pay my vows to the **L**,	**Ps 116:18**	3068
O Jerusalem. Praise the **L**!	**Ps 116:19**	3050
Praise the **L**, all nations;	**Ps 117:1**	3068
the truth of the **L** is everlasting.	**Ps 117:2**	3068
LORD is everlasting. Praise the **L**!	**Ps 117:2**	3050
Give thanks to the **L**,	**Ps 118:1**	3068
Oh let those who fear the **L** say,	**Ps 118:4**	3068
my distress I called upon the **L**;	**Ps 118:5**	3050
The **L** answered me *and set me* in a	**Ps 118:5**	3050
The **L** is for me; I will not fear;	**Ps 118:6**	3068
The **L** is for me among those who	**Ps 118:7**	3068
It is better to take refuge in the **L**	**Ps 118:8**	3068
It is better to take refuge in the **L**	**Ps 118:9**	3068
In the name of the **L** I will surely	**Ps 118:10**	3068
In the name of the **L** I will surely	**Ps 118:11**	3068
In the name of the **L** I will surely	**Ps 118:12**	3068
was falling, But the **L** helped me.	**Ps 118:13**	3068
The **L** is my strength and song, And	**Ps 118:14**	3050
hand of the **L** does valiantly.	**Ps 118:15**	3068
right hand of the **L** is exalted;	**Ps 118:16**	3068
hand of the **L** does valiantly.	**Ps 118:16**	3068
And tell of the works of the **L**.	**Ps 118:17**	3050
The **L** has disciplined me severely,	**Ps 118:18**	3050
I shall give thanks to the **L**.	**Ps 118:19**	3050
This is the gate of the **L**;	**Ps 118:20**	3068
is the day which the **L** has made;	**Ps 118:24**	3068
O **L**, do save, we beseech You;	**Ps 118:25**	3068
O **L**, we beseech You, do send	**Ps 118:25**	3068
who comes in the name of the **L**;	**Ps 118:26**	3068
you from the house of the **L**.	**Ps 118:26**	3068
The **L** is God, and He has given us	**Ps 118:27**	3068
Give thanks to the **L**,	**Ps 118:29**	3068
Who walk in the law of the **L**.	**Ps 119:1**	3068
Blessed are You, O **L**;	**Ps 119:12**	3068
O **L**, do not put me to shame!	**Ps 119:31**	3068

Teach me, O **L**, the way of Your	**Ps 119:33**	3068
also come to me, O **L**,	**Ps 119:41**	3068
Your ordinances from of old, O **L**,	**Ps 119:52**	3068
O **L**, I remember Your name in the	**Ps 119:55**	3068
The **L** is my portion;	**Ps 119:57**	3068
full of Your lovingkindness, O **L**;	**Ps 119:64**	3068
dealt well with Your servant, O **L**,	**Ps 119:65**	3068
I know, O **L**, that Your judgments	**Ps 119:75**	3068
Forever, O **L**, Your word is settled	**Ps 119:89**	3068
Revive me, O **L**, according to Your	**Ps 119:107**	3068
offerings of my mouth, O **L**,	**Ps 119:108**	3068
It is time for the **L** to act,	**Ps 119:126**	3068
Righteous are You, O **L**,	**Ps 119:137**	3068
answer me, O **L**! I will observe Your	**Ps 119:145**	3068
Revive me, O **L**, according to Your	**Ps 119:149**	3068
You are near, O **L**,	**Ps 119:151**	3068
Great are Your mercies, O **L**;	**Ps 119:156**	3068
Revive me, O **L**, according to Your	**Ps 119:159**	3068
I hope for Your salvation, O **L**,	**Ps 119:166**	3068
Let my cry come before You, O **L**;	**Ps 119:169**	3068
I long for Your salvation, O **L**,	**Ps 119:174**	3068
In my trouble I cried to the **L**,	**Ps 120:1**	3068
Deliver my soul, O **L**,	**Ps 120:2**	3068
My help *comes* from the **L**,	**Ps 121:2**	3068
The **L** is your keeper;	**Ps 121:5**	3068
The **L** is your shade on your right	**Ps 121:5**	3068
The **L** will protect you from all	**Ps 121:7**	3068
The **L** will guard your going out	**Ps 121:8**	3068
"Let us go to the house of the **L**."	**Ps 122:1**	3068
even the tribes of the **L**	**Ps 122:4**	3050
give thanks to the name of the **L**.	**Ps 122:4**	3068
L our God, I will seek your good.	**Ps 122:9**	3068
So our eyes *look* to the **L** our God,	**Ps 123:2**	3068
Be gracious to us, O **L**,	**Ps 123:3**	3068
been the **L** who was on our side,"	**Ps 124:1**	3068
been the **L** who was on our side When	**Ps 124:2**	3068
Blessed be the **L**, Who has not	**Ps 124:6**	3068
Our help is in the name of the **L**,	**Ps 124:8**	3068
trust in the **L** Are as Mount Zion,	**Ps 125:1**	3068
So the **L** surrounds His people From	**Ps 125:2**	3068
Do good, O **L**, to those who are	**Ps 125:4**	3068
The **L** will lead them away with the	**Ps 125:5**	3068
When the **L** brought back the	**Ps 126:1**	3068
"The **L** has done great things for	**Ps 126:2**	3068
L has done great things for us;	**Ps 126:3**	3068
Restore our captivity, O **L**,	**Ps 126:4**	3068
Unless the **L** builds the house,	**Ps 127:1**	3068
Unless the **L** guards the city, The	**Ps 127:1**	3068
children are a gift of the **L**,	**Ps 127:3**	3068
is everyone who fears the **L**,	**Ps 128:1**	3068
man be blessed Who fears the **L**.	**Ps 128:4**	3068
The **L** bless you from Zion, And may	**Ps 128:5**	3068
The **L** is righteous;	**Ps 129:4**	3068
"The blessing of the **L** be upon you;	**Ps 129:8**	3068
bless you in the name of the **L**."	**Ps 129:8**	3068
depths I have cried to You, O **L**.	**Ps 130:1**	3068
L, hear my voice!	**Ps 130:2**	136
If You, **L**, should mark	**Ps 130:3**	3050
should mark iniquities, O **L**,	**Ps 130:3**	136
I wait for the **L**, my soul does	**Ps 130:5**	3068
My soul *waits* for the **L** More than	**Ps 130:6**	136
O Israel, hope in the **L**;	**Ps 130:7**	3068
with the **L** there is lovingkindness,	**Ps 130:7**	3068
O **L**, my heart is not proud, nor my	**Ps 131:1**	3068
hope in the **L** From this time forth	**Ps 131:3**	3068
Remember, O **L**, on David's behalf,	**Ps 132:1**	3068
How he swore to the **L**	**Ps 132:2**	3068
Until I find a place for the **L**,	**Ps 132:5**	3068
Arise, O **L**, to Your resting place,	**Ps 132:8**	3068
The **L** has sworn to David A truth	**Ps 132:11**	3068
For the **L** has chosen Zion;	**Ps 132:13**	3068
For there the **L** commanded the	**Ps 133:3**	3068
Behold, bless the **L**,	**Ps 134:1**	3068
the LORD, all servants of the **L**,	**Ps 134:1**	3068
by night in the house of the **L**!	**Ps 134:1**	3068
to the sanctuary And bless the **L**.	**Ps 134:2**	3068
May the **L** bless you from Zion, He	**Ps 134:3**	3068
Praise the **L**! Praise the name of the	**Ps 135:1**	3050
Praise the name of the **L**;	**Ps 135:1**	3068
Praise *Him,* O servants of the **L**,	**Ps 135:1**	3068
who stand in the house of the **L**,	**Ps 135:2**	3068
Praise the **L**, for the LORD is good;	**Ps 135:3**	3050
the LORD, for the **L** is good;	**Ps 135:3**	3068
L has chosen Jacob for Himself,	**Ps 135:4**	3050
For I know that the **L** is great And	**Ps 135:5**	3068
And that our **L** is above all gods.	**Ps 135:5**	136
Whatever the **L** pleases, He does,	**Ps 135:6**	3068
Your name, O **L**, is everlasting, Your	**Ps 135:13**	3068
everlasting, Your remembrance, O **L**,	**Ps 135:13**	3068
For the **L** will judge His people And	**Ps 135:14**	3068
O house of Israel, bless the **L**;	**Ps 135:19**	3068
O house of Aaron, bless the **L**;	**Ps 135:19**	3068
O house of Levi, bless the **L**;	**Ps 135:20**	3068
You who revere the **L**,	**Ps 135:20**	3068
who revere the LORD, bless the **L**.	**Ps 135:20**	3068
Blessed be the **L** from Zion, Who	**Ps 135:21**	3068
dwells in Jerusalem. Praise the **L**!	**Ps 135:21**	3050
Give thanks to the **L**,	**Ps 136:1**	3068
Give thanks to the **L** of lords,	**Ps 136:3**	113
Remember, O **L**, against the sons of	**Ps 137:7**	3068
will give thanks to You, O **L**,	**Ps 138:4**	3068
will sing of the ways of the **L**,	**Ps 138:5**	3068
For great is the glory of the **L**.	**Ps 138:5**	3068
For though the **L** is exalted, Yet	**Ps 138:6**	3068
The **L** will accomplish what	**Ps 138:8**	3068
Your lovingkindness, O **L**,	**Ps 138:8**	3068
O **L**, You have searched me and	**Ps 139:1**	3068
Behold, O **L**, You know it all.	**Ps 139:4**	3068
not hate those who hate You, O **L**?	**Ps 139:21**	3068

Rescue me, O **L**, from evil men;	**Ps 140:1**	3068
Keep me, O **L**, from the hands of	**Ps 140:4**	3068
I said to the **L**,	**Ps 140:6**	3068
Give ear, O **L**, to the voice of my	**Ps 140:6**	3068
"O GOD the **L**, the strength of my	**Ps 140:7**	136
"Do not grant, O **L**, the desires	**Ps 140:8**	3068
I know that the **L** will maintain	**Ps 140:12**	3068
O **L**, I call upon You;	**Ps 141:1**	3068
Set a guard, O **L**, over my mouth;	**Ps 141:3**	3068
are toward You, O GOD, the **L**;	**Ps 141:8**	136
cry aloud with my voice to the **L**;	**Ps 142:1**	3068
supplication with my voice to the **L**.	**Ps 142:1**	3068
I cried out to You, O **L**;	**Ps 142:5**	3068
Hear my prayer, O **L**,	**Ps 143:1**	3068
Answer me quickly, O **L**,	**Ps 143:7**	3068
Deliver me, O **L**, from my enemies;	**Ps 143:9**	3068
For the sake of Your name, O **L**,	**Ps 143:11**	3068
Blessed be the **L**, my rock, Who	**Ps 144:1**	3068
O **L**, what is man, that You take	**Ps 144:3**	3068
Bow Your heavens, O **L**,	**Ps 144:5**	3068
are the people whose God is the **L**!	**Ps 144:15**	3068
Great is the **L**, and highly to be	**Ps 145:3**	3068
The **L** is gracious and merciful;	**Ps 145:8**	3068
The **L** is good to all, And His	**Ps 145:9**	3068
shall give thanks to You, O **L**,	**Ps 145:10**	3068
The **L** sustains all who fall And	**Ps 145:14**	3068
L is righteous in all His ways And	**Ps 145:17**	3068
The **L** is near to all who call upon	**Ps 145:18**	3068
The **L** keeps all who love Him,	**Ps 145:20**	3068
will speak the praise of the **L**,	**Ps 145:21**	3068
Praise the **L**! Praise the LORD,	**Ps 146:1**	3050
Praise the **L**, O my soul!	**Ps 146:1**	3068
I will praise the **L** while I live;	**Ps 146:2**	3068
Whose hope is in the **L** his God,	**Ps 146:5**	3068
The **L** sets the prisoners free.	**Ps 146:7**	3068
The **L** opens *the eyes of* the blind;	**Ps 146:8**	3068
The **L** raises up those who are	**Ps 146:8**	3068
The **L** loves the righteous;	**Ps 146:8**	3068
The **L** protects the strangers;	**Ps 146:9**	3068
The **L** will reign forever, Your God,	**Ps 146:10**	3068
to all generations. Praise the **L**!	**Ps 146:10**	3050
Praise the **L**! For it is good to sing	**Ps 147:1**	3050
The **L** builds up Jerusalem;	**Ps 147:2**	3068
Great is our **L** and abundant in	**Ps 147:5**	136
The **L** supports the afflicted;	**Ps 147:6**	3068
Sing to the **L** with thanksgiving;	**Ps 147:7**	3068
The **L** favors those who fear Him,	**Ps 147:11**	3068
Praise the **L**, O Jerusalem!	**Ps 147:12**	3068
have not known them. Praise the **L**!	**Ps 147:20**	3050
Praise the **L**! Praise the LORD from	**Ps 148:1**	3050
Praise the **L** from the heavens;	**Ps 148:1**	3068
Let them praise the name of the **L**,	**Ps 148:5**	3068
Praise the **L** from the earth, Sea	**Ps 148:7**	3068
Let them praise the name of the **L**,	**Ps 148:13**	3068
a people near to Him. Praise the **L**!	**Ps 148:14**	3050
Praise the **L**! Sing to the LORD	**Ps 149:1**	3050
Sing to the **L** a new song, *And* His	**Ps 149:1**	3068
L takes pleasure in His people;	**Ps 149:4**	3068
for all His godly ones. Praise the **L**!	**Ps 149:9**	3050
Praise the **L**! Praise God in His	**Ps 150:1**	3050
that has breath praise the **L**.	**Ps 150:6**	3050
praise the LORD. Praise the **L**!	**Ps 150:6**	3050
The fear of the **L** is the beginning	**Pr 1:7**	3068
did not choose the fear of the **L**.	**Pr 1:29**	3068
will discern the fear of the **L** And	**Pr 2:5**	3068
For the **L** gives wisdom;	**Pr 2:6**	3068
Trust in the **L** with all your heart And	**Pr 3:5**	3068
Fear the **L** and turn away from evil.	**Pr 3:7**	3068
Honor the **L** from your wealth And	**Pr 3:9**	3068
do not reject the discipline of the **L** Or	**Pr 3:11**	3068
For whom the **L** loves He reproves,	**Pr 3:12**	3068
The **L** by wisdom founded the earth,	**Pr 3:19**	3068
For the **L** will be your confidence And	**Pr 3:26**	3068
devious are an abomination to the **L**;	**Pr 3:32**	3068
The curse of the **L** is on the house	**Pr 3:33**	3068
man are before the eyes of the **L**,	**Pr 5:21**	3068
are six things which the **L** hates,	**Pr 6:16**	3068
"The fear of the **L** is to hate evil;	**Pr 8:13**	3068
"The **L** possessed me at the	**Pr 8:22**	3068
And obtains favor from the **L**.	**Pr 8:35**	3068
The fear of the **L** is the beginning	**Pr 9:10**	3068
The **L** will not allow the righteous	**Pr 10:3**	3068
blessing of the **L** that makes rich,	**Pr 10:22**	3068
The fear of the **L** prolongs life,	**Pr 10:27**	3068
The way of the **L** is a stronghold	**Pr 10:29**	3068
is an abomination to the **L**,	**Pr 11:1**	3068
heart are an abomination to the **L**,	**Pr 11:20**	3068
man will obtain favor from the **L**,	**Pr 12:2**	3068
lips are an abomination to the **L**,	**Pr 12:22**	3068
in his uprightness fears the **L**,	**Pr 14:2**	3068
In the fear of the **L** there is strong	**Pr 14:26**	3068
The fear of the **L** is a fountain of	**Pr 14:27**	3068
eyes of the **L** are in every place,	**Pr 15:3**	3068
wicked is an abomination to the **L**,	**Pr 15:8**	3068
wicked is an abomination to the **L**,	**Pr 15:9**	3068
and Abaddon *lie open* before the **L**,	**Pr 15:11**	3068
a little with the fear of the **L**	**Pr 15:16**	3068
The **L** will tear down the house of	**Pr 15:25**	3068
plans are an abomination to the **L**,	**Pr 15:26**	3068
The **L** is far from the wicked, But	**Pr 15:29**	3068
The fear of the **L** is the instruction	**Pr 15:33**	3068
answer of the tongue is from the **L**.	**Pr 16:1**	3068
But the **L** weighs the motives.	**Pr 16:2**	3068
Commit your works to the **L**	**Pr 16:3**	3068
The **L** has made everything for its	**Pr 16:4**	3068
heart is an abomination to the **L**;	**Pr 16:5**	3068
by the fear of the **L** one keeps away	**Pr 16:6**	3068
a man's ways are pleasing to the **L**,	**Pr 16:7**	3068
way, But the **L** directs his steps.	**Pr 16:9**	3068

and scales belong to the L;	Pr 16:11	3068
blessed is he who trusts in the L.	Pr 16:20	3068
its every decision is from the L.	Pr 16:33	3068
for gold, But the L tests hearts.	Pr 17:3	3068
alike are an abomination to the L.	Pr 17:15	3068
name of the L is a strong tower;	Pr 18:10	3068
And obtains favor from the L.	Pr 18:22	3068
And his heart rages against the L.	Pr 19:3	3068
But a prudent wife is from the L.	Pr 19:14	3068
to a poor man lends to the L,	Pr 19:17	3068
the counsel of the L will stand.	Pr 19:21	3068
The fear of the L *leads* to life,	Pr 19:23	3068
of them are abominable to the L.	Pr 20:10	3068
eye, The L has made both of them.	Pr 20:12	3068
Wait for the L, and He will save	Pr 20:22	3068
are an abomination to the L,	Pr 20:23	3068
Man's steps are *ordained* by the L,	Pr 20:24	3068
of man is the lamp of the L,	Pr 20:27	3068
of water in the hand of the L;	Pr 21:1	3068
eyes, But the L weighs the hearts.	Pr 21:2	3068
justice Is desired by the L more	Pr 21:3	3068
And no counsel against the L.	Pr 21:30	3068
But victory belongs to the L.	Pr 21:31	3068
The L is the maker of them all.	Pr 22:2	3068
and the fear of the L Are riches,	Pr 22:4	3068
eyes of the L preserve knowledge,	Pr 22:12	3068
cursed of the L will fall into it.	Pr 22:14	3068
that your trust may be in the L,	Pr 22:19	3068
For the L will plead their case And	Pr 22:23	3068
live in the fear of the L always.	Pr 23:17	3068
the L will see *it* and be displeased,	Pr 24:18	3068
My son, fear the L and the king;	Pr 24:21	3068
head, And the L will reward you.	Pr 25:22	3068
those who seek the L understand all	Pr 28:5	3068
who trusts in the L will prosper.	Pr 28:25	3068
The L gives light to the eyes of	Pr 29:13	3068
he who trusts in the L will be	Pr 29:25	3068
justice for man *comes* from the L.	Pr 29:26	3068
deny *You* and say, "Who is the L?"	Pr 30:9	3068
vain, *But* a woman who fears the L,	Pr 31:30	3068
of fire, The *very* flame of the L.	SS 8:6	3050
For the L speaks,	Is 1:2	3068
They have abandoned the L,	Is 1:4	3068
Unless the L of hosts Had left us	Is 1:9	3068
Hear the word of the L,	Is 1:10	3068
Says the L. "I have had enough of	Is 1:11	3068
us reason together," Says the L,	Is 1:18	3068
the mouth of the L has spoken.	Is 1:20	3068
Therefore the L GOD of hosts, The	Is 1:24	136
those who forsake the L will come	Is 1:28	3068
house of the L Will be established	Is 2:2	3068
us go up to the mountain of the L,	Is 2:3	3068
the word of the L from Jerusalem.	Is 2:3	3068
let us walk in the light of the L.	Is 2:5	3068
From the terror of the L and from	Is 2:10	3068
And the L alone will be exalted in	Is 2:11	3068
For the L of hosts will have a day	Is 2:12	3068
And the L alone will be exalted in	Is 2:17	3068
ground Before the terror of the L And	Is 2:19	3068
Before the terror of the L and the	Is 2:21	3068
the L GOD of hosts is going to	Is 3:1	136
their actions are against the L,	Is 3:8	3068
The L arises to contend, And	Is 3:13	3068
The L enters into judgment with	Is 3:14	3068
Declares the L GOD of hosts.	Is 3:15	136
Moreover, the L said,	Is 3:16	3068
Therefore the L will afflict the scalp	Is 3:17	136
the L will make their foreheads bare	Is 3:17	3068
In that day the L will take away	Is 3:18	136
In that day the Branch of the L	Is 4:2	3068
When the L has washed away the	Is 4:4	136
then the L will create over the	Is 4:5	3068
For the vineyard of the L of hosts	Is 5:7	3068
my ears the L of hosts *has sworn,*	Is 5:9	3068
attention to the deeds of the L,	Is 5:12	3068
But the L of hosts will be exalted	Is 5:16	3068
the law of the L of hosts And	Is 5:24	3068
anger of the L has burned against	Is 5:25	3068
I saw the L sitting on a throne,	Is 6:1	136
Holy, Holy, is the L of hosts,	Is 6:3	3068
seen the King, the L of hosts."	Is 6:5	3068
Then I heard the voice of the L,	Is 6:8	136
Then I said, "L, how long?"	Is 6:11	136
"The L has removed men far away,	Is 6:12	3068
Then the L said to Isaiah,	Is 7:3	3068
thus says the L GOD:	Is 7:7	136
Then the L spoke again to Ahaz,	Is 7:10	3068
for yourself from the L your God;	Is 7:11	3068
not ask, nor will I test the L!"	Is 7:12	3068
L Himself will give you a sign:	Is 7:14	136
"The L will bring on you, on your	Is 7:17	3068
that day the L will whistle for the	Is 7:18	3068
day the L will shave with a razor,	Is 7:20	136
Then the L said to me,	Is 8:1	3068
Then the L said to me,	Is 8:3	3068
Again the L spoke to me further,	Is 8:5	3068
the L is about to bring on them	Is 8:7	136
For thus the L spoke to me with	Is 8:11	3068
"It is the L of hosts whom you	Is 8:13	3068
And I will wait for the L who is	Is 8:17	3068
I and the children whom the L has	Is 8:18	3068
in Israel from the L of hosts,	Is 8:18	3068
The zeal of the L of hosts will	Is 9:7	3068
L sends a message against Jacob,	Is 9:8	136
Therefore the L raises against	Is 9:11	3068
Nor do they seek the L of hosts.	Is 9:13	3068
So the L cuts off head and tail	Is 9:14	3068
Therefore the L does not take	Is 9:17	136
By the fury of the L of hosts the	Is 9:19	3068
the L has completed all His work on	Is 10:12	136
Therefore the L, the GOD of hosts,	Is 10:16	136
but will truly rely on the L,	Is 10:20	3068
the L GOD of hosts will execute in	Is 10:23	136
thus says the L GOD of hosts,	Is 10:24	136
The L of hosts will arouse a	Is 10:26	3068
Behold, the L, the GOD of hosts,	Is 10:33	113
Spirit of the L will rest on Him,	Is 11:2	3068
knowledge and the fear of the L.	Is 11:2	3068
will delight in the fear of the L,	Is 11:3	3068
be full of the knowledge of the L	Is 11:9	3068
L Will again recover the second time	Is 11:11	136
And the L will utterly destroy The	Is 11:15	3068
"I will give thanks to You, O L;	Is 12:1	3068
the L GOD is my strength and song,	Is 12:2	3050
"Give thanks to the L,	Is 12:4	3068
Praise the L in song, For He has	Is 12:5	3068
The L of hosts is mustering the	Is 13:4	3068
The L and His instruments of	Is 13:5	3068
for the day of the L is near!	Is 13:6	3068
the day of the L is coming,	Is 13:9	3068
At the fury of the L of hosts	Is 13:13	3068
L will have compassion on Jacob and	Is 14:1	3068
an inheritance in the land of the L	Is 14:2	3068
in the day when the L gives you rest	Is 14:3	3068
"The L has broken the staff of	Is 14:5	3068
them," declares the L of hosts,	Is 14:22	3068
and posterity," declares the L.	Is 14:22	3068
declares the L of hosts.	Is 14:23	3068
The L of hosts has sworn saying,	Is 14:24	3068
"For the L of hosts has planned,	Is 14:27	3068
That the L has founded Zion, And	Is 14:32	3068
L spoke earlier concerning Moab.	Is 16:13	3068
But now the L speaks, saying,	Is 16:14	3068
Israel," Declares the L of hosts.	Is 17:3	3068
a fruitful tree, Declares the L,	Is 17:6	3068
For thus the L has told me,	Is 18:4	3068
of homage will be brought to the L	Is 18:7	3068
of the name of the L of hosts,	Is 18:7	3068
the L is riding on a swift cloud and	Is 19:1	3068
them," declares the L GOD of hosts.	Is 19:4	136
let them understand what the L	Is 19:12	3068
The L has mixed within her a	Is 19:14	3068
of the hand of the L of hosts,	Is 19:16	3068
because of the purpose of the L of	Is 19:17	3068
allegiance to the L of hosts;	Is 19:18	3068
there will be an altar to the L in the	Is 19:19	3068
a pillar to the L near its border.	Is 19:19	3068
sign and a witness to the L of hosts	Is 19:20	3068
cry to the L because of oppressors,	Is 19:20	3068
Thus the L will make Himself known	Is 19:21	3068
will know the L in that day.	Is 19:21	3068
a vow to the L and perform it.	Is 19:21	3068
The L will strike Egypt,	Is 19:22	3068
so they will return to the L,	Is 19:22	3068
whom the L of hosts has blessed,	Is 19:25	3068
at that time the L spoke through	Is 20:2	3068
L said, "Even as My servant Isaiah	Is 20:3	3068
For thus the L says to me,	Is 21:6	136
"O L, I stand continually by day	Is 21:8	136
I have heard from the L of hosts,	Is 21:10	3068
For thus the L said to me,	Is 21:16	136
the L God of Israel has spoken."	Is 21:17	3068
For the L GOD of hosts has a day	Is 22:5	136
in that day the L GOD of hosts called	Is 22:12	136
But the L of hosts revealed	Is 22:14	3068
you die," says the L GOD of hosts.	Is 22:14	136
Thus says the L GOD of hosts,	Is 22:15	136
L is about to hurl you headlong,	Is 22:17	3068
that day," declares the L of hosts,	Is 22:25	3068
cut off, for the L has spoken."	Is 22:25	3068
The L of hosts has planned it,	Is 23:9	3068
The L has given a command	Is 23:11	3068
years that the L will visit Tyre.	Is 23:17	3068
wages will be set apart to the L;	Is 23:18	3068
dwell in the presence of the L.	Is 23:18	3068
the L lays the earth waste,	Is 24:1	3068
for the L has spoken this word.	Is 24:3	3068
concerning the majesty of the L.	Is 24:14	3068
glorify the L in the east,	Is 24:15	3068
in the east, The name of the L,	Is 24:15	3068
That the L will punish the host of	Is 24:21	3068
For the L of hosts will reign on	Is 24:23	3068
O L, You are my God;	Is 25:1	3068
The L of hosts will prepare a	Is 25:6	3068
And the L GOD will wipe tears away	Is 25:8	136
For the L has spoken.	Is 25:8	3068
is the L for whom we have waited;	Is 25:9	3068
the hand of the L will rest on this	Is 25:10	3068
But *the* L will lay low his pride	Is 25:11	
"Trust in the L forever, For in	Is 26:4	3068
For in GOD the L, *we have* an	Is 26:4	3068
the way of Your judgments, O L,	Is 26:8	3068
not perceive the majesty of the L.	Is 26:10	3068
O L, Your hand is lifted up *yet*	Is 26:11	3068
L, You will establish peace for	Is 26:12	3068
O L our God, other masters besides	Is 26:13	3068
have increased the nation, O L,	Is 26:15	3068
O L, they sought You in distress;	Is 26:16	3068
Thus were we before You, O L.	Is 26:17	3068
the L is about to come out from	Is 26:21	3068
the L will punish Leviathan the	Is 27:1	3068
"I, the L, am its keeper;	Is 27:3	3068
that day the L will start *His*	Is 27:12	3068
Egypt will come and worship the L	Is 27:13	3068
L has a strong and mighty *agent;*	Is 28:2	136
In that day the L of hosts will	Is 28:5	3068
the word of the L to them will be,	Is 28:13	3068
Therefore, hear the word of the L,	Is 28:14	3068
Therefore thus says the L GOD,	Is 28:16	136
For the L will rise up as *at* Mount	Is 28:21	3068
heard from the L GOD of hosts Of	Is 28:22	136
also comes from the L of hosts,	Is 28:29	3068
From the L of hosts you will be	Is 29:6	3068
For the L has poured over you a	Is 29:10	3068
Then the L said,	Is 29:13	136
hide their plans from the L,	Is 29:15	3068
increase their gladness in the L,	Is 29:19	3068
Therefore thus says the L,	Is 29:22	3068
children," declares the L,	Is 30:1	3068
To the instruction of the L;	Is 30:9	3068
For thus the L GOD, the Holy One	Is 30:15	136
the L longs to be gracious to you,	Is 30:18	3068
For the L is a God of justice;	Is 30:18	3068
Although the L has given you bread	Is 30:20	136
on the day the L binds up the	Is 30:26	3068
the L comes from a remote place;	Is 30:27	3068
To go to the mountain of the L,	Is 30:29	3068
And the L will cause His voice of	Is 30:30	3068
at the voice of the L Assyria will be	Is 30:31	3068
Which the L will lay on him,	Is 30:32	3068
The breath of the L,	Is 30:33	3068
One of Israel, nor seek the L!	Is 31:1	3068
the L will stretch out His hand,	Is 31:3	3068
For thus says the L to me,	Is 31:4	3068
So will the L of hosts come down	Is 31:4	3068
the L of hosts will protect Jerusalem	Is 31:5	3068
at the standard," Declares the L,	Is 31:9	3068
and to speak error against the L,	Is 32:6	3068
O L, be gracious to us;	Is 33:2	3068
The L is exalted, for He dwells on	Is 33:5	3068
The fear of the L is his treasure.	Is 33:6	3068
"Now I will arise," says the L,	Is 33:10	3068
But there the majestic *One,* the L,	Is 33:21	3068
For the L is our judge, The LORD	Is 33:22	3068
our judge, The L is our lawgiver,	Is 33:22	3068
our lawgiver, The L is our king;	Is 33:22	3068
sword of the L is filled with blood	Is 34:6	3068
the L has a sacrifice in Bozrah And	Is 34:6	3068
For the L has a day of vengeance,	Is 34:8	3068
Seek from the book of the L,	Is 34:16	3068
They will see the glory of the L,	Is 35:2	3068
the ransomed of the L will return And	Is 35:10	3068
'We trust in the L our God,' is it	Is 36:7	3068
The L said to me,	Is 36:10	3068
Hezekiah make you trust in the L,	Is 36:15	3068
"The L will surely deliver us,	Is 36:15	3068
"The L will deliver us."	Is 36:18	3068
that the L would deliver	Is 36:20	3068
and entered the house of the L.	Is 37:1	3068
'Perhaps the L your God will hear	Is 37:4	3068
which the L your God has heard.	Is 37:4	3068
'Thus says the L,	Is 37:6	3068
he went up to the house of the L	Is 37:14	3068
and spread it out before the L.	Is 37:14	3068
Hezekiah prayed to the L saying,	Is 37:15	3068
"O L of hosts, the God of Israel,	Is 37:16	3068
"Incline Your ear, O L,	Is 37:17	3068
open Your eyes, O L,	Is 37:17	3068
"Truly, O L, the kings of Assyria	Is 37:18	3068
"Now, O L our God, deliver us	Is 37:20	3068
know that You alone, L, are God."	Is 37:20	3068
"Thus says the L, the God of	Is 37:21	3068
that the L has spoken against him:	Is 37:22	3068
you have reproached the L,	Is 37:24	136
zeal of the L of hosts will perform	Is 37:32	3068
thus says the L concerning the	Is 37:33	3068
come to this city,' declares the L.	Is 37:34	3068
Then the angel of the L went out and	Is 37:36	3068
"Thus says the L,	Is 38:1	3068
to the wall and prayed to the L,	Is 38:2	3068
"Remember now, O L, I beseech	Is 38:3	3068
the word of the L came to Isaiah,	Is 38:4	3068
'Thus says the L, the God of your	Is 38:5	3068
be the sign to you from the L,	Is 38:7	3068
that the L will do this thing that	Is 38:7	3068
"I will not see the L,	Is 38:11	3050
The L in the land of the living;	Is 38:11	3050
O L, I am oppressed, be my	Is 38:14	3068
"O L, by *these* things *men* live,	Is 38:16	136
"The L will surely save me;	Is 38:20	3068
our life at the house of the L."	Is 38:20	3068
go up to the house of the L?"	Is 38:22	3068
"Hear the word of the L of hosts,	Is 39:5	3068
nothing will be left,' says the L.	Is 39:6	3068
"The word of the L which you have	Is 39:8	3068
"Clear the way for the L in the	Is 40:3	3068
glory of the L will be revealed,	Is 40:5	3068
the mouth of the L has spoken."	Is 40:5	3068
the breath of the L blows upon it;	Is 40:7	3068
the L GOD will come with might,	Is 40:10	136
has directed the Spirit of the L,	Is 40:13	3068
"My way is hidden from the L,	Is 40:27	3068
The Everlasting God, the L,	Is 40:28	3068
for the L Will gain new strength;	Is 40:31	3068
'I, the L, am the first, and with	Is 41:4	3068
"For I am the L your God, who	Is 41:13	3068
I will help you," declares the L,	Is 41:14	3068
But you will rejoice in the L,	Is 41:16	3068
I, the L, will answer them Myself,	Is 41:17	3068
the hand of the L has done this,	Is 41:20	3068
"Present your case," the L says.	Is 41:21	3068
Thus says God the L,	Is 42:5	3068
"I am the L, I have called you in	Is 42:6	3068
"I am the L, that is My name;	Is 42:8	3068
Sing to the L a new song, *Sing* His	Is 42:10	3068
Let them give glory to the L And	Is 42:12	3068
L will go forth like a warrior,	Is 42:13	3068

so blind as the servant of the **L**?	**Is 42:19**	3068
The **L** was pleased for His	**Is 42:21**	3068
Was it not the **L**, against whom we	**Is 42:24**	3068
But now, thus says the **L**,	**Is 43:1**	3068
"For I am the **L** your God, The	**Is 43:3**	3068
are My witnesses," declares the **L**,	**Is 43:10**	3068
"I, even I, am the **L**,	**Is 43:11**	3068
are My witnesses," declares the **L**,	**Is 43:12**	3068
Thus says the **L** your Redeemer, the	**Is 43:14**	3068
"I am the **L**, your Holy One, The	**Is 43:15**	3068
Thus says the **L**, Who makes a way	**Is 43:16**	3068
Thus says the **L** who made you And	**Is 44:2**	3068
'Belonging to the **L**,'	**Is 44:5**	3068
"Thus says the **L**, the King of	**Is 44:6**	3068
And his Redeemer, the **L** of hosts:	**Is 44:6**	3068
O heavens, for the **L** has done *it!*	**Is 44:23**	3068
For the **L** has redeemed Jacob And	**Is 44:23**	3068
Thus says the **L**, your Redeemer,	**Is 44:24**	3068
"I, the **L**, am the maker of all	**Is 44:24**	3068
says the **L** to Cyrus His anointed,	**Is 45:1**	3068
you may know that it is I, The **L**,	**Is 45:3**	3068
"I am the **L**, and there is no other;	**Is 45:5**	3068
I am the **L**, and there is no other,	**Is 45:6**	3068
I am the **L** who does all these.	**Is 45:7**	3068
I, the **L**, have created it.	**Is 45:8**	3068
Thus says the **L**, the Holy One of	**Is 45:11**	3068
or reward," says the **L** of hosts.	**Is 45:13**	3068
Thus says the **L**,	**Is 45:14**	3068
Israel has been saved by the **L**	**Is 45:17**	3068
For thus says the **L**,	**Is 45:18**	3068
"I am the **L**, and there is none	**Is 45:18**	3068
I, the **L**, speak righteousness	**Is 45:19**	3068
Is it not I, the **L**?	**Is 45:21**	3068
'Only in the **L** are righteousness	**Is 45:24**	3068
"In the **L** all the offspring of	**Is 45:25**	3068
the **L** of hosts is His name,	**Is 47:4**	3068
Who swear by the name of the **L**	**Is 48:1**	3068
The **L** of hosts is His name.	**Is 48:2**	3068
The **L** loves him; he will carry out	**Is 48:14**	3068
And now the **L** GOD has sent Me, and	**Is 48:16**	136
Thus says the **L**, your Redeemer,	**Is 48:17**	3068
"I am the **L** your God, who teaches	**Is 48:17**	3068
"The **L** has redeemed His servant	**Is 48:20**	3068
peace for the wicked," says the **L**.	**Is 48:22**	3068
The **L** called Me from the womb;	**Is 49:1**	3068
justice *due* to Me is with the **L**,	**Is 49:4**	3068
And now says the **L**,	**Is 49:5**	3068
am honored in the sight of the **L**,	**Is 49:5**	3068
Thus says the **L**, the Redeemer of	**Is 49:7**	3068
Because of the **L** who is faithful,	**Is 49:7**	3068
Thus says the **L**,	**Is 49:8**	3068
the **L** has comforted His people And	**Is 49:13**	3068
"The **L** has forsaken me, And the	**Is 49:14**	3068
me, And the **L** has forgotten me."	**Is 49:14**	136
As I live," declares the **L**,	**Is 49:18**	3068
Thus says the **L** GOD,	**Is 49:22**	136
And *you* will know that I am the **L**;	**Is 49:23**	3068
Surely, thus says the **L**,	**Is 49:25**	3068
know that I, the **L**, am your Savior And	**Is 49:26**	3068
Thus says the **L**,	**Is 50:1**	3068
The **L** GOD has given Me the tongue	**Is 50:4**	136
The **L** GOD has opened My ear;	**Is 50:5**	136
For the **L** GOD helps Me, Therefore,	**Is 50:7**	136
Behold, the **L** GOD helps Me;	**Is 50:9**	136
Who is among you that fears the **L**,	**Is 50:10**	3068
Let him trust in the name of the **L**	**Is 50:10**	3068
righteousness, Who seek the **L**:	**Is 51:1**	3068
Indeed, the **L** will comfort Zion;	**Is 51:3**	3068
desert like the garden of the **L**;	**Is 51:3**	3068
put on strength, O arm of the **L**;	**Is 51:9**	3068
the ransomed of the **L** will return And	**Is 51:11**	3068
have forgotten the **L** your Maker,	**Is 51:13**	3068
"For I am the **L** your God, who	**Is 51:15**	3068
(the **L** of hosts is His name).	**Is 51:15**	3068
a net, Full of the wrath of the **L**,	**Is 51:20**	3068
Thus says your **L**, the LORD, even	**Is 51:22**	136
Thus says your Lord, the **L**,	**Is 51:22**	3068
For thus says the **L**,	**Is 52:3**	3068
For thus says the **L** GOD,	**Is 52:4**	136
do I have here," declares the **L**,	**Is 52:5**	3068
Again the **L** declares,	**Is 52:5**	3068
own eyes When the **L** restores Zion.	**Is 52:8**	3068
the **L** has comforted His people,	**Is 52:9**	3068
The **L** has bared His holy arm In	**Is 52:10**	3068
who carry the vessels of the **L**.	**Is 52:11**	3068
For the **L** will go before you, And	**Is 52:12**	3068
the arm of the **L** been revealed?	**Is 53:1**	3068
But the **L** has caused the iniquity	**Is 53:6**	3068
the **L** was pleased To crush Him,	**Is 53:10**	3068
good pleasure of the **L** will prosper	**Is 53:10**	3068
of the married woman," says the **L**.	**Is 54:1**	3068
Whose name is the **L** of hosts;	**Is 54:5**	3068
"For the **L** has called you, Like a	**Is 54:6**	3068
on you," Says the **L** your Redeemer.	**Is 54:8**	3068
the **L** who has compassion on you.	**Is 54:10**	3068
your sons will be taught of the **L**;	**Is 54:13**	3068
heritage of the servants of the **L**,	**Is 54:17**	3068
is from Me," declares the **L**.	**Is 54:17**	3068
to you, Because of the **L** your God,	**Is 55:5**	3068
Seek the **L** while He may be found;	**Is 55:6**	3068
And let him return to the **L**,	**Is 55:7**	3068
your ways My ways," declares the **L**.	**Is 55:8**	3068
it will be a memorial to the **L**,	**Is 55:13**	3068
Thus says the **L**,	**Is 56:1**	3068
has joined himself to the **L** say,	**Is 56:3**	3068
"The **L** will surely separate me	**Is 56:3**	3068
For thus says the **L**,	**Is 56:4**	3068
who join themselves to the **L**,	**Is 56:6**	3068
and to love the name of the **L**,	**Is 56:6**	3068
The **L** GOD, who gathers the	**Is 56:8**	136
to him who is near," Says the **L**,	**Is 57:19**	3068
even an acceptable day to the **L**?	**Is 58:5**	3068
of the **L** will be your rear guard.	**Is 58:8**	3068
will call, and the **L** will answer;	**Is 58:9**	3068
the **L** will continually guide you,	**Is 58:11**	3068
the holy *day* of the **L** honorable,	**Is 58:13**	3068
you will take delight in the **L**,	**Is 58:14**	3068
the mouth of the **L** has spoken."	**Is 58:14**	3068
Transgressing and denying the **L**,	**Is 59:13**	3068
Now the **L** saw, And it was	**Is 59:15**	3068
So they will fear the name of the **L**	**Is 59:19**	3068
Which the wind of the **L** drives.	**Is 59:19**	3068
in Jacob," declares the **L**.	**Is 59:20**	3068
My covenant with them," says the **L**:	**Is 59:21**	3068
offspring's offspring," says the **L**,	**Is 59:21**	3068
glory of the **L** has risen upon you.	**Is 60:1**	3068
But the **L** will rise upon you And	**Is 60:2**	3068
good news of the praises of the **L**.	**Is 60:6**	3068
For the name of the **L** your God,	**Is 60:9**	3068
will call you the city of the **L**,	**Is 60:14**	3068
know that I, the **L**, am your Savior And	**Is 60:16**	3068
have the **L** for an everlasting light,	**Is 60:19**	3068
have the **L** for an everlasting light,	**Is 60:20**	3068
I, the **L**, will hasten it in its	**Is 60:22**	3068
Spirit of the **L** GOD is upon me,	**Is 61:1**	136
Because the **L** has anointed me To	**Is 61:1**	3068
the favorable year of the **L** And	**Is 61:2**	3068
The planting of the **L**,	**Is 61:3**	3068
be called the priests of the **L**;	**Is 61:6**	3068
For I, the **L**, love justice, I hate	**Is 61:8**	3068
offspring *whom* the **L** has blessed.	**Is 61:9**	3068
I will rejoice greatly in the **L**,	**Is 61:10**	3068
So the **L** GOD will cause	**Is 61:11**	136
the mouth of the **L** will designate.	**Is 62:2**	3068
of beauty in the hand of the **L**,	**Is 62:3**	3068
For the **L** delights in you, And *to*	**Is 62:4**	3068
You who remind the **L**,	**Is 62:6**	3068
The **L** has sworn by His right hand	**Is 62:8**	3068
it will eat it and praise the **L**;	**Is 62:9**	3068
the **L** has proclaimed to the end of	**Is 62:11**	3068
people, The redeemed of the **L**";	**Is 62:12**	3068
of the lovingkindnesses of the **L**,	**Is 63:7**	3068
of the LORD, the praises of the **L**,	**Is 63:7**	3068
to all that the **L** has granted us,	**Is 63:7**	3068
Spirit of the **L** gave them rest.	**Is 63:14**	3068
You, O **L**, are our Father, Our	**Is 63:16**	3068
Why, O **L**, do You cause us to	**Is 63:17**	3068
But now, O **L**, You are our Father,	**Is 64:8**	3068
not be angry beyond measure, O **L**,	**Is 64:9**	3068
restrain Yourself at these things, O **L**?	**Is 64:12**	3068
fathers together," says the **L**.	**Is 65:7**	3068
Thus says the **L**,	**Is 65:8**	3068
"But you who forsake the **L**,	**Is 65:11**	3068
Therefore, thus says the **L** GOD,	**Is 65:13**	136
ones, And the **L** GOD will slay you.	**Is 65:15**	136
of those blessed by the **L**,	**Is 65:23**	3068
all My holy mountain," says the **L**.	**Is 65:25**	3068
Thus says the **L**,	**Is 66:1**	3068
came into being," declares the **L**.	**Is 66:2**	3068
Hear the word of the **L**,	**Is 66:5**	3068
'Let the **L** be glorified, that we	**Is 66:5**	3068
The voice of the **L** who is	**Is 66:6**	3068
and not give delivery?" says the **L**.	**Is 66:9**	3068
For thus says the **L**,	**Is 66:12**	3068
And the hand of the **L** will be	**Is 66:14**	3068
the **L** will come in fire And His	**Is 66:15**	3068
For the **L** will execute judgment by	**Is 66:16**	3068
those slain by the **L** will be many.	**Is 66:16**	3068
an end altogether," declares the **L**.	**Is 66:17**	3068
as a grain offering to the **L**,	**Is 66:20**	3068
mountain Jerusalem," says the **L**,	**Is 66:20**	3068
vessel to the house of the **L**.	**Is 66:20**	3068
and for Levites," says the **L**.	**Is 66:21**	3068
endure before Me," declares the **L**,	**Is 66:22**	3068
to bow down before Me," says the **L**.	**Is 66:23**	3068
to whom the word of the **L** came in	**Jer 1:2**	3068
word of the **L** came to me saying,	**Jer 1:4**	3068
Then I said, "Alas, **L** GOD! Behold,	**Jer 1:6**	136
But the **L** said to me,	**Jer 1:7**	3068
to deliver you," declares the **L**.	**Jer 1:8**	3068
Then the **L** stretched out His hand	**Jer 1:9**	3068
my mouth, and the **L** said to me,	**Jer 1:9**	3068
word of the **L** came to me saying,	**Jer 1:11**	3068
Then the **L** said to me,	**Jer 1:12**	3068
The word of the **L** came to me a	**Jer 1:13**	3068
Then the **L** said to me,	**Jer 1:14**	3068
of the north," declares the **L**;	**Jer 1:15**	3068
to deliver you," declares the **L**.	**Jer 1:19**	3068
word of the **L** came to me saying,	**Jer 2:1**	3068
'Thus says the **L**,	**Jer 2:2**	3068
"Israel was holy to the **L**,	**Jer 2:3**	3068
upon them," declares the **L**.' "	**Jer 2:3**	3068
Hear the word of the **L**,	**Jer 2:4**	3068
Thus says the **L**,	**Jer 2:5**	3068
'Where is the **L** Who brought us up	**Jer 2:6**	3068
priests did not say, 'Where is the **L**?'	**Jer 2:8**	3068
contend with you," declares the **L**,	**Jer 2:9**	3068
be very desolate," declares the **L**.	**Jer 2:12**	3068
By your forsaking the **L** your God	**Jer 2:17**	3068
For you to forsake the **L** your God,	**Jer 2:19**	3068
you," declares the **L** GOD of hosts.	**Jer 2:19**	136
is before Me," declares the **L** GOD.	**Jer 2:22**	136
against Me," declares the **L**.	**Jer 2:29**	3068
heed the word of the **L**.	**Jer 2:31**	3068
For the **L** has rejected those in	**Jer 2:37**	3068
you turn to Me," declares the **L**.	**Jer 3:1**	3068
Then the **L** said to me in the days	**Jer 3:6**	3068
in deception," declares the **L**.	**Jer 3:10**	3068
And the **L** said to me,	**Jer 3:11**	3068
faithless Israel,' declares the **L**;	**Jer 3:12**	3068
For I am gracious,' declares the **L**;	**Jer 3:12**	3068
you have transgressed against the **L**	**Jer 3:13**	3068
obeyed My voice,' declares the **L**.	**Jer 3:13**	3068
O faithless sons,' declares the **L**;	**Jer 3:14**	3068
in the land," declares the **L**,	**Jer 3:16**	3068
'The ark of the covenant of the **L**.'	**Jer 3:16**	3068
'The Throne of the **L**,'	**Jer 3:17**	3068
Jerusalem, for the name of the **L**;	**Jer 3:17**	3068
O house of Israel," declares the **L**.	**Jer 3:20**	3068
have forgotten the **L** their God.	**Jer 3:21**	3068
For You are the **L** our God.	**Jer 3:22**	3068
in the **L** our God Is the salvation	**Jer 3:23**	3068
have sinned against the **L** our God,	**Jer 3:25**	3068
the voice of the **L** our God."	**Jer 3:25**	3068
return, O Israel," declares the **L**,	**Jer 4:1**	3068
'As the **L** lives,' In truth, in	**Jer 4:2**	3068
For thus says the **L** to the men of	**Jer 4:3**	3068
"Circumcise yourselves to the **L**	**Jer 4:4**	3068
fierce anger of the **L** Has not turned	**Jer 4:8**	3068
about in that day," declares the **L**,	**Jer 4:9**	3068
Then I said, "Ah, **L** GOD!	**Jer 4:10**	136
against Me,' declares the **L**.	**Jer 4:17**	3068
were pulled down Before the **L**,	**Jer 4:26**	3068
For thus says the **L**,	**Jer 4:27**	3068
'As the **L** lives,' Surely they	**Jer 5:2**	3068
O **L**, do not Your eyes *look* for	**Jer 5:3**	3068
they do not know the way of the **L**	**Jer 5:4**	3068
For they know the way of the **L**	**Jer 5:5**	3068
these *people*," declares the **L**,	**Jer 5:9**	3068
with Me," declares the **L**.	**Jer 5:11**	3068
have lied about the **L** And said,	**Jer 5:12**	3068
Therefore, thus says the **L**,	**Jer 5:14**	3068
O house of Israel," declares the **L**.	**Jer 5:15**	3068
in those days," declares the **L**,	**Jer 5:18**	3068
'Why has the **L** our God done all	**Jer 5:19**	3068
'Do you not fear Me?' declares the **L**.	**Jer 5:22**	3068
"Let us now fear the **L** our God,	**Jer 5:24**	3068
punish these *people?*' declares the **L**,	**Jer 5:29**	3068
For thus says the **L** of hosts,	**Jer 6:6**	3068
Thus says the **L** of hosts,	**Jer 6:9**	3068
the word of the **L** has become a	**Jer 6:10**	3068
I am full of the wrath of the **L**;	**Jer 6:11**	3068
of the land," declares the **L**.	**Jer 6:12**	3068
shall be cast down," says the **L**.	**Jer 6:15**	3068
Thus says the **L**,	**Jer 6:16**	3068
Therefore, thus says the **L**,	**Jer 6:21**	3068
Thus says the **L**,	**Jer 6:22**	3068
Because the **L** has rejected them.	**Jer 6:30**	3068
that came to Jeremiah from the **L**,	**Jer 7:1**	3068
'Hear the word of the **L**,	**Jer 7:2**	3068
these gates to worship the **L**!' "	**Jer 7:2**	3068
Thus says the **L** of hosts, the God	**Jer 7:3**	3068
'This is the temple of the **L**,	**Jer 7:4**	3068
of the LORD, the temple of the **L**,	**Jer 7:4**	3068
of the LORD, the temple of the **L**.'	**Jer 7:4**	3068
I, have seen *it*," declares the **L**.	**Jer 7:11**	3068
all these things," declares the **L**,	**Jer 7:13**	3068
"Do they spite Me?" declares the **L**.	**Jer 7:19**	3068
Therefore thus says the **L** GOD,	**Jer 7:20**	136
Thus says the **L** of hosts, the God	**Jer 7:21**	3068
that did not obey the voice of the **L**	**Jer 7:28**	3068
For the **L** has rejected and	**Jer 7:29**	3068
evil in My sight," declares the **L**,	**Jer 7:30**	3068
days are coming," declares the **L**,	**Jer 7:32**	3068
"At that time," declares the **L**,	**Jer 8:1**	3068
them," declares the **L** of hosts.	**Jer 8:3**	3068
'Thus says the **L**,	**Jer 8:4**	3068
not know The ordinance of the **L**.	**Jer 8:7**	3068
And the law of the **L** is with us'?	**Jer 8:8**	3068
have rejected the word of the **L**,	**Jer 8:9**	3068
be brought down," Says the **L**.	**Jer 8:12**	3068
snatch them away," declares the **L**;	**Jer 8:13**	3068
Because the **L** our God has doomed	**Jer 8:14**	3068
For we have sinned against the **L**.	**Jer 8:14**	3068
will bite you," declares the **L**.	**Jer 8:17**	3068
"Is the **L** not in Zion?	**Jer 8:19**	3068
do not know Me," declares the **L**.	**Jer 9:3**	3068
refuse to know Me," declares the **L**.	**Jer 9:6**	3068
thus says the **L** of hosts,	**Jer 9:7**	3068
for these things?" declares the **L**.	**Jer 9:9**	3068
the mouth of the **L** has spoken,	**Jer 9:12**	3068
L said, "Because they have forsaken	**Jer 9:13**	3068
thus says the **L** of hosts,	**Jer 9:15**	3068
Thus says the **L** of hosts,	**Jer 9:17**	3068
Now hear the word of the **L**,	**Jer 9:20**	3068
"Thus says the **L**,	**Jer 9:22**	3068
Thus says the **L**,	**Jer 9:23**	3068
L who exercises lovingkindness,	**Jer 9:24**	3068
in these things," declares the **L**.	**Jer 9:24**	3068
days are coming," declares the **L**,	**Jer 9:25**	3068
word which the **L** speaks to you,	**Jer 10:1**	3068
Thus says the **L**,	**Jer 10:2**	3068
There is none like You, O **L**;	**Jer 10:6**	3068
But the **L** is the true God;	**Jer 10:10**	3068
The **L** of hosts is His name.	**Jer 10:16**	3068
For thus says the **L**,	**Jer 10:18**	3068
stupid And have not sought the **L**;	**Jer 10:21**	3068
I know, O **L**, that a man's way is	**Jer 10:23**	3068
Correct me, O **L**, but with justice;	**Jer 10:24**	3068
which came to Jeremiah from the **L**,	**Jer 11:1**	3068
'Thus says the **L**, the God of	**Jer 11:3**	3068
I said, "Amen, O **L**."	**Jer 11:5**	3068
And the **L** said to me,	**Jer 11:6**	3068
Then the **L** said to me,	**Jer 11:9**	3068
Therefore thus says the **L**,	**Jer 11:11**	3068
The **L** called your name,	**Jer 11:16**	3068
The **L** of hosts, who planted	**Jer 11:17**	3068

the **L** made it known to me and I	**Jer 11:18**	3068
But, O **L** of hosts, who judges	**Jer 11:20**	3068
Therefore thus says the **L**	**Jer 11:21**	3068
not prophesy in the name of the **L**,	**Jer 11:21**	3068
thus says the **L** of hosts,	**Jer 11:22**	3068
Righteous are You, O **L**,	**Jer 12:1**	3068
But You know me, O **L**;	**Jer 12:3**	3068
For a sword of the **L** is devouring	**Jer 12:12**	3068
Because of the fierce anger of the **L**.	**Jer 12:13**	3068
Thus says the **L** concerning all My	**Jer 12:14**	3068
'As the **L** lives,' even as they	**Jer 12:16**	3068
and destroy it," declares the **L**.	**Jer 12:17**	3068
Thus the **L** said to me,	**Jer 13:1**	3068
the **L** and put it around my waist.	**Jer 13:2**	3068
of the **L** came to me a second time,	**Jer 13:3**	3068
as the **L** had commanded me.	**Jer 13:5**	3068
many days the **L** said to me,	**Jer 13:6**	3068
Then the word of the **L** came to me,	**Jer 13:8**	3068
"Thus says the **L**,	**Jer 13:9**	3068
Judah cling to Me,' declares the **L**,	**Jer 13:11**	3068
'Thus says the **L**, the God of	**Jer 13:12**	3068
'Thus says the **L**,	**Jer 13:13**	3068
the sons together," declares the **L**.	**Jer 13:14**	3068
be haughty, For the **L** has spoken.	**Jer 13:15**	3068
Give glory to the **L** your God,	**Jer 13:16**	3068
the flock of the **L** has been taken	**Jer 13:17**	3068
to you From Me," declares the **L**,	**Jer 13:25**	3068
as the word of the **L** to Jeremiah	**Jer 14:1**	3068
O **L**, act for Your name's sake!	**Jer 14:7**	3068
Yet You are in our midst, O **L**,	**Jer 14:9**	3068
Thus says the **L** to this people,	**Jer 14:10**	3068
the **L** does not accept them;	**Jer 14:10**	3068
So the **L** said to me,	**Jer 14:11**	3068
"Ah, **L** GOD!" I said, "Look,	**Jer 14:13**	136
Then the **L** said to me,	**Jer 14:14**	3068
"Therefore thus says the **L**	**Jer 14:15**	3068
We know our wickedness, O **L**,	**Jer 14:20**	3068
Is it not You, O **L** our God?	**Jer 14:22**	3068
Then the **L** said to me,	**Jer 15:1**	3068
'Thus says the **L**: "Those *destined* for	**Jer 15:2**	3068
kinds *of doom*," declares the **L**:	**Jer 15:3**	3068
have forsaken Me," declares the **L**,	**Jer 15:6**	3068
their enemies," declares the **L**.	**Jer 15:9**	3068
L said, "Surely I will set you free	**Jer 15:11**	3068
You who know, O **L**,	**Jer 15:15**	3068
by Your name, O **L** God of hosts.	**Jer 15:16**	3068
Therefore, thus says the **L**,	**Jer 15:19**	3068
And deliver you," declares the **L**.	**Jer 15:20**	3068
of the **L** also came to me saying,	**Jer 16:1**	3068
For thus says the **L** concerning the	**Jer 16:3**	3068
For thus says the **L**,	**Jer 16:5**	3068
from this people," declares the **L**,	**Jer 16:5**	3068
For thus says the **L** of hosts,	**Jer 16:9**	3068
'For what reason has the **L**	**Jer 16:10**	3068
committed against the **L** our God?'	**Jer 16:10**	3068
have forsaken Me,' declares the **L**,	**Jer 16:11**	3068
days are coming," declares the **L**,	**Jer 16:14**	3068
'As the **L** lives, who brought up	**Jer 16:14**	3068
'As the **L** lives, who brought up	**Jer 16:15**	3068
many fishermen," declares the **L**,	**Jer 16:16**	3068
O **L**, my strength and my	**Jer 16:19**	3068
know that My name is the **L**."	**Jer 16:21**	3068
Thus says the **L**,	**Jer 17:5**	3068
whose heart turns away from the **L**.	**Jer 17:5**	3068
the man who trusts in the **L** And	**Jer 17:7**	3068
the LORD And whose trust is the **L**.	**Jer 17:7**	3068
"I, the **L**, search the heart, I	**Jer 17:10**	3068
O **L**, the hope of Israel, All who	**Jer 17:13**	3068
fountain of living water, even the **L**.	**Jer 17:13**	3068
Heal me, O **L**, and I will be healed;	**Jer 17:14**	3068
"Where is the word of the **L**?	**Jer 17:15**	3068
Thus the **L** said to me,	**Jer 17:19**	3068
'Listen to the word of the **L**,	**Jer 17:20**	3068
'Thus says the **L**,	**Jer 17:21**	3068
attentively to Me," declares the **L**,	**Jer 17:24**	3068
to the house of the **L**.	**Jer 17:26**	3068
to Jeremiah from the **L** saying,	**Jer 18:1**	3068
word of the **L** came to me saying,	**Jer 18:5**	3068
as this potter *does?*" declares the **L**.	**Jer 18:6**	3068
'Thus says the **L**,	**Jer 18:11**	3068
"Therefore thus says the **L**,	**Jer 18:13**	3068
Do give heed to me, O **L**,	**Jer 18:19**	3068
Yet You, O **L**, know All their	**Jer 18:23**	3068
Thus says the **L**,	**Jer 19:1**	3068
'Hear the word of the **L**,	**Jer 19:3**	3068
thus says the **L** of hosts, the God	**Jer 19:3**	3068
days are coming," declares the **L**,	**Jer 19:6**	3068
'Thus says the **L** of hosts,	**Jer 19:11**	3068
its inhabitants," declares the **L**,	**Jer 19:12**	3068
the **L** had sent him to prophesy;	**Jer 19:14**	3068
"Thus says the **L** of hosts, the	**Jer 19:15**	3068
officer in the house of the **L**,	**Jer 20:1**	3068
which was by the house of the **L**.	**Jer 20:2**	3068
not the name the **L** has called you,	**Jer 20:3**	3068
"For thus says the **L**,	**Jer 20:4**	3068
O **L**, You have deceived me and I	**Jer 20:7**	3068
Because for me the word of the **L**	**Jer 20:8**	3068
But the **L** is with me like a dread	**Jer 20:11**	3068
Yet, O **L** of hosts, You who test	**Jer 20:12**	3068
Sing to the **L**, praise the LORD!	**Jer 20:13**	3068
Sing to the LORD, praise the **L**!	**Jer 20:13**	3068
the **L** overthrew without relenting,	**Jer 20:16**	3068
which came to Jeremiah from the **L**	**Jer 21:1**	3068
inquire of the **L** on our behalf,	**Jer 21:2**	3068
perhaps the **L** will deal with us	**Jer 21:2**	3068
'Thus says the **L** God of Israel,	**Jer 21:4**	3068
"Then afterwards," declares the **L**,	**Jer 21:7**	3068
'Thus says the **L**,	**Jer 21:8**	3068
and not for good," declares the **L**.	**Jer 21:10**	3068
'Hear the word of the **L**,	**Jer 21:11**	3068
O house of David, thus says the **L**:	**Jer 21:12**	3068
O rocky plain," declares the **L**,	**Jer 21:13**	3068
of your deeds," declares the **L**,	**Jer 21:14**	3068
Thus says the **L**,	**Jer 22:1**	3068
'Hear the word of the **L**,	**Jer 22:2**	3068
'Thus says the **L**,	**Jer 22:3**	3068
I swear by Myself," declares the **L**,	**Jer 22:5**	3068
For thus says the **L** concerning the	**Jer 22:6**	3068
L done thus to this great city?'	**Jer 22:8**	3068
they forsook the covenant of the **L**	**Jer 22:9**	3068
For thus says the **L** in regard to	**Jer 22:11**	3068
means to know Me?" Declares the **L**.	**Jer 22:16**	3068
Therefore thus says the **L** in	**Jer 22:18**	3068
"As I live," declares the **L**,	**Jer 22:24**	3068
land, Hear the word of the **L**!	**Jer 22:29**	3068
"Thus says the **L**,	**Jer 22:30**	3068
of My pasture!" declares the **L**.	**Jer 23:1**	3068
Therefore thus says the **L** God of	**Jer 23:2**	3068
of your deeds," declares the **L**.	**Jer 23:2**	3068
any be missing," declares the **L**.	**Jer 23:4**	3068
days are coming," declares the **L**,	**Jer 23:5**	3068
'The **L** our righteousness.'	**Jer 23:6**	3068
days are coming," declares the **L**,	**Jer 23:7**	3068
'As the **L** lives, who brought up	**Jer 23:7**	3068
'As the **L** lives, who brought up	**Jer 23:8**	3068
Because of the **L** And because of	**Jer 23:9**	3068
their wickedness," declares the **L**.	**Jer 23:11**	3068
their punishment," declares the **L**.	**Jer 23:12**	3068
"Therefore thus says the **L** of	**Jer 23:15**	3068
Thus says the **L** of hosts,	**Jer 23:16**	3068
Not from the mouth of the **L**.	**Jer 23:16**	3068
'The **L** has said,	**Jer 23:17**	3068
has stood in the council of the **L**,	**Jer 23:18**	3068
of the **L** has gone forth in wrath,	**Jer 23:19**	3068
"The anger of the **L** will not turn	**Jer 23:20**	3068
a God who is near," declares the **L**,	**Jer 23:23**	3068
I do not see him?" declares the **L**.	**Jer 23:24**	3068
and the earth?" declares the **L**.	**Jer 23:24**	3068
common with grain?" declares the **L**.	**Jer 23:28**	3068
My word like fire?" declares the **L**,	**Jer 23:29**	3068
the prophets," declares the **L**,	**Jer 23:30**	3068
the prophets," declares the **L**,	**Jer 23:31**	3068
tongues and declare, '*The* **L** declares.'	**Jer 23:31**	3068
false dreams," declares the **L**,	**Jer 23:32**	3068
slightest benefit," declares the **L**.	**Jer 23:32**	3068
'What is the oracle of the **L**?'	**Jer 23:33**	3068
L declares, 'I will abandon you.'	**Jer 23:33**	3068
'The oracle of the **L**,'	**Jer 23:34**	3068
'What has the **L** answered?'	**Jer 23:35**	3068
'What has the **L** spoken?'	**Jer 23:35**	3068
remember the oracle of the **L**,	**Jer 23:36**	3068
of the living God, the **L** of hosts,	**Jer 23:36**	3068
'What has the **L** answered you?'	**Jer 23:37**	3068
'What has the **L** spoken?'	**Jer 23:37**	3068
'The oracle of the **L**!'	**Jer 23:38**	3068
surely thus says the **L**,	**Jer 23:38**	3068
"The oracle of the **L**!"	**Jer 23:38**	3068
'The oracle of the **L**!	**Jer 23:38**	3068
them to Babylon, the **L** showed me:	**Jer 24:1**	3068
set before the temple of the **L**!	**Jer 24:1**	3068
Then the **L** said to me,	**Jer 24:3**	3068
Then the word of the **L** came to me,	**Jer 24:4**	3068
"Thus says the **L** God of Israel,	**Jer 24:5**	3068
heart to know Me, for I am the **L**;	**Jer 24:7**	3068
indeed, thus says the **L**	**Jer 24:8**	3068
the word of the **L** has come to me,	**Jer 25:3**	3068
"And the **L** has sent to you all	**Jer 25:4**	3068
dwell on the land which the **L** has	**Jer 25:5**	3068
listened to Me," declares the **L**,	**Jer 25:7**	3068
thus says the **L** of hosts,	**Jer 25:8**	3068
of the north,' declares the **L**,	**Jer 25:9**	3068
and that nation,' declares the **L**,	**Jer 25:12**	3068
For thus the **L**, the God of Israel,	**Jer 25:15**	3068
to whom the **L** sent me drink it:	**Jer 25:17**	3068
'Thus says the **L** of hosts, the God	**Jer 25:27**	3068
'Thus says the **L** of hosts:	**Jer 25:28**	3068
earth," declares the **L** of hosts.'	**Jer 25:29**	3068
'The **L** will roar from on high And	**Jer 25:30**	3068
Because the **L** has a controversy	**Jer 25:31**	3068
to the sword,' declares the **L**."	**Jer 25:31**	3068
Thus says the **L** of hosts,	**Jer 25:32**	3068
"Those slain by the **L** on that	**Jer 25:33**	3068
the **L** is destroying their pasture,	**Jer 25:36**	3068
of the fierce anger of the **L**.	**Jer 25:37**	3068
Judah, this word came from the **L**,	**Jer 26:1**	3068
"Thus says the **L**,	**Jer 26:2**	3068
'Thus says the **L**,	**Jer 26:4**	3068
these words in the house of the **L**.	**Jer 26:7**	3068
finished speaking all that the **L**	**Jer 26:8**	3068
in the name of the **L** saying,	**Jer 26:9**	3068
Jeremiah in the house of the **L**.	**Jer 26:9**	3068
king's house to the house of the **L**	**Jer 26:10**	3068
"The **L** sent me to prophesy	**Jer 26:12**	3068
obey the voice of the **L** your God;	**Jer 26:13**	3068
and the **L** will change His mind	**Jer 26:13**	3068
for truly the **L** has sent me to you	**Jer 26:15**	3068
us in the name of the **L** our God."	**Jer 26:16**	3068
'Thus the **L** of hosts has said,	**Jer 26:18**	3068
Did he not fear the **L** and entreat	**Jer 26:19**	3068
and entreat the favor of the **L**,	**Jer 26:19**	3068
and the **L** changed His mind about	**Jer 26:19**	3068
prophesied in the name of the **L**,	**Jer 26:20**	3068
word came to Jeremiah from the **L**,	**Jer 27:1**	3068
thus says the **L** to	**Jer 27:2**	3068
'Thus says the **L** of hosts, the God	**Jer 27:4**	3068
with pestilence," declares the **L**,	**Jer 27:8**	3068
on its land," declares the **L**,	**Jer 27:11**	3068
as the **L** has spoken to that nation	**Jer 27:13**	3068
not sent them," declares the **L**,	**Jer 27:15**	3068
"Thus says the **L**:	**Jer 27:16**	3068
if the word of the **L** is with them,	**Jer 27:18**	3068
them now entreat the **L** of hosts that	**Jer 27:18**	3068
are left in the house of the **L**,	**Jer 27:18**	3068
"For thus says the **L** of hosts	**Jer 27:19**	3068
"Yes, thus says the **L** of hosts,	**Jer 27:21**	3068
are left in the house of the **L** and	**Jer 27:21**	3068
day I visit them,' declares the **L**.	**Jer 27:22**	3068
spoke to me in the house of the **L**	**Jer 28:1**	3068
"Thus says the **L** of hosts, the	**Jer 28:2**	3068
went to Babylon,' declares the **L**,	**Jer 28:4**	3068
standing in the house of the **L**,	**Jer 28:5**	3068
May the **L** do so;	**Jer 28:6**	3068
may the **L** confirm your words which	**Jer 28:6**	3068
one whom the **L** has truly sent."	**Jer 28:9**	3068
"Thus says the **L**,	**Jer 28:11**	3068
word of the **L** came to Jeremiah after	**Jer 28:12**	3068
'Thus says the **L**,	**Jer 28:13**	3068
'For thus says the **L** of hosts,	**Jer 28:14**	3068
Hananiah, the **L** has not sent you,	**Jer 28:15**	3068
"Therefore thus says the **L**,	**Jer 28:16**	3068
rebellion against the **L**.' "	**Jer 28:16**	3068
"Thus says the **L** of hosts, the	**Jer 29:4**	3068
and pray to the **L** on its behalf;	**Jer 29:7**	3068
"For thus says the **L** of hosts,	**Jer 29:8**	3068
not sent them," declares the **L**.	**Jer 29:9**	3068
"For thus says the **L**,	**Jer 29:10**	3068
I have for you,' declares the **L**,	**Jer 29:11**	3068
be found by you,' declares the **L**,	**Jer 29:14**	3068
I have driven you,' declares the **L**,	**Jer 29:14**	3068
'The **L** has raised up prophets for	**Jer 29:15**	3068
for thus says the **L** concerning the	**Jer 29:16**	3068
thus says the **L** of hosts,	**Jer 29:17**	3068
to My words,' declares the **L**,	**Jer 29:19**	3068
did not listen,' declares the **L**.	**Jer 29:19**	3068
therefore, hear the word of the **L**,	**Jer 29:20**	3068
"Thus says the **L** of hosts, the	**Jer 29:21**	3068
"May the **L** make you like Zedekiah	**Jer 29:22**	3068
am a witness," declares the **L**.' "	**Jer 29:23**	3068
"Thus says the **L** of hosts, the	**Jer 29:25**	3068
"The **L** has made you priest	**Jer 29:26**	3068
be the overseer in the house of the **L**	**Jer 29:26**	3068
the word of the **L** to Jeremiah,	**Jer 29:30**	3068
'Thus says the **L** concerning	**Jer 29:31**	3068
therefore thus says the **L**,	**Jer 29:32**	3068
do to My people," declares the **L**,	**Jer 29:32**	3068
rebellion against the **L**." ' "	**Jer 29:32**	3068
which came to Jeremiah from the **L**,	**Jer 30:1**	3068
"Thus says the **L**, the God of	**Jer 30:2**	3068
days are coming,' declares the **L**,	**Jer 30:3**	3068
The **L** says, 'I will also bring them	**Jer 30:3**	3068
are the words which the **L** spoke	**Jer 30:4**	3068
"For thus says the **L**,	**Jer 30:5**	3068
that day,' declares the **L** of hosts,	**Jer 30:8**	3068
they shall serve the **L** their God and	**Jer 30:9**	3068
Jacob My servant,' declares the **L**,	**Jer 30:10**	3068
'For I am with you,' declares the **L**,	**Jer 30:11**	3068
"For thus says the **L**,	**Jer 30:12**	3068
of your wounds,' declares the **L**,	**Jer 30:17**	3068
"Thus says the **L**,	**Jer 30:18**	3068
to approach Me?' declares the **L**.	**Jer 30:21**	3068
Behold, the tempest of the **L**!	**Jer 30:23**	3068
anger of the **L** will not turn back Until	**Jer 30:24**	3068
"At that time," declares the **L**,	**Jer 31:1**	3068
Thus says the **L**,	**Jer 31:2**	3068
The **L** appeared to him from afar,	**Jer 31:3**	3068
up *to* Zion, To the **L** our God.' "	**Jer 31:6**	3068
For thus says the **L**,	**Jer 31:7**	3068
'O **L**, save Your people, The remnant	**Jer 31:7**	3068
Hear the word of the **L**,	**Jer 31:10**	3068
For the **L** has ransomed Jacob And	**Jer 31:11**	3068
be radiant over the bounty of the **L**	**Jer 31:12**	3068
with My goodness," declares the **L**.	**Jer 31:14**	3068
Thus says the **L**,	**Jer 31:15**	3068
Thus says the **L**,	**Jer 31:16**	3068
will be rewarded," declares the **L**,	**Jer 31:16**	3068
for your future," declares the **L**,	**Jer 31:17**	3068
For You are the **L** my God.	**Jer 31:18**	3068
have mercy on him," declares the **L**.	**Jer 31:20**	3068
For the **L** has created a new thing	**Jer 31:22**	3068
Thus says the **L** of hosts, the God	**Jer 31:23**	3068
'The **L** bless you, O abode of	**Jer 31:23**	3068
days are coming," declares the **L**,	**Jer 31:27**	3068
and to plant," declares the **L**.	**Jer 31:28**	3068
days are coming," declares the **L**,	**Jer 31:31**	3068
a husband to them," declares the **L**.	**Jer 31:32**	3068
after those days," declares the **L**,	**Jer 31:33**	3068
'Know the **L**,' for they will all	**Jer 31:34**	3068
greatest of them," declares the **L**,	**Jer 31:34**	3068
Thus says the **L**, Who gives the sun	**Jer 31:35**	3068
The **L** of hosts is His name:	**Jer 31:35**	3068
From before Me," declares the **L**,	**Jer 31:36**	3068
Thus says the **L**,	**Jer 31:37**	3068
they have done," declares the **L**.	**Jer 31:37**	3068
days are coming," declares the **L**,	**Jer 31:38**	3068
the city will be rebuilt for the **L**	**Jer 31:38**	3068
the east, shall be holy to the **L**;	**Jer 31:40**	3068
that came to Jeremiah from the **L**	**Jer 32:1**	3068
'Thus says the **L**,	**Jer 32:3**	3068
until I visit him," declares the **L**.	**Jer 32:5**	3068
"The word of the **L** came to me,	**Jer 32:6**	3068
according to the word of the **L** and	**Jer 32:8**	3068
that this was the word of the **L**.	**Jer 32:8**	3068
'Thus says the **L** of hosts, the God	**Jer 32:14**	3068
'For thus says the **L** of hosts,	**Jer 32:15**	3068
of Neriah, then I prayed to the **L**,	**Jer 32:16**	3068
L GOD! Behold, You have made	**Jer 32:17**	136
The **L** of hosts is His name;	**Jer 32:18**	3068

Context	Reference	Number
'You have said to me, O L God,	Jer 32:25	136
word of the L came to Jeremiah,	Jer 32:26	3068
"Behold, I am the L,	Jer 32:27	3068
Therefore thus says the L,	Jer 32:28	3068
of their hands," declares the L.	Jer 32:30	3068
"Now therefore thus says the L	Jer 32:36	3068
"For thus says the L,	Jer 32:42	3068
their fortunes,' declares the L."	Jer 32:44	3068
Then the word of the L came to	Jer 33:1	3068
says the L who made *the earth,*	Jer 33:2	3068
L who formed it to establish it,	Jer 33:2	3068
establish it, the L is His name,	Jer 33:2	3068
"For thus says the L God of	Jer 33:4	3068
"Thus says the L,	Jer 33:10	3068
"Give thanks to the L of hosts,	Jer 33:11	3068
Lord of hosts, For the L is good,	Jer 33:11	3068
offering into the house of the L.	Jer 33:11	3068
as they were at first,' says the L.	Jer 33:11	3068
"Thus says the L of hosts,	Jer 33:12	3068
one who numbers them,' says the L.	Jer 33:13	3068
days are coming,' declares the L,	Jer 33:14	3068
the L is our righteousness.'	Jer 33:16	3068
"For thus says the L,	Jer 33:17	3068
word of the L came to Jeremiah,	Jer 33:19	3068
"Thus says the L,	Jer 33:20	3068
word of the L came to Jeremiah,	Jer 33:23	3068
two families which the L chose,	Jer 33:24	3068
"Thus says the L,	Jer 33:25	3068
which came to Jeremiah from the L,	Jer 34:1	3068
"Thus says the L God of Israel,	Jer 34:2	3068
"Thus says the L, 'Behold, I	Jer 34:2	3068
"Yet hear the word of the L,	Jer 34:4	3068
Thus says the L concerning you,	Jer 34:4	3068
they will lament for you, "Alas, l!"	Jer 34:5	113
spoken the word," declares the L.	Jer 34:5	3068
which came to Jeremiah from the L	Jer 34:8	3068
Then the word of the L came to	Jer 34:12	3068
came to Jeremiah from the L,	Jer 34:12	3068
"Thus says the L God of Israel,	Jer 34:13	3068
"Therefore thus says the L,	Jer 34:17	3068
a release to you,' declares the L,	Jer 34:17	3068
going to command,' declares the L,	Jer 34:22	3068
which came to Jeremiah from the L	Jer 35:1	3068
them into the house of the L,	Jer 35:2	3068
them into the house of the L,	Jer 35:4	3068
word of the L came to Jeremiah,	Jer 35:12	3068
"Thus says the L of hosts, the	Jer 35:13	3068
to My words?" declares the L.	Jer 35:13	3068
"Therefore thus says the L,	Jer 35:17	3068
"Thus says the L of hosts, the	Jer 35:18	3068
thus says the L of hosts,	Jer 35:19	3068
word came to Jeremiah from the L,	Jer 36:1	3068
Jeremiah all the words of the L which	Jer 36:4	3068
cannot go into the house of the L.	Jer 36:5	3068
at my dictation the words of the L	Jer 36:6	3068
supplication will come before the L,	Jer 36:7	3068
the wrath that the L has pronounced	Jer 36:7	3068
words of the L in the Lord's house.	Jer 36:8	3068
proclaimed a fast before the L.	Jer 36:9	3068
of Jeremiah in the house of the L	Jer 36:10	3068
the words of the L from the book,	Jer 36:11	3068
the prophet, but the L hid them.	Jer 36:26	3068
Then the word of the L came to	Jer 36:27	3068
'Thus says the L,	Jer 36:29	3068
'Therefore thus says the L	Jer 36:30	3068
land listened to the words of the L	Jer 37:2	3068
"Please pray to the L our God on	Jer 37:3	3068
the word of the L came to Jeremiah	Jer 37:6	3068
"Thus says the L God of Israel,	Jer 37:7	3068
"Thus says the L,	Jer 37:9	3068
"Is there a word from the L?"	Jer 37:17	3068
please listen, O my l the king;	Jer 37:20	113
"Thus says the L,	Jer 38:2	3068
"Thus says the L,	Jer 38:3	3068
"My l the king, these men have	Jer 38:9	113
that is in the house of the L;	Jer 38:14	3068
"As the L lives, who made this	Jer 38:16	3068
"Thus says the L God of hosts,	Jer 38:17	3068
obey the L in what I am saying to	Jer 38:20	3068
the word which the L has shown me:	Jer 38:21	3068
Now the word of the L had come to	Jer 39:15	3068
'Thus says the L of hosts, the God	Jer 39:16	3068
you on that day," declares the L,	Jer 39:17	3068
trusted in Me," declares the L.' "	Jer 39:18	3068
which came to Jeremiah from the L	Jer 40:1	3068
"The L your God promised this	Jer 40:2	3068
and the L has brought *it* on and	Jer 40:3	3068
you *people* sinned against the L	Jer 40:3	3068
to bring to the house of the L.	Jer 41:5	3068
and pray for us to the L your God,	Jer 42:2	3068
that the L your God may tell us	Jer 42:3	3068
I am going to pray to the L your	Jer 42:4	3068
message which the L will answer you	Jer 42:4	3068
"May the L be a true and faithful	Jer 42:5	3068
L your God will send you to us.	Jer 42:5	3068
we will listen to the voice of the L	Jer 42:6	3068
to the voice of the L our God."	Jer 42:6	3068
word of the L came to Jeremiah.	Jer 42:7	3068
"Thus says the L the God of	Jer 42:9	3068
be afraid of him,' declares the L,	Jer 42:11	3068
to the voice of the L your God,	Jer 42:13	3068
case listen to the word of the L,	Jer 42:15	3068
Thus says the L of hosts, the God	Jer 42:15	3068
For thus says the L of hosts,	Jer 42:18	3068
The L has spoken to you, O remnant	Jer 42:19	3068
you who sent me to the L your God,	Jer 42:20	3068
"Pray for us to the L our God;	Jer 42:20	3068
and whatever the L our God says,	Jer 42:20	3068
have not obeyed the L your God,	Jer 42:21	3068
whom the L their God had sent,	Jer 43:1	3068
all the words of the L their God	Jer 43:1	3068
The L our God has not sent you to	Jer 43:2	3068
did not obey the voice of the L to	Jer 43:4	3068
did not obey the voice of the L)	Jer 43:7	3068
L came to Jeremiah in Tahpanhes,	Jer 43:8	3068
"Thus says the L of hosts, the God	Jer 43:10	3068
"Thus says the L of hosts, the	Jer 44:2	3068
then thus says the L God of hosts,	Jer 44:7	3068
thus says the L of hosts,	Jer 44:11	3068
spoken to us in the name of the L,	Jer 44:16	3068
land, did not the L remember them and	Jer 44:21	3068
"So the L was no longer able to	Jer 44:22	3068
sinned against the L and not obeyed	Jer 44:23	3068
not obeyed the voice of the L or	Jer 44:23	3068
"Hear the word of the L,	Jer 44:24	3068
thus says the L of hosts, the God	Jer 44:25	3068
hear the word of the L,	Jer 44:26	3068
by My great name,' says the L,	Jer 44:26	3068
"As the L God lives."	Jer 44:26	136
the sign to you,' declares the L,	Jer 44:29	3068
"Thus says the L,	Jer 44:30	3068
the L the God of Israel to you,	Jer 45:2	3068
the L has added sorrow to my pain;	Jer 45:3	3068
'Thus says the L,	Jer 45:4	3068
on all flesh,' declares the L,	Jer 45:5	3068
as the word of the L to Jeremiah	Jer 46:1	3068
is on every side!" Declares the L.	Jer 46:5	3068
day belongs to the L God of hosts,	Jer 46:10	136
slaughter for the L God of hosts,	Jer 46:10	136
the L spoke to Jeremiah the prophet	Jer 46:13	3068
the L has thrust them down.	Jer 46:15	3068
King Whose name is the L of hosts,	Jer 46:18	3068
down her forest," declares the L;	Jer 46:23	3068
The L of hosts, the God of Israel,	Jer 46:25	3068
the days of old," declares the L.	Jer 46:26	3068
do not fear," declares the L,	Jer 46:28	3068
which came as the word of the L	Jer 47:1	3068
Thus says the L: "Behold, waters are	Jer 47:2	3068
For the L is going to destroy the	Jer 47:4	3068
"Ah, sword of the L,	Jer 47:6	3068
When the L has given it an order?	Jer 47:7	3068
Thus says the L of hosts, the God	Jer 48:1	3068
be destroyed, As the L has said.	Jer 48:8	3068
days are coming," declares the L,	Jer 48:12	3068
whose name is the L of hosts.	Jer 48:15	3068
his arm broken," declares the L.	Jer 48:25	3068
has become arrogant toward the L;	Jer 48:26	3068
"I know his fury," declares the L,	Jer 48:30	3068
an end of Moab," declares the L,	Jer 48:35	3068
vessel," declares the L.	Jer 48:38	3068
For thus says the L:	Jer 48:40	3068
has become arrogant toward the L.	Jer 48:42	3068
of Moab," declares the L.	Jer 48:43	3068
their punishment," declares the L.	Jer 48:44	3068
the latter days," declares the L.	Jer 48:47	3068
Thus says the L: "Does Israel have	Jer 49:1	3068
days are coming," declares the L,	Jer 49:2	3068
of his possessors," Says the L.	Jer 49:2	3068
you," Declares the L God of hosts,	Jer 49:5	136
the sons of Ammon," Declares the L.	Jer 49:6	3068
Thus says the L of hosts,	Jer 49:7	3068
For thus says the L,	Jer 49:12	3068
sworn by Myself," declares the L,	Jer 49:13	3068
I have heard a message from the L,	Jer 49:14	3068
down from there," declares the L.	Jer 49:16	3068
with its neighbors," says the L,	Jer 49:18	3068
Therefore hear the plan of the L	Jer 49:20	3068
that day," declares the L of hosts.	Jer 49:26	3068
Thus says the L,	Jer 49:28	3068
of Hazor," declares the L;	Jer 49:30	3068
lives securely," declares the L.	Jer 49:31	3068
from every side," declares the L.	Jer 49:32	3068
as the word of the L to Jeremiah	Jer 49:34	3068
"Thus says the L of hosts,	Jer 49:35	3068
My fierce anger,' declares the L,	Jer 49:37	3068
king and princes,' Declares the L.	Jer 49:38	3068
fortunes of Elam,' " Declares the L.	Jer 49:39	3068
the L spoke concerning Babylon,	Jer 50:1	3068
and at that time," declares the L,	Jer 50:4	3068
be the L their God they will seek.	Jer 50:4	3068
may join themselves to the L *in* an	Jer 50:5	3068
they have sinned against the L *who*	Jer 50:7	3068
of righteousness, Even the L,	Jer 50:7	3068
will have enough," declares the L.	Jer 50:10	3068
the L she will not be inhabited,	Jer 50:13	3068
For she has sinned against the L.	Jer 50:14	3068
this is the vengeance of the L:	Jer 50:15	3068
thus says the L of hosts,	Jer 50:18	3068
and at that time,' declares the L,	Jer 50:20	3068
destroy them," declares the L,	Jer 50:21	3068
engaged in conflict with the L."	Jer 50:24	3068
The L has opened His armory And	Jer 50:25	3068
For it is a work of the L God of	Jer 50:25	136
the vengeance of the L our God,	Jer 50:28	3068
has become arrogant against the L,	Jer 50:29	3068
in that day," declares the L.	Jer 50:30	3068
one," Declares the L God of hosts,	Jer 50:31	136
Thus says the L of hosts,	Jer 50:33	3068
the L of hosts is His name;	Jer 50:34	3068
the Chaldeans," declares the L,	Jer 50:35	3068
its neighbors," declares the L,	Jer 50:40	3068
Therefore hear the plan of the L	Jer 50:45	3068
Thus says the L: "Behold, I am	Jer 51:1	3068
By his God, the L of hosts,	Jer 51:5	3068
a golden cup in the hand of the L,	Jer 51:7	3068
The L has brought about our	Jer 51:10	3068
in Zion The work of the L our God!	Jer 51:10	3068
The L has aroused the spirit of	Jer 51:11	3068
For it is the vengeance of the L,	Jer 51:11	3068
For the L has both purposed and	Jer 51:12	3068
L of hosts has sworn by Himself:	Jer 51:14	3068
The L of hosts is His name.	Jer 51:19	3068
before your eyes," declares the L.	Jer 51:24	3068
the whole earth," declares the L,	Jer 51:25	3068
desolate forever," declares the L.	Jer 51:26	3068
purposes of the L against Babylon	Jer 51:29	3068
For thus says the L of hosts,	Jer 51:33	3068
Therefore thus says the L,	Jer 51:36	3068
And not wake up," declares the L.	Jer 51:39	3068
From the fierce anger of the L.	Jer 51:45	3068
from the north," Declares the L.	Jer 51:48	3068
Remember the L from afar, And let	Jer 51:50	3068
days are coming," declares the L,	Jer 51:52	3068
will come to her," declares the L.	Jer 51:53	3068
the L is going to destroy Babylon,	Jer 51:55	3068
For the L is a God of recompense,	Jer 51:56	3068
whose name is the L of hosts.	Jer 51:57	3068
Thus says the L of hosts,	Jer 51:58	3068
'You, O L, have promised	Jer 51:62	3068
He did evil in the sight of the L	Jer 52:2	3068
For through the anger of the L	Jer 52:3	3068
He burned the house of the L,	Jer 52:13	3068
belonged to the house of the L	Jer 52:17	3068
which were in the house of the L,	Jer 52:17	3068
had made for the house of the L	Jer 52:20	3068
For the L has caused her grief	La 1:5	3068
"See, O L, my affliction, For the	La 1:9	3068
"See, O L, and look, For I am	La 1:11	3068
Which the L inflicted on the day	La 1:12	3068
The L has given me into the hands	La 1:14	136
"The L has rejected all my strong	La 1:15	136
The L has trodden *as in* a wine	La 1:15	136
The L has commanded concerning	La 1:17	3068
"The L is righteous;	La 1:18	3068
"See, O L, for I am in distress;	La 1:20	3068
How the L has covered the daughter	La 2:1	136
The L has swallowed up;	La 2:2	136
The L has become like an enemy.	La 2:5	136
The L has caused to be forgotten	La 2:6	3068
The L has rejected His altar, He	La 2:7	136
made a noise in the house of the L	La 2:7	3068
The L determined to destroy The	La 2:8	3068
find No vision from the L.	La 2:9	3068
The L has done what He purposed;	La 2:17	3068
Their heart cried out to the L,	La 2:18	136
Before the presence of the L;	La 2:19	136
See, O L, and look!	La 2:20	3068
slain In the sanctuary of the L?	La 2:20	136
And *so has* my hope from the L."	La 3:18	3068
"The L is my portion,"	La 3:24	3068
The L is good to those who wait	La 3:25	3068
For the salvation of the L.	La 3:26	3068
For the L will not reject forever,	La 3:31	136
things the L does not approve.	La 3:36	136
Unless the L has commanded *it?*	La 3:37	136
ways, And let us return to the L.	La 3:40	3068
Until the L looks down And sees	La 3:50	3068
I called on Your name, O L,	La 3:55	3068
O L, You have pleaded my soul's	La 3:58	136
O L, You have seen my oppression;	La 3:59	3068
have heard their reproach, O L,	La 3:61	3068
You will recompense them, O L,	La 3:64	3068
From under the heavens of the L!	La 3:66	3068
The L has accomplished His wrath,	La 4:11	3068
presence of the L has scattered them	La 4:16	3068
Remember, O L, what has befallen	La 5:1	3068
You, O L, rule forever;	La 5:19	3068
Restore us to You, O L,	La 5:21	3068
the word of the L came expressly	Ezk 1:3	3068
the hand of the L came upon him.)	Ezk 1:3	3068
likeness of the glory of the L.	Ezk 1:28	3068
'Thus says the L God.'	Ezk 2:4	136
'Thus says the L God.' "	Ezk 3:11	136
Blessed be the glory of the L in His	Ezk 3:12	3068
hand of the L was strong on me.	Ezk 3:14	3068
days the word of the L came to me,	Ezk 3:16	3068
The hand of the L was on me there,	Ezk 3:22	3068
glory of the L was standing there,	Ezk 3:23	3068
'Thus says the L God.'	Ezk 3:27	136
Then the L said,	Ezk 4:13	3068
But I said, "Ah, L God! Behold,	Ezk 4:14	136
"Thus says the L God,	Ezk 5:5	136
"Therefore, thus says the L God,	Ezk 5:7	136
therefore, thus says the L God,	Ezk 5:8	136
'So as I live,' declares the L God,	Ezk 5:11	136
will know that I, the L, have spoken	Ezk 5:13	3068
I, the L, have spoken.	Ezk 5:15	3068
I, the L, have spoken.' "	Ezk 5:17	3068
word of the L came to me saying,	Ezk 6:1	3068
listen to the word of the L God!	Ezk 6:3	136
says the L God to the mountains,	Ezk 6:3	136
and you will know that I am the L.	Ezk 6:7	3068
they will know that I am the L;	Ezk 6:10	3068
"Thus says the L God,	Ezk 6:11	136
you will know that I am the L,	Ezk 6:13	3068
will know that I am the L.	Ezk 6:14	3068
word of the L came to me saying,	Ezk 7:1	3068
the L God to the land of Israel,	Ezk 7:2	136
you will know that I am the L!'	Ezk 7:4	3068
"Thus says the L God,	Ezk 7:5	136
know that I, the L, do the smiting.	Ezk 7:9	3068
in the day of the wrath of the L.	Ezk 7:19	3068
will know that I am the L.' "	Ezk 7:27	3068
the hand of the L God fell on me	Ezk 8:1	136
'The L does not see us;	Ezk 8:12	3068
the L has forsaken the land.' "	Ezk 8:12	3068
entrance to the temple of the L,	Ezk 8:16	3068

their backs to the temple of the **L**	**Ezk 8:16**	3068
The **L** said to him,	**Ezk 9:4**	3068
cried out saying, "Alas, **L** GOD!	**Ezk 9:8**	136
'The **L** has forsaken the land, and	**Ezk 9:9**	3068
the land, and the **L** does not see!'	**Ezk 9:9**	3068
Then the glory of the **L** went up	**Ezk 10:4**	3068
brightness of the glory of the **L**.	**Ezk 10:4**	3068
Then the glory of the **L** departed	**Ezk 10:18**	3068
the Spirit of the **L** fell upon me,	**Ezk 11:5**	3068
'Thus says the **L**,	**Ezk 11:5**	3068
'Therefore, thus says the **L** GOD,	**Ezk 11:7**	136
upon you," the **L** GOD declares.	**Ezk 11:8**	136
so you shall know that I am the **L**.	**Ezk 11:10**	3068
you will know that I am the **L**;	**Ezk 11:12**	3068
loud voice and said, "Alas, **L** GOD!	**Ezk 11:13**	136
Then the word of the **L** came to me,	**Ezk 11:14**	3068
'Go far from the **L**;	**Ezk 11:15**	3068
'Thus says the **L** GOD,	**Ezk 11:16**	136
'Thus says the **L** GOD,	**Ezk 11:17**	136
their heads," declares the **L** GOD.	**Ezk 11:21**	136
The glory of the **L** went up	**Ezk 11:23**	3068
things that the **L** had shown me.	**Ezk 11:25**	3068
word of the **L** came to me,	**Ezk 12:1**	3068
the word of the **L** came to me,	**Ezk 12:8**	3068
'Thus says the **L** GOD,	**Ezk 12:10**	136
"So they will know that I am the **L**	**Ezk 12:15**	3068
and may know that I am the **L**."	**Ezk 12:16**	3068
word of the **L** came to me saying,	**Ezk 12:17**	3068
'Thus says the **L** GOD concerning	**Ezk 12:19**	136
So you will know that I am the **L**."	**Ezk 12:20**	3068
word of the **L** came to me,	**Ezk 12:21**	3068
'Thus says the **L** GOD,	**Ezk 12:23**	136
"For I the **L** will speak, and	**Ezk 12:25**	3068
it," declares the **L** GOD.' "	**Ezk 12:25**	136
word of the **L** came to me,	**Ezk 12:26**	3068
'Thus says the **L** GOD,	**Ezk 12:28**	136
be performed," ' " declares the **L** GOD.	**Ezk 12:28**	136
word of the **L** came to me saying,	**Ezk 13:1**	3068
'Listen to the word of the **L**!	**Ezk 13:2**	3068
'Thus says the **L** GOD,	**Ezk 13:3**	136
in the battle on the day of the **L**.	**Ezk 13:5**	3068
'The **L** declares,' when the LORD	**Ezk 13:6**	3068
when the **L** has not sent them;	**Ezk 13:6**	3068
'The **L** declares,' but it is not I	**Ezk 13:7**	3068
Therefore, thus says the **L** GOD,	**Ezk 13:8**	136
against you," declares the **L** GOD.	**Ezk 13:8**	136
you may know that I am the **L** GOD.	**Ezk 13:9**	136
Therefore, thus says the **L** GOD,	**Ezk 13:13**	136
And you will know that I am the **L**.	**Ezk 13:14**	3068
is no peace,' declares the **L** GOD.	**Ezk 13:16**	136
'Thus says the **L** GOD,	**Ezk 13:18**	136
Therefore, thus says the **L** GOD,	**Ezk 13:20**	136
and you will know that I am the **L**.	**Ezk 13:21**	3068
you will know that I am the **L**."	**Ezk 13:23**	3068
word of the **L** came to me,	**Ezk 14:2**	3068
'Thus says the **L** GOD,	**Ezk 14:4**	136
I the **L** will be brought to give	**Ezk 14:4**	3068
'Thus says the **L** GOD,	**Ezk 14:6**	136
I the **L** will be brought to answer	**Ezk 14:7**	3068
So you will know that I am the **L**.	**Ezk 14:8**	3068
to speak a word, it is I, the **L**,	**Ezk 14:9**	3068
their God," ' declares the **L** GOD."	**Ezk 14:11**	136
word of the **L** came to me saying,	**Ezk 14:12**	3068
themselves," declares the **L** GOD.	**Ezk 14:14**	136
as I live," declares the **L** GOD,	**Ezk 14:16**	136
as I live," declares the **L** GOD,	**Ezk 14:18**	136
as I live," declares the **L** GOD,	**Ezk 14:20**	136
For thus says the **L** GOD,	**Ezk 14:21**	136
I did to it," declares the **L** GOD.	**Ezk 14:23**	136
word of the **L** came to me,	**Ezk 15:1**	3068
"Therefore, thus says the **L** GOD,	**Ezk 15:6**	136
you will know that I am the **L**,	**Ezk 15:7**	3068
unfaithfully,' " declares the **L** GOD.	**Ezk 15:8**	136
word of the **L** came to me,	**Ezk 16:1**	3068
'Thus says the **L** GOD to Jerusalem,	**Ezk 16:3**	136
became Mine," declares the **L** GOD.	**Ezk 16:8**	136
on you," declares the **L** GOD.	**Ezk 16:14**	136
it happened," declares the **L** GOD.	**Ezk 16:19**	136
declares the **L** GOD),	**Ezk 16:23**	136
is your heart," declares the **L** GOD,	**Ezk 16:30**	136
O harlot, hear the word of the **L**.	**Ezk 16:35**	3068
Thus says the **L** GOD,	**Ezk 16:36**	136
your own head," declares the **L** GOD,	**Ezk 16:43**	136
"As I live," declares the **L** GOD,	**Ezk 16:48**	136
and abominations," the **L** declares.	**Ezk 16:58**	3068
For thus says the **L** GOD,	**Ezk 16:59**	136
you shall know that I am the **L**,	**Ezk 16:62**	3068
you have done," the **L** GOD declares.	**Ezk 16:63**	136
word of the **L** came to me saying,	**Ezk 17:1**	3068
'Thus says the **L** GOD,	**Ezk 17:3**	136
'Thus says the **L** GOD,	**Ezk 17:9**	136
word of the **L** came to me,	**Ezk 17:11**	3068
'As I live,' declares the **L** GOD,	**Ezk 17:16**	136
Therefore, thus says the **L** GOD,	**Ezk 17:19**	136
know that I, the **L**, have spoken."	**Ezk 17:21**	3068
Thus says the **L** GOD,	**Ezk 17:22**	136
field will know that I am the **L**;	**Ezk 17:24**	3068
I am the **L**; I have spoken, and I	**Ezk 17:24**	3068
word of the **L** came to me,	**Ezk 18:1**	3068
"As I live," declares the **L** GOD,	**Ezk 18:3**	136
surely live," declares the **L** GOD.	**Ezk 18:9**	136
of the wicked," declares the **L** GOD,	**Ezk 18:23**	136
'The way of the **L** is not right.'	**Ezk 18:25**	136
'The way of the **L** is not right.'	**Ezk 18:29**	136
his conduct," declares the **L** GOD.	**Ezk 18:30**	136
who dies," declares the **L** GOD.	**Ezk 18:32**	136
Israel came to inquire of the **L**,	**Ezk 20:1**	3068
word of the **L** came to me saying,	**Ezk 20:2**	3068
'Thus says the **L** GOD,	**Ezk 20:3**	136
As I live," declares the **L** GOD,	**Ezk 20:3**	136
'Thus says the **L** GOD,	**Ezk 20:5**	136
them, saying, I am the **L** your God,	**Ezk 20:5**	3068
I am the **L** your God.'	**Ezk 20:7**	3068
I am the **L** who sanctifies them.	**Ezk 20:12**	3068
'I am the **L** your God;	**Ezk 20:19**	3068
know that I am the **L** your God.'	**Ezk 20:20**	3068
might know that I am the **L**." '	**Ezk 20:26**	3068
'Thus says the **L** GOD,	**Ezk 20:27**	136
'Thus says the **L** GOD,	**Ezk 20:30**	136
As I live," declares the **L** GOD,	**Ezk 20:31**	136
"As I live," declares the **L** GOD,	**Ezk 20:33**	136
with you," declares the **L** GOD.	**Ezk 20:36**	136
you will know that I am the **L**.	**Ezk 20:38**	3068
of Israel," thus says the **L** GOD,	**Ezk 20:39**	136
of Israel," declares the **L** GOD,	**Ezk 20:40**	136
"And you will know that I am the **L**,	**Ezk 20:42**	3068
you will know that I am the **L** when	**Ezk 20:44**	3068
of Israel," declares the **L** GOD.' "	**Ezk 20:44**	136
word of the **L** came to me,	**Ezk 20:45**	3068
'Hear the word of the **L**:	**Ezk 20:47**	3068
thus says the **L** GOD,	**Ezk 20:47**	136
All flesh will see that I, the **L**,	**Ezk 20:48**	3068
Ah **L** GOD! They are saying of me,	**Ezk 20:49**	136
word of the **L** came to me saying,	**Ezk 21:1**	3068
'Thus says the **L**,	**Ezk 21:3**	3068
that I, the **L**, have drawn My sword	**Ezk 21:5**	3068
will happen,' declares the **L** GOD."	**Ezk 21:7**	136
word of the **L** came to me,	**Ezk 21:8**	3068
'Thus says the **L**.'	**Ezk 21:9**	3068
declares the **L** GOD.	**Ezk 21:13**	136
I, the **L**, have spoken."	**Ezk 21:17**	3068
word of the **L** came to me saying,	**Ezk 21:18**	3068
"Therefore, thus says the **L** GOD,	**Ezk 21:24**	136
thus says the **L** GOD,	**Ezk 21:26**	136
'Thus says the **L** GOD concerning	**Ezk 21:28**	136
for I, the **L**, have spoken.	**Ezk 21:32**	3068
word of the **L** came to me,	**Ezk 22:1**	3068
'Thus says the **L** GOD,	**Ezk 22:3**	136
forgotten Me," declares the **L** GOD.	**Ezk 22:12**	136
I, the **L**, have spoken and will	**Ezk 22:14**	3068
will know that I am the **L**.	**Ezk 22:16**	3068
word of the **L** came to me,	**Ezk 22:17**	3068
"Therefore, thus says the **L** GOD,	**Ezk 22:19**	136
I, the **L**, have poured out My wrath	**Ezk 22:22**	3068
word of the **L** came to me,	**Ezk 22:23**	3068
'Thus says the **L** GOD,' when the	**Ezk 22:28**	136
GOD,' when the **L** has not spoken.	**Ezk 22:28**	3068
their heads," declares the **L** GOD.	**Ezk 22:31**	136
of the **L** came to me again,	**Ezk 23:1**	3068
O Oholibah, thus says the **L** GOD,	**Ezk 23:22**	136
"For thus says the **L** GOD,	**Ezk 23:28**	136
'Thus says the **L** GOD,	**Ezk 23:32**	136
I have spoken,' declares the **L** GOD.	**Ezk 23:34**	136
'Therefore, thus says the **L** GOD,	**Ezk 23:35**	136
Moreover, the **L** said to me,	**Ezk 23:36**	3068
"For thus says the **L** GOD,	**Ezk 23:46**	136
will know that I am the **L** GOD.' "	**Ezk 23:49**	136
L came to me in the ninth year,	**Ezk 24:1**	3068
'Thus says the **L** GOD,	**Ezk 24:3**	136
'Therefore, thus says the **L** GOD,	**Ezk 24:6**	136
'Therefore, thus says the **L** GOD,	**Ezk 24:9**	136
"I, the **L**, have spoken;	**Ezk 24:14**	3068
judge you," declares the **L** GOD.' "	**Ezk 24:14**	136
word of the **L** came to me saying,	**Ezk 24:15**	3068
word of the **L** came to me saying,	**Ezk 24:20**	3068
"Thus says the **L** GOD,	**Ezk 24:21**	136
will know that I am the **L** GOD.	**Ezk 24:24**	136
will know that I am the **L**.' "	**Ezk 24:27**	3068
word of the **L** came to me saying,	**Ezk 25:1**	3068
'Hear the word of the **L** GOD!	**Ezk 25:3**	136
Thus says the **L** GOD,	**Ezk 25:3**	136
you will know that I am the **L**."	**Ezk 25:5**	3068
'For thus says the **L** GOD,	**Ezk 25:6**	136
you will know that I am the **L**."	**Ezk 25:7**	3068
'Thus says the **L** GOD,	**Ezk 25:8**	136
they will know that I am the **L**."	**Ezk 25:11**	3068
'Thus says the **L** GOD,	**Ezk 25:12**	136
therefore thus says the **L** GOD,	**Ezk 25:13**	136
My vengeance," declares the **L** GOD.	**Ezk 25:14**	136
'Thus says the **L** GOD,	**Ezk 25:15**	136
therefore thus says the **L** GOD,	**Ezk 25:16**	136
they will know that I am the **L** when	**Ezk 25:17**	3068
word of the **L** came to me saying,	**Ezk 26:1**	3068
therefore thus says the **L** GOD,	**Ezk 26:3**	136
I have spoken,' declares the **L** GOD,	**Ezk 26:5**	136
will know that I am the **L**.' "	**Ezk 26:6**	3068
For thus says the **L** GOD,	**Ezk 26:7**	136
more, for I the **L** have spoken,"	**Ezk 26:14**	3068
have spoken," declares the **L** GOD.	**Ezk 26:14**	136
Thus says the **L** GOD to Tyre,	**Ezk 26:15**	136
For thus says the **L** GOD,	**Ezk 26:19**	136
found again," declares the **L** GOD.	**Ezk 26:21**	136
word of the **L** came to me saying,	**Ezk 27:1**	3068
'Thus says the **L** GOD,	**Ezk 27:3**	136
word of the **L** came again to me	**Ezk 28:1**	3068
'Thus says the **L** GOD,	**Ezk 28:2**	136
Therefore thus says the **L** GOD,	**Ezk 28:6**	136
declares the **L** GOD!	**Ezk 28:10**	136
word of the **L** came to me saying,	**Ezk 28:11**	3068
'Thus says the **L** GOD,	**Ezk 28:12**	136
word of the **L** came to me saying,	**Ezk 28:20**	3068
'Thus says the **L** GOD,	**Ezk 28:22**	136
they will know that I am the **L** when	**Ezk 28:22**	3068
they will know that I am the **L**.	**Ezk 28:23**	3068
will know that I am the **L** GOD."	**Ezk 28:24**	136
'Thus says the **L** GOD,	**Ezk 28:25**	136
that I am the **L** their God.	**Ezk 28:26**	3068
word of the **L** came to me saying,	**Ezk 29:1**	3068
'Thus says the **L** GOD,	**Ezk 29:3**	136
Egypt will know that I am the **L**,	**Ezk 29:6**	3068
'Therefore thus says the **L** GOD,	**Ezk 29:8**	136
they will know that I am the **L**.	**Ezk 29:9**	3068
'For thus says the **L** GOD,	**Ezk 29:13**	136
know that I am the **L** GOD.	**Ezk 29:16**	136
word of the **L** came to me saying,	**Ezk 29:17**	3068
Therefore thus says the **L** GOD,	**Ezk 29:19**	136
acted for Me," declares the **L** GOD.	**Ezk 29:20**	136
they will know that I am the **L**."	**Ezk 29:21**	3068
word of the **L** came again to me	**Ezk 30:1**	3068
'Thus says the **L** GOD,	**Ezk 30:2**	136
Even the day of the **L** is near;	**Ezk 30:3**	3068
'Thus says the **L**,	**Ezk 30:6**	3068
by the sword," Declares the **L** GOD.	**Ezk 30:6**	136
they will know that I am the **L**,	**Ezk 30:8**	3068
'Thus says the **L** GOD,	**Ezk 30:10**	136
I the **L** have spoken."	**Ezk 30:12**	3068
'Thus says the **L** GOD,	**Ezk 30:13**	136
will know that I am the **L**.	**Ezk 30:19**	3068
word of the **L** came to me saying,	**Ezk 30:20**	3068
"Therefore thus says the **L** GOD,	**Ezk 30:22**	136
they will know that I am the **L**,	**Ezk 30:25**	3068
will know that I am the **L**.' "	**Ezk 30:26**	3068
word of the **L** came to me saying,	**Ezk 31:1**	3068
'Therefore thus says the **L** GOD,	**Ezk 31:10**	136
'Thus says the **L** GOD,	**Ezk 31:15**	136
declares the **L** GOD."	**Ezk 31:18**	136
word of the **L** came to me saying,	**Ezk 32:1**	3068
Thus says the **L** GOD,	**Ezk 32:3**	136
on your land," Declares the **L** GOD.	**Ezk 32:8**	136
For thus says the **L** GOD,	**Ezk 32:11**	136
run like oil," Declares the **L** GOD.	**Ezk 32:14**	136
they shall know that I am the **L**.	**Ezk 32:15**	3068
chant it," declares the **L** GOD.	**Ezk 32:16**	136
word of the **L** came to me saying,	**Ezk 32:17**	3068
all his army," declares the **L** GOD.	**Ezk 32:31**	136
his hordes," declares the **L** GOD.	**Ezk 32:32**	136
word of the **L** came to me,	**Ezk 33:1**	3068
declares the **L** GOD,	**Ezk 33:11**	136
'The way of the **L** is not right,	**Ezk 33:17**	136
'The way of the **L** is not right.'	**Ezk 33:20**	136
Now the hand of the **L** had been	**Ezk 33:22**	3068
word of the **L** came to me saying,	**Ezk 33:23**	3068
'Thus says the **L** GOD,	**Ezk 33:25**	136
'Thus says the **L** GOD,	**Ezk 33:27**	136
they will know that I am the **L**,	**Ezk 33:29**	3068
is which comes forth from the **L**.'	**Ezk 33:30**	3068
word of the **L** came to me saying,	**Ezk 34:1**	3068
'Thus says the **L** GOD,	**Ezk 34:2**	136
shepherds, hear the word of the **L**:	**Ezk 34:7**	3068
"As I live," declares the **L** GOD,	**Ezk 34:8**	136
shepherds, hear the word of the **L**:	**Ezk 34:9**	3068
'Thus says the **L** GOD,	**Ezk 34:10**	136
For thus says the **L** GOD,	**Ezk 34:11**	136
them to rest," declares the **L** GOD.	**Ezk 34:15**	136
My flock, thus says the **L** GOD,	**Ezk 34:17**	136
thus says the **L** GOD to them,	**Ezk 34:20**	136
"And I, the **L**, will be their God,	**Ezk 34:24**	3068
I the **L** have spoken.	**Ezk 34:24**	3068
they will know that I am the **L**,	**Ezk 34:27**	3068
will know that I, the **L** their God,	**Ezk 34:30**	3068
are My people," declares the **L** GOD.	**Ezk 34:30**	136
I am your God," declares the **L** GOD.	**Ezk 34:31**	136
word of the **L** came to me saying,	**Ezk 35:1**	3068
'Thus says the **L** GOD,	**Ezk 35:3**	136
you will know that I am the **L**.	**Ezk 35:4**	3068
as I live," declares the **L** GOD,	**Ezk 35:6**	136
you will know that I am the **L**.	**Ezk 35:9**	3068
them,' although the **L** was there,	**Ezk 35:10**	3068
as I live," declares the **L** GOD,	**Ezk 35:11**	136
"Then you will know that I, the **L**,	**Ezk 35:12**	3068
'Thus says the **L** GOD,	**Ezk 35:14**	136
will know that I am the **L**."	**Ezk 35:15**	3068
of Israel, hear the word of the **L**.	**Ezk 36:1**	3068
'Thus says the **L** GOD,	**Ezk 36:2**	136
'Thus says the **L** GOD,	**Ezk 36:3**	136
hear the word of the **L** GOD.	**Ezk 36:4**	136
Thus says the **L** GOD to the	**Ezk 36:4**	136
therefore thus says the **L** GOD,	**Ezk 36:5**	136
"Thus says the **L** GOD,	**Ezk 36:6**	136
"Therefore thus says the **L** GOD,	**Ezk 36:7**	136
you will know that I am the **L**.	**Ezk 36:11**	3068
'Thus says the **L** GOD,	**Ezk 36:13**	136
of children,' declares the **L** GOD.	**Ezk 36:14**	136
longer," declares the **L** GOD.' "	**Ezk 36:15**	136
word of the **L** came to me saying,	**Ezk 36:16**	3068
'These are the people of the **L**;	**Ezk 36:20**	3068
'Thus says the **L** GOD,	**Ezk 36:22**	136
will know that I am the **L**,"	**Ezk 36:23**	3068
I am the LORD," declares the **L** GOD,	**Ezk 36:23**	136
for your sake," declares the **L** GOD,	**Ezk 36:32**	136
'Thus says the **L** GOD,	**Ezk 36:33**	136
I, the **L**, have rebuilt the ruined	**Ezk 36:36**	3068
I, the **L**, have spoken and will do	**Ezk 36:36**	3068
'Thus says the **L** GOD,	**Ezk 36:37**	136
will know that I am the **L**.	**Ezk 36:38**	3068
The hand of the **L** was upon me, and	**Ezk 37:1**	3068
by the Spirit of the **L** and set me	**Ezk 37:1**	3068
"O **L** GOD, You know."	**Ezk 37:3**	136
bones, hear the word of the **L**.'	**Ezk 37:4**	3068
says the **L** GOD to these bones,	**Ezk 37:5**	136
you will know that I am the **L**.' "	**Ezk 37:6**	3068
'Thus says the **L** GOD,	**Ezk 37:9**	136
'Thus says the **L** GOD,	**Ezk 37:12**	136
you will know that I am the **L**,	**Ezk 37:13**	3068
I, the **L**, have spoken and done it,"	**Ezk 37:14**	3068
and done it," declares the **L**.' "	**Ezk 37:14**	3068
word of the **L** came again to me	**Ezk 37:15**	3068

'Thus says the L God,	Ezk 37:19	136
'Thus says the L God,	Ezk 37:21	136
I am the L who sanctifies Israel,	Ezk 37:28	3068
word of the L came to me saying,	Ezk 38:1	3068
'Thus says the L God,	Ezk 38:3	136
'Thus says the L God,	Ezk 38:10	136
'Thus says the L God,	Ezk 38:14	136
'Thus says the L God,	Ezk 38:17	136
of Israel," declares the L God,	Ezk 38:18	136
My mountains," declares the L God.	Ezk 38:21	136
will know that I am the L."	Ezk 38:23	3068
'Thus says the L God,	Ezk 39:1	136
have spoken," declares the L God.	Ezk 39:5	136
they will know that I am the L.	Ezk 39:6	3068
nations will know that I am the L,	Ezk 39:7	3068
shall be done," declares the L God.	Ezk 39:8	136
them," declares the L God.	Ezk 39:10	136
Myself," declares the L God.	Ezk 39:13	136
son of man, thus says the L God,	Ezk 39:17	136
men of war," declares the L God.	Ezk 39:20	136
know that I am the L their God	Ezk 39:22	3068
Therefore thus says the L God,	Ezk 39:25	136
will know that I am the L their God	Ezk 39:28	3068
of Israel," declares the L God.	Ezk 39:29	136
hand of the L was upon me and He	Ezk 40:1	3068
the sons of Levi come near to the L	Ezk 40:46	3068
the table that is before the L."	Ezk 41:22	3068
priests who are near to the L shall	Ezk 42:13	3068
And the glory of the L came into	Ezk 43:4	3068
glory of the L filled the house.	Ezk 43:5	3068
"Son of man, thus says the L God,	Ezk 43:18	136
to Me,' declares the L God,	Ezk 43:19	136
shall present them before the L,	Ezk 43:24	3068
up as a burnt offering to the L.	Ezk 43:24	3068
accept you,' declares the L God."	Ezk 43:27	136
The L said to me,	Ezk 44:2	3068
for the L God of Israel has	Ezk 44:2	3068
prince to eat bread before the L;	Ezk 44:3	3068
the glory of the L filled the house	Ezk 44:4	3068
LORD filled the house of the L,	Ezk 44:4	3068
The L said to me,	Ezk 44:5	3068
the L and concerning all its laws;	Ezk 44:5	3068
'Thus says the L God,	Ezk 44:6	136
'Thus says the L God,	Ezk 44:9	136
against them," declares the L God,	Ezk 44:12	136
and the blood," declares the L God.	Ezk 44:15	136
sin offering," declares the L God.	Ezk 44:27	136
shall offer an allotment to the L,	Ezk 45:1	3068
come near to minister to the L,	Ezk 45:4	3068
'Thus says the L God,	Ezk 45:9	136
My people," declares the L God.	Ezk 45:9	136
for them," declares the L God.	Ezk 45:15	136
'Thus says the L God,	Ezk 45:18	136
provide as a burnt offering to the L	Ezk 45:23	3068
'Thus says the L God,	Ezk 46:1	136
doorway of that gate before the L	Ezk 46:3	3068
shall offer to the L on the sabbath	Ezk 46:4	3068
come before the L at the appointed	Ezk 46:9	3068
as a freewill offering to the L,	Ezk 46:12	3068
a burnt offering to the L daily;	Ezk 46:13	3068
a grain offering to the L	Ezk 46:14	3068
'Thus says the L God,	Ezk 46:16	136
Thus says the L God,	Ezk 47:13	136
inheritance," declares the L God.	Ezk 47:23	136
that you shall set apart to the L	Ezk 48:9	3068
the sanctuary of the L shall be in its	Ezk 48:10	3068
for it is holy to the L.	Ezk 48:14	3068
portions," declares the L God.	Ezk 48:29	136
'The L is there.'"	Ezk 48:35	3068
The L gave Jehoiakim king of	Da 1:2	136
"I am afraid of my l the king,	Da 1:10	113
God of gods and a L of kings	Da 2:47	4756
'My l, *if only* the dream applied	Da 4:19	4756
which has come upon my l the king:	Da 4:24	4756
yourself against the L of heaven;	Da 5:23	4756
revealed as the word of the L to	Da 9:2	3068
So I gave my attention to the L	Da 9:3	136
I prayed to the L my God and	Da 9:4	3068
"Alas, O L, the great and awesome	Da 9:4	136
Righteousness belongs to You, O L	Da 9:7	136
"Open shame belongs to us, O L,	Da 9:8	3068
"To the L our God	Da 9:9	136
obeyed the voice of the L our God,	Da 9:10	3068
sought the favor of the L our God	Da 9:13	3068
the L has kept the calamity in	Da 9:14	3068
for the L our God is righteous	Da 9:14	3068
"And now, O L our God, who have	Da 9:15	136
"O L, in accordance with all Your	Da 9:16	136
and for Your sake, O L,	Da 9:17	136
"O L, hear! O Lord, forgive! O	Da 9:19	136
O L, forgive! O Lord, listen and	Da 9:19	136
O L, listen and take action!	Da 9:19	136
supplication before the L my God	Da 9:20	3068
"O my l, as a result of the	Da 10:16	113
how can such a servant of my l talk	Da 10:17	113
of my lord talk with such as my l?	Da 10:17	113
"May my l speak, for you have	Da 10:19	113
"My l, what *will be* the outcome	Da 12:8	113
The word of the L which came to	Hos 1:1	3068
the L first spoke through Hosea,	Hos 1:2	3068
Hosea, the L said to Hosea,	Hos 1:2	3068
harlotry, forsaking the L."	Hos 1:2	3068
And the L said to him,	Hos 1:4	3068
And the L said to him,	Hos 1:6	3068
deliver them by the L their God,	Hos 1:7	3068
the L said, "Name him Lo-ammi,	Hos 1:9	3068
she forgot Me," declares the L.	Hos 2:13	3068
about in that day," declares the L,	Hos 2:16	3068
Then you will know the L.	Hos 2:20	3068
I will respond," declares the L.	Hos 2:21	3068
Then the L said to me,	Hos 3:1	3068
as the L loves the sons of Israel,	Hos 3:1	3068
seek the L their God and David	Hos 3:5	3068
they will come trembling to the L	Hos 3:5	3068
Listen to the word of the L,	Hos 4:1	3068
For the L has a case against the	Hos 4:1	3068
have stopped giving heed to the L.	Hos 4:10	3068
"As the L lives!"	Hos 4:15	3068
Can the L now pasture them Like a	Hos 4:16	3068
them, And they do not know the L.	Hos 5:4	3068
flocks and herds To seek the L,	Hos 5:6	3068
dealt treacherously against the L,	Hos 5:7	3068
"Come, let us return to the L.	Hos 6:1	3068
let us press on to know the L.	Hos 6:3	3068
returned to the L their God,	Hos 7:10	3068
comes against the house of the L,	Hos 8:1	3068
L has taken no delight in them.	Hos 8:13	3068
out drink offerings of wine to the L,	Hos 9:4	3068
will not enter the house of the L.	Hos 9:4	3068
on the day of the feast of the L?	Hos 9:5	3068
Give them, O L	Hos 9:14	3068
The L will break down their altars	Hos 10:2	
king, For we do not revere the L.	Hos 10:3	3068
For it is time to seek the L Until	Hos 10:12	3068
They will walk after the L,	Hos 11:10	3068
in their houses, declares the L.	Hos 11:11	3068
L also has a dispute with Judah,	Hos 12:2	3068
Even the L, the God of hosts,	Hos 12:5	3068
The L is His name.	Hos 12:5	3068
But I *have been* the L your God	Hos 12:9	3068
the L brought Israel from Egypt,	Hos 12:13	3068
So his L will leave his bloodguilt	Hos 12:14	136
Yet I *have been* the L your God	Hos 13:4	3068
The wind of the L coming up from	Hos 13:15	3068
Return, O Israel, to the L your God	Hos 14:1	3068
with you and return to the L.	Hos 14:2	3068
For the ways of the L are right,	Hos 14:9	3068
word of the L that came to Joel,	Jl 1:1	3068
cut off From the house of the L.	Jl 1:9	3068
mourn, The ministers of the L.	Jl 1:9	3068
To the house of the L your God,	Jl 1:14	3068
your God, And cry out to the L.	Jl 1:14	3068
For the day of the L is near,	Jl 1:15	3068
To You, O L, I cry;	Jl 1:19	3068
For the day of the L is coming;	Jl 2:1	3068
The L utters His voice before	Jl 2:11	3068
The day of the L is indeed great	Jl 2:11	3068
"Yet even now," declares the L,	Jl 2:12	3068
Now return to the L your God, For	Jl 2:13	3068
a drink offering For the L your God?	Jl 2:14	3068
"Spare Your people, O L,	Jl 2:17	3068
L will be zealous for His land And	Jl 2:18	3068
The L will answer and say to	Jl 2:19	3068
For the L has done great things.	Jl 2:21	3068
And be glad in the L your God;	Jl 2:23	3068
praise the name of the L your God,	Jl 2:26	3068
And that I am the L your God,	Jl 2:27	3068
and awesome day of the L comes.	Jl 2:31	3068
whoever calls on the name of the L	Jl 2:32	3068
who escape, As the L has said,	Jl 2:32	3068
the survivors whom the L calls.	Jl 2:32	3068
nation," for the L has spoken.	Jl 3:8	3068
Bring down, O L, Your mighty ones.	Jl 3:11	3068
For the day of the L is near in	Jl 3:14	3068
The L roars from Zion And	Jl 3:16	3068
But the L is a refuge for His	Jl 3:16	3068
know that I am the L your God,	Jl 3:17	3068
go out from the house of the L	Jl 3:18	3068
avenged, For the L dwells in Zion.	Jl 3:21	3068
"The L roars from Zion And from	Am 1:2	3068
Thus says the L,	Am 1:3	3068
will go exiled to Kir," Says the L.	Am 1:5	3068
Thus says the L,	Am 1:6	3068
will perish," Says the L God.	Am 1:8	136
Thus says the L,	Am 1:9	3068
Thus says the L,	Am 1:11	3068
Thus says the L,	Am 1:13	3068
his princes together," says the L.	Am 1:15	3068
Thus says the L,	Am 2:1	3068
her princes with him," says the L.	Am 2:3	3068
Thus says the L,	Am 2:4	3068
they rejected the law of the L And	Am 2:4	3068
Thus says the L,	Am 2:6	3068
O sons of Israel?" declares the L.	Am 2:11	3068
naked in that day," declares the L.	Am 2:16	3068
the L has spoken against you,	Am 3:1	3068
in a city has not the L done it?	Am 3:6	3068
Surely the L God does nothing	Am 3:7	136
The L God has spoken!	Am 3:8	136
do what is right," declares the L,	Am 3:10	3068
Therefore, thus says the L God,	Am 3:11	136
Thus says the L,	Am 3:12	3068
of Jacob," Declares the L God,	Am 3:13	136
come to an end," Declares the L.	Am 3:15	3068
L God has sworn by His holiness,	Am 4:2	136
be cast to Harmon," declares the L.	Am 4:3	3068
of Israel," Declares the L God.	Am 4:5	136
returned to Me," declares the L.	Am 4:6	3068
returned to Me," declares the L.	Am 4:8	3068
returned to Me," declares the L.	Am 4:9	3068
returned to Me," declares the L.	Am 4:10	3068
returned to Me," declares the L.	Am 4:11	3068
The L God of hosts is His name.	Am 4:13	3068
For thus says the L God,	Am 5:3	136
says the L to the house of Israel,	Am 5:4	3068
"Seek the L that you may live,	Am 5:6	3068
of the earth, The L is His name.	Am 5:8	3068
the L God of hosts be with you,	Am 5:14	3068
Perhaps the L God of hosts May be	Am 5:15	3068
thus says the L God of hosts,	Am 5:16	3068
says the LORD God of hosts, the L,	Am 5:16	136
the midst of you," says the L.	Am 5:17	3068
are longing for the day of the L,	Am 5:18	3068
will the day of the L *be* to you?	Am 5:18	3068
the day of the L *be* darkness instead	Am 5:20	3068
exile beyond Damascus," says the L,	Am 5:27	3068
The L God has sworn by Himself,	Am 6:8	136
the L God of hosts has declared:	Am 6:8	3068
of the L is not to be mentioned."	Am 6:10	3068
the L is going to command that the	Am 6:11	3068
declares the L God of hosts,	Am 6:14	3068
Thus the L God showed me, and	Am 7:1	136
"L God, please pardon!	Am 7:2	136
The L changed His mind about this.	Am 7:3	3068
"It shall not be," said the L.	Am 7:3	3068
Thus the L God showed me, and	Am 7:4	136
the L God was calling to contend	Am 7:4	136
"L God, please stop!	Am 7:5	136
The L changed His mind about this.	Am 7:6	3068
too shall not be," said the L God.	Am 7:6	136
the L was standing by a vertical	Am 7:7	136
The L said to me,	Am 7:8	3068
Then the L said,	Am 7:8	136
"But the L took me from following	Am 7:15	3068
the flock and the L said to me,	Am 7:15	3068
"Now hear the word of the L:	Am 7:16	3068
"Therefore, thus says the L,	Am 7:17	3068
Thus the L God showed me, and	Am 8:1	136
Then the L said to me,	Am 8:2	3068
in that day," declares the L God.	Am 8:3	136
The L has sworn by the pride of	Am 8:7	3068
in that day," declares the L God,	Am 8:9	136
are coming," declares the L God,	Am 8:11	136
for hearing the words of the L.	Am 8:11	3068
and fro to seek the word of the L,	Am 8:12	3068
the L standing beside the altar,	Am 9:1	136
The L God of hosts, The One	Am 9:5	136
of the earth, The L is His name.	Am 9:6	3068
O sons of Israel?" declares the L.	Am 9:7	3068
eyes of the L God are on the sinful	Am 9:8	136
house of Jacob," Declares the L.	Am 9:8	3068
Declares the L who does this.	Am 9:12	3068
days are coming," declares the L,	Am 9:13	3068
given them," Says the L your God.	Am 9:15	3068
Thus says the L God concerning	Ob 1:1	136
We have heard a report from the L,	Ob 1:1	3068
bring you down," declares the L.	Ob 1:4	3068
I not on that day," declares the L,	Ob 1:8	3068
the day of the L draws near on all	Ob 1:15	3068
of Esau," For the L has spoken.	Ob 1:18	3068
The word of the L came to Jonah	Jon 1:1	3068
from the presence of the L.	Jon 1:3	3068
from the presence of the L.	Jon 1:3	3068
The L hurled a great wind on	Jon 1:4	3068
and I fear the L God of heaven who	Jon 1:9	3068
from the presence of the L,	Jon 1:10	3068
they called on the L and said,	Jon 1:14	3068
"We earnestly pray, O L,	Jon 1:14	3068
for You, O L, have done as You	Jon 1:14	3068
Then the men feared the L greatly,	Jon 1:16	3068
they offered a sacrifice to the L and	Jon 1:16	3068
And the L appointed a great fish	Jon 1:17	3068
Then Jonah prayed to the L his God	Jon 2:1	3068
I called out of my distress to the L,	Jon 2:2	3068
my life from the pit, O L my God.	Jon 2:6	3068
fainting away, I remembered the L,	Jon 2:7	3068
Salvation is from the L."	Jon 2:9	3068
Then the L commanded the fish, and	Jon 2:10	3068
the word of the L came to Jonah	Jon 3:1	3068
according to the word of the L.	Jon 3:3	3068
He prayed to the L and said,	Jon 4:2	3068
"Please L, was not this what I	Jon 4:2	3068
"Therefore now, O L,	Jon 4:3	3068
The L said, "Do you have	Jon 4:4	3068
So the L God appointed a plant and	Jon 4:6	3068
Then the L said,	Jon 4:10	3068
The word of the L which came *to*	Mi 1:1	3068
L God be a witness against you,	Mi 1:2	136
you, The L from His holy temple.	Mi 1:2	136
the L is coming forth from His	Mi 1:3	3068
calamity has come down from the L	Mi 1:12	3068
Therefore thus says the L,	Mi 2:3	3068
by lot in the assembly of the L.	Mi 2:5	3068
'Is the Spirit of the L impatient?	Mi 2:7	3068
them, And the L at their head."	Mi 2:13	3068
Then they will cry out to the L,	Mi 3:4	3068
Thus says the L concerning the	Mi 3:5	3068
With the Spirit of the L	Mi 3:8	3068
Yet they lean on the L saying,	Mi 3:11	3068
"Is not the L in our midst?	Mi 3:11	3068
mountain of the house of the L Will	Mi 4:1	3068
go up to the mountain of the L	Mi 4:2	3068
the word of the L from Jerusalem.	Mi 4:2	3068
mouth of the L of hosts has spoken.	Mi 4:4	3068
walk In the name of the L our God	Mi 4:5	3068
"In that day," declares the L,	Mi 4:6	3068
And the L will reign over them in	Mi 4:7	3068
There the L will redeem you From	Mi 4:10	3068
do not know the thoughts of the L,	Mi 4:12	3068
That you may devote to the L their	Mi 4:13	3068
wealth to the L of all the earth.	Mi 4:13	136
flock In the strength of the L,	Mi 5:4	3068
In the majesty of the name of the L	Mi 5:4	3068
many peoples Like dew from the L,	Mi 5:7	3068
be in that day," declares the L,	Mi 5:10	3068
Hear now what the L is saying,	Mi 6:1	3068
to the indictment of the L,	Mi 6:2	3068

L has a case against His people;	Mi 6:2	3068
the righteous acts of the **L**."	Mi 6:5	3068
With what shall I come to the **L**	Mi 6:6	3068
Does the **L** take delight in	Mi 6:7	3068
And what does the **L** require of you	Mi 6:8	3068
The voice of the **L** will call to	Mi 6:9	3068
will watch expectantly for the **L**;	Mi 7:7	3068
darkness, the **L** is a light for me.	Mi 7:8	3068
I will bear the indignation of the **L**	Mi 7:9	3068
"Where is the **L** your God?"	Mi 7:10	3068
To the **L** our God they will come in	Mi 7:17	3068
jealous and avenging God is the **L**;	Na 1:2	3068
The **L** is avenging and wrathful.	Na 1:2	3068
The **L** takes vengeance on His	Na 1:2	3068
The **L** is slow to anger and great	Na 1:3	3068
And the **L** will by no means leave	Na 1:3	3068
The **L** is good, A stronghold in the	Na 1:7	3068
Whatever you devise against the **L**,	Na 1:9	3068
who plotted evil against the **L**,	Na 1:11	3068
Thus says the **L**,	Na 1:12	3068
The **L** has issued a command	Na 1:14	3068
For the **L** will restore the	Na 2:2	3068
you," declares the **L** of hosts.	Na 2:13	3068
you," declares the **L** of hosts;	Na 3:5	3068
How long, O **L**, will I call for	Hab 1:2	3068
Are You not from everlasting, O **L**,	Hab 1:12	3068
You, O **L**, have appointed them to	Hab 1:12	3068
Then the **L** answered me and said,	Hab 2:2	3068
"Is it not indeed from the **L** of hosts	Hab 2:13	3068
knowledge of the glory of the **L**,	Hab 2:14	3068
"But the **L** is in His holy temple.	Hab 2:20	3068
L, I have heard the report about You	Hab 3:2	3068
O **L**, revive Your work in the midst	Hab 3:2	3068
Did the **L** rage against the rivers,	Hab 3:8	3068
Yet I will exult in the **L**,	Hab 3:18	3068
The **L** GOD is my strength, And He	Hab 3:19	136
The word of the **L** which came to	Zph 1:1	3068
face of the earth," declares the **L**.	Zph 1:2	3068
face of the earth," declares the **L**.	Zph 1:3	3068
who bow down *and* swear to the **L**	Zph 1:5	3068
turned back from following the **L**,	Zph 1:6	3068
those who have not sought the **L** or	Zph 1:6	3068
Be silent before the **L** GOD!	Zph 1:7	136
For the day of the **L** is near,	Zph 1:7	3068
the **L** has prepared a sacrifice,	Zph 1:7	3068
fill the house of their **l** with violence	Zph 1:9	113
"On that day," declares the **L**,	Zph 1:10	3068
'The **L** will not do good or evil!'	Zph 1:12	3068
Near is the great day of the **L**,	Zph 1:14	3068
Listen, the day of the **L**!	Zph 1:14	3068
they have sinned against the **L**;	Zph 1:17	3068
anger of the **L** comes upon you,	Zph 2:2	3068
Seek the **L**, All you humble of the	Zph 2:3	3068
The word of the **L** is against you,	Zph 2:5	3068
For the **L** their God will care for	Zph 2:7	3068
I live," declares the **L** of hosts,	Zph 2:9	3068
the people of the **L** of hosts.	Zph 2:10	3068
The **L** will be terrifying to them,	Zph 2:11	3068
She did not trust in the **L**,	Zph 3:2	3068
The **L** is righteous within her;	Zph 3:5	3068
wait for Me," declares the **L**,	Zph 3:8	3068
may call on the name of the **L**,	Zph 3:9	3068
take refuge in the name of the **L**.	Zph 3:12	3068
The **L** has taken away *His* judgments	Zph 3:15	3068
The King of Israel, the **L**,	Zph 3:15	3068
"The **L** your God is in your midst,	Zph 3:17	3068
before your eyes," Says the **L**.	Zph 3:20	3068
the word of the **L** came by the	Hg 1:1	3068
"Thus says the **L** of hosts,	Hg 1:2	3068
for the house of the **L** to be rebuilt.	Hg 1:2	3068
Then the word of the **L** came by	Hg 1:3	3068
thus says the **L** of hosts,	Hg 1:5	3068
Thus says the **L** of hosts,	Hg 1:7	3068
it and be glorified," says the **L**.	Hg 1:8	3068
declares the **L** of hosts,	Hg 1:9	3068
obeyed the voice of the **L** their	Hg 1:12	3068
as the **L** their God had sent him.	Hg 1:12	3068
people showed reverence for the **L**.	Hg 1:12	3068
Haggai, the messenger of the **L**,	Hg 1:13	3068
spoke by the commission of the **L**	Hg 1:13	3068
"'I am with you,' declares the **L**."	Hg 1:13	3068
So the **L** stirred up the spirit of	Hg 1:14	3068
on the house of the **L** of hosts,	Hg 1:14	3068
the word of the **L** came by Haggai	Hg 2:1	3068
Zerubbabel,' declares the **L**,	Hg 2:4	3068
land take courage,' declares the **L**,	Hg 2:4	3068
am with you,' declares the **L** of hosts.	Hg 2:4	3068
"For thus says the **L** of hosts,	Hg 2:6	3068
with glory,' says the **L** of hosts.	Hg 2:7	3068
is Mine,' declares the **L** of hosts.	Hg 2:8	3068
the former,' says the **L** of hosts,	Hg 2:9	3068
peace,' declares the **L** of hosts."	Hg 2:9	3068
the word of the **L** came to Haggai	Hg 2:10	3068
"Thus says the **L** of hosts,	Hg 2:11	3068
nation before Me,' declares the **L**,	Hg 2:14	3068
on another in the temple of the **L**,	Hg 2:15	3068
come back to Me,' declares the **L**.	Hg 2:17	3068
the temple of the **L** was founded,	Hg 2:18	3068
Then the word of the **L** came a	Hg 2:20	3068
that day,' declares the **L** of hosts,	Hg 2:23	3068
My servant,' declares the **L**,	Hg 2:23	3068
you,'" declares the **L** of hosts.	Hg 2:23	3068
L came to Zechariah the prophet,	Zch 1:1	3068
"The **L** was very angry with your	Zch 1:2	3068
'Thus says the **L** of hosts,	Zch 1:3	3068
to Me," declares the **L** of hosts,	Zch 1:3	3068
to you," says the **L** of hosts.	Zch 1:3	3068
'Thus says the **L** of hosts,	Zch 1:4	3068
give heed to Me," declares the **L**.	Zch 1:4	3068
'As the **L** of hosts purposed to do	Zch 1:6	3068
the word of the **L** came to Zechariah	Zch 1:7	3068
"My **l**, what are these?"	Zch 1:9	113
L has sent to patrol the earth."	Zch 1:10	3068
So they answered the angel of the **L**	Zch 1:11	3068
angel of the **L** said,	Zch 1:12	3068
"O **L** of hosts, how long will You	Zch 1:12	3068
The **L** answered the angel who	Zch 1:13	3068
'Thus says the **L** of hosts,	Zch 1:14	3068
'Therefore thus says the **L**,	Zch 1:16	3068
in it," declares the **L** of hosts,	Zch 1:16	3068
'Thus says the **L** of hosts,	Zch 1:17	3068
and the **L** will again comfort Zion	Zch 1:17	3068
the **L** showed me four craftsmen.	Zch 1:20	3068
'For I,' declares the **L**,	Zch 2:5	3068
land of the north," declares the **L**,	Zch 2:6	3068
of the heavens," declares the **L**.	Zch 2:6	3068
For thus says the **L** of hosts,	Zch 2:8	3068
that the **L** of hosts has sent Me.	Zch 2:9	3068
in your midst," declares the **L**.	Zch 2:10	3068
nations will join themselves to the **L**	Zch 2:11	3068
the **L** of hosts has sent Me to you.	Zch 2:11	3068
"The **L** will possess Judah as	Zch 2:12	3068
silent, all flesh, before the **L**;	Zch 2:13	3068
before the angel of the **L**,	Zch 3:1	3068
The **L** said to Satan,	Zch 3:2	3068
"The **L** rebuke you, Satan!	Zch 3:2	3068
the **L** who has chosen Jerusalem	Zch 3:2	3068
angel of the **L** was standing by.	Zch 3:5	3068
angel of the **L** admonished Joshua	Zch 3:6	3068
"Thus says the **L** of hosts,	Zch 3:7	3068
on it,' declares the **L** of hosts,	Zch 3:9	3068
that day,' declares the **L** of hosts,	Zch 3:10	3068
"What are these, my **l**?"	Zch 4:4	113
And I said, "No, my **l**."	Zch 4:5	113
the word of the **L** to Zerubbabel	Zch 4:6	3068
by My Spirit,' says the **L** of hosts.	Zch 4:6	3068
word of the **L** came to me,	Zch 4:8	3068
the **L** of hosts has sent me to you.	Zch 4:9	3068
eyes of the **L** which range to and fro	Zch 4:10	3068
And I said, "No, my **l**."	Zch 4:13	113
standing by the **L** of the whole earth	Zch 4:14	136
go forth," declares the **L** of hosts,	Zch 5:4	3068
"What are these, my **l**?"	Zch 6:4	113
standing before the **L** of all the earth	Zch 6:5	136
The word of the **L** also came to me	Zch 6:9	3068
'Thus says the **L** of hosts,	Zch 6:12	3068
He will build the temple of the **L**.	Zch 6:12	3068
will build the temple of the **L**,	Zch 6:13	3068
in the temple of the **L** to Helem,	Zch 6:14	3068
and build the temple of the **L**."	Zch 6:15	3068
the **L** of hosts has sent me to you.	Zch 6:15	3068
completely obey the **L** your God.	Zch 6:15	3068
the word of the **L** came to	Zch 7:1	3068
men to seek the favor of the **L**,	Zch 7:2	3068
to the house of the **L** of hosts,	Zch 7:3	3068
word of the **L** of hosts came to me	Zch 7:4	3068
the words which the **L** proclaimed	Zch 7:7	3068
word of the **L** came to Zechariah	Zch 7:8	3068
"Thus has the **L** of hosts said,	Zch 7:9	3068
words which the **L** of hosts had sent	Zch 7:12	3068
wrath came from the **L** of hosts.	Zch 7:12	3068
not listen," says the **L** of hosts;	Zch 7:13	3068
the word of the **L** of hosts came	Zch 8:1	3068
"Thus says the **L** of hosts,	Zch 8:2	3068
"Thus says the **L**,	Zch 8:3	3068
and the mountain of the **L** of hosts	Zch 8:3	3068
"Thus says the **L** of hosts,	Zch 8:4	3068
"Thus says the **L** of hosts,	Zch 8:6	3068
declares the **L** of hosts.	Zch 8:6	3068
"Thus says the **L** of hosts,	Zch 8:7	3068
"Thus says the **L** of hosts,	Zch 8:9	3068
house of the **L** of hosts was laid,	Zch 8:9	3068
days,' declares the **L** of hosts.	Zch 8:11	3068
"For thus says the **L** of hosts,	Zch 8:14	3068
Me to wrath,' says the **L** of hosts,	Zch 8:14	3068
are what I hate,' declares the **L**."	Zch 8:17	3068
the **L** of hosts came to me,	Zch 8:18	3068
"Thus says the **L** of hosts,	Zch 8:19	3068
"Thus says the **L** of hosts,	Zch 8:20	3068
to entreat the favor of the **L**,	Zch 8:21	3068
LORD, and to seek the **L** of hosts;	Zch 8:21	3068
nations will come to seek the **L** of	Zch 8:22	3068
to entreat the favor of the **L**.'	Zch 8:22	3068
"Thus says the **L** of hosts,	Zch 8:23	3068
The burden of the word of the **L** is	Zch 9:1	3068
of Israel, are toward the **L**),	Zch 9:1	3068
the **L** will dispossess her And cast	Zch 9:4	136
Then the **L** will appear over them,	Zch 9:14	3068
the **L** GOD will blow the trumpet,	Zch 9:14	136
The **L** of hosts will defend them.	Zch 9:15	3068
And the **L** their God will save them	Zch 9:16	3068
Ask rain from the **L** at the time of	Zch 10:1	3068
The **L** who makes the storm clouds;	Zch 10:1	3068
For the **L** of hosts has visited His	Zch 10:3	3068
for the **L** *will be* with them;	Zch 10:5	3068
them, For I am the **L** their God and	Zch 10:6	3068
Their heart will rejoice in the **L**.	Zch 10:7	3068
I will strengthen them in the **L**,	Zch 10:12	3068
they will walk," declares the **L**.	Zch 10:12	3068
Thus says the **L** my God,	Zch 11:4	3068
'Blessed be the **L**, for I have	Zch 11:5	3068
of the land," declares the **L**;	Zch 11:6	3068
that it was the word of the **L**.	Zch 11:11	3068
Then the **L** said to me,	Zch 11:13	3068
the potter in the house of the **L**.	Zch 11:13	3068
The **L** said to me,	Zch 11:15	3068
word of the **L** concerning Israel.	Zch 12:1	3068
L who stretches out the heavens,	Zch 12:1	3068
"In that day," declares the **L**,	Zch 12:4	3068
Jerusalem through the **L** of hosts,	Zch 12:5	3068
"The **L** also will save the tents	Zch 12:7	3068
"In that day the **L** will defend	Zch 12:8	3068
the angel of the **L** before them.	Zch 12:8	3068
that day," declares the **L** of hosts,	Zch 13:2	3068
spoken falsely in the name of the **L**'	Zch 13:3	3068
Declares the **L** of hosts.	Zch 13:7	3068
in all the land," Declares the **L**,	Zch 13:8	3068
'The **L** is my God.'"	Zch 13:9	3068
a day is coming for the **L** when the	Zch 14:1	3068
Then the **L** will go forth and fight	Zch 14:3	3068
Then the **L**, my God, will come, *and*	Zch 14:5	3068
day which is known to the **L**,	Zch 14:7	3068
And the **L** will be king over all	Zch 14:9	3068
day the **L** will be *the only* one,	Zch 14:9	3068
plague with which the **L** will strike	Zch 14:12	3068
a great panic from the **L** will fall	Zch 14:13	3068
worship the King, the **L** of hosts,	Zch 14:16	3068
worship the King, the **L** of hosts,	Zch 14:17	3068
plague with which the **L** smites the	Zch 14:18	3068
"HOLY TO THE **L**." And the cooking	Zch 14:20	3068
will be holy to the **L** of hosts;	Zch 14:21	3068
in the house of the **L** of hosts	Zch 14:21	3068
oracle of the word of the **L** to Israel	Mal 1:1	3068
"I have loved you," says the **L**.	Mal 1:2	3068
Jacob's brother?" declares the **L**.	Mal 1:2	3068
thus says the **L** of hosts,	Mal 1:4	3068
toward whom the **L** is indignant	Mal 1:4	3068
"The **L** be magnified beyond the	Mal 1:5	3068
says the **L** of hosts to you, O	Mal 1:6	3068
table of the **L** is to be despised.'	Mal 1:7	3068
says the **L** of hosts.	Mal 1:8	3068
says the **L** of hosts.	Mal 1:9	3068
with you," says the **L** of hosts,	Mal 1:10	3068
the nations," says the **L** of hosts.	Mal 1:11	3068
'The table of the **L** is defiled,	Mal 1:12	136
sniff at it," says the **L** of hosts,	Mal 1:13	3068
that from your hand?" says the **L**.	Mal 1:13	3068
a blemished animal to the **L**,	Mal 1:14	136
a great King," says the **L** of hosts,	Mal 1:14	3068
to My name," says the **L** of hosts,	Mal 2:2	3068
with Levi," says the **L** of hosts.	Mal 2:4	3068
the messenger of the **L** of hosts.	Mal 2:7	3068
of Levi," says the **L** of hosts.	Mal 2:8	3068
sanctuary of the **L** which He loves and	Mal 2:11	3068
may the **L** cut off from the tents	Mal 2:12	3068
an offering to the **L** of hosts.	Mal 2:12	3068
cover the altar of the **L** with tears,	Mal 2:13	3068
Because the **L** has been a witness	Mal 2:14	3068
"For I hate divorce," says the **L**,	Mal 2:16	3068
with wrong," says the **L** of hosts.	Mal 2:16	3068
wearied the **L** with your words.	Mal 2:17	3068
is good in the sight of the **L**,	Mal 2:17	3068
And the **L**, whom you seek, will	Mal 3:1	113
He is coming," says the **L** of hosts.	Mal 3:1	3068
they may present to the **L** offerings	Mal 3:3	3068
will be pleasing to the **L**	Mal 3:4	3068
not fear Me," says the **L** of hosts.	Mal 3:5	3068
"For I, the **L**, do not change;	Mal 3:6	3068
to you," says the **L** of hosts.	Mal 3:7	3068
now in this," says the **L** of hosts,	Mal 3:10	3068
its grapes," says the **L** of hosts.	Mal 3:11	3068
land," says the **L** of hosts.	Mal 3:12	3068
arrogant against Me," says the **L**.	Mal 3:13	3068
in mourning before the **L** of hosts?	Mal 3:14	3068
those who feared the **L** spoke to one	Mal 3:16	3068
the **L** gave attention and heard *it*,	Mal 3:16	3068
for those who fear the **L** and who	Mal 3:16	3068
will be Mine," says the **L** of hosts,	Mal 3:17	3068
them ablaze," says the **L** of hosts,	Mal 4:1	3068
am preparing," says the **L** of hosts.	Mal 4:3	3068
great and terrible day of the **L**.	Mal 4:5	3068
an angel of the **L** appeared to him	Mt 1:20	*2962*
spoken by the **L** through the prophet	Mt 1:22	*2962*
the angel of the **L** commanded him,	Mt 1:24	*2962*
angel of the **L** appeared to Joseph	Mt 2:13	*2962*
what had been spoken by the **L**	Mt 2:15	*2962*
an angel of the **L** appeared in a	Mt 2:19	*2962*
'MAKE READY THE WAY OF THE **L**,	Mt 3:3	*2962*
THE **L** YOUR GOD TO THE TEST.'"	Mt 4:7	*2962*
'YOU SHALL WORSHIP THE **L** YOUR GOD,	Mt 4:10	*2962*
SHALL FULFILL YOUR VOWS TO THE **L**.'	Mt 5:33	*2962*
'**L**, Lord,' will enter the kingdom	Mt 7:21	*2962*
'Lord, **L**,' will enter the kingdom	Mt 7:21	*2962*
'**L**, Lord, did we not prophesy in	Mt 7:22	*2962*
'Lord, **L**, did we not prophesy in	Mt 7:22	*2962*
"**L**, if You are willing, You can	Mt 8:2	*2962*
"**L**, my servant is lying paralyzed	Mt 8:6	*2962*
"**L**, I am not worthy for You to	Mt 8:8	*2962*
"**L**, permit me first to go and	Mt 8:21	*2962*
"Save *us*, **L**; we are perishing!"	Mt 8:25	*2962*
They said to Him, "Yes, **L**."	Mt 9:28	*2962*
beseech the **L** of the harvest to send	Mt 9:38	*2962*
Father, **L** of heaven and earth,	Mt 11:25	*2962*
Son of Man is **L** of the Sabbath."	Mt 12:8	*2962*
"**L**, if it is You, command me to	Mt 14:28	*2962*
he cried out, "**L**, save me!"	Mt 14:30	*2962*
"Have mercy on me, **L**,	Mt 15:22	*2962*
before Him, saying, "**L**, help me!"	Mt 15:25	*2962*
"Yes, **L**; but even the dogs feed on	Mt 15:27	*2962*
"God forbid *it*, **L**!	Mt 16:22	*2962*
"**L**, it is good for us to be here;	Mt 17:4	*2962*
"**L**, have mercy on my son, for he	Mt 17:15	*2962*
"**L**, how often shall my brother	Mt 18:21	*2962*
his **l** commanded him to be sold,	Mt 18:25	*2962*
"And the **l** of that slave felt	Mt 18:27	*2962*
to their **l** all that had happened.	Mt 18:31	*2962*
summoning him, his **l** said to him,	Mt 18:32	*2962*

"And his **l**, moved with anger,	**Mt 18:34**	*2962*
rulers of the Gentiles **l** it over them,	**Mt 20:25**	*2634b*
"**L**, have mercy on us, Son of	**Mt 20:30**	*2962*
"**L**, Son of David, have mercy on us!"	**Mt 20:31**	*2962*
"**L**, *we want* our eyes to be opened."	**Mt 20:33**	*2962*
'The **L** has need of them,' and	**Mt 21:3**	*2962*
He who comes in the name of the **L**;	**Mt 21:9**	*2962*
This came about from the **L**,	**Mt 21:42**	*2962*
"'You shall love the **L** your God	**Mt 22:37**	*2962*
David in the Spirit call Him '**L**,'	**Mt 22:43**	*2962*
'The **L** said to my Lord,	**Mt 22:44**	*2962*
'The Lord said to my **L**,	**Mt 22:44**	*2962*
'**L**,' how is He his son?"	**Mt 22:45**	*2962*
comes in the name of the **L**!' "	**Mt 23:39**	*2962*
know which day your **L** is coming.	**Mt 24:42**	*2962*
'**L**, lord, open up for us.'	**Mt 25:11**	*2962*
'Lord, **l**, open up for us.'	**Mt 25:11**	*2962*
'**L**, when did we see You hungry,	**Mt 25:37**	*2962*
'**L**, when did we see You hungry, or	**Mt 25:44**	*2962*
"Surely not I, **L**?"	**Mt 26:22**	*2962*
Field, as the **L** directed me."	**Mt 27:10**	*2962*
for an angel of the **L** descended	**Mt 28:2**	*2962*
'Make ready the way of the **L**,	**Mk 1:3**	*2962*
Son of Man is **L** even of the Sabbath	**Mk 2:28**	*2962*
things the **L** has done for you,	**Mk 5:19**	*2962*
"Yes, **L**, *but* even the dogs under	**Mk 7:28**	*2962*
rulers of the Gentiles **l** it over them;	**Mk 10:42**	*2634b*
'The **L** has need of it';	**Mk 11:3**	*2962*
He who comes in the name of the **L**;	**Mk 11:9**	*2962*
This came about from the **L**,	**Mk 12:11**	*2962*
The **L** our God is one Lord;	**Mk 12:29**	*2962*
The Lord our God is one **L**;	**Mk 12:29**	*2962*
you shall love the **L** your God	**Mk 12:30**	*2962*
'The **L** said to my Lord,	**Mk 12:36**	*2962*
'The Lord said to my **L**,	**Mk 12:36**	*2962*
"David himself calls Him '**L**';	**Mk 12:37**	*2962*
the **L** had shortened *those* days,	**Mk 13:20**	*2962*
the **L** Jesus had spoken to them,	**Mk 16:19**	*2962*
while the **L** worked with them,	**Mk 16:20**	*2962*
and requirements of the **L**.	**Lk 1:6**	*2962*
to enter the temple of the **L** and	**Lk 1:9**	*2962*
an angel of the **L** appeared to him,	**Lk 1:11**	*2962*
be great in the sight of the **L**;	**Lk 1:15**	*2962*
sons of Israel back to the **L** their God.	**Lk 1:16**	*2962*
a people prepared for the **L**."	**Lk 1:17**	*2962*
"This is the way the **L** has dealt	**Lk 1:25**	*2962*
The **L** *is* with you."	**Lk 1:28**	*2962*
and the **L** God will give Him the	**Lk 1:32**	*2962*
"Behold, the bondslave of the **L**;	**Lk 1:38**	*2962*
mother of my **L** would come to me?	**Lk 1:43**	*2962*
had been spoken to her by the **L**."	**Lk 1:45**	*2962*
"My soul exalts the **L**,	**Lk 1:46**	*2962*
the **L** had displayed His great mercy	**Lk 1:58**	*2962*
of the **L** was certainly with him.	**Lk 1:66**	*2962*
"Blessed *be* the **L** God of Israel,	**Lk 1:68**	*2962*
before the **L** to prepare His ways;	**Lk 1:76**	*2962*
an angel of the **L** suddenly stood	**Lk 2:9**	*2962*
glory of the **L** shone around them;	**Lk 2:9**	*2962*
you a Savior, who is Christ the **L**.	**Lk 2:11**	*2962*
the **L** has made known to us."	**Lk 2:15**	*2962*
to present Him to the **L**	**Lk 2:22**	*2962*
it is written in the Law of the **L**,	**Lk 2:23**	*2962*
shall be called holy to the **L**"),	**Lk 2:23**	*2962*
what was said in the Law of the **L**,	**Lk 2:24**	*2962*
"Now **L**, You are releasing Your	**Lk 2:29**	*1203*
according to the Law of the **L**,	**Lk 2:39**	*2962*
'Make ready the way of the **L**,	**Lk 3:4**	*2962*
shall worship the **L** your God	**Lk 4:8**	*2962*
the **L** your God to the test.' "	**Lk 4:12**	*2962*
"The Spirit of the **L** is upon Me,	**Lk 4:18**	*2962*
the favorable year of the **L**."	**Lk 4:19**	*2962*
me **L**, for I am a sinful man,	**Lk 5:8**	*2962*
"**L**, if You are willing, You can	**Lk 5:12**	*2962*
and the power of the **L** was *present*	**Lk 5:17**	*2962*
Son of Man is **L** of the Sabbath."	**Lk 6:5**	*2962*
'**L**, Lord,' and do not do what I	**Lk 6:46**	*2962*
'Lord, **L**,' and do not do what I	**Lk 6:46**	*2962*
"**L**, do not trouble Yourself	**Lk 7:6**	*2962*
When the **L** saw her, He felt	**Lk 7:13**	*2962*
John sent them to the **L**,	**Lk 7:19**	*2962*
"**L**, do You want us to command	**Lk 9:54**	*2962*
"**L**, permit me first to go and bury	**Lk 9:59**	*2962*
"I will follow You, **L**;	**Lk 9:61**	*2962*
the **L** appointed seventy others,	**Lk 10:1**	*2962*
beseech the **L** of the harvest to send	**Lk 10:2**	*2962*
"**L**, even the demons are subject	**Lk 10:17**	*2962*
O Father, **L** of heaven and earth,	**Lk 10:21**	*2962*
You shall love the **L** your God	**Lk 10:27**	*2962*
"**L**, do You not care that my	**Lk 10:40**	*2962*
the **L** answered and said to her,	**Lk 10:41**	*2962*
"**L**, teach us to pray just as John	**Lk 11:1**	*2962*
But the **L** said to him,	**Lk 11:39**	*2962*
"**L**, are You addressing this	**Lk 12:41**	*2962*
L said, "Who then is the faithful	**Lk 12:42**	*2962*
But the **L** answered him and said,	**Lk 13:15**	*2962*
"**L**, are there *just* a few who are	**Lk 13:23**	*2962*
'**L**, open up to us!'	**Lk 13:25**	*2962*
comes in the name of the **L**!' "	**Lk 13:35**	*2962*
The apostles said to the **L**,	**Lk 17:5**	*2962*
And the **L** said, "If you had faith	**Lk 17:6**	*2962*
"Where, **L**?" And He said to them,	**Lk 17:37**	*2962*
And the **L** said, "Hear what the	**Lk 18:6**	*2962*
"**L**, *I want* to regain my sight!"	**Lk 18:41**	*2962*
Zaccheus stopped and said to the **L**	**Lk 19:8**	*2962*
"Behold, **L**, half of my possessions	**Lk 19:8**	*2962*
'The **L** has need of it.' "	**Lk 19:31**	*2962*
"The **L** has need of it."	**Lk 19:34**	*2962*
who comes in the name of the **L**;	**Lk 19:38**	*2962*
he calls the **L** the God of Abraham,	**Lk 20:37**	*2962*
'The **L** said to my Lord,	**Lk 20:42**	*2962*
'The Lord said to my **L**,	**Lk 20:42**	*2962*
"Therefore David calls Him '**L**,'	**Lk 20:44**	*2962*
kings of the Gentiles **l** it over them;	**Lk 22:25**	*2961*
"**L**, with You I am ready to go	**Lk 22:33**	*2962*
"**L**, look, here are two swords."	**Lk 22:38**	*2962*
"**L**, shall we strike with the	**Lk 22:49**	*2962*
The **L** turned and looked at Peter.	**Lk 22:61**	*2962*
remembered the word of the **L**,	**Lk 22:61**	*2962*
not find the body of the **L** Jesus.	**Lk 24:3**	*2962*
"The **L** has really risen and has	**Lk 24:34**	*2962*
'Make straight the way of the **L**,'	**Jn 1:23**	*2962*
Therefore when the **L** knew that the	**Jn 4:1**	*2962*
for an angel of the **L** went down at	**Jn 5:4**	*2962*
after the **L** had given thanks.	**Jn 6:23**	*2962*
"**L**, always give us this bread."	**Jn 6:34**	*2962*
"**L**, to whom shall we go?	**Jn 6:68**	*2962*
She said, "No one, **L**." And Jesus	**Jn 8:11**	*2962*
"Who is He, **L**, that I may	**Jn 9:36**	*2962*
"**L**, I believe."	**Jn 9:38**	*2962*
who anointed the **L** with ointment,	**Jn 11:2**	*2962*
"**L**, behold, he whom You love is	**Jn 11:3**	*2962*
"**L**, if he has fallen asleep, he	**Jn 11:12**	*2962*
"**L**, if You had been here, my	**Jn 11:21**	*2962*
"Yes, **L**; I have believed that You	**Jn 11:27**	*2962*
"**L**, if You had been here, my	**Jn 11:32**	*2962*
"**L**, come and see."	**Jn 11:34**	*2962*
"**L**, by this time there will be a	**Jn 11:39**	*2962*
He who comes in the name of the **L**,	**Jn 12:13**	*2962*
"**L**, who has believed our report?	**Jn 12:38**	*2962*
the arm of the **L** been revealed?"	**Jn 12:38**	*2962*
"**L**, do You wash my feet?"	**Jn 13:6**	*2962*
"**L**, *then wash* not only my feet, but also	**Jn 13:9**	*2962*
"You call Me Teacher and **L**;	**Jn 13:13**	*2962*
"If I then, the **L** and the Teacher,	**Jn 13:14**	*2962*
"**L**, who is it?"	**Jn 13:25**	*2962*
"**L**, where are You going?"	**Jn 13:36**	*2962*
"**L**, why can I not follow You	**Jn 13:37**	*2962*
"**L**, we do not know where You are	**Jn 14:5**	*2962*
"**L**, show us the Father, and it is	**Jn 14:8**	*2962*
"**L**, what then has happened that	**Jn 14:22**	*2962*
taken away the **L** out of the tomb,	**Jn 20:2**	*2962*
"Because they have taken away my **L**,	**Jn 20:13**	*2962*
"I have seen the **L**,"	**Jn 20:18**	*2962*
rejoiced when they saw the **L**.	**Jn 20:20**	*2962*
"We have seen the **L**!"	**Jn 20:25**	*2962*
"My **L** and my God!"	**Jn 20:28**	*2962*
"It is the **L**." So when Simon	**Jn 21:7**	*2962*
Peter heard that it was the **L**,	**Jn 21:7**	*2962*
knowing that it was the **L**.	**Jn 21:12**	*2962*
"Yes, **L**; You know that I love You	**Jn 21:15**	*2962*
"Yes, **L**; You know that I love You	**Jn 21:16**	*2962*
"**L**, You know all things;	**Jn 21:17**	*2962*
"**L**, who is the one who betrays	**Jn 21:20**	*2962*
"**L**, and what about this man?"	**Jn 21:21**	*2962*
"**L**, is it at this time You are	**Ac 1:6**	*2962*
L Jesus went in and out among us	**Ac 1:21**	*2962*
"You, **L**, who know the hearts	**Ac 1:24**	*2962*
glorious day of the **L** shall come.	**Ac 2:20**	*2962*
who calls on the name of the **L**	**Ac 2:21**	*2962*
saw the **L** always in my presence;	**Ac 2:25**	*2962*
'The **L** said to my Lord	**Ac 2:34**	*2962*
'The Lord said to my **L**	**Ac 2:34**	*2962*
has made Him both **L** and Christ	**Ac 2:36**	*2962*
L our God will call to Himself."	**Ac 2:39**	*2962*
the **L** was adding to their number	**Ac 2:47**	*2962*
come from the presence of the **L**;	**Ac 3:19**	*2962*
'The **L** God will raise up for you	**Ac 3:22**	*2962*
"O **L**, it is You who made	**Ac 4:24**	*1203*
gathered together Against the **L**	**Ac 4:26**	*2962*
"And now, **L**, take note of their	**Ac 4:29**	*2962*
the resurrection of the **L** Jesus,	**Ac 4:33**	*2962*
to put the Spirit of the **L** to the test?	**Ac 5:9**	*2962*
all the more believers in the **L**,	**Ac 5:14**	*2962*
during the night an angel of the **L**	**Ac 5:19**	*2962*
there came the voice of the **L**:	**Ac 7:31**	*2962*
'But the **L** said to him,	**Ac 7:33**	*2962*
you build for Me?' says the **L**	**Ac 7:49**	*2962*
Stephen as he called on *the* **L**	**Ac 7:59**	
"**L** Jesus, receive my spirit!"	**Ac 7:59**	*2962*
"**L**, do not hold this sin against	**Ac 7:60**	*2962*
baptized in the name of the **L** Jesus.	**Ac 8:16**	*2962*
and pray the **L** that, if possible,	**Ac 8:22**	*2962*
"Pray to the **L** for me yourselves,	**Ac 8:24**	*2962*
and spoken the word of the **L**,	**Ac 8:25**	*2962*
an angel of the **L** spoke to Philip	**Ac 8:26**	*2962*
Spirit of the **L** snatched Philip away	**Ac 8:39**	*2962*
against the disciples of the **L**,	**Ac 9:1**	*2962*
"Who are You, **L**?"	**Ac 9:5**	*2962*
and the **L** said to him in a vision,	**Ac 9:10**	*2962*
"Here I am, **L**."	**Ac 9:10**	*2962*
And the **L** *said* to him,	**Ac 9:11**	*2962*
"**L**, I have heard from many about	**Ac 9:13**	*2962*
But the **L** said to him,	**Ac 9:15**	*2962*
"Brother Saul, the **L** Jesus,	**Ac 9:17**	*2962*
how he had seen the **L** on the road,	**Ac 9:27**	*2962*
out boldly in the name of the **L**.	**Ac 9:28**	*2962*
going on in the fear of the **L** and	**Ac 9:31**	*2962*
saw him, and they turned to the **L**.	**Ac 9:35**	*2962*
Joppa, and many believed in the **L**.	**Ac 9:42**	*2962*
"What is it, **L**?" And he said to him	**Ac 10:4**	*2962*
"By no means, **L**, for I have never	**Ac 10:14**	*2962*
have been commanded by the **L**."	**Ac 10:33**	*2962*
Jesus Christ (He is **L** of all)	**Ac 10:36**	*2962*
'By no means, **L**, for nothing	**Ac 11:8**	*2962*
I remembered the word of the **L**,	**Ac 11:16**	*2962*
believing in the **L** Jesus Christ,	**Ac 11:17**	*2962*
also, preaching the **L** Jesus.	**Ac 11:20**	*2962*
the hand of the **L** was with them,	**Ac 11:21**	*2962*
who believed turned to the **L**.	**Ac 11:21**	*2962*
heart to remain *true* to the **L**;	**Ac 11:23**	*2962*
numbers were brought to the **L**.	**Ac 11:24**	*2962*
angel of the **L** suddenly appeared and	**Ac 12:7**	*2962*
the **L** has sent forth His angel and	**Ac 12:11**	*2962*
L had led him out of the prison.	**Ac 12:17**	*2962*
an angel of the **L** struck him	**Ac 12:23**	*2962*
the word of the **L** continued to grow	**Ac 12:24**	*2962*
ministering to the **L** and fasting,	**Ac 13:2**	*2962*
the straight ways of the **L**?	**Ac 13:10**	*2962*
the hand of the **L** is upon you,	**Ac 13:11**	*2962*
amazed at the teaching of the **L**.	**Ac 13:12**	*2962*
assembled to hear the word of the **L**.	**Ac 13:44**	*2316*
"For so the **L** has commanded us,	**Ac 13:47**	*2962*
and glorifying the word of the **L**;	**Ac 13:48**	*2962*
the word of the **L** was being spread	**Ac 13:49**	*2962*
boldly *with reliance* upon the **L**,	**Ac 14:3**	*2962*
the **L** in whom they had believed.	**Ac 14:23**	*2962*
through the grace of the **L** Jesus,	**Ac 15:11**	*2962*
rest of mankind may seek the **L**,	**Ac 15:17**	*2962*
Says the **L**, who makes these things	**Ac 15:18**	*2962*
the name of our **L** Jesus Christ.	**Ac 15:26**	*2962*
others also, the word of the **L**.	**Ac 15:35**	*2962*
we proclaimed the word of the **L**,	**Ac 15:36**	*2962*
brethren to the grace of the **L**.	**Ac 15:40**	*2962*
and the **L** opened her heart to	**Ac 16:14**	*2962*
judged me to be faithful to the **L**,	**Ac 16:15**	*2962*
"Believe in the **L** Jesus, and you	**Ac 16:31**	*2962*
And they spoke the word of the **L**	**Ac 16:32**	*2962*
since He is **L** of heaven and earth,	**Ac 17:24**	*2962*
in the **L** with all his household,	**Ac 18:8**	*2962*
And the **L** said to Paul in the	**Ac 18:9**	*2962*
instructed in the way of the **L**;	**Ac 18:25**	*2962*
baptized in the name of the **L** Jesus.	**Ac 19:5**	*2962*
in Asia heard the word of the **L**,	**Ac 19:10**	*2962*
spirits the name of the **L** Jesus,	**Ac 19:13**	*2962*
the **L** Jesus was being magnified.	**Ac 19:17**	*2962*
So the word of the **L** was growing	**Ac 19:20**	*2962*
serving the **L** with all humility	**Ac 20:19**	*2962*
and faith in our **L** Jesus Christ.	**Ac 20:21**	*2962*
which I received from the **L** Jesus,	**Ac 20:24**	*2962*
remember the words of the **L** Jesus,	**Ac 20:35**	*2962*
for the name of the **L** Jesus."	**Ac 21:13**	*2962*
"The will of the **L** be done!"	**Ac 21:14**	*2962*
'Who are You, **L**?'	**Ac 22:8**	*2962*
'What shall I do, **L**?'	**Ac 22:10**	*2962*
And the **L** said to me,	**Ac 22:10**	*2962*
'**L**, they themselves understand	**Ac 22:19**	*2962*
the **L** stood at his side and said,	**Ac 23:11**	*2962*
about him to write to my **l**.	**Ac 25:26**	*2962*
'Who are You, **L**?'	**Ac 26:15**	*2962*
And the **L** said, 'I am Jesus whom	**Ac 26:15**	*2962*
and teaching concerning the **L** Jesus	**Ac 28:31**	*2962*
of holiness, Jesus Christ our **L**,	**Ro 1:4**	*2962*
our Father and the **L** Jesus Christ.	**Ro 1:7**	*2962*
L will not take into account."	**Ro 4:8**	*2962*
raised Jesus our **L** from the dead,	**Ro 4:24**	*2962*
God through our **L** Jesus Christ,	**Ro 5:1**	*2962*
in God through our **L** Jesus Christ,	**Ro 5:11**	*2962*
life through Jesus Christ our **L**.	**Ro 5:21**	*2962*
is eternal life in Christ Jesus our **L**.	**Ro 6:23**	*2962*
to God through Jesus Christ our **L**!	**Ro 7:25**	*2962*
which is in Christ Jesus our **L**.	**Ro 8:39**	*2962*
for the **L** will execute His word	**Ro 9:28**	*2962*
"Unless the **L** of Sabaoth had left	**Ro 9:29**	*2962*
confess with your mouth Jesus *as* **L**,	**Ro 10:9**	*2962*
for the same **L** is Lord of all,	**Ro 10:12**	
for the same *Lord* is **L** of all,	**Ro 10:12**	*2962*
the name of the **L** will be saved."	**Ro 10:13**	*2962*
"**L**, who has believed our report?"	**Ro 10:16**	*2962*
"**L**, they have killed Your	**Ro 11:3**	*2962*
who has known the mind of the **L**,	**Ro 11:34**	*2962*
fervent in spirit, serving the **L**;	**Ro 12:11**	*2962*
is Mine, I will repay," says the **L**.	**Ro 12:19**	*2962*
But put on the **L** Jesus Christ, and	**Ro 13:14**	*2962*
the **L** is able to make him stand.	**Ro 14:4**	*2962*
the day, observes it for the **L**,	**Ro 14:6**	*2962*
he who eats, does so for the **L**,	**Ro 14:6**	*2962*
not, for the **L** he does not eat,	**Ro 14:6**	*2962*
for if we live, we live for the **L**,	**Ro 14:8**	*2962*
or if we die, we die for the **L**;	**Ro 14:8**	*2962*
L both of the dead and of the living	**Ro 14:9**	*2961*
"As I live, says the **L**,	**Ro 14:11**	*2962*
I know and am convinced in the **L**	**Ro 14:14**	*2962*
and Father of our **L** Jesus Christ.	**Ro 15:6**	*2962*
"Praise the **L** all you Gentiles,	**Ro 15:11**	*2962*
by our **L** Jesus Christ and by the	**Ro 15:30**	*2962*
that you receive her in the **L** in a	**Ro 16:2**	*2962*
Ampliatus, my beloved in the **L**.	**Ro 16:8**	*2962*
of Narcissus, who are in the **L**.	**Ro 16:11**	*2962*
and Tryphosa, workers in the **L**.	**Ro 16:12**	*2962*
who has worked hard in the **L**.	**Ro 16:12**	*2962*
Rufus, a choice man in the **L**,	**Ro 16:13**	*2962*
slaves, not of our **L** Christ but of	**Ro 16:18**	*2962*
grace of our **L** Jesus be with you.	**Ro 16:20**	*2962*
this letter, greet you in the **L**.	**Ro 16:22**	*2962*
L Jesus Christ be with you all.	**Ro 16:24**	*2962*
the name of our **L** Jesus Christ,	**1Co 1:2**	*2962*
Lord Jesus Christ, their **L** and ours:	**1Co 1:2**	
our Father and the **L** Jesus Christ.	**1Co 1:3**	*2962*
revelation of our **L** Jesus Christ,	**1Co 1:7**	*2962*
in the day of our **L** Jesus Christ.	**1Co 1:8**	*2962*
with His Son, Jesus Christ our **L**.	**1Co 1:9**	*2962*
by the name of our **L** Jesus Christ,	**1Co 1:10**	*2962*
him who boasts, boast in the **L**."	**1Co 1:31**	*2962*
not have crucified the **L** of glory;	**1Co 2:8**	*2962*
who has known the mind of the **L**,	**1Co 2:16**	*2962*
L gave *opportunity* to each one.	**1Co 3:5**	*2962*

"THE **L** KNOWS THE REASONINGS of 1Co 3:20 2962
the one who examines me is the **L**. 1Co 4:4 2962
but wait until the **L** comes who 1Co 4:5 2962
and faithful child in the **L**, 1Co 4:17 2962
come to you soon, if the **L** wills, 1Co 4:19 2962
In the name of our **L** Jesus, 1Co 5:4 2962
with the power of our **L** Jesus, 1Co 5:4 2962
saved in the day of the **L** Jesus. 1Co 5:5 2962
in the name of the **L** Jesus Christ and 1Co 6:11 2962
not for immorality, but for the **L**, 1Co 6:13 2962
and the **L** is for the body. 1Co 6:13 2962
Now God has not only raised the **L**, 1Co 6:14 2962
to the **L** is one spirit *with Him.* 1Co 6:17 2962
instructions, not I, but the **L**, 1Co 7:10 2962
But to the rest I say, not the **L**, 1Co 7:12 2962
as the **L** has assigned to each one, 1Co 7:17 2962
was called in the **L** while a slave, 1Co 7:22 2962
I have no command of the **L**, 1Co 7:25 2962
the mercy of the **L** is trustworthy. 1Co 7:25 2962
about the things of the **L**, 1Co 7:32 2962
the Lord, how he may please the **L**; 1Co 7:32 2962
about the things of the **L**, 1Co 7:34 2962
undistracted devotion to the **L**. 1Co 7:35 2962
to whom she wishes, only in the **L**. 1Co 7:39 2962
and one **L**, Jesus Christ, by whom 1Co 8:6 2962
Have I not seen Jesus our **L**? 1Co 9:1 2962
Are you not my work in the **L**? 1Co 9:1 2962
seal of my apostleship in the **L**. 1Co 9:2 2962
and the brothers of the **L** and 1Co 9:5 2962
So also the **L** directed those who 1Co 9:14 2962
Nor let us try the **L**, 1Co 10:9 2962
You cannot drink the cup of the **L** 1Co 10:21 2962
cannot partake of the table of the **L** 1Co 10:21 2962
do we provoke the **L** to jealousy? 1Co 10:22 2962
However, in the **L**, neither is woman 1Co 11:11 2962
For I received from the **L** that 1Co 11:23 2962
that the **L** Jesus in the night in 1Co 11:23 2962
of the **L** in an unworthy manner, 1Co 11:27 2962
the body and the blood of the **L**. 1Co 11:27 2962
we are disciplined by the **L** so 1Co 11:32 2962
no one can say, "Jesus is **L**," except 1Co 12:3 2962
of ministries, and the same **L**. 1Co 12:5 2962
WILL NOT LISTEN TO ME," says the **L**. 1Co 14:21 2962
I have in Christ Jesus our **L**, 1Co 15:31 2962
victory through our **L** Jesus Christ. 1Co 15:57 2962
abounding in the work of the **L**, 1Co 15:58 2962
your toil is not *in* vain in the **L**. 1Co 15:58 2962
for some time, if the **L** permits. 1Co 16:7 2962
greet you heartily in the **L**, 1Co 16:19 2962
If anyone does not love the **L**, 1Co 16:22 2962
grace of the **L** Jesus be with you. 1Co 16:23 2962
our Father and the **L** Jesus Christ. 2Co 1:2 2962
and Father of our **L** Jesus Christ, 2Co 1:3 2962
ours, in the day of our **L** Jesus. 2Co 1:14 2962
Not that we **l** it over your faith, 2Co 1:24 2961
a door was opened for me in the **L**, 2Co 2:12 2962
but whenever a person turns to the **L**, 2Co 3:16 2962
Now the **L** is the Spirit, 2Co 3:17 2962
and where the Spirit of the **L** is, 2Co 3:17 2962
as in a mirror the glory of the **L**, 2Co 3:18 2962
to glory, just as from the **L**, 2Co 3:18 2962
ourselves but Christ Jesus as **L**, 2Co 4:5 2962
knowing that He who raised the **L** 2Co 4:14 2962
the body we are absent from the **L** 2Co 5:6 2962
body and to be at home with the **L**. 2Co 5:8 2962
knowing the fear of the **L**, 2Co 5:11 2962
MIDST AND BE SEPARATE," says the **L**. 2Co 6:17 2962
to Me," Says the **L** Almighty. 2Co 6:18 2962
L and to us by the will of God. 2Co 8:5 2962
the grace of our **L** Jesus Christ, 2Co 8:9 2962
us for the glory of the **L** Himself, 2Co 8:19 2962
not only in the sight of the **L**, 2Co 8:21 2962
which the **L** gave for building you 2Co 10:8 2962
BOASTS IS TO BOAST IN THE **L**. 2Co 10:17 2962
but he whom the **L** commends. 2Co 10:18 2962
I am not saying as the **L** would, 2Co 11:17 2962
The God and Father of the **L** Jesus, 2Co 11:31 2962
visions and revelations of the **L**. 2Co 12:1 2962
Concerning this I implored the **L** 2Co 12:8 2962
the authority which the **L** gave me for 2Co 13:10 2962
The grace of the **L** Jesus Christ, 2Co 13:14 2962
Father and the **L** Jesus Christ, Ga 1:3 2962
I have confidence in you in the **L** that Ga 5:10 2962
the cross of our **L** Jesus Christ, Ga 6:14 2962
The grace of our **L** Jesus Christ be Ga 6:18 2962
our Father and the **L** Jesus Christ. Eph 1:2 2962
and Father of our **L** Jesus Christ, Eph 1:3 2962
L Jesus which *exists* among you and Eph 1:15 2962
the God of our **L** Jesus Christ, Eph 1:17 2962
into a holy temple in the **L**, Eph 2:21 2962
carried out in Christ Jesus our **L**, Eph 3:11 2962
Therefore I, the prisoner of the **L**, Eph 4:1 2962
one **L**, one faith, one baptism, Eph 4:5 2962
and affirm together with the **L**, Eph 4:17 2962
but now you are Light in the **L**; Eph 5:8 2962
learn what is pleasing to the **L**. Eph 5:10 2962
what the will of the **L** is. Eph 5:17 2962
melody with your heart to the **L**; Eph 5:19 2962
name of our **L** Jesus Christ to God, Eph 5:20 2962
to your own husbands, as to the **L**. Eph 5:22 2962
obey your parents in the **L**, Eph 6:1 2962
discipline and instruction of the **L**. Eph 6:4 2962
will render service, as to the **L**, Eph 6:7 2962
he will receive back from the **L**, Eph 6:8 2962
Finally, be strong in the **L** and Eph 6:10 2962
and faithful minister in the **L**, Eph 6:21 2962
the Father and the **L** Jesus Christ. Eph 6:23 2962
those who love our **L** Jesus Christ Eph 6:24 2962
our Father and the **L** Jesus Christ. Php 1:2 2962
trusting in the **L** because of my Php 1:14 2962
confess that Jesus Christ is **L**, Php 2:11 2962
But I hope in the **L** Jesus to send Php 2:19 2962
and I trust in the **L** that I myself Php 2:24 2962
Receive him then in the **L** with all joy, Php 2:29 2962
my brethren, rejoice in the **L**. Php 3:1 2962
value of knowing Christ Jesus my **L**, Php 3:8 2962
for a Savior, the **L** Jesus Christ; Php 3:20 2962
in this way stand firm in the **L**, Php 4:1 2962
to live in harmony in the **L**. Php 4:2 2962
Rejoice in the **L** always; Php 4:4 2962
be known to all men. The **L** is near. Php 4:5 2962
But I rejoiced in the **L** greatly, Php 4:10 2962
The grace of the **L** Jesus Christ be Php 4:23 2962
the Father of our **L** Jesus Christ, Col 1:3 2962
walk in a manner worthy of the **L**, Col 1:10 2962
have received Christ Jesus the **L**, Col 2:6 2962
just as the **L** forgave you, so also Col 3:13 2962
do all in the name of the **L** Jesus, Col 3:17 2962
husbands, as is fitting in the **L**. Col 3:18 2962
for this is well-pleasing to the **L**. Col 3:20 2962
sincerity of heart, fearing the **L**. Col 3:22 2962
as for the **L** rather than for men, Col 3:23 2962
knowing that from the **L** you will Col 3:24 2962
It is the **L** Christ whom you serve. Col 3:24 2962
and fellow bond-servant in the **L**, Col 4:7 2962
which you have received in the **L**, Col 4:17 2962
the Father and the **L** Jesus Christ: 1Th 1:1 2962
steadfastness of hope in our **L** Jesus 1Th 1:3 2962
imitators of us and of the **L**, 1Th 1:6 2962
the **L** has sounded forth from you, 1Th 1:8 2962
the **L** Jesus and the prophets, 1Th 2:15 2962
of our **L** Jesus at His coming? 1Th 2:19 2962
live, if you stand firm in the **L**. 1Th 3:8 2962
Jesus our **L** direct our way to you; 1Th 3:11 2962
may the **L** cause you to increase 1Th 3:12 2962
our **L** Jesus with all His saints. 1Th 3:13 2962
and exhort you in the **L** Jesus, 1Th 4:1 2962
by *the authority of* the **L** Jesus. 1Th 4:2 2962
L is *the* avenger in all these things, 1Th 4:6 2962
say to you by the word of the **L**, 1Th 4:15 2962
remain until the coming of the **L**, 1Th 4:15 2962
For the **L** Himself will descend 1Th 4:16 2962
clouds to meet the **L** in the air, 1Th 4:17 2962
we shall always be with the **L**. 1Th 4:17 2962
the day of the **L** will come just like 1Th 5:2 2962
through our **L** Jesus Christ, 1Th 5:9 2962
in the **L** and give you instruction, 1Th 5:12 2962
the coming of our **L** Jesus Christ. 1Th 5:23 2962
I adjure you by the **L** to have this 1Th 5:27 2962
The grace of our **L** Jesus Christ be 1Th 5:28 2962
our Father and the **L** Jesus Christ: 2Th 1:1 2962
the Father and the **L** Jesus Christ. 2Th 1:2 2962
when the **L** Jesus will be revealed 2Th 1:7 2962
obey the gospel of our **L** Jesus. 2Th 1:8 2962
away from the presence of the **L** 2Th 1:9 2962
L Jesus will be glorified in you, 2Th 1:12 2962
of our God and *the* **L** Jesus Christ. 2Th 1:12 2962
the coming of our **L** Jesus Christ and 2Th 2:1 2962
that the day of the **L** has come. 2Th 2:2 2962
be revealed whom the **L** will slay 2Th 2:8 2962
you, brethren beloved by the **L**, 2Th 2:13 2962
the glory of our **L** Jesus Christ. 2Th 2:14 2962
Now may our **L** Jesus Christ Himself 2Th 2:16 2962
word of the **L** will spread rapidly 2Th 3:1 2962
But the **L** is faithful, and He will 2Th 3:3 2962
We have confidence in the **L** 2Th 3:4 2962
May the **L** direct your hearts 2Th 3:5 2962
in the name of our **L** Jesus Christ, 2Th 3:6 2962
exhort in the **L** Jesus Christ to work 2Th 3:12 2962
Now may the **L** of peace Himself 2Th 3:16 2962
The **L** be with you all! 2Th 3:16 2962
L Jesus Christ be with you all. 2Th 3:18 2962
the Father and Christ Jesus our **L**. 1Tm 1:2 2962
I thank Christ Jesus our **L**, 1Tm 1:12 2962
the grace of our **L** was more than 1Tm 1:14 2962
words, those of our **L** Jesus Christ, 1Tm 6:3 2962
appearing of our **L** Jesus Christ, 1Tm 6:14 2962
the King of kings and **L** of lords, 1Tm 6:15 2962
the Father and Christ Jesus our **L**. 2Tm 1:2 2962
ashamed of the testimony of our **L** or 2Tm 1:8 2962
The **L** grant mercy to the house of 2Tm 1:16 2962
the **L** grant to him to find mercy 2Tm 1:18 2962
find mercy from the **L** on that day 2Tm 1:18 2962
the **L** will give you understanding 2Tm 2:7 2962
"The **L** knows those who are His," 2Tm 2:19 2962
who names the name of the **L** 2Tm 2:19 2962
call on the **L** from a pure heart. 2Tm 2:22 2962
out of them all the **L** rescued me! 2Tm 3:11 2962
the **L**, the righteous Judge, will 2Tm 4:8 2962
the **L** will repay him according to 2Tm 4:14 2962
But the **L** stood with me and 2Tm 4:17 2962
The **L** will rescue me from every 2Tm 4:18 2962
The **L** be with your spirit. 2Tm 4:22 2962
our Father and the **L** Jesus Christ. Phm 1:3 2962
which you have toward the **L** Jesus and Phm 1:5 2962
both in the flesh and in the **L**. Phm 1:16 2962
let me benefit from you in the **L**; Phm 1:20 2962
The grace of the **L** Jesus Christ be Phm 1:25 2962
"YOU, **L**, IN THE BEGINNING LAID Heb 1:10 2962
at the first spoken through the **L**, Heb 2:3 2962
our **L** was descended from Judah, Heb 7:14 2962
"THE **L** HAS SWORN AND WILL NOT Heb 7:21 2962
tabernacle, which the **L** pitched, Heb 8:2 2962
DAYS ARE COMING, SAYS THE **L**, Heb 8:8 2962
DID NOT CARE FOR THEM, SAYS THE **L**. Heb 8:9 2962
AFTER THOSE DAYS, SAYS THE **L**: Heb 8:10 2962
'KNOW THE **L**,' FOR ALL WILL KNOW Heb 8:11 2962
THEM AFTER THOSE DAYS, SAYS THE **L**: Heb 10:16 2962
"THE **L** WILL JUDGE HIS PEOPLE." Heb 10:30 2962
LIGHTLY THE DISCIPLINE OF THE **L**, Heb 12:5 2962
WHOM THE **L** LOVES HE DISCIPLINES, Heb 12:6 2962
without which no one will see the **L**. Heb 12:14 2962
"THE **L** IS MY HELPER, I WILL NOT Heb 13:6 2962
covenant, *even* Jesus our **L**, Heb 13:20 2962
of God and of the **L** Jesus Christ, Jas 1:1 2962
will receive anything from the **L**, Jas 1:7 2962
the crown of life which *the* **L** has Jas 1:12
faith in our glorious **L** Jesus Christ Jas 2:1 2962
With it we bless *our* **L** and Father, Jas 3:9 2962
in the presence of the **L**, Jas 4:10 2962
"If the **L** wills, we will live Jas 4:15 2962
the ears of the **L** of Sabaoth. Jas 5:4 2962
until the coming of the **L**. Jas 5:7 2962
the coming of the **L** is near. Jas 5:8 2962
who spoke in the name of the **L**. Jas 5:10 2962
that the **L** is full of compassion Jas 5:11 2962
him with oil in the name of the **L**; Jas 5:14 2962
sick, and the **L** will raise him up, Jas 5:15 2962
and Father of our **L** Jesus Christ, 1Pe 1:3 2962
WORD OF THE **L** ENDURES FOREVER." 1Pe 1:25 2962
have tasted the kindness of the **L**. 1Pe 2:3 2962
obeyed Abraham, calling him **l**, 1Pe 3:6 2962
OF THE **L** ARE TOWARD THE RIGHTEOUS, 1Pe 3:12 2962
L IS AGAINST THOSE WHO DO EVIL." 1Pe 3:12 2962
Christ as **L** in your hearts, 1Pe 3:15 2962
of God and of Jesus our **L**; 2Pe 1:2 2962
knowledge of our **L** Jesus Christ. 2Pe 1:8 2962
kingdom of our **L** and Savior Jesus 2Pe 1:11 2962
as also our **L** Jesus Christ has 2Pe 1:14 2962
and coming of our **L** Jesus Christ, 2Pe 1:16 2962
L knows how to rescue the godly 2Pe 2:9 2962
against them before the **L**. 2Pe 2:11 2962
of the **L** and Savior Jesus Christ, 2Pe 2:20 2962
commandment of the **L** and Savior 2Pe 3:2 2962
with the **L** one day is like a thousand 2Pe 3:8 2962
L is not slow about His promise, 2Pe 3:9 2962
day of the **L** will come like a thief, 2Pe 3:10 2962
patience of our **L** *as* salvation; 2Pe 3:15 2962
grace and knowledge of our **L** and 2Pe 3:18 2962
and deny our only Master and **L**, Jude 1:4 2962
the **L**, after saving a people out of Jude 1:5 2962
"The **L** rebuke you!" Jude 1:9 2962
the **L** came with many thousands of Jude 1:14 2962
apostles of our **L** Jesus Christ, Jude 1:17 2962
for the mercy of our **L** Jesus Christ Jude 1:21 2962
through Jesus Christ our **L**, *be* glory Jude 1:25 2962
and the Omega," says the **L** God, Rv 1:8 2962
"HOLY, HOLY, HOLY *is* THE **L** GOD, Rv 4:8 2962
are You, our **L** and our God, Rv 4:11 2962
"How long, O **L**, holy and true, Rv 6:10 1203
"My **l**, you know." Rv 7:14 2962
stand before the **L** of the earth. Rv 11:4 2962
where also their **L** was crucified. Rv 11:8 2962
has become *the kingdom* of our **L** and Rv 11:15 2962
"We give You thanks, O **L** God, Rv 11:17 2962
who die in the **L** from now on!" Rv 14:13 2962
marvelous are Your works, O **L** God, Rv 15:3 2962
"Who will not fear, O **L**, Rv 15:4 2962
"Yes, O **L** God, the Almighty, true Rv 16:7 2962
He is **L** of lords and King of kings, Rv 17:14 2962
L God who judges her is strong. Rv 18:8 2962
For the **L** our God, the Almighty, Rv 19:6 2962
AND **L** OF LORDS." Rv 19:16 2962
L God the Almighty and the Lamb Rv 21:22 2962
the **L** God will illumine them; Rv 22:5 2962
and the **L**, the God of the spirits Rv 22:6 2962
Amen. Come, **L** Jesus. Rv 22:20 2962
grace of the **L** Jesus be with all. Rv 22:21 2962

LORDING

nor yet as **l** it over those 1Pe 5:3 2634b

LORD'S

thus the **L** blessing was upon all Gn 39:5 3068
silver or gold from your **l** house? Gn 44:8 113
and we also will be my **l** slaves." Gn 44:9 113
behold, we are my **l** slaves, Gn 44:16 113
please speak a word in my **l** ears, Gn 44:18 113
spent, and the cattle are my **l**. Gn 47:18 113
know that the earth is the **L**. Ex 9:29 3068
it is the **L** Passover. Ex 12:11 3068
we had died by the **L** hand Ex 16:3 3068
bring it as the **L** contribution: Ex 35:5 3068
came *and* brought the **L** contribution Ex 35:21 3068
brought the **L** contribution; Ex 35:24 3068
all fat is the **L**. Lv 3:16 3068
against the **L** holy things, Lv 5:15 3068
L anointing oil is upon you." Lv 10:7 3068
left over from the **L** offerings Lv 10:12 3068
out of the **L** offerings by fire; Lv 10:13 3068
to offer the **L** offerings by fire; Lv 21:21 3068
'The **L** appointed times which Lv 23:2 3068
at twilight is the **L** Passover. Lv 23:5 3068
from the **L** offerings by fire, Lv 24:9 3068
whether ox or sheep, it is the **L**. Lv 27:26 3068
fruit of the tree, is the **L**; Lv 27:30 3068
the **L** making your thigh waste away Nu 5:21 3068
Israel would keep the **L** charge Nu 9:19 3068
they kept the **L** charge, Nu 9:23 3068
"Is the **L** power limited? Nu 11:23 3068
the **L** people were prophets, Nu 11:29 3068
caused the death of the **L** people." Nu 16:41 3068
you shall give the **L** offering to Aaron Nu 18:28 3068
you brought the **L** assembly into Nu 20:4 3068
first month shall be the **L** Passover. Nu 28:16 3068
the **L** vengeance on Midian. Nu 31:3 3068
L levy of the sheep was 675 Nu 31:37 3068
from which the **L** levy was 72; Nu 31:38 3068

from which the **L** levy was 61;	Nu 31:39	3068
from whom the **L** levy was 32 persons.	Nu 31:40	3068
levy *which was* the **L** offering	Nu 31:41	3068
L anger burned in that day,	Nu 32:10	3068
L anger burned against Israel,	Nu 32:13	3068
to keep the **L** commandments	Dt 10:13	3068
the **L** remission has been proclaimed.	Dt 15:2	3068
they shall eat the **L** offerings	Dt 18:1	3068
the **L** portion is His people;	Dt 32:9	3068
captain of the **L** host said to Joshua,	Jos 5:15	3068
where the **L** tabernacle stands,	Jos 22:19	3068
it shall be the **L**, and I will offer it	Jg 11:31	3068
you are going has the **L** approval."	Jg 18:6	3068
the pillars of the earth are the **L**,	1Sa 2:8	3068
I hear the **L** people circulating.	1Sa 2:24	3068
he repeated them in the **L** hearing.	1Sa 8:21	3068
"Surely the **L** anointed is before Him."	1Sa 16:6	3068
the battle is the **L** and He will	1Sa 17:47	3068
man for me and fight the **L** battles."	1Sa 18:17	3068
to my lord, the **L** anointed,	1Sa 24:6	3068
since he is the **L** anointed."	1Sa 24:6	3068
for he is the **L** anointed.'	1Sa 24:10	3068
wash the feet of my **l** servants."	1Sa 25:41	113
his hand against the **L** anointed	1Sa 26:9	3068
my hand against the **L** anointed;	1Sa 26:11	3068
not guard your lord, the **L** anointed.	1Sa 26:16	3068
my hand against the **L** anointed.	1Sa 26:23	3068
to destroy the **L** anointed?"	2Sa 1:14	3068
'I have killed the **L** anointed.' "	2Sa 1:16	3068
the **L** outburst against Uzzah,	2Sa 6:8	3068
on his bed with his **l** servants,	2Sa 11:13	113
named him Jedidiah for the **L** sake.	2Sa 12:25	3068
he cursed the **L** anointed?"	2Sa 19:21	3068
take your **l** servants and pursue him	2Sa 20:6	113
they would be the **L** people,	2Ki 11:17	3068
"The **L** arrow of victory,	2Ki 13:17	3068
come up without the **L** approval	2Ki 18:25	3068
the **L** outburst against Uzza;	1Ch 13:11	3068
are they not all my **l** servants?	1Ch 21:3	113
glory of the LORD filled the **L** house.	2Ch 7:2	3068
they would be the **L** people.	2Ch 23:16	3068
the **L** throne is in heaven;	Ps 11:4	3068
For the kingdom is the **L**	Ps 22:28	3068
earth is the **L**, and all it contains,	Ps 24:1	3068
In the courts of the **L** house,	Ps 116:19	3068
This is the **L** doing; It is marvelous	Ps 118:23	3068
sing the **L** song In a foreign land?	Ps 137:4	3068
the **L** indignation is against all	Is 34:2	3068
come up without the **L** approval	Is 36:10	3068
she has received of the **L** hand	Is 40:2	3068
"This one will say, 'I am the **L**';	Is 44:5	3068
You who have drunk from the **L** hand	Is 51:17	3068
the **L** hand is not so short	Is 59:1	3068
For they are not the **L**.	Jer 5:10	3068
"Stand in the gate of the **L** house	Jer 7:2	3068
he stood in the court of the **L** house	Jer 19:14	3068
I took the cup from the **L** hand	Jer 25:17	3068
'Stand in the court of the **L** house,	Jer 26:2	3068
have come to worship *in* the **L** house all	Jer 26:2	3068
the New Gate of the **L** *house.*	Jer 26:10	3068
the vessels of the **L** house	Jer 27:16	3068
the vessels of the **L** house,	Jer 28:3	3068
bring back the vessels of the **L** house	Jer 28:6	3068
people in the **L** house on a fast day.	Jer 36:6	3068
words of the LORD in the **L** house.	Jer 36:8	3068
the New Gate of the **L** house,	Jer 36:10	3068
who does the **L** work negligently,	Jer 48:10	3068
this is the **L** time of vengeance;	Jer 51:6	3068
The holy places of the **L** house.	Jer 51:51	3068
survived In the day of the **L** anger.	La 2:22	3068
The **L** lovingkindnesses indeed	La 3:22	3068
the **L** anointed, Was captured	La 4:20	3068
entrance of the gate of the **L** house	Ezk 8:14	3068
into the inner court of the **L** house.	Ezk 8:16	3068
the east gate of the **L** house,	Ezk 10:19	3068
to the east gate of the **L** house	Ezk 11:1	3068
They will not remain in the **L** land,	Hos 9:3	3068
Let the priests, the **L** ministers,	Jl 2:17	3068
the kingdom will be the **L**.	Ob 1:21	3068
The cup in the **L** right hand	Hab 2:16	3068
on the day of the **L** sacrifice	Zph 1:8	3068
On the day of the **L** wrath;	Zph 1:18	3068
day of the **L** anger comes upon you.	Zph 2:2	3068
hidden In the day of the **L** anger.	Zph 2:3	3068
the cooking pots in the **L** house	Zch 14:20	3068
before he had seen the **L** Christ.	Lk 2:26	*2962*
who was seated at the **L** feet,	Lk 10:39	*2962*
we live or die, we are the **L**.	Ro 14:8	*2962*
while a slave, is the **L** freedman;	1Co 7:22	*2962*
FOR THE EARTH IS THE **L**, AND ALL IT	1Co 10:26	*2962*
it is not to eat the **L** Supper,	1Co 11:20	*2960*
proclaim the **L** death until He comes	1Co 11:26	*2962*
to you are the **L** commandment.	1Co 14:37	*2962*
for he is doing the **L** work,	1Co 16:10	*2962*
except James, the **L** brother.	Ga 1:19	*2962*
The **L** bond-servant must not be	2Tm 2:24	*2962*
the outcome of the **L** dealings,	Jas 5:11	*2962*
Submit yourselves for the **L** sake	1Pe 2:13	*2962*
I was in the Spirit on the **L** day,	Rv 1:10	*2960*
LORDS		
"Now behold, my **l**, please turn	Gn 19:2	136
Lot said to them, "Oh no, my **l**!	Gn 19:18	136
the God of gods and the Lord of **l**,	Dt 10:17	113
the five **l** of the Philistines:	Jos 13:3	5633a
the five **l** of the Philistines and	Jg 3:3	5633a
The **l** of the Philistines came	Jg 16:5	5633a
Then the **l** of the Philistines	Jg 16:8	5633a
called the **l** of the Philistines,	Jg 16:18	5633a
Then the **l** of the Philistines came	Jg 16:18	5633a
Now the **l** of the Philistines	Jg 16:23	5633a
l of the Philistines were there.	Jg 16:27	5633a
house fell on the **l** and all the people	Jg 16:30	5633a
gathered all the **l** of the Philistines	1Sa 5:8	5633a
gathered all the **l** of the Philistines	1Sa 5:11	5633a
number of the **l** of the Philistines,	1Sa 6:4	5633a
was on all of you and on your **l**.	1Sa 6:4	5633a
the **l** of the Philistines followed them	1Sa 6:12	5633a
five **l** of the Philistines saw it,	1Sa 6:16	5633a
Philistines belonging to the five **l**,	1Sa 6:18	5633a
the **l** of the Philistines went up	1Sa 7:7	5633a
And the **l** of the Philistines were	1Sa 29:2	5633a
pleasing in the sight of the **l**.	1Sa 29:6	5633a
not displease the **l** of the Philistines	1Sa 29:7	5633a
for the **l** of the Philistines after	1Ch 12:19	5633a
Give thanks to the Lord of **l**,	Ps 136:3	113
The **l** of the nations have trampled	Is 16:8	1167
gave a banquet for his **l** and military	Mk 6:21	*3175*
there are many gods and many **l**,	1Co 8:5	*2962*
the King of kings and Lord of **l**,	1Tm 6:15	*2961*
He is Lord of **l** and King of kings,	Rv 17:14	*2962*
AND LORD OF **L**."	Rv 19:16	*2962*
LO-RUHAMAH		
"Name her **L**, for I will no longer	Hos 1:6	3819
When she had weaned **L**,	Hos 1:8	3819
LOSE		
fall upon you and you will **l** your life,	Jg 18:25	622
a lion, will completely **l** heart;	2Sa 17:10	4549
"Foreigners **l** heart, And come	2Sa 22:46	5034b
be strong and do not **l** courage,	2Ch 15:7	3027, 7503
caused its owners to **l** their lives,	Jb 31:39	5301
Bashan and Carmel **l** *their foliage.*	Is 33:9	5287
And the stars **l** their brightness.	Jl 2:10	622
And the stars **l** their brightness.	Jl 3:15	622
for it is better for you to **l** one of	Mt 5:29	*622*
for it is better for you to **l** one of	Mt 5:30	*622*
who has found his life will **l** it,	Mt 10:39	*622*
you, he shall not **l** his reward."	Mt 10:42	*622*
to save his life will **l** it;	Mt 16:25	*622*
to save his life will **l** it	Mk 8:35	*622*
to you, he will not **l** his reward.	Mk 9:41	*622*
to save his life will **l** it,	Lk 9:24	*622*
seeks to keep his life will **l** it,	Lk 17:33	*622*
ought to pray and not to **l** heart,	Lk 18:1	*1457b*
that He has given Me I **l** nothing,	Jn 6:39	*622*
received mercy, we do not **l** heart,	2Co 4:1	*1457b*
Therefore we do not **l** heart,	2Co 4:16	*1457b*
Let us not **l** heart in doing good,	Ga 6:9	*1457b*
Therefore I ask you not to **l** heart	Eph 3:13	*1457b*
that they will not **l** heart.	Col 3:21	*120b*
will not grow weary and **l** heart.	Heb 12:3	*1590*
not **l** what we have accomplished,	2Jn 1:8	*622*
LOSES		
if a man **l** the hair of his head,	Lv 13:40	4803
A fool always **l** his temper, But a	Pr 29:11	3318
but whoever **l** his life for My sake	Mt 16:25	*622*
but whoever **l** his life for My sake	Mk 8:35	*622*
whoever **l** his life for My sake,	Lk 9:24	*622*
world, and **l** or forfeits himself?	Lk 9:25	*622*
ten silver coins and **l** one coin,	Lk 15:8	*622*
whoever **l** *his life* will preserve it.	Lk 17:33	*622*
"He who loves his life **l** it,	Jn 12:25	*622*
LOSS		
I bore the **l** of it myself.	Gn 31:39	2398
shall only pay for his **l** of time,	Ex 21:19	7674
with *the* **l** *of* his firstborn he	Jos 6:26	
and with *the* **l** *of* his youngest	Jos 6:26	
he laid its foundations with the **l**	1Ki 16:34	
and set up its gates with the **l** *of*	1Ki 16:34	
visit your abode and fear no **l**.	Jb 5:24	2398
Without mishap and without **l**,	Ps 144:14	3318
Nor know **l** of children.'	Is 47:8	7908
L of children and widowhood.	Is 47:9	7908
that the king might not suffer **l**.	Da 6:2	5142
at a **l** *to know* of which one He was	Jn 13:22	*639*
Being at a **l** how to investigate such	Ac 25:20	*639*
with damage and great **l**,	Ac 27:10	*2209*
and incurred this damage and **l**.	Ac 27:21	*2209*
will be no **l** of life among you,	Ac 27:22	*580*
is burned up, he will suffer **l**;	1Co 3:15	*2210*
you might not suffer **l** in anything	2Co 7:9	*2210*
those things I have counted as **l** for	Php 3:7	*2209*
I count all things to be **l** in view	Php 3:8	*2209*
have suffered the **l** of all things,	Php 3:8	*2210*
LOST		
any **l** thing about which one says,	Ex 22:9	9
or has found what was **l** and lied	Lv 6:3	9
or the **l** thing which he found,	Lv 6:4	9
anything **l** by your countryman,	Dt 22:3	9
which he has **l** and you have found.	Dt 22:3	6
of Kish, Saul's father, were **l**.	1Sa 9:3	6
which were **l** three days ago,	1Sa 9:20	6
had died in Hebron, he **l** courage,	2Sa 4:1	7503
like the army that you have **l**,	1Ki 20:25	5307
saw *it,* they **l** their confidence;	Ne 6:16	5307
I have gone astray like a **l** sheep;	Ps 119:176	6
and a time to give up as **l**;	Ec 3:6	6
When those riches were **l** through a	Ec 5:14	6
one among them has **l** her young.	SS 4:2	7909b
one among them has **l** her young.	SS 6:6	7909b
not going to be **l** to the priest,	Jer 18:18	6
have **l** the abundance it produced.	Jer 48:36	6
good counsel been **l** to the prudent?	Jer 49:7	6
"My people have become **l** sheep;	Jer 50:6	6
but the law will be **l** from the priest	Ezk 7:26	6
she waited, *That* her hope was **l**,	Ezk 19:5	6
nor have you sought for the **l**;	Ezk 34:4	6
"I will seek the **l**, bring back	Ezk 34:16	6
l sheep of the house of Israel.	Mt 10:6	*622*
he who has **l** his life for My sake	Mt 10:39	*622*
l sheep of the house of Israel."	Mt 15:24	*622*
come to save that which was **l**.	Mt 18:11	*622*
the skins, and the wine is **l** and	Mk 2:22	*622*
"He has **l** His senses."	Mk 3:21	*1839*
sheep and has **l** one of them,	Lk 15:4	*622*
and go after the one which is **l** until	Lk 15:4	*622*
have found my sheep which was **l**!'	Lk 15:6	*622*
found the coin which I had **l**!'	Lk 15:9	*622*
he was **l** and has been found.'	Lk 15:24	*622*
and *was* **l** and has been found.' "	Lk 15:32	*622*
seek and to save that which was **l**."	Lk 19:10	*622*
fragments so that nothing will be **l**."	Jn 6:12	*622*
You have given Me I **l** not one."	Jn 18:9	*622*
LOT		
and Haran became the father of **L**.	Gn 11:27	3876
his son, and **L** the son of Haran,	Gn 11:31	3876
and **L** went with him.	Gn 12:4	3876
Sarai his wife and **L** his nephew,	Gn 12:5	3876
belonged to him, and **L** with him.	Gn 13:1	3876
Now **L**, who went with Abram, also	Gn 13:5	3876
So Abram said to **L**,	Gn 13:8	3876
L lifted up his eyes and saw	Gn 13:10	3876
So **L** chose for himself all the	Gn 13:11	3876
and **L** journeyed eastward.	Gn 13:11	3876
while **L** settled in the cities of	Gn 13:12	3876
after **L** had separated from him,	Gn 13:14	3876
They also took **L**,	Gn 14:12	3876
brought back his relative **L** with his	Gn 14:16	3876
L was sitting in the gate of Sodom.	Gn 19:1	3876
When **L** saw *them,* he rose to meet	Gn 19:1	3876
they called to **L** and said to him,	Gn 19:5	3876
But **L** went out to them at the	Gn 19:6	3876
So they pressed hard against **L** and	Gn 19:9	3876
brought **L** into the house with them,	Gn 19:10	3876
Then the *two* men said to **L**,	Gn 19:12	3876
L went out and spoke to his	Gn 19:14	3876
dawned, the angels urged **L**,	Gn 19:15	3876
But **L** said to them,	Gn 19:18	3876
the earth when **L** came to Zoar.	Gn 19:23	3876
and sent **L** out of the midst of the	Gn 19:29	3876
the cities in which **L** lived.	Gn 19:29	3876
L went up from Zoar, and	Gn 19:30	3876
Thus both the daughters of **L** were	Gn 19:36	3876
one **l** for the LORD and the other	Lv 16:8	1486
and the other **l** for the scapegoat.	Lv 16:8	1486
on which the **l** for the LORD fell,	Lv 16:9	1486
the **l** for the scapegoat fell shall	Lv 16:10	1486
the land shall be divided by **l**.	Nu 26:55	1486
"According to the selection by **l**,	Nu 26:56	1486
by **l** according to your families;	Nu 33:54	1486
Wherever the **l** falls to anyone,	Nu 33:54	1486
that you are to apportion by **l**	Nu 34:13	1486
to give the land by **l** to the sons of	Nu 36:2	1486
I have given Ar to the sons of **L**	Dt 2:9	3876
I have given it to the sons of **L**	Dt 2:19	3876
tribe which the LORD takes *by* **l**	Jos 7:14	
by the **l** of their inheritance, as	Jos 14:2	1486
l for the tribe of the sons of Judah	Jos 15:1	1486
Then the **l** for the sons of Joseph	Jos 16:1	1486
the **l** for the tribe of Manasseh,	Jos 17:1	1486
So *the* **l** was *made* for	Jos 17:2	
"Why have you given me only one **l**	Jos 17:14	1486
you shall not have one **l** *only,*	Jos 17:17	1486
Now the **l** of the tribe of the sons	Jos 18:11	1486
and the territory of their **l** lay	Jos 18:11	1486
Then the second **l** fell to Simeon,	Jos 19:1	1486
Now the third **l** came up for the	Jos 19:10	1486
The fourth **l** fell to Issachar, to	Jos 19:17	1486
Now the fifth **l** fell to the tribe	Jos 19:24	1486
sixth **l** fell to the sons of Naphtali;	Jos 19:32	1486
The seventh **l** fell to the tribe of	Jos 19:40	1486
by **l** in Shiloh before the LORD at	Jos 19:51	1486
Then the **l** came out for the	Jos 21:4	1486
received thirteen cities by **l** from	Jos 21:4	1486
received ten cities by **l** from the	Jos 21:5	1486
thirteen cities by **l** from the families	Jos 21:6	1486
Now the sons of Israel gave by **l**	Jos 21:8	1486
Levi, for the **l** was theirs first.	Jos 21:10	1486
and their **l** was twelve cities.	Jos 21:40	1486
we will go up against it by **l**.	Jg 20:9	1486
tribe of Benjamin was taken by **l**.	1Sa 10:20	
"Give a perfect **l**."	1Sa 14:41	
(for theirs was the *first* **l**),	1Ch 6:54	1486
sons of Kohath *were given* by **l**,	1Ch 6:61	1486
sons of Merari *were given* by **l**,	1Ch 6:63	1486
They gave by **l** from the tribe	1Ch 6:65	1486
Thus they were divided by **l**,	1Ch 24:5	1486
first **l** came out for Jehoiarib,	1Ch 24:7	1486
first **l** came out for Asaph to Joseph,	1Ch 25:9	1486
l to the east fell to Shelemiah.	1Ch 26:14	1486
and his **l** came out to the north.	1Ch 26:14	1486
Ahasuerus, Pur, that is the **l**,	Es 3:7	1486
and had cast Pur, that is the **l**,	Es 9:24	1486
You support my **l**.	Ps 16:5	1486
become a help to the children of **L**	Ps 83:8	3876
Throw in your **l** with us, We shall	Pr 1:14	1486
The **l** is cast into the lap, But	Pr 16:33	1486
The *cast* **l** puts an end to strife	Pr 18:18	1486
his activities, for that is his **l**.	Ec 3:22	2506
And the **l** of those who pillage us.	Is 17:14	1486
He has cast the **l** for them,	Is 34:17	1486
Is your portion, they are your **l**;	Is 57:6	1486
"This is your **l**, the portion	Jer 13:25	1486
when you divide by **l** the land	Ezk 45:1	5307
divide it by **l** for an inheritance	Ezk 47:22	5307
divide by **l** to the tribes of Israel	Ezk 48:29	5307

cast lots and the l fell on Jonah. Jon 1:7 1486
by l in the assembly of the LORD. Mi 2:5 1486
he was chosen by l to enter the Lk 1:9 *2975*
same as happened in the days of L: Lk 17:28 *3091*
day that L went out from Sodom Lk 17:29 *3091*
them, and the l fell to Matthias; Ac 1:26 *2819*
and *if* He rescued righteous L, 2Pe 2:7 *3091*

LOTAN
L and Shobal and Zibeon and Anah, Gn 36:20 3877
The sons of L were Hori and Hemam; Gn 36:22 3877
chief L, chief Shobal, chief Gn 36:29 3877
The sons of Seir *were* L, 1Ch 1:38 3877
The sons of L *were* Hori and Homam; 1Ch 1:39 3877

LOTAN'S
and L sister was Timna. Gn 36:22 3877
and L sister *was* Timna. 1Ch 1:39 3877

LOT'S
and the herdsmen of L livestock. Gn 13:7 3876
"Remember L wife. Lk 17:32 *3091*

LOTS
shall cast l for the two goats, Lv 16:8 1486
I will cast l for you here Jos 18:6 1486
then I will cast l for you here Jos 18:8 1486
And Joshua cast l for them in Jos 18:10 1486
Saul said, "Cast l between me 1Sa 14:42
These also cast l just as their 1Ch 24:31 1486
They cast l for their duties, 1Ch 25:8 1486
They cast l, the small and the 1Ch 26:13 1486
they cast l *for* his son Zechariah, 1Ch 26:14 1486
Likewise we cast l for the supply Ne 10:34 1486
people cast l to bring one out of ten Ne 11:1 1486
"You would even cast l for Jb 6:27
And for my clothing they cast l. Ps 22:18 1486
have also cast l for My people, Jl 3:3 1486
And cast l for Jerusalem Ob 1:11 1486
let us cast l so we may learn on Jon 1:7 1486
cast l and the lot fell on Jonah. Jon 1:7 1486
They cast l for her honorable men, Na 3:10 1486
among themselves by casting l Mt 27:35 *2819*
themselves, casting l for them Mk 15:24 *2819*
And they cast l, dividing up His Lk 23:34 *2819*
us not tear it, but cast l for it, Jn 19:24 *2975*
AND FOR MY CLOTHING THEY CAST L." Jn 19:24 *2819*
And they drew l for them, and the Ac 1:26 *2819*

LOTUS
"Under the l plants he lies down, Jb 40:21 6628
"The l plants cover him with shade; Jb 40:22 6628

LOUD
and a very l trumpet sound, Ex 19:16 2389
the men of Israel with a l voice, Dt 27:14 7311
she cried out with a l voice; 1Sa 28:12 1419
was weeping with a l voice, 2Sa 15:23 1419
face and cried out with a l voice, 2Sa 19:4 1419
assembly of Israel with a l voice, 1Ki 8:55 1419
"Call out with a l voice, for he 1Ki 18:27 1419
So they cried with a l voice and 1Ki 18:28 1419
cried with a l voice in Judean, 2Ki 18:28 1419
oath to the LORD with a l voice, 2Ch 15:14 1419
of Israel, with a very l voice. 2Ch 20:19 1419
with l instruments to the LORD. 2Ch 30:21 5797
They called this out with a l voice 2Ch 32:18 1419
wept with a l voice when the Ezr 3:12 1419
the people shouted with a l shout, Ezr 3:13 1419
replied with a l voice, Ezr 10:12 1419
they cried with a l voice to the LORD Ne 9:4 1419
Shout l, O Philistia, because of Ps 60:8 7321
Praise Him with l cymbals; Ps 150:5 8087a
a l voice early in the morning, Pr 27:14 1419
and earthquake and l noise, Is 29:6 1419
cried with a l voice in Judean and Is 36:13 1419
He will make *her* l noise vanish Jer 51:55 1419
cry in My ears with a l voice, Ezk 8:18 1419
my hearing with a l voice saying, Ezk 9:1 1419
cried out with a l voice and said, Ezk 11:13 1419
And a l crash from the hills. Zph 1:10 1419
Jesus cried out with a l voice, Mt 27:46 *3173*
cried out again with a l voice, Mt 27:50 *3173*
spirit cried out with a l voice and Mk 1:26 *3173*
and shouting with a l voice, Mk 5:7 *3173*
Jesus cried out with a l voice, Mk 15:34 *3173*
And Jesus uttered a l cry, Mk 15:37 *3173*
And she cried out with a l voice and Lk 1:42 *3173*
and he cried out with a l voice, Lk 4:33 *3173*
before Him, and said in a l voice, Lk 8:28 *3173*
glorifying God with a l voice, Lk 17:15 *3173*
praise God joyfully with a l voice Lk 19:37 *3173*
were insistent, with l voices asking Lk 23:23 *3173*
Jesus, crying out with a l voice, Lk 23:46 *3173*
He cried out with a l voice, Jn 11:43 *3173*
But they cried out with a l voice, Ac 7:57 *3173*
he cried out with a l voice, Ac 7:60 *3173*
and made l lamentation over him. Ac 8:2 *3173*
of them shouting with a l voice; Ac 8:7 *3173*
said with a l voice, Ac 14:10 *3173*
But Paul cried out with a l voice, Ac 16:28 *3173*
defense, Festus said in a l voice, Ac 26:24 *3173*
supplications with l crying and tears Heb 5:7 *2478*
and I heard behind me a l voice Rv 1:10 *3173*
angel proclaiming with a l voice, Rv 5:2 *3173*
saying with a l voice, Rv 5:12 *3173*
and they cried out with a l voice, Rv 6:10 *3173*
and he cried out with a l voice to Rv 7:2 *3173*
and they cry out with a l voice, Rv 7:10 *3173*
midheaven, saying with a l voice, Rv 8:13 *3173*
and he cried out with a l voice, Rv 10:3 *3173*
And they heard a l voice from Rv 11:12 *3173*
there were l voices in heaven, Rv 11:15 *3173*
Then I heard a l voice in heaven, Rv 12:10 *3173*
and like the sound of l thunder, Rv 14:2 *3173*
and he said with a l voice, Rv 14:7 *3173*
them, saying with a l voice, Rv 14:9 *3173*
crying out with a l voice to Him Rv 14:15 *3173*
and he called with a l voice to Rv 14:18 *3173*
I heard a l voice from the temple, Rv 16:1 *3173*
and a l voice came out of the Rv 16:17 *3173*
a l voice of a great multitude in Rv 19:1 *3173*
and he cried out with a l voice, Rv 19:17 *3173*
I heard a l voice from the throne, Rv 21:3 *3173*

LOUDER
of the trumpet grew l and louder, Ex 19:19 2388
of the trumpet grew louder and l, Ex 19:19 3966

LOUDLY
so l that the Egyptians heard *it*, Gn 45:2 6963
city and wailed l and bitterly. Es 4:1 1419
"Cry l, do not hold back; Is 58:1 1627
roared at him, They have roared l. Jer 2:15
5414, 6963
Then the herald l proclaimed: Da 3:4 2429
"Now, why do you cry out l? Mi 4:9 7452
and *people* l weeping and wailing. Mk 5:38 *4183*
l declaring that he ought not to Ac 25:24 *994*

LOUDNESS
Because of the l of my groaning My Ps 102:5 6963

LOUD-SOUNDING
of music, harps, lyres, l cymbals, 1Ch 15:16 8085
with trumpets, with l cymbals, 1Ch 15:28 8085
also Asaph *played* l cymbals, 1Ch 16:5 8085

LOVE
son, your only son, whom you l, Gn 22:2 157
a savory dish for me such as I l, Gn 27:4 157
few days because of his l for her. Gn 29:20 160
surely now my husband will l me." Gn 29:32 157
who l Me and keep My commandments. Ex 20:6 157
'I l my master, my wife and my Ex 21:5 157
shall l your neighbor as yourself; Lv 19:18 157
and you shall l him as yourself, Lv 19:34 157
who l Me and keep My commandments. Dt 5:10 157
"You shall l the LORD your God Dt 6:5 157
"The LORD did not set His l on you Dt 7:7 2836a
l Him and keep His commandments; Dt 7:9 157
"He will l you and bless you Dt 7:13 157
to walk in all His ways and l Him, Dt 10:12 157
LORD set His affection to l them, Dt 10:15 157
and shows His l for the alien by Dt 10:18 157
"So show your l for the alien, Dt 10:19 157
therefore l the LORD your God, Dt 11:1 157
to l the LORD your God and to Dt 11:13 157
to do, to l the LORD your God, Dt 11:22 157
find out if you l the LORD your God Dt 13:3 157
you today, to l the LORD your God, Dt 19:9 157
to l the LORD your God with all Dt 30:6 157
you today to l the LORD your God, Dt 30:16 157
to l the LORD your God and walk in Jos 22:5 157
yourselves to l the LORD your God. Jos 23:11 157
But let those who l Him be like Jg 5:31 157
only hate me, and you do not l me; Jg 14:16 157
"How can you say, 'I l you,' when Jg 16:15 157
you, and all his servants l you; 1Sa 18:22 157
again because of his l for him, 1Sa 20:17 160
Your l to me was more wonderful 2Sa 1:26 160
wonderful Than the l of women. 2Sa 1:26 160
"I am in l with Tamar, the sister 2Sa 13:4 157
the l with which he had loved her. 2Sa 13:15 160
and by hating those who l you. 2Sa 19:6 157
Solomon held fast to these in l. 1Ki 11:2 157
"Should you help the wicked and l 2Ch 19:2 157
l Him and keep His commandments, Ne 1:5 157
those I l have turned against me. Jb 19:19 157
With the pinion and plumage of l, Jb 39:13 2623
How long will you l what is Ps 4:2 157
who l Your name may exult in You. Ps 5:11 157
"I l You, O LORD, my strength." Ps 18:1 7355
I l the habitation of Your house And Ps 26:8 157
O l the LORD, all you His godly Ps 31:23 157
Let those who l Your salvation say Ps 40:16 157
You l evil more than good, Ps 52:3 157
You l all words that devour, O Ps 52:4 157
who l His name will dwell in it. Ps 69:36 157
let those who l Your salvation say Ps 70:4 157
Hate evil, you who l the LORD, Ps 97:10 157
for my l they act as my accusers; Ps 109:4 160
evil for good And hatred for my l. Ps 109:5 160
I l the LORD, because He hears My Ps 116:1 157
in Your commandments, Which I l. Ps 119:47 157
to Your commandments, Which I l; Ps 119:48 157
O how I l Your law! Ps 119:97 157
are double-minded, But I l Your law. Ps 119:113 157
Therefore I l Your testimonies. Ps 119:119 157
I l Your commandments Above gold, Ps 119:127 157
manner with those who l Your name. Ps 119:132 157
Consider how I l Your precepts; Ps 119:159 157
falsehood, *But* I l Your law. Ps 119:163 157
who l Your law have great peace, Ps 119:165 157
And I l them exceedingly. Ps 119:167 157
"May they prosper who l you. Ps 122:6 157
The LORD keeps all who l Him, Ps 145:20 157
will you l being simple-minded? Pr 1:22 157
L her, and she will watch over you. Pr 4:6 157
Be exhilarated always with her l. Pr 5:19 160
drink our fill of l until morning; Pr 7:18 1730
"I l those who love me; Pr 8:17 157
"I love those who l me; Pr 8:17 157
endow those who l me with wealth, Pr 8:21 157
All those who hate me l death." Pr 8:36 157
a wise man and he will l you. Pr 9:8 157
But l covers all transgressions. Pr 10:12 160
But those who l the rich are many. Pr 14:20 157
scoffer does not l one who reproves Pr 15:12 157
a dish of vegetables where l is Than Pr 15:17 160
conceals a transgression seeks l, Pr 17:9 160
those who l it will eat its fruit. Pr 18:21 157
Do not l sleep, or you will become Pr 20:13 157
rebuke Than l that is concealed. Pr 27:5 160
A time to l and a time to hate; Ec 3:8 157
whether *it will be* l or hatred; Ec 9:1 160
Indeed their l, their hate and Ec 9:6 160
the woman whom you l all the days Ec 9:9 157
For your l is better than wine. SS 1:2 1730
Therefore the maidens l you. SS 1:3 157
will extol your l more than wine. SS 1:4 1730
Rightly do they l you." SS 1:4 157
hall, And his banner over me is l. SS 2:4 160
do not arouse or awaken *my* l SS 2:7 160
will not arouse or awaken *my* l Until SS 3:5 160
"How beautiful is your l, SS 4:10 1730
much better is your l than wine, SS 4:10 1730
and how delightful you are, *My* l, SS 7:6 160
There I will give you my l. SS 7:12 1730
Do not arouse or awaken *my* l Until SS 8:4 160
For l is as strong as death, SS 8:6 160
"Many waters cannot quench l, SS 8:7 160
all the riches of his house for l, SS 8:7 160
Since you are honored and I l you, Is 43:4 157
and to l the name of the LORD, Is 56:6 157
lying down, who l to slumber; Is 56:10 157
For I, the LORD, l justice, Is 61:8 157
In His l and in His mercy He Is 63:9 160
for her, all you who l her; Is 66:10 157
youth, The l of your betrothals, Jer 2:2 160
you prepare your way To seek l! Jer 2:33 160
And My people l it so! Jer 5:31 157
loved you with an everlasting l; Jer 31:3 160
you were at the time for l; Ezk 16:8 1730
came to her to the bed of l and Ezk 23:17 1730
l Him and keep His commandments, Da 9:4 157
l a woman *who* is loved by *her* Hos 3:1 157
other gods and l raisin cakes." Hos 3:1 157
Their rulers dearly l shame. Hos 4:18 157
I will l them no more; Hos 9:15 157
cords of a man, with bonds of l, Hos 11:4 160
apostasy, I will l them freely, Hos 14:4 157
For so you l *to do*, you sons of Am 4:5 157
Hate evil, l good, And establish Am 5:15 157
"You who hate good and l evil, Mi 3:2 157
But to do justice, to l kindness, Mi 6:8 157
He delights in unchanging l. Mi 7:18 2617a
Jacob *And* unchanging l to Abraham, Mi 7:20 2617a
joy, He will be quiet in His l, Zph 3:17 160
another, and do not l perjury; Zch 8:17 157
so l truth and peace.' Zch 8:19 157
'YOU SHALL L YOUR NEIGHBOR and Mt 5:43 *25*
"But I say to you, l your enemies and Mt 5:44 *25*
"For if you l those who love you, Mt 5:46 *25*
"For if you love those who l you, Mt 5:46 *25*
for they l to stand and pray in Mt 6:5 *5368*
will hate the one and l the other, Mt 6:24 *25*
L YOUR NEIGHBOR AS YOURSELF." Mt 19:19 *25*
"'YOU SHALL L THE LORD YOUR GOD Mt 22:37 *25*
L YOUR NEIGHBOR AS YOURSELF.' Mt 22:39 *25*
"They l the place of honor at Mt 23:6 *5368*
most people's l will grow cold. Mt 24:12 *26*
at him, Jesus felt a l for him and Mk 10:21 *25*
YOU SHALL L THE LORD YOUR GOD Mk 12:30 *25*
L YOUR NEIGHBOR AS YOURSELF.' Mk 12:31 *25*
AND TO L HIM WITH ALL THE HEART Mk 12:33 *25*
AND TO L ONE'S NEIGHBOR AS HIMSELF, Mk 12:33 *25*
to you who hear, l your enemies, Lk 6:27 *25*
"If you l those who love you, Lk 6:32 *25*
"If you love those who l you, Lk 6:32 *25*
sinners l those who love them. Lk 6:32 *25*
sinners love those who l them. Lk 6:32 *25*
"But l your enemies, and do good, Lk 6:35 *25*
them will l him more?" Lk 7:42 *25*
"YOU SHALL L THE LORD YOUR GOD Lk 10:27 *25*
disregard justice and the l of God; Lk 11:42 *26*
For you l the chief seats in the Lk 11:43 *25*
hate the one and l the other, Lk 16:13 *25*
and l respectful greetings in the Lk 20:46 *5368*
have the l of God in yourselves. Jn 5:42 *26*
were your Father, you would l Me, Jn 8:42 *25*
behold, he whom You l is sick." Jn 11:3 *5368*
to you, that you l one another, Jn 13:34 *25*
you, that you also l one another. Jn 13:34 *25*
if you have l for one another." Jn 13:35 *26*
"If you l Me, you will keep My Jn 14:15 *25*
by My Father, and I will l him and Jn 14:21 *25*
and My Father will l him, Jn 14:23 *25*
not l Me does not keep My words; Jn 14:24 *25*
may know that I l the Father, Jn 14:31 *25*
I have also loved you; abide in My l Jn 15:9 *26*
you will abide in My l; Jn 15:10 *26*
commandments and abide in His l. Jn 15:10 *26*
that you l one another, Jn 15:12 *25*
"Greater l has no one than this, Jn 15:13 *26*
you, that you l one another. Jn 15:17 *25*
world, the world would l its own; Jn 15:19 *5368*
that the l with which You Jn 17:26 *26*
do you l Me more than these?" Jn 21:15 *25*
You know that I l You." Jn 21:15 *5368*
"Simon, *son* of John, do you l Me?" Jn 21:16 *25*
You know that I l You." Jn 21:16 *5368*
"Simon, *son* of John, do you l Me?" Jn 21:17 *5368*
the third time, "Do you l Me?" Jn 21:17 *5368*
You know that I l You." Jn 21:17 *5368*
the l of God has been poured out Ro 5:5 *26*

demonstrates His own l toward us, Ro 5:8 26
for good to those who l God, Ro 8:28 25
separate us from the l of Christ? Ro 8:35 26
to separate us from the l of God, Ro 8:39 26
Let l *be* without hypocrisy. Ro 12:9 26
to one another in brotherly l; Ro 12:10 5360
to anyone except to l one another; Ro 13:8 25
L YOUR NEIGHBOR AS YOURSELF." Ro 13:9 25
L does no wrong to a neighbor; Ro 13:10 26
l is the fulfillment of Ro 13:10 26
no longer walking according to l. Ro 14:15 26
Christ and by the l of the Spirit, Ro 15:30 26
THAT GOD HAS PREPARED FOR THOSE WHO L 1Co 2:9 25
with l and a spirit of gentleness? 1Co 4:21 26
makes arrogant, but l edifies. 1Co 8:1 26
and of angels, but do not have l, 1Co 13:1 26
mountains, but do not have l, 1Co 13:2 26
to be burned, but do not have l, 1Co 13:3 26
L is patient, love is kind *and* is 1Co 13:4 26
Love is patient, l is kind 1Co 13:4 26
l does not brag *and* is not arrogant, 1Co 13:4 26
L never fails; but if *there are gifts* 1Co 13:8 26
But now faith, hope, l, 1Co 13:13 26
but the greatest of these is l. 1Co 13:13 26
Pursue l, yet desire earnestly 1Co 14:1 26
Let all that you do be done in l. 1Co 16:14 26
If anyone does not l the Lord, 1Co 16:22 5368
My l be with you all in Christ 1Co 16:24 26
but that you might know the l 2Co 2:4 26
you to reaffirm *your* l for him. 2Co 2:8 26
For the l of Christ controls us, 2Co 5:14 26
in the Holy Spirit, in genuine l, 2Co 6:6 26
and in the l we inspired in you, 2Co 8:7 26
the sincerity of your l also. 2Co 8:8 26
show them the proof of your l and 2Co 8:24 26
Because I do not l you? 2Co 11:11 25
If I l you more, am I to be 2Co 12:15 25
of l and peace will be with you. 2Co 13:11 26
Jesus Christ, and the l of God, 2Co 13:14 26
but faith working through l. Ga 5:6 26
but through l serve one another. Ga 5:13 26
L YOUR NEIGHBOR AS YOURSELF." Ga 5:14 25
But the fruit of the Spirit is l, Ga 5:22 26
holy and blameless before Him. In l Eph 1:4 26
and your l for all the saints, Eph 1:15 26
great l with which He loved us, Eph 2:4 26
being rooted and grounded in l, Eph 3:17 26
and to know the l of Christ which Eph 3:19 26
tolerance for one another in l, Eph 4:2 26
but speaking the truth in l, Eph 4:15 26
the building up of itself in l. Eph 4:16 26
and walk in l, just as Christ also Eph 5:2 26
Husbands, l your wives, just as Eph 5:25 25
So husbands ought also to l their Eph 5:28 25
l his own wife even as himself, Eph 5:33 25
to the brethren, and l with faith, Eph 6:23 26
those who l our Lord Jesus Christ Eph 6:24 25
Jesus Christ with incorruptible l. Eph 6:24
that your l may abound still more Php 1:9 26
the latter *do it* out of l, Php 1:16 26
if there is any consolation of l, Php 2:1 26
same mind, maintaining the same l, Php 2:2 26
l which you have for all the saints; Col 1:4 26
us of your l in the Spirit. Col 1:8 26
having been knit together in l, Col 2:2 26
Beyond all these things *put on* l, Col 3:14 26
Husbands, l your wives and do not Col 3:19 25
labor of l and steadfastness of hope 1Th 1:3 26
us good news of your faith and l, 1Th 3:6 26
and abound in l for one another, 1Th 3:12 26
Now as to the l of the brethren, 1Th 4:9 5360
taught by God to l one another; 1Th 4:9 25
on the breastplate of faith and l, 1Th 5:8 26
you esteem them very highly in l 1Th 5:13 26
and the l of each one of you 2Th 1:3 26
did not receive the l of the truth so 2Th 2:10 26
direct your hearts into the l of God 2Th 3:5 26
But the goal of our instruction is l 1Tm 1:5 26
with the faith and l which are 1Tm 1:14 26
continue in faith and l and sanctity 1Tm 2:15 26
free from the l of money. 1Tm 3:3 866
but *rather* in speech, conduct, l, 1Tm 4:12 26
For the l of money is a root of 1Tm 6:10 5365
godliness, faith, l, 1Tm 6:11 26
but of power and l and discipline. 2Tm 1:7 26
and l which are in Christ Jesus. 2Tm 1:13 26
righteousness, faith, l *and* peace, 2Tm 2:22 26
purpose, faith, patience, l, 2Tm 3:10 26
sensible, sound in faith, in l, Ti 2:2 26
young women to l their husbands, Ti 2:4 5362
husbands, to l their children, Ti 2:4 5388
and *His* l for mankind appeared, Ti 3:4 5363
Greet those who l us in *the* faith. Ti 3:15 5368
because I hear of your l and Phm 1:5 26
much joy and comfort in your l, Phm 1:7 26
to forget your work and the l which Heb 6:10 26
stimulate one another to l Heb 10:24 26
Let l of the brethren continue. Heb 13:1 5360
is free from the l of money, Heb 13:5 866
has promised to those who l Him. Jas 1:12 25
He promised to those who l Him? Jas 2:5 25
L YOUR NEIGHBOR AS YOURSELF," Jas 2:8 25
you have not seen Him, you l Him, 1Pe 1:8 25
for a sincere l of the brethren, 1Pe 1:22 5360
l one another from the heart, 1Pe 1:22 25
l the brotherhood, fear God, honor 1Pe 2:17 25
"THE ONE WHO DESIRES LIFE, TO L AND 1Pe 3:10 25
fervent in your l for one another, 1Pe 4:8 26
l covers a multitude of sins. 1Pe 4:8 26
Greet one another with a kiss of l. 1Pe 5:14 26
and in *your* brotherly kindness, l. 2Pe 1:7 26
in him the l of God has truly been 1Jn 2:5 26
Do not l the world nor the things 1Jn 2:15 25
the l of the Father is not in him. 1Jn 2:15 26
See how great a l the Father has 1Jn 3:1 26
one who does not l his brother. 1Jn 3:10 25
that we should l one another; 1Jn 3:11 25
life, because we l the brethren. 1Jn 3:14 25
He who does not l abides in death. 1Jn 3:14 25
We know l by this, that He laid 1Jn 3:16 26
does the l of God abide in him? 1Jn 3:17 26
us not l with word or with tongue, 1Jn 3:18 25
Jesus Christ, and l one another, 1Jn 3:23 25
Beloved, let us l one another, for 1Jn 4:7 25
one another, for l is from God; 1Jn 4:7 26
who does not l does not know God, 1Jn 4:8 25
does not know God, for God is l. 1Jn 4:8 26
the l of God was manifested in us, 1Jn 4:9 26
In this is l, not that we loved 1Jn 4:10 26
we also ought to l one another. 1Jn 4:11 25
if we l one another, God abides in 1Jn 4:12 25
us, and His l is perfected in us. 1Jn 4:12 26
the l which God has for us. 1Jn 4:16 26
God is l, and the one who abides 1Jn 4:16 26
one who abides in l abides in God, 1Jn 4:16 26
By this, l is perfected with us, 1Jn 4:17 26
There is no fear in l; 1Jn 4:18 26
but perfect l casts out fear, 1Jn 4:18 26
one who fears is not perfected in l. 1Jn 4:18 26
We l, because He first loved us. 1Jn 4:19 25
If someone says, "I l God," and 1Jn 4:20 25
for the one who does not l his 1Jn 4:20 25
cannot l God whom he has not seen. 1Jn 4:20 25
the one who loves God should l his 1Jn 4:21 25
that we l the children of God, 1Jn 5:2 25
when we l God and observe His 1Jn 5:2 25
For this is the l of God, that we 1Jn 5:3 26
her children, whom I l in truth, 2Jn 1:1 25
Son of the Father, in truth and l. 2Jn 1:3 26
beginning, that we l one another. 2Jn 1:5 25
And this is l, that we walk 2Jn 1:6 26
beloved Gaius, whom I l in truth. 3Jn 1:1 25
they have testified to your l before 3Jn 1:6 26
peace and l be multiplied to you. Jude 1:2 26
who are hidden reefs in your l feasts Jude 1:12 26
keep yourselves in the l of God, Jude 1:21 26
that you have left your first l. Rv 2:4 26
and your l and faith and service Rv 2:19 26
'Those whom I l, I reprove and Rv 3:19 5368
not l their life even when faced Rv 12:11 25

LOVED

she became his wife, and he l her; Gn 24:67 157
Now Isaac l Esau, because he had a Gn 25:28 157
but Rebekah l Jacob. Gn 25:28 157
savory food such as his father l. Gn 27:14 157
Now Jacob l Rachel, so he said, Gn 29:18 157
indeed he l Rachel more than Leah, Gn 29:30 157
and he l the girl and spoke Gn 34:3 157
l Joseph more than all his sons, Gn 37:3 157
l him more than all his brothers; Gn 37:4 157
"Because He l your fathers, Dt 4:37 157
but because the LORD l you and Dt 7:8 157
the one l and the other unloved, Dt 21:15 157
and *both* the l and the unloved Dt 21:15 157
he cannot make the son of the l Dt 21:16 157
he l a woman in the valley of Sorek, Jg 16:4 157
a double portion, for he l Hannah, 1Sa 1:5 157
him; and Saul l him greatly 1Sa 16:21 157
and Jonathan l him as himself. 1Sa 18:1 157
David because he l him as himself. 1Sa 18:3 157
But all Israel and Judah l David, 1Sa 18:16 157
Michal, Saul's daughter, l David. 1Sa 18:20 157
Michal, Saul's daughter, l him, 1Sa 18:28 157
he l him as he loved his own life. 1Sa 20:17 157
he loved him as he l his own life. 1Sa 20:17 157
Now the LORD l him 2Sa 12:24 157
and Amnon the son of David l her. 2Sa 13:1 157
the love with which he had l her. 2Sa 13:15 157
Now Solomon l the LORD, walking in 1Ki 3:3 157
because the LORD l Israel forever, 1Ki 10:9 157
Now King Solomon l many foreign 1Ki 11:1 157
because your God l Israel 2Ch 9:8 157
Rehoboam l Maacah the daughter 2Ch 11:21 157
fertile fields, for he l the soil. 2Ch 26:10 157
like him, and he was l by his God, Ne 13:26 157
The king l Esther more than Es 2:17 157
My l ones and my friends stand Ps 38:11 157
You have l righteousness and Ps 45:7 157
of Judah, Mount Zion which He l. Ps 78:68 157
"Because he has l Me, therefore I Ps 91:14 2836a
He also l cursing, so it came to Ps 109:17 157
And he who speaks right is l. Pr 16:13 157
with them, You have l their bed, Is 57:8 157
For I have l strangers, And after Jer 2:25 157
host of heaven, which they have l and Jer 8:2 157
"Even so they have l to wander; Jer 14:10 157
l you with an everlasting love; Jer 31:3 157
all those whom you l *and* all those Ezk 16:37 157
a woman *who is* l by *her* husband, Hos 3:1 157
You have l *harlots'* earnings on Hos 9:1 157
detestable as that which they l. Hos 9:10 157
When Israel *was* a youth I l him, Hos 11:1 157
"I have l you," says the LORD. But Mal 1:2 157
"How have You l us?" Mal 1:2 157
"Yet I have l Jacob; Mal 1:2 157
been forgiven, for she l much; Lk 7:47 25
"For God so l the world, that He Jn 3:16 25
and men l the darkness rather than Jn 3:19 25
Now Jesus l Martha and her Jn 11:5 25
"See how He l him!" Jn 11:36 5368
for they l the approval of men Jn 12:43 25
l His own who were in the world, Jn 13:1 25
the world, He l them to the end. Jn 13:1 25
of His disciples, whom Jesus l. Jn 13:23 25
one another, even as I have l you, Jn 13:34 25
loves Me will be l by My Father, Jn 14:21 25
If you l Me, you would have Jn 14:28 25
"Just as the Father has l Me, Jn 15:9 25
has loved Me, I have also l you; Jn 15:9 25
one another, just as I have l you. Jn 15:12 25
loves you, because you have l Me and Jn 16:27 5368
and l them, even as You have loved Jn 17:23 25
even as You have l Me. Jn 17:23 25
for You l Me before the foundation of Jn 17:24 25
so that the love with which You l Me Jn 17:26 25
disciple whom He l standing nearby Jn 19:26 25
the other disciple whom Jesus l, Jn 20:2 5368
whom Jesus l said to Peter, Jn 21:7 25
whom Jesus l following *them* Jn 21:20 25
conquer through Him who l us. Ro 8:37 25
"JACOB I L, BUT ESAU I HATED." Ro 9:13 25
more, am I to be l less? 2Co 12:15 25
faith in the Son of God, who l me and Ga 2:20 25
His great love with which He l us, Eph 2:4 25
love, just as Christ also l you and Eph 5:2 25
just as Christ also l the church Eph 5:25 25
who has l us and given us eternal 2Th 2:16 25
to all who have l His appearing. 2Tm 4:8 25
having l this present world, 2Tm 4:10 25
"YOU HAVE L RIGHTEOUSNESS AND Heb 1:9 25
l the wages of unrighteousness; 2Pe 2:15 25
this is love, not that we l God, 1Jn 4:10 25
but that He l us and sent His Son 1Jn 4:10 25
Beloved, if God so l us, 1Jn 4:11 25
We love, because He first l us. 1Jn 4:19 25
make them know that I have l you. Rv 3:9 25

LOVELINESS

and all its l is like the flower Is 40:6 2617a

LOVELY

How l are Your dwelling places, O Ps 84:1 3039
praises to His name, for it is l. Ps 135:3 5273a
"I am black but l, O daughters of SS 1:5 5000
"Your cheeks are l with ornaments, SS 1:10 4998
is sweet, And your form is l." SS 2:14 5000
thread, And your mouth is l. SS 4:3 5000
my darling, As l as Jerusalem, SS 6:4 5000
How l on the mountains Are the Is 52:7 4998
and he was l in the sight of God, Ac 7:20 791
whatever is pure, whatever is l, Php 4:8 4375

LOVER

removed l and friend far from me; Ps 88:18 157
treacherously departs from her l, Jer 3:20 7453

LOVERS

Drink and imbibe deeply, O l." SS 5:1 1730
But you are a harlot *with* many l; Jer 3:1 7453
Your l despise you; Jer 4:30 5689
For all your l have been crushed. Jer 22:20 157
And your l will go into captivity; Jer 22:22 157
'All your l have forgotten you, Jer 30:14 157
to comfort her Among all her l. La 1:2 157
"I called to my l, *but* they La 1:19 157
but you give your gifts to all your l Ezk 16:33 157
through your harlotries with your l Ezk 16:36 157
l with whom you took pleasure, Ezk 16:37 157
give you into the hands of your l, Ezk 16:39
will also no longer pay your l. Ezk 16:41 868
and she lusted after her l, Ezk 23:5 157
I gave her into the hand of her l, Ezk 23:9 157
I will arouse your l against you, Ezk 23:22 157
'I will go after my l, Hos 2:5 157
"She will pursue her l, Hos 2:7 157
lewdness In the sight of her l, Hos 2:10 157
wages Which my l have given me.' Hos 2:12 157
and jewelry, And follow her l, Hos 2:13 157
Ephraim has hired l. Hos 8:9 158
Pharisees, who were l of money, Lk 16:14 5366
For men will be l of self, lovers 2Tm 3:2 5367
be lovers of self, l of money, 2Tm 3:2 5366
l of pleasure rather than lovers 2Tm 3:4 5369
of pleasure rather than l of God, 2Tm 3:4 5377

LOVE'S

yet for l sake I rather appeal *to* Phm 1:9 26

LOVES

for your father, such as he l. Gn 27:9 157
his mother, and his father l him.' Gn 44:20 157
he l you and your household, Dt 15:16 157
because the LORD your God l you. Dt 23:5 157
"Indeed, He l the people; Dt 33:3 2245
who l you and is better to you Ru 4:15 157
"Because the LORD l His people, 2Ch 2:11 157
one who l violence His soul hates. Ps 11:5 157
He l righteousness; Ps 11:7 157
He l righteousness and justice; Ps 33:5 157
And l *length of* days that he may Ps 34:12 157
For the LORD l justice And does Ps 37:28 157
The glory of Jacob whom He l. Ps 47:4 157
The LORD l the gates of Zion More Ps 87:2 157
strength of the King l justice; Ps 99:4 157
pure, Therefore Your servant l it. Ps 119:140 157
The LORD l the righteous; Ps 146:8 157
For whom the LORD l He reproves, Pr 3:12 157
Whoever l discipline loves knowledge Pr 12:1 157
Whoever loves discipline l knowledge Pr 12:1 157
But he who l him disciplines him Pr 13:24 157
l one who pursues righteousness. Pr 15:9 157
A friend l at all times, And a Pr 17:17 157

who l transgression loves strife;	Pr 17:19	157
who loves transgression l strife;	Pr 17:19	157
He who gets wisdom l his own soul;	Pr 19:8	157
He who l pleasure *will become* a	Pr 21:17	157
He who l wine and oil will not	Pr 21:17	157
He who l purity of heart *And* whose	Pr 22:11	157
l wisdom makes his father glad,	Pr 29:3	157
He who l money will not be	Ec 5:10	157
nor he who l abundance *with its*	Ec 5:10	157
"Tell me, O you whom my soul l,	SS 1:7	157
night I sought him Whom my soul l;	SS 3:1	157
I must seek him whom my soul l.'	SS 3:2	157
'Have you seen him whom my soul l?'	SS 3:3	157
When I found him whom my soul l;	SS 3:4	157
Everyone l a bribe And chases	Is 1:23	157
The LORD l him; he will carry out	Is 48:14	157
as the LORD l the sons of Israel,	Hos 3:1	157
a trained heifer that l to thresh,	Hos 10:11	157
false balances, He l to oppress.	Hos 12:7	157
sanctuary of the LORD which He l and	Mal 2:11	157
"He who l father or mother more	Mt 10:37	*5368*
and he who l son or daughter more	Mt 10:37	*5368*
for he l our nation and it was he	Lk 7:5	*25*
he who is forgiven little, l little."	Lk 7:47	*25*
"The Father l the Son and has	Jn 3:35	*25*
"For the Father l the Son, and	Jn 5:20	*5368*
"For this reason the Father l Me,	Jn 10:17	*25*
"He who l his life loses it,	Jn 12:25	*5368*
and keeps them is the one who l Me;	Jn 14:21	*25*
and he who l Me will be loved by	Jn 14:21	*25*
"If anyone l Me, he will keep My	Jn 14:23	*25*
for the Father Himself l you,	Jn 16:27	*5368*
for he who l his neighbor has	Ro 13:8	*25*
but if anyone l God, he is known	1Co 8:3	*25*
for God l a cheerful giver.	2Co 9:7	*25*
who l his own wife loves himself;	Eph 5:28	*25*
who loves his own wife l himself;	Eph 5:28	*25*
WHOM THE LORD L HE DISCIPLINES,	Heb 12:6	*25*
The one who l his brother abides	1Jn 2:10	*25*
If anyone l the world, the love of	1Jn 2:15	*25*
everyone who l is born of God	1Jn 4:7	*25*
that the one who l God should love	1Jn 4:21	*25*
and whoever l the Father loves the	1Jn 5:1	*25*
Father l the *child* born of Him.	1Jn 5:1	*25*
who l to be first among them,	3Jn 1:9	*5383*
To Him who l us and released us	Rv 1:5	*25*
everyone who l and practices lying.	Rv 22:15	*5368*
LOVESICK		
me with apples, Because I am l.	SS 2:5	2470a, 160
what you will tell him: For I am l."	SS 5:8	2470a, 160
LOVING		
by l the LORD your God, by obeying	Dt 30:20	157
by l those who hate you, and by	2Sa 19:6	157
As a l hind and a graceful doe,	Pr 5:19	158
but hospitable, l what is good,	Ti 1:8	*5358*
LOVINGKINDNESS		
and you have magnified your l,	Gn 19:19	2617a
and show l to my master Abraham.	Gn 24:12	2617a
You have shown l to my master."	Gn 24:14	2617a
who has not forsaken His l and His	Gn 24:27	2617a
I am unworthy of all the l and of	Gn 32:10	2617a
"In Your l You have led the	Ex 15:13	2617a
but showing l to thousands, to	Ex 20:6	2617a
and abounding in l and truth;	Ex 34:6	2617a
who keeps l for thousands, who	Ex 34:7	2617a
slow to anger and abundant in l,	Nu 14:18	2617a
to the greatness of Your l,	Nu 14:19	2617a
but showing l to thousands, to	Dt 5:10	2617a
who keeps His covenant and His l	Dt 7:9	2617a
His covenant and His l which He	Dt 7:12	2617a
you not show me the l of the LORD,	1Sa 20:14	2617a
off your l from my house forever,	1Sa 20:15	2617a
the LORD show l and truth to you;	2Sa 2:6	2617a
My l shall not depart from him,	2Sa 7:15	2617a
king, And shows l to His anointed,	2Sa 22:51	2617a
"You have shown great l to Your	1Ki 3:6	2617a
reserved for him this great l,	1Ki 3:6	2617a
showing l to Your servants who walk	1Ki 8:23	2617a
For His l is everlasting.	1Ch 16:34	2617a
because His l is everlasting.	1Ch 16:41	2617a
will not take My l away from him,	1Ch 17:13	2617a
with my father David with great l,	2Ch 1:8	2617a
good for His l is everlasting,"	2Ch 5:13	2617a
keeping covenant and *showing* l to	2Ch 6:14	2617a
Your l to Your servant David."	2Ch 6:42	2617a
truly His l is everlasting."	2Ch 7:3	2617a
"for His l is everlasting"	2Ch 7:6	2617a
LORD, for His l is everlasting."	2Ch 20:21	2617a
His l is upon Israel forever."	Ezr 3:11	2617a
and has extended l to me before	Ezr 7:28	2617a
but has extended l to us in the	Ezr 9:9	2617a
who preserves the covenant and l	Ne 1:5	2617a
Slow to anger and abounding in l;	Ne 9:17	2617a
God, who keeps covenant and l,	Ne 9:32	2617a
to the greatness of Your l.	Ne 13:22	2617a
'You have granted me life and l;	Jb 10:12	2617a
or for His world, Or for l,	Jb 37:13	2617a
by Your abundant l I will enter	Ps 5:7	2617a
Save me because of Your l.	Ps 6:4	2617a
But I have trusted in Your l;	Ps 13:5	2617a
Wondrously show Your l,	Ps 17:7	2617a
king, And shows l to His anointed,	Ps 18:50	2617a
And through the l of the Most High	Ps 21:7	2617a
Surely goodness and l will follow	Ps 23:6	2617a
According to Your l remember me	Ps 25:7	2617a
All the paths of the LORD are l	Ps 25:10	2617a

For Your l is before my eyes, And I	Ps 26:3	2617a
will rejoice and be glad in Your l,	Ps 31:7	2617a
Save me in Your l.	Ps 31:16	2617a
His l to me in a besieged city.	Ps 31:21	2617a
in the LORD, l shall surround him.	Ps 32:10	2617a
is full of the l of the LORD.	Ps 33:5	2617a
Him, On those who hope for His l,	Ps 33:18	2617a
Let Your l, O LORD, be upon us,	Ps 33:22	2617a
Your l, O LORD, extends to the	Ps 36:5	2617a
How precious is Your l,	Ps 36:7	2617a
Your l to those who know You,	Ps 36:10	2617a
I have not concealed Your l and Your	Ps 40:10	2617a
Your l and Your truth will	Ps 40:11	2617a
will command His l in the daytime;	Ps 42:8	2617a
redeem us for the sake of Your l.	Ps 44:26	2617a
We have thought on Your l,	Ps 48:9	2617a
to me, O God, according to Your l;	Ps 51:1	2617a
The l of God *endures* all day long.	Ps 52:1	2617a
in the l of God forever and ever.	Ps 52:8	2617a
send forth His l and His truth.	Ps 57:3	2617a
For Your l is great to the heavens And	Ps 57:10	2617a
My God in His l will meet me;	Ps 59:10	2617a
sing of Your l in the morning,	Ps 59:16	2617a
the God who shows me l.	Ps 59:17	2617a
Appoint l and truth that they may	Ps 61:7	2617a
And l is Yours, O Lord, For You	Ps 62:12	2617a
Because Your l is better than life,	Ps 63:3	2617a
away my prayer Nor His l from me.	Ps 66:20	2617a
O God, in the greatness of Your l,	Ps 69:13	2617a
me, O LORD, for Your l is good;	Ps 69:16	2617a
Has His l ceased forever?	Ps 77:8	2617a
Show us Your l, O LORD, And grant	Ps 85:7	2617a
L and truth have met together;	Ps 85:10	2617a
abundant in l to all who call upon	Ps 86:5	2617a
For Your l toward me is great, And	Ps 86:13	2617a
anger and abundant in l and truth.	Ps 86:15	2617a
Your l be declared in the grave,	Ps 88:11	2617a
sing of the l of the LORD forever;	Ps 89:1	2617a
"L will be built up forever;	Ps 89:2	2617a
L and truth go before You.	Ps 89:14	2617a
and My l will be with him,	Ps 89:24	2617a
"My l I will keep for him	Ps 89:28	2617a
will not break off My l from him,	Ps 89:33	2617a
satisfy us in the morning with Your l	Ps 90:14	2617a
To declare Your l in the morning And	Ps 92:2	2617a
Your l, O LORD, will hold me up.	Ps 94:18	2617a
He has remembered His l and His	Ps 98:3	2617a
His l is everlasting And His	Ps 100:5	2617a
I will sing of l and justice, To	Ps 101:1	2617a
crowns you with l and compassion;	Ps 103:4	2617a
Slow to anger and abounding in l.	Ps 103:8	2617a
His l toward those who fear Him.	Ps 103:11	2617a
But the l of the LORD is from	Ps 103:17	2617a
For His l is everlasting.	Ps 106:1	2617a
to the greatness of His l.	Ps 106:45	2617a
For His l is everlasting.	Ps 107:1	2617a
give thanks to the LORD for His l,	Ps 107:8	2617a
give thanks to the LORD for His l,	Ps 107:15	2617a
give thanks to the LORD for His l,	Ps 107:21	2617a
give thanks to the LORD for His l,	Ps 107:31	2617a
Your l is great above the heavens,	Ps 108:4	2617a
there be none to extend l to him,	Ps 109:12	2617a
he did not remember to show l,	Ps 109:16	2617a
Because Your l is good, deliver me;	Ps 109:21	2617a
Save me according to Your l.	Ps 109:26	2617a
name give glory Because of Your l,	Ps 115:1	2617a
For His l is great toward us, And	Ps 117:2	2617a
For His l is everlasting.	Ps 118:1	2617a
"His l is everlasting."	Ps 118:2	2617a
"His l is everlasting."	Ps 118:3	2617a
"His l is everlasting."	Ps 118:4	2617a
For His l is everlasting.	Ps 118:29	2617a
The earth is full of Your l,	Ps 119:64	2617a
O may Your l comfort me, According	Ps 119:76	2617a
Revive me according to Your l,	Ps 119:88	2617a
Your servant according to Your l And	Ps 119:124	2617a
Hear my voice according to Your l;	Ps 119:149	2617a
me, O LORD, according to Your l.	Ps 119:159	2617a
For with the LORD there is l,	Ps 130:7	2617a
For His l is everlasting.	Ps 136:1	2617a
of gods, For His l is everlasting.	Ps 136:2	2617a
lords, For His l is everlasting.	Ps 136:3	2617a
wonders, For His l is everlasting;	Ps 136:4	2617a
skill, For His l is everlasting;	Ps 136:5	2617a
waters, For His l is everlasting;	Ps 136:6	2617a
lights, For His l is everlasting:	Ps 136:7	2617a
by day, For His l is everlasting,	Ps 136:8	2617a
night, For His l is everlasting.	Ps 136:9	2617a
For His l is everlasting,	Ps 136:10	2617a
midst, For His l is everlasting,	Ps 136:11	2617a
arm, For His l is everlasting.	Ps 136:12	2617a
asunder, For His l is everlasting,	Ps 136:13	2617a
of it, For His l is everlasting;	Ps 136:14	2617a
Red Sea, For His l is everlasting.	Ps 136:15	2617a
For His l is everlasting;	Ps 136:16	2617a
kings, For His l is everlasting,	Ps 136:17	2617a
kings, For His l is everlasting:	Ps 136:18	2617a
For His l is everlasting,	Ps 136:19	2617a
Bashan, For His l is everlasting,	Ps 136:20	2617a
For His l is everlasting,	Ps 136:21	2617a
servant, For His l is everlasting.	Ps 136:22	2617a
estate, For His l is everlasting,	Ps 136:23	2617a
For His l is everlasting;	Ps 136:24	2617a
flesh, For His l is everlasting.	Ps 136:25	2617a
heaven, For His l is everlasting.	Ps 136:26	2617a
Your name for Your l and Your truth;	Ps 138:2	2617a
Your l, O LORD, is everlasting;	Ps 138:8	2617a
Let me hear Your l in the morning;	Ps 143:8	2617a
And in Your l, cut off my enemies	Ps 143:12	2617a

My l and my fortress, My	Ps 144:2	2617a
Slow to anger and great in l.	Ps 145:8	2617a
Him, Those who wait for His l.	Ps 147:11	2617a
By l and truth iniquity is atoned	Pr 16:6	2617a
will even be established in l,	Is 16:5	2617a
But with everlasting l I will have	Is 54:8	2617a
My l will not be removed from you,	Is 54:10	2617a
I am the LORD who exercises l,	Jer 9:24	2617a
"*My* l and compassion.	Jer 16:5	2617a
Therefore I have drawn you with l.	Jer 31:3	2617a
who shows l to thousands, but	Jer 32:18	2617a
good, For His l is everlasting";	Jer 33:11	2617a
According to His abundant l.	La 3:32	2617a
who keeps His covenant and l for	Da 9:4	2617a
justice, In l and in compassion,	Hos 2:19	2617a
Slow to anger, abounding in l And	Jl 2:13	2617a
slow to anger and abundant in l,	Jon 4:2	2617a
LOVINGKINDNESSES		
O LORD, Your compassion and Your l,	Ps 25:6	2617a
Where are Your former l,	Ps 89:49	2617a
And consider the l of the LORD.	Ps 107:43	2617a
May Your l also come to me, O LORD,	Ps 119:41	2617a
make mention of the l of the LORD,	Is 63:7	2617a
to the abundance of His l.	Is 63:7	2617a
The LORD's l indeed never cease,	La 3:22	2617a
LOVINGLY		
With its interior l fitted out By	SS 3:10	160
LOW		
bowed l and worshiped the LORD.	Gn 24:26	6915
I bowed l and worshiped the LORD,	Gn 24:48	6915
then they bowed l and worshiped.	Ex 4:31	6915
the people bowed l and worshiped.	Ex 12:27	6915
Moses made haste to bow l	Ex 34:8	6915
brought very l because of Midian,	Jg 6:6	1809
You have brought me very l,	Jg 11:35	3766
He brings l, He also exalts.	1Sa 2:7	8213
and bowed l and did homage to the	1Ch 29:20	6915
then they bowed l and worshiped	Ne 8:6	6915
Or does the ox l over his fodder?	Jb 6:5	1600
they are brought l and like	Jb 24:24	4355
who is proud, and make him l.	Jb 40:11	8213
laid l even at the sight of him?	Jb 41:9	2904
O LORD, confront him, bring him l;	Ps 17:13	3766
Both l and high, Rich and poor	Ps 49:2	1121, 120
Men of l degree are only vanity and	Ps 62:9	1121, 120
For we are brought very l.	Ps 79:8	1809
I was brought l, and He saved me.	Ps 116:6	1809
Who remembered us in our l estate,	Ps 136:23	8216
my cry, For I am brought very l;	Ps 142:6	1809
A man's pride will bring him l,	Pr 29:23	8213
sound of the grinding mill is l,	Ec 12:4	8217
'Since you were laid l,	Is 14:8	7901
But *the Lord* will lay l his pride	Is 25:11	8213
walls He will bring down, Lay l	Is 25:12	8213
brought l those who dwell on high,	Is 26:5	7817
He lays it l, He lays it low to	Is 26:5	8213
low, He lays it l to the ground,	Is 26:5	8213
Then you will be brought l;	Is 29:4	8213
the city will be utterly laid l.	Is 32:19	8213
every mountain and hill be made l;	Is 40:4	8213
and became a l, spreading vine with	Ezk 17:6	8217
the high tree, exalt the l tree,	Ezk 17:24	8217
Exalt that which is l and	Ezk 21:26	8217
AND HILL WILL BE BROUGHT L;	Lk 3:5	*5013*
were laid l in the wilderness.	1Co 10:5	*2693*
LOWER		
you shall make it with l,	Gn 6:16	8482
it appears to be l than the skin,	Lv 13:20	8217
not l than the skin and is faded,	Lv 13:21	8217
but you will go down l and lower.	Dt 28:43	4295
but you will go down lower and l.	Dt 28:43	4295
as far as the l end of the Sea of	Jos 13:27	
from the l end of the Salt Sea,	Jos 15:2	
upper springs and the l springs.	Jos 15:19	8482
of l Beth-horon even to Gezer,	Jos 16:3	8481
lies on the south of l Beth-horon.	Jos 18:13	8481
upper springs and the l springs.	Jg 1:15	8482
rebuilt Gezer and the l Beth-horon	1Ki 9:17	8481
who built l and upper Beth-horon,	1Ch 7:24	8481
upper Beth-horon and l Beth-horon,	2Ch 8:5	8481
Even as hard as a l millstone.	Jb 41:24	8482
have made him a little l than God,	Ps 8:5	2637
l in the presence of the prince,	Pr 25:7	8213
the waters of the l pool.	Is 22:9	8481
you l parts of the earth;	Is 44:23	8481
dwell in the l parts of the earth,	Ezk 26:20	8482
to the l parts of the earth,	Ezk 32:24	8482
pavement (*that is,* the l pavement)	Ezk 40:18	8481
width from the front of the l gate to	Ezk 40:19	8481
l and middle ones in the building.	Ezk 42:5	8481
more than the l and middle ones.	Ezk 42:6	8481
the l ledge *shall be* two cubits and	Ezk 43:14	8481
into the l parts of the earth?	Eph 4:9	*2737a*
A LITTLE WHILE L THAN THE ANGELS;	Heb 2:7	*1642*
a little while l than the angels,	Heb 2:9	*1642*
LOWERED		
she quickly l her jar to her hand,	Gn 24:18	3381
l her jar from her *shoulder,*	Gn 24:46	3381
each man l his sack to the ground,	Gn 44:11	3381
l by four corners to the ground,	Ac 10:11	*2524*
l by four corners from the sky;	Ac 11:5	*2524*
LOWERING		
the wall, l him in a large basket.	Ac 9:25	*2524, 5465*

LOWEST
And burns to the **l** part of Sheol, Dt 32:22 8482
The **l** story *was* five cubits wide, 1Ki 6:6 8481
The doorway for the **l** side chamber 1Ki 6:8 8484
then I stationed *men* in the **l** parts Ne 4:13 8482
You have put me in the **l** pit, Ps 88:6 8482
name, O LORD, Out of the **l** pit. La 3:55 8482
"It will be the **l** of the kingdoms, Ezk 29:15 8217
thus one went up from the **l** *story* Ezk 41:7 8481
LOWING
along the highway, **l** as they went, 1Sa 6:12 1600
the **l** of the oxen which I hear?" 1Sa 15:14 6963
the **l** of the cattle is not heard; Jer 9:10 6963
LOWLAND
in the hill country and in the **l** Dt 1:7 8219
in the hill country and in the **l** Jos 9:1 8219
l and the slopes and all their kings. Jos 10:40 8219
south of Chinneroth and in the **l** Jos 11:2 8219
all that land of Goshen, the **l**, Jos 11:16 8219
hill country of Israel and its **l** Jos 11:16 8219
in the hill country, in the **l**, Jos 12:8 8219
In the **l**: Eshtaol and Zorah and Jos 15:33 8219
and in the Negev and in the **l**. Jg 1:9 8219
sycamore trees that are in the **l**. 1Ki 10:27 8219
plentiful as sycamores in the **l**. 2Ch 1:15 8219
sycamore trees that are in the **l**. 2Ch 9:27 8219
both in the **l** and in the plain. 2Ch 26:10 8219
the **l** and of the Negev of Judah, 2Ch 28:18 8219
the land of Benjamin, from the **l**, Jer 17:26 8219
country, in the cities of the **l** and Jer 32:44 8219
country, in the cities of the **l**, Jer 33:13 8219
LOWLIEST
And sets over it the **l** of men." Da 4:17 8215
LOWLY
He sets on high those who are **l**, Jb 5:11 8217
is exalted, Yet He regards the **l**, Ps 138:6 8217
be humble in spirit with the **l** Pr 16:19 6041
A poor man who oppresses the **l** Is Pr 28:3 1800b
And *also* with the contrite and **l** Is 57:15 8217
In order to revive the spirit of the **l** Is 57:15 8217
"Take a **l** seat, For your Jer 13:18 8213
there they will be a **l** kingdom. Ezk 29:14 8217
among you A humble and **l** people, Zph 3:12 1800b
in mind, but associate with the **l**. Ro 12:16 *5011*
LOYAL
and do not blot out my **l** deeds Ne 13:14 2617a
LOYALTY
"Is this your **l** to your friend? 2Sa 16:17 2617a
Many a man proclaims his own **l**, Pr 20:6 2617a
L and truth preserve the king, And Pr 20:28 2617a
He who pursues righteousness and **l** Pr 21:21 2617a
your **l** is like a morning cloud And Hos 6:4 2617a
I delight in **l** rather than sacrifice, Hos 6:6 2617a
LUBIM
the **L**, the Sukkiim and the 2Ch 12:3 3864
"Were not the Ethiopians and the **L** 2Ch 16:8 3864
Put and **L** were among her helpers. Na 3:9 3864
LUCIUS
was called Niger, and **L** of Cyrene, Ac 13:1 *3066*
so do **L** and Jason and Sosipater, Ro 16:21 *3066*
LUD
and Arpachshad and **L** and Aram. Gn 10:22 3865
the father of the people of **L**, 1Ch 1:11 3866
were Elam, Asshur, Arpachshad, **L**, 1Ch 1:17 3865
Tarshish, Put, **L**, Meshech, Rosh, Is 66:19 3865
and **L** and Put were in your army, Ezk 27:10 3865
"Ethiopia, Put, **L**, all Arabia, Ezk 30:5 3865
LUDIM
Mizraim became the father of **L** Gn 10:13 3866
LUHITH
go up the ascent of **L** weeping; Is 15:5 3872
"For by the ascent of **L** They will Jer 48:5 3872
LUKE
L, the beloved physician, sends Col 4:14 *3065*
Only **L** is with me. 2Tm 4:11 *3065*
as do Mark, Aristarchus, Demas, **L**, Phm 1:24 *3065*
LUKEWARM
'So because you are **l**, Rv 3:16 *5513*
LUMINARIES
the **l** will dwindle. Zch 14:6 3368
LUMP
to make from the same **l** one vessel Ro 9:21 *5445*
of dough is holy, the **l** is also; Ro 11:16 *5445*
leavens the whole **l** *of dough?* 1Co 5:6 *5445*
leaven so that you may be a new **l**, 1Co 5:7 *5445*
leavens the whole **l** *of dough.* Ga 5:9 *5445*
LUNATIC
mercy on my son, for he is a **l** and Mt 17:15 *4583*
LUNCH
asked Him to have **l** with him; Lk 11:37 *709*
LUNCHEON
"When you give a **l** or a dinner, Lk 14:12 *712*
LURK
They attack, they **l**, Ps 56:6 6845
LURKED
I have **l** at my neighbor's doorway, Jb 31:9 693
LURKING
in the **l** places of the villages; Ps 10:8 3993
a young lion **l** in hiding places. Ps 17:12 3427
LURKS
He **l** in a hiding place as a lion Ps 10:9 693
He **l** to catch the afflicted; Ps 10:9 693
squares, And **l** by every corner. Pr 7:12 693
Surely she **l** as a robber, And Pr 23:28 693

LUST
and poured out their **l** on her. Ezk 23:8 8457
more corrupt in her **l** than she, Ezk 23:11 5691
l for her has already committed adultery Mt 5:28 *1937*
away and enticed by his own **l**. Jas 1:14 *1939*
Then when **l** has conceived, it Jas 1:15 *1939*
You **l** and do not have; Jas 4:2 *1937*
that is in the world by **l**. 2Pe 1:4 *1939*
the **l** of the flesh and the lust of 1Jn 2:16 *1939*
lust of the flesh and the **l** of the eyes 1Jn 2:16 *1939*
LUSTED
and she **l** after her lovers, after Ezk 23:5 5689
and with all whom she **l** after, Ezk 23:7 5689
the Assyrians, after whom she **l**. Ezk 23:9 5689
"She **l** after the Assyrians, Ezk 23:12 5689
"When she saw them she **l** Ezk 23:16 5689
"She **l** after their paramours, Ezk 23:20 5689
LUSTFUL
"For that would be a **l** crime; Jb 31:11 2154
"As for your adulteries and your **l** Jer 13:27
the Egyptians, your **l** neighbors, Ezk 16:26 1320, 1432
for they do the **l** desires Ezk 33:31 5690
not in **l** passion, like the Gentiles 1Th 4:5 *1939*
LUSTS
the **l** of their hearts to impurity, Ro 1:24 *1939*
body so that you obey its **l**, Ro 6:12 *1939*
for the flesh in regard to *its* **l**. Ro 13:14 *1939*
lived in the **l** of our flesh, Eph 2:3 *1939*
accordance with the **l** of deceit, Eph 4:22 *1939*
Now flee from youthful **l** and 2Tm 2:22 *1939*
enslaved to various **l** and pleasures, Ti 3:3 *1939*
do not be conformed to the former **l** 1Pe 1:14 *1939*
to abstain from fleshly **l** which 1Pe 2:11 *1939*
flesh no longer for the **l** of men, 1Pe 4:2 *1939*
pursued a course of sensuality, **l**, 1Pe 4:3 *1939*
following after their own **l**, 2Pe 3:3 *1939*
is passing away, and *also* its **l**; 1Jn 2:17 *1939*
following after their *own* **l**; Jude 1:16 *1939*
after their own ungodly **l**." Jude 1:18 *1939*
LUSTY
"They were well-fed **l** horses, Jer 5:8 7904
LUTE
With the ten-stringed **l** and Ps 92:3
LUXURIANT
hill and beneath every **l** tree. 1Ki 14:23 7488
like a **l** tree in its native soil. Ps 37:35 7488
Indeed, our couch is **l**! SS 1:16 7488
the oaks, Under every **l** tree, Is 57:5 7488
Israel is a **l** vine; Hos 10:1 1238a
I am like a **l** cypress; Hos 14:8 7488
LUXURIOUS
And jackals in their **l** palaces. Is 13:22 6027
and all things that were **l** and Rv 18:14 *3045*
LUXURIOUSLY
Who clothed you **l** in scarlet, 2Sa 1:24 5730a
You have lived **l** on the earth and Jas 5:5 *5171*
LUXURY
L is not fitting for a fool; Pr 19:10 8588
are splendidly clothed and live in **l** Lk 7:25 *5172*
LUZ
the name of the city had been **L**. Gn 28:19 3870
So Jacob came to **L** Gn 35:6 3870
"God Almighty appeared to me at **L** Gn 48:3 3870
It went from Bethel to **L**, Jos 16:2 3870
there the border continued to **L**, Jos 18:13 3870
to Luz, to the side of **L** Jos 18:13 3870
name of the city was formerly **L**). Jg 1:23 3870
named it **L** which is its name to this Jg 1:26 3870
LYCAONIA
of it and fled to the cities of **L**, Ac 14:6 *3071*
LYCAONIAN
voice, saying in the **L** language, Ac 14:11 *3072*
LYCIA
Pamphylia, we landed at Myra in **L**. Ac 27:5 *3073*
LYDDA
also to the saints who lived at **L**. Ac 9:32 *3069*
who lived at **L** and Sharon saw him, Ac 9:35 *3069*
Since **L** was near Joppa, the Ac 9:38 *3069*
LYDIA
A woman named **L**, Ac 16:14 *3070*
prison and entered *the house of* **L**, Ac 16:40 *3070*
LYDIANS
L, that handle *and* bend the bow. Jer 46:9 3866
LYE
snow And cleanse my hands with **l**, Jb 9:30 1253a
smelt away your dross as with **l** And Is 1:25 1253a
"Although you wash yourself with **l** Jer 2:22 5427
LYING
of sheep were **l** there beside it, Gn 29:2 7257
Israel by **l** with Jacob's daughter, Gn 34:7 7901
L down between the sheepfolds. Gn 49:14 7257
you **l** *helpless* under its load, Ex 23:5 7257
or threw something at him **l** in wait Nu 35:20 6660
at him without **l** in wait, Nu 35:22 6660
is found **l** in the open country Dt 21:1 5307
is found **l** with a married woman, Dt 22:22 7901
dew, And from the deep **l** beneath, Dt 33:13 7257
and behold Sisera was **l** dead with Jg 4:22 5307
sons of the east were **l** in the valley Jg 7:12 5307
men **l** in wait in an inner room. Jg 16:9 693
were **l** in wait in the inner room. Jg 16:12 693
his concubine was **l** at the doorway Jg 19:27 5307
had not known a man by **l** with him; Jg 21:12 4904
behold, a woman was **l** at his feet. Ru 3:8 7901

as Eli was **l** down in his place 1Sa 3:2 7901
and Samuel was **l** down in the 1Sa 3:3 7901
l in ambush as *it is* this day?" 1Sa 22:13 693
though you are **l** in wait for my 1Sa 24:11 6658a
was **l** in the circle of the camp, 1Sa 26:5 7901
and the people were **l** around him. 1Sa 26:7 7901
was **l** on his bed in his bedroom, 2Sa 4:7 7901
Amnon's house, and he was **l** down. 2Sa 13:8 7901
to Jezreel, for Joram was **l** there. 2Ki 9:16 7901
they *were* corpses **l** on the ground, 2Ch 20:24 5307
Let the **l** lips be mute, Which Ps 31:18 8267
spoken against me with a **l** tongue. Ps 109:2 8267
my soul, O LORD, from **l** lips, Ps 120:2 8267
scrutinize my path and my **l** down, Ps 139:3 7250
Haughty eyes, a **l** tongue, And Pr 6:17 8267
He who conceals hatred *has* **l** lips, Pr 10:18 8267
a **l** tongue is only for a moment. Pr 12:19 8267
L lips are an abomination to the Pr 12:22 8267
Much less are **l** lips to a prince. Pr 17:7 8267
by a **l** tongue Is a fleeting vapor, Pr 21:6 8267
A **l** tongue hates those it crushes, Pr 26:28 8267
unable to bark, Dreamers **l** down, Is 56:10 7901
uttering from the heart **l** words. Is 59:13 8267
They watch like fowlers **l** in wait; Jer 5:26 7918
the **l** pen of the scribes Has made Jer 8:8 8267
He is to me like a bear **l** in wait, La 3:10 693
They see falsehood and **l** divination Ezk 13:6 3577
false vision and speak a **l** divination Ezk 13:7 3577
visions and utter **l** divinations. Ezk 13:9 3577
by your **l** to My people who listen Ezk 13:19 3576
speak **l** and corrupt words before me Da 2:9 3538a
Your nobles are **l** down. Na 3:18 7931
And the diviners see **l** visions And Zch 10:2 8267
my servant is **l** paralyzed at home, Mt 8:6 *906*
saw his mother-in-law **l** sick in bed Mt 8:14 *906*
to Him a paralytic **l** on a bed Mt 9:2 *906*
see the place where He was **l**. Mt 28:6 *2749*
was **l** sick with a fever; Mk 1:30 *2621*
on which the paralytic was **l**. Mk 2:4 *2621*
she found the child **l** on the bed, Mk 7:30 *906*
in cloths and **l** in a manger." Lk 2:12 *2749*
boats **l** at the edge of the lake; Lk 5:2 *2476*
and picked up what he had been **l** on, Lk 5:25 *2621*
When Jesus saw him **l** Jn 5:6 *2621*
and a stone was **l** against it. Jn 11:38 *1945*
saw the linen wrappings **l** *there* Jn 20:5 *2749*
the linen wrappings **l** *there,* Jn 20:6 *2749*
not **l** with the linen wrappings, Jn 20:7 *2749*
the body of Jesus had been **l**. Jn 20:12 *2749*
more than forty of them are **l** in wait Ac 23:21 *1748*
l *in bed* afflicted with *recurrent* fever Ac 28:8 *2621*
the truth in Christ, I am not **l**, Ro 9:1 *5574*
forever, knows that I am not **l**. 2Co 11:31 *5574*
you before God that I am not **l**.) Ga 1:20 *5574*
am telling the truth, I am not **l**) 1Tm 2:7 *5574*
who practices abomination and **l**, Rv 21:27 *5579*
who loves and practices **l**. Rv 22:15 *5579*
LYRE
all those who play the **l** and pipe. Gn 4:21 3658
songs, with timbrel and with **l**; Gn 31:27 3658
flute, and a **l** before them, 1Sa 10:5 3658
thanks to the LORD with the **l**; Ps 33:2 3658
upon the **l** I shall praise You, Ps 43:4 3658
Awake, harp and **l**! I will awaken Ps 57:8 3658
I will sing praises with the **l**, Ps 71:22 3658
sweet sounding **l** with the harp. Ps 81:2 3658
With resounding music upon the **l**. Ps 92:3 3658
praises to the LORD with the **l**, Ps 98:5 3658
the **l** and the sound of melody. Ps 98:5 3658
Awake, harp and **l**; Ps 108:2 3658
Sing praises to our God on the **l**, Ps 147:7 3658
praises to Him with timbrel and **l**. Ps 149:3 3658
Praise Him with harp and **l**. Ps 150:3 3658
are *accompanied* by **l** and harp, Is 5:12 3658
the sound of the horn, flute, **l**, Da 3:5 7030
the sound of the horn, flute, **l**, Da 3:7 7030
the sound of the horn, flute, **l**, Da 3:10 7030
the sound of the horn, flute, **l**, Da 3:15 7030
LYRES
made of fir wood, and with **l**, 2Sa 6:5 3658
also **l** and harps for the singers; 1Ki 10:12 3658
might, even with songs and with **l**, 1Ch 13:8 3658
instruments of music, harps, **l**, 1Ch 15:16 3658
with **l** tuned to the sheminith. 1Ch 15:21 3658
cymbals, with harps and **l**. 1Ch 15:28 3658
musical instruments, harps, **l**; 1Ch 16:5 3658
who *were* to prophesy with **l**, 1Ch 25:1 3658
LORD, with cymbals, harps and **l**, 1Ch 25:6 3658
linen, with cymbals, harps and **l**, 2Ch 5:12 3658
and **l** and harps for the singers; 2Ch 9:11 3658
came to Jerusalem with harps, **l** and 2Ch 20:28 3658
cymbals, with harps and with **l**, 2Ch 29:25 3658
of cymbals, harps and **l**. Ne 12:27 3658
the music of tambourines and **l**; Is 30:32 3658
LYSANIAS
and **L** was tetrarch of Abilene, Lk 3:1 *3078*
LYSIAS
"Claudius **L**, to the most Ac 23:26 *3079*
"But **L** the commander came along, Ac 24:7 *3079*
"When **L** the commander comes down, Ac 24:22 *3079*
LYSTRA
cities of Lycaonia, **L** and Derbe, Ac 14:6 *3082*
At **L** a man was sitting Ac 14:8 *3082*
they returned to **L** and to Iconium Ac 14:21 *3082*
Paul came also to Derbe and to **L**. Ac 16:1 *3082*
who were in **L** and Iconium. Ac 16:2 *3082*
at Antioch, at Iconium *and* at **L**; 2Tm 3:11 *3082*

M

MAACAH
Gaham and Tahash and **M**. Gn 22:24 4601
the third, Absalom the son of **M**, 2Sa 3:3 4601
and the king of **M** with 1,000 men, 2Sa 10:6 4601
and the men of Tob and **M** *were* by 2Sa 10:8 4601
ran away to Achish son of **M**, 1Ki 2:39 4601
was **M** the daughter of Abishalom. 1Ki 15:2 4601
was **M** the daughter of Abishalom. 1Ki 15:10 4601
He also removed **M** his mother 1Ki 15:13 4601
M, Caleb's concubine, bore Sheber 1Ch 2:48 4601
third *was* Absalom the son of **M**, 1Ch 3:2 4601
Shuppim, whose sister's name was **M**. 1Ch 7:15 4601
M the wife of Machir bore a son, 1Ch 7:16 4601
lived, and his wife's name was **M**; 1Ch 8:29 4601
lived, and his wife's name was **M**, 1Ch 9:35 4601
Hanan the son of **M** and Joshaphat 1Ch 11:43 4601
and the king of **M** and his people, 1Ch 19:7 4601
Shephatiah the son of **M**; 1Ch 27:16 4601
he took **M** the daughter of Absalom, 2Ch 11:20 4601
Rehoboam loved **M** the daughter 2Ch 11:21 4601
appointed Abijah the son of **M** 2Ch 11:22 4601
He also removed **M**, 2Ch 15:16 4601

MAACATH
for Geshur and **M** live among Israel Jos 13:13 4601

MAACATHITE
son of Ahasbai, the son of the **M**, 2Sa 23:34 4602
and Jaazaniah the son of the **M**, 2Ki 25:23 4602
the Garmite and Eshtemoa the **M**. 1Ch 4:19 4602
and Jezaniah the son of the **M**, Jer 40:8 4602

MAACATHITES
border of the Geshurites and the **M**, Dt 3:14 4602
border of the Geshurites and the **M**, Jos 12:5 4602
territory of the Geshurites and **M**, Jos 13:11 4602
the Geshurites or the **M**; Jos 13:13 4602

MAADAI
of the sons of Bani: **M**, Amram, Uel Ezr 10:34 4572

MAADIAH
Mijamin, **M**, Bilgah, Ne 12:5 4573

MAAI
Azarel, Milalai, Gilalai, **M**, Ne 12:36 4597

MAARATH
and **M** and Beth-anoth and Eltekon; Jos 15:59 4638

MAAREH-GEBA
out of their place, even out of **M**. Jg 20:33 4626, 1387

MAASAI
Malchijah, and **M** the son of Adiel, 1Ch 9:12 4640

MAASEIAH
Jehiel, Unni, Eliab, Benaiah, **M**, 1Ch 15:18 4641
Jehiel, Unni, Eliab, **M** and 1Ch 15:20 4641
son of Obed, **M** the son of Adaiah, 2Ch 23:1 4641
the scribe and **M** the official, 2Ch 26:11 4641
of Ephraim, slew **M** the king's son and 2Ch 28:7 4641
and **M** an official of the city, 2Ch 34:8 4641
M, Eliezer, Jarib and Gedaliah. Ezr 10:18 4641
M, Elijah, Shemaiah, Jehiel and Ezr 10:21 4641
Elioenai, **M**, Ishmael, Nethanel, Ezr 10:22 4641
Adna, Chelal, Benaiah, **M**, Ezr 10:30 4641
After them Azariah the son of **M**, Ne 3:23 4641
Hilkiah, and **M** on his right hand; Ne 8:4 4641
Akkub, Shabbethai, Hodiah, **M**, Ne 8:7 4641
Rehum, Hashabnah, **M**, Ne 10:25 4641
and **M** the son of Baruch, the son Ne 11:5 4641
the son of Kolaiah, the son of **M**, Ne 11:7 4641
and the priests, Eliakim, **M**, Ne 12:41 4641
and **M**, Shemaiah, Eleazar, Uzzi, Ne 12:42 4641
the priest, the son of **M**, Jer 21:1 4641
concerning Zedekiah the son of **M**, Jer 29:21 4641
and to Zephaniah the son of **M**, Jer 29:25 4641
chamber of **M** the son of Shallum, Jer 35:4 4641
and Zephaniah the son of **M**, Jer 37:3 4641

MAATH
the son of **M**, the son of Lk 3:26 *3092*

MAAZ
firstborn of Jerahmeel, were **M**, 1Ch 2:27 4619

MAAZIAH
Delaiah, the twenty-fourth for **M**. 1Ch 24:18 4590
M, Bilgai, Shemaiah. Ne 10:8 4590

MACEDONIA
a man of **M** was standing Ac 16:9 *3110*
"Come over to **M** and help us." Ac 16:9 *3109*
we sought to go into **M**, Ac 16:10 *3109*
leading city of the district of **M**, Ac 16:12 *3109*
and Timothy came down from **M**, Ac 18:5 *3109*
had passed through **M** and Achaia, Ac 19:21 *3109*
And having sent into **M** two of Ac 19:22 *3109*
Paul's traveling companions from **M**. Ac 19:29 *3110*
of them, he left to go to **M**. Ac 20:1 *3109*
he decided to return through **M**. Ac 20:3 *3109*
For **M** and Achaia have been pleased Ro 15:26 *3109*
come to you after I go through **M**, 1Co 16:5 *3109*
for I am going through **M**; 1Co 16:5 *3109*
that is, to pass your way into **M**, 2Co 1:16 *3109*
and again from **M** to come to you, 2Co 1:16 *3109*
my leave of them, I went on to **M**. 2Co 2:13 *3109*
when we came into **M** our flesh had 2Co 7:5 *3109*
been given in the churches of **M**, 2Co 8:1 *3109*
for when the brethren came from **M** 2Co 11:9 *3109*
gospel, after I left **M**, Php 4:15 *3109*
the believers in **M** and in Achaia. 1Th 1:7 *3109*
you, not only in **M** and Achaia, 1Th 1:8 *3109*
all the brethren who are in all **M**. 1Th 4:10 *3109*
urged you upon my departure for **M**, 1Tm 1:3 *3109*

MACEDONIAN
Aristarchus, a **M** of Thessalonica. Ac 27:2 *3110*

MACEDONIANS
which I boast about you to the **M**, 2Co 9:2 *3110*
otherwise if any **M** come with me and 2Co 9:4 *3110*

MACHBANNAI
the tenth, **M** the eleventh. 1Ch 12:13 4344

MACHBENA
Sheva the father of **M** and 1Ch 2:49 4343

MACHI
tribe of Gad, Geuel the son of **M**. Nu 13:15 4352

MACHIR
also the sons of **M**, Gn 50:23 4353
of **M**, the family of the Machirites; Nu 26:29 4353
and **M** became the father of Gilead: Nu 26:29 4353
the son of Gilead, the son of **M**, Nu 27:1 4353
The sons of **M** the son of Nu 32:39 4353
Gilead to **M** the son of Manasseh, Nu 32:40 4353
the sons of Gilead, the son of **M**, Nu 36:1 4353
"To **M** I gave Gilead. Dt 3:15 4353
the sons of **M** the son of Manasseh, Jos 13:31 4353
for half of the sons of **M** according Jos 13:31 4353
To **M** the firstborn of Manasseh, Jos 17:1 4353
the son of Gilead, the son of **M**, Jos 17:3 4353
From **M** commanders came down, And Jg 5:14 4353
M the son of Ammiel in Lo-debar." 2Sa 9:4 4353
the house of **M** the son of Ammiel, 2Sa 9:5 4353
M the son of Ammiel from Lo-debar, 2Sa 17:27 4353
daughter of **M** the father of Gilead, 1Ch 2:21 4353
All these were the sons of **M**, 1Ch 2:23 4353
she bore **M** the father of Gilead. 1Ch 7:14 4353
M took a wife for Huppim and 1Ch 7:15 4353
Maacah the wife of **M** bore a son, 1Ch 7:16 4353
the sons of Gilead the son of **M**, 1Ch 7:17 4353

MACHIRITES
of Machir, the family of the **M**; Nu 26:29 4354

MACHNADEBAI
M, Shashai, Sharai, Ezr 10:40 4367

MACHPELAH
me the cave of **M** which he owns, Gn 23:9 4375
So Ephron's field, which was in **M**, Gn 23:17 4375
cave of the field at **M** facing Mamre Gn 23:19 4375
buried him in the cave of **M**, Gn 25:9 4375
cave that is in the field of **M**, Gn 49:30 4375
cave of the field of **M** before Mamre Gn 50:13 4375

MAD
You shall be driven **m** by the sight Dt 28:34 7696
did this **m** fellow come to you?" 2Ki 9:11 7696
For oppression makes a wise man **m**, Ec 7:7 1984b
will drink and stagger and go **m** Jer 25:16 1984b
they are **m** over fearsome idols. Jer 50:38 1984b
Therefore the nations are going **m**. Jer 51:7 1984b
great learning is driving you **m**." Ac 26:24 *3130*
will they not say that you are **m**? 1Co 14:23 *3105*

MADAI
were Gomer and Magog and **M** Gn 10:2 4074
of Japheth *were* Gomer, Magog, **M**, 1Ch 1:5 4074

MADE
God **m** the expanse, and Gn 1:7 6213a
God **m** the two great lights, Gn 1:16 6213a
He **m** the stars also. Gn 1:16
God **m** the beasts of the earth Gn 1:25 6213a
God saw all that He had **m**, Gn 1:31 6213a
work which God had created and **m**. Gn 2:3 6213a
the LORD God **m** earth and heaven. Gn 2:4 6213a
field which the LORD God had **m**. Gn 3:1 6213a
and **m** themselves loin coverings. Gn 3:7 6213a
The LORD God **m** garments of Gn 3:21 6213a
He **m** him in the likeness of God. Gn 5:1 6213a
that He had **m** man on the earth, Gn 6:6 6213a
I am sorry that I have **m** them." Gn 6:7 6213a
living thing that I have **m**." Gn 7:4 6213a
window of the ark which he had **m**; Gn 8:6 6213a
For in the image of God He **m** man. Gn 9:6 6213a
which he had **m** there formerly; Gn 13:4 6213a
m war with Bera king of Sodom, Gn 14:2 6213a
'I have **m** Abram rich.' Gn 14:23 6238
the LORD **m** a covenant with Abram, Gn 15:18 3772
For I have **m** you the father of a Gn 17:5 5414
So they **m** their father drink wine Gn 19:33
So they **m** their father drink wine Gn 19:35
"God has **m** laughter for me; Gn 21:6 6213a
and Abraham **m** a great feast on the Gn 21:8 6213a
and the two of them **m** a covenant. Gn 21:27 3772
So they **m** a covenant at Beersheba; Gn 21:32 3772
He **m** the camels kneel down Gn 24:11
m his journey successful or not. Gn 24:21 6743b
"My master **m** me swear, Gn 24:37
last the LORD has **m** room for us, Gn 26:22 7337
Then he **m** them a feast, and they Gn 26:30 6213a
and his mother **m** savory food such Gn 27:14 6213a
and the bread, which she had **m**, Gn 27:17 6213a
Then he also **m** savory food, and Gn 27:31 6213a
"Behold, I have **m** him your Gn 27:37 7760
Then Jacob **m** a vow, saying, Gn 28:20 5087
men of the place and **m** a feast. Gn 29:22 6213a
and **m** the flocks face toward the Gn 30:40 5414
father he has **m** all this wealth." Gn 31:1 6213a
a pillar, where you **m** a vow to Me; Gn 31:13 5087
So they took stones and **m** a heap, Gn 31:46 6213a
and **m** booths for his livestock; Gn 33:17 6213a
and he **m** him a varicolored tunic. Gn 37:3 6213a
breach you have **m** for yourself!" Gn 38:29 6555
he **m** him overseer over his house, Gn 39:4 6485
he **m** him overseer in his house and Gn 39:5 6485
he did, the LORD **m** to prosper. Gn 39:23 6743b
he **m** a feast for all his servants; Gn 40:20 6213a
"God has **m** me forget all my Gn 41:51
"God has **m** me fruitful in the Gn 41:52 6509
m himself known to his brothers. Gn 45:1 3045
and He has **m** me a father to Gn 45:8 7760
"God has **m** me lord of all Egypt; Gn 45:9 7760
Joseph **m** it a statute Gn 47:26 7760
'My father **m** me swear, saying, Gn 50:5
your father, as he **m** you swear." Gn 50:6
Joseph **m** the sons of Israel swear, Gn 50:25
and they **m** their lives bitter with Ex 1:14 4843
"Who **m** you a prince or a judge Ex 2:14 7760
"Who has **m** man's mouth? Ex 4:11 7760
for you have **m** us odious in Ex 5:21 887
and **m** supplication to the LORD. Ex 8:30 6279
m his servants and his livestock flee Ex 9:20
I **m** a mockery of the Egyptians and Ex 10:2 5953a
and **m** supplication to the LORD. Ex 10:18 6279
for he had **m** the sons of Israel Ex 13:19
So he **m** his chariot ready and took Ex 14:6 631
He **m** them drive with difficulty; Ex 14:25
You have **m** for Your dwelling, Ex 15:17 6466
There He **m** for them a statute and Ex 15:25 7760
and **m** them heads over the people, Ex 18:25 5414
LORD **m** the heavens and the earth, Ex 20:11 6213a
the sabbath day and **m** it holy. Ex 20:11 6942
shall be **m** by the two of them that Ex 22:11 1961
which the LORD has **m** with you in Ex 24:8 3772
are to be **m** of hammered work; Ex 25:31 6213a
be **m** from a talent of pure gold, Ex 25:39 6213a
it shall be **m** with cherubim, the Ex 26:31 6213a
atonement was **m** at their ordination Ex 29:33 3722a
days the LORD **m** heaven and earth, Ex 31:17 6213a
tool and **m** it into a molten calf; Ex 32:4 6213a
Aaron **m** a proclamation and said, Ex 32:5 7121
m for themselves a molten calf, Ex 32:8 6213a
He took the calf which they had **m** Ex 32:20 6213a
and **m** the sons of Israel drink *it*. Ex 32:20
m a god of gold for themselves. Ex 32:31 6213a
with the calf which Aaron had **m**. Ex 32:35 6213a
Moses **m** haste to bow low Ex 34:8 4116
I have **m** a covenant with you and Ex 34:27 3772
m the tabernacle with ten curtains; Ex 36:8 6213a
skillful workman, Bezalel **m** them. Ex 36:8 6213a
He **m** loops of blue on the edge Ex 36:11 6213a
He **m** fifty loops in the one Ex 36:12 6213a
he **m** fifty loops on the edge of the Ex 36:12 6213a
He **m** fifty clasps of gold and Ex 36:13 6213a
Then he **m** curtains of goats' *hair* Ex 36:14 6213a
he **m** eleven curtains in all. Ex 36:14 6213a
he **m** fifty loops on the edge of Ex 36:17 6213a
and he **m** fifty loops on the edge Ex 36:17 6213a
He **m** fifty clasps of bronze to Ex 36:18 6213a
He **m** a covering for the tent Ex 36:19 6213a
Then he **m** the boards for the Ex 36:20 6213a
m the boards for the tabernacle: Ex 36:23 6213a
and he **m** forty sockets of silver Ex 36:24 6213a
north side, he **m** twenty boards, Ex 36:25 6213a
to the west, he **m** six boards. Ex 36:27 6213a
He **m** two boards for the Ex 36:28 6213a
Then he **m** bars of acacia wood, Ex 36:31 6213a
He **m** the middle bar to pass Ex 36:33 6213a
and **m** their rings of gold *as* holders Ex 36:34 6213a
he **m** the veil of blue and purple Ex 36:35 6213a
he **m** it with cherubim, the work of Ex 36:35 6213a
m four pillars of acacia for it, Ex 36:36 6213a
He **m** a screen for the doorway Ex 36:37 6213a
and *he* **m** its five pillars with Ex 36:38
Bezalel **m** the ark of acacia wood; Ex 37:1 6213a
and **m** a gold molding for it all Ex 37:2 6213a
He **m** poles of acacia wood and Ex 37:4 6213a
He **m** a mercy seat of pure gold, Ex 37:6 6213a
He **m** two cherubim of gold; Ex 37:7 6213a
he **m** them of hammered work at the Ex 37:7 6213a
he **m** the cherubim *of one piece* Ex 37:8 6213a
he **m** the table of acacia wood, Ex 37:10 6213a
and **m** a gold molding for it all Ex 37:11 6213a
He **m** a rim for it of a Ex 37:12 6213a
and **m** a gold molding for its rim Ex 37:12 6213a
He **m** the poles of acacia wood Ex 37:15 6213a
He **m** the utensils which were Ex 37:16 6213a
he **m** the lampstand of pure gold. Ex 37:17 6213a
He **m** the lampstand of hammered Ex 37:17 6213a
He **m** its seven lamps with its Ex 37:23 6213a
He **m** it and all its utensils from Ex 37:24 6213a
Then he **m** the altar of incense of Ex 37:25 6213a
and he **m** a gold molding for it all Ex 37:26 6213a
He **m** two golden rings for it Ex 37:27 6213a
He **m** the poles of acacia wood Ex 37:28 6213a
And he **m** the holy anointing oil Ex 37:29 6213a
Then he **m** the altar of burnt Ex 38:1 6213a
m its horns on its four corners, Ex 38:2 6213a
m all the utensils of the altar, Ex 38:3 6213a
he **m** all its utensils of bronze. Ex 38:3 6213a
He **m** for the altar a grating Ex 38:4 6213a
He **m** the poles of acacia wood Ex 38:6 6213a
He **m** it hollow with planks. Ex 38:7 6213a
he **m** the laver of bronze with its Ex 38:8 6213a
Then he **m** the court: Ex 38:9 6213a
m of bronze; the hooks of Ex 38:10
m all that the LORD had commanded Ex 38:22 6213a
he **m** hooks for the pillars and Ex 38:28 6213a
their tops and **m** bands for them. Ex 38:28 2836b
With it he **m** the sockets to Ex 38:30 6213a
they **m** finely woven garments for Ex 39:1 6213a
He **m** the ephod of gold, *and* of Ex 39:2 6213a
They **m** attaching shoulder pieces Ex 39:4 6213a
They **m** the onyx stones, set in Ex 39:6 6213a
He **m** the breastpiece, the work Ex 39:8 6213a
m the breastpiece folded double, Ex 39:9 6213a

Context	Reference	Number
They **m** on the breastpiece	**Ex 39:15**	6213a
They **m** two gold filigree	**Ex 39:16**	6213a
They **m** two gold rings and	**Ex 39:19**	6213a
they **m** two gold rings and placed	**Ex 39:20**	6213a
Then he **m** the robe of the ephod of	**Ex 39:22**	6213a
They **m** pomegranates of blue	**Ex 39:24**	6213a
They also **m** bells of pure gold,	**Ex 39:25**	6213a
They **m** the tunics of finely	**Ex 39:27**	6213a
They **m** the plate of the holy	**Ex 39:30**	6213a
your offering is a grain offering **m**	**Lv 2:5**	
your offering is a grain offering **m**	**Lv 2:7**	
shall be **m** of fine flour with oil.	**Lv 2:7**	6213a
grain offering which is **m** of these	**Lv 2:8**	6213a
the LORD, shall be **m** with leaven,	**Lv 2:11**	6213a
has committed is **m** known to him,	**Lv 4:23**	3045
has committed is **m** known to him,	**Lv 4:28**	3045
moreover, you will be **m** unclean:	**Lv 11:24**	2930
any article of which use is **m**	**Lv 11:32**	6213a
or in any article **m** of leather,	**Lv 13:48**	4399
shall be **m** for you to cleanse you;	**Lv 16:30**	3722a
has **m** naked his blood relative;	**Lv 20:19**	6168
if one touches anything **m** unclean	**Lv 22:4**	
things by which he is **m** unclean,	**Lv 22:5**	2930
any man by whom he is **m** unclean,	**Lv 22:5**	2930
m of two-tenths *of an ephah;*	**Lv 23:17**	
the LORD might be **m** clear to them.	**Lv 24:12**	6567a
of your yoke and **m** you walk erect.	**Lv 26:13**	
it is **m** desolate without them.	**Lv 26:43**	8074
restitution may be **m** for the wrong,	**Nu 5:8**	7725
restitution which is **m** for the wrong	**Nu 5:8**	7725
by which atonement is **m** for him.	**Nu 5:8**	3722a
'When he has **m** her drink the	**Nu 5:27**	
m from wine or strong drink,	**Nu 6:3**	
fathers' households, **m** an offering	**Nu 7:2**	7126
Moses, so he **m** the lampstand.	**Nu 8:4**	6213a
Aaron also **m** atonement for them to	**Nu 8:21**	3722a
and **m** all the congregation grumble	**Nu 14:36**	
let them be **m** into hammered sheets	**Nu 16:38**	6213a
and **m** atonement for the people.	**Nu 16:47**	3722a
have you **m** us come up from Egypt,	**Nu 20:5**	
So Israel **m** a vow to the LORD and	**Nu 21:2**	5087
And Moses **m** a bronze serpent and	**Nu 21:9**	6213a
you have **m** a mockery of me!	**Nu 22:29**	5953a
m atonement for the sons of Israel.'	**Nu 25:13**	3722a
So they **m** war against Midian, just	**Nu 31:7**	6633
and He **m** them wander in the	**Nu 32:13**	
no expiation can be **m** for the land	**Nu 35:33**	3722a
brethren have **m** our hearts melt,	**Dt 1:28**	
spirit and **m** his heart obstinate,	**Dt 2:30**	553
your God which He **m** with you,	**Dt 4:23**	3772
God **m** a covenant with us at Horeb.	**Dt 5:2**	3772
of my hand **m** me this wealth.'	**Dt 8:17**	6213a
which the LORD had **m** with you,	**Dt 9:9**	3772
m a molten image for themselves.'	**Dt 9:12**	6213a
m for yourselves a molten calf;	**Dt 9:16**	6213a
thing, the calf which you had **m**,	**Dt 9:21**	6213a
"So I **m** an ark of acacia wood and	**Dt 10:3**	6213a
tablets in the ark which I had **m**;	**Dt 10:5**	6213a
and now the LORD your God has **m**	**Dt 10:22**	7760
when He **m** the water of the Red Sea	**Dt 11:4**	
above all nations which He has **m**,	**Dt 26:19**	6213a
which He had **m** with them at Horeb.	**Dt 29:1**	3772
which He **m** with them when He	**Dt 29:25**	3772
covenant which I have **m** with them.	**Dt 31:16**	3772
He has **m** you and established you.	**Dt 32:6**	6213a
"He **m** him ride on the high places	**Dt 32:13**	
He **m** him suck honey from the rock,	**Dt 32:13**	
Then he forsook God who **m** him,	**Dt 32:15**	6213a
m Him jealous with strange *gods;*	**Dt 32:16**	7065
'They have **m** Me jealous with *what*	**Dt 32:21**	7065
to you which you have **m** us swear,	**Jos 2:17**	
oath which you have **m** us swear."	**Jos 2:20**	
So Joshua **m** himself flint knives	**Jos 5:3**	6213a
Then Joshua **m** them take an oath at	**Jos 6:26**	
burned Ai and **m** it a heap forever,	**Jos 8:28**	7760
Joshua **m** peace with them and	**Jos 9:15**	6213a
them and **m** a covenant with them,	**Jos 9:15**	3772
they had **m** a covenant with them,	**Jos 9:16**	3772
But Joshua **m** them that day hewers	**Jos 9:27**	5414
Gibeon had **m** peace with Israel	**Jos 10:1**	7999b
for it has **m** peace with Joshua and	**Jos 10:4**	7999b
There was not a city which **m** peace	**Jos 11:19**	7999b
m the heart of the people melt with	**Jos 14:8**	
So *the lot* was **m** for the rest	**Jos 17:2**	
promises which the LORD had **m** to	**Jos 21:45**	1696
"For the LORD has **m** the Jordan a	**Jos 22:25**	5414
of the LORD which our fathers **m**,	**Jos 22:28**	6213a
So Joshua **m** a covenant with the	**Jos 24:25**	3772
and **m** for them a statute and an	**Jos 24:25**	7760
Ehud **m** himself a sword which	**Jg 3:16**	6213a
sons of Israel **m** for themselves the	**Jg 6:2**	6213a
Gideon **m** it into an ephod, and	**Jg 8:27**	6213a
Baals, and **m** Baal-berith their god.	**Jg 8:33**	7760
they went and **m** Abimelech king,	**Jg 9:6**	4427a
one stone, and have **m** Abimelech,	**Jg 9:18**	4427a
m him head and chief over them;	**Jg 11:11**	7760
Jephthah **m** a vow to the LORD and	**Jg 11:30**	5087
to the vow which he had **m**;	**Jg 11:39**	5087
and Samson **m** a feast there, for	**Jg 14:10**	6213a
She **m** him sleep on her knees,	**Jg 16:19**	
m him stand between the pillars.	**Jg 16:25**	
who **m** them into a graven image	**Jg 17:4**	6213a
he **m** an ephod and household idols	**Jg 17:5**	6213a
and as he **m** his journey, he came	**Jg 17:8**	6213a
have taken away my gods which I **m**,	**Jg 18:24**	6213a
Then they took what Micah had **m**	**Jg 18:27**	6213a
graven image which he had **m**,	**Jg 18:31**	6213a
LORD had **m** a breach in the tribes	**Jg 21:15**	6213a
She **m** a vow and said,	**1Sa 1:11**	5087
and there they **m** Saul king before	**1Sa 11:15**	4427a
Jonathan and his armor bearer **m**	**1Sa 14:14**	5221
"I regret that I have **m** Saul king,	**1Sa 15:11**	4427a
you were **m** the head of the tribes	**1Sa 15:17**	
your sword has **m** women childless,	**1Sa 15:33**	7921
He had **m** Saul king over Israel.	**1Sa 15:35**	4427a
and **m** him pass before Samuel.	**1Sa 16:8**	
Next Jesse **m** Shammah pass by.	**1Sa 16:9**	
Thus Jesse **m** seven of his sons	**1Sa 16:10**	
Then Jonathan **m** a covenant with	**1Sa 18:3**	3772
So Jonathan **m** a *covenant* with the	**1Sa 20:16**	3772
Jonathan **m** David vow again	**1Sa 20:17**	
the two of them **m** a covenant	**1Sa 23:18**	3772
Philistines have **m** a raid on the land	**1Sa 23:27**	6584
"Where have you **m** a raid today?"	**1Sa 27:10**	6584
"He has surely **m** himself odious	**1Sa 27:12**	887
that the Amalekites had **m** a raid	**1Sa 30:1**	6584
"We **m** a raid on the Negev of the	**1Sa 30:14**	6584
that he **m** it a statute and an	**1Sa 30:25**	7760
He **m** him king over Gilead,	**2Sa 2:9**	4427a
And David **m** a feast for Abner and	**2Sa 3:20**	6213a
and King David **m** a covenant with	**2Sa 5:3**	3772
with all kinds of *instruments* **m**	**2Sa 6:5**	
m a revelation to Your servant,	**2Sa 7:27**	1540
So David **m** a name *for himself* when	**2Sa 8:13**	6213a
they **m** peace with Israel and	**2Sa 10:19**	7999b
before him, and he **m** him drunk;	**2Sa 11:13**	7937
m them pass through the brickkiln.	**2Sa 12:31**	
Tamar that he **m** himself ill,	**2Sa 13:2**	2470a
kneaded *it,* **m** cakes in his sight,	**2Sa 13:8**	3823b
took the cakes which she had **m**	**2Sa 13:10**	6213a
the people have **m** me afraid;	**2Sa 14:15**	3372a
you have **m** yourself odious to your	**2Sa 16:21**	887
the sons of Israel **m** a covenant with	**2Sa 21:2**	7650
He **m** darkness canopies around Him,	**2Sa 22:12**	7896
"You have also **m** my enemies turn	**2Sa 22:41**	5414
He has **m** an everlasting covenant	**2Sa 23:5**	7760
King David has **m** Solomon king.	**1Ki 1:43**	4427a
have **m** him ride on the king's mule.	**1Ki 1:44**	
has **m** me a house as He promised,	**1Ki 2:24**	6213a
You have **m** Your servant king in	**1Ki 3:7**	4427a
offerings and **m** peace offerings,	**1Ki 3:15**	6213a
and **m** a feast for all his	**1Ki 3:15**	6213a
and the two of them **m** a covenant.	**1Ki 5:12**	3772
he **m** windows with *artistic* frames.	**1Ki 6:4**	6213a
he **m** side chambers all around.	**1Ki 6:5**	6213a
for on the outside he **m** offsets *in*	**1Ki 6:6**	5414
he **m** two cherubim of olive wood,	**1Ki 6:23**	6213a
he **m** doors of olive wood,	**1Ki 6:31**	6213a
So *he* **m** two doors of olive wood,	**1Ki 6:32**	
So also he **m** for the entrance of	**1Ki 6:33**	6213a
Then he **m** the hall of pillars;	**1Ki 7:6**	6213a
He **m** the hall of the throne	**1Ki 7:7**	6213a
He also **m** a house like this hall	**1Ki 7:8**	6213a
He also **m** two capitals of molten	**1Ki 7:16**	6213a
So he **m** the pillars, and two rows	**1Ki 7:18**	6213a
Now he **m** the sea of cast *metal* ten	**1Ki 7:23**	6213a
brim was **m** like the brim of a cup,	**1Ki 7:26**	4639
he **m** the ten stands of bronze;	**1Ki 7:27**	6213a
He **m** the ten stands like this:	**1Ki 7:37**	6213a
He **m** ten basins of bronze, one	**1Ki 7:38**	6213a
Now Hiram **m** the basins and the	**1Ki 7:40**	6213a
utensils which Hiram **m** for King	**1Ki 7:45**	6213a
Solomon **m** all the furniture	**1Ki 7:48**	6213a
and the cherubim **m** a covering over	**1Ki 8:7**	5526a
where the LORD **m** a covenant with	**1Ki 8:9**	3772
which He **m** with our fathers when	**1Ki 8:21**	3772
neighbor and is **m** to take an oath,	**1Ki 8:31**	5377
whatever prayer or supplication is **m**	**1Ki 8:38**	1961
m supplication before the LORD,	**1Ki 8:59**	2603a
which you have **m** before Me;	**1Ki 9:3**	2603a
forever, therefore He **m** you king,	**1Ki 10:9**	7760
The king **m** of the almug trees	**1Ki 10:12**	6213a
King Solomon **m** 200 large	**1Ki 10:16**	6213a
He **m** 300 shields of beaten gold,	**1Ki 10:17**	
the king **m** a great throne of ivory	**1Ki 10:18**	6213a
it was **m** for any other kingdom.	**1Ki 10:20**	6213a
The king **m** silver *as common* as	**1Ki 10:27**	5414
and he **m** cedars as plentiful as	**1Ki 10:27**	5414
"Your father **m** our yoke hard;	**1Ki 12:4**	7185
'Your father **m** our yoke heavy, now	**1Ki 12:10**	3513
"My father **m** your yoke heavy, but	**1Ki 12:14**	3513
King Rehoboam **m** haste to mount	**1Ki 12:18**	553
and **m** him king over all Israel.	**1Ki 12:20**	4427a
and **m** two golden calves,	**1Ki 12:28**	6213a
And he **m** houses on high places,	**1Ki 12:31**	6213a
and **m** priests from among all the	**1Ki 12:31**	6213a
to the calves which he had **m**.	**1Ki 12:32**	6213a
of the high places which he had **m**.	**1Ki 12:32**	6213a
the altar which he had **m** in Bethel	**1Ki 12:33**	6213a
but again he **m** priests of the high	**1Ki 13:33**	6213a
m you leader over My people Israel,	**1Ki 14:7**	5414
and have gone and **m** for yourself	**1Ki 14:9**	6213a
because they have **m** their Asherim,	**1Ki 14:15**	6213a
with which he **m** Israel to sin."	**1Ki 14:16**	
how he **m** war and how he reigned,	**1Ki 14:19**	3898a
of gold which Solomon had **m**.	**1Ki 14:26**	6213a
King Rehoboam **m** shields of bronze	**1Ki 14:27**	6213a
the idols which his fathers had **m**.	**1Ki 15:12**	6213a
m a horrid image as an Asherah;	**1Ki 15:13**	6213a
Then King Asa **m** a proclamation to	**1Ki 15:22**	8085
in his sin which he **m** Israel sin.	**1Ki 15:26**	
sinned, and which he **m** Israel sin,	**1Ki 15:30**	
in his sin which he **m** Israel sin.	**1Ki 15:34**	
m you leader over My people Israel,	**1Ki 16:2**	5414
and have **m** My people Israel sin,	**1Ki 16:2**	
and which they **m** Israel sin,	**1Ki 16:13**	
Therefore all Israel **m** Omri,	**1Ki 16:16**	4427a
in his sins which he **m** Israel sin,	**1Ki 16:26**	
Ahab also **m** the Asherah.	**1Ki 16:33**	6213a
he **m** the kingdom or nation swear	**1Ki 18:10**	
about the altar which they **m**.	**1Ki 18:26**	6213a
he **m** a trench around the altar,	**1Ki 18:32**	6213a
as my father **m** in Samaria."	**1Ki 20:34**	7760
So he **m** a covenant with him and	**1Ki 20:34**	3772
and *because* you have **m** Israel sin.	**1Ki 21:22**	
son of Chenaanah **m** horns of iron	**1Ki 22:11**	6213a
m peace with the king of Israel.	**1Ki 22:44**	7999b
Jehoshaphat **m** ships of Tarshish to	**1Ki 22:48**	6213a
of Baal which his father had **m**.	**2Ki 3:2**	6213a
of Nebat, which he **m** Israel sin;	**2Ki 3:3**	
and they **m** a circuit of seven	**2Ki 3:9**	5437
it in there, and **m** the iron float.	**2Ki 6:6**	
and **m** a king over themselves.	**2Ki 8:20**	4427a
And they **m** his chariot ready.	**2Ki 9:21**	631
So he **m** him ride in his chariot.	**2Ki 10:16**	
and **m** it a latrine to this day.	**2Ki 10:27**	7760
of Nebat, which he **m** Israel sin,	**2Ki 10:29**	
Jeroboam, which he **m** Israel sin.	**2Ki 10:31**	
Then he **m** a covenant with them and	**2Ki 11:4**	3772
they **m** him king and anointed him,	**2Ki 11:12**	4427a
Then Jehoiada **m** a covenant between	**2Ki 11:17**	3772
But there were not **m** for the house	**2Ki 12:13**	6213a
servants arose and **m** a conspiracy and	**2Ki 12:20**	7194
Nebat, with which he **m** Israel sin;	**2Ki 13:2**	
with which he **m** Israel sin,	**2Ki 13:6**	
m them like the dust at threshing.	**2Ki 13:7**	7760
Nebat, with which he **m** Israel sin,	**2Ki 13:11**	
and **m** him king in the place of his	**2Ki 14:21**	4427a
of Nebat, which he **m** Israel sin.	**2Ki 14:24**	
of Nebat, which he **m** Israel sin.	**2Ki 15:9**	
and his conspiracy which he **m**,	**2Ki 15:15**	7194
of Nebat, which he **m** Israel sin.	**2Ki 15:18**	
of Nebat, which he **m** Israel sin.	**2Ki 15:24**	
of Nebat, which he **m** Israel sin.	**2Ki 15:28**	
And Hoshea the son of Elah **m** a	**2Ki 15:30**	7194
m his son pass through the fire,	**2Ki 16:3**	
thus Urijah the priest **m** *it,*	**2Ki 16:11**	6213a
which He **m** with their fathers and	**2Ki 17:15**	3772
and **m** for themselves molten	**2Ki 17:16**	6213a
and **m** an Asherah and worshiped all	**2Ki 17:16**	6213a
Then they **m** their sons and their	**2Ki 17:17**	
they **m** Jeroboam the son of Nebat	**2Ki 17:21**	4427a
and **m** them commit a great sin.	**2Ki 17:21**	
every nation still **m** gods of its own	**2Ki 17:29**	6213a
which the people of Samaria had **m**,	**2Ki 17:29**	6213a
men of Babylon **m** Succoth-benoth,	**2Ki 17:30**	6213a
the men of Cuth **m** Nergal,	**2Ki 17:30**	6213a
the men of Hamath **m** Ashima,	**2Ki 17:30**	6213a
the Avvites **m** Nibhaz and Tartak;	**2Ki 17:31**	6213a
with whom the LORD **m** a covenant	**2Ki 17:35**	3772
covenant that I have **m** with you,	**2Ki 17:38**	3772
bronze serpent that Moses had **m**,	**2Ki 18:4**	6213a
You have **m** heaven and earth.	**2Ki 19:15**	6213a
how he **m** the pool and the conduit and	**2Ki 20:20**	6213a
altars for Baal and **m** an Asherah,	**2Ki 21:3**	6213a
m his son pass through the fire,	**2Ki 21:6**	
image of Asherah that he had **m**,	**2Ki 21:7**	6213a
also **m** Judah sin with his idols;	**2Ki 21:11**	
his sin with which he **m** Judah sin,	**2Ki 21:16**	
people of the land **m** Josiah his son	**2Ki 21:24**	4427a
'Only no accounting shall be **m**	**2Ki 22:7**	
and **m** a covenant before the LORD,	**2Ki 23:3**	3772
the vessels that were **m** for Baal,	**2Ki 23:4**	6213a
which the kings of Judah had **m**,	**2Ki 23:12**	6213a
altars which Manasseh had **m** in the	**2Ki 23:12**	6213a
son of Nebat, who **m** Israel sin,	**2Ki 23:15**	
Nebat, who made Israel sin, had **m**,	**2Ki 23:15**	6213a
Israel had **m** provoking the LORD;	**2Ki 23:19**	6213a
and anointed him and **m** him king	**2Ki 23:30**	4427a
Pharaoh Neco **m** Eliakim the son	**2Ki 23:34**	4427a
had **m** in the temple of the LORD,	**2Ki 24:13**	6213a
of Babylon **m** his uncle Mattaniah king	**2Ki 24:17**	4427a
stands which Solomon had **m** for the	**2Ki 25:16**	6213a
Saul they **m** war with the Hagrites,	**1Ch 5:10**	6213a
They **m** war against the Hagrites,	**1Ch 5:19**	6213a
and David **m** a covenant with them	**1Ch 11:3**	3772
and **m** them captains of the band.	**1Ch 12:18**	5414
Philistines had come and **m** a raid	**1Ch 14:9**	6584
The Philistines **m** yet another	**1Ch 14:13**	6584
LORD our God **m** an outburst on us,	**1Ch 15:13**	6555
covenant which He **m** with Abraham,	**1Ch 16:16**	3772
idols, But the LORD **m** the heavens.	**1Ch 16:26**	6213a
"For Your people Israel You **m** Your	**1Ch 17:22**	5414
with which Solomon **m** the bronze	**1Ch 18:8**	6213a
had **m** themselves odious to David,	**1Ch 19:6**	887
they **m** peace with David and served	**1Ch 19:19**	7999b
Moses had **m** in the wilderness,	**1Ch 21:29**	6213a
So David **m** ample preparations	**1Ch 22:5**	3559
he **m** his son Solomon king over	**1Ch 23:1**	4427a
which David **m** for giving praise.	**1Ch 23:5**	6213a
his father **m** him first),	**1Ch 26:10**	7760
And King David **m** them overseers of	**1Ch 26:32**	6485
I had **m** preparations to build *it.*	**1Ch 28:2**	3559
"the LORD **m** me understand in	**1Ch 28:19**	
for they **m** their offering to the	**1Ch 29:9**	5068
for which I have **m** provision."	**1Ch 29:19**	3559
they **m** sacrifices to the LORD and	**1Ch 29:21**	2076
And they **m** Solomon the son of	**1Ch 29:22**	4427a
the LORD had **m** in the wilderness.	**2Ch 1:3**	6213a
son of Uri, the son of Hur, had **m**,	**2Ch 1:5**	6213a
and have **m** me king in his place.	**2Ch 1:8**	4427a
for You have **m** me king over a	**2Ch 1:9**	4427a
over whom I have **m** you king,	**2Ch 1:11**	4427a
The king **m** silver and gold as	**2Ch 1:15**	5414
and he **m** cedars as plentiful as	**2Ch 1:15**	5414
He has **m** you king over them."	**2Ch 2:11**	5414
who has **m** heaven and earth,	**2Ch 2:12**	6213a

he **m** the room of the holy of holies: **2Ch 3:8** 6213a
Then he **m** two sculptured cherubim **2Ch 3:10** 6213a
He **m** the veil of violet, **2Ch 3:14** 6213a
He also **m** two pillars for the **2Ch 3:15** 6213a
m chains in the inner sanctuary and **2Ch 3:16** 6213a
and he **m** one hundred pomegranates **2Ch 3:16** 6213a
Then he **m** a bronze altar, twenty **2Ch 4:1** 6213a
Also he **m** the cast *metal* sea, ten **2Ch 4:2** 6213a
brim was **m** like the brim of a cup, **2Ch 4:5** 4639
m ten basins in which to wash, **2Ch 4:6** 6213a
he **m** the ten golden lampstands **2Ch 4:7** 6213a
He also **m** ten tables and placed **2Ch 4:8** 6213a
And he **m** one hundred golden bowls. **2Ch 4:8** 6213a
Then he **m** the court of the priests **2Ch 4:9** 6213a
Huram also **m** the pails, the **2Ch 4:11** 6213a
He also **m** the stands and he made **2Ch 4:14** 6213a
and he **m** the basins on the stands, **2Ch 4:14** 6213a
Huram-abi **m** of polished bronze for **2Ch 4:16** 6213a
Thus Solomon **m** all these utensils **2Ch 4:18** 6213a
Solomon also **m** all the things that **2Ch 4:19** 6213a
so that the cherubim **m** a covering **2Ch 5:8** 3680
where the LORD **m** a covenant with **2Ch 5:10** 3772
He **m** with the sons of Israel." **2Ch 6:11** 3772
Solomon had **m** a bronze platform, **2Ch 6:13** 6213a
and is **m** to take an oath, **2Ch 6:22** 5377
whatever prayer or supplication is **m** **2Ch 6:29** 1961
which King David had **m** for giving **2Ch 7:6** 6213a
bronze altar which Solomon had **m** **2Ch 7:7** 6213a
therefore He **m** you king over them, **2Ch 9:8** 5414
the king **m** steps for the house of **2Ch 9:11** 6213a
King Solomon **m** 200 large shields **2Ch 9:15** 6213a
He **m** 300 shields of beaten gold, **2Ch 9:16**
the king **m** a great throne of ivory **2Ch 9:17** 6213a
nothing like *it* was **m** for any *other* **2Ch 9:19** 6213a
The king **m** silver *as common* as **2Ch 9:27** 5414
and he **m** cedars as plentiful as **2Ch 9:27** 5414
"Your father **m** our yoke hard; **2Ch 10:4** 7185
'Your father **m** our yoke heavy, but **2Ch 10:10** 3513
"My father **m** your yoke heavy, but **2Ch 10:14** 3513
And King Rehoboam **m** haste to mount **2Ch 10:18** 553
and for the calves which he had **m**. **2Ch 11:15** 6213a
shields which Solomon had **m**. **2Ch 12:9** 6213a
King Rehoboam **m** shields of bronze **2Ch 12:10** 6213a
which Jeroboam **m** for gods for you. **2Ch 13:8** 6213a
and **m** for yourselves priests like **2Ch 13:9** 6213a
they **m** an oath to the LORD with a **2Ch 15:14** 7650
m a horrid image as an Asherah, **2Ch 15:16** 6213a
they **m** a very great fire for him. **2Ch 16:14** 8313
m his position over Israel firm. **2Ch 17:1** 2388
son of Chenaanah **m** horns of iron **2Ch 18:10** 6213a
for the LORD had **m** them to rejoice **2Ch 20:27**
they **m** the ships in Ezion-geber. **2Ch 20:36** 6213a
his father and **m** himself secure, **2Ch 21:4** 2388
which He had **m** with David, **2Ch 21:7** 3772
he **m** high places in the mountains **2Ch 21:11** 6213a
And his people **m** no fire for him **2Ch 21:19** 6213a
inhabitants of Jerusalem **m** Ahaziah, **2Ch 22:1** 4427a
Then all the assembly **m** a covenant **2Ch 23:3** 3772
him the testimony and **m** him king. **2Ch 23:11** 4427a
Then Jehoiada **m** a covenant between **2Ch 23:16** 3772
and they **m** a chest and set it **2Ch 24:8** 6213a
They **m** a proclamation in Judah **2Ch 24:9** 5414
and it was **m** into utensils for the **2Ch 24:14** 6213a
and **m** him king in the place of his **2Ch 26:1** 4427a
In Jerusalem he **m** engines *of* **2Ch 26:15** 6213a
m molten images for the Baals. **2Ch 28:2** 6213a
and **m** altars for himself in every **2Ch 28:24** 6213a
he **m** high places to burn incense to **2Ch 28:25** 6213a
He has **m** them an object of terror, **2Ch 29:8** 5414
so that He **m** them a horror, **2Ch 30:7** 5414
and **m** weapons and shields in great **2Ch 32:5** 6213a
and he **m** for himself treasuries **2Ch 32:27** 6213a
He **m** cities for himself and **2Ch 32:29** 6213a
for the Baals and **m** Asherim, **2Ch 33:3** 6213a
He **m** his sons pass through the fire **2Ch 33:6**
he had **m** in the house of God, **2Ch 33:7** 6213a
Ophel *with it* and **m** it very high. **2Ch 33:14** 1361b
which his father Manasseh had **m**, **2Ch 33:22** 6213a
people of the land **m** Josiah his son **2Ch 33:25** 4427a
and **m** a covenant before the LORD **2Ch 34:31** 3772
he **m** all who were present in **2Ch 34:32**
and **m** all who were present in **2Ch 34:33**
m them an ordinance in Israel; **2Ch 35:25** 5414
and **m** him king in place of his **2Ch 36:1** 4427a
The king of Egypt **m** Eliakim **2Ch 36:4** 4427a
and he **m** his kinsman Zedekiah king **2Ch 36:10** 4427a
had **m** him swear *allegiance* by God. **2Ch 36:13**
so that a search may be **m** in the **Ezr 4:15** 5648
and a search has been **m** and it has **Ezr 4:19** 1240
and search was **m** in the archives, **Ezr 6:1** 1240
his house shall be **m** a refuse heap **Ezr 6:11** 5648
rose and **m** the leading priests, **Ezr 10:5**
They **m** a proclamation **Ezr 10:7** 5674a
Uriah the son of Hakkoz **m** repairs. **Ne 3:4** 2388
the son of Meshezabel **m** repairs. **Ne 3:4** 2388
the son of Baana *also* **m** repairs. **Ne 3:4** 2388
to him the Tekoites **m** repairs, **Ne 3:5** 2388
also **m** repairs for the official **Ne 3:7** 2388
of the goldsmiths **m** repairs. **Ne 3:8** 2388
one of the perfumers, **m** repairs, **Ne 3:8** 2388
district of Jerusalem, **m** repairs. **Ne 3:9** 2388
m repairs opposite his house. **Ne 3:10** 2388
the son of Hashabneiah **m** repairs. **Ne 3:10** 2388
district of Jerusalem, **m** repairs, **Ne 3:12** 2388
m repairs as far as *a point* **Ne 3:16** 2388
Palal the son of Uzai **m** *repairs* **Ne 3:25**
him Pedaiah the son of Parosh **m** **Ne 3:25**
temple servants living in Ophel **m** **Ne 3:26**
which they had **m** for the purpose. **Ne 8:4** 6213a

which had been **m** known to them. **Ne 8:12** 3045
them and **m** booths for themselves, **Ne 8:16** 6213a
m booths and lived in them. **Ne 8:17** 6213a
You have **m** the heavens, The **Ne 9:6** 6213a
And **m** a covenant with him To give **Ne 9:8** 3772
And **m** a name for Yourself as *it is* **Ne 9:10** 6213a
"So You **m** known to them Your holy **Ne 9:14** 3045
"Even when they **m** for themselves **Ne 9:18** 6213a
"You **m** their sons numerous as **Ne 9:23** 7235a
hair, and **m** them swear by God, **Ne 13:25**
God **m** him king over all Israel; **Ne 13:26** 5414
and **m** her queen instead of Vashti. **Es 2:17** 4427a
he also **m** a holiday for the **Es 2:18** 6213a
Esther had not yet **m** known her **Es 2:20**
"Have a gallows fifty cubits high **m** **Es 5:14** 6213a
Haman, so he had the gallows **m**. **Es 5:14** 6213a
which Haman **m** for Mordecai who **Es 7:9** 6213a
they rested and **m** it a day of feasting **Es 9:17** 6213a
m it a day of feasting and rejoicing. **Es 9:18** 6213a
and **m** a custom for themselves and **Es 9:27** 6901
"Have You not **m** a hedge about him **Jb 1:10** 7753
formed three bands and **m** a raid on **Jb 1:17** 7760
and they **m** an appointment together **Jb 2:11** 3259
And **m** all my bones shake. **Jb 4:14**
fashioned and **m** me altogether, **Jb 10:8** 6213a
now, that You have **m** me as clay; **Jb 10:9** 6213a
And **m** his thighs heavy with flesh. **Jb 15:27** 6213a
has **m** me a byword of the people, **Jb 17:6** 3322
is God *who* has **m** my heart faint, **Jb 23:16**
The poor of the land are **m** to hide **Jb 24:4**
as a hut *which* the watchman has **m**. **Jb 27:18** 6213a
And I **m** the widow's heart sing for **Jb 29:13**
"I have **m** a covenant with my eyes; **Jb 31:1** 3772
He who **m** me in the womb make him, **Jb 31:15** 6213a
"The Spirit of God has **m** me, **Jb 33:4** 6213a
"From the breath of God ice is **m**, **Jb 37:10** 5414
When I **m** a cloud its garment And **Jb 38:9** 7760
God has **m** her forget wisdom, **Jb 39:17**
which I **m** as well as you; **Jb 40:15** 6213a
is like him, One **m** without fear. **Jb 41:33** 6213a
has bent His bow and **m** it ready. **Ps 7:12** 3559
fallen into the hole which he **m**. **Ps 7:15** 6466
m him a little lower than God, **Ps 8:5** 2637
down in the pit which they have **m**; **Ps 9:15** 6213a
The LORD has **m** Himself known; **Ps 9:16** 3045
He **m** darkness His hiding place, **Ps 18:11** 7896
You have also **m** my enemies turn **Ps 18:40** 5414
You **m** me trust *when* upon my **Ps 22:9**
m my mountain to stand strong; **Ps 30:7**
And to the Lord I **m** supplication: **Ps 30:8** 2603a
For He has **m** marvelous His **Ps 31:21** 6381
of the LORD the heavens were **m**, **Ps 33:6** 6213a
have **m** my days *as* handbreadths, **Ps 39:5** 5414
man who has **m** the LORD his trust, **Ps 40:4** 7760
instruments have **m** You glad. **Ps 45:8** 8055
The nations **m** an uproar, the **Ps 46:6** 1993
m Himself known as a stronghold. **Ps 48:3**
Those who have **m** a covenant with **Ps 50:5** 3772
You have **m** the land quake, You **Ps 60:2**
You have **m** Your people experience **Ps 60:3**
You **m** men ride over our heads; We **Ps 66:12**
When I **m** sackcloth my clothing, I **Ps 69:11** 5414
I have **m** the Lord GOD my refuge, **Ps 73:28** 7896
You have **m** summer and winter. **Ps 74:17** 3335
You have **m** known Your strength **Ps 77:14** 3045
And He **m** the waters stand up like **Ps 78:13**
And **m** the tribes of Israel dwell **Ps 78:55**
And You have **m** them to drink **Ps 80:5** 8248
the son of man whom You **m** strong **Ps 80:17** 553
All nations whom You have **m** shall **Ps 86:9** 6213a
You have **m** me an object of **Ps 88:8** 7896
Will Your wonders be **m** known in **Ps 88:12** 3045
have **m** a covenant with My chosen; **Ps 89:3** 3772
have **m** all his enemies rejoice. **Ps 89:42**
have not **m** him stand in battle. **Ps 89:43**
You have **m** his splendor to cease And **Ps 89:44**
For you have **m** the LORD, my **Ps 91:9** 7760
have **m** me glad by what You have **Ps 92:4** 8055
is His, for it was He who **m** it, **Ps 95:5** 6213a
idols, But the LORD **m** the heavens. **Ps 96:5** 6213a
LORD has **m** known His salvation; **Ps 98:2** 3045
It is He who has **m** us, **Ps 100:3** 6213a
He **m** known His ways to Moses, His **Ps 103:7** 3045
He **m** the moon for the seasons; **Ps 104:19** 6213a
In wisdom You have **m** them all; **Ps 104:24** 6213a
covenant which He **m** with Abraham, **Ps 105:9** 3772
He **m** him lord of his house And **Ps 105:21** 7760
And **m** them stronger than their **Ps 105:24** 6105a
He sent darkness and **m** *it* dark; **Ps 105:28** 2821
They **m** a calf in Horeb And **Ps 106:19** 6213a
He also **m** them *objects* of **Ps 106:46** 5414
m His wonders to be remembered; **Ps 111:4** 6213a
He has **m** known to His people the **Ps 111:6** 5046
is the day which the LORD has **m**; **Ps 118:24** 6213a
In which You have **m** me hope. **Ps 119:49**
Your hands **m** me and fashioned me; **Ps 119:73** 6213a
the LORD, Who **m** heaven and earth. **Ps 121:2** 6213a
the LORD, Who **m** heaven and earth. **Ps 124:8** 6213a
Zion, He who **m** heaven and earth. **Ps 134:3** 6213a
Him who **m** the heavens with skill, **Ps 136:5** 6213a
To Him who **m** *the* great lights, For **Ps 136:7** 6213a
And **m** Israel pass through the **Ps 136:14**
You **m** me bold with strength in my **Ps 138:3** 7292
I am fearfully and wonderfully **m**; **Ps 139:14**
from You, When I was **m** in secret, **Ps 139:15** 6213a
He has **m** me dwell in dark places, **Ps 143:3**
Who **m** heaven and earth, The sea **Ps 146:6** 6213a
He has **m** a decree which will not **Ps 148:6** 5414
yet **m** the earth and the fields, **Pr 8:26** 6213a

When He **m** firm the skies above, **Pr 8:28** 553
the soul of the diligent is **m** fat. **Pr 13:4** 1878
the hearts of fools it is **m** known. **Pr 14:33** 3045
The LORD has **m** everything for its **Pr 16:4** 6466
eye, The LORD has **m** both of them. **Pr 20:12** 6213a
I **m** gardens and parks for myself and **Ec 2:5** 6213a
I **m** ponds of water for myself from **Ec 2:6** 6213a
He has **m** everything appropriate in **Ec 3:11** 6213a
God has **m** the one as well as the **Ec 7:14** 6213a
only this, that God **m** men upright, **Ec 7:29** 6213a
m me caretaker of the vineyards, **SS 1:6** 7760
"King Solomon has **m** for himself a **SS 3:9** 6213a
"He **m** its posts of silver, Its **SS 3:10** 6213a
"You have **m** my heart beat faster, **SS 4:9**
You have **m** my heart beat faster **SS 4:9**
That which their fingers have **m**. **Is 2:8** 6213a
they **m** for themselves to worship, **Is 2:20** 6213a
'Even you have been **m** weak as we, **Is 14:10** 2470a
the man who **m** the earth tremble, **Is 14:16**
Who **m** the world like a wilderness **Is 14:17** 7760
I have **m** the shouting to cease. **Is 16:10**
to that which his fingers have **m**, **Is 17:8** 6213a
the manufacturers of linen **m** from **Is 19:9**
I have **m** an end of all the **Is 21:2** 7673a
And you **m** a reservoir between the **Is 22:11** 6213a
did not depend on Him who **m** it, **Is 22:11** 6213a
He has **m** the kingdoms tremble; **Is 23:11**
its palaces, they **m** it a ruin. **Is 23:13** 7760
You have **m** a city into a heap, **Is 25:2** 7760
"We have **m** a covenant with death, **Is 28:15** 3772
And with Sheol we have **m** a pact. **Is 28:15** 6213a
For we have **m** falsehood our refuge **Is 28:15** 7760
Or your fetters will be **m** stronger; **Is 28:22** 2388
Who has **m** *His* counsel wonderful **Is 28:29** 6381
what is **m** would say to its maker, **Is 29:16** 4639
He has **m** it deep and large, A pyre **Is 30:33** 6009
sinful hands have **m** for you as a sin. **Is 31:7** 6213a
You have **m** heaven and earth. **Is 37:16** 6213a
every mountain and hill be **m** low; **Is 40:4** 8213
"Behold, I have **m** you a new, **Is 41:15** 7760
have formed, even whom I have **m**." **Is 43:7** 6213a
Thus says the LORD who **m** you And **Is 44:2** 6213a
"It is I who **m** the earth, and **Is 45:12** 6213a
God who formed the earth and **m** it, **Is 45:18** 6213a
aged you **m** your yoke very heavy. **Is 47:6** 3513
He **m** the water flow out of the rock **Is 48:21**
has **m** My mouth like a sharp sword, **Is 49:2** 7760
He has also **m** Me a select arrow, **Is 49:2** 7760
Who **m** the depths of the sea a **Is 51:10** 7760
son of man who is **m** like grass, **Is 51:12** 5414
even **m** your back like the ground And **Is 51:23** 7760
m him a witness to the peoples, **Is 55:4** 5414
You have **m** a grain offering. **Is 57:6** 5927
mountain You have **m** your bed. **Is 57:7** 7760
have gone up and **m** your bed wide. **Is 57:8** 7337
And you have **m** an agreement for **Is 57:8** 3772
And **m** *them* go down to Sheol. **Is 57:9**
the breath *of those whom* I have **m**. **Is 57:16** 6213a
your iniquities have **m** a separation **Is 59:2** 914
They have **m** their paths crooked, **Is 59:8** 6140
And **m** them drunk in My wrath, **Is 63:6**
"For My hand **m** all these things, **Is 66:2** 6213a
hand of the LORD will be **m** known **Is 66:14** 3045
m you today as a fortified city and **Jer 1:18** 5414
inheritance you **m** an abomination. **Jer 2:7** 7760
And they have **m** his land a waste; **Jer 2:15** 7896
gods Which you **m** for yourself? **Jer 2:28** 6213a
miss *it*, nor will it be **m** again. **Jer 3:16** 6213a
m their faces harder than rock; **Jer 5:3** 2388
"I have **m** you an assayer *and* a **Jer 6:27** 5414
I **m** My name dwell at the first, **Jer 7:12**
pen of the scribes Has **m** *it* into a lie. **Jer 8:8** 6213a
He who **m** the earth by His power, **Jer 10:12** 6213a
which I **m** with their fathers." **Jer 11:10** 3772
LORD **m** it known to me and I knew **Jer 11:18** 3045
They have **m** My pleasant field A **Jer 12:10** 5414
"It has been **m** a desolation, **Jer 12:11** 7760
whole land has been **m** desolate, **Jer 12:11** 8074
so I **m** the whole household of Israel **Jer 13:11**
and have **m** this an alien place **Jer 19:4** 5235a
And **m** him very happy. **Jer 20:15**
m all the nations to whom the LORD **Jer 25:17**
"And the peaceful folds are **m** silent **Jer 25:37** 1826a
"I have **m** the earth, the men and **Jer 27:5** 6213a
m instead of them yokes of iron." **Jer 28:13** 6213a
have **m** this people trust in a lie. **Jer 28:15**
"The LORD has **m** you priest **Jer 29:26** 5414
and he has **m** you trust in a lie," **Jer 29:31**
not like the covenant which I **m** **Jer 31:32** 3772
You have **m** the heavens and the **Jer 32:17** 6213a
You have **m** a name for Yourself, **Jer 32:20** 6213a
therefore You have **m** all this **Jer 32:23**
says the LORD who **m** *the earth*, **Jer 33:2** 6213a
King Zedekiah had **m** a covenant **Jer 34:8** 3772
'I **m** a covenant with your **Jer 34:13** 3772
and you had **m** a covenant before Me **Jer 34:15** 3772
covenant which they **m** before Me, **Jer 34:18** 3772
had **m** king in the land of Judah, **Jer 37:1** 4427a
which they had **m** into the prison. **Jer 37:15** 6213a
lives, who **m** this life for us, **Jer 38:16** 6213a
Asa had **m** on account of Baasha, **Jer 41:9** 6213a
we **m** for her *sacrificial* cakes **Jer 44:19** 6213a
And I have **m** the wine to cease **Jer 48:33**
m you small among the nations, **Jer 49:15** 5414
They have **m** them turn aside *on* the **Jer 50:6**
be **m** for the iniquity of Israel, **Jer 50:20** 1245
He who **m** the earth by His power, **Jer 51:15** 6213a
which King Solomon had **m** for the **Jer 52:20** 6213a
He has **m** me desolate, Faint all **La 1:13** 5414

He has **m** my strength fail.	**La 1:14**	
They have **m** a noise in the house	**La 2:7**	5414
He has driven me and **m** me walk In	**La 3:2**	
In dark places He has **m** me dwell,	**La 3:6**	
He has **m** my chain heavy.	**La 3:7**	3513
He has **m** my paths crooked.	**La 3:9**	5753a
He has **m** me desolate.	**La 3:11**	8074
He **m** the arrows of His quiver To	**La 3:13**	
He has **m** me drunk with wormwood.	**La 3:15**	7301
He has **m** me cower in the dust.	**La 3:16**	
m *us mere* offscouring and refuse	**La 3:45**	7760
I have **m** your face as hard as	**Ezk 3:8**	5414
than flint I have **m** your forehead.	**Ezk 3:9**	5414
me and **m** me stand on my feet,	**Ezk 3:24**	
trumpet and **m** everything ready,	**Ezk 7:14**	3559
and they **m** the images of their	**Ezk 7:20**	6213a
intact, it is not **m** into anything.	**Ezk 15:5**	6213a
can it still be **m** into anything!	**Ezk 15:5**	6213a
"I **m** you numerous like plants of	**Ezk 16:7**	5414
m for yourself high places of	**Ezk 16:16**	6213a
also took your beautiful jewels **m**	**Ezk 16:17**	
and **m** for yourself male images	**Ezk 16:17**	6213a
and **m** yourself a high place in every	**Ezk 16:24**	6213a
and **m** your beauty abominable,	**Ezk 16:25**	8581
m your high place in every square,	**Ezk 16:31**	6213a
Thus you have **m** your sisters	**Ezk 16:51**	6663
you have **m** judgment favorable for	**Ezk 16:52**	6419
m your sisters appear righteous.	**Ezk 16:52**	6663
family and **m** a covenant with him,	**Ezk 17:13**	3772
her cubs And **m** him a young lion.	**Ezk 19:5**	7760
m Myself known to them in the land	**Ezk 20:5**	3045
in whose sight I **m** Myself known to	**Ezk 20:9**	3045
also they **m** their soothing aroma and	**Ezk 20:28**	7760
is **m** *for striking* like lightning,	**Ezk 21:15**	6213a
'Because you have **m** your iniquity	**Ezk 21:24**	
by your idols which you have **m**.	**Ezk 22:4**	6213a
therefore I have **m** you a reproach	**Ezk 22:4**	6213a
they have **m** many widows in the	**Ezk 22:25**	7235a
they have **m** no distinction between	**Ezk 22:26**	914
of Israel when it was **m** desolate,	**Ezk 25:3**	8074
"They have **m** all *your* planks of	**Ezk 27:5**	1129
from Bashan they have **m** your oars;	**Ezk 27:6**	6213a
'Because you have **m** your heart	**Ezk 28:6**	5414
is mine, and I myself have **m** *it*.'	**Ezk 29:3**	6213a
they have been *only* a staff **m**	**Ezk 29:6**	
and **m** all their loins quake."	**Ezk 29:7**	
'The Nile is mine, and I have **m** *it*,'	**Ezk 29:9**	6213a
Nebuchadnezzar king of Babylon **m**	**Ezk 29:18**	
every head was **m** bald and every	**Ezk 29:18**	7139
'The waters **m** it grow, the deep	**Ezk 31:4**	
made it grow, the deep **m** it high.	**Ezk 31:4**	7311
'I **m** it beautiful with the	**Ezk 31:9**	6213a
up, and I **m** Lebanon mourn for it,	**Ezk 31:15**	
"I **m** the nations quake at the	**Ezk 31:16**	
when I **m** it go down to Sheol	**Ezk 31:16**	
"They have **m** a bed for her among	**Ezk 32:25**	5414
yet he will be **m** to lie down among	**Ezk 32:32**	
"For good reason they have **m** you	**Ezk 36:3**	8074
I **m** them go into exile among the	**Ezk 39:28**	
He **m** the side pillars sixty	**Ezk 40:14**	6213a
m for the court all around;	**Ezk 40:17**	6213a
for they **m** My covenant void	**Ezk 44:7**	6565a
were **m** under the rows round about.	**Ezk 46:23**	6213a
sea, being **m** to flow into the sea,	**Ezk 47:8**	
But Daniel **m** up his mind that he	**Da 1:8**	7760
houses will be **m** a rubbish heap.	**Da 2:5**	7761
Even now You have **m** known to me	**Da 2:23**	3046
For You have **m** known to us the	**Da 2:23**	3046
and He has **m** known to King	**Da 2:28**	3046
who reveals mysteries has **m** known	**Da 2:29**	3046
"The head of that statue *was* **m**	**Da 2:32**	
the great God has **m** known to the	**Da 2:45**	3046
and he **m** him ruler over the whole	**Da 2:48**	7981
And Daniel **m** request of the king,	**Da 2:49**	1156
the king **m** an image of gold,	**Da 3:1**	5648
have **m** a decree that every man who	**Da 3:10**	7761
worship the image that I have **m**,	**Da 3:15**	5648
furnace had been **m** extremely hot,	**Da 3:22**	228
"I saw a dream and it **m** me fearful;	**Da 4:5**	1763
heart was **m** like *that of* beasts,	**Da 5:21**	7739a
m to stand on two feet like a man;	**Da 7:4**	6966
So he told me and **m** known to me	**Da 7:16**	3046
touched me and **m** me stand upright.	**Da 8:18**	
who was **m** king over the kingdom of	**Da 9:1**	4427a
and have **m** a name for Yourself,	**Da 9:15**	6213a
"After an alliance is **m** with	**Da 11:23**	2266
they have **m** idols for themselves,	**Hos 8:4**	6213a
A craftsman **m** it, so it is not God;	**Hos 8:6**	6213a
his fruit, The more altars he **m**;	**Hos 10:1**	7235a
better he **m** the *sacred* pillars.	**Hos 10:1**	3190
Idols skillfully **m** from their silver,	**Hos 13:2**	
It has **m** my vine a waste And my	**Jl 1:7**	7760
you **m** the Nazirites drink wine,	**Am 2:12**	
unless they have **m** an appointment?	**Am 3:3**	3259
And I **m** the stench of your camp	**Am 4:10**	
He who **m** the Pleiades and Orion	**Am 5:8**	6213a
gods which you **m** for yourselves.	**Am 5:26**	6213a
who **m** the sea and the dry land."	**Jon 1:9**	6213a
sacrifice to the LORD and **m** vows.	**Jon 1:16**	5087
There he **m** a shelter for himself	**Jon 4:5**	6213a
m men like the fish of the sea,	**Hab 1:14**	6213a
Your bow was **m** bare, The rods of	**Hab 3:9**	5783
He has **m** my feet like hinds' *feet*,	**Hab 3:19**	7760
I have **m** their streets desolate,	**Zph 3:6**	2717b
'As for the promise which I **m** you	**Hg 2:5**	3772
"They **m** their hearts	**Zch 7:12**	7760
m the pleasant land desolate."	**Zch 7:14**	7760
I had **m** with all the peoples.	**Zch 11:10**	3772
have **m** his mountains a desolation and	**Mal 1:3**	7760
"So I also have **m** you despised	**Mal 2:9**	5414
how can it be **m** salty *again?*	**Mt 5:13**	*233*
your faith has **m** you well."	**Mt 9:22**	*4982*
At once the woman was **m** well.	**Mt 9:22**	*4982*
He **m** the disciples get into the boat and	**Mt 14:22**	*315*
he had, and repayment to be **m**.	**Mt 18:25**	*591*
beginning **M** THEM MALE AND FEMALE	**Mt 19:4**	*4160*
eunuchs who were **m** eunuchs by men;	**Mt 19:12**	*2134*
and there are *also* eunuchs who **m**	**Mt 19:12**	*2134*
and you have **m** them equal to us	**Mt 20:12**	*4160*
be **m** secure until the third day,	**Mt 27:64**	*805*
they went and **m** the grave secure,	**Mt 27:66**	*805*
"The Sabbath was **m** for man, and	**Mk 2:27**	*1096*
your faith has **m** you well;	**Mk 5:34**	*4982*
Jesus **m** His disciples get into the boat	**Mk 6:45**	*315*
God **M** THEM MALE AND FEMALE.	**Mk 10:6**	*4160*
your faith has **m** you well."	**Mk 10:52**	*4982*
But you have **m** it A ROBBERS' DEN."	**Mk 11:17**	*4160*
destroy this temple **m** with hands,	**Mk 14:58**	*5499*
build another **m** without hands.' "	**Mk 14:58**	*886*
how Jesus had **m** the remark to him,	**Mk 14:72**	*3004*
But Jesus **m** no further answer;	**Mk 15:5**	*611*
And they **m** signs to his father, as	**Lk 1:62**	*1770*
the Lord has **m** known to us."	**Lk 2:15**	*1107*
they **m** known the statement which	**Lk 2:17**	*1107*
statement which He had **m** to them.	**Lk 2:50**	*2980*
demon-possessed had been **m** well.	**Lk 8:36**	*4982*
your faith has **m** you well;	**Lk 8:48**	*4982*
and she will be **m** well."	**Lk 8:50**	*4982*
did not He who **m** the outside make	**Lk 11:40**	*4160*
immediately she was **m** erect again and	**Lk 13:13**	*461*
your faith has **m** you well."	**Lk 17:19**	*4982*
your faith has **m** you well."	**Lk 18:42**	*4982*
your mina has **m** ten minas more.'	**Lk 19:16**	*4333*
mina, master, has **m** five minas.'	**Lk 19:18**	*4160*
but you have **m** it a ROBBERS' DEN."	**Lk 19:46**	*4160*
insurrection **m** in the city,	**Lk 23:19**	*1096*
and the world was **m** through Him,	**Jn 1:10**	*1096*
And He **m** a scourge of cords, and	**Jn 2:15**	*4160*
this joy of mine has been **m** full.	**Jn 3:29**	*4137*
where He had **m** the water wine.	**Jn 4:46**	*4160*
stepped in was **m** well from	**Jn 5:4**	*1096*
"He who **m** me well was the one who	**Jn 5:11**	*4160*
it was Jesus who had **m** him well.	**Jn 5:15**	*4160*
I **m** an entire man well on the	**Jn 7:23**	*4160*
ground, and **m** clay of the spittle,	**Jn 9:6**	*4160*
man who is called Jesus **m** clay,	**Jn 9:11**	*4160*
on the day when Jesus **m** the clay and	**Jn 9:14**	*4160*
So they **m** Him a supper there, and	**Jn 12:2**	*4160*
and *that* your joy may be **m** full.	**Jn 15:11**	*4137*
My Father I have **m** known to you.	**Jn 15:15**	*1107*
that your joy may be **m** full.	**Jn 16:24**	*4137*
have My joy **m** full in themselves.	**Jn 17:13**	*4137*
I have **m** Your name known to them,	**Jn 17:26**	*1107*
there, having **m** a charcoal fire,	**Jn 18:18**	*4160*
He **m** Himself out *to be* the Son of	**Jn 19:7**	*4160*
Pilate **m** efforts to release Him,	**Jn 19:12**	*2212*
outer garments and **m** four parts,	**Jn 19:23**	*4160*
'LET HIS HOMESTEAD BE **M** DESOLATE,	**Ac 1:20**	*1096*
M KNOWN TO ME THE WAYS OF LIFE;	**Ac 2:28**	*1107*
God has **m** Him both Lord and	**Ac 2:36**	*4160*
power or piety we had **m** him walk?	**Ac 3:12**	*4160*
which God **m** with your fathers,	**Ac 3:25**	*1303*
to how this man has been **m** well,	**Ac 4:9**	*4982*
it is You who **M** THE HEAVEN	**Ac 4:24**	*4160*
and he **m** him governor over Egypt	**Ac 7:10**	*2525*
m himself known to his brothers,	**Ac 7:13**	*1107*
M YOU A RULER AND JUDGE OVER US?	**Ac 7:27**	*2525*
'WHO **M** YOU A RULER AND A JUDGE?'	**Ac 7:35**	*2525*
"At that time they **m** a calf	**Ac 7:41**	*3447*
WHICH YOU **M** TO WORSHIP.	**Ac 7:43**	*4160*
dwell in *houses* **m** by *human* hands;	**Ac 7:48**	*5499*
HAND WHICH **M** ALL THESE THINGS?'	**Ac 7:50**	*4160*
and **m** loud lamentation over him.	**Ac 8:2**	*4160*
m their way to Phoenicia and Cyprus	**Ac 11:19**	*1330*
but prayer for him was being **m**	**Ac 12:5**	*1096*
and **m** the people great during	**Ac 13:17**	*5312*
of the promise **m** to the fathers,	**Ac 13:32**	*1096*
And when an attempt was **m** by both	**Ac 14:5**	*1096*
that he had faith to be **m** well,	**Ac 14:9**	*4982*
WHO **M** THE HEAVEN AND THE EARTH	**Ac 14:15**	*4160*
city and had **m** many disciples,	**Ac 14:21**	*3100*
days God **m** a choice among you,	**Ac 15:7**	*1586*
and He **m** no distinction between us	**Ac 15:9**	*1252*
"The God who **m** the world and all	**Ac 17:24**	*4160*
not dwell in temples **m** with hands;	**Ac 17:24**	*5499*
He **m** from one *man* every nation of	**Ac 17:26**	*4160*
who **m** silver shrines of Artemis,	**Ac 19:24**	*4160*
gods **m** with hands are no gods *at*	**Ac 19:26**	*1096*
Holy Spirit has **m** you overseers,	**Ac 20:28**	*5087*
promise **m** by God to our fathers;	**Ac 26:6**	*1096*
for God **m** it evident to them.	**Ro 1:19**	*5319*
through what has been **m**,	**Ro 1:20**	*4161*
faith is **m** void and the promise is	**Ro 4:14**	*2758*
OF MANY NATIONS HAVE I **M** YOU")	**Ro 4:17**	*5087*
the many were **m** sinners,	**Ro 5:19**	*2525*
One the many will be **m** righteous.	**Ro 5:19**	*2525*
you also were **m** to die to the Law	**Ro 7:4**	*2289*
been **m** known to all the nations,	**Ro 16:26**	*1107*
but that you be **m** complete in the same	**1Co 1:10**	*2675*
of Christ would not be **m** void.	**1Co 1:17**	*2758*
Has not God **m** foolish the wisdom	**1Co 1:20**	*3471*
I have **m** myself a slave to all,	**1Co 9:19**	*1402*
were all **m** to drink of one Spirit.	**1Co 12:13**	*4222*
is **m** to another who is seated,	**1Co 14:30**	*601*
in Christ all will be **m** alive.	**1Co 15:22**	*2227*
no collections be **m** when I come.	**1Co 16:2**	*1096*
but the one whom I **m** sorrowful?	**2Co 2:2**	*3076*
that you would be **m** sorrowful,	**2Co 2:4**	*3076*
who also **m** us adequate *as* servants	**2Co 3:6**	*2427*
God, a house not **m** with hands,	**2Co 5:1**	*886*
men, but we are **m** manifest to God;	**2Co 5:11**	*5319*
and I hope that we are **m** manifest	**2Co 5:11**	*5319*
He **m** Him who knew no sin *to be* sin	**2Co 5:21**	*4160*
not that you were **m** sorrowful,	**2Co 7:9**	*3076*
but that you were **m** sorrowful to	**2Co 7:9**	*3076*
for you were **m** sorrowful according	**2Co 7:9**	*3076*
m known to you in the sight of God.	**2Co 7:12**	*5319*
he had previously **m** a beginning,	**2Co 8:6**	*4278*
may not be **m** empty in this case,	**2Co 9:3**	*2758*
in every way we have **m** *this*	**2Co 11:6**	*5319*
pray for, that you be **m** complete.	**2Co 13:9**	*2676*
brethren, rejoice, be **m** complete,	**2Co 13:11**	*2675*
to whom the promise had been **m**.	**Ga 3:19**	*1861*
He **m** known to us the mystery of	**Eph 1:9**	*1107*
m us alive together with Christ	**Eph 2:5**	*4806*
peace, who **m** both *groups into* one and	**Eph 2:14**	*4160*
was **m** known to me the mystery,	**Eph 3:3**	*1107*
not **m** known to the sons of men,	**Eph 3:5**	*1107*
of which I was **m** a minister,	**Eph 3:7**	*1096*
be **m** known through the church	**Eph 3:10**	*1107*
being **m** in the likeness of men.	**Php 2:7**	*1096*
your requests be **m** known to God.	**Php 4:6**	*1107*
having **m** peace through the blood	**Col 1:20**	*1517*
which I, Paul, was **m** a minister.	**Col 1:23**	*1096*
Of *this church* I was **m** a minister	**Col 1:25**	*1096*
in Him you have been **m** complete,	**Col 2:10**	*4137*
a circumcision **m** without hands,	**Col 2:11**	*886*
He **m** you alive together with Him,	**Col 2:13**	*4806*
He **m** a public display of them,	**Col 2:15**	*1165*
law is not **m** for a righteous person,	**1Tm 1:9**	*2749*
previously **m** concerning you,	**1Tm 1:18**	*4254*
be **m** on behalf of all men,	**1Tm 2:1**	*4160*
and you **m** the good confession in	**1Tm 6:12**	*3670*
by His grace we would be **m** heirs	**Ti 3:7**	*1096*
through whom also He **m** the world.	**Heb 1:2**	*4160*
He had **m** purification of sins,	**Heb 1:3**	*4160*
"YOU HAVE **M** HIM FOR A LITTLE	**Heb 2:7**	*1642*
But we do see Him who was **m**	**Heb 2:9**	*1642*
He had to be **m** like His brethren	**Heb 2:17**	*3666*
And having been **m** perfect, He	**Heb 5:9**	*5048*
m partakers of the Holy Spirit,	**Heb 6:4**	*1096*
when God **m** the promise to Abraham,	**Heb 6:13**	*1861*
life, but **m** like the Son of God,	**Heb 7:3**	*871*
(for the Law **m** nothing perfect),	**Heb 7:19**	*5048*
appoints a Son, **m** perfect forever.	**Heb 7:28**	*5048*
NOT LIKE THE COVENANT WHICH I **M**	**Heb 8:9**	*4160*
He has **m** the first obsolete.	**Heb 8:13**	*3822*
tabernacle, not **m** with hands,	**Heb 9:11**	*5499*
be the death of the one who **m** it.	**Heb 9:16**	*1303*
while the one who **m** it lives.	**Heb 9:17**	*1303*
enter a holy place **m** with hands,	**Heb 9:24**	*5499*
BE **M** A FOOTSTOOL FOR HIS FEET.	**Heb 10:13**	*5087*
by being **m** a public spectacle	**Heb 10:33**	*2301*
so that what is seen was not **m** out	**Heb 11:3**	*1096*
m mention of the exodus of the	**Heb 11:22**	*3421*
from weakness were **m** strong,	**Heb 11:34**	*1412*
us they would not be **m** perfect.	**Heb 11:40**	*5048*
spirits of *the* righteous **m** perfect,	**Heb 12:23**	*5048*
m distinctions among yourselves,	**Jas 2:4**	*1252*
been **m** in the likeness of God;	**Jas 3:9**	*1096*
which He has **m** to dwell in us"?	**Jas 4:5**	*2733b*
you **m** careful searches and inquiries,	**1Pe 1:10**	*1567a, 1830*
flesh, but **m** alive in the spirit;	**1Pe 3:18**	*2227*
m proclamation to the spirits *now* in	**1Pe 3:19**	*2784*
Jesus Christ has **m** clear to me.	**2Pe 1:14**	*1213*
when we **m** known to you the power	**2Pe 1:16**	*1107*
an utterance as this was **m** to Him	**2Pe 1:17**	*5342*
heard this utterance **m** from heaven	**2Pe 1:18**	*5342*
So we have the prophetic word **m**	**2Pe 1:19**	
no prophecy was ever **m** by an act	**2Pe 1:21**	*5342*
having **m** them an example to those	**2Pe 2:6**	*5087*
so that our joy may be **m** complete.	**1Jn 1:4**	*4137*
promise which He Himself **m** to us:	**1Jn 2:25**	*1861*
not believe God has **m** Him a liar,	**1Jn 5:10**	*4160*
face, so that your joy may be **m** full.	**2Jn 1:12**	*4137*
and He has **m** us *to be* a kingdom,	**Rv 1:6**	*4160*
when it has been **m** to glow in a	**Rv 1:15**	*4448*
"You have **m** them *to be* a	**Rv 5:10**	*4160*
the sun became black as sackcloth **m**	**Rv 6:12**	
washed their robes and **m** them white	**Rv 7:14**	*3021*
because they were **m** bitter.	**Rv 8:11**	*4087*
eaten it, my stomach was **m** bitter.	**Rv 10:10**	*4087*
worship Him who **m** the heaven	**Rv 14:7**	*4160*
she who has **m** all the nations drink	**Rv 14:8**	*4222*
who dwell on the earth were **m** drunk	**Rv 17:2**	*3184*
of ivory and every article **m** from	**Rv 18:12**	
His bride has **m** herself ready."	**Rv 19:7**	*2090*
m ready as a bride adorned for her	**Rv 21:2**	*2090*

MADLY

Go up, you horses, and drive **m**,	**Jer 46:9**	1984b
chariots race **m** in the streets,	**Na 2:4**	1984b

MADMAN

you see the man behaving as a **m**.	**1Sa 21:14**	7696
one to act the **m** in my presence?	**1Sa 21:15**	7696
Like a **m** who throws Firebrands,	**Pr 26:18**	3858b
LORD over every **m** who prophesies,	**Jer 29:26**	7696

MADMANNAH

and Ziklag and **M** and Sansannah,	**Jos 15:31**	4089
also bore Shaaph the father of **M**,	**1Ch 2:49**	4089

MADMEN

"Do I lack **m**, that you have	**1Sa 21:15**	7696
You too, **M**, will be silenced;	**Jer 48:2**	4086

MADMENAH

M has fled.	**Is 10:31**	4088

MADNESS
"The LORD will smite you with **m** Dt 28:28 7697
wisdom and to know **m** and folly; Ec 1:17 1947
I said of laughter, "It is **m**," Ec 2:2 1984b
to consider wisdom, **m** and folly; Ec 2:12 1947
of folly and the foolishness of **m**. Ec 7:25 1947
and the end of it is wicked **m**. Ec 10:13 1948
and his rider with **m**. Zch 12:4 7697
restrained the **m** of the prophet. 2Pe 2:16 *3913*

MADON
that he sent to Jobab king of **M** Jos 11:1 4068
the king of **M**, one; Jos 12:19 4068

MAGADAN
boat and came to the region of **M**. Mt 15:39 *3093*

MAGBISH
the sons of **M**, 156; Ezr 2:30 4019

MAGDALENE
Among them was Mary **M**, Mt 27:56 *3094*
And Mary **M** was there, and the Mt 27:61 *3094*
Mary **M** and the other Mary came to Mt 28:1 *3094*
distance, among whom were Mary **M**, Mk 15:40 *3094*
Mary **M** and Mary the *mother* of Mk 15:47 *3094*
When the Sabbath was over, Mary **M**, Mk 16:1 *3094*
week, He first appeared to Mary **M**, Mk 16:9 *3094*
Mary who was called **M**, Lk 8:2 *3094*
Now they were Mary **M** and Joanna Lk 24:10 *3094*
the *wife* of Clopas, and Mary **M**. Jn 19:25 *3094*
Mary **M** came early to the tomb, Jn 20:1 *3094*
Mary **M** came, announcing to the Jn 20:18 *3094*

MAGDIEL
chief **M**, chief Iram. Gn 36:43 4025
chief **M**, chief Iram. 1Ch 1:54 4025

MAGGOT
How much less man, *that* **m**, Jb 25:6 7415

MAGGOTS
M are spread out *as your bed* Is 14:11 7415

MAGI
m from the east arrived in Mt 2:1 *3097*
Then Herod secretly called the **m** and Mt 2:7 *3097*
the **m** left for their own country by Mt 2:12
that he had been tricked by the **m**, Mt 2:16 *3097*
he had determined from the **m**. Mt 2:16 *3097*

MAGIC
"Woe to the women who sew **m** Ezk 13:18
I am against your **m** bands by Ezk 13:20
was practicing **m** in the city and Ac 8:9 *3096*
astonished them with his **m** arts. Ac 8:11 *3095*
And many of those who practiced **m** Ac 19:19 *4021*

MAGICIAN
asked anything like this of any **m**, Da 2:10 2749
as Paphos, they found a **m**, Ac 13:6 *3097*
But Elymas the **m** Ac 13:8 *3097*

MAGICIANS
and called for all the **m** of Egypt, Gn 41:8 2748
Then I told it to the **m**, Gn 41:24 2748
and they also, the **m** of Egypt, Ex 7:11 2748
But the **m** of Egypt did the same Ex 7:22 2748
The **m** did the same with their Ex 8:7 2748
The **m** tried with their secret Ex 8:18 2748
Then the **m** said to Pharaoh, Ex 8:19 2748
The **m** could not stand before Ex 9:11 2748
for the boils were on the **m** as Ex 9:11 2748
ten times better than all the **m** Da 1:20 2748
king gave orders to call in the **m**, Da 2:2 2748
neither wise men, conjurers, **m** Da 2:27 2749
"Then the **m**, the conjurers, the Da 4:7 2749
'O Belteshazzar, chief of the **m**, Da 4:9 2749
appointed him chief of the **m**, Da 5:11 2749

MAGISTRATE
opponent to appear before the **m**, Lk 12:58 *758*

MAGISTRATES
appoint **m** and judges that they may Ezr 7:25 8200
the **m** and all the rulers of the Da 3:2 8614
the **m** and all the rulers of the Da 3:3 8614
had brought them to the chief **m**, Ac 16:20 *4755*
chief **m** tore their robes off them and Ac 16:22 *4755*
the chief **m** sent their policemen, Ac 16:35 *4755*
chief **m** have sent to release you. Ac 16:36 *4755*
these words to the chief **m**. Ac 16:38 *4755*

MAGNIFICENCE
even be dethroned from her **m**." Ac 19:27 *3168*

MAGNIFICENT
In a **m** bowl she brought him curds. Jg 5:25 117
the LORD shall be exceedingly **m**, 1Ch 22:5 1431
that **m** price at which I was valued Zch 11:13 145
to us His precious and **m** promises, 2Pe 1:4 *3176*

MAGNIFICENTLY
the ones near, **m** dressed, Ezk 23:12 4358

MAGNIFIED
you have **m** your lovingkindness, Gn 19:19 1431
that Your name may be **m** forever, 2Sa 7:26 1431
name be established and **m** forever, 1Ch 17:24 1431
instance where the king had **m** him and Es 5:11 1431
that they have **m** themselves. Jb 36:9 1396
"The LORD be **m**, Who delights in Ps 35:27 1431
say continually, "The LORD be **m**!" Ps 40:16 1431
say continually, "Let God be **m**." Ps 70:4 1431
For You have **m** Your word according Ps 138:2 1431
I have **m** and increased wisdom more Ec 1:16 1431
For the enemy has **m** himself!" La 1:9 1431
did as he pleased and **m** *himself*. Da 8:4 1431
male goat **m** *himself* exceedingly. Da 8:8 1431
It even **m** *itself* to be equal with Da 8:11 1431
will not be **m** above Judah. Zch 12:7 1431
"The LORD be **m** beyond the border Mal 1:5 1431
of the Lord Jesus was being **m**. Ac 19:17 *3170*

MAGNIFY
"What is man that You **m** him, Jb 7:17 1431
O **m** the LORD with me, And let us Ps 34:3 1431
dishonor who **m** themselves over me. Ps 35:26 1431
would **m** themselves against me." Ps 38:16 1431
And **m** Him with thanksgiving. Ps 69:30 1431
"I will **m** Myself, sanctify Ezk 38:23 1431
he will **m** *himself* in his heart, Da 8:25 1431
and **m** himself above every god and Da 11:36 1431
he will **m** himself above *them* all. Da 11:37 1431
of Gentiles, I **m** my ministry, Ro 11:13 *1392*

MAGNITUDE
Because of the **m** of your iniquity Jer 13:22 7230

MAGOG
sons of Japheth *were* Gomer and **M** Gn 10:2 4031
The sons of Japheth *were* Gomer, **M**, 1Ch 1:5 4031
face toward Gog of the land of **M**, Ezk 38:2 4031
"And I will send fire upon **M** and Ezk 39:6 4031
corners of the earth, Gog and **M**, Rv 20:8 *3098*

MAGOR-MISSABIB
LORD has called you, but rather **M**. Jer 20:3 4036

MAGPIASH
M, Meshullam, Hezir, Ne 10:20 4047

MAHALALEEL
the son of Jared, the son of **M**, Lk 3:37 *3121*

MAHALALEL
years, and became the father of **M**. Gn 5:12 4111
after he became the father of **M**, Gn 5:13 4111
M lived sixty-five years, and Gn 5:15 4111
Then **M** lived eight hundred and Gn 5:16 4111
So all the days of **M** were eight Gn 5:17 4111
Kenan, **M**, Jared, 1Ch 1:2 4111
son of Shephatiah, the son of **M**, Ne 11:4 4111

MAHALATH
he had, **M** the daughter of Ishmael, Gn 28:9 4258
Then Rehoboam took as a wife **M** 2Ch 11:18 4258

MAHANAIM
So he named that place **M**. Gn 32:2 4266
M as far as the border of Debir; Jos 13:26 4266
Their territory was from **M**, Jos 13:30 4266
and **M** with its pasture lands, Jos 21:38 4266
Saul and brought him over to **M**. 2Sa 2:8 4266
went out from **M** to Gibeon with the 2Sa 2:12 4266
walked all morning, and came to **M**. 2Sa 2:29 4266
Then David came to **M**. 2Sa 17:24 4266
Now when David had come to **M**, 2Sa 17:27 4266
the king while he stayed at **M**, 2Sa 19:32 4266
curse on the day I went to **M**. 1Ki 2:8 4266
Ahinadab the son of Iddo, *in* **M**; 1Ki 4:14 4266
lands, **M** with its pasture lands, 1Ch 6:80 4266

MAHANEH-DAN
the LORD began to stir him in **M**, Jg 13:25 4265
called that place **M** to this day; Jg 18:12 4265

MAHARAI
the Ahohite, **M** the Netophathite, 2Sa 23:28 4121
M the Netophathite, Heled the son 1Ch 11:30 4121
tenth month *was* **M** the Netophathite 1Ch 27:13 4121

MAHATH
the son of Elkanah, the son of **M**, 1Ch 6:35 4287
M, the son of Amasai and Joel the 2Ch 29:12 4287
Jozabad, Eliel, Ismachiah, **M** and 2Ch 31:13 4287

MAHAVITE
the **M** and Jeribai and Joshaviah, 1Ch 11:46 4233

MAHAZIOTH
Joshbekashah, Mallothi, Hothir, **M**. 1Ch 25:4 4238
for the twenty-third to **M**, 1Ch 25:30 4238

MAHER-SHALAL-HAS
LORD said to me, "Name him **M**; Is 8:3 4122

MAHLAH
daughters of Zelophehad were **M**, Nu 26:33 4244
M, Noah and Hoglah and Milcah Nu 27:1 4244
M, Tirzah, Hoglah, Milcah and Nu 36:11 4244
M and Noah, Hoglah, Milcah and Jos 17:3 4244
bore Ishhod and Abiezer and **M**. 1Ch 7:18 4244

MAHLI
The sons of Merari: **M** and Mushi. Ex 6:19 4249
by their families: **M** and Mushi. Nu 3:20 4249
sons of Merari *were* **M** and Mushi. 1Ch 6:19 4249
The sons of Merari *were* **M**, 1Ch 6:29 4249
the son of **M**, the son of Mushi, 1Ch 6:47 4249
sons of Merari were **M** and Mushi. 1Ch 23:21 4249
sons of **M** *were* Eleazar and Kish. 1Ch 23:21 4249
M, Eder and Jeremoth. 1Ch 23:23 4249
The sons of Merari, **M** and Mushi; 1Ch 24:26 4249
By **M**: Eleazar, who had no sons. 1Ch 24:28 4249
M, Eder and Jerimoth. 1Ch 24:30 4249
a man of insight of the sons of **M**, Ezr 8:18 4249

MAHLITES
Of Merari *was* the family of the **M** Nu 3:33 4250
Hebronites, the family of the **M**, Nu 26:58 4250

MAHLON
his two sons *were* **M** and Chilion, Ru 1:2 4248
Then both **M** and Chilion also died, Ru 1:5 4248
that belonged to Chilion and **M**. Ru 4:9 4248
the Moabitess, the widow of **M**, Ru 4:10 4248

MAHOL
Calcol and Darda, the sons of **M**; 1Ki 4:31 4235

MAHSEIAH
the son of Neriah, the son of **M**, Jer 32:12 4271
son of Neriah, the grandson of **M**, Jer 51:59 4271

MAID
Egyptian **m** whose name was Hagar. Gn 16:1 8198
Please go in to my **m**; Gn 16:2 8198
took Hagar the Egyptian, her **m**, Gn 16:3 8198
I gave my **m** into your arms, Gn 16:5 8198
"Behold, your **m** is in your power; Gn 16:6 8198
"Hagar, Sarai's **m**, where have you Gn 16:8 8198
"Drive out this **m** and her son, Gn 21:10 519
for the son of this **m** shall not be Gn 21:10 519
because of the lad and your **m**; Gn 21:12 519
the **m** I will make a nation also, Gn 21:13 519
whom Hagar the Egyptian, Sarah's **m**, Gn 25:12 8198
Laban also gave his **m** Zilpah to Gn 29:24 8198
to his daughter Leah as a **m**. Gn 29:24 8198
Laban also gave his **m** Bilhah to Gn 29:29 8198
to his daughter Rachel as her **m**. Gn 29:29 8198
"Here is my **m** Bilhah, go in to Gn 30:3 519
gave him her **m** Bilhah as a wife, Gn 30:4 8198
Rachel's **m** Bilhah conceived Gn 30:7 8198
she took her **m** Zilpah and gave her Gn 30:9 8198
Leah's **m** Zilpah bore Jacob a son. Gn 30:10 8198
Leah's **m** Zilpah bore Jacob a Gn 30:12 8198
I gave my **m** to my husband." Gn 30:18 8198
and the sons of Bilhah, Rachel's **m**: Gn 35:25 8198
and the sons of Zilpah, Leah's **m**: Gn 35:26 8198
among the reeds and sent her **m**, Ex 2:5 519
"I am Ruth your **m**. Ru 3:9 519
spread your covering over your **m**, Ru 3:9 519
your maidservant is a **m** to wash 1Sa 25:41 8189
the eyes of a **m** to the hand of her Ps 123:2 8189
And the way of a man with a **m**. Pr 30:19 5959
master, the **m** like her mistress, Is 24:2 8198

MAIDEN
that the **m** who comes out to draw, Gn 24:43 5959
A **m**, two maidens for every warrior; Jg 5:30 7358

MAIDENS
her **m** walking alongside the Nile; Ex 2:5 5291
A maiden, two **m** for every warrior; Jg 5:30 7358
with her five **m** who attended her; 1Sa 25:42 5291
Then Esther's **m** and her eunuchs Es 4:4 5291
I and my **m** also will fast in the Es 4:16 5291
Or will you bind him for your **m**? Jb 41:5 5291
of the **m** beating tambourines. Ps 68:25 5959
She has sent out her **m**, Pr 9:3 5291
And sustenance for your **m**. Pr 27:27 5291
household And portions to her **m**. Pr 31:15 5291
Therefore the **m** love you. SS 1:3 5959
So is my darling among the **m**." SS 2:2 1323
concubines, And **m** without number; SS 6:8 5959
The **m** saw her and called her SS 6:9 1323
slay old men, young men, **m**, Ezk 9:6 1330

MAIDS
Abimelech and his wife and his **m**, Gn 20:17 519
and gold, and servants and **m**, Gn 24:35 8198
Then Rebekah arose with her **m**, Gn 24:61 5291
and into the tent of the two **m**, Gn 31:33 519
his two **m** and his eleven children, Gn 32:22 8198
Leah and Rachel and the two **m**. Gn 33:1 8198
the **m** and their children in front, Gn 33:2 8198
m came near with their children, Gn 33:6 8198
this one, but stay here with my **m**. Ru 2:8 5291
that you go out with his **m**, Ru 2:22 5291
she stayed close by the **m** of Boaz Ru 2:23 5291
kinsman, with whose **m** you were? Ru 3:2 5291
today in the eyes of his servants' **m** 2Sa 6:20 519
the **m** of whom you have spoken, 2Sa 6:22 519
choice **m** from the king's palace and Es 2:9 5291
and transferred her and her **m** to Es 2:9 5291
and my **m** consider me a stranger. Jb 19:15 519

MAIDSERVANT
you shall do likewise to your **m**. Dt 15:17 519
made Abimelech, the son of his **m**, Jg 9:18 519
bread and wine for me, your **m**, Jg 19:19 519
have spoken kindly to your **m**, Ru 2:13 8198
look on the affliction of Your **m** and 1Sa 1:11 519
remember me, and not forget Your **m**, 1Sa 1:11 519
but will give Your **m** a son, 1Sa 1:11 519
your **m** as a worthless woman, 1Sa 1:16 519
your **m** find favor in your sight." 1Sa 1:18 8198
please let your **m** speak to you, 1Sa 25:24 519
and listen to the words of your **m**. 1Sa 25:24 519
but I your **m** did not see the young 1Sa 25:25 519
this gift which your **m** has brought 1Sa 25:27 8198
the transgression of your **m**; 1Sa 25:28 519
my lord, then remember your **m**." 1Sa 25:31 519
your **m** is a maid to wash the feet 1Sa 25:41 519
"Behold, your **m** has obeyed you, 1Sa 28:21 8198
listen to the voice of your **m**, 1Sa 28:22 8198
"Your **m** had two sons, but the 2Sa 14:6 8198
family has risen against your **m**, 2Sa 14:7 8198
"Please let your **m** speak a word 2Sa 14:12 8198
so your **m** said, 'Let me now speak 2Sa 14:15 8198
will perform the request of his **m**. 2Sa 14:15 519
the king will hear and deliver his **m** 2Sa 14:16 519
"Then your **m** said, 2Sa 14:17 8198
words in the mouth of your **m**; 2Sa 14:19 8198
and a **m** would go and tell them, 2Sa 17:17 8198
"Listen to the words of your **m**." 2Sa 20:17 519
my lord, O king, sworn to your **m**, 1Ki 1:13 519
you swore to your **m** by the LORD 1Ki 1:17 519
from beside me while your **m** slept, 1Ki 3:20 519
"Your **m** has nothing in the house 2Ki 4:2 8198
of God, do not lie to your **m**." 2Ki 4:16 8198
a **m** when she supplants her mistress Pr 30:23 8198

MAIDSERVANTS
I am not like one of your **m**." Ru 2:13 8198

MAIL
like the opening of a coat of **m**, Ex 28:32 8473
as the opening of a coat of **m**, Ex 39:23 8473
Who can come within his double **m**? Jb 41:13 7448

MAIMED
that are blind or fractured or **m** Lv 22:22 2782

MAIN
He overlaid the **m** room with **2Ch 3:5** 1419
on their feet facing the **m** room. **2Ch 3:13**
'Go therefore to the **m** highways, **Mt 22:9** *1327b*
Now the **m** point in what has been **Heb 8:1** *2774*

MAINLAND
her daughters who are on the **m** **Ezk 26:6** 7704
daughters on the **m** with the sword; **Ezk 26:8** 7704

MAINTAIN
supplication, and **m** their cause. **1Ki 8:45** 6213a
dwelling place, and **m** their cause, **1Ki 8:49** 6213a
that He may **m** the cause of His **1Ki 8:59** 6213a
supplication, and **m** their cause. **2Ch 6:35** 6213a
supplications, and **m** their cause and **2Ch 6:39** 6213a
not **m** his position before me. **Ps 101:7** 3559
He will **m** his cause in judgment. **Ps 112:5** 3557
will **m** the cause of the afflicted And **Ps 140:12** 6213a
them **m** his life by his iniquity. **Ezk 7:13** 2388
to **m** always a blameless conscience **Ac 24:16** *2192*
we **m** that a man is justified by faith **Ro 3:28** *3049*
m these *principles* without bias, **1Tm 5:21** *5442*
For when they **m** this, it escapes **2Pe 3:5** *2309*

MAINTAINED
For You have **m** my just cause; **Ps 9:4** 6213a
And he **m** his fury forever. **Am 1:11** 8104
of the testimony which they had **m**; **Rv 6:9** *2192*

MAINTAINING
of the same mind, **m** the same love, **Php 2:2** *2192*

MAINTENANCE
a suit of clothes, and your **m**." **Jg 17:10** 4241

MAJESTIC
right hand, O LORD, is **m** in power, **Ex 15:6** 142
Who is like You, **m** in holiness, **Ex 15:11** 142
He thunders with His **m** voice, **Jb 37:4** 1347b
His **m** snorting is terrible. **Jb 39:20** 1935
m is Your name in all the earth, **Ps 8:1** 117
m is Your name in all the earth! **Ps 8:9** 117
They are the **m** ones in whom is all **Ps 16:3** 117
The voice of the LORD is **m**. **Ps 29:4** 1926
More **m** than the mountains of prey. **Ps 76:4** 117
Splendid and **m** is His work, **Ps 111:3** 1926
But there the **m** *One,* the LORD, **Is 33:21** 117
This One who is **m** in His apparel, **Is 63:1** 1921
them like His **m** horse in battle. **Zch 10:3** 1935
was made to Him by the **M** Glory, **2Pe 1:17** *3169*

MAJESTIES
when they revile angelic **m**, **2Pe 2:10** *1391*
authority, and revile angelic **m**. **Jude 1:8** *1391*

MAJESTY
the firstborn of his ox, **m** is his, **Dt 33:17** 1926
And through the skies in His **m**. **Dt 33:26** 1346
help And the sword of your **m**! **Dt 33:29** 1346
Splendor and **m** are before Him, **1Ch 16:27** 1926
glory and the victory and the **m**, **1Ch 29:11** 1935
and bestowed on him royal **m** which **1Ch 29:25** 1935
the splendor of his great **m** for many **Es 1:4** 1420
"Will not His **m** terrify you, And **Jb 13:11** 7613
because of His **m** I can do nothing. **Jb 31:23** 7613
Around God is awesome **m**. **Jb 37:22** 1935
clothe yourself with honor and **m**. **Jb 40:10** 1926
You crown him with glory and **m**! **Ps 8:5** 1926
and **m** You place upon him. **Ps 21:5** 1926
One, *In* Your splendor and Your **m**! **Ps 45:3** 1926
And in Your **m** ride on victoriously, **Ps 45:4** 1926
His **m** is over Israel And His **Ps 68:34** 1346
And Your **m** to their children. **Ps 90:16** 1926
LORD reigns, He is clothed with **m**; **Ps 93:1** 1348
Splendor and **m** are before Him, **Ps 96:6** 1926
are clothed with splendor and **m**, **Ps 104:1** 1926
On the glorious splendor of Your **m** **Ps 145:5** 1935
the glory of the **m** of Your kingdom. **Ps 145:12** 1926
and from the splendor of His **m**. **Is 2:10** 1347b
And the splendor of His **m**, **Is 2:19** 1347b
LORD and the splendor of His **m**, **Is 2:21** 1347b
west concerning the **m** of the LORD. **Is 24:14** 1347b
not perceive the **m** of the LORD. **Is 26:10** 1348
to it, The **m** of Carmel and Sharon. **Is 35:2** 1926
of the LORD, The **m** of our God. **Is 35:2** 1926
He has no *stately* form or **m** That **Is 53:2** 1926
All her **m** Has departed from **La 1:6** 1926
and your **m** has become great and **Da 4:22** 7238
power and for the glory of my **m**?' **Da 4:30** 1923
And my **m** and splendor were **Da 4:36** 1923
m to Nebuchadnezzar your father. **Da 5:18** 1923
In the **m** of the name of the LORD **Mi 5:4** 1347b
the right hand of the **M** on high, **Heb 1:3** *3172*
throne of the **M** in the heavens, **Heb 8:1** *3172*
but we were eyewitnesses of His **m**. **2Pe 1:16** *3168*
be glory, **m**, dominion and authority, **Jude 1:25** *3172*

MAJOR
and let it be that every **m** dispute **Ex 18:22** 1419

MAJORITY
and the **m** did not know for what **Ac 19:32** *4183*
the **m** reached a decision to put **Ac 27:12** *4183*
which *was inflicted* by the **m**, **2Co 2:6** *4183*

MAKAZ
Ben-deker in **M** and Shaalbim and **1Ki 4:9** 4739

MAKE
"Let Us **m** man in Our image, **Gn 1:26** 6213a
m him a helper suitable for him." **Gn 2:18** 6213a
tree was desirable to **m** *one* wise, **Gn 3:6**
"**M** for yourself an ark of gopher **Gn 6:14** 6213a
you shall **m** the ark with rooms, **Gn 6:14** 6213a
"This is how you shall **m** it: **Gn 6:15** 6213a
"You shall **m** a window for the **Gn 6:16** 6213a
you shall **m** it with lower, second, **Gn 6:16** 6213a
let us **m** bricks and burn *them* **Gn 11:3** 3835b
and let us **m** for ourselves a name, **Gn 11:4** 6213a
And I will **m** you a great nation, **Gn 12:2** 6213a
bless you, And **m** your name great; **Gn 12:2** 1431
"I will **m** your descendants as **Gn 13:16** 7760
I will **m** you exceedingly fruitful, **Gn 17:6** 6509
and I will **m** nations of you, **Gn 17:6** 5414
him, and will **m** him fruitful and **Gn 17:20** 6509
and I will **m** him a great nation. **Gn 17:20** 5414
knead *it* and **m** bread cakes." **Gn 18:6** 6213a
let us **m** our father drink wine, **Gn 19:32**
let us **m** him drink wine tonight **Gn 19:34**
the maid I will **m** a nation also, **Gn 21:13** 7760
I will **m** a great nation of him." **Gn 21:18** 7760
I will **m** you swear by the LORD, **Gn 24:3**
you to **m** your journey successful, **Gn 24:40**
if now You will **m** my journey on **Gn 24:42**
and let us **m** a covenant with you, **Gn 26:28** 3772
m you fruitful and multiply you, **Gn 28:3** 6509
"So now come, let us **m** a covenant, **Gn 31:44** 3772
and **m** your descendants as the sand **Gn 32:12** 7760
and **m** an altar there to God, who **Gn 35:1** 6213a
I will **m** an altar there to God, **Gn 35:3** 6213a
a Hebrew to us to **m** sport of us; **Gn 39:14** 6711
came in to me to **m** sport of me; **Gn 39:17** 6711
"I would **m** mention today of my **Gn 41:9**
and slay an animal and **m** ready; **Gn 43:16** 3559
I will **m** you a great nation there. **Gn 46:3** 7760
will **m** you fruitful and numerous, **Gn 48:4** 6509
I will **m** you a company of peoples, **Gn 48:4** 5414
'May God **m** you like Ephraim and **Gn 48:20** 7760
straw to **m** brick as previously; **Ex 5:7** 3835b
they keep saying to us, '**M** bricks!' **Ex 5:16** 6213a
I did not **m** Myself known to them. **Ex 6:3** 3045
"See, I **m** you *as* God to Pharaoh, **Ex 7:1** 5414
and **m** frogs come up on the land of **Ex 8:5**
M supplication for me." **Ex 8:28** 6279
and I shall **m** supplication to the **Ex 8:29** 6279
LORD will **m** a distinction between **Ex 9:4** 6395
"**M** supplication to the LORD, for **Ex 9:28** 6279
and **m** supplication to the LORD **Ex 10:17** 6279
and **m** known the statutes of God **Ex 18:16** 3045
and **m** known to them the way in **Ex 18:20** 3045
shall not **m** for yourself an idol, **Ex 20:4** 6213a
shall not **m** *other gods* besides Me; **Ex 20:23** 6213a
you shall not **m** for yourselves. **Ex 20:23** 6213a
shall **m** an altar of earth for Me, **Ex 20:24** 6213a
If you **m** an altar of stone for Me, **Ex 20:25** 6213a
of the pit shall **m** restitution; **Ex 21:34** 7999a
He shall surely **m** restitution; **Ex 22:3** 7999a
he shall **m** restitution from the **Ex 22:5** 7999a
fire shall surely **m** restitution. **Ex 22:6** 7999a
and he shall not **m** restitution. **Ex 22:11** 7999a
shall **m** restitution to its owner. **Ex 22:12** 7999a
he shall not **m** restitution for **Ex 22:13** 7999a
it, he shall **m** full restitution. **Ex 22:14** 7999a
it, he shall not **m** restitution; **Ex 22:15** 7999a
and I will **m** all your enemies turn **Ex 23:27** 5414
"You shall **m** no covenant with **Ex 23:32** 3772
they will **m** you sin against Me; **Ex 23:33**
shall **m** a gold molding around it. **Ex 25:11** 6213a
"You shall **m** poles of acacia **Ex 25:13** 6213a
shall **m** a mercy seat of pure gold, **Ex 25:17** 6213a
"You shall **m** two cherubim of gold, **Ex 25:18** 6213a
m them of hammered work at the two **Ex 25:18** 6213a
"**M** one cherub at one end and one **Ex 25:19** 6213a
you shall **m** the cherubim *of one* **Ex 25:19** 6213a
shall **m** a table of acacia wood, **Ex 25:23** 6213a
and **m** a gold border around it. **Ex 25:24** 6213a
"You shall **m** for it a rim of **Ex 25:25** 6213a
and you shall **m** a gold border for **Ex 25:25** 6213a
"You shall **m** four gold rings **Ex 25:26** 6213a
"You shall **m** the poles of **Ex 25:28** 6213a
"You shall **m** its dishes and **Ex 25:29** 6213a
you shall **m** them of pure gold. **Ex 25:29** 6213a
shall **m** a lampstand of pure gold. **Ex 25:31** 6213a
shall **m** its lamps seven *in number;* **Ex 25:37** 6213a
"See that you **m** *them* after **Ex 25:40** 6213a
"Moreover you shall **m** the **Ex 26:1** 6213a
you shall **m** them with cherubim, **Ex 26:1** 6213a
"You shall **m** loops of blue on **Ex 26:4** 6213a
and likewise you shall **m** *them* on **Ex 26:4** 6213a
"You shall **m** fifty loops in the **Ex 26:5** 6213a
and you shall **m** fifty loops on the **Ex 26:5** 6213a
You shall **m** fifty clasps of gold, **Ex 26:6** 6213a
"Then you shall **m** curtains of **Ex 26:7** 6213a
shall **m** eleven curtains in all. **Ex 26:7** 6213a
"You shall **m** fifty loops on **Ex 26:10** 6213a
shall **m** fifty clasps of bronze, **Ex 26:11** 6213a
"You shall **m** a covering for **Ex 26:14** 6213a
"Then you shall **m** the boards for **Ex 26:15** 6213a
m the boards for the tabernacle: **Ex 26:18** 6213a
"You shall **m** forty sockets of **Ex 26:19** 6213a
the west, you shall **m** six boards. **Ex 26:22** 6213a
"You shall **m** two boards for **Ex 26:23** 6213a
you shall **m** bars of acacia wood, **Ex 26:26** 6213a
and **m** their rings of gold *as* holders **Ex 26:29** 6213a
"You shall **m** a veil of blue **Ex 26:31** 6213a
"You shall **m** a screen for the **Ex 26:36** 6213a
"You shall **m** five pillars of **Ex 26:37** 6213a
shall **m** the altar of acacia wood, **Ex 27:1** 6213a
m its horns on its four corners; **Ex 27:2** 6213a
"You shall **m** its pails for **Ex 27:3** 6213a
you shall **m** all its utensils **Ex 27:3** 6213a
"You shall **m** for it a grating **Ex 27:4** 6213a
and on the net you shall **m** four **Ex 27:4** 6213a
You shall **m** poles for the altar, **Ex 27:6** 6213a
"You shall **m** it hollow with planks; **Ex 27:8** 6213a
the mountain, so they shall **m** *it.* **Ex 27:8** 6213a
m the court of the tabernacle. **Ex 27:9** 6213a
to **m** a lamp burn continually. **Ex 27:20**
"You shall **m** holy garments **Ex 28:2** 6213a
that they **m** Aaron's garments to **Ex 28:3** 6213a
the garments which they shall **m**: **Ex 28:4** 6213a
and they shall **m** holy garments for **Ex 28:4** 6213a
shall also **m** the ephod of gold, **Ex 28:6** 6213a
shall **m** filigree *settings* of gold, **Ex 28:13** 6213a
m them of twisted cordage work, **Ex 28:14** 6213a
shall **m** a breastpiece of judgment, **Ex 28:15** 6213a
work of the ephod you shall **m** it: **Ex 28:15** 6213a
fine twisted linen you shall **m** it. **Ex 28:15** 6213a
"You shall **m** on the **Ex 28:22** 6213a
"You shall **m** on the **Ex 28:23** 6213a
"You shall **m** two rings of **Ex 28:26** 6213a
"You shall **m** two rings of **Ex 28:27** 6213a
"You shall **m** the robe of the **Ex 28:31** 6213a
"You shall **m** on its hem **Ex 28:33** 6213a
"You shall also **m** a plate of pure **Ex 28:36** 6213a
shall **m** a turban of fine linen, **Ex 28:39** 6213a
linen, and you shall **m** a sash, **Ex 28:39** 6213a
Aaron's sons you shall **m** tunics; **Ex 28:40** 6213a
you shall also **m** sashes for them, **Ex 28:40** 6213a
and you shall **m** caps for them, **Ex 28:40** 6213a
"You shall **m** for them linen **Ex 28:42** 6213a
shall **m** them of fine wheat flour. **Ex 29:2** 6213a
altar when you **m** atonement for it, **Ex 29:36** 3722a
seven days you shall **m** atonement **Ex 29:37** 3722a
you shall **m** an altar as a place **Ex 30:1** 6213a
you shall **m** it of acacia wood. **Ex 30:1** 6213a
and you shall **m** a gold molding all **Ex 30:3** 6213a
"You shall **m** two gold rings **Ex 30:4** 6213a
you shall **m** *them* on its two side **Ex 30:4** 6213a
"You shall **m** the poles of **Ex 30:5** 6213a
"Aaron shall **m** atonement on **Ex 30:10** 3722a
he shall **m** atonement on it with **Ex 30:10** 3722a
to **m** atonement for yourselves. **Ex 30:15** 3722a
to **m** atonement for yourselves." **Ex 30:16** 3722a
shall also **m** a laver of bronze, **Ex 30:18** 6213a
m of these a holy anointing oil, **Ex 30:25** 6213a
body, nor shall you **m** *any* like it in **Ex 30:32** 6213a
"With it you shall **m** incense, **Ex 30:35** 6213a
"The incense which you shall **m**, **Ex 30:37** 6213a
you shall not **m** in the same **Ex 30:37** 6213a
"Whoever shall **m** *any* like it, to **Ex 30:38** 6213a
to **m** artistic designs for work in **Ex 31:4** 2803
m all that I have commanded you: **Ex 31:6** 6213a
they are to **m** *them* according to **Ex 31:11** 6213a
m us a god who will go before us; **Ex 32:1** 6213a
I will **m** of you a great nation." **Ex 32:10** 6213a
'**M** a god for us who will go before **Ex 32:23** 6213a
I can **m** atonement for your sin." **Ex 32:30** 3722a
"I Myself will **m** all My goodness **Ex 33:19**
I am going to **m** a covenant. **Ex 34:10** 3772
"Watch yourself that you **m** no **Ex 34:12** 3772
you might **m** a covenant with the **Ex 34:15** 3772
m for yourself no molten gods. **Ex 34:17** 6213a
and **m** all that the LORD has **Ex 35:10** 6213a
who could **m** a contribution of silver **Ex 35:24** 7311
to **m** designs for working in gold **Ex 35:32** 2803
him to **m** atonement on his behalf. **Lv 1:4** 3722a
priest shall **m** atonement for them, **Lv 4:20** 3722a
Thus the priest shall **m** atonement **Lv 4:26** 3722a
priest shall **m** atonement for him, **Lv 4:31** 3722a
Thus the priest shall **m** atonement **Lv 4:35** 3722a
So the priest shall **m** atonement on **Lv 5:6** 3722a
So the priest shall **m** atonement on **Lv 5:10** 3722a
'So the priest shall **m** atonement **Lv 5:13** 3722a
"He shall **m** restitution for **Lv 5:16** 7999a
The priest shall then **m** atonement **Lv 5:16** 3722a
So the priest shall **m** atonement **Lv 5:18** 3722a
m restitution for it in full and **Lv 6:5** 7999a
and the priest shall **m** atonement **Lv 6:7** 3722a
to **m** atonement in the holy place **Lv 6:30** 3722a
it, to **m** atonement for it. **Lv 8:15** 3722a
to **m** atonement on your behalf. **Lv 8:34** 3722a
that you may **m** atonement for **Lv 9:7** 3722a
m the offering for the people, **Lv 9:7** 6213a
that you may **m** atonement for them, **Lv 9:7** 3722a
and so as to **m** a distinction **Lv 10:10** 914
to **m** atonement for them before the **Lv 10:17** 3722a
hoof but do not **m** a split *hoof,* **Lv 11:26** 8156
and you shall not **m** yourselves **Lv 11:43** 2930
And you shall not **m** yourselves **Lv 11:44** 2930
to **m** a distinction between the **Lv 11:47** 914
the LORD and **m** atonement for her, **Lv 12:7** 3722a
priest shall **m** atonement for her, **Lv 12:8** 3722a
So the priest shall **m** atonement on **Lv 14:18** 3722a
and **m** atonement for the one to be **Lv 14:19** 3722a
priest shall **m** atonement for him, **Lv 14:20** 3722a
offering to **m** atonement for him, **Lv 14:21** 3722a
to **m** atonement on his behalf **Lv 14:29** 3722a
So the priest shall **m** atonement **Lv 14:31** 3722a
seventh day and **m** an inspection. **Lv 14:39** 7200
shall come in and **m** an inspection. **Lv 14:44** 7200
shall **m** atonement for the house, **Lv 14:53** 3722a
So the priest shall **m** atonement on **Lv 15:15** 3722a
So the priest shall **m** atonement on **Lv 15:30** 3722a
that he may **m** atonement for **Lv 16:6** 3722a
fell, and **m** it a sin offering. **Lv 16:9** 6213a
the LORD, to **m** atonement upon it, **Lv 16:10** 3722a
and **m** atonement for himself and **Lv 16:11** 3722a
m atonement for the holy place, **Lv 16:16** 3722a
to **m** atonement in the holy place, **Lv 16:17** 3722a
that he may **m** atonement for **Lv 16:17** 3722a
the LORD and **m** atonement for it, **Lv 16:18** 3722a
and **m** atonement for himself and **Lv 16:24** 3722a
to **m** atonement in the holy place, **Lv 16:27** 3722a
father's place shall **m** atonement: **Lv 16:32** 3722a

and **m** atonement for the holy	Lv 16:33	3722a
and he shall **m** atonement for the	Lv 16:33	3722a
He shall also **m** atonement for the	Lv 16:33	3722a
to **m** atonement for the sons of	Lv 16:34	3722a
to **m** atonement for your souls;	Lv 17:11	3722a
or **m** for yourselves molten gods;	Lv 19:4	6213a
'The priest shall also **m** atonement	Lv 19:22	3722a
'You shall not **m** any cuts in your	Lv 19:28	5414
nor **m** any tattoo marks on	Lv 19:28	5414
'You are therefore to **m** a distinction	Lv 20:25	914
and you shall not **m** yourselves	Lv 20:25	8262
not **m** any baldness on their heads,	Lv 21:5	7139
nor **m** any cuts in their flesh.	Lv 21:5	8295
nor **m** of them an offering by fire	Lv 22:22	5414
shall **m** a proclamation as well;	Lv 23:21	7121
to **m** atonement on your behalf	Lv 23:28	3722a
to **m** a lamp burn continually.	Lv 24:2	
life of an animal shall **m** it good,	Lv 24:18	7999a
kills an animal shall **m** it good,	Lv 24:21	7999a
'If you **m** a sale, moreover, to	Lv 25:14	4376
shall not **m** for yourselves idols,	Lv 26:1	6213a
m you fruitful and multiply you,	Lv 26:9	
I will **m** My dwelling among you,	Lv 26:11	5414
I will also **m** your sky like iron	Lv 26:19	5414
will **m** your sanctuaries desolate,	Lv 26:31	8074
'I will **m** the land desolate so	Lv 26:32	8074
then **m** amends for their iniquity,	Lv 26:41	7521
and will **m** up for its sabbaths	Lv 26:43	7521
and **m** a list of their names.	Nu 3:40	5375
and he shall **m** restitution in full	Nu 5:7	7725
"the LORD **m** you a curse and an	Nu 5:21	5414
and **m** your abdomen swell and your	Nu 5:22	
'Then he shall **m** the woman drink	Nu 5:24	
shall **m** the woman drink the water.	Nu 5:26	
he shall then **m** the woman stand	Nu 5:30	
'He shall not **m** himself unclean	Nu 6:7	2930
and **m** atonement for him concerning	Nu 6:11	3722a
The LORD **m** His face shine on you,	Nu 6:25	215
to **m** atonement for the Levites.	Nu 8:12	3722a
and to **m** atonement on behalf of	Nu 8:19	3722a
"**M** yourself two trumpets of silver,	Nu 10:2	6213a
of hammered work you shall **m** them;	Nu 10:2	6213a
it in the pot and **m** cakes with it;	Nu 11:8	6213a
shall **m** Myself known to him in a	Nu 12:6	3045
M an effort then to get some of	Nu 13:20	2388
and I will **m** you into a nation	Nu 14:12	6213a
then **m** an offering by fire to the	Nu 15:3	6213a
to **m** a soothing aroma to the LORD,	Nu 15:3	6213a
wishes to **m** an offering by fire,	Nu 15:14	6213a
'Then the priest shall **m** atonement	Nu 15:25	3722a
'The priest shall **m** atonement	Nu 15:28	3722a
they shall **m** for themselves tassels	Nu 15:38	6213a
and **m** atonement for them,	Nu 16:46	3722a
"**M** a fiery *serpent,* and set it on	Nu 21:8	6213a
spoken, and will He not **m** it good?	Nu 23:19	6965
offering to **m** atonement for you.	Nu 28:22	3722a
male goat to **m** atonement for you.	Nu 28:30	3722a
offering, to **m** atonement for you,	Nu 29:5	3722a
to **m** atonement for ourselves	Nu 31:50	3722a
but **m** them known to your sons and	Dt 4:9	3045
act corruptly and **m** a graven image	Dt 4:16	6213a
m for yourselves a graven image	Dt 4:23	6213a
and **m** an idol in the form of	Dt 4:25	6213a
"The LORD did not **m** this covenant	Dt 5:3	3772
shall not **m** for yourself an idol,	Dt 5:8	6213a
You shall **m** no covenant with them	Dt 7:2	3772
you will **m** their name perish from	Dt 7:24	
that He might **m** you understand	Dt 8:3	
is giving you power to **m** wealth,	Dt 8:18	6213a
and I will **m** of you a nation	Dt 9:14	6213a
and **m** an ark of wood for yourself.	Dt 10:1	6213a
on you and **m** you increase,	Dt 13:17	
which you shall **m** for yourself.	Dt 16:21	6213a
m his brothers' hearts melt like his	Dt 20:8	
If it agrees to **m** peace with you	Dt 20:11	6030a
if it does not **m** peace with you,	Dt 20:12	7999b
to **m** war against it in order to	Dt 20:19	3898a
he cannot **m** the son of the loved	Dt 21:16	1069
shall **m** a parapet for your roof,	Dt 22:8	6213a
"You shall **m** yourself tassels on	Dt 22:12	6213a
you **m** a vow to the LORD your God,	Dt 23:21	5087
"When you **m** your neighbor a loan	Dt 24:10	5383
and the man to whom you **m** the loan	Dt 24:11	5383
the judge shall then **m** him lie	Dt 25:2	
will **m** you abound in prosperity,	Dt 28:11	
m you the head and not the tail,	Dt 28:13	5414
"The LORD will **m** the pestilence	Dt 28:21	
"The LORD will **m** the rain of your	Dt 28:24	5414
to **m** you perish and destroy you;	Dt 28:63	
Moses to **m** with the sons of Israel	Dt 29:1	3772
to get it for us and **m** us hear it,	Dt 30:12	
to get it for us and **m** us hear it,	Dt 30:13	
So I will **m** them jealous with	Dt 32:21	
will **m** My arrows drunk with blood,	Dt 32:42	
you will **m** your way prosperous,	Jos 1:8	6743b
"**M** for yourself flint knives and	Jos 5:2	6213a
m a long blast with the ram's horn,	Jos 6:5	4900
and **m** the camp of Israel accursed	Jos 6:18	7760
m all the people toil up there,	Jos 7:3	
therefore, **m** a covenant with us."	Jos 9:6	3772
shall we **m** a covenant with you?"	Jos 9:7	3772
then, **m** a covenant with us."	Jos 9:11	3772
So your sons may **m** our sons stop	Jos 22:25	
gods, or **m** *anyone* swear *by them,*	Jos 23:7	
you shall **m** no covenant with the	Jg 2:2	3772
please let me **m** a test once more	Jg 6:39	5254
for my son to **m** a graven image and	Jg 17:3	6213a
they would **m** a great cloud of	Jg 20:38	
but do not **m** yourself known to the	Ru 3:3	3045

May the LORD **m** the woman who is	Ru 4:11	5414
long will you **m** yourself drunk?	1Sa 1:14	7937
heap To **m** them sit with nobles,	1Sa 2:8	
And his mother would **m** him a	1Sa 2:19	6213a
"So you shall **m** likenesses of	1Sa 6:5	6213a
to **m** his weapons of war and	1Sa 8:12	6213a
"**M** a covenant with us and we will	1Sa 11:1	3772
m *it* with you on this condition,	1Sa 11:2	3772
m it a reproach on all Israel."	1Sa 11:2	7760
to **m** you a people for Himself.	1Sa 12:22	6213a
the Hebrews will **m** swords or spears."	1Sa 13:19	6213a
m his father's house free in Israel."	1Sa 17:25	6213a
Now Saul planned to **m** David fall	1Sa 18:25	
send to you and **m** it known to you?	1Sa 20:12	1540
if I do not **m** it known to you and	1Sa 20:13	1540
Will he **m** you all commanders of	1Sa 22:7	7760
"Go now, **m** more sure, and	1Sa 23:22	3559
m for my lord an enduring house,	1Sa 25:28	6213a
m you my bodyguard for life."	1Sa 28:2	7760
m known to me what I should do."	1Sa 28:15	3045
"**M** the man go back, that he may	1Sa 29:4	
For with what could this *man* **m**	1Sa 29:4	7521
me through and **m** sport of me."	1Sa 31:4	5953a
M your covenant with me, and	2Sa 3:12	3772
I will **m** a covenant with you, but	2Sa 3:13	3772
they may **m** a covenant with you,	2Sa 3:21	3772
and I will **m** you a great name,	2Sa 7:9	6213a
the LORD will **m** a house for you.	2Sa 7:11	6213a
and to **m** a name for Himself,	2Sa 7:23	7760
m your battle against the city	2Sa 11:25	2388
"He must **m** restitution for	2Sa 12:6	7999a
Tamar come and **m** me a couple of	2Sa 13:6	3823b
I today **m** you wander with us,	2Sa 15:20	
m the counsel of Ahithophel	2Sa 15:31	5528
And how can I **m** atonement that you	2Sa 21:3	3722a
Will He not indeed **m** *it* grow?	2Sa 23:5	
and **m** his throne greater than the	1Ki 1:37	1431
'May your God **m** the name of	1Ki 1:47	3190
"Did I not **m** you swear by the	1Ki 2:42	
and I will **m** them into rafts *to go*	1Ki 5:9	7760
pray and **m** supplication to You	1Ki 8:33	2603a
and repent and **m** supplication to	1Ki 8:47	2603a
and **m** them *objects of* compassion	1Ki 8:50	5414
m slaves of the sons of Israel;	1Ki 9:22	5414
but I will **m** him ruler all the	1Ki 11:34	7896
had come to Shechem to **m** him king.	1Ki 12:1	4427a
now you **m** it lighter for us!'	1Ki 12:10	7043
and I will **m** a clean sweep of the	1Ki 14:10	1197a
and I will **m** your house like the	1Ki 16:3	5414
the son of Ginath, to **m** him king;	1Ki 16:21	4427a
but **m** me a little bread cake from	1Ki 17:13	6213a
and afterward you may **m** *one* for	1Ki 17:13	6213a
if I do not **m** your life as the	1Ki 19:2	7760
and you shall **m** streets for	1Ki 20:34	7760
and I will **m** your house like the	1Ki 21:22	5414
'**M** this valley full of trenches.'	2Ki 3:16	6213a
let us **m** a little walled upper	2Ki 4:10	6213a
"Am I God, to kill and to **m** alive,	2Ki 5:7	2421a
and let us **m** a place there for	2Ki 6:2	6213a
LORD should **m** windows in heaven,	2Ki 7:2	6213a
LORD should **m** windows in heaven,	2Ki 7:19	6213a
'I will **m** the house of Ahab	2Ki 9:9	5414
do, we will not **m** any man king;	2Ki 10:5	4427a
m a bargain with my master the	2Ki 18:23	6148
Hezekiah **m** you trust in the LORD,	2Ki 18:30	
"**M** your peace with me and come	2Ki 18:31	6213a
And I will **m** him fall by the sword	2Ki 19:7	
"And I will not **m** the feet of	2Ki 21:8	
that no man might **m** his son or his	2Ki 23:10	
and to **m** atonement for Israel,	1Ch 6:49	3722a
with all Israel, to **m** him king,	1Ch 11:10	4427a
by name to come and **m** David king.	1Ch 12:31	4427a
to **m** David king over all Israel;	1Ch 12:38	4427a
were of one mind to **m** David king.	1Ch 12:38	4427a
M known His deeds among the	1Ch 16:8	3045
and I will **m** you a name like the	1Ch 17:8	6213a
to **m** known all these great things.	1Ch 17:19	3045
to **m** You a name by great and	1Ch 17:21	7760
large quantities of iron to **m** the nails	1Ch 22:3	
I will **m** preparation for it."	1Ch 22:5	3559
me to **m** *me* king over all Israel.	1Ch 28:4	4427a
it lies in Your hand to **m** great and	1Ch 29:12	1431
m *their* offerings willingly to	1Ch 29:17	5068
and who knows how to **m** engravings,	2Ch 2:7	6605b
and *who knows how* to **m** all kinds	2Ch 2:14	6605b
supervisors to **m** the people work.	2Ch 2:18	
singers were to **m** themselves heard	2Ch 5:13	8085
and pray and **m** supplication before	2Ch 6:24	2603a
and repent and **m** supplication to	2Ch 6:37	2603a
and I will **m** it a proverb and a	2Ch 7:20	5414
But Solomon did not **m** slaves for	2Ch 8:9	5414
had come to Shechem to **m** him king.	2Ch 10:1	4427a
but you **m** it lighter for us.'	2Ch 10:10	7043
for he *intended* to **m** him king.	2Ch 11:22	4427a
did not **m** war against Jehoshaphat.	2Ch 17:10	3898a
came to **m** war against Jehoshaphat.	2Ch 20:1	
him to **m** ships to go to Tarshish,	2Ch 20:36	6213a
it is in my heart to **m** a covenant	2Ch 29:10	3772
month they began to **m** the heaps,	2Ch 31:7	3245
he intended to **m** war on Jerusalem,	2Ch 32:2	
to **m** beams for the houses	2Ch 34:11	7136b
king of Egypt came up to **m** war at	2Ch 35:20	3898a
in order to **m** war with him;	2Ch 35:22	3898a
to **m** war on the plain of Megiddo.	2Ch 35:22	3898a
a decree to **m** these men stop *work,*	Ezr 4:21	
"So now let us **m** a covenant with	Ezr 10:3	3772
m confession to the LORD God of	Ezr 10:11	5414
m Your servant successful today and	Ne 1:11	6743b
timber to **m** beams for the gates of	Ne 2:8	7136b

of *other* leafy trees, to **m** booths,	Ne 8:15	6213a
You did not **m** an end of them	Ne 9:31	6213a
to **m** atonement for Israel,	Ne 10:33	3722a
the king's edict which he will **m**	Es 1:20	6213a
Esther did not **m** known her people	Es 2:10	5046
that she should not **m** *them* known.	Es 2:10	5046
m the fourteenth day of the month	Es 9:19	6213a
that they should **m** them days of	Es 9:22	6213a
M known to me my rebellion and my	Jb 13:23	3045
And **m** me to inherit the	Jb 13:26	
m the clean out of the unclean?	Jb 14:4	5414
"They **m** night into day, *saying,*	Jb 17:12	7760
home, I **m** my bed in the darkness;	Jb 17:13	7502
disquieting thoughts **m** me respond,	Jb 20:2	
profit if you **m** your ways perfect?	Jb 22:3	8552
liar, And **m** my speech worthless?"	Jb 24:25	7760
He who made me in the womb **m** him,	Jb 31:15	6213a
to **m** the seeds of grass to sprout?	Jb 38:27	
"Do you **m** him leap like the locust?	Jb 39:20	
who is proud, and **m** him low.	Jb 40:11	8213
he **m** many supplications to you,	Jb 41:3	7235a
"Will he **m** a covenant with you?	Jb 41:4	3772
"The arrow cannot **m** him flee;	Jb 41:28	
m me to dwell in safety.	Ps 4:8	
M Your way straight before me.	Ps 5:8	3474
Every night I **m** my bed swim, I	Ps 6:6	
To **m** the enemy and the revengeful	Ps 8:2	
You **m** him to rule over the	Ps 8:6	
They **m** ready their arrow upon the	Ps 11:2	3559
m known to me the path of life;	Ps 16:11	3045
You **m** him most blessed forever;	Ps 21:6	7896
You **m** him joyful with	Ps 21:6	2302b
You will **m** them as a fiery oven in	Ps 21:9	7896
You will **m** them turn their back;	Ps 21:12	7896
M me know Your ways, O LORD;	Ps 25:4	
He will **m** them know His covenant.	Ps 25:14	
M Your face to shine upon Your	Ps 31:16	
will **m** its boast in the LORD;	Ps 34:2	1984b
M haste to help me, O Lord, my	Ps 38:22	2363a
"LORD, **m** me to know my end And	Ps 39:4	
they **m** an uproar for nothing;	Ps 39:6	1993
M me not the reproach of the	Ps 39:8	7760
M haste, O LORD, to help me.	Ps 40:13	2363a
You **m** us a reproach to our	Ps 44:13	7760
m us a byword among the nations,	Ps 44:14	7760
m them princes in all the earth.	Ps 45:16	7896
streams **m** glad the city of God,	Ps 46:4	8055
part You will **m** me know wisdom.	Ps 51:6	
M me to hear joy and gladness, Let	Ps 51:8	
who would not **m** God his refuge,	Ps 52:7	7760
So they will **m** him stumble;	Ps 64:8	
You **m** the dawn and the	Ps 65:8	
M His praise glorious.	Ps 66:2	7760
I shall **m** *an offering of* bulls	Ps 66:15	6213a
m their loins shake continually.	Ps 69:23	
m mention of Your righteousness,	Ps 71:16	2142
M vows to the LORD your God and	Ps 76:11	5087
You **m** us an object of	Ps 80:6	7760
behold, Your enemies **m** an uproar	Ps 83:2	1993
They **m** shrewd plans against Your	Ps 83:3	6191
Against You they **m** a covenant:	Ps 83:5	3772
M their nobles like Oreb and Zeeb And	Ps 83:11	7896
m them like the whirling dust,	Ps 83:13	7896
of Baca they **m** it a spring	Ps 84:6	7896
will **m** His footsteps into a way.	Ps 85:13	7760
M glad the soul of Your servant,	Ps 86:4	8055
To all generations I will **m** known	Ps 89:1	3045
"I also shall **m** him *My* firstborn,	Ps 89:27	5414
M us glad according to the days	Ps 90:15	8055
may **m** *his* face glisten with oil,	Ps 104:15	
M known His deeds among the	Ps 105:1	3045
That He might **m** His power known.	Ps 106:8	3045
Until I **m** Your enemies a footstool	Ps 110:1	7896
To **m** *them* sit with princes, With	Ps 113:8	
m a sound with their throat.	Ps 115:7	1897
who **m** them will become like them,	Ps 115:8	6213a
M me understand the way of Your	Ps 119:27	
M me walk in the path of Your	Ps 119:35	
m me wiser than my enemies,	Ps 119:98	2449
M Your face shine upon Your servant,	Ps 119:135	
who **m** them will be like them,	Ps 135:18	6213a
If I **m** my bed in Sheol, behold,	Ps 139:8	3331
I **m** supplication with my voice to	Ps 142:1	2603a
To **m** known to the sons of men Your	Ps 145:12	3045
I will **m** my words known to you.	Pr 1:23	3045
M your ear attentive to wisdom,	Pr 2:2	7181
And He will **m** your paths straight.	Pr 3:6	3474
unless they **m** *someone* stumble.	Pr 4:16	
And **m** war by wise guidance.	Pr 20:18	6213a
And after the vows to **m** inquiry.	Pr 20:25	1239
who oppresses the poor to **m** more	Pr 22:16	7235a
To **m** you know the certainty of the	Pr 22:21	
And **m** it ready for yourself in the	Pr 24:27	6257
Oil and perfume **m** the heart glad,	Pr 27:9	8055
wise, my son, and **m** my heart glad,	Pr 27:11	8055
they **m** their houses in the rocks;	Pr 30:26	7760
When you **m** a vow to God, do not be	Ec 5:4	5087
flies **m** a perfumer's oil stink,	Ec 10:1	
creature will **m** the matter known.	Ec 10:20	5046
do you **m** *it* lie down at noon?	SS 1:7	
"We will **m** for you ornaments of	SS 1:11	6213a
"The watchmen who **m** the rounds in	SS 3:3	5437
M my garden breathe out *fragrance,*	SS 4:16	
"The watchmen who **m** the rounds in	SS 5:7	5437
yourselves, **m** yourselves clean;	Is 1:16	2135
He arises to **m** the earth tremble.	Is 2:19	6206
He arises to **m** the earth tremble.	Is 2:21	6206
And I will **m** mere lads their	Is 3:4	5414
will **m** their foreheads bare."	Is 3:17	6168

Context	Reference	Number
“Let Him **m** speed, let Him hasten	**Is 5:19**	4116
and **m** for ourselves a breach in	**Is 7:6**	1234
m *it* deep as Sheol or high as	**Is 7:11**	6009
later on He shall **m** *it* glorious,	**Is 9:1**	3513
Nor **m** a decision by what His ears	**Is 11:3**	3198
And **m** *men* walk over dry-shod.	**Is 11:15**	
M known His deeds among the	**Is 12:4**	3045
M *them* remember that His name is	**Is 12:4**	
anger, To **m** the land a desolation;	**Is 13:9**	7760
I will **m** mortal man scarcer than	**Is 13:12**	3365
I will **m** the heavens tremble,	**Is 13:13**	
m *their flocks* lie down there.	**Is 13:20**	
will **m** myself like the Most High.’	**Is 14:14**	1819
“I will also **m** it a possession	**Is 14:23**	7760
“Give *us* advice, **m** a decision;	**Is 16:3**	6213a
will **m** Himself known to Egypt,	**Is 19:21**	3045
and will **m** a vow to the LORD and	**Is 19:21**	5087
God of Israel, I **m** known to you.	**Is 21:10**	5046
m the path of the righteous level.	**Is 26:7**	6424
Let him **m** peace with Me,	**Is 27:5**	6213a
Me, Let him **m** peace with Me.”	**Is 27:5**	6213a
Women come *and* **m** a fire with them,	**Is 27:11**	215
will **m** justice the measuring line And	**Is 28:17**	7760
“He did not **m** me”;	**Is 29:16**	6213a
but not Mine, And **m** an alliance,	**Is 30:1**	5259
The tree snake will **m** its nest and	**Is 34:15**	7077
come **m** a bargain with my master	**Is 36:8**	6148
Hezekiah **m** you trust in the LORD,	**Is 36:15**	
‘**M** your peace with me and come out	**Is 36:16**	6213a
And I will **m** him fall by the sword	**Is 37:7**	
night You **m** an end of me.	**Is 38:12**	7999a
night You **m** an end of me.	**Is 38:13**	7999a
M smooth in the desert a highway	**Is 40:3**	3474
And will **m** the hills like chaff.	**Is 41:15**	7760
I will **m** the wilderness a pool of	**Is 41:18**	7760
Nor **m** His voice heard in the street.	**Is 42:2**	8085
will **m** the rivers into coastlands And	**Is 42:15**	7760
I will **m** darkness into light	**Is 42:16**	7760
To **m** the law great and glorious.	**Is 42:21**	1431
m a roadway in the wilderness,	**Is 43:19**	7760
Then I **m** the rest of it into an	**Is 44:19**	6213a
And I will **m** your rivers dry.	**Is 44:27**	3001
you and **m** the rough places smooth;	**Is 45:2**	3474
And I will **m** all his ways smooth;	**Is 45:13**	3474
They will **m** supplication to you:	**Is 45:14**	6419
Me And **m** Me equal and compare Me,	**Is 46:5**	7737a
and He will **m** his ways successful.	**Is 48:15**	6743b
I will also **m** You a light of the	**Is 49:6**	5414
to **m** *them* inherit the desolate	**Is 49:8**	
I will **m** all My mountains a road,	**Is 49:11**	7760
M room for me that I may live *here*.’	**Is 49:20**	5066
I **m** the rivers a wilderness;	**Is 50:2**	7760
And **m** sackcloth their covering.”	**Is 50:3**	7760
wilderness He will **m** like Eden,	**Is 51:3**	7760
will **m** your battlements of rubies,	**Is 54:12**	7760
I will **m** an everlasting covenant	**Is 55:3**	3772
And **m** them joyful in My house of	**Is 56:7**	8055
to **m** your voice heard on high.	**Is 58:4**	8085
And I will **m** you ride on the	**Is 58:14**	
coastlands He will **m** recompense.	**Is 59:18**	7999a
m the place of My feet glorious.	**Is 60:13**	3513
I will **m** you an everlasting pride,	**Is 60:15**	7760
will **m** peace your administrators And	**Is 60:17**	7760
And **m** an everlasting covenant	**Is 61:8**	3772
I shall **m** mention of the	**Is 63:7**	2142
m for Himself an everlasting name,	**Is 63:12**	6213a
To **m** for Yourself a glorious name.	**Is 63:14**	6213a
To **m** Your name known to Your	**Is 64:2**	3045
and the new earth Which I **m**	**Is 66:22**	6213a
his place To **m** your land a waste.	**Jer 4:7**	7760
In vain you **m** yourself beautiful.	**Jer 4:30**	3302
not **m** you a complete destruction.	**Jer 5:18**	6213a
And **m** you a desolation, A land	**Jer 6:8**	7760
m cakes for the queen of heaven;	**Jer 7:18**	6213a
“Then I will **m** to cease from the	**Jer 7:34**	
will **m** Jerusalem a heap of ruins,	**Jer 9:11**	5414
And I will **m** the cities of Judah a	**Jer 9:11**	5414
“Let them **m** haste and take	**Jer 9:18**	4116
gods that did not **m** the heavens	**Jer 10:11**	5648
m the cities of Judah A desolation,	**Jer 10:22**	7760
to **m** an end of them by the sword,	**Jer 14:12**	3615
“I will **m** them an object of	**Jer 15:4**	5414
cause the enemy to **m** supplication	**Jer 15:11**	6293
“Then I will **m** you to this people	**Jer 15:20**	5414
Can man **m** gods for himself?	**Jer 16:20**	6213a
I am going to **m** them know	**Jer 16:21**	
I will **m** them know My power	**Jer 16:21**	
And I will **m** you serve your	**Jer 17:4**	
as it pleased the potter to **m**.	**Jer 18:4**	6213a
To **m** their land a desolation, *An*	**Jer 18:16**	7760
“I will **m** void the counsel	**Jer 19:7**	1238b
“I will also **m** this city a desolation	**Jer 19:8**	7760
“I will **m** them eat the flesh	**Jer 19:9**	
“so as to **m** this city like Topheth.	**Jer 19:12**	5414
I am going to **m** you a terror to	**Jer 20:4**	5414
I will **m** you like a wilderness,	**Jer 22:6**	7896
And **m** them drink poisonous water,	**Jer 23:15**	
who intend to **m** My people forget	**Jer 23:27**	
‘I will **m** them a terror *and an*	**Jer 24:9**	5414
destroy them and **m** them a horror	**Jer 25:9**	7760
m it an everlasting desolation.	**Jer 25:12**	7760
kings will **m** slaves of them,	**Jer 25:14**	5647
and its princes, to **m** them a ruin,	**Jer 25:18**	5414
I will **m** this house like Shiloh,	**Jer 26:6**	5414
and this city I will **m** a curse to	**Jer 26:6**	5414
“**M** for yourself bonds and yokes	**Jer 27:2**	6213a
kings will **m** him their servant.	**Jer 27:7**	5647
I will **m** them like split-open figs	**Jer 29:17**	5414
and I will **m** them a terror to all	**Jer 29:18**	5414
“May the LORD **m** you like Zedekiah	**Jer 29:22**	7760
no longer **m** them their slaves.	**Jer 30:8**	5647
And no one will **m** him afraid.	**Jer 30:10**	2729
I will **m** them walk by streams of	**Jer 31:9**	
“when I will **m** a new covenant	**Jer 31:31**	3772
this is the covenant which I will **m**	**Jer 31:33**	3772
place and **m** them dwell in safety.	**Jer 32:37**	
I will **m** an everlasting covenant	**Jer 32:40**	3772
of Judah which are broken down *to* **m**	**Jer 33:4**	
all the peace that I **m** for it.’	**Jer 33:9**	6213a
and I will **m** you a terror to all	**Jer 34:17**	5414
and I will **m** the cities of Judah a	**Jer 34:22**	5414
and will **m** man and beast to cease	**Jer 36:29**	
and do not **m** me return to the	**Jer 37:20**	
not to **m** me return to the house of	**Jer 38:26**	
“**M** your baggage ready for exile,	**Jer 46:19**	6213a
For I will **m** a full end of all	**Jer 46:28**	6213a
I will not **m** a full end of you;	**Jer 46:28**	6213a
“**M** him drunk, for he has become	**Jer 48:26**	7937
“I will **m** an end of Moab,”	**Jer 48:35**	7673a
Though you **m** your nest as high as	**Jer 49:16**	1361b
I will **m** him run away from it,	**Jer 49:19**	
surely He will **m** their pasture	**Jer 49:20**	8074
m her land an object of horror,	**Jer 50:3**	7896
I will **m** them run away from it,	**Jer 50:44**	
surely He will **m** their pasture	**Jer 50:45**	8074
I will **m** you a burnt out mountain.	**Jer 51:25**	5414
To **m** the land of Babylon A	**Jer 51:29**	7760
up her sea And **m** her fountain dry.	**Jer 51:36**	3001
their banquet And **m** them drunk,	**Jer 51:39**	7937
And I will **m** what he has	**Jer 51:44**	
And He will **m** *her* loud noise	**Jer 51:55**	6
“I will **m** her princes and	**Jer 51:57**	7937
become drunk and **m** yourself naked.	**La 4:21**	6168
I will **m** your tongue stick to the	**Ezk 3:26**	
m them into bread for yourself;	**Ezk 4:9**	6213a
I will **m** you a desolation and a	**Ezk 5:14**	5414
and I will **m** your slain fall in	**Ezk 6:4**	
m the land more desolate and waste	**Ezk 6:14**	5414
m it an abhorrent thing to them.	**Ezk 7:20**	5414
‘**M** the chain, for the land is full	**Ezk 7:23**	6213a
I will also **m** the pride of the	**Ezk 7:24**	
“I will **m** this proverb cease so	**Ezk 12:23**	
“I will **m** a violent wind break	**Ezk 13:13**	
and **m** veils for the heads of	**Ezk 13:18**	6213a
and **m** him a sign and a proverb,	**Ezk 14:8**	7760
be taken from it to **m** anything,	**Ezk 15:3**	6213a
‘Thus I will **m** the land desolate,	**Ezk 15:8**	5414
m known to Jerusalem her	**Ezk 16:2**	3045
your harlotry to **m** Me angry.	**Ezk 16:26**	3707
tree and **m** the dry tree flourish.	**Ezk 17:24**	
And **m** yourselves a new heart and a	**Ezk 18:31**	6213a
M them know the abominations of	**Ezk 20:4**	
so that I might **m** them desolate,	**Ezk 20:26**	8074
I will **m** you pass under the rod,	**Ezk 20:37**	
‘Sharpened to **m** a slaughter,	**Ezk 21:10**	2873
m two ways for the sword of the	**Ezk 21:19**	7760
And **m** a signpost;	**Ezk 21:19**	1254a
m it at the head of the way to the	**Ezk 21:19**	1254a
a ruin, a ruin, I will **m** it.	**Ezk 21:27**	7760
‘Thus I will **m** your lewdness and	**Ezk 23:27**	
m lewdness cease from the land,	**Ezk 23:48**	
M it boil vigorously.	**Ezk 24:5**	
I also will **m** the pile great.	**Ezk 24:9**	1431
m no mourning for the dead.	**Ezk 24:17**	6213a
and **m** their dwellings among you;	**Ezk 25:4**	5414
“I will **m** Rabbah a pasture	**Ezk 25:5**	5414
and **m** you perish from the lands;	**Ezk 25:7**	
from her and **m** her a bare rock.	**Ezk 26:4**	5414
he will **m** siege walls against you,	**Ezk 26:8**	5414
“Also they will **m** a spoil of your	**Ezk 26:12**	7997b
“I will **m** you a bare rock;	**Ezk 26:14**	5414
I **m** you a desolate city,	**Ezk 26:19**	5414
and I will **m** you dwell in the	**Ezk 26:20**	
from Lebanon to **m** a mast for you.	**Ezk 27:5**	6213a
And they will **m** their voice heard	**Ezk 27:30**	8085
“Also they will **m** themselves bald	**Ezk 27:31**	7139
Although you **m** your heart like the	**Ezk 28:2**	5414
And **m** the fish of your rivers	**Ezk 29:4**	
and I will **m** the land of Egypt an	**Ezk 29:10**	5414
“So I will **m** the land of Egypt a	**Ezk 29:12**	5414
m them return to the land of Pathros	**Ezk 29:14**	7725
And I will **m** them so small that	**Ezk 29:15**	4591
“On that day I will **m** a horn	**Ezk 29:21**	
“I will also **m** the hordes of	**Ezk 30:10**	
I will **m** the Nile canals dry And	**Ezk 30:12**	5414
And I will **m** the land desolate And	**Ezk 30:12**	8074
m the images cease from Memphis.	**Ezk 30:13**	
“I will **m** Pathros desolate,	**Ezk 30:14**	8074
m the sword fall from his hand.	**Ezk 30:22**	
“I will also **m** the land drink the	**Ezk 32:6**	
m many peoples appalled at you,	**Ezk 32:10**	8074
“Then I will **m** their waters	**Ezk 32:14**	
“When I **m** the land of Egypt a	**Ezk 32:15**	5414
Go down and **m** your bed with the	**Ezk 32:19**	7901
them and **m** him their watchman,	**Ezk 33:2**	5414
“I will **m** the land a desolation	**Ezk 33:28**	5414
when I **m** the land a desolation and	**Ezk 33:29**	5414
m them cease from feeding sheep.	**Ezk 34:10**	
“I will **m** a covenant of peace	**Ezk 34:25**	3772
“I will **m** them and the places	**Ezk 34:26**	5414
and no one will **m** *them* afraid.	**Ezk 34:28**	2729
m you a desolation and a waste.	**Ezk 35:3**	5414
“I will **m** Mount Seir a waste	**Ezk 35:7**	5414
m you an everlasting desolation and	**Ezk 35:9**	5414
so I will **m** Myself known among	**Ezk 35:11**	3045
I will **m** you a desolation.	**Ezk 35:14**	6213a
on you, **m** flesh grow back on you,	**Ezk 37:6**	
of Judah, and **m** them one stick,	**Ezk 37:19**	6213a
m them one nation in the land,	**Ezk 37:22**	6213a
m a covenant of peace with them;	**Ezk 37:26**	3772
and **m** Myself known in the sight of	**Ezk 38:23**	3045
“My holy name I will **m** known	**Ezk 39:7**	3045
and **m** fires with the weapons and	**Ezk 39:9**	1197a
years they will **m** fires of them.	**Ezk 39:9**	1197a
will **m** fires with the weapons;	**Ezk 39:10**	1197a
seven months they will **m** a search.	**Ezk 39:14**	2713
land with no one to **m** *them* afraid.	**Ezk 39:26**	2729
m known to them the design of the	**Ezk 43:11**	3045
cleanse it and **m** atonement for it.	**Ezk 43:20**	3722a
seven days they shall **m** atonement	**Ezk 43:26**	3722a
to **m** atonement for them,”	**Ezk 45:15**	3722a
to **m** atonement for the house of	**Ezk 45:17**	3722a
shall **m** atonement for the house.	**Ezk 45:20**	3722a
Then you would **m** me forfeit my	**Da 1:10**	
if you do not **m** known to me the	**Da 2:5**	3046
do not **m** the dream known to me,	**Da 2:9**	3046
who can **m** the interpretation known	**Da 2:25**	3046
“Are you able to **m** known to me	**Da 2:26**	3046
I **m** a decree that any people,	**Da 3:29**	7761
that they might **m** known to me the	**Da 4:6**	3046
they could not **m** its interpretation	**Da 4:7**	3046
to **m** known to me the interpretation;	**Da 4:18**	3046
or **m** known its interpretation	**Da 5:8**	3046
m its interpretation known to me,	**Da 5:15**	3046
m its interpretation known to me,	**Da 5:16**	3046
m the interpretation known to him.	**Da 5:17**	3046
“I **m** a decree that in all the	**Da 6:26**	7761
he will intend to **m** alterations in	**Da 7:25**	8133
transgression, to **m** an end of sin,	**Da 9:24**	8552
sin, to **m** atonement for iniquity,	**Da 9:24**	3722a
“And he will **m** a firm covenant	**Da 9:27**	1396
will be no strength to **m** a stand.	**Da 11:15**	5975
to refine, purge and **m** them pure	**Da 11:35**	3835a
will also **m** her like a wilderness,	**Hos 2:3**	7760
M her like desert land And	**Hos 2:3**	7896
And I will **m** them a forest, And	**Hos 2:12**	7760
In that day I will also **m** a covenant	**Hos 2:18**	3772
will **m** them lie down in safety.	**Hos 2:18**	
wickedness they **m** the king glad,	**Hos 7:3**	8055
worthless oaths they **m** covenants;	**Hos 10:4**	3772
How can I **m** you like Admah?	**Hos 11:8**	5414
I will **m** you live in tents again,	**Hos 12:9**	
m for themselves molten images,	**Hos 13:2**	6213a
m Your inheritance a reproach,	**Jl 2:17**	5414
I will never again **m** you a reproach	**Jl 2:19**	5414
“Then I will **m** up to you for the	**Jl 2:25**	7999a
freewill offerings, **m** them known.	**Am 4:5**	8085
I will **m** you go into exile beyond	**Am 5:27**	
To **m** the bushel smaller and the	**Am 8:5**	6994
“That I will **m** the sun go down	**Am 8:9**	
m the earth dark in broad daylight.	**Am 8:9**	2821
And I will **m** it like *a time of*	**Am 8:10**	7760
And **m** gardens and eat their fruit.	**Am 9:14**	6213a
m you small among the nations;	**Ob 1:2**	5414
For I will **m** Samaria a heap of	**Mi 1:6**	7760
of her images I will **m** desolate,	**Mi 1:7**	7760
I must **m** a lament like the jackals	**Mi 1:8**	6213a
M yourself bald and cut off your	**Mi 1:16**	7139
m known to Jacob his rebellious act,	**Mi 3:8**	5046
With no one to **m** *them* afraid,	**Mi 4:4**	2729
“I will **m** the lame a remnant And	**Mi 4:7**	7760
For your horn I will **m** iron And	**Mi 4:13**	7760
And your hoofs I will **m** bronze,	**Mi 4:13**	7760
“So also I will **m** *you* sick,	**Mi 6:13**	2470a
will **m** a complete end of its site,	**Na 1:8**	6213a
He will **m** a complete end of it.	**Na 1:9**	6213a
throw filth on you And **m** you vile,	**Na 3:6**	5034a
Why do You **m** me see iniquity,	**Hab 1:3**	7200
to you who **m** your neighbors drink,	**Hab 2:15**	
your venom even to **m** *them* drunk	**Hab 2:15**	7937
the midst of the years **m** it known;	**Hab 3:2**	3045
For He will **m** a complete end,	**Zph 1:18**	6213a
He will **m** Nineveh a desolation,	**Zph 2:13**	7760
With no one to **m** them tremble.”	**Zph 3:13**	
I will **m** you like a signet *ring*,	**Hg 2:23**	7760
“I will **m** it go forth,”	**Zch 5:4**	
and gold, **m** an *ornate* crown and	**Zch 6:11**	6213a
will **m** you like a warrior’s sword.	**Zch 9:13**	7760
will **m** the young men flourish,	**Zch 9:17**	
And will **m** them like His majestic	**Zch 10:3**	7760
I am going to **m** Jerusalem a cup	**Zch 12:2**	7760
I will **m** Jerusalem a heavy stone	**Zch 12:3**	7760
“In that day I will **m** the clans	**Zch 12:6**	7760
‘**M** READY THE WAY OF THE LORD	**Mt 3:3**	*2090*
LORD, **M** HIS PATHS STRAIGHT!’ ”	**Mt 3:3**	*4160*
and I will **m** you fishers of men.”	**Mt 4:19**	*4160*
“**M** friends quickly with your	**Mt 5:25**	*2132*
‘YOU SHALL NOT **M** FALSE VOWS, BUT	**Mt 5:33**	*1964*
I say to you, **m** no oath at all,	**Mt 5:34**	*3660*
shall you **m** an oath by your head,	**Mt 5:36**	*3660*
cannot **m** one hair white or black.	**Mt 5:36**	*4160*
are willing, You can **m** me clean.”	**Mt 8:2**	*2511*
“Either **m** the tree good and its	**Mt 12:33**	*4160*
or **m** the tree bad and its fruit	**Mt 12:33**	*4160*
I will **m** three tabernacles here,	**Mt 17:4**	*4160*
for a pretense you **m** long prayers;	**Mt 23:14**	*4336*
sea and land to **m** one proselyte;	**Mt 23:15**	*4160*
you **m** him twice as much a son of	**Mt 23:15**	*4160*
were going away to **m** the purchase,	**Mt 25:10**	*59*
m it *as* secure as you know how.”	**Mt 27:65**	*805*
m disciples of all the nations,	**Mt 28:19**	*3100*
‘**M** READY THE WAY OF THE LORD	**Mk 1:3**	*2090*
LORD, **M** HIS PATHS STRAIGHT.’ ”	**Mk 1:3**	*4160*
m you become fishers of men.”	**Mk 1:17**	*4160*
are willing, You can **m** me clean.”	**Mk 1:40**	*2511*
and His disciples began to **m** their	**Mk 2:23**	*4160*
“Why **m** a commotion and weep?	**Mk 5:39**	*2350b*

let us **m** three tabernacles, **Mk 9:5** *4160*
what will you **m** it salty *again?* **Mk 9:50** *741*
so as to **m** ready a people prepared **Lk 1:17** *2090*
'**M** READY THE WAY OF THE LORD **Lk 3:4** *2090*
THE LORD, **M** HIS PATHS STRAIGHT. **Lk 3:4** *4160*
are willing, You can **m** me clean." **Lk 5:12** *2511*
and **m** an offering for your **Lk 5:14** *4374*
"You cannot **m** the attendants of **Lk 5:34** *4160*
let us **m** three tabernacles: **Lk 9:33** *4160*
to **m** arrangements for Him. **Lk 9:52** *2090*
the outside **m** the inside also? **Lk 11:40** *4160*
m yourselves money belts which do not **Lk 12:33** *4160*
m an effort to settle with him, **Lk 12:58** *1325*
And they could **m** no reply to this. **Lk 14:6** *470*
they all alike began to **m** excuses. **Lk 14:18** *3868*
m me as one of your hired men." **Lk 15:19** *4160*
m friends for yourselves by means **Lk 16:9** *4160*
you, the things which **m** for peace! **Lk 19:42**
UNTIL I **M** YOUR ENEMIES A **Lk 20:43** *5087*
"So **m** up your minds not to **Lk 21:14** *5087*
charges which you **m** against Him. **Lk 23:14** *2723*
'**M** STRAIGHT THE WAY OF THE LORD,' **Jn 1:23** *2116*
take Him by force to **m** Him king, **Jn 6:15** *4160*
and the truth will **m** you free." **Jn 8:32** *1659*
do You **m** Yourself out *to be?* **Jn 8:53** *4160*
a man, **m** Yourself out *to be* God." **Jn 10:33** *4160*
to him and **m** Our abode with him. **Jn 14:23** *4160*
"They will **m** you outcasts from **Jn 16:2** *4160*
to them, and will **m** it known, **Jn 17:26** *1107*
YOU WILL **M** ME FULL OF GLADNESS **Ac 2:28** *4137*
UNTIL I **M** YOUR ENEMIES A **Ac 2:35** *5087*
'**M** FOR US GODS WHO WILL GO **Ac 7:40** *4160*
directed *him* to **m** it according to the **Ac 7:44** *4160*
get up and **m** your bed." **Ac 9:34** *4766*
used to **m** while she was with them. **Ac 9:39** *4160*
will you not cease to **m** crooked **Ac 13:10** *1294*
to **m** a defense to the assembly. **Ac 19:33** *626*
'**M** haste, and get out of Jerusalem **Ac 22:18** *4692*
nation, I cheerfully **m** my defense, **Ac 24:10** *626*
before you and to **m** accusation, **Ac 24:19** *2723*
has an opportunity to **m** his defense **Ac 25:16**
and *proceeded* to **m** his defense: **Ac 26:1** *626*
to **m** my defense before you today; **Ac 26:2** *626*
unceasingly I **m** mention of you, **Ro 1:9** *4160*
"Why did you **m** me like this," **Ro 9:20** *4160*
to **m** from the same lump one vessel **Ro 9:21** *4160*
wrath and to **m** His power known, **Ro 9:22** *1107*
to **m** known the riches of His **Ro 9:23** *1107*
"I WILL **M** YOU JEALOUS BY THAT **Ro 10:19** *3863*
the Gentiles, to **m** them jealous. **Ro 11:11** *3863*
and **m** no provision for the flesh **Ro 13:14** *4160*
the Lord is able to **m** him stand. **Ro 14:4** *2476*
pursue the things which **m** for peace **Ro 14:19**
been pleased to **m** a contribution for **Ro 15:26** *4160*
and **m** them members of a prostitute? **1Co 6:15** *4160*
they did not **m** full use of it; **1Co 7:31** *2710*
any man **m** my boast an empty one. **1Co 9:15** *2758*
so as not to **m** full use of my **1Co 9:18** *2710*
discipline my body and **m** it my slave, **1Co 9:27** *1396*
Therefore I **m** known to you that **1Co 12:3** *1107*
Now I **m** known to you, brethren, **1Co 15:1** *1107*
those who ought to **m** me rejoice; **2Co 2:3** *1163*
M room for us *in your hearts* **2Co 7:2** *5562*
we *wish to* **m** known to you the **2Co 8:1** *1107*
able to **m** all grace abound to you, **2Co 9:8** *4052*
Those who desire to **m** a good **Ga 6:12** *2146a*
might **m** the two into one new man, **Eph 2:15** *2936*
to **m** known with boldness the **Eph 6:19** *1107*
will **m** everything known to you. **Eph 6:21** *1107*
m my joy complete by being of the **Php 2:2** *4137*
to whom God willed to **m** known **Col 1:27** *1107*
that I may **m** it clear in **Col 4:4** *5319*
and to **m** it your ambition to lead **1Th 4:11** *5389*
which they **m** confident assertions. **1Tm 1:7** *1226*
to **m** some return to their parents; **1Tm 5:4** *591*
they will not **m** further progress; **2Tm 3:9** *4298*
M every effort to come to me soon; **2Tm 4:9** *4704*
M every effort to come before **2Tm 4:21** *4704*
m every effort to come to me at **Ti 3:12** *4704*
UNTIL I **M** YOUR ENEMIES A **Heb 1:13** *5087*
to **m** propitiation for the sins of **Heb 2:17** *2433*
lives to **m** intercession for them. **Heb 7:25** *1793*
"THAT YOU **M** all things ACCORDING **Heb 8:5** *4160*
IS THE COVENANT THAT I WILL **M** **Heb 8:10** *1303*
cannot **m** the worshiper perfect in **Heb 9:9** *5048*
m perfect those who draw near. **Heb 10:1** *5048*
COVENANT THAT I WILL **M** WITH **Heb 10:16** *1303*
those who say such things **m** it clear **Heb 11:14** *1718*
m straight paths for your feet, **Heb 12:13** *4160*
M *sure that* your character is **Heb 13:5**
in peace by those who **m** peace. **Jas 3:18** *4160*
in business and **m** a profit." **Jas 4:13** *4160*
always *being* ready to **m** a defense **1Pe 3:15**
M sure that none of you suffers as a **1Pe 4:15** *3361*
to **m** certain about His calling **2Pe 1:10** *4160*
have not sinned, we **m** Him a liar and **1Jn 1:10** *4160*
Little children, **m** sure no one **1Jn 3:7**
that he should **m** request for this. **1Jn 5:16** *2065*
and to **m** you stand in the presence **Jude 1:24** *2476*
and I will **m** war against them with **Rv 2:16** *4170*
I will **m** them come and bow down **Rv 3:9** *4160*
and **m** *them* know that I have loved **Rv 3:9**
I will **m** him a pillar in the **Rv 3:12** *4160*
it will **m** your stomach bitter, **Rv 10:9** *4087*
of the abyss will **m** war with them, **Rv 11:7** *4160*
and went off to **m** war with the **Rv 12:17** *4160*
It was also given to him to **m** war **Rv 13:7** *4160*
to **m** an image to the beast who had **Rv 13:14** *4160*
and will **m** her desolate and naked, **Rv 17:16** *4160*
many as **m** their living by the sea, **Rv 18:17** *2038b*
assembled to **m** war against Him who **Rv 19:19** *4160*

MAKER

Can a man be pure before his **M**? **Jb 4:17** 6213a
Else my **M** would soon take me away. **Jb 32:22** 6213a
'Where is God my **M**, Who gives **Jb 35:10** 6213a
ascribe righteousness to my **M**. **Jb 36:3** 6466
Let his **m** bring near his sword. **Jb 40:19** 6213a
us kneel before the LORD our **M**. **Ps 95:6** 6213a
the LORD, **M** of heaven and earth. **Ps 115:15** 6213a
Let Israel be glad in his **M**; **Ps 149:2** 6213a
oppresses the poor taunts his **M**, **Pr 14:31** 6213a
mocks the poor taunts his **M**; **Pr 17:5** 6213a
The LORD is the **m** of them all. **Pr 22:2** 6213a
man will have regard for his **M** And **Is 17:7** 6213a
Therefore their **M** will not have **Is 27:11** 6213a
what is made would say to its **m**, **Is 29:16** 6213a
I, the LORD, am the **m** of all things, **Is 44:24** 6213a
the one who quarrels with his **M** **Is 45:9** 3335
the Holy One of Israel, and his **M**: **Is 45:11** 3335
have forgotten the LORD your **M**, **Is 51:13** 6213a
"For your husband is your **M**, **Is 54:5** 6213a
For the **M** of all is He, And Israel **Jer 10:16** 3335
For the **M** of all is He, And of the **Jer 51:19** 3335
forgotten his **M** and built palaces; **Hos 8:14** 6213a
the idol when its **m** has carved it, **Hab 2:18** 3335
For *its* **m** trusts in his *own* **Hab 2:18** 3335

MAKERS

of every work and **m** of designs. **Ex 35:35** 2803

MAKES

Or who **m** *him* mute or deaf, or **Ex 4:11** 7760
LORD **m** a distinction between Egypt **Ex 11:7** 6395
the priest who **m** atonement with it **Lv 7:7** 3722a
comes in and **m** an inspection and **Lv 14:48** 7200
of the life that **m** atonement.' **Lv 17:11** 3722a
'When a man **m** a difficult vow, he **Lv 27:2** 6381
a man or woman **m** a special vow, **Nu 6:2** 6381
"If a man **m** a vow to the LORD, or **Nu 30:2** 5087
if a woman **m** a vow to the LORD, **Nu 30:3** 5087
the LORD **m** to perish before you, **Dt 8:20** 6
who **m** his son or his daughter pass **Dt 18:10**
with you, but **m** war against you, **Dt 20:12** 6213a
who **m** an idol or a molten image, **Dt 27:15** 6213a
"The LORD kills and **m** alive; **1Sa 2:6** 2421a
"The LORD **m** poor and rich; **1Sa 2:7** 3423
my son **m** *a covenant* with the son of **1Sa 22:8** 3772
"He **m** my feet like hinds' *feet,* **2Sa 22:34** 7737b
And Your help **m** me great. **2Sa 22:36** 7235a
Who **m** the Bear, Orion and the **Jb 9:9** 6213a
"He **m** counselors walk barefoot And **Jb 12:17**
barefoot And **m** fools of judges. **Jb 12:17** 1984b
"He **m** priests walk barefoot And **Jb 12:19**
"He **m** the nations great, then **Jb 12:23** 7679
And **m** them wander in a pathless **Jb 12:24**
And He **m** them stagger like a **Jb 12:25**
of my understanding **m** me answer. **Jb 20:3**
And **m** him find it according to his **Jb 34:11**
And **m** us wiser than the birds of **Jb 35:11** 2449
And **m** the lightning of His cloud **Jb 37:15**
mounts up And **m** his nest on high? **Jb 39:27** 7311
"He **m** the depths boil like a pot; **Jb 41:31**
He **m** the sea like a jar of **Jb 41:31** 7760
"Behind him he **m** a wake to shine; **Jb 41:32**
He **m** His arrows fiery shafts. **Ps 7:13** 6466
strength And **m** my way blameless? **Ps 18:32** 5414
He **m** my feet like hinds' *feet,* And **Ps 18:33** 7737b
And Your gentleness **m** me great. **Ps 18:35** 7235a
m me lie down in green pastures; **Ps 23:2**
He **m** Lebanon skip like a calf, **Ps 29:6**
of the LORD **m** the deer to calve And **Ps 29:9**
He **m** wars to cease to the end of **Ps 46:9**
wine to drink that **m** us stagger. **Ps 60:3**
God **m** a home for the lonely; **Ps 68:6** 3427
He **m** the clouds His chariot; **Ps 104:3** 7760
He **m** the winds His messengers, **Ps 104:4** 6213a
And wine which **m** man's heart glad, **Ps 104:15** 8055
there He **m** the hungry to dwell, **Ps 107:36**
And **m** them wander in a pathless **Ps 107:40**
And **m** *his* families like a flock. **Ps 107:41** 7760
He **m** the barren woman abide in the **Ps 113:9**
Who **m** lightnings for the rain, **Ps 135:7** 6213a
Who **m** grass to grow on the **Ps 147:8**
He **m** peace in your borders; **Ps 147:14** 7760
A wise son **m** a father glad, But a **Pr 10:1** 8055
the hand of the diligent **m** rich. **Pr 10:4** 6238
blessing of the LORD that **m** rich, **Pr 10:22** 6238
down, But a good word **m** it glad. **Pr 12:25** 8055
Hope deferred **m** the heart sick, **Pr 13:12** 2470a
the wise **m** knowledge acceptable, **Pr 15:2** 3190
A joyful heart **m** a cheerful face, **Pr 15:13** 3190
A wise son **m** a father glad, But a **Pr 15:20** 8055
He **m** even his enemies to be at **Pr 16:7** 7999b
A man's gift **m** room for him And **Pr 18:16** 7337
discretion **m** him slow to anger, **Pr 19:11** 748
witness **m** a mockery of justice, **Pr 19:28** 3917b
the upright, he **m** his way sure. **Pr 21:29** 3559
wealth certainly **m** itself wings Like **Pr 23:5** 6213a
But he who **m** haste to be rich will **Pr 28:20** 213
loves wisdom **m** his father glad, **Pr 29:3** 8055
strength And **m** her arms strong. **Pr 31:17** 553
She **m** coverings for herself; **Pr 31:22** 6213a
m linen garments and sells *them,* **Pr 31:24** 6213a
For oppression **m** a wise man mad, **Ec 7:7** 1984b
enjoyment, and wine **m** life merry, **Ec 10:19** 8055
activity of God who **m** all things. **Ec 11:5** 6213a
When he **m** all the altar stones **Is 27:9** 7760
Who **m** the judges of the earth **Is 40:23** 6213a
m them like dust with his sword, **Is 41:2** 5414
Who **m** a way through the sea And a **Is 43:16** 5414
and **m** it like the form of a man, **Is 44:13** 6213a
a fir, and the rain **m** it grow. **Is 44:14** 1431
he also **m** a fire to bake bread. **Is 44:15** 8026b
He also **m** a god and worships it; **Is 44:15** 6466
he **m** it a graven image and falls **Is 44:15** 6213a
the rest of it he **m** into a god, **Is 44:17** 6213a
goldsmith, and he **m** it *into* a god; **Is 46:6** 6213a
As he **m** ready to destroy? **Is 51:13** 3559
aside from evil **m** himself a prey. **Is 59:15** 7997b
m Jerusalem a praise in the earth. **Is 62:7** 7760
He **m** lightning for the rain, And **Jer 10:13** 6213a
light He **m** it into deep darkness, **Jer 13:16** 7760
mankind And **m** flesh his strength, **Jer 17:5** 7760
laid, *So* is he who **m** a fortune, **Jer 17:11** 6213a
He **m** lightning for the rain And **Jer 51:16** 6213a
time will come, and that **m** idols, **Ezk 22:3** 6213a
themselves with *anything which* **m** **Ezk 44:18**
anyone who **m** a petition to any god **Da 6:7** 1156
man who **m** a petition to any god **Da 6:12** 1156
will come one who **m** desolate, **Da 9:27** 8074
out on the one who **m** desolate." **Da 9:27** 8074
he **m** a covenant with Assyria, **Hos 12:1** 3772
He who **m** dawn into darkness And **Am 4:13** 6213a
He rebukes the sea and **m** it dry; **Na 1:4** 3001
And **m** himself rich with loans?' **Hab 2:6** 3513
And **m** me walk on my high places. **Hab 3:19**
The LORD who **m** the storm clouds; **Zch 10:1** 6213a
If your right eye **m** you stumble, **Mt 5:29** *4624*
If your right hand **m** you stumble, **Mt 5:30** *4624*
unchastity, **m** her commit adultery; **Mt 5:32** *4160*
He **m** even the deaf to hear and **Mk 7:37** *4160*
with a spirit which **m** him mute; **Mk 9:17**
"So if the Son **m** you free, you will **Jn 8:36** *1659*
everyone who **m** himself out *to be* a **Jn 19:12** *4160*
LORD, WHO **M** THESE THINGS KNOWN **Ac 15:18** *4160*
Knowledge **m** arrogant, but love **1Co 8:1** *5448*
who then **m** me glad but the one **2Co 2:2** *2165*
what they were **m** no difference to **Ga 2:6** *1308*
"WHO **M** HIS ANGELS WINDS, AND HIS **Heb 1:7** *4160*
world **m** himself an enemy of God. **Jas 4:4** *2525*
And he **m** the earth and those who **Rv 13:12** *4160*
so that he even **m** fire come down **Rv 13:13** *4160*

MAKHELOTH

from Haradah and camped at **M**. **Nu 33:25** 4722
They journeyed from **M** and **Nu 33:26** 4722

MAKING

covenant which I am **m** between Me **Gn 9:12** 5414
by **m** me odious among the **Gn 34:30** 887
which they were **m** previously, **Ex 5:8** 6213a
today in **m** brick as previously?" **Ex 5:14** 3835b
m frogs come up on the land of **Ex 8:7**
after **m** the sin offering and the **Lv 9:22** 6213a
a hoof, thus **m** split hoofs, **Lv 11:3** 8156
the hoof, thus **m** a split hoof, **Lv 11:7** 8156
your daughter by **m** her a harlot, **Lv 19:29** 2181
down with no one **m** *you* tremble. **Lv 26:6**
be **m** amends for their iniquity, **Lv 26:43** 7521
the LORD's **m** your thigh waste away **Nu 5:21** 5414
which they are **m** against Me. **Nu 14:27** 3885b
m atonement for him that he may be **Nu 15:28** 3722a
the city that is **m** war with you **Dt 20:20** 6213a
LORD your God is **m** with you today, **Dt 29:12** 3772
am I **m** this covenant and this oath, **Dt 29:14** 3772
and integrity in **m** Abimelech king, **Jg 9:16** 4427a
me wrong by **m** war against me; **Jg 11:27** 3898a
by **m** yourselves fat with the **1Sa 2:29** 1254b
Abner was **m** himself strong in the **2Sa 3:6** 2388
m them lie down on the ground; **2Sa 8:2**
"Why is the city **m** such an uproar?" **1Ki 1:41** 1993
"Now I am **m** one request of you; **1Ki 2:16** 7592
"I am **m** one small request of you; **1Ki 2:20** 7592
sin which he did, **m** Israel sin. **1Ki 16:19**
of a medium, **m** inquiry *of it,* **1Ch 10:13** 1875
Ezra was praying and **m** confession, **Ezr 10:1** 3034
We are **m** an agreement in writing; **Ne 9:38** 3772
LORD is sure, **m** wise the simple. **Ps 19:7** 2449
upon a rock **m** my footsteps firm. **Ps 40:2** 3559
Who are **m** their paths straight: **Pr 9:15** 3474
to fail, **M** fools out of diviners, **Is 44:25** 1984b
Or the thing you are **m** *say,* **Is 45:9** 6467
earth And **m** it bear and sprout, **Is 55:10**
I am **m** My words in your mouth fire **Jer 5:14** 5414
he was, **m** something on the wheel. **Jer 18:3** 6213a
But the vessel that he was **m** of clay **Jer 18:4** 6213a
secure, with no one **m** *him* tremble. **Jer 46:27**
after piece, Without **m** a choice. **Ezk 24:6** 5307
m the interpretation known to the **Da 2:30** 3046
and found Daniel **m** petition **Da 6:11** 1156
but keeps **m** his petition three **Da 6:13** 1156
down and **m** a request of Him. **Mt 20:20** *154*
but you are **m** it a ROBBERS' DEN." **Mt 21:13** *4160*
and he kept **m** signs to them, and **Lk 1:22** *1269*
stop **m** My Father's house a place **Jn 2:16** *4160*
Jesus was **m** and baptizing more **Jn 4:1** *4160*
Father, **m** Himself equal with God. **Jn 5:18** *4160*
while they were **m** preparations, **Ac 10:10** *3903*
always in my prayers **m** request, **Ro 1:10** *1189a*
and **m** me a prisoner of the law of **Ro 7:23** *163*
as though God were **m** an appeal **2Co 5:20** *3870*
as poor yet **m** many rich, **2Co 6:10** *4148*
m mention *of you* in my prayers; **Eph 1:16** *4160*
m the most of your time, because **Eph 5:16** *1805*
singing and **m** melody with your **Eph 5:19** *5567*
m the most of the opportunity. **Col 4:5** *1805*
m mention *of you* in our prayers; **1Th 1:2** *4160*
women **m** a claim to godliness. **1Tm 2:10** *1861*
m mention of you in my prayers, **Phm 1:4** *4160*

while I was **m** every effort to **Jude 1:3** *4160*
"Behold, I am **m** all things new." **Rv 21:5** *4160*

MAKKEDAH
them as far as Azekah and **M**. **Jos 10:10** 4719
themselves in the cave at **M**. **Jos 10:16** 4719
found hidden in the cave at **M**." **Jos 10:17** 4719
the camp to Joshua at **M** in peace. **Jos 10:21** 4719
Now Joshua captured **M** on that day, **Jos 10:28** 4719
Thus he did to the king of **M** just **Jos 10:28** 4719
him passed on from **M** to Libnah, **Jos 10:29** 4719
the king of **M**, one; **Jos 12:16** 4719
Beth-dagon and Naamah and **M**; **Jos 15:41** 4719

MALACHI
of the LORD to Israel through **M**. **Mal 1:1** 4401

MALCAM
father of Jobab, Zibia, Mesha, **M**, **1Ch 8:9** 4445a
Why then has **M** taken possession of **Jer 49:1** 4445a
For **M** will go into exile Together **Jer 49:3** 4445a

MALCHIEL
sons of Beriah: Heber and **M**. **Gn 46:17** 4439
of **M**, the family of the **Nu 26:45** 4439
sons of Beriah *were* Heber and **M**, **1Ch 7:31** 4439

MALCHIELITES
of Malchiel, the family of the **M**. **Nu 26:45** 4440

MALCHIJAH
the son of Baaseiah, the son of **M**, **1Ch 6:40** 4441
the son of Pashhur, the son of **M**, **1Ch 9:12** 4441
the fifth for **M**, the sixth for **1Ch 24:9** 4441
there were Ramiah, Izziah, **M**, **Ezr 10:25** 4441
Malchijah, Mijamin, Eleazar, **M** and **Ezr 10:25** 4441
Eliezer, Isshijah, **M**, **Ezr 10:31** 4441
M the son of Harim and Hasshub the **Ne 3:11** 4441
M the son of Rechab, the **Ne 3:14** 4441
After him **M**, one of the goldsmiths, **Ne 3:31** 4441
and Pedaiah, Mishael, **M**, **Ne 8:4** 4441
Pashhur, Amariah, **M**, **Ne 10:3** 4441
the son of Pashhur, the son of **M**, **Ne 11:12** 4441
Eleazar, Uzzi, Jehohanan, **M**, **Ne 12:42** 4441
sent to him Pashhur the son of **M**, **Jer 21:1** 4441
and Pashhur the son of **M** heard the **Jer 38:1** 4441
the cistern *of* **M** the king's son, **Jer 38:6** 4441

MALCHIRAM
and **M**, Pedaiah, Shenazzar, **1Ch 3:18** 4443

MALCHI-SHUA
were Jonathan and Ishvi and **M**; **1Sa 14:49** 4444
Abinadab and **M** the sons of Saul. **1Sa 31:2** 4444
became the father of Jonathan, **M**, **1Ch 8:33** 4444
became the father of Jonathan, **M**, **1Ch 9:39** 4444
down Jonathan, Abinadab and **M**, **1Ch 10:2** 4444

MALCHUS
and the slave's name was **M**. **Jn 18:10** *3124*

MALE
m and female He created them. **Gn 1:27** 2145
He created them **m** and female, and **Gn 5:2** 2145
they shall be **m** and female. **Gn 6:19** 2145
by sevens, a **m** and his female; **Gn 7:2** 376
not clean two, a **m** and his female; **Gn 7:2** 376
the sky, by sevens, **m** and female, **Gn 7:3** 2145
ark to Noah by twos, **m** and female, **Gn 7:9** 2145
m and female of all flesh, **Gn 7:16** 2145
donkeys and **m** and female servants **Gn 12:16** 5650
every **m** among you shall be **Gn 17:10** 2145
"And every **m** among you who is **Gn 17:12** 2145
"But an uncircumcised **m** who is **Gn 17:14** 2145
every **m** among the men of Abraham's **Gn 17:23** 2145
oxen and **m** and female servants, **Gn 20:14** 5650
the striped and spotted **m** goats and **Gn 30:35** 8495
female and **m** servants and camels **Gn 30:43** 5650
the **m** goats which were mating *were* **Gn 31:10** 6260
all the **m** goats which are mating **Gn 31:12** 6260
flocks and **m** and female servants; **Gn 32:5** 5650
female goats and twenty **m** goats, **Gn 32:14** 8495
female donkeys and ten **m** donkeys. **Gn 32:15** 5895
every **m** of you be circumcised, **Gn 34:15** 2145
every **m** among us be circumcised **Gn 34:22** 2145
and every **m** was circumcised, **Gn 34:24** 2145
city unawares, and killed every **m**. **Gn 34:25** 2145
tunic, and slaughtered a **m** goat and **Gn 37:31** 8163b
be an unblemished **m** a year old; **Ex 12:5** 2145
your **m** or your female servant or **Ex 20:10** 5650
neighbor's wife or his **m** servant **Ex 20:17** 5650
not to go free as the **m** slaves do. **Ex 21:7** 5650
a man strikes his **m** or female slave **Ex 21:20** 5650
the eye of his **m** or female slave, **Ex 21:26** 5650
a tooth of his **m** or female slave, **Ex 21:27** 5650
the ox gores a **m** or female slave, **Ex 21:32** 5650
to Me, and all your **m** livestock, **Ex 34:19** 2145
offer it, a **m** without defect; **Lv 1:3** 2145
shall offer it a **m** without defect. **Lv 1:10** 2145
of the herd, whether **m** or female, **Lv 3:1** 2145
he shall offer it, **m** or female, **Lv 3:6** 2145
a goat, a **m** without defect. **Lv 4:23** 2145
hand on the head of the **m** goat and **Lv 4:24** 8163b
'Every **m** among the sons of Aaron **Lv 6:18** 2145
'Every **m** among the priests may eat **Lv 6:29** 2145
'Every **m** among the priests may eat **Lv 7:6** 2145
'Take a **m** goat for a sin offering, **Lv 9:3** 8163b
gives birth and bears a **m** *child,* **Lv 12:2** 2145
a child, whether a **m** or a female. **Lv 12:7** 2145
take two **m** lambs without defect, **Lv 14:10** 3532
the priest shall take the one **m** lamb **Lv 14:12** 3532
"Next he shall slaughter the **m** lamb **Lv 14:13** 3532
then he is to take one **m** lamb for **Lv 14:21** 3532
whether a **m** or a female, **Lv 15:33** 2145
two **m** goats for a sin offering and **Lv 16:5** 8163b
a **m** as one lies with a female; **Lv 18:22** 2145
a **m** as those who lie with a woman, **Lv 20:13** 2145

a **m** without defect from the cattle, **Lv 22:19** 2145
you shall offer a **m** lamb one year **Lv 23:12** 3532
year old **m** lambs without defect, **Lv 23:18** 3532
'You shall also offer one **m** goat **Lv 23:19** 8163b
and two **m** lambs one year old for a **Lv 23:19** 3532
and your **m** and female slaves, **Lv 25:6** 5650
'As for your **m** and female slaves **Lv 25:44** 5650
may acquire **m** and female slaves **Lv 25:44** 5650
'If your valuation is of the **m** **Lv 27:3** 2145
then your valuation for the **m** shall **Lv 27:5** 2145
five shekels of silver for the **m**, **Lv 27:6** 2145
old and upward, if it is a **m**, **Lv 27:7** 2145
to the number of names, every **m**, **Nu 1:2** 2145
every **m** from twenty years old and **Nu 1:20** 2145
every **m** from twenty years old and **Nu 1:22** 2145
every **m** from a month old and **Nu 3:15** 2145
in the numbering of every **m** from a **Nu 3:22** 2145
In the numbering of every **m** from a **Nu 3:28** 2145
in the numbering of every **m** from a **Nu 3:34** 2145
m from a month old and upward, **Nu 3:39** 2145
"Number every firstborn **m** of the **Nu 3:40** 2145
shall send away both **m** and female; **Nu 5:3** 2145
and shall bring a **m** lamb a year **Nu 6:12** 3532
one **m** lamb a year old without **Nu 6:14** 3532
one ram, one **m** lamb one year old, **Nu 7:15** 3532
one **m** goat for a sin offering; **Nu 7:16** 8163b
two oxen, five rams, five **m** goats, **Nu 7:17** 6260
goats, five **m** lambs one year old. **Nu 7:17** 3532
one ram, one **m** lamb one year old, **Nu 7:21** 3532
one **m** goat for a sin offering; **Nu 7:22** 8163b
two oxen, five rams, five **m** goats, **Nu 7:23** 6260
goats, five **m** lambs one year old. **Nu 7:23** 3532
one ram, one **m** lamb one year old, **Nu 7:27** 3532
one **m** goat for a sin offering; **Nu 7:28** 8163b
two oxen, five rams, five **m** goats, **Nu 7:29** 6260
goats, five **m** lambs one year old. **Nu 7:29** 3532
one ram, one **m** lamb one year old, **Nu 7:33** 3532
one **m** goat for a sin offering; **Nu 7:34** 8163b
two oxen, five rams, five **m** goats, **Nu 7:35** 6260
goats, five **m** lambs one year old. **Nu 7:35** 3532
one ram, one **m** lamb one year old, **Nu 7:39** 3532
one **m** goat for a sin offering; **Nu 7:40** 8163b
two oxen, five rams, five **m** goats, **Nu 7:41** 6260
goats, five **m** lambs one year old. **Nu 7:41** 3532
one ram, one **m** lamb one year old, **Nu 7:45** 3532
one **m** goat for a sin offering; **Nu 7:46** 8163b
two oxen, five rams, five **m** goats, **Nu 7:47** 6260
goats, five **m** lambs one year old. **Nu 7:47** 3532
one ram, one **m** lamb one year old, **Nu 7:51** 3532
one **m** goat for a sin offering; **Nu 7:52** 8163b
two oxen, five rams, five **m** goats, **Nu 7:53** 6260
goats, five **m** lambs one year old. **Nu 7:53** 3532
one ram, one **m** lamb one year old, **Nu 7:57** 3532
one **m** goat for a sin offering; **Nu 7:58** 8163b
two oxen, five rams, five **m** goats, **Nu 7:59** 6260
goats, five **m** lambs one year old. **Nu 7:59** 3532
one ram, one **m** lamb one year old, **Nu 7:63** 3532
one **m** goat for a sin offering; **Nu 7:64** 8163b
two oxen, five rams, five **m** goats, **Nu 7:65** 6260
goats, five **m** lambs one year old. **Nu 7:65** 3532
one ram, one **m** lamb one year old, **Nu 7:69** 3532
one **m** goat for a sin offering; **Nu 7:70** 8163b
two oxen, five rams, five **m** goats, **Nu 7:71** 6260
goats, five **m** lambs one year old. **Nu 7:71** 3532
one ram, one **m** lamb one year old, **Nu 7:75** 3532
one **m** goat for a sin offering; **Nu 7:76** 8163b
two oxen, five rams, five **m** goats, **Nu 7:77** 6260
goats, five **m** lambs one year old. **Nu 7:77** 3532
one ram, one **m** lamb one year old, **Nu 7:81** 3532
one **m** goat for a sin offering; **Nu 7:82** 8163b
two oxen, five rams, five **m** goats, **Nu 7:83** 6260
goats, five **m** lambs one year old. **Nu 7:83** 3532
the **m** lambs one year old with **Nu 7:87** 3532
and the **m** goats for a sin offering **Nu 7:87** 8163b
all the rams 60, the **m** goats 60, **Nu 7:88** 6260
60, the **m** lambs one year old 60. **Nu 7:88** 3532
ram, or for each of the **m** lambs, **Nu 15:11** 3532
and one **m** goat for a sin offering. **Nu 15:24** 8163b
every **m** shall eat it. **Nu 18:10** 2145
m from a month old and upward, **Nu 26:62** 2145
two **m** lambs one year old without **Nu 28:3** 3532
two **m** lambs one year old without **Nu 28:9** 3532
seven **m** lambs one year old without **Nu 28:11** 3532
'And one **m** goat for a sin offering **Nu 28:15** 8163b
and seven **m** lambs one year old, **Nu 28:19** 3532
and one **m** goat for a sin offering to **Nu 28:22** 8163b
ram, seven **m** lambs one year old; **Nu 28:27** 3532
one **m** goat to make atonement for **Nu 28:30** 8163b
and seven **m** lambs one year old **Nu 29:2** 3532
one **m** goat for a sin offering, **Nu 29:5** 8163b
ram, seven **m** lambs one year old, **Nu 29:8** 3532
one **m** goat for a sin offering, **Nu 29:11** 8163b
fourteen **m** lambs one year old, **Nu 29:13** 3532
and one **m** goat for a sin offering, **Nu 29:16** 8163b
fourteen **m** lambs one year old **Nu 29:17** 3532
and one **m** goat for a sin offering, **Nu 29:19** 8163b
fourteen **m** lambs one year old **Nu 29:20** 3532
and one **m** goat for a sin offering, **Nu 29:22** 8163b
fourteen **m** lambs one year old **Nu 29:23** 3532
and one **m** goat for a sin offering, **Nu 29:25** 8163b
fourteen **m** lambs one year old **Nu 29:26** 3532
and one **m** goat for a sin offering, **Nu 29:28** 8163b
fourteen **m** lambs one year old **Nu 29:29** 3532
and one **m** goat for a sin offering, **Nu 29:31** 8163b
fourteen **m** lambs one year old **Nu 29:32** 3532
and one **m** goat for a sin offering, **Nu 29:34** 8163b
seven **m** lambs one year old without **Nu 29:36** 3532
and one **m** goat for a sin offering, **Nu 29:38** 8163b
Moses, and they killed every **m**. **Nu 31:7** 2145

every **m** among the little ones, **Nu 31:17** 2145
the likeness of **m** or female, **Dt 4:16** 2145
your daughter or your **m** servant **Dt 5:14** 5650
so that your **m** servant and your **Dt 5:14** 5650
m servant or his female servant, **Dt 5:21** 5650
there will be no **m** or female **Dt 7:14**
your **m** and female servants, **Dt 12:12** 5650
and your **m** and female servants, **Dt 12:18** 5650
and your **m** and female servants **Dt 16:11** 5650
and your **m** and female servants **Dt 16:14** 5650
or has his **m** organ cut off shall **Dt 23:1** 8212
enemies as **m** and female slaves, **Dt 28:68** 5650
were the **m** descendants of Manasseh **Jos 17:2** 2145
your **m** servants and your female **1Sa 8:16** 5650
one **m** of any who belong to him." **1Sa 25:22**
8366, 7023
morning light *as much as* one **m**." **1Sa 25:34**
8366, 7023
had struck down every **m** in Edom **1Ki 11:15** 2145
he had cut off every **m** in Edom), **1Ki 11:16** 2145
off from Jeroboam every **m** person, **1Ki 14:10**
8366, 7023
m cult prostitutes in the land. **1Ki 14:24** 6945
He also put away the **m** cult **1Ki 15:12** 6945
he did not leave a single **m**, **1Ki 16:11**
8366, 7023
will cut off from Ahab every **m**, **1Ki 21:21**
8366, 7023
oxen and **m** and female servants? **2Ki 5:26** 5650
cut off from Ahab every **m** person **2Ki 9:8**
8366, 7023
also broke down the houses of the **m** **2Ki 23:7**
7,700 rams and 7,700 **m** goats. **2Ch 17:11** 8495
Jerusalem for **m** and female slaves. **2Ch 28:10** 5650
and seven **m** goats for a sin offering **2Ch 29:21** 6842
Then they brought the **m** goats of **2Ch 29:23** 8163b
to distribute portions to every **m** **2Ch 31:19** 2145
And all the **m** and female singers **2Ch 35:25**
their **m** and female servants who **Ezr 2:65** 5650
for all Israel 12 **m** goats, **Ezr 6:17** 6841
12 **m** goats for a sin offering, **Ezr 8:35** 6842
their **m** and their female servants, **Ne 7:67** 5650
they had 245 **m** and female singers. **Ne 7:67**
the claim of my **m** or female slaves **Jb 31:13** 5650
Nor **m** goats out of your folds. **Ps 50:9** 6260
Or drink the blood of **m** goats? **Ps 50:13** 6260
an offering of bulls with **m** goats. **Ps 66:15** 6260
strutting rooster, the **m** goat also, **Pr 30:31** 8495
I bought **m** and female slaves and **Ec 2:7** 5650
for myself **m** and female singers **Ec 2:8**
as **m** servants and female servants; **Is 14:2** 5650
and see If a **m** can give birth. **Jer 30:6** 2145
man should set free his **m** servant **Jer 34:9** 5650
man should set free his **m** servant **Jer 34:10** 5650
and took back the **m** servants **Jer 34:11** 5650
them into subjection for **m** servants **Jer 34:11** 5650
each man took back his **m** servant **Jer 34:16** 5650
into subjection to be your **m** servants **Jer 34:16** 5650
Be also like **m** goats at the head **Jer 50:8** 6260
Like rams together with **m** goats. **Jer 51:40** 6260
and made for yourself **m** images **Ezk 16:17** 2145
between the rams and the **m** goats. **Ezk 34:17** 6260
offer a **m** goat without blemish **Ezk 43:22** 8163b
a **m** goat daily for a sin offering. **Ezk 45:23** 8163b
a **m** goat was coming from the west **Da 8:5** 6842
Then the **m** goat magnified *himself* **Da 8:8** 6842
Even on the **m** and female servants **Jl 2:29** 5650
And I will punish the **m** goats; **Zch 10:3** 6260
swindler who has a **m** in his flock and **Mal 1:14** 2145
slew all the **m** children who were in **Mt 2:16** *3816*
beginning MADE THEM **M** AND FEMALE **Mt 19:4** *733b*
God MADE THEM **M** AND FEMALE. **Mk 10:6** *733b*
"EVERY *firstborn* **M** THAT OPENS **Lk 2:23** *733b*
there is neither **m** nor female; **Ga 3:28** *733b*
gave birth to a son, a **m** *child,* **Rv 12:5** *733b*
who gave birth to the **m** *child.* **Rv 12:13** *733b*

MALES
let all his **m** be circumcised, **Ex 12:48** 2145
the **m** belong to the LORD. **Ex 13:12** 2145
I sacrifice to the LORD the **m**, **Ex 13:15** 2145
"Three times a year all your **m** **Ex 23:17** 2138
"Three times a year all your **m** **Ex 34:23** 2138
and all the firstborn **m** by the **Nu 3:43** 2145
all the firstborn **m** that are born of **Dt 15:19** 2145
"Three times in a year all your **m** **Dt 16:16** 2138
who came out of Egypt who were **m**, **Jos 5:4** 2145
to the **m** from thirty years old and **2Ch 31:16** 2145
Zechariah and with him 150 **m** *who* **Ezr 8:3** 2145
of Zerahiah and 200 **m** with him; **Ezr 8:4** 2145
of Jahaziel and 300 **m** with him; **Ezr 8:5** 2145
son of Jonathan and 50 **m** with him; **Ezr 8:6** 2145
son of Athaliah and 70 **m** with him; **Ezr 8:7** 2145
son of Michael and 80 **m** with him; **Ezr 8:8** 2145
son of Jehiel and 218 **m** with him; **Ezr 8:9** 2145
of Josiphiah and 160 **m** with him; **Ezr 8:10** 2145
son of Bebai and 28 **m** with him; **Ezr 8:11** 2145
of Hakkatan and 110 **m** with him; **Ezr 8:12** 2145
and Shemaiah, and 60 **m** with them; **Ezr 8:13** 2145
and Zabbud, and 70 **m** with them. **Ezr 8:14** 2145

MALICE
But Jesus perceived their **m**, **Mt 22:18** *4189*
envy, murder, strife, deceit, **m**; **Ro 1:29** *2550*
the leaven of **m** and wickedness, **1Co 5:8** *2549*
away from you, along with all **m**. **Eph 4:31** *2549*
anger, wrath, **m**, slander, *and* **Col 3:8** *2549*
spending our life in **m** and envy, **Ti 3:3** *2549*
putting aside all **m** and all deceit **1Pe 2:1** *2549*

MALICIOUS
a wicked man to be a **m** witness. Ex 23:1 2555
"If a **m** witness rises up against Dt 19:16 2555
M witnesses rise up; Ps 35:11 2555
be dignified, not **m** gossips, 1Tm 3:11 *1228*
irreconcilable, **m** gossips, 2Tm 3:3 *1228*
in their behavior, not **m** gossips nor Ti 2:3 *1228*
MALICIOUSLY
who hate me without cause wink **m**. Ps 35:19 7169, 5869
men who had **m** accused Daniel, Da 6:24 399, 7170
MALIGN
how much more *will they* **m** Mt 10:25
to **m** no one, to be peaceable, Ti 3:2 *987*
of dissipation, and they **m** *you;* 1Pe 4:4 *987*
MALIGNANCY
is used, the mark is a leprous **m**, Lv 13:51 3992
occurs, for it is a leprous **m**; Lv 13:52 3992
MALIGNANT
it is a **m** mark in the house; Lv 14:44 3992
it became a loathsome and **m** sore Rv 16:2 *4190*
MALIGNED
the way of the truth will be **m**; 2Pe 2:2 *987*
MALLOTHI
and Romamti-ezer, Joshbekashah, **M**, 1Ch 25:4 4413
for the nineteenth to **M**, 1Ch 25:26 4413
MALLOW
Who pluck **m** by the bushes, And Jb 30:4 4408
MALLUCH
the son of Abdi, the son of **M**, 1Ch 6:44 4409
Meshullam, **M** and Adaiah, Jashub, Ezr 10:29 4409
Benjamin, **M** *and* Shemariah; Ezr 10:32 4409
Hattush, Shebaniah, **M**, Ne 10:4 4409
M, Harim, Baanah. Ne 10:27 4409
Amariah, **M**, Hattush, Ne 12:2 4409
MALLUCHI
M, Jonathan; of Shebaniah, Joseph; Ne 12:14 4424b
MALTA
out that the island was called **M**. Ac 28:1 *3194*
MAMRE
came and dwelt by the oaks of **M**, Gn 13:18 4471
by the oaks of **M** the Amorite, Gn 14:13 4471
went with me, Aner, Eshcol, and **M**; Gn 14:24 4471
appeared to him by the oaks of **M**, Gn 18:1 4471
was in Machpelah, which faced **M**, Gn 23:17 4471
the field at Machpelah facing **M** Gn 23:19 4471
of Zohar the Hittite, facing **M**, Gn 25:9 4471
father Isaac at **M** of Kiriath-arba Gn 35:27 4471
of Machpelah, which is before **M**, Gn 49:30 4471
the field of Machpelah before **M**, Gn 50:13 4471
MAN
"Let Us make **m** in Our image, Gn 1:26 120
God created **m** in His own image, Gn 1:27 120
was no **m** to cultivate the ground. Gn 2:5 120
formed **m** of dust from the ground, Gn 2:7 120
and **m** became a living being. Gn 2:7 120
placed the **m** whom He had formed. Gn 2:8 120
Then the LORD God took the **m** and Gn 2:15 120
The LORD God commanded the **m**, Gn 2:16 120
is not good for the **m** to be alone; Gn 2:18 120
and brought *them* to the **m** to see Gn 2:19 120
the **m** called a living creature, Gn 2:19 120
m gave names to all the cattle, Gn 2:20 120
a deep sleep to fall upon the **m**, Gn 2:21 120
rib which He had taken from the **m**, Gn 2:22 120
the man, and brought her to the **m**. Gn 2:22 120
The **m** said, "This is now bone of my Gn 2:23 120
Because she was taken out of **M**." Gn 2:23 376
a **m** shall leave his father and his Gn 2:24 376
the **m** and his wife were both naked Gn 2:25 120
and the **m** and his wife hid Gn 3:8 120
Then the LORD God called to the **m**, Gn 3:9 120
m said, "The woman whom You Gn 3:12 120
the **m** called his wife's name Eve, Gn 3:20 120
the **m** has become like one of Us, Gn 3:22 120
So He drove the **m** out; Gn 3:24 120
the **m** had relations with his wife Gn 4:1 120
I have killed a **m** for wounding me; Gn 4:23 376
In the day when God created **m**, Gn 5:1 120
He blessed them and named them **M** Gn 5:2 120
shall not strive with **m** forever, Gn 6:3 120
that the wickedness of **m** was great Gn 6:5 120
that He had made **m** on the earth, Gn 6:6 120
"I will blot out **m** whom I have Gn 6:7 120
from **m** to animals to creeping Gn 6:7 120
Noah was a righteous **m**, Gn 6:9 376
from **m** to animals to creeping Gn 7:23 120
curse the ground on account of **m**, Gn 8:21 120
And from *every* **m**, from every man's Gn 9:5 120
I will require the life of **m**. Gn 9:5 120
By **m** his blood shall be shed, Gn 9:6 120
For in the image of God He made **m**. Gn 9:6 120
"This **m** will not be your heir; Gn 15:4 376
He will be a wild donkey of a **m**, Gn 16:12 120
born to a **m** one hundred years old? Gn 17:17 1121
who have not had relations with **m**; Gn 19:8 376
and there is not a **m** on earth to Gn 19:31 376
you are a dead **m** because of the Gn 20:3 376
no **m** had had relations with her; Gn 24:16 376
m was gazing at her in silence, Gn 24:21 376
the **m** took a gold ring Gn 24:22 376
Then the **m** bowed low and worshiped Gn 24:26 376
outside to the **m** at the spring. Gn 24:29 376
"This is what the **m** said to me," Gn 24:30 376
man said to me," he went to the **m**; Gn 24:30 376
So the **m** entered the house. Gn 24:32 376
"Will you go with this **m**?" Gn 24:58 376
the camels and followed the **m**. Gn 24:61 376
"Who is that **m** walking in the Gn 24:65 376
an old **m** and satisfied *with life;* Gn 25:8 2205
skillful hunter, a **m** of the field, Gn 25:27 376
but Jacob was a peaceful **m**, Gn 25:27 376
"He who touches this **m** or his wife Gn 26:11 376
and the **m** became rich, and Gn 26:13 376
Esau my brother is a hairy **m** and I Gn 27:11 376
a hairy man and I am a smooth **m**. Gn 27:11 376
to give her to another **m**; Gn 29:19 376
m became exceedingly prosperous, Gn 30:43 376
although no **m** is with us, Gn 31:50 376
and a **m** wrestled with him until Gn 32:24 376
m did not delay to do the thing, Gn 34:19 5288
his people, an old **m** of ripe age; Gn 35:29 2205
A **m** found him, and behold, he Gn 37:15 376
and the **m** asked him, Gn 37:15 376
Then the **m** said, Gn 37:17 376
"I am with child by the **m** to whom Gn 38:25 376
so he became a successful **m**. Gn 39:2 376
each **m** with his *own* dream *and* each Gn 40:5 376
look for a **m** discerning and wise, Gn 41:33 376
"Can we find a **m** like this, in Gn 41:38 376
"We are all sons of one **m**; Gn 42:11 376
of one **m** in the land of Canaan; Gn 42:13 376
"The **m**, the lord of the land, Gn 42:30 376
"The **m**, the lord of the land, Gn 42:33 376
"The **m** solemnly warned us, Gn 43:3 376
for the **m** said to us, Gn 43:5 376
by telling the **m** whether you still Gn 43:6 376
"The **m** questioned particularly Gn 43:7 376
carry down to the **m** as a present, Gn 43:11 376
also, and arise, return to the **m**; Gn 43:13 376
compassion in the sight of the **m**, Gn 43:14 376
So the **m** did as Joseph said, and Gn 43:17 376
Then the **m** brought the men into Gn 43:24 376
each **m** lowered his sack to the Gn 44:11 376
and each **m** opened his sack. Gn 44:11 376
and when each **m** loaded his donkey, Gn 44:13 376
Do you not know that such a **m** as I Gn 44:15 376
The **m** in whose possession the cup Gn 44:17 376
So there was no **m** with him when Gn 45:1 376
Now a **m** from the house of Levi Ex 2:1 376
that you have left the **m** behind? Ex 2:20 376
was willing to dwell with the **m**, Ex 2:21 376
there were gnats on **m** and beast. Ex 8:17 120
there were gnats on **m** and beast. Ex 8:18 120
breaking out with sores on **m** and Ex 9:9 120
breaking out with sores on **m** and Ex 9:10 120
Every **m** and beast that is found in Ex 9:19 120
on **m** and on beast and on every Ex 9:22 120
land of Egypt, both **m** and beast; Ex 9:25 120
long will this **m** be a snare to us? Ex 10:7 376
each **m** ask from his neighbor Ex 11:2 376
the **m** Moses *himself* was greatly Ex 11:3 376
bark, whether against **m** or beast, Ex 11:7 376
to what each **m** should eat, Ex 12:4 376
land of Egypt, both **m** and beast; Ex 12:12 120
of Israel, both of **m** and beast; Ex 13:2 120
and every firstborn of **m** among Ex 13:13 120
of **m** and the firstborn of beast. Ex 13:15 120
every **m** as much as he should eat; Ex 16:16 376
every **m** gathered as much as he Ex 16:18 376
"Let no **m** leave any of it until Ex 16:19 376
every **m** as much as he should eat; Ex 16:21 376
Remain every **m** in his place; Ex 16:29 376
let no **m** go out of his place on Ex 16:29 376
between a **m** and his neighbor and Ex 18:16 376
whether beast or **m**, Ex 19:13 376
out as a free **m** without payment. Ex 21:2 2670
I will not go out as a free **m**,' Ex 21:5 2670
"If a **m** sells his daughter as Ex 21:7 376
"He who strikes a **m** so that he Ex 21:12 376
a **m** acts presumptuously toward his Ex 21:14 376
"He who kidnaps a **m**, Ex 21:16 376
"If a **m** strikes his male or Ex 21:20 376
"If a **m** strikes the eye of Ex 21:26 376
ox gores a **m** or a woman to death, Ex 21:28 376
it and it kills a **m** or a woman, Ex 21:29 376
"If a **m** opens a pit, or digs Ex 21:33 376
"If a **m** steals an ox or a sheep and Ex 22:1 376
"If a **m** lets a field or vineyard Ex 22:5 376
"If a **m** gives his neighbor money Ex 22:7 376
a **m** gives his neighbor a donkey, Ex 22:10 376
"If a **m** borrows *anything* from Ex 22:14 376
"If a **m** seduces a virgin who Ex 22:16 376
not join your hand with a wicked **m** Ex 23:1 7563
nor shall you be partial to a poor **m** Ex 23:3 1800b
from every **m** whose heart moves him Ex 25:2 376
the **m** who brought us up from the Ex 32:1 376
the **m** who brought us up from the Ex 32:23 376
'Every **m** *of you* put his sword upon Ex 32:27 376
and kill every **m** his brother, Ex 32:27 376
brother, and every **m** his friend, Ex 32:27 376
and every **m** his neighbor.' " Ex 32:27 376
for every **m** has been against his son Ex 32:29 376
just as a **m** speaks to his friend. Ex 33:11 376
Joshua, the son of Nun, a young **m**, Ex 33:11 5288
for no **m** can see Me and live!" Ex 33:20 120
"No **m** is to come up with you, Ex 34:3 376
nor let any **m** be seen anywhere on Ex 34:3 376
and no **m** shall covet your land Ex 34:24 376
every skillful **m** among you come, Ex 35:10 2450, 3820
so *did* every **m** who presented an Ex 35:22 376
Every **m**, who had in his Ex 35:23 376
and every **m** who had in his Ex 35:24 376
"Let no **m** or woman any longer Ex 36:6 376
'When any **m** of you brings an Lv 1:2 120
in whatever matter a **m** may speak Lv 5:4 120
any one of the things a **m** may do; Lv 6:3 120
"When a **m** has on the skin of his Lv 13:2 120
infection of leprosy is on a **m**, Lv 13:9 120
"Now if a **m** or woman has an Lv 13:29 376
"When a **m** or a woman has Lv 13:38 376
if a **m** loses the hair of his head, Lv 13:40 376
he is a leprous **m**, he is unclean. Lv 13:44 376
shall present the **m** to be cleansed Lv 14:11 376
m has a discharge from his body, Lv 15:2 376
which the **m** with the discharge has Lv 15:6
'Or if the **m** with the discharge Lv 15:8
'Now when the **m** with the discharge Lv 15:13
'Now if a **m** has a seminal emission, Lv 15:16 376
'If a **m** lies with a woman *so that* Lv 15:18 376
'If a **m** actually lies with Lv 15:24 376
the **m** who has a seminal emission Lv 15:32
m who lies with an unclean woman. Lv 15:33 376
of a **m** who *stands* in readiness. Lv 16:21 376
"Any **m** from the house of Israel Lv 17:3 376
is to be reckoned to that **m**. Lv 17:4 376
He has shed blood and that **m** shall Lv 17:4 376
'Any **m** from the house of Israel, Lv 17:8 376
that **m** also shall be cut off from Lv 17:9 376
any **m** from the house of Israel, Lv 17:10 376
any **m** from the sons of Israel, Lv 17:13 376
a **m** may live if he does them; Lv 18:5 120
The wages of a hired **m** are not to Lv 19:13 7916
'You shall not curse a deaf **m**, Lv 19:14 2795
'Now if a **m** lies carnally with a Lv 19:20 376
is a slave acquired for *another* **m**, Lv 19:20 376
'Any **m** from the sons of Israel or Lv 20:2 376
will also set My face against that **m** Lv 20:3 376
should ever disregard that **m** when Lv 20:4 376
that **m** and against his family, Lv 20:5 376
there is a **m** who commits adultery Lv 20:10 376
m who lies with his father's wife, Lv 20:11 376
m who lies with his daughter-in-law, Lv 20:12 376
m who lies with a male as those Lv 20:13 376
m who marries a woman and her Lv 20:14 376
is a **m** who lies with an animal, Lv 20:15 376
there is a **m** who takes his sister, Lv 20:17 376
there is a **m** who lies with a menstruous Lv 20:18 376
is a **m** who lies with his uncle's wife Lv 20:20 376
a **m** who takes his brother's wife, Lv 20:21 376
m or a woman who is a medium or Lv 20:27 376
'No **m** of your offspring throughout Lv 21:17 376
a blind **m**, or a lame man, or he Lv 21:18 376
a blind man, or a lame **m**, Lv 21:18 6455
or a **m** who has a broken foot or Lv 21:19 376
'No **m** among the descendants of Lv 21:21 376
'If any **m** among all your Lv 22:3 376
'No **m** of the descendants of Aaron Lv 22:4 376
or if a **m** has a seminal emission, Lv 22:4 376
if a **m** touches any teeming things by Lv 22:5 376
any **m** by whom he is made unclean, Lv 22:5 120
hired **m** shall not eat of the holy *gift*. Lv 22:10 7916
'But if a **m** eats a holy *gift* Lv 22:14 376
'Any **m** of the house of Israel or Lv 22:18 376
'When a **m** offers a sacrifice Lv 22:21 376
son and a **m** of Israel struggled with Lv 24:10 376
'If a **m** takes the life of any Lv 24:17 376
'If a **m** injures his neighbor, Lv 24:19 376
just as he has injured a **m**, Lv 24:20 120
kills a **m** shall be put to death. Lv 24:21 120
hired **m** and your foreign resident, Lv 25:6 7916
'Or in case a **m** has no kinsman, Lv 25:26 376
to the **m** to whom he sold it, Lv 25:27 376
if a **m** sells a dwelling house in a Lv 25:29 376
'He shall be with you as a hired **m**, Lv 25:40 7916
It is like the days of a hired **m** *that* Lv 25:50 7916
'Like a **m** hired year by year he Lv 25:53 7916
'When a **m** makes a difficult vow, Lv 27:2 376
'Now if a **m** consecrates his house Lv 27:14 376
if a **m** consecrates to the LORD Lv 27:16 376
has sold the field to another **m**, Lv 27:20 376
the LORD, no **m** may consecrate it; Lv 27:26 376
anything which a **m** sets apart to Lv 27:28 376
of **m** or animal or of the fields of Lv 27:28 120
a **m** wishes to redeem part of his Lv 27:31 376
there shall be a **m** of each tribe, Nu 1:4 376
camp, each **m** by his own camp, Nu 1:52 376
and each **m** by his own standard, Nu 1:52 376
set out, every **m** in his place by Nu 2:17 376
firstborn in Israel, from **m** to beast. Nu 3:13 120
and you shall assign *each* **m** by Nu 4:32 376
'When a **m** or woman commits any of Nu 5:6 376
'But if the **m** has no relative to Nu 5:8 376
any **m** gives to the priest, Nu 5:10 376
and a **m** has intercourse with her Nu 5:13 376
the **m** shall then bring his wife to Nu 5:15 376
"If no **m** has lain with you and if Nu 5:19 376
m other than your husband has had Nu 5:20 376
a **m** and he is jealous of his wife, Nu 5:30 376
the **m** will be free from guilt, Nu 5:31 376
a **m** or woman makes a special vow, Nu 6:2 376
'But if a **m** dies very suddenly Nu 6:9 376
each **m** according to his service." Nu 7:5 376
'But the **m** who is clean and is not Nu 9:13 376
That **m** will bear his sin. Nu 9:13 376
each **m** at the doorway of his tent; Nu 11:10 376
m ran and told Moses and said, Nu 11:27 5288
(Now the **m** Moses was very humble, Nu 12:3 376
more than any **m** who was on the Nu 12:3 120
you shall send a **m** from each of Nu 13:2 376
You slay this people as one **m**, Nu 14:15 376
they found a **m** gathering wood on Nu 15:32 376
m shall surely be put to death; Nu 15:35 376

and the **m** whom the LORD chooses	**Nu 16:7**	376
of all flesh, when one **m** sins,	**Nu 16:22**	376
the rod of the **m** whom I choose will	**Nu 17:5**	376
looked, and each **m** took his rod.	**Nu 17:9**	376
of all flesh, whether **m** or animal,	**Nu 18:15**	120
of **m** you shall surely redeem,	**Nu 18:15**	120
'Now a **m** who is clean shall gather	**Nu 19:9**	376
the body of a **m** who has died,	**Nu 19:13**	120
the law when a **m** dies in a tent:	**Nu 19:14**	120
'But the **m** who is unclean and does	**Nu 19:20**	376
that if a serpent bit any **m**,	**Nu 21:9**	376
"God is not a **m**, that He should lie	**Nu 23:19**	376
He should lie, Nor a son of **m**,	**Nu 23:19**	120
oracle of the **m** whose eye is opened	**Nu 24:3**	1397
oracle of the **m** whose eye is opened	**Nu 24:15**	1397
the **m** of Israel into the tent and	**Nu 25:8**	376
the **m** of Israel and the woman,	**Nu 25:8**	376
the name of the slain **m** of Israel	**Nu 25:14**	376
But among these there was not a **m**	**Nu 26:64**	376
And not a **m** was left of them,	**Nu 26:65**	376
'If a **m** dies and has no son, then	**Nu 27:8**	376
appoint a **m** over the congregation,	**Nu 27:16**	376
of Nun, a **m** in whom is the Spirit,	**Nu 27:18**	376
"If a **m** makes a vow to the LORD,	**Nu 30:2**	376
as between a **m** and his wife,	**Nu 30:16**	376
the prey, both of **m** and of beast.	**Nu 31:11**	120
woman who has known **m** intimately.	**Nu 31:17**	376
who have not known **m** intimately,	**Nu 31:18**	2145
captured, both of **m** and of animal;	**Nu 31:26**	120
who had not known **m** intimately,	**Nu 31:35**	2145
fifty, both of **m** and of animals,	**Nu 31:47**	120
charge, and no **m** of us is missing.	**Nu 31:49**	376
to the LORD what each **m** found,	**Nu 31:50**	376
taken booty, every **m** for himself.	**Nu 31:53**	376
a **m** and his fellow countryman,	**Dt 1:16**	376
You shall not fear **m**,	**Dt 1:17**	376
of your men, one **m** for each tribe.	**Dt 1:23**	376
you, just as a **m** carries his son,	**Dt 1:31**	376
And every **m** of you girded on his	**Dt 1:41**	376
return every **m** to his possession which	**Dt 3:20**	376
that God created **m** on the earth,	**Dt 4:32**	120
seen today that God speaks with **m**,	**Dt 5:24**	120
no **m** will be able to stand before	**Dt 7:24**	376
m does not live by bread alone,	**Dt 8:3**	120
but **m** lives by everything that	**Dt 8:3**	120
just as a **m** disciplines his son.	**Dt 8:5**	376
"No **m** will be able to stand before you;	**Dt 11:25**	376
every **m** *doing* whatever is right in	**Dt 12:8**	376
"If there is a poor **m** with you,	**Dt 15:7**	34
your kinsman, a Hebrew **m** or woman,	**Dt 15:12**	5680
double the service of a hired **m**;	**Dt 15:18**	7916
"Every **m** shall give as he is able,	**Dt 16:17**	376
a **m** or a woman who does what is	**Dt 17:2**	376
then you shall bring out that **m** or	**Dt 17:5**	376
that is, the **m** or the woman,	**Dt 17:5**	376
The **m** who acts presumptuously by	**Dt 17:12**	376
to the judge, that **m** shall die;	**Dt 17:12**	376
as when *a* **m** goes into the forest	**Dt 19:5**	
there is a **m** who hates his neighbor	**Dt 19:11**	376
witness shall not rise up against a **m**	**Dt 19:15**	376
a **m** to accuse him of wrongdoing,	**Dt 19:16**	376
'Who is the **m** that has built a new	**Dt 20:5**	376
battle and another **m** would dedicate it.	**Dt 20:5**	376
'Who is the **m** that has planted	**Dt 20:6**	376
another **m** would begin to use its fruit.	**Dt 20:6**	376
'And who is the **m** that is engaged	**Dt 20:7**	376
battle and another **m** would marry her.'	**Dt 20:7**	376
'Who is the **m** that is afraid and	**Dt 20:8**	376
For is the tree of the field a **m**,	**Dt 20:19**	120
which is nearest to the slain **m**,	**Dt 21:3**	2491a
city which is nearest to the slain **m**	**Dt 21:6**	2491a
"If a **m** has two wives, the one	**Dt 21:15**	376
"If any **m** has a stubborn and	**Dt 21:18**	376
"If a **m** has committed a sin	**Dt 21:22**	376
a **m** put on a woman's clothing;	**Dt 22:5**	1397
"If any **m** takes a wife and goes	**Dt 22:13**	376
my daughter to this **m** for a wife,	**Dt 22:16**	376
shall take the **m** and chastise him,	**Dt 22:18**	376
"If a **m** is found lying with a	**Dt 22:22**	376
die, the **m** who lay with the woman,	**Dt 22:22**	376
who is a virgin engaged to a **m**,	**Dt 22:23**	376
and *another* **m** finds her in the	**Dt 22:23**	376
cry out in the city, and the **m**,	**Dt 22:24**	376
m finds the girl who is engaged,	**Dt 22:25**	376
the **m** forces her and lies with her,	**Dt 22:25**	376
the **m** who lies with her shall die.	**Dt 22:25**	376
for just as a **m** rises against his	**Dt 22:26**	376
a **m** finds a girl who is a virgin,	**Dt 22:28**	376
then the **m** who lay with her shall	**Dt 22:29**	376
"A **m** shall not take his father's wife	**Dt 22:30**	376
"If there is among you any **m** who	**Dt 23:10**	376
a **m** takes a wife and marries her,	**Dt 24:1**	376
"When a **m** takes a new wife, he	**Dt 24:5**	376
"If a **m** is caught kidnapping any	**Dt 24:7**	376
the **m** to whom you make the loan	**Dt 24:11**	376
"If he is a poor **m**,	**Dt 24:12**	376
wicked **m** deserves to be beaten,	**Dt 25:2**	7563
outside *the family* to a strange **m**.	**Dt 25:5**	376
"But if the **m** does not desire to	**Dt 25:7**	376
'Thus it is done to the **m** who does	**Dt 25:9**	376
two men, a **m** and his countryman,	**Dt 25:11**	376
'Cursed is the **m** who makes an idol	**Dt 27:15**	376
as the blind **m** gropes in darkness,	**Dt 28:29**	5787
but another **m** will violate her;	**Dt 28:30**	376
"The **m** who is refined and very	**Dt 28:54**	376
not be among you a **m** or woman,	**Dt 29:18**	376
jealousy will burn against that **m**,	**Dt 29:20**	376
When He separated the sons of **m**,	**Dt 32:8**	120
Both young **m** and virgin,	**Dt 32:25**	970
nursling with the **m** of gray hair.	**Dt 32:25**	376
Moses the **m** of God blessed the sons	**Dt 33:1**	376
Your Urim *belong* to Your godly **m**,	**Dt 33:8**	376
but no **m** knows his burial place to	**Dt 34:6**	376
"No **m** will *be able to* stand	**Jos 1:5**	376
no courage remained in any **m**	**Jos 2:11**	376
of Israel, one **m** for each tribe.	**Jos 3:12**	376
the people, one **m** from each tribe,	**Jos 4:2**	376
of Israel, one **m** from each tribe;	**Jos 4:4**	376
a **m** was standing opposite him with	**Jos 5:13**	376
go up every **m** straight ahead."	**Jos 6:5**	376
the city, every **m** straight ahead,	**Jos 6:20**	376
in the city, both **m** and woman,	**Jos 6:21**	376
"Cursed before the LORD is the **m**	**Jos 6:26**	376
takes shall come near **m** by man.	**Jos 7:14**	1397
takes shall come near man by **m**.	**Jos 7:14**	1397
of the Zerahites near **m** by man,	**Jos 7:17**	1397
of the Zerahites near man by **m**,	**Jos 7:17**	1397
his household near **m** by man;	**Jos 7:18**	1397
his household near man by **m**;	**Jos 7:18**	1397
So not a **m** was left in Ai or	**Jos 8:17**	376
no **m** had wielded an iron *tool;*	**Jos 8:31**	
LORD listened to the voice of a **m**;	**Jos 10:14**	376
they struck every **m** with the edge	**Jos 11:14**	120
LORD spoke to Moses the **m** of God	**Jos 14:6**	376
the greatest **m** among the Anakim.	**Jos 14:15**	120
Bashan, because he was a **m** of war.	**Jos 17:1**	376
And that **m** did not perish alone in	**Jos 22:20**	376
no **m** has stood before you to this	**Jos 23:9**	376
saw a **m** coming out of the city and	**Jg 1:24**	376
the **m** and all his family go free.	**Jg 1:25**	376
The **m** went into the land of	**Jg 1:26**	376
the Benjamite, a left-handed **m**.	**Jg 3:15**	376
Now Eglon was a very fat **m**.	**Jg 3:17**	376
you the **m** whom you are seeking."	**Jg 4:22**	376
shall defeat Midian as one **m**."	**Jg 6:16**	376
people go, each **m** to his home."	**Jg 7:7**	376
a **m** was relating a dream to his	**Jg 7:13**	376
the son of Joash, a **m** of Israel;	**Jg 7:14**	376
for as the **m**, so is his strength."	**Jg 8:21**	376
you, or that one **m** rule over you?'	**Jg 9:2**	376
he called quickly to the young **m**,	**Jg 9:54**	5288
the young **m** pierced him through,	**Jg 9:54**	5288
the son of Dodo, a **m** of Issachar,	**Jg 10:1**	376
"Who is the **m** who will begin to	**Jg 10:18**	376
and she had no relations with a **m**.	**Jg 11:39**	376
There was a certain **m** of Zorah,	**Jg 13:2**	376
"A **m** of God came to me and his	**Jg 13:6**	376
please let the **m** of God whom You	**Jg 13:8**	376
the **m** who came the *other* day has	**Jg 13:10**	376
he came to the **m** he said to him,	**Jg 13:11**	376
the **m** who spoke to the woman?"	**Jg 13:11**	376
weak and be like any *other* **m**."	**Jg 16:7**	120
weak and be like any *other* **m**."	**Jg 16:11**	120
weak and be like any other **m**."	**Jg 16:13**	120
weak and be like any *other* **m**."	**Jg 16:17**	120
and called for a **m** and had him	**Jg 16:19**	376
a **m** of the hill country of Ephraim	**Jg 17:1**	376
And the **m** Micah had a shrine and	**Jg 17:5**	376
every **m** did what was right in his	**Jg 17:6**	376
a young **m** from Bethlehem in Judah,	**Jg 17:7**	5288
Then the **m** departed from the city,	**Jg 17:8**	376
Levite agreed to live with the **m**,	**Jg 17:11**	376
and the young **m** became to him like	**Jg 17:11**	5288
and the young **m** became his priest	**Jg 17:12**	5288
the voice of the young **m**,	**Jg 18:3**	5288
came to the house of the young **m**,	**Jg 18:15**	5288
be a priest to the house of one **m**,	**Jg 18:19**	376
the girl's father said to the **m**,	**Jg 19:6**	376
Then the **m** arose to go, but his	**Jg 19:7**	376
When the **m** arose to go along with	**Jg 19:9**	376
But the **m** was not willing to spend	**Jg 19:10**	376
an old **m** was coming out of the	**Jg 19:16**	376
Now the **m** was from the hill	**Jg 19:16**	376
and the old **m** said,	**Jg 19:17**	376
no **m** will take me into his house.	**Jg 19:18**	376
young **m** who is with your servants;	**Jg 19:19**	5288
The old **m** said,	**Jg 19:20**	376
the owner of the house, the old **m**,	**Jg 19:22**	376
"Bring out the **m** who came into	**Jg 19:22**	376
Then the **m**, the owner of the house,	**Jg 19:23**	376
this **m** has come into my house,	**Jg 19:23**	376
an act of folly against this **m**."	**Jg 19:24**	376
So the **m** seized his concubine and	**Jg 19:25**	376
the **m** arose and went to his home.	**Jg 19:28**	376
as one **m** to the LORD at Mizpah.	**Jg 20:1**	376
all the people arose as one **m**,	**Jg 20:8**	376
against the city, united as one **m**.	**Jg 20:11**	376
you shall utterly destroy every **m**	**Jg 21:11**	2145
woman who has lain with a **m**."	**Jg 21:11**	2145
not known a **m** by lying with him;	**Jg 21:12**	376
take for each **m** *of Benjamin* a wife	**Jg 21:22**	376
every **m** to his tribe and family,	**Jg 21:24**	376
a certain **m** of Bethlehem in Judah	**Ru 1:1**	376
The name of the **m** *was* Elimelech,	**Ru 1:2**	376
her husband, a **m** of great wealth,	**Ru 2:1**	376
"The name of the **m** with whom I	**Ru 2:19**	376
"The **m** is our relative, he is one	**Ru 2:20**	376
not make yourself known to the **m**	**Ru 3:3**	376
m was startled and bent forward;	**Ru 3:8**	376
all that the **m** had done for her.	**Ru 3:16**	376
for the **m** will not rest until he	**Ru 3:18**	376
a **m** removed his sandal and gave it	**Ru 4:7**	376
a certain **m** from Ramathaim-zophim	**1Sa 1:1**	376
Now this **m** would go up from his	**1Sa 1:3**	376
Then the **m** Elkanah went up with	**1Sa 1:21**	376
not by might shall a **m** prevail.	**1Sa 2:9**	376
any **m** was offering a sacrifice,	**1Sa 2:13**	376
say to the **m** who was sacrificing,	**1Sa 2:15**	376
If the **m** said to him,	**1Sa 2:16**	376
"If one **m** sins against another,	**1Sa 2:25**	376
but if a **m** sins against the LORD,	**1Sa 2:25**	376
Then a **m** of God came to Eli and	**1Sa 2:27**	376
not be an old **m** in your house.	**1Sa 2:31**	2205
and an old **m** will not be in your	**1Sa 2:32**	2205
'Yet I will not cut off every **m** of	**1Sa 2:33**	376
and every **m** fled to his tent;	**1Sa 4:10**	376
Now a **m** of Benjamin ran from the	**1Sa 4:12**	376
the **m** came to tell *it* in the city,	**1Sa 4:13**	376
the **m** came hurriedly and told Eli.	**1Sa 4:14**	376
The **m** said to Eli,	**1Sa 4:16**	376
"Go every **m** to his city."	**1Sa 8:22**	376
Now there was a **m** of Benjamin	**1Sa 9:1**	376
a Benjamite, a mighty **m** of valor.	**1Sa 9:1**	1368
a choice and handsome **m**,	**1Sa 9:2**	
there is a **m** of God in this city,	**1Sa 9:6**	376
city, and the **m** is held in honor;	**1Sa 9:6**	376
we go, what shall we bring the **m**?	**1Sa 9:7**	376
present to bring to the **m** of God.	**1Sa 9:7**	376
I will give *it* to the **m** of God and	**1Sa 9:8**	376
when a **m** went to inquire of God,	**1Sa 9:9**	376
the city where the **m** of God was.	**1Sa 9:10**	376
you a **m** from the land of Benjamin,	**1Sa 9:16**	376
the **m** of whom I spoke to you!	**1Sa 9:17**	376
and be changed into another **m**.	**1Sa 10:6**	376
A **m** there said,	**1Sa 10:12**	376
"Has the **m** come here yet?"	**1Sa 10:22**	376
and they came out as one **m**.	**1Sa 11:7**	376
"Not a **m** shall be put to death	**1Sa 11:13**	376
Himself a **m** after His own heart,	**1Sa 13:14**	376
m who was carrying his armor,	**1Sa 14:1**	5288
Jonathan said to the young **m** who	**1Sa 14:6**	5288
m who eats food before evening,	**1Sa 14:24**	376
no **m** put his hand to his mouth,	**1Sa 14:26**	
be the **m** who eats food today.' "	**1Sa 14:28**	376
let us not leave a **m** of them."	**1Sa 14:36**	376
any mighty **m** or any valiant man,	**1Sa 14:52**	376
any mighty man or any valiant **m**,	**1Sa 14:52**	1121
but put to death both **m** and woman,	**1Sa 15:3**	376
for He is not a **m** that He should	**1Sa 15:29**	120
for God *sees* not as **m** sees,	**1Sa 16:7**	120
for **m** looks at the outward	**1Sa 16:7**	120
Let them seek a **m** who is a	**1Sa 16:16**	376
for me now a **m** who can play well and	**1Sa 16:17**	376
musician, a mighty **m** of valor,	**1Sa 16:18**	1368
in speech, and a handsome **m**;	**1Sa 16:18**	376
Choose a **m** for yourselves and let	**1Sa 17:8**	376
give me a **m** that we may fight	**1Sa 17:10**	376
all the men of Israel saw the **m**,	**1Sa 17:24**	376
you seen this **m** who is coming up?	**1Sa 17:25**	376
king will enrich the **m** who kills him	**1Sa 17:25**	376
the **m** who kills this Philistine and	**1Sa 17:26**	376
be done for the **m** who kills him."	**1Sa 17:27**	376
whose son is this young **m**?"	**1Sa 17:55**	5288
"Whose son are you, young **m**?"	**1Sa 17:58**	5288
only be a valiant **m** for me and	**1Sa 18:17**	1121
a poor **m** and lightly esteemed?"	**1Sa 18:23**	376
see the **m** behaving as a madman.	**1Sa 21:14**	376
"For if a **m** finds his enemy, will	**1Sa 24:19**	376
Now *there was* a **m** in Maon whose	**1Sa 25:2**	376
and the **m** was very rich, and he	**1Sa 25:2**	376
but the **m** was harsh and evil in	**1Sa 25:3**	376
So each **m** girded on his sword.	**1Sa 25:13**	376
such a worthless **m** that no one can	**1Sa 25:17**	1121
vain I have guarded all that this **m**	**1Sa 25:21**	
pay attention to this worthless **m**,	**1Sa 25:25**	376
said to Abner, "Are you not a **m**?	**1Sa 26:15**	376
"The LORD will repay each **m**	**1Sa 26:23**	376
not leave a **m** or a woman alive,	**1Sa 27:9**	376
not leave a **m** or a woman alive to	**1Sa 27:11**	376
"An old **m** is coming up, and he is	**1Sa 28:14**	376
"Make the **m** go back, that he may	**1Sa 29:4**	376
For with what could this **m** make	**1Sa 29:4**	
"I am a young **m** of Egypt, a	**1Sa 30:13**	5288
and not a **m** of them escaped,	**1Sa 30:17**	376
every **m** his wife and his children,	**1Sa 30:22**	376
a **m** came out of the camp from	**2Sa 1:2**	376
said to the young **m** who told him,	**2Sa 1:5**	5288
The young **m** who told him said,	**2Sa 1:6**	5288
said to the young **m** who told him,	**2Sa 1:13**	5288
a prince and a great **m** has fallen	**2Sa 3:38**	1419
men have killed a righteous **m**	**2Sa 4:11**	376
And this is the custom of **m**,	**2Sa 7:19**	120
"The rich **m** had a great many	**2Sa 12:2**	6223
"But the poor **m** had nothing	**2Sa 12:3**	
"Now a traveler came to the rich **m**,	**2Sa 12:4**	376
prepared it for the **m** who had come	**2Sa 12:4**	376
anger burned greatly against the **m**,	**2Sa 12:5**	376
surely the **m** who has done this	**2Sa 12:5**	376
then said to David, "You are the **m**!	**2Sa 12:7**	376
and Jonadab was a very shrewd **m**.	**2Sa 13:3**	376
young **m** who attended him and said,	**2Sa 13:17**	5288
And the young **m** who was the	**2Sa 13:34**	5288
the **m** who would destroy both me	**2Sa 14:16**	376
bring back the young **m** Absalom."	**2Sa 14:21**	5288
when any **m** had a suit to come to	**2Sa 15:2**	376
but no **m** listens to you on the	**2Sa 15:3**	
then every **m** who has any suit or	**2Sa 15:4**	376
a **m** came near to prostrate himself	**2Sa 15:5**	376
m of the family of the house of Saul	**2Sa 16:5**	376
out, get out, you **m** of bloodshed,	**2Sa 16:7**	376
for you are a **m** of bloodshed!"	**2Sa 16:8**	376
depends on the **m** you seek;	**2Sa 17:3**	376
knows that your father is a mighty **m**	**2Sa 17:10**	1121
to the house of a **m** in Bahurim,	**2Sa 17:18**	376
Now Amasa was the son of a **m** whose	**2Sa 17:25**	376
sake with the young **m** Absalom."	**2Sa 18:5**	5288
When a certain **m** saw *it,* he told	**2Sa 18:10**	376

said to the **m** who had told him,	**2Sa 18:11**	376
The **m** said to Joab,	**2Sa 18:12**	376
for me the young **m** Absalom!'	**2Sa 18:12**	5288
not the **m** to carry news this day,	**2Sa 18:20**	376
behold, a **m** running by himself.	**2Sa 18:24**	376
watchman saw another **m** running;	**2Sa 18:26**	376
another **m** running by himself."	**2Sa 18:26**	376
good **m** and comes with good news."	**2Sa 18:27**	376
well with the young **m** Absalom?"	**2Sa 18:29**	5288
well with the young **m** Absalom?"	**2Sa 18:32**	5288
for evil, be as that young **m**!"	**2Sa 18:32**	5288
not a **m** will pass the night with you,	**2Sa 19:7**	376
of all the men of Judah as one **m**,	**2Sa 19:14**	376
Should any **m** be put to death in	**2Sa 19:22**	376
for he was a very great **m**.	**2Sa 19:32**	376
Every **m** to his tents, O Israel!"	**2Sa 20:1**	376
m saw that all the people stood still	**2Sa 20:12**	376
But a **m** from the hill country of	**2Sa 20:21**	376
to put any **m** to death in Israel."	**2Sa 21:4**	376
"The **m** who consumed us and who	**2Sa 21:5**	376
where there was a **m** of *great* stature	**2Sa 21:20**	376
You rescue me from the violent **m**.	**2Sa 22:49**	376
The **m** who was raised on high	**2Sa 23:1**	1397
But the **m** who touches them Must be	**2Sa 23:7**	376
the son of a valiant **m** of Kabzeel,	**2Sa 23:20**	376
an Egyptian, an impressive **m**.	**2Sa 23:21**	376
let me fall into the hand of **m**."	**2Sa 24:14**	120
And he was also a very handsome **m**,	**1Ki 1:6**	2896a
a valiant **m** and bring good news."	**1Ki 1:42**	376
"If he is a worthy **m**,	**1Ki 1:52**	1121
therefore, and show yourself a **m**.	**1Ki 2:2**	376
lack a **m** on the throne of Israel.'	**1Ki 2:4**	376
unpunished, for you are a wise **m**;	**1Ki 2:9**	376
each **m** had to provide for a month	**1Ki 4:7**	
every **m** under his vine and his fig	**1Ki 4:25**	376
and his father was a **m** of Tyre,	**1Ki 7:14**	376
not lack a **m** to sit on the throne of	**1Ki 8:25**	376
"If a **m** sins against his neighbor	**1Ki 8:31**	376
supplication is made by any **m** *or*	**1Ki 8:38**	120
there is no **m** who does not sin)	**1Ki 8:46**	120
lack a **m** on the throne of Israel.'	**1Ki 9:5**	376
They brought every **m** his gift,	**1Ki 10:25**	376
Now the **m** Jeroboam was a valiant	**1Ki 11:28**	376
that the young **m** was industrious,	**1Ki 11:28**	5288
God came to Shemaiah the **m** of God,	**1Ki 12:22**	376
return every **m** to his house, for	**1Ki 12:24**	376
there came a **m** of God from Judah	**1Ki 13:1**	376
heard the saying of the **m** of God,	**1Ki 13:4**	376
sign which the **m** of God had given	**1Ki 13:5**	376
said to the **m** of God,	**1Ki 13:6**	376
the **m** of God entreated the LORD,	**1Ki 13:6**	376
the king said to the **m** of God,	**1Ki 13:7**	376
But the **m** of God said to the king,	**1Ki 13:8**	376
deeds which the **m** of God had done	**1Ki 13:11**	376
the way which the **m** of God	**1Ki 13:12**	376
So he went after the **m** of God and	**1Ki 13:14**	376
"Are you the **m** of God	**1Ki 13:14**	376
the **m** of God who came from Judah,	**1Ki 13:21**	376
"It is the **m** of God, who	**1Ki 13:26**	376
took up the body of the **m** of God	**1Ki 13:29**	376
in which the **m** of God is buried;	**1Ki 13:31**	376
I have to do with you, O **m** of God?	**1Ki 17:18**	376
I know that you are a **m** of God and	**1Ki 17:24**	376
how this **m** is looking for trouble;	**1Ki 20:7**	
They killed each his **m**;	**1Ki 20:20**	376
Then a **m** of God came near and	**1Ki 20:28**	376
Now a certain **m** of the sons of the	**1Ki 20:35**	376
But the **m** refused to strike him.	**1Ki 20:35**	376
Then he found another **m** and said,	**1Ki 20:37**	376
And the **m** struck him, wounding him.	**1Ki 20:37**	376
a **m** turned aside and brought a man	**1Ki 20:39**	376
and brought a **m** to me and said,	**1Ki 20:39**	376
'Guard this **m**; if for any reason he	**1Ki 20:39**	376
m whom I had devoted to destruction	**1Ki 20:42**	376
"There is yet one **m** by whom we	**1Ki 22:8**	376
"Put this **m** in prison and feed	**1Ki 22:27**	
Now a certain **m** drew his bow at	**1Ki 22:34**	376
"Every **m** to his city and every	**1Ki 22:36**	376
city and every **m** to his country."	**1Ki 22:36**	376
"A **m** came up to meet us and said	**2Ki 1:6**	376
"What kind of **m** was he who came	**2Ki 1:7**	376
"*He was* a hairy **m** with a leather	**2Ki 1:8**	376
"O **m** of God, the king says,	**2Ki 1:9**	376
"If I am a **m** of God, let fire	**2Ki 1:10**	376
"O **m** of God, thus says the king,	**2Ki 1:11**	376
"If I am a **m** of God, let fire	**2Ki 1:12**	376
"O **m** of God, please let my life	**2Ki 1:13**	376
she came and told the **m** of God.	**2Ki 4:7**	376
I perceive that this is a holy **m**	**2Ki 4:9**	376
"No, my lord, O **m** of God, do not	**2Ki 4:16**	376
him on the bed of the **m** of God,	**2Ki 4:21**	376
run to the **m** of God and return."	**2Ki 4:22**	376
to the **m** of God to Mount Carmel.	**2Ki 4:25**	376
When the **m** of God saw her	**2Ki 4:25**	376
came to the **m** of God to the hill,	**2Ki 4:27**	376
but the **m** of God said,	**2Ki 4:27**	376
if you meet any **m**, do not salute	**2Ki 4:29**	376
"O **m** of God, there is death in	**2Ki 4:40**	376
Now a **m** came from Baal-shalishah,	**2Ki 4:42**	376
and brought the **m** of God bread of	**2Ki 4:42**	376
was a great **m** with his master,	**2Ki 5:1**	376
The **m** was also a valiant warrior,	**2Ki 5:1**	376
that this **m** is sending *word* to me	**2Ki 5:7**	
to me to cure a **m** of his leprosy?	**2Ki 5:7**	376
when Elisha the **m** of God heard	**2Ki 5:8**	376
to the word of the **m** of God;	**2Ki 5:14**	376
the **m** of God with all his company,	**2Ki 5:15**	376
servant of Elisha the **m** of God,	**2Ki 5:20**	376
when the **m** turned from his chariot	**2Ki 5:26**	376
Then the **m** of God said,	**2Ki 6:6**	376
The **m** of God sent *word* to the	**2Ki 6:9**	376
which the **m** of God had told him;	**2Ki 6:10**	376
attendant of the **m** of God had risen	**2Ki 6:15**	376
you to the **m** whom you seek."	**2Ki 6:19**	376
king sent a **m** from his presence;	**2Ki 6:32**	376
answered the **m** of God and said,	**2Ki 7:2**	376
no one there, nor the voice of **m**,	**2Ki 7:10**	120
just as the **m** of God had said,	**2Ki 7:17**	376
m of God had spoken to the king,	**2Ki 7:18**	376
answered the **m** of God and said,	**2Ki 7:19**	376
to the word of the **m** of God,	**2Ki 8:2**	376
the servant of the **m** of God,	**2Ki 8:4**	376
"The **m** of God has come here."	**2Ki 8:7**	376
hand and go to meet the **m** of God,	**2Ki 8:8**	376
ashamed, and the **m** of God wept.	**2Ki 8:11**	376
So the young **m**, the servant of the	**2Ki 9:4**	5288
know *very well* the **m** and his talk."	**2Ki 9:11**	376
each **m** took his garment and placed	**2Ki 9:13**	376
do, we will not make any **m** king;	**2Ki 10:5**	376
was not a **m** left who did not come.	**2Ki 10:21**	376
So the **m** of God was angry with him	**2Ki 13:19**	376
As they were burying a **m**,	**2Ki 13:21**	376
the **m** into the grave of Elisha.	**2Ki 13:21**	376
And when the **m** touched the bones	**2Ki 13:21**	376
from each **m** fifty shekels of	**2Ki 15:20**	376
on which if a **m** leans, it will go	**2Ki 18:21**	376
"Tell the **m** who sent you to me,	**2Ki 22:15**	376
that no **m** might make his son or	**2Ki 23:10**	376
which the **m** of God proclaimed,	**2Ki 23:16**	376
"It is the grave of the **m** of God	**2Ki 23:17**	376
the son of a valiant **m** of Kabzeel,	**1Ch 11:22**	376
a **m** of *great* stature five cubits	**1Ch 11:23**	376
a mighty **m** among the thirty,	**1Ch 12:4**	1368
Zadok, a young **m** mighty of valor,	**1Ch 12:28**	5288
of Israel, both **m** and woman,	**1Ch 16:3**	376
He permitted no **m** to oppress them,	**1Ch 16:21**	376
standard of a **m** of high degree,	**1Ch 17:17**	120
where there was a **m** of *great* stature	**1Ch 20:6**	376
not let me fall into the hand of **m**."	**1Ch 21:13**	120
to you, who shall be a **m** of rest;	**1Ch 22:9**	376
But *as for* Moses the **m** of God,	**1Ch 23:14**	376
was the mighty **m** of the thirty,	**1Ch 27:6**	1368
a counselor, a **m** of understanding,	**1Ch 27:32**	376
a **m** of war and have shed blood.'	**1Ch 28:3**	376
and every willing **m** of any skill	**1Ch 28:21**	5081
for the temple is not for **m**,	**1Ch 29:1**	120
me a skilled **m** to work in gold,	**2Ch 2:7**	376
sending Huram-abi, a skilled **m**,	**2Ch 2:13**	376
nor did I choose any **m** for a leader	**2Ch 6:5**	376
not lack a **m** to sit on the throne of	**2Ch 6:16**	376
"If a **m** sins against his neighbor and	**2Ch 6:22**	376
supplication is made by any **m** or	**2Ch 6:29**	120
there is no **m** who does not sin)	**2Ch 6:36**	120
lack a **m** *to be* ruler in Israel.'	**2Ch 7:18**	376
the **m** of God had so commanded.	**2Ch 8:14**	376
They brought every **m** his gift,	**2Ch 9:24**	376
Every **m** to your tents, O Israel;	**2Ch 10:16**	376
came to Shemaiah the **m** of God,	**2Ch 11:2**	376
return every **m** to his house, for	**2Ch 11:4**	376
let not **m** prevail against You."	**2Ch 14:11**	582
small or great, **m** or woman.	**2Ch 15:13**	376
"There is yet one **m** by whom we	**2Ch 18:7**	376
"Put this **m** in prison and feed	**2Ch 18:26**	
A certain **m** drew his bow at	**2Ch 18:33**	376
for you do not judge for **m** but for	**2Ch 19:6**	120
Every **m** of Judah and Jerusalem	**2Ch 20:27**	376
m with his weapons in his hand;	**2Ch 23:7**	376
m with his weapon in his hand,	**2Ch 23:10**	376
But a **m** of God came to him saying,	**2Ch 25:7**	376
Amaziah said to the **m** of God,	**2Ch 25:9**	376
And the **m** of God answered,	**2Ch 25:9**	376
And Zichri, a mighty **m** of Ephraim,	**2Ch 28:7**	1368
to the law of Moses the **m** of God;	**2Ch 30:16**	376
'Tell the **m** who sent you to Me,	**2Ch 34:23**	376
compassion on young **m** or virgin,	**2Ch 36:17**	970
man or virgin, old **m** or infirm;	**2Ch 36:17**	2205
together as one **m** to Jerusalem.	**Ezr 3:1**	376
in the law of Moses, the **m** of God.	**Ezr 3:2**	376
any **m** who violates this edict,	**Ezr 6:11**	606
leading **m** at the place Casiphia;	**Ezr 8:17**	7218
they brought us a **m** of insight	**Ezr 8:18**	376
him compassion before this **m**."	**Ne 1:11**	376
"Let each **m** with his servant	**Ne 4:22**	376
"Thus may God shake out every **m**	**Ne 5:13**	376
"Should a **m** like me flee?	**Ne 6:11**	376
he was a faithful **m** and feared God	**Ne 7:2**	376
all the people gathered as one **m**	**Ne 8:1**	376
if a **m** observes them he shall live.	**Ne 9:29**	120
prescribed by David the **m** of God.	**Ne 12:24**	376
instruments of David the **m** of God.	**Ne 12:36**	376
that every **m** should be the master	**Es 1:22**	376
for any **m** or woman who comes to	**Es 4:11**	376
"What is to be done for the **m**	**Es 6:6**	376
"For the **m** whom the king desires	**Es 6:7**	376
array the **m** whom the king desires to	**Es 6:9**	376
'Thus it shall be done to the **m**	**Es 6:9**	376
"Thus it shall be done to the **m**	**Es 6:11**	376
for the **m** Mordecai became greater	**Es 9:4**	376
There was a **m** in the land of Uz whose	**Jb 1:1**	376
was Job; and that **m** was blameless,	**Jb 1:1**	376
and that **m** was the greatest of all	**Jb 1:3**	376
earth, a blameless and upright **m**,	**Jb 1:8**	376
a blameless and upright **m** fearing	**Jb 2:3**	376
all that a **m** has he will give for his	**Jb 2:4**	376
given to a **m** whose way is hidden,	**Jb 3:23**	1397
Can a **m** be pure before his Maker?	**Jb 4:17**	1397
"For anger slays the foolish **m**,	**Jb 5:2**	191
For **m** is born for trouble, As	**Jb 5:7**	120
happy is the **m** whom God reproves,	**Jb 5:17**	582
"For the despairing **m** *there*	**Jb 6:14**	4523
"Is not **m** forced to labor on	**Jb 7:1**	582
days like the days of a hired **m**?	**Jb 7:1**	7916
And as a hired **m** who eagerly waits	**Jb 7:2**	7916
is **m** that You magnify him,	**Jb 7:17**	582
"Lo, God will not reject *a* **m** *of*	**Jb 8:20**	
can a **m** be in the right before God?	**Jb 9:2**	582
He is not a **m** as I am that I may	**Jb 9:32**	376
Or do You see as a **m** sees?	**Jb 10:4**	582
And a talkative **m** be acquitted?	**Jb 11:2**	376
foal of a wild donkey is born a **m**.	**Jb 11:12**	120
The just *and* blameless **m** is a	**Jb 12:4**	
He imprisons a **m**, and there can be	**Jb 12:14**	376
them stagger like a drunken **m**.	**Jb 12:25**	7910
deceive Him as one deceives a **m**?	**Jb 13:9**	582
For a godless **m** may not come	**Jb 13:16**	2611
"**M**, who is born of woman, Is	**Jb 14:1**	120
fulfills his day like a hired **m**.	**Jb 14:6**	7916
"But **m** dies and lies prostrate.	**Jb 14:10**	1397
M expires, and where is he?	**Jb 14:10**	120
So **m** lies down and does not rise.	**Jb 14:12**	376
"If a **m** dies, will he live *again?*	**Jb 14:14**	1397
Should a wise **m** answer with windy	**Jb 15:2**	2450
"Were you the first **m** to be born,	**Jb 15:7**	120
"What is **m**, that he should be pure,	**Jb 15:14**	582
M, who drinks iniquity like water!	**Jb 15:16**	376
m writhes in pain all *his* days,	**Jb 15:20**	7563
"O that a **m** might plead with God	**Jb 16:21**	1397
with God As a **m** with his neighbor!	**Jb 16:21**	1121, 120
I do not find a wise **m** among you.	**Jb 17:10**	2450
the establishment of **m** on earth,	**Jb 20:4**	120
"As for me, is my complaint to **m**?	**Jb 21:4**	120
Can a vigorous **m** be of use to God,	**Jb 22:2**	1397
Or a wise **m** be useful to himself?	**Jb 22:2**	
the earth belongs to the mighty **m**,	**Jb 22:8**	376
And the honorable **m** dwells in it.	**Jb 22:8**	
"How then can a **m** be just with God?	**Jb 25:4**	582
How much less **m**, *that* maggot, And	**Jb 25:6**	582
that maggot, And the son of **m**,	**Jb 25:6**	120
portion of a wicked **m** from God,	**Jb 27:13**	120
"**M** puts an end to darkness,	**Jb 28:3**	
"**M** does not know its value, Nor	**Jb 28:13**	582
"And to **m** He said,	**Jb 28:28**	120
"But it is a spirit in **m**,	**Jb 32:8**	582
God will rout him, not **m**.'	**Jb 32:13**	376
Nor flatter *any* **m**.	**Jb 32:21**	120
this, For God is greater than **m**.	**Jb 33:12**	582
may turn **m** aside *from his* conduct,	**Jb 33:17**	120
conduct, And keep **m** from pride;	**Jb 33:17**	1397
"**M** is also chastened with pain on	**Jb 33:19**	
remind a **m** what is right for him,	**Jb 33:23**	120
restore His righteousness to **m**.	**Jb 33:26**	582
"What **m** is like Job, Who drinks	**Jb 34:7**	1397
'It profits a **m** nothing When he is	**Jb 34:9**	1397
He pays a **m** according to his work,	**Jb 34:11**	120
And **m** would return to dust.	**Jb 34:15**	120
His eyes are upon the ways of a **m**,	**Jb 34:21**	376
not *need to* consider a **m** further,	**Jb 34:23**	376
in regard to both nation and **m**?	**Jb 34:29**	120
to me, And a wise **m** who hears me,	**Jb 34:34**	1397
wickedness is for a **m** like yourself,	**Jb 35:8**	376
righteousness is for a son of **m**.	**Jb 35:8**	120
M beholds from afar.	**Jb 36:25**	120
down, They drip upon **m** abundantly.	**Jb 36:28**	120
"He seals the hand of every **m**,	**Jb 37:7**	120
Or should a **m** say that he would be	**Jb 37:20**	376
"Now gird up your loins like a **m**,	**Jb 38:3**	1397
On a desert without a **m** in it,	**Jb 38:26**	120
"Now gird up your loins like a **m**;	**Jb 40:7**	1397
Job died, an old **m** and full of days.	**Jb 42:17**	2205
How blessed is the **m** who does not	**Ps 1:1**	376
set apart the godly **m** for Himself;	**Ps 4:3**	2623
the **m** of bloodshed and deceit.	**Ps 5:6**	376
who blesses the righteous **m**,	**Ps 5:12**	6662
If a **m** does not repent, He will	**Ps 7:12**	
What is **m** that You take	**Ps 8:4**	582
And the son of **m** that You	**Ps 8:4**	120
O LORD, do not let **m** prevail;	**Ps 9:19**	582
m curses *and* spurns the LORD.	**Ps 10:3**	1214
that **m** who is of the earth will	**Ps 10:18**	582
for the godly **m** ceases to be,	**Ps 12:1**	2623
You rescue me from the violent **m**.	**Ps 18:48**	376
as a strong **m** to run his course.	**Ps 19:5**	1368
But I am a worm and not a **m**,	**Ps 22:6**	376
Who is the **m** who fears the LORD?	**Ps 25:12**	376
I am forgotten as a dead **m**,	**Ps 31:12**	4191
from the conspiracies of **m**;	**Ps 31:20**	376
How blessed is the **m** to whom the	**Ps 32:2**	120
m cried, and the LORD heard him	**Ps 34:6**	6041
is the **m** who takes refuge in Him!	**Ps 34:8**	1397
Who is the **m** who desires life And	**Ps 34:12**	376
LORD, You preserve **m** and beast.	**Ps 36:6**	120
Because of the **m** who carries out	**Ps 37:7**	376
and the wicked **m** will be no more;	**Ps 37:10**	7563
The steps of a **m** are established by	**Ps 37:23**	1397
violent **m** Spreading himself like a	**Ps 37:35**	7563
Mark the blameless **m**,	**Ps 37:37**	8535
For the **m** of peace will have a	**Ps 37:37**	376
But I, like a deaf **m**, do not hear;	**Ps 38:13**	2795
m who does not open his mouth.	**Ps 38:13**	483
I am like a **m** who does not hear,	**Ps 38:14**	376
every **m** at his best is a mere breath.	**Ps 39:5**	120
every **m** walks about as a phantom;	**Ps 39:6**	376
You chasten a **m** for iniquity;	**Ps 39:11**	376
every **m** is a mere breath.	**Ps 39:11**	120
How blessed is the **m** who has made	**Ps 40:4**	1397
from the deceitful and unjust **m**!	**Ps 43:1**	376

No **m** can by any means redeem *his*	Ps 49:7	376
But **m** in *his* pomp will not endure;	Ps 49:12	120
be afraid when a **m** becomes rich,	Ps 49:16	376
M in *his* pomp, yet without	Ps 49:20	120
do you boast in evil, O mighty **m**?	Ps 52:1	1368
the **m** who would not make God his	Ps 52:7	1397
But it is you, a **m** my equal,	Ps 55:13	582
O God, for **m** has trampled upon me;	Ps 56:1	582
What can *mere* **m** do to me?	Ps 56:4	1320
What can **m** do to me?	Ps 56:11	120
For deliverance by **m** is in vain.	Ps 60:11	120
How long will you assail a **m**,	Ps 62:3	376
For You recompense a **m**	Ps 62:12	376
and the heart of a **m** are deep.	Ps 64:6	376
m will be glad in the LORD and	Ps 64:10	6662
of the wrongdoer and ruthless **m**,	Ps 71:4	2556c
how the foolish **m** reproaches You	Ps 74:22	5036
the wrath of **m** shall praise You;	Ps 76:10	120
M did eat the bread of angels;	Ps 78:25	376
be upon the **m** of Your right hand,	Ps 80:17	376
Upon the son of **m** whom You made	Ps 80:17	120
the **m** whose strength is in You,	Ps 84:5	120
blessed is the **m** who trusts in You!	Ps 84:12	120
my soul, for I am a godly **m**;	Ps 86:2	2623
become like a **m** without strength,	Ps 88:4	1397
What **m** can live and not see death?	Ps 89:48	1397
You turn **m** back into dust	Ps 90:3	582
A senseless **m** has no knowledge,	Ps 92:6	376
does a stupid **m** understand this:	Ps 92:6	3684
The righteous **m** will flourish like	Ps 92:12	6662
Even He who teaches **m** knowledge?	Ps 94:10	120
The LORD knows the thoughts of **m**,	Ps 94:11	120
is the **m** whom You chasten,	Ps 94:12	1397
As for **m**, his days are like grass;	Ps 103:15	582
And vegetation for the labor of **m**,	Ps 104:14	120
M goes forth to his work And to	Ps 104:23	120
He permitted no **m** to oppress them,	Ps 105:14	120
He sent a **m** before them, Joseph,	Ps 105:17	376
and staggered like a drunken **m**,	Ps 107:27	7910
For deliverance by **m** is in vain.	Ps 108:12	120
Appoint a wicked **m** over him,	Ps 109:6	7563
the afflicted and needy **m**,	Ps 109:16	376
is the **m** who fears the LORD,	Ps 112:1	376
the **m** who is gracious and lends;	Ps 112:5	376
What can **m** do to me?	Ps 118:6	120
in the LORD Than to trust in **m**.	Ps 118:8	120
can a young **m** keep his way pure?	Ps 119:9	5288
me from the oppression of **m**,	Ps 119:134	120
m whose quiver is full of them;	Ps 127:5	1397
m be blessed Who fears the LORD.	Ps 128:4	1397
of Egypt, Both of **m** and beast.	Ps 135:8	120
hunt the violent **m** speedily."	Ps 140:11	376
sight no **m** living is righteous.	Ps 143:2	2416a
O LORD, what is **m**, that You take	Ps 144:3	120
Or the son of **m**, that You think	Ps 144:3	582
M is like a mere breath;	Ps 144:4	120
not trust in princes, In mortal **m**,	Ps 146:3	120
take pleasure in the legs of a **m**.	Ps 147:10	376
A wise **m** will hear and increase in	Pr 1:5	2450
And a **m** of understanding will	Pr 1:5	
the **m** who speaks perverse things;	Pr 2:12	376
repute In the sight of God and **m**.	Pr 3:4	120
blessed is the **m** who finds wisdom And	Pr 3:13	120
And the **m** who gains understanding.	Pr 3:13	120
contend with a **m** without cause,	Pr 3:30	120
Do not envy a **m** of violence And	Pr 3:31	376
For the ways of a **m** are before the	Pr 5:21	376
And your need like an armed **m**.	Pr 6:11	376
A worthless person, a wicked **m**,	Pr 6:12	376
Can a **m** take fire in his bosom And	Pr 6:27	376
Or can a **m** walk on hot coals And	Pr 6:28	376
For jealousy enrages a **m**,	Pr 6:34	1397
youths A young **m** lacking sense,	Pr 7:7	5288
Blessed is the **m** who listens to me,	Pr 8:34	120
he who reproves a wicked **m** *gets*	Pr 9:7	7563
Reprove a wise **m** and he will love	Pr 9:8	2450
Give *instruction* to a wise **m** and	Pr 9:9	2450
Teach a righteous **m** and he will	Pr 9:9	6662
is wisdom to a **m** of understanding.	Pr 10:23	376
When a wicked **m** dies, *his*	Pr 11:7	120
godless **m** destroys his neighbor,	Pr 11:9	2611
a **m** of understanding keeps silent.	Pr 11:12	376
The merciful **m** does himself good,	Pr 11:17	376
But the cruel **m** does himself harm.	Pr 11:17	394
the evil **m** will not go unpunished,	Pr 11:21	7451a
The generous **m** will be prosperous,	Pr 11:25	5315
A good **m** will obtain favor from	Pr 12:2	2896a
will condemn a **m** who devises evil.	Pr 12:2	376
A **m** will not be established by	Pr 12:3	120
A **m** will be praised according to	Pr 12:8	376
A righteous **m** has regard for the	Pr 12:10	6662
The wicked **m** desires the booty of	Pr 12:12	
An evil **m** is ensnared by the	Pr 12:13	7451a
A **m** will be satisfied with good by	Pr 12:14	376
wise **m** is he who listens to counsel.	Pr 12:15	2450
But a prudent **m** conceals dishonor.	Pr 12:16	6175
A prudent **m** conceals knowledge,	Pr 12:23	120
A lazy **m** does not roast his prey,	Pr 12:27	7423b
possession of a **m** *is* diligence.	Pr 12:27	120
A righteous **m** hates falsehood, But	Pr 13:5	6662
But a wicked **m** acts disgustingly	Pr 13:5	7563
prudent **m** acts with knowledge,	Pr 13:16	6175
A good **m** leaves an inheritance to	Pr 13:22	2896a
is a way *which seems* right to a **m**,	Pr 14:12	376
good **m** will *be satisfied* with his.	Pr 14:14	376
the sensible **m** considers his steps.	Pr 14:15	6175
A wise **m** is cautious and turns	Pr 14:16	2450
A quick-tempered **m** acts foolishly,	Pr 14:17	
And a **m** of evil devices is hated.	Pr 14:17	376
A hot-tempered **m** stirs up strife,	Pr 15:18	376
a foolish **m** despises his mother.	Pr 15:20	120
But a **m** of understanding walks	Pr 15:21	376
A **m** has joy in an apt answer, And	Pr 15:23	376
plans of the heart belong to **m**,	Pr 16:1	120
All the ways of a **m** are clean in his	Pr 16:2	376
The mind of **m** plans his way, But	Pr 16:9	120
But a wise **m** will appease it.	Pr 16:14	376
is a way *which seems* right to a **m**,	Pr 16:25	376
A worthless **m** digs up evil, While	Pr 16:27	376
A perverse **m** spreads strife, And a	Pr 16:28	376
A **m** of violence entices his neighbor	Pr 16:29	376
A rebellious **m** seeks only evil, So	Pr 17:11	4805
Let a **m** meet a bear robbed of her	Pr 17:12	376
A **m** lacking in sense pledges And	Pr 17:18	120
A wicked **m** receives a bribe from	Pr 17:23	7563
spirit is a **m** of understanding.	Pr 17:27	376
When a wicked **m** comes, contempt	Pr 18:3	7563
the heart of **m** is haughty,	Pr 18:12	376
spirit of a **m** can endure his sickness,	Pr 18:14	376
The poor **m** utters supplications,	Pr 18:23	7326
But the rich **m** answers roughly.	Pr 18:23	6223
A **m** of *too many* friends *comes* to ruin,	Pr 18:24	376
Better is a poor **m** who walks in	Pr 19:1	
foolishness of **m** ruins his way,	Pr 19:3	120
poor **m** is separated from his friend.	Pr 19:4	1800b
seek the favor of a generous **m**,	Pr 19:6	5081
And every **m** is a friend to him who	Pr 19:6	3605
the brothers of a poor **m** hate him;	Pr 19:7	7326
And an idle **m** will suffer hunger.	Pr 19:15	5315
One who is gracious to a poor **m**	Pr 19:17	1800b
A **m** *of* great anger will bear	Pr 19:19	
desirable in a **m** is his kindness,	Pr 19:22	120
better to be a poor **m** than a liar.	Pr 19:22	
from strife is an honor for a **m**,	Pr 20:3	376
plan in the heart of a **m** is *like* deep	Pr 20:5	376
a **m** of understanding draws it out.	Pr 20:5	376
a **m** proclaims his own loyalty,	Pr 20:6	120
But who can find a trustworthy **m**?	Pr 20:6	376
A righteous **m** who walks in his	Pr 20:7	6662
by falsehood is sweet to a **m**,	Pr 20:17	376
How then can **m** understand his way?	Pr 20:24	120
is a trap for a **m** to say rashly,	Pr 20:25	120
spirit of **m** is the lamp of the LORD,	Pr 20:27	120
The way of a guilty **m** is crooked,	Pr 21:8	376
A **m** who wanders from the way of	Pr 21:16	120
pleasure *will become* a poor **m**;	Pr 21:17	376
But a foolish **m** swallows it up.	Pr 21:20	120
A wise **m** scales the city of the	Pr 21:22	2450
But the **m** who listens *to the truth*	Pr 21:28	376
A wicked **m** displays a bold face, But	Pr 21:29	376
the words of the treacherous **m**.	Pr 22:12	
associate with a **m** *given* to anger;	Pr 22:24	1167
Or go with a hot-tempered **m**,	Pr 22:24	376
you see a **m** skilled in his work?	Pr 22:29	376
If you are a **m** of *great* appetite.	Pr 23:2	1167
not eat the bread of a selfish **m**,	Pr 23:6	7451a
A wise **m** is strong, And a man of	Pr 24:5	1397
a **m** of knowledge increases power.	Pr 24:5	376
render to **m** according to his work?	Pr 24:12	120
Do not lie in wait, O wicked **m**,	Pr 24:15	7563
a righteous **m** falls seven times,	Pr 24:16	6662
will be no future for the evil **m**;	Pr 24:20	7451a
to the **m** according to his work."	Pr 24:29	376
vineyard of the **m** lacking sense,	Pr 24:30	120
And your want like an armed **m**.	Pr 24:34	376
a **m** who boasts of his gifts falsely.	Pr 25:14	376
a **m** who bears false witness against	Pr 25:18	376
a faithless **m** in time of trouble.	Pr 25:19	
m who gives way before the wicked.	Pr 25:26	6662
m who has no control over his spirit.	Pr 25:28	376
you see a **m** wise in his own eyes?	Pr 26:12	376
the **m** who deceives his neighbor,	Pr 26:19	376
a contentious **m** to kindle strife.	Pr 26:21	376
A sated **m** loathes honey, But to a	Pr 27:7	5315
to a famished **m** any bitter thing is	Pr 27:7	5315
is a **m** who wanders from his home.	Pr 27:8	376
m sees evil *and* hides himself,	Pr 27:12	6175
iron, So one **m** sharpens another.	Pr 27:17	376
So the heart of **m** *reflects* man.	Pr 27:19	120
So the heart of man *reflects* **m**.	Pr 27:19	120
are the eyes of **m** ever satisfied.	Pr 27:20	120
But by a **m** of understanding *and*	Pr 28:2	120
A poor **m** who oppresses the lowly	Pr 28:3	1397
rich **m** is wise in his own eyes,	Pr 28:11	376
blessed is the **m** who fears always,	Pr 28:14	120
A **m** who is laden with the guilt of	Pr 28:17	120
m will abound with blessings,	Pr 28:20	376
of bread a **m** will transgress.	Pr 28:21	1397
A **m** with an evil eye hastens after	Pr 28:22	376
He who rebukes a **m** will afterward	Pr 28:23	120
the companion of a **m** who destroys.	Pr 28:24	376
An arrogant **m** stirs up strife, But	Pr 28:25	
A **m** who hardens *his* neck after	Pr 29:1	376
But when a wicked **m** rules,	Pr 29:2	7563
A **m** who loves wisdom makes his	Pr 29:3	376
But a **m** who takes bribes	Pr 29:4	376
A **m** who flatters his neighbor Is	Pr 29:5	1397
an evil **m** is ensnared,	Pr 29:6	376
When a wise **m** has a controversy	Pr 29:9	376
a controversy with a foolish **m**,	Pr 29:9	376
foolish **m** either rages or laughs,	Pr 29:9	
But a wise **m** holds it back.	Pr 29:11	2450
The poor **m** and the oppressor have	Pr 29:13	376
see a **m** who is hasty in his words?	Pr 29:20	376
An angry **m** stirs up strife, And a	Pr 29:22	376
m abounds in transgression.	Pr 29:22	1167
The fear of **m** brings a snare, But	Pr 29:25	120
justice for **m** *comes* from the LORD.	Pr 29:26	376
An unjust **m** is abominable to the	Pr 29:27	376
The **m** declares to Ithiel, to	Pr 30:1	1397
I am more stupid than any **m**,	Pr 30:2	376
not have the understanding of a **m**.	Pr 30:2	120
There is a kind of **m** who curses	Pr 30:11	
There is a kind of **m** whose teeth	Pr 30:14	
And the way of a **m** with a maid.	Pr 30:19	1397
What advantage does **m** have in all	Ec 1:3	120
M is not able to tell *it*.	Ec 1:8	376
for what *will* the **m** *do* who will	Ec 2:12	120
of the wise **m** *as* with the fool,	Ec 2:16	2450
the wise **m** and the fool alike die!	Ec 2:16	2450
to the **m** who will come after me.	Ec 2:18	120
he will be a wise **m** or a fool?	Ec 2:19	2450
a **m** who has labored with wisdom,	Ec 2:21	120
For what does a **m** get in all his	Ec 2:22	120
There is nothing better for a **m**	Ec 2:24	120
yet so that **m** will not find out	Ec 3:11	120
that every **m** who eats and drinks	Ec 3:13	120
righteous **m** and the wicked man,"	Ec 3:17	6662
righteous man and the wicked **m**,"	Ec 3:17	7563
is no advantage for **m** over beast,	Ec 3:19	120
the breath of **m** ascends upward	Ec 3:21	120
nothing is better than that **m** should	Ec 3:22	120
between a **m** and his neighbor.	Ec 4:4	376
a certain **m** without a dependent,	Ec 4:8	259
sleep of the working **m** is pleasant,	Ec 5:12	
full stomach of the rich **m** does not	Ec 5:12	6223
as a **m** is born, thus will he die.	Ec 5:16	
as for every **m** to whom God has	Ec 5:19	120
a **m** to whom God has given riches	Ec 6:2	376
If a **m** fathers a hundred *children*	Ec 6:3	376
"Even if the *other* **m** lives a	Ec 6:6	
the wise **m** have over the fool?	Ec 6:8	2450
advantage does the poor **m** have,	Ec 6:8	6041
named, and it is known what **m** is;	Ec 6:10	120
What *then* is the advantage to a **m**?	Ec 6:11	120
good for a **m** during *his* lifetime,	Ec 6:12	120
For who can tell a **m** what will be	Ec 6:12	120
that is the end of every **m**,	Ec 7:2	120
to listen to the rebuke of a wise **m**	Ec 7:5	2450
For oppression makes a wise **m** mad,	Ec 7:7	2450
m will not discover anything *that*	Ec 7:14	120
a righteous **m** who perishes in his	Ec 7:15	6662
a wicked **m** who prolongs *his life* in	Ec 7:15	7563
Wisdom strengthens a wise **m** more	Ec 7:19	2450
there is not a righteous **m** on	Ec 7:20	120
have found one **m** among a thousand,	Ec 7:28	120
Who is like the wise **m** and who	Ec 8:1	2450
No **m** has authority to restrain the	Ec 8:8	120
wherein a **m** has exercised authority	Ec 8:9	120
authority over *another* **m** to his hurt.	Ec 8:9	120
But it will not be well for the evil **m**	Ec 8:13	7563
nothing good for a **m** under the sun	Ec 8:15	120
I concluded that **m** cannot discover	Ec 8:17	120
though **m** should seek laboriously,	Ec 8:17	120
and though the wise **m** should say,	Ec 8:17	2450
M does not know whether *it will be*	Ec 9:1	120
for the **m** who offers a sacrifice	Ec 9:2	
As the good **m** is, so is the sinner;	Ec 9:2	2896a
m does not know his time:	Ec 9:12	120
there was found in it a poor wise **m**	Ec 9:15	376
Yet no one remembered that poor **m**.	Ec 9:15	376
But the wisdom of the poor **m** is	Ec 9:16	4542
mouth of a wise **m** are gracious,	Ec 10:12	2450
No **m** knows what will happen, and	Ec 10:14	120
rooms do not curse a rich **m**,	Ec 10:20	6223
if a **m** should live many years,	Ec 11:8	120
Rejoice, young **m**, during your	Ec 11:9	970
For **m** goes to his eternal home	Ec 12:5	120
In addition to being a wise **m**,	Ec 12:9	2450
Each **m** has his sword at his side,	SS 3:8	376
If a **m** were to give all the riches	SS 8:7	376
The strong **m** will become tinder,	Is 1:31	2634
So the *common* **m** has been humbled	Is 2:9	120
m *of importance* has been abased,	Is 2:9	376
proud look of **m** will be abased And	Is 2:11	120
loftiness of **m** will be humbled,	Is 2:11	376
The pride of **m** will be humbled	Is 2:17	120
Stop regarding **m**, whose breath *of*	Is 2:22	120
The mighty **m** and the warrior, The	Is 3:2	1368
of fifty and the honorable **m**,	Is 3:3	
When a **m** lays hold of his brother	Is 3:6	376
women will take hold of one **m**	Is 4:1	376
So the *common* **m** will be humbled and	Is 5:15	120
and the **m** of *importance* abased,	Is 5:15	376
Because I am a **m** of unclean lips,	Is 6:5	376
a **m** may keep alive a heifer and a	Is 7:21	376
head is the elder and honorable **m**,	Is 9:15	
No **m** spares his brother.	Is 9:19	376
And like a mighty **m** I brought down	Is 10:13	47
be as when a sick **m** wastes away.	Is 10:18	5263
mortal **m** scarcer than pure gold And	Is 13:12	582
the **m** who made the earth tremble,	Is 14:16	376
as a hired **m** would count them,	Is 16:14	7916
In that day **m** will have regard for	Is 17:7	120
a drunken **m** staggers in his vomit.	Is 19:14	7910
year, as a hired **m** would count it,	Is 21:16	7916
about to hurl you headlong, O **m**.	Is 22:17	1397
will be as when a hungry **m** dreams	Is 29:8	7457
Or as when a thirsty **m** dreams	Is 29:8	6771
will flee at the threat of one **m**;	Is 30:17	
For in that day every **m** will cast	Is 31:7	376
will fall by a sword not of **m**,	Is 31:8	376
a sword not of **m** will devour him.	Is 31:8	120
the noble **m** devises noble plans;	Is 32:8	5081
cities, He has no regard for **m**.	Is 33:8	582
on which if a **m** leans, it will go	Is 36:6	376
I will look on **m** no more among	Is 38:11	120

arouse *His* zeal like a **m** of war. **Is 42:13** 376
horse, The army and the mighty **m** **Is 43:17** 5808
The **m** shapes iron into a cutting **Is 44:12**
and makes it like the form of a **m**, **Is 44:13** 376
of a man, like the beauty of **m**, **Is 44:13** 120
becomes *something* for a **m** to burn, **Is 44:15** 120
the earth, and created **m** upon it. **Is 45:12** 120
The **m** of My purpose from a far **Is 46:11** 376
and will not spare a **m**." **Is 47:3** 120
prey be taken from the mighty **m**, **Is 49:24** 1368
the mighty **m** will be taken away, **Is 49:25** 1368
"Why was there no **m** when I came? **Is 50:2** 376
Do not fear the reproach of **m**, **Is 51:7** 582
that you are afraid of **m** who dies And **Is 51:12** 582
son of **m** who is made like grass, **Is 51:12** 120
was marred more than any **m** And **Is 52:14** 376
forsaken of men, A **m** of sorrows and **Is 53:3** 376
He was with a rich **m** in His death, **Is 53:9** 6223
the unrighteous **m** his thoughts; **Is 55:7** 376
blessed is the **m** who does this, **Is 56:2** 582
the son of **m** who takes hold of it; **Is 56:2** 120
The righteous **m** perishes, and no **Is 57:1** 6662
and no **m** takes it to heart; **Is 57:1** 376
righteous **m** is taken away from evil, **Is 57:1** 6662
a day for a **m** to humble himself? **Is 58:5** 120
And He saw that there was no **m**, **Is 59:16** 376
For *as* a young **m** marries a virgin, **Is 62:5** 970
peoples there was no **m** with Me. **Is 63:3** 376
Or an old **m** who does not live out **Is 65:20** 2205
an ox is *like* one who slays a **m**; **Is 66:3** 376
one crossed And where no **m** dwelt?' **Jer 2:6** 120
him And belongs to another **m**, **Jer 3:1** 376
and behold, there was no **m**, **Jer 4:25** 120
forsaken, And no **m** dwells in them. **Jer 4:29** 376
open squares, If you can find a **m**, **Jer 5:1** 376
Arrayed as a **m** for the battle **Jer 6:23** 376
between a **m** and his neighbor, **Jer 7:5** 376
on **m** and on beast and on the trees **Jer 7:20** 120
No **m** repented of his wickedness, **Jer 8:6** 376
wise **m** that may understand this? **Jer 9:12** 376
not a wise **m** boast of his wisdom, **Jer 9:23** 2450
the mighty **m** boast of his might, **Jer 9:23** 1368
not a rich **m** boast of his riches; **Jer 9:23** 6223
Every **m** is stupid, devoid of **Jer 10:14** 120
Nor is it in a **m** who walks to direct **Jer 10:23** 376
"Cursed is the **m** who does not **Jer 11:3** 376
Because no **m** lays it to heart. **Jer 12:11** 376
clings to the waist of a **m**, **Jer 13:11** 376
"Why are You like a **m** dismayed, **Jer 14:9** 376
Like a mighty **m** who cannot save? **Jer 14:9** 1368
against the mother of a young **m**, **Jer 15:8** 970
As a **m** of strife and a man of **Jer 15:10** 376
a **m** of contention to all the land! **Jer 15:10** 376
Can **m** make gods for himself? **Jer 16:20** 120
"Cursed is the **m** who trusts in **Jer 17:5** 1397
"Blessed is the **m** who trusts in **Jer 17:7** 1397
to each **m** according to his ways, **Jer 17:10** 376
Cursed be the **m** who brought the **Jer 20:15** 376
But let that **m** be like the cities **Jer 20:16** 376
of this city, both **m** and beast; **Jer 21:6** 120
"Is this **m** Coniah a despised, **Jer 22:28** 376
'Write this **m** down childless, A **Jer 22:30** 376
A **m** who will not prosper in his **Jer 22:30** 1397
no **m** of his descendants will prosper **Jer 22:30** 376
I have become like a drunken **m**, **Jer 23:9** 376
Even like a **m** overcome with wine, **Jer 23:9** 1397
a **m** hide himself in hiding places So **Jer 23:24** 376
upon that **m** and his household. **Jer 23:34** 376
"A death sentence for this **m**! **Jer 26:11** 376
"No death sentence for this **m**! **Jer 26:16** 376
there was also a **m** who prophesied **Jer 26:20** 376
m *With* his hands on his loins, **Jer 30:6** 1397
A woman will encompass a **m**." **Jer 31:22** 1397
with the seed of **m** and with the seed **Jer 31:27** 120
each **m** who eats the sour grapes, **Jer 31:30** 120
each **m** his neighbor and each man **Jer 31:34** 376
neighbor and each **m** his brother, **Jer 31:34** 376
a desolation, without **m** or beast; **Jer 32:43** 120
without **m** and without beast," **Jer 33:10** 120
without **m** and without inhabitant **Jer 33:10** 120
is waste, without **m** or beast, **Jer 33:12** 120
'David shall never lack a **m** to sit **Jer 33:17** 376
Levitical priests shall never lack a **m** **Jer 33:18** 376
that each **m** should set free his **Jer 34:9** 376
and each **m** his female servant, **Jer 34:9** 376
a Hebrew **m** or a Hebrew woman; **Jer 34:9** 5680
each **m** should set free his male servant **Jer 34:10** 376
and each **m** his female servant, **Jer 34:10** 376
each **m** proclaiming release to his **Jer 34:15** 376
and each **m** took back his male **Jer 34:16** 376
and each **m** his female servant whom **Jer 34:16** 376
release each **m** to his brother and **Jer 34:17** 376
and each **m** to his neighbor. **Jer 34:17** 376
the son of Igdaliah, the **m** of God, **Jer 35:4** 376
now every **m** from his evil way and **Jer 35:15** 376
shall not lack a **m** to stand before Me **Jer 35:19** 376
m will turn from his evil way; **Jer 36:3** 376
m and beast to cease from it?" **Jer 36:29** 120
among them, each **m** in his tent, **Jer 37:10** 376
"Now let this **m** be put to death, **Jer 38:4** 376
for this **m** is not seeking the **Jer 38:4** 376
"Let no **m** know about these words **Jer 38:24** 376
Nethaniah, and not a **m** will know! **Jer 40:15** 376
to cut off from you **m** and woman, **Jer 44:7** 376
by the mouth of any **m** of Judah **Jer 44:26** 376
Let not the swift **m** flee, **Jer 46:6** 7031
man flee, Nor the mighty **m** escape; **Jer 46:6** 1368
nor will a son of **m** reside in it. **Jer 49:18** 120
will a son of **m** reside in it." **Jer 49:33** 120
m and beast have wandered off, **Jer 50:3** 120
"No **m** will live there, Nor will **Jer 50:40** 376
will *any* son of **m** reside in it. **Jer 50:40** 120
Marshalled like a **m** for the battle **Jer 50:42** 376
with you I shatter **m** and woman, **Jer 51:22** 376
you I shatter old **m** and youth, **Jer 51:22** 376
you I shatter young **m** and virgin, **Jer 51:22** 970
A land in which no **m** lives And **Jer 51:43** 376
through which no son of **m** passes. **Jer 51:43** 120
in it, whether **m** or beast, **Jer 51:62** 120
As they faint like a wounded **m** In **La 2:12** 2491a
I am the **m** who has seen affliction **La 3:1** 1397
It is good for a **m** that he should **La 3:27** 1397
To deprive a **m** of justice In the **La 3:35** 1397
To defraud a **m** in his lawsuit **La 3:36** 120
any living mortal, or *any* **m**, **La 3:39** 1397
faces, *each* had the face of a **m**; **Ezk 1:10** 120
figure with the appearance of a **m**. **Ezk 1:26** 120
"Son of **m**, stand on your feet **Ezk 2:1** 120
"Son of **m**, I am sending you to **Ezk 2:3** 120
"And you, son of **m**, neither fear **Ezk 2:6** 120
"Now you, son of **m**, listen to **Ezk 2:8** 120
"Son of **m**, eat what you find; **Ezk 3:1** 120
"Son of **m**, feed your stomach and **Ezk 3:3** 120
"Son of **m**, go to the house of **Ezk 3:4** 120
"Son of **m**, take into your heart **Ezk 3:10** 120
"Son of **m**, I have appointed you a **Ezk 3:17** 120
wicked **m** shall die in his iniquity, **Ezk 3:18** 7563
when a righteous **m** turns away from **Ezk 3:20** 6662
if you have warned the righteous **m** **Ezk 3:21** 6662
"As for you, son of **m**, **Ezk 3:25** 120
cannot be a **m** who rebukes them, **Ezk 3:26** 376
"Now you son of **m**, get yourself a **Ezk 4:1** 120
"Son of **m**, behold, I am going to **Ezk 4:16** 120
"As for you, son of **m**, **Ezk 5:1** 120
"Son of **m**, set your face toward **Ezk 6:2** 120
"And you, son of **m**, thus says the **Ezk 7:2** 120
likeness as the appearance of a **m**; **Ezk 8:2** 784
"Son of **m**, raise your eyes now **Ezk 8:5** 120
"Son of **m**, do you see what they **Ezk 8:6** 120
"Son of **m**, now dig through the **Ezk 8:8** 120
each **m** with his censer in his hand and **Ezk 8:11** 376
"Son of **m**, do you see what the **Ezk 8:12** 120
each **m** in the room of his carved **Ezk 8:12** 376
"Do you see *this*, son of **m**? **Ezk 8:15** 120
"Do you see *this*, son of **m**? **Ezk 8:17** 120
and among them was a certain **m** **Ezk 9:2** 376
And He called to the **m** clothed in **Ezk 9:3** 376
touch any **m** on whom is the mark; **Ezk 9:6** 376
the **m** clothed in linen at whose **Ezk 9:11** 376
He spoke to the **m** clothed in linen **Ezk 10:2** 376
of the temple when the **m** entered, **Ezk 10:3** 376
commanded the **m** clothed in linen, **Ezk 10:6** 376
second face *was* the face of a **m**, **Ezk 10:14** 120
"Son of **m**, these are the men who **Ezk 11:2** 120
prophesy against them, son of **m**, **Ezk 11:4** 120
"Son of **m**, your brothers, your **Ezk 11:15** 120
"Son of **m**, you live in the midst **Ezk 12:2** 120
"Therefore, son of **m**, prepare for **Ezk 12:3** 120
"Son of **m**, has not the house of **Ezk 12:9** 120
"Son of **m**, eat your bread with **Ezk 12:18** 120
"Son of **m**, what is this proverb **Ezk 12:22** 120
"Son of **m**, behold, the house of **Ezk 12:27** 120
"Son of **m**, prophesy against the **Ezk 13:2** 120
"Now you, son of **m**, set your face **Ezk 13:17** 120
"Son of **m**, these men have set up **Ezk 14:3** 120
"Any **m** of the house of Israel who **Ezk 14:4** 376
I will set My face against that **m** **Ezk 14:8** 376
"Son of **m**, if a country sins **Ezk 14:13** 120
cut off from it both **m** and beast, **Ezk 14:13** 120
and cut off **m** and beast from it,' **Ezk 14:17** 120
to cut off **m** and beast from it, **Ezk 14:19** 120
to cut off **m** and beast from it! **Ezk 14:21** 120
"Son of **m**, how is the wood of the **Ezk 15:2** 120
"Son of **m**, make known to **Ezk 16:2** 120
"Son of **m**, propound a riddle and **Ezk 17:2** 120
"But if a **m** is righteous and **Ezk 18:5** 376
if a **m** does not oppress anyone, **Ezk 18:7** 376
true justice between **m** and man, **Ezk 18:8** 376
true justice between man and **m**, **Ezk 18:8** 376
"But if the wicked **m** turns from **Ezk 18:21** 7563
"But when a righteous **m** turns **Ezk 18:24** 6662
abominations that a wicked **m** does, **Ezk 18:24** 7563
"When a righteous **m** turns away **Ezk 18:26** 6662
when a wicked **m** turns away from **Ezk 18:27** 7563
"Son of **m**, speak to the elders of **Ezk 20:3** 120
will you judge them, son of **m**? **Ezk 20:4** 120
by which, if a **m** observes them, **Ezk 20:11** 120
by which, if a **m** observes them, **Ezk 20:13** 120
by which, *if* a **m** observes them, **Ezk 20:21** 120
"Therefore, son of **m**, speak to the **Ezk 20:27** 120
"Son of **m**, set your face toward **Ezk 20:46** 120
"Son of **m**, set your face toward **Ezk 21:2** 120
"As for you, son of **m**, groan with **Ezk 21:6** 120
"Son of **m**, prophesy and say, **Ezk 21:9** 120
'Cry out and wail, son of **m**; **Ezk 21:12** 120
"You therefore, son of **m**, prophesy and **Ezk 21:14** 120
"As for you, son of **m**, make two **Ezk 21:19** 120
"And you, son of **m**, prophesy and **Ezk 21:28** 120
"And you, son of **m**, will you **Ezk 22:2** 120
"Son of **m**, the house of Israel **Ezk 22:18** 120
"Son of **m**, say to her, **Ezk 22:24** 120
"I searched for a **m** among **Ezk 22:30** 376
"Son of **m**, there were two women, **Ezk 23:2** 120
"Son of **m**, will you judge Oholah **Ezk 23:36** 120
"Son of **m**, write the name of the **Ezk 24:2** 120
"Son of **m**, behold, I am about to **Ezk 24:16** 120
'As for you, son of **m**, **Ezk 24:25** 120
"Son of **m**, set your face toward **Ezk 25:2** 120
and cut off **m** and beast from it. **Ezk 25:13** 120
"Son of **m**, because Tyre has said **Ezk 26:2** 120
"And you, son of **m**, take up a **Ezk 27:2** 120
"Son of **m**, say to the leader of **Ezk 28:2** 120
Yet you are a **m** and not God, **Ezk 28:2** 120
Though you are a **m** and not God, **Ezk 28:9** 120
"Son of **m**, take up a lamentation **Ezk 28:12** 120
"Son of **m**, set your face toward **Ezk 28:21** 120
"Son of **m**, set your face against **Ezk 29:2** 120
cut off from you **m** and beast. **Ezk 29:8** 120
"Son of **m**, Nebuchadnezzar king of **Ezk 29:18** 120
"Son of **m**, prophesy and say, **Ezk 30:2** 120
"Son of **m**, I have broken the arm **Ezk 30:21** 120
with the groanings of a wounded **m**. **Ezk 30:24** 2491a
"Son of **m**, say to Pharaoh king of **Ezk 31:2** 120
"Son of **m**, take up a lamentation **Ezk 32:2** 120
moment, every **m** for his own life, **Ezk 32:10** 376
foot of **m** will not muddy them **Ezk 32:13** 120
"Son of **m**, wail for the hordes **Ezk 32:18** 120
"Son of **m**, speak to the sons of **Ezk 33:2** 120
the people of the land take one **m** **Ezk 33:2** 376
"Now as for you, son of **m**, **Ezk 33:7** 120
'O wicked **m**, you will surely die,' **Ezk 33:8** 7563
wicked **m** shall die in his iniquity, **Ezk 33:8** 7563
a wicked **m** to turn from his way and **Ezk 33:9** 7563
"Now as for you, son of **m**, **Ezk 33:10** 120
"And you, son of **m**, say to your **Ezk 33:12** 120
'The righteousness of a righteous **m** **Ezk 33:12** 6662
whereas a righteous **m** will not be **Ezk 33:12** 6662
if a wicked **m** restores a pledge, **Ezk 33:15** 7563
"Son of **m**, they who live in these **Ezk 33:24** 120
"But as for you, son of **m**, **Ezk 33:30** 120
"Son of **m**, prophesy against the **Ezk 34:2** 120
"Son of **m**, set your face against **Ezk 35:2** 120
"And you, son of **m**, prophesy to **Ezk 36:1** 120
will multiply on you **m** and beast; **Ezk 36:11** 120
"Son of **m**, when the house of **Ezk 36:17** 120
"Son of **m**, can these bones live?" **Ezk 37:3** 120
to the breath, prophesy, son of **m**, **Ezk 37:9** 120
"Son of **m**, these bones are the **Ezk 37:11** 120
"And you, son of **m**, take for **Ezk 37:16** 120
"Son of **m**, set your face toward **Ezk 38:2** 120
"Therefore prophesy, son of **m**, **Ezk 38:14** 120
"And you, son of **m**, prophesy **Ezk 39:1** 120
"As for you, son of **m**, **Ezk 39:17** 120
there was a **m** whose appearance was **Ezk 40:3** 376
The **m** said to me, **Ezk 40:4** 376
"Son of **m**, see with your eyes, **Ezk 40:4** 120
while a **m** was standing beside me. **Ezk 43:6** 376
"Son of **m**, *this is* the place of **Ezk 43:7** 120
"As for you, son of **m**, **Ezk 43:10** 120
"Son of **m**, thus says the Lord **Ezk 43:18** 120
"Son of **m**, mark well, see with **Ezk 44:5** 120
When the **m** went out toward the **Ezk 47:3** 376
"Son of **m**, have you seen *this?*" **Ezk 47:6** 120
"There is not a **m** on earth who **Da 2:10** 606
"I have found a **m** among the **Da 2:25** 1400
more than *in any other* living **m**, **Da 2:30** 2417
have made a decree that every **m** **Da 3:10** 606
mind be changed from *that of* a **m** And **Da 4:16** 606
"Any **m** who can read this **Da 5:7** 606
"There is a **m** in your kingdom in **Da 5:11** 1400
to any god or **m** besides you, **Da 6:7** 606
m who makes a petition to any god **Da 6:12** 606
to any god or **m** besides you, **Da 6:12** 606
to stand on two feet like a **m**; **Da 7:4** 606
eyes like the eyes of a **m** and **Da 7:8** 606
One like a Son of **M** was coming, **Da 7:13** 606
me was one who looked like a **m**. **Da 8:15** 1397
I heard the voice of a **m** between **Da 8:16** 120
give this **m** an understanding of **Da 8:16**
"Son of **m**, understand that the **Da 8:17** 120
in prayer, then the **m** Gabriel, **Da 9:21** 376
was a certain **m** dressed in linen, **Da 10:5** 376
"O Daniel, **m** of high esteem, **Da 10:11** 376
"O **m** of high esteem, do not be **Da 10:19** 376
said to the **m** dressed in linen, **Da 12:6** 376
I heard the **m** dressed in linen, **Da 12:7** 376
harlot, nor shall you have a **m**; **Hos 3:3** 376
And as raiders wait for a **m**, **Hos 6:9** 376
fool, The inspired **m** is demented, **Hos 9:7** 376
them until not a **m** is left. **Hos 9:12** 120
I led them with cords of a **m**, **Hos 11:4** 120
For I am God and not **m**, **Hos 11:9** 376
"I am a mighty **m**." **Jl 3:10** 1368
And a **m** and his father resort to **Am 2:7** 376
Nor the mighty **m** save his life. **Am 2:14** 1368
declares to **m** what are His thoughts **Am 4:13** 120
As when a **m** flees from a lion And **Am 5:19** 376
and every **m** cried to his god, **Jon 1:5** 376
Each **m** said to his mate, **Jon 1:7** 376
Do not let **m**, beast, herd, or **Jon 3:7** 120
"But both **m** and beast must be **Jon 3:8** 120
They rob a **m** and his house, A man **Mi 2:2** 1397
house, A **m** and his inheritance. **Mi 2:2** 376
"If a **m** walking after wind and **Mi 2:11** 376
vegetation Which do not wait for **m** **Mi 5:7** 376
He has told you, O **m**, **Mi 6:8** 120
there yet a **m** in the wicked house, **Mi 6:10** 376
m speaks the desire of his soul; **Mi 7:3** 1419
M the fortress, watch the road; **Na 2:1** 5341
wine betrays the haughty **m**, **Hab 2:5** 1397
"I will remove **m** and beast; **Zph 1:3** 120
I will cut off **m** from the face of the **Zph 1:3** 120
Without a **m**, without an inhabitant. **Zph 3:6** 376
'If a **m** carries holy meat in the **Hg 2:12** 376
a **m** was riding on a red horse, **Zch 1:8** 376
And the **m** who was standing among **Zch 1:10** 376
so that no **m** lifts up his head; **Zch 1:21** 376

there was a **m** with a measuring	**Zch 2:1**	376
"Run, speak to that young **m**,	**Zch 2:4**	5288
and roused me, as a **m** who is	**Zch 4:1**	376
"Behold, a **m** whose name is Branch	**Zch 6:12**	376
each **m** with his staff in his hand	**Zch 8:4**	376
wage for **m** or any wage for animal;	**Zch 8:10**	120
vegetation in the field to *each* **m**.	**Zch 10:1**	376
Ephraim will be like a mighty **m**,	**Zch 10:7**	1368
forms the spirit of **m** within him,	**Zch 12:1**	120
for a **m** sold me as a slave in my	**Zch 13:5**	120
My Shepherd, And against the **m**,	**Zch 13:7**	1397
"*As* for the **m** who does this, may	**Mal 2:12**	376
"Will a **m** rob God?	**Mal 3:8**	120
spare them as a **m** spares his own	**Mal 3:17**	376
her husband, being a righteous **m** and	**Mt 1:19**	1342
'**M** SHALL NOT LIVE ON BREAD ALONE,	**Mt 4:4**	444
"Or what **m** is there among you who	**Mt 7:9**	444
them, may be compared to a wise **m**	**Mt 7:24**	435
them, will be like a foolish **m** who	**Mt 7:26**	435
I also am a **m** under authority,	**Mt 8:9**	444
M has nowhere to lay His head."	**Mt 8:20**	444
"What kind of a **m** is this, that	**Mt 8:27**	444
the Son of **M** has authority on earth	**Mt 9:6**	444
He saw a **m** called Matthew, sitting	**Mt 9:9**	444
a mute, demon-possessed **m** was	**Mt 9:32**	444
was cast out, the mute **m** spoke;	**Mt 9:33**	2974
Israel until the Son of **M** comes.	**Mt 10:23**	444
TO SET A **M** AGAINST HIS FATHER,	**Mt 10:35**	444
and he who receives a righteous **m**	**Mt 10:41**	1342
in the name of a righteous **m**	**Mt 10:41**	1342
A **m** dressed in soft *clothing?*	**Mt 11:8**	444
Son of **M** came eating and drinking,	**Mt 11:19**	444
a gluttonous **m** and a drunkard,	**Mt 11:19**	444
Son of **M** is Lord of the Sabbath."	**Mt 12:8**	444
a **m** *was there* whose hand was	**Mt 12:10**	444
"What **m** is there among you	**Mt 12:11**	444
valuable then is a **m** than a sheep!	**Mt 12:12**	444
Then He said to the **m**,	**Mt 12:13**	444
m *who was* blind and mute was	**Mt 12:22**	
so that the mute **m** spoke and saw.	**Mt 12:22**	2974
"This **m** cannot be the Son of David,	**Mt 12:23**	
"This **m** casts out demons only by	**Mt 12:24**	3778
he first binds the strong **m**?	**Mt 12:29**	
speaks a word against the Son of **M**,	**Mt 12:32**	444
"The good **m** brings out of *his* good	**Mt 12:35**	444
and the evil **m** brings out of *his* evil	**Mt 12:35**	444
so will the Son of **M** be three	**Mt 12:40**	444
unclean spirit goes out of a **m**,	**Mt 12:43**	444
m becomes worse than the first.	**Mt 12:45**	444
this is the **m** who hears the word and	**Mt 13:20**	
this is the **m** who hears the word,	**Mt 13:22**	
this is the **m** who hears the word	**Mt 13:23**	
m who sowed good seed in his field.	**Mt 13:24**	444
a **m** took and sowed in his field;	**Mt 13:31**	444
the good seed is the Son of **M**,	**Mt 13:37**	444
Son of **M** will send forth His angels,	**Mt 13:41**	444
field, which a **m** found and hid	**Mt 13:44**	444
"Where *did* this **m** *get* this	**Mt 13:54**	3778
did this **m** *get* all these things?"	**Mt 13:56**	3778
into the mouth *that* defiles the **m**,	**Mt 15:11**	444
the mouth, this defiles the **m**."	**Mt 15:11**	444
if a blind **m** guides a blind man,	**Mt 15:14**	5185
if a blind man guides a blind **m**,	**Mt 15:14**	5185
the heart, and those defile the **m**.	**Mt 15:18**	444
are the things which defile the **m**;	**Mt 15:20**	444
hands does not defile the **m**."	**Mt 15:20**	444
people say that the Son of **M** is?"	**Mt 16:13**	444
"For what will it profit a **m**	**Mt 16:26**	444
a **m** give in exchange for his soul?	**Mt 16:26**	444
"For the Son of **M** is going to	**Mt 16:27**	444
EVERY **M** ACCORDING TO HIS DEEDS.	**Mt 16:27**	1538
Son of **M** coming in His kingdom."	**Mt 16:28**	444
Son of **M** has risen from the dead."	**Mt 17:9**	444
So also the Son of **M** is going to	**Mt 17:12**	444
the crowd, a **m** came up to Jesus,	**Mt 17:14**	444
"The Son of **M** is going to be	**Mt 17:22**	444
but woe to that **m** through whom the	**Mt 18:7**	444
"For the Son of **M** has come to	**Mt 18:11**	444
If any **m** has a hundred sheep, and	**Mt 18:12**	444
"Is it lawful *for a* **m** to divorce	**Mt 19:3**	
'FOR THIS REASON A **M** SHALL LEAVE	**Mt 19:5**	444
together, let no **m** separate."	**Mt 19:6**	444
relationship of the **m** with his wife	**Mt 19:10**	444
The young **m** said to Him,	**Mt 19:20**	3495
the young **m** heard this statement,	**Mt 19:22**	3495
it is hard for a rich **m** to enter	**Mt 19:23**	4145
rich **m** to enter the kingdom of God	**Mt 19:24**	4145
when the Son of **M** will sit on His	**Mt 19:28**	444
to this last **m** the same as to you.	**Mt 20:14**	2078
and the Son of **M** will be delivered	**Mt 20:18**	444
of **M** did not come to be served,	**Mt 20:28**	444
A **m** had two sons, and he came to	**Mt 21:28**	444
"The **m** came to the second and said	**Mt 21:30**	
a **m** there who was not dressed in	**Mt 22:11**	444
And the **m** was speechless.	**Mt 22:12**	
'IF A **M** DIES HAVING NO CHILDREN,	**Mt 22:24**	5100
the coming of the Son of **M** be.	**Mt 24:27**	444
Son of **M** will appear in the sky,	**Mt 24:30**	444
and they will see the SON OF **M**	**Mt 24:30**	444
"For the coming of the Son of **M**	**Mt 24:37**	444
the coming of the Son of **M** be.	**Mt 24:39**	444
for the Son of **M** is coming at an	**Mt 24:44**	444
like a **m** *about* to go on a journey,	**Mt 25:14**	444
'Master, I knew you to be a hard **m**,	**Mt 25:24**	444
the Son of **M** comes in His glory,	**Mt 25:31**	444
and the Son of **M** is *to be*	**Mt 26:2**	444
"Go into the city to a certain **m**,	**Mt 26:18**	1170
"The Son of **M** is *to* go, just as	**Mt 26:24**	444
but woe to that **m** by whom the Son	**Mt 26:24**	444
by whom the Son of **M** is betrayed!	**Mt 26:24**	444
that **m** if he had not been born."	**Mt 26:24**	444
and the Son of **M** is being betrayed	**Mt 26:45**	444
"This **m** stated,	**Mt 26:61**	3778
you will see THE SON OF **M** SITTING	**Mt 26:64**	444
m was with Jesus of Nazareth."	**Mt 26:71**	3778
"I do not know the **m**."	**Mt 26:72**	444
"I do not know the **m**!"	**Mt 26:74**	444
to do with that righteous **M**;	**Mt 27:19**	1342
found a **m** of Cyrene named Simon,	**Mt 27:32**	444
"This **m** is calling for Elijah."	**Mt 27:47**	3778
came a rich **m** from Arimathea,	**Mt 27:57**	444
This **m** went to Pilate and asked	**Mt 27:58**	3778
a **m** in their synagogue with an unclean	**Mk 1:23**	444
"Why does this **m** speak that way?	**Mk 2:7**	3778
the Son of **M** has authority on earth	**Mk 2:10**	444
"The Sabbath was made for **m**,	**Mk 2:27**	444
man, and not **m** for the Sabbath.	**Mk 2:27**	444
the Son of **M** is Lord even of the	**Mk 2:28**	444
a **m** was there whose hand was	**Mk 3:1**	444
to the **m** with the withered hand,	**Mk 3:3**	444
of heart, He said to the **m**,	**Mk 3:5**	444
he first binds the strong **m**,	**Mk 3:27**	2478
a **m** who casts seed upon the soil;	**Mk 4:26**	444
immediately a **m** from the tombs	**Mk 5:2**	444
"Come out of the **m**, you unclean	**Mk 5:8**	444
m who had been demon-possessed	**Mk 5:15**	
mind, the very **m** who had had the	**Mk 5:15**	
happened to the demon-possessed **m**,	**Mk 5:16**	
the **m** who had been demon-possessed	**Mk 5:18**	
"Where did this **m** *get* these	**Mk 6:2**	3778
he was a righteous and holy **m**,	**Mk 6:20**	435
'If a **m** says to *his* father or *his*	**Mk 7:11**	444
there is nothing outside the **m**	**Mk 7:15**	444
of the **m** are what defile the man.	**Mk 7:15**	444
of the man are what defile the **m**.	**Mk 7:15**	444
whatever goes into the **m** from	**Mk 7:18**	444
"That which proceeds out of the **m**,	**Mk 7:20**	444
man, that is what defiles the **m**.	**Mk 7:20**	444
from within and defile the **m**."	**Mk 7:23**	444
And they brought a blind **m** to Jesus	**Mk 8:22**	5185
Taking the blind **m** by the hand,	**Mk 8:23**	5185
Son of **M** must suffer many things	**Mk 8:31**	444
what does it profit a **m** to gain the	**Mk 8:36**	444
a **m** give in exchange for his soul?	**Mk 8:37**	444
the Son of **M** will also be ashamed	**Mk 8:38**	444
Son of **M** rose from the dead.	**Mk 9:9**	444
written of the Son of **M** that He	**Mk 9:12**	444
"The Son of **M** is to be delivered	**Mk 9:31**	444
lawful for a **m** to divorce a wife.	**Mk 10:2**	435
They said, "Moses permitted *a* **m**	**Mk 10:4**	
"FOR THIS REASON A **M** SHALL LEAVE	**Mk 10:7**	444
together, let no **m** separate."	**Mk 10:9**	444
her husband and marries another **m**,	**Mk 10:12**	243
a **m** ran up to Him and knelt before	**Mk 10:17**	1520
rich **m** to enter the kingdom of God."	**Mk 10:25**	4145
and the Son of **M** will be delivered	**Mk 10:33**	444
of **M** did not come to be served,	**Mk 10:45**	444
So they called the blind **m**,	**Mk 10:49**	5185
And the blind **m** said to Him,	**Mk 10:51**	5185
"A **M** PLANTED A VINEYARD AND PUT	**Mk 12:1**	444
they will see THE SON OF **M** COMING	**Mk 13:26**	444
"*It is* like a **m** away on a journey,	**Mk 13:34**	444
and a **m** will meet you carrying a	**Mk 14:13**	444
"For the Son of **M** *is to* go just	**Mk 14:21**	444
but woe to that **m** by whom the Son	**Mk 14:21**	444
by whom the Son of **M** is betrayed!	**Mk 14:21**	444
that **m** if he had not been born."	**Mk 14:21**	444
the Son of **M** is being betrayed	**Mk 14:41**	444
A young **m** was following Him,	**Mk 14:51**	3495
and you shall see THE SON OF **M**	**Mk 14:62**	444
this **m** you are talking about!"	**Mk 14:71**	444
The **m** named Barabbas had been	**Mk 15:7**	
for them *to decide* what each **m**	**Mk 15:24**	5100
"Truly this **m** was the Son of God!"	**Mk 15:39**	444
a young **m** sitting at the right,	**Mk 16:5**	3495
For I am an old **m** and my wife is	**Lk 1:18**	4246
to a **m** whose name was Joseph,	**Lk 1:27**	435
there was a **m** in Jerusalem whose	**Lk 2:25**	444
this **m** was righteous and devout,	**Lk 2:25**	444
"The **m** who has two tunics	**Lk 3:11**	
M SHALL NOT LIVE ON BREAD ALONE.'	**Lk 4:4**	444
In the synagogue there was a **m**	**Lk 4:33**	444
from me Lord, for I am a sinful **m**,	**Lk 5:8**	435
there was a **m** covered with leprosy;	**Lk 5:12**	435
on a bed a **m** who was paralyzed;	**Lk 5:18**	444
"Who is this **m** who speaks	**Lk 5:21**	
the Son of **M** has authority on earth	**Lk 5:24**	444
Son of **M** is Lord of the Sabbath."	**Lk 6:5**	444
a **m** there whose right hand was	**Lk 6:6**	444
to the **m** with the withered hand,	**Lk 6:8**	435
for the sake of the Son of **M**.	**Lk 6:22**	444
blind **m** cannot guide a blind man,	**Lk 6:39**	5185
blind man cannot guide a blind **m**,	**Lk 6:39**	5185
"The good **m** out of the good	**Lk 6:45**	444
and the evil **m** out of the evil	**Lk 6:45**	
he is like a **m** building a house,	**Lk 6:48**	444
is like a **m** who built a house on	**Lk 6:49**	444
I also am a **m** placed under authority,	**Lk 7:8**	444
a dead **m** was being carried out,	**Lk 7:12**	
"Young **m**, I say to you, arise!"	**Lk 7:14**	3495
The dead **m** sat up and began	**Lk 7:15**	3498
A **m** dressed in soft clothing?	**Lk 7:25**	444
The Son of **M** has come eating and	**Lk 7:34**	444
'Behold, a gluttonous **m** and	**Lk 7:34**	444
"If this **m** were a prophet He	**Lk 7:39**	3778
"Who is this **m** who even forgives	**Lk 7:49**	
He was met by a **m** from the	**Lk 8:27**	435
unclean spirit to come out of the **m**.	**Lk 8:29**	444
the demons came out of the **m**	**Lk 8:33**	444
and found the **m** from whom the	**Lk 8:35**	444
the **m** who was demon-possessed	**Lk 8:36**	
But the **m** from whom the demons had	**Lk 8:38**	435
there came a **m** named Jairus,	**Lk 8:41**	435
m about whom I hear such things?"	**Lk 9:9**	3778
Son of **M** must suffer many things and	**Lk 9:22**	444
"For what is a **m** profited if he	**Lk 9:25**	444
the Son of **M** will be ashamed of him	**Lk 9:26**	444
a **m** from the crowd shouted	**Lk 9:38**	435
for the Son of **M** is going to be	**Lk 9:44**	444
for the Son of **M** did not come to	**Lk 9:56**	444
M has nowhere to lay His head."	**Lk 9:58**	444
"If a **m** of peace is there,	**Lk 10:6**	5207
"A **m** was going down from	**Lk 10:30**	444
m who fell into the robbers' *hands*	**Lk 10:36**	
had gone out, the mute **m** spoke;	**Lk 11:14**	2974
"When a strong **m**, fully armed,	**Lk 11:21**	
unclean spirit goes out of a **m**,	**Lk 11:24**	444
last state of that **m** becomes worse	**Lk 11:26**	444
Son of **M** be to this generation.	**Lk 11:30**	444
the Son of **M** will confess him	**Lk 12:8**	444
speaks a word against the Son of **M**,	**Lk 12:10**	444
"**M**, who appointed Me a judge or	**Lk 12:14**	444
land of a rich **m** was very	**Lk 12:16**	444
"So is the **m** who stores up treasure	**Lk 12:21**	
for the Son of **M** is coming at an	**Lk 12:40**	444
"A **m** had a fig tree which	**Lk 13:6**	5100
which a **m** took and threw into his	**Lk 13:19**	444
a **m** suffering from dropsy.	**Lk 14:2**	444
'Give *your* place to this **m**,'	**Lk 14:9**	3778
A **m** was giving a big dinner,	**Lk 14:16**	444
'This **m** began to build and was not	**Lk 14:30**	444
"This **m** receives sinners and eats	**Lk 15:2**	3778
"What **m** among you, if he has a	**Lk 15:4**	444
"A **m** had two sons	**Lk 15:11**	444
"There was a rich **m** who had a	**Lk 16:1**	444
"Now there was a rich **m**,	**Lk 16:19**	444
a poor **m** named Lazarus	**Lk 16:20**	4434
the poor **m** died and was carried	**Lk 16:22**	4434
rich **m** also died and was buried.	**Lk 16:22**	4145
one of the days of the Son of **M**,	**Lk 17:22**	444
will the Son of **M** be in His day.	**Lk 17:24**	444
also in the days of the Son of **M**:	**Lk 17:26**	444
day that the Son of **M** is revealed.	**Lk 17:30**	444
fear God and did not respect **m**.	**Lk 18:2**	444
I do not fear God nor respect **m**,	**Lk 18:4**	444
However, when the Son of **M** comes,	**Lk 18:8**	444
this **m** went to his house	**Lk 18:14**	3778
rich **m** to enter the kingdom of God	**Lk 18:25**	4145
the Son of **M** will be accomplished.	**Lk 18:31**	444
blind **m** was sitting by the road begging	**Lk 18:35**	5185
a **m** called by the name of Zaccheus	**Lk 19:2**	435
guest of a **m** who is a sinner."	**Lk 19:7**	435
"For the Son of **M** has come to	**Lk 19:10**	444
not want this **m** to reign over us.'	**Lk 19:14**	3778
because you are an exacting **m**;	**Lk 19:21**	444
you know that I am an exacting **m**,	**Lk 19:22**	444
"A **m** planted a vineyard and	**Lk 20:9**	444
they will see THE SON OF **M** COMING	**Lk 21:27**	444
to stand before the Son of **M**."	**Lk 21:36**	444
a **m** will meet you carrying a	**Lk 22:10**	444
the Son of **M** is going as it has	**Lk 22:22**	444
that **m** by whom He is betrayed!"	**Lk 22:22**	444
betraying the Son of **M** with a kiss?	**Lk 22:48**	444
"This **m** was with Him too."	**Lk 22:56**	3778
But Peter said, "**M**, I am not!"	**Lk 22:58**	444
passed, another **m** *began* to insist,	**Lk 22:59**	243
this **m** also was with Him,	**Lk 22:59**	3778
"**M**, I do not know what you are	**Lk 22:60**	444
THE SON OF **M** WILL BE SEATED AT	**Lk 22:69**	444
"We found this **m** misleading our	**Lk 23:2**	3778
"I find no guilt in this **m**."	**Lk 23:4**	444
whether the **m** was a Galilean.	**Lk 23:6**	444
"You brought this **m** to me as one	**Lk 23:14**	444
I have found no guilt in this **m**	**Lk 23:14**	444
"Away with this **m**, and release	**Lk 23:18**	3778
"Why, what evil has this **m** done?	**Lk 23:22**	3778
And he released the **m** they were	**Lk 23:25**	
they seized a **m**, Simon of Cyrene,	**Lk 23:26**	5100
this **m** has done nothing wrong."	**Lk 23:41**	3778
"Certainly this **m** was innocent."	**Lk 23:47**	444
And a **m** named Joseph, who	**Lk 23:50**	435
Council, a good and righteous **m**	**Lk 23:50**	435
a **m** from Arimathea, a city of	**Lk 23:51**	
this **m** went to Pilate and asked	**Lk 23:52**	3778
saying that the Son of **M** must be	**Lk 24:7**	444
There came a **m** sent from God,	**Jn 1:6**	444
the world, enlightens every **m**.	**Jn 1:9**	444
the flesh nor of the will of **m**,	**Jn 1:13**	435
a **M** who has a higher rank than I,	**Jn 1:30**	435
and descending on the Son of **M**."	**Jn 1:51**	444
m serves the good wine first,	**Jn 2:10**	444
anyone to testify concerning **m**,	**Jn 2:25**	444
for He Himself knew what was in **m**.	**Jn 2:25**	444
there was a **m** of the Pharisees,	**Jn 3:1**	444
this **m** came to Jesus by night and	**Jn 3:2**	3778
can a **m** be born when he is old?	**Jn 3:4**	444
from heaven: the Son of **M**.	**Jn 3:13**	444
so must the Son of **M** be lifted up;	**Jn 3:14**	444
"A **m** can receive nothing unless	**Jn 3:27**	444
see a **m** who told me all the things	**Jn 4:29**	444
The **m** believed the word that Jesus	**Jn 4:50**	444
A **m** was there who had	**Jn 5:5**	444
The sick **m** answered Him,	**Jn 5:7**	
I have no **m** to put me into the	**Jn 5:7**	444
Immediately the **m** became well,	**Jn 5:9**	444
So the Jews were saying to the **m** who	**Jn 5:10**	
"Who is the **m** who said to you,	**Jn 5:12**	444

But the **m** who was healed did not know Jn 5:13 *3778*
The **m** went away, and told the Jews Jn 5:15 *444*
because He is *the* Son of **M**. Jn 5:27 *444*
which I receive is not from **m**, Jn 5:34 *444*
the Son of **M** will give to you, Jn 6:27 *444*
this **m** give us *His* flesh to eat?" Jn 6:52 *3778*
you eat the flesh of the Son of **M** Jn 6:53 *444*
Son of **M** ascending to where He was Jn 6:62 *444*
"He is a good **m**"; Jn 7:12 *18*
"How has this **m** become learned, Jn 7:15 *3778*
on *the* Sabbath you circumcise a **m**. Jn 7:22 *444*
"If a **m** receives circumcision on Jn 7:23 *444*
because I made an entire **m** well on Jn 7:23 *444*
m whom they are seeking to kill? Jn 7:25
we know where this **m** is from; Jn 7:27 *3778*
and no **m** laid his hand on Him, Jn 7:30 *3762*
signs than those which this **m** has, Jn 7:31 *3778*
"Where does this **m** intend to go Jn 7:35 *3778*
"Never has a **m** spoken the way this Jn 7:46 *444*
man spoken the way this **m** speaks." Jn 7:46 *444*
"Our Law does not judge a **m** unless Jn 7:51 *444*
"When you lift up the Son of **M**, Jn 8:28 *444*
a **m** who has told you the truth, Jn 8:40 *444*
by, He saw a **m** blind from birth. Jn 9:1 *444*
who sinned, this **m** or his parents, Jn 9:2 *3778*
"*It was* neither *that* this **m** sinned, Jn 9:3 *3778*
m who is called Jesus made clay, Jn 9:11 *444*
They brought to the Pharisees the **m** Jn 9:13 *444*
"This **m** is not from God, because Jn 9:16 *444*
"How can a **m** who is a sinner Jn 9:16 *444*
said to the blind **m** again, Jn 9:17 *5185*
called the **m** who had been blind, Jn 9:24 *444*
we know that this **m** is a sinner." Jn 9:24 *444*
but as for this **m**, we do not know Jn 9:29 *3778*
The **m** answered and said to them, Jn 9:30 *444*
"If this **m** were not from God, He Jn 9:33 *3778*
"Do you believe in the Son of **M**?" Jn 9:35 *444*
and because You, being a **m**, Jn 10:33 *444*
John said about this **m** was true." Jn 10:41 *3778*
Now a certain **m** was sick, Lazarus Jn 11:1 *5100*
"Could not this **m**, who opened the Jn 11:37 *3778*
who opened the eyes of the blind **m**, Jn 11:37 *3778*
kept this **m** also from dying?" Jn 11:37 *3778*
The **m** who had died came forth, bound Jn 11:44
this **m** is performing many signs. Jn 11:47 *444*
one **m** die for the people, Jn 11:50 *444*
for the Son of **M** to be glorified. Jn 12:23 *444*
'The Son of **M** must be lifted up'? Jn 12:34 *444*
Who is this Son of **M**?" Jn 12:34 *444*
"Now is the Son of **M** glorified, Jn 13:31 *444*
it was expedient for one **m** to die Jn 18:14 *444*
do you bring against this **M**?" Jn 18:29 *444*
"If this **M** were not an evildoer, Jn 18:30 *3778*
"Not this **M**, but Barabbas." Jn 18:40 *3778*
Pilate said to them, "Behold, the **M**!" Jn 19:5 *444*
"If you release this **M**, Jn 19:12 *3778*
and broke the legs of the first **m** and Jn 19:32 *4413*
"Lord, and what about this **m**?" Jn 21:21 *3778*
(Now this **m** acquired a field with Ac 1:18 *3778*
'LET ANOTHER **M** TAKE HIS OFFICE.' Ac 1:20 *2087*
a **m** attested to you by God with Ac 2:22 *435*
this **M**, delivered over by Ac 2:23
And a **m** who had been lame Ac 3:2 *435*
this **m** whom you see and know; Ac 3:16
for a benefit done to a sick **m**, Ac 4:9 *444*
to how this **m** has been made well, Ac 4:9 *3778*
by this *name* this **m** stands here Ac 4:10 *3778*
And seeing the **m** who had been Ac 4:14 *444*
no longer to any **m** in this name." Ac 4:17 *444*
the **m** was more than forty years old Ac 4:22 *444*
But a **m** named Ananias, Ac 5:1 *435*
"After this **m**, Judas of Galilee Ac 5:37 *3778*
a **m** full of faith and of the Holy Ac 6:5 *435*
"This **m** incessantly speaks against Ac 6:13 *444*
a **m** of power in words and deeds. Ac 7:22 *1415*
"This **m** led them out, performing Ac 7:36 *3778*
Son of **M** standing at the right hand Ac 7:56 *444*
the feet of a young **m** named Saul. Ac 7:58 *3494*
there was a **m** named Simon, Ac 8:9 *435*
"This **m** is what is called the Ac 8:10 *3778*
for a **m** from Tarsus named Saul, Ac 9:11
seen in a vision a **m** named Ananias Ac 9:12 *435*
have heard from many about this **m**, Ac 9:13 *435*
he found a **m** named Aeneas, Ac 9:33 *444*
m at Caesarea named Cornelius, Ac 10:1 *435*
a devout **m** and one who feared God Ac 10:2 *2152*
and send for a **m** *named* Simon, Ac 10:5 *5100*
a righteous and God-fearing **m** well Ac 10:22 *435*
I too am *just a* **m**." Ac 10:26 *444*
unlawful it is for a **m** who is a Jew Ac 10:28 *435*
not call any **m** unholy or unclean. Ac 10:28 *444*
a **m** stood before me in shining Ac 10:30 *435*
the **m** who fears Him and does what Ac 10:35
for he was a good **m**, Ac 11:24 *435*
voice of a god and not of a **m**!" Ac 12:22 *444*
Paulus, a **m** of intelligence. Ac 13:7 *435*
This **m** summoned Barnabas and Saul Ac 13:7 *3778*
a **m** of the tribe of Benjamin, Ac 13:21 *435*
son of Jesse, A **M** AFTER MY HEART, Ac 13:22 *435*
"From the descendants of this **m**, Ac 13:23 *3778*
At Lystra a **m** was sitting Ac 14:8 *435*
This **m** was listening to Paul as he Ac 14:9 *3778*
Paul wanted this **m** to go with him; Ac 16:3 *3778*
a **m** of Macedonia was Ac 16:9 *435*
and He made from one **m** every Ac 17:26
by the art and thought of **m**. Ac 17:29 *444*
through a **M** whom He has appointed, Ac 17:31 *435*
a **m** named Titius Justus, Ac 18:7 *5100*
and no **m** will attack you in order Ac 18:10 *3762*
"This **m** persuades men to worship Ac 18:13 *3778*
by birth, an eloquent **m**, Ac 18:24 *435*
This **m** had been instructed in the Ac 18:25 *3778*
And the **m**, in whom was the evil Ac 19:16 *444*
For a **m** named Demetrius, a Ac 19:24 *5100*
what **m** is there after all who does Ac 19:35 *444*
have a complaint against any **m**, Ac 19:38 *5100*
And there was a young **m** Ac 20:9 *3494*
this **m** had four virgin daughters Ac 21:9 *3778*
will bind the **m** who owns this belt Ac 21:11 *435*
This is the **m** who preaches to all Ac 21:28 *444*
a **m** who was devout by the standard Ac 22:12 *435*
to scourge a **m** who is a Roman Ac 22:25 *444*
For this **m** is a Roman." Ac 22:26 *444*
"We find nothing wrong with this **m**; Ac 23:9 *444*
this young **m** to the commander, Ac 23:17 *3494*
asked me to lead this young **m** to you Ac 23:18 *3495*
the commander let the young **m** go, Ac 23:22 *3495*
"When this **m** was arrested by the Ac 23:27 *435*
would be a plot against the **m**, Ac 23:30 *435*
we have found this **m** a real pest Ac 24:5 *435*
is anything wrong about the **m**, Ac 25:5 *435*
a **m** who was left as a prisoner Ac 25:14 *435*
hand over any **m** before the accused Ac 25:16 *444*
and ordered the **m** to be brought before Ac 25:17 *435*
and about a dead **m**, Ac 25:19 *5100*
would like to hear the **m** myself." Ac 25:22 *444*
you see this **m** about whom all Ac 25:24 *3778*
"This **m** is not doing anything Ac 26:31 *444*
"This **m** might have been set free Ac 26:32 *444*
"Undoubtedly this **m** is a murderer, Ac 28:4 *444*
to the leading **m** of the island, Ac 28:7 *4413*
"BUT THE RIGHTEOUS **M** SHALL Ro 1:17
image in the form of corruptible **m** Ro 1:23 *444*
But do you suppose this, O **m**, Ro 2:3 *444*
for every soul of **m** who does evil, Ro 2:9 *444*
So if the uncircumcised **m** Ro 2:26 *203*
though every **m** *be found* a liar, Ro 3:4 *444*
a **m** is justified by faith apart from Ro 3:28 *444*
blessing on the **m** to whom God Ro 4:6 *444*
"BLESSED IS THE **M** WHOSE SIN THE Ro 4:8 *435*
will hardly die for a righteous **m**; Ro 5:7 *1342*
though perhaps for the good **m** Ro 5:7 *18*
just as through one **m** sin entered Ro 5:12 *444*
gift by the grace of the one **M**, Ro 5:15 *444*
she is joined to another **m**, Ro 7:3 *435*
though she is joined to another **m**. Ro 7:3 *435*
the law of God in the inner **m**, Ro 7:22 *444*
Wretched **m** that I am! Ro 7:24 *444*
she had conceived *twins* by one **m**, Ro 9:10 *1520*
m who wills or the man who runs, Ro 9:16
man who wills or the **m** who runs, Ro 9:16
On the contrary, who are you, O **m**, Ro 9:20 *444*
m who practices the righteousness Ro 10:5 *444*
the **m** who eats and gives offense. Ro 14:20 *444*
Rufus, a choice **m** in the Lord, Ro 16:13 *1588*
Where is the wise **m**? 1Co 1:20 *4680*
that no **m** may boast before God. 1Co 1:29 *4561*
HAVE NOT ENTERED THE HEART OF **M**, 1Co 2:9 *444*
knows the *thoughts* of a **m** except 1Co 2:11 *444*
a man except the spirit of the **m** which 1Co 2:11 *444*
But a natural **m** does not accept 1Co 2:14 *444*
But each **m** must be careful how he 1Co 3:10 *1538*
For no **m** can lay a foundation 1Co 3:11 *3762*
Now if any **m** builds on the 1Co 3:12 *5100*
any **m** destroys the temple of God, 1Co 3:17 *5100*
Let no **m** deceive himself. 1Co 3:18 *3367*
If any **m** among you thinks that he 1Co 3:18 *5100*
Let a **m** regard us in this manner, 1Co 4:1 *444*
REMOVE THE WICKED **M** FROM 1Co 5:13 *4190*
there is not among you one wise **m** 1Co 6:5 *4680*
a **m** commits is outside the body, 1Co 6:18 *444*
m sins against his own body. 1Co 6:18
good for a **m** not to touch a woman. 1Co 7:1 *444*
each **m** is to have his own wife, 1Co 7:2 *1538*
each **m** has his own gift from God, 1Co 7:7 *1538*
any **m** called *when he was already* 1Co 7:18 *5100*
Each **m** must remain in that 1Co 7:20 *1538*
good for a **m** to remain as he is. 1Co 7:26 *444*
But if any **m** thinks that he is 1Co 7:36 *5100*
any **m** make my boast an empty one. 1Co 9:15
you but such as is common to **m**; 1Co 10:13 *442*
Christ is the head of every **m**, 1Co 11:3 *435*
and the **m** is the head of a woman, 1Co 11:3 *435*
Every **m** who has *something* on his 1Co 11:4 *435*
For a **m** ought not to have his head 1Co 11:7 *435*
but the woman is the glory of **m**. 1Co 11:7 *435*
m does not originate from woman, 1Co 11:8 *435*
from woman, but woman from **m**; 1Co 11:8 *435*
for indeed **m** was not created for 1Co 11:9 *435*
neither is woman independent of **m**, 1Co 11:11 *435*
nor is **m** independent of woman. 1Co 11:11 *435*
the woman originates from the **m**, 1Co 11:12 *435*
so also the **m** *has his birth* 1Co 11:12 *435*
you that if a **m** has long hair, 1Co 11:14 *435*
But a **m** must examine himself, and 1Co 11:28 *444*
when I became a **m**, I did away with 1Co 13:11 *435*
or an ungifted **m** enters, 1Co 14:24 *2399*
For since by a **m** *came* death, by a 1Co 15:21 *444*
by a **m** also *came* the resurrection 1Co 15:21 *444*
"The first **M**, Adam, BECAME A 1Co 15:45 *444*
The first **m** is from the earth, 1Co 15:47 *444*
the second **m** is from heaven. 1Co 15:47 *444*
though our outer **m** is decaying, 2Co 4:16 *444*
our inner **m** is being renewed day by 2Co 4:16 *2080*
I know a **m** in Christ who fourteen 2Co 12:2 *444*
such a **m** was caught up to the third 2Co 12:2 *5108*
And I know how such a **m** 2Co 12:3 *444*
a **m** is not permitted to speak. 2Co 12:4 *444*
behalf of such a **m** I will boast; 2Co 12:5 *5108*
men nor through the agency of **m**, Ga 1:1 *444*
if any **m** is preaching to you a Ga 1:9 *5100*
by me is not according to **m**. Ga 1:11 *444*
For I neither received it from **m**, Ga 1:12 *444*
a **m** is not justified by the works of Ga 2:16 *444*
RIGHTEOUS **M** SHALL LIVE BY FAITH." Ga 3:11 *1342*
there is neither slave nor free **m**, Ga 3:28 *1658*
every **m** who receives circumcision, Ga 5:3 *444*
for whatever a **m** sows, this he Ga 6:7 *444*
might make the two into one new **m**, Eph 2:15 *444*
through His Spirit in the inner **m**, Eph 3:16 *444*
of the Son of God, to a mature **m**, Eph 4:13 *435*
or impure person or covetous **m**, Eph 5:5 *4123*
FOR THIS REASON A **M** SHALL LEAVE HIS Eph 5:31 *444*
Being found in appearance as a **m**, Php 2:8 *444*
admonishing every **m** and teaching Col 1:28 *444*
teaching every **m** with all wisdom, Col 1:28 *444*
every **m** complete in Christ. Col 1:28 *444*
and that no **m** transgress and 1Th 4:6
he who rejects *this* is not rejecting **m** 1Th 4:8 *444*
the **m** of lawlessness is revealed, 2Th 2:3 *444*
God and men, *the* **m** Christ Jesus, 1Tm 2:5 *444*
or exercise authority over a **m**, 1Tm 2:12 *435*
if any **m** aspires to the office of 1Tm 3:1 *5100*
(but if a **m** does not know how to 1Tm 3:5 *5100*
Do not sharply rebuke an older **m**, 1Tm 5:1 *4245*
having been the wife of one **m**, 1Tm 5:9 *435*
from these things, you **m** of God, 1Tm 6:11 *444*
whom no **m** has seen or can see. 1Tm 6:16 *444*
that the **m** of God may be adequate, 2Tm 3:17 *444*
if any **m** is above reproach, Ti 1:6 *5100*
Reject a factious **m** after a first Ti 3:10 *444*
a **m** is perverted and is sinning, Ti 3:11 *5108*
IS **M**, THAT YOU REMEMBER HIM? Heb 2:6 *444*
OR THE SON OF **M**, THAT YOU ARE Heb 2:6 *444*
great this **m** was to whom Abraham, Heb 7:4 *3778*
which the Lord pitched, not **m**. Heb 8:2 *444*
there was born even of one **m**, Heb 11:12 *1520*
WHAT WILL **M** DO TO ME?" Heb 13:6 *444*
For that **m** ought not to expect that he Jas 1:7 *444*
being a double-minded **m**, Jas 1:8 *435*
rich **m** *is to glory* in his humiliation, Jas 1:10 *4145*
so too the rich **m** in the midst of Jas 1:11 *4145*
is a **m** who perseveres under trial; Jas 1:12 *435*
for the anger of **m** does not Jas 1:20 *435*
he is like a **m** who looks at his Jas 1:23 *435*
this **m** will be blessed in what he Jas 1:25 *3778*
For if a **m** comes into your Jas 2:2 *435*
comes in a poor **m** in dirty clothes, Jas 2:2 *4434*
place," and you say to the poor **m**, Jas 2:3 *4434*
you have dishonored the poor **m**. Jas 2:6 *4434*
that a **m** is justified by works and Jas 2:24 *444*
what he says, he is a perfect **m**, Jas 3:2 *435*
and put to death the righteous **m**; Jas 5:6
effective prayer of a righteous **m** can Jas 5:16 *1342*
was a **m** with a nature like ours, Jas 5:17 *444*
OF THE GODLESS **M** AND THE SINNER? 1Pe 4:18 *765*
he saw and heard *that* righteous **m**, 2Pe 2:8 *1342*
speaking with a voice of a **m**, 2Pe 2:16 *444*
for by what a **m** is overcome, by 2Pe 2:19 *5100*
one like a son of **m**, Rv 1:13 *444*
I fell at His feet like a dead **m**. Rv 1:17 *3498*
had a face like that of a **m**, Rv 4:7 *444*
strong and every slave and free **m** hid Rv 6:15 *1658*
of a scorpion when it stings a **m**. Rv 9:5 *444*
for the number is that of a **m**; Rv 13:18 *444*
the cloud *was* one like a son of **m**, Rv 14:14 *444*
blood like *that* of a dead **m**; Rv 16:3 *3498*
since **m** came to be upon the earth, Rv 16:18 *444*
render to every **m** according to what Rv 22:12 *1538*

MANAEN
and **M** who had been brought up with Ac 13:1 *3127*

MANAGE
know how to **m** his own household, 1Tm 3:5 *4291b*

MANAGEMENT
Give an accounting of your **m**, for Lk 16:2 *3622*
since my master is taking the **m** away Lk 16:3 *3622*
so that when I am removed from the **m** Lk 16:4 *3622*

MANAGER
"There was a rich man who had a **m**, Lk 16:1 *3623*
and this **m** was reported to him as Lk 16:1
for you can no longer be **m**.' Lk 16:2 *3621*
"The **m** said to himself, 'What Lk 16:3 *3623*
his master praised the unrighteous **m** Lk 16:8 *3623*

MANAGERS
but he is under guardians and **m** Ga 4:2 *3623*
and good **m** of *their* children and 1Tm 3:12 *4291b*

MANAGES
one who **m** his own household well, 1Tm 3:4 *4291b*

MANAHATH
Alvan and **M** and Ebal, Shepho and Gn 36:23 4506a
The sons of Shobal *were* Alian, **M**, 1Ch 1:40 4506a
they carried them into exile to **M**, 1Ch 8:6 4506b

MANAHATHITES
Haroeh, half of the **M**, 1Ch 2:52 4506c
Atroth-beth-joab and half of the **M**, 1Ch 2:54 4506c

MANASSEH
Joseph named the firstborn **M**, Gn 41:51 4519
of Egypt were born **M** and Ephraim, Gn 46:20 4519
two sons **M** and Ephraim with him. Gn 48:1 4519
Ephraim and **M** shall be mine, as Gn 48:5 4519
and **M** with his left hand toward Gn 48:13 4519
although **M** was the firstborn. Gn 48:14 4519
make you like Ephraim and **M**!'" Gn 48:20 4519
Thus he put Ephraim before **M**. Gn 48:20 4519
the sons of Machir, the son of **M**, Gn 50:23 4519

of **M**, Gamaliel the son of Pedahzur; **Nu 1:10** 4519
Of the sons of **M**, their **Nu 1:34** 4519
numbered men of the tribe of **M** **Nu 1:35** 4519
to him *shall be* the tribe of **M**, **Nu 2:20** 4519
and the leader of the sons of **M**: **Nu 2:20** 4519
Pedahzur, leader of the sons of **M**; **Nu 7:54** 4519
the tribal army of the sons of **M**; **Nu 10:23** 4519
of Joseph, from the tribe of **M**, **Nu 13:11** 4519
according to their families: **M** and **Nu 26:28** 4519
sons of **M**: of Machir, the family of **Nu 26:29** 4519
These are the families of **M**; **Nu 26:34** 4519
the son of Machir, the son of **M**, **Nu 27:1** 4519
families of **M** the son of Joseph, **Nu 27:1** 4519
to the half-tribe of Joseph's son **M**, **Nu 32:33** 4519
The sons of Machir the son of **M** **Nu 32:39** 4519
Gilead to Machir the son of **M**, **Nu 32:40** 4519
son of **M** went and took its towns, **Nu 32:41** 4519
and the half-tribe of **M** have **Nu 34:14** 4519
tribe of the sons of **M** a leader, **Nu 34:23** 4519
the son of Machir, the son of **M**, **Nu 36:1** 4519
the sons of **M** the son of Joseph, **Nu 36:12** 4519
Og, I gave to the half-tribe of **M**, **Dt 3:13** 4519
Jair the son of **M** took all the **Dt 3:14** 4519
those are the thousands of **M**." **Dt 33:17** 4519
and the land of Ephraim and **M**, **Dt 34:2** 4519
Gadites and to the half-tribe of **M**, **Jos 1:12** 4519
the half-tribe of **M** crossed over **Jos 4:12** 4519
half-tribe of **M** as a possession. **Jos 12:6** 4519
tribes and the half-tribe of **M**." **Jos 13:7** 4519
inheritance to the half-tribe of **M**; **Jos 13:29** 4519
for the half-tribe of the sons of **M** **Jos 13:29** 4519
the sons of Machir the son of **M**, **Jos 13:31** 4519
were two tribes, **M** and Ephraim, **Jos 14:4** 4519
The sons of Joseph, **M** and Ephraim, **Jos 16:4** 4519
the inheritance of the sons of **M**, **Jos 16:9** 4519
was the lot for the tribe of **M**, **Jos 17:1** 4519
To Machir the firstborn of **M**, **Jos 17:1** 4519
made for the rest of the sons of **M** **Jos 17:2** 4519
these *were* the male descendants of **M** **Jos 17:2** 4519
the son of Machir, the son of **M**, **Jos 17:3** 4519
Thus there fell ten portions to **M**, **Jos 17:5** 4519
because the daughters of **M** **Jos 17:6** 4519
to the rest of the sons of **M**. **Jos 17:6** 4519
The border of **M** ran from Asher **Jos 17:7** 4519
The land of Tappuah belonged to **M**, **Jos 17:8** 4519
but Tappuah on the border of **M** **Jos 17:8** 4519
to Ephraim among the cities of **M**), **Jos 17:9** 4519
and the border of **M** *was* on the **Jos 17:9** 4519
Ephraim and the north side to **M**, **Jos 17:10** 4519
M had Beth-shean and its towns and **Jos 17:11** 4519
But the sons of **M** could not take **Jos 17:12** 4519
house of Joseph, to Ephraim and **M**, **Jos 17:17** 4519
half-tribe of **M** also have received **Jos 18:7** 4519
in Bashan from the tribe of **M**. **Jos 20:8** 4519
Dan and from the half-tribe of **M**, **Jos 21:5** 4519
from the half-tribe of **M** in Bashan. **Jos 21:6** 4519
From the half-tribe of **M**, **Jos 21:25** 4519
Levites, from the half-tribe of **M**, **Jos 21:27** 4519
Gadites and the half-tribe of **M**, **Jos 22:1** 4519
Now to the one half-tribe of **M** **Jos 22:7** 4519
the half-tribe of **M** returned *home* **Jos 22:9** 4519
half-tribe of **M** built an altar there **Jos 22:10** 4519
half-tribe of **M** have built an altar at **Jos 22:11** 4519
of Gad and to the half-tribe of **M**, **Jos 22:13** 4519
of Gad and to the half-tribe of **M**, **Jos 22:15** 4519
and the half-tribe of **M** answered and **Jos 22:21** 4519
of Gad and the sons of **M** spoke, **Jos 22:30** 4519
sons of Gad and to the sons of **M**, **Jos 22:31** 4519
But **M** did not take possession of **Jg 1:27** 4519
my family is the least in **M**, **Jg 6:15** 4519
He sent messengers throughout **M**, **Jg 6:35** 4519
from Naphtali and Asher and all **M**, **Jg 7:23** 4519
he passed through Gilead and **M**; **Jg 11:29** 4519
Ephraim *and* in the midst of **M**." **Jg 12:4** 4519
the son of Gershom, the son of **M**, **Jg 18:30** 4519
(the towns of Jair, the son of **M**, **1Ki 4:13** 4519
and **M** his son became king in his **2Ki 20:21** 4519
M was twelve years old when he **2Ki 21:1** 4519
and **M** seduced them to do evil more **2Ki 21:9** 4519
"Because **M** king of Judah has done **2Ki 21:11** 4519
M shed very much innocent blood **2Ki 21:16** 4519
Now the rest of the acts of **M** and **2Ki 21:17** 4519
And **M** slept with his fathers and **2Ki 21:18** 4519
LORD, as **M** his father had done. **2Ki 21:20** 4519
and the altars which **M** had made in **2Ki 23:12** 4519
with which **M** had provoked Him. **2Ki 23:26** 4519
sight because of the sins of **M**, **2Ki 24:3** 4519
son, Hezekiah his son, **M** his son, **1Ch 3:13** 4519
Gadites and the half-tribe of **M**, **1Ch 5:18** 4519
half-tribe of **M** lived in the land; **1Ch 5:23** 4519
Gadites and the half-tribe of **M**, **1Ch 5:26** 4519
from the half-tribe, the half of **M**, **1Ch 6:61** 4519
of Naphtali, and the tribe of **M**, **1Ch 6:62** 4519
and from the half-tribe of **M**: **1Ch 6:70** 4519
the family of the half-tribe of **M**: **1Ch 6:71** 4519
The sons of **M** *were* Asriel, whom **1Ch 7:14** 4519
the son of Machir, the son of **M**, **1Ch 7:17** 4519
the borders of the sons of **M**, **1Ch 7:29** 4519
Ephraim and **M** lived in Jerusalem: **1Ch 9:3** 4519
M also some defected to David when **1Ch 12:19** 4519
there defected to him from **M**: **1Ch 12:20** 4519
of thousands who belonged to **M**. **1Ch 12:20** 4519
Of the half-tribe of **M** 18,000, **1Ch 12:31** 4519
Gadites and of the half-tribe of **M**, **1Ch 12:37** 4519
for the half-tribe of **M**, **1Ch 27:20** 4519
for the half-tribe of **M** in Gilead, **1Ch 27:21** 4519
and those from Ephraim, **M** and **2Ch 15:9** 4519
letters also to Ephraim and **M**, **2Ch 30:1** 4519
the country of Ephraim and **M**, **2Ch 30:10** 4519
Nevertheless some men of Asher, **M** **2Ch 30:11** 4519
even many from Ephraim and **M**, **2Ch 30:18** 4519
as well as in Ephraim and **M**, **2Ch 31:1** 4519
son **M** became king in his place. **2Ch 32:33** 4519
M was twelve years old when he **2Ch 33:1** 4519
Thus **M** misled Judah and the **2Ch 33:9** 4519
LORD spoke to **M** and his people, **2Ch 33:10** 4519
and they captured **M** with hooks, **2Ch 33:11** 4519
Then **M** knew that the LORD *was* God. **2Ch 33:13** 4519
the rest of the acts of **M** even his **2Ch 33:18** 4519
So **M** slept with his fathers, and **2Ch 33:20** 4519
the LORD as **M** his father had done, **2Ch 33:22** 4519
which his father **M** had made, **2Ch 33:22** 4519
the LORD as his father **M** had done, **2Ch 33:23** 4519
In the cities of **M**, **2Ch 34:6** 4519
had collected from **M** and Ephraim, **2Ch 34:9** 4519
Mattaniah, Bezalel, Binnui and **M**; **Ezr 10:30** 4519
Zabad, Eliphelet, Jeremai, **M** **Ezr 10:33** 4519
"Gilead is Mine, and **M** is Mine; **Ps 60:7** 4519
Before Ephraim and Benjamin and **M**, **Ps 80:2** 4519
"Gilead is Mine, **M** is Mine; **Ps 108:8** 4519
M *devours* Ephraim, and Ephraim **Is 9:21** 4519
devours Ephraim, and Ephraim **M**, **Is 9:21** 4519
because of **M**, the son of Hezekiah, **Jer 15:4** 4519
the east side to the west side, **M**, **Ezk 48:4** 4519
"Beside the border of **M**, **Ezk 48:5** 4519
Hezekiah was the father of **M**, **Mt 1:10** *3128*
M the father of Amon, and Amon **Mt 1:10** *3128*
the tribe of **M** twelve thousand, **Rv 7:6** *3128*

MANASSEH'S
and his left hand on **M** head, **Gn 48:14** 4519
it from Ephraim's head to **M** head. **Gn 48:17** 4519

MANASSITES
and Golan in Bashan for the **M**. **Dt 4:43** 4520
and the half-tribe of the **M**. **Dt 29:8** 4520
and the Reubenites and the **M**, **2Ki 10:33** 4520
Gadites and the half-tribe of the **M** **1Ch 26:32** 4520

MANCHILD
"I have gotten a **m** with *the help of* **Gn 4:1** 376

MANDRAKES
went and found **m** in the field, **Gn 30:14** 1736
give me some of your son's **m**." **Gn 30:14** 1736
would you take my son's **m** also?" **Gn 30:15** 1736
in return for your son's **m**." **Gn 30:15** 1736
surely hired you with my son's **m**." **Gn 30:16** 1736
"The **m** have given forth fragrance; **SS 7:13** 1736

MANE
Do you clothe his neck with a **m**? **Jb 39:19** 7483

MANEH
fifteen shekels shall be your **m**. **Ezk 45:12** 4488

MANGER
will he spend the night at your **m**? **Jb 39:9** 18
Where no oxen are, the **m** is clean, **Pr 14:4** 18
owner, And a donkey its master's **m**, **Is 1:3** 18
in cloths, and laid Him in a **m**, **Lk 2:7** *5336*
in cloths and lying in a **m**." **Lk 2:12** *5336*
and the baby as He lay in the **m**. **Lk 2:16** *5336*

MANHOOD
during the days of young **m**. **Ec 11:9** 979
bed, You have looked on *their* **m**. **Is 57:8** 3027

MANIFEST
And I will **m** My holiness in her. **Ezk 28:22** 6942
and will **m** My holiness in them in **Ezk 28:25** 6942
I BECAME **M** TO THOSE WHO DID NOT **Ro 10:20** *1717*
men, but we are made **m** to God; **2Co 5:11** *5319*
made **m** also in your consciences. **2Co 5:11** *5319*

MANIFESTATION
each one is given the **m** of the Spirit **1Co 12:7** *5321*
but by the **m** of truth commending **2Co 4:2** *5321*

MANIFESTED
that He might be **m** to Israel, **Jn 1:31** *5319*
Cana of Galilee, and **m** His glory, **Jn 2:11** *5319*
m as having been wrought in God." **Jn 3:21** *5319*
"I have **m** Your name to the men whom **Jn 17:6** *5319*
After these things Jesus **m** Himself **Jn 21:1** *5319*
and He **m** *Himself* in this way. **Jn 21:1** *5319*
that Jesus was **m** to the disciples, **Jn 21:14** *5319*
righteousness of God has been **m**, **Ro 3:21** *5319*
but now is **m**, and by the **Ro 16:26** *5319*
being **m** that you are a letter of **2Co 3:3** *5319*
Jesus also may be **m** in our body. **2Co 4:10** *5319*
also may be **m** in our mortal flesh. **2Co 4:11** *5319*
but has now been **m** to His saints, **Col 1:26** *5319*
but at the proper time **m**, **Ti 1:3** *5319*
He has been **m** to put away sin **Heb 9:26** *5319*
and the life was **m**, **1Jn 1:2** *5319*
with the Father and was **m** to us **1Jn 1:2** *5319*
this the love of God was **m** in us, **1Jn 4:9** *5319*

MANIFESTS
and **m** through us the sweet aroma **2Co 2:14** *5319*

MANIFOLD
so that the **m** wisdom of God **Eph 3:10** *4182*
stewards of the **m** grace of God. **1Pe 4:10** *4164*

MANKIND
swarms upon the earth, and all **m**; **Gn 7:21** 120
commits any of the sins of **m**, **Nu 5:6** 120
"But will God indeed dwell with **m** **2Ch 6:18** 120
'Can **m** be just before God? **Jb 4:17** 582
thing, And the breath of all **m**? **Jb 12:10** 376, 1320
Nor are they plagued like **m**. **Ps 73:5** 120
And **m** than the gold of Ophir. **Is 13:12** 120
And the needy of **m** will rejoice **Is 29:19** 120
All **m** will come to bow down before **Is 66:23** 1320
will be an abhorrence to all **m**." **Is 66:24** 1320
"Cursed is the man who trusts in **m** **Jer 17:5** 120
day both in Israel and among **m**; **Jer 32:20** 120
All **m** is stupid, devoid of **Jer 51:17** 120
High is ruler over the realm of **m**, **Da 4:17** 606
that you be driven away from **m** and **Da 4:25** 606
High is ruler over the realm of **m** and **Da 4:25** 606
you will be driven away from **m**, **Da 4:32** 606
High is ruler over the realm of **m** and **Da 4:32** 606
and he was driven away from **m** and **Da 4:33** 606
"He was also driven away from **m**, **Da 5:21** 606
God is ruler over the realm of **m** and **Da 5:21** 606
will pour out My Spirit on all **m**; **Jl 2:28** 1320
FORTH OF MY SPIRIT ON ALL **M**; **Ac 2:17** *4561*
THE REST OF **M** MAY SEEK THE LORD, **Ac 15:17** *444*
every nation of **m** to live on all **Ac 17:26** *444*
and *His* love for **m** appeared, **Ti 3:4** *5363*
that they would kill a third of **m**. **Rv 9:15** *444*
A third of **m** was killed by these **Rv 9:18** *444*
The rest of **m**, who were not **Rv 9:20** *444*

MANNA
The house of Israel named it **m**, **Ex 16:31** 4478a
jar and put an omerful of **m** in it, **Ex 16:33** 4478a
of Israel ate the **m** forty years, **Ex 16:35** 4478a
they ate the **m** until they came to **Ex 16:35** 4478a
at all to look at except this **m**." **Nu 11:6** 4478a
Now the **m** was like coriander seed, **Nu 11:7** 4478a
night, the **m** would fall with it. **Nu 11:9** 4478a
fed you with **m** which you did not **Dt 8:3** 4478a
"In the wilderness He fed you **m** **Dt 8:16** 4478a
The **m** ceased on the day after **Jos 5:12** 4478a
sons of Israel no longer had **m**, **Jos 5:12** 4478a
Your **m** You did not withhold from **Ne 9:20** 4478a
He rained down **m** upon them to eat **Ps 78:24** 4478a
fathers ate the **m** in the wilderness; **Jn 6:31** *3131*
fathers ate the **m** in the wilderness, **Jn 6:49** *3131*
was a golden jar holding the **m**, **Heb 9:4** *3131*
I will give *some* of the hidden **m**, **Rv 2:17** *3131*

MANNER
in to us after the **m** of the earth. **Gn 19:31** 1870
for the **m** of women is upon me." **Gn 31:35** 1870
"After this **m** you shall speak to **Gn 32:19** 1697
'Now you shall eat it in this **m**: **Ex 12:11** 3602
shall do these things in this **m**, **Nu 15:13** 3602
'After this **m** you shall present daily, **Nu 28:24** 428
"This is the **m** of remission: **Dt 15:2** 1697
city in the same **m** seven times; **Jos 6:15** 4941
this stronghold in an orderly **m**, **Jg 6:26** 4634
after the **m** of the Sidonians, **Jg 18:7** 4941
and this was the **m** *of* attestation **Ru 4:7**
for in this **m** the virgin daughters **2Sa 13:18** 3651
king and speak to him in this **m**." **2Sa 14:3** 1697
In this **m** Absalom dealt with **2Sa 15:6** 1697
to the priests and Levites in any **m** **2Ch 8:15** 1697
to me four times in this **m**, **Ne 6:4** 1697
sent his servant to me in the same **m** **Ne 6:5** 1697
After Your **m** with those who love **Ps 119:132** 4941
inhabitants will die in like **m**; **Is 51:6** 3654
defile yourselves after the **m** of your **Ezk 20:30** 1870
among you after the **m** of Egypt; **Am 4:10** 1870
the same **m** the one who *had received* **Mt 25:17** *5615*
the Son also does in like **m**. **Jn 5:19** *3668*
and spoke in such a **m** that a large **Ac 14:1** *3779*
in this **m** you must help the weak **Ac 20:35** *3779*
my **m** of life from my youth up, **Ac 26:4** *981*
Lord in a **m** worthy of the saints, **Ro 16:2** *516*
Let a man regard us in this **m**, **1Co 4:1** *3779*
own gift from God, one in this **m**, **1Co 7:7** *3779*
each, in this **m** let him walk. **1Co 7:17** *3779*
cup of the Lord in an unworthy **m**, **1Co 11:27** *371*
done properly and in an orderly **m**. **1Co 14:40** *5010*
of my former **m** of life in Judaism, **Ga 1:13** *391*
eagerly sought in a commendable **m**, **Ga 4:18** *2570*
implore you to walk in a **m** worthy **Eph 4:1** *516*
to your former **m** of life, **Eph 4:22** *391*
Only conduct yourselves in a **m** **Php 1:27** *516*
walk in a **m** worthy of the Lord, **Col 1:10** *516*
so that you would walk in a **m** worthy **1Th 2:12** *516*
in an undisciplined **m** among you, **2Th 3:7** *812*
walk in the same **m** as He walked. **1Jn 2:6** *3779*
on their way in a **m** worthy of God. **3Jn 1:6** *516*

MANOAH
of the Danites, whose name was **M**; **Jg 13:2** 4495
M entreated the LORD and said, **Jg 13:8** 4495
God listened to the voice of **M**; **Jg 13:9** 4495
M her husband was not with her. **Jg 13:9** 4495
M arose and followed his wife, **Jg 13:11** 4495
M said, "Now when your words **Jg 13:12** 4495
the angel of the LORD said to **M**, **Jg 13:13** 4495
M said to the angel of the LORD, **Jg 13:15** 4495
The angel of the LORD said to **M**, **Jg 13:16** 4495
For **M** did not know that he was the **Jg 13:16** 4495
M said to the angel of the LORD, **Jg 13:17** 4495
So **M** took the young goat with the grain **Jg 13:19** 4495
while **M** and his wife looked on. **Jg 13:19** 4495
When **M** and his wife saw *this*, they **Jg 13:20** 4495
did not appear to **M** or his wife **Jg 13:21** 4495
Then **M** knew that he was the angel **Jg 13:21** 4495
So **M** said to his wife, **Jg 13:22** 4495
in the tomb of **M** his father. **Jg 16:31** 4495

MAN'S
the intent of **m** heart is evil from his **Gn 8:21** 120
from every **m** brother I will **Gn 9:5** 376
"Whoever sheds **m** blood, By man **Gn 9:6** 120
"Now therefore, restore the **m** wife, **Gn 20:7** 376
restore every **m** money in his sack, **Gn 42:25** 376
every **m** bundle of money *was* in his **Gn 42:35** 376
each **m** money was in the mouth of **Gn 43:21** 376
and put each **m** money in the mouth **Gn 44:1** 376
for we cannot see the **m** face **Gn 44:26** 376

“Who has made **m** mouth? **Ex 4:11** 120
m slave purchased with money, **Ex 12:44** 376
“If one **m** ox hurts another’s **Ex 21:35** 376
that it grazes in another **m** field, **Ex 22:5**
and it is stolen from the **m** house, **Ex 22:7** 376
who presents any **m** burnt offering, **Lv 7:8** 376
adultery with another **m** wife, **Lv 20:10** 376
every **m** holy *gifts* shall be his; **Nu 5:10** 376
‘If any **m** wife goes astray and is **Nu 5:12** 376
serve gods, the work of **m** hands, **Dt 4:28** 120
“A woman shall not wear **m** clothing, **Dt 22:5** 1397
goes and becomes another **m** *wife,* **Dt 24:2** 376
the **m** house where her master was, **Jg 19:26** 376
taken anything from any **m** hand.” **1Sa 12:4** 376
m sword was against his fellow, **1Sa 14:20** 376
no **m** heart fail on account of him; **1Sa 17:32** 120
(now the **m** name was Nabal, and his **1Sa 25:3** 376
Rather he took the poor **m** ewe lamb **2Sa 12:4** 376
a cloud as small as a **m** hand is **1Ki 18:44** 376
the money of each **m** assessment **2Ki 12:4** 376
money which any **m** heart prompts **2Ki 12:4** 376
a mortal, Or Your years as **m** years, **Jb 10:5** 1397
So You destroy **m** hope. **Jb 14:19** 582
is the wicked **m** portion from God, **Jb 20:29** 120
‘God stores away a **m** iniquity for **Jb 21:19**
And wine which makes **m** heart glad, **Ps 104:15** 582
And food which sustains **m** heart. **Ps 104:15** 582
and gold, The work of **m** hands. **Ps 115:4** 120
and gold, The work of **m** hands. **Ps 135:15** 120
The rich **m** wealth is his fortress, **Pr 10:15** 6223
the deeds of a **m** hands will return to **Pr 12:14** 120
Anxiety in a **m** heart weighs it down, **Pr 12:25** 376
fruit of a **m** mouth he enjoys good, **Pr 13:2** 376
ransom of a **m** life is his wealth, **Pr 13:8** 376
a **m** ways are pleasing to the LORD, **Pr 16:7** 376
words of a **m** mouth are deep waters **Pr 18:4** 376
rich **m** wealth is his strong city, **Pr 18:11** 6223
A **m** gift makes room for him And **Pr 18:16** 120
With the fruit of a **m** mouth his **Pr 18:20** 376
A **m** discretion makes him slow to **Pr 19:11** 120
Many plans are in a **m** heart, **Pr 19:21** 376
M steps are *ordained* by the LORD, **Pr 20:24** 1397
m way is right in his own eyes, **Pr 21:2** 376
So a **m** counsel is sweet to his **Pr 27:9** 5315
A **m** pride will bring him low, But **Pr 29:23** 120
The wise **m** eyes are in his head, **Ec 2:14** 2450
All a **m** labor is for his mouth and **Ec 6:7** 120
A **m** wisdom illumines him and **Ec 8:1** 120
a **m** trouble is heavy upon him. **Ec 8:6** 120
A wise **m** heart *directs him* toward **Ec 10:2** 2450
but the foolish **m** heart *directs* **Ec 10:2** 3684
limp, And every **m** heart will melt. **Is 13:7** 582
that a **m** way is not in himself, **Jer 10:23** 120
because every **m** own word will **Jer 23:36** 376
to have the form of a **m** hand under **Ezk 10:8** 120
“A **m** foot will not pass through **Ezk 29:11** 120
“Every **m** sword will be against **Ezk 38:21** 376
through and anyone sees a **m** bone, **Ezk 39:15** 120
and in the **m** hand was a measuring **Ezk 40:5** 376
a **m** face toward the palm tree on **Ezk 41:19** 120
Suddenly the fingers of a **m** hand **Da 5:5** 606
determined to follow **m** command. **Hos 5:11**
perish on account of this **m** life **Jon 1:14** 376
A **m** enemies are the men of his own **Mi 7:6** 376
A **M** ENEMIES WILL BE THE MEMBERS OF **Mt 10:36** *444*
receive a righteous **m** reward. **Mt 10:41** *1342*
can anyone enter the strong **m** house **Mt 12:29** *2478*
mind on God’s interests, but **m**.” **Mt 16:23** *444*
“I am innocent of this **M** blood; **Mt 27:24** *3778*
no one can enter the strong **m** house **Mk 3:27** *2478*
mind on God’s interests, but **m**.” **Mk 8:33** *444*
IF A **M** BROTHER DIES and leaves **Mk 12:19** *5100*
falling from the rich **m** table; **Lk 16:21** *4145*
IF A **M** BROTHER DIES, having a wife, **Lk 20:28** *5100*
not also *one* of this **m** disciples, **Jn 18:17** *444*
to bring this **m** blood upon us.” **Ac 5:28** *444*
me and we entered the **m** house. **Ac 11:12** *435*
as through the one **m** disobedience **Ro 5:19** *444*
build on another **m** foundation; **Ro 15:20** *245*
each **m** work will become evident; **1Co 3:13** *1538*
test the quality of each **m** work. **1Co 3:13** *1538*
If any **m** work which he has built **1Co 3:14** *5100*
If any **m** work is burned up, he **1Co 3:15** *5100*
and then each **m** praise will come **1Co 4:5** *1538*
but the other **m**; for why is my **1Co 10:29**
sake, but woman for the **m** sake. **1Co 11:9** *435*
m conscience in the sight of God. **2Co 4:2** *444*
though it is *only* a **m** covenant, **Ga 3:15** *444*
this **m** religion is worthless. **Jas 1:26** *3778*

MANSLAYER
shall give for the **m** to flee to; **Nu 35:6** 7523
that the **m** who has killed any **Nu 35:11** 7523
so that the **m** will not die until he **Nu 35:12** 7523
The congregation shall deliver the **m** **Nu 35:25** 7523
‘But if the **m** at any time goes **Nu 35:26** 7523
and the blood avenger kills the **m**, **Nu 35:27** 7523
the **m** shall return to the land of his **Nu 35:28** 7523
that a **m** might flee there, who **Dt 4:42** 7523
so that any **m** may flee there. **Dt 19:3** 7523
the **m** who may flee there and live: **Dt 19:4** 7523
the **m** in the heat of his anger, **Dt 19:6** 7523
that the **m** who kills any person **Jos 20:3** 7523
not deliver the **m** into his hand, **Jos 20:5** 7523
Then the **m** shall return to his own **Jos 20:6** 7523
the city of refuge for the **m**, **Jos 21:13** 7523
the city of refuge for the **m**, **Jos 21:21** 7523
the city of refuge for the **m**, **Jos 21:27** 7523
the city of refuge for the **m**, **Jos 21:32** 7523
the city of refuge for the **m**, **Jos 21:38** 7523

MANTELET
to her wall, And the **m** is set up. **Na 2:5** 5527a

MANTLE
I saw among the spoil a beautiful **m** **Jos 7:21** 155
son of Zerah, the silver, the **m**, **Jos 7:24** 155
he wrapped his face in his **m** **1Ki 19:13** 155
to him and threw his **m** on him. **1Ki 19:19** 155
Elijah took his **m** and folded **2Ki 2:8** 155
m of Elijah that fell from him and **2Ki 2:13** 155
m of Elijah that fell from him and **2Ki 2:14** 155
wrapped Himself with zeal as a **m**. **Is 59:17** 4598
The **m** of praise instead of a **Is 61:3** 4594
LIKE A **M** YOU WILL ROLL THEM UP; **Heb 1:12** *4018*

MANUFACTURERS
the **m** of linen made from combed **Is 19:9** 5647
The **m** of idols will go away **Is 45:16** 2796

MANURE
down in the water of a **m** pile. **Is 25:10** 4087
for the soil or for the **m** pile; **Lk 14:35** *2874a*

MANY
will come out with **m** possessions. **Gn 15:14** 1419
they will be too **m** to count.” **Gn 16:10** 7230
of the Philistines for **m** days. **Gn 21:34** 7227a
and mourned for his son **m** days. **Gn 37:34** 7227a
“How **m** years have you lived?” **Gn 47:8** 4100
to preserve **m** people alive. **Gn 50:20** 7227a
in *the course of* those **m** days **Ex 2:23** 7227a
the people of the land are now **m**, **Ex 5:5** 7227a
There had never been so **m** locusts, **Ex 10:14**
nor would there be so **m** again. **Ex 10:14**
to gaze, and **m** of them perish. **Ex 19:21** 7227a
on *all* fours, whatever has **m** feet, **Lv 11:42** 7235a
a discharge of her blood **m** days, **Lv 15:25** 7227a
‘If there are still **m** years, **Lv 25:51** 7227a
over the tabernacle for **m** days, **Nu 9:19** 7227a
weak, whether they are few or **m**. **Nu 13:18** 7227a
that **m** people of Israel died. **Nu 21:6** 7227a
And his seed *will be* by **m** waters, **Nu 24:7** 7227a
“So you remained in Kadesh **m** days, **Dt 1:46** 7227a
and circled Mount Seir for **m** days. **Dt 2:1** 7227a
besides a great **m** unwalled towns. **Dt 3:5** 7235a
clears away **m** nations before you, **Dt 7:1** 7227a
and you will lend to **m** nations, **Dt 15:6** 7227a
and you will rule over **m** nations, **Dt 15:6** 7227a
with **m** more stripes than these and **Dt 25:3** 7227a
and you shall lend to **m** nations, **Dt 28:12** 7227a
and **m** evils and troubles will **Dt 31:17** 7227a
when **m** evils and troubles have **Dt 31:21** 7227a
as **m** people as the sand that is on **Jos 11:4** 7227a
with very **m** horses and chariots. **Jos 11:4** 7227a
brothers these **m** days to this day, **Jos 22:3** 7227a
iron, and with very **m** clothes; **Jos 22:8** 7235a
Now it came about after **m** days, **Jos 23:1** 7227a
his **m** *troops* to the river Kishon, **Jg 4:7** 1995
people who are with you are too **m** **Jg 7:2** 7227a
“The people are still too **m**; **Jg 7:4** 7227a
descendants, for he had **m** wives. **Jg 8:30** 7227a
and **m** fell wounded up to the **Jg 9:40** 7227a
country, Who has slain **m** of us.” **Jg 16:24** 7235a
she who has **m** children languishes. **1Sa 2:5** 7227a
to save by **m** or by few.” **1Sa 14:6** 7227a
There are **m** servants today who are **1Sa 25:10** 7231
and also **m** of the people have **2Sa 1:4** 7235a
down **m** of Benjamin and Abner’s men, **2Sa 2:31**
had a great **m** flocks and herds. **2Sa 12:2** 7235a
to you **m** more things like these! **2Sa 12:8**
m people were coming from the road **2Sa 13:34** 7227a
been mourning for the dead **m** days; **2Sa 14:2** 7227a
He drew me out of **m** waters. **2Sa 22:17** 7227a
a hundred times as **m** as they are, **2Sa 24:3**
Shimei lived in Jerusalem **m** days. **1Ki 2:38** 7227a
a great people who are too **m** to be **1Ki 3:8** 7230
because *they were* too **m**; **1Ki 7:47** 7230
sacrificing so **m** sheep and oxen **1Ki 8:5** 7230
Solomon loved **m** foreign women **1Ki 11:1** 7227a
and he and her household ate for **m** **1Ki 17:15**
Now it happened *after* **m** days **1Ki 18:1** 7227a
prepare it first for you are **m**, **1Ki 18:25** 7227a
“How **m** times must I adjure you to **1Ki 22:16**
5704, 4100
and her witchcrafts are so **m**?” **2Ki 9:22** 7227a
“With my **m** chariots I came up to **2Ki 19:23** 7230
his brothers did not have **m** sons, **1Ch 4:27** 7227a
For **m** fell slain, because the war **1Ch 5:22** 7227a
for they had **m** wives and sons. **1Ch 7:4** 7235a
father Ephraim mourned **m** days, **1Ch 7:22** 7227a
and had **m** sons and grandsons, **1Ch 8:40** 7235a
a hundred times as **m** as they are! **1Ch 21:3**
there are **m** workmen with you, **1Ch 22:15** 7230
and Beriah did not have **m** sons, **1Ch 23:11** 7235a
the sons of Rehabiah were very **m**. **1Ch 23:17** 7235a
(for the LORD has given me **m** sons), **1Ch 28:5** 7227a
sacrificing so **m** sheep and oxen that **2Ch 5:6** 7230
And he sought **m** wives *for them.* **2Ch 11:23** 1995
and so **m** Ethiopians fell that they **2Ch 14:13**
“For **m** days Israel was **2Ch 15:3** 7227a
for **m** disturbances afflicted all **2Ch 15:5** 7227a
for **m** defected to him from Israel **2Ch 15:9** 7230
with very **m** chariots and horsemen? **2Ch 16:8** 7235a
And Ahab slaughtered **m** sheep and **2Ch 18:2** 7230
“How **m** times must I adjure you to **2Ch 18:15**
5704, 4100
gave them **m** gifts of silver, **2Ch 21:3** 7227a
As to his sons and the **m** oracles **2Ch 24:27** 7230
wilderness and hewed **m** cisterns, **2Ch 26:10** 7227a
There *were* also **m** burnt offerings **2Ch 29:35** 7230
Now **m** people were gathered at **2Ch 30:13** 7227a
For *there were* **m** in the assembly **2Ch 30:17** 7227a
even **m** from Ephraim and Manasseh, **2Ch 30:18** 7227a
So **m** people assembled and stopped **2Ch 32:4** 7227a
And **m** were bringing gifts to the **2Ch 32:23** 7227a
Yet **m** of the priests and Levites **Ezr 3:12** 7227a
while **m** shouted aloud for joy, **Ezr 3:12** 7227a
temple that was built **m** years ago, **Ezr 5:11** 7690
“But there are **m** people; it is **Ezr 10:13** 7227a
our sons and our daughters are **m**; **Ne 5:2** 7227a
Also in those days **m** letters went **Ne 6:17** 7235a
For **m** in Judah were bound by oath **Ne 6:18** 7227a
man and feared God more than **m**. **Ne 7:2** 7227a
And **m** times You rescued them **Ne 9:28** 7227a
bore with them for **m** years, **Ne 9:30** 7227a
Yet among the **m** nations there was **Ne 13:26** 7227a
of his great majesty for **m** days, **Es 1:4** 7227a
m young ladies were gathered to **Es 2:8** 7227a
and **m** lay on sackcloth and ashes. **Es 4:3** 7227a
And **m** among the peoples of the **Es 8:17** 7227a
the Jews and in favor with his **m** **Es 10:3** 7230
donkeys, and very **m** servants; **Jb 1:3** 7227a
“Behold you have admonished **m**, **Jb 4:3** 7227a
that your descendants will be **m**, **Jb 5:25** 7227a
And **m** would entreat your favor. **Jb 11:19** 7227a
“How **m** are my iniquities and sins? **Jb 13:23** 4100
“I have heard **m** such things; **Jb 16:2** 7227a
And **m** such *decrees* are with Him **Jb 23:14** 7227a
“Though his sons are **m**, **Jb 27:14** 7235a
And if your transgressions are **m**, **Jb 35:6** 7231
he make **m** supplications to you, **Jb 41:3** 7235a
M are rising up against me. **Ps 3:1** 7227a
M are saying of my soul, **Ps 3:2** 7227a
M are saying, “Who will show us **Ps 4:6** 7227a
He drew me out of **m** waters. **Ps 18:16** 7227a
M bulls have surrounded me; **Ps 22:12** 7227a
upon my enemies, for they are **m**, **Ps 25:19** 7231
The LORD is over **m** waters. **Ps 29:3** 7227a
For I have heard the slander of **m**, **Ps 31:13** 7227a
M are the sorrows of the wicked, **Ps 32:10** 7227a
M are the afflictions of the **Ps 34:19** 7227a
Than the abundance of **m** wicked. **Ps 37:16** 7227a
And **m** are those who hate me **Ps 38:19** 7231
M will see and fear And will **Ps 40:3** 7227a
M, O LORD my God, are the wonders **Ps 40:5** 7227a
For they are **m** *who strive* with me. **Ps 55:18** 7227a
m who fight proudly against me. **Ps 56:2** 7227a
years will be as **m** generations. **Ps 61:6** 1755
A mountain *of* **m** peaks is **Ps 68:15**
O mountains with **m** peaks, **Ps 68:16**
I have become a marvel to **m**, **Ps 71:7** 7227a
me **m** troubles and distresses Will **Ps 71:20** 7227a
the reproach of all the **m** peoples, **Ps 89:50** 7227a
More than the sounds of **m** waters, **Ps 93:4** 7227a
Let the **m** islands be glad. **Ps 97:1** 7227a
O LORD, how **m** are Your works! **Ps 104:24** 7231
M times He would deliver them; **Ps 106:43** 7227a
the midst of **m** I will praise Him. **Ps 109:30** 7227a
How **m** are the days of Your servant? **Ps 119:84** 4100
M are my persecutors and my **Ps 119:157** 7227a
“**M** times they have persecuted me **Ps 129:1** 7227a
“**M** times they have persecuted me **Ps 129:2** 7227a
He smote **m** nations And slew **Ps 135:10** 7227a
the years of your life will be **m**. **Pr 4:10** 7235a
satisfied though you give **m** gifts. **Pr 6:35** 7235a
her **m** persuasions she entices him; **Pr 7:21** 7230
For **m** are the victims she has cast **Pr 7:26** 7227a
When there are **m** words, **Pr 10:19** 7230
The lips of the righteous feed **m**, **Pr 10:21** 7227a
But those who love the rich are **m**. **Pr 14:20** 7227a
with **m** counselors they succeed. **Pr 15:22** 7230
A man of *too* **m** friends *comes* **Pr 18:24**
Wealth adds **m** friends, But a poor **Pr 19:4** 7227a
M will seek the favor of a **Pr 19:6** 7227a
M plans are in a man’s heart, **Pr 19:21** 7227a
M a man proclaims his own loyalty, **Pr 20:6** 7230
of a land **m** are its princes, **Pr 28:2** 7227a
shuts his eyes will have **m** curses. **Pr 28:27** 7227a
M seek the ruler’s favor, But **Pr 29:26** 7227a
“**M** daughters have done nobly, But **Pr 31:29** 7227a
the pleasures of men—**m** concubines. **Ec 2:8** 7705
voice of a fool through **m** words. **Ec 5:3** 7230
For in **m** dreams and in many words **Ec 5:7** 7230
and in **m** words there is emptiness. **Ec 5:7** 7235a
children and lives **m** years, **Ec 6:3** 7227a
many years, however **m** they be, **Ec 6:3** 7227a
m words which increase futility. **Ec 6:11** 7235a
have **m** times cursed others. **Ec 7:22** 7227a
they have sought out **m** devices.” **Ec 7:29** 7227a
folly is set in **m** exalted places **Ec 10:6** 7227a
for you will find it after **m** days. **Ec 11:1** 7230
if a man should live **m** years, **Ec 11:8** 7235a
of darkness, for they will be **m**. **Ec 11:8** 7235a
out and arranged **m** proverbs. **Ec 12:9** 7235a
the writing of **m** books is endless, **Ec 12:12** 7235a
“**M** waters cannot quench love, Nor **SS 8:7** 7227a
And **m** peoples will come and say, **Is 2:3** 7227a
render decisions for **m** peoples; **Is 2:4** 7227a
m houses shall become desolate, **Is 5:9** 7227a
the forsaken places are **m** in the **Is 6:12** 7231
“**M** will stumble over them, Then **Is 8:15** 7227a
destroy And to cut off **m** nations. **Is 10:7**
3808, 4592
mountains, Like that of **m** people! **Is 13:4** 7227a
the uproar of **m** peoples Who roar **Is 17:12** 7227a
on like the rumbling of **m** waters, **Is 17:13** 7227a
wall of the city of David were **m**; **Is 22:9** 7231
And *were* on **m** waters. **Is 23:3** 7227a
strings skillfully, sing **m** songs, **Is 23:16** 7235a
after **m** days they *will be* punished. **Is 24:22** 7230
in chariots because they are **m** And **Is 31:1** 7227a

‘With my **m** chariots I came up to	**Is 37:24**	7230
You have seen **m** things, but you do	**Is 42:20**	7227a
In spite of your **m** sorceries,	**Is 47:9**	7230
And in your **m** sorceries	**Is 47:12**	7230
are wearied with your **m** counsels;	**Is 47:13**	7230
Just as **m** were astonished at you,	**Is 52:14**	7227a
Thus He will sprinkle **m** nations,	**Is 52:15**	7227a
My Servant, will justify the **m**,	**Is 53:11**	7227a
Yet He Himself bore the sin of **m**,	**Is 53:12**	7227a
The desolations of **m** generations.	**Is 61:4**	1755
those slain by the LORD will be **m**.	**Is 66:16**	7231
you are a harlot *with* **m** lovers;	**Jer 3:1**	7227a
their transgressions are **m**,	**Jer 5:6**	7231
your gods are as **m** as your cities,	**Jer 11:13**	4557
and as **m** as the streets of	**Jer 11:13**	4557
When she has done **m** vile deeds?	**Jer 11:15**	7227a
“**M** shepherds have ruined My	**Jer 12:10**	7227a
After **m** days the LORD said to	**Jer 13:6**	7227a
Truly our apostasies have been **m**,	**Jer 14:7**	7231
going to send for **m** fishermen,”	**Jer 16:16**	7227a
I will send for **m** hunters,	**Jer 16:16**	7227a
I have heard the whispering of **m**,	**Jer 20:10**	7227a
“**M** nations will pass by this city;	**Jer 22:8**	7227a
‘(For **m** nations and great kings	**Jer 25:14**	7227a
then **m** nations and great kings	**Jer 27:7**	7227a
prophesied against **m** lands and	**Jer 28:8**	7227a
that you may live **m** days in the	**Jer 35:7**	7227a
and **m** similar words were added to	**Jer 36:32**	7227a
and Jeremiah stayed there **m** days.	**Jer 37:16**	7227a
we are left *but* a few out of **m**,	**Jer 42:2**	7235a
And their **m** cattle for booty,	**Jer 49:32**	1995
“Summon **m** against Babylon, All	**Jer 50:29**	7227a
And a great nation and **m** kings	**Jer 50:41**	7227a
O you who dwell by **m** waters,	**Jer 51:13**	7227a
waves will roar like **m** waters;	**Jer 51:55**	7227a
For my groans are **m** and	**La 1:22**	7227a
nor to **m** peoples of unintelligible	**Ezk 3:6**	7227a
he sees is for **m** years *from now,*	**Ezk 12:27**	7227a
on you in the sight of **m** women.	**Ezk 16:41**	7227a
and a full plumage of **m** colors came	**Ezk 17:3**	7553
nor by **m** people can it be raised	**Ezk 17:9**	7227a
give him horses and **m** troops.	**Ezk 17:15**	7227a
siege walls to cut off **m** lives.	**Ezk 17:17**	7227a
and **m** fall at all their gates.	**Ezk 21:15**	7235a
made **m** widows in the midst of her.	**Ezk 22:25**	7235a
bring up **m** nations against you,	**Ezk 26:3**	7227a
of the peoples to **m** coastlands,	**Ezk 27:3**	7227a
M coastlands were your market;	**Ezk 27:15**	7227a
work, and in carpets of **m** colors	**Ezk 27:24**	1264
the seas, You satisfied **m** peoples;	**Ezk 27:33**	7227a
And its boughs became **m** and its	**Ezk 31:5**	7235a
of **m** waters as it spread them out.	**Ezk 31:5**	7227a
its roots extended to **m** waters.	**Ezk 31:7**	7227a
And *its* **m** waters were stopped up,	**Ezk 31:15**	7227a
you With a company of **m** peoples,	**Ezk 32:3**	7227a
trouble the hearts of **m** peoples when	**Ezk 32:9**	7227a
make **m** peoples appalled at you,	**Ezk 32:10**	7227a
its cattle from beside **m** waters;	**Ezk 32:13**	7227a
so to us who are **m** the land has	**Ezk 33:24**	7227a
m on the surface of the valley;	**Ezk 37:2**	7227a
m peoples with you.	**Ezk 38:6**	7227a
“After **m** days you will be summoned;	**Ezk 38:8**	7227a
have been gathered from **m** nations	**Ezk 38:8**	7227a
troops, and **m** peoples with you.”	**Ezk 38:9**	7227a
north, you and **m** peoples with you,	**Ezk 38:15**	7227a
who prophesied in those days for **m**	**Ezk 38:17**	
on the **m** peoples who are with him,	**Ezk 38:22**	7227a
known in the sight of **m** nations;	**Ezk 38:23**	7227a
in the sight of the **m** nations.	**Ezk 39:27**	7227a
was like the sound of **m** waters;	**Ezk 43:2**	7227a
there *were* very **m** trees on the one	**Ezk 47:7**	7227a
And there will be very **m** fish,	**Ezk 47:9**	7227a
the fish of the Great Sea, very **m**.	**Ezk 47:10**	7227a
Daniel and gave him **m** great gifts,	**Da 2:48**	7690
destroy **m** while *they are* at ease.	**Da 8:25**	7227a
to **m** days *in the future*.”	**Da 8:26**	7227a
covenant with the **m** for one week,	**Da 9:27**	7227a
“Now in those times **m** will rise	**Da 11:14**	7227a
to the coastlands and capture **m**.	**Da 11:18**	7227a
but **m** will fall down slain.	**Da 11:26**	7227a
will give understanding to the **m**;	**Da 11:33**	7227a
by captivity and by plunder for **m**	**Da 11:33**	
and **m** will join with them in	**Da 11:34**	7227a
cause them to rule over the **m**,	**Da 11:39**	7227a
with horsemen and with **m** ships;	**Da 11:40**	7227a
Land, and **m** *countries* will fall;	**Da 11:41**	7227a
wrath to destroy and annihilate **m**.	**Da 11:44**	7227a
“**M** of those who sleep in the dust of	**Da 12:2**	7227a
who lead the **m** to righteousness,	**Da 12:3**	7227a
m will go back and forth, and	**Da 12:4**	7227a
“**M** will be purged, purified and	**Da 12:10**	7227a
“You shall stay with me for **m** days.	**Hos 3:3**	7227a
for **m** days without king or prince,	**Hos 3:4**	7227a
it To the years of **m** generations.	**Jl 2:2**	1755
Your **m** gardens and vineyards,	**Am 4:9**	7235a
are **m** and your sins are great,	**Am 5:12**	7227a
“**M** *will be* the corpses;	**Am 8:3**	7227a
left hand, as well as **m** animals?”	**Jon 4:11**	7227a
M nations will come and say, “Come	**Mi 4:2**	7227a
He will judge between **m** peoples	**Mi 4:3**	7227a
“And now **m** nations have been	**Mi 4:11**	7227a
That you may pulverize **m** peoples,	**Mi 4:13**	7227a
of Jacob Will be among **m** peoples	**Mi 5:7**	7227a
Among **m** peoples Like a lion among	**Mi 5:8**	7227a
at full *strength* and likewise **m**,	**Na 1:12**	7227a
spears gleaming, **M** slain,	**Na 3:3**	7230
of the **m** harlotries of the harlot,	**Na 3:4**	7230
“Because you have looted **m** nations,	**Hab 2:8**	7227a
house By cutting off **m** peoples;	**Hab 2:10**	7227a
horses, On the surge of **m** waters.	**Hab 3:15**	7227a
“**M** nations will join themselves to	**Zch 2:11**	7227a
as I have done these **m** years?”	**Zch 7:3**	4100
even the inhabitants of **m** cities.	**Zch 8:20**	7227a
‘So **m** peoples and mighty nations	**Zch 8:22**	7227a
he turned **m** back from iniquity.	**Mal 2:6**	7227a
m to stumble by the instruction;	**Mal 2:8**	7227a
But when he saw **m** of the Pharisees	**Mt 3:7**	*4183*
will be heard for their **m** words.	**Mt 6:7**	*4180*
and there are **m** who enter through it.	**Mt 7:13**	*4183*
“**M** will say to Me on that day,	**Mt 7:22**	*4183*
in Your name perform **m** miracles?’	**Mt 7:22**	*4183*
m will come from east and west,	**Mt 8:11**	*4183*
to Him **m** who were demon-possessed;	**Mt 8:16**	*4183*
a herd of **m** swine feeding	**Mt 8:30**	*4183*
behold, **m** tax collectors and sinners	**Mt 9:10**	*4183*
are more valuable than **m** sparrows.	**Mt 10:31**	*4183*
M followed Him, and He healed them	**Mt 12:15**	*4183*
m things to them in parables,	**Mt 13:3**	*4183*
that **m** prophets and righteous men	**Mt 13:17**	*4183*
And He did not do **m** miracles there	**Mt 13:58**	*4183*
and as **m** as touched *it* were cured.	**Mt 14:36**	*3745*
blind, mute, and **m** others,	**Mt 15:30**	*4183*
“Where would we get so **m** loaves	**Mt 15:33**	*5118*
“How **m** loaves do you have?”	**Mt 15:34**	*4214*
how **m** baskets *full* you picked up?	**Mt 16:9**	*4214*
m large baskets *full* you picked up?	**Mt 16:10**	*4214*
and suffer **m** things from the	**Mt 16:21**	*4183*
will receive **m** times as much,	**Mt 19:29**	*4179*
“But **m** *who are* first will be last;	**Mt 19:30**	*4183*
to give His life a ransom for **m**.”	**Mt 20:28**	*4183*
and as **m** as you find *there,*	**Mt 22:9**	*3745*
“For **m** are called, but few *are*	**Mt 22:14**	*4183*
“For **m** will come in My name,	**Mt 24:5**	*4183*
am the Christ,’ and will mislead **m**.	**Mt 24:5**	*4183*
“At that time **m** will fall	**Mt 24:10**	*4183*
“**M** false prophets will arise	**Mt 24:11**	*4183*
will arise and will mislead **m**.	**Mt 24:11**	*4183*
put you in charge of **m** things;	**Mt 25:21**	*4183*
put you in charge of **m** things;	**Mt 25:23**	*4183*
out for **m** for forgiveness of sins.	**Mt 26:28**	*4183*
m false witnesses came forward.	**Mt 26:60**	*4183*
“Do You not hear how **m** things	**Mt 27:13**	*4214*
and **m** bodies of the saints who had	**Mt 27:52**	*4183*
the holy city and appeared to **m**.	**Mt 27:53**	*4183*
M women were there looking on from	**Mt 27:55**	*4183*
And He healed **m** who were ill with	**Mk 1:34**	*4183*
diseases, and cast out **m** demons;	**Mk 1:34**	*4183*
And **m** were gathered together, so	**Mk 2:2**	*4183*
and **m** tax collectors and sinners	**Mk 2:15**	*4183*
for there were **m** of them, and they	**Mk 2:15**	*4183*
for He had healed **m**,	**Mk 3:10**	*4183*
them **m** things in parables,	**Mk 4:2**	*4183*
With **m** such parables He was	**Mk 4:33**	*4183*
“My name is Legion; for we are **m**.”	**Mk 5:9**	*4183*
much at the hands of **m** physicians,	**Mk 5:26**	*4183*
the **m** listeners were astonished,	**Mk 6:2**	*4183*
And they were casting out **m** demons	**Mk 6:13**	*4183*
m sick people and healing them.	**Mk 6:13**	*4183*
were **m** *people* coming and going,	**Mk 6:31**	*4183*
them going, and **m** recognized *them*	**Mk 6:33**	*4183*
He began to teach them **m** things.	**Mk 6:34**	*4183*
“How **m** loaves do you have?	**Mk 6:38**	*4214*
and as **m** as touched it were being	**Mk 6:56**	*3745*
and there are **m** other things which	**Mk 7:4**	*4183*
you do **m** things such as that.”	**Mk 7:13**	*4183*
“How **m** loaves do you have?”	**Mk 8:5**	*4214*
how **m** baskets full of broken pieces	**Mk 8:19**	*4214*
how **m** large baskets full of broken	**Mk 8:20**	*4214*
the Son of Man must suffer **m** things	**Mk 8:31**	*4183*
He will suffer **m** things and be	**Mk 9:12**	*4183*
“But **m** *who are* first will be last	**Mk 10:31**	*4183*
to give His life a ransom for **m**.”	**Mk 10:45**	*4183*
M were sternly telling him to be	**Mk 10:48**	*4183*
And **m** spread their coats in the	**Mk 11:8**	*4183*
and *so with* **m** others, beating	**Mk 12:5**	*4183*
and **m** rich people were putting in	**Mk 12:41**	*4183*
“**M** will come in My name, saying,	**Mk 13:6**	*4183*
and will mislead **m**.	**Mk 13:6**	*4183*
which is poured out for **m**.	**Mk 14:24**	*4183*
For **m** were giving false testimony	**Mk 14:56**	*4183*
how **m** charges they bring	**Mk 15:4**	*4214*
and *there were* **m** other women who	**Mk 15:41**	*4183*
inasmuch as **m** have undertaken to	**Lk 1:1**	*4183*
and **m** will rejoice at his birth.	**Lk 1:14**	*4183*
turn **m** of the sons of Israel	**Lk 1:16**	*4183*
the fall and rise of **m** in Israel,	**Lk 2:34**	*4183*
from **m** hearts may be revealed.”	**Lk 2:35**	*4183*
So with **m** other exhortations he	**Lk 3:18**	*4183*
there were **m** widows in Israel in	**Lk 4:25**	*4183*
“And there were **m** lepers in Israel	**Lk 4:27**	*4183*
Demons also were coming out of **m**,	**Lk 4:41**	*4183*
He cured **m** *people* of diseases and	**Lk 7:21**	*4183*
gave sight to **m** *who were* blind.	**Lk 7:21**	*4183*
say to you, her sins, which are **m**,	**Lk 7:47**	*4183*
and **m** others who were contributing	**Lk 8:3**	*4183*
For it had seized him **m** times;	**Lk 8:29**	*4183*
for **m** demons had entered him.	**Lk 8:30**	*4183*
Now there was a herd of **m** swine	**Lk 8:32**	*2425*
Son of Man must suffer **m** things and	**Lk 9:22**	*4183*
that **m** prophets and kings wished	**Lk 10:24**	*4183*
and bothered about so **m** things;	**Lk 10:41**	*4183*
Him closely on **m** subjects,	**Lk 11:53**	*4183*
after so **m** thousands of people	**Lk 12:1**	*3461*
are more valuable than **m** sparrows.	**Lk 12:7**	*4183*
you have **m** goods laid up for many	**Lk 12:19**	*4183*
goods laid up for **m** years *to come*	**Lk 12:19**	*4183*
his will, will receive **m** lashes,	**Lk 12:47**	*4183*
for **m**, I tell you, will seek to	**Lk 13:24**	*4183*
a big dinner, and he invited **m**;	**Lk 14:16**	*4183*
“And not **m** days later, the	**Lk 15:13**	*4183*
‘How **m** of my father’s hired men	**Lk 15:17**	*4214*
m years I have been serving you and	**Lk 15:29**	*5118*
“But first He must suffer **m** things	**Lk 17:25**	*4183*
who will not receive **m** times as	**Lk 18:30**	*4179*
for **m** will come in My name,	**Lk 21:8**	*4183*
saying **m** other things against Him.	**Lk 22:65**	*4183*
But as **m** as received Him, to them	**Jn 1:12**	*3745*
the feast, **m** believed in His name,	**Jn 2:23**	*4183*
m of the Samaritans believed in Him	**Jn 4:39**	*4183*
M more believed because of His word;	**Jn 4:41**	*4183*
what are these for so **m** people?”	**Jn 6:9**	*5118*
Therefore **m** of His disciples, when	**Jn 6:60**	*4183*
this **m** of His disciples withdrew and	**Jn 6:66**	*4183*
But **m** of the crowd believed in	**Jn 7:31**	*4183*
“I have **m** things to speak and to	**Jn 8:26**	*4183*
things, **m** came to believe in Him.	**Jn 8:30**	*4183*
M of them were saying, “He has a	**Jn 10:20**	*4183*
“I showed you **m** good works from	**Jn 10:32**	*4183*
M came to Him and were saying,	**Jn 10:41**	*4183*
M believed in Him there.	**Jn 10:42**	*4183*
and **m** of the Jews had come to	**Jn 11:19**	*4183*
Therefore **m** of the Jews who came to	**Jn 11:45**	*4183*
this man is performing **m** signs.	**Jn 11:47**	*4183*
and **m** went up to Jerusalem out of	**Jn 11:55**	*4183*
him **m** of the Jews were going away	**Jn 12:11**	*4183*
performed so **m** signs before them,	**Jn 12:37**	*5118*
m even of the rulers believed in Him	**Jn 12:42**	*4183*
house are **m** dwelling places;	**Jn 14:2**	*4183*
have **m** more things to say to you,	**Jn 16:12**	*4183*
Therefore **m** of the Jews read	**Jn 19:20**	*4183*
Therefore **m** other signs Jesus also	**Jn 20:30**	*4183*
and although there were so **m**,	**Jn 21:11**	*5118*
m other things which Jesus did,	**Jn 21:25**	*4183*
suffering, by **m** convincing proofs,	**Ac 1:3**	*4183*
Holy Spirit not **m** days from now.”	**Ac 1:5**	*4183*
as **m** as the Lord our God will	**Ac 2:39**	*3745*
And with **m** other words he solemnly	**Ac 2:40**	*4183*
and **m** wonders and signs were	**Ac 2:43**	*4183*
But **m** of those who had heard the	**Ac 4:4**	*4183*
m signs and wonders were taking	**Ac 5:12**	*4183*
and a great **m** of the priests were	**Ac 6:7**	*3793*
case of **m** who had unclean spirits,	**Ac 8:7**	*4183*
and **m** who had been paralyzed and	**Ac 8:7**	*4183*
to **m** villages of the Samaritans.	**Ac 8:25**	*4183*
have heard from **m** about this man,	**Ac 9:13**	*4183*
When **m** days had elapsed, the	**Ac 9:23**	*2425*
Joppa, and **m** believed in the Lord.	**Ac 9:42**	*4183*
Peter stayed **m** days in Joppa with a	**Ac 9:43**	*2425*
gave **m** alms to the *Jewish* people and	**Ac 10:2**	*4183*
and found **m** people assembled.	**Ac 10:27**	*4183*
where **m** were gathered together and	**Ac 12:12**	*2425*
and for **m** days He appeared to	**Ac 13:31**	*4183*
m of the Jews and of the	**Ac 13:43**	*4183*
and as **m** as had been appointed to	**Ac 13:48**	*3745*
city and had made **m** disciples,	**Ac 14:21**	*2425*
“Through **m** tribulations we must	**Ac 14:22**	*4183*
and preaching with **m** others also,	**Ac 15:35**	*4183*
continued doing this for **m** days.	**Ac 16:18**	*4183*
had struck them with **m** blows,	**Ac 16:23**	*4183*
Therefore **m** of them believed, along	**Ac 17:12**	*4183*
and **m** of the Corinthians when they	**Ac 18:8**	*4183*
I have **m** people in this city.”	**Ac 18:10**	*4183*
having remained **m** days longer,	**Ac 18:18**	*2425*
M also of those who had believed	**Ac 19:18**	*4183*
And **m** of those who practiced magic	**Ac 19:19**	*2425*
There were **m** lamps in the	**Ac 20:8**	*2425*
how **m** thousands there are among	**Ac 21:20**	*4214*
“Knowing that for **m** years you	**Ac 24:10**	*4183*
bringing **m** and serious charges	**Ac 25:7**	*4183*
they were spending **m** days there,	**Ac 25:14**	*4183*
I had to do **m** things hostile to the	**Ac 26:9**	*4183*
did I lock up **m** of the saints in	**Ac 26:10**	*4183*
sailed slowly for a good **m** days,	**Ac 27:7**	*2425*
sun nor stars appeared for **m** days,	**Ac 27:20**	*4183*
us with **m** marks of respect;	**Ac 28:10**	*4183*
FATHER OF **M** NATIONS HAVE I MADE	**Ro 4:17**	*4183*
become a father of **m** nations according	**Ro 4:18**	*4183*
of the one the **m** died,	**Ro 5:15**	*4183*
Jesus Christ, abound to the **m**.	**Ro 5:15**	*4183*
free gift *arose* from **m** transgressions	**Ro 5:16**	*4183*
the **m** were made sinners,	**Ro 5:19**	*4183*
One the **m** will be made righteous.	**Ro 5:19**	*4183*
be the firstborn among **m** brethren;	**Ro 8:29**	*4183*
For just as we have **m** members in	**Ro 12:4**	*4183*
so we, who are **m**, are one body in	**Ro 12:5**	*4183*
and since I have had for **m** years a	**Ro 15:23**	*2425*
has also been a helper of **m**,	**Ro 16:2**	*4183*
not **m** wise according to the flesh,	**1Co 1:26**	*4183*
to the flesh, not **m** mighty,	**1Co 1:26**	*4183*
not many mighty, not **m** noble;	**1Co 1:26**	*4183*
yet *you would* not *have* **m** fathers,	**1Co 4:15**	*4183*
there are **m** gods and many lords,	**1Co 8:5**	*4183*
there are many gods and **m** lords,	**1Co 8:5**	*4183*
bread, we who are **m** are one body;	**1Co 10:17**	*4183*
profit but the *profit* of the **m**,	**1Co 10:33**	*4183*
m among you are weak and sick,	**1Co 11:30**	*4183*
body is one and *yet* has **m** members,	**1Co 12:12**	*4183*
of the body, though they are **m**,	**1Co 12:12**	*4183*
the body is not one member, but **m**.	**1Co 12:14**	*4183*
But now there are **m** members,	**1Co 12:20**	*4183*
a great **m** kinds of languages in	**1Co 14:10**	*5118*
me, and there are **m** adversaries.	**1Co 16:9**	*4183*
that thanks may be given by **m**	**2Co 1:11**	*4183*
on us through *the prayers of* **m**	**2Co 1:11**	*4183*
m as are the promises of God,	**2Co 1:20**	*3745*
heart I wrote to you with **m** tears;	**2Co 2:4**	*4183*
For we are not like **m**,	**2Co 2:17**	*4183*

as poor yet making **m** rich, 2Co 6:10 *4183*
and found diligent in **m** things, 2Co 8:22 *4183*
through **m** thanksgivings to God. 2Co 9:12 *4183*
m boast according to the flesh, 2Co 11:18 *4183*
through **m** sleepless nights, 2Co 11:27 *4178*
and I may mourn over **m** of those 2Co 12:21 *4183*
beyond **m** of my contemporaries Ga 1:14 *4183*
Did you suffer so **m** things in vain Ga 3:4 *5118*
For as **m** as are of the works of Ga 3:10 *3745*
"And to seeds," as *referring* to **m**, Ga 3:16 *4183*
us therefore, as **m** as are perfect, Php 3:15 *3745*
For **m** walk, of whom I often told Php 3:18 *4183*
and **m** foolish and harmful desires 1Tm 6:9 *4183*
pierced themselves with **m** griefs. 1Tm 6:10 *4183*
in the presence of **m** witnesses. 1Tm 6:12 *4183*
me in the presence of **m** witnesses, 2Tm 2:2 *4183*
For there are **m** rebellious men, Ti 1:10 *4183*
in **m** portions and in many ways, Heb 1:1 *4181*
in many portions and in **m** ways, Heb 1:1 *4187*
in bringing **m** sons to glory, Heb 2:10 *4183*
once to bear the sins of **m**, Heb 9:28 *4183*
as **m** *descendants* AS THE STARS Heb 11:12
trouble, and by it **m** be defiled; Heb 12:15 *4183*
Let not **m** *of you* become teachers, Jas 3:1 *4183*
For we all stumble in **m** *ways.* Jas 3:2 *4183*
M will follow their sensuality, 2Pe 2:2 *4183*
now **m** antichrists have appeared; 1Jn 2:18 *4183*
because **m** false prophets have gone 1Jn 4:1 *4183*
For **m** deceivers have gone out into 2Jn 1:7 *4183*
have **m** things to write to you, I 2Jn 1:12 *4183*
I had **m** things to write to you, 3Jn 1:13 *4183*
with **m** thousands of His holy ones, Jude 1:14 *3461*
was like the sound of **m** waters. Rv 1:15 *4183*
and I heard the voice of **m** angels Rv 5:11 *4183*
and **m** men died from the waters, Rv 8:11 *4183*
of **m** horses rushing to battle. Rv 9:9 *4183*
prophesy again concerning **m** peoples Rv 10:11 *4183*
as **m** as do not worship the image Rv 13:15 *3745*
like the sound of **m** waters and Rv 14:2 *4183*
great harlot who sits on **m** waters, Rv 17:1 *4183*
and as **m** as make their living by Rv 18:17 *3745*
and like the sound of **m** waters Rv 19:6 *4183*
and on His head *are* **m** diadems; Rv 19:12 *4183*

MAOCH
with him, to Achish the son of **M**, 1Sa 27:2 4582

MAON
M, Carmel and Ziph and Juttah, Jos 15:55 4584
men were in the wilderness of **M**, 1Sa 23:24 4584
and stayed in the wilderness of **M**. 1Sa 23:25 4584
David in the wilderness of **M**. 1Sa 23:25 4584
in **M** whose business was in Carmel; 1Sa 25:2 4584
The son of Shammai was **M**, 1Ch 2:45 4584
and **M** *was* the father of Bethzur. 1Ch 2:45 4584

MAONITES
and the **M** oppressed you, Jg 10:12 4584

MAR
and **m** every good piece of land 2Ki 3:19 3510

MARA
call me **M**, for the Almighty has Ru 1:20 4755

MARAH
When they came to **M**, Ex 15:23 4785
could not drink the waters of **M**, Ex 15:23 4785
therefore it was named **M**. Ex 15:23 4785
of Etham and camped at **M**. Nu 33:8 4785
They journeyed from **M** and Nu 33:9 4785

MARALAH
went up to the west and to **M**, Jos 19:11 4831

MARANATHA
the Lord, he is to be accursed. **M**. 1Co 16:22 *3134*

MARAUDING
and became leader of a **m** band, 1Ki 11:24 1416
And the **m** bands of Arameans did 2Ki 6:23 1416
a man, behold, they saw a **m** band; 2Ki 13:21 1416

MARBLE
on silver rings and **m** columns, Es 1:6 8337b
a mosaic pavement of porphyry, **m**, Es 1:6 8337b
wood and bronze and iron and **m**, Rv 18:12 *3139*

MARCH
the order of **m** of the sons of Israel Nu 10:28 4550
"You shall **m** around the city, Jos 6:3 5437
m around the city seven times, Jos 6:4 5437
"Go forward, and **m** around the city Jos 6:7 5437
'Go and **m** to Mount Tabor, and take Jg 4:6 4900
O my soul, **m** on with strength. Jg 5:21 1869
And they **m** him before the king of Jb 18:14 6805
which are stately in *their* **m**, Pr 30:29 6806
That the mighty men may **m** forward: Jer 46:9 3318
And they each **m** in line, Nor do Jl 2:7 1980
They **m** everyone in his path; Jl 2:8 1980
steel When he is prepared *to* **m**, Na 2:3
They stumble in their **m**, Na 2:5 1979
people Who **m** throughout the earth Hab 1:6 1980
And will **m** in the storm winds of Zch 9:14 1980

MARCHED
they **m** around the city once and Jos 6:14 5437
and **m** around the city in the same Jos 6:15 5437
m around the city seven times. Jos 6:15 5437
When You **m** from the field of Edom, Jg 5:4 6805
When You **m** through the wilderness, Ps 68:7 6805
In indignation You **m** through Hab 3:12 6805

MARCHES
one **m** to *the sound of* the flute, Is 30:29 1980

MARCHING
the Egyptians were **m** after them, Ex 14:10 5265
by **m** all night from Gilgal. Jos 10:9 5927
when you hear the sound of **m** in 2Sa 5:24 6807a
when you hear the sound of **m** in 1Ch 14:15 6807a
M in the greatness of His strength? Is 63:1 6808

MARDUK
to shame, **M** has been shattered; Jer 50:2 4781

MARE
my darling, you are like My **m** SS 1:9 5484

MARESHAH
and Keilah and Achzib and **M**; Jos 15:44 4762
and his son was **M**, the father of 1Ch 2:42 4762
Lecah and Laadah the father of **M**, 1Ch 4:21 4762
Gath, **M**, Ziph, 2Ch 11:8 4762
300 chariots, and he came to **M**. 2Ch 14:9 4762
in the valley of Zephathah at **M**. 2Ch 14:10 4762
Eliezer the son of Dodavahu of **M** 2Ch 20:37 4762
possession, O inhabitant of **M**. Mi 1:15 4762

MARK
at the **m** on the skin of the body, Lv 13:3 5061
the **m** has not spread on the skin, Lv 13:6 5061
garment has a **m** of leprosy in it, Lv 13:47 5061
if the **m** is greenish or reddish in Lv 13:49 5061
it is a leprous **m** and shall be Lv 13:49 5061
the priest shall look at the **m** and Lv 13:50 5061
quarantine the article with the **m** Lv 13:50 5061
look at the **m** on the seventh day; Lv 13:51 5061
the **m** has spread in the garment, Lv 13:51 5061
the **m** is a leprous malignancy, Lv 13:51 5061
of leather in which the **m** occurs, Lv 13:52 5061
m has not spread in the garment, Lv 13:53 5061
the thing in which the **m** occurs and Lv 13:54 5061
article with the **m** has been washed, Lv 13:55 5061
and if the **m** has not changed its Lv 13:55 5061
even though the **m** has not spread, Lv 13:55 5061
and if the **m** has faded after it Lv 13:56 5061
article with the **m** shall be burned Lv 13:57 5061
leather from which the **m** has departed Lv 13:58 5061
This is the law for the **m** of leprosy Lv 13:59 5061
and I put a **m** of leprosy on a Lv 14:34 5061
'*Something* like a **m** *of leprosy* has Lv 14:35 5061
priest goes in to look at the **m**, Lv 14:36 5061
"So he shall look at the **m**, Lv 14:37 5061
the **m** on the walls of the house has Lv 14:37 5061
If the **m** has indeed spread in the Lv 14:39 5061
tear out the stones with the **m** in them Lv 14:40 5061
m breaks out again in the house after Lv 14:43 5061
that the **m** has indeed spread in the Lv 14:44 5061
it is a malignant **m** in the house; Lv 14:44 6883
and the **m** has not indeed spread in Lv 14:48 5061
because the **m** has not reappeared. Lv 14:48 5061
This is the law for any **m** of leprosy Lv 14:54 5061
move your neighbor's boundary **m**, Dt 19:14
moves his neighbor's boundary **m**.' Dt 27:17
And commands it to strike the **m**. Jb 36:32 6293
M the blameless man, and behold Ps 37:37 8104
You, LORD, should **m** iniquities, Ps 130:3 8104
put a **m** on the foreheads of the men Ezk 9:4 8420a
touch any man on whom is the **m**; Ezk 9:6 8420a
"You shall **m** a way for the sword Ezk 21:20 7760
it became your distinguishing **m**; Ezk 27:7 5251
"Son of man, **m** well, see with Ezk 44:5 7760
and **m** well the entrance of the Ezk 44:5 7760
of John who was also called **M**, Ac 12:12 *3138*
them John, who was also called **M**. Ac 12:25 *3138*
wanted to take John, called **M**, Ac 15:37 *3138*
and Barnabas took **M** with him and Ac 15:39 *3138*
and *also* Barnabas's cousin **M** Col 4:10 *3138*
distinguishing **m** in every letter; 2Th 3:17 *4592*
Pick up **M** and bring him with you, 2Tm 4:11 *3138*
as do **M**, Aristarchus, Demas, Luke, Phm 1:24 *3138*
greetings, and *so does* my son, **M**. 1Pe 5:13 *3138*
be given a **m** on their right hand or Rv 13:16 *5480*
except the one who has the **m**, Rv 13:17 *5480*
and receives a **m** on his forehead Rv 14:9 *5480*
receives the **m** of his name." Rv 14:11 *5480*
the people who had the **m** of the beast Rv 16:2 *5480*
who had received the **m** of the beast Rv 19:20 *5480*
and had not received the **m** on Rv 20:4 *5480*

MARKED
When He **m** out the foundations of Pr 8:29 2710
And **m** off the heavens by the span, Is 40:12 8505
m out for this condemnation, Jude 1:4 *4270*

MARKER
then he will set up a **m** by it Ezk 39:15 6725

MARKET
And she was the **m** of nations. Is 23:3 5504
Many coastlands were your **m**; Ezk 27:15 5506
that we may open the wheat **m**, Am 8:5
children sitting in the **m** places, Mt 11:16 *58*
standing idle in the **m** place; Mt 20:3 *58*
greetings in the **m** places, Mt 23:7 *58*
laying the sick in the **m** places, Mk 6:56 *58*
when they come from the **m** place, Mk 7:4 *58*
greetings in the **m** places, Mk 12:38 *58*
like children who sit in the **m** place Lk 7:32 *58*
greetings in the **m** places. Lk 11:43 *58*
greetings in the **m** places, Lk 20:46 *58*
and dragged them into the **m** place Ac 16:19 *58*
some wicked men from the **m** place, Ac 17:5 *60*
and in the **m** place every day with Ac 17:17 *58*
came from there as far as the **M** of Ac 28:15 *5410*
that is sold in the meat **m** without 1Co 10:25 *3111*

MARKS
make any tattoo **m** on yourselves: Lv 19:28 3793
honored us with many **m** of respect; Ac 28:10 *5092*

MAROTH
M Becomes weak waiting for good, Mi 1:12 4796

MARRED
was **m** more than any man And Is 52:14 4893b

MARRIAGE
please give her to him in **m**. Gn 34:8 802
but give me the girl in **m**." Gn 34:12 802
Let us take their daughters in **m**, Gn 34:21 802
a relative by **m** among his people, Lv 21:4 1167
he gave in **m** outside *the family,* Jg 12:9
his daughter to Benjamin in **m**." Jg 21:1 802
them any of our daughters in **m**?" Jg 21:7 802
Then Solomon formed a **m** alliance 1Ki 3:1 2859
he gave him in **m** the sister of his 1Ki 11:19 802
your daughter to my son in **m**.' 2Ki 14:9 802
to Jarha his servant in **m**. 1Ch 2:35 802
he allied himself by **m** with Ahab. 2Ch 18:1 2859
your daughter to my son in **m**.' 2Ch 25:18 802
neither marry nor are given in **m**, Mt 22:30 *1061a*
marrying and giving in **m**, Mt 24:38 *1061a*
neither marry nor are given in **m**, Mk 12:25 *1061a*
husband seven years after her **m**, Lk 2:36 *3932*
they were being given in **m**, Lk 17:27 *1061a*
this age marry and are given in **m**, Lk 20:34 *1061b*
neither marry nor are given in **m**; Lk 20:35 *1061a*
virgin *daughter* in **m** does well, 1Co 7:38 *1061a*
not give her in **m** will do better. 1Co 7:38 *1061a*
men who forbid **m** *and advocate* 1Tm 4:3 *1060*
M *is to be held* in honor among all, Heb 13:4 *1062*
and the **m** bed *is to be* Heb 13:4
for the **m** of the Lamb has come and Rv 19:7 *1062*
invited to the **m** supper of the Lamb Rv 19:9 *1062*

MARRIED
you have taken, for she is **m**." Gn 20:3 1167, 1166
Esau was forty years old he **m** Judith Gn 26:34 3947, 802
and Esau went to Ishmael, and **m**, Gn 28:9 3947, 802
went and **m** a daughter of Levi. Ex 2:1 3947
m his father's sister Jochebed, Ex 6:20 3947, 802
Aaron **m** Elisheba, the daughter Ex 6:23 3947, 802
Aaron's son Eleazar **m** one of Ex 6:25 3947, 802
priest's daughter is **m** to a layman, Lv 22:12 802
the Cushite woman whom he had **m** Nu 12:1 3947
(for he had **m** a Cushite woman); Nu 12:1 3947
of Zelophehad **m** their uncles' sons. Nu 36:11 802
They **m** *those* from the families of Nu 36:12 802
to a woman and has not **m** her? Dt 20:7 3947
man is found lying with a **m** woman, Dt 22:22 1166, 1167
wife of the deceased shall not be **m** Dt 25:5
he also **m** Basemath the daughter of 1Ki 4:15 3947
daughter, whom Solomon had **m**. 1Ki 7:8 3947
that he **m** Jezebel the daughter of 1Ki 16:31 3947, 802
When Azubah died, Caleb **m** Ephrath, 1Ch 2:19 3947
he **m** when he was sixty years old; 1Ch 2:21 3947
and have **m** foreign women from the Ezr 10:2 3427
unfaithful and have **m** foreign wives Ezr 10:10 3427
who have **m** foreign wives come Ezr 10:14 3427
all the men who had **m** foreign wives Ezr 10:17 3427
who had **m** foreign wives were found Ezr 10:18 3427
All these had **m** foreign wives, and Ezr 10:44 5375
and his son Jehohanan had **m** the Ne 6:18 3947
the Jews had **m** women from Ashdod, Ne 13:23 3427
Than the sons of the **m** woman," Is 54:1 1166
is in her," And your land, "**M**"; Is 62:4 1166
And *to Him* your land will be **m**. Is 62:4 1166
m the daughter of a foreign god. Mal 2:11 1166
and the first **m** and died, and Mt 22:25 *1060*
For they all had **m** her." Mt 22:28
Philip, because he had **m** her. Mk 6:17 *1060*
"The second one **m** her, and died Mk 12:21 *2983*
For all seven had **m** her." Mk 12:23
'I have **m** a wife, and for that Lk 14:20 *1060*
and the third **m** her; and in the same Lk 20:31 *2983*
For all seven had **m** her." Lk 20:33
For the **m** woman is bound by law to Ro 7:2 *5220*
But to the **m** I give instructions, 1Co 7:10 *1060*
but one who is **m** is concerned 1Co 7:33 *1060*
but one who is **m** is concerned 1Co 7:34 *1060*
free to be **m** to whom she wishes, 1Co 7:39 *1060*
of Christ, they want to get **m**, 1Tm 5:11 *1060*
I want younger *widows* to get **m**, 1Tm 5:14 *1060*

MARRIES
man who **m** a woman and her mother, Lv 20:14 3947
"When a man takes a wife and **m** her, Dt 24:1 1166
For *as* a young man **m** a virgin, Is 62:5 1166
and whoever **m** a divorced woman Mt 5:32 *1060*
and **m** another woman commits Mt 19:9 *1060*
"Whoever divorces his wife and **m** Mk 10:11 *1060*
her husband and **m** another man, Mk 10:12 *1060*
who divorces his wife and **m** another Lk 16:18 *1060*
and he who **m** one who is divorced Lk 16:18 *1060*
and if a virgin **m**, she has not 1Co 7:28 *1060*

MARROW
And the **m** of his bones is moist, Jb 21:24 4221
satisfied as with **m** and fatness, Ps 63:5 2459
aged wine, choice pieces with **m**, Is 25:6 4229c
and spirit, of both joints and **m**, Heb 4:12 *3452*

MARRY
who were to **m** his daughters, Gn 19:14 3947
to **m** off the younger before the Gn 29:26 5414
'You shall not **m** a woman in Lv 18:18 3947
to **m** a virgin of his own people, Lv 21:14 3947
if she should **m** while under her Nu 30:6 1961, 376

“But if they **m** one of the sons of Nu 36:3 1961, 802
‘Let them **m** whom they wish; Nu 36:6 1961, 802
only they must **m** within the family Nu 36:6 1961, 802
battle and another man would **m** her.’ Dt 20:7 3947
a virgin, So your sons will **m** you; Is 62:5 1166
“And they shall not **m** a widow or Ezk 44:22 3947
this, it is better not to **m**.” Mt 19:10 1060
AS NEXT OF KIN SHALL **M** HIS WIFE, Mt 22:24 1918
the resurrection they neither **m** nor Mt 22:30 1060
HIS BROTHER SHOULD **M** THE WIFE Mk 12:19 2983
neither **m** nor are given in marriage Mk 12:25 1060
HIS BROTHER SHOULD **M** THE WIFE Lk 20:28 2983
The sons of this age **m** and are given Lk 20:34 1060
neither **m** nor are given in marriage; Lk 20:35 1060
not have self-control, let them **m**; 1Co 7:9 1060
it is better to **m** than to burn 1Co 7:9 1060
But if you **m**, 1Co 7:28 1060
he does not sin; let her **m**. 1Co 7:36 1060

MARRYING
you therefore refrain from **m**? Ru 1:13 1166, 1961, 376
our God by **m** foreign women?” Ne 13:27 3427
m and giving in marriage, Mt 24:38 1060
they were drinking, they were **m**, Lk 17:27 1060

MARSENA
Admatha, Tarshish, Meres, **M** and Es 1:14 4826

MARSH
and they grazed in the **m** grass. Gn 41:2 260
and they grazed in the **m** grass. Gn 41:18 260
“Can the papyrus grow up without a **m**? Jb 8:11 1207
the covert of the reeds and the **m**. Jb 40:21 1207

MARSHAL
Appoint a **m** against her, Bring up Jer 51:27 2951

MARSHALLED
M like a man for the battle Jer 50:42 6186a

MARSHALS
Your **m** are like hordes of Na 3:17 2951

MARSHES
they have burned the **m** with fire, Jer 51:32 98
and **m** will not become fresh; Ezk 47:11 1207

MARTHA
M welcomed Him into her home. Lk 10:38 3136
But **M** was distracted with all her Lk 10:40 3136
“**M**, Martha, you are worried and Lk 10:41 3136
“Martha, **M**, you are worried and Lk 10:41 3136
village of Mary and her sister **M**. Jn 11:1 3136
Now Jesus loved **M** and her sister Jn 11:5 3136
the Jews had come to **M** and Mary, Jn 11:19 3136
M therefore, when she heard that Jn 11:20 3136
M then said to Jesus, Jn 11:21 3136
M said to Him, “I know that he will Jn 11:24 3136
in the place where **M** met Him. Jn 11:30 3136
M, the sister of the deceased, said to Jn 11:39 3136
a supper there, and **M** was serving; Jn 12:2 3136

MARTIAL
sons of Israel went up in **m** array Ex 13:18 2571

MARVEL
I have become a **m** to many, Ps 71:7 4159
so that you will **m**. Jn 5:20 2296
“Do not **m** at this; Jn 5:28 2296
“I did one deed, and you all **m**. Jn 7:21 2296
‘BEHOLD, YOU SCOFFERS, AND **M**, Ac 13:41 2296

MARVELED
Now when Jesus heard this, He **m** and Mt 8:10 2296
m as they saw the mute speaking, Mt 15:31 2296
Jesus heard this, He **m** at him, Lk 7:9 2296
“When Moses saw it, he **m** at Ac 7:31 2296
and to be **m** at among all who have 2Th 1:10 2296

MARVELING
was **m** at all that He was doing, Lk 9:43 2296
m at what had happened. Lk 24:12 2296

MARVELOUS
aside now and see this **m** sight, Ex 3:3 1419
He has made **m** His lovingkindness Ps 31:21 6381
It is **m** in our eyes. Ps 118:23 6381
with this people, wondrously **m**; Is 29:14 6381
LORD, AND IT IS **M** IN OUR EYES’? Mt 21:42 2298
LORD, AND IT IS **M** IN OUR EYES’?” Mk 12:11 2298
out of darkness into His **m** light; 1Pe 2:9 2298
sign in heaven, great and **m**, Rv 15:1 2298
“Great and **m** are Your works, O Rv 15:3 2298

MARVELOUSLY
was **m** helped until he was strong. 2Ch 26:15 6381
again deal **m** with this people, Is 29:14 6381

MARVELS
His **m** and the judgments from His 1Ch 16:12 4159
And His **m** in the field of Zoan, Ps 78:43 4159
wonders which He has done, His **m** and Ps 105:5 4159

MARY
the father of Joseph the husband of **M**, Mt 1:16 3137
M had been betrothed to Joseph, Mt 1:18 3137
not be afraid to take **M** as your wife Mt 1:20 3137
and took **M** as his wife, Mt 1:24
saw the Child with **M** His mother; Mt 2:11 3137
Is not His mother called **M**, Mt 13:55 3137
Among them was **M** Magdalene, and Mt 27:56 3137
and **M** the mother of James Mt 27:56 3137
And **M** Magdalene was there, and the Mt 27:61 3137
was there, and the other **M**, Mt 27:61 3137
M Magdalene and the other Mary Mt 28:1 3137
other **M** came to look at the grave. Mt 28:1 3137
this the carpenter, the son of **M**, Mk 6:3 3137
among whom were **M** Magdalene, Mk 15:40 3137
and **M** the mother of James the Less Mk 15:40 3137
M Magdalene and Mary the Mk 15:47 3137
and **M** the mother of Joses were Mk 15:47 3137
the Sabbath was over, **M** Magdalene, Mk 16:1 3137
and **M** the mother of James, Mk 16:1 3137
He first appeared to **M** Magdalene, Mk 16:9 3137
and the virgin’s name was **M**. Lk 1:27 3137
“Do not be afraid, **M**; Lk 1:30 3137
M said to the angel, Lk 1:34 3137
M said, “Behold, the bondslave Lk 1:38 3137
Now at this time **M** arose and went Lk 1:39 3137
M said: “My soul exalts the Lord, Lk 1:46 3137
And **M** stayed with her about three Lk 1:56 3137
order to register along with **M**, Lk 2:5 3137
found their way to **M** and Joseph, Lk 2:16 3137
M treasured all these things, Lk 2:19 3137
them and said to **M** His mother, Lk 2:34 3137
M who was called Magdalene, from Lk 8:2 3137
She had a sister called **M**, Lk 10:39 3137
for **M** has chosen the good part, Lk 10:42 3137
Now they were **M** Magdalene and Lk 24:10 3137
Joanna and **M** the mother of James; Lk 24:10 3137
village of **M** and her sister Martha. Jn 11:1 3137
It was the **M** who anointed the Jn 11:2 3137
the Jews had come to Martha and **M**, Jn 11:19 3137
but **M** stayed at the house. Jn 11:20 3137
away and called **M** her sister, Jn 11:28 3137
M got up quickly and went out, Jn 11:31 3137
when **M** came where Jesus was, Jn 11:32 3137
the Jews who came to **M**, and Jn 11:45 3137
M then took a pound of very Jn 12:3 3137
sister, **M** the wife of Clopas, Jn 19:25 3137
wife of Clopas, and **M** Magdalene. Jn 19:25 3137
M Magdalene came early to the tomb Jn 20:1 3137
But **M** was standing outside the Jn 20:11 3137
Jesus said to her, “**M**!” Jn 20:16 3137
M Magdalene came, announcing to Jn 20:18 3137
women, and **M** the mother of Jesus, Ac 1:14 3137
the house of **M**, the mother of John Ac 12:12 3137
Greet **M**, who has worked hard for Ro 16:6 3137

MARY’S
When Elizabeth heard **M** greeting, Lk 1:41 3137

MASH
were Uz and Hul and Gether and **M**. Gn 10:23 4851

MASHAL
M with its pasture lands, Abdon 1Ch 6:74 4913

MASONRY
There was a row of **m** round Ezk 46:23

MASONS
and to the **m** and the stonecutters, 2Ki 12:12 1443
and the builders and the **m** 2Ki 22:6 1443
with cedar trees, **m** and carpenters, 1Ch 14:1 2796, 7023
and **m** of stone and carpenters, 1Ch 22:15 2796
and they hired **m** and carpenters to 2Ch 24:12 2672
money to the **m** and carpenters, Ezr 3:7 2672

MASREKAH
Samlah of **M** became king in his Gn 36:36 4957
Samlah of **M** became king in his 1Ch 1:47 4957

MASS
around Him, A **m** of waters, 2Sa 22:12 2841
When the dust hardens into a **m** And Jb 38:38 4165
height with the **m** of its branches. Ezk 19:11 7230
Many slain, a **m** of corpses, Na 3:3 3514

MASSA
and Mishma and Dumah and **M**, Gn 25:14 4854
Mishma, Dumah, **M**, Hadad, Tema, 1Ch 1:30 4854

MASSAH
He named the place **M** and Ex 17:7 4532
the test, as you tested Him at **M**. Dt 6:16 4532
“Again at Taberah and at **M** and at Dt 9:22 4532
man, Whom You proved at **M**, Dt 33:8 4532
in the day of **M** in the wilderness, Ps 95:8 4532

MASSED
They have **m** themselves against me. Jb 16:10 4390

MASSES
“You shall not follow the **m** in doing Ex 23:2 7227a

MASSIVE
headlong at Him With his **m** shield. Jb 15:26 5672, 1354

MAST
who lies down on the top of a **m**. Pr 23:34 2260a
hold the base of its **m** firmly, Is 33:23 8650
from Lebanon to make a **m** for you. Ezk 27:5 8650

MASTER
is for you, but you must **m** it.” Gn 4:7 4910
under the thigh of Abraham his **m**, Gn 24:9 113
camels from the camels of his **m**, Gn 24:10 113
“O LORD, the God of my **m** Abraham, Gn 24:12 113
lovingkindness to my **m** Abraham. Gn 24:12 113
shown lovingkindness to my **m**.” Gn 24:14 113
the LORD, the God of my **m** Abraham, Gn 24:27 113
and His truth toward my **m**; Gn 24:27 113
The LORD has greatly blessed my **m**, Gn 24:35 113
bore a son to my **m** in her old age, Gn 24:36 113
“My **m** made me swear, saying, Gn 24:37 113
“I said to my **m**, Gn 24:39 113
‘O LORD, the God of my **m** Abraham, Gn 24:42 113
the LORD, the God of my **m** Abraham, Gn 24:48 113
deal kindly and truly with my **m**, Gn 24:49 113
“Send me away to my **m**.” Gn 24:54 113
me away that I may go to my **m**.” Gn 24:56 113
And the servant said, “He is my **m**.” Gn 24:65 113
Be **m** of your brothers, And may Gn 27:29 1376
“Behold, I have made him your **m**, Gn 27:37 1376
And he was in the house of his **m**, Gn 39:2 113
Now his **m** saw that the LORD was Gn 39:3 113
my **m** does not concern himself with Gn 39:8 113
beside her until his **m** came home. Gn 39:16 113
his **m** heard the words of his wife, Gn 39:19 113
So Joseph’s **m** took him and put him Gn 39:20 113
“If his **m** gives him a wife, and Ex 21:4 113
children shall belong to her **m**, Ex 21:4 113
‘I love my **m**, my wife and my Ex 21:5 113
then his **m** shall bring him to God, Ex 21:6 113
And his **m** shall pierce his ear Ex 21:6 113
she is displeasing in the eyes of her **m** Ex 21:8 113
the owner shall give his or her **m** Ex 21:32 113
“You shall not hand over to his **m** Dt 23:15 113
who has escaped from his **m** to you. Dt 23:15 113
m had fallen to the floor dead. Jg 3:25 113
“Turn aside, my **m**, turn aside to Jg 4:18 113
and the servant said to his **m**, Jg 19:11 113
However, his **m** said to him, Jg 19:12 113
of the man’s house where her **m** was, Jg 19:26 113
When her **m** arose in the morning Jg 19:27 113
up the arrow and came to his **m**. 1Sa 20:38 113
are each breaking away from his **m**. 1Sa 25:10 113
the wilderness to greet our **m**, 1Sa 25:14 113
for evil is plotted against our **m** and 1Sa 25:17 113
and my **m** left me behind when I 1Sa 30:13 113
deliver me into the hands of my **m**, 1Sa 30:15 113
“Is this you, Elijah my **m**?” 1Ki 18:7 113
Go, say to your **m**, 1Ki 18:8 113
where my **m** has not sent to search 1Ki 18:10 113
‘Go, say to your **m**, 1Ki 18:11 113
“Has it not been told to my **m** 1Ki 18:13 113
‘Go, say to your **m**, 1Ki 18:14 113
the LORD said, ‘These have no **m**. 1Ki 22:17 113
the LORD will take away your **m** 2Ki 2:3 113
the LORD will take away your **m** 2Ki 2:5 113
let them go and search for your **m**; 2Ki 2:16 113
Aram, was a great man with his **m**, 2Ki 5:1 113
“I wish that my **m** were with the 2Ki 5:3 113
Naaman went in and told his **m**, 2Ki 5:4 113
when my **m** goes into the house of 2Ki 5:18 113
my **m** has spared this Naaman the 2Ki 5:20 113
My **m** has sent me, saying 2Ki 5:22 113
he went in and stood before his **m**. 2Ki 5:25 113
“Alas, my **m**! For it was borrowed.” 2Ki 6:5 113
“Alas, my **m**! What shall we do?” 2Ki 6:15 113
eat and drink and go to their **m**.” 2Ki 6:22 113
away, and they went to their **m**. 2Ki 6:23 113
from Elisha and returned to his **m**, 2Ki 8:14 113
strike the house of Ahab your **m**, 2Ki 9:7 113
came out to the servants of his **m**, 2Ki 9:11 113
I conspired against my **m** and killed 2Ki 10:9 113
with my **m** the king of Assyria, 2Ki 18:23 113
“Has my **m** sent me only to your 2Ki 18:27 113
my master sent me only to your **m** 2Ki 18:27 113
whom his **m** the king of Assyria has 2Ki 19:4 113
“Thus you shall say to your **m**, 2Ki 19:6 113
he may defect to his **m** Saul.” 1Ch 12:19 113
up and rebelled against his **m**, 2Ch 13:6 113
the LORD said, ‘These have no **m**. 2Ch 18:16 113
that every man should be the **m** in Es 1:22 8323
And the slave is free from his **m**. Jb 3:19 113
look to the hand of their **m**, Ps 123:2 113
I was beside Him, as a **m** workman; Pr 8:30 525
cares for his **m** will be honored. Pr 27:18 113
Do not slander a slave to his **m**, Pr 30:10 113
into the hand of a cruel **m**, Is 19:4 113
priest, the servant like his **m**, Is 24:2 113
with my **m** the king of Assyria, Is 36:8 113
“Has my **m** sent me only to your Is 36:12 113
only to your **m** and to you to speak Is 36:12 113
whom his **m** the king of Assyria has Is 37:4 113
“Thus you shall say to your **m**, Is 37:6 113
‘For I am a **m** to you, And I will Jer 3:14 1166
not lament for him: ‘Alas for the **m**!’ Jer 22:18 113
his father, and a servant his **m**. Mal 1:6 113
And if I am a **m**, where is My Mal 1:6 113
teacher, nor a slave above his **m**. Mt 10:24 2962
teacher, and the slave like his **m**. Mt 10:25 2962
slave whom his **m** put in charge of Mt 24:45 2962
slave whom his **m** finds so doing Mt 24:46 2962
My **m** is not coming for a long time Mt 24:48 2962
the **m** of that slave will come on a Mt 24:50 2962
the **m** of those slaves came and Mt 25:19 2962
‘**M**, you entrusted five talents to Mt 25:20 2962
“His **m** said to him, Mt 25:21 2962
enter into the joy of your **m**.’ Mt 25:21 2962
‘**M**, you entrusted two talents to me. Mt 25:22 2962
“His **m** said to him, Mt 25:23 2962
enter into the joy of your **m**.’ Mt 25:23 2962
‘**M**, I knew you to be a hard man, Mt 25:24 2962
his **m** answered and said to him, Mt 25:26 2962
when the **m** of the house is coming, Mk 13:35 2962
“**M**, we worked hard all night and Lk 5:5 1988b
“**M**, Master, we are perishing!” Lk 8:24 1988b
“Master, **M**, we are perishing!” Lk 8:24 1988b
“**M**, the people are crowding Lk 8:45 1988b
“**M**, it is good for us to be here; Lk 9:33 1988b
“**M**, we saw someone casting out Lk 9:49 1988b
like men who are waiting for their **m** Lk 12:36 2962
those slaves whom the **m** will find Lk 12:37 2962
whom his **m** will put in charge of Lk 12:42 2962
m finds so doing when he comes. Lk 12:43 2962
m will be a long time in coming,’ Lk 12:45 2962
the **m** of that slave will come on a Lk 12:46 2962
back and reported this to his **m**. Lk 14:21 2962
‘**M**, what you commanded has been Lk 14:22 2962
“And the **m** said to the slave, Lk 14:23 2962
since my **m** is taking the Lk 16:3 2962
‘How much do you owe my **m**?’ Lk 16:5 2962

“And his **m** praised the Lk 16:8 *2962*
“Jesus, **M**, have mercy on us!” Lk 17:13 *1988b*
‘**M**, your mina has made ten minas Lk 19:16 *2962*
‘Your mina, **m**, has made five minas.’ Lk 19:18 *2962*
‘**M**, here is your mina, which I kept Lk 19:20 *2962*
‘**M**, he has ten minas *already*.’ Lk 19:25 *2962*
a slave is not greater than his **m**, Jn 13:16 *2962*
does not know what his **m** is doing; Jn 15:15 *2962*
slave is not greater than his **m**.’ Jn 15:20 *2962*
death no longer is **m** over Him. Ro 6:9 *2961*
For sin shall not be **m** over you, Ro 6:14 *2961*
To his own **m** he stands or falls; Ro 14:4 *2962*
like a wise **m** builder I laid a 1Co 3:10 *753*
their **M** and yours is in heaven, Eph 6:9 *2962*
that you too have a **M** in heaven. Col 4:1 *2962*
sanctified, useful to the **M**, 2Tm 2:21 *1203*
denying the **M** who bought them, 2Pe 2:1 *1203*
and deny our only **M** and Lord, Jude 1:4 *1203*

MASTERED
but I will not be **m** by anything. 1Co 6:12 *1850*

MASTER'S
good things of his **m** in his hand; Gn 24:10 113
to the house of my **m** brothers.” Gn 24:27 113
“Now Sarah my **m** wife bore a son Gn 24:36 113
LORD has appointed for my **m** son.’ Gn 24:44 113
take the daughter of my **m** kinsman Gn 24:48 113
let her be the wife of your **m** son, Gn 24:51 113
m wife looked with desire at Joseph, Gn 39:7 113
he refused and said to his **m** wife, Gn 39:8 113
him in confinement in his **m** house, Gn 40:7 113
I have given to your **m** grandson. 2Sa 9:9 113
your **m** grandson may have food; 2Sa 9:10 113
Mephibosheth your **m** grandson 2Sa 9:10 113
‘I also gave you your **m** house and 2Sa 12:8 113
and your **m** wives into your care, 2Sa 12:8 113
“And where is your **m** son?” 2Sa 16:3 113
sound of his **m** feet behind him?” 2Ki 6:32 113
it well, Zimri, your **m** murderer?” 2Ki 9:31 113
since your **m** sons are with you, 2Ki 10:2 113
best and fittest of your **m** sons, 2Ki 10:3 113
and fight for your **m** house.” 2Ki 10:3 113
the heads of the men, your **m** sons, 2Ki 10:6 113
of the least of my **m** servants, 2Ki 18:24 113
owner, And a donkey its **m** manger, Is 1:3 1167
be, You shame of your **m** house.’ Is 22:18 113
of the least of my **m** servants and Is 36:9 113
the ground and hid his **m** money. Mt 25:18 *2962*
“And that slave who knew his **m** will Lk 12:47 *2962*
each one of his **m** debtors, Lk 16:5 *2962*

MASTERS
not support the work of their **m**. Ne 3:5 113
he refreshes the soul of his **m**. Pr 25:13 113
and **m** of *these* collections are Ec 12:11 1167
m besides You have ruled us; Is 26:13 113
in ashes, you **m** of the flock; Jer 25:34 117
escape from the **m** of the flock. Jer 25:35 117
the wailing of the **m** of the flock! Jer 25:36 117
“Command them *to go* to their **m**, Jer 27:4 113
thus you shall say to your **m**, Jer 27:4 113
Her adversaries have become her **m**, La 1:5 7218
“No one can serve two **m**; Mt 6:24 *2962*
“No servant can serve two **m**; Lk 16:13 *2962*
who was bringing her **m** much profit Ac 16:16 *2962*
But when her **m** saw that their hope Ac 16:19 *2962*
are your **m** according to the flesh, Eph 6:5 *2962*
And **m**, do the same things to Eph 6:9 *2962*
those who are your **m** on earth, Col 3:22 *2962*
M, grant to your slaves justice Col 4:1 *2962*
regard their own **m** as worthy of all 1Tm 6:1 *1203*
Those who have believers as their **m** 1Tm 6:2 *1203*
to their own **m** in everything, Ti 2:9 *1203*
Servants, be submissive to your **m** 1Pe 2:18 *1203*

MASTERS'
on the crumbs which fall from their **m** Mt 15:27 *2962*

MASTERY
hoped to gain the **m** over them, Es 9:1 7980
gained the **m** over those who hated Es 9:1 7980

MATCH
is no secret that is a **m** for you. Ezk 28:3 6004
in God's garden could not **m** it; Ezk 31:8 6004
trees could not **m** its branches. Ezk 31:8 6004
from the new will not **m** the old. Lk 5:36 *4856*

MATE
so that they might **m** by the rods; Gn 30:41 3179
before an animal to **m** with it; Lv 18:23 7250
any animal to **m** with it, Lv 20:16 7250
None will lack its **m**. Is 34:16 7468
Each man said to his **m**, Jon 1:7 7453

MATED
they **m** when they came to drink. Gn 30:38 2552
So the flocks **m** by the rods, and Gn 30:39 2552

MATERIAL
blue, purple and scarlet **m**, Ex 25:4
and blue and purple and scarlet **m**; Ex 26:1
of blue and purple and scarlet **m** Ex 26:31
of blue and purple and scarlet **m** Ex 26:36
of blue and purple and scarlet **m** Ex 27:16
and the purple and the scarlet **m** Ex 28:5
blue and purple *and* scarlet **m** Ex 28:6
its workmanship, of the same **m**: Ex 28:8
of blue and purple and scarlet **m** Ex 28:8
of blue and purple and scarlet **m** Ex 28:15
of blue and purple and scarlet **m**, Ex 28:33
and blue, purple and scarlet **m**, Ex 35:6
blue and purple and scarlet **m** Ex 35:23
blue and purple *and* scarlet **m** Ex 35:25
whose heart moved them to bring **m** Ex 35:29
and in purple *and* in scarlet **m**, Ex 35:35
For the **m** they had was sufficient Ex 36:7 4399
and blue and purple and scarlet **m**, Ex 36:8
of blue and purple and scarlet **m**, Ex 36:35
of blue and purple and scarlet **m**, Ex 36:37
of blue and purple and scarlet **m** Ex 38:18
blue and in purple and in scarlet **m**, Ex 38:23
the blue and purple and scarlet **m**, Ex 39:1
of blue and purple and scarlet **m**, Ex 39:2
and the purple and the scarlet **m**, Ex 39:3
its workmanship, of the same **m**: Ex 39:5
of blue and purple and scarlet **m** Ex 39:5
of blue and purple and scarlet **m** Ex 39:8
of blue and purple and scarlet **m** Ex 39:24
and blue and purple and scarlet **m**, Ex 39:29
of two kinds of **m** mixed together. Lv 19:19 8162
over them a cloth of scarlet **m**, Nu 4:8
cedar wood and hyssop and scarlet **m** Nu 19:6
not wear a **m** mixed of wool and Dt 22:11 8162
minister to them also in **m** things. Ro 15:27 *4559*
we reap **m** things from you? 1Co 9:11 *4559*
The **m** of the wall was jasper; Rv 21:18 *1746b*

MATES
“His ox **m** without fail; Jb 21:10 5674a

MATING
the stronger of the flock were **m**, Gn 30:41 3179
at the time when the flock were **m** Gn 31:10 3179
goats which were **m** *were* striped, Gn 31:10 5927
goats which are **m** are striped, Gn 31:12 5927

MATRED
was Mehetabel, the daughter of **M**, Gn 36:39 4308
was Mehetabel, the daughter of **M**, 1Ch 1:50 4308

MATRITE
and the **M** family was taken. 1Sa 10:21 4309

MATTAN
and killed **M** the priest of Baal 2Ki 11:18 4977
and killed **M** the priest of Baal 2Ch 23:17 4977
Now Shephatiah the son of **M**, Jer 38:1 4977

MATTANAH
wilderness *they continued* to **M**, Nu 21:18 4980
and from **M** to Nahaliel, and from Nu 21:19 4980

MATTANIAH
made his uncle **M** king in his place, 2Ki 24:17 4983
and Galal and **M** the son of Mica, 1Ch 9:15 4983
Bukkiah, **M**, Uzziel, Shebuel and 1Ch 25:4 4983
the ninth to **M**, his sons and his 1Ch 25:16 4983
the son of Jeiel, the son of **M**, 2Ch 20:14 4983
sons of Asaph, Zechariah and **M**; 2Ch 29:13 4983
M, Zechariah, Jehiel, Abdi, Ezr 10:26 4983
Elioenai, Eliashib, **M**, Ezr 10:27 4983
Chelal, Benaiah, Maaseiah, **M**, Ezr 10:30 4983
M, Mattenai, Jaasu, Ezr 10:37 4983
and **M** the son of Mica, the son of Ne 11:17 4983
son of Hashabiah, the son of **M**, Ne 11:22 4983
and **M** *who was* in charge of the Ne 12:8 4983
M, Bakbukiah, Obadiah, Ne 12:25 4983
the son of Shemaiah, the son of **M**, Ne 12:35 4983
the son of Zaccur, the son of **M**; Ne 13:13 4983

MATTATHA
the son of Menna, the son of **M**, Lk 3:31 *3160*

MATTATHIAS
the son of **M**, the son of Amos, Lk 3:25 *3161*
the son of Maath, the son of **M**, Lk 3:26 *3161*

MATTATTAH
Mattenai, **M**, Zabad, Eliphelet, Ezr 10:33 4992

MATTENAI
M, Mattattah, Zabad, Eliphelet, Ezr 10:33 4982
Mattaniah, **M**, Jaasu, Ezr 10:37 4982
of Joiarib, **M**; of Jedaiah, Uzzi; Ne 12:19 4982

MATTER
The **m** distressed Abraham Gn 21:11 1697
“What is the **m** with you, Hagar? Gn 21:17
swore to him concerning this **m**. Gn 24:9 1697
“The **m** comes from the LORD; Gn 24:50 1697
small **m** for you to take my husband Gn 30:15 4592
that the **m** is determined by God, Gn 41:32 1697
“Surely the **m** has become known.” Ex 2:14 1697
When Pharaoh heard of this **m**, Ex 2:15 1697
whoever has a legal **m**, Ex 24:14 1697
and the **m** escapes the notice of Lv 4:13 1697
in whatever **m** a man may speak Lv 5:4
each day's **m** on its own day Lv 23:37 1697
against the LORD in the **m** of Peor, Nu 31:16 1697
Speak to Me no more of this **m**. Dt 3:26 1697
it is true *and* the **m** established Dt 13:14 1697
witnesses a **m** shall be confirmed. Dt 19:15 1697
“What is *the* **m** with you, that Jg 18:23
‘What is *the* **m** with you?’” Jg 18:24
you know how the **m** turns out; Ru 3:18 1697
exchange *of land* to confirm any **m**: Ru 4:7 1697
tell him about the **m** of the kingdom 1Sa 10:16 1697
“What is *the* **m** with the people 1Sa 11:5
and David knew about the **m**. 1Sa 20:39 1697
king has commissioned me with a **m** 1Sa 21:2 1697
the **m** on which I am sending 1Sa 21:2 1697
because the king's **m** was urgent.” 1Sa 21:8 1697
who will listen to you in this **m**? 1Sa 30:24 1697
do not take this **m** to heart.” 2Sa 13:20 1697
then are you angry about this **m**? 2Sa 19:42 1697
“In this **m** may the LORD pardon 2Ki 5:18 1697
pardon your servant in this **m**.” 2Ki 5:18 1697
“What is the **m** with you?” 2Ki 6:28
and you shall do the **m** quickly.” 2Ch 24:5 1697
Even *in the* **m** *of* the envoys of 2Ch 32:31
negligent in carrying out this **m**; Ezr 4:22
us his decision concerning this **m**.” Ezr 5:17
sought our God concerning this **m**, Ezr 8:23
When I heard about this **m**, Ezr 9:3 1697
For *this* **m** is your responsibility, Ezr 10:4 1697
trembling because of this **m** and Ezr 10:9 1697
transgressed greatly in this **m**. Ezr 10:13 1697
this **m** is turned away from us.” Ezr 10:14 1697
tenth month to investigate the **m**. Ezr 10:16 1697
And the **m** pleased the king, and he Es 2:4 1697
and the **m** *seems* proper to the king Es 8:5 1697
“If *it is a* **m** of power, behold, Jb 9:19
And if *it is a* **m** of justice, who Jb 9:19
who is trustworthy conceals a **m**. Pr 11:13 1697
But he who repeats a **m** separates Pr 17:9 1697
the glory of God to conceal a **m**, Pr 25:2 1697
of kings is to search out a **m**. Pr 25:2 1697
time for every **m** and for every deed Ec 3:17 2656
bring up a **m** in the presence of God Ec 5:2 1697
The end of a **m** is better than its Ec 7:8 1697
knows the interpretation of a **m**? Ec 8:1 1697
Do not join in an evil **m**, Ec 8:3 1697
creature will make the **m** known. Ec 10:20 1697
What is the **m** with you now, that Is 22:1
And without succeeding *in the* **m** Is 55:11
to give him an answer in the **m** Ezk 14:4
Were your harlotries so small a **m**? Ezk 16:20
So he listened to them in this **m** and Da 1:14 1697
As for every **m** of wisdom and Da 1:20 1697
could declare the **m** for the king, Da 2:10 4406
informed Daniel about the **m**. Da 2:15 4406
Mishael and Azariah, about the **m**, Da 2:17 4406
made known to us the king's **m**.” Da 2:23 4406
an answer concerning this **m** Da 3:16 6600
but I kept the **m** to myself.” Da 7:28 4406
rulers are a laughing **m** to them. Hab 1:10
And He was stating the **m** plainly. Mk 8:32 *3056*
have no part or portion in this **m**, Ac 8:21 *3056*
came together to look into this **m**. Ac 15:6 *3056*
a **m** of wrong or of vicious crime, Ac 18:14 *5100*
in whatever **m** she may have need Ro 16:2 *4229*
to be innocent in the **m**. 2Co 7:11 *4229*
I give *my* opinion in this **m**, 2Co 8:10
be regarded just as we are in the **m** 2Co 11:12
shared with me in the **m** of giving Php 4:15 *3056*
and defraud his brother in the **m** 1Th 4:6 *4229*
no prophecy of Scripture is *a* **m** 2Pe 1:20

MATTERS
King David heard of all these **m**, 2Sa 13:21 1697
in all **m** concerning the people. Ne 11:24 1697
do I involve myself in great **m**, Ps 131:1
discuss **m** of justice with You: Jer 12:1 4941
all these **m** were being talked about Lk 1:65 *4487*
why do you worry about other **m**? Lk 12:26 *3062*
to be a judge of these **m**.” Ac 18:15
yourself concerning all these **m** you Ac 24:8
a loss how to investigate such **m**, Ac 25:20
and there stand trial on these **m**. Ac 25:20
“For the king knows about these **m**, Ac 26:26
How much more **m** of this life? 1Co 6:3 *982*
dealing with **m** of this life, 1Co 6:4 *982*
but *what* **m** *is* the keeping of 1Co 7:19
The remaining **m** I will arrange 1Co 11:34
These are **m** which have, to be Col 2:23 *3056*
m about which they make confident 1Tm 1:7

MATTHAN
Eleazar the father of **M**, Mt 1:15 *3157*
and **M** the father of Jacob. Mt 1:15 *3157*

MATTHAT
the son of **M**, the son of Levi, the Lk 3:24 *3158*
the son of Jorim, the son of **M**, Lk 3:29 *3103a*

MATTHEW
there, He saw a man called **M**, Mt 9:9 *3102b*
Thomas and **M** the tax collector; Mt 10:3 *3102b*
Philip, and Bartholomew, and **M**, Mk 3:18 *3102b*
and **M** and Thomas; Lk 6:15 *3102b*
and Thomas, Bartholomew and **M**, Ac 1:13 *3102b*

MATTHIAS
who was also called Justus), and **M**. Ac 1:23 *3103b*
for them, and the lot fell to **M**; Ac 1:26 *3103b*

MATTITHIAH
M, one of the Levites, who was 1Ch 9:31 4993
Unni, Eliab, Benaiah, Maaseiah, **M**, 1Ch 15:18 4993
and **M**, Eliphelehu, Mikneiah, 1Ch 15:21 4993
Jeiel, Shemiramoth, Jehiel, **M**, 1Ch 16:5 4993
Shimei, Hashabiah and **M**, 1Ch 25:3 4993
for the fourteenth, **M**, 1Ch 25:21 4993
sons of Nebo *there were* Jeiel, **M**, Ezr 10:43 4993
And beside him stood **M**, Ne 8:4 4993

MATTOCK
to sharpen his plowshare, his **m**, 1Sa 13:20 855a

MATTOCKS
shekel for the plowshares, the **m**, 1Sa 13:21 855a

MATURE
then the **m** grain in the head. Mk 4:28 *4134*
wisdom among those who are **m**; 1Co 2:6 *5046*
infants, but in your thinking be **m**. 1Co 14:20 *5046*
of the Son of God, to a **m** man, Eph 4:13 *5046*
But solid food is for the **m**, Heb 5:14 *5046*

MATURITY
in his **m** he contended with God. Hos 12:3 202
life, and bring no fruit to **m**. Lk 8:14 *5052*
the Christ, let us press on to **m**, Heb 6:1 *5047*

MAULING
m him *as it leaves*. Lk 9:39 *4937*

MAY
of the garden you **m** eat freely; Gn 2:16
the trees of the garden we **m** eat; Gn 3:2
m breed abundantly on the earth, Gn 8:17
“**M** God enlarge Japheth, And let Gn 9:27

so that it **m** go well with me	Gn 12:13	
that I **m** live on account of you."	Gn 12:13	
how **m** I know that I will possess	Gn 15:8	
"**M** the wrong done me be upon you.	Gn 16:5	
M the LORD judge between you and	Gn 16:5	
that you **m** refresh yourselves;	Gn 18:5	
after that you **m** go on, since you	Gn 18:5	
so that he **m** command his children	Gn 18:19	
so that the LORD **m** bring	Gn 18:19	
"Oh **m** the Lord not be angry, and	Gn 18:30	4994
"Oh **m** the Lord not be angry, and	Gn 18:32	4994
m rise early and go on your way."	Gn 19:2	
we **m** have relations with them."	Gn 19:5	
that my life **m** be saved."	Gn 19:20	
that we **m** preserve our family	Gn 19:32	
that we **m** preserve our family	Gn 19:34	
that it **m** be a witness to me,	Gn 21:30	
m bury my dead out of my sight."	Gn 23:4	
that he **m** give me the cave of	Gn 23:9	
me that I **m** bury my dead there."	Gn 23:13	
now **m** it be that the girl to whom	Gn 24:14	
down your jar so that I **m** drink,'	Gn 24:14	
water your camels also'—**m**	Gn 24:14	
and **m** it be that the maiden who	Gn 24:43	
that I **m** turn to the right hand or	Gn 24:49	
afterward she **m** go."	Gn 24:55	
away that I **m** go to my master."	Gn 24:56	
"**M** you, our sister, Become	Gn 24:60	
And **m** your descendants possess The	Gn 24:60	
and bring it to me that I **m** eat,	Gn 27:4	
soul **m** bless you before I die."	Gn 27:4	
savory dish for me, that I **m** eat,	Gn 27:7	
that I **m** prepare them *as* a savory	Gn 27:9	
it to your father, that he **m** eat,	Gn 27:10	
he **m** bless you before his death."	Gn 27:10	
of my game, that you **m** bless me."	Gn 27:19	
come close, that I **m** feel you,	Gn 27:21	
son's game, that I **m** bless you."	Gn 27:25	
Now **m** God give you of the dew of	Gn 27:28	
M peoples serve you, And nations	Gn 27:29	
And **m** your mother's sons bow down	Gn 27:29	
son's game, that you **m** bless me."	Gn 27:31	
"**M** God Almighty bless you and make	Gn 28:3	
you **m** become a company of peoples.	Gn 28:3	
"**M** He also give you the blessing	Gn 28:4	
that you **m** possess the land of	Gn 28:4	
that I **m** go in to her."	Gn 29:21	
her that she **m** bear on my knees,	Gn 30:3	
her I too **m** have children."	Gn 30:3	
"Therefore he **m** lie with you	Gn 30:15	
"**M** the LORD give me another son."	Gn 30:24	
that I **m** go to my own place and to	Gn 30:25	
that they **m** decide between us two.	Gn 31:37	
"**M** the LORD watch between you and	Gn 31:49	
m find favor in your sight.	Gn 32:5	
he too **m** die like his brothers."	Gn 38:11	
me, that you **m** come in to me?"	Gn 38:16	
so that we **m** live and not die."	Gn 42:2	
afraid that harm **m** befall him."	Gn 42:4	
of you that he **m** get your brother,	Gn 42:16	
that your words **m** be tested,	Gn 42:16	
me, so your words **m** be verified,	Gn 42:20	
I **m** know that you are not spies,	Gn 42:34	
and you **m** trade in the land.' "	Gn 42:34	
"You **m** put my two sons to death	Gn 42:37	
go, that we **m** live and not die,	Gn 43:8	
you **m** hold me responsible for him.	Gn 43:9	
and **m** God Almighty grant you	Gn 43:14	
that he **m** seek occasion against us	Gn 43:18	
"**M** God be gracious to you, my son."	Gn 43:29	
m your servant please speak a word	Gn 44:18	
me that I **m** set my eyes on him.'	Gn 44:21	
you **m** live in the land of Goshen;	Gn 46:34	
seed, that we **m** live and not die,	Gn 47:19	
that the land **m** not be desolate."	Gn 47:19	
for you, and you **m** sow the land.	Gn 47:23	
me, please, that I **m** bless them."	Gn 48:9	
And **m** my name live on in them, And	Gn 48:16	
And **m** they grow into a multitude	Gn 48:16	
'**M** God make you like Ephraim and	Gn 48:20	
that I **m** tell you what will befall	Gn 49:1	
M they be on the head of Joseph,	Gn 49:26	
she **m** nurse the child for you?"	Ex 2:7	
so that you **m** bring My people,	Ex 3:10	
Now they **m** say to me,	Ex 3:13	
m sacrifice to the LORD our God.'	Ex 3:18	
For they **m** say, 'The LORD has not	Ex 4:1	
"that they **m** believe that the	Ex 4:5	
they **m** believe the witness of the	Ex 4:8	
that I **m** return to my brethren who	Ex 4:18	
My son go that he **m** serve Me';	Ex 4:23	
'Let My people go that they **m**	Ex 5:1	
m sacrifice to the LORD our God,	Ex 5:3	
"**M** the LORD look upon you and	Ex 5:21	
that I **m** multiply My signs and My	Ex 7:3	
that it **m** become a serpent.' "	Ex 7:9	
they **m** serve Me in the wilderness.	Ex 7:16	
water, that they **m** become blood;	Ex 7:19	
people go, that they **m** serve Me.	Ex 8:1	
they **m** sacrifice to the LORD."	Ex 8:8	
they **m** be left only in the Nile?"	Ex 8:9	
"**M** *it be* according to your word,	Ex 8:10	
that you **m** know that there is no	Ex 8:10	
that it **m** become gnats through all	Ex 8:16	
people go, that they **m** serve Me.	Ex 8:20	
in order that you **m** know that I,	Ex 8:22	
that you **m** sacrifice to the LORD	Ex 8:28	
that the swarms of insects **m** depart	Ex 8:29	
people go, that they **m** serve Me.	Ex 9:1	
people go, that they **m** serve Me.	Ex 9:13	
so that you **m** know that there is	Ex 9:14	
hail **m** fall on all the land of Egypt,	Ex 9:22	
that you **m** know that the earth is	Ex 9:29	
that I **m** perform these signs of	Ex 10:1	
and that you **m** tell in the hearing	Ex 10:2	
you **m** know that I am the LORD."	Ex 10:2	
people go, that they **m** serve Me.	Ex 10:3	
they **m** serve the LORD their God.	Ex 10:7	
"Thus **m** the LORD be with you, if	Ex 10:10	
m come up on the land of Egypt and	Ex 10:12	
that there **m** be darkness over the	Ex 10:21	
even a darkness which **m** be felt."	Ex 10:21	
your little ones **m** go with you."	Ex 10:24	
that we **m** sacrifice *them* to the	Ex 10:25	
that you **m** understand how the LORD	Ex 11:7	
you **m** take it from the sheep or	Ex 12:5	
that alone **m** be prepared by you.	Ex 12:16	
him, then he **m** eat of it.	Ex 12:44	
uncircumcised person **m** eat of it.	Ex 12:48	
that the law of the LORD **m** be in	Ex 13:9	
that we **m** serve the Egyptians'?	Ex 14:12	
that the waters **m** come back over	Ex 14:26	
every day, that I **m** test them,	Ex 16:4	
that they **m** see the bread that I	Ex 16:32	
"Give us water that we **m** drink."	Ex 17:2	
of it, that the people **m** drink."	Ex 17:6	
m hear when I speak with you and	Ex 19:9	
m also believe in you forever."	Ex 19:9	
that your days **m** be prolonged in	Ex 20:12	
the fear of Him **m** remain with you,	Ex 20:20	
with you, so that you **m** not sin."	Ex 20:20	
woman, he **m** not reduce her food,	Ex 21:10	
you a place to which he **m** flee.	Ex 21:13	
even from My altar, that he **m** die.	Ex 21:14	
woman's husband **m** demand of him,	Ex 21:22	
the needy of your people **m** eat;	Ex 23:11	
the beast of the field **m** eat.	Ex 23:11	
your ox and your donkey **m** rest,	Ex 23:12	
stranger, **m** refresh themselves.	Ex 23:12	
the land **m** not become desolate and	Ex 23:29	
for Me, that I **m** dwell among them.	Ex 25:8	
with them the table **m** be carried.	Ex 25:28	
he **m** minister as priest to Me.	Ex 28:3	
he **m** minister as priest to Me.	Ex 28:4	
its two ends, that it **m** be joined.	Ex 28:7	
m be accepted before the LORD.	Ex 28:38	
that they **m** serve Me as priests.	Ex 28:41	
they **m** be anointed and ordained.	Ex 29:29	
that it **m** be a memorial for the	Ex 30:16	
them, that they **m** be most holy;	Ex 30:29	
they **m** minister as priests to Me.	Ex 30:30	
that he **m** work in all *kinds of*	Ex 31:5	
that they **m** make all that I have	Ex 31:6	
that you **m** know that I am the LORD	Ex 31:13	
'For six days work **m** be done,	Ex 31:15	
that My anger **m** burn against them and	Ex 32:10	
them and that I **m** destroy them;	Ex 32:10	
He **m** bestow a blessing upon you	Ex 32:29	
I **m** know what I shall do with you.	Ex 33:5	
know Your ways that I **m** know You,	Ex 33:13	
that I **m** find favor in Your sight.	Ex 33:13	
m be distinguished from all the	Ex 33:16	
even the flocks and the herds **m**	Ex 34:3	
"For six days work **m** be done,	Ex 35:2	
he **m** minister as a priest to Me.	Ex 40:13	
they **m** minister as priests to Me;	Ex 40:15	
he **m** be accepted before the LORD.	Lv 1:3	
that it **m** be accepted for him to	Lv 1:4	
whatever *sort* his uncleanness **m**	Lv 5:3	
in whatever matter a man **m** speak	Lv 5:4	
any one of the things a man **m** do;	Lv 6:3	
he **m** have done to incur guilt."	Lv 6:7	
among the sons of Aaron **m** eat it;	Lv 6:18	
among the priests **m** eat of it;	Lv 6:29	
among the priests **m** eat of it.	Lv 7:6	
day what is left of it **m** be eaten;	Lv 7:16	
who is clean **m** eat *such* flesh.	Lv 7:19	
beasts **m** be put to any other use,	Lv 7:24	
that the breast **m** be presented as	Lv 7:30	
glory of the LORD **m** appear to you.	Lv 9:6	
that you **m** make atonement for	Lv 9:7	
you **m** make atonement for them,	Lv 9:7	
you **m** eat in a clean place,	Lv 10:14	
the creatures which you **m** eat	Lv 11:2	
among the animals, that you **m** eat.	Lv 11:3	
'These you **m** eat, whatever is in	Lv 11:9	
seas or in the rivers, you **m** eat.	Lv 11:9	
you **m** not eat of their flesh, and	Lv 11:11	
'Yet these you **m** eat among all the	Lv 11:21	
'These of them you **m** eat:	Lv 11:22	
of them **m** fall when they are dead	Lv 11:32	
into which one of them **m** fall,	Lv 11:33	
'Any of the food which **m** be eaten,	Lv 11:34	
and any liquid which **m** be drunk in	Lv 11:34	
on which part of their carcass **m** fall	Lv 11:35	
afterward, he **m** enter the camp,	Lv 14:8	
that he **m** make atonement for	Lv 16:6	
that the cloud of incense **m** cover	Lv 16:13	
that he **m** make atonement for	Lv 16:17	
you, that you **m** humble your souls;	Lv 16:31	
sons of Israel **m** bring their sacrifices	Lv 17:5	
they **m** bring them in to the LORD,	Lv 17:5	
'No person among you **m** eat blood,	Lv 17:12	
nor **m** any alien who sojourns among	Lv 17:12	
beast or a bird which **m** be eaten,	Lv 17:13	
a man **m** live if he does them;	Lv 18:5	
it so that you **m** be accepted.	Lv 19:5	
m surely reprove your neighbor,	Lv 19:17	
that its yield **m** increase for you;	Lv 19:25	
for her he **m** defile himself.	Lv 21:3	
by harlotry, these he **m** not take;	Lv 21:14	
'He **m** eat the food of his God,	Lv 21:22	
m eat of the holy *gifts* until he	Lv 22:4	
his money, that one **m** eat of it,	Lv 22:11	
in his house **m** eat of his food.	Lv 22:11	
you **m** present it for a freewill	Lv 22:23	
it so that you **m** be accepted.	Lv 22:29	
'For six days work **m** be done,	Lv 23:3	
so that your generations **m** know	Lv 23:43	
that it **m** be a memorial portion	Lv 24:7	
you **m** live securely on the land.	Lv 25:18	
that he **m** return to his property.	Lv 25:28	
belongs to the Levites **m** be	Lv 25:33	
that he **m** live with you.	Lv 25:35	
your countryman **m** live with you.	Lv 25:36	
that he **m** return to the property	Lv 25:41	
and female slaves whom you **m** have	Lv 25:44	
you **m** acquire male and female slaves	Lv 25:44	
you that you **m** gain acquisition,	Lv 25:45	
also **m** become your possession.	Lv 25:45	
'You **m** even bequeath them to your	Lv 25:46	
One of his brothers **m** redeem him,	Lv 25:48	
or his uncle's son, **m** redeem him,	Lv 25:49	
from his family **m** redeem him;	Lv 25:49	
he prospers, he **m** redeem himself.	Lv 25:49	
so that you **m** lie down with no one	Lv 26:6	
'As for those of you who **m** be left,	Lv 26:36	
'So those of you who **m** be left	Lv 26:39	
price to it, so that it **m** be his.	Lv 27:15	
to it, so that it **m** pass to him.	Lv 27:19	
man, it **m** no longer be redeemed;	Lv 27:20	
the LORD, no man **m** consecrate it;	Lv 27:26	
'No one who **m** have been set apart	Lv 27:29	
the priest, that they **m** serve him.	Nu 3:6	
that they **m** keep their priesthood,	Nu 3:10	
that they **m** live and not die when	Nu 4:19	
restitution **m** be made for the wrong	Nu 5:8	
the Nazirite **m** drink wine.'	Nu 6:20	
that they **m** be used in the service	Nu 7:5	
that they **m** qualify to perform the	Nu 8:11	
"Then after that the Levites **m** go	Nu 8:15	
"They **m**, however, assist their	Nu 8:26	
he **m**, however, observe the Passover	Nu 9:10	
that you **m** be remembered before	Nu 10:9	
'Give us meat that we **m** eat!'	Nu 11:13	
they **m** eat for a whole month.'	Nu 11:21	
she **m** be received again."	Nu 12:14	
they **m** spy out the land of Canaan,	Nu 13:2	
or one who **m** be among you	Nu 15:14	
for him that he **m** be forgiven.	Nu 15:28	
so that you **m** remember to do	Nu 15:40	
that I **m** consume them instantly."	Nu 16:21	
"The earth **m** swallow us up!"	Nu 16:34	
that I **m** consume them instantly."	Nu 16:45	
that you **m** put an end to their	Nu 17:10	
that they **m** be joined with you and	Nu 18:2	
an outsider **m** not come near you.	Nu 18:4	
household who is clean **m** eat it.	Nu 18:11	
household who is clean **m** eat it.	Nu 18:13	
'You **m** eat it anywhere, you	Nu 18:31	
eyes, that it **m** yield its water.	Nu 20:8	
m remove the serpents from us."	Nu 21:7	
that I **m** give them water."	Nu 21:16	
perhaps I **m** be able to defeat them	Nu 22:6	
you as the LORD **m** speak to me."	Nu 22:8	
I **m** be able to fight against them and	Nu 22:11	
place from where you **m** see them,	Nu 23:13	
LORD **m** turn away from Israel."	Nu 25:4	
"**M** the LORD, the God of the	Nu 27:16	
of the sons of Israel **m** obey *him*.	Nu 27:20	
her husband **m** confirm it or her	Nu 30:13	
it or her husband **m** annul it.	Nu 30:13	
that they **m** go against Midian to	Nu 31:3	
afterward you **m** enter the camp."	Nu 31:24	
unintentionally **m** flee there.	Nu 35:11	
unintentionally **m** flee there.	Nu 35:15	
city of refuge to which he **m** flee,	Nu 35:26	
that he **m** return to live in the	Nu 35:32	
each **m** possess the inheritance of his	Nu 36:8	
'**M** the LORD, the God of your	Dt 1:11	
they **m** search out the land for us,	Dt 1:22	
them with money so that you **m** eat,	Dt 2:6	
with money so that you **m** drink.	Dt 2:6	
me food for money so that I **m** eat,	Dt 2:28	
water for money so that I **m** drink,	Dt 2:28	
that you **m** possess his land.'	Dt 2:31	
Then you **m** return every man to his	Dt 3:20	
so that you **m** live and go in	Dt 4:1	
that you **m** keep the commandments	Dt 4:2	
that I **m** let them hear My words so	Dt 4:10	
they **m** learn to fear Me all the days	Dt 4:10	
that they **m** teach their children.'	Dt 4:10	
that it **m** go well with you and	Dt 4:40	
and that you **m** live long on the	Dt 4:40	
that you **m** learn them and observe	Dt 5:1	
servant **m** rest as well as you.	Dt 5:14	
that your days **m** be prolonged and	Dt 5:16	
and that it **m** go well with you on	Dt 5:16	
that it **m** be well with them and	Dt 5:29	
that I **m** speak to you all the	Dt 5:31	
that they **m** observe *them* in the	Dt 5:31	
commanded you, that you **m** live and	Dt 5:33	
and that it **m** be well with you,	Dt 5:33	
and that you **m** prolong *your* days	Dt 5:33	
and that your days **m** be prolonged.	Dt 6:2	
that it **m** be well with you and	Dt 6:3	
and that you **m** multiply greatly,	Dt 6:3	

that it **m** be well with you and	Dt 6:18
you **m** go in and possess the good	Dt 6:18
do, that you **m** live and multiply,	Dt 8:1
you **m** say in your heart,	Dt 8:17
that He **m** confirm His covenant	Dt 8:18
so that you **m** drive them out and	Dt 9:3
that I **m** destroy them and blot out	Dt 9:14
which You brought us **m** say,	Dt 9:28
that they **m** go in and possess the	Dt 10:11
so that you **m** be strong and go in	Dt 11:8
so that you **m** prolong *your* days on	Dt 11:9
that you **m** gather in your grain	Dt 11:14
days of your sons **m** be multiplied	Dt 11:21
you **m** slaughter and eat meat	Dt 12:15
unclean and the clean **m** eat of it,	Dt 12:15
to eat meat, *then* you **m** eat meat,	Dt 12:20
then you **m** slaughter of your herd	Dt 12:21
and you **m** eat within your gates	Dt 12:21
and the clean alike **m** eat of it.	Dt 12:22
so that it **m** be well with	Dt 12:25
your holy things which you **m** have	Dt 12:26
so that it **m** be well with	Dt 12:28
gods, that I also **m** do likewise?'	Dt 12:30
in order that the LORD **m** turn from	Dt 13:17
are the animals which you **m** eat:	Dt 14:4
among the animals, that you **m** eat.	Dt 14:6
"These you **m** eat of all that are in	Dt 14:9
has fins and scales you **m** eat,	Dt 14:9
"You **m** eat any clean bird.	Dt 14:11
"You **m** eat any clean bird.	Dt 14:20
You **m** give it to the alien who is	Dt 14:21
in your town, so that he **m** eat it,	Dt 14:21
or you **m** sell it to a foreigner,	Dt 14:21
so that you **m** learn to fear	Dt 14:23
"You **m** spend the money for	Dt 14:26
the LORD your God **m** bless you	Dt 14:29
"From a foreigner you **m** exact *it,*	Dt 15:3
he **m** cry to the LORD against you,	Dt 15:9
the unclean and the clean alike **m**	Dt 15:22
so that you **m** remember all	Dt 16:3
that you **m** live and possess the	Dt 16:20
you **m** not put a foreigner over	Dt 17:15 3201
that he **m** learn to fear the LORD	Dt 17:19
that his heart **m** not be lifted up	Dt 17:20
that he **m** not turn aside from the	Dt 17:20
he and his sons **m** continue long in	Dt 17:20
"You **m** say in your heart,	Dt 18:21
that any manslayer **m** flee there.	Dt 19:3
who **m** flee there and live:	Dt 19:4
he **m** flee to one of these cities	Dt 19:5
avenger of blood, that he **m** die.	Dt 19:12
that it **m** go well with you.	Dt 19:13
so that they **m** not teach you	Dt 20:18
for you **m** eat from them, and you	Dt 20:19
that you **m** construct siegeworks	Dt 20:20
and after that you **m** go in to her	Dt 21:13
the young you **m** take for yourself,	Dt 22:7
order that it **m** be well with you and	Dt 22:7
and that you **m** prolong your days.	Dt 22:7
m enter the assembly of the LORD.	Dt 23:8
he **m** not reenter the camp.	Dt 23:10
at sundown he **m** reenter the camp.	Dt 23:11
that **m** be loaned at interest.	Dt 23:19
"You **m** charge interest to a	Dt 23:20
so that the LORD your God **m** bless	Dt 23:20
then you **m** eat grapes until you	Dt 23:24
then you **m** pluck the heads with	Dt 23:25
that he **m** sleep in his cloak and	Dt 24:13
the LORD your God **m** bless you	Dt 24:19
"He **m** beat him forty times *but* no	Dt 25:3
that your days **m** be prolonged in	Dt 25:15
that they **m** eat in your towns and	Dt 26:12
so that you **m** enter the land	Dt 27:3
you **m** prosper in all that you do.	Dt 29:9
that you **m** enter into the covenant	Dt 29:12
in order that He **m** establish you	Dt 29:13
people and that He **m** be your God,	Dt 29:13
that we **m** observe all the words of	Dt 29:29
soul, so that you **m** live.	Dt 30:6
us hear it, that we **m** observe it?'	Dt 30:12
us hear it, that we **m** observe it?'	Dt 30:13
your heart, that you **m** observe it.	Dt 30:14
that you **m** live and multiply,	Dt 30:16
and that the LORD your God **m** bless	Dt 30:16
life in order that you **m** live,	Dt 30:19
that you **m** live in the land which	Dt 30:20
so that they **m** hear and	Dt 31:12
that I **m** commission him."	Dt 31:14
so that this song **m** be a	Dt 31:19
that it **m** remain there as a	Dt 31:26
that I **m** speak these words in	Dt 31:28
"**M** Reuben live and not die, Nor	Dt 33:6
And **m** You be a help against his	Dt 33:7
"**M** the beloved of the LORD dwell	Dt 33:12
M he be favored by his brothers,	Dt 33:24
And **m** he dip his foot in oil.	Dt 33:24
m have success wherever you go.	Jos 1:7
so that you **m** be careful to do	Jos 1:8
m the LORD your God be with you as	Jos 1:17
afterward you **m** go on your way."	Jos 2:16
that you **m** know the way by which	Jos 3:4
that they **m** know that just as I	Jos 3:7
all the peoples of the earth **m** know	Jos 4:24
so that you **m** fear the LORD your	Jos 4:24
each tribe that I **m** send them,	Jos 18:4
and that they **m** arise and walk	Jos 18:4
premeditation, **m** flee there,	Jos 20:3
so that he **m** dwell among them.	Jos 20:4
unintentionally **m** flee there,	Jos 20:9
knows, and **m** Israel itself know.	Jos 22:22
it, **m** the LORD Himself require it.	Jos 22:23
come your sons **m** say to our sons,	Jos 22:24
So your sons **m** make our sons stop	Jos 22:25
so that you **m** not turn aside from	Jos 23:6
we **m** fight against the Canaanites;	Jg 1:3
"Bring out your son, that he **m** die,	Jg 6:30
me that I **m** speak once more;	Jg 6:39
you **m** go down against the camp."	Jg 7:11
Shechem, that God **m** listen to you.	Jg 9:7
m fire come out from the bramble	Jg 9:15
that we **m** fight against the sons of	Jg 11:6
that you **m** go with us and fight	Jg 11:8
m the LORD, the Judge, judge today	Jg 11:27
that I **m** go to the mountains and	Jg 11:37
he **m** teach us what to do for the boy	Jg 13:8
that we **m** prepare a young goat	Jg 13:15
come *to pass,* we **m** honor you?"	Jg 13:17
your riddle, that we **m** hear it."	Jg 14:13
we **m** give you into the hands of the	Jg 15:12
and how we **m** overpower him	Jg 16:5
that we **m** bind him to afflict him.	Jg 16:5
you **m** be bound to afflict you."	Jg 16:6
tell me how you **m** be bound."	Jg 16:10
tell me how you **m** be bound."	Jg 16:13
for Samson, that he **m** amuse us."	Jg 16:25
that I **m** lean against them."	Jg 16:26
that I **m** at once be avenged of the	Jg 16:28
stay wherever I **m** find *a place.*"	Jg 17:9
that we **m** know whether our way on	Jg 18:5
bread, and afterward you **m** go."	Jg 19:5
here that your heart **m** be merry.	Jg 19:9
Then tomorrow you **m** arise early	Jg 19:9
journey so that you **m** go home."	Jg 19:9
we **m** have relations with him."	Jg 19:22
you **m** ravish them and do to them	Jg 19:24
they **m** punish *them* for all the	Jg 20:10
that we **m** put them to death and	Jg 20:13
"Let us flee that we **m** draw them	Jg 20:32
M the LORD deal kindly with you as	Ru 1:8
"**M** the LORD grant that you may	Ru 1:9
LORD grant that you **m** find rest,	Ru 1:9
that they **m** be your husbands?	Ru 1:11
Thus **m** the LORD do to me, and	Ru 1:17
in whose sight I **m** find favor."	Ru 2:2
"**M** the LORD be with you."	Ru 2:4
"**M** the LORD bless you."	Ru 2:4
"**M** the LORD reward your work, and	Ru 2:12
that you **m** eat of the bread and	Ru 2:14
and leave *it* that she **m** glean,	Ru 2:16
M he who took notice of you be	Ru 2:19
"**M** he be blessed of the LORD who	Ru 2:20
you, that it **m** be well with you?	Ru 3:1
"**M** you be blessed of the LORD, my	Ru 3:10
but if not, tell me that I **m** know;	Ru 4:4
you **m** *have* my right of redemption,	Ru 4:6
M the LORD make the woman who is	Ru 4:11
and **m** you achieve wealth in	Ru 4:11
m your house be like the house of	Ru 4:12
and **m** his name become famous in	Ru 4:14
"**M** he also be to you a restorer	Ru 4:15
and **m** the God of Israel grant your	1Sa 1:17
that he **m** appear before the LORD	1Sa 1:22
m the LORD confirm His word."	1Sa 1:23
"**M** the LORD give you children	1Sa 2:20
I **m** eat a piece of bread.	1Sa 2:36
M God do so to you, and more also,	1Sa 3:17
that it **m** come among us and	1Sa 4:3
Then send it away that it **m** go.	1Sa 6:8
that He **m** save us from the hand of	1Sa 7:8
we also **m** be like all the nations,	1Sa 8:20
that our king **m** judge us and go	1Sa 8:20
"Get up, that I **m** send you away."	1Sa 9:26
that I **m** proclaim the word of God	1Sa 9:27
that we **m** send messengers	1Sa 11:3
and you **m** do to us whatever seems	1Sa 11:10
that we **m** put them to death."	1Sa 11:12
that I **m** plead with you before the	1Sa 12:7
that He **m** send thunder and rain.	1Sa 12:17
your God, so that we **m** not die;	1Sa 12:19
"**M** God do this *to me* and more	1Sa 14:44
me, that I **m** worship the LORD."	1Sa 15:25
I **m** worship the LORD your God."	1Sa 15:30
a man that we **m** fight together."	1Sa 17:10
"Go, and **m** the LORD be with you."	1Sa 17:37
that all the earth **m** know that	1Sa 17:46
and that all this assembly **m** know	1Sa 17:47
that she **m** become a snare to him,	1Sa 18:21
Philistines **m** be against him."	1Sa 18:21
time you **m** be my son-in-law today."	1Sa 18:21
bed, that I **m** put him to death."	1Sa 19:15
that I **m** hide myself in the field	1Sa 20:5
m the LORD do so to Jonathan and	1Sa 20:13
you away, that you **m** go in safety.	1Sa 20:13
And **m** the LORD be with you as He	1Sa 20:13
of the LORD, that I **m** not die?	1Sa 20:14
"**M** the LORD require *it* at the	1Sa 20:16
away that I **m** see my brothers.'	1Sa 20:29
"**M** you be blessed of the LORD,	1Sa 23:21
"**M** the LORD judge between you and	1Sa 24:12
and **m** the LORD avenge me on you;	1Sa 24:12
and **m** He see and plead my cause and	1Sa 24:15
M the LORD therefore reward you	1Sa 24:19
"**M** God do so to the enemies of	1Sa 25:22
so **m** my life be highly valued in	1Sa 26:24
and **m** He deliver me from all	1Sa 26:24
the country, that I **m** live there;	1Sa 27:5
m go to her and inquire of her."	1Sa 28:7
that you **m** make known to me what I	1Sa 28:15
of bread before you that *you* **m**	1Sa 28:22
that he **m** return to his place	1Sa 29:4
or in the battle he **m** become an	1Sa 29:4
that you **m** not displease the lords	1Sa 29:7
that I **m** not go and fight against	1Sa 29:8
m lead *them* away and depart."	1Sa 30:22
"**M** you be blessed of the LORD	2Sa 2:5
"Now **m** the LORD show	2Sa 2:6
"**M** God do so to Abner, and more	2Sa 3:9
they **m** make a covenant with you,	2Sa 3:21
and that you **m** be king over all	2Sa 3:21
"**M** it fall on the head of Joab	2Sa 3:29
and **m** there not fail from the	2Sa 3:29
"**M** God do so to me, and more	2Sa 3:35
M the LORD repay the evildoer	2Sa 3:39
that they **m** live in their own	2Sa 7:10
Your name **m** be magnified forever,	2Sa 7:26
and **m** the house of Your servant	2Sa 7:26
m it please You to bless the	2Sa 7:29
it **m** continue forever before You.	2Sa 7:29
and with Your blessing **m** the house	2Sa 7:29
that I **m** show him kindness for	2Sa 9:1
I **m** show the kindness of God?"	2Sa 9:3
your master's grandson **m** have food;	2Sa 9:10
and **m** the LORD do what is good in	2Sa 10:12
he **m** be struck down and die."	2Sa 11:15
the LORD **m** be gracious to me,	2Sa 12:22
to me, that the child **m** live.'	2Sa 12:22
that I **m** see *it* and eat from her hand.	2Sa 13:5
that I **m** eat from her hand."	2Sa 13:6
that I **m** eat from your hand."	2Sa 13:10
that we **m** put him to death for the	2Sa 14:7
m the LORD your God be with you.' "	2Sa 14:17
that I **m** send you to the king,	2Sa 14:32
wherever my lord the king **m** be,	2Sa 15:21
I **m** arise and pursue David tonight.	2Sa 17:1
M God do so to me, and more also,	2Sa 19:13
donkey for myself that I **m** ride on it	2Sa 19:26
that I **m** die in my own city near	2Sa 19:37
here that I **m** speak with you.' "	2Sa 20:16
that you **m** bless the inheritance	2Sa 21:3
m know the number of the people."	2Sa 24:2
"Now **m** the LORD your God add to	2Sa 24:3
m be held back from the people."	2Sa 24:21
"**M** the LORD your God accept you."	2Sa 24:23
my lord the king **m** keep warm."	1Ki 1:2
"**M** my lord King David live	1Ki 1:31
Thus **m** the LORD, the God of my	1Ki 1:36
the king, so **m** He be with Solomon,	1Ki 1:37
'**M** your God make the name of	1Ki 1:47
that you **m** succeed in all that you	1Ki 2:3
so that the LORD **m** carry out His	1Ki 2:4
that he **m** give me Abishag the	1Ki 2:17
"**M** God do so to me and more also,	1Ki 2:23
that you **m** remove from me and from	1Ki 2:31
m there be peace from the LORD	1Ki 2:33
that Your eyes **m** be open toward	1Ki 8:29
that they **m** fear You all the days	1Ki 8:40
of the earth **m** know Your name,	1Ki 8:43
and that they **m** know that this	1Ki 8:43
they **m** have compassion on them	1Ki 8:50
that Your eyes **m** be open to the	1Ki 8:52
"**M** the LORD our God be with us,	1Ki 8:57
m He not leave us or forsake us,	1Ki 8:57
m incline our hearts to Himself,	1Ki 8:58
"And **m** these words of mine, with	1Ki 8:59
that He **m** maintain the cause of	1Ki 8:59
earth **m** know that the LORD is God;	1Ki 8:60
that I **m** go to my own country."	1Ki 11:21
that My servant David **m** have a	1Ki 11:36
that we **m** answer this people	1Ki 12:9
my hand **m** be restored to me."	1Ki 13:6
m eat bread and drink water.' "	1Ki 13:18
water in a jar, that I **m** drink."	1Ki 17:10
I **m** go in and prepare for me and	1Ki 17:12
son, that we **m** eat it and die."	1Ki 17:12
and afterward you **m** make *one* for	1Ki 17:13
that this people **m** know that You,	1Ki 18:37
"So **m** the gods do to me and even	1Ki 19:2
"**M** the gods do so to me and more	1Ki 20:10
that I **m** have it for a vegetable	1Ki 21:2
here that we **m** inquire of him?"	1Ki 22:7
by whom we **m** inquire of the LORD,	1Ki 22:8
we **m** inquire of the LORD by him?"	2Ki 3:11
that I **m** run to the man of God and	2Ki 4:22
for the people that they **m** eat."	2Ki 4:41
to the people that they **m** eat."	2Ki 4:42
to the people that they **m** eat,	2Ki 4:43
you **m** cure him of his leprosy."	2Ki 5:6
m the LORD pardon your servant:	2Ki 5:18
for ourselves where we **m** live."	2Ki 6:2
is, that I **m** send and take him."	2Ki 6:13
open his eyes that he **m** see."	2Ki 6:17
of these *men,* that they **m** see."	2Ki 6:20
that they **m** eat and drink and go	2Ki 6:22
your son that we **m** eat him today,	2Ki 6:28
'Give your son, that we **m** eat him';	2Ki 6:29
"**M** God do so to me and more also,	2Ki 6:31
that I **m** avenge the blood of My	2Ki 9:7
wherever any damage **m** be found.	2Ki 12:5
that you **m** live and not die."	2Ki 18:32
the earth **m** know that You alone,	2Ki 19:19
priest that he **m** count the money	2Ki 22:4
harm that *it* **m** not pain me!"	1Ch 4:10
m the God of our fathers look on	1Ch 12:17
he **m** defect to his master Saul."	1Ch 12:19
lands, that they **m** meet with us;	1Ch 13:2
that you **m** bring up the ark of the	1Ch 15:12
that they **m** dwell in their own	1Ch 17:9

it **m** continue forever before You; 1Ch 17:27
and **m** the LORD do what is good in 1Ch 19:13
word that I **m** know their number." 1Ch 21:2
"**M** the LORD add to His people a 1Ch 21:3
that I **m** build on it an altar to 1Ch 21:22
m be restrained from the people." 1Ch 21:22
with you that you **m** be successful, 1Ch 22:11
so that you **m** keep the law of the 1Ch 22:12
prepared, and you **m** add to them. 1Ch 22:14
and **m** the LORD be with you." 1Ch 22:16
so that you **m** bring the ark of the 1Ch 22:19
you **m** possess the good land 1Ch 28:8
that I **m** go out and come in before 2Ch 1:10
that you **m** rule My people over 2Ch 1:11
design which **m** be assigned to him, 2Ch 2:14
you **m** carry it up to Jerusalem." 2Ch 2:16
that Your eye **m** be open toward 2Ch 6:20
that they **m** fear You, to walk in 2Ch 6:31
of the earth **m** know Your name, 2Ch 6:33
and that they **m** know that this 2Ch 6:33
that My name **m** be there forever, 2Ch 7:16
give that we **m** answer this people, 2Ch 10:9
they **m** learn *the difference between* 2Ch 12:8
even he **m** become a priest of *what* 2Ch 13:9
He **m** strongly support those whose 2Ch 16:9
here that we **m** inquire of him?" 2Ch 18:6
by whom we **m** inquire of the LORD, 2Ch 18:7
m not be guilty before the LORD, 2Ch 19:10
and wrath **m** *not* come on you and 2Ch 19:10
they **m** enter, for they are holy. 2Ch 23:6
"**M** the LORD see and avenge!" 2Ch 24:22
to them that they **m** help me." 2Ch 28:23
burning anger **m** turn away from us. 2Ch 29:10
that He **m** return to those of you 2Ch 30:6
anger **m** turn away from you. 2Ch 30:8
"**M** the good LORD pardon 2Ch 30:18
m the LORD his God be with him, 2Ch 36:23
His people, **m** his God be with him! Ezr 1:3
at whatever place he **m** live, Ezr 1:4
so that a search **m** be made in the Ezr 4:15
that this city **m** not be rebuilt Ezr 4:21
that they **m** offer acceptable Ezr 6:10
"**M** the God who has caused His name Ezr 6:12
to go to Jerusalem, **m** go with you. Ezr 7:13
you **m** do according to the will of Ezr 7:18
you **m** have occasion to provide, Ezr 7:20
God of heaven, **m** require of you, Ezr 7:21
that they **m** judge all the people Ezr 7:25
and you **m** teach anyone who is Ezr 7:25
that our God **m** enlighten our eyes Ezr 9:8
that you **m** be strong and eat the Ezr 9:12
m Your ear be attentive to the Ne 1:11
tombs, that I **m** rebuild it." Ne 2:5
that they **m** allow me to pass Ne 2:7
that he **m** give me timber to make Ne 2:8
every place where you **m** turn," Ne 4:12
they **m** be a guard for us by night Ne 4:22
grain that we **m** eat and live." Ne 5:2
that they **m** be sold to us?" Ne 5:8
"Thus **m** God shake out every man Ne 5:13
m he be shaken out and emptied." Ne 5:13
O **m** Your glorious name be blessed Ne 9:5
that Vashti **m** no longer come into Es 1:19
they **m** gather every beautiful young Es 2:3
golden scepter so that he **m** live. Es 4:11
m the king and Haman come this day Es 5:4
that we **m** do as Esther desires." Es 5:5
m the king and Haman come to the Es 5:8
signet ring **m** not be revoked." Es 8:8
"**M** that day be darkness; Jb 3:4
a man as I am that I **m** answer Him, Jb 9:32
That we **m** go to court together. Jb 9:32
Who **m** lay his hand upon us both. Jb 9:33
me that I **m** have a little cheer Jb 10:20
before me so that I **m** speak; Jb 13:13
Then let come on me what **m**. Jb 13:13
m not come before His presence. Jb 13:16
Your gaze from him that he **m** rest, Jb 14:6
you **m** know there is judgment." Jb 19:29
"He **m** flee from the iron weapon, Jb 20:24
"Bear with me that I **m** speak; Jb 21:3
after I have spoken, you **m** mock. Jb 21:3
repay him so that he **m** know *it.* Jb 21:19
"**M** my enemy be as the wicked And Jb 27:7
He **m** prepare *it,* but the just will Jb 27:17
M my wife grind for another, And Jb 31:10
abundant *in years* **m** not be wise, Jb 32:9
Nor **m** elders understand justice. Jb 32:9
"Let me speak that I **m** get relief; Jb 32:20
That He **m** turn man aside *from his* Jb 33:17
That he **m** see His face with joy, Jb 33:26
And He **m** restore His righteousness Jb 33:26
That he **m** be enlightened with the Jb 33:30
the workers of iniquity **m** hide Jb 34:22
man, That all men **m** know His work. Jb 37:7
That it **m** do whatever He commands Jb 37:12
you **m** take it to its territory And Jb 38:20
you **m** discern the paths to its home? Jb 38:20
that they **m** go And say to you, Jb 38:35
forgets that a foot **m** crush them, Jb 39:15
that a wild beast **m** trample them. Jb 39:15
Me that you **m** be justified? Jb 40:8
I **m** not do with you *according to* Jb 42:8
For His wrath **m** soon be kindled. Ps 2:12
And **m** You shelter them, That Ps 5:11
who love Your name **m** exult in You. Ps 5:11
That I **m** tell of all Your praises, Ps 9:14
Zion I **m** rejoice in Your salvation. Ps 9:14
M the LORD cut off all flattering Ps 12:3

O Lord, who **m** abide in Your tent? Ps 15:1
Who **m** dwell on Your holy hill? Ps 15:1
M the LORD answer you in the day Ps 20:1
M the name of the God of Jacob set Ps 20:1
M He send you help from the Ps 20:2
M He remember all your meal Ps 20:3
M He grant you your heart's Ps 20:4
M the LORD fulfill all your Ps 20:5
M the King answer us in the day we Ps 20:9
Who **m** ascend into the hill of the Ps 24:3
And who **m** stand in His holy place? Ps 24:3
That the King of glory **m** come in! Ps 24:7
That the King of glory **m** come in! Ps 24:9
That I **m** proclaim with the voice Ps 26:7
That I **m** dwell in the house of the Ps 27:4
Weeping **m** last for the night, But Ps 30:5
my soul **m** sing praise to You and Ps 30:12
in a time when You **m** be found; Ps 32:6
length of days that he **m** see good? Ps 34:12
"**M** they not rejoice over me, *Who,* Ps 38:16
That I **m** not sin with my tongue; Ps 39:1
from me, that I **m** smile *again* Before Ps 39:13
raise me up, That I **m** repay them. Ps 41:10
That you **m** tell *it* to the next Ps 48:13
M our God come and not keep Ps 50:3
my mouth **m** declare Your praise. Ps 51:15
So that I **m** walk before God In the Ps 56:13
them that they **m** be no more; Ps 59:13
m know that God rules in Jacob To Ps 59:13
That it **m** be displayed because of Ps 60:4
That Your beloved **m** be delivered, Ps 60:5
truth that they **m** preserve him. Ps 61:7
That I **m** pay my vows day by day. Ps 61:8
a man, That you **m** murder *him,* Ps 62:3
Your way **m** be known on the earth, Ps 67:2
the ends of the earth **m** fear Him. Ps 67:7
that the LORD God **m** dwell *there.* Ps 68:18
your foot **m** shatter *them* in blood, Ps 68:23
The tongue of your dogs **m** *have* Ps 68:23
M those who wait for You not be Ps 69:6
M those who seek You not be Ps 69:6
M I be delivered from my foes and Ps 69:14
M the flood of water not overflow Ps 69:15
M their table before them become a Ps 69:22
m *it become* a trap. Ps 69:22
M their eyes grow dim so that they Ps 69:23
And **m** Your burning anger overtake Ps 69:24
M their camp be desolate; Ps 69:25
M none dwell in their tents. Ps 69:25
And **m** they not come into Your Ps 69:27
M they be blotted out of the book Ps 69:28
And **m** they not be recorded with Ps 69:28
M Your salvation, O God, set me Ps 69:29
they **m** dwell there and possess it. Ps 69:35
to which I **m** continually come; Ps 71:3
M You increase my greatness And Ps 71:21
M he judge Your people with Ps 72:2
M he vindicate the afflicted of Ps 72:4
M he come down like rain upon the Ps 72:6
his days **m** the righteous flourish, Ps 72:7
M he also rule from sea to sea And Ps 72:8
So **m** he live, and may the gold of Ps 72:15
and **m** the gold of Sheba be given Ps 72:15
M there be abundance of grain in Ps 72:16
And **m** those from the city flourish Ps 72:16
M his name endure forever; Ps 72:17
M his name increase as long as the Ps 72:17
And **m** the whole earth be filled Ps 72:19
My flesh and my heart **m** fail, Ps 73:26
That I **m** tell of all Your works. Ps 73:28
And who **m** stand in Your presence Ps 76:7
And Your footprints **m** not be known. Ps 77:19
That they **m** arise and tell *them* to Ps 78:6
That they **m** seek Your name, Ps 83:16
That they **m** know that You alone, Ps 83:18
where she **m** lay her young, Ps 84:3
That Your people **m** rejoice in You? Ps 85:6
That glory **m** dwell in our land. Ps 85:9
That those who hate me **m** see *it* and Ps 86:17
That we **m** present to You a heart Ps 90:12
That we **m** sing for joy and be glad Ps 90:14
under His wings you **m** seek refuge; Ps 91:4
A thousand **m** fall at your side And Ps 91:7
That You **m** grant him relief from Ps 94:13
land, that they **m** dwell with me; Ps 101:6
to be created **m** praise the LORD. Ps 102:18
That *men* **m** tell of the name of the Ps 102:21
that they **m** not pass over, Ps 104:9
So that he **m** bring forth food from Ps 104:14
So that he **m** make *his* face glisten Ps 104:15
That I **m** see the prosperity of Your Ps 106:5
That I **m** rejoice in the gladness Ps 106:5
I **m** glory with Your inheritance. Ps 106:5
m establish an inhabited city, Ps 107:36
That Your beloved **m** be delivered, Ps 108:6
That He **m** cut off their memory Ps 109:15
M the LORD give you increase, You Ps 115:14
M you be blessed of the LORD, Ps 115:15
Oh **m** *it be* in the presence of Ps 116:14
Oh **m** *it be* in the presence of Ps 116:18
Oh that my ways **m** be established Ps 119:5
That I **m** not sin against You. Ps 119:11
That I **m** live and keep Your word. Ps 119:17
that I **m** behold Wonderful things Ps 119:18
that I **m** observe Your law And Ps 119:34
M Your lovingkindnesses also come Ps 119:41
That I **m** learn Your statutes. Ps 119:71
that I **m** learn Your commandments. Ps 119:73
M those who fear You see me and Ps 119:74

O **m** Your lovingkindness comfort me, Ps 119:76 4994
M Your compassion come to me that I Ps 119:77
come to me that I **m** live, Ps 119:77
M the arrogant be ashamed, for Ps 119:78
M those who fear You turn to me, Ps 119:79
M my heart be blameless in Your Ps 119:80
So that I **m** keep the testimony of Ps 119:88
evil way, That I **m** keep Your word. Ps 119:101
That I **m** observe the commandments Ps 119:115
to Your word, that I **m** live; Ps 119:116
Uphold me that I **m** be safe, Ps 119:117
That I **m** have regard for Your Ps 119:117
That I **m** know Your testimonies. Ps 119:125
man, That I **m** keep Your precepts. Ps 119:134
me understanding that I **m** live. Ps 119:144
That I **m** meditate on Your word. Ps 119:148
soul live that it **m** praise You, Ps 119:175
"**M** they prosper who love you. Ps 122:6
"**M** peace be within your walls, Ps 122:7
"**M** peace be within you." Ps 122:8
And **m** you see the prosperity of Ps 128:5
m you see your children's children. Ps 128:6
M all who hate Zion Be put to Ps 129:5
with You, That You **m** be feared. Ps 130:4
M the LORD bless you from Zion, He Ps 134:3
M my right hand forget *her skill.* Ps 137:5
M my tongue cling to the roof of Ps 137:6
M the mischief of their lips cover Ps 140:9
"**M** burning coals fall upon them; Ps 140:10
M they be cast into the fire, Into Ps 140:10
"**M** a slanderer not be established Ps 140:11
M evil hunt the violent man Ps 140:11
M my prayer be counted as incense Ps 141:2
that I **m** give thanks to Your name; Ps 142:7
the mountains, that they **m** smoke. Ps 144:5
that you **m** gain understanding, Pr 4:1
That you **m** observe discretion And Pr 5:2
And your lips **m** reserve knowledge. Pr 5:2
m keep you from an adulteress, Pr 7:5
That I **m** fill their treasuries. Pr 8:21
laughter the heart **m** be in pain, Pr 14:13
And the end of joy **m** be grief. Pr 14:13
one **m** avoid the snares of death. Pr 14:27
he **m** keep away from Sheol below. Pr 15:24
m be wise the rest of your days. Pr 19:20
So that one **m** sleep satisfied, Pr 19:23
and the naive **m** become shrewd, Pr 19:25
That they **m** be ready on your lips. Pr 22:18
that your trust **m** be in the LORD, Pr 22:19
truth That you **m** correctly answer Pr 22:21
a ruler **m** be persuaded, Pr 25:15
not know what a day **m** bring forth. Pr 27:1
That I **m** reply to him who Pr 27:11
lizard you **m** grasp with the hands, Pr 30:28
so that he **m** give to one who is good Ec 2:26
a face is sad a heart **m** be happy. Ec 7:3
times and **m** lengthen his *life,* Ec 8:12
He who digs a pit **m** fall into it, Ec 10:8
and a serpent **m** bite him who Ec 10:8
He who quarries stones **m** be hurt Ec 10:9
he who splits logs **m** be endangered Ec 10:9
misfortune **m** occur on the earth. Ec 11:2
"**M** he kiss me with the kisses of SS 1:2
M you come with me from Lebanon. SS 4:8
M my beloved come into his garden SS 4:16
That we **m** seek him with you?" SS 6:1
back, that we **m** gaze at you!" SS 6:13
m your breasts be like clusters of SS 7:8 4994
He **m** teach us concerning His ways Is 2:3
And that we **m** walk in His paths." Is 2:3
is lifted up, That he **m** be abased. Is 2:12
that they **m** pursue strong drink, Is 5:11
evening that wine **m** inflame them! Is 5:11
hasten His work, that we **m** see *it;* Is 5:19
come to pass, that we **m** know *it!"* Is 5:19
a man **m** keep alive a heifer and a Is 7:21
that widows **m** be their spoil And Is 10:2
that they **m** plunder the orphans. Is 10:2
m be like the sand of the sea, Is 10:22
m enter the doors of the nobles. Is 13:2
M the offspring of evildoers not Is 14:20
its palm branch or bulrush, **m** do. Is 19:15
drink, for tomorrow we **m** die." Is 22:13
songs, That you **m** be remembered. Is 23:16
is shut up so that none **m** enter. Is 24:10
that the righteous nation **m** enter, Is 26:2
they **m** go and stumble backward, Is 28:13
That it **m** serve in the time to Is 30:8
no one there *Whom* they **m** proclaim Is 34:12
the earth **m** know that You alone, Is 37:20
to the boil, that he **m** recover." Is 38:21
That they **m** see and recognize, And Is 41:20
were, That we **m** consider them and Is 41:22
That we **m** know that you are gods; Is 41:23
that we **m** anxiously look about us Is 41:23
from former times, that we **m** say, Is 41:26
look, you blind, that you **m** see. Is 42:18
that the peoples **m** be assembled. Is 43:9
that they **m** be justified, Is 43:9
that you **m** know and believe Me And Is 43:10
cause, that you **m** be proved right. Is 43:26
man, so that it **m** sit in a house. Is 44:13
that you **m** know that it is I, Is 45:3
That men **m** know from the rising to Is 45:6
Though one **m** cry to it, it cannot Is 46:7
Perhaps you **m** cause trembling. Is 47:12
My salvation **m** reach to the end of Is 49:6
Even these **m** forget, but I will Is 49:15
room for me that I **m** live *here.*' Is 49:20

That I **m** know how to sustain the Is 50:4
'Lie down that we **m** walk over *you.*' Is 51:23
m see The salvation of our God. Is 52:10
"For the mountains **m** be removed Is 54:10
be removed and the hills **m** shake, Is 54:10
Listen, that you **m** live; Is 55:3
Seek the LORD while He **m** be found; Is 55:6
So that *men* **m** bring to you the Is 60:11
My hands, That I **m** be glorified. Is 60:21
the LORD, that He **m** be glorified. Is 61:3
nations **m** tremble at Your presence! Is 64:2
where is a place that I **m** rest? Is 66:1
that we **m** see your joy.' Is 66:5
That you **m** nurse and be satisfied Is 66:11
That you **m** suck and be delighted Is 66:11
O Jerusalem, That you **m** be saved. Jer 4:14
the orphan, that they **m** prosper; Jer 5:28
give warning That they **m** hear? Jer 6:10
you **m** know and assay their way." Jer 6:27
you **m** do all these abominations?' Jer 7:10
you, that it **m** be well with you.' Jer 7:23
wise man that **m** understand this? Jer 9:12
has spoken, that he **m** declare it? Jer 9:12
mourning women, that they **m** come; Jer 9:17
wailing women, that they **m** come! Jer 9:17
us, That our eyes **m** shed tears And Jer 9:18
distress, That they **m** be found." Jer 10:18
they **m** say nice things to you." Jer 12:6
face, That your shame **m** be seen. Jer 13:26
They for their part **m** turn to you, Jer 15:19
M an outcry be heard from their Jer 18:22
But **m** they be overthrown before Jer 18:23
so that we **m** prevail against him Jer 20:10
That My wrath **m** not go forth like Jer 21:12
m devour all its environs. Jer 21:14
has a dream **m** relate *his* dream, Jer 23:28
that I **m** repent of the calamity Jer 26:3
in order that I **m** drive you out and Jer 27:15
you out and that you **m** perish, Jer 27:15
in Jerusalem **m** not go to Babylon. Jer 27:18
M the LORD do so; Jer 28:6
m the LORD confirm your words Jer 28:6
that they **m** serve Nebuchadnezzar Jer 28:14
they **m** bear sons and daughters; Jer 29:6
"**M** the LORD make you like Jer 29:22
me back that I **m** be restored, Jer 31:18
that they **m** last a long time." Jer 32:14
way, that they **m** fear Me always, Jer 32:39
then My covenant **m** also be broken Jer 33:21
that you **m** live many days in the Jer 35:7
scribe, that I **m** not die there." Jer 37:20
for they **m** give me over into their Jer 38:19
that it **m** go well with you and you Jer 38:20
go well with you and you **m** live. Jer 38:20
that it **m** go well with you. Jer 40:9
that the LORD your God **m** tell us Jer 42:3
"**M** the LORD be a true and Jer 42:5
so that it **m** go well with us Jer 42:6
so that you **m** know that My words Jer 44:29
all the places where you **m** go.'" Jer 45:5
the mighty men **m** march forward: Jer 46:9
That you **m** be like a juniper in Jer 48:6
they will come that they **m** join Jer 50:5
that He **m** bring rest to the earth, Jer 50:34
to Babylon that they **m** winnow her Jer 51:2
her And **m** devastate her land; Jer 51:2
Perhaps she **m** be healed. Jer 51:8
"**M** the violence *done* to me and to Jer 51:35
"**M** my blood be upon the Jer 51:35
that they **m** become jubilant And Jer 51:39
And **m** sleep a perpetual sleep Jer 51:39
That they **m** sleep a perpetual Jer 51:57
That they **m** become like me. La 1:21
O LORD, that we **m** be restored; La 5:21
feet that I **m** speak with you!" Ezk 2:1
his wicked way that he **m** live, Ezk 3:18
that your altars **m** become waste Ezk 6:6
your idols **m** be broken and brought Ezk 6:6
your incense altars **m** be cut down, Ezk 6:6
and your works **m** be blotted out. Ezk 6:6
that they **m** walk in My statutes Ezk 11:20
they **m** tell all their abominations Ezk 12:16
and **m** know that I am the LORD." Ezk 12:16
you **m** know that I am the Lord GOD. Ezk 13:9
the house of Israel **m** no longer stray Ezk 14:11
they **m** see all your nakedness. Ezk 16:37
that you **m** bear your humiliation and Ezk 16:54
you **m** remember and be ashamed and Ezk 16:63
that it **m** bring forth boughs and Ezk 17:23
"Then he **m** have a violent son who Ezk 18:10
so that iniquity **m** not become a Ezk 18:30
that you **m** know that I am the LORD Ezk 20:20
be polished, that it **m** be handled; Ezk 21:11
that *their* hearts **m** melt, Ezk 21:15
that they **m** be seized. Ezk 21:23
that it **m** be like lightning Ezk 21:28
they **m** deal with you in wrath. Ezk 23:25
that all women **m** be admonished and Ezk 23:48
"That it **m** cause wrath to come up Ezk 24:8
rock, That it **m** not be covered." Ezk 24:8
on its coals So that it **m** be hot Ezk 24:11
may be hot And its bronze **m** glow Ezk 24:11
its filthiness **m** be melted in it, Ezk 24:11
before kings, That they **m** see you. Ezk 28:17
it **m** be strong to hold the sword. Ezk 30:21
trees by the waters **m** not be exalted Ezk 31:14
so that they **m** live securely in Ezk 34:25
enter you that you **m** come to life. Ezk 37:5
in you that you **m** come alive; Ezk 37:6

they **m** become one in your hand. Ezk 37:17
so that the nations **m** know Ezk 38:16
you **m** eat flesh and drink blood. Ezk 39:17
that they **m** be ashamed of their Ezk 43:10
so that they **m** observe its whole Ezk 43:11
husband, they **m** defile themselves. Ezk 44:25
in order that they **m** not bring Ezk 46:20
that I **m** know that you can declare Da 2:9
and that you **m** understand the Da 2:30
"**M** your peace abound! Da 4:1
In order that the living **m** know Da 4:17
m my advice be pleasing to you: Da 4:27
in case there **m** be a prolonging of Da 4:27
so that it **m** not be changed, Da 6:8
which **m** not be revoked." Da 6:8
which **m** not be revoked." Da 6:12
king establishes **m** be changed." Da 6:15
"**M** your peace abound! Da 6:25
"**M** my lord speak, for you have Da 10:19
that he **m** again wage war up to his Da 11:10
day, That we **m** live before Him. Hos 6:2
it **m** consume its palatial dwellings. Hos 8:14
he **m** save you in all your cities, Hos 13:10
m present the fruit of our lips. Hos 14:2
a girl for wine that they **m** drink. Jl 3:3
"Bring now, that we **m** drink!" Am 4:1
"Seek Me that you **m** live. Am 5:4
"Seek the LORD that you **m** live, Am 5:6
and not evil, that you **m** live; Am 5:14
And thus **m** the LORD God of hosts Am 5:14
Perhaps the LORD God of hosts **M** be Am 5:15
be over, So that we **m** sell grain, Am 8:5
that we **m** open the wheat *market,* Am 8:5
m sell the refuse of the wheat?" Am 8:6
That they **m** possess the remnant of Am 9:12
So that everyone **m** be cut off Ob 1:9
let us cast lots so we **m** learn on Jon 1:7
that the sea **m** become calm for us?" Jon 1:11
each **m** turn from his wicked way Jon 3:8
"Who knows, God **m** turn and Jon 3:9
That He **m** teach us about His ways Mi 4:2
And that we **m** walk in His paths." Mi 4:2
That you **m** pulverize many peoples, Mi 4:13
That you **m** devote to the LORD Mi 4:13
how I **m** reply when I am reproved. Hab 2:1
That the one who reads it **m** run. Hab 2:2
m call on the name of the LORD, Zph 3:9
that I **m** be pleased with it and be Hg 1:8
"that I **m** return to you," Zch 1:3
you that you **m** become a blessing. Zch 8:13
That a fire **m** feed on your cedars. Zch 11:1
that the sheep **m** be scattered; Zch 13:7
"They **m** build, but I will tear Mal 1:4
that He **m** be gracious to us? Mal 1:9
covenant **m** continue with Levi," Mal 2:4
m the LORD cut off from the tents Mal 2:12
so that they **m** present to the LORD Mal 3:3
that there **m** be food in My house, Mal 3:10
I too **m** come and worship Him." Mt 2:8
that they **m** see your good works, Mt 5:16
m not hand you over to the judge, Mt 5:25
so that you **m** be sons of Mt 5:45
that they **m** be honored by men. Mt 6:2
on the street corners so that they **m** Mt 6:5
them, **m** be compared to a wise man Mt 7:24
"But so that you **m** know Mt 9:6
"The kingdom of heaven **m** be Mt 13:24
you **m** uproot the wheat with them. Mt 13:29
that they **m** go into the villages Mt 14:15
EVERY FACT **M** BE CONFIRMED. Mt 18:16
about anything that they **m** ask, Mt 18:19
kingdom of heaven **m** be compared Mt 18:23
do that I **m** obtain eternal life?" Mt 19:16
these two sons of mine **m** sit one Mt 20:21
of heaven **m** be compared to a king who Mt 22:2
outside of it **m** become clean also. Mt 23:26
that upon you **m** fall *the guilt of* Mt 23:35
all **m** fall away because of You, Mt 26:33
you **m** not enter into temptation; Mt 26:41
otherwise His disciples **m** come Mt 27:64
so that I **m** preach there also; Mk 1:38
"But so that you **m** know Mk 2:10
THEY **M** SEE AND NOT PERCEIVE Mk 4:12
THEY **M** HEAR AND NOT UNDERSTAND Mk 4:12
swine so that we **m** enter them." Mk 5:12
send them away so that they **m** go Mk 6:36
"Grant that we **m** sit, Mk 10:37
"**M** no one ever eat fruit from you Mk 11:14
it **m** not happen in the winter. Mk 13:18
room in which I **m** eat the Passover Mk 14:14
"*Even* though all **m** fall away, yet Mk 14:29
you **m** not come into temptation; Mk 14:38
so that we **m** see and believe!" Mk 15:32
so that you **m** know the exact truth Lk 1:4
m it be done to me according to your Lk 1:38
from many hearts **m** be revealed." Lk 2:35
"But, so that you **m** know Lk 5:24
so that SEEING THEY **M** NOT SEE, Lk 8:10
AND HEARING THEY **M** NOT UNDERSTAND. Lk 8:10
those who come in **m** see the light. Lk 8:16
that they **m** go into the Lk 9:12
those who enter **m** see the light. Lk 11:33
m be charged against this Lk 11:50
so that they **m** immediately open Lk 12:36
m not drag you before the judge, Lk 12:58
you **m** have been invited by him, Lk 14:8
you comes, he **m** say to you, Lk 14:10
otherwise they **m** also invite you in Lk 14:12
in, so that my house **m** be filled. Lk 14:23

that he **m** dip the tip of his Lk 16:24
m cross over from there to us.' Lk 16:26
that he **m** warn them, so that they Lk 16:28
and afterward you **m** eat and drink'? Lk 17:8
they said, "**M** it never be!" Lk 20:16
praying that you **m** have Lk 21:36
for us, so that we **m** eat it." Lk 22:8
room in which I **m** eat the Passover Lk 22:11
that you **m** eat and drink at My Lk 22:30
you, that your faith **m** not fail; Lk 22:32
you **m** not enter into temptation." Lk 22:40
you **m** not enter into temptation." Lk 22:46
so that we **m** give an answer to Jn 1:22
that his deeds **m** be manifested as Jn 3:21
he who reaps **m** rejoice together. Jn 4:36
these things so that you **m** be saved. Jn 5:34
come to Me so that you **m** have life. Jn 5:40
to buy bread, so that these **m** eat?" Jn 6:5
that we **m** work the works of God?" Jn 6:28
You do for a sign, so that we **m** see, Jn 6:30
that one **m** eat of it and not die. Jn 6:50
that Your disciples also **m** see Jn 7:3
but whenever the Christ **m** come, Jn 7:27
Lord, that I **m** believe in Him?" Jn 9:36
that those who do not see **m** see, Jn 9:39
those who see **m** become blind." Jn 9:39
I came that they **m** have life, Jn 10:10
My life so that I **m** take it again. Jn 10:17
that you **m** know and understand Jn 10:38
Son of God **m** be glorified by it." Jn 11:4
I **m** awaken him out of sleep." Jn 11:11
not there, so that you **m** believe; Jn 11:15
also go, so that we **m** die with Him." Jn 11:16
that they **m** believe that You Jn 11:42
so that she **m** keep it for Jn 12:7
that you **m** become sons of Light." Jn 12:36
that the Scripture **m** be fulfilled, Jn 13:18
occur, you **m** believe that I am *He.* Jn 13:19
where I am, *there* you **m** be also. Jn 14:3
Father **m** be glorified in the Son. Jn 14:13
that He **m** be with you forever; Jn 14:16
it happens, you **m** believe. Jn 14:29
m know that I love the Father, Jn 14:31
it so that it **m** bear more fruit. Jn 15:2
to you so that My joy **m** be in you, Jn 15:11
and *that* your joy **m** be made full. Jn 15:11
in My name He **m** give to you. Jn 15:16
that you **m** be kept from stumbling. Jn 16:1
you **m** remember that I told you of Jn 16:4
that your joy **m** be made full. Jn 16:24
you, so that in Me you **m** have peace. Jn 16:33
Son, that the Son **m** glorify You, Jn 17:1
given Him, He **m** give eternal life. Jn 17:2
life, that they **m** know You, Jn 17:3
have given Me, that they **m** be one even Jn 17:11
that they **m** have My joy made full Jn 17:13
also **m** be sanctified in truth. Jn 17:19
that they **m** all be one; Jn 17:21
You, that they also **m** be in Us, Jn 17:21
that the world **m** believe that You Jn 17:21
that they **m** be one, just as We are Jn 17:22
that they **m** be perfected in unity, Jn 17:23
m know that You sent Me, Jn 17:23
so that they **m** see My glory Jn 17:24
You loved Me **m** be in them, Jn 17:26
that you **m** know that I find no Jn 19:4
truth, so that you also **m** believe. Jn 19:35
you **m** believe that Jesus is the Christ Jn 20:31
you **m** have life in His name. Jn 20:31
I **m** confidently say to you Ac 2:29 *1832*
that your sins **m** be wiped away, Ac 3:19
times of refreshing **m** come from the Ac 3:19
and that He **m** send Jesus, the Ac 3:20
bond-servants **m** speak Your word Ac 4:29
or else you **m** even be found Ac 5:39
we **m** put in charge of this task. Ac 6:3
hands **m** receive the Holy Spirit." Ac 8:19
"**M** your silver perish with you, Ac 8:20
of your heart **m** be forgiven you. Ac 8:22
you have said **m** come upon me." Ac 8:24
with all your heart, you **m**." Ac 8:37 *1832*
so that you **m** regain your sight and Ac 9:17
the Prophets **m** not come upon *you:* Ac 13:40
THAT YOU **M** BRING SALVATION Ac 13:47
REST OF MANKIND **M** SEEK THE LORD, Ac 15:17
"**M** we know what this new teaching Ac 17:19 *1410*
so that I **m** finish my course Ac 20:24
that they **m** shave their heads; Ac 21:24
"**M** I say something to you?" Ac 21:37 *1832*
I **m** not weary you any further, Ac 24:4
I **m** have something to write. Ac 25:26
so that they **m** turn from darkness Ac 26:18
that they **m** receive forgiveness of sins Ac 26:18
God I **m** succeed in coming to you. Ro 1:10
I **m** impart some spiritual gift to you, Ro 1:11
to you, that you **m** be established; Ro 1:11
that I **m** be encouraged together Ro 1:12
been prevented so far) so that I **m** Ro 1:13
M it never be! Rather, let God be Ro 3:4
"THAT YOU **M** BE JUSTIFIED IN YOUR Ro 3:4
M it never be! For otherwise, Ro 3:6
"Let us do evil that good **m** come"? Ro 3:8
Law, so that every mouth **m** be closed Ro 3:19
world **m** become accountable to God; Ro 3:19
Law through faith? **M** it never be! Ro 3:31
in order that *it* **m** *be* in Ro 4:16
we to continue in sin so that grace **m** Ro 6:1
M it never be! How shall we who Ro 6:2
but under grace? **M** it never be! Ro 6:15

Is the Law sin? **M** it never be! **Ro 7:7**
cause of death for me? **M** it never be **Ro 7:13**
we **m** also be glorified with *Him.* **Ro 8:17**
with God, is there? **M** it never be! **Ro 9:14**
His people, has He? **M** it never be! **Ro 11:1**
so as to fall, did they? **M** it never be **Ro 11:11**
they also **m** now be shown mercy. **Ro 11:31**
up all in disobedience so that He **m** **Ro 11:32**
m prove what the will of God is, **Ro 12:2**
faith that he **m** eat all things, **Ro 14:2**
Now **m** the God who gives **Ro 15:5**
that with one accord you **m** with **Ro 15:6**
Now **m** the God of hope fill you **Ro 15:13**
my offering of the Gentiles **m** **Ro 15:16**
that I **m** be rescued from those **Ro 15:31**
my service for Jerusalem **m** prove **Ro 15:31**
so that I **m** come to you in joy by **Ro 15:32**
matter she **m** have need of you; **Ro 16:2**
so that He **m** nullify the things that **1Co 1:28**
so that no man **m** boast before God. **1Co 1:29**
so that we **m** know the things freely **1Co 2:12**
so that he **m** become wise. **1Co 3:18**
me it is a very small thing that I **m** **1Co 4:3**
so that in us you **m** learn not to **1Co 4:6**
that his spirit **m** be saved in the **1Co 5:5**
leaven so that you **m** be a new lump, **1Co 5:7**
members of a prostitute? **M** it never be! **1Co 6:15**
you **m** devote yourselves to prayer, **1Co 7:5**
Lord, how he **m** please the Lord; **1Co 7:32**
world, how he **m** please his wife, **1Co 7:33**
that she **m** be holy both in body **1Co 7:34**
how she **m** please her husband. **1Co 7:34**
I **m** offer the gospel without **1Co 9:18**
so that I **m** win more. **1Co 9:19**
that I **m** by all means save some. **1Co 9:22**
that I **m** become a fellow partaker **1Co 9:23**
Run in such a way that you **m** win. **1Co 9:24**
of the many, so that they **m** be saved. **1Co 10:33**
m become evident among you. **1Co 11:19**
so that there **m** be no division in **1Co 12:25**
but *that* the members **m** have **1Co 12:25**
especially that you **m** prophesy. **1Co 14:1**
the church **m** receive edifying. **1Co 14:5**
a tongue pray that he **m** interpret. **1Co 14:13**
that I **m** instruct others also, **1Co 14:19**
that all **m** learn and all may **1Co 14:31**
may learn and all **m** be exhorted; **1Co 14:31**
to Him, so that God **m** be all in all. **1Co 15:28**
aside and save, as he **m** prosper, **1Co 16:2**
I arrive, whomever you **m** approve, **1Co 16:3**
that you **m** send me on my way **1Co 16:6**
send me on my way wherever I **m** go. **1Co 16:6**
in peace, so that he **m** come to me; **1Co 16:11**
that thanks **m** be given by many **2Co 1:11**
also **m** be manifested in our body. **2Co 4:10**
life of Jesus also **m** be manifested **2Co 4:11**
m cause the giving of thanks to **2Co 4:15**
that each one **m** be recompensed for **2Co 5:10**
so *there* **m** *be* also **2Co 8:11**
m become *a supply* for your need, **2Co 8:14**
need, that there **m** be equality; **2Co 8:14**
that our boasting about you **m** not **2Co 9:3**
I was saying, you **m** be prepared; **2Co 9:3**
you **m** have an abundance for every **2Co 9:8**
that I **m** cut off opportunity from **2Co 11:12**
that I also **m** boast a little. **2Co 11:16**
the power of Christ **m** dwell in me. **2Co 12:9**
But be that as it **m**, **2Co 12:16**
I **m** find you to be not what I wish **2Co 12:20**
m be found by you to be not what **2Co 12:20**
my God **m** humiliate me before you, **2Co 12:21**
and I **m** mourn over many of those **2Co 12:21**
we ourselves **m** appear approved, **2Co 13:7**
but that you **m** do what is right, **2Co 13:7**
even though we **m** appear unapproved. **2Co 13:7**
that we **m** be justified by faith in **Ga 2:16**
a minister of sin? **M** it never be! **Ga 2:17**
the promises of God? **M** it never be! **Ga 3:21**
that we **m** be justified by faith. **Ga 3:24**
so that you **m** not do the things **Ga 5:17**
that they **m** boast in your flesh. **Ga 6:13**
But **m** it never be that I would **Ga 6:14**
m give to you a spirit of wisdom **Eph 1:17**
of your heart **m** be enlightened, **Eph 1:18**
so that no one **m** boast. **Eph 2:9**
so that Christ **m** dwell in your **Eph 3:17**
m be able to comprehend with all **Eph 3:18**
that you **m** be filled up to all the **Eph 3:19**
THAT IT **M** BE WELL WITH YOU, AND **Eph 6:3**
YOU **M** LIVE LONG ON THE EARTH. **Eph 6:3**
that utterance **m** be given to me in **Eph 6:19**
proclaiming it I **m** speak boldly, **Eph 6:20**
m know about my circumstances, **Eph 6:21**
so that you **m** know about us, **Eph 6:22**
and that he **m** comfort your hearts. **Eph 6:22**
that your love **m** abound still more **Php 1:9**
so that you **m** approve the things **Php 1:10**
confidence in me **m** abound in Christ **Php 1:26**
so that I also **m** be encouraged **Php 2:19**
you see him again you **m** rejoice **Php 2:28**
I **m** be less concerned *about you.* **Php 2:28**
so that I **m** gain Christ, **Php 3:8**
and **m** be found in Him, not having **Php 3:9**
that I **m** know Him and the power **Php 3:10**
in order that I **m** attain to the **Php 3:11**
that I **m** lay hold of that for which **Php 3:12**
that you **m** be filled with the knowledge **Col 1:9**
that we **m** present every man **Col 1:28**
that their hearts **m** be encouraged, **Col 2:2**
so that we **m** speak forth the **Col 4:3**
that I **m** make it clear in **Col 4:4**
that you **m** know about our **Col 4:8**
that he **m** encourage your hearts; **Col 4:8**
that you **m** stand perfect and fully **Col 4:12**
the Lord, that you **m** fulfill it." **Col 4:17**
to the Gentiles so that they **m** be **1Th 2:16**
earnestly that we **m** see your face, **1Th 3:10**
and **m** complete what is lacking in **1Th 3:10**
Now **m** our God and Father Himself **1Th 3:11**
and **m** the Lord cause you to **1Th 3:12**
so that He **m** establish your hearts **1Th 3:13**
Now **m** the God of peace Himself **1Th 5:23**
and **m** your spirit and soul and **1Th 5:23**
in order that they all **m** be judged **2Th 2:12**
that you **m** gain the glory of our **2Th 2:14**
Now **m** our Lord Jesus Christ **2Th 2:16**
M the Lord direct your hearts into **2Th 3:5**
Now **m** the Lord of peace Himself **2Th 3:16**
so that you **m** instruct **1Tm 1:3**
so that we **m** lead a tranquil **1Tm 2:2**
so that they **m** be above reproach. **1Tm 5:7**
so that it **m** assist those who are **1Tm 5:16**
so that they **m** take hold of that **1Tm 6:19**
so that I **m** be filled with joy. **2Tm 1:4**
so that he **m** please the one who **2Tm 2:4**
that they also **m** obtain the **2Tm 2:10**
if perhaps God **m** grant them **2Tm 2:25**
and they **m** come to their senses **2Tm 2:26**
that the man of God **m** be adequate, **2Tm 3:17**
m it not be counted against them. **2Tm 4:16**
that they **m** be sound in the faith, **Ti 1:13**
that they **m** encourage the young **Ti 2:4**
your faith **m** become effective **Phm 1:6**
any one of you **m** seem to have come **Heb 4:1**
that we **m** receive mercy and find **Heb 4:16**
those who have been called **m** **Heb 9:15**
And according to the Law, *one* **m** **Heb 9:22**
you **m** receive what was promised. **Heb 10:36**
that we **m** share His holiness. **Heb 12:10**
is lame **m** not be put out of joint, **Heb 12:13**
which cannot be shaken **m** remain. **Heb 12:27**
by which we **m** offer to God an **Heb 12:28**
I **m** be restored to you the sooner. **Heb 13:19**
you **m** be perfect and complete, **Jas 1:4**
But someone **m** *well* say, **Jas 2:18**
you **m** spend *it* on your pleasures. **Jas 4:3**
you yourselves **m** not be judged; **Jas 5:9**
you **m** not fall under judgment. **Jas 5:12**
another so that you **m** be healed. **Jas 5:16**
M grace and peace be yours in **1Pe 1:2**
m be found to result in praise and **1Pe 1:7**
m grow in respect to salvation, **1Pe 2:2**
that you **m** proclaim the **1Pe 2:9**
m because of your good deeds, **1Pe 2:12**
by doing right you **m** silence the **1Pe 2:15**
they **m** be won without a word by **1Pe 3:1**
they **m** live in the spirit **1Pe 4:6**
that in all things God **m** be glorified **1Pe 4:11**
you **m** rejoice with exultation. **1Pe 4:13**
He **m** exalt you at the proper time, **1Pe 5:6**
that by them you **m** become **2Pe 1:4**
too **m** have fellowship with us; **1Jn 1:3**
that our joy **m** be made complete. **1Jn 1:4**
things to you so that you **m** not sin. **1Jn 2:1**
we **m** have confidence and not **1Jn 2:28**
that we **m** have confidence in the **1Jn 4:17**
so that you **m** know that you **1Jn 5:13**
given us understanding so that we **m** **1Jn 5:20**
that you **m** receive a full reward. **2Jn 1:8**
that your joy **m** be made full. **2Jn 1:12**
m prosper and be in good health, **3Jn 1:2**
that we **m** be fellow workers with **3Jn 1:8**
M mercy and peace and love be **Jude 1:2**
by fire so that you **m** become rich, **Rv 3:18**
that you **m** clothe yourself, **Rv 3:18**
anoint your eyes so that you **m** see. **Rv 3:18**
they **m** rest from their labors, **Rv 14:13**
with it He **m** strike down the nations, **Rv 19:15**
so that you **m** eat the flesh **Rv 19:18**
that they **m** have the right to the **Rv 22:14**
and **m** enter by the gates into the **Rv 22:14**

MEADOW

planted in a pleasant **m** like Tyre; **Hos 9:13** 5116a

MEADOWS

The **m** are clothed with flocks And **Ps 65:13** 3733b

MEAL

and called his kinsmen to the **m**; **Gn 31:54** 398, 3899
and they ate the **m** and spent the **Gn 31:54** 3899
Then they sat down to eat a **m**. **Gn 37:25** 3899
that they were to eat a **m** there. **Gn 43:25** 3899
and said, "Serve the **m**." **Gn 43:31** 3899
all the elders of Israel to eat a **m** **Ex 18:12** 3899
or burnt offering or **m** offering; **Ex 30:9** 4503
burnt offering and the **m** offering, **Ex 40:29** 4503
one-tenth of an ephah of barley **m**; **Nu 5:15** 7058
son of Jesse not come to the **m**, **1Sa 20:27** 3899
of fine flour and sixty kors of **m**, **1Ki 4:22** 7058
But he said, "Now bring **m**." **2Ki 4:41** 7058
burnt offering and his **m** offering, **2Ki 16:13** 4503
the evening **m** offering and the king's **2Ki 16:15** 4503
burnt offering and his **m** offering, **2Ki 16:15** 4503
m offering and their drink **2Ki 16:15** 4503
He remember all your **m** offerings And **Ps 20:3** 4503
Sacrifice and **m** offering You have **Ps 40:6** 4503
Men prepare a **m** for enjoyment, and **Ec 10:19** 3899
"Take the millstones and grind **m**. **Is 47:2** 7058
that they could not even eat a **m**. **Mk 3:20** *740*
ceremonially washed before the **m**. **Lk 11:38** *712*
his own birthright for a *single* **m**. **Heb 12:16** *1035*

MEALS

and had his **m** in the king's **2Ki 25:29** 3899
and had his **m** in the king's **Jer 52:33** 3899
they were taking their **m** together **Ac 2:46** *5160*

MEALTIME

At **m** Boaz said to her, **Ru 2:14** 6256, 400

MEAN

"What do these seven ewe lambs **m**, **Gn 21:29**
"What do you **m** by all this **Gn 33:8**
'What does this rite **m** to you?' **Ex 12:26**
the statutes and the judgments **m** **Dt 6:20**
'What do these stones **m** to you?' **Jos 4:6**
shout in the camp of the Hebrews **m**? **1Sa 4:6**
the noise of this commotion **m**?" **1Sa 4:14**
"What do you **m** by crushing My **Is 3:15**
'Do you not know what these things **m**?' **Ezk 17:12**
"What do you **m** by using this **Ezk 18:2**
that you are doing **m** for us?" **Ezk 24:19**
to us what you **m** by these?' **Ezk 37:18**
"What does this **m**?" **Ac 2:12** *2309, 1510*
'YOU DO NOT **M** TO KILL ME AS YOU **Ac 7:28** *2309*
know what these things **m**." **Ac 17:20** *2309, 1510*
Now I **m** this, that each one of you **1Co 1:12** *3004*
I *did* not at all **m** with **1Co 5:10**
What do I **m** then? **1Co 10:19** *5346*
I **m** not your own conscience, but **1Co 10:29** *3004*
what does it **m** except that He also **Eph 4:9** *1510*
this *will* **m** fruitful labor for me; **Php 1:22**

MEANING

asking him the exact **m** of all this. **Da 7:16** 3330a
the exact **m** of the fourth beast, **Da 7:19** 3321
and *the* **m** of the ten horns that **Da 7:20**
and *the* **m** *of* this statement was **Lk 18:34**
world, and no *kind* is without **m**. **1Co 14:10** *880*
do not know the **m** of the language, **1Co 14:11** *1411*

MEANINGLESS

one in the right with **m** arguments. **Is 29:21** 8414
by Him as less than nothing and **m**. **Is 40:17** 8414
makes the judges of the earth **m**. **Is 40:23** 8414
praying, do not use **m** repetition as **Mt 6:7** *945*

MEANS

it **m** that the matter is **Gn 41:32**
by no **m** leave *the guilty* unpunished, **Ex 34:7** 5352
'But if his **m** are insufficient for **Lv 5:11** 3027
poor and his **m** are insufficient, **Lv 14:21** 3027
pigeons which are within his **m**, **Lv 14:22** 3027
pigeons, which are within his **m**. **Lv 14:30** 3027
m are limited for his cleansing." **Lv 14:32** 3027
but so recovers his **m** as to find **Lv 25:26** 3027
if he has not found sufficient **m** to **Lv 25:28** 3027
his **m** with regard to you falter, **Lv 25:35** 3027
'Now if the **m** of a stranger or of **Lv 25:47** 3027
if he is not redeemed by these **m**, **Lv 25:54**
according to the **m** of the one who **Lv 27:8** 3027, 5381
"We should by all **m** go up and **Nu 13:30** 5927
He will by no **m** clear *the guilty,* **Nu 14:18** 5352
shall by no **m** see the land which I **Nu 14:23** 518
but by all **m** cross over, **2Sa 17:16** 5674a
child, and by no **m** kill him." **1Ki 3:26** 4191
child, and by no **m** kill him. **1Ki 3:27** 4191
and by the same **m** they exported **1Ki 10:29** 3651, 3027
and by the same **m** they exported **2Ch 1:17** 3651, 3027
he gave praise by their **m**, **2Ch 7:6** 3027
out on Jerusalem by **m** of Shishak. **2Ch 12:7** 3027
can by any **m** redeem *his* brother Or **Ps 49:7** 6299
terror to understand what it **m**." **Is 28:19** 8052
not that what it **m** to know Me?" **Jer 22:16**
by no **m** leave you unpunished.' **Jer 30:11** 5352
by no **m** leave you unpunished." **Jer 46:28** 5352
by no **m** leave *the guilty* unpunished **Na 1:3** 5352
NAME IMMANUEL," which translated **m**, **Mt 1:23** *1510*
ARE BY NO **M** LEAST AMONG THE **Mt 2:6** *3760*
"But go and learn what this **m**: **Mt 9:13** *1510*
"But if you had known what this **m**, **Mt 12:7** *1510*
"But since he did not have *the* **m** **Mt 18:25**
which **m** Place of a Skull, **Mt 27:33** *3004*
gave the name Boanerges, which **m**, **Mk 3:17** *1510*
(which translated **m**, **Mk 5:41** *1510*
support out of their private **m**. **Lk 8:3** *5225*
since they do not have *the* **m** to **Lk 14:14**
make friends for yourselves by **m** **Lk 16:9** *1537*
"Rabbi (which translated **m** Teacher), **Jn 1:38** *3004*
(which translated **m** Christ). **Jn 1:41** *1510*
(which **m**, Teacher). **Jn 20:16** *3004*
translated **m** Son of Encouragement **Ac 4:36** *1510*
"By no **m**, Lord, for I have never **Ac 10:14** *3365*
'By no **m**, Lord, for nothing unholy **Ac 11:8** *3365*
that any of the disciples had **m**, **Ac 11:29** *2141*
that I may by all **m** save some. **1Co 9:22** *3843*
it to Abraham by **m** of a promise. **Ga 3:18** *1223*
nor uncircumcision **m** anything, **Ga 5:6** *2480*
how to get along with humble **m**, **Php 4:12** *5013*
but rather by **m** of good works, as **1Tm 2:10** *1223*
by **m** of the hypocrisy of liars **1Tm 4:2** *1722*
m of the word of God and prayer. **1Tm 4:5** *1223*
that godliness is a **m** of gain. **1Tm 6:5** *4200*
actually is a **m** of great gain when **1Tm 6:6** *4200*

MEANT
As for you, you **m** evil against me, **Gn 50:20** 2803
but God **m** it for good in order to **Gn 50:20** 2803
"This is what the LORD **m**: **Ex 16:23** 1696
those who are **m** for death *will* **Jer 43:11**
another what rising from the dead **m**. **Mk 9:10** *1510*
Him as to what this parable **m**. **Lk 8:9** *1510*
Now He **m** Judas *the son* of Simon **Jn 6:71** *3004*

MEANWHILE
M, the man was gazing at her in **Gn 24:21**
M, the Midianites sold him in **Gn 37:36**
They, **m**, will be making amends **Lv 26:43**
M David took more concubines and **2Sa 5:13**
M, David and all the house of **2Sa 6:5**
M, Pharaoh's army had set out from **Jer 37:5**
M the disciples were urging Him, **Jn 4:31** *3342*

MEARAH
M that belongs to the Sidonians, **Jos 13:4** 4632

MEASURE
measuring *it*, for it was beyond **m**. **Gn 41:49** 4557
"You shall also **m** outside the **Nu 35:5** 4058
go out and **m** *the distance* to the cities **Dt 21:2** 4058
you shall have a full and just **m**, **Dt 25:15** 374
of about 2,000 cubits by **m**. **Jos 3:4** 4060a
the cherubim were of the same **m** **1Ki 6:25** 4060a
of stone cut according to **m**, **1Ki 7:9** 4060a
stones, stone cut according to **m**, **1Ki 7:11** 4060a
one casting, one **m** and one form. **1Ki 7:37** 4060a
a **m** of fine flour will be *sold* for a **2Ki 7:1** 5429
Then a **m** of fine flour *was sold* **2Ki 7:16** 5429
a **m** of fine flour for a shekel, **2Ki 7:18** 5429
but I will grant them some **m** of **2Ch 12:7**
"Its **m** is longer than the earth And **Jb 11:9** 4055
And meted out the waters by **m**, **Jb 28:25** 4060a
and **m** out the valley of Succoth. **Ps 60:6** 4058
them to drink tears in large **m**. **Ps 80:5** 7991a
And **m** out the valley of Succoth. **Ps 108:7** 4058
and opened its mouth without **m**; **Is 5:14** 2706
the dust of the earth by the **m**, **Is 40:12** 7991a
They will come on you in full **m** **Is 47:9** 8537
Do not be angry beyond **m**, **Is 64:9** 3966
silent and afflict us beyond **m**? **Is 64:12** 3966
Therefore I will **m** their former **Is 65:7** 4058
end has come, The **m** of your end. **Jer 51:13** 520
be the sixth part of a hin by **m**; **Ezk 4:11** 4884
drink water by **m** and in horror, **Ezk 4:16** 4884
and let them **m** the plan. **Ezk 43:10** 4058
shall **m** a length of 25,000 *cubits* **Ezk 45:3** 4058
to the eastern sea you shall **m**. **Ezk 47:18** 4058
And a short **m** *that is* cursed? **Mi 6:10** 374
"To **m** Jerusalem, to see how wide **Zch 2:2** 4058
and by your standard of **m**, it **Mt 7:2** *3354*
m *of the guilt* of your fathers. **Mt 23:32** *3358*
By your standard of **m** it will be **Mk 4:24** *3354*
good **m**—pressed down, shaken **Lk 6:38** *3358*
For by your standard of **m** it will **Lk 6:38** *3354*
for He gives the Spirit without **m**. **Jn 3:34** *3358*
has allotted to each a **m** of faith. **Ro 12:3** *3358*
they **m** themselves by themselves and **2Co 10:12** *3354*
we will not boast beyond *our* **m**, **2Co 10:13** *280*
but within the **m** of the sphere **2Co 10:13** *3358*
God apportioned to us as a **m**, **2Co 10:13** *3358*
not boasting beyond *our* **m**, **2Co 10:15** *280*
the church of God beyond **m** and **Ga 1:13** *5236*
to the **m** of Christ's gift. **Eph 4:7** *3358*
to the **m** of the stature which **Eph 4:13** *3358*
fill up the **m** of their sins. **1Th 2:16** *378*
and peace be yours in the fullest **m**. **1Pe 1:2** *4129*
"Get up and **m** the temple of God **Rv 11:1** *3354*
the temple and do not **m** it, **Rv 11:2** *3354*
gold measuring rod to **m** the city, **Rv 21:15** *3354*

MEASURED
When they **m** it with an omer, he **Ex 16:18** 4058
and he **m** six *measures* of barley **Ru 3:15** 4058
Moab, and **m** them with the line, **2Sa 8:2** 4058
and he **m** two lines to put to death **2Sa 8:2** 4058
m the circumference of both. **1Ki 7:15** 5437
Who has **m** the waters in the hollow **Is 40:12** 4058
the portion **m** to you From Me," **Jer 13:25** 4055
"If the heavens above can be **m** And **Jer 31:37** 4058
the sand of the sea cannot be **m**, **Jer 33:22** 4058
So he **m** the thickness of the wall, **Ezk 40:5** 4058
and **m** the threshold of the gate, **Ezk 40:6** 4058
Then he **m** the porch of the gate **Ezk 40:8** 4058
He **m** the porch of the gate, **Ezk 40:9** 4058
And he **m** the width of the gateway, **Ezk 40:11** 4058
He **m** the gate from the roof of **Ezk 40:13** 4058
Then he **m** the width from the front **Ezk 40:19** 4058
he **m** its length and its width. **Ezk 40:20** 4058
and he **m** a hundred cubits from **Ezk 40:23** 4058
and he **m** its side pillars and its **Ezk 40:24** 4058
and he **m** from gate to gate toward **Ezk 40:27** 4058
and he **m** the south gate according **Ezk 40:28** 4058
And he **m** the gate according to **Ezk 40:32** 4058
and he **m** *it* according to those **Ezk 40:35** 4058
He **m** the court, a *perfect* **Ezk 40:47** 4058
m *each* side pillar of the porch, **Ezk 40:48** 4058
the nave and **m** the side pillars; **Ezk 41:1** 4058
And he **m** the length of the nave, **Ezk 41:2** 4058
m each side pillar of the doorway, **Ezk 41:3** 4058
He **m** its length, twenty **Ezk 41:4** 4058
Then he **m** the wall of the temple, **Ezk 41:5** 4058
Then he **m** the temple, a hundred **Ezk 41:13** 4058
He **m** the length of the building **Ezk 41:15** 4058
he also **m** the inner nave **Ezk 41:15**
the east and **m** it all around. **Ezk 42:15** 4058
He **m** on the east side with the **Ezk 42:16** 4058
He **m** on the north side five **Ezk 42:17** 4058
On the south side he **m** five **Ezk 42:18** 4058
and **m** five hundred reeds with the **Ezk 42:19** 4058
He **m** it on the four sides; **Ezk 42:20** 4058
his hand, he **m** a thousand cubits, **Ezk 47:3** 4058
Again he **m** a thousand and led me **Ezk 47:4** 4058
Again he **m** a thousand and led me **Ezk 47:4** 4058
Again he **m** a thousand; **Ezk 47:5** 4058
Which cannot be **m** or numbered; **Hos 1:10** 4058
of measure, it will be **m** to you. **Mt 7:2** *3354*
of measure it will be **m** to you; **Mk 4:24** *3354*
it will be **m** to you in return." **Lk 6:38** *488*
and he **m** the city with the rod, **Rv 21:16** *3354*
And he **m** its wall, seventy-two **Rv 21:17** *3354*

MEASUREMENT
wrong in judgment, in **m** of weight, **Lv 19:35** 4060a
them for an inheritance by **m**, **Ps 78:55** 2256a
the three of them had the same **m**. **Ezk 40:10** 4060a
also had the same **m** on each side. **Ezk 40:10** 4060a
had the same **m** as the first gate. **Ezk 40:21** 4060a
around inside and outside, by **m**. **Ezk 41:17** 4060a
the north side, 4,500 *cubits* by **m**, **Ezk 48:30** 4060a
the south side, 4,500 *cubits* by **m**, **Ezk 48:33** 4060a

MEASUREMENTS
curtains shall have the same **m**. **Ex 26:2** 4060a
curtains shall have the same **m**. **Ex 26:8** 4060a
all the curtains had the same **m**. **Ex 36:9** 4060a
eleven curtains had the same **m**. **Ex 36:15** 4060a
Who set its **m**? Since you know. **Jb 38:5** 4461
ornaments *had* the same **m** as the gate **Ezk 40:22** 4060a
porches according to those same **m**. **Ezk 40:24** 4060a
gate according to those same **m**. **Ezk 40:28** 4060a
were according to those same **m**. **Ezk 40:29** 4060a
gate according to those same **m**. **Ezk 40:32** 4060a
were according to those same **m**. **Ezk 40:33** 4060a
it according to those same **m**, **Ezk 40:35** 4060a
are the **m** of the altar by cubits **Ezk 43:13** 4060a
"These *shall be* its **m**: **Ezk 48:16** 4060a
yards, *according to* human **m**, **Rv 21:17** *3358*
which are *also* angelic **m**. **Rv 21:17**

MEASURES
prepare three **m** of fine flour, **Gn 18:6** 5429
have in your house differing **m**, **Dt 25:14** 374
and he measured six **m** of barley **Ru 3:15**
She said, "These six **m** of **Ru 3:17**
and five **m** of roasted grain and **1Sa 25:18** 5429
enough to hold two **m** of seed. **1Ki 18:32** 5429
and two **m** of barley for a shekel, **2Ki 7:1** 5429
and two **m** of barley for a shekel, **2Ki 7:16** 5429
"Two **m** of barley for a shekel and **2Ki 7:18** 5429
and all **m** of volume and size. **1Ch 23:29** 4060a
Differing weights and differing **m**, **Pr 20:10** 374
to a *grain* heap of twenty **m**, **Hg 2:16**
to the wine vat to draw fifty **m**, **Hg 2:16** 6333b
'A hundred **m** of oil.' **Lk 16:6** *943*
'A hundred **m** of wheat.' **Lk 16:7** *2884*

MEASURING
of the sea, until he stopped **m** *it*, **Gn 41:49** 5608
I will make justice the **m** line And **Is 28:17** 6957b
shapes wood, he extends a **m** line; **Is 44:13** 6957b
"The **m** line will go out **Jer 31:39** 4060a
of flax and a **m** rod in his hand; **Ezk 40:3** 4060a
hand was a **m** rod of six cubits, **Ezk 40:5** 4060a
he had finished the **m** the inner house, **Ezk 42:15** 4060a
the **m** reed five hundred reeds by **Ezk 42:16** 4060a
five hundred reeds by the **m** reed. **Ezk 42:16** 4060a
five hundred reeds by the **m** reed. **Ezk 42:17** 4060a
hundred reeds with the **m** reed; **Ezk 42:18** 4060a
hundred reeds with the **m** reed. **Ezk 42:19** 4060a
parceled up by a **m** line **Am 7:17**
no one stretching a **m** line For you **Mi 2:5** 2256a
"and a **m** line will be stretched **Zch 1:16** 6957b
a man with a **m** line in his hand. **Zch 2:1** 4060a
was given me a **m** rod like a staff; **Rv 11:1** *2563*
a gold **m** rod to measure the city, **Rv 21:15** *2563*

MEAT
when we sat by the pots of **m**, **Ex 16:3** 1320
gives you **m** to eat in the evening, **Ex 16:8** 1320
'At twilight you shall eat **m**, **Ex 16:12** 1320
"Who will give us **m** to eat? **Nu 11:4** 1320
"Where am I to get **m** to give to all **Nu 11:13** 1320
'Give us **m** that we may eat!' **Nu 11:13** 1320
for tomorrow, and you shall eat **m**; **Nu 11:18** 1320
someone would give us **m** to eat! **Nu 11:18** 1320
will give you **m** and you shall eat. **Nu 11:18** 1320
'I will give them **m**, so that **Nu 11:21** 1320
m was still between their teeth, **Nu 11:33** 1320
"Their **m** shall be yours; **Nu 18:18** 1320
eat **m** within any of your gates, **Dt 12:15** 1320
'I will eat **m**,' because you desire **Dt 12:20** 1320
meat,' because you desire to eat **m**, **Dt 12:20** 1320
to eat meat, *then* you may eat **m**, **Dt 12:20** 1320
he put the **m** in a basket and the **Jg 6:19** 1320
"Take the **m** and the unleavened **Jg 6:20** 1320
the **m** and the unleavened bread; **Jg 6:21** 1320
the **m** and the unleavened bread. **Jg 6:21** 1320
come while the **m** was boiling, **1Sa 2:13** 1320
"Give the priest **m** for roasting, **1Sa 2:15** 1320
will not take boiled **m** from you, **1Sa 2:15** 1320
and my **m** that I have slaughtered **1Sa 25:11** 2878
The ravens brought him bread and **m** **1Ki 17:6** 1320
and bread and **m** in the evening, **1Ki 17:6** 1320
a loaf of bread and a portion *of* **m** **1Ch 16:3**
not been satisfied with his **m**? **Jb 31:31** 1320
He provide **m** for His people?" **Ps 78:20** 7607
rained **m** upon them like the dust, **Ps 78:27** 7607
Or with gluttonous eaters of **m**; **Pr 23:20** 1320
Eating of **m** and drinking of wine: **Is 22:13** 1320
he eats **m** as he roasts a roast and **Is 44:16** 1320
I roast **m** and eat *it*. **Is 44:19** 1320
broth of unclean **m** is *in* their pots. **Is 65:4** 6292
unclean **m** ever entered my mouth." **Ezk 4:14** 1320
"You eat **m** with the blood *in* **Ezk 33:25**
'Arise, devour much **m**!' **Da 7:5** 1321
nor did **m** or wine enter my mouth, **Da 10:3** 1320
will take you away with **m** hooks, **Am 4:2** 6793a
the pot And as **m** in a kettle." **Mi 3:3** 1320
holy **m** in the fold of his garment, **Hg 2:12** 1320
abstain from **m** sacrificed to idols **Ac 21:25** *3588*
not to eat **m** or to drink wine, **Ro 14:21** *2907*
stumble, I will never eat **m** again, **1Co 8:13** *2907*
that is sold in the **m** market without **1Co 10:25** *3111*
"This is **m** sacrificed to idols," **1Co 10:28**

MEBUNNAI
the Anathothite, **M** the Hushathite, **2Sa 23:27** 4012

MECHERATHITE
Hepher the **M**, Ahijah the Pelonite, **1Ch 11:36** 4382

MECONAH
in Ziklag, in **M** and in its towns, **Ne 11:28** 4368

MEDAD
Eldad and the name of the other **M**. **Nu 11:26** 4312
Eldad and **M** are prophesying in the **Nu 11:27** 4312

MEDAN
Zimran and Jokshan and **M** and **Gn 25:2** 4091
she bore, *were* Zimran, Jokshan, **M**, **1Ch 1:32** 4091

MEDDLER
or evildoer, or a troublesome **m**; **1Pe 4:15** *244*

MEDDLES
m with strife not belonging to him. **Pr 26:17** 5674b

MEDE
So Darius the **M** received the **Da 5:31** 4077
In the first year of Darius the **M**, **Da 11:1** 4075

MEDEBA
to Nophah, Which *reaches* to **M**." **Nu 21:30** 4311
valley, and all the plain of **M**, **Jos 13:9** 4311
the valley and all the plain by **M**; **Jos 13:16** 4311
who came and camped before **M**. **1Ch 19:7** 4311
Moab wails over Nebo and **M**; **Is 15:2** 4311

MEDES
Gozan, and in the cities of the **M**. **2Ki 17:6** 4074
Gozan, and in the cities of the **M**, **2Ki 18:11** 4074
to stir up the **M** against them, **Is 13:17** 4074
the spirit of the kings of the **M**, **Jer 51:11** 4074
against her, The kings of the **M**, **Jer 51:28** 4074
given over to the **M** and Persians." **Da 5:28** 4076
to the law of the **M** and Persians, **Da 6:8** 4076
to the law of the **M** and Persians, **Da 6:12** 4076
that it is a law of the **M** and **Da 6:15** 4076
"Parthians and **M** and Elamites, **Ac 2:9** *3370*

MEDIA
which is in the province of **M**, **Ezr 6:2** 4076
the army *officers* of Persia and **M**, **Es 1:3** 4074
the seven princes of Persia and **M** **Es 1:14** 4074
This day the ladies of Persia and **M** **Es 1:18** 4074
written in the laws of Persia and **M** **Es 1:19** 4074
of the Kings of **M** and Persia? **Es 10:2** 4074
Go up, Elam, lay siege, **M**; **Is 21:2** 4074
of Elam and all the kings of **M**; **Jer 25:25** 4074
the kings of **M** and Persia. **Da 8:20** 4074

MEDIAN
son of Ahasuerus, of **M** descent, **Da 9:1** 4074

MEDIATE
another, God will **m** for him; **1Sa 2:25** 6419

MEDIATOR
"If there is an angel *as* **m** for him, **Jb 33:23** 3917b
angels by the agency of a **m**, **Ga 3:19** *3316*
Now a **m** is not for one *party only;* **Ga 3:20** *3316*
one **m** also between God and men, **1Tm 2:5** *3316*
also the **m** of a better covenant, **Heb 8:6** *3316*
He is the **m** of a new covenant, **Heb 9:15** *3316*
to Jesus, the **m** of a new covenant, **Heb 12:24** *3316*

MEDICINE
A joyful heart is good **m**, **Pr 17:22** 1456

MEDITATE
to **m** in the field toward evening; **Gn 24:63** 7742
you shall **m** on it day and night, **Jos 1:8** 1897
M in your heart upon your bed, and **Ps 4:4** 559
the LORD And to **m** in His temple. **Ps 27:4** 1239
I **m** on You in the night watches, **Ps 63:6** 1897
I will **m** with my heart, **Ps 77:6** 7878
I will **m** on all Your work And muse **Ps 77:12** 1897
I will **m** on Your precepts And **Ps 119:15** 7878
So I will **m** on Your wonders. **Ps 119:27** 7878
And I will **m** on Your statutes. **Ps 119:48** 7878
But I shall **m** on Your precepts. **Ps 119:78** 7878
watches, That I may **m** on Your word. **Ps 119:148** 7878
I **m** on all Your doings; **Ps 143:5** 1897
on Your wonderful works, I will **m**. **Ps 145:5** 7878
Your heart will **m** on terror: **Is 33:18** 1897

MEDITATES
And in His law he **m** day and night. **Ps 1:2** 1897
me, Your servant **m** on Your statutes. **Ps 119:23** 7878

MEDITATION
And hinder **m** before God. **Jb 15:4** 7881
and the **m** of my heart Be acceptable **Ps 19:14** 1902
And the **m** of my heart *will be* **Ps 49:3** 1900
Let my **m** be pleasing to Him; **Ps 104:34** 7879
It is my **m** all the day. **Ps 119:97** 7881
For Your testimonies are my **m**. **Ps 119:99** 7881

MEDIUM
'Now a man or a woman who is a **m** **Lv 20:27** 178
or one who casts a spell, or a **m**, **Dt 18:11** 7592, 178

“Seek for me a woman who is a **m**,	**1Sa 28:7**	1172, 178
is a woman who is a **m** at En-dor.”	**1Sa 28:7**	1172, 178
because he asked counsel of a **m**,	**1Ch 10:13**	178

MEDIUMS

'Do not turn to **m** or spiritists;	**Lv 19:31**	178
who turns to **m** and to spiritists,	**Lv 20:6**	178
those who were **m** and spiritists.	**1Sa 28:3**	178
m and spiritists from the land.	**1Sa 28:9**	178
and dealt with **m** and spiritists.	**2Ki 21:6**	178
Josiah removed the **m** and the	**2Ki 23:24**	178
and dealt with **m** and spiritists.	**2Ch 33:6**	178
“Consult the **m** and the spiritists	**Is 8:19**	178
the dead And to **m** and spiritists.	**Is 19:3**	178

MEEK

am **m** when face to face with you,	**2Co 10:1**	*5011*

MEEKNESS

of truth and **m** *and* righteousness;	**Ps 45:4**	6038
by the **m** and gentleness of Christ	**2Co 10:1**	*4240*

MEET

to **m** him at the valley of Shaveh	**Gn 14:17**	7122
ran from the tent door to **m** them and	**Gn 18:2**	7122
he rose to **m** them and bowed down	**Gn 19:1**	7122
Then the servant ran to **m** her,	**Gn 24:17**	7122
walking in the field to **m** us?”	**Gn 24:65**	7122
sister's son, he ran to **m** him,	**Gn 29:13**	7122
Leah went out to **m** him and said,	**Gn 30:16**	7122
furthermore he is coming to **m** you,	**Gn 32:6**	7122
ran to **m** him and embraced him,	**Gn 33:4**	7122
to Goshen to **m** his father Israel;	**Gn 46:29**	7122
behold, he is coming out to **m** you;	**Ex 4:14**	7122
“Go to **m** Moses in the wilderness.”	**Ex 4:27**	7122
to **m** him on the bank of the Nile;	**Ex 7:15**	7122
went out to **m** his father-in-law,	**Ex 18:7**	7122
people out of the camp to **m** God,	**Ex 19:17**	7122
“If you **m** your enemy's ox or his	**Ex 23:4**	6293
“There I will **m** with you;	**Ex 25:22**	3259
the LORD, where I will **m** with you,	**Ex 29:42**	3259
m there with the sons of Israel,	**Ex 29:43**	3259
where I will **m** with you.	**Ex 30:6**	3259
in the tent of meeting where I will **m**	**Ex 30:36**	3259
the testimony, where I **m** with you.	**Nu 17:4**	3259
out to **m** him at the city of Moab,	**Nu 22:36**	7122
perhaps the LORD will come to **m** me	**Nu 23:3**	7122
your burnt offering while I myself **m**	**Nu 23:15**	7136a
out to **m** them outside the camp.	**Nu 31:13**	7122
came out to **m** us in battle at Jahaz.	**Dt 2:32**	7122
out to **m** us in battle at Edrei.	**Dt 3:1**	7122
because they did not **m** you with	**Dt 23:4**	6923
came out to **m** us for battle,	**Dt 29:7**	7122
come out to **m** us as at the first,	**Jos 8:5**	7122
went out to **m** Israel in battle,	**Jos 8:14**	7122
and go to **m** them and say to them,	**Jos 9:11**	7122
of these kings having agreed to **m**,	**Jos 11:5**	3259
to **m** Israel in battle in order	**Jos 11:20**	7122
Jael went out to **m** Sisera,	**Jg 4:18**	7122
came out to **m** him and said to him,	**Jg 4:22**	7122
and they came up to **m** them.	**Jg 6:35**	7122
to **m** me when I return in peace	**Jg 11:31**	7122
daughter was coming out to **m** him	**Jg 11:34**	7122
saw him, he was glad to **m** him.	**Jg 19:3**	7122
Now Israel went out to **m** the	**1Sa 4:1**	7122
drew up in battle array to **m** Israel.	**1Sa 4:2**	7122
up to God at Bethel will **m** you,	**1Sa 10:3**	4672
that you will **m** a group of	**1Sa 10:5**	6293
out to **m** him *and* to greet him.	**1Sa 13:10**	7122
rose early in the morning to **m** Saul	**1Sa 15:12**	7122
came trembling to **m** him and said,	**1Sa 16:4**	7122
and came and drew near to **m** David,	**1Sa 17:48**	7122
battle line to **m** the Philistine.	**1Sa 17:48**	7122
and dancing, to **m** King Saul,	**1Sa 18:6**	7122
came trembling to **m** David and	**1Sa 21:1**	7122
and went to **m** the Philistines;	**1Sa 23:28**	7122
who sent you this day to **m** me,	**1Sa 25:32**	7122
you had come quickly to **m** me,	**1Sa 25:34**	7122
and they went out to **m** David and	**1Sa 30:21**	7122
to **m** the people who were with him,	**1Sa 30:21**	7122
Saul came out to **m** David and said,	**2Sa 6:20**	7122
it to David, he sent to **m** them,	**2Sa 10:5**	7122
to **m** David and fought against him.	**2Sa 10:17**	7122
to **m** the servants of David.	**2Sa 18:9**	7122
in order to go to **m** the king,	**2Sa 19:15**	7122
the men of Judah to **m** King David.	**2Sa 19:16**	7122
go down to **m** my lord the king.”	**2Sa 19:20**	7122
of Saul came down to **m** the king;	**2Sa 19:24**	7122
came from Jerusalem to **m** the king,	**2Sa 19:25**	7122
in Gibeon, Amasa came to **m** them.	**2Sa 20:8**	6440
And the king arose to **m** her,	**1Ki 2:19**	7122
So Obadiah went to **m** Ahab and	**1Ki 18:16**	7122
and Ahab went to **m** Elijah.	**1Ki 18:16**	7122
provisioned and went to **m** them;	**1Ki 20:27**	7122
go down to **m** Ahab king of Israel,	**1Ki 21:18**	7122
go up to **m** the messengers of the	**2Ki 1:3**	7122
came up to **m** us and said to us,	**2Ki 1:6**	7122
he who came up to **m** you and spoke	**2Ki 1:7**	7122
And they came to **m** him and bowed	**2Ki 2:15**	7122
run now to **m** her and say to her,	**2Ki 4:26**	7122
if you **m** any man, do not salute	**2Ki 4:29**	4672
he returned to **m** him and told him,	**2Ki 4:31**	7122
down from the chariot to **m** him	**2Ki 5:21**	7122
turned from his chariot to **m** you?	**2Ki 5:26**	7122
hand and go to **m** the man of God,	**2Ki 8:8**	7122
So Hazael went to **m** him and took a	**2Ki 8:9**	7122
send him to **m** them and let him say	**2Ki 9:17**	7122
a horseman went to **m** him and said,	**2Ki 9:18**	7122
and they went out to **m** Jehu and	**2Ki 9:21**	7122
the son of Rechab *coming* to **m** him;	**2Ki 10:15**	7122
to **m** Tiglath-pileser king of Assyria,	**2Ki 16:10**	7122
And King Josiah went to **m** him,	**2Ki 23:29**	7122
David went out to **m** them,	**1Ch 12:17**	6440
lands, that they may **m** with us;	**1Ch 13:2**	6908
And he sent to **m** them, for the men	**1Ch 19:5**	7122
So Asa went out to **m** him,	**2Ch 14:10**	6440
went out to **m** Asa and said to him,	**2Ch 15:2**	6440
went out to **m** him and said to King	**2Ch 19:2**	6440
and he went out to **m** the army	**2Ch 28:9**	6440
let us **m** together at Chephirim in	**Ne 6:2**	3259
us **m** together in the house of God,	**Ne 6:10**	3259
they did not **m** the sons of Israel	**Ne 13:2**	6923
“By day they **m** with darkness, And	**Jb 5:14**	6298
He goes out to **m** the weapons.	**Jb 39:21**	7122
For You **m** him with the	**Ps 21:3**	6923
to **m** those who pursue me;	**Ps 35:3**	7122
in His lovingkindness will **m** me;	**Ps 59:10**	6923
compassion come quickly to **m** us,	**Ps 79:8**	6923
behold, a woman *comes* to **m** him,	**Pr 7:10**	7122
I have come out to **m** you,	**Pr 7:15**	7122
Where the paths **m**, she takes her	**Pr 8:2**	1007a
a man **m** a bear robbed of her cubs,	**Pr 17:12**	6298
“Go out now to **m** Ahaz, you and	**Is 7:3**	7122
over you to **m** you when you come;	**Is 14:9**	7122
Tema, **M** the fugitive with bread.	**Is 21:14**	6923
creatures will **m** with the wolves,	**Is 34:14**	6298
You **m** him who rejoices in	**Is 64:5**	6293
those prophets shall **m** their end!	**Jer 14:15**	8552
went out from Mizpah to **m** them,	**Jer 41:6**	7122
and they will all **m** their end in	**Jer 44:12**	8552
sword *and* **m** their end by famine.	**Jer 44:12**	8552
will **m** their end by the sword and by	**Jer 44:27**	8552
One courier runs to **m** another,	**Jer 51:31**	7122
And one messenger to **m** another,	**Jer 51:31**	7122
to you, Prepare to **m** your God,	**Am 4:12**	7122
angel was coming out to **m** him,	**Zch 2:3**	7122
whole city came out to **m** Jesus;	**Mt 8:34**	*5222*
and went out to **m** the bridegroom.	**Mt 25:1**	*5222*
Come out to **m** *him.*'	**Mt 25:6**	*529*
and a man will **m** you carrying a	**Mk 14:13**	*528*
out to **m** another king in battle,	**Lk 14:31**	*4820*
a man will **m** you carrying a	**Lk 22:10**	*4876*
Jesus was coming, went to **m** Him,	**Jn 11:20**	*5221*
palm trees and went out to **m** Him,	**Jn 12:13**	*5222*
of Appius and Three Inns to **m** us;	**Ac 28:15**	*529*
Therefore when you **m** together,	**1Co 11:20**	*4905*
clouds to **m** the Lord in the air,	**1Th 4:17**	*529*
in good deeds to **m** pressing needs,	**Ti 3:14**	

MEETING

“In the tent of **m**, outside the	**Ex 27:21**	4150
when they enter the tent of **m**,	**Ex 28:43**	4150
to the doorway of the tent of **m** and	**Ex 29:4**	4150
the bull before the tent of **m**,	**Ex 29:10**	4150
at the doorway of the tent of **m**.	**Ex 29:11**	4150
he enters the tent of **m** to minister	**Ex 29:30**	4150
at the doorway of the tent of **m**.	**Ex 29:32**	4150
of the tent of **m** before the LORD,	**Ex 29:42**	4150
the tent of **m** and the altar;	**Ex 29:44**	4150
for the service of the tent of **m**,	**Ex 30:16**	4150
the tent of **m** and the altar,	**Ex 30:18**	4150
when they enter the tent of **m**,	**Ex 30:20**	4150
With it you shall anoint the tent of **m**	**Ex 30:26**	4150
the testimony in the tent of **m** where	**Ex 30:36**	4150
the tent of **m**, and the ark of	**Ex 31:7**	4150
and he called it the tent of **m**.	**Ex 33:7**	4150
LORD would go out to the tent of **m**	**Ex 33:7**	4150
for the work of the tent of **m** and for	**Ex 35:21**	4150
at the doorway of the tent of **m**.	**Ex 38:8**	4150
to the doorway of the tent of **m**,	**Ex 38:30**	4150
of the tent of **m** was completed;	**Ex 39:32**	4150
the tabernacle, for the tent of **m**;	**Ex 39:40**	4150
the tabernacle of the tent of **m**.	**Ex 40:2**	4150
the tabernacle of the tent of **m**.	**Ex 40:6**	4150
the tent of **m** and the altar and	**Ex 40:7**	4150
to the doorway of the tent of **m**	**Ex 40:12**	4150
he put the table in the tent of **m** on	**Ex 40:22**	4150
the lampstand in the tent of **m**,	**Ex 40:24**	4150
gold altar in the tent of **m** in front	**Ex 40:26**	4150
the tabernacle of the tent of **m**,	**Ex 40:29**	4150
the tent of **m** and the altar and	**Ex 40:30**	4150
When they entered the tent of **m**,	**Ex 40:32**	4150
the cloud covered the tent of **m**,	**Ex 40:34**	4150
was not able to enter the tent of **m**	**Ex 40:35**	4150
spoke to him from the tent of **m**,	**Lv 1:1**	4150
at the doorway of the tent of **m**,	**Lv 1:3**	4150
at the doorway of the tent of **m**.	**Lv 1:5**	4150
at the doorway of the tent of **m**,	**Lv 3:2**	4150
and slay it before the tent of **m**,	**Lv 3:8**	4150
and slay it before the tent of **m**,	**Lv 3:13**	4150
the doorway of the tent of **m** before	**Lv 4:4**	4150
and bring it to the tent of **m**,	**Lv 4:5**	4150
before the LORD in the tent of **m**;	**Lv 4:7**	4150
at the doorway of the tent of **m**.	**Lv 4:7**	4150
and bring it before the tent of **m**.	**Lv 4:14**	4150
of the bull to the tent of **m**;	**Lv 4:16**	4150
before the LORD in the tent of **m**;	**Lv 4:18**	4150
at the doorway of the tent of **m**.	**Lv 4:18**	4150
it in the court of the tent of **m**.	**Lv 6:16**	4150
in the court of the tent of **m**.	**Lv 6:26**	4150
blood is brought into the tent of **m**	**Lv 6:30**	4150
at the doorway of the tent of **m**.”	**Lv 8:3**	4150
at the doorway of the tent of **m**.	**Lv 8:4**	4150
at the doorway of the tent of **m**,	**Lv 8:31**	4150
outside the doorway of the tent of **m**	**Lv 8:33**	4150
“At the doorway of the tent of **m**,	**Lv 8:35**	4150
to the front of the tent of **m**,	**Lv 9:5**	4150
and Aaron went into the tent of **m**.	**Lv 9:23**	4150
from the doorway of the tent of **m**,	**Lv 10:7**	4150
when you come into the tent of **m**,	**Lv 10:9**	4150
at the doorway of the tent of **m** a	**Lv 12:6**	4150
at the doorway of the tent of **m**.	**Lv 14:11**	4150
at the doorway of the tent of **m**,	**Lv 14:23**	4150
to the doorway of the tent of **m** and	**Lv 15:14**	4150
to the doorway of the tent of **m**.	**Lv 15:29**	4150
at the doorway of the tent of **m**.	**Lv 16:7**	4150
thus he shall do for the tent of **m**	**Lv 16:16**	4150
no one shall be in the tent of **m**	**Lv 16:17**	4150
and the tent of **m** and the altar,	**Lv 16:20**	4150
Aaron shall come into the tent of **m** and	**Lv 16:23**	4150
the tent of **m** and for the altar.	**Lv 16:33**	4150
to the doorway of the tent of **m**	**Lv 17:4**	4150
at the doorway of the tent of **m** to	**Lv 17:5**	4150
at the doorway of the tent of **m**,	**Lv 17:6**	4150
to the doorway of the tent of **m** to	**Lv 17:9**	4150
to the doorway of the tent of **m**,	**Lv 19:21**	4150
veil of testimony in the tent of **m**,	**Lv 24:3**	4150
of Sinai, in the tent of **m**,	**Nu 1:1**	4150
shall camp around the tent of **m** at	**Nu 2:2**	4150
“Then the tent of **m** shall set out	**Nu 2:17**	4150
congregation before the tent of **m**,	**Nu 3:7**	4150
the furnishings of the tent of **m**,	**Nu 3:8**	4150
the sons of Gershon in the tent of **m**	**Nu 3:25**	4150
for the doorway of the tent of **m**,	**Nu 3:25**	4150
the tent of **m** toward the sunrise,	**Nu 3:38**	4150
to do the work in the tent of **m**.	**Nu 4:3**	4150
of Kohath in the tent of **m**,	**Nu 4:4**	4150
These are the things in the tent of **m**	**Nu 4:15**	4150
to do the work in the tent of **m**.	**Nu 4:23**	4150
and the tent of **m** *with* its covering	**Nu 4:25**	4150
for the doorway of the tent of **m**,	**Nu 4:25**	4150
the Gershonites in the tent of **m**,	**Nu 4:28**	4150
to do the work of the tent of **m**.	**Nu 4:30**	4150
their service in the tent of **m**:	**Nu 4:31**	4150
their service in the tent of **m**,	**Nu 4:33**	4150
service for work in the tent of **m**.	**Nu 4:35**	4150
who was serving in the tent of **m**,	**Nu 4:37**	4150
service for work in the tent of **m**.	**Nu 4:39**	4150
who was serving in the tent of **m**,	**Nu 4:41**	4150
service for work in the tent of **m**.	**Nu 4:43**	4150
work of carrying in the tent of **m**.	**Nu 4:47**	4150
to the doorway of the tent of **m**.	**Nu 6:10**	4150
to the doorway of the tent of **m**.	**Nu 6:13**	4150
at the doorway of the tent of **m**,	**Nu 6:18**	4150
in the service of the tent of **m**,	**Nu 7:5**	4150
when Moses went into the tent of **m**	**Nu 7:89**	4150
the Levites before the tent of **m**.	**Nu 8:9**	4150
may go in to serve the tent of **m**.	**Nu 8:15**	4150
sons of Israel at the tent of **m** and	**Nu 8:19**	4150
perform their service in the tent of **m**	**Nu 8:22**	4150
in the work of the tent of **m**.	**Nu 8:24**	4150
their brothers in the tent of **m**,	**Nu 8:26**	4150
at the doorway of the tent of **m**.	**Nu 10:3**	4150
and bring them to the tent of **m**,	**Nu 11:16**	4150
three come out to the tent of **m**.”	**Nu 12:4**	4150
the LORD appeared in the tent of **m**	**Nu 14:10**	4150
at the doorway of the tent of **m**,	**Nu 16:18**	4150
at the doorway of the tent of **m**.	**Nu 16:19**	4150
they turned toward the tent of **m**,	**Nu 16:42**	4150
to the front of the tent of **m**,	**Nu 16:43**	4150
at the doorway of the tent of **m**,	**Nu 16:50**	4150
then deposit them in the tent of **m**	**Nu 17:4**	4150
the obligations of the tent of **m**,	**Nu 18:4**	4150
the service for the tent of **m**.	**Nu 18:6**	4150
the service of the tent of **m**.	**Nu 18:21**	4150
not come near the tent of **m** again,	**Nu 18:22**	4150
the service of the tent of **m**,	**Nu 18:23**	4150
for your service in the tent of **m**.	**Nu 18:31**	4150
toward the front of the tent of **m**	**Nu 19:4**	4150
to the doorway of the tent of **m** and	**Nu 20:6**	4150
at the doorway of the tent of **m**.	**Nu 25:6**	4150
at the doorway of the tent of **m**,	**Nu 27:2**	4150
and brought it to the tent of **m** as	**Nu 31:54**	4150
yourselves at the tent of **m**,	**Dt 31:14**	4150
themselves at the tent of **m**.	**Dt 31:14**	4150
and set up the tent of **m** there;	**Jos 18:1**	4150
at the doorway of the tent of **m**.	**Jos 19:51**	4150
at the doorway of the tent of **m**.	**1Sa 2:22**	4150
tent of **m** and all the holy utensils,	**1Ki 8:4**	4150
the tabernacle of the tent of **m**,	**1Ch 6:32**	4150
of the entrance of the tent of **m**.	**1Ch 9:21**	4150
to keep charge of the tent of **m**,	**1Ch 23:32**	4150
for God's tent of **m** was there,	**2Ch 1:3**	4150
altar which *was* at the tent of **m**,	**2Ch 1:6**	4150
was at Gibeon, from the tent of **m**,	**2Ch 1:13**	4150
brought up the ark and the tent of **m**	**2Ch 5:5**	4150
to the house of **m** for all living.	**Jb 30:23**	4150
in the midst of Your **m** place;	**Ps 74:4**	4150
have burned all the **m** places of God	**Ps 74:8**	4150
destroyed His appointed **m** place.	**La 2:6**	4150
Now when *the* **m** *of* the synagogue	**Ac 13:43**	

MEETS

brother Esau **m** you and asks you,	**Gn 32:17**	6298
put him to death when he **m** him.	**Nu 35:19**	6293
murderer to death when he **m** him.	**Nu 35:21**	6293
from a lion And a bear **m** him,	**Am 5:19**	6293
accused **m** his accusers face to face and	**Ac 25:16**	*2192*

MEGIDDO

the king of **M**, one;	**Jos 12:21**	4023b
inhabitants of **M** and its towns,	**Jos 17:11**	4023b
inhabitants of **M** and its villages;	**Jg 1:27**	4023b
At Taanach near the waters of **M**;	**Jg 5:19**	4023b
son of Ahilud, *in* Taanach and **M**,	**1Ki 4:12**	4023b
the wall of Jerusalem, Hazor, **M**,	**1Ki 9:15**	4023b
But he fled to **M** and died there.	**2Ki 9:27**	4023b
Neco saw him he killed him at **M**.	**2Ki 23:29**	4023b
his body in a chariot from **M**,	**2Ki 23:30**	4023b
with its towns, **M** with its towns,	**1Ch 7:29**	4023b

to make war on the plain of **M**. 2Ch 35:22 4023b
of Hadadrimmon in the plain of **M**. Zch 12:11 4023b

MEHETABEL
and his wife's name was **M**, Gn 36:39 4105
was Pai, and his wife's name was **M**, 1Ch 1:50 4105
the son of Delaiah, son of **M**, Ne 6:10 4105

MEHIDA
sons of Bazluth, the sons of **M**, Ezr 2:52 4240
sons of Bazlith, the sons of **M**, Ne 7:54 4240

MEHIR
of Shuhah became the father of **M**, 1Ch 4:11 4243

MEHOLATHITE
given to Adriel the **M** for a wife. 1Sa 18:19 4259
Adriel the son of Barzillai the **M**. 2Sa 21:8 4259

MEHUJAEL
and Irad became the father of **M**, Gn 4:18 4232
and **M** became the father of Gn 4:18 4232

MEHUMAN
merry with wine, he commanded **M**, Es 1:10 4104

ME-JARKON
and **M** and Rakkon, with the Jos 19:46 4313

MELATIAH
Next to them **M** the Gibeonite and Ne 3:7 4424a

MELCHI
the son of Levi, the son of **M**, Lk 3:24 *3197*
the son of **M**, the son of Addi, the Lk 3:28 *3197*

MELCHIZEDEK
And **M** king of Salem brought out Gn 14:18 4442
According to the order of **M**." Ps 110:4 4442
ACCORDING TO THE ORDER OF **M**." Heb 5:6 *3198*
according to the order of **M**. Heb 5:10 *3198*
according to the order of **M**. Heb 6:20 *3198*
For this **M**, king of Salem, priest Heb 7:1 *3198*
of his father when **M** met him. Heb 7:10 *3198*
arise according to the order of **M**, Heb 7:11 *3198*
according to the likeness of **M**, Heb 7:15 *3198*
ACCORDING TO THE ORDER OF **M**." Heb 7:17 *3198*

MELEA
the son of **M**, the son of Menna, Lk 3:31 *3190*

MELECH
The sons of Micah *were* Pithon, **M**, 1Ch 8:35 4429
The sons of Micah *were* Pithon, **M**, 1Ch 9:41 4429

MELODY
With the lyre and the sound of **m**. Ps 98:5 2172
Thanksgiving and sound of a **m**. Is 51:3 2172
m with your heart to the Lord; Eph 5:19 *5567*

MELONS
the cucumbers and the **m** and the Nu 11:5 20

MELT
when the sun grew hot, it would **m**. Ex 16:21 4549
brethren have made our hearts **m**, Dt 1:28 4549
brothers' hearts **m** like his heart.' Dt 20:8 4549
heart of the people **m** with fear; Jos 14:8 4529
earth and all who dwell in it **m**; Ps 75:3 4127
will gnash his teeth and **m** away; Ps 112:10 4549
limp, And every man's heart will **m**. Is 13:7 4549
M away, O Philistia, all of you; Is 14:31 4127
the heart of the Egyptians will **m** Is 19:1 4549
and every heart will **m**, Ezk 21:7 4549
that *their* hearts may **m**, Ezk 21:15 4127
blow fire on it in order to **m** *it*, Ezk 22:20 5413
I will lay you *there* and **m** you. Ezk 22:20 5413
The mountains will **m** under Him And Mi 1:4 4549
elements will **m** with intense heat! 2Pe 3:12 *5080*

MELTED
inhabitants of Canaan have **m** away. Ex 15:15 4127
the land have **m** away before you. Jos 2:9 4127
our hearts **m** and no courage Jos 2:11 4549
have **m** away before us." Jos 2:24 4127
had crossed, that their hearts **m**, Jos 5:1 4549
the people **m** and became as water. Jos 7:5 4549
and behold, the multitude **m** away; 1Sa 14:16 4127
It is **m** within me. Ps 22:14 4549
He raised His voice, the earth **m**. Ps 46:6 4127
The mountains **m** like wax at the Ps 97:5 4549
Their soul **m** away in *their* misery. Ps 107:26 4127
you will be **m** in the midst of it. Ezk 22:21 5413
'As silver is **m** in the furnace, so Ezk 22:22 2046
you will be **m** in the midst of it; Ezk 22:22 5413
And its filthiness may be **m** in it, Ezk 24:11 5413

MELTING
Hearts are **m** and knees knocking! Na 2:10 4549

MELTS
of ice *And* into which the snow **m**. Jb 6:16 5956
snail which **m** away as it goes along, Ps 58:8 8557
As wax **m** before the fire, *So* let Ps 68:2 4549
sends forth His word and **m** them; Ps 147:18 4529
who touches the land so that it **m**, Am 9:5 4127

MEMBER
which has an overgrown or stunted **m**, Lv 22:23
a prominent **m** of the Council, Mk 15:43 *1010*
who was a **m** of the Council, Lk 23:50 *1010*
For the body is not one **m**, 1Co 12:14 *3196*
If they were all one **m**, 1Co 12:19 *3196*
more abundant honor to that **m** 1Co 12:24
And if one **m** suffers, all the 1Co 12:26 *3196*
if *one* **m** is honored, all the 1Co 12:26 *3196*

MEMBERS
And all my **m** are as a shadow. Jb 17:7 3338
will they malign the **m** of his household! Mt 10:25
WILL BE THE **M** OF HIS HOUSEHOLD. Mt 10:36
for from now on five **m** in one Lk 12:52
go on presenting the **m** of your body Ro 6:13 *3196*
m *as* instruments of righteousness to Ro 6:13 *3196*
For just as you presented your **m** Ro 6:19 *3196*
your **m** as slaves to righteousness, Ro 6:19 *3196*
were at work in the **m** of our body Ro 7:5 *3196*
different law in the **m** of my body, Ro 7:23 *3196*
the law of sin which is in my **m**. Ro 7:23 *3196*
as we have many **m** in one body Ro 12:4 *3196*
m do not have the same function, Ro 12:4 *3196*
and individually **m** one of another. Ro 12:5 *3196*
that your bodies are **m** of Christ? 1Co 6:15 *3196*
I then take away the **m** of Christ 1Co 6:15 *3196*
and make them **m** of a prostitute? 1Co 6:15 *3196*
body is one and *yet* has many **m**, 1Co 12:12 *3196*
and all the **m** of the body, 1Co 12:12 *3196*
But now God has placed the **m**, 1Co 12:18 *3196*
But now there are many **m**, 1Co 12:20 *3196*
it is much truer that the **m** of the 1Co 12:22 *3196*
and those **m** of the body which we 1Co 12:23
and our less presentable **m** become 1Co 12:23
whereas our more presentable **m** have 1Co 12:24
but *that* the **m** may have the 1Co 12:25 *3196*
suffers, all the **m** suffer with it; 1Co 12:26 *3196*
all the **m** rejoice with it. 1Co 12:26 *3196*
body, and individually **m** of it. 1Co 12:27 *3196*
heirs and fellow **m** of the body, Eph 3:6 *4954*
for we are **m** of one another. Eph 4:25 *3196*
because we are **m** of His body. Eph 5:30 *3196*
consider the **m** of your earthly body Col 3:5 *3196*
the tongue is set among our **m** as Jas 3:6 *3196*
pleasures that wage war in your **m**? Jas 4:1 *3196*

MEMORABLE
m sayings are proverbs of ashes, Jb 13:12 2146

MEMORANDUM
was written in it as follows: "**M** Ezr 6:2 1799a

MEMORIAL
'Now this day will be a **m** to you, Ex 12:14 2146
"Write this in a book as a **m** and Ex 17:14 2146
as stones of **m** for the sons of Israel, Ex 28:12 2146
LORD on his two shoulders for a **m**. Ex 28:12 2146
a **m** before the LORD continually. Ex 28:29 2146
that it may be a **m** for the sons of Ex 30:16 2146
m stones for the sons of Israel, Ex 39:7 2146
as its **m** portion on the altar, Lv 2:2 234
the grain offering its **m** portion, Lv 2:9 234
offer up in smoke its **m** portion, Lv 2:16 234
take his handful of it as its **m** portion Lv 5:12 234
as its **m** offering to the LORD. Lv 6:15 234
may be a **m** portion for the bread, Lv 24:7 234
jealousy, a grain offering of **m**, Nu 5:15 2146
grain offering of **m** in her hands, Nu 5:18 2146
of the grain offering as its **m** offering Nu 5:26 234
as a **m** for the sons of Israel before the Nu 31:54 2146
So these stones shall become a **m** to Jos 4:7 2146
right or **m** in Jerusalem." Ne 2:20 2146
And it will be a **m** to the LORD, Is 55:13 8034
My house and within My walls a **m**, Is 56:5 3027
have ascended as a **m** before God. Ac 10:4 *3422*

MEMORIAL-NAME
this is My **m** to all generations. Ex 3:15 2143

MEMORY
m of Amalek from under heaven." Ex 17:14 2143
the **m** of Amalek from under heaven; Dt 25:19 2143
remove the **m** of them from men." Dt 32:26 2143
m fade from their descendants. Es 9:28 2143
"**M** of him perishes from the Jb 18:17 2143
The very **m** of them has perished. Ps 9:6 2143
cut off the **m** of them from the earth. Ps 34:16 2143
cut off their **m** from the earth; Ps 109:15 2143
the **m** of Your abundant goodness Ps 145:7 2143
The **m** of the righteous is blessed, Pr 10:7 2143
reward, for their **m** is forgotten. Ec 9:5 2143
Your name, even Your **m**, Is 26:8 2143
also be spoken of in **m** of her." Mt 26:13 *3422*
also be spoken of in **m** of her." Mk 14:9 *3422*

MEMPHIS
The princes of **M** are deluded; Is 19:13 5297
"Also the men of **M** and Tahpanhes Jer 2:16 5297
living in Migdol, Tahpanhes, **M**, Jer 44:1 5297
Proclaim also in **M** and Tahpanhes; Jer 46:14 5297
For **M** will become a desolation; Jer 46:19 5297
And make the images cease from **M**. Ezk 30:13 5297
And **M** *will have* distresses daily. Ezk 30:16 5297
gather them up, **M** will bury them. Hos 9:6 4644

MEMUCAN
Tarshish, Meres, Marsena and **M**, Es 1:14 4462
the king and the princes, **M** said, Es 1:16 4462
and the king did as **M** proposed. Es 1:21 4462

MEN
Then **m** began to call upon Gn 4:26
when **m** began to multiply on the Gn 6:1 120
the daughters of **m** were beautiful; Gn 6:2 120
came in to the daughters of **m**, Gn 6:4 120
were the mighty **m** who *were* of old, Gn 6:4 1368
men who *were* of old, **m** of renown. Gn 6:4 376
which the sons of **m** had built. Gn 11:5 120
commanded *his* **m** concerning him; Gn 12:20 376
Now the **m** of Sodom were wicked Gn 13:13 376
captive, he led out his trained **m**, Gn 14:14 2593
what the young **m** have eaten, Gn 14:24 5288
share of the **m** who went with me, Gn 14:24 376
among the **m** of Abraham's household, Gn 17:23 376
All the **m** of his household, Gn 17:27 376
m were standing opposite him; Gn 18:2 376
Then the **m** rose up from there, and Gn 18:16 376
Then the **m** turned away from there Gn 18:22 376
they lay down, the **m** of the city, Gn 19:4 376
men of the city, the **m** of Sodom, Gn 19:4 376
are the **m** who came to you tonight? Gn 19:5 376
only do nothing to these **m**, Gn 19:8 376
But the **m** reached out their hands Gn 19:10 376
They struck the **m** who were at Gn 19:11 376
Then the *two* **m** said to Lot, Gn 19:12 376
So the **m** seized his hand and the Gn 19:16 376
and the **m** were greatly frightened. Gn 20:8 376
before all **m** you are cleared." Gn 20:16 3605
took two of his young **m** with him Gn 22:3 5288
Abraham said to his young **m**, Gn 22:5 5288
Abraham returned to his young **m**, Gn 22:19 5288
and the daughters of the **m** of the Gn 24:13 376
feet of the **m** who were with him. Gn 24:32 376
Then he and the **m** who were with Gn 24:54 376
with Abraham's servant and his **m**. Gn 24:59 376
When the **m** of the place asked Gn 26:7 376
"the **m** of the place might kill me Gn 26:7 376
gathered all the **m** of the place and Gn 29:22 376
and four hundred **m** are with him." Gn 32:6 376
have striven with God and with **m** Gn 32:28 376
and four hundred **m** with him. Gn 33:1 376
and the **m** were grieved, and they Gn 34:7 376
and spoke to the **m** of their city, Gn 34:20 376
"These **m** are friendly with us; Gn 34:21 376
m consent to us to live with us, Gn 34:22 376
and my **m** being few in number, they Gn 34:30 4962
He asked the **m** of her place, Gn 38:21 376
the **m** of the place said, Gn 38:22 376
and none of the **m** of the household Gn 39:11 376
called to the **m** of her household and Gn 39:14 376
of Egypt, and all its wise **m**. Gn 41:8 2450
we are honest **m**, your servants are Gn 42:11 3653a
if you are honest **m**, Gn 42:19 3653a
'We are honest **m**; we are not spies. Gn 42:31 3653a
will know that you are honest **m**: Gn 42:33 3653a
you are not spies, but honest **m**. Gn 42:34 3653a
So the **m** took this present, and Gn 43:15 376
"Bring the **m** into the house, and Gn 43:16 376
m are to dine with me at noon." Gn 43:16 376
brought the **m** to Joseph's house. Gn 43:17 376
Now the **m** were afraid, because Gn 43:18 376
Then the man brought the **m** into Gn 43:24 376
and the **m** looked at one another in Gn 43:33 376
was light, the **m** were sent away, Gn 44:3 376
"Up, follow the **m**; Gn 44:4 376
and the **m** are shepherds, for they Gn 46:32 376
five **m** from among his brothers and Gn 47:2 376
you know any capable **m** among them, Gn 47:6 376
in their anger they slew **m**, Gn 49:6 376
for all the **m** who were seeking Ex 4:19 376
"Let the labor be heavier on the **m**, Ex 5:9 376
for *the* wise **m** and *the* sorcerers, Ex 7:11 2450
Let the **m** go, that they may serve Ex 10:7 376
Go now, the **m** *among you*, and serve Ex 10:11 1397
six hundred thousand **m** on foot, Ex 12:37 1397
"Choose **m** for us and go out, Ex 17:9 376
the people able **m** who fear God, Ex 18:21 376
able men who fear God, **m** of truth, Ex 18:21 376
chose able **m** out of all Israel and Ex 18:25 376
"If **m** have a quarrel and one Ex 21:18 376
"If **m** struggle with each Ex 21:22 376
"You shall be holy **m** to Me, Ex 22:31 376
young **m** of the sons of Israel, Ex 24:5 5288
m of the people fell that day. Ex 32:28 376
moved them, both **m** and women, Ex 35:22 376
Israelites, all the **m** and women, Ex 35:29 376
And all the skillful **m** who were Ex 36:4 2450
All the skillful **m** among those Ex 36:8 2450, 3820
old and upward, for 603,550 **m**. Ex 38:26
(for the **m** of the land who have Lv 18:27 376
the kind which **m** can present as an Lv 27:9
kind which **m** do not present as an Lv 27:11
apart among **m** shall be ransomed; Lv 27:29 120
"These then are the names of the **m** Nu 1:5 376
So Moses and Aaron took these **m** Nu 1:17 376
their numbered **m** of the tribe of Nu 1:21
households, their numbered **m**, Nu 1:22
their numbered **m** of the tribe of Nu 1:23
their numbered **m** of the tribe of Nu 1:25
their numbered **m** of the tribe of Nu 1:27
their numbered **m** of the tribe of Nu 1:29
their numbered **m** of the tribe of Nu 1:31
their numbered **m** of the tribe of Nu 1:33
their numbered **m** of the tribe of Nu 1:35
their numbered **m** of the tribe of Nu 1:37
their numbered **m** of the tribe of Nu 1:39
their numbered **m** of the tribe of Nu 1:41
their numbered **m** of the tribe of Nu 1:43
the leaders of Israel, twelve **m**, Nu 1:44 376
So all the numbered **m** of the sons Nu 1:45
all the numbered **m** were 603,550. Nu 1:46
his army, even their numbered **m**, Nu 2:4
his army, even their numbered **m**, Nu 2:6
and his army, even his numbered **m**, Nu 2:8
numbered **m** of the camp of Judah: Nu 2:9
his army, even their numbered **m**, Nu 2:11
his army, even their numbered **m**, Nu 2:13
his army, even their numbered **m**, Nu 2:15
numbered **m** of the camp of Reuben: Nu 2:16
his army, even their numbered **m**, Nu 2:19
his army, even their numbered **m**, Nu 2:21
his army, even their numbered **m**, Nu 2:23
numbered **m** of the camp of Ephraim: Nu 2:24
his army, even their numbered **m**, Nu 2:26
his army, even their numbered **m**, Nu 2:28
his army, even their numbered **m**, Nu 2:30
the numbered **m** of the camp of Dan Nu 2:31
These are the numbered **m** of the Nu 2:32
the numbered **m** of the camps Nu 2:32
Their numbered **m**, in the numbering Nu 3:22

even their numbered **m** *were* 7,500.	**Nu 3:22**	
Their numbered **m** in the numbering	**Nu 3:34**	
All the numbered **m** of the Levites,	**Nu 3:39**	
for their numbered **m** were 22,273.	**Nu 3:43**	
m by their families were 2,750.	**Nu 4:36**	
m of the Kohathite families,	**Nu 4:37**	
The numbered **m** of the sons of	**Nu 4:38**	
numbered **m** by their families,	**Nu 4:40**	
These are the numbered **m** of the	**Nu 4:41**	
The numbered **m** of the families	**Nu 4:42**	
m by their families were 3,200.	**Nu 4:44**	
These are the numbered **m** of the	**Nu 4:45**	
All the numbered **m** of the Levites,	**Nu 4:46**	
Their numbered **m** were 8,580.	**Nu 4:48**	
thus *these were* his numbered **m**,	**Nu 4:49**	
who were over the numbered **m**).	**Nu 7:2**	
among the **m** and among the animals;	**Nu 8:17**	120
But there were *some* **m** who were	**Nu 9:6**	376
Those **m** said to him,	**Nu 9:7**	376
"Gather for Me seventy **m** from the	**Nu 11:16**	376
he gathered seventy **m** of the elders	**Nu 11:24**	376
two **m** had remained in the camp;	**Nu 11:26**	376
"Send out for yourself **m** so that	**Nu 13:2**	376
all of them **m** who were heads of	**Nu 13:3**	376
These are the names of the **m** whom	**Nu 13:16**	376
carried it on a pole between two **m**,	**Nu 13:23**	
m who had gone up with him said,	**Nu 13:31**	376
we saw in it are **m** of *great* size.	**Nu 13:32**	376
"Surely all the **m** who have seen	**Nu 14:22**	376
even all your numbered **m**,	**Nu 14:29**	
As for the **m** whom Moses sent to	**Nu 14:36**	376
even those **m** who brought out the	**Nu 14:37**	376
m who went to spy out the land.	**Nu 14:38**	376
in the assembly, **m** of renown.	**Nu 16:2**	376
you put out the eyes of these **m**?	**Nu 16:14**	376
from the tents of these wicked **m**,	**Nu 16:26**	376
these **m** die the death of all men or	**Nu 16:29**	428
these men die the death of all **m** or	**Nu 16:29**	120
if they suffer the fate of all **m**,	**Nu 16:29**	120
these **m** have spurned the LORD."	**Nu 16:30**	376
all the **m** who belonged to Korah with	**Nu 16:32**	120
m who were offering the incense.	**Nu 16:35**	376
"As for the censers of these **m**	**Nu 16:38**	2400, 5315
the **m** who were burned had offered,	**Nu 16:39**	376
"Who are these **m** with you?"	**Nu 22:9**	376
"If the **m** have come to call you,	**Nu 22:20**	376
"Go with the **m**, but you shall	**Nu 22:35**	376
"Each of you slay his **m** who have	**Nu 25:5**	376
when the fire devoured 250 **m**,	**Nu 26:10**	376
"Arm **m** from among you for the	**Nu 31:3**	376
m of war who had gone to battle,	**Nu 31:21**	376
m of war who went out to battle,	**Nu 31:28**	376
which the **m** of war had plundered	**Nu 31:32**	5971a
from the **m** who had gone to war	**Nu 31:42**	376
have taken a census of **m** of war	**Nu 31:49**	376
The **m** of war had taken booty,	**Nu 31:53**	376
of the **m** who came up from Egypt,	**Nu 32:11**	376
place, a brood of sinful **m**,	**Nu 32:14**	376
and all of you armed **m** cross over	**Nu 32:21**	
"These are the names of the **m** who	**Nu 34:17**	376
"These are the names of the **m**:	**Nu 34:19**	376
experienced **m** from your tribes,	**Dt 1:13**	376
tribes, wise and experienced **m**,	**Dt 1:15**	376
'Let us send **m** before us, that	**Dt 1:22**	376
me and I took twelve of your **m**,	**Dt 1:23**	376
'Not one of these **m**,	**Dt 1:35**	376
generation of the **m** of war perished	**Dt 2:14**	376
all the **m** of war had finally perished	**Dt 2:16**	376
time and utterly destroyed the **m**,	**Dt 2:34**	4962
Heshbon, utterly destroying the **m**,	**Dt 3:6**	4962
all you valiant **m** shall cross over	**Dt 3:18**	1121
all the **m** who followed Baal-peor,	**Dt 4:3**	376
some worthless **m** have gone out	**Dt 13:13**	376
both the **m** who have the dispute	**Dt 19:17**	376
you shall strike all the **m** in it	**Dt 20:13**	2138
all the **m** of his city shall stone him	**Dt 21:21**	376
and the **m** of her city shall stone	**Dt 22:21**	376
If there is a dispute between **m** and	**Dt 25:1**	376
"If *two* **m**, a man and his	**Dt 25:11**	376
the **m** of Israel with a loud voice,	**Dt 27:14**	376
even all the **m** of Israel,	**Dt 29:10**	376
"Then **m** will say, 'Because	**Dt 29:25**	
the **m** and the women and children	**Dt 31:12**	376
the memory of them from **m**,"	**Dt 32:26**	582
and not die, Nor his **m** be few."	**Dt 33:6**	4962
the son of Nun sent two **m** as spies	**Jos 2:1**	376
m from the sons of Israel have	**Jos 2:2**	376
"Bring out the **m** who have come to	**Jos 2:3**	376
taken the two **m** and hidden them,	**Jos 2:4**	376
"Yes, the **m** came to me, but I did	**Jos 2:4**	376
at dark, that the **m** went out;	**Jos 2:5**	376
I do not know where the **m** went.	**Jos 2:5**	376
So the **m** pursued them on the road	**Jos 2:7**	376
and said to the **m**,	**Jos 2:9**	376
So the **m** said to her,	**Jos 2:14**	376
The **m** said to her,	**Jos 2:17**	376
Then the two **m** returned and came	**Jos 2:23**	376
take for yourselves twelve **m** from	**Jos 3:12**	376
twelve **m** from the people,	**Jos 4:2**	376
So Joshua called the twelve **m** whom	**Jos 4:4**	376
who were males, all the **m** of war,	**Jos 5:4**	376
m of war who came out of Egypt,	**Jos 5:6**	376
m of war circling the city once.	**Jos 6:3**	376
and let the armed **m** go on before	**Jos 6:7**	
The armed **m** went before the	**Jos 6:9**	
and the armed **m** went before them and	**Jos 6:13**	
two **m** who had spied out the land,	**Jos 6:22**	376
So the young **m** who were spies went	**Jos 6:23**	5288

Joshua sent **m** from Jericho to Ai,	**Jos 7:2**	376
So the **m** went up and spied out Ai.	**Jos 7:2**	376
three thousand **m** need go up to Ai;	**Jos 7:3**	376
m from the people went up there,	**Jos 7:4**	376
but they fled from the **m** of Ai.	**Jos 7:4**	376
The **m** of Ai struck down about	**Jos 7:5**	376
down about thirty-six of their **m**,	**Jos 7:5**	376
and Joshua chose 30,000 **m**,	**Jos 8:3**	376
And he took about 5,000 **m** and set	**Jos 8:12**	376
that the **m** of the city hurried and	**Jos 8:14**	376
The **m** *in* ambush rose quickly from	**Jos 8:19**	
m of Ai turned back and looked,	**Jos 8:20**	376
and all Israel saw that the **m** *in*	**Jos 8:21**	
turned back and slew the **m** of Ai.	**Jos 8:21**	376
fell that day, both **m** and women,	**Jos 8:25**	376
to him and to the **m** of Israel,	**Jos 9:6**	376
m of Israel said to the Hivites,	**Jos 9:7**	376
So the **m** *of Israel* took some of	**Jos 9:14**	376
Ai, and all its **m** *were* mighty.	**Jos 10:2**	376
Then the **m** of Gibeon sent *word* to	**Jos 10:6**	376
and assign **m** by it to guard them,	**Jos 10:18**	376
called for all the **m** of Israel,	**Jos 10:24**	376
said to the chiefs of the **m**	**Jos 10:24**	376
"Provide for yourselves three **m**	**Jos 18:4**	376
Then the **m** arose and went, and	**Jos 18:8**	376
So the **m** went and passed through	**Jos 18:9**	376
your **m** puts to flight a thousand,	**Jos 23:10**	376
defeated ten thousand **m** at Bezek.	**Jg 1:4**	376
all robust and valiant **m**;	**Jg 3:29**	376
and take with you ten thousand **m**	**Jg 4:6**	376
ten thousand **m** went up with him;	**Jg 4:10**	376
with ten thousand **m** following him.	**Jg 4:14**	376
Gideon took ten **m** of his servants	**Jg 6:27**	376
the **m** of the city to do it by day,	**Jg 6:27**	376
When the **m** of the city arose early	**Jg 6:28**	376
the **m** of the city said to Joash,	**Jg 6:30**	376
hand to their mouth, was 300 **m**;	**Jg 7:6**	376
"I will deliver you with the 300 **m**	**Jg 7:7**	376
So the 300 **m** took the people's	**Jg 7:8**	
sent all the *other* **m** of Israel,	**Jg 7:8**	376
his tent, but retained the 300 **m**;	**Jg 7:8**	376
the 300 **m** into three companies,	**Jg 7:16**	376
So Gideon and the hundred **m** who	**Jg 7:19**	376
The **m** of Israel were summoned	**Jg 7:23**	376
the **m** of Ephraim were summoned and	**Jg 7:24**	376
Then the **m** of Ephraim said to him,	**Jg 8:1**	376
Gideon and the 300 **m** who were	**Jg 8:4**	376
He said to the **m** of Succoth,	**Jg 8:5**	376
and the **m** of Penuel answered him	**Jg 8:8**	376
as the **m** of Succoth had answered.	**Jg 8:8**	376
he spoke also to the **m** of Penuel,	**Jg 8:9**	376
armies with them, about 15,000 **m**,	**Jg 8:10**	
and its elders, seventy-seven **m**.	**Jg 8:14**	376
came to the **m** of Succoth and said,	**Jg 8:15**	376
bread to your **m** who are weary?' "	**Jg 8:15**	376
the **m** of Succoth with them.	**Jg 8:16**	376
and killed the **m** of the city.	**Jg 8:17**	376
"What kind of **m** *were* they whom	**Jg 8:18**	376
the **m** of Israel said to Gideon,	**Jg 8:22**	376
is better for you, that seventy **m**,	**Jg 9:2**	376
the sons of Jerubbaal, seventy **m**,	**Jg 9:5**	376
All the **m** of Shechem and all	**Jg 9:6**	1167
"Listen to me, O **m** of Shechem,	**Jg 9:7**	1167
with which God and **m** are honored,	**Jg 9:9**	376
new wine, which cheers God and **m**,	**Jg 9:13**	376
have killed his sons, seventy **m**,	**Jg 9:18**	376
king over the **m** of Shechem,	**Jg 9:18**	1167
the **m** of Shechem and Beth-millo;	**Jg 9:20**	1167
and let fire come out from the **m**	**Jg 9:20**	1167
Abimelech and the **m** of Shechem;	**Jg 9:23**	1167
the **m** of Shechem dealt treacherously	**Jg 9:23**	1167
them, and on the **m** of Shechem,	**Jg 9:24**	1167
m of Shechem set men in ambush	**Jg 9:25**	1167
men of Shechem set **m** in ambush	**Jg 9:25**	
and the **m** of Shechem put their	**Jg 9:26**	1167
Serve the **m** of Hamor the father of	**Jg 9:28**	376
the mountains as *if they were* **m**."	**Jg 9:36**	376
all the **m** of the tower of Shechem	**Jg 9:49**	376
about a thousand **m** and women.	**Jg 9:49**	376
and all the **m** and women with all	**Jg 9:51**	376
When the **m** of Israel saw that	**Jg 9:55**	376
the **m** of Shechem on their heads,	**Jg 9:57**	376
the **m** of Ephraim were summoned,	**Jg 12:1**	376
gathered all the **m** of Gilead and	**Jg 12:4**	376
the **m** of Gilead defeated Ephraim,	**Jg 12:4**	376
the **m** of Gilead would say to him,	**Jg 12:5**	376
the young **m** customarily did this.	**Jg 14:10**	970
So the **m** of the city said to him	**Jg 14:18**	376
The **m** of Judah said,	**Jg 15:10**	376
Then 3,000 **m** of Judah went down to	**Jg 15:11**	376
and killed a thousand **m** with it.	**Jg 15:15**	376
I have killed a thousand **m**."	**Jg 15:16**	376
Now she had **m** lying in wait in an	**Jg 16:9**	
For the **m** were lying in wait in	**Jg 16:12**	
the house was full of **m** and women,	**Jg 16:27**	376
And about 3,000 **m** and women were	**Jg 16:27**	376
five **m** out of their whole number,	**Jg 18:2**	376
valiant **m** from Zorah and Eshtaol,	**Jg 18:2**	376
Then the five **m** departed and came	**Jg 18:7**	376
six hundred **m** armed with weapons	**Jg 18:11**	376
Then the five **m** who went to spy	**Jg 18:14**	376
The six hundred **m** armed with	**Jg 18:16**	376
Now the five **m** who went to spy out	**Jg 18:17**	376
m armed with weapons of war.	**Jg 18:17**	376
the **m** who *were* in the houses near	**Jg 18:22**	376
or else fierce **m** will fall upon you and	**Jg 18:25**	376
m of the place were Benjamites.	**Jg 19:16**	376
celebrating, behold, the **m** of the city,	**Jg 19:22**	376
But the **m** would not listen to him.	**Jg 19:25**	376

"But the **m** of Gibeah rose up	**Jg 20:5**	1167
"And we will take 10 **m** out of 100	**Jg 20:10**	376
Thus all the **m** of Israel were	**Jg 20:11**	376
Then the tribes of Israel sent **m**	**Jg 20:12**	376
"Now then, deliver up the **m**,	**Jg 20:13**	376
26,000 **m** who draw the sword,	**Jg 20:15**	376
who were numbered, 700 choice **m**.	**Jg 20:15**	376
700 choice **m** were left-handed;	**Jg 20:16**	376
Then the **m** of Israel besides	**Jg 20:17**	376
400,000 **m** who draw the sword;	**Jg 20:17**	376
all these were **m** of war.	**Jg 20:17**	376
The **m** of Israel went out to	**Jg 20:20**	376
and the **m** of Israel arrayed for	**Jg 20:20**	376
on that day 22,000 **m** of Israel.	**Jg 20:21**	376
But the people, the **m** of Israel,	**Jg 20:22**	376
18,000 **m** of the sons of Israel;	**Jg 20:25**	376
set **m** in ambush around Gibeah.	**Jg 20:29**	
field, about thirty **m** of Israel.	**Jg 20:31**	376
Then all the **m** of Israel arose	**Jg 20:33**	376
and the **m** of Israel in ambush	**Jg 20:33**	
When ten thousand choice **m** from	**Jg 20:34**	376
25,100 **m** of Benjamin that day,	**Jg 20:35**	376
When the **m** of Israel gave ground	**Jg 20:36**	376
they relied on the **m** in ambush	**Jg 20:36**	
the **m** in ambush hurried and rushed	**Jg 20:37**	
the **m** in ambush also deployed and	**Jg 20:37**	
sign between the **m** of Israel and the	**Jg 20:38**	376
and the **m** in ambush was that they	**Jg 20:38**	
Then the **m** of Israel turned in the	**Jg 20:39**	376
and kill about thirty **m** of Israel,	**Jg 20:39**	376
Then the **m** of Israel turned, and	**Jg 20:41**	376
the **m** of Benjamin were terrified;	**Jg 20:41**	376
their backs before the **m** of Israel	**Jg 20:42**	376
Thus 18,000 **m** of Benjamin fell;	**Jg 20:44**	376
were 25,000 **m** who draw the sword;	**Jg 20:46**	376
But 600 **m** turned and fled toward	**Jg 20:47**	376
The **m** of Israel then turned back	**Jg 20:48**	376
m of Israel had sworn in Mizpah,	**Jg 21:1**	376
first by not going after young **m**,	**Ru 3:10**	970
He took ten **m** of the elders of	**Ru 4:2**	376
the sons of Eli were worthless **m**;	**1Sa 2:12**	1121
Thus the sin of the young **m** was	**1Sa 2:17**	5288
for the **m** despised the offering of	**1Sa 2:17**	376
both with the LORD and with **m**.	**1Sa 2:26**	376
who killed about four thousand **m**	**1Sa 4:2**	376
"Take courage and be **m**,	**1Sa 4:9**	376
therefore, be **m** and fight."	**1Sa 4:9**	376
m of Ashdod saw that it was so,	**1Sa 5:7**	376
and He smote the **m** of the city,	**1Sa 5:9**	376
And the **m** who did not die were	**1Sa 5:12**	376
Then the **m** did so, and took two	**1Sa 6:10**	376
and the **m** of Beth-shemesh offered	**1Sa 6:15**	376
He struck down some of the **m**	**1Sa 6:19**	376
down of all the people, 50,070 **m**,	**1Sa 6:19**	376
The **m** of Beth-shemesh said,	**1Sa 6:20**	376
And the **m** of Kiriath-jearim came	**1Sa 7:1**	376
The **m** of Israel went out of	**1Sa 7:11**	376
best young **m** and your donkeys and	**1Sa 8:16**	970
So Samuel said to the **m** of Israel,	**1Sa 8:22**	376
invited, who were about thirty **m**.	**1Sa 9:22**	376
then you will find two **m** close to	**1Sa 10:2**	376
and there three **m** going up to God	**1Sa 10:3**	376
and the valiant **m** whose hearts	**1Sa 10:26**	
But certain worthless **m** said,	**1Sa 10:27**	1121
the **m** of Jabesh said to Nahash,	**1Sa 11:1**	376
him the words of the **m** of Jabesh.	**1Sa 11:5**	376
and the **m** of Judah 30,000.	**1Sa 11:8**	376
say to the **m** of Jabesh-gilead,	**1Sa 11:9**	376
went and told the **m** of Jabesh;	**1Sa 11:9**	376
Then the **m** of Jabesh said,	**1Sa 11:10**	376
Bring the **m**, that we may put them	**1Sa 11:12**	376
the **m** of Israel rejoiced greatly.	**1Sa 11:15**	376
for himself 3,000 **m** of Israel;	**1Sa 13:2**	
When the **m** of Israel saw that they	**1Sa 13:6**	376
with him, about six hundred **m**.	**1Sa 13:15**	376
with him *were* about six hundred **m**,	**1Sa 14:2**	376
m and reveal ourselves to them.	**1Sa 14:8**	376
So the **m** of the garrison hailed	**1Sa 14:12**	376
twenty **m** within about half a furrow	**1Sa 14:14**	376
When all the **m** of Israel who had	**1Sa 14:22**	376
Now the **m** of Israel were	**1Sa 14:24**	376
soldiers and 10,000 **m** of Judah.	**1Sa 15:4**	376
one of the young **m** said,	**1Sa 16:18**	5288
and the **m** of Israel were gathered and	**1Sa 17:2**	376
Saul, advanced *in years* among **m**.	**1Sa 17:12**	376
Saul and they and all the **m** of Israel	**1Sa 17:19**	376
all the **m** of Israel saw the man,	**1Sa 17:24**	376
The **m** of Israel said,	**1Sa 17:25**	376
to the **m** who were standing by him,	**1Sa 17:26**	376
heard when he spoke to the **m**;	**1Sa 17:28**	376
The **m** of Israel and Judah	**1Sa 17:52**	376
Saul set him over the **m** of war.	**1Sa 18:5**	376
rose up and went, he and his **m**,	**1Sa 18:27**	376
hundred **m** among the Philistines.	**1Sa 18:27**	376
the young **m** to a certain place.'	**1Sa 21:2**	5288
if only the young **m** have kept	**1Sa 21:4**	5288
vessels of the young **m** were holy,	**1Sa 21:5**	5288
about four hundred **m** with him.	**1Sa 22:2**	376
David and the **m** who were with him	**1Sa 22:6**	376
m who wore the linen ephod.	**1Sa 22:18**	376
of the sword, both **m** and women,	**1Sa 22:19**	376
But David's **m** said to him,	**1Sa 23:3**	376
So David and his **m** went to Keilah	**1Sa 23:5**	376
Keilah to besiege David and his **m**.	**1Sa 23:8**	376
"Will the **m** of Keilah surrender	**1Sa 23:11**	1167
"Will the **m** of Keilah surrender	**1Sa 23:12**	1167
and my **m** into the hand of Saul?"	**1Sa 23:12**	376
Then David and his **m**,	**1Sa 23:13**	376
Now David and his **m** were in the	**1Sa 23:24**	376

Saul and his **m** went to seek *him*, 1Sa 23:25 376
and David and his **m** on the other 1Sa 23:26 376
for Saul and his **m** were 1Sa 23:26 376
David and his **m** to seize them. 1Sa 23:26 376
thousand chosen **m** from all Israel and 1Sa 24:2 376
and went to seek David and his **m** 1Sa 24:2 376
Now David and his **m** were sitting 1Sa 24:3 376
The **m** of David said to him, 1Sa 24:4 376
So he said to his **m**, 1Sa 24:6 376
David persuaded his **m** with 1Sa 24:7 376
do you listen to the words of **m**, 1Sa 24:9 120
his **m** went up to the stronghold. 1Sa 24:22 376
So David sent ten young **m**; 1Sa 25:5 5288
and David said to the young **m**, 1Sa 25:5 5288
'Ask your young **m** and they will tell 1Sa 25:8 5288
young **m** find favor in your eyes, 1Sa 25:8 5288
When David's young **m** came, 1Sa 25:9 5288
to **m** whose origin I do not know?" 1Sa 25:11 376
So David's young **m** retraced their 1Sa 25:12 5288
David said to his **m**, 1Sa 25:13 376
and about four hundred **m** went up 1Sa 25:13 376
one of the young **m** told Abigail, 1Sa 25:14 5288
"Yet the **m** were very good to us, 1Sa 25:15 376
She said to her young **m**, 1Sa 25:19 5288
his **m** were coming down toward her; 1Sa 25:20 376
young **m** of my lord whom you sent. 1Sa 25:25 5288
the young **m** who accompany my lord. 1Sa 25:27 5288
three thousand chosen **m** of Israel, 1Sa 26:2 376
but if it is **m**, cursed are they 1Sa 26:19
1121, 120
the young **m** come over and take it. 1Sa 26:22 5288
six hundred **m** who were with him, 1Sa 27:2 376
with Achish at Gath, he and his **m**, 1Sa 27:3 376
Now David and his **m** went up and 1Sa 27:8 376
me in the camp, you and your **m**." 1Sa 28:1 376
and went, he and two **m** with him, 1Sa 28:8 376
David and his **m** were proceeding on 1Sa 29:2 376
not *be* with the heads of these **m**? 1Sa 29:4 376
David arose early, he and his **m**, 1Sa 29:11 376
David and his **m** came to Ziklag 1Sa 30:1 376
David and his **m** came to the city, 1Sa 30:3 376
six hundred **m** who were with him, 1Sa 30:9 376
pursued, he and four hundred **m**, 1Sa 30:10 376
m who rode on camels and fled. 1Sa 30:17 5288
David came to the two hundred **m** 1Sa 30:21
Then all the wicked and worthless **m** 1Sa 30:22 376
and his **m** were accustomed to go." 1Sa 30:31 376
and the **m** of Israel fled from 1Sa 31:1 376
all his **m** on that day together. 1Sa 31:6 376
When the **m** of Israel who were 1Sa 31:7 376
saw that the **m** of Israel had fled 1Sa 31:7 376
m rose and walked all night, 1Sa 31:12 376
did all the **m** who *were* with him. 2Sa 1:11 376
David called one of the young **m** 2Sa 1:15 5288
David brought up his **m** who *were* 2Sa 2:3
Then the **m** of Judah came and there 2Sa 2:4 376
"It was the **m** of Jabesh-gilead 2Sa 2:4 376
to the **m** of Jabesh-gilead, 2Sa 2:5 376
"Now let the young **m** arise and 2Sa 2:14 5288
and Abner and the **m** of Israel were 2Sa 2:17 376
one of the young **m** for yourself, 2Sa 2:21 5288
Abner and his **m** then went through 2Sa 2:29 376
many of Benjamin and Abner's **m**, 2Sa 2:31 376
three hundred and sixty **m** died. 2Sa 2:31 376
Then Joab and his **m** went all night 2Sa 2:32 376
Then Abner and twenty **m** with him 2Sa 3:20 376
Abner and the **m** who were with him. 2Sa 3:20 376
and these **m** the sons of Zeruiah 2Sa 3:39 376
m who were commanders of bands: 2Sa 4:2 376
when wicked **m** have killed a 2Sa 4:11 376
Then David commanded the young **m**, 2Sa 4:12 5288
Now the king and his **m** went to 2Sa 5:6 376
David and his **m** carried them away. 2Sa 5:21 376
all the chosen **m** of Israel, 2Sa 6:1
of Israel, both to **m** and women, 2Sa 6:19 376
the great **m** who are on the earth. 2Sa 7:9 1419
I will correct him with the rod of **m** 2Sa 7:14 376
and the strokes of the sons of **m**, 2Sa 7:14 120
for the **m** were greatly humiliated. 2Sa 10:5 376
the king of Maacah with 1,000 **m**, 2Sa 10:6 376
and the **m** of Tob with 12,000 men. 2Sa 10:6 382a
and the men of Tob with 12,000 **m**. 2Sa 10:6 376
and all the army, the mighty **m**. 2Sa 10:7 1368
the **m** of Tob and Maacah *were* by 2Sa 10:8 382a
from all the choice **m** of Israel, 2Sa 10:9
he knew there *were* valiant **m**. 2Sa 11:16 376
The **m** of the city went out and 2Sa 11:17 376
"The **m** prevailed against us and 2Sa 11:23 376
"There were two **m** in one city, 2Sa 12:1 376
have put to death all the young **m**, 2Sa 13:32 5288
and fifty **m** as runners before him. 2Sa 15:1 376
the hearts of the **m** of Israel. 2Sa 15:6 376
Then two hundred **m** went with 2Sa 15:11 376
m of Israel are with Absalom." 2Sa 15:13 376
six hundred **m** who had come with 2Sa 15:18 376
the Gittite passed over with all his **m** 2Sa 15:22 376
fruit for the young **m** to eat, 2Sa 16:2 5288
the mighty **m** were at his right hand 2Sa 16:6 1368
David and his **m** went on the way; 2Sa 16:13 376
all the people, the **m** of Israel, 2Sa 16:15 376
all the **m** of Israel have chosen, 2Sa 16:18 376
"Please let me choose 12,000 **m** 2Sa 17:1 376
"You know your father and his **m**, 2Sa 17:8 376
are mighty **m** and they are fierce, 2Sa 17:8 1368
who are with him are valiant **m**. 2Sa 17:10 1121
and of all the **m** who are with him, 2Sa 17:12 376
and all the **m** of Israel said, 2Sa 17:14 376
and all the **m** of Israel with him. 2Sa 17:24 376
that day was great, 20,000 **m**. 2Sa 18:7

And ten young **m** who carried Joab's 2Sa 18:15 5288
who has delivered up the **m** who 2Sa 18:28 376
of all the **m** of Judah as one man, 2Sa 19:14 376
the **m** of Judah to meet King David. 2Sa 19:16 376
a thousand **m** of Benjamin with him, 2Sa 19:17 376
dead **m** before my lord the king; 2Sa 19:28 376
the voice of singing **m** and women? 2Sa 19:35
all the **m** of Israel came to the 2Sa 19:41 376
the **m** of Judah stolen you away, 2Sa 19:41 376
m with him over the Jordan?" 2Sa 19:41 376
Then all the **m** of Judah answered 2Sa 19:42 376
of Judah answered the **m** of Israel, 2Sa 19:42 376
But the **m** of Israel answered the 2Sa 19:43 376
answered the **m** of Judah and said, 2Sa 19:43 376
Yet the words of the **m** of Judah 2Sa 19:43 376
than the words of the **m** of Israel. 2Sa 19:43 376
So all the **m** of Israel withdrew 2Sa 20:2 376
but the **m** of Judah remained 2Sa 20:2 376
"Call out the **m** of Judah for me 2Sa 20:4 376
So Amasa went to call out *the* **m** *of* 2Sa 20:5
So Joab's **m** went out after him, 2Sa 20:7 376
Pelethites and all the mighty **m**; 2Sa 20:7 1368
stood by him one of Joab's young **m**, 2Sa 20:11 5288
all the **m** passed on after Joab to 2Sa 20:13 376
m from his sons be given to us, 2Sa 21:6 376
son from the **m** of Jabesh-gilead, 2Sa 21:12 1167
Then the **m** of David swore to him, 2Sa 21:17 376
'He who rules over **m** righteously, 2Sa 23:3 120
of the mighty **m** whom David had: 2Sa 23:8 1368
one of the three mighty **m** with 2Sa 23:9 1368
and the **m** of Israel had withdrawn. 2Sa 23:9 376
Then three of the thirty chief **m** 2Sa 23:13 7218
So the three mighty **m** broke 2Sa 23:16 1368
Shall I drink the blood of the **m** 2Sa 23:17 376
things the three mighty **m** did. 2Sa 23:17 1368
as well as the three mighty **m**. 2Sa 23:22 1368
valiant **m** who drew the sword, 2Sa 24:9 376
and the **m** of Judah were five 2Sa 24:9 376
were five hundred thousand **m**. 2Sa 24:9 376
and seventy thousand **m** of the 2Sa 24:15 376
with fifty **m** to run before him. 1Ki 1:5 376
mighty **m** who belonged to David, 1Ki 1:8 1368
sons, and all the **m** of Judah, 1Ki 1:9 376
prophet, Benaiah, the mighty **m**, 1Ki 1:10 1368
because he fell upon two **m** more 1Ki 2:32 376
the **m** subject to forced labor. 1Ki 4:6 4522
For he was wiser than all **m**, 1Ki 4:31 120
M came from all peoples to hear 1Ki 4:34
forced laborers numbered 30,000 **m**. 1Ki 5:13 376
All the **m** of Israel assembled 1Ki 8:2 376
the hearts of all the sons of **m**, 1Ki 8:39 120
for they were **m** of war, his 1Ki 9:22 376
"How blessed are your **m**, 1Ki 10:8 376
and they took **m** with them from 1Ki 11:18 376
He gathered **m** to himself and 1Ki 11:24 376
and consulted with the young **m** who 1Ki 12:8 3206
The young **m** who grew up with 1Ki 12:10 3206
to the advice of the young **m**, 1Ki 12:14 3206
chosen **m** who were warriors, 1Ki 12:21
m passed by and saw the body 1Ki 13:25 376
but Baal's prophets are 450 **m**. 1Ki 18:22 376
'By the young **m** of the rulers of 1Ki 20:14 5288
mustered the young **m** of the rulers 1Ki 20:15 5288
The young **m** of the rulers of 1Ki 20:17 5288
"**M** have come out from Samaria." 1Ki 20:17 376
the young **m** of the rulers of the 1Ki 20:19 5288
wall fell on 27,000 **m** who were left. 1Ki 20:30 376
Now the **m** took this as an omen, 1Ki 20:33 376
seat two worthless **m** before him, 1Ki 21:10 376
So the **m** of his city, the elders 1Ki 21:11 376
Then the two worthless **m** came in 1Ki 21:13 376
worthless **m** testified against him, 1Ki 21:13 376
together, about four hundred **m**, 1Ki 22:6 376
fifty **m** of the sons of the prophets 2Ki 2:7 376
with your servants fifty strong **m**, 2Ki 2:16 376
They sent therefore fifty **m**; 2Ki 2:17 376
the **m** of the city said to Elisha, 2Ki 2:19 376
with him 700 **m** who drew swords, 2Ki 3:26 376
poured *it* out for the **m** to eat. 2Ki 4:40 376
I set this before a hundred **m**?" 2Ki 4:43 376
just now two young **m** of the sons 2Ki 5:22 5288
the house, and he sent the **m** away, 2Ki 5:24 376
open the eyes of these **m**, that 2Ki 6:20
were four leprous **m** at the entrance 2Ki 7:3 376
let some **m** take five of 2Ki 7:13
their young **m** you will kill with the 2Ki 8:12 970
my voice, take the heads of the **m**, 2Ki 10:6 376
were with the great **m** of the city, 2Ki 10:6 1419
and all his great **m** and his 2Ki 10:11 1419
the pit of Beth-eked, forty-two **m**; 2Ki 10:14 376
for himself eighty **m** outside, 2Ki 10:24 376
"The one who permits any of the **m** 2Ki 10:24 376
And each one of them took his **m** 2Ki 11:9 376
not require an accounting from the **m** 2Ki 12:15 376
from all the mighty **m** of wealth, 2Ki 15:20 1368
were fifty **m** of the Gileadites, 2Ki 15:25 376
The king of Assyria brought **m** 2Ki 17:24
The **m** of Babylon made 2Ki 17:30 376
the **m** of Cuth made Nergal, 2Ki 17:30 376
the **m** of Hamath made Ashima, 2Ki 17:30 376
not to the **m** who sit on the wall, 2Ki 18:27 376
when **m** rose early in the morning, 2Ki 19:35
"What did these **m** say, and from 2Ki 20:14 376
and all the **m** of Judah and all 2Ki 23:2 376
And the **m** of the city told him, 2Ki 23:17 376
and all the mighty **m** of valor, 2Ki 24:14 1368
and the leading **m** of the land, 2Ki 24:15 193b
All the **m** of valor, seven 2Ki 24:16 376
and all the **m** of war *fled* by night 2Ki 25:4 376

who was overseer of the **m** of war, 2Ki 25:19 376
sixty **m** of the people of the land 2Ki 25:19 376
of the forces, they and *their* **m**, 2Ki 25:23 376
the Maacathite, they and their **m**. 2Ki 25:23 376
them and their **m** and said to them, 2Ki 25:24 376
came with ten **m** and struck 2Ki 25:25 376
These are the **m** of Recah. 1Ch 4:12 376
and Jokim, the **m** of Cozeba, Joash, 1Ch 4:22 376
five hundred **m** went to Mount Seir, 1Ch 4:42 376
Manasseh, *consisting* of valiant **m**, 1Ch 5:18 1121
m who bore shield and sword and 1Ch 5:18 376
2,000 donkeys; and 100,000 **m**. 1Ch 5:21
5315, 120
and Jahdiel, mighty **m** of valor, 1Ch 5:24 376
mighty men of valor, famous **m**, 1Ch 5:24 376
m of valor in their generations; 1Ch 7:2 1368
all five of them *were* chief **m**. 1Ch 7:3 7218
Issachar *were* mighty **m** of valor, 1Ch 7:5 1368
households, mighty **m** of valor, 1Ch 7:7 1368
20,200 mighty **m** of valor. 1Ch 7:9 1368
17,200 mighty **m** of valor, 1Ch 7:11 1368
and Ezer and Elead whom the **m** of 1Ch 7:21 376
choice and mighty **m** of valor, 1Ch 7:40 1368
for service in war was 26,000 **m**. 1Ch 7:40 376
to their generations, chief **m** who 1Ch 8:28 7218
of Ulam were mighty **m** of valor, 1Ch 8:40 376
1,760 very able **m** for the work of 1Ch 9:13 1368
to their generations, chief **m**, 1Ch 9:34 7218
and the **m** of Israel fled before 1Ch 10:1 376
When all the **m** of Israel who were 1Ch 10:7 376
all the valiant **m** arose and took 1Ch 10:12 376
of the mighty **m** whom David had, 1Ch 11:10 1368
of the mighty **m** whom David had: 1Ch 11:11 1368
who *was* one of the three mighty **m**. 1Ch 11:12 1368
Now three of the thirty chief **m** 1Ch 11:15 7218
Shall I drink the blood of these **m** 1Ch 11:19 376
things the three mighty **m** did. 1Ch 11:19 1368
as well as the three mighty **m**. 1Ch 11:24 1368
Now the mighty **m** of the armies 1Ch 11:26 1368
mighty **m** who helped *him* in war. 1Ch 12:1 1368
the wilderness, mighty **m** of valor, 1Ch 12:8 1368
men of valor, **m** trained for war, 1Ch 12:8 376
they were all mighty **m** of valor, 1Ch 12:21 1368
For day by day **m** came to David to 1Ch 12:22
Simeon, mighty **m** of valor for war, 1Ch 12:25 1368
Ephraim 20,800, mighty **m** of valor, 1Ch 12:30 1368
m in their fathers' households. 1Ch 12:30 376
m who understood the times, 1Ch 12:32
All these, being **m** of war who 1Ch 12:38 376
killed 22,000 **m** of the Arameans. 1Ch 18:5 376
went and told David about the **m**. 1Ch 19:5 376
for the **m** were greatly humiliated. 1Ch 19:5 376
and all the army, the mighty **m**. 1Ch 19:8 1368
all the choice **m** of Israel 1Ch 19:10
1,100,000 **m** who drew the sword; 1Ch 21:5 376
was 470,000 **m** who drew the sword. 1Ch 21:5 376
70,000 **m** of Israel fell. 1Ch 21:14 376
and all **m** who are skillful in 1Ch 22:15 2450
number by census of **m** was 38,000. 1Ch 23:3 1397
Since more chief **m** were found from 1Ch 24:4 1397
for they were mighty **m** of valor. 1Ch 26:6 1368
and Semachiah, were valiant **m**. 1Ch 26:7 1121
m with strength for the service, 1Ch 26:8 376
sons and relatives, 18 valiant **m**. 1Ch 26:9 1121
of the gatekeepers, the chief **m**, 1Ch 26:12 1397
his relatives, 1,700 capable **m**, 1Ch 26:30 1121
and **m** of outstanding capability 1Ch 26:31 1368
and his relatives, capable **m**, 1Ch 26:32 1121
the officials and the mighty **m**, 1Ch 28:1 1368
men, even all the valiant **m**. 1Ch 28:1 1368
All the officials, the mighty **m**, 1Ch 29:24 1368
assigned 70,000 **m** to carry loads and 2Ch 2:2 376
and 80,000 **m** to quarry *stone* in 2Ch 2:2 376
to *work* with the skilled **m** whom I 2Ch 2:7 2450
him, *to work* with your skilled **m** and 2Ch 2:14 2450
All the **m** of Israel assembled 2Ch 5:3 376
know the hearts of the sons of **m**, 2Ch 6:30 120
they were **m** of war, his chief 2Ch 8:9 376
"How blessed are your **m**, 2Ch 9:7 376
and consulted with the young **m** who 2Ch 10:8 3206
The young **m** who grew up with 2Ch 10:10 3206
to the advice of the young **m**, 2Ch 10:14 3206
chosen **m** who were warriors, 2Ch 11:1
warriors, 400,000 chosen **m**, 2Ch 13:3 376
800,000 chosen **m** *who were* valiant 2Ch 13:3 376
worthless **m** gathered about him, 2Ch 13:7 376
the **m** of Judah raised a war cry, 2Ch 13:15 376
the **m** of Judah raised the war cry, 2Ch 13:15 376
chosen **m** of Israel fell slain. 2Ch 13:17 376
of a million **m** and 300 chariots, 2Ch 14:9
of Judah, and warriors, valiant **m**, 2Ch 17:13 1368
the prophets, four hundred **m**, 2Ch 18:5 376
for the band of **m** who came with 2Ch 22:1
And each one of them took his **m** 2Ch 23:8 376
came with a small number of **m**; 2Ch 24:24 376
found them to be 300,000 choice **m**, 2Ch 25:5
engines *of war* invented by skillful **m** 2Ch 26:15
priests of the LORD, valiant **m**. 2Ch 26:17 1121
120,000 in one day, all valiant **m**, 2Ch 28:6 1121
So the armed **m** left the captives 2Ch 28:14
the **m** who were designated by name 2Ch 28:15 376
Nevertheless some **m** of Asher, 2Ch 30:11 376
there were **m** who were designated 2Ch 31:19 376
The **m** did the work faithfully 2Ch 34:12 376
the LORD and all the **m** of Judah, 2Ch 34:30 376
Chaldeans who slew their young **m** 2Ch 36:17 970
let the **m** of that place support Ezr 1:4 376
of the **m** of the people of Israel: Ezr 2:2 376
the **m** of Bethlehem, 123; Ezr 2:21 1121

the **m** of Netophah, 56;	**Ezr 2:22**	376
the **m** of Anathoth, 128;	**Ezr 2:23**	376
the **m** of Michmas, 122;	**Ezr 2:27**	376
the **m** of Bethel and Ai, 223;	**Ezr 2:28**	376
the **m** of Jericho, 345;	**Ezr 2:34**	1121
they had 200 singing **m** and women.	**Ezr 2:65**	
m who had seen the first temple,	**Ezr 3:12**	2205
the secretaries, the **m** of Erech,	**Ezr 4:9**	756
the Babylonians, the **m** of Susa,	**Ezr 4:9**	7801
the **m** in the region beyond the	**Ezr 4:11**	606
decree to make these **m** stop *work,*	**Ezr 4:21**	1400
what the names of the **m** were	**Ezr 5:4**	1400
write down the names of the **m** who	**Ezr 5:10**	1400
I gathered leading **m** from Israel to	**Ezr 7:28**	7218
and Meshullam, leading **m**,	**Ezr 8:16**	7218
and his sons and brothers, 18 **m**;	**Ezr 8:18**	
his brothers and their sons, 20 **m**;	**Ezr 8:19**	
of God, a very large assembly, **m**,	**Ezr 10:1**	376
So all the **m** of Judah and Benjamin	**Ezr 10:9**	376
And Ezra the priest selected **m** *who*	**Ezr 10:16**	376
the **m** who had married foreign wives	**Ezr 10:17**	376
and some **m** from Judah came;	**Ne 1:2**	376
the night, I and a few **m** with me.	**Ne 2:12**	376
to him the **m** of Jericho built,	**Ne 3:2**	376
the **m** of Gibeon and of Mizpah,	**Ne 3:7**	376
and the house of the mighty **m**.	**Ne 3:16**	1368
the priests, the **m** of the valley,	**Ne 3:22**	376
of his brothers and the wealthy **m**	**Ne 4:2**	
then I stationed **m** in the lowest	**Ne 4:13**	
m of the guard who followed me,	**Ne 4:23**	376
of **m** of the people of Israel:	**Ne 7:7**	376
the **m** of Bethlehem and Netophah,	**Ne 7:26**	376
the **m** of Anathoth, 128;	**Ne 7:27**	376
the **m** of Beth-azmaveth, 42;	**Ne 7:28**	376
the **m** of Kiriath-jearim,	**Ne 7:29**	376
the **m** of Ramah and Geba, 621;	**Ne 7:30**	376
the **m** of Michmas, 122;	**Ne 7:31**	376
the **m** of Bethel and Ai, 123;	**Ne 7:32**	376
the **m** of the other Nebo, 52;	**Ne 7:33**	376
the **m** of Jericho, 345;	**Ne 7:36**	1121
the law before the assembly of **m**,	**Ne 8:2**	376
in the presence of **m** and women,	**Ne 8:3**	376
And the people blessed all the **m**	**Ne 11:2**	376
in Jerusalem were 468 able **m**.	**Ne 11:6**	376
On that day **m** were also appointed	**Ne 12:44**	376
Also **m** of Tyre were living there	**Ne 13:16**	6876
Then the king said to the wise **m**	**Es 1:13**	2450
Then his wise **m** and Zeresh his	**Es 6:13**	2450
been sold as slaves, **m** and women,	**Es 7:4**	
and destroyed five hundred **m**,	**Es 9:6**	376
killed and destroyed five hundred **m**	**Es 9:12**	376
killed three hundred **m** in Susa,	**Es 9:15**	376
greatest of all the **m** of the east.	**Jb 1:3**	1121
night, When deep sleep falls on **m**,	**Jb 4:13**	376
I done to You, O watcher of **m**?	**Jb 7:20**	120
"Shall your boasts silence **m**?	**Jb 11:3**	4962
"For He knows false **m**,	**Jb 11:11**	4962
"Wisdom is with aged **m**,	**Jb 12:12**	3453
What wise **m** have told, And have	**Jb 15:18**	2450
And I am one at whom **m** spit.	**Jb 17:6**	
"Have you not asked wayfaring **m**,	**Jb 21:29**	
M will keep watch over *his*	**Jb 21:32**	
all **m** will follow after him,	**Jb 21:33**	120
cause, And stripped **m** naked.	**Jb 22:6**	
path Which wicked **m** have trod,	**Jb 22:15**	4962
"From the city **m** groan, And the	**Jb 24:12**	4962
"**M** will clap their hands at him	**Jb 27:23**	
and swing to and fro far from **m**.	**Jb 28:4**	582
young **m** saw me and hid themselves,	**Jb 29:8**	5288
And the old **m** arose *and* stood.	**Jb 29:8**	3453
"Have the **m** of my tent not said,	**Jb 31:31**	4962
three **m** ceased answering Job,	**Jb 32:1**	376
answer in the mouth of the three **m**	**Jb 32:5**	376
When sound sleep falls on **m**,	**Jb 33:15**	376
Then He opens the ears of **m**,	**Jb 33:16**	376
"He will sing to **m** and say,	**Jb 33:27**	376
does all these oftentimes with **m**,	**Jb 33:29**	1397
"Hear my words, you wise **m**,	**Jb 34:2**	2450
iniquity, And walks with wicked **m**?	**Jb 34:8**	376
to me, you **m** of understanding.	**Jb 34:10**	376
"He breaks in pieces mighty **m**	**Jb 34:24**	3524
So that godless **m** would not rule	**Jb 34:30**	120
"**M** of understanding will say to	**Jb 34:34**	376
Because he answers like wicked **m**.	**Jb 34:36**	376
Because of the pride of evil **m**.	**Jb 35:12**	7451a
His work, Of which **m** have sung.	**Jb 36:24**	376
"All **m** have seen it;	**Jb 36:25**	120
man, That all **m** may know His work.	**Jb 37:7**	376
"Now **m** do not see the light	**Jb 37:21**	
"Therefore **m** fear Him;	**Jb 37:24**	376
O sons of **m**, how long will my	**Ps 4:2**	376
nations know that they are but **m**.	**Ps 9:20**	582
His eyelids test the sons of **m**.	**Ps 11:4**	120
from among the sons of **m**.	**Ps 12:1**	120
is exalted among the sons of **m**.	**Ps 12:8**	120
from heaven upon the sons of **m** To	**Ps 14:2**	120
As for the deeds of **m**,	**Ps 17:4**	120
From **m** with Your hand, O LORD, From	**Ps 17:14**	4962
hand, O LORD, From **m** of the world,	**Ps 17:14**	4962
from among the sons of **m**.	**Ps 21:10**	120
and not a man, A reproach of **m** and	**Ps 22:6**	120
I do not sit with deceitful **m**,	**Ps 26:4**	4962
Nor my life with **m** of bloodshed,	**Ps 26:9**	376
in You, Before the sons of **m**!	**Ps 31:19**	120
He sees all the sons of **m**;	**Ps 33:13**	120
And the children of **m** take refuge	**Ps 36:7**	120
are fairer than the sons of **m**;	**Ps 45:2**	120
For he sees *that even* wise **m** die;	**Ps 49:10**	2450
himself—And though **m** praise	**Ps 49:18**	
from heaven upon the sons of **m** To	**Ps 53:2**	120
And violent **m** have sought my life;	**Ps 54:3**	6184
M of bloodshed and deceit will not	**Ps 55:23**	376
forth fire, *Even* the sons of **m**,	**Ps 57:4**	120
you judge uprightly, O sons of **m**?	**Ps 58:1**	120
m will say, "Surely there is a reward	**Ps 58:11**	120
And save me from **m** of bloodshed.	**Ps 59:2**	376
m launch an attack against me,	**Ps 59:3**	5794
That **m** may know that God rules in	**Ps 59:13**	
M of low degree are only vanity and	**Ps 62:9**	
		1121, 120
vanity and **m** of rank are a lie;	**Ps 62:9**	
		1121, 376
Then all **m** will fear, And they	**Ps 64:9**	120
hear prayer, To You all **m** come.	**Ps 65:2**	1320
in *His* deeds toward the sons of **m**.	**Ps 66:5**	120
made **m** ride over our heads;	**Ps 66:12**	582
You have received gifts among **m**,	**Ps 68:18**	120
And let **m** bless themselves by	**Ps 72:17**	
are not in trouble *as other* **m**,	**Ps 73:5**	582
M declare Your wondrous works.	**Ps 75:1**	
subdued the choice **m** of Israel.	**Ps 78:31**	977
tent which He had pitched among **m**,	**Ps 78:60**	120
Fire devoured His young **m**,	**Ps 78:63**	970
"Nevertheless you will die like **m** And	**Ps 82:7**	120
m have risen up against me,	**Ps 86:14**	2086
of violent **m** have sought my life,	**Ps 86:14**	6184
have created all the sons of **m**!	**Ps 89:47**	120
"Return, O children of **m**."	**Ps 90:3**	120
That **m** may tell of the name of	**Ps 102:21**	
they were only a few **m** in number,	**Ps 105:12**	4962
for His wonders to the sons of **m**!	**Ps 107:8**	120
for His wonders to the sons of **m**!	**Ps 107:15**	120
for His wonders to the sons of **m**!	**Ps 107:21**	120
for His wonders to the sons of **m**!	**Ps 107:31**	120
the chief **m** over a broad country.	**Ps 110:6**	7218
He has given to the sons of **m**.	**Ps 115:16**	120
"All **m** are liars."	**Ps 116:11**	120
M who are not in accord with Your	**Ps 119:85**	
side When **m** rose up against us	**Ps 124:2**	120
me, therefore, **m** of bloodshed.	**Ps 139:19**	376
Rescue me, O LORD, from evil **m**;	**Ps 140:1**	376
Preserve me from violent **m**	**Ps 140:1**	120
Preserve me from violent **m** Who	**Ps 140:4**	376
wickedness With **m** who do iniquity;	**Ps 141:4**	376
M shall speak of the power of Your	**Ps 145:6**	
to the sons of **m** Your mighty acts And	**Ps 145:12**	120
Both young **m** and virgins;	**Ps 148:12**	970
Old **m** and children.	**Ps 148:12**	2205
will walk in the way of good **m** And	**Pr 2:20**	2896a
not proceed in the way of evil **m**.	**Pr 4:14**	7451a
M do not despise a thief if he	**Pr 6:30**	
"To you, O **m**, I call, And my	**Pr 8:4**	376
And my voice is to the sons of **m**.	**Pr 8:4**	120
my delight in the sons of **m**.	**Pr 8:31**	120
Wise **m** store up knowledge, But	**Pr 10:14**	2450
And the hope of strong **m** perishes.	**Pr 11:7**	202
And ruthless **m** attain riches.	**Pr 11:16**	6184
desires the booty of evil **m**,	**Pr 12:12**	7451a
He who walks with wise **m** will be	**Pr 13:20**	2450
How much more the hearts of **m**!	**Pr 15:11**	
		1121, 120
are the crown of old **m**,	**Pr 17:6**	2205
And brings him before great **m**.	**Pr 18:16**	1419
glory of young **m** is their strength,	**Pr 20:29**	970
honor of old **m** is their gray hair.	**Pr 20:29**	2205
will not stand before obscure **m**.	**Pr 22:29**	2823
increases the faithless among **m**.	**Pr 23:28**	120
Do not be envious of evil **m**,	**Pr 24:1**	376
evil, **M** will call a schemer.	**Pr 24:8**	
scoffer is an abomination to **m**.	**Pr 24:9**	120
the **m** of Hezekiah, king of Judah,	**Pr 25:1**	376
not stand in the place of great **m**;	**Pr 25:6**	1419
wiser in his own eyes Than seven **m**	**Pr 26:16**	
Evil **m** do not understand justice,	**Pr 28:5**	376
wicked rise, **m** hide themselves.	**Pr 28:12**	120
wicked rise, **m** hide themselves;	**Pr 28:28**	120
But wise **m** turn away anger.	**Pr 29:8**	2450
M of bloodshed hate the blameless,	**Pr 29:10**	376
earth And the needy from among **m**.	**Pr 30:14**	120
sons of **m** to be afflicted with.	**Ec 1:13**	120
good there is for the sons of **m** to do	**Ec 2:3**	120
female singers and the pleasures of **m**	**Ec 2:8**	1121, 120
which God has given the sons of **m**	**Ec 3:10**	120
so worked that **m** should fear Him.	**Ec 3:14**	
myself concerning the sons of **m**,	**Ec 3:18**	120
For the fate of the sons of **m** and	**Ec 3:19**	120
sun and it is prevalent among **m**	**Ec 6:1**	120
this, that God made **m** upright,	**Ec 7:29**	120
hearts of the sons of **m** among them	**Ec 8:11**	120
there are righteous **m** to whom it	**Ec 8:14**	6662
there are evil **m** to whom it	**Ec 8:14**	7563
and explain it that righteous **m**,	**Ec 9:1**	6662
it that righteous men, wise **m**,	**Ec 9:1**	2450
that there is one fate for all **m**.	**Ec 9:3**	3605
of the sons of **m** are full of evil and	**Ec 9:3**	120
nor favor to **m** of ability;	**Ec 9:11**	
so the sons of **m** are ensnared at	**Ec 9:12**	120
There was a small city with few **m**	**Ec 9:14**	376
while rich **m** sit in humble places.	**Ec 10:6**	6223
M prepare a meal for enjoyment,	**Ec 10:19**	
house tremble, and mighty **m** stoop,	**Ec 12:3**	376
m are afraid of a high place and	**Ec 12:5**	
words of wise **m** are like goads,	**Ec 12:11**	2450
is my beloved among the young **m**.	**SS 2:3**	1121
Sixty mighty **m** around it, Of the	**SS 3:7**	1368
it, Of the mighty **m** of Israel.	**SS 3:7**	1368
the round shields of the mighty **m**.	**SS 4:4**	1368
the loftiness of **m** will be abased;	**Is 2:17**	376
M will go into caves of the rocks	**Is 2:19**	
In that day **m** will cast away to	**Is 2:20**	120
Your **m** will fall by the sword And	**Is 3:25**	4962
of Jerusalem and **m** of Judah,	**Is 5:3**	376
m of Judah His delightful plant.	**Is 5:7**	376
their honorable **m** are famished,	**Is 5:13**	4962
valiant **m** in mixing strong drink,	**Is 5:22**	376
"The LORD has removed **m** far away,	**Is 6:12**	120
for you to try the patience of **m**,	**Is 7:13**	376
As **m** rejoice when they divide the	**Is 9:3**	
take pleasure in their young **m**,	**Is 9:17**	970
it into seven streams And make **m**	**Is 11:15**	
bows will mow down the young **m**,	**Is 13:18**	5288
the armed **m** of Moab cry aloud;	**Is 15:4**	
How can you **m** say to Pharaoh,	**Is 19:11**	
Well then, where are your wise **m**?	**Is 19:12**	2450
the mighty **m** of the sons of Kedar,	**Is 21:17**	1368
I have neither brought up young **m**	**Is 23:4**	970
are burned, and few **m** are left.	**Is 24:6**	582
wisdom of their wise **m** will perish,	**Is 29:14**	2450
discerning **m** will be concealed.	**Is 29:14**	
Now the Egyptians are **m** and	**Is 31:3**	120
m will become forced laborers.	**Is 31:8**	970
rushing about **m** rush about on it.	**Is 33:4**	
their brave **m** cry in the streets,	**Is 33:7**	691
not to the **m** who sit on the wall,	**Is 36:12**	376
when **m** arose early in the morning,	**Is 37:36**	
"O Lord, by *these* things **m**	**Is 38:16**	
"What did these **m** say, and from	**Is 39:3**	376
vigorous young **m** stumble badly,	**Is 40:30**	970
you worm Jacob, you **m** of Israel;	**Is 41:14**	4962
I will give *other* **m** in your place	**Is 43:4**	120
craftsmen themselves are mere **m**.	**Is 44:11**	120
Causing wise **m** to draw back And	**Is 44:25**	2450
That **m** may know from the rising to	**Is 45:6**	
And the Sabeans, **m** of stature,	**Is 45:14**	376
M will come to Him,	**Is 45:24**	
His form more than the sons of **m**.	**Is 52:14**	120
He was despised and forsaken of **m**,	**Is 53:3**	376
one from whom **m** hide their face He	**Is 53:3**	
grave was assigned with wicked **m**,	**Is 53:9**	7563
And devout **m** are taken away, while	**Is 57:1**	376
grope along the wall like blind **m**,	**Is 59:10**	5787
are vigorous *we are* like dead **m**.	**Is 59:10**	
So that **m** may bring to you	**Is 60:11**	
and look On the corpses of the **m**	**Is 66:24**	376
"Also the **m** of Memphis and	**Jer 2:16**	1121
the **m** of Judah and to Jerusalem,	**Jer 4:3**	376
M of Judah and inhabitants of	**Jer 4:4**	376
grave, All of them are mighty **m**.	**Jer 5:16**	1368
m are found among My people,	**Jer 5:26**	7563
They set a trap, They catch **m**.	**Jer 5:26**	376
the gathering of young **m** together;	**Jer 6:11**	970
"Do **m** fall and not get up	**Jer 8:4**	
"The wise **m** are put to shame,	**Jer 8:9**	2450
An assembly of treacherous **m**.	**Jer 9:2**	
The young **m** from the town squares.	**Jer 9:21**	970
'The corpses of **m** will fall like	**Jer 9:22**	120
all the wise **m** of the nations And	**Jer 10:7**	2450
are all the work of skilled **m**.	**Jer 10:9**	2450
and speak to the **m** of Judah and to	**Jer 11:2**	376
been found among the **m** of Judah	**Jer 11:9**	376
LORD concerning the **m** of Anathoth,	**Jer 11:21**	376
The young **m** will die by the sword,	**Jer 11:22**	970
bring disaster on the **m** of Anathoth	**Jer 11:23**	376
Because **m** have said, "He will	**Jer 12:4**	
lent, nor have **m** lent money to me,	**Jer 15:10**	
"Both great **m** and small will die	**Jer 16:6**	1419
"**M** will not break *bread* in	**Jer 16:7**	
and their princes, the **m** of Judah and	**Jer 17:25**	376
speak to the **m** of Judah and	**Jer 18:11**	376
their **m** also be smitten to death,	**Jer 18:21**	376
Their young **m** struck down by the	**Jer 18:21**	970
sight of the **m** who accompany you	**Jer 19:10**	376
"You **m** who say, 'Who will come	**Jer 21:13**	
"For if you **m** will indeed perform	**Jer 22:4**	
King Jehoiakim and all his mighty **m**	**Jer 26:21**	1368
King Jehoiakim sent **m** to Egypt:	**Jer 26:22**	376
m with him *went* into Egypt.	**Jer 26:22**	376
the **m** and the beasts which are on	**Jer 27:5**	120
And the young **m** and the old,	**Jer 31:13**	970
to all the ways of the sons of **m**,	**Jer 32:19**	120
their prophets, the **m** of Judah and	**Jer 32:32**	376
'**M** will buy fields for money,	**Jer 32:44**	
the corpses of **m** whom I have slain	**Jer 33:5**	120
'I will give the **m** who have	**Jer 34:18**	376
Then I set before the **m** of the	**Jer 35:5**	1121
'Go and say to the **m** of Judah and	**Jer 35:13**	376
and the **m** of Judah all the calamity	**Jer 36:31**	376
only wounded **m** left among them,	**Jer 37:10**	376
he is discouraging the **m** of war	**Jer 38:4**	376
these **m** have acted wickedly in all	**Jer 38:9**	376
"Take thirty **m** from here under	**Jer 38:10**	376
So Ebed-melech took the **m** under	**Jer 38:11**	376
m who are seeking your life."	**Jer 38:16**	376
and all the **m** of war saw them,	**Jer 39:4**	376
the hand of the **m** whom you dread.	**Jer 39:17**	376
in the field, they and their **m**,	**Jer 40:7**	376
he had put him in charge of the **m**,	**Jer 40:7**	376
Maacathite, *both* they and their **m**.	**Jer 40:8**	376
swore to them and to their **m**,	**Jer 40:9**	376
of the king, along with ten **m**,	**Jer 41:1**	376
the ten **m** who were with him arose	**Jer 41:2**	376
were found there, the **m** of war.	**Jer 41:3**	376
that eighty **m** came from Shechem,	**Jer 41:5**	376
the **m** that were with him slaughtered	**Jer 41:7**	376
But ten **m** who were found among	**Jer 41:8**	376
corpses of the **m** whom he had struck	**Jer 41:9**	376
So they took all the **m** and went to	**Jer 41:12**	376

m and went to the sons of Ammon.	Jer 41:15	376
that is, the **m** who were soldiers,	Jer 41:16	376
"So all the **m** who set their mind	Jer 42:17	376
the arrogant **m** said to Jeremiah,	Jer 43:2	376
the **m**, the women, the children,	Jer 43:6	1397
Then all the **m** who were aware that	Jer 44:15	376
to all the people, to the **m** and women	Jer 44:20	1397
and all the **m** of Judah who are in	Jer 44:27	376
And their mighty **m** are defeated	Jer 46:5	1368
the mighty **m** may march forward:	Jer 46:9	1368
And the **m** will cry out, And every	Jer 47:2	120
And **m** valiant for battle'?	Jer 48:14	376
and **m** have gone up to his cities;	Jer 48:15	376
His choicest young **m** have also	Jer 48:15	970
I will moan for the **m** of Kir-heres.	Jer 48:31	376
like flutes for the **m** of Kir-heres.	Jer 48:36	376
So the hearts of the mighty **m** of	Jer 48:41	1368
the nations, Despised among **m**.	Jer 49:15	120
the hearts of the mighty **m** of Edom	Jer 49:22	1368
young **m** will fall in her streets,	Jer 49:26	970
all the **m** of war will be silenced in	Jer 49:26	376
And devastate the **m** of the east.	Jer 49:28	1121
young **m** will fall in her streets,	Jer 50:30	970
all her **m** of war will be silenced in	Jer 50:30	376
her officials and her wise **m**!	Jer 50:35	2450
A sword against her mighty **m**,	Jer 50:36	1368
So do not spare her young **m**;	Jer 51:3	970
sentries, Place **m** in ambush!	Jer 51:12	
The mighty **m** of Babylon have	Jer 51:30	1368
And the **m** of war are terrified.	Jer 51:32	376
And her mighty **m** will be captured,	Jer 51:56	1368
her princes and her wise **m** drunk,	Jer 51:57	2450
her prefects and her mighty **m**,	Jer 51:57	1368
and all the **m** of war fled and went	Jer 52:7	376
who was overseer of the **m** of war,	Jer 52:25	376
and sixty **m** of the people of the	Jer 52:25	376
Lord has rejected all my strong **m**	La 1:15	47
against me To crush my young **m**;	La 1:15	970
young **m** Have gone into captivity.	La 1:18	970
young **m** Have fallen by the sword.	La 2:21	970
Or grieve the sons of **m**.	La 3:33	376
M among the nations said, "They	La 4:15	
m worked at the grinding mill,	La 5:13	970
gate, Young **m** from their music.	La 5:14	970
were about twenty-five **m** with	Ezk 8:16	376
six **m** came from the direction of	Ezk 9:2	376
put a mark on the foreheads of the **m**	Ezk 9:4	376
"Utterly slay old **m**,	Ezk 9:6	2205
"Utterly slay old men, young **m**,	Ezk 9:6	970
m at the entrance of the gate,	Ezk 11:1	376
these are the **m** who devise iniquity	Ezk 11:2	376
these **m** have set up their idols in	Ezk 14:3	376
even *though* these three **m**,	Ezk 14:14	376
these three **m** were in its midst,	Ezk 14:16	376
these three **m** were in its midst,	Ezk 14:18	376
or can **m** take a peg from it on	Ezk 15:3	
"**M** give gifts to all harlots, but	Ezk 16:33	
All the choice **m** in all his troops	Ezk 17:21	4005
He devoured **m**.	Ezk 19:3	120
He devoured **m**.	Ezk 19:6	120
you into the hand of brutal **m**,	Ezk 21:31	376
"Slanderous **m** have been in you	Ezk 22:9	376
all of them desirable young **m**,	Ezk 23:6	970
were the choicest **m** of Assyria;	Ezk 23:7	1121
in her youth **m** had lain with her,	Ezk 23:8	
all of them desirable young **m**.	Ezk 23:12	970
she saw **m** portrayed on the wall,	Ezk 23:14	376
desirable young **m**, governors and	Ezk 23:23	970
of them, officers and **m** of renown,	Ezk 23:23	7121
sent for **m** who come from afar,	Ezk 23:40	376
with **m** of the common sort.	Ezk 23:42	376
they, righteous **m**, will judge them	Ezk 23:45	376
and do not eat the bread of **m**."	Ezk 24:17	376
you will not eat the bread of **m**.	Ezk 24:22	376
m enter a city that is breached.	Ezk 26:10	
Your wise **m**, O Tyre, were aboard;	Ezk 27:8	2450
"The elders of Gebal and her wise **m**	Ezk 27:9	2450
were in your army, your **m** of war.	Ezk 27:10	376
with the lives of **m** and vessels of	Ezk 27:13	120
all your **m** of war who are in you,	Ezk 27:27	376
the land into the hands of evil **m**.	Ezk 30:12	7451a
"The young **m** of On and of	Ezk 30:17	970
beneath, among the sons of **m**,	Ezk 31:14	120
you are **m**, and I am your God,"	Ezk 34:31	120
'I will multiply **m** on you,	Ezk 36:10	120
I will cause **m**—My people Israel	Ezk 36:12	120
"You are a devourer of **m** and have	Ezk 36:13	120
you will no longer devour **m** and	Ezk 36:14	120
increase their **m** like a flock.	Ezk 36:37	120
cities be filled with flocks of **m**.	Ezk 36:38	120
and all the **m** who are on the face	Ezk 38:20	120
"They will set apart **m** who	Ezk 39:14	376
will eat the flesh of mighty **m**	Ezk 39:18	1368
mighty **m** and all the men of war,"	Ezk 39:20	1368
mighty men and all the **m** of war,"	Ezk 39:20	376
destroy all the wise **m** of Babylon.	Da 2:12	2445
that the wise **m** should be slain;	Da 2:13	2445
to slay the wise **m** of Babylon;	Da 2:14	2445
the rest of the wise **m** of Babylon.	Da 2:18	2445
He gives wisdom to wise **m** And	Da 2:21	2445
knowledge to **m** of understanding.	Da 2:21	
to destroy the wise **m** of Babylon;	Da 2:24	2445
not destroy the wise **m** of Babylon!	Da 2:24	2445
king has inquired, neither wise **m**,	Da 2:27	2445
and wherever the sons of **m** dwell,	Da 2:38	606
with one another in the seed of **m**;	Da 2:43	606
over all the wise **m** of Babylon.	Da 2:48	2445
nations and **m** *of every* language,	Da 3:4	
nations and **m** *of every* language	Da 3:7	
These **m**, O king, have disregarded	Da 3:12	1400
m were brought before the king.	Da 3:13	1400
Then these **m** were tied up in their	Da 3:21	1400
those **m** who carried up Shadrach,	Da 3:22	1400
But these three **m**, Shadrach,	Da 3:23	1400
"Was it not three **m** we cast bound	Da 3:24	1400
I see four **m** loosed *and* walking	Da 3:25	1400
saw in regard to these **m** that the fire	Da 3:27	1400
no effect on the bodies of these **m**	Da 3:27	1400
and **m** *of every* language that live	Da 4:1	
all the wise **m** of Babylon,	Da 4:6	2445
sets over it the lowliest of **m**."	Da 4:17	606
none of the wise **m** of my kingdom	Da 4:18	2445
and said to the wise **m** of Babylon,	Da 5:7	2445
Then all the king's wise **m** came in,	Da 5:8	2445
the wise **m** *and* the conjurers were	Da 5:15	2445
nations and **m** *of every* language	Da 5:19	
Then these **m** said,	Da 6:5	1400
Then these **m** came by agreement and	Da 6:11	1400
Then these **m** came by agreement to	Da 6:15	1400
and they brought those **m** who had	Da 6:24	1400
nations and **m** *of every* language	Da 6:25	
m are to fear and tremble before the	Da 6:26	
nations and **m** *of every* language	Da 7:14	
mighty **m** and the holy people.	Da 8:24	6099
to the **m** of Judah, the inhabitants of	Da 9:7	376
while the **m** who were with me did	Da 10:7	376
For *the* **m** themselves go apart	Hos 4:14	
m who sacrifice kiss the calves!"	Hos 13:2	120
dries up From the sons of **m**.	Jl 1:12	120
They run like mighty **m**,	Jl 2:7	1368
Your old **m** will dream dreams,	Jl 2:28	2205
Your young **m** will see visions.	Jl 2:28	970
rouse the mighty **m**!	Jl 3:9	1368
of your young **m** to be Nazirites.	Am 2:11	970
Do two **m** walk together unless they	Am 3:3	
I slew your young **m** by the sword	Am 4:10	970
m of the foremost of nations,	Am 6:1	
if ten **m** are left in one house,	Am 6:9	376
young **m** will faint from thirst.	Am 8:13	970
"All the **m** allied with you Will	Ob 1:7	376
And the **m** at peace with you Will	Ob 1:7	376
"Destroy wise **m** from Edom And	Ob 1:8	2450
your mighty **m** will be dismayed,	Ob 1:9	1368
the **m** became extremely frightened	Jon 1:10	376
For the **m** knew that he was fleeing	Jon 1:10	376
the **m** rowed *desperately* to return	Jon 1:13	376
the **m** feared the LORD greatly,	Jon 1:16	376
and let **m** call on God earnestly	Jon 3:8	
pasture They will be noisy with **m**.	Mi 2:12	120
shepherds and eight leaders of **m**.	Mi 5:5	120
man Or delay for the sons of **m**.	Mi 5:7	120
"For the rich **m** of *the* city are	Mi 6:12	6223
is no upright *person* among **m**.	Mi 7:2	120
are the **m** of his own household.	Mi 7:6	376
shields of his mighty **m** are *colored*	Na 2:3	1368
cast lots for her honorable **m**,	Na 3:10	
great **m** were bound with fetters.	Na 3:10	1419
made **m** like the fish of the sea,	Hab 1:14	120
the **m** Who are stagnant in spirit,	Zph 1:12	376
I will bring distress on **m** So	Zph 1:17	120
are reckless, treacherous **m**;	Zph 3:4	376
on what the ground produces, on **m**,	Hg 1:11	120
multitude of **m** and cattle within it.	Zch 2:4	120
they are **m** who are a symbol,	Zch 3:8	376
m to seek the favor of the LORD,	Zch 7:2	376
'Old **m** and old women will again	Zch 8:4	2205
I set all **m** one against another.	Zch 8:10	120
ten **m** from all the nations will grasp	Zch 8:23	376
resting place (for the eyes of **m**,	Zch 9:1	120
will make the young **m** flourish,	Zch 9:17	970
"They will be as mighty **m**,	Zch 10:5	1368
I will cause the **m** to fall,	Zch 11:6	120
and **m** will call them the wicked	Mal 1:4	
and **m** should seek instruction from	Mal 2:7	
I will make you fishers of **m**."	Mt 4:19	*444*
out and trampled under foot by **m**.	Mt 5:13	*444*
"Let your light shine before **m** in	Mt 5:16	*444*
before **m** to be noticed by them;	Mt 6:1	*444*
that they may be honored by **m**.	Mt 6:2	*444*
corners so that they may be seen by **m**.	Mt 6:5	*444*
noticed by **m** when they are fasting.	Mt 6:16	*444*
your fasting will not be noticed by **m**,	Mt 6:18	*444*
afraid, you **m** of little faith?"	Mt 8:26	*3640b*
The **m** were amazed, and said,	Mt 8:27	*444*
two **m** who were demon-possessed met	Mt 8:28	
who had given such authority to **m**.	Mt 9:8	*444*
there, two blind **m** followed Him,	Mt 9:27	*5185*
house, the blind **m** came up to Him,	Mt 9:28	*5185*
beware of **m**, for they will hand	Mt 10:17	*444*
who confesses Me before **m**,	Mt 10:32	*444*
whoever denies Me before **m**,	Mt 10:33	*444*
As these **m** were going *away,*	Mt 11:7	
and violent **m** take it by force.	Mt 11:12	*973*
"The **m** of Nineveh will stand up	Mt 12:41	*435*
m desired to see what you see,	Mt 13:17	*1342*
"But while his **m** were sleeping, his	Mt 13:25	*444*
about five thousand **m** who ate,	Mt 14:21	*435*
m of that place recognized Him,	Mt 14:35	*435*
DOCTRINES THE PRECEPTS OF **M**.' "	Mt 15:9	*444*
who ate were four thousand **m**,	Mt 15:38	*435*
"You **m** of little faith, why do	Mt 16:8	*3640b*
be delivered into the hands of **m**;	Mt 17:22	*444*
Not all **m** *can* accept this statement,	Mt 19:11	*3956*
who were made eunuchs by **m**;	Mt 19:12	*444*
last **m** have worked *only* one hour,	Mt 20:12	*2078*
m exercise authority over them.	Mt 20:25	*3173*
two blind **m** sitting by the road,	Mt 20:30	*5185*
source, from heaven or from **m**?"	Mt 21:25	*444*
'From **m**,' we fear the people;	Mt 21:26	*444*
their deeds to be noticed by **m**;	Mt 23:5	*444*
places, and being called Rabbi by **m**	Mt 23:7	*444*
"You fools and blind **m**!	Mt 23:17	*5185*
"You blind **m**, which is more	Mt 23:19	*5185*
outwardly appear righteous to **m**,	Mt 23:28	*444*
prophets and wise **m** and scribes;	Mt 23:34	*4680*
there will be two **m** in the field;	Mt 24:40	*1417*
you **m** could not keep watch with	Mt 26:40	
m are testifying against You?"	Mt 26:62	*3778*
of him and became like dead **m**.	Mt 28:4	*3498*
make you become fishers of **m**."	Mk 1:17	*444*
a paralytic, carried by four **m**.	Mk 2:3	*5064*
shall be forgiven the sons of **m**,	Mk 3:28	*444*
They went out and preached that **m**	Mk 6:12	
and the leading **m** of Galilee;	Mk 6:21	*4413*
thousand **m** who ate the loaves.	Mk 6:44	*435*
AS DOCTRINES THE PRECEPTS OF **M**.'	Mk 7:7	*444*
you hold to the tradition of **m**."	Mk 7:8	*444*
within, out of the heart of **m**,	Mk 7:21	*444*
"I see **m**, for I see *them*	Mk 8:24	*444*
be delivered into the hands of **m**,	Mk 9:31	*444*
m exercise authority over them.	Mk 10:42	*3173*
of John from heaven, or from **m**?	Mk 11:30	*444*
"But shall we say, 'From **m**'?"	Mk 11:32	*444*
m are testifying against You?"	Mk 14:60	*3778*
take away my disgrace among **m**."	Lk 1:25	*444*
among **m** with whom He is pleased."	Lk 2:14	*444*
and in favor with God and **m**.	Lk 2:52	*444*
now on you will be catching **m**."	Lk 5:10	*444*
some **m** *were* carrying on a bed a	Lk 5:18	*435*
"Blessed are you when **m** hate you,	Lk 6:22	*444*
you when all **m** speak well of you,	Lk 6:26	*444*
is kind to ungrateful and evil **m**.	Lk 6:35	
For **m** do not gather figs from	Lk 6:44	
When the **m** came to Him,	Lk 7:20	*435*
compare the **m** of this generation,	Lk 7:31	*444*
there were about five thousand **m**.)	Lk 9:14	*435*
two **m** were talking with Him;	Lk 9:30	*435*
and the two **m** standing with Him.	Lk 9:32	*435*
delivered into the hands of **m**."	Lk 9:44	*444*
rise up with the **m** of this generation	Lk 11:31	*435*
"The **m** of Nineveh will stand up	Lk 11:32	*435*
For you weigh **m** down with burdens	Lk 11:46	*444*
who confesses Me before **m**,	Lk 12:8	*444*
but he who denies Me before **m**	Lk 12:9	*444*
clothe you? You **m** of little faith!	Lk 12:28	*3640b*
"Be like **m** who are waiting	Lk 12:36	*444*
beat the slaves, *both* **m** and women,	Lk 12:45	*3816*
all the **m** who live in Jerusalem?	Lk 13:4	*444*
none of those **m** who were invited	Lk 14:24	*435*
strong enough with ten thousand **m**	Lk 14:31	
m have more than enough bread,	Lk 15:17	*3407*
me as one of your hired **m**."	Lk 15:19	*3407*
yourselves in the sight of **m**,	Lk 16:15	*444*
which is highly esteemed among **m**	Lk 16:15	*444*
ten leprous **m** who stood at a	Lk 17:12	*435*
"Two **m** will be in the field;	Lk 17:36	*1417*
"Two **m** went up into the temple to	Lk 18:10	*444*
and the leading **m** among the people	Lk 19:47	*4413*
of John from heaven or from **m**?"	Lk 20:4	*444*
if we say, 'From **m**,' all the people	Lk 20:6	*444*
m fainting from fear and the	Lk 21:26	*444*
Now the **m** who were holding Jesus	Lk 22:63	*435*
two **m** suddenly stood near them in	Lk 24:4	*435*
the **m** said to them, "Why do you	Lk 24:5	
into the hands of sinful **m**,	Lk 24:7	*444*
"O foolish **m** and slow of heart to	Lk 24:25	*453*
and the life was the Light of **m**.	Jn 1:4	*444*
to them, for He knew all **m**,	Jn 2:24	*3956*
and **m** loved the darkness rather	Jn 3:19	*444*
place where **m** ought to worship."	Jn 4:20	
into the city and said to the **m**,	Jn 4:28	*444*
"I do not receive glory from **m**;	Jn 5:41	*444*
So the **m** sat down, in number about	Jn 6:10	*435*
the testimony of two **m** is true.	Jn 8:17	*444*
this, all **m** will believe in Him,	Jn 11:48	*3956*
will draw all **m** to Myself."	Jn 12:32	*3956*
for they loved the approval of **m**	Jn 12:43	*444*
"By this all **m** will know that you	Jn 13:35	*3956*
"I have manifested Your name to the **m**	Jn 17:6	*444*
Him, and with Him two other **m**,	Jn 19:18	*243*
two **m** in white clothing stood	Ac 1:10	*435*
"**M** of Galilee, why do you stand	Ac 1:11	*435*
the **m** who have accompanied us	Ac 1:21	*435*
So they put forward two **m**,	Ac 1:23	*1417*
who know the hearts of all **m**,	Ac 1:24	*3956*
living in Jerusalem, devout **m** from	Ac 2:5	*435*
"**M** of Judea and all you who live	Ac 2:14	*435*
"For these **m** are not drunk, as	Ac 2:15	*3778*
YOUR YOUNG **M** SHALL SEE VISIONS,	Ac 2:17	*3495*
YOUR OLD **M** SHALL DREAM DREAMS;	Ac 2:17	*4245*
BONDSLAVES, BOTH **M** AND WOMEN,	Ac 2:18	*1401*
"**M** of Israel, listen to these	Ac 2:22	*435*
of godless **m** and put *Him* to death.	Ac 2:23	*459*
"**M** of Israel, why are you amazed	Ac 3:12	*435*
and the number of the **m** came to be	Ac 4:4	*435*
that has been given among **m** by	Ac 4:12	*444*
were uneducated and untrained **m**,	Ac 4:13	*444*
"What shall we do with these **m**?	Ac 4:16	*444*
You have not lied to **m** but	Ac 5:4	*444*
young **m** got up and covered him up,	Ac 5:6	*3501b*
m came in and found her dead,	Ac 5:10	*3495*
Lord, multitudes of **m** and women,	Ac 5:14	*435*
The **m** whom you put in prison are	Ac 5:25	*435*
"We must obey God rather than **m**.	Ac 5:29	*444*
gave orders to put the **m** outside for	Ac 5:34	*444*
"**M** of Israel, take care what you	Ac 5:35	*435*
you propose to do with these **m**.	Ac 5:35	*444*

four hundred **m** joined up with him. **Ac 5:36** *435*
stay away from these **m** and let **Ac 5:38** *444*
plan or action is of **m**, **Ac 5:38** *444*
seven **m** of good reputation, **Ac 6:3** *435*
But some **m** from what was called **Ac 6:9** *5100*
they secretly induced **m** to say, **Ac 6:11** *435*
'**M**, you are brethren, why do you **Ac 7:26** *435*
"You **m** who are stiff-necked and **Ac 7:51** *435*
Some devout **m** buried Stephen, **Ac 8:2** *435*
and dragging off **m** and women, **Ac 8:3** *435*
being baptized, **m** and women alike. **Ac 8:12** *435*
to the Way, both **m** and women, **Ac 9:2** *435*
The **m** who traveled with him **Ac 9:7** *435*
was there, sent two **m** to him, **Ac 9:38** *435*
"Now dispatch *some* **m** to Joppa and **Ac 10:5** *435*
the **m** who had been sent by **Ac 10:17** *435*
three **m** are looking for you. **Ac 10:19** *435*
Peter went down to the **m** and said, **Ac 10:21** *435*
"You went to uncircumcised **m** and **Ac 11:3** *435*
at that moment three **m** appeared **Ac 11:11** *435*
of them, **m** of Cyprus and Cyrene, **Ac 11:20** *435*
"**M** of Israel, and you who fear **Ac 13:16** *435*
and the leading **m** of the city, **Ac 13:50** *4413*
like **m** and have come down to us." **Ac 14:11** *444*
"**M**, why are you doing these **Ac 14:15** *435*
also **m** of the same nature as you, **Ac 14:15** *444*
Some **m** came down from Judea **Ac 15:1** *5100*
to choose **m** from among them to **Ac 15:22** *435*
leading **m** among the brethren, **Ac 15:22** *435*
to select **m** to send to you with **Ac 15:25** *435*
m who have risked their lives for **Ac 15:26** *444*
"These **m** are bond-servants of the **Ac 16:17** *444*
"These **m** are throwing our city **Ac 16:20** *444*
"Release those **m**." **Ac 16:35** *444*
without trial, **m** who are Romans, **Ac 16:37** *444*
wicked **m** from the market place, **Ac 17:5** *435*
"These **m** who have upset the world **Ac 17:6** *3778*
of prominent Greek women and **m**. **Ac 17:12** *435*
"**M** of Athens, I observe that you **Ac 17:22** *435*
God is now declaring to **m** that all **Ac 17:30** *444*
furnished proof to all **m** by raising **Ac 17:31** *3956*
some **m** joined him and believed, **Ac 17:34** *435*
"This man persuades **m** to worship **Ac 18:13** *444*
There were in all about twelve **m**. **Ac 19:7** *435*
"**M**, you know that our prosperity **Ac 19:25** *435*
"**M** of Ephesus, what man is there **Ac 19:35** *435*
"For you have brought these **m** **Ac 19:37** *435*
am innocent of the blood of all **m**. **Ac 20:26** *3956*
your own selves **m** will arise, **Ac 20:30** *435*
and to the **m** who were with me. **Ac 20:34**
have four **m** who are under a vow; **Ac 21:23** *435*
Then Paul took the **m**, **Ac 21:26** *435*
"**M** of Israel, come to our aid! **Ac 21:28** *435*
m everywhere against our people and **Ac 21:28** *3956*
the four thousand **m** of the Assassins **Ac 21:38** *435*
both **m** and women into prisons, **Ac 22:4** *435*
will be a witness for Him to all **m** **Ac 22:15** *444*
which these **m** cherish themselves, **Ac 24:15** *3778*
both before God and before **m**. **Ac 24:16** *444*
"Or else let these **m** themselves **Ac 24:20** *3778*
m of the Jews brought charges **Ac 25:2** *4413*
m among you go there with me, **Ac 25:5** *1415*
true of which these **m** accuse me, **Ac 25:11** *3778*
and the prominent **m** of the city, **Ac 25:23** *435*
"**M**, I perceive that the voyage **Ac 27:10** *435*
"**M**, you ought to have followed my **Ac 27:21** *435*
keep up your courage, **m**, **Ac 27:25** *435*
"Unless these **m** remain in the **Ac 27:31** *3778*
were the leading **m** of the Jews, **Ac 28:17** *4413*
and unrighteousness of **m** who **Ro 1:18** *444*
m abandoned the natural function **Ro 1:27** *733b*
m with **m** committing indecent **Ro 1:27** *733b*
men with **m** committing indecent **Ro 1:27** *733b*
God will judge the secrets of **m** **Ro 2:16** *444*
and his praise is not from **m**, **Ro 2:29** *444*
sin, and so death spread to all **m**, **Ro 5:12** *444*
resulted condemnation to all **m**, **Ro 5:18** *444*
justification of life to all **m**. **Ro 5:18** *444*
KEPT for Myself SEVEN THOUSAND M **Ro 11:4** *435*
is right in the sight of all **m**. **Ro 12:17** *444*
on you, be at peace with all **m**. **Ro 12:18** *444*
to God and approved by **m**. **Ro 14:18** *444*
For such **m** are slaves, not of our **Ro 16:18** *5108*
foolishness of God is wiser than **m**, **1Co 1:25** *444*
weakness of God is stronger than **m**. **1Co 1:25** *444*
not rest on the wisdom of **m**, **1Co 2:5** *444*
For who among **m** knows the *thoughts* **1Co 2:11** *444*
speak to you as to spiritual **m**, **1Co 3:1** *4152*
men, but as to **m** of flesh, **1Co 3:1** *4560*
are you not walking like mere **m**? **1Co 3:3** *444*
am of Apollos," are you not *mere* **m**? **1Co 3:4** *444*
So then let no one boast in **m**. **1Co 3:21** *444*
of all, as **m** condemned to death; **1Co 4:9** *1935*
world, both to angels and to **m**. **1Co 4:9** *444*
Yet I wish that all **m** were even as I **1Co 7:7** *444*
do not become slaves of **m**. **1Co 7:23** *444*
not all **m** have this knowledge; **1Co 8:7** *3956*
For though I am free from all **m**, **1Co 9:19**
I have become all things to all **m**, **1Co 9:22** *3956*
I speak as to wise **m**; **1Co 10:15** *5429*
I also please all **m** in all things, **1Co 10:33** *3956*
the tongues of **m** and of angels, **1Co 13:1** *444*
in a tongue does not speak to **m** but **1Co 14:2** *444*
one who prophesies speaks to **m** **1Co 14:3** *444*
"BY M OF STRANGE TONGUES AND BY **1Co 14:21** *2084*
ungifted **m** or unbelievers enter, **1Co 14:23** *2399*
we are of all **m** most to be pitied. **1Co 15:19** *444*
but there is one *flesh* of **m**, **1Co 15:39** *444*
firm in the faith, act like **m**, **1Co 16:13** *407*

you also be in subjection to such **m** **1Co 16:16** *5108*
Therefore acknowledge such **m**. **1Co 16:18** *5108*
hearts, known and read by all **m**; **2Co 3:2** *444*
fear of the Lord, we persuade **m**, **2Co 5:11** *444*
Lord, but also in the sight of **m**. **2Co 8:21** *444*
For such **m** are false apostles, **2Co 11:13** *5108*
Paul, an apostle (not *sent* from **m** nor **Ga 1:1** *444*
am I now seeking the favor of **m**, **Ga 1:10** *444*
Or am I striving to please **m**? **Ga 1:10** *444*
If I were still trying to please **m**, **Ga 1:10** *444*
coming of certain **m** from James, **Ga 2:12** *5100*
not made known to the sons of **m**, **Eph 3:5** *444*
AND HE GAVE GIFTS TO M." **Eph 4:8** *444*
of doctrine, by the trickery of **m**, **Eph 4:14** *444*
walk, not as unwise **m** but as wise, **Eph 5:15** *781*
as to the Lord, and not to **m**, **Eph 6:7** *444*
being made in the likeness of **m**. **Php 2:7** *444*
hold **m** like him in high regard; **Php 2:29** *5108*
gentle *spirit* be known to all **m**. **Php 4:5** *444*
according to the tradition of **m**, **Col 2:8** *444*
commandments and teachings of **m**? **Col 2:22** *444*
as those who *merely* please **m**, **Col 3:22** *441*
as for the Lord rather than for **m**, **Col 3:23** *444*
what kind of **m** we proved to be **1Th 1:5** *3634*
speak, not as pleasing **m**, but God **1Th 2:4** *444*
nor did we seek glory from **m**, **1Th 2:6** *444*
accepted *it* not *as* the word of **m**, **1Th 2:13** *444*
to God, but hostile to all **m**, **1Th 2:15** *444*
from perverse and evil **m**; **2Th 3:2** *444*
may instruct certain **m** not to teach **1Tm 1:3** *5100*
For some **m**, straying from these **1Tm 1:6** *5100*
and immoral **m** and homosexuals and **1Tm 1:10** *4205*
be made on behalf of all **m**, **1Tm 2:1** *444*
who desires all **m** to be saved and **1Tm 2:4** *444*
mediator also between God and **m**, **1Tm 2:5** *444*
want the **m** in every place to pray, **1Tm 2:8** *435*
likewise *must be* **m** of dignity, **1Tm 3:8** *4586*
These **m** must also first be tested; **1Tm 3:10**
m who forbid marriage **1Tm 4:3**
God, who is the Savior of all **m**, **1Tm 4:10** *444*
to the younger **m** as brothers, **1Tm 5:1** *3501b*
sins of some **m** are quite evident, **1Tm 5:24** *444*
and constant friction between **m** of **1Tm 6:5** *444*
m into ruin and destruction. **1Tm 6:9** *444*
these to faithful **m** **2Tm 2:2** *444*
m who have gone astray from **2Tm 2:18**
For **m** will be lovers of self, **2Tm 3:2** *444*
Avoid such **m** as these. **2Tm 3:5**
so these **m** also oppose the truth, **2Tm 3:8**
the truth, **m** of depraved mind, **2Tm 3:8** *444*
But evil **m** and impostors will **2Tm 3:13** *444*
For there are many rebellious **m**, **Ti 1:10** *506*
of **m** who turn away from the truth. **Ti 1:14** *444*
Older **m** are to be temperate, **Ti 2:2** *4246*
urge the young **m** to be sensible; **Ti 2:6** *3501b*
bringing salvation to all **m**, **Ti 2:11** *444*
every consideration for all **m**. **Ti 3:2** *444*
are good and profitable for **m**. **Ti 3:8** *444*
high priest taken from among **m** **Heb 5:1** *444*
of **m** in things pertaining to God, **Heb 5:1** *444*
For **m** swear by one greater *than* **Heb 6:16** *444*
this case mortal **m** receive tithes, **Heb 7:8** *444*
m as high priests who are weak, **Heb 7:28** *444*
is valid *only* when **m** are dead, **Heb 9:17**
it is appointed for **m** to die once **Heb 9:27** *444*
it the **m** of old gained approval. **Heb 11:2** *4245*
(**m** of whom the world was not **Heb 11:38**
Pursue peace with all **m**, **Heb 12:14** *3956*
and with it we curse **m**, **Jas 3:9** *444*
stone which has been rejected by **m**, **1Pe 2:4** *444*
the ignorance of foolish **m**. **1Pe 2:15** *444*
Act as free **m**, and do not use your **1Pe 2:16** *1658*
no longer for the lusts of **m**, **1Pe 4:2** *444*
they are judged in the flesh as **m**, **1Pe 4:6** *444*
You younger **m**, likewise, be subject **1Pe 5:5** *3501b*
but **m** moved by the Holy Spirit **2Pe 1:21** *444*
sensual conduct of unprincipled **m** **2Pe 2:7** *113*
and destruction of ungodly **m**. **2Pe 3:7** *444*
by the error of unprincipled **m** and **2Pe 3:17** *113*
I am writing to you, young **m**, **1Jn 2:13** *3495*
I have written to you, young **m**, **1Jn 2:14** *3495*
If we receive the testimony of **m**, **1Jn 5:9** *444*
we ought to support such **m**, **3Jn 1:8** *5108*
Yet in the same way these **m**, **Jude 1:8** *3778*
But these **m** revile the things **Jude 1:10** *3778*
These are the **m** who are hidden **Jude 1:12** *3778*
It was also about these **m** *that* **Jude 1:14**
and that you cannot tolerate evil **m**, **Rv 2:2** *2556*
purchased for God with Your blood **m** **Rv 5:9**
and that **m** would slay one another; **Rv 6:4**
kings of the earth and the great **m** **Rv 6:15** *3175*
and many **m** died from the waters, **Rv 8:11** *444*
but only the **m** who do not have the **Rv 9:4** *444*
m will seek death and will not find **Rv 9:6** *444*
faces were like the faces of **m**. **Rv 9:7** *444*
power to hurt **m** for five months. **Rv 9:10** *444*
to the earth in the presence of **m**. **Rv 13:13** *444*
and the free **m** and the slaves, **Rv 13:16** *1658*
have been purchased from among **m** **Rv 14:4** *444*
given to it to scorch **m** with fire. **Rv 16:8** *444*
M were scorched with fierce heat; **Rv 16:9** *444*
naked and **m** will not see his shame.") **Rv 16:15**
came down from heaven upon **m**; **Rv 16:21** *444*
and **m** blasphemed God because of **Rv 16:21** *444*
have passed away from you and **m** **Rv 18:14**
were the great **m** of the earth, **Rv 18:23** *3175*
the flesh of mighty **m** and the flesh **Rv 19:18** *2478*
on them and the flesh of all **m**, **Rv 19:18** *3956*
all men, both free **m** and slaves, **Rv 19:18** *1658*

the tabernacle of God is among **m**, **Rv 21:3** *444*

MENAHEM
Then **M** son of Gadi went up from **2Ki 15:14** 4505
Then **M** struck Tiphsah and all who **2Ki 15:16** 4505
M son of Gadi became king over **2Ki 15:17** 4505
and **M** gave Pul a thousand talents **2Ki 15:19** 4505
M exacted the money from Israel, **2Ki 15:20** 4505
the acts of **M** and all that he did, **2Ki 15:21** 4505
And **M** slept with his fathers, and **2Ki 15:22** 4505
Pekahiah son of **M** became king over **2Ki 15:23** 4505

MENDED
wineskins worn-out and torn and **m**, **Jos 9:4** 6887a

MENDING
their father, **m** their nets; **Mt 4:21** *2675*
were also in the boat **m** the nets. **Mk 1:19** *2675*

MENĒ
'**M**, MENĒ, TEKĒL, UPHARSIN.' **Da 5:25** 4484
'MENĒ, **M**, TEKĒ, UPHARSIN.' **Da 5:25** 4484
'**M**'—God has numbered your **Da 5:26** 4484

MENNA
the son of Melea, the son of **M**, **Lk 3:31** *3303b*

MEN-PLEASERS
not by way of eyeservice, as **m**, **Eph 6:6** *441*

MEN'S
"Fill the **m** sacks with food, as **Gn 44:1** 376
not gods but the work of **m** hands, **2Ki 19:18** 120
of the earth, the work of **m** hands. **2Ch 32:19** 120
not gods but the work of **m** hands, **Is 37:19** 120
and lay them on **m** shoulders, **Mt 23:4** *444*
dead **m** bones and all uncleanness. **Mt 23:27** *3498*
did not come to destroy **m** lives, **Lk 9:56** *444*
the motives of **m** hearts; **1Co 4:5**
that is, in other **m** labors, **2Co 10:15** *245*

MENSTRUAL
in her **m** impurity for seven days; **Lv 15:19** 5079
her **m** impurity shall be unclean, **Lv 15:20** 5079
so that her **m** impurity is on him, **Lv 15:24** 5079
at the period of her **m** impurity, **Lv 15:25** 5079
as though in her **m** impurity; **Lv 15:25** 5079
who is ill because of **m** impurity, **Lv 15:33** 5079
nakedness during her **m** impurity. **Lv 18:19** 5079
a woman during her **m** period **Ezk 18:6** 5079
who was unclean in her **m** impurity. **Ezk 22:10** 5079

MENSTRUATION
as in the days of her **m** she shall be **Lv 12:2** 5079, 1738
for two weeks, as in her **m**; **Lv 12:5** 5079
shall be to her like her bed at **m**; **Lv 15:26** 5079

MENSTRUOUS
a man who lies with a **m** woman and **Lv 20:18** 1739

MENTION
make **m** today of my *own* offenses. **Gn 41:9** 2142
do not **m** the name of other gods, **Ex 23:13** 2142
you, or **m** the name of their gods, **Jos 23:7** 2142
there is no **m** of You in death; **Ps 6:5** 2143
will make **m** of Your righteousness, **Ps 71:16** 2142
"I shall **m** Rahab and Babylon **Ps 87:4** 2142
make **m** of the lovingkindnesses of **Is 63:7** 2142
how unceasingly I make **m** of you, **Ro 1:9** *3417*
making **m** *of you* in my prayers; **Eph 1:16** *3417*
making **m** *of you* in our prayers; **1Th 1:2** *3417*
about things not proper *to* **m**. **1Tm 5:13**
making **m** of you in my prayers, **Phm 1:4** *3417*
not to **m** to you that you owe **Phm 1:19** *3004*
made **m** of the exodus of the sons **Heb 11:22** *3421*

MENTIONED
cities which are *here* **m** by name **Jos 21:9** 7121
When he **m** the ark of God, Eli **1Sa 4:18** 2142
of the kingdom which Samuel had **m**. **1Sa 10:16** 559
these **m** by name *were* leaders in **1Ch 4:38** 935
these cities which are **m** by name. **1Ch 6:65** 7121
"Coral and crystal are not to be **m**; **Jb 28:18** 2142
the offspring of evildoers not be **m** **Is 14:20** 7121
everyone to whom it is **m** will be in **Is 19:17** 2142
will be **m** by their names no more. **Hos 2:17** 2142
name of the LORD is not to be **m**." **Am 6:10** 2142

MENTIONING
me a kindness by **m** me to Pharaoh and **Gn 40:14** 2142

MEONOTHAI
sons of Othniel *were* Hathath and **M**. **1Ch 4:13** 4587
M became the father of Ophrah, **1Ch 4:14** 4587

MEPHAATH
and Jahaz and Kedemoth and **M**, **Jos 13:18** 4158
and **M** with its pasture lands; **Jos 21:37** 4158
and **M** with its pasture lands; **1Ch 6:79** 4158
upon Holon, Jahzah and against **M**, **Jer 48:21** 4158

MEPHIBOSHETH
And his name was **M**. **2Sa 4:4** 4648
M, the son of Jonathan the son **2Sa 9:6** 4648
And David said, "**M**." **2Sa 9:6** 4648
M your master's grandson shall eat **2Sa 9:10** 4648
So **M** ate at David's table as one **2Sa 9:11** 4648
M had a young son whose name **2Sa 9:12** 4648
house of Ziba were servants to **M**. **2Sa 9:12** 4648
So **M** lived in Jerusalem, for he **2Sa 9:13** 4648
Ziba the servant of **M** met him with **2Sa 16:1** 4648
all that belongs to **M** is yours." **2Sa 16:4** 4648
Then **M** the son of Saul came down **2Sa 19:24** 4648
"Why did you not go with me, **M**?" **2Sa 19:25** 4648
M said to the king, **2Sa 19:30** 4648
But the king spared **M**, **2Sa 21:7** 4648
and **M** whom she had borne to Saul, **2Sa 21:8** 4648

MERAB
the name of the firstborn **M** and **1Sa 14:49** 4764
"Here is my older daughter **M**; **1Sa 18:17** 4764
when **M**, Saul's daughter, should **1Sa 18:19** 4764

sons of **M** the daughter of Saul, 2Sa 21:8 4764

MERAIAH

households were: of Seraiah, **M**; Ne 12:12 4811

MERAIOTH

Zerahiah became the father of **M**, 1Ch 6:6 4812
M became the father of Amariah, 1Ch 6:7 4812
M his son, Amariah his son, Ahitub 1Ch 6:52 4812
the son of Zadok, the son of **M**, 1Ch 9:11 4812
Amariah, son of Azariah, son of **M**, Ezr 7:3 4812
the son of Zadok, the son of **M**, Ne 11:11 4812
of Harim, Adna; of **M**, Helkai; Ne 12:15 4812

MERARI

Gershon, Kohath, and **M**. Gn 46:11 4847
Gershon and Kohath and **M**; Ex 6:16 4847
The sons of **M**: Ex 6:19 4847
Gershon and Kohath and **M**. Nu 3:17 4847
the sons of **M** by their families: Nu 3:20 4847
Of **M** *was* the family of the Nu 3:33 4847
these *were* the families of **M**. Nu 3:33 4847
households of the families of **M** Nu 3:35 4847
appointed duties of the sons of **M** Nu 3:36 4847
"*As for* the sons of **M**, Nu 4:29 4847
of the families of the sons of **M**, Nu 4:33 4847
the sons of **M** by their families, Nu 4:42 4847
of the families of the sons of **M**, Nu 4:45 4847
oxen he gave to the sons of **M**, Nu 7:8 4847
sons of Gershon and the sons of **M**, Nu 10:17 4847
of **M**, the family of the Merarites. Nu 26:57 4847
The sons of **M** according to their Jos 21:7 4847
To the families of the sons of **M**, Jos 21:34 4847
the cities of the sons of **M** according Jos 21:40 4847
Levi *were* Gershon, Kohath and **M**. 1Ch 6:1 4847
Levi *were* Gershom, Kohath and **M**. 1Ch 6:16 4847
sons of **M** *were* Mahli and Mushi. 1Ch 6:19 4847
The sons of **M** *were* Mahli, Libni 1Ch 6:29 4847
were their kinsmen the sons of **M**: 1Ch 6:44 4847
the son of Mushi, the son of **M**, 1Ch 6:47 4847
the sons of **M** *were given* by lot, 1Ch 6:63 4847
of *the Levites*, the sons of **M**, 1Ch 6:77 4847
of Hashabiah, of the sons of **M**; 1Ch 9:14 4847
of the sons of **M**, Asaiah the 1Ch 15:6 4847
of the sons of **M** their relatives, 1Ch 15:17 4847
Gershon, Kohath, and **M**. 1Ch 23:6 4847
sons of **M** were Mahli and Mushi. 1Ch 23:21 4847
The sons of **M**, Mahli and Mushi; 1Ch 24:26 4847
sons of **M**: by Jaaziah *were* Beno, 1Ch 24:27 4847
one of the sons of **M** had sons: 1Ch 26:10 4847
of Korah and of the sons of **M**. 1Ch 26:19 4847
and from the sons of **M**, 2Ch 29:12 4847
the Levites of the sons of **M**, 2Ch 34:12 4847
and Jeshaiah of the sons of **M**, Ezr 8:19 4847

MERARITES

of Merari, the family of the **M**. Nu 26:57 4848

MERATHAIM

"Against the land of **M**, Jer 50:21 4850

MERCENARIES

"Also her **m** in her midst Are like Jer 46:21 7917a

MERCHANDISE

imported fish and all kinds of **m**, Ne 13:16 4377
and merchants of every kind of **m** Ne 13:20 4465
and the **m** of Cush And the Sabeans, Is 45:14 5504
your riches and a prey of your **m**, Ezk 26:12 7404
you in order to deal in your **m**. Ezk 27:9 4627
of bronze they paid for your **m**. Ezk 27:13 4627
and balm they paid for your **m**. Ezk 27:17 4627
and sweet cane were among your **m**. Ezk 27:19 4627
cords, *which were* among your **m**. Ezk 27:24 4819
were the carriers for your **m**. Ezk 27:25 4627
"Your wealth, your wares, your **m**, Ezk 27:27 4627
of seams, your dealers in **m** And Ezk 27:27 4627
abundance of your wealth and your **m** Ezk 27:33 4627
Your **m** and all your company Have Ezk 27:34 4627
He would not permit anyone to carry **m** Mk 11:16 *4632*

MERCHANT

She is like **m** ships; Pr 31:14 5503
With all scented powders of the **m**? SS 3:6 7402
m of the peoples to many Ezk 27:3 7402
A **m**, in whose hands are false Hos 12:7 3669b
is like a **m** seeking fine pearls, Mt 13:45 *1713*

MERCHANTS

the traders and the wares of the **m** 1Ki 10:15 7402
and the king's **m** procured *them* 1Ki 10:28 5503
which the traders and **m** brought; 2Ch 9:14 5503
the temple servants and of the **m**, Ne 3:31 7402
and the **m** carried out repairs. Ne 3:32 7402
and **m** of every kind of merchandise Ne 13:20 4376
Will they divide him among the **m**? Jb 41:6 3669b
of the coastland, You **m** of Sidon; Is 23:2 5503
of crowns, Whose **m** were princes, Is 23:8 5503
your harlotry with the land of **m**, Ezk 16:29 3667b
and brought it to a land of **m**; Ezk 17:4 3667b
m among the peoples hiss at you; Ezk 27:36 5503
and Dedan and the **m** of Tarshish Ezk 38:13 5503
and the **m** of the earth have become Rv 18:3 *1713*
"And the **m** of the earth weep and Rv 18:11 *1713*
"The **m** of these things, who Rv 18:15 *1713*
for your **m** were the great men of Rv 18:23 *1713*

MERCIES

of the LORD for His **m** are great, 2Sa 24:14 7356
LORD, for His **m** are very great. 1Ch 21:13 7356
Great are Your **m**, O LORD; Ps 119:156 7356
And His **m** are over all His works. Ps 145:9 7356
to the faithful **m** shown to David. Is 55:3 2617a
brethren, by the **m** of God, Ro 12:1 *3628*
of **m** and God of all comfort, 2Co 1:3 *3628*

MERCIFUL

the house of Israel are **m** kings, 1Ki 20:31 2617a
O Lord, are a God **m** and gracious, Ps 86:15 7349
The LORD is gracious and **m**; Ps 145:8 7349
The **m** man does himself good, But Pr 11:17 2617a
"Blessed are the **m**, for they Mt 5:7 *1655*
"Be **m**, just as your Father is Lk 6:36 *3629*
just as your Father is **m**. Lk 6:36 *3629*
'God, be **m** to me, the sinner!' Lk 18:13 *2433*
become a **m** and faithful high priest Heb 2:17 *1655*
I WILL BE **M** TO THEIR INIQUITIES, Heb 8:12 *2436*
is full of compassion and *is* **m**. Jas 5:11 *3629*

MERCILESS

judgment *will be* **m** to one who has Jas 2:13 *415b*

MERCY

shall make a **m** seat of pure gold, Ex 25:17 3727
at the two ends of the **m** seat. Ex 25:18 3727
with the **m** seat at its two ends. Ex 25:19 3727
covering the **m** seat with their wings Ex 25:20 3727
to be *turned* toward the **m** seat. Ex 25:20 3727
put the **m** seat on top of the ark, Ex 25:21 3727
and from above the **m** seat, Ex 25:22 3727
"You shall put the **m** seat on Ex 26:34 3727
in front of the **m** seat that is Ex 30:6 3727
testimony, and the **m** seat upon it, Ex 31:7 3727
the ark and its poles, the **m** seat, Ex 35:12 3727
He made a **m** seat of pure gold, Ex 37:6 3727
at the two ends of the **m** seat; Ex 37:7 3727
with the **m** seat at the two ends. Ex 37:8 3727
the **m** seat with their wings, Ex 37:9 3727
cherubim were toward the **m** seat. Ex 37:9 3727
and its poles and the **m** seat; Ex 39:35 3727
put the **m** seat on top of the ark. Ex 40:20 3727
the **m** seat which is on the ark, Lv 16:2 3727
in the cloud over the **m** seat. Lv 16:2 3727
cover the **m** seat that is on *the ark* Lv 16:13 3727
on the **m** seat on the east *side;* Lv 16:14 3727
also in front of the **m** seat he Lv 16:14 3727
and sprinkle it on the **m** seat and Lv 16:15 3727
seat and in front of the **m** seat. Lv 16:15 3727
above the **m** seat that was on the ark Nu 7:89 3727
burning anger and show **m** to you, Dt 13:17 7356
that they might receive no **m**, Jos 11:20 8467
m and truth be with you." 2Sa 15:20 2617a
and the room for the **m** seat; 1Ch 28:11 3727
have to implore the **m** of my judge. Jb 9:15 2603a
Without **m** He splits my kidneys Jb 16:13 2550
You did not show **m** to them, Is 47:6 7356
and in His **m** He redeemed them, Is 63:9 2551
They are cruel and have no **m**; Jer 6:23 7355
I will surely have **m** on him," Jer 31:20 7355
and will have **m** on them.' " Jer 33:26 7355
They are cruel and have no **m**. Jer 50:42 7355
m on the whole house of Israel; Ezk 39:25 7355
by showing **m** to *the* poor, Da 4:27 2604
For in You the orphan finds **m**." Hos 14:3 7355
In wrath remember **m**. Hab 3:2 7355
for they shall receive **m**. Mt 5:7 *1653*
"Have **m** on us, Son of David!" Mt 9:27 *1653*
"Have **m** on me, Lord, Son of Mt 15:22 *1653*
"Lord, have **m** on my son, for he Mt 17:15 *1653*
have had **m** on your fellow slave, Mt 18:33 *1653*
the same way that I had **m** on you?' Mt 18:33 *1653*
"Lord, have **m** on us, Son of David!" Mt 20:30 *1653*
"Lord, Son of David, have **m** on us!" Mt 20:31 *1653*
justice and **m** and faithfulness; Mt 23:23 *1656*
you, and *how* He had **m** on you." Mk 5:19 *1653*
Son of David, have **m** on me!" Mk 10:47 *1653*
"Son of David, have **m** on me!" Mk 10:48 *1653*
"AND HIS **M** IS UPON GENERATION Lk 1:50 *1656*
servant, In remembrance of His **m**, Lk 1:54 *1656*
displayed His great **m** toward her; Lk 1:58 *1656*
To show **m** toward our fathers, And Lk 1:72 *1656*
of the tender **m** of our God, Lk 1:78 *1656*
"The one who showed **m** toward him." Lk 10:37 *1656*
'Father Abraham, have **m** on me, Lk 16:24 *1653*
"Jesus, Master, have **m** on us!" Lk 17:13 *1653*
Son of David, have **m** on me!" Lk 18:38 *1653*
"Son of David, have **m** on me!" Lk 18:39 *1653*
HAVE **M** ON WHOM I HAVE MERCY, Ro 9:15 *1653*
HAVE MERCY ON WHOM I HAVE **M**. Ro 9:15 *1653*
who runs, but on God who has **m**. Ro 9:16 *1653*
then He has **m** on whom He desires, Ro 9:18 *1653*
of His glory upon vessels of **m**, Ro 9:23 *1656*
m because of their disobedience, Ro 11:30 *1653*
that because of the **m** shown to you Ro 11:31 *1656*
you they also may now be shown **m**. Ro 11:31 *1653*
that He may show **m** to all. Ro 11:32 *1653*
he who shows **m**, with cheerfulness. Ro 12:8 *1653*
Gentiles to glorify God for His **m**; Ro 15:9 *1656*
the **m** of the Lord is trustworthy. 1Co 7:25 *1653*
this ministry, as we received **m**, 2Co 4:1 *1653*
rule, peace and **m** *be* upon them, Ga 6:16 *1656*
But God, being rich in **m**, Eph 2:4 *1656*
of death, but God had **m** on him, Php 2:27 *1653*
m *and* peace from God the Father 1Tm 1:2 *1656*
Yet I was shown **m** 1Tm 1:13 *1653*
Yet for this reason I found **m**, 1Tm 1:16 *1653*
m *and* peace from God the Father 2Tm 1:2 *1656*
The Lord grant **m** to the house of 2Tm 1:16 *1656*
the Lord grant to him to find **m** 2Tm 1:18 *1656*
but according to His **m**, Ti 3:5 *1656*
that we may receive **m** and find Heb 4:16 *1656*
of glory overshadowing the **m** seat; Heb 9:5 *2435*
dies without **m** on *the testimony of* Heb 10:28 *3628*
to one who has shown no **m**; Jas 2:13 *1656*
m triumphs over judgment. Jas 2:13 *1656*
full of **m** and good fruits, Jas 3:17 *1656*
who according to His great **m** has 1Pe 1:3 *1656*
you had NOT RECEIVED **M**, 1Pe 2:10 *1653*
but now you have RECEIVED **M**. 1Pe 2:10 *1653*
m *and* peace will be with us, 2Jn 1:3 *1656*
May **m** and peace and love be Jude 1:2 *1656*
for the **m** of our Lord Jesus Christ Jude 1:21 *1656*
And have **m** on some, who are Jud 1:22 *1653*
and on some have **m** with fear, Judq:23 *1653*

MERE

every man at his best is a **m** breath. Ps 39: 3605
Surely every man is a **m** breath. Ps 39:1 1892
What can **m** man do to me? Ps 56:4
That they are a **m** breath. Ps 94:11
Man is like a **m** breath; Ps 144:4 *1892*
But **m** talk *leads* only to poverty. Pr 14:23 8193
And I will make **m** lads their Is 3:4
The princes of Zoan are **m** fools; Is 19:11 389
craftsmen themselves are **m** men. Is 44:11 480
You have made us **m** offscouring La 3:45
They speak **m** words, With Hos 10:4
their journey, except a **m** staff Mk 6:8 *41*
are you not walking like **m** men? 1Co 3:3
are you not **m** men? 1Co 3:4
things which are a **m** shadow of Col 2:17
which give rise to **m** speculation 1Tm 1:4
a **m** copy of the true one, but Heb 9:24

MERED

The sons of Ezrah *were* Jether, **M**, 1Ch 4:17 47
daughter of Pharaoh, whom **M** took) 1Ch 4:17 47

MERELY

"Your servant would **m** cross over 2Sa 19:36 459
the earth, But He **m** blows on them, Is 40:24 157
"Yet you have not **m** walked in Ezk 16:47
"But all these things are **m** Mt 24:8
These things are **m** the beginning Mk 13:8
do not **m** look out for your own Php 2:4
as those who **m** please men, but Col 3:22
and not **m** idle, but also gossips 1Tm 5:13 *3441*
m hearers who delude themselves. Jas 1:22 *3441*
Your adornment must not be **m** 1Pe 3:3

MEREMOTH

into the hand of **M** the son of Uriah Ezr 8:33 4822
Vaniah, **M**, Eliashib, Ezr 10:36 4822
Next to them **M** the son of Uriah Ne 3:4 4822
After him **M** the son of Uriah the Ne 3:21 4822
Harim, **M**, Obadiah, Ne 10:5 4822
Shecaniah, Rehum, **M**, Ne 12:3 4822

MERES

Shethar, Admatha, Tarshish, **M**, Es 1:14 4825

MERIBAH

He named the place Massah and **M** Ex 17:7 4809
Those *were* the waters of **M**, Nu 20:13 4809
My command at the waters of **M**. Nu 20:24 4809
are the waters of **M** of Kadesh in Nu 27:14 4809
contended at the waters of **M**; Dt 33:8 4809
I proved you at the waters of **M**. Ps 81:7 4809
not harden your hearts, as at **M**, Ps 95:8 4809
Him to wrath at the waters of **M**, Ps 106:32 4809

MERIBAH-KADESH

sons of Israel at the waters of **M**, Dt 32:51 4809, 6946

MERIBATH-KADESH

Tamar as far as the waters of **M**, Ezk 47:19 4809, 6946
be from Tamar to the waters of **M**, Ezk 48:28 4809, 6946

MERIB-BAAL

The son of Jonathan *was* **M**, 1Ch 8:34 4807
and **M** became the father of Micah. 1Ch 8:34 4807
The son of Jonathan *was* **M**; 1Ch 9:40 4807
and **M** became the father of Micah. 1Ch 9:40 4807

MERITS

on account of any **m** of our own, Da 9:18 6666

MERODACH-BALADAN

At that time **M** son of Baladan, Is 39:1 4757

MEROM

together at the waters of **M**, Jos 11:5 4792
them suddenly by the waters of **M**, Jos 11:7 4792

MERONOTHITE

Jehdeiah the **M** had charge of the 1Ch 27:30 4824
the Gibeonite and Jadon the **M**, Ne 3:7 4824

MEROZ

'Curse **M**,' said the angel of the Jg 5:23 4789

MERRY

night, and let your heart be **m**." Jg 19:6 3190
here that your heart may be **m**. Jg 19:9 3190
and drunk and his heart was **m**, Ru 3:7 3190
And Nabal's heart was **m** within him, 1Sa 25:36 2895
when Amnon's heart is **m** with wine, 2Sa 13:28 2895
heart of the king was **m** with wine, Es 1:10 2895
to eat and to drink and to be **m**, Ec 8:15 8055
enjoyment, and wine makes life **m**, Ec 10:19 8055
take your ease, eat, drink *and* be **m**. Lk 12:19 *2165*

MERRY-HEARTED

The vine decays, All the **m** sigh. Is 24:7 8056, 3820

MERRYMAKERS

I did not sit in the circle of **m**, Jer 15:17 7832
go forth to the dances of the **m**. Jer 31:4 7832

MESHA

from **M** as you go toward Sephar, Gn 10:30 4852
Now **M** king of Moab was a sheep 2Ki 3:4 4338
Jerahmeel, *were* **M** his firstborn, 1Ch 2:42 4337
the father of Jobab, Zibia, **M**, 1Ch 8:9 4331

MESHACH

Hananiah Shadrach, to Mishael **M** and Da 1:7 4335
M and Abed-nego over the Da 2:49 4336

namely Shadrach, **M** and Abed-nego. **Da 3:12** 4336
to bring Shadrach, **M** and Abed-nego; **Da 3:13** 4336
it true, Shadrach, **M** and Abed-nego, **Da 3:14** 4336
M and Abed-nego replied **Da 3:16** 4336
toward Shadrach, **M** and Abed-nego. **Da 3:19** 4336
tie up Shadrach, **M** and Abed-nego in **Da 3:20** 4336
up Shadrach, **M** and Abed-nego. **Da 3:22** 4336
men, Shadrach, **M** and Abed-nego, **Da 3:23** 4336
"Shadrach, **M** and Abed-nego, come **Da 3:26** 4336
Shadrach, **M** and Abed-nego came **Da 3:26** 4336
God of Shadrach, **M** and Abed-nego, **Da 3:28** 4336
God of Shadrach, **M** and Abed-nego **Da 3:29** 4336
caus[illegible] Shadrach, **M** and Abed-nego **Da 3:30** 4336

MESHECH
Ja[illegible] and Tubal and **M** and Tiras. **Gn 10:2** 4902
M[illegible]g, Madai, Javan, Tubal, **M** and **1Ch 1:5** 4902
[illegible] Aram, Uz, Hul, Gether and **M**. **1Ch 1:17** 4902
[illegible]e is me, for I sojourn in **M**, **Ps 120:5** 4902
[illegible]shish, Put, Lud, **M**, **Is 66:19** 4902
[illegible]van, Tubal and **M**, **Ezk 27:13** 4902
M, Tubal and all their hordes **Ezk 32:26** 4902
[illegible]f Magog, the prince of Rosh, **M** and **Ezk 38:2** 4902
[illegible]ou, O Gog, prince of Rosh, **M** and **Ezk 38:3** 4902
you, O Gog, prince of Rosh, **M** and **Ezk 39:1** 4902

MESHELEMIAH
Zechariah the son of **M** was **1Ch 9:21** 4920
the Korahites, **M** the son of Kore, **1Ch 26:1** 4920
M had sons: Zechariah the firstborn, **1Ch 26:2** 4920
M had sons and relatives, 18 **1Ch 26:9** 4920

MESHEZABEL
the son of **M** made repairs. **Ne 3:4** 4898
M, Zadok, Jaddua, **Ne 10:21** 4898
Pethahiah the son of **M**, **Ne 11:24** 4898

MESHILLEMITH
son of Meshullam, the son of **M**, **1Ch 9:12** 4919

MESHILLEMOTH
Johanan, Berechiah the son of **M**, **2Ch 28:12** 4919
the son of Ahzai, the son of **M**, **Ne 11:13** 4919

MESHOBAB
M and Jamlech and Joshah the **1Ch 4:34** 4877

MESHULLAM
Azaliah the son of **M** the scribe, **2Ki 22:3** 4918
of Zerubbabel *were* **M** and Hananiah, **1Ch 3:19** 4918
households *were* Michael, **M**, **1Ch 5:13** 4918
Zebadiah, **M**, Hizki, Heber, **1Ch 8:17** 4918
Benjamin *were* Sallu the son of **M**, **1Ch 9:7** 4918
and **M** the son of Shephatiah, **1Ch 9:8** 4918
the son of Hilkiah, the son of **M**, **1Ch 9:11** 4918
the son of Jahzerah, the son of **M**, **1Ch 9:12** 4918
M of the sons of the Kohathites, **2Ch 34:12** 4918
Nathan, Zechariah and **M**, **Ezr 8:16** 4918
with **M** and Shabbethai the Levite **Ezr 10:15** 4918
M, Malluch and Adaiah, Jashub, **Ezr 10:29** 4918
And next to him **M** the son of **Ne 3:4** 4918
M the son of Besodeiah repaired the **Ne 3:6** 4918
After him **M** the son of Berechiah **Ne 3:30** 4918
of **M** the son of Berechiah. **Ne 6:18** 4918
Zechariah *and* **M** on his left hand. **Ne 8:4** 4918
M, Abijah, Mijamin, **Ne 10:7** 4918
Magpiash, **M**, Hezir, **Ne 10:20** 4918
Sallu the son of **M**, **Ne 11:7** 4918
the son of Hilkiah, the son of **M**, **Ne 11:11** 4918
of Ezra, **M**; of Amariah, Jehohanan; **Ne 12:13** 4918
of Iddo, Zechariah; of Ginnethon, **M**; **Ne 12:16** 4918
Bakbukiah, Obadiah, **M**, **Ne 12:25** 4918
with Azariah, Ezra, **M**, **Ne 12:33** 4918

MESHULLEMETH
and his mother's name *was* **M** the **2Ki 21:19** 4922

MESOPOTAMIA
and he arose and went to **M**, **Gn 24:10** 763
the son of Beor from Pethor of **M**, **Dt 23:4** 763
of Cushan-rishathaim king of **M**; **Jg 3:8** 763
gave Cushan-rishathaim king of **M** **Jg 3:10** 763
chariots and horsemen from **M**, **1Ch 19:6** 763
and Elamites, and residents of **M**, **Ac 2:9** 3318
father Abraham when he was in **M**, **Ac 7:2** 3318

MESSAGE
So they sent *a* **m** to Joseph, **Gn 50:16**
now send *the* **m** by whomever You **Ex 4:13**
"I have a secret **m** for you, O **Jg 3:19** 1697
"I have a **m** from God for you." **Jg 3:20** 1697
the **m** which Jephthah sent him. **Jg 11:28** 1697
"I have heard *the* **m** which you **1Ki 5:8**
I am sent to you *with* a harsh **m**. **1Ki 14:6**
So Ahab sent *a* **m** among all **1Ki 18:20**
When *Ben-hadad* heard this **m**, **1Ki 20:12** 1697
then Sanballat and Geshem sent *a* **m** **Ne 6:2**
Then I sent *a* **m** to him saying, **Ne 6:8**
sends a **m** by the hand of a fool. **Pr 26:6** 1697
The Lord sends a **m** against Jacob, **Is 9:8** 1697
to whom would He interpret the **m**? **Is 28:9** 8052
Who has believed our **m**? **Is 53:1** 8052
m which the LORD will answer you **Jer 42:4** 1697
act in accordance with the whole **m** **Jer 42:5** 1697
"As for the **m** that you have **Jer 44:16** 1697
is the **m** which Jeremiah the **Jer 45:1** 1697
This is the **m** which the LORD spoke **Jer 46:13** 1697
I have heard a **m** from the LORD, **Jer 49:14** 8052
The **m** which Jeremiah the prophet **Jer 51:59** 1697
you will hear a **m** from My mouth and **Ezk 33:7** 1697
and hear what the **m** is which comes **Ezk 33:30** 1697
the interpretation of the **m**. **Da 5:15** 4406
is the interpretation of the **m**: **Da 5:26** 4406
so give heed to the **m** and gain **Da 9:23** 1697
Persia a **m** was revealed to Daniel, **Da 10:1** 1697
and the **m** was true and *one of* **Da 10:1** 1697
but he understood the **m** and had an **Da 10:1** 1697
his wife sent him *a* **m**, saying, **Mt 27:19**
for His **m** was with authority. **Lk 4:32** 3056
one another saying, "What is this **m**? **Lk 4:36** 3056
who had heard the **m** believed; **Ac 4:4** 3056
temple the whole **m** of this Life." **Ac 5:20** 4487
his house and hear a **m** from you." **Ac 10:22** 4487
those who were listening to the **m**. **Ac 10:44** 3056
to us the **m** of this salvation has **Ac 13:26** 3056
the brethren with a lengthy **m**. **Ac 15:32** 3056
he prolonged his **m** until midnight. **Ac 20:7** 3056
the foolishness of the **m** preached **1Co 1:21** 2782
and my **m** and my preaching were not **1Co 2:4** 3056
after listening to the **m** of truth, **Eph 1:13** 3056
or a **m** or a letter as if from us, **2Th 2:2** 3056
This is the **m** we have heard **1Jn 1:5** 31a
For this is the **m** which you have **1Jn 3:11** 31a

MESSAGES
They sent **m** to me four times in **Ne 6:4**

MESSENGER
But a **m** came to Saul, saying, **1Sa 23:27** 4397
He charged the **m**, **2Sa 11:19** 4397
So the **m** departed and came and **2Sa 11:22** 4397
The **m** said to David, **2Sa 11:23** 4397
Then David said to the **m**, **2Sa 11:25** 4397
Then a **m** came to David, saying, **2Sa 15:13** 5046
Then Jezebel sent a **m** to Elijah, **1Ki 19:2** 4397
Then the **m** who went to summon **1Ki 22:13** 4397
Elisha sent a **m** to him, **2Ki 5:10** 4397
but before the **m** came to him, he **2Ki 6:32** 4397
Look, when the **m** comes, shut the **2Ki 6:32** 4397
behold, the **m** came down to him and **2Ki 6:33** 4397
"The **m** came to them, but he did **2Ki 9:18** 4397
When the **m** came and told him, **2Ki 10:8** 4397
Then the **m** who went to summon **2Ch 18:12** 4397
a **m** came to Job and said, **Jb 1:14** 4397
A wicked **m** falls into adversity, **Pr 13:17** 4397
cruel **m** will be sent against him. **Pr 17:11** 4397
faithful **m** to those who send him, **Pr 25:13** 6735a
say in the presence of the **m** *of God* **Ec 5:6** 4397
'I will give a **m** of good news.' **Is 41:27** 1319
Or so deaf as My **m** whom I send? **Is 42:19** 4397
And one **m** to meet another, **Jer 51:31** 5046
from afar, to whom a **m** was sent; **Ezk 23:40** 4397
Then Haggai, the **m** of the LORD, **Hg 1:13** 4397
he is the **m** of the LORD of hosts. **Mal 2:7** 4397
"Behold, I am going to send My **m**, **Mal 3:1** 4397
and the **m** of the covenant, in whom **Mal 3:1** 4397
I SEND MY **M** AHEAD OF YOU, WHO **Mt 11:10** 32a
I SEND MY **M** AHEAD OF YOU, WHO **Mk 1:2** 32a
I SEND MY **M** AHEAD OF YOU, WHO **Lk 7:27** 32a
a thorn in the flesh, a **m** of Satan **2Co 12:7** 32a
your **m** and minister to my need; **Php 2:25** 652

MESSENGERS
Then Jacob sent **m** before him to **Gn 32:3** 4397
The **m** returned to Jacob, **Gn 32:6** 4397
then sent **m** to the king of Edom: **Nu 20:14** 4397
Then Israel sent **m** to Sihon, **Nu 21:21** 4397
sent **m** to Balaam the son of Beor, **Nu 22:5** 4397
your **m** whom you had sent to me, **Nu 24:12** 4397
"So I sent **m** from the wilderness **Dt 2:26** 4397
she hid the **m** whom we sent. **Jos 6:17** 4397
for she hid the **m** whom Joshua sent **Jos 6:25** 4397
So Joshua sent **m**, and they ran to **Jos 7:22** 4397
He sent **m** throughout Manasseh, **Jg 6:35** 4397
and he sent **m** to Asher, Zebulun, **Jg 6:35** 4397
Gideon sent **m** throughout all **Jg 7:24** 4397
sent **m** to Abimelech deceitfully, **Jg 9:31** 4397
Now Jephthah sent **m** to the king of **Jg 11:12** 4397
Ammon said to the **m** of Jephthah, **Jg 11:13** 4397
But Jephthah sent **m** again to the **Jg 11:14** 4397
Israel sent **m** to the king of Edom, **Jg 11:17** 4397
m to Sihon king of the Amorites, **Jg 11:19** 4397
So they sent **m** to the inhabitants **1Sa 6:21** 4397
that we may send **m** throughout the **1Sa 11:3** 4397
Then the **m** came to Gibeah of Saul **1Sa 11:4** 4397
of Israel by the hand of **m**, **1Sa 11:7** 4397
They said to the **m** who had come, **1Sa 11:9** 4397
So the **m** went and told the men of **1Sa 11:9** 4397
So Saul sent **m** to Jesse and said, **1Sa 16:19** 4397
m to David's house to watch him, **1Sa 19:11** 4397
When Saul sent **m** to take David, **1Sa 19:14** 4397
Then Saul sent **m** to see David, **1Sa 19:15** 4397
When the **m** entered, behold, the **1Sa 19:16** 4397
Then Saul sent **m** to take David, **1Sa 19:20** 4397
of God came upon the **m** of Saul; **1Sa 19:20** 4397
it was told Saul, he sent other **m**, **1Sa 19:21** 4397
Saul sent **m** again the third time, **1Sa 19:21** 4397
David sent **m** from the wilderness **1Sa 25:14** 4397
and she followed the **m** of David and **1Sa 25:42** 4397
sent **m** to the men of Jabesh-gilead, **2Sa 2:5** 4397
sent **m** to David in his place, **2Sa 3:12** 4397
So David sent **m** to Ish-bosheth, **2Sa 3:14** 4397
from David, he sent **m** after Abner, **2Sa 3:26** 4397
Then Hiram king of Tyre sent **m** to **2Sa 5:11** 4397
David sent **m** and took her, and **2Sa 11:4** 4397
Joab sent **m** to David and said, **2Sa 12:27** 4397
Then he sent **m** to the city to Ahab **1Ki 20:2** 4397
Then the **m** returned and said, **1Ki 20:5** 4397
So he said to the **m** of Ben-hadad, **1Ki 20:9** 4397
And the **m** departed and brought him **1Ki 20:9** 4397
So he sent **m** and said to them, **2Ki 1:2** 4397
go up to meet the **m** of the king of **2Ki 1:3** 4397
When the **m** returned to him he said **2Ki 1:5** 4397
sent **m** to inquire of Baal-zebub, **2Ki 1:16** 4397
the **m** returned and told the king. **2Ki 7:15** 4397
Then Amaziah sent **m** to Jehoash, **2Ki 14:8** 4397
So Ahaz sent **m** to Tiglath-pileser **2Ki 16:7** 4397
who had sent **m** to So king of Egypt **2Ki 17:4** 4397
sent **m** again to Hezekiah saying, **2Ki 19:9** 4397
the letter from the hand of the **m** **2Ki 19:14** 4397
Through your **m** you have **2Ki 19:23** 4397
his head and his armor and sent **m** **1Ch 10:9**
Hiram king of Tyre sent **m** to David **1Ch 14:1** 4397
So David sent **m** to console him **1Ch 19:2** 4397
defeated by Israel, they sent **m** and **1Ch 19:16** 4397
But Neco sent **m** to him, saying, **2Ch 35:21** 4397
to them again and again by His **m**, **2Ch 36:15** 4397
continually mocked the **m** of God, **2Ch 36:16** 4397
So I sent **m** to them, saying, **Ne 6:3** 4397
He makes the winds His **m**, **Ps 104:4** 4397
fury of a king is *like* **m** of death, **Pr 16:14** 4397
one answer the **m** of the nation? **Is 14:32** 4397
Go, swift **m**, to a nation tall and **Is 18:2** 4397
Your **m** crossed the sea **Is 23:2** 4390
he heard *it* he sent **m** to Hezekiah, **Is 37:9** 4397
the letter from the hand of the **m** **Is 37:14** 4397
performing the purpose of His **m**. **Is 44:26** 4397
by the **m** who come to Jerusalem **Jer 27:3** 4397
and sent **m** to them in Chaldea. **Ezk 23:16** 4397
"On that day **m** will go forth from **Ezk 30:9** 4397
the voice of your **m** be heard." **Na 2:13** 4397
When the **m** of John had left, **Lk 7:24** 32a
and He sent **m** on ahead of Him, **Lk 9:52** 32a
they are **m** of the churches, **2Co 8:23** 652
when she received the **m** and sent **Jas 2:25** 32a

MESSIAH
until **M** the Prince *there will be* seven **Da 9:25** 4899
M will be cut off and have nothing, **Da 9:26** 4899
of the genealogy of Jesus the **M**, **Mt 1:1** 5547
who is called the **M**. **Mt 1:16** 5547
the deportation to Babylon to the **M**, **Mt 1:17** 5547
he inquired of them where the **M** was **Mt 2:4** 5547
"We have found the **M**" **Jn 1:41** 3323
"I know that **M** is coming **Jn 4:25** 3323

MET
his way, the angels of God **m** him. **Gn 32:1** 6293
all this company which I have **m**?" **Gn 33:8** 6298
God of the Hebrews, has **m** with us. **Ex 3:18** 7136a
LORD **m** him and sought to put him **Ex 4:24** 6298
and **m** him at the mountain of God and **Ex 4:27** 6298
God of the Hebrews has **m** with us. **Ex 5:3** 7122
they **m** Moses and Aaron as they **Ex 5:20** 6293
Now God **m** Balaam, and he said to **Nu 23:4** 7136a
Then the LORD **m** Balaam and put a **Nu 23:16** 7136a
how he **m** you along the way and **Dt 25:18** 7136a
Philistines shouted as they **m** him. **Jg 15:14** 7122
behold, a group of prophets **m** him; **1Sa 10:10** 7122
down toward her; so she **m** them. **1Sa 25:20** 6298
and **m** them by the pool of Gibeon; **2Sa 2:13** 6298
Archite **m** him with his coat torn and **2Sa 15:32** 7122
the servant of Mephibosheth **m** him **2Sa 16:1** 7122
a lion **m** him on the way and killed **1Ki 13:24** 4672
on the way, behold, Elijah **m** him, **1Ki 18:7** 7122
Jehu **m** the relatives of Ahaziah **2Ki 10:13** 4672
he **m** Jehonadab the son of Rechab **2Ki 10:15** 4672
Lovingkindness and truth have **m** **Ps 85:10** 6298
as he **m** them, he said to them, **Jer 41:6** 6298
and have **m** our end by the sword **Jer 44:18** 8552
who were demon-possessed **m** Him **Mt 8:28** 5221
Jesus **m** them and greeted them. **Mt 28:9** 5221
with an unclean spirit **m** Him, **Mk 5:2** 5221
He was **m** by a man from the **Lk 8:27** 5221
mountain, a large crowd **m** Him. **Lk 9:37** 4876
men who stood at a distance **m** Him; **Lk 17:12** 528
now going down, *his* slaves **m** him, **Jn 4:51** 5221
in the place where Martha **m** Him. **Jn 11:30** 5221
also the people went and **m** Him, **Jn 12:18** 5221
often **m** there with His disciples. **Jn 18:2** 4863
Peter entered, Cornelius **m** him, **Ac 10:25** 4876
year they **m** with the church and **Ac 11:26** 4863
a spirit of divination **m** us, **Ac 16:16** 5221
And when he **m** us at Assos, we took **Ac 20:14** 4820
striking a reef where two seas **m**, **Ac 27:41** 1337
who **m** Abraham as he was returning **Heb 7:1** 4876
his father when Melchizedek **m** him. **Heb 7:10** 4876

METAL
Now he made the sea of cast **m** ten **1Ki 7:23**
and he set the sea *of cast* **m** on **1Ki 7:39**
Also he made the cast **m** sea, **2Ch 4:2**
A calf of molten **m** And said, **Ne 9:18** 4541a
And he who smooths **m** with **Is 41:7**
something like glowing **m** in the **Ezk 1:4** 2830
like glowing **m** that looked like fire **Ezk 1:27** 2830
like the appearance of glowing **m**. **Ezk 8:2** 2830
Also their gods with their **m** images **Da 11:8** 5257a

METED
And **m** out the waters by measure, **Jb 28:25** 8505

METHUSELAH
years, and became the father of **M**. **Gn 5:21** 4968
after he became the father of **M**, **Gn 5:22** 4968
M lived one hundred and **Gn 5:25** 4968
Then **M** lived seven hundred and **Gn 5:26** 4968
So all the days of **M** were nine **Gn 5:27** 4968
Enoch, **M**, Lamech, **1Ch 1:3** 4968
the son of **M**, the son of Enoch, **Lk 3:37** 3103c

METHUSHAEL
Mehujael became the father of **M**, **Gn 4:18** 4967
and **M** became the father of Lamech. **Gn 4:18** 4967

MEUNIM
the sons of Asnah, the sons of **M**, **Ezr 2:50** 4586
the sons of Besai, the sons of **M**, **Ne 7:52** 4586

MEUNITES
and the **M** who were found there, **1Ch 4:41** 4586
together with some of the **M**, **2Ch 20:1** 4586
who lived in Gur-baal, and the **M**. **2Ch 26:7** 4586

MEZAHAB
daughter of Matred, daughter of **M**. **Gn 36:39** 4314
of Matred, the daughter of **M**. **1Ch 1:50** 4314

MEZOBAITE
Eliel and Obed and Jaasiel the **M**. **1Ch 11:47** 4677

MIBHAR
of Nathan, **M** the son of Hagri, **1Ch 11:38** 4006

MIBSAM
and Kedar and Adbeel and **M** **Gn 25:13** 4017
Nebaioth, then Kedar, Adbeel, **M**, **1Ch 1:29** 4017
Shallum his son, **M** his son, **1Ch 4:25** 4017

MIBZAR
chief Kenaz, chief Teman, chief **M**, **Gn 36:42** 4014
chief Kenaz, chief Teman, chief **M**, **1Ch 1:53** 4014

MICA
had a young son whose name was **M**. **2Sa 9:12** 4316
Galal and Mattaniah the son of **M**, **1Ch 9:15** 4316
M, Rehob, Hashabiah, **Ne 10:11** 4316
and Mattaniah the son of **M**, **Ne 11:17** 4316
son of Mattaniah, the son of **M**, **Ne 11:22** 4316

MICAH
of Ephraim whose name was **M**. **Jg 17:1** 4321
and they were in the house of **M**. **Jg 17:4** 4321
And the man **M** had a shrine and he **Jg 17:5** 4318
of Ephraim to the house of **M**, **Jg 17:8** 4318
M said to him, "Where do you come **Jg 17:9** 4318
M then said to him, **Jg 17:10** 4318
So **M** consecrated the Levite, and **Jg 17:12** 4318
and lived in the house of **M**. **Jg 17:12** 4318
M said, "Now I know that the LORD **Jg 17:13** 4318
of Ephraim, to the house of **M**, **Jg 18:2** 4318
they were near the house of **M**, **Jg 18:3** 4318
"Thus and so has **M** done to me, **Jg 18:4** 4318
and came to the house of **M**. **Jg 18:13** 4318
the Levite, to the house of **M**, **Jg 18:15** 4318
some distance from the house of **M**, **Jg 18:22** 4318
who turned around and said to **M**, **Jg 18:23** 4318
and when **M** saw that they were too **Jg 18:26** 4318
Then they took what **M** had made and **Jg 18:27** 4318
M his son, Reaiah his son, Baal **1Ch 5:5** 4318
Merib-baal became the father of **M**. **1Ch 8:34** 4318
The sons of **M** *were* Pithon, **1Ch 8:35** 4318
Merib-baal became the father of **M**. **1Ch 9:40** 4318
The sons of **M** *were* Pithon, **1Ch 9:41** 4318
The sons of Uzziel *were* **M** the first **1Ch 23:20** 4318
Of the sons of Uzziel, **M**; **1Ch 24:24** 4318
of the sons of **M**, Shamir. **1Ch 24:24** 4318
The brother of **M**, Isshiah; **1Ch 24:25** 4318
of Shaphan, Abdon the son of **M**, **2Ch 34:20** 4318
"**M** of Moresheth prophesied in the **Jer 26:18** 4318
word of the LORD which came *to* **M** **Mi 1:1** 4318

MICAH'S
When these went into **M** house **Jg 18:18** 4318
who *were* in the houses near **M** house **Jg 18:22** 4318
M graven image which he had made **Jg 18:31** 4318

MICAIAH
He is **M** son of Imlah." **1Ki 22:8** 4321
"Bring quickly **M** son of Imlah." **1Ki 22:9** 4321
messenger who went to summon **M** **1Ki 22:13** 4321
But **M** said, "As the LORD lives, **1Ki 22:14** 4321
"**M**, shall we go to Ramoth-gilead **1Ki 22:15** 4321
M said, "Therefore, hear the word **1Ki 22:19** 4321
struck **M** on the cheek and said, **1Ki 22:24** 4321
M said, "Behold, you shall see **1Ki 22:25** 4321
"Take **M** and return him to Amon **1Ki 22:26** 4321
M said, "If you indeed return safely **1Ki 22:28** 4321
of Shaphan, Achbor the son of **M**, **2Ki 22:12** 4320
and his mother's name was **M** the **2Ch 13:2** 4322
Zechariah, Nethanel and **M**, **2Ch 17:7** 4322
He is **M**, son of Imla." **2Ch 18:7** 4321
"Bring quickly **M**, Imla's son." **2Ch 18:8** 4321
messenger who went to summon **M** **2Ch 18:12** 4321
But **M** said, "As the LORD lives, **2Ch 18:13** 4321
"**M**, shall we go to Ramoth-gilead **2Ch 18:14** 4318
M said, "Therefore, hear the word **2Ch 18:18** 4321
struck **M** on the cheek and said, **2Ch 18:23** 4321
M said, "Behold, you will see **2Ch 18:24** 4321
"Take **M** and return him to Amon **2Ch 18:25** 4321
M said, "If you indeed return safely, **2Ch 18:27** 4321
son of Mattaniah, the son of **M**, **Ne 12:35** 4320
Eliakim, Maaseiah, Miniamin, **M**, **Ne 12:41** 4320
Now when **M** the son of Gemariah, **Jer 36:11** 4321
M declared to them all the **Jer 36:13** 4321

MICE
golden tumors and five golden **m** **1Sa 6:4** 5909
likenesses of your **m** that ravage the **1Sa 6:5** 5909
and the box with the golden **m** and **1Sa 6:11** 5909
and the golden **m**, *according* to the **1Sa 6:18** 5909
flesh, detestable things and **m**, **Is 66:17** 5909

MICHAEL
of Asher, Sethur the son of **M**; **Nu 13:13** 4317
their fathers' households *were* **M**, **1Ch 5:13** 4317
the son of Gilead, the son of **M**, **1Ch 5:14** 4317
the son of **M**, the son of Baaseiah, **1Ch 6:40** 4317
And the sons of Izrahiah *were* **M**, **1Ch 7:3** 4317
M, Ishpah and Joha *were* the sons **1Ch 8:16** 4317
Adnah, Jozabad, Jediael, **M**, **1Ch 12:20** 4317
for Issachar, Omri the son of **M**; **1Ch 27:18** 4317
Jehiel, Zechariah, Azaryahu, **M** and **2Ch 21:2** 4317
son of **M** and 80 males with him; **Ezr 8:8** 4317
behold, **M**, one of the chief princes **Da 10:13** 4317
these *forces* except **M** your prince. **Da 10:21** 4317
M, the great prince who stands **Da 12:1** 4317
But **M** the archangel, when he **Jude 1:9** *3413*
M and his angels waging war with **Rv 12:7** *3413*

MICHAL
and the name of the younger **M**. **1Sa 14:49** 4324
Now **M**, Saul's daughter, loved **1Sa 18:20** 4324
So Saul gave him **M** his daughter **1Sa 18:27** 4324
M, Saul's daughter, loved him, **1Sa 18:28** 4324
But **M**, David's wife, told him, **1Sa 19:11** 4324
So **M** let David down through a **1Sa 19:12** 4324
M took the household idol and **1Sa 19:13** 4324
So Saul said to **M**, **1Sa 19:17** 4324
And **M** said to Saul, **1Sa 19:17** 4324
Now Saul had given **M** his daughter, **1Sa 25:44** 4324
my face unless you first bring **M**, **2Sa 3:13** 4324
"Give me my wife **M**, to whom I was **2Sa 3:14** 4324
M the daughter of Saul looked out **2Sa 6:16** 4324
M the daughter of Saul came out to **2Sa 6:20** 4324
So David said to **M**, **2Sa 6:21** 4324
M the daughter of Saul had no child **2Sa 6:23** 4324
that **M** the daughter of Saul looked **1Ch 15:29** 4324

MICHMAS
the men of **M**, 122; **Ezr 2:27** 4363
the men of **M**, 122; **Ne 7:31** 4363

MICHMASH
2,000 were with Saul in **M** **1Sa 13:2** 4363
and they came up and camped in **M**, **1Sa 13:5** 4363
Philistines were assembling at **M**, **1Sa 13:11** 4363
while the Philistines camped at **M**. **1Sa 13:16** 4363
went out to the pass of **M**. **1Sa 13:23** 4363
crag rose on the north opposite **M**, **1Sa 14:5** 4363
that day from **M** to Aijalon. **1Sa 14:31** 4363
from Geba *onward*, at **M** and Aija, **Ne 11:31** 4363
At **M** he deposited his baggage. **Is 10:28** 4363

MICHMETHATH
went westward at **M** on the north, **Jos 16:6** 4366
to **M** which was east of Shechem; **Jos 17:7** 4366

MICHRI
the son of Uzzi, the son of **M**, **1Ch 9:8** 4381

MIDDAY
while he was taking his **m** rest. **2Sa 4:5** 6672a
When **m** was past, **1Ki 18:29** 6672a
Gate from early morning until **m**, **Ne 8:3** 4276, 3117
And your gloom *will become* like **m**. **Is 58:10** 6672a
stumble at **m** as in the twilight, **Is 59:10** 6672a
at **m**, O King, I saw on the way a **Ac 26:13** *2250, 3319*

MIDDIN
Beth-arabah, **M** and Secacah, **Jos 15:61** 4081

MIDDLE
which is in the **m** of the garden, **Gn 3:3** 8432
"The **m** bar in the center of **Ex 26:28** 8484
opening at its top in the **m** of it; **Ex 28:32** 8432
He made the **m** bar to pass **Ex 36:33** 8484
the **m** of the valley as a border **Dt 3:16** 8432
booty into the **m** of its open square **Dt 13:16** 8432
on dry ground in the **m** of the Jordan **Jos 3:17** 8432
here out of the **m** of the Jordan, **Jos 4:3** 8432
your God into the **m** of the Jordan, **Jos 4:5** 8432
stones from the **m** of the Jordan, **Jos 4:8** 8432
twelve stones in the **m** of the Jordan **Jos 4:9** 8432
were standing in the **m** of the Jordan **Jos 4:10** 8432
come up from the **m** of the Jordan, **Jos 4:18** 8432
sun stopped in the **m** of the sky and **Jos 10:13** 2677
both the **m** of the valley and half **Jos 12:2** 8432
which is in the **m** of the valley, **Jos 13:9** 8432
city which is in the **m** of the valley **Jos 13:16** 8432
at the beginning of the **m** watch, **Jg 7:19** 8484
torch in the **m** between two tails. **Jg 15:4** 8432
Samson grasped the two **m** pillars **Jg 16:29** 8432
It happened in the **m** of the night **Ru 3:8** 2677
Joab took him aside into the **m** of **2Sa 3:27** 8432
They came to the **m** of the house as **2Sa 4:6** 8432
cut off their garments in the **m** as **2Sa 10:4** 2677
his blood in the **m** of the highway. **2Sa 20:12** 8432
killed a lion in the **m** of a pit on a **2Sa 23:20** 8432
is in the **m** of the valley of Gad and **2Sa 24:5** 8432
"So she arose in the **m** of the night **1Ki 3:20** 8432
and the **m** *was* six cubits wide, **1Ki 6:6** 8484
by winding stairs to the **m** *story,* **1Ki 6:8** 8484
and from the **m** to the third. **1Ki 6:8** 8484
king consecrated the **m** of the court **1Ki 8:64** 8432
had gone out of the **m** court, **2Ki 20:4** 8484
cut off their garments in the **m** as **1Ch 19:4** 2677
consecrated the **m** of the court **2Ch 7:7** 8432
In the **m** of the night and *in* the **Pr 7:9** 380
who lies down in the **m** of the sea, **Pr 23:34** 3820
way of a ship in the **m** of the sea, **Pr 30:19** 3820
He built a tower in the **m** of it And **Is 5:2** 8432
refuse in the **m** of the streets. **Is 5:25** 7130
spread out his hands in the **m** of it **Is 25:11** 7130
"In the **m** of my life I am to **Is 38:10** 1824
in and sat down at the **M** Gate: **Jer 39:3** 8432
it into the **m** of the Euphrates, **Jer 51:63** 8432
and its **m** part has been charred, **Ezk 15:4** 8432
me down in the **m** of the valley; **Ezk 37:1** 8432
lower and **m** ones in the building. **Ezk 42:5** 8484
more than the lower and **m** ones. **Ezk 42:6** 8484
sanctuary shall be in the **m** of it. **Ezk 48:8** 8432
the house shall be in the **m** of it. **Ezk 48:21** 8432
which are in the **m** of that which **Ezk 48:22** 8432
but in the **m** of the week he will **Da 9:27** 2677
her down into the **m** of the ephah **Zch 5:8** 8432
Mount of Olives will be split in its **m** **Zch 14:4** 2677
the boat was in the **m** of the sea, **Mk 6:47** *3319*
into the **m** *of the crowd,* in **Lk 5:19** *3319*
a fire in the **m** of the courtyard **Lk 22:55** *3319*
headlong, he burst open in the **m** **Ac 1:18** *3319*
and in the **m** of the lampstands **Rv 1:13** *3319*
in the **m** of its street. **Rv 22:2** *3319*

MIDHEAVEN
and I heard an eagle flying in **m**, **Rv 8:13** *3321*
I saw another angel flying in **m**, **Rv 14:6** *3321*
to all the birds which fly in **m**, **Rv 19:17** *3321*

MIDIAN
Medan and **M** and Ishbak and Shuah. **Gn 25:2** 4080
The sons of **M** *were* Ephah and **Gn 25:4** 4080
defeated **M** in the field of Moab, **Gn 36:35** 4080
and settled in the land of **M**, **Ex 2:15** 4080
priest of **M** had seven daughters; **Ex 2:16** 4080
his father-in-law, the priest of **M**; **Ex 3:1** 4080
Now the LORD said to Moses in **M**, **Ex 4:19** 4080
Now Jethro, the priest of **M**, **Ex 18:1** 4080
Moab said to the elders of **M**, **Nu 22:4** 4080
elders of **M** departed with the *fees* **Nu 22:7** 4080
of a father's household in **M**. **Nu 25:15** 4080
the daughter of the leader of **M**, **Nu 25:18** 4080
war, that they may go against **M** to **Nu 31:3** 4080
execute the LORD's vengeance on **M**. **Nu 31:3** 4080
So they made war against **M**, **Nu 31:7** 4080
They killed the kings of **M** **Nu 31:8** 4080
Hur and Reba, the five kings of **M**; **Nu 31:8** 4080
women of **M** and their little ones; **Nu 31:9** 4080
Moses struck with the chiefs of **M**, **Jos 13:21** 4080
into the hands of **M** seven years. **Jg 6:1** 4080
power of **M** prevailed against Israel. **Jg 6:2** 4080
Because of **M** the sons of Israel **Jg 6:2** 4080
was brought very low because of **M**, **Jg 6:6** 4080
cried to the LORD on account of **M**, **Jg 6:7** 4080
and given us into the hand of **M**." **Jg 6:13** 4080
deliver Israel from the hand of **M**. **Jg 6:14** 4080
you shall defeat **M** as one man." **Jg 6:16** 4080
and the camp of **M** was on the north **Jg 7:1** 4080
for Me to give **M** into their hands, **Jg 7:2** 4080
the camp of **M** was below him in **Jg 7:8** 4080
was tumbling into the camp of **M**, **Jg 7:13** 4080
God has given **M** and all the camp **Jg 7:14** 4080
the camp of **M** into your hands." **Jg 7:15** 4080
all Manasseh, and they pursued **M**. **Jg 7:23** 4080
"Come down against **M** and take the **Jg 7:24** 4080
captured the two leaders of **M**, **Jg 7:25** 4080
of Zeeb, while they pursued **M**; **Jg 7:25** 4080
you went to fight against **M**?" **Jg 8:1** 4080
"God has given the leaders of **M**, **Jg 8:3** 4080
and Zalmunna, the kings of **M**." **Jg 8:5** 4080
and captured the two kings of **M**, **Jg 8:12** 4080
delivered us from the hand of **M**." **Jg 8:22** 4080
which *were* on the kings of **M**, **Jg 8:26** 4080
So **M** was subdued before the sons **Jg 8:28** 4080
delivered you from the hand of **M**; **Jg 9:17** 4080
arose from **M** and came to Paran; **1Ki 11:18** 4080
were Zimran, Jokshan, Medan, **M**, **1Ch 1:32** 4080
The sons of **M** were Ephah, **1Ch 1:33** 4080
defeated **M** in the field of Moab, **1Ch 1:46** 4080
Deal with them as with **M**, **Ps 83:9** 4080
oppressor, as at the battle of **M**. **Is 9:4** 4080
slaughter of **M** at the rock of Oreb; **Is 10:26** 4080
The young camels of **M** and Ephah; **Is 60:6** 4080
The tent curtains of the land of **M** **Hab 3:7** 4080
BECAME AN ALIEN IN THE LAND OF **M**, **Ac 7:29** *3099*

MIDIANITE
Then some **M** traders passed by, so **Gn 37:28** 4084
to Hobab the son of Reuel the **M**, **Nu 10:29** 4084
to his relatives a **M** woman, **Nu 25:6** 4084
who was slain with the **M** woman, **Nu 25:14** 4084
The name of the **M** woman who **Nu 25:15** 4084

MIDIANITES
M sold him in Egypt to Potiphar, **Gn 37:36** 4084
hostile to the **M** and strike them; **Nu 25:17** 4084
for the sons of Israel on the **M**; **Nu 31:2** 4084
that the **M** would come up with the **Jg 6:3** 4080
in order to save *it* from the **M**. **Jg 6:11** 4080
Then all the **M** and the Amalekites **Jg 6:33** 4080
will give the **M** into your hands; **Jg 7:7** 4080
Now the **M** and the Amalekites and **Jg 7:12** 4080

MIDNIGHT
'About **m** I am going out into the **Ex 11:4** 2676, 3915
Now it came about at **m** that the **Ex 12:29** 2677, 3915
Now Samson lay until **m**, **Jg 16:3** 2677, 3915
and at **m** he arose and took hold of **Jg 16:3** 2677, 3915
and at **m** People are shaken and **Jb 34:20** 2676, 3915
At **m** I shall rise to give thanks **Ps 119:62** 2676, 3915
"But at **m** there was a shout, **Mt 25:6** *3319, 3571*
whether in the evening, at **m**, **Mk 13:35** *3317*
friend, and goes to him at **m** **Lk 11:5** *3317*
But about **m** Paul and Silas were **Ac 16:25** *3317*
he prolonged his message until **m**. **Ac 20:7** *3317*
about **m** the sailors *began* to **Ac 27:27** *3319, 3571*

MIDST
an expanse in the **m** of the waters, **Gn 1:6** 8432
life also in the **m** of the garden, **Gn 2:9** 8432
Lot out of the **m** of the overthrow, **Gn 19:29** 8432
multitude in the **m** of the earth." **Gn 48:16** 7130
blazing fire from the **m** of a bush; **Ex 3:2** 8432
to him from the **m** of the bush and **Ex 3:4** 8432
which I shall do in the **m** of it; **Ex 3:20** 7130
the sons of Israel from their **m**." **Ex 7:5** 8432
the LORD, am in the **m** of the land. **Ex 8:22** 7130
continually in the **m** of the hail, **Ex 9:24** 8432
am going out into the **m** of Egypt, **Ex 11:4** 8432

shall go through the **m** of the sea on	Ex 14:16	8432
went through the **m** of the sea on	Ex 14:22	8432
after them into the **m** of the sea.	Ex 14:23	8432
the Egyptians in the **m** of the sea.	Ex 14:27	8432
dry land through the **m** of the sea,	Ex 14:29	8432
dry land through the **m** of the sea.	Ex 15:19	8432
will remove sickness from your **m**.	Ex 23:25	7130
to Moses from the **m** of the cloud.	Ex 24:16	8432
Moses entered the **m** of the cloud as	Ex 24:18	8432
for I will not go up in your **m**,	Ex 33:3	7130
I go up in your **m** for one moment,	Ex 33:5	7130
let the Lord go along in our **m**,	Ex 34:9	7130
or it will become a snare in your **m**.	Ex 34:12	7130
them in the **m** of their impurities.	Lv 16:16	8432
will be no immorality in your **m**.	Lv 20:14	8432
the Levites in the **m** of the camps;	Nu 2:17	8432
camp where I dwell in their **m**."	Nu 5:3	8432
which I have performed in their **m**?	Nu 14:11	7130
brought up this people from their **m**,	Nu 14:13	7130
LORD, are in the **m** of this people,	Nu 14:14	7130
them, and the LORD is in their **m**;	Nu 16:3	8432
from the **m** of the assembly.	Nu 16:33	8432
censers out of the **m** of the blaze,	Nu 16:37	996
ran into the **m** of the assembly,	Nu 16:47	8432
into the **m** of the burning heifer.	Nu 19:6	8432
off from the **m** of the assembly,	Nu 19:20	8432
from the **m** of the congregation and	Nu 25:7	8432
passed through the **m** of the sea into	Nu 33:8	8432
live, in the **m** of which I dwell;	Nu 35:34	8432
the **m** of the sons of Israel.' "	Nu 35:34	8432
spoke to you from the **m** of the fire	Dt 4:12	8432
at Horeb from the **m** of the fire,	Dt 4:15	8432
speaking from the **m** of the fire,	Dt 4:33	8432
His words from the **m** of the fire.	Dt 4:36	8432
mountain from the **m** of the fire,	Dt 5:4	8432
mountain from the **m** of the fire,	Dt 5:22	8432
voice from the **m** of the darkness,	Dt 5:23	8432
His voice from the **m** of the fire;	Dt 5:24	8432
speaking from the **m** of the fire,	Dt 5:26	8432
in the **m** of you is a jealous God;	Dt 6:15	7130
the LORD your God is in your **m**,	Dt 7:21	7130
from the **m** of the fire on the day	Dt 9:10	8432
from the **m** of the fire on the day	Dt 10:4	8432
which He did in the **m** of Egypt	Dt 11:3	8432
and the widow who are in your **m**,	Dt 16:11	7130
"If there is found in your **m**,	Dt 17:2	7130
shall purge the evil from your **m**.	Dt 17:7	7130
in his kingdom in the **m** of Israel.	Dt 17:20	7130
yourself in the **m** of your land,	Dt 19:2	8432
not be shed in the **m** of your land	Dt 19:10	7130
in the **m** of Your people Israel.'	Dt 21:8	7130
of innocent blood from your **m**,	Dt 21:9	7130
shall remove the evil from your **m**,	Dt 21:21	7130
God walks in the **m** of your camp	Dt 23:14	7130
"He shall live with you in your **m**,	Dt 23:16	7130
came through the **m** of the nations	Dt 29:16	7130
into the **m** of which they are going,	Dt 31:16	7130
in the **m** of the sons of Israel	Dt 32:51	8432
in the **m** of the sons of Israel.	Dt 32:51	8432
the **m** of ten thousand holy ones;	Dt 33:2	
"Pass through the **m** of the camp	Jos 1:11	7130
went through the **m** of the camp;	Jos 3:2	7130
in the **m** of Israel to this day,	Jos 6:25	7130
things under the ban from your **m**.	Jos 7:12	7130
things under the ban in your **m**,	Jos 7:13	7130
under the ban from your **m**."	Jos 7:13	7130
that night in the **m** of the valley.	Jos 8:13	8432
were *trapped* in the **m** of Israel,	Jos 8:22	8432
the **m** of the inheritance of the sons	Jos 16:9	8432
in the **m** of Ephraim to this day,	Jos 16:10	7130
in the **m** of the inheritance of the sons	Jos 19:1	8432
in the **m** of Judah's inheritance.	Jos 19:9	8432
an inheritance in their **m** to Joshua	Jos 19:49	8432
in the **m** of the possession of the sons	Jos 21:41	8432
we know that the LORD is in our **m**,	Jos 22:31	8432
Egypt by what I did in its **m**;	Jos 24:5	7130
peoples through whose **m** we passed.	Jos 24:17	7130
foreign gods which are in your **m**,	Jos 24:23	7130
in the **m** of Ephraim *and* in the	Jg 12:4	8432
and in the **m** of Manasseh."	Jg 12:4	8432
destroyed them in the **m** of them.	Jg 20:42	8432
they came into the **m** of the camp	1Sa 11:11	8432
him in the **m** of his brothers;	1Sa 16:13	7130
he raved in the **m** of the house,	1Sa 18:10	8432
fallen in the **m** of the battle!	2Sa 1:25	8432
was yet alive in the **m** of the oak.	2Sa 18:14	3820
his stand in the **m** of the plot,	2Sa 23:12	8432
servant is in the **m** of Your people	1Ki 3:8	8432
in the **m** of the inner house,	1Ki 6:27	8432
from the **m** of the iron furnace),	1Ki 8:51	8432
went out into the **m** of the battle;	1Ki 20:39	7130
they were in the **m** of Samaria.	2Ki 6:20	8432
their stand in the **m** of the plot and	1Ch 11:14	8432
had set it in the **m** of the court;	2Ch 6:13	8432
Then in the **m** of the assembly the	2Ch 20:14	8432
passed through the **m** of the sea on	Ne 9:11	8432
and went out into the **m** of the city	Es 4:1	8432
In the **m** of the assembly I will	Ps 22:22	8432
God is in the **m** of her, she will	Ps 46:5	7130
O God, In the **m** of Your temple.	Ps 48:9	7130
and mischief are in her **m**.	Ps 55:10	7130
Destruction is in her **m**;	Ps 55:11	7130
is in their dwelling, in their **m**.	Ps 55:15	7130
have fallen into the **m** of it.	Ps 57:6	8432
In the **m** of the maidens beating	Ps 68:25	8432
in the **m** of Your meeting place;	Ps 74:4	7130
deliverance in the **m** of the earth.	Ps 74:12	7130
them fall in the **m** of their camp,	Ps 78:28	7130
He judges in the **m** of the rulers.	Ps 82:1	7130
take me away in the **m** of my days,	Ps 102:24	2677
in the **m** of many I will praise Him.	Ps 109:30	8432
"Rule in the **m** of Your enemies."	Ps 110:2	7130
In the **m** of you, O Jerusalem.	Ps 116:19	8432
signs and wonders into your **m**,	Ps 135:9	8432
brought Israel out from their **m**,	Ps 136:11	8432
Israel pass through the **m** of it,	Ps 136:14	8432
in the **m** of it We hung our harps.	Ps 137:2	8432
Though I walk in the **m** of trouble,	Ps 138:7	7130
Keep them in the **m** of your heart.	Pr 4:21	8432
utter ruin In the **m** of the assembly	Pr 5:14	8432
In the **m** of the paths of justice,	Pr 8:20	8432
bloodshed of Jerusalem from her **m**,	Is 4:4	7130
live alone in the **m** of the land!	Is 5:8	7130
are many in the **m** of the land.	Is 6:12	7130
Tabeel as king in the **m** of it,"	Is 7:6	8432
in the **m** of the whole land.	Is 10:23	7130
great in your **m** is the Holy One of	Is 12:6	7130
in the **m** of the land of Egypt,	Is 19:19	8432
a blessing in the **m** of the earth,	Is 19:24	7130
thus it will be in the **m** of the earth	Is 24:13	7130
the work of My hands, in his **m**,	Is 29:23	7130
springs in the **m** of the valleys;	Is 41:18	8432
Go out of the **m** of her, purify	Is 52:11	8432
you remove the yoke from your **m**,	Is 58:9	8432
in the **m** of the peoples.	Is 61:9	8432
His Holy Spirit in the **m** of them,	Is 63:11	7130
Benjamin, From the **m** of Jerusalem!	Jer 6:1	7130
In whose **m** there is only oppression.	Jer 6:6	7130
dwelling is in the **m** of deceit;	Jer 9:6	8432
be built up in the **m** of My people.	Jer 12:16	8432
Yet You are in our **m**,	Jer 14:9	7130
In the **m** of his days it will	Jer 17:11	2677
let your prophets who are in your **m**	Jer 29:8	7130
shall come forth from their **m**;	Jer 30:21	7130
her mercenaries in her **m** Are like	Jer 46:21	7130
And a flame from the **m** of Sihon,	Jer 48:45	996
"Wander away from the **m** of Babylon	Jer 50:8	8432
who are in the **m** of her,	Jer 50:37	8432
Flee from the **m** of Babylon, And	Jer 51:6	8432
"Come forth from her **m**,	Jer 51:45	8432
all her slain will fall in her **m**.	Jer 51:47	8432
were found in the **m** of the city.	Jer 52:25	8432
her In the **m** of distress.	La 1:3	996
all my strong men In my **m**;	La 1:15	7130
refuse In the **m** of the peoples.	La 3:45	7130
Who have shed in her **m** The blood	La 4:13	7130
and in its **m** something like	Ezk 1:4	8432
glowing metal in the **m** of the fire.	Ezk 1:4	8432
In the **m** of the living beings	Ezk 1:13	
your abominations are in your **m**;	Ezk 7:9	8432
"Go through the **m** of the city,	Ezk 9:4	8432
even through the **m** of Jerusalem,	Ezk 9:4	8432
are being committed in its **m**."	Ezk 9:4	8432
you have laid in the **m** of the city	Ezk 11:7	8432
you out of the **m** of the city and	Ezk 11:9	8432
will you be flesh in the **m** of it,	Ezk 11:11	8432
went up from the **m** of the city and	Ezk 11:23	8432
in the **m** of the rebellious house,	Ezk 12:2	8432
you will be consumed in its **m**.	Ezk 13:14	8432
Daniel and Job were in its **m**,	Ezk 14:14	8432
these three men were in its **m**,	Ezk 14:16	8432
these three men were in its **m**,	Ezk 14:18	8432
Daniel and Job were in its **m**,	Ezk 14:20	8432
in the **m** of the land of Egypt.	Ezk 20:8	8432
will be in the **m** of the land.	Ezk 21:32	8432
"A city shedding blood in her **m**,	Ezk 22:3	8432
they have oppressed in your **m**;	Ezk 22:7	8432
In your **m** they have committed acts	Ezk 22:9	8432
you into the **m** of Jerusalem.	Ezk 22:19	8432
you will be melted in the **m** of it.	Ezk 22:21	8432
you will be melted in the **m** of it;	Ezk 22:22	8432
conspiracy of her prophets in her **m** like	Ezk 22:25	8432
made many widows in the **m** of her.	Ezk 22:25	8432
"For her blood is in her **m**;	Ezk 24:7	8432
of nets in the **m** of the sea,	Ezk 26:5	8432
the slaughter occurs in your **m**?	Ezk 26:15	8432
your company that is in your **m**,	Ezk 27:27	8432
who is silent in the **m** of the sea?	Ezk 27:32	8432
Have fallen in the **m** of you.	Ezk 27:34	8432
in the **m** of the stones of fire.	Ezk 28:14	8432
From the **m** of the stones of fire.	Ezk 28:16	8432
brought fire from the **m** of you;	Ezk 28:18	8432
I will be glorified in your **m**.	Ezk 28:22	8432
And the wounded will fall in her **m**	Ezk 28:23	8432
that lies in the **m** of his rivers,	Ezk 29:3	8432
up out of the **m** of your rivers,	Ezk 29:4	8432
in the **m** of desolated lands.	Ezk 29:12	8432
in the **m** of cities that are	Ezk 29:12	8432
will open your mouth in their **m**.	Ezk 29:21	8432
In the **m** of the desolated lands;	Ezk 30:7	8432
In the **m** of the devastated cities.	Ezk 30:7	8432
lie in the **m** of the uncircumcised,	Ezk 31:18	8432
fall in the **m** of those who are slain	Ezk 32:20	8432
his helpers from the **m** of Sheol,	Ezk 32:21	8432
were put in the **m** of the slain.	Ezk 32:25	8432
"But in the **m** of the uncircumcised	Ezk 32:28	8432
a prophet has been in their **m**."	Ezk 33:33	8432
you have profaned in their **m**.	Ezk 36:23	8432
My sanctuary in their **m** forever.	Ezk 37:26	8432
My sanctuary is in their **m** forever."	Ezk 37:28	8432
in the **m** of My people Israel;	Ezk 39:7	8432
the aliens who stay in your **m**,	Ezk 47:22	8432
who bring forth sons in your **m**.	Ezk 47:22	8432
of the LORD shall be in its **m**.	Ezk 48:10	8432
and the city shall be in its **m**.	Ezk 48:15	8432
m of a furnace of blazing fire."	Da 3:6	1459
m of a furnace of blazing fire.	Da 3:11	1459
m of a furnace of blazing fire;	Da 3:15	1459
the **m** of the furnace of blazing fire.	Da 3:21	1459
fell into the **m** of the furnace of	Da 3:23	1459
bound into the **m** of the fire?"	Da 3:24	1459
in the **m** of the fire without harm,	Da 3:25	1459
came out of the **m** of the fire.	Da 3:26	1459
was a tree in the **m** of the earth	Da 4:10	1459
not man, the Holy One in your **m**,	Hos 11:9	7130
know that I am in the **m** of Israel,	Jl 2:27	7130
also cut off the judge from her **m** And	Am 2:3	7130
her and *the* oppressions in her **m**.	Am 3:9	7130
will pass through the **m** of you,"	Am 5:17	7130
calves from the **m** of the stall,	Am 6:4	8432
line In the **m** of My people Israel.	Am 7:8	7130
in the **m** of the house of Israel;	Am 7:10	7130
Like a flock in the **m** of its pasture	Mi 2:12	8432
"Is not the LORD in our **m**?	Mi 3:11	7130
your vileness will be in your **m**.	Mi 6:14	7130
In the **m** of a fruitful field.	Mi 7:14	8432
your people are women in your **m**!	Na 3:13	7130
Your work in the **m** of the years,	Hab 3:2	7130
the **m** of the years make it known;	Hab 3:2	7130
Flocks will lie down in her **m**,	Zph 2:14	8432
remove from your **m** Your proud,	Zph 3:11	7130
of Israel, the LORD, is in your **m**;	Zph 3:15	7130
"The LORD your God is in your **m**,	Zph 3:17	7130
My Spirit is abiding in your **m**;	Hg 2:5	8432
I will be the glory in her **m**.' "	Zch 2:5	8432
and I will dwell in your **m**,"	Zch 2:10	8432
Then I will dwell in your **m**,	Zch 2:11	8432
will dwell in the **m** of Jerusalem.	Zch 8:3	8432
will live in the **m** of Jerusalem;	Zch 8:8	8432
out as sheep in the **m** of wolves;	Mt 10:16	*3319*
My name, I am there in their **m**."	Mt 18:20	*3319*
sitting in the **m** of the teachers,	Lk 2:46	*3319*
But passing through their **m**,	Lk 4:30	*3319*
had thrown him down in the **m**	Lk 4:35	*3319*
out as lambs in the **m** of wolves.	Lk 10:3	*3319*
the kingdom of God is in your **m**."	Lk 17:21	*1787*
are in the **m** of the city must	Lk 21:21	*3319*
He Himself stood in their **m**	Lk 24:36	*3319*
when it was now the **m** of the feast	Jn 7:14	*3322*
Jesus came and stood in their **m** and	Jn 20:19	*3319*
been shut, and stood in their **m** and	Jn 20:26	*3319*
stood up in the **m** of the brethren	Ac 1:15	*3319*
performed through Him in your **m**,	Ac 2:22	*3319*
stood in the **m** of the Areopagus	Ac 17:22	*3319*
So Paul went out of their **m**.	Ac 17:33	*3319*
Paul stood up in their **m** and said,	Ac 27:21	*3319*
deed would be removed from your **m**.	1Co 5:2	*3319*
FROM THEIR **M** AND BE SEPARATE,"	2Co 6:17	*3319*
above reproach in the **m** of a crooked	Php 2:15	*3319*
faith in the **m** of all your persecutions	2Th 1:4	
IN THE **M** OF THE CONGREGATION I	Heb 2:12	*3319*
rich man in the **m** of his pursuits	Jas 1:11	

MIDWIFE

labor the **m** said to her,	Gn 35:17	3205
and the **m** took and tied a scarlet	Gn 38:28	3205
before the **m** can get to them."	Ex 1:19	3205

MIDWIVES

of Egypt spoke to the Hebrew **m**,	Ex 1:15	3205
But the **m** feared God, and did not	Ex 1:17	3205
king of Egypt called for the **m** and	Ex 1:18	3205
The **m** said to Pharaoh,	Ex 1:19	3205
So God was good to the **m**,	Ex 1:20	3205
Because the **m** feared God,	Ex 1:21	3205

MIGDAL-EL

and Yiron and **M**, Horem and	Jos 19:38	4027

MIGDAL-GAD

Zenan and Hadashah and **M**,	Jos 15:37	4028

MIGDOL

Pi-hahiroth, between **M** and the sea;	Ex 14:2	4024
and they camped before **M**.	Nu 33:7	4024
Egypt, those who were living in **M**,	Jer 44:1	4024
in Egypt and proclaim in **M**,	Jer 46:14	4024
from **M** *to* Syene and even to the	Ezk 29:10	4024
From **M** *to* Syene They will fall	Ezk 30:6	4024

MIGHT

he **m** stretch out his hand, and take	Gn 3:22	6435
that Ishmael **m** live before You!"	Gn 17:18	
m kill me on account of Rebekah,	Gn 26:7	
'I **m** die on account of her.' "	Gn 26:9	6435
One of the people **m** easily have lain	Gn 26:10	
so that they **m** mate by the rods;	Gn 30:41	
so that I **m** have sent you away	Gn 31:27	
m rescue him out of their hands,	Gn 37:22	
My **m** and the beginning of my	Gn 49:3	3581b
"The people **m** change their minds	Ex 13:17	6435
they **m** travel by day and by night.	Ex 13:21	
Egypt, that I **m** dwell among them;	Ex 29:46	
and I **m** destroy you on the way."	Ex 33:3	6435
otherwise you **m** make a covenant with	Ex 34:15	6435
and someone **m** invite you to eat of	Ex 34:15	
and you **m** take some of his daughters	Ex 34:16	
and his daughters **m** play the harlot	Ex 34:16	
the LORD **m** be made clear to them.	Lv 24:12	
nations, that I **m** be their God.	Lv 26:45	
by which he **m** die, and *as a result*	Nu 35:18	
that you **m** perform them in the	Dt 4:14	
that you **m** know that the LORD,	Dt 4:35	
that a manslayer **m** flee there,	Dt 4:42	
to one of these cities he **m** live:	Dt 4:42	
that you **m** do *them* in the land	Dt 6:1	
grandson **m** fear the LORD your God,	Dt 6:2	
all your soul and with all your **m**.	Dt 6:5	3966
forty years, that He **m** humble you,	Dt 8:2	
that He **m** make you understand that	Dt 8:3	
that He **m** humble you and that He	Dt 8:16	
humble you and that He **m** test you,	Dt 8:16	

otherwise the avenger of blood **m** **Dt 19:6**
otherwise he **m** die in the battle **Dt 20:5**
otherwise he **m** die in the battle **Dt 20:6**
otherwise he **m** die in the battle **Dt 20:7**
so that he **m** not make his **Dt 20:8**
in order that you **m** know that I am **Dt 29:6**
that he **m** utterly destroy them, **Jos 11:20**
that they **m** receive no mercy, **Jos 11:20**
mercy, but that he **m** destroy them, **Jos 11:20**
sons of Israel **m** be taught war, **Jg 3:2**
the rising of the sun in its **m**." **Jg 5:31** 1369
seventy sons of Jerubbaal **m** come, **Jg 9:24**
and their blood **m** be laid on **Jg 9:24**
who **m** pass by them along the road; **Jg 9:25**
And he bent with all his **m** so that **Jg 16:30** 3581b
sons, that he **m** become his priest. **Jg 17:5**
stay wherever he **m** find *a place;* **Jg 17:8**
m return from the land of Moab, **Ru 1:6**
For not by **m** shall a man prevail. **1Sa 2:9** 3581b
he **m** go ahead of us and pass on, **1Sa 9:27**
he **m** become the king's son-in-law. **1Sa 18:27**
that they **m** bring it from the house **2Sa 6:3**
before the LORD with all *his* **m**, **2Sa 6:14** 5797
since he **m** do *himself* harm!" **2Sa 12:18**
LORD **m** bring calamity on Absalom. **2Sa 17:14**
a house that My name **m** be there, **1Ki 8:16**
that He **m** establish His word, **1Ki 12:15**
all the acts of Asa and all his **m** **1Ki 15:23** 1369
Baasha and what he did and his **m**, **1Ki 16:5** 1369
he did and his **m** which he showed, **1Ki 16:27** 1369
for himself that he **m** die, **1Ki 19:4**
and his **m** which he showed and how **1Ki 22:45** 1369
so that he **m** destroy the **2Ki 10:19**
and all that he did and all his **m**, **2Ki 10:34** 1369
and all that he did and his **m**, **2Ki 13:8** 1369
Joash and all that he did and his **m** **2Ki 13:12** 1369
and his **m** and how he fought with **2Ki 14:15** 1369
and all that he did and his **m**, **2Ki 14:28** 1369
so that his hand **m** be with him **2Ki 15:19**
acts of Hezekiah and all his **m**, **2Ki 20:20** 1369
that they **m** provoke Me to anger **2Ki 22:17**
that no man **m** make his son or his **2Ki 23:10**
that he **m** confirm the words of the **2Ki 23:24**
all his soul and with all his **m**, **2Ki 23:25** 3966
that he **m** not reign in Jerusalem; **2Ki 23:33**
and that Your hand **m** be with me, **1Ch 4:10**
before God with all *their* **m**, **1Ch 13:8** 5797
and in Your hand is power and **m**; **1Ch 29:12** 1369
a house that My name **m** be there, **2Ch 6:5**
Jerusalem that My name **m** be there, **2Ch 6:6**
place, You and the ark of Your **m**; **2Ch 6:41** 5797
the LORD **m** establish His word, **2Ch 10:15**
Power and **m** are in Your hand so **2Ch 20:6** 1369
that He **m** deliver them into the **2Ch 25:20**
that they **m** devote themselves to **2Ch 31:4**
so that they **m** take the city. **2Ch 32:18**
that He **m** know all that was in his **2Ch 32:31**
that they **m** provoke Me to anger **2Ch 34:25**
burnt offerings that *they* **m** give them **2Ch 35:12**
and that we **m** write down the names **Ezr 5:10**
that we **m** humble ourselves before **Ezr 8:21**
and our houses that we **m** get grain **Ne 5:3**
that I **m** become frightened and act **Ne 6:13**
so that they **m** have an evil report **Ne 6:13**
they **m** gain insight into the words **Ne 8:13**
So that they **m** return to You, **Ne 9:26**
that they **m** bring it to the house **Ne 10:34**
and that they **m** bring the **Ne 10:35**
that they **m** celebrate the dedication **Ne 12:27**
m remove his sackcloth from him, **Es 4:4**
he **m** show Esther and inform her, **Es 4:8**
or province which **m** attack them, **Es 8:11**
"Oh that my request **m** come to pass, **Jb 6:8**
"But would that God **m** speak, **Jb 11:5**
"With Him are wisdom and **m**; **Jb 12:13** 1369
"O that a man **m** plead with God As **Jb 16:21**
"Oh that I knew where I **m** find Him, **Jb 23:3**
Him, That I **m** come to His seat! **Jb 23:3**
With the **m** of Your hand You persecute **Jb 30:21** 6108
And that He **m** hear the cry of the **Jb 34:28**
That it **m** take hold of the ends of **Jb 38:13**
"Do you give the horse *his* **m**? **Jb 39:19** 1369
His strength, Being girded with **m**; **Ps 65:6** 1369
He rules by His **m** forever; **Ps 66:7** 1369
the generation to come **m** know, **Ps 78:6**
they **m** be destroyed forevermore. **Ps 92:7**
That he **m** teach his elders wisdom. **Ps 105:22**
That they **m** take possession of *the* **Ps 105:44**
So that they **m** keep His statutes And **Ps 105:45**
That He **m** make His power known. **Ps 106:8**
there anything of which one **m** say, **Ec 1:10**
do, do *it* with *all* your **m**; **Ec 9:10** 3581b
Otherwise they **m** see with their eyes, **Is 6:10**
we have waited that He **m** save us. **Is 25:9**
who are near, acknowledge My **m**." **Is 33:13** 1369
the Lord GOD will come with **m**, **Is 40:10** 2389
Because of the greatness of His **m** **Is 40:26** 202
who lacks **m** He increases power. **Is 40:29** 202
the beginning, that we **m** know? **Is 41:26**
that Israel **m** be gathered to Him **Is 49:5**
mountains **m** quake at Your presence **Is 64:1**
That I **m** weep day and night For **Jer 9:1**
That I **m** leave my people And go **Jer 9:2**
not the mighty man boast of his **m**, **Jer 9:23** 1369
great, and great is Your name in **m**. **Jer 10:6** 1369
'that they **m** be for Me a people, **Jer 13:11**
know My power and My **m**; **Jer 16:21** 1369
"At one moment I **m** speak **Jer 18:7**
"Or at another moment I **m** speak **Jer 18:9**
is evil And their **m** is not right. **Jer 23:10** 1369
"in order that you **m** provoke Me **Jer 25:7**
so that you **m** be cut off and **Jer 44:8**
of Elam, The finest of their **m**. **Jer 49:35** 1369
exalted the **m** of your adversaries. **La 2:17** 7161
every passer-by who **m** be *willing.* **Ezk 16:15**
you **m** play the harlot with them. **Ezk 16:17**
was planted, that he **m** water it. **Ezk 17:7**
m yield branches and bear fruit **Ezk 17:8**
the kingdom **m** be in subjection, **Ezk 17:14**
his covenant that it **m** continue. **Ezk 17:14**
to Egypt that they **m** give him horses **Ezk 17:15**
that they **m** know that I am the **Ezk 20:12**
so that I **m** make them desolate, **Ezk 20:26**
m know that I am the LORD."' **Ezk 20:26**
who for *all* their **m** are laid with **Ezk 32:29** 1369
the terror resulting from their **m**, **Ezk 32:30** 1369
around, that they **m** be fastened, **Ezk 41:6**
that he **m** not defile himself. **Da 1:8**
in order that he **m** declare the **Da 2:16**
so that they **m** request **Da 2:18**
that they **m** make known to me the **Da 4:6**
by the **m** of my power and for the **Da 4:30** 8632a
his concubines **m** drink from them. **Da 5:2**
that they **m** read this inscription **Da 5:15**
satraps **m** be accountable to them, **Da 6:2**
that the king **m** not suffer loss. **Da 6:2**
men of every language **M** serve Him. **Da 7:14**
That they **m** be cut off. **Hos 8:4**
you **m** take possession of the land **Am 2:10**
So that you **m** know the **Mi 6:5**
see and be ashamed Of all their **m**. **Mi 7:16** 1369
Ethiopia was *her* **m**, **Na 3:9** 6109
'Not by **m** nor by power, but by My **Zch 4:6** 2428
end that the temple **m** be built. **Zch 8:9**
that you **m** not uselessly kindle **Mal 1:10**
so that they **m** accuse Him. **Mt 12:10**
Him, *as to* how they **m** destroy Him. **Mt 12:14**
they **m** just touch the fringe of His **Mt 14:36**
for they **m** faint on the way." **Mt 15:32**
so that He **m** lay His hands on them **Mt 19:13**
they **m** trap Him in what He said. **Mt 22:15**
otherwise a riot **m** occur among **Mt 26:5**
"For this *perfume* **m** have been sold **Mt 26:9** *1410*
that they **m** put Him to death. **Mt 26:59**
so that they **m** accuse Him. **Mk 3:2**
Him, *as to* how they **m** destroy Him. **Mk 3:6**
OTHERWISE THEY **M** RETURN AND BE **Mk 4:12**
Him that he **m** accompany Him. **Mk 5:18**
they **m** just touch the fringe of His **Mk 6:56**
to Him so that He **m** touch them; **Mk 10:13**
otherwise there **m** be a riot of **Mk 14:2**
"For this perfume **m** have been sold **Mk 14:5** *1410*
possible, the hour **m** pass Him by. **Mk 14:35**
that they **m** come and anoint Him. **Mk 16:1**
enemies, **M** serve Him without fear, **Lk 1:74**
they **m** find *reason* to accuse Him. **Lk 6:7**
together what they **m** do to Jesus. **Lk 6:11**
Him that he **m** accompany Him; **Lk 8:38**
which of them **m** be the greatest. **Lk 9:46**
catch *Him* in something He **m** say. **Lk 11:54**
that I **m** celebrate with my friends; **Lk 15:29**
that he **m** know what business they **Lk 19:15**
not find anything that they **m** do, **Lk 19:48**
m catch Him in some statement, **Lk 20:20**
how they **m** put Him to death; **Lk 22:2**
how he **m** betray Him to them. **Lk 22:4**
which one of them it **m** be who was **Lk 22:23**
that all **m** believe through him. **Jn 1:7**
that He **m** be manifested to Israel, **Jn 1:31**
but that the world **m** be saved through **Jn 3:17**
m have grounds for accusing Him. **Jn 8:6**
works of God **m** be displayed in him **Jn 9:3**
order that He **m** also gather together **Jn 11:52**
report it, so that they **m** seize Him. **Jn 11:57**
but that they **m** also see Lazarus, **Jn 12:9**
defiled, but **m** eat the Passover. **Jn 18:28**
that their legs **m** be broken, **Jn 19:31**
and *that* they **m** be taken away. **Jn 19:31**
he **m** take away the body of Jesus; **Jn 19:38**
with all, as anyone **m** have need. **Ac 2:45**
shadow **m** fall on any one of them. **Ac 5:15**
that they **m** be stoned). **Ac 5:26**
and asked that he **m** find a **Ac 7:46**
they **m** receive the Holy Spirit. **Ac 8:15**
m bring them bound to Jerusalem. **Ac 9:2**
so that he **m** regain his sight." **Ac 9:12**
so that they **m** put him to death; **Ac 9:24**
the vision which he had seen **m** be, **Ac 10:17**
these things **m** be spoken to them **Ac 13:42**
they **m** grope for Him and find Him, **Ac 17:27**
so that he **m** find out the reason why **Ac 22:24**
that he **m** have him brought to **Ac 25:3**
this day, **m** become such as I am, **Ac 26:29**
"This man **m** have been set free if **Ac 26:32** *1410*
fearing that they **m** run aground on **Ac 27:17**
Fearing that we **m** run aground **Ac 27:29**
OTHERWISE THEY **M** SEE WITH THEIR EYES, **Ac 28:27**
that he **m** be the father of all who **Ro 4:11**
m be credited to them, **Ro 4:11**
so that he **m** become a father **Ro 4:18**
we too **m** walk in newness of life. **Ro 6:4**
body of sin **m** be done away with, **Ro 6:6**
that you **m** be joined to another, **Ro 7:4**
that we **m** bear fruit for God. **Ro 7:4**
in order that it **m** be shown to be **Ro 7:13**
of the Law **m** be fulfilled in us, **Ro 8:4**
THAT MY NAME **M** BE PROCLAIMED **Ro 9:17**
if somehow I **m** move to jealousy my **Ro 11:14**
off so that I **m** be grafted in." **Ro 11:19**
IT **M** BE PAID BACK TO HIM AGAIN? **Ro 11:35**
that He **m** be Lord both of the dead **Ro 14:9**
of the Scriptures we **m** have hope. **Ro 15:4**
so that we also **m** reign with you. **1Co 4:8**
as a Jew, so that I **m** win Jews; **1Co 9:20**
that I **m** win those who are under **1Co 9:20**
I **m** win those who are without law. **1Co 9:21**
weak, that I **m** win the weak; **1Co 9:22**
you **m** twice receive a blessing; **2Co 1:15**
but that you **m** know the love which **2Co 2:4**
such a one **m** be overwhelmed **2Co 2:7**
that I **m** put you to the test, **2Co 2:9**
that they **m** not see the light of **2Co 4:4**
so that they who live **m** no longer **2Co 5:15**
that we **m** become the righteousness **2Co 5:21**
so that you **m** not suffer loss **2Co 7:9**
earnestness on our behalf **m** be made **2Co 7:12**
through His poverty **m** become rich. **2Co 8:9**
I **m** present you *as* a pure virgin. **2Co 11:2**
myself so that you **m** be exalted, **2Co 11:7**
times that it **m** leave me. **2Co 12:8**
that He **m** rescue us from this **Ga 1:4**
I **m** preach Him among the Gentiles, **Ga 1:16**
for fear that I **m** be running, **Ga 2:2**
so that we **m** *go* to **Ga 2:9**
to the Law, so that I **m** live to God. **Ga 2:19**
the blessing of Abraham **m** come to **Ga 3:14**
m be given to those who believe. **Ga 3:22**
so that He **m** redeem those **Ga 4:5**
we **m** receive the adoption as sons. **Ga 4:5**
working of the strength of His **m** **Eph 1:19** *2479*
He **m** show the surpassing riches of **Eph 2:7**
m make the two into one new man, **Eph 2:15**
and **m** reconcile them both in one **Eph 2:16**
wisdom of God **m** now be made **Eph 3:10**
that He **m** fill all things.) **Eph 4:10**
that He **m** sanctify her, having **Eph 5:26**
that He **m** present to Himself the **Eph 5:27**
and in the strength of His **m**. **Eph 6:10** *2479*
although I myself **m** have confidence **Php 3:4**
according to His glorious **m**, **Col 1:11** *2904*
that I **m** fully carry out the **Col 1:25**
we **m** have asserted our authority. **1Th 2:6**
the tempter **m** have tempted you, **1Th 3:5**
Jesus Christ **m** demonstrate His **1Tm 1:16**
m be fully accomplished, **2Tm 4:17**
and that all the Gentiles **m** hear; **2Tm 4:17**
that on your behalf he **m** minister **Phm 1:13**
God He **m** taste death for everyone. **Heb 2:9**
that through death He **m** render **Heb 2:14**
and **m** free those who through **Heb 2:15**
that He **m** become a merciful and **Heb 2:17**
m obtain a better resurrection; **Heb 11:35**
that He **m** sanctify the people **Heb 13:12**
that we **m** die to sin and live to **1Pe 2:24**
that you **m** inherit a blessing. **1Pe 3:9**
so that He **m** bring us to God, **1Pe 3:18**
whereas angels who are greater in **m** **2Pe 2:11** *2479*
so that we **m** live through Him. **1Jn 4:9**
riches and wisdom and **m** and honor **Rv 5:12** *2479*
and honor and power and **m**, **Rv 7:12** *2479*
that he **m** add it to the prayers of **Rv 8:3**
gave birth he **m** devour her child. **Rv 12:4**
so that he **m** cause her to be swept **Rv 12:15**

MIGHTIER

of Israel are more and **m** than we. **Ex 1:9** 6099
nation greater and **m** than they." **Nu 14:12** 6099
nations greater and **m** than you, **Dt 4:38** 6099
nations greater and **m** than you, **Dt 9:1** 6099
a nation **m** and greater than they.' **Dt 9:14** 6099
nations greater and **m** than you. **Dt 11:23** 6099
is coming after me is **m** than I, **Mt 3:11** *2478*
me One is coming who is **m** than I, **Mk 1:7** *2478*
but One is coming who is **m** than I, **Lk 3:16** *2478*

MIGHTILY

Spirit of the LORD came upon him **m** **Jg 14:6** 6743a
Spirit of the LORD came upon him **m** **Jg 14:19** 6743a
Spirit of the LORD came upon him **m** **Jg 15:14** 6743a
of the LORD will come upon you **m**, **1Sa 10:6** 6743a
the Spirit of God came upon him **m**, **1Sa 10:10** 6743a
Spirit of God came upon Saul **m** **1Sa 11:6** 6743a
the Spirit of the LORD came **m** upon **1Sa 16:13** 6743a
spirit from God came **m** upon Saul, **1Sa 18:10** 6743a
good news, Lift up your voice **m**, **Is 40:9** 3581b
He will roar **m** against His fold. **Jer 25:30** 7580
Lord was growing **m** and prevailing. **Ac 19:20** *2904*
power, which **m** works within me. **Col 1:29** *1411*

MIGHTY

were the **m** men who *were* of old, **Gn 6:4** 1368
he became a **m** one on the earth. **Gn 10:8** 1368
He was a **m** hunter before the LORD; **Gn 10:9** 1368
a **m** hunter before the LORD." **Gn 10:9** 1368
become a great and **m** nation, **Gn 18:18** 6099
lord, you are a **m** prince among us; **Gn 23:6** 430
"With **m** wrestlings I have **Gn 30:8** 430
the hands of the **M** One of Jacob **Gn 49:24** 46
and became exceedingly **m**, **Ex 1:7** 6105a
multiplied, and became very **m**. **Ex 1:20** 6105a
sank like lead in the **m** waters. **Ex 15:10** 117
great power and with a **m** hand? **Ex 32:11** 2389
me since they are too **m** for me; **Nu 22:6** 6099
do such works and **m** acts as Yours? **Dt 3:24** 1369
by war and by a **m** hand and by an **Dt 4:34** 2389
brought you out of there by a **m** hand **Dt 5:15** 2389
us from Egypt with a **m** hand. **Dt 6:21** 2389
LORD brought you out by a **m** hand and **Dt 7:8** 2389
the **m** hand and the outstretched arm **Dt 7:19** 2389

out of Egypt with a **m** hand.	**Dt 9:26**	2389
great, the **m**, and the awesome God	**Dt 10:17**	1368
His greatness, His **m** hand and	**Dt 11:2**	2389
a great, **m** and populous nation.	**Dt 26:5**	6099
us out of Egypt with a **m** hand	**Dt 26:8**	2389
and for all the **m** power and for	**Dt 34:12**	2389
that the hand of the LORD is **m**,	**Jos 4:24**	2389
than Ai, and all its men *were* **m**.	**Jos 10:2**	1368
"The **M** One, God, the LORD, the	**Jos 22:22**	410
One, God, the LORD, the **M** One,	**Jos 22:22**	410
"The bows of the **m** are shattered,	**1Sa 2:4**	1368
us from the hand of these **m** gods?	**1Sa 4:8**	117
of a Benjamite, a **m** man of valor.	**1Sa 9:1**	1368
saw any **m** man or any valiant man,	**1Sa 14:52**	1368
musician, a **m** man of valor,	**1Sa 16:18**	1368
How have the **m** fallen!	**2Sa 1:19**	1368
the shield of the **m** was defiled,	**2Sa 1:21**	1368
the slain, from the fat of the **m**,	**2Sa 1:22**	1368
"How have the **m** fallen in the	**2Sa 1:25**	1368
"How have the **m** fallen, And the	**2Sa 1:27**	1368
Joab and all the army, the **m** men.	**2Sa 10:7**	1368
all the **m** men were at his right hand	**2Sa 16:6**	1368
they are **m** men and they are fierce,	**2Sa 17:8**	1368
knows that your father is a **m** man	**2Sa 17:10**	1368
the Pelethites and all the **m** men;	**2Sa 20:7**	1368
names of the **m** men whom David had:	**2Sa 23:8**	1368
one of the three **m** men with David	**2Sa 23:9**	1368
So the three **m** men broke through	**2Sa 23:16**	1368
These things the three **m** men did.	**2Sa 23:17**	1368
of Kabzeel, who had done **m** deeds,	**2Sa 23:20**	7227a
a name as well as the three **m** men.	**2Sa 23:22**	1368
the **m** men who belonged to David,	**1Ki 1:8**	1368
the prophet, Benaiah, the **m** men,	**1Ki 1:10**	1368
of Your great name and Your **m** hand,	**1Ki 8:42**	2389
even from all the **m** men of wealth,	**2Ki 15:20**	1368
and all the **m** men of valor,	**2Ki 24:14**	1368
began to be a **m** one in the earth.	**1Ch 1:10**	1368
and Jahdiel, **m** men of valor,	**1Ch 5:24**	1368
sons of Tola *were* **m** men of valor	**1Ch 7:2**	1368
of Issachar *were* **m** men of valor,	**1Ch 7:5**	1368
households, **m** men of valor,	**1Ch 7:7**	1368
households, 20,200 **m** men of valor.	**1Ch 7:9**	1368
households, 17,200 **m** men of valor,	**1Ch 7:11**	1368
houses, choice and **m** men of valor,	**1Ch 7:40**	1368
sons of Ulam were **m** men of valor,	**1Ch 8:40**	1368
heads of the **m** men whom David had,	**1Ch 11:10**	1368
list of the **m** men whom David had:	**1Ch 11:11**	1368
who *was* one of the three **m** men.	**1Ch 11:12**	1368
These things the three **m** men did.	**1Ch 11:19**	1368
man of Kabzeel, **m** in deeds,	**1Ch 11:22**	7227a
a name as well as the three **m** men.	**1Ch 11:24**	1368
Now the **m** men of the armies *were*	**1Ch 11:26**	1368
the **m** men who helped *him* in war.	**1Ch 12:1**	1368
a **m** man among the thirty,	**1Ch 12:4**	1368
in the wilderness, **m** men of valor,	**1Ch 12:8**	1368
for they were all **m** men of valor,	**1Ch 12:21**	1368
of Simeon, **m** men of valor for war,	**1Ch 12:25**	1368
Zadok, a young man of **m** valor,	**1Ch 12:28**	1368
of Ephraim 20,800, **m** men of valor,	**1Ch 12:30**	1368
Joab and all the army, the **m** men.	**1Ch 19:8**	1368
for they were **m** men of valor.	**1Ch 26:6**	1368
was the **m** man of the thirty,	**1Ch 27:6**	1368
with the officials and the **m** men,	**1Ch 28:1**	1368
All the officials, the **m** men,	**1Ch 29:24**	1368
great name's sake and Your **m** hand	**2Ch 6:32**	2389
So Jotham became **m** because he	**2Ch 27:6**	2388
And Zichri, a **m** man of Ephraim,	**2Ch 28:7**	1368
who destroyed every **m** warrior,	**2Ch 32:21**	1368
that **m** kings have ruled over	**Ezr 4:20**	8624
before all the king's **m** princes.	**Ezr 7:28**	1368
pool and the house of the **m** men.	**Ne 3:16**	1368
great, the **m**, and the awesome God	**Ne 9:32**	1368
the poor from the hand of the **m**.	**Jb 5:15**	2389
words of your mouth be a **m** wind?	**Jb 8:2**	3524
"Wise in heart and **m** in strength,	**Jb 9:4**	533
the earth belongs to the **m** man,	**Jb 22:8**	2220
But His **m** thunder, who can	**Jb 26:14**	1369
you condemn the righteous **m** One,	**Jb 34:17**	3524
m are taken away without a hand.	**Jb 34:20**	47
in pieces **m** men without inquiry,	**Jb 34:24**	3524
help because of the arm of the **m**.	**Jb 35:9**	7227a
God is **m** but does not despise *any;*	**Jb 36:5**	3524
is **m** in strength of understanding.	**Jb 36:5**	3524
his limbs, Or his **m** strength,	**Jb 41:12**	1369
he raises himself up, the **m** fear;	**Jb 41:25**	410
unfortunate fall by his **m** ones.	**Ps 10:10**	6099
me, for they were too **m** for me.	**Ps 18:17**	553
The LORD strong and **m**,	**Ps 24:8**	1368
and mighty, The LORD **m** in battle.	**Ps 24:8**	1368
to the LORD, O sons of the **m**,	**Ps 29:1**	410
The king is not saved by a **m** army;	**Ps 33:16**	7230
will praise You among a **m** throng.	**Ps 35:18**	6099
Your sword on *Your* thigh, O **M** One,	**Ps 45:3**	1368
The **M** One, God, the LORD, has	**Ps 50:1**	410
Why do you boast in evil, O **m** man?	**Ps 52:1**	1368
forth with His voice, a **m** voice.	**Ps 68:33**	5797
with the **m** deeds of the Lord GOD;	**Ps 71:16**	1369
And Your paths in the **m** waters,	**Ps 77:19**	7227a
Who among the sons of the **m** is like	**Ps 89:6**	410
hosts, who is like You, O **m** LORD?	**Ps 89:8**	2626
Your enemies with Your **m** arm.	**Ps 89:10**	5797
Your hand is **m**, Your right hand is	**Ps 89:13**	5810
"I have given help to one who is **m**;	**Ps 89:19**	1368
Than the **m** breakers of the sea,	**Ps 93:4**	117
of the sea, The LORD on high is **m**.	**Ps 93:4**	117
you His angels, **M** in strength,	**Ps 103:20**	1368
speak of the **m** deeds of the LORD,	**Ps 106:2**	1369
descendants will be **m** on earth;	**Ps 112:2**	1368
And vowed to the **M** One of Jacob,	**Ps 132:2**	46
place for the **M** One of Jacob."	**Ps 132:5**	46
many nations And slew **m** kings,	**Ps 135:10**	6099
And slew **m** kings, For His	**Ps 136:18**	117
And shall declare Your **m** acts.	**Ps 145:4**	1369
to the sons of men Your **m** acts And	**Ps 145:12**	1369
Praise Him in His **m** expanse.	**Ps 150:1**	5797
Praise Him for His **m** deeds;	**Ps 150:2**	1369
slow to anger is better than the **m**,	**Pr 16:32**	1368
And decides between the **m** ones	**Pr 18:18**	6099
wise man scales the city of the **m** And	**Pr 21:22**	1368
The shephanim are not **m** people,	**Pr 30:26**	6099
The lion *which* is **m** among beasts	**Pr 30:30**	1368
house tremble, and **m** men stoop,	**Ec 12:3**	2428
Sixty **m** men around it, Of the	**SS 3:7**	1368
around it, Of the **m** men of Israel.	**SS 3:7**	1368
the round shields of the **m** men.	**SS 4:4**	1368
The **M** One of Israel,	**Is 1:24**	46
The **m** man and the warrior, The	**Is 3:2**	1368
sword And your **m** ones in battle.	**Is 3:25**	1369
the LORD spoke to me with **m** power	**Is 8:11**	2393
called Wonderful Counselor, **M** God,	**Is 9:6**	1368
And like a **m** man I brought down	**Is 10:13**	3524
remnant of Jacob, to the **m** God.	**Is 10:21**	1368
Lebanon will fall by the **M** One.	**Is 10:34**	117
I have even called My **m** warriors,	**Is 13:3**	1368
on like the rumbling of **m** waters!	**Is 17:12**	3524
a **m** king will rule over them,"	**Is 19:4**	5794
the **m** men of the sons of Kedar,	**Is 21:17**	1368
His fierce and great and **m** sword,	**Is 27:1**	2389
the Lord has a strong and **m** *agent;*	**Is 28:2**	533
a storm of **m** overflowing waters,	**Is 28:2**	3524
And on which no **m** ship will pass	**Is 33:21**	117
And a path through the **m** waters,	**Is 43:16**	5794
the horse, The army and the **m** man	**Is 43:17**	5808
the prey be taken from the **m** man,	**Is 49:24**	1368
captives of the **m** man will be taken	**Is 49:25**	1368
Redeemer, the **M** One of Jacob."	**Is 49:26**	46
your Redeemer, the **M** One of Jacob.	**Is 60:16**	46
And the least one a **m** nation.	**Is 60:22**	6099
in righteousness, **m** to save."	**Is 63:1**	7227a
are Your zeal and Your **m** deeds?	**Is 63:15**	1369
open grave, All of them are **m** men.	**Jer 5:16**	1368
not the **m** man boast of his might,	**Jer 9:23**	1368
Like a **m** man who cannot save?	**Jer 14:9**	1368
has been crushed with a **m** blow,	**Jer 14:17**	1419
an outstretched hand and a **m** arm,	**Jer 21:5**	2389
King Jehoiakim and all his **m** men	**Jer 26:21**	1368
after them, O great and **m** God.	**Jer 32:18**	1368
great in counsel and **m** in deed,	**Jer 32:19**	7227a
will tell you great and **m** things,	**Jer 33:3**	1219
And their **m** men are defeated And	**Jer 46:5**	1368
man flee, Nor the **m** man escape;	**Jer 46:6**	1368
That the **m** men may march forward:	**Jer 46:9**	1368
have your **m** ones become prostrate?	**Jer 46:15**	47
'We are **m** warriors, And men	**Jer 48:14**	1368
'How has the **m** scepter been broken	**Jer 48:17**	5797
So the hearts of the **m** men of Moab	**Jer 48:41**	1368
the hearts of the **m** men of Edom	**Jer 49:22**	1368
A sword against her **m** men,	**Jer 50:36**	1368
The **m** men of Babylon have ceased	**Jer 51:30**	1368
And her **m** men will be captured,	**Jer 51:56**	1368
her prefects and her **m** men,	**Jer 51:57**	1368
also took away the **m** of the land,	**Ezk 17:13**	352c
'Pharaoh with *his* **m** army and	**Ezk 17:17**	1419
"surely with a **m** hand and with an	**Ezk 20:33**	2389
with a **m** hand and with an	**Ezk 20:34**	2389
city, Which was **m** on the sea,	**Ezk 26:17**	2389
nor their well-watered **m** ones stand	**Ezk 31:14**	352c
"By the swords of the **m** ones I	**Ezk 32:12**	1368
"The strong among the **m** ones	**Ezk 32:21**	1368
a great assembly and a **m** army;	**Ezk 38:15**	7227a
"You will eat the flesh of **m** men	**Ezk 39:18**	1368
m men and all the men of war,"	**Ezk 39:20**	1368
signs And how **m** are His wonders!	**Da 4:3**	8624
and rushed at him in his **m** wrath.	**Da 8:6**	3581b
But as soon as he was **m**,	**Da 8:8**	6105a
"His power will be **m**,	**Da 8:24**	6105a
destroy **m** men and the holy people.	**Da 8:24**	6099
of the land of Egypt with a **m** hand	**Da 9:15**	2389
"And a **m** king will arise, and he	**Da 11:3**	1368
large and **m** army for war;	**Da 11:25**	6099
my land, **M** and without number;	**Jl 1:6**	6099
So there is a great and **m** people;	**Jl 2:2**	6099
a **m** people arranged for battle.	**Jl 2:5**	6099
They run like **m** men,	**Jl 2:7**	1368
Prepare a war; rouse the **m** men!	**Jl 3:9**	1368
Let the weak say, "I am a **m** man."	**Jl 3:10**	1368
Bring down, O LORD, Your **m** ones.	**Jl 3:11**	1368
Nor the **m** man save his life.	**Am 2:14**	1368
"Then your **m** men will be dismayed	**Ob 1:9**	1368
decisions for **m**, distant nations.	**Mi 4:3**	6099
shields of his **m** men are *colored* red	**Na 2:3**	1368
'So many peoples and **m** nations	**Zch 8:22**	6099
"They will be as **m** men,	**Zch 10:5**	1368
"Ephraim will be like a **m** man,	**Zch 10:7**	1368
"For the **M** One has done great	**Lk 1:49**	*1415*
"He has done **m** deeds with His arm;	**Lk 1:51**	*2904*
who was a prophet **m** in deed and	**Lk 24:19**	*1415*
speaking of the **m** deeds of God."	**Ac 2:11**	*3167*
and he was **m** in the Scriptures.	**Ac 18:24**	*1415*
flesh, not many **m**, not many noble;	**1Co 1:26**	*1415*
not weak toward you, but **m** in you.	**2Co 13:3**	*1414*
with His **m** angels in flaming fire,	**2Th 1:7**	*1411*
were made strong, became **m** in war,	**Heb 11:34**	*2478*
under the **m** hand of God,	**1Pe 5:6**	*2900*
an earthquake *was it, and* so **m**.	**Rv 16:18**	*3173*
And he cried out with a **m** voice,	**Rv 18:2**	*2478*
the sound of **m** peals of thunder,	**Rv 19:6**	*2478*
and the flesh of **m** men and the flesh	**Rv 19:18**	*2478*

MIGRATION

Observe the time of their **m**;	**Jer 8:7**	935

MIGRON

pomegranate tree which is in **M**.	**1Sa 14:2**	4051
Aiath, He has passed through **M**;	**Is 10:28**	4051

MIJAMIN

for Malchijah, the sixth for **M**,	**1Ch 24:9**	4326
were Ramiah, Izziah, Malchijah, **M**,	**Ezr 10:25**	4326
Meshullam, Abijah, **M**,	**Ne 10:7**	4326
M, Maadiah, Bilgah,	**Ne 12:5**	4326

MIKLOTH

M became the father of Shimeah.	**1Ch 8:32**	4732
Gedor, Ahio, Zechariah and **M**.	**1Ch 9:37**	4732
M became the father of Shimeam.	**1Ch 9:38**	4732
month, **M** *being* the chief officer;	**1Ch 27:4**	4732

MIKNEIAH

Mattithiah, Eliphelehu, **M**,	**1Ch 15:18**	4737
and Mattithiah, Eliphelehu, **M**,	**1Ch 15:21**	4737

MILALAI

his kinsmen, Shemaiah, Azarel, **M**,	**Ne 12:36**	4450

MILCAH

and the name of Nahor's wife was **M**,	**Gn 11:29**	4435
Haran, the father of **M** and Iscah.	**Gn 11:29**	4435
M also has borne children to your	**Gn 22:20**	4435
these eight **M** bore to Nahor,	**Gn 22:23**	4435
was born to Bethuel the son of **M**,	**Gn 24:15**	4435
daughter of Bethuel, the son of **M**,	**Gn 24:24**	4435
Nahor's son, whom **M** bore to him';	**Gn 24:47**	4435
Noah, Hoglah, **M** and Tirzah.	**Nu 26:33**	4435
Noah and Hoglah and **M** and Tirzah.	**Nu 27:1**	4435
Tirzah, Hoglah, **M** and Noah,	**Nu 36:11**	4435
and Noah, Hoglah, **M** and Tirzah.	**Jos 17:3**	4435

MILCH

prepare a new cart and two **m** cows	**1Sa 6:7**	5783
and took two **m** cows and hitched	**1Sa 6:10**	5763

MILCOM

after **M** the detestable idol of the	**1Ki 11:5**	4445b
M the god of the sons of Ammon;	**1Ki 11:33**	4445b
and for **M** the abomination of the	**2Ki 23:13**	4445b
to the LORD and *yet* swear by **M**,	**Zph 1:5**	4445b

MILDEW

sword and with blight and with **m**,	**Dt 28:22**	3420
if there is blight *or* **m**,	**1Ki 8:37**	3420
if there is blight or **m**,	**2Ch 6:28**	3420
you with scorching *wind* and **m**;	**Am 4:9**	3420
your hands with blasting wind, **m** and	**Hg 2:17**	3420

MILE

forces you to go one **m**,	**Mt 5:41**	*3400*

MILES

was about seven **m** from Jerusalem.	**Lk 24:13**	*4712*
had rowed about three or four **m**,	**Jn 6:19**	*4712*
near Jerusalem, about two **m** off;	**Jn 11:18**	*4712*
for a distance of two hundred **m**.	**Rv 14:20**	*4712*
with the rod, fifteen hundred **m**.	**Rv 21:16**	*4712*

MILETUS

the day following we came to **M**.	**Ac 20:15**	*3399*
From **M** he sent to Ephesus and	**Ac 20:17**	*3399*
but Trophimus I left sick at **M**.	**2Tm 4:20**	*3399*

MILITARY

Joab was dressed in his **m** attire,	**2Sa 20:8**	
appointed **m** officers over the people	**2Ch 32:6**	4421
for his lords and **m** commanders	**Mk 6:21**	*5506*

MILK

He took curds and **m** and the	**Gn 18:8**	2461
wine, And his teeth white from **m**.	**Gn 49:12**	2461
a land flowing with **m** and honey,	**Ex 3:8**	2461
land flowing with **m** and honey."	**Ex 3:17**	2461
a land flowing with **m** and honey,	**Ex 13:5**	2461
not to boil a young goat in the **m**	**Ex 23:19**	2461
a land flowing with **m** and honey;	**Ex 33:3**	2461
not boil a young goat in its mother's **m**."	**Ex 34:26**	2461
a land flowing with **m** and honey."	**Lv 20:24**	2461
does flow with **m** and honey,	**Nu 13:27**	2461
land which flows with **m** and honey.	**Nu 14:8**	2461
up out of a land flowing with **m** and	**Nu 16:13**	2461
a land flowing with **m** and honey,	**Nu 16:14**	2461
a land flowing with **m** and honey.	**Dt 6:3**	2461
a land flowing with **m** and honey.	**Dt 11:9**	2461
not boil a young goat in its mother's **m**.	**Dt 14:21**	2461
a land flowing with **m** and honey.	**Dt 26:9**	2461
a land flowing with **m** and honey.	**Dt 26:15**	2461
a land flowing with **m** and honey,	**Dt 27:3**	2461
the land flowing with **m** and honey,	**Dt 31:20**	2461
Curds of cows, and **m** of the flock,	**Dt 32:14**	2461
a land flowing with **m** and honey.	**Jos 5:6**	2461
bottle of **m** and gave him a drink;	**Jg 4:19**	2461
for water *and* she gave him **m**;	**Jg 5:25**	2461
'Did You not pour me out like **m** And	**Jb 10:10**	2461
be goats' **m** enough for your food,	**Pr 27:27**	2461
the churning of **m** produces butter,	**Pr 30:33**	2461
Honey and **m** are under your tongue,	**SS 4:11**	2461
I have drunk my wine and my **m**.	**SS 5:1**	2461
streams of water, Bathed in **m**,	**SS 5:12**	2461
the **m** produced he will eat curds,	**Is 7:22**	2461
Those *just* weaned from **m**?	**Is 28:9**	2461
buy wine and **m** Without money and	**Is 55:1**	2461
will also suck the **m** of nations And	**Is 60:16**	2461
a land flowing with **m** and honey,	**Jer 11:5**	2461
a land flowing with **m** and honey.	**Jer 32:22**	2461
snow, They were whiter than **m**;	**La 4:7**	2461
them, flowing with **m** and honey,	**Ezk 20:6**	2461
them, flowing with **m** and honey,	**Ezk 20:15**	2461
eat your fruit and drink your **m**.	**Ezk 25:4**	2461
And the hills will flow with **m**,	**Jl 3:18**	2461
I gave you **m** to drink, not solid	**1Co 3:2**	*1051*
does not use the **m** of the flock?	**1Co 9:7**	*1051*

come to need **m** and not solid food. **Heb 5:12** *1051*
everyone who partakes *only* of **m** is **Heb 5:13** *1051*
long for the pure **m** of the word, **1Pe 2:2** *1051*

MILKING
thirty **m** camels and their colts, **Gn 32:15** 3243

MILL
sound of the grinding **m** is low, **Ec 12:4** 2913
men worked at the grinding **m**, **La 5:13** 2911a
women *will be* grinding at the **m**; **Mt 24:41** *3458*
and the sound of a **m** will not be **Rv 18:22** *3458*

MILLET
beans, lentils, **m** and spelt, **Ezk 4:9** 1764

MILLION
army of a **m** men and 300 chariots, **2Ch 14:9** 505
of the horsemen was two hundred **m**; **Rv 9:16** *1365a, 3461*

MILLO
all around from the **M** and inward. **2Sa 5:9** 4407
of the LORD, his own house, the **M**, **1Ki 9:15** 4407
for her, then he built the **M**. **1Ki 9:24** 4407
Solomon built the **M**, **1Ki 11:27** 4407
down Joash at the house of **M** **2Ki 12:20** 4407
M even to the surrounding area; **1Ch 11:8** 4407
the **M** *in* the city of David, **2Ch 32:5** 4407

MILLSTONE
handmill or an upper **m** in pledge, **Dt 24:6** 7393
an upper **m** on Abimelech's head, **Jg 9:53** 7393
Did not a woman throw an upper **m** **2Sa 11:21** 7393
Even as hard as a lower **m**. **Jb 41:24** 6400
a heavy **m** hung around his neck, **Mt 18:6** *3458*
a heavy **m** hung around his neck, **Mk 9:42** *3458*
if a **m** were hung around his neck **Lk 17:2** *3037, 3457a*
angel took up a stone like a great **m** **Rv 18:21** *3457b*

MILLSTONES
slave girl who is behind the **m**; **Ex 11:5** 7347
grind *it* between two **m** or beat *it* in **Nu 11:8** 7347
"Take the **m** and grind meal. **Is 47:2** 7347
the sound of the **m** and the light of **Jer 25:10** 7347

MINA
your **m** has made ten minas more.' **Lk 19:16** *3414*
'Your **m**, master, has made five **Lk 19:18** *3414*
'Master, here is your **m**, **Lk 19:20** *3414*
'Take the **m** away from him and **Lk 19:24** *3414*

MINAS
three **m** of gold on each shield, **1Ki 10:17** 4488
gold drachmas and 5,000 silver **m** **Ezr 2:69** 4488
gold drachmas and 2,200 silver **m**. **Ne 7:71** 4488
gold drachmas and 2,000 silver **m** and **Ne 7:72** 4488
his slaves, and gave them ten **m** and **Lk 19:13** *3414*
your mina has made ten **m** more.' **Lk 19:16** *3414*
mina, master, has made five **m**.' **Lk 19:18** *3414*
it to the one who has the ten **m**.' **Lk 19:24** *3414*
'Master, he has ten **m** *already*.' **Lk 19:25** *3414*

MINCING
eyes, And go along with **m** steps And **Is 3:16** 2952

MIND
but his father kept the saying *in* **m**. **Gn 37:11**
keep me in **m** when it goes well with **Gn 40:14**
Take heed, for evil is in your **m**. **Ex 10:10** 6440
change Your **m** about *doing* harm **Ex 32:12** 5162
So the LORD changed His **m** about **Ex 32:14** 5162
and you call *them* to **m** in all **Dt 30:1** 3824
tell you all that is on your **m**. **1Sa 9:19** 3824
ago, do not set your **m** on them, **1Sa 9:20** 3820
will not lie or change His **m**; **1Sa 15:29** 5162
man that He should change His **m**." **1Sa 15:29** 5162
"Go, do all that is in your **m**, **2Sa 7:3** 3824
discernment and breadth of **m**, **1Ki 4:29** 3820
"If this is your **m**, *then* let no **2Ki 9:15** 5315
were of one **m** to make David king. **1Ch 12:38** 3820
a whole heart and a willing **m**; **1Ch 28:9** 5315
the plan of all that he had in **m**, **1Ch 28:12** 7307
"Because you had this in **m**, **2Ch 1:11** 3824
God was putting into my **m** to do **Ne 2:12** 3820
for the people had a **m** to work. **Ne 4:6** 3820
inventing them in your own **m**." **Ne 6:8** 3820
And their **m** prepares deception." **Jb 15:35** 990
Or given understanding to the **m**? **Jb 38:36** 7907
my **m** instructs me in the night. **Ps 16:7** 3629
Test my **m** and my heart. **Ps 26:2** 3629
forgotten as a dead man, out of **m**; **Ps 31:12** 3820
conspired together with one **m**; **Ps 83:5** 3820
sworn and will not change His **m**, **Ps 110:4** 5162
of perverse **m** will be despised. **Pr 12:8** 3820
The **m** of the intelligent seeks **Pr 15:14** 3820
The **m** of man plans his way, But **Pr 16:9** 3820
who has a crooked **m** finds no good, **Pr 17:20** 3820
But only in revealing his own **m**. **Pr 18:2** 3820
The **m** of the prudent acquires **Pr 18:15** 3820
And apply your **m** to my knowledge; **Pr 22:17** 3820
your **m** will utter perverse things. **Pr 23:33** 3820
And I set my **m** to seek and explore **Ec 1:13** 3820
and my **m** has observed a wealth of **Ec 1:16** 3820
And I set my **m** to know wisdom and **Ec 1:17** 3820
I explored with my **m** *how* to **Ec 2:3** 3820
while my **m** was guiding *me* wisely, **Ec 2:3** 3820
even at night his **m** does not rest. **Ec 2:23** 3820
The **m** of the wise is in the house **Ec 7:4** 3820
While the **m** of fools is in the **Ec 7:4** 3820
I directed my **m** to know, to **Ec 7:25** 3820
and applied my **m** to every deed that **Ec 8:9** 3820
My **m** reels, horror overwhelms me; **Is 21:4** 3824
"The steadfast of **m** You will **Is 26:3** 3336
who err in **m** will know the truth, **Is 29:24** 7307
The **m** of the hasty will **Is 32:4** 3824
not call to **m** the former things, **Is 43:18** 2142
Recall it to **m**, you transgressors. **Is 46:8** 3820
not be remembered or come to **m**. **Is 65:17** 3820
And it will not come to **m**, **Jer 3:16** 3820
And I will not change My **m**, **Jer 4:28** 5162
and it did not come into My **m**. **Jer 7:31** 3820
their lips But far from their **m**. **Jer 12:2** 3629
search the heart, I test the **m**, **Jer 17:10** 3629
of, nor did it *ever* enter My **m**; **Jer 19:5** 3820
Who see the **m** and the heart; **Jer 20:12** 3629
and the LORD will change His **m** **Jer 26:13** 5162
and the LORD changed His **m** about **Jer 26:19** 5162
Direct your **m** to the highway, The **Jer 31:21** 3820
nor had it entered My **m** that they **Jer 32:35** 3820
come with me to Babylon, never **m**. **Jer 40:4** 2308
really set your **m** to enter Egypt and **Jer 42:15** 6440
"So all the men who set their **m** **Jer 42:17** 6440
who have set their **m** on entering the **Jer 44:12** 6440
did not *all this* come into His **m**? **Jer 44:21** 3820
And let Jerusalem come to your **m**. **Jer 51:50** 3824
This I recall to my **m**, **La 3:21** 3820
into your **m** will not come about, **Ezk 20:32** 7307
bringing to **m** the iniquity of **Ezk 29:16** 2142
thoughts will come into your **m** and **Ezk 38:10** 3824
But Daniel made up his **m** that he **Da 1:8** 3820
in your **m** *while* on your bed. **Da 2:28** 7217
understand the thoughts of your **m**. **Da 2:30** 3825
visions in my **m** kept alarming me. **Da 4:5** 7217
in my **m** *as I lay* on my bed: **Da 4:10** 7217
in my **m** *as I lay* on my bed, **Da 4:13** 7217
m be changed from *that of* a man And **Da 4:16** 3825
let a beast's **m** be given to him, **Da 4:16** 3825
set *his* **m** on delivering Daniel; **Da 6:14** 1079
saw a dream and visions in his **m** **Da 7:1** 7217
a human **m** also was given to it. **Da 7:4** 3825
visions in my **m** kept alarming me. **Da 7:15** 7217
The LORD changed His **m** about this. **Am 7:3** 5162
The LORD changed His **m** about this. **Am 7:6** 5162
but if not, never **m**!" **Zch 11:12** 2308
setting your **m** on God's interests, **Mt 16:23** *5426*
YOUR SOUL, AND WITH ALL YOUR M.' **Mt 22:37** *1271*
down, clothed and in his right **m**, **Mk 5:15** *4993*
setting your **m** on God's interests, **Mk 8:33** *5426*
YOUR SOUL, AND WITH ALL YOUR M, **Mk 12:30** *1271*
All who heard them kept them in **m**, **Lk 1:66** *2588*
Jesus, clothed and in his right **m**; **Lk 8:35** *4993*
STRENGTH, AND WITH ALL YOUR M; **Lk 10:27** *1271*
These all with one **m** were **Ac 1:14** *3661*
with one **m** in the temple, **Ac 2:46** *3661*
his **m** to visit his brethren, **Ac 7:23** *2588*
Peter was greatly perplexed in **m** **Ac 10:17** *1438*
"You are out of your **m**!" **Ac 12:15** *3105*
to us, having become of one **m**, **Ac 15:25** *3661*
"Paul, you are out of your **m**! **Ac 26:24** *3105*
"I am not out of my **m**, **Ac 26:25** *3105*
gave them over to a depraved **m**, **Ro 1:28** *3563*
war against the law of my **m** and **Ro 7:23** *3563*
I myself with my **m** am serving the **Ro 7:25** *3563*
the **m** set on the flesh is death, **Ro 8:6** *5427*
but the **m** set on the Spirit is **Ro 8:6** *5427*
because the **m** set on the flesh is **Ro 8:7** *5427*
knows what the **m** of the Spirit is, **Ro 8:27** *5427*
HAS KNOWN THE M OF THE LORD, **Ro 11:34** *3563*
by the renewing of your **m**, **Ro 12:2** *3563*
of the same **m** toward one another; **Ro 12:16** *5426*
do not be haughty in **m**, **Ro 12:16** *5426*
be fully convinced in his own **m**. **Ro 14:5** *3563*
be of the same **m** with one another **Ro 15:5** *5426*
same **m** and in the same judgment. **1Co 1:10** *3563*
HAS KNOWN THE M OF THE LORD, **1Co 2:16** *3563*
But we have the **m** of Christ. **1Co 2:16** *3563*
prays, but my **m** is unfruitful. **1Co 14:14** *3563*
and I will pray with the **m** also; **1Co 14:15** *3563*
and I will sing with the **m** also. **1Co 14:15** *3563*
to speak five words with my **m** so **1Co 14:19** *3563*
if we are of sound **m**, **2Co 5:13** *4993*
desires of the flesh and of the **m**, **Eph 2:3** *1271*
walk, in the futility of their **m**, **Eph 4:17** *3563*
renewed in the spirit of your **m**, **Eph 4:23** *3563*
with one **m** striving together for **Php 1:27** *5590*
complete by being of the same **m**, **Php 2:2** *5426*
but with humility of **m** **Php 2:3** *5012a*
If anyone else has a **m** to put **Php 3:4** *1380*
alienated and hostile in **m**, **Col 1:21** *1271*
without cause by his fleshly **m**, **Col 2:18** *3563*
Set your **m** on the things above, **Col 3:2** *5426*
constantly bearing in **m** your work **1Th 1:3** *3421*
friction between men of depraved **m** **1Tm 6:5** *3563*
the truth, men of depraved **m**, **2Tm 3:8** *3563*
both their **m** and their conscience **Ti 1:15** *3563*
AND WILL NOT CHANGE HIS M, **Heb 7:21** *3338*
ON THEIR M I WILL WRITE THEM," **Heb 10:16** *1271*
be able to call these things to **m**. **2Pe 1:15** *3420*
your sincere **m** by way of reminder, **2Pe 3:1** *1271*
"Here is the **m** which has wisdom. **Rv 17:9** *3563*

MINDFUL
needy, Let the Lord be **m** of me. **Ps 40:17** 2803
He is **m** that we are *but* dust. **Ps 103:14** 2142
The LORD has been **m** of us; **Ps 115:12** 2142
For I am **m** of the sincere faith **2Tm 1:5** *5280*

MINDS
change their **m** when they see war, **Ex 13:17** 5162
bring forth words from their **m**? **Jb 8:10** 3820
God tries the hearts and **m**. **Ps 7:9** 3629
For their **m** devise violence, And **Pr 24:2** 3820
and the deception of their own **m**. **Jer 14:14** 3820
"So make up your **m** not to prepare **Lk 21:14** *2588*
m to understand the Scriptures, **Lk 24:45** *3563*
stirred up the **m** of the Gentiles and **Ac 14:2** *5590*
they changed their **m** and *began* to **Ac 28:6** *3328*
set their **m** on the things of the flesh **Ro 8:5** *5426*
But their **m** were hardened; **2Co 3:14** *3540*
blinded the **m** of the unbelieving so **2Co 4:4** *3540*
your **m** will be led astray from **2Co 11:3** *3540*
who set their **m** on earthly things. **Php 3:19** *5426*
hearts and your **m** in Christ Jesus. **Php 4:7** *3540*
I WILL PUT MY LAWS INTO THEIR M, **Heb 8:10** *1271*
Therefore, prepare your **m** for action, **1Pe 1:13** *1271*
He who searches the **m** and hearts; **Rv 2:23** *3510*

MINE
flocks, and all that you see is **m**. **Gn 31:43**
I came to you in Egypt, are **m**; **Gn 48:5**
Ephraim and Manasseh shall be **m**, **Gn 48:5**
these signs of **M** among them, **Ex 10:1**
peoples, for all the earth is **M**; **Ex 19:5**
apart from the peoples to be **M**. **Lv 20:26**
permanently, for the land is **M**; **Lv 25:23**
So the Levites shall be **M**. **Nu 3:12**
"For all the firstborn are **M**; **Nu 3:13**
They shall be **M**; I am the LORD." **Nu 3:13**
And the Levites shall be **M**; **Nu 3:45**
and the Levites shall be **M**. **Nu 8:14**
among the sons of Israel is **M**, **Nu 8:17**
impress these words of **m** on your **Dt 11:18**
'Vengeance is **M**, and retribution, **Dt 32:35**
"See, Joab's field is next to **m**, **2Sa 14:30**
"You know that the kingdom was **m** **1Ki 2:15**
"He shall be neither **m** nor yours; **1Ki 3:26**
"And may these words of **m**, **1Ki 8:59**
'Your silver and your gold are **m**; **1Ki 20:3**
wives and children are also **m**.' " **1Ki 20:3**
"Surely there is a **m** for silver And **Jb 28:1** 4161
is under the whole heaven is **M**. **Jb 41:11**
every beast of the forest is **M**, **Ps 50:10**
that moves in the field is **M**. **Ps 50:11** 5973
For the world is **M**, **Ps 50:12**
For no guilt of **m**, they run **Ps 59:4**
"Gilead is **M**, and Manasseh is **Ps 60:7**
"Gilead is Mine, and Manasseh is **M**; **Ps 60:7**
"Gilead is **M**, Manasseh is Mine; **Ps 108:8**
"Gilead is Mine, Manasseh is **M**; **Ps 108:8**
This has become **m**, That I observe **Ps 119:56**
my enemies, For they are ever **m**. **Ps 119:98**
prepared a lamp for **M** anointed. **Ps 132:17**
"Counsel is **m** and sound wisdom; **Pr 8:14**
I am understanding, power is **m**. **Pr 8:14**
"My beloved is **m**, and I am his; **SS 2:16**
my beloved's and my beloved is **m**, **SS 6:3**
"Who execute a plan, but not **M**, **Is 30:1** 4480
called you by name; you are **M**! **Is 43:1**
mountain of **M** in the countryside, **Jer 17:3**
word will stand, **M** or theirs. **Jer 44:28** 4480
with you so that you became **M**," **Ezk 16:8**
"Behold, all souls are **M**; **Ezk 18:4**
well as the soul of the son is **M**. **Ezk 18:4**
And they became **M**, and they bore **Ezk 23:4**
played the harlot while she was **M**; **Ezk 23:5** 8478
'My Nile is **m**, and I myself have **Ezk 29:3**
'The Nile is **m**, and I have made **Ezk 29:9**
and these two lands will be **m**, **Ezk 35:10**
'The silver is **M** and the gold is **Hg 2:8**
silver is Mine and the gold is **M**,' **Hg 2:8**
"They will be **M**," **Mal 3:17**
who hears these words of **M** and **Mt 7:24** *1473*
who hears these words of **M** and **Mt 7:26** *1473*
these two sons of **m** may sit one **Mt 20:21** *1473*
on *My* left, this is not **M** to give, **Mt 20:23** *1699*
it to one of these brothers of **M**, **Mt 25:40** *1473*
on *My* left, this is not **M** to give; **Mk 10:40** *1699*
a friend of **m** has come to me from **Lk 11:6** *1473*
for this son of **m** was dead and **Lk 15:24** *1473*
me, and all that is **m** is yours. **Lk 15:31** *1699*
"But these enemies of **m**, **Lk 19:27** *1473*
of the one betraying Me is with **M** on **Lk 22:21** *1700*
this joy of **m** has been made full. **Jn 3:29** *1699*
"My teaching is not **M**, **Jn 7:16** *1699*
then you are truly disciples of **M**; **Jn 8:31** *1473*
the word which you hear is not **M**, **Jn 14:24** *1699*
for He will take of **M** **Jn 16:14** *1699*
things that the Father has are **M**; **Jn 16:15** *1699*
I said that He takes of **M** **Jn 16:15** *1699*
all things that are **M** are Yours, **Jn 17:10** *1699*
Mine are Yours, and Yours are **M**; **Jn 17:10** *1699*
he is a chosen instrument of **M**, **Ac 9:15** *1473*
other's faith, both yours and **m**. **Ro 1:12** *1473*
"VENGEANCE IS M, I WILL REPAY," **Ro 12:19** *1699*
the Lord, also his mother and **m**. **Ro 16:13** *1699*
this boasting of **m** will not be **2Co 11:10** *1519, 1473*
"VENGEANCE IS M, I WILL REPAY." **Heb 10:30** *1699*

MINGLED
And **m** my drink with weeping **Ps 102:9** 4537
But they **m** with the nations And **Ps 106:35** 6148

MINIAMIN
Under his authority *were* Eden, **M**, **2Ch 31:15** 4509
of **M**, of Moadiah, Piltai; **Ne 12:17** 4509
the priests, Eliakim, Maaseiah, **M**, **Ne 12:41** 4509

MINISTER
sons of Israel, to **m** as priest to Me **Ex 28:1** 3547
that he may **m** as priest to Me. **Ex 28:3** 3547
that he may **m** as priest to Me. **Ex 28:4** 3547
the altar to **m** in the holy place, **Ex 28:43** 8334
them to **m** as priests to Me: **Ex 29:1** 3547
of meeting to **m** in the holy place. **Ex 29:30** 8334
his sons to **m** as priests to Me. **Ex 29:44** 3547
when they approach the altar to **m**, **Ex 30:20** 8334
that they may **m** as priests to Me. **Ex 30:30** 3547

of his sons, to **m** as priests.' " Ex 35:19 3547
of his sons, to **m** as priests. Ex 39:41 3547
that he may **m** as a priest to Me. Ex 40:13 3547
that they may **m** as priests to Me; Ex 40:15 3547
the sanctuary with which they **m**, Nu 3:31 8334
the congregation to **m** to them; Nu 16:9 8334
stood before it to **m** in those Jg 20:28 8334
priests could not stand to **m** because 1Ki 8:11 8334
of God and to **m** to Him forever." 1Ch 15:2 8334
to **m** before the ark continually, 1Ch 16:37 8334
to **m** to Him and to bless in His 1Ch 23:13 8334
to **m** in the house of the LORD. 1Ch 26:12 8334
stand to **m** because of the cloud, 2Ch 5:14 8334
to stand before Him, to **m** to Him, 2Ch 29:11 8334
to **m** and to give thanks and to 2Ch 31:2 8334
way is the one who will **m** to me. Ps 101:6 8334
to the LORD, To **m** to Him, Is 56:6 8334
rams of Nebaioth will **m** to you; Is 60:7 8334
And their kings will **m** to you; Is 60:10 8334
and the Levites who **m** to Me.' " Jer 33:22 8334
near to the LORD to **m** to Him." Ezk 40:46 8334
their garments in which they **m**, Ezk 42:14 8334
who draw near to Me to **m** to Me,' Ezk 43:19 8334
stand before them to **m** to them. Ezk 44:11 8334
shall come near to Me to **m** to Me; Ezk 44:15 8334
come near to My table to **m** to Me Ezk 44:16 8334
inner court to **m** in the sanctuary, Ezk 44:27 8334
who come near to **m** to the LORD, Ezk 45:4 8334
angels came and *began* to **m** to Him. Mt 4:11 *1247*
used to follow Him and **m** to Him; Mk 15:41 *1247*
to appoint you a **m** and a witness Ac 26:16 *5257*
it is a **m** of God to you for good. Ro 13:4 *1249*
for it is a **m** of God, an avenger Ro 13:4 *1249*
to be a **m** of Christ Jesus to the Ro 15:16 *3011*
they are indebted to **m** to them Ro 15:27 *3008*
is Christ then a **m** of sin? Ga 2:17 *1249*
of which I was made a **m**, Eph 3:7 *1249*
and faithful **m** in the Lord, Eph 6:21 *1249*
your messenger and **m** to my need; Php 2:25 *3011*
of which I, Paul, was made a **m**. Col 1:23 *1249*
Of *this church* I was made a **m** Col 1:25 *1249*
that on your behalf he might **m** to Phm 1:13 *1247*
a **m** in the sanctuary and in the Heb 8:2 *3011*

MINISTERED
his son **m** as priest in his place. Dt 10:6 3547
But the boy **m** to the LORD before 1Sa 2:11 8334
and followed Elijah and **m** to him. 1Ki 19:21 8334
They **m** with song before the 1Ch 6:32 8334
"Because they **m** to them before Ezk 44:12 8334
two of those who **m** to him, Ac 19:22 *1247*
these hands **m** to my *own* needs Ac 20:34 *5256*
in having **m** and in still ministering Heb 6:10 *1247*

MINISTERING
garments for **m** in the holy place, Ex 35:19 8334
garments for **m** in the holy place as Ex 39:1 8334
the woven garments for **m** in the Ex 39:41 8334
Now Samuel was **m** before the LORD, 1Sa 2:18 8334
was **m** to the LORD before Eli. 1Sa 3:1 8334
the Shunammite was **m** to the king. 1Ki 1:15 8334
m before the priests according to the 2Ch 8:14 8334
are **m** to the LORD as priests, 2Ch 13:10 8334
Ahaziah's brothers **m** to Ahaziah, 2Ch 22:8 8334
the priests and the **m** Levites; 2Ch 23:6 8334
who are **m** in the house of our God. Ne 10:36 8334
sanctuary, the priests who are **m**, Ne 10:39 8334
of the house and **m** in the house; Ezk 44:11 8334
they are **m** in the gates of the inner Ezk 44:17 8334
garments in which they have been **m** Ezk 44:19 8334
Jesus from Galilee while **m** to Him Mt 27:55 *1247*
and the angels were **m** to Him. Mk 1:13 *1247*
were **m** to the Lord and fasting, Ac 13:2 *3008*
any of his friends from **m** to him. Ac 24:23 *5256*
m as a priest the gospel of God, Ro 15:16 *2418*
Are they not all **m** spirits, Heb 1:14 *3010*
and in still **m** to the saints. Heb 6:10 *1247*
Every priest stands daily **m** Heb 10:11 *3008*

MINISTERS
It shall be on Aaron when he **m**; Ex 28:35 8334
and David's sons were chief **m**. 2Sa 8:18 3548
as **m** before the ark of the LORD, 1Ch 16:4 8334
of his **m** and their attire, 2Ch 9:4 8334
to be His **m** and burn incense." 2Ch 29:11 8334
to bring **m** to us for the house of Ezr 8:17 8334
messengers, Flaming fire His **m**. Ps 104:4 8334
All his **m** *become* wicked. Pr 29:12 8334
will be spoken of *as* **m** of our God. Is 61:6 8334
with the Levitical priests, My **m**. Jer 33:21 8334
they shall be **m** in My sanctuary, Ezk 44:11 8334
priests, the **m** of the sanctuary, Ezk 45:4 8334
the Levites, the **m** of the house, Ezk 45:5 8334
the **m** of the house shall boil the Ezk 46:24 8334
priests mourn, The **m** of the LORD. Jl 1:9 8334
Wail, O **m** of the altar! Jl 1:13 8334
night in sackcloth O **m** of my God, Jl 1:13 8334
Let the priests, the LORD's **m**, Jl 2:17 8334
AND HIS **M** A FLAME OF FIRE." Heb 1:7 *3011*

MINISTRIES
And there are varieties of **m**, 1Co 12:5 *1248*

MINISTRY
to their offices for their **m**. 1Ch 24:3 5656
were their offices for their **m** when 1Ch 24:19 5656
When He began His **m**, Lk 3:23
received his share in this **m**." Ac 1:17 *1248*
to occupy this **m** and apostleship Ac 1:25 *1248*
and to the **m** of the word." Ac 6:4 *1248*
and the **m** which I received from Ac 20:24 *1248*
among the Gentiles through his **m**. Ac 21:19 *1248*
of Gentiles, I magnify my **m**, Ro 11:13 *1248*
themselves for **m** to the saints), 1Co 16:15 *1248*
But if the **m** of death, in letters 2Co 3:7 *1248*
how will the **m** of the Spirit fail 2Co 3:8 *1248*
the **m** of condemnation has glory, 2Co 3:9 *1248*
does the **m** of righteousness abound 2Co 3:9 *1248*
Therefore, since we have this **m**, 2Co 4:1 *1248*
gave us the **m** of reconciliation, 2Co 5:18 *1248*
so that the **m** will not be discredited, 2Co 6:3 *1248*
to you about this **m** to the saints; 2Co 9:1 *1248*
For the **m** of this service is not 2Co 9:12 *1248*
Because of the proof given by this **m** 2Co 9:13 *1248*
"Take heed to the **m** which you Col 4:17 *1248*
of an evangelist, fulfill your **m**. 2Tm 4:5 *1248*
has obtained a more excellent **m**, Heb 8:6 *3009*
vessels of the **m** with the blood. Heb 9:21 *3009*

MINNI
of Ararat, **M** and Ashkenaz; Jer 51:27 4508

MINNITH
from Aroer to the entrance of **M**, Jg 11:33 4511
with the wheat of **M**, Ezk 27:17 4511

MINOR
but every **m** dispute they Ex 18:22 6996b
but every **m** dispute they Ex 18:26 6996b

MINSTREL
"But now bring me a **m**." 2Ki 3:15 5059
it came about, when the **m** played, 2Ki 3:15 5059

MINT
you tithe of **m** and dill and cummin, Mt 23:23 *2238*
For you pay tithe of **m** and rue and Lk 11:42 *2238*

MIRACLE
'Work a **m**,' then you shall say to Ex 7:9 4159
And He could do no **m** there except Mk 6:5 *1411*
who will perform a **m** in My name, Mk 9:39 *1411*
a noteworthy **m** has taken place Ac 4:16 *4592*
m of healing had been performed. Ac 4:22 *4592*

MIRACLES
and strike Egypt with all My **m** Ex 3:20 6381
I will perform **m** which have not Ex 34:10 6381
And where are all His **m** which our Jg 6:13 6381
And His **m** that He had shown them. Ps 78:11 6381
them, And **m** in the land of Ham. Ps 105:27 4159
of Egypt, I will show you **m**." Mi 7:15 6381
and in Your name perform many **m**?' Mt 7:22 *1411*
in which most of His **m** were done, Mt 11:20 *1411*
For if the **m** had occurred in Tyre Mt 11:21 *1411*
for if the **m** had occurred in Sodom Mt 11:23 *1411*
And He did not do many **m** there Mt 13:58 *1411*
and such **m** as these performed by Mk 6:2 *1411*
For if the **m** had been performed in Lk 10:13 *1411*
for all the **m** which they had seen, Lk 19:37 *1411*
man attested to you by God with **m** Ac 2:22 *1411*
signs and great **m** taking place, Ac 8:13 *1411*
m by the hands of Paul, Ac 19:11 *1411*
and to another the effecting of **m**, 1Co 12:10 *1411*
prophets, third teachers, then **m**, 1Co 12:28 *1411*
All are not *workers of* **m**, 1Co 12:29 *1411*
by signs and wonders and **m**. 2Co 12:12 *1411*
the Spirit and works **m** among you, Ga 3:5 *1411*
signs and wonders and by various **m** Heb 2:4 *1411*

MIRACULOUS
this wisdom and *these* **m** powers? Mt 13:54 *1411*
why **m** powers are at work in him." Mt 14:2 *1411*
m powers are at work in Him." Mk 6:14 *1411*

MIRE
them as the **m** of the streets. 2Sa 22:43 2916
"He has cast me into the **m**, Jb 30:19 2563a
like a threshing sledge on the **m**. Jb 41:30 2916
them out as the **m** of the streets. Ps 18:42 2916
I have sunk in deep **m**, Ps 69:2 3121
Deliver me from the **m** and Ps 69:14 2916
your feet were sunk in the **m**, Jer 38:22 1206
down Like **m** of the streets. Mi 7:10 2916
gold like the **m** of the streets. Zch 9:3 2916
in the **m** of the streets in battle; Zch 10:5 2916
returns to wallowing in the **m**." 2Pe 2:22 *1004*

MIRIAM
M the prophetess, Aaron's Ex 15:20 4813
M answered them, Ex 15:21 4813
Then **M** and Aaron spoke against Nu 12:1 4813
said to Moses and Aaron and to **M**, Nu 12:4 4813
tent, and He called Aaron and **M**. Nu 12:5 4813
the tent, behold, **M** *was* leprous, Nu 12:10 4813
As Aaron turned toward **M**, Nu 12:10 4813
So **M** was shut up outside the camp Nu 12:15 4813
on until **M** was received again. Nu 12:15 4813
Now **M** died there and was buried Nu 20:1 4813
and Moses and their sister **M**. Nu 26:59 4813
what the LORD your God did to **M** Dt 24:9 4813
and she conceived *and bore* **M**, 1Ch 4:17 4813
of Amram *were* Aaron, Moses and **M**. 1Ch 6:3 4813
before you Moses, Aaron and **M**. Mi 6:4 4813

MIRMAH
Sachia, **M**. These were his sons, 1Ch 8:10 4821

MIRROR
the skies, Strong as a molten **m**? Jb 37:18 7209
For now we see in a **m** dimly, 1Co 13:12 *2072*
as in a **m** the glory of the Lord, 2Co 3:18 *2734*
looks at his natural face in a **m**; Jas 1:23 *2072*

MIRRORS
from the **m** of the serving women Ex 38:8 4759b
hand **m**, undergarments, turbans and Is 3:23 1549

MIRTH
of us songs, And our tormentors **m**, Ps 137:3 8057

MIRY
of destruction, out of the **m** clay, Ps 40:2 3121

MISCARRIAGE
"Or like a **m** which is discarded, Jb 3:16 5309
"Better the **m** than he, Ec 6:3 5309

MISCARRIAGES
Like the **m** of a woman which never Ps 58:8 5309

MISCARRIED
and your female goats have not **m**, Gn 31:38 7921

MISCARRYING
no one **m** or barren in your land; Ex 23:26 7921
them a **m** womb and dry breasts. Hos 9:14 7921

MISCHIEF
conceive **m** and bring forth iniquity, Jb 15:35 5999
wickedness, And he conceives **m** and Ps 7:14 5999
m will return upon his own head, Ps 7:16 5999
his tongue is **m** and wickedness. Ps 10:7 5999
for You have beheld **m** and Ps 10:14 5999
iniquity and **m** are in her midst. Ps 55:10 5999
One which devises **m** by decree? Ps 94:20 5999
the **m** of their lips cover them. Ps 140:9 5999
They conceive **m** and bring forth Is 59:4 5999

MISDEED
themselves tell what **m** they found Ac 24:20 *92*

MISERABLE
and we loathe this **m** food." Nu 21:5 7052
and **m** and chronic sicknesses. Dt 28:59 7451a
Be **m** and mourn and weep; Jas 4:9 *5003*
m and poor and blind and naked, Rv 3:17 *1652*

MISERIES
your **m** which are coming upon you. Jas 5:1 *5004*

MISERY
bear the **m** of Israel no longer. Jg 10:16 5999
disgrace and conscious of my **m**. Jb 10:15 6040a
death, Prisoners in **m** and chains, Ps 107:10 6040a
Their soul melted away in *their* **m**. Ps 107:26 7463a
bowed down Through oppression, **m** Ps 107:39 7463a
AND **M** ARE IN THEIR PATHS, Ro 3:16 *5004*

MISFORTUNE
"He has not observed **m** in Jacob; Nu 23:21 205
there is neither adversary nor **m**. 1Ki 5:4 6294, 7451a
because **m** had come upon his house. 1Ch 7:23 7463a
what **m** may occur on the earth. Ec 11:2 7463a
M will not come on us, Jer 5:12 7463a
will change His mind about the **m** Jer 26:13 7463a
LORD changed His mind about the **m** Jer 26:19 7463a
and were well off and saw no **m**. Jer 44:17 7463a
brother's day, The day of his **m**. Ob 1:12 5235b

MISFORTUNES
'I will heap **m** on them; Dt 32:23 7463a

MISGIVINGS
and accompany them without **m**, Ac 10:20 *1252*
told me to go with them without **m**. Ac 11:12 *1252*

MISGUIDED
gently with the ignorant and **m**, Heb 5:2 *4105*

MISHAEL
M and Elzaphan and Sithri. Ex 6:22 4332
called also to **M** and Elzaphan, Lv 10:4 4332
and Pedaiah, **M**, Malchijah, Hashum, Ne 8:4 4332
Daniel, Hananiah, **M** and Azariah. Da 1:6 4332
Hananiah Shadrach, to **M** Meshach and Da 1:7 4332
Daniel, Hananiah, **M** and Azariah. Da 1:11 4332
Daniel, Hananiah, **M** and Azariah; Da 1:19 4332
friends, Hananiah, **M** and Azariah, Da 2:17 4331

MISHAL
and Allammelech and Amad and **M**; Jos 19:26 4861
gave **M** with its pasture lands, Jos 21:30 4861

MISHAM
The sons of Elpaal *were* Eber, **M**, 1Ch 8:12 4936

MISHAP
bear Without **m** and without loss, Ps 144:14 6556

MISHMA
and **M** and Dumah and Massa, Gn 25:14 4927
M, Dumah, Massa, Hadad, Tema, 1Ch 1:30 4927
son, Mibsam his son, **M** his son. 1Ch 4:25 4927
sons of **M** *were* Hammuel his son, 1Ch 4:26 4927

MISHMANNAH
M the fourth, Jeremiah the fifth, 1Ch 12:10 4925

MISHRAITES
the Shumathites and the **M**; 1Ch 2:53 4954

MISJUDGE
That their adversaries would **m**, Dt 32:27 5235a

MISLEAD
deceive you or **m** you like this, 2Ch 32:15 5496
'*Beware* that Hezekiah does not **m** Is 36:18 5496
'I am the Christ,' and will **m** many. Mt 24:5 *4105*
will arise and will **m** many. Mt 24:11 *4105*
so as to **m**, if possible, even the elect Mt 24:24 *4105*
saying, 'I am *He!*' and will **m** many. Mk 13:6 *4105*

MISLEADER
misled and the **m** belong to Him. Jb 12:16 7686

MISLEADING
'Is not Hezekiah **m** you to give 2Ch 32:11 5496
seen for you false and **m** oracles. La 2:14 4065
"We found this man **m** our nation Lk 23:2 *1294*

MISLEADS
who **m** a blind *person* on the road.' Dt 27:18 7686
listen to Hezekiah when he **m** you, 2Ki 18:32 5496
"See to it that no one **m** you. Mt 24:4 *4105*
"See to it that no one **m** you. Mk 13:5 *4105*

MISLED
Thus Manasseh **m** Judah and the 2Ch 33:9 8582
The **m** and the misleader belong to Jb 12:16 7683
Have **m** and overpowered you; Jer 38:22 5496
they have **m** My people by saying, Ezk 13:10 2937

"See to it that you are not **m**; Lk 21:8 *4105*

MISPAR
Reelaiah, Mordecai, Bilshan, **M**, Ezr 2:2 4558

MISPERETH
Nahamani, Mordecai, Bilshan, **M**, Ne 7:7 4559

MISREPHOTH-MAIM
as far as Great Sidon and **M** and the Jos 11:8 4956
country from Lebanon as far as **M**, Jos 13:6 4956

MISS
sling a stone at a hair and not **m**. Jg 20:16 2398
nor did we **m** anything as long as 1Sa 25:15 6485
remember it, nor will they **m** *it*, Jer 3:16 6485

MISSED
and you will be **m** because your 1Sa 20:18 6485
nor have they **m** anything all the 1Sa 25:7 6485
nothing was **m** of all that belonged 1Sa 25:21 6485

MISSES
"If your father **m** me at all, then 1Sa 20:6 6485

MISSING
our charge, and no man of us is **m**. Nu 31:49 6485
so that one tribe should be **m** Jg 21:3 6485
But nothing of theirs was **m**, 1Sa 30:19 5737c
servants besides Asahel were **m**. 2Sa 2:30 6485
if for any reason he is **m**, 1Ki 20:39 6485
let no one be **m**, for I have a 2Ki 10:19 6485
whoever is **m** shall not live." 2Ki 10:19 6485
Not one of these will be **m**; Is 34:16 5737c
of *His* power, Not one *of them* is **m**. Is 40:26 5737c
be terrified, nor will any be **m**," Jer 23:4 6485

MISSION
and the LORD sent you on a **m**, 1Sa 15:18 1870
the **m** on which the LORD sent me, 1Sa 15:20 1870
when they had fulfilled their **m**, Ac 12:25 *1248*

MIST
But a **m** used to rise from the earth Gn 2:6 108
They distill rain from the **m**, Jb 36:27 108
And your sins like a heavy **m**. Is 44:22 6051
a **m** and a darkness fell upon him, Ac 13:11 *887*

MISTAKE
perhaps it was a **m**. Gn 43:12 4870
messenger *of God* that it was a **m**. Ec 5:6 7684

MISTAKEN
"You are **m**, not understanding the Mt 22:29 *4105*
"Is this not the reason you are **m**, Mk 12:24 *4105*
you are greatly **m**." Mk 12:27 *4105*

MISTREAT
"If you **m** my daughters, or if you Gn 31:50 6031a
for money, you shall not **m** her, Dt 21:14 6014b
you shall not **m** him. Dt 23:16 3238
Also do not **m** *or* do violence to Jer 22:3 3238
you, pray for those who **m** you. Lk 6:28 *1908*
to the church in order to **m** them. Ac 12:1 *2559*
rulers, to **m** and to stone them, Ac 14:5 *5195*

MISTREATED
slaves and **m** them and killed them. Mt 22:6 *5195*
be mocked and **m** and spit upon, Lk 18:32 *5195*
AND **M** FOR FOUR HUNDRED YEARS. Ac 7:6 *2559*
and **m** our fathers so that they Ac 7:19 *2559*
suffered and been **m** in Philippi, 1Th 2:2 *5195*

MISTRESS
her **m** was despised in her sight. Gn 16:4 1404
from the presence of my **m** Sarai." Gn 16:8 1404
"Return to your **m**, and submit Gn 16:9 1404
of the woman, the **m** of the house, 1Ki 17:17 1172
She said to her **m**, 2Ki 5:3 1404
of a maid to the hand of her **m**, Ps 123:2 1404
when she supplants her **m**. Pr 30:23 1404
his master, the maid like her **m**, Is 24:2 1404
charming one, the **m** of sorceries, Na 3:4 1172

MISTS
water and **m** driven by a storm, 2Pe 2:17 *3658*

MITHKAH
from Terah and camped at **M**. Nu 33:28 4989
They journeyed from **M** and Nu 33:29 4989

MITHNITE
son of Maacah and Joshaphat the **M**, 1Ch 11:43 4981

MITHREDATH
by the hand of **M** the treasurer, Ezr 1:8 4990
days of Artaxerxes, Bishlam, **M**, Ezr 4:7 4990

MITYLENE
took him on board and came to **M**. Ac 20:14 *3412*

MIX
'Whoever shall **m** *any* like it or Ex 30:33 7543
flesh well And **m** in the spices, Ezk 24:10 7543
Who **m** in your venom even to make Hab 2:15 5596
mixed, **m** twice as much for her. Rv 18:6 *2767*

MIXED
A **m** multitude also went up Ex 12:38 6154a
and unleavened cakes **m** with oil, Ex 29:2 1101a
of bread and one cake of bread **m** Ex 29:23
fine flour **m** with one-fourth of a hin Ex 29:40 1101a
cakes of fine flour **m** with oil, Lv 2:4 1101a
flour, unleavened, **m** with oil; Lv 2:5 1101a
'Every grain offering, **m** with oil Lv 7:10 1101a
offer unleavened cakes **m** with oil, Lv 7:12 1101a
stirred fine flour **m** with oil. Lv 7:12 1101a
cake and one cake of bread **m** *with* Lv 8:26
and a grain offering **m** with oil; Lv 9:4 1101a
m with oil for a grain offering, Lv 14:10 1101a
m with oil for a grain offering, Lv 14:21 1101a
two kinds of material **m** together. Lv 19:19 8162
an ephah of fine flour **m** with oil, Lv 23:13 1101a
cakes of fine flour **m** with oil Nu 6:15 1101a
full of fine flour **m** with oil for a Nu 7:13 1101a
full of fine flour **m** with oil for a Nu 7:19 1101a
full of fine flour **m** with oil for a Nu 7:25 1101a
full of fine flour **m** with oil for a Nu 7:31 1101a
full of fine flour **m** with oil for a Nu 7:37 1101a
full of fine flour **m** with oil for a Nu 7:43 1101a
full of fine flour **m** with oil for a Nu 7:49 1101a
full of fine flour **m** with oil for a Nu 7:55 1101a
full of fine flour **m** with oil for a Nu 7:61 1101a
full of fine flour **m** with oil for a Nu 7:67 1101a
full of fine flour **m** with oil for a Nu 7:73 1101a
full of fine flour **m** with oil for a Nu 7:79 1101a
offering, fine flour **m** with oil; Nu 8:8 1101a
fine flour **m** with one-fourth of a hin Nu 15:4 1101a
fine flour **m** with one-third of a hin Nu 15:6 1101a
flour **m** with one-half a hin of oil; Nu 15:9 1101a
m with a fourth of a hin of beaten Nu 28:5 1101a
an ephah of fine flour **m** with oil as Nu 28:9 1101a
m with oil for a grain offering, Nu 28:12 1101a
m with oil for a grain offering, Nu 28:12 1101a
flour **m** with oil for a grain offering Nu 28:13 1101a
shall offer fine flour **m** with oil: Nu 28:20 1101a
offering, fine flour **m** with oil: Nu 28:28 1101a
offering, fine flour **m** with oil: Nu 29:3 1101a
offering, fine flour **m** with oil: Nu 29:9 1101a
offering, fine flour **m** with oil: Nu 29:14 1101a
wear a material **m** of wool and linen Dt 22:11 8162
It is well **m**, and He pours out of Ps 75:8 4538
her food, she has **m** her wine; Pr 9:2 4537
And drink of the wine I have **m**. Pr 9:5 4537
Those who go to taste **m** wine. Pr 23:30 4469
goblet Which never lacks **m** wine; SS 7:2 4197
The LORD has **m** within her a spirit Is 19:14 4537
fill *cups* with **m** wine for Destiny, Is 65:11 4469
saw the iron **m** with common clay. Da 2:41 6151
saw the iron **m** with common clay, Da 2:43 6151
they gave Him wine to drink **m** with Mt 27:34 *3396*
to give Him wine **m** with myrrh; Mk 15:23 *4669*
Galileans whose blood Pilate had **m** Lk 13:1 *3396*
came hail and fire, **m** with blood, Rv 8:7 *3396*
which is **m** in full strength in the Rv 14:10 *2767*
like a sea of glass **m** with fire, Rv 15:2 *3396*
in the cup which she has **m**, Rv 18:6 *2767*

MIXES
Ephraim **m** himself with the nations; Hos 7:8 1101a

MIXING
prepared the **m** of the spices. 1Ch 9:30 4842
And valiant men in **m** strong drink, Is 5:22 4537

MIXTURE
a holy anointing oil, a perfume **m**, Ex 30:25 4842
bringing a **m** of myrrh and aloes, Jn 19:39 *3395*

MIZAR
the peaks of Hermon, from Mount **M**. Ps 42:6 4706

MIZPAH
and **M**, for he said, Gn 31:49 4709
together and camped in **M**. Jg 10:17 4709
his words before the LORD at **M**. Jg 11:11 4709
he passed through **M** of Gilead, Jg 11:29 4708
and from **M** of Gilead he went on to Jg 11:29 4708
Jephthah came to his house at **M**, Jg 11:34 4709
as one man to the LORD at **M**. Jg 20:1 4709
sons of Israel had gone up to **M**.) Jg 20:3 4709
the men of Israel had sworn in **M**, Jg 21:1 4709
did not come up to the LORD at **M**, Jg 21:5 4709
not come up to the LORD at **M**?" Jg 21:8 4709
"Gather all Israel to **M** and 1Sa 7:5 4708
They gathered to **M**, 1Sa 7:6 4709
judged the sons of Israel at **M**. 1Sa 7:6 4709
sons of Israel had gathered to **M**, 1Sa 7:7 4709
The men of Israel went out of **M** 1Sa 7:11 4709
and set it between **M** and Shen, 1Sa 7:12 4709
to Bethel and Gilgal and **M**, 1Sa 7:16 4709
people together to the LORD at **M**; 1Sa 10:17 4709
went from there to **M** of Moab; 1Sa 22:3 4708
with them Geba of Benjamin and **M**. 1Ki 15:22 4709
they came to Gedaliah to **M**, 2Ki 25:23 4709
Chaldeans who were with him at **M**. 2Ki 25:25 4709
with them he fortified Geba and **M**. 2Ch 16:6 4709
the men of Gibeon and of **M**, Ne 3:7 4709
the official of the district of **M**, Ne 3:15 4709
son of Jeshua, the official of **M**, Ne 3:19 4709
Then Jeremiah went to **M** to Jer 40:6 4709
So they came to Gedaliah at **M**, Jer 40:8 4709
I am going to stay at **M** to stand Jer 40:10 4709
land of Judah, to Gedaliah at **M**, Jer 40:12 4709
the field came to Gedaliah at **M**, Jer 40:13 4709
spoke secretly to Gedaliah in **M**, Jer 40:15 4709
came to **M** to Gedaliah the son of Jer 41:1 4709
eating bread together there in **M**, Jer 41:1 4709
him, *that is* with Gedaliah at **M**, Jer 41:3 4709
went out from **M** to meet them, Jer 41:6 4709
of the people who were in **M**, Jer 41:10 4709
all the people who were left in **M**, Jer 41:10 4709
Ishmael had taken captive from **M** Jer 41:14 4709
took from **M** all the remnant of the Jer 41:16 4709
For you have been a snare at **M** And Hos 5:1 4709

MIZPEH
foot of Hermon in the land of **M**. Jos 11:3 4709
and the valley of **M** to the east; Jos 11:8 4708
and Dilean and **M** and Joktheel, Jos 15:38 4708
and **M** and Chephirah and Mozah, Jos 18:26 4708

MIZRAIM
Cush and **M** and Put and Canaan. Gn 10:6 4714
M became the father of Ludim Gn 10:13 4714
The sons of Ham *were* Cush, **M**, 1Ch 1:8 4714
M became the father of the 1Ch 1:11 4714

MIZZAH
Nahath and Zerah, Shammah and **M**. Gn 36:13 4199
Zerah, chief Shammah, chief **M**. Gn 36:17 4199
Nahath, Zerah, Shammah and **M**. 1Ch 1:37 4199

MNASON
with us, taking us to **M** of Cyprus, Ac 21:16 *3416*

MOAB
bore a son, and called his name **M**; Gn 19:37 4124
defeated Midian in the field of **M**, Gn 36:35 4124
The leaders of **M**, trembling grips Ex 15:15 4124
wilderness which is opposite **M**, Nu 21:11 4124
for the Arnon is the border of **M**, Nu 21:13 4124
Moab, between **M** and the Amorites. Nu 21:13 4124
And leans to the border of **M**." Nu 21:15 4124
valley that is in the land of **M**, Nu 21:20 4124
fought against the former king of **M** Nu 21:26 4124
It devoured Ar of **M**, Nu 21:28 4124
"Woe to you, O **M**! You are ruined Nu 21:29 4124
and camped in the plains of **M** Nu 22:1 4124
So **M** was in great fear because of Nu 22:3 4124
and **M** was in dread of the sons of Nu 22:3 4124
M said to the elders of Midian, Nu 22:4 4124
Zippor was king of **M** at that time. Nu 22:4 4124
So the elders of **M** and the elders Nu 22:7 4124
leaders of **M** stayed with Balaam. Nu 22:8 4124
the son of Zippor, king of **M**, Nu 22:10 4124
The leaders of **M** arose and went to Nu 22:14 4124
and went with the leaders of **M**. Nu 22:21 4124
out to meet him at the city of **M**, Nu 22:36 4124
he and all the leaders of **M**. Nu 23:6 4124
and the leaders of **M** with him. Nu 23:17 4124
crush through the forehead of **M**, Nu 24:17 4124
harlot with the daughters of **M**. Nu 25:1 4124
spoke with them in the plains of **M** Nu 26:3 4124
in the plains of **M** by the Jordan at Nu 26:63 4124
to the camp at the plains of **M**, Nu 31:12 4124
at Iye-abarim, at the border of **M**. Nu 33:44 4124
and camped in the plains of **M** by Nu 33:48 4124
as Abel-shittim in the plains of **M**. Nu 33:49 4124
spoke to Moses in the plains of **M** Nu 33:50 4124
spoke to Moses in the plains of **M** Nu 35:1 4124
in the plains of **M** by the Jordan Nu 36:13 4124
the Jordan in the land of **M**, Dt 1:5 4124
by the way of the wilderness of **M**. Dt 2:8 4124
'Do not harass **M**, nor provoke them Dt 2:9 4124
cross over Ar, the border of **M**. Dt 2:18 4124
sons of Israel in the land of **M**, Dt 29:1 4124
in the land of **M** opposite Jericho, Dt 32:49 4124
the plains of **M** to Mount Nebo, Dt 34:1 4124
died there in the land of **M**, Dt 34:5 4124
in the valley in the land of **M**, Dt 34:6 4124
wept for Moses in the plains of **M** Dt 34:8 4124
an inheritance in the plains of **M**, Jos 13:32 4124
the son of Zippor, king of **M**, Jos 24:9 4124
strengthened Eglon the king of **M** Jg 3:12 4124
Israel served Eglon the king of **M** Jg 3:14 4124
by him to Eglon the king of **M**. Jg 3:15 4124
the tribute to Eglon king of **M**. Jg 3:17 4124
fords of the Jordan opposite **M**, Jg 3:28 4124
So **M** was subdued that day under Jg 3:30 4124
the gods of Sidon, the gods of **M**, Jg 10:6 4124
did not take away the land of **M** nor Jg 11:15 4124
they also sent to the king of **M**, Jg 11:17 4124
land of Edom and the land of **M**, Jg 11:18 4124
to the east side of the land of **M**, Jg 11:18 4124
did not enter the territory of **M**, Jg 11:18 4124
for the Arnon *was* the border of **M**. Jg 11:18 4124
the son of Zippor, king of **M**? Jg 11:25 4124
went to sojourn in the land of **M** Ru 1:1 4124
entered the land of **M** and remained Ru 1:2 4124
might return from the land of **M**, Ru 1:6 4124
she had heard in the land of **M** that Ru 1:6 4124
who returned from the land of **M**. Ru 1:22 4124
with Naomi from the land of **M**. Ru 2:6 4124
has come back from the land of **M**, Ru 4:3 4124
into the hand of the king of **M**, 1Sa 12:9 4124
enemies on every side, against **M**, 1Sa 14:47 4124
went from there to Mizpah of **M**; 1Sa 22:3 4124
and he said to the king of **M**, 1Sa 22:3 4124
he left them with the king of **M**; 1Sa 22:4 4124
He defeated **M**, and measured 2Sa 8:2 4124
from Aram and **M** and the sons of 2Sa 8:12 4124
killed the two *sons of* Ariel of **M**. 2Sa 23:20 4124
Chemosh the detestable idol of **M**, 1Ki 11:7 4124
Sidonians, Chemosh the god of **M**, 1Ki 11:33 4124
Now **M** rebelled against Israel 2Ki 1:1 4124
king of **M** was a sheep breeder, 2Ki 3:4 4124
the king of **M** rebelled against the 2Ki 3:5 4124
king of **M** has rebelled against me. 2Ki 3:7 4124
go with me to fight against **M**?" 2Ki 3:7 4124
to give them into the hand of **M**." 2Ki 3:10 4124
to give them into the hand of **M**." 2Ki 3:13 4124
Now therefore, **M**, to the spoil!" 2Ki 3:23 4124
When the king of **M** saw that the 2Ki 3:26 4124
for Chemosh the abomination of **M**, 2Ki 23:13 4124
defeated Midian in the field of **M**, 1Ch 1:46 4124
Joash, Saraph, who ruled in **M**, 1Ch 4:22 4124
of children in the country of **M** after 1Ch 8:8 4124
down the two *sons of* Ariel of **M**. 1Ch 11:22 4124
He defeated **M**, and the 1Ch 18:2 4124
from Edom, **M**, the sons of Ammon, 1Ch 18:11 4124
sons of **M** and the sons of Ammon, 2Ch 20:1 4124
behold, the sons of Ammon and **M** 2Ch 20:10 4124
against the sons of Ammon, **M** and 2Ch 20:22 4124
For the sons of Ammon and **M** rose 2Ch 20:23 4124
women from Ashdod, Ammon *and* **M**. Ne 13:23 4125
"**M** is My washbowl; Ps 60:8 4124
M and the Hagrites; Ps 83:6 4124
"**M** is My washbowl; Ps 108:9 4124
They will possess Edom and **M**, Is 11:14 4124
The oracle concerning **M**. Is 15:1 4124

Ar of **M** is devastated *and* ruined; Is 15:1 4124
Kir of **M** is devastated *and* ruined. Is 15:1 4124
M wails over Nebo and Medeba; Is 15:2 4124
the armed men of **M** cry aloud; Is 15:4 4124
My heart cries out for **M**; Is 15:5 4124
gone around the territory of **M**, Is 15:8 4124
A lion upon the fugitives of **M** and Is 15:9 4124
The daughters of **M** will be at the Is 16:2 4124
the outcasts of **M** stay with you; Is 16:4 4124
We have heard of the pride of **M**, Is 16:6 4124
Therefore **M** will wail; Is 16:7 4124
everyone of **M** will wail. Is 16:7 4124
heart intones like a harp for **M** And Is 16:11 4124
about when **M** presents himself, Is 16:12 4124
LORD spoke earlier concerning **M**. Is 16:13 4124
the glory of **M** will be degraded Is 16:14 4124
And **M** will be trodden down in his Is 25:10 4124
and the sons of Ammon, and **M** and Jer 9:26 4124
Edom, **M** and the sons of Ammon; Jer 25:21 4124
king of Edom, to the king of **M**, Jer 27:3 4124
also all the Jews who were in **M** Jer 40:11 4124
Concerning **M**. Thus says the LORD Jer 48:1 4124
"There is praise for **M** no longer; Jer 48:2 4124
"**M** is broken, Her little ones Jer 48:4 4124
"Give wings to **M**, For she will Jer 48:9 4124
"**M** has been at ease since his Jer 48:11 4124
"And **M** will be ashamed of Jer 48:13 4124
"**M** has been destroyed and men Jer 48:15 4124
"The disaster of **M** will soon come, Jer 48:16 4124
destroyer of **M** has come up against Jer 48:18 4124
"**M** has been put to shame, for it Jer 48:20 4124
Arnon That **M** has been destroyed. Jer 48:20 4124
all the cities of the land of **M**, Jer 48:24 4124
"The horn of **M** has been cut off and Jer 48:25 4124
so **M** will wallow in his vomit, and Jer 48:26 4124
the crags, O inhabitants of **M**, Jer 48:28 4124
"We have heard of the pride of **M** Jer 48:29 4124
"Therefore I will wail for **M**, Jer 48:31 4124
Even for all **M** will I cry out; Jer 48:31 4124
field, even from the land of **M**. Jer 48:33 4124
"I will make an end of **M**," Jer 48:35 4124
My heart wails for **M** like flutes; Jer 48:36 4124
"On all the housetops of **M** and in Jer 48:38 4124
broken **M** like an undesirable vessel Jer 48:38 4124
How **M** has turned his back Jer 48:39 4124
So **M** will become a laughingstock Jer 48:39 4124
spread out his wings against **M**. Jer 48:40 4124
the hearts of the mighty men of **M** Jer 48:41 4124
"**M** will be destroyed from Jer 48:42 4124
upon you, O inhabitant of **M**," Jer 48:43 4124
shall bring upon her, *even* upon **M**, Jer 48:44 4124
it has devoured the forehead of **M** Jer 48:45 4124
"Woe to you, **M**! Jer 48:46 4124
Yet I will restore the fortunes of **M** Jer 48:47 4124
Thus far the judgment on **M**. Jer 48:47 4124
"Because **M** and Seir say, Ezk 25:8 4124
deprive the flank of **M** of *its* cities, Ezk 25:9 4124
I will execute judgments on **M**, Ezk 25:11 4124
M and the foremost of the sons of Da 11:41 4124
"For three transgressions of **M** Am 2:1 4124
"So I will send fire upon **M** And Am 2:2 4124
And **M** will die amid tumult, With Am 2:2 4124
What Balak king of **M** counseled Mi 6:5 4124
"I have heard the taunting of **M** Zph 2:8 4124
"Surely **M** will be like Sodom And Zph 2:9 4124

MOABITE
"No Ammonite or **M** shall enter the Dt 23:3 4125
for themselves **M** women *as* wives; Ru 1:4 4125
"She is the young **M** woman who Ru 2:6 4125
M, Ammonite, Edomite, Sidonian, 1Ki 11:1 4125
sons of Elnaam, and Ithmah the **M**, 1Ch 11:46 4125
no Ammonite or **M** should ever enter Ne 13:1 4125

MOABITES
the father of the **M** to this day. Gn 19:37 4124
Rephaim, but the **M** call them Emim. Dt 2:11 4125
the **M** who live in Ar did for me, Dt 2:29 4125
enemies the **M** into your hands." Jg 3:28 4124
at that time about ten thousand **M**, Jg 3:29 4124
the **M** became servants to David, 2Sa 8:2 4124
also give the **M** into your hand. 2Ki 3:18 4124
Now all the **M** heard that the kings 2Ki 3:21 4124
and the **M** saw the water opposite 2Ki 3:22 4124
Israelites arose and struck the **M**, 2Ki 3:24 4124
into the land, slaughtering the **M**. 2Ki 3:24 4124
Now the bands of the **M** would 2Ki 13:20 4124
bands of Arameans, bands of **M**, 2Ki 24:2 4124
the **M** became servants to David, 1Ch 18:2 4124
Jebusites, the Ammonites, the **M**, Ezr 9:1 4125

MOABITESS
returned, and with her Ruth the **M**, Ru 1:22 4125
And Ruth the **M** said to Naomi, Ru 2:2 4125
Then Ruth the **M** said, Ru 2:21 4125
you must also acquire Ruth the **M**, Ru 4:5 4125
I have acquired Ruth the **M**, Ru 4:10 4125
the son of Shimrith the **M**. 2Ch 24:26 4125

MOAB'S
M king from the mountains of the Nu 23:7 4124

MOADIAH
of Miniamin, of **M**, Piltai; Ne 12:17 4573

MOAN
You will **m** for the raisin cakes Is 16:7 1897
so I twitter; I **m** like a dove; Is 38:14 1897
bears, And **m** sadly like doves; Is 59:11 1897
I will **m** for the men of Kir-heres. Jer 48:31 1897

MOANING
daughter of Judah Mourning and **m**. La 2:5 592
are **m** like the sound of doves, Na 2:7 5090b

MOAT
be built again, with plaza and **m**, Da 9:25 2742c

MOB
formed a **m** and set the city in an Ac 17:5 *3792*
because of the violence of the **m**; Ac 21:35 *3793*

MOBILIZE
"His sons will **m** and assemble Da 11:10 1624
so the king of the South will **m** an Da 11:25 1624

MOCK
after I have spoken, you may **m**. Jb 21:3 3932
are glad, And the innocent **m** them, Jb 22:19 3932
"But now those younger than I **m** me, Jb 30:1 7832
They **m** and wickedly speak of Ps 73:8 4167
I will **m** when your dread comes, Pr 1:26 3932
Fools **m** at sin, But among the Pr 14:9 3917b
who are far from you will **m** you, Ezk 22:5 7046
"They **m** at kings And rulers are Hab 1:10 7046
to **m** and scourge and crucify *Him*, Mt 20:19 *1702*
"They will **m** Him and spit on Him, Mk 10:34 *1702*

MOCKED
noon, that Elijah **m** them and said, 1Ki 18:27 2048
city and **m** him and said to him, 2Ki 2:23 7046
'She has despised you and **m** you, 2Ki 19:21 3932
laughed them to scorn and **m** them. 2Ch 30:10 3932
m the messengers of God, 2Ch 36:16 3931
m us and despised us and said, Ne 2:19 3932
and very angry and **m** the Jews. Ne 4:1 3932
"She has despised you and **m** you, Is 37:22 3932
saw her, They **m** at her ruin. La 1:7 7832
knelt down before Him and **m** Him, Mt 27:29 *1702*
After they had **m** Him, Mt 27:31 *1702*
After they had **m** Him, Mk 15:20 *1702*
be **m** and mistreated and spit upon, Lk 18:32 *1702*
The soldiers also **m** Him, Lk 23:36 *1702*
Do not be deceived, God is not **m**; Ga 6:7 *3456*

MOCKER
Wine is a **m**, strong drink a brawler Pr 20:1 3917b

MOCKERS
"Surely **m** are with me, And my eye Jb 17:2 2049
m will come with *their* mocking, 2Pe 3:3 *1703*
"In the last time there will be **m**, Jude 1:18 *1703*

MOCKERY
how I made a **m** of the Egyptians and Ex 10:2 5953a
"Because you have made a **m** of me! Nu 22:29 5953a
witness makes a **m** of justice, Pr 19:28 3917b
They are worthless, a work of **m**; Jer 10:15 8595
They are worthless, a work of **m**; Jer 51:18 8595
m *and* insinuations against him And Hab 2:6 4426

MOCKING
whom she had borne to Abraham, **m**. Gn 21:9 6711
Their **m** song all the day. La 3:14
I am their **m** song. La 3:63 4485
nations and a **m** to all the lands. Ezk 22:4 7048
scribes and elders, were **m** *Him* Mt 27:41 *1702*
were **m** *Him* among themselves and Mk 15:31 *1702*
Jesus in custody were **m** Him and Lk 22:63 *1702*
Him with contempt and **m** Him, Lk 23:11 *1702*
But others were **m** and saying, Ac 2:13 *1315b*
mockers will come with *their* **m**, 2Pe 3:3 *1701a*

MOCKINGS
experienced **m** and scourgings, Heb 11:36 *1701b*

MOCKS
He **m** the despair of the innocent. Jb 9:23 3932
He who **m** the poor taunts his Pr 17:5 3932
The eye that **m** a father And Pr 30:17 3932
all day long; Everyone **m** me. Jer 20:7 3932

MODE
boy's **m** of life and his vocation?" Jg 13:12 4941

MODEL
pattern of the altar and its **m**, 2Ki 16:10 8403
and gold for the **m** of the chariot, 1Ch 28:18 8403
to offer ourselves as a **m** for you, 2Th 3:9 *5179b*

MODERATE
When a **m** south wind came up, Ac 27:13 *5285*

MODESTLY
proper clothing, **m** and discreetly, 1Tm 2:9 *127*

MOIST
And the marrow of his bones is **m**, Jb 21:24 8248

MOISTEN
a hin of oil to **m** the fine flour, Ezk 46:14 7450

MOISTURE
with **m** He loads the thick cloud; Jb 37:11 7377
away, because it had no **m**. Lk 8:6 *2429*

MOLADAH
Amam and Shema and **M**, Jos 15:26 4137
Beersheba or Sheba and **M**, Jos 19:2 4137
They lived at Beersheba, **M** and 1Ch 4:28 4137
and in Jeshua, in **M** and Beth-pelet, Ne 11:26 4137

MOLD
Take hold of the brick **m**! Na 3:14 4404

MOLDED
thing **m** will not say to the molder, Ro 9:20 *4110*

MOLDER
thing molded will not say to the **m**, Ro 9:20 *4111*

MOLDING
you shall make a gold **m** around it. Ex 25:11 2213
make a gold **m** all around for it. Ex 30:3 2213
two gold rings for it under its **m**; Ex 30:4 2213
made a gold **m** for it all around. Ex 37:2 2213
made a gold **m** for it all around. Ex 37:11 2213
a gold **m** for its rim all around. Ex 37:12 2213
made a gold **m** for it all around. Ex 37:26 2213
golden rings for it under its **m**, Ex 37:27 2213

MOLE
the **m**, and the mouse, and the Lv 11:29 2467

MOLECH
your offspring to offer them to **M**, Lv 18:21 4432
gives any of his offspring to **M**, Lv 20:2 4432
given some of his offspring to **M**, Lv 20:3 4432
gives any of his offspring to **M**, Lv 20:4 4432
by playing the harlot after **M**. Lv 20:5 4432
and for **M** the detestable idol of 1Ki 11:7 4432
pass through the fire for **M**. 2Ki 23:10 4432
to pass through *the fire* to **M**, Jer 32:35 4432

MOLES
men will cast away to the **m** and the Is 2:20 2663c

MOLID
and she bore him Ahban and **M**. 1Ch 2:29 4140a

MOLOCH
TOOK ALONG THE TABERNACLE OF **M** Ac 7:43 *3434*

MOLTEN
tool and made it into a **m** calf; Ex 32:4 4541a
have made for themselves a **m** calf, Ex 32:8 4541a
shall make for yourself no **m** gods. Ex 34:17 4541a
or make for yourselves **m** gods; Lv 19:4 4541a
and destroy all their **m** images and Nu 33:52 4541a
made a **m** image for themselves.' Dt 9:12 4541a
had made for yourselves a **m** calf; Dt 9:16 4541a
who makes an idol or a **m** image, Dt 27:15 4541a
make a graven image and a **m** image; Jg 17:3 4541a
into a graven image and a **m** image, Jg 17:4 4541a
and a graven image and a **m** image? Jg 18:14 4541a
household idols and the **m** image, Jg 18:17 4541a
household idols and the **m** image, Jg 18:18 4541a
He also made two capitals of **m** 1Ki 7:16 3332
m images to provoke Me to anger, 1Ki 14:9 4541a
and made for themselves **m** images, 2Ki 17:16 4541a
also made **m** images for the Baals. 2Ch 28:2 4541a
carved images and the **m** images. 2Ch 34:3 4541a
and the **m** images he broke in 2Ch 34:4 4541a
A calf of **m** metal And said, Ne 9:18 4541a
the skies, Strong as a **m** mirror? Jb 37:18 3332
in Horeb And worshiped a **m** image. Ps 106:19 4541a
your **m** images plated with gold. Is 30:22 4541a
m images are wind and emptiness. Is 41:29 5262b
in idols, Who say to **m** images, Is 42:17 4541a
my **m** image have commanded them.' Is 48:5 5262b
For his **m** images are deceitful, Jer 10:14 5262b
For his **m** images are deceitful, Jer 51:17 5262b
And make for themselves **m** images, Hos 13:2 4541a

MOMENT
I go up in your midst for one **m**, Ex 33:5 7281
see the holy *objects* even for a **m**, Nu 4:20 1104
"But now for a brief **m** grace has Ezr 9:8 7281
morning And try him every **m**? Jb 7:18 7281
"In a **m** they die, and at midnight Jb 34:20 7281
For His anger is but for a **m**, Ps 30:5 7281
How they are destroyed in a **m**! Ps 73:19 7281
a lying tongue is only for a **m**. Pr 12:19 7280a
I water it every **m**. Is 27:3 7281
"For a brief **m** I forsook you, But Is 54:7 7281
I hid My face from you for a **m**, Is 54:8 7281
"At one **m** I might speak Jer 18:7 7281
"Or at another **m** I might speak Jer 18:9 7281
Which was overthrown as in a **m**, La 4:6 7281
on the ground, tremble every **m** and Ezk 26:16 7281
and they will tremble every **m**, Ezk 32:10 7281
that at the **m** you hear the sound Da 3:5 5732
at the **m** you hear the sound of the Da 3:15 5732
servant was healed that *very* **m**. Mt 8:13 *5610*
At that very **m** she came up and Lk 2:38 *5610*
of the world in a **m** of time. Lk 4:5 *4743*
at that **m** three men appeared Ac 11:11 *1824*
And it came out at that very **m**. Ac 16:18 *5610*
in a **m**, in the twinkling of an eye, 1Co 15:52 *823*
according to the need *of the* **m**, Eph 4:29
discipline for the **m** seems not to be Heb 12:11 *3918b*

MOMENTARY
And the joy of the godless **m**? Jb 20:5
5704, 7281
For **m**, light affliction is 2Co 4:17 *3910*

MONEY
bought with **m** from any foreigner, Gn 17:12 3701
or who is bought with your **m** Gn 17:13 3701
all who were bought with his **m**, Gn 17:23 3701
or bought with **m** from a foreigner, Gn 17:27 3701
for one hundred pieces of **m**. Gn 33:19 7192
restore every man's **m** in his sack, Gn 42:25 3701
the lodging place, he saw his **m**; Gn 42:27 3701
"My **m** has been returned, and Gn 42:28 3701
man's bundle of **m** *was* in his sack; Gn 42:35 3701
father saw their bundles of **m**, Gn 42:35 3701
Take double *the* **m** in your hand, Gn 43:12 3701
and take back in your hand the **m** Gn 43:12 3701
took double *the* **m** in their hand, Gn 43:15 3701
"*It is* because of the **m** that was Gn 43:18 3701
each man's **m** was in the mouth of Gn 43:21 3701
mouth of his sack, our **m** in full. Gn 43:21 3701
other **m** in our hand to buy food; Gn 43:22 3701
know who put our **m** in our sacks." Gn 43:22 3701
treasure in your sacks; I had your **m** Gn 43:23 3701
put each man's **m** in the mouth of Gn 44:1 3701
and his **m** for the grain." Gn 44:2 3701
the **m** which we found in the mouth Gn 44:8 3701
Joseph gathered all the **m** that Gn 47:14 3701
brought the **m** into Pharaoh's house. Gn 47:14 3701
When the **m** was all spent in Gn 47:15 3701

For *our* **m** is gone." **Gn 47:15** 3701
livestock, since *your* **m** is gone." **Gn 47:16** 3701
my lord that our **m** is all spent, **Gn 47:18** 3701
every man's slave purchased with **m**, **Ex 12:44** 3701
for nothing, without *payment of* **m**. **Ex 21:11** 3701
he shall give **m** to its owner, and **Ex 21:34** 3701
man gives his neighbor **m** or goods **Ex 22:7** 3701
he shall pay **m** equal to the dowry **Ex 22:17** 3701
"If you lend **m** to My people, to **Ex 22:25** 3701
You shall take the atonement **m** **Ex 30:16** 3701
slave as *his* property with his **m**, **Lv 22:11** 3701
and give the **m**, the ransom of **Nu 3:48** 3701
So Moses took the ransom **m** from **Nu 3:49** 3701
he took the **m** in terms of the shekel **Nu 3:50** 3701
Moses gave the ransom **m** to Aaron **Nu 3:51** 3701
shall buy food from them with **m** **Dt 2:6** 3701
purchase water from them with **m** **Dt 2:6** 3701
'You will sell me food for **m** so that I **Dt 2:28** 3701
give me water for **m** so that I may **Dt 2:28** 3701
then you shall exchange *it* for **m**, **Dt 14:25** 3701
and bind the **m** in your hand and go **Dt 14:25** 3701
"You may spend the **m** for **Dt 14:26** 3701
certainly not sell her for **m**, **Dt 21:14** 3701
interest on **m**, food, *or* anything **Dt 23:19** 3701
for one hundred pieces of **m**; **Jos 24:32** 7192
and brought the **m** in their hands. **Jg 16:18** 3701
give you the price of it in **m**." **1Ki 21:2** 3701
'Give me your vineyard for **m**; **1Ki 21:6** 3701
he refused to give you for **m**; **1Ki 21:15** 3701
Is it a time to receive **m** and to **2Ki 5:26** 3701
"All the **m** of the sacred things **2Ki 12:4** 3701
house of the LORD, in current **m**, **2Ki 12:4** 3701
both the **m** of each man's assessment **2Ki 12:4** 3701
all the **m** which any man's heart **2Ki 12:4** 3701
no *more* **m** from your acquaintances, **2Ki 12:7** 3701
take no *more* **m** from the people, **2Ki 12:8** 3701
put in it all the **m** which was brought **2Ki 12:9** 3701
there was much **m** in the chest, **2Ki 12:10** 3701
and counted the **m** which was found **2Ki 12:10** 3701
They gave the **m** which was **2Ki 12:11** 3701
or vessels of silver from the **m** **2Ki 12:13** 3701
men into whose hand they gave the **m** **2Ki 12:15** 3701
The **m** from the guilt offerings and **2Ki 12:16** 3701
and the **m** from the sin offerings was **2Ki 12:16** 3701
Menahem exacted the **m** from Israel, **2Ki 15:20** 3701
high priest that he may count the **m** **2Ki 22:4** 3701
the **m** delivered into their hands, **2Ki 22:7** 3701
the **m** that was found in the house, **2Ki 22:9** 3701
the **m** at the command of Pharaoh. **2Ki 23:35** 3701
and collect **m** from all Israel to **2Ch 24:5** 3701
they saw that there was much **m**, **2Ch 24:11** 3701
did daily and collected much **m**. **2Ch 24:11** 3701
m before the king and Jehoiada; **2Ch 24:14** 3701
delivered the **m** that was brought **2Ch 34:9** 3701
When they were bringing out the **m** **2Ch 34:14** 3701
"They have also emptied out the **m** **2Ch 34:17** 3701
m to the masons and carpenters, **Ezr 3:7** 3701
with this **m**, therefore, you shall **Ezr 7:17** 3702
"We have borrowed **m** for the **Ne 5:4** 3701
are lending them **m** and grain. **Ne 5:10** 3701
part of the **m** and of the grain, **Ne 5:11** 3701
and the exact amount of **m** that **Es 4:7** 3701
I have eaten its fruit without **m**, **Jb 31:39** 3701
each one gave him one piece of **m**, **Jb 42:11** 7192
not put out his **m** at interest, **Ps 15:5** 3701
He has taken a bag of **m** with him, **Pr 7:20** 3701
He who loves **m** will not be **Ec 5:10** 3701
will not be satisfied with **m**, **Ec 5:10** 3701
just as **m** is protection, **Ec 7:12** 3701
and **m** is the answer to everything. **Ec 10:19** 3701
outer tunics, cloaks, **m** purses, **Is 3:22** 2754
bought Me not sweet cane with **m**, **Is 43:24** 3701
you will be redeemed without **m**." **Is 52:3** 3701
And you who have no **m** come, **Is 55:1** 3701
milk Without **m** and without cost. **Is 55:1** 3701
you spend **m** for what is not bread, **Is 55:2** 3701
lent, nor have men lent **m** to me, **Jer 15:10**
"Buy for yourself the field with **m** and **Jer 32:25** 3701
'Men will buy fields for **m**, **Jer 32:44** 3701
in every square, in disdaining **m**, **Ezk 16:31** 868
give **m** and no money is given you; **Ezk 16:34** 868
give money and no **m** is given you; **Ezk 16:34** 868
if he does not lend **m** on interest **Ezk 18:8**
he lends **m** on interest and takes **Ezk 18:13**
they sell the righteous for **m** **Am 2:6** 3701
So as to buy the helpless for **m** **Am 8:6** 3701
And her prophets divine for **m**. **Mi 3:11** 3701
or copper for your **m** belts, **Mt 10:9** *5475*
and overturned the tables of the **m** **Mt 21:12** *2855a*
the ground and hid his master's **m**. **Mt 25:18** *694*
to have put my **m** in the bank, **Mt 25:27** *694*
arrival I would have received my **m** **Mt 25:27**
sold for a high price and *the* **m** **Mt 26:9**
with the **m** bought the Potter's Field **Mt 27:7** *846*
a large sum of **m** to the soldiers, **Mt 28:12** *694*
And they took the **m** and did as **Mt 28:15** *694*
bread, no bag, no **m** in their belt **Mk 6:8** *5475*
and overturned the tables of the **m** **Mk 11:15** *2855a*
were putting **m** into the treasury; **Mk 12:41** *5475*
and *the* **m** given to the poor." **Mk 14:5**
this, and promised to give him **m**. **Mk 14:11** *694*
not take **m** from anyone by force, **Lk 3:14** *1286*
nor a bag, nor bread, nor **m**; **Lk 9:3** *694*
"Carry no **m** belt, no bag, no shoes; **Lk 10:4** *905*
make yourselves **m** belts which do not **Lk 12:33** *905*
Pharisees, who were lovers of **m**, **Lk 16:14** *5366*
to whom he had given the **m**, **Lk 19:15** *694*
did you not put my **m** in the bank, **Lk 19:23** *694*
glad and agreed to give him **m**. **Lk 22:5** *694*
"When I sent you out without **m** belt **Lk 22:35** *905*
whoever has a **m** belt is to take it **Lk 22:36** *905*
and the **m** changers seated *at their* **Jn 2:14** *2773*
out the coins of the **m** changers **Jn 2:15** *2855a*
a thief, and as he had the **m** box, **Jn 12:6** *1101*
because Judas had the **m** box, **Jn 13:29** *1101*
sold it and brought the **m** and laid **Ac 4:37** *5536*
had purchased for a sum of **m** **Ac 7:16** *694*
apostles' hands, he offered them **m**, **Ac 8:18** *5536*
obtain the gift of God with **m**! **Ac 8:20** *5536*
citizenship with a large sum of **m**." **Ac 22:28** *2774*
that **m** would be given him by Paul; **Ac 24:26** *5536*
free from the love of **m**. **1Tm 3:3** *866*
For the love of **m** is a root of all **1Tm 6:10** *5365*
be lovers of self, lovers of **m**, **2Tm 3:2** *5366*
is free from the love of **m**, **Heb 13:5** *866*

MONEYLENDER

"A **m** had two debtors: **Lk 7:41** *1157*

MONGREL

And a **m** race will dwell in Ashdod, **Zch 9:6** 4464

MONSTER

"Am I the sea, or the sea **m**, **Jb 7:12** 8577
the night **m** will settle there And **Is 34:14** 3917a
He has swallowed me like a **m**, **Jer 51:34** 8577
The great **m** that lies in the midst **Ezk 29:3** 8577
you are like the **m** in the seas; **Ezk 32:2** 8577
NIGHTS IN THE BELLY OF THE SEA **M**, **Mt 12:40** *2785*

MONSTERS

God created the great sea **m** and **Gn 1:21** 8577
heads of the sea **m** in the waters. **Ps 74:13** 8577
the earth, Sea **m** and all deeps; **Ps 148:7** 8577

MONSTROUS

and will speak **m** things against **Da 11:36** 6381

MONTH

of Noah's life, in the second **m**, **Gn 7:11** 2320
on the seventeenth day of the **m**, **Gn 7:11** 2320
In the seventh **m**, **Gn 8:4** 2320
on the seventeenth day of the **m**, **Gn 8:4**
steadily until the tenth **m**; **Gn 8:5** 2320
in the tenth **m**, on the first day **Gn 8:5**
month, on the first day of the **m**, **Gn 8:5** 2320
in the first **m**, on the first of **Gn 8:13**
month, on the first of the **m**, **Gn 8:13**
In the second **m**, **Gn 8:14** 2320
on the twenty-seventh day of the **m**, **Gn 8:14** 2320
And he stayed with him a **m**. **Gn 29:14** 2320
"This **m** shall be the beginning of **Ex 12:2** 2320
be the first **m** of the year to you. **Ex 12:2** 2320
'On the tenth of this **m** they are **Ex 12:3** 2320
the fourteenth day of the same **m**, **Ex 12:6** 2320
'In the first **m**, on **Ex 12:18**
fourteenth day of the **m** at evening, **Ex 12:18** 2320
twenty-first day of the **m** at evening. **Ex 12:18** 2320
"On this day in the **m** of Abib, **Ex 13:4** 2320
shall observe this rite in this **m**. **Ex 13:5** 2320
the second **m** after their departure **Ex 16:1** 2320
In the third **m** after the sons of **Ex 19:1** 2320
the appointed time in the **m** Abib, **Ex 23:15** 2320
appointed time in the **m** of Abib, **Ex 34:18** 2320
for in the **m** of Abib you **Ex 34:18** 2320
"On the first day of the first **m** **Ex 40:2** 2320
in the first **m** of the second year, **Ex 40:17** 2320
year, on the first *day* of the **m**, **Ex 40:17** 2320
in the seventh **m**, on the tenth day **Lv 16:29** 2320
month, on the tenth day of the **m**, **Lv 16:29** 2320
'In the first **m**, on the fourteenth **Lv 23:5** 2320
on the fourteenth day of the **m** at **Lv 23:5** 2320
on the fifteenth day of the same **m** **Lv 23:6** 2320
seventh **m** on the first of the month you **Lv 23:24** 2320
seventh month on the first of the **m** you **Lv 23:24** 2320
seventh **m** is the day of atonement; **Lv 23:27** 2320
on the ninth of the **m** at evening, **Lv 23:32** 2320
'On the fifteenth of this seventh **m** **Lv 23:34** 2320
fifteenth day of the seventh **m**, **Lv 23:39** 2320
celebrate it in the seventh **m**. **Lv 23:41** 2320
on the tenth day of the seventh **m**; **Lv 25:9** 2320
a **m** even up to five years old, **Lv 27:6** 2320
on the first of the second **m**, **Nu 1:1**
on the first of the second **m**. **Nu 1:18** 2320
every male from a **m** old and upward **Nu 3:15** 2320
male from a **m** old and upward, **Nu 3:22** 2320
male from a **m** old and upward, **Nu 3:28** 2320
male from a **m** old and upward, **Nu 3:34** 2320
male from a **m** old and upward, **Nu 3:39** 2320
of Israel from a **m** old and upward, **Nu 3:40** 2320
of names from a **m** old and upward, **Nu 3:43** 2320
in the first **m** of the second year **Nu 9:1** 2320
"On the fourteenth day of this **m**, **Nu 9:3** 2320
the Passover in the first **m**, on **Nu 9:5**
on the fourteenth day of the **m**, **Nu 9:5** 2320
'In the second **m** on the fourteenth **Nu 9:11** 2320
Whether it was two days or a **m** or **Nu 9:22** 2320
the second year, in the second **m**, **Nu 10:11** 2320
month, on the twentieth of the **m**, **Nu 10:11** 2320
but a whole **m**, until it comes out **Nu 11:20** 2320
that they may eat for a whole **m**.' **Nu 11:21** 2320
a **m** old you shall redeem them, **Nu 18:16** 2320
wilderness of Zin in the first **m**; **Nu 20:1** 2320
male from a **m** old and upward, **Nu 26:62** 2320
this is the burnt offering of each **m** **Nu 28:14** 2320
m shall be the LORD's Passover. **Nu 28:16** 2320
day of this **m** *shall be* a feast, **Nu 28:17** 2320
'Now in the seventh **m**, **Nu 29:1** 2320
month, on the first day of the **m**, **Nu 29:1** 2320
on the tenth day of this seventh **m** **Nu 29:7** 2320
on the fifteenth day of the seventh **m** **Nu 29:12** 2320
from Rameses in the first **m**, **Nu 33:3** 2320
the fifteenth day of the first **m**; **Nu 33:3** 2320
on the first *day* in the fifth **m**. **Nu 33:38** 2320
the first *day* of the eleventh **m**, **Dt 1:3** 2320
"Observe the **m** of Abib and **Dt 16:1** 2320
for in the **m** of Abib the LORD your **Dt 16:1** 2320
her father and mother a full **m**; **Dt 21:13** 3391
the Jordan on the tenth of the first **m** **Jos 4:19** 2320
the fourteenth day of the **m** **Jos 5:10** 2320
to provide for a **m** in the year. **1Ki 4:7** 2320
Solomon's table, each in his **m**; **1Ki 4:27** 2320
to Lebanon, 10,000 a **m** in relays; **1Ki 5:14** 2320
a **m** *and* two months at home. **1Ki 5:14** 2320
in the **m** of Ziv which is the **1Ki 6:1** 2320
month of Ziv which is the second **m**, **1Ki 6:1** 2320
LORD was laid, in the **m** of Ziv. **1Ki 6:37** 3391
eleventh year, in the **m** of Bul, **1Ki 6:38** 3391
of Bul, which is the eighth **m**, **1Ki 6:38** 2320
at the feast, in the **m** Ethanim, **1Ki 8:2** 3391
Ethanim, which is the seventh **m**. **1Ki 8:2** 2320
instituted a feast in the eighth **m** **1Ki 12:32** 2320
on the fifteenth day of the **m**, **1Ki 12:32** 2320
the fifteenth day in the eighth **m**, **1Ki 12:33** 2320
even in the **m** which he had devised **1Ki 12:33** 2320
and he reigned one **m** in Samaria. **2Ki 15:13** 3391
on the tenth day of the tenth **m**, **2Ki 25:1** 2320
On the ninth day of the *fourth* **m** **2Ki 25:3** 2320
on the seventh day of the fifth **m**, **2Ki 25:8** 2320
it came about in the seventh **m**, **2Ki 25:25** 2320
king of Judah, in the twelfth **m**, **2Ki 25:27** 2320
on the twenty-seventh *day* of the **m**, **2Ki 25:27** 2320
who crossed the Jordan in the first **m** **1Ch 12:15** 2320
came in and went out **m** by month **1Ch 27:1** 2320
came in and went out month by **m** **1Ch 27:1** 2320
first division for the first **m**; **1Ch 27:2** 2320
of the army for the first **m**. **1Ch 27:3** 2320
of the division for the second **m**, **1Ch 27:4** 2320
army for the third **m** *was* Benaiah, **1Ch 27:5** 2320
The fourth for the fourth **m** *was* **1Ch 27:7** 2320
The fifth for the fifth **m** *was* the **1Ch 27:8** 2320
The sixth for the sixth **m** *was* Ira **1Ch 27:9** 2320
The seventh for the seventh **m** *was* **1Ch 27:10** 2320
The eighth for the eighth **m** *was* **1Ch 27:11** 2320
The ninth for the ninth **m** *was* **1Ch 27:12** 2320
The tenth for the tenth **m** *was* **1Ch 27:13** 2320
The eleventh for the eleventh **m** **1Ch 27:14** 2320
The twelfth for the twelfth **m** *was* **1Ch 27:15** 2320
in the second **m** of the fourth year **2Ch 3:2** 2320
feast, that is *in* the seventh **m**. **2Ch 5:3** 2320
twenty-third day of the seventh **m** **2Ch 7:10** 2320
third **m** of the fifteenth year of Asa's **2Ch 15:10** 2320
year of his reign, in the first **m**, **2Ch 29:3** 2320
on the first *day* of the first **m**, **2Ch 29:17** 2320
and on the eighth day of the **m** **2Ch 29:17** 2320
the sixteenth day of the first **m**. **2Ch 29:17** 2320
the Passover in the second **m**, **2Ch 30:2** 2320
Unleavened Bread in the second **m**, **2Ch 30:13** 2320
on the fourteenth of the second **m**. **2Ch 30:15** 2320
m they began to make the heaps, **2Ch 31:7** 2320
finished *them* by the seventh **m**. **2Ch 31:7** 2320
the fourteenth *day* of the first **m**. **2Ch 35:1** 2320
Now when the seventh **m** came, **Ezr 3:1** 2320
first day of the seventh **m** they began **Ezr 3:6** 2320
God at Jerusalem in the second **m**, **Ezr 3:8** 2320
on the third day of the **m** Adar; **Ezr 6:15** 3393
on the fourteenth of the first **m**. **Ezr 6:19** 2320
came to Jerusalem in the fifth **m**. **Ezr 7:8** 2320
For on the first of the first **m** he **Ezr 7:9** 2320
the fifth **m** he came to Jerusalem, **Ezr 7:9** 2320
on the twelfth of the first **m** to go to **Ezr 8:31** 2320
It was the ninth **m** on the twentieth **Ezr 10:9** 2320
month on the twentieth of the **m**, **Ezr 10:9** 2320
tenth **m** to investigate the matter. **Ezr 10:16** 2320
wives by the first day of the first **m**. **Ezr 10:17** 2320
Now it happened in the **m** Chislev, **Ne 1:1** 2320
And it came about in the **m** Nisan, **Ne 2:1** 2320
on the twenty-fifth of *the* **m** Elul, **Ne 6:15**
And when the seventh **m** came, **Ne 7:73** 2320
on the first day of the seventh **m**. **Ne 8:2** 2320
during the feast of the seventh **m**. **Ne 8:14** 2320
this **m** the sons of Israel assembled **Ne 9:1** 2320
tenth **m** which is the month Tebeth, **Es 2:16** 2320
tenth month which is the **m** Tebeth, **Es 2:16** 2320
In the first **m**, which is the month **Es 3:7** 2320
first month, which is the **m** Nisan, **Es 3:7** 2320
day to day and from **m** *to month*, **Es 3:7** 2320
from day to day and from month *to* **m**, **Es 3:7**
to month, until the twelfth **m**, **Es 3:7** 2320
twelfth month, that is the **m** Adar. **Es 3:7** 2320
the thirteenth day of the first **m**, **Es 3:12** 2320
thirteenth *day* of the twelfth **m**, **Es 3:13** 2320
month, which is the **m** Adar, **Es 3:13** 2320
at that time in the third **m** **Es 8:9** 2320
third month (that is, the **m** Sivan), **Es 8:9** 2320
thirteenth *day* of the twelfth **m** **Es 8:12** 2320
month (that is, the **m** Adar). **Es 8:12** 2320
Now in the twelfth **m** **Es 9:1** 2320
month (that is, the **m** Adar), **Es 9:1** 2320
on the fourteenth day of the **m** Adar **Es 9:15** 2320
the thirteenth day of the **m** Adar, **Es 9:17** 2320
and the fourteenth of the same **m**, **Es 9:18**
make the fourteenth day of the **m** **Es 9:19** 2320
the fourteenth day of the **m** Adar, **Es 9:21** 2320
the fifteenth day of the same **m**, **Es 9:21**
and *it was a* **m** which was turned **Es 9:22** 2320
exile of Jerusalem in the fifth **m**. **Jer 1:3** 2320
In her **m** they will find her. **Jer 2:24** 2320
the fourth year, in the fifth **m**, **Jer 28:1** 2320
in the same year in the seventh **m**. **Jer 28:17** 2320

king of Judah, in the ninth **m**, **Jer 36:9** 2320
the winter house in the ninth **m**, **Jer 36:22** 2320
king of Judah, in the tenth **m**, **Jer 39:1** 2320
year of Zedekiah, in the fourth **m**, **Jer 39:2** 2320
month, in the ninth *day* of the **m**, **Jer 39:2** 2320
In the seventh **m** Ishmael the son **Jer 41:1** 2320
on the tenth *day* of the tenth **m**, **Jer 52:4** 2320
On the ninth *day* of the fourth **m** **Jer 52:6** 2320
on the tenth *day* of the fifth **m**, **Jer 52:12** 2320
king of Judah, in the twelfth **m**, **Jer 52:31** 2320
on the twenty-fifth of the **m**, **Jer 52:31** 2320
on the fifth *day* of the fourth **m**, **Ezk 1:1** 2320
(On the fifth of the **m** in the **Ezk 1:2** 2320
on the fifth *day* of the sixth **m**, **Ezk 8:1** 2320
in the fifth **m**, on the tenth of **Ezk 20:1**
month, on the tenth of the **m**, **Ezk 20:1** 2320
in the ninth year, in the tenth **m**, **Ezk 24:1** 2320
month, on the tenth of the **m**, **Ezk 24:1** 2320
year, on the first of the **m**, **Ezk 26:1** 2320
In the tenth year, in the tenth **m**, **Ezk 29:1**
month, on the twelfth of the **m**, **Ezk 29:1** 2320
in the first **m**, on the first of **Ezk 29:17**
month, on the first of the **m**, **Ezk 29:17** 2320
in the first **m**, on the seventh **Ezk 30:20**
month, on the seventh of the **m**, **Ezk 30:20** 2320
in the third **m**, on the first of **Ezk 31:1**
month, on the first of the **m**, **Ezk 31:1** 2320
in the twelfth **m**, on the first **Ezk 32:1**
month, on the first of the **m**, **Ezk 32:1** 2320
year, on the fifteenth of the **m**, **Ezk 32:17** 2320
on the fifth of the tenth **m**, **Ezk 33:21** 2320
the year, on the tenth of the **m**, **Ezk 40:1** 2320
"In the first **m**, on the first **Ezk 45:18**
month, on the first of the **m**, **Ezk 45:18** 2320
shall do on the seventh *day* of the **m** **Ezk 45:20** 2320
"In the first **m**, on **Ezk 45:21**
on the fourteenth day of the **m**, **Ezk 45:21** 2320
"In the seventh **m**, on **Ezk 45:25**
on the fifteenth day of the **m**, **Ezk 45:25** 2320
They will bear every **m** because **Ezk 47:12** 2320
twenty-fourth day of the first **m**, **Da 10:4** 2320
on the first day of the sixth **m**, **Hg 1:1** 2320
sixth **m** in the second year of Darius **Hg 1:15** 2320
the twenty-first of the seventh **m**, **Hg 2:1** 2320
On the twenty-fourth of the ninth **m**, **Hg 2:10** 2320
twenty-fourth day of the ninth **m**; **Hg 2:18** 2320
twenty-fourth *day* of the **m**, **Hg 2:20** 2320
In the eighth **m** of the second year **Zch 1:1** 2320
twenty-fourth day of the eleventh **m**, **Zch 1:7** 2320
month, which is the **m** Shebat, **Zch 1:7** 2320
on the fourth *day* of the ninth **m**, **Zch 7:1** 2320
I weep in the fifth **m** and abstain, **Zch 7:3** 2320
the three shepherds in one **m**, **Zch 11:8** 3391
Now in the sixth **m** the angel **Lk 1:26** *3376*
barren is now in her sixth **m**. **Lk 1:36** *3376*
the hour and day and **m** and year, **Rv 9:15** *3376*
fruit, yielding its fruit every **m**; **Rv 22:2** *3376*

MONTHS

about three **m** later that Judah was **Gn 38:24** 2320
she hid him for three **m**. **Ex 2:2** 3391
be the beginning of **m** for you; **Ex 12:2** 2320
and on the first *days* of your **m**, **Nu 10:10** 2320
at the beginning of each of your **m** **Nu 28:11** 2320
throughout the **m** of the year. **Nu 28:14** 2320
with the choice produce of the **m**. **Dt 33:14** 3391
let me alone two **m**, **Jg 11:37** 2320
So he sent her away for two **m**; **Jg 11:38** 2320
At the end of two **m** she returned **Jg 11:39** 2320
was there for a period of four **m**. **Jg 19:2** 2320
at the rock of Rimmon four **m**. **Jg 20:47** 2320
country of the Philistines seven **m**. **1Sa 6:1** 2320
Philistines was a year and four **m**. **1Sa 27:7** 2320
Judah was seven years and six **m**. **2Sa 2:11** 2320
over Judah seven years and six **m**, **2Sa 5:5** 2320
of Obed-edom the Gittite three **m**, **2Sa 6:11** 2320
the end of nine **m** and twenty days. **2Sa 24:8** 2320
Or will you flee three **m** before **2Sa 24:13** 2320
Lebanon a month *and* two **m** at home. **1Ki 5:14** 2320
and all Israel stayed there six **m**, **1Ki 11:16** 2320
over Israel in Samaria *for* six **m**. **2Ki 15:8** 2320
he reigned three **m** in Jerusalem; **2Ki 23:31** 2320
he reigned three **m** in Jerusalem; **2Ki 24:8** 2320
he reigned seven years and six **m**. **1Ch 3:4** 2320
of Obed-edom in his house three **m**; **1Ch 13:14** 2320
or three **m** to be swept away before **1Ch 21:12** 2320
throughout all the **m** of the year, **1Ch 27:1** 2320
he reigned three **m** in Jerusalem. **2Ch 36:2** 2320
three **m** and ten days in Jerusalem, **2Ch 36:9** 2320
after the end of her twelve **m** **Es 2:12** 2320
six **m** with oil of myrrh and six **Es 2:12** 2320
six **m** with spices and the cosmetics **Es 2:12** 2320
not come into the number of the **m**. **Jb 3:6** 3391
So am I allotted **m** of vanity, **Jb 7:3** 3391
The number of his **m** is with You; **Jb 14:5** 2320
the number of his **m** is cut off? **Jb 21:21** 2320
"Oh that I were as in **m** gone by, **Jb 29:2** 3391
"Can you count the **m** they fulfill, **Jb 39:2** 3391
"For seven **m** the house of Israel **Ezk 39:12** 2320
seven **m** they will make a search. **Ezk 39:14** 2320
"Twelve **m** later he was walking on **Da 4:29** 3393
were still three **m** until harvest. **Am 4:7** 2320
mourned in the fifth and seventh **m** **Zch 7:5**
seventh and the fast of the tenth **m** **Zch 8:19**
kept herself in seclusion for five **m**, **Lk 1:24** *3376*
Mary stayed with her about three **m** **Lk 1:56** *3376*
shut up for three years and six **m**, **Lk 4:25** *3376*
'There are yet four **m**, **Jn 4:35** *5072*
three **m** in his father's home. **Ac 7:20** *3376*
he settled *there* a year and six **m**, **Ac 18:11** *3376*
speaking out boldly for three **m**, **Ac 19:8** *3376*
And *there* he spent three **m**, **Ac 20:3** *3376*
At the end of three **m** we set **Ac 28:11** *3376*
days and **m** and seasons and years. **Ga 4:10** *3376*
hidden for three **m** by his parents, **Heb 11:23** *5150*
earth for three years and six **m**. **Jas 5:17** *3376*
anyone, but to torment for five **m**; **Rv 9:5** *3376*
power to hurt men for five **m**. **Rv 9:10** *3376*
foot the holy city for forty-two **m**. **Rv 11:2** *3376*
authority to act for forty-two **m** was **Rv 13:5** *3376*

MONUMENT

behold, he set up a **m** for himself, **1Sa 15:12** 3027
and it is called Absalom's **M** to this **2Sa 18:18** 3027
"What is this **m** that I see?" **2Ki 23:17** 6725

MONUMENTS

and adorn the **m** of the righteous, **Mt 23:29** *3419*

MOON

the sun and the **m** and eleven stars **Gn 37:9** 3394
the burnt offering of the new **m** and **Nu 29:6** 2320
the sun and the **m** and the stars, **Dt 4:19** 3394
the **m** or any of the heavenly host, **Dt 17:3** 3394
O **m** in the valley of Aijalon." **Jos 10:12** 3394
stood still, and the **m** stopped, **Jos 10:13** 3394
"Behold, tomorrow is the new **m**, **1Sa 20:5** 2320
"Tomorrow is the new **m**, **1Sa 20:18** 2320
and when the new **m** came, **1Sa 20:24** 2320
day, the second *day* of the new **m**, **1Sa 20:27** 2320
on the second day of the new **m**, **1Sa 20:34** 2320
It is neither new **m** nor sabbath." **2Ki 4:23** 2320
to the sun and to the **m** and to the **2Ki 23:5** 3394
offering, the sabbaths, the new **m**, **Ne 10:33** 2320
"If even the **m** has no brightness **Jb 25:5** 3394
obscures the face of the full **m** And **Jb 26:9** 3677
shone Or the **m** going in splendor, **Jb 31:26** 3394
Your fingers, The **m** and the stars, **Ps 8:3** 3394
sun *endures*, And as long as the **m**, **Ps 72:5** 3394
of peace till the **m** is no more. **Ps 72:7** 3394
Blow the trumpet at the new **m**, **Ps 81:3** 2320
at the new moon, At the full **m**, **Ps 81:3** 3677
be established forever like the **m**, **Ps 89:37** 3394
He made the **m** for the seasons; **Ps 104:19** 3394
you by day, Nor the **m** by night. **Ps 121:6** 3394
The **m** and stars to rule by night, **Ps 136:9** 3394
Praise Him, sun and **m**; **Ps 148:3** 3394
At the full **m** he will come home." **Pr 7:20** 3677
before the sun and the light, the **m** **Ec 12:2** 3394
dawn, As beautiful as the full **m**, **SS 6:10** 3842
New **m** and sabbath, the calling of **Is 1:13** 2320
"I hate your new **m** *festivals* and **Is 1:14** 2320
And the **m** will not shed its light. **Is 13:10** 3394
Then the **m** will be abashed and the **Is 24:23** 3842
The light of the **m** will be as **Is 30:26** 3842
will the **m** give you light; **Is 60:19** 3394
no longer set, Nor will your **m** wane; **Is 60:20** 3394
shall be from new **m** to new moon **Is 66:23** 2320
new **m** And from sabbath to sabbath, **Is 66:23** 2320
spread them out to the sun, the **m** and **Jer 8:2** 3394
And the fixed order of the **m** and **Jer 31:35** 3394
the **m** will not give its light. **Ezk 32:7** 3394
opened on the day of the new **m**. **Ezk 46:1** 2320
"On the day of the new **m** *he* **Ezk 46:6** 2320
Now the new **m** will devour them **Hos 5:7** 2320
The sun and the **m** grow dark And **Jl 2:10** 3394
darkness And the **m** into blood **Jl 2:31** 3394
The sun and **m** grow dark And the **Jl 3:15** 3394
"When will the new **m** be over, **Am 8:5** 2320
Sun *and* **m** stood in their places; **Hab 3:11** 3394
AND THE **M** WILL NOT GIVE ITS LIGHT, **Mt 24:29** *4582*
AND THE **M** WILL NOT GIVE ITS LIGHT, **Mk 13:24** *4582*
be signs in sun and **m** and stars, **Lk 21:25** *4582*
DARKNESS AND THE **M** INTO BLOOD, **Ac 2:20** *4582*
sun, and another glory of the **m**, **1Co 15:41** *4582*
or a new **m** or a Sabbath day **Col 2:16** *3501a*
and the whole **m** became like blood; **Rv 6:12** *4582*
third of the sun and a third of the **m** **Rv 8:12** *4582*
the sun, and the **m** under her feet, **Rv 12:1** *4582*
has no need of the sun or of the **m** **Rv 21:23** *4582*

MOONS

the new **m** and the fixed festivals **1Ch 23:31** 2320
on sabbaths and on new **m** and on **2Ch 2:4** 2320
for the sabbaths, the new **m** and **2Ch 8:13** 2320
new **m** and for the fixed festivals, **2Ch 31:3** 2320
also for the new **m** and for all the **Ezr 3:5** 2320
Those who predict by the new **m**, **Is 47:13** 2320
at the feasts, on the new **m** and **Ezk 45:17** 2320
on the sabbaths and on the new **m**. **Ezk 46:3** 2320
her gaiety, Her feasts, her new **m**, **Hos 2:11** 2320

MOORED

at Gennesaret, and **m** to the shore. **Mk 6:53** *4358*

MORAL

could lift up your face without **m** **Jb 11:15**
in your faith supply **m** excellence, **2Pe 1:5** *703*
and in *your* **m** excellence, **2Pe 1:5** *703*

MORALS

"Bad company corrupts good **m**." **1Co 15:33** *2239*

MORBID

but he has a **m** interest in **1Tm 6:4** *3552*

MORDECAI

Nehemiah, Seraiah, Reelaiah, **M**, **Ezr 2:2** 4782
Azariah, Raamiah, Nahamani, **M**, **Ne 7:7** 4782
in Susa a Jew whose name was **M**, **Es 2:5** 4782
M took her as his own daughter. **Es 2:7** 4782
for **M** had instructed her that she **Es 2:10** 4782
Every day **M** walked back and **Es 2:11** 4782
daughter of Abihail the uncle of **M** **Es 2:15** 4782
then **M** was sitting at the king's **Es 2:19** 4782
even as **M** had commanded her; **Es 2:20** 4782
for Esther did what **M** told her as **Es 2:20** 4782
while **M** was sitting at the king's **Es 2:21** 4782
But the plot became known to **M** and **Es 2:22** 4782
But **M** neither bowed down nor paid **Es 3:2** 4782
were at the king's gate said to **M**, **Es 3:3** 4782
When Haman saw that **M** neither **Es 3:5** 4782
disdained to lay hands on **M** alone, **Es 3:6** 4782
told him *who* the people of **M** *were;* **Es 3:6** 4782
all the Jews, the people of **M**, **Es 3:6** 4782
When **M** learned all that had been **Es 4:1** 4782
And she sent garments to clothe **M** **Es 4:4** 4782
and ordered him *to go* to **M** to **Es 4:5** 4782
So Hathach went out to **M** to the **Es 4:6** 4782
M told him all that had **Es 4:7** 4782
and ordered him *to reply* to **M**: **Es 4:10** 4782
They related Esther's words to **M**. **Es 4:12** 4782
M told *them* to reply to Esther, **Es 4:13** 4782
Esther told *them* to reply to **M**, **Es 4:15** 4782
So **M** went away and did just as **Es 4:17** 4782
Haman saw **M** in the king's gate and **Es 5:9** 4782
was filled with anger against **M**. **Es 5:9** 4782
every time I see **M** the Jew sitting at **Es 5:13** 4782
the king to have **M** hanged on it; **Es 5:14** 4782
found written what **M** had reported **Es 6:2** 4782
or dignity has been bestowed on **M** **Es 6:3** 4782
speak to the king about hanging **M** **Es 6:4** 4782
said, and do so for **M** the Jew, **Es 6:10** 4782
robe and the horse, and arrayed **M**, **Es 6:11** 4782
Then **M** returned to the king's gate. **Es 6:12** 4782
"If **M**, before whom you have begun **Es 6:13** 4782
which Haman made for **M** who spoke **Es 7:9** 4782
which he had prepared for **M**, **Es 7:10** 4782
and **M** came before the king, for **Es 8:1** 4782
away from Haman, and gave it to **M**. **Es 8:2** 4782
set **M** over the house of Haman. **Es 8:2** 4782
to Queen Esther and to **M** the Jew, **Es 8:7** 4782
all that **M** commanded to the Jews, **Es 8:9** 4782
Then **M** went out from the presence **Es 8:15** 4782
the dread of **M** had fallen on them. **Es 9:3** 4782
M was great in the king's house, **Es 9:4** 4782
man **M** became greater and greater. **Es 9:4** 4782
Then **M** recorded these events, and **Es 9:20** 4782
and what **M** had written to them. **Es 9:23** 4782
of Abihail, with **M** the Jew, **Es 9:29** 4782
just as **M** the Jew and Queen Esther **Es 9:31** 4782
account of the greatness of **M** to **Es 10:2** 4782
For **M** the Jew was second *only* to **Es 10:3** 4782

MORDECAI'S

informed the king in **M** name. **Es 2:22** 4782
see whether **M** reason would stand; **Es 3:4** 4782
and related **M** words to Esther. **Es 4:9** 4782

MORE

Now the serpent was **m** crafty than **Gn 3:1** 4480
Cursed are you **m** than all cattle, **Gn 3:14** 4480
m than every beast of the field; **Gn 3:14** 4480
"For after seven **m** days, I will **Gn 7:4** 5750
The water prevailed **m** and more **Gn 7:19** 3966
The water prevailed more and **m** **Gn 7:19** 3966
he loved Rachel **m** than Leah, **Gn 29:30** 4480
Now he was **m** respected than all **Gn 34:19** 4480
loved Joseph **m** than all his sons, **Gn 37:3** 4480
loved him **m** than all his brothers; **Gn 37:4** 4480
brothers, they hated him even **m**. **Gn 37:5**
3254, 5750
So they hated him even **m** for his **Gn 37:8**
3254, 5750
"She is **m** righteous than I, **Gn 38:26** 4480
within three **m** days Pharaoh will **Gn 40:13** 5750
within three **m** days Pharaoh will **Gn 40:19** 5750
Joseph is no **m**, and Simeon is no **Gn 42:36** 369
is no more, and Simeon is no **m**, **Gn 42:36** 369
one portion **m** than your brothers, **Gn 48:22** 5921
Israel are **m** and mightier than we. **Ex 1:9** 7227a
But the **m** they afflicted them, the **Ex 1:12** 3512c
the **m** they multiplied and the more **Ex 1:12** 3651
and the **m** they spread out, **Ex 1:12** 3651
and what is **m**, he even drew the **Ex 2:19** 1571
"One **m** plague I will bring on **Ex 11:1** 5750
little **m** and they will stone me." **Ex 17:4** 5750
"The rich shall not pay **m** and **Ex 30:15** 7235a
"The people are bringing much **m** **Ex 36:5** 7235a
were restrained from bringing *any* **m**. **Ex 36:6**
m than enough for all the work, **Ex 36:7** 3498
in full and add to it one-fifth **m**. **Lv 6:5** 3254
isolate him for seven **m** days. **Lv 13:5** 8145
with the scale seven **m** days. **Lv 13:33** 8145
quarantine it for seven **m** days. **Lv 13:54** 8145
I will punish you seven times **m** for **Lv 26:18** 3254
in the work and not work any **m**. **Nu 8:25** 5750
m than any man who was on the face **Nu 12:3** 4480
m numerous and more distinguished **Nu 22:15** 4480
m distinguished than the former. **Nu 22:15** 4480
to add still **m** to the burning anger **Nu 32:14** 5750
He will once **m** abandon them in the **Nu 32:15**
3254, 5750
you shall give **m** inheritance, **Nu 33:54** 7235a
you shall take **m** from the larger **Nu 35:8** 7235a
you a thousand-fold **m** than you are and **Dt 1:11** 3254
Speak to Me no **m** of this matter. **Dt 3:26**
3254, 5750
a great voice, and He added no **m**. **Dt 5:22** 3254
because you were **m** in number **Dt 7:7** 7231
add three **m** cities for yourself, **Dt 19:9** 5750
and people **m** numerous than you, **Dt 20:1** 7227a
may beat him forty times *but* no **m**, **Dt 25:3** 3254
with many **m** stripes than these and **Dt 25:3** 3254
multiply you **m** than your fathers. **Dt 30:5** 4480

how much **m**, then, after my death?	Dt 31:27	637, 3588
"**M** blessed than sons is Asher;	Dt 33:24	4480
there were **m** who died from the	Jos 10:11	7227a
m corruptly than their fathers,	Jg 2:19	4480
me that I may speak once **m**;	Jg 6:39	6471
a test once **m** with the fleece,	Jg 6:39	6471
Is not her younger sister **m** beautiful	Jg 15:2	4480, 2896a
"Come up once **m**, for he has told	Jg 16:18	6471
were **m** than those whom he killed in	Jg 16:30	7227a
go with her, she said no **m** to her.	Ru 1:18	
"Boast no **m** so very proudly, Do	1Sa 2:3	7235a
May God do so to you, and **m** also,	1Sa 3:17	3254
there was not a **m** handsome person	1Sa 9:2	4480, 2896a
"How much **m**, if only the people	1Sa 14:30	637, 3588
"May God do this *to me* and **m** also,	1Sa 14:44	3254
m can he have but the kingdom?"	1Sa 18:8	5750
Saul was even **m** afraid of David.	1Sa 18:29	3254, 5750
that David behaved himself **m**	1Sa 18:30	4480
LORD do so to Jonathan and **m** also,	1Sa 20:13	3254
wept together, but David *wept* the **m**.	1Sa 20:41	1431
how much **m** then today will their	1Sa 21:5	637, 3588
How much **m** then if we go to Keilah	1Sa 23:3	637, 3588
David inquired of the LORD once **m**.	1Sa 23:4	3254, 5750
"Go now, make **m** sure, and	1Sa 23:22	5750
"You are **m** righteous than I;	1Sa 24:17	4480
the enemies of David, and **m** also,	1Sa 25:22	3254
Your love to me was **m** wonderful	2Sa 1:26	4480
God do so to Abner, and **m** also,	2Sa 3:9	3254
"May God do so to me, and **m** also,	2Sa 3:35	3254
"How much **m**, when wicked men have	2Sa 4:11	637, 3588
Meanwhile David took **m** concubines	2Sa 5:13	5750
and **m** sons and daughters were born	2Sa 5:13	5750
"I will be **m** lightly esteemed	2Sa 6:22	5750
afflict them any **m** as formerly,	2Sa 7:10	3254
what **m** can David say to You?	2Sa 7:20	5750
have added to you many **m** things	2Sa 12:8	
how much **m** now this Benjamite?	2Sa 16:11	637, 3588
and the forest devoured **m** people	2Sa 18:8	7235a
son of Zadok said once **m** to Joab,	2Sa 18:22	3254, 5750
May God do so to me, and **m** also,	2Sa 19:13	3254
have **m** *claim* on David than you.	2Sa 19:43	4480
will do us **m** harm than Absalom;	2Sa 20:6	4480
"May God do so to me and **m** also,	1Ki 2:23	3254
he fell upon two men **m** righteous	1Ki 2:32	4480
for seven days and seven **m** days,	1Ki 8:65	
there was no **m** spirit in her.	1Ki 10:5	5750
you also have done **m** evil than all	1Ki 14:9	4480
provoked Him to jealousy **m** than all	1Ki 14:22	4480
and acted **m** wickedly than all who	1Ki 16:25	4480
m than all who were before him.	1Ki 16:30	4480
Thus Ahab did **m** to provoke the	1Ki 16:33	3254
may the gods do to me and even **m**,	1Ki 19:2	3254
the gods do so to me and **m** also,	1Ki 20:10	3254
And he saw Elijah no **m**.	2Ki 2:12	5750
"There is not one vessel **m**."	2Ki 4:6	5750
How much **m** *then,* when he says to	2Ki 5:13	637, 3588
there, **m** than once or twice.	2Ki 6:10	
m than those who are with them."	2Ki 6:16	7227a
"May God do so to me and **m** also,	2Ki 6:31	3254
but they found nothing **m** of her than	2Ki 9:35	3588, 518
Now therefore take no **m** money	2Ki 12:7	
agreed that they would take no **m**	2Ki 12:8	
of the army not **m** than fifty horsemen	2Ki 13:7	3588, 518
to do evil **m** than the nations whom	2Ki 21:9	4480
having done wickedly **m** than all	2Ki 21:11	4480
was **m** honorable than his brothers,	1Ch 4:9	4480
David took **m** wives at Jerusalem,	1Ch 14:3	5750
father of **m** sons and daughters.	1Ch 14:3	5750
"What **m** can David still *say* to	1Ch 17:18	3254
m bronze than could be weighed;	1Ch 22:3	7230
Since **m** chief men were found from	1Ch 24:4	7227a
daughter of Absalom **m** than all his	2Ch 11:21	4480
And there was no **m** war until the	2Ch 15:19	
m than they could carry.	2Ch 20:25	
"The LORD has much **m** to give you	2Ch 25:9	7235a
King Ahaz became yet **m** unfaithful	2Ch 28:22	3254
the Levites were **m** conscientious to	2Ch 29:34	4480
Jerusalem to do **m** evil than the	2Ch 33:9	4480
man and feared God **m** than many.	Ne 7:2	4480
another who is **m** worthy than she.	Es 1:19	4480
loved Esther **m** than all the women,	Es 2:17	4480
with him **m** than all the virgins,	Es 2:17	4480
escape any **m** than all the Jews.	Es 4:13	4480
king desire to honor **m** than me?"	Es 6:6	3148
it **m** than for hidden treasures,	Jb 3:21	4480
'How much **m** those who dwell in	Jb 4:19	637
mouth **m** than my necessary food.	Jb 23:12	4480
'My righteousness is **m** than God's'?	Jb 35:2	4480
I have, **m** than if I had sinned?'	Jb 35:3	4480
us **m** than the beasts of the earth And	Jb 35:11	4480
yet **m** to be said in God's behalf.	Jb 36:2	5750
Even twice, and I will add nothing **m**."	Jb 40:5	
days of Job **m** than his beginning;	Jb 42:12	4480
M than when their grain and new	Ps 4:7	4480
They are **m** desirable than gold,	Ps 19:10	4480
and the wicked man will be no **m**;	Ps 37:10	369
passed away, and lo, he was no **m**;	Ps 37:36	369
Before I depart and am no **m**."	Ps 39:13	369
They are **m** numerous than the hairs	Ps 40:12	4480
You love evil **m** than good,	Ps 52:3	4480
Falsehood **m** than speaking what is	Ps 52:3	4480
them that they may be no **m**;	Ps 59:13	369
are **m** than the hairs of my head;	Ps 69:4	7231
will praise You yet **m** and more.	Ps 71:14	3254
will praise You yet more and **m**.	Ps 71:14	3254
of peace till the moon is no **m**.	Ps 72:7	1097
M majestic than the mountains of	Ps 76:4	4480
name of Israel be remembered no **m**	Ps 83:4	5750
LORD loves the gates of Zion **M** than	Ps 87:2	4480
Whom You remember no **m**,	Ps 88:5	5750
M than the sounds of many waters,	Ps 93:4	4480
has passed over it, it is no **m**,	Ps 103:16	369
earth And let the wicked be no **m**.	Ps 104:35	5750
m insight than all my teachers,	Ps 119:99	4480
I understand **m** than the aged,	Ps 119:100	4480
and what **m** shall be done to you,	Ps 120:3	3254
My soul *waits* for the Lord **M** than	Ps 130:6	4480
m *than* the watchmen for the morning.	Ps 130:6	
She is **m** precious than jewels;	Pr 3:15	4480
passes, the wicked is no **m**,	Pr 10:25	369
and *yet* increases all the **m**,	Pr 11:24	5750
much **m** the wicked and the sinner!	Pr 11:31	637
are overthrown and are no **m**,	Pr 12:7	
How much **m** the hearts of men!	Pr 15:11	637
How much **m** do his friends abandon	Pr 19:7	637
knowledge are a **m** precious thing.	Pr 20:15	637
justice Is desired by the LORD **m**	Pr 21:3	4480
How much **m** when he brings it with	Pr 21:27	637, 3588
to be **m** desired than great wealth,	Pr 22:1	4480
He who oppresses the poor to make **m**	Pr 22:16	7235a
is **m** hope for a fool than for him.	Pr 26:12	4480
rebukes a man will afterward find **m**	Pr 28:23	
is **m** hope for a fool than for him.	Pr 29:20	4480
Surely I am **m** stupid than any man,	Pr 30:2	4480
And remember his trouble no **m**.	Pr 31:7	5750
increased wisdom **m** than all who	Ec 1:16	5921
I became great and increased **m** than	Ec 2:9	4480
m than the living who are still living.	Ec 4:2	4480
Wisdom strengthens a wise man **m**	Ec 7:19	4480
And I discovered **m** bitter than	Ec 7:26	4480
then he must exert **m** strength.	Ec 10:10	
will extol your love **m** than wine.	SS 1:4	4480
"What **m** was there to do for My	Is 5:4	5750
field, Until there is no **m** room,	Is 5:8	657
But there will be no **m** gloom for	Is 9:1	
Before morning they are no **m**.	Is 17:14	369
dry, be driven away, and be no **m**.	Is 19:7	369
Tarshish, There is no **m** restraint.	Is 23:10	5750
"You shall exult no **m**,	Is 23:12	3254, 5750
palace of strangers is a city no **m**,	Is 25:2	4480
Let us hear no **m** about the Holy	Is 30:11	7673a
I will look on man no **m** among the	Is 38:11	5750
was marred **m** than any man And	Is 52:14	4480
His form **m** than the sons of men.	Is 52:14	4480
will be **m** numerous Than the sons	Is 54:1	4480
widowhood you will remember no **m**.	Is 54:4	5750
will be like today, only **m** so."	Is 56:12	1419, 3499a, 3966
Israel has proved herself **m** righteous	Jer 3:11	4480
did **m** evil than their fathers.	Jer 7:26	4480
have gone from me and are no **m**;	Jer 10:20	369
his name be remembered no **m**."	Jer 11:19	5750
"Their widows will be **m** numerous	Jer 15:8	4480
even **m** than your forefathers;	Jer 16:12	4480
"The heart is **m** deceitful than	Jer 17:9	4480
and rise no **m** because of the sword	Jer 25:27	
children, Because they are no **m**."	Jer 31:15	369
their sin I will remember no **m**."	Jer 31:34	5750
there is no **m** bread in the city."	Jer 38:9	5750
you will see this place no **m**."	Jer 42:18	5750
"Surely it will no **m** be found,	Jer 46:23	
are *now* **m** numerous than locusts	Jer 46:23	4480
"**M** than the weeping for Jazer I	Jer 48:32	4480
And his neighbors, and he is no **m**.	Jer 49:10	369
The law is no **m**. Also, her prophets	La 2:9	369
were **m** ruddy *in* body than corals,	La 4:7	4480
Our fathers sinned, *and* are no **m**;	La 5:7	369
against My ordinances **m** wickedly	Ezk 5:6	4480
against My statutes **m** than the lands	Ezk 5:6	4480
'Because you have **m** turmoil than	Ezk 5:7	4480
make the land **m** desolate and waste	Ezk 6:14	4480
"How much **m** when I send My four	Ezk 14:21	637, 3588
will be pacified and angry no **m**.	Ezk 16:42	5750
you acted **m** corruptly in all your	Ezk 16:47	4480
multiplied your abominations **m**	Ezk 16:51	4480
you acted **m** abominably than they,	Ezk 16:52	4480
they are **m** in the right than you.	Ezk 16:52	4480
his voice would be heard no **m**	Ezk 19:9	5750
rod which despises will be no **m**?"	Ezk 21:13	
This also will be no **m** until	Ezk 21:27	
m corrupt in her lust than she,	Ezk 23:11	4480
and her harlotries were **m** than the	Ezk 23:11	4480
of your harps will be heard no **m**.	Ezk 26:13	5750
You will be built no **m**,	Ezk 26:14	5750
on you and you will be no **m**;	Ezk 26:21	369
"And there will be no **m** for the	Ezk 28:24	5750
because the galleries took **m** *space*	Ezk 42:5	4480
m than the lower and middle ones.	Ezk 42:6	4480
see your faces looking **m** haggard	Da 1:10	4480
me **m** than *in any other* living man,	Da 2:30	4481
to heat the furnace seven times **m**	Da 3:19	5922
three **m** kings are going to arise	Da 11:2	5750
a fourth will gain far **m** riches than	Da 11:2	1419
and fall and be found no **m**.	Da 11:19	
be mentioned by their names no **m**.	Hos 2:17	5750
The **m** they multiplied, the more	Hos 4:7	
the **m** they sinned against Me;	Hos 4:7	3651
I will love them no **m**;	Hos 9:15	3254
The **m** his fruit, The more altars	Hos 10:1	7230
his fruit, The **m** altars he made;	Hos 10:1	7235a
The **m** they called them, The more	Hos 11:2	
them, The **m** they went from them;	Hos 11:2	3651
And now they sin **m** and more,	Hos 13:2	3254
And now they sin more and **m**,	Hos 13:2	3254
what **m** have I to do with idols?	Hos 14:8	5750
strangers will pass through it no **m**.	Jl 3:17	5750
city in which there are **m** than 120,000	Jon 4:11	7235a
you will have fortune-tellers no **m**.	Mi 5:12	
You have increased your traders **m**	Na 3:16	4480
up Those **m** righteous than they?	Hab 1:13	4480
You will fear disaster no **m**.	Zph 3:15	5750
'Once **m** in a little while, I am	Hg 2:6	5750
BECAUSE THEY WERE NO **M**."	Mt 2:18	
what **m** are you doing *than others?*	Mt 5:47	*4053*
Is not life **m** than food, and the	Mt 6:25	*4183*
and the body **m** than clothing?	Mt 6:25	*4183*
you not worth much **m** than they?	Mt 6:26	*1308*
will He not much **m** *clothe* you?	Mt 6:30	*3123*
how much **m** will your Father who	Mt 7:11	*3123*
it will be **m** tolerable for *the*	Mt 10:15	*414*
how much **m** *will they malign*	Mt 10:25	*3123*
are **m** valuable than many sparrows.	Mt 10:31	*1308*
m than Me is not worthy of Me;	Mt 10:37	*5228*
m than Me is not worthy of Me.	Mt 10:37	*5228*
and one who is **m** than a prophet.	Mt 11:9	*4053*
it will be **m** tolerable for Tyre	Mt 11:22	*414*
be **m** tolerable for the land of Sodom	Mt 11:24	*414*
"How much **m** valuable then is a	Mt 12:12	*1308*
spirits **m** wicked than itself,	Mt 12:45	*4190*
"For whoever has, to him **m**	Mt 13:12	
he rejoices over it **m** than over	Mt 18:13	*3123*
you, take one or two **m** with you,	Mt 18:16	*2089*
thought that they would receive **m**;	Mt 20:10	*4183*
but they cried out all the **m**,	Mt 20:31	*3173*
Which is **m** important, the gold or	Mt 23:17	*3173*
blind men, which is **m** important,	Mt 23:19	*3173*
them, and gained five **m** talents.	Mt 25:16	*243*
the two *talents* gained two **m**.	Mt 25:17	*243*
up and brought five **m** talents,	Mt 25:20	*243*
I have gained five **m** talents.'	Mt 25:20	*243*
See, I have gained two **m** talents.'	Mt 25:22	*243*
"For to everyone who has, **m**	Mt 25:29	
saying the same thing once **m**.	Mt 26:44	*3825*
m than twelve legions of angels?	Mt 26:53	*4183*
But they kept shouting all the **m**,	Mt 27:23	*4057*
and **m** will be given you besides.	Mk 4:24	*4369*
"For whoever has, to him **m**	Mk 4:25	
but the **m** He ordered them, the	Mk 7:36	*3745*
the **m** widely they continued to	Mk 7:36	*3123*
and did not have **m** than one loaf	Mk 8:14	*1508*
He once **m** *began* to teach them.	Mk 10:1	*3825*
even **m** astonished and said to Him,	Mk 10:26	*4057*
but he kept crying out all the **m**,	Mk 10:48	*3123*
"He had one **m** *to send,* a beloved	Mk 12:6	*2089*
is much **m** than all burnt offerings	Mk 12:33	*4053*
to ask Him any **m** questions.	Mk 12:34	*3765*
this poor widow put in **m** than all	Mk 12:43	*4183*
once **m** to say to the bystanders,	Mk 14:69	*3825*
But they shouted all the **m**,	Mk 15:14	*4057*
"Collect no **m** than what you have	Lk 3:13	*4183*
and one who is **m** than a prophet.	Lk 7:26	*4053*
them will love him **m**?"	Lk 7:42	*4183*
the one whom he forgave **m**."	Lk 7:43	*4183*
to him **m** shall be given;	Lk 8:18	
m than five loaves and two fish,	Lk 9:13	*4183*
it will be **m** tolerable in that day	Lk 10:12	*414*
"But it will be **m** tolerable for	Lk 10:14	*414*
and whatever **m** you spend, when I	Lk 10:35	*4325*
how much **m** will *your* heavenly	Lk 11:13	*3123*
other spirits **m** evil than itself,	Lk 11:26	*4190*
that have no **m** that they can do.	Lk 12:4	*4057*
are **m** valuable than many sparrows.	Lk 12:7	*1308*
"For life is **m** than food, and the	Lk 12:23	*4183*
and the body **m** than clothing.	Lk 12:23	*4183*
how much **m** valuable you are than	Lk 12:24	*3123*
how much **m** *will He clothe* you?	Lk 12:28	*3123*
of him they will ask all the **m**.	Lk 12:48	*4057*
for someone **m** distinguished than	Lk 14:8	*1784*
there will be **m** joy in heaven	Lk 15:7	
men have **m** than enough bread,	Lk 15:17	*4052*
the sons of this age are **m** shrewd	Lk 16:8	*5429*
but he kept crying out all the **m**,	Lk 18:39	*3123*
your mina has made ten minas **m**.'	Lk 19:16	*4333*
m shall be given, but from the one	Lk 19:26	
widow put in **m** than all *of them;*	Lk 21:3	*4183*
and said, "Stop! No **m** of this."	Lk 22:51	*2193*
baptizing **m** disciples than John	Jn 4:1	*4183*
m believed because of His word;	Jn 4:41	*4183*
seeking all the **m** to kill Him,	Jn 5:18	*3123*
He will not perform **m** signs than	Jn 7:31	*4183*
From now on sin no **m**."	Jn 8:11	*3371*
"I will not speak much **m** with you,	Jn 14:30	*3765*
it so that it may bear **m** fruit.	Jn 15:2	*4183*
have many **m** things to say to you,	Jn 16:12	*2089*
statement, he was *even* **m** afraid;	Jn 19:8	*3123*
do you love Me **m** than these?"	Jn 21:15	*4183*
for the man was **m** than forty years	Ac 4:22	*4183*
all the **m** believers in the Lord,	Ac 5:14	*3123*
and as he approached to look **m**	Ac 7:31	
Now these were **m** noble-minded than	Ac 17:11	*2104b*

him the way of God **m** accurately. Ac 18:26 *199*
'It is **m** blessed to give than to Ac 20:35 *3123*
dialect, they became even **m** quiet; Ac 22:2 *3123*
There were **m** than forty who Ac 23:13 *4183*
by a **m** thorough investigation; Ac 23:15 *199*
somewhat **m** thoroughly about him. Ac 23:20 *199*
for **m** than forty of them are lying Ac 23:21 *4183*
no **m** than twelve days ago I went Ac 24:11 *4183*
a **m** exact knowledge about the Way, Ac 24:22 *199*
After he had spent not **m** than Ac 25:6 *4183*
But the centurion was **m** persuaded Ac 27:11 *3123*
Much **m** then, having now been Ro 5:9 *3123*
much **m**, having been reconciled, Ro 5:10 *3123*
much **m** did the grace of God and Ro 5:15 *3123*
much **m** those who receive the Ro 5:17 *3123*
grace abounded all the **m**, Ro 5:20 *5248*
much **m** will their fulfillment be! Ro 11:12 *3123*
how much **m** will these who are the Ro 11:24 *3123*
not to think **m** highly of himself than Ro 12:3 *5252*
How much **m** matters of this life? 1Co 6:3 *3386*
the right over you, do we not **m**? 1Co 9:12 *3123*
to all, so that I may win **m**. 1Co 9:19 *4183*
these we bestow **m** abundant honor, 1Co 12:23 *4053*
become much **m** presentable, 1Co 12:23 *4053*
whereas our **m** presentable members 1Co 12:24 *4053*
giving **m** abundant honor to that 1Co 12:24 *4053*
show you a still **m** excellent way. 1Co 12:31 *5236*
even **m** that you would prophesy; 1Co 14:5 *3123*
I speak in tongues **m** than you all; 1Co 14:18 *3123*
appeared to **m** than five hundred 1Co 15:6 *1883*
I labored even **m** than all of them, 1Co 15:10 *4053*
fail to be even **m** with glory? 2Co 3:8 *3123*
much **m** does the ministry of 2Co 3:9 *3123*
much **m** that which remains *is* in 2Co 3:11 *3123*
grace which is spreading to **m** and 2Co 4:15 *4183*
spreading to more and **m** people may 2Co 4:15
so that I rejoiced even **m**. 2Co 7:7 *3123*
even much **m** for the joy of Titus, 2Co 7:13 *4057*
abounds all the **m** toward you, 2Co 7:15 *4053*
things, but now even **m** diligent because 2Co 8:22 *4183*
sphere, enlarged even **m** by you, 2Co 10:15 *4050*
I **m** so; in far more labors, 2Co 11:23 *5228*
in far **m** labors, in far more 2Co 11:23 *4057*
labors, in far **m** imprisonments, 2Co 11:23 *4057*
credit me with **m** than he sees *in* me 2Co 12:6 *5228*
If I love you **m**, 2Co 12:15 *4057*
being **m** extremely zealous for my Ga 1:14 *4053*
and returned once **m** to Damascus. Ga 1:17 *3825*
FOR **M** NUMEROUS ARE THE CHILDREN Ga 4:27 *4183*
Now to Him who is able to do far **m** Eph 3:20 *5238b*
that your love may abound still **m** Php 1:9 *3123*
love may abound still more and **m** in Php 1:9 *3123*
have far **m** courage to speak the Php 1:14 *4057*
is **m** necessary for your sake. Php 1:24 *316*
regard one another as **m** important Php 2:3 *5242*
but now much **m** in my absence, Php 2:12 *3123*
I have sent him all the **m** eagerly Php 2:28 *4709*
confidence in the flesh, I far **m**: Php 3:4 *3123*
M than that, I count all things to Php 3:8 *3304*
a gift **m** than once for my needs. Php 4:16 *2532, 1364*
were all the **m** eager with great 1Th 2:17 *4053*
I, Paul, **m** than once 1Th 2:18 *2532, 1364*
that you excel still **m**. 1Th 4:1 *3123*
you, brethren, to excel still **m**, 1Th 4:10 *3123*
of our Lord was **m** than abundant, 1Tm 1:14 *5250*
but must serve them all the **m**, 1Tm 6:2 *3123*
as a slave, but **m** than a slave, Phm 1:16 *5228*
to me, but how much **m** to you, Phm 1:16 *3123*
will do even **m** than what I say. Phm 1:21 *5228*
a **m** excellent name than they. Heb 1:4 *1313*
worthy of **m** glory than Moses, Heb 3:3 *4183*
house has **m** honor than the house. Heb 3:3 *4183*
desiring even **m** to show to the Heb 6:17 *4053*
so much the **m** also Jesus has Heb 7:22 *2596*
obtained a **m** excellent ministry, Heb 8:6 *1313*
I WILL REMEMBER THEIR SINS NO **M**." Heb 8:12 *2089*
greater and **m** perfect tabernacle, Heb 9:11 *5046*
much **m** will the blood of Christ, Heb 9:14 *3123*
DEEDS I WILL REMEMBER NO **M**." Heb 10:17 *2089*
and all the **m** as you see the day Heb 10:25 *3123*
And what **m** shall I say? Heb 11:32 *2089*
"YET ONCE **M** I WILL SHAKE NOT Heb 12:26 *530*
"Yet once **m**," denotes the removing Heb 12:27 *530*
I urge *you* all the **m** to do this, Heb 13:19 *4053*
being **m** precious than gold which 1Pe 1:7 *4186*
be all the **m** diligent to make 2Pe 1:10 *3123*
the prophetic word *made* **m** sure, 2Pe 1:19 *949*
no one buys their cargoes any **m** Rv 18:11 *3765*

MOREH

site of Shechem, to the oak of **M**. Gn 12:6 4176
Gilgal, beside the oaks of **M**? Dt 11:30 4176
by the hill of **M** in the valley. Jg 7:1 4176

MOREOVER

M, the angel of the LORD said to Gn 16:10
M, whenever the stronger Gn 30:41
She said, **m**, "Will you give a pledge Gn 38:17
M, it took place while she was Gn 38:28
M, Pharaoh said to Joseph, Gn 41:44
And **m**, behold, he is coming out to Ex 4:14 1571
"**M**, he shall speak for you to the Ex 4:16
M, the foremen of the sons of Ex 5:14
'**M**, there shall be a great cry in Ex 11:6
'**M**, they shall take some of the Ex 12:7
"**M** you shall make the tabernacle Ex 26:1
"**M**, you shall make an altar as a Ex 30:1
M, the LORD spoke to Moses, Ex 30:22
M, You have said, Ex 33:12
M, he made fifty loops on the edge Ex 36:17
M, he made the veil of blue and Ex 36:35
M, he made the laver of bronze Ex 38:8
M, from the blue and purple and Ex 39:1
"**M**, you shall set the gold altar Ex 40:5
'Every grain offering of yours, **m**, Lv 2:13
'**M**, if his offering is a goat, Lv 3:12
doorway of the tent of meeting, **m**, Lv 8:35
"You shall eat it, **m**, Lv 10:13
'These, **m**, you shall detest among Lv 11:13
'By these, **m**, you will be made Lv 11:24
'Everything, **m**, on which part of Lv 11:35
"**M**, the rest of the oil that is Lv 14:29
"**M**, whoever goes into the house Lv 14:46
'This, **m**, shall be his uncleanness Lv 15:3
'Anyone, **m**, who touches his bed Lv 15:5
'**M**, he shall take some of the Lv 16:14
'**M**, you shall not follow the Lv 20:23
reap the harvest of your land, **m**, Lv 23:22
'**M**, the one who blasphemes the Lv 24:16
'If you make a sale, **m**, Lv 25:14
'The land, **m**, shall not be sold Lv 25:23
'**M**, I will make My dwelling among Lv 26:11
'Every valuation of yours, **m**, Lv 27:25
"With you, **m**, there shall be a Nu 1:4
'**M**, the man will be free from Nu 5:31
"The priestly sons of Aaron, **m**, Nu 10:8
and **m**, we saw the descendants of Nu 13:28 1571
"**M**, you shall speak to the Nu 18:26
"**M**, he shall stand before Eleazar Nu 27:21
'**M**, you shall not take ransom for Nu 35:31
'**M**, your little ones who you said Dt 1:39
"**M** the hand of the LORD was Dt 2:15 1571
"**M**, the LORD showed great and Dt 6:22
"**M**, the LORD your God will send Dt 7:20 1571
"I, **m**, stayed on the mountain Dt 10:10
"**M**, he shall not multiply horses Dt 17:16 7534
"**M**, you shall build there an Dt 27:5
"**M**, it shall eat the offspring of Dt 28:51
"**M**, the LORD will scatter you Dt 28:64
m, you have seen their abominations Dt 29:17
"**M** the LORD your God will Dt 30:6
m, all the inhabitants of the land Jos 2:24 1571
"You shall, **m**, command the Jos 3:8
M, they have also put *them* among Jos 7:11
M, the Jordan was its border on Jos 18:20
"**M**, I have acquired Ruth the Ru 4:10 1571
"**M**, may your house be like the Ru 4:12
"**M**, as for me, far be it from me 1Sa 12:23 1571
"**M** the LORD will also give over 1Sa 28:19
M David was greatly distressed 1Sa 30:6
"**M**, the archers shot at your 2Sa 11:24
M, Absalom would say, 2Sa 15:4
M, Hushai said, "You know your 2Sa 17:8
"**M**, he has slandered your servant 2Sa 19:27
"**M**, the king's servants came to 1Ki 1:47 1571
M, the king made a great throne of 1Ki 10:18
"**M**, the LORD will raise up for 1Ki 14:14
M, the word of the LORD through 1Ki 16:7 1571
M, Jehoshaphat said to the king of 1Ki 22:5
M, they did not require an 2Ki 12:15
M, they built for themselves high 2Ki 17:9
M, Manasseh shed very much 2Ki 21:16 1571
M, Shaphan the scribe told the 2Ki 22:10
M, Josiah removed the mediums and 2Ki 23:24 1571
M those who were near to them, 1Ch 12:40
M, I tell you that the LORD will 1Ch 17:10
M Abishai the son of Zeruiah 1Ch 18:12
"**M**, there are many workmen with 1Ch 22:15
M, David and the commanders of the 1Ch 25:1
"**M**, in my delight in the house of 1Ch 29:3 5750
M, the king made a great throne of 2Ch 9:17
M, the priests and the Levites who 2Ch 11:13
M, they made an oath to the LORD 2Ch 15:14
M, Jehoshaphat said to the king of 2Ch 18:4
M, he made high places in the 2Ch 21:11 1571
M, Jehoiada placed the offices of 2Ch 23:18
M, Amaziah assembled Judah and 2Ch 25:5
M, Uzziah built towers in 2Ch 26:9
M, Uzziah had an army ready for 2Ch 26:11
M, Uzziah prepared for all the 2Ch 26:14
M, he built cities in the hill 2Ch 27:4
M, he burned incense in the valley 2Ch 28:3
M, when Ahaz gathered together the 2Ch 28:24
"**M**, all the utensils which King 2Ch 29:19
M, King Hezekiah and the officials 2Ch 29:30
M, he did not humble himself 2Ch 33:23
M, Shaphan the scribe told the 2Ch 34:18
M, he made all who were present in 2Ch 34:32
"**M**, stand in the holy place 2Ch 35:5
"**M**, I issue a decree concerning Ezr 6:8
M, next to him the Tekoites made Ne 3:5
M, from the day that I was Ne 5:14 1571
M, *there were* at my table one Ne 5:17
M, they were speaking about his Ne 6:19 1571
M, all men will follow after him, Jb 21:33
M, they are brought low and like Jb 24:24
M, it would be an iniquity Jb 31:11
M, by them Your servant is warned; Ps 19:11 1571
m, that every man who eats and Ec 3:13 1571
M, man does not know his time: Ec 9:12 3588, 1571
M, the LORD said, Is 3:16
M, he will seek justice And be Is 16:5
"**M**, I will deliver the Egyptians Is 19:4
M, the manufacturers of linen made Is 19:9
"**M**, I will make your battlements Is 54:12
M, the LORD made it known to me Jer 11:18
"**M** you shall not go into a house Jer 16:8
"**M**, among the prophets of Samaria Jer 23:13
'**M**, I will take from them the Jer 25:10
M Jeremiah said to King Zedekiah, Jer 37:18
M, He said to me, Ezk 3:10
"**M**, I will make your tongue stick Ezk 3:26
M, He said to me, Ezk 4:16
'**M**, I will make you a desolation Ezk 5:14
'**M**, I will send on you famine and Ezk 5:17
M, the word of the LORD came to me Ezk 7:1
M, the sound of the wings of the Ezk 10:5
M, the Spirit lifted me up and Ezk 11:1
M, the word of the LORD came to me Ezk 12:17
"**M**, you took your sons and Ezk 16:20
"**M**, you played the harlot with Ezk 16:28
M, the word of the LORD came to me Ezk 17:11
M, the LORD said to me, Ezk 23:36
M, the word of the LORD came to me Ezk 27:1
"**M**, in their wailing they will Ezk 27:32
"**M**, I will make the Nile canals Ezk 30:12
M, the word of the LORD came to me Ezk 35:1
"**M**, I will give you a new heart Ezk 36:26
"**M**, I will save you from all your Ezk 36:29
"**M**, they shall teach My people Ezk 44:23
"**M**, they shall not sell or Ezk 48:14
"**M**, the thing which the king Da 2:11
"**M**, we have not listened to Your Da 9:6
m, he will repay him for his scorn. Da 11:18 1115
M, the pride of Israel testifies Hos 5:5
M, he makes a covenant with Hos 12:1
"**M**, what are you to Me, O Tyre, Jl 3:4 1571
M, Israel will certainly go from Am 7:17
M, I will bring on you The one who Mi 1:15 5750
"**M**, their wealth will become Zph 1:13
M, the king will perish from Gaza, Zch 9:5
M MY FLESH ALSO WILL LIVE IN HOPE; Ac 2:26 *2089, 1161*
In this case, **m**, it is required of 1Co 4:2 *3062*
M we are even found *to be* false 1Co 15:15 *1161*

MORESHETH

"Micah of **M** prophesied in the Jer 26:18 4183
Micah of **M** in the days of Jotham, Mi 1:1 4183

MORESHETH-GATH

give parting gifts On behalf of **M**; Mi 1:14 4182

MORIAH

Isaac, and go to the land of **M**, Gn 22:2 4179
the LORD in Jerusalem on Mount **M**, 2Ch 3:1 4179

MORNING

there was evening and there was **m**, Gn 1:5 1242
there was evening and there was **m**, Gn 1:8 1242
There was evening and there was **m**, Gn 1:13 1242
There was evening and there was **m**, Gn 1:19 1242
There was evening and there was **m**, Gn 1:23 1242
there was evening and there was **m**, Gn 1:31 1242
When **m** dawned, the angels Gn 19:15 7837
Now Abraham arose early in the **m** Gn 19:27 1242
So Abimelech arose early in the **m** Gn 20:8 1242
So Abraham rose early in the **m** and Gn 21:14 1242
in the **m** and saddled his donkey, Gn 22:3 1242
When they arose in the **m**, Gn 24:54 1242
In the **m** they arose early and Gn 26:31 1242
So Jacob rose early in the **m**, Gn 28:18 1242
So it came about in the **m** that, Gn 29:25 1242
Early in the **m** Laban arose, Gn 31:55 1242
Joseph came to them in the **m** and Gn 40:6 1242
m his spirit was troubled, Gn 41:8 1242
In the **m** he devours the prey, And Gn 49:27 1242
"Go to Pharaoh in the **m** as he is Ex 7:15 1242
"Rise early in the **m** and present Ex 8:20 1242
"Rise up early in the **m** and stand Ex 9:13 1242
and when it was **m**, the east wind Ex 10:13 1242
not leave any of it over until **m**, Ex 12:10 1242
whatever is left of it until **m**, Ex 12:10 1242
the door of his house until **m**. Ex 12:22 1242
At the **m** watch, Ex 14:24 1242
and in the **m** you will see the Ex 16:7 1242
and bread to the full in the **m**; Ex 16:8 1242
and in the **m** you shall be filled Ex 16:12 1242
and in the **m** there was a layer of Ex 16:13 1242
no man leave any of it until **m**." Ex 16:19 1242
and some left part of it until **m**, Ex 16:20 1242
They gathered it **m** by morning, Ex 16:21 1242
They gathered it morning by **m**, Ex 16:21 1242
put aside to be kept until **m**." Ex 16:23 1242
So they put it aside until **m**, Ex 16:24 1242
from the **m** until the evening. Ex 18:13 1242
about you from **m** until evening?" Ex 18:14 1242
on the third day, when it was **m**, Ex 19:16 1242
feast to remain overnight until **m**. Ex 23:18 1242
Then he arose early in the **m**, Ex 24:4 1242
from evening to **m** before the LORD; Ex 27:21 1242
any of the bread remains until **m**, Ex 29:34 1242
one lamb you shall offer in the **m** and Ex 29:39 1242
same drink offering as in the **m**, Ex 29:41 1242
every **m** when he trims the lamps. Ex 30:7 1242
"So be ready by **m**, and come up in Ex 34:2 1242
come up in the **m** to Mount Sinai, Ex 34:2 1242
the **m** and went up to Mount Sinai, Ex 34:4 1242
Passover to be left over until **m**. Ex 34:25 1242
to him freewill offerings every **m**. Ex 36:3 1242
the altar all night until the **m**, Lv 6:9 1242
shall burn wood on it every **m**; Lv 6:12 1242
half of it in the **m** and half of it in Lv 6:20 1242
not leave any of it over until **m**. Lv 7:15 1242
the burnt offering of the **m**, Lv 9:17 1242
remain with you all night until **m**. Lv 19:13 1242
shall leave none of it until **m**; Lv 22:30 1242
to **m** before the LORD continually; Lv 24:3 1242

shall leave none of it until **m**,	**Nu 9:12**	1242
fire over the tabernacle, until **m**.	**Nu 9:15**	1242
remained from evening until **m**,	**Nu 9:21**	1242
the cloud was lifted in the **m**,	**Nu 9:21**	1242
In the **m**, however, they rose up	**Nu 14:40**	1242
m the LORD will show who is His,	**Nu 16:5**	1242
So Balaam arose in the **m** and said	**Nu 22:13**	1242
So Balaam arose in the **m**,	**Nu 22:21**	1242
in the **m** that Balak took Balaam and	**Nu 22:41**	1242
shall offer the one lamb in the **m** and	**Nu 28:4**	1242
as the grain offering of the **m** and	**Nu 28:8**	1242
the burnt offering of the **m**,	**Nu 28:23**	1242
shall remain overnight until **m**.	**Dt 16:4**	1242
In the **m** you are to return to	**Dt 16:7**	1242
"In the **m** you shall say,	**Dt 28:67**	1242
'Would that it were **m**!'	**Dt 28:67**	1242
Then Joshua rose early in the **m**;	**Jos 3:1**	1242
Now Joshua rose early in the **m**,	**Jos 6:12**	1242
'In the **m** then you shall come near	**Jos 7:14**	1242
So Joshua arose early in the **m** and	**Jos 7:16**	1242
in the **m** and mustered the people,	**Jos 8:10**	1242
men of the city arose early in the **m**,	**Jg 6:28**	1242
him shall be put to death by **m**.	**Jg 6:31**	1242
next **m** and squeezed the fleece,	**Jg 6:38**	4283
"In the **m**, as soon as the sun	**Jg 9:33**	1242
"*Let us wait* until the **m** light,	**Jg 16:2**	1242
day they got up early in the **m**,	**Jg 19:5**	1242
day he arose to go early in the **m**,	**Jg 19:8**	1242
and abused her all night until **m**,	**Jg 19:25**	1242
When her master arose in the **m** and	**Jg 19:27**	1242
the **m** and camped against Gibeah.	**Jg 20:19**	1242
has remained from the **m** until now;	**Ru 2:7**	1242
this night, and when **m** comes,	**Ru 3:13**	1242
Lie down until **m**."	**Ru 3:13**	1242
So she lay at his feet until **m** and	**Ru 3:14**	1242
m and worshiped before the LORD,	**1Sa 1:19**	1242
So Samuel lay down until **m**.	**1Sa 3:15**	1242
Ashdodites arose early the next **m**,	**1Sa 5:3**	4283
when they arose early the next **m**,	**1Sa 5:4**	1242
and in the **m** I will let you go,	**1Sa 9:19**	1242
The next **m** Saul put the people	**1Sa 11:11**	4283
midst of the camp at the **m** watch and	**1Sa 11:11**	1242
among them until the **m** light,	**1Sa 14:36**	1242
rose early in the **m** to meet Saul;	**1Sa 15:12**	1242
m and evening for forty days and	**1Sa 17:16**	7925
So David arose early in the **m** and	**1Sa 17:20**	1242
please be on guard in the **m**,	**1Sa 19:2**	1242
to put him to death in the **m**.	**1Sa 19:11**	1242
Now it came about in the **m** that	**1Sa 20:35**	1242
if by **m** I leave *as much as* one	**1Sa 25:22**	1242
the **m** light *as much as* one male."	**1Sa 25:34**	1242
anything at all until the **m** light.	**1Sa 25:36**	1242
But in the **m**, when the wine	**1Sa 25:37**	1242
"Now then arise early in the **m**	**1Sa 29:10**	1242
as you have arisen early in the **m**	**1Sa 29:10**	1242
and his men, to depart in the **m** to	**1Sa 29:11**	1242
would have gone away in the **m**,	**2Sa 2:27**	1242
crossed the Jordan, walked all **m**,	**2Sa 2:29**	1338
Now in the **m** David wrote	**2Sa 11:14**	1242
you so depressed **m** after morning?	**2Sa 13:4**	1242
you so depressed morning after **m**?	**2Sa 13:4**	1242
light of the **m** *when* the sun rises,	**2Sa 23:4**	1242
the sun rises, A **m** without clouds,	**2Sa 23:4**	1242
When David arose in the **m**,	**2Sa 24:11**	1242
the **m** until the appointed time,	**2Sa 24:15**	1242
I rose in the **m** to nurse my son,	**1Ki 3:21**	1242
looked at him carefully in the **m**,	**1Ki 3:21**	1242
brought him bread and meat in the **m**	**1Ki 17:6**	1242
of Baal from **m** until noon saying,	**1Ki 18:26**	1242
It happened in the **m** about the	**2Ki 3:20**	1242
They rose early in the **m**,	**2Ki 3:22**	1242
if we wait until **m** light,	**2Ki 7:9**	1242
entrance of the gate until **m**."	**2Ki 10:8**	1242
Now in the **m** he went out	**2Ki 10:9**	1242
burn the **m** burnt offering and the	**2Ki 16:15**	1242
and when men rose early in the **m**,	**2Ki 19:35**	1242
charge of opening *it* **m** by morning.	**1Ch 9:27**	1242
charge of opening *it* morning by **m**.	**1Ch 9:27**	1242
continually **m** and evening,	**1Ch 16:40**	1242
They are to stand every **m** to	**1Ch 23:30**	1242
burnt offerings **m** and evening,	**2Ch 2:4**	1242
"Every **m** and evening they	**2Ch 13:11**	1242
They rose early in the **m** and	**2Ch 20:20**	1242
the **m** and evening burnt offerings,	**2Ch 31:3**	1242
burnt offerings **m** and evening.	**Ezr 3:3**	1242
Gate from early **m** until midday,	**Ne 8:3**	216
and in the **m** she would return to the	**Es 2:14**	1242
the **m** ask the king to have Mordecai	**Es 5:14**	1242
rising up early in the **m** and	**Jb 1:5**	1242
'Between **m** and evening they are	**Jb 4:20**	1242
You examine him every **m**	**Jb 7:18**	1242
Darkness would be like the **m**.	**Jb 11:17**	1242
"For the **m** is the same to him as	**Jb 24:17**	1242
When the **m** stars sang together And	**Jb 38:7**	1242
ever in your life commanded the **m**,	**Jb 38:12**	1242
are like the eyelids of the **m**.	**Jb 41:18**	7837
In the **m**, O LORD, You will hear	**Ps 5:3**	1242
In the **m** I will order *my prayer* to	**Ps 5:3**	1242
But a shout of joy *comes* in the **m**.	**Ps 30:5**	1242
God will help her when **m** dawns.	**Ps 46:5**	1242
shall rule over them in the **m**,	**Ps 49:14**	1242
Evening and **m** and at noon, I will	**Ps 55:17**	1242
of Your lovingkindness in the **m**,	**Ps 59:16**	1242
day long And chastened every **m**.	**Ps 73:14**	1242
the **m** my prayer comes before You.	**Ps 88:13**	1242
In the **m** they are like grass which	**Ps 90:5**	1242
In the **m** it flourishes and	**Ps 90:6**	1242
in the **m** with Your lovingkindness,	**Ps 90:14**	1242
Your lovingkindness in the **m** And	**Ps 92:2**	1242
Every **m** I will destroy all the	**Ps 101:8**	1242
More than the watchmen for the **m**;	**Ps 130:6**	1242
more than the watchmen for the **m**;	**Ps 130:6**	1242
hear Your lovingkindness in the **m**;	**Ps 143:8**	1242
us drink our fill of love until **m**;	**Pr 7:18**	1242
with a loud voice early in the **m**,	**Pr 27:14**	1242
and whose princes feast in the **m**.	**Ec 10:16**	1242
Sow your seed in the **m** and	**Ec 11:6**	1242
for you do not know whether **m** or	**Ec 11:6**	2088
who rise early in the **m** that they may	**Is 5:11**	1242
from heaven, O star of the **m**,	**Is 14:12**	1966
And in the **m** you bring your seed	**Is 17:11**	1242
Before **m** they are no more.	**Is 17:14**	1242
"**M** comes but also night.	**Is 21:12**	1242
For **m** after morning it will pass	**Is 28:19**	1242
after **m** it will pass through,	**Is 28:19**	1242
Be their strength every **m**,	**Is 33:2**	1242
and when men arose early in the **m**,	**Is 37:36**	1242
"I composed *my soul* until **m**.	**Is 38:13**	1242
He awakens *Me* **m** by morning, He	**Is 50:4**	1242
He awakens *Me* morning by **m**,	**Is 50:4**	1242
m And a shout of alarm at noon;	**Jer 20:16**	1242
"Administer justice every **m**;	**Jer 21:12**	1242
They are new every **m**;	**La 3:23**	1242
In the **m** the word of the LORD	**Ezk 12:8**	1242
So I spoke to the people in the **m**,	**Ezk 24:18**	1242
in the **m** I did as I was commanded.	**Ezk 24:18**	1242
the time *they* came to me in the **m**;	**Ezk 33:22**	1242
m by morning you shall provide it.	**Ezk 46:13**	1242
morning by **m** you shall provide it.	**Ezk 46:13**	1242
offering with it **m** by morning,	**Ezk 46:14**	1242
offering with it morning by **m**,	**Ezk 46:14**	1242
and the oil, **m** by morning,	**Ezk 46:15**	1242
and the oil, morning by **m**,	**Ezk 46:15**	1242
your loyalty is like a **m** cloud And	**Hos 6:4**	1242
m it burns like a flaming fire.	**Hos 7:6**	1242
they will be like the **m** cloud And	**Hos 13:3**	1242
Bring your sacrifices every **m**,	**Am 4:4**	1242
And changes deep darkness into **m**,	**Am 5:8**	1242
When **m** comes, they do it, For it	**Mi 2:1**	1242
They leave nothing for the **m**.	**Zph 3:3**	1242
Every **m** He brings His justice to	**Zph 3:5**	1242
And in the **m**, '*There will be* a storm	**Mt 16:3**	*4404*
who went out early in the **m** to hire	**Mt 20:1**	*4404*
Now in the **m**, when He was returning	**Mt 21:18**	*4404*
Now when **m** came, all the chief	**Mt 27:1**	*4405*
In the early **m**,	**Mk 1:35**	*4404*
As they were passing by in the **m**,	**Mk 11:20**	*4404*
when the rooster crows, or in the **m**	**Mk 13:35**	*4404*
Early in the **m** the chief	**Mk 15:1**	*4404*
people would get up early in the **m**	**Lk 21:38**	*3719*
were at the tomb early in the **m**,	**Lk 24:22**	*3720*
m He came again into the temple,	**Jn 8:2**	*3722*
Prophets, from **m** until evening.	**Ac 28:23**	*4404*
the **m** star arises in your hearts.	**2Pe 1:19**	*5459*
and I will give him the **m** star.	**Rv 2:28**	*4407*
of David, the bright **m** star."	**Rv 22:16**	*4407*

MORNINGS

"For 2,300 evenings *and* **m**;	**Da 8:14**	1242
The vision of the evenings and **m**	**Da 8:26**	1242

MORSEL

Or have eaten my **m** alone,	**Jb 31:17**	6595
Better is a dry **m** and quietness	**Pr 17:1**	6595
vomit up the **m** you have eaten,	**Pr 23:8**	6595
dip the **m** and give it to him."	**Jn 13:26**	*5596*
So when He had dipped the **m**,	**Jn 13:26**	*5596*
After the **m**, Satan then	**Jn 13:27**	*5596*
after receiving the **m** he went out	**Jn 13:30**	*5596*

MORSELS

of a whisperer are like dainty **m**,	**Pr 18:8**	3859
of a whisperer are like dainty **m**,	**Pr 26:22**	3859

MORTAL

'Are Your days as the days of a **m**,	**Jb 10:5**	582
Do not trust in princes, In **m** man,	**Ps 146:3**	1121
make **m** man scarcer than pure gold	**Is 13:12**	582
Why should *any* living **m**,	**La 3:39**	120
whose dwelling place is not with **m**	**Da 2:11**	
do not let sin reign in your **m** body	**Ro 6:12**	*2349*
will also give life to your **m** bodies	**Ro 8:11**	*2349*
this **m** must put on immortality.	**1Co 15:53**	*2349*
m will have put on immortality,	**1Co 15:54**	*2349*
may be manifested in our **m** flesh.	**2Co 4:11**	*2349*
what is **m** will be swallowed up by	**2Co 5:4**	*2349*
In this case **m** men receive tithes,	**Heb 7:8**	*599*

MORTALLY

those days Hezekiah became **m** ill.	**2Ki 20:1**	4191
those days Hezekiah became **m** ill;	**2Ch 32:24**	4191
those days Hezekiah became **m** ill.	**Is 38:1**	4191
And the **m** wounded will groan	**Jer 51:52**	2491a

MORTAR

stone, and they used tar for **m**.	**Gn 11:3**	2563a
hard labor in **m** and bricks and at all	**Ex 1:14**	2563a
millstones or beat *it* in the **m**,	**Nu 11:8**	4085
Though you pound a fool in a **m**	**Pr 27:22**	4388
will come upon rulers as *upon* **m**,	**Is 41:25**	2563a
and hide them in the **m** in the brick	**Jer 43:9**	4423
Go into the clay and tread the **m**!	**Na 3:14**	2563a
"Wail, O inhabitants of the **M**,	**Zph 1:11**	4389

MORTGAGING

"We are **m** our fields, our	**Ne 5:3**	6148

MOSAIC

on a **m** pavement of porphyry,	**Es 1:6**	7531b

MOSERAH

out from Beeroth Bene-jaakan to **M**.	**Dt 10:6**	4149

MOSEROTH

from Hashmonah and camped at **M**.	**Nu 33:30**	4149
They journeyed from **M** and	**Nu 33:31**	4149

MOSES

And she named him **M**,	**Ex 2:10**	4872
those days, when **M** had grown up,	**Ex 2:11**	4872
Then **M** was afraid and said,	**Ex 2:14**	4872
this matter, he tried to kill **M**.	**Ex 2:15**	4872
But **M** fled from the presence of	**Ex 2:15**	4872
but **M** stood up and helped them and	**Ex 2:17**	4872
M was willing to dwell with	**Ex 2:21**	4872
gave his daughter Zipporah to **M**.	**Ex 2:21**	4872
Now **M** was pasturing the flock of	**Ex 3:1**	4872
So **M** said, "I must turn aside now and	**Ex 3:3**	4872
the midst of the bush and said, "**M**,	**Ex 3:4**	4872
M!" And he said, "Here I am."	**Ex 3:4**	4872
Then **M** hid his face, for he was	**Ex 3:6**	4872
But **M** said to God,	**Ex 3:11**	4872
Then **M** said to God,	**Ex 3:13**	4872
God said to **M**,	**Ex 3:14**	4872
God, furthermore, said to **M**,	**Ex 3:15**	4872
Then **M** said,	**Ex 4:1**	4872
and **M** fled from it.	**Ex 4:3**	4872
But the LORD said to **M**,	**Ex 4:4**	4872
Then **M** said to the LORD,	**Ex 4:10**	4872
of the LORD burned against **M**,	**Ex 4:14**	4872
Then **M** departed and returned to	**Ex 4:18**	4872
And Jethro said to **M**,	**Ex 4:18**	4872
Now the LORD said to **M** in Midian,	**Ex 4:19**	4872
So **M** took his wife and his sons	**Ex 4:20**	4872
M also took the staff of God in	**Ex 4:20**	4872
The LORD said to **M**,	**Ex 4:21**	4872
"Go to meet **M** in the wilderness."	**Ex 4:27**	4872
M told Aaron all the words of	**Ex 4:28**	4872
Then **M** and Aaron went and	**Ex 4:29**	4872
which the LORD had spoken to **M**.	**Ex 4:30**	4872
And afterward **M** and Aaron came and	**Ex 5:1**	4872
"**M** and Aaron, why do you draw the	**Ex 5:4**	4872
they met **M** and Aaron as they were	**Ex 5:20**	4872
M returned to the LORD and said,	**Ex 5:22**	4872
Then the LORD said to **M**,	**Ex 6:1**	4872
God spoke further to **M** and said to	**Ex 6:2**	4872
So **M** spoke thus to the sons of	**Ex 6:9**	4872
but they did not listen to **M** on	**Ex 6:9**	4872
Now the LORD spoke to **M**,	**Ex 6:10**	4872
But **M** spoke before the LORD,	**Ex 6:12**	4872
the LORD spoke to **M** and to Aaron,	**Ex 6:13**	4872
and she bore him Aaron and **M**;	**Ex 6:20**	4872
Aaron and **M** to whom the LORD said,	**Ex 6:26**	4872
it was *the same* **M** and Aaron.	**Ex 6:27**	4872
spoke to **M** in the land of Egypt,	**Ex 6:28**	4872
that the LORD spoke to **M**,	**Ex 6:29**	4872
But **M** said before the LORD,	**Ex 6:30**	4872
Then the LORD said to **M**,	**Ex 7:1**	4872
So **M** and Aaron did *it;*	**Ex 7:6**	4872
M was eighty years old and	**Ex 7:7**	4872
Now the LORD spoke to **M** and Aaron,	**Ex 7:8**	4872
So **M** and Aaron came to Pharaoh,	**Ex 7:10**	4872
Then the LORD said to **M**,	**Ex 7:14**	4872
Then the LORD said to **M**,	**Ex 7:19**	4872
So **M** and Aaron did even as the	**Ex 7:20**	4872
Then the LORD said to **M**,	**Ex 8:1**	4872
Then the LORD said to **M**,	**Ex 8:5**	4872
called for **M** and Aaron and said,	**Ex 8:8**	4872
M said to Pharaoh,	**Ex 8:9**	4872
Then **M** and Aaron went out from	**Ex 8:12**	4872
and **M** cried to the LORD concerning	**Ex 8:12**	4872
did according to the word of **M**,	**Ex 8:13**	4872
Then the LORD said to **M**,	**Ex 8:16**	4872
Now the LORD said to **M**,	**Ex 8:20**	4872
called for **M** and Aaron and said,	**Ex 8:25**	4872
But **M** said, "It is not right to do so,	**Ex 8:26**	4872
M said, "Behold, I am going out	**Ex 8:29**	4872
So **M** went out from Pharaoh and	**Ex 8:30**	4872
The LORD did as **M** asked,	**Ex 8:31**	4872
Then the LORD said to **M**,	**Ex 9:1**	4872
Then the LORD said to **M** and Aaron,	**Ex 9:8**	4872
and let **M** throw it toward the sky	**Ex 9:8**	4872
and **M** threw it toward the sky, and	**Ex 9:10**	4872
before **M** because of the boils,	**Ex 9:11**	4872
just as the LORD had spoken to **M**.	**Ex 9:12**	4872
Then the LORD said to **M**,	**Ex 9:13**	4872
Now the LORD said to **M**,	**Ex 9:22**	4872
M stretched out his staff	**Ex 9:23**	4872
Then Pharaoh sent for **M** and Aaron,	**Ex 9:27**	4872
M said to him,	**Ex 9:29**	4872
So **M** went out of the city from	**Ex 9:33**	4872
as the LORD had spoken through **M**.	**Ex 9:35**	4872
Then the LORD said to **M**,	**Ex 10:1**	4872
M and Aaron went to Pharaoh	**Ex 10:3**	4872
So **M** and Aaron were brought back	**Ex 10:8**	4872
M said, "We shall go with our	**Ex 10:9**	4872
Then the LORD said to **M**,	**Ex 10:12**	4872
So **M** stretched out his staff over	**Ex 10:13**	4872
hurriedly called for **M** and Aaron,	**Ex 10:16**	4872
Then the LORD said to **M**,	**Ex 10:21**	4872
So **M** stretched out his hand toward	**Ex 10:22**	4872
Then Pharaoh called to **M**,	**Ex 10:24**	4872
M said, "You must also let us have	**Ex 10:25**	4872
M said, "You are right; I shall	**Ex 10:29**	4872
Now the LORD said to **M**,	**Ex 11:1**	4872
the man **M** *himself* was greatly	**Ex 11:3**	4872
M said, "Thus says the LORD,	**Ex 11:4**	4872
Then the LORD said to **M**,	**Ex 11:9**	4872
M and Aaron performed all	**Ex 11:10**	4872
Now the LORD said to **M** and Aaron	**Ex 12:1**	4872
Then **M** called for all the elders	**Ex 12:21**	4872
LORD had commanded **M** and Aaron,	**Ex 12:28**	4872
for **M** and Aaron at night and said,	**Ex 12:31**	4872
done according to the word of **M**,	**Ex 12:35**	4872
The LORD said to **M** and Aaron,	**Ex 12:43**	4872
LORD had commanded **M** and Aaron.	**Ex 12:50**	4872

Then the LORD spoke to **M**,	**Ex 13:1**	4872
M said to the people,	**Ex 13:3**	4872
M took the bones of Joseph	**Ex 13:19**	4872
Now the LORD spoke to **M**,	**Ex 14:1**	4872
Then they said to **M**,	**Ex 14:11**	4872
But **M** said to the people,	**Ex 14:13**	4872
Then the LORD said to **M**,	**Ex 14:15**	4872
Then **M** stretched out his hand over	**Ex 14:21**	4872
Then the LORD said to **M**,	**Ex 14:26**	4872
So **M** stretched out his hand over	**Ex 14:27**	4872
in the LORD and in His servant **M**.	**Ex 14:31**	4872
Then **M** and the sons of Israel sang	**Ex 15:1**	4872
M led Israel from the Red Sea,	**Ex 15:22**	4872
So the people grumbled at **M**,	**Ex 15:24**	4872
M and Aaron in the wilderness.	**Ex 16:2**	4872
Then the LORD said to **M**,	**Ex 16:4**	4872
So **M** and Aaron said to all the	**Ex 16:6**	4872
M said, "*This will happen* when	**Ex 16:8**	4872
Then **M** said to Aaron, "Say	**Ex 16:9**	4872
And the LORD spoke to **M**,	**Ex 16:11**	4872
And **M** said to them,	**Ex 16:15**	4872
M said to them,	**Ex 16:19**	4872
But they did not listen to **M**,	**Ex 16:20**	4872
and **M** was angry with them.	**Ex 16:20**	4872
the congregation came and told **M**,	**Ex 16:22**	4872
until morning, as **M** had ordered,	**Ex 16:24**	4872
M said, "Eat it today, for today is a	**Ex 16:25**	4872
Then the LORD said to **M**,	**Ex 16:28**	4872
M said, "This is what the LORD has	**Ex 16:32**	4872
M said to Aaron,	**Ex 16:33**	4872
As the LORD commanded **M**,	**Ex 16:34**	4872
people quarreled with **M** and said,	**Ex 17:2**	4872
And **M** said to them,	**Ex 17:2**	4872
they grumbled against **M** and said,	**Ex 17:3**	4872
So **M** cried out to the LORD,	**Ex 17:4**	4872
Then the LORD said to **M**,	**Ex 17:5**	4872
And **M** did so in the sight of the	**Ex 17:6**	4872
So **M** said to Joshua,	**Ex 17:9**	4872
Joshua did as **M** told him,	**Ex 17:10**	4872
and **M**, Aaron, and Hur went up to	**Ex 17:10**	4872
about when **M** held his hand up,	**Ex 17:11**	4872
Then the LORD said to **M**,	**Ex 17:14**	4872
M built an altar and named it	**Ex 17:15**	4872
for **M** and for Israel His people,	**Ex 18:1**	4872
for **M** said, "I have been a	**Ex 18:3**	
came with his sons and his wife to **M**	**Ex 18:5**	4872
He sent word to **M**,	**Ex 18:6**	4872
Then **M** went out to meet his	**Ex 18:7**	4872
M told his father-in-law all	**Ex 18:8**	4872
that **M** sat to judge the people,	**Ex 18:13**	4872
and the people stood about **M** from	**Ex 18:13**	4872
M said to his father-in-law,	**Ex 18:15**	4872
So **M** listened to his	**Ex 18:24**	4872
M chose able men out of all	**Ex 18:25**	4872
dispute they would bring to **M**,	**Ex 18:26**	4872
Then **M** bade his father-in-law	**Ex 18:27**	4872
M went up to God, and the LORD	**Ex 19:3**	4872
So **M** came and called the elders of	**Ex 19:7**	4872
And **M** brought back the words of	**Ex 19:8**	4872
The LORD said to **M**,	**Ex 19:9**	4872
Then **M** told the words of the	**Ex 19:9**	4872
The LORD also said to **M**,	**Ex 19:10**	4872
So **M** went down from the mountain	**Ex 19:14**	4872
And **M** brought the people out of	**Ex 19:17**	4872
M spoke and God answered him with	**Ex 19:19**	4872
M to the top of the mountain,	**Ex 19:20**	4872
of the mountain, and **M** went up.	**Ex 19:20**	4872
Then the LORD spoke to **M**,	**Ex 19:21**	4872
M said to the LORD,	**Ex 19:23**	4872
So **M** went down to the people and	**Ex 19:25**	4872
Then they said to **M**,	**Ex 20:19**	4872
M said to the people,	**Ex 20:20**	4872
while **M** approached the thick cloud	**Ex 20:21**	4872
Then the LORD said to **M**,	**Ex 20:22**	4872
Then He said to **M**,	**Ex 24:1**	4872
"**M** alone, however, shall come	**Ex 24:2**	4872
Then **M** came and recounted to the	**Ex 24:3**	4872
M wrote down all the words of	**Ex 24:4**	4872
M took half of the blood and	**Ex 24:6**	4872
So **M** took the blood and sprinkled	**Ex 24:8**	4872
Then **M** went up with Aaron, Nadab	**Ex 24:9**	4872
Now the LORD said to **M**,	**Ex 24:12**	4872
M arose with Joshua his servant,	**Ex 24:13**	4872
and **M** went up to the mountain of	**Ex 24:13**	4872
Then **M** went up to the mountain,	**Ex 24:15**	4872
to **M** from the midst of the cloud.	**Ex 24:16**	4872
M entered the midst of the	**Ex 24:18**	4872
and **M** was on the mountain forty	**Ex 24:18**	4872
Then the LORD spoke to **M**,	**Ex 25:1**	4872
The LORD also spoke to **M**,	**Ex 30:11**	4872
The LORD spoke to **M**,	**Ex 30:17**	4872
Moreover, the LORD spoke to **M**,	**Ex 30:22**	4872
Then the LORD said to **M**,	**Ex 30:34**	4872
Now the LORD spoke to **M**,	**Ex 31:1**	4872
The LORD spoke to **M**,	**Ex 31:12**	4872
He gave **M** the two tablets of the	**Ex 31:18**	4872
Now when the people saw that **M**	**Ex 32:1**	4872
as for this **M**, the man who brought	**Ex 32:1**	4872
Then the LORD spoke to **M**,	**Ex 32:7**	4872
The LORD said to **M**,	**Ex 32:9**	4872
Then **M** entreated the LORD his God,	**Ex 32:11**	4872
Then **M** turned and went down from	**Ex 32:15**	4872
as they shouted, he said to **M**,	**Ex 32:17**	4872
as soon as **M** came near the camp,	**Ex 32:19**	
Then **M** said to Aaron,	**Ex 32:21**	4872
for this **M**, the man who brought us	**Ex 32:23**	4872
Now when **M** saw that the people	**Ex 32:25**	4872
M stood in the gate of the camp,	**Ex 32:26**	4872
sons of Levi did as **M** instructed,	**Ex 32:28**	4872
M said, "Dedicate yourselves today	**Ex 32:29**	4872
day **M** said to the people,	**Ex 32:30**	4872
Then **M** returned to the LORD, and	**Ex 32:31**	4872
The LORD said to **M**,	**Ex 32:33**	4872
Then the LORD spoke to **M**,	**Ex 33:1**	4872
For the LORD had said to **M**,	**Ex 33:5**	4872
Now **M** used to take the tent and	**Ex 33:7**	4872
whenever **M** went out to the tent,	**Ex 33:8**	4872
after **M** until he entered the tent.	**Ex 33:8**	4872
Whenever **M** entered the tent,	**Ex 33:9**	4872
and the LORD would speak with **M**.	**Ex 33:9**	4872
used to speak to **M** face to face,	**Ex 33:11**	4872
When **M** returned to the camp, his	**Ex 33:11**	
Then **M** said to the LORD,	**Ex 33:12**	4872
The LORD said to **M**,	**Ex 33:17**	4872
M said, "I pray You, show me Your	**Ex 33:18**	
Now the LORD said to **M**,	**Ex 34:1**	4872
and **M** rose up early in the morning	**Ex 34:4**	4872
M made haste to bow low toward	**Ex 34:8**	4872
Then the LORD said to **M**,	**Ex 34:27**	4872
when **M** was coming down	**Ex 34:29**	4872
that **M** did not know that the skin	**Ex 34:29**	4872
and all the sons of Israel saw **M**,	**Ex 34:30**	4872
Then **M** called to them, and Aaron	**Ex 34:31**	4872
and **M** spoke to them.	**Ex 34:31**	4872
When **M** had finished speaking with	**Ex 34:33**	4872
But whenever **M** went in before the	**Ex 34:34**	4872
of Israel would see the face of **M**,	**Ex 34:35**	4872
So **M** would replace the veil over	**Ex 34:35**	4872
Then **M** assembled all the	**Ex 35:1**	4872
M spoke to all the	**Ex 35:4**	4872
commanded through **M** to be done,	**Ex 35:29**	4872
Then **M** said to the sons of Israel,	**Ex 35:30**	4872
Then **M** called Bezalel and Oholiab	**Ex 36:2**	4872
They received from **M** all the	**Ex 36:3**	4872
and they said to **M**,	**Ex 36:5**	4872
So **M** issued a command, and a	**Ex 36:6**	4872
according to the command of **M**,	**Ex 38:21**	4872
all that the LORD had commanded **M**.	**Ex 38:22**	4872
just as the LORD had commanded **M**.	**Ex 39:1**	4872
just as the LORD had commanded **M**.	**Ex 39:5**	4872
just as the LORD had commanded **M**.	**Ex 39:7**	4872
just as the LORD had commanded **M**.	**Ex 39:21**	4872
just as the LORD had commanded **M**.	**Ex 39:26**	4872
just as the LORD had commanded **M**.	**Ex 39:29**	4872
just as the LORD had commanded **M**.	**Ex 39:31**	4872
all that the LORD had commanded **M**;	**Ex 39:32**	4872
They brought the tabernacle to **M**,	**Ex 39:33**	4872
all that the LORD had commanded **M**.	**Ex 39:42**	4872
And **M** examined all the work and	**Ex 39:43**	4872
So **M** blessed them.	**Ex 39:43**	4872
Then the LORD spoke to **M**,	**Ex 40:1**	4872
Thus **M** did; according to all that	**Ex 40:16**	4872
M erected the tabernacle and	**Ex 40:18**	4872
just as the LORD had commanded **M**.	**Ex 40:19**	4872
just as the LORD had commanded **M**.	**Ex 40:21**	4872
just as the LORD had commanded **M**.	**Ex 40:23**	4872
just as the LORD had commanded **M**.	**Ex 40:25**	4872
just as the LORD had commanded **M**.	**Ex 40:27**	4872
just as the LORD had commanded **M**.	**Ex 40:29**	4872
From it **M** and Aaron and his	**Ex 40:31**	4872
just as the LORD had commanded **M**.	**Ex 40:32**	4872
Thus **M** finished the work.	**Ex 40:33**	4872
M was not able to enter the	**Ex 40:35**	4872
Then the LORD called to **M** and	**Lv 1:1**	4872
Then the LORD spoke to **M**,	**Lv 4:1**	4872
Then the LORD spoke to **M**,	**Lv 5:14**	4872
Then the LORD spoke to **M**,	**Lv 6:1**	4872
Then the LORD spoke to **M**,	**Lv 6:8**	4872
Then the LORD spoke to **M**,	**Lv 6:19**	4872
Then the LORD spoke to **M**,	**Lv 6:24**	4872
Then the LORD spoke to **M**,	**Lv 7:22**	4872
Then the LORD spoke to **M**,	**Lv 7:28**	4872
which the LORD commanded **M** at	**Lv 7:38**	4872
Then the LORD spoke to **M**,	**Lv 8:1**	4872
So **M** did just as the LORD	**Lv 8:4**	4872
M said to the congregation,	**Lv 8:5**	4872
Then **M** had Aaron and his sons come	**Lv 8:6**	4872
just as the LORD had commanded **M**.	**Lv 8:9**	4872
M then took the anointing oil and	**Lv 8:10**	4872
Next **M** had Aaron's sons come near	**Lv 8:13**	4872
just as the LORD had commanded **M**.	**Lv 8:13**	4872
Next **M** slaughtered *it* and took the	**Lv 8:15**	4872
and **M** offered it up in smoke on	**Lv 8:16**	4872
just as the LORD had commanded **M**.	**Lv 8:17**	4872
M slaughtered *it* and sprinkled	**Lv 8:19**	4872
M offered up the head and the	**Lv 8:20**	4872
M offered up the whole ram in	**Lv 8:21**	4872
just as the LORD had commanded **M**.	**Lv 8:21**	4872
M slaughtered *it* and took some	**Lv 8:23**	4872
and **M** put some of the blood on the	**Lv 8:24**	4872
M then sprinkled *the rest of* the	**Lv 8:24**	4872
Then **M** took them from their hands	**Lv 8:28**	4872
M also took the breast and	**Lv 8:29**	4872
just as the LORD had commanded **M**.	**Lv 8:29**	4872
So **M** took some of the anointing	**Lv 8:30**	4872
M said to Aaron and to his sons,	**Lv 8:31**	4872
the LORD had commanded through **M**.	**Lv 8:36**	4872
M called Aaron and his sons	**Lv 9:1**	4872
So they took what **M** had commanded	**Lv 9:5**	4872
M said, "This is the thing which	**Lv 9:6**	4872
M then said to Aaron,	**Lv 9:7**	4872
just as the LORD had commanded **M**.	**Lv 9:10**	4872
the LORD, just as **M** had commanded.	**Lv 9:21**	4872
M and Aaron went into the tent	**Lv 9:23**	4872
Then **M** said to Aaron,	**Lv 10:3**	4872
M called also to Mishael and	**Lv 10:4**	4872
of the camp, as **M** had said.	**Lv 10:5**	4872
Then **M** said to Aaron and to his	**Lv 10:6**	4872
did according to the word of **M**.	**Lv 10:7**	4872
has spoken to them through **M**."	**Lv 10:11**	4872
Then **M** spoke to Aaron, and to his	**Lv 10:12**	4872
But **M** searched carefully for the	**Lv 10:16**	4872
But Aaron spoke to **M**,	**Lv 10:19**	4872
When **M** heard *that,* it seemed	**Lv 10:20**	4872
spoke again to **M** and to Aaron,	**Lv 11:1**	4872
Then the LORD spoke to **M**,	**Lv 12:1**	4872
the LORD spoke to **M** and to Aaron,	**Lv 13:1**	4872
Then the LORD spoke to **M**,	**Lv 14:1**	4872
further spoke to **M** and to Aaron,	**Lv 14:33**	4872
LORD also spoke to **M** and to Aaron,	**Lv 15:1**	4872
Now the LORD spoke to **M** after the	**Lv 16:1**	4872
The LORD said to **M**:	**Lv 16:2**	4872
just as the LORD had commanded **M**,	**Lv 16:34**	4872
Then the LORD spoke to **M**,	**Lv 17:1**	4872
Then the LORD spoke to **M**,	**Lv 18:1**	4872
Then the LORD spoke to **M**,	**Lv 19:1**	4872
Then the LORD spoke to **M**,	**Lv 20:1**	4872
Then the LORD said to **M**,	**Lv 21:1**	4872
Then the LORD spoke to **M**,	**Lv 21:16**	4872
So **M** spoke to Aaron and to his	**Lv 21:24**	4872
Then the LORD spoke to **M**,	**Lv 22:1**	4872
Then the LORD spoke to **M**,	**Lv 22:17**	4872
Then the LORD spoke to **M**,	**Lv 22:26**	4872
The LORD spoke again to **M**,	**Lv 23:1**	4872
Then the LORD spoke to **M**,	**Lv 23:9**	4872
Again the LORD spoke to **M**,	**Lv 23:23**	4872
The LORD spoke to **M**,	**Lv 23:26**	4872
Again the LORD spoke to **M**,	**Lv 23:33**	4872
So **M** declared to the sons of	**Lv 23:44**	4872
Then the LORD spoke to **M**,	**Lv 24:1**	4872
So they brought him to **M**.	**Lv 24:11**	4872
Then the LORD spoke to **M**,	**Lv 24:13**	4872
M spoke to the sons of Israel,	**Lv 24:23**	4872
just as the LORD had commanded **M**.	**Lv 24:23**	4872
then spoke to **M** at Mount Sinai,	**Lv 25:1**	4872
Israel through **M** at Mount Sinai.	**Lv 26:46**	4872
Again, the LORD spoke to **M**,	**Lv 27:1**	4872
commanded **M** for the sons of Israel	**Lv 27:34**	4872
to **M** in the wilderness of Sinai,	**Nu 1:1**	4872
So **M** and Aaron took these men who	**Nu 1:17**	4872
just as the LORD had commanded **M**.	**Nu 1:19**	4872
whom **M** and Aaron numbered,	**Nu 1:44**	4872
For the LORD had spoken to **M**,	**Nu 1:48**	4872
which the LORD had commanded **M**,	**Nu 1:54**	4872
the LORD spoke to **M** and to Aaron,	**Nu 2:1**	4872
just as the LORD had commanded **M**.	**Nu 2:33**	4872
to all that the LORD commanded **M**,	**Nu 2:34**	4872
the generations of Aaron and **M**	**Nu 3:1**	4872
LORD spoke with **M** on Mount Sinai.	**Nu 3:1**	4872
Then the LORD spoke to **M**,	**Nu 3:5**	4872
Again the LORD spoke to **M**,	**Nu 3:11**	4872
to **M** in the wilderness of Sinai,	**Nu 3:14**	4872
So **M** numbered them according to	**Nu 3:16**	4872
are **M** and Aaron and his sons,	**Nu 3:38**	4872
whom **M** and Aaron numbered at the	**Nu 3:39**	4872
Then the LORD said to **M**,	**Nu 3:40**	4872
So **M** numbered all the firstborn	**Nu 3:42**	4872
Then the LORD spoke to **M**,	**Nu 3:44**	4872
So **M** took the ransom money from	**Nu 3:49**	4872
Then **M** gave the ransom money to	**Nu 3:51**	4872
just as the LORD had commanded **M**.	**Nu 3:51**	4872
the LORD spoke to **M** and to Aaron,	**Nu 4:1**	4872
the LORD spoke to **M** and to Aaron,	**Nu 4:17**	4872
Then the LORD spoke to **M**,	**Nu 4:21**	4872
So **M** and Aaron and the leaders of	**Nu 4:34**	4872
whom **M** and Aaron numbered	**Nu 4:37**	4872
commandment of the LORD through **M**.	**Nu 4:37**	4872
whom **M** and Aaron numbered	**Nu 4:41**	4872
whom **M** and Aaron numbered	**Nu 4:45**	4872
commandment of the LORD through **M**.	**Nu 4:45**	4872
whom **M** and Aaron and the leaders	**Nu 4:46**	4872
commandment of the LORD through **M**,	**Nu 4:49**	4872
just as the LORD had commanded **M**.	**Nu 4:49**	4872
Then the LORD spoke to **M**,	**Nu 5:1**	4872
just as the LORD had spoken to **M**,	**Nu 5:4**	4872
Then the LORD spoke to **M**,	**Nu 5:5**	4872
Then the LORD spoke to **M**,	**Nu 5:11**	4872
Again the LORD spoke to **M**,	**Nu 6:1**	4872
Then the LORD spoke to **M**,	**Nu 6:22**	4872
on the day that **M** had finished	**Nu 7:1**	4872
Then the LORD spoke to **M**,	**Nu 7:4**	4872
So **M** took the carts and the oxen and	**Nu 7:6**	4872
Then the LORD said to **M**,	**Nu 7:11**	4872
Now when **M** went into the tent of	**Nu 7:89**	4872
Then the LORD spoke to **M**,	**Nu 8:1**	4872
just as the LORD had commanded **M**.	**Nu 8:3**	4872
which the LORD had shown **M**,	**Nu 8:4**	4872
Again the LORD spoke to **M**,	**Nu 8:5**	4872
Thus did **M** and Aaron and all the	**Nu 8:20**	4872
that the LORD had commanded **M**	**Nu 8:20**	4872
just as the LORD had commanded **M**	**Nu 8:22**	4872
Now the LORD spoke to **M**,	**Nu 8:23**	4872
to **M** in the wilderness of Sinai,	**Nu 9:1**	4872
So **M** told the sons of Israel to	**Nu 9:4**	4872
all that the LORD had commanded **M**,	**Nu 9:5**	4872
before **M** and Aaron on that day.	**Nu 9:6**	4872
M therefore said to them,	**Nu 9:8**	4872
Then the LORD spoke to **M**,	**Nu 9:9**	4872
the command of the LORD through **M**.	**Nu 9:23**	4872
The LORD spoke further to **M**,	**Nu 10:1**	4872
commandment of the LORD through **M**.	**Nu 10:13**	4872
Then **M** said to Hobab the son of	**Nu 10:29**	4872
when the ark set out that **M** said,	**Nu 10:35**	4872
people therefore cried out to **M**,	**Nu 11:2**	4872
Moses, and **M** prayed to the LORD and	**Nu 11:2**	4872
Now **M** heard the people weeping	**Nu 11:10**	4872
greatly, and **M** was displeased.	**Nu 11:10**	4872

So **M** said to the LORD,	**Nu 11:11**	4872
The LORD therefore said to **M**,	**Nu 11:16**	4872
But **M** said, "The people, among	**Nu 11:21**	4872
The LORD said to **M**,	**Nu 11:23**	4872
So **M** went out and told the people	**Nu 11:24**	4872
young man ran and told **M** and said,	**Nu 11:27**	4872
the attendant of **M** from his youth,	**Nu 11:28**	4872
"**M**, my lord, restrain them."	**Nu 11:28**	4872
But **M** said to him,	**Nu 11:29**	4872
Then **M** returned to the camp, *both*	**Nu 11:30**	4872
Miriam and Aaron spoke against **M**	**Nu 12:1**	4872
LORD indeed spoken only through **M**?	**Nu 12:2**	4872
(Now the man **M** was very humble,	**Nu 12:3**	4872
said to **M** and Aaron and to Miriam,	**Nu 12:4**	4872
"Not so, with My servant **M**,	**Nu 12:7**	4872
against My servant, against **M**?"	**Nu 12:8**	4872
Then Aaron said to **M**,	**Nu 12:11**	4872
M cried out to the LORD,	**Nu 12:13**	4872
But the LORD said to **M**,	**Nu 12:14**	4872
Then the LORD spoke to **M** saying,	**Nu 13:1**	4872
So **M** sent them from the wilderness	**Nu 13:3**	4872
whom **M** sent to spy out the land;	**Nu 13:16**	4872
M called Hoshea the son of Nun,	**Nu 13:16**	4872
When **M** sent them to spy out the	**Nu 13:17**	4872
they proceeded to come to **M** and	**Nu 13:26**	4872
Caleb quieted the people before **M** and	**Nu 13:30**	4872
grumbled against **M** and Aaron;	**Nu 14:2**	4872
Then **M** and Aaron fell on their	**Nu 14:5**	4872
The LORD said to **M**,	**Nu 14:11**	4872
But **M** said to the LORD,	**Nu 14:13**	4872
The LORD spoke to **M** and Aaron,	**Nu 14:26**	4872
As for the men whom **M** sent to spy	**Nu 14:36**	4872
When **M** spoke these words to	**Nu 14:39**	4872
But **M** said, "Why then are you	**Nu 14:41**	4872
of the LORD nor **M** left the camp.	**Nu 14:44**	4872
Now the LORD spoke to **M**,	**Nu 15:1**	4872
Then the LORD spoke to **M**,	**Nu 15:17**	4872
which the LORD has spoken to **M**,	**Nu 15:22**	4872
LORD has commanded you through **M**,	**Nu 15:23**	4872
wood brought him to **M** and Aaron and	**Nu 15:33**	4872
Then the LORD said to **M**,	**Nu 15:35**	4872
just as the LORD had commanded **M**.	**Nu 15:36**	4872
The LORD also spoke to **M**,	**Nu 15:37**	4872
and they rose up before **M**,	**Nu 16:2**	4872
together against **M** and Aaron,	**Nu 16:3**	4872
When **M** heard *this*, he fell on his	**Nu 16:4**	4872
Then **M** said to Korah,	**Nu 16:8**	4872
Then **M** sent a summons to Dathan	**Nu 16:12**	4872
Then **M** became very angry and said	**Nu 16:15**	4872
M said to Korah,	**Nu 16:16**	4872
tent of meeting, with **M** and Aaron.	**Nu 16:18**	4872
the LORD spoke to **M** and Aaron,	**Nu 16:20**	4872
Then the LORD spoke to **M**,	**Nu 16:23**	4872
Then **M** arose and went to Dathan	**Nu 16:25**	4872
M said, "By this you shall know	**Nu 16:28**	4872
Then the LORD spoke to **M**,	**Nu 16:36**	4872
LORD had spoken to him through **M**.	**Nu 16:40**	4872
grumbled against **M** and Aaron,	**Nu 16:41**	4872
had assembled against **M** and Aaron,	**Nu 16:42**	4872
Then **M** and Aaron came to the front	**Nu 16:43**	4872
and the LORD spoke to **M**,	**Nu 16:44**	4872
M said to Aaron,	**Nu 16:46**	4872
Aaron took *it* as **M** had spoken,	**Nu 16:47**	4872
Then Aaron returned to **M** at the	**Nu 16:50**	4872
Then the LORD spoke to **M**,	**Nu 17:1**	4872
M therefore spoke to the sons of	**Nu 17:6**	4872
So **M** deposited the rods before the	**Nu 17:7**	4872
M went into the tent of the testimony	**Nu 17:8**	4872
M then brought out all the rods	**Nu 17:9**	4872
But the LORD said to **M**,	**Nu 17:10**	4872
Thus **M** did; just as the LORD had	**Nu 17:11**	4872
the sons of Israel spoke to **M**,	**Nu 17:12**	4872
Then the LORD spoke to **M**,	**Nu 18:25**	4872
the LORD spoke to **M** and Aaron,	**Nu 19:1**	4872
themselves against **M** and Aaron.	**Nu 20:2**	4872
thus contended with **M** and spoke,	**Nu 20:3**	4872
Then **M** and Aaron came in from the	**Nu 20:6**	4872
and the LORD spoke to **M**,	**Nu 20:7**	4872
So **M** took the rod from before the	**Nu 20:9**	4872
and **M** and Aaron gathered the	**Nu 20:10**	4872
Then **M** lifted up his hand and	**Nu 20:11**	4872
But the LORD said to **M** and Aaron,	**Nu 20:12**	4872
From Kadesh **M** then sent messengers	**Nu 20:14**	4872
Then the LORD spoke to **M** and Aaron	**Nu 20:23**	4872
So **M** did just as the LORD had	**Nu 20:27**	4872
After **M** had stripped Aaron of	**Nu 20:28**	4872
Then **M** and Eleazar came down from	**Nu 20:28**	4872
people spoke against God and **M**,	**Nu 21:5**	4872
So the people came to **M** and said,	**Nu 21:7**	4872
And **M** interceded for the people.	**Nu 21:7**	4872
Then the LORD said to **M**,	**Nu 21:8**	4872
And **M** made a bronze serpent and	**Nu 21:9**	4872
the well where the LORD said to **M**,	**Nu 21:16**	4872
M sent to spy out Jazer, and	**Nu 21:32**	4872
But the LORD said to **M**,	**Nu 21:34**	4872
The LORD said to **M**,	**Nu 25:4**	4872
So **M** said to the judges of Israel,	**Nu 25:5**	4872
in the sight of **M** and in the sight	**Nu 25:6**	4872
Then the LORD spoke to **M**,	**Nu 25:10**	4872
Then the LORD spoke to **M**,	**Nu 25:16**	4872
that the LORD spoke to **M** and to	**Nu 26:1**	4872
So **M** and Eleazar the priest spoke	**Nu 26:3**	4872
as the LORD has commanded **M**."	**Nu 26:4**	4872
who contended against **M** and	**Nu 26:9**	4872
Then the LORD spoke to **M**,	**Nu 26:52**	4872
and **M** and their sister Miriam.	**Nu 26:59**	4872
by **M** and Eleazar the priest,	**Nu 26:63**	4872
by **M** and Aaron the priest,	**Nu 26:64**	4872
They stood before **M** and before	**Nu 27:2**	4872
So **M** brought their case before	**Nu 27:5**	4872
Then the LORD spoke to **M**,	**Nu 27:6**	4872
just as the LORD commanded **M**.' "	**Nu 27:11**	4872
Then the LORD said to **M**,	**Nu 27:12**	4872
Then **M** spoke to the LORD, saying,	**Nu 27:15**	4872
So the LORD said to **M**,	**Nu 27:18**	4872
M did just as the LORD	**Nu 27:22**	4872
as the LORD had spoken through **M**.	**Nu 27:23**	4872
Then the LORD spoke to **M**,	**Nu 28:1**	4872
M spoke to the sons of Israel	**Nu 29:40**	4872
all that the LORD had commanded **M**.	**Nu 29:40**	4872
Then **M** spoke to the heads of the	**Nu 30:1**	4872
which the LORD commanded **M**,	**Nu 30:16**	4872
Then the LORD spoke to **M**,	**Nu 31:1**	4872
M spoke to the people, saying,	**Nu 31:3**	4872
M sent them, a thousand from	**Nu 31:6**	4872
just as the LORD had commanded **M**,	**Nu 31:7**	4872
and the prey and the spoil to **M**,	**Nu 31:12**	4872
M and Eleazar the priest and	**Nu 31:13**	4872
M was angry with the officers	**Nu 31:14**	4872
And **M** said to them,	**Nu 31:15**	4872
which the LORD has commanded **M**:	**Nu 31:21**	4872
Then the LORD spoke to **M**,	**Nu 31:25**	4872
M and Eleazar the priest did	**Nu 31:31**	4872
just as the LORD had commanded **M**.	**Nu 31:31**	4872
M gave the levy *which was* the	**Nu 31:41**	4872
just as the LORD had commanded **M**.	**Nu 31:41**	4872
which **M** separated from the men who	**Nu 31:42**	4872
M took one drawn out of every	**Nu 31:47**	4872
just as the LORD had commanded **M**.	**Nu 31:47**	4872
of hundreds, approached **M**,	**Nu 31:48**	4872
and they said to **M**,	**Nu 31:49**	4872
M and Eleazar the priest took	**Nu 31:51**	4872
So **M** and Eleazar the priest took	**Nu 31:54**	4872
sons of Reuben came and spoke to **M**	**Nu 32:2**	4872
But **M** said to the sons of Gad and	**Nu 32:6**	4872
So **M** said to them,	**Nu 32:20**	4872
and the sons of Reuben spoke to **M**,	**Nu 32:25**	4872
So **M** gave command concerning them	**Nu 32:28**	4872
M said to them,	**Nu 32:29**	4872
So **M** gave to them, to the sons of	**Nu 32:33**	4872
So **M** gave Gilead to Machir the son	**Nu 32:40**	4872
the leadership of **M** and Aaron.	**Nu 33:1**	4872
M recorded their starting	**Nu 33:2**	4872
Then the LORD spoke to **M** in the	**Nu 33:50**	4872
Then the LORD spoke to **M**,	**Nu 34:1**	4872
So **M** commanded the sons of Israel,	**Nu 34:13**	4872
Then the LORD spoke to **M**,	**Nu 34:16**	4872
Now the LORD spoke to **M** in the	**Nu 35:1**	4872
Then the LORD spoke to **M**,	**Nu 35:9**	4872
before **M** and before the leaders,	**Nu 36:1**	4872
Then **M** commanded the sons of	**Nu 36:5**	4872
Just as the LORD had commanded **M**,	**Nu 36:10**	4872
to the sons of Israel through **M**	**Nu 36:13**	4872
These are the words which **M** spoke	**Dt 1:1**	4872
M spoke to the children of	**Dt 1:3**	4872
M undertook to expound this law,	**Dt 1:5**	4872
Then **M** set apart three cities	**Dt 4:41**	4872
M set before the sons of Israel;	**Dt 4:44**	4872
M spoke to the sons of Israel,	**Dt 4:45**	4872
whom **M** and the sons of Israel	**Dt 4:46**	4872
Then **M** summoned all Israel and	**Dt 5:1**	4872
Then **M** and the elders of Israel	**Dt 27:1**	4872
Then **M** and the Levitical priests	**Dt 27:9**	4872
M also charged the people on that	**Dt 27:11**	4872
LORD commanded **M** to make with	**Dt 29:1**	4872
And **M** summoned all Israel and said	**Dt 29:2**	4872
So **M** went and spoke these words to	**Dt 31:1**	4872
Then **M** called to Joshua and said	**Dt 31:7**	4872
So **M** wrote this law and gave it to	**Dt 31:9**	4872
Then **M** commanded them, saying,	**Dt 31:10**	4872
Then the LORD said to **M**,	**Dt 31:14**	4872
So **M** and Joshua went and presented	**Dt 31:14**	4872
The LORD said to **M**,	**Dt 31:16**	4872
So **M** wrote this song the same day,	**Dt 31:22**	4872
when **M** finished writing the words	**Dt 31:24**	4872
that **M** commanded the Levites who	**Dt 31:25**	4872
Then **M** spoke in the hearing of all	**Dt 31:30**	4872
Then **M** came and spoke all the	**Dt 32:44**	4872
When **M** had finished speaking all	**Dt 32:45**	4872
spoke to **M** that very same day,	**Dt 32:48**	4872
M the man of God blessed the sons	**Dt 33:1**	4872
"**M** charged us with a law, A	**Dt 33:4**	4872
Now **M** went up from the plains of	**Dt 34:1**	4872
So **M** the servant of the LORD died	**Dt 34:5**	4872
Although **M** was one hundred and	**Dt 34:7**	4872
So the sons of Israel wept for **M**	**Dt 34:8**	4872
and mourning for **M** came to an end.	**Dt 34:8**	4872
for **M** had laid his hands on him;	**Dt 34:9**	4872
did as the LORD had commanded **M**.	**Dt 34:9**	4872
has risen in Israel like **M**,	**Dt 34:10**	4872
the great terror which **M** performed	**Dt 34:12**	4872
after the death of **M** the servant of	**Jos 1:1**	4872
"**M** My servant is dead;	**Jos 1:2**	4872
it to you, just as I spoke to **M**.	**Jos 1:3**	4872
Just as I have been with **M**,	**Jos 1:5**	4872
which **M** My servant commanded you;	**Jos 1:7**	4872
"Remember the word which **M** the	**Jos 1:13**	4872
M gave you beyond the Jordan,	**Jos 1:14**	4872
and possess that which **M** the	**Jos 1:15**	4872
"Just as we obeyed **M** in all things,	**Jos 1:17**	4872
God be with you as He was with **M**.	**Jos 1:17**	4872
that just as I have been with **M**,	**Jos 3:7**	4872
all that **M** had commanded Joshua.	**Jos 4:10**	4872
just as **M** had spoken to them;	**Jos 4:12**	4872
M all the days of his life.	**Jos 4:14**	4872
just as **M** the servant of the LORD	**Jos 8:31**	4872
in the book of the law of **M**,	**Jos 8:31**	4872
the stones a copy of the law of **M**,	**Jos 8:32**	4872
just as **M** the servant of the LORD	**Jos 8:33**	4872
word of all that **M** had commanded	**Jos 8:35**	4872
M to give you all the land,	**Jos 9:24**	4872
just as **M** the servant of the LORD	**Jos 11:12**	4872
LORD had commanded **M** his servant,	**Jos 11:15**	4872
servant, so **M** commanded Joshua,	**Jos 11:15**	4872
all that the LORD had commanded **M**.	**Jos 11:15**	4872
just as the LORD had commanded **M**.	**Jos 11:20**	4872
all that the LORD had spoken to **M**,	**Jos 11:23**	4872
M the servant of the LORD and the	**Jos 12:6**	4872
and **M** the servant of the LORD gave	**Jos 12:6**	4872
their inheritance which **M** gave them	**Jos 13:8**	4872
just as **M** the servant of the LORD	**Jos 13:8**	4872
for **M** struck them and dispossessed	**Jos 13:12**	4872
So **M** gave *an inheritance* to the	**Jos 13:15**	4872
whom **M** struck with the chiefs of	**Jos 13:21**	4872
M also gave *an inheritance* to the	**Jos 13:24**	4872
M also gave *an inheritance* to the	**Jos 13:29**	4872
These are *the territories* which **M**	**Jos 13:32**	4872
M did not give an inheritance;	**Jos 13:33**	4872
as the LORD commanded through **M**,	**Jos 14:2**	4872
For **M** had given the inheritance of	**Jos 14:3**	4872
just as the LORD had commanded **M**,	**Jos 14:5**	4872
word which the LORD spoke to **M**	**Jos 14:6**	4872
"I was forty years old when **M** the	**Jos 14:7**	4872
"So **M** swore on that day, saying,	**Jos 14:9**	4872
the LORD spoke this word to **M**,	**Jos 14:10**	4872
as I was in the day **M** sent me;	**Jos 14:11**	4872
"The LORD commanded **M** to give us	**Jos 17:4**	4872
which **M** the servant of the LORD	**Jos 18:7**	4872
of which I spoke to you through **M**,	**Jos 20:2**	4872
M to give us cities to live in,	**Jos 21:2**	4872
the LORD had commanded through **M**.	**Jos 21:8**	4872
"You have kept all that **M** the	**Jos 22:2**	4872
which **M** the servant of the LORD	**Jos 22:4**	4872
law which **M** the servant of the LORD	**Jos 22:5**	4872
M had given *a possession* in Bashan,	**Jos 22:7**	4872
the command of the LORD through **M**.	**Jos 22:9**	4872
in the book of the law of **M**,	**Jos 23:6**	4872
'Then I sent **M** and Aaron, and I	**Jos 24:5**	4872
to Caleb, as **M** had promised;	**Jg 1:20**	4872
commanded their fathers through **M**.	**Jg 3:4**	4872
of Hobab the father-in-law of **M**,	**Jg 4:11**	4872
"It is the LORD who appointed **M**	**1Sa 12:6**	4872
then the LORD sent **M** and Aaron who	**1Sa 12:8**	4872
what is written in the Law of **M**,	**1Ki 2:3**	4872
stone which **M** put there at Horeb,	**1Ki 8:9**	4872
spoke through **M** Your servant,	**1Ki 8:53**	4872
He promised through **M** His servant.	**1Ki 8:56**	4872
in the book of the Law of **M**,	**2Ki 14:6**	4872
bronze serpent that **M** had made,	**2Ki 18:4**	4872
which the LORD had commanded **M**.	**2Ki 18:6**	4872
even all that **M** the servant of the	**2Ki 18:12**	4872
My servant **M** commanded them."	**2Ki 21:8**	4872
according to all the law of **M**;	**2Ki 23:25**	4872
children of Amram *were* Aaron, **M** and	**1Ch 6:3**	4872
all that **M** the servant of God had	**1Ch 6:49**	4872
with the poles thereon, as **M** had	**1Ch 15:15**	4872
M had made in the wilderness,	**1Ch 21:29**	4872
commanded **M** concerning Israel.	**1Ch 22:13**	4872
sons of Amram were Aaron and **M**.	**1Ch 23:13**	4872
But *as for* **M** the man of God, his	**1Ch 23:14**	4872
The sons of **M** *were* Gershom and	**1Ch 23:15**	4872
the son of Gershom, the son of **M**,	**1Ch 26:24**	4872
which **M** the servant of the LORD	**2Ch 1:3**	4872
which **M** put *there* at Horeb,	**2Ch 5:10**	4872
according to the commandment of **M**,	**2Ch 8:13**	4872
as it is written in the law of **M**	**2Ch 23:18**	4872
the levy *fixed by* **M** the servant of the	**2Ch 24:6**	4872
levy *fixed by* **M** the servant of God	**2Ch 24:9**	4872
in the law in the book of **M**,	**2Ch 25:4**	4872
to the law of **M** the man of God;	**2Ch 30:16**	4872
the ordinances *given* through **M**."	**2Ch 33:8**	4872
of the law of the LORD *given* by **M**.	**2Ch 34:14**	4872
to the word of the LORD by **M**."	**2Ch 35:6**	4872
as it is written in the book of **M**.	**2Ch 35:12**	4872
as it is written in the law of **M**,	**Ezr 3:2**	4872
as it is written in the book of **M**.	**Ezr 6:18**	4873
a scribe skilled in the law of **M**,	**Ezr 7:6**	4872
You commanded Your servant **M**.	**Ne 1:7**	4872
You commanded Your servant **M**,	**Ne 1:8**	4872
to bring the book of the law of **M**,	**Ne 8:1**	4872
LORD had commanded through **M**	**Ne 8:14**	4872
and law, Through Your servant **M**.	**Ne 9:14**	4872
law, which was given through **M**,	**Ne 10:29**	4872
read aloud from the book of **M** in	**Ne 13:1**	4872
flock By the hand of **M** and Aaron.	**Ps 77:20**	4872
M and Aaron were among His	**Ps 99:6**	4872
He made known His ways to **M**,	**Ps 103:7**	4872
He sent **M** His servant, *And* Aaron	**Ps 105:26**	4872
became envious of **M** in the camp,	**Ps 106:16**	4872
Had not **M** His chosen one stood in	**Ps 106:23**	4872
went hard with **M** on their account;	**Ps 106:32**	4872
remembered the days of old, of **M**.	**Is 63:11**	4872
arm to go at the right hand of **M**,	**Is 63:12**	4872
"Even though **M** and Samuel were to	**Jer 15:1**	4872
the law of **M** the servant of God,	**Da 9:11**	4872
"As it is written in the law of **M**,	**Da 9:13**	4872
slavery, And I sent before you **M**,	**Mi 6:4**	4872
"Remember the law of **M** My servant,	**Mal 4:4**	4872
the offering that **M** commanded,	**Mt 8:4**	*3475*
M and Elijah appeared to them,	**Mt 17:3**	*3475*
here, one for You, and one for **M**,	**Mt 17:4**	*3475*
"Why then did **M** command to GIVE	**Mt 19:7**	*3475*
M permitted you to divorce your	**Mt 19:8**	*3475*
"Teacher, **M** said, 'IF A MAN DIES HAVING	**Mt 22:24**	*3475*
themselves in the chair of **M**;	**Mt 23:2**	*3475*
your cleansing what **M** commanded,	**Mk 1:44**	*3475*
"For **M** said, 'HONOR YOUR FATHER	**Mk 7:10**	*3475*

appeared to them along with **M**;	**Mk 9:4**	*3475*
one for You, and one for **M**,	**Mk 9:5**	*3475*
"What did **M** command you?"	**Mk 10:3**	*3475*
"**M** permitted *a man* TO WRITE A	**Mk 10:4**	*3475*
M wrote for us that IF A MAN'S	**Mk 12:19**	*3475*
have you not read in the book of **M**	**Mk 12:26**	*3475*
to the law of **M** were completed,	**Lk 2:22**	*3475*
cleansing, just as **M** commanded,	**Lk 5:14**	*3475*
and they were **M** and Elijah,	**Lk 9:30**	*3475*
one for You, and one for **M**,	**Lk 9:33**	*3475*
'They have **M** and the Prophets;	**Lk 16:29**	*3475*
not listen to **M** and the Prophets,	**Lk 16:31**	*3475*
M wrote for us that IF A MAN'S	**Lk 20:28**	*3475*
dead are raised, even **M** showed,	**Lk 20:37**	*3475*
with **M** and with all the prophets,	**Lk 24:27**	*3475*
written about Me in the Law of **M**	**Lk 24:44**	*3475*
For the Law was given through **M**;	**Jn 1:17**	*3475*
"We have found Him of whom **M** in	**Jn 1:45**	*3475*
"As **M** lifted up the serpent	**Jn 3:14**	*3475*
the one who accuses you is **M**,	**Jn 5:45**	*3475*
"For if you believed **M**,	**Jn 5:46**	*3475*
it is not **M** who has given you the	**Jn 6:32**	*3475*
"Did not **M** give you the Law, and	**Jn 7:19**	*3475*
M has given you circumcision	**Jn 7:22**	*3475*
(not because it is from **M**,	**Jn 7:22**	*3475*
the Law of **M** will not be broken,	**Jn 7:23**	*3475*
"Now in the Law **M** commanded us to	**Jn 8:5**	*3475*
But we are disciples of **M**.	**Jn 9:28**	*3475*
"We know that God has spoken to **M**,	**Jn 9:29**	*3475*
"**M** said, 'THE LORD GOD WILL	**Ac 3:22**	*3475*
words against **M** and *against* God."	**Ac 6:11**	*3475*
which **M** handed down to us."	**Ac 6:14**	*3475*
was at this time that **M** was born;	**Ac 7:20**	*3475*
"**M** was educated in all the	**Ac 7:22**	*3475*
"At this remark, **M** FLED	**Ac 7:29**	*3475*
"When **M** saw it, he marveled	**Ac 7:31**	*3475*
M shook with fear and would	**Ac 7:32**	*3475*
"This **M** whom they disowned,	**Ac 7:35**	*3475*
"This is the **M** who said to the	**Ac 7:37**	*3475*
FOR THIS **M** WHO LED US OUT OF THE	**Ac 7:40**	*3475*
just as He who spoke to **M** directed	**Ac 7:44**	*3475*
not be freed through the Law of **M**.	**Ac 13:39**	*3475*
according to the custom of **M**,	**Ac 15:1**	*3475*
them to observe the Law of **M**."	**Ac 15:5**	*3475*
"For **M** from ancient generations	**Ac 15:21**	*3475*
among the Gentiles to forsake **M**,	**Ac 21:21**	*3475*
what the Prophets and **M** said was	**Ac 26:22**	*3475*
Law of **M** and from the Prophets,	**Ac 28:23**	*3475*
death reigned from Adam until **M**,	**Ro 5:14**	*3475*
For He says to **M**,	**Ro 9:15**	*3475*
For **M** writes that the man who	**Ro 10:5**	*3475*
First **M** says,	**Ro 10:19**	*3475*
For it is written in the Law of **M**,	**1Co 9:9**	*3475*
M in the cloud and in the sea;	**1Co 10:2**	*3475*
not look intently at the face of **M**	**2Co 3:7**	*3475*
and *are* not like **M**, *who* used to put	**2Co 3:13**	*3475*
to this day whenever **M** is read,	**2Co 3:15**	*3475*
as Jannes and Jambres opposed **M**,	**2Tm 3:8**	*3475*
as **M** also was in all His house.	**Heb 3:2**	*3475*
worthy of more glory than **M**,	**Heb 3:3**	*3475*
Now **M** was faithful in all His	**Heb 3:5**	*3475*
who came out of Egypt *led* by **M**?	**Heb 3:16**	*3475*
M spoke nothing concerning priests.	**Heb 7:14**	*3475*
just as **M** was warned *by God* when	**Heb 8:5**	*3475*
commandment had been spoken by **M**	**Heb 9:19**	*3475*
who has set aside the Law of **M** dies	**Heb 10:28**	*3475*
By faith **M**, when he was born, was	**Heb 11:23**	*3475*
By faith **M**, when he had grown up,	**Heb 11:24**	*3475*
M said, "I AM FULL OF FEAR and	**Heb 12:21**	*3475*
and argued about the body of **M**,	**Jude 1:9**	*3475*
And they sang the song of **M**,	**Rv 15:3**	*3475*

MOSES'

foreskin and threw it at **M** feet,	**Ex 4:25**	
But **M** hands were heavy. Then they	**Ex 17:12**	
of Midian, **M** father-in-law,	**Ex 18:1**	4872
Jethro, **M** father-in-law, took	**Ex 18:2**	4872
took **M** wife Zipporah, after he had	**Ex 18:2**	4872
Then Jethro, **M** father-in-law,	**Ex 18:5**	4872
Then Jethro, **M** father-in-law,	**Ex 18:12**	4872
to eat a meal with **M** father-in-law	**Ex 18:12**	4872
Now when **M** father-in-law saw all	**Ex 18:14**	4872
M father-in-law said to him,	**Ex 18:17**	4872
and **M** anger burned, and he threw	**Ex 32:19**	4872
of the testimony *were* in **M** hand	**Ex 34:29**	4872
that the skin of **M** face shone. So	**Ex 34:35**	4872
of Israel departed from **M** presence.	**Ex 35:20**	4872
it was **M** portion of the ram of	**Lv 8:29**	4872
M father-in-law, "We are setting	**Nu 10:29**	4872
son of Nun, **M** servant,	**Jos 1:1**	4872
of the Kenite, **M** father-in-law,	**Jg 1:16**	4872

MOST

now he was a priest of God **M** High.	**Gn 14:18**	5945b
"Blessed be Abram of God **M** High,	**Gn 14:19**	5945b
And blessed be God **M** High,	**Gn 14:20**	5945b
have sworn to the LORD God **M** High,	**Gn 14:22**	5945b
then the altar shall be **m** holy,	**Ex 29:37**	6944
It is **m** holy to the LORD."	**Ex 30:10**	6944
them, that they may be **m** holy;	**Ex 30:29**	6944
it shall be **m** holy to you.	**Ex 30:36**	6944
and the altar shall be **m** holy.	**Ex 40:10**	6944
a thing **m** holy, of the offerings	**Lv 2:3**	6944
a thing **m** holy of the offerings	**Lv 2:10**	6944
it is **m** holy, like the sin	**Lv 6:17**	6944
slain before the LORD; it is **m** holy.	**Lv 6:25**	6944
the priests may eat of it; it is **m** holy.	**Lv 6:29**	6944
law of the guilt offering; it is **m** holy	**Lv 7:1**	6944
eaten in a holy place; it is **m** holy.	**Lv 7:6**	6944
the altar, for it is **m** holy.	**Lv 10:12**	6944
For it is **m** holy, and He gave it	**Lv 10:17**	6944
belongs to the priest; it is **m** holy.	**Lv 14:13**	6944
of the **m** holy and of the holy,	**Lv 21:22**	6944
for it is **m** holy to him from the	**Lv 24:9**	6944
destruction is **m** holy to the LORD.	**Lv 27:28**	6944
concerning the **m** holy things.	**Nu 4:4**	6944
they approach the **m** holy *objects:*	**Nu 4:19**	6944
be yours from the **m** holy *gifts reserved*	**Nu 18:9**	6944
shall be **m** holy for you and for	**Nu 18:9**	6944
the **m** holy *gifts* you shall eat it;	**Nu 18:10**	6944
knows the knowledge of the **M** High,	**Nu 24:16**	5945b
"When the **M** High gave the nations	**Dt 32:8**	5945b
"**M** blessed of women is Jael, The	**Jg 5:24**	
M blessed is she of women in the	**Jg 5:24**	
And the **M** High uttered His voice.	**2Sa 22:14**	5945b
He was **m** honored of the thirty,	**2Sa 23:19**	4480
even as the **m** holy place.	**1Ki 6:16**	6944
the inner house, the **m** holy place,	**1Ki 7:50**	6944
of the house, to the **m** holy place,	**1Ki 8:6**	6944
your **m** beautiful wives and	**1Ki 20:3**	
all the work of the **m** holy place,	**1Ch 6:49**	6944
second *rank* he was the **m** honored and	**1Ch 11:21**	
apart to sanctify him as **m** holy,	**1Ch 23:13**	6944
the LORD and the **m** holy things.	**2Ch 31:14**	6944
should not eat from the **m** holy things	**Ezr 2:63**	6944
the **m** remote part of the heavens,	**Ne 1:9**	7097a
should not eat from the **m** holy things	**Ne 7:65**	6944
to one of the king's **m** noble princes	**Es 6:9**	
to the name of the LORD **M** High.	**Ps 7:17**	5945b
sing praise to Your name, O **M** High.	**Ps 9:2**	5945b
And the **M** High uttered His voice,	**Ps 18:13**	5945b
You make him **m** blessed forever;	**Ps 21:6**	1293
the **M** High he will not be shaken.	**Ps 21:7**	5945b
dwelling places of the **M** High.	**Ps 46:4**	5945b
the LORD **M** High is to be feared,	**Ps 47:2**	5945b
And pay your vows to the **M** High;	**Ps 50:14**	5945b
I will cry to God **M** High,	**Ps 57:2**	5945b
there knowledge with the **M** High?"	**Ps 73:11**	5945b
hand of the **M** High has changed."	**Ps 77:10**	5945b
against the **M** High in the desert.	**Ps 78:17**	5945b
the **M** High God their Redeemer.	**Ps 78:35**	5945b
rebelled against the **M** High God And	**Ps 78:56**	5945b
all of you are sons of the **M** High.	**Ps 82:6**	5945b
Are the **M** High over all the earth.	**Ps 83:18**	5945b
And the **M** High Himself will	**Ps 87:5**	5945b
dwells in the shelter of the **M** High	**Ps 91:1**	5945b
LORD, my refuge, *Even* the **M** High,	**Ps 91:9**	5945b
praises to Your name, O **M** High;	**Ps 92:1**	5945b
LORD **M** High over all the earth;	**Ps 97:9**	5945a
spurned the counsel of the **M** High.	**Ps 107:11**	5945b
know, **M** beautiful among women,	**SS 1:8**	
O **m** beautiful among women?	**SS 5:9**	
gone, O **m** beautiful among women?	**SS 6:1**	
will make myself like the **M** High.'	**Is 14:14**	5945b
Those who are **m** helpless will eat,	**Is 14:30**	1060
The **m** beautiful inheritance of the	**Jer 3:19**	6635
only son, A lamentation **m** bitter.	**Jer 6:26**	8563
Has done a **m** appalling thing.	**Jer 18:13**	3966
Yet **m** assuredly I will make you	**Jer 22:6**	518, 3808
In the presence of the **M** High,	**La 3:35**	5945b
not from the mouth of the **M** High	**La 3:38**	5945b
The **m** ruthless of the nations.	**Ezk 28:7**	6184
The **m** ruthless of the nations,	**Ezk 30:11**	6184
"This is the **m** holy *place*."	**Ezk 41:4**	6944
LORD shall eat the **m** holy things.	**Ezk 42:13**	6944
they shall lay the **m** holy things,	**Ezk 42:13**	6944
all around *shall be* **m** holy.	**Ezk 43:12**	6944
to the things that are **m** holy;	**Ezk 44:13**	6944
the sanctuary, the **m** holy place.	**Ezk 45:3**	6944
of the land, a **m** holy place,	**Ezk 48:12**	6944
you servants of the **M** High God,	**Da 3:26**	5943
the **M** High God has done for me.	**Da 4:2**	5943
the **M** High is ruler over the realm	**Da 4:17**	5943
this is the decree of the **M** High,	**Da 4:24**	5943
the **M** High is ruler over the realm	**Da 4:25**	5943
the **M** High is ruler over the realm	**Da 4:32**	5943
and I blessed the **M** High and	**Da 4:34**	5943
M High God granted sovereignty,	**Da 5:18**	5943
M High God is ruler over the realm	**Da 5:21**	5943
He will speak out against the **M** High	**Da 7:25**	5943
and to anoint the **m** holy *place*.	**Da 9:24**	6944
The **m** upright like a thorn hedge.	**Mi 7:4**	
which **m** of His miracles were done,	**Mt 11:20**	*4183*
M of the crowd spread their coats in	**Mt 21:8**	*4183*
m people's love will grow cold.	**Mt 24:12**	*4183*
other, Jesus, Son of the **M** High God?	**Mk 5:7**	*5310*
like a corpse that **m** *of them* said,	**Mk 9:26**	*4183*
order, **m** excellent Theophilus;	**Lk 1:3**	*2903*
be called the Son of the **M** High;	**Lk 1:32**	*5310*
of the **M** High will overshadow you;	**Lk 1:35**	*5310*
called the prophet of the **M** High;	**Lk 1:76**	*5310*
you will be sons of the **M** High;	**Lk 6:35**	*5310*
other, Jesus, Son of the **M** High God?	**Lk 8:28**	*5310*
the **M** High does not dwell in	**Ac 7:48**	*5310*
"I **m** certainly understand *now*	**Ac 10:34**	*225*
bond-servants of the **M** High God,	**Ac 16:17**	*5310*
to the **m** excellent governor Felix,	**Ac 23:26**	*2903*
and everywhere, **m** excellent Felix,	**Ac 24:3**	*2903*
of my mind, **m** excellent Festus,	**Ac 26:25**	*2903*
with **m** of them God was not	**1Co 10:5**	*4183*
be by two or at the **m** three,	**1Co 14:27**	*4183*
time, **m** of whom remain until now,	**1Co 15:6**	*4183*
we are of all men **m** to be pitied.	**1Co 15:19**	*1652*
zeal has stirred up **m** of them.	**2Co 9:2**	*4183*
to the **m** eminent apostles.	**2Co 11:5**	*5244b*
M gladly, therefore, I will rather	**2Co 12:9**	*2234*
to the **m** eminent apostles,	**2Co 12:11**	*5244b*
I will **m** gladly spend and be	**2Co 12:15**	*2234*
making the **m** of your time, because	**Eph 5:16**	*1805*
and that **m** of the brethren,	**Php 1:14**	*4183*
making the **m** of the opportunity.	**Col 4:5**	*1805*
keep praying **m** earnestly that we	**1Th 3:10**	*5238b*
Salem, priest of the **M** High God,	**Heb 7:1**	*5310*
up on your **m** holy faith,	**Jude 1:20**	*40*

MOTH

Who are crushed before the **m**!	**Jb 4:19**	6211
You consume as a **m** what is	**Ps 39:11**	6211
The **m** will eat them.	**Is 50:9**	6211
m will eat them like a garment,	**Is 51:8**	6211
I am like a **m** to Ephraim And	**Hos 5:12**	6211
earth, where **m** and rust destroy,	**Mt 6:19**	*4597*
where neither **m** nor rust destroys,	**Mt 6:20**	*4597*
thief comes near nor **m** destroys.	**Lk 12:33**	*4597*

MOTH-EATEN

thing, Like a garment that is **m**.	**Jb 13:28**	6211, 398
and your garments have become **m**.	**Jas 5:2**	*4598*

MOTHER

shall leave his father and his **m**,	**Gn 2:24**	517
she was the **m** of all *the* living.	**Gn 3:20**	517
and she shall be *a* **m** *of* nations;	**Gn 17:16**	
but not the daughter of my **m**,	**Gn 20:12**	517
and his **m** took a wife for him from	**Gn 21:21**	517
to her brother and to her **m**.	**Gn 24:53**	517
But her brother and her **m** said,	**Gn 24:55**	517
her into his **m** Sarah's tent,	**Gn 24:67**	517
Jacob answered his **m** Rebekah,	**Gn 27:11**	517
But his **m** said to him,	**Gn 27:13**	517
them, and brought *them* to his **m**;	**Gn 27:14**	517
and his **m** made savory food such as	**Gn 27:14**	517
Rebekah, the **m** of Jacob and Esau.	**Gn 28:5**	517
had obeyed his father and his **m**	**Gn 28:7**	517
and brought them to his **m** Leah.	**Gn 30:14**	517
Shall I and your **m** and your	**Gn 37:10**	517
so he alone is left of his **m**,	**Gn 44:20**	517
girl went and called the child's **m**.	**Ex 2:8**	517
"Honor your father and your **m**,	**Ex 20:12**	517
He who strikes his father or his **m**	**Ex 21:15**	517
He who curses his father or his **m**	**Ex 21:17**	517
It shall be with its **m** seven days;	**Ex 22:30**	517
boil a young goat in the milk of its **m**.	**Ex 23:19**	517
that is, the nakedness of your **m**.	**Lv 18:7**	517
She is your **m**; you are not to	**Lv 18:7**	517
reverence his **m** and his father,	**Lv 19:3**	517
who curses his father or his **m**,	**Lv 20:9**	517
he has cursed his father or his **m**,	**Lv 20:9**	517
man who marries a woman and her **m**,	**Lv 20:14**	517
his **m** and his father and his son	**Lv 21:2**	517
even for his father or his **m**;	**Lv 21:11**	517
remain seven days with its **m**,	**Lv 22:27**	517
for his father or for his **m**,	**Nu 6:7**	517
'Honor your father and your **m**,	**Dt 5:16**	517
mourn her father and **m** a full	**Dt 21:13**	517
will not obey his father or his **m**,	**Dt 21:18**	517
his father and **m** shall seize him,	**Dt 21:19**	517
and the **m** sitting on the young or	**Dt 22:6**	517
not take the **m** with the young;	**Dt 22:6**	517
you shall certainly let the **m** go,	**Dt 22:7**	517
then the girl's father and her **m**	**Dt 22:15**	517
he who dishonors his father or **m**.'	**Dt 27:16**	517
daughter of his father or of his **m**.'	**Dt 27:22**	517
Who said of his father and his **m**,	**Dt 33:9**	517
and spare my father and my **m** and	**Jos 2:13**	517
father and your **m** and your brothers	**Jos 2:18**	517
Rahab and her father and her **m**	**Jos 6:23**	517
Until I arose, a **m** in Israel.	**Jg 5:7**	517
m of Sisera through the lattice,	**Jg 5:28**	517
my brothers, the sons of my **m**.	**Jg 8:19**	517
back and told his father and **m**,	**Jg 14:2**	517
his father and his **m** said to him,	**Jg 14:3**	517
his father and **m** did not know that	**Jg 14:4**	517
to Timnah with his father and **m**,	**Jg 14:5**	517
he did not tell his father or **m** what	**Jg 14:6**	517
When he came to his father and **m**,	**Jg 14:9**	517
not told *it* to my father or **m**;	**Jg 14:16**	517
He said to his **m**,	**Jg 17:2**	517
And his **m** said, "Blessed be my son	**Jg 17:2**	517
hundred *pieces* of silver to his **m**,	**Jg 17:3**	517
to his mother, and his **m** said,	**Jg 17:3**	517
he returned the silver to his **m**,	**Jg 17:4**	517
his **m** took two hundred *pieces* of	**Jg 17:4**	517
your **m** and the land of your birth,	**Ru 2:11**	517
And his **m** would make him a little	**1Sa 2:19**	517
your **m** be childless among women."	**1Sa 15:33**	517
let my father and my **m** come *and*	**1Sa 22:3**	517
sister of Zeruiah, Joab's **m**.	**2Sa 17:25**	517
the grave of my father and my **m**.	**2Sa 19:37**	517
destroy a city, even a **m** in Israel.	**2Sa 20:19**	517
to Bathsheba the **m** of Solomon,	**1Ki 1:11**	517
to Bathsheba the **m** of Solomon.	**1Ki 2:13**	517
had a throne set for the king's **m**,	**1Ki 2:19**	517
"Ask, my **m**, for I will not refuse	**1Ki 2:20**	517
answered and said to his **m**,	**1Ki 2:22**	517
by no means kill him. She is his **m**."	**1Ki 3:27**	517
his **m** from *being* queen mother,	**1Ki 15:13**	517
his mother from *being* queen **m**,	**1Ki 15:13**	1377
the house and gave him to his **m**;	**1Ki 17:23**	517
let me kiss my father and my **m**,	**1Ki 19:20**	517
in the way of his **m** and in the way	**1Ki 22:52**	517
not like his father and his **m**;	**2Ki 3:2**	517
and to the prophets of your **m**."	**2Ki 3:13**	517
"Carry him to his **m**."	**2Ki 4:19**	517
him and brought him to his **m**,	**2Ki 4:20**	517
The **m** of the lad said,	**2Ki 4:30**	517
the harlotries of your **m** Jezebel	**2Ki 9:22**	517
and the sons of the queen **m**."	**2Ki 10:13**	1377

When Athaliah the **m** of Ahaziah saw	**2Ki 11:1**	517
he and his **m** and his servants and	**2Ki 24:12**	517
also the king's **m** and the king's	**2Ki 24:15**	517
she was the **m** of Onam.	**1Ch 2:26**	517
and his **m** named him Jabez saying,	**1Ch 4:9**	517
removed Maacah, the **m** of King Asa,	**2Ch 15:16**	517
Asa, from the *position of* queen **m**,	**2Ch 15:16**	1377
for his **m** was his counselor to do	**2Ch 22:3**	517
Now when Athaliah the **m** of Ahaziah	**2Ch 22:10**	517
for she had no father or **m**.	**Es 2:7**	517
when her father and her **m** died,	**Es 2:7**	517
'my **m** and my sister';	**Jb 17:14**	517
"A **m** will forget him;	**Jb 24:20**	7358
father and my **m** have forsaken me,	**Ps 27:10**	517
as one who sorrows for a **m**.	**Ps 35:14**	517
And in sin my **m** conceived me.	**Ps 51:5**	517
the sin of his **m** be blotted out.	**Ps 109:14**	517
house *As* a joyful **m** of children.	**Ps 113:9**	517
weaned child *rests* against his **m**,	**Ps 131:2**	517
the only son in the sight of my **m**,	**Pr 4:3**	517
forsake the teaching of your **m**;	**Pr 6:20**	517
a foolish son is a grief to his **m**.	**Pr 10:1**	517
But a foolish man despises his **m**.	**Pr 15:20**	517
his father *and* drives *his* **m** away	**Pr 19:26**	517
He who curses his father or his **m**,	**Pr 20:20**	517
not despise your **m** when she is old.	**Pr 23:22**	517
your father and your **m** be glad,	**Pr 23:25**	517
He who robs his father or his **m** And	**Pr 28:24**	517
his own way brings shame to his **m**.	**Pr 29:15**	517
father And does not bless his **m**.	**Pr 30:11**	517
mocks a father And scorns a **m**,	**Pr 30:17**	517
the oracle which his **m** taught him:	**Pr 31:1**	517
With which his **m** has crowned him	**SS 3:11**	517
bring you Into the house of my **m**,	**SS 8:2**	517
your **m** was in labor with you,	**SS 8:5**	517
to cry out 'My father' or 'My **m**,'	**Is 8:4**	517
From the body of My **m** He named	**Is 49:1**	517
By which I have sent your **m** away?	**Is 50:1**	517
your **m** was sent away.	**Is 50:1**	517
"As one whom his **m** comforts, so I	**Is 66:13**	517
Say to the king and the queen **m**,	**Jer 13:18**	1377
against the **m** of a young man,	**Jer 15:8**	517
Woe to me, my **m**, that you have	**Jer 15:10**	517
to drink for anyone's father or **m**.	**Jer 16:7**	517
not be blessed when my **m** bore me!	**Jer 20:14**	517
my **m** would have been my grave,	**Jer 20:17**	517
"I will hurl you and your **m** who	**Jer 22:26**	517
King Jeconiah and the queen **m**,	**Jer 29:2**	1377
Your **m** will be greatly ashamed,	**Jer 50:12**	517
an Amorite and your **m** a Hittite.	**Ezk 16:3**	517
'Like **m**, like daughter.'	**Ezk 16:44**	517
"You are the daughter of your **m**,	**Ezk 16:45**	517
Your **m** was a Hittite and your	**Ezk 16:45**	517
'What was your **m**? A lioness among	**Ezk 19:2**	517
'Your **m** was like a vine in your	**Ezk 19:10**	517
have treated father and **m** lightly	**Ezk 22:7**	517
two women, the daughters of one **m**;	**Ezk 23:2**	517
however, for father, for **m**,	**Ezk 44:25**	517
"Contend with your **m**,	**Hos 2:2**	517
"For their **m** has played the harlot;	**Hos 2:5**	517
And I will destroy your **m**.	**Hos 4:5**	517
Daughter rises up against her **m**,	**Mi 7:6**	517
then his father and **m** who gave	**Zch 13:3**	517
and his father and **m** who gave	**Zch 13:3**	517
when His **m** Mary had been betrothed	**Mt 1:18**	*3384*
they saw the Child with Mary His **m**;	**Mt 2:11**	*3384*
Take the Child and His **m**	**Mt 2:13**	*3384*
took the Child and His **m**	**Mt 2:14**	*3384*
take the Child and His **m**,	**Mt 2:20**	*3384*
took the Child and His **m**,	**Mt 2:21**	*3384*
AND A DAUGHTER AGAINST HER **M**,	**Mt 10:35**	*3384*
"He who loves father or **m** more	**Mt 10:37**	*3384*
His **m** and brothers were standing	**Mt 12:46**	*3384*
Your **m** and Your brothers are	**Mt 12:47**	*3384*
is My **m** and who are My brothers?"	**Mt 12:48**	*3384*
"Behold My **m** and My brothers!	**Mt 12:49**	*3384*
is My brother and sister and **m**."	**Mt 12:50**	*3384*
Is not His **m** called Mary, and His	**Mt 13:55**	*3384*
Having been prompted by her **m**,	**Mt 14:8**	*3384*
and she brought it to her **m**.	**Mt 14:11**	*3384*
'HONOR YOUR FATHER AND **M**,'	**Mt 15:4**	*3384*
WHO SPEAKS EVIL OF FATHER OR **M**	**Mt 15:4**	*3384*
says to *his* father or **m**,	**Mt 15:5**	*3384*
not to honor his father or his **m**.'	**Mt 15:6**	*3384*
MAN SHALL LEAVE HIS FATHER AND **M**	**Mt 19:5**	*3384*
HONOR YOUR FATHER AND **M**	**Mt 19:19**	*3384*
or brothers or sisters or father or **m**	**Mt 19:29**	*3384*
Then the **m** of the sons of Zebedee	**Mt 20:20**	*3384*
Mary the **m** of James and Joseph,	**Mt 27:56**	*3384*
and the **m** of the sons of Zebedee.	**Mt 27:56**	*3384*
His **m** and His brothers arrived,	**Mk 3:31**	*3384*
Your **m** and Your brothers are	**Mk 3:32**	*3384*
"Who are My **m** and My brothers?"	**Mk 3:33**	*3384*
"Behold My **m** and My brothers!	**Mk 3:34**	*3384*
he is My brother and sister and **m**."	**Mk 3:35**	*3384*
took along the child's father and **m**	**Mk 5:40**	*3384*
she went out and said to her **m**,	**Mk 6:24**	*3384*
and the girl gave it to her **m**.	**Mk 6:28**	*3384*
'HONOR YOUR FATHER AND YOUR **M**';	**Mk 7:10**	*3384*
WHO SPEAKS EVIL OF FATHER OR **M**,	**Mk 7:10**	*3384*
a man says to *his* father or *his* **m**,	**Mk 7:11**	*3384*
anything for *his* father or *his* **m**;	**Mk 7:12**	*3384*
MAN SHALL LEAVE HIS FATHER AND **M**,	**Mk 10:7**	*3384*
HONOR YOUR FATHER AND **M**.' "	**Mk 10:19**	*3384*
left house or brothers or sisters or **m**	**Mk 10:29**	*3384*
the **m** of James the Less and Joses,	**Mk 15:40**	*3384*
Mary Magdalene and Mary the **m** of	**Mk 15:47**	
and Mary the **m** of James,	**Mk 16:1**	
m of my Lord would come to me?	**Lk 1:43**	*3384*
But his **m** answered and said,	**Lk 1:60**	*3384*
And His father and **m** were amazed	**Lk 2:33**	*3384*
them and said to Mary His **m**,	**Lk 2:34**	*3384*
and His **m** said to Him,	**Lk 2:48**	*3384*
and His **m** treasured all *these*	**Lk 2:51**	*3384*
out, the only son of his **m**,	**Lk 7:12**	*3384*
And *Jesus* gave him back to his **m**.	**Lk 7:15**	*3384*
His **m** and brothers came to Him,	**Lk 8:19**	*3384*
"Your **m** and Your brothers are	**Lk 8:20**	*3384*
"My **m** and My brothers are these	**Lk 8:21**	*3384*
James, and the girl's father and **m**.	**Lk 8:51**	*3384*
m against daughter and daughter	**Lk 12:53**	*3384*
daughter and daughter against **m**	**Lk 12:53**	*3384*
does not hate his own father and **m**	**Lk 14:26**	*3384*
HONOR YOUR FATHER AND **M**.' "	**Lk 18:20**	*3384*
Magdalene and Joanna and Mary the **m**	**Lk 24:10**	*3384*
and the **m** of Jesus was there;	**Jn 2:1**	*3384*
out, the **m** of Jesus said to Him,	**Jn 2:3**	*3384*
His **m** said to the servants,	**Jn 2:5**	*3384*
down to Capernaum, He and His **m** and	**Jn 2:12**	*3384*
whose father and **m** we know?	**Jn 6:42**	*3384*
by the cross of Jesus were His **m**,	**Jn 19:25**	*3384*
When Jesus then saw His **m**,	**Jn 19:26**	*3384*
standing nearby, He said to His **m**,	**Jn 19:26**	*3384*
"Behold, your **m**!"	**Jn 19:27**	*3384*
women, and Mary the **m** of Jesus,	**Ac 1:14**	*3384*
the **m** of John who was also called	**Ac 12:12**	*3384*
in the Lord, also his **m** and mine.	**Ro 16:13**	*3384*
Jerusalem above is free; she is our **m**.	**Ga 4:26**	*3384*
MAN SHALL LEAVE HIS FATHER AND **M**	**Eph 5:31**	*3384*
HONOR YOUR FATHER AND **M**	**Eph 6:2**	*3384*
as a nursing **m** tenderly cares for	**1Th 2:7**	
Lois and your **m** Eunice,	**2Tm 1:5**	*3384*
Without father, without **m**,	**Heb 7:3**	*282*
THE **M** OF HARLOTS AND OF THE	**Rv 17:5**	*3384*

MOTHER-IN-LAW

'Cursed is he who lies with his **m**.'	**Dt 27:23**	2860b
and Orpah kissed her **m**,	**Ru 1:14**	2545
"All that you have done for your **m**	**Ru 2:11**	2545
her **m** saw what she had gleaned.	**Ru 2:18**	2545
Her **m** then said to her,	**Ru 2:19**	2545
So she told her **m** with whom she	**Ru 2:19**	2545
And she lived with her **m**.	**Ru 2:23**	2545
Then Naomi her **m** said to her,	**Ru 3:1**	2545
all that her **m** had commanded her.	**Ru 3:6**	2545
When she came to her **m**,	**Ru 3:16**	2545
not go to your **m** empty-handed.' "	**Ru 3:17**	2545
Daughter-in-law against her **m**;	**Mi 7:6**	2545
He saw his **m** lying sick in bed	**Mt 8:14**	*3994*
A DAUGHTER-IN-LAW AGAINST HER **M**;	**Mt 10:35**	*3994*
m was lying sick with a fever;	**Mk 1:30**	*3994*
Now Simon's **m** was suffering from a	**Lk 4:38**	*3994*
m against daughter-in-law and	**Lk 12:53**	*3994*
and daughter-in-law against **m**."	**Lk 12:53**	*3994*

MOTHER-OF-PEARL

pavement of porphyry, marble, **m** and	**Es 1:6**	1858

MOTHER'S

girl ran and told her **m** household	**Gn 24:28**	517
was comforted after his **m** death.	**Gn 24:67**	517
may your **m** sons bow down to you.	**Gn 27:29**	517
house of Bethuel your **m** father;	**Gn 28:2**	517
daughters of Laban your **m** brother.	**Gn 28:2**	517
daughter of Laban his **m** brother,	**Gn 29:10**	517
the sheep of Laban his **m** brother,	**Gn 29:10**	517
the flock of Laban his **m** brother.	**Gn 29:10**	517
his brother Benjamin, his **m** son,	**Gn 43:29**	517
not boil a young goat in its **m** milk."	**Ex 34:26**	517
daughter or your **m** daughter,	**Lv 18:9**	517
the nakedness of your **m** sister,	**Lv 18:13**	517
for she is your **m** blood relative.	**Lv 18:13**	517
daughter or his **m** daughter,	**Lv 20:17**	517
the nakedness of your **m** sister	**Lv 20:19**	517
(Now his **m** name was Shelomith, the	**Lv 24:11**	517
when he comes from his **m** womb!"	**Nu 12:12**	517
"If your brother, your **m** son,	**Dt 13:6**	517
not boil a young goat in its **m** milk.	**Dt 14:21**	517
to Shechem to his **m** relatives,	**Jg 9:1**	517
of the household of his **m** father,	**Jg 9:1**	517
And his **m** relatives spoke all	**Jg 9:3**	517
a Nazirite to God from my **m** womb.	**Jg 16:17**	517
return each of you to her **m** house.	**Ru 1:8**	517
to the shame of your **m** nakedness?	**1Sa 20:30**	517
servant, whose **m** name was Zeruah,	**1Ki 11:26**	517
And his **m** name was Naamah the	**1Ki 14:21**	517
and his **m** name was Naamah the	**1Ki 14:31**	517
and his **m** name was Maacah the	**1Ki 15:2**	517
and his **m** name was Maacah the	**1Ki 15:10**	517
And his **m** name was Azubah the	**1Ki 22:42**	517
And his **m** name *was* Athaliah the	**2Ki 8:26**	517
m name was Zibiah of Beersheba.	**2Ki 12:1**	517
And his **m** name was Jehoaddin of	**2Ki 14:2**	517
and his **m** name was Jecoliah of	**2Ki 15:2**	517
and his **m** name *was* Jerusha the	**2Ki 15:33**	517
and his **m** name was Abi the	**2Ki 18:2**	517
and his **m** name was Hephzibah.	**2Ki 21:1**	517
and his **m** name *was* Meshullemeth	**2Ki 21:19**	517
and his **m** name *was* Jedidah the	**2Ki 22:1**	517
and his **m** name was Hamutal the	**2Ki 23:31**	517
and his **m** name *was* Zebidah the	**2Ki 23:36**	517
and his **m** name *was* Nehushta the	**2Ki 24:8**	517
and his **m** name was Hamutal the	**2Ki 24:18**	517
And his **m** name was Naamah the	**2Ch 12:13**	517
and his **m** name was Micaiah the	**2Ch 13:2**	517
And his **m** name *was* Azubah the	**2Ch 20:31**	517
And his **m** name was Athaliah, the	**2Ch 22:2**	517
his **m** name *was* Zibiah from	**2Ch 24:1**	517
And his **m** name was Jehoaddan of	**2Ch 25:1**	517
and his **m** name was Jechiliah of	**2Ch 26:3**	517
And his **m** name was Jerushah the	**2Ch 27:1**	517
And his **m** name *was* Abijah, the	**2Ch 29:1**	517
"Naked I came from my **m** womb,	**Jb 1:21**	517
not shut the opening of my **m** womb,	**Jb 3:10**	
me trust *when* upon my **m** breasts.	**Ps 22:9**	517
have been my God from my **m** womb.	**Ps 22:10**	517
You slander your own **m** son.	**Ps 50:20**	517
And an alien to my **m** sons.	**Ps 69:8**	517
are He who took me from my **m** womb;	**Ps 71:6**	517
You wove me in my **m** womb.	**Ps 139:13**	517
do not forsake your **m** teaching;	**Pr 1:8**	517
he had come naked from his **m** womb,	**Ec 5:15**	517
My **m** sons were angry with me;	**SS 1:6**	517
I had brought him to my **m** house,	**SS 3:4**	517
She is her **m** only *daughter;*	**SS 6:9**	517
to me Who nursed at my **m** breasts.	**SS 8:1**	517
and his **m** name was Hamutal the	**Jer 52:1**	517
born that way from their **m** womb;	**Mt 19:12**	*3384*
Spirit while yet in his **m** womb.	**Lk 1:15**	*3384*
time into his **m** womb and be born,	**Jn 3:4**	*3384*
His mother, and His **m** sister,	**Jn 19:25**	*3384*
had been lame from his **m** womb	**Ac 3:2**	*3384*
in his feet, lame from his **m** womb,	**Ac 14:8**	*3384*
set me apart *even* from my **m** womb	**Ga 1:15**	*3384*

MOTHERS

me *and* the **m** with the children.	**Gn 32:11**	517
concerning their **m** who bear them,	**Jer 16:3**	517
They say to their **m**,	**La 2:12**	517
a father, Our **m** are like widows.	**La 5:3**	517
When **m** were dashed in pieces with	**Hos 10:14**	517
and **m** and children and farms,	**Mk 10:30**	*3384*
those who kill their fathers or **m**,	**1Tm 1:9**	*3389*
the older women as **m**,	**1Tm 5:2**	*3384*

MOTHERS'

life is poured out On their **m** bosom.	**La 2:12**	517

MOTIONED

and having **m** with his hand,	**Ac 19:33**	*2678*
m to the people with his hand;	**Ac 21:40**	*2678*

MOTIONING

But **m** to them with his hand to be	**Ac 12:17**	*2678*
stood up, and **m** with his hand said	**Ac 13:16**	*2678*

MOTIONLESS

of Your arm they are **m** as stone;	**Ex 15:16**	1826a

MOTIVES

sight, But the LORD weighs the **m**.	**Pr 16:2**	7307
and disclose the **m** of *men's* hearts;	**1Co 4:5**	*1012*
If from human **m** I fought with wild	**1Co 15:32**	*2596*
ambition rather than from pure **m**,	**Php 1:17**	*55*
and become judges with evil **m**?	**Jas 2:4**	*1261*
because you ask with wrong **m**,	**Jas 4:3**	*2560*

MOTTLED

were striped, speckled, and **m**.	**Gn 31:10**	1261
are striped, speckled, and **m**;	**Gn 31:12**	1261

MOUNDS

any cities that stood on their **m**,	**Jos 11:13**	8510

MOUNT

and the Horites in their **M** Seir,	**Gn 14:6**	2022
"In the **m** of the LORD it will be	**Gn 22:14**	2022
he was camped, at the **m** of God.	**Ex 18:5**	2022
LORD will come down on **M** Sinai	**Ex 19:11**	2022
Now **M** Sinai *was* all in smoke	**Ex 19:18**	2022
The LORD came down on **M** Sinai,	**Ex 19:20**	2022
people cannot come up to **M** Sinai,	**Ex 19:23**	2022
glory of the LORD rested on **M** Sinai	**Ex 24:16**	2022
and they shall **m** its lamps so as	**Ex 25:37**	5927
shall **m** on it four rows of stones;	**Ex 28:17**	4390, 4396
speaking with him upon **M** Sinai,	**Ex 31:18**	2022
ornaments, from **M** Horeb *onward.*	**Ex 33:6**	2022
come up in the morning to **M** Sinai,	**Ex 34:2**	2022
morning and went up to **M** Sinai,	**Ex 34:4**	2022
was coming down from **M** Sinai	**Ex 34:29**	2022
LORD had spoken to him on **M** Sinai.	**Ex 34:32**	2022
in the lampstand and **m** its lamps.	**Ex 40:4**	5927
LORD commanded Moses at **M** Sinai	**Lv 7:38**	2022
then spoke to Moses at **M** Sinai,	**Lv 25:1**	2022
Israel through Moses at **M** Sinai.	**Lv 26:46**	2022
for the sons of Israel at **M** Sinai.	**Lv 27:34**	2022
LORD spoke with Moses on **M** Sinai.	**Nu 3:1**	2022
'When you **m** the lamps, the seven	**Nu 8:2**	5927
they set out from the **m** of the LORD	**Nu 10:33**	2022
whole congregation, came to **M** Hor.	**Nu 20:22**	2022
spoke to Moses and Aaron at **M** Hor	**Nu 20:23**	2022
and bring them up to **M** Hor;	**Nu 20:25**	2022
and they went up to **M** Hor in the	**Nu 20:27**	2022
they set out from **M** Hor by the way	**Nu 21:4**	2022
which was ordained in **M** Sinai as a	**Nu 28:6**	2022
and camped at **M** Shepher.	**Nu 33:23**	2022
They journeyed from **M** Shepher and	**Nu 33:24**	2022
from Kadesh and camped at **M** Hor,	**Nu 33:37**	2022
Aaron the priest went up to **M** Hor	**Nu 33:38**	2022
years old when he died on **M** Hor.	**Nu 33:39**	2022
Then they journeyed from **M** Hor and	**Nu 33:41**	2022
line from the Great Sea to **M** Hor.	**Nu 34:7**	2022
line from **M** Hor to the Lebo-hamath,	**Nu 34:8**	2022
the way of **M** Seir to Kadesh-barnea.	**Dt 1:2**	2022
and circled **M** Seir for many days.	**Dt 2:1**	2022
M Seir to Esau as a possession.	**Dt 2:5**	2022
the valley of Arnon to **M** Hermon	**Dt 3:8**	2022
of Arnon, even as far as **M** Sion	**Dt 4:48**	2022
place the blessing on **M** Gerizim	**Dt 11:29**	2022
Gerizim and the curse on **M** Ebal.	**Dt 11:29**	2022
you shall set up on **M** Ebal,	**Dt 27:4**	2022
on **M** Gerizim to bless the people:	**Dt 27:12**	2022
these shall stand on **M** Ebal:	**Dt 27:13**	2022
mountain of the Abarim, **M** Nebo,	**Dt 32:49**	2022
Aaron your brother died on **M** Hor	**Dt 32:50**	2022

He shone forth from **M** Paran,	**Dt 33:2**	2022
from the plains of Moab to **M** Nebo,	**Dt 34:1**	2022
the God of Israel, in **M** Ebal,	**Jos 8:30**	2022
of them *stood* in front of **M** Gerizim	**Jos 8:33**	2022
half of them in front of **M** Ebal,	**Jos 8:33**	2022
from **M** Halak, that rises toward	**Jos 11:17**	2022
Lebanon at the foot of **M** Hermon.	**Jos 11:17**	2022
of the Arnon as far as **M** Hermon,	**Jos 12:1**	2022
and ruled over **M** Hermon and	**Jos 12:5**	2022
of Lebanon even as far as **M** Halak,	**Jos 12:7**	2022
M Hermon as far as Lebo-hamath.	**Jos 13:5**	2022
and Maacathites, and all **M** Hermon,	**Jos 13:11**	2022
to the cities of **M** Ephron,	**Jos 15:9**	2022
from Baalah westward to **M** Seir,	**Jos 15:10**	2022
slope of **M** Jearim on the north	**Jos 15:10**	2022
and continued to **M** Baalah	**Jos 15:11**	2022
Esau, and to Esau I gave **M** Seir to	**Jos 24:4**	2022
Ephraim, on the north of **M** Gaash.	**Jos 24:30**	2022
persisted in living in **M** Heres,	**Jg 1:35**	2022
of Ephraim, north of **M** Gaash.	**Jg 2:9**	2022
Hivites who lived in **M** Lebanon,	**Jg 3:3**	2022
from **M** Baal-hermon as far as	**Jg 3:3**	2022
'Go and march to **M** Tabor, and take	**Jg 4:6**	2022
of Abinoam had gone up to **M** Tabor.	**Jg 4:12**	2022
So Barak went down from **M** Tabor	**Jg 4:14**	2022
and depart from **M** Gilead.' "	**Jg 7:3**	2022
and stood on the top of **M** Gerizim,	**Jg 9:7**	2022
So Abimelech went up to **M** Zalmon,	**Jg 9:48**	2022
and fell slain on **M** Gilboa.	**1Sa 31:1**	2022
his three sons fallen on **M** Gilboa.	**1Sa 31:8**	2022
I happened to be on **M** Gilboa,	**2Sa 1:6**	2022
David went up the ascent of the **M**	**2Sa 15:30**	2022
made haste to **m** his chariot to flee	**1Ki 12:18**	5927
to me all Israel at **M** Carmel,	**1Ki 18:19**	2022
the prophets together at **M** Carmel.	**1Ki 18:20**	2022
He went from there to **M** Carmel,	**2Ki 2:25**	2022
to the man of God to **M** Carmel.	**2Ki 4:25**	2022
and out of **M** Zion survivors.	**2Ki 19:31**	2022
on the right of the **m** of destruction	**2Ki 23:13**	2022
five hundred men went to **M** Seir,	**1Ch 4:42**	2022
and **M** Hermon they were numerous.	**1Ch 5:23**	2022
and fell slain on **M** Gilboa.	**1Ch 10:1**	2022
and his sons fallen on **M** Gilboa.	**1Ch 10:8**	2022
the LORD in Jerusalem on **M** Moriah,	**2Ch 3:1**	2022
made haste to **m** his chariot to flee	**2Ch 10:18**	5927
Then Abijah stood on **M** Zemaraim,	**2Ch 13:4**	2022
sons of Ammon and Moab and **M** Seir,	**2Ch 20:10**	2022
sons of Ammon, Moab and **M** Seir,	**2Ch 20:22**	2022
against the inhabitants of **M** Seir	**2Ch 20:23**	2022
was no place for my **m** to pass.	**Ne 2:14**	929
You came down on **M** Sinai,	**Ne 9:13**	2022
the peaks of Hermon, from **M** Mizar.	**Ps 42:6**	2022
earth, Is **M** Zion *in* the far north,	**Ps 48:2**	2022
Let **M** Zion be glad, Let the	**Ps 48:11**	2022
this **M** Zion, where You have dwelt.	**Ps 74:2**	2022
of Judah, **M** Zion which He loved.	**Ps 78:68**	2022
as **M** Zion, which cannot be moved but	**Ps 125:1**	2022
That have descended from **M** Gilead.	**SS 4:1**	2022
create over the whole area of **M** Zion	**Is 4:5**	2022
of hosts, who dwells on **M** Zion.	**Is 8:18**	2022
work on **M** Zion and on Jerusalem,	**Is 10:12**	2022
And I will sit on the **m** of assembly	**Is 14:13**	2022
of the LORD of hosts, *even* **M** Zion.	**Is 18:7**	2022
reign on **M** Zion and in Jerusalem,	**Is 24:23**	2022
LORD will rise up as *at* **M** Perazim,	**Is 28:21**	2022
be Who wage war against **M** Zion.	**Is 29:8**	2022
war on **M** Zion and on its hill."	**Is 31:4**	2022
and out of **M** Zion survivors.	**Is 37:32**	2022
will **m** up *with* wings like eagles,	**Is 40:31**	5927
wickedness from **M** Ephraim.	**Jer 4:15**	2022
the horses, And **m** the steeds,	**Jer 46:4**	5927
will **m** up and swoop like an eagle and	**Jer 49:22**	5927
Because of **M** Zion which lies	**La 5:18**	2022
man, set your face against **M** Seir,	**Ezk 35:2**	2022
"Behold, I am against you, **M** Seir,	**Ezk 35:3**	2022
M Seir a waste and a desolation and	**Ezk 35:7**	2022
will be a desolation, O **M** Seir,	**Ezk 35:15**	2022
My fury will **m** up in My anger.	**Ezk 38:18**	5927
For on **M** Zion and in Jerusalem	**Jl 2:32**	2022
"But on **M** Zion there will be	**Ob 1:17**	2022
The deliverers will ascend **M** Zion	**Ob 1:21**	2022
in **M** Zion From now on and forever.	**Mi 4:7**	2022
And the Holy One from **M** Paran.	**Hab 3:3**	2022
will stand on the **M** of Olives,	**Zch 14:4**	2022
and the **M** of Olives will be split	**Zch 14:4**	2022
to Bethphage, at the **M** of Olives,	**Mt 21:1**	*3735*
He was sitting on the **M** of Olives,	**Mt 24:3**	*3735*
they went out to the **M** of Olives.	**Mt 26:30**	*3735*
and Bethany, near the **M** of Olives,	**Mk 11:1**	*3735*
He was sitting on the **M** of Olives	**Mk 13:3**	*3735*
they went out to the **M** of Olives.	**Mk 14:26**	*3735*
near the **m** that is called Olivet,	**Lk 19:29**	*3735*
the descent of the **M** of Olives,	**Lk 19:37**	*3735*
on the **m** that is called Olivet.	**Lk 21:37**	*3735*
was His custom to the **M** of Olives;	**Lk 22:39**	*3735*
But Jesus went to the **M** of Olives.	**Jn 8:1**	*3735*
from the **m** called Olivet,	**Ac 1:12**	*3735*
HIM IN THE WILDERNESS OF **M** Sinai,	**Ac 7:30**	*3735*
was speaking to him on **M** Sinai,	**Ac 7:38**	*3735*
one *proceeding* from **M** Sinai	**Ga 4:24**	*3735*
this Hagar is **M** Sinai in Arabia and	**Ga 4:25**	*3735*
But you have come to **M** Zion and to	**Heb 12:22**	*3735*
the Lamb *was* standing on **M** Zion,	**Rv 14:1**	*3735*

MOUNTAIN

to the **m** on the east of Bethel,	**Gn 12:8**	2022
offered a sacrifice on the **m**,	**Gn 31:54**	2022
meal and spent the night on the **m**.	**Gn 31:54**	2022
and came to Horeb, the **m** of God.	**Ex 3:1**	2022
you shall worship God at this **m**."	**Ex 3:12**	2022
went and met him at the **m** of God and	**Ex 4:27**	2022
in the **m** of Your inheritance,	**Ex 15:17**	2022
Israel camped in front of the **m**.	**Ex 19:2**	2022
the LORD called to him from the **m**,	**Ex 19:3**	2022
do not go up on the **m** or touch the	**Ex 19:12**	2022
whoever touches the **m** shall surely	**Ex 19:12**	2022
they shall come up to the **m**."	**Ex 19:13**	2022
So Moses went down from the **m** to	**Ex 19:14**	2022
and a thick cloud upon the **m** and	**Ex 19:16**	2022
they stood at the foot of the **m**.	**Ex 19:17**	2022
and the whole **m** quaked violently.	**Ex 19:18**	2022
Mount Sinai, to the top of the **m**;	**Ex 19:20**	2022
called Moses to the top of the **m**,	**Ex 19:20**	2022
about the **m** and consecrate it.' "	**Ex 19:23**	2022
of the trumpet and the **m** smoking;	**Ex 20:18**	2022
built an altar at the foot of the **m**	**Ex 24:4**	2022
"Come up to Me on the **m** and	**Ex 24:12**	2022
and Moses went up to the **m** of God.	**Ex 24:13**	2022
Then Moses went up to the **m**,	**Ex 24:15**	2022
and the cloud covered the **m**.	**Ex 24:15**	2022
a consuming fire on the **m** top.	**Ex 24:17**	2022
the cloud as he went up to the **m**;	**Ex 24:18**	2022
Moses was on the **m** forty days and	**Ex 24:18**	2022
which was shown to you on the **m**.	**Ex 25:40**	2022
you have been shown in the **m**.	**Ex 26:30**	2022
as it was shown to you in the **m**,	**Ex 27:8**	2022
delayed to come down from the **m**,	**Ex 32:1**	2022
down from the **m** with the two tablets	**Ex 32:15**	2022
shattered them at the foot of the **m**.	**Ex 32:19**	2022
there to Me on the top of the **m**.	**Ex 34:2**	2022
any man be seen anywhere on the **m**;	**Ex 34:3**	2022
not graze in front of that **m**."	**Ex 34:3**	2022
as he was coming down from the **m**),	**Ex 34:29**	2022
Aaron died there on the **m** top.	**Nu 20:28**	2022
and Eleazar came down from the **m**.	**Nu 20:28**	2022
"Go up to this **m** of Abarim, and	**Nu 27:12**	2022
have stayed long enough at this **m**.	**Dt 1:6**	2022
have circled this **m** long enough.	**Dt 2:3**	2022
and stood at the foot of the **m**,	**Dt 4:11**	2022
and the **m** burned with fire to the	**Dt 4:11**	2022
the **m** from the midst of the fire,	**Dt 5:4**	2022
the fire and did not go up the **m**.	**Dt 5:5**	2022
the **m** from the midst of the fire,	**Dt 5:22**	2022
while the **m** was burning with fire,	**Dt 5:23**	2022
"When I went up to the **m** to	**Dt 9:9**	2022
on the **m** forty days and nights;	**Dt 9:9**	2022
LORD had spoken with you at the **m**	**Dt 9:10**	2022
I turned and came down from the **m**	**Dt 9:15**	2022
while the **m** was burning with fire,	**Dt 9:15**	2022
brook that came down from the **m**.	**Dt 9:21**	2022
ones, and come up to Me on the **m**,	**Dt 10:1**	2022
and went up on the **m** with the two	**Dt 10:3**	2022
LORD had spoken to you on the **m**	**Dt 10:4**	2022
I turned and came down from the **m** and	**Dt 10:5**	2022
stayed on the **m** forty days and	**Dt 10:10**	2022
the antelope and the **m** sheep.	**Dt 14:5**	2169
"Go up to this **m** of the Abarim,	**Dt 32:49**	2022
die on the **m** where you ascend,	**Dt 32:50**	2022
"They will call peoples *to the* **m**;	**Dt 33:19**	2022
border went up to the top of the **m**	**Jos 15:8**	2022
From the top of the **m** the	**Jos 15:9**	2022
of the **m** which is opposite Hebron.	**Jg 16:3**	2022
Philistines stood on the **m** on one side	**1Sa 17:3**	2022
stood on the **m** on the other side,	**1Sa 17:3**	2022
Saul went on one side of the **m**,	**1Sa 23:26**	2022
men on the other side of the **m**;	**1Sa 23:26**	2022
down by the hidden part of the **m**,	**1Sa 25:20**	2022
and stood on top of the **m** at a	**1Sa 26:13**	2022
behind him by the side of the **m**.	**2Sa 13:34**	2022
they hanged them in the **m** before	**2Sa 21:9**	2022
the **m** which is east of Jerusalem,	**1Ki 11:7**	2022
nights to Horeb, the **m** of God.	**1Ki 19:8**	2022
stand on the **m** before the LORD."	**1Ki 19:11**	2022
on some **m** or into some valley."	**2Ki 2:16**	2022
the **m** was full of horses and	**2Ki 6:17**	2022
graves that *were* there on the **m**,	**2Ki 23:16**	2022
altars which he had built on the **m**	**2Ch 33:15**	2022
"But the falling **m** crumbles away,	**Jb 14:18**	2022
"They are wet with the **m** rains And	**Jb 24:8**	2022
the time the **m** goats give birth?	**Jb 39:1**	
		3277, 5553
My King Upon Zion, My holy **m**."	**Ps 2:6**	2022
He answered me from His holy **m**.	**Ps 3:4**	2022
"Flee *as* a bird to your **m**;	**Ps 11:1**	2022
have made my **m** to stand strong;	**Ps 30:7**	2022
the city of our God, His holy **m**.	**Ps 48:1**	2022
A **m** of God is the mountain of	**Ps 68:15**	2022
mountain of God is the **m** of Bashan	**Ps 68:15**	2022
A **m** *of many* peaks is the mountain	**Ps 68:15**	2022
of many peaks is the **m** of Bashan.	**Ps 68:15**	2022
At the **m** which God has desired for	**Ps 68:16**	2022
I will go my way to the **m** of myrrh	**SS 4:6**	2022
The **m** of the house of the LORD	**Is 2:2**	2022
let us go up to the **m** of the LORD,	**Is 2:3**	2022
at the **m** of the daughter of Zion,	**Is 10:32**	2022
hurt or destroy in all My holy **m**,	**Is 11:9**	2022
to the **m** of the daughter of Zion.	**Is 16:1**	2022
left together for **m** birds of prey,	**Is 18:6**	2022
of walls And a crying to the **m**.	**Is 22:5**	2022
banquet for all peoples on this **m**;	**Is 25:6**	2022
And on this **m** He will swallow up	**Is 25:7**	2022
of the LORD will rest on this **m**,	**Is 25:10**	2022
LORD in the holy **m** at Jerusalem.	**Is 27:13**	2022
you are left as a flag on a **m** top And	**Is 30:17**	2022
On every lofty **m** and on every	**Is 30:25**	2022
flute, To go to the **m** of the LORD,	**Is 30:29**	2022
And every **m** and hill be made low;	**Is 40:4**	2022
Get yourself up on a high **m**,	**Is 40:9**	2022
those I will bring to My holy **m** And	**Is 56:7**	2022
lofty **m** You have made your bed.	**Is 57:7**	2022
And will possess My holy **m**."	**Is 57:13**	2022
the LORD, Who forget My holy **m**,	**Is 65:11**	2022
evil or harm in all My holy **m**,"	**Is 65:25**	2022
camels, to My holy **m** Jerusalem,"	**Is 66:20**	2022
them from every **m** and every hill and	**Jer 16:16**	2022
O **m** of Mine in the countryside, I	**Jer 17:3**	2022
And the **m** of the house as the high	**Jer 26:18**	2022
They have gone along from **m** to	**Jer 50:6**	2022
I am against you, O destroying **m**,	**Jer 51:25**	2022
And I will make you a burnt out **m**.	**Jer 51:25**	2022
the **m** which is east of the city.	**Ezk 11:23**	2022
plant *it* on a high and lofty **m**.	**Ezk 17:22**	2022
high **m** of Israel I will plant it,	**Ezk 17:23**	2022
and does not eat at the **m** *shrines*	**Ezk 18:6**	2022
is, he even eats at the **m** *shrines*,	**Ezk 18:11**	2022
"He does not eat at the **m** *shrines*	**Ezk 18:15**	2022
"For on My holy **m**, on the high	**Ezk 20:40**	2022
on the high **m** of Israel,"	**Ezk 20:40**	2022
they have eaten at the **m** *shrines*.	**Ezk 22:9**	2022
You were on the holy **m** of God;	**Ezk 28:14**	2022
you as profane From the **m** of God.	**Ezk 28:16**	2022
be on the **m** heights of Israel.	**Ezk 34:14**	2022
and set me on a very high **m**,	**Ezk 40:2**	2022
m all around *shall be* most holy.	**Ezk 43:12**	2022
became a great **m** and filled the	**Da 2:35**	2906
a stone was cut out of the **m**	**Da 2:45**	2906
Your city Jerusalem, Your holy **m**;	**Da 9:16**	2022
in behalf of the holy **m** of my God,	**Da 9:20**	2022
the seas and the beautiful Holy **M**;	**Da 11:45**	2022
And sound an alarm on My holy **m**!	**Jl 2:1**	2022
God, Dwelling in Zion, My holy **m**.	**Jl 3:17**	2022
who are on the **m** of Samaria,	**Am 4:1**	2022
feel secure in the **m** of Samaria,	**Am 6:1**	2022
understanding from the **m** of Esau?	**Ob 1:8**	2022
may be cut off from the **m** of Esau	**Ob 1:9**	2022
just as you drank on My holy **m**,	**Ob 1:16**	2022
Negev will possess the **m** of Esau,	**Ob 1:19**	2022
Mount Zion To judge the **m** of Esau,	**Ob 1:21**	2022
And the **m** of the temple *will*	**Mi 3:12**	2022
That the **m** of the house of the LORD	**Mi 4:1**	2022
"Come and let us go up to the **m**	**Mi 4:2**	2022
from sea to sea and **m** to mountain.	**Mi 7:12**	2022
from sea to sea and mountain to **m**.	**Mi 7:12**	2022
again be haughty On My holy **m**.	**Zph 3:11**	2022
'What are you, O great **m**?	**Zch 4:7**	2022
and the **m** of the LORD of hosts	**Zch 8:3**	2022
hosts *will be called* the Holy **M**.'	**Zch 8:3**	2022
so that half of the **m** will move	**Zch 14:4**	2022
devil took Him to a very high **m** and	**Mt 4:8**	*3735*
crowds, He went up on the **m**;	**Mt 5:1**	*3735*
When Jesus came down from the **m**,	**Mt 8:1**	*3735*
up on the **m** by Himself to pray;	**Mt 14:23**	*3735*
and having gone up on the **m**,	**Mt 15:29**	*3735*
them up on a high **m** by themselves.	**Mt 17:1**	*3735*
they were coming down from the **m**,	**Mt 17:9**	*3735*
seed, you will say to this **m**,	**Mt 17:20**	*3735*
but even if you say to this **m**,	**Mt 21:21**	*3735*
the **m** which Jesus had designated.	**Mt 28:16**	*3735*
And He went up on the **m** and	**Mk 3:13**	*3735*
of swine feeding nearby on the **m**.	**Mk 5:11**	*3735*
He left for the **m** to pray.	**Mk 6:46**	*3735*
them up on a high **m** by themselves.	**Mk 9:2**	*3735*
they were coming down from the **m**,	**Mk 9:9**	*3735*
to you, whoever says to this **m**,	**Mk 11:23**	*3735*
M AND HILL WILL BE BROUGHT LOW;	**Lk 3:5**	*3735*
that He went off to the **m** to pray,	**Lk 6:12**	*3735*
many swine feeding there on the **m**;	**Lk 8:32**	*3735*
and went up on the **m** to pray.	**Lk 9:28**	*3735*
they came down from the **m**,	**Lk 9:37**	*3735*
"Our fathers worshiped in this **m**,	**Jn 4:20**	*3735*
is coming when neither in this **m** nor	**Jn 4:21**	*3735*
Then Jesus went up on the **m**,	**Jn 6:3**	*3735*
withdrew again to the **m** by Himself	**Jn 6:15**	*3735*
WHICH WAS SHOWN YOU ON THE **M**."	**Heb 8:5**	*3735*
For you have not come to *a* **m** that	**Heb 12:18**	
"IF EVEN A BEAST TOUCHES THE **M**,	**Heb 12:20**	*3735*
we were with Him on the holy **m**.	**2Pe 1:18**	*3735*
and every **m** and island were moved	**Rv 6:14**	*3735*
like a great **m** burning with fire	**Rv 8:8**	*3735*
the Spirit to a great and high **m**,	**Rv 21:10**	*3735*

MOUNTAINS

so that all the high **m** everywhere	**Gn 7:19**	2022
higher, and the **m** were covered.	**Gn 7:20**	2022
ark rested upon the **m** of Ararat.	**Gn 8:4**	2022
the tops of the **m** became visible.	**Gn 8:5**	2022
escape to the **m**,	**Gn 19:17**	2022
but I cannot escape to the **m**,	**Gn 19:19**	2022
up from Zoar, and stayed in the **m**,	**Gn 19:30**	2022
the **m** of which I will tell you."	**Gn 22:2**	2022
to kill them in the **m** and to destroy	**Ex 32:12**	2022
Moab's king from the **m** of the East,	**Nu 23:7**	2022
and camped in the **m** of Abarim,	**Nu 33:47**	2022
journeyed from the **m** of Abarim and	**Nu 33:48**	2022
on the high **m** and on the hills and	**Dt 12:2**	2022
on fire the foundations of the **m**.	**Dt 32:22**	2022
the best things of the ancient **m**,	**Dt 33:15**	2022
"The **m** quaked at the presence of	**Jg 5:5**	2022
the dens which were in the **m**	**Jg 6:2**	2022
against him on the tops of the **m**,	**Jg 9:25**	2022
down from the tops of the **m**."	**Jg 9:36**	2022
You are seeing the shadow of the **m**	**Jg 9:36**	2022
that I may go to the **m** and weep	**Jg 11:37**	2022
and wept on the **m** because of her	**Jg 11:38**	2022
one hunts a partridge in the **m**."	**1Sa 26:20**	2022
"O **m** of Gilboa, Let not dew or	**2Sa 1:21**	2022
80,000 hewers *of stone* in the **m**,	**1Ki 5:15**	2022
strong wind was rending the **m**	**1Ki 19:11**	2022
"Their gods are gods of the **m**,	**1Ki 20:23**	2022

"The LORD is a god of *the* **m**, 1Ki 20:28 2022
saw all Israel Scattered on the **m**, 1Ki 22:17 2022
I came up to the heights of the **m**, 2Ki 19:23 2022
as swift as the gazelles on the **m**. 1Ch 12:8 2022
men to quarry *stone* in the **m** and 2Ch 2:2 2022
80,000 to quarry *stones* in the **m** and 2Ch 2:18 2022
saw all Israel Scattered on the **m**, 2Ch 18:16 2022
high places in the **m** of Judah, 2Ch 21:11 2022
"*It is God* who removes the **m**, Jb 9:5 2022
He overturns the **m** at the base. Jb 28:9 2022
"He explores the **m** for his pasture And Jb 39:8 2022
"Surely the **m** bring him food, And Jb 40:20 2022
And the foundations of the **m** were Ps 18:7 2022
righteousness is like the **m** of God; Ps 36:6 2022
And though the **m** slip into the Ps 46:2 2022
the **m** quake at its swelling pride. Ps 46:3 2022
"I know every bird of the **m**, Ps 50:11 2022
establishes the **m** by His strength, Ps 65:6 2022
with envy, O **m** with *many* peaks, Ps 68:16 2022
the **m** bring peace to the people, Ps 72:3 2022
in the earth on top of the **m**; Ps 72:16 2022
More majestic than the **m** of prey. Ps 76:4 2022
m were covered with its shadow, Ps 80:10 2022
a flame that sets the **m** on fire, Ps 83:14 2022
His foundation is in the holy **m**. Ps 87:1 2022
Before the **m** were born Or You Ps 90:2 2022
The peaks of the **m** are His also. Ps 95:4 2022
The **m** melted like wax at the Ps 97:5 2022
Let the **m** sing together for joy Ps 98:8 2022
waters were standing above the **m**. Ps 104:6 2022
The **m** rose; the valleys sank down Ps 104:8 2022
They flow between the **m**; Ps 104:10 2022
He waters the **m** from His upper Ps 104:13 2022
The high **m** are for the wild goats; Ps 104:18 2022
He touches the **m**, and they smoke. Ps 104:32 2022
The **m** skipped like rams, The Ps 114:4 2022
O **m**, that you skip like rams? Ps 114:6 2022
I will lift up my eyes to the **m**; Ps 121:1 2022
As the **m** surround Jerusalem, So Ps 125:2 2022
Coming down upon the **m** of Zion; Ps 133:3 2022
Touch the **m**, that they may smoke. Ps 144:5 2022
Who makes grass to grow on the **m**. Ps 147:8 2022
M and all hills; Fruit trees and all Ps 148:9 2022
"Before the **m** were settled, Pr 8:25 2022
herbs of the **m** are gathered in, Pr 27:25 2022
he is coming, Climbing on the **m**, SS 2:8 2022
a young stag on the **m** of Bether." SS 2:17 2022
of lions, From the **m** of leopards. SS 4:8 2022
a young stag On the **m** of spices." SS 8:14 2022
established as the chief of the **m**, Is 2:2 2022
Against all the lofty **m**, Is 2:14 2022
them down. And the **m** quaked Is 5:25 2022
A sound of tumult on the **m**, Is 13:4 2022
and I will trample him on My **m**. Is 14:25 2022
chaff in the **m** before the wind, Is 17:13 2022
as a standard is raised on the **m**, Is 18:3 2022
And the **m** will be drenched with Is 34:3 2022
I came up to the heights of the **m**, Is 37:24 2022
And weighed the **m** in a balance And Is 40:12 2022
You will thresh the **m** and Is 41:15 2022
for joy from the tops of the **m**. Is 42:11 2022
"I will lay waste the **m** and hills And Is 42:15 2022
forth into a shout of joy, you **m**, Is 44:23 2022
"I will make all My **m** a road, Is 49:11 2022
forth into joyful shouting, O **m**! Is 49:13 2022
How lovely on the **m** Are the feet Is 52:7 2022
"For the **m** may be removed and the Is 54:10 2022
The **m** and the hills will break forth Is 55:12 2022
the **m** might quake at Your presence Is 64:1 2022
the **m** quaked at Your presence. Is 64:3 2022
they have burned incense on the **m** And Is 65:7 2022
And an heir of My **m** from Judah; Is 65:9 2022
a deception, A tumult *on* the **m**. Jer 3:23 2022
I looked on the **m**, and behold, Jer 4:24 2022
"For the **m** I will take up a weeping Jer 9:10 2022
your feet stumble On the dusky **m**, Jer 13:16 2022
looms up like Tabor among the **m**, Jer 46:18 2022
made them turn aside *on* the **m**; Jer 50:6 2022
They chased us on the **m**, La 4:19 2022
set your face toward the **m** of Israel, Ezk 6:2 2022
'**M** of Israel, listen to the word Ezk 6:3 2022
Thus says the Lord GOD to the **m**, Ezk 6:3 2022
hill, on all the tops of the **m**, Ezk 6:13 2022
than joyful shouting on the **m**. Ezk 7:7 2022
the **m** like doves of the valleys, Ezk 7:16 2022
heard no more On the **m** of Israel. Ezk 19:9 2022
on the **m** and in all the valleys Ezk 31:12 2022
I will lay your flesh on the **m** And Ezk 32:5 2022
of your blood As far as the **m**, Ezk 32:6 2022
the **m** of Israel will be desolate so Ezk 33:28 2022
all the **m** and on every high hill; Ezk 34:6 2022
will feed them on the **m** of Israel, Ezk 34:13 2022
rich pasture on the **m** of Israel. Ezk 34:14 2022
I will fill its **m** with its slain; Ezk 35:8 2022
against the **m** of Israel saying, Ezk 35:12 2022
to the **m** of Israel and say, Ezk 36:1 2022
'O **m** of Israel, hear the word of Ezk 36:1 2022
'Therefore, O **m** of Israel, hear Ezk 36:4 2022
GOD to the **m** and to the hills, Ezk 36:4 2022
and say to the **m** and to the hills, Ezk 36:6 2022
'But you, O **m** of Israel, you will Ezk 36:8 2022
in the land, on the **m** of Israel; Ezk 37:22 2022
from many nations to the **m** of Israel Ezk 38:8 2022
the **m** also will be thrown down, Ezk 38:20 2022
a sword against him on all My **m**," Ezk 38:21 2022
bring you against the **m** of Israel. Ezk 39:2 2022
"You will fall on the **m** of Israel, Ezk 39:4 2022
sacrifice on the **m** of Israel, Ezk 39:17 2022
offer sacrifices on the tops of the **m** Hos 4:13 2022
Then they will say to the **m**, Hos 10:8 2022
As the dawn is spread over the **m**, Jl 2:2 2022
They leap on the tops of the **m**, Jl 2:5 2022
The **m** will drip with sweet wine, Jl 3:18 2022
"Assemble yourselves on the **m** of Am 3:9 2022
He who forms **m** and creates the Am 4:13 2022
When the **m** will drip sweet wine And Am 9:13 2022
"I descended to the roots of the **m**. Jon 2:6 2022
The **m** will melt under Him And the Mi 1:4 2022
established as the chief of the **m**. Mi 4:1 2022
plead your case before the **m**, Mi 6:1 2022
"Listen, you **m**, to the indictment Mi 6:2 2022
M quake because of Him And the Na 1:5 2022
on the **m** the feet of him who Na 1:15 2022
people are scattered on the **m** And Na 3:18 2022
the perpetual **m** were shattered, Hab 3:6 2022
The **m** saw You *and* quaked; Hab 3:10 2022
"Go up to the **m**, bring wood and Hg 1:8 2022
a drought on the land, on the **m**, Hg 1:11 2022
forth from between the two **m**; Zch 6:1 2022
and the **m** *were* bronze mountains. Zch 6:1 2022
and the mountains *were* bronze **m**. Zch 6:1 2022
will flee by the valley of My **m**, Zch 14:5 2022
of the **m** will reach to Azel; Zch 14:5 2022
I have made his **m** a desolation and Mal 1:3 2022
leave the ninety-nine on the **m** and Mt 18:12 *3735*
who are in Judea must flee to the **m**. Mt 24:16 *3735*
among the tombs and in the **m**, Mk 5:5 *3735*
who are in Judea must flee to the **m**. Mk 13:14 *3735*
who are in Judea must flee to the **m**. Lk 21:21 *3735*
they will begin TO SAY TO THE **M**, Lk 23:30 *3735*
have all faith, so as to remove **m**, 1Co 13:2 *3735*
wandering in deserts and **m** and Heb 11:38 *3735*
and among the rocks of the **m**; Rv 6:15 *3735*
said to the **m** and to the rocks, Rv 6:16 *3735*
away, and the **m** were not found. Rv 16:20 *3735*
seven **m** on which the woman sits, Rv 17:9 *3735*

MOUNTED
and they **m** the camels and followed Gn 24:61 7392
his sons and **m** them on a donkey, Ex 4:20 7392
they **m** four rows of stones on it. Ex 39:10 4390
filigree *settings* when they were **m**. Ex 39:13 4396
he **m** its lamps at the front of the Nu 8:3 5927
and each **m** his mule and fled. 2Sa 13:29 7392
And anger also **m** against Israel, Ps 78:21 5927
Humble, and **m** on a donkey, Zch 9:9 7392
M ON A DONKEY, EVEN ON A COLT, Mt 21:5 *1910*

MOUNTS
your command that the eagle **m** up And Jb 39:27 1361b
also to provide **m** to put Paul on Ac 23:24 *2934*

MOURN
m for Sarah and to weep for her. Gn 23:2 5594
and **m** her father and mother a full Dt 21:13 1058
old prophet to **m** and to bury him. 1Ki 13:29 5594
shall **m** for him and bury him, 1Ki 14:13 5594
do not **m** or weep." Ne 8:9 56
those who **m** are lifted to safety. Jb 5:11 6937
A time to **m** and a time to dance. Ec 3:4 5594
And her gates will lament and **m**, Is 3:26 56
cast a line into the Nile will **m**, Is 19:8 56
Who will **m** for you? Is 51:19 5110
To comfort all who **m**, Is 61:2 57
To grant those who **m** *in* Zion, Is 61:3 57
with her, all you who **m** over her, Is 66:10 56
"For this the earth shall **m** And Jer 4:28 56
M as for an only son, A Jer 6:26 60
I **m**, dismay has taken hold of me. Jer 8:21 6937
How long is the land to **m** And the Jer 12:4 56
Jerusalem, Or who will **m** for you, Jer 15:5 5110
weep for the dead or **m** for him, Jer 22:10 5110
"**M** for him, all you who *live* Jer 48:17 5110
buyer rejoice nor the seller **m**; Ezk 7:12 56
'The king will **m**, the prince will Ezk 7:27 56
but you shall not **m** and Ezk 24:16 5594
You will not **m** and you will not Ezk 24:23 5594
up, and I made Lebanon **m** for it, Ezk 31:15 6937
Indeed, its people will **m** for it, Hos 10:5 56
The priests **m**, The ministers of Jl 1:9 56
the shepherds' pasture grounds **m**, Am 1:2 56
And everyone who dwells in it **m**? Am 8:8 56
And all those who dwell in it **m**, Am 9:5 56
and they will **m** for Him, as one Zch 12:10 5594
"The land will **m**, Zch 12:12 5594
'Blessed are those who **m**, Mt 5:4 *3996*
cannot **m** as long as the bridegroom Mt 9:15 *3996*
sang a dirge, and you did not **m**.' Mt 11:17 *2875*
the tribes of the earth will **m**, Mt 24:30 *2875*
now, for you shall **m** and weep. Lk 6:25 *3996*
and I may **m** over many of those who 2Co 12:21 *3996*
Be miserable and **m** and weep; Jas 4:9 *3996*
tribes of the earth will **m** over Him. Rv 1:7 *2875*
of the earth weep and **m** over her, Rv 18:11 *3996*

MOURNED
and **m** for his son many days. Gn 37:34 56
of Israel, the people **m** greatly. Nu 14:39 56
and the people **m** because the LORD 1Sa 6:19 56
gathered together and **m** for him, 1Sa 25:1 5594
They **m** and wept and fasted 2Sa 1:12 5594
was dead, she **m** for her husband. 2Sa 11:26 5594
And *David* **m** for his son every day. 2Sa 13:37 56
own grave, and they **m** over him, 1Ki 13:30 5594
Israel buried him and **m** for him, 1Ki 14:18 5594
Their father Ephraim **m** many days, 1Ch 7:22 56
Judah and Jerusalem **m** for Josiah. 2Ch 35:24 56
sat down and wept and **m** for days; Ne 1:4 56
'When you fasted and **m** in the Zch 7:5 5594
arrogant and have not **m** instead, 1Co 5:2 *3996*

MOURNER
"Please pretend to be a **m**, 2Sa 14:2 56

MOURNERS
As one who comforted the **m**. Jb 29:25 57
while **m** go about in the street. Ec 12:5 5594
comfort to him and to his **m**, Is 57:18 57
And professional **m** to lamentation. Am 5:16 3045

MOURNERS'
will be like **m** bread; Hos 9:4 205

MOURNING
days of **m** for my father are near; Gn 27:41 60
down to Sheol in **m** for my son." Gn 37:35 57
and when the time of **m** was ended, Gn 38:12 5162
the days of **m** for him were past, Gn 50:4 1068
seven days **m** for his father. Gn 50:10 60
saw the **m** at the threshing floor Gn 50:11 60
a grievous **m** for the Egyptians." Gn 50:11 60
this sad word, they went into **m**, Ex 33:4 56
'I have not eaten of it while **m**, Dt 26:14 205
and **m** for Moses came to an end. Dt 34:8 60
When the *time of* **m** was over, 2Sa 11:27 60
and put on **m** garments now, 2Sa 14:2 60
has been **m** for the dead many days; 2Sa 14:2 56
turned to **m** for all the people, 2Sa 19:2 60
for he was **m** over the unfaithfulness Ezr 10:6 56
there was great **m** among the Jews, Es 4:3 60
But Haman hurried home, **m**, Es 6:12 57
and from **m** into a holiday; Es 9:22 60
"I go about **m** without comfort; Jb 30:28 6937
'Therefore my harp is turned to **m**, Jb 30:31 60
turned for me my **m** into dancing; Ps 30:11 4553
I bowed down **m**, as one who sorrows Ps 35:14 6937
I go **m** all day long. Ps 38:6 6937
Why do I go **m** because of the Ps 42:9 6937
Why do I go **m** because of the Ps 43:2 6937
It is better to go to a house of **m** Ec 7:2 60
of the wise is in the house of **m**; Ec 7:4 60
be *a city of* lamenting and **m**; Is 29:2 592
days of your **m** will be over. Is 60:20 60
The oil of gladness instead of **m**, Is 61:3 60
"Consider and call for the **m** women, Jer 9:17 6969
They sit on the ground in **m**, Jer 14:2 6937
"Do not enter a house of **m**, Jer 16:5 4798
not break *bread* in **m** for them, Jer 16:7 60
For I will turn their **m** into joy And Jer 31:13 60
The roads of Zion are in **m** Because La 1:4 57
daughter of Judah **M** and moaning. La 2:5 592
dancing has been turned into **m**. La 5:15 60
it were lamentations, **m** and woe. Ezk 2:10 1899
of the valleys, all of them **m**, Ezk 7:16 1993
make no **m** for the dead. Ezk 24:17 60
bitterness of soul With bitter **m**. Ezk 27:31 4553
had been **m** for three entire weeks. Da 10:2 56
And with fasting, weeping and **m**; Jl 2:12 4553
They also call the farmer to **m** And Am 5:16 60
I will turn your festivals into **m** Am 8:10 60
like *a time of* **m** for an only son, Am 8:10 60
And a **m** like the ostriches. Mi 1:8 60
will be great **m** in Jerusalem, Zch 12:11 4553
like the **m** of Hadadrimmon in the Zch 12:11 4553
in **m** before the LORD of hosts? Mal 3:14 6941
IN RAMAH, WEEPING AND GREAT **M**, Mt 2:18 *3602*
while they were **m** and weeping. Mk 16:10 *3996*
who were **m** and lamenting Him. Lk 23:27 *2875*
to us your longing, your **m**, 2Co 7:7 *3602*
your laughter be turned into **m** and Jas 4:9 *3997*
degree give her torment and **m**; Rv 18:7 *3997*
and will never see **m**.' Rv 18:7 *3997*
come, pestilence and **m** and famine, Rv 18:8 *3997*
fear of her torment, weeping and **m**, Rv 18:15 *3996*
were crying out, weeping and **m**, Rv 18:19 *3996*
there will no longer be *any* **m**, Rv 21:4 *3997*

MOURNS
is weeping and **m** for Absalom." 2Sa 19:1 56
him, And he **m** only for himself." Jb 14:22 56
The earth **m** *and* withers, the world Is 24:4 56
The new wine **m**, The vine decays, Is 24:7 56
The land **m** *and* pines away, Lebanon Is 33:9 56
Desolate, it **m** before Me; Jer 12:11 56
"Judah **m** And her gates languish Jer 14:2 56
the land **m** because of the curse. Jer 23:10 56
Therefore the land **m**, Hos 4:3 56
The field is ruined, The land **m**; Jl 1:10 56
for Him, as one **m** for an only son, Zch 12:10 5594

MOUSE
the mole, and the **m**, Lv 11:29 5909

MOUTH
which has opened its **m** to receive Gn 4:11 6310
stone on the **m** of the well was large Gn 29:2 6310
the stone from the **m** of the well and Gn 29:3 6310
in its place on the **m** of the well. Gn 29:3 6310
the stone from the **m** of the well; Gn 29:8 6310
the stone from the **m** of the well and Gn 29:10 6310
it was in the **m** of his sack. Gn 42:27 6310
returned in the **m** of your sacks; Gn 43:12 6310
money was in the **m** of his sack, Gn 43:21 6310
man's money in the **m** of his sack. Gn 44:1 6310
the **m** of the sack of the youngest, Gn 44:2 6310
which we found in the **m** of our sacks Gn 44:8 6310
is my **m** which is speaking to you. Gn 45:12 6310
"Who has made man's **m**? Ex 4:11 6310
I, even I, will be with your **m**, Ex 4:12 6310
to him and put the words in his **m**; Ex 4:15 6310
will be with your **m** and his mouth, Ex 4:15 6310
will be with your mouth and his **m**, Ex 4:15 6310
he will be as a **m** for you Ex 4:16 6310
law of the LORD may be in your **m**; Ex 13:9 6310
nor let *them* be heard from your **m**. Ex 23:13 6310

With him I speak **m** to mouth,	**Nu 12:8**	6310
With him I speak mouth to **m**,	**Nu 12:8**	6310
the ground opens its **m** and swallows	**Nu 16:30**	6310
its **m** and swallowed them up,	**Nu 16:32**	6310
LORD opened the **m** of the donkey,	**Nu 22:28**	6310
The word that God puts in my **m**,	**Nu 22:38**	6310
put a word in Balaam's **m** and said,	**Nu 23:5**	6310
what the LORD puts in my **m**?"	**Nu 23:12**	6310
and put a word in his **m** and said,	**Nu 23:16**	6310
and the earth opened its **m** and	**Nu 26:10**	6310
to all that proceeds out of his **m**.	**Nu 30:2**	6310
proceeds out of the **m** of the LORD.	**Dt 8:3**	6310
opened its **m** and swallowed them,	**Dt 11:6**	6310
and I will put My words in his **m**,	**Dt 18:18**	6310
you, in your **m** and in your heart,	**Dt 30:14**	6310
the earth hear the words of my **m**.	**Dt 32:1**	6310
law shall not depart from your **m**,	**Jos 1:8**	6310
let a word proceed out of your **m**,	**Jos 6:10**	6310
stones against the **m** of the cave,	**Jos 10:18**	6310
"Open the **m** of the cave and bring	**Jos 10:22**	6310
stones over the **m** of the cave,	**Jos 10:27**	6310
as far as the **m** of the Jordan.	**Jos 15:5**	7097a
of the sea at the **m** of the Jordan.	**Jos 15:5**	7097a
putting their hand to their **m**,	**Jg 7:6**	6310
hand over your **m** and come with us,	**Jg 18:19**	6310
LORD, that Eli was watching her **m**.	**1Sa 1:12**	6310
My **m** speaks boldly against my	**1Sa 2:1**	6310
let arrogance come out of your **m**;	**1Sa 2:3**	6310
but no man put his hand to his **m**,	**1Sa 14:26**	6310
and put his hand to his **m**,	**1Sa 14:27**	6310
him, and rescued *it* from his **m**;	**1Sa 17:35**	6310
your **m** has testified against you,	**2Sa 1:16**	6310
So Joab put the words in her **m**.	**2Sa 14:3**	6310
in the **m** of your maidservant;	**2Sa 14:19**	6310
and spread it over the well's **m** and	**2Sa 17:19**	6440
there is good news in his **m**."	**2Sa 18:25**	6310
Fire from His **m** devoured;	**2Sa 22:9**	6310
who spoke with His **m** to my father	**1Ki 8:15**	6310
You have spoken with Your **m** and	**1Ki 8:24**	6310
word of the LORD in your **m** is truth	**1Ki 17:24**	6310
every **m** that has not kissed him."	**1Ki 19:18**	6310
in the **m** of all his prophets.'	**1Ki 22:22**	6310
the **m** of all these your prophets;	**1Ki 22:23**	6310
and put his **m** on his mouth and his	**2Ki 4:34**	6310
and put his mouth on his **m** and his	**2Ki 4:34**	6310
and the judgments from His **m**,	**1Ch 16:12**	6310
who spoke with His **m** to my father	**2Ch 6:4**	6310
You have spoken with Your **m** and	**2Ch 6:15**	6310
in the **m** of all his prophets.'	**2Ch 18:21**	6310
in the **m** of these your prophets,	**2Ch 18:22**	6310
words of Neco from the **m** of God,	**2Ch 35:22**	6310
of the LORD by the **m** of Jeremiah,	**2Ch 36:21**	6310
of the LORD by the **m** of Jeremiah	**2Ch 36:22**	6310
of the LORD by the **m** of Jeremiah,	**Ezr 1:1**	6310
did not withhold from their **m**,	**Ne 9:20**	6310
the word went out of the king's **m**,	**Es 7:8**	6310
Afterward Job opened his **m** and	**Jb 3:1**	6310
saves from the sword of their **m**,	**Jb 5:15**	6310
unrighteousness must shut its **m**.	**Jb 5:16**	6310
I will not restrain my **m**;	**Jb 7:11**	6310
words of your **m** be a mighty wind?	**Jb 8:2**	6310
yet fill your **m** with laughter And	**Jb 8:21**	6310
righteous, my **m** will condemn me;	**Jb 9:20**	6310
"For your guilt teaches your **m**,	**Jb 15:5**	6310
"Your own **m** condemns you, and not	**Jb 15:6**	6310
such words to go out of your **m**?	**Jb 15:13**	6310
breath of His **m** he will go away.	**Jb 15:30**	6310
"I could strengthen you with my **m**,	**Jb 16:5**	6310
have gaped at me with their **m**,	**Jb 16:10**	6310
I have to implore him with my **m**.	**Jb 19:16**	6310
"Though evil is sweet in his **m**	**Jb 20:12**	6310
let it go, But holds it in his **m**,	**Jb 20:13**	2441
And put *your* hand over *your* **m**.	**Jb 21:5**	6310
receive instruction from His **m** And	**Jb 22:22**	6310
Him And fill my **m** with arguments.	**Jb 23:4**	6310
I have treasured the words of His **m**	**Jb 23:12**	6310
opened their **m** as for the spring rain	**Jb 29:23**	6310
my hand threw a kiss from my **m**,	**Jb 31:27**	6310
I have not allowed my **m** to sin By	**Jb 31:30**	2441
no answer in the **m** of the three men	**Jb 32:5**	6310
"Behold now, I open my **m**,	**Jb 33:2**	6310
mouth, My tongue in my **m** speaks.	**Jb 33:2**	2441
So Job opens his **m** emptily;	**Jb 35:16**	6310
you from the **m** of distress,	**Jb 36:16**	6310
rumbling that goes out from His **m**.	**Jb 37:2**	6310
I lay my hand on my **m**.	**Jb 40:4**	6310
though the Jordan rushes to his **m**.	**Jb 40:23**	6310
"Out of his **m** go burning torches;	**Jb 41:19**	6310
And a flame goes forth from his **m**.	**Jb 41:21**	6310
From the **m** of infants and nursing	**Ps 8:2**	6310
His **m** is full of curses and deceit	**Ps 10:7**	6310
that my **m** will not transgress.	**Ps 17:3**	6310
With their **m** they speak proudly.	**Ps 17:10**	6310
And fire from His **m** devoured;	**Ps 18:8**	6310
Let the words of my **m** and the	**Ps 19:14**	6310
They open wide their **m** at me,	**Ps 22:13**	6310
Save me from the lion's **m**;	**Ps 22:21**	6310
breath of His **m** all their host.	**Ps 33:6**	6310
shall continually be in my **m**.	**Ps 34:1**	6310
opened their **m** wide against me;	**Ps 35:21**	6310
The words of his **m** are wickedness	**Ps 36:3**	6310
m of the righteous utters wisdom,	**Ps 37:30**	6310
mute man who does not open his **m**.	**Ps 38:13**	6310
And in whose **m** are no arguments.	**Ps 38:14**	6310
will guard my **m** as with a muzzle	**Ps 39:1**	6310
become mute, I do not open my **m**,	**Ps 39:9**	6310
He put a new song in my **m**,	**Ps 40:3**	6310
My **m** will speak wisdom,	**Ps 49:3**	6310
And to take My covenant in your **m**?	**Ps 50:16**	6310
"You let your **m** loose in evil And	**Ps 50:19**	6310
That my **m** may declare Your praise.	**Ps 51:15**	6310
Give ear to the words of my **m**.	**Ps 54:2**	6310
shatter their teeth in their **m**;	**Ps 58:6**	6310
they belch forth with their **m**;	**Ps 59:7**	6310
On account of the sin of their **m** *and*	**Ps 59:12**	6310
They bless with their **m**,	**Ps 62:4**	6310
And my **m** offers praises with	**Ps 63:5**	6310
my **m** spoke when I was in distress.	**Ps 66:14**	6310
I cried to Him with my **m**,	**Ps 66:17**	6310
Nor the pit shut its **m** on me.	**Ps 69:15**	6310
My **m** is filled with Your praise And	**Ps 71:8**	6310
My **m** shall tell of Your	**Ps 71:15**	6310
set their **m** against the heavens,	**Ps 73:9**	6310
your ears to the words of my **m**.	**Ps 78:1**	6310
I will open my **m** in a parable;	**Ps 78:2**	6310
they deceived Him with their **m** And	**Ps 78:36**	6310
Open your **m** wide and I will fill it.	**Ps 81:10**	6310
known Your faithfulness with my **m**.	**Ps 89:1**	6310
the judgments uttered by His **m**,	**Ps 105:5**	6310
all unrighteousness shuts its **m**.	**Ps 107:42**	6310
wicked and deceitful **m** against me;	**Ps 109:2**	6310
With my **m** I will give thanks	**Ps 109:30**	6310
of All the ordinances of Your **m**.	**Ps 119:13**	6310
word of truth utterly out of my **m**,	**Ps 119:43**	6310
The law of Your **m** is better to me	**Ps 119:72**	6310
I may keep the testimony of Your **m**.	**Ps 119:88**	6310
Yes, sweeter than honey to my **m**!	**Ps 119:103**	6310
the freewill offerings of my **m**,	**Ps 119:108**	6310
I opened my **m** wide and panted, For	**Ps 119:131**	6310
our **m** was filled with laughter And	**Ps 126:2**	6310
tongue cling to the roof of my **m**	**Ps 137:6**	2441
have heard the words of Your **m**.	**Ps 138:4**	6310
Set a guard, O LORD, over my **m**;	**Ps 141:3**	6310
been scattered at the **m** of Sheol.	**Ps 141:7**	6310
of aliens, Whose **m** speaks deceit And	**Ps 144:11**	6310
My **m** will speak the praise of the	**Ps 145:21**	6310
high praises of God *be* in their **m**,	**Ps 149:6**	1627
From His **m** *come* knowledge and	**Pr 2:6**	6310
turn away from the words of my **m**.	**Pr 4:5**	6310
Put away from you a deceitful **m** And	**Pr 4:24**	6310
not depart from the words of my **m**.	**Pr 5:7**	6310
snared with the words of your **m**,	**Pr 6:2**	6310
caught with the words of your **m**,	**Pr 6:2**	6310
the one who walks with a perverse **m**,	**Pr 6:12**	6310
attention to the words of my **m**.	**Pr 7:24**	6310
"For my **m** will utter truth;	**Pr 8:7**	2441
of my **m** are in righteousness;	**Pr 8:8**	6310
the evil way And the perverted **m**,	**Pr 8:13**	6310
But the **m** of the wicked conceals	**Pr 10:6**	6310
The **m** of the righteous is a fountain	**Pr 10:11**	6310
But the **m** of the wicked conceals	**Pr 10:11**	6310
But with the **m** of the foolish,	**Pr 10:14**	6310
The **m** of the righteous flows with	**Pr 10:31**	6310
But the **m** of the wicked what	**Pr 10:32**	6310
With *his* **m** the godless man	**Pr 11:9**	6310
m of the wicked it is torn down.	**Pr 11:11**	6310
But the **m** of the upright will	**Pr 12:6**	6310
fruit of a man's **m** he enjoys good,	**Pr 13:2**	6310
guards his **m** preserves his life;	**Pr 13:3**	6310
In the **m** of the foolish is a rod	**Pr 14:3**	6310
But the **m** of fools spouts folly.	**Pr 15:2**	6310
But the **m** of fools feeds on folly.	**Pr 15:14**	6310
But the **m** of the wicked pours out	**Pr 15:28**	6310
His **m** should not err in judgment.	**Pr 16:10**	6310
heart of the wise instructs his **m**	**Pr 16:23**	6310
words of a man's **m** are deep waters;	**Pr 18:4**	6310
strife, And his **m** calls for blows.	**Pr 18:6**	6310
A fool's **m** is his ruin, And his	**Pr 18:7**	6310
With the fruit of a man's **m** his	**Pr 18:20**	6310
not even bring it back to his **m**.	**Pr 19:24**	6310
And the **m** of the wicked spreads	**Pr 19:28**	6310
his **m** will be filled with gravel.	**Pr 20:17**	6310
who guards his **m** and his tongue,	**Pr 21:23**	6310
The **m** of an adulteress is a deep	**Pr 22:14**	6310
does not open his **m** in the gate.	**Pr 24:7**	6310
So is a proverb in the **m** of fools.	**Pr 26:7**	6310
So is a proverb in the **m** of fools.	**Pr 26:9**	6310
weary of bringing it to his **m** again.	**Pr 26:15**	6310
And a flattering **m** works ruin.	**Pr 26:28**	6310
praise you, and not your own **m**;	**Pr 27:2**	6310
She eats and wipes her **m**,	**Pr 30:20**	6310
evil, put your hand on your **m**.	**Pr 30:32**	6310
Open your **m** for the mute, For the	**Pr 31:8**	6310
Open your **m**, judge righteously,	**Pr 31:9**	6310
She opens her **m** in wisdom, And the	**Pr 31:26**	6310
All a man's labor is for his **m** and	**Ec 6:7**	6310
Words from the **m** of a wise man	**Ec 10:12**	6310
kiss me with the kisses of his **m**!	**SS 1:2**	6310
thread, And your **m** is lovely.	**SS 4:3**	4057a
"His **m** is *full of* sweetness.	**SS 5:16**	2441
And your **m** like the best wine!"	**SS 7:9**	2441
the **m** of the LORD has spoken.	**Is 1:20**	6310
and opened its **m** without measure;	**Is 5:14**	6310
He touched my **m** *with it* and said,	**Is 6:7**	6310
every **m** is speaking foolishness.	**Is 9:17**	6310
the earth with the rod of His **m**,	**Is 11:4**	6310
For His **m** has commanded, And His	**Is 34:16**	6310
the **m** of the LORD has spoken."	**Is 40:5**	6310
The word has gone forth from My **m**	**Is 45:23**	6310
ago And they went forth from My **m**,	**Is 48:3**	6310
has made My **m** like a sharp sword,	**Is 49:2**	6310
"I have put My words in your **m** and	**Is 51:16**	6310
Yet He did not open His **m**;	**Is 53:7**	6310
So He did not open His **m**.	**Is 53:7**	6310
Nor was there any deceit in His **m**.	**Is 53:9**	6310
be which goes forth from My **m**;	**Is 55:11**	6310
your **m** And stick out your tongue?	**Is 57:4**	6310
the **m** of the LORD has spoken."	**Is 58:14**	6310
words which I have put in your **m** shall	**Is 59:21**	6310
shall not depart from your **m**,	**Is 59:21**	6310
nor from the **m** of your offspring,	**Is 59:21**	6310
nor from the **m** of your offspring's	**Is 59:21**	6310
the **m** of the LORD will designate.	**Is 62:2**	6310
out His hand and touched my **m**,	**Jer 1:9**	6310
I have put My words in your **m**.	**Jer 1:9**	6310
am making My words in your **m** fire	**Jer 5:14**	6310
and has been cut off from their **m**.	**Jer 7:28**	6310
With his **m** one speaks peace to his	**Jer 9:8**	6310
whom the **m** of the LORD has spoken,	**Jer 9:12**	6310
ear receive the word of His **m**;	**Jer 9:20**	6310
Not from the **m** of the LORD.	**Jer 23:16**	6310
invoked again by the **m** of any man	**Jer 44:26**	6310
nests Beyond the **m** of the chasm.	**Jer 48:28**	6310
has swallowed come out of his **m**;	**Jer 51:44**	6310
Let him put his **m** in the dust,	**La 3:29**	6310
Is it not from the **m** of the Most	**La 3:38**	6310
cleaves To the roof of its **m** because	**La 4:4**	2441
Open your **m** and eat what I am	**Ezk 2:8**	6310
So I opened my **m**, and He fed me	**Ezk 3:2**	6310
and it was sweet as honey in my **m**.	**Ezk 3:3**	6310
you hear a word from My **m**,	**Ezk 3:17**	6310
tongue stick to the roof of your **m**	**Ezk 3:26**	2441
speak to you, I will open your **m** and	**Ezk 3:27**	6310
unclean meat ever entered my **m**."	**Ezk 4:14**	6310
and never open your **m** anymore	**Ezk 16:63**	6310
rams, to open the **m** for slaughter,	**Ezk 21:22**	6310
'On that day your **m** will be opened	**Ezk 24:27**	6310
will open your **m** in their midst.	**Ezk 29:21**	6310
you will hear a message from My **m** and	**Ezk 33:7**	6310
And He opened my **m** at the time	**Ezk 33:22**	6310
so my **m** was opened and I was no	**Ezk 33:22**	6310
desires *expressed* by their **m**,	**Ezk 33:31**	6310
deliver My flock from their **m**,	**Ezk 34:10**	6310
"While the word *was* in the king's **m**,	**Da 4:31**	6433
and laid over the **m** of the den;	**Da 6:17**	6433
were in its **m** between its teeth;	**Da 7:5**	6433
and a **m** uttering great *boasts*.	**Da 7:8**	6433
and a **m** uttering great *boasts*	**Da 7:20**	6433
nor did meat or wine enter my **m**,	**Da 10:3**	6310
then I opened my **m** and spoke and	**Da 10:16**	6310
the names of the Baals from her **m**,	**Hos 2:17**	6310
slain them by the words of My **m**;	**Hos 6:5**	6310
wine That is cut off from your **m**.	**Jl 1:5**	6310
shepherd snatches from the lion's **m**	**Am 3:12**	6310
For the **m** of the LORD of hosts has	**Mi 4:4**	6310
tongue is deceitful in their **m**.	**Mi 6:12**	6310
will put *their* hand on *their* **m**,	**Mi 7:16**	6310
they fall into the eater's **m**.	**Na 3:12**	6310
words from the **m** of the prophets,	**Zch 8:9**	6310
remove their blood from their **m** And	**Zch 9:7**	6310
their tongue will rot in their **m**.	**Zch 14:12**	6310
"True instruction was in his **m** and	**Mal 2:6**	6310
seek instruction from his **m**;	**Mal 2:7**	6310
PROCEEDS OUT OF THE **M** OF GOD.' "	**Mt 4:4**	*4750*
opened His **m** and *began* to teach	**Mt 5:2**	*4750*
For the **m** speaks out of that which	**Mt 12:34**	*4750*
"I WILL OPEN MY **M** IN PARABLES;	**Mt 13:35**	*4750*
enters into the **m** *that* defiles the man,	**Mt 15:11**	*4750*
but what proceeds out of the **m**,	**Mt 15:11**	*4750*
everything that goes into the **m**	**Mt 15:17**	*4750*
the things that proceed out of the **m**	**Mt 15:18**	*4750*
and when you open its **m**,	**Mt 17:27**	*4750*
so that BY THE **M** OF TWO OR THREE	**Mt 18:16**	*4750*
'OUT OF THE **M** OF INFANTS AND	**Mt 21:16**	*4750*
the ground and he foams *at the* **m**,	**Mk 9:18**	
rolling around and foaming *at the* **m**.	**Mk 9:20**	
And at once his **m** was opened and	**Lk 1:64**	*4750*
As He spoke by the **m** of His holy	**Lk 1:70**	*4750*
for his **m** speaks from that which	**Lk 6:45**	*4750*
convulsion with foaming *at the* **m**;	**Lk 9:39**	
heard it ourselves from His own **m**.	**Lk 22:71**	*4750*
and brought it up to His **m**.	**Jn 19:29**	*4750*
the **m** of David concerning Judas,	**Ac 1:16**	*4750*
by the **m** of all the prophets,	**Ac 3:18**	*4750*
spoke by the **m** of His holy prophets	**Ac 3:21**	*4750*
through the **m** of our father David	**Ac 4:25**	*4750*
SILENT, SO HE DOES NOT OPEN HIS **M**.	**Ac 8:32**	*4750*
Then Philip opened his **m**,	**Ac 8:35**	*4750*
Opening his **m**, Peter said:	**Ac 10:34**	*4750*
or unclean has ever entered my **m**.'	**Ac 11:8**	*4750*
that by my **m** the Gentiles would	**Ac 15:7**	*4750*
the same things by word *of* **m**.	**Ac 15:27**	
when Paul was about to open his **m**,	**Ac 18:14**	*4750*
to hear an utterance from His **m**.	**Ac 22:14**	*4750*
beside him to strike him on the **m**.	**Ac 23:2**	*4750*
"WHOSE **M** IS FULL OF CURSING AND	**Ro 3:14**	*4750*
Law, so that every **m** may be closed	**Ro 3:19**	*4750*
IN YOUR **M** AND IN YOUR HEART"	**Ro 10:8**	*4750*
confess with your **m** Jesus *as* Lord,	**Ro 10:9**	*4750*
and with the **m** he confesses,	**Ro 10:10**	*4750*
Our **m** has spoken freely to you, O	**2Co 6:11**	*4750*
word proceed from your **m**,	**Eph 4:29**	*4750*
to me in the opening of my **m**,	**Eph 6:19**	*4750*
and abusive speech from your **m**.	**Col 3:8**	*4750*
will slay with the breath of His **m**	**2Th 2:8**	*4750*
whether by word *of* **m** or by letter	**2Th 2:15**	
was rescued out of the lion's **m**.	**2Tm 4:17**	*4750*
from the same **m** come *both* blessing	**Jas 3:10**	*4750*
WAS ANY DECEIT FOUND IN HIS **M**;	**1Pe 2:22**	*4750*
and out of His **m** came a sharp	**Rv 1:16**	*4750*
them with the sword of My **m**.	**Rv 2:16**	*4750*
cold, I will spit you out of My **m**.	**Rv 3:16**	*4750*
in your **m** it will be sweet as honey.	**Rv 10:9**	*4750*
and in my **m** it was sweet as honey;	**Rv 10:10**	*4750*
fire flows out of their **m** and	**Rv 11:5**	*4750*
water like a river out of his **m**	**Rv 12:15**	*4750*
and the earth opened its **m** and	**Rv 12:16**	*4750*

the dragon poured out of his **m**. Rv 12:16 *4750*
his **m** like the mouth of a lion. Rv 13:2 *4750*
his mouth like the **m** of a lion. Rv 13:2 *4750*
There was given to him a **m** Rv 13:5 *4750*
opened his **m** in blasphemies against Rv 13:6 *4750*
And no lie was found in their **m**; Rv 14:5 *4750*
coming out of the **m** of the dragon Rv 16:13 *4750*
out of the **m** of the beast and out Rv 16:13 *4750*
out of the **m** of the false prophet, Rv 16:13 *4750*
From His **m** comes a sharp sword, Rv 19:15 *4750*
m of Him who sat on the horse, Rv 19:21 *4750*

MOUTHS
And put *their* hands on their **m**; Jb 29:9 6310
For the **m** of those who speak lies Ps 63:11 6310
While their food was in their **m**, Ps 78:30 6310
They have **m**, but they cannot speak; Ps 115:5 6310
They have **m**, but they do not speak; Ps 135:16 6310
any breath at all in their **m**. Ps 135:17 6310
Whose **m** speak deceit, And whose Ps 144:8 6310
shut their **m** on account of Him; Is 52:15 6310
that has proceeded from our **m**, Jer 44:17 6310
you have spoken with your **m** and Jer 44:25 6310
opened their **m** wide against you; La 2:16 6310
have opened their **m** against us. La 3:46 6310
His angel and shut the lions' **m** and Da 6:22 6133
him who puts nothing in their **m** They Mi 3:5 6310
they will all cover *their* **m** Mi 3:7 8222
deceitful tongue Be found in their **m** Zph 3:13 6310
promises, shut the **m** of lions, Heb 11:33 *4750*
horses' **m** so that they will obey us, Jas 3:3 *4750*
and out of their **m** proceed fire Rv 9:17 *4750*
which proceeded out of their **m**. Rv 9:18 *4750*
is in their **m** and in their tails; Rv 9:19 *4750*

MOVE
in the morning, they would **m** out; Nu 9:21 5265
and the people did not **m** on until Nu 12:15 5265
m your neighbor's boundary mark, Dt 19:14 5472
David was unwilling to **m** the ark 2Sa 6:10 5493
"For the eyes of the LORD **m** to 2Ch 16:9 7751a
Were He to **m** past *me,* I would not Jb 9:11 2498
There the ships **m** along, *And* Ps 104:26 1980
Do not **m** the ancient boundary Pr 22:28 5472
Do not **m** the ancient boundary Or Pr 23:10 5472
It does not **m** from its place. Is 46:7 4185
For they **m** on like an army And Jer 46:22 1980
like those who **m** a boundary; Hos 5:10 5472
half of the mountain will **m** toward Zch 14:4 4185
'**M** from here to there,' and it Mt 17:20 *3327*
here to there,' and it will **m**; Mt 17:20 *3327*
m them with *so much as* a finger. Mt 23:4 *2795*
'Friend, **m** up higher'; Lk 14:10 *4320*
God had him **m** to this country in Ac 7:4 *3351*
in Him we live and **m** and exist, Ac 17:28 *2795*
if somehow I might **m** to jealousy Ro 11:14 *3863*

MOVED
flesh that **m** on the earth perished, Gn 7:21 7430
and **m** his tents as far as Sodom. Gn 13:12 167
Then Abram **m** his tent and came and Gn 13:18 167
He **m** away from there and dug Gn 26:22 6275
"They have **m** from here; Gn 37:17 5265
of Israel, **m** and went behind them; Ex 14:19 5265
and the pillar of cloud **m** from Ex 14:19 5265
everyone whose spirit **m** him came Ex 35:21 5068
Then all whose hearts **m** them, Ex 35:22 5081
whose heart **m** them to bring Ex 35:29 5068
So they **m** out for the first time Nu 10:13 5265
the people **m** out from Hazeroth and Nu 12:16 5265
Israel **m** out and camped in Oboth. Nu 21:10 5265
for the LORD was **m** to pity by Jg 2:18 5162
The king was deeply **m** and went 2Sa 18:33 7264
was **m** by prayer for the land. 2Sa 21:14 6279
was **m** by prayer for the land, 2Sa 24:25 6279
established, it will not be **m**. 1Ch 16:30 4131
their own place and not be **m** again; 1Ch 17:9 7264
and **m** David to number Israel. 1Ch 21:1 5496
He was **m** by his entreaty and heard 2Ch 33:13 6279
the rock to be **m** from its place? Jb 18:4 6275
"I will not be **m**; Ps 10:6 4131
"I will never be **m**." Ps 30:6 4131
midst of her, she will not be **m**; Ps 46:5 4131
established, it will not be **m**. Ps 93:1 4131
established, it will not be **m**; Ps 96:10 4131
as Mount Zion, which cannot be **m** but Ps 125:1 4131
of the righteous will not be **m**. Pr 12:3 4131
And all the hills **m** to and fro. Jer 4:24 7043
faces did not turn when they **m**, Ezk 1:9 1980
Whenever they **m**, they moved in any Ezk 1:17 1980
they **m** in any of their four Ezk 1:17 1980
without turning as they **m**. Ezk 1:17 1980
Whenever the living beings **m**, Ezk 1:19 1980
moved, the wheels **m** with them. Ezk 1:19 1980
When they **m**, they went in *any of* Ezk 10:11 1980
Now when the cherubim **m**, Ezk 10:16 1980
"And his lord, **m** with anger, Mt 18:34 *3710*
M with compassion, Jesus touched Mt 20:34 *4697*
M with compassion, Jesus stretched Mk 1:41 *4697*
He was deeply **m** in spirit and Jn 11:33 *1690*
again being deeply **m** within, Jn 11:38 *1690*
and not **m** away from the hope of Col 1:23 *3334*
but men **m** by the Holy Spirit spoke 2Pe 1:21 *5342*
island were **m** out of their places. Rv 6:14 *2795*

MOVES
and every living creature that **m**, Gn 1:21 7430
thing that **m** on the earth." Gn 1:28 7430
to every thing that **m** on the earth Gn 1:30 7430
everything that **m** on the earth, Gn 8:19 7430
from every man whose heart **m** him Ex 25:2 5068
living thing that **m** in the waters and Lv 11:46 7430
m his neighbor's boundary mark.' Dt 27:17 5472
And the rock **m** from its place; Jb 14:18 6275
that **m** in the field is Mine. Ps 50:11 2123a
and everything that **m** in them. Ps 69:34 7430
whatever **m** in the field feeds on it. Ps 80:13 2123a
"Its sound **m** along like a serpent; Jer 46:22 1980
Their horde of faces **m** forward. Hab 1:9

MOVING
and the Spirit of God was **m** over Gn 1:2 7363b
"Every **m** thing that is alive Gn 9:3 7431
her heart, only her lips were **m**, 1Sa 1:13 5128
but I have been **m** about in a tent, 2Sa 7:6 1980
Do not keep **m** from house to house. Lk 10:7 *3327*
waiting for the **m** of the waters; Jn 5:3 *2796a*
them, **m** about freely in Jerusalem, Ac 9:28 *1531, 2532, 1607*

MOW
bows will **m** down the young men, Is 13:18 7376

MOWED
of the laborers who **m** your fields, Jas 5:4 *270*

MOWING
spring crop *was* after the king's **m**. Am 7:1 1488

MOWN
down like rain upon the **m** grass, Ps 72:6 1488

MOZA
Caleb's concubine, bore Haran, **M** and 1Ch 2:46 4162
and Zimri became the father of **M**. 1Ch 8:36 4162
M became the father of Binea; 1Ch 8:37 4162
and Zimri became the father of **M**, 1Ch 9:42 4162
and **M** became the father of Binea 1Ch 9:43 4162

MOZAH
and Mizpeh and Chephirah and **M**, Jos 18:26 4681

MUCH
ever so **m** bridal payment and gift, Gn 34:12 7235a, 3966
five times as **m** as any of theirs. Gn 43:34 7235a
with food, as **m** as they can carry, Gn 44:1 3512c
twice as **m** as they gather daily." Ex 16:5 834
every man as **m** as he should eat; Ex 16:16 6310
some gathered **m** and *some* little. Ex 16:17 7235a
who had gathered **m** had no excess, Ex 16:18 7235a
gathered as **m** as he should eat. Ex 16:18 6310
every man as **m** as he should eat; Ex 16:21 6310
they gathered twice as **m** bread, Ex 16:22 4932
of fragrant cinnamon half as **m**, Ex 30:23 4276
"The people are bringing **m** more Ex 36:5 7235a
(I know that you have **m** livestock) shall Dt 3:19 7227a
"You shall bring out **m** seed to Dt 28:38 7227a
how **m** more, then, after my death? Dt 31:27 637, 3588
and very **m** of the land remains to Jos 13:1 7235a
riches and with very **m** livestock, Jos 22:8 7227a
then take as **m** as you desire," 1Sa 2:16 3512c
"How **m** more, if only the people 1Sa 14:30 637, 3588
"Has the LORD as **m** delight in 1Sa 15:22
how **m** more then today will their 1Sa 21:5 637, 3588
How **m** more then if we go to Keilah 1Sa 23:3 637, 3588
if by morning I leave *as* **m** *as* one 1Sa 25:22
Nabal until the morning light as **m** 1Sa 25:34
accomplish **m** and surely prevail." 1Sa 26:25 6213a
and brought **m** spoil with them; 2Sa 3:22 7227a
"How **m** more, when wicked men have 2Sa 4:11 637, 3588
how **m** more now this Benjamite? 2Sa 16:11 637, 3588
So Hiram gave Solomon as **m** as he 1Ki 5:10 3605
how **m** less this house which I have 1Ki 8:27 637, 3588
very **m** gold and precious stones. 1Ki 10:2 7227a
and mules, so **m** year by year. 1Ki 10:25 1697
m for you to go up to Jerusalem; 1Ki 12:28 7227a
How **m** more *then,* when he says to 2Ki 5:13 637, 3588
Jehu will serve him **m**. 2Ki 10:18 7235a
there was **m** money in the chest, 2Ki 12:10 7227a
He did **m** evil in the sight of the 2Ki 21:6 7235a
shed very **m** innocent blood 2Ki 21:16 7235a
'You have shed **m** blood and have 1Ch 22:8 7230
so **m** blood on the earth before Me. 1Ch 22:8 7227a
how **m** less this house which I have 2Ch 6:18 637, 3588
and mules, so **m** year by year. 2Ch 9:24 1697
they carried away very **m** plunder. 2Ch 14:13 7235a
for there was **m** plunder in them. 2Ch 14:14 7227a
spoil, they found **m** among them, 2Ch 20:25 7230
the spoil because there was so **m**. 2Ch 20:25 7227a
they saw that there was **m** money, 2Ch 24:11 7227a
did daily and collected **m** money. 2Ch 24:11 7230
m more to give you than this." 2Ch 25:9 7235a
of them and plundered **m** spoil. 2Ch 25:13 7227a
cisterns, for he had **m** livestock, 2Ch 26:10 7227a
How **m** less will your God deliver 2Ch 32:15 637, 3588
m evil in the sight of the LORD, 2Ch 33:6 7235a
Then I was very **m** afraid. Ne 2:2 7235a
failing, Yet there is **m** rubbish; Ne 4:10 7235a
'How **m** more those who dwell in Jb 4:19 637
How **m** less one who is detestable Jb 15:16 637, 3588
How **m** less man, *that* maggot, And Jb 25:6 637, 3588
because my hand had secured *so* **m**; Jb 31:25 3524
"How **m** less when you say you do Jb 35:14 637
than gold, yes, than **m** fine gold; Ps 19:10 7227a
burden they weigh too **m** for me. Ps 38:4 3515
As **m** as in all riches. Ps 119:14 5921
How **m** more the wicked and the Pr 11:31 637, 3588
But **m** revenue *comes* by the Pr 14:4 7230
How **m** more the hearts of men! Pr 15:11 637, 3588
How **m** better it is to get wisdom Pr 16:16
M less are lying lips to a prince. Pr 17:7 637, 3588
How **m** more do his friends abandon Pr 19:7 637, 3588
M less for a slave to rule over Pr 19:10 637, 3588
How **m** more when he brings it with Pr 21:27 637, 3588
It is not good to eat **m** honey, Pr 25:27 7235a
who hardens *his* neck after **m** reproof Pr 29:1
in **m** wisdom there is much grief, Ec 1:18 7230
in much wisdom there is **m** grief, Ec 1:18 7230
the dream comes through **m** effort and Ec 5:3 7230
whether he eats little or **m**; Ec 5:12 7235a
but one sinner destroys **m** good. Ec 9:18 7235a
m better is your love than wine, SS 4:10
yourself with lye And use **m** soap, Jer 2:22 7235a
go around so **m** Changing your way? Jer 2:36 3966
"How **m** more when I send My four Ezk 14:21 637
How **m** less, when the fire has Ezk 15:5 637
with great wings and **m** plumage; Ezk 17:7 7227a
and held in derision; It contains **m**. Ezk 23:32 4767
lambs as **m** as he is able to give, Ezk 46:5 3027
with the lambs as **m** as he is able, Ezk 46:7 3027
lambs as **m** as one is able to give, Ezk 46:11 3027
'Arise, devour **m** meat!' Da 7:5 7690
with a great army and **m** equipment. Da 11:13 7227a
return to his land with **m** plunder; Da 11:28 1419
"You have sown **m**, but harvest Hg 1:6 7235a
"*You* look for **m**, but behold, *it* Hg 1:9 7235a
you not worth **m** more than they? Mt 6:26 *3123*
will He not **m** more *clothe* you? Mt 6:30 *4183*
how **m** more will your Father who Mt 7:11 *4214*
how **m** more *will they malign* Mt 10:25 *4214*
"How **m** more valuable then is a Mt 12:12 *4214*
where they did not have **m** soil; Mt 13:5 *4183*
so **m** that he promised with an Mt 14:7
he was one who owned **m** property. Mt 19:22 *4183*
will receive many times as **m**, Mt 19:29 *4179*
unwilling to move them with *so* **m** *as* Mt 23:4
as **m** a son of hell as yourselves. Mt 23:15 *1362*
where it did not have **m** soil; Mk 4:5 *4183*
so **m** that the boat was already filling Mk 4:37
They became very **m** afraid and Mk 4:41 *3173*
and had endured **m** at the hands of Mk 5:26 *4183*
the boy became so **m** like a corpse Mk 9:26 *5616*
he was one who owned **m** property. Mk 10:22 *4183*
receive a hundred times as **m** now Mk 10:30 *1542*
is **m** more than all burnt offerings Mk 12:33 *4053*
been forgiven, for she loved **m**; Lk 7:47 *4183*
up and give him as **m** as he needs. Lk 11:8 *3745*
how **m** more will *your* heavenly Lk 11:13 *4214*
how **m** more valuable you are than Lk 12:24 *4214*
how **m** more *will He clothe* you? Lk 12:28 *4214*
From everyone who has been given **m**, Lk 12:48 *4183*
m will be required; and to whom they Lk 12:48 *4183*
and to whom they entrusted **m**, Lk 12:48 *4183*
'How **m** do you owe my master?' Lk 16:5 *4214*
'And how **m** do you owe?' Lk 16:7 *4214*
thing is faithful also in **m**; Lk 16:10 *4183*
thing is unrighteous also in **m**. Lk 16:10 *4183*
receive many times as **m** at this time Lk 18:30 *4179*
will give back four times as **m**." Lk 19:8 *5073*
because there was **m** water there; Jn 3:23 *4183*
there was **m** grass in the place. Jn 6:10 *4183*
of the fish as **m** as they wanted. Jn 6:11 *3745*
There was **m** grumbling among Jn 7:12 *4183*
but if it dies, it bears **m** fruit. Jn 12:24 *4183*
"I will not speak **m** more with you, Jn 14:30 *4183*
and I in him, he bears **m** fruit, Jn 15:5 *4183*
this, that you bear **m** fruit, Jn 15:8 *4183*
was **m** rejoicing in that city. Ac 8:8 *4183*
how **m** harm he did to Your saints at Ac 9:13 *3745*
for I will show him how **m** he must Ac 9:16 *3745*
gaze on him and being **m** alarmed, Ac 10:4 *1719*
After there had been **m** debate, Ac 15:7 *4183*
m profit by fortune-telling. Ac 16:16 *4183*
and had given them **m** exhortation, Ac 20:2 *4183*
have through you attained **m** peace, Ac 24:2 *4183*
and with **m** violence took him out Ac 24:7 *4183*
M more then, having now been Ro 5:9 *4183*
the death of His Son, **m** more, Ro 5:10 *4183*
m more did the grace of God and Ro 5:15 *4183*
m more those who receive the Ro 5:17 *4183*
endured with **m** patience vessels of Ro 9:22 *4183*
how **m** more will their fulfillment Ro 11:12 *4214*
how **m** more will these who are the Ro 11:24 *4214*
and in fear and in **m** trembling, 1Co 2:3 *4183*
How **m** more matters of this life? 1Co 6:3 *3386*
is it too **m** if we reap 1Co 9:11 *3173*
it is **m** truer that the members of 1Co 12:22 *4183*
less presentable members become **m** 1Co 12:23 *622*
For out of **m** affliction and 2Co 2:4 *4183*
in order not to say too **m** 2Co 2:5 *1912*
m more does the ministry of 2Co 3:9 *4183*
m more that which remains *is* in 2Co 3:11 *4183*
servants of God, in **m** endurance, 2Co 6:4 *4183*
even **m** more for the joy of Titus, 2Co 7:13 *3123*
begging us with **m** urging for the 2Co 8:4 *4183*
gathered **M** DID NOT HAVE TOO MUCH, 2Co 8:15 *4183*

gathered MUCH DID NOT HAVE TOO **m**, 2Co 8:15 *4121*
Christ, for *that* is very **m** better; Php 1:23 *4183*
but now **m** more in my absence, Php 2:12 *4183*
received the word in **m** tribulation 1Th 1:6 *4183*
gospel of God amid **m** opposition. 1Th 2:2 *4183*
to **m** wine or fond of sordid gain, 1Tm 3:8 *4183*
the coppersmith did me **m** harm; 2Tm 4:14 *4183*
gossips nor enslaved to **m** wine, Ti 2:3 *4183*
m joy and comfort in your love, Phm 1:7 *4183*
to me, but how **m** more to you, Phm 1:16 *4214*
as **m** better than the angels, Heb 1:4 *5118*
we must pay **m** closer attention to Heb 2:1 *4057*
by just so **m** as the builder of the Heb 3:3 *3745*
Concerning him we have **m** to say, Heb 5:11 *4183*
so **m** the more also Jesus has Heb 7:22 *5118*
by as **m** as He is also the mediator Heb 8:6 *3745*
m more will the blood of Christ, Heb 9:14 *4214*
How **m** severer punishment do you Heb 10:29 *4214*
shall we not **m** rather be subject Heb 12:9 *4183*
m less *will* we *escape* who turn Heb 12:25 *4183*
a righteous man can accomplish **m**. Jas 5:16 *4183*
and **m** incense was given to him, Rv 8:3 *4183*
has mixed, mix twice as **m** for her. Rv 18:6 *1362*

MUD
them down like **m** in the streets. Is 10:6 2563a
its waters toss up refuse and **m**. Is 57:20 2916
there was no water but only **m**, Jer 38:6 2916
mud, and Jeremiah sank into the **m**. Jer 38:6 2916

MUDDIED
And **m** the waters with your feet And Ezk 32:2 1804

MUDDY
of man will not **m** them anymore Ezk 32:13 1804
hoofs of beasts will not **m** them. Ezk 32:13 1804

MULBERRY
you would say to this **m** tree, Lk 17:6 *4807*

MULE
and each mounted his **m** and fled. 2Sa 13:29 6505
For Absalom was riding on *his* **m**, 2Sa 18:9 6505
and the **m** went under the thick 2Sa 18:9 6505
while the **m** that was under him kept 2Sa 18:9 6505
my son Solomon ride on my own **m**, 1Ki 1:33 6506
had Solomon ride on King David's **m**, 1Ki 1:38 6506
have made him ride on the king's **m**. 1Ki 1:44 6506
the **m** which have no understanding, Ps 32:9 6505
be the plague on the horse, the **m**, Zch 14:15 6505

MULES
weapons, spices, horses, and **m**, 1Ki 10:25 6505
and keep the horses and **m** alive, 1Ki 18:5 6505
food on donkeys, camels, **m** and 1Ch 12:40 6505
weapons, spices, horses and **m**, 2Ch 9:24 6505
Their horses were 736; their **m**, 245; Ezr 2:66 6505
Their horses were 736; their **m**, 245; Ne 7:68 6505
in chariots, in litters, on **m** and Is 66:20 6505
war horses and **m** for your wares. Ezk 27:14 6505

MULES'
at least be given two **m** load 2Ki 5:17 6505

MULTIPLIED
and increased greatly, and **m**, Ex 1:7 7235a
the more they **m** and the more they Ex 1:12 7235a
to the midwives, and the people **m**, Ex 1:20 7235a
will be **m** in the land of Egypt." Ex 11:9 7235a
'The LORD your God has **m** you, Dt 1:10 7235a
and the days of your sons may be **m** Dt 11:21 7235a
and **m** his descendants and gave him Jos 24:3 7235a
had done, but Amon **m** guilt. 2Ch 33:23 7235a
for another *god* will be **m**; Ps 16:4 7235a
For by me your days will be **m**, Pr 9:11 7235a
are your **m** sacrifices to Me?" Is 1:11 7230
Then I blessed him and **m** him." Is 51:2 7235a
transgressions are **m** before You, Is 59:12 7231
are **m** and increased in the land," Jer 3:16 7235a
In vain have you **m** remedies; Jer 46:11 7235a
And **m** in the daughter of Judah La 2:5 7235a
have **m** your slain in this city, Ezk 11:6 7235a
and **m** your harlotry to make Me Ezk 16:26 7235a
"You also **m** your harlotry with Ezk 16:29 7235a
for you have **m** your abominations Ezk 16:51 7235a
"Yet she **m** her harlotries, Ezk 23:19 7235a
and have **m** your words against Me; Ezk 35:13 6280
The more they **m**, the more they Hos 4:7 7231
Ephraim has **m** altars for sin, Hos 8:11 7235a
And Judah has **m** fortified cities, Hos 8:14 7235a
people increased and **m** in Egypt, Ac 7:17 *4129*
continued to grow and to be **m**. Ac 12:24 *4129*
Grace and peace be **m** to you in the 2Pe 1:2 *4129*
and peace and love be **m** to you. Jude 1:2 *4129*

MULTIPLIES
multiply, and all that you have **m**, Dt 8:13 7235a
And **m** my wounds without cause. Jb 9:17 7235a
And **m** his words against God.'" Jb 34:37 7235a
He **m** words without knowledge." Jb 35:16 3527
Yet the fool **m** words. Ec 10:14 7235a
He **m** lies and violence. Hos 12:1 7235a

MULTIPLY
"Be fruitful and **m**, and fill the Gn 1:22 7235a
and let birds **m** on the earth." Gn 1:22 7235a
"Be fruitful and **m**, and fill the Gn 1:28 7235a
greatly **m** Your pain in childbirth, Gn 3:16 7235a
to **m** on the face of the land, Gn 6:1 7231
be fruitful and **m** on the earth." Gn 8:17 7235a
"Be fruitful and **m**, and fill the Gn 9:1 7235a
"As for you, be fruitful and **m**; Gn 9:7 7235a
earth abundantly and **m** in it." Gn 9:7 7235a
"I will greatly **m** your descendants Gn 16:10 7235a
And I will **m** you exceedingly." Gn 17:2 7235a
and will **m** him exceedingly. Gn 17:20 7235a
and I will greatly **m** your seed as Gn 22:17 7235a
"I will **m** your descendants as Gn 26:4 7235a
bless you, and **m** your descendants, Gn 26:24 7235a
and make you fruitful and **m** you, Gn 28:3 7235a
Be fruitful and **m**; Gn 35:11 7235a
they will **m** and in the event of war, Ex 1:10 7235a
I may **m** My signs and My wonders Ex 7:3 7235a
'I will **m** your descendants as the Ex 32:13 7235a
and make you fruitful and **m** you, Lv 26:9 7235a
you and that you may **m** greatly, Dt 6:3 7235a
love you and bless you and **m** you; Dt 7:13 7235a
to do, that you may live and **m**, Dt 8:1 7235a
when your herds and your flocks **m**, Dt 8:13 7235a
and your silver and gold **m**, Dt 8:13 7235a
he shall not **m** horses for himself, Dt 17:16 7235a
to return to Egypt to **m** horses, Dt 17:16 7235a
"He shall not **m** wives for himself, Dt 17:17 7235a
you to prosper you, and **m** you, Dt 28:63 7235a
and **m** you more than your fathers. Dt 30:5 7235a
that you may live and **m**, Dt 30:16 7235a
family **m** like the sons of Judah. 1Ch 4:27 7235a
m Israel as the stars of heaven. 1Ch 27:23 7235a
And I shall **m** *my* days as the sand. Jb 29:18 7235a
my anxious thoughts **m** within me, Ps 94:19 7230
blesses them and they **m** greatly, Ps 107:38 7235a
Yes, even though you **m** prayers, Is 1:15 7235a
You shall **m** the nation, You Is 9:3 7235a
and they will be fruitful and **m**. Jer 23:3 7235a
and **m** there and do not decrease. Jer 29:6 7235a
And I will **m** them and they will Jer 30:19 7235a
so I will **m** the descendants of Jer 33:22 7235a
every passer-by to **m** your harlotry. Ezk 16:25 7235a
'I will **m** men on you, all the Ezk 36:10 7235a
'I will **m** on you man and beast; Ezk 36:11 7235a
will call for the grain and **m** it, Ezk 36:29 7235a
"I will **m** the fruit of the tree Ezk 36:30 7235a
And I will place them and **m** them, Ezk 37:26 7235a
In Gilgal **m** transgression! Am 4:4 7235a
M yourself like the creeping locust Na 3:15 3513
M yourself like the swarming locust Na 3:15 3513
will supply and **m** your seed for 2Co 9:10 *4129*
YOU AND I WILL SURELY **M** YOU." Heb 6:14 *4129*

MULTITUDE
be the father of a **m** of nations. Gn 17:4 1995
you the father of a **m** of nations. Gn 17:5 1995
came and it has increased to a **m** Gn 30:30 7230
a **m** in the midst of the earth." Gn 48:16 7230
shall become a **m** of nations." Gn 48:19 4393
A mixed **m** also went up with them, Ex 12:38 7227a
a **m** in order to pervert *justice;* Ex 23:2 7227a
and behold, the **m** melted away; 1Sa 14:16 1995
people, to all the **m** of Israel, 2Sa 6:19 1995
'Have you seen all this great **m**? 1Ki 20:13 1995
all this great **m** into your hand, 1Ki 20:28 1995
be in any case like all the **m** of Israel 2Ki 7:13 1995
be in any case like all the **m** of Israel 2Ki 7:13 1995
being a great **m** and *having* with 2Ch 13:8 1995
Your name have come against this **m**. 2Ch 14:11 1995
"A great **m** is coming against you 2Ch 20:2 1995
great **m** who are coming against us; 2Ch 20:12 1995
dismayed because of this great **m**, 2Ch 20:15 1995
they looked toward the **m**, 2Ch 20:24 1995
For a **m** of the people, *even* many 2Ch 30:18 4768
"Shall a **m** of words go unanswered, Jb 11:2 7230
Because I feared the great **m**, Jb 31:34 1995
the **m** of oppressions they cry out; Jb 35:9 7230
In the **m** of their transgressions Ps 5:10 7230
a **m** keeping festival. Ps 42:4 1995
In a **m** of people is a king's glory, Pr 14:28 7230
their **m** is parched with thirst. Is 5:13 1995
And Jerusalem's splendor, her **m**, Is 5:14 1995
But the **m** of your enemies will Is 29:5 1995
And the **m** of the ruthless ones Is 29:5 1995
And the **m** of all the nations who Is 29:7 1995
the **m** of all the nations will be Is 29:8 1995
"A **m** of camels will cover you, Is 60:6 8229
of the **m** of her transgressions; La 1:5 7230
for wrath is against all their **m**. Ezk 7:12 1995
all their **m** will not be averted, Ezk 7:13 1995
My wrath is against all their **m**. Ezk 7:14 1995
in view of the **m** of his idols, Ezk 14:4 7230
sound of a carefree **m** was with her; Ezk 23:42 1995
"Because of the **m** of his horses, Ezk 26:10 8229
"By the **m** of your iniquities, In Ezk 28:18 7230
with the **m** of its branches, Ezk 31:9 7230
and assemble a **m** of great forces; Da 11:10 1995
the latter will raise a great **m**, Da 11:11 1995
but *that* **m** will be given into the Da 11:11 1995
"When the **m** is carried away, his Da 11:12 1995
raise a greater **m** than the former, Da 11:13 1995
the **m** of men and cattle within it. Zch 2:4 7230
a great **m** from Galilee followed; Mk 3:7 *4128*
And the whole **m** of the people were Lk 1:10 *4128*
m of the heavenly host praising God Lk 2:13 *4128*
lay a **m** of those who were sick, Jn 5:3 *4128*
for the **m** of the people kept Ac 21:36 *4128*
death and will cover a **m** of sins. Jas 5:20 *4128*
because love covers a **m** of sins. 1Pe 4:8 *4128*
I looked, and behold, a great **m** which Rv 7:9 *3793*
loud voice of a great **m** in heaven, Rv 19:1 *3793*
the voice of a great **m** and like the Rv 19:6 *3793*

MULTITUDES
M, multitudes in the valley of Jl 3:14 1995
m in the valley of decision! Jl 3:14 1995
in the Lord, **m** of men and women, Ac 5:14 *4128*
and **m** and nations and tongues. Rv 17:15 *3793*

MUPPIM
and Rosh, **M** and Huppim and Ard. Gn 46:21 4649

MURDER
"You shall not **m**. Ex 20:13 7523
'You shall not **m**. Dt 5:17 7523
assail a man, That you may **m** *him*, Ps 62:3 7523
the stranger And **m** the orphans. Ps 94:6 7523
"Will you steal, **m**, and commit Jer 7:9 7523
There is swearing, deception, **m**, Hos 4:2 7523
priests **m** on the way to Shechem; Hos 6:9 7523
'YOU SHALL NOT COMMIT **M**' and Mt 5:21 *5407*
'Whoever commits **m** shall be liable Mt 5:21 *5407*
"YOU SHALL NOT COMMIT **M**; Mt 19:18 *5407*
'DO NOT **M**, DO NOT COMMIT Mk 10:19 *5407*
committed **m** in the insurrection. Mk 15:7 *5408*
NOT COMMIT ADULTERY, DO NOT **M**, Lk 18:20 *5407*
made in the city, and for **m**.) Lk 23:19 *5408*
prison for insurrection and **m**, Lk 23:25 *5408*
still breathing threats and **m** Ac 9:1 *5408*
full of envy, **m**, strife, deceit, Ro 1:29 *5408*
ADULTERY, YOU SHALL NOT **M**, Ro 13:9 *5407*
"DO NOT COMMIT **M**." Jas 2:11 *5407*
commit adultery, but do commit **m**, Jas 2:11 *5407*
and do not have; *so* you commit **m**. Jas 4:2 *5407*

MURDERED
husband of the woman who was **m**, Jg 20:4 7523
"Have you **m** and also taken 1Ki 21:19 7523
had shown him, but he **m** his son. 2Ch 24:22 2026
the priest, and **m** him on his bed. 2Ch 24:25 2026
sons of those who **m** the prophets. Mt 23:31 *5407*
whom you **m** between the temple and Mt 23:35 *5407*

MURDERER
so that he died, he is a **m**; Nu 35:16 7523
m shall surely be put to death. Nu 35:16 7523
as a result he died, he is a **m**; Nu 35:17 7523
m shall surely be put to death. Nu 35:17 7523
as a result he died, he is a **m**; Nu 35:18 7523
m shall surely be put to death. Nu 35:18 7523
himself shall put the **m** to death; Nu 35:19 7523
surely be put to death, he is a **m**; Nu 35:21 7523
the **m** to death when he meets him. Nu 35:21 7523
the **m** shall be put to death at the Nu 35:30 7523
of a **m** who is guilty of death, Nu 35:31 7523
a **m** has sent to take away my head? 2Ki 6:32 7523
it well, Zimri, your master's **m**?" 2Ki 9:31 2026
"The **m** arises at dawn; Jb 24:14 7523
He was a **m** from the beginning, and Jn 8:44 *443*
asked for a **m** to be granted to you, Ac 3:14 *5406*
"Undoubtedly this man is a **m**, Ac 28:4 *5406*
none of you suffers as a **m**, 1Pe 4:15 *5406*
who hates his brother is a **m**; 1Jn 3:15 *443*
no **m** has eternal life abiding in him. 1Jn 3:15 *443*

MURDERERS
once lodged in her, But now **m**. Is 1:21 7523
woe is me, for I faint before **m**." Jer 4:31 2026
his armies and destroyed those **m** Mt 22:7 *5406*
and **m** you have now become; Ac 7:52 *5406*
their fathers or mothers, for **m** 1Tm 1:9 *409*
m and immoral persons and sorcerers Rv 21:8 *5406*
and the **m** and the idolaters, Rv 22:15 *5406*

MURDERS
against his neighbor and **m** him, Dt 22:26 7523
the heart come evil thoughts, **m**, Mt 15:19 *5408*
thoughts, fornications, thefts, **m**, Mk 7:21 *5408*
and they did not repent of their **m** Rv 9:21 *5408*

MURMUR
at noon, I will complain and **m**, Ps 55:17 1993

MUSCLES
his power in the **m** of his belly. Jb 40:16 8306

MUSE
all Your work And **m** on Your deeds. Ps 77:12 7878
I **m** on the work of Your hands. Ps 143:5 7878

MUSHI
The sons of Merari: Mahli and **M**. Ex 6:19 4187
by their families: Mahli and **M**. Nu 3:20 4187
sons of Merari *were* Mahli and **M**. 1Ch 6:19 4187
the son of Mahli, the son of **M**, 1Ch 6:47 4187
sons of Merari were Mahli and **M**. 1Ch 23:21 4187
The sons of **M** *were* three: 1Ch 23:23 4187
The sons of Merari, Mahli and **M**; 1Ch 24:26 4187
The sons of **M**: 1Ch 24:30 4187

MUSHITES
Mahlites and the family of the **M**; Nu 3:33 4188
the Mahlites, the family of the **M**, Nu 26:58 4188

MUSIC
singers, with instruments of **m**, 1Ch 15:16 7892a
and cymbals and instruments of **m**, 2Ch 5:13 7892a
the instruments of **m** to the LORD, 2Ch 7:6 7892a
With resounding **m** upon the lyre. Ps 92:3 1902
'Your pomp *and* the **m** of your harps Is 14:11 1998
Will be with *the* **m** *of* tambourines Is 30:32
the gate, Young men from their **m**. La 5:14 5058
bagpipe and all kinds of **m**, Da 3:5 2170
bagpipe and all kinds of **m**, Da 3:7 2170
and bagpipe and all kinds of **m**, Da 3:10 2170
and bagpipe and all kinds of **m**, Da 3:15 2170
the house, he heard **m** and dancing. Lk 15:25 *4858*

MUSICAL
with joy and with **m** instruments. 1Sa 18:6 7991b
and Jeiel, with **m** instruments, 1Ch 16:5
the singers with *their* **m** instruments 2Ch 23:13 7892a
The Levites stood with the **m** 2Ch 29:26
were skillful with **m** instruments. 2Ch 34:12 7892a
with the **m** instruments of David Ne 12:36 7892a

MUSICIAN
Bethlehemite who is a skillful **m**, 1Sa 16:18 5059

MUSICIANS
singers went on, the **m** after *them*, Ps 68:25 5059

"And the sound of harpists and **m** Rv 18:22 *3451*

MUSING

While I was **m** the fire burned; Ps 39:3 1901

MUST

is for you, but you **m** master it." Gn 4:7
"You **m** come in to me, for I have Gn 30:16
"If *it* **m** *be* so, then do this: Gn 43:11
"Now you **m** tell my father of all Gn 45:13
and you **m** hurry and bring my Gn 45:13
"I **m** turn aside now and see this Ex 3:3
m deliver the quota of bricks." Ex 5:18
"You **m** not reduce *your* daily Ex 5:19
"We **m** go a three days' journey Ex 8:27
we **m** hold a feast to the LORD." Ex 10:9
"You **m** also let us have Ex 10:25
what **m** be eaten by every person, Ex 12:16
he **m** pay a dowry for her *to be* his Ex 22:16
but you **m** certainly not eat it. Lv 7:24
for you to be accepted—*it* **m** *be* Lv 22:19
it **m** be perfect to be accepted; Lv 22:21
which is made for the wrong **m** *go* Nu 5:8
the tabernacle of the LORD, **m** die. Nu 17:13
"**M** I not be careful to speak what Nu 23:12
the LORD speaks, that I **m** do'?" Nu 23:26
only they **m** marry within the Nu 36:6
then he **m** go outside the camp; Dt 23:10
therefore your camp **m** be holy; Dt 23:14
and He **m** not see anything indecent Dt 23:14
you **m** not forget. Dt 25:19
that you **m** turn away this day from Jos 22:18
They said, "*There* **m** *be* an Jg 21:17
you **m** also acquire Ruth the Ru 4:5
"They **m** surely burn the fat 1Sa 2:16
of Israel **m** not remain with us, 1Sa 5:7
because he **m** bless the sacrifice; 1Sa 9:13
"You **m** not turn aside, for 1Sa 12:21
Here I am, I **m** die!" 1Sa 14:43
"**M** Jonathan die, who has brought 1Sa 14:45
him to me, for he **m** surely die." 1Sa 20:31 1121
lives, *all* of you **m** surely die, 1Sa 26:16 1121
'He **m** not go up with us to the 1Sa 29:9
"You **m** not do so, my brothers, 1Sa 30:23
"He **m** make restitution for 2Sa 12:6
man who touches them **M** be armed 2Sa 23:7
you **m** surely let me go." 1Ki 11:22
"You **m** not go up and fight 1Ki 12:24
"How many times **m** I adjure you to 1Ki 22:16
you **m** go *to be* with your fathers, 1Ch 17:11
"How many times **m** I adjure you to 2Ch 18:15
"You **m** not bring the captives in 2Ch 28:13
unrighteousness **m** shut its mouth. Jb 5:16
For you **m** choose, and not I; Jb 34:33
Him, and you **m** wait for Him! Jb 35:14
I **m** lie among those who breathe Ps 57:4
all the wicked of the earth **m** drain Ps 75:8
he is found, he **m** repay sevenfold; Pr 6:31
He **m** give all the substance of his Pr 6:31
for I **m** leave it to the man who Ec 2:18
then he **m** exert more strength. Ec 10:10
'I **m** arise now and go about the SS 3:2
I **m** seek him whom my soul loves.' SS 3:2
They **m** not arise and take Is 14:21
of Arabia you **m** spend the night, Is 21:13
"You **m** not see *visions*"; Is 30:10
"You **m** not prophesy to us what is Is 30:10
How long **m** I see the standard And Jer 4:21
They **m** be carried, Because they Jer 10:5 5375
is a sickness, And I **m** bear it." Jer 10:19
for you, you **m** not turn to them. Jer 15:19
seized him, saying, "You **m** die! Jer 26:8 4191
that you **m** tread down with your Ezk 34:18
that you **m** foul the rest Ezk 34:18
they **m** eat what you tread down Ezk 34:19
Now they **m** bear their guilt. Hos 10:2
beast **m** be covered with sackcloth; Jon 3:8
of this I **m** lament and wail, Mi 1:8
wail, I **m** go barefoot and naked; Mi 1:8
I **m** make a lament like the jackals Mi 1:8
Because I **m** wait quietly for the Hab 3:16
that He **m** go to Jerusalem, Mt 16:21 *1163*
he **m** deny himself, and take up his Mt 16:24
say that Elijah **m** come first?" Mt 17:10 *1163*
for *those things* **m** take place, Mt 24:6 *1163*
then those who are in Judea **m** flee to Mt 24:16
"Whoever is on the housetop **m** not go Mt 24:17
"Whoever is in the field **m** not turn Mt 24:18
"For this reason you also **m** be ready; Mt 24:44
that it **m** happen this way?" Mt 26:54 *1163*
Son of Man **m** suffer many things Mk 8:31 *1163*
he **m** deny himself, and take up his Mk 8:34
say that Elijah **m** come first?" Mk 9:11 *1163*
those things **m** take place; Mk 13:7 *1163*
"The gospel **m** first be preached Mk 13:10 *1163*
then those who are in Judea **m** flee to Mk 13:14
one who is on the housetop **m** not Mk 13:15
and the one who is in the field **m** not Mk 13:16
"I **m** preach the kingdom of God to Lk 4:43 *1163*
m be put into fresh wineskins. Lk 5:38 *992*
Son of Man **m** suffer many things and Lk 9:22 *1163*
he **m** deny himself, and take up his Lk 9:23
"Nevertheless I **m** journey on Lk 13:33 *1163*
"But first He **m** suffer many Lk 17:25 *1163*
and whose goods are in the house **m** Lk 17:31
the one who is in the field **m** not Lk 17:31
today I **m** stay at your house." Lk 19:5 *1163*
these things **m** take place first, Lk 21:9 *1163*
"Then those who are in Judea **m** flee Lk 21:21
who are in the midst of the city **m** Lk 21:21
those who are in the country **m** not Lk 21:21
one who is the greatest among you **m** Lk 22:26
is written **m** be fulfilled in Me, Lk 22:37 *1163*
the Son of Man **m** be delivered into Lk 24:7 *1163*
and the Psalms **m** be fulfilled." Lk 24:44 *1163*
'You **m** be born again.' Jn 3:7 *1163*
so **m** the Son of Man be lifted up; Jn 3:14 *1163*
"He **m** increase, but I must Jn 3:30 *1163*
must increase, but I **m** decrease. Jn 3:30
m worship in spirit and truth." Jn 4:24 *1163*
"We **m** work the works of Him who Jn 9:4 *1163*
I **m** bring them also, and they Jn 10:16 *1163*
"If anyone serves Me, he **m** follow Jn 12:26
'The Son of Man **m** be lifted up'? Jn 12:34 *1163*
He **m** rise again from the dead. Jn 20:9 *1163*
up from us—one of these **m** Ac 1:22
whom heaven **m** receive until *the* Ac 3:21 *1163*
men by which we **m** be saved." Ac 4:12 *1163*
"We **m** obey God rather than men. Ac 5:29 *1163*
will be told you what you **m** do." Ac 9:6 *1163*
he **m** suffer for My name's sake." Ac 9:16 *1163*
we **m** enter the kingdom of God." Ac 14:22 *1163*
"Sirs, what **m** I do to be saved?" Ac 16:30 *1163*
been there, I **m** also see Rome." Ac 19:21 *1163*
in this manner you **m** help the weak Ac 20:35 *1163*
so you **m** witness at Rome also." Ac 23:11 *1163*
you **m** stand before Caesar; Ac 27:24 *1163*
"But we **m** run aground on a Ac 27:26 *1163*
according to the flesh, you **m** die; Ro 8:13 *3195*
Each person **m** be fully convinced in Ro 14:5
But each man **m** be careful how he 1Co 3:10
he **m** become foolish, so that he may 1Co 3:18
The husband **m** fulfill his duty to his 1Co 7:3 *3782*
(but if she does leave, she **m** 1Co 7:11
he **m** not divorce her. 1Co 7:12
she **m** not send her husband away. 1Co 7:13
Each man **m** remain in that condition 1Co 7:20
past her youth, and if it **m** be so, 1Co 7:36 *3784*
m also be factions among you, 1Co 11:19 *1163*
But a man **m** examine himself, and in 1Co 11:28
and one **m** interpret; 1Co 14:27
but if there is no interpreter, he **m** 1Co 14:28
the first one **m** keep silent. 1Co 14:30
But all things **m** be done properly 1Co 14:40
For He **m** reign until He has put 1Co 15:25 *1163*
m put on the imperishable, 1Co 15:53 *1163*
this mortal **m** put on immortality. 1Co 15:53
For we **m** all appear before the 2Co 5:10 *1163*
Each one **m** *do* just as he has 2Co 9:7
To *my* shame I **m** say that we 2Co 11:21
But each one **m** examine his own work, Ga 6:4
He who steals **m** steal no longer; but Eph 4:28
but rather he **m** labor, performing Eph 4:28
immorality or any impurity or greed **m** Eph 5:3
and *there* **m** *be no* filthiness Eph 5:4
and the wife **m** *see to it* that she Eph 5:33
A woman **m** quietly receive instruction 1Tm 2:11
overseer, then, **m** be above reproach 1Tm 3:2 *1163*
He **m** be one who manages his own 1Tm 3:4
And he **m** have a good reputation 1Tm 3:7 *1163*
Deacons likewise **m** *be* men of 1Tm 3:8
These men **m** also first be tested; 1Tm 3:10
Women **m** likewise *be* dignified, 1Tm 3:11
Deacons **m** be husbands of *only* one 1Tm 3:12
they **m** first learn to practice piety 1Tm 5:4
she **m** assist them and the church must 1Tm 5:16
she must assist them and the church **m** 1Tm 5:16
who have believers as their masters **m** 1Tm 6:2
but **m** serve them all the more, 1Tm 6:2
bond-servant **m** not be quarrelsome, 2Tm 2:24 *1163*
the overseer **m** be above reproach Ti 1:7 *1163*
who **m** be silenced because they are Ti 1:11 *1163*
Our people **m** also learn to engage in Ti 3:14
we **m** pay much closer attention to Heb 2:1 *1163*
there **m** of necessity be the death Heb 9:16
comes to God **m** believe that He is and Heb 11:6 *1163*
But he **m** ask in faith without any Jas 1:6
But everyone **m** be quick to hear, Jas 1:19
Then he **m** pray. Is anyone Jas 5:13
Then he **m** call for the elders of Jas 5:14
Your adornment **m** not be *merely* 1Pe 3:3
M KEEP HIS TONGUE FROM EVIL AND HIS 1Pe 3:10
"HE **M** TURN AWAY FROM EVIL AND DO 1Pe 3:11
HE **M** SEEK PEACE AND PURSUE IT. 1Pe 3:11
things which **m** soon take place; Rv 1:1 *1163*
m take place after these things." Rv 4:1 *1163*
"You **m** prophesy again concerning Rv 10:11 *1163*
he **m** be killed in this way. Rv 11:5 *1163*
with the sword he **m** be killed. Rv 13:10 *1163*
comes, he **m** remain a little while. Rv 17:10 *1163*
he **m** be released for a short time. Rv 20:3 *1163*
things which **m** soon take place. Rv 22:6 *1163*

MUSTACHE

and he shall cover his **m** and cry, Lv 13:45 8222
for his feet, nor trimmed his **m**, 2Sa 19:24 8222
feet, and do not cover *your* **m** and Ezk 24:17 8222
you will not cover *your* **m** and Ezk 24:22 8222

MUSTARD

kingdom of heaven is like a **m** seed, Mt 13:31 *4615*
faith the size of a **m** seed, Mt 17:20 *4615*
"*It is* like a **m** seed, which, when Mk 4:31 *4615*
"It is like a **m** seed, which a man Lk 13:19 *4615*
"If you had faith like a **m** seed, Lk 17:6 *4615*

MUSTER

and **m** an army like the army that 1Ki 20:25 4487
This was their **m** according to 2Ch 17:14 6486
to the number of their **m**, 2Ch 26:11 6486
"Now **m** yourselves in troops, Mi 5:1 1413

MUSTERED

in the morning and **m** the people, Jos 8:10 6485
Then he **m** the young men of the 1Ki 20:15 6485
after them he **m** all the people, 1Ki 20:15 6485
Ben-hadad **m** the Arameans and 1Ki 20:26 6485
The sons of Israel were **m** and 1Ki 20:27 6485
at that time and **m** all Israel. 2Ki 3:6 6485
who **m** the people of the land; 2Ki 25:19 6633
army who **m** the people of the land, Jer 52:25 6633

MUSTERING

LORD of hosts is **m** the army for Is 13:4 6485

MUTE

Or who makes *him* **m** or deaf, or Ex 4:11 483
Let the lying lips be **m**, Which speak Ps 31:18 481
And *I am* like a **m** man who does Ps 38:13 483
I was **m** and silent, I refrained Ps 39:2 481
"I have become **m**, I do not open my Ps 39:9 481
Open your mouth for the **m**, Pr 31:8 483
And the tongue of the **m** will shout Is 35:6 483
All of them are **m** dogs unable to bark, Is 56:10 483
of your mouth so that you will be **m** Ezk 3:26 481
and you will speak and be **m** no longer. Ezk 24:27 481
To a **m** stone, 'Arise!' *And* Hab 2:19 1748
As they were going out, a **m**, Mt 9:32 *2974*
After the demon was cast out, the **m** Mt 9:33 *2974*
man *who was* blind and **m** was Mt 12:22 *2974*
so that the **m** man spoke and saw. Mt 12:22 *2974*
m, and many others, and they laid Mt 15:30 *2974*
the crowd marveled as they saw the **m** Mt 15:31 *2974*
makes even the deaf to hear and the **m** Mk 7:37 *216*
with a spirit which makes him **m**; Mk 9:17 *216*
"You deaf and **m** spirit, I command Mk 9:25 *216*
signs to them, and remained **m**. Lk 1:22 *2974*
and it was **m**; when the demon had Lk 11:14 *2974*
the **m** man spoke; and the crowds were Lk 11:14 *2974*
you were led astray to the **m** 1Co 12:2 *880*
for a **m** donkey, speaking with a 2Pe 2:16 *880*

MUTILATE

you would even **m** themselves. Ga 5:12 *609*

MUTTER

Nor will my tongue **m** deceit. Jb 27:4 1897
spiritists who whisper and **m**," Is 8:19 1897

MUTTERING

m these things about Him, Jn 7:32 *1111*

MUTTERS

Your tongue **m** wickedness. Is 59:3 1897

MUZZLE

not **m** the ox while he is threshing. Dt 25:4 2629
I will guard my mouth as with a **m** Ps 39:1 4269
YOU SHALL NOT **M** THE OX WHILE HE 1Co 9:9 *2778a*
YOU SHALL NOT **M** THE OX WHILE HE 1Tm 5:18 *5392*

MYRA

we landed at **M** in Lycia. Ac 27:5 *3460*

MYRIAD

To the **m** thousands of Israel." Nu 10:36 7233

MYRIADS

The chariots of God are **m**, Ps 68:17 7239
And **m** upon myriads were standing Da 7:10 7240
And myriads upon **m** were standing Da 7:10 7240
Jerusalem, and to **m** of angels, Heb 12:22 *3461*
number of them was **m** of myriads, Rv 5:11 *3461*
number of them was myriads of **m**, Rv 5:11 *3461*

MYRRH

aromatic gum and balm and **m**, Gn 37:25 3910
little honey, aromatic gum and **m**, Gn 43:11 3910
of flowing **m** five hundred *shekels*, Ex 30:23 4753
six months with oil of **m** and six Es 2:12 4753
with **m** and aloes *and* cassia; Ps 45:8 4753
"I have sprinkled my bed With **m**, Pr 7:17 4753
"My beloved is to me a pouch of **m** SS 1:13 4753
Perfumed with **m** and frankincense, SS 3:6 4753
will go my way to the mountain of **m** SS 4:6 4753
of frankincense, **M** and aloes, SS 4:14 4753
my **m** along with my balsam. SS 5:1 4753
And my hands dripped with **m**, SS 5:5 4753
And my fingers with liquid **m**, SS 5:5 4753
lilies Dripping with liquid **m**. SS 5:13 4753
of gold, frankincense, and **m**. Mt 2:11 *4666*
to give Him wine mixed with **m**; Mk 15:23 *4669*
bringing a mixture of **m** and aloes, Jn 19:39 *4666*

MYRTLE

wild olive branches, **m** branches, Ne 8:15 1918
wilderness, The acacia and the **m** Is 41:19 1918
of the nettle the **m** will come up, Is 55:13 1918
he was standing among the **m** trees Zch 1:8 1918
who was standing among the **m** trees Zch 1:10 1918
was standing among the **m** trees and Zch 1:11 1918

MYSELF

because I was naked; so I hid **m**." Gn 3:10
I **M** do establish My covenant with Gn 9:9 589
"By **M** I have sworn, declares the Gn 22:16
and I will bring upon **m** a curse Gn 27:12
I bore the loss of it **m**. Gn 31:39 595
"I **m** will be surety for him; Gn 43:9 595
I dug for **m** in the land of Canaan, Gn 50:5
I did not make **M** known to them. Ex 6:3
Tomorrow I will station **m** on the Ex 17:9 5324
wings, and brought you to **M**. Ex 19:4
I **M** have appointed with him Ex 31:6 589
"I **M** will make all My goodness Ex 33:19 589
then I **M** will set My face against Lv 20:5 589
and I **M** will give it to you to Lv 20:24 589
I sanctified to **M** all the firstborn Nu 3:13
I have taken them for **M** instead of Nu 8:16
of Egypt I sanctified them for **M**. Nu 8:17
make **M** known to him in a vision. Nu 12:6

Thus I will lessen from upon **M** **Nu 17:5**
I **M** have taken your fellow Levites **Nu 18:6** 589
I **M** have given you charge of My **Nu 18:8** 589
beside your burnt offering while I **m** **Nu 23:15** 595
name, I **M** will require *it* of him. **Dt 18:19** 595
at other times and shake **m** free." **Jg 16:20**
"I cannot redeem *it* for **m**, **Ru 4:6**
'Did I *not* indeed reveal **M** to the **1Sa 2:27**
I will raise up for **M** a faithful priest **1Sa 2:35**
So I forced **m** and offered the **1Sa 13:12**
I have avenged **m** on my enemies." **1Sa 14:24**
a king for **M** among his sons." **1Sa 16:1**
that I may hide **m** in the field **1Sa 20:5**
from avenging **m** by my own hand. **1Sa 25:33**
or I will capture the city **m** **2Sa 12:28** 589
have not I **m** commanded you? **2Sa 13:28** 595
And Ziba said, "I prostrate **m**; **2Sa 16:4**
"I **m** will surely go out with you **2Sa 18:2** 589
'I will saddle a donkey for **m** that **2Sa 19:26**
And I kept **m** from my iniquity. **2Sa 22:24**
have chosen for **M** to put My name. **1Ki 11:36**
will surely show **m** to him today." **1Ki 18:15**
disguise **m** and go into the battle, **1Ki 22:30**
I bow **m** in the house of Rimmon, **2Ki 5:18**
I bow **m** in the house of Rimmon, **2Ki 5:18**
for **M** as a house of sacrifice. **2Ch 7:12**
disguise **m** and go into battle, **2Ch 18:29**
I consulted with **m** and **Ne 5:7**
I also applied **m** to the work on this **Ne 5:16**
So that I am a burden to **m**? **Jb 7:20**
I do not take notice of **m**; **Jb 9:21** 5315
"If I should wash **m** with snow And **Jb 9:30**
But I am not like that in **m**. **Jb 9:35**
Whom I **m** shall behold, And whom my **Jb 19:27** 589
I would bind it to **m** like a crown. **Jb 31:36**
And I kept **m** from my iniquity. **Ps 18:23**
me, Then I could hide **m** from him. **Ps 55:12**
of old, O LORD, And comfort **m**. **Ps 119:52**
do I involve **m** in great matters, **Ps 131:1**
I said to **m**, "Behold, I have **Ec 1:16** 3820
I said to **m**, "Come now, I will test **Ec 2:1** 3820
I built houses for **m**, **Ec 2:4**
myself, I planted vineyards for **m**; **Ec 2:4**
I made gardens and parks for **m** and **Ec 2:5**
I made ponds of water for **m** from **Ec 2:6**
I collected for **m** silver and gold and **Ec 2:8**
I provided for **m** male and female **Ec 2:8**
Then I said to **m**, **Ec 2:15** 3820
So I said to **m**, "This too is vanity." **Ec 2:15** 3820
I said to **m**, "God will judge both **Ec 3:17** 3820
I said to **m** concerning the sons of **Ec 3:18** 3820
and depriving **m** of pleasure?" **Ec 4:8** 5315
And avenge **M** on My foes. **Is 1:24**
I will take to **M** faithful witnesses **Is 8:2**
I will make **m** like the Most High.' **Is 14:14**
I, the LORD, will answer them **M**, **Is 41:17**
have kept still and restrained **M**. **Is 42:14**
"The people whom I formed for **M** Will **Is 43:21**
Stretching out the heavens by **M** And **Is 44:24** 905
"I have sworn by **M**, The word has **Is 45:23**
I **M** have created the smith who **Is 54:16** 595
"I permitted **M** to be sought by **Is 65:1**
I permitted **M** to be found by those **Is 65:1**
as this Shall I not avenge **M**? **Jer 5:9** 5315
as this Shall I not avenge **M**?' **Jer 5:29** 5315
as this Shall I not avenge **M**? **Jer 9:9** 5315
"So I **M** have also stripped your **Jer 13:26** 589
"I **M** will war against you **Jer 21:5** 589
obey these words, I swear by **M**," **Jer 22:5**
'I will build **m** a roomy house With **Jer 22:14**
"Then I **M** will gather the **Jer 23:3** 589
"For I have sworn by **M**," **Jer 49:13**
I **M** am going to bring a sword on **Ezk 6:3** 589
made **M** known to them in the land **Ezk 20:5**
in whose sight I made **M** known to **Ezk 20:9**
and I will prove **M** holy among you **Ezk 20:41**
is mine, and I **m** have made *it*.' **Ezk 29:3** 589
I **M** will search for My sheep and **Ezk 34:11** 589
so I will make **M** known among them **Ezk 35:11**
M holy among you in their sight. **Ezk 36:23**
"I will magnify **M**, **Ezk 38:23**
will magnify Myself, sanctify **M**, **Ezk 38:23**
and make **M** known in the sight of **Ezk 38:23**
on the day that I glorify **M**," **Ezk 39:13**
which I **m** have built as a royal **Da 4:30** 576
but I kept the matter to **m**." **Da 7:28** 3821
and I **m** was beside the Ulai Canal. **Da 8:2** 589
I will sow her for **M** in the land. **Hos 2:23**
So I bought her for **m** for fifteen **Hos 3:2**
rich, I have found wealth for **m**; **Hos 12:8**
And bow **m** before the God on high? **Mi 6:6**
post And station **m** on the rampart; **Hab 2:1**
And I took for **m** two staffs: **Zch 11:7**
consider **m** worthy to come to You, **Lk 7:7** *1683*
"I **m** had John beheaded; **Lk 9:9** *1473*
hands and My feet, that it is I **M**; **Lk 24:39** *846*
"I **m** have seen, and have testified **Jn 1:34** *1473*
until now, and I **M** am working." **Jn 5:17** *1473*
"If I *alone* testify about **M**, **Jn 5:31** *1683*
and I **M** will raise him up on the **Jn 6:40** *1473*
"Did I **M** not choose you, the **Jn 6:70** *1473*
of God or *whether* I speak from **M**. **Jn 7:17** *1683*
and I have not come of **M**, **Jn 7:28** *1683*
"Even if I testify about **M**, **Jn 8:14** *1683*
"I am He who testifies about **M**, **Jn 8:18** *1683*
"If I glorify **M**, My glory is nothing **Jn 8:54** *1683*
earth, will draw all men to **M**." **Jn 12:32** *1683*
come again and receive you to **M** **Jn 14:3** *1683*
him and will disclose **M** to him." **Jn 14:21** *1683*
"For their sakes I sanctify **M**, **Jn 17:19** *1683*
BE IN BONDAGE I **M** WILL JUDGE,' **Ac 7:7** *1473*
for I have sent them **M**." **Ac 10:20** *1473*
life of any account as dear to **m**, **Ac 20:24** *1683*
would like to hear the man **m**." **Ac 25:22** *846*
the Jews, I consider **m** fortunate, **Ac 26:2** *1683*
I thought to **m** that I had to do **Ac 26:9** *1683*
I **m** with my mind am serving the **Ro 7:25** *846*
could wish that I **m** were accursed, **Ro 9:3** *846*
"I HAVE KEPT for **M** SEVEN THOUSAND **Ro 11:4** *1683*
I **m** also am convinced that you **Ro 15:14** *846*
helper of many, and of **m** as well. **Ro 16:2** *1473*
in fact, I do not even examine **m**. **1Co 4:3** *1683*
am conscious of nothing against **m**, **1Co 4:4** *1683*
to **m** and Apollos for your sakes, **1Co 4:6** *1683*
that all men were even as I **m** am. **1Co 7:7** *1683*
men, I have made **m** a slave to all, **1Co 9:19** *1683*
though not being **m** under the Law, **1Co 9:20** *846*
I **m** will not be disqualified. **1Co 9:27** *846*
I **m** urge you by the meekness and **2Co 10:1** *846*
For I consider **m** not in the least **2Co 11:5**
m so that you might be exalted, **2Co 11:7** *1683*
kept **m** from being a burden to you, **2Co 11:9** *1683*
I am just as bold **m**. **2Co 11:21** *1473*
to keep me from exalting **m**, **2Co 12:7**
to keep me from exalting **m**! **2Co 12:7**
except that I **m** did not become a **2Co 12:13** *846*
as it may, I did not burden you **m**; **2Co 12:16** *1473*
I prove **m** to be a transgressor. **Ga 2:18** *1683*
I **m** also will be coming shortly. **Php 2:24** *846*
although I **m** might have confidence **Php 3:4** *1473*
m as having laid hold of *it* yet; **Php 3:13** *1683*

MYSIA
and after they came to **M**, **Ac 16:7** *3465*
and passing by **M**, they came down **Ac 16:8** *3465*

MYSTERIES
"He reveals **m** from the darkness And **Jb 12:22** 6013
is a God in heaven who reveals **m**, **Da 2:28** 7328
and He who reveals **m** has made **Da 2:29** 7328
Lord of kings and a revealer of **m**, **Da 2:47** 7328
the **m** of the kingdom of heaven, **Mt 13:11** *3466*
know the **m** of the kingdom of God, **Lk 8:10** *3466*
and stewards of the **m** of God. **1Co 4:1** *3466*
and know all **m** and all knowledge; **1Co 13:2** *3466*
but in *his* spirit he speaks **m**. **1Co 14:2** *3466*

MYSTERIOUS
been is remote and exceedingly **m**. **Ec 7:24** 6013

MYSTERY
God of heaven concerning this **m**, **Da 2:18** 7328
Then the **m** was revealed to Daniel **Da 2:19** 7328
"As for the **m** about which the **Da 2:27** 7328
this **m** has not been revealed to me **Da 2:30** 7328
have been able to reveal this **m**." **Da 2:47** 7328
is in you and no **m** baffles you, **Da 4:9** 7328
given the **m** of the kingdom of God, **Mk 4:11** *3466*
to be uninformed of this **m** **Ro 11:25** *3466*
revelation of the **m** which has been **Ro 16:25** *3466*
but we speak God's wisdom in a **m**, **1Co 2:7** *3466*
Behold, I tell you a **m**; **1Co 15:51** *3466*
known to us the **m** of His will, **Eph 1:9** *3466*
there was made known to me the **m**, **Eph 3:3** *3466*
my insight into the **m** of Christ, **Eph 3:4** *3466*
m which for ages has been hidden **Eph 3:9** *3466*
This **m** is great; but I am speaking **Eph 5:32** *3466*
with boldness the **m** of the gospel, **Eph 6:19** *3466*
the **m** which has been hidden from **Col 1:26** *3466*
of this **m** among the Gentiles, **Col 1:27** *3466*
in a true knowledge of God's **m**, **Col 2:2** *3466*
may speak forth the **m** of Christ, **Col 4:3** *3466*
For the **m** of lawlessness is **2Th 2:7** *3466*
but holding to the **m** of the faith **1Tm 3:9** *3466*
great is the **m** of godliness: **1Tm 3:16** *3466*
"As for the **m** of the seven stars **Rv 1:20** *3466*
then the **m** of God is finished, **Rv 10:7** *3466*
forehead a name *was* written, a **m**, **Rv 17:5** *3466*
I will tell you the **m** of the woman **Rv 17:7** *3466*

MYSTICALLY
which **m** is called Sodom and Egypt, **Rv 11:8** *4153*

MYTHS
to **m** and endless genealogies, **1Tm 1:4** *3454*
truth and will turn aside to **m**. **2Tm 4:4** *3454*
not paying attention to Jewish **m** **Ti 1:14** *3454*

N

NAAM
of Jephunneh *were* Iru, Elah and **N**; **1Ch 4:15** 5277

NAAMAH
and the sister of Tubal-cain was **N**. **Gn 4:22** 5279a
Beth-dagon and **N** and Makkedah; **Jos 15:41** 5279b
mother's name was **N** the Ammonitess. **1Ki 14:21** 5279a
mother's name was **N** the Ammonitess. **1Ki 14:31** 5279a
mother's name was **N** the Ammonitess. **2Ch 12:13** 5279a

NAAMAN
and Becher and Ashbel, Gera and **N**, **Gn 46:21** 5283
The sons of Bela were Ard and **N**: **Nu 26:40** 5283
of **N**, the family of the Naamites. **Nu 26:40** 5283
Now **N**, captain of the army of the **2Ki 5:1** 5283
N went in and told his master, **2Ki 5:4**
I have sent **N** my servant to you, **2Ki 5:6** 5283
So **N** came with his horses and his **2Ki 5:9** 5283
But **N** was furious and went away **2Ki 5:11** 5283
N said, "If not, please let your **2Ki 5:17** 5283
has spared this **N** the Aramean, **2Ki 5:20** 5283
So Gehazi pursued **N**. **2Ki 5:21** 5283
When **N** saw one running after him, **2Ki 5:21** 5283
N said, "Be pleased to take two **2Ki 5:23** 5283
the leprosy of **N** shall cling to **2Ki 5:27** 5283
Abishua, **N**, Ahoah, **1Ch 8:4** 5283
namely, **N**, Ahijah and Gera **1Ch 8:7** 5283
cleansed, but only **N** the Syrian." **Lk 4:27** *3483b*

NAAMAN'S
and she waited on **N** wife. **2Ki 5:2** 5283

NAAMATHITE
the Shuhite and Zophar the **N**; **Jb 2:11** 5284
Then Zophar the **N** answered, **Jb 11:1** 5284
Then Zophar the **N** answered, **Jb 20:1** 5284
Zophar the **N** went and did as the **Jb 42:9** 5284

NAAMITES
of Naaman, the family of the **N**. **Nu 26:40** 5280

NAARAH
from Janoah to Ataroth and to **N**, **Jos 16:7** 5292
Tekoa, had two wives, Helah and **N**. **1Ch 4:5** 5292
N bore him Ahuzzam, Hepher, **1Ch 4:6** 5292
These were the sons of **N**. **1Ch 4:6** 5292

NAARAI
the Carmelite, **N** the son of Ezbai, **1Ch 11:37** 5293

NAARAN
with its towns, and to the east **N**, **1Ch 7:28** 5295

NABAL
(now the man's name was **N**, **1Sa 25:3** 5037
that **N** was shearing his sheep. **1Sa 25:4** 5037
visit **N** and greet him in my name; **1Sa 25:5** 5037
they spoke to **N** according to all **1Sa 25:9** 5037
But **N** answered David's servants and **1Sa 25:10** 5037
she did not tell her husband **N**. **1Sa 25:19** 5037
to this worthless man, **N**, **1Sa 25:25** 5037
N is his name and folly is with **1Sa 25:25** 5037
evil against my lord, be as **N**. **1Sa 25:26** 5037
there would not have been left to **N** **1Sa 25:34** 5037
Then Abigail came to **N**, **1Sa 25:36** 5037
when the wine had gone out of **N**, **1Sa 25:37** 5037
the LORD struck **N** **1Sa 25:38** 5037
When David heard that **N** was dead, **1Sa 25:39** 5037
of my reproach from the hand of **N** and **1Sa 25:39** 5037
evildoing of **N** on his own head." **1Sa 25:39** 5037
the widow of **N** the Carmelite. **1Sa 30:5** 5037
the widow of **N** the Carmelite. **2Sa 2:2** 5037
the widow of **N** the Carmelite; **2Sa 3:3** 5037

NABAL'S
young men told Abigail, **N** wife, **1Sa 25:14** 5037
And **N** heart was merry within him, **1Sa 25:36** 5037
Abigail the Carmelitess, **N** widow. **1Sa 27:3** 5037

NABOTH
that **N** the Jezreelite had a vineyard **1Ki 21:1** 5022
Ahab spoke to **N**, **1Ki 21:2** 5022
But **N** said to Ahab, **1Ki 21:3** 5022
N the Jezreelite had spoken to him; **1Ki 21:4** 5022
I spoke to **N** the Jezreelite and **1Ki 21:6** 5022
vineyard of **N** the Jezreelite." **1Ki 21:7** 5022
were living with **N** in his city. **1Ki 21:8** 5022
seat **N** at the head of the people; **1Ki 21:9** 5022
N at the head of the people. **1Ki 21:12** 5022
against him, even against **N**, **1Ki 21:13** 5022
"**N** cursed God and the king." **1Ki 21:13** 5022
"**N** has been stoned and is dead." **1Ki 21:14** 5022
N had been stoned and was dead, **1Ki 21:15** 5022
possession of the vineyard of **N**, **1Ki 21:15** 5022
for **N** is not alive, but dead." **1Ki 21:15** 5022
When Ahab heard that **N** was dead, **1Ki 21:16** 5022
the vineyard of **N** the Jezreelite, **1Ki 21:16** 5022
he is in the vineyard of **N** where **1Ki 21:18** 5022
the dogs licked up the blood of **N** **1Ki 21:19** 5022
the property of **N** the Jezreelite. **2Ki 9:21** 5022
of the field of **N** the Jezreelite, **2Ki 9:25** 5022
of **N** and the blood of his sons,' **2Ki 9:26** 5022

NACON
came to the threshing floor of **N**, **2Sa 6:6** 5225b

NADAB
and she bore him **N** and Abihu, **Ex 6:23** 5070
N and Abihu and seventy of the **Ex 24:1** 5070
went up with Aaron, **N** and Abihu, **Ex 24:9** 5070
Aaron, **N** and Abihu, Eleazar and **Ex 28:1** 5070
Now **N** and Abihu, the sons of **Lv 10:1** 5070
N the firstborn, and Abihu, **Nu 3:2** 5070
But **N** and Abihu died before the **Nu 3:4** 5070
To Aaron were born **N** and Abihu, **Nu 26:60** 5070
But **N** and Abihu died when they **Nu 26:61** 5070
N his son reigned in his place. **1Ki 14:20** 5070
Now **N** the son of Jeroboam became **1Ki 15:25** 5070
while **N** and all Israel were laying **1Ki 15:27** 5070
the acts of **N** and all that he did, **1Ki 15:31** 5070
of Shammai *were* **N** and Abishur. **1Ch 2:28** 5070
sons of **N** *were* Seled and Appaim, **1Ch 2:30** 5070
And the sons of Aaron *were* **N**, **1Ch 6:3** 5070
Abdon, then Zur, Kish, Baal, **N**, **1Ch 8:30** 5070
then Zur, Kish, Baal, Ner, **N**, **1Ch 9:36** 5070
the sons of Aaron *were* **N**, **1Ch 24:1** 5070
But **N** and Abihu died before their **1Ch 24:2** 5070

NAGGAI
the son of Hesli, the son of **N**, **Lk 3:25** *3477*

NAHALAL
Included also *were* Kattah and **N** **Jos 19:15** 5096
lands, **N** with its pasture lands; **Jos 21:35** 5096

NAHALIEL
and from Mattanah to **N**, **Nu 21:19** 5160
to Nahaliel, and from **N** to Bamoth, **Nu 21:19** 5160

NAHALOL
Kitron, or the inhabitants of **N**; **Jg 1:30** 5096

NAHAM
wife of Hodiah, the sister of **N**, **1Ch 4:19** 5163
NAHAMANI
Nehemiah, Azariah, Raamiah, **N**, **Ne 7:7** 5167
NAHARAI
the Ammonite, **N** the Beerothite, **2Sa 23:37** 5171
the Ammonite, **N** the Berothite, **1Ch 11:39** 5171
NAHASH
Now **N** the Ammonite came up and **1Sa 11:1** 5176
all the men of Jabesh said to **N**, **1Sa 11:1** 5176
But **N** the Ammonite said to them, **1Sa 11:2** 5176
N the king of the sons of Ammon **1Sa 12:12** 5176
kindness to Hanun the son of **N**, **2Sa 10:2** 5176
in to Abigail the daughter of **N**, **2Sa 17:25** 5176
Shobi the son of **N** from Rabbah of **2Sa 17:27** 5176
N the king of the sons of Ammon **1Ch 19:1** 5176
kindness to Hanun the son of **N**, **1Ch 19:2** 5176
NAHATH
N and Zerah, Shammah and Mizzah. **Gn 36:13** 5184
chief **N**, chief Zerah, chief **Gn 36:17** 5184
The sons of Reuel *were* **N**, **1Ch 1:37** 5184
were Zophai his son and **N** his son, **1Ch 6:26** 5184
Jehiel, Azaziah, **N**, **2Ch 31:13** 5184
NAHBI
of Naphtali, **N** the son of Vophsi; **Nu 13:14** 5147
NAHOR
years, and became the father of **N**; **Gn 11:22** 5152
after he became the father of **N**, **Gn 11:23** 5152
N lived twenty-nine years, and **Gn 11:24** 5152
and **N** lived one hundred and **Gn 11:25** 5152
the father of Abram, **N** and Haran. **Gn 11:26** 5152
the father of Abram, **N** and Haran; **Gn 11:27** 5152
and **N** took wives for themselves. **Gn 11:29** 5152
borne children to your brother **N**: **Gn 22:20** 5152
these eight Milcah bore to **N**, **Gn 22:23** 5152
to Mesopotamia, to the city of **N**. **Gn 24:10** 5152
the wife of Abraham's brother **N**, **Gn 24:15** 5152
of Milcah, whom she bore to **N**." **Gn 24:24** 5152
"Do you know Laban the son of **N**?" **Gn 29:5** 5152
God of Abraham and the God of **N**, **Gn 31:53** 5152
of Abraham and the father of **N**, **Jos 24:2** 5152
Serug, **N**, Terah, **1Ch 1:26** 5152
the son of Terah, the son of **N**, **Lk 3:34** *3493*
NAHOR'S
and the name of **N** wife was Milcah, **Gn 11:29** 5152
'The daughter of Bethuel, **N** son, **Gn 24:47** 5152
NAHSHON
of Amminadab, the sister of **N**, **Ex 6:23** 5177
of Judah, **N** the son of Amminadab; **Nu 1:7** 5177
N the son of Amminadab, **Nu 2:3** 5177
day was **N** the son of Amminadab, **Nu 7:12** 5177
of **N** the son of Amminadab. **Nu 7:17** 5177
with **N** the son of Amminadab, **Nu 10:14** 5177
and to Amminadab was born **N**, **Ru 4:20** 5177
born Nahshon, and to **N**, Salmon, **Ru 4:20** 5177
Amminadab became the father of **N**, **1Ch 2:10** 5177
N became the father of Salma, **1Ch 2:11** 5177
Amminadab the father of **N**, **Mt 1:4** *3476*
and **N** the father of Salmon. **Mt 1:4** *3476*
the son of Salmon, the son of **N**, **Lk 3:32** *3476*
NAHUM
book of the vision of **N** the Elkoshite. **Na 1:1** 5151
the son of Amos, the son of **N**, **Lk 3:25** *3486*
NAILED
you **n** to a cross by the hands of **Ac 2:23** *4362*
the way, having **n** it to the cross. **Col 2:14** *4338*
NAILS
shave her head and trim her **n**. **Dt 21:12** 6856
iron to make the **n** for the doors **1Ch 22:3** 4548
weight of the **n** was fifty shekels **2Ch 3:9** 4548
collections are like well-driven **n**; **Ec 12:11** 4548
And he fastens it with **n**, **Is 41:7** 4548
They fasten it with **n** and with **Jer 10:4** 4548
and his **n** like birds' *claws.* **Da 4:33** 2953
in His hands the imprint of the **n**, **Jn 20:25** *2247*
my finger into the place of the **n**, **Jn 20:25** *2247*
NAIN
afterwards He went to a city called **N**; **Lk 7:11** *3484*
NAIOTH
and Samuel went and stayed in **N**. **1Sa 19:18** 5121
"Behold, David is at **N** in Ramah." **1Sa 19:19** 5121
"Behold, they are at **N** in Ramah." **1Sa 19:22** 5121
He proceeded there to **N** in Ramah; **1Sa 19:23** 5121
until he came to **N** in Ramah. **1Sa 19:23** 5121
Then David fled from **N** in Ramah, **1Sa 20:1** 5121
NAIVE
To give prudence to the **n**, **Pr 1:4** 6612a
"How long, O **n** ones, will you **Pr 1:22** 6612a
waywardness of the **n** will kill them, **Pr 1:32** 6612a
And I saw among the **n**, **Pr 7:7** 6612a
"O **n** ones, understand prudence; **Pr 8:5** 6612a
"Whoever is **n**, let him turn in **Pr 9:4** 6612a
She is **n** and knows nothing. **Pr 9:13** 6615
"Whoever is **n**, let him turn in **Pr 9:16** 6612a
The **n** believes everything, But the **Pr 14:15** 6612a
The **n** inherit foolishness, But the **Pr 14:18** 6612a
and the **n** may become shrewd, **Pr 19:25** 6612a
is punished, the **n** becomes wise; **Pr 21:11** 6612a
But the **n** go on, and are punished **Pr 22:3** 6612a
The **n** proceed *and* pay the penalty. **Pr 27:12** 6612a
everyone who goes astray or is **n**; **Ezk 45:20** 6612a
NAKED
the man and his wife were both **n** **Gn 2:25** 6174
and they knew that they were **n**; **Gn 3:7** 5903
and I was afraid because I was **n**; **Gn 3:10** 5903
"Who told you that you were **n**? **Gn 3:11** 5903
one has made **n** his blood relative; **Lv 20:19** 6168
lay down **n** all that day and all that **1Sa 19:24** 6174
all their **n** ones from the spoil; **2Ch 28:15** 4636
"**N** I came from my mother's womb, **Jb 1:21** 6174
womb, And **n** I shall return there. **Jb 1:21** 6174
without cause, And stripped men **n**. **Jb 22:6** 6174
"They spend the night **n**, **Jb 24:7** 6174
to go about **n** without clothing, **Jb 24:10** 6174
"**N** is Sheol before Him, **Jb 26:6** 6174
had come **n** from his mother's womb, **Ec 5:15** 6174
he did so, going **n** and barefoot. **Is 20:2** 6174
My servant Isaiah has gone **n** and **Is 20:3** 6174
young and old, **n** and barefoot with **Is 20:4** 6174
When you see the **n**, **Is 58:7** 6174
become drunk and make yourself **n**. **La 4:21** 6168
Yet you were **n** and bare. **Ezk 16:7** 5903
when you were **n** and bare and **Ezk 16:22** 5903
and will leave you **n** and bare. **Ezk 16:39** 5903
and covers the **n** with clothing, **Ezk 18:7** 5903
and covers the **n** with clothing, **Ezk 18:16** 5903
and leave you **n** and bare. **Ezk 23:29** 5903
Or I will strip her **n** And expose her **Hos 2:3** 6174
will flee **n** in that day," **Am 2:16** 6174
wail, I must go barefoot and **n**; **Mi 1:8** 6174
n, and you clothed Me; **Mt 25:36** *1131*
invite You in, or **n**, and clothe You? **Mt 25:38** *1131*
n, and you did not clothe Me; **Mt 25:43** *1131*
or thirsty, or a stranger, or **n**, **Mt 25:44** *1131*
but a linen sheet over *his* **n** *body* **Mk 14:51** *1131*
linen sheet and escaped **n**. **Mk 14:52** *1131*
out of that house **n** and wounded. **Ac 19:16** *1131*
put it on, will not be found **n**. **2Co 5:3** *1131*
and poor and blind and **n**, **Rv 3:17** *1131*
not walk about **n** and men will not see **Rv 16:15** *1131*
and will make her desolate and **n**, **Rv 17:16** *1131*
NAKEDNESS
Canaan, saw the **n** of his father, **Gn 9:22** 6172
and covered the **n** of their father; **Gn 9:23** 6172
they did not see their father's **n**. **Gn 9:23** 6172
your **n** will not be exposed on it.' **Ex 20:26** 6172
relative of his to uncover **n**; **Lv 18:6** 6172
not uncover the **n** of your father, **Lv 18:7** 6172
that is, the **n** of your mother. **Lv 18:7** 6172
you are not to uncover her **n**. **Lv 18:7** 6172
the **n** of your father's wife; **Lv 18:8** 6172
it is your father's **n**. **Lv 18:8** 6172
'The **n** of your sister, *either* your **Lv 18:9** 6172
their **n** you shall not uncover. **Lv 18:9** 6172
'The **n** of your son's daughter or **Lv 18:10** 6172
their **n** you shall not uncover; **Lv 18:10** 6172
for their **n** is yours. **Lv 18:10** 6172
'The **n** of your father's wife's **Lv 18:11** 6172
you shall not uncover her **n**. **Lv 18:11** 6172
the **n** of your father's sister; **Lv 18:12** 6172
the **n** of your mother's sister, **Lv 18:13** 6172
the **n** of your father's brother; **Lv 18:14** 6172
the **n** of your daughter-in-law; **Lv 18:15** 6172
wife, you shall not uncover her **n**. **Lv 18:15** 6172
the **n** of your brother's wife; **Lv 18:16** 6172
it is your brother's **n**. **Lv 18:16** 6172
shall not uncover the **n** of a woman **Lv 18:17** 6172
daughter, to uncover her **n**; **Lv 18:17** 6172
she is alive, to uncover her **n**. **Lv 18:18** 6172
n during her menstrual impurity. **Lv 18:19** 6172
he has uncovered his father's **n**; **Lv 20:11** 6172
her **n** and she sees his nakedness, **Lv 20:17** 6172
her nakedness and she sees his **n**, **Lv 20:17** 6172
He has uncovered his sister's **n**; **Lv 20:17** 6172
woman and uncovers her **n**, **Lv 20:18** 6172
'You shall also not uncover the **n** **Lv 20:19** 6172
he has uncovered his uncle's **n**; **Lv 20:20** 6172
he has uncovered his brother's **n**. **Lv 20:21** 6172
you, in hunger, in thirst, in **n**, **Dt 28:48** 5903
to the shame of your mother's **n**? **1Sa 20:30** 6172
"Your **n** will be uncovered, Your **Is 47:3** 6172
her Because they have seen her **n**; **La 1:8** 6172
skirt over you and covered your **n**. **Ezk 16:8** 6172
and your **n** uncovered through your **Ezk 16:36** 6172
expose your **n** to them that they may **Ezk 16:37** 6172
them that they may see all your **n**. **Ezk 16:37** 6172
have uncovered *their* fathers' **n**; **Ezk 22:10** 6172
"They uncovered her **n**; **Ezk 23:10** 6172
harlotries and uncovered her **n**; **Ezk 23:18** 6172
And the **n** of your harlotries will **Ezk 23:29** 6172
and My flax *Given* to cover her **n**. **Hos 2:9** 6172
of Shaphir, in shameful **n**. **Mi 1:11** 6181
And show to the nations your **n** And **Na 3:5** 4626
drunk So as to look on their **n**! **Hab 2:15** 4589
drink and expose your *own* **n**. **Hab 2:16** 6188
or persecution, or famine, or **n**, **Ro 8:35** *1132*
that the shame of your **n** will not be **Rv 3:18** *1132*
NAME
The **n** of the first is Pishon; **Gn 2:11** 8034
n of the second river is Gihon; **Gn 2:13** 8034
n of the third river is Tigris; **Gn 2:14** 8034
a living creature, that was its **n**. **Gn 2:19** 8034
the man called his wife's **n** Eve, **Gn 3:20** 8034
called the **n** of the city Enoch, **Gn 4:17** 8034
Enoch, after the **n** of his son. **Gn 4:17** 8034
the **n** of the one was Adah, and the **Gn 4:19** 8034
the **n** of the other, Zillah. **Gn 4:19** 8034
His brother's **n** was Jubal; **Gn 4:21** 8034
and he called his **n** Enosh. **Gn 4:26** 8034
to call upon the **n** of the LORD. **Gn 4:26** 8034
Now he called his **n** Noah, **Gn 5:29** 8034
the **n** of the one *was* Peleg, for in **Gn 10:25** 8034
and his brother's **n** *was* Joktan. **Gn 10:25** 8034
and let us make for ourselves a **n**, **Gn 11:4** 8034
Therefore its **n** was called Babel, **Gn 11:9** 8034
The **n** of Abram's wife was Sarai; **Gn 11:29** 8034
the **n** of Nahor's wife was Milcah, **Gn 11:29** 8034
bless you, And make your **n** great; **Gn 12:2** 8034
and called upon the **n** of the LORD. **Gn 12:8** 8034
Abram called on the **n** of the LORD. **Gn 13:4** 8034
Egyptian maid whose **n** was Hagar. **Gn 16:1** 8034
And you shall call his **n** Ishmael, **Gn 16:11** 8034
she called the **n** of the LORD who **Gn 16:13** 8034
and Abram called the **n** of his son, **Gn 16:15** 8034
shall your **n** be called Abram, **Gn 17:5** 8034
But your **n** shall be Abraham; **Gn 17:5** 8034
you shall not call her **n** Sarai, **Gn 17:15** 8034
Sarai, but Sarah *shall be* her **n**. **Gn 17:15** 8034
and you shall call his **n** Isaac; **Gn 17:19** 8034
the **n** of the town was called Zoar. **Gn 19:22** 8034
bore a son, and called his **n** Moab; **Gn 19:37** 8034
a son, and called his **n** Ben-ammi; **Gn 19:38** 8034
Abraham called the **n** of his son **Gn 21:3** 8034
he called on the **n** of the LORD, **Gn 21:33** 8034
Abraham called the **n** of that place **Gn 22:14** 8034
His concubine, whose **n** was Reumah, **Gn 22:24** 8034
had a brother whose **n** was Laban; **Gn 24:29** 8034
another wife, whose **n** was Keturah. **Gn 25:1** 8034
heel, so his **n** was called Jacob; **Gn 25:26** 8034
Therefore his **n** was called Edom **Gn 25:30** 8034
and called upon the **n** of the LORD, **Gn 26:25** 8034
therefore the **n** of the city is **Gn 26:33** 8034
called the **n** of that place Bethel; **Gn 28:19** 8034
the **n** of the city had been Luz. **Gn 28:19** 8034
the **n** of the older was Leah, and **Gn 29:16** 8034
the **n** of the younger was Rachel. **Gn 29:16** 8034
"**N** me your wages, and I will give **Gn 30:28** 5344a
"What is your **n**?" **Gn 32:27** 8034
"Your **n** shall no longer be Jacob, **Gn 32:28** 8034
"Please tell me your **n**." **Gn 32:29** 8034
"Why is it that you ask my **n**?" **Gn 32:29** 8034
God said to him, "Your **n** is Jacob; **Gn 35:10** 8034
But Israel shall be your **n**." **Gn 35:10** 8034
the **n** of his city was Dinhabah. **Gn 36:32** 8034
and the **n** of his city was Avith. **Gn 36:35** 8034
and the **n** of his city was Pau; **Gn 36:39** 8034
and his wife's **n** was Mehetabel, **Gn 36:39** 8034
Adullamite, whose **n** was Hirah. **Gn 38:1** 8034
Canaanite whose **n** was Shua; **Gn 38:2** 8034
firstborn, and her **n** *was* Tamar. **Gn 38:6** 8034
And may my **n** live on in them, And **Gn 48:16** 8034
they may say to me, 'What is His **n**?' **Ex 3:13** 8034
This is My **n** forever, and this is **Ex 3:15** 8034
came to Pharaoh to speak in Your **n**, **Ex 5:23** 8034
as God Almighty, *but by* My **n**, **Ex 6:3** 8034
My **n** through all the earth. **Ex 9:16** 8034
The LORD is His **n**. **Ex 15:3** 8034
n of the LORD your God in vain, **Ex 20:7** 8034
who takes His **n** in vain. **Ex 20:7** 8034
I cause My **n** to be remembered, **Ex 20:24** 8034
not mention the **n** of other gods, **Ex 23:13** 8034
since My **n** is in him. **Ex 23:21** 8034
to his **n** for the twelve tribes. **Ex 28:21** 8034
"See, I have called by **n** Bezalel, **Ex 31:2** 8034
'I have known you by **n**, **Ex 33:12** 8034
and I have known you by **n**." **Ex 33:17** 8034
will proclaim the **n** of the LORD **Ex 33:19** 8034
he called upon the **n** of the LORD. **Ex 34:5** 8034
for the LORD, whose **n** is Jealous, **Ex 34:14** 8034
by **n** Bezalel the son of Uri, **Ex 35:30** 8034
with its **n** for the twelve tribes. **Ex 39:14** 8034
you profane the **n** of your God; **Lv 18:21** 8034
shall not swear falsely by My **n**, **Lv 19:12** 8034
as to profane the **n** of your God; **Lv 19:12** 8034
and to profane My holy **n**. **Lv 20:3** 8034
not profane the **n** of their God, **Lv 21:6** 8034
so as not to profane My holy **n**; **Lv 22:2** 8034
You shall not profane My holy **n**, **Lv 22:32** 8034
woman blasphemed the **N** and cursed. **Lv 24:11** 8034
(Now his mother's **n** was Shelomith, **Lv 24:11** 8034
who blasphemes the **n** of the LORD **Lv 24:16** 8034
native, when he blasphemes the **N**, **Lv 24:16** 8034
men who had been designated by **n**, **Nu 1:17** 8034
shall assign *each man* by **n** the items **Nu 4:32** 8034
invoke My **n** on the sons of Israel, **Nu 6:27** 8034
So the **n** of that place was called **Nu 11:3** 8034
the **n** of one was Eldad and the **Nu 11:26** 8034
and the **n** of the other Medad. **Nu 11:26** 8034
So the **n** of that place was called **Nu 11:34** 8034
You shall write each **n** on his rod, **Nu 17:2** 8034
write Aaron's **n** on the rod of Levi; **Nu 17:3** 8034
Thus the **n** of the place was called **Nu 21:3** 8034
Now the **n** of the slain man of Israel **Nu 25:14** 8034
The **n** of the Midianite woman **Nu 25:15** 8034
The **n** of the daughter of Asher **Nu 26:46** 8034
The **n** of Amram's wife was Jochebed, **Nu 26:59** 8034
"Why should the **n** of our father **Nu 27:4** 8034
called it Nobah after his own **n**. **Nu 32:42** 8034
that is, Bashan, after his own **n**, **Dt 3:14** 8034
n of the LORD your God in vain, **Dt 5:11** 8034
who takes His **n** in vain. **Dt 5:11** 8034
worship Him and swear by His **n**. **Dt 6:13** 8034
that you will make their **n** perish **Dt 7:24** 8034
blot out their **n** from under heaven; **Dt 9:14** 8034
to bless in His **n** until this day. **Dt 10:8** 8034
Him, and you shall swear by His **n**. **Dt 10:20** 8034
obliterate their **n** from that place. **Dt 12:3** 8034
His **n** there for His dwelling, **Dt 12:5** 8034
will choose for His **n** to dwell, **Dt 12:11** 8034
your God chooses to put His **n** **Dt 12:21** 8034
He chooses to establish His **n**, **Dt 14:23** 8034
LORD your God chooses to set His **n** **Dt 14:24** 8034
LORD chooses to establish His **n**. **Dt 16:2** 8034

God chooses to establish His **n**. **Dt 16:6** 8034
God chooses to establish His **n**. **Dt 16:11** 8034
serve in the **n** of the LORD forever. **Dt 18:5** 8034
serve in the **n** of the LORD his God, **Dt 18:7** 8034
which he shall speak in My **n**, **Dt 18:19** 8034
a word presumptuously in My **n** **Dt 18:20** 8034
speaks in the **n** of other gods, **Dt 18:20** 8034
speaks in the **n** of the LORD, **Dt 18:22** 8034
and to bless in the **n** of the LORD; **Dt 21:5** 8034
assume the **n** of his dead brother, **Dt 25:6** 8034
that his **n** will not be blotted out **Dt 25:6** 8034
a **n** for his brother in Israel; **Dt 25:7** 8034
In Israel his **n** shall be called, **Dt 25:10** 8034
God chooses to establish His **n**. **Dt 26:2** 8034
are called by the **n** of the LORD, **Dt 28:10** 8034
fear this honored and awesome **n**, **Dt 28:58** 8034
blot out his **n** from under heaven. **Dt 29:20** 8034
"For I proclaim the **n** of the LORD; **Dt 32:3** 8034
of a harlot whose **n** was Rahab, **Jos 2:1** 8034
So the **n** of that place is called **Jos 5:9** 8034
and cut off our **n** from the earth. **Jos 7:9** 8034
will You do for Your great **n**?" **Jos 7:9** 8034
Therefore the **n** of that place has **Jos 7:26** 8034
Now the **n** of Hebron was formerly **Jos 14:15** 8034
now the **n** of Debir formerly was **Jos 15:15** 8034
after the **n** of Dan their father. **Jos 19:47** 8034
cities which are *here* mentioned by **n** **Jos 21:9** 8034
or mention the **n** of their gods, **Jos 23:7** 8034
now the **n** of Hebron formerly *was* **Jg 1:10** 8034
now the **n** of Debir formerly *was* **Jg 1:11** 8034
n of the city was called Hormah. **Jg 1:17** 8034
n of the city was formerly Luz). **Jg 1:23** 8034
it Luz which is its **n** to this day. **Jg 1:26** 8034
the Danites, whose **n** was Manoah; **Jg 13:2** 8034
from, nor did he tell me his **n**. **Jg 13:6** 8034
"What is your **n**, so that when **Jg 13:17** 8034
"Why do you ask my **n**, **Jg 13:18** 8034
of Sorek, whose **n** was Delilah. **Jg 16:4** 8034
of Ephraim whose **n** was Micah. **Jg 17:1** 8034
They called the **n** of the city Dan, **Jg 18:29** 8034
after the **n** of Dan their father **Jg 18:29** 8034
the **n** of the city formerly was **Jg 18:29** 8034
The **n** of the man *was* Elimelech, **Ru 1:2** 8034
and the **n** of his wife, Naomi; **Ru 1:2** 8034
the **n** of the one was Orpah and the **Ru 1:4** 8034
Orpah and the **n** of the other Ruth. **Ru 1:4** 8034
of Elimelech, whose **n** was Boaz. **Ru 2:1** 8034
"The **n** of the man with whom I **Ru 2:19** 8034
to raise up the **n** of the deceased on **Ru 4:5** 8034
to raise up the **n** of the deceased **Ru 4:10** 8034
so that the **n** of the deceased will **Ru 4:10** 8034
may his **n** become famous in Israel. **Ru 4:14** 8034
The neighbor women gave him a **n**, **Ru 4:17** 8034
and his **n** was Elkanah the son of **1Sa 1:1** 8034
the **n** of one was Hannah and the **1Sa 1:2** 8034
and the **n** of the other Peninnah; **1Sa 1:2** 8034
the **n** of his firstborn was Joel, **1Sa 8:2** 8034
and the **n** of his second, Abijah; **1Sa 8:2** 8034
whose **n** was Kish the son of Abiel, **1Sa 9:1** 8034
He had a son whose **n** was Saul, **1Sa 9:2** 8034
people on account of His great **n**, **1Sa 12:22** 8034
and the **n** of the one was Bozez, **1Sa 14:4** 8034
and the **n** of the other Seneh. **1Sa 14:4** 8034
the **n** of the firstborn Merab and **1Sa 14:49** 8034
and the **n** of the younger Michal. **1Sa 14:49** 8034
The **n** of Saul's wife was **1Sa 14:50** 8034
And the **n** of the captain of his **1Sa 14:50** 8034
in Judah, whose **n** was Jesse, **1Sa 17:12** 8034
you in the **n** of the LORD of hosts, **1Sa 17:45** 8034
So his **n** was highly esteemed. **1Sa 18:30** 8034
each other in the **n** of the LORD, **1Sa 20:42** 8034
and his **n** was Doeg the Edomite, **1Sa 21:7** 8034
that you will not destroy my **n** from **1Sa 24:21** 8034
(now the man's **n** was Nabal, and **1Sa 25:3** 8034
and his wife's **n** was Abigail. **1Sa 25:3** 8034
visit Nabal and greet him in my **n**; **1Sa 25:5** 8034
to all these words in David's **n**; **1Sa 25:9** 8034
Nabal, for as his **n** is, so is he. **1Sa 25:25** 8034
Nabal is his **n** and folly is with him; **1Sa 25:25** 8034
up for me whom I shall **n** to you." **1Sa 28:8** 559
a concubine whose **n** was Rizpah, **2Sa 3:7** 8034
the **n** of the one was Baanah and **2Sa 4:2** 8034
and the **n** of the other Rechab, **2Sa 4:2** 8034
And his **n** was Mephibosheth. **2Sa 4:4** 8034
of God which is called by the **N**, **2Sa 6:2** 8034
the very **n** of the LORD of hosts **2Sa 6:2** 8034
in the **n** of the LORD of hosts. **2Sa 6:18** 8034
and I will make you a great **n**, **2Sa 7:9** 8034
"He shall build a house for My **n**, **2Sa 7:13** 8034
and to make a **n** for Himself, **2Sa 7:23** 8034
Your **n** may be magnified forever, **2Sa 7:26** 8034
So David made a **n** *for himself* when **2Sa 8:13** 8034
house of Saul whose **n** was Ziba, **2Sa 9:2** 8034
had a young son whose **n** was Mica. **2Sa 9:12** 8034
sister whose **n** was Tamar, **2Sa 13:1** 8034
had a friend whose **n** was Jonadab, **2Sa 13:3** 8034
to leave my husband neither **n** nor **2Sa 14:7** 8034
one daughter whose **n** was Tamar; **2Sa 14:27** 8034
house of Saul whose **n** was Shimei, **2Sa 16:5** 8034
whose **n** was Ithra the Israelite, **2Sa 17:25** 8034
"I have no son to preserve my **n**." **2Sa 18:18** 8034
named the pillar after his own **n**, **2Sa 18:18** 8034
to be there whose **n** was Sheba, **2Sa 20:1** 8034
Sheba the son of Bichri by **n**, **2Sa 20:21** 8034
And I will sing praises to Your **n**. **2Sa 22:50** 8034
and had a **n** as well as the three. **2Sa 23:18** 8034
and had a **n** as well as the three **2Sa 23:22** 8034
God make the **n** of Solomon better **1Ki 1:47** 8034
name of Solomon better than your **n** **1Ki 1:47** 8034

no house built for the **n** of the LORD **1Ki 3:2** 8034
build a house for the **n** of the LORD **1Ki 5:3** 8034
for the **n** of the LORD my God, **1Ki 5:5** 8034
he will build the house for My **n**.' **1Ki 5:5** 8034
a house that My **n** might be there, **1Ki 8:16** 8034
a house for the **n** of the LORD, **1Ki 8:17** 8034
heart to build a house for My **n**, **1Ki 8:18** 8034
will build the house for My **n**.' **1Ki 8:19** 8034
the house for the **n** of the LORD, **1Ki 8:20** 8034
'My **n** shall be there,' to listen **1Ki 8:29** 8034
confess Your **n** and pray and make **1Ki 8:33** 8034
confess Your **n** and turn from their sin **1Ki 8:35** 8034
Your great **n** and Your mighty hand, **1Ki 8:42** 8034
of the earth may know Your **n**, **1Ki 8:43** 8034
I have built is called by Your **n**. **1Ki 8:43** 8034
which I have built for Your **n**, **1Ki 8:44** 8034
which I have built for Your **n**; **1Ki 8:48** 8034
by putting My **n** there forever, **1Ki 9:3** 8034
which I have consecrated for My **n**, **1Ki 9:7** 8034
concerning the **n** of the LORD, **1Ki 10:1** 8034
whose mother's **n** was Zeruah, **1Ki 11:26** 8034
chosen for Myself to put My **n**. **1Ki 11:36** 8034
the house of David, Josiah by **n**; **1Ki 13:2** 8034
of Israel to put His **n** there. **1Ki 14:21** 8034
n was Naamah the Ammonitess. **1Ki 14:21** 8034
n was Naamah the Ammonitess. **1Ki 14:31** 8034
and his mother's **n** was Maacah the **1Ki 15:2** 8034
and his mother's **n** was Maacah the **1Ki 15:10** 8034
Samaria, after the **n** of Shemer, **1Ki 16:24** 8034
you call on the **n** of your god, **1Ki 18:24** 8034
I will call on the **n** of the LORD, **1Ki 18:24** 8034
and call on the **n** of your god, **1Ki 18:25** 8034
called on the **n** of Baal from morning **1Ki 18:26** 8034
"Israel shall be your **n**." **1Ki 18:31** 8034
an altar in the **n** of the LORD, **1Ki 18:32** 8034
So she wrote letters in Ahab's **n** and **1Ki 21:8** 8034
the truth in the **n** of the LORD?" **1Ki 22:16** 8034
And his mother's **n** was Azubah the **1Ki 22:42** 8034
cursed them in the **n** of the LORD. **2Ki 2:24** 8034
call on the **n** of the LORD his God, **2Ki 5:11** 8034
And his mother's **n** *was* Athaliah **2Ki 8:26** 8034
mother's **n** was Zibiah of Beersheba. **2Ki 12:1** 8034
n was Jehoaddin of Jerusalem. **2Ki 14:2** 8034
the **n** of Israel from under heaven, **2Ki 14:27** 8034
n was Jecoliah of Jerusalem. **2Ki 15:2** 8034
and his mother's **n** *was* Jerusha the **2Ki 15:33** 8034
and his mother's **n** was Abi the **2Ki 18:2** 8034
and his mother's **n** was Hephzibah. **2Ki 21:1** 8034
"In Jerusalem I will put My **n**." **2Ki 21:4** 8034
Israel, I will put My **n** forever. **2Ki 21:7** 8034
and his mother's **n** *was* **2Ki 21:19** 8034
and his mother's **n** was Jedidah the **2Ki 22:1** 8034
'My **n** shall be there.' " **2Ki 23:27** 8034
and his mother's **n** was Hamutal the **2Ki 23:31** 8034
and changed his **n** to Jehoiakim. **2Ki 23:34** 8034
and his mother's **n** *was* Zebidah the **2Ki 23:36** 8034
and his mother's **n** *was* Nehushta **2Ki 24:8** 8034
and changed his **n** to Zedekiah. **2Ki 24:17** 8034
and his mother's **n** was Hamutal the **2Ki 24:18** 8034
Eber, the **n** of the one was Peleg, **1Ch 1:19** 8034
and his brother's **n** was Joktan. **1Ch 1:19** 8034
the **n** of his city was Dinhabah. **1Ch 1:43** 8034
and the **n** of his city *was* Avith. **1Ch 1:46** 8034
and the **n** of his city was Pai, and **1Ch 1:50** 8034
and his wife's **n** was Mehetabel, **1Ch 1:50** 8034
another wife, whose **n** was Atarah; **1Ch 2:26** 8034
n of Abishur's wife *was* Abihail, **1Ch 2:29** 8034
servant whose **n** was Jarha. **1Ch 2:34** 8034
and the **n** of their sister *was* **1Ch 4:3** 8034
these mentioned by **n** *were* leaders **1Ch 4:38** 8034
These, recorded by **n**, **1Ch 4:41** 8034
cities which are mentioned by **n**. **1Ch 6:65** 8034
whose sister's **n** was Maacah. **1Ch 7:15** 8034
n of the second was Zelophehad, **1Ch 7:15** 8034
the **n** of his brother *was* Sheresh, **1Ch 7:16** 8034
lived, and his wife's **n** was Maacah; **1Ch 8:29** 8034
lived, and his wife's **n** was Maacah, **1Ch 9:35** 8034
he had a **n** as well as the thirty. **1Ch 11:20** 8034
and had a **n** as well as the three **1Ch 11:24** 8034
by **n** to come and make David king. **1Ch 12:31** 8034
cherubim, where His **n** is called. **1Ch 13:6** 8034
the people in the **n** of the LORD. **1Ch 16:2** 8034
to the LORD, call upon His **n**; **1Ch 16:8** 8034
Glory in His holy **n**; **1Ch 16:10** 8034
to the LORD the glory due His **n**; **1Ch 16:29** 8034
To give thanks to Your holy **n**, **1Ch 16:35** 8034
chosen, who were designated by **n**, **1Ch 16:41** 8034
and I will make you a **n** like the **1Ch 17:8** 8034
a name like the **n** of the great ones **1Ch 17:8** 8034
make You a **n** by great and terrible **1Ch 17:21** 8034
"Let Your **n** be established and **1Ch 17:24** 8034
he spoke in the **n** of the LORD. **1Ch 21:19** 8034
build a house to the **n** of the LORD **1Ch 22:7** 8034
shall not build a house to My **n**, **1Ch 22:8** 8034
for his **n** shall be Solomon, and I **1Ch 22:9** 8034
'He shall build a house for My **n**, **1Ch 22:10** 8034
be built for the **n** of the LORD." **1Ch 22:19** 8034
Him and to bless in His **n** forever. **1Ch 23:13** 8034
You shall not build a house for My **n** **1Ch 28:3** 8034
You, and praise Your glorious **n**. **1Ch 29:13** 8034
build You a house for Your holy **n**, **1Ch 29:16** 8034
a house for the **n** of the LORD and **2Ch 2:1** 8034
build a house for the **n** of the LORD **2Ch 2:4** 8034
a house that My **n** might be there, **2Ch 6:5** 8034
that My **n** might be there, **2Ch 6:6** 8034
a house for the **n** of the LORD, **2Ch 6:7** 8034
heart to build a house for My **n**, **2Ch 6:8** 8034
shall build the house for My **n**.' **2Ch 6:9** 8034
the house for the **n** of the LORD, **2Ch 6:10** 8034

that *You would* put Your **n** there, **2Ch 6:20** 8034
return *to You* and confess Your **n**, **2Ch 6:24** 8034
this place and confess Your **n**, **2Ch 6:26** 8034
of the earth may know Your **n**, **2Ch 6:33** 8034
I have built is called by Your **n**. **2Ch 6:33** 8034
which I have built for Your **n**, **2Ch 6:34** 8034
which I have built for Your **n**, **2Ch 6:38** 8034
My people who are called by My **n** **2Ch 7:14** 8034
that My **n** may be there forever, **2Ch 7:16** 8034
which I have consecrated for My **n** **2Ch 7:20** 8034
of Israel, to put His **n** there. **2Ch 12:13** 8034
And his mother's **n** was Naamah **2Ch 12:13** 8034
and his mother's **n** was Micaiah the **2Ch 13:2** 8034
and in Your **n** have come against **2Ch 14:11** 8034
the truth in the **n** of the LORD?" **2Ch 18:15** 8034
You a sanctuary there for Your **n**, **2Ch 20:8** 8034
(for Your **n** is in this house) **2Ch 20:9** 8034
And his mother's **n** *was* Azubah the **2Ch 20:31** 8034
And his mother's **n** was Athaliah, **2Ch 22:2** 8034
his mother's **n** *was* Zibiah from **2Ch 24:1** 8034
And his mother's **n** was Jehoaddan **2Ch 25:1** 8034
and his mother's **n** was Jechiliah **2Ch 26:3** 8034
And his mother's **n** was Jerushah **2Ch 27:1** 8034
LORD was there, whose **n** *was* Oded; **2Ch 28:9** 8034
who were designated by **n** arose, **2Ch 28:15** 8034
And his mother's **n** *was* Abijah, the **2Ch 29:1** 8034
designated by **n** to distribute portions **2Ch 31:19** 8034
My **n** shall be in Jerusalem forever." **2Ch 33:4** 8034
Israel, I will put My **n** forever; **2Ch 33:7** 8034
the **n** of the LORD God of Israel, **2Ch 33:18** 8034
and changed his **n** to Jehoiakim. **2Ch 36:4** 8034
and he was called by their **n**. **Ezr 2:61** 8034
in the **n** of the God of Israel, **Ezr 5:1** 8036
to one whose **n** was Sheshbazzar, **Ezr 5:14** 8036
God who has caused His **n** to dwell **Ezr 6:12** 8036
all of them designated by **n**. **Ezr 8:20** 8034
households, all of them by **n**. **Ezr 10:16** 8034
chosen to cause My **n** to dwell.' **Ne 1:9** 8034
who delight to revere Your **n**; **Ne 1:11** 8034
O may Your glorious **n** be blessed **Ne 9:5** 8034
And gave him the **n** Abraham. **Ne 9:7** 8034
a **n** for Yourself as *it is* this day. **Ne 9:10** 8034
in Susa a Jew whose **n** was Mordecai, **Es 2:5** 8034
in her and she was summoned by **n**. **Es 2:14** 8034
informed the king in Mordecai's **n**. **Es 2:22** 8034
written in the **n** of King Ahasuerus **Es 3:12** 8034
as you see fit, in the king's **n**, **Es 8:8** 8034
which is written in the **n** of the king **Es 8:8** 8034
wrote in the **n** of King Ahasuerus, **Es 8:10** 8034
days Purim after the **n** of Pur. **Es 9:26** 8034
the land of Uz whose **n** was Job **Jb 1:1** 8034
Blessed be the **n** of the LORD." **Jb 1:21** 8034
the earth, And he has no **n** abroad. **Jb 18:17** 8034
"Fools, even those without a **n**, **Jb 30:8** 8034
who love Your **n** may exult in You. **Ps 5:11** 8034
to the **n** of the LORD Most High. **Ps 7:17** 8034
majestic is Your **n** in all the earth, **Ps 8:1** 8034
majestic is Your **n** in all the earth! **Ps 8:9** 8034
I will sing praise to Your **n**, **Ps 9:2** 8034
out their **n** forever and ever. **Ps 9:5** 8034
those who know Your **n** will put their **Ps 9:10** 8034
And I will sing praises to Your **n**. **Ps 18:49** 8034
May the **n** of the God of Jacob set **Ps 20:1** 8034
And in the **n** of our God we will **Ps 20:5** 8034
will boast in the **n** of the LORD, **Ps 20:7** 8034
will tell of Your **n** to my brethren; **Ps 22:22** 8034
the LORD the glory due to His **n**; **Ps 29:2** 8034
And give thanks to His holy **n**. **Ps 30:4** 2143
Because we trust in His holy **n**. **Ps 33:21** 8034
And let us exalt His **n** together. **Ps 34:3** 8034
will he die, and his **n** perish?" **Ps 41:5** 8034
Through Your **n** we will trample down **Ps 44:5** 8034
will give thanks to Your **n** forever. **Ps 44:8** 8034
we had forgotten the **n** of our God Or **Ps 44:20** 8034
I will cause Your **n** to be **Ps 45:17** 8034
As is Your **n**, O God, So is Your **Ps 48:10** 8034
done *it*, And I will wait on Your **n**, **Ps 52:9** 8034
Save me, O God, by Your **n**, **Ps 54:1** 8034
I will give thanks to Your **n**, **Ps 54:6** 8034
inheritance of those who fear Your **n**. **Ps 61:5** 8034
will sing praise to Your **n** forever, **Ps 61:8** 8034
I will lift up my hands in Your **n**. **Ps 63:4** 8034
Sing the glory of His **n**; **Ps 66:2** 8034
They will sing praises to Your **n**." **Ps 66:4** 8034
to God, sing praises to His **n**; **Ps 68:4** 8034
the deserts, Whose **n** is the LORD, **Ps 68:4** 8034
praise the **n** of God with song And **Ps 69:30** 8034
who love His **n** will dwell in it. **Ps 69:36** 8034
May his **n** endure forever; **Ps 72:17** 8034
May his **n** increase as long as the **Ps 72:17** 8034
blessed be His glorious **n** forever; **Ps 72:19** 8034
defiled the dwelling place of Your **n**. **Ps 74:7** 8034
And the enemy spurn Your **n** forever? **Ps 74:10** 8034
foolish people has spurned Your **n**. **Ps 74:18** 8034
afflicted and needy praise Your **n**. **Ps 74:21** 8034
we give thanks, For Your **n** is near; **Ps 75:1** 8034
His **n** is great in Israel. **Ps 76:1** 8034
which do not call upon Your **n**. **Ps 79:6** 8034
salvation, for the glory of Your **n**; **Ps 79:9** 8034
us, and we will call upon Your **n**. **Ps 80:18** 8034
That the **n** of Israel be remembered **Ps 83:4** 8034
That they may seek Your **n**, **Ps 83:16** 8034
You alone, whose **n** is the LORD, **Ps 83:18** 8034
And they shall glorify Your **n**. **Ps 86:9** 8034
Unite my heart to fear Your **n**. **Ps 86:11** 8034
And will glorify Your **n** forever. **Ps 86:12** 8034
and Hermon shout for joy at Your **n**. **Ps 89:12** 8034
In Your **n** they rejoice all the day, **Ps 89:16** 8034
in My **n** his horn will be exalted. **Ps 89:24** 8034

high, because he has known My **n**.	Ps 91:14	8034
And to sing praises to Your **n**,	Ps 92:1	8034
Sing to the LORD, bless His **n**;	Ps 96:2	8034
to the LORD the glory of His **n**;	Ps 96:8	8034
And give thanks to His holy **n**.	Ps 97:12	2143
praise Your great and awesome **n**;	Ps 99:3	8034
among those who called on His **n**;	Ps 99:6	8034
Give thanks to Him, bless His **n**.	Ps 100:4	8034
Those who deride me have used my **n**	Ps 102:8	8034
And Your **n** to all generations.	Ps 102:12	2143
nations will fear the **n** of the LORD And	Ps 102:15	8034
tell of the **n** of the LORD in Zion And	Ps 102:21	8034
is within me, *bless* His holy **n**.	Ps 103:1	8034
to the LORD, call upon His **n**;	Ps 105:1	8034
Glory in His holy **n**;	Ps 105:3	8034
saved them for the sake of His **n**,	Ps 106:8	8034
To give thanks to Your holy **n** And	Ps 106:47	8034
let their **n** be blotted out.	Ps 109:13	8034
Holy and awesome is His **n**.	Ps 111:9	8034
Praise the **n** of the LORD.	Ps 113:1	8034
Blessed be the **n** of the LORD From	Ps 113:2	8034
n of the LORD is to be praised.	Ps 113:3	8034
But to Your **n** give glory Because of	Ps 115:1	8034
I called upon the **n** of the LORD:	Ps 116:4	8034
And call upon the **n** of the LORD.	Ps 116:13	8034
And call upon the **n** of the LORD.	Ps 116:17	8034
In the **n** of the LORD I will surely	Ps 118:10	8034
In the **n** of the LORD I will surely	Ps 118:11	8034
In the **n** of the LORD I will surely	Ps 118:12	8034
who comes in the **n** of the LORD;	Ps 118:26	8034
I remember Your **n** in the night,	Ps 119:55	8034
manner with those who love Your **n**.	Ps 119:132	8034
give thanks to the **n** of the LORD.	Ps 122:4	8034
Our help is in the **n** of the LORD,	Ps 124:8	8034
bless you in the **n** of the LORD."	Ps 129:8	8034
Praise the **n** of the LORD;	Ps 135:1	8034
Sing praises to His **n**,	Ps 135:3	8034
Your **n**, O LORD, is everlasting, Your	Ps 135:13	8034
And give thanks to Your **n** for Your	Ps 138:2	8034
Your word according to all Your **n**.	Ps 138:2	8034
And Your enemies take *Your* **n** in	Ps 139:20	8034
righteous will give thanks to Your **n**;	Ps 140:13	8034
that I may give thanks to Your **n**;	Ps 142:7	8034
For the sake of Your **n**,	Ps 143:11	8034
will bless Your **n** forever and ever.	Ps 145:1	8034
praise Your **n** forever and ever.	Ps 145:2	8034
bless His holy **n** forever and ever.	Ps 145:21	8034
Let them praise the **n** of the LORD,	Ps 148:5	8034
Let them praise the **n** of the LORD,	Ps 148:13	8034
LORD, For His **n** alone is exalted;	Ps 148:13	8034
them praise His **n** with dancing;	Ps 149:3	8034
But the **n** of the wicked will rot.	Pr 10:7	8034
n of the LORD is a strong tower;	Pr 18:10	8034
A *good* **n** is to be more desired	Pr 22:1	8034
What is His **n** or His son's name?	Pr 30:4	8034
What is His name or His son's **n**?	Pr 30:4	8034
And profane the **n** of my God.	Pr 30:9	8034
and its **n** is covered in obscurity.	Ec 6:4	8034
A good **n** is better than a good	Ec 7:1	8034
Your **n** is *like* purified oil;	SS 1:3	8034
only let us be called by your **n**;	Is 4:1	8034
and she will call His **n** Immanuel.	Is 7:14	8034
"**N** him Maher-shalal-hash-baz;	Is 8:3	7121, 8034
And His **n** will be called Wonderful	Is 9:6	8034
thanks to the LORD, call on His **n**.	Is 12:4	8034
remember that His **n** is exalted."	Is 12:4	8034
off from Babylon **n** and survivors,	Is 14:22	8034
place of the **n** of the LORD of hosts,	Is 18:7	8034
in the east, The **n** of the LORD,	Is 24:15	8034
You, I will give thanks to Your **n**;	Is 25:1	8034
Your **n**, even Your memory, is the	Is 26:8	8034
You alone we confess Your **n**.	Is 26:13	8034
midst, They will sanctify My **n**;	Is 29:23	8034
the **n** of the LORD comes from a	Is 30:27	8034
by number, He calls them all by **n**;	Is 40:26	8034
of the sun he will call on My **n**;	Is 41:25	8034
"I am the LORD, that is My **n**;	Is 42:8	8034
I have called you by **n**;	Is 43:1	8034
Everyone who is called by My **n**,	Is 43:7	8034
one will call on the **n** of Jacob;	Is 44:5	8034
will **n** Israel's name with honor.	Is 44:5	3655
will name Israel's **n** with honor.	Is 44:5	8034
Israel, who calls you by your **n**.	Is 45:3	8034
I have also called you by your **n**;	Is 45:4	8034
the LORD of hosts is His **n**,	Is 47:4	8034
Who swear by the **n** of the LORD And	Is 48:1	8034
The LORD of hosts is His **n**.	Is 48:2	8034
the sake of My **n** I delay My wrath,	Is 48:9	8034
For how can *My* **n** be profaned?	Is 48:11	
Their **n** would never be cut off or	Is 48:19	8034
Let him trust in the **n** of the LORD	Is 50:10	8034
(the LORD of hosts is His **n**).	Is 51:15	8034
and My **n** is continually blasphemed	Is 52:5	8034
My people shall know My **n**;	Is 52:6	8034
Whose **n** is the LORD of hosts;	Is 54:5	8034
And a **n** better than that of sons	Is 56:5	8034
n which will not be cut off.	Is 56:5	8034
and to love the **n** of the LORD,	Is 56:6	8034
lives forever, whose **n** is Holy,	Is 57:15	8034
So they will fear the **n** of the LORD	Is 59:19	8034
For the **n** of the LORD your God,	Is 60:9	8034
you will be called by a new **n** Which	Is 62:2	8034
make for Himself an everlasting **n**,	Is 63:12	8034
To make for Yourself a glorious **n**.	Is 63:14	8034
Our Redeemer from of old is Your **n**.	Is 63:16	8034
who were not called by Your **n**.	Is 63:19	8034
Your **n** known to Your adversaries,	Is 64:2	8034
is no one who calls on Your **n**,	Is 64:7	8034

nation which did not call on My **n**.	Is 65:1	8034
n for a curse to My chosen ones,	Is 65:15	8034
servants will be called by another **n**.	Is 65:15	8034
offspring and your **n** will endure.	Is 66:22	8034
Jerusalem, for the **n** of the LORD;	Jer 3:17	8034
house, which is called by My **n**,	Jer 7:10	8034
house, which is called by My **n**,	Jer 7:11	8034
I made My **n** dwell at the first,	Jer 7:12	8034
the house which is called by My **n**,	Jer 7:14	8034
the house which is called by My **n**,	Jer 7:30	8034
and great is Your **n** in might.	Jer 10:6	8034
The LORD of hosts is His **n**.	Jer 10:16	8034
families that do not call Your **n**;	Jer 10:25	8034
The LORD called your **n**,	Jer 11:16	8034
his **n** be remembered no more."	Jer 11:19	8034
not prophesy in the **n** of the LORD,	Jer 11:21	8034
of My people, to swear by My **n**,	Jer 12:16	8034
LORD, And we are called by Your **n**;	Jer 14:9	8034
are prophesying falsehood in My **n**.	Jer 14:14	8034
who are prophesying in My **n**,	Jer 14:15	8034
For I have been called by Your **n**,	Jer 15:16	8034
know that My **n** is the LORD."	Jer 16:21	8034
not the **n** the LORD has called you,	Jer 20:3	8034
Him Or speak anymore in His **n**,"	Jer 20:9	8034
His **n** by which He will be called,	Jer 23:6	8034
said who prophesy falsely in My **n**,	Jer 23:25	8034
to make My people forget My **n**	Jer 23:27	8034
forgot My **n** because of Baal?	Jer 23:27	8034
this city which is called by My **n**,	Jer 25:29	8034
in the **n** of the LORD saying,	Jer 26:9	8034
us in the **n** of the LORD our God."	Jer 26:16	8034
prophesied in the **n** of the LORD,	Jer 26:20	8034
"but they prophesy falsely in My **n**,	Jer 27:15	8034
prophesy falsely to you in My **n**;	Jer 29:9	8034
to you falsely in My **n**,	Jer 29:21	8034
have spoken words in My **n** falsely,	Jer 29:23	8034
you have sent letters in your own **n**	Jer 29:25	8034
The LORD of hosts is His **n**:	Jer 31:35	8034
The LORD of hosts is His **n**;	Jer 32:18	8034
You have made a **n** for Yourself,	Jer 32:20	8034
the house which is called by My **n**,	Jer 32:34	8034
establish it, the LORD is His **n**,	Jer 33:2	8034
'It will be to Me a **n** of joy,	Jer 33:9	8034
and this is *the* **n** by which she	Jer 33:16	
the house which is called by My **n**.	Jer 34:15	8034
"Yet you turned and profaned My **n**,	Jer 34:16	8034
of the guard whose **n** was Irijah,	Jer 37:13	8034
spoken to us in the **n** of the LORD,	Jer 44:16	8034
I have sworn by My great **n**,'	Jer 44:26	8034
'never shall My **n** be invoked again	Jer 44:26	8034
King Whose **n** is the LORD of hosts,	Jer 46:18	8034
whose **n** is the LORD of hosts.	Jer 48:15	8034
Even all of you who know his **n**;	Jer 48:17	8034
the LORD of hosts is His **n**;	Jer 50:34	8034
The LORD of hosts is His **n**.	Jer 51:19	8034
whose **n** is the LORD of hosts.	Jer 51:57	8034
and his mother's **n** was Hamutal the	Jer 52:1	8034
I called on Your **n**, O LORD, Out of	La 3:55	8034
"As *the* **n** *of* your sister Sodom	Ezk 16:56	
"But I acted for the sake of My **n**,	Ezk 20:9	8034
"But I acted for the sake of My **n**,	Ezk 20:14	8034
and acted for the sake of My **n**,	Ezk 20:22	8034
n is called Bamah to this day."	Ezk 20:29	8034
and My holy **n** you will profane no	Ezk 20:39	8034
of man, write the **n** of the day,	Ezk 24:2	8034
went, they profaned My holy **n**,	Ezk 36:20	8034
"But I had concern for My holy **n**,	Ezk 36:21	8034
about to act, but for My holy **n**,	Ezk 36:22	8034
vindicate the holiness of My great **n**	Ezk 36:23	8034
"My holy **n** I will make known	Ezk 39:7	8034
will not let My holy **n** be profaned	Ezk 39:7	8034
the **n** of *the* city will be Hamonah.	Ezk 39:16	8034
I will be jealous for My holy **n**.	Ezk 39:25	8034
will not again defile My holy **n**,	Ezk 43:7	8034
And they have defiled My holy **n** by	Ezk 43:8	8034
and the **n** of the city from *that*	Ezk 48:35	8034
and to Daniel he assigned *the* **n**	Da 1:7	
"Let the **n** of God be blessed	Da 2:20	8036
Daniel, whose **n** was Belteshazzar,	Da 2:26	8036
whose **n** is Belteshazzar according	Da 4:8	8036
according to the **n** of my god,	Da 4:8	8036
Daniel, whose **n** is Belteshazzar,	Da 4:19	8036
who spoke in Your **n** to our kings,	Da 9:6	8034
and have made a **n** for Yourself,	Da 9:15	8034
the city which is called by Your **n**;	Da 9:18	8034
are called by Your **n**."	Da 9:19	8034
LORD said to him, "**N** him Jezreel;	Hos 1:4	7121, 8034
"**N** her Lo-ruhamah, for I will no	Hos 1:6	7121, 8034
"**N** him Lo-ammi, for you are not	Hos 1:9	7121, 8034
The LORD is His **n**.	Hos 12:5	2143
praise the **n** of the LORD your God,	Jl 2:26	8034
n of the LORD Will be delivered;	Jl 2:32	8034
In order to profane My holy **n**.	Am 2:7	8034
The LORD God of hosts is His **n**.	Am 4:13	8034
of the earth, The LORD is His **n**.	Am 5:8	8034
LORD, whose **n** is the God of hosts.	Am 5:27	8034
For the **n** of the LORD is not to be	Am 6:10	8034
of the earth, The LORD is His **n**.	Am 9:6	8034
nations who are called by My **n**,"	Am 9:12	8034
walk Each in the **n** of his god,	Mi 4:5	8034
we will walk In the **n** of the LORD	Mi 4:5	8034
In the majesty of the **n** of the LORD	Mi 5:4	8034
it is sound wisdom to fear Your **n**:	Mi 6:9	8034
n will no longer be perpetuated.	Na 1:14	8034
may call on the **n** of the LORD,	Zph 3:9	8034
take refuge in the **n** of the LORD.	Zph 3:12	8034

one who swears falsely by My **n**;	Zch 5:4	8034
"Behold, a man whose **n** is Branch,	Zch 6:12	8034
And in His **n** they will walk,"	Zch 10:12	8034
spoken falsely in the **n** of the LORD';	Zch 13:3	8034
They will call on My **n**,	Zch 13:9	8034
only one, and His **n** *the only* one.	Zch 14:9	8034
you, O priests who despise My **n**.	Mal 1:6	8034
'How have we despised Your **n**?'	Mal 1:6	8034
My **n** *will be* great among the	Mal 1:11	8034
is going to be offered to My **n**,	Mal 1:11	8034
for My **n** *will be* great among the	Mal 1:11	8034
My **n** is feared among the nations."	Mal 1:14	8034
to heart to give honor to My **n**,"	Mal 2:2	8034
Me and stood in awe of My **n**.	Mal 2:5	8034
the LORD and who esteem His **n**.	Mal 3:16	8034
"But for you who fear My **n**,	Mal 4:2	8034
and you shall call His **n** Jesus,	Mt 1:21	3686
THEY SHALL CALL HIS N IMMANUEL,"	Mt 1:23	3686
and he called His **n** Jesus.	Mt 1:25	3686
is in heaven, Hallowed be Your **n**.	Mt 6:9	3686
did we not prophesy in Your **n**,	Mt 7:22	3686
and in Your **n** cast out demons,	Mt 7:22	3686
in Your **n** perform many miracles?'	Mt 7:22	3686
hated by all because of My **n**,	Mt 10:22	3686
a prophet in *the* **n** of a prophet	Mt 10:41	3686
man in the **n** of a righteous man	Mt 10:41	3686
whoever in the **n** of a disciple gives	Mt 10:42	3686
IN HIS N THE GENTILES WILL HOPE."	Mt 12:21	3686
receives one such child in My **n**	Mt 18:5	3686
have gathered together in My **n**,	Mt 18:20	3686
WHO COMES IN THE N OF THE LORD;	Mt 21:9	3686
COMES IN THE N OF THE LORD!'"	Mt 23:39	3686
"For many will come in My **n**,	Mt 24:5	3686
by all nations because of My **n**.	Mt 24:9	3686
baptizing them in the **n** of the	Mt 28:19	3686
(to whom He gave the **n** Peter),	Mk 3:16	3686
(to them He gave the **n** Boanerges,	Mk 3:17	3686
"What is your **n**?"	Mk 5:9	3686
"My **n** is Legion; for we are many."	Mk 5:9	3686
for His **n** had become well known;	Mk 6:14	3686
like this in My **n** receives Me;	Mk 9:37	3686
casting out demons in Your **n**,	Mk 9:38	3686
will perform a miracle in My **n**,	Mk 9:39	3686
of your **n** as *followers* of Christ,	Mk 9:41	3686
WHO COMES IN THE N OF THE LORD;	Mk 11:9	3686
"Many will come in My **n**,	Mk 13:6	3686
hated by all because of My **n**,	Mk 13:13	3686
in My **n** they will cast out demons,	Mk 16:17	3686
of Aaron, and her **n** was Elizabeth.	Lk 1:5	3686
and you will give him the **n** John.	Lk 1:13	3686
to a man whose **n** was Joseph,	Lk 1:27	3686
and the virgin's **n** was Mary.	Lk 1:27	3686
a son, and you shall **n** Him Jesus.	Lk 1:31	3686
And holy is His **n**.	Lk 1:49	3686
who is called by that **n**."	Lk 1:61	3686
wrote as follows, "His **n** is John."	Lk 1:63	3686
His **n** was *then* called Jesus,	Lk 2:21	3686
Jesus, the **n** given by the angel	Lk 2:21	2564
in Jerusalem whose **n** was Simeon;	Lk 2:25	3686
and scorn your **n** as evil,	Lk 6:22	3686
"What is your **n**?"	Lk 8:30	3686
Whoever receives this child in My **n**	Lk 9:48	3686
casting out demons in Your **n**;	Lk 9:49	3686
are subject to us in Your **n**."	Lk 10:17	3686
'Father, hallowed be Your **n**.	Lk 11:2	3686
COMES IN THE N OF THE LORD!'"	Lk 13:35	3686
a man called by the **n** of Zaccheus;	Lk 19:2	3686
WHO COMES IN THE N OF THE LORD;	Lk 19:38	3686
for many will come in My **n**,	Lk 21:8	3686
hated by all because of My **n**.	Lk 21:17	3686
would be proclaimed in His **n** to all	Lk 24:47	3686
sent from God, whose **n** was John.	Jn 1:6	3686
to those who believe in His **n**,	Jn 1:12	3686
the feast, many believed in His **n**,	Jn 2:23	3686
n of the only begotten Son of God.	Jn 3:18	3686
"I have come in My Father's **n**,	Jn 5:43	3686
another comes in his own **n**,	Jn 5:43	3686
and he calls his own sheep by **n** and	Jn 10:3	3686
works that I do in My Father's **n**,	Jn 10:25	3686
WHO COMES IN THE N OF THE LORD,	Jn 12:13	3686
"Father, glorify Your **n**."	Jn 12:28	3686
"Whatever you ask in My **n**,	Jn 14:13	3686
"If you ask Me anything in My **n**,	Jn 14:14	3686
whom the Father will send in My **n**,	Jn 14:26	3686
you ask of the Father in My **n** He	Jn 15:16	3686
in My **n**, He will give it to you.	Jn 16:23	3686
have asked for nothing in My **n**;	Jn 16:24	3686
"In that day you will ask in My **n**,	Jn 16:26	3686
"I have manifested Your **n** to the men	Jn 17:6	3686
Holy Father, keep them in Your **n**,	Jn 17:11	3686
the **n** which You have given Me,	Jn 17:11	
in Your **n** which You have given Me;	Jn 17:12	3686
I have made Your **n** known to them,	Jn 17:26	3686
and the slave's **n** was Malchus.	Jn 18:10	3686
you may have life in His **n**.	Jn 20:31	3686
WHO CALLS ON THE N OF THE LORD	Ac 2:21	3686
be baptized in the **n** of Jesus Christ	Ac 2:38	3686
In the **n** of Jesus Christ the	Ac 3:6	3686
on the basis of faith in His **n**,	Ac 3:16	3686
it is the **n** of Jesus which has	Ac 3:16	3686
"By what power, or in what **n**,	Ac 4:7	3686
n of Jesus Christ the Nazarene,	Ac 4:10	3686
raised from the dead—by this **n**	Ac 4:10	
for there is no other **n** under	Ac 4:12	3686
speak no longer to any man in this **n**."	Ac 4:17	3686
or teach at all in the **n** of Jesus.	Ac 4:18	3686
the **n** of Your holy servant Jesus."	Ac 4:30	3686
to continue teaching in this **n**,	Ac 5:28	3686
not to speak in the **n** of Jesus,	Ac 5:40	3686

worthy to suffer shame for *His* **n**. **Ac 5:41** 3686
of God and the **n** of Jesus Christ, **Ac 8:12** 3686
in the **n** of the Lord Jesus. **Ac 8:16** 3686
to bind all who call on Your **n**." **Ac 9:14** 3686
to bear My **n** before the Gentiles **Ac 9:15** 3686
those who called on this **n**, **Ac 9:21** 3686
spoken out boldly in the **n** of Jesus. **Ac 9:27** 3686
out boldly in the **n** of the Lord. **Ac 9:28** 3686
through His **n** everyone who believes **Ac 10:43** 3686
baptized in the **n** of Jesus Christ. **Ac 10:48** 3686
prophet whose **n** was Bar-Jesus, **Ac 13:6** 3686
(for so his **n** is translated) **Ac 13:8** 3686
the Gentiles a people for His **n**. **Ac 15:14** 3686
GENTILES WHO ARE CALLED BY MY N,' **Ac 15:17** 3686
the **n** of our Lord Jesus Christ. **Ac 15:26** 3686
"I command you in the **n** of Jesus **Ac 16:18** 3686
baptized in the **n** of the Lord Jesus. **Ac 19:5** 3686
attempted to **n** over those who had **Ac 19:13** 3687
spirits the **n** of the Lord Jesus, **Ac 19:13** 3686
the **n** of the Lord Jesus was being **Ac 19:17** 3686
for the **n** of the Lord Jesus." **Ac 21:13** 3686
away your sins, calling on His **n**.' **Ac 22:16** 3686
to the **n** of Jesus of Nazareth. **Ac 26:9** 3686
But if you bear the **n** "Jew" **Ro 2:17** 2028
THE N OF GOD IS BLASPHEMED AMONG **Ro 2:24** 3686
THAT MY N MIGHT BE PROCLAIMED **Ro 9:17** 3686
THE N OF THE LORD WILL BE SAVED." **Ro 10:13** 3686
AND I WILL SING TO YOUR N." **Ro 15:9** 3686
the **n** of our Lord Jesus Christ, **1Co 1:2** 3686
by the **n** of our Lord Jesus Christ, **1Co 1:10** 3686
you baptized in the **n** of Paul? **1Co 1:13** 3686
say you were baptized in my **n**. **1Co 1:15** 3686
In the **n** of our Lord Jesus, when **1Co 5:4** 3686
in the **n** of the Lord Jesus Christ and **1Co 6:11** 3686
and every **n** that is named, **Eph 1:21** 3686
heaven and on earth derives its **n**, **Eph 3:15** 3687
in the **n** of our Lord Jesus Christ **Eph 5:20** 3686
the **n** which is above every name, **Php 2:9** 3686
the name which is above every **n**, **Php 2:9** 3686
that at the **n** of Jesus EVERY KNEE **Php 2:10** 3686
do all in the **n** of the Lord Jesus, **Col 3:17** 3686
so that the **n** of our Lord **2Th 1:12** 3686
in the **n** of our Lord Jesus Christ, **2Th 3:6** 3686
n of God and *our* doctrine will not **1Tm 6:1** 3686
who names the **n** of the Lord **2Tm 2:19** 3686
a more excellent **n** than they. **Heb 1:4** 3686
PROCLAIM YOUR N TO MY BRETHREN, **Heb 2:12** 3686
which you have shown toward His **n**, **Heb 6:10** 3686
by the translation *of his* **n**, **Heb 7:2**
of lips that give thanks to His **n**. **Heb 13:15** 3686
n by which you have been called? **Jas 2:7** 3686
who spoke in the **n** of the Lord. **Jas 5:10** 3686
him with oil in the **n** of the Lord; **Jas 5:14** 3686
are reviled for the **n** of Christ, **1Pe 4:14** 3686
but is to glorify God in this **n**. **1Pe 4:16** 3686
in the **n** of His Son Jesus Christ, **1Jn 3:23** 3686
in the **n** of the Son of God, **1Jn 5:13** 3686
went out for the sake of the **N**, **3Jn 1:7** 3686
Greet the friends by **n**. **3Jn 1:15** 3686
and you hold fast My **n**, **Rv 2:13** 3686
and a new **n** written on the stone **Rv 2:17** 3686
you have a **n** that you are alive, **Rv 3:1** 3686
erase his **n** from the book of life, **Rv 3:5** 3686
confess his **n** before My Father and **Rv 3:5** 3686
My word, and have not denied My **n**. **Rv 3:8** 3686
write on him the **n** of My God, **Rv 3:12** 3686
and the **n** of the city of My God, **Rv 3:12** 3686
heaven from My God, and My new **n**. **Rv 3:12** 3686
he who sat on it had the **n** Death; **Rv 6:8** 3686
The **n** of the star is called **Rv 8:11** 3686
his **n** in Hebrew is Abaddon, and in **Rv 9:11** 3686
the Greek he has the **n** Apollyon. **Rv 9:11** 3686
and those who fear Your **n**, **Rv 11:18** 3686
blaspheme His **n** and His tabernacle, **Rv 13:6** 3686
whose **n** has not been written from **Rv 13:8** 3686
either the **n** of the beast or the **Rv 13:17** 3686
the beast or the number of his **n**. **Rv 13:17** 3686
having His **n** and the name of His **Rv 14:1** 3686
having His name and the **n** of His **Rv 14:1** 3686
receives the mark of his **n**." **Rv 14:11** 3686
and the number of his **n**, **Rv 15:2** 3686
fear, O Lord, and glorify Your **n**? **Rv 15:4** 3686
and they blasphemed the **n** of God **Rv 16:9** 3686
on her forehead a **n** *was* written, **Rv 17:5** 3686
whose **n** has not been written in **Rv 17:8** 3686
and He has a **n** written *on Him* **Rv 19:12** 3686
His **n** is called The Word of God. **Rv 19:13** 3686
on His thigh He has a **n** written, **Rv 19:16** 3686
if anyone's **n** was not found written **Rv 20:15**
His **n** *will be* on their foreheads. **Rv 22:4** 3686

NAMED

birth to a son, and **n** him Seth, **Gn 4:25** 7121, 8034
and He blessed them and **n** them Man **Gn 5:2** 7121, 8034
to his image, and **n** him Seth. **Gn 5:3** 7121, 8034
Isaac your descendants shall be **n**. **Gn 21:12** 7121
for Ephron the silver which he had **n** **Gn 23:16** 1696
and they **n** him Esau. **Gn 25:25** 7121, 8034
So he **n** the well Esek, because **Gn 26:20** 7121, 8034
over it too, so he **n** it Sitnah. **Gn 26:21** 7121, 8034
so he **n** it Rehoboth, for he said, **Gn 26:22** 7121, 8034
"Is he not rightly **n** Jacob, **Gn 27:36** 7121, 8034
and bore a son and **n** him Reuben, **Gn 29:32** 7121, 8034
So she **n** him Simeon. **Gn 29:33** 7121, 8034
Therefore he was **n** Levi. **Gn 29:34** 7121, 8034
Therefore she **n** him Judah. **Gn 29:35** 7121, 8034
Therefore she **n** him Dan. **Gn 30:6** 7121
And she **n** him Naphtali. **Gn 30:8** 7121
So she **n** him Gad. **Gn 30:11** 7121
So she **n** him Asher. **Gn 30:13** 7121
So she **n** him Issachar. **Gn 30:18** 7121
So she **n** him Zebulun. **Gn 30:20** 7121
bore a daughter and **n** her Dinah. **Gn 30:21** 7121, 8034
She **n** him Joseph, saying, **Gn 30:24** 7121, 8034
Therefore it was **n** Galeed, **Gn 31:48** 7121, 8034
So he **n** that place Mahanaim. **Gn 32:2** 7121, 8034
So Jacob **n** the place Peniel, for **Gn 32:30** 7121, 8034
therefore the place is **n** Succoth. **Gn 33:17** 7121, 8034
it was **n** Allon-bacuth. **Gn 35:8** 7121, 8034
So Jacob **n** the place where God had **Gn 35:15** 7121, 8034
that she **n** him Ben-oni; **Gn 35:18** 7121, 8034
and bore a son and he **n** him Er. **Gn 38:3** 7121, 8034
and bore a son and **n** him Onan. **Gn 38:4** 7121, 8034
another son and **n** him Shelah; **Gn 38:5** 7121, 8034
So he was **n** Perez. **Gn 38:29** 7121, 8034
and he was **n** Zerah. **Gn 38:30** 7121, 8034
Pharaoh **n** Joseph Zaphenath-paneah; **Gn 41:45** 7121, 8034
Joseph **n** the firstborn Manasseh, **Gn 41:51** 7121, 8034
He **n** the second Ephraim, **Gn 41:52** 7121, 8034
Therefore it was **n** Abel-mizraim, **Gn 50:11** 7121, 8034
one of whom was **n** Shiphrah and **Ex 1:15** 8034
and the other was **n** Puah; **Ex 1:15** 8034
And she **n** him Moses, and said, **Ex 2:10** 7121, 8034
to a son, and he **n** him Gershom, **Ex 2:22** 7121, 8034
therefore it was **n** Marah. **Ex 15:23** 7121, 8034
The house of Israel **n** it manna, **Ex 16:31** 7121, 8034
He **n** the place Massah and **Ex 17:7** 7121, 8034
and **n** it The LORD is My Banner; **Ex 17:15** 7121, 8034
sons, of whom one was **n** Gershom, **Ex 18:3** 8034
The other was **n** Eliezer, **Ex 18:4** 8034
and built a city and **n** it Luz **Jg 1:26** 7121, 8034
So they **n** that place Bochim; **Jg 2:5** 7121, 8034
LORD and **n** it The LORD is Peace. **Jg 6:24** 7121
on that day he **n** him Jerubbaal, **Jg 6:32** 7121
him a son, and he **n** him Abimelech. **Jg 8:31** 8034, 7760
birth to a son and **n** him Samson; **Jg 13:24** 7121, 8034
and he **n** that place Ramath-lehi. **Jg 15:17** 7121
Therefore he **n** it En-hakkore, **Jg 15:19** 7121, 8034
So they **n** him Obed. **Ru 4:17** 7121, 8034
and she **n** him Samuel, *saying,* **1Sa 1:20** 7121, 8034
and Shen, and **n** it Ebenezer, **1Sa 7:12** 7121, 8034
of the Philistines **n** Goliath, **1Sa 17:4** 8034
Philistine from Gath **n** Goliath, **1Sa 17:23** 8034
the son of Ahitub, **n** Abiathar, **1Sa 22:20** 8034
he **n** that place Baal-perazim. **2Sa 5:20** 7121, 8034
to a son, and he **n** him Solomon. **2Sa 12:24** 7121, 8034
and he **n** him Jedidiah for the **2Sa 12:25** 7121, 8034
myself and it will be **n** after me." **2Sa 12:28** 7121, 8034
n the pillar after his own name, **2Sa 18:18** 7121
the right pillar and **n** it Jachin, **1Ki 7:21** 7121, 8034
up the left pillar and **n** it Boaz. **1Ki 7:21** 7121, 8034
and **n** the city which he built **1Ki 16:24** 7121, 8034
and **n** it Joktheel to this day. **2Ki 14:7** 7121, 8034
sons of Jacob, whom He **n** Israel; **2Ki 17:34** 7760, 8034
and his mother **n** him Jabez saying, **1Ch 4:9** 7121, 8034
bore a son, and she **n** him Peresh; **1Ch 7:16** 7121, 8034
bore a son, and he **n** him Beriah, **1Ch 7:23** 7121, 8034
they **n** that place Baal-perazim. **1Ch 14:11** 7121, 8034
were **n** among the tribe of Levi. **1Ch 23:14** 7121
and **n** the one on the right Jachin **2Ch 3:17** 7121, 8034
Therefore they have **n** that place **2Ch 20:26** 7121, 8034
Gileadite, and was **n** after them. **Ne 7:63** 7121, 8034
He **n** the first Jemimah, and **Jb 42:14** 7121, 8034
exists has already been **n**, **Ec 6:10** 7121, 8034
O house of Jacob, who are **n** Israel **Is 48:1** 7121, 8034
the body of My mother He **n** Me. **Is 49:1** 2142, 8034
city, **n** for the tribes of Israel, **Ezk 48:31** 5921, 8034
whom the king **n** Belteshazzar. **Da 5:12** 8036
to Daniel, who was **n** Belteshazzar; **Da 10:1** 7121, 8034
of the high priest, **n** Caiaphas; **Mt 26:3** 3004
of the twelve, **n** Judas Iscariot, **Mt 26:14** 3004
found a man of Cyrene **n** Simon, **Mt 27:32** 3686
rich man from Arimathea, **n** Joseph, **Mt 27:57** 5122
officials **n** Jairus came up, **Mk 5:22** 3686
a blind beggar **n** Bartimaeus, **Mk 10:46**
They came to a place **n** Gethsemane; **Mk 14:32** 3686
The man **n** Barabbas had been **Mk 15:7** 3004
was a priest **n** Zacharias, **Lk 1:5** 3686
noticed a tax collector **n** Levi sitting **Lk 5:27** 3686
them, whom He also **n** as apostles: **Lk 6:13** 3687
Simon, whom He also **n** Peter, **Lk 6:14** 3687
And there came a man **n** Jairus, **Lk 8:41** 3686
and a woman **n** Martha welcomed Him **Lk 10:38** 3686
a poor man **n** Lazarus was **Lk 16:20** 3686
And a man **n** Joseph, **Lk 23:50** 3686
very day to a village **n** Emmaus, **Lk 24:13** 3686
One *of them,* **n** Cleopas, **Lk 24:18** 3686
man of the Pharisees, **n** Nicodemus, **Jn 3:1** 3686
But a man **n** Ananias, **Ac 5:1** 3686
But a Pharisee **n** Gamaliel, **Ac 5:34** 3686
at the feet of a young man **n** Saul. **Ac 7:58** 2564
there was a man **n** Simon, **Ac 8:9** 3686
disciple at Damascus **n** Ananias; **Ac 9:10** 3686
for a man from Tarsus **n** Saul, **Ac 9:11** 3686
has seen in a vision a man **n** Ananias **Ac 9:12** 3686
he found a man **n** Aeneas, **Ac 9:33** 3686
was a disciple **n** Tabitha **Ac 9:36** 3686
many days in Joppa with a tanner **n** **Ac 9:43**
man at Caesarea **n** Cornelius, **Ac 10:1** 3686
men to Joppa and send for a man **n** **Ac 10:5**
he is staying with a tanner **n** **Ac 10:6**
One of them **n** Agabus stood up **Ac 11:28** 3686
a servant-girl **n** Rhoda came **Ac 12:13** 3686
disciple was there, **n** Timothy, **Ac 16:1** 3686
A woman **n** Lydia, **Ac 16:14** 3686
n Damaris and others with them. **Ac 17:34** 3686
he found a Jew **n** Aquila, **Ac 18:2** 3686
of a man **n** Titius Justus, **Ac 18:7** 3686
Now a Jew **n** Apollos, **Ac 18:24** 3686
For a man **n** Demetrius, **Ac 19:24** 3686
was a young man **n** Eutychus **Ac 20:9** 3686
a prophet **n** Agabus came **Ac 21:10** 3686
with an attorney **n** Tertullus, **Ac 24:1**
of the Augustan cohort **n** Julius. **Ac 27:1** 3686
man of the island, **n** Publius, **Ac 28:7** 3686
YOUR DESCENDANTS WILL BE N." **Ro 9:7** 2564
not where Christ was *already* **n**, **Ro 15:20** 3687
and every name that is **n**, **Eph 1:21** 3687
or greed must not even be **n** among you, **Eph 5:3** 3687

NAMELY

of years, **n**, forty-nine years. **Lv 25:8**
Of the sons of Joseph, **n**, **Nu 1:32**
n, Kiriath-arba, *Arba being* **Jos 15:13**
n, Terah, the father of Abraham **Jos 24:2**
n, you shall not see my face unless **2Sa 3:13** 559
n, 'all the king's sons are dead,' **2Sa 13:33** 559
n, Ishmael the son of Nethaniah, **2Ki 25:23**
away into exile, **n** the Reubenites, **1Ch 5:26**
n, Naaman, Ahijah and Gera **1Ch 8:7**
n, the Jehielites, *were* **1Ch 26:21**
n, 3,000 talents of gold, of **1Ch 29:4**
n, from their descendants who were **2Ch 8:8**
n, for the morning and evening **2Ch 31:3**
the son of Israel, **n**, Sherebiah, **Ezr 8:18**
n, words of peace and truth, **Es 9:30**
the prescribed portion of oil (**n**, **Ezk 45:14**
n for the priests, toward **Ezk 48:10**
n Shadrach, Meshach **Da 3:12**
n, that horn which had eyes and a **Da 7:20**
of Jerusalem, **n**, seventy years. **Da 9:2**
n, that God was in Christ **2Co 5:19** 5613
n, that Achaia has been prepared **2Co 9:2**
n, if any man is above reproach, **Ti 1:6**
n, Jesus, because of **Heb 2:9**

NAME'S

from a far country for Your **n** sake **1Ki 8:41** 8034
for Your great **n** sake and Your mighty **2Ch 6:32** 8034
of righteousness For His **n** sake. **Ps 23:3** 8034
For Your **n** sake, O LORD, Pardon my **Ps 25:11** 8034
For Your **n** sake You will lead me **Ps 31:3** 8034
forgive our sins for Your **n** sake. **Ps 79:9** 8034

kindly with me for Your **n** sake; Ps 109:21 8034
who exclude you for My **n** sake, Is 66:5 8034
us, O LORD, act for Your **n** sake! Jer 14:7 8034
despise *us,* for Your own **n** sake; Jer 14:21 8034
have dealt with you for My **n** sake, Ezk 20:44 8034
children or farms for My **n** sake, Mt 19:29 *3686*
kings and governors for My **n** sake. Lk 21:12 *3686*
they will do to you for My **n** sake, Jn 15:21 *3686*
he must suffer for My **n** sake." Ac 9:16 *3686*
all the Gentiles for His **n** sake, Ro 1:5 *3686*
been forgiven you for His **n** sake. 1Jn 2:12 *3686*
and have endured for My **n** sake, Rv 2:3 *3686*

NAMES
The man gave **n** to all the cattle, Gn 2:20 8034
are the **n** of the sons of Ishmael, Gn 25:13 8034
the sons of Ishmael, by their **n**, Gn 25:13 8034
of Ishmael and these are their **n**, Gn 25:16 8034
and he gave them the same **n** which Gn 26:18 8034
These are the **n** of Esau's sons: Gn 36:10 8034
Now these are the **n** of the chiefs Gn 36:40 8034
and their localities, by their **n**: Gn 36:40 8034
are the **n** of the sons of Israel, Gn 46:8 8034
be called by the **n** of their brothers Gn 48:6 8034
And the **n** of my fathers Abraham Gn 48:16 8034
these are the **n** of the sons of Israel Ex 1:1 8034
These are the **n** of the sons of Levi Ex 6:16 8034
them the **n** of the sons of Israel, Ex 28:9 8034
six of their **n** on the one stone and Ex 28:10 8034
and the **n** of the remaining six on Ex 28:10 8034
to the **n** of the sons of Israel; Ex 28:11 8034
and Aaron shall bear their **n** Ex 28:12 8034
to the **n** of the sons of Israel: Ex 28:21 8034
twelve, according to their **n**; Ex 28:21 8034
"Aaron shall carry the **n** of Ex 28:29 8034
to the **n** of the sons of Israel. Ex 39:6 8034
to the **n** of the sons of Israel; Ex 39:14 8034
twelve, corresponding to their **n**, Ex 39:14 8034
according to the number of **n**, Nu 1:2 8034
"These then are the **n** of the men Nu 1:5 8034
according to the number of **n**, Nu 1:18 8034
according to the number of **n**, Nu 1:20 8034
men, according to the number of **n**, Nu 1:22 8034
according to the number of **n**, Nu 1:24 8034
according to the number of **n**, Nu 1:26 8034
according to the number of **n**, Nu 1:28 8034
according to the number of **n**, Nu 1:30 8034
according to the number of **n**, Nu 1:32 8034
according to the number of **n**, Nu 1:34 8034
according to the number of **n**, Nu 1:36 8034
according to the number of **n**, Nu 1:38 8034
according to the number of **n**, Nu 1:40 8034
according to the number of **n**, Nu 1:42 8034
are the **n** of the sons of Aaron: Nu 3:2 8034
are the **n** of the sons of Aaron, Nu 3:3 8034
are the sons of Levi by their **n**: Nu 3:17 8034
are the **n** of the sons of Gershon Nu 3:18 8034
and make a list of their **n**. Nu 3:40 8034
firstborn males by the number of **n** Nu 3:43 8034
These then *were* their **n**: Nu 13:4 8034
These are the **n** of the men whom Nu 13:16 8034
n of the daughters of Zelophehad Nu 26:33 8034
according to the number of **n**. Nu 26:53 8034
to the **n** of the tribes of their fathers. Nu 26:55 8034
these are the **n** of his daughters: Nu 27:1 8034
their **n** being changed Nu 32:38 8034
and they gave *other* **n** to the Nu 32:38 8034
"These are the **n** of the men who Nu 34:17 8034
"These are the **n** of the men: Nu 34:19 8034
these are the **n** of his daughters: Jos 17:3 8034
and the **n** of his two sons *were* Ru 1:2 8034
and the **n** of his two daughters 1Sa 14:49 8034
And the **n** of his three sons who 1Sa 17:13 8034
the **n** of those who were born to him 2Sa 5:14 8034
like the **n** of the great men who 2Sa 7:9 8034
These are the **n** of the mighty men 2Sa 23:8 8034
These are their **n**: 1Ki 4:8 8034
are the **n** of the sons of Gershom: 1Ch 6:17 8034
six sons, and these *were* their **n**: 1Ch 8:38 8034
had six sons whose **n** are these: 1Ch 9:44 8034
These are the **n** of the children born 1Ch 14:4 8034
the number of **n** by their census, 1Ch 23:24 8034
what the **n** of the men were who Ezr 5:4 8036
"We also asked them their **n** so as to Ezr 5:10 8036
n of the men who were at their head. Ezr 5:10 8036
last ones, these being their **n**, Ezr 8:13 8034
on the sealed document *are the* **n** *of* Ne 9:38
on the sealed document *were the* **n** Ne 10:1
will I take their **n** upon my lips. Ps 16:4 8034
called their lands after their own **n**. Ps 49:11 8034
He gives **n** to all of them. Ps 147:4 8034
"Haughty," "Scoffer," are his **n**, Pr 21:24 8034
"Their **n** were Oholah the Ezk 23:4 8034
And *as for* their **n**, Ezk 23:4 8034
"Now these are the **n** of the tribes: Ezk 48:1 8034
officials assigned *new* **n** to them; Da 1:7 8034
the **n** of the Baals from her mouth, Hos 2:17 8034
be mentioned by their **n** no more. Hos 2:17 8034
And the **n** of the idolatrous priests Zph 1:4 8034
the **n** of the idols from the land, Zch 13:2 8034
Now the **n** of the twelve apostles Mt 10:2 *3686*
your **n** are recorded in heaven." Lk 10:20 *3686*
words and **n** and your own law, Ac 18:15 *3686*
whose **n** are in the book of life. Php 4:3 *3686*
"Everyone who **n** the name of 2Tm 2:19 *3687*
on his heads *were* blasphemous **n**. Rv 13:1 *3686*
beast, full of blasphemous **n**, Rv 17:3 *3686*
and **n** *were* written on them, which Rv 21:12 *3686*
which are *the* **n** of the twelve Rv 21:12
the twelve **n** of the twelve apostles Rv 21:14 *3686*
but only those whose **n** are written Rv 21:27

NAOMI
and the name of his wife, N; Ru 1:2 5281
And N said to her two Ru 1:8 5281
But N said, "Return, my daughters. Ru 1:11 5281
and the women said, "Is this N?" Ru 1:19 5281
"Do not call me N; call me Mara, Ru 1:20 5281
Why do you call me N, Ru 1:21 5281
So N returned, and with her Ruth Ru 1:22 5281
N had a kinsman of her husband, Ru 2:1 5281
And Ruth the Moabitess said to N, Ru 2:2 5281
with N from the land of Moab. Ru 2:6 5281
She also took *it* out and gave N Ru 2:18
N said to her daughter-in-law, Ru 2:20 5281
Again N said to her, Ru 2:20 5281
N said to Ruth her Ru 2:22 5281
N her mother-in-law said to her, Ru 3:1 5281
"N, who has come back from the Ru 4:3 5281
buy the field from the hand of N, Ru 4:5 5281
I have bought from the hand of N Ru 4:9 5281
Then the women said to N, Ru 4:14 5281
Then N took the child and laid him Ru 4:16 5281
"A son has been born to N!" Ru 4:17 5281

NAOMI'S
Then Elimelech, N husband, died; Ru 1:3 5281

NAPHETH
and its towns, the third is N. Jos 17:11 5316

NAPHISH
and Tema, Jetur, N and Kedemah. Gn 25:15 5305
Jetur, N and Kedemah; 1Ch 1:31 5305
against the Hagrites, Jetur, N and 1Ch 5:19 5305

NAPHTALI
And she named him N. Gn 30:8 5321
Bilhah, Rachel's maid: Dan and N; Gn 35:25 5321
The sons of N: Gn 46:24 5321
"N is a doe let loose, He gives Gn 49:21 5321
Dan and N, Gad and Asher. Ex 1:4 5321
of N, Ahira the son of Enan. Nu 1:15 5321
Of the sons of N, their Nu 1:42 5321
numbered men of the tribe of N Nu 1:43 5321
"Then *comes* the tribe of N, Nu 2:29 5321
and the leader of the sons of N: Nu 2:29 5321
of Enan, leader of the sons of N; Nu 7:78 5321
the tribal army of the sons of N. Nu 10:27 5321
from the tribe of N, Nu 13:14 5321
sons of N according to their Nu 26:48 5321
the families of N according to their Nu 26:50 5321
tribe of the sons of N a leader, Nu 34:28 5321
Gad, Asher, Zebulun, Dan, and N. Dt 27:13 5321
Of N he said, Dt 33:23 5321
"O N, satisfied with favor, And Dt 33:23 5321
and all N and the land of Ephraim Dt 34:2 5321
sixth lot fell to the sons of N; Jos 19:32 5321
to the sons of N according to their Jos 19:32 5321
the tribe of the sons of N according Jos 19:39 5321
in Galilee in the hill country of N Jos 20:7 5321
and from the tribe of N and from Jos 21:6 5321
From the tribe of N, Jos 21:32 5321
N did not drive out the Jg 1:33 5321
thousand men from the sons of N Jg 4:6 5321
Zebulun and N together to Kedesh, Jg 4:10 5321
lives *even* to death, And N also, Jg 5:18 5321
to Asher, Zebulun, and N, Jg 6:35 5321
from N and Asher and all Manasseh, Jg 7:23 5321
Ahimaaz, in N 1Ki 4:15 5321
a widow's son from the tribe of N, 1Ki 7:14 5321
besides all the land of N. 1Ki 15:20 5321
and Galilee, all the land of N; 2Ki 15:29 5321
Dan, Joseph, Benjamin, N, 1Ch 2:2 5321
tribe of Asher, the tribe of N, 1Ch 6:62 5321
and from the tribe of N: 1Ch 6:76 5321
The sons of N *were* Jahziel, Guni, 1Ch 7:13 5321
Of N *there were* 1,000 captains, 1Ch 12:34 5321
far as Issachar and Zebulun and N, 1Ch 12:40 5321
for N, Jeremoth the son of Azriel; 1Ch 27:19 5321
and all the store cities of N. 2Ch 16:4 5321
Ephraim, Simeon, even as far as N, 2Ch 34:6 5321
of Zebulun, the princes of N. Ps 68:27 5321
and the land of N with contempt, Is 9:1 5321
the east side to the west side, N, Ezk 48:3 5321
"Beside the border of N, Ezk 48:4 5321
the gate of N, one. Ezk 48:34 5321
in the region of Zebulun and N. Mt 4:13 *3508*
OF ZEBULUN AND THE LAND OF N, Mt 4:15 *3508*
the tribe of N twelve thousand, Rv 7:6 *3508*

NAPHTUH
the people of Lud, Anam, Lehab, N, 1Ch 1:11 5320

NAPHTUHIM
and Anamim and Lehabim and N Gn 10:13 5320

NARCISSUS
Greet those of the *household* of N, Ro 16:11 *3488*

NARD
fruits, henna with **n** plants, SS 4:13 5373
N and saffron, calamus and SS 4:14 5373
of very costly perfume of pure **n**; Mk 14:3 *3487*
of very costly perfume of pure **n**, Jn 12:3 *3487*

NARROW
in a **n** path of the vineyards, Nu 22:24 4934
and stood in a **n** place where there Nu 22:26 6862a
country of Ephraim is too **n** for you Jos 17:15 213
an adulterous woman is a **n** well. Pr 23:27 6862a
"Enter through the **n** gate; Mt 7:13 *4728*
the way is **n** that leads to life, Mt 7:14 *2346*
"Strive to enter through the **n** door; Lk 13:24 *4728*

NATHAN
Shammua, Shobab, N, 2Sa 5:14 5416
the king said to N the prophet, 2Sa 7:2 5416
N said to the king, 2Sa 7:3 5416
the word of the LORD came to N, 2Sa 7:4 5416
this vision, so N spoke to David. 2Sa 7:17 5416
Then the LORD sent N to David. 2Sa 12:1 5416
against the man, and he said to N, 2Sa 12:5 5416
N then said to David, 2Sa 12:7 5416
Then David said to N, 2Sa 12:13 5416
And N said to David, 2Sa 12:13 5416
So N went to his house. 2Sa 12:15 5416
sent *word* through N the prophet, 2Sa 12:25 5416
Igal the son of N of Zobah, Bani 2Sa 23:36 5416
son of Jehoiada, N the prophet, 1Ki 1:8 5416
he did not invite N the prophet, 1Ki 1:10 5416
Then N spoke to Bathsheba the 1Ki 1:11 5416
the king, N the prophet came in. 1Ki 1:22 5416
"Here is N the prophet." 1Ki 1:23 5416
Then N said, "My lord the king, 1Ki 1:24 5416
Zadok the priest, N the prophet, 1Ki 1:32 5416
Zadok the priest and N the prophet 1Ki 1:34 5416
Zadok the priest, N the prophet, 1Ki 1:38 5416
Zadok the priest, N the prophet, 1Ki 1:44 5416
Zadok the priest and N the prophet 1Ki 1:45 5416
son of N *was* over the deputies; 1Ki 4:5 5416
and Zabud the son of N, a priest, 1Ki 4:5 5416
Attai became the father of N, 1Ch 2:36 5416
and N became the father of Zabad, 1Ch 2:36 5416
Shimea, Shobab, N and Solomon, 1Ch 3:5 5416
Joel the brother of N, 1Ch 11:38 5416
Shammua, Shobab, N, 1Ch 14:4 5416
that David said to N the prophet, 1Ch 17:1 5416
Then N said to David, 1Ch 17:2 5416
that the word of God came to N, 1Ch 17:3 5416
this vision, so N spoke to David. 1Ch 17:15 5416
the chronicles of N the prophet and 1Ch 29:29 5416
in the records of N the prophet, 2Ch 9:29 5416
king's seer, and of N the prophet; 2Ch 29:25 5416
Elnathan, Jarib, Elnathan, N, Ezr 8:16 5416
Shelemiah, N, Adaiah, Ezr 10:39 5416
family of the house of N by itself and Zch 12:12 5416
the son of Mattatha, the son of N, Lk 3:31 *3481*

NATHANAEL
Philip found N and said to him, Jn 1:45 *3482*
N said to him, Jn 1:46 *3482*
Jesus saw N coming to Him, and Jn 1:47 *3482*
N said to Him, "How do You know Jn 1:48 *3482*
N answered Him, "Rabbi, You are Jn 1:49 *3482*
Didymus, and N of Cana in Galilee, Jn 21:2 *3482*

NATHAN-MELECH
by the chamber of N the official, 2Ki 23:11 5419

NATION
And I will make you a great **n**, Gn 12:2 1471
judge the **n** whom they will serve, Gn 15:14 1471
and I will make him a great **n**. Gn 17:20 1471
become a great and mighty **n**, Gn 18:18 1471
"Lord, will You slay a **n**, Gn 20:4 1471
of the maid I will make a **n** also, Gn 21:13 1471
I will make a great **n** of him." Gn 21:18 1471
A **n** and a company of nations shall Gn 35:11 1471
I will make you a great **n** there. Gn 46:3 1471
land of Egypt since it became a **n**. Ex 9:24 1471
kingdom of priests and a holy **n**.' Ex 19:6 1471
I will make of you a great **n**." Ex 32:10 1471
too, that this **n** is Your people." Ex 33:13 1471
the **n** which has been before you. Lv 18:28 1471
shall not follow the customs of the **n** Lv 20:23 1471
and I will make you into a **n** Nu 14:12 1471
'Surely this great **n** is a wise and Dt 4:6 1471
"For what great **n** is there that Dt 4:7 1471
"Or what great **n** is there that Dt 4:8 1471
tried to go to take for himself a **n** Dt 4:34 1471
from within *another* **n** by trials, Dt 4:34 1471
a **n** mightier and greater than they.' Dt 9:14 1471
a great, mighty and populous **n**. Dt 26:5 1471
to a **n** which neither you nor your Dt 28:36 1471
bring a **n** against you from afar, Dt 28:49 1471
a **n** whose language you shall not Dt 28:49 1471
a **n** of fierce countenance who Dt 28:50 1471
them to anger with a foolish **n**, Dt 32:21 1471
they are a **n** lacking in counsel, Dt 32:28 1471
until all the **n** had finished crossing Jos 3:17 1471
when all the **n** had finished crossing Jos 4:1 1471
all the **n**, *that is,* the men of war Jos 5:6 1471
finished circumcising all the **n**, Jos 5:8 1471
Until the **n** avenged themselves of Jos 10:13 1471
"Because this **n** has transgressed Jg 2:20 1471
"And what one **n** on the earth is 2Sa 7:23 1471
there is no **n** or kingdom where my 1Ki 18:10 1471
he made the kingdom or **n** swear 1Ki 18:10 1471
But every **n** still made gods of its 2Ki 17:29 1471
every **n** in their cities in which 2Ki 17:29 1471
wandered about from nation to nation, 1Ch 16:20 1471
wandered about from nation to **n**, 1Ch 16:20 1471
"And what one **n** in the earth is 1Ch 17:21 1471
"N was crushed by nation, and city 2Ch 15:6 1471
"Nation was crushed by **n**, 2Ch 15:6 1471
for no god of any **n** or kingdom was 2Ch 32:15 1471
for the welfare of his whole **n**. Es 10:3 2233
is, in regard to both **n** and man? Jb 34:29 1471
is the **n** whose God is the LORD, Ps 33:12 1471
my case against an ungodly **n**; Ps 43:1 1471
and let us wipe them out as a **n**, Ps 83:4 1471
wandered about from **n** to nation, Ps 105:13 1471
wandered about from nation to **n**, Ps 105:13 1471
rejoice in the gladness of Your **n**, Ps 106:5 1471
He has not dealt thus with any **n**; Ps 147:20 1471
Righteousness exalts a **n**, Pr 14:34 1471
Alas, sinful **n**, People weighed Is 1:4 1471
N will not lift up sword against Is 2:4 1471

will not lift up sword against **n**, **Is 2:4** 1471
lift up a standard to the distant **n**, **Is 5:26** 1471
You shall multiply the **n**, **Is 9:3** 1471
I send it against a godless **n** And **Is 10:6** 1471
answer the messengers of the **n**? **Is 14:32** 1471
to a **n** tall and smooth, **Is 18:2** 1471
n Whose land the rivers divide. **Is 18:2** 1471
wide, A powerful and oppressive **n**, **Is 18:7** 1471
that the righteous **n** may enter, **Is 26:2** 1471
You have increased the **n**, **Is 26:15** 1471
O LORD, You have increased the **n**, **Is 26:15** 1471
that I established the ancient **n**. **Is 44:7** 5971a
One, To the One abhorred by the **n**, **Is 49:7** 1471
And give ear to Me, O My **n**; **Is 51:4** 3816
you will call a **n** you do not know, **Is 55:5** 1471
And a **n** which knows you not will **Is 55:5** 1471
a **n** that has done righteousness And **Is 58:2** 1471
"For the **n** and the kingdom which **Is 60:12** 1471
And the least one a mighty **n**. **Is 60:22** 1471
a **n** which did not call on My name. **Is 65:1** 1471
a **n** be brought forth all at once? **Is 66:8** 1471
"Has a **n** changed gods When they **Jer 2:11** 1471
"And on a **n** such as this Shall I **Jer 5:9** 1471
I am bringing a **n** against you from **Jer 5:15** 1471
"It is an enduring **n**, **Jer 5:15** 1471
nation, It is an ancient **n**, **Jer 5:15** 1471
A **n** whose language you do not **Jer 5:15** 1471
'On a **n** such as this Shall I not **Jer 5:29** 1471
And a great **n** will be aroused from **Jer 6:22** 1471
'This is the **n** that did not obey **Jer 7:28** 1471
"On a **n** such as this Shall I not **Jer 9:9** 1471
listen, then I will uproot that **n**, **Jer 12:17** 1471
I might speak concerning a **n** **Jer 18:7** 1471
if that **n** against which I have **Jer 18:8** 1471
I might speak concerning a **n** **Jer 18:9** 1471
the king of Babylon and that **n**,' **Jer 25:12** 1471
is going forth From **n** to nation, **Jer 25:32** 1471
is going forth From nation to **n**, **Jer 25:32** 1471
that the **n** or the kingdom which **Jer 27:8** 1471
will punish that **n** with the sword, **Jer 27:8** 1471
"But the **n** which will bring its **Jer 27:11** 1471
as the LORD has spoken to that **n** **Jer 27:13** 1471
being a **n** before Me forever." **Jer 31:36** 1471
are they as a **n** in their sight. **Jer 33:24** 1471
us cut her off from *being* a **n**!' **Jer 48:2** 1471
up against a **n** which is at ease, **Jer 49:31** 1471
And there will be no **n** To which **Jer 49:36** 1471
"For a **n** has come up against her **Jer 50:3** 1471
And a great **n** and many kings Will **Jer 50:41** 1471
For a **n** that could not save. **La 4:17** 1471
bereaved your **n** of children," **Ezk 36:13** 1471
longer bereave your **n** of children,' **Ezk 36:14** 1471
nor will you cause your **n** to stumble **Ezk 36:15** 1471
will make them one **n** in the land, **Ezk 37:22** 1471
any people, **n** or tongue that speaks **Da 3:29** 524
which will arise from *his* **n**, **Da 8:22** 1471
since there was a **n** until that time; **Da 12:1** 1471
For a **n** has invaded my land, **Jl 1:6** 1471
to the Sabeans, to a distant **n**," **Jl 3:8** 1471
going to raise up a **n** against you, **Am 6:14** 1471
N will not lift up sword against **Mi 4:3** 1471
will not lift up sword against **n**, **Mi 4:3** 1471
And the outcasts a strong **n**, **Mi 4:7** 1471
yes, gather, O **n** without shame, **Zph 2:1** 1471
The **n** of the Cherethites! **Zph 2:5** 1471
remainder of My **n** will inherit them **Zph 2:9** 1471
And so is this **n** before Me,' **Hg 2:14** 1471
robbing Me, the whole **n** *of you!* **Mal 3:9** 1471
"For **n** will rise against nation, **Mt 24:7** *1484*
"For nation will rise against **n**, **Mt 24:7** *1484*
"For **n** will rise up against nation, **Mk 13:8** *1484*
"For nation will rise up against **n**, **Mk 13:8** *1484*
for he loves our **n** and **Lk 7:5** *1484*
"**N** will rise against nation and **Lk 21:10** *1484*
"Nation will rise against **n** and **Lk 21:10** *1484*
We found this man misleading our **n** **Lk 23:2** *1484*
away both our place and our **n**." **Jn 11:48** *1484*
the whole **n** not perish." **Jn 11:50** *1484*
Jesus was going to die for the **n**, **Jn 11:51** *1484*
and not for the **n** only, but in **Jn 11:52** *1484*
Your own **n** and the chief priests **Jn 18:35** *1484*
men from every **n** under heaven. **Ac 2:5** *1484*
"'AND WHATEVER **N** TO WHICH THEY **Ac 7:7** *1484*
of by the entire **n** of the Jews, **Ac 10:22** *1484*
in every **n** the man who fears Him **Ac 10:35** *1484*
every **n** of mankind to live on all **Ac 17:26** *1484*
are being carried out for this **n**, **Ac 24:2** *1484*
you have been a judge to this **n**, **Ac 24:10** *1484*
I came to bring alms to my **n** and **Ac 24:17** *1484*
among my *own* **n** and at Jerusalem; **Ac 26:4** *1484*
I had any accusation against my **n**. **Ac 28:19** *1484*
JEALOUS BY THAT WHICH IS NOT A **N**, **Ro 10:19** *1484*
BY A **N** WITHOUT UNDERSTANDING **Ro 10:19** *1484*
Look at the **n** Israel; **1Co 10:18** *4561*
eighth day, of the **n** of Israel, **Php 3:5** *1085*
A ROYAL PRIESTHOOD, A HOLY **N**, **1Pe 2:9** *1484*
tribe and tongue and people and **n**. **Rv 5:9** *1484*
from every **n** and *all* tribes and **Rv 7:9** *1484*
and tongue and **n** was given to him. **Rv 13:7** *1484*
and to every **n** and tribe and **Rv 14:6** *1484*

NATIONS

coastlands of the **n** were separated **Gn 10:5** 1471
to their families, into their **n**. **Gn 10:5** 1471
by their lands, by their **n**. **Gn 10:20** 1471
their lands, according to their **n**. **Gn 10:31** 1471
to their genealogies, by their **n**; **Gn 10:32** 1471
the **n** were separated on the earth **Gn 10:32** 1471
be the father of a multitude of **n**. **Gn 17:4** 1471
the father of a multitude of **n**. **Gn 17:5** 1471
and I will make **n** of you, **Gn 17:6** 1471
and she shall be *a mother of* **n**; **Gn 17:16** 1471
all the **n** of the earth will be blessed **Gn 18:18** 1471
all the **n** of the earth shall be blessed **Gn 22:18** 1471
"Two **n** are in your womb; **Gn 25:23** 1471
all the **n** of the earth shall be blessed **Gn 26:4** 1471
serve you, And **n** bow down to you; **Gn 27:29** 3816
company of **n** shall come from you, **Gn 35:11** 1471
shall become a multitude of **n**." **Gn 48:19** 1471
the earth nor among any of the **n**; **Ex 34:10** 1471
"For I will drive out **n** before **Ex 34:24** 1471
for by all these the **n** which I am **Lv 18:24** 1471
the pagan **n** that are around you. **Lv 25:44** 1471
I will scatter among the **n** and **Lv 26:33** 1471
'But you will perish among the **n**, **Lv 26:38** 1471
of Egypt in the sight of the **n**, **Lv 26:45** 1471
the **n** who have heard of Your fame **Nu 14:15** 1471
will not be reckoned among the **n**. **Nu 23:9** 1471
devour the **n** *who are* his adversaries **Nu 24:8** 1471
"Amalek was the first of the **n**, **Nu 24:20** 1471
left few in number among the **n** where **Dt 4:27** 1471
n greater and mightier than you, **Dt 4:38** 1471
clears away many **n** before you, **Dt 7:1** 1471
n greater and stronger than you, **Dt 7:1** 1471
'These **n** are greater than I; **Dt 7:17** 1471
your God will clear away these **n** **Dt 7:22** 1471
"Like the **n** that the LORD makes **Dt 8:20** 1471
n greater and mightier than you, **Dt 9:1** 1471
because of the wickedness of these **n** **Dt 9:4** 1471
because of the wickedness of these **n** **Dt 9:5** 1471
the LORD will drive out all these **n** **Dt 11:23** 1471
n greater and mightier than you. **Dt 11:23** 1471
the **n** whom you shall dispossess **Dt 12:2** 1471
your God cuts off before you the **n** **Dt 12:29** 1471
'How do these **n** serve their gods, **Dt 12:30** 1471
you, and you will lend to many **n**, **Dt 15:6** 1471
and you will rule over many **n**, **Dt 15:6** 1471
like all the **n** who are around me,' **Dt 17:14** 1471
the detestable things of those **n**. **Dt 18:9** 1471
those **n**, which you shall dispossess, **Dt 18:14** 1471
the LORD your God cuts off the **n**, **Dt 19:1** 1471
not of the cities of these **n** nearby. **Dt 20:15** 1471
above all **n** which He has made, **Dt 26:19** 1471
high above all the **n** of the earth. **Dt 28:1** 1471
and you shall lend to many **n**, **Dt 28:12** 1471
Among those **n** you shall find no rest **Dt 28:65** 1471
we came through the midst of the **n** **Dt 29:16** 1471
go and serve the gods of those **n**; **Dt 29:18** 1471
"All the **n** will say, **Dt 29:24** 1471
all **n** where the LORD your God has **Dt 30:1** 1471
will destroy these **n** before you, **Dt 31:3** 1471
High gave the **n** their inheritance, **Dt 32:8** 1471
"Rejoice, O **n**, *with* His people; **Dt 32:43** 1471
to all these **n** because of you, **Jos 23:3** 1471
I have apportioned to you these **n** **Jos 23:4** 1471
all the **n** which I have cut off, **Jos 23:4** 1471
will not associate with these **n**, **Jos 23:7** 1471
has driven out great and strong **n** **Jos 23:9** 1471
and cling to the rest of these **n**, **Jos 23:12** 1471
drive these **n** out from before you; **Jos 23:13** 1471
the **n** which Joshua left when he died, **Jg 2:21** 1471
LORD allowed those **n** to remain, **Jg 2:23** 1471
are the **n** which the LORD left, **Jg 3:1** 1471
These **n** *are:* the five lords of **Jg 3:3**
us to judge us like all the **n**." **1Sa 8:5** 1471
we also may be like all the **n**, **1Sa 8:20** 1471
from Egypt, *from* **n** and their gods? **2Sa 7:23** 1471
all the **n** which he had subdued: **2Sa 8:11** 1471
have kept me as head of the **n**; **2Sa 22:44** 1471
to You, O LORD, among the **n**, **2Sa 22:50** 1471
known in all the surrounding **n**. **1Ki 4:31** 1471
from the **n** concerning which the **1Ki 11:2** 1471
the **n** which the LORD dispossessed **1Ki 14:24** 1471
n whom the LORD had driven out **2Ki 16:3** 1471
the **n** whom the LORD had driven out **2Ki 17:8** 1471
as the **n** *did* which the LORD had **2Ki 17:11** 1471
after the **n** which surrounded them, **2Ki 17:15** 1471
"The **n** whom you have carried away **2Ki 17:26** 1471
n from among whom they had been **2Ki 17:33** 1471
So while these **n** feared the LORD, **2Ki 17:41** 1471
'Has any one of the gods of the **n** **2Ki 18:33** 1471
'Did the gods of those **n** which my **2Ki 19:12** 1471
devastated the **n** and their lands **2Ki 19:17** 1471
the **n** whom the LORD dispossessed **2Ki 21:2** 1471
to do evil more than the **n** whom the **2Ki 21:9** 1471
the fear of him on all the **n**. **1Ch 14:17** 1471
Tell of His glory among the **n**, **1Ch 16:24** 1471
And let them say among the **n**, **1Ch 16:31** 1471
us and deliver us from the **n**, **1Ch 16:35** 1471
in driving out **n** from before Your **1Ch 17:21** 1471
had carried away from all the **n**: **1Ch 18:11** 1471
over all the kingdoms of the **n**? **2Ch 20:6** 1471
the **n** whom the LORD had driven out **2Ch 28:3** 1471
Were the gods of the **n** of the lands **2Ch 32:13** 1471
n which my fathers utterly destroyed **2Ch 32:14** 1471
"As the gods of the **n** of the lands **2Ch 32:17** 1471
in the sight of all **n** thereafter. **2Ch 32:23** 1471
the **n** whom the LORD dispossessed **2Ch 33:2** 1471
the **n** whom the LORD destroyed **2Ch 33:9** 1471
all the abominations of the **n**; **2Ch 36:14** 1471
and the rest of the **n** which the **Ezr 4:10** 524
the impurity of the **n** of the land **Ezr 6:21** 1471
brothers who were sold to the **n**; **Ne 5:8** 1471
because of the reproach of the **n**, **Ne 5:9** 1471
us from the **n** that were around us. **Ne 5:17** 1471
"It is reported among the **n**, **Ne 6:6** 1471
all the **n** surrounding us saw *it*, **Ne 6:16** 1471
among the many **n** there was no **Ne 13:26** 1471
"He makes the **n** great, then **Jb 12:23** 1471
He enlarges the **n**, then leads them **Jb 12:23** 1471
Why are the **n** in an uproar And **Ps 2:1** 1471
give the **n** as Your inheritance, **Ps 2:8** 1471
You have rebuked the **n**, **Ps 9:5** 1471
The **n** have sunk down in the pit **Ps 9:15** 1471
Even all the **n** who forget God. **Ps 9:17** 1471
Let the **n** be judged before You. **Ps 9:19** 1471
the **n** know that they are but men. **Ps 9:20** 1471
N have perished from His land. **Ps 10:16** 1471
have placed me as head of the **n**; **Ps 18:43** 1471
give thanks to You among the **n**, **Ps 18:49** 1471
of the **n** will worship before You. **Ps 22:27** 1471
LORD's And He rules over the **n**. **Ps 22:28** 1471
LORD nullifies the counsel of the **n**; **Ps 33:10** 1471
own hand drove out the **n**; **Ps 44:2** 1471
And have scattered us among the **n**. **Ps 44:11** 1471
You make us a byword among the **n**, **Ps 44:14** 1471
The **n** made an uproar, the kingdoms **Ps 46:6** 1471
I will be exalted among the **n**, **Ps 46:10** 1471
under us And **n** under our feet. **Ps 47:3** 3816
God reigns over the **n**, **Ps 47:8** 1471
sing praises to You among the **n**. **Ps 57:9** 3816
Israel, Awake to punish all the **n**; **Ps 59:5** 1471
You scoff at all the **n**. **Ps 59:8** 1471
His eyes keep watch on the **n**; **Ps 66:7** 1471
earth, Your salvation among all **n**. **Ps 67:2** 1471
the **n** be glad and sing for joy; **Ps 67:4** 3816
And guide the **n** on the earth. **Ps 67:4** 3816
down before him, All **n** serve him. **Ps 72:11** 1471
Let all **n** call him blessed. **Ps 72:17** 1471
also drove out the **n** before them And **Ps 78:55** 1471
the **n** have invaded Your **Ps 79:1** 1471
upon the **n** which do not know You, **Ps 79:6** 1471
Why should the **n** say, **Ps 79:10** 1471
be known among the **n** in our sight, **Ps 79:10** 1471
You drove out the **n** **Ps 80:8** 1471
You who possesses all the **n**. **Ps 82:8** 1471
All **n** whom You have made shall **Ps 86:9** 1471
He who chastens the **n**, **Ps 94:10** 1471
Tell of His glory among the **n**, **Ps 96:3** 1471
Say among the **n**, **Ps 96:10** 1471
in the sight of the **n**. **Ps 98:2** 1471
So the **n** will fear the name of the **Ps 102:15** 1471
gave them also the lands of the **n**, **Ps 105:44** 1471
would cast their seed among the **n** And **Ps 106:27** 1471
But they mingled with the **n** And **Ps 106:35** 1471
gave them into the hand of the **n**, **Ps 106:41** 1471
And gather us from among the **n**, **Ps 106:47** 1471
sing praises to You among the **n**. **Ps 108:3** 3816
He will judge among the **n**, **Ps 110:6** 1471
giving them the heritage of the **n**. **Ps 111:6** 1471
The LORD is high above all **n**; **Ps 113:4** 1471
Why should the **n** say, **Ps 115:2** 1471
Praise the LORD, all **n**; **Ps 117:1** 1471
All **n** surrounded me; **Ps 118:10** 1471
Then they said among the **n**, **Ps 126:2** 1471
He smote many **n** And slew mighty **Ps 135:10** 1471
idols of the **n** are *but* silver and gold, **Ps 135:15** 1471
To execute vengeance on the **n** And **Ps 149:7** 1471
will curse him, **n** will abhor him; **Pr 24:24** 3816
And all the **n** will stream to it. **Is 2:2** 1471
And He will judge between the **n**, **Is 2:4** 1471
to destroy And to cut off many **n**. **Is 10:7** 1471
The **n** will resort to the root of Jesse, **Is 11:10** 1471
will lift up a standard for the **n** And **Is 11:12** 1471
kingdoms, Of **n** gathered together! **Is 13:4** 1471
Which subdued the **n** in anger with **Is 14:6** 1471
kings of the **n** from their thrones. **Is 14:9** 1471
You who have weakened the **n**! **Is 14:12** 1471
the kings of the **n** lie in glory, **Is 14:18** 1471
stretched out against all the **n**. **Is 14:26** 1471
The lords of the **n** have trampled **Is 16:8** 1471
And the rumbling of **n** Who rush on **Is 17:12** 3816
The **n** rumble on like the rumbling **Is 17:13** 3816
And she was the market of **n**. **Is 23:3** 1471
Cities of ruthless **n** will revere You. **Is 25:3** 1471
which is stretched over all **n**. **Is 25:7** 1471
the **n** who wage war against Ariel, **Is 29:7** 1471
multitude of all the **n** will be **Is 29:8** 1471
To shake the **n** back and forth in a **Is 30:28** 1471
lifting up of Yourself **n** disperse. **Is 33:3** 1471
Draw near, O **n**, to hear; **Is 34:1** 1471
indignation is against all the **n**, **Is 34:2** 1471
Has any one of the gods of the **n** **Is 36:18** 1471
'Did the gods of those **n** which my **Is 37:12** 1471
n are like a drop from a bucket, **Is 40:15** 1471
the **n** are as nothing before Him, **Is 40:17** 1471
He delivers up **n** before him And **Is 41:2** 1471
will bring forth justice to the **n**. **Is 42:1** 1471
the people, As a light to the **n**, **Is 42:6** 1471
All the **n** have gathered together **Is 43:9** 1471
hand, To subdue **n** before him And **Is 45:1** 1471
together, you fugitives of the **n**; **Is 45:20** 1471
I will also make You a light of the **n** **Is 49:6** 1471
I will lift up My hand to the **n** And **Is 49:22** 1471
arm In the sight of all the **n**, **Is 52:10** 1471
Thus He will sprinkle many **n**, **Is 52:15** 1471
your descendants will possess **n** And **Is 54:3** 1471
"**N** will come to your light, **Is 60:3** 1471
wealth of the **n** will come to you. **Is 60:5** 1471
bring to you the wealth of the **n**, **Is 60:11** 1471
And the **n** will be utterly ruined. **Is 60:12** 1471
"You will also suck the milk of **n** And **Is 60:16** 1471
You will eat the wealth of **n**, **Is 61:6** 1471
will be known among the **n**, **Is 61:9** 1471
To spring up before all the **n**. **Is 61:11** 1471
The **n** will see your righteousness, **Is 62:2** 1471
the **n** may tremble at Your presence! **Is 64:2** 1471
glory of the **n** like an overflowing **Is 66:12** 1471

to gather all **n** and tongues.	**Is 66:18**	1471
send survivors from them to the **n**:	**Is 66:19**	1471
will declare My glory among the **n**.	**Is 66:19**	1471
bring all your brethren from all the **n**	**Is 66:20**	1471
appointed you a prophet to the **n**."	**Jer 1:5**	1471
appointed you this day over the **n**	**Jer 1:10**	1471
all the **n** will be gathered to it,	**Jer 3:17**	1471
beautiful inheritance of the **n**!'	**Jer 3:19**	1471
n will bless themselves in Him,	**Jer 4:2**	1471
And a destroyer of **n** has set out;	**Jer 4:7**	1471
"Report *it* to the **n**,	**Jer 4:16**	1471
"Therefore hear, O **n**,	**Jer 6:18**	1471
I will scatter them among the **n**,	**Jer 9:16**	1471
for all the **n** are uncircumcised,	**Jer 9:26**	1471
"Do not learn the way of the **n**,	**Jer 10:2**	1471
the **n** are terrified by them;	**Jer 10:2**	1471
not fear You, O King of the **n**?	**Jer 10:7**	1471
among all the wise men of the **n** And	**Jer 10:7**	1471
n cannot endure His indignation.	**Jer 10:10**	1471
on the **n** that do not know You And	**Jer 10:25**	1471
the idols of the **n** who give rain?	**Jer 14:22**	1471
To You the **n** will come From the	**Jer 16:19**	1471
'Ask now among the **n**,	**Jer 18:13**	1471
"Many **n** will pass by this city;	**Jer 22:8**	1471
against all these **n** round about;	**Jer 25:9**	1471
and these **n** will serve the king	**Jer 25:11**	1471
has prophesied against all the **n**.	**Jer 25:13**	1471
'(For many **n** and great kings will	**Jer 25:14**	1471
from My hand and cause all the **n**	**Jer 25:15**	1471
the **n** to whom the LORD sent me	**Jer 25:17**	1471
LORD has a controversy with the **n**.	**Jer 25:31**	1471
to all the **n** of the earth.	**Jer 26:6**	1471
"All the **n** shall serve him and	**Jer 27:7**	1471
then many **n** and great kings will	**Jer 27:7**	1471
from the neck of all the **n**.'"	**Jer 28:11**	1471
iron on the neck of all these **n**,	**Jer 28:14**	1471
and will gather you from all the **n**	**Jer 29:14**	1471
the **n** where I have driven them,	**Jer 29:18**	1471
the **n** where I have scattered you,	**Jer 30:11**	1471
shout among the chief of the **n**;	**Jer 31:7**	1471
Hear the word of the LORD, O **n**,	**Jer 31:10**	1471
before all the **n** of the earth which	**Jer 33:9**	1471
Judah, and concerning all the **n**,	**Jer 36:2**	1471
the **n** to which they had been driven	**Jer 43:5**	1471
among all the **n** of the earth?	**Jer 44:8**	1471
the prophet concerning the **n**.	**Jer 46:1**	1471
The **n** have heard of your shame,	**Jer 46:12**	1471
all the **n** Where I have driven you,	**Jer 46:28**	1471
And an envoy is sent among the **n**,	**Jer 49:14**	1471
I have made you small among the **n**,	**Jer 49:15**	1471
"Declare and proclaim among the **n**.	**Jer 50:2**	1471
A horde of great **n** from the land of	**Jer 50:9**	1471
she will be the least of the **n**,	**Jer 50:12**	1471
An object of horror among the **n**!	**Jer 50:23**	1471
an outcry is heard among the **n**.	**Jer 50:46**	1471
The **n** have drunk of her wine;	**Jer 51:7**	1471
Therefore the **n** are going mad.	**Jer 51:7**	1471
And with you I shatter **n**,	**Jer 51:20**	1471
land, Blow a trumpet among the **n**!	**Jer 51:27**	1471
Consecrate the **n** against her,	**Jer 51:27**	1471
Consecrate the **n** against her, The	**Jer 51:28**	1471
an object of horror among the **n**!	**Jer 51:41**	1471
n will no longer stream to him.	**Jer 51:44**	1471
And the **n** become exhausted *only*	**Jer 51:58**	3816
Who was *once* great among the **n**!	**La 1:1**	1471
She dwells among the **n**,	**La 1:3**	1471
seen the **n** enter her sanctuary,	**La 1:10**	1471
and her princes are among the **n**;	**La 2:9**	1471
Men among the **n** said,	**La 4:15**	1471
We shall live among the **n**."	**La 4:20**	1471
the **n** where I will banish them."	**Ezk 4:13**	1471
set her at the center of the **n**,	**Ezk 5:5**	1471
ordinances more wickedly than the **n**	**Ezk 5:6**	1471
you have more turmoil than the **n**	**Ezk 5:7**	1471
nor observed the ordinances of the **n**	**Ezk 5:7**	1471
among you in the sight of the **n**.	**Ezk 5:8**	1471
among the **n** which surround you,	**Ezk 5:14**	1471
horror to the **n** who surround you when	**Ezk 5:15**	1471
who escaped the sword among the **n**	**Ezk 6:8**	1471
the **n** to which they will be carried	**Ezk 6:9**	1471
I will bring the worst of the **n**,	**Ezk 7:24**	1471
the ordinances of the **n** around you.	**Ezk 11:12**	1471
removed them far away among the **n**	**Ezk 11:16**	1471
when I scatter them among the **n**	**Ezk 12:15**	1471
among the **n** where they go,	**Ezk 12:16**	1471
the **n** on account of your beauty,	**Ezk 16:14**	1471
'Then **n** heard about him;	**Ezk 19:4**	1471
'Then **n** set against him On every	**Ezk 19:8**	1471
not be profaned in the sight of the **n**	**Ezk 20:9**	1471
not be profaned in the sight of the **n**,	**Ezk 20:14**	1471
not be profaned in the sight of the **n**	**Ezk 20:22**	1471
I would scatter them among the **n**	**Ezk 20:23**	1471
'We will be like the **n**,	**Ezk 20:32**	1471
among you in the sight of the **n**.	**Ezk 20:41**	1471
have made you a reproach to the **n** and	**Ezk 22:4**	1471
I will scatter you among the **n**	**Ezk 22:15**	1471
yourself in the sight of the **n**,	**Ezk 22:16**	1471
have played the harlot with the **n**,	**Ezk 23:30**	1471
will give you for spoil to the **n**.	**Ezk 25:7**	1471
house of Judah is like all the **n**,'	**Ezk 25:8**	1471
will not be remembered among the **n**.	**Ezk 25:10**	1471
will bring up many **n** against you,	**Ezk 26:3**	1471
she will become spoil for the **n**.	**Ezk 26:5**	1471
you, The most ruthless of the **n**.	**Ezk 28:7**	1471
in them in the sight of the **n**,	**Ezk 28:25**	1471
scatter the Egyptians among the **n**	**Ezk 29:12**	1471
again lift itself up above the **n**.	**Ezk 29:15**	1471
they will not rule over the **n**.	**Ezk 29:15**	1471
clouds, A time *of doom* for the **n**.	**Ezk 30:3**	1471
him, The most ruthless of the **n**,	**Ezk 30:11**	1471
scatter the Egyptians among the **n**	**Ezk 30:23**	1471
I scatter the Egyptians among the **n**	**Ezk 30:26**	1471
all great **n** lived under its shade.	**Ezk 31:6**	1471
the hand of a despot of the **n**;	**Ezk 31:11**	1471
Alien tyrants of the **n** have cut it	**Ezk 31:12**	1471
"I made the **n** quake at the sound	**Ezk 31:16**	1471
lived under its shade among the **n**.	**Ezk 31:17**	1471
yourself to a young lion of the **n**,	**Ezk 32:2**	1471
your destruction among the **n**,	**Ezk 32:9**	1471
all of them are tyrants of the **n**,	**Ezk 32:12**	1471
daughters of the **n** shall chant it.	**Ezk 32:16**	1471
the daughters of the powerful **n**,	**Ezk 32:18**	1471
will no longer be a prey to the **n**,	**Ezk 34:28**	1471
the insults of the **n** anymore.	**Ezk 34:29**	1471
'These two **n** and these two lands	**Ezk 35:10**	1471
a possession of the rest of the **n** and	**Ezk 36:3**	1471
a derision to the rest of the **n** which	**Ezk 36:4**	1471
spoken against the rest of the **n**,	**Ezk 36:5**	1471
endured the insults of the **n**.'	**Ezk 36:6**	1471
'I have sworn that surely the **n**	**Ezk 36:7**	1471
hear insults from the **n** anymore,	**Ezk 36:15**	1471
"Also I scattered them among the **n** and	**Ezk 36:19**	1471
came to the **n** where they went,	**Ezk 36:20**	1471
Israel had profaned among the **n**	**Ezk 36:21**	1471
among the **n** where you went.	**Ezk 36:22**	1471
has been profaned among the **n**,	**Ezk 36:23**	1471
Then the **n** will know that I am	**Ezk 36:23**	1471
"For I will take you from the **n**,	**Ezk 36:24**	1471
disgrace of famine among the **n**.	**Ezk 36:30**	1471
"Then the **n** that are left round	**Ezk 36:36**	1471
among the **n** where they have gone,	**Ezk 37:21**	1471
and they will no longer be two **n** and	**Ezk 37:22**	1471
"And the **n** will know that I am	**Ezk 37:28**	1471
have been gathered from many **n**	**Ezk 38:8**	5971a
were brought out from the **n**,	**Ezk 38:8**	5971a
who are gathered from the **n**,	**Ezk 38:12**	1471
so that the **n** may know Me	**Ezk 38:16**	1471
known in the sight of many **n**;	**Ezk 38:23**	1471
n will know that I am the LORD,	**Ezk 39:7**	1471
I will set My glory among the **n**;	**Ezk 39:21**	1471
and all the **n** will see My judgment	**Ezk 39:21**	1471
"The **n** will know that the	**Ezk 39:23**	1471
them in the sight of the many **n**.	**Ezk 39:27**	1471
them go into exile among the **n**,	**Ezk 39:28**	1471
n and *men of every* language,	**Da 3:4**	524
n and *men of every* language fell	**Da 3:7**	524
the king to all the peoples, **n**,	**Da 4:1**	524
on him, all the peoples, **n** and	**Da 5:19**	524
king wrote to all the peoples, **n** and	**Da 6:25**	524
kingdom, That all the peoples, **n** and	**Da 7:14**	524
Ephraim mixes himself with the **n**;	**Hos 7:8**	5971a
They are now among the **n** Like a	**Hos 8:8**	1471
they hire *allies* among the **n**,	**Hos 8:10**	1471
with exultation like the **n**!	**Hos 9:1**	5971a
will be wanderers among the **n**.	**Hos 9:17**	1471
a reproach, A byword among the **n**.	**Jl 2:17**	1471
make you a reproach among the **n**.	**Jl 2:19**	1471
I will gather all the **n** And	**Jl 3:2**	1471
they have scattered among the **n**;	**Jl 3:2**	1471
Proclaim this among the **n**:	**Jl 3:9**	1471
and come, all you surrounding **n**,	**Jl 3:11**	1471
Let the **n** be aroused And come up	**Jl 3:12**	1471
to judge All the surrounding **n**.	**Jl 3:12**	1471
men of the foremost of **n**,	**Am 6:1**	1471
n As *grain* is shaken in a sieve,	**Am 9:9**	1471
the **n** who are called by My name,"	**Am 9:12**	1471
envoy has been sent among the **n**	**Ob 1:1**	1471
I will make you small among the **n**;	**Ob 1:2**	1471
the LORD draws near on all the **n**.	**Ob 1:15**	1471
All the **n** will drink continually.	**Ob 1:16**	1471
Many **n** will come and say,	**Mi 4:2**	1471
decisions for mighty, distant **n**.	**Mi 4:3**	1471
now many **n** have been assembled	**Mi 4:11**	1471
of Jacob Will be among the **n**,	**Mi 5:8**	1471
On the **n** which have not obeyed."	**Mi 5:15**	1471
N will see and be ashamed Of all	**Mi 7:16**	1471
Who sells **n** by her harlotries And	**Na 3:4**	1471
And show to the **n** your nakedness	**Na 3:5**	1471
"Look among the **n**!	**Hab 1:5**	1471
slay **n** without sparing?	**Hab 1:17**	1471
He also gathers to himself all **n**	**Hab 2:5**	1471
"Because you have looted many **n**,	**Hab 2:8**	1471
And **n** grow weary for nothing?	**Hab 2:13**	3816
He looked and startled the **n**.	**Hab 3:6**	1471
In anger You trampled the **n**.	**Hab 3:12**	1471
of the **n** will bow down to Him,	**Zph 2:11**	1471
"I have cut off **n**;	**Zph 3:6**	1471
My decision is to gather **n**,	**Zph 3:8**	1471
'I will shake all the **n**;	**Hg 2:7**	1471
come with the wealth of all **n**,	**Hg 2:7**	1471
power of the kingdoms of the **n**;	**Hg 2:22**	1471
angry with the **n** who are at ease;	**Zch 1:15**	1471
to throw down the horns of the **n**	**Zch 1:21**	1471
against the **n** which plunder you,	**Zch 2:8**	1471
"Many **n** will join themselves	**Zch 2:11**	1471
the **n** whom they have not known.	**Zch 7:14**	1471
as you were a curse among the **n**,	**Zch 8:13**	1471
'So many peoples and mighty **n** will	**Zch 8:22**	1471
ten men from all the **n** will grasp the	**Zch 8:23**	1471
And He will speak peace to the **n**;	**Zch 9:10**	1471
And all the **n** of the earth will be	**Zch 12:3**	1471
the **n** that come against Jerusalem.	**Zch 12:9**	1471
gather all the **n** against Jerusalem	**Zch 14:2**	1471
forth and fight against those **n**,	**Zch 14:3**	1471
the wealth of all the surrounding **n**	**Zch 14:14**	1471
all the **n** that went against Jerusalem	**Zch 14:16**	1471
LORD smites the **n** who do not go up	**Zch 14:18**	1471
and the punishment of all the **n**	**Zch 14:19**	1471
My name *will be* great among the **n**,	**Mal 1:11**	1471
name *will be* great among the **n**,"	**Mal 1:11**	1471
My name is feared among the **n**."	**Mal 1:14**	1471
All the **n** will call you blessed,	**Mal 3:12**	1471
will be hated by all **n** because of	**Mt 24:9**	*1484*
world as a testimony to all the **n**,	**Mt 24:14**	*1484*
the **n** will be gathered before Him;	**Mt 25:32**	*1484*
and make disciples of all the **n**,	**Mt 28:19**	*1484*
A HOUSE OF PRAYER FOR ALL THE **N**'?	**Mk 11:17**	*1484*
first be preached to all the **n**.	**Mk 13:10**	*1484*
the **n** of the world eagerly seek;	**Lk 12:30**	*1484*
be led captive into all the **n**;	**Lk 21:24**	*1484*
and on the earth dismay among **n**,	**Lk 21:25**	*1484*
in His name to all the **n**,	**Lk 24:47**	*1484*
n whom God drove out before our	**Ac 7:45**	*1484*
seven **n** in the land of Canaan,	**Ac 13:19**	*1484*
all the **n** to go their own ways;	**Ac 14:16**	*1484*
OF MANY **N** HAVE I MADE YOU")	**Ro 4:17**	*1484*
might become a father of many **n**	**Ro 4:18**	*1484*
has been made known to all the **n**,	**Ro 16:26**	*1484*
ALL THE **N** WILL BE BLESSED IN YOU.	**Ga 3:8**	*1484*
by angels, Proclaimed among the **n**,	**1Tm 3:16**	*1484*
I WILL GIVE AUTHORITY OVER THE **N**;	**Rv 2:26**	*1484*
and **n** and tongues and kings."	**Rv 10:11**	*1484*
for it has been given to the **n**;	**Rv 11:2**	*1484*
and **n** *will* look at their dead bodies	**Rv 11:9**	*1484*
"And the **n** were enraged, and Your	**Rv 11:18**	*1484*
rule all the **n** with a rod of iron;	**Rv 12:5**	*1484*
she who has made all the **n** drink	**Rv 14:8**	*1484*
are Your ways, King of the **n**!	**Rv 15:3**	*1484*
FOR ALL THE **N** WILL COME AND	**Rv 15:4**	*1484*
and the cities of the **n** fell.	**Rv 16:19**	*1484*
and multitudes and **n** and tongues.	**Rv 17:15**	*1484*
"For all the **n** have drunk of the	**Rv 18:3**	*1484*
n were deceived by your sorcery.	**Rv 18:23**	*1484*
that with it He may strike down the **n**,	**Rv 19:15**	*1484*
not deceive the **n** any longer,	**Rv 20:3**	*1484*
and will come out to deceive the **n**	**Rv 20:8**	*1484*
The **n** will walk by its light,	**Rv 21:24**	*1484*
and the honor of the **n** into it;	**Rv 21:26**	*1484*
were for the healing of the **n**.	**Rv 22:2**	*1484*

NATIVE

he is an alien or a **n** of the land.	**Ex 12:19**	249
he shall be like a **n** of the land.	**Ex 12:48**	249
same law shall apply to the **n** as to	**Ex 12:49**	249
not do any work, whether the **n**,	**Lv 16:29**	249
whether he is a **n** or an alien,	**Lv 17:15**	249
neither the **n**, nor the alien who	**Lv 18:26**	249
be to you as the **n** among you,	**Lv 19:34**	249
The alien as well as the **n**,	**Lv 24:16**	249
for the stranger as well as the **n**,	**Lv 24:22**	249
and for the **n** of the land.'"	**Nu 9:14**	249
'All who are **n** shall do these	**Nu 15:13**	249
for him who is **n** among the sons of	**Nu 15:29**	249
whether he is **n** or an alien,	**Nu 15:30**	249
the stranger as well as the **n**.	**Jos 8:33**	249
a luxuriant tree in its **n** soil.	**Ps 37:35**	249
never return Or see his **n** land.	**Jer 22:10**	4138
To our own people and our **n** land	**Jer 46:16**	4138
Hellenistic *Jews* against the **n**	**Ac 6:1**	
Jew named Aquila, a **n** of Pontus,	**Ac 18:2**	*1085*

NATIVE-BORN

all the **n** in Israel shall live in	**Lv 23:42**	249
as the **n** among the sons of Israel;	**Ezk 47:22**	249

NATIVES

The **n** showed us extraordinary	**Ac 28:2**	*915*
When the **n** saw the creature	**Ac 28:4**	*915*

NATURAL

bird or beast that has died a **n** death	**Ezk 44:31**	5038
for my **n** color turned to a deathly	**Da 10:8**	1935
women exchanged the **n** function	**Ro 1:26**	*5446*
men abandoned the **n** function of the	**Ro 1:27**	*5446*
God did not spare the **n** branches,	**Ro 11:21**	*5449*
n *branches* be grafted into their own	**Ro 11:24**	*2596, 5449*
But a **n** man does not accept the	**1Co 2:14**	*5591*
it is sown a **n** body, it is raised	**1Co 15:44**	*5591*
If there is a **n** body, there is	**1Co 15:44**	*5591*
spiritual is not first, but the **n**;	**1Co 15:46**	*5591*
looks at his **n** face in a mirror;	**Jas 1:23**	*1078*
but is earthly, **n**, demonic.	**Jas 3:15**	*5591*

NATURALLY

with a sword or who has died **n**,	**Nu 19:16**	
or the one slain or the one dying **n**	**Nu 19:18**	

NATURE

he speaks from his own **n**, for he	**Jn 8:44**	
are also men of the same **n** as you,	**Ac 14:15**	*3663*
think that the Divine **N** is like gold	**Ac 17:29**	*2304*
His eternal power and divine **n**,	**Ro 1:20**	*2305*
what is by **n** a wild olive tree,	**Ro 11:24**	*5449*
were grafted contrary to **n** into a	**Ro 11:24**	*5449*
Does not even **n** itself teach you	**1Co 11:14**	*5449*
"We *are* Jews by **n** and not	**Ga 2:15**	*5449*
to those which by **n** are no gods.	**Ga 4:8**	*5449*
and were by **n** children of wrath,	**Eph 2:3**	*5449*
the exact representation of His **n**,	**Heb 1:3**	*5287*
was a man with a **n** like ours,	**Jas 5:17**	*3663*
become partakers of *the* divine **n**,	**2Pe 1:4**	*5449*

NAVE

porch in front of the **n** of the house	**1Ki 6:3**	1964
the **n** and the inner sanctuary;	**1Ki 6:5**	1964
the **n** in front of *the inner sanctuary*	**1Ki 6:17**	1964
he made for the entrance of the **n**	**1Ki 6:33**	1964
the pillars at the porch of the **n**;	**1Ki 7:21**	1964
doors of the house, *that is*, of the **n**,	**1Ki 7:50**	1964
doors of the house, *that is*, of the **n**,	**2Ch 4:22**	1964
he brought me to the **n** and	**Ezk 41:1**	1964

he measured the length of the **n**, Ezk 41:2
twenty cubits, before the **n**; Ezk 41:4 1964
he also *measured* the inner **n** and Ezk 41:15 1964
as well as *on* the wall of the **n**. Ezk 41:20 1964
doorposts of the **n** were square; Ezk 41:21 1964
The **n** and the sanctuary each Ezk 41:23 1964
on them, on the doors of the **n**, Ezk 41:25 1964

NAVEL
"Your **n** is *like* a round goblet SS 7:2 8270
were born your **n** cord was not cut, Ezk 16:4 8270

NAZARENE
"He shall be called a **N**." Mt 2:23 *3480*
he heard that it was Jesus the **N**, Mk 10:47 *3479*
"You also were with Jesus the **N**." Mk 14:67 *3479*
you are looking for Jesus the **N**, Mk 16:6 *3479*
"The things about Jesus the **N**, Lk 24:19 *3479*
They answered Him, "Jesus the **N**." Jn 18:5 *3480*
And they said, "Jesus the **N**." Jn 18:7 *3480*
"JESUS THE **N**, THE KING Jn 19:19 *3480*
Jesus the **N**, a man attested to you Ac 2:22 *3480*
In the name of Jesus Christ the **N** Ac 3:6 *3480*
by the name of Jesus Christ the **N**, Ac 4:10 *3480*
heard him say that this **N**, Jesus, Ac 6:14 *3480*
'I am Jesus the **N**, whom you are Ac 22:8 *3480*

NAZARENES
a ringleader of the sect of the **N**. Ac 24:5 *3480*

NAZARETH
and lived in a city called **N** Mt 2:23 *3478*
and leaving **N**, He came and settled Mt 4:13 *3478*
Jesus, from **N** in Galilee." Mt 21:11 *3478*
"This man was with Jesus of **N**." Mt 26:71 *3480*
days Jesus came from **N** in Galilee Mk 1:9 *3478*
have with each other, Jesus of **N**? Mk 1:24 *3479*
to a city in Galilee called **N**, Lk 1:26 *3478*
from Galilee, from the city of **N**, Lk 2:4 *3478*
Galilee, to their own city of **N**. Lk 2:39 *3478*
down with them and came to **N** Lk 2:51 *3478*
And He came to **N**, where He had Lk 4:16 *3478*
have with each other, Jesus of **N**? Lk 4:34 *3479*
that Jesus of **N** was passing by. Lk 18:37 *3480*
the Prophets wrote—Jesus of **N**, Jn 1:45 *3478*
Can any good thing come out of **N** Jn 1:46 *3478*
"*You know of* Jesus of **N**, Ac 10:38 *3478*
hostile to the name of Jesus of **N**. Ac 26:9 *3480*

NAZIRITE
a special vow, the vow of a **N**, Nu 6:2 5139
to the LORD his days as a **N**, Nu 6:12 5145
'Now this is the law of the **N** when Nu 6:13 5139
'The **N** shall then shave his Nu 6:18 5139
shall put *them* on the hands of the **N** Nu 6:19 5139
afterward the **N** may drink wine.' Nu 6:20 5139
"This is the law of the **N** who Nu 6:21 5139
shall be a **N** to God from the womb; Jg 13:5 5139
for the boy shall be a **N** to God Jg 13:7 5139
a **N** to God from my mother's womb. Jg 16:17 5139

NAZIRITES
some of your young men to be **N**. Am 2:11 5139
"But you made the **N** drink wine, Am 2:12 5139

NEAH
to Rimmon which stretches to **N**. Jos 19:13 5269

NEAPOLIS
and on the day following to **N**; Ac 16:11 *3496*

NEAR
about when he came **n** to Egypt, Gn 12:11 7126
Abraham came **n** and said, Gn 18:23 5066
Lot and came **n** to break the door. Gn 19:9 5066
this town is **n** *enough* to flee to, Gn 19:20 7138
Now Abimelech had not come **n** her; Gn 20:4 7126
of mourning for my father are **n**; Gn 27:41 7126
until he came **n** to his brother. Gn 33:3 5066
maids came **n** with their children, Gn 33:6 5066
Leah likewise came **n** with her Gn 33:7 5066
Joseph came **n** with Rachel, Gn 33:7 5066
under the oak which was **n** Shechem. Gn 35:4 5973
came **n** to Joseph's house steward, Gn 43:19 5066
of Goshen, and you shall be **n** me, Gn 45:10 7138
the time for Israel to die drew **n**, Gn 47:29 7126
"Do not come **n** here; Ex 3:5 7126
let him come **n** to celebrate it; Ex 12:48 7126
Philistines, even though it was **n**; Ex 13:17 7138
As Pharaoh drew **n**, Ex 14:10 7126
not come **n** the other all night. Ex 14:20 7126
'Come **n** before the LORD, for He Ex 16:9 7126
do not go **n** a woman." Ex 19:15 5066
the priests who come **n** to the LORD Ex 19:22 5066
however, shall come **n** to the LORD, Ex 24:2 5066
LORD, but they shall not come **n**, Ex 24:2 5066
"Then bring **n** to yourself Aaron Ex 28:1 7126
is **n** the ark of the testimony, Ex 30:6 5921
as soon as Moses came **n** the camp, Ex 32:19 7126
they were afraid to come **n** him. Ex 34:30 5066
all the sons of Israel came **n**, Ex 34:32 5066
had Aaron and his sons come **n** and Lv 8:6 7126
Moses had Aaron's sons come **n** Lv 8:13 7126
He also had Aaron's sons come **n**; Lv 8:24 7126
came **n** and stood before the LORD. Lv 9:5 7126
"Come **n** to the altar and offer Lv 9:7 7126
So Aaron came **n** to the altar and Lv 9:8 7126
'By those who come **n** Me I will be Lv 10:3 7138
who is **n** to him because she has Lv 21:3 7138
is to come **n** to offer the LORD's Lv 21:21 5066
not come **n** to offer the food of his Lv 21:21 5066
go in to the veil or come **n** the altar Lv 21:23 5066
who comes **n** shall be put to death. Nu 1:51 7131
"Bring the tribe of Levi **n** and Nu 3:6 7126
layman who comes **n** shall be put Nu 3:10 7131
layman coming **n** was to be put to Nu 3:38 7131
'Then the priest shall bring her **n** Nu 5:16 7126
shall not go **n** to a dead person. Nu 6:6
their coming **n** to the sanctuary." Nu 8:19 5066
and will bring *him* **n** to Himself; Nu 16:5 7126
He will bring **n** to Himself. Nu 16:5 7126
Israel, to bring you **n** to Himself, Nu 16:9 7126
and that He has brought you **n**, Nu 16:10 7126
descendants of Aaron should come **n** Nu 16:40 7126
"Everyone who comes **n**, Nu 17:13 7131
who comes **n** to the tabernacle of Nu 17:13 7131
n to the furnishings of the sanctuary Nu 18:3 7126
an outsider may not come **n** you. Nu 18:4 7126
outsider who comes **n** shall be put Nu 18:7 7131
Israel shall not come **n** the tent of Nu 18:22 7126
at Pethor, which is **n** the River, Nu 22:5 5921
I behold him, but not **n**; Nu 24:17 7138
the son of Joseph, came **n**; Nu 27:1 7126
Then they came **n** to him and said, Nu 32:16 5066
came **n** and spoke before Moses and Nu 36:1 7126
"Only you did not go **n** to the Dt 2:37 7126
nation is there that has a god so **n** Dt 4:7 7138
"You came **n** and stood at the Dt 4:11 7126
with fire, you came **n** to me, Dt 5:23 7126
'Go **n** and hear all that the LORD Dt 5:27 7126
around you, **n** you or far from you, Dt 13:7 7138
year, the year of remission, is **n**,' Dt 15:9 7126
come **n** and speak to the people. Dt 20:2 5066
the sons of Levi, shall come **n**, Dt 21:5 5066
If your countryman is not **n** you, Dt 22:2 7138
this woman, *but* when I came **n** her, Dt 22:14 7126
wife of one comes **n** to deliver her Dt 25:11 7126
"But the word is very **n** you, Dt 30:14 7138
the time for you to die is **n**; Dt 31:14 7126
the day of their calamity is **n**, Dt 32:35 7138
Do not come **n** it, that you may Jos 3:4 7126
to Ai, which is **n** Beth-aven, Jos 7:2 5973
you shall come **n** by your tribes. Jos 7:14 7126
by lot shall come **n** by families, Jos 7:14 7126
takes shall come **n** by households, Jos 7:14 7126
takes shall come **n** man by man. Jos 7:14 7126
and brought Israel **n** by tribes, Jos 7:16 7126
He brought the family of Judah **n**, Jos 7:17 7126
of the Zerahites **n** man by man, Jos 7:17 7126
his household **n** man by man; Jos 7:18 7126
were with him went up and drew **n** Jos 8:11 5066
"Come **n**, put your feet on the Jos 10:24 7126
So they came **n** and put their feet Jos 10:24 7126
Judah drew **n** to Joshua in Gilgal, Jos 14:6 5066
They came **n** before Eleazar the Jos 17:4 7126
n the hill which *lies* on the south Jos 18:13 5921
in Zaanannim, which is **n** Kedesh. Jg 4:11 854
Taanach **n** the waters of Megiddo; Jg 5:19 5921
they were **n** the house of Micah, Jg 18:3 5973
were in the houses **n** Micah's house Jg 18:22 5973
the valley which is **n** Beth-rehob. Jg 18:28
When they *were* **n** Jebus, the day Jg 19:11 5973
and the sun set on them **n** Gibeah Jg 19:14 681a
"Shall we again draw **n** for battle Jg 20:23 5066
drew **n** to battle against Israel. 1Sa 7:10 5066
all the tribes of Israel **n**, 1Sa 10:20 7126
he brought the tribe of Benjamin **n** 1Sa 10:21 7126
"Let us draw **n** to God here." 1Sa 14:36 7126
"Draw **n** here, all you chiefs of 1Sa 14:38 5066
and came and drew **n** to meet David, 1Sa 17:48 7126
people who were with him drew **n** 2Sa 10:13 5066
you go so **n** to the city to fight? 2Sa 11:20 5066
Why did you go so **n** the wall?' 2Sa 11:21 5066
in Baal-hazor, which is **n** Ephraim, 2Sa 13:23 5973
a man came **n** to prostrate himself 2Sa 15:5 7126
n the grave of my father and my 2Sa 19:37 5973
As David's time to die drew **n**, 1Ki 2:1 7126
land of the enemy, far off or **n**; 1Ki 8:46 7138
be **n** to the LORD our God day and 1Ki 8:59 7138
which is **n** Eloth on the shore of 1Ki 9:26 854
came **n** to all the people and said, 1Ki 18:21 5066
to all the people, "Come **n** to me." 1Ki 18:30 5066
So all the people came **n** to him. 1Ki 18:30 5066
the prophet came **n** and said, 1Ki 18:36 5066
came **n** to the king of Israel and 1Ki 20:22 5066
Then a man of God came **n** and spoke 1Ki 20:28 5066
son of Chenaanah came **n** and struck 1Ki 22:24 5066
Gehazi came **n** to push her away; 2Ki 4:27 5066
came **n** and spoke to him and said, 2Ki 5:13 5066
Moreover those who were **n** to them, 1Ch 12:40 7138
people who were with him drew **n** 1Ch 19:14 5066
captive to a land far off or **n**, 2Ch 6:36 7138
son of Chenaanah came **n** and struck 2Ch 18:23 5066
come **n** and bring sacrifices and 2Ch 29:31 5066
Ammonite *was* **n** him and he said, Ne 4:3 681a
the Jews who lived **n** them came Ne 4:12 681a
while the trumpeter *stood* **n** me. Ne 4:18 681a
So Esther came **n** and touched the Es 5:2 7126
of King Ahasuerus, both **n** and far, Es 9:20 7138
'The light is **n**,' Jb 17:12 7138
"Then his soul draws **n** to the pit, Jb 33:22 7126
Let his maker bring **n** his sword. Jb 40:19 5066
"One is so **n** to another That no Jb 41:16 5066
not far from me, for trouble is **n**; Ps 22:11 7138
they will not come **n** to you. Ps 32:9 7126
LORD is **n** to the brokenhearted And Ps 34:18 7138
choose and bring **n** *to You* Ps 65:4 7126
draw **n** to my soul *and* redeem it; Ps 69:18 7126
we give thanks, For Your name is **n**; Ps 75:1 7138
His salvation is **n** to those who fear Ps 85:9 7138
And my life has drawn **n** to Sheol. Ps 88:3 5060
will any plague come **n** your tent. Ps 91:10 7126
they drew **n** to the gates of death. Ps 107:18 5060
follow after wickedness draw **n**; Ps 119:150 7126
You are **n**, O LORD, And all Your Ps 119:151 7138
LORD is **n** to all who call upon Him, Ps 145:18 7138
sons of Israel, a people **n** to Him. Ps 148:14 7138
do not go **n** the door of her house, Pr 5:8 7126
through the street **n** her corner; Pr 7:8 681a
Better is a neighbor who is **n** than a Pr 27:10 7138
and draw **n** to listen rather than Ec 5:1 7138
years draw **n** when you will say, Ec 12:1 5060
the Holy One of Israel draw **n** And Is 5:19 7126
for the day of the LORD is **n**! Is 13:6 7138
a pillar to the LORD **n** its border. Is 19:19 681a
this people draw **n** with their words Is 29:13 5066
And you who are **n**, acknowledge My Is 33:13 7138
Draw **n**, O nations, to hear; Is 34:1 7126
They have drawn **n** and have come. Is 41:5 7126
Draw **n** together, you fugitives of Is 45:20 5066
"I bring **n** My righteousness, it Is 46:13 7126
"Come **n** to Me, listen to this: Is 48:16 7126
He who vindicates Me is **n**; Is 50:8 7138
Let him draw **n** to Me. Is 50:8 5066
"My righteousness is **n**, Is 51:5 7138
for it will not come **n** you. Is 54:14 7126
Call upon Him while He is **n**. Is 55:6 7138
who is far and to him who is **n**," Is 57:19 7138
to yourself, do not come **n** me, Is 65:5 5066
You are **n** to their lips But far Jer 12:2 7138
"Am I a God who is **n**," Jer 23:23 7138
the kings of the north, **n** and far, Jer 25:26 7138
And I will bring him **n** and Jer 30:21 7126
n the chamber of the officials, Jer 35:4 681a
And draw **n** for the battle! Jer 46:3 5066
of the land of Moab, far and **n**. Jer 48:24 7138
drew **n** when I called on You; La 3:57 7126
Our end drew **n**, Our days were La 4:18 7126
who is **n** will fall by the sword, Ezk 6:12 7138
The time has come, the day is **n** Ezk 7:7 7138
"Draw **n**, O executioners of the Ezk 9:1 7126
'*The time* is not **n** to build houses. Ezk 11:3 7138
"The days draw **n** as well as the Ezk 12:23 7126
day **n** and have come to your years; Ezk 22:4 7126
"Those who are **n** and those who Ezk 22:5 7138
and officials, the ones **n**, Ezk 23:12 7138
"For the day is **n**, Even the day Ezk 30:3 7138
Even the day of the LORD is **n**; Ezk 30:3 7138
who from the sons of Levi come **n** Ezk 40:46 7131
the priests who are **n** to the LORD Ezk 42:13 7138
draw **n** to Me to minister to Me,' Ezk 43:19 7138
"And they shall not come **n** to Me Ezk 44:13 5066
come **n** to any of My holy things, Ezk 44:13 5066
come **n** to Me to minister to Me; Ezk 44:15 7126
they shall come **n** to My table to Ezk 44:16 7126
come **n** to minister to the LORD, Ezk 45:4 7131
Then Nebuchadnezzar came **n** to the Da 3:26 7127
he had come **n** the den to Daniel, Da 6:20 7127
he came **n** to where I was standing, Da 8:17 681a
For the day of the LORD is **n**, Jl 1:15 7138
the LORD is coming; Surely it is **n**, Jl 2:1 7138
Let all the soldiers draw **n**, Jl 3:9 5066
day of the LORD is **n** in the valley Jl 3:14 7138
you bring **n** the seat of violence? Am 6:3 5066
LORD draws **n** on all the nations. Ob 1:15 7138
For the day of the LORD is **n**, Zph 1:7 7138
N is the great day of the LORD, Zph 1:14 7138
LORD, **N** and coming very quickly; Zph 1:14 7138
She did not draw **n** to her God. Zph 3:2 7126
I will draw **n** to you for judgment; Mal 3:5 7126
leaves, you know that summer is **n**; Mt 24:32 *1451*
things, recognize that He is **n**, Mt 24:33 *1451*
"My time is **n**; I *am to* keep Mt 26:18 *1451*
no longer room, not even **n** the door; Mk 2:2 *4314*
Bethany, **n** the Mount of Olives, Mk 11:1 *4314*
leaves, you know that summer is **n**. Mk 13:28 *1451*
happening, recognize that He is **n**, Mk 13:29 *1451*
kingdom of God has come **n** to you.' Lk 10:9 *1448*
the kingdom of God has come **n**.' Lk 10:11 *1448*
in heaven, where no thief comes **n** nor Lk 12:33 *1448*
coming **n** Him to listen to Him. Lk 15:1 *1448*
and when he came **n**, Lk 18:40 *1448*
because He was **n** Jerusalem, Lk 19:11 *1451*
n the mount that is called Olivet, Lk 19:29 *4314*
n the descent of the Mount of Lk 19:37 *4314*
'The time is **n**.' Do not go after Lk 21:8 *1448*
recognize that her desolation is **n**. Lk 21:20 *1448*
your redemption is drawing **n**." Lk 21:28 *1448*
yourselves that summer is now **n**. Lk 21:30 *1451*
that the kingdom of God is **n**. Lk 21:31 *1451*
stood **n** them in dazzling clothing; Lk 24:4 *2186*
The Passover of the Jews was **n**, Jn 2:13 *1451*
was baptizing in Aenon **n** Salim, Jn 3:23 *1451*
n the parcel of ground that Jacob Jn 4:5 *4139*
of the Jews, was **n**. Jn 6:4 *1451*
the sea and drawing **n** to the boat; Jn 6:19 *1451*
boats from Tiberias **n** to the place Jn 6:23 *1451*
Feast of Booths, was **n**. Jn 7:2 *1451*
Now Bethany was **n** Jerusalem, about Jn 11:18 *1451*
to the country **n** the wilderness, Jn 11:54 *1451*
Now the Passover of the Jews was **n**, Jn 11:55 *1451*
was crucified was **n** the city; Jn 19:20 *1451*
Olivet, which is **n** Jerusalem, Ac 1:12 *1451*
Since Lydda was **n** Joppa, Ac 9:38 *1451*
to me, and standing **n** said to me, Ac 22:13 *2186*
him before he comes **n** *the place*." Ac 23:15 *1448*
n which was the city of Lasea. Ac 27:8 *1451*
THE WORD IS **N** YOU, in your mouth Ro 10:8 *1451*
and the day is **n**. Therefore let us Ro 13:12 *1448*
brought **n** by the blood of Christ. Eph 2:13 *1451*
AND PEACE TO THOSE WHO WERE **N**; Eph 2:17 *1451*
be known to all men. The Lord is **n**. Php 4:5 *1451*
Therefore let us draw **n** with Heb 4:16 *4334*
through which we draw **n** to God. Heb 7:19 *1448*

who draw **n** to God through Him,	**Heb 7:25**	*4334*
make perfect those who draw **n**.	**Heb 10:1**	*4334*
let us draw **n** with a sincere heart	**Heb 10:22**	*4334*
as you see the day drawing **n**.	**Heb 10:25**	*1448*
Draw **n** to God and He will draw	**Jas 4:8**	*1448*
to God and He will draw **n** to you.	**Jas 4:8**	*1448*
for the coming of the Lord is **n**.	**Jas 5:8**	*1448*
The end of all things is **n**;	**1Pe 4:7**	*1448*
for the time is **n**.	**Rv 1:3**	*1451*
of this book, for the time is **n**.	**Rv 22:10**	*1451*

NEARBY

of the cities of these nations **n**.	**Dt 20:15**	2008
those who are **n** and those who are	**Da 9:7**	7138
go somewhere else to the towns **n**,	**Mk 1:38**	*2192*
was a large herd of swine feeding **n**	**Mk 5:11**	*1563*
one of the officers standing **n** struck	**Jn 18:22**	*3936*
disciple whom He loved standing **n**,	**Jn 19:26**	*3936*
since the tomb was **n**,	**Jn 19:42**	*1451*

NEARER

And he came **n** and nearer.	**2Sa 18:25**	1980
And he came nearer and **n**.	**2Sa 18:25**	7131
salvation is **n** to us than when we	**Ro 13:11**	*1451*

NEAREST

he and his neighbor **n** to his house	**Ex 12:4**	7138
his relatives who are **n** to him,	**Lv 21:2**	7138
then his **n** kinsman is to come and	**Lv 25:25**	7138
his **n** relative in his own family,	**Nu 27:11**	7138
city which is **n** to the slain man,	**Dt 21:3**	7138
that city which is **n** to the slain man	**Dt 21:6**	7138

NEARIAH

Hattush, Igal, Bariah, **N** and	**1Ch 3:22**	5294
The sons of **N** *were* Elioenai,	**1Ch 3:23**	5294
to Mount Seir, with Pelatiah, **N**,	**1Ch 4:42**	5294

NEARLY

of it, for the oxen **n** upset *it*.	**2Sa 6:6**	
ark, because the oxen **n** upset *it*.	**1Ch 13:9**	
and the day is now **n** over."	**Lk 24:29**	*2827*
The next Sabbath **n** the whole city	**Ac 13:44**	*4975*

NEARNESS

for me, the **n** of God is my good;	**Ps 73:28**	7132
They delight in the **n** of God.	**Is 58:2**	7132

NEBAI

Hariph, Anathoth, **N**,	**Ne 10:19**	5109

NEBAIOTH

N, the firstborn of Ishmael, and	**Gn 25:13**	5032
Abraham's son, the sister of **N**.	**Gn 28:9**	5032
daughter, the sister of **N**.	**Gn 36:3**	5032
the firstborn of Ishmael *was* **N**,	**1Ch 1:29**	5032
rams of **N** will minister to you;	**Is 60:7**	5032

NEBALLAT

Hadid, Zeboim, **N**,	**Ne 11:34**	5041

NEBAT

Then Jeroboam the son of **N**,	**1Ki 11:26**	5028
Jeroboam the son of **N** heard *of it*,	**1Ki 12:2**	5028
to Jeroboam the son of **N**.	**1Ki 12:15**	5028
of King Jeroboam, the son of **N**,	**1Ki 15:1**	5028
house of Jeroboam the son of **N**.	**1Ki 16:3**	5028
the way of Jeroboam the son of **N**	**1Ki 16:26**	5028
the sins of Jeroboam the son of **N**,	**1Ki 16:31**	5028
house of Jeroboam the son of **N**,	**1Ki 21:22**	5028
the way of Jeroboam the son of **N**,	**1Ki 22:52**	5028
the sins of Jeroboam the son of **N**,	**2Ki 3:3**	5028
house of Jeroboam the son of **N**,	**2Ki 9:9**	5028
the sins of Jeroboam the son of **N**,	**2Ki 10:29**	5028
the sins of Jeroboam the son of **N**,	**2Ki 13:2**	5028
the sins of Jeroboam the son of **N**,	**2Ki 13:11**	5028
the sins of Jeroboam the son of **N**,	**2Ki 14:24**	5028
the sins of Jeroboam the son of **N**,	**2Ki 15:9**	5028
the sins of Jeroboam the son of **N**,	**2Ki 15:18**	5028
the sins of Jeroboam son of **N**,	**2Ki 15:24**	5028
the sins of Jeroboam the son of **N**,	**2Ki 15:28**	5028
made Jeroboam the son of **N** king.	**2Ki 17:21**	5028
place which Jeroboam the son of **N**,	**2Ki 23:15**	5028
concerning Jeroboam the son of **N**?	**2Ch 9:29**	5028
Jeroboam the son of **N** heard *of it*	**2Ch 10:2**	5028
to Jeroboam the son of **N**.	**2Ch 10:15**	5028
"Yet Jeroboam the son of **N**,	**2Ch 13:6**	5028

NEBO

Elealeh, Sebam, **N** and Beon,	**Nu 32:3**	5015a
and **N** and Baal-meon	**Nu 32:38**	5015a
the mountains of Abarim, before **N**.	**Nu 33:47**	5015a
mountain of the Abarim, Mount **N**,	**Dt 32:49**	5015a
the plains of Moab to Mount **N**,	**Dt 34:1**	5015a
in Aroer, even to **N** and Baal-meon.	**1Ch 5:8**	5015a
the sons of **N**, 52;	**Ezr 2:29**	5015a
Of the sons of **N** *there were* Jeiel,	**Ezr 10:43**	5015a
the men of the other **N**,	**Ne 7:33**	5015a
Moab wails over **N** and Medeba;	**Is 15:2**	5015a
Bel has bowed down, **N** stoops over;	**Is 46:1**	5015b
"Woe to **N**, for it has been	**Jer 48:1**	5015a
against Dibon, **N** and	**Jer 48:22**	5015a

NEBUCHADNEZZAR

days **N** king of Babylon came up,	**2Ki 24:1**	5019
At that time the servants of **N**	**2Ki 24:10**	5019
And **N** the king of Babylon came to	**2Ki 24:11**	5019
N king of Babylon came,	**2Ki 25:1**	5019
was the nineteenth year of King **N**,	**2Ki 25:8**	5019
whom **N** king of Babylon had left,	**2Ki 25:22**	5019
Jerusalem away into exile by **N**.	**1Ch 6:15**	5019
N king of Babylon came up against	**2Ch 36:6**	5019
N also brought *some* of the	**2Ch 36:7**	5019
N sent and brought him to Babylon	**2Ch 36:10**	5019
He also rebelled against King **N**	**2Ch 36:13**	5019
which **N** had carried away from	**Ezr 1:7**	5019
exiles whom **N** the king of Babylon	**Ezr 2:1**	5019
the hand of **N** king of Babylon,	**Ezr 5:12**	5020
which **N** had taken from the temple	**Ezr 5:14**	5020
which **N** took from the temple in	**Ezr 6:5**	5020
exiles whom **N** the king of Babylon	**Ne 7:6**	5019
whom **N** the king of Babylon had	**Es 2:6**	5019
for **N** king of Babylon is warring	**Jer 21:2**	5019
the hand of **N** king of Babylon,	**Jer 21:7**	5019
the hand of **N** king of Babylon and	**Jer 22:25**	5019
After **N** king of Babylon had	**Jer 24:1**	5019
first year of **N** king of Babylon),	**Jer 25:1**	5019
I will send to **N** king of Babylon,	**Jer 25:9**	5019
the hand of **N** king of Babylon,	**Jer 27:6**	5019
not serve him, **N** king of Babylon,	**Jer 27:8**	5019
which **N** king of Babylon did not	**Jer 27:20**	5019
which **N** king of Babylon took away	**Jer 28:3**	5019
the yoke of **N** king of Babylon from	**Jer 28:11**	5019
they may serve **N** king of Babylon;	**Jer 28:14**	5019
people whom **N** had taken into exile	**Jer 29:1**	5019
to Babylon to **N** king of Babylon,	**Jer 29:3**	5019
the hand of **N** king of Babylon,	**Jer 29:21**	5019
was the eighteenth year of **N**.	**Jer 32:1**	5019
the hand of **N** king of Babylon,	**Jer 32:28**	5019
when **N** king of Babylon and all his	**Jer 34:1**	5019
when **N** king of Babylon came up	**Jer 35:11**	5019
N king of Babylon had made king	**Jer 37:1**	5019
N king of Babylon and all his army	**Jer 39:1**	5019
brought him up to **N** king of Babylon	**Jer 39:5**	5019
Now **N** king of Babylon gave orders	**Jer 39:11**	5019
and get **N** the king of Babylon,	**Jer 43:10**	5019
to the hand of **N** king of Babylon,	**Jer 44:30**	5019
which **N** king of Babylon defeated	**Jer 46:2**	5019
the coming of **N** king of Babylon	**Jer 46:13**	5019
even into the hand of **N** king of	**Jer 46:26**	5019
which **N** king of Babylon defeated.	**Jer 49:28**	5019
"For **N** king of Babylon has formed	**Jer 49:30**	5019
his bones is **N** king of Babylon.	**Jer 50:17**	5019
"**N** king of Babylon has devoured	**Jer 51:34**	5019
that **N** king of Babylon came,	**Jer 52:4**	5019
was the nineteenth year of King **N**,	**Jer 52:12**	5019
whom **N** carried away into exile:	**Jer 52:28**	5019
of **N** 832 persons from Jerusalem;	**Jer 52:29**	5019
in the twenty-third year of **N**,	**Jer 52:30**	5019
from the north **N** king of Babylon,	**Ezk 26:7**	5019
N king of Babylon made his army	**Ezk 29:18**	5019
of Egypt to **N** king of Babylon.	**Ezk 29:19**	5019
By the hand of **N** king of Babylon.	**Ezk 30:10**	5019
N king of Babylon came to	**Da 1:1**	5019
officials presented them before **N**.	**Da 1:18**	5019
the second year of the reign of **N**,	**Da 2:1**	5019
of Nebuchadnezzar, **N** had dreams;	**Da 2:1**	5019
and He has made known to King **N**	**Da 2:28**	5020
Then King **N** fell on his face and	**Da 2:46**	5020
N the king made an image of gold,	**Da 3:1**	5020
Then **N** the king sent *word* to	**Da 3:2**	5020
image that **N** the king had set up.	**Da 3:2**	5020
image that **N** the king had set up;	**Da 3:3**	5020
the image that **N** had set up.	**Da 3:3**	5020
image that **N** the king has set up.	**Da 3:5**	5020
image that **N** the king had set up.	**Da 3:7**	5020
responded and said to **N** the king:	**Da 3:9**	5020
Then **N** in rage and anger gave	**Da 3:13**	5020
N responded and said to them,	**Da 3:14**	5020
"O **N**, we do not need to give you	**Da 3:16**	5020
Then **N** was filled with wrath, and	**Da 3:19**	5020
Then **N** the king was astounded and	**Da 3:24**	5020
Then **N** came near to the door of	**Da 3:26**	5020
N responded and said,	**Da 3:28**	5020
N the king to all the peoples,	**Da 4:1**	5020
"I, **N**, was at ease in my house	**Da 4:4**	5020
'This is the dream *which* I, King **N**,	**Da 4:18**	5020
"All *this* happened to **N** the king.	**Da 4:28**	5020
'King **N**, to you it is declared:	**Da 4:31**	5020
word concerning **N** was fulfilled;	**Da 4:33**	5020
at the end of that period, I, **N**,	**Da 4:34**	5020
"Now I, **N**, praise, exalt and honor	**Da 4:37**	5020
vessels which **N** his father had taken	**Da 5:2**	5020
And King **N**, your father, your	**Da 5:11**	5020
and majesty to **N** your father.	**Da 5:18**	5020

NEBUSHAZBAN

word, along with **N** the Rab-saris,	**Jer 39:13**	5021

NEBUZARADAN

N the captain of the guard,	**2Ki 25:8**	5018
N the captain of the guard carried	**2Ki 25:11**	5018
N the captain of the guard	**2Ki 25:20**	5018
N the captain of the bodyguard	**Jer 39:9**	5018
N the captain of the bodyguard	**Jer 39:10**	5018
N the captain of the bodyguard,	**Jer 39:11**	5018
So **N** the captain of the bodyguard	**Jer 39:13**	5018
after **N** captain of the bodyguard	**Jer 40:1**	5018
whom **N** the captain of the	**Jer 41:10**	5018
N the captain of the bodyguard had	**Jer 43:6**	5018
N the captain of the bodyguard,	**Jer 52:12**	5018
Then **N** the captain of the guard	**Jer 52:15**	5018
But **N** the captain of the guard	**Jer 52:16**	5018
N the captain of the guard	**Jer 52:26**	5018
N the captain of the guard carried	**Jer 52:30**	5018

NECESSARY

of His mouth more than my **n** food.	**Jb 23:12**	2706
but *only* one thing is **n**,	**Lk 10:42**	*5532*
"Was it not **n** for the Christ to	**Lk 24:26**	*1163*
"Therefore it is **n** that of the	**Ac 1:21**	*1163*
"It was **n** that the word of God	**Ac 13:46**	*316*
"It is **n** to circumcise them and	**Ac 15:5**	*1163*
it is **n** to be in subjection,	**Ro 13:5**	*318*
which seem to be weaker are **n**;	**1Co 12:22**	*316*
So I thought it **n** to urge the	**2Co 9:5**	*316*
Boasting is **n**, though it is not	**2Co 12:1**	*1163*
the flesh is more **n** for your sake.	**Php 1:24**	*316*
it **n** to send to you Epaphroditus,	**Php 2:25**	*316*
n that this *high priest* also have	**Heb 8:3**	*316*
Therefore it was **n** for the copies	**Heb 9:23**	*318*
them what is **n** for *their* body,	**Jas 2:16**	*2006*
now for a little while, if **n**,	**1Pe 1:6**	*1189b*

NECESSITY

of **n** there takes place a change of	**Heb 7:12**	*318*
there must of **n** be the death of	**Heb 9:16**	*318*
I felt the **n** to write to you	**Jude 1:3**	*318*

NECK

and on the smooth part of his **n**.	**Gn 27:16**	6677
break his yoke from your **n**."	**Gn 27:40**	6677
and fell on his **n** and kissed him,	**Gn 33:4**	6677
the gold necklace around his **n**.	**Gn 41:42**	6677
he fell on his brother Benjamin's **n**	**Gn 45:14**	6677
and Benjamin wept on his **n**.	**Gn 45:14**	6677
he fell on his **n** and wept on his	**Gn 46:29**	6677
and wept on his **n** a long time.	**Gn 46:29**	6677
shall be on the **n** of your enemies;	**Gn 49:8**	6203
it, then you shall break its **n**;	**Ex 13:13**	6202
it, then you shall break its **n**.	**Ex 34:20**	6202
its head at the front of its **n**,	**Lv 5:8**	6203
heart, and stiffen your **n** no longer.	**Dt 10:16**	6203
and shall break the heifer's **n** there	**Dt 21:4**	6202
whose **n** was broken in the valley;	**Dt 21:6**	6202
He will put an iron yoke on your **n**	**Dt 28:48**	6677
on the **n** of the spoiler?'	**Jg 5:30**	6677
and besides the **n** bands that *were*	**Jg 8:26**	6060
and his **n** was broken and he died,	**1Sa 4:18**	4665
stiffened their **n** like their fathers,	**2Ki 17:14**	6203
stiffen your **n** like your fathers,	**2Ch 30:8**	6203
But he stiffened his **n** and	**2Ch 36:13**	6203
shoulder and stiffened their **n**,	**Ne 9:29**	6203
He has grasped me by the **n** and	**Jb 16:12**	6203
Do you clothe his **n** with a mane?	**Jb 39:19**	6677
"In his **n** lodges strength, And	**Jb 41:22**	6677
head And ornaments about your **n**.	**Pr 1:9**	1621
Bind them around your **n**,	**Pr 3:3**	1621
soul And adornment to your **n**.	**Pr 3:22**	1621
Tie them around your **n**.	**Pr 6:21**	1621
A man who hardens *his* **n** after much	**Pr 29:1**	6203
Your **n** with strings of beads."	**SS 1:10**	6677
"Your **n** is like the tower of	**SS 4:4**	6677
"Your **n** is like a tower of ivory,	**SS 7:4**	6677
It will reach even to the **n**;	**Is 8:8**	6677
and his yoke from your **n**,	**Is 10:27**	6677
torrent, Which reaches to the **n**,	**Is 30:28**	6677
And your **n** is an iron sinew And	**Is 48:4**	6203
from the chains around your **n**,	**Is 52:2**	6677
like the one who breaks a dog's **n**;	**Is 66:3**	6202
their ear, but stiffened their **n**;	**Jer 7:26**	6203
and yokes and put them on your **n**,	**Jer 27:2**	6677
and which will not put its **n** under	**Jer 27:8**	6677
nation which will bring its **n** under	**Jer 27:11**	6677
took the yoke from the **n** of Jeremiah	**Jer 28:10**	6677
from the **n** of all the nations.' "	**Jer 28:11**	6677
off the **n** of the prophet Jeremiah,	**Jer 28:12**	6677
on the **n** of all these nations,	**Jer 28:14**	6677
break his yoke from off their **n** and	**Jer 30:8**	6677
They have come upon my **n**;	**La 1:14**	6677
and a necklace around your **n**.	**Ezk 16:11**	1627
a necklace of gold around his **n**,	**Da 5:7**	6676
a necklace of gold around your **n**,	**Da 5:16**	6676
a necklace of gold around his **n**.	**Da 5:29**	6676
come over her fair **n** *with a yoke*;	**Hos 10:11**	6677
To lay him open from thigh to **n**.	**Hab 3:13**	6677
millstone hung around his **n**,	**Mt 18:6**	*5137*
heavy millstone hung around his **n**,	**Mk 9:42**	*5137*
a millstone were hung around his **n**	**Lk 17:2**	*5137*
placing upon the **n** of the disciples	**Ac 15:10**	*5137*

NECKLACE

put the gold **n** around his neck.	**Gn 41:42**	7242
Therefore pride is their **n**;	**Ps 73:6**	6059
With a single strand of your **n**.	**SS 4:9**	6701b
hands and a **n** around your neck.	**Ezk 16:11**	7242
have a **n** of gold around his neck,	**Da 5:7**	2002
wear a **n** of gold around your neck,	**Da 5:16**	2002
put a **n** of gold around his neck,	**Da 5:29**	2002

NECKLACES

signet rings, earrings and **n**,	**Nu 31:50**	3558

NECKS

feet on the **n** of these kings."	**Jos 10:24**	6677
and put their feet on their **n**.	**Jos 10:24**	6677
which were on their camels' **n**.	**Jg 8:21**	6677
that *were* on their camels' **n**.	**Jg 8:26**	6677
but stiffened their **n** in order not	**Jer 17:23**	6203
stiffened their **n** so as not to heed	**Jer 19:15**	6203
"Bring your **n** under the yoke of	**Jer 27:12**	6677
Our pursuers are at our **n**;	**La 5:5**	6677
the **n** of the wicked who are slain,	**Ezk 21:29**	6677
which you cannot remove your **n**;	**Mi 2:3**	6677
for my life risked their own **n**,	**Ro 16:4**	*5137*

NECO

Pharaoh **N** king of Egypt went up	**2Ki 23:29**	6549
and when *Pharaoh* **N** saw him he	**2Ki 23:29**	
Pharaoh **N** imprisoned him at	**2Ki 23:33**	6549
Pharaoh **N** made Eliakim the son	**2Ki 23:34**	6549
to give it to Pharaoh **N**.	**2Ki 23:35**	6549
N king of Egypt came up to make	**2Ch 35:20**	5224
But **N** sent messengers to him,	**2Ch 35:21**	
words of **N** from the mouth of God,	**2Ch 35:22**	5224
But **N** took Joahaz his brother and	**2Ch 36:4**	5224
army of Pharaoh **N** king of Egypt,	**Jer 46:2**	6549

NEDABIAH

Jekamiah, Hoshama and **N**.	**1Ch 3:18**	5072

NEED

But he said, "What **n** is there?	**Gn 33:15**	
the priest **n** not seek for the	**Lv 13:36**	
in the house **n** not become unclean;	**Lv 14:36**	

for his **n** *in* whatever he lacks.	**Dt 15:8**	4270
three thousand men **n** go up to Ai;	**Jos 7:3**	
the Levites will no longer **n** to	**1Ch 23:26**	
timber you **n** from Lebanon and	**2Ch 2:16**	6878
'You **n** not fight in this	**2Ch 20:17**	
"For He does not **n** *to* consider a	**Jb 34:23**	
And your **n** like an armed man.	**Pr 6:11**	4270
But the stomach of the wicked is in **n**.	**Pr 13:25**	2637
Eat *only* what you **n**,	**Pr 25:16**	1767
we do not **n** to give you an answer	**Da 3:16**	2818
"I have **n** to be baptized by You,	**Mt 3:14**	*5532*
your Father knows what you **n** before	**Mt 6:8**	*5532*
knows that you **n** all these things.	**Mt 6:32**	*5535*
who are healthy who **n** a physician,	**Mt 9:12**	*5532*
"They do not **n** to go away;	**Mt 14:16**	*5532*
'The Lord has **n** of them,' and	**Mt 21:3**	*5532*
further **n** do we have of witnesses?	**Mt 26:65**	*5532*
who are healthy who **n** a physician,	**Mk 2:17**	*5532*
he was in **n** and he and his companions	**Mk 2:25**	*5532*
'The Lord has **n** of it';	**Mk 11:3**	*5532*
further **n** do we have of witnesses?	**Mk 14:63**	*5532*
who are well who **n** a physician,	**Lk 5:31**	*5532*
curing those who had **n** of healing.	**Lk 9:11**	*5532*
knows that you **n** these things.	**Lk 12:30**	*5535*
and I **n** to go out and look at it;	**Lk 14:18**	*318*
persons who **n** no repentance.	**Lk 15:7**	*5532*
'The Lord has **n** of it.' "	**Lk 19:31**	*5532*
"The Lord has **n** of it."	**Lk 19:34**	*5532*
further **n** do we have of testimony?	**Lk 22:71**	*5532*
and because He did not **n** anyone to	**Jn 2:25**	*5532*
we have **n** of for the feast";	**Jn 13:29**	*5532*
no **n** for anyone to question You;	**Jn 16:30**	*5532*
with all, as anyone might have **n**.	**Ac 2:45**	*5532*
distributed to each as any had **n**.	**Ac 4:35**	*5532*
matter she may have **n** of you;	**Ro 16:2**	*5535*
"I have no **n** of you";	**1Co 12:21**	*5532*
"I have no **n** of you."	**1Co 12:21**	*5532*
presentable members have no **n**	**1Co 12:24**	*5532*
Or do we **n**, as some, letters of	**2Co 3:1**	*5535*
being a supply for their **n**,	**2Co 8:14**	*5303*
may become *a supply* for your **n**,	**2Co 8:14**	*5303*
I ask that when I am present I **n**	**2Co 10:2**	
was present with you and was in **n**,	**2Co 11:9**	*5302*
they fully supplied my **n**,	**2Co 11:9**	*5303*
so that when present I **n** not use	**2Co 13:10**	
to share with one who has **n**.	**Eph 4:28**	*5532*
according to the **n** *of the moment,*	**Eph 4:29**	*5532*
messenger and minister to my **n**;	**Php 2:25**	*5532*
having abundance and suffering **n**.	**Php 4:12**	*5302*
that we have no **n** to say anything.	**1Th 1:8**	*5532*
no **n** for *anyone* to write to you,	**1Th 4:9**	*5532*
outsiders and not be in any **n**.	**1Th 4:12**	*5532*
you have no **n** of anything to be	**1Th 5:1**	*5532*
who does not **n** to be ashamed,	**2Tm 2:15**	*422*
find grace to help in time of **n**.	**Heb 4:16**	*2121*
you have **n** again for someone to	**Heb 5:12**	*5532*
come to **n** milk and not solid food.	**Heb 5:12**	*5532*
what further **n** *was there* for	**Heb 7:11**	*5532*
who does not **n** daily, like those	**Heb 7:27**	*318*
For you have **n** of endurance, so	**Heb 10:36**	*5532*
clothing and in **n** of daily food,	**Jas 2:15**	*3007*
have no **n** for anyone to teach you;	**1Jn 2:27**	*5532*
and sees his brother in **n** and	**1Jn 3:17**	*5532*
wealthy, and have **n** of nothing,"	**Rv 3:17**	*5532*
And the city has no **n** of the sun	**Rv 21:23**	*5532*
not have **n** of the light of a lamp	**Rv 22:5**	*5532*

NEEDED

to the seed **n** for it:	**Lv 27:16**	
"Whatever is **n**, both young	**Ezr 6:9**	2819a
100 baths of oil, and salt as **n**.	**Ezr 7:22**	3792
hands, as though He **n** anything,	**Ac 17:25**	*4326*
they supplied *us* with all we **n**.	**Ac 28:10**	*5532*
He would have **n** to suffer often	**Heb 9:26**	*1163*

NEEDLE

to go through the eye of a **n**,	**Mt 19:24**	*4476*
camel to go through the eye of a **n**	**Mk 10:25**	*4476*
to go through the eye of a **n** than	**Lk 18:25**	*956a*

NEEDLESSLY

the Law, then Christ died **n**."	**Ga 2:21**	*1431*

NEEDS

let me *take care of* all your **n**;	**Jg 19:20**	4270
is asleep and **n** to be awakened."	**1Ki 18:27**	
the **n** for the house of your God,	**Ezr 7:20**	2819b
up and give him as much as he **n**.	**Lk 11:8**	*5535*
bathed **n** only to wash his feet,	**Jn 13:10**	*5532*
these hands ministered to my *own* **n**	**Ac 20:34**	*5532*
to the **n** of the saints,	**Ro 12:13**	*5532*
supplying the **n** of the saints,	**2Co 9:12**	*5303*
a gift more than once for my **n**.	**Php 4:16**	*5532*
And my God will supply all your **n**	**Php 4:19**	*5532*
in good deeds to meet pressing **n**,	**Ti 3:14**	*5532*

NEEDY

to your **n** *brother* in his dispute.	**Ex 23:6**	34
that the **n** of your people may eat;	**Ex 23:11**	34
for the **n** and for the stranger.	**Lv 19:10**	6041
them for the **n** and the alien.	**Lv 23:22**	6041
to your **n** and poor in your land.'	**Dt 15:11**	6041
a hired servant *who is* poor and **n**,	**Dt 24:14**	34
He lifts the **n** from the ash heap	**1Sa 2:8**	34
push the **n** aside from the road;	**Jb 24:4**	34
He kills the poor and the **n**,	**Jb 24:14**	34
"I was a father to the **n**,	**Jb 29:16**	34
Was not my soul grieved for the **n**?	**Jb 30:25**	34
Or that the **n** had no covering,	**Jb 31:19**	34
n will not always be forgotten,	**Ps 9:18**	34
because of the groaning of the **n**,	**Ps 12:5**	34
and the **n** from him who robs him?"	**Ps 35:10**	34
cast down the afflicted and the **n**,	**Ps 37:14**	34
Since I am afflicted and **n**,	**Ps 40:17**	34
For the LORD hears the **n** And	**Ps 69:33**	34
But I am afflicted and **n**;	**Ps 70:5**	34
Save the children of the **n** And	**Ps 72:4**	34
deliver the **n** when he cries for help,	**Ps 72:12**	34
have compassion on the poor and **n**,	**Ps 72:13**	34
the lives of the **n** he will save.	**Ps 72:13**	34
afflicted and **n** praise Your name.	**Ps 74:21**	34
Rescue the weak and **n**;	**Ps 82:4**	34
For I am afflicted and **n**.	**Ps 86:1**	34
But He sets the **n** securely on high	**Ps 107:41**	34
the afflicted and **n** man,	**Ps 109:16**	34
For I am afflicted and **n**,	**Ps 109:22**	34
stands at the right hand of the **n**,	**Ps 109:31**	34
And lifts the **n** from the ash heap,	**Ps 113:7**	34
I will satisfy her **n** with bread.	**Ps 132:15**	34
he who is gracious to the **n** honors	**Pr 14:31**	34
earth And the **n** from among men.	**Pr 30:14**	34
the rights of the afflicted and **n**.	**Pr 31:9**	34
stretches out her hands to the **n**.	**Pr 31:20**	34
So as to deprive the **n** of justice And	**Is 10:2**	1800b
the **n** will lie down in security;	**Is 14:30**	34
defense for the **n** in his distress,	**Is 25:4**	34
And the **n** of mankind will rejoice	**Is 29:19**	34
the **n** one speaks what is right.	**Is 32:7**	34
afflicted and **n** are seeking water,	**Is 41:17**	34
He has delivered the soul of the **n** one	**Jer 20:13**	34
the cause of the afflicted and **n**;	**Jer 22:16**	34
she did not help the poor and **n**.	**Ezk 16:49**	34
oppresses the poor and **n**,	**Ezk 18:12**	34
they have wronged the poor and **n**	**Ezk 22:29**	34
And the **n** for a pair of sandals.	**Am 2:6**	34
oppress the poor, who crush the **n**,	**Am 4:1**	34
Hear this, you who trample the **n**,	**Am 8:4**	34
And the **n** for a pair of sandals,	**Am 8:6**	34
was not a **n** person among them,	**Ac 4:34**	*1729b*

NEGEV

on, continuing toward the **N**.	**Gn 12:9**	5045
Abram went up from Egypt to the **N**,	**Gn 13:1**	5045
from the **N** as far as Bethel,	**Gn 13:3**	5045
there toward the land of the **N**,	**Gn 20:1**	5045
for he was living in the **N**.	**Gn 24:62**	5045
"Go up there into the **N**;	**Nu 13:17**	5045
When they had gone up into the **N**,	**Nu 13:22**	5045
Amalek is living in the land of the **N**	**Nu 13:29**	5045
king of Arad, who lived in the **N**,	**Nu 21:1**	5045
in the **N** in the land of Canaan,	**Nu 33:40**	5045
and in the **N** and by the seacoast,	**Dt 1:7**	5045
and the **N** and the plain in the	**Dt 34:3**	5045
the hill country and the **N** and the	**Jos 10:40**	5045
the hill country and all the **N**,	**Jos 11:16**	5045
in the wilderness, and in the **N**;	**Jos 12:8**	5045
have given me the land of the **N**,	**Jos 15:19**	5045
as Baalath-beer, Ramah of the **N**.	**Jos 19:8**	7437b
and in the **N** and in the lowland.	**Jg 1:9**	5045
have given me the land of the **N**,	**Jg 1:15**	5045
"Against the **N** of Judah and	**1Sa 27:10**	5045
against the **N** of the Jerahmeelites	**1Sa 27:10**	5045
against the **N** of the Kenites."	**1Sa 27:10**	5045
a raid on the **N** and on Ziklag,	**1Sa 30:1**	5045
raid on the **N** of the Cherethites,	**1Sa 30:14**	5045
to Judah, and on the **N** of Caleb,	**1Sa 30:14**	5045
those who were in Ramoth of the **N**,	**1Sa 30:27**	7418
the lowland and of the **N** of Judah,	**2Ch 28:18**	5045
As windstorms in the **N** sweep on,	**Is 21:1**	5045
concerning the beasts of the **N**.	**Is 30:6**	5045
cities of the **N** have been locked up,	**Jer 13:19**	5045
the hill country and from the **N**,	**Jer 17:26**	5045
and in the cities of the **N**;	**Jer 32:44**	5045
lowland, in the cities of the **N**,	**Jer 33:13**	5045
against the forest land of the **N**,	**Ezk 20:46**	5045
and say to the forest of the **N**,	**Ezk 20:47**	5045
Then *those of* the **N** will possess	**Ob 1:19**	5045
Will possess the cities of the **N**.	**Ob 1:20**	5045
and the **N** and the foothills were	**Zch 7:7**	5045

NEGLECT

"Also you shall not **n** the Levite	**Dt 14:27**	5800a
You are not allowed to **n** *them.*	**Dt 22:3**	5956
will not **n** the house of our God.	**Ne 10:39**	5800a
and be wise, And do not **n** *it.*	**Pr 8:33**	6544a
for they **n** their appearance so	**Mt 6:16**	*853*
not desirable for us to **n** the word	**Ac 6:2**	*2641*
n the spiritual gift within you,	**1Tm 4:14**	*272*
if we **n** so great a salvation?	**Heb 2:3**	*272*
Do not **n** to show hospitality to	**Heb 13:2**	*1950*
do not **n** doing good and sharing,	**Heb 13:16**	*1950*

NEGLECTED

"You **n** the Rock who begot you,	**Dt 32:18**	7876
And you **n** all my counsel And did	**Pr 1:25**	6544a
She *lies* **n** on her land;	**Am 5:2**	5203
n the weightier provisions of the law:	**Mt 23:23**	*863*
I have never **n** a command of yours;	**Lk 15:29**	*3928*

NEGLECTING

have done without **n** the others.	**Mt 23:23**	*863*
"**N** the commandment of God, you	**Mk 7:8**	*863*
have done without **n** the others.	**Lk 11:42**	*3935*

NEGLECTS

and yet **n** to observe the Passover,	**Nu 9:13**	2308
will come to him who **n** discipline,	**Pr 13:18**	6544a
who **n** discipline despises himself,	**Pr 15:32**	6544a

NEGLIGENCE

and no **n** or corruption was *to be*	**Da 6:4**	7960

NEGLIGENT

"My sons, do not be **n** now,	**2Ch 29:11**	7951
n in carrying out this *matter;*	**Ezr 4:22**	7960
is he who works with a **n** hand,	**Pr 10:4**	7423b

NEGLIGENTLY

the one who does the LORD's work **n**,	**Jer 48:10**	7423b

NEHELAMITE

To Shemaiah the **N** you shall speak,	**Jer 29:24**	5161
LORD concerning Shemaiah the **N**,	**Jer 29:31**	5161
the **N** and his descendants;	**Jer 29:32**	5161

NEHEMIAH

came with Zerubbabel, Jeshua, **N**,	**Ezr 2:2**	5166
words of **N** the son of Hacaliah.	**Ne 1:1**	5166
After him **N** the son of Azbuk,	**Ne 3:16**	5166
came with Zerubbabel, Jeshua, **N**,	**Ne 7:7**	5166
Then **N**, who was the governor, and	**Ne 8:9**	5166
N the governor, the son of	**Ne 10:1**	5166
and in the days of **N** the governor	**Ne 12:26**	5166
N gave the portions due the singers	**Ne 12:47**	5166

NEHUM

Bilshan, Mispereth, Bigvai, **N**,	**Ne 7:7**	5149

NEHUSHTA

and his mother's name *was* **N** the	**2Ki 24:8**	5179b

NEHUSHTAN

and it was called **N**.	**2Ki 18:4**	5180

NEIEL

northward to Beth-emek and **N**;	**Jos 19:27**	5272b

NEIGH

heifer And **n** like stallions,	**Jer 50:11**	6670a

NEIGHBOR

"But every woman shall ask of her **n**	**Ex 3:22**	7934
each man ask from his **n** and each	**Ex 11:2**	7453
each woman from her **n** for articles	**Ex 11:2**	7468
he and his **n** nearest to his house	**Ex 12:4**	7934
I judge between a man and his **n** and	**Ex 18:16**	7453
bear false witness against your **n**.	**Ex 20:16**	7453
anything that belongs to your **n**."	**Ex 20:17**	7453
acts presumptuously toward his **n**,	**Ex 21:14**	7453
"If a man gives his **n** money or	**Ex 22:7**	7453
condemn shall pay double to his **n**.	**Ex 22:9**	7453
"If a man gives his **n** a donkey,	**Ex 22:10**	7453
a man borrows *anything* from his **n**,	**Ex 22:14**	7453
friend, and every man his **n**.' "	**Ex 32:27**	7453
'You shall not oppress your **n**,	**Lv 19:13**	7453
you are to judge your **n** fairly.	**Lv 19:15**	5997
to act against the life of your **n**;	**Lv 19:16**	7453
you may surely reprove your **n**,	**Lv 19:17**	5997
you shall love your **n** as yourself;	**Lv 19:18**	7453
'If a man injures his **n**,	**Lv 24:19**	5997
who unintentionally slew his **n**	**Dt 4:42**	7453
bear false witness against your **n**.	**Dt 5:20**	7453
anything that belongs to your **n**.'	**Dt 5:21**	7453
what he has loaned to his **n**;	**Dt 15:2**	7453
exact it of his **n** and his brother,	**Dt 15:2**	7453
if there is a man who hates his **n**	**Dt 19:11**	7453
against his **n** and murders him,	**Dt 22:26**	7453
make your **n** a loan of any sort,	**Dt 24:10**	7453
he who strikes his **n** in secret.'	**Dt 27:24**	7453
because he struck his **n** without	**Jos 20:5**	7453
The **n** women gave him a name,	**Ru 4:17**	7934
to your **n**, who is better than you.	**1Sa 15:28**	7453
your hand and given it to your **n**,	**1Sa 28:17**	7453
his **n** and is made to take an oath,	**1Ki 8:31**	7453
"If a man sins against his **n** and	**2Ch 6:22**	7453
with God As a man with his **n**!	**Jb 16:21**	7453
tongue, Nor does evil to his **n**,	**Ps 15:3**	7453
Whoever secretly slanders his **n**,	**Ps 101:5**	7453
Do not say to your **n**,	**Pr 3:28**	7453
Do not devise harm against your **n**,	**Pr 3:29**	7453
you have become surety for your **n**,	**Pr 6:1**	7453
have come into the hand of your **n**,	**Pr 6:3**	7453
yourself, and importune your **n**.	**Pr 6:3**	7453
the godless man destroys his **n**,	**Pr 11:9**	7453
He who despises his **n** lacks sense,	**Pr 11:12**	7453
The righteous is a guide to his **n**,	**Pr 12:26**	7453
The poor is hated even by his **n**,	**Pr 14:20**	7453
He who despises his **n** sins,	**Pr 14:21**	7453
A man of violence entices his **n** And	**Pr 16:29**	7453
guarantor in the presence of his **n**.	**Pr 17:18**	7453
His **n** finds no favor in his eyes.	**Pr 21:10**	7453
against your **n** without cause,	**Pr 24:28**	7453
When your **n** humiliates you?	**Pr 25:8**	7453
Argue your case with your **n**,	**Pr 25:9**	7453
bears false witness against his **n**.	**Pr 25:18**	7453
So is the man who deceives his **n**,	**Pr 26:19**	7453
Better is a **n** who is near than a	**Pr 27:10**	7934
A man who flatters his **n** Is	**Pr 29:5**	7453
rivalry between a man and his **n**.	**Ec 4:4**	7453
by another, and each one by his **n**;	**Is 3:5**	7453
brother and each against his **n**,	**Is 19:2**	7453
Each one helps his **n** And	**Is 41:6**	7453
N and friend will perish."	**Jer 6:21**	7934
justice between a man and his **n**,	**Jer 7:5**	7453
be on guard against his **n**,	**Jer 9:4**	7453
every **n** goes about as a slanderer.	**Jer 9:4**	7453
"Everyone deceives his **n** And	**Jer 9:5**	7453
mouth one speaks peace to his **n**,	**Jer 9:8**	7453
And everyone her **n** a dirge.	**Jer 9:20**	7468
say to his **n** and to his brother,	**Jer 23:35**	7453
his **n** and each man his brother,	**Jer 31:34**	7453
man proclaiming release to his **n**,	**Jer 34:15**	7453
brother and each man to his **n**.	**Jer 34:17**	7453
Do not trust in a **n**;	**Mi 7:5**	7453
will invite his **n** to *sit* under *his* vine	**Zch 3:10**	7453
'YOU SHALL LOVE YOUR **N**	**Mt 5:43**	*4139*
SHALL LOVE YOUR **N** AS YOURSELF."	**Mt 19:19**	*4139*
SHALL LOVE YOUR **N** AS YOURSELF.'	**Mt 22:39**	*4139*
SHALL LOVE YOUR **N** AS YOURSELF.'	**Mk 12:31**	*4139*
AND TO LOVE ONE'S **N** AS HIMSELF,	**Mk 12:33**	*4139*
AND YOUR **N** AS YOURSELF."	**Lk 10:27**	*4139*
"And who is my **n**?"	**Lk 10:29**	*4139*

proved to be a **n** to the man who fell **Lk 10:36** *4139*
injuring his **n** pushed him away, **Ac 7:27** *4139*
loves his **n** has fulfilled *the* law. **Ro 13:8** *2087*
SHALL LOVE YOUR N AS YOURSELF." **Ro 13:9** *4139*
Love does no wrong to a **n**; **Ro 13:10** *4139*
of us is to please his **n** for his good, **Ro 15:2** *4139*
when he has a case against his **n**, **1Co 6:1** *2087*
his own *good,* but that of his **n**. **1Co 10:24** *2087*
SHALL LOVE YOUR N AS YOURSELF." **Ga 5:14** *4139*
EACH ONE *of you* WITH HIS N, **Eph 4:25** *4139*
SHALL LOVE YOUR N AS YOURSELF," **Jas 2:8** *4139*
but who are you who judge your **n**? **Jas 4:12** *4139*

NEIGHBORHOOD
Now in the **n** of that place were **Ac 28:7** *4012*

NEIGHBOR'S
"You shall not covet your **n** house; **Ex 20:17** 7453
you shall not covet your **n** wife or **Ex 20:17** 7453
laid his hands on his **n** property. **Ex 22:8** 7453
not laid hands on his **n** property; **Ex 22:11** 7453
take your **n** cloak as a pledge, **Ex 22:26** 7453
have intercourse with your **n** wife, **Lv 18:20** 5997
'You shall not covet your **n** wife, **Dt 5:21** 7453
you shall not desire your **n** house, **Dt 5:21** 7453
not move your **n** boundary mark, **Dt 19:14** 7453
he has violated his **n** wife. **Dt 22:24** 7453
"When you enter your **n** vineyard, **Dt 23:24** 7453
you enter your **n** standing grain, **Dt 23:25** 7453
a sickle in your **n** standing grain. **Dt 23:25** 7453
he who moves his **n** boundary mark.' **Dt 27:17** 7453
Or I have lurked at my **n** doorway, **Jb 31:9** 7453
the one who goes in to his **n** wife; **Pr 6:29** 7453
foot rarely be in your **n** house, **Pr 25:17** 7453
one neighing after his **n** wife. **Jer 5:8** 7453
Who uses his **n** services without **Jer 22:13** 7453
of Israel, or defile his **n** wife or **Ezk 18:6** 7453
shrines, and defiles his **n** wife, **Ezk 18:11** 7453
of Israel, or defile his **n** wife, **Ezk 18:15** 7453
abomination with his **n** wife and **Ezk 22:11** 7453
each of you defiles his **n** wife. **Ezk 33:26** 7453

NEIGHBORS
and to all their **n** in the Arabah, **Dt 1:7** 7934
that they heard that they were **n** **Jos 9:16** 7138
for yourself from all your **n**, **2Ki 4:3** 7934
Who speak peace with their **n**, **Ps 28:3** 7453
a reproach, Especially to my **n**, **Ps 31:11** 7934
You make us a reproach to our **n**, **Ps 44:13** 7934
have become a reproach to our **n**, **Ps 79:4** 7934
And return to our **n** sevenfold into **Ps 79:12** 7934
an object of contention to our **n**, **Ps 80:6** 7934
He has become a reproach to his **n**. **Ps 89:41** 7934
all My wicked **n** who strike at the **Jer 12:14** 7934
with his relatives And his **n**, **Jer 49:10** 7934
Sodom and Gomorrah with its **n**," **Jer 49:18** 7934
Sodom And Gomorrah with its **n**," **Jer 50:40** 7934
the Egyptians, your lustful **n**, **Ezk 16:26** 7934
you have injured your **n** for gain by **Ezk 22:12** 7453
after the Assyrians, *her* **n**, **Ezk 23:5** 7138
"Woe to you who make your **n** drink, **Hab 2:15** 7453
Her **n** and her relatives heard **Lk 1:58** *4040*
or your relatives or rich **n**, **Lk 14:12** *1069*
together his friends and his **n**, **Lk 15:6** *1069*
calls together her friends and **n**, **Lk 15:9** *1069*
Therefore the **n**, and those who **Jn 9:8** *1069*

NEIGHBORS'
adultery with their **n** wives **Jer 29:23** 7453

NEIGHING
one **n** after his neighbor's wife. **Jer 5:8** 6670a
At the sound of the **n** of his stallions **Jer 8:16** 4684

NEIGHINGS
adulteries and your *lustful* **n**, **Jer 13:27** 4684

NEITHER
n shall there again be a flood to **Gn 9:11** 3808
will be **n** plowing nor harvesting. **Gn 45:6** 369
n recently nor in time past, **Ex 4:10** 1571
something which **n** your fathers nor **Ex 10:6** 3808
n you nor your sons with you, **Lv 10:9**
n the native, nor the alien who **Lv 18:26**
you shall eat **n** bread nor roasted **Lv 23:14** 3808
n the ark of the covenant of the **Nu 14:44** 3808
which **n** see nor hear nor eat nor **Dt 4:28** 3808
I **n** ate bread nor drank water. **Dt 9:9** 3808
I **n** ate bread nor drank water, **Dt 9:18** 3808
you **n** believed Him nor listened to **Dt 9:23** 3808
(whom **n** you nor your fathers have **Dt 13:6** 3808
to a nation which **n** you nor your **Dt 28:36** 3808
but you will **n** drink of the wine **Dt 28:39** 3808
drunk **n** wine nor strong drink, **1Sa 1:15** 3808
Therefore **n** the priests of Dagon **1Sa 5:5** 3808
that **n** sword nor spear was found **1Sa 13:22** 3808
n you nor your kingdom will be **1Sa 20:31** 3808
For I brought **n** my sword nor my **1Sa 21:8** 1571, 3808
so as to leave my husband **n** name **2Sa 14:7** 1115
and he had **n** cared for his feet **2Sa 19:24** 3808
and she allowed **n** the birds of the **2Sa 21:10** 3808
"He shall be **n** mine nor yours; **1Ki 3:26** 1571, 3808
is **n** adversary nor misfortune. **1Ki 5:4** 369
and there was **n** hammer nor axe nor **1Ki 6:7** 3808
n of his relatives nor of his **1Ki 16:11** 3808
be **n** dew nor rain these years, **1Ki 17:1** 518
It is **n** new moon nor sabbath." **2Ki 4:23** 3808
for there was **n** bond nor free, nor **2Ki 14:26** 657
they would **n** listen nor do *it.* **2Ki 18:12** 3808
So **n** I, my brothers, my servants, **Ne 4:23** 369
n I nor my kinsmen have eaten the **Ne 5:14** 3808
n bowed down nor paid homage. **Es 3:2** 3808
Mordecai **n** bowed down nor paid **Es 3:5** 369
Israel Will **n** slumber nor sleep. **Ps 121:4** 3808
N have I learned wisdom, Nor do I **Pr 30:3** 3808
me, Give me **n** poverty nor riches; **Pr 30:8** 408
having **n** a son nor a brother, **Ec 4:8** 1571, 369
and **n** is bread to the wise nor **Ec 9:11** 1571, 3808
house there is **n** bread nor cloak; **Is 3:7** 369
have **n** travailed nor given birth, **Is 23:4** 3808
I have **n** brought up young men *nor* **Is 23:4** 3808
have **n** heard My fame nor seen My **Is 66:19** 3808
whom **n** they nor their fathers have **Jer 9:16** 3808
I have **n** sent them nor commanded **Jer 14:14** 3808
will be no one to bury them—**n** **Jer 14:16**
not known, **n** you nor your fathers; **Jer 16:13**
that **n** they nor their forefathers **Jer 19:4** 3808
But **n** he nor his servants nor the **Jer 37:2** 3808
n they, you, nor your fathers. **Jer 44:3**
For **n** Israel nor Judah has been **Jer 51:5** 3808
n fear them nor fear their words, **Ezk 2:6** 408
n fear their words nor be dismayed **Ezk 2:6** 408
And **n** by great strength nor by **Ezk 17:9** 3808
holy name, **n** they nor their kings, **Ezk 43:7** 3808
the king has inquired, **n** wise men, **Da 2:27** 3809
N their silver nor their gold Will **Zph 1:18** 1571, 3808
to the LORD, **n** day nor night, **Zch 14:7** 3808
leave them **n** root nor branch." **Mal 4:1** 3808
where **n** moth nor rust destroys, **Mt 6:20** *3777*
John came **n** eating nor drinking, **Mt 11:18** *3383*
"**N** will I tell you by what authority **Mt 21:27** *3761*
in the resurrection they **n** marry nor **Mt 22:30** *3777*
n will your Father who is in **Mk 11:26** *3761*
rise from the dead, they **n** marry nor **Mk 12:25** *3777*
"I **n** know nor understand what you **Mk 14:68** *3777*
for *your* journey, **n** a staff, **Lk 9:3** *3383*
ravens, for they **n** sow nor reap; **Lk 12:24** *3777*
they **n** toil nor spin; **Lk 12:27** *3777*
n marry nor are given in marriage; **Lk 20:35** *3777*
is coming when **n** in this mountain nor **Jn 4:21** *3777*
n heard His voice at any time nor **Jn 5:37** *3777*
"You know **n** Me nor My Father; **Jn 8:19** *3777*
"*It was* **n** *that* this man sinned, **Jn 9:3** *3777*
abides in the vine, so **n** *can* you unless **Jn 15:4** *3761*
HE WAS N ABANDONED TO HADES, **Ac 2:31** *3777*
sight, and **n** ate nor drank. **Ac 9:9** *3756*
recognizing **n** Him nor the **Ac 13:27**
a yoke which **n** our fathers nor we **Ac 15:10** *3777*
these men *here* who are **n** robbers **Ac 19:37** *3777*
saying that they would **n** eat nor **Ac 23:12** *3383*
"**N** in the temple, nor in **Ac 24:12** *3777*
Since **n** sun nor stars appeared **Ac 27:20** *3383*
"We have **n** received letters from **Ac 28:21** *3777*
n death, nor life, nor angels, nor **Ro 8:38** *3777*
So then **n** the one who plants nor **1Co 3:7** *3777*
n fornicators, nor idolaters, nor **1Co 6:9** *3777*
are **n** the worse if we do not eat, **1Co 8:8** *3777*
n is woman independent of man, **1Co 11:11** *3777*
For I **n** received it from man, nor **Ga 1:12** *3761*
There is **n** Jew nor Greek, there is **Ga 3:28** *3756, 1762*
there is **n** slave nor free man, **Ga 3:28** *3756, 1762*
man, there is **n** male nor female; **Ga 3:28** *3756, 1762*
For in Christ Jesus **n** circumcision **Ga 5:6** *3777*
For **n** is circumcision anything, **Ga 6:15** *3777*
having **n** beginning of days nor end **Heb 7:3** *3383*
they render you **n** useless nor **2Pe 1:8** *3756*
that you are **n** cold nor hot; **Rv 3:15** *3777*
are lukewarm, and **n** hot nor cold, **Rv 3:16** *3777*
which can **n** see nor hear nor walk; **Rv 9:20** *3777*

NEKODA
the sons of Rezin, the sons of **N**, **Ezr 2:48** 5353
the sons of Tobiah, the sons of **N**, **Ezr 2:60** 5353
the sons of Rezin, the sons of **N**, **Ne 7:50** 5353
the sons of Tobiah, the sons of **N**, **Ne 7:62** 5353

NEMUEL
N and Dathan and Abiram. **Nu 26:9** 5241
of **N**, the family of the Nemuelites; **Nu 26:12** 5241
sons of Simeon *were* **N** and Jamin, **1Ch 4:24** 5241

NEMUELITES
of Nemuel, the family of the **N**; **Nu 26:12** 5242

NEPHEG
Korah and **N** and Zichri. **Ex 6:21** 5298
Ibhar, Elishua, **N**, Japhia, **2Sa 5:15** 5298
Nogah, **N** and Japhia, **1Ch 3:7** 5298
Nogah, **N**, Japhia, **1Ch 14:6** 5298

NEPHEW
took Sarai his wife and Lot his **n**, **Gn 12:5** 1121, 251
They also took Lot, Abram's **n**, **Gn 14:12** 1121, 251

NEPHILIM
The **N** were on the earth in those **Gn 6:4** 5303
"There also we saw the **N** **Nu 13:33** 5303
sons of Anak are part of the **N**); **Nu 13:33** 5303

NEPHISIM
the sons of Meunim, the sons of **N**, **Ezr 2:50** 5304

NEPHTOAH
to the spring of the waters of **N** **Jos 15:9** 5318
the fountain of the waters of **N**. **Jos 18:15** 5318

NEPHUSHESIM
the sons of Meunim, the sons of **N**, **Ne 7:52** 5304

NER
his army was Abner the son of **N**, **1Sa 14:50** 5369
and **N** the father of Abner *was* the **1Sa 14:51** 5369
Saul lay, and Abner the son of **N**, **1Sa 26:5** 5369
people and to Abner the son of **N**, **1Sa 26:14** 5369
But Abner the son of **N**, **2Sa 2:8** 5369
Now Abner the son of **N**, **2Sa 2:12** 5369
the son of **N** came to the king, **2Sa 3:23** 5369
"You know Abner the son of **N**, **2Sa 3:25** 5369
the blood of Abner the son of **N**. **2Sa 3:28** 5369
put Abner the son of **N** to death. **2Sa 3:37** 5369
of Israel, to Abner the son of **N**, **1Ki 2:5** 5369
Abner the son of **N**, **1Ki 2:32** 5369
N became the father of Kish, **1Ch 8:33** 5369
Abdon, then Zur, Kish, Baal, **N**, **1Ch 9:36** 5369
N became the father of Kish, **1Ch 9:39** 5369
Abner the son of **N** and Joab **1Ch 26:28** 5369

NEREUS
and Julia, **N** and his sister, **Ro 16:15** *3517*

NERGAL
the men of Cuth made **N**, **2Ki 17:30** 5370

NERGAL-SAR-EZER
N, Samgar-nebu, Sar-sekim the **Jer 39:3** 5371
the Rab-saris, **N** *the* Rab-mag, **Jer 39:3** 5371
the Rab-saris, and **N** the Rab-mag, **Jer 39:13** 5371

NERI
son of Shealtiel, the son of **N**, **Lk 3:27** *3518*

NERIAH
purchase to Baruch the son of **N**, **Jer 32:12** 5374
purchase to Baruch the son of **N**, **Jer 32:16** 5374
called Baruch the son of **N**, **Jer 36:4** 5374
Baruch the son of **N** did **Jer 36:8** 5374
So Baruch the son of **N** took the **Jer 36:14** 5374
gave it to Baruch the son of **N**, **Jer 36:32** 5374
but Baruch the son of **N** is **Jer 43:3** 5374
prophet and Baruch the son of **N** **Jer 43:6** 5374
spoke to Baruch the son of **N**, **Jer 45:1** 5374
commanded Seraiah the son of **N**, **Jer 51:59** 5374

NEST
And your **n** is set in the cliff. **Nu 24:21** 7064
come upon a bird's **n** along the way, **Dt 22:6** 7064
"Like an eagle that stirs up its **n**, **Dt 32:11** 7064
'I shall die in my **n**, **Jb 29:18** 7064
up And makes his **n** on high? **Jb 39:27** 7064
And the swallow a **n** for herself, **Ps 84:3** 7064
a bird that wanders from her **n**, **Pr 27:8** 7064
riches of the peoples like a **n**, **Is 10:14** 7064
make its **n** and lay *eggs* there, **Is 34:15** 7077
make your **n** as high as an eagle's, **Jer 49:16** 7064
birds of every kind will **n** under it; **Ezk 17:23** 7931
they will **n** in the shade of its **Ezk 17:23** 7931
you set your **n** among the stars, **Ob 1:4** 7064
To put his **n** on high **Hab 2:9** 7064
AIR come and N IN ITS BRANCHES." **Mt 13:32** *2681*
THE AIR can N UNDER ITS SHADE." **Mk 4:32** *2681*

NESTED
dwell in Lebanon, **N** in the cedars, **Jer 22:23** 7077
birds of the heavens **n** in its boughs, **Ezk 31:6** 7077
BIRDS OF THE AIR N IN ITS BRANCHES." **Lk 13:19** *2681*

NESTLINGS
like fleeing birds *or* scattered **n**, **Is 16:2** 7064

NESTS
Where the birds build their **n**, **Ps 104:17** 7077
n Beyond the mouth of the chasm. **Jer 48:28** 7077
and the birds of the air *have* **n**, **Mt 8:20** *2682*
and the birds of the air *have* **n**, **Lk 9:58** *2682*

NET
and on the **n** you shall make four **Ex 27:4** 7568
that the **n** will reach halfway up **Ex 27:5** 7568
thrown into the **n** by his own feet, **Jb 18:8** 7568
And has closed His **n** around me. **Jb 19:6** 4685b
In the **n** which they hid, their own **Ps 9:15** 7568
when he draws him into his **n**. **Ps 10:9** 7568
will pluck my feet out of the **n**. **Ps 25:15** 7568
You will pull me out of the **n** **Ps 31:4** 7568
cause they hid their **n** for me; **Ps 35:7** 7568
the **n** which he hid catch himself; **Ps 35:8** 7568
have prepared a **n** for my steps; **Ps 57:6** 7568
You brought us into the **n**; **Ps 66:11** 4686a
have spread a **n** by the wayside; **Ps 140:5** 7568
the *baited* **n** In the sight of any bird; **Pr 1:17** 7568
Is spreading a **n** for his steps. **Pr 29:5** 7568
fish caught in a treacherous **n** and **Ec 9:12** 4685c
street, Like an antelope in a **n**, **Is 51:20** 4364b
He has spread a **n** for my feet; **La 1:13** 7568
"I will also spread My **n** over him, **Ezk 12:13** 7568
"I will spread My **n** over him, **Ezk 17:20** 7568
And they spread their **n** over him; **Ezk 19:8** 7568
"Now I will spread My **n** over you **Ezk 32:3** 7568
they shall lift you up in My **n**. **Ezk 32:3** 2764b
And a **n** spread out on Tabor. **Hos 5:1** 7568
go, I will spread My **n** over them; **Hos 7:12** 7568
of them hunts the other with a **n**. **Mi 7:2** 2764b
hook, Drag them away with their **n**, **Hab 1:15** 2764b
them together in their fishing **n**. **Hab 1:15** 4365a
they offer a sacrifice to their **n** and **Hab 1:16** 2764b
burn incense to their fishing **n**; **Hab 1:16** 4365a
Will they therefore empty their **n** **Hab 1:17** 2764b
brother, casting a **n** into the sea; **Mt 4:18** *293b*
of Simon, casting a **n** in the sea; **Mk 1:16** *293a*
"Cast the **n** on the right-hand **Jn 21:6** *1350*
away, dragging the **n** *full* of fish. **Jn 21:8** *1350*
went up and drew the **n** to land, **Jn 21:11** *1350*
were so many, the **n** was not torn. **Jn 21:11** *1350*

NETAIM
the inhabitants of **N** and Gederah; **1Ch 4:23** 5196

NETHANEL
of Issachar, **N** the son of Zuar; **Nu 1:8** 5417

N the son of Zuar, Nu 2:5 5417
the second day N the son of Zuar, Nu 7:18 5417
the offering of N the son of Zuar. Nu 7:23 5417
and N the son of Zuar, over the Nu 10:15 5417
N the fourth, Raddai the fifth, 1Ch 2:14 5417
Shebaniah, Joshaphat, N, 1Ch 15:24 5417
Shemaiah, the son of N the scribe, 1Ch 24:6 5417
Sacar the fourth, N the fifth, 1Ch 26:4 5417
Ben-hail, Obadiah, Zechariah, N and 2Ch 17:7 5417
Conaniah also, and Shemaiah and N, 2Ch 35:9 5417
Elioenai, Maaseiah, Ishmael, N, Ezr 10:22 5417
Hilkiah, Hashabiah; of Jedaiah, N. Ne 12:21 5417
Azarel, Milalai, Gilalai, Maai, N, Ne 12:36 5417

NETHANIAH
namely, Ishmael the son of N, 2Ki 25:23 5418
month, that Ishmael the son of N, 2Ki 25:25 5418
Zaccur, Joseph, N and Asharelah; 1Ch 25:2 5418
the fifth to N, his sons and his 1Ch 25:12 5418
them the Levites, Shemaiah, N, 2Ch 17:8 5418
sent Jehudi the son of N, Jer 36:14 5418
along with Ishmael the son of N, Jer 40:8 5418
the son of N to take your life?" Jer 40:14 5418
go and kill Ishmael the son of N, Jer 40:15 5418
month Ishmael the son of N, Jer 41:1 5418
Ishmael the son of N and the ten Jer 41:2 5418
Then Ishmael the son of N went out Jer 41:6 5418
Ishmael the son of N and the men Jer 41:7 5418
son of N filled it with the slain. Jer 41:9 5418
thus Ishmael the son of N took Jer 41:10 5418
Ishmael the son of N had done. Jer 41:11 5418
to fight with Ishmael the son of N Jer 41:12 5418
But Ishmael the son of N escaped Jer 41:15 5418
from Ishmael the son of N, Jer 41:16 5418
since Ishmael the son of N had Jer 41:18 5418

NETHER
powerful nations, to the n world, Ezk 32:18 8482

NETHINIM
Levites, singers, doorkeepers, N or Ezr 7:24 5412

NETOPHAH
the men of N, 56; Ezr 2:22 5199
the men of Bethlehem and N, Ne 7:26 5199

NETOPHATHITE
Zalmon the Ahohite, Maharai the N, 2Sa 23:28 5200
Heleb the son of Baanah the N, 2Sa 23:29 5200
the son of Tanhumeth the N, 2Ki 25:23 5200
Maharai the N, Heled the son of 1Ch 11:30 5200
Heled the son of Baanah the N, 1Ch 11:30 5200
Maharai the N of the Zerahites; 1Ch 27:13 5200
month *was* Heldai the N of Othniel; 1Ch 27:15 5200
and the sons of Ephai the N, Jer 40:8 5200

NETOPHATHITES
of Salma *were* Bethlehem and the N, 1Ch 2:54 5200
lived in the villages of the N, 1Ch 9:16 5200
and from the villages of the N, Ne 12:28 5200

NETS
There were n of network and 1Ki 7:17 7639
the wicked fall into their own n, Ps 141:10 4364a
woman whose heart is snares and n, Ec 7:26 2764b
those who spread n on the waters Is 19:8 4365b
They brought him in hunting n So Ezk 19:9 4685c
be a place for the spreading of n Ezk 26:5 2764b
be a place for the spreading of n. Ezk 26:14 2764b
be a place for the spreading of n. Ezk 47:10 2764b
Immediately they left their n Mt 4:20 *1350*
their father, mending their n; Mt 4:21 *1350*
left their n and followed Him. Mk 1:18 *1350*
also in the boat mending the n. Mk 1:19 *1350*
of them and were washing their n. Lk 5:2 *1350*
and let down your n for a catch." Lk 5:4 *1350*
do as You say *and* let down the n." Lk 5:5 *1350*
and their n *began* to break; Lk 5:6 *1350*

NETTLE
instead of the n the myrtle will Is 55:13 5636

NETTLES
Under the n they are gathered Jb 30:7 2738
Its surface was covered with n, Pr 24:31 2738
N and thistles in its fortified Is 34:13 7057
possessed by n and salt pits, Zph 2:9 2738

NETWORK
for it a grating of n of bronze, Ex 27:4 7568
a grating of bronze n beneath, Ex 38:4 7568
There were nets of n and twisted 1Ki 7:17 7639
and two rows around on the one n 1Ki 7:18 7639
projection which was beside the n; 1Ki 7:20 7639
rows of pomegranates for each n 1Ki 7:42 7639
with a n and pomegranates on the 2Ki 25:17 7639
pillar was like these with n. 2Ki 25:17 7639
rows of pomegranates for each n 2Ch 4:13 7639
with n and pomegranates upon the Jer 52:22 7639
a hundred on the n all around. Jer 52:23 7639

NETWORKS
and the two n to cover the two 1Ki 7:41 7639
pomegranates for the two n, 1Ki 7:42 7639
and the two n to cover the two 2Ch 4:12 7639
pomegranates for the two n, 2Ch 4:13 7639

NEVER
"I will n again curse the ground Gn 8:21 3808, 5750
and I will n again destroy every Gn 8:21 3808, 5750
and all flesh shall n again be cut Gn 9:11 3808
and n again shall the water become Gn 9:15 3808
such as I had n seen for ugliness Gn 41:19 3808
"I n expected to see your face, Gn 48:11 3808
Lord, I have n been eloquent, Ex 4:10 3808
There had n been so *many* locusts, Ex 10:14 3808
I shall n see your face again!" Ex 10:29 3808
and such as shall n be again. Ex 11:6 3808
you will n see them again forever. Ex 14:13 3808, 5750
on which a yoke has n been placed. Nu 19:2 3808
and will n again do such a wicked Dt 13:11 3808
It shall n be rebuilt. Dt 13:16 3808
will n cease *to be* in the land; Dt 15:11 3808
shall n again return that way.' Dt 17:16 3808
and will n again do such an evil Dt 19:20 3808
"You shall n seek their peace or Dt 23:6 3808, 5769
and you will n be anything but Dt 28:33 7534
'You will n see it again!' Dt 28:68 3808
shall n be willing to forgive him, Dt 29:20 3808
you shall n cease being slaves, Jos 9:23 3808
will n break My covenant with you, Jg 2:1 3808, 5769
"A razor has n come on my head, Jg 16:17 3808
razor shall n come on his head." 1Sa 1:11 3808
on which there has n been a yoke; 1Sa 6:7 3808
shall n depart from your house, 2Sa 12:10 3808, 5704, 5769
His father had n crossed him 1Ki 1:6 3808
N again did such abundance of 1Ki 10:10 3808
there had n been spice like that 2Ch 9:9 3808
for he n prophesies good 2Ch 18:7 369
and n seek their peace or their Ezr 9:12 3808
be, As infants that n saw light. Jb 3:16 3808
You n turn Your gaze away from me, Jb 7:19 3808
deny him, *saying,* 'I n saw you.' Jb 8:18 3808
N even tasting *anything* good. Jb 21:25 3808
"He lies down rich, but n again; Jb 27:19 3808
He will n see it." Ps 10:11 1077, 5331
these things will n be shaken. Ps 15:5 3808, 5769
"I will n be moved." Ps 30:6 1077, 5769
Let me n be ashamed; Ps 31:1 408, 5769
their faces will n be ashamed. Ps 34:5 408
They will n see the light. Ps 49:19 3808, 5704, 5331
He will n allow the righteous to Ps 55:22 3808, 5769
of a woman which n see the sun. Ps 58:8 1077
Let me n be ashamed. Ps 71:1 408, 5769
And will He n be favorable again? Ps 77:7 3808
For he will n be shaken; Ps 112:6 5769, 3808
I will n forget Your precepts, For Ps 119:93 5769, 3808
The righteous will n be shaken, Pr 10:30 5769, 1077
Sheol and Abaddon are n satisfied, Pr 27:20 3808
who gives to the poor will n want, Pr 28:27 369
that is n satisfied with water, Pr 30:16 3808
with water, And fire that n says, Pr 30:16 3808
them is the one who has n existed, Ec 4:3 3808
who has n seen the evil activity Ec 4:3 3808
not satisfied with riches *and he* n Ec 4:8
"It n sees the sun and it never Ec 6:5 3808
the sun and it n knows *anything;* Ec 6:5 3808
does good and who n sins. Ec 7:20 3808
one should n sleep day or night), Ec 8:16 369
goblet Which n lacks mixed wine; SS 7:2 408
And n again will they learn war. Is 2:4 3808
such days as have n come since Is 7:17 3808
will n again rely on the one who Is 10:20 3808
It will n be inhabited or lived in Is 13:20 3808, 5331
And it will fall, n to rise again. Is 24:20 3808
no more, It will n be rebuilt. Is 25:2 5769, 3808
Its stakes will n be pulled up Is 33:20 1077, 5331
Their name would n be cut off or Is 48:19 3808
anger; You will n drink it again. Is 51:22 3808
all night they will n keep silent. Is 62:6 3808
"I will n again give your grain Is 62:8 518
those over whom You have n ruled, Is 63:19 3808, 4480, 5769
which I n commanded or spoke of, Jer 19:5 3808
n return Or see his native land. Jer 22:10 3808, 5750
"He will n return there; Jer 22:11 3808, 5750
And they will n languish again. Jer 31:12 3808, 5750
'David shall n lack a man to sit Jer 33:17 3808
and the Levitical priests shall n Jer 33:18 3808
come with me to Babylon, n mind. Jer 40:4 2308
'n shall My name be invoked again Jer 44:26 518
And it will n again be inhabited Jer 50:39 3808
lovingkindnesses indeed n cease, La 3:22 3808
cease, For His compassions n fail. La 3:22 3808
Behold, I have n been defiled; Ezk 4:14 3808
I have n eaten what died of itself Ezk 4:14 3808
like of which I will n do again. Ezk 5:9 3808
should n come about nor happen. Ezk 16:16 3808
and n open your mouth anymore Ezk 16:63 3808
you will n be found again," Ezk 26:21 3808, 5769
and it will n again lift itself up Ezk 29:15 3808
"And it will n again be the Ezk 29:16 3808
n again bereave them of children.' Ezk 36:12 3808, 5750
kingdom which will n be destroyed, Da 2:44 5957, 3809
accomplish what his fathers n did, Da 11:24 3808
time of distress such as n occurred Da 12:1 3808
There has n been *anything* like it, Jl 2:2 3808, 4480, 5769
And I will n again make you a Jl 2:19 3808
My people will n be put to shame. Jl 2:26 3808, 5769
My people will n be put to shame. Jl 2:27 3808, 5769
will n forget any of their deeds. Am 8:7 518, 5331
become as if they had n existed. Ob 1:16 3808
n again will they train for war. Mi 4:3 3808
For n again will the wicked one Na 1:15 3808, 5750
Her prey n departs. Na 3:1 3808
ignored And justice is n upheld. Hab 1:4 3808, 5331
And he is like death, n satisfied. Hab 2:5 3808
And you will n again be haughty On Zph 3:11 3808, 5750
but if not, n mind!" Zch 11:12 2308
will declare to them, 'I n knew you; Mt 7:23 *3763*
This shall n happen to You." Mt 16:22 *3756, 3361*
have you n read, Mt 21:16 *3763*
"Did you n read in the Scriptures, Mt 21:42 *3763*
of You, I will n fall away." Mt 26:33 *3763*
have n seen anything like this." Mk 2:12 *3763*
"Have you n read what David did Mk 2:25 *3763*
the Holy Spirit n has forgiveness, Mk 3:29 *3756, 1519, 165*
created until now, and n will. Mk 13:19 *3756, 3361*
I will n again drink of the fruit Mk 14:25 *3756, 3361*
She n left the temple, serving Lk 2:37 *3756*
and I have n neglected a command Lk 15:29 *3763*
you have n given me a young goat, Lk 15:29 *3763*
heard it, they said, "May it n be!" Lk 20:16 *3361*
I shall n again eat it until it is Lk 22:16 *3756, 3361*
barren, and the wombs that n bore, Lk 23:29 *3756*
and the breasts that n nursed.' Lk 23:29 *3756*
I will give him shall n thirst; Jn 4:14 *3756, 3361*
who believes in Me will n thirst. Jn 6:35 *3756, 3361*
learned, having n been educated?" Jn 7:15 *3361*
"N has a man spoken the way this Jn 7:46 *3763*
n yet been enslaved to anyone; Jn 8:33 *3762, 4455*
My word he will n see death." Jn 8:51 *3756, 3361*
word, he will n taste of death.' Jn 8:52 *3756, 3361*
it has n been heard that anyone Jn 9:32 *3756*
to them, and they will n perish; Jn 10:28 *3756, 3361*
and believes in Me will n die. Jn 11:26 *3756, 3361*
"N shall You wash my feet!" Jn 13:8 *3756, 3361*
for I have n eaten anything unholy Ac 10:14 *3763*
A WORK WHICH YOU WILL N BELIEVE, Ac 13:41 *3756, 3361*
mother's womb, who had n walked. Ac 14:8 *3763*
May it n be! Rather, let God be Ro 3:4 *3361*
May it n be! For otherwise, Ro 3:6 *3361*
Law through faith? May it n be! Ro 3:31 *3361*
May it n be! How shall we who died Ro 6:2 *3361*
from the dead, is n to die again; Ro 6:9 *3765*
law but under grace? May it n be! Ro 6:15 *3361*
Is the Law sin? May it n be! Ro 7:7 *3361*
a cause of death for me? May it n be! Ro 7:13 *3361*
with God, is there? May it n be! Ro 9:14 *3361*
I say, surely they have n heard, Ro 10:18 *3361, 3756*
His people, has He? May it n be! Ro 11:1 *3361*
so as to fall, did they? May it n be! Ro 11:11 *3361*
N pay back evil for evil to anyone. Ro 12:17 *3367*
N take your own revenge, beloved, Ro 12:19 *3361*
members of a prostitute? May it n be! 1Co 6:15 *3361*
stumble, I will n eat meat again, 1Co 8:13 *3756, 3361*
Love n fails; but if *there are gifts of* 1Co 13:8 *3763*
then a minister of sin? May it n be! Ga 2:17 *3361*
the promises of God? May it n be! Ga 3:21 *3361*
may it n be that I would boast, Ga 6:14 *3361*
we n came with flattering speech, 1Th 2:5 *3777, 4218*
n able to come to the knowledge of 2Tm 3:7 *3368*
for it is n in force while the one Heb 9:17 *3379*
can n, by the same sacrifices Heb 10:1 *3763*
which can n take away sins; Heb 10:11 *3763*
"I WILL N DESERT YOU, NOR WILL I Heb 13:5 *3756, 3361*
these things, you will n stumble; 2Pe 1:10 *3756, 3361, 4218*
adultery that n cease from sin, 2Pe 2:14 *180*
and will n see mourning.' Rv 18:7 *3756*
its gates will n be closed; Rv 21:25 *3756*

NEVERTHELESS
n his days shall be one hundred Gn 6:3
n in the day when I punish, I will Ex 32:34
'N, you are not to eat of these, Lv 11:4 389
'N a spring or a cistern Lv 11:36 389
'N, anything which a man sets Lv 27:28 389

“N, the people who live in the Nu 13:28 657, 3588
n the firstborn of man you shall Nu 18:15 389
“N Kain will be consumed; Nu 24:22 3588, 518
“N, you are not to eat of these Dt 14:7 389
“N, the LORD your God was not Dt 23:5
“N my brethren who went up with Jos 14:8
n, the honor shall not be yours on Jg 4:9 657, 3588
N, the people refused to listen to 1Sa 8:19
N Saul did not speak anything that 1Sa 20:26
“N, as the LORD God of Israel 1Sa 25:34 199
N, you are not pleasing in the 1Sa 29:6
n the commanders of the 1Sa 29:9 389
N, David captured the stronghold 2Sa 5:7
n Mephibosheth your master's 2Sa 9:10
N he would not drink it, but 2Sa 23:16
N, the king's word prevailed 2Sa 24:4
‘N you shall not build the house, 1Ki 8:19 7534
“N I did not believe the reports, 1Ki 10:7
“N I will not do it in your days 1Ki 11:12 389
n you must surely let me go.” 1Ki 11:22 3588
‘N I will not take the whole 1Ki 11:34
n the heart of Asa was wholly 1Ki 15:14 7534
N, if you see me when I am taken 2Ki 2:10
N, he clung to the sins of 2Ki 3:3 7534
N they did not turn away from the 2Ki 13:6 389
N the priests of the high places 2Ki 23:9 389
N David captured the stronghold of 1Ch 11:5
n David would not drink it, but 1Ch 11:18
N, the king's word prevailed 1Ch 21:4
‘N you shall not build the house, 2Ch 6:9 7534
“N I did not believe their 2Ch 9:6
n Asa's heart was blameless all 2Ch 15:17 7534
N some men of Asher, Manasseh and 2Ch 30:11 389
N the people still sacrificed in 2Ch 33:17 61
“N, in Your great compassion You Ne 9:31
n the foreign women caused even Ne 13:26 1571
N I will argue my ways before Him. Jb 13:15 389
“N the righteous will hold to Jb 17:9
N You heard the voice of my Ps 31:22 403
N I am continually with You; Ps 73:23
“N you will die like men And Ps 82:7 403
N He saved them for the sake of Ps 106:8
N He looked upon their distress When Ps 106:44
“N you will be thrust down to Is 14:15 389
“N hear the word of the LORD, all Jer 44:26 3651
“N, I will restore their Ezk 16:53
“N, I will remember My covenant Ezk 16:60
n, a great dread fell on them, and Da 10:7 61
N, I will not totally destroy the Am 9:8 657, 3588
N I will look again toward Your Jon 2:4 389
“N I say to you, it will be more Mt 11:22 *4133*
“N I say to you that it will be Mt 11:24 *4133*
n I tell you, hereafter you will Mt 26:64 *4133*
“N do not rejoice in this, that Lk 10:20 *4133*
“N I must journey on today and Lk 13:33 *4133*
N many even of the rulers believed Jn 12:42 *3676, 3305*
N death reigned from Adam until Ro 5:14 *235*
N, we did not use this right, but 1Co 9:12 *235*
N, with most of them God was not 1Co 10:5 *235*
n, crafty fellow that I am, I took 2Co 12:16 *235*
n knowing that a man is not Ga 2:16 *1161*
N, each individual among you Eph 5:33 *4133*
N, you have done well to share Php 4:14 *4133*
body, n I am with you in spirit, Col 2:5 *235*
N, the firm foundation of God 2Tm 2:19 *3305*
‘N what you have, hold fast until Rv 2:25 *4133*

NEW

an abundance of grain and n wine; Gn 27:28 8492
and n wine I have sustained him. Gn 27:37 8492
Now a n king arose over Egypt, who Ex 1:8 2319
in the fire, grits of n growth, Lv 2:14 3759
nor roasted grain nor n growth. Lv 23:14 3759
a n grain offering to the LORD. Lv 23:16 2319
out the old because of the n. Lv 26:10 2319
LORD brings about an entirely n thing Nu 16:30 1278
when you present a n grain offering Nu 28:26 2319
the burnt offering of the n moon and Nu 29:6 2320
and your n wine and your oil, Dt 7:13 8492
and your n wine and your oil. Dt 11:14 8492
tithe of your grain or n wine Dt 12:17 8492
tithe of your grain, your n wine, Dt 14:23 8492
fruits of your grain, your n wine, Dt 18:4 8492
the man that has built a n house Dt 20:5 2319
“When you build a n house, Dt 22:8 2319
“When a man takes a n wife, Dt 24:5 2319
also leaves you no grain, n wine, Dt 28:51 8492
not known, N *gods* who came lately, Dt 32:17 2319
In a land of grain and n wine; Dt 33:28 8492
wineskins which we filled were n, Jos 9:13 2319
“N gods were chosen; Jg 5:8 2319
‘Shall I leave my n wine, Jg 9:13 8492
they bound him with two n ropes Jg 15:13 2319
If they bind me tightly with n ropes Jg 16:11 2319
So Delilah took n ropes and bound Jg 16:12 2319
prepare a n cart and two milch cows 1Sa 6:7 2319
“Behold, tomorrow is the n moon, 1Sa 20:5 2320
“Tomorrow is the n moon, and you 1Sa 20:18 2320
and when the n moon came, the king 1Sa 20:24 2320
day, the second *day* of the n moon, 1Sa 20:27 2320
on the second day of the n moon, 1Sa 20:34 2320
placed the ark of God on a n cart 2Sa 6:3 2319
Abinadab, were leading the n cart. 2Sa 6:3 2319
weight, was girded with a n *sword,* 2Sa 21:16 2319
clothed himself with a n cloak; 1Ki 11:29 2319
Ahijah took hold of the n cloak 1Ki 11:30 2319
“Bring me a n jar, and put salt 2Ki 2:20 2319
is neither n moon nor sabbath.” 2Ki 4:23 2320
land, a land of grain and n wine, 2Ki 18:32 8492
carried the ark of God on a n cart 1Ch 13:7 2319
the n moons and the fixed 1Ch 23:31 2320
on sabbaths and on n moons and on 2Ch 2:4 2320
for the sabbaths, the n moons and 2Ch 8:13 2320
of the LORD before the n court, 2Ch 20:5 2319
for the sabbaths and for the n moons 2Ch 31:3 2320
the first fruits of grain, n wine, 2Ch 31:5 8492
also for the n moons and for all Ezr 3:5 2320
and of the grain, the n wine and Ne 5:11 8492
the sabbaths, the n moon, Ne 10:33 2320
the n wine and the oil to the Ne 10:37 8492
the grain, the n wine and the oil to Ne 10:39 8492
‘My glory is *ever* n with me, Jb 29:20 2319
Like n wineskins it is about to Jb 32:19 2319
their grain and n wine abound. Ps 4:7 8492
Sing to Him a n song; Ps 33:3 2319
He put a n song in my mouth, a Ps 40:3 2319
Blow the trumpet at the n moon, Ps 81:3 2320
Sing to the LORD a n song; Ps 96:1 2319
O sing to the LORD a n song, Ps 98:1 2319
I will sing a n song to You, O Ps 144:9 2319
Sing to the LORD a n song, Ps 149:1 2319
vats will overflow with n wine. Pr 3:10 8492
disappears, the n growth is seen, Pr 27:25 1877
there is nothing n under the sun. Ec 1:9 2319
“See this, it is n”? Ec 1:10 2319
all choice *fruits,* Both n and old, SS 7:13 2319
N moon and sabbath, the calling of Is 1:13 2320
“I hate your n moon *festivals* and Is 1:14 2320
The n wine mourns, The vine Is 24:7 8492
land, a land of grain and n wine, Is 36:17 8492
for the LORD Will gain n strength; Is 40:31 2498
let the peoples gain n strength; Is 41:1 2498
a n, sharp threshing sledge with Is 41:15 2319
to pass, Now I declare n things; Is 42:9 2319
Sing to the LORD a n song, Is 42:10 2319
“Behold, I will do something n, Is 43:19 2319
Those who predict by the n moons, Is 47:13 2320
I proclaim to you n things from this Is 48:6 2319
you will be called by a n name Which Is 62:2 2319
will foreigners drink your n wine for Is 62:8 8492
n wine is found in the cluster, Is 65:8 8492
create n heavens and a new earth; Is 65:17 2319
create new heavens and a n earth; Is 65:17 2319
will flourish like the n grass; Is 66:14 1877
as the n heavens and the new earth Is 66:22 2319
as the new heavens and the n earth Is 66:22 2319
shall be from n moon to new moon Is 66:23 2320
shall be from new moon to n moon Is 66:23 2320
others, Their fields to n owners; Jer 8:10 3423
of the N Gate of the LORD's *house.* Jer 26:10 2319
Over the grain and the n wine Jer 31:12 8492
For the LORD has created a n thing Jer 31:22 2319
“when I will make a n covenant Jer 31:31 2319
of the N Gate of the LORD's house, Jer 36:10 2319
They are n every morning; La 3:23 2319
and put a n spirit within them. Ezk 11:19 2319
a n heart and a new spirit! Ezk 18:31 2319
a new heart and a n spirit! Ezk 18:31 2319
I will give you a n heart and put Ezk 36:26 2319
and put a n spirit within you; Ezk 36:26 2319
at the feasts, on the n moons and Ezk 45:17 2320
opened on the day of the n moon. Ezk 46:1 2320
the sabbaths and on the n moons. Ezk 46:3 2320
“On the day of the n moon *he* Ezk 46:6 2320
of the officials assigned n names Da 1:7
it In the n grass of the field; Da 4:15 1883
it in the n grass of the field, Da 4:23 1883
gave her the grain, the n wine and Hos 2:8 8492
time And My n wine in its season. Hos 2:9 8492
gaiety, Her feasts, her n moons, Hos 2:11 2320
to the grain, to the n wine and Hos 2:22 8492
and n wine take away the Hos 4:11 8492
Now the n moon will devour them Hos 5:7 2320
For the sake of grain and n wine Hos 7:14 8492
And the n wine will fail them. Hos 9:2 8492
is ruined, The n wine dries up, Jl 1:10 8492
going to send you grain, n wine and Jl 2:19 8492
overflow with the n wine and oil. Jl 2:24 8492
“When will the n moon be over, So Am 8:5 2320
on the grain, on the n wine, Hg 1:11 8492
flourish, and n wine the virgins. Zch 9:17 8492
people put n wine into old wineskins; Mt 9:17 *3501b*
put n wine into fresh wineskins, Mt 9:17 *3501b*
his treasure things n and old.” Mt 13:52 *2537*
day when I drink it n with you in My Mt 26:29 *2537*
and laid it in his own n tomb, Mt 27:60 *2537*
A n teaching with authority! Mk 1:27 *2537*
away from it, the n from the old, Mk 2:21 *2537*
puts n wine into old wineskins; Mk 2:22 *3501b*
n wine into fresh wineskins.” Mk 2:22 *3501b*
when I drink it n in the kingdom Mk 14:25 *2537*
they will speak with n tongues; Mk 16:17 *2537*
piece of cloth from a n garment and Lk 5:36 *2537*
otherwise he will both tear the n, Lk 5:36 *2537*
from the n will not match the old. Lk 5:36 *2537*
puts n wine into old wineskins; Lk 5:37 *3501b*
the n wine will burst the skins and Lk 5:37 *3501b*
“But n wine must be put into Lk 5:38 *3501b*
drinking old *wine* wishes for n; Lk 5:39 *3501b*
you is the n covenant in My blood. Lk 22:20 *2537*
“A n commandment I give to you, Jn 13:34 *2537*
and in the garden a n tomb in Jn 19:41 *2537*
“May we know what this n teaching Ac 17:19 *2537*
telling or hearing something n.) Ac 17:21 *2537*
leaven so that you may be a n lump, 1Co 5:7 *3501b*
cup is the n covenant in My blood; 1Co 11:25 *2537*
as servants of a n covenant, 2Co 3:6 *2537*
is in Christ, *he is* a n creature; 2Co 5:17 *2537*
behold, n things have come. 2Co 5:17 *2537*
uncircumcision, but a n creation. Ga 6:15 *2537*
might make the two into one n man, Eph 2:15 *2537*
and put on the n self, which in Eph 4:24 *2537*
or a n moon or a Sabbath day Col 2:16 *3501a*
and have put on the n self who is Col 3:10 *3501b*
and not a n convert, so that he 1Tm 3:6 *3504*
WHEN I WILL EFFECT A N COVENANT Heb 8:8 *2537*
When He said, “A n *covenant,*” Heb 8:13 *2537*
is the mediator of a n covenant, Heb 9:15 *2537*
by a n and living way which He Heb 10:20 *4372*
the mediator of a n covenant, Heb 12:24 *3501b*
for n heavens and a new earth, 2Pe 3:13 *2537*
for new heavens and a n earth, 2Pe 3:13 *2537*
writing a n commandment to you, 1Jn 2:7 *2537*
am writing a n commandment to you, 1Jn 2:8 *2537*
writing to you a n commandment, 2Jn 1:5 *2537*
and a n name written on the stone Rv 2:17 *2537*
city of My God, the n Jerusalem, Rv 3:12 *2537*
heaven from My God, and My n name. Rv 3:12 *2537*
And they sang a n song, saying, Rv 5:9 *2537*
And they sang a n song before the Rv 14:3 *2537*
I saw a n heaven and a new earth; Rv 21:1 *2537*
I saw a new heaven and a n earth; Rv 21:1 *2537*
I saw the holy city, n Jerusalem, Rv 21:2 *2537*
I am making all things n.” Rv 21:5 *2537*

NEWBORN

like n babies, long for the pure 1Pe 2:2 *738*

NEWLY

“Your teeth are like a flock of n SS 4:2

NEWNESS

so we too might walk in n of life. Ro 6:4 *2538*
we serve in n of the Spirit and not Ro 7:6 *2538*

NEWS

the n of Jacob his sister's son, Gn 29:13 8088
Now when the n was heard in Gn 45:16 6963
one who brought the n replied 1Sa 4:17 1319
and when she heard the n that the 1Sa 4:19 8052
All Israel heard the n that 1Sa 13:4 559
and bring back n of them. 1Sa 17:18 6161
to carry the good n to the house 1Sa 31:9 1319
thought he was bringing good n, 2Sa 4:10 1319
the reward I gave him for *his* n. 2Sa 4:10 1309
bring the king n that the LORD has 2Sa 18:19 1319
not the man to carry n this day, 2Sa 18:20 1309
but you shall carry n another day; 2Sa 18:20 1319
you shall carry no n today because 2Sa 18:20 1319
there is good n in his mouth.” 2Sa 18:25 1309
one also is bringing good n.” 2Sa 18:26 1319
good man and comes with good n.” 2Sa 18:27 1309
my lord the king receive good n, 2Sa 18:31 1319
a valiant man and bring good n.” 1Ki 1:42 1319
Now the n came to Joab, for Joab 1Ki 2:28 8052
This day is a day of good n, 2Ki 7:9 1309
to carry the good n to their idols 1Ch 10:9 1319
Good n puts fat on the bones. Pr 15:30 8052
So is good n from a distant land. Pr 25:25 8052
O Zion, bearer of good n, Is 40:9 1319
O Jerusalem, bearer of good n; Is 40:9 1319
will give a messenger of good n.’ Is 41:27 1319
the feet of him who brings good n, Is 52:7 1319
And brings good n of happiness, Is 52:7 1319
good n of the praises of the LORD. Is 60:6 1319
To bring good n to the afflicted; Is 61:1 1319
who brought the n To my father, Jer 20:15 1319
shame, For they have heard bad n; Jer 49:23 8052
‘Because of the n that is coming; Ezk 21:7 8052
the feet of him who brings good n, Na 1:15 1319
The n about Him spread throughout Mt 4:24 *189*
n spread throughout all that land. Mt 9:26 *5345*
n about Him throughout all that land. Mt 9:31 *1310*
tetrarch heard the n about Jesus, Mt 14:1 *189*
Immediately the n about Him Mk 1:28 *189*
freely and to spread the n around, Mk 1:45 *3056*
you and to bring you this good n. Lk 1:19 *2097*
I bring you good n of great joy Lk 2:10 *2097*
and n about Him spread through all Lk 4:14 *5345*
But the n about Him was spreading Lk 5:15 *3056*
believed Philip preaching the good n Ac 8:12 *2097*
The n about them reached the Ac 11:22 *3056*
“And we preach to you the good n Ac 13:32 *2097*
THE FEET OF THOSE WHO BRING GOOD N OF Ro 10:15 *2097*
they did not all heed the good n; Ro 10:16 *2098*
WHO HAD NO N OF HIM SHALL SEE, Ro 15:21 *312*
us good n of your faith and love, 1Th 3:6 *2097*
we have had good n preached to us, Heb 4:2 *2097*
who formerly had good n preached Heb 4:6 *2097*

NEXT

to you at this season n year.” Gn 17:21 312
return to you at this time n year; Gn 18:10 2416a
to you, at this time n year, Gn 18:14 2416a
and Leah and her children n, Gn 33:2 314
to him the n year and said to him, Gn 47:18 8145
He went out the n day, Ex 2:13 8145
LORD did this thing on the n day, Ex 9:6 4283
It came about the n day that Ex 18:13 4283
So the n day they rose early and Ex 32:6 4283
On the n day Ex 32:30 4283
edge which was n to the ephod. Ex 39:19 413, 5676
on undergarments n to his flesh; Lv 6:10 5921
and on the n day what is left of Lv 7:16 4283
N Moses had Aaron's sons come near Lv 8:13
N Moses slaughtered *it* and took Lv 8:15
N he presented the grain offering, Lv 9:17
“N he shall slaughter the male Lv 14:13

“The priest shall **n** offer the sin Lv 14:19
“**N** he shall slaughter the lamb of Lv 14:25
shall be **n** to his body, Lv 16:4 5921
day you offer *it,* and the **n** day; Lv 19:6 4283
“Those who camp **n** to him Nu 2:5 5921
“Those who camp **n** to him Nu 2:12 5921
“**N** to him *shall be* the tribe of Nu 2:20 5921
“Those who camp **n** to him Nu 2:27 5921
N the standard of the camp of Nu 10:18
N the standard of the camp of the Nu 10:22
and all night and all the **n** day, Nu 11:32 4283
But on the **n** day all the Nu 16:41 4283
Now on the **n** day Nu 17:8 4283
‘**N** Eleazar the priest shall take Nu 19:4
on the **n** day after the Passover Nu 33:3 4283
When he arose early the **n** morning Jg 6:38 4283
Now it came about the **n** day, Jg 9:42 4283
It came about the **n** day that Jg 21:4 4283
arose early the **n** morning, 1Sa 5:3 4283
they arose early the **n** morning, 1Sa 5:4 4283
The **n** morning 1Sa 11:11 4283
N Jesse made Shammah pass by. 1Sa 16:9
Now it came about on the **n** day 1Sa 18:10 4283
It came about the **n** day, 1Sa 20:27 4283
Israel and I will be **n** to you; 1Sa 23:17 4932
until the evening of the **n** day; 1Sa 30:17 4283
It came about on the **n** day 1Sa 31:8 4283
in Jerusalem that day and the **n**. 2Sa 11:12 4283
“See, Joab's field is **n** to mine, 2Sa 14:30 413
n year you will embrace a son.” 2Ki 4:16 2416a
a son at that season the **n** year, 2Ki 4:17 2416a
and I said to her on the **n** day, 2Ki 6:29 312
It came about the **n** day, 1Ch 10:8 4283
On the **n** day they made 1Ch 29:21 4283
and **n** to him *was* Johanan the 2Ch 17:15 5921, 3027
and **n** to him Amasiah the son of 2Ch 17:16 5921, 3027
and **n** to him Jehozabad, and with 2Ch 17:18 5921, 3027
N to him the men of Jericho built, Ne 3:2 3027
and **n** to them Zaccur the son of Ne 3:2 5921, 3027
N to them Meremoth the son of Uriah Ne 3:4 3027
And **n** to him Meshullam the son of Ne 3:4 5921, 3027
And **n** to him Zadok the son of Ne 3:4 5921, 3027
n to him the Tekoites made Ne 3:5 5921, 3027
N to them Melatiah the Gibeonite Ne 3:7 5921, 3027
N to him Uzziel the son of Ne 3:8 5921, 3027
And **n** to him Hananiah, one of the Ne 3:8 5921, 3027
N to them Rephaiah the son of Hur, Ne 3:9 5921
N to them Jedaiah the son of Ne 3:10 5921, 3027
And **n** to him Hattush the son of Ne 3:10 5921, 3027
N to him Shallum the son of Hallohesh, Ne 3:12 5921
N to him Hashabiah, the official Ne 3:17 5921, 3027
N to him Ezer the son of Jeshua, Ne 3:19 5921
may tell *it* to the **n** generation. Ps 48:13 314
On the **n** day, Jer 20:3 4283
Now it happened on the **n** day after Jer 41:4 8145
were on each side **n** to the gate; Ezk 40:41 3802
And their sons the **n** generation. Jl 1:3 312
a worm when dawn came the **n** day and Jon 4:7 4283
you in one city, flee to the **n**; Mt 10:23 *2087*
AS **N** OF KIN SHALL MARRY HIS WIFE, Mt 22:24
Now on the **n** day, the day Mt 27:62 *1887*
On the **n** day, when they had Mk 11:12 *1887*
On the **n** day, Lk 9:37 *1836*
“On the **n** day he took out two Lk 10:35 *839*
and if it bears fruit **n** year, Lk 13:9 *1519, 3195*
today and tomorrow and the **n** *day* Lk 13:33 *2192*
The **n** day he saw Jesus coming to Jn 1:29 *1887*
Again the **n** day John was standing Jn 1:35 *1887*
The **n** day He purposed to go into Jn 1:43 *1887*
The **n** day the crowd that stood Jn 6:22 *1887*
On the **n** day the large crowd Jn 12:12 *1887*
put them in jail until the **n** day, Ac 4:3 *839*
On the **n** day, Ac 4:5 *839*
On the **n** day, as they were on Ac 10:9 *1887*
And on the **n** day he got up and went Ac 10:23 *1887*
be spoken to them the **n** Sabbath. Ac 13:42 *3342*
The **n** Sabbath nearly the whole Ac 13:44 *2064*
The **n** day he went away with Ac 14:20 *1887*
house was **n** to the synagogue. Ac 18:7 *4927*
intending to leave the **n** day, Ac 20:7 *1887*
n day we crossed over to Samos; Ac 20:15 *2087*
the **n** day to Rhodes and from there Ac 21:1 *1836*
On the **n** day we left and Ac 21:8 *1887*
Paul took the men, and the **n** day, Ac 21:26 *2192*
But on the **n** day, wishing to know Ac 22:30 *1887*
But the **n** day, leaving the Ac 23:32 *1887*
and on the **n** day he took his seat Ac 25:6 *1887*
but on the **n** day I took my seat on Ac 25:17 *1836*
on the **n** day when Agrippa came Ac 25:23 *1887*
The **n** day we put in at Sidon; Ac 27:3 *2087*
The **n** day as we were being Ac 27:18 *1836*

NEZIAH
the sons of **N**, the sons of Hatipha. Ezr 2:54 5335
the sons of **N**, the sons of Hatipha. Ne 7:56 5335

NEZIB
and Iphtah and Ashnah and **N**, Jos 15:43 5334

NIBHAZ
and the Avvites made **N** and Tartak; 2Ki 17:31 5026

NIBSHAN
and **N** and the City of Salt and Jos 15:62 5044

NICANOR
Spirit, and Philip, Prochorus, **N**, Ac 6:5 *3527*

NICE
they may say **n** things to you.” Jer 12:6 2899b

NICODEMUS
a man of the Pharisees, named **N**, Jn 3:1 *3530*
N said to Him, “How can a man be Jn 3:4 *3530*
N said to Him, Jn 3:9 *3530*
N (he who came to Him before, being Jn 7:50 *3530*
N, who had first come to Him Jn 19:39 *3530*

NICOLAITANS
that you hate the deeds of the **N**, Rv 2:6 *3531*
way hold the teaching of the **N**. Rv 2:15 *3531*

NICOLAS
Nicanor, Timon, Parmenas and **N**, Ac 6:5 *3532*

NICOPOLIS
every effort to come to me at **N**, Ti 3:12 *3533*

NIGER
and Simeon who was called **N**, Ac 13:1 *3526*

NIGHT
day, and the darkness He called **n**. Gn 1:5 3915
to separate the day from the **n**, Gn 1:14 3915
the lesser light to govern the **n**; Gn 1:16 3915
and to govern the day and the **n**, Gn 1:18 3915
And day and **n** Shall not cease.” Gn 8:22 3915
his forces against them by **n**, Gn 14:15 3915
servant's house, and spend the **n**, Gn 19:2 3885a
shall spend the **n** in the square.” Gn 19:2 3885a
made their father drink wine that **n**, Gn 19:33 3915
I lay last **n** with my father; Gn 19:34 570
made their father drink wine that **n** Gn 19:35 3915
to Abimelech in a dream of the **n**, Gn 20:3 3915
him ate and drank and spent the **n**. Gn 24:54 3885a
LORD appeared to him the same **n** Gn 26:24 3915
place and spent the **n** there, Gn 28:11 3885a
So he lay with her that **n**. Gn 30:16 3915
the Aramean in a dream of the **n** and Gn 31:24 3915
of your father spoke to me last **n**, Gn 31:29 570
stolen by day or stolen by **n**. Gn 31:39 3915
consumed me and the frost by **n**, Gn 31:40 3915
so He rendered judgment last **n**.” Gn 31:42 570
and spent the **n** on the mountain. Gn 31:54 3885a
So he spent the **n** there. Gn 32:13 3915
himself spent that **n** in the camp. Gn 32:21 3915
Now he arose that same **n** and took Gn 32:22 3915
jail, both had a dream the same **n**, Gn 40:5 3915
“We had a dream on the same **n**, Gn 41:11 3915
spoke to Israel in visions of the **n** Gn 46:2 3915
land all that day and all that **n**; Ex 10:13 3915
shall eat the flesh that *same* **n**, Ex 12:8 3915
the land of Egypt on that **n**, Ex 12:12 3915
Pharaoh arose in the **n**, Ex 12:30 3915
he called for Moses and Aaron at **n** Ex 12:31 3915
It is a **n** to be observed for the Ex 12:42 3915
this **n** is for the LORD, to be Ex 12:42 3915
pillar of fire by **n** to give them light, Ex 13:21 3915
they might travel by day and by **n**. Ex 13:21 3915
day, nor the pillar of fire by **n**, Ex 13:22 3915
darkness, yet it gave light at **n**. Ex 14:20 3915
did not come near the other all **n**. Ex 14:20 3915
back by a strong east wind all **n** and Ex 14:21 3915
and there was fire in it by **n**, Ex 40:38 3915
the altar all **n** until the morning, Lv 6:9 3915
remain day and **n** for seven days and Lv 8:35 3915
with you all **n** until morning. Lv 19:13 3885a
and the appearance of fire by **n**. Nu 9:16 3915
remained in the daytime and at **n**, Nu 9:21 3915
the dew fell on the camp at **n**, Nu 11:9 3915
and all **n** and all the next day, Nu 11:32 3915
cried, and the people wept that **n**. Nu 14:1 3915
day and in a pillar of fire by **n**. Nu 14:14 3915
“Spend the **n** here, and I will Nu 22:8 3915
God came to Balaam at **n** and said Nu 22:20 3915
in fire by **n** and cloud by day, Dt 1:33 3915
God brought you out of Egypt by **n**. Dt 16:1 3915
shall not hang all **n** on the tree, Dt 21:23 3885a
you will be in dread **n** and day, Dt 28:66 3915
shall meditate on it day and **n**, Jos 1:8 3915
camp and spent the **n** in the camp. Jos 6:11 3885a
warriors, and sent them out at **n**. Jos 8:3 3915
spent that **n** among the people. Jos 8:9 3915
that **n** in the midst of the valley. Jos 8:13 3915
by marching all **n** from Gilgal. Jos 10:9 3915
Now on the same **n** Jg 6:25 3915
do it by day, he did it by **n**. Jg 6:27 3915
God did so that **n**; Jg 6:40 3915
Now the same **n** it came about that Jg 7:9 3915
“Now therefore, arise by **n**, Jg 9:32 3915
people who *were* with him arose by **n** Jg 9:34 3915
lay in wait for him all **n** at the gate Jg 16:2 3915
And they kept silent all **n**, Jg 16:2 3915
“Please be willing to spend the **n**, Jg 19:6 3885a
that he spent the **n** there again. Jg 19:7 3885a
please spend the **n**. Jg 19:9 3885a
spend the **n** here that your heart Jg 19:9 3885a
was not willing to spend the **n**, Jg 19:10 3885a
Jebusites and spend the **n** in it.” Jg 19:11 3885a
spend the **n** in Gibeah or Ramah.” Jg 19:13 3885a
into *his* house to spend the **n**. Jg 19:15 3885a
spend the **n** in the open square.” Jg 19:20 3885a
abused her all **n** until morning, Jg 19:25 3915
with my concubine to spend the **n** Jg 20:4 3885a
surrounded the house at **n** because Jg 20:5 3915
It happened in the middle of the **n** Ru 3:8 3915
“Remain this **n**, and when morning Ru 3:13 3915
So all the people that **n** brought 1Sa 14:34 3915
go down after the Philistines by **n** 1Sa 14:36 3915
and cried out to the LORD all **n**. 1Sa 15:11 3915
what the LORD said to me last **n**.” 1Sa 15:16 3915
And David fled and escaped that **n**. 1Sa 19:10 3915
naked all that day and all that **n**. 1Sa 19:24 3915
a wall to us both by **n** and by day, 1Sa 25:16 3915
Abishai came to the people by **n**, 1Sa 26:7 3915
and they came to the woman by **n**; 1Sa 28:8 3915
eaten no food all day and all **n**. 1Sa 28:20 3915
they arose and went away that **n**. 1Sa 28:25 3915
valiant men rose and walked all **n**, 1Sa 31:12 3915
through the Arabah all that **n**; 2Sa 2:29 3915
Then Joab and his men went all **n** 2Sa 2:32 3915
by way of the Arabah all **n**. 2Sa 4:7 3915
But in the same **n** 2Sa 7:4 3915
went and lay all **n** on the ground. 2Sa 12:16 3885a
not spend the **n** with the people. 2Sa 17:8 3885a
‘Do not spend the **n** at the fords 2Sa 17:16 3915
a man will pass the **n** with you, 2Sa 19:7 3915
nor the beasts of the field by **n**. 2Sa 21:10 3915
to Solomon in a dream at **n**; 1Ki 3:5 3915
“This woman's son died in the **n**, 1Ki 3:19 3915
“So she arose in the middle of the **n** 1Ki 3:20 3915
open toward this house **n** and day, 1Ki 8:29 3915
to the LORD our God day and **n**, 1Ki 8:59 3915
came by **n** and surrounded the city. 2Ki 6:14 3915
in the **n** and said to his servants, 2Ki 7:12 3915
he arose by **n** and struck the Edomites 2Ki 8:21 3915
Then it happened that **n** that the 2Ki 19:35 3915
and all the men of war *fled* by **n** 2Ki 25:4 3915
They spent the **n** around the house 1Ch 9:27 3885a
engaged in their work day and **n**. 1Ch 9:33 3915
It came about the same **n** that 1Ch 17:3 3915
In that **n** God appeared to Solomon 2Ch 1:7 3915
open toward this house day and **n**, 2Ch 6:20 3915
to Solomon at **n** and said to him, 2Ch 7:12 3915
he arose by **n** and struck down the 2Ch 21:9 3915
offerings and the fat until **n**; 2Ch 35:14 3915
before You now, day and **n**, Ne 1:6 3915
And I arose in the **n**, Ne 2:12 3915
So I went out at **n** by the Valley Ne 2:13 3915
So I went up at **n** by the ravine Ne 2:15 3915
up a guard against them day and **n**. Ne 4:9 3915
spend the **n** within Jerusalem Ne 4:22 3885a
us by **n** and a laborer by day.” Ne 4:22 3915
are coming to kill you at **n**.” Ne 6:10 3915
And with a pillar of fire by **n** To Ne 9:12 3915
way, Nor the pillar of fire by **n**, Ne 9:19 3915
spent the **n** outside Jerusalem. Ne 13:20 3885a
spend the **n** in front of the wall? Ne 13:21 3885a
or drink for three days, **n** or day. Es 4:16 3915
During that **n** the king could not Es 6:1 3915
n *which* said, ‘A boy is conceived.’ Jb 3:3 3915
“*As for* that **n**, let darkness Jb 3:6 3915
“Behold, let that **n** be barren; Jb 3:7 3915
from the visions of the **n**, Jb 4:13 3915
And grope at noon as in the **n**. Jb 5:14 3915
But the **n** continues, And I am Jb 7:4 6153
“They make **n** into day, *saying,* Jb 17:12 3915
like a vision of the **n** he is chased Jb 20:8 3915
“They spend the **n** naked, without Jb 24:7 3885a
needy, And at **n** he is as a thief. Jb 24:14 3915
tempest steals him away in the **n**. Jb 27:20 3915
And dew lies all **n** on my branch. Jb 29:19 3885a
gnaw the dry ground by **n** in waste Jb 30:3 570
At **n** it pierces my bones within me, Jb 30:17 3915
“In a dream, a vision of the **n**, Jb 33:15 3915
And He overthrows *them* in the **n**, Jb 34:25 3915
Maker, Who gives songs in the **n**, Jb 35:10 3915
“Do not long for the **n**, Jb 36:20 3915
he spend the **n** at your manger? Jb 39:9 3885a
in His law he meditates day and **n**. Ps 1:2 3915
Every **n** I make my bed swim, I Ps 6:6 3915
my mind instructs me in the **n**. Ps 16:7 3915
You have visited *me* by **n**; Ps 17:3 3915
And **n** to night reveals knowledge. Ps 19:2 3915
And night to **n** reveals knowledge. Ps 19:2 3915
And by **n**, but I have no rest. Ps 22:2 3915
Weeping may last for the **n**, Ps 30:5 6153
day and **n** Your hand was heavy Ps 32:4 3915
tears have been my food day and **n**, Ps 42:3 3915
His song will be with me in the **n**, Ps 42:8 3915
Day and **n** they go around her upon Ps 55:10 3915
meditate on You in the **n** watches, Ps 63:6
Yours is the day, Yours also is the **n**; Ps 74:16 3915
In the **n** my hand was stretched out Ps 77:2 3915
I will remember my song in the **n**; Ps 77:6 3915
all the **n** with a light of fire. Ps 78:14 3915
by day and in the **n** before You. Ps 88:1 3915
passes by, Or *as* a watch in the **n**. Ps 90:4 3915
not be afraid of the terror by **n**, Ps 91:5 3915
And Your faithfulness by **n**, Ps 92:2 3915
appoint darkness and it becomes **n**, Ps 104:20 3915
And fire to illumine by **n**. Ps 105:39 3915
I remember Your name in the **n**, Ps 119:55 3915
My eyes anticipate the **n** watches, Ps 119:148
you by day, Nor the moon by **n**. Ps 121:6 3915
by **n** in the house of the LORD! Ps 134:1 3915
The moon and stars to rule by **n**, Ps 136:9 3915
the light around me will be **n**,” Ps 139:11 3915
And the **n** is as bright as the day. Ps 139:12 3915
of the **n** and *in* the darkness. Pr 7:9 3915
rises also while it is still **n** And Pr 31:15 3915
Her lamp does not go out at **n**. Pr 31:18 3915

even at **n** his mind does not rest. Ec 2:23 3915
one should never sleep day or **n**), Ec 8:16 3915
lies all **n** between my breasts. SS 1:13 3885a
"On my bed **n** after night I sought SS 3:1 3915
"On my bed night after **n** I sought SS 3:1 3915
against the terrors of the **n**. SS 3:8 3915
My locks with the damp of the **n**.' SS 5:2 3915
us spend the **n** in the villages. SS 7:11 3885a
brightness of a flaming fire by **n**; Is 4:5 3915
Surely in a **n** Ar of Moab is Is 15:1 3915
Surely in a **n** Kir of Moab is Is 15:1 3915
your shadow like **n** at high noon; Is 16:3 3915
every **n** at my guard post. Is 21:8 3915
"Watchman, how far gone is the **n**? Is 21:11 3915
Watchman, how far gone is the **n**?" Is 21:11 3915
"Morning comes but also **n**. Is 21:12 3915
of Arabia you must spend the **n**, Is 21:13 3885a
At **n** my soul longs for You, Is 26:9 3915
damage it, I guard it **n** and day. Is 27:3 3915
anytime during the day or **n**, Is 28:19 3915
like a dream, a vision of the **n**. Is 29:7 3915
You will have songs as in the **n** Is 30:29 3915
It will not be quenched **n** or day; Is 34:10 3915
the **n** monster will settle there Is 34:14 3917a
From day until **n** You make Is 38:12 3915
From day until **n** You make Is 38:13 3915
They will not be closed day or **n**, Is 60:11 3915
all **n** they will never keep silent. Is 62:6 3915
and spend the **n** in secret places; Is 65:4 3885a
by **n** And destroy her palaces!" Jer 6:5 3915
That I might weep day and **n** For Jer 9:1 3915
has pitched his *tent* for the **n**? Jer 14:8 3885a
flow down with tears **n** and day, Jer 14:17 3915
will serve other gods day and **n**, Jer 16:13 3915
moon and the stars for light by **n**, Jer 31:35 3915
day and My covenant for the **n**, Jer 33:20 3915
so that day and **n** will not be at Jer 33:20 3915
covenant *for* day and **n** *stand* not, Jer 33:25 3915
of the day and the frost of the **n**. Jer 36:30 3915
fled and went out of the city at **n** Jer 39:4 3915
If thieves *came* by **n**, Jer 49:9 3915
and went forth from the city at **n** Jer 52:7 3915
She weeps bitterly in the **n** And La 1:2 3915
run down like a river day and **n**; La 2:18 3915
cry aloud in the **n** At the La 2:19 3915
At the beginning of the **n** watches; La 2:19 3915
revealed to Daniel in a **n** vision. Da 2:19 3916
That same **n** Belshazzar the Da 5:30 3916
palace and spent the **n** fasting, Da 6:18 1006b
"I was looking in my vision by **n**, Da 7:2 3916
I kept looking in the **n** visions, Da 7:7 3916
"I kept looking in the **n** visions, Da 7:13 3916
also will stumble with you by **n**; Hos 4:5 3915
Their anger smolders all **n**, Hos 7:6 3915
Come, spend the **n** in sackcloth O Jl 1:13 3885a
Who also darkens day *into* **n**, Am 5:8 3915
thieves came to you, If robbers by **n** Ob 1:5 3915
Therefore *it will be* **n** for you Mi 3:6 3915
I saw at **n**, and behold, a man was Zch 1:8 3915
and it will spend the **n** within Zch 5:4 3885a
to the LORD, neither day nor **n**, Zch 14:7 3915
and His mother while it was still **n**, Mt 2:14 *3571*
watch of the **n** He came to them, Mt 14:25 *3571*
and spent the **n** there. Mt 21:17 *835*
at what time of the **n** the thief was Mt 24:43 *5438*
fall away because of Me this **n**, Mt 26:31 *3571*
I say to you that this *very* **n**, Mt 26:34 *3571*
for last **n** I suffered greatly in a Mt 27:19 *4594*
'His disciples came by **n** and stole Mt 28:13 *3571*
to bed at **n** and gets up by day, Mk 4:27 *3571*
n and day, he was screaming Mk 5:5 *3571*
about the fourth watch of the **n** He Mk 6:48 *3571*
that this very **n**, Mk 14:30 *3571*
watch over their flock by **n**. Lk 2:8 *3571*
serving **n** and day with fastings Lk 2:37 *3571*
"Master, we worked hard all **n** and Lk 5:5 *3571*
the whole **n** in prayer to God. Lk 6:12 *1273*
This *very* **n** your soul is required of Lk 12:20 *3571*
on that **n** there will be two in Lk 17:34 *3571*
elect who cry to Him day and **n**, Lk 18:7 *3571*
He would go out and spend the **n** Lk 21:37 *835*
this man came to Jesus by **n** Jn 3:2 *3571*
n is coming when no one can work. Jn 9:4 *3571*
"But if anyone walks in the **n**, Jn 11:10 *3571*
went out immediately; and it was **n**. Jn 13:30 *3571*
who had first come to Him by **n**, Jn 19:39 *3571*
and that **n** they caught nothing. Jn 21:3 *3571*
the **n** an angel of the Lord opened Ac 5:19 *3571*
also watching the gates day and **n** Ac 9:24 *3571*
but his disciples took him by **n** and Ac 9:25 *3571*
On the very **n** when Herod was Ac 12:6 *3571*
vision appeared to Paul in the **n**: Ac 16:9 *3571*
he took them that *very* hour of the **n** Ac 16:33 *3571*
Paul and Silas away by **n** to Berea, Ac 17:10 *3571*
said to Paul in the **n** by a vision, Ac 18:9 *3571*
remembering that **n** and day for a Ac 20:31 *3571*
on the **n** *immediately* following, Ac 23:11 *3571*
of the **n** to proceed to Caesarea, Ac 23:23 *3571*
brought him by **n** to Antipatris. Ac 23:31 *3571*
earnestly serve *God* **n** and day. Ac 26:7 *3571*
"For this very **n** an angel of the Ac 27:23 *3571*
when the fourteenth **n** came, Ac 27:27 *3571*
The **n** is almost gone, and the day Ro 13:12 *3571*
in the **n** in which He was betrayed 1Co 11:23 *3571*
a **n** and a day I have spent in the 2Co 11:25 *3574*
how working **n** and day so as not to 1Th 2:9 *3571*
as we **n** and day keep praying most 1Th 3:10 *3571*
come just like a thief in the **n**. 1Th 5:2 *3571*
We are not of **n** nor of darkness; 1Th 5:5 *3571*
who sleep do their sleeping at **n**, 1Th 5:7 *3571*
who get drunk get drunk at **n**. 1Th 5:7 *3571*
we *kept* working **n** and day 2Th 3:8 *3571*
entreaties and prayers **n** and day. 1Tm 5:5 *3571*
you in my prayers **n** and day, 2Tm 1:3 *3571*
day and **n** they do not cease to say, Rv 4:8 *3571*
serve Him day and **n** in His temple; Rv 7:15 *3571*
of it, and the **n** in the same way. Rv 8:12 *3571*
them before our God day and **n**. Rv 12:10 *3571*
they have no rest day and **n**, Rv 14:11 *3571*
day and **n** forever and ever. Rv 20:10 *3571*
(for there will be no **n** there) Rv 21:25 *3571*
there will no longer be *any* **n**; Rv 22:5 *3571*

NIGHTS
the earth forty days and forty **n**; Gn 7:4 3915
earth for forty days and forty **n**. Gn 7:12 3915
mountain forty days and forty **n**. Ex 24:18 3915
the LORD forty days and forty **n**; Ex 34:28 3915
on the mountain forty days and **n**; Dt 9:9 3915
at the end of forty days and **n** Dt 9:11 3915
as at the first, forty days and **n**; Dt 9:18 3915
the LORD the forty days and **n**, Dt 9:25 3915
forty days and forty **n** like the first Dt 10:10 3915
water for three days and three **n**. 1Sa 30:12 3915
forty days and forty **n** to Horeb, 1Ki 19:8 3915
with him for seven days and seven **n** Jb 2:13 3915
And **n** of trouble are appointed me. Jb 7:3 3915
the fish three days and three **n**. Jon 1:17 3915
had fasted forty days and forty **n**, Mt 4:2 *3571*
JONAH WAS THREE DAYS AND THREE N IN Mt 12:40 *3571*
three days and three **n** in the heart Mt 12:40 *3571*
through many sleepless **n**, 2Co 11:27 *70*

NILE
behold, he was standing by the **N**. Gn 41:1 2975
from the **N** there came up seven Gn 41:2 2975
came up after them from the **N**, Gn 41:3 2975
other cows on the bank of the **N**. Gn 41:3 2975
was standing on the bank of the **N**; Gn 41:17 2975
and sleek came up out of the **N**, Gn 41:18 2975
born you are to cast into the **N**, Ex 1:22 2975
the reeds by the bank of the **N**. Ex 2:3 2975
came down to bathe at the **N**, Ex 2:5 2975
maidens walking alongside the **N**; Ex 2:5 2975
shall take some water from the **N** Ex 4:9 2975
the water which you take from the **N** Ex 4:9 2975
to meet him on the bank of the **N**; Ex 7:15 2975
will strike the water that is in the **N** Ex 7:17 2975
fish that are in the **N** will die, Ex 7:18 2975
die, and the **N** will become foul, Ex 7:18 2975
drinking water from the **N**. Ex 7:18 2975
the water that *was* in the **N**, Ex 7:20 2975
all the water that *was* in the **N** Ex 7:20 2975
The fish that *were* in the **N** died, Ex 7:21 2975
Nile died, and the **N** became foul, Ex 7:21 2975
could not drink water from the **N**. Ex 7:21 2975
all the Egyptians dug around the **N** Ex 7:24 2975
not drink of the water of the **N**. Ex 7:24 2975
after the LORD had struck the **N**. Ex 7:25 2975
"The **N** will swarm with frogs, Ex 8:3 2975
they may be left only in the **N**?" Ex 8:9 2975
they will be left only in the **N**." Ex 8:11 2975
staff with which you struck the **N**, Ex 17:5 2975
The bulrushes by the **N**, Is 19:7 2975
by the edge of the **N** And all the Is 19:7 2975
fields by the **N** Will become dry, Is 19:7 2975
cast a line into the **N** will mourn, Is 19:8 2975
The grain of the **N**, Is 23:3 7883
Overflow your land like the **N**, Is 23:10 2975
To drink the waters of the **N**? Jer 2:18 7883
Who is this that rises like the **N**, Jer 46:7 2975
Egypt rises like the **N**, Jer 46:8 2975
'My **N** is mine, and I myself have Ezk 29:3 2975
'The **N** is mine, and I have made Ezk 29:9 2975
I will make the **N** canals dry And Ezk 30:12 2975
all of it will rise up like the **N**, Am 8:8 2975
And subside like the **N** of Egypt. Am 8:8 2975
And all of it rises up like the **N** Am 9:5 2975
And subsides like the **N** of Egypt; Am 9:5 2975
situated by the waters of the **N**, Na 3:8 2975
the depths of the **N** will dry up; Zch 10:11 2975

NIMRAH
"Ataroth, Dibon, Jazer, **N**, Nu 32:3 5247

NIMRIM
For the waters of **N** are desolate. Is 15:6 5249
waters of **N** will become desolate. Jer 48:34 5249

NIMROD
Now Cush became the father of **N**; Gn 10:8 5248
"Like **N** a mighty hunter before Gn 10:9 5248
Cush became the father of **N**; 1Ch 1:10 5248
The land of **N** at its entrances; Mi 5:6 5248

NIMSHI
and Jehu the son of **N** you shall 1Ki 19:16 5250
son of Jehoshaphat the son of **N**, 2Ki 9:2 5250
son of **N** conspired against Joram. 2Ki 9:14 5250
the driving of Jehu the son of **N**, 2Ki 9:20 5250
Jehoram against Jehu the son of **N**, 2Ch 22:7 5250

NINE
were **n** hundred and thirty years, Gn 5:5 8672
were **n** hundred and twelve years, Gn 5:8 8672
were **n** hundred and five years, Gn 5:11 8672
were **n** hundred and ten years, Gn 5:14 8672
were **n** hundred and sixty-two years, Gn 5:20 8672
n hundred and sixty-nine years, Gn 5:27 8672
were **n** hundred and fifty years, Gn 9:29 8672
Peleg lived two hundred and **n** years Gn 11:19 8672
n bulls, two rams, fourteen male Nu 29:26 8672
give to the **n** and a half tribes. Nu 34:13 8672
Its length was **n** cubits and its Dt 3:11 8672
an inheritance to the **n** tribes and Jos 13:7 8672
the **n** tribes and the half-tribe. Jos 14:2 8672
n cities with their villages. Jos 15:44 8672
n cities with their villages. Jos 15:54 8672
n cities from these two tribes. Jos 21:16 8672
he had **n** hundred iron chariots, Jg 4:3 8672
chariots, **n** hundred iron chariots, Jg 4:13 8672
end of **n** months and twenty days. 2Sa 24:8 8672
in Samaria, *and reigned* **n** years. 2Ki 17:1 8672
Eliada and Eliphelet, **n**. 1Ch 3:8 8672
But the **n**—where are they? Lk 17:17 *1767*

NINETEEN
lived one hundred and **n** years Gn 11:25 8672, 6240
n cities with their villages. Jos 19:38 8672, 6240
n of David's servants besides 2Sa 2:30 8672, 6240

NINETEENTH
the **n** year of King Nebuchadnezzar, 2Ki 25:8 8672, 6240
the **n** for Pethahiah, the twentieth 1Ch 24:16 8672, 6240
for the **n** to Mallothi, his sons 1Ch 25:26 8672, 6240
the **n** year of King Nebuchadnezzar, Jer 52:12 8672, 6240

NINE-TENTHS
n *remained* in the *other* cities. Ne 11:1 8672

NINETY
Enosh lived **n** years, and Gn 5:9 8673
will Sarah, who is **n** years old, Gn 17:17 8673
three hundred and **n** days; Ezk 4:5 8673
side, three hundred and **n** days. Ezk 4:9 8673
and its length *was* **n** cubits. Ezk 41:12 8673

NINETY-EIGHT
Now Eli was **n** years old, and his 1Sa 4:15 8673, 8083

NINETY-FIVE
were eight hundred and **n** years, Gn 5:17 8673, 2568
lived five hundred and **n** years after Gn 5:30 8673, 2568

NINETY-NINE
Now when Abram was **n** years old, Gn 17:1 8673, 8672
Now Abraham was **n** years old when Gn 17:24 8673, 8672
does he not leave the **n** on the Mt 18:12 *1752b, 1767*
the **n** which have not gone astray. Mt 18:13 *1752b, 1767*
leave the **n** in the open pasture and Lk 15:4 *1752b, 1767*
than over **n** righteous persons who Lk 15:7 *1752b, 1767*

NINETY-SIX
There were **n** exposed pomegranates; Jer 52:23 8673, 8337a

NINEVEH
built **N** and Rehoboth-Ir and Calah, Gn 10:11 5210
and Resen between **N** and Calah; Gn 10:12 5210
and returned *home,* and lived at **N**. 2Ki 19:36 5210
and returned *home* and lived at **N**. Is 37:37 5210
"Arise, go to **N** the great city and Jon 1:2 5210
go to **N** the great city and Jon 3:2 5210
So Jonah arose and went to **N** Jon 3:3 5210
N was an exceedingly great city, Jon 3:3 5210
days and **N** will be overthrown." Jon 3:4 5210
the people of **N** believed in God; Jon 3:5 5210
the word reached the king of **N**, Jon 3:6 5210
"In **N** by the decree of the king Jon 3:7 5210
Should I not have compassion on **N**, Jon 4:11 5210
The oracle of **N**. Na 1:1 5210
Though **N** *was* like a pool of water Na 2:8 5210
'**N** is devastated! Who will grieve Na 3:7 5210
And He will make **N** a desolation, Zph 2:13 5210
"The men of **N** will stand up with Mt 12:41 *3536*
"The men of **N** will stand up with Lk 11:32 *3536*

NINEVITES
as Jonah became a sign to the **N**, Lk 11:30 *3536*

NINTH
on the **n** of the month at evening, Lv 23:32 8672
the **n** year when its crop comes in. Lv 25:22 8671
On the **n** day *it was* Abidan the son Nu 7:60 8671
In the **n** year of Hoshea, the king 2Ki 17:6 8671
n year of Hoshea king of Israel, 2Ki 18:10 8672
Now in the **n** year of his reign, 2Ki 25:1 8671
On the **n** day of the *fourth* month 2Ki 25:3 8672
Johanan the eighth, Elzabad the **n**, 1Ch 12:12 8671
the **n** for Jeshua, the tenth for 1Ch 24:11 8671
the **n** to Mattaniah, his sons and 1Ch 25:16 8671
The **n** for the ninth month *was* 1Ch 27:12 8671
The ninth for the **n** month *was* 1Ch 27:12 8671
It was the **n** month on the Ezr 10:9 8671
king of Judah, in the **n** month, Jer 36:9 8671
the winter house in the **n** month, Jer 36:22 8671
captured in the **n** year of Zedekiah Jer 39:1 8671
month, in the **n** *day* of the month, Jer 39:2 8672
about in the **n** year of his reign, Jer 52:4 8671
On the **n** *day* of the fourth month Jer 52:6 8672
the LORD came to me in the **n** year, Ezk 24:1 8671
the twenty-fourth of the **n** *month,* Hg 2:10 8671
twenty-fourth day of the **n** *month;* Hg 2:18 8671
on the fourth *day* of the **n** month, Zch 7:1 8671
about the sixth and the **n** hour, Mt 20:5 *1729a*

all the land until the **n** hour. **Mt 27:45** *1729a*
About the **n** hour Jesus cried **Mt 27:46** *1729a*
the whole land until the **n** hour. **Mk 15:33** *1729a*
At the **n** hour Jesus cried out **Mk 15:34** *1729a*
the whole land until the **n** hour, **Lk 23:44** *1729a*
up to the temple at the **n** *hour,* **Ac 3:1** *1729a*
About the **n** hour of the day he **Ac 10:3** *1729a*
in my house during the **n** hour; **Ac 10:30** *1729a*
the **n**, topaz; the tenth, chrysoprase; **Rv 21:20** *1729a*

NIP
n its head at the front of its neck, **Lv 5:8** 4454

NISAN
And it came about in the month **N**, **Ne 2:1** 5212
first month, which is the month **N**, **Es 3:7** 5212

NISROCH
in the house of **N** his god, **2Ki 19:37** 5268
in the house of **N** his god, **Is 37:38** 5268

NO
Now **n** shrub of the field was yet **Gn 2:5** 2962, 3605
and **n** plant of the field had yet **Gn 2:5** 2962, 3605
was **n** man to cultivate the ground. **Gn 2:5** 369
for his offering He had **n** regard. **Gn 4:5** 3808
it will **n** longer yield its **Gn 4:12** 3808
so that **n** one finding him would slay **Gn 4:15** 3605
but the dove found **n** resting place **Gn 8:9** 3808
Sarai was barren; she had **n** child. **Gn 11:30** 369
be **n** strife between you and me, **Gn 13:8** 408
You have given **n** offspring to me, **Gn 15:3** 3808
wife had borne him **n** *children,* **Gn 16:1** 3808
"**N** longer shall your name be **Gn 17:5** 3808
"**N**, but Sarah your wife will **Gn 17:19** 61
"**N**, but you did laugh." **Gn 18:15** 3808
"**N**, but we shall spend the night **Gn 19:2** 3808
"Oh **n**, my lords! **Gn 19:18** 408
is **n** fear of God in this place, **Gn 20:11** 369
"**N**, my lord, hear me; **Gn 23:11** 3808
and **n** man had had relations with **Gn 24:16** 3808
that you will do us **n** harm, **Gn 26:29** 518
that she bore Jacob **n** children, **Gn 30:1** 3808
although **n** man is with us, **Gn 31:50** 369
"Your name shall **n** longer be **Gn 32:28** 3808
"**N**, please, if now I have found **Gn 33:10** 408
shall **n** longer be called Jacob, **Gn 35:10** 3808
"Shed **n** blood. Throw him into this **Gn 37:22** 408
been **n** temple prostitute here." **Gn 38:21** 3808
been **n** temple prostitute here.' " **Gn 38:22** 3808
"There is **n** one greater in this **Gn 39:9** 369
there is **n** one to interpret it." **Gn 40:8** 369
but there was **n** one who could **Gn 41:8** 369
dream, but **n** one can interpret it; **Gn 41:15** 369
but there was **n** one who could **Gn 41:24** 369
there is **n** one so discerning and **Gn 41:39** 369
yet without your permission **n** one **Gn 41:44** 3808
"**N**, my lord, but your servants **Gn 42:10** 3808
"**N**, but you have come to look at **Gn 42:12** 3808
father today, and one is **n** longer alive." **Gn 42:13** 369
one is **n** longer alive, and the youngest **Gn 42:32** 369
Joseph is **n** more, and Simeon is no more, **Gn 42:36** 369
is no more, and Simeon is **n** more, **Gn 42:36** 369
So there was **n** man with him when **Gn 45:1** 3808
for there is **n** pasture for your **Gn 47:4** 369
there was **n** food in all the land, **Gn 47:13** 369
when she could hide him **n** longer, **Ex 2:3** 3808
he saw there was **n** one *around,* **Ex 2:12** 369
"You are **n** longer to give the **Ex 5:7** 3808
pay **n** attention to false words." **Ex 5:9** 408
is **n** straw given to your servants, **Ex 5:16** 369
for you will be given **n** straw, **Ex 5:18** 3808
with **n** concern even for this. **Ex 7:23** 3808
is **n** one like the LORD our God. **Ex 8:10** 369
so that **n** swarms of insects will **Ex 8:22** 1115
is **n** one like Me in all the earth. **Ex 9:14** 369
but he who paid **n** regard to the **Ex 9:21** 3808
of Israel *were,* there was **n** hail. **Ex 9:26** 3808
go, and you shall stay **n** longer." **Ex 9:28** 3808
and there will be hail **n** longer, **Ex 9:29** 3808
rain **n** longer poured on the earth. **Ex 9:33** 3808
so that **n** one will be able to see **Ex 10:5** 3808
and **n** plague will befall you to **Ex 12:13** 3808
n work at all shall be done on **Ex 12:16** 3808
be **n** leaven found in your houses; **Ex 12:19** 3808
for there was **n** home where there **Ex 12:30** 369
n foreigner is to eat of it; **Ex 12:43** 3605, 3808
But **n** uncircumcised person may eat **Ex 12:48** 3605, 3808
"Is it because there were **n** graves **Ex 14:11** 369
the wilderness and found **n** water. **Ex 15:22** 3808
had gathered much had **n** excess, **Ex 16:18** 3808
had gathered little had **n** lack; **Ex 16:18** 3808
"Let **n** man leave any of it until **Ex 16:19** 408
let **n** man go out of his place on **Ex 16:29** 408
n water for the people to drink. **Ex 17:1** 369
'**N** hand shall touch him, but he **Ex 19:13** 3808
shall have **n** other gods before Me. **Ex 20:3** 3808
two, **n** vengeance shall be taken; **Ex 21:21** 3808
yet there is **n** injury, **Ex 21:22** 3808
yet there is no f injury, he **Ex 21:22**
there will be **n** bloodguiltiness on **Ex 22:2** 369
away while **n** one is looking, **Ex 22:10** 369
"There shall be **n** one miscarrying **Ex 23:26** 3808
"You shall make **n** covenant with **Ex 23:32** 3808
that there will be **n** plague among **Ex 30:12** 3808
for **n** man can see Me and live!" **Ex 33:20** 3808
"**N** man is to come up with you, nor **Ex 34:3** 3808
yet He will by **n** means leave *the* **Ex 34:7** 3808
"Watch yourself that you make **n** **Ex 34:12** 6435
make for yourself **n** molten gods. **Ex 34:17** 3808
and **n** man shall covet your land **Ex 34:24** 3808
"Let **n** man or woman any longer **Ex 36:6** 408
'**N** grain offering, which you bring **Lv 2:11** 3605, 3808
'But **n** sin offering of which any **Lv 6:30** 3605, 3808
there are **n** white hairs in it and **Lv 13:21** 369
there is **n** white hair in the bright **Lv 13:26** 369
and it is **n** deeper than the skin, **Lv 13:26** 369
to be **n** deeper than the skin and **Lv 13:31** 369
and there is **n** black hair in it, **Lv 13:31** 369
and **n** yellowish hair has grown in **Lv 13:32** 3808
scale is **n** deeper than the skin, **Lv 13:32** 369
to be **n** deeper than the skin, **Lv 13:34** 369
n one shall be in the tent of **Lv 16:17** 3808
"They shall **n** longer sacrifice **Lv 17:7** 3808
'**N** person among you may eat blood, **Lv 17:12** 3605, 3808
shall do **n** injustice in judgment; **Lv 19:15** 3808
who has in **n** way been redeemed nor **Lv 19:20** 3808
'You shall do **n** wrong in judgment, **Lv 19:35** 3808
will be **n** immorality in your midst. **Lv 20:14** 3808
'**N** one shall defile himself for a **Lv 21:1** 3808
him because she has had **n** husband; **Lv 21:3** 3808
'**N** man of your offspring **Lv 21:17** 3808
'For **n** one who has a defect shall **Lv 21:18** 3808, 3605
'**N** man among the descendants of **Lv 21:21** 3808, 3605
'**N** man of the descendants of **Lv 22:4** 376, 3808
'**N** layman, however, is to eat the **Lv 22:10** 3808
and has **n** child and returns to her **Lv 22:13** 369
but **n** layman shall eat of it. **Lv 22:13** 3808, 3605
there shall be **n** defect in it. **Lv 22:21** 3808, 3605
You shall do **n** laborious work. **Lv 23:21** 3808, 3605
"You shall do **n** work at all. **Lv 23:31** 3808, 3605
do **n** laborious work of any kind. **Lv 23:35** 3808, 3605
You shall do **n** laborious work. **Lv 23:36** 3808, 3605
'Or in case a man has **n** kinsman, **Lv 25:26** 3808
which have **n** surrounding wall **Lv 25:31** 369
with **n** one making *you* tremble. **Lv 26:6** 369
and **n** sword will pass through your **Lv 26:6** 3808
flee when **n** one is pursuing you. **Lv 26:17** 369
and even when **n** one is pursuing they **Lv 26:36** 369
sword, although **n** one is pursuing; **Lv 26:37** 369
and you will have **n** *strength* to **Lv 26:37**
man, it may **n** longer be redeemed; **Lv 27:20** 3808
the LORD, **n** man may consecrate it; **Lv 27:26** 3808
'**N** one who may have been set apart **Lv 27:29** 3808, 3605
that there will be **n** wrath on the **Nu 1:53** 3808
and they had **n** children. **Nu 3:4** 3808
'But if the man has **n** relative to **Nu 5:8** 369
and there is **n** witness against her **Nu 5:13** 369
"If **n** man has lain with you and **Nu 5:19** 3808
he shall drink **n** vinegar, whether **Nu 6:3** 3808
n razor shall pass over his head. **Nu 6:5** 3808
that there will be **n** plague among **Nu 8:19** 3808
they *themselves* shall do **n** work. **Nu 8:26** 3808
will by **n** means clear *the guilty,* **Nu 14:18** 3808
shall by **n** means see the land **Nu 14:23** 518
that **n** layman who is not of the **Nu 16:40** 3808
that there will **n** longer be wrath **Nu 18:5** 3808
have **n** inheritance in their land nor **Nu 18:20** 3808
they shall have **n** inheritance. **Nu 18:23** 3808
'They shall have **n** inheritance **Nu 18:24** 3808
will bear **n** sin by reason of it **Nu 18:32** 3808
red heifer in which is **n** defect **Nu 19:2** 369
has **n** covering tied down on it, **Nu 19:15** 369
was **n** water for the congregation, **Nu 20:2** 3808
For there is **n** food and no water, **Nu 21:5** 369
For there is no food and **n** water, **Nu 21:5** 369
there was **n** remnant left him; **Nu 21:35** 1115
place where there was **n** way to turn **Nu 22:26** 369
And he said, "**N**." **Nu 22:30** 3808
"For there is **n** omen against **Nu 23:23** 3808
the son of Hepher had **n** sons, **Nu 26:33** 3808
since **n** inheritance was given to them **Nu 26:62** 3808
in his own sin, and he had **n** sons. **Nu 27:3** 3808
his family because he had **n** son? **Nu 27:4** 369
'If a man dies and has **n** son, **Nu 27:8** 369
'If he has **n** daughter, then **Nu 27:9** 369
'If he has **n** brothers, then **Nu 27:10** 369
'If his father has **n** brothers, **Nu 27:11** 369
sheep which have **n** shepherd." **Nu 27:17** 369
you shall do **n** laborious work. **Nu 28:18** 3808, 3605
you shall do **n** laborious work. **Nu 28:25** 3808, 3605
you shall do **n** laborious work. **Nu 28:26** 3808, 3605
you shall do **n** laborious work. **Nu 29:1** 3808, 3605
you shall do **n** laborious work, and **Nu 29:12** 3808, 3605
you shall do **n** laborious work. **Nu 29:35** 3808, 3605
and **n** man of us is missing. **Nu 31:49** 3808
the people had **n** water to drink. **Nu 33:14** 3808
but **n** person shall be put to death **Nu 35:30** 3808
n expiation can be made for the land **Nu 35:33** 3808
"Thus **n** inheritance of the sons **Nu 36:7** 3808
"Thus **n** inheritance shall be **Nu 36:9** 3808
have **n** knowledge of good or evil, **Dt 1:39** 3808
We left **n** survivor. **Dt 2:34** 3808
n city that was too high for us; **Dt 2:36** 3808
them until **n** survivor was left. **Dt 3:3** 1115
Speak to Me **n** more of this matter. **Dt 3:26** 408
but you saw **n** form—only a voice. **Dt 4:12** 369
there is **n** other besides Him. **Dt 4:35** 369
there is **n** other. **Dt 4:39** 369
shall have **n** other gods before Me. **Dt 5:7** 3808
great voice, and He added **n** more. **Dt 5:22** 3808
You shall make **n** covenant with **Dt 7:2** 3808
them and show **n** favor to them. **Dt 7:2** 3808
there will be **n** male or female **Dt 7:14** 3808
n man will be able to stand before **Dt 7:24** 3808
ground where there was **n** water; **Dt 8:15** 369
and stiffen your neck **n** longer. **Dt 10:16** 3808
so that there will be **n** rain **Dt 11:17** 3808
"**N** man will be able to stand before **Dt 11:25** 3808
since he has **n** portion or **Dt 12:12** 369
for he has **n** portion or **Dt 14:27** 369
because he has **n** portion or **Dt 14:29** 369
there will be **n** poor among you, **Dt 15:4** 3808
"Beware that there is **n** base thought **Dt 15:9** 6435
"For seven days **n** leaven shall be **Dt 16:4** 3808
you shall do **n** work *on it.* **Dt 16:8** 3808
shall have **n** portion or **Dt 18:1** 3808
"They shall have **n** inheritance **Dt 18:2** 3808
away, and pay **n** attention to them; **Dt 22:1** 5956
way, and pay **n** attention to them; **Dt 22:4** 5956
there is **n** sin in the girl worthy **Dt 22:26** 369
but there was **n** one to save her. **Dt 22:27** 369
"**N** one who is emasculated or has **Dt 23:1** 3808
"**N** one of illegitimate birth **Dt 23:2** 3808
"**N** Ammonite or Moabite shall **Dt 23:3** 3808
that she finds **n** favor in his eyes **Dt 24:1** 3808
"**N** one shall take a handmill or **Dt 24:6** 3808
beat him forty times *but* **n** more, **Dt 25:3** 3808
one of them dies and has **n** son, **Dt 25:5** 369
be **n** one to frighten *them* away. **Dt 28:26** 369
will have **n** respect for the old, **Dt 28:50** 3808
who also leaves you **n** grain, **Dt 28:51** 3808
nations you shall find **n** rest, **Dt 28:65** 3808
and there will be **n** resting place **Dt 28:65** 3808
have **n** assurance of your life. **Dt 28:66** 3808
but there will be **n** buyer." **Dt 28:68** 369
and **n** grass grows in it, **Dt 29:23** 3808, 3605
I am **n** longer able to come and go, **Dt 31:2** 3808
there was **n** foreign god with him. **Dt 32:12** 369
Sons in whom is **n** faithfulness. **Dt 32:20** 3808
there is **n** understanding in them. **Dt 32:28** 369
He, And there is **n** god besides Me; **Dt 32:39** 369
And there is **n** one who can deliver **Dt 32:39** 369
but **n** man knows his burial place **Dt 34:6** 3808
Since that time **n** prophet has risen in **Dt 34:10** 3808
"**N** man will *be able to* stand **Jos 1:5** 3808
n courage remained in any man **Jos 2:11** 3808
was **n** spirit in them any longer because **Jos 5:1** 3808
sons of Israel **n** longer had manna, **Jos 5:12** 3808
"**N**; rather I indeed come now *as* **Jos 5:14** 3808
n one went out and no one came in. **Jos 6:1** 369
no one went out and **n** one came in. **Jos 6:1** 369
and they had **n** place to flee this **Jos 8:20** 3808
until **n** one was left of those who **Jos 8:22** 1115
n man had wielded an iron *tool;* **Jos 8:31** 3808
There was **n** day like that **Jos 10:14** 3808
N one uttered a word against any **Jos 10:21** 3808
He left **n** survivor. **Jos 10:28** 3808
He left **n** survivor in it. **Jos 10:30** 3808
until he had left him **n** survivor. **Jos 10:33** 1115
He left **n** survivor, according to **Jos 10:37** 3808
He left **n** survivor. **Jos 10:39** 3808
He left **n** survivor, but he utterly **Jos 10:40** 3808
until **n** survivor was left to them. **Jos 11:8** 1115
there was **n** one left who breathed. **Jos 11:11** 3808, 3605
They left **n** one who breathed. **Jos 11:14** 3808
that they might receive **n** mercy, **Jos 11:20** 1115
There were **n** Anakim left in the **Jos 11:22** 3808
the son of Manasseh, had **n** sons, **Jos 17:3** 3808
Levites have **n** portion among you, **Jos 18:7** 369
and **n** one of all their enemies **Jos 21:44** 3808
you have **n** portion in the LORD." **Jos 22:25** 369
have **n** portion in the LORD." **Jos 22:27** 369
n man has stood before you to this **Jos 23:9** 3808
"**N**, but we will serve the LORD." **Jos 24:21** 3808
you shall make **n** covenant with the **Jg 2:2** 3808
so that they could **n** longer stand **Jg 2:14** 3808
I also will **n** longer drive out **Jg 2:21** 3808
and **n** one escaped. **Jg 3:29** 3808
that you shall say, '**N**.' " **Jg 4:20** 369
They took **n** plunder in silver. **Jg 5:19** 3808
and leave **n** sustenance in Israel **Jg 6:4** 3808
in Israel as well as **n** sheep, **Jg 6:4**
I will **n** longer deliver you. **Jg 10:13** 3808
the misery of Israel **n** longer. **Jg 10:16** 7114a
besides her he had **n** son or daughter. **Jg 11:34** 369
she had **n** relations with a man. **Jg 11:39** 3808
you an Ephraimite?" If he said, "**N**," **Jg 12:5** 3808
barren and had borne **n** *children.* **Jg 13:2** 3808
barren and have borne **n** *children,* **Jg 13:3** 3808
and **n** razor shall come upon his **Jg 13:5** 3808
"Is there **n** woman among the **Jg 14:3** 369
"**N**, but we will bind you fast and **Jg 15:13** 3808
days there was **n** king in Israel; **Jg 17:6** 369
days there was **n** king of Israel; **Jg 18:1** 369

for there was **n** ruler humiliating **Jg 18:7** 369
and had **n** dealings with anyone. **Jg 18:7** 369
a place where there is **n** lack of **Jg 18:10** 369
there was **n** one to deliver *them,* **Jg 18:28** 369
they had **n** dealings with anyone, **Jg 18:28** 369
when there was **n** king in Israel, **Jg 19:1** 369
for **n** one took them into *his* house **Jg 19:15** 369
and **n** man will take me into his **Jg 19:18** 369
there is **n** lack of anything." **Jg 19:19** 369
"**N**, my fellows, please do not act **Jg 19:23** 408
let us go," but there was **n** answer. **Jg 19:28** 369
n one had come to the camp from **Jg 21:8** 3808
days there was **n** king in Israel; **Jg 21:25** 369
And they said to her, "**N**, but **Ru 1:10**
N, my daughters; for it is harder for **Ru 1:13** 408
with her, she said **n** more to her. **Ru 1:18** 2308
is **n** one but you to redeem *it,* **Ru 4:4** 369
but Hannah had **n** children. **1Sa 1:2** 369
"**N**, my lord, I am a woman **1Sa 1:15** 369
and her face was **n** longer *sad.* **1Sa 1:18** 3808
"There is **n** one holy like the **1Sa 2:2** 369
there is **n** one besides You, **1Sa 2:2** 369
"Boast **n** more so very proudly, Do **1Sa 2:3** 408
"**N**, but you shall give *it to me* **1Sa 2:16** 3808
"**N**, my sons; for the report is not **1Sa 2:24** 408
"**N**, but there shall be a king **1Sa 8:19** 3808
there is **n** present to bring to the man **1Sa 9:7** 369
'**N**, but set a king over us!' **1Sa 10:19** 3808
Surely there is **n** one like him **1Sa 10:24** 369
if there is **n** one to deliver us, **1Sa 11:3** 369
so that **n** two of them were left **1Sa 11:11** 3808
'**N**, but a king shall reign over **1Sa 12:12** 3808
Now **n** blacksmith could be found in **1Sa 13:19** 3808
n man put his hand to his mouth, **1Sa 14:26** 369
"Let **n** man's heart fail on **1Sa 17:32** 408
there was **n** sword in David's hand. **1Sa 17:50** 369
is safety for you and **n** harm, **1Sa 20:21** 369
you alone and **n** one with you?" **1Sa 21:1** 369
'Let **n** one know anything about the **1Sa 21:2** 408
"There is **n** ordinary bread on **1Sa 21:4** 369
for there was **n** bread there but **1Sa 21:6** 3808
there is **n** other except it here." **1Sa 21:9** 369
there is **n** one who discloses to me **1Sa 22:8** 369
n evil or rebellion in my hands, **1Sa 24:11** 369
man that **n** one can speak to him." **1Sa 25:17** 4480
away, but **n** one saw or knew *it,* **1Sa 26:12** 369
I would have **n** attachment with the **1Sa 26:19** 4480
so he **n** longer searched for him. **1Sa 27:4** 3808
n punishment shall come upon **1Sa 28:10** 518
from me and **n** longer answers me, **1Sa 28:15** 3808
also there was **n** strength in him, **1Sa 28:20** 3808
n food all day and all night. **1Sa 28:20** 3808
and I have found **n** fault in him **1Sa 29:3** 3808
was **n** strength in them to weep. **1Sa 30:4** 369
and pursued Israel **n** longer, **2Sa 2:28** 3808
n longer answer Abner a word, **2Sa 3:11** 3808
the daughter of Saul had **n** child **2Sa 6:23** 3808
and there is **n** God besides You, **2Sa 7:22** 369
this thing and had **n** compassion." **2Sa 12:6** 3808
"**N**, my brother, do not violate **2Sa 13:12** 408
"**N**, because this wrong in sending **2Sa 13:16** 408
"**N**, my son, we should not all go, **2Sa 13:25** 408
there was **n** one to separate them, **2Sa 14:6** 369
n one can turn to the right or to **2Sa 14:19** 518
was **n** one as handsome as Absalom, **2Sa 14:25** 3808
head there was **n** defect in him. **2Sa 14:25** 3808
but **n** man listens to you on the **2Sa 15:3** 369
'I have **n** delight in you,' behold, **2Sa 15:26** 3808
Then Hushai said to Absalom, "**N**! **2Sa 16:18** 3808
have **n** son to preserve my name." **2Sa 18:18** 369
you shall carry **n** news today **2Sa 18:20** 3808
will have **n** reward for going?" **2Sa 18:22** 369
"We have **n** portion in David, Nor **2Sa 20:1** 369
"We have **n** *concern* of silver or **2Sa 21:4** 369
"**N**, but I will surely buy *it* from **2Sa 24:24** 3808
replied to Adonijah, "**N**! **1Ki 1:43** 61
"**N**, for I will die here." **1Ki 2:30** 3808
because there was **n** house built **1Ki 3:2** 3808
been **n** one like you before you, **1Ki 3:12** 3808
n stranger with us in the house, **1Ki 3:18** 369
Then the other woman said, "**N**! **1Ki 3:22** 3808
But the first woman said, "**N**! **1Ki 3:22** 3808
and the other says, '**N**! **1Ki 3:23** 3808
child, and by **n** means kill him." **1Ki 3:26** 408
child, and by **n** means kill him. **1Ki 3:27** 3808
there is **n** one among us who knows **1Ki 5:6** 369
was cedar, there was **n** stone seen. **1Ki 6:18** 369
there is **n** God like You in heaven **1Ki 8:23** 369
are shut up and there is **n** rain, **1Ki 8:35** 3808
there is **n** man who does not sin) **1Ki 8:46** 369
there is **n** one else. **1Ki 8:60** 369
there was **n** more spirit in her. **1Ki 10:5** 3808
We have **n** inheritance in the son **1Ki 12:16** 3808
'You shall eat **n** bread, nor drink **1Ki 13:9** 3808
'You shall eat **n** bread, nor drink **1Ki 13:17** 3808
"Eat **n** bread and drink no water"; **1Ki 13:22** 408
"Eat no bread and drink **n** water"; **1Ki 13:22** 408
there was **n** rain in the land. **1Ki 17:7** 3808
your God lives, I have **n** bread, **1Ki 17:12** 518
there was **n** breath left in him. **1Ki 17:17** 3808
there is **n** nation or kingdom where **1Ki 18:10** 518
the wood, but put **n** fire *under it;* **1Ki 18:23** 3808
god, but put **n** fire *under it.*" **1Ki 18:25** 3808
was **n** voice and no one answered. **1Ki 18:26** 369
was no voice and **n** one answered. **1Ki 18:26** 369
but there was **n** voice, no one **1Ki 18:29** 369
was no voice, **n** one answered, **1Ki 18:29** 369
and **n** one paid attention. **1Ki 18:29** 369
away his face and ate **n** food. **1Ki 21:4** 3808

Surely there was **n** one like Ahab **1Ki 21:25** 3808
Like sheep which have **n** shepherd. **1Ki 22:17** 369
'These have **n** master. **1Ki 22:17** 3808
Now there was **n** king in Edom; **1Ki 22:47** 369
'Is it because there is **n** God in **2Ki 1:3** 369
'Is it because there is **n** God in **2Ki 1:6** 369
is it because there is **n** God in Israel **2Ki 1:16** 369
And because he had **n** son, **2Ki 1:17** 3808
And he saw Elijah **n** more. **2Ki 2:12** 3808
and there was **n** water for the army **2Ki 3:9** 3808
"**N**, for the LORD has called these **2Ki 3:13** 408
n son and her husband is old." **2Ki 4:14** 369
"**N**, my lord, O man of God, do not **2Ki 4:16** 408
but there was **n** sound or response. **2Ki 4:31** 369
Then there was **n** harm in the pot. **2Ki 4:41** 3808
there is **n** God in all the earth, **2Ki 5:15** 369
for your servant will **n** longer offer **2Ki 5:17** 3808
"**N**, my lord, O king; **2Ki 6:12** 3808
behold, there was **n** one there. **2Ki 7:5** 369
and behold, there was **n** one there, **2Ki 7:10** 369
then let **n** one escape *or* leave the **2Ki 9:15** 408
let **n** one be missing, for I have a **2Ki 10:19** 408
Now therefore take **n** *more* money **2Ki 12:7** 408
take **n** *more* money from the people, **2Ki 12:8** 1115
offered **n** tribute to the king of Assyria **2Ki 17:4** 3808
there is **n** strength to *deliver.* **2Ki 19:3** 369
n, but let the shadow turn **2Ki 20:10** 3808
"Only **n** accounting shall be made **2Ki 22:7** 3808
that **n** man might make his son or **2Ki 23:10** 1115
let **n** one disturb his bones." **2Ki 23:18** 408
Before him there was **n** king **2Ki 23:25** 3808
there was **n** food for the people **2Ki 25:3** 3808
Now Sheshan had **n** sons, only **1Ch 2:34** 3808
there is **n** wrong in my hands, **1Ch 12:17** 3808
"**N** one is to carry the ark of God **1Ch 15:2** 3808
permitted **n** man to oppress them, **1Ch 16:21** 3808
ones, And do My prophets **n** harm." **1Ch 16:22** 408
"**N**, but I will surely buy *it* for **1Ch 21:24** 3808
and the iron there is **n** limit. **1Ch 22:16** 369
and Eliezer had **n** other sons, but **1Ch 23:17** 3808
Eleazar died and had **n** sons, **1Ch 23:22** 3808
the Levites will **n** longer need to **1Ch 23:26** 369
their father and had **n** sons. **1Ch 24:2** 3808
Eleazar, who had **n** sons. **1Ch 24:28** 3808
a shadow, and there is **n** hope. **1Ch 29:15** 369
there is **n** god like You in heaven **2Ch 6:14** 369
heavens are shut up and there is **n** rain **2Ch 6:26** 3808
there is **n** man who does not sin) **2Ch 6:36** 369
heavens so that there is **n** rain, **2Ch 7:13** 3808
We have **n** inheritance in the son **2Ch 10:16** 3808
a priest of *what are* **n** gods. **2Ch 13:9** 3808
and there was **n** one at war with **2Ch 14:6** 369
there is **n** one besides You to **2Ch 14:11** 369
and those who have **n** strength; **2Ch 14:11** 369
there was **n** peace to him who went out **2Ch 15:5** 369
And there was **n** more war until the **2Ch 15:19** 3808
Like sheep which have **n** shepherd; **2Ch 18:16** 369
'These have **n** master. **2Ch 18:16** 3808
have **n** part in unrighteousness or **2Ch 19:7** 369
that **n** one can stand against You. **2Ch 20:6** 369
the ground, and **n** one had escaped. **2Ch 20:24** 369
so that **n** son was left to him **2Ch 21:17** 3808
And his people made **n** fire for him **2Ch 21:19** 3808
he departed with **n** one's regret, **2Ch 21:20** 3808
So there was **n** one of the house of **2Ch 22:9** 369
"But let **n** one enter the house of **2Ch 23:6** 408
so that **n** one would enter *who was* **2Ch 23:19** 3808
have **n** honor from the LORD God." **2Ch 26:18** 3808
for **n** god of any nation or kingdom **2Ch 32:15** 3808, 3605
But Hezekiah gave **n** return for the **2Ch 32:25** 3808
people, but they paid **n** attention. **2Ch 33:10** 3808
burden on *your* shoulders **n** longer. **2Ch 35:3** 369
people, until there was **n** remedy. **2Ch 36:16** 369
and had **n** compassion on young man **2Ch 36:17** 3808
as a result you will have **n** **Ezr 4:16** 3809
is **n** remnant nor any who escape? **Ezr 9:14** 369
for **n** one can stand before You **Ezr 9:15** 369
there was **n** animal with me except **Ne 2:12** 369
was **n** place for my mount to pass. **Ne 2:14** 369
we will **n** longer be a reproach." **Ne 2:17** 3808
and build, but you have **n** portion, **Ne 2:20** 369
and *that* **n** breach remained in it, **Ne 6:1** 3808
n Ammonite or Moabite should ever **Ne 13:1** 3808
n load would enter on the sabbath **Ne 13:19** 3808
nations there was **n** king like him, **Ne 13:26** 3808
the law, there was **n** compulsion, **Es 1:8** 369
that Vashti may **n** longer come **Es 1:19** 3808
for she had **n** father or mother. **Es 2:7** 369
for **n** one was to enter the king's **Es 4:2** 369
"Even Esther the queen let **n** one **Es 5:12** 3808
and **n** one could stand before them, **Es 9:2** 3808
is **n** one like him on the earth, **Jb 1:8** 369
is **n** one like him on the earth, **Jb 2:3** 369
with **n** one speaking a word to him, **Jb 2:13** 369
Let **n** joyful shout enter it. **Jb 3:7** 408
puts **n** trust even in His servants; **Jb 4:18** 3808
And there is **n** deliverer. **Jb 5:4** 369
visit your abode and fear **n** loss. **Jb 5:24** 3808
now, let there be **n** injustice; **Jb 6:29** 408
who sees me will behold me **n** longer; **Jb 7:8** 3808
tent of the wicked will be **n** longer." **Jb 8:22** 369
They flee away, they see **n** good. **Jb 9:25** 3808
"There is **n** umpire between us, **Jb 9:33** 3808
is **n** deliverance from Your hand. **Jb 10:7** 369
I had died and **n** eye had seen me! **Jb 10:18** 3808
there will be **n** escape for them; **Jb 11:20** 6
a man, and there can be **n** release. **Jb 12:14** 3808
grope in darkness with **n** light, **Jb 12:25** 3808

the clean out of the unclean? **N** one! **Jb 14:4** 3808
Until the heavens are **n** longer, **Jb 14:12** 1115
He puts **n** trust in His holy ones, **Jb 15:15** 3808
And **n** alien passed among them. **Jb 15:19** 3808
In houses **n** one would inhabit, **Jb 15:28** 3808
"Is there **n** limit to windy words? **Jb 16:3**
there is **n** violence in my hands, **Jb 16:17** 3808
be **n** *resting* place for my cry. **Jb 16:18** 408
I shall go the way of **n** return. **Jb 16:22** 3808
flame of his fire gives **n** light. **Jb 18:5** 3808
earth, And he has **n** name abroad. **Jb 18:17** 3808
"He has **n** offspring or posterity **Jb 18:19** 3808
but I get **n** answer; **Jb 19:7** 3808
for help, but there is **n** justice. **Jb 19:7** 369
eye which saw him sees him **n** longer, **Jb 20:9** 3808
his place **n** longer beholds him. **Jb 20:9** 3808
"Because he knew **n** quiet within **Jb 20:20** 3808
you have given **n** water to drink, **Jb 22:7** 3808
N, surely He would pay attention **Jb 23:6** 3808
have **n** covering against the cold. **Jb 24:7** 369
'**N** eye will see me.' **Jb 24:15** 3808
till he is **n** longer remembered. **Jb 24:20** 3808
And does **n** good for the widow. **Jb 24:21** 3808
but **n** one has assurance of life. **Jb 24:22** 3808
"If even the moon has **n** brightness **Jb 25:5** 3808
Him, And Abaddon has **n** covering. **Jb 26:6** 369
opens his eyes, and it is **n** longer. **Jb 27:19** 369
"The path **n** bird of prey knows, **Jb 28:7** 3808
And the orphan who had **n** helper. **Jb 29:12** 3808
destruction; **N** one restrains them. **Jb 30:13** 3808
And my gnawing *pains* take **n** rest. **Jb 30:17** 3808
Or that the needy had **n** covering, **Jb 31:19** 369
"**N**, I have not allowed my mouth **Jb 31:30** 3808
because they had found **n** answer, **Jb 32:3** 3808
Elihu saw that there was **n** answer **Jb 32:5** 369
there was **n** one who refuted Job, **Jb 32:12** 369
are dismayed, they **n** longer answer; **Jb 32:15** 3808
they stop *and* **n** longer answer? **Jb 32:16** 3808
"Let me now be partial to **n** one, **Jb 32:21** 408
n fear of me should terrify you, **Jb 33:7** 3808
and there is **n** guilt in me. **Jb 33:9** 3808
Or twice, *yet* **n** one notices it. **Jb 33:14** 3808
Who shows **n** partiality to princes Nor **Jb 34:19** 3808
"There is **n** darkness or deep **Jb 34:22** 369
had **n** regard for any of His ways; **Jb 34:27** 3808
"But **n** one says, **Jb 35:10** 3808
a broad place with **n** constraint; **Jb 36:16** 3808
far you shall come, but **n** farther; **Jb 38:11** 3808
"**N** one is so fierce that he dares **Jb 41:10** 3808
That **n** air can come between them. **Jb 41:16** 3808
And that **n** purpose of Yours can be **Jb 42:2** 3808
In all the land **n** women were **Jb 42:15** 3808
is **n** deliverance for him in God." **Ps 3:2** 369
N evil dwells with You. **Ps 5:4** 3808
is **n** mention of You in death; **Ps 6:5** 369
"There is **n** God." **Ps 10:4** 369
the earth will **n** longer cause terror. **Ps 10:18** 1077
"There is **n** God." **Ps 14:1** 369
There is **n** one who does good. **Ps 14:1** 369
There is **n** one who does good, not **Ps 14:3** 369
I have **n** good besides You." **Ps 16:2** 1077
There is **n** speech, nor are there **Ps 19:3** 369
And by night, but I have **n** rest. **Ps 22:2** 3808
shadow of death, I fear **n** evil, **Ps 23:4** 3808
in whose spirit there is **n** deceit! **Ps 32:2** 369
mule which have **n** understanding, **Ps 32:9** 369
who fear Him there is **n** want. **Ps 34:9** 369
is **n** fear of God before his eyes. **Ps 36:1** 369
and the wicked man will be **n** more; **Ps 37:10** 369
away, and lo, he was **n** more; **Ps 37:36** 369
There is **n** soundness in my flesh **Ps 38:3** 369
There is **n** health in my bones **Ps 38:3** 369
there is **n** soundness in my flesh. **Ps 38:7** 369
in whose mouth are **n** arguments. **Ps 38:14** 369
Before I depart and am **n** more." **Ps 39:13** 369
N man can by any means redeem *his* **Ps 49:7** 3808
So that they have **n** habitation. **Ps 49:14** 4480
"I shall take **n** young bull out of **Ps 50:9** 3808
"There is **n** God," **Ps 53:1** 369
There is **n** one who does good. **Ps 53:1** 369
There is **n** one who does good, not **Ps 53:3** 369
workers of wickedness **n** knowledge, **Ps 53:4** 3808
great fear *where* **n** fear had been; **Ps 53:5** 3808
With whom there is **n** change, **Ps 55:19** 369
N, in heart you work **Ps 58:2** 637
For **n** guilt of *mine,* they run and **Ps 59:4** 1097
them that they may be **n** more; **Ps 59:13** 369
weary land where there is **n** water. **Ps 63:1** 1097
mire, and there is **n** foothold; **Ps 69:2** 369
for there is **n** one to deliver." **Ps 71:11** 369
of peace till the moon is **n** more. **Ps 72:7** 1097
also, and him who has **n** helper. **Ps 72:12** 369
there are **n** pains in their death, **Ps 73:4** 369
There is **n** longer any prophet, Nor **Ps 74:9** 369
His virgins had **n** wedding songs. **Ps 78:63** 3808
And there was **n** one to bury them. **Ps 79:3** 369
there be **n** strange god among you; **Ps 81:9** 3808
of Israel be remembered **n** more." **Ps 83:4** 3808
N good thing does He withhold from **Ps 84:11** 3808
is **n** one like You among the gods, **Ps 86:8** 369
Whom You remember **n** more, **Ps 88:5** 3808
N evil will befall you, Nor will **Ps 91:10** 3808
A senseless man has **n** knowledge, **Ps 92:6** 3808
there is **n** unrighteousness in Him. **Ps 92:15** 3808
I will set **n** worthless thing **Ps 101:3** 3808
I will know **n** evil. **Ps 101:4** 3808
N one who has a haughty look and **Ps 101:5** 3808
has passed over it, it is **n** more, **Ps 103:16** 369
place acknowledges it **n** longer. **Ps 103:16** 3808

And let the wicked be **n** more. Ps 104:35 369
permitted **n** man to oppress them, Ps 105:14 3808
ones, And do My prophets **n** harm." Ps 105:15 408
They also do **n** unrighteousness; Ps 119:3 3808
For there is **n** one who regards me; Ps 142:4 369
There is **n** escape for me; Ps 142:4 6
N one cares for my soul. Ps 142:4 369
sight **n** man living is righteous. Ps 143:2 3808
there be **n** outcry in our streets! Ps 144:14 369
man, in whom there is **n** salvation. Ps 146:3 369
my hand and **n** one paid attention; Pr 1:24 369
cause, If he has done you **n** harm. Pr 3:30 3808
Give **n** sleep to your eyes, Nor Pr 6:4 369
Which, having **n** chief, Officer or Pr 6:7 369
and there will be **n** healing. Pr 6:15 369
were **n** depths I was brought forth, Pr 8:24 369
there were **n** springs abounding Pr 8:24 369
rich, And He adds **n** sorrow to it. Pr 10:22 3808
passes, the wicked is **n** more, Pr 10:25 369
Where there is **n** guidance the Pr 11:14 369
are overthrown and are **n** more, Pr 12:7 369
N harm befalls the righteous, But Pr 12:21
3808, 3605
in *its* pathway there is **n** death. Pr 12:28 408
But the poor hears **n** rebuke. Pr 13:8 3808
Where **n** oxen are, the manger is Pr 14:4 369
buy wisdom, When he has **n** sense? Pr 17:16 369
has a crooked mind finds **n** good, Pr 17:20 3808
the father of a fool has **n** joy. Pr 17:21 3808
finds **n** favor in his eyes. Pr 21:10 3808
There is **n** wisdom and no Pr 21:30 369
There is no wisdom and **n** Pr 21:30 369
And **n** counsel against the LORD. Pr 21:30 369
will be **n** future for the evil man; Pr 24:20 3808
who has **n** control over his spirit. Pr 25:28 369
And where there is **n** whisperer, Pr 26:20 369
flee when **n** one is pursuing, Pr 28:1 369
driving rain which leaves **n** food. Pr 28:3 369
let **n** one support him. Pr 28:17 408
or laughs, and there is **n** rest. Pr 29:9 369
Where there is **n** vision, the Pr 29:18 369
there will be **n** response. Pr 29:19 369
"I have done **n** wrong." Pr 30:20 3808
The locusts have **n** king, Pr 30:27 369
And remember his trouble **n** more. Pr 31:7 3808
And he will have **n** lack of gain. Pr 31:11 3808
n remembrance of earlier things; Ec 1:11 369
will be for them **n** remembrance Ec 1:11 3808
there was **n** profit under the sun. Ec 2:11 369
For there is **n** lasting remembrance Ec 2:16 369
is **n** advantage for man over beast, Ec 3:19 369
they had **n** one to comfort *them;* Ec 4:1 369
they had **n** one to comfort *them.* Ec 4:1 369
there was **n** end to all his labor. Ec 4:8 369
an old and foolish king who **n** longer Ec 4:13 3808
There is **n** end to all the people, Ec 4:16 369
for *He takes* **n** delight in fools. Ec 5:4 369
command experiences **n** trouble, Ec 8:5 3808
If **n** one knows what will happen, Ec 8:7 369
N man has authority to restrain Ec 8:8 369
is **n** discharge in the time of war, Ec 8:8 369
and they will **n** longer have a Ec 9:6 369
for there is **n** activity or Ec 9:10 369
n one remembered that poor man. Ec 9:15 3808
there is **n** profit for the charmer. Ec 10:11 369
N man knows what will happen, and Ec 10:14 3808
"I have **n** delight in them"; Ec 12:1 369
And there is **n** blemish in you. SS 4:7 369
N one would despise me, either. SS 8:1 3808
sister, And she has **n** breasts; SS 8:8 369
And I take **n** pleasure in the blood Is 1:11 3808
your worthless offerings **n** longer, Is 1:13 3808
Or as a garden that has **n** water. Is 1:30 369
there is **n** end to their treasures; Is 2:7 369
there is **n** end to their chariots. Is 2:7 369
the clouds to rain **n** rain on it." Is 5:6 4480
field, Until there is **n** more room, Is 5:8 657
N one in it is weary or stumbles, Is 5:27 369
it off with **n** one to deliver *it.* Is 5:29 369
have **n** fear and do not be Is 7:4 408
so that it is **n** longer a people), Is 7:8 4480
it is because they have **n** dawn. Is 8:20 369
But there will be **n** *more* gloom for Is 9:1 3808
There will be **n** end to the Is 9:7 369
N man spares his brother. Is 9:19 3808
n *tree* cutter comes up against us.' Is 14:8 3808
there is **n** straggler in his ranks. Is 14:31 369
died out, There is **n** green thing. Is 15:6 3808
there will be **n** cries of joy or jubilant Is 16:10 3808
N treader treads out wine in the Is 16:10 3808
will be **n** one to frighten *them.* Is 17:2 369
Before morning they are **n** more. Is 17:14 369
be driven away, and be **n** more. Is 19:7 369
There will be **n** work for Egypt Is 19:15 3808
When he opens **n** one will shut, Is 22:22 369
When he shuts **n** one will open. Is 22:22 369
There is **n** more restraint. Is 23:10 369
"You shall exult **n** more, O Is 23:12 3808
even there you will find **n** rest." Is 23:12 3808
palace of strangers is a city **n** more, Is 25:2 4480
And will **n** longer cover her slain. Is 26:21 3808
So that **n** one will damage it, I Is 27:3
"I have **n** wrath. Is 27:4 369
"He has **n** understanding"? Is 29:16 3808
Let us hear **n** more about the Holy Is 30:11
7673a, 4480
"**N**, for we will flee on horses," Is 30:16 3808
Jerusalem, you will weep **n** longer. Is 30:19 3808
will **n** longer hide Himself, Is 30:20 3808

N longer will the fool be called Is 32:5 3808
cities, He has **n** regard for man. Is 33:8 3808
hands so that they hold **n** bribe; Is 33:15 4480
will **n** longer see a fierce people, Is 33:19 3808
speech which **n** one comprehends, Is 33:19 4480
tongue which **n** one understands. Is 33:19 369
which **n** boat with oars will go, Is 33:21 1077
on which **n** mighty ship will pass Is 33:21 3808
And **n** resident will say, Is 33:24 1077
there is **n** one there *Whom* they may Is 34:12 369
N lion will be there, Nor will any Is 35:9 3808
there is **n** strength to deliver. Is 37:3 369
I will look on man **n** more among Is 38:11 3808
Behold, you are of **n** account, Is 41:24 369
there was **n** one who declared, Is 41:26 369
there was **n** one who proclaimed, Is 41:26 369
was **n** one who heard your words. Is 41:26 369
"But when I look, there is **n** one, Is 41:28 369
is **n** counselor among them Who, Is 41:28 369
him, but he paid **n** attention. Is 42:25 3808
Before Me there was **n** God formed, Is 43:10 3808
And there is **n** savior besides Me. Is 43:11 369
there was **n** strange *god* among you; Is 43:12 369
And there is **n** God besides Me. Is 44:6 369
precious things are of **n** profit; Is 44:9 1077
a god or cast an idol to **n** profit? Is 44:10 1115
drinks **n** water and becomes weary. Is 44:12 3808
N one recalls, nor is there Is 44:19 3808
am the LORD, and there is **n** other; Is 45:5 369
Besides Me there is **n** God. Is 45:5 369
That there is **n** one besides Me. Is 45:6 657
am the LORD, and there is **n** other, Is 45:6 369
are making *say,* 'He has **n** hands'? Is 45:9 369
is none else, **N** other God.' " Is 45:14 657
They have **n** knowledge, Who carry Is 45:20 3808
there is **n** other God besides Me, Is 45:21 369
I am God, and there is **n** other. Is 45:22 369
I am God, and there is **n** other; Is 46:9 369
God, and there is **n** one like Me, Is 46:9 657
For you shall **n** longer be called Is 47:1 3808
For you will **n** longer be called The Is 47:5 3808
am, and there is **n** one besides me. Is 47:8 657
'**N** one sees me,' Your wisdom and Is 47:10 369
and there is **n** one besides me.' Is 47:10 657
There will be **n** coal to warm by Is 47:14 369
"There is **n** peace for the wicked," Is 48:22 369
And have **n** compassion on the son Is 49:15 4480
"Why was there **n** man when I came? Is 50:2 369
Or have I **n** power to deliver? Is 50:2 369
walks in darkness and has **n** light? Is 50:10 369
unclean Will **n** longer come into you. Is 52:1 3808
He has **n** *stately* form or majesty Is 53:2 3808
Because He had done **n** violence, Is 53:9 3808
one, you who have borne **n** *child;* Is 54:1 3808
you will remember **n** more. Is 54:4 3808
"**N** weapon that is formed against Is 54:17
3605, 3808
And you who have **n** money come, Is 55:1 369
who have **n** understanding; Is 56:11 3808
and **n** man takes it to heart; Is 57:1 369
away, while **n** one understands. Is 57:1 369
"There is **n** peace," Is 57:21 369
N one sues righteously and no one Is 59:4 369
and **n** one pleads honestly. Is 59:4 369
is **n** justice in their tracks; Is 59:8 369
grope like those who have **n** eyes; Is 59:10 369
sight that there was **n** justice. Is 59:15 369
And He saw that there was **n** man, Is 59:16 369
that there was **n** one to intercede; Is 59:16 369
hated With **n** one passing through, Is 60:15 369
"**N** longer will you have the sun Is 60:19 3808
"Your sun will **n** longer set, Is 60:20 3808
It will **n** longer be said to you, Is 62:4 3808
LORD, take **n** rest for yourselves; Is 62:6 408
And give Him **n** rest until He Is 62:7 408
peoples there was **n** man with Me. Is 63:3 369
and there was **n** one to help, Is 63:5 369
and there was **n** one to uphold; Is 63:5 369
is **n** one who calls on Your name, Is 64:7 369
And there will **n** longer be heard Is 65:19 3808
"**N** longer will there be in it an Is 65:20 3808
They will do **n** evil or harm in Is 65:25 3808
I called, but **n** one answered; Is 66:4 369
Through a land that **n** one crossed Jer 2:6 3808
crossed And where **n** man dwelt?' Jer 2:6 3808
cisterns That can hold **n** water. Jer 2:13 3808
'It is hopeless! **N**! Jer 2:25 3808
They accepted **n** chastening. Jer 2:30 3808
We will **n** longer come to You'? Jer 2:31 3808
And there has been **n** spring rain. Jer 3:3 3808
they will **n** longer say, Jer 3:16 3808
And have **n** understanding. Jer 4:22 3808
the heavens, and they had **n** light. Jer 4:23 369
and behold, there was **n** man, Jer 4:25 369
And **n** man dwells in them. Jer 4:29 369
They have **n** delight in it. Jer 6:10 3808
peace,' But there is **n** peace. Jer 6:14 369
They are cruel and have **n** mercy; Jer 6:23 3808
in deceptive words to **n** avail. Jer 7:8 1115
it will **n** longer be called Topheth, Jer 7:32 3808
because there is **n** *other* place. Jer 7:32 369
and **n** one will frighten *them away.* Jer 7:33 369
N man repented of his wickedness, Jer 8:6 369
peace,' But there is **n** peace. Jer 8:11 369
will be **n** grapes on the vine And Jer 8:13 369
vine And **n** figs on the fig tree, Jer 8:13 369
waited for peace, but **n** good *came;* Jer 8:15 369
for which there is **n** charm, Jer 8:17 369
Is there **n** balm in Gilead? Jer 8:22 369

Is there **n** physician there? Jer 8:22 369
so that **n** one passes through, Jer 9:10 1097
so that **n** one passes through? Jer 9:12 1097
But **n** one will gather *them.*' " Jer 9:22 369
fear them, For they can do **n** harm, Jer 10:5 3808
And there is **n** breath in them. Jer 10:14 3808
have gone from me and are **n** more. Jer 10:20 369
There is **n** one to stretch out my Jer 10:20 369
his name be remembered **n** more." Jer 11:19 3808
Because **n** man lays it to heart. Jer 12:11 369
There is **n** peace for anyone. Jer 12:12 369
strained themselves to **n** profit. Jer 12:13 3808
And there is **n** one to open *them;* Jer 13:19 369
to the cisterns and found **n** water. Jer 14:3 3808
there has been **n** rain on the land; Jer 14:4 3808
young, Because there is **n** grass. Jer 14:5 3808
fail For there is **n** vegetation. Jer 14:6 369
'There will be **n** sword or famine Jer 14:15 3808
there will be **n** one to bury them Jer 14:16 369
for I will grant you **n** favor.' Jer 16:13 3808
"when it will **n** longer be said, Jer 16:14 3808
Futility and things of **n** profit." Jer 16:19 369
"to bring **n** load in through the Jer 17:24 1115
day holy by doing **n** work on it, Jer 17:24
1115, 3605
give **n** heed to any of his words." Jer 18:18 408
"when this place will **n** longer be Jer 19:6 3808
there is **n** *other* place for burial. Jer 19:11 369
For **n** man of his descendants will Jer 22:30 3808
"when they will **n** longer say, Jer 23:7 3808
So that **n** one has turned back from Jer 23:14 1115
"For you will **n** longer remember Jer 23:36 3808
hands, and I will do you **n** harm.' Jer 25:6 3808
and rise **n** more because of the Jer 25:27 3808
"**N** death sentence for this man! Jer 26:16 369
Of dread, and there is **n** peace. Jer 30:5 369
n longer make them their slaves. Jer 30:8 3808
And **n** one will make him afraid. Jer 30:10 369
by **n** means leave you unpunished.' Jer 30:11 3808
is **n** one to plead your cause; Jer 30:13 369
N healing for *your* sore, No Jer 30:13
for *your* sore, **N** recovery for you. Jer 30:13 369
n one cares for her." Jer 30:17 369
Because they are **n** more." Jer 31:15 369
sin I will remember **n** more." Jer 31:34 3808
n longer are they as a nation in Jer 33:24 4480
so that **n** one should keep them, a Jer 34:9 1115
so that **n** one should keep them any Jer 34:10 1115
"He shall have **n** one to sit on Jer 36:30 3808
there was **n** water but only mud, Jer 38:6 369
is **n** more bread in the city." Jer 38:9 369
"Let **n** man know about these words Jer 38:24 408
when **n** one knew about *it,* Jer 41:4 3808
"**N**, but we will go to the land of Jer 42:14 3808
and they will have **n** survivors or Jer 42:17 3808
you will see this place **n** more." Jer 42:18 3808
in ruins and **n** one lives in them, Jer 44:2 369
'So there will be **n** refugees or Jer 44:14 3808
well off and saw **n** misfortune. Jer 44:17 3808
was **n** longer able to endure *it,* Jer 44:22 3808
and have found **n** rest." Jer 45:3 3808
There is **n** healing for you. Jer 46:11 369
"Surely it will **n** *more* be found, Jer 46:23 3808
with **n** one making *him* tremble. Jer 46:27 369
by **n** means leave you unpunished." Jer 46:28 3808
"There is praise for Moab **n** longer; Jer 48:2 369
city, So that **n** city will escape; Jer 48:8 3808
N one will tread *them* with Jer 48:33 3808
"Does Israel have **n** sons? Jer 49:1 369
Or has he **n** heirs? Jer 49:1 369
With **n** one to gather the fugitives Jer 49:5 369
n longer any wisdom in Teman? Jer 49:7 369
his neighbors, and he is **n** more. Jer 49:10 369
"**n** one will live there, nor will Jer 49:18 3808
"It has **n** gates or bars; Jer 49:31 3808
N one will live there, Nor will a Jer 49:33 3808
And there will be **n** nation To Jer 49:36 3808
there will be **n** inhabitant in it. Jer 50:3 3808
every side, Let there be **n** escape. Jer 50:29 408
fall With **n** one to raise him up; Jer 50:32 369
"**N** man will live there, Nor will Jer 50:40 3808
They are cruel and have **n** mercy. Jer 50:42 3808
And there is **n** breath in them. Jer 51:17 3808
A land in which **n** man lives And Jer 51:43
3808, 3605
through which **n** son of man passes. Jer 51:43 3808
will **n** longer stream to him. Jer 51:44 3808
there was **n** food for the people Jer 52:6 3808
nations, *But* she has found **n** rest; La 1:3 3808
n one comes to the appointed feasts. La 1:4 1097
deer That have found **n** pasture; La 1:6 3808
adversary And **n** one helped her. La 1:7 369
She has **n** comforter. La 1:9 369
There is **n** one to comfort her; La 1:17 369
There is **n** one to comfort me; La 1:21 369
The law is **n** more. La 2:9 369
find **N** vision from the LORD. La 2:9 3808
Give yourself **n** relief, La 2:18 408
Let your eyes have **n** rest. La 2:18 408
And there was **n** one who escaped or La 2:22 3808
So that **n** prayer can pass through. La 3:44 4480
But **n** one breaks *it* for them. La 4:4 369
n hands were turned toward her. La 4:6 3808
n one could touch their garments. La 4:14 3808
He will exile you **n** longer. La 4:22 3808
worn out, there is **n** rest for us. La 5:5 3808
fathers sinned, *and* are **n** more; La 5:7 369
There is **n** one to deliver us from La 5:8 3808
have **n** pity and I will not spare. Ezk 5:11 3808

My eye will have **n** pity on you,	**Ezk 7:4**	3808
'My eye will show **n** pity nor	**Ezk 7:9**	3808
but **n** one is going to the battle,	**Ezk 7:14**	369
have **n** pity nor will I spare;	**Ezk 8:18**	3808
have **n** pity nor will I spare,	**Ezk 9:10**	3808
they will **n** longer use it as a proverb	**Ezk 12:23**	3808
"For there will **n** longer be any	**Ezk 12:24**	3808
It will **n** longer be delayed, for	**Ezk 12:25**	3808
They will have **n** place in the	**Ezk 13:9**	3808
'Peace!' when there is **n** peace.	**Ezk 13:10**	369
for her when there is **n** peace,'	**Ezk 13:16**	369
and they will **n** longer be in your	**Ezk 13:21**	3808
you women will **n** longer see false	**Ezk 13:23**	3808
Israel may **n** longer stray from Me	**Ezk 14:11**	3808
and **n** longer defile themselves	**Ezk 14:11**	3808
so that **n** one would pass through it	**Ezk 14:15**	1097
"**N** eye looked with pity on you to	**Ezk 16:5**	3808
in that **n** one plays the harlot as	**Ezk 16:34**	3808
money and **n** money is given you;	**Ezk 16:34**	3808
also **n** longer pay your lovers.	**Ezk 16:41**	3808
be pacified and angry **n** more.	**Ezk 16:42**	3808
"For I have **n** pleasure in the	**Ezk 18:32**	3808
his voice would be heard **n** more	**Ezk 19:9**	3808
holy name you will profane **n** longer	**Ezk 20:39**	3808
which despises will be **n** more?"	**Ezk 21:13**	3808
this *will* **n** longer *be* the same.	**Ezk 21:26**	3808
This also will be **n** more until	**Ezk 21:27**	3808
they have made **n** distinction	**Ezk 22:26**	3808
but I found **n** one.	**Ezk 22:30**	3808
make **n** mourning for the dead.	**Ezk 24:17**	3808
will speak and be mute **n** longer.	**Ezk 24:27**	3808
your harps will be heard **n** more.	**Ezk 26:13**	3808
You will be built **n** more,	**Ezk 26:14**	3808
on you and you will be **n** more;	**Ezk 26:21**	369
There is **n** secret that is a match	**Ezk 28:3**	
		3605, 3808
"And there will be **n** more for the	**Ezk 28:24**	3808
But he and his army had **n** wages	**Ezk 29:18**	3808
And there will **n** longer be a prince	**Ezk 30:13**	3808
N tree in God's garden could	**Ezk 31:8**	
		3605, 3808
'I take **n** pleasure in the death of	**Ezk 33:11**	518
and I was **n** longer speechless.	**Ezk 33:22**	3808
so that **n** one will pass through.	**Ezk 33:28**	369
and there was **n** one to search or	**Ezk 34:6**	369
and they will **n** longer be a prey;	**Ezk 34:22**	3808
"They will **n** longer be a prey	**Ezk 34:28**	3808
and **n** one will make *them* afraid.	**Ezk 34:28**	369
you will **n** longer devour men and	**Ezk 36:14**	3808
and **n** longer bereave your nation	**Ezk 36:14**	3808
but there was **n** breath in them.	**Ezk 37:8**	369
they will **n** longer be two nations and	**Ezk 37:22**	3808
will no longer be two nations and **n**	**Ezk 37:22**	3808
"They will **n** longer defile	**Ezk 37:23**	3808
walls and having **n** bars or gates,	**Ezk 38:11**	369
with **n** one to make *them* afraid.	**Ezk 39:26**	369
were in three stories and had **n** pillars	**Ezk 42:6**	369
and **n** one shall enter by it,	**Ezk 44:2**	3808
"**N** foreigner uncircumcised in	**Ezk 44:9**	
		3605, 3808
give them **n** possession in Israel	**Ezk 44:28**	3808
shall **n** longer oppress My people,	**Ezk 45:8**	3808
N one shall return by way of the	**Ezk 46:9**	3808
youths in whom was **n** defect,	**Da 1:4**	369, 3605
inasmuch as **n** great king or ruler	**Da 2:10**	
		3606, 3809
and there is **n** one else who could	**Da 2:11**	3809
the fire had **n** effect on the bodies of	**Da 3:27**	3809
inasmuch as there is **n** other god	**Da 3:29**	3809
in you and **n** mystery baffles you,	**Da 4:9**	
		3606, 3809
And **n** one can ward off His hand Or	**Da 4:35**	3809
could find **n** ground of accusation	**Da 6:4**	
		3606, 3809
and **n** negligence or corruption was	**Da 6:4**	
		3606, 3809
Judah, pays **n** attention to you,	**Da 6:13**	3809
n injunction or statute which the king	**Da 6:15**	
		3606, 3809
and **n** entertainment was brought	**Da 6:18**	3809
king, I have committed **n** crime."	**Da 6:22**	3809
and **n** injury whatever was found on	**Da 6:23**	
		3606, 3809
and **n** *other* beasts could stand	**Da 8:4**	3808
had **n** strength to withstand him.	**Da 8:7**	3808
yet **n** strength was left in me, for	**Da 10:8**	3808
pallor, and I retained **n** strength.	**Da 10:8**	3808
and I have retained **n** strength.	**Da 10:16**	3808
remains just now **n** strength in me,	**Da 10:17**	3808
Yet there is **n** one who stands	**Da 10:21**	369
be **n** strength to make a stand.	**Da 11:15**	369
and **n** one will *be able to* withstand	**Da 11:16**	369
and fall and be found **n** more.	**Da 11:19**	3808
"He will show **n** regard for	**Da 11:37**	3808
his end, and **n** one will help him.	**Da 11:45**	369
for I will **n** longer have compassion	**Hos 1:6**	3808
have **n** compassion on her children,	**Hos 2:4**	3808
And **n** one will rescue her out of	**Hos 2:10**	3808
And will **n** longer call Me Baali.	**Hos 2:16**	3808
mentioned by their names **n** more.	**Hos 2:17**	3808
Because there is **n** faithfulness or	**Hos 4:1**	369
Yet let **n** one find fault, and let	**Hos 4:4**	408
The standing grain has **n** heads;	**Hos 8:7**	369
It yields **n** grain.	**Hos 8:7**	1097
a vessel in which **n** one delights.	**Hos 8:8**	369
LORD has taken **n** delight in them.	**Hos 8:13**	3808
N birth, no pregnancy and no	**Hos 9:11**	4480
n pregnancy and no conception!	**Hos 9:11**	4480
no pregnancy and **n** conception!	**Hos 9:11**	4480
I will love them **n** more;	**Hos 9:15**	3808
dried up, They will bear **n** fruit.	**Hos 9:16**	1097
"We have **n** king, For we do not	**Hos 10:3**	369
they will find in me **N** iniquity,	**Hos 12:8**	3808
For there is **n** savior besides Me.	**Hos 13:4**	369
there is **n** pasture for them;	**Jl 1:18**	369
your God, And there is **n** other;	**Jl 2:27**	369
will pass through it **n** more.	**Jl 3:17**	3808
in the forest when he has **n** prey?	**Am 3:4**	369
ground when there is **n** bait in it?	**Am 3:5**	369
gloom with **n** brightness in it?	**Am 5:20**	3808
And that one will say, "**N** one."	**Am 6:10**	657
I will spare them **n** longer.	**Am 7:8**	3808
"But **n** longer prophesy at Bethel,	**Am 7:13**	3808
I will spare them **n** longer.	**Am 8:2**	3808
(There is **n** understanding in him.)	**Ob 1:7**	369
n survivor of the house of Esau,"	**Ob 1:18**	3808
you will have **n** one stretching a	**Mi 2:5**	3808
For this is **n** place of rest	**Mi 2:10**	3808
there is **n** answer from God.	**Mi 3:7**	369
With **n** one to make *them* afraid,	**Mi 4:4**	369
Is there **n** king among you, Or has	**Mi 4:9**	369
will have fortune-tellers **n** more.	**Mi 5:12**	3808
So that you will **n** longer bow down	**Mi 5:13**	3808
is **n** upright *person* among men.	**Mi 7:2**	369
And the LORD will by **n** means leave	**Na 1:3**	3808
you, I will afflict you **n** longer.	**Na 1:12**	3808
name will **n** longer be perpetuated.	**Na 1:14**	3808
"Stop, stop," But **n** one turns back.	**Na 2:8**	369
For there is **n** limit to the treasure	**Na 2:9**	369
and **n** longer will the voice of	**Na 2:13**	3808
there is **n** one to regather *them.*	**Na 3:18**	369
is **n** relief for your breakdown,	**Na 3:19**	369
is **n** breath at all inside it.	**Hab 2:19**	369
And there be **n** fruit on the vines,	**Hab 3:17**	369
And the fields produce **n** food,	**Hab 3:17**	3808
there be **n** cattle in the stalls,	**Hab 3:17**	369
that there will be **n** inhabitant.	**Zph 2:5**	369
and there is **n** one besides me."	**Zph 2:15**	657
She heeded **n** voice,	**Zph 3:2**	3808
She accepted **n** instruction.	**Zph 3:2**	3808
He will do **n** injustice.	**Zph 3:5**	3808
But the unjust knows **n** shame.	**Zph 3:5**	3808
desolate, With **n** one passing by;	**Zph 3:6**	1097
"In that day you will feel **n** shame	**Zph 3:11**	3808
will do **n** wrong And tell no lies,	**Zph 3:13**	3808
will do no wrong And tell **n** lies,	**Zph 3:13**	3808
With **n** one to make them tremble."	**Zph 3:13**	369
You will fear disaster **n** more.	**Zph 3:15**	3808
but **n** one is warm *enough;*	**Hg 1:6**	369
priests answered, "**N**."	**Hg 2:12**	3808
will You have **n** compassion for	**Zch 1:12**	3808
so that **n** man lifts up his head;	**Zch 1:21**	3808
And I said, "**N**, my lord."	**Zch 4:5**	3808
And I said, "**N**, my lord."	**Zch 4:13**	3808
so that **n** one went back and forth,	**Zch 7:14**	4480
there was **n** wage for man or any	**Zch 8:10**	3808
was **n** peace because of his enemies,	**Zch 8:10**	3808
And **n** oppressor will pass over	**Zch 9:8**	3808
because there is **n** shepherd.	**Zch 10:2**	369
***n** room* can be found for them.	**Zch 10:10**	3808
own shepherds have **n** pity on them.	**Zch 11:5**	3808
"For I will **n** longer have pity	**Zch 11:6**	3808
they will **n** longer be remembered;	**Zch 13:2**	3808
day there will be **n** light;	**Zch 14:6**	3808
and there will **n** longer be a curse,	**Zch 14:11**	3808
there will be **n** rain on them.	**Zch 14:17**	3808
then ***n** rain will fall* on them;	**Zch 14:18**	3808
And there will **n** longer be a	**Zch 14:21**	3808
because He **n** longer regards the	**Mal 2:13**	369
and let **n** one deal treacherously	**Mal 2:15**	408
ARE BY **N** MEANS LEAST AMONG THE	**Mt 2:6**	*3760*
BECAUSE THEY WERE **N** MORE."	**Mt 2:18**	*3756*
It is **n** longer good for anything,	**Mt 5:13**	*3762*
I say to you, make **n** oath at all,	**Mt 5:34**	*3361*
statement be, 'Yes, yes' *or* '**N**, no';	**Mt 5:37**	*3756*
statement be, 'Yes, yes' *or* 'No, **n**';	**Mt 5:37**	*3756*
otherwise you have **n** reward with	**Mt 6:1**	*3756*
"**N** one can serve two masters;	**Mt 6:24**	*3762*
"See that you tell **n** one;	**Mt 8:4**	*3367*
n one could pass by that way.	**Mt 8:28**	*3361*
"But **n** one puts a patch of	**Mt 9:16**	*3762*
"See that **n** one knows *about this!*"	**Mt 9:30**	*3367*
and **n** one knows the Son except	**Mt 11:27**	*3762*
and *yet* **n** sign will be given to	**Mt 12:39**	*3756*
because they had **n** depth of soil.	**Mt 13:5**	*3361*
and because they had **n** root,	**Mt 13:6**	*3361*
yet he has **n** *firm* root in himself,	**Mt 13:21**	*3756*
"But he said, '**N**; for while you are	**Mt 13:29**	*3756*
yourselves that you have **n** bread?	**Mt 16:8**	*3756*
tell **n** one that He was the Christ.	**Mt 16:20**	*3367*
they saw **n** one except Jesus	**Mt 17:8**	*3762*
"Tell the vision to **n** one until	**Mt 17:9**	*3367*
they are **n** longer two,	**Mt 19:6**	*3765*
together, let **n** man separate."	**Mt 19:6**	*3361*
'Because **n** one hired us.'	**Mt 20:7**	*3762*
'Friend, I am doing you **n** wrong;	**Mt 20:13**	*3756*
"**N** longer shall there ever be *any*	**Mt 21:19**	*3756*
n attention and went their way,	**Mt 22:5**	*272*
God in truth, and defer to **n** one;	**Mt 22:16**	*3762*
(who say there is **n** resurrection)	**Mt 22:23**	*3361*
'IF A MAN DIES HAVING **N** CHILDREN,	**Mt 22:24**	*3361*
and having **n** children left his	**Mt 22:25**	*3361*
N one was able to answer Him a word,	**Mt 22:46**	*3762*
"See to it that **n** one misleads you.	**Mt 24:4**	*3361*
n life would have been saved;	**Mt 24:22**	
		3756, 3956
of that day and hour **n** one knows,	**Mt 24:36**	*3762*
lamps, they took **n** oil with them,	**Mt 25:3**	*3756*
'**N**, there will not be enough for	**Mt 25:9**	*3379*
where you scattered **n** *seed.*	**Mt 25:24**	*3756*
gather where I scattered **n** *seed.*	**Mt 25:26**	*3756*
n longer publicly enter a city,	**Mk 1:45**	*3371*
so that there was **n** longer room,	**Mk 2:2**	*3371*
"**N** one sews a patch of unshrunk	**Mk 2:21**	*3762*
"**N** one puts new wine into old	**Mk 2:22**	*3762*
"But **n** one can enter the strong	**Mk 3:27**	*3762*
up because it had **n** depth of soil.	**Mk 4:5**	*3361*
and because it had **n** root,	**Mk 4:6**	*3361*
choked it, and it yielded **n** crop.	**Mk 4:7**	*3756*
have **n** *firm* root in themselves,	**Mk 4:17**	*3756*
Do you still have **n** faith?"	**Mk 4:40**	*3768*
And **n** one was able to bind him	**Mk 5:3**	
		3761, 3762
and **n** one was strong enough to	**Mk 5:4**	*3762*
allowed **n** one to accompany Him,	**Mk 5:37**	
		3756, 3762
that **n** one should know about this,	**Mk 5:43**	*3367*
And He could do **n** miracle there	**Mk 6:5**	
		3756, 3762
n bread, no bag, no money in their	**Mk 6:8**	*3361*
no bread, **n** bag, no money in their	**Mk 6:8**	*3361*
no bag, **n** money in their belt	**Mk 6:8**	*3361*
you **n** longer permit him to do	**Mk 7:12**	*3765*
He wanted **n** one to know *of it*	**Mk 7:24**	*3762*
n sign will be given to this	**Mk 8:12**	*1487*
the fact that they had **n** bread.	**Mk 8:16**	*3756*
the fact that you have **n** bread?	**Mk 8:17**	*3756*
them to tell **n** one about Him.	**Mk 8:30**	*3367*
as **n** launderer on earth can whiten	**Mk 9:3**	*3756*
and saw **n** one with them anymore,	**Mk 9:8**	*3762*
for there is **n** one who will	**Mk 9:39**	*3762*
they are **n** longer two,	**Mk 10:8**	*3765*
together, let **n** man separate."	**Mk 10:9**	*3361*
N one is good except God alone.	**Mk 10:18**	*3762*
there is **n** one who has left house	**Mk 10:29**	*3762*
on which **n** one yet has ever sat;	**Mk 11:2**	*3762*
"May **n** one ever eat fruit from	**Mk 11:14**	*3367*
are truthful and defer to **n** one;	**Mk 12:14**	*3762*
say that there is **n** resurrection)	**Mk 12:18**	*3361*
behind a wife AND LEAVES **N** CHILD,	**Mk 12:19**	*3361*
and died leaving **n** children.	**Mk 12:20**	*3756*
died leaving behind **n** children;	**Mk 12:21**	*3361*
and *so* all seven left **n** children.	**Mk 12:22**	*3756*
There is **n** other commandment	**Mk 12:31**	*3756*
THERE IS **N** ONE ELSE BESIDES HIM;	**Mk 12:32**	*3756*
n one would venture to ask Him any	**Mk 12:34**	*3762*
"See to it that **n** one misleads you.	**Mk 13:5**	*3361*
n life would have been saved;	**Mk 13:20**	
		3756, 3956
of that day or hour **n** one knows,	**Mk 13:32**	*3762*
But Jesus made **n** further answer;	**Mk 15:5**	
		3762, 3765
But they had **n** child, because	**Lk 1:7**	*3756*
he will drink **n** wine or liquor,	**Lk 1:15**	
		3756, 3361
and His kingdom will have **n** end."	**Lk 1:33**	*3756*
N indeed; but he shall be called John	**Lk 1:60**	*3780*
"There is **n** one among your	**Lk 1:61**	*3762*
was **n** room for them in the inn.	**Lk 2:7**	*3756*
"Collect **n** more than what you	**Lk 3:13**	*3367*
"**N** doubt you will quote this	**Lk 4:23**	*3843*
n prophet is welcome in his home	**Lk 4:24**	*3762*
And He ordered him to tell **n** one,	**Lk 5:14**	*3367*
"**N** one tears a piece of cloth from a new	**Lk 5:36**	*3762*
"And **n** one puts new wine into old	**Lk 5:37**	*3762*
"And **n** one, after drinking old	**Lk 5:39**	*3762*
"For there is **n** good tree which	**Lk 6:43**	*3756*
there is **n** one greater than John;	**Lk 7:28**	*3762*
n bread and drinking no wine,	**Lk 7:33**	*3361*
no bread and drinking **n** wine,	**Lk 7:33**	*3383*
you gave Me **n** water for My feet,	**Lk 7:44**	*3756*
"You gave Me **n** kiss;	**Lk 7:45**	*3756*
away, because it had **n** moisture.	**Lk 8:6**	*3361*
and these have **n** *firm* root;	**Lk 8:13**	*3756*
and bring **n** fruit to maturity.	**Lk 8:14**	*3756*
"Now **n** one after lighting a lamp	**Lk 8:16**	*3762*
to tell **n** one what had happened.	**Lk 8:56**	*3367*
"We have **n** more than five loaves	**Lk 9:13**	*3756*
and reported to **n** one in those	**Lk 9:36**	*3762*
"**N** one, after putting his hand to	**Lk 9:62**	*3762*
"Carry **n** money belt, no bag, no	**Lk 10:4**	*3361*
"Carry no money belt, **n** bag, no	**Lk 10:4**	*3361*
"Carry no money belt, no bag, **n**	**Lk 10:4**	*3361*
and greet **n** one on the way.	**Lk 10:4**	*3367*
and **n** one knows who the Son is	**Lk 10:22**	*3762*
and *yet* **n** sign will be given to	**Lk 11:29**	*3756*
"**N** one, after lighting a lamp,	**Lk 11:33**	*3762*
of light, with **n** dark part in it,	**Lk 11:36**	
		3361, 5100
that have **n** more that they can do.	**Lk 12:4**	
		3361, 5100
I have **n** place to store my crops?'	**Lk 12:17**	*3756*
they have **n** storeroom nor barn,	**Lk 12:24**	*3756*
heaven, where **n** thief comes near nor	**Lk 12:33**	*3756*
I tell you, **n**, but rather division;	**Lk 12:51**	*3780*
"I tell you, **n**, but unless you	**Lk 13:3**	*3780*
"I tell you, **n**, but unless you	**Lk 13:5**	*3780*
they could make **n** reply to this.	**Lk 14:6**	*3756*
persons who need **n** repentance.	**Lk 15:7**	*3756*
and **n** one was giving *anything* to	**Lk 15:16**	*3762*
I am **n** longer worthy to be	**Lk 15:19**	*3765*
I am **n** longer worthy to be called	**Lk 15:21**	*3765*
for you can **n** longer be manager.'	**Lk 16:2**	*3756*
'**N** servant can serve two masters;	**Lk 16:13**	*3756*
'**N**, father Abraham, but if someone	**Lk 16:30**	*3780*
"Was **n** one found who returned	**Lk 17:18**	*3756*
N one is good except God alone.	**Lk 18:19**	*3762*

there is **n** one who has left house	**Lk 18:29**	*3762*
on which **n** one yet has ever sat;	**Lk 19:30**	*3762*
say that there is **n** resurrection),	**Lk 20:27**	*3361*
seven died, leaving **n** children.	**Lk 20:31**	*3756*
They said, "**N**, nothing."	**Lk 22:35**	*3762*
and whoever has **n** *sword* is to sell	**Lk 22:36**	*3361*
N more of this."	**Lk 22:51**	*2193*
"I find **n** guilt in this man."	**Lk 23:4**	*3762*
I have found **n** guilt in this man	**Lk 23:14**	*3762*
"**N**, nor has Herod, for he sent	**Lk 23:15**	*235*
in Him **n** guilt *demanding* death;	**Lk 23:22**	*3762*
rock, where **n** one had ever lain.	**Lk 23:53**	*3756*
N one has seen God at any time;	**Jn 1:18**	*3762*
And he answered, "**N**."	**Jn 1:21**	*3756*
indeed, in whom there is **n** deceit!"	**Jn 1:47**	*3756*
"They have **n** wine."	**Jn 2:3**	*3756*
for **n** one can do these signs that	**Jn 3:2**	*3762*
"**N** one has ascended into heaven,	**Jn 3:13**	*3762*
and **n** one receives His testimony.	**Jn 3:32**	*3762*
have **n** dealings with Samaritans.)	**Jn 4:9**	*3756*
"I have **n** husband."	**Jn 4:17**	*3756*
'I have **n** husband';	**Jn 4:17**	*3756*
yet **n** one said, "What do You seek?"	**Jn 4:27**	*3762*
"**N** one brought Him *anything* to	**Jn 4:33**	*3361*
"It is **n** longer because of what	**Jn 4:42**	*3765*
has **n** honor in his own country.	**Jn 4:44**	*3756*
I have **n** man to put me into the	**Jn 5:7**	*3756*
was **n** other small boat there,	**Jn 6:22**	*3756*
"**N** one can come to Me unless the	**Jn 6:44**	*3762*
you have **n** life in yourselves.	**Jn 6:53**	*3756*
you, that **n** one can come to Me unless	**Jn 6:65**	*3762*
"For **n** one does anything in	**Jn 7:4**	*3762*
"**N**, on the contrary, He leads the	**Jn 7:12**	*3756*
Yet **n** one was speaking openly of	**Jn 7:13**	*3762*
there is **n** unrighteousness in Him.	**Jn 7:18**	*3756*
n one knows where He is from."	**Jn 7:27**	*3762*
and **n** man laid his hand on Him,	**Jn 7:30**	*3762*
Him, but **n** one laid hands on Him.	**Jn 7:44**	*3762*
"**N** one of the rulers or Pharisees	**Jn 7:48**	*3361*
n prophet arises out of Galilee."	**Jn 7:52**	*3756*
Did **n** one condemn you?"	**Jn 8:10**	*3762*
She said, "**N** one, Lord."	**Jn 8:11**	*3762*
From now on sin **n** more."	**Jn 8:11**	*3371*
and **n** one seized Him, because His	**Jn 8:20**	*3762*
My word has **n** place in you.	**Jn 8:37**	*3756*
because there is **n** truth in him.	**Jn 8:44**	*3756*
is coming when **n** one can work.	**Jn 9:4**	*3762*
"**N**, but he is like him."	**Jn 9:9**	*3780*
were blind, you would have **n** sin;	**Jn 9:41**	*3756*
"**N** one has taken it away from Me,	**Jn 10:18**	*3762*
and **n** one will snatch them out of	**Jn 10:28**	*3756*
and **n** one is able to snatch *them*	**Jn 10:29**	*3762*
"While John performed **n** sign,	**Jn 10:41**	*3762*
Jesus **n** longer continued	**Jn 11:54**	*3765*
you, you have **n** part with Me."	**Jn 13:8**	*3756*
Now **n** one of those reclining *at*	**Jn 13:28**	*3762*
n one comes to the Father but	**Jn 14:6**	*3762*
the world will **n** longer see Me,	**Jn 14:19**	*3765*
"Greater love has **n** one than this,	**Jn 15:13**	*3762*
"**N** longer do I call you slaves,	**Jn 15:15**	*3765*
they have **n** excuse for their sin.	**Jn 15:22**	*3756*
the works which **n** one else did,	**Jn 15:24**	*3762*
and you **n** longer see Me;	**Jn 16:10**	*3765*
and you will **n** longer see Me;	**Jn 16:16**	*3765*
she **n** longer remembers the anguish	**Jn 16:21**	*3765*
and **n** one *will* take your joy away from	**Jn 16:22**	*3762*
when I will **n** longer speak to you	**Jn 16:25**	*3765*
and have **n** need for anyone to	**Jn 16:30**	*3756*
"I am **n** longer in the world;	**Jn 17:11**	*3765*
"I find **n** guilt in Him.	**Jn 18:38**	*3762*
know that I find **n** guilt in Him."	**Jn 19:4**	*3762*
Him, for I find **n** guilt in Him."	**Jn 19:6**	*3756*
But Jesus gave him **n** answer.	**Jn 19:9**	*3756*
would have **n** authority over Me,	**Jn 19:11**	
		3756, 3762
Man, you are **n** friend of Caesar;	**Jn 19:12**	*3756*
"We have **n** king but Caesar."	**Jn 19:15**	*3756*
in which **n** one had yet been laid.	**Jn 19:41**	*3762*
They answered Him, "**N**."	**Jn 21:5**	*3756*
AND LET N ONE DWELL IN IT';	**Ac 1:20**	*3361*
there is salvation in **n** one else;	**Ac 4:12**	
		3756, 3762
there is **n** other name under heaven	**Ac 4:12**	*3761*
let us warn them to speak **n** longer	**Ac 4:17**	*3371*
(finding **n** basis on which	**Ac 4:21**	*3367*
up, we found **n** one inside."	**Ac 5:23**	*3762*
He gave him **n** inheritance in it,	**Ac 7:5**	*3756*
and *yet,* even when he had **n** child,	**Ac 7:5**	*3756*
and our fathers could find **n** food.	**Ac 7:11**	*3756*
"You have **n** part or portion in	**Ac 8:21**	*3756*
and the eunuch **n** longer saw him,	**Ac 8:39**	*3765*
the voice but seeing **n** one.	**Ac 9:7**	*3367*
"By **n** means, Lord, for I have	**Ac 10:14**	*3365*
n *longer* consider unholy."	**Ac 10:15**	*3361*
"Surely **n** one can refuse the	**Ac 10:47**	*3385*
'By **n** means, Lord, for nothing	**Ac 11:8**	*3365*
n longer consider unholy.'	**Ac 11:9**	*3361*
to **n** one except to Jews alone.	**Ac 11:19**	*3367*
there was **n** small disturbance	**Ac 12:18**	*3756*
"And though they found **n** ground	**Ac 13:28**	*3367*
dead, **n** longer to return to decay,	**Ac 13:34**	*3371*
At Lystra a man was sitting who had **n**	**Ac 14:8**	*102*
and He made **n** distinction between	**Ac 15:9**	*3762*
to whom we gave **n** instruction	**Ac 15:24**	*3756*
to lay upon you **n** greater burden	**Ac 15:28**	*3367*
sending us away secretly? **N** indeed!	**Ac 16:37**	*3756*
and **n** man will attack you in order	**Ac 18:10**	*3762*
"**N**, we have not even heard	**Ac 19:2**	*3761*
there occurred **n** small disturbance	**Ac 19:23**	*3756*
was bringing **n** little business to	**Ac 19:24**	*3756*
made with hands are **n** gods *at all.*	**Ac 19:26**	*3756*
there is **n** *real* cause *for it,*	**Ac 19:40**	*3367*
kingdom, will **n** longer see my face.	**Ac 20:25**	*3765*
"I have coveted **n** one's silver or	**Ac 20:33**	*3762*
a citizen of **n** insignificant city;	**Ac 21:39**	*3756*
say that there is **n** resurrection,	**Ac 23:8**	*3361*
"Tell **n** one that you have	**Ac 23:22**	*3367*
but under **n** accusation deserving	**Ac 23:29**	*3367*
n more than twelve days ago I went	**Ac 24:11**	*3756*
"I have committed **n** offense	**Ac 25:8**	*3777*
I have done **n** wrong to *the* Jews,	**Ac 25:10**	*3762*
n one can hand me over to them.	**Ac 25:11**	*3762*
n small storm was assailing *us,*	**Ac 27:20**	*3756*
will be **n** loss of life among you,	**Ac 27:22**	*3762*
into the fire and suffered **n** harm.	**Ac 28:5**	*3762*
was **n** ground for putting me to death.	**Ac 28:18**	*3367*
Therefore you have **n** excuse,	**Ro 2:1**	*379*
there is **n** partiality with God.	**Ro 2:11**	*3756*
N FEAR OF GOD BEFORE THEIR EYES."	**Ro 3:18**	*3756*
n flesh will be justified in His sight;	**Ro 3:20**	
		3756, 3956
for there is **n** distinction;	**Ro 3:22**	*3756*
N, but by a law of faith.	**Ro 3:27**	*3780*
wrath, but where there is **n** law,	**Ro 4:15**	*3756*
there also is **n** violation.	**Ro 4:15**	*3756*
not imputed when there is **n** law.	**Ro 5:13**	*3361*
would **n** longer be slaves to sin;	**Ro 6:6**	*3371*
death **n** longer is master over Him.	**Ro 6:9**	*3765*
n longer am I the one doing it,	**Ro 7:17**	*3765*
I am **n** longer the one doing it,	**Ro 7:20**	*3765*
is now **n** condemnation	**Ro 8:1**	*3762*
There is **n** injustice with God, is	**Ro 9:14**	*3361*
For there is **n** distinction between	**Ro 10:12**	*3756*
is **n** longer on the basis of works,	**Ro 11:6**	*3765*
otherwise grace is **n** longer grace.	**Ro 11:6**	*3765*
is **n** authority except from God,	**Ro 13:1**	*3756*
want to have **n** fear of authority?	**Ro 13:3**	*3361*
Love does **n** wrong to a neighbor;	**Ro 13:10**	*3756*
and make **n** provision for the flesh	**Ro 13:14**	*3361*
you are **n** longer walking according	**Ro 14:15**	*3765*
WHO HAD N NEWS OF HIM SHALL SEE,	**Ro 15:21**	*3756*
with **n** further place for me in	**Ro 15:23**	*3371*
there be **n** divisions among you,	**1Co 1:10**	*3361*
that **n** one would say you were	**1Co 1:15**	*3361*
n man may boast before God.	**1Co 1:29**	
		3361, 3956
so the *thoughts* of God **n** one knows	**1Co 2:11**	*3762*
he himself is appraised by **n** one.	**1Co 2:15**	*3762*
For **n** man can lay a foundation	**1Co 3:11**	*3762*
Let **n** man deceive himself.	**1Co 3:18**	*3367*
So then let **n** one boast in men.	**1Co 3:21**	*3367*
so that **n** one of you will	**1Co 4:6**	*3361*
are of **n** account in the church?	**1Co 6:4**	*1848*
I have **n** command of the Lord,	**1Co 7:25**	*3756*
heart, being under **n** constraint,	**1Co 7:37**	*3361*
we know that there is **n** such thing	**1Co 8:4**	*3762*
and that there is **n** God but one.	**1Co 8:4**	*3762*
that we will cause **n** hindrance to	**1Co 9:12**	
		3361, 5100
N temptation has overtaken you but	**1Co 10:13**	*3756*
N, but I *say* that the things	**1Co 10:20**	
Let **n** one seek his own *good,* but	**1Co 10:24**	*3367*
Give **n** offense either to Jews or	**1Co 10:32**	*677*
we have **n** other practice,	**1Co 11:16**	*3756*
that **n** one speaking by the Spirit	**1Co 12:3**	*3762*
and **n** one can say, "Jesus is Lord,"	**1Co 12:3**	*3762*
"I have **n** need of you";	**1Co 12:21**	*3756*
"I have **n** need of you."	**1Co 12:21**	*3756*
presentable members have **n** need	**1Co 12:24**	*3756*
may be **n** division in the body,	**1Co 12:25**	*3361*
for **n** one understands, but in *his*	**1Co 14:2**	*3762*
and **n** *kind* is without meaning.	**1Co 14:10**	*3762*
but if there is **n** interpreter, he	**1Co 14:28**	*3361*
is **n** resurrection of the dead?	**1Co 15:12**	*3756*
is **n** resurrection of the dead,	**1Co 15:13**	*3756*
for some have **n** knowledge of God.	**1Co 15:34**	*56*
that **n** collections be made when I	**1Co 16:2**	*3361*
So let **n** one despise him.	**1Co 16:11**	*3361*
me there will be yes, yes and **n**,	**2Co 1:17**	*3756*
yes and no, **n** *at the same time?*	**2Co 1:17**	*3756*
our word to you is not yes and **n**.	**2Co 1:18**	*3756*
was not yes and **n**, but is yes in Him.	**2Co 1:19**	*3756*
so that **n** advantage would be taken	**2Co 2:11**	*3361*
I had **n** rest for my spirit, not	**2Co 2:13**	*3756*
in this case has **n** glory because	**2Co 3:10**	*3756*
n longer live for themselves,	**2Co 5:15**	*3371*
n one according to the flesh;	**2Co 5:16**	*3762*
now we know *Him in this way* **n**	**2Co 5:16**	*3765*
n sin *to be* sin on our behalf,	**2Co 5:21**	*3361*
n cause for offense in anything,	**2Co 6:3**	*3367*
we wronged **n** one, we corrupted no	**2Co 7:2**	*3367*
no one, we corrupted **n** one,	**2Co 7:2**	*3762*
one, we took advantage of **n** one.	**2Co 7:2**	*3762*
Macedonia our flesh had **n** rest,	**2Co 7:5**	*3762*
WHO *gathered* LITTLE HAD N LACK."	**2Co 8:15**	*3756*
taking precaution so that **n** one	**2Co 8:20**	*3361*
N wonder, for even Satan disguises	**2Co 11:14**	*3756*
I say, let **n** one think me foolish;	**2Co 11:16**	*3361*
so that **n** one will credit me with	**2Co 12:6**	*3361*
for in **n** respect was I inferior to	**2Co 12:11**	*3762*
pray to God that you do **n** wrong;	**2Co 13:7**	*3361*
what they were makes **n** difference	**Ga 2:6**	*3762*
God shows **n** partiality)	**Ga 2:6**	*3756*
Law **n** flesh will be justified.	**Ga 2:16**	
		3756, 3956
and it is **n** longer I who live, but	**Ga 2:20**	*3765*
Now that **n** one is justified by the	**Ga 3:11**	*3762*
n one sets it aside or adds	**Ga 3:15**	*3762*
it is **n** longer based on a promise;	**Ga 3:18**	*3765*
we are **n** longer under a tutor.	**Ga 3:25**	*3765*
you are **n** longer a slave,	**Ga 4:7**	*3765*
those which by nature are **n** gods.	**Ga 4:8**	*3361*
You have done me **n** wrong;	**Ga 4:12**	*3762*
Christ will be of **n** benefit to you.	**Ga 5:2**	*3762*
that you will adopt **n** other view;	**Ga 5:10**	*3762*
against such things there is **n** law.	**Ga 5:23**	*3756*
on let **n** one cause trouble for me,	**Ga 6:17**	*3367*
of works, so that **n** one may boast.	**Eph 2:9**	*3361*
having **n** hope and without God in	**Eph 2:12**	*3361*
are **n** longer strangers and aliens,	**Eph 2:19**	*3765*
we are **n** longer to be children,	**Eph 4:14**	*3371*
that you walk **n** longer just as the	**Eph 4:17**	*3371*
He who steals must steal **n** longer;	**Eph 4:28**	*3371*
Let **n** unwholesome word proceed	**Eph 4:29**	
		3361, 3956
and *there must be* **n** filthiness	**Eph 5:4**	
that **n** immoral or impure person or	**Eph 5:5**	
		3756, 3956
Let **n** one deceive you with empty	**Eph 5:6**	*3367*
having **n** spot or wrinkle or any	**Eph 5:27**	*3361*
n one ever hated his own flesh,	**Eph 5:29**	*3762*
there is **n** partiality with Him.	**Eph 6:9**	*3756*
in **n** way alarmed by *your*	**Php 1:28**	*3367*
For I have **n** one *else* of kindred	**Php 2:20**	*3762*
things *again* is **n** trouble to me,	**Php 3:1**	*3756*
and put **n** confidence in the flesh,	**Php 3:3**	*3756*
n church shared with me in the	**Php 4:15**	*3762*
I say this so that **n** one will	**Col 2:4**	*3367*
See to it that **n** one takes you	**Col 2:8**	*3361*
Therefore **n** one is to act as your	**Col 2:16**	*3361*
Let **n** one keep defrauding you of	**Col 2:18**	*3367*
but are of **n** value against fleshly	**Col 2:23**	
		3756, 5100
n *distinction between* Greek and Jew	**Col 3:11**	*3756*
we have **n** need to say anything.	**1Th 1:8**	*3361*
when we could endure *it* **n** longer,	**1Th 3:1**	*3371*
so that **n** one would be disturbed by	**1Th 3:3**	*3367*
when I could endure *it* **n** longer,	**1Th 3:5**	*3371*
and that **n** man transgress and	**1Th 4:6**	*3361*
you have **n** need for *anyone* to	**1Th 4:9**	*3756*
as do the rest who have **n** hope.	**1Th 4:13**	*3361*
you have **n** need of anything to be	**1Th 5:1**	*3756*
See that **n** one repays another with	**1Th 5:15**	*3361*
Let **n** one in any way deceive you,	**2Th 2:3**	*3361*
life, doing **n** work at all,	**2Th 3:11**	*3367*
Let **n** one look down on your	**1Tm 4:12**	*3367*
the enemy **n** occasion for reproach;	**1Tm 5:14**	*3367*
N longer drink water *exclusively,*	**1Tm 5:23**	*3371*
whom **n** man has seen or can see.	**1Tm 6:16**	*3762*
N soldier in active service	**2Tm 2:4**	*3762*
first defense **n** one supported me,	**2Tm 4:16**	*3762*
Let **n** one disregard you.	**Ti 2:15**	*3367*
to malign **n** one, to be	**Ti 3:2**	*3367*
n longer as a slave, but more than	**Phm 1:16**	*3765*
so that **n** one will fall, through	**Heb 4:11**	*3361*
And there is **n** creature hidden	**Heb 4:13**	*3756*
And **n** one takes the honor to	**Heb 5:4**	*3756*
He could swear by **n** one greater,	**Heb 6:13**	*3762*
from which **n** one has officiated at	**Heb 7:13**	*3762*
n occasion sought for a second.	**Heb 8:7**	*3756*
WILL REMEMBER THEIR SINS N MORE."	**Heb 8:12**	
		3756, 3361
of blood there is **n** forgiveness.	**Heb 9:22**	*3756*
would **n** longer have had	**Heb 10:2**	*3367*
SIN YOU HAVE TAKEN N PLEASURE.	**Heb 10:6**	*3756*
DEEDS I WILL REMEMBER N MORE."	**Heb 10:17**	
		3756, 3361
is **n** longer *any* offering for sin.	**Heb 10:18**	*3765*
there **n** longer remains a sacrifice	**Heb 10:26**	*3765*
MY SOUL HAS N PLEASURE IN HIM.	**Heb 10:38**	*3756*
which **n** one will see the Lord.	**Heb 12:14**	*3762*
See to it that **n** one comes short	**Heb 12:15**	*3361*
that **n** root of bitterness springing up	**Heb 12:15**	*3361*
that *there be* **n** immoral or godless	**Heb 12:16**	
		3361, 5100
he found **n** place for repentance,	**Heb 12:17**	*3756*
begged that **n** further word be	**Heb 12:19**	*3361*
tabernacle have **n** right to eat.	**Heb 13:10**	*3756*
Let **n** one say when he is tempted,	**Jas 1:13**	*3367*
with whom there is **n** variation or	**Jas 1:17**	*3756*
to one who has shown **n** mercy;	**Jas 2:13**	*3361*
he has faith but he has **n** works?	**Jas 2:14**	*3361*
Even so faith, if it has **n** works,	**Jas 2:17**	*3361*
But **n** one can tame the tongue;	**Jas 3:8**	*3762*
the Scripture speaks to **n** purpose:	**Jas 4:5**	*2761*
and your **n**, no, so that you may not	**Jas 5:12**	*3756*
n, so that you may not fall under	**Jas 5:12**	*3756*
WHO COMMITTED N SIN, NOR WAS ANY	**1Pe 2:22**	*3756*
suffering, He uttered **n** threats,	**1Pe 2:23**	*3756*
n longer for the lusts of men,	**1Pe 4:2**	*3371*
that **n** prophecy of Scripture is *a*	**2Pe 1:20**	
		3956, 3756
for **n** prophecy was ever made by an	**2Pe 1:21**	*3756*
where they have **n** knowledge,	**2Pe 2:12**	*50*
in Him there is **n** darkness at all.	**1Jn 1:5**	*3756*
If we say that we have **n** sin,	**1Jn 1:8**	*3756*
is **n** cause for stumbling in him.	**1Jn 2:10**	*3756*
and because **n** lie is of the truth.	**1Jn 2:21**	
		3956, 3756
n need for anyone to teach you;	**1Jn 2:27**	*3756*
and in Him there is **n** sin.	**1Jn 3:5**	*3756*
N one who abides in Him sins;	**1Jn 3:6**	
		3956, 3756
n one who sins has seen Him or	**1Jn 3:6**	
		3956, 3756
children, make sure **n** one deceives you;	**1Jn 3:7**	*3367*

N one who is born of God practices 1Jn 3:9 *3956, 3756*
and you know that **n** murderer has 1Jn 3:15 *3956, 3756*
N one has seen God at any time; 1Jn 4:12 *3762*
There is **n** fear in love; 1Jn 4:18 *3756*
n one who is born of God sins; 1Jn 5:18 *3956, 3756*
I have **n** greater joy than this, to 3Jn 1:4 *3756*
n one knows but he who receives it.' Rv 2:17 *3762*
I place **n** other burden on you. Rv 2:24 *3756*
who opens and **n** one will shut, Rv 3:7 *3762*
and who shuts and **n** one opens, Rv 3:7 *3762*
an open door which **n** one can shut, Rv 3:8 *3762*
so that **n** one will take your crown. Rv 3:11 *3367*
And **n** one in heaven or on the Rv 5:3 *3762*
because **n** one was found worthy to Rv 5:4 *3762*
so that **n** wind would blow on the Rv 7:1 *3361*
multitude which **n** one could count, Rv 7:9 *3762*
"They will hunger **n** longer, Rv 7:16 *3756*
there will be delay **n** longer, Rv 10:6 *3765*
and there was **n** longer a place Rv 12:8 *3761*
and *he provides* that **n** one will Rv 13:17 *3761*
and **n** one could learn the song Rv 14:3 *3762*
n lie was found in their mouth; Rv 14:5 *3756*
they have **n** rest day and night, Rv 14:11 *3756*
and **n** one was able to enter the Rv 15:8 *3762*
because **n** one buys their cargoes Rv 18:11 *3762*
and *men* will **n** longer find them. Rv 18:14 *3765*
and **n** craftsman of any craft will Rv 18:22 *3756, 3361, 3956*
which **n** one knows except Himself. Rv 19:12 *3762*
the second death has **n** power, Rv 20:6 *3756*
and **n** place was found for them. Rv 20:11 *3756*
and there is **n** longer *any* sea. Rv 21:1 *3756*
there will **n** longer be *any* death; Rv 21:4 *3756*
will **n** longer be *any* mourning, Rv 21:4 *3756*
I saw **n** temple in it, for the Rv 21:22 *3756*
And the city has **n** need of the sun Rv 21:23 *3756*
(for there will be **n** night there) Rv 21:25 *3756*
and nothing unclean, and **n** one who Rv 21:27 *3756, 3361*
There will **n** longer be any curse; Rv 22:3 *3756*
there will **n** longer be *any* night; Rv 22:5 *3756*

NOADIAH
of Jeshua and **N** the son of Binnui. Ezr 8:33 5129
and also **N** the prophetess and the Ne 6:14 5129

NOAH
Now he called his name **N**, Gn 5:29 5146
after he became the father of **N**, Gn 5:30 5146
N was five hundred years old, Gn 5:32 5146
and **N** became the father of Shem, Gn 5:32 5146
But **N** found favor in the eyes of Gn 6:8 5146
records of the generations of **N**. Gn 6:9 5146
N was a righteous man, blameless Gn 6:9 5146
N walked with God. Gn 6:9 5146
N became the father of three Gn 6:10 5146
Then God said to **N**, Gn 6:13 5146
Thus **N** did; according to all that Gn 6:22 5146
Then the LORD said to **N**, Gn 7:1 5146
N did according to all that Gn 7:5 5146
Now **N** was six hundred years old Gn 7:6 5146
Then **N** and his sons and his wife Gn 7:7 5146
went into the ark to **N** by twos, Gn 7:9 5146
female, as God had commanded **N**. Gn 7:9 5146
N and Shem and Ham and Japheth, Gn 7:13 5146
Ham and Japheth, the sons of **N**, Gn 7:13 5146
So they went into the ark to **N**, Gn 7:15 5146
and only **N** was left, together with Gn 7:23 5146
But God remembered **N** and all the Gn 8:1 5146
that **N** opened the window of the Gn 8:6 5146
So **N** knew that the water was Gn 8:11 5146
Then **N** removed the covering of the Gn 8:13 5146
Then God spoke to **N**, Gn 8:15 5146
So **N** went out, and his sons and Gn 8:18 5146
Then **N** built an altar to the LORD, Gn 8:20 5146
And God blessed **N** and his sons Gn 9:1 5146
to **N** and to his sons with him, Gn 9:8 5146
And God said to **N**, Gn 9:17 5146
Now the sons of **N** who came out of Gn 9:18 5146
These three *were* the sons of **N**, Gn 9:19 5146
Then **N** began farming and planted a Gn 9:20 5146
When **N** awoke from his wine, he Gn 9:24 5146
N lived three hundred and Gn 9:28 5146
So all the days of **N** were nine Gn 9:29 5146
Ham, and Japheth, the sons of **N**; Gn 10:1 5146
are the families of the sons of **N**, Gn 10:32 5146
of Zelophehad were Mahlah, **N**, Nu 26:33 5270
N and Hoglah and Milcah and Tirzah. Nu 27:1 5270
Tirzah, Hoglah, Milcah and **N**, Nu 36:11 5270
Mahlah and **N**, Hoglah, Milcah and Jos 17:3 5270
N, Shem, Ham and Japheth. 1Ch 1:4 5146
this is like the days of **N** to Me, Is 54:9 5146
the waters of **N** Would not flood Is 54:9 5146
these three men, **N**, Daniel and Job Ezk 14:14 5146
even *though* **N**, Daniel and Job Ezk 14:20 5146
will be just like the days of **N**. Mt 24:37 *3575*
the day that **N** entered the ark, Mt 24:38 *3575*
the son of Shem, the son of **N**, Lk 3:36 *3575*
as it happened in the days of **N**, Lk 17:26 *3575*
the day that **N** entered the ark, Lk 17:27 *3575*
By faith **N**, being warned *by God* Heb 11:7 *3575*
God kept waiting in the days of **N**, 1Pe 3:20 *3575*
ancient world, but preserved **N**, 2Pe 2:5 *3575*

NOAH'S
the six hundredth year of **N** life, Gn 7:11 5146
and **N** wife and the three wives of Gn 7:13 5146

NO-AMON
Are you better than **N**, Na 3:8 4996, 528

NOB
came to **N** to Ahimelech the priest; 1Sa 21:1 5011
saw the son of Jesse coming to **N**, 1Sa 22:9 5011
the priests who were in **N**; 1Sa 22:11 5011
And he struck **N** the city of the 1Sa 22:19 5011
at Anathoth, **N**, Ananiah, Ne 11:32 5011
Yet today he will halt at **N**; Is 10:32 5011

NOBAH
N went and took Kenath and its Nu 32:42 5025
called it **N** after his own name. Nu 32:42 5025
on the east of **N** and Jogbehah, Jg 8:11 5025

NOBILITY
whose king is of **n** and whose Ec 10:17 1121, 2715

NOBLE
to one of the king's most **n** princes Es 6:9 6579
daughters are among Your **n** ladies; Ps 45:9 3368
for I will speak **n** things; Pr 8:6 5057
to strike the **n** for *their* uprightness. Pr 17:26 5081
the chariots of my **n** people." SS 6:12 5081
longer will the fool be called **n**, Is 32:5 5081
But the **n** man devises noble plans; Is 32:8 5081
But the noble man devises **n** plans; Is 32:8 5082
And by **n** plans he stands. Is 32:8 5082
not many mighty, not many **n**; 1Co 1:26 *2104b*

NOBLEMAN
'Where is the house of the **n**, Jb 21:28 5081
"A **n** went to a distant Lk 19:12 *2104b, 444*

NOBLE-MINDED
more **n** than those in Thessalonica, Ac 17:11 *2104b*

NOBLES
the **n** of the sons of Israel; Ex 24:11 678
Which the **n** of the people dug, Nu 21:18 5081
"Then survivors came down to the **n**; Jg 5:13 117
ash heap To make them sit with **n**, 1Sa 2:8 5081
the **n** who were living with Naboth 1Ki 21:8 2715
and the **n** who lived in his city, 1Ki 21:11 2715
the captains of hundreds, the **n**, 2Ch 23:20 117
told the Jews, the priests, the **n**, Ne 2:16 2715
but their **n** did not support the Ne 3:5 117
fear, I rose and spoke to the **n**, Ne 4:14 2715
I said to the **n**, Ne 4:19 2715
and contended with the **n** and the Ne 5:7 2715
from the **n** of Judah to Tobiah, Ne 6:17 2715
into my heart to assemble the **n**, Ne 7:5 2715
with their kinsmen, their **n**, Ne 10:29 117
Then I reprimanded the **n** of Judah Ne 13:17 2715
officers of Persia and Media, the **n** and Es 1:3 6579
"He pours contempt on **n** And Jb 12:21 5081
The voice of the **n** was hushed, Jb 29:10 5057
'Worthless one,' To **n**, Jb 34:18 5081
Make their **n** like Oreb and Zeeb And Ps 83:11 5081
And their **n** with fetters of iron, Ps 149:8 3513
"By me princes rule, and **n**, Pr 8:16 5081
they may enter the doors of the **n**. Is 13:2 5081
Its **n**—there is no one there *Whom* Is 34:12 2715
"Their **n** have sent their Jer 14:3 117
all the **n** of Judah and Jerusalem. Jer 27:20 2715
also slew all the **n** of Judah. Jer 39:6 2715
of the royal family and of the **n**, Da 1:3 6579
and my **n** began seeking me out; Da 4:36 7261
feast for a thousand of his **n**, Da 5:1 7261
so that the king and his **n**, Da 5:2 7261
and the king and his **n**, Da 5:3 7261
paler, and his **n** were perplexed. Da 5:9 7261
the words of the king and his **n**; Da 5:10 7261
before you, and you and your **n**, Da 5:23 7261
with the signet rings of his **n**, Da 6:17 7261
the decree of the king and his **n**: Jon 3:7 1419
He remembers his **n**; Na 2:5 117
Your **n** are lying down. Na 3:18 117

NOBLY
"Many daughters have done **n**, Pr 31:29 2428

NOBODY
apostles, even though I am a **n**. 2Co 12:11 *3762*

NOCTURNAL
unclean because of a **n** emission, Dt 23:10 3915

NOD
and settled in the land of **N**, Gn 4:16 5113

NODAB
Hagrites, Jetur, Naphish and **N**. 1Ch 5:19 5114

NODDED
governor had **n** for him to speak, Ac 24:10 *3506*

NOGAH
N, Nepheg and Japhia, 1Ch 3:7 5052
N, Nepheg, Japhia, 1Ch 14:6 5052

NOHAH
N the fourth and Rapha the fifth. 1Ch 8:2 5119

NOISE
Philistines heard the **n** of the shout, 1Sa 4:6 6963
"What *does* the **n** of this great shout 1Sa 4:6 6963
Eli heard the **n** of the outcry, 1Sa 4:14 6963
the **n** of this commotion *mean?*" 1Sa 4:14 6963
that the earth shook at their **n**. 1Ki 1:40 6963
is the **n** which you have heard. 1Ki 1:45 6963
Athaliah heard the **n** of the guard 2Ki 11:13 6963
Athaliah heard the **n** of the people 2Ch 23:12 6963
"Its **n** declares His presence; Jb 36:33 7452
You who were full of **n**, Is 22:2 8663
ceases, The **n** of revelers stops, Is 24:8 7588
thunder and earthquake and loud **n**, Is 29:6 6963
voice nor disturbed at their **n**, Is 31:4 1995
With the **n** of a great tumult He Jer 11:16 6963
king of Egypt *is but* a big **n**; Jer 46:17 7588
the **n** of the galloping hoofs of his Jer 47:3 6963
quaked at the **n** of their downfall. Jer 49:21 6963
The **n** of it has been heard at the Jer 49:21 6963
"The **n** of battle is in the land, Jer 50:22 6963
make *her* loud **n** vanish from her. Jer 51:55 6963
They have made a **n** in the house of La 2:7 6963
walls will shake at the **n** of cavalry Ezk 26:10 6963
as I prophesied, there was a **n**, Ezk 37:7 6963
With a **n** as of chariots They leap Jl 2:5 6963
away from Me the **n** of your songs; Am 5:23 1995
The **n** of the whip, The noise of Na 3:2 6963
The **n** of the rattling of the wheel, Na 3:2 6963
from heaven a **n** like a violent rushing Ac 2:2 *2279*

NOISY
At the head of the **n** *streets* she cries Pr 1:21 1993
pasture They will be **n** with men. Mi 2:12 1949
and the crowd in **n** disorder, Mt 9:23 *2350b*
a **n** gong or a clanging cymbal. 1Co 13:1 *2278*

NOMADS
n of the desert bow before him, Ps 72:9 6716b

NON
N his son and Joshua his son. 1Ch 7:27 5126

NONE
n of us will refuse you his grave Gn 23:6 376, 3808
is **n** other than the house of God, Gn 28:17 369
and **n** of the men of the household Gn 39:11 369, 376
n of your labor will be reduced.' " Ex 5:11 369
and **n** of you shall go outside the Ex 12:22 3808, 376
I will put **n** of the diseases on Ex 15:26 3605, 3808
the sabbath, there will be **n**." Ex 16:26 3808
out to gather, but they found **n**. Ex 16:27 3808
And **n** shall appear before Me Ex 23:15 3808
n of them put on his ornaments. Ex 33:4 3808, 376
N shall appear before Me Ex 34:20 3808
'**N** of you shall approach any blood Lv 18:6 376, 3808
shall leave **n** of it until morning; Lv 22:30 3808
shall leave **n** of it until morning, Nu 9:12 3808
n of her vows or her obligations Nu 30:5 3605, 3808
'**N** of the men who came up from Nu 32:11 518
and **n** of the flesh which you Dt 16:4 3808
n of his *descendants,* even to the Dt 23:2 3808
n of their *descendants,* even to Dt 23:3 3808
"**N** of the daughters of Israel Dt 23:17 3808
continually, with **n** to save you. Dt 28:29 369
and you will have **n** to save you. Dt 28:31 369
there is **n** *remaining,* bond or free. Dt 32:36 657
is **n** like the God of Jeshurun, Dt 33:26 369
"**N** of us shall give his daughter Jg 21:1 376, 3808
him and let **n** of his words fail. 1Sa 3:19 3808, 3605
So **n** of the people tasted food. 1Sa 14:24 3808, 3605
"There is **n** like it; 1Sa 21:9 369
and there is **n** of you who is sorry 1Sa 22:8 369
for there is **n** like You, and 2Sa 7:22 369
for *otherwise* **n** of us will escape 2Sa 15:14 3808
looked, but there was **n** to save; 2Sa 22:42 369
N was of silver; it was not considered 1Ki 10:21 369
N but the tribe of Judah followed 1Ki 12:20 3808
to all Judah—**n** was exempt 1Ki 15:22 369
Jezreel, and **n** shall bury *her.*' " 2Ki 9:10 369
and he left **n** of them. 2Ki 10:14 3808, 376
you **n** of the servants of the LORD, 2Ki 10:23 6435
let **n** come out." 2Ki 10:25 376, 408
n was left except the tribe of 2Ki 17:18 3808
after him there was **n** like him 2Ki 18:5 3808
N remained except the poorest 2Ki 24:14 3808
"O LORD, there is **n** like You, 1Ch 17:20 369
such as **n** of the kings who were 2Ch 1:12 3808
and **n** like that was seen before in 2Ch 9:11 3808
me, **n** of us removed our clothes, Ne 4:23 369
and **n** of them was able to speak Ne 13:24 369
Let it wait for light but have **n**, Jb 3:9 369
long for death, but there is **n**, Jb 3:21 369
And shall you scoff and **n** rebuke? Jb 11:3 369
lie down and **n** would disturb *you,* Jb 11:19 369
away, while there is **n** to deliver. Ps 7:2 369
wickedness until You find **n**. Ps 10:15 1077
for help, but there was **n** to save, Ps 18:41 369
For there is **n** to help. Ps 22:11 369
n of those who wait for You will Ps 25:3 3605, 3808
And **n** of those who take refuge in Ps 34:22 3808, 3605
There is **n** to compare with You. Ps 40:5 369
pieces, and there will be **n** to deliver. Ps 50:22 369
for sympathy, but there was **n**, Ps 69:20 369
And for comforters, but I found **n**. Ps 69:20 3808
May **n** dwell in their tents. Ps 69:25 408
And **n** of the warriors could use Ps 76:5 3808, 3605
And forget **n** of His benefits; Ps 103:2 408, 3605
stumbled and there was **n** to help. Ps 107:12 369
Let there be **n** to extend Ps 109:12 408
N who go to her return again, Nor Pr 2:19 3605, 3808

scoffer seeks wisdom and *finds* **n**,	**Pr 14:6**	369
there will be **n** to quench *them.*	**Is 1:31**	369
or stumbles, **N** slumbers or sleeps;	**Is 5:27**	3808
like sheep with **n** to gather *them,*	**Is 13:14**	369
is shut up so that **n** may enter.	**Is 24:10**	4480
N will pass through it forever	**Is 34:10**	369
N will lack its mate.	**Is 34:16**	802, 3808
are seeking water, but there is **n**,	**Is 41:17**	369
Your ears are open, but **n** hears.	**Is 42:20**	3808
a prey with **n** to deliver *them,*	**Is 42:22**	369
them, And a spoil, with **n** to say,	**Is 42:22**	369
And there will be **n** after Me.	**Is 43:10**	3808
And there is **n** who can deliver out	**Is 43:13**	369
any *other* Rock? I know of **n**.' "	**Is 44:8**	1077
is with you, and there is **n** else,	**Is 45:14**	369
am the LORD, and there is **n** else.	**Is 45:18**	369
There is **n** except Me.	**Is 45:21**	369
There is **n** to save you.	**Is 47:15**	369
called, *why* was there **n** to answer?	**Is 50:2**	369
There is **n** to guide her among all	**Is 51:18**	369
hope for justice, but there is **n**,	**Is 59:11**	369
fire And burn with **n** to quench it,	**Jer 4:4**	369
There is **n** like You, O LORD;	**Jer 10:6**	369
kingdoms, There is **n** like You.	**Jer 10:7**	369
And burn with **n** to extinguish *it,*	**Jer 21:12**	369
day is great, There is **n** like it;	**Jer 30:7**	369
for **n** will return except *a few*	**Jer 44:14**	3808
of Israel, but there will be **n**;	**Jer 50:20**	369
She has **n** to comfort her Among all	**La 1:2**	369
N of them *shall remain,* none of	**Ezk 7:11**	3808
remain, **n** of their people,	**Ezk 7:11**	3808
people, **n** of their wealth,	**Ezk 7:11**	3808
seek peace, but there will be **n**.	**Ezk 7:25**	369
"**N** of My words will be delayed	**Ezk 12:28**	3808, 3605
n of his righteous deeds will be	**Ezk 33:13**	3605, 3808
"**N** of his sins that he has	**Ezk 33:16**	3605, 3808
leave **n** of them there any longer.	**Ezk 39:28**	3808
inasmuch as **n** of the wise men of	**Da 4:18**	3606, 3809
and there was **n** to rescue the ram	**Da 8:7**	3808
and there was **n** to explain *it.*	**Da 8:27**	369
n of the wicked will understand,	**Da 12:10**	3808, 3605
fault, and let **n** offer reproof;	**Hos 4:4**	408, 376
and there will be **n** to deliver.	**Hos 5:14**	369
N of them calls on Me.	**Hos 7:7**	369
One on high, **N** at all exalts *Him.*	**Hos 11:7**	3808
There is **n** to raise her up.	**Am 5:2**	369
with **n** to quench *it* for Bethel,	**Am 5:6**	369
tears, And there is **n** to rescue.	**Mi 5:8**	369
'Also let **n** of you devise evil in	**Zch 8:17**	376, 408
to share with him who has **n**;	**Lk 3:11**	*3361*
yet Elijah was sent to **n** of them,	**Lk 4:26**	*3762*
and **n** of them was cleansed, but	**Lk 4:27**	*3762*
n of those men who were invited	**Lk 14:24**	*3762*
"So then, **n** of you can be My	**Lk 14:33**	*3956, 3756*
and *that* **n** may cross over from	**Lk 16:26**	*3366*
disciples understood **n** of these things,	**Lk 18:34**	*3762*
wisdom which **n** of your opponents	**Lk 21:15**	*3756, 537a*
yet **n** of you carries out the Law?	**Jn 7:19**	*3762*
and **n** of you asks Me,	**Jn 16:5**	*3762*
N of the disciples ventured to	**Jn 21:12**	*3762*
But **n** of the rest dared to associate	**Ac 5:13**	*3762*
but if **n** of those things is *true*	**Ac 25:11**	*3762*
n of these things escape his notice;	**Ac 26:26**	*3756, 3762*
that **n** *of them* would swim away	**Ac 27:42**	*3361, 5100*
"THERE IS **N** RIGHTEOUS, NOT EVEN	**Ro 3:10**	*3756*
THERE IS **N** WHO UNDERSTANDS,	**Ro 3:11**	*3756*
THERE IS **N** WHO SEEKS FOR GOD;	**Ro 3:11**	*3756*
THERE IS **N** WHO DOES GOOD, THERE	**Ro 3:12**	*3756*
I baptized **n** of you except Crispus	**1Co 1:14**	*3762*
the wisdom which **n** of the rulers	**1Co 2:8**	*3762*
should be as though they had **n**;	**1Co 7:29**	*3361*
But I have used **n** of these things.	**1Co 9:15**	*3762*
so that **n** of you will be hardened by	**Heb 3:13**	*5100, 1438*
Make sure that **n** of you suffers as a	**1Pe 4:15**	*5100, 3361*

NON-EXISTENT

you will be as nothing and **n**.	**Is 41:12**	657

NONSENSE

For a fool speaks **n**,	**Is 32:6**	5039
these words appeared to them as **n**,	**Lk 24:11**	*3026*

NOON

men are to dine with me at **n**."	**Gn 43:16**	6672a
present for Joseph's coming at **n**;	**Gn 43:25**	6672a
and you will grope at **n**,	**Dt 28:29**	6672a
Baal from morning until **n** saying,	**1Ki 18:26**	6672a
It came about at **n**,	**1Ki 18:27**	6672a
They went out at **n**,	**1Ki 20:16**	6672a
mother, he sat on her lap until **n**,	**2Ki 4:20**	6672a
And grope at **n** as in the night.	**Jb 5:14**	6672a
Evening and morning and at **n**,	**Ps 55:17**	6672a
destruction that lays waste at **n**.	**Ps 91:6**	6672a
do you make *it* lie down at **n**?	**SS 1:7**	6672a
your shadow like night at high **n**;	**Is 16:3**	6672a
Arise, and let us attack at **n**.	**Jer 6:4**	6672a
morning And a shout of alarm at **n**;	**Jer 20:16**	6672a
I will make the sun go down at **n**	**Am 8:9**	6672a
Ashdod will be driven out at **n** And	**Zph 2:4**	6672a

NOONDAY

life would be brighter than **n**;	**Jb 11:17**	6672a
light And your judgment as the **n**.	**Ps 37:6**	6672a
of a young man, A destroyer at **n**;	**Jer 15:8**	6672a

NOONTIME

way, approaching Damascus about **n**,	**Ac 22:6**	*3314*

NOOSE

"A **n** for him is hidden in the	**Jb 18:10**	2256a

NOPHAH

Then we have laid waste even to **N**,	**Nu 21:30**	5302

NOR

n between my herdsmen and your	**Gn 13:8**	
n did I hear of it until today."	**Gn 21:26**	571, 3808
n have I eaten the rams of your	**Gn 31:38**	3808
be neither plowing **n** harvesting.	**Gn 45:6**	369
n have they attained the years	**Gn 47:9**	3808
N the ruler's staff from between	**Gn 49:10**	3808
neither recently **n** in time past,	**Ex 4:10**	1571
n since You have spoken to Your	**Ex 4:10**	1571
your fathers **n** your grandfathers	**Ex 10:6**	3808
n would there be so *many* again.	**Ex 10:14**	3808
n did anyone rise from his place	**Ex 10:23**	3808
n had they prepared any provisions	**Ex 12:39**	1571, 3808
n are you to break any bone of it.	**Ex 12:46**	3808
n shall any leaven be seen among	**Ex 13:7**	3808
n the pillar of fire by night,	**Ex 13:22**	3808
foul **n** was there any worm in it.	**Ex 16:24**	3808
n curse a ruler of your people.	**Ex 22:28**	3808
n shall you testify in a dispute	**Ex 23:2**	3808
n shall you be partial to a poor	**Ex 23:3**	3808
n let *them* be heard from your	**Ex 23:13**	3808
n is the fat of My feast to remain	**Ex 23:18**	3808
worship their gods, **n** serve them,	**Ex 23:24**	3808
n do according to their deeds;	**Ex 23:24**	3808
n shall the people come up with	**Ex 24:2**	3808
n shall you make *any* like it in	**Ex 30:32**	3808
N is it the sound of the cry of	**Ex 32:18**	369
n let any man be seen anywhere on	**Ex 34:3**	408
earth **n** among any of the nations;	**Ex 34:10**	3808
n is the sacrifice of the Feast of	**Ex 34:25**	3808
your heads **n** tear your clothes,	**Lv 10:6**	3808
neither you **n** your sons with you,	**Lv 10:9**	408
flesh **n** touch their carcasses;	**Lv 11:8**	3808
thing, **n** enter the sanctuary until	**Lv 12:4**	3808
n may any alien who sojourns among	**Lv 17:12**	3808
n are you to do what is done in	**Lv 18:3**	3808
n shall you take her son's	**Lv 18:17**	3808
n shall you profane the name of	**Lv 18:21**	3808
n shall any woman stand before an	**Lv 18:23**	3808
n the alien who sojourns among you	**Lv 18:26**	
n shall you gather the gleanings of	**Lv 19:9**	3808
'**N** shall you glean your vineyard,	**Lv 19:10**	3808
n shall you gather the fallen	**Lv 19:10**	3808
shall not steal, **n** deal falsely,	**Lv 19:11**	3808
falsely, **n** lie to one another.	**Lv 19:11**	3808
oppress your neighbor, **n** rob *him.*	**Lv 19:13**	3808
n place a stumbling block before	**Lv 19:14**	3808
to the poor **n** defer to the great,	**Lv 19:15**	3808
n bear any grudge against the sons	**Lv 19:18**	3808
n wear a garment upon you of two	**Lv 19:19**	3808
redeemed **n** given her freedom,	**Lv 19:20**	3808
n practice divination or	**Lv 19:26**	3808
n harm the edges of your beard.	**Lv 19:27**	3808
n make any tattoo marks on	**Lv 19:28**	3808
n shave off the edges of their	**Lv 21:5**	3808
n make any cuts in their flesh.	**Lv 21:5**	3808
n shall they take a woman divorced	**Lv 21:7**	3808
uncover his head **n** tear his clothes;	**Lv 21:10**	3808
n shall he approach any dead	**Lv 21:11**	3808
n defile himself *even* for his	**Lv 21:11**	3808
n shall he go out of the	**Lv 21:12**	3808
n profane the sanctuary of his God,	**Lv 21:12**	3808
n make of them an offering by fire	**Lv 22:22**	3808
n shall you accept any such from	**Lv 22:25**	3808
n roasted grain nor new growth.	**Lv 23:14**	3808
nor roasted grain **n** new growth.	**Lv 23:14**	3808
n gather the gleaning of your	**Lv 23:22**	3808
your field **n** prune your vineyard.	**Lv 25:4**	3808
not sow, **n** reap its aftergrowth,	**Lv 25:11**	3808
n gather in *from* its untrimmed	**Lv 25:11**	3808
at interest, **n** your food for gain.	**Lv 25:37**	3808
n shall you set up for yourselves	**Lv 26:1**	3808
n shall you place a figured stone	**Lv 26:1**	3808
n will I so abhor them as to	**Lv 26:44**	3808
or bad, **n** shall he exchange it;	**Lv 27:33**	3808
n shall you take their census	**Nu 1:49**	3808
on it **n** put frankincense on it,	**Nu 5:15**	3808
n shall he drink any grape juice nor	**Nu 6:3**	3808
n eat fresh or dried grapes.	**Nu 6:3**	3808
morning, **n** break a bone of it;	**Nu 9:12**	3808
eat, not one day, **n** two days,	**Nu 11:19**	3808
day, nor two days, **n** five days,	**Nu 11:19**	3808
days, nor five days, **n** ten days,	**Nu 11:19**	3808
days, nor ten days, **n** twenty days,	**Nu 11:19**	3808
n shall any of those who spurned	**Nu 14:23**	3808
of the LORD **n** Moses left the camp.	**Nu 14:44**	3808
n have you given us an inheritance	**Nu 16:14**	3808
n have I done harm to any of them."	**Nu 16:15**	3808
n own any portion among them;	**Nu 18:20**	3808
n is there water to drink."	**Nu 20:5**	369
He should lie, **N** a son of man,	**Nu 23:19**	3808
N has He seen trouble in Israel;	**Nu 23:21**	3808
N is there any divination against	**Nu 23:23**	3808
them at all **n** bless them at all!"	**Nu 23:25**	3808
his enemy **n** seeking his injury,	**Nu 35:23**	3808
'Do not be shocked, **n** fear them.	**Dt 1:29**	3808
"Do not go up **n** fight, for I am	**Dt 1:42**	3808
to your voice **n** give ear to you.	**Dt 1:45**	3808
Moab, **n** provoke them to war,	**Dt 2:9**	408
do not harass them **n** provoke them,	**Dt 2:19**	408
you, **n** take away from it,	**Dt 4:2**	3808
see **n** hear nor eat nor smell.	**Dt 4:28**	3808
see nor hear **n** eat nor smell.	**Dt 4:28**	3808
see nor hear nor eat **n** smell.	**Dt 4:28**	3808
He will not fail you **n** destroy you	**Dt 4:31**	3808
n forget the covenant with your fathers	**Dt 4:31**	3808
n shall you take their daughters	**Dt 7:3**	3808
not set His love on you **n** choose you	**Dt 7:7**	3808
n shall you serve their gods, for	**Dt 7:16**	3808
on them, **n** take it for yourselves,	**Dt 7:25**	3808
not know, **n** did your fathers know,	**Dt 8:3**	3808
n did your foot swell these forty	**Dt 8:4**	3808
I neither ate bread **n** drank water.	**Dt 9:9**	3808
I neither ate bread **n** drank water,	**Dt 9:18**	3808
Him **n** listened to His voice.	**Dt 9:23**	3808
show partiality **n** take a bribe.	**Dt 10:17**	3808
not add to **n** take away from it.	**Dt 12:32**	3808
you **n** your fathers have known,	**Dt 13:6**	3808
n shall you spare or conceal him.	**Dt 13:8**	3808
n shave your forehead for the sake	**Dt 14:1**	3808
flesh **n** touch their carcasses.	**Dt 14:8**	3808
n close your hand from your poor	**Dt 15:7**	3808
n shear the firstborn of your	**Dt 15:19**	3808
the LORD your God, **n** to the judge,	**Dt 17:12**	176
n shall he cause the people to	**Dt 17:16**	3808
n shall he greatly increase silver	**Dt 17:17**	3808
this blood, **n** did our eyes see *it.*	**Dt 21:7**	3808
n shall a man put on a woman's	**Dt 22:5**	3808
n shall any of the sons of Israel	**Dt 23:17**	3808
army **n** be charged with any duty;	**Dt 24:5**	3808
n shall sons be put to death for	**Dt 24:16**	3808
n take a widow's garment in pledge.	**Dt 24:17**	3808
n have I removed any of it while I	**Dt 26:14**	3808
n offered any of it to the dead.	**Dt 26:14**	3808
you **n** your fathers have known,	**Dt 28:36**	3808
of the wine **n** gather *the grapes,*	**Dt 28:39**	3808
old, **n** show favor to the young.	**Dt 28:50**	3808
n the increase of your herd or the	**Dt 28:51**	3808
a heart to know, **n** eyes to see,	**Dt 29:4**	3808
nor eyes to see, **n** ears to hear.	**Dt 29:4**	3808
n have you drunk wine or strong	**Dt 29:6**	3808
for you, **n** is it out of reach.	**Dt 30:11**	3808
"**N** is it beyond the sea, that you	**Dt 30:13**	3808
and not die, **N** his men be few."	**Dt 33:6**	408
N did he regard his own sons,	**Dt 33:9**	3808
was not dim, **n** his vigor abated.	**Dt 34:7**	3808
shout **n** let your voice be heard nor	**Jos 6:10**	3808
n let a word proceed out of your	**Jos 6:10**	3808
n yet the work which He had done	**Jg 2:10**	1571
you, **n** shall my son rule over you;	**Jg 8:23**	3808
n did they show kindness to the	**Jg 8:35**	3808
n the land of the sons of Ammon.	**Jg 11:15**	3808
drink, **n** eat any unclean thing.	**Jg 13:4**	408
from, **n** did he tell me his name.	**Jg 13:6**	3808
drink **n** eat any unclean thing,	**Jg 13:7**	408
vine **n** drink wine or strong drink,	**Jg 13:14**	408
drink, **n** eat any unclean thing;	**Jg 13:14**	408
n would He have shown us all these	**Jg 13:23**	3808
n would He have let us hear *things*	**Jg 13:23**	3808
n will any of us return to his	**Jg 20:8**	3808
n did you give *them* to them,	**Jg 21:22**	3588, 3808
drunk neither wine **n** strong drink,	**1Sa 1:15**	3808
N is there any rock like our God.	**1Sa 2:2**	369
n had the word of the LORD yet	**1Sa 3:7**	2962
neither the priests of Dagon **n** all	**1Sa 5:5**	3808
neither sword **n** spear was found	**1Sa 13:22**	3808
neither you **n** your kingdom will be	**1Sa 20:31**	3808
my sword **n** my weapons with me,	**1Sa 21:8**	1571
n have they missed anything all	**1Sa 25:7**	3808
n did we miss anything as long as	**1Sa 25:15**	3808
saw or knew *it,* **n** did any awake,	**1Sa 26:12**	369
be on you, **n** fields of offerings;	**2Sa 1:21**	408
n did they continue to fight	**2Sa 2:28**	3808
bound, **n** your feet put in fetters;	**2Sa 3:34**	3808
n will the wicked afflict them any	**2Sa 7:10**	3808
my husband neither name **n** remnant	**2Sa 14:7**	1115
n remember what your servant did	**2Sa 19:19**	408
his feet, **n** trimmed his mustache,	**2Sa 19:24**	3808
mustache, **n** washed his clothes,	**2Sa 19:24**	3808
N do we have inheritance in the	**2Sa 20:1**	3808
n is it for us to put any man to	**2Sa 21:4**	369
n the beasts of the field by night.	**2Sa 21:10**	3808
n have asked riches for yourself,	**1Ki 3:11**	3808
n have you asked for the life of	**1Ki 3:11**	3808
n shall one like you arise after	**1Ki 3:12**	3808
"He shall be neither mine **n** yours;	**1Ki 3:26**	3808
is neither adversary **n** misfortune.	**1Ki 5:4**	369
and there was neither hammer **n** axe	**1Ki 6:7**	3808
neither hammer nor axe **n** any iron	**1Ki 6:7**	3808
n have they been seen to this day.	**1Ki 10:12**	3808
n shall they associate with you,	**1Ki 11:2**	3808
n would I eat bread or drink water	**1Ki 13:8**	3808
shall eat no bread, **n** drink water,	**1Ki 13:9**	3808
nor drink water, **n** return by the	**1Ki 13:9**	3808
return with you, **n** go with you,	**1Ki 13:16**	3808
n will I eat bread or drink water	**1Ki 13:16**	3808
eat no bread, **n** drink water there;	**1Ki 13:17**	3808
eaten the body **n** torn the donkey.	**1Ki 13:28**	3808
of his relatives **n** of his friends.	**1Ki 16:11**	
be neither dew **n** rain these years,	**1Ki 17:1**	
n shall the jar of oil be empty,	**1Ki 17:14**	3808
n did the jar of oil become empty,	**1Ki 17:16**	3808
I would not look at you **n** see you.	**2Ki 3:14**	518
not see wind **n** shall you see rain;	**2Ki 3:17**	3808

is neither new moon **n** sabbath." 2Ki 4:23 3808
n will he sacrifice to other gods, 2Ki 5:17 3808
not the way, **n** is this the city; 2Ki 6:19 3808
no one there, **n** the voice of man, 2Ki 7:10 369
n repair the damages of the house. 2Ki 12:8 1115
n the sons be put to death for the 2Ki 14:6 3808
for there was neither bond **n** free, 2Ki 14:26 657
n was there any helper for Israel. 2Ki 14:26 369
n do they follow their statutes or 2Ki 17:34 369
n bow down yourselves to them nor 2Ki 17:35 3808
n serve them nor sacrifice 2Ki 17:35 3808
serve them **n** sacrifice to them. 2Ki 17:35 3808
n shall you fear other gods. 2Ki 17:38 3808
n *among those* who were before him. 2Ki 18:5 3808
would neither listen **n** do *it.* 2Ki 18:12 3808
n let Hezekiah make you trust in 2Ki 18:30 408
his house **n** in all his dominion 2Ki 20:13 3808
n did he turn aside to the right 2Ki 22:2 3808
n in all the days of the kings of 2Ki 23:22 3808
n did any like him arise after him. 2Ki 23:25 3808
n did all their family multiply 1Ch 4:27 3808
n is there any God besides You, 1Ch 17:20 369
do not fear **n** be dismayed. 1Ch 22:13 408
do not fear **n** be dismayed, for the 1Ch 28:20 408
He will not fail you **n** forsake you 1Ch 28:20 3808
n have you even asked for long 2Ch 1:11 3808
n those who will come after you." 2Ch 1:12 3808
n did I choose any man for a 2Ch 6:5 3808
n do we know what to do, but our 2Ch 20:12 3808
n sons be put to death for 2Ch 25:4 3808
the LORD is not with Israel **n** 2Ch 25:7
n had the people been gathered to 2Ch 30:3 3808
n because of all the horde 2Ch 32:7
n had any of the kings of Israel 2Ch 35:18 3808
n did he listen to the words of 2Ch 35:22 3808
n take their daughters to your sons, Ezr 9:12 408
is no remnant **n** any who escape? Ezr 9:14 369
did not eat bread **n** drink water, Ezr 10:6 3808
N *can* the task *be done* in one or Ezr 10:13 3808
the commandments, **n** the statutes, Ne 1:7 3808
n the ordinances which You Ne 1:7 3808
n had I as yet told the Jews, the Ne 2:16 3808
n the men of the guard who Ne 4:23 369
neither I **n** my kinsmen have eaten Ne 5:14 3808
N the pillar of fire by night, Ne 9:19 3808
wear out, **n** did their feet swell. Ne 9:21 3808
n take of their daughters for your Ne 13:25 518
neither bowed down **n** paid homage. Es 3:2 3808
bowed down **n** paid homage to him, Es 3:5 369
Job did not sin **n** did he blame God. Jb 1:22 3808
care for it, **N** light shine on it. Jb 3:4 408
"I am not at ease, **n** am I quiet, Jb 3:26 3808
N does trouble sprout from the ground, Jb 5:6 3808
N will his place know him anymore. Jb 7:10 3808
N let me alone until I swallow my Jb 7:19 3808
N will He support the evildoers. Jb 8:20 3808
n be aroused out of his sleep. Jb 14:12 3808
rich, **n** will his wealth endure; Jb 15:29 3808
N any survivor where he sojourned. Jb 18:19 369
N deep gloom *which* covers me. Jb 23:17 3808
its ways **N** abide in its paths. Jb 24:13 3808
N will my tongue mutter deceit. Jb 27:4 518
N has the falcon's eye caught Jb 28:7 3808
N has the *fierce* lion passed over Jb 28:8 3808
N is it found in the land of the Jb 28:13 3808
N can silver be weighed as its Jb 28:15 3808
N can it be exchanged for articles Jb 28:17 3808
N can it be valued in pure gold. Jb 28:19 3808
N may elders understand justice. Jb 32:9 3808
N will I reply to him with your Jb 32:14 3808
N flatter *any* man. Jb 32:21 3808
N should my pressure weigh heavily Jb 33:7 3808
N regards the rich above the poor, Jb 34:19 3808
rule **N** be snares of the people. Jb 34:30 4480
N will the Almighty regard it. Jb 35:13 3808
N has He acknowledged Jb 35:15 3808
N the spear, the dart or the Jb 41:26 1097
N stand in the path of sinners, Ps 1:1 3808
N sit in the seat of scoffers! Ps 1:1 3808
N sinners in the assembly of the Ps 1:5 3808
anger, **N** chasten me in Your wrath. Ps 6:1 408
N the hope of the afflicted perish Ps 9:18
N does evil to his neighbor, Ps 15:3 3808
N takes up a reproach against his Ps 15:3 3808
N does he take a bribe against the Ps 15:5 3808
N will I take their names upon my Ps 16:4 1077
N will You allow Your Holy One to Ps 16:10 3808
is no speech, **n** are there words; Ps 19:3 369
For He has not despised **n** abhorred Ps 22:24 3808
N has He hidden His face from him; Ps 22:24 3808
men, **N** will I go with pretenders. Ps 26:4 3808
N my life with men of bloodshed, Ps 26:9 408
Do not abandon me **n** forsake me, Ps 27:9 408
the LORD **N** the deeds of His hands, Ps 28:5 3808
N does it deliver anyone by its Ps 33:17 3808
N let those who hate me without cause Ps 35:19
n to those who lapse into Ps 40:4
my bow, **N** will my sword save me. Ps 44:6 3808
N male goats out of your folds. Ps 50:9
N is it one who hates me who has Ps 55:12 3808
for my transgression **n** for my sin, Ps 59:3 3808
N His lovingkindness from me. Ps 66:20 3808
the flood of water not overflow me **N** Ps 69:15 408
N the pit shut its mouth on me. Ps 69:15 408
N are they plagued like mankind. Ps 73:5 3808
N is there any among us who knows Ps 74:9 3808
from the east, **n** from the west, Ps 75:6 3808
N from the desert *comes* exaltation; Ps 75:6 3808
N were they faithful in His Ps 78:37 3808
N shall you worship any foreign Ps 81:9 3808
do not know **n** do they understand; Ps 82:5 3808
N are there any works like Yours. Ps 86:8 369
N the son of wickedness afflict Ps 89:22 3808
N deal falsely in My faithfulness. Ps 89:33 3808
N will I alter the utterance of My Ps 89:34 3808
N will any plague come near your Ps 91:10 3808
N does a stupid man understand Ps 92:6 3808
N does the God of Jacob pay heed." Ps 94:7 3808
N will He forsake His inheritance. Ps 94:14 3808
N will He keep *His anger* forever. Ps 103:9 3808
N rewarded us according to our Ps 103:10 3808
N any to be gracious to his Ps 109:12 408
N *do* any who go down into silence; Ps 115:17 3808
Will neither slumber **n** sleep. Ps 121:4 3808
you by day, **N** the moon by night. Ps 121:6 3808
N do those who pass by say, Ps 129:8 3808
is not proud, **n** my eyes haughty; Ps 131:1 3808
N do I involve myself in great Ps 131:1 3808
enter my house, **N** lie on my bed; Ps 132:3 518
N is there any breath at all in Ps 135:17 369
N do they reach the paths of life. Pr 2:19 3808
N of the onslaught of the wicked Pr 3:25 408
n turn away from the words of my Pr 4:5 408
Do not turn to the right **n** to the left; Pr 4:27 408
N inclined my ear to my Pr 5:13 3808
eyes, **N** slumber to your eyelids; Pr 6:4 408
N let her capture you with her Pr 6:25 408
N will he be satisfied though you Pr 6:35 3808
N the first dust of the world. Pr 8:26 3808
N to strike the noble for *their* Pr 17:26
N to thrust aside the righteous Pr 18:5
men, **N** desire to be with them; Pr 24:1 408
N is it glory to search out one's Pr 25:27 3808
N are the eyes of man ever Pr 27:20 3808
N does a crown *endure* to all Pr 27:24 518
N do I have the knowledge of the Pr 30:3 3808
Give me neither poverty **n** riches; Pr 30:8 408
N is the ear filled with hearing. Ec 1:8 3808
having neither a son **n** a brother, Ec 4:8 369
n he who loves abundance *with its* Ec 5:10 3808
n have they any longer a reward, Ec 9:5 369
wise **n** wealth to the discerning Ec 9:11
3808, 1571
n favor to men of ability; Ec 9:11
3808, 1571
love, **N** will rivers overflow it; SS 8:7 3808
or bandaged, **N** softened with oil. Is 1:6 3808
N does the widow's plea come Is 1:23 3808
there is neither bread **n** cloak; Is 3:7 369
N do they consider the work of His Is 5:12 3808
N is the belt at its waist undone, Is 5:27 3808
undone, **N** its sandal strap broken. Is 5:27 3808
not stand **n** shall it come to pass. Is 7:7 3808
not ask, **n** will I test the LORD!" Is 7:12 3808
N do they seek the LORD of hosts. Is 9:13 3808
N does He have pity on their Is 9:17 3808
N does it plan so in its heart, Is 10:7 3808
N make a decision by what His ears Is 11:3 3808
N will their eye pity children. Is 13:18
N will the Arab pitch *his* tent Is 13:20 3808
N will shepherds make *their flocks* Is 13:20 3808
N will he look to that which his Is 17:8 3808
sword, **N** did they die in battle. Is 22:2 3808
N did you take into consideration Is 22:11 3808
neither travailed **n** given birth, Is 23:4 3808
have neither brought up young men **n** Is 23:4
N were inhabitants of the world born. Is 26:18 1077
N is the cartwheel driven over Is 28:27 3808
n shall his face now turn pale; Is 29:22 3808
One of Israel, **n** seek the LORD! Is 31:1 3808
voice **n** disturbed at their noise, Is 31:4 3808
N any of its cords be torn apart. Is 33:20 1077
firmly, **N** spread out the sail. Is 33:23 1077
N will any vicious beast go up on Is 35:9 1077
n let Hezekiah make you trust in Is 36:15 408
his house **n** in all his dominion Is 39:2
N its beasts enough for a burnt Is 40:16 369
N make His voice heard in the Is 42:2 3808
N My praise to graven images. Is 42:8 3808
N will the flame burn you. Is 43:2 3808
N have you honored Me with your Is 43:23 3808
N wearied you with incense. Is 43:23 3808
N have you filled Me with the fat of Is 43:24 3808
do not know, **n** do they understand, Is 44:18 3808
n is there knowledge or Is 44:19 3808
he cannot deliver himself, **n** say, Is 44:20 3808
N remember the outcome of them. Is 47:7 3808
N know loss of children.' Is 47:8 3808
There will be no coal to warm by **N** Is 47:14
not in truth **n** in righteousness. Is 48:1 3808
"They will not hunger or thirst, **N** Is 49:10 3808
disobedient **N** did I turn back. Is 50:5 3808
N be dismayed at their revilings. Is 51:7 408
n will his bread be lacking. Is 51:14 3808
N is there one to take her by the Is 51:18 369
haste, **N** will you go as fugitives; Is 52:12 3808
N appearance that we should be Is 53:2 3808
N was there any deceit in His Is 53:9 3808
with you **N** will I rebuke you. Is 54:9 4480
N are your ways My ways," declares Is 55:8 3808
N let the eunuch say, "Behold, I Is 56:3 408
remember Me **N** give *Me* a thought? Is 57:11 3808
"For I will not contend forever, **N** Is 57:16 3808
N is His ear so dull That it cannot Is 59:1 3808
N will they cover themselves with Is 59:6 3808
n from the mouth of your Is 59:21 3808
n from the mouth of your Is 59:21 3808
N devastation or destruction Is 60:18 3808
N for brightness will the moon Is 60:19 3808
"Your sun will no longer set, **N** Is 60:20 3808
N to your land will it any longer Is 62:4 3808
N will foreigners drink your new Is 62:8 518
N has the eye seen a God besides You, Is 64:4 408
N remember iniquity forever; Is 64:9 1755
heard My fame **n** seen My glory. Is 66:19 3808
to mind, **n** will they remember it, Jer 3:16 3808
remember it, **n** will they miss *it,* Jer 3:16 3808
miss *it,* **n** will it be made again. Jer 3:16 3808
n will they walk anymore after Jer 3:17 3808
My mind, **n** will I turn from it." Jer 4:28 3808
N can you understand what they say. Jer 5:15 3808
n walk after other gods to your Jer 7:6 3808
My voice **n** walked according to it, Jer 9:13 3808
they **n** their fathers have known; Jer 9:16 3808
no harm, **N** can they do any good." Jer 10:5
1571, 369
N is it in a man who walks to Jer 10:23 3808
n lift up a cry or prayer for them; Jer 11:14 408
"I will not show pity **n** be sorry Jer 13:14 3808
nor be sorry **n** have compassion Jer 13:14 3808
the sword **n** will you have famine, Jer 14:13 3808
I have neither sent them **n** Jer 14:14 3808
commanded them **n** spoken to them; Jer 14:14 3808
n their wives, nor their sons, Jer 14:16
nor their wives, **n** their sons, Jer 14:16 369
nor their sons, **n** their daughters Jer 14:16 369
lent, **n** have men lent money to me, Jer 15:10 3808
of merrymakers, **N** did I exult. Jer 15:17 3808
n have sons or daughters in this place Jer 16:2 3808
n will anyone gash himself or Jer 16:6 3808
n give them a cup of consolation Jer 16:7 3808
known, neither you **n** your fathers; Jer 16:13 3808
n is their iniquity concealed from Jer 16:17 3808
of drought **N** cease to yield fruit. Jer 17:8 3808
N have I longed for the woeful day; Jer 17:16 3808
on the sabbath day **n** do any work, Jer 17:22 3808
the priest, **n** counsel to the sage, Jer 18:18 3808
n the *divine* word to the prophet! Jer 18:18 3808
that neither they **n** their forefathers Jer 19:4 3808
n the kings of Judah had *ever* known, Jer 19:4 3808
of, **n** did it *ever* enter My mind; Jer 19:5 3808
n have pity nor compassion." Jer 21:7 3808
nor have pity **n** compassion." Jer 21:7 3808
afraid any longer, **n** be terrified, Jer 23:4 3808
terrified, **n** will any be missing," Jer 23:4 3808
n do they furnish this people the Jer 23:32 3808
n inclined your ear to hear, Jer 25:4 3808
n had it entered My mind that they Jer 32:35 3808
n to build ourselves houses to Jer 35:9 1115
n did they rend their garments. Jer 36:24 3808
But neither he **n** his servants nor Jer 37:2 3808
his servants **n** the people of the land Jer 37:2 3808
n will I give you over to the hand of Jer 38:16 518
neither they, you, **n** your fathers. Jer 44:3 3808
n have they feared nor walked in Jer 44:10 3808
nor have they feared **n** walked in Jer 44:10 3808
man flee, **N** the mighty man escape; Jer 46:6 408
do not fear, **N** be dismayed, Jer 46:27 408
vessel, **N** has he gone into exile. Jer 48:11 3808
n will a son of man reside in it. Jer 49:18 3808
N will a son of man reside in it." Jer 49:33 3808
N will *any* son of man reside in it. Jer 50:40 3808
N let him rise up in his Jer 51:3 413
For neither Israel **n** Judah has Jer 51:5 3808
corner **N** a stone for foundations, Jer 51:26 3808
N *did* any of the inhabitants of La 4:12 3808
fear them **n** fear their words, Ezk 2:6 408
n be dismayed at their presence, Ezk 2:6 408
n to many peoples of Ezk 3:6 3808
n has any unclean meat ever Ezk 4:14 3808
n observed My ordinances, Ezk 5:7 3808
n observed the ordinances of the Ezk 5:7 3808
pity on you, **n** will I spare *you,* Ezk 7:4 3808
will show no pity **n** will I spare. Ezk 7:9 3808
n anything eminent among them. Ezk 7:11 3808
buyer rejoice **n** the seller mourn; Ezk 7:12 408
n will any of them maintain his Ezk 7:13 3808
n can they fill their stomachs, Ezk 7:19 3808
will have no pity **n** will I spare; Ezk 8:18 3808
will have no pity **n** will I spare, Ezk 9:10 3808
n will you be flesh in the midst Ezk 11:11 3808
n have you executed My ordinances, Ezk 11:12 3808
n did you build the wall around Ezk 13:5 3808
n will they be written down in the Ezk 13:9 3808
n will they enter the land of Ezk 13:9 3808
n were you washed with water for Ezk 16:4 3808
should never come about **n** happen. Ezk 16:16 3808
by great strength **n** by many people Ezk 17:9 3808
n will the father bear the Ezk 18:20 3808
n did they forsake the idols of Ezk 20:8 3808
n were they careful to observe My Ezk 20:21 3808
n set their top among the clouds, Ezk 31:14 3808
n their well-watered mighty ones Ezk 31:14 3808
"**N** do they lie beside the fallen Ezk 32:27 3808
n have you sought for the lost; Ezk 34:4 3808
n will you bear disgrace from the Ezk 36:15 3808
n will you cause your nation to Ezk 36:15 3808
name, neither they **n** their kings, Ezk 43:7 3808
n come near to any of My holy Ezk 44:13 3808
"**N** shall any of the priests drink Ezk 44:21 3808
magicians **n** diviners are able to Da 2:27
n was the hair of their head singed, Da 3:27 3809
n were their trousers damaged, Da 3:27 3809
n had the smell of fire *even* come Da 3:27 3809
n was there anyone to rescue from Da 8:4 369
n have we obeyed the voice of the Da 9:10 3808
n did meat or wine enter my mouth, Da 10:3 3808

n did I use any ointment at all until	**Da 10:3**	3808
n has any breath been left in me."	**Da 10:17**	3808
n according to his authority which	**Da 11:4**	3808
n will he remain with his power,	**Da 11:6**	3808
not in anger **n** in battle.	**Da 11:20**	3808
never did, **n** his ancestors;	**Da 11:24**	3808
n will he show regard for any	**Da 11:37**	3808
harlot, **n** shall you have a man;	**Hos 3:3**	3808
their God, **N** have they sought Him,	**Hos 7:10**	3808
N will we say again,	**Hos 14:3**	3808
N will there be again after it To	**Jl 2:2**	3808
N do they deviate from their paths.	**Jl 2:7**	3808
N the mighty man save his life.	**Am 2:14**	3808
N will he who rides the horse save	**Am 2:15**	3808
Gilgal, **N** cross over to Beersheba;	**Am 5:5**	3808
N do I delight in your solemn	**Am 5:21**	3808
n am I the son of a prophet;	**Am 7:14**	3808
n shall you speak against the house	**Am 7:16**	3808
Neither their silver **n** their gold	**Zph 1:18**	1571
N will a deceitful tongue Be found	**Zph 3:13**	3808
'Not by might **n** by power, but by	**Zch 4:6**	3808
to the LORD, neither day **n** night,	**Zch 14:7**	3808
"**n** will I accept an offering from	**Mal 1:10**	3808
n will your vine in the field cast	**Mal 3:11**	3808
them neither root **n** branch."	**Mal 4:1**	3808
n does *anyone* light a lamp	**Mt 5:15**	*3761*
"**N** shall you make an oath by your	**Mt 5:36**	*3383*
neither moth **n** rust destroys,	**Mt 6:20**	*3777*
n for your body, *as to* what you	**Mt 6:25**	*3366*
n reap nor gather into barns, and	**Mt 6:26**	*3761*
reap **n** gather into barns,	**Mt 6:26**	*3761*
they do not toil **n** do they spin,	**Mt 6:28**	*3761*
bushes **n** figs from thistles,	**Mt 7:16**	*2228*
n can a bad tree produce good	**Mt 7:18**	*3761*
"**N** do *people* put new wine into old	**Mt 9:17**	*3761*
receive you, **n** heed your words,	**Mt 10:14**	*3366*
n a slave above his master.	**Mt 10:24**	*3761*
came neither eating **n** drinking,	**Mt 11:18**	*3383*
n does anyone know the Father except	**Mt 11:27**	*3761*
him to eat **n** for those with him,	**Mt 12:4**	*3761*
"HE WILL NOT QUARREL, **N** CRY OUT;	**Mt 12:19**	*3761*
N WILL ANYONE HEAR HIS VOICE IN	**Mt 12:19**	*3761*
do not hear, **n** do they understand.	**Mt 13:13**	*3761*
not understanding the Scriptures **n**	**Mt 22:29**	*3366*
marry **n** are given in marriage,	**Mt 22:30**	*3777*
n did anyone dare from that day on	**Mt 22:46**	*3761*
n do you allow those who are	**Mt 23:13**	*3761*
the world until now, **n** ever will.	**Mt 24:21**	*3761*
the angels of heaven, **n** the Son,	**Mt 24:36**	*3761*
do not know the day **n** the hour.	**Mt 25:13**	*3761*
n has *anything* been secret, but	**Mk 4:22**	*3761*
"**N** will I tell you by what authority	**Mk 11:33**	*3761*
marry **n** are given in marriage,	**Mk 12:25**	*3777*
the angels in heaven, **n** the Son,	**Mk 13:32**	*3761*
"I neither know **n** understand what	**Mk 14:68**	*3777*
n, on the other hand, a bad tree	**Lk 6:43**	*3761*
n do they pick grapes from a briar	**Lk 6:44**	*3761*
n *anything* secret that will not	**Lk 8:17**	*3761*
journey, neither a staff, **n** a bag,	**Lk 9:3**	*3383*
a staff, nor a bag, **n** bread,	**Lk 9:3**	*3383*
nor a bag, nor bread, **n** money;	**Lk 9:3**	*3383*
a cellar **n** under a basket,	**Lk 11:33**	*3761*
n for your body, *as to* what you	**Lk 12:22**	*3366*
for they neither sow **n** reap;	**Lk 12:24**	*3777*
they have no storeroom **n** barn	**Lk 12:24**	*3761*
they neither toil **n** spin;	**Lk 12:27**	*3777*
thief comes near **n** moth destroys.	**Lk 12:33**	*3761*
n will they say,	**Lk 17:21**	*3761*
I do not fear God **n** respect man,	**Lk 18:4**	*3761*
And Jesus said to them, "**N** will I	**Lk 20:8**	*3761*
marry **n** are given in marriage;	**Lk 20:35**	*3777*
"No, **n** has Herod, for he sent Him	**Lk 23:15**	*3761*
blood **n** of the will of the flesh	**Jn 1:13**	*3761*
the flesh **n** of the will of man,	**Jn 1:13**	*3761*
you are not the Christ, **n** Elijah,	**Jn 1:25**	*3761*
nor Elijah, **n** the Prophet?"	**Jn 1:25**	*3761*
n come all the way here to draw."	**Jn 4:15**	*3366*
in this mountain **n** in Jerusalem	**Jn 4:21**	*3777*
at any time **n** seen His form.	**Jn 5:37**	*3777*
was not there, **n** His disciples,	**Jn 6:24**	*3761*
"You know neither Me **n** My Father;	**Jn 8:19**	*3777*
this man sinned, **n** his parents;	**Jn 9:3**	*3777*
n do you take into account that it	**Jn 11:50**	*3761*
n *is* one who is sent greater than	**Jn 13:16**	*3761*
be troubled, **n** let it be fearful.	**Jn 14:27**	*3366*
N ALLOW YOUR HOLY ONE TO	**Ac 2:27**	*3761*
N DID His flesh SUFFER DECAY.	**Ac 2:31**	*3777*
sight, and neither ate **n** drank.	**Ac 9:9**	*3761*
n the utterances of the prophets	**Ac 13:27**	*2532*
n we have been able to bear?	**Ac 15:10**	*3777*
n is He served by human hands, as	**Ac 17:25**	*3761*
n blasphemers of our goddess.	**Ac 19:37**	*3777*
n to walk according to the customs.	**Ac 21:21**	*3366*
is no resurrection, **n** an angel,	**Ac 23:8**	*3383*
nor an angel, **n** a spirit,	**Ac 23:8**	*3383*
n drink until they had killed Paul.	**Ac 23:12**	*3383*
the temple, **n** in the synagogues,	**Ac 24:12**	*3777*
n in the city *itself* did they find	**Ac 24:12**	*3777*
"**N** can they prove to you	**Ac 24:13**	*3761*
n stars appeared for many days,	**Ac 27:20**	*3383*
n have any of the brethren come	**Ac 28:21**	*3777*
n is circumcision that which is	**Ro 2:28**	*3761*
that neither death, **n** life,	**Ro 8:38**	*3777*
neither death, nor life, **n** angels,	**Ro 8:38**	*3777*
nor angels, **n** principalities,	**Ro 8:38**	*3777*
principalities, **n** things present,	**Ro 8:38**	*3777*
things present, **n** things to come,	**Ro 8:38**	*3777*
nor things to come, **n** powers,	**Ro 8:38**	*3777*
n height, nor depth, nor any other	**Ro 8:39**	*3777*
nor height, **n** depth, nor any other	**Ro 8:39**	*3777*
depth, **n** any other created thing,	**Ro 8:39**	*3777*
n are they all children because they	**Ro 9:7**	*3761*
age **n** of the rulers of this age,	**1Co 2:6**	*3761*
one who plants **n** the one who waters	**1Co 3:7**	*3777*
n with the leaven of malice and	**1Co 5:8**	*3366*
neither fornicators, **n** idolaters,	**1Co 6:9**	*3777*
nor idolaters, **n** adulterers,	**1Co 6:9**	*3777*
nor adulterers, **n** effeminate,	**1Co 6:9**	*3777*
nor effeminate, **n** homosexuals,	**1Co 6:9**	*3777*
n thieves, nor *the* covetous, nor	**1Co 6:10**	*3777*
nor thieves, **n** *the* covetous, nor	**1Co 6:10**	*3777*
nor *the* covetous, **n** drunkards,	**1Co 6:10**	*3756*
nor drunkards, **n** revilers,	**1Co 6:10**	*3756*
nor revilers, **n** swindlers,	**1Co 6:10**	*3756*
eat, **n** the better if we do eat.	**1Co 8:8**	*3777*
N let us act immorally, as some of	**1Co 10:8**	*3366*
N let us try the Lord, as some of	**1Co 10:9**	*3366*
N grumble, as some of them did,	**1Co 10:10**	*3366*
n is man independent of woman.	**1Co 11:11**	*3777*
n have the churches of God.	**1Co 11:16**	*3761*
n does the perishable inherit the	**1Co 15:50**	*3761*
n for the sake of the one offended,	**2Co 7:12**	*3761*
men **n** through the agency of man,	**Ga 1:1**	*3761*
it from man, **n** was I taught it,	**Ga 1:12**	*3777*
n did I go up to Jerusalem to	**Ga 1:17**	*3761*
There is neither Jew **n** Greek,	**Ga 3:28**	*3761*
there is neither slave **n** free man,	**Ga 3:28**	*3761*
there is neither male **n** female;	**Ga 3:28**	*2532*
n uncircumcision means anything,	**Ga 5:6**	*3777*
anything, **n** uncircumcision,	**Ga 6:15**	*3777*
not run in vain **n** toil in vain.	**Php 2:16**	*3761*
n with a pretext for greed	**1Th 2:5**	*3777*
n did we seek glory from men,	**1Th 2:6**	*3777*
We are not of night **n** of darkness;	**1Th 5:5**	*3761*
n did we eat anyone's bread	**2Th 3:8**	*3761*
n to pay attention to myths and	**1Tm 1:4**	*3366*
gossips **n** enslaved to much wine,	**Ti 2:3**	*3366*
beginning of days **n** end of life,	**Heb 7:3**	*3383*
n was it that He would offer	**Heb 9:25**	*3761*
N HAVE YOU TAKEN PLEASURE *in them*"	**Heb 10:8**	*3761*
N FAINT WHEN YOU ARE REPROVED BY	**Heb 12:5**	*3366*
YOU, **N** WILL I EVER FORSAKE YOU,"	**Heb 13:5**	*3761*
N *can* salt water produce fresh.	**Jas 3:12**	*3777*
N WAS ANY DECEIT FOUND IN HIS	**1Pe 2:22**	*3761*
n yet as lording it over those	**1Pe 5:3**	*3366*
render you neither useless **n** unfruitful	**2Pe 1:8**	*3761*
world **n** the things in the world.	**1Jn 2:15**	*3366*
n the one who does not love his	**1Jn 3:10**	*2532*
that you are neither cold **n** hot;	**Rv 3:15**	*3777*
lukewarm, and neither hot **n** cold,	**Rv 3:16**	*3777*
"They will hunger no longer, **n**	**Rv 7:16**	*3761*
n will the sun beat down on them,	**Rv 7:16**	*3761*
sun beat down on them, **n** any heat;	**Rv 7:16**	*3761*
of the earth, **n** any green thing,	**Rv 9:4**	*3761*
nor any green thing, **n** any tree,	**Rv 9:4**	*3761*
can neither see **n** hear nor walk;	**Rv 9:20**	*3777*
can neither see nor hear **n** walk;	**Rv 9:20**	*3777*
not repent of their murders **n** of their	**Rv 9:21**	*3777*
their sorceries **n** of their immorality	**Rv 9:21**	*3777*
immorality **n** of their thefts.	**Rv 9:21**	*3777*
of a lamp **n** the light of the sun,	**Rv 22:5**	*2532*

NORMAL

and the sea returned to its **n** state	**Ex 14:27**	386
it out, and it was restored to **n**,	**Mt 12:13**	*5199*

NORTH

as Hobah, which is **n** of Damascus.	**Gn 14:15**	8040
and to the **n** and to the south;	**Gn 28:14**	6828
of the tabernacle, on the **n** side,	**Ex 26:20**	6828
shall put the table on the **n** side.	**Ex 26:35**	6828
"Likewise for the **n** side in	**Ex 27:11**	6828
of the tabernacle, on the **n** side,	**Ex 36:25**	6828
For the **n** side *there were* one	**Ex 38:11**	6828
on the **n** side of the tabernacle,	**Ex 40:22**	6828
"On the **n** side *shall be* the	**Nu 2:25**	6828
'And this shall be your **n** border:	**Nu 34:7**	6828
This shall be your **n** border.	**Nu 34:9**	6828
on the **n** side two thousand cubits,	**Nu 35:5**	6828
mountain long enough. *Now* turn **n**,	**Dt 2:3**	6828
the west and **n** and south and east,	**Dt 3:27**	6828
and camped on the **n** side of Ai.	**Jos 8:11**	6828
was on the **n** side of the city,	**Jos 8:13**	6828
were of the **n** in the hill country,	**Jos 11:2**	6828
as the border of Ekron to the **n**	**Jos 13:3**	6828
And the border of the **n** side was	**Jos 15:5**	6828
continued on the **n** of Beth-arabah,	**Jos 15:6**	6828
valley of Rephaim toward the **n**.	**Jos 15:8**	6828
slope of Mount Jearim on the **n**	**Jos 15:10**	6828
westward at Michmethath on the **n**,	**Jos 16:6**	6828
was on the **n** side of the brook and	**Jos 17:9**	6828
and the **n** side to Manasseh,	**Jos 17:10**	6828
the **n** and to Issachar on the east.	**Jos 17:10**	6828
stay in their territory on the **n**.	**Jos 18:5**	6828
on the **n** side was from the Jordan,	**Jos 18:12**	6828
to the side of Jericho on the **n**,	**Jos 18:12**	6828
at the **n** bay of the Salt Sea,	**Jos 18:19**	6828
around it on the **n** to Hannathon,	**Jos 19:14**	6828
then it proceeded on **n** to Cabul,	**Jos 19:27**	8040
Ephraim, on the **n** of Mount Gaash.	**Jos 24:30**	6828
of Ephraim, **n** of Mount Gaash.	**Jg 2:9**	6828
camp of Midian was on the **n** side	**Jg 7:1**	6828
which is on the **n** side of Bethel,	**Jg 21:19**	6828
rose on the **n** opposite Michmash,	**1Sa 14:5**	6828
three facing **n**, three facing west,	**1Ki 7:25**	6828
put it on the **n** side of *his* altar.	**2Ki 16:14**	6828
four sides, to the east, west, **n** and	**1Ch 9:24**	6828
and his lot came out to the **n**.	**1Ch 26:14**	6828
six Levites, on the **n** four daily,	**1Ch 26:17**	6828
twelve oxen, three facing the **n**,	**2Ch 4:4**	6828
stretches out the **n** over empty space	**Jb 26:7**	6828
storm, And out of the **n** the cold.	**Jb 37:9**	2219
Out of the **n** comes golden *splendor;*	**Jb 37:22**	6828
earth, Is Mount Zion *in* the far **n**,	**Ps 48:2**	6828
The **n** and the south, You have	**Ps 89:12**	6828
From the **n** and from the south.	**Ps 107:3**	6828
The **n** wind brings forth rain, And	**Pr 25:23**	6828
south, Then turning toward the **n**,	**Ec 1:6**	6828
toward the south or toward the **n**,	**Ec 11:3**	6828
"Awake, O **n** *wind,* And come, *wind*	**SS 4:16**	6828
assembly In the recesses of the **n**.	**Is 14:13**	6828
For smoke comes from the **n**,	**Is 14:31**	6828
"I have aroused one from the **n**,	**Is 41:25**	6828
"I will say to the **n**,	**Is 43:6**	6828
come from the **n** and from the west,	**Is 49:12**	6828
pot, facing away from the **n**."	**Jer 1:13**	6828
"Out of the **n** the evil will break	**Jer 1:14**	6828
of the kingdoms of the **n**,"	**Jer 1:15**	6828
these words toward the **n** and say,	**Jer 3:12**	6828
come together from the land of the **n**	**Jer 3:18**	6828
For I am bringing evil from the **n**,	**Jer 4:6**	6828
For evil looks down from the **n**,	**Jer 6:1**	6828
people is coming from the **n** land,	**Jer 6:22**	6828
commotion out of the land of the **n**	**Jer 10:22**	6828
and see Those coming from the **n**.	**Jer 13:20**	6828
smash iron, Iron from the **n**,	**Jer 15:12**	6828
sons of Israel from the land of the **n**	**Jer 16:15**	6828
household of Israel from *the* **n** land	**Jer 23:8**	6828
take all the families of the **n**,'	**Jer 25:9**	6828
and all the kings of the **n**,	**Jer 25:26**	6828
bringing them from the **n** country,	**Jer 31:8**	6828
In the **n** beside the river Euphrates	**Jer 46:6**	6828
of the **n** by the river Euphrates.	**Jer 46:10**	6828
But a horsefly is coming from the **n**	**Jer 46:20**	6828
power of the people of the **n**."	**Jer 46:24**	6828
waters are going to rise from the **n**	**Jer 47:2**	6828
come up against her out of the **n**;	**Jer 50:3**	6828
nations from the land of the **n**,	**Jer 50:9**	6828
a people is coming from the **n**,	**Jer 50:41**	6828
will come to her from the **n**,"	**Jer 51:48**	6828
storm wind was coming from the **n**,	**Ezk 1:4**	6828
of the **n** gate of the inner *court,*	**Ezk 8:3**	6828
your eyes now toward the **n**."	**Ezk 8:5**	6828
So I raised my eyes toward the **n**,	**Ezk 8:5**	6828
to the **n** of the altar gate *was*	**Ezk 8:5**	6828
house which *was* toward the **n**;	**Ezk 8:14**	6828
of the upper gate which faces **n**,	**Ezk 9:2**	6828
lives **n** of you with her daughters;	**Ezk 16:46**	8040
south to **n** will be burned by it.	**Ezk 20:47**	6828
against all flesh from south *to* **n**.	**Ezk 21:4**	6828
I will bring upon Tyre from the **n**	**Ezk 26:7**	6828
also are the chiefs of the **n**,	**Ezk 32:30**	6828
from the remote parts of the **n**	**Ezk 38:6**	6828
out of the remote parts of the **n**,	**Ezk 38:15**	6828
from the remotest parts of the **n** and	**Ezk 39:2**	6828
cubits on the east and on the **n**.	**Ezk 40:19**	6828
the outer court which faced the **n**,	**Ezk 40:20**	6828
a gate opposite the gate on the **n**	**Ezk 40:23**	6828
Then he brought me to the **n** gate;	**Ezk 40:35**	6828
up to the gateway toward the **n**,	**Ezk 40:40**	6828
was at the side of the **n** gate,	**Ezk 40:44**	6828
the south gate facing toward the **n**.	**Ezk 40:44**	6828
chamber which faces toward the **n**	**Ezk 40:46**	6828
consisted of one doorway toward the **n**	**Ezk 41:11**	6828
outer court, the way toward the **n**;	**Ezk 42:1**	6828
the building toward the **n**.	**Ezk 42:1**	6828
a hundred cubits, *was* the **n** door;	**Ezk 42:2**	6828
and their openings *were* on the **n**.	**Ezk 42:4**	6828
the chambers which *were* on the **n**,	**Ezk 42:11**	6828
"The **n** chambers *and* the south	**Ezk 42:13**	6828
He measured on the **n** side five	**Ezk 42:17**	6828
He brought me by way of the **n** gate	**Ezk 44:4**	6828
he who enters by way of the **n** gate	**Ezk 46:9**	6828
shall go out by way of the **n** gate.	**Ezk 46:9**	6828
for the priests, which faced **n**;	**Ezk 46:19**	6828
brought me out by way of the **n** gate	**Ezk 47:2**	6828
on the **n** side, from the Great Sea	**Ezk 47:15**	6828
and on the **n** toward the north is	**Ezk 47:17**	6828
the **n** is the border of Hamath.	**Ezk 47:17**	6828
This is the **n** side.	**Ezk 47:17**	6828
from the **n** border to the eastern	**Ezk 47:18**	
toward the **n** beside Hamath,	**Ezk 48:1**	6828
the **n** 25,000 *cubits in length,*	**Ezk 48:10**	6828
the **n** side 4,500 *cubits,* the south	**Ezk 48:16**	6828
on the **n** 250 *cubits,* on the south	**Ezk 48:17**	6828
on the **n** side, 4,500 *cubits* by	**Ezk 48:30**	6828
Israel, three gates toward the **n**:	**Ezk 48:31**	6828
South will come to the king of the **N**	**Da 11:6**	6828
the fortress of the king of the **N**,	**Da 11:7**	6828
from *attacking* the king of the **N**	**Da 11:8**	6828
and fight with the king of the **N**.	**Da 11:11**	6828
"For the king of the **N** will again	**Da 11:13**	6828
"Then the king of the **N** will come,	**Da 11:15**	6828
and the king of the **N** will storm	**Da 11:40**	6828
and from the **N** will disturb him,	**Da 11:44**	6828
And from the **n** even to the east;	**Am 8:12**	6828
against the **n** And destroy Assyria,	**Zph 2:13**	6828
Flee from the land of the **n**,"	**Zch 2:6**	6828
are going forth to the **n** country;	**Zch 6:6**	6828
who are going to the land of the **n**	**Zch 6:8**	6828
My wrath in the land of the **n**."	**Zch 6:8**	6828
mountain will move toward the **n**	**Zch 14:4**	6828
and west and from **n** and south,	**Lk 13:29**	*1005*
three gates on the **n** and three gates	**Rv 21:13**	*1005*

NORTHERN

from the **n** extremity, beside the	**Ezk 48:1**	6828
remove the **n** *army* far from you,	**Jl 2:20**	6830

NORTHWARD		
n and southward and eastward and	Gn 13:14	6828
of the altar **n** before the LORD,	Lv 1:11	6828
on the **n** side of the tabernacle.	Nu 3:35	6828
and turned **n** toward Gilgal which	Jos 15:7	6828
proceeded to the side of Ekron **n**.	Jos 15:11	6828
is in the valley of Rephaim **n**;	Jos 18:16	6828
It extended **n** and went to	Jos 18:17	6828
the side in front of the Arabah **n** and	Jos 18:18	6828
to the side of Beth-hoglah **n**;	Jos 18:19	6828
Iphtahel **n** to Beth-emek and Neiel;	Jos 19:27	6828
I saw the ram butting westward, **n**,	Da 8:4	6828
NORTHWEST		
of Crete, facing southwest and **n**,	Ac 27:12	*5566*
NOSE		
and I put the ring on her **n**,	Gn 24:47	639
I will put My hook in your **n**,	2Ki 19:28	639
barbs can anyone pierce *his* **n**?	Jb 40:24	639
"Can you put a rope in his **n** Or	Jb 41:2	639
pressing the **n** brings forth blood;	Pr 30:33	639
Your **n** is like the tower of Lebanon,	SS 7:4	639
finger rings, **n** rings,	Is 3:21	639
I will put My hook in your **n** And	Is 37:29	639
are putting the twig to their **n**.	Ezk 8:17	639
will remove your **n** and your ears;	Ezk 23:25	639
NOSES		
They have **n**, but they cannot smell;	Ps 115:6	639
NOSTRIL		
"I also put a ring in your **n**,	Ezk 16:12	639
NOSTRILS		
breathed into his **n** the breath of life;	Gn 2:7	639
all in whose **n** was the breath of	Gn 7:22	639
At the blast of Your **n** the waters	Ex 15:8	639
until it comes out of your **n** and	Nu 11:20	639
"Smoke went up out of His **n**,	2Sa 22:9	639
At the blast of the breath of His **n**.	2Sa 22:16	639
And the breath of God is in my **n**,	Jb 27:3	639
"Out of his **n** smoke goes forth As	Jb 41:20	5156
Smoke went up out of His **n**,	Ps 18:8	639
At the blast of the breath of Your **n**.	Ps 18:15	639
whose breath *of life* is in his **n**;	Is 2:22	639
These are smoke in My **n**,	Is 65:5	639
The breath of our **n**,	La 4:20	639
of your camp rise up in your **n**;	Am 4:10	639
NOTE		
the LORD took **n** of Sarah as He	Gn 21:1	6485
Now all the people took **n** *of it,*	2Sa 3:36	5234
then You would take **n** of me,	Jb 10:14	8104
And look now and take **n**.	Jer 5:1	3045
and they were taking **n** of him as	Ac 3:10	*1921*
Lord, take **n** of their threats,	Ac 4:29	*1896*
since you can take **n** of the fact	Ac 24:11	*1921*
take special **n** of that person and do	2Th 3:14	*4593*
NOTEWORTHY		
a **n** miracle has taken place through	Ac 4:16	*1110*
NOTHING		
and now **n** which they purpose to do	Gn 11:6	3808, 3605
"I will take **n** except what the	Gn 14:24	1107
only do **n** to these men, inasmuch	Gn 19:8	408, 1697
against the lad, and do **n** to him;	Gn 22:12	408, 3972
and have done to you **n** but good and	Gn 26:29	7534
you therefore serve me for **n**?	Gn 29:15	2600
has withheld **n** from me except you,	Gn 39:9	3808, 3972
and even here I have done **n** that	Gn 40:15	3808, 3972
There is **n** left for my lord except	Gn 47:18	3808
so that **n** will die of all that	Ex 9:4	3808, 1697
Thus **n** green was left on tree or	Ex 10:15	3808, 3605
And **n** leavened shall be eaten.	Ex 13:3	3808
and **n** leavened shall be seen among	Ex 13:7	3808
her, then she shall go out for **n**,	Ex 21:11	2600
if he owns **n**, then he shall be	Ex 22:3	369
There is **n** at all to look at	Nu 11:6	369
and touch **n** that belongs to them,	Nu 16:26	408, 3605
pass through on my feet, **n** *else*."	Nu 20:19	369, 1697
'Let **n**, I beg you, hinder you from	Nu 22:16	408
and her father says **n** to her,	Nu 30:4	2790b
says **n** to her on the day he hears *it,*	Nu 30:7	2790b
n to her *and* did not forbid her,	Nu 30:11	2790b
says **n** to her from day to day,	Nu 30:14	2790b
because he said **n** to her on the	Nu 30:14	2790b
"**N** from that which is put under	Dt 13:17	3808
poor brother, and you give him **n**;	Dt 15:9	3808
"But you shall do **n** to the girl;	Dt 22:26	3808, 1697
but there will be **n** you can do.	Dt 28:32	369
eat, since he has **n** *else* left,	Dt 28:55	1097, 3605
he left **n** undone of all that the	Jos 11:15	3808, 1697
"This is **n** less than the sword of	Jg 7:14	369
young goat though he had **n** in his hand;	Jg 14:6	3972, 369
"**N** like this has *ever* happened or	Jg 19:30	3808
him everything and hid **n** from him.	1Sa 3:18	3808
n like this has happened before.	1Sa 4:7	3808
you have found **n** in my hand."	1Sa 12:5	3808, 3972
my father does **n** either great or	1Sa 20:2	3808, 1697
your servant knows **n** at all of this	1Sa 22:15	3808
so that **n** was missed of all that	1Sa 25:21	3808, 3972
There is **n** better for me than to	1Sa 27:1	369
But **n** of theirs was missing,	1Sa 30:19	3808
"But the poor man had **n** except	2Sa 12:3	369, 3605
grain on it, so that **n** was known.	2Sa 17:19	3808, 1697
there is **n** hidden from the king),	2Sa 18:13	3605, 1697, 3808
princes and servants are **n** to you;	2Sa 19:6	369
household was **n** but dead men	2Sa 19:28	3808
the LORD my God which cost me **n**."	2Sa 24:24	2600
they left **n** lacking.	1Ki 4:27	3808, 1697
There was **n** in the ark except the	1Ki 8:9	369
n was hidden from the king which	1Ki 10:3	3808, 1697
n like *it* was made for any other	1Ki 10:20	3808
And he answered, "**N**;	1Ki 11:22	3808
and looked and said, "There is **n**."	1Ki 18:43	369, 3972
and we are still doing **n** to take	1Ki 22:3	2814
to speak to me **n** but the truth	1Ki 22:16	3808
"Your maidservant has **n** in the	2Ki 4:2	369, 3605
whom I stand, I will take **n**."	2Ki 5:16	518
but they found **n** more of her than	2Ki 9:35	3808
earth **n** of the word of the LORD,	2Ki 10:10	3808
There was **n** in his house nor in	2Ki 20:13	3808, 1697
there is **n** among my treasuries	2Ki 20:15	3808, 1697
n shall be left,' says the LORD.	2Ki 20:17	3808, 1697
burnt offering which costs me **n**."	1Ch 21:24	2600
There was **n** in the ark except the	2Ch 5:10	369
n was hidden from Solomon which he	2Ch 9:2	3808, 1697
n like *it* was made for any *other*	2Ch 9:19	3808
to speak to me **n** but the truth	2Ch 18:15	3808
because there was **n** like this in	2Ch 30:26	3808
"You have **n** in common with us in	Ezr 4:3	3808
This is **n** but sadness of heart."	Ne 2:2	369
back and will require **n** from them;	Ne 5:12	3808
to him who has **n** prepared;	Ne 8:10	369
"**N** has been done for him."	Es 6:3	3808, 1697
"Does Job fear God for **n**?	Jb 1:9	2600
They go up into **n** and perish.	Jb 6:18	8414
are *only* of yesterday and know **n**,	Jb 8:9	3808
"There dwells in his tent **n** of his;	Jb 18:15	1097
"**N** remains for him to devour,	Jb 20:21	369
space And hangs the earth on **n**.	Jb 26:7	1099
because of His majesty I can do **n**.	Jb 31:23	3808
profits a man **n** When he is pleased	Jb 34:9	3808
and I will add **n** more."	Jb 40:5	3808
"**N** on earth is like him, One made	Jb 41:33	369
is **n** reliable in what they say;	Ps 5:9	369
have tested me and You find **n**;	Ps 17:3	1077
there is **n** hidden from its heat.	Ps 19:6	369
And my lifetime as **n** in Your sight;	Ps 39:5	369
Surely they make an uproar for **n**;	Ps 39:6	1892
when he dies he will carry **n** away;	Ps 49:17	3808, 3605
besides You, I desire **n** on earth.	Ps 73:25	3808
And **n** causes them to stumble.	Ps 119:165	369
n you desire compares with her.	Pr 3:15	3605, 3808
is **n** crooked or perverted in them.	Pr 8:8	369
She is naive and knows **n**.	Pr 9:13	1077, 4100
of the sluggard craves and *gets* **n**,	Pr 13:4	369
pretends to be rich, but has **n**;	Pr 13:7	369, 3605
insolence comes **n** but strife,	Pr 13:10	7534
begs during the harvest and has **n**.	Pr 20:4	369
If you have **n** with which to pay,	Pr 22:27	369
He hears the oath but tells **n**.	Pr 29:24	3808
So there is **n** new under the sun.	Ec 1:9	369, 3605
There is **n** better for a man *than*	Ec 2:24	369
I know that there is **n** better for	Ec 3:12	369
there is **n** to add to it and there	Ec 3:14	369
it and there is **n** to take from it,	Ec 3:14	369
I have seen that **n** is better	Ec 3:22	369
then there was **n** to support him.	Ec 5:14	369, 3972
He will take **n** from the fruit of	Ec 5:15	3972, 3808
lacks **n** of all that he desires;	Ec 6:2	369
for there is **n** good for a man	Ec 8:15	369
the head There is **n** sound in it,	Is 1:6	369
N *remains* but to crouch among the	Is 10:4	1115
And all its princes will be **n**.	Is 34:12	657
There was **n** in his house nor in	Is 39:2	3808, 1697
there is **n** among my treasuries	Is 39:4	3808, 1697
n will be left,' says the LORD.	Is 39:6	3808, 1697
the nations are as **n** before Him,	Is 40:17	369
as less than **n** and meaningless.	Is 40:17	657
He *it is* who reduces rulers to **n**,	Is 40:23	369
who contend with you will be as **n** and	Is 41:11	369
who war with you will be as **n** and	Is 41:12	369
And your work amounts to **n**;	Is 41:24	657
My strength for **n** and vanity;	Is 49:4	8414
"You were sold for **n** and you will	Is 52:3	2600
out from there, Touch **n** unclean;	Is 52:11	408
are blind, All of them know **n**.	Is 56:10	3808
anger, or You will bring me to **n**.	Jer 10:24	4591
waited for peace, but **n** good *came;*	Jer 14:19	369
have inherited **n** but falsehood,	Jer 16:19	389
N is too difficult for You,	Jer 32:17	3808, 3605, 1697
they have done **n** of all that You	Jer 32:23	3808
the king can *do* **n** against you."	Jer 38:5	369, 1697
of the poorest people who had **n**,	Jer 39:10	369, 3972
him, and do **n** harmful to him,	Jer 39:12	408, 3972
idle boasts have accomplished **n**.	Jer 48:30	3808
destroy her, Let **n** be left to her.	Jer 50:26	408
So the peoples will toil for **n**,	Jer 51:58	1767, 7385b
there will be **n** dwelling in it,	Jer 51:62	1115
Is it **n** to all you who pass this way?	La 1:12	3808
their own spirit and have seen **n**.	Ezk 13:3	1115
of the earth are accounted as **n**,	Da 4:35	3809
so that **n** would be changed in	Da 6:17	3809, 6640
will be cut off and have **n**,	Da 9:26	369
them, And **n** at all escapes them.	Jl 2:3	3808
earth when it captures **n** at all?	Am 3:5	3808
Surely the Lord GOD does **n** Unless	Am 3:7	3808, 1697
him who puts **n** in their mouths They	Mi 3:5	3808
prowled, With **n** to disturb *them?*	Na 2:11	369
And nations grow weary for **n**?	Hab 2:13	7385b
They leave **n** for the morning.	Zph 3:3	3808
seem to you like **n** in comparison?	Hg 2:3	369
"**N** like this has ever been seen in	Mt 9:33	*3763*
n concealed that will not be revealed,	Mt 10:26	*3762*
now three days and have **n** to eat;	Mt 15:32	*3756, 5100*
and **n** will be impossible to you.	Mt 17:20	*3762*
found **n** on it except leaves only;	Mt 21:19	*3762*
swears by the temple, *that* is **n**;	Mt 23:16	*3762*
swears by the altar, *that* is **n**,	Mt 23:18	*3762*
and you gave Me **n** to eat; I was	Mt 25:42	*3756*
and you gave Me **n** to drink;	Mt 25:42	*3756*
n to do with that righteous Man;	Mt 27:19	*3367*
saw that he was accomplishing **n**,	Mt 27:24	*3762*
"See that you say **n** to anyone;	Mk 1:44	*3367*
n is hidden, except to be revealed;	Mk 4:22	*3756, 5100*
should take **n** for *their* journey,	Mk 6:8	*3367*
there is **n** outside the man which	Mk 7:15	*3762*
crowd and they had **n** to eat,	Mk 8:1	*3361, 5100*
now three days and have **n** to eat	Mk 8:2	*3756, 5100*
came to it, He found **n** but leaves,	Mk 11:13	*3762*
wearing **n** *but* a linen sheet over	Mk 14:51	
and they said **n** to anyone, for	Mk 16:8	*3762*
n will be impossible with God."	Lk 1:37	*3756, 3956, 4487*
And He ate **n** during those days,	Lk 4:2	*3756, 3762*
hard all night and caught **n**,	Lk 5:5	*3762*
and lend, expecting **n** in return;	Lk 6:35	*3367*
"For **n** is hidden that will not	Lk 8:17	*3756*
"Take **n** for *your* journey, neither	Lk 9:3	*3367*
the enemy, and **n** will injure you.	Lk 10:19	*3762*
and I have **n** to set before him';	Lk 11:6	*3756*
"But there is **n** covered up that	Lk 12:2	*3762*
They said, "*No*, **n**."	Lk 22:35	*3762*
but He answered him **n**.	Lk 23:9	*3762*
n deserving death has been done by	Lk 23:15	*3762*
but this man has done **n** wrong."	Lk 23:41	*3762*
apart from Him **n** came into being	Jn 1:3	*3761, 1520*
"A man can receive **n** unless	Jn 3:27	*3756, 3762*
You have **n** to draw with and the	Jn 4:11	*3777*
so that **n** worse happens to you."	Jn 5:14	*3361, 5100*
you, the Son can do **n** of Himself,	Jn 5:19	*3756, 3762*
"I can do **n** on My own initiative.	Jn 5:30	*3756, 3762*
fragments so that **n** will be lost."	Jn 6:12	*3361, 5100*
all that He has given Me I lose **n**,	Jn 6:39	*3361*
the flesh profits **n**;	Jn 6:63	*3762*
and they are saying **n** to Him.	Jn 7:26	*3762*
and I do **n** on My own initiative,	Jn 8:28	*3762*
"If I glorify Myself, My glory is **n**;	Jn 8:54	*3762*
not from God, He could do **n**."	Jn 9:33	*3756, 3762*
"You know **n** at all,	Jn 11:49	*3762*
is coming, and he has **n** in Me;	Jn 14:30	*3756, 3762*
for apart from Me you can do **n**.	Jn 15:5	*3756, 3762*
you have asked for **n** in My name;	Jn 16:24	*3762*
and I spoke **n** in secret.	Jn 18:20	*3762*
and that night they caught **n**.	Jn 21:3	*3762*
them, they had **n** to say in reply.	Ac 4:14	*3762*
him were dispersed and came to **n**.	Ac 5:36	*3762*
EGYPT WHO KNEW **N** ABOUT JOSEPH.	Ac 7:18	*3756*
so that **n** of what you have said	Ac 8:24	*3367*
eyes were open, he could see **n**;	Ac 9:8	*3762*
for **n** unholy or unclean has ever	Ac 11:8	*3763*
to spend their time in **n** other than	Ac 17:21	*3762*

to keep calm and to do **n** rash. Ac 19:36 *3367*
there is **n** to the things which they Ac 21:24 *3762*
"We find **n** wrong with this man; Ac 23:9 *3762*
taste **n** until we have killed Paul. Ac 23:14 *3367*
had committed **n** worthy of death; Ac 25:25 *3367*
"Yet I have **n** definite about him Ac 25:26 *3756*
stating **n** but what the Prophets Ac 26:22 *3762*
without eating, having taken **n**. Ac 27:33 *3367*
had seen **n** unusual happen to him, Ac 28:6 *3367*
I had done **n** against our people or Ac 28:17 *3762*
I know that **n** good dwells in me, Ro 7:18 *3756*
it does not bear the sword for **n**; Ro 13:4 *1500*
Owe **n** to anyone except to love one Ro 13:8 *3367*
Jesus that **n** is unclean in itself; Ro 14:14 *3762*
to know **n** among you except Jesus 1Co 2:2 *3756, 5100*
am conscious of **n** against myself, 1Co 4:4 *3762*
Circumcision is **n**, and 1Co 7:19 *3762*
nothing, and uncircumcision is **n**, 1Co 7:19 *3762*
the gospel, I have **n** to boast of, 1Co 9:16 *3756*
God and shame those who have **n**? 1Co 11:22 *3361*
but do not have love, I am **n**. 1Co 13:2 *3762*
do not have love, it profits me **n**. 1Co 13:3 *3762*
For we write **n** else to you than 2Co 1:13 *3756*
as having **n** yet possessing all things. 2Co 6:10 *3367*
For we can do **n** against the truth, 2Co 13:8 *3756, 5100*
of reputation contributed **n** to me. Ga 2:6 *3762*
thinks he is something when he is **n**, Ga 6:3 *3367*
Do **n** from selfishness or empty Php 2:3 *3367*
Be anxious for **n**, but in Php 4:6 *3367*
is good, and **n** is to be rejected if 1Tm 4:4 *3762*
But have **n** to do with worldly 1Tm 4:7 *3868*
doing **n** in a *spirit of* partiality. 1Tm 5:21 *3367*
he is conceited *and* understands **n**; 1Tm 6:4 *3367*
we have brought **n** into the world, 1Tm 6:7 *3762*
and unbelieving, **n** is pure, Ti 1:15 *3762*
having **n** bad to say about us. Ti 2:8 *3367*
way so that **n** is lacking for them. Ti 3:13 *3367*
He left **n** that is not subject to him. Heb 2:8 *3762*
Moses spoke **n** concerning priests. Heb 7:14 *3762*
(for the Law made **n** perfect), Heb 7:19 *3762*
perfect and complete, lacking in **n**. Jas 1:4 *3367*
accepting **n** from the Gentiles. 3Jn 1:7 *3367*
wealthy, and have need of **n**," Rv 3:17 *3762*
and **n** unclean, and no one who Rv 21:27 *3956*

NOTHINGNESS
kept my soul from the pit of **n**, Is 38:17 1097

NOTICE
of Israel, and God took **n** *of them.* Ex 2:25 3045
escapes the **n** of the assembly, Lv 4:13 5869
that you should take **n** of me, Ru 2:10 5234
he who took **n** of you be blessed." Ru 2:19 5234
shall **n** the place where he lies, Ru 3:4 3045
I do not take **n** of myself; Jb 9:21 3045
due me escapes the **n** of my God"? Is 40:27 5674a
ourselves and You do not **n**?' Is 58:3 3045
O LORD, Remember me, take **n** of me, Jer 15:15 6485
but do not **n** the log that is in Mt 7:3 *2657*
yet He could not escape **n**. Mk 7:24 *2990*
but do not **n** the log that is in Lk 6:41 *2657*
saw that she had not escaped **n**, Lk 8:47 *2990*
giving **n** of the completion of the Ac 21:26 *1229*
none of these things escape his **n**; Ac 26:26 *2990*
Take **n** that our brother Timothy Heb 13:23 *1097*
it escapes their **n** that by the 2Pe 3:5 *2990*
let this one *fact* escape your **n**, 2Pe 3:8 *2990*

NOTICED
Then I **n** from the appearance of Ezk 1:27 7200
before men to be **n** by them; Mt 6:1 *2300*
appearance so that they will be **n** by Mt 6:16 *5316*
so that your fasting will not be **n** by Mt 6:18 *5316*
do all their deeds to be **n** by men; Mt 23:5 *2300*
and **n** a tax collector named Levi sitting Lk 5:27 *2300*
He **n** how they had been picking out Lk 14:7 *1907*

NOTICES
once, Or twice, *yet* no one **n** it. Jb 33:14 7789

NOTIFIED
you have **n** me of these things." Ac 23:22 *1718*

NOTIFY
you and the Council **n** the Ac 23:15 *1718*

NOTORIOUS
holding a **n** prisoner, Mt 27:16 *1978*

NOURISHED
ewe lamb Which he bought and **n**; 2Sa 12:3 2421a
constantly **n** on the words of the 1Tm 4:6 *1789*
so that there she would be **n** for Rv 12:6 *5142*
where she was **n** for a time and Rv 12:14 *5142*

NOURISHES
own flesh, but **n** and cherishes it, Eph 5:29 *1625*

NOURISHMENT
"Who prepares for the raven its **n** When Jb 38:41 6718b

NOW
N no shrub of the field was yet in Gn 2:5
N a river flowed out of Eden to Gn 2:10
"This is **n** bone of my bones, And Gn 2:23 6471
N the serpent was more crafty than Gn 3:1
N the man called his wife's name Gn 3:20
and **n**, he might stretch out his Gn 3:22 6258
N the man had relations with his Gn 4:1
"**N** you are cursed from the ground, Gn 4:11 6258
N to Enoch was born Irad, Gn 4:18
N he called his name Noah, saying, Gn 5:29
N it came about, when men began to Gn 6:1
N the earth was corrupt in the Gn 6:11
N Noah was six hundred years old Gn 7:6
N it came about in the six hundred Gn 8:13
"**N** behold, I Myself do establish Gn 9:9
N the sons of Noah who came out of Gn 9:18
N these are *the records of* the Gn 10:1
N Cush became the father of Nimrod; Gn 10:8
N their settlement extended from Gn 10:30
N the whole earth used the same Gn 11:1
and **n** nothing which they purpose Gn 11:6 6258
N these are *the records of* the Gn 11:27
N the LORD said to Abram, Gn 12:1
N Abram was seventy-five years old Gn 12:4
N the Canaanite *was* then in the Gn 12:6
N there was a famine in the land; Gn 12:10
"See **n**, I know that you are a Gn 12:11 4994
N then, here is your wife, take Gn 12:19 6258
N Abram was very rich in Gn 13:2
N Lot, who went with Abram, also Gn 13:5
N the Canaanite and the Perizzite Gn 13:7
N the men of Sodom were wicked Gn 13:13
"**N** lift up your eyes and look Gn 13:14 4994
N the valley of Siddim was full of Gn 14:10
N he was living by the oaks of Gn 14:13
n he was a priest of God Most High. Gn 14:18
"**N** look toward the heavens, and Gn 15:5 4994
N when the sun was going down, a Gn 15:12
N Sarai, Abram's wife had borne Gn 16:1
"**N** behold, the LORD has prevented Gn 16:2 4994
N the angel of the LORD found her Gn 16:7
N when Abram was ninety-nine years Gn 17:1
"**N** as for you, you shall keep My Gn 17:9
N Abraham was ninety-nine years Gn 17:24
N the LORD appeared to him by the Gn 18:1
if **n** I have found favor in Your Gn 18:3 4994
N Abraham and Sarah were old, Gn 18:11
"I will go down **n**, and see if Gn 18:21 4994
"**N** behold, I have ventured to Gn 18:27 4994
"**N** behold, I have ventured to Gn 18:31 4994
N the two angels came to Sodom in Gn 19:1
"**N** behold, my lords, please turn Gn 19:2 4994
"**N** behold, I have two daughters Gn 19:8 4994
n we will treat you worse than Gn 19:9 6258
"**N** behold, your servant has found Gn 19:19 4994
n behold, this town is near *enough* Gn 19:20 4994
N Abraham arose early in the Gn 19:27
N Abraham journeyed from there Gn 20:1
N Abimelech had not come near her; Gn 20:4
"**N** therefore, restore the man's Gn 20:7 6258
N Abraham was one hundred years Gn 21:5
N Sarah saw the son of Hagar the Gn 21:9
N it came about at that time that Gn 21:22
n therefore, swear to me here by Gn 21:23 6258
N it came about after these Gn 22:1
"Take **n** your son, your only son, Gn 22:2 4994
for **n** I know that you fear God, Gn 22:12 6258
N it came about after these Gn 22:20
N Sarah lived one hundred and Gn 23:1
N Ephron was sitting among the Gn 23:10
N Abraham was old, advanced in age; Gn 24:1
n may it be that the girl to whom Gn 24:14
N when she had finished giving him Gn 24:19
N Rebekah had a brother whose name Gn 24:29
"**N** Sarah my master's wife bore a Gn 24:36
if **n** You will make my journey on Gn 24:42 4994
"So **n** if you are going to deal Gn 24:49 6258
N Isaac had come from going to Gn 24:62
N Abraham took another wife, whose Gn 25:1
N Abraham gave all that he had to Gn 25:5
N these are *the records of* the Gn 25:12
N these are *the records of* the Gn 25:19
N the first came forth red, all Gn 25:25
N Isaac loved Esau, because he had Gn 25:28
N there was a famine in the land, Gn 26:1
N Isaac sowed in that land and Gn 26:12
N all the wells which his father's Gn 26:15
'Let there **n** be an oath between Gn 26:28 4994
are **n** the blessed of the LORD.'" Gn 26:29 6258
N it came about on the same day, Gn 26:32
N it came about, when Isaac was Gn 27:1
"Behold **n**, I am old *and* I do not Gn 27:2 4994
"**N** then, please take your gear, Gn 27:3 6258
"**N** therefore, my son, listen to Gn 27:8 6258
"Go **n** to the flock and bring me Gn 27:9 4994
N may God give you of the dew of Gn 27:28
N it came about, as soon as Isaac Gn 27:30
n he has taken away my blessing." Gn 27:36 6258
N as for you then, what can I do, Gn 27:37
N when the words of her elder son Gn 27:42
"**N** therefore, my son, obey my Gn 27:43 6258
N Esau saw that Isaac had blessed Gn 28:6
N the stone on the mouth of the Gn 29:2
N Laban had two daughters; Gn 29:16
N Jacob loved Rachel, so he said, Gn 29:18
N in the evening Gn 29:23
N the LORD saw that Leah was Gn 29:31
n my husband will love me." Gn 29:32 6258
"**N** this time my husband will Gn 29:34 6258
N when Rachel saw that she bore Gn 30:1
N in the days of wheat harvest Gn 30:14
n my husband will dwell with me, Gn 30:20 6471
N it came about when Rachel had Gn 30:25
"If **n** it pleases you, *stay with* Gn 30:27 4994
But **n**, when shall I provide for my Gn 30:30 6258
N Jacob heard the words of Laban's Gn 31:1
'Lift up **n** your eyes and see Gn 31:12 4994
n arise, leave this land, and Gn 31:13 6258
n then, do whatever God has said Gn 31:16 6258
N Jacob had pitched his tent in Gn 31:25
N you have done foolishly. Gn 31:28 6258
"**N** you have indeed gone away because Gn 31:30 6258
N Rachel had taken the household Gn 31:34
surely **n** you would have sent me Gn 31:42 6258
"So **n** come, let us make a covenant Gn 31:44 6258
N Laban called it Jegar-sahadutha, Gn 31:47
N as Jacob went on his way, the Gn 32:1
with Laban, and stayed until **n**; Gn 32:4 6258
and **n** I have become two companies. Gn 32:10 6258
N he arose that same night and Gn 32:22
N the sun rose upon him just as he Gn 32:31
if **n** I have found favor in your Gn 33:10 4994
N Jacob came safely to the city of Gn 33:18
N Dinah the daughter of Leah, whom Gn 34:1
N Jacob heard that he had defiled Gn 34:5
N the sons of Jacob came in from Gn 34:7
N their words seemed reasonable to Gn 34:18
N he was more respected than all Gn 34:19
N it came about on the third day, Gn 34:25
N Deborah, Rebekah's nurse, died, Gn 35:8
for **n** you have another son." Gn 35:17 1571, 2088
N there were twelve sons of Jacob Gn 35:22
N the days of Isaac were one Gn 35:28
N these are *the records of* the Gn 36:1
N these are the kings who reigned Gn 36:31
N these are the names of the Gn 36:40
N Jacob lived in the land where Gn 37:1
N Israel loved Joseph more than Gn 37:3
N he had still another dream, and Gn 37:9
"Go **n** and see about the welfare Gn 37:14 4994
"**N** then, come and let us kill him Gn 37:20 6258
N the pit was empty, without any Gn 37:24
N Reuben returned to the pit, and Gn 37:29
N Judah took a wife for Er his Gn 38:6
N after a considerable time Shua's Gn 38:12
"Here **n**, let me come in to you"; Gn 38:16 4994
N it was about three months later Gn 38:24
N Joseph had been taken down to Gn 39:1
N his master saw that the LORD was Gn 39:3
N Joseph was handsome in form and Gn 39:6
N it happened one day that he went Gn 39:11
N when his master Gn 39:19
"**N** Pharaoh's cup was in my hand; Gn 40:11
N it happened at the end of two Gn 41:1
N in the morning Gn 41:8
"**N** a Hebrew youth *was* with us Gn 41:12
N Joseph said to Pharaoh, Gn 41:25
"**N** as for the repeating of the Gn 41:32
"**N** let Pharaoh look for a man Gn 41:33 6258
N the proposal seemed good to Gn 41:37
N Joseph was thirty years old when Gn 41:46
N before the year of famine came, Gn 41:50
N Jacob saw that there was grain Gn 42:1
N Joseph was the ruler over the Gn 42:6
N Joseph said to them on the third Gn 42:18
N comes the reckoning for his Gn 42:22 1571, 2009
N it came about as they were Gn 42:35
N the famine was severe in the Gn 43:1
by **n** we could have returned twice." Gn 43:10 6258
N the men were afraid, because Gn 43:18
N they were seated before him, the Gn 43:33
"**N** let it also be according to Gn 44:10 6258
N his brother is dead, so he alone Gn 44:20
"**N**, therefore, when I come to Gn 44:30 6258
"**N**, therefore, please let your Gn 44:33 6258
"**N** do not be grieved or angry with Gn 45:5 6258
"**N**, therefore, it was not you who Gn 45:8 6258
"**N** you must tell my father of all Gn 45:13
N when the news was heard in Gn 45:16
"**N** you are ordered, Gn 45:19
N these are the names of the sons Gn 46:8
N to Joseph in the land of Egypt Gn 46:20
N he sent Judah before him to Gn 46:28
"**N** let me die, since I have seen Gn 46:30 6471
from our youth even until **n**, Gn 46:34 6258
N, therefore, please let your Gn 47:4 6258
N there was no food in all the Gn 47:13
n, *here* is seed for you, and you Gn 47:23 1887
N Israel lived in the land of Gn 47:27
place **n** your hand under my thigh Gn 47:29 4994
N it came about after these things Gn 48:1
"**N** your two sons, who were born to Gn 48:5 6258
"**N** as for me, when I came from Gn 48:7
N the eyes of Israel were *so* dim Gn 48:10
N forty days were required for it, Gn 50:3
"If **n** I have found favor in your Gn 50:4 4994
N therefore, please let me go up and Gn 50:5 6258
N when the inhabitants of the Gn 50:11
And **n**, please forgive the Gn 50:17 6258
N Joseph stayed in Egypt, he and Gn 50:22
N these are the names of the sons Ex 1:1
N a new king arose over Egypt, who Ex 1:8
N a man from the house of Levi Ex 2:1
N it came about in those days, Ex 2:11
N the priest of Midian had seven Ex 2:16
N it came about in *the course of* Ex 2:23
N Moses was pasturing the flock of Ex 3:1
"I must turn aside **n** and Ex 3:3 4994
"**N**, behold, the cry of the sons of Ex 3:9 6258
"Therefore, come **n**, and I will Ex 3:10 6258
N they may say to me, Ex 3:13
So **n**, please, let us go a three Ex 3:18 6258
"**N** put your hand into your bosom." Ex 4:6 4994
"**N** then go, and I, even I, will Ex 4:12 6258
n send *the message* by whomever Ex 4:13 4994
N the LORD said to Moses in Ex 4:19
N it came about at the lodging Ex 4:24
N the LORD said to Aaron, Ex 4:27
the people of the land are **n** many, Ex 5:5 6258
"So go **n** *and* work; Ex 5:18 6258

Context	Reference	Number
"N you shall see what I will do	Ex 6:1	6258
N the LORD spoke to Moses, saying,	Ex 6:10	
N it came about on the day when	Ex 6:28	
N the LORD spoke to Moses and	Ex 7:8	
you have not listened until n."	Ex 7:16	3541
N the LORD said to Moses,	Ex 8:20	
"For *if by* n I had put forth My	Ex 9:15	6258
from the day it was founded until n.	Ex 9:18	6258
"N therefore send, bring your	Ex 9:19	6258
N the LORD said to Moses,	Ex 9:22	
(N the flax and the barley were	Ex 9:31	
Go n, the men *among you,* and serve	Ex 10:11	4994
"N therefore, please forgive my	Ex 10:17	6258
N the LORD said to Moses,	Ex 11:1	
"Speak n in the hearing of the	Ex 11:2	4994
N the LORD said to Moses and Aaron	Ex 12:1	
'N if the household is too small	Ex 12:4	
'N you shall eat it in this manner:	Ex 12:11	
'N this day will be a memorial to	Ex 12:14	
N it came about at midnight that	Ex 12:29	
N the sons of Israel had done	Ex 12:35	
N the sons of Israel journeyed	Ex 12:37	
N the time that the sons of Israel	Ex 12:40	
"N when the LORD	Ex 13:11	
N when Pharaoh had	Ex 13:17	
N the LORD spoke to Moses, saying,	Ex 14:1	
N on the sixth day	Ex 16:22	
(N an omer is a tenth of an ephah.)	Ex 16:36	
"Why, n, have you brought us up	Ex 17:3	2088
N Jethro, the priest of Midian,	Ex 18:1	
"N I know that the LORD is	Ex 18:11	6258
N when Moses' father-in-law saw	Ex 18:14	
"N listen to me: I will give you	Ex 18:19	6258
'N then, if you will indeed obey	Ex 19:5	6258
N Mount Sinai *was* all in smoke	Ex 19:18	
"N these are the ordinances which	Ex 21:1	
"N concerning everything which I	Ex 23:13	
N the LORD said to Moses,	Ex 24:12	
"N this is what you shall do to	Ex 29:1	
"N this is what you shall offer	Ex 29:38	
N the LORD spoke to Moses, saying,	Ex 31:1	
N when the people saw that Moses	Ex 32:1	
N when Aaron saw *this,* he built an	Ex 32:5	
"N then let Me alone, that My	Ex 32:10	6258
N when Joshua heard the sound of	Ex 32:17	
N when Moses saw that the people	Ex 32:25	
and n I am going up to the LORD,	Ex 32:30	6258
"But n, if You will, forgive	Ex 32:32	6258
"But go n, lead the people where	Ex 32:34	6258
N therefore, put off your	Ex 33:5	6258
N Moses used to take the tent and	Ex 33:7	
"N therefore, I pray You, if I	Ex 33:13	6258
N the LORD said to Moses,	Ex 34:1	
"If n I have found favor in Your	Ex 34:9	4994
"N Bezalel and Oholiab, and every	Ex 36:1	
N Bezalel made the ark of acacia	Ex 37:1	
N Bezalel the son of Uri, the son	Ex 38:22	
N in the first month	Ex 40:17	
'N when anyone presents a grain	Lv 2:1	
'N when you bring an offering of a	Lv 2:4	
'N if your offering is a grain	Lv 2:7	
'N if his offering is a sacrifice	Lv 3:1	
'N if the whole congregation of	Lv 4:13	
'N if anyone of the common people	Lv 4:27	
'N if a person sins after he	Lv 5:1	
"N if a person sins and does any	Lv 5:17	
'N this is the law of the grain	Lv 6:14	
'N this is the law of the guilt	Lv 7:1	
'N this is the law of the	Lv 7:11	
'N *as for* the flesh of the	Lv 7:15	
N it came about on the eighth day	Lv 9:1	
they n placed the portions of fat	Lv 9:20	
N Nadab and Abihu, the sons of	Lv 10:1	
'N these are to you the unclean	Lv 11:29	
'N every swarming thing that	Lv 11:41	
"N if a man or woman has an	Lv 13:29	
"N if a man loses the hair of his	Lv 13:40	
N he shall be brought to the	Lv 14:2	
N afterward, he may enter the	Lv 14:8	
"N on the eighth day he is to	Lv 14:10	
'N when the man with the discharge	Lv 15:13	
'N if a man has a seminal emission,	Lv 15:16	
'N if a woman has a discharge of	Lv 15:25	
N the LORD spoke to Moses after	Lv 16:1	
"N you shall have this as a	Lv 16:34	
'N when you offer a sacrifice of	Lv 19:5	
'N when you reap the harvest of	Lv 19:9	
'N if a man lies carnally with a	Lv 19:20	
'N a man or a woman who is a	Lv 20:27	
'N on the day when you wave the	Lv 23:12	
'N on the first day you shall take	Lv 23:40	
N the son of an Israelite woman,	Lv 24:10	
(N his mother's name was	Lv 24:11	
'N in case a countryman of yours	Lv 25:35	
'N if the means of a stranger or	Lv 25:47	
'N if it is an animal of the kind	Lv 27:9	
'N if a man consecrates his house	Lv 27:14	
N the sons of Reuben, Israel's	Nu 1:20	
N the LORD spoke to Moses and to	Nu 2:1	
"N those who camp on the east	Nu 2:3	
N these are *the records of* the	Nu 3:1	
"N, behold, I have taken the	Nu 3:12	
N the duties of the sons of	Nu 3:25	
N their duties *involved* the ark,	Nu 3:31	
N the appointed duties of the sons	Nu 3:36	
N those who were to camp before	Nu 3:38	
"N this is the duty of their	Nu 4:31	
'N this is the law of the Nazirite	Nu 6:13	
N on the day that	Nu 7:1	
N the one who presented his	Nu 7:12	
N when Moses went into the tent of	Nu 7:89	
N this was the workmanship of the	Nu 8:4	
"N the Levites shall lay their	Nu 8:12	
N the LORD spoke to Moses, saying,	Nu 8:23	
"N, let the sons of Israel observe	Nu 9:2	
N on the day that the tabernacle	Nu 9:15	
N in the second year,	Nu 10:11	
N the people became like those who	Nu 11:1	
but n our appetite is gone.	Nu 11:6	6258
N the manna was like coriander	Nu 11:7	
N Moses heard the people weeping	Nu 11:10	
N you shall see whether My word	Nu 11:23	6258
(n they were among those who had	Nu 11:26	
N there went forth a wind from the	Nu 11:31	
(N the man Moses was very humble,	Nu 12:3	
He said, "Hear n My words:	Nu 12:6	4994
N the time was the time of the	Nu 13:20	
(N Hebron was built seven years	Nu 13:22	
"N if You slay this people	Nu 14:15	
"But n, I pray, let the power of	Nu 14:17	6258
people, from Egypt even until n."	Nu 14:19	2008
"N the Amalekites and the	Nu 14:25	
N the LORD spoke to Moses, saying,	Nu 15:1	
N while the sons of Israel were in	Nu 15:32	
N Korah the son of Izhar, the son	Nu 16:1	
"Hear n, you sons of Levi,	Nu 16:8	4994
"Depart n from the tents of these	Nu 16:26	4994
N on the next day	Nu 17:8	
"N behold, I Myself have given	Nu 18:8	
'N a man who is clean shall gather	Nu 19:9	
N Miriam died there and was buried	Nu 20:1	
"Listen n, you rebels;	Nu 20:10	4994
n behold, we are at Kadesh, a town	Nu 20:16	
N when they set out from Kadesh,	Nu 20:22	
N the sons of Israel moved out and	Nu 21:10	
N Balak the son of Zippor saw all	Nu 22:2	
"N this horde will lick up all	Nu 22:4	6258
"N, therefore, please come, curse	Nu 22:6	6258
n come, curse them for me;	Nu 22:11	6258
"N please, you also stay here	Nu 22:19	6258
N he was riding on his donkey and	Nu 22:22	
I would have killed you by n."	Nu 22:29	6258
surely have killed you just n,	Nu 22:33	6258
N then, if it is displeasing to	Nu 22:34	6258
"Behold, I have come n to you!	Nu 22:38	6258
N God met Balaam, and he said to	Nu 23:4	
"Therefore, flee to your place n.	Nu 24:11	6258
"And n, behold, I am going to my	Nu 24:14	6258
'I see him, but not n;	Nu 24:17	6258
N the name of the slain man of	Nu 25:14	
N the sons of Israel who came out	Nu 26:4	
N Zelophehad the son of Hepher had	Nu 26:33	
'N in the seventh month, on the	Nu 29:1	
"N therefore, kill every male	Nu 31:17	6258
N the booty that remained from the	Nu 31:32	
n the congregation's half was	Nu 31:43	
N the sons of Reuben and the sons	Nu 32:1	
"N why are you discouraging the	Nu 32:7	
"N behold, you have risen up in	Nu 32:14	
n it was there that the people had	Nu 33:14	
N the Canaanite, the king of Arad	Nu 33:40	
N the LORD spoke to Moses in the	Nu 35:1	
mountain long enough. N turn north,	Dt 2:3	
'N arise and cross over the brook	Dt 2:13	6258
"N the time that it took for us	Dt 2:14	
"N, O Israel, listen to	Dt 4:1	6258
"N the LORD was angry with me on	Dt 4:21	
ask n concerning the former days	Dt 4:32	4994
N this is the law which Moses set	Dt 4:44	
'N then why should we die?	Dt 5:25	6258
"N this is the commandment, the	Dt 6:1	
(N the sons of Israel set out from	Dt 10:6	
"N, Israel, what does the LORD	Dt 10:12	6258
and n the LORD your God has made	Dt 10:22	6258
"N it shall come about when he	Dt 17:18	
"N this shall be the priests' due	Dt 18:3	
"N if a Levite comes from any of	Dt 18:6	
"N this is the case of the	Dt 19:4	
'N behold, I have brought the first	Dt 26:10	6258
"N it shall be, if you diligently	Dt 28:1	
"N not with you alone am I making	Dt 29:14	
"N the generation to come, your	Dt 29:22	
"N therefore, write this song for	Dt 31:19	6258
'See n that I, I am He, And there	Dt 32:39	6258
N this is the blessing with which	Dt 33:1	
N Moses went up from the plains of	Dt 34:1	
N Joshua the son of Nun was filled	Dt 34:9	
N it came about after the death of	Jos 1:1	
n therefore arise, cross this	Jos 1:2	6258
N before they lay down, she came	Jos 2:8	
"N therefore, please swear to me	Jos 2:12	6258
N the pursuers had sought *them* all	Jos 2:22	
N the LORD said to Joshua,	Jos 3:7	
"N then, take for yourselves	Jos 3:12	6258
N when all the	Jos 4:1	
N the LORD said to Joshua,	Jos 4:15	
N the people came up from the	Jos 4:19	
N it came about when all the kings	Jos 5:1	
N when they had	Jos 5:8	
N it came about when Joshua was by	Jos 5:13	
rather I indeed come n *as* captain	Jos 5:14	6258
N Jericho was tightly shut because	Jos 6:1	
N Joshua rose early in the	Jos 6:12	
N Joshua sent men from Jericho to	Jos 7:2	
and tell me n what you have done.	Jos 7:19	4994
N the LORD said to Joshua,	Jos 8:1	
N Joshua rose early in the morning	Jos 8:10	
N *there was* a valley between him	Jos 8:11	
N when Israel had	Jos 8:24	
N it came about when all the kings	Jos 9:1	
n therefore, make a covenant with	Jos 9:6	6258
n then, make a covenant with us."	Jos 9:11	6258
but n behold, it is dry and has	Jos 9:12	6258
N their cities *were* Gibeon and	Jos 9:17	
and n we cannot touch them.	Jos 9:19	6258
"N therefore, you are cursed, and	Jos 9:23	6258
"N behold, we are in your hands;	Jos 9:25	6258
N it came about when Adoni-zedek	Jos 10:1	
N these five kings had fled and	Jos 10:16	
N Joshua captured Makkedah on that	Jos 10:28	
N these are the kings of the land	Jos 12:1	
N these are the kings of the land	Jos 12:7	
N Joshua was old *and* advanced in	Jos 13:1	
"N therefore, apportion this land	Jos 13:7	6258
N these are *the territories* which	Jos 14:1	
"N behold, the LORD has let me	Jos 14:10	6258
and n behold, I am eighty-five	Jos 14:10	6258
was then, so my strength is n,	Jos 14:11	6258
"N then, give me this hill	Jos 14:12	6258
N the name of Hebron was formerly	Jos 14:15	
N the lot for the tribe of the	Jos 15:1	
N he gave to Caleb the son of	Jos 15:13	
n the name of Debir formerly was	Jos 15:15	
N the cities at the extremity of	Jos 15:21	
N as for the Jebusites, the	Jos 15:63	
N *this* was the territory of the	Jos 16:5	
N *this* was the lot for the tribe	Jos 17:1	
N the lot of the tribe of the sons	Jos 18:11	
N the cities of the tribe of the	Jos 18:21	
N the third lot came up for the	Jos 19:10	
N the fifth lot fell to the tribe	Jos 19:24	
'N if the avenger of blood pursues	Jos 20:5	
N the sons of Israel gave by lot	Jos 21:8	
"And n the LORD your God has	Jos 22:4	6258
turn n and go to your tents,	Jos 22:4	6258
N to the one half-tribe of	Jos 22:7	
n you have delivered the sons of	Jos 22:31	227
N it came about after many days,	Jos 23:1	
"N behold, today I am going the	Jos 23:14	
"N, therefore, fear the LORD and	Jos 24:14	6258
"N therefore, put away the	Jos 24:23	6258
N they buried the bones of Joseph,	Jos 24:32	
N it came about after the death of	Jg 1:1	
(n the name of Hebron formerly *was*	Jg 1:10	
(n the name of Debir formerly *was*	Jg 1:11	
N the LORD was with Judah, and	Jg 1:19	
(n the name of the city was formerly	Jg 1:23	
N the angel of the LORD came up	Jg 2:1	
N these are the nations which the	Jg 3:1	
N the sons of Israel again did	Jg 3:12	
N Eglon was a very fat man.	Jg 3:17	
N Ehud escaped while they were	Jg 3:26	
N Deborah, a prophetess, the wife	Jg 4:4	
N she sent and summoned Barak the	Jg 4:6	
N Heber the Kenite had separated	Jg 4:11	
N Sisera fled away on foot to the	Jg 4:17	
N it came about when the sons of	Jg 6:7	
But n the LORD has abandoned us	Jg 6:13	6258
"If n I have found favor in Your	Jg 6:17	4994
For n I have seen the angel of the	Jg 6:22	5921, 3651
N on the same night	Jg 6:25	
let it n be dry only on the fleece,	Jg 6:39	4994
"N therefore come, proclaim in	Jg 7:3	6258
N the number of those who lapped,	Jg 7:6	
N the same night it came about	Jg 7:9	
N the Midianites and the	Jg 7:12	
"What have I done n in comparison	Jg 8:2	6258
N Zebah and Zalmunna were in	Jg 8:10	
N Gideon had seventy sons who were	Jg 8:30	
"Speak, n, in the hearing of all	Jg 9:2	4994
N when they told Jotham, he went	Jg 9:7	
"N therefore, if you have dealt	Jg 9:16	6258
N Abimelech ruled over Israel	Jg 9:22	
N Gaal the son of Ebed came with	Jg 9:26	
"N therefore, arise by night, you	Jg 9:32	6258
N Gaal the son of Ebed went out	Jg 9:35	
boasting n with which you said,	Jg 9:38	645
Go out n and fight with them!"	Jg 9:38	6258
N it came about the next day, that	Jg 9:42	
N after Abimelech died, Tola the	Jg 10:1	
N Jephthah the Gileadite was a	Jg 11:1	
to me n when you are in trouble?"	Jg 11:7	6258
reason we have n returned to you,	Jg 11:8	6258
N Jephthah sent messengers to the	Jg 11:12	
return them peaceably n."	Jg 11:13	6258
'Since n the LORD, the God of	Jg 11:23	6258
'N are you any better than Balak	Jg 11:25	6258
N the Spirit of the LORD came upon	Jg 11:29	
N she was his one *and* only child;	Jg 11:34	
say to him, "Say n, 'Shibboleth.' "	Jg 12:6	4994
N Ibzan of Bethlehem judged Israel	Jg 12:8	
N Elon the Zebulunite judged	Jg 12:11	
N Abdon the son of Hillel the	Jg 12:13	
N the sons of Israel again did	Jg 13:1	
"Behold n, you are barren and	Jg 13:3	4994
"N therefore, be careful not to	Jg 13:4	6258
and n you shall not drink wine or	Jg 13:7	6258
"N when your words come *to pass,*	Jg 13:12	6258
N the angel of the LORD did	Jg 13:21	
n therefore, get her for me as a	Jg 14:2	6258
N at that time the Philistines	Jg 14:4	
"Let me n propound a riddle to you;	Jg 14:12	4994
and n I shall die of thirst and	Jg 15:18	6258
N Samson went to Gaza and saw a	Jg 16:1	
N Samson lay until midnight, and	Jg 16:3	
N she had *men* lying in wait in an	Jg 16:9	

n please tell me how you may be	**Jg 16:10**	6258
"Up to **n** you have deceived me and	**Jg 16:13**	2008
N the lords of the Philistines	**Jg 16:23**	
N the house was full of men and	**Jg 16:27**	
N there was a man of the hill	**Jg 17:1**	
n therefore, I will return them to	**Jg 17:3**	6258
N there was a young *man* from	**Jg 17:7**	
"**N** I know that the LORD will	**Jg 17:13**	6258
N therefore, consider what you	**Jg 18:14**	6258
N the five men who went to spy out	**Jg 18:17**	
N it came about in those days,	**Jg 19:1**	
N on the fourth day	**Jg 19:5**	
"Behold **n**, the day has drawn to a	**Jg 19:9**	4994
N the man was from the hill	**Jg 19:16**	
But I am **n** going to my house,	**Jg 19:18**	
(**N** the sons of Benjamin heard that	**Jg 20:3**	
"But **n** this is the thing which we	**Jg 20:9**	6258
"**N** then, deliver up the men, the	**Jg 20:13**	6258
N the sons of Israel arose, went	**Jg 20:18**	
N the appointed sign between the	**Jg 20:38**	
N the men of Israel had sworn in	**Jg 21:1**	
else you would **n** be guilty.' "	**Jg 21:22**	6256
N it came about in the days when	**Ru 1:1**	
N they entered the land of Moab	**Ru 1:2**	
N Naomi had a kinsman of her	**Ru 2:1**	
N behold, Boaz came from Bethlehem	**Ru 2:4**	
remained from the morning until **n**;	**Ru 2:7**	6258
"**N** is not Boaz our kinsman, with	**Ru 3:2**	6258
"**N**, my daughter, do not fear.	**Ru 3:11**	6258
"**N** it is true I am a close relative;	**Ru 3:12**	6258
N Boaz went up to the gate and sat	**Ru 4:1**	
N this was *the custom* in former	**Ru 4:7**	
N these are the generations of	**Ru 4:18**	
N there was a certain man from	**1Sa 1:1**	
N this man would go up from his	**1Sa 1:3**	
N Eli the priest was sitting on	**1Sa 1:9**	
N it came about, as she continued	**1Sa 1:12**	
for I have spoken until **n** out of	**1Sa 1:16**	2008
N when she had weaned him, she	**1Sa 1:24**	
N the sons of Eli were worthless	**1Sa 2:12**	
"No, but you shall give *it to me* **n**;	**1Sa 2:16**	6258
N Samuel was ministering before	**1Sa 2:18**	
N Eli was very old;	**1Sa 2:22**	
N the boy Samuel was growing in	**1Sa 2:26**	
but **n** the LORD declares,	**1Sa 2:30**	6258
N the boy Samuel was ministering	**1Sa 3:1**	
n his eyesight had begun to grow dim	**1Sa 3:2**	
N Samuel did not yet know the	**1Sa 3:7**	
N Israel went out to meet the	**1Sa 4:1**	
N a man of Benjamin ran from the	**1Sa 4:12**	
N Eli was ninety-eight years old,	**1Sa 4:15**	
N his daughter-in-law, Phinehas's	**1Sa 4:19**	
N the Philistines took the ark of	**1Sa 5:1**	
N the hand of the LORD was heavy	**1Sa 5:6**	
N the ark of the LORD had been in	**1Sa 6:1**	
"**N** therefore, take and prepare a	**1Sa 6:7**	6258
N *the people of* Beth-shemesh were	**1Sa 6:13**	
N when the Philistines heard that	**1Sa 7:7**	
N Samuel was offering up the burnt	**1Sa 7:10**	
N Samuel judged Israel all the	**1Sa 7:15**	
N the name of his firstborn was	**1Sa 8:2**	
N appoint a king for us to judge	**1Sa 8:5**	6258
"**N** then, listen to their voice;	**1Sa 8:9**	6258
N after Samuel had heard all the	**1Sa 8:21**	
N there was a man of Benjamin	**1Sa 9:1**	
N the donkeys of Kish, Saul's	**1Sa 9:3**	
Take **n** with you one of the servants,	**1Sa 9:3**	4994
"Behold **n**, there is a man of God	**1Sa 9:6**	4994
N let us go there, perhaps he can	**1Sa 9:6**	6258
a prophet **n** was formerly called a	**1Sa 9:9**	3117
Hurry **n**, for he has come into the	**1Sa 9:12**	6258
N therefore, go up for you will	**1Sa 9:13**	6258
N a day before Saul's coming, the	**1Sa 9:15**	
on, but you remain standing **n**,	**1Sa 9:27**	3117
N behold, your father has ceased	**1Sa 10:2**	
he prophesied **n** with the prophets,	**1Sa 10:11**	2009
"**N**, who is their father?"	**1Sa 10:12**	
N Saul's uncle said to him and his	**1Sa 10:14**	
N therefore, present yourselves	**1Sa 10:19**	6258
N Nahash the Ammonite came up and	**1Sa 11:1**	
N behold, Saul was coming from the	**1Sa 11:5**	
"**N**, here is the king walking before	**1Sa 12:2**	6258
"So **n**, take your stand, that I	**1Sa 12:7**	6258
but **n** deliver us from the hands of	**1Sa 12:10**	6258
"**N** therefore, here is the king	**1Sa 12:13**	6258
"Even **n**, take your stand and see	**1Sa 12:16**	6258
N Saul chose for himself 3,000 men	**1Sa 13:2**	
N the Philistines assembled to	**1Sa 13:5**	
N he waited seven days, according	**1Sa 13:8**	
'**N** the Philistines will come down	**1Sa 13:12**	6258
for **n** the LORD would have	**1Sa 13:13**	6258
n your kingdom shall not endure.	**1Sa 13:14**	6258
N Saul and his son Jonathan and	**1Sa 13:16**	
N no blacksmith could be found in	**1Sa 13:19**	
N the day came that Jonathan, the	**1Sa 14:1**	
N Saul's watchmen in Gibeah of	**1Sa 14:16**	
"Number **n** and see who has gone	**1Sa 14:17**	4994
N the Hebrews *who* were with the	**1Sa 14:21**	
N the men of Israel were	**1Sa 14:24**	
See **n**, how my eyes have brightened	**1Sa 14:29**	4994
For **n** the slaughter among the	**1Sa 14:30**	6258
N when Saul had taken the kingdom	**1Sa 14:47**	
N the sons of Saul were Jonathan	**1Sa 14:49**	
N the war against the Philistines	**1Sa 14:52**	
n therefore, listen to the words	**1Sa 15:1**	6258
'**N** go and strike Amalek and	**1Sa 15:3**	6258
"**N** therefore, please pardon my	**1Sa 15:25**	6258
but please honor me **n** before the	**1Sa 15:30**	6258
N the LORD said to Samuel,	**1Sa 16:1**	
N he was ruddy, with beautiful	**1Sa 16:12**	
N the Spirit of the LORD departed	**1Sa 16:14**	
"Behold **n**, an evil spirit from	**1Sa 16:15**	4994
"Let our lord **n** command your	**1Sa 16:16**	4994
for me **n** a man who can play well and	**1Sa 16:17**	4994
"Let David **n** stand before me,	**1Sa 16:22**	4994
N the Philistines gathered their	**1Sa 17:1**	
N David was the son of the	**1Sa 17:12**	
N the three oldest followed Saul,	**1Sa 17:14**	
"Take **n** for your brothers an	**1Sa 17:17**	4994
N Eliab his oldest brother heard	**1Sa 17:28**	
"What have I done **n**?	**1Sa 17:29**	6258
N when Saul saw David going out	**1Sa 17:55**	
N it came about when he had	**1Sa 18:1**	
N what more can he have but the	**1Sa 18:8**	
N it came about on the next day	**1Sa 18:10**	
N Saul was afraid of David, for	**1Sa 18:12**	
N Michal, Saul's daughter, loved	**1Sa 18:20**	
n therefore, become the king's	**1Sa 18:22**	6258
N Saul planned to make David fall	**1Sa 18:25**	
N Saul told Jonathan his son and	**1Sa 19:1**	
N therefore, please be on guard in	**1Sa 19:2**	6258
N there was an evil spirit from	**1Sa 19:9**	
N David fled and escaped and came	**1Sa 19:18**	
And **n**, if I have found favor in	**1Sa 20:29**	6258
Therefore **n**, send and bring him to	**1Sa 20:31**	6258
N it came about in the morning	**1Sa 20:35**	
find **n** the arrows which I am about	**1Sa 20:36**	4994
"**N** therefore, what do you have on	**1Sa 21:3**	6258
N one of the servants of Saul was	**1Sa 21:7**	
"**N** is there not a spear or a	**1Sa 21:8**	
N there were about four hundred	**1Sa 22:2**	
N Saul was sitting in Gibeah,	**1Sa 22:6**	
"Hear **n**, O Benjamites!	**1Sa 22:7**	4994
"Listen **n**, son of Ahitub."	**1Sa 22:12**	4994
N it came about, when Abiathar the	**1Sa 23:6**	
N David knew that Saul was	**1Sa 23:9**	
N David became aware that Saul had	**1Sa 23:15**	
"**N** then, O king, come down	**1Sa 23:20**	6258
"Go **n**, make more sure, and	**1Sa 23:22**	4994
N David and his men were in the	**1Sa 23:24**	
N when Saul returned	**1Sa 24:1**	
N David and his men were sitting	**1Sa 24:3**	
N afterward David arose and went	**1Sa 24:8**	
"**N**, my father, see!	**1Sa 24:11**	
"**N**, behold, I know that you will	**1Sa 24:20**	6258
"So **n** swear to me by the LORD	**1Sa 24:21**	6258
N *there was* a man in Maon whose	**1Sa 25:2**	
(**n** the man's name was Nabal, and	**1Sa 25:3**	
'**N** I have heard that you have	**1Sa 25:7**	6258
n your shepherds have been with us	**1Sa 25:7**	6258
"**N** therefore, know and consider	**1Sa 25:17**	6258
N David had said,	**1Sa 25:21**	
"**N** therefore, my lord, as the	**1Sa 25:26**	6258
own hand, **n** then let your enemies and	**1Sa 25:26**	6258
"**N** let this gift which your	**1Sa 25:27**	6258
N Saul had given Michal his	**1Sa 25:44**	
n therefore, please let me strike	**1Sa 26:8**	6258
but **n** please take the spear that	**1Sa 26:11**	6258
And **n**, see where the king's spear	**1Sa 26:16**	6258
"**N** therefore, please let my lord	**1Sa 26:19**	6258
"**N** then, do not let my blood fall	**1Sa 26:20**	6258
N let one of the young men come	**1Sa 26:22**	
"**N** behold, as your life was	**1Sa 26:24**	
"**N** I will perish one day by the	**1Sa 27:1**	6258
N it was told Saul that David had	**1Sa 27:4**	
"If **n** I have found favor in your	**1Sa 27:5**	4994
N David and his men went up and	**1Sa 27:8**	
N Achish said, "Where have you	**1Sa 27:10**	
N it came about in those days that	**1Sa 28:1**	
N Samuel was dead, and all Israel	**1Sa 28:3**	
"So **n** also, please listen to the	**1Sa 28:22**	6258
N the Philistines gathered	**1Sa 29:1**	
"**N** therefore return and go in	**1Sa 29:7**	6258
"**N** then arise early in the	**1Sa 29:10**	6258
N David's two wives had been taken	**1Sa 30:5**	
N they found an Egyptian in the	**1Sa 30:11**	
N when David came to Ziklag, he	**1Sa 30:26**	
N the Philistines were fighting	**1Sa 31:1**	
N when the inhabitants of	**1Sa 31:11**	
N it came about after the death of	**2Sa 1:1**	
"**N** may the LORD show	**2Sa 2:6**	6258
"**N** therefore, let your hands be	**2Sa 2:7**	6258
N Abner the son of Ner, went out	**2Sa 2:12**	
"**N** let the young men arise and	**2Sa 2:14**	4994
N the three sons of Zeruiah were	**2Sa 2:18**	
N there was a long war between the	**2Sa 3:1**	
N Saul had a concubine whose name	**2Sa 3:7**	
N Abner had consultation with the	**2Sa 3:17**	
"**N** then, do *it!* For the LORD has	**2Sa 3:18**	6258
N all the people took note *of it,*	**2Sa 3:36**	
N when Ish-bosheth, Saul's son,	**2Sa 4:1**	
N Jonathan, Saul's son, had a son	**2Sa 4:4**	
N when they came into the house,	**2Sa 4:7**	
shall I not **n** require his blood	**2Sa 4:11**	6258
N the king and his men went to	**2Sa 5:6**	
N these are the names of those who	**2Sa 5:14**	
N the Philistines came and spread	**2Sa 5:18**	
N the Philistines came up once	**2Sa 5:22**	
N David again gathered all the	**2Sa 6:1**	
N it was told King David, saying,	**2Sa 6:12**	
N it came about when the king	**2Sa 7:1**	
"See **n**, I dwell in a house of	**2Sa 7:2**	4994
"**N** therefore, thus you shall say	**2Sa 7:8**	6258
"**N** therefore, O LORD God, the	**2Sa 7:25**	6258
"**N**, O Lord GOD, You are God,	**2Sa 7:28**	6258
"**N** therefore, may it please You	**2Sa 7:29**	6258
N after this it came about that	**2Sa 8:1**	
N when Toi king of Hamath heard	**2Sa 8:9**	
N there was a servant of the house	**2Sa 9:2**	
N Ziba had fifteen sons and twenty	**2Sa 9:10**	
N he was lame in both feet.	**2Sa 9:13**	
N it happened afterwards that the	**2Sa 10:1**	
N when the sons of Ammon saw that	**2Sa 10:6**	
N when Joab saw that the battle	**2Sa 10:9**	
N when it was told David, he	**2Sa 10:17**	
N when evening came David arose	**2Sa 11:2**	
N when they told David, saying,	**2Sa 11:10**	
N David called him, and he ate and	**2Sa 11:13**	
N in the morning	**2Sa 11:14**	
N when the wife of Uriah heard	**2Sa 11:26**	
"**N** a traveler came to the rich	**2Sa 12:4**	
'**N** therefore, the sword shall	**2Sa 12:10**	6258
"But **n** he has died;	**2Sa 12:23**	6258
N the LORD loved him	**2Sa 12:24**	
N Joab fought against Rabbah of	**2Sa 12:26**	
"**N** therefore, gather the rest of	**2Sa 12:28**	6258
N it was after this that Absalom	**2Sa 13:1**	
"Go **n** to your brother Amnon's	**2Sa 13:7**	4994
N therefore, please speak to the	**2Sa 13:13**	6258
"**N** throw this woman out of my	**2Sa 13:17**	4994
N she had on a long-sleeved	**2Sa 13:18**	
But **n** keep silent, my sister, he	**2Sa 13:20**	6258
N when King David heard of all	**2Sa 13:21**	
N it came about after two full	**2Sa 13:23**	
"Behold **n**, your servant has	**2Sa 13:24**	4994
"See **n**, when Amnon's heart is	**2Sa 13:28**	4994
N it was while they were on the	**2Sa 13:30**	
"**N** therefore, do not let my lord	**2Sa 13:33**	6258
N Absalom had fled.	**2Sa 13:34**	
N Absalom fled and went to Talmai	**2Sa 13:37**	
N Joab the son of Zeruiah	**2Sa 14:1**	
and put on mourning garments **n**,	**2Sa 14:2**	4994
N when the woman of Tekoa spoke to	**2Sa 14:4**	
"**N** behold, the whole family has	**2Sa 14:7**	
"**N** the reason I have come to	**2Sa 14:15**	6258
'Let me **n** speak to the king,	**2Sa 14:15**	4994
"Behold **n**, I will surely do this	**2Sa 14:21**	4994
N in all Israel was no one as	**2Sa 14:25**	
N Absalom lived two full years in	**2Sa 14:28**	
N therefore, let me see the king's face	**2Sa 14:32**	6258
N it came about after this that	**2Sa 15:1**	
N it came about at the end of	**2Sa 15:7**	
N all his servants passed on	**2Sa 15:18**	
N behold, Zadok also *came,* and all	**2Sa 15:24**	
N someone told David, saying,	**2Sa 15:31**	
past, so I will **n** be your servant,'	**2Sa 15:34**	6258
N when David had passed a little	**2Sa 16:1**	
Let me go over **n** and cut off his	**2Sa 16:9**	4994
how much more **n** this Benjamite?	**2Sa 16:11**	6258
N it came about when Hushai the	**2Sa 16:16**	
"**N** call Hushai the Archite also,	**2Sa 17:5**	4994
he has **n** hidden himself in one of	**2Sa 17:9**	6258
"**N** therefore, send quickly and	**2Sa 17:16**	6258
N Jonathan and Ahimaaz were	**2Sa 17:17**	
N when Ahithophel saw that his	**2Sa 17:23**	
N Amasa was the son of a man whose	**2Sa 17:25**	
N when David had come to Mahanaim,	**2Sa 17:27**	
therefore **n** it is better that you	**2Sa 18:3**	6258
N Absalom happened to meet the	**2Sa 18:9**	
"**N** behold, you saw *him!*	**2Sa 18:11**	
N Absalom in his lifetime had	**2Sa 18:18**	
N Ahimaaz the son of Zadok said	**2Sa 18:22**	
N David was sitting between the	**2Sa 18:24**	
"**N** therefore arise, go out and	**2Sa 19:7**	6258
you from your youth until **n**."	**2Sa 19:7**	6258
N Israel had fled, each to his	**2Sa 19:8**	
but **n** he has fled out of the land	**2Sa 19:9**	6258
N then, why are you silent about	**2Sa 19:10**	6258
N Barzillai the Gileadite had come	**2Sa 19:31**	
N Barzillai was very old, being	**2Sa 19:32**	
"I am **n** eighty years old.	**2Sa 19:35**	3117
N the king went on to Gilgal, and	**2Sa 19:40**	
N a worthless fellow happened to	**2Sa 20:1**	
"**N** Sheba the son of Bichri will	**2Sa 20:6**	6258
N Joab was dressed in his military	**2Sa 20:8**	
N there stood by him one of Joab's	**2Sa 20:11**	
N he went through all the tribes	**2Sa 20:14**	
N Joab was over the whole army of	**2Sa 20:23**	
N there was a famine in the days	**2Sa 21:1**	
n the Gibeonites were not of the sons	**2Sa 21:2**	
N when the Philistines were at war	**2Sa 21:15**	
N it came about after this that	**2Sa 21:18**	
N these are the last words of	**2Sa 23:1**	
N after him was Shammah the son of	**2Sa 23:11**	
N the Egyptian *had* a spear in his	**2Sa 23:21**	
N again the anger of the LORD	**2Sa 24:1**	
"Go about **n** through all the	**2Sa 24:2**	4994
"**N** may the LORD your God add to	**2Sa 24:3**	
N David's heart troubled him after	**2Sa 24:10**	
But **n**, O LORD, please take away	**2Sa 24:10**	6258
N consider and see what answer I	**2Sa 24:13**	6258
Let us **n** fall into the hand of the	**2Sa 24:14**	4994
N relax your hand!"	**2Sa 24:16**	6258
N King David was old, advanced in	**1Ki 1:1**	
N Adonijah the son of Haggith	**1Ki 1:5**	
"So **n** come, please let me give	**1Ki 1:12**	6258
N the king was very old, and	**1Ki 1:15**	
"**N**, behold, Adonijah is king;	**1Ki 1:18**	6258
and **n**, my lord the king, you do	**1Ki 1:18**	6258
"As for you **n**, my lord the	**1Ki 1:20**	
N Adonijah and all the guests who	**1Ki 1:41**	
N it was told Solomon, saying,	**1Ki 1:51**	
"**N** you also know what Joab the	**1Ki 2:5**	
n it was he who cursed me with a	**1Ki 2:8**	
"**N** therefore, do not let him go	**1Ki 2:9**	6258
N Adonijah the son of Haggith came	**1Ki 2:13**	
"**N** I am making one request of you;	**1Ki 2:16**	6258

"**N** therefore, as the LORD lives, **1Ki 2:24** 6258
N the news came to Joab, for Joab **1Ki 2:28**
N the king sent and called for **1Ki 2:36**
N Solomon loved the LORD, walking **1Ki 3:3**
"**N**, O LORD my God, You have **1Ki 3:7** 6258
N King Solomon was king over all **1Ki 4:1**
N Solomon ruled over all the **1Ki 4:21**
N God gave Solomon wisdom and very **1Ki 4:29**
N Hiram king of Tyre sent his **1Ki 5:1**
"But **n** the LORD my God has given **1Ki 5:4** 6258
"**N** therefore, command that they **1Ki 5:6** 6258
N King Solomon levied forced **1Ki 5:13**
N Solomon had 70,000 transporters, **1Ki 5:15**
N it came about in the four **1Ki 6:1**
N the word of the LORD came to **1Ki 6:11**
N Solomon was building his own **1Ki 7:1**
N King Solomon sent and brought **1Ki 7:13**
N he made the sea of cast *metal* **1Ki 7:23**
N each stand had four bronze **1Ki 7:30**
N *there were* four supports at the **1Ki 7:34**
N Hiram made the basins and the **1Ki 7:40**
"**N** it was in the heart of my **1Ki 8:17**
"**N** the LORD has fulfilled His **1Ki 8:20**
"**N** therefore, O LORD, the God of **1Ki 8:25** 6258
"**N** therefore, O God of Israel, **1Ki 8:26** 6258
N the king and all Israel with him **1Ki 8:62**
N it came about when Solomon had **1Ki 9:1**
N this is the account of the **1Ki 9:15**
N three times in a year Solomon **1Ki 9:25**
N when the queen of Sheba heard **1Ki 10:1**
N the weight of gold which came in **1Ki 10:14**
N Solomon gathered chariots and **1Ki 10:26**
N King Solomon loved many foreign **1Ki 11:1**
N the LORD was angry with Solomon **1Ki 11:9**
N Hadad found great favor before **1Ki 11:19**
N this was the reason why he **1Ki 11:27**
N the man Jeroboam was a valiant **1Ki 11:28**
N Ahijah had clothed himself with **1Ki 11:29**
N the rest of the acts of Solomon **1Ki 11:41**
N when Jeroboam the **1Ki 12:2**
n therefore lighten the hard service **1Ki 12:4** 6258
n you make it lighter for us!' **1Ki 12:10**
N look after your own house, David!" **1Ki 12:16** 6258
N when Rehoboam had come to **1Ki 12:21**
"**N** the kingdom will return to the **1Ki 12:26** 6258
N this thing became a sin, for the **1Ki 12:30**
N behold, there came a man of God **1Ki 13:1**
N when the king **1Ki 13:4**
N an old prophet was living in **1Ki 13:11**
N his sons had seen the way which **1Ki 13:12**
N it came about, as they were **1Ki 13:20**
N when he had gone, a lion met him **1Ki 13:24**
N when the prophet who brought him **1Ki 13:26**
"Arise **n**, and disguise yourself **1Ki 14:2** 4994
N Ahijah could not see, for his **1Ki 14:4**
N the LORD had said to Ahijah, **1Ki 14:5**
"**N** you, arise, go to your house. **1Ki 14:12**
Jeroboam this day and from **n** on. **1Ki 14:14** 6258
N the rest of the acts of **1Ki 14:19**
N Rehoboam the son of Solomon **1Ki 14:21**
N it happened in the fifth year **1Ki 14:25**
N the rest of the acts of Rehoboam **1Ki 14:29**
N in the eighteenth year of King **1Ki 15:1**
N the rest of the acts of Abijam **1Ki 15:7**
N there was war between Asa and **1Ki 15:16**
N the rest of all the acts of Asa **1Ki 15:23**
N Nadab the son of Jeroboam became **1Ki 15:25**
N the rest of the acts of Nadab **1Ki 15:31**
N the word of the LORD came to **1Ki 16:1**
N the rest of the acts of Baasha **1Ki 16:5**
N he *was* at Tirzah drinking **1Ki 16:9**
N the rest of the acts of Elah and **1Ki 16:14**
N the people were camped against **1Ki 16:15**
N the rest of the acts of Zimri **1Ki 16:20**
N the rest of the acts of Omri **1Ki 16:27**
N Ahab the son of Omri became king **1Ki 16:29**
N Elijah the Tishbite, who was of **1Ki 17:1**
N it came about after these **1Ki 17:17**
"**N** I know that you are a man of **1Ki 17:24** 6258
N it happened *after* many days **1Ki 18:1**
N the famine *was* severe in Samaria. **1Ki 18:2**
(**N** Obadiah feared the LORD greatly; **1Ki 18:3**
N as Obadiah was on the way, **1Ki 18:7**
"And **n** you are saying, **1Ki 18:11** 6258
"And **n** you are saying, **1Ki 18:14** 6258
"**N** then send *and* gather to me all **1Ki 18:19** 6258
"**N** let them give us two oxen; **1Ki 18:23**
N Elijah said to Ahab, **1Ki 18:41**
"Go up **n**, look toward the sea." **1Ki 18:43** 4994
N Ahab told Jezebel all that **1Ki 19:1**
n, O LORD, take my life, for I am **1Ki 19:4** 6258
N Ben-hadad king of Aram gathered **1Ki 20:1**
N behold, a prophet approached **1Ki 20:13**
N the servants of the king of Aram **1Ki 20:23**
"Behold **n**, we have heard that the **1Ki 20:31** 4994
N the men took this as an omen, **1Ki 20:33**
N a certain man of the sons of the **1Ki 20:35**
N it came about after these **1Ki 21:1**
"Do you **n** reign over Israel? **1Ki 21:7** 6258
N she wrote in the letters, **1Ki 21:9**
N the king of Israel said to his **1Ki 22:3**
N the king of Israel and **1Ki 22:10**
"Behold **n**, the words of the **1Ki 22:13** 4994
"**N** therefore, behold, the LORD **1Ki 22:23** 6258
N the king of Aram had commanded **1Ki 22:31**
N a certain man drew his bow at **1Ki 22:34**
n the harlots bathed themselves *there* **1Ki 22:38**
N the rest of the acts of Ahab and **1Ki 22:39**
N Jehoshaphat the son of Asa **1Ki 22:41**
N the rest of the acts of **1Ki 22:45**
N there was no king in Edom; **1Ki 22:47**
N Moab rebelled against Israel **2Ki 1:1**
"**N** therefore thus says the LORD, **2Ki 1:4**
but **n** let my life be precious in **2Ki 1:14** 6258
N the rest of the acts of Ahaziah **2Ki 1:18**
N fifty men of the sons of the **2Ki 2:7**
N when the sons of the prophets **2Ki 2:15**
"Behold **n**, there are with your **2Ki 2:16** 4994
"Behold **n**, the situation of this **2Ki 2:19**
N Jehoram the son of Ahab became **2Ki 3:1**
N Mesha king of Moab was a sheep **2Ki 3:4**
N Elisha said to the king of **2Ki 3:13**
"But **n** bring me a minstrel." **2Ki 3:15** 6258
N all the Moabites heard that the **2Ki 3:21**
N therefore, Moab, to the spoil!" **2Ki 3:23** 6258
N a certain woman of the wives of **2Ki 4:1**
N there came a day when Elisha **2Ki 4:8**
"Behold **n**, I perceive that this **2Ki 4:9** 4994
"Say **n** to her, 'Behold, you have **2Ki 4:13** 4994
run **n** to meet her and say to her, **2Ki 4:26** 6258
But he said, "**N** bring meal." **2Ki 4:41**
N a man came from Baal-shalishah, **2Ki 4:42**
N Naaman, captain of the army of **2Ki 5:1**
N the Arameans had gone out in **2Ki 5:2**
"Go **n**, and I will send a letter **2Ki 5:5** 935
"And **n** as this letter comes to **2Ki 5:6** 6258
But consider **n**, and see how he is **2Ki 5:7** 4994
N let him come to me, and he shall **2Ki 5:8** 4994
"Behold **n**, I know that there is **2Ki 5:15** 4994
a present from your servant **n**." **2Ki 5:15** 6258
just **n** two young men of the sons **2Ki 5:22** 6258
N the sons of the prophets said to **2Ki 6:1**
"Behold **n**, the place before you **2Ki 6:1** 4994
N the king of Aram was warring **2Ki 6:8**
N the heart of the king of Aram **2Ki 6:11**
N when the attendant of the man of **2Ki 6:15**
N it came about after this, that **2Ki 6:24**
n he was passing by on the wall **2Ki 6:30**
N Elisha was sitting in his house, **2Ki 6:32**
N there were four leprous men at **2Ki 7:3**
N therefore come, and let us go **2Ki 7:4** 6258
N therefore come, let us go and **2Ki 7:9** 6258
"I will **n** tell you what the **2Ki 7:12** 4994
N the king appointed the royal **2Ki 7:17**
"**N** behold, if the LORD should **2Ki 7:19**
N Elisha spoke to the woman whose **2Ki 8:1**
N the king was talking with **2Ki 8:4**
she left the land even until **n**." **2Ki 8:6** 6258
N Ben-hadad king of Aram was sick, **2Ki 8:7**
N in the fifth year of Joram the **2Ki 8:16**
N Elisha the prophet called one of **2Ki 9:1**
N Jehu came out to the servants of **2Ki 9:11**
"It is a lie, tell us **n**." **2Ki 9:12** 4994
N Joram with all Israel was **2Ki 9:14**
N the watchman was standing on the **2Ki 9:17**
N then, take and cast him into the **2Ki 9:26** 6258
N in the eleventh year of Joram, **2Ki 9:29**
"See **n** to this cursed woman and **2Ki 9:34** 4994
N Ahab had seventy sons in Samaria. **2Ki 10:1**
"**N**, when this letter comes to you, **2Ki 10:2** 6258
N the king's sons, seventy persons, **2Ki 10:6**
N in the morning **2Ki 10:9**
N when he had departed from there, **2Ki 10:15**
"**N**, summon all the prophets of Baal, **2Ki 10:19** 6258
N Jehu had stationed for himself **2Ki 10:24**
N the rest of the acts of Jehu and **2Ki 10:34**
N the time which Jehu reigned over **2Ki 10:36**
N in the seventh year Jehoiada **2Ki 11:4**
N therefore take no *more* money **2Ki 12:7** 6258
N the rest of the acts of Joash **2Ki 12:19**
N the rest of the acts of **2Ki 13:8**
N the rest of the acts of Joash **2Ki 13:12**
But **n** you shall strike Aram *only* **2Ki 13:19** 6258
N the bands of the Moabites would **2Ki 13:20**
N Hazael king of Aram had **2Ki 13:22**
cast them from His presence until **n**. **2Ki 13:23** 6258
N it came about, as soon as the **2Ki 14:5**
N the rest of the acts of Jehoash **2Ki 14:15**
N the rest of the acts of Amaziah, **2Ki 14:18**
N the rest of the acts of Jeroboam **2Ki 14:28**
N the rest of the acts of Azariah **2Ki 15:6**
N the rest of the acts of **2Ki 15:11**
N the rest of the acts of Shallum **2Ki 15:15**
N the rest of the acts of Menahem **2Ki 15:21**
N the rest of the acts of Pekahiah **2Ki 15:26**
N the rest of the acts of Pekah **2Ki 15:31**
N the rest of the acts of Jotham **2Ki 15:36**
N King Ahaz went to Damascus to **2Ki 16:10**
N the rest of the acts of Ahaz **2Ki 16:19**
N *this* came about because the **2Ki 17:7**
N it came about in the third year **2Ki 18:1**
N in the fourth year **2Ki 18:9**
N in the fourteenth year of King **2Ki 18:13**
"Say **n** to Hezekiah, **2Ki 18:19** 4994
N on whom do you rely, **2Ki 18:20** 6258
"**N** behold, you rely on the staff **2Ki 18:21** 6258
"**N** therefore, come, make a **2Ki 18:23** 6258
"Have I **n** come up without the **2Ki 18:25** 6258
n to your servants in Aramaic, **2Ki 18:26** 4994
"**N**, O LORD our God, I pray, **2Ki 19:19** 6258
N I have brought it to pass, That **2Ki 19:25** 6258
"Remember **n**, O LORD, I beseech **2Ki 20:3** 4994
N Hezekiah said to Isaiah, **2Ki 20:8**
N the rest of the acts of Hezekiah **2Ki 20:20**
N the LORD spoke through His **2Ki 21:10**
N the rest of the acts of Manasseh **2Ki 21:17**
N the rest of the acts of Amon **2Ki 21:25**
N in the eighteenth year **2Ki 22:3**
(**n** she lived in Jerusalem in the **2Ki 22:14**
N when Josiah turned, he saw the **2Ki 23:16**
N the rest of the acts of Josiah **2Ki 23:28**
N the rest of the acts of **2Ki 24:5**
N in the ninth year **2Ki 25:1**
N on the seventh day of the fifth **2Ki 25:8**
N the bronze pillars which were in **2Ki 25:13**
N *as for* the people who were left **2Ki 25:22**
N it came about in the **2Ki 25:27**
N these are the kings who reigned **1Ch 1:43**
N the chiefs of Edom were: **1Ch 1:51**
N the sons of Hezron, who were **1Ch 2:9**
N Caleb the son of Hezron had sons **1Ch 2:18**
N the sons of Jerahmeel the **1Ch 2:25**
N Sheshan had no sons, only **1Ch 2:34**
N the sons of Caleb, the brother **1Ch 2:42**
N these were the sons of David who **1Ch 3:1**
N Solomon's son *was* Rehoboam, **1Ch 3:10**
N Jabez called on the God of **1Ch 4:10**
N the sons of Kenaz *were* Othniel **1Ch 4:13**
N Shimei had sixteen sons and six **1Ch 4:27**
N the sons of Reuben the **1Ch 5:1**
N the sons of Gad lived opposite **1Ch 5:11**
N the sons of the half-tribe of **1Ch 5:23**
N these are those whom David **1Ch 6:31**
N these are their settlements **1Ch 6:54**
N some of the families of the sons **1Ch 6:66**
N the sons of Issachar *were* four: **1Ch 7:1**
N in Gibeon, *Jeiel*, the father of **1Ch 8:29**
N the first who lived in their **1Ch 9:2**
N the gatekeepers *were* Shallum and **1Ch 9:17**
being stationed until **n** at the **1Ch 9:18** 2008
N some of them had charge of the **1Ch 9:28**
N these are the singers, heads of **1Ch 9:33**
N the Philistines fought against **1Ch 10:1**
N David had said, **1Ch 11:6**
N these are the heads of the **1Ch 11:10**
N three of the thirty chief men **1Ch 11:15**
N in the Egyptian's hand *was* a **1Ch 11:23**
N the mighty men of the armies **1Ch 11:26**
N these are the ones who came to **1Ch 12:1**
N these are the numbers of the **1Ch 12:23**
N Jehoiada was the leader of *the* **1Ch 12:27**
for until **n** the greatest part of **1Ch 12:29** 2008
N Hiram king of Tyre sent **1Ch 14:1**
N the Philistines had come and **1Ch 14:9**
N *David* built houses for himself **1Ch 15:1**
N David was clothed with a robe of **1Ch 15:27**
"**N**, therefore, thus shall you say **1Ch 17:7** 6258
"**N**, O LORD, let the word that **1Ch 17:23** 6258
"**N**, O LORD, You are God, **1Ch 17:26** 6258
"And **n** it has pleased You to **1Ch 17:27** 6258
N after this it came about that **1Ch 18:1**
N when Tou king of Hamath heard **1Ch 18:9**
N it came about after this, that **1Ch 19:1**
N when Joab saw that the battle **1Ch 19:10**
N it came about after this, that **1Ch 20:4**
But **n**, please take away the **1Ch 21:8** 6258
N, therefore, consider what answer **1Ch 21:12** 6258
"It is enough; **n** relax your hand." **1Ch 21:15** 6258
N Ornan turned back and saw the **1Ch 21:20**
n I will make preparation for it **1Ch 22:5** 4994
"**N**, my son, the LORD be with you **1Ch 22:11** 6258
"**N** behold, with great pains I **1Ch 22:14**
"**N** set your heart and your soul **1Ch 22:19** 6258
N when David reached old age, he **1Ch 23:1**
N the divisions of the descendants **1Ch 24:1**
N the first lot came out for **1Ch 24:7**
N for the rest of the sons of Levi: **1Ch 24:20**
N the first lot came out for Asaph **1Ch 25:9**
N *this is* the enumeration of the **1Ch 27:1**
N in charge of the tribes of **1Ch 27:16**
N Azmaveth the son of Adiel had **1Ch 27:25**
N David assembled at Jerusalem all **1Ch 28:1**
and My ordinances, as is done **n**.' **1Ch 28:7** 3117
"So **n**, in the sight of all **1Ch 28:8** 6258
"Consider **n**, for the LORD has **1Ch 28:10** 6258
"**N** behold, *there are* the **1Ch 28:21**
"**N** with all my ability I have **1Ch 29:2**
"**N** therefore, our God, we thank **1Ch 29:13** 6258
so **n** with joy I have seen Your **1Ch 29:17** 6258
"**N** bless the LORD your God." **1Ch 29:20** 4994
N David the son of Jesse reigned **1Ch 29:26**
N the acts of King David, from **1Ch 29:29**
N Solomon the son of David **2Ch 1:1**
N the bronze altar, which Bezalel **2Ch 1:5**
"**N**, O LORD God, Your promise to my **2Ch 1:9** 6258
"Give me **n** wisdom and knowledge, **2Ch 1:10** 6258
N Solomon decided to build a house **2Ch 2:1**
"**N** send me a skilled man to work in **2Ch 2:7** 6258
"**N** behold, I will give to your **2Ch 2:10**
"**N** I am sending Huram-abi, a **2Ch 2:13** 6258
N then, let my lord send to his **2Ch 2:15** 6258
N these are the foundations which **2Ch 3:3**
N he made the room of the holy of **2Ch 3:8**
N figures like oxen *were* under it **2Ch 4:3**
"**N** it was in the heart of my **2Ch 6:7**
"**N** the LORD has fulfilled His **2Ch 6:10**
N Solomon had made a bronze **2Ch 6:13** 3588
"**N** therefore, O LORD, the God of **2Ch 6:16** 6258
"**N** therefore, O LORD, the God of **2Ch 6:17** 6258
"**N**, O my God, I pray, let **2Ch 6:40** 6258
"**N** therefore arise, O LORD God, **2Ch 6:41** 6258
N when Solomon had finished **2Ch 7:1**
"**N** My eyes will be open and My **2Ch 7:15** 6258
"For **n** I have chosen and **2Ch 7:16** 6258
N it came about at the end of the **2Ch 8:1**
N according to the ordinance of **2Ch 8:14**
N when the queen of Sheba heard of **2Ch 9:1**

N the weight of gold which came to	**2Ch 9:13**	
N Solomon had 4,000 stalls for	**2Ch 9:25**	
N the rest of the acts of Solomon,	**2Ch 9:29**	
n therefore lighten the hard service	**2Ch 10:4**	6258
N look after your own house, David."	**2Ch 10:16**	6258
N when Rehoboam had come to	**2Ch 11:1**	
N Rehoboam was forty-one years old	**2Ch 12:13**	3588
N the acts of Rehoboam, from first	**2Ch 12:15**	
N there was war between Abijah	**2Ch 13:2**	
"So **n** you intend to resist the	**2Ch 13:8**	6258
"**N** behold, God is with us at *our*	**2Ch 13:12**	
N the rest of the acts of Abijah,	**2Ch 13:22**	
N Asa had an army of 300,000 from	**2Ch 14:8**	
N Zerah the Ethiopian came out	**2Ch 14:9**	
N the Spirit of God came on	**2Ch 15:1**	
N when Asa heard these words and	**2Ch 15:8**	
n on you will surely have wars."	**2Ch 16:9**	6258
N, the acts of Asa from first to	**2Ch 16:11**	2009
N the dread of the LORD was on all	**2Ch 17:10**	
N Jehoshaphat had great riches and	**2Ch 18:1**	
N the king of Israel and	**2Ch 18:9**	
"**N** therefore, behold, the LORD has	**2Ch 18:22**	6258
N the king of Aram had commanded	**2Ch 18:30**	
"**N** then let the fear of the LORD	**2Ch 19:7**	6258
N it came about after this that	**2Ch 20:1**	
'**N** behold, the sons of Ammon	**2Ch 20:10**	6258
N Jehoshaphat reigned over Judah.	**2Ch 20:31**	
N the rest of the acts of	**2Ch 20:34**	
N when Jehoram had taken over the	**2Ch 21:4**	
N it came about in the course of	**2Ch 21:19**	
N the destruction of Ahaziah was	**2Ch 22:7**	
N when Athaliah the mother of	**2Ch 22:10**	
N in the seventh year Jehoiada	**2Ch 23:1**	
N it came about after this that	**2Ch 24:4**	
N when Jehoiada reached a ripe old	**2Ch 24:15**	
N it happened at the turn of the	**2Ch 24:23**	
N these are those who conspired	**2Ch 24:26**	
N it came about as soon as the	**2Ch 25:3**	
N Amaziah strengthened himself and	**2Ch 25:11**	
N after Amaziah came	**2Ch 25:14**	
N stay at home; for why should you	**2Ch 25:19**	6258
N the rest of the acts of Amaziah,	**2Ch 25:26**	
N he went out and warred against	**2Ch 26:6**	
N the rest of the acts of Uzziah,	**2Ch 26:22**	
N the rest of the acts of Jotham,	**2Ch 27:7**	
"**N** you are proposing to subjugate	**2Ch 28:10**	6258
"**N** therefore, listen to me and	**2Ch 28:11**	6258
N in the time of his distress this	**2Ch 28:22**	
N the rest of his acts and all his	**2Ch 28:26**	
Consecrate yourselves **n**,	**2Ch 29:5**	6258
"**N** it is in my heart to make a	**2Ch 29:10**	6258
"My sons, do not be negligent **n**,	**2Ch 29:11**	6258
N they began the consecration on	**2Ch 29:17**	
N at the completion of the burnt	**2Ch 29:29**	
"**N** *that* you have consecrated	**2Ch 29:31**	6258
N Hezekiah sent to all Israel and	**2Ch 30:1**	
'**N** do not stiffen your neck like	**2Ch 30:8**	6258
N many people were gathered at	**2Ch 30:13**	
N when all this was finished, all	**2Ch 31:1**	
N when Hezekiah saw that	**2Ch 32:2**	
'**N** therefore, do not let Hezekiah	**2Ch 32:15**	6258
N Hezekiah had immense riches and	**2Ch 32:27**	
N the rest of the acts of Hezekiah	**2Ch 32:32**	
N after this he built the outer	**2Ch 33:14**	
N the rest of the acts of Manasseh	**2Ch 33:18**	
N in the eighteenth year of his	**2Ch 34:8**	
n she lived in Jerusalem in the Second	**2Ch 34:22**	
N serve the LORD your God and His	**2Ch 35:3**	6258
"**N** slaughter the Passover *animals,*	**2Ch 35:6**	
N the rest of the acts of Josiah	**2Ch 35:26**	
N the rest of the acts of	**2Ch 36:8**	
N in the first year of Cyrus king	**2Ch 36:22**	
N in the first year of Cyrus king	**Ezr 1:1**	
N this *was* their number:	**Ezr 1:9**	
N these are the people of the	**Ezr 2:1**	
N these are those who came up from	**Ezr 2:59**	
N the priests and the Levites,	**Ezr 2:70**	
N when the seventh month came, and	**Ezr 3:1**	
N in the second year of their	**Ezr 3:8**	
N when the builders had laid the	**Ezr 3:10**	
N when the enemies of Judah and	**Ezr 4:1**	
N in the reign of Ahasuerus, in	**Ezr 4:6**	
of the region beyond the River. **N**	**Ezr 4:10**	3706
region beyond the River, and **n**	**Ezr 4:11**	3706
"**N** let it be known to the king,	**Ezr 4:13**	3705
"**N** because we are in the service	**Ezr 4:14**	3705
beyond the River: "Peace. And **n**	**Ezr 4:17**	3706
n issue a decree to make these men	**Ezr 4:21**	3705
and from then until **n** it has been	**Ezr 5:16**	3705
"**N** if it pleases the king, let a	**Ezr 5:17**	3705
"**N** *therefore,* Tattenai, governor	**Ezr 6:6**	3705
N after these things, in the reign	**Ezr 7:1**	
N this is the copy of the decree	**Ezr 7:11**	
God of heaven, perfect *peace.* And **n**	**Ezr 7:12**	3706
N these are the heads of their	**Ezr 8:1**	
N I assembled them at the river	**Ezr 8:15**	
N when these things had been	**Ezr 9:1**	
"But **n** for a brief moment grace	**Ezr 9:8**	6258
"**N**, our God, what shall we say	**Ezr 9:10**	6258
'So **n** do not give your daughters	**Ezr 9:12**	6258
N while Ezra was praying and	**Ezr 10:1**	
yet **n** there is hope for Israel in	**Ezr 10:2**	6258
"So **n** let us make a covenant with	**Ezr 10:3**	6258
"**N** therefore, make confession to	**Ezr 10:11**	6258
N it happened in the month	**Ne 1:1**	
let Your ear **n** be attentive and	**Ne 1:6**	4994
which I am praying before You **n**,	**Ne 1:6**	3117
N I was the cupbearer to the king.	**Ne 1:11**	
N I had not been sad in his	**Ne 2:1**	
N the king had sent with me	**Ne 2:9**	
N the sons of Hassenaah built the	**Ne 3:3**	
N it came about that when	**Ne 4:1**	
N Tobiah the Ammonite *was* near him	**Ne 4:3**	
N when Sanballat,	**Ne 4:7**	
N there was a great outcry of the	**Ne 5:1**	
"**N** our flesh is like the flesh of	**Ne 5:5**	6258
n would you even sell your	**Ne 5:8**	
N that which was prepared for each	**Ne 5:18**	
N when it was	**Ne 6:1**	
And **n** it will be reported to the	**Ne 6:7**	6258
So come **n**, let us take counsel	**Ne 6:7**	6258
But **n**, *O God,* strengthen my hands.	**Ne 6:9**	6258
N when the wall was	**Ne 7:1**	
N the city was large and spacious,	**Ne 7:4**	
N the priests, the Levites, the	**Ne 7:73**	
N on the twenty-fourth day of this	**Ne 9:1**	
N on the Levites' platform stood	**Ne 9:4**	
"**N** therefore, our God, the great,	**Ne 9:32**	6258
"**N** because of all this We are	**Ne 9:38**	
N on the sealed document *were the*	**Ne 10:1**	
N the rest of the people, the	**Ne 10:28**	
N the leaders of the people lived	**Ne 11:1**	
N these are the heads of the	**Ne 11:3**	
N these are the sons of Benjamin:	**Ne 11:7**	
N from the Levites:	**Ne 11:15**	
N the overseer of the Levites in	**Ne 11:22**	
N as for the villages with their	**Ne 11:25**	
N these are the priests and the	**Ne 12:1**	
N in the days of Joiakim,	**Ne 12:12**	
N at the dedication of the wall of	**Ne 12:27**	
N prior to this, Eliashib the	**Ne 13:4**	
N it took place in the days of	**Es 1:1**	
N there was at the citadel in	**Es 2:5**	
N the young lady was beautiful of	**Es 2:7**	
N the young lady pleased him and	**Es 2:9**	
N when the turn of each young lady	**Es 2:12**	
N when the turn of Esther, the	**Es 2:15**	
N when the plot was investigated	**Es 2:23**	
N it was when they had spoken	**Es 3:4**	
N it came about on the third day	**Es 5:1**	
N Haman had just entered the outer	**Es 6:4**	
N the king and Haman came to drink	**Es 7:1**	
N if we had only been sold as	**Es 7:4**	
N when the king returned from the	**Es 7:8**	
"**N** you write to the Jews as you	**Es 8:8**	
N in the twelfth month	**Es 9:1**	
N what is your petition?	**Es 9:12**	
N the rest of the Jews who *were* in	**Es 9:16**	
N King Ahasuerus laid a tribute on	**Es 10:1**	
N there was a day when the sons of	**Jb 1:6**	
But put forth Your hand **n** and touch	**Jb 1:11**	4994
N on the day when his	**Jb 1:13**	
"However, put forth Your hand **n**,	**Jb 2:5**	4994
N when Job's three friends heard	**Jb 2:11**	
"For **n** I would have lain down and	**Jb 3:13**	6258
"But **n** it has come to you, and	**Jb 4:5**	6258
"Remember **n**, who *ever* perished	**Jb 4:7**	4994
"**N** a word was brought to me	**Jb 4:12**	
"Call **n**, is there anyone who will	**Jb 5:1**	4994
"Indeed, you have **n** become such,	**Jb 6:21**	6258
"**N** please look at me, And *see*	**Jb 6:28**	6258
"Desist **n**, let there be no	**Jb 6:29**	4994
For **n** I will lie down in the dust;	**Jb 7:21**	6258
Surely **n** He would rouse Himself	**Jb 8:6**	6258
"**N** my days are swifter than a	**Jb 9:25**	
'Remember **n**, that You have made	**Jb 10:9**	4994
"But **n** ask the beasts, and let	**Jb 12:7**	4994
"Behold **n**, I have prepared my	**Jb 13:18**	4994
"For **n** You number my steps,	**Jb 14:16**	6258
"But **n** He has exhausted me;	**Jb 16:7**	6258
"Even **n**, behold, my witness is in	**Jb 16:19**	6258
"Lay down, **n**, a pledge for me	**Jb 17:3**	4994
"But come again all of you **n**,	**Jb 17:10**	4994
Where **n** is my hope?	**Jb 17:15**	645
"Yield **n** and be at peace with Him;	**Jb 22:21**	4994
"**N** if it is not so, who can prove	**Jb 24:25**	
n those younger than I mock me,	**Jb 30:1**	6258
"And **n** I have become their taunt,	**Jb 30:9**	6258
"And **n** my soul is poured out	**Jb 30:16**	6258
N Elihu had waited to speak to Job	**Jb 32:4**	
"Let me **n** be partial to no one,	**Jb 32:21**	4994
"However **n**, Job, please hear my	**Jb 33:1**	
"Behold **n**, I open my mouth, My	**Jb 33:2**	4994
"And **n**, because He has not visited	**Jb 35:15**	6258
"**N** men do not see the light which is	**Jb 37:21**	6258
"**N** gird up your loins like a man,	**Jb 38:3**	4994
"**N** gird up your loins like a man;	**Jb 40:7**	4994
"Behold **n**, Behemoth, which I made	**Jb 40:15**	4994
"Behold **n**, his strength in his	**Jb 40:16**	4994
'Hear, **n**, and I will speak;	**Jb 42:4**	4994
But **n** my eye sees You;	**Jb 42:5**	6258
"**N** therefore, take for yourselves	**Jb 42:8**	6258
N therefore, O kings, show	**Ps 2:10**	6258
of the needy, **N** I will arise,"	**Ps 12:5**	6258
have **n** surrounded us in our steps;	**Ps 17:11**	6258
N I know that the LORD saves His	**Ps 20:6**	6258
And **n** my head will be lifted up	**Ps 27:6**	6258
N as for me, I said in my	**Ps 30:6**	
I have been young and **n** I am old	**Ps 37:25**	1571
"And **n**, Lord, for what do I wait?	**Ps 39:7**	6258
"**N** consider this, you who forget	**Ps 50:22**	4994
And **n** all its carved work They	**Ps 74:6**	6258
O God *of* hosts, turn again **n**,	**Ps 80:14**	4994
"Where, **n**, is their God?"	**Ps 115:2**	4994
astray, But **n** I keep Your word.	**Ps 119:67**	6258
I will **n** say, "May peace be within	**Ps 122:8**	4994
was on our side," Let Israel **n** say,	**Ps 124:1**	4994
my youth up," Let Israel **n** say,	**Ps 129:1**	4994
N then, *my* sons, listen to me And	**Pr 5:7**	6258
She is **n** in the streets, now in	**Pr 7:12**	6471
in the streets, **n** in the squares,	**Pr 7:12**	6471
N therefore, *my* sons, listen to	**Pr 7:24**	6258
"**N** therefore, *O* sons, listen to	**Pr 8:32**	6258
"Come **n**, I will test you with	**Ec 2:1**	4994
arise **n** and go about the city;	**SS 3:2**	4994
"Come **n**, and let us reason	**Is 1:18**	4994
lodged in her, But **n** murderers.	**Is 1:21**	6258
N it will come about that In the	**Is 2:2**	
N it will come about that instead	**Is 3:24**	
Let me sing **n** for my well-beloved	**Is 5:1**	4994
"And **n**, O inhabitants of Jerusalem	**Is 5:3**	6258
"So **n** let Me tell you what I am	**Is 5:5**	6258
N it came about in the days of	**Is 7:1**	
"Go out **n** to meet Ahaz, you and	**Is 7:3**	4994
(**n** within another 65 years Ephraim	**Is 7:8**	
"Listen **n**, O house of David!	**Is 7:13**	4994
N in that day a man	**Is 7:21**	
"**N** therefore, behold, the Lord is	**Is 8:7**	
N what will you do in the day of	**Is 10:3**	
N in that day the remnant	**Is 10:20**	
But **n** the LORD speaks, saying,	**Is 16:14**	6258
N in that day the glory	**Is 17:4**	
"**N** behold, here comes a troop of	**Is 21:9**	
What is the matter with you **n**,	**Is 22:1**	645
N in that day Tyre	**Is 23:15**	
And **n** do not carry on as scoffers,	**Is 28:22**	6258
"Jacob shall not **n** be ashamed,	**Is 29:22**	6258
nor shall his face **n** turn pale;	**Is 29:22**	6258
N go, write it on a tablet before	**Is 30:8**	6258
N the Egyptians are men and not	**Is 31:3**	
"**N** I will arise,"	**Is 33:10**	6258
"**N** I will be exalted, now I will	**Is 33:10**	6258
be exalted, **n** I will be lifted up.	**Is 33:10**	6258
N in the fourteenth year	**Is 36:1**	
"Say **n** to Hezekiah,	**Is 36:4**	4994
N on whom do you rely,	**Is 36:5**	6258
"**N** therefore, come make a bargain	**Is 36:8**	6258
"Have I **n** come up without the	**Is 36:10**	6258
Speak **n** to your servants in Aramaic,	**Is 36:11**	4994
"**N**, O LORD our God, deliver us	**Is 37:20**	6258
N I have brought it to pass, That	**Is 37:26**	6258
"Remember **n**, O LORD, I beseech	**Is 38:3**	4994
N Isaiah had said,	**Is 38:21**	
to pass, **N** I declare new things;	**Is 42:9**	
N like a woman in labor I will	**Is 42:14**	
But **n**, thus says the LORD, your	**Is 43:1**	6258
new, **N** it will spring forth;	**Is 43:19**	6258
"But **n** listen, O Jacob, My	**Is 44:1**	6258
"**N**, then, hear this, you sensual one	**Is 47:8**	6258
"Stand *fast* **n** in your spells And	**Is 47:12**	4994
Let **n** the astrologers, Those who	**Is 47:13**	4994
are created **n** and not long ago;	**Is 48:7**	6258
And **n** the Lord GOD has sent Me,	**Is 48:16**	6258
And **n** says the LORD, who formed Me	**Is 49:5**	6258
Surely **n** you will be too cramped	**Is 49:19**	6258
"**N** therefore, what do I have	**Is 52:5**	6258
N the LORD saw, And it was	**Is 59:15**	
"from **n** and forever."	**Is 59:21**	6258
But **n**, O LORD, You are our Father	**Is 64:8**	6258
Behold, look **n**, all of us are Your	**Is 64:9**	4994
N the word of the LORD came to me	**Jer 1:4**	
"**N**, gird up your loins and	**Jer 1:17**	
"**N** behold, I have made you today	**Jer 1:18**	
N the word of the LORD came to me	**Jer 2:1**	
"But **n** what are you doing on the	**Jer 2:18**	6258
"Have you not just **n** called to Me,	**Jer 3:4**	6258
n I will also pronounce judgments	**Jer 4:12**	6258
"Report *it* to the nations, **n**!	**Jer 4:16**	2009
And look **n** and take note.	**Jer 5:1**	4994
'**N** hear this, O foolish	**Jer 5:21**	4994
"Let us **n** fear the LORD our God,	**Jer 5:24**	4994
N blow a trumpet in Tekoa And	**Jer 6:1**	
"But go **n** to My place which was	**Jer 7:12**	4994
"And **n**, because you have done all	**Jer 7:13**	6258
N hear the word of the LORD, O you	**Jer 9:20**	3588
n He will remember their iniquity	**Jer 14:10**	6258
"**N** when you tell	**Jer 16:10**	
word of the LORD? Let it come **n**!"	**Jer 17:15**	4994
"So **n** then, speak to the men of	**Jer 18:11**	6258
'Ask **n** among the nations, Who ever	**Jer 18:13**	4994
"**N** when this people or the	**Jer 23:33**	
'Turn **n** everyone from his evil way	**Jer 25:5**	4994
"**N** therefore amend your ways and	**Jer 26:13**	6258
"**N** I have given all these lands into	**Jer 27:6**	6258
n shortly be brought again from	**Jer 27:16**	6258
them **n** entreat the LORD of hosts that	**Jer 27:18**	4994
N in the same year,	**Jer 28:1**	
"Yet hear **n** this word which I am	**Jer 28:7**	4994
"Listen **n**, Hananiah, the LORD has	**Jer 28:15**	4994
N these are the words of the	**Jer 29:1**	
n then, why have you not rebuked	**Jer 29:27**	6258
N these are the words which the	**Jer 30:4**	
'Ask **n**, and see If a male can	**Jer 30:6**	4994
N at that time the army of the	**Jer 32:2**	
"**N** therefore thus says the LORD	**Jer 32:36**	6258
Turn **n** every man from his evil way and	**Jer 35:15**	4994
N in the fifth year	**Jer 36:9**	
N when Micaiah the son of	**Jer 36:11**	
N the king was sitting in the	**Jer 36:22**	
N Zedekiah the son of Josiah whom	**Jer 37:1**	
N Jeremiah was *still* coming in and	**Jer 37:4**	
N it happened when the army of	**Jer 37:11**	
N King Zedekiah sent and took him	**Jer 37:17**	
"But **n**, please listen, O my lord	**Jer 37:20**	6258
N Shephatiah the son of Mattan,	**Jer 38:1**	
"**N** let this man be put to death,	**Jer 38:4**	4994
N in the cistern there was no	**Jer 38:6**	

N the king was sitting in the Gate Jer 38:7
"N put these worn-out clothes and Jer 38:12 4994
Tell us n what you said to the king and Jer 38:25 4994
N when Jerusalem was Jer 39:1
N Nebuchadnezzar king of Babylon Jer 39:11
N the word of the LORD had come to Jer 39:15
N the captain of the bodyguard had Jer 40:2
"But n, behold, I am freeing you Jer 40:4 6258
N all the commanders of the forces Jer 40:7
"N as for me, behold, I am going Jer 40:10
N Johanan the son of Kareah and Jer 40:13
N it happened on the next day Jer 41:4
N as for the cistern where Ishmael Jer 41:9
N as soon as all Jer 41:13
as your own eyes n see us, Jer 42:2
N at the end of ten Jer 42:7
whom you are n fearing; do not Jer 42:11
you should n clearly understand Jer 42:22 6258
'N then thus says the LORD God of Jer 44:7 6258
Even though they are n more Jer 46:23
"N was not Israel a laughingstock Jer 48:27
N so that your heart does not grow Jer 51:46
(N Seraiah was quartermaster.) Jer 51:59
N it came about in the ninth year Jer 52:4
N on the tenth *day* of the fifth Jer 52:12
N the bronze pillars which Jer 52:17
N a capital of bronze was on it; Jer 52:22
N it came about in the Jer 52:31
Hear n, all peoples, And behold my La 1:18 4994
N it came about in the thirtieth Ezk 1:1
N as I looked at the living Ezk 1:15
N over the heads of the living Ezk 1:22
N above the expanse that was over Ezk 1:26
"N you, son of man, listen to Ezk 2:8
"N you son of man, get yourself a Ezk 4:1
"N behold, I will put ropes on Ezk 4:8
for from my youth until n I have Ezk 4:14 6258
'N the end is upon you, and I Ezk 7:3 6258
"N I will shortly pour out My Ezk 7:8 6258
"Son of man, raise your eyes n Ezk 8:5 4994
Son of man, n dig through the wall. Ezk 8:8 4994
N the cherubim were standing on Ezk 10:3
N when the cherubim moved, the Ezk 10:16
N it came about as I prophesied, Ezk 11:13
he sees is for many years *from* n, Ezk 12:27
"N you, son of man, set your face Ezk 13:17
"Behold n, I have stretched out Ezk 16:27
"N your older sister is Samaria, Ezk 16:46
so n you have become the reproach Ezk 16:57 6256
N the word of the LORD came to me Ezk 17:1
"Say n to the rebellious house, Ezk 17:12 4994
'N he despised the oath by Ezk 17:18
"N behold, he has a son who has Ezk 18:14
Hear n, O house of Israel! Ezk 18:25 4994
'And n it is planted in the Ezk 19:13 6258
N in the seventh year, Ezk 20:1
N the word of the LORD came to me Ezk 20:45
"N her sister Oholibah saw *this,* Ezk 23:11
bear n the *punishment* of your Ezk 23:35 1571
'Will they n commit adultery with Ezk 23:43 6258
N in the eleventh year, Ezk 26:1
n *that* she is laid waste,' Ezk 26:2
'N the coastlands will tremble On Ezk 26:18 6258
'N that you are broken by the seas Ezk 27:34 6256
N in the twenty-seventh year, in Ezk 29:17
"N I will spread My net over you Ezk 32:3
"N as for you, son of man, I have Ezk 33:7
"N as for you, son of man, say to Ezk 33:10
N in the twelfth year Ezk 33:21
N the hand of the LORD had been Ezk 33:22
'Come n and hear what the message Ezk 33:30 4994
the waste places which are n Ezk 38:12
"N I will restore the fortunes Ezk 39:25 6258
N the upper chambers *were* smaller Ezk 42:5
N when he had finished measuring Ezk 42:15
"N let them put away their Ezk 43:9 6258
"N the altar hearth *shall be* Ezk 43:16
N when I had returned, behold, on Ezk 47:7
"N these are the names of the Ezk 48:1
N among them from the sons of Da 1:6
N God granted Daniel favor and Da 1:9
N in the second year of the reign Da 2:1
Even n You have made known to me Da 2:23 3705
n we will tell its interpretation Da 2:36
"N if you are ready, at the Da 3:15 3705
'N *these were* the visions in my Da 4:10
N you, Belteshazzar, tell *me* its Da 4:18
break away n from your sins by Da 4:27
"N I, Nebuchadnezzar, praise, Da 4:37 3705
Let Daniel n be summoned and he Da 5:12 3705
"N I have heard about you that a Da 5:14
"Just n the wise men *and* the Da 5:15 3705
N if you are able to read the Da 5:16 3705
"N this is the inscription that Da 5:25
concerning him that he n had Da 5:29
"N, O king, establish the injunction Da 6:8 3705
N when Daniel knew that the Da 6:10
(n in his roof chamber he had Da 6:10
N the two horns *were* long, but one Da 8:3
N while he was talking with me, I Da 8:18
"And n, O Lord our God, who have Da 9:15 6258
let n Your anger and Your wrath Da 9:16 4994
"So n, our God, listen to the Da 9:17 6258
N while I was speaking and Da 9:20
I have n come forth to give you Da 9:22 6258
N I, Daniel, alone saw the vision, Da 10:7
for I have n been sent to you." Da 10:11 6258
"N I have come to give you an Da 10:14
remains just n no strength in me, Da 10:17 6258
N as soon as he spoke to me, Da 10:19
But I shall n return to fight Da 10:20 6258
"And n I will tell you the truth. Da 11:2 6258
"N in those times many will rise Da 11:14
"N when they fall they will be Da 11:34
"N at that time Michael, the Da 12:1
it was better for me then than n!' Hos 2:7 6258
Can the LORD n pasture them Like a Hos 4:16 6258
For n, O Ephraim, you have played Hos 5:3 6258
N the new moon will devour them Hos 5:7 6258
N their deeds are all around them; Hos 7:2 6258
They are n among the nations Like Hos 8:8 6258
nations, N I will gather them up; Hos 8:10 6258
N He will remember their iniquity, Hos 8:13 6258
N they must bear their guilt. Hos 10:2 6258
Surely n they will say, Hos 10:3 6258
N Jacob fled to the land of Aram, Hos 12:12
And n they sin more and more, And Hos 13:2 6258
Where n is your king That he may Hos 13:10 645
"Yet even n," declares the LORD, Jl 2:12 6258
N return to the LORD your God, Jl 2:13
"Bring n, that we may drink!" Am 4:1
they will n go into exile at the Am 6:7 6258
"N hear the word of the LORD: Am 7:16 6258
Then they said to him, "Tell us, n! Jon 1:8 4994
N the word of the LORD came to Jon 3:1
N Nineveh was an exceedingly great Jon 3:3
"Therefore n, O LORD, please take Jon 4:3 6258
"Hear n, heads of Jacob And Mi 3:1 4994
N hear this, heads of the house of Mi 3:9 4994
Mount Zion From n on and forever. Mi 4:7 6258
"N, why do you cry out loudly? Mi 4:9 6258
For n you will go out of the city, Mi 4:10 6258
"And n many nations have been Mi 4:11 6258
"N muster yourselves in troops, Mi 5:1 6258
Hear n what the LORD is saying, Mi 6:1 4994
remember n What Balak king of Moab Mi 6:5 4994
"So n, I will break his yoke bar Na 1:13 6258
her days, N they are fleeing; Na 2:8
N you yourself drink and expose Hab 2:16 1571
N therefore, thus says the LORD of Hg 1:5 6258
"Speak n to Zerubbabel the son of Hg 2:2 4994
And how do you see it n? Hg 2:3 6258
'But n take courage, Zerubbabel,' Hg 2:4 6258
'Ask n the priests *for* a ruling: Hg 2:11 4994
'But n, do consider from this day Hg 2:15 6258
"Return n from your evil ways and Zch 1:4 4994
N Joshua was clothed with filthy Zch 3:3
'N listen, Joshua the high priest, Zch 3:8 4994
"Lift up n your eyes and see Zch 5:5 4994
N I lifted up my eyes again and Zch 6:1
"N the crown will become a Zch 6:14
N *the town of* Bethel had sent Zch 7:2
'But n I will not treat the Zch 8:11 6258
For n I have seen with My eyes. Zch 9:8 6258
N this will be the plague with Zch 14:12
"But n will you not entreat God's Mal 1:9 6258
"And n this commandment is for Mal 2:1 6258
My house, and test Me n in this," Mal 3:10 4994
'So n we call the arrogant blessed; Mal 3:15 6258
N the birth of Jesus Christ was as Mt 1:18 *1161*
N all this took place to fulfill what Mt 1:22 *1161*
N after Jesus was born in Mt 2:1 *1161*
N when they had gone, behold, Mt 2:13 *1161*
N in those days John the Baptist Mt 3:1 *1161*
N John himself had a garment of Mt 3:4 *1161*
N when Jesus heard that John had been Mt 4:12 *1161*
N as Jesus was walking by the Sea of Mt 4:18
N when Jesus heard *this,* He Mt 8:10 *1161*
N when Jesus saw a crowd around Mt 8:18 *1161*
N there was a herd of many swine Mt 8:30 *1161*
N the names of the twelve apostles Mt 10:2 *1161*
N when John, while imprisoned, heard Mt 11:2 *1161*
the days of John the Baptist until n Mt 11:12 *737*
"N when the unclean spirit goes Mt 12:43 *1161*
Nheard *about John,* HE WITHDREW Mt 14:13 *1161*
have remained with Me n three days Mt 15:32 *2235*
N when Jesus came into the Mt 16:13 *1161*
N in the morning, when He was Mt 21:18 *1161*
"N there were seven brothers with Mt 22:25 *1161*
N while the Pharisees were gathered Mt 22:41 *1161*
from n on you will not see Me Mt 23:39 *737*
beginning of the world until n, Mt 24:21 *3568*
"N learn the parable from the fig Mt 24:32 *1161*
"N while the bridegroom was Mt 25:5 *1161*
"N after a long time the master Mt 25:19 *1161*
N when Jesus was in Bethany, at Mt 26:6 *1161*
N on the first *day* of Unleavened Mt 26:17 *1161*
N when evening came, Jesus was Mt 26:20 *1161*
from n on until that day when I Mt 26:29 *737*
N he who was betraying Him gave Mt 26:48 *1161*
N the chief priests and the whole Mt 26:59 *1161*
you have n heard the blasphemy; Mt 26:65 *3568*
N Peter was sitting outside in the Mt 26:69 *1161*
N when morning came, all the Mt 27:1 *1161*
N Jesus stood before the governor, Mt 27:11 *1161*
N at *the* feast the governor was Mt 27:15 *1161*
let Him n come down from the cross Mt 27:42 *3568*
LET GOD RESCUE *Him* n, Mt 27:43 *3568*
N from the sixth hour darkness Mt 27:45 *1161*
N the centurion, and those who Mt 27:54 *1161*
N on the next day, the day Mt 27:62 *1161*
N after the Sabbath, as it began Mt 28:1 *1161*
N while they were on their way, Mt 28:11 *1161*
N after John had been taken into Mk 1:14
N Simon's mother-in-law was lying Mk 1:30 *1161*
N there was a large herd of swine Mk 5:11 *1161*
N the woman was a Gentile, of the Mk 7:26 *1161*
remained with Me n three days and Mk 8:2 *2235*
receive a hundred times as much n Mk 10:30 *3568*
which God created until n, Mk 13:19 *3568*
"N learn the parable from the fig Mk 13:28 *1161*
N the Passover and Unleavened Mk 14:1 *1161*
N he who was betraying Him had Mk 14:44 *1161*
N the chief priests and the whole Mk 14:55 *1161*
N at *the* feast he used to release Mk 15:6 *1161*
n come down from the cross, Mk 15:32 *3568*
N after He had risen early on the Mk 16:9 *1161*
N it happened *that* while he was Lk 1:8 *1161*
N in the sixth month the angel Lk 1:26 *1161*
barren is n in her sixth month. Lk 1:36
N at this time Mary arose and went Lk 1:39 *1161*
N the time had come for Elizabeth Lk 1:57 *1161*
N in those days Lk 2:1 *1161*
"N Lord, You are releasing Your Lk 2:29 *3568*
N His parents went to Jerusalem every Lk 2:41
N in the fifteenth year of the Lk 3:1 *1161*
N while the people were in a state Lk 3:15 *1161*
N when all the people Lk 3:21 *1161*
N Simon's mother-in-law was Lk 4:38 *1161*
N it happened that while the Lk 5:1 *1161*
from n on you will be catching men." Lk 5:10 *3568*
N it happened that He was Lk 6:1 *1161*
"Blessed *are* you who hunger n, Lk 6:21 *3568*
Blessed *are* you who weep n, Lk 6:21 *3568*
"Woe to you who are well-fed n, Lk 6:25 *3568*
Woe *to you* who laugh n, Lk 6:25 *3568*
N Jesus *started* on His way with Lk 7:6 *1161*
N when Jesus heard this, He Lk 7:9 *1161*
N as He approached the gate of the Lk 7:12 *1161*
N one of the Pharisees was Lk 7:36 *1161*
N when the Pharisee who had Lk 7:39 *1161*
"N the parable is this: Lk 8:11 *1161*
"N no one after lighting a lamp Lk 8:16 *1161*
N on one of *those* days Lk 8:22 *1161*
N there was a herd of many swine Lk 8:32 *1161*
N they were all weeping and Lk 8:52 *1161*
N Herod the tetrarch heard of all Lk 9:7 *1161*
N the day was ending, and the twelve Lk 9:12
N Peter and his companions had Lk 9:32 *1161*
N after this the Lord appointed Lk 10:1 *1161*
N as they were traveling along, He Lk 10:38 *1161*
"N suppose one of you fathers is Lk 11:11 *1161*
N when He had spoken, a Pharisee Lk 11:37 *1161*
"N you Pharisees clean the Lk 11:39 *3568*
and n who will own what you have Lk 12:20
for from n on five *members* in one Lk 12:52 *3568*
N on the same occasion there were Lk 13:1 *1161*
'Come; for everything is ready n.' Lk 14:17 *2235*
N large crowds were going Lk 14:25 *1161*
N all the tax collectors and the Lk 15:1 *1161*
"N when he had spent everything, Lk 15:14 *1161*
"N his older son was in the Lk 15:25 *1161*
N He was also saying to the Lk 16:1 *1161*
N the Pharisees, who were lovers Lk 16:14 *1161*
"N there was a rich man, Lk 16:19 *1161*
"N the poor Lk 16:22 *1161*
but n he is being comforted here, Lk 16:25 *3568*
N one of them, when he saw that he Lk 17:15 *1161*
N having been questioned by the Lk 17:20 *1161*
N He was telling them a parable to Lk 18:1 *1161*
n, will not God bring about justice Lk 18:7 *1161*
N hearing a crowd going by, he Lk 18:36 *1161*
But n they have been hidden from Lk 19:42 *3568*
N there came to Him some of the Lk 20:27 *1161*
"N there were seven brothers; Lk 20:29 *3767*
"N He is not the God of the dead but Lk 20:38 *1161*
yourselves that summer is n near. Lk 21:30 *2235*
N during the day He was teaching Lk 21:37 *1161*
N the Feast of Unleavened Bread, Lk 22:1 *1161*
from n on until the kingdom of God Lk 22:18 *3568*
"But n, whoever has a money belt Lk 22:36 *3568*
N an angel from heaven appeared to Lk 22:43 *1161*
N the men who were holding Jesus in Lk 22:63
"But from n on THE SON OF MAN Lk 22:69 *3568*
N Herod was very glad when he saw Lk 23:8 *1161*
N Herod and Pilate became friends Lk 23:12 *1161*
N he was obliged to release to Lk 23:17 *1161*
N there was also an inscription Lk 23:38 *1161*
It was n about the sixth hour, Lk 23:44 *2235*
N when the centurion saw what had Lk 23:47 *1161*
N the women who had come with Him Lk 23:55 *1161*
N they were Mary Magdalene and Lk 24:10 *1161*
and the day is n nearly over." Lk 24:29 *2235*
N He said to them, Lk 24:44 *1161*
N they had been sent from the Jn 1:24 *2532*
N Philip was from Bethsaida, of Jn 1:44 *1161*
N there were six stone waterpots Jn 2:6 *1161*
"Draw *some* out n and take it to Jn 2:8 *3568*
have kept the good wine until n." Jn 2:10 *737*
N when He was in Jerusalem at the Jn 2:23 *1161*
N there was a man of the Jn 3:1 *1161*
the one whom you n have is not Jn 4:18 *3568*
"But an hour is coming, and n is, Jn 4:23 *3568*
As he was n going down, *his* Jn 4:51 *2235*
N there is in Jerusalem by the Jn 5:2 *1161*
N it was the Sabbath on that day. Jn 5:9 *1161*
"My Father is working until n, Jn 5:17 *737*
you, an hour is coming and n is, Jn 5:25 *3568*
N the Passover, the feast of the Jn 6:4 *1161*
N there was much grass in the Jn 6:10 *1161*
N when evening came, His disciples Jn 6:16 *1161*
How does He n say, Jn 6:42 *3568*
N He meant Judas *the son* of Simon Jn 6:71 *1161*
N the feast of the Jews, the Feast Jn 7:2 *1161*
when it was n the midst of the feast Jn 7:14 *2235*
N on the last day, the great *day* Jn 7:37 *1161*
"N in the Law Moses commanded us Jn 8:5 *1161*

From **n** on sin no more."	**Jn 8:11**	*3568*
"**N** we know that You have a demon.	**Jn 8:52**	*3568*
N it was a Sabbath on the day when	**Jn 9:14**	*1161*
Then how does he **n** see?"	**Jn 9:19**	*737*
but how he **n** sees, we do not know;	**Jn 9:21**	*3568*
though I was blind, **n** I see."	**Jn 9:25**	*737*
N a certain man was sick, Lazarus	**Jn 11:1**	*1161*
N Jesus loved Martha and *her*	**Jn 11:5**	*1161*
Jews were just **n** seeking to stone	**Jn 11:8**	*3568*
N Jesus had spoken of his death,	**Jn 11:13**	*1161*
N Bethany was near Jerusalem,	**Jn 11:18**	*1161*
"Even **n** I know that whatever You	**Jn 11:22**	*3568*
N Jesus had not yet come into the	**Jn 11:30**	*1161*
N it was a cave, and a stone was	**Jn 11:38**	*1161*
N he did not say this on his own	**Jn 11:51**	*1161*
N the Passover of the Jews was near	**Jn 11:55**	*1161*
N the chief priests and the	**Jn 11:57**	*1161*
N he said this, not because he was	**Jn 12:6**	*1161*
N there were some Greeks among	**Jn 12:20**	*1161*
"**N** My soul has become troubled;	**Jn 12:27**	*3568*
"**N** judgment is upon this world;	**Jn 12:31**	*3568*
n the ruler of this world will be	**Jn 12:31**	*3568*
N before the Feast of the	**Jn 13:1**	*1161*
"What I do you do not realize **n**,	**Jn 13:7**	*737*
"From **n** on I am telling you	**Jn 13:19**	*737*
N no one of those reclining *at the*	**Jn 13:28**	*1161*
"**N** is the Son of Man glorified,	**Jn 13:31**	*3568*
to the Jews, **n** I also say to you,	**Jn 13:33**	*737*
I go, you cannot follow Me **n**;	**Jn 13:36**	*3568*
why can I not follow You right **n**?	**Jn 13:37**	*737*
from **n** on you know Him, and have	**Jn 14:7**	*737*
"**N** I have told you before it happens,	**Jn 14:29**	*3568*
but **n** they have no excuse for	**Jn 15:22**	*3568*
but **n** they have both seen and	**Jn 15:24**	*3568*
n I am going to Him who sent Me;	**Jn 16:5**	*3568*
you, but you cannot bear *them* **n**.	**Jn 16:12**	*737*
"Therefore you too have grief **n**;	**Jn 16:22**	*3568*
"Until **n** you have asked for nothing	**Jn 16:24**	*737*
"Lo, **n** You are speaking plainly and	**Jn 16:29**	*3568*
"**N** we know that You know all	**Jn 16:30**	*3568*
"Do you **n** believe?	**Jn 16:31**	*737*
"**N**, Father, glorify Me together	**Jn 17:5**	*3568*
"**N** they have come to know that	**Jn 17:7**	*3568*
"But **n** I come to You;	**Jn 17:13**	*3568*
N Judas also, who was betraying	**Jn 18:2**	*1161*
N Caiaphas was the one who had	**Jn 18:14**	*1161*
N that disciple was known to the	**Jn 18:15**	*1161*
N the slaves and the officers were	**Jn 18:18**	*1161*
N Simon Peter was standing and	**Jn 18:25**	*1161*
N Barabbas was a robber.	**Jn 18:40**	*1161*
N it was the day of preparation	**Jn 19:14**	*1161*
n the tunic was seamless, woven in	**Jn 19:23**	*1161*
N in the place where He was	**Jn 19:41**	*1161*
N on the first *day* of the week	**Jn 20:1**	*1161*
But when the day was **n** breaking,	**Jn 21:4**	*2235*
fish which you have **n** caught."	**Jn 21:10**	*3568*
This is **n** the third time that	**Jn 21:14**	*2235*
N this He said, signifying by what	**Jn 21:19**	*1161*
Spirit not many days from **n**."	**Ac 1:5**	*3326, 3778*
(**N** this man acquired a field with	**Ac 1:18**	*3767*
N there were Jews living in	**Ac 2:5**	*1161*
N when they heard *this*, they were	**Ac 2:37**	*1161*
N Peter and John were going up to	**Ac 3:1**	*1161*
"And **n**, brethren, I know that you	**Ac 3:17**	*3568*
N as they observed the confidence	**Ac 4:13**	*1161*
"And **n**, Lord, take note of their	**Ac 4:29**	*3568*
N Joseph, a Levite of Cyprian birth,	**Ac 4:36**	
N there elapsed an interval of	**Ac 5:7**	*1161*
N when the high priest and his	**Ac 5:21**	*1161*
N when the captain of the temple	**Ac 5:24**	*1161*
N at this time while the disciples	**Ac 6:1**	*1161*
country in which you are **n** living.	**Ac 7:4**	*3568*
"**N** a famine came over all Egypt	**Ac 7:11**	*1161*
COME **N**, AND I WILL SEND YOU TO	**Ac 7:34**	*3568*
and murderers you have **n** become;	**Ac 7:52**	*3568*
N when they heard this, they were	**Ac 7:54**	*1161*
N there was a man named	**Ac 8:9**	*1161*
N when the apostles in Jerusalem	**Ac 8:14**	*1161*
N when Simon saw that the Spirit	**Ac 8:18**	*1161*
N the passage of Scripture which	**Ac 8:32**	*1161*
N Saul, still breathing threats	**Ac 9:1**	*1161*
N there was a disciple at	**Ac 9:10**	*1161*
N for several days he was with the	**Ac 9:19**	*1161*
N as Peter was traveling	**Ac 9:32**	*1161*
N in Joppa there was a disciple	**Ac 9:36**	*1161*
N *there was* a man at	**Ac 10:1**	*1161*
"**N** dispatch *some* men to Joppa	**Ac 10:5**	*3568*
N while Peter was greatly	**Ac 10:17**	*1161*
N Cornelius was waiting for them and	**Ac 10:24**	*1161*
N then, we are all here present	**Ac 10:33**	*3568*
"I most certainly understand **n**	**Ac 10:34**	
N the apostles and the brethren	**Ac 11:1**	*1161*
N at this time some prophets came	**Ac 11:27**	*1161*
N about that time Herod the king	**Ac 12:1**	*1161*
N it was during the days of	**Ac 12:3**	*1161*
"**N** I know for sure that the Lord	**Ac 12:11**	*3568*
N when day came, there was no	**Ac 12:18**	*1161*
N he was very angry with the	**Ac 12:20**	*1161*
N there were at Antioch, in the	**Ac 13:1**	*1161*
"**N**, behold, the hand of the Lord	**Ac 13:11**	*3568*
N Paul and his companions put out	**Ac 13:13**	*1161*
are **n** His witnesses to the people.	**Ac 13:31**	*3568*
N when *the meeting of* the	**Ac 13:43**	*1161*
"**N** therefore why do you put God	**Ac 15:10**	*3568*
N while they were passing through	**Ac 16:4**	*1161*
N when day came, the chief	**Ac 16:35**	*1161*
Therefore come out **n** and go in peace."	**Ac 16:36**	*3568*
and **n** are they sending us away	**Ac 16:37**	*3568*
N when they had traveled through	**Ac 17:1**	*1161*
N these were more noble-minded	**Ac 17:11**	*1161*
N those who escorted Paul brought	**Ac 17:15**	*1161*
N while Paul was waiting for them	**Ac 17:16**	*1161*
(**N** all the Athenians and the	**Ac 17:21**	*1161*
God is **n** declaring to men that all	**Ac 17:30**	*3568*
N when they heard of the	**Ac 17:32**	*1161*
n on I will go to the Gentiles."	**Ac 18:6**	*3568*
N he himself entered the synagogue	**Ac 18:19**	*1161*
N a Jew named Apollos, an	**Ac 18:24**	*1161*
N after these things were	**Ac 19:21**	*1161*
"And **n**, behold, bound by the Spirit,	**Ac 20:22**	*3568*
"And **n**, behold, I know that all	**Ac 20:25**	*3568*
"And **n** I commend you to God and	**Ac 20:32**	*3568*
N this man had four virgin	**Ac 21:9**	*1161*
defense which I **n** *offer* to you."	**Ac 22:1**	*3570*
'**N** why do you delay? Get up and be	**Ac 22:16**	*3568*
"**N** therefore, you and the Council	**Ac 23:15**	*3568*
and **n** they are ready and waiting	**Ac 23:21**	*3568*
charges of which they **n** accuse me.	**Ac 24:13**	*3570*
"**N** after several years I came to	**Ac 24:17**	*1161*
N when several days had elapsed,	**Ac 25:13**	*1161*
"And **n** I am standing trial for	**Ac 26:6**	*3568*
and the voyage was **n** dangerous,	**Ac 27:9**	*2235*
"*Yet* **n** I urge you to keep up	**Ac 27:22**	*3568*
N in the neighborhood of that	**Ac 28:7**	*1161*
if perhaps **n** at last by the will	**Ro 1:10**	*2235*
N we know that whatever the Law	**Ro 3:19**	*1161*
But **n** apart from the Law *the*	**Ro 3:21**	*3570*
N to the one who works, his wage	**Ro 4:4**	*1161*
his own body, **n** as good as dead	**Ro 4:19**	
N not for his sake only was it	**Ro 4:23**	*1161*
n been justified by His blood,	**Ro 5:9**	*3568*
n received the reconciliation.	**Ro 5:11**	*3568*
N if we have died with Christ, we	**Ro 6:8**	*1161*
so **n** present your members as	**Ro 6:19**	*3568*
things of which you are **n** ashamed?	**Ro 6:21**	*3568*
But **n** having been freed from sin	**Ro 6:22**	*3570*
But **n** we have been released from	**Ro 7:6**	*3570*
So **n**, no longer am I the one doing	**Ro 7:17**	*3570*
is **n** no condemnation	**Ro 8:1**	*3568*
pains of childbirth together until **n**.	**Ro 8:22**	*3568*
N if their transgression is riches	**Ro 11:12**	*1161*
but **n** have been shown mercy	**Ro 11:30**	*3568*
also **n** have been disobedient,	**Ro 11:31**	*3568*
they also may **n** be shown mercy.	**Ro 11:31**	*3568*
for **n** salvation is nearer to us	**Ro 13:11**	*3568*
N accept the one who is weak in	**Ro 14:1**	*1161*
N we who are strong ought to bear	**Ro 15:1**	*1161*
N may the God who gives	**Ro 15:5**	*1161*
N may the God of hope fill you	**Ro 15:13**	*1161*
but **n**, with no further place for	**Ro 15:23**	*3570*
but **n**, I am going to Jerusalem	**Ro 15:25**	*3570*
N I urge you, brethren, by our	**Ro 15:30**	*1161*
N the God of peace be with you all.	**Ro 15:33**	*1161*
N I urge you, brethren, keep your	**Ro 16:17**	*1161*
N to Him who is able to establish	**Ro 16:25**	*1161*
but **n** is manifested, and by the	**Ro 16:26**	*3568*
N I exhort you, brethren, by the	**1Co 1:10**	*1161*
N I mean this, that each one of	**1Co 1:12**	*1161*
N I did baptize also the household	**1Co 1:16**	*1161*
N we have received, not the spirit	**1Co 2:12**	*1161*
even **n** you are not yet able,	**1Co 3:2**	*3568*
N he who plants and he who waters	**1Co 3:8**	*1161*
N if any man builds on the	**1Co 3:12**	*1161*
N these things, brethren, I have	**1Co 4:6**	*1161*
dregs of all things, *even* until **n**.	**1Co 4:13**	*737*
N some have become arrogant, as	**1Co 4:18**	*1161*
N God has not only raised the Lord	**1Co 6:14**	*1161*
N concerning the things about	**1Co 7:1**	*1161*
are unclean, but **n** they are holy.	**1Co 7:14**	*3568*
N concerning virgins I have no	**1Co 7:25**	*1161*
so that from **n** on those who have	**1Co 7:29**	*3062*
N concerning things sacrificed to	**1Co 8:1**	*1161*
accustomed to the idol until **n**,	**1Co 8:7**	*737*
N these things happened as	**1Co 10:6**	*1161*
N these things happened to them as	**1Co 10:11**	*1161*
N I praise you because you	**1Co 11:2**	*1161*
N concerning spiritual *gifts*,	**1Co 12:1**	*1161*
N there are varieties of gifts,	**1Co 12:4**	*1161*
But **n** God has placed the members,	**1Co 12:18**	*3568*
But **n** there are many members, but	**1Co 12:20**	*3568*
N you are Christ's body, and	**1Co 12:27**	*1161*
For **n** we see in a mirror dimly,	**1Co 13:12**	*737*
n I know in part, but then I will	**1Co 13:12**	*737*
But **n** faith, hope, love,	**1Co 13:13**	*3570*
N I wish that you all spoke in	**1Co 14:5**	*1161*
But **n**, brethren, if I come to you	**1Co 14:6**	*3568*
N I make known to you, brethren,	**1Co 15:1**	*1161*
time, most of whom remain until **n**,	**1Co 15:6**	*737*
N if Christ is preached, that He	**1Co 15:12**	*1161*
But **n** Christ has been raised from	**1Co 15:20**	*3570*
N I say this, brethren, that flesh	**1Co 15:50**	*1161*
N concerning the collection for	**1Co 16:1**	*1161*
wish to see you **n** *just* in passing;	**1Co 16:7**	*737*
N if Timothy comes, see that he is	**1Co 16:10**	*1161*
not at all *his* desire to come **n**,	**1Co 16:12**	*3568*
N I urge you, brethren	**1Co 16:15**	*1161*
N He who establishes us with you	**2Co 1:21**	*1161*
N when I came to Troas for the	**2Co 2:12**	*1161*
N the Lord is the Spirit,	**2Co 3:17**	*1161*
N He who prepared us for this very	**2Co 5:5**	*1161*
from **n** on we recognize no one	**2Co 5:16**	*3568*
yet **n** we know *Him in this way*	**2Co 5:16**	*3568*
N all *these* things are from God,	**2Co 5:18**	*1161*
Behold, **n** is "THE ACCEPTABLE TIME,"	**2Co 6:2**	*3568*
behold, **n** is "THE DAY OF SALVATION"	**2Co 6:2**	*3568*
N in a like exchange	**2Co 6:13**	*1161*
I **n** rejoice, not that you were	**2Co 7:9**	*3568*
N, brethren, we *wish to* make known	**2Co 8:1**	*1161*
But **n** finish doing it also,	**2Co 8:11**	*3570*
things, but **n** even more diligent because	**2Co 8:22**	*3570*
N this *I say*, he who sows	**2Co 9:6**	*1161*
N He who supplies seed to the	**2Co 9:10**	*1161*
N I, Paul, myself urge you by the	**2Co 10:1**	*1161*
though **n** absent I say in advance	**2Co 13:2**	*3568*
N we pray to God that you do no	**2Co 13:7**	*1161*
said before, so I say again **n**,	**Ga 1:9**	*737*
am I **n** seeking the favor of men,	**Ga 1:10**	*737*
(**N** in what I am writing to you, I	**Ga 1:20**	*1161*
n preaching the faith which he once	**Ga 1:23**	*3568*
the *life* which I **n** live in the flesh	**Ga 2:20**	*3568*
n being perfected by the flesh?	**Ga 3:3**	*3568*
N that no one is justified by the	**Ga 3:11**	*1161*
N the promises were spoken to	**Ga 3:16**	*1161*
N a mediator is not for one *party*	**Ga 3:20**	*1161*
But **n** that faith has come, we are	**Ga 3:25**	*1161*
N I say, as long as the heir is a	**Ga 4:1**	*1161*
n that you have come to know God	**Ga 4:9**	*3568*
could wish to be present with you **n**	**Ga 4:20**	*737*
N this Hagar is Mount Sinai in	**Ga 4:25**	*3568*
to the Spirit, so it is **n** also.	**Ga 4:29**	*3568*
N the deeds of the flesh are evident,	**Ga 5:19**	*1161*
N those who belong to Christ Jesus	**Ga 5:24**	*1161*
From **n** on let no one cause trouble	**Ga 6:17**	*3062*
of the spirit that is **n** working in	**Eph 2:2**	*3568*
But **n** in Christ Jesus you who	**Eph 2:13**	*3570*
as it has **n** been revealed to His	**Eph 3:5**	*3568*
wisdom of God might **n** be made	**Eph 3:10**	*3568*
N to Him who is able to do	**Eph 3:20**	*1161*
(**N** this *expression*, "He ascended,"	**Eph 4:9**	*1161*
but **n** you are Light in the Lord;	**Eph 5:8**	*3568*
gospel from the first day until **n**.	**Php 1:5**	*3568*
N I want you to know, brethren,	**Php 1:12**	*1161*
all boldness, Christ will even **n**,	**Php 1:20**	*3568*
saw in me, and **n** hear *to be* in me.	**Php 1:30**	*3568*
but **n** much more in my absence,	**Php 2:12**	*3568*
you, and **n** tell you even weeping,	**Php 3:18**	*3568*
that **n** at last you have revived	**Php 4:10**	*2235*
N to our God and Father *be* the	**Php 4:20**	*1161*
yet He has **n** reconciled you in His	**Col 1:22**	*3570*
N I rejoice in my sufferings for	**Col 1:24**	*3568*
n been manifested to His saints,	**Col 1:26**	*3568*
having been firmly rooted *and* **n**	**Col 2:7**	
But **n** you also, put them all aside:	**Col 3:8**	*3570*
But **n** that Timothy has come to us	**1Th 3:6**	*737*
for **n** we *really* live, if you stand	**1Th 3:8**	*3568*
N may our God and Father Himself	**1Th 3:11**	*1161*
N as to the love of the brethren,	**1Th 4:9**	*1161*
N as to the times and the epochs,	**1Th 5:1**	*1161*
N may the God of peace Himself	**1Th 5:23**	*1161*
N we request you, brethren, with	**2Th 2:1**	*1161*
And you know what restrains him **n**,	**2Th 2:6**	*3568*
only he who **n** restrains *will do so*	**2Th 2:7**	*737*
N may our Lord Jesus Christ	**2Th 2:16**	*1161*
N we command you, brethren, in the	**2Th 3:6**	*1161*
N such persons we command and	**2Th 3:12**	*1161*
N may the Lord of peace Himself	**2Th 3:16**	*1161*
N to the King eternal, immortal,	**1Tm 1:17**	*1161*
N she who is a widow indeed and	**1Tm 5:5**	*1161*
but **n** has been revealed by the	**2Tm 1:10**	*3568*
N in a large house there are not	**2Tm 2:20**	*1161*
N flee from youthful lusts and	**2Tm 2:22**	*1161*
N you followed my teaching, conduct,	**2Tm 3:10**	
and **n** also a prisoner of Christ	**Phm 1:9**	*3570*
but **n** is useful both to you and to	**Phm 1:11**	*3570*
But **n** we do not yet see all things	**Heb 2:8**	*3568*
N Moses was faithful in all His	**Heb 3:5**	*2532*
N observe how great this man was	**Heb 7:4**	*1161*
N if perfection was through the	**Heb 7:11**	*3767*
N the main point in what has been	**Heb 8:1**	*1161*
N if He were on earth, He would	**Heb 8:4**	*3767*
But **n** He has obtained a more	**Heb 8:6**	*3568*
N even the first *covenant* had	**Heb 9:1**	*3767*
we cannot **n** speak in detail.	**Heb 9:5**	*3568*
N when these things have been so	**Heb 9:6**	*1161*
n to appear in the presence of God	**Heb 9:24**	*3568*
but **n** once at the consummation of	**Heb 9:26**	*3570*
N where there is forgiveness of	**Heb 10:18**	*1161*
N faith is the assurance of *things*	**Heb 11:1**	*1161*
earth then, but **n** He has promised,	**Heb 12:26**	*3568*
N the God of peace, who brought up	**Heb 13:20**	*1161*
N if you do not commit adultery,	**Jas 2:11**	*1161*
N if we put the bits into the	**Jas 3:3**	*1161*
Come **n**, you who say,	**Jas 4:13**	*3568*
Come **n**, you rich, weep and howl	**Jas 5:1**	*3568*
even though **n** for a little while,	**1Pe 1:6**	*737*
and though you do not see Him **n**,	**1Pe 1:8**	*737*
which **n** have been announced to	**1Pe 1:12**	*3568*
but **n** you are THE PEOPLE OF GOD;	**1Pe 2:10**	*3568*
but **n** you have RECEIVED MERCY.	**1Pe 2:10**	*3568*
but **n** you have returned to the	**1Pe 2:25**	*3568*
made proclamation to the spirits **n**	**1Pe 3:19**	
baptism **n** saves you	**1Pe 3:21**	*3568*
N for this very reason also,	**2Pe 1:5**	*1161*
This is **n**, beloved, the second letter	**2Pe 3:1**	*2235*
both **n** and to the day of eternity.	**2Pe 3:18**	*3568*
is in the darkness until **n**.	**1Jn 2:9**	*737*
n many antichrists have appeared;	**1Jn 2:18**	*3568*
N, little children, abide in Him,	**1Jn 2:28**	*3568*
Beloved, **n** we are children of God,	**1Jn 3:2**	*3568*
and **n** it is already in the world.	**1Jn 4:3**	*3568*
N I ask you, lady, not as though	**2Jn 1:5**	*3568*
N I desire to remind you, though	**Jude 1:5**	*1161*
N to Him who is able to keep you	**Jude 1:24**	*1161*
before all time and **n** and forever.	**Jude 1:25**	*3568*
"**N** the salvation, and the power,	**Rv 12:10**	*737*
who die in the Lord from **n** on!'"	**Rv 14:13**	*737*

NOWHERE
"Your servant went **n**." 2Ki 5:25 3808, 575
Son of Man has **n** to lay His head." Mt 8:20 *3756, 4226*
Son of Man has **n** to lay His head." Lk 9:58 *3756, 4226*

NULLIFIED
is made void and the promise is **n**; Ro 4:14 *2673*

NULLIFIES
LORD **n** the counsel of the nations; Ps 33:10 6565a

NULLIFY
not **n** the faithfulness of God, Ro 3:3 *2673*
we then **n** the Law through faith? Ro 3:31 *2673*
He may **n** the things that are, 1Co 1:28 *2673*
"I do not **n** the grace of God, Ga 2:21 *114*
by God, so as to **n** the promise. Ga 3:17 *2673*

NUMBER
can **n** the dust of the earth, Gn 13:16 4487
and my men being few in **n**, Gn 34:30 4557
loins of Jacob were seventy in **n**, Ex 1:5 5315
to the **n** of persons *in them;* Ex 12:4 4373
a very large **n** of livestock. Ex 12:38 3515
apiece according to the **n** of persons Ex 16:16 4557
I will fulfill the **n** of your days. Ex 23:26 4557
you shall make its lamps seven *in* **n**; Ex 25:37
of the sons of Israel to **n** them, Ex 30:12 6485
to the LORD, when you **n** them, Ex 30:12 6485
plague among them when you **n** them. Ex 30:12 6485
This is the **n** of the things for Ex 38:21 6491a
the **n** of years after the jubilee, Lv 25:15 4557
to the **n** of years of crops. Lv 25:15 4557
a **n** of crops he is selling to you. Lv 25:16 4557
correspond to the **n** of years. Lv 25:50 4557
destroy your cattle and reduce your **n** Lv 26:22
according to the **n** of names, Nu 1:2 4557
Aaron shall **n** them by their armies. Nu 1:3 6485
according to the **n** of names, Nu 1:18 4557
according to the **n** of names, Nu 1:20 4557
men, according to the **n** of names, Nu 1:22 4557
according to the **n** of names, Nu 1:24 4557
according to the **n** of names, Nu 1:26 4557
according to the **n** of names, Nu 1:28 4557
according to the **n** of names, Nu 1:30 4557
according to the **n** of names, Nu 1:32 4557
according to the **n** of names, Nu 1:34 4557
according to the **n** of names, Nu 1:36 4557
according to the **n** of names, Nu 1:38 4557
according to the **n** of names, Nu 1:40 4557
according to the **n** of names, Nu 1:42 4557
the tribe of Levi you shall not **n**, Nu 1:49 6485
"**N** the sons of Levi by their Nu 3:15 6485
old and upward you shall **n**." Nu 3:15 6485
"**N** every firstborn male of the Nu 3:40 6485
firstborn males by the **n** of names Nu 3:43 4557
fifty years old, you shall **n** them; Nu 4:23 6485
shall **n** them by their families, Nu 4:29 6485
fifty years old, you shall **n** them, Nu 4:30 6485
according to your complete **n** from Nu 14:29 4557
'According to the **n** of days which Nu 14:34 4557
to the **n** that you prepare, Nu 15:12 4557
for everyone according to their **n**. Nu 15:12 4557
Or **n** the fourth part of Israel? Nu 23:10 4557
according to the **n** of names. Nu 26:53 4557
n according to the ordinance; Nu 29:18 4557
n according to the ordinance; Nu 29:21 4557
n according to the ordinance; Nu 29:24 4557
n according to the ordinance; Nu 29:27 4557
n according to the ordinance; Nu 29:30 4557
n according to the ordinance; Nu 29:33 4557
n according to the ordinance; Nu 29:37 4557
the **n** of sheep was 337,500, Nu 31:36 4557
exceedingly large **n** of livestock. Nu 32:1 6099
day like the stars of heaven in **n**. Dt 1:10 7230
left few in **n** among the nations where Dt 4:27 4557
more in **n** than any of the peoples, Dt 7:7 7231
the **n** of stripes according to his guilt. Dt 25:2 4557
and sojourned there, few in **n**; Dt 26:5 4962
"Then you shall be left few in **n**, Dt 28:62 4962
to the **n** of the sons of Israel. Dt 32:8 4557
according to the **n** of the tribes Jos 4:5 4557
according to the **n** of the tribes Jos 4:8 4557
would come in like locusts for **n**, Jg 6:5 7230
Now the **n** of those who lapped, Jg 7:6 4557
and their camels were without **n**, Jg 7:12 4557
five men out of their whole **n**, Jg 18:2 7098
to their **n** from those who danced, Jg 21:23 4557
the **n** of the lords of the Philistines, 1Sa 6:4 4557
according to the **n** of all the cities 1Sa 6:18 4557
"**N** now and see who has gone from 1Sa 14:17 6485
gave them in full **n** to the king, 1Sa 18:27
The **n** of days that David lived 1Sa 27:7 4557
on each foot, twenty-four in **n**; 2Sa 21:20 4557
"Go, **n** Israel and Judah." 2Sa 24:1 4487
I may know the **n** of the people." 2Sa 24:2 4557
n of the registration of the people 2Sa 24:9 4557
in from Ophir a very great **n** *of* 1Ki 10:11
n of the tribes of the sons of Jacob, 1Ki 18:31 4557
tore up forty-two lads of their **n**. 2Ki 2:24
their **n** in the days of David was 1Ch 7:2 4557
the **n** of them enrolled by genealogy 1Ch 7:40 4557
When they were only a few in **n**, 1Ch 16:19 4557
and moved David to **n** Israel. 1Ch 21:1 4487
n Israel from Beersheba even to 1Ch 21:2 5608
me *word* that I may know their **n**." 1Ch 21:2 4557
Joab gave the **n** of the census 1Ch 21:5 4557
n Levi and Benjamin among them, 1Ch 21:6 6485
timbers of cedar logs beyond **n**, 1Ch 22:4 4557
n by census of men was 38,000. 1Ch 23:3 4557
in the **n** of names by their census, 1Ch 23:24 4557
festivals in the **n** *set* by the ordinance 1Ch 23:31 4557
and the **n** of those who performed 1Ch 25:1 4557
Their **n** who were trained in singing 1Ch 25:7 4557
capable men, *were* 2,700 in **n**, 1Ch 26:32
and the **n** was not included in the 1Ch 27:24 4557
him from Egypt were without **n**: 2Ch 12:3 4557
came with a small **n** of men; 2Ch 24:24
to the **n** of their muster, 2Ch 26:11 4557
The total **n** of the heads of the 2Ch 26:12 4557
from him a great **n** of captives and 2Ch 28:5
The **n** of the burnt offerings 2Ch 29:32 4557
and a large **n** of priests consecrated 2Ch 30:24 7230
weapons and shields in great **n**. 2Ch 32:5 7230
Now this *was* their **n**: Ezr 1:9 4557
n of the men of the people of Israel Ezr 2:2 4557
fixed **n** of burnt offerings daily, Ezr 3:4 4557
to the **n** of the tribes of Israel. Ezr 6:17 4510
The **n** of men of the people of Israel Ne 7:7 4557
his riches, and the **n** of his sons, Es 5:11 7230
n of those who were killed Es 9:11 4557
according to the **n** of them all; Jb 1:5 4557
not come into the **n** of the months. Jb 3:6 4557
things, Wonders without **n**. Jb 5:9 4557
And wondrous works without **n**. Jb 9:10 4557
The **n** of his months is with You; Jb 14:5 4557
"For now You **n** my steps, Jb 14:16 5608
the **n** of his months is cut off? Jb 21:21 4557
"Is there any **n** to His troops? Jb 25:3 4557
see my ways And **n** all my steps? Jb 31:4 5608
declare to Him the **n** of my steps; Jb 31:37 4557
n of His years is unsearchable. Jb 36:26 4557
And the **n** of your days is great! Jb 38:21 4557
evils beyond **n** have surrounded me; Ps 40:12 4557
So teach us to **n** our days, That we Ps 90:12 4487
In which are swarms without **n**, Ps 104:25 4557
they were only a few men in **n**, Ps 105:12 4557
And young locusts, even without **n**, Ps 105:34 4557
He counts the **n** of the stars; Ps 147:4 4557
concubines, And maidens without **n**; SS 6:8 4557
trees of his forest will be so small in **n** Is 10:19 4557
the remainder of the **n** of bowmen, Is 21:17 4557
who leads forth their host by **n**, Is 40:26 4557
For *according to* the **n** of your cities Jer 2:28 4557
have forgotten Me Days without **n**. Jer 2:32 4557
to the land of Judah few in **n**. Jer 44:28 4557
than locusts And are without **n**. Jer 46:23 4557
the **n** of days that you lie on it. Ezk 4:4 4557
"For I have assigned you a **n** of days Ezk 4:5 4557
eat it according to the **n** of the days Ezk 4:9 4557
"Take also a few in **n** from them Ezk 5:3 4557
which are four *in* **n**, are four Da 7:17
Daniel, observed in the books the **n** Da 9:2 4557
Yet the **n** of the sons of Israel Hos 1:10 4557
my land, Mighty and without **n**; Jl 1:6 4557
a great **n** of people heard of all that Mk 3:8 *4128*
after spending the full **n** of days, Lk 2:43 *5048*
belonging to the **n** of the twelve. Lk 22:3 *706*
down, in **n** about five thousand. Jn 6:10 *706*
in because of the great **n** of fish. Jn 21:6 *4128*
Lord was adding to their **n** day by day Ac 2:47 *846*
and the **n** of the men came to be Ac 4:4 *706*
were constantly added to *their* **n**, Ac 5:14
the disciples were increasing *in* **n**, Ac 6:1
the **n** of the disciples continued to Ac 6:7 *706*
and a large **n** who believed turned Ac 11:21 *706*
spoke in such a manner that a large **n** Ac 14:1 *4128*
some of our **n** to whom we gave no Ac 15:24 *1473*
and were increasing in **n** daily. Ac 16:5 *706*
along with a large **n** of Ac 17:4 *3756*
and a **n** of the leading women. Ac 17:4 *3756, 3641*
a **n** of prominent Greek women and Ac 17:12 *3756, 3641*
away a considerable **n** of people, Ac 19:26 *3793*
"THOUGH THE **N** OF THE SONS OF Ro 9:27 *706*
are weak and sick, and a **n** sleep. 1Co 11:30 *2425*
beaten times without **n**, 2Co 11:23 *5234*
who is one of your **n**. They will Col 4:9
Epaphras, who is one of your **n**, Col 4:12 *4771*
AS THE STARS OF HEAVEN IN **N**, Heb 11:12 *4128*
and the **n** of them was myriads of Rv 5:11 *706*
until *the* **n** *of* their fellow Rv 6:11
the **n** of those who were sealed, Rv 7:4 *706*
The **n** of the armies of the horsemen Rv 9:16 *706*
I heard the **n** of them. Rv 9:16 *706*
of the beast or the **n** of his name. Rv 13:17 *706*
calculate the **n** of the beast, Rv 13:18 *706*
beast, for the **n** is that of a man; Rv 13:18 *706*
his **n** is six hundred and sixty-six. Rv 13:18 *706*
image and the **n** of his name, Rv 15:2 *706*
the **n** of them is like the sand of Rv 20:8 *706*

NUMBERED
your descendants can also be **n**. Gn 13:16 4487
is too great to be **n**.'" Gn 32:12 5608
all his sons and his daughters **n** Gn 46:15
"What everyone who is **n** shall give: Ex 30:13 6485
"Everyone who is **n**, from twenty Ex 30:14 6485
as they were **n** according to the Ex 38:21 6485
those of the congregation who were **n** Ex 38:25 6485
passed over to those who were **n**, Ex 38:26 6485
So he **n** them in the wilderness of Nu 1:19 6485
their **n** men of the tribe of Nu 1:21 6485
fathers' households, their **n** men, Nu 1:22 6485
their **n** men of the tribe of Nu 1:23 6485
their **n** men of the tribe of Gad Nu 1:25 6485
their **n** men of the tribe of Nu 1:27 6485
their **n** men of the tribe of Nu 1:29 6485
their **n** men of the tribe of Nu 1:31 6485
their **n** men of the tribe of Nu 1:33 6485
their **n** men of the tribe of Nu 1:35 6485
their **n** men of the tribe of Nu 1:37 6485
their **n** men of the tribe of Dan Nu 1:39 6485
their **n** men of the tribe of Nu 1:41 6485
their **n** men of the tribe of Nu 1:43 6485
These are the ones who were **n**, Nu 1:44 6485
numbered, whom Moses and Aaron **n**, Nu 1:44 6485
all the **n** men of the sons of Israel Nu 1:45 6485
even all the **n** men were 603,550. Nu 1:46 6485
Levites, however, were not **n** among Nu 1:47 6485
and his army, even their **n** men, Nu 2:4 6485
and his army, even their **n** men, Nu 2:6 6485
and his army, even his **n** men, Nu 2:8 6485
of the **n** men of the camp of Judah: Nu 2:9 6485
and his army, even their **n** men, Nu 2:11 6485
and his army, even their **n** men, Nu 2:13 6485
and his army, even their **n** men, Nu 2:15 6485
the **n** men of the camp of Reuben: Nu 2:16 6485
and his army, even their **n** men, Nu 2:19 6485
and his army, even their **n** men, Nu 2:21 6485
and his army, even their **n** men, Nu 2:23 6485
the **n** men of the camp of Ephraim: Nu 2:24 6485
and his army, even their **n** men, Nu 2:26 6485
and his army, even their **n** men, Nu 2:28 6485
and his army, even their **n** men, Nu 2:30 6485
of the **n** men of the camp of Dan Nu 2:31 6485
are the **n** men of the sons of Israel Nu 2:32 6485
the total of the **n** men of the Nu 2:32 6485
not **n** among the sons of Israel, Nu 2:33 6485
So Moses **n** them according to the Nu 3:16 6485
Their **n** men, in the numbering of Nu 3:22 6485
even their **n** men *were* 7,500. Nu 3:22 6485
Their **n** men in the numbering of Nu 3:34 6485
All the **n** men of the Levites, whom Nu 3:39 6485
whom Moses and Aaron **n** at the Nu 3:39 6485
So Moses **n** all the firstborn Nu 3:42 6485
for their **n** men were 22,273. Nu 3:43 6485
n the sons of the Kohathites by their Nu 4:34 6485
Their **n** men by their families Nu 4:36 6485
n men of the Kohathite families, Nu 4:37 6485
whom Moses and Aaron **n** according Nu 4:37 6485
The **n** men of the sons of Gershon Nu 4:38 6485
Their **n** men by their families, Nu 4:40 6485
These are the **n** men of the Nu 4:41 6485
whom Moses and Aaron **n** according Nu 4:41 6485
The **n** men of the families of Nu 4:42 6485
Their **n** men by their families Nu 4:44 6485
These are the **n** men of the Nu 4:45 6485
whom Moses and Aaron **n** according Nu 4:45 6485
All the **n** men of the Levites, whom Nu 4:46 6485
Aaron and the leaders of Israel **n**, Nu 4:46 6485
Their **n** men were 8,580. Nu 4:48 6485
LORD through Moses, they were **n**, Nu 4:49 6485
thus *these were* his **n** men, Nu 4:49 6485
the ones who were over the **n** men). Nu 7:2 6485
wilderness, even all your **n** men, Nu 14:29 6485
who were **n** of them were 43,730. Nu 26:7 6485
to those who were **n** of them, Nu 26:18 6485
to those who were **n** of them, Nu 26:22 6485
to those who were **n** of them, Nu 26:25 6485
to those who were **n** of them, Nu 26:27 6485
who were **n** of them were 52,700. Nu 26:34 6485
to those who were **n** of them, Nu 26:37 6485
who were **n** of them were 45,600. Nu 26:41 6485
to those who were **n** of them, Nu 26:43 6485
to those who were **n** of them, Nu 26:47 6485
who were **n** of them were 45,400. Nu 26:50 6485
who were **n** of the sons of Israel, Nu 26:51 6485
to those who were **n** of them. Nu 26:54 6485
are those who were **n** of the Levites Nu 26:57 6485
who were **n** of them were 23,000, Nu 26:62 6485
for they were not **n** among the sons Nu 26:62 6485
n by Moses and Eleazar the priest, Nu 26:63 6485
who **n** the sons of Israel in the Nu 26:63 6485
n by Moses and Aaron the priest, Nu 26:64 6485
who **n** the sons of Israel in the Nu 26:64 6485
day the sons of Benjamin were **n**, Jg 20:15 6485
inhabitants of Gibeah who were **n**, Jg 20:15 6485
of Israel besides Benjamin were **n**, Jg 20:17 6485
For when the people were **n**, Jg 21:9 6485
He **n** them in Bezek; 1Sa 11:8 6485
And Saul **n** the people who were 1Sa 13:15 6485
And when they had **n**, behold, 1Sa 14:17 6485
the people and **n** them in Telaim, 1Sa 15:4 6485
Then David **n** the people who were 2Sa 18:1 6485
him after he had **n** the people. 2Sa 24:10 5608
people who are too many to be **n** 1Ki 3:8 4487
the forced laborers **n** 30,000 men. 1Ki 5:13 1961
and the pomegranates **n** two 1Ki 7:20
They could not be counted or **n**. 1Ki 8:5 4487
The Levites were **n** from thirty 1Ch 23:3 5608
of David the sons of Levi *were* **n** 1Ch 23:27 4557
Solomon **n** all the aliens who 2Ch 2:17 5608
they could not be counted or **n**. 2Ch 5:6 4487
of gold and silver **n** 5,400. Ezr 1:11
The whole assembly **n** 42,360, Ezr 2:64 259
and female servants who **n** 7,337; Ezr 2:65
Everything *was* **n** and weighed, and Ezr 8:34 4557
And **n** are the years stored up for Jb 15:20 4557
And was **n** with the transgressors; Is 53:12 4487
all the pomegranates **n** a hundred Jer 52:23
of the gate toward the east **n** Ezk 40:10
God has **n** your kingdom and put Da 5:26 4483
Which cannot be measured or **n**; Hos 1:10 5608
very hairs of your head are all **n**. Mt 10:30 *705*
He was **n** with transgressors." Mk 15:28 *3049*
very hairs of your head are all **n**. Lk 12:7 *705*

AND HE WAS **N** WITH TRANSGRESSORS Lk 22:37 *3049*

NUMBERING
in the **n** of every male from a Nu 3:22 4557
In the **n** of every male from a Nu 3:28 4557
men in the **n** of every male Nu 3:34 4557
each division **n** 24,000: 1Ch 27:1
n 30,000 plus 3,000 bulls; 2Ch 35:7 4557

NUMBERS
n of the divisions equipped for war, 1Ch 12:23 4557
away large **n** of sheep and camels. 2Ch 14:15 7230
themselves in sufficient **n**, 2Ch 30:3 1767
in great **n** as it was prescribed. 2Ch 30:5 7230
the hands of the one who **n** them,' Jer 33:13 4487
n were brought to the Lord. Ac 11:24 *3793*
church and taught considerable **n**; Ac 11:26 *3793*
to him at his lodging in large **n**; Ac 28:23 *4183*
one hand, existed in greater **n** because Heb 7:23 *4183*

NUMEROUS
were fruitful and became very **n**. Gn 47:27 7235a
I will make you fruitful and **n**, Gn 48:4 7235a
they were very **n**. Ex 10:14 3515
of the field become too **n** for you. Ex 23:29 7231
of the people, for they were **n**; Nu 22:3 7227a
more **n** and more distinguished than Nu 22:15 7227a
a people as great, **n**, and tall as the Dt 2:10 7227a
a people as great, **n**, and tall as the Dt 2:21 7227a
wild beasts would grow too **n** for you. Dt 7:22 7235a
you as **n** as the stars of heaven. Dt 10:22 7230
and people more **n** than you, Dt 20:1 7227a
whereas you were as **n** as the stars of Dt 28:62 7230
since I am a **n** people whom the Jos 17:14 7227a
"If you are a **n** people, go up to Jos 17:15 7227a
a **n** people and have great power; Jos 17:17 7227a
in the valley as **n** as locusts; Jg 7:12 7230
as **n** as the sand on the seashore. Jg 7:12 7230
Judah and Israel *were* as **n** as the 1Ki 4:20 7227a
and Mount Hermon they were **n**. 1Ch 5:23 7235a
as **n** as the dust of the earth. 2Ch 1:9 7227a
sons **n** as the stars of heaven, Ne 9:23 7235a
They would be too **n** to count. Ps 40:5 6105a
more **n** than the hairs of my head, Ps 40:12 6105a
down, And **n** are all her slain. Pr 7:26 6099
more **n** Than the sons of the married Is 54:1 7227a
are many, Their apostasies are **n**. Jer 5:6 6105a
"Their widows will be more **n** Jer 15:8 6105a
is great *And* your sins are **n**. Jer 30:14 6105a
is great *And* your sins are **n**, Jer 30:15 6105a
they are *now* more **n** than locusts Jer 46:23 7231
made you **n** like plants of the field. Ezk 16:7 7233
in your way, in your **n** warriors, Hos 10:13 7230
prophets, And I gave **n** visions, Hos 12:10 7235a
will be as **n** as they were before. Zch 10:8 7235a
FOR MORE **N** ARE THE CHILDREN OF Ga 4:27 *4183*

NUN
his servant Joshua, the son of **N**, Ex 33:11 5126
Then Joshua the son of **N**, Nu 11:28 5126
of Ephraim, Hoshea the son of **N**; Nu 13:8 5126
Moses called Hoshea the son of **N**, Nu 13:16 5126
Joshua the son of **N** and Caleb Nu 14:6 5126
Jephunneh and Joshua the son of **N**. Nu 14:30 5126
But Joshua the son of **N** and Caleb Nu 14:38 5126
and Joshua the son of **N**. Nu 26:65 5126
"Take Joshua the son of **N**, Nu 27:18 5126
Kenizzite and Joshua the son of **N**, Nu 32:12 5126
and to Joshua the son of **N**, Nu 32:28 5126
priest and Joshua the son of **N**. Nu 34:17 5126
'Joshua the son of **N**, Dt 1:38 5126
commissioned Joshua the son of **N**, Dt 31:23 5126
he, with Joshua the son of **N**. Dt 32:44 5126
Now Joshua the son of **N** was filled Dt 34:9 5126
LORD spoke to Joshua the son of **N**, Jos 1:1 5126
Then Joshua the son of **N** sent two Jos 2:1 5126
and came to Joshua the son of **N**, Jos 2:23 5126
So Joshua the son of **N** called the Jos 6:6 5126
priest, and Joshua the son of **N**, Jos 14:1 5126
and before Joshua the son of **N** and Jos 17:4 5126
midst to Joshua the son of **N**. Jos 19:49 5126
the priest, and Joshua the son of **N** Jos 19:51 5126
Joshua the son of **N**, and the heads Jos 21:1 5126
things that Joshua the son of **N**, Jos 24:29 5126
Then Joshua the son of **N**, Jg 2:8 5126
He spoke by Joshua the son of **N**. 1Ki 16:34 5126
Joshua the son of **N** to that day. Ne 8:17 5126

NURSE
that Sarah would **n** children? Gn 21:7 3243
away their sister Rebekah and her **n** Gn 24:59 3243
Now Deborah, Rebekah's **n**, died, Gn 35:8 3243
a **n** for you from the Hebrew women Ex 2:7 3243
she may **n** the child for you?" Ex 2:7 3243
"Take this child away and **n** him Ex 2:9 3243
as a **n** carries a nursing infant, Nu 11:12 539
him in her lap, and became his **n**. Ru 4:16 539
and his **n** took him up and fled. 2Sa 4:4 539
attend the king and become his **n**; 1Ki 1:2 5532a
became the king's **n** and served him, 1Ki 1:4 5532a
I rose in the morning to **n** my son, 1Ki 3:21 3243
him and his **n** in the bedroom. 2Ki 11:2 3243
him and his **n** in the bedroom. 2Ch 22:11 3243
That you may **n** and be satisfied Is 66:11 3243
the breast, They **n** their young; La 4:3 3243

NURSED
woman took the child and **n** him. Ex 2:9 5134
n her son until she weaned him. 1Sa 1:23 3243
to me Who **n** at my mother's breasts. SS 8:1 3243
And you will be **n**, Is 66:12 3243
and the breasts at which You **n**." Lk 11:27 *2337*
and the breasts that never **n**.' Lk 23:29 *5142*

NURSES
And their princesses your **n**. Is 49:23 3243

NURSING
herds which are **n** are a care to me. Gn 33:13 5763
as a nurse carries a **n** infant, Nu 11:12 3243
the mouth of infants and **n** babes Ps 8:2 3243
The **n** child will play by the Is 11:8 3243
He will gently lead the **n** *ewes*. Is 40:11 5763
"Can a woman forget her **n** child And Is 49:15 5764
the children and the **n** infants. Jl 2:16 3243, 7699a
OF THE MOUTH OF INFANTS AND **N** Mt 21:16 *2337*
are pregnant and to those who are **n** Mt 24:19 *2337*
are pregnant and to those who are **n** Mk 13:17 *2337*
are pregnant and to those who are **n** Lk 21:23 *2337*
as a **n** *mother* tenderly cares for 1Th 2:7 *5162*

NURSLING
The **n** with the man of gray hair. Dt 32:25 3243

NURTURED
and he was **n** three months in his Ac 7:20 *397*
away and **n** him as her own son. Ac 7:21 *397*

NUT
went down to the orchard of **n** trees SS 6:11 93

NUTS
myrrh, pistachio **n** and almonds. Gn 43:11 992

NYMPHA
who are in Laodicea and also **N** Col 4:15 *3564*

O

O
"**O** Lord GOD, what will You give Gn 15:2
"**O** Lord GOD, how may I know that Gn 15:8
"**O** LORD, the God of my master Gn 24:12
'**O** LORD, the God of my master Gn 24:42
me, *even* me also, **O** my father!" Gn 27:34
me, *even* me also, **O** my father." Gn 27:38
"**O** God of my father Abraham and Gn 32:9
God of my father Isaac, **O** LORD, Gn 32:9
and hear, **O** sons of Jacob; Gn 49:2
"For Your salvation I wait, **O** LORD. Gn 49:18
"**O** Lord, why have You brought Ex 5:22
"Your right hand, **O** LORD, is Ex 15:6
in power, Your right hand, **O** LORD, Ex 15:6
like You among the gods, **O** LORD? Ex 15:11
Your people pass over, **O** LORD, Ex 15:16
inheritance, The place, **O** LORD, Ex 15:17
dwelling, The sanctuary, **O** Lord, Ex 15:17
"This is your god, **O** Israel, Ex 32:4
'This is your god, **O** Israel, Ex 32:8
"**O** LORD, why does Your anger Ex 32:11
found favor in Your sight, **O** Lord, Ex 34:9
Moses said, "Rise up, **O** LORD! Nu 10:35
"**O** LORD, *To* the myriad thousands of Nu 10:36
"**O** God, heal her, I pray!" Nu 12:13
You, **O** LORD, are in the midst of Nu 14:14
You, **O** LORD, are seen eye to eye, Nu 14:14
"**O** God, God of the spirits Nu 16:22
"Spring up, **O** well! Nu 21:17
"Woe to you, **O** Moab! Nu 21:29
are ruined, **O** people of Chemosh! Nu 21:29
"Arise, **O** Balak, and hear; Nu 23:18
Give ear to me, **O** son of Zippor! Nu 23:18
How fair are your tents, **O** Jacob, Nu 24:5
O Jacob, Your dwellings, **O** Israel! Nu 24:5
'**O** Lord GOD, You have begun to Dt 3:24
"Now, **O** Israel, listen to the Dt 4:1
"Hear, **O** Israel, the statutes and Dt 5:1
"**O** Israel, you should listen and Dt 6:3
"Hear, **O** Israel! The LORD is our Dt 6:4
"Hear, **O** Israel! You are crossing Dt 9:1
'**O** Lord GOD, do not destroy Your Dt 9:26
'Hear, **O** Israel, you are Dt 20:3
whom You have redeemed, **O** LORD, Dt 21:8
which You, **O** LORD have given me.' Dt 26:10
"Be silent and listen, **O** Israel! Dt 27:9
"Give ear, **O** heavens, and let me Dt 32:1
LORD, **O** foolish and unwise people? Dt 32:6
"Rejoice, **O** nations, *with* His Dt 32:43
"Hear, **O** LORD, the voice of Dt 33:7
"**O** LORD, bless his substance, And Dt 33:11
"**O** Naphtali, satisfied with Dt 33:23
"Blessed are you, **O** Israel; Dt 33:29
"Alas, **O** Lord GOD, why did You Jos 7:7
"**O** Lord, what can I say since Jos 7:8 994a
the ban in your midst, **O** Israel. Jos 7:13
"**O** sun, stand still at Gibeon, Jos 10:12
O moon in the valley of Aijalon." Jos 10:12
secret message for you, **O** king." Jg 3:19
"Hear, **O** kings; give ear, O rulers! Jg 5:3
give ear, **O** rulers! Jg 5:3
your captives, **O** son of Abinoam. Jg 5:12
O my soul, march on with strength. Jg 5:21
All your enemies perish, **O** LORD; Jg 5:31
is with you, **O** valiant warrior." Jg 6:12
"**O** my lord, if the LORD is with Jg 6:13 994a
"**O** Lord, how shall I deliver Jg 6:15 994a
"Alas, **O** Lord GOD! Jg 6:22
"Listen to me, **O** men of Shechem, Jg 9:7
of Ephraim, **O** Gileadites, Jg 12:4
"**O** Lord, please let the man of Jg 13:8 994a
"**O** Lord GOD, please remember me Jg 16:28
me just this time, **O** God, Jg 16:28
"Why, **O** LORD, God of Israel, has Jg 21:3
"**O** LORD of hosts, if You will 1Sa 1:11
courage and be men, **O** Philistines, 1Sa 4:9
"By your life, **O** king, I do not 1Sa 17:55
"Hear now, **O** Benjamites! 1Sa 22:7
"**O** LORD God of Israel, Your 1Sa 23:10
O LORD God of Israel, I pray, tell 1Sa 23:11
"Now then, **O** king, come down 1Sa 23:20
"Your beauty, **O** Israel, is slain 2Sa 1:19
"**O** mountains of Gilboa, Let not 2Sa 1:21
"**O** daughters of Israel, weep over 2Sa 1:24
"Who am I, **O** Lord GOD, and what 2Sa 7:18
in Your eyes, **O** Lord GOD, 2Sa 7:19
is the custom of man, **O** Lord GOD. 2Sa 7:19
know Your servant, **O** Lord GOD! 2Sa 7:20
reason You are great, **O** Lord GOD; 2Sa 7:22
people forever, and You, **O** LORD, 2Sa 7:24
"Now therefore, **O** LORD God, the 2Sa 7:25
"For You, **O** LORD of hosts, the 2Sa 7:27
"Now, **O** Lord GOD, You are 2Sa 7:28
For You, **O** Lord GOD, have spoken; 2Sa 7:29
"**O** son of the king, why are you 2Sa 13:4
herself and said, "Help, **O** king." 2Sa 14:4
"**O** my lord, the king, the 2Sa 14:9
favor in your sight, **O** my lord, 2Sa 14:22
"**O** LORD, I pray, make the counsel 2Sa 15:31
'I will be your servant, **O** king; 2Sa 15:34
favor in your sight, **O** my lord, 2Sa 16:4
to do with you, **O** sons of Zeruiah? 2Sa 16:10
"**O** my son Absalom, my son, my son 2Sa 18:33
died instead of you, **O** Absalom, 2Sa 18:33
"**O** my son Absalom, O Absalom, my 2Sa 19:4
"O my son Absalom, **O** Absalom, 2Sa 19:4
to do with you, **O** sons of Zeruiah, 2Sa 19:22
"**O** my lord, the king, my servant 2Sa 19:26
Every man to his tents, **O** Israel!" 2Sa 20:1
"For You are my lamp, **O** LORD; 2Sa 22:29
will give thanks to You, **O** LORD, 2Sa 22:50
"Be it far from me, **O** LORD, 2Sa 23:17
But now, **O** LORD, please take away 2Sa 24:10
"Everything, **O** king, Araunah 2Sa 24:23
'Have you not, my lord, **O** king, 1Ki 1:13
"Now, **O** LORD my God, You 1Ki 3:7
"**O** LORD, the God of Israel, there 1Ki 8:23
"Now therefore, **O** LORD, the God 1Ki 8:25
"Now therefore, **O** God of Israel, 1Ki 8:26
his supplication, **O** LORD my God, 1Ki 8:28
forth from Egypt, **O** Lord GOD." 1Ki 8:53
To your tents, **O** Israel! 1Ki 12:16
behold your gods, **O** Israel, 1Ki 12:28
"**O** altar, altar, thus says the 1Ki 13:2
have to do with you, **O** man of God? 1Ki 17:18
"**O** LORD my God, have You also 1Ki 17:20
"**O** LORD my God, I pray You, let 1Ki 17:21
"**O** Baal, answer us." 1Ki 18:26
"**O** LORD, the God of Abraham, 1Ki 18:36
"Answer me, **O** LORD, answer me, 1Ki 18:37
people may know that You, **O** LORD, 1Ki 18:37
now, **O** LORD, take my life, for I 1Ki 19:4
to your word, my lord, **O** king; 1Ki 20:4
"Have you found me, **O** my enemy?" 1Ki 21:20
"**O** man of God, the king says, 2Ki 1:9
"**O** man of God, thus says the 2Ki 1:11
"**O** man of God, please let my life 2Ki 1:13
"No, my lord, **O** man of God, do 2Ki 4:16
"**O** man of God, there is death in 2Ki 4:40
"No, my lord, **O** king; 2Ki 6:12
"**O** LORD, I pray, open his eyes 2Ki 6:17
"**O** LORD, open the eyes of these 2Ki 6:20
"Help, my lord, **O** king!" 2Ki 6:26
"My lord, **O** king, this is the 2Ki 8:5
have a word for you, **O** captain." 2Ki 9:5
"For you, **O** captain." 2Ki 9:5
"*There is* treachery, **O** Ahaziah!" 2Ki 9:23
"**O** LORD, the God of Israel, who 2Ki 19:15
"Incline Your ear, **O** LORD, 2Ki 19:16
open Your eyes, **O** LORD, 2Ki 19:16
"Truly, **O** LORD, the kings of 2Ki 19:17
"Now, **O** LORD our God, I pray, 2Ki 19:19
may know that You alone, **O** LORD, 2Ki 19:19
"Remember now, **O** LORD, I beseech 2Ki 20:3 577
"*We* are yours, **O** David, And with 1Ch 12:18
And with you, **O** son of Jesse! 1Ch 12:18
O seed of Israel His servant, Sons 1Ch 16:13
LORD, **O** families of the peoples, 1Ch 16:28
O give thanks to the LORD, for *He* 1Ch 16:34
"Save us, **O** God of our salvation, 1Ch 16:35
"Who am I, **O** LORD God, and what 1Ch 17:16
small thing in Your eyes, **O** God; 1Ch 17:17
a man of high degree, **O** LORD God. 1Ch 17:17
"**O** LORD, for Your servant's sake, 1Ch 17:19
"**O** LORD, there is none like You, 1Ch 17:20
people forever, and You, **O** LORD, 1Ch 17:22
"Now, **O** LORD, let the word 1Ch 17:23
"For You, **O** my God, have 1Ch 17:25
"Now, **O** LORD, You are God, 1Ch 17:26
for You, **O** LORD, have blessed, 1Ch 17:27
O LORD my God, please let Your hand 1Ch 21:17
O LORD God of Israel our father, 1Ch 29:10
"Yours, **O** LORD, is the greatness 1Ch 29:11
Yours is the dominion, **O** LORD, 1Ch 29:11
"**O** LORD our God, all this 1Ch 29:16
"Since I know, **O** my God, that 1Ch 29:17
"**O** LORD, the God of Abraham, 1Ch 29:18
"Now, **O** LORD God, Your promise to 2Ch 1:9
"**O** LORD, the God of Israel, there 2Ch 6:14
"Now therefore, **O** LORD, the God 2Ch 6:16
"Now therefore, **O** LORD, the God 2Ch 6:17
his supplication, **O** LORD my God, 2Ch 6:19
"Now, **O** my God, I pray, let 2Ch 6:40
"Now therefore arise, **O** LORD God, 2Ch 6:41

let Your priests, O LORD God, 2Ch 6:41
"O LORD God, do not turn away the 2Ch 6:42
Every man to your tents, O Israel; 2Ch 10:16
O sons of Israel, do not fight 2Ch 13:12
so help us, O LORD our God, for we 2Ch 14:11
O LORD, You are our God; 2Ch 14:11
"O LORD, the God of our fathers, 2Ch 20:6
"Did You not, O our God, drive 2Ch 20:7
"O our God, will You not judge 2Ch 20:12
behalf, O Judah and Jerusalem.' 2Ch 20:17
O Judah and inhabitants of 2Ch 20:20
"O king, do not let the army of 2Ch 25:7
"Listen to me, O Levites. 2Ch 29:5
"O sons of Israel, return to the 2Ch 30:6
with each other, O King of Judah? 2Ch 35:21
"O my God, I am ashamed and Ezr 9:6
"O LORD God of Israel, You are Ezr 9:15
You, O LORD God of heaven, Ne 1:5
"O Lord, I beseech You, may Ne 1:11 577
Hear, O our God, how we are Ne 4:4
Remember me, O my God, for good, Ne 5:19
O *God,* strengthen my hands. Ne 6:9
Remember, O my God, Tobiah and Ne 6:14
O may Your glorious name be blessed Ne 9:5
Remember me for this, O my God, Ne 13:14
this also remember me, O my God, Ne 13:22
Remember them, O my God, because Ne 13:29
Remember me, O my God, for good. Ne 13:31
found favor in your sight, O king, Es 7:3
I done to You, O watcher of men? Jb 7:20
"O that you would be completely Jb 13:5 4310
"O earth, do not cover my blood, Jb 16:18
"O that a man might plead with Jb 16:21
"O you who tear yourself in your Jb 18:4
me, pity me, O you my friends, Jb 19:21
"Pay attention, O Job, listen to Jb 33:31
"Listen to this, O Job, Stand and Jb 37:14
Now therefore, O kings, show Ps 2:10
warning, O judges of the earth. Ps 2:10
O Lord, how my adversaries have Ps 3:1
But You, O LORD, are a shield Ps 3:3
Arise, O LORD; save me, O my God! Ps 3:7
save me, O my God! Ps 3:7
I call, O God of my righteousness! Ps 4:1
O sons of men, how long will my Ps 4:2
Your countenance upon us, O LORD! Ps 4:6
and sleep, For You alone, O LORD, Ps 4:8
Give ear to my words, O LORD, Ps 5:1
In the morning, O LORD, You will Ps 5:3
O LORD, lead me in Your Ps 5:8
Hold them guilty, O God; Ps 5:10
blesses the righteous man, O LORD, Ps 5:12
O Lord, do not rebuke me in Your Ps 6:1
Be gracious to me, O LORD, Ps 6:2
Heal me, O LORD, for my bones are Ps 6:2
But You, O LORD—how long? Ps 6:3
Return, O LORD, rescue my soul; Ps 6:4
O Lord my God, in You I have Ps 7:1
O LORD my God, if I have done Ps 7:3
Arise, O LORD, in Your anger; Ps 7:6
Vindicate me, O LORD, according to Ps 7:8
O let the evil of the wicked come Ps 7:9 4994
O LORD, our Lord, How majestic is Ps 8:1
O LORD, our Lord, How majestic is Ps 8:9
praise to Your name, O Most High. Ps 9:2
For You, O LORD, have not Ps 9:10
Be gracious to me, O LORD; Ps 9:13
Arise, O LORD, do not let man Ps 9:19
Put them in fear, O LORD; Ps 9:20
do You stand afar off, O LORD? Ps 10:1
Arise, O LORD; O God, lift up Your Ps 10:12
O God, lift up Your hand. Ps 10:12
O LORD, You have heard the desire Ps 10:17
You, O LORD, will keep them; Ps 12:7
How long, O LORD? Ps 13:1
Consider *and* answer me, O LORD my Ps 13:3
O Lord, who may abide in Your tent? Ps 15:1
Preserve me, O God, for I take Ps 16:1
Hear a just cause, O LORD, Ps 17:1
for You will answer me, O God; Ps 17:6
O Savior of those who take refuge Ps 17:7
Arise, O LORD, confront him, bring Ps 17:13
From men with Your hand, O LORD, Ps 17:14
"I love You, O LORD, my strength." Ps 18:1
laid bare At Your rebuke, O LORD, Ps 18:15
to You among the nations, O LORD, Ps 18:49
acceptable in Your sight, O LORD, Ps 19:14
Save, O LORD; May the King Ps 20:9
O LORD, in Your strength the king Ps 21:1
Be exalted, O LORD, Ps 21:13
O my God, I cry by day, but You Ps 22:2
O You who are enthroned upon the Ps 22:3
But You, O LORD, be not far off; Ps 22:19
O You my help, hasten to my Ps 22:19
Lift up your heads, O gates, Ps 24:7
And be lifted up, O ancient doors, Ps 24:7
Lift up your heads, O gates, Ps 24:9
And lift *them* up, O ancient doors, Ps 24:9
To You, O LORD, I lift up my soul. Ps 25:1
O my God, in You I trust, Do not Ps 25:2
Make me know Your ways, O LORD; Ps 25:4
Remember, O LORD, Your compassion Ps 25:6
me, For Your goodness' sake, O LORD. Ps 25:7
For Your name's sake, O LORD, Ps 25:11
Redeem Israel, O God, Out of all Ps 25:22
Vindicate me, O LORD, for I have Ps 26:1
Examine me, O LORD, and try me; Ps 26:2
will go about Your altar, O LORD, Ps 26:6
O LORD, I love the habitation of Ps 26:8

Hear, O LORD, when I cry with my Ps 27:7
"Your face, O LORD, I shall seek." Ps 27:8
forsake me, O God of my salvation! Ps 27:9
Teach me Your way, O LORD, Ps 27:11
To You, O LORD, I call; Ps 28:1
to the LORD, O sons of the mighty, Ps 29:1
I will extol You, O LORD, Ps 30:1
O LORD my God, I cried to You for Ps 30:2
O LORD, You have brought up my Ps 30:3
O LORD, by Your favor You have Ps 30:7
To You, O LORD, I called, And to Ps 30:8
"Hear, O LORD, and be gracious to Ps 30:10
O LORD, be my helper." Ps 30:10
O LORD my God, I will give thanks Ps 30:12
In You, O LORD, I have taken Ps 31:1
You have ransomed me, O LORD, Ps 31:5
Be gracious to me, O LORD, Ps 31:9
for me, I trust in You, O LORD, Ps 31:14
me not be put to shame, O LORD, Ps 31:17
O love the LORD, all you His godly Ps 31:23
in the LORD, O you righteous ones; Ps 33:1
Let Your lovingkindness, O LORD, Ps 33:22
O magnify the LORD with me, And Ps 34:3
O taste and see that the LORD is Ps 34:8
O fear the LORD, you His saints; Ps 34:9
Contend, O LORD, with those who Ps 35:1
You have seen it, O LORD, Ps 35:22
O Lord, do not be far from me. Ps 35:22
Judge me, O LORD my God, according Ps 35:24
Your lovingkindness, O LORD, Ps 36:5
O LORD, You preserve man and Ps 36:6
is Your lovingkindness, O God! Ps 36:7
O continue Your lovingkindness to Ps 36:10
O Lord, rebuke me not in Your wrath, Ps 38:1
For I hope in You, O LORD; Ps 38:15
You will answer, O Lord my God. Ps 38:15
Do not forsake me, O LORD; Ps 38:21
O my God, do not be far from me! Ps 38:21
Make haste to help me, O Lord, Ps 38:22
"Hear my prayer, O LORD, and give Ps 39:12
Many, O LORD my God, are the Ps 40:5
delight to do Your will, O my God; Ps 40:8
will not restrain my lips, O LORD, Ps 40:9
You, O LORD, will not withhold Ps 40:11
Be pleased, O LORD, to deliver me; Ps 40:13
Make haste, O LORD, to help me. Ps 40:13
Do not delay, O my God. Ps 40:17
"O LORD, be gracious to me; Ps 41:4
But You, O LORD, be gracious to Ps 41:10
So my soul pants for You, O God. Ps 42:1
Why are you in despair, O my soul? Ps 42:5
O my God, my soul is in despair Ps 42:6
Why are you in despair, O my soul? Ps 42:11
Vindicate me, O God, and plead my Ps 43:1
O deliver me from the deceitful Ps 43:1
O send out Your light and Your Ps 43:3
lyre I shall praise You, O God, Ps 43:4
Why are you in despair, O my soul? Ps 43:5
O God, we have heard with our Ps 44:1
You are my King, O God; Ps 44:4
why do You sleep, O Lord? Ps 44:23
sword on *Your* thigh, O Mighty One, Ps 45:3
Your throne, O God, is forever and Ps 45:6
Listen, O daughter, give attention Ps 45:10
O clap your hands, all peoples; Ps 47:1
on Your lovingkindness, O God, Ps 48:9
As is Your name, O God, So is Your Ps 48:10
"Hear, O My people, and I will Ps 50:7
O Israel, I will testify against Ps 50:7
Be gracious to me, O God, Ps 51:1
Create in me a clean heart, O God, Ps 51:10
me from bloodguiltiness, O God, Ps 51:14
O Lord, open my lips, That my Ps 51:15
and a contrite heart, O God, Ps 51:17
you boast in evil, O mighty man? Ps 52:1
a sharp razor, O worker of deceit. Ps 52:2
that devour, O deceitful tongue. Ps 52:4
Save me, O God, by Your name, And Ps 54:1
Hear my prayer, O God; Ps 54:2
give thanks to Your name, O LORD, Ps 54:6
Give ear to my prayer, O God; Ps 55:1
Confuse, O Lord, divide their Ps 55:9
But You, O God, will bring them Ps 55:23
Be gracious to me, O God, for man has Ps 56:1
anger put down the peoples, O God! Ps 56:7
vows are *binding* upon me, O God; Ps 56:12
Be gracious to me, O God, Ps 57:1
exalted above the heavens, O God; Ps 57:5
My heart is steadfast, O God, Ps 57:7
will give thanks to You, O Lord, Ps 57:9
exalted above the heavens, O God; Ps 57:11
speak righteousness, O gods? Ps 58:1
judge uprightly, O sons of men? Ps 58:1
O God, shatter their teeth in Ps 58:6
fangs of the young lions, O LORD. Ps 58:6
me from my enemies, O my God; Ps 59:1
nor for my sin, O LORD, Ps 59:3
You, O LORD God of hosts, the Ps 59:5
But You, O LORD, laugh at Ps 59:8
and bring them down, O Lord, Ps 59:11
O my strength, I will sing praises Ps 59:17
O God, You have rejected us. Ps 60:1
You have been angry; O, restore us. Ps 60:1
Shout loud, O Philistia, because Ps 60:8
Have not You Yourself, O God, Ps 60:10
go forth with our armies, O God? Ps 60:10
O give us help against the Ps 60:11
Hear my cry, O God; Ps 61:1
You have heard my vows, O God; Ps 61:5

Trust in Him at all times, O people; Ps 62:8
lovingkindness is Yours, O Lord, Ps 62:12
O God, You are my God; Ps 63:1
Hear my voice, O God, in my Ps 64:1
You, *and* praise in Zion, O God, Ps 65:1
O You who hear prayer, To Ps 65:2
O God of our salvation, Ps 65:5
Bless our God, O peoples, And Ps 66:8
For You have tried us, O God; Ps 66:10
the peoples praise You, O God; Ps 67:3
the peoples praise You, O God; Ps 67:5
O God, when You went forth Ps 68:7
abroad a plentiful rain, O God; Ps 68:9
Your goodness for the poor, O God. Ps 68:10
envy, O mountains with *many* peaks, Ps 68:16
have seen Your procession, O God, Ps 68:24
Show Yourself strong, O God, Ps 68:28
to God, O kingdoms of the earth, Ps 68:32
O God, *You are* awesome from Your Ps 68:35
Save me, O God, For the waters Ps 69:1
O God, it is You who knows my Ps 69:5
through me, O Lord GOD of hosts; Ps 69:6
through me, O God of Israel, Ps 69:6
me, my prayer is to You, O LORD, Ps 69:13
O God, in the greatness of Your Ps 69:13
Answer me, O LORD, for Your Ps 69:16
May Your salvation, O God, Ps 69:29
O God, *hasten* to deliver me; Ps 70:1
O LORD, hasten to my help! Ps 70:1
Hasten to me, O God! Ps 70:5
O LORD, do not delay. Ps 70:5
In You, O LORD, I have taken Ps 71:1
Rescue me, O my God, out of the Ps 71:4
O Lord GOD, *You are* my confidence Ps 71:5
O God, do not be far from me; Ps 71:12
O my God, hasten to my help! Ps 71:12
O God, You have taught me from Ps 71:17
when *I am* old and gray, O God, Ps 71:18
For Your righteousness, O God, Ps 71:19
O God, who is like You? Ps 71:19
a harp, *Even* Your truth, O my God; Ps 71:22
lyre, O Holy One of Israel. Ps 71:22
the king Your judgments, O God, Ps 72:1
a dream when one awakes, O Lord, Ps 73:20
O God, why have You rejected *us* Ps 74:1
How long, O God, will the Ps 74:10
Remember this, O LORD, that the Ps 74:18
Arise, O God, *and* plead Your Ps 74:22
We give thanks to You, O God, Ps 75:1
At Your rebuke, O God of Jacob, Ps 76:6
Your way, O God, is holy; Ps 77:13
The waters saw You, O God; Ps 77:16
Listen, O my people, to my Ps 78:1
O God, the nations have invaded Ps 79:1
How long, O LORD? Ps 79:5
Help us, O God of our salvation, Ps 79:9
they have reproached You, O Lord. Ps 79:12
O God, restore us And cause Your Ps 80:3
O LORD God *of* hosts, How long will Ps 80:4
O God *of* hosts, restore us And Ps 80:7
O God *of* hosts, turn again now, we Ps 80:14
O LORD God of hosts, restore us; Ps 80:19
"Hear, O My people, and I will Ps 81:8
O Israel, if you would listen to Ps 81:8
Arise, O God, judge the earth! Ps 82:8
O God, do not remain quiet; Ps 83:1
Do not be silent and, O God, Ps 83:1
O my God, make them like the Ps 83:13
they may seek Your name, O LORD. Ps 83:16
dwelling places, O LORD of hosts! Ps 84:1
Your altars, O LORD of hosts, Ps 84:3
O LORD God of hosts, hear my Ps 84:8
Give ear, O God of Jacob! Ps 84:8
Behold our shield, O God, Ps 84:9
O LORD of hosts, How blessed is Ps 84:12
O Lord, You showed favor to Ps 85:1
us, O God of our salvation, Ps 85:4
us Your lovingkindness, O LORD, Ps 85:7
Incline Your ear, O LORD, Ps 86:1
O You my God, save Your servant Ps 86:2
Be gracious to me, O Lord, Ps 86:3
to You, O Lord, I lift up my soul Ps 86:4
Give ear, O LORD, to my prayer; Ps 86:6
like You among the gods, O Lord, Ps 86:8
and worship before You, O Lord, Ps 86:9
Teach me Your way, O LORD; Ps 86:11
thanks to You, O Lord my God, Ps 86:12
O God, arrogant men have risen up Ps 86:14
But You, O Lord, are a God Ps 86:15
You, O LORD, have helped me Ps 86:17
are spoken of you, O city of God. Ps 87:3
O Lord, the God of my salvation, I Ps 88:1
upon You every day, O LORD; Ps 88:9
But I, O LORD, have cried out to Ps 88:13
O LORD, why do You reject my Ps 88:14
will praise Your wonders, O LORD; Ps 89:5
O LORD God of hosts, who is like Ps 89:8
who is like You, O mighty LORD? Ps 89:8
O LORD, they walk in the light of Ps 89:15
How long, O LORD? Ps 89:46
former lovingkindnesses, O Lord, Ps 89:49
Remember, O Lord, the reproach of Ps 89:50
enemies have reproached, O LORD, Ps 89:51
"Return, O children of men." Ps 90:3
Do return, O LORD; Ps 90:13
O satisfy us in the morning with Ps 90:14
praises to Your name, O Most High; Ps 92:1
For You, O LORD, have made me Ps 92:4
How great are Your works, O LORD! Ps 92:5

But You, O LORD, are on high	Ps 92:8	
behold, Your enemies, O LORD,	Ps 92:9	
The floods have lifted up, O LORD,	Ps 93:3	
Holiness befits Your house, O LORD,	Ps 93:5	
O Lord, God of vengeance,	Ps 94:1	
Rise up, O Judge of the earth,	Ps 94:2	
How long shall the wicked, O LORD,	Ps 94:3	
They crush Your people, O LORD,	Ps 94:5	
whom You chasten, O LORD,	Ps 94:12	
Your lovingkindness, O LORD,	Ps 94:18	
O come, let us sing for joy to the	Ps 95:1	
LORD, O families of the peoples,	Ps 96:7	
Because of Your judgments, O LORD.	Ps 97:8	
O sing to the LORD a new song, For	Ps 98:1	
O LORD our God, You answered	Ps 99:8	
and justice, To You, O LORD,	Ps 101:1	
Hear my prayer, O LORD!	Ps 102:1	
But You, O LORD, abide	Ps 102:12	
"O my God, do not take me away in	Ps 102:24	
Bless the LORD, O my soul,	Ps 103:1	
Bless the LORD, O my soul, And	Ps 103:2	
Bless the LORD, O my soul!	Ps 103:22	
Bless the LORD, O my soul!	Ps 104:1	
O LORD my God, You are very great;	Ps 104:1	
O LORD, how many are Your works!	Ps 104:24	
Bless the LORD, O my soul.	Ps 104:35	
O seed of Abraham, His servant, O	Ps 105:6	
His servant, O sons of Jacob,	Ps 105:6	
Remember me, O LORD, in *Your* favor	Ps 106:4	
Save us, O LORD our God, And	Ps 106:47	
My heart is steadfast, O God;	Ps 108:1	
will give thanks to You, O LORD,	Ps 108:3	
Be exalted, O God, above the	Ps 108:5	
Have not You Yourself, O God,	Ps 108:11	
go forth with our armies, O God?	Ps 108:11	
O God of my praise, Do not be	Ps 109:1	
But You, O GOD, the Lord, deal	Ps 109:21	
Help me, O LORD my God;	Ps 109:26	
Praise, O servants of the LORD,	Ps 113:1	
What ails you, O sea, that you	Ps 114:5	
O Jordan, that you turn back?	Ps 114:5	
O mountains, that you skip like	Ps 114:6	
O hills, like lambs?	Ps 114:6	
Tremble, O earth, before the Lord,	Ps 114:7	
Not to us, O LORD, not to us, But	Ps 115:1	
O Israel, trust in the LORD;	Ps 115:9	
O house of Aaron, trust in the	Ps 115:10	
"O LORD, I beseech You, save my	Ps 116:4	
Return to your rest, O my soul,	Ps 116:7	
O LORD, surely I am Your servant, I	Ps 116:16	577
In the midst of you, O Jerusalem.	Ps 116:19	
O LORD, do save, we beseech You;	Ps 118:25	577
O LORD, we beseech You, do send	Ps 118:25	577
Blessed are You, O LORD;	Ps 119:12	
O LORD, do not put me to shame!	Ps 119:31	
Teach me, O LORD, the way of Your	Ps 119:33	
also come to me, O LORD,	Ps 119:41	
ordinances from of old, O LORD,	Ps 119:52	
O LORD, I remember Your name in	Ps 119:55	
of Your lovingkindness, O LORD;	Ps 119:64	
well with Your servant, O LORD,	Ps 119:65	
I know, O LORD, that Your judgments	Ps 119:75	
O may Your lovingkindness comfort	Ps 119:76	4994
Forever, O LORD, Your word is	Ps 119:89	
O how I love Your law!	Ps 119:97	
Revive me, O LORD, according to	Ps 119:107	
O accept the freewill offerings of	Ps 119:108	4994
offerings of my mouth, O LORD,	Ps 119:108	
Righteous are You, O LORD,	Ps 119:137	
answer me, O LORD!	Ps 119:145	
Revive me, O LORD, according to	Ps 119:149	
You are near, O LORD, And all Your	Ps 119:151	
Great are Your mercies, O LORD;	Ps 119:156	
Revive me, O LORD, according to	Ps 119:159	
I hope for Your salvation, O LORD,	Ps 119:166	
my cry come before You, O LORD;	Ps 119:169	
I long for Your salvation, O LORD,	Ps 119:174	
Deliver my soul, O LORD,	Ps 120:2	
Within your gates, O Jerusalem,	Ps 122:2	
O You who are enthroned in the	Ps 123:1	
Be gracious to us, O LORD,	Ps 123:3	
Do good, O LORD, to those who are	Ps 125:4	
Restore our captivity, O LORD,	Ps 126:4	
I have cried to You, O LORD.	Ps 130:1	
should mark iniquities, O Lord,	Ps 130:3	
O Israel, hope in the LORD;	Ps 130:7	
O Lord, my heart is not proud, nor	Ps 131:1	
O Israel, hope in the LORD From	Ps 131:3	
Remember, O LORD, on David's	Ps 132:1	
Arise, O LORD, to Your resting	Ps 132:8	
Him, O servants of the LORD,	Ps 135:1	
wonders into your midst, O Egypt,	Ps 135:9	
Your name, O LORD, is everlasting,	Ps 135:13	
Your remembrance, O LORD,	Ps 135:13	
O house of Israel, bless the LORD;	Ps 135:19	
O house of Aaron, bless the LORD;	Ps 135:19	
O house of Levi, bless the LORD;	Ps 135:20	
If I forget you, O Jerusalem,	Ps 137:5	
Remember, O LORD, against the sons	Ps 137:7	
O daughter of Babylon, you	Ps 137:8	
will give thanks to You, O LORD,	Ps 138:4	
Your lovingkindness, O LORD,	Ps 138:8	
O Lord, You have searched me and	Ps 139:1	
word on my tongue, Behold, O LORD,	Ps 139:4	
are Your thoughts to me, O God!	Ps 139:17	
O that You would slay the	Ps 139:19	518
would slay the wicked, O God;	Ps 139:19	
hate those who hate You, O LORD?	Ps 139:21	
Search me, O God, and know my	Ps 139:23	

Rescue me, O LORD, from evil men;	Ps 140:1	
Keep me, O LORD, from the hands of	Ps 140:4	
Give ear, O LORD, to the voice of	Ps 140:6	
"O GOD the Lord, the strength of	Ps 140:7	
"Do not grant, O LORD, the	Ps 140:8	
O Lord, I call upon You;	Ps 141:1	
Set a guard, O LORD, over my mouth;	Ps 141:3	
my eyes are toward You, O GOD,	Ps 141:8	
I cried out to You, O LORD;	Ps 142:5	
Hear my prayer, O LORD, Give ear	Ps 143:1	
Answer me quickly, O LORD,	Ps 143:7	
Deliver me, O LORD, from my	Ps 143:9	
For the sake of Your name, O LORD,	Ps 143:11	
O LORD, what is man, that You	Ps 144:3	
Bow Your heavens, O LORD,	Ps 144:5	
sing a new song to You, O God;	Ps 144:9	
I will extol You, my God, O King,	Ps 145:1	
shall give thanks to You, O LORD,	Ps 145:10	
Praise the LORD, O my soul!	Ps 146:1	
reign forever, Your God, O Zion,	Ps 146:10	
Praise the LORD, O Jerusalem!	Ps 147:12	
Praise your God, O Zion!	Ps 147:12	
"How long, O naive ones, will you	Pr 1:22	
Hear, O sons, the instruction	Pr 4:1	
Go to the ant, O sluggard, Observe	Pr 6:6	
will you lie down, O sluggard?	Pr 6:9	
"To you, O men, I call, And my	Pr 8:4	
"O naive ones, understand prudence;	Pr 8:5	
And, O fools, understand wisdom.	Pr 8:5	
"Now therefore, O sons, listen	Pr 8:32	
Do not lie in wait, O wicked man,	Pr 24:15	
What, O my son? And what, O son	Pr 31:2	
And what, O son of my womb?	Pr 31:2	
And what, O son of my vows?	Pr 31:2	
It is not for kings, O Lemuel,	Pr 31:4	
Woe to you, O land, whose king is	Ec 10:16	
Blessed are you, O land,	Ec 10:17	
lovely, O daughters of Jerusalem,	SS 1:5	
Tell me, O you whom my soul loves	SS 1:7	
you, O daughters of Jerusalem,	SS 2:7	
"O my dove, in the clefts of the	SS 2:14	
you, O daughters of Jerusalem,	SS 3:5	
"Go forth, O daughters of Zion,	SS 3:11	
"Awake, O north *wind,* And come,	SS 4:16	
and imbibe deeply, O lovers."	SS 5:1	
you, O daughters of Jerusalem,	SS 5:8	
O most beautiful among women?	SS 5:9	
O daughters of Jerusalem."	SS 5:16	
O most beautiful among women?	SS 6:1	
back, come back, O Shulammite;	SS 6:13	
in sandals, O prince's daughter!	SS 7:1	
swear, O daughters of Jerusalem,	SS 8:4	
"O you who sit in the gardens, *My*	SS 8:13	
Listen, O heavens, and hear, O	Is 1:2	
O heavens, and hear, O earth;	Is 1:2	
O My people! Their oppressors are	Is 3:12	
O My people! Those who guide you	Is 3:12	
O inhabitants of Jerusalem and men	Is 5:3	
"Listen now, O house of David!	Is 7:13	
breadth of your land, O Immanuel.	Is 8:8	
"Be broken, O peoples, and be	Is 8:9	
For though your people, O Israel,	Is 10:22	
"O My people who dwell in Zion,	Is 10:24	
your voice, O daughter of Gallim!	Is 10:30	
will give thanks to You, O LORD;	Is 12:1	
for joy, O inhabitant of Zion,	Is 12:6	
heaven, O star of the morning,	Is 14:12	
"Do not rejoice, O Philistia, all	Is 14:29	
"Wail, O gate; cry, O city;	Is 14:31	
cry, O city; Melt away, O Philistia,	Is 14:31	
Melt away, O Philistia, all of you;	Is 14:31	
my tears, O Heshbon and Elealeh;	Is 16:9	
"O Lord, I stand continually by	Is 21:8	
O my threshed *people,* and my	Is 21:10	
night, O caravans of Dedanites.	Is 21:13	
O inhabitants of the land of Tema,	Is 21:14	
about to hurl you headlong, O man.	Is 22:17	
Wail, O ships of Tarshish, For	Is 23:1	
Be ashamed, O Sidon;	Is 23:4	
O inhabitants of the coastland.	Is 23:6	
the Nile, O daughter of Tarshish,	Is 23:10	
O crushed virgin daughter of Sidon.	Is 23:12	
Wail, O ships of Tarshish, For	Is 23:14	
the city, O forgotten harlot;	Is 23:16	
you, O inhabitant of the earth.	Is 24:17	
O Lord, You are my God;	Is 25:1	
O Upright One, make the path of	Is 26:7	
the way of Your judgments, O LORD,	Is 26:8	
O LORD, Your hand is lifted up *yet*	Is 26:11	
O LORD our God, other masters	Is 26:13	
have increased the nation, O LORD,	Is 26:15	
O LORD, they sought You in	Is 26:16	
Thus were we before You, O LORD.	Is 26:17	
up one by one, O sons of Israel.	Is 27:12	
the word of the LORD, O scoffers,	Is 28:14	
Woe, O Ariel, Ariel the city *where*	Is 29:1	
O people in Zion, inhabitant in	Is 30:19	
deeply defected, O sons of Israel.	Is 31:6	
troubled, O complacent *daughters;*	Is 32:10	
Woe to you, O destroyer, While you	Is 33:1	
O LORD, be gracious to us;	Is 33:2	
Draw near, O nations, to hear;	Is 34:1	
and listen, O peoples!	Is 34:1	
"O LORD of hosts, the God of	Is 37:16	
"Incline Your ear, O LORD,	Is 37:17	
open Your eyes, O LORD,	Is 37:17	
"Truly, O LORD, the kings of	Is 37:18	
"Now, O LORD our God, deliver	Is 37:20	
"Remember now, O LORD, I beseech	Is 38:3	577

O Lord, I am oppressed, be my	Is 38:14
"O Lord, by *these* things *men* live,	Is 38:16
O restore me to health and let me	Is 38:16
"Comfort, O comfort My people,"	Is 40:1
up on a high mountain, O Zion,	Is 40:9
your voice mightily, O Jerusalem,	Is 40:9
Why do you say, O Jacob, and	Is 40:27
O Jacob, and assert, O Israel,	Is 40:27
the LORD, your Creator, O Jacob,	Is 43:1
And He who formed you, O Israel,	Is 43:1
have not called on Me, O Jacob;	Is 43:22
have become weary of Me, O Israel.	Is 43:22
"But now listen, O Jacob, My	Is 44:1
'Do not fear, O Jacob My servant;	Is 44:2
"Remember these things, O Jacob,	Is 44:21
you, you are My servant, O Israel,	Is 44:21
Shout for joy, O heavens, for the	Is 44:23
O forest, and every tree in it;	Is 44:23
"Drip down, O heavens, from	Is 45:8
hides Himself, O God of Israel,	Is 45:15
"Listen to Me, O house of Jacob,	Is 46:3
O virgin daughter of Babylon;	Is 47:1
O daughter of the Chaldeans!	Is 47:1
O daughter of the Chaldeans,	Is 47:5
"Hear this, O house of Jacob, who	Is 48:1
"Listen to Me, O Jacob, even	Is 48:12
Listen to Me, O islands, And pay	Is 49:1
Shout for joy, O heavens!	Is 49:13
And rejoice, O earth!	Is 49:13
into joyful shouting, O mountains!	Is 49:13
"Pay attention to Me, O My people,	Is 51:4
And give ear to Me, O My nation;	Is 51:4
on strength, O arm of the LORD;	Is 51:9
Arise, O Jerusalem, You who have	Is 51:17
yourself in your strength, O Zion;	Is 52:1
beautiful garments, O Jerusalem,	Is 52:1
rise up, O captive Jerusalem;	Is 52:2
neck, O captive daughter of Zion.	Is 52:2
"Shout for joy, O barren one, you	Is 54:1
"O afflicted one, storm-tossed,	Is 54:11
On your walls, O Jerusalem, I have	Is 62:6
You, O LORD, are our Father, Our	Is 63:16
Why, O LORD, do You cause us to	Is 63:17
But now, O LORD, You are our	Is 64:8
be angry beyond measure, O LORD,	Is 64:9
Yourself at these things, O LORD?	Is 64:12
of the LORD, O house of Jacob,	Jer 2:4
"Be appalled, O heavens, at this,	Jer 2:12
cities Are your gods, O Judah.	Jer 2:28
"O generation, heed the word of	Jer 2:31
'Return, O faithless sons,'	Jer 3:14
with Me, O house of Israel,"	Jer 3:20
"Return, O faithless sons, I will	Jer 3:22
"If you will return, O Israel,"	Jer 4:1
your heart from evil, O Jerusalem,	Jer 4:14
Because you have heard, O my soul,	Jer 4:19
And you, O desolate one, what will	Jer 4:30
O LORD, do not Your eyes *look* for	Jer 5:3
from afar, O house of Israel,"	Jer 5:15
O foolish and senseless people,	Jer 5:21
for safety, O sons of Benjamin,	Jer 6:1
"Be warned, O Jerusalem, Or I	Jer 6:8
"Therefore hear, O nations, And	Jer 6:18
nations, And know, O congregation,	Jer 6:18
"Hear, O earth: behold, I am	Jer 6:19
Against you, O daughter of Zion!"	Jer 6:23
O daughter of my people, put on	Jer 6:26
the word of the LORD, O you women,	Jer 9:20
speaks to you, O house of Israel.	Jer 10:1
There is none like You, O LORD;	Jer 10:6
fear You, O King of the nations?	Jer 10:7
I know, O LORD, that a man's way	Jer 10:23
Correct me, O LORD, but with	Jer 10:24
said, "Amen, O LORD."	Jer 11:5
as many as your cities, O Judah;	Jer 11:13
But, O LORD of hosts, who judges	Jer 11:20
Righteous are You, O LORD,	Jer 12:1
But You know me, O LORD;	Jer 12:3
Woe to you, O Jerusalem!	Jer 13:27
testify against us, O LORD,	Jer 14:7
"O Hope of Israel, Its Savior in	Jer 14:8
Yet You are in our midst, O LORD,	Jer 14:9
We know our wickedness, O LORD,	Jer 14:20
Is it not You, O LORD our God?	Jer 14:22
have pity on you, O Jerusalem,	Jer 15:5
You who know, O LORD,	Jer 15:15
by Your name, O LORD God of hosts.	Jer 15:16
O LORD, my strength and my	Jer 16:19
O mountain of Mine in the	Jer 17:3
O LORD, the hope of Israel, All	Jer 17:13
Heal me, O LORD, and I will be	Jer 17:14
"Can I not, O house of Israel,	Jer 18:6
you in My hand, O house of Israel.	Jer 18:6
Do give heed to me, O LORD,	Jer 18:19
Yet You, O LORD, know All	Jer 18:23
O kings of Judah and inhabitants	Jer 19:3
O LORD, You have deceived me and	Jer 20:7
Yet, O LORD of hosts, You who	Jer 20:12
O house of David, thus says the	Jer 21:12
am against you, O valley dweller,	Jer 21:13
O valley dweller, O rocky plain,"	Jer 21:13
word of the LORD, O king of Judah,	Jer 22:2
"O land, land, land, Hear the	Jer 22:29
'Fear not, O Jacob My servant,	Jer 30:10
'And do not be dismayed, O Israel;	Jer 30:10
be rebuilt, O virgin of Israel!	Jer 31:4
'O LORD, save Your people, The	Jer 31:7
the word of the LORD, O nations,	Jer 31:10
Return, O virgin of Israel, Return	Jer 31:21

and there, **O** faithless daughter? Jer 31:22
you, **O** abode of righteousness, Jer 31:23
of righteousness, **O** holy hill!' Jer 31:23
them, **O** great and mighty God. Jer 32:18
You have said to me, **O** Lord GOD, Jer 32:25
LORD, **O** Zedekiah king of Judah! Jer 34:4
please listen, **O** my lord the king; Jer 37:20
of the LORD, **O** remnant of Judah. Jer 42:15
spoken to you, **O** remnant of Judah, Jer 42:19
God of Israel to you, **O** Baruch: Jer 45:2
balm, **O** virgin daughter of Egypt! Jer 46:11
O daughter dwelling in Egypt, Jer 46:19
as for you, **O** Jacob My servant, Jer 46:27
fear, Nor be dismayed, **O** Israel! Jer 46:27
"**O** Jacob My servant, do not fear," Jer 46:28
O remnant of their valley, How Jer 47:5
O daughter dwelling in Dibon, Jer 48:18
keep watch, **O** inhabitant of Aroer; Jer 48:19
the crags, **O** inhabitants of Moab, Jer 48:28
weep for you, **O** vine of Sibmah! Jer 48:32
upon you, **O** inhabitant of Moab," Jer 48:43
"Wail, **O** Heshbon, for Ai has been Jer 49:3
Cry out, **O** daughters of Rabbah, Jer 49:3
O backsliding daughter Who trusts Jer 49:4
depths, **O** inhabitants of Dedan, Jer 49:8
O you who live in the clefts of Jer 49:16
depths, **O** inhabitants of Hazor," Jer 49:30
O you who pillage My heritage, Jer 50:11
you were also caught, **O** Babylon, Jer 50:24
am against you, **O** arrogant one," Jer 50:31
you, **O** daughter of Babylon. Jer 50:42
O you who dwell by many waters, Jer 51:13
you, **O** destroying mountain, Jer 51:25
'You, **O** LORD, have promised Jer 51:62
"See, **O** LORD, my affliction, For La 1:9
"See, **O** LORD, and look, For I am La 1:11
"See, **O** LORD, for I am in La 1:20
you, **O** daughter of Jerusalem? La 2:13
you, **O** virgin daughter of Zion? La 2:13
"**O** wall of the daughter of Zion, La 2:18
See, **O** LORD, and look! La 2:20
I called on Your name, **O** LORD, La 3:55
O Lord, You have pleaded my soul's La 3:58
O LORD, You have seen my La 3:59
have heard their reproach, **O** LORD, La 3:61
You will recompense them, **O** LORD, La 3:64
and be glad, **O** daughter of Edom, La 4:21
completed, **O** daughter of Zion; La 4:22
your iniquity, **O** daughter of Edom; La 4:22
Remember, **O** LORD, what has La 5:1
You, **O** LORD, rule forever; La 5:19
Restore us to You, **O** LORD, La 5:21
to you, **O** inhabitant of the land. Ezk 7:7
near, **O** executioners of the city, Ezk 9:1
in your days, **O** rebellious house, Ezk 12:25
"**O** Israel, your prophets have Ezk 13:4
will come, and you, **O** hailstones, Ezk 13:11
Therefore, **O** harlot, hear the word Ezk 16:35
Hear now, **O** house of Israel! Ezk 18:25
ways not right, **O** house of Israel? Ezk 18:29
will judge you, **O** house of Israel, Ezk 18:30
will you die, **O** house of Israel? Ezk 18:31
of by you, **O** house of Israel? Ezk 20:31
"As for you, **O** house of Israel," Ezk 20:39
deeds, **O** house of Israel," Ezk 20:44
'And you, **O** slain, wicked one, the Ezk 21:25
"Therefore, **O** Oholibah, thus says Ezk 23:22
'Behold, I am against you, **O** Tyre, Ezk 26:3
have perished, **O** inhabited one, Ezk 26:17
From the seas, **O** renowned city, Ezk 26:17
"**O** Tyre, you have said, Ezk 27:3
Your wise men, **O** Tyre, were aboard; Ezk 27:8
destroyed you, **O** covering cherub, Ezk 28:16
"Behold, I am against you, **O** Sidon, Ezk 28:22
'**O** wicked man, you will surely Ezk 33:8
will you die, **O** house of Israel?' Ezk 33:11
O house of Israel, Ezk 33:20
be a desolation, **O** Mount Seir, Ezk 35:15
'**O** mountains of Israel, hear the Ezk 36:1
'Therefore, **O** mountains of Israel, Ezk 36:4
'But you, **O** mountains of Israel, Ezk 36:8
for your sake, **O** house of Israel, Ezk 36:22
your ways, **O** house of Israel!" Ezk 36:32
"**O** Lord GOD, You know." Ezk 37:3
'**O** dry bones, hear the word of the Ezk 37:4
from the four winds, **O** breath, Ezk 37:9
"Behold, I am against you, **O** Gog, Ezk 38:3
you before their eyes, **O** Gog." Ezk 38:16
"Behold, I am against you, **O** Gog, Ezk 39:1
abominations, **O** house of Israel, Ezk 44:6
"**O** king, live forever! Da 2:4
"To You, **O** God of my fathers, I Da 2:23
"As for you, **O** king, *while* on Da 2:29
"You, **O** king, were looking and Da 2:31
"You, **O** king, are the king of Da 2:37
the command is given, **O** peoples, Da 3:4
"**O** king, live forever! Da 3:9
"You, **O** king, have made Da 3:10
These men, **O** king, have Da 3:12
"**O** Nebuchadnezzar, we do not need Da 3:16
us out of your hand, **O** king. Da 3:17
let it be known to you, **O** king, Da 3:18
"Certainly, **O** king." Da 3:24
'**O** Belteshazzar, chief of the Da 4:9
it is you, **O** king; Da 4:22
is the interpretation, **O** king, Da 4:24
'Therefore, **O** king, may my advice Da 4:27
"**O** king, live forever! Da 5:10
"**O** king, the Most High God Da 5:18
god or man besides you, **O** king, Da 6:7
"Now, **O** king, establish the Da 6:8
god or man besides you, **O** king, Da 6:12
pays no attention to you, **O** king, Da 6:13
"Recognize, **O** king, that it is a Da 6:15
"**O** king, live forever! Da 6:21
and also toward you, **O** king, Da 6:22
"Alas, **O** Lord, the great and Da 9:4
belongs to You, **O** Lord, Da 9:7
"Open shame belongs to us, **O** Lord, Da 9:8
"And now, **O** Lord our God, who Da 9:15
"**O** Lord, in accordance with all Da 9:16
and for Your sake, **O** Lord, Da 9:17
"**O** my God, incline Your ear and Da 9:18
"**O** Lord, hear! O Lord, forgive! Da 9:19
"O Lord, hear! **O** Lord, forgive! Da 9:19
O Lord, listen and take action! Da 9:19
For Your own sake, **O** my God, Da 9:19
"**O** Daniel, I have now come forth Da 9:22
"**O** Daniel, man of high esteem, Da 10:11
"**O** my lord, as a result of the Da 10:16
"**O** man of high esteem, do not be Da 10:19
of the LORD, **O** sons of Israel, Hos 4:1
Hear this, **O** priests! Hos 5:1
Give heed, **O** house of Israel! Hos 5:1
Listen, **O** house of the king! Hos 5:1
For now, **O** Ephraim, you have Hos 5:3
shall I do with you, **O** Ephraim? Hos 6:4
What shall I do with you, **O** Judah? Hos 6:4
Also, **O** Judah, there is a harvest Hos 6:11
has rejected your calf, **O** Samaria, Hos 8:5
Do not rejoice, **O** Israel, with Hos 9:1
Give them, **O** LORD Hos 9:14
Gibeah you have sinned, **O** Israel; Hos 10:9
How can I give you up, **O** Ephraim? Hos 11:8
How can I surrender you, **O** Israel? Hos 11:8
It is your destruction, **O** Israel, Hos 13:9
O Death, where are your thorns? Hos 13:14
O Sheol, where is your sting? Hos 13:14
Return, **O** Israel, to the LORD your Hos 14:1
O Ephraim, what more have I to do Hos 14:8
Hear this, **O** elders, And listen, Jl 1:2
Be ashamed, **O** farmers, Wail, O Jl 1:11
O farmers, Wail, **O** vinedressers, Jl 1:11
sackcloth And lament, **O** priests; Jl 1:13
Wail, **O** ministers of the altar! Jl 1:13
sackcloth **O** ministers of my God, Jl 1:13
To You, **O** LORD, I cry; Jl 1:19
"Spare Your people, **O** LORD, Jl 2:17
Do not fear, **O** land, rejoice and Jl 2:21
So rejoice, **O** sons of Zion, And be Jl 2:23
what are you to Me, **O** Tyre, Jl 3:4
Bring down, **O** LORD, Your mighty Jl 3:11
this not so, **O** sons of Israel?" Am 2:11
thus I will do to you, **O** Israel; Am 4:12
to meet your God, **O** Israel." Am 4:12
you as a dirge, **O** house of Israel: Am 5:1
like a fire, **O** house of Joseph, Am 5:6
forty years, **O** house of Israel? Am 5:25
against you, **O** house of Israel," Am 6:14
'As your god lives, **O** Dan,' Am 8:14
to Me, **O** sons of Israel?" Am 9:7
O how you will be ruined! Ob 1:5
"**O** how Esau will be ransacked, Ob 1:6
men will be dismayed, **O** Teman, Ob 1:9
"We earnestly pray, **O** LORD, Jon 1:14 577
for You, **O** LORD, have done as Jon 1:14
life from the pit, **O** LORD my God. Jon 2:6
"Therefore now, **O** LORD, please Jon 4:3
Hear, **O** peoples, all of you; Mi 1:2
Listen, **O** earth and all it contains, Mi 1:2
O inhabitant of Lachish Mi 1:13
O inhabitant of Mareshah. Mi 1:15
it being said, **O** house of Jacob: Mi 2:7
He has told you, **O** man, Mi 6:8
"Hear, **O** tribe. Who has appointed Mi 6:9
not rejoice over me, **O** my enemy. Mi 7:8
Celebrate your feasts, **O** Judah; Na 1:15
are sleeping, **O** king of Assyria; Na 3:18
How long, **O** LORD, will I call for Hab 1:2
You not from everlasting, **O** LORD, Hab 1:12
You, **O** LORD, have appointed them Hab 1:12
And You, **O** Rock, have established Hab 1:12
O LORD, revive Your work in the Hab 3:2
"Wail, **O** inhabitants of the Zph 1:11
gather, **O** nation without shame, Zph 2:1
the LORD is against you, **O** Canaan, Zph 2:5
"You also, **O** Ethiopians, will be Zph 2:12
Shout for joy, **O** daughter of Zion! Zph 3:14
Shout *in triumph,* **O** Israel! Zph 3:14
heart, **O** daughter of Jerusalem! Zph 3:14
"Do not be afraid, **O** Zion; Zph 3:16
O *Zion; The* reproach *of* Zph 3:18
"**O** LORD of hosts, how long will Zch 1:12
and be glad, **O** daughter of Zion; Zch 2:10
'What are you, **O** great mountain? Zch 4:7
O house of Judah and house of Zch 8:13
greatly, **O** daughter of Zion! Zch 9:9
triumph, **O** daughter of Jerusalem! Zch 9:9
O prisoners who have the hope; Zch 9:12
I will stir up your sons, **O** Zion, Zch 9:13
Zion, against your sons, **O** Greece; Zch 9:13
Open your doors, **O** Lebanon, Zch 11:1
Wail, **O** cypress, for the cedar has Zch 11:2
Wail, **O** oaks of Bashan, For the Zch 11:2
"Awake, **O** sword, against My Zch 13:7
O priests who despise My name. Mal 1:6
commandment is for you, **O** priests. Mal 2:1
therefore you, **O** sons of Jacob, Mal 3:6
"**O** woman, your faith is great; Mt 15:28 *5599*
"**O** unbelieving generation, how Mk 9:19 *5599*
'HEAR, **O** ISRAEL! THE LORD OUR Mk 12:29
"I praise You, **O** Father, Lord of Lk 10:21
"**O** Jerusalem, Jerusalem, *the city* Lk 13:34
"**O** foolish men and slow of heart Lk 24:25 *5599*
"**O** righteous Father, although the Jn 17:25
"**O** Lord, it is You who MADE Ac 4:24
WAS IT, **O** HOUSE OF ISRAEL? Ac 7:42
wrong or of vicious crime, **O** Jews, Ac 18:14 *5599*
And for this hope, **O** King, Ac 26:7
at midday, **O** King, I saw on the Ac 26:13
But do you suppose this, **O** man, Ro 2:3 *5599*
the contrary, who are you, **O** man, Ro 9:20 *5599*
"REJOICE, **O** GENTILES, WITH HIS Ro 15:10
For how do you know, **O** wife, 1Co 7:16
Or how do you know, **O** husband, 1Co 7:16
"**O** DEATH, WHERE IS YOUR VICTORY? 1Co 15:55
O DEATH, WHERE IS YOUR STING?" 1Co 15:55
freely to you, **O** Corinthians, 2Co 6:11
O Timothy, guard what has been 1Tm 6:20 *5599*
"YOUR THRONE, **O** GOD, IS FOREVER Heb 1:8
TO DO YOUR WILL, **O** GOD.' " Heb 10:7
"How long, **O** Lord, holy and true, Rv 6:10
"We give You thanks, **O** Lord God, Rv 11:17
O heavens and you who dwell in Rv 12:12
are Your works, **O** Lord God, Rv 15:3
"Who will not fear, **O** Lord, Rv 15:4
who are and who were, **O** Holy One, Rv 16:5
"Yes, **O** Lord God, the Almighty, Rv 16:7
"Rejoice over her, **O** heaven, Rv 18:20

OAK

of Shechem, to the **o** of Moreh. Gn 12:6 436
the **o** which was near Shechem. Gn 35:4 424
buried below Bethel under the **o**; Gn 35:8 437
from the **o** in Zaanannim and Jos 19:33 436
stone and set it up there under the **o** Jos 24:26 427
as far away as the **o** in Zaanannim, Jg 4:11 436
under the **o** that was in Ophrah, Jg 6:11 424
them out to him under the **o** and Jg 6:19 424
by the **o** of the pillar which was Jg 9:6 436
by the way of the diviners' **o**." Jg 9:37 436
come as far as the **o** of Tabor, 1Sa 10:3 436
the thick branches of a great **o**. 2Sa 18:9 424
And his head caught fast in the **o**, 2Sa 18:9 424
I saw Absalom hanging in an **o**." 2Sa 18:10 424
yet alive in the midst of the **o**. 2Sa 18:14 424
and found him sitting under an **o**; 1Ki 13:14 424
their bones under the **o** in Jabesh, 1Ch 10:12 424
Like an **o** whose leaf fades away Or Is 1:30 424
Like a terebinth or an **o** Whose Is 6:13 437
and takes a cypress or an **o** and Is 44:14 437
green tree and under every leafy **o** Ezk 6:13 424
Under **o**, poplar and terebinth, Hos 4:13 437

OAKS

came and dwelt by the **o** of Mamre, Gn 13:18 436
by the **o** of Mamre the Amorite, Gn 14:13 436
appeared to him by the **o** of Mamre, Gn 18:1 436
Gilgal, beside the **o** of Moreh? Dt 11:30 436
you will be ashamed of the **o** which Is 1:29 352d
up, Against all the **o** of Bashan, Is 2:13 437
inflame yourselves among the **o**, Is 57:5 352d
will be called **o** of righteousness, Is 61:3 352d
"Of **o** from Bashan they have made Ezk 27:6 437
cedars And he *was* strong as the **o**; Am 2:9 437
Wail, O **o** of Bashan, For the Zch 11:2 437

OAR

"All who handle the **o**, Ezk 27:29 4880a

OARS

On which no boat with **o** will go, Is 33:21 7885
from Bashan they have made your **o**; Ezk 27:6 4880b
Seeing them straining at the **o**, Mk 6:48 *1643*

OATH

there the two of them took an **o**. Gn 21:31 7650
you will be free from this my **o**; Gn 24:8 7621
then you will be free from my **o**, Gn 24:41 423
you, you will be free from my **o**.' Gn 24:41 423
and I will establish the **o** which I Gn 26:3 7621
'Let there now be an **o** between us, Gn 26:28 423
which He promised on **o** to Abraham, Gn 50:24 7650
an **o** before the LORD shall be made Ex 22:11 7621
may speak thoughtlessly with an **o**, Lv 5:4 7621
The priest shall have her take an **o** Nu 5:19 7650
swear with the **o** of the curse, Nu 5:21 7621
"the LORD make you a curse and an **o** Nu 5:21 7621
land which He promised them by **o**, Nu 14:16 7650
or takes an **o** to bind himself with Nu 30:2 7621
by an obligation with an **o**, Nu 30:10 7621
every binding **o** to humble herself, Nu 30:13 7621
and He was angry and took an **o**, Dt 1:34 7650
the LORD loved you and kept the **o** Dt 7:8 7621
in order to confirm the **o** which Dt 9:5 1697
and into His **o** which the LORD your Dt 29:12 423
I making this covenant and this **o**, Dt 29:14 423
"We *shall be* free from this **o** to Jos 2:17 7621
o which you have made us swear." Jos 2:20 7621
made them take an **o** at that time, Jos 6:26 7650
of the congregation swore *an* **o** to Jos 9:15 7621
the **o** which we swore to them." Jos 9:20 7621
For they had taken a great **o** Jg 21:5 7621
Saul had put the people under **o**, 1Sa 14:24 422
for the people feared the **o**. 1Sa 14:26 7621
his father put the people under **o**; 1Sa 14:27 7650
strictly put the people under **o**, 1Sa 14:28 7650
because of the **o** of the LORD which 2Sa 21:7 7621
you not kept the **o** of the LORD, 1Ki 2:43 7621
neighbor and is made to take an **o**, 1Ki 8:31 423

and he comes *and* takes an **o** before 1Ki 8:31 422
under **o** in the house of the LORD, 2Ki 11:4 7650
with Abraham, And His **o** to Isaac. 1Ch 16:16 7621
and is made to take an **o**, 2Ch 6:22 423
and he comes *and* takes an **o** before 2Ch 6:22 422
o to the LORD with a loud voice, 2Ch 15:14 7650
Judah rejoiced concerning the **o**, 2Ch 15:15 7621
take **o** that they would do Ezr 10:5 7650
so they took the **o**. Ezr 10:5 7650
So I called the priests and took an **o** Ne 5:12 7650
For many in Judah were bound by **o** Ne 6:18 7621
and an **o** to walk in God's law, Ne 10:29 7621
with Abraham, And His **o** to Isaac. Ps 105:9 7621
He hears the **o** but tells nothing. Pr 29:24 423
king because of the **o** before God. Ec 8:2 7621
in order to confirm the **o** which I Jer 11:5 7621
the **o** by breaking the covenant. Ezk 16:59 423
with him, putting him under **o**. Ezk 17:13 423
the throne, whose **o** he despised and Ezk 17:16 423
the **o** by breaking the covenant, Ezk 17:18 423
surely My **o** which he despised and Ezk 17:19 423
along with the **o** which is written Da 9:11 7621
go up to Beth-aven And take the **o**: Hos 4:15 7650
I say to you, make no **o** at all, Mt 5:34 *3660*
shall you make an **o** by your head, Mt 5:36 *3660*
that he promised with an **o** to Mt 14:7 *3727*
And again he denied *it* with an **o**, Mt 26:72 *3727*
The **o** which He swore to Abraham Lk 1:73 *3727*
GOD HAD SWORN TO HIM WITH AN **O** Ac 2:30 *3727*
and bound themselves under an **o**, Ac 23:12 *332*
bound ourselves under a solemn **o** Ac 23:14 *332*
with them an **o** *given* as confirmation Heb 6:16 *3727*
His purpose, interposed with an **o**, Heb 6:17 *3727*
as *it was* not without an **o** Heb 7:20 *3728*
became priests without an **o**, Heb 7:21 *3728*
but He with an **o** through the One Heb 7:21 *3728*
are weak, but the word of the **o**, Heb 7:28 *3728*
or by earth or with any other **o**; Jas 5:12 *3727*

OATHS
they arose early and exchanged **o**; Gn 26:31 7650
they have *sworn* solemn **o**. Ezk 21:23 7621
worthless **o** they make covenants; Hos 10:4 422
it to be given because of his **o**, Mt 14:9 *3727*
yet because of his **o** and because Mk 6:26 *3727*

OBADIAH
O who *was* over the household. 1Ki 18:3 5662
(Now **O** feared the LORD greatly; 1Ki 18:3 5662
O took a hundred prophets and 1Ki 18:4 5662
Then Ahab said to **O**, 1Ki 18:5 5662
and **O** went another way by himself. 1Ki 18:6 5662
Now as **O** was on the way, behold, 1Ki 18:7 5662
So **O** went to meet Ahab and told 1Ki 18:16 5662
the sons of Arnan, the sons of **O**, 1Ch 3:21 5662
sons of Izrahiah *were* Michael, **O**, 1Ch 7:3 5662
Ishmael, Sheariah, **O** and Hanan. 1Ch 8:38 5662
and **O** the son of Shemaiah, the son 1Ch 9:16 5662
and Sheariah and **O** and Hanan. 1Ch 9:44 5662
Ezer *was* the first, **O** the second, 1Ch 12:9 5662
Zebulun, Ishmaiah the son of **O**; 1Ch 27:19 5662
he sent his officials, Ben-hail, **O**, 2Ch 17:7 5662
Jahath and **O**, the Levites of the 2Ch 34:12 5662
O the son of Jehiel and 218 males Ezr 8:9 5662
Harim, Meremoth, **O**, Ne 10:5 5662
Mattaniah, Bakbukiah, **O**, Ne 12:25 5662
The vision of **O**. Thus says the Lord Ob 1:1 5662

OBAL
and **O** and Abimael and Sheba Gn 10:28 5745

OBED
So they named him **O**. Ru 4:17 5744
was born Boaz, and to Boaz, **O**, Ru 4:21 5744
and to **O** was born Jesse, and to Ru 4:22 5744
Boaz became the father of **O**, 1Ch 2:12 5744
and **O** became the father of Jesse; 1Ch 2:12 5744
and Ephlal became the father of **O**, 1Ch 2:37 5744
and **O** became the father of Jehu, 1Ch 2:38 5744
and **O** and Jaasiel the Mezobaite. 1Ch 11:47 5744
Shemaiah *were* Othni, Rephael, **O** and 1Ch 26:7 5744
of Johanan, Azariah the son of **O**, 2Ch 23:1 5744
Boaz was the father of **O** by Ruth, Mt 1:5 *2492b*
and **O** the father of Jesse. Mt 1:5 *2492b*
the son of Jesse, the son of **O**, Lk 3:32 *2492b*

OBED-EDOM
to the house of **O** the Gittite. 2Sa 6:10 5654
in the house of **O** the Gittite three 2Sa 6:11 5654
blessed **O** and all his household. 2Sa 6:11 5654
of **O** and all that belongs to him, 2Sa 6:12 5654
the ark of God from the house of **O** 2Sa 6:12 5654
to the house of **O** the Gittite. 1Ch 13:13 5654
of **O** in his house three months; 1Ch 13:14 5654
family of **O** with all that he had. 1Ch 13:14 5654
Eliphelehu, Mikneiah, **O** and 1Ch 15:18 5654
Eliphelehu, Mikneiah, **O**, 1Ch 15:21 5654
O and Jehiah also *were* gatekeepers 1Ch 15:24 5654
LORD from the house of **O** with joy. 1Ch 15:25 5654
Mattithiah, Eliab, Benaiah, **O** and 1Ch 16:5 5654
and **O** with his 68 relatives; 1Ch 16:38 5654
O, also the son of Jeduthun, and 1Ch 16:38 5654
O had sons: Shemaiah the firstborn, 1Ch 26:4 5654
All these *were* of the sons of **O**; 1Ch 26:8 5654
for the service, 62 from **O**. 1Ch 26:8 5654
For **O** *it fell* to the south, and to 1Ch 26:15 5654
found in the house of God with **O**, 2Ch 25:24 5654

OBEDIENCE
him *shall be* the **o** of the peoples. Gn 49:10 3349
"Foreigners pretend **o** to me; 2Sa 22:45 3584
enemies will give feigned **o** to You. Ps 66:3 3584
the LORD would pretend **o** to Him, Ps 81:15 3584
the **o** of faith among all the Gentiles for Ro 1:5 *5218*
even so through the **o** of the One Ro 5:19 *5218*
to someone *as* slaves for **o**, Ro 6:16 *5218*
of **o** resulting in righteousness? Ro 6:16 *5218*
resulting in the **o** of the Gentiles Ro 15:18 *5218*
report of your **o** has reached to all; Ro 16:19 *5218*
nations, *leading* to **o** of faith; Ro 16:26 *5218*
as he remembers the **o** of you all, 2Co 7:15 *5218*
they will glorify God for *your* **o** 2Co 9:13 *5292*
captive to the **o** of Christ, 2Co 10:5 *5218*
whenever your **o** is complete. 2Co 10:6 *5218*
Having confidence in your **o**, Phm 1:21 *5218*
He learned **o** from the things which Heb 5:8 *5218*
in **o** to the truth purified your souls 1Pe 1:22 *5218*

OBEDIENT
we will do, and we will be **o**!" Ex 24:7 8085
were becoming **o** to the faith. Ac 6:7 *5219*
were unwilling to be **o** to him, Ac 7:39 *5255*
you became **o** from the heart to Ro 6:17 *5219*
whether you are **o** in all things. 2Co 2:9 *5255*
be **o** to those who are your masters Eph 6:5 *5219*
becoming **o** to the point of death, Php 2:8 *5255*
o to your parents in all things, Col 3:20 *5219*
rulers, to authorities, to be **o**, Ti 3:1 *3980*
As **o** children, do not be conformed 1Pe 1:14 *5218*

OBEDIENTLY
if you listen **o** to my commandments Dt 11:13 8085
if only you listen **o** to the voice Dt 15:5 8085

OBELISKS
also shatter the **o** of Heliopolis, Jer 43:13 4676

OBEY
only **o** my voice, and go, get *them* Gn 27:13 8085
"Now therefore, my son, **o** my voice, Gn 27:43 8085
o His voice to let Israel go? Ex 5:2 8085
o My voice and keep My covenant, Ex 19:5 8085
guard before him and **o** his voice; Ex 23:21 8085
"But if you truly **o** his voice Ex 23:22 8085
'But if you do not **o** Me and do not Lv 26:14 8085
these things you do not **o** Me, Lv 26:18 8085
Me and are unwilling to **o** Me, Lv 26:21 8085
in spite of this you do not **o** Me, Lv 26:27 8085
of the sons of Israel may **o** *him*. Nu 27:20 8085
not **o** his father or his mother, Dt 21:18 8085, 6963
and rebellious, he will not **o** us, Dt 21:20 8085, 6963
therefore **o** the LORD your God, Dt 27:10 8085, 6963
diligently **o** the LORD your God, Dt 28:1 8085, 6963
if you **o** the LORD your God: Dt 28:2 8085, 6963
you do not **o** the LORD your God, Dt 28:15 8085, 6963
because you would not **o** the LORD Dt 28:45 8085, 6963
you did not **o** the LORD your God. Dt 28:62 8085, 6963
o Him with all your heart and soul Dt 30:2 8085, 6963
"And you shall again **o** the LORD, Dt 30:8 8085, 6963
if you **o** the LORD your God to keep Dt 30:10 8085, 6963
turns away and you will not **o**, Dt 30:17 8085
in all things, so we will **o** you; Jos 1:17 8085
and does not **o** your words Jos 1:18 8085
our God and we will **o** His voice." Jos 24:24 8085
o the commandments of the LORD, Jg 3:4 8085
you not **o** the voice of the LORD, 1Sa 15:19 8085
"I did **o** the voice of the LORD, 1Sa 15:20 8085
to **o** is better than sacrifice, 1Sa 15:22 8085
"As you did not **o** the LORD and 1Sa 28:18 8085, 6963
As soon as they hear, they **o** me. 2Sa 22:45 8085
because they did not **o** the voice 2Ki 18:12 8085
because she did not **o** the command Es 1:15 6213a
As soon as they hear, they **o** me; Ps 18:44 8085
And Israel did not **o** Me. Ps 81:11 14
"If you consent and **o**, Is 1:19 8085
And whose law they did not **o**? Is 42:24 8085
'**O** My voice, and I will be your Jer 7:23 8085
did not **o** or incline their ear, Jer 7:24 8085
'This is the nation that did not **o** Jer 7:28 8085
did not **o** or incline their ear, Jer 11:8 8085
"But if you will not **o** these words, Jer 22:5 8085
and **o** the voice of the LORD your Jer 26:13 8085
o Your voice or walk in Your law; Jer 32:23 8085
but your forefathers did not **o** Me or Jer 34:14 8085
Please **o** the LORD in what I am Jer 38:20 8085, 6963
did not **o** the voice of the LORD to Jer 43:4 8085
did not **o** the voice of the LORD) Jer 43:7 8085
dominions will serve and **o** Him.' Da 7:27 8086
completely **o** the LORD your God. Zch 6:15 8085, 6963
the winds and the sea **o** Him?" Mt 8:27 *5219*
unclean spirits, and they **o** Him." Mk 1:27 *5219*
even the wind and the sea **o** Him?" Mk 4:41 *5219*
and the water, and they **o** Him?" Lk 8:25 *5219*
and it would **o** you. Lk 17:6 *5219*
not **o** the Son will not see life, Jn 3:36 *544*
"We must **o** God rather than men. Ac 5:29 *3980*
God has given to those who **o** Him. Ac 5:32 *3980*
ambitious and do not **o** the truth, Ro 2:8 *544*
the truth, but **o** unrighteousness, Ro 2:8 *3982*
body so that you **o** its lusts, Ro 6:12 *5219*
are slaves of the one whom you **o**, Ro 6:16 *5219*
o your parents in the Lord, Eph 6:1 *5219*
in all things **o** those who are your Col 3:22 *5219*
not **o** the gospel of our Lord Jesus. 2Th 1:8 *5219*
not **o** our instruction in this letter, 2Th 3:14 *5219*
He became to all those who **o** Him Heb 5:9 *5219*
O your leaders and submit *to them* Heb 13:17 *3982*
mouths so that they will **o** us, Jas 3:3 *3982*
to **o** Jesus Christ and be 1Pe 1:2 *5218*
who do not **o** the gospel of God? 1Pe 4:17 *544*

OBEYED
because you have **o** My voice." Gn 22:18 8085
Abraham **o** Me and kept My charge, Gn 26:5 8085, 6963
and that Jacob had **o** his father Gn 28:7 8085
"Just as we **o** Moses in all Jos 1:17 8085
But you have not **o** Me; Jg 2:2 8085, 6963
But you have not **o** Me. Jg 6:10 8085, 6963
your maidservant has **o** you, 1Sa 28:21 8085, 6963
prospered, and all Israel **o** him. 1Ch 29:23 8085
tree, And you have not **o** My voice,' Jer 3:13 8085
not **o** the voice of the LORD our God." Jer 3:25 8085
and have not **o** My voice nor walked Jer 9:13 8085
That you have not **o** My voice. Jer 22:21 8085
'Because you have not **o** My words, Jer 25:8 8085
officials and all the people **o** who Jer 34:10 8085
they **o**, and set *them free*. Jer 34:10 8085
'You have not **o** Me in proclaiming Jer 34:17 8085
"We have **o** the voice of Jonadab Jer 35:8 8085
only dwelt in tents, and have **o** and Jer 35:10 8085
they have **o** their father's command. Jer 35:14 8085
'Because you have **o** the command of Jer 35:18 8085
you have not **o** the LORD your God, Jer 42:21 8085, 6963
and not **o** the voice of the LORD or Jer 44:23 8085
nor have we **o** the voice of the LORD Da 9:10 8085
done, but we have not **o** His voice. Da 9:14 8085
On the nations which have not **o**." Mi 5:15 8085
o the voice of the LORD their God Hg 1:12 8085
just as you have always **o**, Php 2:12 *5219*
o by going out to a place which he Heb 11:8 *5219*
as Sarah **o** Abraham, calling him 1Pe 3:6 *5219*

OBEYING
the LORD your God, by **o** His voice, Dt 30:20 8085
in **o** the commandments of the LORD; Jg 2:17 8085
As in **o** the voice of the LORD? 1Sa 15:22 8085
His word, **O** the voice of His word! Ps 103:20 8085
in My sight by not **o** My voice, Jer 18:10 8085
and turned aside, not **o** Your voice; Da 9:11 8085
who hindered you from **o** the truth? Ga 5:7 *3982*

OBEYS
That **o** the voice of His servant, Is 50:10 8085

OBIL
O the Ishmaelite had charge of 1Ch 27:30 179

OBJECT
he struck him down with an iron **o**, Nu 35:16 3627
him with a wooden **o** in the hand, Nu 35:18 3627
or with any deadly **o** of stone, Nu 35:23
He has made them an **o** of terror, 2Ch 29:8 2113
an **o** of dread to my acquaintances; Ps 31:11 6343
You make us an **o** of contention to Ps 80:6 4066
made me an **o** of loathing to them; Ps 88:8 8441
I will make them an **o** of horror Jer 15:4 2113
An **o** *of* perpetual hissing; Jer 18:16
this city a desolation and an **o** *of* Jer 19:8
become a curse, an **o** of horror, Jer 42:18 8047
become a curse, an **o** of horror, Jer 44:12 8047
ruin, an **o** of horror and a curse, Jer 44:22 8047
o of terror to all around him." Jer 48:39 4288
Bozrah will become an **o** of horror, Jer 49:13 8047
Edom will become an **o** of horror; Jer 49:17 8047
will make her land an **o** of horror, Jer 50:3 8047
Babylon has become An **o** of horror Jer 50:23 8047
An **o** of horror and hissing, Jer 51:37 8047
Babylon has become an **o** of horror Jer 51:41 8047
cities have become an **o** of horror, Jer 51:43 8047
a warning and an **o** of horror to Ezk 5:15 4923
from every kind of desirable **o**. Na 2:9 3627
and I gave them to him *as an* **o** *of* Mal 2:5
and an **o** like a great sheet Ac 10:11 *4632*
the **o** was taken up into the sky. Ac 10:16 *4632*
an **o** coming down like a Ac 11:5 *4632*
so-called god or **o** of worship, 2Th 2:4 *4574*

OBJECTED
"But when the Jews **o**, Ac 28:19 *483*

OBJECTION
I came without even raising any **o** Ac 10:29 *369*

OBJECTS
have finished covering the holy **o** Nu 4:15
that they will not touch the holy **o** Nu 4:15
when they approach the most holy **o**: Nu 4:19
shall not go in to see the holy **o** Nu 4:20
was the service of the holy **o**, Nu 7:9
carrying the holy **o**; Nu 10:21
and make them **o** *of* compassion 1Ki 8:50
He also made them **o** of compassion Ps 106:46
examining the **o** of your worship, Ac 17:23 *4574*

OBLIGATED
by the gold of the temple is **o**.' Mt 23:16 *3784*
by the offering on it, he is **o**.' Mt 23:18 *3784*
is **o** to offer *sacrifices* for sins, Heb 5:3 *3784*

OBLIGATION
for the **o** of the sons of Israel; Nu 3:38 4931
the tent of meeting, to keep an **o**, Nu 18:3 4931
"And they shall thus attend to your **o** Nu 18:3 4931
and the **o** of all the tent, Nu 18:3 4931

to bind himself with a binding o, Nu 30:2 632
and binds herself by an o in her Nu 30:3 632
her father hears her vow and her o Nu 30:4 632
and every o by which she has bound Nu 30:4 632
herself by an o with an oath, Nu 30:10 632
and every o by which she bound Nu 30:11 632
or concerning the o of herself shall Nu 30:12 632
and be free of o toward the LORD Nu 32:22 5355a
We also placed ourselves under o Ne 10:32 4687
I am under o both to Greeks and to Ro 1:14 *3781*
So then, brethren, we are under o, Ro 8:12 *3781*
is under o to keep the whole Law. Ga 5:3 *3781*

OBLIGATIONS
the Levites concerning their o." Nu 8:26 4931
to the o of the tent of meeting, Nu 18:4 4931
attend to the o of the sanctuary and Nu 18:5 4931
sanctuary and the o of the altar, Nu 18:5 4931
none of her vows or her o by which Nu 30:5 632
her o by which she has bound herself Nu 30:7 632
or all her o which are on her; Nu 30:14 632
the house of the LORD for his daily o 2Ch 31:16 1697

OBLIGED
Now he was o to release to them Lk 23:17 *2192, 318*

OBLIGING
o them to celebrate the fourteenth Es 9:21 6965, 5921

OBLITERATE
o their name from that place. Dt 12:3 6

OBOTH
Israel moved out and camped in O. Nu 21:10 88
They journeyed from O and Nu 21:11 88
from Punon and camped at O. Nu 33:43 88
They journeyed from O and Nu 33:44 88

OBSCURE
He will not stand before o men. Pr 22:29 2823

OBSCURED
the sun was o; Lk 23:45 *1587*

OBSCURES
"He o the face of the full moon And Jb 26:9 270

OBSCURITY
comes in futility and goes into o; Ec 6:4 2822
and its name is covered in o. Ec 6:4 2822

OBSERVANCE
Tomorrow is a sabbath o, Ex 16:23 7677

OBSERVE
o the *Feast of* Unleavened Bread, Ex 12:17 8104
therefore you shall o this day Ex 12:17 8104
"And you shall o this event as an Ex 12:24 8104
you shall o this rite. Ex 12:25 8104
shall o this rite in this month. Ex 13:5 5647
o the Feast of Unleavened Bread; Ex 23:15 8104
"Also *you shall* o the Feast of Ex 23:16
'You shall surely o My sabbaths; Ex 31:13 8104
you are to o the sabbath, Ex 31:14 8104
of Israel shall o the sabbath, Ex 31:16 8104
"Be sure to o what I am Ex 34:11 8104
o the Feast of Unleavened Bread. Ex 34:18 8104
'You shall thus o all My statutes and Lv 19:37 8104
'You shall thus o My statutes and Lv 25:18 6213a
it will o the rest which it did not Lv 26:35 7673a
it did not o on your sabbaths, Lv 26:35 7673a
let the sons of Israel o the Nu 9:2 6213a
shall o it at its appointed time; Nu 9:3 6213a
you shall o it according to all Nu 9:3 6213a
sons of Israel to o the Passover. Nu 9:4 6213a
could not o Passover on that day; Nu 9:6 6213a
o the Passover to the LORD. Nu 9:10 6213a
day at twilight, they shall o it; Nu 9:11 6213a
of the Passover they shall o it. Nu 9:12 6213a
yet neglects to o the Passover, Nu 9:13 6213a
do not o all these commandments, Nu 15:22 6213a
and you shall o a feast to the Nu 29:12 2287
learn them and o them carefully. Dt 5:1 8104
'O the sabbath day to keep it holy, Dt 5:12 8104
you to o the sabbath day. Dt 5:15 6213a
that they may o *them* in the land Dt 5:31 6213a
"So you shall o to do just as the Dt 5:32 6213a
as to o all these statutes, Dt 6:24 6213a
careful to o all this commandment Dt 6:25 6213a
o in the land which the LORD, Dt 12:1 8104
to o carefully all this Dt 15:5 6213a
"O the month of Abib and Dt 16:1 8104
be careful to o these statutes. Dt 16:12 6213a
and you shall be careful to o Dt 17:10 6213a
carefully all this commandment which Dt 19:9 8104
that you diligently o and do Dt 24:8 8104
you today, to o *them* carefully, Dt 28:13 6213a
to o to do all His commandments Dt 28:15 6213a
"If you are not careful to o all Dt 28:58 6213a
may o all the words of this law. Dt 29:29 6213a
and o all His commandments which I Dt 30:8 6213a
us hear it, that we may o it?' Dt 30:12 6213a
us hear it, that we may o it?' Dt 30:13 6213a
in your heart, that you may o it. Dt 30:14 6213a
to o all the words of this law. Dt 31:12 6213a
command your sons to o carefully, Dt 32:46 6213a
very careful to o the commandment Jos 22:5 6213a
let her o all that I commanded." Jg 13:14 8104
not o what the LORD had commanded. 1Ki 11:10 8104
"Please o and see how this man is 1Ki 20:7 3045
and o and see what you have to do; 1Ki 20:22 3045
you, you shall o to do forever; 2Ki 17:37 8104
if only they will o to do 2Ki 21:8 8104
if you are careful to o the statutes 1Ch 22:13 6213a
o and seek after all the 1Ch 28:8 8104
to o the law and the commandment. 2Ch 14:4 6213a
if only they will o to do all that 2Ch 33:8 8104
"Whoever will not o the law Ezr 7:26 5648
and to keep and to o all the Ne 10:29 6213a
and they do not o the king's laws, Es 3:8 6213a
my steps, You do not o my sin. Jb 14:16 8104
Do you o the calving of the deer? Jb 39:1 8104
keep His statutes And o His laws, Ps 105:45 5341
are those who o His testimonies, Ps 119:2 5341
from me, For I o Your testimonies. Ps 119:22 5341
And I shall o it to the end. Ps 119:33 5341
that I may o Your law And Ps 119:34 5341
mine, That I o Your precepts. Ps 119:56 5341
my heart I will o Your precepts. Ps 119:69 5341
may o the commandments of my God. Ps 119:115 5341
I will o Your statutes. Ps 119:145 5341
That you may o discretion And Pr 5:2 8104
sluggard, O her ways and be wise, Pr 6:6 7200
o the commandment of your father And Pr 6:20 5341
year, o *your* feasts on schedule. Is 29:1 5362b
things, but you do not o *them;* Is 42:20 8104
And send to Kedar and o closely And Jer 2:10 995
O the time of their migration; Jer 8:7 8104
keep My ordinances and o them. Ezk 20:19 6213a
they careful to o My ordinances, Ezk 20:21 6213a
be careful to o My ordinances. Ezk 36:27 6213a
and keep My statutes and o them. Ezk 37:24 6213a
so that they may o its whole design Ezk 43:11 8104
your God, O kindness and justice, Hos 12:6 8104
"Look among the nations! O! Hab 1:5 5027
O how the lilies of the field grow; Mt 6:28 *2648*
all that they tell you, do and o, Mt 23:3 *5083*
to o all that I commanded you; Mt 28:20 *5083*
they have received in order to o, Mk 7:4 *2902*
hear the word of God and o it." Lk 11:28 *5442*
who o it begin to ridicule him, Lk 14:29 *2334*
them to o the Law of Moses." Ac 15:5 *5083*
were in Jerusalem, for them to o. Ac 16:4 *5442*
lawful for us to accept or to o, Ac 16:21 *4160*
I o that you are very religious in Ac 17:22 *2334*
did o a bay with a beach, Ac 27:39 *2657*
You o days and months and seasons Ga 4:10 *3906*
and o those who walk according to Php 3:17 *4648*
Now o how great this man was to Heb 7:4 *2334*
your good deeds, as they o *them,* 1Pe 2:12 *2029*
as they o your chaste and 1Pe 3:2 *2029*
love God and o His commandments. 1Jn 5:2 *4160*

OBSERVED
to them in the morning and o them, Gn 40:6 7200
and he o seven days mourning for Gn 50:10 6213a
It is a night to be o for the LORD Ex 12:42 8107
to be o by all the sons of Israel Ex 12:42 8107
They o the Passover in the Nu 9:5 6213a
"He has not o misfortune in Jacob; Nu 23:21 5027
his own sons, For they o Your word, Dt 33:9 8104
they o the Passover on the evening Jos 5:10 6213a
Solomon o the feast at that time, 1Ki 8:65 6213a
who o My commandments and My 1Ki 11:34 8104
and have not o the commandment 1Ki 13:21 8104
this Passover was o to the LORD in 2Ki 23:23 6213a
So Solomon o the feast at that 2Ch 7:8 6213a
of the altar they o seven days and 2Ch 7:9 6213a
have not o the word of the LORD, 2Ch 34:21 8104
The exiles o the Passover on Ezr 6:19 6213a
And they o the Feast of Unleavened Ezr 6:22 6213a
I o the people and the priests, Ezr 8:15 995
Because I have o Your precepts. Ps 119:100 5341
my mind has o a wealth of wisdom Ec 1:16 7200
o what this people have spoken, Jer 33:24 7200
his sons not to drink wine, are o. Jer 35:14 6965
have o the command of their father Jer 35:16 6965
My statutes, nor o My ordinances, Ezk 5:7 6213a
nor o the ordinances of the nations Ezk 5:7 6213a
a son who has o all his father's sins Ezk 18:14 7200
o all My statutes and done them, Ezk 18:19 8104
they had not o My ordinances, Ezk 20:24 6213a
appearance be o in your presence and Da 1:13 7200
o in the books the number of the Da 9:2 995
works of the house of Ahab are o; Mi 6:16 8104
They came to Jesus and o the Mk 5:15 *2334*
is not coming with signs to be o; Lk 17:20 *3907*
when they o what had happened, Lk 23:48 *2334*
o the confidence of Peter and John and Ac 4:13 *2334*
and as he o signs and great miracles Ac 8:13 *2334*

OBSERVES
and o the Passover to the LORD, Nu 9:14 6213a
if a man o them he shall live. Ne 9:29 6213a
Therefore my soul o them. Ps 119:129 5341
o all My statutes and practices justice Ezk 18:21 8104
by which, if a man o them, Ezk 20:11 6213a
by which, if a man o them, Ezk 20:13 6213a
by which, *if* a man o them, Ezk 20:21 6213a
He who o the day, observes it for Ro 14:6 *5426*
the day, o it for the Lord, Ro 14:6 *5426*

OBSERVING
by carefully o all the words of Dt 17:19 6213a
what is right in My sight and o 1Ki 11:33
right in My sight by o My statutes 1Ki 11:38 8104
and o does not do likewise. Ezk 18:14 7200
While I was o, behold, a male goat Da 8:5 995
o the traditions of the elders; Mk 7:3 *2902*
and *began* o how the people were Mk 12:41 *2334*
o His signs which He was doing. Jn 2:23 *2334*
fixed my gaze on it and was o it Ac 11:6 *2657*
being provoked within him as he was o Ac 17:16 *2334*

OBSOLETE
covenant," He has made the first o. Heb 8:13 *3822*
But whatever is becoming o and Heb 8:13 *3822*

OBSTACLE
Remove *every* o out of the way of Is 57:14 4383
and I place an o before him, Ezk 3:20 4383
not to put an o or a stumbling block Ro 14:13 *4348*

OBSTINATE
and behold, they are an o people. Ex 32:9 7186, 6203
because you are an o people, Ex 33:3 7186, 6203
'You are an o people; Ex 33:5 7186, 6203
even though the people are so o, Ex 34:9 7186, 6203
his spirit and made his heart o, Dt 2:30 553
"Because I know that you are o, Is 48:4 7186
who are stubborn and o children, Ezk 2:4 2389, 3820
house of Israel is stubborn and o. Ezk 3:7 7186, 3820
TO A DISOBEDIENT AND O PEOPLE." Ro 10:21 *483*

OBSTRUCTS
whether his body o its discharge. Lv 15:3 2856

OBTAIN
I will o children through her." Gn 16:2 1129
man will o favor from the LORD, Pr 12:2 6329
But a humble spirit will o honor. Pr 29:23 8551
They will o gladness and joy, And Is 51:11 5381
Go up to Gilead and o balm, Jer 46:11 3947
over him and o dominion; Da 11:5 4910
I do that I may o eternal life?" Mt 19:16 *2192*
o false testimony against Jesus, Mt 26:59 *2212*
trying to o testimony against Jesus Mk 14:55 *2212*
o the gift of God with money! Ac 8:20 *2932*
may o some fruit among you also, Ro 1:13 *2192*
o for themselves a high standing 1Tm 3:13 *4046*
that they also may o the salvation 2Tm 2:10 *5177*
might o a better resurrection; Heb 11:35 *5177*
You are envious and cannot o; Jas 4:2 *2013*
to o an inheritance *which is* 1Pe 1:4

OBTAINED
court, she o favor in his sight; Es 5:2 5375
Wealth o by fraud dwindles, Pr 13:11
Bread o by falsehood is sweet to a Pr 20:17
on her who had not o compassion, Hos 2:23 7355
"So, having o help from God, Ac 26:22 *5177*
we have o our introduction by faith Ro 5:2 *2192*
is seeking, it has not o, Ro 11:7 *2013*
but those who were chosen o it, Ro 11:7 *2013*
also we have o an inheritance, Eph 1:11 *2820*
Not that I have already o *it* or Php 3:12 *2983*
waited, he o the promise. Heb 6:15 *2013*
has o a more excellent ministry, Heb 8:6 *5177*
all, having o eternal redemption. Heb 9:12 *2147*
through which he o the testimony Heb 11:4 *3140*
for he o the witness that before Heb 11:5 *3140*
acts of righteousness, o promises, Heb 11:33 *2013*

OBTAINING
but for o salvation through our 1Th 5:9 *4047*
o as the outcome of your faith the 1Pe 1:9 *2865*

OBTAINS
life And o favor from the LORD. Pr 8:35 6329
thing And o favor from the LORD. Pr 18:22 6329

OBVIOUS
for their folly will be o to all, 2Tm 3:9 *1552*
the children of the devil are o: 1Jn 3:10 *5318*

OCCASION
that he may seek o against us and Gn 43:18 1556
seeking an o against the Philistines. Jg 14:4 8385b
for yourself what the o requires, 1Sa 10:7 3027
you have given o to the enemies of 2Sa 12:14
which you may have o to provide, Ezr 7:20 5308
has become an o of stumbling. Ezk 7:19 4383
Now on the same o there were some Lk 13:1 *2540*
giving you an o to be proud of us, 2Co 5:12 *874*
give the enemy no o for reproach; 1Tm 5:14 *874*
been no o sought for a second. Heb 8:7 *5117*

OCCUPANTS
great and fine ones, without o. Is 5:9 3427

OCCUPATION
calls you and says, 'What is your o?' Gn 46:33 4639
"What is your o?" Gn 47:3 4639
What is your o? And where do you Jon 1:8 4399

OCCUPIED
either he is o or gone aside, or 1Ki 18:27 7879
so that they o their tents 1Ch 5:10 3427
because God keeps him o with the Ec 5:20 6030b
in which they found me o in Ac 24:18
those who were so o were not Heb 13:9 *4043*

OCCUPY
Begin to o, that you may possess Dt 2:31 3423
of men with which to o themselves. Ec 3:10 6030b
Who o the height of the hill. Jer 49:16 8610
you proceed to o the last place. Lk 14:9 *2722*
to o this ministry and apostleship Ac 1:25 *2983*

OCCUR
which will o in the land of Egypt, Gn 41:36 1961
Tomorrow this sign will o. Ex 8:23 1961
of the later things which will o, Ec 1:11 1961
him to see what will o after him? Ec 3:22 1961
misfortune may o on the earth. Ec 11:2 1961
going to let you know what will o Da 8:19 1961
Then their confusion will o. Mi 7:4 1961
a riot might o among the people." Mt 26:5 *1096*
to pass, so that when it does o, Jn 13:19 *1096*
and Your purpose predestined to o. Ac 4:28 *1096*

OCCURRED
that had o in the days of Abraham. Gn 26:1 1961
which o in the land of Egypt and Gn 41:48 1961
be a time of distress such as never o Da 12:1 1961
For if the miracles had o in Tyre Mt 11:21 *1096*
in Tyre and Sidon which o in you, Mt 11:21 *1096*
for if the miracles had o in Sodom Mt 11:23 *1096*
occurred in Sodom which o in you, Mt 11:23 *1096*
such as has not o since the Mt 24:21 *1096*
behold, a severe earthquake had o, Mt 28:2 *1096*
time of tribulation such as has not o Mk 13:19 *1096*
and when a flood o, the torrent Lk 6:48 *1096*
in Tyre and Sidon which o in you, Lk 10:13 *1096*
a severe famine o in that country, Lk 15:14 *1096*
So a division o in the crowd because Jn 7:43 *1096*
A division o again among the Jews Jn 10:19 *1096*
And when this sound o, Ac 2:6 *1096*
because of the persecution that o in Ac 11:19 *1096*
And there o such a sharp disagreement Ac 15:39 *1096*
About that time there o no small Ac 19:23 *1096*
As he said this, there o a Ac 23:7 *1096*
And there o a great uproar; and some Ac 23:9 *1096*

OCCURS
there o a reddish-white infection, Lv 13:42 1961
of leather in which the mark o, Lv 13:52 1961
the thing in which the mark o and Lv 13:54
the slaughter o in your midst? Ezk 26:15 2026
If a calamity o in a city has not Am 3:6 1961

OCEAN
abundant drink like the o depths. Ps 78:15 8415

OCHRAN
of Asher, Pagiel the son of O; Nu 1:13 5918
Pagiel the son of O, Nu 2:27 5918
day *it was* Pagiel the son of O, Nu 7:72 5918
offering of Pagiel the son of O. Nu 7:77 5918
and Pagiel the son of O over the Nu 10:26 5918

ODED
God came on Azariah the son of O, 2Ch 15:1 5752
the son of O the prophet spoke, 2Ch 15:8 5752
LORD was there, whose name *was* O; 2Ch 28:9 5752

ODIOUS
by making me o among the Gn 34:30 887
for you have made us o in Ex 5:21 887, 7381b
had become o to the Philistines. 1Sa 13:4 887
made himself o among his people 1Sa 27:12 887
that they had become o to David, 2Sa 10:6 887
made yourself o to your father. 2Sa 16:21 887
had made themselves o to David, 1Ch 19:6 887

OFF
cut o by the water of the flood, Gn 9:11 3772
shall be cut o from his people; Gn 17:14 3772
walking with them to send them o. Gn 18:16
to marry o the younger before the Gn 29:26 5414
birds will eat your flesh o you." Gn 40:19 4480, 5921
Then Pharaoh took o his signet ring Gn 41:42 5493
the city, *and* were not far o, Gn 44:4
and they lived o the allotment Gn 47:22 398
a flint and cut o her son's foreskin Ex 4:25 3772
have been cut o from the earth. Ex 9:15 3582
person shall be cut o from Israel. Ex 12:15 3772
that person shall be cut o from Ex 12:19 3772
be cut o from his people.'" Ex 30:33 3772
shall be cut o from his people." Ex 30:38 3772
be cut o from among his people. Ex 31:14 3772
"Tear o the gold rings which are Ex 32:2 6561
all the people tore o the gold rings Ex 32:3 6561
has any gold, let them tear it o.' Ex 32:24 6561
put o your ornaments from you, Ex 33:5 3381
take o the veil until he came out; Ex 34:34 5493
screened o the ark of the testimony, Ex 40:21 5526a
to the altar, and wring o its head Lv 1:15 4454
'Then he shall take o his garments Lv 6:11 6584
shall be cut o from his people. Lv 7:20 3772
be cut o from his people.'" Lv 7:21 3772
shall be cut o from his people. Lv 7:25 3772
be cut o from his people.'" Lv 7:27 3772
clothes and shave o all his hair and Lv 14:8 1548
he shall shave o all his hair: Lv 14:9 1548
dump the plaster that they scrape o Lv 14:41 7096
then he shall count o for himself Lv 15:13
count o for herself seven days; Lv 15:28
and take o the linen garments Lv 16:23 6584
be cut o from among his people. Lv 17:4 3772
shall be cut o from his people. Lv 17:9 3772
cut him o from among his people. Lv 17:10 3772
whoever eats it shall be cut o.' Lv 17:14 3772
be cut o from among their people. Lv 18:29 3772
shall be cut o from his people. Lv 19:8 3772
shall not round o the side-growth Lv 19:27
cut him o from among his people, Lv 20:3 3772
and I will cut o from among their Lv 20:5 3772
cut him o from among his people. Lv 20:6 3772
and they shall be cut o in the Lv 20:17 3772
be cut o from among their people. Lv 20:18 3772
shave o the edges of their beards, Lv 21:5 1548
shall be cut o from before Me; Lv 22:3 3772
he shall be cut o from his people. Lv 23:29 3772
'You are also to count o seven Lv 25:8
be cut o from among the Levites. Nu 4:18 3772
he shall wash them o into the water Nu 5:23 4229a
then be cut o from his people, Nu 9:13 3772
be cut o from among his people. Nu 15:30 3772
person shall be completely cut o; Nu 15:31 3772
person shall be cut o from Israel. Nu 19:13 3772
that person shall be cut o from Nu 19:20 3772
not turn o into field or vineyard; Nu 21:22
the donkey turned o from the way Nu 22:23
wipe you o the face of the earth. Dt 6:15 4480, 5921
"When the LORD your God cuts o Dt 12:29 3772
LORD your God cuts o the nations, Dt 19:1 3772
and the iron *head* slips o the handle Dt 19:5 5394
or has his male organ cut o shall Dt 23:1 3772
pull his sandal o his foot and spit in Dt 25:9 4480, 5921
then you shall cut o her hand; Dt 25:12 7112
oil, for your olives will drop o. Dt 28:40 5394
of the Jordan will be cut o, Jos 3:13 3772
Salt Sea, were completely cut o. Jos 3:16 3772
the waters of the Jordan were cut o Jos 4:7 3772
waters of the Jordan were cut o.' Jos 4:7 3772
and cut o our name from the earth. Jos 7:9 3772
and cut o the Anakim from the hill Jos 11:21 3772
"How long will you put o entering Jos 18:3 7503
the nations which I have cut o, Jos 23:4 3772
until you perish from o this good Jos 23:13 5921
He has destroyed you from o this Jos 23:15 5921
you will perish quickly from o the Jos 23:16 5921
and cut o his thumbs and big toes. Jg 1:6 7112
their thumbs and their big toes cut o Jg 1:7 7112
shave o the seven locks of his hair. Jg 16:19 1548
grow again after it was shaved o. Jg 16:22 1548
tribe is cut o from Israel today. Jg 21:6 1438
will not be cut o from his brothers Ru 4:10 3772
'Yet I will not cut o every man of 1Sa 2:33 3772
Eli fell o the seat backward 1Sa 4:18 4480, 5921
hands *were* cut o on the threshold; 1Sa 5:4 3772
And David took them o. 1Sa 17:39 4480, 5921
him, and cut o his head with it. 1Sa 17:51 3772
He also stripped o his clothes, 1Sa 19:24 6584
"You shall not cut o your 1Sa 20:15 3772
not even when the LORD cuts o 1Sa 20:15 3772
cut o the edge of Saul's robe secretly 1Sa 24:4 3772
had cut o the edge of Saul's *robe.* 1Sa 24:5 3772
For in that I cut o the edge of 1Sa 24:11 3772
not cut o my descendants after me and 1Sa 24:21 3772
how he has cut o those who are 1Sa 28:9 3772
carried *them* o and went their way. 1Sa 30:2 5090a
They cut o his head and 1Sa 31:9 3772
head and stripped o his weapons, 1Sa 31:9 6584
and cut o their hands and feet and 2Sa 4:12 7112
and have cut o all your enemies 2Sa 7:9 3772
and shaved o half of their beards, 2Sa 10:4 1548
and cut o their garments in the 2Sa 10:4 3772
go over now and cut o his head." 2Sa 16:9 5493
And they cut o the head of Sheba 2Sa 20:22 3772
land of the enemy, far o or near; 1Ki 8:46
then I will cut o Israel from the 1Ki 9:7 3772
he had cut o every male in Edom), 1Ki 11:16 3772
it from o the face of the earth. 1Ki 13:34 5921
and will cut o from Jeroboam every 1Ki 14:10 3772
who will cut o the house of Jeroboam 1Ki 14:14 3772
boast like him who takes *it* o.'" 1Ki 20:11 6605a
will cut o from Ahab every male, 1Ki 21:21 3772
him the place, he cut o a stick and 2Ki 6:6 7094
and I will cut o from Ahab every 2Ki 9:8 3772
to cut o *portions* from Israel; 2Ki 10:32 7096
cut o the borders of the stands, 2Ki 16:17 7112
At that time Hezekiah cut o *the* 2Ki 18:16 7112
And I will cast o Jerusalem, this 2Ki 23:27 3988a
and have cut o all your enemies 1Ch 17:8 3772
and cut o their garments in the 1Ch 19:4 3772
captive to a land far o or near, 2Ch 6:36
to cut o the house of Ahab. 2Ch 22:7 3772
cut o from the house of the LORD. 2Ch 26:21 1504
warriors to cut o the *supply of* water 2Ch 32:3 5640
Please, let us leave o this usury. Ne 5:10
The king took o his signet ring Es 8:2 5493
would loose His hand and cut me o! Jb 6:9 1214
I will leave o my *sad* countenance Jb 9:27
"He will drop o his unripe grape Jb 15:33 2554
And will cast o his flower like Jb 15:33 7993
And his branch is cut o above. Jb 18:16 4448c
number of his months is cut o? Jb 21:21 2686a
'Truly our adversaries are cut o, Jb 22:20 3582
drags o the valiant by His power; Jb 24:22
the heads of grain they are cut o. Jb 24:24 4448c
of the godless when he is cut o, Jb 27:8 1214
have cast o the bridle before me. Jb 30:11 7971
my arm be broken o at the elbow. Jb 31:22 7665
"Who can strip o his outer armor? Jb 41:13 1540
Why do You stand afar o, Ps 10:1
LORD cut o all flattering lips, Ps 12:3 3772
But You, O LORD, be not far o; Ps 22:19
am cut o from before Your eyes"; Ps 31:22 1629a
To cut o the memory of them from Ps 34:16 3772
For evildoers will be cut o, Ps 37:9 3772
those cursed by Him will be cut o. Ps 37:22 3772
of the wicked will be cut o. Ps 37:28 3772
When the wicked are cut o, Ps 37:34 3772
of the wicked will be cut o. Ps 37:38 3772
And my kinsmen stand afar o. Ps 38:11
flow away like water that runs o; Ps 58:7 1980
cast me o in the time of old age; Ps 71:9 7993
horns of the wicked He will cut o, Ps 75:10 1438
will cut o the spirit of princes; Ps 76:12 1219
And they are cut o from Your hand. Ps 88:5 1504
will not break o My lovingkindness Ps 89:33
But You have cast o and rejected, Ps 89:38 2186a
So as to cut o from the city of Ps 101:8 3772
Let his posterity be cut o; Ps 109:13 3772
cut o their memory from the earth; Ps 109:15 3772
I am shaken o like the locust. Ps 109:23 5287
the LORD I will surely cut them o. Ps 118:10 4135
the LORD I will surely cut them o. Ps 118:11 4135
the LORD I will surely cut them o. Ps 118:12 4135
lovingkindness, cut o my enemies Ps 143:12 6789
will be cut o from the land And Pr 2:22 3772
And your hope will not be cut o. Pr 23:18 3772
And your hope will not be cut o. Pr 24:14 3772
takes o a garment on a cold day, Pr 25:20 5710a
He cuts o *his own* feet *and* drinks Pr 26:6 7096
But better o than both of them is Ec 4:3
it is better o than he. Ec 6:5
"I have taken o my dress, How can SS 5:3 6584
carries *it* o with no one to deliver *it.* Is 5:29 6403
cuts o head and tail from Israel, Is 9:14 3772
They slice o *what is* on the Is 9:20 1504
And to cut o many nations. Is 10:7 3772
will lop o the boughs with a Is 10:33 5586
who harass Judah will be cut o; Is 11:13 3772
"and will cut o from Babylon name Is 14:22 3772
And it will kill o your survivors. Is 14:30
is bald *and* every beard is cut o. Is 15:2 1639
carry o over the brook of Arabim. Is 15:7
Then He will cut o the sprigs with Is 18:5 3772
and take your shoes o your feet." Is 20:2 4480
it will even break o and fall, Is 22:25 1438
load hanging on it will be cut o, Is 22:25 3772
limbs are dry, they are broken o; Is 27:11
intent on doing evil will be cut o; Is 29:20 3772
corpses will give o their stench, Is 34:3 5927
He cuts me o from the loom; Is 38:12 1214
marked o the heavens by the span, Is 40:12 8505
My righteousness, it is not far o; Is 46:13
your veil, strip o the skirt, Is 47:2 2834
you, In order not to cut you o. Is 48:9 3772
Their name would never be cut o Is 48:19 3772
o out of the land of the living For Is 53:8 1504
sign which will not be cut o." Is 55:13 3772
name which will not be cut o. Is 56:5 3772
your yoke *And* tore o your bonds; Jer 2:20 5423
daughter of Zion, I will cut o. Jer 6:2 1820
has been cut o from their mouth. Jer 7:28 3772
'Cut o your hair and cast *it* away, Jer 7:29 1494
cut o the children from the streets, Jer 9:21 3772
him o from the land of the living, Jer 11:19 3772
Drag them o like sheep for the Jer 12:3 5423
stripped your skirts o over your face Jer 13:26 2834
sword to slay, the dogs to drag o, Jer 15:3
Dragged o and thrown out beyond Jer 22:19
hand, yet I would pull you o; Jer 22:24 5423
"And not a God far o? Jer 23:23 4480, 7350
had broken the yoke from o the neck Jer 28:12 5921
break his yoke from o their neck and Jer 30:8 5921
neck and will tear o their bonds; Jer 30:8 5423
declare in the coastlands afar o, Jer 31:10 4801
also cast o all the offspring of Israel Jer 31:37 3988a
with their beards shaved o and their Jer 41:5 1548
to cut o from you man and woman, Jer 44:7 3772
so that you might be cut o and Jer 44:8 3772
for woe, even to cut o all Judah. Jer 44:11 3772
plenty of food and were well o Jer 44:17 2896a
To cut o from Tyre and Sidon Every Jer 47:4 3772
us cut her o from *being* a nation!' Jer 48:2 3772
And Chemosh will go o into exile Jer 48:7 3318
"The horn of Moab has been cut o and Jer 48:25 1438
surely they will drag them o, Jer 49:20 5498
They will carry o for themselves Jer 49:29 5375
man and beast have wandered o, Jer 50:3
"Cut o the sower from Babylon And Jer 50:16 3772
earth Has been cut o and broken! Jer 50:23 1438
surely they will drag them o, Jer 50:45 5498
concerning this place to cut it o, Jer 51:62 3772
cut o All the strength of Israel; La 2:3 1438
over my head; I said, "I am cut o!" La 3:54 1504
is far o will die by the plague, Ezk 6:12 7350
and he prophesies of times far o.' Ezk 12:27 7350
"I will also tear o your veils Ezk 13:21
cut him o from among My people. Ezk 14:8 3772
cut o from it both man and beast, Ezk 14:13 3772
and cut o man and beast from it,' Ezk 14:17 3772
to cut o man and beast from it, Ezk 14:19 3772
to cut o man and beast from it! Ezk 14:21 3772
washed o your blood from you and Ezk 16:9 7857
"He plucked o the topmost of its Ezk 17:4 6998
up its roots and cut o its fruit, Ezk 17:9 7082
siege walls to cut o many lives. Ezk 17:17 3772
was torn o So that it withered; Ezk 19:12 6561
and cut o from you the righteous Ezk 21:3 3772
"Because I will cut o from you Ezk 21:4 3772
the turban and take o the crown; Ezk 21:26 7311
I will cut you o from the peoples Ezk 25:7 3772
and cut o man and beast from it. Ezk 25:13 3772
even cut o the Cherethites and Ezk 25:16 3772
strip o their embroidered garments. Ezk 26:16 6584
cut o from you man and beast. Ezk 29:8 3772
And he will carry o her wealth and Ezk 29:19 5375
cut o the hordes of Thebes. Ezk 30:15 3772
and I will cut o from it the one Ezk 35:7 3772
We are completely cut o.' Ezk 37:11 1504
it will block o those who would pass Ezk 39:11 2629
they shall put o their garments in Ezk 44:19 6584
the tree and cut o its branches, Da 4:14 7113
Strip o its foliage and scatter Da 4:14 5426
can ward o His hand Or say to Him, Da 4:35 4223
Then the king went o to his palace Da 6:18 236
will be cut o and have nothing, Da 9:26 3772
That they might be cut o. Hos 8:4 3772
Samaria will be cut o *with* her king Like Hos 10:7 1820
Israel will be completely cut o. Hos 10:15 1820

That is cut o from your mouth. Jl 1:5 3772
cut o From the house of the LORD. Jl 1:9 3772
food been cut o before our eyes, Jl 1:16 3772
And cut o the inhabitant from the Am 1:5 3772
cut o the inhabitant from Ashdod, Am 1:8 3772
cut o the judge from her midst And Am 2:3 3772
horns of the altar will be cut o And Am 3:14 1438
Do you put o the day of calamity, Am 6:3 5077
So that everyone may be cut o Ob 1:9 3772
And you will be cut o forever. Ob 1:10 3772
strangers carried o his wealth, Ob 1:11 7617
yourself bald and cut o your hair, Mi 1:16 1494
You strip the robe o the garment From Mi 2:8 6584
Who tear o their skin from them Mi 3:2 1497
Strip o their skin from them, Mi 3:3 6584
all your enemies will be cut o. Mi 5:9 3772
"That I will cut o your horses Mi 5:10 3772
"I will also cut o the cities of Mi 5:11 3772
cut o sorceries from your hand, Mi 5:12 3772
"I will cut o your carved images Mi 5:13 3772
they will be cut o and pass away. Na 1:12 1494
And I will tear o your shackles." Na 1:13 5423
I will cut o idol and image From Na 1:14 3772
He is cut o completely. Na 1:15 3772
cut o your prey from the land, Na 2:13 3772
house By cutting o many peoples; Hab 2:10 7096
flock should be cut o from the fold And Hab 3:17 1504
cut o man from the face of the earth Zph 1:3 3772
I will cut o the remnant of Baal Zph 1:4 3772
weigh out silver will be cut o. Zph 1:11 3772
"I have cut o nations; Zph 3:6 3772
So her dwelling will not be cut o Zph 3:7 3772
"Those who are far o will Zch 6:15
cut o the pride of the Philistines. Zch 9:6 3772
cut o the chariot from Ephraim And Zch 9:10 3772
And the bow of war will be cut o. Zch 9:10 3772
fat *sheep* and tear o their hoofs. Zch 11:16 6561
I will cut o the names of the idols Zch 13:2 3772
in it will be cut o *and* perish; Zch 13:8 3772
will not be cut o from the city. Zch 14:2 3772
may the LORD cut o from the tents Mal 2:12 3772
hand makes you stumble, cut it o and Mt 5:30 1581
shake the dust o your feet. Mt 10:14 1621
REED HE WILL NOT BREAK O, Mt 12:20
house and carry o his property, Mt 12:29 726
cut it o and throw it from you; Mt 18:8 1581
because you shut o the kingdom of Mt 23:13
high priest and cut o his ear. Mt 26:51 851
o Him and put His *own* garments back Mt 27:31 1562
And He went o with him; Mk 5:24 565
shake the dust o the soles of Mk 6:11 1621
causes you to stumble, cut it o; Mk 9:43 609
causes you to stumble, cut it o; Mk 9:45 609
went o to the chief priests in Mk 14:10 565
high priest and cut o his ear. Mk 14:47 851
Him, they took the purple robe o Him Mk 15:20 1562
He went o to the mountain to pray, Lk 6:12 1831
shake the dust o your feet as Lk 9:5 660
we wipe o *in protest* against you; Lk 10:11 631
while he was still a long way o, Lk 15:20 568
in water and cool o my tongue, Lk 16:24
priest and cut o his right ear. Lk 22:50 851
spoke to him and started o. Jn 4:50
near Jerusalem, about two miles o; Jn 11:18 575
slave, and cut o his right ear; Jn 18:10 609
of the one whose ear Peter cut o, Jn 18:26 609
and for all who are far o, Ac 2:39 3112
'TAKE O THE SANDALS FROM YOUR Ac 7:33 3089
and dragging o men and women, he Ac 8:3
they sent Barnabas o to Antioch. Ac 11:22 1821
And his chains fell o his hands. Ac 12:7 1601b
But they shook o the dust of their Ac 13:51 1621
magistrates tore their robes o them and Ac 16:22 4048
and started o for Damascus in Ac 22:5
throwing o their cloaks and tossing Ac 22:23 4496
about the Way, put them o, Ac 24:22 306
difficulty had arrived o Cnidus, Ac 27:7 2596
the shelter of Crete, o Salmone; Ac 27:7 2596
And casting o the anchors, they Ac 27:40 4014
he shook the creature o into the fire Ac 28:5 660
of the branches were broken o, Ro 11:17 1575
o so that I might be grafted in." Ro 11:19 1575
were broken o for their unbelief, Ro 11:20 1575
otherwise you also will be cut o. Ro 11:22 1581
cut o from what is by nature a wild Ro 11:24 1581
let her also have her hair cut o; 1Co 11:6 2751
her hair cut o or her head shaved, 1Co 11:6 2751
that I may cut o opportunity from 2Co 11:12 1581
you who formerly were far o have Eph 2:13 3112
and its flower falls o and Jas 1:11 1601b
WITHERS, AND THE FLOWER FALLS O, 1Pe 1:24 1601b
and went o to make war with the Rv 12:17 565

OFFEND

I will not o *anymore;* Jb 34:31 2254b
"However, so that we do not o them, Mt 17:27 4624

OFFENDED

the king of Egypt o their lord, Gn 40:1 2398
A brother o *is harder to be won* Pr 18:19 6586
Pharisees were o when they heard this Mt 15:12 4624
nor for the sake of the one o, 2Co 7:12 91

OFFENDER

and he said to the o, Ex 2:13 7563
it was not for the sake of the o nor 2Co 7:12 91

OFFENDERS

Solomon will be considered o." 1Ki 1:21 2400

OFFENSE

all on the third day, it is an o; Lv 19:7 6292
a ram of the flock for their o. Ezr 10:19 818
"And blessed is he who does not take o Mt 11:6 4624
And they took o at Him. Mt 13:57 4624
And they took o at Him. Mk 6:3 4624
"Blessed is he who does not take o Lk 7:23 4624
"I have committed no o either Ac 25:8 264
in the likeness of the o of Adam, Ro 5:14 3847
OF STUMBLING AND A ROCK OF O, Ro 9:33 4625
for the man who eats and gives o. Ro 14:20 4348
Give no o either to Jews or to 1Co 10:32 677
giving no cause for o in anything, 2Co 6:3 4349
OF STUMBLING AND A ROCK OF O"; 1Pe 2:8 4625

OFFENSES

make mention today of my *own* o. Gn 41:9 2399
because composure allays great o. Ec 10:4 2399

OFFENSIVE

It shall be an o thing, and the Lv 7:18 6292
"My breath is o to my wife, And I Jb 19:17 2114b
of Samaria I saw an o thing: Jer 23:13 8604
speaks anything o against the God Da 3:29 7960

OFFER

and o him there as a burnt offering Gn 22:2 5927
"You shall not o the blood of My Ex 23:18 2076
o them up in smoke on the altar. Ex 29:13 6999
"You shall o up in smoke the Ex 29:18 6999
and o them up in smoke on the Ex 29:25 6999
"Each day you shall o a bull Ex 29:36 6213a
is what you shall o on the altar: Ex 29:38 6213a
lamb you shall o in the morning and Ex 29:39 6213a
lamb you shall o at twilight; Ex 29:39 6213a
lamb you shall o at twilight, Ex 29:41 6213a
and shall o with it the Ex 29:41 6213a
You shall not o any strange incense Ex 30:9 5927
"You shall not o the blood of My Ex 34:25 7819
from the herd, he shall o it, Lv 1:3 7126
he shall o it at the doorway of Lv 1:3 7126
shall o up the blood and sprinkle Lv 1:5 7126
And the priest shall o up in smoke Lv 1:9 6999
shall o it a male without defect. Lv 1:10 7126
And the priest shall o all of it, Lv 1:13 7126
and o it up in smoke on the altar; Lv 1:13 6999
and o it up in smoke on the altar; Lv 1:15 6999
And the priest shall o it up in Lv 1:17 6999
And the priest shall o *it up* in Lv 2:2 6999
and shall o *it* up in smoke on the Lv 2:9 6999
for you shall not o up in smoke Lv 2:11 6999
your offerings you shall o salt. Lv 2:13 7126
The priest shall o up in smoke Lv 2:16 6999
he is going to o out of the herd, Lv 3:1 7126
he shall o it without defect Lv 3:1 7126
'Then Aaron's sons shall o *it* up Lv 3:5 6999
is from the flock, he shall o it, Lv 3:6 7126
to o a lamb for his offering, Lv 3:7 7126
he shall o it before the LORD, Lv 3:7 7126
o *it* up in smoke on the altar Lv 3:11 6999
he shall o it before the LORD, Lv 3:12 7126
The priest shall o them up in smoke Lv 3:16 6999
then let him o to the LORD a bull Lv 4:3 7126
the priest is to o them up in smoke Lv 4:10 6999
then the assembly shall o a bull Lv 4:14 7126
and o it up in smoke on the altar. Lv 4:19 6999
All its fat he shall o up in smoke Lv 4:26 6999
the priest shall o it up in smoke Lv 4:31 6999
o them up in smoke on the altar, Lv 4:35 6999
who shall o first that which is Lv 5:8 7126
and o *it* up in smoke on the altar, Lv 5:12 6999
and o up in smoke the fat portions Lv 6:12 6999
o *it* up in smoke on the altar, Lv 6:15 6999
place among his sons shall o it. Lv 6:22 6213a
he shall o from it all its fat: Lv 7:3 7126
'The priest shall o them up in Lv 7:5 6999
he shall o unleavened cakes mixed Lv 7:12 7126
'The priest shall o up the fat Lv 7:31 6999
and o *them* before the LORD. Lv 9:2 7126
"Come near to the altar and o Lv 9:7 6213a
'Then he shall o it before the LORD Lv 12:7 7126
The priest shall next o the sin offering Lv 14:19 6213a
"The priest shall o up the Lv 14:20 5927
and the priest shall o them for a Lv 14:24 5130
"He shall then o one of the Lv 14:30 6213a
"*He shall* o what he can afford, Lv 14:31
and the priest shall o them, Lv 15:15 6213a
'The priest shall o the one Lv 15:30 6213a
"Then Aaron shall o the bull for Lv 16:6 7126
"Then Aaron shall o the goat on Lv 16:9 7126
"Then Aaron shall o the bull of Lv 16:11 7126
altar, he shall o the live goat. Lv 16:20 7126
and come forth and o his burnt Lv 16:24 6213a
"Then he shall o up in smoke the Lv 16:25 6999
and o up the fat in smoke as a Lv 17:6 6999
of meeting to o it to the LORD, Lv 17:9 6213a
offspring to o them to Molech, Lv 18:21 5674a
you o a sacrifice of peace offerings Lv 19:5 2076
you shall o it so that you may be Lv 19:5 2076
be eaten the same day you o *it,* Lv 19:6 2077
to o the food of his God. Lv 21:17 7126
to o the LORD's offerings by fire; Lv 21:21 7126
near to o the food of his God. Lv 21:21 7126
Israel which they o to the LORD, Lv 22:15 7311
has a defect, you shall not o, Lv 22:20 7126
you shall not o to the LORD, Lv 22:22 7126
cut, you shall not o to the LORD, Lv 22:24 7126
you shall o a male lamb one year Lv 23:12 6213a
'You shall also o one male goat Lv 23:19 6213a
which they o to the priest, Nu 5:9 7126
and o *it* up in smoke on the altar, Nu 5:26 6999
'The priest shall o one for a Nu 6:11 6213a
and shall o his sin offering and his Nu 6:16 6213a
'He shall also o the ram for a Nu 6:17 6213a
the priest shall likewise o its Nu 6:17 6213a
then o the one for a sin offering Nu 8:12 6213a
and for the drink offering you shall o Nu 15:7 7126
then you shall o with the bull a Nu 15:9 7126
and you shall o as the drink offering Nu 15:10 7126
o one bull for a burnt offering, Nu 15:24 6213a
then he shall o a one year old Nu 15:27 7126
animal, which they o to the LORD, Nu 18:15 7126
and shall o up their fat in smoke Nu 18:17 6999
the sons of Israel o to the LORD, Nu 18:19 7311
they o as an offering to the LORD, Nu 18:24 7311
which you shall o to the LORD: Nu 28:3 7126
shall o the one lamb Nu 28:4 6213a
lamb you shall o at twilight; Nu 28:4 6213a
lamb you shall o at twilight; Nu 28:8 6213a
as its drink offering, you shall o it, Nu 28:8 6213a
shall o fine flour mixed with oil: Nu 28:20 6213a
o for each of the seven lambs; Nu 28:21 6213a
'You shall o a burnt offering Nu 28:27 7126
'You shall o a burnt offering Nu 29:2 6213a
'O one male goat for a sin Nu 29:5
"Be careful that you do not o Dt 12:13 5927
you shall o your burnt offerings, Dt 12:14 5927
you shall o your burnt offerings, Dt 12:27 6213a
from those who o a sacrifice, Dt 18:3 2076
it, you shall o it terms of peace. Dt 20:10 7121
you shall o on it burnt offerings Dt 27:6 5927
And there you will o yourselves Dt 28:68 4376
they will o righteous sacrifices; Dt 33:19 2076
or if to o a burnt offering or Jos 22:23 5927
or if to o sacrifices of peace Jos 22:23 6213a
and take a second bull and o a Jg 6:26 5927
o it up as a burnt offering." Jg 11:31 5927
offering, *then* o it to the LORD." Jg 13:16 5927
Philistines assembled to o a great Jg 16:23 2076
to o to the LORD the yearly sacrifice 1Sa 1:21 2076
husband to o the yearly sacrifice. 1Sa 2:19 2076
I will come down to you to o burnt 1Sa 10:8 5927
o up what is good in his sight. 2Sa 24:22 5927
for I will not o burnt offerings 2Sa 24:24 5927
"If this people go up to o 1Ki 12:27 6213a
for your servant will no longer o 2Ki 5:17 6213a
Then they went in to o sacrifices 2Ki 10:24 6213a
o a prayer for the remnant that is 2Ki 19:4 5375
to o burnt offerings to the LORD 1Ch 16:40 5927
"I o you three things; 1Ch 21:10 5186
or o a burnt offering which costs 1Ch 21:24 5927
and to o all burnt offerings to 1Ch 23:31 5927
able to o as generously as this? 1Ch 29:14 5068
and to o burnt offerings morning 2Ch 2:4
to o burnt offerings of the 2Ch 23:18 5927
o *them* on the altar of the LORD. 2Ch 29:21 5927
Then Hezekiah gave the order to o 2Ch 29:27 5927
and to o burnt offerings on the 2Ch 35:16 5927
to o burnt offerings on it, Ezr 3:2 5927
to o burnt offerings to the LORD, Ezr 3:6 5927
o acceptable sacrifices to the God Ezr 6:10 7127
offerings and o them on the altar Ezr 7:17 7127
Can they o sacrifices? Ne 4:2 2076
'O a bribe for me from your Jb 6:22 7809
and o up a burnt offering for Jb 42:8 5927
O the sacrifices of righteousness, Ps 4:5 2076
And I will o in His tent Ps 27:6 2076
O to God a sacrifice of thanksgiving Ps 50:14 2076
I shall o to You burnt offerings Ps 66:15 5927
kings of Sheba and Seba o gifts. Ps 72:10 7126
also o sacrifices of thanksgiving, Ps 107:22 2076
o a sacrifice of thanksgiving, Ps 116:17 2076
"I was due to o peace offerings; Pr 7:14 2077
than to o the sacrifice of fools; Ec 5:1 5414
o a prayer for the remnant that is Is 37:4 5375
also went up there to o sacrifice. Is 57:7 2076
falsely, and o sacrifices to Baal and Jer 7:9 6999
and when they o burnt offering and Jer 14:12 5927
before Me to o burnt offerings, Jer 33:18 5927
O complaint in view of his sins? La 3:39 596
Even jackals o the breast, They La 4:3 2502a
you would o before them for a Ezk 16:19 5414
"When you o your gifts, when Ezk 20:31 5375
to o burnt offerings on it and to Ezk 43:18 5927
'On the second day you shall o Ezk 43:22 7126
And they shall o them up as a Ezk 43:24 5927
the priests shall o your burnt Ezk 43:27 6213a
to o Me the fat and the blood," Ezk 44:15 7126
he shall o his sin offering," Ezk 44:27 7126
shall o an allotment to the LORD, Ezk 45:1 7311
is the offering that you shall o: Ezk 45:13 7311
which the prince shall o to the LORD Ezk 46:4 7126
the day of the new moon *he shall* o Ezk 46:6
When she used to o sacrifices to them Hos 2:13 6999
fault, and let none o reproof; Hos 4:4 3198
They o sacrifices on the tops of Hos 4:13 2076
o sacrifices with temple prostitutes; Hos 4:14 2076
"O a thank offering also from Am 4:5 6999
"Even though you o up to Me burnt Am 5:22 5927
they o a sacrifice to their net And Hab 1:16 2076
and what they o there is unclean. Hg 2:14 7126
Why not o it to your governor? Mal 1:8 7126
and o for your cleansing what Moses Mk 1:44 4374
appearance's sake o long prayers; Mk 12:40 4336
and to o a sacrifice according to Lk 2:24 1325
of John often fast and o prayers, Lk 5:33 4160
the cheek, o him the other also; Lk 6:29 3930
appearance's sake o long prayers. Lk 20:47 4336
to o sacrifice with the crowds. Ac 14:13 2380
hear my defense which I now o to Ac 22:1
I may o the gospel without charge, 1Co 9:18 5087
to o ourselves as a model for you, 2Th 3:9 1325
in order to o both gifts and Heb 5:1 4374

to **o** *sacrifices* for sins, **Heb 5:3** *4374*
high priests, to **o** up sacrifices, **Heb 7:27** *399*
to **o** both gifts and sacrifices; **Heb 8:3** *4374*
priest also have something to **o**. **Heb 8:3** *4374*
who **o** the gifts according to the Law **Heb 8:4** *4374*
it that He would **o** Himself often, **Heb 9:25** *4374*
which they **o** continually year by year, **Heb 10:1** *4374*
may **o** to God an acceptable service **Heb 12:28** *3000*
continually **o** up a sacrifice of praise **Heb 13:15** *399*
to **o** up spiritual sacrifices **1Pe 2:5** *399*

OFFERED

o burnt offerings on the altar. **Gn 8:20** 5927
and **o** him up for a burnt offering **Gn 22:13** 5927
o a sacrifice on the mountain, **Gn 31:54** 2076
and **o** sacrifices to the God of his **Gn 46:1** 2076
and they **o** burnt offerings and **Ex 24:5** 5927
was **o** from the ram of ordination, **Ex 29:27** 7311
rose early and **o** burnt offerings, **Ex 32:6** 5927
and **o** on it the burnt offering and **Ex 40:29** 5927
o up in smoke to the LORD. **Lv 6:22** 6999
offering by fire is **o** to the LORD, **Lv 7:25** 7126
o it up in smoke on the altar. **Lv 8:16** 6999
Moses **o** up the head and the pieces **Lv 8:20** 6999
Moses **o** up the whole ram in smoke **Lv 8:21** 6999
and **o** them up in smoke on the altar **Lv 8:28** 6999
he then **o** up in smoke on the altar **Lv 9:10** 6999
o *them* up in smoke on the altar. **Lv 9:13** 6999
and **o** *them* up in smoke with the **Lv 9:14** 6999
slaughtered it and **o** it for sin, **Lv 9:15** 2398
o it according to the ordinance. **Lv 9:16** 6213a
and **o** *it* up in smoke on the altar, **Lv 9:17** 6999
o them up in smoke on the altar. **Lv 9:20** 6999
o strange fire before the LORD, **Lv 10:1** 7126
"The thigh **o** by lifting up and **Lv 10:15** 8641
up and the breast **o** by waving they **Lv 10:15** 8573
they **o** strange fire before the LORD **Nu 3:4** 7126
together with the breast **o** by waving **Nu 6:20** 8573
and the thigh **o** by lifting up; **Nu 6:20** 8641
The leaders **o** the dedication *offering* **Nu 7:10** 7126
so the leaders **o** their offering **Nu 7:10** 7126
the men who were burned had **o**, **Nu 16:39** 7126
you have **o** from it the best of it, **Nu 18:30** 7311
when you have **o** the best of it. **Nu 18:32** 7311
and Balak and Balaam **o** up a bull **Nu 23:2** 5927
and I have **o** up a bull and a ram **Nu 23:4** 5927
and built seven altars and **o** a **Nu 23:14** 5927
and **o** up a bull and a ram on *each* **Nu 23:30** 5927
o strange fire before the LORD. **Nu 26:61** 7126
it shall be **o** with its drink offering in **Nu 28:15** 6213a
which they **o** up to the LORD, **Nu 31:52** 7311
nor **o** any of it to the dead. **Dt 26:14** 5414
and they **o** burnt offerings on it **Jos 8:31** 5927
the second bull was **o** on the altar **Jg 6:28** 5927
and **o** it on the rock to the LORD, **Jg 13:19** 5927
And they **o** burnt offerings and **Jg 20:26** 5927
and **o** burnt offerings and peace **Jg 21:4** 5927
and **o** the cows as a burnt offering **1Sa 6:14** 5927
and the men of Beth-shemesh **o** **1Sa 6:15** 5927
Samuel took a suckling lamb and **o** it **1Sa 7:9** 5927
There they also **o** sacrifices of **1Sa 11:15** 2076
And he **o** the burnt offering. **1Sa 13:9** 5927
myself and **o** the burnt offering." **1Sa 13:12** 5927
and David **o** burnt offerings and **2Sa 6:17** 5927
and **o** burnt offerings and peace **2Sa 24:25** 5927
Solomon **o** a thousand burnt **1Ki 3:4** 5927
and **o** burnt offerings and made **1Ki 3:15** 5927
him **o** sacrifice before the LORD. **1Ki 8:62** 2076
Solomon **o** for the sacrifice of **1Ki 8:63** 2076
offerings, which he **o** to the LORD, **1Ki 8:63** 2076
because there he **o** the burnt **1Ki 8:64** 6213a
Solomon **o** burnt offerings and peace **1Ki 9:25** 5927
and **o** him as a burnt offering on **2Ki 3:27** 5927
o no tribute to the king of Assyria, **2Ki 17:4** 5927
But Aaron and his sons **o** on the **1Ch 6:49** 6999
and they **o** burnt offerings and **1Ch 16:1** 7126
and **o** burnt offerings and peace **1Ch 21:26** 5927
Jebusite, he **o** sacrifice there. **1Ch 21:28** 2076
over the king's work, **o** willingly; **1Ch 29:6** 5068
because they had **o** so willingly, **1Ch 29:9** 5068
have willingly **o** all these *things;* **1Ch 29:17** 5068
and **o** burnt offerings to the LORD, **1Ch 29:21** 5927
and **o** a thousand burnt offerings **2Ch 1:6** 5927
Your ears attentive to the prayer **o** **2Ch 6:40**
o sacrifice before the LORD. **2Ch 7:4** 2076
o a sacrifice of 22,000 oxen and **2Ch 7:5** 2076
for there he **o** the burnt offerings **2Ch 7:7** 6213a
My ears attentive to the prayer **o** **2Ch 7:15**
Then Solomon **o** burnt offerings to **2Ch 8:12** 5927
And they **o** burnt offerings in the **2Ch 24:14** 5927
o burnt offerings in the holy place **2Ch 29:7** 5927
o willingly for the house of God **Ezr 2:68** 5068
and they **o** burnt offerings on it **Ezr 3:3** 5927
and **o** the fixed number of burnt **Ezr 3:4**
and from everyone who **o** a freewill **Ezr 3:5** 5068
the place where sacrifices are **o**, **Ezr 6:3** 1684
They **o** for the dedication of **Ezr 6:17** 7127
freely **o** to the God of Israel, **Ezr 7:15** 5069
who **o** willingly for the house of **Ezr 7:16** 5069
all Israel present *there* had **o**. **Ezr 8:25** 7311
o burnt offerings to the God of Israel **Ezr 8:35** 7126
they **o** a ram of the flock for **Ezr 10:19**
on that day they **o** great sacrifices **Ne 12:43** 2076
bulls will be **o** on Your altar. **Ps 51:19** 5927
And ate sacrifices **o** to the dead. **Ps 106:28**
have **o** sacrifices to other gods, **Jer 1:16** 6999
where *people* have **o** incense to Baal **Jer 32:29** 6999
places where they **o** soothing aroma **Ezk 6:13** 5414
and **o** My oil and My incense before **Ezk 16:18** 5414
and **o** them up to idols by causing **Ezk 16:21** 5414
and they **o** there their sacrifices and **Ezk 20:28** 2076
even My house, when you **o** My food, **Ezk 44:7** 7126
and they **o** a sacrifice to the LORD **Jon 1:16** 2076
is going to be **o** to My name, **Mal 1:11** 5066, 6999
WAS NOT TO ME THAT YOU **O** VICTIMS **Ac 7:42** *4374*
apostles' hands, he **o** them money, **Ac 8:18** *4374*
was **o** for each one of them. **Ac 21:26** *4374*
He **o** up both prayers and **Heb 5:7** *4374*
once for all when He **o** up Himself. **Heb 7:27** *399*
both gifts and sacrifices are **o** **Heb 9:9** *4374*
through the eternal Spirit **o** Himself **Heb 9:14** *4374*
o once to bear the sins of many, **Heb 9:28** *4374*
would they not have ceased to be **o**, **Heb 10:2** *4374*
(which are **o** according to the Law), **Heb 10:8** *4374*
having **o** one sacrifice for sins **Heb 10:12** *4374*
By faith Abel **o** to God a better **Heb 11:4** *4374*
when he was tested, **o** up Isaac, **Heb 11:17** *4374*
o up Isaac his son on the altar? **Jas 2:21** *399*
and the prayer **o** in faith will **Jas 5:15**

OFFERING

Cain brought an **o** to the LORD **Gn 4:3** 4503
had regard for Abel and for his **o**; **Gn 4:4** 4503
and for his **o** He had no regard. **Gn 4:5** 4503
and offer him there as a burnt **o** **Gn 22:2** 5930a
and he split wood for the burnt **o**, **Gn 22:3** 5930a
took the wood of the burnt **o** and **Gn 22:6** 5930a
where is the lamb for the burnt **o**?" **Gn 22:7** 5930a
Himself the lamb for the burnt **o**, **Gn 22:8** 5930a
a burnt **o** in the place of his son. **Gn 22:13** 5930a
and he poured out a drink **o** on it; **Gn 35:14** 5262a
a burnt **o** and sacrifices for God, **Ex 18:12** 5930a
"You shall not delay *the* **o** *from* **Ex 22:29**
fire outside the camp; it is a sin **o**. **Ex 29:14** 2403b
it is a burnt **o** to the LORD: **Ex 29:18** 5930a
aroma, an **o** by fire to the LORD. **Ex 29:18** 801
them as a wave **o** before the LORD. **Ex 29:24** 8573
in smoke on the altar on the burnt **o** **Ex 29:25** 5930a
it is an **o** by fire to the LORD. **Ex 29:25** 801
it as a wave **o** before the LORD; **Ex 29:26** 8573
consecrate the breast of the wave **o** **Ex 29:27** 8573
and the thigh of the heave **o** **Ex 29:27** 8641
of Israel, for it is a heave **o**; **Ex 29:28** 8641
and it shall be a heave **o** from the **Ex 29:28** 8641
even their heave **o** to the LORD. **Ex 29:28** 8641
a bull as a sin **o** for atonement, **Ex 29:36** 2403b
of a hin of wine for a drink **o** with **Ex 29:40** 5262a
offer with it the same grain **o** and **Ex 29:41** 4503
grain offering and the same drink **o** **Ex 29:41** 5262a
aroma, an **o** by fire to the LORD. **Ex 29:41** 801
"It shall be a continual burnt **o** **Ex 29:42** 5930a
or burnt **o** or meal offering; **Ex 30:9** 5930a
or burnt offering or meal **o**; **Ex 30:9** 4503
shall not pour out a drink **o** **Ex 30:9** 5262a
the blood of the sin **o** of atonement **Ex 30:10** 2403b
by **o** up in smoke a fire *sacrifice* **Ex 30:20** 6999
altar of burnt **o** and all its utensils, **Ex 30:28** 5930a
the altar of burnt **o** also with all its **Ex 31:9** 5930a
burnt **o** with its bronze grating, **Ex 35:16** 5930a
an **o** of gold to the LORD. **Ex 35:22** 8573
brought a freewill **o** to the LORD. **Ex 35:29** 5071
altar of burnt **o** of acacia wood, **Ex 38:1** 5930a
even the gold of the wave **o**, **Ex 38:24** 8573
of the wave **o** was 70 talents and **Ex 38:29** 8573
set the altar of burnt **o** in front of the **Ex 40:6** 5930a
altar of burnt **o** and all its utensils, **Ex 40:10** 5930a
He set the altar of burnt **o** **Ex 40:29** 5930a
the burnt **o** and the meal offering, **Ex 40:29** 5930a
the burnt offering and the meal **o**, **Ex 40:29** 4503
of you brings an **o** to the LORD, **Lv 1:2** 7133a
you shall bring your **o** of animals **Lv 1:2** 7133a
'If his **o** is a burnt offering from **Lv 1:3** 7133a
is a burnt **o** from the herd, **Lv 1:3** 5930a
hand on the head of the burnt **o**, **Lv 1:4** 5930a
'He shall then skin the burnt **o** and **Lv 1:6** 5930a
of it on the altar for a burnt **o**, **Lv 1:9** 5930a
an **o** by fire of a soothing aroma **Lv 1:9** 801
'But if his **o** is from the flock, **Lv 1:10** 7133a
or of the goats, for a burnt **o**, **Lv 1:10** 5930a
it is a burnt **o**, an offering by **Lv 1:13** 5930a
an **o** by fire of a soothing aroma **Lv 1:13** 801
'But if his **o** to the LORD is a **Lv 1:14** 7133a
to the LORD is a burnt **o** of birds, **Lv 1:14** 5930a
then he shall bring his **o** from the **Lv 1:14** 7133a
it is a burnt **o**, an offering by **Lv 1:17** 5930a
an **o** by fire of a soothing aroma **Lv 1:17** 801
o as an offering to the LORD, **Lv 2:1** 4503
offering as an **o** to the LORD, **Lv 2:1** 7133a
his **o** shall be of fine flour, **Lv 2:1** 7133a
an **o** by fire of a soothing aroma **Lv 2:2** 801
o belongs to Aaron and his sons: **Lv 2:3** 4503
you bring an **o** of a grain offering **Lv 2:4** 7133a
of a grain **o** baked in an oven, **Lv 2:4** 4503
'If your **o** is a grain offering **Lv 2:5** 7133a
is a grain **o** *made* on the griddle, **Lv 2:5** 4503
and pour oil on it; it is a grain **o**. **Lv 2:6** 4503
'Now if your **o** is a grain offering **Lv 2:7** 7133a
is a grain **o** *made* in a pan, **Lv 2:7** 4503
'When you bring in the grain **o** **Lv 2:8** 4503
then shall take up from the grain **o** **Lv 2:9** 4503
as an **o** by fire of a soothing aroma **Lv 2:9** 801
The remainder of the grain **o** belongs **Lv 2:10** 4503
'No grain **o**, which you bring to **Lv 2:11** 4503
honey as an **o** by fire to the LORD. **Lv 2:11** 801
'As an **o** of first fruits you **Lv 2:12** 7133a
'Every grain **o** of yours, moreover, **Lv 2:13** 7133a, 4503
not be lacking from your grain **o**; **Lv 2:13** 4503
a grain **o** of early ripened things **Lv 2:14** 4503
for the grain **o** of your early **Lv 2:14** 4503
and lay incense on it; it is a grain **o**. **Lv 2:15** 4503
as an **o** by fire to the LORD. **Lv 2:16** 801
his **o** is a sacrifice of peace offerings **Lv 3:1** 7133a
lay his hand on the head of his **o** **Lv 3:2** 7133a
present an **o** by fire to the LORD, **Lv 3:3** 801
smoke on the altar on the burnt **o**, **Lv 3:5** 5930a
is an **o** by fire of a soothing aroma **Lv 3:5** 801
o for a sacrifice of peace offerings **Lv 3:6** 7133a
going to offer a lamb for his **o**, **Lv 3:7** 7133a
lay his hand on the head of his **o** and **Lv 3:8** 7133a
bring as an **o** by fire to the LORD, **Lv 3:9** 801
as food, an **o** by fire to the LORD. **Lv 3:11** 801
'Moreover, if his **o** is a goat, **Lv 3:12** 7133a
present his **o** as an offering by fire **Lv 3:14** 7133a
as an **o** by fire to the LORD, **Lv 3:14** 801
an **o** by fire for a soothing aroma; **Lv 3:16** 801
a sin **o** for the sin he has committed. **Lv 4:3** 2403b
at the base of the altar of burnt **o** **Lv 4:7** 5930a
the fat of the bull of the sin **o**: **Lv 4:8** 2403b
in smoke on the altar of burnt **o**. **Lv 4:10** 5930a
a bull of the herd for a sin **o** and **Lv 4:14** 2403b
at the base of the altar of burnt **o** **Lv 4:18** 5930a
he did with the bull of the sin **o**; **Lv 4:20** 2403b
it is the sin **o** for the assembly. **Lv 4:21** 2403b
he shall bring for his **o** a goat, **Lv 4:23** 7133a
slay the burnt **o** before the LORD; **Lv 4:24** 5930a
before the LORD; it is a sin **o**. **Lv 4:24** 2403b
of the sin **o** with his finger and **Lv 4:25** 2403b
the horns of the altar of burnt **o**; **Lv 4:25** 5930a
the base of the altar of burnt **o**. **Lv 4:25** 5930a
he shall bring for his **o** a goat, **Lv 4:28** 7133a
his hand on the head of the sin **o** and **Lv 4:29** 2403b
and slay the sin **o** at the place of **Lv 4:29** 2403b
at the place of the burnt **o**. **Lv 4:29** 5930a
the horns of the altar of burnt **o**; **Lv 4:30** 5930a
lamb as his **o** for a sin offering, **Lv 4:32** 7133a
lamb as his offering for a sin **o**, **Lv 4:32** 2403b
his hand on the head of the sin **o** and **Lv 4:33** 2403b
and slay it for a sin **o** in the **Lv 4:33** 2403b
place where they slay the burnt **o**. **Lv 4:33** 5930a
take some of the blood of the sin **o** **Lv 4:34** 2403b
the horns of the altar of burnt **o**, **Lv 4:34** 5930a
'He shall also bring his guilt **o** **Lv 5:6** 817
a lamb or a goat as a sin **o**. **Lv 5:6** 2403b
he shall bring to the LORD his guilt **o** **Lv 5:7** 817
one for a sin **o** and the other for **Lv 5:7** 2403b
and the other for a burnt **o**. **Lv 5:7** 5930a
offer first that which is for the sin **o** **Lv 5:8** 2403b
sin **o** on the side of the altar, **Lv 5:9** 2403b
the base of the altar: it is a sin **o**. **Lv 5:9** 2403b
he shall then prepare as a burnt **o** **Lv 5:10** 5930a
o for that which he has sinned, **Lv 5:11** 7133a
ephah of fine flour for a sin **o**; **Lv 5:11** 2403b
incense on it, for it is a sin **o**. **Lv 5:11** 2403b
of the LORD by fire: it is a sin **o**. **Lv 5:12** 2403b
the priest's, like the grain **o**.' " **Lv 5:13** 4503
bring his guilt **o** to the LORD: **Lv 5:15** 817
of the sanctuary, for a guilt **o**. **Lv 5:15** 817
him with the ram of the guilt **o**, **Lv 5:16** 817
to your valuation, for a guilt **o**. **Lv 5:18** 817
"It is a guilt **o**; he was certainly **Lv 5:19** 817
the day *he presents* his guilt **o**. **Lv 6:5** 819
priest his guilt **o** to the LORD, **Lv 6:6** 817
to your valuation, for a guilt **o**, **Lv 6:6** 817
'This is the law for the burnt **o**: **Lv 6:9** 5930a
the burnt **o** itself *shall remain* on **Lv 6:9** 5930a
reduces the burnt **o** on the altar and **Lv 6:10** 5930a
shall lay out the burnt **o** on it, **Lv 6:12** 5930a
this is the law of the grain **o**: **Lv 6:14** 4503
of the fine flour of the grain **o**, **Lv 6:15** 4503
incense that is on the grain **o**, **Lv 6:15** 4503
as its memorial **o** to the LORD. **Lv 6:15** 234
the sin **o** and the guilt offering. **Lv 6:17** 2403b
the sin offering and the guilt **o**. **Lv 6:17** 817
"This is the **o** which Aaron and **Lv 6:20** 7133a
fine flour as a regular grain **o**, **Lv 6:20** 4503
You shall present the grain **o** in **Lv 6:21** 4503
"So every grain **o** of the priest **Lv 6:23** 4503
'This is the law of the sin **o**: **Lv 6:25** 2403b
the place where the burnt **o** is slain **Lv 6:25** 5930a
sin **o** shall be slain before the LORD; **Lv 6:25** 2403b
'But no sin **o** of which any of the **Lv 6:30** 2403b
this is the law of the guilt **o**; **Lv 7:1** 817
the place where they slay the burnt **o** **Lv 7:2** 5930a
they are to slay the guilt **o**, **Lv 7:2** 817
altar as an **o** by fire to the LORD; **Lv 7:5** 801
by fire to the LORD; it is a guilt **o**. **Lv 7:5** 817
guilt **o** is like the sin offering, **Lv 7:7** 817
guilt offering is like the sin **o**, **Lv 7:7** 2403b
who presents any man's burnt **o**, **Lv 7:8** 5930a
burnt **o** which he has presented. **Lv 7:8** 5930a
grain **o** that is baked in the oven and **Lv 7:9** 4503
'Every grain **o**, mixed with oil **Lv 7:10** 4503
present his **o** with cakes of leavened **Lv 7:13** 7133a
one of every **o** as a contribution to **Lv 7:14** 7133a
be eaten on the day of his **o**; **Lv 7:15** 7133a
'But if the sacrifice of his **o** is **Lv 7:16** 7133a
is a votive or a freewill **o**, **Lv 7:16** 5071
an **o** by fire is offered to the LORD, **Lv 7:25** 801
shall bring his **o** to the LORD from **Lv 7:29** 7133a
as a wave **o** before the LORD. **Lv 7:30** 8573
I have taken the breast of the wave **o** **Lv 7:34** 8573
This is the law of the burnt **o**, **Lv 7:37** 5930a
the grain **o** and the sin offering **Lv 7:37** 4503
the grain offering and the sin **o** **Lv 7:37** 2403b
and the sin offering and the guilt **o** **Lv 7:37** 817
the ordination **o** and the sacrifice **Lv 7:37** 4394
oil and the bull of the sin **o**, **Lv 8:2** 2403b

he brought the bull of the sin **o**,	Lv 8:14	2403b
the head of the bull of the sin **o**.	Lv 8:14	2403b
presented the ram of the burnt **o**,	Lv 8:18	5930a
a burnt **o** for a soothing aroma;	Lv 8:21	5930a
it was an **o** by fire to the LORD,	Lv 8:21	801
them as a wave **o** before the LORD.	Lv 8:27	8573
on the altar with the burnt **o**.	Lv 8:28	5930a
ordination **o** for a soothing aroma;	Lv 8:28	4394
it was an **o** by fire to the LORD.	Lv 8:28	801
it for a wave **o** before the LORD;	Lv 8:29	8573
in the basket of the ordination **o**,	Lv 8:31	4394
for a sin **o** and a ram for a burnt	Lv 9:2	2403b
offering and a ram for a burnt **o**,	Lv 9:2	5930a
'Take a male goat for a sin **o**,	Lv 9:3	2403b
without defect, for a burnt **o**,	Lv 9:3	5930a
and a grain **o** mixed with oil;	Lv 9:4	4503
sin **o** and your burnt offering,	Lv 9:7	2403b
sin offering and your burnt **o**,	Lv 9:7	5930a
then make the **o** for the people,	Lv 9:7	7133a
the sin **o** which was for himself.	Lv 9:8	2403b
lobe of the liver of the sin **o**,	Lv 9:10	2403b
Then he slaughtered the burnt **o**;	Lv 9:12	5930a
They handed the burnt **o** to him	Lv 9:13	5930a
with the burnt **o** on the altar.	Lv 9:14	5930a
Then he presented the people's **o**,	Lv 9:15	7133a
sin **o** which was for the people,	Lv 9:15	2403b
He also presented the burnt **o**,	Lv 9:16	5930a
Next he presented the grain **o**,	Lv 9:17	4503
the burnt **o** of the morning.	Lv 9:17	5930a
as a wave **o** before the LORD,	Lv 9:21	8573
stepped down after making the sin **o**	Lv 9:22	2403b
burnt **o** and the peace offerings.	Lv 9:22	5930a
and consumed the burnt **o**	Lv 9:24	5930a
"Take the grain **o** that is left	Lv 10:12	4503
"The breast of the wave **o**,	Lv 10:14	8573
o you may eat in a clean place,	Lv 10:14	8641
as a wave **o** before the LORD;	Lv 10:15	8573
for the goat of the sin **o**,	Lv 10:16	2403b
eat the sin **o** at the holy place?	Lv 10:17	2403b
they presented their sin **o** and their	Lv 10:19	2403b
and their burnt **o** before the LORD.	Lv 10:19	5930a
me, if I had eaten a sin **o** today,	Lv 10:19	2403b
a one year old lamb for a burnt **o** and	Lv 12:6	5930a
or a turtledove for a sin **o**.	Lv 12:6	2403b
the one for a burnt **o** and the	Lv 12:8	5930a
and the other for a sin **o**;	Lv 12:8	2403b
mixed with oil for a grain **o**,	Lv 14:10	4503
lamb and bring it for a guilt **o**,	Lv 14:12	817
them as a wave **o** before the LORD.	Lv 14:12	8573
The sin **o** and the burnt offering,	Lv 14:13	2403b
the sin offering and the burnt **o**,	Lv 14:13	5930a
for the guilt **o**, like the sin offering,	Lv 14:13	817
guilt offering, like the sin **o**,	Lv 14:13	2403b
some of the blood of the guilt **o**,	Lv 14:14	817
foot, on the blood of the guilt **o**;	Lv 14:17	817
"The priest shall next offer the sin **o**	Lv 14:19	2403b
he shall slaughter the burnt **o**.	Lv 14:19	5930a
The priest shall offer up the burnt **o**	Lv 14:20	5930a
and the grain **o** on the altar.	Lv 14:20	4503
take one male lamb for a guilt **o**	Lv 14:21	817
wave **o** to make atonement for him,	Lv 14:21	8573
flour mixed with oil for a grain **o**,	Lv 14:21	4503
the one shall be a sin **o** and the	Lv 14:22	2403b
offering and the other a burnt **o**.	Lv 14:22	5930a
take the lamb of the guilt **o** and	Lv 14:24	817
them for a wave **o** before the LORD.	Lv 14:24	8573
slaughter the lamb of the guilt **o**;	Lv 14:25	817
take some of the blood of the guilt **o**	Lv 14:25	817
place of the blood of the guilt **o**.	Lv 14:28	817
can afford, the one for a sin **o** and	Lv 14:31	2403b
and the other for a burnt **o**,	Lv 14:31	5930a
together with the grain **o**.	Lv 14:31	4503
shall offer them, one for a sin **o** and	Lv 15:15	2403b
and the other for a burnt **o**.	Lv 15:15	5930a
priest shall offer the one for a sin **o**	Lv 15:30	2403b
and the other for a burnt **o**.	Lv 15:30	5930a
with a bull for a sin **o** and a ram	Lv 16:3	2403b
offering and a ram for a burnt **o**.	Lv 16:3	5930a
two male goats for a sin **o** and one	Lv 16:5	2403b
and one ram for a burnt **o**.	Lv 16:5	5930a
the sin **o** which is for himself,	Lv 16:6	2403b
LORD fell, and make it a sin **o**.	Lv 16:9	2403b
of the sin **o** which is for himself and	Lv 16:11	2403b
of the sin **o** which is for himself.	Lv 16:11	2403b
the sin **o** which is for the people,	Lv 16:15	2403b
and come forth and offer his burnt **o**	Lv 16:24	5930a
and the burnt **o** of the people and	Lv 16:24	5930a
the fat of the sin **o** on the altar.	Lv 16:25	2403b
"But the bull of the sin **o** and	Lv 16:27	2403b
and the goat of the sin **o**,	Lv 16:27	2403b
to present *it* as an **o** to the LORD	Lv 17:4	7133a
who offers a burnt **o** or sacrifice,	Lv 17:8	5930a
'He shall bring his guilt **o** to	Lv 19:21	817
of meeting, a ram for a guilt **o**.	Lv 19:21	817
ram of the guilt **o** before the LORD	Lv 19:22	817
holy, an **o** of praise to the LORD.	Lv 19:24	1974
not eat of the **o** of the *gifts*.	Lv 22:12	8641
in Israel who presents his **o**,	Lv 22:18	7133a
present to the LORD for a burnt **o**	Lv 22:18	5930a
special vow or for a freewill **o**,	Lv 22:21	5071
nor make of them an **o** by fire on	Lv 22:22	801
may present it for a freewill **o**,	Lv 22:23	5071
for **o** as the food of your God;	Lv 22:25	7126
of an **o** by fire to the LORD.	Lv 22:27	801
present an **o** by fire to the LORD.	Lv 23:8	801
defect for a burnt **o** to the LORD.	Lv 23:12	5930a
'Its grain **o** shall then be	Lv 23:13	4503
an **o** by fire to the LORD *for* a	Lv 23:13	801
with its drink **o**, a fourth of a hin	Lv 23:13	5262a

have brought in the **o** of your God,	Lv 23:14	7133a
in the sheaf of the wave **o**;	Lv 23:15	8573
present a new grain **o** to the LORD.	Lv 23:16	4503
two *loaves* of bread for a wave **o**,	Lv 23:17	8573
are to be a burnt **o** to the LORD,	Lv 23:18	5930a
their grain **o** and their drink	Lv 23:18	4503
an **o** by fire of a soothing aroma	Lv 23:18	801
also offer one male goat for a sin **o**	Lv 23:19	2403b
bread of the first fruits for a wave **o**	Lv 23:20	8573
an **o** by fire to the LORD.' "	Lv 23:25	801
present an **o** by fire to the LORD.	Lv 23:27	801
present an **o** by fire to the LORD.	Lv 23:36	801
present an **o** by fire to the LORD;	Lv 23:36	801
even an **o** by fire to the LORD.	Lv 24:7	801
can present as an **o** to the LORD,	Lv 27:9	7133a
not present as an **o** to the LORD,	Lv 27:11	7133a
bowls and the jars for the drink **o**,	Nu 4:7	5262a
incense and the continual grain **o**	Nu 4:16	4503
and shall bring *as* an **o** for her	Nu 5:15	7133a
for it is a grain **o** of jealousy,	Nu 5:15	4503
jealousy, a grain **o** of memorial,	Nu 5:15	4503
grain **o** of memorial in her hands,	Nu 5:18	4503
which is the grain **o** of jealousy,	Nu 5:18	4503
priest shall take the grain **o** of jealousy	Nu 5:25	4503
and he shall wave the grain **o**	Nu 5:25	4503
take a handful of the grain **o** as its	Nu 5:26	4503
as its memorial **o** and offer *it* up	Nu 5:26	234
The priest shall offer one for a sin **o**	Nu 6:11	2403b
and *the* other for a burnt **o**,	Nu 6:11	5930a
lamb a year old for a guilt **o**;	Nu 6:12	817
he shall bring the **o** to the	Nu 6:13	
shall present his **o** to the LORD:	Nu 6:14	7133a
year old without defect for a burnt **o**	Nu 6:14	5930a
a year old without defect for a sin **o**	Nu 6:14	2403b
ram without defect for a peace **o**,	Nu 6:14	8002
along with their grain **o** and their	Nu 6:15	4503
grain offering and their drink **o**.	Nu 6:15	4503
his sin **o** and his burnt offering.	Nu 6:16	2403b
his sin offering and his burnt **o**.	Nu 6:16	5930a
its grain **o** and its drink offering.	Nu 6:17	4503
its grain offering and its drink **o**.	Nu 6:17	5262a
them for a wave **o** before the LORD.	Nu 6:20	8573
Nazirite who vows his **o** to the LORD	Nu 6:21	7133a
fathers' households, made an **o**	Nu 7:2	7126
brought their **o** before the LORD,	Nu 7:3	7133a
leaders offered the dedication **o**	Nu 7:10	
offered their **o** before the altar.	Nu 7:10	7133a
"Let them present their **o**,	Nu 7:11	7133a
Now the one who presented his **o** on	Nu 7:12	7133a
and his **o** *was* one silver dish	Nu 7:13	7133a
mixed with oil for a grain **o**;	Nu 7:13	4503
lamb one year old, for a burnt **o**;	Nu 7:15	5930a
one male goat for a sin **o**;	Nu 7:16	2403b
This *was* the **o** of Nahshon the son	Nu 7:17	7133a
leader of Issachar, presented *an* **o**;	Nu 7:18	
he presented as his **o** one silver	Nu 7:19	7133a
mixed with oil for a grain **o**;	Nu 7:19	4503
lamb one year old, for a burnt **o**;	Nu 7:21	5930a
one male goat for a sin **o**;	Nu 7:22	2403b
the **o** of Nethanel the son of Zuar.	Nu 7:23	7133a
his **o** *was* one silver dish whose	Nu 7:25	7133a
flour mixed with oil for a grain **o**;	Nu 7:25	4503
lamb one year old, for a burnt **o**;	Nu 7:27	5930a
one male goat for a sin **o**;	Nu 7:28	2403b
the **o** of Eliab the son of Helon.	Nu 7:29	7133a
his **o** *was* one silver dish whose	Nu 7:31	7133a
flour mixed with oil for a grain **o**;	Nu 7:31	4503
lamb one year old, for a burnt **o**;	Nu 7:33	5930a
one male goat for a sin **o**;	Nu 7:34	2403b
o of Elizur the son of Shedeur.	Nu 7:35	7133a
his **o** *was* one silver dish whose	Nu 7:37	7133a
flour mixed with oil for a grain **o**;	Nu 7:37	4503
lamb one year old, for a burnt **o**;	Nu 7:39	5930a
one male goat for a sin **o**;	Nu 7:40	2403b
This *was* the **o** of Shelumiel the	Nu 7:41	7133a
his **o** *was* one silver dish whose	Nu 7:43	7133a
flour mixed with oil for a grain **o**;	Nu 7:43	4503
lamb one year old, for a burnt **o**;	Nu 7:45	5930a
one male goat for a sin **o**;	Nu 7:46	2403b
o of Eliasaph the son of Deuel.	Nu 7:47	7133a
his **o** *was* one silver dish whose	Nu 7:49	7133a
flour mixed with oil for a grain **o**;	Nu 7:49	4503
lamb one year old, for a burnt **o**;	Nu 7:51	5930a
one male goat for a sin **o**;	Nu 7:52	2403b
This *was* the **o** of Elishama the son	Nu 7:53	7133a
his **o** *was* one silver dish whose	Nu 7:55	7133a
flour mixed with oil for a grain **o**;	Nu 7:55	4503
lamb one year old, for a burnt **o**;	Nu 7:57	5930a
one male goat for a sin **o**;	Nu 7:58	2403b
This *was* the **o** of Gamaliel the son	Nu 7:59	7133a
his **o** *was* one silver dish whose	Nu 7:61	7133a
flour mixed with oil for a grain **o**;	Nu 7:61	4503
lamb one year old, for a burnt **o**;	Nu 7:63	5930a
one male goat for a sin **o**;	Nu 7:64	2403b
o of Abidan the son of Gideoni.	Nu 7:65	7133a
his **o** *was* one silver dish whose	Nu 7:67	7133a
flour mixed with oil for a grain **o**;	Nu 7:67	4503
lamb one year old, for a burnt **o**;	Nu 7:69	5930a
one male goat for a sin **o**;	Nu 7:70	2403b
This *was* the **o** of Ahiezer the son	Nu 7:71	7133a
his **o** *was* one silver dish whose	Nu 7:73	7133a
flour mixed with oil for a grain **o**;	Nu 7:73	4503
lamb one year old, for a burnt **o**;	Nu 7:75	5930a
one male goat for a sin **o**;	Nu 7:76	2403b
the **o** of Pagiel the son of Ochran.	Nu 7:77	7133a
his **o** *was* one silver dish whose	Nu 7:79	7133a
flour mixed with oil for a grain **o**;	Nu 7:79	4503
lamb one year old, for a burnt **o**;	Nu 7:81	5930a
one male goat for a sin **o**;	Nu 7:82	2403b

the **o** of Ahira the son of Enan.	Nu 7:83	7133a
This *was* the dedication **o** for	Nu 7:84	
oxen for the burnt **o** twelve bulls,	Nu 7:87	5930a
old with their grain **o** twelve,	Nu 7:87	4503
the male goats for a sin **o** twelve;	Nu 7:87	2403b
This *was* the dedication **o** for	Nu 7:88	
them take a bull with its grain **o**,	Nu 8:8	4503
bull you shall take for a sin **o**.	Nu 8:8	2403b
a wave **o** from the sons of Israel,	Nu 8:11	8573
then offer the one for a sin **o** and	Nu 8:12	2403b
other for a burnt **o** to the LORD,	Nu 8:12	5930a
them as a wave **o** to the LORD.	Nu 8:13	8573
them and present them as a wave **o**;	Nu 8:15	8573
them as a wave **o** before the LORD.	Nu 8:21	8573
restrained from presenting the **o**	Nu 9:7	7133a
for he did not present the **o** of	Nu 9:13	7133a
make an **o** by fire to the LORD,	Nu 15:3	801
a burnt **o** or a sacrifice to	Nu 15:3	5930a
freewill **o** or in your appointed times	Nu 15:3	5071
'The one who presents his **o**	Nu 15:4	7133a
shall present to the LORD a grain **o**	Nu 15:4	4503
shall prepare wine for the drink **o**,	Nu 15:5	5262a
the burnt **o** or for the sacrifice,	Nu 15:5	5930a
prepare as a grain **o** two-tenths *of an*	Nu 15:6	4503
and for the drink **o** you shall offer	Nu 15:7	5262a
bull as a burnt **o** or a sacrifice,	Nu 15:8	5930a
you shall offer with the bull a grain **o**	Nu 15:9	4503
and you shall offer as the drink **o**	Nu 15:10	5262a
a hin of wine as an **o** by fire,	Nu 15:10	801
in presenting an **o** by fire,	Nu 15:13	801
he *wishes to* make an **o** by fire,	Nu 15:14	801
shall lift up an **o** to the LORD.	Nu 15:19	8641
you shall lift up a cake as an **o**;	Nu 15:20	8641
as the **o** of the threshing floor,	Nu 15:20	8641
an **o** throughout your generations.	Nu 15:21	8641
offer one bull for a burnt **o**,	Nu 15:24	5930a
to the LORD, with its grain **o** and	Nu 15:24	4503
its grain offering and its drink **o**,	Nu 15:24	5262a
and one male goat for a sin **o**.	Nu 15:24	2403b
and they have brought their **o**,	Nu 15:25	7133a
an **o** by fire to the LORD,	Nu 15:25	801
and their sin **o** before the LORD,	Nu 15:25	2403b
year old female goat for a sin **o**.	Nu 15:27	2403b
"Do not regard their **o**!	Nu 16:15	4503
fifty men who were **o** the incense.	Nu 16:35	7126
every **o** of theirs, even every	Nu 18:9	7133a
even every grain **o** and every sin	Nu 18:9	4503
sin **o** and every guilt offering,	Nu 18:9	2403b
sin offering and every guilt **o**,	Nu 18:9	817
is yours, the **o** of their gift,	Nu 18:11	8641
fat in smoke *as* an **o** by fire,	Nu 18:17	801
like the breast of a wave **o** and like	Nu 18:18	8573
they offer as an **o** to the LORD,	Nu 18:24	8641
present an **o** from it to the LORD,	Nu 18:26	8641
'Your **o** shall be reckoned to	Nu 18:27	8641
an **o** to the LORD from your tithes,	Nu 18:28	8641
the LORD'S **o** to Aaron the priest.	Nu 18:28	8641
present every **o** due to the LORD,	Nu 18:29	8641
"Stand beside your burnt **o**,	Nu 23:3	5930a
was standing beside his burnt **o**,	Nu 23:6	5930a
"Stand here beside your burnt **o** while	Nu 23:15	5930a
was standing beside his burnt **o**,	Nu 23:17	5930a
shall be careful to present My **o**,	Nu 28:2	7133a
'This is the **o** by fire which you	Nu 28:3	801
as a continual burnt **o** every day.	Nu 28:3	5930a
ephah of fine flour for a grain **o**,	Nu 28:5	4503
'It is a continual burnt **o** which	Nu 28:6	5930a
aroma, an **o** by fire to the LORD.	Nu 28:6	801
'Then the drink **o** with it *shall be*	Nu 28:7	5262a
place you shall pour out a drink **o** of	Nu 28:7	5262a
as the grain **o** of the morning and	Nu 28:8	4503
of the morning and as its drink **o**,	Nu 28:8	5262a
you shall offer it, an **o** by fire,	Nu 28:8	801
flour mixed with oil as a grain **o**,	Nu 28:9	4503
offering, and its drink **o**:	Nu 28:9	5262a
This is the burnt **o** of every sabbath	Nu 28:10	5930a
continual burnt **o** and its drink offering.	Nu 28:10	5930a
burnt offering and its drink **o**.	Nu 28:10	5262a
present a burnt **o** to the LORD:	Nu 28:11	5930a
flour mixed with oil for a grain **o**,	Nu 28:12	4503
flour mixed with oil for a grain **o**,	Nu 28:12	4503
oil for a grain **o** for each lamb,	Nu 28:13	4503
for a burnt **o** of a soothing aroma,	Nu 28:13	5930a
aroma, an **o** by fire to the LORD.	Nu 28:13	801
this is the burnt **o** of each month	Nu 28:14	5930a
male goat for a sin **o** to the LORD;	Nu 28:15	2403b
it shall be offered with its drink **o**	Nu 28:15	5262a
addition to the continual burnt **o**.	Nu 28:15	5930a
You shall present an **o** by fire,	Nu 28:19	801
by fire, a burnt **o** to the LORD:	Nu 28:19	5930a
'For their grain **o**,	Nu 28:20	4503
and one male goat for a sin **o** to	Nu 28:22	2403b
the burnt **o** of the morning,	Nu 28:23	5930a
which is for a continual burnt **o**.	Nu 28:23	5930a
days, the food of the **o** by fire,	Nu 28:24	801
shall be presented with its drink **o**	Nu 28:24	5262a
addition to the continual burnt **o**.	Nu 28:24	5930a
when you present a new grain **o** to	Nu 28:26	4503
'You shall offer a burnt **o** for	Nu 28:27	5930a
and their grain **o**, fine flour	Nu 28:28	4503
burnt **o** and its grain offering,	Nu 28:31	5930a
burnt offering and its grain **o**,	Nu 28:31	4503
'You shall offer a burnt **o** as	Nu 29:2	5930a
also their grain **o**,	Nu 29:3	4503
Offer one male goat for a sin **o**,	Nu 29:5	2403b
the burnt **o** of the new moon and	Nu 29:6	5930a
of the new moon and its grain **o**,	Nu 29:6	4503
burnt **o** and its grain offering,	Nu 29:6	5930a
burnt offering and its grain **o**,	Nu 29:6	4503

aroma, an **o** by fire to the LORD.	**Nu 29:6**	801
'You shall present a burnt **o**	**Nu 29:8**	5930a
and their grain **o**, fine flour	**Nu 29:9**	4503
one male goat for a sin **o**,	**Nu 29:11**	2403b
besides the sin **o** of atonement and	**Nu 29:11**	2403b
burnt **o** and its grain offering,	**Nu 29:11**	5930a
burnt offering and its grain **o**,	**Nu 29:11**	4503
'You shall present a burnt **o**,	**Nu 29:13**	5930a
an **o** by fire as a soothing aroma	**Nu 29:13**	801
and their grain **o**, fine flour	**Nu 29:14**	4503
and one male goat for a sin **o**,	**Nu 29:16**	2403b
besides the continual burnt **o**,	**Nu 29:16**	5930a
its grain **o** and its drink offering.	**Nu 29:16**	4503
its grain offering and its drink **o**.	**Nu 29:16**	5262a
and their grain **o** and their	**Nu 29:18**	4503
and one male goat for a sin **o**,	**Nu 29:19**	2403b
burnt **o** and its grain offering,	**Nu 29:19**	5930a
burnt offering and its grain **o**,	**Nu 29:19**	4503
and their grain **o** and their	**Nu 29:21**	4503
and one male goat for a sin **o**,	**Nu 29:22**	2403b
besides the continual burnt **o** and	**Nu 29:22**	5930a
and its grain **o** and its drink offering.	**Nu 29:22**	4503
its grain offering and its drink **o**.	**Nu 29:22**	5262a
their grain **o** and their drink	**Nu 29:24**	4503
and one male goat for a sin **o**,	**Nu 29:25**	2403b
besides the continual burnt **o**,	**Nu 29:25**	5930a
its grain **o** and its drink offering.	**Nu 29:25**	4503
its grain offering and its drink **o**.	**Nu 29:25**	5262a
and their grain **o** and their	**Nu 29:27**	4503
and one male goat for a sin **o**,	**Nu 29:28**	2403b
besides the continual burnt **o** and	**Nu 29:28**	5930a
and its grain **o** and its drink offering.	**Nu 29:28**	4503
its grain offering and its drink **o**.	**Nu 29:28**	5262a
and their grain **o** and their	**Nu 29:30**	4503
and one male goat for a sin **o**,	**Nu 29:31**	2403b
besides the continual burnt **o**,	**Nu 29:31**	5930a
its grain **o** and its drink offerings.	**Nu 29:31**	4503
and their grain **o** and their	**Nu 29:33**	4503
and one male goat for a sin **o**,	**Nu 29:34**	2403b
besides the continual burnt **o**,	**Nu 29:34**	5930a
its grain **o** and its drink offering.	**Nu 29:34**	4503
its grain offering and its drink **o**.	**Nu 29:34**	5262a
'But you shall present a burnt **o**,	**Nu 29:36**	5930a
a burnt offering, an **o** by fire,	**Nu 29:36**	801
their grain **o** and their drink	**Nu 29:37**	4503
and one male goat for a sin **o**,	**Nu 29:38**	2403b
besides the continual burnt **o** and	**Nu 29:38**	5930a
and its grain **o** and its drink offering.	**Nu 29:38**	4503
its grain offering and its drink **o**.	**Nu 29:38**	5262a
the priest, as an **o** to the LORD.	**Nu 31:29**	8641
the LORD's **o** to Eleazar the priest,	**Nu 31:41**	8641
"So we have brought as an **o** to	**Nu 31:50**	7133a
All the gold of the **o** which	**Nu 31:52**	8641
burnt **o** to the LORD your God;	**Dt 13:16**	3632
of a freewill **o** of your hand,	**Dt 16:10**	5071
LORD your God for any votive **o**,	**Dt 23:18**	5088
And drank the wine of their drink **o**?	**Dt 32:38**	5257a
a burnt **o** or grain offering on it,	**Jos 22:23**	5930a
a burnt offering or grain **o** on it,	**Jos 22:23**	4503
not for burnt **o** or for sacrifice;	**Jos 22:26**	5930a
not for burnt **o** or for sacrifice;	**Jos 22:28**	5930a
by building an altar for burnt **o**,	**Jos 22:29**	5930a
for grain **o** or for sacrifice,	**Jos 22:29**	4503
out my **o** and lay it before You."	**Jg 6:18**	4503
and offer a burnt **o** with the wood	**Jg 6:26**	5930a
I will offer it up as a burnt **o**."	**Jg 11:31**	5930a
but if you prepare a burnt **o**,	**Jg 13:16**	5930a
took the young goat with the grain **o**	**Jg 13:19**	4503
would not have accepted a burnt **o**	**Jg 13:23**	5930a
and a grain **o** from our hands,	**Jg 13:23**	4503
When any man was **o** a sacrifice,	**1Sa 2:13**	2076
men despised the **o** of the LORD.	**1Sa 2:17**	4503
you kick at My sacrifice and at My **o**	**1Sa 2:29**	4503
of every **o** of My people Israel?'	**1Sa 2:29**	4503
for by sacrifice or **o** forever."	**1Sa 3:14**	4503
surely return to Him a guilt **o**.	**1Sa 6:3**	817
o which we shall return to Him?"	**1Sa 6:4**	817
as a guilt **o** in a box by its side.	**1Sa 6:8**	817
the cows as a burnt **o** to the LORD.	**1Sa 6:14**	5930a
for a guilt **o** to the LORD:	**1Sa 6:17**	817
for a whole burnt **o** to the LORD;	**1Sa 7:9**	5930a
Samuel was **o** up the burnt offering,	**1Sa 7:10**	5927
Samuel was offering up the burnt **o**,	**1Sa 7:10**	5930a
burnt **o** and the peace offerings."	**1Sa 13:9**	5930a
And he offered the burnt **o**.	**1Sa 13:9**	5930a
he finished **o** the burnt offering,	**1Sa 13:10**	5927
he finished offering the burnt **o**,	**1Sa 13:10**	5930a
myself and offered the burnt **o**."	**1Sa 13:12**	5930a
against me, let Him accept an **o**;	**1Sa 26:19**	4503
When David had finished **o** the	**2Sa 6:18**	5927
burnt **o** and the peace offering,	**2Sa 6:18**	5930a
burnt offering and the peace **o**,	**2Sa 6:18**	8002
while he was **o** the sacrifices.	**2Sa 15:12**	2076
"I am **o** you three things;	**2Sa 24:12**	5190
Look, the oxen for the burnt **o**,	**2Sa 24:22**	5930a
there he offered the burnt **o**	**1Ki 8:64**	5930a
and the grain **o** and the fat	**1Ki 8:64**	4503
was too small to hold the burnt **o**	**1Ki 8:64**	5930a
the grain **o** and the fat of the peace	**1Ki 8:64**	4503
time of the **o** of the *evening* sacrifice;	**1Ki 18:29**	5927
on the burnt **o** and on the wood."	**1Ki 18:34**	5930a
of the **o** of the *evening* sacrifice,	**1Ki 18:36**	5927
and consumed the burnt **o** and the	**1Ki 18:38**	5930a
about the time of **o** the sacrifice,	**2Ki 3:20**	5927
him as a burnt **o** on the wall.	**2Ki 3:27**	5930a
servant will no longer offer burnt **o**	**2Ki 5:17**	5930a
had finished **o** the burnt offering,	**2Ki 10:25**	6213a
had finished offering the burnt **o**,	**2Ki 10:25**	5930a
his burnt **o** and his meal offering,	**2Ki 16:13**	5930a
his burnt offering and his meal **o**,	**2Ki 16:13**	4503
and poured his drink **o** and sprinkled	**2Ki 16:13**	5262a
burn the morning burnt **o**	**2Ki 16:15**	5930a
evening meal **o** and the king's burnt	**2Ki 16:15**	4503
burnt **o** and his meal offering,	**2Ki 16:15**	5930a
burnt offering and his meal **o**,	**2Ki 16:15**	4503
with the burnt **o** of all the people	**2Ki 16:15**	5930a
their meal **o** and their drink	**2Ki 16:15**	4503
on it all the blood of the burnt **o**	**2Ki 16:15**	5930a
o and on the altar of incense,	**1Ch 6:49**	5930a
When David had finished **o** the	**1Ch 16:2**	5927
burnt **o** and the peace offerings,	**1Ch 16:2**	5930a
Bring an **o**, and come before Him;	**1Ch 16:29**	4503
on the altar of burnt **o** continually	**1Ch 16:40**	5930a
and the wheat for the grain **o**;	**1Ch 21:23**	4503
burnt **o** which costs me nothing."	**1Ch 21:24**	5930a
heaven on the altar of burnt **o**.	**1Ch 21:26**	5930a
and the altar of burnt **o** *were* in	**1Ch 21:29**	5930a
the altar of burnt **o** for Israel."	**1Ch 22:1**	5930a
and the fine flour for a grain **o**,	**1Ch 23:29**	4503
for they made their **o** to the LORD	**1Ch 29:9**	5068
to rinse things for the burnt **o**;	**2Ch 4:6**	5930a
the burnt **o** and the sacrifices,	**2Ch 7:1**	5930a
not able to contain the burnt **o**,	**2Ch 7:7**	5930a
the burnt offering, the grain **o** and	**2Ch 7:7**	4503
o *them* up according to the	**2Ch 8:13**	5927
for the service and the burnt **o**,	**2Ch 24:14**	5930a
burnt **o** with all of its utensils,	**2Ch 29:18**	5930a
goats for a sin **o** for the kingdom,	**2Ch 29:21**	2403b
brought the male goats of the sin **o**	**2Ch 29:23**	2403b
for the king ordered the burnt **o**	**2Ch 29:24**	5930a
and the sin **o** for all Israel.	**2Ch 29:24**	2403b
to offer the burnt **o** on the altar.	**2Ch 29:27**	5930a
When the burnt **o** began, the song	**2Ch 29:27**	5930a
until the burnt **o** was finished.	**2Ch 29:28**	5930a
were for a burnt **o** to the LORD.	**2Ch 29:32**	5930a
a freewill **o** to the people,	**2Ch 35:8**	5071
were **o** the burnt offerings and the	**2Ch 35:14**	5927
together with a freewill **o** for the	**Ezr 1:4**	5071
that was given as a freewill **o**.	**Ezr 1:6**	5068
there was a continual burnt **o**,	**Ezr 3:5**	5930a
offered a freewill **o** to the LORD.	**Ezr 3:5**	5071
a burnt **o** to the God of heaven,	**Ezr 6:9**	5928
a sin **o** for all Israel 12 male goats,	**Ezr 6:17**	2409
with the freewill **o** of the people	**Ezr 7:16**	5069
the **o** for the house of our God	**Ezr 8:25**	8641
silver and the gold are a freewill **o**	**Ezr 8:28**	5071
lambs, 12 male goats for a sin **o**,	**Ezr 8:35**	2403b
all as a burnt **o** to the LORD.	**Ezr 8:35**	5930a
sat appalled until the evening **o**.	**Ezr 9:4**	4503
at the evening **o** I arose from my	**Ezr 9:5**	4503
for the continual grain **o**,	**Ne 10:33**	4503
for the continual burnt **o**,	**Ne 10:33**	5930a
and **o** burnt offerings *according to*	**Jb 1:5**	5927
offer up a burnt **o** for yourselves,	**Jb 42:8**	5930a
And find your burnt **o** acceptable!	**Ps 20:3**	5930a
and meal **o** You have not desired;	**Ps 40:6**	4503
Burnt **o** and sin offering You have	**Ps 40:6**	5930a
and sin **o** You have not required.	**Ps 40:6**	2401
You are not pleased with burnt **o**.	**Ps 51:16**	5930a
burnt **o** and whole burnt offering;	**Ps 51:19**	5930a
burnt offering and whole burnt **o**;	**Ps 51:19**	3632
I shall make *an* **o** *of* bulls with	**Ps 66:15**	
Bring an **o** and come into His	**Ps 96:8**	4503
up of my hands as the evening **o**.	**Ps 141:2**	4503
even worship with sacrifice and **o**,	**Is 19:21**	4503
its beasts enough for a burnt **o**.	**Is 40:16**	5930a
is too impoverished for *such* an **o**	**Is 40:20**	8641
would render Himself *as* a guilt **o**,	**Is 53:10**	817
to them you have poured out a drink **o**,	**Is 57:6**	5262a
offering, You have made a grain **o**.	**Is 57:6**	4503
I hate robbery in burnt **o**;	**Is 61:8**	5930a
O sacrifices in gardens and	**Is 65:3**	2076
He who offers a grain **o** *is like*	**Is 66:3**	4503
nations as a grain **o** to the LORD,	**Is 66:20**	4503
the sons of Israel bring their grain **o**	**Is 66:20**	4503
Me by **o** up sacrifices to Baal.	**Jer 11:17**	6999
offer burnt **o** and grain offering,	**Jer 14:12**	5930a
offer burnt offering and grain **o**,	**Jer 14:12**	4503
o into the house of the LORD.	**Jer 33:11**	8426
the pans and the drink **o** bowls, what	**Jer 52:19**	4518
the provocation of their **o**.	**Ezk 20:28**	7133a
there they rinse the burnt **o**.	**Ezk 40:38**	5930a
on which to slaughter the burnt **o**,	**Ezk 40:39**	5930a
the burnt offering, the sin **o** and	**Ezk 40:39**	2403b
the sin offering and the guilt **o**.	**Ezk 40:39**	817
For the burnt **o** *there were*	**Ezk 40:42**	5930a
the burnt **o** and the sacrifice.	**Ezk 40:42**	5930a
the tables *was* the flesh of the **o**.	**Ezk 40:43**	7133a
the most holy things, the grain **o**,	**Ezk 42:13**	4503
the grain offering, the sin **o** and	**Ezk 42:13**	2403b
the sin offering and the guilt **o**;	**Ezk 42:13**	817
'a young bull for a sin **o**.	**Ezk 43:19**	2403b
also take the bull for the sin **o**,	**Ezk 43:21**	2403b
goat without blemish for a sin **o**,	**Ezk 43:22**	2403b
them up as a burnt **o** to the LORD.	**Ezk 43:24**	5930a
prepare daily a goat for a sin **o**;	**Ezk 43:25**	2403b
they shall slaughter the burnt **o**	**Ezk 44:11**	5930a
he shall offer his sin **o**,"	**Ezk 44:27**	2403b
"They shall eat the grain **o**,	**Ezk 44:29**	4503
eat the grain offering, the sin **o** and	**Ezk 44:29**	2403b
the sin offering and the guilt **o**;	**Ezk 44:29**	817
is the **o** that you shall offer:	**Ezk 45:13**	8641
for a grain **o**, for a burnt offering and	**Ezk 45:15**	4503
a grain offering, for a burnt **o** and	**Ezk 45:15**	5930a
this **o** for the prince in Israel.	**Ezk 45:16**	8641
he shall provide the sin **o**,	**Ezk 45:17**	2403b
the sin offering, the grain **o**,	**Ezk 45:17**	4503
the grain offering, the burnt **o** and	**Ezk 45:17**	5930a
take some of the blood from the sin **o**	**Ezk 45:19**	2403b
of the land a bull for a sin **o**.	**Ezk 45:22**	2403b
he shall provide as a burnt **o** to the	**Ezk 45:23**	5930a
and a male goat daily for a sin **o**.	**Ezk 45:23**	2403b
as a grain **o** an ephah with a bull,	**Ezk 45:24**	4503
this, seven days for the sin **o**,	**Ezk 45:25**	2403b
for the sin offering, the burnt **o**,	**Ezk 45:25**	5930a
the burnt offering, the grain **o** and	**Ezk 45:25**	4503
burnt **o** and his peace offerings,	**Ezk 46:2**	5930a
"The burnt **o** which the prince	**Ezk 46:4**	5930a
and the grain **o** shall be an ephah	**Ezk 46:5**	4503
and the grain **o** with the lambs as	**Ezk 46:5**	4503
"And he shall provide a grain **o**,	**Ezk 46:7**	4503
grain **o** shall be an ephah with a bull	**Ezk 46:11**	4503
the prince provides a freewill **o**,	**Ezk 46:12**	5071
a freewill offering, a burnt **o**,	**Ezk 46:12**	5930a
as a freewill **o** to the LORD,	**Ezk 46:12**	5071
And he shall provide his burnt **o**	**Ezk 46:12**	5930a
for a burnt **o** to the LORD daily;	**Ezk 46:13**	5930a
provide a grain **o** with it morning by	**Ezk 46:14**	4503
a grain **o** to the LORD continually	**Ezk 46:14**	4503
provide the lamb, the grain **o** and	**Ezk 46:15**	4503
for a continual burnt **o**."	**Ezk 46:15**	5930a
the guilt **o** and the sin offering	**Ezk 46:20**	817
the guilt offering and the sin **o**	**Ezk 46:20**	2403b
where they shall bake the grain **o**,	**Ezk 46:20**	4503
to him an **o** and fragrant incense.	**Da 2:46**	4504
about the time of the evening **o**.	**Da 9:21**	4503
a stop to sacrifice and grain **o**;	**Da 9:27**	4503
The grain **o** and the drink offering are	**Jl 1:9**	4503
The grain offering and the drink **o**	**Jl 1:9**	5262a
For the grain **o** and the drink offering	**Jl 1:13**	4503
the grain offering and the drink **o**	**Jl 1:13**	5262a
Even a grain **o** and a drink offering For	**Jl 2:14**	4503
Even a grain offering and a drink **o**	**Jl 2:14**	5262a
"Offer a thank **o** also from that	**Am 4:5**	8426
"Take *an* **o** from the exiles,	**Zch 6:10**	
With such an **o** on your part, will	**Mal 1:9**	
'nor will I accept an **o** from you.	**Mal 1:10**	4503
name, and a grain **o** *that is* pure;	**Mal 1:11**	4503
so you bring the **o**!	**Mal 1:13**	4503
an **o** to the LORD of hosts.	**Mal 2:12**	4503
He no longer regards the **o** or accepts	**Mal 2:13**	4503
Then the **o** of Judah and Jerusalem	**Mal 3:4**	4503
presenting your **o** at the altar,	**Mt 5:23**	*1435*
your **o** there before the altar and	**Mt 5:24**	*1435*
and then come and present your **o**.	**Mt 5:24**	*1435*
the **o** that Moses commanded,	**Mt 8:4**	*1435*
whoever swears by the **o** on it,	**Mt 23:18**	*1435*
the **o**, or the altar that sanctifies	**Mt 23:19**	*1435*
the altar that sanctifies the **o**?	**Mt 23:19**	*1435*
at the hour of the incense **o**.	**Lk 1:10**	
and make an **o** for your cleansing,	**Lk 5:14**	*4374*
of their surplus put into the **o**;	**Lk 21:4**	*1435*
coming up to Him, **o** Him sour wine,	**Lk 23:36**	*4374*
think that he is **o** service to God.	**Jn 16:2**	*4374*
crowds from **o** sacrifice to them.	**Ac 14:18**	*2380*
of sinful flesh and *as an* **o** for	**Ro 8:3**	
that *my* **o** of the Gentiles may	**Ro 15:16**	*4376*
an **o** and a sacrifice to God as a	**Eph 5:2**	*4376*
always **o** prayer with joy in my	**Php 1:4**	*4160*
I am being poured out as a drink **o**	**Php 2:17**	*4689*
being poured out as a drink **o**,	**2Tm 4:6**	*4689*
AND **O** YOU HAVE NOT DESIRED,	**Heb 10:5**	*4376*
sanctified through the **o** of the body	**Heb 10:10**	*4376*
o time after time the same sacrifices,	**Heb 10:11**	*4374*
For by one **o** He has perfected for	**Heb 10:14**	*4376*
there is no longer *any* **o** for sin.	**Heb 10:18**	*4376*
was **o** up his only begotten *son;*	**Heb 11:17**	*4374*
place by the high priest *as an* **o**	**Heb 13:11**	

OFFERINGS

and offered burnt **o** on the altar.	**Gn 8:20**	5930a
us have sacrifices and burnt **o**,	**Ex 10:25**	5930a
burnt **o** and your peace offerings,	**Ex 20:24**	5930a
burnt offerings and your peace **o**,	**Ex 20:24**	8002
and they offered burnt **o** and	**Ex 24:5**	5930a
bulls as peace **o** to the LORD.	**Ex 24:5**	8002
with which to pour drink **o**;	**Ex 25:29**	5258a
the sacrifices of their peace **o**,	**Ex 29:28**	8002
rose early and offered burnt **o**,	**Ex 32:6**	5930a
offerings, and brought peace **o**;	**Ex 32:6**	8002
to him freewill **o** every morning.	**Ex 36:3**	5071
with which to pour out drink **o**, of	**Ex 37:16**	5258a
of the **o** to the LORD by fire.	**Lv 2:3**	801
of the **o** to the LORD by fire.	**Lv 2:10**	801
with all your **o** you shall offer salt.	**Lv 2:13**	7133a
is a sacrifice of peace **o**,	**Lv 3:1**	8002
From the sacrifice of the peace **o**	**Lv 3:3**	8002
o to the LORD is from the flock,	**Lv 3:6**	8002
'From the sacrifice of peace **o**	**Lv 3:9**	8002
ox of the sacrifice of peace **o**),	**Lv 4:10**	8002
fat of the sacrifice of peace **o**.	**Lv 4:26**	8002
from the sacrifice of peace **o**;	**Lv 4:31**	8002
from the sacrifice of the peace **o**,	**Lv 4:35**	8002
on the **o** by fire to the LORD.	**Lv 4:35**	801
with the **o** of the LORD by fire:	**Lv 5:12**	801
fat portions of the peace **o** on it.	**Lv 6:12**	8002
as their share from My **o** by fire;	**Lv 6:17**	801
from the **o** by fire to the LORD.	**Lv 6:18**	801
the law of the sacrifice of peace **o**	**Lv 7:11**	8002
of his peace **o** for thanksgiving,	**Lv 7:13**	8002
the blood of the peace **o**.	**Lv 7:14**	8002
sacrifice of his thanksgiving peace **o**,	**Lv 7:15**	8002
flesh of the sacrifice of his peace **o**	**Lv 7:18**	8002
peace **o** which belong to the LORD,	**Lv 7:20**	8002
peace **o** which belong to the LORD,	**Lv 7:21**	8002
who offers the sacrifice of his peace **o**	**Lv 7:29**	8002
from the sacrifice of his peace **o**.	**Lv 7:29**	8002
to bring **o** by fire to the LORD.	**Lv 7:30**	801

the sacrifices of your peace **o**.	**Lv 7:32**	8002
blood of the peace **o** and the fat,	**Lv 7:33**	8002
the sacrifices of their peace **o**,	**Lv 7:34**	8002
from the **o** by fire to the LORD,	**Lv 7:35**	801
and the sacrifice of peace **o**,	**Lv 7:37**	8002
the sons of Israel to present their **o**	**Lv 7:38**	7133a
and an ox and a ram for peace **o**,	**Lv 9:4**	8002
peace **o** which was for the people;	**Lv 9:18**	8002
burnt offering and the peace **o**.	**Lv 9:22**	8002
left over from the LORD'S **o** by fire	**Lv 10:12**	801
due out of the LORD'S **o** by fire;	**Lv 10:13**	801
the peace **o** of the sons of Israel.	**Lv 10:14**	8002
shall bring along with the **o** by fire	**Lv 10:15**	801
sacrifices of peace **o** to the LORD.	**Lv 17:5**	8002
sacrifice of peace **o** to the LORD,	**Lv 19:5**	8002
present the **o** by fire to the LORD,	**Lv 21:6**	801
near to offer the LORD'S **o** by fire;	**Lv 21:21**	801
votive or any of their freewill **o**,	**Lv 22:18**	5071
a man offers a sacrifice of peace **o**	**Lv 22:21**	8002
grain offering and their drink **o**, an	**Lv 23:18**	5262a
old for a sacrifice of peace **o**.	**Lv 23:19**	8002
to present **o** by fire to the	**Lv 23:37**	801
burnt **o** and grain offerings,	**Lv 23:37**	5930a
grain **o**, sacrifices and drink	**Lv 23:37**	4503
sacrifices and drink **o**, *each*	**Lv 23:37**	5262a
all your votive and freewill **o**,	**Lv 23:38**	5071
to him from the LORD'S **o** by fire,	**Lv 24:9**	801
sacrifice of peace **o** to the LORD,	**Nu 6:17**	8002
is under the sacrifice of peace **o**.	**Nu 6:18**	8002
and for the sacrifice of peace **o**,	**Nu 7:17**	8002
and for the sacrifice of peace **o**,	**Nu 7:23**	8002
and for the sacrifice of peace **o**,	**Nu 7:29**	8002
and for the sacrifice of peace **o**,	**Nu 7:35**	8002
and for the sacrifice of peace **o**,	**Nu 7:41**	8002
and for the sacrifice of peace **o**,	**Nu 7:47**	8002
and for the sacrifice of peace **o**,	**Nu 7:53**	8002
and for the sacrifice of peace **o**,	**Nu 7:59**	8002
and for the sacrifice of peace **o**,	**Nu 7:65**	8002
and for the sacrifice of peace **o**,	**Nu 7:71**	8002
and for the sacrifice of peace **o**,	**Nu 7:77**	8002
and for the sacrifice of peace **o**,	**Nu 7:83**	8002
the sacrifice of peace **o** 24 bulls,	**Nu 7:88**	8002
the trumpets over your burnt **o**,	**Nu 10:10**	5930a
the sacrifices of your peace **o**;	**Nu 10:10**	8002
vow, or for peace **o** to the LORD,	**Nu 15:8**	8002
have given you charge of My **o**,	**Nu 18:8**	8641
the wave **o** of the sons of Israel;	**Nu 18:11**	8573
"All the **o** of the holy *gifts*,	**Nu 18:19**	8641
My food for My **o** by fire,	**Nu 28:2**	801
'Their drink **o** shall be half a hin	**Nu 28:14**	5262a
present *them* with their drink **o**.	**Nu 28:31**	5262a
and their drink **o**, according to	**Nu 29:6**	5262a
offering, and their drink **o**.	**Nu 29:11**	5262a
grain offering and their drink **o** for	**Nu 29:18**	5262a
offering, and their drink **o**.	**Nu 29:19**	5262a
grain offering and their drink **o** for	**Nu 29:21**	5262a
grain offering and their drink **o** for	**Nu 29:24**	5262a
grain offering and their drink **o** for	**Nu 29:27**	5262a
grain offering and their drink **o** for	**Nu 29:30**	5262a
its grain offering and its drink **o**.	**Nu 29:31**	5262a
grain offering and their drink **o** for	**Nu 29:33**	5262a
grain offering and their drink **o** for	**Nu 29:37**	5262a
votive **o** and your freewill offerings,	**Nu 29:39**	5088
offerings and your freewill **o**,	**Nu 29:39**	5071
for your burnt **o** and for your	**Nu 29:39**	5930a
your grain **o** and for your drink	**Nu 29:39**	4503
grain offerings and for your drink **o**	**Nu 29:39**	5262a
drink offerings and for your peace **o**.' "	**Nu 29:39**	8002
you shall bring your burnt **o**,	**Dt 12:6**	5930a
of your hand, your votive **o**,	**Dt 12:6**	5088
votive offerings, your freewill **o**,	**Dt 12:6**	5071
your burnt **o** and your sacrifices,	**Dt 12:11**	5930a
and all your choice votive **o** which	**Dt 12:11**	5088
o in every *cultic* place you see,	**Dt 12:13**	5930a
you shall offer your burnt **o**,	**Dt 12:14**	5930a
of your votive **o** which you vow,	**Dt 12:17**	5088
which you vow, or your freewill **o**,	**Dt 12:17**	5071
you may have and your votive **o**,	**Dt 12:26**	5088
"And you shall offer your burnt **o**,	**Dt 12:27**	5930a
LORD'S **o** by fire and His portion.	**Dt 18:1**	801
it burnt **o** to the LORD your God;	**Dt 27:6**	5930a
sacrifice peace **o** and eat there,	**Dt 27:7**	8002
And whole burnt **o** on Your altar.	**Dt 33:10**	3632
offered burnt **o** on it to the LORD,	**Jos 8:31**	5930a
the LORD, and sacrificed peace **o**.	**Jos 8:31**	8002
the **o** by fire to the LORD, the God	**Jos 13:14**	801
offer sacrifices of peace **o** on it,	**Jos 22:23**	8002
LORD before Him with our burnt **o**,	**Jos 22:27**	5930a
sacrifices and with our peace **o**,	**Jos 22:27**	8002
And they offered burnt **o** and peace	**Jg 20:26**	5930a
and peace **o** before the LORD.	**Jg 20:26**	8002
burnt **o** and peace offerings.	**Jg 21:4**	5930a
burnt offerings and peace **o**.	**Jg 21:4**	8002
house of your father all the fire **o**	**1Sa 2:28**	
men of Beth-shemesh offered burnt **o**	**1Sa 6:15**	5930a
come down to you to offer burnt **o**	**1Sa 10:8**	5930a
offerings and sacrifice peace **o**.	**1Sa 10:8**	8002
of peace **o** before the LORD;	**1Sa 11:15**	8002
burnt offering and the peace **o**."	**1Sa 13:9**	8002
delight in burnt **o** and sacrifices	**1Sa 15:22**	5930a
rain be on you, nor fields of **o**;	**2Sa 1:21**	8641
and David offered burnt **o** and	**2Sa 6:17**	5930a
and peace **o** before the LORD.	**2Sa 6:17**	8002
for I will not offer burnt **o** to	**2Sa 24:24**	5930a
burnt **o** and peace offerings.	**2Sa 24:25**	5930a
burnt offerings and peace **o**.	**2Sa 24:25**	8002
a thousand burnt **o** on that altar.	**1Ki 3:4**	5930a
burnt **o** and made peace offerings,	**1Ki 3:15**	5930a
burnt offerings and made peace **o**,	**1Ki 3:15**	8002

for the sacrifice of peace **o**,	**1Ki 8:63**	8002
and the fat of the peace **o**;	**1Ki 8:64**	8002
and the fat of the peace **o**.	**1Ki 8:64**	8002
Solomon offered burnt **o** and peace	**1Ki 9:25**	5930a
offered burnt offerings and peace **o**	**1Ki 9:25**	8002
to offer sacrifices and burnt **o**.	**1Ki 10:24**	5930a
The money from the guilt **o** and the	**2Ki 12:16**	817
and the money from the sin **o** was	**2Ki 12:16**	2403b
blood of his peace **o** on the altar.	**2Ki 16:13**	8002
their meal offering and their drink **o**;	**2Ki 16:15**	5262a
and they offered burnt **o** and peace	**1Ch 16:1**	5930a
offerings and peace **o** before God.	**1Ch 16:1**	8002
burnt offering and the peace **o**,	**1Ch 16:2**	8002
to offer burnt **o** to the LORD on	**1Ch 16:40**	5930a
I will give the oxen for burnt **o**	**1Ch 21:23**	5930a
burnt **o** and peace offerings.	**1Ch 21:26**	5930a
burnt offerings and peace **o**.	**1Ch 21:26**	8002
to offer all burnt **o** to the LORD,	**1Ch 23:31**	5930a
make *their* **o** willingly to You.	**1Ch 29:17**	5068
and offered burnt **o** to the LORD,	**1Ch 29:21**	5930a
with their drink **o** and sacrifices in	**1Ch 29:21**	5262a
offered a thousand burnt **o** on it.	**2Ch 1:6**	5930a
offer burnt **o** morning and evening,	**2Ch 2:4**	5930a
for there he offered the burnt **o**	**2Ch 7:7**	5930a
and the fat of the peace **o** because	**2Ch 7:7**	8002
Then Solomon offered burnt **o** to	**2Ch 8:12**	5930a
LORD burnt **o** and fragrant incense,	**2Ch 13:11**	5930a
to offer the burnt **o** of the LORD,	**2Ch 23:18**	5930a
And they offered burnt **o** in the	**2Ch 24:14**	5930a
or offered burnt **o** in the holy place	**2Ch 29:7**	5930a
at the completion of the burnt **o**,	**2Ch 29:29**	5927
thank **o** to the house of the LORD."	**2Ch 29:31**	8426
brought sacrifices and thank **o**,	**2Ch 29:31**	8426
who were willing *brought* burnt **o**.	**2Ch 29:31**	5930a
The number of the burnt **o**	**2Ch 29:32**	5930a
unable to skin all the burnt **o**;	**2Ch 29:34**	5930a
There *were* also many burnt **o**	**2Ch 29:35**	5930a
with the fat of the peace **o** and with	**2Ch 29:35**	8002
the libations for the burnt **o**.	**2Ch 29:35**	5930a
burnt **o** to the house of the LORD.	**2Ch 30:15**	5930a
sacrificing peace **o** and giving	**2Ch 30:22**	8002
burnt **o** and for peace offerings,	**2Ch 31:2**	5930a
burnt offerings and for peace **o**,	**2Ch 31:2**	8002
portion of his goods for the burnt **o**,	**2Ch 31:3**	5930a
the morning and evening burnt **o**,	**2Ch 31:3**	5930a
and the burnt **o** for the sabbaths	**2Ch 31:3**	5930a
was over the freewill **o** of God,	**2Ch 31:14**	5071
peace **o** and thank offerings on it;	**2Ch 33:16**	8002
peace offerings and thank **o** on it;	**2Ch 33:16**	8426
and young goats, all for the Passover **o**,	**2Ch 35:7**	6453
gave to the priests for the Passover **o**	**2Ch 35:8**	6453
to the Levites for the Passover **o**	**2Ch 35:9**	6453
Then they removed the burnt **o** that	**2Ch 35:12**	5930a
offering the burnt **o** and the fat	**2Ch 35:14**	5930a
and to offer burnt **o** on the altar	**2Ch 35:16**	5930a
of Israel to offer burnt **o** on it,	**Ezr 3:2**	5930a
offered burnt **o** on it to the LORD,	**Ezr 3:3**	5930a
LORD, burnt **o** morning and evening.	**Ezr 3:3**	5930a
the fixed number of burnt **o** daily,	**Ezr 3:4**	5930a
to offer burnt **o** to the LORD,	**Ezr 3:6**	5930a
with their grain **o** and their	**Ezr 7:17**	4504
grain offerings and their drink **o**	**Ezr 7:17**	5261
offered burnt **o** to the God of Israel:	**Ezr 8:35**	5930a
for the holy things and for the sin **o**	**Ne 10:33**	2403b
formerly they put the grain **o**,	**Ne 13:5**	4503
the grain **o** and the frankincense.	**Ne 13:9**	4503
and offering burnt **o** *according to* the	**Jb 1:5**	5930a
I shall not pour out their drink **o** of	**Ps 16:4**	5262a
May He remember all your meal **o** And	**Ps 20:3**	4503
burnt **o** are continually before Me.	**Ps 50:8**	5930a
I will render thank **o** to You.	**Ps 56:12**	8426
come into Your house with burnt **o**;	**Ps 66:13**	5930a
to You burnt **o** of fat beasts,	**Ps 66:15**	5930a
accept the freewill **o** of my mouth,	**Ps 119:108**	5071
"I was due to offer peace **o**;	**Pr 7:14**	8002
had enough of burnt **o** of rams And	**Is 1:11**	5930a
"Bring your worthless **o** no longer,	**Is 1:13**	4503
to Me the sheep of your burnt **o**,	**Is 43:23**	5930a
I have not burdened you with **o**,	**Is 43:23**	4503
Their burnt **o** and their sacrifices	**Is 56:7**	5930a
Your burnt **o** are not acceptable And	**Jer 6:20**	5930a
and *they* pour out drink **o** to	**Jer 7:18**	5262a
"Add your burnt **o** to your sacrifices	**Jer 7:21**	5930a
concerning burnt **o** and sacrifices.	**Jer 7:22**	5930a
from the Negev, bringing burnt **o**,	**Jer 17:26**	5930a
sacrifices, grain **o** and incense,	**Jer 17:26**	4503
in the fire as burnt **o** to Baal,	**Jer 19:5**	5930a
heavenly host and poured out drink **o**	**Jer 19:13**	5262a
on their roofs and poured out drink **o**	**Jer 32:29**	5262a
a man before Me to offer burnt **o**,	**Jer 33:18**	5930a
burnt offerings, to burn grain **o** and	**Jer 33:18**	4503
having grain **o** and incense in	**Jer 41:5**	4503
of heaven and pouring out drink **o** to	**Jer 44:17**	5262a
of heaven and pouring out drink **o** to	**Jer 44:18**	5262a
heaven and were pouring out drink **o**	**Jer 44:19**	5262a
in her image and poured out drink **o**	**Jer 44:19**	5262a
queen of heaven and pour out drink **o**	**Jer 44:25**	5262a
there they poured out their drink **o**.	**Ezk 20:28**	5262a
to offer burnt **o** on it and to	**Ezk 43:18**	5930a
offer your burnt **o** on the altar,	**Ezk 43:27**	5930a
on the altar, and your peace **o**;	**Ezk 43:27**	8002
a burnt offering and for peace **o**,	**Ezk 45:15**	8002
part *to provide* the burnt **o**,	**Ezk 45:17**	5930a
the burnt offerings, the grain **o** and	**Ezk 45:17**	4503
the grain offerings and the drink **o**,	**Ezk 45:17**	5262a
burnt offering and the peace **o**,	**Ezk 45:17**	8002
burnt offering and his peace **o**,	**Ezk 46:2**	8002
or peace **o** *as* a freewill offering	**Ezk 46:12**	8002
his burnt offering and his peace **o**	**Ezk 46:12**	8002

of God rather than burnt **o**.	**Hos 6:6**	5930a
They will not pour out drink **o** of	**Hos 9:4**	5258a
leavened, And proclaim freewill **o**,	**Am 4:5**	5071
burnt **o** and your grain offerings,	**Am 5:22**	5930a
burnt offerings and your grain **o**,	**Am 5:22**	4503
at the peace **o** of your fatlings.	**Am 5:22**	8002
present Me with sacrifices and grain **o**	**Am 5:25**	4503
Shall I come to Him with burnt **o**,	**Mi 6:6**	5930a
dispersed ones, Will bring My **o**.	**Zph 3:10**	4503
to the LORD **o** in righteousness.	**Mal 3:3**	4503
we robbed You?' In tithes and **o**.	**Mal 3:8**	8641
than all burnt **o** and sacrifices."	**Mk 12:33**	*3646*
to my nation and to present **o**;	**Ac 24:17**	*4376*
IN WHOLE BURNT **O** AND *sacrifices*	**Heb 10:6**	*3646*
SACRIFICES AND **O** AND WHOLE BURNT	**Heb 10:8**	*4376*
AND WHOLE BURNT **O** AND *sacrifices*	**Heb 10:8**	*3646*

OFFERS

priest who **o** it for sin shall eat it.	**Lv 6:26**	2398
'If he **o** it by way of thanksgiving,	**Lv 7:12**	7126
the day that he **o** his sacrifice,	**Lv 7:16**	7126
he who **o** it will not be accepted,	**Lv 7:18**	7126
o the sacrifice of his peace offerings	**Lv 7:29**	7126
o the blood of the peace offerings	**Lv 7:33**	7126
o a burnt offering or sacrifice,	**Lv 17:8**	5927
for he **o** the food of your God;	**Lv 21:8**	7126
'When a man **o** a sacrifice of	**Lv 22:21**	7126
He who **o** a sacrifice of thanksgiving	**Ps 50:23**	2076
mouth **o** praises with joyful lips.	**Ps 63:5**	1984b
for the man who **o** a sacrifice and	**Ec 9:2**	2076
He who **o** a grain offering *is like*	**Is 66:3**	5927
a grain offering *is like one who* **o**	**Is 66:3**	
"the one who **o** *sacrifice* on the	**Jer 48:35**	5927
which he **o** for himself and for the	**Heb 9:7**	*4374*

OFFICE

head and restore you to your **o**;	**Gn 40:13**	3653b
restored the chief cupbearer to his **o**,	**Gn 40:21**	4945b
he restored me in my **o**,	**Gn 41:13**	3653b
priest or the judge who is *in* **o**	**Dt 17:9**	
and the judges who will be *in* **o**	**Dt 19:17**	
priest who is in **o** at that time and	**Dt 26:3**	
those who wield the staff of **o**.	**Jg 5:14**	5613b
their **o** according to their order.	**1Ch 6:32**	5656
appointed in their **o** of trust.	**1Ch 9:22**	
Levites, were in an **o** of trust,	**1Ch 9:26**	
For their **o** is to assist the sons	**1Ch 23:28**	4612
Let another take his **o**.	**Ps 109:8**	6486
"I will depose you from your **o**,	**Is 22:19**	4673
to the custom of the priestly **o**,	**Lk 1:9**	*2405*
'LET ANOTHER MAN TAKE HIS **O**.'	**Ac 1:20**	*1984*
man aspires to the **o** of overseer,	**1Tm 3:1**	*1984*
sons of Levi who receive the priest's **o**	**Heb 7:5**	*2405*

OFFICER

in Egypt to Potiphar, Pharaoh's **o**,	**Gn 37:36**	5631
an Egyptian **o** of Pharaoh,	**Gn 39:1**	5631
king of Israel called an **o** and said,	**1Ki 22:9**	5631
The royal **o** on whose hand the	**2Ki 7:2**	7991c
Now the king appointed the royal **o**	**2Ki 7:17**	7991c
Then the royal **o** answered the man	**2Ki 7:19**	7991c
appointed for her a certain **o**,	**2Ki 8:6**	5631
Then *Jehu* said to Bidkar his **o**,	**2Ki 9:25**	7991c
Then Pekah son of Remaliah, his **o**,	**2Ki 15:25**	7991c
the chief **o** of the house of God;	**1Ch 9:11**	5057
Moses, was **o** over the treasures.	**1Ch 26:24**	5057
month, Mikloth *being* the chief **o**;	**1Ch 27:4**	5057
chief **o** for the Reubenites was	**1Ch 27:16**	5057
king of Israel called an **o** and said,	**2Ch 18:8**	5631
chest was brought in to the king's **o**	**2Ch 24:11**	6496
the chief priest's **o** would come,	**2Ch 24:11**	6496
and Conaniah the Levite *was* the **o**	**2Ch 31:12**	5057
the *chief* **o** of the house of God.	**2Ch 31:13**	5057
commander and **o** in the camp of the	**2Ch 32:21**	8269
having no chief, **O** or ruler,	**Pr 6:7**	7860
chief **o** in the house of the LORD,	**Jer 20:1**	6496
the judge, and the judge to the **o**,	**Mt 5:25**	*5257*
and the judge turn you over to the **o**,	**Lk 12:58**	*4233*
and the **o** throw you into prison.	**Lk 12:58**	*4233*

OFFICERS

of Egypt with **o** over all of them.	**Ex 14:7**	7991c
his **o** are drowned in the Red Sea.	**Ex 15:4**	7991c
the elders of the people and their **o**	**Nu 11:16**	7860
was angry with the **o** of the army,	**Nu 31:14**	6485
Then the **o** who were over the	**Nu 31:48**	6485
of tens, and **o** for your tribes.	**Dt 1:15**	7860
appoint for yourself judges and **o**	**Dt 16:18**	7860
"The **o** also shall speak to the	**Dt 20:5**	7860
"Then the **o** shall speak further	**Dt 20:8**	7860
When the **o** have finished speaking	**Dt 20:9**	7860
tribes, your elders and your **o**,	**Dt 29:10**	7860
elders of your tribes and your **o**,	**Dt 31:28**	7860
commanded the **o** of the people,	**Jos 1:10**	7860
o went through the midst of the camp	**Jos 3:2**	7860
All Israel with their elders and **o** and	**Jos 8:33**	7860
and their judges and their **o**,	**Jos 23:2**	7860
and their judges and their **o**;	**Jos 24:1**	7860
give to his **o** and to his servants.	**1Sa 8:15**	5631
o who *were* over Solomon's work,	**1Ki 9:23**	5324
to the guard and to the royal **o**,	**2Ki 10:25**	7991c
and the royal **o** threw *them* out,	**2Ki 10:25**	7991c
o over the house of the LORD.	**2Ki 11:18**	6486
with the three **o** of the temple.	**2Ki 25:18**	8104
and 6,000 *were* **o** and judges,	**1Ch 23:4**	7860
for they were **o** of the sanctuary	**1Ch 24:5**	8269
of the sanctuary and **o** of God,	**1Ch 24:5**	8269
for Israel, as **o** and judges.	**1Ch 26:29**	7860
and their **o** who served the king in	**1Ch 27:1**	7860
were the chief **o** of King Solomon,	**2Ch 8:10**	5333
put **o** in them and stores of food,	**2Ch 11:11**	5057
the Levites shall be **o** before you.	**2Ch 19:11**	7860

All the **o** and all the people 2Ch 24:10 8269
of Hananiah, one of the king's **o**. 2Ch 26:11 8269
before the **o** and all the assembly. 2Ch 28:14 8269
he decided with his **o** and his 2Ch 32:3 8269
appointed military **o** over the people 2Ch 32:6 8269
His **o** also contributed a freewill 2Ch 35:8 8269
and Jozabad, the **o** of the Levites, 2Ch 35:9 8269
treasures of the king and of his **o**, 2Ch 36:18 8269
king had sent with me **o** of the army Ne 2:9 8269
the army **o** of Persia and Media, Es 1:3
of Jerusalem, the court **o** and Jer 34:19 5631
to the **o** of the king of Babylon, Jer 38:17 8269
to the **o** of the king of Babylon, Jer 38:18 8269
to the **o** of the king of Babylon; Jer 38:22 8269
leading **o** of the king of Babylon; Jer 39:13 7227b
one of the chief **o** of the king, Jer 41:1 7227b
and into the hand of his **o**. Jer 46:26 5650
with the three **o** of the temple. Jer 52:24 8104
heads, all of them looking like **o**, Ezk 23:15 7991c
all of them, **o** and men of renown, Ezk 23:23 7991c
with the **o** to see the outcome. Mt 26:58 *5257*
and he was sitting with the **o** and Mk 14:54 *5257*
And the **o** received Him with slaps Mk 14:65 *5257*
discussed with the chief priests and **o** Lk 22:4 *4755*
Jesus said to the chief priests and **o** Lk 22:52 *4755*
the Pharisees sent **o** to seize Him. Jn 7:32 *5257*
The **o** then came to the chief Jn 7:45 *5257*
o answered, "Never has a man spoken Jn 7:46 *5257*
and **o** from the chief priests and Jn 18:3 *5257*
commander and the **o** of the Jews, Jn 18:12 *5257*
and the **o** were standing *there,* Jn 18:18 *5257*
o standing nearby struck Jesus, Jn 18:22 *5257*
chief priests and the **o** saw Him, Jn 19:6 *5257*
But the **o** who came did not find Ac 5:22 *5257*
the captain went along with the **o** Ac 5:26 *5257*

OFFICES
assign me to one of the priest's **o** 1Sa 2:36 3550
divided them according to their **o** 1Ch 24:3 6486
were their **o** for their ministry when 1Ch 24:19 6486
Jehoiada placed the **o** of the house 2Ch 23:18 6486
He set the priests in their **o** 2Ch 35:2 4931
will be between the two **o**." Zch 6:13

OFFICIAL
"How then can you repulse one **o** 2Ki 18:24 6346
the chamber of Nathan-melech the **o**, 2Ki 23:11 5631
From the city he took one **o** 2Ki 25:19 5631
the scribe and Maaseiah the **o**, 2Ch 26:11 7860
and Maaseiah an **o** of the city, 2Ch 34:8 8269
the Ammonite **o** heard *about it,* Ne 2:10 5650
and Tobiah the Ammonite **o**, Ne 2:19 5650
also made repairs for the **o** seat Ne 3:7 3678
the **o** of half the district of Ne 3:9 8269
the **o** of half the district of Ne 3:12 8269
the **o** of the district of Ne 3:14 8269
the **o** of the district of Mizpah, Ne 3:15 8269
o of half the district of Ne 3:16 8269
the **o** of half the district of Ne 3:17 8269
o of *the other* half of the Ne 3:18 8269
son of Jeshua, the **o** of Mizpah, Ne 3:19 8269
the king had given orders to each **o** Es 1:8 7227b
o watches over another official, Ec 5:8 1364
official watches over another **o**, Ec 5:8 1364
"How then can you repulse one **o** Is 36:9 6346
He also took from the city one **o** Jer 52:25 5631
a *synagogue* **o** came Mt 9:18 *758*
from the *house of* the synagogue **o**, Mk 5:35 *752*
spoken, said to the synagogue **o**, Mk 5:36 *752*
to the house of the synagogue **o**; Mk 5:38 *752*
and he was an **o** of the synagogue; Lk 8:41 *758*
from *the house of* the synagogue **o**, Lk 8:49 *752*
But the synagogue **o**, Lk 13:14 *752*
And there was a royal **o** Jn 4:46 *937*
The royal **o** said to Him, Jn 4:49 *937*
eunuch, a court **o** of Candace, Ac 8:27 *1413*

OFFICIAL'S
When Jesus came into the **o** house, Mt 9:23 *758*

OFFICIALS
Pharaoh's **o** saw her and Gn 12:15 8269
Pharaoh was furious with his two **o**, Gn 40:2 5631
He asked Pharaoh's **o** who were Gn 40:7 5631
These were his **o**: 1Ki 4:2 8269
two or three **o** looked down at him. 2Ki 9:32 5631
and they will become **o** in the 2Ki 20:18 5631
and his captains and his **o**. 2Ki 24:12 5631
and the king's wives and his **o** 2Ki 24:15 5631
at Jerusalem all the **o** of Israel, 1Ch 28:1 8269
with the **o** and the mighty men, 1Ch 28:1 5631
The **o** also and all the people will 1Ch 28:21 8269
All the **o**, the mighty men, and 1Ch 29:24 8269
year of his reign he sent his **o**, 2Ch 17:7 8269
o of Judah came and bowed down 2Ch 24:17 8269
destroyed all the **o** of the people 2Ch 24:23 8269
King Hezekiah and the **o** ordered 2Ch 29:30 8269
scribes and **o** and gatekeepers. 2Ch 34:13 7860
Jehiel, the **o** of the house of God, 2Ch 35:8 5057
all the **o** of the priests and the 2Ch 36:14 8269
and the lesser governors, the **o**, Ezr 4:9 2967
and his colleagues the **o**, Ezr 5:6 671a
the **o** of *the provinces* beyond the Ezr 6:6 671a
The **o** did not know where I had Ne 2:16 5461
the priests, the nobles, the **o** or Ne 2:16 5461
and spoke to the nobles, the **o** and Ne 4:14 5461
I said to the nobles, the **o** and Ne 4:19 5461
one hundred and fifty Jews and **o**, Ne 5:17 5461
to assemble the nobles, the **o** and Ne 7:5 5461
So did I and half of the **o** with me; Ne 12:40 5461
So I reprimanded the **o** and said, Ne 13:11 5461
two of the king's **o** from those who Es 2:21 5631
and there are higher **o** over them. Ec 5:8 1364
and they will become **o** in the Is 39:7 5631
and the **o** of Judah with the Jer 24:1 8269
Zedekiah king of Judah and his **o**, Jer 24:8 8269
When the **o** of Judah heard these Jer 26:10 8269
to the **o** and to all the people, Jer 26:11 8269
all the **o** and to all the people, Jer 26:12 8269
Then the **o** and all the people said Jer 26:16 8269
men and all the **o** heard his words, Jer 26:21 8269
and the queen mother, the court **o**, Jer 29:2 5631
the **o** and all the people obeyed who Jer 34:10 8269
the **o** of Judah and the officials Jer 34:19 8269
of Judah and the **o** of Jerusalem, Jer 34:19 8269
Zedekiah king of Judah and his **o** Jer 34:21 8269
was near the chamber of the **o**, Jer 35:4 8269
all the **o** were sitting there Jer 36:12 8269
of Hananiah, and all the *other* **o**. Jer 36:12 8269
Then all the **o** sent Jehudi the son Jer 36:14 8269
Then the **o** said to Baruch, Jer 36:19 8269
the **o** who stood beside the king. Jer 36:21 8269
Jeremiah and brought him to the **o**. Jer 37:14 8269
Then the **o** were angry at Jeremiah Jer 37:15 8269
Then the **o** said to the king, Jer 38:4 8269
"But if the **o** hear that I have Jer 38:25 8269
Then all the **o** came to Jeremiah Jer 38:27 8269
Then all the **o** of the king of Jer 39:3 8269
all the **o** of the king of Babylon. Jer 39:3 8269
against her **o** and her wise men! Jer 50:35 8269
it is against all the **o** of Israel. Ezk 21:12 5387a
in purple, governors and **o**, Ezk 23:6 5461
the Assyrians, governors and **o**, Ezk 23:12 5461
men, governors and **o** all of them, Ezk 23:23 5461
Ashpenaz, the chief of his **o**, Da 1:3 5631
the **o** assigned *new* names to them; Da 1:7 5631
from the commander of the **o** that Da 1:8 5631
sight of the commander of the **o**, Da 1:9 5631
commander of the **o** said to Daniel, Da 1:10 5631
the **o** had appointed over Daniel, Da 1:11 5631
the commander of the **o** presented Da 1:18 5631
said to his high **o**, Da 3:24 1907
the king's high **o** gathered around Da 3:27 1907
the high **o** and the governors have Da 6:7 1907
synagogue **o** named Jairus came up, Mk 5:22 *752*
the synagogue **o** sent to them, Ac 13:15 *752*

OFFICIATED
from which no one has **o** at the altar. Heb 7:13 *4337*

OFFSCOURING
made us mere **o** and refuse La 3:45 5501a

OFFSETS
for on the outside he made **o** *in* 1Ki 6:6 4052

OFFSPRING
me another **o** in place of Abel, Gn 4:25 2233
to keep **o** alive on the face of all Gn 7:3 2233
"Since You have given no **o** to me, Gn 15:3 2233
falsely with me or with my **o** Gn 21:23 5209
and raise up **o** for your brother." Gn 38:8 2233
knew that the **o** would not be his; Gn 38:9 2233
not to give **o** to his brother. Gn 38:9 2233
"But your **o** that have been born Gn 48:6 4138
the first **o** of every womb among Ex 13:2 6363a
LORD the first **o** of every womb, Ex 13:12 6363a
and the first **o** of every beast Ex 13:12 6363a
"But every first **o** of a donkey Ex 13:13 6363a
males, the first **o** of every womb, Ex 13:15 6363a
"The first **o** from every womb Ex 34:19 6363a
the first **o** from cattle and sheep. Ex 34:19 6363a
a lamb the first **o** from a donkey; Ex 34:20 6363a
of your **o** to offer them to Molech, Lv 18:21 2233
who gives any of his **o** to Molech, Lv 20:2 2233
has given some of his **o** to Molech, Lv 20:3 2233
he gives any of his **o** to Molech, Lv 20:4 2233
not profane his **o** among his people; Lv 21:15 2233
'No man of your **o** throughout their Lv 21:17 2233
"Blessed *shall be* the **o** of your body Dt 28:4 6529
ground and the **o** of your beasts, Dt 28:4 6529
in the **o** of your body and in the Dt 28:11 6529
in the **o** of your beast and in the Dt 28:11 6529
"Cursed *shall be* the **o** of your body Dt 28:18 6529
it shall eat the **o** of your herd Dt 28:51 6529
shall eat the **o** of your own body, Dt 28:53 6529
in the **o** of your body and in the Dt 30:9 6529
and in the **o** of your cattle and in the Dt 30:9 6529
through the **o** which the LORD will Ru 4:12 2233
and destroyed all the royal **o**. 2Ki 11:1 2233
the royal **o** of the house of Judah. 2Ch 22:10 2233
your **o** as the grass of the earth. Jb 5:25 6631
o or posterity among his people, Jb 18:19 5209
And their **o** before their eyes, Jb 21:8 6631
"Their **o** become strong, they grow Jb 39:4 1121
Their **o** You will destroy from the Ps 21:10 6529
with iniquity, **O** of evildoers, Is 1:4 2233
May the **o** of evildoers not be Is 14:20 2233
and survivors, **o** and posterity," Is 14:22 5209
of his father's house, **o** and issue, Is 22:24 6631
spread out the earth and its **o**, Is 42:5 6631
I will bring your **o** from the east, Is 43:5 2233
will pour out My Spirit on your **o** And Is 44:3 6631
I did not say to the **o** of Jacob, Is 45:19 2233
the **o** of Israel Will be justified and Is 45:25 2233
sand, And your **o** like its grains; Is 48:19 6631, 4578
guilt offering, He will see *His* **o**, Is 53:10 2233
O of an adulterer and a prostitute. Is 57:3 2233
children of rebellion, **O** of deceit, Is 57:4 2233
nor from the mouth of your **o**, Is 59:21 2233
the mouth of your offspring's **o**," Is 59:21 2233
Then their **o** will be known among Is 61:9 2233
the **o** *whom* the LORD has blessed. Is 61:9 2233
I will bring forth **o** from Jacob, Is 65:9 2233
o of those blessed by the LORD, Is 65:23 2233
your **o** and your name will endure. Is 66:22 2233
brothers, all the **o** of Ephraim. Jer 7:15 2233
And your **o** from the land of their Jer 30:10 2233
"Then the **o** of Israel also will Jer 31:36 2233
I will also cast off all the **o** of Israel Jer 31:37 2233
His **o** has been destroyed along Jer 49:10 2233
Should women eat their **o**, La 2:20 6529
who are from the **o** of Zadok, Ezk 43:19 2233
from the **o** of the house of Israel, Ezk 44:22 2233
I am going to rebuke your **o**, Mal 2:3 2233
do while he was seeking a godly **o**? Mal 2:15 2233

OFFSPRING'S
the mouth of your **o** offspring," Is 59:21 2233

OFTEN
as **o** as she went up to the house 1Sa 1:7 1767
it happened as **o** as they went out, 1Sa 18:30 1767
as **o** as the king entered the house 1Ki 14:28 1767
so it was, as **o** as he passed by, 2Ki 4:8 1767
As **o** as the king entered the house 2Ch 12:11 1767
"How **o** is the lamp of the wicked Jb 21:17 4100
o as the trumpet *sounds* he says, Jb 39:25 1767
And **o** He restrained His anger And Ps 78:38 7235a
How **o** they rebelled against Him in Ps 78:40 4100
For he will not **o** consider the Ec 5:20 7235a
"As **o** as it passes through, it Is 28:19 1767
as **o** as I have spoken against him, Jer 31:20 1767
for he **o** falls into the fire and Mt 17:15 *4178*
the fire and **o** into the water. Mt 17:15 *4178*
how **o** shall my brother sin against Mt 18:21 *4212*
How **o** I wanted to gather your Mt 23:37 *4212*
because he had **o** been bound with Mk 5:4 *4178*
"It has **o** thrown him both Mk 9:22 *4178*
But Jesus Himself would **o** slip Lk 5:16
"The disciples of John **o** fast and Lk 5:33 *4437*
How **o** I wanted to gather your Lk 13:34 *4212*
for Jesus had **o** met there with His Jn 18:2 *4178*
he also used to send for him quite **o** Ac 24:26 *4437*
And as I punished them **o** in all the Ac 26:11 *4178*
that **o** I have planned to come to Ro 1:13 *4178*
I have **o** been prevented from coming Ro 15:22 *4183*
do this, as **o** as you drink *it,* in 1Co 11:25 *3740*
For as **o** as you eat this bread and 1Co 11:26 *3740*
whom we have **o** tested and found 2Co 8:22 *4178*
number, **o** in danger of death. 2Co 11:23 *4178*
hunger and thirst, **o** without food, 2Co 11:27 *4178*
many walk, of whom I **o** told you, Php 3:18 *4178*
Onesiphorus, for he **o** refreshed me 2Tm 1:16 *4178*
drinks the rain which **o** falls on it Heb 6:7 *4178*
it that He would offer Himself **o**, Heb 9:25 *4178*
He would have needed to suffer **o** Heb 9:26 *4178*
every plague, as **o** as they desire. Rv 11:6 *3740*

OFTENTIMES
God does all these **o** with men, Jb 33:29 6471, 7969

OG
and **O** the king of Bashan went out Nu 21:33 5747
the Amorites and the kingdom of **O**, Nu 32:33 5747
Heshbon, and **O** the king of Bashan, Dt 1:4 5747
went up the road to Bashan, and **O**, Dt 3:1 5747
the LORD our God delivered **O** also, Dt 3:3 5747
Argob, the kingdom of **O** in Bashan. Dt 3:4 5747
cities of the kingdom of **O** in Dt 3:10 5747
(For only **O** king of Bashan was Dt 3:11 5747
and all Bashan, the kingdom of **O**, Dt 3:13 5747
and the land of **O** king of Bashan, Dt 4:47 5747
O the king of Bashan came out to Dt 29:7 5747
just as He did to Sihon and **O**, Dt 31:4 5747
beyond the Jordan, to Sihon and **O**, Jos 2:10 5747
of Heshbon and to **O** king of Bashan Jos 9:10 5747
the territory of **O** king of Bashan, Jos 12:4 5747
all the kingdom of **O** in Bashan, Jos 13:12 5747
the kingdom of **O** king of Bashan, Jos 13:30 5747
of the kingdom of **O** in Bashan, Jos 13:31 5747
Amorites and of **O** king of Bashan; 1Ki 4:19 5747
the land of **O** the king of Bashan. Ne 9:22 5747
And **O**, king of Bashan, And all Ps 135:11 5747
And **O**, king of Bashan, For His Ps 136:20 5747

OH
"**O** that Ishmael might live before Gn 17:18 3863
"**O** may the Lord not be angry, and Gn 18:30 4994
"**O** may the Lord not be angry, and Gn 18:32 4994
"**O** no, my lords! Gn 19:18 4994
"**O**, my lord, we indeed came down Gn 43:20 994a
"**O** my lord, may your servant Gn 44:18 994a
"**O** that someone would give us Nu 11:18 4310
"**O**, my lord, I beg you, do not Nu 12:11 994a
"**O**, do not let her be like one Nu 12:12 4994
'**O** that they had such a heart in Dt 5:29 4310, 5414
"**O**, my lord! As your soul lives, 1Sa 1:26 994a
"**O** that one would appoint me 2Sa 15:4 4310
"**O** that someone would give me 2Sa 23:15 4310
"**O**, my lord, this woman and I 1Ki 3:17 994a
"**O**, my lord, give her the living 1Ki 3:26 994a
"**O** that You would bless me 1Ch 4:10 518
"**O** that someone would give me 1Ch 11:17 4310
O give thanks to the LORD, call 1Ch 16:8
"**O** that my grief were actually Jb 6:2 3863
"**O** that my request might come to Jb 6:8 4310, 5414
"**O** that You would hide me in Jb 14:13 4310, 5414
"**O** that my words were written! Jb 19:23 4310, 5414
O that they were inscribed in a Jb 19:23 4310, 5414

“**O** that I knew where I might find **Jb 23:3** 4310, 5414
“**O** that I were as in months gone **Jb 29:2** 4310, 5414
“**O** that I had one to hear me! **Jb 31:35** 4310, 5414
O, that the salvation of Israel **Ps 14:7** 4310, 5414
O, that the salvation of Israel **Ps 53:6** 4310, 5414
“**O**, that I had wings like a dove! **Ps 55:6** 4310, 5414
O draw near to my soul *and* redeem **Ps 69:18**
O, give ear, Shepherd of Israel, **Ps 80:1**
“**O** that My people would listen to **Ps 81:13** 3863
O grant Your strength to Your **Ps 86:16**
O give thanks to the LORD, call **Ps 105:1**
O give thanks to the LORD, for He **Ps 106:1**
O give thanks to the LORD, for He **Ps 107:1**
O give us help against the **Ps 108:12**
O *may it be* in the presence of all **Ps 116:14** 4994
O *may it be* in the presence of all **Ps 116:18** 4994
O let Israel say, **Ps 118:2** 4994
O let the house of Aaron say, **Ps 118:3** 4994
O let those who fear the LORD say, **Ps 118:4** 4994
O that my ways may be established **Ps 119:5** 305
O hold *them* back. **Pr 24:11** 518
o how lofty are his eyes! **Pr 30:13**
O, may your breasts be like clusters **SS 7:8** 4994
“**O** that you were like a brother **SS 8:1** 4310, 5414
o land of whirring wings Which **Is 18:1**
O, that You would rend the **Is 64:1** 3863
O, my heart! My heart is pounding **Jer 4:19** 7023
O that my head were waters And **Jer 9:1** 4310, 5414
O that I had in the desert A **Jer 9:2** 4310
O turn back, each of you from his **Jer 18:11** 4994
“**O**, do not do this abominable **Jer 44:4** 4994
O, that You would bring the day **La 1:21**
“**O** that there were one among you **Mal 1:10** 4310
O, the depth of the riches both of **Ro 11:33** *5599*

OHAD
Jemuel and Jamin and **O** and Jachin **Gn 46:10** 161
Jemuel and Jamin and **O** and Jachin **Ex 6:15** 161

OHEL
and Hashubah, **O**, Berechiah, **1Ch 3:20** 169

OHOLAH
“Their names were **O** the elder **Ezk 23:4** 170
as for their names, Samaria is **O** and **Ezk 23:4** 170
“**O** played the harlot while **Ezk 23:5** 170
will you judge **O** and Oholibah? **Ezk 23:36** 170
they went in to **O** and to Oholibah, **Ezk 23:44** 170

OHOLIAB
Myself have appointed with him **O**, **Ex 31:6** 171
his heart to teach, both he and **O**, **Ex 35:34** 171
“Now Bezalel and **O**, and every **Ex 36:1** 171
Then Moses called Bezalel and **O** **Ex 36:2** 171
With him *was* **O** **Ex 38:23** 171

OHOLIBAH
Oholah the elder and **O** her sister. **Ezk 23:4** 172
is Oholah and Jerusalem is **O**. **Ezk 23:4** 172
“Now her sister **O** saw *this,* yet **Ezk 23:11** 172
“Therefore, O **O**, thus says the **Ezk 23:22** 172
man, will you judge Oholah and **O**? **Ezk 23:36** 172
they went in to Oholah and to **O**, **Ezk 23:44** 172

OHOLIBAMAH
and **O** the daughter of Anah and the **Gn 36:2** 173
and **O** bore Jeush and Jalam and **Gn 36:5** 173
were the sons of Esau's wife **O**, **Gn 36:14** 173
are the sons of Esau's wife **O**: **Gn 36:18** 173
descended from Esau's wife **O**, **Gn 36:18** 173
and **O**, the daughter of Anah. **Gn 36:25** 173
chief **O**, chief Elah, chief Pinon, **Gn 36:41** 173
chief **O**, chief Elah, chief Pinon, **1Ch 1:52** 173

OIL
a pillar and poured **o** on its top. **Gn 28:18** 8081
he also poured **o** on it. **Gn 35:14** 8081
o for lighting, spices for the **Ex 25:6** 8081
spices for the anointing **o** and for **Ex 25:6** 8081
bring you clear **o** of beaten olives **Ex 27:20** 8081
and unleavened cakes mixed with **o**, **Ex 29:2** 8081
unleavened wafers spread with **o**; **Ex 29:2** 8081
you shall take the anointing **o** and **Ex 29:7** 8081
altar and some of the anointing **o**, **Ex 29:21** 8081
and one cake of bread *mixed with* **o** **Ex 29:23** 8081
one-fourth of a hin of beaten **o**. **Ex 29:40** 8081
sanctuary, and of olive **o** a hin. **Ex 30:24** 8081
make of these a holy anointing **o**, **Ex 30:25** 8081
it shall be a holy anointing **o**. **Ex 30:25** 8081
'This shall be a holy anointing **o** **Ex 30:31** 8081
the anointing **o** also, and the **Ex 31:11** 8081
and **o** for lighting, and spices for **Ex 35:8** 8081
and spices for the anointing **o**, **Ex 35:8** 8081
its lamps and the **o** for the light; **Ex 35:14** 8081
o and the fragrant incense, **Ex 35:15** 8081
o for the light and for the anointing **Ex 35:28** 8081
for the light and for the anointing **o** **Ex 35:28** 8081
the holy anointing **o** and the pure, **Ex 37:29** 8081
utensils, and the **o** for the light; **Ex 39:37** 8081
o and the fragrant incense, **Ex 39:38** 8081
“Then you shall take the anointing **o** **Ex 40:9** 8081
and he shall pour **o** on it and put **Lv 2:1** 8081
handful of its fine flour and of its **o** **Lv 2:2** 8081
cakes of fine flour mixed with **o**, **Lv 2:4** 8081
unleavened wafers spread with **o**. **Lv 2:4** 8081
flour, unleavened, mixed with **o**; **Lv 2:5** 8081
it into bits and pour **o** on it; **Lv 2:6** 8081
be made of fine flour with **o**. **Lv 2:7** 8081
put **o** on it and lay incense on it; **Lv 2:15** 8081
part of its grits and its **o** with **Lv 2:16** 8081
o on it or place incense on it, **Lv 5:11** 8081
with its **o** and all the incense **Lv 6:15** 8081
be prepared with **o** on a griddle. **Lv 6:21** 8081
'Every grain offering, mixed with **o** **Lv 7:10** 8081
unleavened cakes mixed with **o**, **Lv 7:12** 8081
unleavened wafers spread with **o**, **Lv 7:12** 8081
stirred fine flour mixed with **o**. **Lv 7:12** 8081
the garments and the anointing **o** **Lv 8:2** 8081
Moses then took the anointing **o** **Lv 8:10** 8081
he poured some of the anointing **o** **Lv 8:12** 8081
bread *mixed with* **o** and one wafer, **Lv 8:26** 8081
Moses took some of the anointing **o** **Lv 8:30** 8081
and a grain offering mixed with **o**; **Lv 9:4** 8081
LORD's anointing **o** is upon you.” **Lv 10:7** 8081
mixed with **o** for a grain offering, **Lv 14:10** 8081
grain offering, and one log of **o**; **Lv 14:10** 8081
guilt offering, with the log of **o**, **Lv 14:12** 8081
also take some of the log of **o**, **Lv 14:15** 8081
the **o** that is in his left palm, **Lv 14:16** 8081
sprinkle some of the **o** seven times **Lv 14:16** 8081
remaining **o** which is in his palm, **Lv 14:17** 8081
the **o** that is in the priest's palm, **Lv 14:18** 8081
mixed with **o** for a grain offering, **Lv 14:21** 8081
a grain offering, and a log of **o**, **Lv 14:21** 8081
guilt offering and the log of **o**, **Lv 14:24** 8081
some of the **o** into his left palm; **Lv 14:26** 8081
the priest shall sprinkle some of the **o** **Lv 14:27** 8081
put some of the **o** that is in his palm **Lv 14:28** 8081
the rest of the **o** that is in the **Lv 14:29** 8081
the anointing **o** has been poured and **Lv 21:10** 8081
anointing **o** of his God is on him; **Lv 21:12** 8081
ephah of fine flour mixed with **o**, **Lv 23:13** 8081
they bring to you clear **o** from beaten **Lv 24:2** 8081
its trays and all its **o** vessels, **Nu 4:9** 8081
the son of Aaron the priest is the **o** **Nu 4:16** 8081
grain offering and the anointing **o** **Nu 4:16** 8081
he shall not pour **o** on it nor **Nu 5:15** 8081
cakes of fine flour mixed with **o** **Nu 6:15** 8081
unleavened wafers spread with **o** **Nu 6:15** 8081
mixed with **o** for a grain offering; **Nu 7:13** 8081
mixed with **o** for a grain offering; **Nu 7:19** 8081
mixed with **o** for a grain offering; **Nu 7:25** 8081
mixed with **o** for a grain offering; **Nu 7:31** 8081
mixed with **o** for a grain offering; **Nu 7:37** 8081
mixed with **o** for a grain offering; **Nu 7:43** 8081
mixed with **o** for a grain offering; **Nu 7:49** 8081
mixed with **o** for a grain offering; **Nu 7:55** 8081
mixed with **o** for a grain offering; **Nu 7:61** 8081
mixed with **o** for a grain offering; **Nu 7:67** 8081
mixed with **o** for a grain offering; **Nu 7:73** 8081
mixed with **o** for a grain offering; **Nu 7:79** 8081
offering, fine flour mixed with **o**; **Nu 8:8** 8081
the taste of cakes baked with **o**. **Nu 11:8** 8081
with one-fourth of a hin of **o**, **Nu 15:4** 8081
mixed with one-third of a hin of **o**; **Nu 15:6** 8081
mixed with one-half a hin of **o**; **Nu 15:9** 8081
“All the best of the fresh **o** and **Nu 18:12** 3323
a fourth of a hin of beaten **o**. **Nu 28:5** 8081
mixed with **o** as a grain offering, **Nu 28:9** 8081
mixed with **o** for a grain offering, **Nu 28:12** 8081
mixed with **o** for a grain offering, **Nu 28:12** 8081
flour mixed with **o** for a grain offering **Nu 28:13** 8081
offer fine flour mixed with **o**: **Nu 28:20** 8081
offering, fine flour mixed with **o**: **Nu 28:28** 8081
offering, fine flour mixed with **o**: **Nu 29:3** 8081
offering, fine flour mixed with **o**: **Nu 29:9** 8081
offering, fine flour mixed with **o**: **Nu 29:14** 8081
who was anointed with the holy **o**. **Nu 35:25** 8081
and your new wine and your **o**, **Dt 7:13** 3323
a land of olive **o** and honey; **Dt 8:8** 8081
and your new wine and your **o**. **Dt 11:14** 3323
of your grain or new wine or **o**, **Dt 12:17** 3323
your grain, your new wine, your **o**, **Dt 14:23** 3323
grain, your new wine, and your **o**, **Dt 18:4** 3323
not anoint yourself with the **o**, **Dt 28:40** 8081
leaves you no grain, new wine, or **o**, **Dt 28:51** 3323
rock, And **o** from the flinty rock, **Dt 32:13** 8081
And may he dip his foot in **o**. **Dt 33:24** 8081
Then Samuel took the flask of **o**, **1Sa 10:1** 8081
Fill your horn with **o** and **1Sa 16:1** 8081
Then Samuel took the horn of **o** and **1Sa 16:13** 8081
shield of Saul, not anointed with **o**. **2Sa 1:21** 8081
and do not anoint yourself with **o**, **2Sa 14:2** 8081
the priest then took the horn of **o** **1Ki 1:39** 8081
and twenty kors of beaten **o**; **1Ki 5:11** 8081
bowl and a little **o** in the jar; **1Ki 17:12** 8081
nor shall the jar of **o** be empty, **1Ki 17:14** 8081
nor did the jar of **o** become empty, **1Ki 17:16** 8081
in the house except a jar of **o**.” **2Ki 4:2** 8081
And the **o** stopped. **2Ki 4:6** 8081
“Go, sell the **o** and pay your **2Ki 4:7** 8081
take this flask of **o** in your hand and **2Ki 9:1** 8081
“Then take the flask of **o** and **2Ki 9:3** 8081
he poured the **o** on his head and **2Ki 9:6** 8081
and the spices and the precious **o** **2Ki 20:13** 8081
wine and the **o** and the frankincense **1Ch 9:29** 8081
and bunches of raisins, wine, **o**, **1Ch 12:40** 8081
had charge of the stores of **o**. **1Ch 27:28** 8081
of wine and 20,000 baths of **o**.” **2Ch 2:10** 8081
wheat and barley, **o** and wine, **2Ch 2:15** 8081
and stores of food, **o** and wine. **2Ch 11:11** 8081
anointed them *with* **o**, led all **2Ch 28:15** 8081
fruits of grain, new wine, **o**, **2Ch 31:5** 3323
the produce of grain, wine and **o**, **2Ch 32:28** 3323
and **o** to the Sidonians and to the **Ezr 3:7** 8081
salt, wine and anointing **o**, **Ezr 6:9** 4887
100 baths of wine, 100 baths of **o**, **Ezr 7:22** 4887
and the **o** that you are exacting **Ne 5:11** 3323
the new wine and the **o** to the **Ne 10:37** 3323
the grain, the new wine and the **o** to **Ne 10:39** 3323
and **o** prescribed for the Levites, **Ne 13:5** 3323
wine and **o** into the storehouses. **Ne 13:12** 3323
six months with **o** of myrrh and six **Es 2:12** 8081
“Within the walls they produce **o**; **Jb 24:11** 6671
poured out for me streams of **o**! **Jb 29:6** 8081
You have anointed my head with **o**; **Ps 23:5** 8081
the **o** of joy above Your fellows. **Ps 45:7** 8081
His words were softer than **o**, **Ps 55:21** 8081
With My holy **o** I have anointed him **Ps 89:20** 8081
I have been anointed with fresh **o**. **Ps 92:10** 8081
may make *his* face glisten with **o**, **Ps 104:15** 8081
water And like **o** into his bones. **Ps 109:18** 8081
like the precious **o** upon the head, **Ps 133:2** 8081
It is **o** upon the head; **Ps 141:5** 8081
And smoother than **o** is her speech; **Pr 5:3** 8081
He who loves wine and **o** will not **Pr 21:17** 8081
and **o** in the dwelling of the wise, **Pr 21:20** 8081
O and perfume make the heart glad, **Pr 27:9** 8081
And grasps **o** with his right hand. **Pr 27:16** 8081
let not **o** be lacking on your head. **Ec 9:8** 8081
flies make a perfumer's **o** stink, **Ec 10:1** 8081
Your name is *like* purified **o**; **SS 1:3** 8081
or bandaged, Nor softened with **o**. **Is 1:6** 8081
up, captains, **o** the shields,” **Is 21:5** 4886
the precious **o** and his whole armory **Is 39:2** 8081
have journeyed to the king with **o** **Is 57:9** 8081
The **o** of gladness instead of **Is 61:3** 8081
and the new wine and the **o**, **Jer 31:12** 3323
in wine and summer fruit and **o** and **Jer 40:10** 8081
o and honey hidden in the field.” **Jer 41:8** 8081
from you and anointed you with **o**. **Ezk 16:9** 8081
You ate fine flour, honey and **o**; **Ezk 16:13** 8081
and offered My **o** and My incense **Ezk 16:18** 8081
which I gave you, fine flour, **o** and **Ezk 16:19** 8081
you had set My incense and My **o**. **Ezk 23:41** 8081
wheat of Minnith, cakes, honey, **o** and **Ezk 27:17** 8081
their rivers to run like **o**,” **Ezk 32:14** 8081
and the prescribed portion of **o** **Ezk 45:14** 8081
(*namely,* the bath of **o**), **Ezk 45:14** 8081
ram and a hin of **o** with an ephah. **Ezk 45:24** 8081
the grain offering and the **o**.” **Ezk 45:25** 8081
and a hin of **o** with an ephah. **Ezk 46:5** 8081
and a hin of **o** with an ephah. **Ezk 46:7** 8081
and a hin of **o** with an ephah. **Ezk 46:11** 8081
of **o** to moisten the fine flour, **Ezk 46:14** 8081
the grain offering and the **o**, **Ezk 46:15** 8081
and my flax, my **o** and my drink.' **Hos 2:5** 8081
grain, the new wine and the **o**, **Hos 2:8** 3323
to the new wine and to the **o**, **Hos 2:22** 3323
And **o** is carried to Egypt. **Hos 12:1** 8081
new wine dries up, Fresh **o** fails. **Jl 1:10** 3323
send you grain, new wine and **o**, **Jl 2:19** 3323
overflow with the new wine and **o**. **Jl 2:24** 3323
rams, In ten thousand rivers of **o**? **Mi 6:7** 8081
will not anoint yourself with **o**; **Mi 6:15** 8081
grain, on the new wine, on the **o**, **Hg 1:11** 3323
fold, or cooked food, wine, **o**, **Hg 2:12** 8081
which empty the golden **o** from **Zch 4:12**
lamps, they took no **o** with them, **Mt 25:3** *1637*
but the prudent took **o** in flasks **Mt 25:4** *1637*
'Give us some of your **o**, **Mt 25:8** *1637*
anointing with **o** many sick people **Mk 6:13** *1637*
“You did not anoint My head with **o**, **Lk 7:46** *1637*
pouring **o** and wine on *them* **Lk 10:34** *1637*
'A hundred measures of **o**.' **Lk 16:6** *1637*
HAS ANOINTED YOU WITH THE **O** OF **Heb 1:9** *1637*
anointing him with **o** in the name **Jas 5:14** *1637*
do not damage the **o** and the wine.” **Rv 6:6** *1637*
frankincense and wine and olive **o** **Rv 18:13** *1637*

OILS
“Your **o** have a pleasing fragrance, **SS 1:3** 8081
the fragrance of your **o** Than all **SS 4:10** 8081
themselves with the finest of **o**, **Am 6:6** 8081

OINTMENT
He makes the sea like a jar of **o**. **Jb 41:31** 4841
good name is better than a good **o**, **Ec 7:1** 8081
mouth, nor did I use any **o** at all until **Da 10:3** 5480a
Mary who anointed the Lord with **o**, **Jn 11:2** *3464*

OLD
Noah was five hundred years **o**, **Gn 5:32** 1121
were the mighty men who *were* of **o**, **Gn 6:4** 5769
Now Noah was six hundred years **o** **Gn 7:6** 1121
Shem was one hundred years **o**, **Gn 11:10** 1121
Abram was seventy-five years **o** **Gn 12:4** 1121
“Bring Me a three year **o** heifer, **Gn 15:9** 8027
and a three year **o** female goat, **Gn 15:9** 8027
goat, and a three year **o** ram, **Gn 15:9** 8027
will be buried at a good **o** age. **Gn 15:15** 7872
Abram was eighty-six years **o** **Gn 16:16** 1121
when Abram was ninety-nine years **o**, **Gn 17:1** 1121
male among you who is eight days **o** **Gn 17:12** 1121
born to a man one hundred years **o**? **Gn 17:17** 1121
will Sarah, who is ninety years **o**, **Gn 17:17** 1323
Abraham was ninety-nine years **o** **Gn 17:24** 1121
Ishmael his son was thirteen years **o** **Gn 17:25** 1121
Now Abraham and Sarah were **o**, **Gn 18:11** 2205
“After I have become **o**, **Gn 18:12** 1086
pleasure, my lord being **o** also?” **Gn 18:12** 2204
bear *a child,* when I am *so* **o**?' **Gn 18:13** 2204
the house, both young and **o**, **Gn 19:4** 2205
“Our father is **o**, and there is **Gn 19:31** 2204
a son to Abraham in his **o** age, **Gn 21:2** 2208
Isaac when he was eight days **o**, **Gn 21:4** 1121

Abraham was one hundred years **o**	**Gn 21:5**	1121
borne him a son in his **o** age."	**Gn 21:7**	2208
Now Abraham was **o**, advanced in age;	**Gn 24:1**	2204
a son to my master in her **o** age,	**Gn 24:36**	2209
his last and died in a ripe **o** age,	**Gn 25:8**	7872
an **o** man and satisfied *with life;*	**Gn 25:8**	2205
years **o** when he took Rebekah,	**Gn 25:20**	1121
o when she gave birth to them.	**Gn 25:26**	1121
When Esau was forty years **o** he	**Gn 26:34**	1121
it came about, when Isaac was **o** and	**Gn 27:1**	2204
I am **o** *and* I do not know the day	**Gn 27:2**	2204
his people, an **o** man of ripe age;	**Gn 35:29**	2205
he was the son of his **o** age;	**Gn 37:3**	2208
Joseph was thirty years **o** when he	**Gn 41:46**	1121
"Is your **o** father well, of whom	**Gn 43:27**	2205
'We have an **o** father and a little	**Gn 44:20**	2205
and a little child of *his* **o** age.	**Gn 44:20**	2208
years **o** and Aaron eighty-three,	**Ex 7:7**	1121
shall go with our young and our **o**;	**Ex 10:9**	2205
be an unblemished male a year **o**;	**Ex 12:5**	1121
two onc year **o** lambs each day,	**Ex 29:38**	1121
from twenty years **o** and over,	**Ex 30:14**	1121
from twenty years **o** and upward,	**Ex 38:26**	1121
calf and a lamb, both one year **o**,	**Lv 9:3**	1121
year **o** lamb for a burnt offering and	**Lv 12:6**	1121
shall offer a male lamb one year **o**	**Lv 23:12**	1121
year **o** male lambs without defect,	**Lv 23:18**	1121
male lambs one year **o** for a sacrifice	**Lv 23:19**	1121
still eat **o** things from the crop,	**Lv 25:22**	3465
eating *the* **o** until the ninth year	**Lv 25:22**	
'You will eat the **o** supply and	**Lv 26:10**	3465
clear out the **o** because of the new.	**Lv 26:10**	3465
twenty years even to sixty years **o**,	**Lv 27:3**	1121
five years even to twenty years **o**	**Lv 27:5**	1121
a month even up to five years **o**,	**Lv 27:6**	1121
are from sixty years **o** and upward,	**Lv 27:7**	1121
from twenty years **o** and upward,	**Nu 1:3**	1121
from twenty years **o** and upward,	**Nu 1:18**	1121
from twenty years **o** and upward,	**Nu 1:20**	1121
from twenty years **o** and upward,	**Nu 1:22**	1121
from twenty years **o** and upward,	**Nu 1:24**	1121
from twenty years **o** and upward,	**Nu 1:26**	1121
from twenty years **o** and upward,	**Nu 1:28**	1121
from twenty years **o** and upward,	**Nu 1:30**	1121
from twenty years **o** and upward,	**Nu 1:32**	1121
from twenty years **o** and upward,	**Nu 1:34**	1121
from twenty years **o** and upward,	**Nu 1:36**	1121
from twenty years **o** and upward,	**Nu 1:38**	1121
from twenty years **o** and upward,	**Nu 1:40**	1121
from twenty years **o** and upward,	**Nu 1:42**	1121
from twenty years **o** and upward,	**Nu 1:45**	1121
o and upward you shall number."	**Nu 3:15**	1121
male from a month **o** and upward,	**Nu 3:22**	1121
male from a month **o** and upward,	**Nu 3:28**	1121
male from a month **o** and upward,	**Nu 3:34**	1121
male from a month **o** and upward,	**Nu 3:39**	1121
Israel from a month **o** and upward,	**Nu 3:40**	1121
names from a month **o** and upward,	**Nu 3:43**	1121
and upward, even to fifty years **o**,	**Nu 4:3**	1121
years and upward to fifty years **o**,	**Nu 4:23**	1121
and upward even to fifty years **o**,	**Nu 4:30**	1121
and upward even to fifty years **o**,	**Nu 4:35**	1121
and upward even to fifty years **o**,	**Nu 4:39**	1121
and upward even to fifty years **o**,	**Nu 4:43**	1121
and upward even to fifty years **o**,	**Nu 4:47**	1121
shall bring a male lamb a year **o**	**Nu 6:12**	1121
one male lamb a year **o** without	**Nu 6:14**	1121
ewe-lamb a year **o** without defect	**Nu 6:14**	1323
one ram, one male lamb one year **o**,	**Nu 7:15**	1121
goats, five male lambs one year **o**.	**Nu 7:17**	1121
one ram, one male lamb one year **o**,	**Nu 7:21**	1121
goats, five male lambs one year **o**.	**Nu 7:23**	1121
one ram, one male lamb one year **o**,	**Nu 7:27**	1121
goats, five male lambs one year **o**.	**Nu 7:29**	1121
one ram, one male lamb one year **o**,	**Nu 7:33**	1121
goats, five male lambs one year **o**.	**Nu 7:35**	1121
one ram, one male lamb one year **o**,	**Nu 7:39**	1121
goats, five male lambs one year **o**.	**Nu 7:41**	1121
one ram, one male lamb one year **o**,	**Nu 7:45**	1121
goats, five male lambs one year **o**.	**Nu 7:47**	1121
one ram, one male lamb one year **o**,	**Nu 7:51**	1121
goats, five male lambs one year **o**.	**Nu 7:53**	1121
one ram, one male lamb one year **o**,	**Nu 7:57**	1121
goats, five male lambs one year **o**.	**Nu 7:59**	1121
one ram, one male lamb one year **o**,	**Nu 7:63**	1121
goats, five male lambs one year **o**.	**Nu 7:65**	1121
one ram, one male lamb one year **o**,	**Nu 7:69**	1121
goats, five male lambs one year **o**.	**Nu 7:71**	1121
one ram, one male lamb one year **o**,	**Nu 7:75**	1121
goats, five male lambs one year **o**.	**Nu 7:77**	1121
one ram, one male lamb one year **o**,	**Nu 7:81**	1121
goats, five male lambs one year **o**.	**Nu 7:83**	1121
the male lambs one year **o** with	**Nu 7:87**	1121
60, the male lambs one year **o** 60.	**Nu 7:88**	1121
from twenty-five years **o** and	**Nu 8:24**	1121
from twenty years **o** and upward,	**Nu 14:29**	1121
shall offer a one year **o** female goat	**Nu 15:27**	1323
a month **o** you shall redeem them,	**Nu 18:16**	1121
from twenty years **o** and upward,	**Nu 26:2**	1121
from twenty years **o** and upward,	**Nu 26:4**	1121
male from a month **o** and upward,	**Nu 26:62**	1121
two male lambs one year **o** without	**Nu 28:3**	1121
lambs one year **o** without defect,	**Nu 28:9**	1121
lambs one year **o** without defect;	**Nu 28:11**	1121
and seven male lambs one year **o**,	**Nu 28:19**	1121
ram, seven male lambs one year **o**;	**Nu 28:27**	1121
lambs one year **o** without defect;	**Nu 29:2**	1121
ram, seven male lambs one year **o**,	**Nu 29:8**	1121
fourteen male lambs one year **o**,	**Nu 29:13**	1121

lambs one year **o** without defect;	**Nu 29:17**	1121
lambs one year **o** without defect;	**Nu 29:20**	1121
lambs one year **o** without defect;	**Nu 29:23**	1121
lambs one year **o** without defect;	**Nu 29:26**	1121
lambs one year **o** without defect;	**Nu 29:29**	1121
lambs one year **o** without defect;	**Nu 29:32**	1121
lambs one year **o** without defect;	**Nu 29:36**	1121
from twenty years **o** and upward,	**Nu 32:11**	1121
years **o** when he died on Mount Hor.	**Nu 33:39**	1121
will have no respect for the **o**,	**Dt 28:50**	2205
hundred and twenty years **o** today;	**Dt 31:2**	1121
"Remember the days of **o**,	**Dt 32:7**	5769
one hundred and twenty years **o**	**Dt 34:7**	1121
both man and woman, young and **o**,	**Jos 6:21**	2205
Now Joshua was **o** *and* advanced in	**Jos 13:1**	2204
"You are **o** *and* advanced in years,	**Jos 13:1**	2204
"I was forty years **o** when Moses	**Jos 14:7**	1121
I am eighty-five years **o** today.	**Jos 14:10**	1121
Joshua was **o**, advanced in years,	**Jos 23:1**	2204
"I am **o**, advanced in years.	**Jos 23:2**	2204
being one hundred and ten years **o**.	**Jos 24:29**	1121
and a second bull seven years **o**,	**Jg 6:25**	
the son of Joash died at a ripe **o** age	**Jg 8:32**	7872
an **o** man was coming out of the	**Jg 19:16**	2205
and the **o** man said,	**Jg 19:17**	2205
The **o** man said,	**Jg 19:20**	2205
the owner of the house, the **o** man,	**Jg 19:22**	2205
for I am too **o** to have a husband.	**Ru 1:12**	2204
and a sustainer of your **o** age;	**Ru 4:15**	7872
Now Eli was very **o**;	**1Sa 2:22**	2204
not be an **o** man in your house.	**1Sa 2:31**	2205
and an **o** man will not be in your	**1Sa 2:32**	2205
Now Eli was ninety-eight years **o**,	**1Sa 4:15**	1121
he died, for he was **o** and heavy.	**1Sa 4:18**	2204
men of the city, both young and **o**,	**1Sa 5:9**	1419
it came about when Samuel was **o**	**1Sa 8:1**	2204
"Behold, you have grown **o**,	**1Sa 8:5**	2204
before you, but I am **o** and gray,	**1Sa 12:2**	2204
years **o** when he began to reign,	**1Sa 13:1**	1121
Jesse was **o** in the days of Saul,	**1Sa 17:12**	2204
"An **o** man is coming up, and he is	**1Sa 28:14**	2205
was forty years **o** when he became	**2Sa 2:10**	1121
He was five years **o** when the	**2Sa 4:4**	1121
David was thirty years **o** when he	**2Sa 5:4**	1121
Now Barzillai was very **o**,	**2Sa 19:32**	2204
very old, being eighty years **o**;	**2Sa 19:32**	1121
"I am now eighty years **o**.	**2Sa 19:35**	1121
Now King David was **o**,	**1Ki 1:1**	2204
Now the king was very **o**,	**1Ki 1:15**	2204
when Solomon was **o**,	**1Ki 11:4**	2209
an **o** prophet was living in Bethel;	**1Ki 13:11**	2205
city where the **o** prophet lived.	**1Ki 13:25**	2205
he came to the city of the **o** prophet	**1Ki 13:29**	2205
years **o** when he became king,	**1Ki 14:21**	1121
But in the time of his **o** age he	**1Ki 15:23**	2209
years **o** when he became king,	**1Ki 22:42**	1121
has no son and her husband is **o**."	**2Ki 4:14**	2204
He was thirty-two years **o** when he	**2Ki 8:17**	1121
Ahaziah *was* twenty-two years **o**	**2Ki 8:26**	1121
Jehoash was seven years **o** when he	**2Ki 11:21**	1121
years **o** when he became king,	**2Ki 14:2**	1121
Azariah, who *was* sixteen years **o**,	**2Ki 14:21**	1121
He was sixteen years **o** when he	**2Ki 15:2**	1121
years **o** when he became king,	**2Ki 15:33**	1121
Ahaz *was* twenty years **o** when he	**2Ki 16:2**	1121
He was twenty-five years **o** when he	**2Ki 18:2**	1121
Manasseh was twelve years **o** when	**2Ki 21:1**	1121
Amon was twenty-two years **o** when	**2Ki 21:19**	1121
eight years **o** when he became king,	**2Ki 22:1**	1121
Jehoahaz was twenty-three years **o**	**2Ki 23:31**	1121
years **o** when he became king,	**2Ki 23:36**	1121
Jehoiachin was eighteen years **o**	**2Ki 24:8**	1121
years **o** when he became king,	**2Ki 24:18**	1121
married when he was sixty years **o**;	**1Ch 2:21**	1121
Now when David reached **o** age,	**1Ch 23:1**	2204
from thirty years **o** and upward,	**1Ch 23:3**	1121
from twenty years **o** and upward.	**1Ch 23:24**	1121
from twenty years **o** and upward.	**1Ch 23:27**	1121
Then he died in a ripe **o** age,	**1Ch 29:28**	7872
the **o** standard *was* sixty cubits,	**2Ch 3:3**	7223
years **o** when he began to reign,	**2Ch 12:13**	1121
years **o** when he became king,	**2Ch 20:31**	1121
years **o** when he became king,	**2Ch 21:5**	1121
years **o** when he became king,	**2Ch 21:20**	1121
years **o** when he became king,	**2Ch 22:2**	1121
seven years **o** when he became king,	**2Ch 24:1**	1121
when Jehoiada reached a ripe **o** age	**2Ch 24:15**	2204
and thirty years **o** at his death.	**2Ch 24:15**	1121
years **o** when he became king,	**2Ch 25:1**	1121
from twenty years **o** and upward and	**2Ch 25:5**	1121
Uzziah, who *was* sixteen years **o**,	**2Ch 26:1**	1121
years **o** when he became king,	**2Ch 26:3**	1121
years **o** when he became king,	**2Ch 27:1**	1121
years **o** when he became king,	**2Ch 27:8**	1121
years **o** when he became king,	**2Ch 28:1**	1121
when he was twenty-five years **o**;	**2Ch 29:1**	1121
to the males from thirty years **o**	**2Ch 31:16**	1121
from twenty years **o** and upwards,	**2Ch 31:17**	1121
years **o** when he became king,	**2Ch 33:1**	1121
years **o** when he became king,	**2Ch 33:21**	1121
eight years **o** when he became king,	**2Ch 34:1**	1121
years **o** when he became king,	**2Ch 36:2**	1121
years **o** when he became king,	**2Ch 36:5**	1121
eight years **o** when he became king,	**2Ch 36:9**	1121
years **o** when he became king,	**2Ch 36:11**	1121
man or virgin, **o** man or infirm;	**2Ch 36:17**	2205
the **o** men who had seen the first	**Ezr 3:12**	2205
of Besodeiah repaired the **O** Gate;	**Ne 3:6**	3465
Gate of Ephraim, by the **O** Gate,	**Ne 12:39**	3465

all the Jews, both young and **o**,	**Es 3:13**	2205
its roots grow **o** in the ground And	**Jb 14:8**	2204
"Do you know this from of **o**,	**Jb 20:4**	5703
And the **o** men arose *and* stood.	**Jb 29:8**	3453
"I am young in years and you are **o**;	**Jb 32:6**	3453
Job died, an **o** man and full of days.	**Jb 42:17**	2205
o because of all my adversaries.	**Ps 6:7**	6275
For they have been from of **o**.	**Ps 25:6**	5769
I have been young and now I am **o**	**Ps 37:25**	2204
in their days, In the days of **o**.	**Ps 44:1**	6924a
one who sits enthroned from of **o**	**Ps 55:19**	6924a
cast me off in the time of **o** age;	**Ps 71:9**	2209
And even when *I am* **o** and gray,	**Ps 71:18**	2209
which You have purchased of **o**,	**Ps 74:2**	6924a
Yet God is my king from of **o**,	**Ps 74:12**	6924a
I have considered the days of **o**,	**Ps 77:5**	6924a
I will remember Your wonders of **o**.	**Ps 77:11**	6924a
I will utter dark sayings of **o**,	**Ps 78:2**	6924a
will still yield fruit in **o** age;	**Ps 92:14**	7872
throne is established from of **o**;	**Ps 93:2**	3975b
"Of **o** You founded the earth,	**Ps 102:25**	6440
Your ordinances from of **o**,	**Ps 119:52**	5769
Of **o** I have known from Your	**Ps 119:152**	6924a
I remember the days of **o**;	**Ps 143:5**	6924a
O men and children.	**Ps 148:12**	2205
of His way, Before His works of **o**.	**Pr 8:22**	6924a
are the crown of **o** men,	**Pr 17:6**	2205
honor of **o** men is their gray hair.	**Pr 20:29**	2205
when he is **o** he will not depart from	**Pr 22:6**	2204
despise your mother when she is **o**.	**Pr 23:22**	2204
yet wise lad is better than an **o**	**Ec 4:13**	2205
all choice *fruits,* Both new and **o**,	**SS 7:13**	3465
the exiles of Cush, young and **o**,	**Is 20:4**	2205
For the waters of the **o** pool.	**Is 22:11**	3465
Who has announced this from of **o**?	**Is 45:21**	6924a
Even to *your* **o** age I will be the	**Is 46:4**	2209
Awake as in the days of **o**,	**Is 51:9**	6924a
carried them all the days of **o**.	**Is 63:9**	5769
people remembered the days of **o**,	**Is 63:11**	5769
Redeemer from of **o** is Your name.	**Is 63:16**	5769
For from days of **o** they have not heard	**Is 64:4**	5769
Or an **o** man who does not live out	**Is 65:20**	2205
be taken, The aged and the very **o**.	**Jer 6:11**	4392, 3117
And the young men and the **o**,	**Jer 31:13**	2205
inhabited as in the days of **o**,"	**Jer 46:26**	6924a
you I shatter **o** man and youth,	**Jer 51:22**	2205
years **o** when he became king,	**Jer 52:1**	1121
things That were from the days of **o**	**La 1:7**	6924a
Which He commanded from days of **o**.	**La 2:17**	6924a
in the streets Lie young and **o**;	**La 2:21**	2205
Renew our days as of **o**,	**La 5:21**	6924a
"Utterly slay **o** men, young men,	**Ezk 9:6**	2205
to the pit, to the people of **o**,	**Ezk 26:20**	5769
you shall provide a lamb a year **o**	**Ezk 46:13**	1121
Your **o** men will dream dreams,	**Jl 2:28**	2205
rebuild it as in the days of **o**;	**Am 9:11**	5769
and Gilead As in the days of **o**.	**Mi 7:14**	5769
forefathers From the days of **o**.	**Mi 7:20**	6924a
'**O** men and old women will again	**Zch 8:4**	2205
'Old men and **o** women will again	**Zch 8:4**	2205
days of **o** and as in former years.	**Mal 3:4**	5769
from two years **o** and under,	**Mt 2:16**	*1332*
of unshrunk cloth on an **o** garment;	**Mt 9:16**	*3820*
people put new wine into **o** wineskins;	**Mt 9:17**	*3820*
his treasure things new and **o**."	**Mt 13:52**	*3820*
of unshrunk cloth on an **o** garment;	**Mk 2:21**	*3820*
away from it, the new from the **o**,	**Mk 2:21**	*3820*
puts new wine into **o** wineskins;	**Mk 2:22**	*3820*
for she was twelve years **o**.	**Mk 5:42**	
like one of the prophets *of* **o**."	**Mk 6:15**	
For I am an **o** man and my wife is	**Lk 1:18**	*4246*
also conceived a son in her **o** age;	**Lk 1:36**	*1094*
of His holy prophets from of **o**	**Lk 1:70**	*165*
and puts it on an **o** garment;	**Lk 5:36**	*3820*
from the new will not match the **o**.	**Lk 5:36**	*3820*
puts new wine into **o** wineskins;	**Lk 5:37**	*3820*
drinking **o** *wine* wishes for new;	**Lk 5:39**	*3820*
'The **o** is good *enough.*' "	**Lk 5:39**	*3820*
daughter, about twelve years **o**,	**Lk 8:42**	
the prophets of **o** had risen again.	**Lk 9:8**	*744*
one of the prophets of **o** has risen	**Lk 9:19**	*744*
can a man be born when he is **o**?	**Jn 3:4**	*1088*
"You are not yet fifty years **o**,	**Jn 8:57**	
but when you grow **o**,	**Jn 21:18**	*1095*
YOUR **O** MEN SHALL DREAM DREAMS;	**Ac 2:17**	*4245*
the man was more than forty years **o**	**Ac 4:22**	
he was about a hundred years **o**,	**Ro 4:19**	*1541*
our **o** self was crucified with *Him,*	**Ro 6:6**	*3820*
Clean out the **o** leaven so that you	**1Co 5:7**	*3820*
the feast, not with **o** leaven,	**1Co 5:8**	*3820*
at the reading of the **o** covenant	**2Co 3:14**	*3820*
the **o** things passed away;	**2Co 5:17**	*744*
of life, you lay aside the **o** self,	**Eph 4:22**	*3820*
o self with its *evil* practices,	**Col 3:9**	*3820*
fables fit only for **o** women.	**1Tm 4:7**	*1126*
is not less than sixty years **o**,	**1Tm 5:9**	
ALL WILL BECOME **O** LIKE A GARMENT,	**Heb 1:11**	*3822*
growing **o** is ready to disappear.	**Heb 8:13**	*1095*
it the men of **o** gained approval.	**Heb 11:2**	*4245*
but an **o** commandment which you	**1Jn 2:7**	*3820*
the **o** commandment is the word	**1Jn 2:7**	*3820*
the serpent of **o** who is called the	**Rv 12:9**	*744*
of the dragon, the serpent of **o**,	**Rv 20:2**	*744*

OLDER

and the **o** brother of Japheth,	**Gn 10:21**	1419
the **o** shall serve the younger."	**Gn 25:23**	7227a
his **o** son Esau and said to him,	**Gn 27:1**	1419
the name of the **o** was Leah, and	**Gn 29:16**	1419

The three **o** sons of Jesse had | 1Sa 17:13 | 1419
"Here is my **o** daughter Merab; | 1Sa 18:17 | 1419
for he is my **o** brother | 1Ki 2:22 | 1419
put on armor and **o** were summoned and | 2Ki 3:21 | 4605
the camp had slain all the **o** *sons.* | 2Ch 22:1 | 7223
the Levites from twenty years and **o** | Ezr 3:8 | 4605
are among us, **O** than your father. | Jb 15:10 | 3524, 3117
because they were years **o** than he. | Jb 32:4 | 2205
"Now your **o** sister is Samaria, | Ezk 16:46 | 1419
both your **o** and your younger; | Ezk 16:61 | 1419
"Now his **o** son was in the field, | Lk 15:25 | *4245*
by one, beginning with the **o** ones, | Jn 8:9 | *4245*
"THE **O** WILL SERVE THE YOUNGER." | Ro 9:12 | *3173*
Do not sharply rebuke an **o** man, | 1Tm 5:1 | *4245*
the **o** women as mothers, *and* the | 1Tm 5:2 | *4245*
O men are to be temperate, | Ti 2:2 | *4246*
O women likewise are to be | Ti 2:3 | *4247*

OLDEST
servant, the **o** of his household, | Gn 24:2 | 2205
o and ending with the youngest, | Gn 44:12 | 1419
Now the three **o** followed Saul, | 1Sa 17:14 | 1419
Now Eliab his **o** brother heard when | 1Sa 17:28 | 1419
Then he took his **o** son who was to | 2Ki 3:27 | 1060
wine in their **o** brother's house, | Jb 1:13 | 1060
wine in their **o** brother's house, | Jb 1:18 | 1060

OLDNESS
Spirit and not in **o** of the letter. | Ro 7:6 | *3821*

OLIVE
beak was a freshly picked **o** leaf. | Gn 8:11 | 2132
your vineyard *and* your **o** grove. | Ex 23:11 | 2132
the sanctuary, and of **o** oil a hin. | Ex 30:24 | 2132
o trees which you did not plant, | Dt 6:11 | 2132
a land of **o** oil and honey; | Dt 8:8 | 2132
"When you beat your **o** tree, | Dt 24:20 | 2132
"You shall have **o** trees | Dt 28:40 | 2132
o groves which you did not plant.' | Jos 24:13 | 2132
them, and they said to the **o** tree, | Jg 9:8 | 2132
"But the **o** tree said to them, | Jg 9:9 | 2132
your vineyards and your **o** groves and | 1Sa 8:14 | 2132
he made two cherubim of **o** wood, | 1Ki 6:23 | 8081
sanctuary he made doors of **o** wood, | 1Ki 6:31 | 8081
So *he made* two doors of **o** wood, | 1Ki 6:32 | 8081
four-sided doorposts of **o** wood | 1Ki 6:33 | 8081
and to receive clothes and **o** groves | 2Ki 5:26 | 2132
a land of **o** trees and honey, | 2Ki 18:32 | 2132
charge of the **o** and sycamore trees | 1Ch 27:28 | 2132
their vineyards, their **o** groves and | Ne 5:11 | 2132
the hills, and bring **o** branches and | Ne 8:15 | 2132
branches and wild **o** branches, | Ne 8:15 | 8081
cisterns, vineyards, **o** groves, | Ne 9:25 | 2132
off his flower like the **o** tree. | Jb 15:33 | 2132
green **o** tree in the house of God; | Ps 52:8 | 2132
like **o** plants Around your table. | Ps 128:3 | 2132
it like the shaking of an **o** tree, | Is 17:6 | 2132
As the shaking of an **o** tree, | Is 24:13 | 2132
and the myrtle and the **o** tree; | Is 41:19 | 8081
"A green **o** tree, beautiful in | Jer 11:16 | 2132
beauty will be like the **o** tree And | Hos 14:6 | 2132
vineyards, fig trees and **o** trees; | Am 4:9 | 2132
You will tread the **o** but will not | Mi 6:15 | 2132
the yield of the **o** should fail And | Hab 3:17 | 2132
the pomegranate and the **o** tree, | Hg 2:19 | 2132
also two **o** trees by it, one on the | Zch 4:3 | 2132
"What are these two **o** trees on | Zch 4:11 | 2132
"What are the two **o** branches | Zch 4:12 | 2132
off, and you, being a wild **o**, | Ro 11:17 | *65*
of the rich root of the **o** tree, | Ro 11:17 | *1636*
what is by nature a wild **o** tree, | Ro 11:24 | *65*
nature into a cultivated **o** tree, | Ro 11:24 | *2565*
be grafted into their own **o** tree? | Ro 11:24 | *1636*
These are the two **o** trees and the | Rv 11:4 | *1636*
and frankincense and wine and **o** oil | Rv 18:13 | *1637*

OLIVES
oil of beaten **o** for the light, | Ex 27:20 | 2132
oil from beaten **o** for the light, | Lv 24:2 | 2132
oil, for your **o** will drop off. | Dt 28:40 | 2132
up the ascent of the *Mount of* **O**, | 2Sa 15:30 | 2132
or three **o** on the topmost bough, | Is 17:6 | 1620
feet will stand on the Mount of **O**, | Zch 14:4 | 2132
and the Mount of **O** will be split | Zch 14:4 | 2132
to Bethphage, at the Mount of **O**, | Mt 21:1 | *1636*
He was sitting on the Mount of **O**, | Mt 24:3 | *1636*
they went out to the Mount of **O**. | Mt 26:30 | *1636*
and Bethany, near the Mount of **O**, | Mk 11:1 | *1636*
Mount of **O** opposite the temple, | Mk 13:3 | *1636*
they went out to the Mount of **O**. | Mk 14:26 | *1636*
the descent of the Mount of **O**, | Lk 19:37 | *1636*
was His custom to the Mount of **O**; | Lk 22:39 | *1636*
But Jesus went to the Mount of **O**. | Jn 8:1 | *1636*
fig tree, my brethren, produce **o**, | Jas 3:12 | *1636*

OLIVET
near the mount that is called **O**, | Lk 19:29 | *1638*
on the mount that is called **O**. | Lk 21:37 | *1638*
Jerusalem from the mount called **O**, | Ac 1:12 | *1638*

OLYMPAS
Nereus and his sister, and **O**, | Ro 16:15 | *3652*

OMAR
The sons of Eliphaz were Teman, **O**, | Gn 36:11 | 201
of Esau, are chief Teman, chief **O**, | Gn 36:15 | 201
The sons of Eliphaz *were* Teman, **O**, | 1Ch 1:36 | 201

OMEGA
"I am the Alpha and the **O**," | Rv 1:8 | *5598*
I am the Alpha and the **O**, | Rv 21:6 | *5598*
"I am the Alpha and the **O**, | Rv 22:13 | *5598*

OMEN
"For there is no **o** against Jacob, | Nu 23:23 | 5173
Now the men took this as an **o**, | 1Ki 20:33 | 5172

OMENS
did not go as at other times to seek **o** | Nu 24:1 | 5173
or one who interprets **o**, | Dt 18:10 | 5172
Causing the **o** of boasters to fail, | Is 44:25 | 226

OMER
you shall take an **o** apiece | Ex 16:16 | 6016b
When they measured it with an **o**, | Ex 16:18 | 6016b
(Now an **o** is a tenth of an ephah.) | Ex 16:36 | 6016b

OMERFUL
'Let an **o** of it be kept throughout | Ex 16:32 | 4393, 6016b
a jar and put an **o** of manna in it, | Ex 16:33 | 4393, 6016b

OMERS
as much bread, two **o** for each one. | Ex 16:22 | 6016b

OMIT
to speak to them. Do not **o** a word! | Jer 26:2 | 1639

OMRI
Therefore all Israel made **O**, | 1Ki 16:16 | 6018
Then **O** and all Israel with him | 1Ki 16:17 | 6018
the *other* half followed **O**. | 1Ki 16:21 | 6018
But the people who followed **O** | 1Ki 16:22 | 6018
And Tibni died and **O** became king. | 1Ki 16:22 | 6018
Judah, **O** became king over Israel | 1Ki 16:23 | 6018
O did evil in the sight of the | 1Ki 16:25 | 6018
Now the rest of the acts of **O** | 1Ki 16:27 | 6018
So **O** slept with his fathers and | 1Ki 16:28 | 6018
Now Ahab the son of **O** became king | 1Ki 16:29 | 6018
and Ahab the son of **O** reigned over | 1Ki 16:29 | 6018
Ahab the son of **O** did evil in | 1Ki 16:30 | 6018
granddaughter of **O** king of Israel. | 2Ki 8:26 | 6018
Joash, Eliezer, Elioenai, **O**, | 1Ch 7:8 | 6018
the son of Ammihud, the son of **O**, | 1Ch 9:4 | 6018
Issachar, **O** the son of Michael; | 1Ch 27:18 | 6018
Athaliah, the granddaughter of **O**. | 2Ch 22:2 | 6018
"The statutes of **O** And all the | Mi 6:16 | 6018

ON
daughter of Potiphera priest of **O** | Gn 41:45 | 204
daughter of Potiphera priest of **O** | Gn 41:50 | 204
daughter of Potiphera, priest of **O** | Gn 46:20 | 204
and **O** the son of Peleth | Nu 16:1 | 203
young men of **O** and of Pi-beseth | Ezk 30:17 | 204

ONAM
Manahath and Ebal, Shepho and **O**. | Gn 36:23 | 208
Manahath, Ebal, Shephi and **O**. | 1Ch 1:40 | 208
she was the mother of **O**. | 1Ch 2:26 | 208
sons of **O** were Shammai and Jada. | 1Ch 2:28 | 208

ONAN
and bore a son and named him **O**. | Gn 38:4 | 209
Then Judah said to **O**, | Gn 38:8 | 209
O knew that the offspring | Gn 38:9 | 209
Er and **O** and Shelah and Perez and | Gn 46:12 | 209
and **O** died in the land of Canaan). | Gn 46:12 | 209
The sons of Judah *were* Er and **O**, | Nu 26:19 | 209
and **O** died in the land of Canaan. | Nu 26:19 | 209
The sons of Judah *were* Er, **O** and | 1Ch 2:3 | 209

ONCE
and I shall speak only this **o**; | Gn 18:32 | 6471
please forgive my sin only this **o**, | Ex 10:17 | 6471
atonement on its horns **o** a year; | Ex 30:10 | 259
o a year throughout your generations | Ex 30:10 | 259
"Go down at **o**, for your people, | Ex 32:7 | 3381
for all their sins **o** every year." | Lv 16:34 | 259
thus with me, please kill me at **o**, | Nu 11:15 | 2026
He will **o** more abandon them in the | Nu 32:15 | 3254, 5750
will push the peoples, All at **o**, | Dt 33:17 | 3164a
men of war circling the city **o**. | Jos 6:3 | 259, 6471
around the city, circling *it* **o**; | Jos 6:11 | 259, 6471
they marched around the city **o** | Jos 6:14 | 259, 6471
me that I may speak **o** more; | Jg 6:39 | 6471
a test **o** more with the fleece, | Jg 6:39 | 6471
"**O** the trees went forth to anoint | Jg 9:8 | 1980
"Come up **o** more, for he has told | Jg 16:18 | 6471
that I may at **o** be avenged of the | Jg 16:28 | 259
up for you will find him at **o**." | 1Sa 9:13 | 3117
David inquired of the LORD **o** more. | 1Sa 23:4 | 3254, 5750
Now the Philistines came up **o** | 2Sa 5:22 | 3254, 5750
son of Zadok said **o** more to Joab, | 2Sa 18:22 | 3254, 5750
at **o** to King David and say to him, | 1Ki 1:13 | 935
o every three years the ships of | 1Ki 10:22 | 259
and walked in the house **o** back and | 2Ki 4:35 | 259
there, more than **o** or twice. | 2Ki 6:10 | 259
o every three years the ships of | 2Ch 9:21 | 259
and **o** in ten days all sorts of | Ne 5:18 | 996
O or twice the traders and | Ne 13:20 | 6471
answer Him **o** in a thousand *times.* | Jb 9:3 | 259
"Indeed God speaks **o**, | Jb 33:14 | 259
"**O** I have spoken, and I will not | Jb 40:5 | 259
O God has spoken; | Ps 62:11 | 259
presence when **o** You are angry? | Ps 76:7 | 3975b
O You spoke in vision to | Ps 89:19 | 227
"**O** I have sworn by My holiness; | Ps 89:35 | 259
A fool's anger is known at **o**, | Pr 12:16 | 3117
who is crooked will fall all at **o**. | Pr 28:18 | 259
Righteousness **o** lodged in her, But | Is 1:21 |
Ariel the city *where* David **o** | Is 29:1 |
I will **o** again deal marvelously | Is 29:14 |
nation be brought forth all at **o**? | Is 66:8 | 259, 6471
"**O** again they will speak this | Jer 31:23 |
has become like a widow Who was **o** | La 1:1 |
was **o** in the land of the living. | Ezk 32:27 |
'**O** more in a little while, I am | Hg 2:6 | 259
"Let us go at **o** to entreat the | Zch 8:21 | 1980
At **o** the woman was made well. | Mt 9:22 | *1565, 5610*
And her daughter was healed at **o**. | Mt 15:28 | *1565, 5610*
him, and the boy was cured at **o**. | Mt 17:18 | *1565, 5610*
And at **o** the fig tree withered. | Mt 21:19 | *3916*
"How did the fig tree wither *all* at **o**?" | Mt 21:20 | *3916*
saying the same thing **o** more. | Mt 26:44 | *3825*
and He will at **o** put at My disposal | Mt 26:53 | *737*
"I want you to give me at **o** the head | Mk 6:25 | *1824*
All at **o** they looked around | Mk 9:8 | *1819*
He **o** more *began* to teach them. | Mk 10:1 | *3825*
o more to say to the bystanders, | Mk 14:69 | *3825*
And at **o** his mouth was opened and | Lk 1:64 | *3916*
"**O** the head of the house gets up | Lk 13:25 | *575, 3739*
'Go out at **o** into the streets and | Lk 14:21 | *5030*
you, when **o** you have turned again, | Lk 22:32 | *4218*
At **o** he took along *some* | Ac 21:32 | *1824*
the man, I sent him to you at **o**, | Ac 23:30 | *1824*
died, He died to sin **o** for all; | Ro 6:10 | *2178*
I was **o** alive apart from the Law; | Ro 7:9 | *4218*
as you **o** were disobedient to God, | Ro 11:30 | *4218*
beaten with rods, **o** I was stoned, | 2Co 11:25 | *530*
and returned **o** more to Damascus. | Ga 1:17 | *3825*
"He who **o** persecuted us is now | Ga 1:23 | *4218*
faith which he **o** tried to destroy." | Ga 1:23 | *4218*
"For if I rebuild what I have **o** | Ga 2:18 |
a gift more than **o** for my needs. | Php 4:16 | *530*
and in them you also **o** walked, | Col 3:7 | *4218*
I, Paul, more than **o** | 1Th 2:18 | *530*
we also **o** were foolish ourselves, | Ti 3:3 | *4218*
those who have **o** been enlightened | Heb 6:4 | *530*
because this He did **o** for all when | Heb 7:27 | *2178*
the high priest *enters* **o** a year, | Heb 9:7 | *530*
entered the holy place **o** for all, | Heb 9:12 | *2178*
but now **o** at the consummation of | Heb 9:26 | *530*
o and after this *comes* judgment, | Heb 9:27 | *530*
o to bear the sins of many, | Heb 9:28 | *530*
having **o** been cleansed, | Heb 10:2 | *530*
body of Jesus Christ **o** for all. | Heb 10:10 | *2178*
"YET **O** MORE I WILL SHAKE NOT | Heb 12:26 | *530*
"Yet **o** more," denotes the removing | Heb 12:27 | *530*
for **o** he has been approved, he | Jas 1:12 |
for **o** he has looked at himself | Jas 1:24 |
for you **o** were NOT A PEOPLE, but | 1Pe 2:10 | *4218*
also died for sins **o** for all, | 1Pe 3:18 | *530*
who **o** were disobedient, when the | 1Pe 3:20 | *4218*
faith which was **o** for all handed | Jude 1:3 | *530*
you know all things **o** for all, | Jude 1:5 | *530*

ONE
and there was morning, **o** day. | Gn 1:5 | 259
heavens be gathered into **o** place, | Gn 1:9 | 259
then He took **o** of his ribs and | Gn 2:21 | 259
and they shall become **o** flesh. | Gn 2:24 | 259
the tree was desirable to make **o** | Gn 3:6 |
the man has become like **o** of Us, | Gn 3:22 | 259
so that no **o** finding him would slay | Gn 4:15 | 3605
the name of the **o** was Adah, and | Gn 4:19 | 259
lived **o** hundred and thirty years, | Gn 5:3 |
lived **o** hundred and five years, | Gn 5:6 |
Jared lived **o** hundred and sixty-two | Gn 5:18 |
Methuselah lived **o** hundred and | Gn 5:25 |
lived **o** hundred and eighty-two | Gn 5:28 |
"This **o** will give us rest from | Gn 5:29 | 2088
be **o** hundred and twenty years." | Gn 6:3 |
earth **o** hundred and fifty days. | Gn 7:24 |
and at the end of **o** hundred and | Gn 8:3 |
every **o** according to his language, | Gn 10:5 | 376
he became a mighty **o** on the earth. | Gn 10:8 | 1368
the name of the **o** *was* Peleg, for | Gn 10:25 | 259
They said to **o** another, | Gn 11:3 | 376
"Behold, they are **o** people, | Gn 11:6 | 259
understand **o** another's speech." | Gn 11:7 | 376
Shem was **o** hundred years old, and | Gn 11:10 |
and Nahor lived **o** hundred and | Gn 11:25 |
the **o** who curses you I will curse. | Gn 12:3 |
o born in my house is my heir." | Gn 15:3 | 1121
but **o** who will come forth from | Gn 15:4 |
born to a man **o** hundred years old? | Gn 17:17 |
"This **o** came in as an alien, and | Gn 19:9 | 259
brought them outside, **o** said, | Gn 19:17 |
Now Abraham was **o** hundred years | Gn 21:5 |
the boy under **o** of the bushes. | Gn 21:15 | 259
burnt offering on **o** of the mountains | Gn 22:2 | 259
Now Sarah lived **o** hundred and | Gn 23:1 |
also'—*may* she *be the* **o** | Gn 24:14 |
o hundred and seventy-five years. | Gn 25:7 |
o hundred and thirty-seven years; | Gn 25:17 |
of Egypt as **o** goes toward Assyria; | Gn 25:18 |
And **o** people shall be stronger | Gn 25:23 |
O of the people might easily have | Gn 26:10 | 259
"Do you have only **o** blessing, | Gn 27:38 | 259
bereaved of you both in **o** day?" | Gn 27:45 | 259
and he took **o** of the stones of the | Gn 28:11 |
"Complete the week of this **o**, | Gn 29:27 | 2088
If you will do this **o** thing for | Gn 30:31 |
and every black **o** among the lambs and | Gn 30:32 | 7716
Every **o** that is not speckled and | Gn 30:33 | 3605
goats, every **o** with white in it, | Gn 30:35 | 3605
"The **o** with whom you find your | Gn 31:32 |
we are absent **o** from the other. | Gn 31:49 | 376
"If Esau comes to the **o** company | Gn 32:8 | 259
He commanded the **o** in front, | Gn 32:17 | 7223
face as **o** sees the face of God, | Gn 33:10 |

And if they are driven hard **o** day, **Gn 33:13** 259
for **o** hundred pieces of money. **Gn 33:19**
sister to **o** who is uncircumcised, **Gn 34:14** 376
live with you and become **o** people. **Gn 34:16** 259
live with us, to become **o** people: **Gn 34:22** 259
were **o** hundred and eighty years. **Gn 35:28**
They said to **o** another, **Gn 37:19** 376
and throw him into **o** of the pits; **Gn 37:20** 259
giving birth, **o** put out a hand, **Gn 38:28**
"This **o** came out first." **Gn 38:28** 2088
no **o** greater in this house than I, **Gn 39:9**
Now it happened **o** day that he went **Gn 39:11** 2088
there is no **o** to interpret it." **Gn 40:8** 369
but there was no **o** who could **Gn 41:8** 369
To each **o** he interpreted according **Gn 41:12** 376
dream, but no **o** can interpret it; **Gn 41:15** 369
no **o** who could explain it to me." **Gn 41:24** 369
dreams are **o** *and the same;* **Gn 41:25** 259
the dreams are **o** *and the same.* **Gn 41:26** 259
there is no **o** so discerning and **Gn 41:39** 369
no **o** shall raise his hand or foot **Gn 41:44** 376
are you staring at **o** another?" **Gn 42:1**
he was the **o** who sold to all the **Gn 42:6**
"We are all sons of **o** man; **Gn 42:11** 259
of **o** man in the land of Canaan; **Gn 42:13** 259
father today, and **o** is no longer alive." **Gn 42:13** 259
"Send **o** of you that he may get **Gn 42:16** 259
let **o** of your brothers be confined **Gn 42:19** 259
Then they said to **o** another, **Gn 42:21** 376
As **o** *of them* opened his sack **Gn 42:27** 259
turned trembling to **o** another, **Gn 42:28** 376
o is no longer alive, and the youngest is **Gn 42:32** 259
leave **o** of your brothers with me **Gn 42:33** 259
at **o** another in astonishment. **Gn 43:33** 376
the **o** from which my lord drinks and **Gn 44:5**
both we and the **o** in whose **Gn 44:16**
and the **o** went out from me, and I **Gn 44:28** 259
If you take this **o** also from me, **Gn 44:29** 2088
are **o** hundred and thirty; **Gn 47:9**
cities from **o** end of Egypt's border **Gn 47:21**
o hundred and forty-seven years. **Gn 47:28**
for this **o** is the firstborn. **Gn 48:18** 2088
"I give you **o** portion more **Gn 48:22** 259
As **o** of the tribes of Israel. **Gn 49:16** 259
hands of the Mighty **O** of Jacob **Gn 49:24** 46
o distinguished among his brothers. **Gn 49:26** 5139
every **o** with the blessing **Gn 49:28** 376
lived **o** hundred and ten years. **Gn 50:22**
age of **o** hundred and ten years; **Gn 50:26**
came each **o** with his household: **Ex 1:1** 376
o of whom was named Shiphrah and **Ex 1:15** 259
is **o** of the Hebrews' children." **Ex 2:6** 4480
a Hebrew, **o** of his brethren. **Ex 2:11** 4480
when he saw there was no **o** *around,* **Ex 2:12** 376
length of Levi's life was **o** hundred **Ex 6:16**
Kohath's life was **o** hundred and **Ex 6:18**
Amram's life was **o** hundred and **Ex 6:20**
o of the daughters of Putiel, **Ex 6:25** 4480
For each **o** threw down his staff **Ex 7:12** 376
is no **o** like the LORD our God. **Ex 8:10** 369
from his people; not **o** remained. **Ex 8:31** 259
of the sons of Israel, not **o** died. **Ex 9:6** 259
not even **o** of the livestock of Israel **Ex 9:7** 259
is no **o** like Me in all the earth. **Ex 9:14** 369
The **o** among the servants of **Ex 9:20** 4480
the LORD is the righteous **o**, **Ex 9:27** 6662
no **o** will be able to see the land. **Ex 10:5**
not **o** locust was left in all the **Ex 10:19** 259
They did not see **o** another, **Ex 10:23** 376
"**O** more plague I will bring on **Ex 11:1** 259
o to take a lamb for themselves, **Ex 12:3** 376
to take **o** according to the number **Ex 12:4**
Thus the **o** did not come near the **Ex 14:20** 2088
not even **o** of them remained. **Ex 14:28** 259
saw *it,* they said to **o** another, **Ex 16:15** 376
much bread, two omers for each **o**. **Ex 16:22** 259
o on one side and one on the other. **Ex 17:12** 259
on **o** side and one on the other. **Ex 17:12** 2088
on one side and **o** on the other. **Ex 17:12** 259
sons, of whom **o** was named Gershom, **Ex 18:3** 259
o strikes the other with a stone or **Ex 21:18** 376
"If **o** man's ox hurts **Ex 21:35** 376
any lost thing about which **o** says, **Ex 22:9**
driven away while no **o** is looking, **Ex 22:10** 369
"If you see the donkey of **o** who **Ex 23:5**
"There shall be no **o** miscarrying **Ex 23:26**
the people answered with **o** voice and **Ex 24:3** 259
and **o** and a half cubits wide, **Ex 25:10**
and **o** and a half cubits high. **Ex 25:10**
and two rings shall be on **o** side **Ex 25:12** 259
long and **o** and a half cubits wide. **Ex 25:17**
"Make **o** cherub at one end and **Ex 25:19** 259
"Make one cherub at **o** end and **Ex 25:19** 2088
end and **o** cherub at the other end; **Ex 25:19** 259
you shall make the cherubim *of* **o** **Ex 25:19**
their wings and facing **o** another; **Ex 25:20** 376
two cubits long and **o** cubit wide **Ex 25:23**
wide and **o** and a half cubits high. **Ex 25:23**
bulbs and its flowers shall be *of* **o** **Ex 25:31**
of the lampstand from its **o** side and **Ex 25:32** 259
almond *blossoms* in the **o** branch, **Ex 25:33** 259
and their branches *shall be of* **o** **Ex 25:36**
all of it shall be **o** piece of **Ex 25:36** 259
shall be joined to **o** another, **Ex 26:3** 802
shall be joined to **o** another. **Ex 26:3** 802
make fifty loops in the **o** curtain, **Ex 26:5** 259
to **o** another with the clasps so **Ex 26:6** 802
"The cubit on **o** side and the **Ex 26:13** 2088
on **o** side and on the other, **Ex 26:13** 2088

and **o** and a half cubits the width **Ex 26:16**
each board, fitted to **o** another; **Ex 26:17** 802
two sockets under **o** board for its **Ex 26:19** 259
two sockets under **o** board and two **Ex 26:21** 259
two sockets under **o** board and two **Ex 26:25** 259
of **o** side of the tabernacle, **Ex 26:26** 259
horns shall be of **o** piece with it, **Ex 27:2**
twisted linen **o** hundred cubits long **Ex 27:9**
hundred cubits long for **o** side; **Ex 27:9** 259
be hangings **o** hundred *cubits* long, **Ex 27:11**
"The hangings for the **o** side **Ex 27:14**
court *shall be* **o** hundred cubits, **Ex 27:18**
six of their names on the **o** stone and **Ex 28:10** 259
take **o** young bull and two rams **Ex 29:1** 259
You shall put them in **o** basket, **Ex 29:3** 259
"You shall also take the **o** ram, **Ex 29:15** 259
and **o** cake of bread and one cake **Ex 29:23** 259
and **o** cake of bread *mixed with* oil **Ex 29:23** 259
and **o** wafer from the basket **Ex 29:23** 259
from the **o** which was for Aaron and **Ex 29:27**
from the **o** which was for his sons. **Ex 29:27**
"For seven days the **o** of his sons **Ex 29:30**
two **o** year old lambs each day, **Ex 29:38**
"The **o** lamb you shall offer in **Ex 29:39** 259
wine for a drink offering with **o** lamb. **Ex 29:40** 259
horns *shall be* of **o** piece with it. **Ex 30:2**
then each **o** of them shall give a **Ex 30:12** 376
written on **o** *side* and the other. **Ex 32:15** 2088
go up in your midst for **o** moment, **Ex 33:5** 259
joined five curtains to **o** another and **Ex 36:10** 259
curtains he joined to **o** another. **Ex 36:10** 259
He made fifty loops in the **o** curtain **Ex 36:12** 259
to **o** another with the clasps, **Ex 36:13** 259
and **o** and a half cubits the width **Ex 36:21**
each board, fitted to **o** another; **Ex 36:22** 259
two sockets under **o** board for its **Ex 36:24** 259
two sockets under **o** board and two **Ex 36:26** 259
of **o** side of the tabernacle, **Ex 36:31** 259
and its width **o** and a half cubits, **Ex 37:1**
its height **o** and a half cubits; **Ex 37:1**
even two rings on **o** side of it, **Ex 37:3** 259
and **o** and a half cubits wide. **Ex 37:6**
o cherub at the one end and one **Ex 37:8** 259
one cherub at the **o** end and **Ex 37:8** 2088
and **o** cherub at the other end; **Ex 37:8** 259
he made the cherubim *of* **o** *piece* **Ex 37:8**
wide and **o** and a half cubits high. **Ex 37:10**
its bulbs and its flowers were *of* **o** **Ex 37:17**
lampstand from the **o** side of it and **Ex 37:18** 259
a bulb and a flower in **o** branch, **Ex 37:19** 259
bulbs and their branches were *of* **o** **Ex 37:22**
its horns were *of* **o** *piece* with it. **Ex 37:25**
its horns being *of* **o** *piece* with **Ex 38:2**
twisted linen, **o** hundred cubits; **Ex 38:9**
side *there were* **o** hundred cubits; **Ex 38:11**
The hangings for the **o** side *of* **Ex 38:14**
for each **o** who passed over to **Ex 38:26** 3605
o hundred sockets for the hundred **Ex 38:27**
does any **o** of all the things which **Lv 4:22** 259
he will be guilty in **o** of these. **Lv 5:4** 259
he becomes guilty in **o** of these, **Lv 5:5** 259
o for a sin offering and the other **Lv 5:7** 259
he has committed from **o** of these, **Lv 5:13** 259
any **o** of the things a man may do; **Lv 6:3** 3605
He shall give it to the **o** to whom **Lv 6:5**
be forgiven for any **o** of the things **Lv 6:7** 259
'Then **o** *of them* shall lift up from **Lv 6:15**
offering, there is **o** law for them; **Lv 7:7** 259
'Of this he shall present **o** of **Lv 7:14** 259
'The **o** among the sons of Aaron who **Lv 7:33**
he took **o** unleavened cake and one **Lv 8:26** 259
and **o** cake of bread *mixed with* oil **Lv 8:26** 259
bread *mixed with* oil and **o** wafer, **Lv 8:26** 259
calf and a lamb, both **o** year old, **Lv 9:3**
and the **o** who picks up their **Lv 11:28**
'Also anything on which **o** of them **Lv 11:32**
into which **o** of them may fall, **Lv 11:33**
the **o** who touches their carcass **Lv 11:36**
'Also if **o** of the animals dies **Lv 11:39**
the **o** who touches its carcass **Lv 11:39**
and the **o** who picks up its carcass **Lv 11:40**
a **o** year old lamb for a burnt **Lv 12:6**
the **o** for a burnt offering and the **Lv 12:8** 259
or to **o** of his sons the priests. **Lv 13:2** 259
for the **o** who is to be cleansed. **Lv 14:4**
also give orders to slay the **o** bird **Lv 14:5** 259
the **o** who is to be cleansed from **Lv 14:7**
"The **o** to be cleansed shall then **Lv 14:8**
grain offering, and **o** log of oil; **Lv 14:10** 259
the priest shall take the **o** male lamb **Lv 14:12** 259
right ear of the **o** to be cleansed, **Lv 14:14**
ear lobe of the **o** to be cleansed, **Lv 14:17**
the head of the **o** to be cleansed. **Lv 14:18**
atonement for the **o** to be cleansed **Lv 14:19**
then he is to take **o** male lamb for **Lv 14:21** 259
the **o** shall be a sin offering and **Lv 14:22** 259
the right ear of the **o** to be cleansed **Lv 14:25**
right ear of the **o** to be cleansed, **Lv 14:28**
the head of the **o** to be cleansed, **Lv 14:29**
"He shall then offer **o** of the **Lv 14:30** 259
afford, the **o** for a sin offering and **Lv 14:31** 259
on behalf of the **o** to be cleansed. **Lv 14:31**
then the **o** who owns the house **Lv 14:35**
and he shall slaughter the **o** bird **Lv 14:50** 259
discharge spits on **o** who is clean, **Lv 15:8**
whomever the **o** with the discharge **Lv 15:11**
offer them, **o** for a sin offering and **Lv 15:15** 259
'The priest shall offer the **o** **Lv 15:30** 259
law for the **o** with a discharge, **Lv 15:32**

and for the **o** who has a discharge, **Lv 15:33**
and **o** ram for a burnt offering. **Lv 16:5** 259
o lot for the LORD and the other **Lv 16:8** 259
no **o** shall be in the tent of **Lv 16:17** 120
"The **o** who released the goat **Lv 16:26**
"Then the **o** who burns them shall **Lv 16:28**
a male as **o** lies with a female; **Lv 18:22**
'Every **o** of you shall reverence **Lv 19:3** 376
falsely, nor lie to **o** another. **Lv 19:11** 376
o who commits adultery with his **Lv 20:10**
for such a **o** has made naked his **Lv 20:19**
'No **o** shall defile himself for a **Lv 21:1**
or **o** who is profaned by harlotry, **Lv 21:14**
'For no **o** who has a defect shall **Lv 21:18** 376
or a hunchback or a dwarf, or **o** **Lv 21:20**
And if **o** touches anything made **Lv 22:4**
his money, that **o** may eat of it, **Lv 22:11** 1931
both it and its young in **o** day. **Lv 22:28** 259
you shall offer a male lamb **o** year **Lv 23:12**
you shall present seven **o** year old **Lv 23:18**
'You shall also offer **o** male goat **Lv 23:19** 259
and two male lambs **o** year old **Lv 23:19**
"Bring the **o** who has cursed **Lv 24:14**
the **o** who blasphemes the name of **Lv 24:16**
'The **o** who takes the life of **Lv 24:18**
'Thus the **o** who kills an animal **Lv 24:21**
but the **o** who kills a man shall be **Lv 24:21**
'There shall be **o** standard for you; **Lv 24:22** 259
they brought the **o** who had cursed **Lv 24:23**
you shall not wrong **o** another. **Lv 25:14** 376
'So you shall not wrong **o** another, **Lv 25:17** 376
rule with severity over **o** another. **Lv 25:46** 376
O of his brothers may redeem him, **Lv 25:48** 259
or **o** of his blood relatives from **Lv 25:49**
down with no **o** making *you* tremble. **Lv 26:6** 369
flee when no **o** is pursuing you. **Lv 26:17** 369
will bake your bread in **o** oven, **Lv 26:26** 259
and even when no **o** is pursuing they **Lv 26:36**
sword, although no **o** is pursuing; **Lv 26:37** 369
to the means of the **o** who vowed, **Lv 27:8**
any such that **o** gives to the LORD **Lv 27:9**
'Yet if the **o** who consecrates it **Lv 27:15**
'If the **o** who consecrates it **Lv 27:19**
to the **o** from whom he bought it, **Lv 27:24**
'No **o** who may have been set apart **Lv 27:29** 3605
tenth **o** shall be holy to the LORD. **Lv 27:32**
each **o** head of his father's **Nu 1:4** 376
set out, every **o** by his family according **Nu 2:34** 376
'The priest shall offer **o** for **Nu 6:11** 259
o male lamb a year old without **Nu 6:14** 259
o ewe-lamb a year old without defect **Nu 6:14** 259
and **o** ram without defect for a peace **Nu 6:14** 259
and **o** unleavened cake out of the **Nu 6:19** 259
basket and **o** unleavened wafer, **Nu 6:19** 259
the leaders and an ox for each **o**, **Nu 7:3** 259
their offering, **o** leader each day, **Nu 7:11** 259
Now the **o** who presented his **Nu 7:12**
and his offering *was* **o** silver dish **Nu 7:13** 259
was **o** hundred and thirty *shekels,* **Nu 7:13**
o silver bowl of seventy shekels, **Nu 7:13** 259
o gold pan of ten *shekels,* full of **Nu 7:14** 259
o bull, one ram, one male lamb one **Nu 7:15** 259
one bull, **o** ram, one male lamb one **Nu 7:15** 259
one ram, **o** male lamb one year old, **Nu 7:15** 259
one ram, one male lamb **o** year old, **Nu 7:15**
o male goat for a sin offering; **Nu 7:16** 259
goats, five male lambs **o** year old. **Nu 7:17**
presented as his offering **o** silver dish **Nu 7:19** 259
was **o** hundred and thirty *shekels,* **Nu 7:19**
o silver bowl of seventy shekels, **Nu 7:19**
o gold pan of ten *shekels,* full of **Nu 7:20** 259
o bull, one ram, one male lamb one **Nu 7:21** 259
one bull, **o** ram, one male lamb one **Nu 7:21** 259
one ram, **o** male lamb one year old, **Nu 7:21** 259
one ram, one male lamb **o** year old, **Nu 7:21**
o male goat for a sin offering; **Nu 7:22** 259
goats, five male lambs **o** year old. **Nu 7:23**
his offering *was* **o** silver dish **Nu 7:25** 259
was **o** hundred and seventy *shekels,* **Nu 7:25**
o silver bowl of seventy shekels, **Nu 7:25** 259
o gold pan of ten *shekels,* full of **Nu 7:26** 259
o young bull, one ram, one male **Nu 7:27** 259
one young bull, **o** ram, one male **Nu 7:27** 259
one ram, **o** male lamb one year old, **Nu 7:27** 259
one ram, one male lamb **o** year old, **Nu 7:27**
o male goat for a sin offering; **Nu 7:28** 259
goats, five male lambs **o** year old. **Nu 7:29**
his offering *was* **o** silver dish **Nu 7:31** 259
was **o** hundred and thirty *shekels,* **Nu 7:31**
o silver bowl of seventy shekels, **Nu 7:31** 259
o gold pan of ten *shekels,* full of **Nu 7:32** 259
o bull, one ram, one male lamb one **Nu 7:33** 259
one bull, **o** ram, one male lamb one **Nu 7:33** 259
one ram, **o** male lamb one year old, **Nu 7:33** 259
one ram, one male lamb **o** year old, **Nu 7:33**
o male goat for a sin offering; **Nu 7:34** 259
goats, five male lambs **o** year old. **Nu 7:35**
his offering *was* **o** silver dish **Nu 7:37** 259
was **o** hundred and thirty *shekels,* **Nu 7:37**
o silver bowl of seventy shekels, **Nu 7:37** 259
o gold pan of ten *shekels,* full of **Nu 7:38** 259
o bull, one ram, one male lamb one **Nu 7:39** 259
one bull, **o** ram, one male lamb one **Nu 7:39** 259
one ram, **o** male lamb one year old, **Nu 7:39** 259
one ram, one male lamb **o** year old, **Nu 7:39**
o male goat for a sin offering; **Nu 7:40** 259
goats, five male lambs **o** year old. **Nu 7:41**
his offering *was* **o** silver dish **Nu 7:43** 259
was **o** hundred and thirty *shekels,* **Nu 7:43**

o silver bowl of seventy shekels,	Nu 7:43	259
o gold pan of ten *shekels,* full of	Nu 7:44	259
o bull, one ram, one male lamb one	Nu 7:45	259
one bull, **o** ram, one male lamb one	Nu 7:45	259
one ram, **o** male lamb one year old,	Nu 7:45	259
one ram, one male lamb **o** year old,	Nu 7:45	
o male goat for a sin offering;	Nu 7:46	259
goats, five male lambs **o** year old.	Nu 7:47	
his offering *was* **o** silver dish	Nu 7:49	259
was **o** hundred and thirty *shekels,*	Nu 7:49	
o silver bowl of seventy shekels,	Nu 7:49	259
o gold pan of ten *shekels,* full of	Nu 7:50	259
o bull, one ram, one male lamb one	Nu 7:51	259
one bull, **o** ram, one male lamb one	Nu 7:51	259
one ram, **o** male lamb one year old,	Nu 7:51	259
one ram, one male lamb **o** year old,	Nu 7:51	
o male goat for a sin offering;	Nu 7:52	259
goats, five male lambs **o** year old.	Nu 7:53	
his offering *was* **o** silver dish	Nu 7:55	259
was **o** hundred and thirty *shekels,*	Nu 7:55	
o silver bowl of seventy shekels,	Nu 7:55	259
o gold pan of ten *shekels,* full of	Nu 7:56	259
o bull, one ram, one male lamb one	Nu 7:57	259
one bull, **o** ram, one male lamb one	Nu 7:57	259
one ram, **o** male lamb one year old,	Nu 7:57	259
one ram, one male lamb **o** year old,	Nu 7:57	
o male goat for a sin offering;	Nu 7:58	259
goats, five male lambs **o** year old.	Nu 7:59	
his offering *was* **o** silver dish	Nu 7:61	259
was **o** hundred and thirty *shekels,*	Nu 7:61	
o silver bowl of seventy shekels,	Nu 7:61	259
o gold pan of ten *shekels,* full of	Nu 7:62	259
o bull, one ram, one male lamb one	Nu 7:63	259
one bull, **o** ram, one male lamb one	Nu 7:63	259
one ram, **o** male lamb one year old,	Nu 7:63	259
one ram, one male lamb **o** year old,	Nu 7:63	
o male goat for a sin offering;	Nu 7:64	259
goats, five male lambs **o** year old.	Nu 7:65	
his offering *was* **o** silver dish	Nu 7:67	259
was **o** hundred and thirty *shekels,*	Nu 7:67	
o silver bowl of seventy shekels,	Nu 7:67	259
o gold pan of ten *shekels,* full of	Nu 7:68	259
o bull, one ram, one male lamb one	Nu 7:69	259
one bull, **o** ram, one male lamb one	Nu 7:69	259
one ram, **o** male lamb one year old,	Nu 7:69	259
one ram, one male lamb **o** year old,	Nu 7:69	
o male goat for a sin offering;	Nu 7:70	259
goats, five male lambs **o** year old.	Nu 7:71	
his offering *was* **o** silver dish	Nu 7:73	259
was **o** hundred and thirty *shekels,*	Nu 7:73	3967
o silver bowl of seventy shekels,	Nu 7:73	259
o gold pan of ten *shekels,* full of	Nu 7:74	259
o bull, one ram, one male lamb one	Nu 7:75	259
one bull, **o** ram, one male lamb one	Nu 7:75	259
one ram, **o** male lamb one year old,	Nu 7:75	259
one ram, one male lamb **o** year old,	Nu 7:75	
o male goat for a sin offering;	Nu 7:76	259
goats, five male lambs **o** year old.	Nu 7:77	
his offering *was* **o** silver dish	Nu 7:79	259
was **o** hundred and thirty *shekels,*	Nu 7:79	
o silver bowl of seventy shekels,	Nu 7:79	259
o gold pan of ten *shekels,* full of	Nu 7:80	259
o bull, one ram, one male lamb one	Nu 7:81	259
one bull, **o** ram, one male lamb one	Nu 7:81	259
one ram, **o** male lamb one year old,	Nu 7:81	259
one ram, one male lamb **o** year old,	Nu 7:81	
o male goat for a sin offering;	Nu 7:82	259
goats, five male lambs **o** year old.	Nu 7:83	
o hundred and thirty *shekels*	Nu 7:85	
the male lambs **o** year old with	Nu 7:87	
60, the male lambs **o** year old 60.	Nu 7:88	
then offer the **o** for a sin	Nu 8:12	259
'If any **o** of you or of your	Nu 9:10	376
you shall have **o** statute, both for	Nu 9:14	259
"Yet if *only* **o** is blown, then the	Nu 10:4	259
'You shall eat, not **o** day,	Nu 11:19	259
the name of **o** was Eldad and the	Nu 11:26	259
"Oh, do not let her be like **o** dead,	Nu 12:12	
every **o** a leader among them."	Nu 13:2	3605
So they said to **o** another,	Nu 14:4	376
You slay this people as **o** man,	Nu 14:15	259
'The **o** who presents his	Nu 15:4	
or **o** who may be among you	Nu 15:14	
there shall be **o** statute for you	Nu 15:15	259
'There is to be **o** law and one	Nu 15:16	259
'There is to be one law and **o**	Nu 15:16	259
offer **o** bull for a burnt offering,	Nu 15:24	259
o male goat for a sin offering.	Nu 15:24	259
if **o** person sins unintentionally,	Nu 15:27	259
then he shall offer a **o** year old	Nu 15:27	
'You shall have **o** law for him who	Nu 15:29	259
that **o** is blaspheming the LORD;	Nu 15:30	1931
are holy, every **o** of them,	Nu 16:3	3605
even the **o** whom He will choose, He	Nu 16:5	
shall be the **o** who is holy.	Nu 16:7	6918
of all flesh, when **o** man sins,	Nu 16:22	259
for there is **o** rod for the head *of*	Nu 17:3	259
'The **o** who burns it shall also	Nu 19:8	
'The **o** who gathers the ashes	Nu 19:10	
'The **o** who touches the corpse of	Nu 19:11	
'That **o** shall purify himself from	Nu 19:12	1931
o who has been slain with a sword	Nu 19:16	2491a
and on the **o** who touched the bone	Nu 19:18	
who touched the bone or the **o** slain	Nu 19:18	2491a
o dying *naturally* or the grave.	Nu 19:18	
"**O** from Jacob shall have	Nu 24:19	
o of the sons of Israel came and	Nu 25:6	376
two male lambs **o** year old without	Nu 28:3	
offer the **o** lamb in the morning and	Nu 28:4	259
lambs **o** year old without defect,	Nu 28:9	
two bulls and **o** ram, seven male	Nu 28:11	259
lambs **o** year old without defect;	Nu 28:11	
for a grain offering, for the **o** ram;	Nu 28:12	259
'And **o** male goat for a sin offering	Nu 28:15	259
two bulls and **o** ram and seven male	Nu 28:19	259
and seven male lambs **o** year old,	Nu 28:19	
o male goat for a sin offering to	Nu 28:22	259
the LORD: two young bulls, **o** ram,	Nu 28:27	259
ram, seven male lambs **o** year old;	Nu 28:27	
bull, two-tenths for the **o** ram,	Nu 28:28	259
o male goat to make atonement for	Nu 28:30	259
o bull, one ram, *and* seven male	Nu 29:2	259
one bull, **o** ram, *and* seven male	Nu 29:2	259
lambs **o** year old without defect;	Nu 29:2	
o male goat for a sin offering,	Nu 29:5	259
o bull, one ram, seven male lambs	Nu 29:8	259
one bull, **o** ram, seven male lambs	Nu 29:8	259
ram, seven male lambs **o** year old,	Nu 29:8	
the bull, two-tenths for the **o** ram,	Nu 29:9	259
o male goat for a sin offering,	Nu 29:11	259
fourteen male lambs **o** year old,	Nu 29:13	
o male goat for a sin offering,	Nu 29:16	259
lambs **o** year old without defect;	Nu 29:17	
o male goat for a sin offering,	Nu 29:19	259
lambs **o** year old without defect;	Nu 29:20	
o male goat for a sin offering,	Nu 29:22	259
lambs **o** year old without defect;	Nu 29:23	
o male goat for a sin offering,	Nu 29:25	259
lambs **o** year old without defect;	Nu 29:26	
o male goat for a sin offering,	Nu 29:28	259
lambs **o** year old without defect;	Nu 29:29	
o male goat for a sin offering,	Nu 29:31	259
lambs **o** year old without defect;	Nu 29:32	
o male goat for a sin offering,	Nu 29:34	259
o bull, one ram, seven male lambs	Nu 29:36	259
one bull, **o** ram, seven male lambs	Nu 29:36	259
lambs **o** year old without defect;	Nu 29:36	
o male goat for a sin offering,	Nu 29:38	259
o in five hundred of the persons	Nu 31:28	259
you shall take **o** drawn out of	Nu 31:30	259
took **o** drawn out of every fifty,	Nu 31:47	259
until every **o** of the sons of Israel	Nu 32:18	376
Aaron was **o** hundred	Nu 33:39	
"You shall take **o** leader of	Nu 34:18	259
the **o** who struck him shall surely	Nu 35:21	
on the testimony of **o** witness.	Nu 35:30	259
"But if they marry **o** of the sons	Nu 36:3	259
shall be wife to **o** of the family	Nu 36:8	259
from **o** tribe to another tribe,	Nu 36:9	259
of your men, **o** man for each tribe.	Dt 1:23	259
'Not **o** of these men, this evil	Dt 1:35	376
God is the **o** fighting for you.'	Dt 3:22	
are alive today, every **o** of you.	Dt 4:4	3605
and *inquire* from **o** end of the	Dt 4:32	
o of these cities he might live:	Dt 4:42	259
LORD is our God, the LORD is **o**!	Dt 6:4	259
LORD chooses in **o** of your tribes,	Dt 12:14	259
from **o** end of the earth to the	Dt 13:7	
"If you hear in **o** of your cities,	Dt 13:12	259
man with you, **o** of your brothers,	Dt 15:7	259
on the evidence of **o** witness.	Dt 17:6	259
o kind of homicide or another,	Dt 17:8	
o kind of lawsuit or another,	Dt 17:8	
o kind of assault or another,	Dt 17:8	
o from among your countrymen you	Dt 17:15	
the fire, **o** who uses divination,	Dt 18:10	
o who practices witchcraft,	Dt 18:10	
or **o** who interprets omens,	Dt 18:10	
or **o** who casts a spell, or a	Dt 18:11	
or **o** who calls up the dead.	Dt 18:11	
may flee to **o** of these cities and live;	Dt 19:5	259
and he flees to **o** of these cities,	Dt 19:11	259
God is the **o** who goes with you,	Dt 20:4	
which are around the slain **o**.	Dt 21:2	2491a
the **o** loved and the other unloved,	Dt 21:15	259
but there was no **o** to save her.	Dt 22:27	
"No **o** who is emasculated or has	Dt 23:1	6481
"No **o** of illegitimate birth shall	Dt 23:2	4464
he shall choose in **o** of your towns	Dt 23:16	259
he shall be free at home **o** year	Dt 24:5	259
"No **o** shall take a handmill or an	Dt 24:6	
whether *he is* **o** of your countrymen	Dt 24:14	
o of your aliens who is in your land	Dt 24:14	
and **o** of them dies and has no son,	Dt 25:5	259
and the wife of **o** comes near to	Dt 25:11	259
hand of the **o** who is striking him,	Dt 25:11	
will come out against you **o** way	Dt 28:7	259
will go out **o** way against them,	Dt 28:25	259
be no **o** to frighten *them* away.	Dt 28:26	369
that he will not give *even* **o** of them	Dt 28:55	259
from **o** end of the earth to the	Dt 28:64	
from the **o** who chops your wood to	Dt 29:11	
to the **o** who draws your water,	Dt 29:11	
the **o** who will cross ahead of you,	Dt 31:3	
God is the **o** who goes with you.	Dt 31:6	
is the **o** who goes ahead of you;	Dt 31:8	
"How could **o** chase a thousand,	Dt 32:30	259
no **o** who can deliver from My hand.	Dt 32:39	369
o distinguished among his brothers.	Dt 33:16	5139
"Blessed is the **o** who enlarges Gad;	Dt 33:20	
Although Moses was **o** hundred and	Dt 34:7	
of Israel, **o** man for each tribe.	Jos 3:12	259
above will stand in **o** heap."	Jos 3:13	259
above stood *and* rose up in **o** heap,	Jos 3:16	259
the people, **o** man from each tribe,	Jos 4:2	259
of Israel, **o** man from each tribe,	Jos 4:4	259
no **o** went out and no one came in.	Jos 6:1	369
no one went out and no **o** came in.	Jos 6:1	369
'It shall be that the **o** who is	Jos 7:15	
no **o** was left of those who survived	Jos 8:22	
with **o** accord to fight with Joshua	Jos 9:2	259
city, like **o** of the royal cities,	Jos 10:2	259
not **o** of them shall stand before	Jos 10:8	376
No **o** uttered a word against any of	Jos 10:21	
kings and their lands at **o** time,	Jos 10:42	259
there was no **o** left who breathed.	Jos 11:11	
They left no **o** who breathed.	Jos 11:14	3605
o of the remnant of Rephaim,	Jos 12:4	
the king of Jericho, **o**;	Jos 12:9	259
of Ai, which is beside Bethel, **o**;	Jos 12:9	259
the king of Jerusalem, **o**;	Jos 12:10	259
the king of Hebron, **o**;	Jos 12:10	259
the king of Jarmuth, **o**;	Jos 12:11	259
the king of Lachish, **o**;	Jos 12:11	259
the king of Eglon, **o**;	Jos 12:12	259
the king of Gezer, **o**;	Jos 12:12	259
the king of Debir, **o**;	Jos 12:13	259
the king of Geder, **o**;	Jos 12:13	259
the king of Hormah, **o**;	Jos 12:14	259
the king of Arad, **o**;	Jos 12:14	259
the king of Libnah, **o**;	Jos 12:15	259
the king of Adullam, **o**;	Jos 12:15	259
the king of Makkedah, **o**;	Jos 12:16	259
the king of Bethel, **o**;	Jos 12:16	259
the king of Tappuah, **o**;	Jos 12:17	259
the king of Hepher, **o**;	Jos 12:17	259
the king of Aphek, **o**;	Jos 12:18	259
the king of Lasharon, **o**;	Jos 12:18	259
the king of Madon, **o**;	Jos 12:19	259
the king of Hazor, **o**;	Jos 12:19	259
the king of Shimron-meron, **o**;	Jos 12:20	259
the king of Achshaph, **o**;	Jos 12:20	259
the king of Taanach, **o**;	Jos 12:21	259
the king of Megiddo, **o**;	Jos 12:21	259
the king of Kedesh, **o**;	Jos 12:22	259
the king of Jokneam in Carmel, **o**;	Jos 12:22	259
of Dor in the heights of Dor, **o**;	Jos 12:23	259
the king of Goiim in Gilgal, **o**;	Jos 12:23	259
the king of Tirzah, **o**:	Jos 12:24	259
"The **o** who attacks Kiriath-sepher	Jos 15:16	
"Why have you given me only **o** lot	Jos 17:14	259
and **o** portion for an inheritance,	Jos 17:14	259
and you shall not have **o** lot *only,*	Jos 17:17	259
shall flee to **o** of these cities,	Jos 20:4	259
until the death of the **o** who is	Jos 20:6	
o of the families of the Kohathites,	Jos 21:10	
o of the families of the Levites,	Jos 21:27	
and no **o** of all their enemies	Jos 21:44	376
Not **o** of the good promises which	Jos 21:45	1697
Now to the **o** half-tribe of	Jos 22:7	
o chief for each father's household	Jos 22:14	259
and each **o** of them *was* the head of	Jos 22:14	376
"The Mighty **O**, God, the LORD, the	Jos 22:22	410
One, God, the LORD, the Mighty **O**,	Jos 22:22	410
"**O** of your men puts to flight a	Jos 23:10	259
not **o** word of all the good words	Jos 23:14	259
for you, not **o** of them has failed.	Jos 23:14	259
being **o** hundred and ten years old.	Jos 24:29	
for **o** hundred pieces of money;	Jos 24:32	
"The **o** who attacks Kiriath-sepher	Jg 1:12	
at the age of **o** hundred and ten.	Jg 2:8	
and no **o** escaped.	Jg 3:29	376
not even **o** was left.	Jg 4:16	259
shall defeat Midian as **o** man."	Jg 6:16	259
They said to **o** another,	Jg 6:29	376
'This **o** shall go with you,' he	Jg 7:4	2088
'This **o** shall not go with you,' he	Jg 7:4	2088
the LORD set the sword of **o**	Jg 7:22	376
o resembling the son of a king."	Jg 8:18	259
and every **o** of them threw an	Jg 8:25	376
you, or that **o** man rule over you?'	Jg 9:2	259
seventy men, on **o** stone.	Jg 9:5	259
his sons, seventy men, on **o** stone,	Jg 9:18	259
and **o** company comes by the way of	Jg 9:37	259
also cut down each **o** his branch	Jg 9:49	376
of Gilead, said to **o** another,	Jg 10:18	376
Now she was his **o** *and* only child;	Jg 11:34	3173
Gileadite died and was buried in **o**	Jg 12:7	
o of the daughters of	Jg 14:1	
o of the daughters of	Jg 14:2	
he tore him as **o** tears a young goat	Jg 14:6	
and put **o** torch in the middle	Jg 15:4	259
the **o** with his right hand and the	Jg 16:29	259
and consecrated **o** of his sons,	Jg 17:5	259
became to him like **o** of his sons.	Jg 17:11	259
be a priest to the house of **o** man,	Jg 18:19	259
there was no **o** to deliver *them,*	Jg 18:28	369
let us approach **o** of these places;	Jg 19:13	259
for no **o** took them into *his* house	Jg 19:15	376
as **o** man to the LORD at Mizpah.	Jg 20:1	259
all the people arose as **o** man,	Jg 20:8	259
"Not **o** of us will go to his tent,	Jg 20:8	376
against the city, united as **o** man.	Jg 20:11	259
each **o** could sling a stone at a	Jg 20:16	2088
o who goes up to Bethel and	Jg 20:31	259
so that **o** tribe should be *missing*	Jg 21:3	259
"**O** tribe is cut off from Israel	Jg 21:6	259
"What **o** is there of the tribes of	Jg 21:8	259
no **o** had come to the camp from	Jg 21:8	376
not **o** of the inhabitants of	Jg 21:9	376
and each **o** of them went out from	Jg 21:24	376
the name of the **o** was Orpah and	Ru 1:4	259
o in whose sight I may find favor."	Ru 2:2	
do not go on from this **o**,	Ru 2:8	2088
not like **o** of your maidservants."	Ru 2:13	259
is **o** of our closest relatives."	Ru 2:20	
before **o** could recognize another;	Ru 3:14	376

is no **o** but you to redeem *it*, Ru 4:4 369
the name of **o** was Hannah and the 1Sa 1:2 259
with a three-year-old bull and **o** 1Sa 1:24 259
"There is no **o** holy like the LORD, 1Sa 2:2 369
there is no **o** besides You, 1Sa 2:2 369
the **o** she dedicated to the LORD." 1Sa 2:20 7596
"If **o** man sins against another, 1Sa 2:25
assign me to **o** of the priest's offices 1Sa 2:36 259
o who came from the battle line. 1Sa 4:16
Then the **o** who brought the news 1Sa 4:17
for **o** plague was on all of you and 1Sa 6:4 259
o for Ashdod, one for Gaza, one 1Sa 6:17 259
one for Ashdod, **o** for Gaza, one 1Sa 6:17 259
one for Gaza, **o** for Ashkelon, 1Sa 6:17 259
one for Ashkelon, **o** for Gath, 1Sa 6:17 259
one for Gath, **o** for Ekron; 1Sa 6:17 259
now with you **o** of the servants, 1Sa 9:3 259
o shall rule over My people." 1Sa 9:17 2088
meet you, **o** carrying three young goats, 1Sa 10:3 259
that the people said to **o** another, 1Sa 10:11 376
no **o** like him among all the people. 1Sa 10:24 369
people away, each **o** to his house. 1Sa 10:25 376
"How can this **o** deliver us?" 1Sa 10:27 2088
the right eye of every **o** of you, 1Sa 11:2 3605
if there is no **o** to deliver us, 1Sa 11:3 369
and they came out as **o** man. 1Sa 11:7 259
o company turned toward Ophrah, to 1Sa 13:17 259
was a sharp crag on the **o** side and 1Sa 14:4 2088
and the name of the **o** was Bozez, 1Sa 14:4
The **o** crag rose on the north 1Sa 14:5 259
Then **o** of the people said, 1Sa 14:28 376
'Each **o** of you bring me his ox or 1Sa 14:34 376
brought each **o** his ox with him and 1Sa 14:34 376
But not **o** of all the people 1Sa 14:39 369
"You shall be on **o** side and I and 1Sa 14:40 259
not **o** hair of his head shall 1Sa 14:45
the **o** whom I designate to you." 1Sa 16:3
"The LORD has not chosen this **o** 1Sa 16:8 2088
"The LORD has not chosen this **o** 1Sa 16:9 2088
Then **o** of the young men said 1Sa 16:18 259
a warrior, **o** prudent in speech, 1Sa 16:18
stood on the mountain on **o** side 1Sa 17:3 2088
Philistine will be like **o** of them, 1Sa 17:36 259
LORD cuts off every **o** of the enemies 1Sa 20:15 376
are you alone and no **o** with you?" 1Sa 21:1 376
'Let no **o** know anything about the 1Sa 21:2 376
Now **o** of the servants of Saul was 1Sa 21:7 376
not sing of this **o** as they danced, 1Sa 21:11 2088
that you have brought this **o** to 1Sa 21:15 2088
Shall this **o** come into my house?" 1Sa 21:15 2088
there is no **o** who discloses to me 1Sa 22:8 369
But **o** son of Ahimelech the son of 1Sa 22:20 259
went on **o** side of the mountain, 1Sa 23:26 2088
o of the young men told Abigail, 1Sa 25:14 259
man that no **o** can speak to him." 1Sa 25:17
o male of any who belong to him." 1Sa 25:22
morning light *as much as* **o** male." 1Sa 25:34
spear to the ground with **o** stroke, 1Sa 26:8 259
away, but no **o** saw or knew *it*, 1Sa 26:12 369
For **o** of the people came to 1Sa 26:15 259
just as **o** hunts a partridge in the 1Sa 26:20
Now let **o** of the young men come 1Sa 26:22 259
perish **o** day by the hand of Saul. 1Sa 27:1 259
in **o** of the cities in the country, 1Sa 27:5 259
each **o** because of his sons and his 1Sa 30:6 376
David called **o** of the young men 2Sa 1:15 259
up to **o** of the cities of Judah?" 2Sa 2:1 259
o on the one side of the pool and 2Sa 2:13 428
one on the **o** side of the pool and 2Sa 2:13 2088
Each **o** of them seized his 2Sa 2:16 376
as swift-footed as **o** of the gazelles 2Sa 2:18 259
o of the young men for yourself, 2Sa 2:21 259
behind Abner and became **o** band, 2Sa 2:25 259
you, but I demand **o** thing of you, 2Sa 3:13 259
o who has a discharge, or who is a 2Sa 3:29
As **o** falls before the wicked, you 2Sa 3:34
the name of the **o** was Baanah and 2Sa 4:2 259
when **o** told me, saying, 2Sa 4:10
the **o** who led Israel out and in. 2Sa 5:2
a cake of bread and **o** of dates and 2Sa 6:19 259
and **o** of raisins to each one. 2Sa 6:19 259
and one of raisins to each **o**. 2Sa 6:19 376
as **o** of the foolish ones shamelessly 2Sa 6:20 259
"Are you the **o** who should build 2Sa 7:5
with **o** of the tribes of Israel, 2Sa 7:7 259
"And what **o** nation on the earth 2Sa 7:23 259
and **o** full line to keep alive. 2Sa 8:2
table as **o** of the king's sons. 2Sa 9:11 259
And **o** said, "Is this not Bathsheba, 2Sa 11:3
devours **o** as well as another; 2Sa 11:25 2088
"There were two men in **o** city, 2Sa 12:1 259
the **o** rich and the other poor. 2Sa 12:1 259
had nothing except **o** little ewe lamb 2Sa 12:3 259
be like **o** of the fools in Israel. 2Sa 13:13 259
sons, and not **o** of them is left." 2Sa 13:30 259
there was no **o** to separate them, 2Sa 14:6 369
so **o** struck the other and killed 2Sa 14:6 259
over the **o** who struck his brother, 2Sa 14:7
not **o** hair of your son shall fall 2Sa 14:11
the king is as **o** who is guilty, 2Sa 14:13 818
not bring back his banished **o**. 2Sa 14:13 5080
o will not be cast out from him. 2Sa 14:14 5080
no **o** can turn to the right or to 2Sa 14:19
was no **o** as handsome as Absalom, 2Sa 14:25 376
o daughter whose name was Tamar; 2Sa 14:27 259
from **o** of the tribes of Israel." 2Sa 15:2 259
"Oh that **o** would appoint me judge 2Sa 15:4
if **o** inquired of the word of God; 2Sa 16:23
he has now hidden himself in **o** of 2Sa 17:9 259
"And even the **o** who is valiant, 2Sa 17:10 1121
"So we shall come to him in **o** of 2Sa 17:12 259
with him, not even **o** will be left. 2Sa 17:12 259
and by dawn not even **o** remained 2Sa 17:22 259
o third under the command of Joab, 2Sa 18:2
o third under the command of 2Sa 18:2
and **o** third under the command of 2Sa 18:2
o also is bringing good news." 2Sa 18:26 2088
first **o** is like the running of Ahimaaz 2Sa 18:27 7223
of all the men of Judah as **o** man, 2Sa 19:14 259
stood by him **o** of Joab's young men, 2Sa 20:11 376
every **o** of them will be thrust 2Sa 23:6 3605
hundred slain *by him* at **o** time; 2Sa 23:8 259
o of the three mighty men with 2Sa 23:9
choose for yourself **o** of them, 2Sa 24:12 259
has granted **o** to sit on my throne 1Ki 1:48
not **o** of his hairs will fall to 1Ki 1:52
Now I am making **o** request of you; 1Ki 2:16 259
am making **o** small request of you; 1Ki 2:20 259
has been no **o** like you before you, 1Ki 3:12
shall **o** like you arise after you. 1Ki 3:12
The **o** woman said, 1Ki 3:17 259
For the living **o** is my son, and 1Ki 3:22 2416a
son, and the dead **o** is your son." 1Ki 3:22
For the dead **o** is your son, and 1Ki 3:22
son, and the living **o** is my son." 1Ki 3:22 2416a
"The **o** says, 'This is my son who is 1Ki 3:23 2088
and your son is the dead **o**'; 1Ki 3:23
For your son is the dead **o**, 1Ki 3:23
and my son is the living **o**.' " 1Ki 3:23 2416a
to the **o** and half to the other." 1Ki 3:25 259
the living **o** spoke to the king, 1Ki 3:26 2416a
Solomon's provision for **o** day 1Ki 4:22 259
for you know that there is no **o** 1Ki 5:6 376
Five cubits *was* the **o** wing of 1Ki 6:24 259
from the end of **o** wing to the end 1Ki 6:24
of the **o** cherub *was* ten cubits, 1Ki 6:26 259
the **o** was touching the *one* wall, 1Ki 6:27 259
wing of the one was touching the **o** 1Ki 6:27
the two leaves of the **o** door turned 1Ki 6:34 259
cubits was the height of **o** pillar, 1Ki 7:15 259
the height of the **o** capital was 1Ki 7:16 259
seven for the **o** capital and seven 1Ki 7:17 259
and two rows around on the **o** 1Ki 7:18 259
all of them had **o** casting, one 1Ki 7:37 259
casting, **o** measure and one form. 1Ki 7:37 259
casting, one measure and **o** form. 1Ki 7:37 259
bronze, **o** basin held forty baths; 1Ki 7:38 259
of the ten stands *was* **o** basin. 1Ki 7:38 259
and the **o** sea and the twelve oxen 1Ki 7:44 259
not **o** word has failed of all His 1Ki 8:56 259
the LORD is God; there is no **o** else. 1Ki 8:60 369
in **o** year was 666 talents of gold, 1Ki 10:14 259
on the **o** side and on the other; 1Ki 10:20 2088
but I will give **o** tribe to your 1Ki 11:13 259
(but he will have **o** tribe, 1Ki 11:32 259
to his son I will give **o** tribe, 1Ki 11:36 259
He set **o** in Bethel, and the 1Ki 12:29 259
before the **o** as far as Dan. 1Ki 12:30 259
as **o** sweeps away dung until it is 1Ki 14:10
and afterward you may make **o** for 1Ki 17:13
Ahab went **o** way by himself and 1Ki 18:6 259
and let them choose **o** ox for 1Ki 18:23 259
"Choose **o** ox for yourselves and 1Ki 18:25 259
was no voice and no **o** answered. 1Ki 18:26 369
there was no voice, no **o** answered, 1Ki 18:29 369
answered, and no **o** paid attention. 1Ki 18:29 369
do not let **o** of them escape." 1Ki 18:40 376
your life as the life of **o** of them 1Ki 19:2 259
the **o** who escapes from the sword 1Ki 19:17
and the **o** who escapes from the 1Ki 19:17
So they camped **o** over against the 1Ki 20:29 428
100,000 foot soldiers in **o** day. 1Ki 20:29 259
"The **o** belonging to Ahab, who 1Ki 21:24
and the **o** who dies in the field 1Ki 21:24
Surely there was no **o** like Ahab 1Ki 21:25
"There is yet **o** man by whom we 1Ki 22:8 259
be like the word of **o** of them, 1Ki 22:13 259
And **o** said this while another said 1Ki 22:20 2088
o of the king of Israel's servants 2Ki 3:11 259
and they have slain **o** another. 2Ki 3:23 376
and each **o** threw a stone on every 2Ki 3:25 376
"There is not **o** vessel more." 2Ki 4:6 369
O day he came there and turned in 2Ki 4:11
"Please send me **o** of the servants 2Ki 4:22 259
the servants and **o** of the donkeys, 2Ki 4:22 259
Then **o** went out into the field to 2Ki 4:39 259
Naaman saw **o** running after him, 2Ki 5:21
o said, "Please be willing to go with 2Ki 6:3 259
But as **o** was felling a beam, the 2Ki 6:5 259
O of his servants said, "No, my 2Ki 6:12 259
and they said to **o** another, 2Ki 7:3 376
behold, there was no **o** there. 2Ki 7:5 376
so that they said to **o** another, 2Ki 7:6 376
entered **o** tent and ate and drank, 2Ki 7:8 259
Then they said to **o** another, 2Ki 7:9 376
and behold, there was no **o** there, 2Ki 7:10 376
O of his servants said, "Please, 2Ki 7:13 259
to life the **o** who was dead, 2Ki 8:5
he reigned **o** year in Jerusalem. 2Ki 8:26 259
o of the sons of the prophets and 2Ki 9:1 259
"For which **o** of us?" 2Ki 9:5
of his master, and **o** said to him, 2Ki 9:11
then let no **o** escape *or* leave the 2Ki 9:15 6412a
the **o** who *was* over the household, 2Ki 10:5
let no **o** be missing, for I have a 2Ki 10:19 376
filled from **o** end to the other. 2Ki 10:21 6310
He said to the **o** who *was* in 2Ki 10:22
"The **o** who permits any of the men 2Ki 10:24 376
o third of you, who come in on the 2Ki 11:5
(**o** third also *shall be* at the gate 2Ki 11:6
and **o** third at the gate behind the 2Ki 11:6
And each **o** of them took his men 2Ki 11:9 376
on the right side as **o** comes into 2Ki 12:9 376
and he reigned **o** month in Samaria. 2Ki 15:13
"Take there **o** of the priests whom 2Ki 17:27 259
So **o** of the priests whom they had 2Ki 17:28 259
"How then can you repulse **o** 2Ki 18:24 259
Has any **o** of the gods of the nations 2Ki 18:33 376
Against the Holy **O** of Israel! 2Ki 19:22 6918
wipe Jerusalem as **o** wipes a dish, 2Ki 21:13
Jerusalem from **o** end to another; 2Ki 21:16 6310
let no **o** disturb his bones." 2Ki 23:18 376
a fine of **o** hundred talents of silver 2Ki 23:33
and the smiths, **o** thousand, 2Ki 24:16
The two pillars, the **o** sea, 2Ki 25:16 259
the **o** pillar was eighteen cubits, 2Ki 25:17 259
From the city he took **o** official who 2Ki 25:19 259
to be a mighty **o** in the earth. 1Ch 1:10 1368
Eber, the name of the **o** was Peleg, 1Ch 1:19 259
Mattithiah, **o** of the Levites, 1Ch 9:31
you *were* the **o** who led out and 1Ch 11:2
hundred whom he killed at **o** time. 1Ch 11:11 259
who *was* **o** of the three mighty men. 1Ch 11:12
were of **o** mind to make David king. 1Ch 12:38 259
"No **o** is to carry the ark of God 1Ch 15:2
And from **o** kingdom to another 1Ch 16:20
gone from tent to tent and from **o** 1Ch 17:5
that I will set up **o** *of* your 1Ch 17:11
"And what **o** nation in the earth 1Ch 17:21 259
o of the descendants of the 1Ch 20:4
choose for yourself **o** of them, 1Ch 21:10 259
I am the **o** who has sinned and done 1Ch 21:17
a father's household, **o** class. 1Ch 23:11 259
by lot, the **o** as the other; 1Ch 24:5 428
o father's household taken for 1Ch 24:6 259
Eleazar and **o** taken for Ithamar. 1Ch 24:6
Also Hosah, **o** of the sons of 1Ch 26:10
for Judah, Elihu, **o** of David's 1Ch 27:18
'Your son Solomon is the **o** who 1Ch 28:6
the wing of **o**, of five cubits, 2Ch 3:11 259
and he made **o** hundred pomegranates 2Ch 3:16
o on the right and the other on 2Ch 3:17 259
and named the **o** on the right 2Ch 3:17
Jachin and the **o** on the left Boaz. 2Ch 3:17
were in two rows, cast in **o** piece. 2Ch 4:3
he made **o** hundred golden bowls. 2Ch 4:8
and the **o** sea with the twelve oxen 2Ch 4:15 259
and with them **o** hundred and twenty 2Ch 5:12
make themselves heard with **o** voice 2Ch 5:13 259
Then she gave the king **o** hundred 2Ch 9:9
in **o** year was 666 talents of gold, 2Ch 9:13 259
on the **o** side and on the other; 2Ch 9:19 2088
and there was no **o** at war with him 2Ch 14:6 369
there is no **o** besides You to help 2Ch 14:11 369
"There is yet **o** man by whom we 2Ch 18:7 259
o of them and speak favorably." 2Ch 18:12 259
And **o** said this while another said 2Ch 18:19 2088
that no **o** can stand against You. 2Ch 20:6 369
they helped to destroy **o** another. 2Ch 20:23 376
the ground, and no **o** had escaped. 2Ch 20:24 369
he reigned **o** year in Jerusalem. 2Ch 22:2 259
was no **o** of the house of Ahaziah 2Ch 22:9 369
o third of you, of the priests and 2Ch 23:4
and **o** third *shall be* at the king's 2Ch 23:5
let no **o** enter the house of the LORD 2Ch 23:6
And each **o** of them took his men 2Ch 23:8 376
so that no **o** would enter *who was* 2Ch 23:19
he was **o** hundred and thirty years 2Ch 24:15
for **o** hundred talents of silver. 2Ch 25:6
Hananiah, **o** of the king's officers. 2Ch 26:11
year **o** hundred talents of silver, 2Ch 27:5
slew in Judah 120,000 in **o** day, 2Ch 28:6 259
also on Judah to give them **o** heart 2Ch 30:12 259
for the **o** with us is greater than 2Ch 32:7
us is greater than the **o** with him. 2Ch 32:7
"You shall worship before **o** altar, 2Ch 32:12 259
a fine of **o** hundred talents of silver 2Ch 36:3
of silver and **o** talent of gold. 2Ch 36:3
people gathered together as **o** man Ezr 3:1 259
to **o** whose name was Sheshbazzar, Ezr 5:14
stones and **o** layer of timbers. Ezr 6:4
for no **o** can stand before You Ezr 9:15 369
of Jehiel, **o** of the sons of Elam, Ezr 10:2
the task *be done* in **o** or two days, Ezr 10:13 259
that Hanani, **o** of my brothers, and Ne 1:2 259
him Hananiah, **o** of the perfumers, Ne 3:8 1121
him Malchijah, **o** of the goldsmiths, Ne 3:31 1121
to the wall, each **o** to his work. Ne 4:15 376
took *their* load with **o** hand doing the Ne 4:17 259
on the wall far from **o** another. Ne 4:19 376
there were at my table **o** hundred Ne 5:17
day was **o** ox *and* six choice sheep, Ne 5:18 259
And could **o** such as I go into the Ne 6:11
And all the people gathered as **o** Ne 8:1 259
contribute yearly **o** third of a shekel Ne 10:32
o out of ten to live in Jerusalem, Ne 11:1 259
Even **o** of the sons of Joiada, the Ne 13:28
the **o** who speaks in the language Es 1:22
old, women and children, in **o** day, Es 3:13 259
for no **o** was to enter the king's gate Es 4:2 369
is not summoned, he has but **o** law, Es 4:11 259
Esther the queen let no **o** but me Es 5:12
to **o** of the king's most noble princes Es 6:9 376
o of the eunuchs who *were* before Es 7:9 259
on **o** day in all the provinces of Es 8:12 259
and no **o** could stand before them, Es 9:2 376
portions *of food* to **o** another. Es 9:19 376

sending portions *of food* to **o** another Es 9:22 376
o who sought the good of his Es 10:3
o who spoke for the welfare of his Es 10:3
in the house of each **o** on his day, Jb 1:4 376
is no **o** like him on the earth, Jb 1:8 369
is no **o** like him on the earth, Jb 2:3 369
as **o** of the foolish women speaks. Jb 2:10 259
came each **o** from his own place, Jb 2:11 376
with no **o** speaking a word to him, Jb 2:13 369
"If **o** ventures a word with you, Jb 4:2
denied the words of the Holy **O**. Jb 6:10 6918
the words of **o** in despair belong to Jb 6:26
"If **o** wished to dispute with Him, Jb 9:3
power, behold, *He is* the strong **o**! Jb 9:19 533
"It is *all* **o**; therefore I say, Jb 9:22 259
The **o** who called on God and He Jb 12:4
deceive Him as **o** deceives a man? Jb 13:9
the clean out of the unclean? No **o**! Jb 14:4 259
o who is detestable and corrupt, Jb 15:16
In houses no **o** would inhabit, Jb 15:28
And I am **o** at whom men spit. Jb 17:6
"**O** dies in his full strength, Jb 21:23 2088
deliver **o** who is not innocent, Jb 22:30
but no **o** has assurance of life. Jb 24:22
"What counsel you have given to **o** Jb 26:3
The blessing of the **o** ready to perish Jb 29:13
As **o** who comforted the mourners. Jb 29:25
destruction; No **o** restrains them. Jb 30:13
does not **o** in a heap of ruins stretch Jb 30:24
wept for the **o** whose life is hard? Jb 30:25
the same **o** fashion us in the womb? Jb 31:15 259
'Who can find **o** who has not been Jb 31:31
"Oh that I had **o** to hear me! Jb 31:35
there was no **o** who refuted Job, Jb 32:12 369
o of you who answered his words. Jb 32:12
"Let me now be partial to no **o**, Jb 32:21 376
Or twice, *yet* no **o** notices it. Jb 33:14
for him, **O** out of a thousand, Jb 33:23 259
"Shall **o** who hates justice rule? Jb 34:17
you condemn the righteous mighty **O**, Jb 34:17 3524
'Worthless **o**,' To nobles, Jb 34:18 1100
"But no **o** says, Jb 35:10
O who is perfect in knowledge is Jb 36:4
wonders of **o** perfect in knowledge, Jb 37:16
"No **o** is so fierce that he dares Jb 41:10
"**O** is so near to another That no Jb 41:16 259
"They are joined **o** to another; Jb 41:17 376
O would think the deep to be Jb 41:32
is like him, **O** made without fear. Jb 41:33
each **o** gave him one piece of money Jb 42:11 376
one gave him **o** piece of money, Jb 42:11 259
and the **O** who lifts my head. Ps 3:3
And the **o** who loves violence His Ps 11:5
They speak falsehood to **o** another; Ps 12:2 376
There is no **o** who does good. Ps 14:1 369
There is no **o** who does good, not Ps 14:3 369
no one who does good, not even **o**. Ps 14:3 259
allow Your Holy **O** to undergo decay. Ps 16:10 2623
is from **o** end of the heavens, Ps 19:6
O thing I have asked from the Ps 27:4 259
Not **o** of them is broken. Ps 34:20 259
as **o** who sorrows for a mother. Ps 35:14 57
LORD is the **O** who holds his hand. Ps 37:24
sword on *Your* thigh, O Mighty **O**, Ps 45:3 1368
The Mighty **O**, God, the LORD, has Ps 50:1 410
There is no **o** who does good. Ps 53:1 369
Every **o** of them has turned aside; Ps 53:3 3605
There is no **o** who does good, not Ps 53:3 369
no one who does good, not even **o**. Ps 53:3 259
Nor is it **o** who hates me who has Ps 55:12
the **o** who sits enthroned from of old Ps 55:19
is the **o** whom You choose Ps 65:4
for there is no **o** to deliver." Ps 71:11 369
the lyre, O Holy **O** of Israel. Ps 71:22 6918
Like a dream when **o** awakes, Ps 73:20
It seems as if **o** had lifted up *His* Ps 74:5
He puts down **o** and exalts another. Ps 75:7 2088
And pained the Holy **O** of Israel. Ps 78:41 6918
And there was no **o** to bury them. Ps 79:3 369
fall like *any* **o** of the princes." Ps 82:7 259
conspired together with **o** mind; Ps 83:5
Every **o** *of them* appears before Ps 84:7
is no **o** like You among the gods, Ps 86:8 369
'This **o** was born there.' " Ps 87:4 2088
o and that one were born in her"; Ps 87:5 376
one and that **o** were born in her"; Ps 87:5 376
"This **o** was born there." Ps 87:6 2088
crushed Rahab like **o** who is slain; Ps 89:10
our king to the Holy **O** of Israel. Ps 89:18 6918
given help to **o** who is mighty; Ps 89:19
exalted **o** chosen from the people. Ps 89:19
O which devises mischief by decree? Ps 94:20
No **o** who has a haughty look and an Ps 101:5
is the **o** who will minister to me. Ps 101:6 1931
From **o** kingdom to another people. Ps 105:13
there was not **o** who stumbled. Ps 105:37 369
the hand of the **o** who hated *them*, Ps 106:10
Not **o** of them was left. Ps 106:11 259
of Aaron, the holy **o** of the LORD, Ps 106:16 6918
Had not Moses His chosen **o** stood Ps 106:23
Blessed is the **o** who comes in the Ps 118:26
every **o** of Your righteous ordinances Ps 119:160 3605
word, As **o** who finds great spoil. Ps 119:162
vowed to the Mighty **O** of Jacob, Ps 132:2 46
place for the Mighty **O** of Jacob." Ps 132:5 46
"Sing us **o** of the songs of Zion." Ps 137:3
of Babylon, you devastated **o**, Ps 137:8
How blessed will be the **o** who Ps 137:8
How blessed will be the **o** who Ps 137:9

as yet there was not **o** of them. Ps 139:16 259
As when **o** plows and breaks open Ps 141:7
For there is no **o** who regards me; Ps 142:4 369
No **o** cares for my soul. Ps 142:4 369
O generation shall praise Your Ps 145:4
us, We shall all have **o** purse," Pr 1:14 259
my hand and no **o** paid attention; Pr 1:24 369
And your years to the cruel **o**; Pr 5:9 394
o who walks with a perverse mouth, Pr 6:12
And **o** who spreads strife among Pr 6:19
For on account of a harlot **o** *is* Pr 6:26
So is the **o** who goes in to his Pr 6:29
The **o** who commits adultery with a Pr 6:32
Or as **o** *in* fetters to Pr 7:22
of the Holy **O** is understanding. Pr 9:10 6918
the lazy **o** to those who send him. Pr 10:26 6102
There is **o** who scatters, and Pr 11:24
And there is **o** who withholds what Pr 11:24
But **o** of perverse mind will be Pr 12:8
There is **o** who speaks rashly like Pr 12:18
The **o** who guards his mouth Pr 13:3
The **o** who opens wide his lips Pr 13:3
the **o** whose way is blameless, Pr 13:6
is **o** who pretends to be rich, Pr 13:7
But the **o** who gathers by labor Pr 13:11
The **o** who despises the word will Pr 13:13
the **o** who fears the commandment Pr 13:13
But knowledge is easy to **o** who has Pr 14:6
o may avoid the snares of death. Pr 14:27
heart of **o** who has understanding, Pr 14:33
But He loves **o** who pursues Pr 15:9
does not love **o** who reproves him, Pr 15:12
the LORD **o** keeps away from evil. Pr 16:6
is a fountain of life to **o** who has it, Pr 16:22
A rebuke goes deeper into **o** who Pr 17:10
of the **o** who has understanding, Pr 17:24
O who is gracious to a poor man lends Pr 19:17
So that **o** may sleep satisfied, Pr 19:23
But reprove **o** who has Pr 19:25
The righteous **o** considers the Pr 21:12 6662
And drowsiness will clothe **o** with Pr 23:21
And you will be like **o** who lies Pr 23:34
Or like **o** who lies down on the top Pr 23:34
O who plans to do evil, Men will Pr 24:8
Like **o** who takes off a garment on Pr 25:20
o who binds a stone in a sling, Pr 26:8
Like **o** who takes a dog by the ears Pr 26:17
iron, So **o** man sharpens another. Pr 27:17
wicked flee when no **o** is pursuing, Pr 28:1 369
let no **o** support him. Pr 28:17
have the knowledge of the Holy **O**. Pr 30:3 6918
anything of which **o** might say, Ec 1:10
that **o** fate befalls them both. Ec 2:14 259
o who has not labored with them. Ec 2:21 120
to **o** who is good in God's sight. Ec 2:26 2896a
As **o** dies so dies the other; Ec 3:19 2088
they had no **o** to comfort *them;* Ec 4:1 369
but they had no **o** to comfort *them.* Ec 4:1 369
is the **o** who has never existed, Ec 4:3
O hand full of rest is better than Ec 4:6
Two are better than **o** because they Ec 4:9 259
the **o** will lift up his companion. Ec 4:10 259
But woe to the **o** who falls when Ec 4:10 259
warm, but how can **o** be warm *alone?* Ec 4:11 259
And if **o** can overpower him who is Ec 4:12 259
for **o** official watches over Ec 5:8
do not all go to **o** place?" Ec 6:6 259
for **o** to listen to the song of fools. Ec 7:5 376
God has made the **o** as well as the Ec 7:14 2088
It is good that you grasp **o** thing and Ec 7:18 2088
for the **o** who fears God comes Ec 7:18
O who is pleasing to God will Ec 7:26 2896a
"*adding* **o** thing to another to Ec 7:27 259
have found **o** man among a thousand, Ec 7:28 259
If no **o** knows what will happen, Ec 8:7 369
o should never sleep day or night), Ec 8:16 369
There is **o** fate for the righteous Ec 9:2 259
for the **o** who does not sacrifice. Ec 9:2
is the **o** who is afraid to swear. Ec 9:2
that there is **o** fate for all men. Ec 9:3 259
Yet no **o** remembered that poor man. Ec 9:15 120
but **o** sinner destroys much good. Ec 9:18 259
and **o** will arise at the sound of Ec 12:4
they are given by **o** Shepherd. Ec 12:11 259
For why should I be like **o** who SS 1:7
'Arise, my darling, my beautiful **o**, SS 2:10 3303
Arise, my darling, my beautiful **o**, SS 2:13 3303
o among them has lost her young. SS 4:2 369
my darling, My dove, my perfect **o**! SS 5:2 8535
o among them has lost her young. SS 6:6 369
But my dove, my perfect **o**, SS 6:9 8535
pure *child* of the **o** who bore her. SS 6:9
No **o** would despise me, either. SS 8:1
in his eyes as **o** who finds peace. SS 8:10
Each **o** was to bring a thousand SS 8:11 376
despised the Holy **O** of Israel, Is 1:4 6918
The Mighty **O** of Israel, Is 1:24 46
be oppressed, Each **o** by another, Is 3:5 376
and each **o** by his neighbor; Is 3:5 376
take hold of **o** man in that day, Is 4:1 259
will yield *only* **o** bath *of wine*, Is 5:10 259
the purpose of the Holy **O** of Israel Is 5:19 6918
the word of the Holy **O** of Israel. Is 5:24 6918
No **o** in it is weary or stumbles, Is 5:27 369
it off with no **o** to deliver *it*. Is 5:29 369
If **o** looks to the land, behold, Is 5:30
And **o** called out to another and Is 6:3 2088
Then **o** of the seraphim flew to me with Is 6:6 259
For every **o** of them is godless and Is 9:17 3605

And as **o** gathers abandoned eggs, Is 10:14
And there was not **o** that flapped Is 10:14
over the **o** who chops with it? Is 10:15
itself over the **o** who wields it? Is 10:15
a fire and his Holy **O** a flame, Is 10:17 6918
rely on the **o** who struck them, Is 10:20
on the LORD, the Holy **O** of Israel. Is 10:20 6918
destruction, **o** that is decreed, Is 10:23
Lebanon will fall by the Mighty **O**. Is 10:34 117
midst is the Holy **O** of Israel. Is 12:6 6918
look at **o** another in astonishment, Is 13:8 376
And each **o** flee to his own land. Is 13:14 376
"How then will **o** answer the Is 14:32
will be no **o** to frighten *them*. Is 17:2 369
will be like **o** gleaning ears of grain Is 17:5
will look to the Holy **O** of Israel. Is 17:7 6918
o will be called the City of Is 19:18 259
o *still* deals treacherously, Is 21:2
And **o** said, "Fallen, fallen is Babylon; Is 21:9
O keeps calling to me from Seir, Is 21:11
When he opens no **o** will shut, Is 22:22 369
When he shuts no **o** will open. Is 22:22 369
years like the days of **o** king. Is 23:15 259
"Glory to the Righteous **O**," Is 24:16 6662
The **o** that remains faithful. Is 26:2
O Upright **O**, make the path of the Is 26:7 3477
So that no **o** will damage it, I guard Is 27:3
you will be gathered up **o** by one, Is 27:12 259
you will be gathered up one by **o**, Is 27:12 259
Which **o** sees, *And* as soon as it is Is 28:4
give it to the **o** who is literate, Is 29:11
given to the **o** who is illiterate, Is 29:12
rejoice in the Holy **O** of Israel. Is 29:19 6918
And defraud the **o** in the right Is 29:21 6662
will sanctify the Holy **O** of Jacob And Is 29:23 6918
more about the Holy **O** of Israel." Is 30:11 6918
thus says the Holy **O** of Israel, Is 30:12 6918
Lord GOD, the Holy **O** of Israel, Is 30:15 6918
O thousand *will flee* at the Is 30:17 259
will flee at the threat of **o** *man* Is 30:17 259
o marches to *the sound of* the flute, Is 30:29
not look to the Holy **O** of Israel, Is 31:1 6918
the needy **o** speaks what is right. Is 32:7 34
speech which no **o** comprehends, Is 33:19
tongue which no **o** understands. Is 33:19 369
But there the majestic **O**, the Is 33:21
Or as **o** withers from the fig tree. Is 34:4
there is no **o** there *Whom* they may Is 34:12 369
there, Every **o** with its kind. Is 34:15 376
Not **o** of these will be missing; Is 34:16 259
"How then can you repulse **o** Is 36:9 259
Has any **o** of the gods of the Is 36:18 376
Against the Holy **O** of Israel! Is 37:23 6918
be *his equal?*" says the Holy **O**. Is 40:25 6918
The **O** who leads forth their host Is 40:26
power, Not **o** *of them* is missing. Is 40:26 376
"Who has aroused **o** from the east Is 41:2
Each **o** helps his neighbor And Is 41:6 376
Redeemer is the Holy **O** of Israel. Is 41:14 6918
glory in the Holy **O** of Israel. Is 41:16 6918
Holy **O** of Israel has created it. Is 41:20 6918
"I have aroused **o** from the north, Is 41:25
there was no **o** who declared, Is 41:26 369
there was no **o** who proclaimed, Is 41:26 369
was no **o** who heard your words. Is 41:26 369
"But when I look, there is no **o**, Is 41:28 376
chosen **o** *in whom* My soul delights. Is 42:1
your God, The Holy **O** of Israel, Is 43:3 6918
Redeemer, the Holy **O** of Israel, Is 43:14 6918
"I am the LORD, your Holy **O**, Is 43:15 6918
o who wipes out your transgressions Is 43:25
"This **o** will say, Is 44:5 2088
And that **o** will call on the name Is 44:5 2088
takes **o** of them and warms himself; Is 44:15
No **o** recalls, nor is there Is 44:19
o who formed you from the womb, Is 44:24
And Israel My chosen **o**, I have Is 45:4
sun That there is no **o** besides Me. Is 45:6 657
The **O** forming light and creating Is 45:7
"Woe to *the* **o** who quarrels with Is 45:9
the LORD, the Holy **O** of Israel, Is 45:11 6918
Though **o** may cry to it, it cannot Is 46:7
am God, and there is no **o** like Me, Is 46:9 657
is His name, The Holy **O** of Israel. Is 47:4 6918
then, hear this, you sensual **o**, Is 47:8 5719
am, and there is no **o** besides me. Is 47:8 657
come on you suddenly in **o** day: Is 47:9 259
'No **o** sees me,' Your wisdom and Is 47:10 369
am, and there is no **o** besides me.' Is 47:10 657
Redeemer, the Holy **O** of Israel, Is 48:17 6918
of Israel *and* its Holy **O**, Is 49:7 6918
its Holy One, To the despised **O**, Is 49:7
To the **O** abhorred by the nation, Is 49:7
the Holy **O** of Israel who has chosen Is 49:7 6918
with the **o** who contends with you, Is 49:25 3401
Redeemer, the Mighty **O** of Jacob." Is 49:26 46
sustain the weary **o** with a word. Is 50:4 3287
When *he was but* **o** I called him, Then I Is 51:2 259
is there **o** to take her by the hand Is 51:18 369
day I am the **o** who is speaking, Is 52:6
o from whom men hide their face He Is 53:3
By His knowledge the Righteous **O**, Is 53:11 6662
"Shout for joy, O barren **o**, Is 54:1 6135
For the sons of the desolate **o** Is 54:1
Redeemer is the Holy **O** of Israel, Is 54:5 6918
"O afflicted **o**, storm-tossed, Is 54:11 6041
Every **o** who thirsts, come to the Is 55:1 3605
God, even the Holy **O** of Israel; Is 55:5 6918
every **o** who keeps from profaning Is 56:6 3605

way, Each **o** to his unjust gain, Is 56:11 376
to his unjust gain, to the last **o**. Is 56:11 7097a
away, while no **o** understands. Is 57:1 369
Each **o** who walked in his upright Is 57:2
and exalted **O** Who lives forever, Is 57:15
No **o** sues righteously and no one Is 59:4 369
and no **o** pleads honestly. Is 59:4 369
that there was no **o** to intercede; Is 59:16 369
And for the Holy **O** of Israel Is 60:9 6918
The Zion of the Holy **O** of Israel. Is 60:14 6918
hated With no **o** passing through, Is 60:15 369
Redeemer, the Mighty **O** of Jacob. Is 60:16 46
"The smallest **o** will become a Is 60:22 6996b
And the least **o** a mighty nation. Is 60:22 6810
This **O** who is majestic in His Is 63:1 2088
o who treads in the wine press? Is 63:2
and there was no **o** to help, Is 63:5 369
and there was no **o** to uphold; Is 63:5 369
behalf of the **o** who waits for Him. Is 64:4
have become like **o** who is unclean, Is 64:6
is no **o** who calls on Your name, Is 64:7 369
found in the cluster, And **o** says, Is 65:8
will die at the age of **o** hundred Is 65:20
the **o** who does not reach the age Is 65:20
does not reach the age of **o** hundred Is 65:20
"But to this **o** I will look, To Is 66:2 2088
an ox is *like* **o** who slays a man; Is 66:3
like the **o** who breaks a dog's neck; Is 66:3
offers a grain offering *is like* **o** Is 66:3
is *like* the **o** who blesses an idol. Is 66:3
I called, but no **o** answered; Is 66:4 369
Can a land be born in **o** day? Is 66:8 259
"As **o** whom his mother comforts, Is 66:13 376
Following **o** in the center, Is 66:17 259
and they will set each **o** his throne Jer 1:15 376
Through a land that no **o** crossed Jer 2:6 376
And I will take you **o** from a city Jer 3:14 259
And you, O desolate **o**, Jer 4:30
The anguish as of **o** giving birth Jer 4:31
If there is **o** who does justice, Jer 5:1
But they too, with **o** accord, Jer 5:5 3162
Each **o** neighing after his Jer 5:8 376
"The comely and dainty **o**, Jer 6:2
and no **o** will frighten *them away.* Jer 7:33 369
Does **o** turn away and not repent? Jer 8:4
o speaks peace to his neighbor, Jer 9:8
so that no **o** passes through, Jer 9:10 376
so that no **o** passes through? Jer 9:12 1097
But no **o** will gather *them.*' " Jer 9:22 369
There is no **o** to stretch out my tent Jer 10:20 369
their ear, but walked, each **o**, Jer 11:8 376
is devouring From **o** end of the land Jer 12:12
each **o** to his inheritance and each Jer 12:15 376
and each **o** to his land. Jer 12:15 376
And there is no **o** to open *them;* Jer 13:19 369
and there will be no **o** to bury them Jer 14:16 369
For You are the **o** who has done Jer 14:22
you are each **o** walking according Jer 16:12 376
"At **o** moment I might speak Jer 18:7
and they will eat **o** another's flesh Jer 19:9 376
even as **o** breaks a potter's vessel, Jer 19:11
o From the hand of evildoers. Jer 20:13 34
and deliver the **o** who has been Jer 22:3
and they will say to **o** another, Jer 22:8 376
for the **o** who goes away; Jer 22:10
So that no **o** has turned back from Jer 23:14 376
which they relate to **o** another, Jer 23:27 376
O basket had very good figs, like Jer 24:2 259
near and far, **o** with another; Jer 25:26 376
o end of the earth to the other. Jer 25:33
the **o** who is pleasing in My sight. Jer 27:5
o whom the LORD has truly sent." Jer 28:9
And no **o** will make him afraid. Jer 30:10 369
'There is no **o** to plead your cause; Jer 30:13 369
With the punishment of a cruel **o**, Jer 30:14 394
your adversaries, every **o** of them, Jer 30:16 3605
no **o** cares for her." Jer 30:17 369
Their leader shall be **o** of them, Jer 30:21
give them **o** heart and one way, Jer 32:39 259
give them one heart and **o** way, Jer 32:39 259
hands of the **o** who numbers them,' Jer 33:13
so that no **o** should keep them, a Jer 34:9 1097
so that no **o** should keep them any Jer 34:10 1097
the LORD, into **o** of the chambers, Jer 35:2 259
not plant a vineyard or own **o**; Jer 35:7
they turned in fear **o** to another and Jer 36:16 376
no **o** to sit on the throne of David, Jer 36:30
of the royal family and **o** of Jer 41:1
put to death the **o** whom the king of Jer 41:2
Gedaliah, when no **o** knew about *it,* Jer 41:4 376
it was the **o** that King Asa had Jer 41:9
in ruins and no **o** lives in them, Jer 44:2 369
For **o** warrior has stumbled over Jer 46:12
have fallen **o** against another. Jer 46:16 376
"Surely **o** shall come *who looms up* Jer 46:18
with no **o** making *him* tremble. Jer 46:27 369
"Cursed be the **o** who does the Jer 48:10
And cursed be the **o** who restrains Jer 48:10
No **o** will tread *them* with shouting, Jer 48:33
"the **o** who offers *sacrifice* on Jer 48:35
o who burns incense to his gods. Jer 48:35
o will fly swiftly like an eagle And Jer 48:40
"The **o** who flees from the terror Jer 48:44
And the **o** who climbs up out of the Jer 48:44
With no **o** to gather the fugitives Jer 49:5 369
and are you the **o** who will be Jer 49:12 1931
"no **o** will live there, nor will a Jer 49:18 376
o will come up like a lion from Jer 49:19
they will call out to **o** another, Jer 49:29

No **o** will live there, Nor will a Jer 49:33 376
And the **o** who wields the sickle at Jer 50:16
The first **o** *who* devoured him was Jer 50:17 7223
and this last **o** *who* has broken his Jer 50:17 314
Against the Holy **O** of Israel. Jer 50:29 6918
I am against you, O arrogant **o**," Jer 50:31
"The arrogant **o** will stumble Jer 50:32
fall With no **o** to raise him up; Jer 50:32 369
o will come up like a lion from Jer 50:44
guilt Before the Holy **O** of Israel. Jer 51:5 6918
O courier runs to meet another, Jer 51:31
And **o** messenger to meet another, Jer 51:31
For the report will come **o** year, Jer 51:46
The two pillars, the **o** sea, Jer 52:20 259
He also took from the city **o** official Jer 52:25 259
no **o** comes to the appointed feasts. La 1:4
adversary And no **o** helped her. La 1:7 369
comforter, **O** who restores my soul. La 1:16
There is no **o** to comfort her; La 1:17 369
There is no **o** to comfort me; La 1:21 369
And there was no **o** who escaped or La 2:22
But no **o** breaks *it* for them. La 4:4 369
no **o** could touch their garments. La 4:14
o to deliver us from their hand. La 5:8 369
their wings touched **o** another; Ezk 1:9 802
there was **o** wheel on the earth Ezk 1:15 259
as if **o** wheel were within another. Ezk 1:16
out straight, **o** toward the other; Ezk 1:23 802
each **o** also had two wings covering Ezk 1:23 376
on the **o** side and on the other. Ezk 1:23 376
living beings touching **o** another and Ezk 3:13 802
turn from **o** side to the other until Ezk 4:8
put them in **o** vessel and make them Ezk 4:9 259
they will be appalled with **o** another Ezk 4:17 376
"**O** third you shall burn in the Ezk 5:2 7992
Then you shall take **o** third and Ezk 5:2 7992
and **o** third you shall scatter to Ezk 5:2 7992
'**O** third of you will die by plague Ezk 5:12 7992
o third will fall by the sword Ezk 5:12 7992
and **o** third I will scatter to Ezk 5:12 7992
but no **o** is going to the battle, Ezk 7:14 369
hands of the **o** clothed in linen, Ezk 10:7
o wheel beside each cherub; Ezk 10:9 259
as if **o** wheel were within another Ezk 10:10
And each **o** had four faces. Ezk 10:14 259
Each **o** had four faces and each one Ezk 10:21 259
four faces and each **o** four wings, Ezk 10:21 259
Each **o** went straight ahead. Ezk 10:22 376
"And I will give them **o** heart, Ezk 11:19 259
so that no **o** would pass through it Ezk 14:15 1097
no **o** plays the harlot as you do, Ezk 16:34
'He took **o** of the royal family Ezk 17:13
of its young twigs a tender **o** and Ezk 17:22 7390
'When she brought up **o** of her cubs, Ezk 19:3 259
the sword for the great **o** slain, Ezk 21:14 1419
both of them will go out of **o** land. Ezk 21:19 259
'And you, O slain, wicked **o**, Ezk 21:25 7563
"**O** has committed abomination with Ezk 22:11 376
but I found no **o**. Ezk 22:30
women, the daughters of **o** mother; Ezk 23:2 259
and you will groan to **o** another. Ezk 24:23 376
you have perished, O inhabited **o**, Ezk 26:17
the people of the land take **o** man Ezk 33:2 259
'Abraham was *only* **o**, Ezk 33:24 259
so that no **o** will pass through. Ezk 33:28 369
of the houses, speak to **o** another, Ezk 33:30 2297
song by **o** who has a beautiful voice Ezk 33:32
o to search or seek *for them.* Ezk 34:6 369
judge between **o** sheep and another, Ezk 34:17
judge between **o** sheep and another. Ezk 34:22
I will set over them **o** shepherd, Ezk 34:23 259
and no **o** will make *them* afraid. Ezk 34:28 369
and I will cut off from it the **o** Ezk 35:7
son of man, take for yourself **o** stick Ezk 37:16 259
o to another into one stick, Ezk 37:17 259
one to another into **o** stick, Ezk 37:17 259
they may become **o** in your hand. Ezk 37:17 259
of Judah, and make them **o** stick, Ezk 37:19 259
and they will be **o** in My hand." Ezk 37:19 259
make them **o** nation in the land, Ezk 37:22 259
and **o** king will be king for all of Ezk 37:22 259
and they will all have **o** shepherd; Ezk 37:24 259
"Are you the **o** of whom I spoke in Ezk 38:17 1931
am the LORD, the Holy **O** in Israel. Ezk 39:7 6918
with no **o** to make *them* afraid. Ezk 39:26 369
the thickness of the wall, **o** rod; Ezk 40:5 259
and the height, **o** rod. Ezk 40:5 259
of the gate, **o** rod in width; Ezk 40:6 259
threshold *was* **o** rod in width. Ezk 40:6 259
was **o** rod long and one rod wide; Ezk 40:7 259
was one rod long and **o** rod wide; Ezk 40:7 259
the gate facing inward *was* **o** rod. Ezk 40:7 259
of the gate facing inward, **o** rod. Ezk 40:8 259
There was a barrier *wall* **o** cubit *wide* Ezk 40:12 259
from the roof of the **o** guardroom to Ezk 40:13
width of twenty-five cubits from **o** Ezk 40:13
its side pillars, **o** on each side. Ezk 40:26 259
as **o** went up to the gateway toward Ezk 40:40
and a half wide and **o** cubit high, Ezk 40:42 259
hooks, **o** handbreadth in length, Ezk 40:43 259
o *of* which was at the side of Ezk 40:44
and **o** at the side of the south gate Ezk 40:44 259
the side pillars, **o** on each side. Ezk 40:49 259
in three stories, **o** above another, Ezk 41:6 6763
and thus **o** went up from the lowest Ezk 41:7
o doorway toward the north and Ezk 41:11 259
toward the palm tree on **o** side and Ezk 41:19
the appearance of **o** doorpost was Ezk 41:21
two *leaves* for **o** door and two Ezk 41:24 259

trees on **o** side and on the other, Ezk 41:26
wide, a way of **o** *hundred* cubits; Ezk 42:4 259
as **o** enters them from the outer Ezk 42:9
toward the east, as **o** enters them. Ezk 42:12
o speaking to me from the house, Ezk 43:6
on its edge round about **o** span; Ezk 43:13 259
two cubits and the width **o** cubit; Ezk 43:14
cubits and the width **o** cubit. Ezk 43:14 259
and no **o** shall enter by it, Ezk 44:2 376
comparable to **o** of the portions, Ezk 45:7 259
and **o** sheep from *each* flock of two Ezk 45:15 259
No **o** shall return by way of the Ezk 46:9
as much as **o** is able to give, Ezk 46:11
inheritance to **o** of his servants, Ezk 46:17 259
on the **o** side and on the other. Ezk 47:7 2088
bank, on **o** side and on the other, Ezk 47:12 2088
each **o** equally with the other; Ezk 47:14 376
from east to west, Dan, **o** *portion.* Ezk 48:1 259
the west side, Asher, **o** *portion.* Ezk 48:2 259
west side, Naphtali, **o** *portion.* Ezk 48:3 259
west side, Manasseh, **o** *portion.* Ezk 48:4 259
the west side, Ephraim, **o** *portion.* Ezk 48:5 259
the west side, Reuben, **o** *portion.* Ezk 48:6 259
the west side, Judah, **o** *portion.* Ezk 48:7 259
in length like **o** of the portions, Ezk 48:8 259
on the **o** side and on the other of Ezk 48:21 2088
west side, Benjamin, **o** *portion.* Ezk 48:23 259
the west side, Simeon, **o** *portion.* Ezk 48:24 259
west side, Issachar, **o** *portion.* Ezk 48:25 259
the west side, Zebulun, **o** *portion.* Ezk 48:26 259
to the west side, Gad, **o** *portion.* Ezk 48:27 259
the gate of Reuben, **o**; Ezk 48:31 259
the gate of Judah, **o**; Ezk 48:31 259
the gate of Levi, **o**. Ezk 48:31 259
the gate of Joseph, **o**; Ezk 48:32 259
the gate of Benjamin, **o**; Ezk 48:32 259
the gate of Dan, **o**. Ezk 48:32 259
the gate of Simeon, **o**; Ezk 48:33 259
the gate of Issachar, **o**; Ezk 48:33 259
the gate of Zebulun, **o**. Ezk 48:33 259
the gate of Gad, **o**; Ezk 48:34 259
the gate of Asher, **o**; Ezk 48:34 259
the gate of Naphtali, **o**. Ezk 48:34 259
not **o** was found like Daniel, Da 1:19
there is only **o** decree for you. Da 2:9 2298
and there is no **o** else who could Da 2:11 321
they will combine with **o** another in Da 2:43
they will not adhere to **o** another, Da 2:43
1836, 5974
an *angelic* watcher, a holy **o**, Da 4:13 6922
saw an *angelic* watcher, a holy **o**, Da 4:23 6922
And no **o** can ward off His hand Or Da 4:35
who is **o** of the exiles from Judah, Da 5:13
(of whom Daniel was **o**), Da 6:2 2298
who is **o** of the exiles from Judah, Da 6:13
is **o** which will not be destroyed, Da 6:26
the sea, different from **o** another. Da 7:3 1668
behold, another beast, a second **o**, Da 7:5
And it was raised up on **o** side, Da 7:5 2298
behold, another **o**, like a leopard, Da 7:6
behold, another horn, a little **o**, Da 7:8 2192
O like a Son of Man was coming, Da 7:13
is **o** Which will not be destroyed. Da 7:14
"I approached **o** of those who were Da 7:16 2298
'But the saints of the Highest **O** Da 7:18 5946
favor of the saints of the Highest **O**, Da 7:22 5946
down the saints of the Highest **O**, Da 7:25 5946
of the saints of the Highest **O**; Da 7:27 5946
subsequent to the **o** which appeared Da 8:1
but **o** *was* longer than the other, Da 8:3 259
with the longer **o** coming up last. Da 8:3 1364
Out of **o** of them came forth a Da 8:9 259
Then I heard a holy **o** speaking, Da 8:13 6918
and another holy **o** said to that Da 8:13 6918
particular **o** who was speaking, Da 8:13 6423
me was **o** who looked like a man. Da 8:15
covenant with the many for **o** week, Da 9:27 259
will come **o** who makes desolate, Da 9:27
destruction, **o** that is decreed, Da 9:27
out on the **o** who makes desolate." Da 9:27
and the message was true and **o** *of* Da 10:1
Michael, **o** of the chief princes, Da 10:13 259
o who resembled a human being was Da 10:16
Then *this* **o** with human appearance Da 10:18
no **o** who stands firmly with me Da 10:21 259
along with **o** of his princes who Da 11:5
her in and the **o** who sired her Da 11:6
"But **o** of the descendants of her Da 11:7
and **o** of them will keep on coming Da 11:10
o will *be able to* withstand him; Da 11:16 369
"Then in his place **o** will arise Da 11:20
his end, and no **o** will help him. Da 11:45 369
o on this bank of the river and Da 12:5 259
And **o** said to the man dressed in Da 12:6
appoint for themselves **o** leader, Hos 1:11 259
And no **o** will rescue her out of My Hos 2:10 376
Yet let no **o** find fault, and let Hos 4:4 376
a vessel in which no **o** delights. Hos 8:8 369
And I became to them as **o** who Hos 11:4
Though they call them to *the* **O** on Hos 11:7
not man, the Holy **O** in your midst, Hos 11:9 6918
the Holy **O** who is faithful. Hos 11:12 6918
even **o** surrounding the land, Am 3:11 5439
walls, Each **o** straight before her, Am 4:3 802
Then I would send rain on **o** city Am 4:7 259
O part would be rained on, While Am 4:7 259
o which goes forth a hundred Am 5:3
if ten men are left in **o** house, Am 6:9 259
and he will say to the **o** who is in Am 6:10

And that **o** will say, **Am 6:10**
And that one will say, "No **o**." **Am 6:10** 657
Or does **o** plow them with oxen? **Am 6:12**
The **O** who touches the land so that **Am 9:5**
The **O** who builds His upper **Am 9:6**
You too were as **o** of them. **Ob 1:11** 259
go through the city **o** day's walk; **Jon 3:4** 259
and **o** who relents concerning **Jon 4:2**
on you The **o** who takes possession, **Mi 1:15**
no **o** stretching a measuring line **Mi 2:5**
good To the **o** walking uprightly? **Mi 2:7**
Each **o** from her pleasant house. **Mi 2:9**
With no **o** to make *them* afraid, **Mi 4:4** 369
From you **O** will go forth for Me to **Mi 5:2**
This **O** will be *our* peace. **Mi 5:5** 2088
From you has gone forth **O** who **Na 1:11**
the wicked **o** pass through you; **Na 1:15**
The **o** who scatters has come up **Na 2:1** 4650
"Stop, stop," But no **o** turns back. **Na 2:8** 369
of the harlot, The charming **o**, **Na 3:4** 2896a
there is no **o** to regather *them*. **Na 3:18** 369
O LORD, my God, my Holy **O**? **Hab 1:12** 6918
That the **o** who reads it may run. **Hab 2:2**
"Behold, as for the proud **o**, **Hab 2:4**
And the Holy **O** from Mount Paran. **Hab 3:3** 6918
end, Indeed a terrifying **o**, **Zph 1:18**
and there is no **o** besides me." **Zph 2:15** 657
desolate, With no **o** passing by; **Zph 3:6** 1097
With no **o** to make them tremble." **Zph 3:13** 369
clothing, but no **o** is warm *enough;* **Hg 1:6** 369
"If **o** who is unclean from a **Hg 2:13**
before **o** stone was placed on **Hg 2:15**
from that time *when* **o** came to a **Hg 2:16**
and *when* **o** came to the wine vat to **Hg 2:16**
on **o** stone are seven eyes. **Zch 3:9** 259
iniquity of that land in **o** day. **Zch 3:9** 259
'every **o** of you will invite his **Zch 3:10** 376
o on the right side of the bowl **Zch 4:3** 259
to the writing on **o** side, **Zch 5:3** 2088
o who swears falsely by My name; **Zch 5:4**
with **o** of which the black horses **Zch 6:6**
in your hearts against **o** another.' **Zch 7:10** 376
so that no **o** went back and forth, **Zch 7:14**
I set all men **o** against another. **Zch 8:10** 376
speak the truth to **o** another; **Zch 8:16** 376
inhabitants of **o** will go to another **Zch 8:21** 259
the **o** I called Favor and the **Zch 11:7** 259
the three shepherds in **o** month, **Zch 11:8** 259
are left eat **o** another's flesh." **Zch 11:9** 802
broken, or sustain the **o** standing, **Zch 11:16**
and the **o** who is feeble among them **Zch 12:8**
Him, as **o** mourns for an only son, **Zch 12:10**
"And **o** will say to him, **Zch 13:6**
day the LORD will be *the only* **o**, **Zch 14:9** 259
only one, and His name *the only* **o**. **Zch 14:9** 259
they will seize **o** another's hand, **Zch 14:13** 376
and the hand of **o** will be lifted **Zch 14:13**
"Oh that there were **o** among you **Mal 1:10**
"My covenant with him was **o** *of* **Mal 2:5**
"Do we not all have **o** father? **Mal 2:10** 259
Has not **o** God created us? **Mal 2:10** 259
"But not **o** has done *so* who has a **Mal 2:15** 259
And what did *that* **o** *do* while he **Mal 2:15** 259
and let no **o** deal treacherously **Mal 2:15**
the LORD spoke to **o** another, **Mal 3:16** 376
between **o** who serves God and one **Mal 3:18**
God and **o** who does not serve Him. **Mal 3:18**
For this is the **o** referred to by **Mt 3:3**
"THE VOICE OF **O** CRYING IN **Mt 3:3**
then annuls **o** of the least of these **Mt 5:19** 1520
for it is better for you to lose **o** of **Mt 5:29** 1520
for it is better for you to lose **o** of **Mt 5:30** 1520
cannot make **o** hair white or black. **Mt 5:36** 1520
forces you to go **o** mile, **Mt 5:41** 1520
"No **o** can serve two masters; **Mt 6:24** 3762
hate the **o** and love the other, **Mt 6:24** 1520
devoted to **o** and despise the other. **Mt 6:24** 1520
clothed himself like **o** of these. **Mt 6:29** 1520
for He was teaching them as **o** **Mt 7:29**
"See that you tell no **o**; **Mt 8:4** 3367
and I say to this **o**, **Mt 8:9** 3778
that no **o** could pass by that way. **Mt 8:28** 5100
no **o** puts a patch of unshrunk cloth **Mt 9:16** 3762
no **o** knows *about this!*" **Mt 9:30** 3367
Iscariot, the **o** who betrayed Him. **Mt 10:4**
but it is the **o** who has endured to **Mt 10:22**
"But whenever they persecute you in **o** **Mt 10:23** 3778
And *yet* not **o** of them will fall to **Mt 10:29** 1520
gives to **o** of these little ones even a **Mt 10:42** 1520
"Are You the Expected **O**, **Mt 11:3**
and **o** who is more than a prophet. **Mt 11:9**
is the **o** about whom it is written, **Mt 11:10**
Yet the **o** who is least in the kingdom **Mt 11:11** 3739
and no **o** knows the Son except the **Mt 11:27** 3762
o who was telling Him and said, **Mt 12:48**
the evil **o** comes and snatches **Mt 13:19**
This is the **o** on whom seed was **Mt 13:19**
"The **o** on whom seed was sown **Mt 13:20**
"And the **o** on whom seed was sown **Mt 13:22**
"And the **o** on whom seed was sown **Mt 13:23**
"The **o** who sows the good seed is **Mt 13:37**
tares are the sons of the evil **o**; **Mt 13:38**
finding **o** pearl of great value, **Mt 13:46** 1520
Jeremiah, or **o** of the prophets." **Mt 16:14** 1520
tell no **o** that He was the Christ. **Mt 16:20** 3367
three tabernacles here, **o** for You, **Mt 17:4** 1520
one for You, and **o** for Moses, **Mt 17:4** 1520
one for Moses, and **o** for Elijah." **Mt 17:4** 1520
they saw no **o** except Jesus Himself **Mt 17:8** 3762
"Tell the vision to no **o** until **Mt 17:9** 3367
whoever receives **o** such child in My **Mt 18:5** 1520
whoever causes **o** of these little ones **Mt 18:6** 1520
for you to enter life with **o** eye, **Mt 18:9** 3442
despise **o** of these little ones, **Mt 18:10** 1520
and **o** of them has gone astray, **Mt 18:12** 1520
search for the **o** that is straying? **Mt 18:12**
o of these little ones perish. **Mt 18:14** 1520
you, take **o** or two more with you, **Mt 18:16** 1520
o who owed him **Mt 18:24** 1520
and found **o** of his fellow slaves who **Mt 18:28** 1520
AND THE TWO SHALL BECOME **O** FLESH'? **Mt 19:5** 1520
are no longer two, but **o** flesh. **Mt 19:6** 1520
There is *only* **O** who is good; **Mt 19:17** 1520
he was **o** who owned much property. **Mt 19:22**
'Because no **o** hired us.' **Mt 20:7** 3762
came, each **o** received a denarius. **Mt 20:9** 303
last men have worked *only* **o** hour, **Mt 20:12** 1520
he answered and said to **o** of them, **Mt 20:13** 1520
o on Your right and one on Your **Mt 20:21** 1520
Your right and **o** on Your left." **Mt 20:21** 1520
"I will also ask you **o** thing, **Mt 21:24** 1520
took his slaves and beat **o**, **Mt 21:35** 3739
went their way, **o** to his own farm, **Mt 22:5** 3739
God in truth, and defer to no **o**; **Mt 22:16** 3762
O of them, a lawyer, asked Him *a* **Mt 22:35** 1520
No **o** was able to answer Him **Mt 22:46** 3762
for **O** is your Teacher, and you are **Mt 23:8** 1520
for **O** is your Father, He who is in **Mt 23:9** 1520
for **O** is your Leader, *that is,* Christ. **Mt 23:10** 1520
sea and land to make **o** proselyte; **Mt 23:15** 1520
and when he becomes **o**, **Mt 23:15**
not **o** stone here will be left **Mt 24:2**
"See to it that no **o** misleads you. **Mt 24:4** 5100
will betray **o** another and hate **Mt 24:10** 240
betray one another and hate **o** another. **Mt 24:10** 240
"But the **o** who endures to the end, **Mt 24:13**
o end of the sky to the other. **Mt 24:31**
of that day and hour no **o** knows, **Mt 24:36** 3762
o will be taken and one will be **Mt 24:40** 1520
will be taken and one **o** will be left. **Mt 24:40** 1520
o will be taken and one will be **Mt 24:41** 1520
will be taken and **o** will be left. **Mt 24:41** 1520
"To **o** he gave five talents, **Mt 25:15** 3739
another, two, and to another, **o**, **Mt 25:15** 1520
o who had received the five talents **Mt 25:16**
o who *had received* the two *talents* **Mt 25:17**
"But he who received the **o** *talent* **Mt 25:18** 1520
"The **o** who had received the **Mt 25:20**
"Also the **o** who *had received* the **Mt 25:22** 3588
"And the **o** also who had received **Mt 25:24**
the **o** talent came up and said, **Mt 25:24** 1520
to the **o** who has the ten talents.' **Mt 25:28**
but from the **o** who does not have, **Mt 25:29**
will separate them from **o** another, **Mt 25:32** 240
it to **o** of these brothers of Mine, **Mt 25:40** 1520
do it to **o** of the least of these, **Mt 25:45** 1520
Then **o** of the twelve, named Judas **Mt 26:14** 1520
that **o** of you will betray Me." **Mt 26:21** 1520
they each **o** began to say to Him, **Mt 26:22** 1520
bowl is the **o** who will betray Me. **Mt 26:23** 3778
not keep watch with Me for **o** hour? **Mt 26:40** 1520
the **o** who betrays Me is at hand!" **Mt 26:46**
behold, Judas, **o** of the twelve, **Mt 26:47** 1520
I kiss, He is the **o**; **Mt 26:48**
o of those who were with Jesus **Mt 26:51** 1520
who is the **o** who hit You?" **Mt 26:68**
"Surely you too are **o** of them; **Mt 26:73**
PRICE OF THE **O** WHOSE PRICE HAD **Mt 27:9**
any **o** prisoner whom they wanted. **Mt 27:15** 1520
o on the right and one on the left. **Mt 27:38** 1520
on the right and **o** on the left. **Mt 27:38** 1520
Immediately **o** of them ran, and **Mt 27:48** 1520
OF **O** CRYING IN THE WILDERNESS, **Mk 1:3**
"After me **O** is coming who is **Mk 1:7**
for He was teaching them as **o** **Mk 1:22**
who You are—the Holy **O** of God!" **Mk 1:24** 40
"No **o** sews a patch of unshrunk **Mk 2:21** 3762
"No **o** puts new wine into old **Mk 2:22** 3762
but **o** *puts* new wine into fresh **Mk 2:22**
"But no **o** can enter the strong **Mk 3:27** 3762
much afraid and said to **o** another, **Mk 4:41** 240
no **o** was able to bind him anymore, **Mk 5:3** 3762
and no **o** was strong enough to **Mk 5:4** 3762
O of the synagogue officials named **Mk 5:22** 1520
allowed no **o** to accompany Him, **Mk 5:37** 3762
that no **o** should know about this, **Mk 5:43** 3367
like **o** of the prophets *of old.*" **Mk 6:15** 1520
He wanted no **o** to know *of it* **Mk 7:24** 3762
They brought to Him **o** who was **Mk 7:32** 2974
did not have more than **o** loaf in the **Mk 8:14** 1520
They *began* to discuss with **o** another **Mk 8:16** 240
but others, **o** of the prophets." **Mk 8:28** 1520
them to tell no **o** about Him. **Mk 8:30** 3367
make three tabernacles, **o** for You, **Mk 9:5** 1520
one for You, and **o** for Moses, **Mk 9:5** 1520
one for Moses, and **o** for Elijah." **Mk 9:5** 1520
and saw no **o** with them anymore, **Mk 9:8** 3762
discussing with **o** another what **Mk 9:10** 1438
And **o** of the crowd answered Him, **Mk 9:17** 1520
they had discussed with **o** another **Mk 9:34** 240
"Whoever receives **o** child like **Mk 9:37** 1520
for there is no **o** who will **Mk 9:39** 3762
"Whoever causes **o** of these **Mk 9:42** 1520
the kingdom of God with **o** eye, **Mk 9:47** 3442
and be at peace with **o** another." **Mk 9:50** 240
AND THE TWO SHALL BECOME **O** FLESH **Mk 10:8** 1520
are no longer two, but **o** flesh. **Mk 10:8** 1520
No **o** is good except God alone. **Mk 10:18** 3762
"**O** thing you lack: **Mk 10:21** 1520
he was **o** who owned much property. **Mk 10:22**
there is no **o** who has left house **Mk 10:29** 3762
o on Your right **Mk 10:37** 1520
Your right and **o** on *Your* left, **Mk 10:37** 1520
on which no **o** yet has ever sat; **Mk 11:2** 444, 3762
no **o** ever eat fruit from you again!" **Mk 11:14** 3367
"I will ask you **o** question, and **Mk 11:29** 1520
another, and that **o** they killed; **Mk 12:5** 2548
"He had **o** more *to send,* a beloved **Mk 12:6** 1520
vine-growers said to **o** another, **Mk 12:7** 1438
are truthful and defer to no **o**; **Mk 12:14** 3762
They brought **o**. And He said to **Mk 12:16**
"The second **o** married her, and **Mk 12:21** 1208
O of the scribes came and heard them **Mk 12:28** 1520
THE LORD OUR GOD IS **O** LORD; **Mk 12:29** 1520
have truly stated that HE IS **O**, **Mk 12:32** 1520
THERE IS NO **O** ELSE BESIDES HIM; **Mk 12:32** 243
no **o** would venture to ask Him any **Mk 12:34** 3762
o of His disciples said to Him, **Mk 13:1** 1520
Not **o** stone will be left upon **Mk 13:2**
"See to it that no **o** misleads you. **Mk 13:5** 5100
but the **o** who endures to the end, **Mk 13:13**
"The **o** who is on the housetop must **Mk 13:15** 3739
the **o** who is in the field must not **Mk 13:16** 3739
of that day or hour no **o** knows, **Mk 13:32** 3762
assigning to each **o** his task, **Mk 13:34** 1538
remarking to **o** another, **Mk 14:4** 1438
Iscariot, who was **o** of the twelve, **Mk 14:10** 1520
that **o** of you will betray Me **Mk 14:18** 1520
o who is eating with Me." **Mk 14:18**
and to say to Him **o** by one, **Mk 14:19** 1520
and to say to Him one by **o**, **Mk 14:19** 1520
"*It is* **o** of the twelve, one who **Mk 14:20**
o who dips with Me in the bowl. **Mk 14:20**
you not keep watch for **o** hour? **Mk 14:37** 1520
the **o** who betrays Me is at hand!" **Mk 14:42**
Judas, **o** of the twelve, came up **Mk 14:43** 1520
Whomever I kiss, He is the **o**; **Mk 14:44**
But **o** of those who stood **Mk 14:47** 1520
the Son of the Blessed **O**?" **Mk 14:61**
o of the servant-girls of the high **Mk 14:66** 1520
"This is **o** of them!" **Mk 14:69**
"Surely you are **o** of them, for **Mk 14:70**
to release for them *any* **o** prisoner **Mk 15:6** 1520
o on His right and one on His left. **Mk 15:27** 1520
on His right and **o** on His left. **Mk 15:27** 1520
They were saying to **o** another, **Mk 16:3** 1438
"Greetings, favored **o**! The Lord *is* with **Lk 1:28**
the Mighty **O** has done great things **Lk 1:49** 1415
"There is no **o** among your **Lk 1:61** 3762
began saying to **o** another, **Lk 2:15** 240
OF **O** CRYING IN THE WILDERNESS, **Lk 3:4**
but **O** is coming who is mightier **Lk 3:16**
who You are—the Holy **O** of God!" **Lk 4:34** 40
talking with **o** another saying, **Lk 4:36** 240
His hands on each **o** of them, **Lk 4:40** 1520
And He got into **o** of the boats, **Lk 5:3** 1520
While He was in **o** of the cities, **Lk 5:12** 1520
And He ordered him to tell no **o**, **Lk 5:14** 3367
O day He was teaching; and there **Lk 5:17** 1520
"No **o** tears a piece of cloth from **Lk 5:36** 3762
"And no **o** puts new wine into old **Lk 5:37** 3762
"And no **o**, after drinking old **Lk 5:39** 3762
"But the **o** who has heard and has **Lk 6:49**
and I say to this **o**, **Lk 7:8** 3778
"Are You the Expected **O**, **Lk 7:19**
'Are You the Expected **O**, **Lk 7:20**
and **o** who is more than a prophet. **Lk 7:26**
is the **o** about whom it is written, **Lk 7:27**
there is no **o** greater than John; **Lk 7:28** 3762
place and call to **o** another, **Lk 7:32** 240
Now **o** of the Pharisees was **Lk 7:36** 5100
o owed five hundred denarii, and **Lk 7:41** 1520
the **o** whom he forgave more." **Lk 7:43**
o city and village to another, **Lk 8:1**
"Now no **o** after lighting a lamp **Lk 8:16** 3762
on **o** of *those* days **Lk 8:22** 1520
and amazed, saying to **o** another, **Lk 8:25** 240
"Who is the **o** who touched Me?" **Lk 8:45**
to tell no **o** what had happened. **Lk 8:56** 3367
that **o** of the prophets of old had **Lk 9:8** 5100
that **o** of the prophets of old has **Lk 9:19** 5100
he is the **o** who will save it. **Lk 9:24**
o for You, and one for Moses, and **Lk 9:33** 1520
one for You, and **o** for Moses, **Lk 9:33** 1520
one for Moses, and **o** for Elijah" **Lk 9:33** 1520
"This is My Son, *My* Chosen **O**; **Lk 9:35**
and reported to no **o** in those days **Lk 9:36** 3762
for the **o** who is least among all of **Lk 9:48** 3588
you, this is the **o** who is great." **Lk 9:48**
"No **o**, after putting his hand to **Lk 9:62** 3762
and greet no **o** on the way. **Lk 10:4** 3367
"The **o** who listens to you listens **Lk 10:16**
the **o** who rejects you rejects Me; **Lk 10:16**
Me rejects the **O** who sent Me." **Lk 10:16**
and no **o** knows who the Son is **Lk 10:22** 3762
o who showed mercy toward him." **Lk 10:37** 1520
but *only* **o** thing is necessary, **Lk 10:42** 1520
o of His disciples said to Him, **Lk 11:1** 5100
o of you has a friend, **Lk 11:5** 5101
"Now suppose **o** of you fathers is **Lk 11:11** 5101
o of the women in the crowd raised **Lk 11:27** 5100
"No **o**, after lighting a lamp, **Lk 11:33** 3762
O of the lawyers said to Him in reply, **Lk 11:45** 5100
burdens with **o** of your fingers. **Lk 11:46** 1520
they were stepping on **o** another, **Lk 12:1** 240
fear the **O** who, after He has killed **Lk 12:5**

Yet not **o** of them is forgotten	**Lk 12:6**	*1520*
for not *even* when **o** has an	**Lk 12:15**	*5100*
clothed himself like **o** of these.	**Lk 12:27**	*1520*
but the **o** who did not know *it,* and	**Lk 12:48**	
in **o** household will be divided,	**Lk 12:52**	*1520*
was teaching in **o** of the synagogues	**Lk 13:10**	*1520*
o city and village to another,	**Lk 13:22**	
into the house of **o** of the leaders	**Lk 14:1**	*5100*
"Which **o** of you will have a son	**Lk 14:5**	
the **o** who has invited you comes,	**Lk 14:10**	
say to the **o** who had invited Him,	**Lk 14:12**	
When **o** of those who were	**Lk 14:15**	*5100*
The first **o** said to him,	**Lk 14:18**	*4413*
"Another **o** said,	**Lk 14:19**	*2087*
"Another **o** said,	**Lk 14:20**	*2087*
"For which **o** of you, when he	**Lk 14:28**	
encounter the **o** coming against him	**Lk 14:31**	
sheep and has lost **o** of them,	**Lk 15:4**	*1520*
and go after the **o** which is lost until	**Lk 15:4**	
heaven over **o** sinner who repents than	**Lk 15:7**	*1520*
ten silver coins and loses **o** coin,	**Lk 15:8**	*1520*
God over **o** sinner who repents."	**Lk 15:10**	*1520*
hired himself out to **o** of the citizens	**Lk 15:15**	*1520*
no **o** was giving *anything* to him.	**Lk 15:16**	*3762*
me as **o** of your hired men."	**Lk 15:19**	*1520*
And he summoned **o** of the servants	**Lk 15:26**	*1520*
each **o** of his master's debtors,	**Lk 16:5**	*1520*
for either he will hate the **o** and	**Lk 16:13**	*1520*
other, or else he will be devoted to **o**	**Lk 16:13**	*1520*
o stroke of a letter of the Law to fail.	**Lk 16:17**	*1520*
he who marries **o** who is divorced	**Lk 16:18**	
cause **o** of these little ones	**Lk 17:2**	*1520*
Now **o** of them, when he saw that he	**Lk 17:15**	*1520*
"Was no **o** found who returned	**Lk 17:18**	
o of the days of the Son of Man,	**Lk 17:22**	*1520*
flashes out of **o** part of the sky,	**Lk 17:24**	
the **o** who is on the housetop	**Lk 17:31**	
the **o** who is in the field must not turn	**Lk 17:31**	
there will be two in **o** bed;	**Lk 17:34**	*1520*
o will be taken and the other	**Lk 17:34**	*1520*
o will be taken and the other	**Lk 17:35**	*1520*
o will be taken and the other will	**Lk 17:36**	*1520*
the temple to pray, **o** a Pharisee and	**Lk 18:10**	*1520*
No **o** is good except God alone.	**Lk 18:19**	*3762*
"**O** thing you still lack;	**Lk 18:22**	*1520*
there is no **o** who has left house	**Lk 18:29**	*3762*
to the **o** who has the ten minas.'	**Lk 19:24**	
but from the **o** who does not have,	**Lk 19:26**	
on which no **o** yet has ever sat;	**Lk 19:30**	
		444, 3762
leave in you **o** stone upon another,	**Lk 19:44**	
On **o** of the days	**Lk 20:1**	*1520*
o who gave You this authority?"	**Lk 20:2**	
and this **o** also they wounded and	**Lk 20:12**	*3778*
him, they reasoned with **o** another,	**Lk 20:14**	*240*
there will not be left **o** stone upon	**Lk 21:6**	
the hand of the **o** betraying Me is	**Lk 22:21**	
which **o** of them it might be who was	**Lk 22:23**	
which **o** of them was regarded to be	**Lk 22:24**	
but the **o** who is the greatest among	**Lk 22:26**	*3739*
the **o** who reclines *at the table*	**Lk 22:27**	
at the table or the **o** who serves?	**Lk 22:27**	
the **o** who reclines *at the table?*	**Lk 22:27**	
am among you as the **o** who serves.	**Lk 22:27**	
no sword is to sell his coat and buy **o**.	**Lk 22:36**	
came, and the **o** called Judas,	**Lk 22:47**	
one called Judas, **o** of the twelve,	**Lk 22:47**	*1520*
And **o** of them struck the	**Lk 22:50**	*1520*
"You are **o** of them too!"	**Lk 22:58**	
who is the **o** who hit You?"	**Lk 22:64**	
Pilate became friends with **o** another	**Lk 23:12**	*240*
as **o** who incites the people to	**Lk 23:14**	
to them at the feast **o** prisoner.	**Lk 23:17**	*1520*
(He was **o** who had been thrown into	**Lk 23:19**	*3748*
o on the right and the other on	**Lk 23:33**	*3739*
the Christ of God, His Chosen **O**."	**Lk 23:35**	*1588*
O of the criminals who were hanged	**Lk 23:39**	*1520*
rock, where no **o** had ever lain.	**Lk 23:53**	*3762*
seek the living **O** among the dead?	**Lk 24:5**	
you are exchanging with **o** another	**Lk 24:17**	*240*
O *of them,* named Cleopas,	**Lk 24:18**	*1520*
"Are You the only **o** visiting	**Lk 24:18**	*3441*
They said to **o** another,	**Lk 24:32**	*240*
No **o** has seen God at any time;	**Jn 1:18**	*3762*
OF **O** CRYING IN THE WILDERNESS,	**Jn 1:23**	
you stands **O** whom you do not know.	**Jn 1:26**	
this is the **O** who baptizes in	**Jn 1:33**	
O of the two who heard John *speak*	**Jn 1:40**	*1520*
for no **o** can do these signs that	**Jn 3:2**	*3762*
to you, unless **o** is born again he	**Jn 3:3**	*5100*
unless **o** is born of water and the	**Jn 3:5**	*5100*
"No **o** has ascended into heaven,	**Jn 3:13**	*3762*
and no **o** receives His testimony.	**Jn 3:32**	*3762*
and the **o** whom you now have is not	**Jn 4:18**	
when that **O** comes, He will declare	**Jn 4:25**	*1565*
yet no **o** said, "What do You seek?"	**Jn 4:27**	*3762*
were saying to **o** another,	**Jn 4:33**	*240*
"No **o** brought Him *anything* to	**Jn 4:33**	*5100*
'**O** sows and another reaps.'	**Jn 4:37**	*243*
O is indeed the Savior of the world."	**Jn 4:42**	*3778*
me well was the **o** who said to me,	**Jn 5:11**	*1565*
you receive glory from **o** another and	**Jn 5:44**	*240*
seek the glory that is from the **o**	**Jn 5:44**	
the **o** who accuses you is Moses, in	**Jn 5:45**	
O of His disciples, Andrew, Simon	**Jn 6:8**	*1520*
no other small boat there, except **o**,	**Jn 6:22**	*1520*
and the **o** who comes to Me I will	**Jn 6:37**	
"No **o** can come to Me unless the	**Jn 6:44**	*3762*
except the **O** who is from God;	**Jn 6:46**	

that **o** may eat of it and not die.	**Jn 6:50**	*5100*
began to argue with **o** another,	**Jn 6:52**	*240*
to you, that no **o** can come to Me unless	**Jn 6:65**	*3762*
that You are the Holy **O** of God."	**Jn 6:69**	*40*
and *yet* **o** of you is a devil?"	**Jn 6:70**	*1520*
Iscariot, for he, **o** of the twelve,	**Jn 6:71**	*1520*
"For no **o** does anything in secret when	**Jn 7:4**	*3762*
Yet no **o** was speaking openly of	**Jn 7:13**	*3762*
He who is seeking the glory of the **O**	**Jn 7:18**	
"I did **o** deed, and you all marvel.	**Jn 7:21**	*1520*
no **o** knows where He is from."	**Jn 7:27**	*3762*
Jews then said to **o** another,	**Jn 7:35**	*1438*
Him, but no **o** laid hands on Him.	**Jn 7:44**	*3762*
"No **o** of the rulers or Pharisees	**Jn 7:48**	*5100*
to Him before, being **o** of them) said	**Jn 7:50**	*1520*
it, they *began* to go out **o** by one,	**Jn 8:9**	*1520*
it, they *began* to go out one by **o**,	**Jn 8:9**	*1520*
Did no **o** condemn you?"	**Jn 8:10**	*3762*
She said, "No **o**, Lord."	**Jn 8:11**	*3762*
and no **o** seized Him, because His	**Jn 8:20**	*3762*
we have **o** Father: God."	**Jn 8:41**	*1520*
"Which **o** of you convicts Me of sin?	**Jn 8:46**	*5101*
there is **O** who seeks and judges.	**Jn 8:50**	
night is coming when no **o** can work.	**Jn 9:4**	*3762*
the **o** who used to sit and beg?"	**Jn 9:8**	
He kept saying, "I am the **o**."	**Jn 9:9**	
very **o** who had received his sight,	**Jn 9:18**	*846*
o thing I do know, that though I	**Jn 9:25**	*1520*
the **o** who is talking with you."	**Jn 9:37**	
become **o** flock *with* one shepherd.	**Jn 10:16**	*1520*
become one flock *with* **o** shepherd.	**Jn 10:16**	*1520*
"No **o** has taken it away from Me,	**Jn 10:18**	*3762*
the sayings of **o** demon-possessed.	**Jn 10:21**	
and no **o** will snatch them out of	**Jn 10:28**	*5100*
and no **o** is able to snatch *them*	**Jn 10:29**	*3762*
"I and the Father are **o**."	**Jn 10:30**	*1520*
But **o** of them, Caiaphas,	**Jn 11:49**	*1520*
o man die for the people,	**Jn 11:50**	*1520*
together into **o** the children of God	**Jn 11:52**	*1520*
and were saying to **o** another as	**Jn 11:56**	*240*
but Lazarus was **o** of those	**Jn 12:2**	*1520*
Iscariot, **o** of His disciples,	**Jn 12:4**	*1520*
Pharisees said to **o** another,	**Jn 12:19**	*1438*
Me sees the **O** who sent Me.	**Jn 12:45**	
My sayings, has **o** who judges him;	**Jn 12:48**	
knew the **o** who was betraying Him;	**Jn 13:11**	
ought to wash **o** another's feet.	**Jn 13:14**	*240*
nor *is* **o** who is sent greater	**Jn 13:16**	*652*
greater than the **o** who sent him.	**Jn 13:16**	
that **o** of you will betray Me."	**Jn 13:21**	*1520*
began looking at **o** another,	**Jn 13:22**	*240*
know of which **o** He was speaking.	**Jn 13:22**	*5101*
Jesus' bosom **o** of His disciples,	**Jn 13:23**	*1520*
"That is the **o** for whom I shall	**Jn 13:26**	
Now no **o** of those reclining *at the*	**Jn 13:28**	*3762*
to you, that you love **o** another,	**Jn 13:34**	*240*
you, that you also love **o** another.	**Jn 13:34**	*240*
if you have love for **o** another."	**Jn 13:35**	*240*
no **o** comes to the Father but	**Jn 14:6**	*3762*
commandments and keeps them is the **o**	**Jn 14:21**	*1565*
that you love **o** another,	**Jn 15:12**	*240*
"Greater love has no **o** than this,	**Jn 15:13**	*3762*
that **o** lay down his life for his	**Jn 15:13**	*5100*
you, that you love **o** another.	**Jn 15:17**	*240*
do not know the **O** who sent Me.	**Jn 15:21**	
the works which no **o** else did,	**Jn 15:24**	*3762*
then said to **o** another,	**Jn 16:17**	*240*
no **o** *will* take your joy away	**Jn 16:22**	*3762*
have given Me, that they may be **o** even	**Jn 17:11**	*1520*
and not **o** of them perished but the	**Jn 17:12**	*3762*
but to keep them from the evil **o**.	**Jn 17:15**	
that they may all be **o**;	**Jn 17:21**	*1520*
that they may be **o**,	**Jn 17:22**	*1520*
they may be one, just as We are **o**;	**Jn 17:22**	*1520*
You have given Me I lost not **o**."	**Jn 18:9**	*3762*
Now Caiaphas was the **o** who had	**Jn 18:14**	
expedient for **o** man to die on behalf	**Jn 18:14**	*1520*
"You are not also **o** of this	**Jn 18:17**	
o of the officers standing nearby struck	**Jn 18:22**	*1520*
"You are not also **o** of His	**Jn 18:25**	
O of the slaves of the high	**Jn 18:26**	*1520*
of the **o** whose ear Peter cut off,	**Jn 18:26**	
two other men, **o** on either side,	**Jn 19:18**	
was seamless, woven in **o** piece.	**Jn 19:23**	*3650*
So they said to **o** another,	**Jn 19:24**	*240*
But **o** of the soldiers pierced His	**Jn 19:34**	*1520*
but a secret **o** for fear of	**Jn 19:38**	
in which no **o** had yet been laid.	**Jn 19:41**	*3762*
in white sitting, **o** at the head and	**Jn 20:12**	*1520*
at the head and **o** at the feet,	**Jn 20:12**	*1520*
But Thomas, **o** of the twelve,	**Jn 20:24**	*1520*
but about **o** hundred yards away,	**Jn 21:8**	*1250*
the **o** who also had leaned back on	**Jn 21:20**	
who is the **o** who betrays You?"	**Jn 21:20**	
These all with **o** mind were	**Ac 1:14**	*3661*
a gathering of about **o** hundred and	**Ac 1:15**	*1540*
AND LET NO **O** DWELL IN IT';	**Ac 1:20**	*3361*
o of these *must* become a witness	**Ac 1:22**	*1520*
show which **o** of these two You	**Ac 1:24**	*1520*
they were all together in **o** place.	**Ac 2:1**	*846*
and they rested on each **o** of them.	**Ac 2:3**	*1520*
because each **o** of them was hearing	**Ac 2:6**	*1520*
perplexity, saying to **o** another,	**Ac 2:12**	*243*
YOUR HOLY **O** TO UNDERGO DECAY.	**Ac 2:27**	*3741*
TO HIM WITH AN OATH TO SEAT **O**	**Ac 2:30**	
with **o** mind in the temple,	**Ac 2:46**	*3661*
the **o** who used to sit at the Beautiful	**Ac 3:10**	
the **o** whom you delivered	**Ac 3:13**	
disowned the Holy and Righteous **O**	**Ac 3:14**	*1342*

the **o** whom God raised from	**Ac 3:15**	
o *of you* from your wicked ways."	**Ac 3:26**	*1538*
there is salvation in no **o** else;	**Ac 4:12**	*3762*
began to confer with **o** another,	**Ac 4:15**	*240*
to God with **o** accord and said,	**Ac 4:24**	*3661*
believed were of **o** heart and soul;	**Ac 4:32**	*1520*
and not **o** *of them* claimed that	**Ac 4:32**	*1520*
with **o** accord in Solomon's portico.	**Ac 5:12**	*3661*
might fall on any **o** of them.	**Ac 5:15**	*5100*
opened up, we found no **o** inside."	**Ac 5:23**	*3762*
"He is the **o** whom God exalted to	**Ac 5:31**	
"And when he saw **o** *of them* being	**Ac 7:24**	*5100*
why do you injure **o** another?'	**Ac 7:26**	*240*
"But the **o** who was injuring his	**Ac 7:27**	
is the **o** whom God sent *to be* both	**Ac 7:35**	*3778*
"This is the **o** who was in the	**Ac 7:38**	
"Which **o** of the prophets did your	**Ac 7:52**	*5101*
the coming of the Righteous **O**,	**Ac 7:52**	*1342*
rushed at him with **o** impulse.	**Ac 7:57**	*3661*
The crowds with **o** accord	**Ac 8:6**	*3661*
hearing the voice but seeing no **o**.	**Ac 9:7**	*3367*
and **o** who feared God with all his	**Ac 10:2**	
I am the **o** you are looking for;	**Ac 10:21**	
God is not **o** to show partiality,	**Ac 10:34**	*4381*
O who has been appointed by God	**Ac 10:42**	
"Surely no **o** can refuse the water	**Ac 10:47**	*5100*
word to no **o** except to Jews alone.	**Ac 11:19**	*3367*
O of them named Agabus stood up and	**Ac 11:28**	*1520*
went out and went along **o** street,	**Ac 12:10**	*1520*
with **o** accord they came to him,	**Ac 12:20**	*3661*
o is coming after me the sandals	**Ac 13:25**	
YOUR HOLY **O** TO UNDERGO DECAY.'	**Ac 13:35**	*3741*
to us, having become of **o** mind,	**Ac 15:25**	*3661*
they separated from **o** another,	**Ac 15:39**	*240*
and He made from **o**	**Ac 17:26**	*1520*
He is not far from each **o** of us;	**Ac 17:27**	*1520*
the Jews with **o** accord rose up	**Ac 18:12**	*3661*
Seven sons of **o** Sceva,	**Ac 19:14**	*5100*
with **o** accord into the theater,	**Ac 19:29**	*3661*
shouting **o** thing and some another,	**Ac 19:32**	*3303a*
bring charges against **o** another.	**Ac 19:38**	*240*
to admonish each **o** with tears.	**Ac 20:31**	*1520*
we said farewell to **o** another.	**Ac 21:5**	*240*
who was **o** of the seven,	**Ac 21:8**	
he *began* to relate **o** by one the	**Ac 21:19**	*1520*
he *began* to relate one by **o** the	**Ac 21:19**	*1520*
was offered for each **o** of them.	**Ac 21:26**	*1520*
shouting **o** thing *and* some another,	**Ac 21:34**	
of the **O** who was speaking to me.	**Ac 22:9**	
will and to see the Righteous **O**	**Ac 22:14**	*1342*
that in **o** synagogue after another	**Ac 22:19**	
o group were Sadducees and the other	**Ac 23:6**	*1520*
Paul called **o** of the centurions	**Ac 23:17**	*1520*
"Tell no **o** that you have notified	**Ac 23:22**	*3367*
other than for this **o** statement	**Ac 24:21**	*1520*
me, no **o** can hand me over to them.	**Ac 25:11**	*3762*
they *began* talking to **o** another,	**Ac 26:31**	*240*
they *began* saying to **o** another,	**Ac 28:4**	*240*
they did not agree with **o** another,	**Ac 28:25**	*240*
Paul had spoken **o** *parting* word,	**Ac 28:25**	*1520*
in their desire toward **o** another,	**Ro 1:27**	*240*
preach that **o** shall not steal,	**Ro 2:21**	
that **o** should not commit adultery,	**Ro 2:22**	
is not a Jew who is **o** outwardly,	**Ro 2:28**	
But he is a Jew who is **o** inwardly;	**Ro 2:29**	
IS NONE RIGHTEOUS, NOT EVEN **O**;	**Ro 3:10**	*1520*
DOES GOOD, THERE IS NOT EVEN **O**."	**Ro 3:12**	*1520*
of the **o** who has faith in Jesus.	**Ro 3:26**	
uncircumcised through faith is **o**.	**Ro 3:30**	*1520*
Now to the **o** who works, his wage	**Ro 4:4**	
But to the **o** who does not work,	**Ro 4:5**	
For **o** will hardly die for a	**Ro 5:7**	*5100*
just as through **o** man sin entered	**Ro 5:12**	*1520*
For if by the transgression of the **o**	**Ro 5:15**	*1520*
gift by the grace of the **o** Man,	**Ro 5:15**	*1520*
came through the **o** who sinned;	**Ro 5:16**	*1520*
for on the **o** hand the judgment	**Ro 5:16**	*3303a*
judgment *arose* from **o** *transgression*	**Ro 5:16**	*1520*
if by the transgression of the **o**,	**Ro 5:17**	*1520*
one, death reigned through the **o**,	**Ro 5:17**	*1520*
will reign in life through the **O**,	**Ro 5:17**	*1520*
So then as through **o** transgression	**Ro 5:18**	*1520*
so through **o** act of righteousness	**Ro 5:18**	*1520*
as through the **o** man's disobedience	**Ro 5:19**	*1520*
so through the obedience of the **O**	**Ro 5:19**	*1520*
are slaves of the **o** whom you obey,	**Ro 6:16**	
no longer am I the **o** doing it,	**Ro 7:17**	
I am no longer the **o** doing it,	**Ro 7:20**	
me, the **o** who wants to do good.	**Ro 7:21**	
on the **o** hand I myself with my	**Ro 7:25**	*3303a*
God is the **o** who justifies;	**Ro 8:33**	
who is the **o** who condemns?	**Ro 8:34**	
she had conceived *twins* by **o** man,	**Ro 9:10**	*1520*
lump **o** vessel for honorable use and	**Ro 9:21**	
		3739, 3303a
we have many members in **o** body	**Ro 12:4**	*1520*
are many, are **o** body in Christ,	**Ro 12:5**	*1520*
individually members **o** of another.	**Ro 12:5**	*1520*
to **o** another in brotherly love;	**Ro 12:10**	*240*
preference to **o** another in honor;	**Ro 12:10**	*240*
of the same mind toward **o** another;	**Ro 12:16**	*240*
on the **o** who practices evil.	**Ro 13:4**	
anyone except to love **o** another;	**Ro 13:8**	*240*
accept the **o** who is weak in faith,	**Ro 14:1**	
O person has faith that he may eat	**Ro 14:2**	
		3739, 3303a
The **o** who eats is not to regard with	**Ro 14:3**	*3739*
is not to regard with contempt the **o**	**Ro 14:3**	*3588*
and the **o** who does not eat is not to	**Ro 14:3**	*3739*

does not eat is not to judge the **o** Ro 14:3 3588
O person regards one day above Ro 14:5
3739, 3303a
person regards **o** day above another, Ro 14:5
For not **o** of us lives for himself, Ro 14:7 3762
and not **o** dies for himself; Ro 14:7 3762
So then each **o** of us will give Ro 14:12 1538
us not judge **o** another anymore, Ro 14:13 240
and the building up of **o** another. Ro 14:19 240
be of the same mind with **o** another Ro 15:5 240
that with **o** accord you may with Ro 15:6 3661
you may with **o** voice glorify the God Ro 15:6 1520
Therefore, accept **o** another, Ro 15:7 240
able also to admonish **o** another. Ro 15:14 240
Greet **o** another with a holy kiss. Ro 16:16 240
that each **o** of you is saying, 1Co 1:12 1538
so that no **o** would say you were 1Co 1:15 5100
no **o** knows except the Spirit of God. 1Co 2:11 3762
yet he himself is appraised by no **o**. 1Co 2:15 3762
For when **o** says, 1Co 3:4 5100
Lord gave *opportunity* to each **o**. 1Co 3:5 1538
So then neither the **o** who plants 1Co 3:7
nor the **o** who waters is anything, 1Co 3:7
plants and he who waters are **o**; 1Co 3:8 1520
other than the **o** which is laid, 1Co 3:11
"*He is* THE **O** WHO CATCHES THE WISE 1Co 3:19
So then let no **o** boast in men. 1Co 3:21 3367
that **o** be found trustworthy. 1Co 4:2 5100
the **o** who examines me is the Lord. 1Co 4:4
so that no **o** of you will 1Co 4:6 1520
in behalf of **o** against the other. 1Co 4:6 1520
so that the **o** who had done 1Co 5:2
decided to deliver such a **o** to Satan 1Co 5:5 5108
even to eat with such a **o**. 1Co 5:11 5108
Does any **o** of you, when he has a 1Co 6:1 5100
that there is not among you **o** wise 1Co 6:5 3762
you have lawsuits with **o** another. 1Co 6:7 1438
the **o** who joins himself to a prostitute 1Co 6:16
to a prostitute is **o** body *with her?* 1Co 6:16 1520
"THE TWO SHALL BECOME **O** FLESH." 1Co 6:16 1520
But the **o** who joins himself to the 1Co 6:17
to the Lord is **o** spirit *with Him.* 1Co 6:17 1520
Stop depriving **o** another, except 1Co 7:5 240
gift from God, **o** in this manner, 1Co 7:7
3588, 3303a
Yet if the unbelieving **o** leaves, 1Co 7:15 571
the Lord has assigned to each **o**, 1Co 7:17 1538
Brethren, each **o** is to remain with 1Co 7:24 1538
but I give an opinion as **o** who by 1Co 7:25
O who is unmarried is concerned 1Co 7:32
but **o** who is married is concerned 1Co 7:33
but **o** who is married is concerned 1Co 7:34
and that there is no God but **o**. 1Co 8:4 1520
yet for us there is *but* **o** God, 1Co 8:6 1520
and **o** Lord, Jesus Christ, by whom 1Co 8:6 1520
any man make my boast an empty **o**. 1Co 9:15
but *only* **o** receives the prize? 1Co 9:24 1520
twenty-three thousand fell in **o** day. 1Co 10:8 1520
Since there is **o** bread, we who are 1Co 10:17 1520
bread, we who are many are **o** body; 1Co 10:17 1520
for we all partake of the **o** bread. 1Co 10:17 1520
Let no **o** seek his own *good,* but 1Co 10:24 3367
If **o** of the unbelievers invites 1Co 10:27 5100
sake of the **o** who informed *you,* 1Co 10:28 1565
for she is **o** and the same as the woman 1Co 11:5 1520
o is inclined to be contentious, 1Co 11:16 5100
each **o** takes his own supper first; 1Co 11:21 1538
and **o** is hungry and another is 1Co 11:21
3739, 3303a
to eat, wait for **o** another. 1Co 11:33 240
that no **o** speaking by the Spirit 1Co 12:3 3762
and no **o** can say, "Jesus is Lord," 1Co 12:3 3762
But to each **o** is given the 1Co 12:7 1538
For to **o** is given the word of 1Co 12:8
3739, 3303a
gifts of healing by the **o** Spirit, 1Co 12:9 1520
But **o** and the same Spirit works 1Co 12:11 1520
distributing to each **o** individually 1Co 12:11 1538
as the body is **o** and *yet* has many 1Co 12:12 1520
though they are many, are **o** body, 1Co 12:12 1520
For by **o** Spirit we were all baptized 1Co 12:13 1520
we were all baptized into **o** body, 1Co 12:13 1520
all made to drink of **o** Spirit. 1Co 12:13 1520
For the body is not **o** member, 1Co 12:14 1520
the members, each **o** of them, 1Co 12:18 1520
If they were all **o** member, 1Co 12:19 1520
are many members, but **o** body. 1Co 12:20 1520
have the same care for **o** another. 1Co 12:25 240
And if **o** member suffers, all the 1Co 12:26 1520
if **o** member is honored, all 1Co 12:26
For **o** who speaks in a tongue does 1Co 14:2
for no **o** understands, but in *his* 1Co 14:2 3762
But **o** who prophesies speaks to men 1Co 14:3
O who speaks in a tongue edifies 1Co 14:4
but **o** who prophesies edifies the 1Co 14:4
and greater is **o** who prophesies 1Co 14:5
than **o** who speaks in tongues, 1Co 14:5
to the **o** who speaks a barbarian, 1Co 14:11
and the **o** who speaks will be a 1Co 14:11
Therefore let **o** who speaks in a 1Co 14:13
how will the **o** who fills the place 1Co 14:16
you assemble, each **o** has a psalm, 1Co 14:26 1538
each in turn, and **o** must interpret; 1Co 14:27 1520
the first **o** must keep silent. 1Co 14:30
For you can all prophesy **o** by one, 1Co 14:31
2596, 1520
For you can all prophesy one by **o**, 1Co 14:31
2596, 1520
five hundred brethren at **o** time, 1Co 15:6 2178
as to **o** untimely born, 1Co 15:8 1626
subjected to the **O** who subjected all 1Co 15:28
but there is **o** *flesh* of men 1Co 15:39 243
the glory of the heavenly is **o**, 1Co 15:40 2087
There is **o** glory of the sun, and 1Co 15:41 243
each **o** of you is to put aside and save, 1Co 16:2 1538
So let no **o** despise him. 1Co 16:11 5100
Greet **o** another with a holy kiss. 1Co 16:20 240
but the **o** whom I made sorrowful? 2Co 2:2
Sufficient for such a **o** is this 2Co 2:6 5108
such a **o** might be overwhelmed 2Co 2:7 5108
But **o** whom you forgive anything, I 2Co 2:10 5100
o an aroma from death to death, 2Co 2:16
3739, 3303a
the **O** who has shone in our hearts 2Co 4:6
that each **o** may be recompensed for 2Co 5:10 1538
this, that **o** died for all, 2Co 5:14 1520
from now on we recognize no **o** 2Co 5:16 3762
we wronged no **o**, we corrupted no 2Co 7:2 3762
wronged no one, we corrupted no **o**, 2Co 7:2 3762
no one, we took advantage of no **o**. 2Co 7:2 3762
for the sake of the **o** offended, 2Co 7:12
that no **o** will discredit us in our 2Co 8:20 5100
Each **o** *must do* just as he has 2Co 9:7 1538
for I betrothed you to **o** husband, 2Co 11:2 1520
For if **o** comes and preaches 2Co 11:4
I say, let no **o** think me foolish; 2Co 11:16 5100
so that no **o** will credit me with 2Co 12:6 5100
Greet **o** another with a holy kiss. 2Co 13:12 240
that no **o** is justified by the Law Ga 3:11 3762
no **o** sets it aside or adds Ga 3:15 3762
to many, but *rather* to **o**, Ga 3:16 1520
mediator is not for **o** *party only;* Ga 3:20 1520
whereas God is *only* **o**. Ga 3:20 1520
for you are all **o** in Christ Jesus. Ga 3:28 1520
o by the bondwoman and one by the Ga 4:22 1520
bondwoman and **o** by the free woman. Ga 4:22 1520
o *proceeding* from Mount Sinai Ga 4:24 1520
THAN OF THE **O** WHO HAS A HUSBAND Ga 4:27
but the **o** who is disturbing you Ga 5:10
but through love serve **o** another. Ga 5:13 240
whole Law is fulfilled in **o** word, Ga 5:14 1520
if you bite and devour **o** another, Ga 5:15 240
that you are not consumed by **o** another. Ga 5:15 240
are in opposition to **o** another, Ga 5:17 240
boastful, challenging **o** another, Ga 5:26 240
one another, envying **o** another. Ga 5:26 240
restore such a **o** in a spirit of Ga 6:1 5108
each **o** looking to yourself, so Ga 6:1
Bear **o** another's burdens, and thereby Ga 6:2 240
each **o** must examine his own work, Ga 6:4 1538
each **o** will bear his own load. Ga 6:5 1538
The **o** who is taught the Ga 6:6
to share all good things with the **o** Ga 6:6
For the **o** who sows to his own Ga 6:8
but the **o** who sows to the Spirit Ga 6:8
on let no **o** cause trouble for me, Ga 6:17 3367
age but also in the **o** to come. Eph 1:21
of works, so that no **o** may boast. Eph 2:9 5100
who made both *groups into* **o** and Eph 2:14 1520
might make the two into **o** new man, Eph 2:15 1520
o body to God through the cross, Eph 2:16 1520
access in **o** Spirit to the Father. Eph 2:18 1520
tolerance for **o** another in love, Eph 4:2 240
There is **o** body and one Spirit, Eph 4:4 1520
There is one body and **o** Spirit, Eph 4:4 1520
called in **o** hope of your calling; Eph 4:4 1520
o Lord, one faith, one baptism, Eph 4:5 1520
one Lord, **o** faith, one baptism, Eph 4:5 1520
one Lord, one faith, **o** baptism, Eph 4:5 1520
o God and Father of all who is Eph 4:6 1520
But to each **o** of us grace was given Eph 4:7 1520
SPEAK TRUTH EACH **O** *of you* Eph 4:25 1538
for we are members of **o** another. Eph 4:25 240
have *something* to share with **o** Eph 4:28 3588
Be kind to **o** another, Eph 4:32 240
no **o** deceive you with empty words, Eph 5:6 3367
speaking to **o** another in psalms Eph 5:19 1438
o another in the fear of Christ. Eph 5:21 240
for no **o** ever hated his own flesh, Eph 5:29 3762
AND THE TWO SHALL BECOME **O** FLESH. Eph 5:31 1520
whatever good thing each **o** does, Eph 6:8 1538
the flaming arrows of the evil **o**. Eph 6:16
you are standing firm in **o** spirit, Php 1:27 1520
with **o** mind striving together for Php 1:27 1520
in spirit, intent on **o** purpose. Php 2:2 1520
regard **o** another as more important Php 2:3
For I have no **o** *else* of kindred Php 2:20 3762
but **o** thing *I do:* Php 3:13 1520
that no **o** will delude you with Col 2:4 3367
that no **o** takes you captive through Col 2:8 5100
Therefore no **o** is to act as your judge Col 2:16 5100
Let no **o** keep defrauding you of Col 2:18 3367
Do not lie to **o** another, since you Col 3:9 240
image of the **O** who created him Col 3:10
bearing with **o** another, and Col 3:13 240
indeed you were called in **o** body; Col 3:15 1520
admonishing **o** another with psalms Col 3:16 1438
brother, who is **o** of your *number.* Col 4:9
Epaphras, who is **o** of your number, Col 4:12
imploring each **o** of you as a father 1Th 2:11 1520
so that no **o** would be disturbed by 1Th 3:3 3367
and abound in love for **o** another, 1Th 3:12 240
taught by God to love **o** another; 1Th 4:9 240
comfort **o** another with these words. 1Th 4:18 240
Therefore encourage **o** another and 1Th 5:11 240
another and build up **o** another, 1Th 5:11 1520
Live in peace with **o** another. 1Th 5:13 1438
See that no **o** repays another with 1Th 5:15 5100
for **o** another and for all people. 1Th 5:15 240
and the love of each **o** of you 2Th 1:3 1520
each one of you toward **o** another 2Th 1:3 240
Let no **o** in any way deceive you, 2Th 2:3 5100
Then that lawless **o** will be revealed 2Th 2:8 459
the **o** whose coming is in accord 2Th 2:9
and protect you from the evil **o**. 2Th 3:3
is good, if **o** uses it lawfully, 1Tm 1:8 5100
For there is **o** God, *and* one 1Tm 2:5 1520
and **o** mediator also between God 1Tm 2:5 1520
reproach, the husband of **o** wife, 1Tm 3:2 1520
He must be **o** who manages his own 1Tm 3:4
be husbands of *only* **o** wife, 1Tm 3:12 1520
how **o** ought to conduct himself 1Tm 3:15
Let no **o** look down on your 1Tm 4:12 3367
having been the wife of **o** man, 1Tm 5:9 1520
o who enlisted him as a soldier. 2Tm 2:4
first defense no **o** supported me, 2Tm 4:16 3762
reproach, the husband of **o** wife, Ti 1:6 1520
O of themselves, a prophet of Ti 1:12 5100
Let no **o** disregard you. Ti 2:15 3367
to malign no **o**, to be Ti 3:2 3367
envy, hateful, hating **o** another. Ti 3:3 240
But **o** has testified somewhere, Heb 2:6 5100
sanctified are all from **o** *Father;* Heb 2:11 1520
not be in any **o** of you an evil, Heb 3:12 5100
encourage **o** another day after day, Heb 3:13 1438
any **o** of you may seem to have Heb 4:1 5100
For the **o** who has entered His rest Heb 4:10
so that no **o** will fall, through Heb 4:11 5100
but **O** who has been tempted in all Heb 4:15
no **o** takes the honor to himself, Heb 5:4 5100
the **O** able to save Him from death, Heb 5:7
And we desire that each **o** of you Heb 6:11 1538
He could swear by no **o** greater, Heb 6:13 3762
by **o** greater *than themselves,* Heb 6:16 3173
o which enters within the veil, Heb 6:19
But the **o** whose genealogy is not Heb 7:6
the **o** who had the promises. Heb 7:6
but in that case **o** *receives them,* Heb 7:8
For the **o** concerning whom these Heb 7:13
no **o** has officiated at the altar. Heb 7:13 3762
For, on the **o** hand, there is a Heb 7:18 3303a
through the **O** who said to Him, Heb 7:21
The *former* priests, on the **o** hand, Heb 7:23 3303a
tabernacle prepared, the outer **o**, Heb 9:2 4387
be the death of the **o** who made it. Heb 9:16
while the **o** who made it lives. Heb 9:17
And according to the Law, **o** *may* Heb 9:22
hands, a *mere* copy of the true **o**, Heb 9:24 228
having offered **o** sacrifice for Heb 10:12 1520
For by **o** offering He has perfected Heb 10:14 1520
stimulate **o** another to love and good Heb 10:24 240
but encouraging **o** *another;* Heb 10:25
possession and a lasting **o**. Heb 10:34
RIGHTEOUS **O** SHALL LIVE BY FAITH; Heb 10:38 1342
there was born even of **o** man, Heb 11:12 1520
country, that is, a heavenly **o**. Heb 11:16 2032
which no **o** will see the Lord. Heb 12:14 3762
See to it that no **o** comes short of Heb 12:15 5100
for the **o** who doubts is like the Jas 1:6
Let no **o** say when he is tempted, Jas 1:13 3367
But each **o** is tempted when he is Jas 1:14 1538
But **o** who looks intently at the Jas 1:25
the **o** who is wearing the fine clothes, Jas 2:3
law and yet stumbles in **o** *point,* Jas 2:10 1520
to **o** who has shown no mercy; Jas 2:13
and **o** of you says to them, Jas 2:16 5100
You believe that God is **o**. Jas 2:19 1520
But no **o** can tame the tongue; Jas 3:8 3762, 444
Do not speak against **o** another, Jas 4:11 240
is *only* **o** Lawgiver and Judge, Jas 4:12 1520
the **O** who is able to save and to Jas 4:12
to **o** who knows *the* right thing to Jas 4:17
brethren, against **o** another, Jas 5:9 240
will restore the **o** who is sick, Jas 5:15
confess your sins to **o** another, Jas 5:16 240
another, and pray for **o** another so Jas 5:16 240
the truth and **o** turns him back, Jas 5:19 5100
like the Holy **O** who called you, 1Pe 1:15 40
the **O** who impartially judges 1Pe 1:17
love **o** another from the heart, 1Pe 1:22 240
to a king as the **o** in authority, 1Pe 2:13
For, "THE **O** WHO DESIRES LIFE, TO 1Pe 3:10 3588
in your love for **o** another, 1Pe 4:8 1438
to **o** another without complaint. 1Pe 4:9 240
o has received a *special* gift, 1Pe 4:10 1538
employ it in serving **o** another as 1Pe 4:10 1438
Whoever speaks, *is to do so* as **o** 1Pe 4:11 5613
serves *is to do so* as **o** who 1Pe 4:11 5613
with humility toward **o** another, 1Pe 5:5 240
Greet **o** another with a kiss of love. 1Pe 5:14 240
do not let this **o** *fact* escape your 2Pe 3:8 1520
with the Lord **o** day is like a thousand 2Pe 3:8 1520
and a thousand years like **o** day. 2Pe 3:8 1520
we have fellowship with **o** another, 1Jn 1:7 240
o who says, "I have come to know 1Jn 2:4
the **o** who says he abides in Him 1Jn 2:6
The **o** who says he is in the Light 1Jn 2:9
The **o** who loves his brother abides 1Jn 2:10
But the **o** who hates his brother is 1Jn 2:11
you have overcome the evil **o**. 1Jn 2:13 4190
and you have overcome the evil **o**. 1Jn 2:14 4190
but the **o** who does the will of God 1Jn 2:17
have an anointing from the Holy **O**, 1Jn 2:20 40
Who is the liar but the **o** who 1Jn 2:22
the **o** who denies the Father and 1Jn 2:22
the **o** who confesses the Son has 1Jn 2:23
No **o** who abides in Him sins; 1Jn 3:6 3956

no **o** who sins has seen Him or	**1Jn 3:6**	*3956*
children, make sure no **o** deceives you;	**1Jn 3:7**	*3367*
the **o** who practices righteousness	**1Jn 3:7**	
the **o** who practices sin is of the	**1Jn 3:8**	
No **o** who is born of God practices	**1Jn 3:9**	*3956*
o who does not love his brother.	**1Jn 3:10**	
that we should love **o** another;	**1Jn 3:11**	*240*
as Cain, *who* was of the evil **o** and	**1Jn 3:12**	*4190*
Jesus Christ, and love **o** another,	**1Jn 3:23**	*240*
The **o** who keeps His commandments	**1Jn 3:24**	
Beloved, let us love **o** another,	**1Jn 4:7**	*240*
The **o** who does not love does not	**1Jn 4:8**	
we also ought to love **o** another.	**1Jn 4:11**	*240*
No **o** has seen God at any time;	**1Jn 4:12**	*3762*
if we love **o** another, God abides	**1Jn 4:12**	*240*
and the **o** who abides in love	**1Jn 4:16**	
o who fears is not perfected in love.	**1Jn 4:18**	
for the **o** who does not love his	**1Jn 4:20**	
that the **o** who loves God should	**1Jn 4:21**	
is the **o** who overcomes the world,	**1Jn 5:5**	
This is the **O** who came by water	**1Jn 5:6**	
The **o** who believes in the Son of	**1Jn 5:10**	
the **o** who does not believe God has	**1Jn 5:10**	
that no **o** who is born of God sins;	**1Jn 5:18**	*3956*
and the evil **o** does not touch him.	**1Jn 5:18**	*4190*
lies in *the power of* the evil **o**.	**1Jn 5:19**	*4190*
but the **o** which we have had from	**2Jn 1:5**	
beginning, that we love **o** another.	**2Jn 1:5**	*240*
the **o** who abides in the teaching,	**2Jn 1:9**	
for the **o** who gives him a greeting	**2Jn 1:11**	
The **o** who does good is of God;	**3Jn 1:11**	
the **o** who does evil has not seen	**3Jn 1:11**	
o like a son of man,	**Rv 1:13**	*3664*
and the living **O**;	**Rv 1:18**	
The **O** who holds the seven stars in	**Rv 2:1**	
the **O** who walks among the seven	**Rv 2:1**	
The **O** who has the sharp two-edged	**Rv 2:12**	
My witness, My faithful **o**,	**Rv 2:13**	*4103*
o knows but he who receives it.'	**Rv 2:17**	*3762*
and I will give to each **o** of you	**Rv 2:23**	*1538*
who opens and no **o** will shut,	**Rv 3:7**	*3762*
and who shuts and no **o** opens,	**Rv 3:7**	*3762*
an open door which no **o** can shut,	**Rv 3:8**	*3762*
so that no **o** will take your crown.	**Rv 3:11**	*3367*
and **O** sitting on the throne.	**Rv 4:2**	
each **o** of them having six wings,	**Rv 4:8**	*1520*
And no **o** in heaven or on the	**Rv 5:3**	*3762*
because no **o** was found worthy to	**Rv 5:4**	*3762*
and **o** of the elders said to me,	**Rv 5:5**	*1520*
the Lamb, each **o** holding a harp	**Rv 5:8**	*1538*
Lamb broke **o** of the seven seals,	**Rv 6:1**	*1520*
and I heard **o** of the four living	**Rv 6:1**	*1520*
that *men* would slay **o** another;	**Rv 6:4**	*240*
o hundred and forty-four thousand	**Rv 7:4**	*1540*
multitude which no **o** could count,	**Rv 7:9**	*3762*
Then **o** of the elders answered,	**Rv 7:13**	*1520*
o saying to the sixth angel who	**Rv 9:14**	
they will send gifts to **o** another,	**Rv 11:10**	*240*
be nourished for **o** thousand two	**Rv 12:6**	*5507*
I saw **o** of his heads as if it	**Rv 13:3**	*1520*
no **o** will be able to buy or to sell	**Rv 13:17**	*5100*
except the **o** who has the mark,	**Rv 13:17**	
and with Him **o** hundred and	**Rv 14:1**	*1540*
and no **o** could learn the song	**Rv 14:3**	*3762*
except the **o** hundred and forty-four	**Rv 14:3**	*1540*
And another angel, a second **o**,	**Rv 14:8**	*1208*
Then another angel, a third **o**,	**Rv 14:9**	*5154*
the cloud *was* **o** like a son of man,	**Rv 14:14**	*3664*
the **o** who has power over fire,	**Rv 14:18**	
Then **o** of the four living creatures	**Rv 15:7**	*1520*
and no **o** was able to enter the	**Rv 15:8**	*3762*
who are and who were, O Holy **O**,	**Rv 16:5**	*3741*
Blessed is the **o** who stays awake	**Rv 16:15**	
about **o** hundred pounds each,	**Rv 16:21**	*5006*
Then **o** of the seven angels who had	**Rv 17:1**	*1520*
five have fallen, **o** is,	**Rv 17:10**	*1520*
is himself also an eighth and is **o**	**Rv 17:11**	
kings with the beast for **o** hour.	**Rv 17:12**	*1520*
"These have **o** purpose, and they	**Rv 17:13**	*1520*
in **o** day her plagues will come,	**Rv 18:8**	*1520*
in **o** hour your judgment has come.'	**Rv 18:10**	*1520*
no **o** buys their cargoes any more	**Rv 18:11**	*3762*
for in **o** hour such great wealth	**Rv 18:17**	*1520*
in **o** hour she has been laid waste!'	**Rv 18:19**	*1520*
which no **o** knows except Himself.	**Rv 19:12**	*3762*
Blessed and holy is the **o** who has	**Rv 20:6**	
every **o** *of them* according to their	**Rv 20:13**	*1538*
I will give to the **o** who thirsts	**Rv 21:6**	
Then **o** of the seven angels who had	**Rv 21:9**	*1520*
The **o** who spoke with me had a	**Rv 21:15**	
each **o** of the gates was a single	**Rv 21:21**	*1520*
no **o** who practices abomination and	**Rv 21:27**	
am the **o** who heard and saw these	**Rv 22:8**	
"Let the **o** who does wrong, still	**Rv 22:11**	
and the **o** who is filthy, still be	**Rv 22:11**	
and let the **o** who is righteous, still	**Rv 22:11**	
and the **o** who is holy, still keep	**Rv 22:11**	
And let the **o** who hears say,	**Rv 22:17**	
And let the **o** who is thirsty come;	**Rv 22:17**	
let the **o** who wishes take the	**Rv 22:17**	

ONE-FIFTH

it in full and add to it **o** more.	**Lv 6:5**	2549
add **o** of it to your valuation.	**Lv 27:13**	2549
o of your valuation price to it,	**Lv 27:15**	2549
o of your valuation price to it,	**Lv 27:19**	2549
valuation and add to it **o** of it;	**Lv 27:27**	2549
tithe, he shall add to it **o** of it.	**Lv 27:31**	2549
his wrong and add to it **o** of it,	**Nu 5:7**	2549

ONE-FOURTH

with **o** of a hin of beaten oil,	**Ex 29:40**	7253
and **o** of a hin of wine for a	**Ex 29:40**	7243
mixed with **o** of a hin of oil,	**Nu 15:4**	
wine for the drink offering, **o** of a hin,	**Nu 15:5**	

ONE-HALF

flour mixed with **o** a hin of oil;	**Nu 15:9**	
drink offering **o** a hin of wine	**Nu 15:10**	

ONE'S

were on **o** left at the city gate.	**2Ki 23:8**	376
and he departed with no **o** regret,	**2Ch 21:20**	
So are the children of **o** youth.	**Ps 127:4**	
glory to search out **o** own glory.	**Pr 25:27**	
and to do good in **o** lifetime;	**Ec 3:12**	
and enjoy oneself in all **o** labor	**Ec 5:18**	
And the day of **o** death is better	**Ec 7:1**	
is better than the day of **o** birth.	**Ec 7:1**	
Even like a wife of **o** youth when	**Is 54:6**	
it for bowing **o** head like a reed And	**Is 58:5**	
Then **o** uncle, or his undertaker,	**Am 6:10**	
again, which **o** wife will she be?	**Mk 12:23**	*846*
TO LOVE **O** NEIGHBOR AS HIMSELF,	**Mk 12:33**	
which **o** wife will she be?	**Lk 20:33**	*846*
no **o** silver or gold or clothes.	**Ac 20:33**	*3762*
judges according to each **o** work,	**1Pe 1:17**	*1538*
a matter of **o** own interpretation,	**2Pe 1:20**	*2398*

ONES

all the black **o** among the sheep,	**Gn 30:35**	2345
their little **o** and their wives,	**Gn 34:29**	2945
as well as you and our little **o**.	**Gn 43:8**	2945
your little **o** and for your wives,	**Gn 45:19**	2945
their little **o** and their wives in	**Gn 46:5**	2945
food, according to their little **o**.	**Gn 47:12**	2945
and as food for your little **o**."	**Gn 47:24**	2945
they left only their little **o** and	**Gn 50:8**	2945
for you and your little **o**."	**Gn 50:21**	2945
They were the **o** who spoke to	**Ex 6:27**	
I and my people are the wicked **o**.	**Ex 9:27**	7563
Who are the **o** that are going?"	**Ex 10:8**	
I let you and your little **o** go!	**Ex 10:10**	2945
your little **o** may go with you."	**Ex 10:24**	2945
stone tablets like the former **o**,	**Ex 34:1**	7223
stone tablets like the former **o**,	**Ex 34:4**	7223
These are the **o** who were numbered,	**Nu 1:44**	
they were the **o** who were over the	**Nu 7:2**	
our little **o** will become plunder;	**Nu 14:3**	2945
and their sons and their little **o**.	**Nu 16:27**	2945
"You are the **o** who have caused	**Nu 16:41**	
of Midian and their little **o**;	**Nu 31:9**	2945
every male among the little **o**,	**Nu 31:17**	2945
and cities for our little **o**;	**Nu 32:16**	2945
while our little **o** live in the	**Nu 32:17**	2945
cities for your little **o**,	**Nu 32:24**	2945
"Our little **o**, our wives, our	**Nu 32:26**	2945
your little **o** who you said would	**Dt 1:39**	2945
your little **o** and your livestock	**Dt 3:19**	2945
tablets of stone like the former **o**,	**Dt 10:1**	7223
tablets of stone like the former **o**,	**Dt 10:3**	7223
are the **o** which you shall not eat:	**Dt 14:12**	
the ground, with young **o** or eggs,	**Dt 22:6**	667
your little **o**, your wives, and the	**Dt 29:11**	2945
the midst of ten thousand holy **o**;	**Dt 33:2**	6944
All Your holy **o** are in Your hand,	**Dt 33:3**	6918
"Your wives, your little **o**,	**Jos 1:14**	2945
with the women and the little **o**	**Jos 8:35**	2945
and put the little **o** and the	**Jg 18:21**	2945
with the women and the little **o**.	**Jg 21:10**	2945
"He keeps the feet of His godly **o**,	**1Sa 2:9**	2623
wicked **o** are silenced in darkness;	**1Sa 2:9**	7563
o shamelessly uncovers himself!"	**2Sa 6:20**	7386
the little **o** who *were* with him.	**2Sa 15:22**	2945
little **o** you will dash in pieces,	**2Ki 8:12**	5768
the **o** who came to David at Ziklag,	**1Ch 12:1**	
These are the **o** who crossed the	**1Ch 12:15**	1992a
Sons of Jacob, His chosen **o**!	**1Ch 16:13**	972
"Do not touch My anointed **o**,	**1Ch 16:22**	4899
the great **o** who are in the earth.	**1Ch 17:8**	1419
godly **o** rejoice in what is good.	**2Ch 6:41**	2623
they clothed all their naked **o** from	**2Ch 28:15**	4636
led all their feeble **o** on donkeys,	**2Ch 28:15**	
the sons of Adonikam, the last **o**,	**Ezr 8:13**	314
safe journey for us, our little **o**,	**Ezr 8:21**	2945
dusty rubble even the burned **o**?"	**Ne 4:2**	
which of the holy **o** will you turn?	**Jb 5:1**	6918
And overthrows the secure **o**.	**Jb 12:19**	386
deprives the trusted **o** of speech And	**Jb 12:20**	
He puts no trust in His holy **o**,	**Jb 15:15**	6918
their little **o** like the flock,	**Jb 21:11**	5759
While countless **o** *go* before him.	**Jb 21:33**	
To nobles, 'Wicked **o**';	**Jb 34:18**	7563
"His young **o** also suck up blood;	**Jb 39:30**	667
unfortunate fall by his mighty **o**.	**Ps 10:10**	6099
o in whom is all my delight.	**Ps 16:3**	117
to the LORD, you His godly **o**,	**Ps 30:4**	2623
the LORD, all you His godly **o**!	**Ps 31:23**	2623
LORD and rejoice, you righteous **o**	**Ps 32:11**	6662
in the LORD, O you righteous **o**;	**Ps 33:1**	6662
And does not forsake His godly **o**;	**Ps 37:28**	2623
My loved **o** and my friends stand	**Ps 38:11**	
"Gather My godly **o** to Me, Those	**Ps 50:5**	2623
in the presence of Your godly **o**.	**Ps 52:9**	2623
killed some of their stoutest **o**,	**Ps 78:31**	
flesh of Your godly **o** to the beasts	**Ps 79:2**	2623
together against Your treasured **o**.	**Ps 83:3**	
to His people, to His godly **o**;	**Ps 85:8**	2623
in the assembly of the holy **o**.	**Ps 89:5**	6918
in the council of the holy **o**,	**Ps 89:7**	6918
spoke in vision to Your godly **o**,	**Ps 89:19**	2623
will you understand, stupid **o**?	**Ps 94:8**	3684
the souls of His godly **o**;	**Ps 97:10**	2623
glad in the LORD, you righteous **o**,	**Ps 97:12**	6662
O sons of Jacob, His chosen **o**!	**Ps 105:6**	972
"Do not touch My anointed **o**,	**Ps 105:15**	4899
His chosen **o** with a joyful shout.	**Ps 105:43**	972
the prosperity of Your chosen **o**,	**Ps 106:5**	972
LORD Is the death of His godly **o**.	**Ps 116:15**	2623
brought back the captive **o** of Zion,	**Ps 126:1**	
And let Your godly **o** sing for joy.	**Ps 132:9**	2623
godly **o** will sing aloud for joy.	**Ps 132:16**	2623
who seizes and dashes your little **o**	**Ps 137:9**	5768
And Your godly **o** shall bless You.	**Ps 145:10**	2623
Praise for all His godly **o**;	**Ps 148:14**	2623
the congregation of the godly **o**.	**Ps 149:1**	2623
He will beautify the afflicted **o** with	**Ps 149:4**	6035
Let the godly **o** exult in glory;	**Ps 149:5**	2623
is an honor for all His godly **o**.	**Ps 149:9**	2623
"How long, O naive **o**,	**Pr 1:22**	6612a
preserves the way of His godly **o**.	**Pr 2:8**	2623
"O naive **o**, understand prudence;	**Pr 8:5**	6612a
And decides between the mighty **o**.	**Pr 18:18**	
and even the **o** who will come later	**Ec 4:16**	314
the grinding **o** stand idle because	**Ec 12:3**	
repentant **o** with righteousness.	**Is 1:27**	
And your mighty **o** in battle.	**Is 3:25**	1369
But it produced *only* worthless **o**.	**Is 5:2**	891
grapes did it produce worthless **o**?	**Is 5:4**	891
desolate, *Even* great and fine **o**,	**Is 5:9**	2896a
take away the rights of the **o** who	**Is 5:23**	
assemble the banished **o** of Israel,	**Is 11:12**	
I have commanded My consecrated **o**,	**Is 13:3**	
warriors, My proudly exulting **o**,	**Is 13:3**	5947
Their little **o** also will be dashed	**Is 13:16**	5768
the multitude of the ruthless **o** like	**Is 29:5**	6184
And young bulls with strong **o**;	**Is 34:7**	47
restore the preserved **o** of Israel;	**Is 49:6**	
Even My chosen **o** shall inherit it,	**Is 65:9**	972
name for a curse to My chosen **o**,	**Is 65:15**	972
And My chosen **o** will wear out the	**Is 65:22**	972
and the **o** who dwell in the land of	**Jer 24:8**	
"For I satisfy the weary **o** and	**Jer 31:25**	5315
your mighty **o** become prostrate?	**Jer 46:15**	47
Her little **o** have sounded out a	**Jer 48:4**	6810
even the little **o** of the flock;	**Jer 49:20**	6810
even the little **o** of the flock;	**Jer 50:45**	6810
Her little **o** have gone away As	**La 1:5**	5768
The **o** whom You commanded	**La 1:10**	
the **o** round about him should be his	**La 1:17**	
When little **o** and infants faint In	**La 2:11**	5768
the life of your little **o** Who are faint	**La 2:19**	5768
little **o** who were born healthy?	**La 2:20**	5768
The little **o** ask for bread, *But* no	**La 4:4**	5768
o were purer than snow,	**La 4:7**	5139
the pride of the strong **o** cease,	**Ezk 7:24**	5794
and officials, the **o** near,	**Ezk 23:12**	7138
o stand *erect* in their height.	**Ezk 31:14**	
"By the swords of the mighty **o** I	**Ezk 32:12**	1368
"The strong among the mighty **o**	**Ezk 32:21**	1368
and middle **o** in the building.	**Ezk 42:5**	8484
more than the lower and middle **o**.	**Ezk 42:6**	8484
You shall say to the rebellious **o**,	**Ezk 44:6**	4805
is a command of the holy **o**,	**Da 4:17**	6922
o and will subdue three kings.	**Da 7:24**	6933
the violent **o** among your people	**Da 11:14**	1121, 6530
slay the precious **o** of their womb.	**Hos 9:16**	4261
little **o** will be dashed in pieces,	**Hos 13:16**	5768
Bring down, O LORD, Your mighty **o**.	**Jl 3:11**	1368
My worshipers, My dispersed **o**,	**Zph 3:10**	
your midst Your proud, exulting **o**,	**Zph 3:11**	5947
"These are the two anointed **o** who	**Zch 4:14**	1121
the white **o** go forth after them,	**Zch 6:6**	3836
o go forth to the south country.	**Zch 6:6**	1261
"When the strong **o** went out, they	**Zch 6:7**	554
turn My hand against the little **o**.	**Zch 13:7**	
come, *and* all the holy **o** with Him!	**Zch 14:5**	6918
gives to one of these little **o** even a	**Mt 10:42**	*3398*
these little **o** who believe in Me	**Mt 18:6**	*3398*
not despise one of these little **o**,	**Mt 18:10**	*3398*
that one of these little **o** perish.	**Mt 18:14**	*3398*
he said to Him, "Which **o**?"	**Mt 19:18**	*4169*
'Depart from Me, accursed **o**,	**Mt 25:41**	
"These are the **o** who are	**Mk 4:15**	
these are the **o** on whom seed was	**Mk 4:16**	
"And others are the **o** on whom	**Mk 4:18**	
are the **o** who have heard the word,	**Mk 4:18**	
"And those are the **o** on whom seed	**Mk 4:20**	
little **o** who believe to stumble,	**Mk 9:42**	*3398*
these are the **o** who have heard,	**Lk 8:14**	
these are the **o** who have heard the	**Lk 8:15**	
"You foolish **o**, did not He who	**Lk 11:40**	*878*
down my barns and build larger **o**,	**Lk 12:18**	*3173*
one of these little **o** to stumble.	**Lk 17:2**	*3398*
one, beginning with the older **o**,	**Jn 8:9**	*4245*
I know the **o** I have chosen;	**Jn 13:18**	*5100*
the very **o** who are now His	**Ac 13:31**	*3748*
from the **o** who live in error,	**2Pe 2:18**	
with many thousands of His holy **o**,	**Jude 1:14**	*40*
are the **o** who cause divisions,	**Jude 1:19**	
"These are the **o** who come out of	**Rv 7:14**	
These are the **o** who have not been	**Rv 14:4**	
These *are* the **o** who follow the	**Rv 14:4**	

ONESELF

to drink and enjoy **o** in all one's	**Ec 5:18**	
blanket is too small to wrap **o** in.	**Is 28:20**	
to keep **o** unstained by the world.	**Jas 1:27**	*1438*

ONESIMUS
and with him **O**, *our* faithful and — **Col 4:9** *3682*
appeal to you for my child **O**, — **Phm 1:10** *3682*

ONESIPHORUS
Lord grant mercy to the house of **O** — **2Tm 1:16** *3683*
Aquila, and the household of **O**. — **2Tm 4:19** *3683*

ONE-TENTH
and there *shall be* **o** *of an ephah* — **Ex 29:40** 6241
and **o** *of an ephah* of fine flour — **Lv 14:21** 259
her **o** of an ephah of barley meal; — **Nu 5:15** 6224
offering of **o** *of an ephah* of fine flour — **Nu 15:4**
and **o** for each of the seven lambs. — **Nu 29:4** 259

ONE-THIRD
mixed with **o** of a hin of oil; — **Nu 15:6**
you shall offer **o** of a hin of wine — **Nu 15:7**

ONIONS
leeks and the **o** and the garlic, — **Nu 11:5** 1211

ONLY
his heart was **o** evil continually. — **Gn 6:5** 7534
and **o** Noah was left, together with — **Gn 7:23** 389
"**O** you shall not eat flesh with — **Gn 9:4** 389
and I shall speak **o** this once; — **Gn 18:32** 389
o do nothing to these men, — **Gn 19:8** 7534
"Take now your son, your **o** son, — **Gn 22:2** 3173
not withheld your son, your **o** son, — **Gn 22:12** 3173
not withheld your son, your **o** son, — **Gn 22:16** 3173
"If you will **o** please listen to me; — **Gn 23:13** 389
o do not take my son back there." — **Gn 24:8** 7534
o obey my voice, and go, get *them* — **Gn 27:13** 389
"Do you have **o** one blessing, my — **Gn 27:38**
for with my staff **o** I crossed — **Gn 32:10**
"**O** on this *condition* will we — **Gn 34:15** 389
"**O** on this *condition* will the men — **Gn 34:22** 389
O let us consent to them, and they — **Gn 34:23** 389
"**O** keep me in mind when it goes — **Gn 40:14**
3588, 518
o in the throne I will be greater — **Gn 41:40** 7534
O the land of the priests he did — **Gn 47:22** 7534
o the land of the priests did not — **Gn 47:26** 7534
they left **o** their little ones and — **Gn 50:8** 7534
they may be left **o** in the Nile?" — **Ex 8:9** 7534
they will be left **o** in the Nile." — **Ex 8:11** 7534
o you shall not go very far away. — **Ex 8:28** 7534
o do not let Pharaoh deal — **Ex 8:29** 7534
O in the land of Goshen, where the — **Ex 9:26** 7534
please forgive my sin **o** this once, — **Ex 10:17** 389
o remove this death from me." — **Ex 10:17** 7534
o let your flocks and your herds — **Ex 10:24** 7534
shall **o** pay for his loss of time, — **Ex 21:19** 7534
for that is his **o** covering; — **Ex 22:27** 905
it is **o** a scab. And he shall — **Lv 13:6**
it is **o** the scar of the boil; — **Lv 13:23**
for it is **o** the scar of the burn. — **Lv 13:28**
o he shall not go in to the veil — **Lv 21:23** 389
"**O** the tribe of Levi you shall — **Nu 1:49** 389
"Yet if **o** one is blown, then — **Nu 10:4**
indeed spoken **o** through Moses? — **Nu 12:2**
7534, 389
"**O** do not rebel against the LORD; — **Nu 14:9** 389
"**O** the Levites shall perform the — **Nu 18:23**
"If **o** we had perished when our — **Nu 20:3** 3863
Let me **o** pass through on my feet, — **Nu 20:19** 7534
but **o** the word which I speak to — **Nu 22:20** 389
but you shall speak **o** the word — **Nu 22:35** 657
o see the extreme end of them and — **Nu 23:13** 657
had no sons, but **o** daughters; — **Nu 26:33** 518
o the gold and the silver, the — **Nu 31:22** 389
o they must marry within the — **Nu 36:6** 389
I will travel **o** on the highway; — **Dt 2:27**
o let me pass through on foot, — **Dt 2:28** 7534
"We took **o** the animals as our — **Dt 2:35** 7534
"**O** you did not go near to the — **Dt 2:37** 7534
(For **o** Og king of Bashan was left — **Dt 3:11** 7534
"**O** give heed to yourself and keep — **Dt 4:9** 7534
but you saw no form—**o** a voice. — **Dt 4:12** 2108
"You shall fear **o** the LORD — **Dt 6:13**
"**O** you shall not eat the blood; — **Dt 12:16** 7534
"**O** be sure not to eat the blood, — **Dt 12:23** 7534
"**O** your holy things which you may — **Dt 12:26** 7534
if **o** you listen obediently to the — **Dt 15:5** 7534
"**O** you shall not eat its blood; — **Dt 15:23** 7534
"Justice, *and* **o** justice, you — **Dt 16:20**
"**O** the women and the children and — **Dt 20:14** 7534
"**O** in the cities of these peoples — **Dt 20:16** 7534
"**O** the trees which you know are — **Dt 20:20** 7534
then **o** the man who lies with her — **Dt 22:25** 905
tail, and you **o** will be above, — **Dt 28:13** 7534
but you shall **o** be oppressed and — **Dt 28:29** 389
"**O** be strong and very courageous; — **Jos 1:7** 7534
o may the LORD your God be with — **Jos 1:17** 7534
o be strong and courageous." — **Jos 1:18** 7534
o on that day they marched around — **Jos 6:15** 7534
o Rahab the harlot and all who are — **Jos 6:17** 7534
o keep yourselves from the things — **Jos 6:18** 7534
O the silver and gold, and articles — **Jos 6:24** 7534
o about two or three thousand men — **Jos 7:3**
o to deliver us into the hand of — **Jos 7:7**
If **o** we had been willing to dwell — **Jos 7:7** 3863
you shall take **o** its spoil and its — **Jos 8:2** 7534
Israel took **o** the cattle and the — **Jos 8:27** 7534
o in Gaza, in Gath, and in Ashdod — **Jos 11:22** 7534
o allot it to Israel for an — **Jos 13:6** 7534
O to the tribe of Levi he did not — **Jos 13:14** 7534
had no sons, **o** daughters; — **Jos 17:3**
3588, 518
"Why have you given me **o** one lot — **Jos 17:14**
you shall not have one lot **o**, — **Jos 17:17**
"**O** be very careful to observe the — **Jos 22:5** 7534

O do not rebel against the LORD, — **Jos 22:19**
o in order that the generations of — **Jg 3:2** 7534
"He is **o** relieving himself in the — **Jg 3:24** 389
If there is dew on the fleece **o**, — **Jg 6:37** 905
let it now be dry **o** on the fleece, — **Jg 6:39** 905
for it was dry **o** on the fleece, — **Jg 6:40** 905
lives, if **o** you had let them live, — **Jg 8:19** 3863
o please deliver us this day." — **Jg 10:15** 389
Now she was his one *and* **o** child; — **Jg 11:34** 7534
"You **o** hate me, and you do not — **Jg 14:16** 7534
O let me *take care of* all your — **Jg 19:20** 7534
her heart, **o** her lips were moving, — **1Sa 1:13** 7534
o may the LORD confirm His word." — **1Sa 1:23** 389
boiled meat from you, **o** raw." — **1Sa 2:15**
3588, 518
o the trunk of Dagon was left to — **1Sa 5:4** 7534
"**O** fear the LORD and serve Him in — **1Sa 12:24** 389
if **o** the people had eaten freely — **1Sa 14:30**
o be a valiant man for me and — **1Sa 18:17** 389
o Jonathan and David knew about — **1Sa 20:39** 389
if **o** the young men have kept — **1Sa 21:4** 389
are dead,' for **o** Amnon is dead." — **2Sa 13:33** 905
"You came **o** yesterday, — **2Sa 15:20**
O hand him over, and I will depart — **2Sa 20:21** 905
after him **o** to strip *the slain.* — **2Sa 23:10** 389
o the two of us in the house. — **1Ki 3:18** 2108
the **o** deputy who *was* in the land. — **1Ki 4:19** 259
if **o** your sons take heed to their — **1Ki 8:25** 7534
to do **o** that which was right in My — **1Ki 14:8** 7534
o a handful of flour in the bowl — **1Ki 17:12**
3588, 518
until in Kir-hareseth **o** they left — **2Ki 3:25**
o the horses tied and the donkeys — **2Ki 7:10**
3588, 518
but **o** the worshipers of Baal." — **2Ki 10:23** 905
O the high places were not taken — **2Ki 12:3** 7534
But now you shall strike Aram **o** — **2Ki 13:19**
O the high places were not taken — **2Ki 14:4** 7534
O the high places were not taken — **2Ki 15:4** 7534
O the high places were not taken — **2Ki 15:35** 7534
o not as the kings of Israel who — **2Ki 17:2** 7534
(but *they are* **o** empty words), — **2Ki 18:20** 389
"Has my master sent me **o** to your — **2Ki 18:27**
if **o** they will observe to do — **2Ki 21:8** 7534
"**O** no accounting shall be made — **2Ki 22:7** 389
Sheshan had no sons, **o** daughters. — **1Ch 2:34**
3588, 518
When they were **o** a few in number, — **1Ch 16:19**
"**O** the LORD give you discretion — **1Ch 22:12** 389
and had no sons, but daughters **o**, — **1Ch 23:22** 518
if **o** your sons take heed to their — **2Ch 6:16** 7534
"With him is **o** an arm of flesh, — **2Ch 32:8**
God left him *alone* **o** to test him, — **2Ch 32:31**
if **o** they will observe to do all — **2Ch 33:8** 7534
although **o** to the LORD their God. — **2Ch 33:17** 7534
O Jonathan the son of Asahel and — **Ezr 10:15** 389
Vashti has wronged not **o** the king — **Es 1:16** 905
if we had **o** been sold as slaves, — **Es 7:4**
For Mordecai the Jew was second **o** — **Es 10:3**
o do not put forth your hand on — **Jb 1:12** 7534
in your power, **o** spare his life." — **Jb 2:6** 389
"For we are **o** of yesterday — **Jb 8:9**
"**O** two things do not do to me, — **Jb 13:20** 389
And he mourns **o** for himself." — **Jb 14:22**
And I have escaped **o** by the skin — **Jb 19:20**
My **o** *life* from the power of the — **Ps 22:20** 3173
ravages, My **o** *life* from the lions. — **Ps 35:17** 3173
not fret; *it leads* **o** to evildoing. — **Ps 37:8** 389
Against You, You **o**, I have sinned — **Ps 51:4** 905
soul *waits* in silence for God **o**; — **Ps 62:1** 389
He **o** is my rock and my salvation, — **Ps 62:2** 389
counseled **o** to thrust him down — **Ps 62:4** 389
soul, wait in silence for God **o**, — **Ps 62:5** 389
He **o** is my rock and my salvation, — **Ps 62:6** 389
Men of low degree are **o** vanity and — **Ps 62:9** 389
O the rebellious dwell in a — **Ps 68:6** 389
You will **o** look on with your eyes And — **Ps 91:8** 7534
It *was* **o** that they might be — **Ps 92:7**
they were **o** a few men in number, — **Ps 105:12**
o son in the sight of my mother, — **Pr 4:3** 3173
desire of the righteous is **o** good, — **Pr 11:23** 389
due, *and yet it results* **o** in want. — **Pr 11:24** 389
a lying tongue is **o** for a moment. — **Pr 12:19** 5704
But mere talk *leads* **o** to poverty. — **Pr 14:23** 389
A rebellious man seeks **o** evil, — **Pr 17:11** 389
But **o** in revealing his own mind. — **Pr 18:2** 518
you will **o** have to do it again. — **Pr 19:19**
the rich, *will* **o** *come to* poverty. — **Pr 22:16** 389
Have you found honey? Eat **o** what — **Pr 25:16**
"Behold, I have found **o** this, — **Ec 7:29** 905
She is her mother's **o** *daughter;* — **SS 6:9** 259
O bruises, welts and raw wounds, — **Is 1:6**
o let us be called by your name; — **Is 4:1** 7534
But it produced **o** worthless ones. — **Is 5:2**
ten acres of vineyard will yield **o** — **Is 5:10**
O a remnant within them will — **Is 10:22**
They could **o** whisper a prayer, — **Is 26:16**
o to wind. We could not — **Is 26:18**
for the war are **o** empty words.' — **Is 36:5** 389
sent me **o** to your master and to you — **Is 36:12**
'**O** in the LORD are righteousness — **Is 45:24** 389
"If **o** you had paid attention to — **Is 48:18** 3863
will be like today, **o** more so." — **Is 56:12**
'**O** acknowledge your iniquity, That — **Jer 3:13** 389
"They are **o** the poor, They are — **Jer 5:4** 389
whose midst there is **o** oppression. — **Jer 6:6** 3605
Mourn as for an **o** son, A — **Jer 6:26** 3173
birth **o** to abandon *her young,* — **Jer 14:5**

o upon your own dishonest gain, — **Jer 22:17**
3588, 518
"**O** know for certain that if you — **Jer 26:15** 389
O I will not destroy you — **Jer 30:11** 389
sons of Judah have been doing **o** evil — **Jer 32:30** 389
sons of Israel have been **o** provoking — **Jer 32:30** 389
"We have **o** dwelt in tents, and — **Jer 35:10**
and there were **o** wounded men left — **Jer 37:10**
there was no water but **o** mud, — **Jer 38:6** 518
For you have **o** deceived — **Jer 42:20**
They would destroy **o** until they — **Jer 49:9**
And the nations become exhausted **o** — **Jer 51:58**
own righteousness they could **o** — **Ezk 14:14**
They would deliver **o** themselves by — **Ezk 14:20**
Because they have been **o** a — **Ezk 29:6**
'Abraham was **o** one, yet he — **Ezk 33:24**
with **o** the wall between Me — **Ezk 43:8**
o trim *the hair of* their heads. — **Ezk 44:20** 3697
inheritance *shall be* **o** his sons'; — **Ezk 46:17** 389
me, there is **o** one decree for you. — **Da 2:9**
if **o** the dream applied to those — **Da 4:19**
against strongholds, but **o** for a time. — **Da 11:24**
And there is **o** hostility in — **Hos 9:8**
"You **o** have I chosen among all — **Am 3:2** 7534
a time of mourning for an **o** son, — **Am 8:10** 3173
Would they not steal **o** until — **Ob 1:5**
measures, there would be **o** ten; — **Hg 2:16**
there would be **o** twenty. — **Hg 2:16**
for while I was **o** a little angry, — **Zch 1:15**
Him, as one mourns for an **o** son, — **Zch 12:10** 3173
that day the LORD will be *the* **o** — **Zch 14:9**
and His name *the* **o** one. — **Zch 14:9**
not **o** are the doers of wickedness — **Mal 3:15** 1571
YOUR GOD, AND SERVE HIM **O**.' " — **Mt 4:10** *3441*
"If you greet **o** your brothers, — **Mt 5:47** *3440*
"If I **o** touch His garment, I — **Mt 9:21** *3440*
casts out demons **o** by Beelzebul — **Mt 12:24**
3756, 1487, 3361
but is **o** temporary, and when — **Mt 13:21**
here **o** five loaves and two fish." — **Mt 14:17**
3756, 1487, 3361
"I was sent **o** to the lost sheep — **Mt 15:24**
3756, 1487, 3361
but **o** those to whom it has been — **Mt 19:11**
There is **o** One who is good; — **Mt 19:17**
men have worked **o** one hour, — **Mt 20:12**
nothing on it except leaves **o**; — **Mt 21:19** *3440*
not **o** do what was done to the fig — **Mt 21:21** *3440*
but are **o** temporary; then, when — **Mk 4:17**
be afraid *any longer,* **o** believe." — **Mk 5:36** *3440*
LORD YOUR GOD AND SERVE HIM **O**.' " — **Lk 4:8** *3441*
none of them, but **o** to Zarephath, — **Lk 4:26**
1487, 3361
but **o** Naaman the Syrian." — **Lk 4:27**
1487, 3361
out, the **o** son of his mother, — **Lk 7:12** *3439*
for he had an **o** daughter, about — **Lk 8:42** *3439*
o believe, and she will be made — **Lk 8:50** *3440*
at my son, for he is my **o** *boy,* — **Lk 9:38** *3439*
and **o** with difficulty does it leave — **Lk 9:39** *3433*
but **o** one thing is necessary, — **Lk 10:42**
we have done **o** that which we — **Lk 17:10**
in, he saw the linen wrappings **o**; — **Lk 24:12** *3441*
"Are You the **o** one visiting — **Lk 24:18** *3441*
glory as of the **o** begotten from the — **Jn 1:14** *3439*
the **o** begotten God who is in the — **Jn 1:18** *3439*
that He gave His **o** begotten Son, — **Jn 3:16** *3439*
name of the **o** begotten Son of God. — **Jn 3:18** *3439*
He not **o** was breaking the Sabbath, — **Jn 5:18** *3440*
that is from the *one and* **o** God? — **Jn 5:44** *3441*
"The thief comes **o** to steal and — **Jn 10:10**
3756, 1487, 3361
and not for the nation **o**, — **Jn 11:52** *3440*
they came, not for Jesus' sake **o**, — **Jn 12:9** *3440*
"Lord, *then wash* not **o** my feet, — **Jn 13:9** *3440*
bathed needs **o** to wash his feet, — **Jn 13:10**
3756, 1487, 3361
may know You, the **o** true God, — **Jn 17:3** *3441*
but **o**, "If I want him to remain — **Jn 21:23**
for it is **o** the third hour of — **Ac 2:15**
o with the baptism of John; — **Ac 18:25** *3440*
and hear that not **o** in Ephesus, — **Ac 19:26** *3440*
"Not **o** is there danger that — **Ac 19:27** *3440*
For I am ready not **o** to be bound, — **Ac 21:13** *3440*
not **o** did I lock up many of the — **Ac 26:10**
2532, 5037
a witness not **o** to the things which — **Ac 26:16** *5037*
a short or long time, not **o** you, — **Ac 26:29** *3440*
not **o** of the cargo and the ship, — **Ac 27:10** *3440*
but **o** of the ship. — **Ac 27:22**
of death, they not **o** do the same, — **Ro 1:32** *3440*
Or is God *the God* of Jews **o**? — **Ro 3:29** *3440*
who not **o** are of the circumcision, — **Ro 4:12** *3440*
not **o** to those who are of the Law, — **Ro 4:16** *3440*
not for his sake **o** was it written that — **Ro 4:23** *3440*
And not **o** this, but we also exult — **Ro 5:3** *3440*
And not **o** this, but we also exult — **Ro 5:11** *3440*
And not **o** this, but also we — **Ro 8:23** *3440*
And not **o** this, but there was — **Ro 9:10** *3440*
called, not from among Jews **o**, — **Ro 9:24** *3440*
not **o** because of wrath, — **Ro 13:5** *3440*
he who is weak eats vegetables **o**. — **Ro 14:2**
to whom not **o** do I give thanks, — **Ro 16:4** *3441*
to the **o** wise God, through Jesus — **Ro 16:27** *3441*
Now God has not **o** raised the Lord, — **1Co 6:14** *2532*
O, as the Lord has assigned to — **1Co 7:17**
1487, 3361
to whom she wishes, **o** in the Lord. — **1Co 7:39** *3440*
Or do **o** Barnabas and I not have a — **1Co 9:6** *3441*

but **o** one receives the prize? **1Co 9:24**
if you bless in the spirit **o**, **1Co 14:16**
Or has it come to you **o**? **1Co 14:36** *3441*
hoped in Christ in this life **o**, **1Co 15:19** *3440*
and not **o** by his coming, but also **2Co 7:7** *3440*
you sorrow, though **o** for a while **2Co 7:8** *2532*
begin a year ago not **o** to do *this,* **2Co 8:10** *3440*
For he not **o** accepted our appeal, **2Co 8:17** *3303a*
and not **o** *this,* but he has also **2Co 8:19** *3440*
not **o** in the sight of the Lord, **2Co 8:21** *3440*
this service is not **o** fully supplying **2Co 9:12** *3440*
but **o** for the truth. **2Co 13:8**
o there are some who are **Ga 1:7** *1487, 3361*
but **o**, they kept hearing, **Ga 1:23** *3440*
They **o** *asked* us to remember the **Ga 2:10** *3440*
This is the **o** thing I want to find **Ga 3:2** *3441*
even though it is **o** a man's **Ga 3:15**
a mediator is not for one *party* **o**; **Ga 3:20**
whereas God is **o** one. **Ga 3:20**
not **o** when I am present with you. **Ga 4:18** *3440*
o *do* not *turn* your freedom into an **Ga 5:13** *3440*
that is named, not **o** in this age but **Eph 1:21** *3440*
but **o** such *a word* as is good for **Eph 4:29** *1487*
For it is **o** right for me to feel **Php 1:7** *2531a*
O that in every way, whether in **Php 1:18** *4133*
O conduct yourselves in a manner **Php 1:27** *3440*
sake, not **o** to believe in Him, **Php 1:29** *3440*
obeyed, not as in my presence **o**, **Php 2:12** *3440*
and not on him **o** but also on me, **Php 2:27** *3441*
these are the **o** fellow workers for **Col 4:11** *3441*
did not come to you in word **o**, **1Th 1:5** *3440*
not **o** in Macedonia and Achaia, **1Th 1:8** *3440*
impart to you not **o** the gospel of God **1Th 2:8** *3440*
as is **o** fitting, because your **2Th 1:3**
For after all it is **o** just for **2Th 1:6**
o he who now restrains *will do so* **2Th 2:7** *3440*
immortal, invisible, the **o** God, **1Tm 1:17** *3441*
Deacons must be husbands of **o** one **1Tm 3:12**
fables fit **o** for old women. **1Tm 4:7** *1126*
discipline is **o** of little profit, **1Tm 4:8**
A widow is to be put on the list **o** **1Tm 5:9**
is the blessed and **o** Sovereign, **1Tm 6:15** *3441*
are not **o** gold and silver vessels, **2Tm 2:20** *3440*
and not **o** to me, but also to all **2Tm 4:8** *3440*
O Luke is with me. **2Tm 4:11** *3441*
For everyone who partakes **o** of **Heb 5:13**
second, **o** the high priest *enters* **Heb 9:7** *3441*
since they *relate* **o** to food and **Heb 9:10** *3440*
For a covenant is valid **o** when **Heb 9:17**
For the Law, since it has **o** a **Heb 10:1**
offering up his **o** begotten *son;* **Heb 11:17** *3439*
I WILL SHAKE NOT **O** THE EARTH, **Heb 12:26** *3440*
There is **o** one Lawgiver and Judge, **Jas 4:12**
not **o** to those who are good and **1Pe 2:18** *3440*
and not for ours **o**, **1Jn 2:2** *3440*
that God has sent His **o** begotten **1Jn 4:9** *3439*
not with the water **o**, **1Jn 5:6** *3440*
and not **o** I, but also all who know **2Jn 1:1** *3441*
and deny our **o** Master and Lord, **Jude 1:4** *3441*
to the **o** God our Savior, through **Jude 1:25** *3441*
but **o** the men who do not have the **Rv 9:4** *1487, 3361*
knowing that he has **o** a short **Rv 12:12**
but **o** those whose names are **Rv 21:27** *1487, 3361*

ONO
and Shemed, who built **O** and Lod, **1Ch 8:12** 207
the sons of Lod, Hadid and **O**, **Ezr 2:33** 207
at Chephirim in the plain of **O**." **Ne 6:2** 207
the sons of Lod, Hadid and **O**, **Ne 7:37** 207
Lod and **O**, the valley of craftsmen. **Ne 11:35** 207

ONSLAUGHT
the **o** of the wicked when it comes; **Pr 3:25** 7724b
those who repel the **o** at the gate. **Is 28:6** 4421

ONTO
vomited Jonah up **o** the dry land. **Jon 2:10** 413
And he went out **o** the porch, **Mk 14:68** *1519*
when He came out **o** the land, **Lk 8:27** *1909*
drive the ship **o** it if they could. **Ac 27:39** *1856*

ONWARD
their ornaments, from Mount Horeb **o**. **Ex 33:6**
and **o** throughout your generations, **Nu 15:23** 1973
Benjamin also *lived* from Geba **o**, **Ne 11:31**
LORD their God from that day **o**. **Ezk 39:22** 1973
be that on the eighth day and **o**, **Ezk 43:27** 1973
now, do consider from this day **o**: **Hg 2:15** 4605
'Do consider from this day **o**, **Hg 2:18** 4605
from Samuel and *his* successors **o**, **Ac 3:24** *2517*
waiting from that time **o** UNTIL HIS **Heb 10:13** *3062*

ONYCHA
spices, stacte and **o** and galbanum, **Ex 30:34** 7827

ONYX
and the **o** stone are there. **Gn 2:12** 7718
o stones and setting stones for **Ex 25:7** 7718
"You shall take two **o** stones **Ex 28:9** 7718
row a beryl and an **o** and a jasper; **Ex 28:20** 7718
and **o** stones and setting stones for **Ex 35:9** 7718
The rulers brought the **o** **Ex 35:27** 7718
They made the **o** stones, **Ex 39:6** 7718
and the fourth row, a beryl, an **o**, **Ex 39:13** 7718
wood, **o** stones and inlaid *stones,* **1Ch 29:2** 7718
the gold of Ophir, In precious **o**, **Jb 28:16** 7718
The beryl, the **o** and the jasper; **Ezk 28:13** 7718

OPEN
in the **o** expanse of the heavens." **Gn 1:20** 6440
fountains of the great deep burst **o**, **Gn 7:11** 1234
and the land shall be **o** before **Gn 34:10**
bird go free over the **o** field. **Lv 14:7** 6440
outside the city into the **o** field. **Lv 14:53** 6440
were sacrificing in the **o** field, **Lv 17:5** 6440
shall be considered as **o** fields; **Lv 25:31** 776
are *they* like **o** camps or with **Nu 13:19**
ground that was under them split **o**; **Nu 16:31** 1234
'Every **o** vessel, which has no **Nu 19:15** 6605a
anyone who in the **o** field touches **Nu 19:16** 6440
booty into the middle of its **o** square **Dt 13:16** 7339
shall freely **o** your hand to him, **Dt 15:8** 6605a
o your hand to your brother, **Dt 15:11** 6605a
person is found lying in the **o** country **Dt 21:1**
o for you His good storehouse, **Dt 28:12** 6605a
"**O** the mouth of the cave and **Jos 10:22** 6605a
o the doors of the roof chamber. **Jg 3:25** 6605a
down in the **o** square of the city, **Jg 19:15** 7339
in the **o** square of the city; **Jg 19:17** 7339
spend the night in the **o** square." **Jg 19:20** 7339
lord are camping in the **o** field. **2Sa 11:11** 6440
from the **o** square of Beth-shan, **2Sa 21:12** 7339
the shape of gourds and **o** flowers; **1Ki 6:18** 6362
palm trees, and **o** flowers, **1Ki 6:29** 6362
palm trees, and **o** flowers, **1Ki 6:32** 6362
palm trees, and **o** flowers; **1Ki 6:35** 6362
that Your eyes may be **o** toward **1Ki 8:29** 6605a
that Your eyes may be **o** to the **1Ki 8:52** 6605a
o his eyes that he may see." **2Ki 6:17** 6491b
"O LORD, **o** the eyes of these *men,* **2Ki 6:20** 6491b
Then **o** the door and flee and do **2Ki 9:3** 6605a
"**O** the window toward the east," **2Ki 13:17** 6605a
because they did not **o** *to him;* **2Ki 15:16** 6605a
o Your eyes, O LORD, and see; **2Ki 19:16** 6491b
that Your eye may be **o** toward **2Ch 6:20** 6605a
I pray, let Your eyes be **o** **2Ch 6:40** 6605a
"Now My eyes will be **o** and My **2Ch 7:15** 6605a
and to plunder and to **o** shame, **Ezr 9:7** 6440
and all the people sat in the **o** **Ezr 10:9** 7339
we are not able to stand in the **o**. **Ezr 10:13** 2351
and Your eyes **o** to hear the prayer **Ne 1:6** 6605a
time with an **o** letter in his hand. **Ne 6:5** 6605a
o them until after the sabbath. **Ne 13:19** 6605a
speak, And **o** His lips against you, **Jb 11:5** 6605a
also **o** Your eyes on him **Jb 14:3** 6491b
mercy He splits my kidneys **o**; **Jb 16:13** 6398
Let me **o** my lips and answer. **Jb 32:20** 6605a
"Behold now, I **o** my mouth, My **Jb 33:2** 6605a
they grow up in the **o** field; **Jb 39:4** 1253b
"Who can **o** the doors of his face? **Jb 41:14** 6605a
Their throat is an **o** grave; **Ps 5:9** 6605a
They **o** wide their mouth at me, As **Ps 22:13** 6475
the righteous And His ears are **o** **Ps 34:15**
mute man who does not **o** his mouth. **Ps 38:13** 6605a
become mute, I do not **o** my mouth, **Ps 39:9** 6605a
O Lord, **o** my lips, That my mouth **Ps 51:15** 6605a
land quake, You have split it **o**; **Ps 60:2** 6480
broke **o** springs and torrents; **Ps 74:15** 1234
You have held my eyelids **o**; I am **Ps 77:4**
I will **o** my mouth in a parable; **Ps 78:2** 6605a
O your mouth wide and I will fill **Ps 81:10** 7337
You **o** Your hand, they are **Ps 104:28** 6605a
O to me the gates of righteousness; **Ps 118:19** 6605a
O my eyes, that I may behold **Ps 119:18** 1540
one plows and breaks **o** the earth, **Ps 141:7** 1234
You **o** Your hand And **Ps 145:16** 6605a
Sheol and Abaddon *lie* **o** before **Pr 15:11**
O your eyes, *and* you will be **Pr 20:13** 6491b
does not **o** his mouth in the gate. **Pr 24:7** 6605a
A lion is in the **o** square!" **Pr 26:13** 7339
Better is **o** rebuke Than love that **Pr 27:5** 1540
O your mouth for the mute, For the **Pr 31:8** 6605a
O your mouth, judge righteously, **Pr 31:9** 6605a
"**O** to me, my sister, my darling, **SS 5:2** 6605a
"I arose to **o** to my beloved; **SS 5:5** 6605a
shut, When he shuts no one will **o**. **Is 22:22** 6605a
"**O** the gates, that the righteous **Is 26:2** 6605a
o Your eyes, O LORD, and see; **Is 37:17** 6491b
will **o** rivers on the bare heights And **Is 41:18** 6605a
To **o** blind eyes, To bring out **Is 42:7** 6491b
Your ears are **o**, but none hears. **Is 42:20** 6491b
To **o** doors before him so that **Is 45:1** 6605a
o up and salvation bear fruit, **Is 45:8** 6605a
long ago your ear has not been **o**, **Is 48:8** 6605a
Yet He did not **o** His mouth; **Is 53:7** 6605a
So He did not **o** His mouth. **Is 53:7** 6605a
Against whom do you **o** wide your **Is 57:4** 7337
Your gates will be **o** continually; **Is 60:11** 6605a
And seek in her **o** squares, If you **Jer 5:1** 7339
"Their quiver is like an **o** grave, **Jer 5:16** 6605a
fall like dung on the **o** field, **Jer 9:22** 6440
up, And there is no one to **o** *them;* **Jer 13:19** 6605a
forsake the rock of the **o** country? **Jer 18:14**
and conditions and the **o** *copy;* **Jer 32:11** 1540
deed of purchase and this **o** deed, **Jer 32:14** 1540
whose eyes are **o** to all the ways **Jer 32:19** 6491b
O up her barns, Pile her up like **Jer 50:26** 6605a
O your mouth and eat what I am **Ezk 2:8** 6475
speak to you, I will **o** your mouth and **Ezk 3:27** 6605a
were thrown out into the **o** field, **Ezk 16:5** 6440
and never **o** your mouth anymore **Ezk 16:63** 6610
to **o** the mouth for slaughter, **Ezk 21:22** 6605a
You will fall on the **o** field; **Ezk 29:5** 6440
will **o** your mouth in their midst. **Ezk 29:21** 5414, 6610
I will cast you on the **o** field. **Ezk 32:4** 6440
and whoever is in the **o** field I **Ezk 33:27** 6440
I will **o** your graves and cause you **Ezk 37:12** 6605a
"You will fall on the **o** field; **Ezk 39:5** 6440
for its **o** space round about. **Ezk 45:2** 4054
for dwellings and for **o** spaces; **Ezk 48:15** 4054
"The city shall have **o** spaces: **Ezk 48:17** 4054
had windows **o** toward Jerusalem); **Da 6:10** 6606
You, O Lord, but to us **o** shame, **Da 9:7** 6440
"**O** shame belongs to us, O Lord, **Da 9:8** 6440
O Your eyes and see our **Da 9:18** 6491b
And I will tear **o** their chests; **Hos 13:8**
pregnant women will be ripped **o**. **Hos 13:16** 1234
Because they ripped **o** the pregnant **Am 1:13** 1234
that we may **o** the wheat *market,* **Am 8:5** 6605a
a heap of ruins in the **o** country, **Mi 1:6**
To lay him **o** from thigh to neck. **Hab 3:13** 6168
O your doors, O Lebanon, That a **Zch 11:1** 6605a
o for you the windows of heaven and **Mal 3:10** 6605a
"I WILL **O** MY MOUTH IN PARABLES; **Mt 13:35** *455*
and when you **o** its mouth, you will **Mt 17:27** *455*
'Lord, lord, **o** up for us.' **Mt 25:11** *455*
so that they may immediately **o** *the* **Lk 12:36** *455*
'Lord, **o** up to us!' **Lk 13:25** *455*
the ninety-nine in the **o** pasture and **Lk 15:4** *2048*
How did He **o** your eyes?" **Jn 9:26** *455*
cannot **o** the eyes of the blind, **Jn 10:21** *455*
he burst **o** in the middle and all **Ac 1:18** *2997*
SO HE DOES NOT **O** HIS MOUTH. **Ac 8:32** *455*
and though his eyes were **o**, **Ac 9:8** *455*
of her joy she did not **o** the gate, **Ac 12:14** *455*
Paul was about to **o** his mouth, **Ac 18:14** *455*
to **o** their eyes so that they may **Ac 26:18** *455*
"THEIR THROAT IS AN **O** GRAVE, **Ro 3:13** *455*
o wide *to us* also. **2Co 6:13** *4115*
o up to us a door for the word, **Col 4:3** *455*
but all things are **o** and laid bare **Heb 4:13** *1131*
of God and put Him to **o** shame. **Heb 6:6** *3856*
an **o** door which no one can shut, **Rv 3:8** *455*
a door *standing* **o** in heaven, **Rv 4:1** *455*
"Who is worthy to **o** the book and **Rv 5:2** *455*
the earth was able to **o** the book **Rv 5:3** *455*
was found worthy to **o** the book or **Rv 5:4** *455*
o the book and its seven seals." **Rv 5:5** *455*
hand a little book which was **o**. **Rv 10:2** *455*
take the book which is **o** in the **Rv 10:8** *455*

OPENED
eat from it your eyes will be **o**, **Gn 3:5** 6491b
the eyes of both of them were **o**, **Gn 3:7** 6491b
which has **o** its mouth to receive **Gn 4:11** 6475
the floodgates of the sky were **o**. **Gn 7:11** 6605a
that Noah **o** the window of the ark **Gn 8:6** 6605a
Then God **o** her eyes and she saw a **Gn 21:19** 6491b
was unloved, and He **o** her womb, **Gn 29:31** 6605a
gave heed to her and **o** her womb. **Gn 30:22** 6605a
then Joseph **o** all the storehouses, **Gn 41:56** 6605a
As one *of them* **o** his sack to **Gn 42:27** 6605a
place, that we **o** our sacks, **Gn 43:21** 6605a
ground, and each man **o** his sack. **Gn 44:11** 6605a
When she **o** *it,* she saw the child, **Ex 2:6** 6605a
and the earth **o** its mouth and **Nu 16:32** 6605a
LORD **o** the mouth of the donkey, **Nu 22:28** 6605a
the LORD **o** the eyes of Balaam, **Nu 22:31** 1540
oracle of the man whose eye is **o**; **Nu 24:3** 8365b
oracle of the man whose eye is **o**, **Nu 24:15** 8365b
and the earth **o** its mouth and **Nu 26:10** 6605a
o its mouth and swallowed them, **Dt 11:6** 6475
they took the key and **o** them, **Jg 3:25** 6605a
So she **o** a bottle of milk and gave **Jg 4:19** 6605a
arose in the morning and **o** the doors **Jg 19:27** 6605a
Then he **o** the doors of the house **1Sa 3:15** 6605a
times and the lad **o** his eyes. **2Ki 4:35** 6491b
And the LORD **o** the servant's eyes and **2Ki 6:17** 6491b
So the LORD **o** their eyes and they **2Ki 6:20** 6491b
Then he **o** the door and fled. **2Ki 9:10** 6605a
toward the east," and he **o** *it.* **2Ki 13:17** 6605a
he **o** the doors of the house of the **2Ch 29:3** 6605a
not let the gates of Jerusalem be **o** **Ne 7:3** 6605a
Ezra **o** the book in the sight **Ne 8:5** 6605a
and when he **o** it, all the people **Ne 8:5** 6605a
Afterward Job **o** his mouth and **Jb 3:1** 6605a
And **o** their mouth as for the **Jb 29:23** 6473
I have **o** my doors to the traveler. **Jb 31:32** 6605a
o their mouth wide against me; **Ps 35:21** 7337
My ears You have **o**; **Ps 40:6** 3738a
above And **o** the doors of heaven; **Ps 78:23** 6605a
He **o** the rock and water flowed **Ps 105:41** 6605a
earth **o** and swallowed up Dathan, **Ps 106:17** 6605a
For they have **o** the wicked and **Ps 109:2** 6605a
I **o** my mouth wide and panted, For **Ps 119:131** 6473
"I **o** to my beloved, But my **SS 5:6** 6605a
budded *And its* blossoms have **o**, **SS 7:12** 6605a
and **o** its mouth without measure; **Is 5:14** 6473
wing or **o** *its* beak or chirped." **Is 10:14** 6475
For the windows above are **o**, **Is 24:18** 6605a
the eyes of the blind will be **o** And **Is 35:5** 6491b
The Lord GOD has **o** My ear; **Is 50:5** 6605a
The LORD has **o** His armory And has **Jer 50:25** 6605a
o their mouths wide against you; **La 2:16** 6475
have **o** their mouths against us. **La 3:46** 6475
were **o** and I saw visions of God. **Ezk 1:1** 6605a
So I **o** my mouth, and He fed me **Ezk 3:2** 6605a
your mouth will be **o** to him who **Ezk 24:27** 6605a
peoples is broken; it has **o** to me. **Ezk 26:2** 5437
And He **o** my mouth at the time *they* **Ezk 33:22** 6605a
so my mouth was **o** and I was no **Ezk 33:22** 6605a
when I have **o** your graves and **Ezk 37:13** 6605a
it shall not be **o**, and no one **Ezk 44:2** 6605a
it shall be **o** on the sabbath day and **Ezk 46:1** 6605a
and **o** on the day of the new moon. **Ezk 46:1** 6605a
facing east shall be **o** for him. **Ezk 46:12** 6605a
court sat, And the books were **o**. **Da 7:10** 6606
then I **o** my mouth and spoke and **Da 10:16** 6605a
The gates of the rivers are **o** And **Na 2:6** 6605a

land are **o** wide to your enemies;	**Na 3:13**	6605a
"In that day a fountain will be **o**	**Zch 13:1**	6605a
and behold, the heavens were **o**,	**Mt 3:16**	*455*
He **o** His mouth and *began* to teach	**Mt 5:2**	*455*
knock, and it will be **o** to you.	**Mt 7:7**	*455*
to him who knocks it will be **o**.	**Mt 7:8**	*455*
And their eyes were **o**.	**Mt 9:30**	*455*
"Lord, *we want* our eyes to be **o**."	**Mt 20:33**	*455*
The tombs were **o**,	**Mt 27:52**	*455*
"Ephphatha!" that is, "Be **o**!"	**Mk 7:34**	*1272*
And his ears were **o**,	**Mk 7:35**	*455*
mouth was **o** and his tongue *loosed,*	**Lk 1:64**	*455*
He was praying, heaven was **o**,	**Lk 3:21**	*455*
And He **o** the book and found the	**Lk 4:17**	*455*
knock, and it will be **o** to you.	**Lk 11:9**	*455*
to him who knocks, it will be **o**.	**Lk 11:10**	*455*
were **o** and they recognized Him;	**Lk 24:31**	*1272*
Then He **o** their minds to	**Lk 24:45**	*1272*
you, you will see the heavens **o**	**Jn 1:51**	*455*
"How then were your eyes **o**?"	**Jn 9:10**	*455*
made the clay and **o** his eyes.	**Jn 9:14**	*455*
about Him, since He **o** your eyes?"	**Jn 9:17**	*455*
or who **o** his eyes, we do not know.	**Jn 9:21**	*455*
He is from, and *yet* He **o** my eyes.	**Jn 9:30**	*455*
o the eyes of a person born blind.	**Jn 9:32**	*455*
o the eyes of the blind man,	**Jn 11:37**	*455*
Lord **o** the gates of the prison,	**Ac 5:19**	*455*
but when we had **o** up, we found no	**Ac 5:23**	*455*
I see the heavens **o** up and the Son	**Ac 7:56**	*1272*
Then Philip **o** his mouth, and	**Ac 8:35**	*455*
And she **o** her eyes, and when she	**Ac 9:40**	*455*
and he saw the sky **o** up,	**Ac 10:11**	*455*
city, which **o** for them by itself;	**Ac 12:10**	*455*
and when they had **o** *the door,*	**Ac 12:16**	*455*
had **o** a door of faith to the Gentiles.	**Ac 14:27**	*455*
and the Lord **o** her heart to	**Ac 16:14**	*1272*
immediately all the doors were **o** and	**Ac 16:26**	*455*
and saw the prison doors **o**,	**Ac 16:27**	*455*
for effective *service* has **o** to me,	**1Co 16:9**	*455*
a door was **o** for me in the Lord,	**2Co 2:12**	*455*
Corinthians, our heart is **o** wide.	**2Co 6:11**	*4115*
He **o** the bottomless pit,	**Rv 9:2**	*455*
of God which is in heaven was **o**;	**Rv 11:19**	*455*
and the earth **o** its mouth and	**Rv 12:16**	*455*
And he **o** his mouth in blasphemies	**Rv 13:6**	*455*
of testimony in heaven was **o**,	**Rv 15:5**	*455*
And I saw heaven **o**,	**Rv 19:11**	*455*
the throne, and books were **o**;	**Rv 20:12**	*455*
and another book was **o**,	**Rv 20:12**	*455*
OPENING		
"There shall be an **o** at its	**Ex 28:32**	6310
around its **o** there shall be a	**Ex 28:32**	6310
like the **o** of a coat of mail,	**Ex 28:32**	6310
and the **o** of the robe was *at the*	**Ex 39:23**	6310
as the **o** of a coat of mail,	**Ex 39:23**	6310
with a binding all around its **o**,	**Ex 39:23**	6310
Its **o** inside the crown at the	**1Ki 7:31**	6310
and its **o** *was* round like the	**1Ki 7:31**	6310
on its **o** *there were* engravings,	**1Ki 7:31**	6310
charge of **o** *it* morning by morning.	**1Ch 9:27**	4668
not shut the **o** of my *mother's* womb,	**Jb 3:10**	1817
the gates, at the **o** to the city,	**Pr 8:3**	6310
And the **o** of my lips *will reveal*	**Pr 8:6**	4669
extended his hand through the **o**,	**SS 5:4**	2356
was an **o** at the head of the way,	**Ezk 42:12**	6607
should delay at the **o** of the womb.	**Hos 13:13**	4866, 1121
and cast the lead weight on its **o**.	**Zch 5:8**	6310
Then, **o** their treasures, they	**Mt 2:11**	*455*
the water, He saw the heavens **o**,	**Mk 1:10**	*4977*
and when they had dug an **o**,	**Mk 2:4**	
night and let him down through *an* **o**	**Ac 9:25**	
O his mouth, Peter said: "I most	**Ac 10:34**	*455*
given to me in the **o** of my mouth,	**Eph 6:19**	*457*
fountain send out from the same **o**	**Jas 3:11**	*3692*
OPENINGS		
and their **o** *were* on the north.	**Ezk 42:4**	6607
to their arrangements and **o**.	**Ezk 42:11**	6607
to the **o** of the chambers which were	**Ezk 42:12**	6607
OPENLY		
I speak mouth to mouth, Even **o**,	**Nu 12:8**	4758
who fear God, who fear Him **o**.	**Ec 8:12**	4480, 6440
no one was speaking **o** of Him for	**Jn 7:13**	*3954*
"I have spoken **o** to the world;	**Jn 18:20**	*3954*
Therefore **o** before the churches	**2Co 8:24**	*4383*
OPENNESS		
the Lord Jesus Christ with all **o**,	**Ac 28:31**	*3954*
OPENS		
"If a man **o** a pit, or digs a	**Ex 21:33**	6605a
the ground **o** its mouth and swallows	**Nu 16:30**	6475
make peace with you and **o** to you,	**Dt 20:11**	6605a
He **o** his eyes, and it is no longer.	**Jb 27:19**	6491b
Then He **o** the ears of men, And	**Jb 33:16**	1540
So Job **o** his mouth emptily;	**Jb 35:16**	6475
"He **o** their ear to instruction,	**Jb 36:10**	1540
And **o** their ear in *time of*	**Jb 36:15**	1540
The LORD **o** *the eyes of* the blind;	**Ps 146:8**	6491b
one who **o** wide his lips comes to	**Pr 13:3**	6589
She **o** her mouth in wisdom, And the	**Pr 31:26**	6605a
When he **o** no one will shut,	**Is 22:22**	6605a
firstborn MALE THAT **O** THE WOMB	**Lk 2:23**	*1272*
"To him the doorkeeper **o**,	**Jn 10:3**	*455*
David, who **o** and no one will shut,	**Rv 3:7**	*455*
shut, and who shuts and no one **o**,	**Rv 3:7**	*455*
hears My voice and **o** the door,	**Rv 3:20**	*455*
OPHEL		
built extensively the wall of **O**.	**2Ch 27:3**	6077
he encircled the **O** *with it* and made	**2Ch 33:14**	6077
servants living in **O** *made repairs*	**Ne 3:26**	6077
tower and as far as the wall of **O**.	**Ne 3:27**	6077
temple servants were living in **O**,	**Ne 11:21**	6077
OPHIR		
and **O** and Havilah and Jobab;	**Gn 10:29**	211
They went to **O** and	**1Ki 9:28**	211
Hiram, which brought gold from **O**,	**1Ki 10:11**	211
brought in from **O** a very great	**1Ki 10:11**	211
of Tarshish to go to **O** for gold,	**1Ki 22:48**	211
O, Havilah and Jobab;	**1Ch 1:23**	211
talents of gold, of the gold of **O**,	**1Ch 29:4**	211
went with Solomon's servants to **O**,	**2Ch 8:18**	211
Solomon who brought gold from **O**,	**2Ch 9:10**	211
And *the gold of* **O** among the stones	**Jb 22:24**	211
cannot be valued in the gold of **O**,	**Jb 28:16**	211
stands the queen in gold from **O**.	**Ps 45:9**	211
And mankind than the gold of **O**.	**Is 13:12**	211
OPHNI		
and Chephar-ammoni and **O** and Geba;	**Jos 18:24**	6078
OPHRAH		
and Avvim and Parah and **O**,	**Jos 18:23**	6084
sat under the oak that was in **O**,	**Jg 6:11**	6084
is still in **O** of the Abiezrites.	**Jg 6:24**	6084
and placed it in his city, **O**,	**Jg 8:27**	6084
Joash, in **O** of the Abiezrites.	**Jg 8:32**	6084
he went to his father's house at **O** and	**Jg 9:5**	6084
one company turned toward **O**,	**1Sa 13:17**	6084
Meonothai became the father of **O**,	**1Ch 4:14**	6084
OPINION		
my share, I also will tell my **o**.	**Jb 32:17**	1843
but I give an **o** as one who by the	**1Co 7:25**	*1106*
But in my **o** she is happier if she	**1Co 7:40**	*1106*
I give *my* **o** in this matter,	**2Co 8:10**	*1106*
OPINIONS		
will you hesitate between two **o**?	**1Ki 18:21**	5589b
of passing judgment on his **o**.	**Ro 14:1**	*1261*
OPPONENT		
of them seized his **o** by the head and	**2Sa 2:16**	7453
wicked And my **o** as the unjust.	**Jb 27:7**	6965
"Make friends quickly with your **o**	**Mt 5:25**	*476*
so that your **o** may not	**Mt 5:25**	*476*
while you are going with your **o**	**Lk 12:58**	*476*
me legal protection from my **o**.'	**Lk 18:3**	*476*
that the **o** will be put to shame,	**Ti 2:8**	*1727*
OPPONENT'S		
thrust his sword in his **o** side;	**2Sa 2:16**	7453
OPPONENTS		
listen to what my **o** are saying!	**Jer 18:19**	3401
all His **o** were being humiliated;	**Lk 13:17**	*480*
none of your **o** will be able to resist	**Lk 21:15**	*480*
in no way alarmed by *your* **o**	**Php 1:28**	*480*
OPPORTUNE		
how to betray Him at an **o** time.	**Mk 14:11**	*2122*
left Him until an **o** time.	**Lk 4:13**	*2540*
here, but your time is always **o**.	**Jn 7:6**	*2092*
OPPORTUNITY		
for a good **o** to betray Jesus.	**Mt 26:16**	*2120*
lead to an **o** for your testimony.	**Lk 21:13**	
and *began* seeking a good **o** to	**Lk 22:6**	*2120*
and has an **o** to make his defense	**Ac 25:16**	*5117*
taking **o** through the commandment,	**Ro 7:8**	*874*
taking an **o** through the commandment,	**Ro 7:11**	*874*
even as the Lord gave **o** to each	**1Co 3:5**	
but he will come when he has **o**.	**1Co 16:12**	*2119*
that I may cut off **o** from those	**2Co 11:12**	*874*
those who desire an **o** to be regarded	**2Co 11:12**	*874*
freedom into an **o** for the flesh,	**Ga 5:13**	*874*
So then, while we have **o**,	**Ga 6:10**	*2540*
and do not give the devil an **o**.	**Eph 4:27**	*5117*
before, but you lacked **o**.	**Php 4:10**	*170*
making the most of the **o**.	**Col 4:5**	*2540*
they would have had **o** to return.	**Heb 11:15**	*2540*
OPPOSE		
repay evil for good, They **o** me,	**Ps 38:20**	7853
will even **o** the Prince of princes,	**Da 8:25**	5975
so these *men* also **o** the truth,	**2Tm 3:8**	*436*
OPPOSED		
They **o** Uzziah the king and	**2Ch 26:18**	5975
Jahzeiah the son of Tikvah **o** this,	**Ezr 10:15**	5975
For on every side they will be **o**	**Jer 51:2**	5921
in Israel, and for a sign to be **o**	**Lk 2:34**	*483*
has **o** the ordinance of God;	**Ro 13:2**	*436*
and they who have **o** will receive	**Ro 13:2**	*436*
to Antioch, I **o** him to his face,	**Ga 2:11**	*436*
as Jannes and Jambres **o** Moses,	**2Tm 3:8**	*436*
for he vigorously **o** our teaching.	**2Tm 4:15**	*436*
"GOD IS **O** TO THE PROUD, BUT GIVES	**Jas 4:6**	*498*
for GOD IS **O** TO THE PROUD,	**1Pe 5:5**	*498*
OPPOSES		
out *to be* a king **o** Caesar."	**Jn 19:12**	*483*
who **o** and exalts himself above	**2Th 2:4**	*480*
OPPOSING		
was **o** them, seeking to turn the	**Ac 13:8**	*436*
o arguments of what is falsely called	**1Tm 6:20**	*477*
OPPOSITE		
and laid each half **o** the other;	**Gn 15:10**	7122
three men were standing **o** him;	**Gn 18:2**	5921
Then she went and sat down **o** him,	**Gn 21:16**	4480, 5048
And she sat **o** him, and lifted up	**Gn 21:16**	4480, 5048
camp in front of Baal-zephon, **o** it,	**Ex 14:2**	5227
the loops shall be **o** each other.	**Ex 26:5**	6901
and the lampstand **o** the table on	**Ex 26:35**	5227
on its two side walls—on **o** sides	**Ex 30:4**	8147
the loops were **o** each other.	**Ex 36:12**	6901
on its two sides—on **o** sides	**Ex 37:27**	8147
the tent of meeting, **o** the table,	**Ex 40:24**	5227
in the wilderness which is **o** Moab,	**Nu 21:11**	5921, 6440
plains of Moab beyond the Jordan **o**	**Nu 22:1**	
land, and they are living **o** me.	**Nu 22:5**	4480, 4136
which are by the Jordan **o** Jericho.	**Nu 31:12**	
the plains of Moab by the Jordan **o**	**Nu 33:48**	
the plains of Moab by the Jordan **o**	**Nu 33:50**	
across the Jordan **o** Jericho,	**Nu 34:15**	
of Moab by the Jordan **o** Jericho,	**Nu 35:1**	
the plains of Moab by the Jordan **o**	**Nu 36:13**	
wilderness, in the Arabah **o** Suph,	**Dt 1:1**	4136
When you come **o** the sons of Ammon,	**Dt 2:19**	4136
remained in the valley **o** Beth-peor.	**Dt 3:29**	4136
Jordan, in the valley **o** Beth-peor,	**Dt 4:46**	4136
who live in the Arabah, **o** Gilgal,	**Dt 11:30**	4136
is in the land of Moab **o** Jericho,	**Dt 32:49**	5921, 6440
top of Pisgah, which is **o** Jericho.	**Dt 34:1**	5921, 6440
in the land of Moab, **o** Beth-peor;	**Dt 34:6**	4136
So the people crossed **o** Jericho.	**Jos 3:16**	5048
a man was standing **o** him with his	**Jos 5:13**	5048
which is **o** the ascent of Adummim,	**Jos 15:7**	5227
which is **o** the ascent of Adummim,	**Jos 18:17**	5227
the fords of the Jordan **o** Moab,	**Jg 3:28**	
the fords of the Jordan **o** Ephraim.	**Jg 12:5**	
of the mountain which is **o** Hebron.	**Jg 16:3**	5921, 6440
and came to *a place* **o** Jebus	**Jg 19:10**	5227
down **o** Gibeah toward the east.	**Jg 20:43**	5227
crag rose on the north **o** Michmash,	**1Sa 14:5**	4136
and the other on the south **o** Geba.	**1Sa 14:5**	4136
window was **o** window in three	**1Ki 7:4**	413
was **o** window in three ranks.	**1Ki 7:5**	4136, 413
and stood **o** *them* at a distance,	**2Ki 2:7**	4480, 5048
who *were* at Jericho **o** *him* saw him,	**2Ki 2:15**	4480, 5048
the water **o** *them* as red as blood.	**2Ki 3:22**	4480, 5048
Now the sons of Gad lived **o** them	**1Ch 5:11**	5048
Jerusalem **o** their *other* relatives.	**1Ch 8:32**	5048
Jerusalem **o** their *other* relatives.	**1Ch 9:38**	5048
Harumaph made repairs **o** his house.	**Ne 3:10**	5048
as *a point* **o** the tombs of David,	**Ne 3:16**	5048
stood **o** them in *their* service	**Ne 12:9**	5048
with their brothers **o** them,	**Ne 12:24**	5048
o the entrance to the palace.	**Es 5:1**	5227
from *one* door to *the* door **o**.	**Ezk 40:13**	5048
had a gate **o** the gate on the north	**Ezk 40:23**	5048
three stories, **o** the threshold,	**Ezk 41:16**	5048
chamber which *was* **o** the separate	**Ezk 42:1**	5048
and **o** the building toward the north.	**Ezk 42:1**	5048
O the twenty *cubits* which belonged	**Ezk 42:3**	5048
and **o** the pavement which belonged	**Ezk 42:3**	5048
which are **o** the separate area,	**Ezk 42:13**	413, 6440
border to a point **o** Lebo-hamath.	**Ezk 47:20**	5227
and began writing **o** the lampstand	**Da 5:5**	6903
"Go into the village **o** you,	**Mt 21:2**	*2713*
other Mary, sitting **o** the grave.	**Mt 27:61**	*561*
"Go into the village **o** you,	**Mk 11:2**	*2713*
And He sat down **o** the treasury,	**Mk 12:41**	*2713*
the Mount of Olives **o** the temple,	**Mk 13:3**	*2713*
the Gerasenes, which is **o** Galilee.	**Lk 8:26**	*495*
arrived the following day **o** Chios;	**Ac 20:15**	*481*
OPPOSITION		
years, and you will know My **o**.	**Nu 14:34**	8569
Because of the **o** of Your hand I am	**Ps 39:10**	8409
for these are in **o** to one another,	**Ga 5:17**	*480*
you the gospel of God amid much **o**.	**1Th 2:2**	*73*
correcting those who are in **o**,	**2Tm 2:25**	*475*
OPPRESS		
not wrong a stranger or **o** him,	**Ex 22:21**	3905
"You shall not **o** a stranger,	**Ex 23:9**	3905
'You shall not **o** your neighbor,	**Lv 19:13**	6231
"You shall not **o** a hired servant	**Dt 24:14**	6231
by which your enemy will **o** you.	**Dt 28:53**	6693
will **o** you in all your towns.	**Dt 28:55**	6693
enemy will **o** you in your towns.	**Dt 28:57**	6693
He permitted no man to **o** them,	**1Ch 16:21**	6231
'Is it right for You indeed to **o**,	**Jb 10:3**	6231
He permitted no man to **o** them,	**Ps 105:14**	6231
Do not let the arrogant **o** me.	**Ps 119:122**	6231
if you do not **o** the alien, the	**Jer 7:6**	6231
if a man does not **o** anyone,	**Ezk 18:7**	3238
or **o** anyone, or retain a pledge,	**Ezk 18:16**	3238
shall no longer **o** My people,	**Ezk 45:8**	3238
are false balances, He loves to **o**.	**Hos 12:7**	6231
of Samaria, Who **o** the poor,	**Am 4:1**	6231
do not **o** the widow or the orphan,	**Zch 7:10**	6231
o the wage earner in his wages,	**Mal 3:5**	6231
Is it not the rich who **o** you and	**Jas 2:6**	*2616a*
OPPRESSED		
enslaved and **o** four hundred years.	**Gn 15:13**	6031a
only be **o** and robbed continually,	**Dt 28:29**	6231
but **o** and crushed continually.	**Dt 28:33**	6231
of those who **o** and afflicted them.	**Jg 2:18**	3905
and he **o** the sons of Israel	**Jg 4:3**	3905
Amalekites and the Maonites **o** you,	**Jg 10:12**	3905
my lord, I am a woman **o** in spirit;	**1Sa 1:15**	7186
Whom have I **o**, or from whose hand	**1Sa 12:3**	7533
have not defrauded us or **o** us	**1Sa 12:4**	7533
how the king of Aram **o** them.	**2Ki 13:4**	3905

Hazael king of Aram had **o** Israel 2Ki 13:22 3905
And Asa **o** some of the people at 2Ch 16:10 7533
of their oppressors who **o** them, Ne 9:27 6887a
They are even **o** in the gate, Jb 5:4 1792
he has **o** *and* forsaken the poor; Jb 20:19 7533
will be a stronghold for the **o**, Ps 9:9 1790
To vindicate the orphan and the **o**, Ps 10:18 1790
Let not the **o** return dishonored; Ps 74:21 1790
And judgments for all who are **o**. Ps 103:6 6231
Their enemies also **o** them, Ps 106:42 3905
Who executes justice for the **o**; Ps 146:7 6231
And behold *I saw* the tears of the **o** Ec 4:1 6231
And the people will be **o**, Is 3:5 5065
O Lord, I am **o**, be my security. Is 38:14 6234
the Assyrian **o** them without cause. Is 52:4 6231
He was **o** and He was afflicted, Yet Is 53:7 5065
yoke, And to let the **o** go free And Is 58:6 7533
"The sons of Israel are **o**, Jer 50:33 6231
alien they have **o** in your midst; Ezk 22:7 6213a, 6233
o the sojourner without justice. Ezk 22:29 6231
Ephraim is **o**, crushed in judgment, Hos 5:11 6231
those Who devour the **o** in secret. Hab 3:14 6041
TO SET FREE THOSE WHO ARE **O**, Lk 4:18 *2352*
o by striking down the Egyptian. Ac 7:24 *2669*
all who were **o** by the devil, Ac 10:38 *2616a*
o by the sensual conduct of 2Pe 2:7 *2669*

OPPRESSES

Fighting all day long he **o** me. Ps 56:1 3905
He who **o** the poor taunts his Pr 14:31 6231
He who **o** the poor to make more for Pr 22:16 6231
A poor man who **o** the lowly Is *like* Pr 28:3 6231
o the poor and needy, commits Ezk 18:12 3238

OPPRESSING

which the Egyptians are **o** them. Ex 3:9 3905
all the kingdoms that were **o** you.' 1Sa 10:18 3905
of the fierceness of the **o** *sword* Jer 25:38 3238

OPPRESSION

I have seen the **o** with which the Ex 3:9 3906
affliction and our toil and our **o**; Dt 26:7 3906
for He saw the **o** of Israel, how 2Ki 13:4 3906
And opens their ear in *time of* **o**. Jb 36:15 3906
full of curses and deceit and **o**; Ps 10:7 8496
because of the **o** of the enemy?" Ps 42:9 3906
because of the **o** of the enemy? Ps 43:2 3906
forget our affliction and our **o**? Ps 44:24 3906
O and deceit do not depart from Ps 55:11 8496
Do not trust in **o** And do not Ps 62:10 6233
rescue their life from **o** and violence Ps 72:14 8496
mock and wickedly speak of **o**; Ps 73:8 6233
and bowed down Through **o**, Ps 107:39 6115
Redeem me from the **o** of man, Ps 119:134 6233
the acts of **o** which were being done Ec 4:1 6217
If you see **o** of the poor and Ec 5:8 6233
For **o** makes a wise man mad, And a Ec 7:7 6233
put your trust in **o** and guile, Is 30:12 6233
bread of privation and water of **o**, Is 30:20 3906
By **o** and judgment He was taken Is 53:8 6115
You will be far from **o**, Is 54:14 6233
our God, Speaking **o** and revolt, Is 59:13 6233
In whose midst there is only **o**. Jer 6:6 6233
on practicing **o** and extortion." Jer 22:17 6233
O LORD, You have seen my **o**; La 3:59 5792
your neighbors for gain by **o**, Ezk 22:12 6233
practiced **o** and committed robbery, Ezk 22:29 6233
SEEN THE **O** OF MY PEOPLE IN EGYPT Ac 7:34 *2561*

OPPRESSIONS

the multitude of **o** they cry out; Jb 35:9 6217
within her and *the* **o** in her midst. Am 3:9 6217

OPPRESSIVE

laid an **o** burden upon our loins. Ps 66:11 4157
A powerful and **o** nation Whose land Is 18:2 4001
and wide, A powerful and **o** nation, Is 18:7 4001

OPPRESSOR

of the needy And crush the **o**. Ps 72:4 6231
A leader who is a great **o** lacks Pr 28:16 4642
man and the **o** have this in common: Pr 29:13 376, 8496
shoulders, The rod of their **o**, Is 9:4 5065
"How the **o** has ceased, *And how* Is 14:4 5065
long because of the fury of the **o**, Is 51:13 6693
But where is the fury of the **o**? Is 51:13 6693
robbed from the power of *his* **o**, Jer 21:12 6231
robbed from the power of *his* **o**. Jer 22:3 6216
Away from the sword of the **o**.' Jer 46:16 3238
From before the sword of the **o** Jer 50:16 3238
who will send an **o** through the Jewel Da 11:20 5065
no **o** will pass over them anymore, Zch 9:8 5065

OPPRESSORS

and from the hands of all your **o**, Jg 6:9 3905
of their **o** who oppressed them, Ne 9:27 6862c
them from the hand of their **o**. Ne 9:27 6862c
Do not leave me to my **o**. Ps 119:121 6231
on the side of their **o** was power, Ec 4:1 6231
Their **o** are children, And women Is 3:12 5065
and will rule over their **o**. Is 14:2 5065
O have completely *disappeared* from Is 16:4 7429
will cry to the LORD because of **o**, Is 19:20 3905
feed your **o** with their own flesh, Is 49:26 3238
And I will punish all their **o**. Jer 30:20 3905
deal at that time With all your **o**, Zph 3:19 6031a

OR

shall not eat from it **o** touch it, Gn 3:3
o you will die.' " Gn 3:3
o if *to* the right, then I will go Gn 13:9
not take a thread **o** a sandal thong Gn 14:23
thong **o** anything that is yours, Gn 14:23
born in the house **o** who is bought Gn 17:12
born in your house **o** who is bought Gn 17:13
who were born in the house **o** Gn 17:27
o you will be swept away in Gn 19:15 6435
o you will be swept away." Gn 19:17 6435
she lay down **o** when she arose. Gn 19:33
she lay down **o** when she arose. Gn 19:35
with me **o** with my offspring Gn 21:23
my offspring **o** with my posterity Gn 21:23
made his journey successful **o** not. Gn 24:21 518
to the right hand **o** the left." Gn 24:49 176
we cannot speak to you bad **o** good. Gn 24:50 176
who touches this man **o** his wife Gn 26:11
are really my son Esau **o** not." Gn 27:21 518
"Give me children, **o** else I die." Gn 30:1
"Do we still have any portion **o** Gn 31:14
to Jacob either good **o** bad." Gn 31:24 5704
speak either good **o** bad to Jacob.' Gn 31:29 5704
stolen by day **o** stolen by night. Gn 31:39
my daughters **o** to their children Gn 31:43 176
o if you take wives besides my Gn 31:50
O are you really going to rule Gn 37:8 518
it is your son's tunic **o** not." Gn 37:32 518
listen to her to lie beside her **o** Gn 39:10
no one shall raise his hand **o** foot Gn 41:44
could we steal silver **o** gold from Gn 44:8 176
'Have you a father **o** a brother?' Gn 44:19 176
grieved **o** angry with yourselves, Gn 45:5
o else they will multiply and in Ex 1:10 6435
you a prince **o** a judge over us? Ex 2:14
me **o** listen to what I say? Ex 4:1
If they will not believe you **o** heed Ex 4:8
two signs **o** heed what you say, Ex 4:9
O who makes *him* mute or deaf, or Ex 4:11 176
Or who makes *him* mute **o** deaf, Ex 4:11 176
mute or deaf, **o** seeing or blind? Ex 4:11 176
mute or deaf, or seeing **o** blind? Ex 4:11 176
pestilence **o** with the sword." Ex 5:3 176
amount either yesterday **o** today Ex 5:14 1571
nothing green was left on tree **o** plant Ex 10:15
bark, whether against man **o** beast, Ex 11:7 5704
from the sheep **o** from the goats. Ex 12:5
it raw **o** boiled at all with water, Ex 12:9
an alien **o** a native of the land. Ex 12:19
"A sojourner **o** a hired servant Ex 12:45
whether **o** not they will walk in My Ex 16:4 518
"Is the LORD among us, **o** not?" Ex 17:7 518
mountain **o** touch the border of it; Ex 19:12
surely be stoned **o** shot through; Ex 19:13 176
whether beast **o** man, he shall not Ex 19:13 518
o else the LORD will break out Ex 19:22 6435
o He will break forth upon them." Ex 19:24 6435
o any likeness of what is in Ex 20:4
heaven above **o** on the earth beneath Ex 20:4
o in the water under the earth. Ex 20:4
not worship them **o** serve them; Ex 20:5
not do any work, you **o** your son or your daughter, Ex 20:10
you or your son **o** your daughter, Ex 20:10
your male **o** your female servant or Ex 20:10
your female servant **o** your cattle Ex 20:10
or your cattle **o** your sojourner Ex 20:10
neighbor's wife **o** his male servant Ex 20:17
his male servant **o** his female servant Ex 20:17
his female servant **o** his ox or his Ex 20:17
or his ox **o** his donkey or anything Ex 20:17
his donkey **o** anything that belongs Ex 20:17
o we will die." Ex 20:19 6435
gods of silver **o** gods of gold, you Ex 20:23
she bears him sons **o** daughters, Ex 21:4 176
him to the door **o** the doorpost. Ex 21:6 176
clothing, **o** her conjugal rights. Ex 21:10
"He who strikes his father **o** Ex 21:15
o he is found in his possession, Ex 21:16
who curses his father **o** his mother Ex 21:17
with a stone **o** with *his* fist, Ex 21:18 176
man strikes his male **o** female slave Ex 21:20 176
however, he survives a day **o** two, Ex 21:21 176
eye of his male **o** female slave, Ex 21:26 176
tooth of his male **o** female slave, Ex 21:27 176
ox gores a man **o** a woman to death, Ex 21:28 176
it and it kills a man **o** a woman, Ex 21:29 176
it gores a son **o** a daughter, Ex 21:31 176
ox gores a male **o** female slave, Ex 21:32 176
the owner shall give his **o** *her* Ex 21:32
o digs a pit and does not cover it Ex 21:33 176
an ox **o** a donkey falls into it, Ex 21:33 176
"**O** *if* it is known that the ox was Ex 21:36 176
"If a man steals an ox **o** a sheep and Ex 22:1 176
and slaughters it **o** sells it, Ex 22:1 176
an ox **o** a donkey or a sheep, Ex 22:4 5704
an ox or a donkey **o** a sheep, Ex 22:4 5704
"If a man lets a field **o** vineyard Ex 22:5 176
stacked grain **o** the standing grain Ex 22:6 176
grain **o** the field *itself* is Ex 22:6 176
money **o** goods to keep *for him* Ex 22:7 176
o for any lost thing about which Ex 22:9
o any animal to keep *for him*, Ex 22:10 176
and it dies **o** is hurt or is driven Ex 22:10 176
and it dies or is hurt **o** is driven Ex 22:10 176
and it is injured **o** dies while its Ex 22:14 176
wrong a stranger **o** oppress him, Ex 22:21
not afflict any widow **o** orphan. Ex 22:22
ox **o** his donkey wandering away, Ex 23:4 176
kill the innocent **o** the righteous, Ex 23:7
miscarrying **o** barren in your land; Ex 23:26
with them **o** with their gods. Ex 23:32
o when they approach the altar to Ex 28:43 176
flesh of ordination **o** any of the bread Ex 29:34
o burnt offering or meal offering; Ex 30:9
or burnt offering **o** meal offering; Ex 30:9
o when they approach the altar to Ex 30:20 176
o whoever puts any of it on a Ex 30:33
o it will become a snare in your Ex 34:12 6435
did not eat bread **o** drink water. Ex 34:28
"Let no man **o** woman any longer Ex 36:6 408
animals from the herd **o** the flock. Lv 1:2
of the sheep **o** of the goats, Lv 1:10 176
turtledoves **o** from young pigeons. Lv 1:14 176
o unleavened wafers spread with Lv 2:4
leaven **o** any honey as an offering Lv 2:11
the herd, whether male **o** female, Lv 3:1 518
he shall offer it, male **o** female, Lv 3:6 176
not eat any fat **o** any blood.' " Lv 3:17
he has seen **o** *otherwise* known, Lv 5:1 176
'**O** if a person touches any unclean Lv 5:2 176
o the carcass of unclean cattle or Lv 5:2 176
o a carcass of unclean swarming Lv 5:2 176
'**O** if he touches human Lv 5:3 176
'**O** if a person swears Lv 5:4 176
his lips to do evil **o** to do good, Lv 5:4 176
a lamb **o** a goat as a sin offering. Lv 5:6 176
turtledoves **o** two young pigeons, Lv 5:7 176
turtledoves **o** two young pigeons, Lv 5:11 176
oil on it **o** place incense on it, Lv 5:11
o a security entrusted *to him*, Lv 6:2 176
to him, **o** through robbery, Lv 6:2 176
o *if* he has extorted from his Lv 6:2 176
o has found what was lost and lied Lv 6:3 176
o what he got by extortion, Lv 6:4 176
o the deposit which was entrusted Lv 6:4 176
o the lost thing which he found, Lv 6:4 176
o anything about which he swore Lv 6:5 176
prepared in a pan **o** on a griddle shall Lv 7:9
offering, mixed with oil **o** dry, Lv 7:10
is a votive **o** a freewill offering, Lv 7:16 176
uncleanness, **o** an unclean animal, Lv 7:21 176
o any unclean detestable thing, Lv 7:21 176
fat *from* an ox, a sheep **o** a goat. Lv 7:23
blood, either of bird **o** animal, Lv 7:26
o you will die; for the LORD's Lv 10:7 6435
"Do not drink wine **o** strong drink, Lv 10:9
o among those which divide the Lv 11:4
in the seas **o** in the rivers, Lv 11:9
hoof, **o** which do not chew cud, Lv 11:26
any wooden article, **o** clothing, Lv 11:32 176
article, or clothing, **o** a skin, Lv 11:32 176
or clothing, or a skin, **o** a sack Lv 11:32 176
oven **o** a stove shall be smashed; Lv 11:35
'Nevertheless a spring **o** a cistern Lv 11:36
for a son **o** for a daughter, Lv 12:6 176
and a young pigeon **o** a turtledove Lv 12:6 176
child, whether a male **o** a female. Lv 12:7 176
turtledoves **o** two young pigeons, Lv 12:8 176
o a scab or a bright spot, Lv 13:2 176
or a scab **o** a bright spot, Lv 13:2 176
o to one of his sons the priests. Lv 13:2 176
"**O** if the raw flesh turns again Lv 13:16 176
a white swelling **o** a reddish-white, Lv 13:19 176
"**O** if the body sustains in its Lv 13:24 176
spot, reddish-white, **o** white, Lv 13:24 176
"Now if a man **o** woman has an Lv 13:29 176
on the head **o** on the beard, Lv 13:29 176
of the head **o** of the beard. Lv 13:30 176
"When a man **o** a woman has Lv 13:38 176
the bald head **o** the bald forehead, Lv 13:42 176
bald head **o** on his bald forehead. Lv 13:42 176
bald head **o** on his bald forehead, Lv 13:43 176
a wool garment **o** a linen garment, Lv 13:47 176
whether in warp **o** woof, of linen Lv 13:48 176
warp or woof, of linen **o** of wool, Lv 13:48 176
in leather **o** in any article made of Lv 13:48 176
if the mark is greenish **o** reddish Lv 13:49 176
in the garment **o** in the leather, Lv 13:49 176
o in the warp or in the woof, Lv 13:49 176
or in the warp **o** in the woof, Lv 13:49 176
woof, **o** in any article of leather, Lv 13:49 176
whether in the warp **o** in the woof, Lv 13:51 176
or in the woof, **o** in the leather, Lv 13:51 176
whether the warp **o** the woof, Lv 13:52 176
or the woof, in wool **o** in linen, Lv 13:52 176
o any article of leather in which Lv 13:52 176
either in the warp **o** in the woof, Lv 13:53 176
woof, **o** in any article of leather, Lv 13:53 176
on the top **o** on the front of it. Lv 13:55 176
the garment **o** out of the leather, Lv 13:56 176
from the warp **o** from the woof; Lv 13:56 176
whether in the warp **o** in the woof, Lv 13:57 176
woof, **o** in any article of leather, Lv 13:57 176
whether the warp **o** the woof, Lv 13:58 176
o any article of leather from Lv 13:58 176
in a garment of wool **o** linen, Lv 13:59 176
whether in the warp **o** in the woof, Lv 13:59 176
woof, **o** in any article of leather, Lv 13:59 176
pronouncing it clean **o** unclean. Lv 13:59 176
and two turtledoves **o** two young Lv 14:22 176
the turtledoves **o** young pigeons, Lv 14:30 176
greenish **o** reddish depressions and Lv 14:37 176
for the leprous garment **o** house, Lv 14:55
o whether his body obstructs its Lv 15:3 176
'**O** if the man with the discharge Lv 15:8
turtledoves **o** two young pigeons, Lv 15:14 176
'As for any garment **o** any leather Lv 15:17
'Whether it be on the bed **o** on the Lv 15:23 176
o if she has a discharge beyond Lv 15:25 176
turtledoves **o** two young pigeons and Lv 15:29 176
whether a male **o** a female, Lv 15:33
o a man who lies with an unclean Lv 15:33
o he will die; for I will appear in Lv 16:2 3808

Context	Reference	No.
o the alien who sojourns among you;	Lv 16:29	
who slaughters an ox o a lamb	Lv 17:3	176
or a lamb o a goat in the camp,	Lv 17:3	176
o who slaughters it outside the	Lv 17:3	176
o from the aliens who sojourn	Lv 17:8	
a burnt offering o sacrifice,	Lv 17:8	176
o from the aliens who sojourn	Lv 17:10	
o from the aliens who sojourn	Lv 17:13	
beast o a bird which may be eaten,	Lv 17:13	176
which dies o is torn *by beasts,*	Lv 17:15	
whether he is a native o an alien,	Lv 17:15	
not wash *them* o bathe his body,	Lv 17:16	
daughter o your mother's daughter,	Lv 18:9	176
born at home o born outside,	Lv 18:9	176
o your daughter's daughter,	Lv 18:10	176
daughter o her daughter's daughter,	Lv 18:17	
'Do not turn to idols o make for	Lv 19:4	
practice divination o soothsaying.	Lv 19:26	
not turn to mediums o spiritists;	Lv 19:31	
measurement of weight, o capacity.	Lv 19:35	
'Any man from the sons of Israel o	Lv 20:2	
curses his father o his mother,	Lv 20:9	
cursed his father o his mother,	Lv 20:9	
daughter o his mother's daughter,	Lv 20:17	176
sister o of your father's sister,	Lv 20:19	
detestable by animal o by bird	Lv 20:25	
or by bird o by anything that creeps	Lv 20:25	
'Now a man o a woman who is a	Lv 20:27	176
who is a medium o a spiritist shall	Lv 20:27	176
even for his father o his mother;	Lv 21:11	
'A widow, o a divorced woman, or	Lv 21:14	
o one who is profaned by harlotry,	Lv 21:14	
a blind man, o a lame man, or he	Lv 21:18	176
o he who has a disfigured *face,*	Lv 21:18	176
face, o any deformed *limb,*	Lv 21:18	176
o a man who has a broken foot or	Lv 21:19	176
has a broken foot o broken hand,	Lv 21:19	176
o a hunchback or a dwarf, or *one*	Lv 21:20	176
or a hunchback o a dwarf, or *one*	Lv 21:20	176
o *one who has* a defect in his eye	Lv 21:20	176
who has a defect in his eye o eczema	Lv 21:20	176
o scabs or crushed testicles.	Lv 21:20	176
or scabs o crushed testicles.	Lv 21:20	176
he shall not go in to the veil o come	Lv 21:23	
is a leper o who has a discharge,	Lv 22:4	176
o if a man has a seminal emission,	Lv 22:4	176
o if a man touches any teeming	Lv 22:5	176
o any man by whom he is made	Lv 22:5	176
which dies o is torn *by beasts,*	Lv 22:8	
a sojourner with the priest o a	Lv 22:10	
becomes a widow o divorced,	Lv 22:13	
'Any man of the house of Israel o	Lv 22:18	
votive o any of their freewill offerings	Lv 22:18	
cattle, the sheep, o the goats.	Lv 22:19	
vow o for a freewill offering,	Lv 22:21	176
of the herd o of the flock,	Lv 22:21	176
'Those *that are* blind o fractured	Lv 22:22	176
or fractured o maimed or having a	Lv 22:22	176
maimed o having a running sore	Lv 22:22	176
a running sore o eczema or scabs,	Lv 22:22	176
a running sore or eczema o scabs,	Lv 22:22	176
'In respect to an ox o a lamb	Lv 22:23	
has an overgrown o stunted *member,*	Lv 22:23	
bruised o crushed or torn or cut,	Lv 22:24	
bruised or crushed o torn or cut,	Lv 22:24	
bruised or crushed or torn o cut,	Lv 22:24	
LORD, o sacrifice in your land,	Lv 22:24	
an ox o a sheep or a goat is born,	Lv 22:27	176
an ox or a sheep o a goat is born,	Lv 22:27	176
whether it is an ox o a sheep,	Lv 22:28	176
o buy from your friend's hand,	Lv 25:14	176
not sow o gather in our crops?"	Lv 25:20	
'O in case a man has no kinsman,	Lv 25:26	
like a stranger o a sojourner,	Lv 25:35	
'Now if the means of a stranger o	Lv 25:47	
o to the descendants of a	Lv 25:47	176
o his uncle, or his uncle's son,	Lv 25:49	176
or his uncle, o his uncle's son,	Lv 25:49	176
o one of his blood relatives	Lv 25:49	176
o if he prospers, he may redeem	Lv 25:49	176
an image o a *sacred* pillar,	Lv 26:1	
o if their uncircumcised heart	Lv 26:41	176
'O if it is a female, then your	Lv 27:4	
not replace it o exchange it,	Lv 27:10	
for a bad, o a bad for a good;	Lv 27:10	176
o if he does exchange animal for	Lv 27:10	
value it as either good o bad;	Lv 27:12	996
value it as either good o bad;	Lv 27:14	996
'O if he consecrates to the LORD a	Lv 27:22	
whether ox o sheep, it is the	Lv 27:26	518
of man o animal or of the fields	Lv 27:28	
of man or animal o of the fields	Lv 27:28	
shall not be sold o redeemed.	Lv 27:28	
land o of the fruit of the tree,	Lv 27:30	
every tenth part of herd o flock,	Lv 27:32	
whether *it is* good o bad,	Lv 27:33	
o if he does exchange it, then	Lv 27:33	
o they will die."	Nu 4:20	
by his serving o carrying;	Nu 4:49	
'When a man o woman commits any of	Nu 5:6	176
o if a spirit of jealousy comes	Nu 5:14	176
o when a spirit of jealousy comes	Nu 5:30	176
a man o woman makes a special vow,	Nu 6:2	176
made from wine o strong drink,	Nu 6:3	
nor eat fresh o dried grapes.	Nu 6:3	
for his father o for his mother,	Nu 6:7	
for his brother o for his sister,	Nu 6:7	
two turtledoves o two young pigeons	Nu 6:10	176
one of you o of your generations	Nu 9:10	176
person, o is on a distant journey,	Nu 9:10	176
o *if it remained* in the daytime	Nu 9:21	176
Whether it was two days o a month	Nu 9:22	176
o a year that the cloud lingered over	Nu 9:22	176
o beat *it* in the mortar,	Nu 11:8	176
O should all the fish of the sea	Nu 11:22	518
will come true for you o not."	Nu 11:23	518
people who live in it are strong o	Nu 13:18	176
weak, whether they are few o many.	Nu 13:18	518
which they live, is it good o bad?	Nu 13:19	518
open camps o with fortifications?	Nu 13:19	518
How is the land, is it fat o lean?	Nu 13:20	518
Are there trees in it o not?	Nu 13:20	518
O would that we had died in this	Nu 14:2	176
"Do not go up, o you will be struck	Nu 14:42	3808
a burnt offering o a sacrifice to	Nu 15:3	176
o as a freewill offering or in	Nu 15:3	176
freewill offering o in your appointed	Nu 15:3	176
from the herd o from the flock.	Nu 15:3	176
offering o for the sacrifice,	Nu 15:5	176
'O for a ram you shall prepare as	Nu 15:6	176
as a burnt offering o a sacrifice,	Nu 15:8	176
o for peace offerings to the LORD,	Nu 15:8	176
done for each ox, o for each ram,	Nu 15:11	176
ram, o for each of the male lambs,	Nu 15:11	176
of the male lambs, o of the goats.	Nu 15:11	176
o one who may be among you	Nu 15:14	176
whether he is native o an alien,	Nu 15:30	
o you will be swept away in all their	Nu 16:26	6435
o if they suffer the fate of all	Nu 16:29	
o both they and you will die.	Nu 18:3	3808
all flesh, whether man o animal,	Nu 18:15	
"But the firstborn of an ox o	Nu 18:17	176
a sheep o the firstborn of a goat,	Nu 18:17	176
o they will bear sin and die.	Nu 18:22	
o the full produce from the wine vat.	Nu 18:27	
of Israel, o you will die.'"	Nu 18:32	3808
a sword o who has died *naturally,*	Nu 19:16	176
o a human bone or a grave,	Nu 19:16	176
or a human bone o a grave,	Nu 19:16	176
one who touched the bone o the one	Nu 19:18	176
one slain o the one dying *naturally*	Nu 19:18	176
one dying *naturally* o the grave.	Nu 19:18	176
o figs or vines or pomegranates,	Nu 20:5	
or figs o vines or pomegranates,	Nu 20:5	
or figs or vines o pomegranates,	Nu 20:5	
through field o through vineyard;	Nu 20:17	
not turning to the right o left,	Nu 20:17	
o I will come out with the sword	Nu 20:18	6435
turn off into field o vineyard;	Nu 21:22	
do anything, either small o great,	Nu 22:18	176
turn to the right hand o the left.	Nu 22:26	
O number the fourth part of Israel?	Nu 23:10	
O has He spoken, and will He not	Nu 23:19	
of the LORD, either good o bad,	Nu 24:13	176
o takes an oath to bind himself	Nu 30:2	176
none of her vows o her obligations	Nu 30:5	
vows o the rash statement of her lips	Nu 30:6	176
of a widow o of a divorced woman,	Nu 30:9	
o bound herself by an obligation	Nu 30:10	176
her vows o concerning the obligation	Nu 30:12	
it o her husband may annul it.	Nu 30:13	
then he confirms all her vows o	Nu 30:14	176
'O if he struck him with a wooden	Nu 35:18	176
o threw something at him lying in	Nu 35:20	176
o if he struck him down with his	Nu 35:21	176
o threw something at him without	Nu 35:22	176
o with any deadly object of stone,	Nu 35:23	176
o the alien who is with him.	Dt 1:16	
Do not fear o be dismayed.'	Dt 1:21	
have no knowledge of good o evil,	Dt 1:39	
aside to the right o to the left.	Dt 2:27	
god is there in heaven o on earth	Dt 3:24	
"O what great nation is there	Dt 4:8	
the likeness of male o female,	Dt 4:16	176
o has *anything* been heard like it?	Dt 4:32	176
"O has a god tried to go to take	Dt 4:34	176
o any likeness *of* what is in	Dt 5:8	
heaven above o on the earth beneath	Dt 5:8	
o in the water under the earth.	Dt 5:8	
not worship them o serve them;	Dt 5:9	
you o your son or your daughter or	Dt 5:14	
you or your son o your daughter or	Dt 5:14	
your daughter o your male servant	Dt 5:14	
male servant o your female servant	Dt 5:14	
your female servant o your ox or	Dt 5:14	
or your ox o your donkey or any	Dt 5:14	
your donkey o any of your cattle	Dt 5:14	
o your sojourner who stays with you,	Dt 5:14	
his field o his male servant or	Dt 5:21	
male servant o his female servant,	Dt 5:21	
his ox o his donkey or anything	Dt 5:21	
his ox or his donkey o anything	Dt 5:21	
aside to the right o to the left.	Dt 5:32	
there will be no male o female	Dt 7:14	
among you o among your cattle.	Dt 7:14	
silver o the gold that is on them,	Dt 7:25	
o you will be snared by it, for it	Dt 7:25	6435
would keep His commandments o not.	Dt 8:2	518
o for the uprightness of your heart	Dt 9:5	
stubbornness of this people o at their	Dt 9:27	
at their wickedness o their sin.	Dt 9:27	
o inheritance with his brothers;	Dt 10:9	
"O the anger of the LORD will be	Dt 11:17	
no portion o inheritance with you.	Dt 12:12	
tithe of your grain o new wine	Dt 12:17	
the tithe of your grain or new wine o	Dt 12:17	
o the firstborn of your herd or	Dt 12:17	
firstborn of your herd o flock,	Dt 12:17	
o any of your votive offerings	Dt 12:17	
vow, o your freewill offerings,	Dt 12:17	
o the contribution of your hand.	Dt 12:17	
as a gazelle o a deer is eaten,	Dt 12:22	
"If a prophet o a dreamer of	Dt 13:1	176
and gives you a sign o a wonder,	Dt 13:1	176
the sign o the wonder comes true,	Dt 13:2	
prophet o that dreamer of dreams;	Dt 13:3	176
"But that prophet o that dreamer	Dt 13:5	176
son, o your son or daughter,	Dt 13:6	176
son, or your son o daughter,	Dt 13:6	176
daughter, o the wife you cherish,	Dt 13:6	176
o your friend who is as your own	Dt 13:6	176
you, near you o far from you,	Dt 13:7	176
not yield to him o listen to him;	Dt 13:8	
nor shall you spare o conceal him.	Dt 13:8	
o among those that divide the hoof	Dt 14:7	
o you may sell it to a foreigner,	Dt 14:21	176
heart desires: for oxen, o sheep,	Dt 14:26	
for oxen, or sheep, o wine,	Dt 14:26	
or sheep, or wine, o strong drink,	Dt 14:26	
o whatever your heart desires;	Dt 14:26	
portion o inheritance among you.	Dt 14:27	
portion o inheritance among you,	Dt 14:29	
kinsman, a Hebrew man o woman,	Dt 15:12	176
such as lameness o blindness,	Dt 15:21	176
o any serious defect, you shall	Dt 15:21	
may eat it, as a gazelle o a deer.	Dt 15:22	
an ox o a sheep which has a blemish	Dt 17:1	
which has a blemish o any defect,	Dt 17:1	
a man o a woman who does what is	Dt 17:2	176
o the sun or the moon or any of	Dt 17:3	
or the sun o the moon or any of	Dt 17:3	176
moon o any of the heavenly host,	Dt 17:3	176
bring out that man o that woman	Dt 17:5	176
that is, the man o the woman,	Dt 17:5	176
two witnesses o three witnesses,	Dt 17:6	176
one kind of homicide o another,	Dt 17:8	
one kind of lawsuit o another,	Dt 17:8	
one kind of assault o another,	Dt 17:8	
to the Levitical priest o the judge	Dt 17:9	
to you, to the right o the left.	Dt 17:11	
o else his heart will turn away; nor	Dt 17:17	3808
to the right o the left,	Dt 17:20	
portion o inheritance with Israel;	Dt 18:1	
sacrifice, either an ox o a sheep,	Dt 18:3	518
his son o his daughter pass through	Dt 18:10	
o one who interprets omens,	Dt 18:10	
interprets omens, o a sorcerer,	Dt 18:10	
o one who casts a spell, or a	Dt 18:11	
one who casts a spell, o a medium,	Dt 18:11	
spell, or a medium, o a spiritist,	Dt 18:11	
o one who calls up the dead.	Dt 18:11	
anymore, o I will die.'	Dt 18:16	3808
o which he speaks in the name	Dt 18:20	
does not come about o come true,	Dt 18:22	
on account of any iniquity o any sin	Dt 19:15	
evidence of two o three witnesses	Dt 19:15	176
Do not be afraid, o panic,	Dt 20:3	
or panic, o tremble before them,	Dt 20:3	
which has not been plowed o sown,	Dt 21:4	
not obey his father o his mother,	Dt 21:18	
ox o his sheep straying away,	Dt 22:1	176
you, o if you do not know him,	Dt 22:2	
o his ox fallen down on the way,	Dt 22:4	176
way, in any tree o on the ground,	Dt 22:6	176
ground, with young ones o eggs,	Dt 22:6	176
on the young o on the eggs,	Dt 22:6	176
o all the produce of the seed which	Dt 22:9	6435
o has his male organ cut off shall	Dt 23:1	
"No Ammonite o Moabite shall	Dt 23:3	
seek their peace o their prosperity	Dt 23:6	
not see anything indecent among you o	Dt 23:14	
hire of a harlot o the wages of a dog	Dt 23:18	
o anything that may be loaned at	Dt 23:19	
o if the latter husband dies who	Dt 24:3	176
o an upper millstone in pledge,	Dt 24:6	
with him violently o sells him,	Dt 24:7	
your countrymen o one of your aliens	Dt 24:14	176
pervert the justice due an alien o	Dt 24:17	
I have not transgressed o forgotten	Dt 26:13	
makes an idol o a molten image,	Dt 27:15	
dishonors his father o mother.'	Dt 27:16	
of his father o of his mother.'	Dt 27:22	176
today, to the right o to the left,	Dt 28:14	
you no grain, new wine, o oil,	Dt 28:51	
your herd o the young of your flock	Dt 28:51	
you o your fathers have not known.	Dt 28:64	
you drunk wine o strong drink,	Dt 29:6	
not be among you a man o woman,	Dt 29:18	176
a man or woman, o family or tribe,	Dt 29:18	176
a man or woman, or family o tribe,	Dt 29:18	176
not be afraid o tremble at them,	Dt 31:6	
will not fail you o forsake you."	Dt 31:6	
will not fail you o forsake you.	Dt 31:8	
Do not fear o be dismayed."	Dt 31:8	
is none *remaining,* bond o free.	Dt 32:36	
I will not fail you o forsake you.	Jos 1:5	
it to the right o to the left,	Jos 1:7	
Do not tremble o be dismayed, for	Jos 1:9	
for us o for our adversaries?"	Jos 5:13	518
only about two o three thousand	Jos 7:3	176
"Do not fear o be dismayed.	Jos 8:1	
not a man was left in Ai o Bethel	Jos 8:17	
no place to flee this way o that,	Jos 8:20	
of those who survived o escaped.	Jos 8:22	
like that before it o after it,	Jos 10:14	
"Do not fear o be dismayed!	Jos 10:25	
the Geshurites o the Maacathites;	Jos 13:13	

their inheritance Beersheba **o** Sheba	Jos 19:2	
o rebel against us by building an	Jos 22:19	
o if in an unfaithful act against	Jos 22:22	
o if to offer a burnt offering or	Jos 22:23	
offering **o** grain offering on it,	Jos 22:23	
o if to offer sacrifices of peace	Jos 22:23	
burnt offering **o** for sacrifice;	Jos 22:26	
say *this* to us **o** to our generations	Jos 22:28	
burnt offering **o** for sacrifice;	Jos 22:28	
grain offering **o** for sacrifice,	Jos 22:29	
to the right hand **o** to the left,	Jos 23:6	
o mention the name of their gods,	Jos 23:7	
gods, **o** make *anyone* swear *by them,*	Jos 23:7	
swear *by them,* **o** serve them,	Jos 23:7	
or serve them, **o** bow down to them.	Jos 23:7	
but not by your sword **o** your bow.	Jos 24:12	
o the gods of the Amorites in	Jos 24:15	
your transgression **o** your sins.	Jos 24:19	
o Taanach and its villages,	Jg 1:27	
o the inhabitants of Dor and its	Jg 1:27	
o the inhabitants of Ibleam and	Jg 1:27	
o the inhabitants of Megiddo and	Jg 1:27	
o the inhabitants of Nahalol;	Jg 1:30	
Acco, **o** the inhabitants of Sidon,	Jg 1:31	
inhabitants of Sidon, **o** of Ahlab,	Jg 1:31	
Sidon, or of Ahlab, **o** of Achzib,	Jg 1:31	
Ahlab, or of Achzib, **o** of Helbah,	Jg 1:31	
Achzib, or of Helbah, **o** of Aphik,	Jg 1:31	
Helbah, or of Aphik, **o** of Rehob.	Jg 1:31	
o the inhabitants of Beth-anath,	Jg 1:33	
practices **o** their stubborn ways.	Jg 2:19	
it as their fathers did, **o** not."	Jg 2:22	518
Not a shield **o** a spear was seen	Jg 5:8	
as well as no sheep, ox, **o** donkey.	Jg 6:4	
for Baal, **o** will you deliver him?	Jg 6:31	518
o that one man rule over you?"	Jg 9:2	518
o did he ever fight against them?	Jg 11:25	518
besides her he had no son **o** daughter.	Jg 11:34	176
not to drink wine **o** strong drink,	Jg 13:4	
shall not drink wine **o** strong drink	Jg 13:7	
nor drink wine **o** strong drink,	Jg 13:14	
appear to Manoah **o** his wife again.	Jg 13:21	
relatives, **o** among all our people,	Jg 14:3	
father **o** mother what he had done.	Jg 14:6	
o we will burn you and	Jg 14:15	6435
not told *it* to my father **o** mother;	Jg 14:16	
o to be priest to a tribe and a	Jg 18:19	176
o else fierce men will fall upon you	Jg 18:25	6435
the night in Gibeah **o** Ramah."	Jg 19:13	176
this has *ever* happened **o** been seen	Jg 19:30	
Benjamin, **o** shall I cease?"	Jg 20:28	518
when their fathers **o** their brothers	Jg 21:22	176
"Do not urge me to leave you **o**	Ru 1:16	
young men, whether poor **o** rich.	Ru 3:10	518
from his brothers **o** from the court	Ru 4:10	
thrust it into the pan, **o** kettle,	1Sa 2:14	176
the pan, or kettle, **o** caldron,	1Sa 2:14	176
pan, or kettle, or caldron, **o** pot;	1Sa 2:14	176
piece of silver **o** a loaf of bread and	1Sa 2:36	
by sacrifice **o** offering forever."	1Sa 3:14	
o you will become slaves to	1Sa 4:9	6435
did not answer **o** pay attention.	1Sa 4:20	
aside to the right **o** to the left.	1Sa 6:12	
o else my father will cease *to be*	1Sa 9:5	6435
o whose donkey have I taken,	1Sa 12:3	
I taken, **o** whom have I defrauded?	1Sa 12:3	
o from whose hand have I taken	1Sa 12:3	
defrauded us **o** oppressed us	1Sa 12:4	
oppressed us **o** taken anything	1Sa 12:4	
which can not profit **o** deliver,	1Sa 12:21	
Hebrews will make swords **o** spears."	1Sa 13:19	176
to save by many **o** by few."	1Sa 14:6	176
you bring me his ox **o** his sheep,	1Sa 14:34	
any mighty man **o** any valiant man,	1Sa 14:52	
will not lie **o** change His mind;	1Sa 15:29	
o at the height of his stature,	1Sa 16:7	
When a lion **o** a bear came and took	1Sa 17:34	
not deliver by sword **o** by spear;	1Sa 17:47	
my life **o** my father's family	1Sa 18:18	
does nothing either great **o** small	1Sa 20:2	176
o he will be grieved.' But truly as	1Sa 20:3	6435
o the third day, behold, if	1Sa 20:12	
meal, either yesterday **o** today?"	1Sa 20:27	1571
bread, **o** whatever can be found."	1Sa 21:3	176
not a spear **o** a sword on hand?	1Sa 21:8	176
who is sorry for me **o** discloses to me	1Sa 22:8	
impute anything to his servant **o**	1Sa 22:15	
no evil **o** rebellion in my hands,	1Sa 24:11	
o a troubled heart to my lord,	1Sa 25:31	
o his day will come that he dies,	1Sa 26:10	176
o he will go down into battle and	1Sa 26:10	176
away, but no one saw **o** knew *it,*	1Sa 26:12	
O what evil is in my hand?	1Sa 26:18	
not leave a man **o** a woman alive,	1Sa 27:9	
not leave a man **o** a woman alive to	1Sa 27:11	
dreams **o** by Urim or by prophets.	1Sa 28:6	1571
dreams or by Urim **o** by prophets.	1Sa 28:6	1571
through prophets **o** by dreams;	1Sa 28:15	1571
these days, **o** *rather* these years,	1Sa 29:3	176
o in the battle he may become an	1Sa 29:4	3808
had not eaten bread **o** drunk water	1Sa 30:12	
that you will not kill me **o** deliver me	1Sa 30:15	
missing, whether small **o** great,	1Sa 30:19	5704
small or great, sons **o** daughters,	1Sa 30:19	
spoil **o** anything that they had	1Sa 30:19	5704
O the daughters of the Philistines	2Sa 1:20	6435
Let not dew **o** rain be on you,	2Sa 1:21	
did not turn to the right **o** to the left	2Sa 2:19	
"Turn to your right **o** to your left,	2Sa 2:21	176
has a discharge, **o** who is a leper,	2Sa 3:29	
o who takes hold of a distaff,	2Sa 3:29	
distaff, **o** who falls by the sword,	2Sa 3:29	
by the sword, **o** who lacks bread."	2Sa 3:29	
if I taste bread **o** anything else	2Sa 3:35	176
"The blind **o** the lame shall not	2Sa 5:8	
from his own flock **o** his own herd,	2Sa 12:4	
o I will capture the city myself	2Sa 12:28	6435
speak to Amnon either good **o** bad;	2Sa 13:22	5704
can turn to the right **o** to the left	2Sa 14:19	
every man who has any suit **o** cause	2Sa 15:4	
o he will overtake us quickly	2Sa 15:14	6435
be, whether for death **o** for life,	2Sa 15:21	518
of the caves **o** in another place;	2Sa 17:9	176
o else the king and all the people	2Sa 17:16	6435
O can your servant taste what I	2Sa 19:35	518
taste what I eat **o** what I drink?	2Sa 19:35	
O can I hear anymore the voice of	2Sa 19:35	518
o has anything been taken for us?"	2Sa 19:42	518
I should swallow up **o** destroy!	2Sa 20:20	
o gold with Saul or his house,	2Sa 21:4	
or gold with Saul **o** his house,	2Sa 21:4	
O will you flee three months	2Sa 24:13	518
O shall there be three days'	2Sa 24:13	
not know how to go out **o** come in.	1Ki 3:7	
too many to be numbered **o** counted.	1Ki 3:8	
could not be counted **o** numbered.	1Ki 8:5	
heaven above **o** on earth beneath,	1Ki 8:23	
if there is blight **o** mildew,	1Ki 8:37	
locust **o** grasshopper, if their	1Ki 8:37	
whatever prayer **o** supplication is	1Ki 8:38	
supplication is made by any man **o**	1Ki 8:38	
land of the enemy, far off **o** near;	1Ki 8:46	176
may He not leave us **o** forsake us,	1Ki 8:57	
"But if you **o** your sons indeed	1Ki 9:6	
nor would I eat bread **o** drink water	1Ki 13:8	
nor will I eat bread **o** drink water	1Ki 13:16	
going out **o** coming in to Asa king of	1Ki 15:17	
there is no nation **o** kingdom where	1Ki 18:10	
he made the kingdom **o** nation swear	1Ki 18:10	
he is occupied **o** gone aside,	1Ki 18:27	
or gone aside, **o** is on a journey,	1Ki 18:27	
o perhaps he is asleep and needs	1Ki 18:27	
"Do not listen **o** consent."	1Ki 20:8	
o if they have come out for war,	1Ki 20:18	
o else you shall pay a talent of	1Ki 20:39	176
o else, if it pleases you, I will	1Ki 21:6	176
to battle **o** shall I refrain?"	1Ki 22:6	518
to battle, **o** shall we refrain?"	1Ki 22:15	518
"Do not fight with small **o** great,	1Ki 22:31	
mountain **o** into some valley."	2Ki 2:16	176
death **o** unfruitfulness any longer.	2Ki 2:21	
no water for the army **o** for the cattle	2Ki 3:9	
o to the captain of the army?' "	2Ki 4:13	176
but there was no sound **o** response.	2Ki 4:31	369
there, more than once **o** twice.	2Ki 6:10	
floor, **o** from the wine press?"	2Ki 6:27	176
then let no one escape **o**	2Ki 9:15	
And two **o** three officials looked	2Ki 9:32	
o vessels of silver from the money	2Ki 12:13	
have struck five **o** six times,	2Ki 13:19	176
o cast them from His presence until	2Ki 13:23	
o their ordinances or the law,	2Ki 17:34	
or their ordinances **o** the law,	2Ki 17:34	
o the commandments which the LORD	2Ki 17:34	
this city **o** shoot an arrow there;	2Ki 19:32	
not come before it with a shield **o**	2Ki 19:32	3808
ten steps **o** go back ten steps?"	2Ki 20:9	518
aside to the right **o** to the left.	2Ki 22:2	
that no man might make his son **o**	2Ki 23:10	
o three months to be swept away	1Ch 21:12	
o else three days of the sword of	1Ch 21:12	
o offer a burnt offering which	1Ch 21:24	
o *what is baked in* the pan or	1Ch 23:29	
in the pan **o** what is well-mixed,	1Ch 23:29	
ask for riches, wealth **o** honor,	2Ch 1:11	
o the life of those who hate you,	2Ch 1:11	
could not be counted **o** numbered.	2Ch 5:6	
like You in heaven **o** on earth,	2Ch 6:14	
if there is blight **o** mildew,	2Ch 6:28	
if there is locust **o** grasshopper,	2Ch 6:28	
o whatever sickness *there is,*	2Ch 6:28	
whatever prayer **o** supplication is	2Ch 6:29	
man **o** by all Your people Israel,	2Ch 6:29	
captive to a land far off **o** near,	2Ch 6:36	176
o if I command the locust to	2Ch 7:13	
o if I send pestilence among My	2Ch 7:13	
o concerning the storehouses.	2Ch 8:15	
up **o** fight against your relatives;	2Ch 11:4	
who went out **o** to him who came in,	2Ch 15:5	
to death, whether small **o** great,	2Ch 15:13	5704
small or great, man **o** woman.	2Ch 15:13	5704
from going out **o** coming in to Asa	2Ch 16:1	
to battle, **o** shall I refrain?"	2Ch 18:5	518
to battle, **o** shall I refrain?"	2Ch 18:14	518
"Do not fight with small **o** great,	2Ch 18:30	
in unrighteousness **o** partiality	2Ch 19:7	
o the taking of a bribe."	2Ch 19:7	
o judgment, or pestilence, or	2Ch 20:9	
sword, *or* judgment, **o** pestilence,	2Ch 20:9	
judgment, or pestilence, **o** famine,	2Ch 20:9	
'Do not fear **o** be dismayed because	2Ch 20:15	
Do not fear **o** be dismayed;	2Ch 20:17	
o offered burnt offerings in the holy	2Ch 29:7	
divisions, whether great **o** small,	2Ch 31:15	
cities, **o** in each and every city,	2Ch 31:19	
do not fear **o** be dismayed because	2Ch 32:7	
you **o** mislead you like this,	2Ch 32:15	
for no god of any nation **o** kingdom	2Ch 32:15	
o from the hand of my fathers.	2Ch 32:15	
aside to the right **o** to the left.	2Ch 34:2	
compassion on young man **o** virgin,	2Ch 36:17	
man or virgin, old man **o** infirm;	2Ch 36:17	
not pay tribute, custom **o** toll,	Ezr 4:13	
overthrow any king **o** people who	Ezr 6:12	
o toll *on* any of the priests,	Ezr 7:24	
o servants of this house of God.	Ezr 7:24	
whether for death **o** for banishment	Ezr 7:26	2006
o for confiscation of goods or for	Ezr 7:26	2006
of goods **o** for imprisonment."	Ezr 7:26	
their peace **o** their prosperity,	Ezr 9:12	
task *be done* in one **o** two days,	Ezr 10:13	
I had gone **o** what I had done;	Ne 2:16	
o the rest who did the work.	Ne 2:16	
have no portion, right **o** memorial	Ne 2:20	
They will not know **o** see until we	Ne 4:11	
houses **o** their descendants,	Ne 7:61	
do not mourn **o** weep."	Ne 8:9	
an end of them **o** forsake them,	Ne 9:31	
not kept Your law **O** paid attention	Ne 9:34	
You **o** turn from their evil deeds.	Ne 9:35	
o take their daughters for our sons.	Ne 10:30	
who bring wares **o** any grain on the	Ne 10:31	
them on the sabbath **o** a holy day;	Ne 10:31	
no Ammonite **o** Moabite should ever	Ne 13:1	
Once **o** twice the traders and	Ne 13:20	
for your sons **o** for yourselves.	Ne 13:25	
for she had no father **o** mother.	Es 2:7	369
known her people **o** her kindred,	Es 2:10	
known her kindred **o** her people,	Es 2:20	
man **o** woman who comes to the king	Es 4:11	
do not eat **o** drink for three days,	Es 4:16	
drink for three days, night **o** day.	Es 4:16	
not stand up **o** tremble before him,	Es 5:9	
"What honor **o** dignity has been	Es 6:3	
people **o** province which might attack	Es 8:11	
o their memory fade from their	Es 9:28	
womb, **O** hide trouble from my eyes.	Jb 3:10	
O with princes who had gold, Who	Jb 3:15	176
"**O** like a miscarriage which is	Jb 3:16	176
O where were the upright destroyed?	Jb 4:7	
O does the ox low over his fodder?	Jb 6:5	518
O is there any taste in the white	Jb 6:6	518
of stones, **O** is my flesh bronze?	Jb 6:12	518
'Give me *something,*' **O**,	Jb 6:22	
O, 'Deliver me from the hand of	Jb 6:23	
from the hand of the adversary,' **O**,	Jb 6:23	
"Am I the sea, **o** the sea monster,	Jb 7:12	518
"Does God pervert justice? **O** does	Jb 8:3	518
O do You see as a man sees?	Jb 10:4	518
mortal, **O** Your years as man's years,	Jb 10:5	518
"If He passes by **o** shuts up, Or	Jb 11:10	
or shuts up, **O** calls an assembly,	Jb 11:10	
"**O** speak to the earth, and let it	Jb 12:8	176
O will you deceive Him as one	Jb 13:9	518
O let me speak, then reply to me.	Jb 13:22	176
O will You pursue the dry chaff?	Jb 13:25	
O they become insignificant, but	Jb 14:21	
O with words which are not	Jb 15:3	
O were you brought forth before	Jb 15:7	
pure, **O** he who is born of a woman,	Jb 15:14	
O what plagues you that you answer?	Jb 16:3	176
O the rock to be moved from its	Jb 18:4	
O posterity among his people,	Jb 18:19	
O does their calamity fall on them?	Jb 21:17	
O a wise man be useful to himself?	Jb 22:2	3588
O profit if you make your ways	Jb 22:3	518
O darkness, so that you cannot	Jb 22:11	176
O how can he be clean who is born	Jb 25:4	
O as a hut *which* the watchman has	Jb 27:18	
In precious onyx, **o** sapphire.	Jb 28:16	
"Gold **o** glass cannot equal it,	Jb 28:17	
O in his disaster therefore cry	Jb 30:24	518
O the heritage of the Almighty	Jb 31:2	
way, **O** my heart followed my eyes,	Jb 31:7	
O if any spot has stuck to my hands,	Jb 31:7	
O I have lurked at my neighbor's	Jb 31:9	
the claim of my male **o** female slaves	Jb 31:13	
O have caused the eyes of the	Jb 31:16	
O have eaten my morsel alone, And	Jb 31:17	
O that the needy had no covering,	Jb 31:19	
O the moon going in splendor,	Jb 31:26	
O exulted when evil befell him?	Jb 31:29	
O have caused its owners to lose	Jb 31:39	
"Indeed God speaks once, **O** twice,	Jb 33:14	
There is no darkness **o** deep shadow	Jb 34:22	
O what does He receive from your	Jb 35:7	176
O all the forces of *your* strength?	Jb 36:19	
for correction, **o** for His world,	Jb 37:13	518
His world, **O** for lovingkindness,	Jb 37:13	518
O should a man say that he would	Jb 37:20	518
O who stretched the line on it?	Jb 38:5	176
O who laid its cornerstone,	Jb 38:6	176
"**O** *who* enclosed the sea with	Jb 38:8	
O walked in the recesses	Jb 38:16	
O have you seen the gates of deep	Jb 38:17	
O have you seen the storehouses of	Jb 38:22	
O the east wind scattered on	Jb 38:24	
O a way for the thunderbolt,	Jb 38:25	
O who has begotten the drops of	Jb 38:28	176
O loose the cords of Orion?	Jb 38:31	176
O fix their rule over the earth?	Jb 38:33	518
O given understanding to the	Jb 38:36	176
O tip the water jars of the	Jb 38:37	
O satisfy the appetite of the	Jb 38:39	
O do you know the time they give	Jb 39:2	
O will he spend the night at your	Jb 39:9	518
O will he harrow the valleys after	Jb 39:10	518

O that a wild beast may trample Jb 39:15
"O do you have an arm like God, Jb 40:9 518
O press down his tongue with a Jb 41:1
O pierce his jaw with a hook? Jb 41:2
O will he speak to you soft words? Jb 41:3 518
O will you bind him for your Jb 41:5
O his head with fishing spears? Jb 41:7
his limbs, O his mighty strength, Jb 41:12
strength, o his orderly frame. Jb 41:12
spear, the dart o the javelin. Jb 41:26
O he will tear my soul like a lion, Ps 7:2 6435
O have plundered him who without Ps 7:4
o I will sleep the *sleep of* death, Ps 13:3 6435
of my youth o my transgressions; Ps 25:7
Do not be as the horse o as the Ps 32:9
it were my friend o brother; Ps 35:14
O his descendants begging bread. Ps 37:25
O let him be condemned when he is Ps 37:33
O extended our hands to a strange Ps 44:20
O give to God a ransom for him Ps 49:7 3808
O drink the blood of male goats? Ps 50:13
O I will tear *you* in pieces, Ps 50:22 6435
O a skillful caster of spells. Ps 58:5
Do not slay them, o my people will Ps 59:11 6435
the LORD better than an ox O Ps 69:31
O has He in anger withdrawn His Ps 77:9 518
O You gave birth to the Ps 90:2
by, O *as* a watch in the night. Ps 90:4
years, O if due to strength, Ps 90:10
O of the arrow that flies by day; Ps 91:5
O of the destruction that lays Ps 91:6
O can show forth all His praise? Ps 106:2
O the binder of sheaves his bosom; Ps 129:7
O in things too difficult for me. Ps 131:1
my eyes O slumber to my eyelids Ps 132:4
O where can I flee from Your Ps 139:7
O I will become like those who go Ps 143:7
O the son of man, that You think Ps 144:3
of the LORD O loathe His reproof, Pr 3:11
O you will give your vigor to others Pr 5:9 6435
having no chief, Officer o ruler, Pr 6:7
O can a man walk on hot coals And Pr 6:28 518
O as *one in* fetters to the Pr 7:22
crooked o perverted in them. Pr 8:8
Do not reprove a scoffer, o he will Pr 9:8 6435
O you will not discern words of Pr 14:7
Do not love sleep, o you will become Pr 20:13 6435
curses his father o his mother, Pr 20:20
himself O who gives to the rich, Pr 22:16
O crush the afflicted at the gate; Pr 22:22
O go with a hot-tempered man, Pr 22:24
O you will learn his ways And find a Pr 22:25 6435
man, O desire his delicacies; Pr 23:6
O go into the fields of the Pr 23:10
O with gluttonous eaters of meat; Pr 23:20
O like one who lies down on the Pr 23:34
O the LORD will see *it* and be Pr 24:18 6435
O be envious of the wicked; Pr 24:19
O he who hears *it* will reproach Pr 25:10 6435
O he will become weary of you Pr 25:17 6435
o *like* vinegar on soda, Is he Pr 25:20
O you will also be like him. Pr 26:4 6435
o who hires those who pass by. Pr 26:10
own friend o your father's friend, Pr 27:10
who robs his father o his mother And Pr 28:24
foolish man either rages o laughs, Pr 29:9
What is His name o His son's name? Pr 30:4
Do not add to His words O He will Pr 30:6 6435
O that I not be in want and steal, Pr 30:9
O he will curse you and you will be Pr 30:10 6435
O if you have plotted *evil,* Pr 30:32
O your ways to that which destroys Pr 31:3
O for rulers to desire strong Pr 31:4
he will be a wise man o a fool? Ec 2:19 176
o impulsive in thought to bring up Ec 5:2
whether he eats little o much; Ec 5:12
o authority over the day of death; Ec 8:8
should never sleep day o night), Ec 8:16
whether *it will be* love o hatred; Ec 9:1 1571
is no activity o planning or knowledge Ec 9:10
there is no activity or planning o Ec 9:10
or knowledge o wisdom in Sheol Ec 9:10
portion to seven, o even to eight, Ec 11:2
the south o toward the north, Ec 11:3
o evening sowing will succeed, Ec 11:6 176
o whether both of them alike will Ec 11:6
hidden, whether it is good o evil. Ec 12:14
o by the hinds of the field, SS 2:7 176
do not arouse o awaken *my* love SS 2:7
is like a gazelle o a young stag. SS 2:9 176
and be like a gazelle O a young SS 2:17 176
o by the hinds of the field, SS 3:5 176
will not arouse o awaken *my* love Until SS 3:5
see whether the vine had budded O SS 6:11
Do not arouse o awaken *my* love Until SS 8:4
And be like a gazelle o a young SS 8:14 176
Not pressed out o bandaged, Is 1:6
blood of bulls, lambs o goats. Is 1:11
O as a garden that has no water. Is 1:30
It will not be pruned o hoed, Is 5:6
No one in it is weary o stumbles, Is 5:27
stumbles, None slumbers o sleeps; Is 5:27
Like a terebinth o an oak Whose Is 6:13
deep as Sheol o high as heaven." Is 7:11 176
cry out 'My father' o 'My mother,' Is 8:4
they fear o be in dread of *it.* Is 8:12
of *His* government o of peace, Is 9:7
on their orphans o their widows; Is 9:17
captives O fall among the slain. Is 10:4
Carchemish, O Hamath like Arpad, Is 10:9 518
Arpad, O Samaria like Damascus? Is 10:9 518
o opened *its* beak or chirped." Is 10:14
or opened *its* beak o chirped." Is 10:14
O like a rod lifting *him who* Is 10:15
They will not hurt o destroy in Is 11:9
O like sheep with none to gather Is 13:14
silver o take pleasure in gold. Is 13:17
It will never be inhabited o lived Is 13:20
Then, like fleeing birds o Is 16:2
cries of joy o jubilant shouting, Is 16:10
O it will be like one gleaning Is 17:5
Two o three olives on the topmost Is 17:6
Four o five on the branches of a Is 17:6
O like branches which they Is 17:9
O like whirling dust before a gale. Is 17:13
for Egypt Which *its* head o tail, Is 19:15
tail, *its* palm branch o bulrush, Is 19:15
without house o harbor; It is Is 23:1
will not be stored up o hoarded, Is 23:18
"O let him rely on My protection, Is 27:5 176
O like the slaughter of His slain, Is 27:7 518
anytime during the day o night, Is 28:19
O your fetters will be made stronger; Is 28:22 6435
O as when a thirsty man dreams Is 29:8
"Who sees us?" o "Who knows us?" Is 29:15
O what is formed say to him who Is 29:16
Who are not for help o profit, Is 30:5
O to scoop water from a cistern." Is 30:14
turn to the right o to the left. Is 30:21
"As the lion o the young lion Is 31:4
O the rogue be spoken of *as* Is 32:5
O as *one* withers from the fig tree. Is 34:4
will not be quenched night o day; Is 34:10
this city o shoot an arrow there; Is 37:33
o throw up a siege ramp against it. Is 37:33 3808
O as His counselor has informed Is 40:13
O what likeness will you compare Is 40:18
Does not become weary o tired. Is 40:28
O announce to us what is coming; Is 41:22 176
Indeed, do good o evil, that we Is 41:23
O from former times, that we may Is 41:26
not cry out o raise *His voice,* Is 42:2
not be disheartened o crushed Until Is 42:4
O so deaf as My messenger whom I Is 42:19
O so blind as the servant of the Is 42:19
O are hidden away in prisons; Is 42:22
O let them hear and say, Is 43:9
O ponder things of the past. Is 43:18
Me, O is there any *other* Rock? Is 44:8
own witnesses fail to see o know, Is 44:9
a god o cast an idol to no profit? Is 44:10
and takes a cypress o an oak and Is 44:14
knowledge o understanding to say, Is 44:19
O the thing you are making *say,* Is 45:9
O to a woman, 'To what are you Is 45:10
Without any payment o reward," Is 45:13
not be put to shame o humiliated Is 45:17
o destroyed from My presence." Is 48:19
"They will not hunger o thirst, Is 49:10
heat o sun strike them down; Is 49:10
O the captives of a tyrant be Is 49:24 518
O to whom of My creditors did I Is 50:1 176
O have I no power to deliver? Is 50:2 518
He has no *stately* form o majesty Is 53:2
will not be closed day o night, Is 60:11
Nor devastation o destruction Is 60:18
days of old they have not heard o Is 64:4 3808
not be remembered o come to mind. Is 65:17
O an old man who does not live out Is 65:20
O bear *children* for calamity; Is 65:23
They will do no evil o harm in all Is 65:25
"O shall I who gives delivery Is 66:9 518
o I will dismay you before them. Jer 1:17 6435
O is he a homeborn servant? Jer 2:14 518
O what are you doing on the road Jer 2:18
O a land of thick darkness? Jer 2:31 518
ornaments, O a bride her attire? Jer 2:32
O else My wrath will go forth like Jer 4:4 6435
not know the way of the LORD O Jer 5:4
we will not see sword o famine. Jer 5:12
"Be warned, O Jerusalem, O I shall Jer 6:8 6435
alien, the orphan, o the widow, Jer 7:6
not lift up cry o prayer for them, Jer 7:16
o command them in the day that I Jer 7:22
did not obey o incline their ear, Jer 7:24
listen to Me o incline their ear, Jer 7:26
their God o accept correction; Jer 7:28
o the valley of the son of Hinnom, Jer 7:32
will not be gathered o buried; Jer 8:2
again O to set up my curtains. Jer 10:20
o You will bring me to nothing. Jer 10:24 6435
did not obey o incline their ear, Jer 11:8
lift up a cry o prayer for them; Jer 11:14
his skin O the leopard his spots? Jer 13:23
stranger in the land O like a traveler Jer 14:8
'There will be no sword o famine Jer 14:15
O if I enter the city, Behold, Jer 14:18
O have You loathed Zion? Jer 14:19 518
O can the heavens grant showers? Jer 14:22 518
O who will mourn for you, Jer 15:5
O who will turn aside to ask about Jer 15:5
Iron from the north, o bronze? Jer 15:12
sons o daughters in this place." Jer 16:2
will not be lamented o buried; Jer 16:4
o go to lament o to console them; Jer 16:5
or go to lament o to console them; Jer 16:5
himself o shave his head for them. Jer 16:6
drink for anyone's father o mother. Jer 16:7
o what is our sin which we have Jer 16:10
o bring anything in through the gates Jer 17:21
not listen o incline their ears, Jer 17:23
not to listen o take correction. Jer 17:23
concerning a nation o concerning a Jer 18:7
to pull down, o to destroy *it;* Jer 18:7
"O at another moment I might Jer 18:9
a nation o concerning a kingdom Jer 18:9
kingdom to build up o to plant *it;* Jer 18:9
O is the cold flowing water *from* a Jer 18:14 518
Do not forgive their iniquity O Jer 18:23
I never commanded o spoke of, Jer 19:5
Topheth o the valley of Ben-hinnom, Jer 19:6
Him O speak anymore in His name," Jer 20:9
O who will enter into our Jer 21:13
Also do not mistreat o do Jer 22:3
stranger, the orphan, o the widow; Jer 22:3
weep for the dead o mourn for him, Jer 22:10
return O see his native land. Jer 22:10
'Alas, my brother!' o, 'Alas, sister!' Jer 22:18
'Alas for the master!' o, 'Alas for his Jer 22:18
O is he an undesirable vessel? Jer 22:28 518
David O ruling again in Judah.'" Jer 22:30
did not send them o command them, Jer 23:32
this people o the prophet or a priest Jer 23:33 176
o a priest asks you saying, Jer 23:33 176
prophet o the priest or the people Jer 23:34
the priest o the people who say, Jer 23:34
o, 'What has the LORD spoken?' Jer 23:35
be lamented, gathered o buried; Jer 25:33
that the nation o the kingdom Jer 27:8
soothsayers o your sorcerers Jer 27:9
o overthrown anymore forever." Jer 31:40
obey Your voice o walk in Your law; Jer 32:23
a desolation, without man o beast; Jer 32:43
is waste, without man o beast, Jer 33:12
a Hebrew man o a Hebrew woman; Jer 34:9
Me o incline their ear to Me. Jer 34:14
not drink wine, you o your sons, Jer 35:6
not plant a vineyard o own one; Jer 35:7
wives, our sons o our daughters, Jer 35:8
not have vineyard o field or seed. Jer 35:9
not have vineyard or field o seed. Jer 35:9
inclined your ear o listened to Me. Jer 35:15
had read three o four columns, Jer 36:23
you, o against your servants, Jer 37:18
servants, o against this people, Jer 37:18
against you o against this land'? Jer 37:19
o else go anywhere it seems right Jer 40:5 176
it is pleasant o unpleasant, Jer 42:6 518
where we will not see war o hear Jer 42:14
of a trumpet o hunger for bread, Jer 42:14
they will have no survivors o refugees Jer 42:17
to death o exile us to Babylon." Jer 43:3
'But they did not listen o incline Jer 44:5
walked in My law o My statutes, Jer 44:10
there will be no refugees o survivors Jer 44:14
of the LORD o walked in His law, Jer 44:23
His statutes o His testimonies, Jer 44:23
word will stand, Mine o theirs. Jer 44:28
O like Carmel by the sea. Jer 46:18
O was he caught among thieves? Jer 48:27 518
O has he no heirs? Jer 49:1 518
"It has no gates o bars; Jer 49:31
never again be inhabited O dwelt in Jer 50:39
in it, whether man o beast, Jer 51:62
was no one who escaped o survived La 2:22
O grieve the sons of men. La 3:33
any living mortal, o *any* man, La 3:39
whether they listen o not Ezk 2:5 518
to them whether they listen o not, Ezk 2:7 518
speech o difficult language, Ezk 3:5
speech o difficult language, Ezk 3:6
of them o be dismayed before them, Ezk 3:9
them, whether they listen o not, Ezk 3:11 518
and you do not warn him o speak Ezk 3:18
wickedness o from his wicked way, Ezk 3:19
died of itself o was torn by beasts, Ezk 4:14
will die by plague o be consumed by Ezk 5:12
false vision o flattering divination Ezk 12:24
visions o practice divination, Ezk 13:23
house of Israel o of the immigrants Ezk 14:7
their sons o *their* daughters. Ezk 14:16 518
"O *if* I should bring a sword on Ezk 14:17 176
their sons o *their* daughters, Ezk 14:18
"O *if* I should send a plague Ezk 14:19 176
either *their* son o *their* daughter. Ezk 14:20 518
o can *men* take a peg from it on Ezk 15:3 518
salt o even wrapped in cloths. Ezk 16:4
adultery o shed blood are judged; Ezk 16:38
merely walked in their ways o done Ezk 16:47
o lift up his eyes to the idols of the Ezk 18:6
o defile his neighbor's wife or Ezk 18:6
o approach a woman during her Ezk 18:6
money on interest o take increase, Ezk 18:8
o lift up his eyes to the idols of the Ezk 18:15
o defile his neighbor's wife, Ezk 18:15
o oppress anyone, or retain a Ezk 18:16
oppress anyone, o retain a pledge, Ezk 18:16
retain a pledge, o commit robbery, Ezk 18:16
does not take interest o increase, Ezk 18:17
fathers o keep their ordinances Ezk 20:18
o defile yourselves with their Ezk 20:18
o according to your corrupt deeds, Ezk 20:44
O shall we rejoice, Ezk 21:10 176
o can your hands be strong in Ezk 22:14 518
land that is not cleansed o rained on Ezk 22:24
to them o remember Egypt anymore.' Ezk 23:27
a prickling brier o a painful thorn Ezk 28:24

be brought together **o** gathered.	Ezk 29:5	
healing **o** wrapped with a bandage,	Ezk 30:21	
no one to search **o** seek *for them.*	Ezk 34:6	
O that you should drink of the	Ezk 34:18	
o with their detestable things,	Ezk 37:23	
o with any of their transgressions;	Ezk 37:23	
walls and having no bars **o** gates,	Ezk 38:11	
o gather firewood from the forests,	Ezk 39:10	
o, eight tables on which they	Ezk 40:41	
shall not marry a widow **o** a divorced	Ezk 44:22	
o a widow who is the widow of a	Ezk 44:22	
o for a sister who has not had a	Ezk 44:25	
priests shall not eat any bird **o** beast	Ezk 44:31	
death **o** has been torn to pieces.	Ezk 44:31	
kor (*which is* ten baths **o**	Ezk 45:14	
who goes astray **o** is naive;	Ezk 45:20	
o peace offerings *as* a freewill	Ezk 46:12	176
not sell **o** exchange any of it,	Ezk 48:14	
o alienate this choice *portion* of	Ezk 48:14	
o with the wine which he drank;	Da 1:8	
inasmuch as no great king **o** ruler	Da 2:10	
any magician, conjurer **o** Chaldean.	Da 2:10	
o the beasts of the field, or	Da 2:38	
the field, **o** the birds of the sky,	Da 2:38	
they do not serve your gods **o**	Da 3:12	
that you do not serve my gods **o**	Da 3:14	
going to serve your gods **o** worship	Da 3:18	
so as not to serve **o** worship any god	Da 3:28	
nation **o** tongue that speaks	Da 3:29	
o its interpretation alarm you.'	Da 4:19	
ward off His hand **O** say to Him,	Da 4:35	
read the inscription **o** make known	Da 5:8	
alarm you **o** your face be pale.	Da 5:10	
o give your rewards to someone	Da 5:17	
do not see, hear **o** understand.	Da 5:23	
o *evidence of* corruption,	Da 6:4	
and no negligence **o** corruption was	Da 6:4	
to any god **o** man besides you,	Da 6:7	
to any god **o** man besides you,	Da 6:12	
o to the injunction which you	Da 6:13	
no injunction **o** statute which the king	Da 6:15	
did meat **o** wine enter my mouth,	Da 10:3	
a stand *for him* **o** be on his side.	Da 11:17	
fathers **o** for the desire of women,	Da 11:37	
battle, horses **o** horsemen."	Hos 1:7	
cannot be measured **o** numbered;	Hos 1:10	
O I will strip her naked And expose	Hos 2:3	6435
many days without king **o** prince,	Hos 3:4	
without sacrifice **o** *sacred* pillar and	Hos 3:4	
without ephod **o** household idols.	Hos 3:4	
there is no faithfulness **o** kindness	Hos 4:1	
O knowledge of God in the land.	Hos 4:1	
O your brides when they commit	Hos 4:14	
go to Gilgal, **O** go up to Beth-aven And	Hos 4:15	
you, **O** to cure you of your wound.	Hos 5:13	
your days **O** in your fathers' days?	Jl 1:2	518
a couple of legs **o** a piece of an ear,	Am 3:12	176
"So two **o** three cities would	Am 4:8	
O He will break forth like a fire,	Am 5:6	6435
And a bear meets him, **O** goes home,	Am 5:19	
O is their territory greater than	Am 6:2	518
Then one's uncle, **o** his undertaker,	Am 6:10	
O does one plow them with oxen?	Am 6:12	518
for bread **o** a thirst for water,	Am 8:11	
flee, **O** a refugee who will escape.	Am 9:1	
will not overtake **o** confront us.'	Am 9:10	
herd, **o** flock taste a thing.	Jon 3:7	
Do not let them eat **o** drink water.	Jon 3:7	
O has your counselor perished,	Mi 4:9	518
man **O** delay for the sons of men.	Mi 5:7	
O a first-ripe fig *which* I	Mi 7:1	
O an image, a teacher of	Hab 2:18	
O *was* Your anger against the	Hab 3:8	518
O *was* Your wrath against the sea,	Hab 3:8	518
sought the LORD **o** inquired of Him	Zph 1:6	
'The LORD will not do good **o** evil!'	Zph 1:12	
with this fold, **o** cooked food,	Hg 2:12	
food, wine, oil, **o** any *other* food,	Hg 2:12	
not listen **o** give heed to Me,"	Zch 1:4	
oppress the widow **o** the orphan,	Zch 7:10	
orphan, the stranger **o** the poor;	Zch 7:10	
for man **o** any wage for animal;	Zch 8:10	
and for him who went out **o** came in	Zch 8:10	
o sustain the one standing,	Zch 11:16	
of Egypt does not go up **o** enter,	Zch 14:18	
O would he receive you kindly?"	Mal 1:8	176
robbery and *what is* lame **o** sick;	Mal 1:13	
o who presents an offering to the	Mal 2:12	
regards the offering **o** accepts *it*	Mal 2:13	
LORD, and He delights in them," **o**,	Mal 2:17	176
to abolish the Law **o** the Prophets;	Mt 5:17	*2228*
not the smallest letter **o** stroke	Mt 5:18	*2228*
o by the earth, for it is the	Mt 5:35	*3383*
of His feet, **o** by Jerusalem,	Mt 5:35	*3383*
make one hair white **o** black.	Mt 5:36	*2228*
yes' **o** 'No, no'; anything	Mt 5:37	
thieves do not break in **o** steal;	Mt 6:20	*3761*
o he will be devoted to one and despise	Mt 6:24	*2228*
will eat **o** what you will drink;	Mt 6:25	*2228*
'What will we eat?' **o**	Mt 6:31	*2228*
'What will we drink?' **o**	Mt 6:31	*2228*
"**O** how can you say to your	Mt 7:4	*2228*
o they will trample them under their	Mt 7:6	*3379*
"**O** what man is there among you who	Mt 7:9	*2228*
"**O** if he asks for a fish, he	Mt 7:10	*2228*
'Your sins are forgiven,' **o** to say,	Mt 9:5	*2228*
'Do not acquire gold, **o** silver,	Mt 10:9	*3366*
silver, **o** copper for your money	Mt 10:9	*3366*
o a bag for *your* journey, or even	Mt 10:10	*3361*
your journey, **o** even two coats,	Mt 10:10	*3366*
or even two coats, **o** sandals,	Mt 10:10	*3366*
two coats, or sandals, **o** a staff;	Mt 10:10	*3366*
whatever city **o** village you enter,	Mt 10:11	*2228*
go out of that house **o** that city,	Mt 10:14	*2228*
about how **o** what you are to say;	Mt 10:19	*2228*
o hidden that will not be known.	Mt 10:26	*2532*
"He who loves father **o** mother	Mt 10:37	*2228*
and he who loves son **o** daughter	Mt 10:37	*2228*
o shall we look for someone else?"	Mt 11:3	*2228*
"**O** have you not read in the Law,	Mt 12:5	*2228*
and any city **o** house divided	Mt 12:25	*2228*
"**O** how can anyone enter the	Mt 12:29	*2228*
in this age **o** in the *age* to come.	Mt 12:32	*3777*
o make the tree bad and its fruit	Mt 12:33	*2228*
and when affliction **o** persecution	Mt 13:21	*2228*
SPEAKS EVIL OF FATHER **O** MOTHER	Mt 15:4	*2228*
says to *his* father **o** mother,	Mt 15:5	*2228*
to honor his father **o** his mother.'	Mt 15:6	*2228*
you not yet understand **o** remember	Mt 16:9	*3761*
"**O** the seven loaves of the four	Mt 16:10	*3761*
Jeremiah, **o** one of the prophets."	Mt 16:14	*2228*
O what will a man give in exchange	Mt 16:26	*2228*
earth collect customs **o** poll-tax,	Mt 17:25	*2228*
their sons **o** from strangers?"	Mt 17:25	*2228*
"If your hand **o** your foot	Mt 18:8	*2228*
you to enter life crippled **o** lame,	Mt 18:8	*2228*
than to have two hands **o** two feet	Mt 18:8	*2228*
you, take one **o** two more with you,	Mt 18:16	*2228*
MOUTH OF TWO **O** THREE WITNESSES	Mt 18:16	*2228*
where two **o** three have gathered	Mt 18:20	*2228*
who has left houses **o** brothers	Mt 19:29	*2228*
brothers **o** sisters or father or mother	Mt 19:29	*2228*
sisters **o** father or mother or children	Mt 19:29	*2228*
father **o** mother or children or farms	Mt 19:29	*2228*
mother **o** children or farms for My	Mt 19:29	*2228*
o farms for My name's sake,	Mt 19:29	*2228*
O is your eye envious because I am	Mt 20:15	*2228*
source, from heaven **o** from men?"	Mt 21:25	*2228*
give a poll-tax to Caesar, **o** not?"	Mt 22:17	*2228*
o the temple that sanctified the	Mt 23:17	*2228*
the offering, **o** the altar that	Mt 23:19	*2228*
be in the winter, **o** on a Sabbath.	Mt 24:20	*3366*
'Behold, here is the Christ,' **o**	Mt 24:23	*2228*
o, 'Behold, He is in the inner	Mt 24:26	
hungry, and feed You, **o** thirsty,	Mt 25:37	*2228*
o naked, and clothe You?	Mt 25:38	*2228*
did we see You sick, **o** in prison,	Mt 25:39	*2228*
did we see You hungry, **o** thirsty,	Mt 25:44	*2228*
hungry, or thirsty, **o** a stranger,	Mt 25:44	*2228*
thirsty, or a stranger, **o** naked,	Mt 25:44	*2228*
or a stranger, or naked, **o** sick,	Mt 25:44	*2228*
or naked, or sick, **o** in prison,	Mt 25:44	*2228*
"**O** do you think that I cannot	Mt 26:53	*2228*
o Jesus who is called Christ?"	Mt 27:17	*2228*
o to say, 'Get up, and pick up your	Mk 2:9	*2228*
lawful to do good **o** to do harm	Mk 3:4	*2228*
Sabbath, to save a life **o** to kill?"	Mk 3:4	*2228*
when affliction **o** persecution arises	Mk 4:17	*2228*
basket, is it, **o** under a bed?	Mk 4:21	*2228*
o by what parable shall we present	Mk 4:30	*2228*
not receive you **o** listen to you,	Mk 6:11	*3366*
He entered villages, **o** cities,	Mk 6:56	*2228*
or cities, **o** countryside,	Mk 6:56	*2228*
SPEAKS EVIL OF FATHER **O** MOTHER,	Mk 7:10	*2228*
says to *his* father **o** *his* mother,	Mk 7:11	*2228*
for *his* father **o** *his* mother;	Mk 7:12	*2228*
Do you not yet see **o** understand?	Mk 8:17	*3761*
no one who has left house **o** brothers	Mk 10:29	*2228*
brothers **o** sisters or mother or father	Mk 10:29	*2228*
sisters **o** mother or father or children	Mk 10:29	*2228*
o father or children or farms,	Mk 10:29	*2228*
or father **o** children or farms,	Mk 10:29	*2228*
or father or children **o** farms,	Mk 10:29	*2228*
o to be baptized with the baptism	Mk 10:38	*2228*
to sit on My right **o** on *My* left,	Mk 10:40	*2228*
o who gave You this authority to	Mk 11:28	*2228*
of John from heaven, **o** from men?	Mk 11:30	*2228*
to pay a poll-tax to Caesar, **o** not?	Mk 12:14	*2228*
we pay **o** shall we not pay?"	Mk 12:15	*2228*
Scriptures **o** the power of God?	Mk 12:24	*3366*
housetop must not go down, **o** go in	Mk 13:15	*3366*
o, 'Behold, *He is* there';	Mk 13:21	
of that day **o** hour no one knows,	Mk 13:32	*2228*
o when the rooster crows	Mk 13:35	*2228*
the rooster crows, **o** in the morning	Mk 13:35	*2228*
he will drink no wine **o** liquor,	Lk 1:15	*2532*
O TWO YOUNG PIGEONS."	Lk 2:24	*2228*
by force, **o** accuse *anyone* falsely,	Lk 3:14	*3366*
have been forgiven you,' **o** to say,	Lk 5:23	*2228*
to do good **o** to do harm on the Sabbath,	Lk 6:9	*2228*
to save a life **o** to destroy it?"	Lk 6:9	*2228*
"**O** how can you say to your	Lk 6:42	
o do we look for someone else?"	Lk 7:19	*2228*
o do we look for someone else?' "	Lk 7:20	*2228*
container, **o** puts it under a bed;	Lk 8:16	*2228*
and loses **o** forfeits himself?	Lk 9:25	*2228*
"**O** *if* he is asked for an egg, he	Lk 11:12	*2228*
about how **o** what you are to speak	Lk 12:11	*2228*
defense, **o** what you are to say;	Lk 12:11	*2228*
who appointed Me a judge **o** arbitrator	Lk 12:14	*2228*
second watch, **o** even in the third,	Lk 12:38	*2579*
us, **o** to everyone *else* as well?"	Lk 12:41	*2228*
o act in accord with his will,	Lk 12:47	*2228*
"**O** do you suppose that those	Lk 13:4	*2228*
ox **o** his donkey from the stall and	Lk 13:15	*2228*
to heal on the Sabbath, **o** not?"	Lk 14:3	*2228*
a son **o** an ox fall into a well,	Lk 14:5	*2228*
you give a luncheon **o** a dinner,	Lk 14:12	*2228*
do not invite your friends **o** your	Lk 14:12	*3366*
or your brothers **o** your relatives	Lk 14:12	*3366*
your relatives **o** rich neighbors,	Lk 14:12	*3366*
"**O** what king, when he sets out to	Lk 14:31	*2228*
"**O** else, while the other is still	Lk 14:32	*1161*
the soil **o** for the manure pile;	Lk 14:35	*3777*
"**O** what woman, if she has ten	Lk 15:8	*2228*
other, **o** else he will be devoted to one	Lk 16:13	*2228*
a slave plowing **o** tending sheep,	Lk 17:7	*2228*
'Look, here *it is!*' **o**, 'There *it is!*'	Lk 17:21	*2228*
o even like this tax collector.	Lk 18:11	*2228*
no one who has left house **o** wife	Lk 18:29	*2228*
house or wife **o** brothers or parents	Lk 18:29	*2228*
or brothers **o** parents or children,	Lk 18:29	*2228*
or brothers or parents **o** children,	Lk 18:29	*2228*
o who is the one who gave You this	Lk 20:2	*2228*
of John from heaven **o** from men?"	Lk 20:4	*2228*
to pay taxes to Caesar, **o** not?"	Lk 20:22	*2228*
will be able to resist **o** refute.	Lk 21:15	*2228*
at the table **o** the one who serves?	Lk 22:27	*2228*
twenty **o** thirty gallons each.	Jn 2:6	*2228*
o, "Why do You speak with her?"	Jn 4:27	*2228*
of the Sea of Galilee (**o** Tiberias).	Jn 6:1	
rowed about three **o** four miles,	Jn 6:19	*2228*
o *whether* I speak from Myself.	Jn 7:17	*2228*
o Pharisees has believed in Him,	Jn 7:48	*2228*
I come from **o** where I am going.	Jn 8:14	*2228*
sinned, this man **o** his parents,	Jn 9:2	*2228*
o who opened his eyes, we do not	Jn 9:21	*2228*
o else, that he should give	Jn 13:29	*2228*
it does not see Him **o** know Him,	Jn 14:17	*3761*
have not known the Father **o** Me.	Jn 16:3	*3761*
o did others tell you about Me?"	Jn 18:34	*2228*
not for you to know times **o** epochs	Ac 1:7	*2228*
at this, **o** why do you gaze at us,	Ac 3:12	*2228*
o piety we had made him walk?	Ac 3:12	*2228*
"By what power, **o** in what name,	Ac 4:7	*2228*
not to speak **o** teach at all in the	Ac 4:18	*3366*
all who were owners of land **o** houses	Ac 4:34	*2228*
sick **o** afflicted with unclean spirits,	Ac 5:16	*2532*
plan **o** action is of men,	Ac 5:38	*2228*
o else you may even be found	Ac 5:39	*3379*
'**O** WHAT PLACE IS THERE FOR MY	Ac 7:49	*2228*
no part **o** portion in this matter,	Ac 8:21	*3761*
Of himself **o** of someone else?"	Ac 8:34	*2228*
with a foreigner **o** to visit him;	Ac 10:28	*2228*
not call any man unholy **o** unclean.	Ac 10:28	*2228*
for nothing unholy **o** unclean has	Ac 11:8	*2228*
for us to accept **o** to observe,	Ac 16:21	*3761*
telling **o** hearing something new.)	Ac 17:21	*2228*
is like gold **o** silver or stone,	Ac 17:29	*2228*
is like gold or silver **o** stone,	Ac 17:29	*2228*
matter of wrong **o** of vicious crime,	Ac 18:14	*2228*
so that handkerchiefs **o** aprons	Ac 19:12	*2228*
no one's silver **o** gold or clothes.	Ac 20:33	*2228*
no one's silver or gold **o** clothes.	Ac 20:33	*2228*
o an angel has spoken to him?"	Ac 23:9	*2228*
under a curse not to eat **o** drink	Ac 23:21	*3383*
deserving death **o** imprisonment.	Ac 23:29	*2228*
with anyone **o** causing a riot.	Ac 24:12	*2228*
without *any* crowd **o** uproar.	Ac 24:18	*3761*
"**O** else let these men themselves	Ac 24:20	*2228*
than eight **o** ten days among them,	Ac 25:6	*2228*
against the Law of the Jews **o** against	Ac 25:8	*3777*
the temple **o** against Caesar."	Ac 25:8	*3777*
whether in a short **o** long time,	Ac 26:29	*2532*
worthy of death **o** imprisonment."	Ac 26:31	*2228*
up **o** suddenly fall down dead.	Ac 28:6	*2228*
o the customs of our fathers,	Ac 28:17	*2228*
o spoken anything bad about you.	Ac 28:21	*2228*
honor Him as God **o** give thanks	Ro 1:21	*2228*
O do you think lightly of the	Ro 2:4	*2228*
accusing **o** else defending them,	Ro 2:15	*2228*
O what is the benefit of	Ro 3:1	*2228*
O is God *the God* of Jews only?	Ro 3:29	*2228*
o on the uncircumcised also?	Ro 4:9	*2228*
was circumcised, **o** uncircumcised?	Ro 4:10	*2228*
For the promise to Abraham **o** to	Ro 4:13	*2228*
O do you not know that all of us	Ro 6:3	*2228*
o of obedience resulting in	Ro 6:16	*2228*
O do you not know, brethren	Ro 7:1	*2228*
Will tribulation, **o** distress,	Ro 8:35	*2228*
or distress, **o** persecution,	Ro 8:35	*2228*
or persecution, **o** famine,	Ro 8:35	*2228*
or famine, **o** nakedness,	Ro 8:35	*2228*
or famine, or nakedness, **o** peril,	Ro 8:35	*2228*
or nakedness, or peril, **o** sword?	Ro 8:35	*2228*
had not done anything good **o** bad,	Ro 9:11	*2228*
man who wills **o** the man who runs,	Ro 9:16	*3761*
O does not the potter have a right	Ro 9:21	*2228*
o 'WHO WILL DESCEND INTO THE	Ro 10:7	*2228*
O do you not know what the	Ro 11:2	*2228*
LORD, **O** WHO BECAME HIS COUNSELOR?	Ro 11:34	*2228*
O WHO HAS FIRST GIVEN TO HIM	Ro 11:35	*2228*
o he who teaches, in his teaching;	Ro 12:7	*1535a*
o he who exhorts, in his	Ro 12:8	*1535a*
his own master he stands **o** falls;	Ro 14:4	*2228*
we live for the Lord, **o** if we die,	Ro 14:8	*5037*
therefore whether we live **o** die,	Ro 14:8	*1437, 5037*
O you again, why do you regard	Ro 14:10	*2228*
not to put an obstacle **o** a stumbling	Ro 14:13	*2228*
not to eat meat **o** to drink wine,	Ro 14:21	*3366*
o *to do anything* by which your	Ro 14:21	*3366*
O were you baptized in the name of	1Co 1:13	*2228*
superiority of speech **o** of wisdom,	1Co 2:1	*2228*
whether Paul **o** Apollos or Cephas	1Co 3:22	*1535a*
whether Paul or Apollos **o** Cephas	1Co 3:22	*1535a*
Apollos or Cephas **o** the world or life	1Co 3:22	*1535a*

or the world **o** life or death or things 1Co 3:22 *1535a*
or life **o** death or things present or 1Co 3:22 *1535a*
or death **o** things present or things 1Co 3:22 *1535a*
things present **o** things to come; 1Co 3:22 *1535a*
by you, **o** by *any* human court; 1Co 4:3 *2228*
come to you with a rod, **o** with love 1Co 4:21 *2228*
o with the covetous and swindlers, 1Co 5:10 *2228*
and swindlers, **o** with idolaters, 1Co 5:10 *2228*
is an immoral person, **o** covetous, 1Co 5:11 *2228*
or covetous, **o** an idolater, 1Co 5:11 *2228*
or an idolater, **o** a reviler, 1Co 5:11 *2228*
or a reviler, **o** a drunkard, 1Co 5:11 *2228*
or a drunkard, **o** a swindler 1Co 5:11 *2228*
O do you not know that the saints 1Co 6:2 *2228*
O do you not know that the 1Co 6:9 *2228*
O do you not know that the one who 1Co 6:16 *2228*
O do you not know that your body 1Co 6:19 *2228*
o else be reconciled to her 1Co 7:11 *2228*
the brother **o** the sister is not 1Co 7:15 *2228*
O how do you know, O husband, 1Co 7:16 *2228*
gods whether in heaven **o** on earth, 1Co 8:5 *1535a*
O do only Barnabas and I not have 1Co 9:6 *2228*
O who tends a flock and does not 1Co 9:7 *2228*
O does not the Law also say these 1Co 9:8 *2228*
O is He speaking altogether for 1Co 9:10 *2228*
o that an idol is anything? 1Co 10:19 *2228*
O do we provoke the Lord to 1Co 10:22 *2228*
eat **o** drink or whatever you do, 1Co 10:31 *1535a*
eat or drink **o** whatever you do, 1Co 10:31 *1535a*
Give no offense either to Jews **o** 1Co 10:32 *2532*
to Greeks **o** to the church of God; 1Co 10:32 *2532*
head while praying **o** prophesying 1Co 11:4 *2228*
while praying **o** prophesying disgraces 1Co 11:5 *2228*
hair cut off **o** her head shaved, 1Co 11:6 *2228*
O do you despise the church of 1Co 11:22 *2228*
whoever eats the bread **o** drinks the 1Co 11:27 *2228*
one body, whether Jews **o** Greeks, 1Co 12:13 *1535a*
or Greeks, whether slaves **o** free, 1Co 12:13 *1535a*
o again the head to the feet, 1Co 12:21 *2228*
a noisy gong **o** a clanging cymbal. 1Co 13:1 *2228*
by way of revelation **o** of knowledge 1Co 14:6 *2228*
o of prophecy or of teaching? 1Co 14:6 *2228*
or of prophecy **o** of teaching? 1Co 14:6 *2228*
things, either flute **o** harp, 1Co 14:7 *1535a*
played on the flute **o** on the harp? 1Co 14:7 *2228*
ungifted men **o** unbelievers enter, 1Co 14:23 *2228*
o an ungifted man enters, 1Co 14:24 *2228*
be by two **o** at the most three, 1Co 14:27 *2228*
Let two **o** three prophets speak, 1Co 14:29 *2228*
O has it come to you only? 1Co 14:36 *2228*
he is a prophet **o** spiritual, 1Co 14:37 *2228*
Whether then *it was* I **o** they, 1Co 15:11 *1535a*
of wheat **o** of something else. 1Co 15:37 *2228*
with you, **o** even spend the winter, 1Co 16:6 *2228*
o if we are comforted, it is for 2Co 1:6 *1535a*
O what I purpose, do I 2Co 1:17 *2228*
O do we need, as some, letters of 2Co 3:1 *2228*
of commendation to you **o** from you? 2Co 3:1 *2228*
o adulterating the word of God, 2Co 4:2 *3366*
whether at home **o** absent, 2Co 5:9 *1535a*
he has done, whether good **o** bad. 2Co 5:10 *1535a*
o what fellowship has light with 2Co 6:14 *2228*
O what harmony has Christ with 2Co 6:15 *1161*
o what has a believer in common 2Co 6:15 *2228*
O what agreement has the temple of 2Co 6:16 *1161*
not grudgingly **o** under compulsion, 2Co 9:7 *2228*
bold to class **o** compare ourselves 2Co 10:12 *2228*
o you receive a different spirit 2Co 11:4 *2228*
o a different gospel which you 2Co 11:4 *2228*
O did I commit a sin in humbling 2Co 11:7 *2228*
o out of the body I do not know, 2Co 12:2 *1535a*
in the body **o** apart from the body 2Co 12:3 *1535a*
he sees *in* me **o** hears from me. 2Co 12:6 *2228*
OF TWO **O** THREE WITNESSES. 2Co 13:1 *2532*
O do you not recognize this about 2Co 13:5 *2228*
if we, **o** an angel from heaven, Ga 1:8 *2228*
the favor of men, **o** of God? Ga 1:10 *2228*
O am I striving to please men? Ga 1:10 *2228*
I might be running, **o** had run, Ga 2:2 *2228*
the Law, **o** by hearing with faith? Ga 3:2 *2228*
the Law, **o** by hearing with faith? Ga 3:5 *2228*
it aside **o** adds conditions to it. Ga 3:15 *2228*
God, **o** rather to be known by God, Ga 4:9 *1161*
you did not despise **o** loathe, Ga 4:14 *3761*
beyond all that we ask **o** think, Eph 3:20 *2228*
immorality **o** any impurity Eph 5:3 *2532*
o greed must not even be named Eph 5:3 *2228*
and silly talk, **o** coarse jesting, Eph 5:4 *2228*
that no immoral **o** impure person or Eph 5:5 *2228*
or impure person **o** covetous man, Eph 5:5 *2228*
spot **o** wrinkle or any such thing; Eph 5:27 *2228*
spot or wrinkle **o** any such thing; Eph 5:27 *2228*
the Lord, whether slave **o** free. Eph 6:8 *1535a*
whether in pretense **o** in truth, Php 1:18 *1535a*
body, whether by life **o** by death. Php 1:20 *1535a*
come and see you **o** remain absent, Php 1:27 *1535a*
from selfishness **o** empty conceit, Php 2:3 *3366*
without grumbling **o** disputing; Php 2:14 *2532*
it **o** have already become perfect, Php 3:12 *2228*
whether thrones **o** dominions or Col 1:16 *1535a*
whether thrones or dominions **o** Col 1:16 *1535a*
or dominions or rulers **o** authorities Col 1:16 *1535a*
on earth **o** things in heaven. Col 1:20 *1535a*
your judge in regard to food **o** drink Col 2:16 *2532*
o in respect to a festival or a new Col 2:16 *2228*
o a new moon or a Sabbath day Col 2:16 *2228*
or a new moon **o** a Sabbath day Col 2:16 *2228*
Whatever you do in word **o** deed, Col 3:17 *2228*
o impurity or by way of deceit; 1Th 2:3 *3761*
or impurity **o** by way of deceit; 1Th 2:3 *3761*
either from you **o** from others, 1Th 2:6 *3777*
hope **o** joy or crown of exultation? 1Th 2:19 *2228*
hope or joy **o** crown of exultation? 1Th 2:19 *2228*
whether we are awake **o** asleep, 1Th 5:10 *1535a*
from your composure **o** be disturbed 2Th 2:2 *3366*
either by a spirit **o** a message or a 2Th 2:2 *3383*
message **o** a letter as if from us, 2Th 2:2 *3383*
so-called god **o** object of worship, 2Th 2:4 *2228*
word *of mouth* **o** by letter from us. 2Th 2:15 *1535a*
what they are saying **o** the matters 1Tm 1:7 *3383*
who kill their fathers **o** mothers, 1Tm 1:9 *2532*
gold **o** pearls or costly garments, 1Tm 2:9 *2228*
gold or pearls **o** costly garments, 1Tm 2:9 *2228*
o exercise authority over a man, 1Tm 2:12 *3761*
not addicted to wine **o** pugnacious, 1Tm 3:3 *3361*
o addicted to much wine or fond of 1Tm 3:8 *3361*
much wine **o** fond of sordid gain, 1Tm 3:8 *3361*
has children **o** grandchildren, 1Tm 5:4 *2228*
basis of two **o** three witnesses. 1Tm 5:19 *2228*
without stain **o** reproach until 1Tm 6:14
whom no man has seen **o** can see. 1Tm 6:16 *3761*
not to be conceited **o** to fix their hope 1Tm 6:17 *3366*
of our Lord **o** of me His prisoner 2Tm 1:8 *3366*
of dissipation **o** rebellion. Ti 1:6 *2228*
I send Artemas **o** Tychicus to you, Ti 3:12 *2228*
in any way **o** owes you anything, Phm 1:18 *2228*
O THE SON OF MAN, THAT YOU ARE Heb 2:6 *2228*
testimony of two **o** three witnesses. Heb 10:28 *2228*
o godless person like Esau, Heb 12:16 *2228*
no variation **o** shifting shadow. Jas 1:17 *2228*
o sit down by my footstool," Jas 2:3 *2228*
If a brother **o** sister is without Jas 2:15 *2228*
olives, **o** a vine produce figs? Jas 3:12 *2228*
O do you think that the Scripture Jas 4:5 *2228*
a brother **o** judges his brother, Jas 4:11 *2228*
"Today **o** tomorrow we will go to Jas 4:13 *2228*
live and also do this **o** that." Jas 4:15 *2228*
either by heaven **o** by earth or Jas 5:12 *3383*
or by earth **o** with any other oath; Jas 5:12 *3383*
seeking to know what person **o** time 1Pe 1:11 *2228*
perishable things like silver **o** gold 1Pe 1:18 *2228*
o to governors as sent by him for 1Pe 2:14 *1535a*
jewelry, **o** putting on dresses; 1Pe 3:3 *2228*
for evil **o** insult for insult, 1Pe 3:9 *2228*
you suffers as a murderer, **o** thief, 1Pe 4:15 *2228*
a murderer, or thief, **o** evildoer, 1Pe 4:15 *2228*
evildoer, **o** a troublesome meddler; 1Pe 4:15 *2228*
these *qualities* is blind **o** 2Pe 1:9
who sins has seen Him **o** knows Him. 1Jn 3:6 *3761*
not love with word **o** with tongue, 1Jn 3:18 *3366*
o else I am coming to you and Rv 2:5 *1161*
o else I am coming to you quickly, Rv 2:16 *1161*
I wish that you were cold **o** hot. Rv 3:15 *2228*
no one in heaven **o** on the earth Rv 5:3 *3761*
on the earth **o** under the earth Rv 5:3 *3761*
open the book **o** to look into it. Rv 5:3 *3777*
open the book **o** to look into it; Rv 5:4 *3777*
earth **o** on the sea or on any tree. Rv 7:1 *3383*
earth or on the sea **o** on any tree. Rv 7:1 *3383*
the earth **o** the sea or the trees until Rv 7:3 *3383*
the earth or the sea **o** the trees until Rv 7:3 *3383*
right hand **o** on their forehead, Rv 13:16 *2228*
will be able to buy **o** to sell, Rv 13:17 *2228*
beast **o** the number of his name. Rv 13:17 *2228*
on his forehead **o** on his hand, Rv 14:9 *2228*
worshiped the beast **o** his image, Rv 20:4 *3761*
longer be *any* mourning, **o** crying, Rv 21:4 *3777*
any mourning, or crying, **o** pain; Rv 21:4 *3777*
o of the moon to shine on it, Rv 21:23 *3761*

ORACLE

"The **o** of Balaam the son of Beor, Nu 24:3 5002
And the **o** of the man whose eye is Nu 24:3 5002
The **o** of him who hears the words Nu 24:4 5002
"The **o** of Balaam the son of Beor, Nu 24:15 5002
And the **o** of the man whose eye is Nu 24:15 5002
The **o** of him who hears the words Nu 24:16 5002
the LORD laid this **o** against him: 2Ki 9:25 4853b
of Agur the son of Jakeh, the **o**. Pr 30:1 4853b
the **o** which his mother taught him: Pr 31:1 4853b
The **o** concerning Babylon which Is 13:1 4853b
that King Ahaz died this **o** came: Is 14:28 4853b
The **o** concerning Moab. Is 15:1 4853b
The **o** concerning Damascus. Is 17:1 4853b
The **o** concerning Egypt. Is 19:1 4853b
The **o** concerning the wilderness of Is 21:1 4853b
The **o** concerning Edom. Is 21:11 4853b
The **o** about Arabia. Is 21:13 4853b
The **o** concerning the valley of Is 22:1 4853b
The **o** concerning Tyre. Is 23:1 4853b
The **o** concerning the beasts of the Is 30:6 4853b
'What is the **o** of the LORD?' Jer 23:33 4853b
you shall say to them, 'What **o**?' Jer 23:33 4853b
'The **o** of the LORD,' I will bring Jer 23:34 4853b
longer remember the **o** of the LORD, Jer 23:36 4853b
man's own word will become the **o**, Jer 23:36 4853b
'The **o** of the LORD!' Jer 23:38 4853b
"The **o** of the LORD!" Jer 23:38 4853b
shall not say, 'The **o** of the LORD! Jer 23:38 4853b
"A sword against the **o** priests, Jer 50:36 907
The **o** of Nineveh. Na 1:1 4853b
The **o** which Habakkuk the prophet Hab 1:1 4853b
The **o** of the word of the LORD to Mal 1:1 4853b

ORACLES

As to his sons and the many **o** 2Ch 24:27 4853b
for you false and misleading **o**. La 2:14 4065
living **o** to pass on to you. Ac 7:38 *3051*
were entrusted with the **o** of God. Ro 3:2 *3051*
principles of the **o** of God, Heb 5:12 *3051*

ORCHARD

"Your shoots are an **o** of SS 4:13 6508
"I went down to the **o** of nut trees SS 6:11 1593

ORDAIN

and **o** them and consecrate them, Ex 28:41
4390, 3027
So you shall **o** Aaron and his sons. Ex 29:9
4390, 3027
shall **o** them through seven days. Ex 29:35
4390, 3027
he will **o** you through seven days. Lv 8:33
4390, 3027

ORDAINED

them they may be anointed and **o**. Ex 29:29
4390, 3027
priest who is anointed and **o** to serve Lv 16:32
4390, 3027
whom he **o** to serve as priests. Nu 3:3
4390, 3027
who can live except God has **o** it? Nu 24:23 7760
offering which was **o** in Mount Sinai Nu 28:6 6213a
For the LORD had **o** to thwart the 2Sa 17:14 6680
any who would, he **o**, 1Ki 13:33
4390, 3027
and the stars, which You have **o**, Ps 8:3 3559
He has **o** His covenant forever; Ps 111:9 6680
You have **o** Your precepts, That we Ps 119:4 6680
The days that were **o** *for me,* Ps 139:16 3335
Man's steps are **o** by the LORD, Pr 20:24
My hands And I **o** all their host. Is 45:12 6680
received the law as **o** by angels, Ac 7:53 *1296*
having been **o** through angels by Ga 3:19 *1299*

ORDEAL

that in a great **o** of affliction 2Co 8:2 *1382*
at the fiery **o** among you, 1Pe 4:12 *4451*

ORDER

in **o** to enter the land of Canaan; Gn 11:31
names, in the **o** of their birth: Gn 25:13 8435
in **o** not to give offspring to his Gn 38:9
in **o** to bring about this present result Gn 50:20 4616
in **o** that you may know that I, Ex 8:22 4616
remain, in **o** to show you My power and Ex 9:16 5668
and in **o** to proclaim My name Ex 9:16 4616
for God has come in **o** to test you, Ex 20:20 5668
and in **o** that the fear of Him may Ex 20:20 5668
multitude in **o** to pervert *justice;* Ex 23:2
Aaron and his sons shall keep it in **o** Ex 27:21 6186a
in **o** that He may bestow a blessing Ex 32:29
set the arrangement of bread in **o** Ex 40:23 6186a
then the priest shall **o** them to Lv 13:54 6680
then the priest shall **o** them to Lv 14:40 6680
Aaron shall keep it in **o** from Lv 24:3 6186a
"He shall keep the lamps in **o** on Lv 24:4 6186a
he shall set it in **o** before the LORD Lv 24:8 6186a
then I will so **o** My blessing for Lv 25:21 6680
This was the **o** of march of the Nu 10:28 4550
in **o** that all the congregation of Nu 27:20 4616
o to deliver him into your hand, Dt 2:30 4616
from there in **o** to bring us in, Dt 6:23 4616
in **o** to confirm the oath which the Dt 9:5 4616
against you in **o** to destroy you, Dt 9:19
in **o** that the LORD may turn from Dt 13:17 4616
in **o** that the LORD your God may Dt 14:29 4616
war against it in **o** to capture it, Dt 20:19
in **o** that it may be well with you and Dt 22:7 4616
in **o** that the LORD your God may Dt 24:19 4616
in **o** that you might know that I am Dt 29:6 4616
in **o** that He may establish you Dt 29:13 4616
in **o** to destroy the watered *land* Dt 29:19 4616
life in **o** that you may live, Dt 30:19 4616
she had laid in **o** on the roof. Jos 2:6 6186a
to meet Israel in battle in **o** that Jos 11:20 4616
in **o** to test Israel by them, Jg 2:22 4616
only in **o** that the generations of Jg 3:2 4616
in **o** to save *it* from the Midianites. Jg 6:11
o to do to him as he did to us." Jg 15:10
to her in **o** to bring her back, Jg 19:3
in **o** to enter *and* lodge in Gibeah. Jg 19:15
in **o** to glean until the end of the Ru 2:23
in **o** to raise up the name of the Ru 4:5
to be my wife in **o** to raise up the Ru 4:10
in **o** to greet his brothers. 1Sa 17:22
down in **o** to see the battle." 1Sa 17:28 4616
in **o** to put him to death in the 1Sa 19:11
in **o** to put hot bread *in its place* 1Sa 21:6
to you in **o** to search the city, 2Sa 10:3 5668
stood beside him in **o** to raise him up 2Sa 12:17
in **o** to change the appearance of 2Sa 14:20 5668
his city, and set his house in **o**, 2Sa 17:23 6680
in **o** to go to meet the king, 2Sa 19:15
in **o** to topple the wall. 2Sa 20:15
o to build an altar to the LORD, 2Sa 24:21
in **o** to fulfill the word of the LORD, 1Ki 2:27
in **o** that *the beams* would not be 1Ki 6:6
in **o** to place there the ark of the 1Ki 6:19
in **o** that all the peoples of the 1Ki 8:43 4616
in **o** to prevent *anyone* from going 1Ki 15:17
'Set your house in **o**, 2Ki 20:1 6680
the second **o** and the doorkeepers, 2Ki 23:4
but he taxed the land in **o** to give 2Ki 23:35
their office according to their **o**. 1Ch 6:32 4941
so David gave the **o** and they were 1Ch 14:12 559
in **o** that all the peoples of the 2Ch 6:33 4616
in **o** to prevent *anyone* from going 2Ch 16:1
according to the **o** of David. 2Ch 23:18 3027
Then Hezekiah gave the **o** to offer 2Ch 29:27 559
in **o** to consecrate *them* to the 2Ch 30:17

As soon as the **o** spread,	2Ch 31:5	1697
Josiah had set the temple in **o**,	2Ch 35:20	3559
himself in **o** to make war with him;	2Ch 35:22	
in **o** to fulfill the word of the LORD	2Ch 36:22	
in **o** to fulfill the word of the LORD	Ezr 1:1	
in **o** that they could reproach me.	Ne 6:13	4616
to enter in **o** to possess The land	Ne 9:15	
in **o** to turn them back to Your law.	Ne 9:29	
an **o** and they cleansed the rooms;	Ne 13:9	559
in **o** to display her beauty to the	Es 1:11	
and to **o** her to go in to the king	Es 4:8	6680
an **o** to bring the book of records,	Es 6:1	559
palace in **o** to speak to the king	Es 6:4	
itself, Of deep shadow without **o**,	Jb 10:22	5468
In the morning I will **o** *my prayer*	Ps 5:3	6186a
state *the case* in **o** before your eyes.	Ps 50:21	6186a
According to the **o** of Melchizedek.	Ps 110:4	1700
"God has surely tested them in **o**	Ec 3:18	
In **o** to go into the caverns of the	Is 2:21	
'**O** on order, order on order, Line	Is 28:10	6673
'Order on **o**, order on order, Line	Is 28:10	6673
'Order on order, **o** on order, Line	Is 28:10	6673
'Order on order, order on **o**,	Is 28:10	6673
"**O** on order, order on order, Line	Is 28:13	6673
"Order on **o**, order on order, Line	Is 28:13	6673
"Order on order, **o** on order, Line	Is 28:13	6673
"Order on order, order on **o**,	Is 28:13	6673
My Spirit, In **o** to add sin to sin;	Is 30:1	4616
'Set your house in **o**,	Is 38:1	6680
let him recount it to Me in **o**,	Is 44:7	6186a
for you, In **o** not to cut you off.	Is 48:9	
In **o** to revive the spirit of the lowly	Is 57:15	
In **o** not to destroy all of them.	Is 65:8	
to other gods in **o** to spite Me.	Jer 7:18	4616
in **o** to confirm the oath which I	Jer 11:5	4616
in **o** not to listen or take correction	Jer 17:23	
"in **o** that you might provoke Me	Jer 25:7	4616
in **o** to remove you far from your	Jer 27:10	4616
in **o** that I may drive you out and	Jer 27:15	4616
And the fixed **o** of the moon and	Jer 31:35	2708
fixed **o** departs From before Me,"	Jer 31:36	2706
in **o** that every man will turn from	Jer 36:3	4616
of Benjamin in **o** to take possession	Jer 37:12	
in **o** to proceed into Egypt	Jer 41:17	
in **o** to reside in the land of	Jer 43:5	
When the LORD has given it an **o**?	Jer 47:7	6680
in **o** to lay hold of the hearts of	Ezk 14:5	4616
in **o** that the house of Israel may	Ezk 14:11	4616
in **o** that you may bear your	Ezk 16:54	4616
in **o** that they might know that I	Ezk 20:26	4616
blow fire on it in **o** to melt *it,*	Ezk 22:20	
lives in **o** to get dishonest gain.	Ezk 22:27	4616
in **o** to deal in your merchandise.	Ezk 27:9	
them in **o** to cleanse the land.	Ezk 39:12	4616
of the ground, in **o** to cleanse it.	Ezk 39:14	
here in **o** to show *it* to you.	Ezk 40:4	4616
in **o** that they may not bring *them*	Ezk 46:20	
in **o** that he might declare the	Da 2:16	
in **o** to cast *them* into the furnace	Da 3:20	
In **o** that the living may know That	Da 4:17	5705, 1701
up in **o** to fulfill the vision,	Da 11:14	
insight will fall, in **o** to refine,	Da 11:35	
to the Greeks in **o** to remove them	Jl 3:6	4616
In **o** to enlarge their borders.	Am 1:13	4616
girl In **o** to profane My holy name.	Am 2:7	4616
in **o** to forestall this I fled to	Jon 4:2	
of Judah in **o** to scatter it."	Zch 1:21	
on a hairy robe in **o** to deceive;	Zch 13:4	4616
unoccupied, swept, and put in **o**.	Mt 12:44	*2885*
around Him in **o** to touch Him.	Mk 3:10	*2443*
have received in **o** to observe,	Mk 7:4	
God in **o** to keep your tradition.	Mk 7:9	*2443*
in **o** to receive *some* of the	Mk 12:2	*2443*
in **o** to trap Him in a statement.	Mk 12:13	*2443*
in **o** to lead astray, if possible, the elect.	Mk 13:22	*4314*
in **o** to betray Him to them.	Mk 14:10	*2443*
it out for you in consecutive **o**,	Lk 1:3	*2517*
the *appointed* **o** of his division,	Lk 1:8	*5010*
in **o** to register along with Mary,	Lk 2:5	
in **o** to throw Him down the cliff.	Lk 4:29	*5620*
in **o** to receive back the same	Lk 6:34	*2443*
it finds it swept and put in **o**.	Lk 11:25	*2885*
have five brothers—in **o** that	Lk 16:28	*3704*
a sycamore tree in **o** to see Him,	Lk 19:4	*2443*
in **o** that they might catch Him in	Lk 20:20	*2443*
but in **o** that He might also gather	Jn 11:52	*2443*
in **o** to beg alms of those who were	Ac 3:2	
in **o** that times of refreshing may	Ac 3:19	*3704*
word of God in **o** to serve tables.	Ac 6:2	
the church in **o** to mistreat them.	Ac 12:1	
to **o** *them* to be beaten with rods.	Ac 16:22	*2753*
will attack you in **o** to harm you,	Ac 18:10	
in **o** to bring even those who were	Ac 22:5	
of the Law **o** me to be struck?"	Ac 23:3	*2753*
in **o** that *it may be* in accordance	Ro 4:16	*2443*
in **o** that our body of sin might be	Ro 6:6	*2443*
in **o** that we might bear fruit for God.	Ro 7:4	*2443*
in **o** that it might be shown to be	Ro 7:13	*2443*
But each in his own **o**:	1Co 15:23	*5001*
in **o** not to say too much	2Co 2:5	*2443*
have sent the brethren, in **o** that	2Co 9:3	*2443*
the Damascenes in **o** to seize me,	2Co 11:32	
in **o** to bring us into bondage.	Ga 2:4	*2443*
in **o** that in Christ Jesus the	Ga 3:14	*2443*
in **o** to be sincere and blameless	Php 1:10	*2443*
in **o** that I may attain to the	Php 3:11	*1513b*
in **o** to present you before Him	Col 1:22	
in **o** that they all may be judged	2Th 2:12	*2443*
in **o** to offer ourselves as a model	2Th 3:9	*2443*
you, we used to give you this **o**:	2Th 3:10	*3853*
you would set in **o** what remains	Ti 1:5	*1930*
to **o** you *to do* what is proper,	Phm 1:8	*2004*
in **o** to offer both gifts and	Heb 5:1	*2443*
TO THE **O** OF MELCHIZEDEK."	Heb 5:6	*5010*
according to the **o** of Melchizedek.	Heb 5:10	*5010*
according to the **o** of Melchizedek.	Heb 6:20	*5010*
according to the **o** of Melchizedek,	Heb 7:11	*5010*
according to the **o** of Aaron?	Heb 7:11	*5010*
TO THE **O** OF MELCHIZEDEK."	Heb 7:17	*5010*
in **o** to establish the second.	Heb 10:9	*2443*
appeared in **o** to take away sins;	1Jn 3:5	*2443*

ORDERED

"Now you are **o**,	Gn 45:19	6680
land of Rameses, as Pharaoh had **o**.	Gn 47:11	6680
until morning, as Moses had **o**,	Ex 16:24	6680
covenant with me, **O** in all things,	2Sa 23:5	6186a
he **o** his ways before the LORD his	2Ch 27:6	3559
And he **o** the priests, the sons of	2Ch 29:21	559
for the king **o** the burnt offering	2Ch 29:24	559
officials **o** the Levites to sing praises	2Ch 29:30	559
and he **o** Judah to serve the LORD	2Ch 33:16	559
at war, and God has **o** me to hurry.	2Ch 35:21	559
and **o** him *to go* to Mordecai to	Es 4:5	6680
and **o** him *to reply* to Mordecai:	Es 4:10	6680
Then the king **o** Ashpenaz, the	Da 1:3	559
and *he* **o** *him* to teach them	Da 1:4	
Pilate **o** it to be given *to him.*	Mt 27:58	*2753*
but the more He **o** them, the more	Mk 7:36	*1291*
He **o** these to be served as well.	Mk 8:7	*3004*
than what you have been **o** to."	Lk 3:13	*1299*
And He **o** him to tell no one,	Lk 5:14	*3853*
kingdom, he **o** that these slaves,	Lk 19:15	*3004*
But when they had **o** them to leave	Ac 4:15	*2753*
o them not to speak in the	Ac 5:40	*3853*
And he **o** the chariot to stop;	Ac 8:38	*2753*
He **o** us to preach to the people,	Ac 10:42	*3853*
And he **o** them to be baptized in	Ac 10:48	*4367*
he examined the guards and **o** that	Ac 12:19	*2753*
and **o** him to be bound with two	Ac 21:33	*2753*
he **o** him to be brought into the	Ac 21:34	*2753*
the commander **o** him to be brought	Ac 22:24	*2753*
he released him and **o** the chief	Ac 22:30	*2753*
o the troops to go down and take	Ac 23:10	*2753*
tribunal and **o** Paul to be brought.	Ac 25:6	*2753*
and **o** the man to be brought before	Ac 25:17	*2753*
I **o** him to be kept in custody	Ac 25:21	*2753*

ORDERING

O the people to sit down on the grass,	Mt 14:19	*2753*
o his accusers to come before you.	Ac 24:8	*2753*

ORDERLY

of this stronghold in an **o** manner,	Jg 6:26	4634
mighty strength, or his **o** frame.	Jb 41:12	2433
to explain to them in **o** sequence,	Ac 11:4	*2517*
but that you yourself also walk **o**,	Ac 21:24	*4748*
done properly and in an **o** manner.	1Co 14:40	*5010*

ORDERS

Then Joseph gave **o** to fill their	Gn 42:25	6680
then the priest shall give **o** to	Lv 14:4	6680
"The priest shall also give **o** to	Lv 14:5	6680
I will give **o** concerning you."	2Sa 14:8	6680
So David gave **o** to gather the	1Ch 22:2	559
Levites in their **o** for the service of	Ezr 6:18	4255a
for so the king had given **o** to	Es 1:8	3245
And to him who **o** *his* way *aright* I	Ps 50:23	7760
king of Babylon gave **o** about	Jer 39:11	6680
gave **o** to call in the magicians,	Da 2:2	559
and gave **o** to destroy all the wise	Da 2:12	560
and gave **o** to present to him an	Da 2:46	560
anger gave **o** to bring Shadrach,	Da 3:13	560
giving **o** to heat the furnace seven	Da 3:19	560
"So I gave **o** to bring into my	Da 4:6	2942
he gave **o** to bring the gold and	Da 5:2	560
Then Belshazzar gave **o**,	Da 5:29	560
Then the king gave **o**,	Da 6:16	560
and gave **o** for Daniel to be taken up	Da 6:23	560
The king then gave **o**,	Da 6:24	560
o to depart to the other side	Mt 8:18	*2753*
give **o** for the grave to be made	Mt 27:64	*2753*
And He gave them strict **o** that no	Mk 5:43	*1291*
He gave them **o** not to tell anyone;	Mk 7:36	*1291*
And He was giving **o** to them,	Mk 8:15	*1291*
He gave them **o** not to relate to	Mk 9:9	*1291*
and He gave **o** for *something* to be	Lk 8:55	*1299*
priests and the Pharisees had given **o**	Jn 11:57	*1785*
He had by the Holy Spirit given **o**	Ac 1:2	*1781*
and sent **o** to the prison house	Ac 5:21	
"We gave you strict **o** not to	Ac 5:28	*3852*
gave **o** to put the men outside	Ac 5:34	*2753*
in accordance with their **o**,	Ac 23:31	*1299*
giving **o** for him to be kept in	Ac 23:35	*2753*
Then he gave **o** to the centurion for	Ac 24:23	*1299*
and gave **o** concerning his bones.	Heb 11:22	*1781*

ORDINANCE

to celebrate it *as* a permanent **o**.	Ex 12:14	2708
your generations as a permanent **o**.	Ex 12:17	2708
you shall observe this event as an **o**	Ex 12:24	2706
"This is the **o** of the Passover:	Ex 12:43	2708
you shall keep this **o** at its	Ex 13:10	2708
burnt offering according to the **o**.	Lv 5:10	4941
o throughout your generations,	Lv 6:18	2706
By a permanent **o** it shall be	Lv 6:22	2706
and offered it according to the **o**.	Lv 9:16	4941
Passover and according to its **o**,	Nu 9:14	4941
'There is to be one law and one **o**	Nu 15:16	4941
its drink offering, according to the **o**,	Nu 15:24	4941
statutory **o** to the sons of Israel,	Nu 27:11	4941
offerings, according to their **o**,	Nu 29:6	4941
their number according to the **o**;	Nu 29:18	4941
their number according to the **o**;	Nu 29:21	4941
their number according to the **o**;	Nu 29:24	4941
their number according to the **o**;	Nu 29:27	4941
their number according to the **o**;	Nu 29:30	4941
their number according to the **o**;	Nu 29:33	4941
their number according to the **o**;	Nu 29:37	4941
shall be for a statutory **o** to you	Nu 35:29	4941
a statute and an **o** in Shechem.	Jos 24:25	4941
and an **o** for Israel to this day.	1Sa 30:25	4941
not seek Him according to the **o**."	1Ch 15:13	4941
set by the **o** concerning them,	1Ch 23:31	4941
the **o** *given* to them through Aaron	1Ch 24:19	4941
to the **o** of his father David,	2Ch 8:14	4941
on the fire according to the **o**,	2Ch 35:13	4941
And they made them an **o** in Israel;	2Ch 35:25	2706
daily, according to the **o**,	Ezr 3:4	4941
assembly according to the **o**.	Ne 8:18	4941
Israel, An **o** of the God of Jacob.	Ps 81:4	4941
An **o** for Israel	Ps 122:4	5715
not forsaken the **o** of their God.	Is 58:2	4941
of the LORD *Or* the **o** of their God.	Jer 5:4	4941
LORD *And* the **o** of their God."	Jer 5:5	4941
do not know The **o** of the LORD.	Jer 8:7	4941
LORD continually by a perpetual **o**.	Ezk 46:14	2708
although they know the **o** of God,	Ro 1:32	*1345*
has opposed the **o** of God;	Ro 13:2	*1296*

ORDINANCES

"Now these are the **o** which you	Ex 21:1	4941
words of the LORD and all the **o**;	Ex 24:3	4941
all My statutes and all My **o**	Lv 19:37	4941
statutes and all My **o** and do them,	Lv 20:22	4941
and if your soul abhors My **o** so as	Lv 26:15	4941
because they rejected My **o** and	Lv 26:43	4941
These are the statutes and **o** and	Lv 26:46	4941
and according to all its **o**."	Nu 9:3	4941
avenger according to these **o**.	Nu 35:24	4941
the **o** which the LORD commanded	Nu 36:13	4941
statutes and the **o** which Moses spoke	Dt 4:45	4941
the statutes and the **o** which I am	Dt 5:1	4941
His commandments and His **o**	Dt 8:11	4941
His charge, His statutes, His **o**,	Dt 11:1	4941
you to do these statutes and **o**.	Dt 26:16	4941
His commandments and His **o**,	Dt 26:17	4941
"They shall teach Your **o** to Jacob,	Dt 33:10	4941
the LORD, And His **o** with Israel."	Dt 33:21	4941
the people the **o** of the kingdom,	1Sa 10:25	4941
"For all His **o** *were* before me,	2Sa 22:23	4941
statutes, His commandments, His **o**,	1Ki 2:3	4941
and execute My **o** and keep all My	1Ki 6:12	4941
and His statutes and His **o**,	1Ki 8:58	4941
will keep My statutes and My **o**,	1Ki 9:4	4941
observing My statutes and My **o**,	1Ki 11:33	4941
statutes or their **o** or the law,	2Ki 17:34	4941
"The statutes and the **o** and	2Ki 17:37	4941
o which the LORD commanded Moses	1Ch 22:13	4941
performs My commandments and My **o**,	1Ch 28:7	4941
will keep My statutes and My **o**,	2Ch 7:17	4941
and commandment, statutes and **o**,	2Ch 19:10	4941
and the **o** *given* through Moses."	2Ch 33:8	4941
His statutes and **o** in Israel.	Ezr 7:10	4941
nor the **o** which You commanded	Ne 1:7	4941
gave them just **o** and true laws,	Ne 9:13	4941
but sinned against Your **o**,	Ne 9:29	4941
Lord, and His **o** and His statutes;	Ne 10:29	4941
"Do you know the **o** of the heavens	Jb 38:33	2708
For all His **o** were before me, And	Ps 18:22	4941
told of All the **o** of Your mouth.	Ps 119:13	4941
After Your **o** at all times.	Ps 119:20	4941
I have placed Your **o** *before me.*	Ps 119:30	4941
I dread, For Your **o** are good.	Ps 119:39	4941
my mouth, For I wait for Your **o**.	Ps 119:43	4941
remembered Your **o** from of old,	Ps 119:52	4941
You Because of Your righteous **o**.	Ps 119:62	4941
this day according to Your **o**,	Ps 119:91	4941
not turned aside from Your **o**,	Ps 119:102	4941
That I will keep Your righteous **o**.	Ps 119:106	4941
O LORD, And teach me Your **o**.	Ps 119:108	4941
me, O LORD, according to Your **o**.	Ps 119:149	4941
Revive me according to Your **o**.	Ps 119:156	4941
of Your righteous **o** is everlasting.	Ps 119:160	4941
You, Because of Your righteous **o**.	Ps 119:164	4941
You, And let Your **o** help me.	Ps 119:175	4941
His statutes and His **o** to Israel.	Ps 147:19	4941
And as for His **o**, they have not	Ps 147:20	4941
'But she has rebelled against My **o**	Ezk 5:6	4941
for they have rejected My **o** and	Ezk 5:6	4941
in My statutes, nor observed My **o**,	Ezk 5:7	4941
nor observed the **o** of the nations	Ezk 5:7	4941
nor have you executed My **o**,	Ezk 11:12	4941
acted according to the **o** of the nations	Ezk 11:12	4941
walk in My statutes and keep My **o** and	Ezk 11:20	4941
if he walks in My statutes and My **o**	Ezk 18:9	4941
or increase, *but* executes My **o**,	Ezk 18:17	4941
and informed them of My **o**,	Ezk 20:11	4941
statutes and they rejected My **o**,	Ezk 20:13	4941
because they rejected My **o**,	Ezk 20:16	4941
of your fathers or keep their **o**	Ezk 20:18	4941
in My statutes and keep My **o**	Ezk 20:19	4941
were they careful to observe My **o**,	Ezk 20:21	4941
they had not observed My **o**,	Ezk 20:24	4941
o by which they could not live;	Ezk 20:25	4941
will be careful to observe My **o**.	Ezk 36:27	4941
and they will walk in My **o** and	Ezk 37:24	4941
shall judge it according to My **o**.	Ezk 44:24	4941
aside from Your commandments and **o**.	Da 9:5	4941
earth Who have carried out His **o**;	Zph 2:3	4941
even the statutes and **o** which I	Mal 4:4	4941

of commandments *contained* in **o**, Eph 2:15 *1378*
ORDINARY
its width four cubits by **o** cubit.) Dt 3:11 376
"There is no **o** bread on hand, but 1Sa 21:4 2455
holy, though it was an **o** journey; 1Sa 21:5 2455
and write on it in **o** letters: Is 8:1 582
ORDINATION
right thigh (for it is a ram of **o**), Ex 29:22 4394
the breast of Aaron's ram of **o**, Ex 29:26 4394
was offered from the ram of **o**, Ex 29:27 4394
"You shall take the ram of **o** Ex 29:31 4394
made at their **o** *and* consecration; Ex 29:33 4390, 3027
"If any of the flesh of **o** or Ex 29:34 4394
the guilt offering and the **o** offering Lv 7:37 4394
the second ram, the ram of **o**, Lv 8:22 4394
o offering for a soothing aroma; Lv 8:28 4394
was Moses' portion of the ram of **o**, Lv 8:29 4394
in the basket of the **o** offering, Lv 8:31 4394
the period of your **o** is fulfilled; Lv 8:33 4394
OREB
two leaders of Midian, **O** and Zeeb, Jg 7:25 6159
they killed **O** at the rock of Oreb, Jg 7:25 6159
they killed Oreb at the rock of **O**, Jg 7:25 6159
and they brought the heads of **O** Jg 7:25 6159
O and Zeeb into your hands; Jg 8:3 6159
Make their nobles like **O** and Zeeb And Ps 83:11 6159
of Midian at the rock of **O**; Is 10:26 6159
OREN
Ram the firstborn, then Bunah, **O**, 1Ch 2:25 767
ORGAN
or has his male **o** cut off shall Dt 23:1 8212
ORIGIN
it to men whose **o** I do not know?" 1Sa 25:11 4480, 2088, 335
begun to fall, is of Jewish **o**, Es 6:13 2233
city, Whose **o** is from antiquity, Is 23:7 6927
"Your **o** and your birth are from Ezk 16:3 4351
created, in the land of your **o**, Ezk 21:30 4351
Pathros, to the land of their **o**, Ezk 29:14 4351
ORIGINATE
and authority **o** with themselves. Hab 1:7 3318
For man does not **o** from woman, 1Co 11:8 *1510*
and all things **o** from God. 1Co 11:12
ORIGINATES
For as the woman **o** from the man, 1Co 11:12
ORION
Who makes the Bear, **O** and Jb 9:9 3685
Pleiades, Or loose the cords of **O**? Jb 38:31 3685
He who made the Pleiades and **O** And Am 5:8 3685
ORNAMENT
earring of gold and an **o** of fine gold Pr 25:12 2481
ORNAMENTED
o it with palm trees and chains. 2Ch 3:5 5927, 5921
ORNAMENTS
and none of them put on his **o**. Ex 33:4 5716
put off your **o** from you, Ex 33:5 5716
Israel stripped themselves of their **o** Ex 33:6 5716
and took the crescent **o** which were Jg 8:21 7720
besides the crescent **o** and the Jg 8:26 7720
Who put **o** of gold on your apparel. 2Sa 1:24 5716
your head And **o** about your neck. Pr 1:9 6060
"Your cheeks are lovely with **o**, SS 1:10 8447
o of gold With beads of silver." SS 1:11 8447
anklets, headbands, crescent **o**, Is 3:18 7720
"Can a virgin forget her **o**, Jer 2:32 5716
decorate *yourself with* **o** of gold, Jer 4:30 5716
the beauty of His **o** into pride, Ezk 7:20 5716
and reached the age for fine **o**; Ezk 16:7 5716
"I adorned you with **o**, Ezk 16:11 5716
and decorated yourselves with **o**; Ezk 23:40 5716
each side pillar *were* palm tree **o**. Ezk 40:16 8561
and its palm tree **o** *had* the same Ezk 40:22 8561
palm tree **o** on its side pillars, Ezk 40:26 8561
palm tree **o** *were* on its side pillars, Ezk 40:31 8561
palm tree **o** *were* on its side pillars, Ezk 40:34 8561
and palm tree **o** *were* on its side Ezk 40:37 8561
ORNAN
threshing floor of **O** the Jebusite. 1Ch 21:15 771
threshing floor of **O** the Jebusite. 1Ch 21:18 771
O turned back and saw the angel, 1Ch 21:20 771
And **O** was threshing wheat. 1Ch 21:20 771
As David came to **O**, 1Ch 21:21 771
to Ornan, **O** looked and saw David, 1Ch 21:21 771
Then David said to **O**, 1Ch 21:22 771
O said to David, 1Ch 21:23 771
But King David said to **O**, 1Ch 21:24 771
So David gave **O** 600 shekels of 1Ch 21:25 771
threshing floor of **O** the Jebusite, 1Ch 21:28 771
threshing floor of **O** the Jebusite. 2Ch 3:1 771
ORNATE
"Take silver and gold, make an **o** Zch 6:11
ORPAH
the name of the one was **O** and the Ru 1:4 6204
and **O** kissed her mother-in-law, Ru 1:14 6204
ORPHAN
shall not afflict any widow or **o**. Ex 22:22 3490
justice for the **o** and the widow, Dt 10:18 3490
the **o** and the widow who are in Dt 14:29 3490
and the stranger and the **o** and the Dt 16:11 3490
the stranger and the **o** and the widow Dt 16:14 3490
the justice due an alien *or* an **o**, Dt 24:17 3490
alien, for the **o**, and for the widow, Dt 24:19 3490
alien, for the **o**, and for the widow. Dt 24:20 3490
alien, for the **o**, and for the widow. Dt 24:21 3490
to the **o** and to the widow, Dt 26:12 3490
the alien, the **o** and the widow, Dt 26:13 3490
justice due an alien, **o**, and widow. Dt 27:19 3490
snatch the **o** from the breast, Jb 24:9 3490
help, And the **o** who had no helper. Jb 29:12 3490
And the **o** has not shared it Jb 31:17 3490
lifted up my hand against the **o**, Jb 31:21 3490
have been the helper of the **o**. Ps 10:14 3490
vindicate the **o** and the oppressed, Ps 10:18 3490
Defend the **o**, Plead for the widow. Is 1:17 3490
They do not defend the **o**, Is 1:23 3490
the cause, The cause of the **o**, Jer 5:28 3490
the alien, the **o**, or the widow, Jer 7:6 3490
the stranger, the **o**, or the widow; Jer 22:3 3490
For in You the **o** finds mercy." Hos 14:3 3490
do not oppress the widow or the **o**, Zch 7:10 3490
in his wages, the widow and the **o**, Mal 3:5 3490
ORPHANS
would even cast *lots* for the **o** And Jb 6:27 3490
strength of the **o** has been crushed. Jb 22:9 3490
drive away the donkeys of the **o**; Jb 24:3 3490
the stranger And murder the **o**. Ps 94:6 3490
pity on their **o** or their widows; Is 9:17 3490
And that they may plunder the **o**. Is 10:2 3490
"Leave your **o** behind, I will keep Jer 49:11 3490
We have become **o** without a father, La 5:3 3490
"I will not leave you as **o**; Jn 14:18 *3737*
visit **o** and widows in their distress, Jas 1:27 *3737*
OSNAPPAR
the great and honorable **O** deported Ezr 4:10 620
OSTRACIZE
you when men hate you, and **o** you, Lk 6:22 *873*
OSTRICH
and the **o** and the owl and the sea Lv 11:16 3284
and the **o**, the owl, the sea gull, Dt 14:15 3284
OSTRICHES
to jackals And a companion of **o**. Jb 30:29 1323, 3284
of owls; **O** also will live there, Is 13:21 3284
of jackals *And* an abode of **o**. Is 34:13 3284
The jackals and the **o**, Is 43:20 3284
The **o** also will live in it, And it Jer 50:39 3284
cruel Like **o** in the wilderness. La 4:3 3283
jackals And a mourning like the **o**. Mi 1:8 3284
OSTRICHES'
"The **o** wings flap joyously With Jb 39:13 7443
OTHER
and the name of the **o**, Zillah. Gn 4:19 8145
and he had **o** sons and daughters. Gn 5:4
and he had **o** sons and daughters. Gn 5:7
and he had **o** sons and daughters. Gn 5:10
and he had **o** sons and daughters. Gn 5:13
and he had **o** sons and daughters. Gn 5:16
and he had **o** sons and daughters. Gn 5:19
and he had **o** sons and daughters. Gn 5:22
and he had **o** sons and daughters. Gn 5:26
and he had **o** sons and daughters. Gn 5:30
and he had **o** sons and daughters. Gn 11:11
and he had **o** sons and daughters. Gn 11:13
and he had **o** sons and daughters. Gn 11:15
and he had **o** sons and daughters. Gn 11:17
and he had **o** sons and daughters. Gn 11:19
and he had **o** sons and daughters. Gn 11:21
and he had **o** sons and daughters. Gn 11:23
and he had **o** sons and daughters. Gn 11:25
Thus they separated from each **o**. Gn 13:11 251
and laid each half opposite the **o**; Gn 15:10 7453
shall be stronger than the **o**; Gn 25:23 3816
is none **o** than the house of God, Gn 28:17 369
and we will give you the **o** also Gn 29:27 2088
when we are absent one from the **o**. Gn 31:49 7453
seven **o** cows came up after them Gn 41:3 312
and they stood by the **o** cows on Gn 41:3
seven **o** cows came up after them, Gn 41:19 312
you your **o** brother and Benjamin. Gn 43:14 312
o money in our hand to buy food; Gn 43:22 312
one end of Egypt's border to the **o**. Gn 47:21 7097a
and the **o** was named Puah; Ex 1:15 8145
Hebrews were fighting with each **o**; Ex 2:13
and all the **o** chariots of Egypt Ex 14:7
did not come near the **o** all night. Ex 14:20 2088
one on one side and one on the **o**. Ex 17:12 2088
The **o** was named Eliezer, for Ex 18:4 259
asked each **o** of their welfare and Ex 18:7 7453
shall have no **o** gods before Me. Ex 20:3 312
'You shall not make **o** *gods* Ex 20:23
one strikes the **o** with a stone or Ex 21:18 7453
"If men struggle with each **o** Ex 21:22
any god, **o** than to the LORD alone, Ex 22:20 1115
do not mention the name of **o** gods, Ex 23:13 312
and the **o** half of the blood he Ex 24:6
and two rings on the **o** side of it. Ex 25:12 8145
end and one cherub at the **o** end; Ex 25:19 259
of the lampstand from its **o** side. Ex 25:32 8145
almond *blossoms* in the **o** branch, Ex 25:33 259
and *the* **o** five curtains *shall* Ex 26:3
loops shall be opposite each **o**. Ex 26:5 259
curtains by themselves and the **o** Ex 26:9
one side and the cubit on the **o**, Ex 26:13 2088
on one side and on the **o**, Ex 26:13 2088
of the **o** side of the tabernacle, Ex 26:27 8145
"And for the **o** side *shall be* Ex 27:15 8145
the remaining six on the **o** stone, Ex 28:10 8145
"You shall put the **o** two ends of Ex 28:25
"Then you shall take the **o** ram, Ex 29:19 8145
and the **o** lamb you shall offer at Ex 29:39 8145
"The **o** lamb you shall offer Ex 29:41 8145
written on one *side* and the **o**. Ex 32:15 2088
may be distinguished from all the **o** Ex 33:16
you shall not worship any **o** god, Ex 34:14 312
curtains to one another and *the* **o** Ex 36:10
the loops were opposite each **o**. Ex 36:12 259
curtains by themselves and *the* **o** Ex 36:16
of the **o** side of the tabernacle, Ex 36:32 8145
and two rings on the **o** side of it. Ex 37:3 8145
end and one cherub at the **o** end; Ex 37:8 2088
with their faces toward each **o**; Ex 37:9 251
lampstand from the **o** side of it; Ex 37:18 8145
a bulb and a flower in the **o** branch Ex 37:19 259
and so for the **o** side. Ex 38:15 8145
They put the **o** two ends of Ex 39:18
and the **o** for a burnt offering. Lv 5:7 259
garments and put on **o** garments, Lv 6:11 312
As for **o** flesh, anyone who is Lv 7:19
beasts may be put to any **o** use, Lv 7:24
'But all **o** winged insects which Lv 11:23
and the **o** for a sin offering; Lv 12:8 259
and the **o** a burnt offering. Lv 14:22 259
and the **o** for a burnt offering, Lv 14:31 259
"Then they shall take **o** stones Lv 14:42 312
and he shall take **o** plaster and Lv 14:42 312
"If, on the **o** hand, the priest Lv 14:48
and the **o** for a burnt offering. Lv 15:15 259
and the **o** for a burnt offering. Lv 15:30 259
and the **o** lot for the scapegoat. Lv 16:8 259
struggled with each **o** in the camp. Lv 24:10
o as if *running* from the sword, Lv 26:37 251
a man **o** than your husband has had Nu 5:20 1107
and *the* **o** for a burnt offering, Nu 6:11 259
o for a burnt offering to the LORD, Nu 8:12 259
Eldad and the name of the **o** Medad. Nu 11:26 8145
and a day's journey on the **o** side, Nu 11:31 3541
camped on the **o** side of the Arnon, Nu 21:13 5676
he did not go as at **o** times to Nu 24:1 6471
and the **o** lamb you shall offer at Nu 28:4 8145
'The **o** lamb you shall offer at Nu 28:8 8145
o side of the Jordan and beyond, Nu 32:19 5676
and they gave **o** names to Nu 32:38
they marry one of the sons of the **o** Nu 36:3
one end of the heavens to the **o**. Dt 4:32 7097a, 8064
there is no **o** besides Him. Dt 4:35 5750
on the earth below; there is no **o**. Dt 4:39 5750
shall have no **o** gods before Me. Dt 5:7 312
'You shall not follow **o** gods, Dt 6:14 312
from following Me to serve **o** gods; Dt 7:4 312
and go after **o** gods and serve them Dt 8:19 312
and serve **o** gods and worship them. Dt 11:16 312
o gods which you have not known. Dt 11:28 312
'Let us go after **o** gods Dt 13:2 312
'Let us go and serve **o** gods' Dt 13:6 312
one end of the earth to the **o** end Dt 13:7
'Let us go and serve **o** gods' Dt 13:13 312
served **o** gods and worshiped them, Dt 17:3 312
speaks in the name of **o** gods, Dt 18:20 312
the one loved and the **o** unloved, Dt 21:15 259
to go after **o** gods to serve them. Dt 28:14 312
and there you shall serve **o** gods, Dt 28:36 312
one end of the earth to the **o** end Dt 28:64
and there you shall serve **o** gods, Dt 28:64 312
served **o** gods and worshiped them, Dt 29:26 312
and worship **o** gods and serve them, Dt 30:17 312
do, for they will turn to **o** gods. Dt 31:18 312
turn to **o** gods and serve them, Dt 31:20 312
With the **o** half-tribe, the Jos 13:8
but to the **o** half Joshua gave *a* Jos 22:7
you, and go and serve **o** gods and Jos 23:16 312
of Nahor, and they served **o** gods. Jos 24:2 312
forsake the LORD to serve **o** gods; Jos 24:16 312
and followed **o** gods from *among* the Jg 2:12 312
they played the harlot after **o** gods Jg 2:17 312
in following **o** gods to serve them Jg 2:19 312
so let all the **o** people go, each Jg 7:7
And Gideon sent all the **o** men of Jg 7:8
the **o** two companies then dashed Jg 9:44
forsaken Me and served **o** gods; Jg 10:13 312
the man who came the **o** day has Jg 13:10
will become weak and be like any **o** Jg 16:7
will become weak and be like any **o** Jg 16:11
weak and be like any **o** man." Jg 16:13
will become weak and be like any **o** Jg 16:17
I will go out as at **o** times and shake Jg 16:20 6471
hand and the **o** with his left. Jg 16:29 259
against Gibeah as at **o** times. Jg 20:30 6471
some of the people as at **o** times, Jg 20:31 6471
up to Bethel and the **o** to Gibeah, Jg 20:31 259
Orpah and the name of the **o** Ruth. Ru 1:4 8145
and the name of the **o** Peninnah; 1Sa 1:2 8145
stood and called as at **o** times, 1Sa 3:10 6471
have forsaken Me and served **o** gods 1Sa 8:8 312
garrison that is on the **o** side." 1Sa 14:1 5676
and a sharp crag on the **o** side, 1Sa 14:4 2088
and the name of the **o** Seneh. 1Sa 14:4 259
the **o** on the south opposite Geba. 1Sa 14:5 259
my son will be on the **o** side." 1Sa 14:40 259
on the mountain on the **o** side, 1Sa 17:3 2088
told Saul, he sent **o** messengers, 1Sa 19:21 312
kissed each **o** and wept together, 1Sa 20:41 7453
to each **o** in the name of the LORD, 1Sa 20:42 8147
there is no **o** except it here." 1Sa 21:9 312
men on the **o** side of the mountain; 1Sa 23:26 2088
David crossed over to the **o** side and 1Sa 26:13 5676
'Go, serve **o** gods.' 1Sa 26:19 312
himself by putting on **o** clothes, 1Sa 28:8 312
the people drove ahead of the **o** 1Sa 30:20
were on the **o** side of the valley, 1Sa 31:7 5676

o on the other side of the pool. 2Sa 2:13 2088
other on the o side of the pool. 2Sa 2:13 2088
and the name of the o Rechab, 2Sa 4:2 8145
city, the one rich and the o poor. 2Sa 12:1 259
the o that you have done to me!" 2Sa 13:16 312
one struck the o and killed him. 2Sa 14:6 259
Then the o woman said, 1Ki 3:22 312
o says, 'No! For your son is the dead 1Ki 3:23 2088
to the one and half to the o." 1Ki 3:25 259
the o said, "He shall be neither mine 1Ki 3:26 2088
as far as the o side of Jokmeam; 1Ki 4:12 5676
cubits the o wing of the cherub; 1Ki 6:24 8145
end of the o wing were ten cubits. 1Ki 6:24
The o cherub was ten cubits; 1Ki 6:25 8145
cubits, and so was the o cherub. 1Ki 6:26 8145
and the wing of the o cherub was 1Ki 6:27 8145
cherub was touching the o wall. 1Ki 6:27 8145
So their wings were touching each o 1Ki 6:27 3671
the two leaves of the o door turned 1Ki 6:34 8145
the o court inward from the hall, 1Ki 7:8 312
the height of the o capital was five 1Ki 7:16 8145
and seven for the o capital. 1Ki 7:17 8145
and so he did for the o capital. 1Ki 7:18 8145
and serve o gods and worship them, 1Ki 9:6 312
and adopted o gods and worshiped 1Ki 9:9 312
on the one side and on the o; 1Ki 10:20 2088
it was made for any o kingdom. 1Ki 10:20
turned his heart away after o gods; 1Ki 11:4 312
he should not go after o gods; 1Ki 11:10 312
Bethel, and the o he put in Dan. 1Ki 12:29 259
gone and made for yourself o gods 1Ki 14:9 312
the o half followed Omri. 1Ki 16:21
and I will prepare the o ox and 1Ki 18:23 259
one over against the o seven days. 1Ki 20:29 428
nor will he sacrifice to o gods, 2Ki 5:17 312
was filled from one end to the o. 2Ki 10:21 6310
and for the o priests and said to 2Ki 12:7
"Come, let us face each o." 2Ki 14:8
Judah faced each o at Beth-shemesh, 2Ki 14:11
Egypt, and they had feared o gods 2Ki 17:7 312
"You shall not fear o gods, 2Ki 17:35 312
and you shall not fear o gods. 2Ki 17:37 312
forget, nor shall you fear o gods. 2Ki 17:38 312
and have burned incense to o gods 2Ki 22:17 312
in Jerusalem opposite their o 1Ch 8:32
of the temple free from o 1Ch 9:33
in Jerusalem opposite their o 1Ch 9:38
From the o side of the Jordan, 1Ch 12:37 5676
and Eliezer had no o sons, 1Ch 23:17 312
divided by lot, the one as the o; 1Ch 24:5 428
wall of the house, and its wing, 2Ch 3:11 312
touched the wing of the o cherub. 2Ch 3:11 312
The wing of the o cherub, 2Ch 3:12 312
and its o wing of five cubits was 2Ch 3:12 312
the right and the o on the left, 2Ch 3:17 259
priests on the o side blew trumpets; 2Ch 7:6 5048
and serve o gods and worship them, 2Ch 7:19 312
and they adopted o gods and 2Ch 7:22 312
on the one side and on the o; 2Ch 9:19 2088
like it was made for any o 2Ch 9:19
of Absalom more than all his o 2Ch 11:21
priests like the peoples of o 2Ch 13:9
"Come, let us face each o." 2Ch 25:17
Judah faced each o at Beth-shemesh, 2Ch 25:21
places to burn incense to o gods, 2Ch 28:25 312
work was completed and until the o 2Ch 29:34
o have burned incense to o gods, 2Ch 34:25 312
"What have we to do with each o, 2Ch 35:21
second kind and 1,000 o articles. Ezr 1:10 312
the sons of the o Elam, 1,254; Ezr 2:31 312
official of the o half of Ne 3:18
work and the o holding a weapon. Ne 4:17 259
the men of the o Nebo, 52; Ne 7:33 312
the sons of the o Elam, 1,254; Ne 7:34 312
palm branches and branches of o Ne 8:15
nine-tenths remained in the o Ne 11:1
different from those of all o Es 3:8
Yet it withers before any o plant. Jb 8:12
each o and cannot be separated. Jb 41:17
its circuit to the o end of them; Ps 19:6
They are not in trouble as o men, Ps 73:5
and peace have kissed each o. Ps 85:10
gates of Zion More than all the o Ps 87:2
As one dies so dies the o; Ec 3:19 2088
"Even if the o man lives a Ec 6:6
has made the one as well as the o Ec 7:14 2088
and also not let go of the o; Ec 7:18 2088
On the o hand, there are evil men Ec 8:14
the sea, on the o side of Jordan, Is 9:1 5676
o masters besides You have ruled Is 26:13
I will give o men in your place Is 43:4
other men in your place and o Is 43:4
Or is there any o Rock? I know Is 44:8
"I am the LORD, and there is no o; Is 45:5 5750
I am the LORD, and there is no o, Is 45:6 5750
there is none else, No o God.'" Is 45:14 657
And there is no o God besides Me, Is 45:21 5750
For I am God, and there is no o. Is 45:22 5750
For I am God, and there is no o; Is 46:9 5750
Let us stand up to each o; Is 50:8 3162
have offered sacrifices to o gods, Jer 1:16 312
after o gods to your own ruin, Jer 7:6 312
o gods that you have not known, Jer 7:9 312
to o gods in order to spite Me. Jer 7:18 312
in Topheth because there is no o Jer 7:32
gone after o gods to serve them; Jer 11:10 312
one end of the land even to the o; Jer 12:12
7097a, 776
have gone after o gods to serve them Jer 13:10 312

I will dash them against each o, Jer 13:14 251
'and have followed o gods and Jer 16:11 312
will serve o gods day and night, Jer 16:13 312
have burned sacrifices in it to o gods Jer 19:4 312
in Topheth because there is no o Jer 19:11
drink offerings to o gods."'" Jer 19:13 312
to o gods and served them."' Jer 22:9 312
"who steal My words from each o. Jer 23:30 7453
the o basket had very bad figs which Jer 24:2 259
and do not go after o gods to Jer 25:6 312
one end of the earth to the o. Jer 25:33
7097a, 776
to o gods to provoke Me to anger. Jer 32:29 312
do not go after o gods to worship Jer 35:15 312
and all the o officials. Jer 36:12
in Edom and who were in all the o Jer 40:11
o gods whom they had not known, Jer 44:3 312
not to burn sacrifices to o gods. Jer 44:5 312
to o gods in the land of Egypt, Jer 44:8 312
were burning sacrifices to o gods, Jer 44:15 312
out straight, one toward the o; Ezk 1:23 269
on the one side and on the o. Ezk 1:23 2008
turn from one side to the o until Ezk 4:8 6654
this lewdness on top of all your o Ezk 16:43
and the o threshold was one rod in Ezk 40:6 259
guardroom to the roof of the o, Ezk 40:13
all around like those o windows; Ezk 40:25
and on the o side of the porch of Ezk 40:40 312
the palm tree on the o side; Ezk 41:19
doorpost was like that of the o. Ezk 41:21
one door and two leaves for the o. Ezk 41:24 312
trees on one side and on the o, Ezk 41:26 6311
They shall put on o garments; Ezk 42:14 312
then they shall put on o garments Ezk 44:19 312
on the one side and on the o. Ezk 47:7 2088
bank, on one side and on the o, Ezk 47:12 2088
each one equally with the o; Ezk 47:14 251
on the one side and on the o of Ezk 48:21 2088
in me more than in any o Da 2:30
their caps and their o clothes, Da 3:21
inasmuch as there is no o god who Da 3:29 321
and the o horn which came up, Da 7:20 321
different from all the o kingdoms Da 7:23
but one was longer than the o, Da 8:3 8145
and no o beasts could stand Da 8:4
and they will speak lies to each o Da 11:27
nor will he show regard for any o Da 11:37
will stretch out his hand against o Da 11:42
the o on that bank of the river. Da 12:5 259
though they turn to o gods and love Hos 3:1 312
They do not crowd each o, Jl 2:8 251
LORD your God, And there is no o; Jl 2:27 5750
On the o hand I am filled with Mi 3:8 199
Each of them hunts the o with a net. Mi 7:2 251
or any o food, will it become Hg 2:12
bowl and the o on its left side." Zch 4:3 259
to the writing on the o side. Zch 5:3
Favor and the o I called Union; Zch 11:7 259
and the o half toward the south. Zch 14:4
the o half toward the western sea; Zch 14:8
"On the o hand, it is written, Mt 4:7 3825
from there He saw two o brothers, Mt 4:21 243
cheek, turn the o to him also. Mt 5:39 243
will hate the one and love the o, Mt 6:24 2087
devoted to one and despise the o. Mt 6:24 2087
orders to depart to the o side Mt 8:18 4008
When He came to the o side Mt 8:28 4008
"What business do we have with each o, Mt 8:29
who call out to the o children, Mt 11:16 2087
restored to normal, like the o. Mt 12:13 243
takes along with it seven o spirits Mt 12:45 2087
and this is smaller than all o Mt 13:32
and go ahead of Him to the o side, Mt 14:22 4008
And the disciples came to the o side Mt 16:5 4008
out the vineyard to o vine-growers who Mt 21:41 243
"Again he sent out o slaves saying, Mt 22:4 243
from one end of the sky to the o. Mt 24:31 206
"Later the o virgins also Mt 25:11 3062
was there, and the o Mary, Mt 27:61 243
Mary Magdalene and the o Mary came Mt 28:1 243
"What business do we have with each o, Mk 1:24
"O seed fell on the rocky Mk 4:5 243
"O seed fell among the thorns, Mk 4:7 243
"O seeds fell into the good soil, Mk 4:8 243
and the desires for o things enter Mk 4:19 3062
"Let us go over to the o side." Mk 4:35 4008
and o boats were with Him. Mk 4:36 243
came to the o side of the sea, Mk 5:1 4008
"What business do we have with each o, Mk 5:7
again in the boat to the o side, Mk 5:21 4008
of Him to the o side to Bethsaida, Mk 6:45 4008
and there are many o things which Mk 7:4 243
and went away to the o side. Mk 8:13 4008
There is no o commandment greater Mk 12:31 243
and there were many o women who Mk 15:41 243
So with many o exhortations he Lk 3:18 2087
What business do we have with each o, Lk 4:34
the kingdom of God to the o cities Lk 4:43 2087
to their partners in the o boat for Lk 5:7 2087
crowd of tax collectors and o people Lk 5:29 243
the cheek, offer him the o also; Lk 6:29 243
nor, on the o hand, a bad tree Lk 6:43 3825
five hundred denarii, and the o fifty. Lk 7:41 2087
"O seed fell on rocky soil, Lk 8:6 2087
"O seed fell among the thorns; Lk 8:7 2087
"O seed fell into the good soil, Lk 8:8 2087
over to the o side of the lake." Lk 8:22 4008
"What business do we have with each o, Lk 8:28
him, he passed by on the o side. Lk 10:31 492

saw him, passed by on the o side. Lk 10:32 492
takes along seven o spirits more evil Lk 11:26 2087
do you worry about o matters? Lk 12:26 3062
were greater sinners than all o Lk 13:2
while the o is still far away, Lk 14:32 846
will hate the one and love the o, Lk 16:13 2087
be devoted to one and despise the o. Lk 16:13 2087
shines to the o part of the sky, Lk 17:24
be taken and the o will be left. Lk 17:34 2087
be taken and the o will be left. Lk 17:35 2087
taken and the o will be left." Lk 17:36 2087
Pharisee and the o a tax collector. Lk 18:10 2087
You that I am not like o people: Lk 18:11 3062
house justified rather than the o; Lk 18:14 1565
saying many o things against Him, Lk 22:65 2087
had been enemies with each o. Lk 23:12 848
the right and the o on the left. Lk 23:33 3739
But the o answered, and rebuking Lk 23:40 2087
also the o women with them were Lk 24:10 3062
they were talking with each o Lk 24:14 240
the o side of the Sea of Galilee Jn 6:1 4008
crowd that stood on the o side Jn 6:22 4008
there was no o small boat there, Jn 6:22 243
There came o small boats from Jn 6:23 243
Him on the o side of the sea, Jn 6:25 4008
sheep, but climbs up some o way, Jn 10:1 237a
"I have o sheep, which are Jn 10:16 243
So the o disciple, who was known Jn 18:16 243
Him, and with Him two o men, Jn 19:18 243
and of the o who was crucified Jn 19:32 243
the o disciple whom Jesus loved, Jn 20:2 243
and the o disciple went forth, Jn 20:3 243
and the o disciple ran ahead Jn 20:4 243
So the o disciple who had first Jn 20:8 243
So the o disciples were Jn 20:25 243
Therefore many o signs Jesus also Jn 20:30 243
But the o disciples came in the Jn 21:8 243
many o things which Jesus did, Jn 21:25 243
and began to speak with o tongues, Ac 2:4 2087
And with many o words he solemnly Ac 2:40 2087
for there is no o name under Ac 4:12 2087
their time in nothing o than telling Ac 17:21 2087
Sadducees and the o Pharisees, Ac 23:6 2087
o than for this one statement Ac 24:21 2228
to deliver Paul and some o prisoners Ac 27:1 2087
but on the o hand the free gift Ro 5:16 1161
the law of God, but on the o, Ro 7:25 1161
depth, nor any o created thing, Ro 8:39 2087
and if there is any o commandment, Ro 13:9 2087
not know whether I baptized any o. 1Co 1:16 243
o than the one which is laid, 1Co 3:11 243
in behalf of one against the o. 1Co 4:6 2087
Flee immorality. Every o sin 1Co 6:18
own conscience, but the o man's; 1Co 10:29 2087
we have no o practice, 1Co 11:16 5108
but the o person is not edified. 1Co 14:17 2087
the o an aroma from life to life. 2Co 2:16 3739
that is, in o men's labors, 2Co 10:15 245
I robbed o churches by taking wages 2Co 11:8 243
I did not see any o of the apostles Ga 1:19 2087
that you will adopt no o view; Ga 5:10 243
which in o generations was not Eph 3:5 2087
tender-hearted, forgiving each o, Eph 4:32 1438
one another, and forgiving each o, Col 3:13 1438
On the o hand, discipline yourself 1Tm 4:7 1161
on the o hand there is a bringing in Heb 7:19 1161
but Jesus, on the o hand, because He Heb 7:24 1161
or by earth or with any o oath; Jas 5:12 243
On the o hand, I am writing a new 1Jn 2:8 3825
I place no o burden on you. Rv 2:24 243
one is, the o has not yet come; Rv 17:10 243

OTHER'S

you, each of us by the o faith, Ro 1:12 240

OTHERS

The o came out from the city Jos 8:22 428
so that o do not fall upon you in Ru 2:22
Assyria and from the hand of all o, 2Ch 32:22
There were o who said, Ne 5:3
and vineyards belong to o." Ne 5:5 312
And out of the dust o will spring. Jb 8:19 312
"O snatch the orphan from the Jb 24:9
"O have been with those who rebel Jb 24:13 1992a
And let o kneel down over her. Jb 31:10 312
And sets o in their place. Jb 34:24 312
And leave their wealth to o. Ps 49:10 312
Or you will give your vigor to o Pr 5:9 312
likewise have many times cursed o. Ec 7:22 312
while o did not deal Is 33:1
o will deal treacherously with Is 33:1
"Yet o I will gather to them, Is 56:8
houses shall be turned over to o, Jer 6:12 312
I will give their wives to o, Jer 8:10 312
As she has done to o, so do to Jer 50:15
to the o He said in my hearing, Ezk 9:5 428
but preserve the lives of o for Ezk 13:18
keep o alive who should not live, Ezk 13:19 5315
for these waters go there and the o Ezk 47:9
was different from all the o, Da 7:19
and given to o besides them. Da 11:4 312
but the o to disgrace and Da 12:2 428
and behold, two o were standing, Da 12:5 312
commandments, and teaches o Mt 5:19 444
what more are you doing than o? Mt 5:47
"For if you forgive o for their Mt 6:14 444
"But if you do not forgive o, then Mt 6:15 444
"O fell on the rocky places, where Mt 13:5 243
"O fell among the thorns, Mt 13:7 243
"And o fell on the good soil and Mt 13:8 243

crippled, blind, mute, and many **o**, **Mt 15:30** *2087*
say John the Baptist; and **o**, Elijah; **Mt 16:14** *243*
but still **o**, Jeremiah, or one of **Mt 16:14** *2087*
saw **o** standing idle in the market **Mt 20:3** *243*
he went out and found **o** standing **Mt 20:6** *243*
and **o** were cutting branches from **Mt 21:8** *243*
done without neglecting the **o**. **Mt 23:23** *2548*
and **o** slapped Him, **Mt 26:67** *3588*
He saved **o**; He cannot save Himself. **Mt 27:42** *243*
"And **o** are the ones on whom seed **Mk 4:18** *243*
But **o** were saying, **Mk 6:15** *243*
And **o** were saying, **Mk 6:15** *243*
and **o** *say* Elijah; **Mk 8:28** *243*
but **o**, one of the prophets." **Mk 8:28** *243*
and **o** *spread* leafy branches which **Mk 11:8** *243*
and *so with* many **o**, **Mk 12:5** *243*
beating some and killing **o**. **Mk 12:5**
3739, 1161
and will give the vineyard to **o**. **Mk 12:9** *243*
He saved **o**; He cannot save Himself. **Mk 15:31** *243*
away and reported it to the **o**, **Mk 16:13** *3062*
"Treat **o** the same way you want them **Lk 6:31** *444*
and many **o** who were contributing **Lk 8:3** *2087*
Elijah had appeared, and by **o** that **Lk 9:8** *243*
the Baptist, and **o** *say* Elijah; **Lk 9:19** *243*
but **o**, that one of the prophets of **Lk 9:19** *243*
this the Lord appointed seventy **o**, **Lk 10:1** *2087*
O, to test *Him*, were demanding **Lk 11:16** *2087*
done without neglecting the **o**. **Lk 11:42** *2548*
and viewed **o** with contempt: **Lk 18:9** *3062*
and will give the vineyard to **o**." **Lk 20:16** *243*
Two **o** also, who were **Lk 23:32** *2087*
"He saved **o**; let Him save Himself **Lk 23:35** *243*
o have labored and you have **Jn 4:38** *243*
o were saying, "No, on the contrary, **Jn 7:12** *243*
O were saying, "This is the Christ." **Jn 7:41** *243*
Still **o** were saying, **Jn 7:41** *3588*
O were saying, "This is he," **Jn 9:9** *243*
still **o** were saying, "No, but he is **Jn 9:9** *243*
But **o** were saying, **Jn 9:16** *243*
O were saying, "These are not the **Jn 10:21** *243*
o were saying, "An angel has spoken **Jn 12:29** *243*
or did **o** tell you about Me?" **Jn 18:34** *243*
and two **o** of His disciples were **Jn 21:2** *243*
But **o** were mocking and saying, **Ac 2:13** *2087*
Paul and Barnabas and some **o** **Ac 15:2** *243*
and preaching with many **o** also, **Ac 15:35** *2087*
a pledge from Jason and the **o**, **Ac 17:9** *3062*
O, "He seems to be a proclaimer of **Ac 17:18**
3588, 1161
some *began* to sneer, but **o** said, **Ac 17:32** *3588*
named Damaris and **o** with them. **Ac 17:34** *2087*
and **o** on various things from the **Ac 27:44**
3739, 1161
spoken, but **o** would not believe. **Ac 28:24** *3588*
If to **o** I am not an apostle, at **1Co 9:2** *243*
If **o** share the right over you, do **1Co 9:12** *243*
after I have preached to **o**, **1Co 9:27** *243*
mind so that I may instruct **o** also, **1Co 14:19** *243*
and let the **o** pass judgment. **1Co 14:29** *243*
proving through the earnestness of **o** **2Co 8:8** *2087*
ease of **o** *and* for your affliction, **2Co 8:13** *243*
but also for the interests of **o**. **Php 2:4** *2087*
men, either from you or from **o**, **1Th 2:6** *243*
so then let us not sleep as **o** do, **1Th 5:6** *3062*
responsibility for the sins of **o**; **1Tm 5:22** *245*
for **o**, their *sins* follow after. **1Tm 5:24** *5100*
who will be able to teach **o** also. **2Tm 2:2** *2087*
and **o** were tortured, not accepting **Heb 11:35** *243*
and **o** experienced mockings and **Heb 11:36** *2087*
of righteousness, with seven **o**, **2Pe 2:5** *3590*
save **o**, snatching them out of the **Jude 1:23**

OTHERWISE
o we will be scattered abroad over **Gn 11:4** 6435
o we will become a laughingstock. **Gn 38:23** 6435
o He will fall upon us with **Ex 5:3** 6435
o you might make a covenant with **Ex 34:15** 6435
whether he has seen or **o** known, **Lv 5:1**
o he will die. **Lv 16:13** 3808
o you will be defeated before your **Dt 1:42** 3808
o the anger of the LORD your God **Dt 6:15** 6435
o, when you have eaten and are **Dt 8:12** 6435
"**O**, you may say in your heart, **Dt 8:17**
'**O** the land from which You brought **Dt 9:28** 6435
o the avenger of blood might pursue **Dt 19:6** 6435
o he might die in the battle **Dt 20:5** 6435
o he might die in the battle **Dt 20:6** 6435
o he might die in the battle **Dt 20:7** 6435
"**O** the Hebrews will make swords or **1Sa 13:19** 6435
"**O** they will tell about us, saying, **1Sa 27:11** 6435
o these uncircumcised will come **1Sa 31:4** 6435
o they will destroy my son." **2Sa 14:11** 3808
for **o** none of us will escape from **2Sa 15:14**
"**O**, if I had dealt treacherously **2Sa 18:13** 176
"**O** it will come about, as soon as **1Ki 1:21**
o these uncircumcised will come **1Ch 10:4** 6435
the Passover **o** than prescribed. **2Ch 30:18** 3808
O they will not come near to you. **Ps 32:9**
in sacrifice, **o** I would give it; **Ps 51:16**
O, what will you do in the end, **Pr 25:8** 6435
O they might see with their eyes, **Is 6:10** 6435
o you have no reward with your **Mt 6:1** *1490b*
o the wineskins burst, and the **Mt 9:17** *1490b*
O THEY WOULD SEE WITH THEIR EYES, **Mt 13:15** *3379*
o a riot might occur among the people." **Mt 26:5**
2443, 3361
o His disciples may come and steal **Mt 27:64** *3379*
o the patch pulls away from it, **Mk 2:21** *1490b*
o the wine will burst the skins, **Mk 2:22** *1490b*
O THEY MIGHT RETURN AND BE FORGIVEN." **Mk 4:12** *3379*
o there might be a riot of the people." **Mk 14:2** *3379*
o he will both tear the new, and **Lk 5:36** *1490b*
o the new wine will burst the **Lk 5:37** *1490b*
o they may also invite you in return **Lk 14:12** *3379*
"**O**, when he has laid a foundation and **Lk 14:29**
2443, 3361
o by continually coming she will wear **Lk 18:5**
2443, 3361
o believe because of the works **Jn 14:11** *1490b*
O THEY MIGHT SEE WITH THEIR EYES, **Ac 28:27** *3379*
o, how will God judge the world? **Ro 3:6** *1893*
works, **o** grace is no longer grace. **Ro 11:6** *1893*
o you also will be cut off. **Ro 11:22** *1893*
for **o** your children are unclean, **1Co 7:14** *1893*
O if you bless in the spirit *only*, **1Co 14:16** *1893*
O, what will those do who are **1Co 15:29** *1893*
o such a one might be overwhelmed by **2Co 2:7** *3381*
o if any Macedonians come with me **2Co 9:4** *3381*
which are **o** cannot be concealed. **1Tm 5:25** *247*
O, He would have needed to suffer **Heb 9:26** *1893*
O, would they not have ceased to **Heb 10:2** *1893*

OTHNI
The sons of Shemaiah *were* **O**, **1Ch 26:7** 6273

OTHNIEL
O the son of Kenaz, the **Jos 15:17** 6274
O the son of Kenaz, Caleb's **Jg 1:13** 6274
deliver them, **O** the son of Kenaz, **Jg 3:9** 6274
And **O** the son of Kenaz died. **Jg 3:11** 6274
sons of Kenaz *were* **O** and Seraiah. **1Ch 4:13** 6274
And the sons of **O** *were* Hathath **1Ch 4:13** 6274
was Heldai the Netophathite of **O**; **1Ch 27:15** 6274

OUGHT
me things that **o** not to be done." **Gn 20:9**
for such a thing **o** not to be done. **Gn 34:7**
and I **o** to sit down to eat with **1Sa 20:5**
will know what you **o** to do to him, **1Ki 2:9**
'Job **o** to be tried to the limit, **Jb 34:36** 994b
'Then you **o** to have put my money **Mt 25:27** *1163*
very hour what you **o** to say." **Lk 12:12** *1163*
that which we **o** to have done.' " **Lk 17:10** *3784*
o to pray and not to lose heart, **Lk 18:1** *1163*
place where men **o** to worship." **Jn 4:20** *1163*
also **o** to wash one another's feet. **Jn 13:14** *3784*
and by that law He **o** to die **Jn 19:7** *3784*
we **o** not to think that the Divine **Ac 17:29** *3784*
you **o** to keep calm and to do **Ac 19:36** *1189b*
who **o** to have been present before **Ac 24:19** *1163*
tribunal, where I **o** to be tried. **Ac 25:10** *1163*
that he **o** not to live any longer. **Ac 25:24** *1163*
you **o** to have followed my advice **Ac 27:21** *1163*
of himself than he **o** to think; **Ro 12:3** *1163*
Now we who are strong **o** to bear **Ro 15:1** *3784*
has not yet known as he **o** to know; **1Co 8:2** *1163*
the plowman **o** to plow in hope, **1Co 9:10** *3784*
o not to have his head covered, **1Co 11:7** *3784*
Therefore the woman **o** to have *a* **1Co 11:10** *3784*
Become sober-minded as you **o**, **1Co 15:34** *1346*
those who **o** to make me rejoice; **2Co 2:3** *1163*
so also the wives **o** *to be* to **Eph 5:24**
So husbands **o** also to love their **Eph 5:28** *3784*
may speak boldly, as I **o** to speak. **Eph 6:20** *1163*
it clear in the way I **o** to speak. **Col 4:4** *1163*
how you **o** to walk and please God **1Th 4:1** *1163*
We **o** always to give thanks to God **2Th 1:3** *3784*
how you **o** to follow our example, **2Th 3:7** *1163*
know how one **o** to conduct himself **1Tm 3:15** *1163*
The hard-working farmer **o** to be **2Tm 2:6** *1163*
by this time you **o** to be teachers, **Heb 5:12** *3784*
For that man **o** not to expect that he **Jas 1:7**
these things **o** not to be this way. **Jas 3:10** *5534*
Instead, *you* **o** to say, "If **Jas 4:15**
what sort of people **o** you to be in **2Pe 3:11** *1163*
o himself to walk in the same manner **1Jn 2:6** *3784*
and we **o** to lay down our lives for **1Jn 3:16** *3784*
us, we also **o** to love one another. **1Jn 4:11** *3784*
we **o** to support such men, **3Jn 1:8** *3784*
o to remember the words that were **Jude 1:17**

OURS
"The water is **o**!" **Gn 26:20**
and all their animals be **o**? **Gn 34:23**
This son of **o** is stubborn and **Dt 21:20**
do not tell this business of **o**; **Jos 2:14**
if you tell this business of **o**, **Jos 2:20**
The land is still **o** because **2Ch 14:7** 6440
and the inheritance will be **o**!' **Mk 12:7** *1473*
that the inheritance will be **o**.' **Lk 20:14** *1473*
trade of **o** fall into disrepute, **Ac 19:27** *1473*
Jesus Christ, their *Lord* and **o**: **1Co 1:2** *1473*
of Christ are **o** in abundance, **2Co 1:5** *1473*
to be proud as you also are **o**, **2Co 1:14** *1473*
was a man with a nature like **o**, **Jas 5:17** *1473*
a faith of the same kind as **o**, **2Pe 1:1** *1473*
and not for **o** only, but also for **1Jn 2:2** *2251*

OURSELVES
"Come, let us build for **o** a city, **Gn 11:4**
and let us make for **o** a name, **Gn 11:4**
we will take your daughters for **o**, **Gn 34:16**
o down before you to the ground?" **Gn 37:10**
And how can we justify **o**? **Gn 44:16**
we **o** do not know with what we **Ex 10:26** 587
atonement for **o** before the LORD." **Nu 31:50** 5315
but we **o** will be armed ready *to go* **Nu 32:17** 587
"We **o** will cross over armed in **Nu 32:32** 5168
have not cleansed **o** to this day, **Jos 22:17**
Let us take to **o** from Shiloh the **1Sa 4:3**
evil by asking for **o** a king." **1Sa 12:19**
to the men and reveal **o** to them. **1Sa 14:8**
and let us show **o** courageous for **2Sa 10:12**
there for **o** where we may live." **2Ki 6:2**
and let us show **o** courageous for **1Ch 19:13**
but we **o** will together build to **Ezr 4:3** 587
we might humble **o** before our God **Ezr 8:21**
And we **o** are unable To rebuild the **Ne 4:10** 587
We also placed **o** under obligation **Ne 10:32**
"Let us choose for **o** what is right; **Jb 34:4**
Let us know among **o** what is good. **Jb 34:4**
Let us possess for **o** The pastures **Ps 83:12**
He who has made us, and not we **o**; **Ps 100:3** 587
Let us delight **o** with caresses. **Pr 7:18**
make for **o** a breach in its walls and **Is 7:6**
have concealed **o** with deception." **Is 28:15**
Yet we **o** esteemed Him stricken, **Is 53:4** 587
Why have we humbled **o** and You **Is 58:3** 5315
a great evil against **o**." **Jer 26:19** 5315
nor to build **o** houses to dwell in; **Jer 35:9**
offerings to her, just as we **o**, **Jer 44:17** 587
strength taken Karnaim for **o**?" **Am 6:13**
For we **o** also forgive everyone who **Lk 11:4** *846*
heard it **o** from His own mouth." **Lk 22:71** *846*
for we have heard for **o** and know **Jn 4:42** *846*
"But we will devote **o** to prayer and **Ac 6:4** *4342*
"We have bound **o** under a solemn **Ac 23:14** *1438*
to it and let **o** be driven along. **Ac 27:15**
And not only this, but also we **o**, **Ro 8:23** *846*
even we **o** groan within ourselves, **Ro 8:23** *846*
even we ourselves groan within **o**, **Ro 8:23** *1438*
strength and not *just* please **o**. **Ro 15:1** *1438*
But if we judged **o** rightly, **1Co 11:31** *1438*
which we **o** are comforted by God. **2Co 1:4** *846*
we had the sentence of death within **o** **2Co 1:9** *1438*
that we would not trust in **o**, **2Co 1:9** *1438*
we have conducted **o** in the world, **2Co 1:12**
we beginning to commend **o** again? **2Co 3:1** *1438*
Not that we are adequate in **o** to **2Co 3:5** *1438*
anything as *coming* from **o**, **2Co 3:5** *1438*
manifestation of truth commending **o** **2Co 4:2** *1438*
preach **o** but Christ Jesus as Lord, **2Co 4:5** *1438*
and **o** as your bond-servants for **2Co 4:5** *1438*
will be of God and not from **o**; **2Co 4:7** *1473*
We are not again commending **o** to **2Co 5:12** *1438*
For if we are beside **o**, it is for God **2Co 5:13** *1839*
commending **o** as servants of God, **2Co 6:4** *1438*
let us cleanse **o** from all **2Co 7:1** *1438*
are not bold to class or compare **o** **2Co 10:12** *1438*
For we are not overextending **o**, **2Co 10:14** *1438*
Did we not conduct **o** in the same **2Co 12:18** *4043*
that we are defending **o** to you. **2Co 12:19**
that we **o** do not fail the test. **2Co 13:6** *1473*
not that we **o** may appear approved, **2Co 13:7** *1473*
we **o** are weak but you are strong; **2Co 13:9** *1473*
we **o** have also been found sinners, **Ga 2:17** *846*
we **o** speak proudly of you among **2Th 1:4** *846*
to offer **o** as a model for you, **2Th 3:9** *1438*
For we also once were foolish **o**, **Ti 3:3** *2249*
conduct **o** honorably in all things. **Heb 13:18**
and we **o** heard this utterance made **2Pe 1:18** *2249*
have no sin, we are deceiving **o** and **1Jn 1:8** *1438*

OUTBREAK
article of leather, it is an **o**; **Lv 13:57** 6524b

OUTBURST
Why this great **o** of anger?' **Dt 29:24** 2750
of the LORD's **o** against Uzzah, **2Sa 6:8**
6555, 6556
of the LORD's **o** against Uzza; **1Ch 13:11**
6555, 6556
the LORD our God made an **o** on us, **1Ch 15:13** 6555
"In an **o** of anger I hid My face **Is 54:8** 7858

OUTBURSTS
strife, jealousy, **o** of anger, **Ga 5:20** *2372*

OUTCAST
'Because they have called you an **o**, **Jer 30:17** 5080
save the lame And gather the **o**, **Zph 3:19** 5080

OUTCASTS
o are at the ends of the earth, **Dt 30:4** 5080
He gathers the **o** of Israel. **Ps 147:2** 5080
Hide the **o**, do not betray the **Is 16:3** 5080
"Let the **o** of Moab stay with you; **Is 16:4** 5080
which the **o** of Elam will not go. **Jer 49:36** 5080
the lame And gather the **o**, **Mi 4:6** 5080
And the **o** a strong nation, **Mi 4:7** 1972
make you **o** from the synagogue, **Jn 16:2** *656*

OUTCOME
consider them and know their **o** **Is 41:22** 319
Nor remember the **o** of them. **Is 47:7** 319
will be the **o** of these *events?*" **Da 12:8** 319
with the officers to see the **o**. **Mt 26:58** *5056*
the **o** of those things is death. **Ro 6:21** *5056*
sanctification, and the **o**, eternal life **Ro 6:22** *5056*
What is *the* **o** then? I will pray **1Co 14:15**
What is *the* **o** then, brethren? **1Co 14:26**
seen the **o** of the Lord's dealings, **Jas 5:11** *5056*
obtaining as the **o** of your faith **1Pe 1:9** *5056*
what *will be* the **o** for those who **1Pe 4:17** *5056*

OUTCRY
"The **o** of Sodom and Gomorrah is **Gn 18:20** 2201
done entirely according to its **o**, **Gn 18:21** 6818
their **o** has become so great before **Gn 19:13** 6818
were around them fled at their **o**, **Nu 16:34** 6963
When Eli heard the noise of the **o**, **1Sa 4:14** 6818
there was a great **o** of the people **Ne 5:1** 6818
had heard their **o** and these words. **Ne 5:6** 2201
Let there be no **o** in our streets! **Ps 144:14** 6682
There is an **o** in the streets **Is 24:11** 6682
an **o** be heard from their houses, **Jer 18:22** 2201

And let him hear an **o** in the **Jer 20:16** 2201
"The sound of an **o** from Horonaim, **Jer 48:3** 6818
the **o** at Heshbon even to Elealeh, **Jer 48:34** 2201
There is an **o**! The noise of it has **Jer 49:21** 6818
an **o** is heard among the nations. **Jer 50:46** 2201
The sound of an **o** from Babylon, **Jer 51:54** 2201
a *single* **o** arose from them all as **Ac 19:34** *5456*
o of those who did the harvesting **Jas 5:4** *995*

OUTDOORS
If I found you **o**, I would kiss you; **SS 8:1** 2351

OUTER
flowers, inner and **o** *sanctuaries.* **1Ki 6:29** 2435
gold, inner and **o** *sanctuaries.* **1Ki 6:30** 2435
and the **o** entry of the king, **2Ki 16:18** 2435
Now after this he built the **o** wall **2Ch 33:14** 2435
Haman had just entered the **o** court **Es 6:4** 2435
"Who can strip off his **o** armor? **Jb 41:13** 6440
festal robes, **o** tunics, cloaks, **Is 3:22** 4595
was heard as far as the **o** court, **Ezk 10:5** 2435
he brought me into the **o** court, **Ezk 40:17** 2435
the **o** court which faced the north, **Ezk 40:20** 2435
porches *were* toward the **o** court; **Ezk 40:31** 2435
porches *were* toward the **o** court; **Ezk 40:34** 2435
pillars *were* toward the **o** court; **Ezk 40:37** 2435
On the **o** side, as one went up **Ezk 40:40** 2351
The thickness of the **o** wall of the **Ezk 41:9** 2351
and the **o** chambers *was* twenty **Ezk 41:10**
brought me out into the **o** court, **Ezk 42:1** 2435
which belonged to the **o** court, **Ezk 42:3** 2435
As for the **o** wall by the side of **Ezk 42:7** 2351
the **o** court facing the chambers, **Ezk 42:7** 2435
in the **o** court *was* fifty cubits; **Ezk 42:8** 2435
one enters them from the **o** court. **Ezk 42:9** 2435
they shall not go out into the **o** court **Ezk 42:14** 2435
of the **o** gate of the sanctuary, **Ezk 44:1** 2435
When they go out into the **o** court, **Ezk 44:19** 2435
into the **o** court to the people, **Ezk 44:19** 2435
not bring *them* out into the **o** court **Ezk 46:20** 2435
he brought me out into the **o** court **Ezk 46:21** 2435
around on the outside to the **o** gate **Ezk 47:2** 2351
be cast out into the **o** darkness; **Mt 8:12** *1857*
and throw him into the **o** darkness; **Mt 22:13** *1857*
slave into the **o** darkness; **Mt 25:30** *1857*
o garments and made four parts, **Jn 19:23** *2440*
DIVIDED MY **O** GARMENTS AMONG **Jn 19:24** *2440*
the Lord, he put his **o** garment on **Jn 21:7** *1903*
but though our **o** man is decaying, **2Co 4:16** *1854*
a tabernacle prepared, the **o** one, **Heb 9:2** *4413*
entering the **o** tabernacle performing **Heb 9:6** *4413*
o tabernacle is still standing, **Heb 9:8** *4413*

OUTERMOST
of the **o** curtain in the *first* set, **Ex 26:4** 259, 4480, 7098
that is **o** in the second set. **Ex 26:4** 7020
that is **o** in the *first* set, **Ex 26:10** 7020
the edge of the curtain *that is* **o** **Ex 26:10**
edge of the **o** curtain in the first set; **Ex 36:11** 7098
that was **o** in the second set. **Ex 36:11** 7020
that was **o** in the *first* set, **Ex 36:17** 7020
the edge of the curtain *that was* **o** **Ex 36:17**

OUTLET
stopped the upper **o** of the waters **2Ch 32:30** 4161

OUTLINES
he **o** it with red chalk. **Is 44:13** 8388b
planes and **o** it with a compass, **Is 44:13** 8388b

OUTNUMBER
count them, they would **o** the sand. **Ps 139:18** 7235a

OUTPOSTS
o of the army that was in the camp. **Jg 7:11** 7097a

OUTRAN
his loins and **o** Ahab to Jezreel. **1Ki 18:46** 7323, 6440

OUTSIDE
and told his two brothers **o**. **Gn 9:22** 2351
And He took him **o** and said, **Gn 15:5** 2351
him out, and put him **o** the city. **Gn 19:16** 4480, 2351
When they had brought them **o**, **Gn 19:17** 2351
He made the camels kneel down **o** the **Gn 24:11** 4480, 2351
and Laban ran **o** to the man at the **Gn 24:29** 2351
Why do you stand **o** since I have **Gn 24:31** 2351
in her hand and fled, and went **o**. **Gn 39:12** 2351
in her hand and had fled **o**, **Gn 39:13** 2351
beside me and fled and went **o**." **Gn 39:15** 2351
garment beside me and fled **o**." **Gn 39:18** 2351
and none of you shall go **o** the door **Ex 12:22** 3318
any of the flesh **o** of the house, **Ex 12:46** 2351
and walks around **o** on his staff, **Ex 21:19** 2351
shall set the table **o** the veil, **Ex 26:35** 4480, 2351
o the veil which is before the **Ex 27:21** 4480, 2351
shall burn with fire **o** the camp; **Ex 29:14** 4480, 2351
the tent and pitch it **o** the camp, **Ex 33:7** 4480, 2351
of meeting which was **o** the camp. **Ex 33:7** 4480, 2351
of the tabernacle, **o** the veil. **Ex 40:22** 4480, 2351
place **o** the camp where the ashes are **Lv 4:12** 4480, 2351
the bull to *a place* **o** the camp and **Lv 4:21** 4480, 2351
ashes **o** the camp to a clean place. **Lv 6:11** 413, 4480, 2351
he burned in the fire **o** the camp, **Lv 8:17** 4480, 2351
"You shall not go **o** the doorway **Lv 8:33** 3318
he burned with fire **o** the camp. **Lv 9:11** 4480, 2351
sanctuary to the **o** of the camp." **Lv 10:4** 4480, 2351
their tunics to the **o** of the camp, **Lv 10:5** 4480, 2351
his dwelling shall be **o** the camp. **Lv 13:46** 4480, 2351
shall go out to the **o** of the camp. **Lv 14:3** 4480, 2351
stay **o** his tent for seven days. **Lv 14:8** 4480, 2351
at an unclean place **o** the city. **Lv 14:40** 4480, 2351
at an unclean place **o** the city. **Lv 14:41** 4480, 2351
o the city to an unclean place. **Lv 14:45** 413, 4480, 2351
o the city into the open field. **Lv 14:53** 413, 4480, 2351
place, shall be taken **o** the camp, **Lv 16:27** 413, 4480, 2351
or who slaughters it **o** the camp, **Lv 17:3** 4480, 2351
whether born at home or born **o**, **Lv 18:9** 2351
"**O** the veil of testimony in the **Lv 24:3** 4480, 2351
the one who has cursed **o** the camp, **Lv 24:14** 413, 4480, 2351
the one who had cursed **o** the camp **Lv 24:23** 413, 4480, 2351
you shall send them **o** the camp so **Nu 5:3** 413, 4480, 2351
did so and sent them **o** the camp; **Nu 5:4** 413, 4480, 2351
shut up for seven days **o** the camp, **Nu 12:14** 4480, 2351
shut up **o** the camp for seven days, **Nu 12:15** 4480, 2351
him with stones **o** the camp." **Nu 15:35** 4480, 2351
brought him **o** the camp and **Nu 15:36** 413, 4480, 2351
and it shall be brought **o** the camp **Nu 19:3** 413, 4480, 2351
them **o** the camp in a clean place, **Nu 19:9** 4480, 2351
went out to meet them **o** the camp. **Nu 31:13** 413, 4480, 2351
you, camp **o** the camp seven days; **Nu 31:19** 4480, 2351
"You shall also measure **o** the city **Nu 35:5** 4480, 2351
o the border of his city of refuge, **Nu 35:27** 4480, 2351
then he must go **o** the camp; **Dt 23:10** 413, 4480, 2351
place **o** the camp and go out there, **Dt 23:12** 4480, 2351
it shall be when you sit down **o**, **Dt 23:13** 2351
"You shall remain **o**, **Dt 24:11** 2351
shall not be *married* **o** *the family* **Dt 25:5** 2351
'**O** the sword will bereave, And **Dt 32:25** 4480, 2351
placed them **o** the camp of Israel. **Jos 6:23** 4480, 2351
he gave in marriage **o** *the family,* **Jg 12:9** 2351
daughters from **o** for his sons. **Jg 12:9** 2351
for on the **o** he made offsets *in* **1Ki 6:6** 2351
sawed with saws, inside and **o**; **1Ki 7:9** 4480, 2351
so on the **o** to the great court. **1Ki 7:9** 2351
but they could not be seen **o**; **1Ki 8:8** 2351
So they took him **o** the city and **1Ki 21:13** 4480, 2351
stationed for himself eighty men **o**, **2Ki 10:24** 2351
and he burned them **o** Jerusalem in **2Ki 23:4** 4480, 2351
o Jerusalem to the brook Kidron, **2Ki 23:6** 4480, 2351
assigned to **o** duties for Israel, **1Ch 26:29** 2435
but they could not be seen **o**; **2Ch 5:9** 2351
made a chest and set it **o** by the gate **2Ch 24:8** 2351
the springs which *were* **o** the city, **2Ch 32:3** 4480, 2351
on it, and *built* another **o** wall and **2Ch 32:5** 2351
and he threw *them* **o** the city. **2Ch 33:15** 2351
in charge of the **o** work of the house **Ne 11:16** 2435
spent the night **o** Jerusalem. **Ne 13:20** 4480, 2351
"The alien has not lodged **o**, **Jb 31:32** 2351
When he goes **o**, he tells it. **Ps 41:6** 2351
courts is better than a thousand **o**. **Ps 84:10**
"There is a lion **o**; **Pr 22:13** 2351
Prepare your work **o** And **Pr 24:27** 2351
who are besieging you **o** the wall; **Jer 21:4** 4480, 2351
'The sword is **o** and the plague **Ezk 7:15** 2351
on the **o** of the temple all around, **Ezk 40:5** 2351
From the **o** to the inner gate **Ezk 40:44** 2351
to the inner house, and on the **o**, **Ezk 41:17** 2351
the wall all around inside and **o**, **Ezk 41:17** 2435
wood on the front of the porch **o**. **Ezk 41:25** 4480, 2351
of the house, **o** the sanctuary. **Ezk 43:21** 4480, 2351
way of the porch of the gate from **o** **Ezk 46:2** 2351
led me around on the **o** to the outer **Ezk 47:2** 2351
thief enters in, Bandits raid **o**, **Hos 7:1** 2351
and brothers were standing **o**, **Mt 12:46** *1854*
standing **o** seeking to speak to You. **Mt 12:47** *1854*
the **o** of the cup and of the dish, **Mt 23:25** *1855*
the **o** of it may become clean also. **Mt 23:26** *1622*
which on the **o** appear beautiful, **Mt 23:27** *1855*
was sitting **o** in the courtyard, **Mt 26:69** *1854*
standing **o** they sent *word* to Him and **Mk 3:31** *1854*
brothers are **o** looking for You." **Mk 3:32** *1854*
those who are **o** get everything in **Mk 4:11** *1854*
there is nothing **o** the man which **Mk 7:15** *1855*
the man from **o** cannot defile him, **Mk 7:18** *1855*
tied at the door, **o** in the street; **Mk 11:4** *1854*
people were in prayer **o** at the hour **Lk 1:10** *1854*
and Your brothers are standing **o**, **Lk 8:20** *1854*
you Pharisees clean the **o** of the cup **Lk 11:39** *1855*
did not He who made the **o** **Lk 11:40** *1855*
to stand **o** and knock on the door, **Lk 13:25** *1854*
would perish **o** of Jerusalem. **Lk 13:33** *1854*
Peter was standing at the door **o**. **Jn 18:16** *1854*
was standing **o** the tomb weeping; **Jn 20:11** *1854*
to put the men **o** for a short time. **Ac 5:34** *1854*
"And after he had been set **o**, **Ac 7:21** *1620*
whose *temple* was just **o** the city, **Ac 14:13** *4253*
we went **o** the gate to a riverside, **Ac 16:13** *1854*
But those who are **o**, **1Co 5:13** *1854*
that a man commits is **o** the body, **1Co 6:18** *1622*
with those **o** *the church,* **1Tm 3:7** *1855*
for sin, are burned **o** the camp. **Heb 13:11** *1854*
own blood, suffered **o** the gate. **Heb 13:12** *1854*
let us go out to Him **o** the camp, **Heb 13:13** *1854*
the court which is **o** the temple and **Rv 11:2** *1855*
wine press was trodden **o** the city, **Rv 14:20** *1855*
O are the dogs and the sorcerers **Rv 22:15** *1854*

OUTSIDER
but an **o** may not come near you. **Nu 18:4** 2114a
but the **o** who comes near shall be **Nu 18:7** 2114a

OUTSIDERS
what have I to do with judging **o**? **1Co 5:12** *3588, 1854*
yourselves with wisdom toward **o**, **Col 4:5** *3588, 1854*
toward **o** and not be in any need. **1Th 4:12** *3588, 1854*

OUTSKIRTS
some of the **o** of the camp. **Nu 11:1** 7097a
when I come to the **o** of the camp, **Jg 7:17** 7097a
came to the **o** of the camp at the **Jg 7:19** 7097a
Saul was staying in the **o** of **1Sa 14:2** 7097a
the **o** of the camp of the Arameans, **2Ki 7:5** 7097a
lepers came to the **o** of the camp, **2Ki 7:8** 7097a

OUTSTANDING
and men of **o** capability were found **1Ch 26:31** 1368
and ruddy, **O** among ten thousand. **SS 5:10** 1713a
who are **o** among the apostles, **Ro 16:7** *1978*

OUTSTRETCHED
will also redeem you with an **o** arm **Ex 6:6** 5186
by an **o** arm and by great terrors, **Dt 4:34** 5186
by a mighty hand and by an **o** arm; **Dt 5:15** 5186
o arm by which the LORD your God **Dt 7:19** 5186
Your great power and Your **o** arm.' **Dt 9:29** 5186
His mighty hand and His **o** arm, **Dt 11:2** 5186
with a mighty hand and an **o** arm **Dt 26:8** 5186
mighty hand, and of Your **o** arm); **1Ki 8:42** 5186
great power and with an **o** arm, **2Ki 17:36** 5186
Your mighty hand and Your **o** arm, **2Ch 6:32** 5186
With a strong hand and an **o** arm, **Ps 136:12** 5186
war against you with an **o** hand and **Jer 21:5** 5186
by My great power and by My **o** arm, **Jer 27:5** 5186
great power and by Your **o** arm! **Jer 32:17** 5186
a strong hand and with an **o** arm and **Jer 32:21** 5186
a mighty hand and with an **o** arm **Ezk 20:33** 5186
o arm and with wrath poured out; **Ezk 20:34** 5186

OUTWARD
extend from the wall of the city **o** **Nu 35:4** 2351
for man looks at the **o** appearance, **1Sa 16:7** 5869
that which is **o** in the flesh. **Ro 2:28** *5318*

OUTWARDLY
you, too, **o** appear righteous to men, **Mt 23:28** *1855*
For he is not a Jew who is one **o**, **Ro 2:28** *1722, 5318*
looking at things as they are **o**. **2Co 10:7** *2596, 4383*

OVEN
there appeared a smoking **o** and a **Gn 15:17** 8574
of a grain offering baked in an **o**, **Lv 2:4** 8574
offering that is baked in the **o** and **Lv 7:9** 8574
an **o** or a stove shall be smashed; **Lv 11:35** 8574
will bake your bread in one **o**, **Lv 26:26** 8574
fiery **o** in the time of your anger; **Ps 21:9** 8574
skin has become as hot as an **o**, **La 5:10** 8574
Like an **o** heated by the baker Who **Hos 7:4** 8574
For their hearts are like an **o** *As* **Hos 7:6** 8574
All of them are hot like an **o**, **Hos 7:7** 8574

OVENS
into your **o** and into your kneading **Ex 8:3** 8574

OVER
was **o** the surface of the deep, **Gn 1:2** 5921
o the surface of the waters. **Gn 1:2** 5921
and let them rule **o** the fish of **Gn 1:26**
and **o** the birds of the sky and over **Gn 1:26**
and **o** the cattle and over all the **Gn 1:26**
the cattle and **o** all the earth, **Gn 1:26**
and **o** every creeping thing that **Gn 1:26**
and rule **o** the fish of the sea and **Gn 1:28**

sea and **o** the birds of the sky and	**Gn 1:28**	
and **o** every living thing that	**Gn 1:28**	
And he will rule **o** you."	**Gn 3:16**	
caused a wind to pass **o** the earth,	**Gn 8:1**	5921
when I bring a cloud **o** the earth,	**Gn 9:14**	5921
o the face of the whole earth."	**Gn 11:4**	5921
o the face of the whole earth;	**Gn 11:8**	5921
o the face of the whole earth.	**Gn 11:9**	5921
The sun had risen **o** the earth when	**Gn 19:23**	5921
and I and the lad will go **o** there;	**Gn 22:5**	5704, 3541
confines of its border, were deeded **o**	**Gn 23:17**	6965
were deeded **o** to Abraham for a	**Gn 23:20**	6965
red, all **o** like a hairy garment;	**Gn 25:25**	
well, and they quarreled **o** it too,	**Gn 26:21**	5921
and they did not quarrel **o** it;	**Gn 26:22**	5921
him just as he crossed **o** Penuel,	**Gn 32:31**	5674a
Jacob set up a pillar **o** her grave;	**Gn 35:20**	5921
king reigned **o** the sons of Israel.	**Gn 36:31**	
you actually going to reign **o** us?	**Gn 37:8**	5921
you really going to rule **o** us?"	**Gn 37:8**	
he made him overseer **o** his house,	**Gn 39:4**	5921
house and **o** all that he owned,	**Gn 39:5**	5921
and set him **o** the land of Egypt.	**Gn 41:33**	5921
"You shall be **o** my house, and	**Gn 41:40**	5921
set you **o** all the land of Egypt."	**Gn 41:41**	5921
set him **o** all the land of Egypt.	**Gn 41:43**	5921
went forth **o** the land of Egypt.	**Gn 41:45**	5921
o all the face of the earth,	**Gn 41:56**	5921
Joseph was the ruler **o** the land;	**Gn 42:6**	5921
was deeply stirred **o** his brother,	**Gn 43:30**	413
and ruler **o** all the land of Egypt.	**Gn 45:8**	
ruler **o** all the land of Egypt."	**Gn 45:26**	
Its branches run **o** a wall.	**Gn 49:22**	5921
and wept **o** him and kissed him.	**Gn 50:1**	5921
Now a new king arose **o** Egypt,	**Ex 1:8**	5921
So they appointed taskmasters **o**	**Ex 1:11**	5921
covered it **o** with tar and pitch.	**Ex 2:3**	
made you a prince or a judge **o** us?	**Ex 2:14**	5921
o the people and their foremen,	**Ex 5:6**	
taskmasters had set **o** them,	**Ex 5:14**	5921
your hand **o** the waters of Egypt,	**Ex 7:19**	5921
waters of Egypt, **o** their rivers,	**Ex 7:19**	5921
their rivers, **o** their streams,	**Ex 7:19**	5921
their streams, and **o** their pools,	**Ex 7:19**	5921
o all their reservoirs of water,	**Ex 7:19**	5921
hand with your staff **o** the rivers,	**Ex 8:5**	5921
o the streams and over the pools,	**Ex 8:5**	5921
over the streams and **o** the pools,	**Ex 8:5**	5921
his hand **o** the waters of Egypt,	**Ex 8:6**	5921
fine dust **o** all the land of Egypt,	**Ex 9:9**	5921
"Stretch out your hand **o** the land	**Ex 10:12**	5921
out his staff **o** the land of Egypt,	**Ex 10:13**	5921
The locusts came up **o** all the	**Ex 10:14**	5921
be darkness **o** the land of Egypt,	**Ex 10:21**	5921
leave any of it **o** until morning,	**Ex 12:10**	3498
I see the blood I will pass **o** you,	**Ex 12:13**	5921
the LORD will pass **o** the door and	**Ex 12:23**	5921
to the LORD who passed **o** the houses	**Ex 12:27**	5921
Egypt with officers **o** all of them.	**Ex 14:7**	5921
your hand **o** the sea and divide it,	**Ex 14:16**	5921
stretched out his hand **o** the sea;	**Ex 14:21**	5921
"Stretch out your hand **o** the sea	**Ex 14:26**	5921
may come back **o** the Egyptians,	**Ex 14:26**	5921
o their chariots and their	**Ex 14:26**	5921
stretched out his hand **o** the sea,	**Ex 14:27**	5921
Until Your people pass **o**,	**Ex 15:16**	5674a
pass **o** whom You have purchased.	**Ex 15:16**	5674a
and all that is left **o** put aside	**Ex 16:23**	5736
Jethro rejoiced **o** all the goodness	**Ex 18:9**	5921
and you shall place *these* **o** them	**Ex 18:21**	5921
and made them heads **o** the people,	**Ex 18:25**	5921
a pit and does not cover it **o**,	**Ex 21:33**	
hair for a tent **o** the tabernacle;	**Ex 26:7**	5921
you shall double **o** the sixth curtain	**Ex 26:9**	3717
The overlapping part that is left **o**	**Ex 26:12**	5736
the half curtain that is left **o**,	**Ex 26:12**	5736
lap **o** the back of the tabernacle.	**Ex 26:12**	5921
of what is left **o** in the length of	**Ex 26:13**	5736
shall lap **o** the sides of the	**Ex 26:13**	5921
breastpiece of judgment **o** his heart	**Ex 28:29**	5921
and they shall be **o** Aaron's heart	**Ex 28:30**	5921
o his heart before the LORD	**Ex 28:30**	5921
is **o** *the ark of* the testimony,	**Ex 30:6**	5921
from twenty years old and **o**,	**Ex 30:14**	4605
it **o** the surface of the water and	**Ex 32:20**	5921
to be left **o** until morning.	**Ex 34:25**	3885a
them, he put a veil **o** his face.	**Ex 34:33**	5921
Moses would replace the veil **o** his	**Ex 34:35**	5921
hair for a tent **o** the tabernacle;	**Ex 36:14**	5921
for each one who passed **o** to those	**Ex 38:26**	5674a
He spread the tent **o** the tabernacle	**Ex 40:19**	5921
taken up from **o** the tabernacle,	**Ex 40:36**	5921
and the suet **o** the wood which is	**Lv 1:8**	5921
leave any of it **o** until morning.	**Lv 7:15**	
but what is left **o** from the flesh	**Lv 7:17**	3498
"Take the grain offering that is left **o**	**Lv 10:12**	3498
vessel **o** running water.	**Lv 14:5**	5921
was slain **o** the running water.	**Lv 14:6**	5921
bird go free **o** the open field.	**Lv 14:7**	5921
vessel **o** running water.	**Lv 14:50**	5921
in the cloud **o** the mercy seat.	**Lv 16:2**	5921
and confess **o** it all the iniquities	**Lv 16:21**	5921
not rule **o** him with severity,	**Lv 25:43**	
rule with severity **o** one another.	**Lv 25:46**	
he shall not rule **o** him with	**Lv 25:53**	
appoint **o** you a sudden terror,	**Lv 26:16**	5921
who hate you will rule **o** you,	**Lv 26:17**	
in it will be appalled **o** it.	**Lv 26:32**	5921
will therefore stumble **o** each other	**Lv 26:37**	
appoint the Levites **o** the tabernacle	**Nu 1:50**	5921
and **o** all its furnishings and over	**Nu 1:50**	5921
and **o** all that belongs to it.	**Nu 1:50**	5921
spread **o** *it* a cloth of pure blue,	**Nu 4:6**	4605
"**O** the table of the bread of the	**Nu 4:7**	5921
"They shall spread **o** them a	**Nu 4:8**	5921
"**O** the golden altar they shall	**Nu 4:11**	5921
and spread a purple cloth **o** it.	**Nu 4:13**	5921
spread a cover of porpoise skin **o** it	**Nu 4:14**	5921
if a spirit of jealousy comes **o** him	**Nu 5:14**	5921
or if a spirit of jealousy comes **o** him	**Nu 5:14**	5921
a spirit of jealousy comes **o** a man	**Nu 5:30**	5921
no razor shall pass **o** his head.	**Nu 6:5**	5921
ones who were **o** the numbered men).	**Nu 7:2**	5921
use a razor **o** their whole body and	**Nu 8:7**	5921
of fire **o** the tabernacle,	**Nu 9:15**	5921
cloud was lifted from **o** the tent,	**Nu 9:17**	5921
cloud settled **o** the tabernacle,	**Nu 9:18**	5921
the cloud lingered **o** the tabernacle	**Nu 9:19**	5921
a few days **o** the tabernacle,	**Nu 9:20**	5921
cloud lingered **o** the tabernacle,	**Nu 9:22**	5921
trumpets **o** your burnt offerings,	**Nu 10:10**	5921
and **o** the sacrifices of your peace	**Nu 10:10**	5921
was lifted from **o** the tabernacle	**Nu 10:11**	5921
the son of Amminadab, **o** its army,	**Nu 10:14**	5921
o the tribal army of the sons of	**Nu 10:15**	5921
the son of Helon **o** the tribal army	**Nu 10:16**	5921
the son of Shedeur, **o** its army,	**Nu 10:18**	5921
son of Zurishaddai **o** the tribal army	**Nu 10:19**	5921
son of Deuel was **o** the tribal army	**Nu 10:20**	5921
the son of Ammihud **o** its army,	**Nu 10:22**	5921
the son of Pedahzur **o** the tribal army	**Nu 10:23**	5921
the son of Gideoni **o** the tribal army	**Nu 10:24**	5921
the son of Ammishaddai **o** its army,	**Nu 10:25**	5921
the son of Ochran **o** the tribal army	**Nu 10:26**	5921
the son of Enan **o** the tribal army	**Nu 10:27**	5921
The cloud of the LORD was **o** them	**Nu 10:34**	5921
had withdrawn from **o** the tent,	**Nu 12:10**	5921
while Your cloud stands **o** them;	**Nu 14:14**	5921
but you would also lord it **o** us?	**Nu 16:13**	5921
and the earth closed **o** them,	**Nu 16:33**	5921
while I myself meet *the LORD* **o**	**Nu 23:15**	3541
appoint a man **o** the congregation,	**Nu 27:16**	5921
were **o** the thousands of the army,	**Nu 31:48**	
the sons of Israel from crossing **o**	**Nu 32:7**	5674a
you armed men cross **o** the Jordan	**Nu 32:21**	5674a
will cross **o** in the presence of	**Nu 32:27**	5674a
will cross with you **o** the Jordan	**Nu 32:29**	5674a
will not cross **o** with you armed,	**Nu 32:30**	5674a
"We ourselves will cross **o** armed	**Nu 32:32**	5674a
'When you cross **o** the Jordan into	**Nu 33:51**	5674a
and appointed them heads **o** you,	**Dt 1:15**	5921
o the brook Zered yourselves.'	**Dt 2:13**	5674a
So we crossed **o** the brook Zered.	**Dt 2:13**	5674a
we crossed **o** the brook Zered was	**Dt 2:14**	5674a
you shall cross **o** Ar, the border	**Dt 2:18**	5674a
until I cross **o** the Jordan into	**Dt 2:29**	5674a
deliver Sihon and his land **o** to you.	**Dt 2:31**	6440
our God delivered him **o** to us,	**Dt 2:33**	6440
our God delivered all **o** to us.	**Dt 2:36**	6440
all you valiant men shall cross **o**	**Dt 3:18**	5674a
cross **o** and see the fair land that	**Dt 3:25**	5674a
you shall not cross **o** this Jordan.	**Dt 3:27**	5674a
you are going **o** to possess it.	**Dt 4:14**	5674a
going **o** the Jordan to possess it.	**Dt 4:26**	5674a
you are going **o** to possess it,	**Dt 6:1**	5674a
You are crossing **o** the Jordan	**Dt 9:1**	5674a
God who is crossing **o** before you	**Dt 9:3**	5674a
and you will rule **o** many nations,	**Dt 15:6**	
but they will not rule **o** you.	**Dt 15:6**	
'I will set a king **o** me like all	**Dt 17:14**	5921
you shall surely set a king **o** you	**Dt 17:15**	5921
shall set as king **o** yourselves;	**Dt 17:15**	5921
may not put a foreigner **o** yourselves	**Dt 17:15**	5921
shall wash their hands **o** the heifer	**Dt 21:6**	5921
not hand **o** to his master a slave	**Dt 23:15**	5462
shall not go **o** the boughs again;	**Dt 24:20**	6287a
you shall not go **o** it again;	**Dt 24:21**	5953b
of this law, when you cross **o**,	**Dt 27:3**	5674a
The heaven which is **o** your head	**Dt 28:23**	5921
king, whom you set **o** you,	**Dt 28:36**	5921
delighted **o** you to prosper you,	**Dt 28:63**	5921
so the LORD will delight **o** you to	**Dt 28:63**	5921
will again rejoice **o** you for good,	**Dt 30:9**	5921
as He rejoiced **o** your fathers;	**Dt 30:9**	5921
its nest, That hovers **o** its young,	**Dt 32:11**	5921
but you shall not go **o** there."	**Dt 34:4**	5674a
and crossed **o** and came to Joshua	**Jos 2:23**	5674a
and cross **o** ahead of the people."	**Jos 3:6**	5674a
o ahead of you into the Jordan.	**Jos 3:11**	5674a
firm, and carry them **o** with you and	**Jos 4:3**	5674a
and they carried them **o** with them	**Jos 4:8**	5674a
Manasseh crossed **o** in battle array	**Jos 4:12**	5674a
went **o** all its banks as before.	**Jos 4:18**	5921
bring this people **o** the Jordan,	**Jos 7:7**	5674a
They raised **o** him a great heap	**Jos 7:26**	5921
and raised **o** it a great heap of	**Jos 8:29**	5921
stones **o** the mouth of the cave,	**Jos 10:27**	5921
and ruled **o** Mount Hermon and	**Jos 12:5**	
the territory **o** against Joppa.	**Jos 19:46**	4136
he prevailed **o** Cushan-rishathaim.	**Jg 3:10**	5921
and the fat closed **o** the blade,	**Jg 3:22**	5704
and they crossed **o** and camped in	**Jg 6:33**	5674a
came to the Jordan *and* crossed **o**,	**Jg 8:4**	5674a
"Rule **o** us, both you and your	**Jg 8:22**	
"I will not rule **o** you, nor shall	**Jg 8:23**	
you, nor shall my son rule **o** you;	**Jg 8:23**	
the LORD shall rule **o** you."	**Jg 8:23**	
the sons of Jerubbaal, rule **o** you,	**Jg 9:2**	
you, or that one man rule **o** you?'	**Jg 9:2**	
forth to anoint a king **o** them,	**Jg 9:8**	5921
said to the olive tree, 'Reign **o** us!'	**Jg 9:8**	5921
and go to wave **o** the trees?'	**Jg 9:9**	5921
'You come, reign **o** us!'	**Jg 9:10**	5921
and go to wave **o** the trees?'	**Jg 9:11**	5921
'You come, reign **o** us!'	**Jg 9:12**	5921
men, and go to wave **o** the trees?'	**Jg 9:13**	5921
'You come, reign **o** us!'	**Jg 9:14**	5921
are anointing me as king **o** you,	**Jg 9:15**	5921
king **o** the men of Shechem,	**Jg 9:18**	5921
ruled **o** Israel three years.	**Jg 9:22**	5921
and crossed **o** into Shechem;	**Jg 9:26**	5674a
chamber on fire **o** those *inside*,	**Jg 9:49**	5921
o all the inhabitants of Gilead."	**Jg 10:18**	
o all the inhabitants of Gilead."	**Jg 11:8**	
made him head and chief **o** them;	**Jg 11:11**	5921
So Jephthah crossed **o** to the sons	**Jg 11:32**	5674a
"Why did you cross **o** to fight	**Jg 12:1**	5674a
o against the sons of Ammon,	**Jg 12:3**	5674a
"Let me cross **o**,"	**Jg 12:5**	5674a
Philistines were ruling **o** Israel.	**Jg 14:4**	
the Philistines are rulers **o** us?	**Jg 15:11**	
put your hand **o** your mouth and	**Jg 18:19**	5921
spread your covering **o** your maid,	**Ru 3:9**	5921
his sons judges **o** Israel.	**1Sa 8:1**	
rejected Me from being king **o** them.	**1Sa 8:7**	5921
the king who will reign **o** them."	**1Sa 8:9**	5921
of the king who will reign **o** you:	**1Sa 8:11**	5921
but there shall be a king **o** us,	**1Sa 8:19**	5921
to be prince **o** My people Israel;	**1Sa 9:16**	5921
This one shall rule **o** My people."	**1Sa 9:17**	
you a ruler **o** His inheritance?	**1Sa 10:1**	5921
'No, but set a king **o** us!'	**1Sa 10:19**	5921
'Shall Saul reign **o** us?'	**1Sa 11:12**	5921
and I have appointed a king **o** you.	**1Sa 12:1**	5921
'No, but a king shall reign **o** us,'	**1Sa 12:12**	5921
the LORD has set a king **o** you.	**1Sa 12:13**	5921
and also the king who reigns **o** you	**1Sa 12:14**	5921
reigned *forty* two years **o** Israel.	**1Sa 13:1**	5921
established your kingdom **o** Israel	**1Sa 13:13**	413
him as ruler **o** His people,	**1Sa 13:14**	5921
"Come and let us cross **o** to the	**1Sa 14:1**	5674a
by which Jonathan sought to cross **o**	**1Sa 14:4**	5674a
"Come and let us cross **o** to the	**1Sa 14:6**	5674a
we will cross **o** to the men and	**1Sa 14:8**	5674a
had taken the kingdom **o** Israel,	**1Sa 14:47**	5921
anoint you as king **o** His people,	**1Sa 15:1**	5921
as king over His people, **o** Israel;	**1Sa 15:1**	5921
LORD anointed you king **o** Israel,	**1Sa 15:17**	5921
you from being king **o** Israel."	**1Sa 15:26**	5921
for Samuel grieved **o** Saul.	**1Sa 15:35**	413
He had made Saul king **o** Israel.	**1Sa 15:35**	5921
"How long will you grieve **o** Saul,	**1Sa 16:1**	413
him from being king **o** Israel?	**1Sa 16:1**	5921
David girded his sword **o** his armor	**1Sa 17:39**	4480, 5921
David prevailed **o** the Philistine	**1Sa 17:50**	4480
David ran and stood **o** the Philistine	**1Sa 17:51**	413
and Saul set him **o** the men of war.	**1Sa 18:5**	5921
standing *and* presiding **o** them,	**1Sa 19:20**	5921
for he was grieved **o** David because	**1Sa 20:34**	413
and he became captain **o** them.	**1Sa 22:2**	5921
who is captain **o** your guard,	**1Sa 22:14**	413
and you will be king **o** Israel and	**1Sa 23:17**	5921
appoints you ruler **o** Israel,	**1Sa 25:30**	5921
David crossed **o** to the other side and	**1Sa 26:13**	5674a
the young men come **o** and take it.	**1Sa 26:22**	5674a
So David arose and crossed **o**,	**1Sa 27:2**	5674a
the LORD will also give **o** Israel	**1Sa 28:19**	
LORD will give **o** the army of Israel	**1Sa 28:19**	
they were spread **o** all the land,	**1Sa 30:16**	5921
this lament **o** Saul and Jonathan	**2Sa 1:17**	5921
daughters of Israel, weep **o** Saul,	**2Sa 1:24**	413
David king **o** the house of Judah.	**2Sa 2:4**	5921
has anointed me king **o** them."	**2Sa 2:7**	5921
and brought him **o** to Mahanaim.	**2Sa 2:8**	5674a
He made him king **o** Gilead,	**2Sa 2:9**	413
king over Gilead, **o** the Ashurites,	**2Sa 2:9**	413
over the Ashurites, **o** Jezreel,	**2Sa 2:9**	413
over Jezreel, **o** Ephraim,	**2Sa 2:9**	5921
over Ephraim, and **o** Benjamin,	**2Sa 2:9**	5921
over Benjamin, even **o** all Israel.	**2Sa 2:9**	5921
old when he became king **o** Israel,	**2Sa 2:10**	5921
David was king in Hebron **o** the	**2Sa 2:11**	5921
So they arose and went **o** by count,	**2Sa 2:15**	5674a
angry **o** the words of Ish-bosheth	**2Sa 3:8**	5921
the throne of David **o** Israel and	**2Sa 3:10**	5921
of David over Israel and **o** Judah,	**2Sa 3:10**	5921
to bring all Israel **o** to you."	**2Sa 3:12**	5437
for David to be king **o** you.	**2Sa 3:17**	5921
king **o** all that your soul desires.	**2Sa 3:21**	
all the people wept again **o** him.	**2Sa 3:34**	5921
when Saul was king **o** us,	**2Sa 5:2**	5921
you will be a ruler **o** Israel.' "	**2Sa 5:2**	5921
they anointed David king **o** Israel.	**2Sa 5:3**	5921
At Hebron he reigned **o** Judah seven	**2Sa 5:5**	5921
years **o** all Israel and Judah.	**2Sa 5:5**	5921
established him as king **o** Israel,	**2Sa 5:12**	5921
had anointed David king **o** Israel,	**2Sa 5:17**	5921
me ruler **o** the people of the LORD,	**2Sa 6:21**	5921
the people of the LORD, **o** Israel;	**2Sa 6:21**	5921
be ruler **o** My people Israel.	**2Sa 7:8**	5921
judges to be **o** My people Israel;	**2Sa 7:11**	5921
LORD of hosts is God **o** Israel';	**2Sa 7:26**	5921
So David reigned **o** all Israel;	**2Sa 8:15**	5921
the son of Zeruiah *was* **o** the army,	**2Sa 8:16**	5921
son of Jehoiada was **o** the Cherethites	**2Sa 8:18**	

When the *time of* mourning was **o**, 2Sa 11:27 5674a
is I who anointed you king **o** Israel 2Sa 12:7 5921
'Hand **o** the one who struck his 2Sa 14:7 5414
David said to Ittai, "Go and pass **o**." 2Sa 15:22 5674a
So Ittai the Gittite passed **o** with 2Sa 15:22 5674a
voice, all the people passed **o**. 2Sa 15:23 5674a
also passed **o** the brook Kidron, 2Sa 15:23 5674a
and all the people passed **o** toward 2Sa 15:23 5674a
"If you pass **o** with me, then you 2Sa 15:33 5674a
Let me go **o** now and cut off his 2Sa 16:9 5674a
but by all means cross **o**, 2Sa 17:16 5674a
and spread it **o** the well's mouth 2Sa 17:19 5921
"Arise and cross **o** the water 2Sa 17:21 5674a
Amasa **o** the army in place of Joab. 2Sa 17:25 5921
set **o** them commanders of thousands 2Sa 18:1 5921
spread **o** the whole countryside, 2Sa 18:8 5921, 6440
and erected **o** him a very great heap 2Sa 18:17 5921
the chamber **o** the gate and wept. 2Sa 18:33 5944
Absalom, whom we anointed **o** us, 2Sa 19:10 5921
to bring **o** the king's household, 2Sa 19:18 5674a
that I am king **o** Israel today?" 2Sa 19:22 5921
king to escort him **o** the Jordan. 2Sa 19:31
"You cross **o** with me and I will 2Sa 19:33 5674a
cross **o** the Jordan with the king. 2Sa 19:36 5674a
him cross **o** with my lord the king, 2Sa 19:37 5674a
"Chimham shall cross **o** with me, 2Sa 19:38 5674a
All the people crossed **o** the Jordan 2Sa 19:39 5674a
men with him **o** the Jordan?" 2Sa 19:41 5674a
and **o** it was a belt with a sword 2Sa 20:8 5921
threw a garment **o** him when he saw 2Sa 20:12 5921
Only hand him **o**, and I will depart 2Sa 20:21 5414
be thrown to you **o** the wall." 2Sa 20:21 1157
was **o** the whole army of Israel, 2Sa 20:23 413
son of Jehoiada was **o** the Cherethites 2Sa 20:23 5921
and Adoram was **o** the forced labor, 2Sa 20:24 5921
By my God I can leap **o** a wall. 2Sa 22:30
'He who rules **o** men righteously, 2Sa 23:3
David appointed him **o** his guard. 2Sa 23:23 413
servants crossing **o** toward him; 2Sa 24:20 5674a
anoint him there as king **o** Israel, 1Ki 1:34 5921
to be ruler **o** Israel and Judah." 1Ki 1:35 5921
reigned **o** Israel *were* forty years: 1Ki 2:11 5921
Jehoiada **o** the army in his place, 1Ki 2:35 5921
out and cross **o** the brook Kidron, 1Ki 2:37 5674a
for she was deeply stirred **o** her son 1Ki 3:26 5921
Solomon was king **o** all Israel. 1Ki 4:1 5921
son of Jehoiada *was* **o** the army; 1Ki 4:4 5921
son of Nathan *was* **o** the deputies; 1Ki 4:5 5921
and Ahishar was **o** the household; 1Ki 4:6 5921
Adoniram the son of Abda *was* **o** the 1Ki 4:6 5921
had twelve deputies **o** all Israel, 1Ki 4:7 5921
Solomon ruled **o** all the kingdoms 1Ki 4:21
o everything west of the River, 1Ki 4:24
o all the kings west of the River; 1Ki 4:24
a wise son **o** this great people." 1Ki 5:7 5921
was **o** the forced laborers. 1Ki 5:14 5921
chief deputies who *were* **o** the project 1Ki 5:16 5921
ruled **o** the people who were doing 1Ki 5:16
year of Solomon's reign **o** Israel, 1Ki 6:1 5921
wings **o** the place of the ark, 1Ki 8:7 413
cherubim made a covering **o** the ark 1Ki 8:7 5921
David to be **o** My people Israel.' 1Ki 8:16 5921
of your kingdom **o** Israel forever, 1Ki 9:5 5921
officers who *were* **o** Solomon's work, 1Ki 9:23 5921
ruled **o** the people doing the work. 1Ki 9:23
Israel and reigned **o** Aram. 1Ki 11:25 5921
appointed him **o** all the forced labor 1Ki 11:28
shall reign **o** whatever you desire, 1Ki 11:37
and you shall be king **o** Israel. 1Ki 11:37 5921
o all Israel was forty years. 1Ki 11:42 5921
of Judah, Rehoboam reigned **o** them. 1Ki 12:17 5921
who was **o** the forced labor, 1Ki 12:18 5921
and made him king **o** all Israel. 1Ki 12:20 5921
own grave, and they mourned **o** him, 1Ki 13:30 5921
I would be king **o** this people. 1Ki 14:2 5921
you leader **o** My people Israel, 1Ki 14:7 5921
raise up for Himself a king **o** Israel 1Ki 14:14 5921
Nebat, Abijam became king **o** Judah. 1Ki 15:1 5921
son of Jeroboam became king **o** Israel 1Ki 15:25 5921
and he reigned **o** Israel two years. 1Ki 15:25 5921
king **o** all Israel at Tirzah, 1Ki 15:33 5921
you leader **o** My people Israel, 1Ki 16:2 5921
became king **o** Israel at Tirzah, 1Ki 16:8 5921
who *was* **o** the household at Tirzah. 1Ki 16:9 5921
o Israel that day in the camp. 1Ki 16:16 5921
the king's house **o** him with fire, 1Ki 16:18 5921
prevailed **o** the people who followed 1Ki 16:22 2388
Judah, Omri became king **o** Israel 1Ki 16:23 5921
the son of Omri became king **o** Israel 1Ki 16:29 5921
Ahab the son of Omri reigned **o** Israel 1Ki 16:29 5921
Obadiah who *was* **o** the household. 1Ki 18:3 5921
shall anoint Hazael king **o** Aram; 1Ki 19:15 5921
you shall anoint king **o** Israel; 1Ki 19:16 5921
And Elijah passed **o** to him and 1Ki 19:19 5674a
o against the other seven days. 1Ki 20:29 5227
himself with a bandage **o** his eyes. 1Ki 20:38 5921
"Do you now reign **o** Israel? 1Ki 21:7 5921
the son of Asa became king **o** Judah 1Ki 22:41 5921
the son of Ahab became king **o** Israel 1Ki 22:51 5921
and he reigned two years **o** Israel. 1Ki 22:51 5921
your master from **o** you today?" 2Ki 2:3 5921
your master from **o** you today?" 2Ki 2:5 5921
of them crossed **o** on dry ground. 2Ki 2:8 5674a
When they had crossed **o**, 2Ki 2:9 5674a
and Elisha crossed **o**. 2Ki 2:14 5674a
the son of Ahab became king **o** Israel 2Ki 3:1 5921
when Elisha passed **o** to Shunem, 2Ki 4:8 5674a
eat and have *some* left **o**.' " 2Ki 4:43 3498

and they ate and had *some* left **o**, 2Ki 4:44 3498
and wave his hand **o** the place and 2Ki 5:11 413
of Aram was enraged **o** this thing; 2Ki 6:11 5921
go **o** to the camp of the Arameans. 2Ki 7:4 5307
me that you will be king **o** Aram." 2Ki 8:13 5921
and made a king **o** themselves. 2Ki 8:20 5921
Then Joram crossed **o** to Zair, 2Ki 8:21 5674a
anointed you king **o** Israel." 2Ki 9:3 5921
you king **o** the people of the LORD, 2Ki 9:6 413
people of the LORD, *even* **o** Israel. 2Ki 9:6 413
anointed you king **o** Israel. 2Ki 9:12 413
Ahab, Ahaziah became king **o** Judah. 2Ki 9:29 5921
the one who *was* **o** the household, 2Ki 10:5 5921
and he who *was* **o** the city, 2Ki 10:5 5921
Jehu reigned **o** Israel in Samaria 2Ki 10:36 5921
Athaliah was reigning **o** the land. 2Ki 11:3 5921
and keep watch **o** the king's house 2Ki 11:5
watch **o** the house for defense. 2Ki 11:6
shall also keep watch **o** the house 2Ki 11:7
who were appointed **o** the army and 2Ki 11:15
officers **o** the house of the LORD. 2Ki 11:18 5921
became king **o** Israel at Samaria, 2Ki 13:1 5921
became king **o** Israel in Samaria, 2Ki 13:10 5921
to him and wept **o** him and said, 2Ki 13:14 5921
even the arrow of victory **o** Aram; 2Ki 13:17
the king's son was **o** the household, 2Ki 15:5 5921
son of Jeroboam became king **o** Israel 2Ki 15:8 5921
son of Gadi became king **o** Israel 2Ki 15:17 5921
became king **o** Israel in Samaria, 2Ki 15:23 5921
became king **o** Israel in Samaria, 2Ki 15:27 5921
became king **o** Israel in Samaria, 2Ki 17:1 5921
Hilkiah, who was **o** the household, 2Ki 18:18 5921
Hilkiah, who was **o** the household, 2Ki 18:37 5921
Eliakim who was **o** the household 2Ki 19:2 5921
'I will stretch **o** Jerusalem 2Ki 21:13 5921
Ahikam, the son of Shaphan **o** them. 2Ki 25:22 5921
Judah prevailed **o** his brothers, 1Ch 5:2
David appointed **o** the service of song 1Ch 6:31 5921
were **o** the work of the service, 1Ch 9:19 5921
had been **o** the camp of the LORD, 1Ch 9:19 5921
was ruler **o** them previously, 1Ch 9:20 5921
and were **o** the chambers and over 1Ch 9:26 5921
o the treasuries in the house of God 1Ch 9:26 5921
also were appointed **o** the furniture 1Ch 9:29 5921
and **o** all the utensils of the sanctuary 1Ch 9:29 5921
and **o** the fine flour and the wine 1Ch 9:29 5921
had the responsibility **o** the things 1Ch 9:31 5921
the Kohathites *were* **o** the showbread 1Ch 9:32 5921
be prince **o** My people Israel.' " 1Ch 11:2 5921
they anointed David king **o** Israel, 1Ch 11:3 5921
David appointed him **o** his guard. 1Ch 11:25 5921
the thirty, and **o** the thirty. 1Ch 12:4 5921
From the Gadites there came **o** 1Ch 12:8 914
to make David king **o** all Israel; 1Ch 12:38 5921
established him as king **o** Israel, 1Ch 14:2 5921
been anointed king **o** all Israel, 1Ch 14:8 5921
and the captains **o** thousands, 1Ch 15:25
be leader **o** My people Israel. 1Ch 17:7 5921
judges *to be* **o** My people Israel. 1Ch 17:10 5921
So David reigned **o** all Israel; 1Ch 18:14 5921
the son of Zeruiah *was* **o** the army, 1Ch 18:15 5921
son of Jehoiada *was* **o** the Cherethites 1Ch 18:17 5921
saw and was sorry **o** the calamity, 1Ch 21:15 5921
hand stretched out **o** Jerusalem. 1Ch 21:16 5921
of his kingdom **o** Israel forever.' 1Ch 22:10 5921
and give you charge **o** Israel, 1Ch 22:12 5921
his son Solomon king **o** Israel. 1Ch 23:1 5921
ruled **o** the house of their father, 1Ch 26:6
was officer **o** the treasures. 1Ch 26:24 5921
and **o** his division was Ammizabad 1Ch 27:6
to be king **o** Israel forever. 1Ch 28:4 5921
me to make *me* king **o** all Israel. 1Ch 28:4 5921
the kingdom of the LORD **o** Israel. 1Ch 28:5 5921
o and above all that I have 1Ch 29:3 4605
the overseers **o** the king's work, 1Ch 29:6
You exalt Yourself as head **o** all. 1Ch 29:11
You, and You rule **o** all, 1Ch 29:12
son of Jesse reigned **o** all Israel. 1Ch 29:26 5921
The period which he reigned **o** Israel 1Ch 29:27 5921
himself securely **o** his kingdom, 2Ch 1:1 5921
You have made me king **o** a people 2Ch 1:9 5921
o whom I have made you king, 2Ch 1:11 5921
and he reigned **o** Israel. 2Ch 1:13 5921
He has made you king **o** them." 2Ch 2:11 5921
wings **o** the place of the ark, 2Ch 5:8 5921
covering **o** the ark and its poles. 2Ch 5:8 5921
for a leader **o** My people Israel; 2Ch 6:5 5921
David to be **o** My people Israel.' 2Ch 6:6 5921
and fifty who ruled **o** the people. 2Ch 8:10
therefore He made you king **o** them, 2Ch 9:8 5921
He was the ruler **o** all the 2Ch 9:26
years in Jerusalem **o** all Israel. 2Ch 9:30 5921
of Judah, Rehoboam reigned **o** them. 2Ch 10:17 5921
who was **o** the forced labor, 2Ch 10:18 5921
Abijah became king **o** Judah. 2Ch 13:1 5921
gave the rule **o** Israel forever to David 2Ch 13:5 5921
made his position **o** Israel firm. 2Ch 17:1 5921
Amariah the chief priest will be **o** you 2Ch 19:11 5921
You not ruler **o** all the kingdoms 2Ch 20:6 5921
them to rejoice **o** their enemies. 2Ch 20:27 4480
Now Jehoshaphat reigned **o** Judah. 2Ch 20:31 5921
taken **o** the kingdom of his father 2Ch 21:4 5921
and set up a king **o** themselves. 2Ch 21:8 5921
Then Jehoram crossed **o** with his 2Ch 21:9 5674a
while Athaliah reigned **o** the land. 2Ch 22:12 5921
who were appointed **o** the army and 2Ch 23:14
assigned **o** the house of the LORD, 2Ch 23:18 5921
his son *was* **o** the king's house 2Ch 26:21 5921
the Ammonites and prevailed **o** them 2Ch 27:5 5921

the people rejoiced **o** what God had 2Ch 29:36 5921
the Levites *were* **o** the slaughter 2Ch 30:17 5921
enough to eat with plenty left **o**, 2Ch 31:10 3498
this great quantity is left **o**." 2Ch 31:10 3498
o the freewill offerings of God, 2Ch 31:14 5921
military officers **o** the people and 2Ch 32:6 5921
to give yourselves **o** to die by hunger 2Ch 32:11
with foremen **o** them to supervise: 2Ch 34:12 5921
were also **o** the burden bearers, 2Ch 34:13 5921
king **o** Judah and Jerusalem, 2Ch 36:4 5921
king **o** Judah and Jerusalem. 2Ch 36:10 5921
kings have ruled **o** Jerusalem, Ezr 4:20 5922
the God of Israel, who was **o** them, Ezr 5:1 5922
and the hand of our God was **o** us, Ezr 8:31 5921
was mourning **o** the unfaithfulness Ezr 10:6 5921
so that they ruled **o** them. Ne 9:28
have set **o** us because of our sins; Ne 9:37 5921
They also rule **o** our bodies And Ne 9:37 5921
And **o** our cattle as they please, Ne 9:37
o the chambers for the stores, Ne 12:44 5921
for Judah rejoiced **o** the priests Ne 12:44 5921
who was appointed **o** the chambers Ne 13:4
God made him king **o** all Israel; Ne 13:26 5921
India to Ethiopia **o** 127 provinces, Es 1:1
authority **o** all the princes who *were* Es 3:1 4480, 5921
who were **o** each province and Es 3:12 5921
the robe and the horse be handed **o** Es 6:9 5414
set Mordecai **o** the house of Haman. Es 8:2 5921
hoped to gain the mastery **o** them, Es 9:1 7980
mastery **o** those who hated them. Es 9:1 7980
dust **o** their heads toward the sky. Jb 2:12 5921
the wild donkey bray **o** *his* grass, Jb 6:5 5921
Or does the ox low **o** his fodder? Jb 6:5 5921
orphans And barter **o** your friend. Jb 6:27 5921
That You set a guard **o** me? Jb 7:12 5921
shoots spread out **o** his garden. Jb 8:16 5921
"God hands me **o** to ruffians And Jb 16:11 5462
"I have sewed sackcloth **o** my skin And Jb 16:15 5921
And put *your* hand **o** *your* mouth. Jb 21:5 5921
Men will keep watch **o** *his* tomb. Jb 21:32 5921
out the north **o** empty space And Jb 26:7 5921
moon And spreads His cloud **o** it. Jb 26:9 5921
has the *fierce* lion passed **o** it. Jb 28:8 5921
in the days when God watched **o** me; Jb 29:2
When His lamp shone **o** my head, Jb 29:3 5921
friendship of God *was* **o** my tent; Jb 29:4 5921
And let others kneel down **o** her. Jb 31:10 5921
life from passing **o** into Sheol. Jb 33:18 5674a
gave Him authority **o** the earth? Jb 34:13 5921
Or fix their rule **o** the earth? Jb 38:33
and rage he races **o** the ground, Jb 39:24
"Will the traders bargain **o** him? Jb 41:6 5921
is king **o** all the sons of pride." Jb 41:34 5921
And **o** them return on high. Ps 7:7 5921
to rule **o** the works of Your hands; Ps 8:6
who is lord **o** us?" Ps 12:4
will my enemy be exalted **o** me? Ps 13:2 5921
And by my God I can leap **o** a wall. Ps 18:29
Let them not rule **o** me; Ps 19:13
will sing for joy **o** your victory, Ps 20:5
LORD's And He rules **o** the nations. Ps 22:28
Do not let my enemies exult **o** me. Ps 25:2
Do not deliver me **o** to the desire Ps 27:12
The LORD is **o** many waters. Ps 29:3 5921
not let my enemies rejoice **o** me. Ps 30:1
me **o** into the hand of the enemy; Ps 31:8 5462
my enemies rejoice **o** me; Ps 35:19
And do not let them rejoice **o** me. Ps 35:24
who magnify themselves **o** me. Ps 35:26 5921
my iniquities are gone **o** my head; Ps 38:4 5674a
am bent **o** and greatly bowed down; Ps 38:6
"May they not rejoice **o** me, Ps 38:16
do not give him **o** to the desire of Ps 41:2
does not shout in triumph **o** me. Ps 41:11 5921
and Your waves have rolled **o** me. Ps 42:7 5921
A great King **o** all the earth. Ps 47:2 5921
God reigns **o** the nations, God sits Ps 47:8 5921
shall rule **o** them in the morning, Ps 49:14
O Edom I shall throw My shoe; Ps 60:8 5921
o to the power of the sword; Ps 63:10 5064
made men ride **o** our heads; Ps 66:12
His majesty is **o** Israel And His Ps 68:34 5921
He gave **o** their cattle also to the Ps 78:48 5462
gave **o** their life to the plague, Ps 78:50 5462
"So I gave them **o** to the Ps 81:12 7971
Are the Most High **o** all the earth. Ps 83:18 5921
Your burning anger has passed **o** me; Ps 88:16 5921
LORD Most High **o** all the earth; Ps 97:9 5921
When the wind has passed **o** it, Ps 103:16 5674a
And His sovereignty rules **o** all. Ps 103:19
boundary that they may not pass **o**, Ps 104:9 5674a
And ruler **o** all his possessions, Ps 105:21
those who hated them ruled **o** them. Ps 106:41
O Edom I shall throw My shoe; Ps 108:9 5921
O Philistia I will shout aloud." Ps 108:9 5921
Appoint a wicked man **o** him, Ps 109:6 5921
the chief men **o** a broad country. Ps 110:6 5921
He has not given me **o** to death. Ps 118:18
any iniquity have dominion **o** me. Ps 119:133
would have swept **o** our soul; Ps 124:4 5921
would have swept **o** our soul." Ps 124:5 5921
Set a guard, O LORD, **o** my mouth; Ps 141:3
Keep watch **o** the door of my lips. Ps 141:3 5921
His mercies are **o** all His works. Ps 145:9 5921
Understanding will watch **o** you, Pr 2:11
her, and she will watch **o** you. Pr 4:6
do not know **o** what they stumble. Pr 4:19
Watch **o** your heart with all Pr 4:23

you sleep, they will watch **o** you;	**Pr 6:22**	5921
rule **o** a son who acts shamefully,	**Pr 17:2**	
for a slave to rule **o** princes.	**Pr 19:10**	
drives the *threshing* wheel **o** them.	**Pr 20:26**	5921
The rich rules **o** the poor, And the	**Pr 22:7**	
Those who linger long **o** wine,	**Pr 23:30**	5921
who has no control **o** his spirit.	**Pr 25:28**	
Is a wicked ruler **o** a poor people.	**Pr 28:15**	5921
been king **o** Israel in Jerusalem.	**Ec 1:12**	5921
who were **o** Jerusalem before me;	**Ec 1:16**	5921
control **o** all the fruit of my labor	**Ec 2:19**	7980
is no advantage for man **o** beast,	**Ec 3:19**	4480
watches **o** another official,	**Ec 5:8**	4480, 5921
there are higher officials **o** them.	**Ec 5:8**	5921
does the wise man have **o** the fool?	**Ec 6:8**	4480
or authority **o** the day of death;	**Ec 8:8**	
o *another* man to his hurt.	**Ec 8:9**	
hall, And his banner **o** me is love.	**SS 2:4**	5921
is past, The rain is **o** *and* gone.	**SS 2:11**	2498
my soul set me **O** the chariots of	**SS 6:12**	
And **o** our doors are all choice	**SS 7:13**	5921
"Put me like a seal **o** your heart,	**SS 8:6**	5921
capricious children will rule **o** them,	**Is 3:4**	
children, And women rule **o** them.	**Is 3:12**	
LORD will create **o** the whole area	**Is 4:5**	5921
o her assemblies a cloud by day,	**Is 4:5**	5921
for **o** all the glory will be a	**Is 4:5**	5921
And it will growl **o** it in that	**Is 5:30**	5921
And it will rise up **o** all its channels	**Is 8:7**	5921
channels and go **o** all its banks.	**Is 8:7**	5921
to strike and a rock to stumble **o**,	**Is 8:14**	
"Many will stumble **o** them,	**Is 8:15**	
throne of David and **o** his kingdom,	**Is 9:7**	5921
Is the axe to boast itself **o** the	**Is 10:15**	5921
itself **o** the one who wields it?	**Is 10:15**	5921
and His staff will be **o** the sea and	**Is 10:26**	5921
He will wave His hand **o** the River	**Is 11:15**	5921
And make *men* walk **o** dry-shod.	**Is 11:15**	
and will rule **o** their oppressors.	**Is 14:2**	
the cypress trees rejoice **o** you,	**Is 14:8**	
Sheol from beneath is excited **o** you	**Is 14:9**	
at you, They will ponder **o** you,	**Is 14:16**	413
Moab wails **o** Nebo and Medeba;	**Is 15:2**	5921
a cry of distress **o** *their* ruin.	**Is 15:5**	
carry off **o** the brook of Arabim.	**Is 15:7**	5921
out *and* passed **o** the sea.	**Is 16:8**	5674a
the shouting **o** your summer fruits	**Is 16:9**	5921
a mighty king will rule **o** them,"	**Is 19:4**	
which He is going to wave **o** them.	**Is 19:16**	5921
Pass **o** to Tarshish;	**Is 23:6**	5674a
stretched His hand out **o** the sea,	**Is 23:11**	5921
Arise, pass **o** to Cyprus;	**Is 23:12**	5674a
when the grape harvest is **o**.	**Is 24:13**	3615
covering which is **o** all peoples,	**Is 25:7**	5921
which is stretched **o** all nations.	**Is 25:7**	5921
is the cartwheel driven **o** cummin;	**Is 28:27**	5921
o you a spirit of deep sleep,	**Is 29:10**	5921
the young lion growls **o** his prey,	**Is 31:4**	5921
He will pass **o** and rescue *it.*	**Is 31:5**	6452a
He has given them **o** to slaughter.	**Is 34:2**	
And He will stretch **o** it the line	**Is 34:11**	5921
Hilkiah, who was **o** the household,	**Is 36:3**	5921
Hilkiah, who was **o** the household,	**Is 36:22**	5921
Then he sent Eliakim who was **o** the	**Is 37:2**	5921
you by the hand and watch **o** you,	**Is 42:6**	
and does his work **o** the coals,	**Is 44:12**	
o *this* half he eats meat as he	**Is 44:16**	5921
for He has smeared **o** their eyes so	**Is 44:18**	2911b
also have baked bread **o** its coals.	**Is 44:19**	5921
come **o** to you and will be yours;	**Is 45:14**	5674a
they will come **o** in chains And	**Is 45:14**	5674a
Bel has bowed down, Nebo stoops **o**;	**Is 46:1**	7164
They stooped **o**, they have bowed	**Is 46:2**	7164
For the redeemed to cross **o**?	**Is 51:10**	5674a
'Lie down that we may walk **o** *you.*'	**Is 51:23**	5674a
street for those who walk **o** *it.*"	**Is 51:23**	5674a
"Those who rule **o** them howl, and	**Is 52:5**	
the days of your mourning will be **o**.	**Is 60:20**	7999a
shout for joy **o** their portion.	**Is 61:7**	
bridegroom rejoices **o** the bride,	**Is 62:5**	5921
So your God will rejoice **o** you.	**Is 62:5**	5921
lift up a standard **o** the peoples.	**Is 62:10**	5921
o whom You have never ruled,	**Is 63:19**	
with her, all you who mourn **o** her,	**Is 66:10**	5921
I have appointed you this day **o**	**Jer 1:10**	5921
the nations and **o** the kingdoms,	**Jer 1:10**	5921
watching **o** My word to perform it."	**Jer 1:12**	5921
Proclaim **o** Jerusalem,	**Jer 4:16**	5921
decree, so it cannot cross **o** it.	**Jer 5:22**	5674a
roar, yet they cannot cross **o** it.	**Jer 5:22**	5674a
And raise a signal **o** Beth-haccerem;	**Jer 6:1**	5921
a grape gatherer **O** the branches."	**Jer 6:9**	5921
houses shall be turned **o** to others,	**Jer 6:12**	5437
"And I set watchmen **o** you,	**Jer 6:17**	5921
will you say when He appoints **o** you	**Jer 13:21**	5921
companions to be head **o** you?	**Jer 13:21**	5921
your skirts off **o** your face,	**Jer 13:26**	5921
appoint **o** them four kinds *of doom,*"	**Jer 15:3**	5921
So I will give **o** their survivors	**Jer 15:9**	
you, They will not prevail **o** you;	**Jer 15:20**	
I will give **o** your wealth and all	**Jer 17:3**	
give their children **o** to famine And	**Jer 18:21**	
and I will give **o** their carcasses	**Jer 19:7**	
So I will give **o** all Judah to the	**Jer 20:4**	
o all the wealth of this city,	**Jer 20:5**	
o to the hand of their enemies,	**Jer 20:5**	
"I will give **o** Zedekiah king of	**Jer 21:7**	
and I will give you **o** into the	**Jer 22:25**	
will also raise up shepherds **o** them	**Jer 23:4**	5921
o every madman who prophesies,	**Jer 29:26**	
'Why do you cry out **o** your injury?	**Jer 30:15**	5921
And they will be radiant **o** the	**Jer 31:12**	413
O the grain and the new wine	**Jer 31:12**	5921
And **o** the young of the flock and	**Jer 31:12**	5921
I have watched **o** them to pluck up,	**Jer 31:28**	5921
o them to build and to plant,"	**Jer 31:28**	5921
rejoice **o** them to do them good and	**Jer 32:41**	5921
o the descendants of Abraham,	**Jer 33:26**	413
are going **o** to the Chaldeans!"	**Jer 37:13**	5307
am not going **o** to the Chaldeans";	**Jer 37:14**	5307
nor will I give you **o** to the hand of	**Jer 38:16**	
o to the hand of the Chaldeans;	**Jer 38:18**	
who have gone **o** to the Chaldeans,	**Jer 38:19**	5307
for they may give me **o** into their	**Jer 38:19**	
"They will not give you **o**.	**Jer 38:20**	
the deserters who had gone **o** to	**Jer 39:9**	5307
appointed **o** the cities of Judah,	**Jer 40:5**	
Gedaliah the son of Ahikam **o** the	**Jer 40:7**	
cities that you have taken **o**."	**Jer 40:10**	8610
he had appointed **o** them Gedaliah	**Jer 40:11**	5921
Babylon had appointed **o** the land.	**Jer 41:2**	
to cross **o** to the sons of Ammon.	**Jer 41:10**	5674a
Babylon had appointed **o** the land.	**Jer 41:18**	
us **o** into the hand of the Chaldeans,	**Jer 43:3**	
set his throne *right* **o** these stones	**Jer 43:10**	4605
he will spread his canopy **o** them.	**Jer 43:10**	5921
meant for death *will be given* **o**	**Jer 43:11**	
I am watching **o** them for harm and	**Jer 44:27**	5921
I am going to give **o** Pharaoh	**Jer 44:30**	
just as I gave **o** Zedekiah king of	**Jer 44:30**	
one warrior has stumbled **o** another,	**Jer 46:12**	
Given **o** to the power of the people	**Jer 46:24**	
"I shall give them **o** to the	**Jer 46:26**	
vessels, and they will tip him **o**,	**Jer 48:12**	6808
is chosen I shall appoint **o** it.	**Jer 49:19**	413
And they are mad **o** fearsome idols.	**Jer 50:38**	
is chosen I will appoint **o** it.	**Jer 50:44**	413
Wail **o** her! Bring balm for her pain;	**Jer 51:8**	5921
with shouts of victory **o** you."	**Jer 51:14**	5921
"The sea has come up **o** Babylon;	**Jer 51:42**	5921
them Will shout for joy **o** Babylon,	**Jer 51:48**	5921
hand **O** all her precious things,	**La 1:10**	5921
And it prevailed **o** *them.* He has	**La 1:13**	
caused the enemy to rejoice **o** you;	**La 2:17**	5921
Waters flowed **o** my head;	**La 3:54**	5921
has been turned **o** to strangers,	**La 5:2**	
Slaves rule **o** us;	**La 5:8**	
Now **o** the heads of the living beings	**Ezk 1:22**	5921
crystal, spread out **o** their heads.	**Ezk 1:22**	5921, 4605
expanse that was **o** their heads;	**Ezk 1:25**	5921
the expanse that was **o** their heads	**Ezk 1:26**	5921
it in their sight **o** human dung."	**Ezk 4:12**	
o which you will prepare your bread.	**Ezk 4:15**	5921
mourning, each **o** his own iniquity.	**Ezk 7:16**	
and groan **o** all the abominations	**Ezk 9:4**	5921
was **o** the heads of the cherubim	**Ezk 10:1**	5921
and scatter *them* **o** the city."	**Ezk 10:2**	5921
temple and stood **o** the cherubim.	**Ezk 10:18**	5921
the God of Israel hovered **o** them.	**Ezk 10:19**	5921
the God of Israel hovered **o** them.	**Ezk 11:22**	5921
and stood **o** the mountain which is	**Ezk 11:23**	5921
"I will also spread My net **o** him,	**Ezk 12:13**	5921
they plaster it **o** with whitewash;	**Ezk 13:10**	2902
who plaster *it* **o** with whitewash,	**Ezk 13:11**	2902
the wall which you plastered **o**	**Ezk 13:14**	2902
plastered it **o** with whitewash;	**Ezk 13:15**	2902
so I spread My skirt **o** you and	**Ezk 16:8**	5921
"I will spread My net **o** him,	**Ezk 17:20**	5921
And they spread their net **o** him;	**Ezk 19:8**	5921
poured out, I shall be king **o** you.	**Ezk 20:33**	5921
They are delivered **o** to the sword	**Ezk 21:12**	
give them **o** to terror and plunder.	**Ezk 23:46**	
lamentation **o** you and say to you,	**Ezk 26:17**	5921
I bring up the deep **o** you	**Ezk 26:19**	5921
man, take up a lamentation **o** Tyre;	**Ezk 27:2**	5921
will make their voice heard **o** you	**Ezk 27:30**	5921
for you And lament **o** you:	**Ezk 27:32**	5921
a lamentation **o** the king of Tyre and	**Ezk 28:12**	5921
they will not rule **o** the nations.	**Ezk 29:15**	5921
have all been given **o** to death,	**Ezk 31:14**	
I closed the deep **o** it and held back	**Ezk 31:15**	5921
take up a lamentation **o** Pharaoh	**Ezk 32:2**	5921
"Now I will spread My net **o** you	**Ezk 32:3**	5921
the heavens I will darken **o** you	**Ezk 32:8**	5921
O Egypt and over all her hordes	**Ezk 32:16**	5921
Over Egypt and **o** all her hordes	**Ezk 32:16**	5921
She is given **o** to the sword;	**Ezk 32:20**	
o all the surface of the earth,	**Ezk 34:6**	5921
I will set **o** them one shepherd,	**Ezk 34:23**	5921
"I will give you **o** to bloodshed,	**Ezk 35:6**	6213a
o the inheritance of the house of	**Ezk 35:15**	
"Prophesy **o** these bones and say	**Ezk 37:4**	5921
servant David will be king **o** them,	**Ezk 37:24**	5921
o the entrance, and to the inner	**Ezk 41:17**	5921
officials had appointed **o** Daniel,	**Da 1:11**	5921
has caused you to rule **o** them all.	**Da 2:38**	
which will rule **o** all the earth.	**Da 2:39**	
o the whole province of Babylon	**Da 2:48**	5922
o all the wise men of Babylon.	**Da 2:48**	5922
o the administration of the province	**Da 2:49**	5922
Jews whom you have appointed **o**	**Da 3:12**	5922
seven periods of time pass **o** him.	**Da 4:16**	5922
is ruler **o** the realm of mankind,	**Da 4:17**	
sets **o** it the lowliest of men."	**Da 4:17**	5922
periods of time pass **o** him,"	**Da 4:23**	5922
periods of time will pass **o** you,	**Da 4:25**	5922
is ruler **o** the realm of mankind and	**Da 4:25**	
periods of time will pass **o** you until	**Da 4:32**	5922
is ruler **o** the realm of mankind and	**Da 4:32**	
is ruler **o** the realm of mankind and	**Da 5:21**	
He sets **o** it whomever He wishes.	**Da 5:21**	5922
given **o** to the Medes and Persians."	**Da 5:28**	
appoint 120 satraps **o** the kingdom,	**Da 6:1**	5922
and **o** them three commissioners	**Da 6:2**	5924
appoint him **o** the entire kingdom.	**Da 6:3**	5922
and laid **o** the mouth of the den;	**Da 6:17**	5922
o the surface of the whole earth	**Da 8:5**	5921
the host will be given **o** *to the horn*	**Da 8:12**	
who was made king **o** the kingdom of	**Da 9:1**	5921
o him and obtain dominion;	**Da 11:5**	5921
cause them to rule **o** the many,	**Da 11:39**	
"But he will gain control **o** the	**Da 11:43**	
and **o** all the precious things of	**Da 11:43**	
guard **o** the sons of your people,	**Da 12:1**	5921
go, I will spread My net **o** them;	**Hos 7:12**	5921
take **o** their treasures of silver;	**Hos 9:6**	3423
priests will cry out **o** it,	**Hos 10:5**	5921
will cry out over it, **O** its glory,	**Hos 10:5**	5921
come **o** her fair neck *with a yoke;*	**Hos 10:11**	5921
My heart is turned **o** within Me,	**Hos 11:8**	2015
dawn is spread **o** the mountains,	**Jl 2:2**	5921
Gilgal, Nor cross **o** to Beersheba;	**Am 5:5**	5674a
Go **o** to Calneh and look, And go	**Am 6:2**	5674a
not grieved **o** the ruin of Joseph.	**Am 6:6**	5921
"When will the new moon be **o**,	**Am 8:5**	5674a
His vaulted dome **o** the earth,	**Am 9:6**	5921
"Do not gloat **o** your brother's day,	**Ob 1:12**	
And do not rejoice **o** the sons of	**Ob 1:12**	
do not gloat **o** their calamity In	**Ob 1:13**	
breakers and billows passed **o** me.	**Jon 2:3**	5921
a plant and it grew up **o** Jonah	**Jon 4:6**	4480, 5921
over Jonah to be a shade **o** his head	**Jon 4:6**	5921
the day will become dark **o** them.	**Mi 3:6**	5921
And the LORD will reign **o** them in	**Mi 4:7**	5921
And let our eyes gloat **o** Zion.'	**Mi 4:11**	
Do not rejoice **o** me, O my enemy.	**Mi 7:8**	
And passes **o** the rebellious act of the	**Mi 7:18**	5921
They stumble **o** the dead bodies!	**Na 3:3**	
lift up your skirts **o** your face,	**Na 3:5**	5921
you Will clap *their* hands **o** you,	**Na 3:19**	5921
things without a ruler **o** them?	**Hab 1:14**	
He will exult **o** you with joy, He	**Zph 3:17**	5921
rejoice **o** you with shouts of joy.	**Zph 3:17**	5921
will be stretched **o** Jerusalem."	**Zch 1:16**	5921
I will wave My hand **o** them so	**Zch 2:9**	5921
o the face of the whole land;	**Zch 5:3**	5921
will pass **o** them anymore,	**Zch 9:8**	5921
Then the LORD will appear **o** them,	**Zch 9:14**	5921
I will watch **o** the house of Judah,	**Zch 12:4**	5921
and they will weep bitterly **o** Him like	**Zch 12:10**	5921
the bitter weeping **o** a firstborn.	**Zch 12:10**	5921
LORD will be king **o** all the earth;	**Zch 14:9**	5921
stood **o** *the place* where the Child was.	**Mt 2:9**	*1883*
Archelaus was reigning **o** Judea	**Mt 2:22**	
that your opponent may not hand you **o**	**Mt 5:25**	
Getting into a boat, Jesus crossed **o**	**Mt 9:1**	*1276*
them authority **o** unclean spirits,	**Mt 10:1**	
for they will hand you **o** to *the*	**Mt 10:17**	
"But when they hand you **o**, do not	**Mt 10:19**	
been handed **o** to Me by My Father;	**Mt 11:27**	*3860*
and from joy **o** it he goes and	**Mt 13:44**	
was left **o** of the broken pieces,	**Mt 14:20**	*4052*
When they had crossed **o**,	**Mt 14:34**	*1276*
was left **o** of the broken pieces,	**Mt 15:37**	*4052*
he rejoices **o** it more than over	**Mt 18:13**	*1909*
he rejoices over it more than **o**	**Mt 18:13**	*1909*
handed him **o** to the torturers	**Mt 18:34**	*3860*
and will hand Him **o** to the Gentiles	**Mt 20:19**	
of the Gentiles lord it **o** them,	**Mt 20:25**	*2634b*
men exercise authority **o** them.	**Mt 20:25**	*2715*
in to look **o** the dinner guests,	**Mt 22:11**	*2300*
the Son of Man is *to be* handed **o**	**Mt 26:2**	
while I go **o** there and pray."	**Mt 26:36**	*565*
because of envy they had handed Him **o**.	**Mt 27:18**	
he handed Him **o** to be crucified.	**Mt 27:26**	
began to keep watch **o** Him there.	**Mt 27:36**	*5083*
with him keeping guard **o** Jesus,	**Mt 27:54**	*5083*
we will win him **o** and keep you out	**Mt 28:14**	*3982*
"Let us go **o** to the other side."	**Mk 4:35**	*1330*
the waves were breaking **o** the boat	**Mk 4:37**	*1911*
When Jesus had crossed **o** again	**Mk 5:21**	*1276*
authority **o** the unclean spirits;	**Mk 6:7**	
When they had crossed **o** they	**Mk 6:53**	*1276*
was left **o** of the broken pieces.	**Mk 8:8**	*4051*
Him to death and will hand Him **o** to	**Mk 10:33**	
of the Gentiles lord it **o** them;	**Mk 10:42**	*2634b*
men exercise authority **o** them.	**Mk 10:42**	*2715*
"When they arrest you and hand you **o**,	**Mk 13:11**	
the vial and poured it **o** His head.	**Mk 14:3**	*2708*
sold for **o** three hundred denarii,	**Mk 14:5**	*1883*
a linen sheet **o** *his* naked *body*	**Mk 14:51**	*1909*
the chief priests had handed Him **o**	**Mk 15:10**	
he handed Him **o** to be crucified.	**Mk 15:15**	
darkness fell **o** the whole land	**Mk 15:33**	*1909*
When the Sabbath was **o**,	**Mk 16:1**	*1230*
He will reign **o** the house of Jacob	**Lk 1:33**	*1909*
watch **o** their flock by night.	**Lk 2:8**	*1909*
for it has been handed **o** to me,	**Lk 4:6**	*3860*
great famine came **o** all the land;	**Lk 4:25**	*1909*
And standing **o** her, He rebuked the	**Lk 4:39**	*1883*
down, shaken together, *and* running **o**.	**Lk 6:38**	*5240*
Him went out all **o** Judea and	**Lk 7:17**	*1722*
lamp covers it **o** with a container,	**Lk 8:16**	
o to the other side of the lake."	**Lk 8:22**	*1330*

and authority **o** all the demons and Lk 9:1 1909
broken pieces which they had left **o** Lk 9:17 4052
and **o** all the power of the enemy, Lk 10:19 1909
been handed **o** to Me by My Father, Lk 10:22 3860
and the people who walk **o** *them* Lk 11:44 1883
Me a judge or arbitrator **o** you?" Lk 12:14 1909
judge turn you **o** to the officer, Lk 12:58 3860
He called her **o** and said to her, Lk 13:12 4377
entire crowd was rejoicing **o** all Lk 13:17 1909
heaven **o** one sinner who repents than Lk 15:7 1909
than **o** ninety-nine righteous Lk 15:7 1909
of God **o** one sinner who repents." Lk 15:10 1909
those who wish to come **o** from here Lk 16:26 1224
may cross **o** from there to us.' Lk 16:26 1276
and will He delay long **o** them? Lk 18:7 1909
"For He will be handed **o** to Lk 18:32
not want this man to reign **o** us.' Lk 19:14 1909
be in authority **o** ten cities.' Lk 19:17 1883
'And you are to be **o** five cities.' Lk 19:19 1883
did not want me to reign **o** them, Lk 19:27 1909
He saw the city and wept **o** it, Lk 19:41 1909
of the Gentiles lord it **o** them; Lk 22:25 2961
those who have authority **o** them Lk 22:25 1850
the people, teaching all **o** Judea, Lk 23:5 2596
and darkness fell **o** the whole land Lk 23:44 1909
and the day is now nearly **o**." Lk 24:29 2827
left **o** by those who had eaten. Jn 6:13 4052
Him authority **o** all flesh, Jn 17:2
o the ravine of the Kidron, Jn 18:1 4008
so that I would not be handed **o** to Jn 18:36
"You would have no authority **o** Me, Jn 19:11 2596
So he then handed Him **o** to them to be Jn 19:16
to them **o** *a period of* forty days and Ac 1:3 1223
this *Man,* delivered **o** by Ac 2:23
and great fear came **o** all who heard Ac 5:5 1909
And great fear came **o** the whole Ac 5:11 1909
and **o** all who heard of these things. Ac 5:11 1909
o Egypt and all his household. Ac 7:10 1909
came **o** all Egypt and Canaan, Ac 7:11 1909
AROSE ANOTHER KING **O** EGYPT Ac 7:18 1909
MADE YOU A RULER AND JUDGE **O** US? Ac 7:27 1909
and made loud lamentation **o** him. Ac 8:2 1909
It became known all **o** Joppa, Ac 9:42 2596
be a great famine all **o** the world. Ac 11:28 1909
door were watching **o** the prison. Ac 12:6 5083
and having won **o** Blastus the Ac 12:20 3982
and having won **o** the crowds, Ac 14:19 3982
"Come **o** to Macedonia and help us." Ac 16:9 1224
attempted to name **o** those who had Ac 19:13 1909
next day we crossed **o** to Samos; Ac 20:15 3846
o the word which he had spoken, Ac 20:38 1909
a ship crossing **o** to Phoenicia, Ac 21:2 1276
When the seven days were almost **o**, Ac 21:27 4931
o questions about their Law, Ac 23:29 4012
me, no one can hand me **o** to them. Ac 25:11
custom of the Romans to hand **o** any Ac 25:16
since even the fast was already **o**, Ac 27:9 3928
Therefore God gave them **o** in the Ro 1:24 3860
gave them **o** to degrading passions; Ro 1:26 3860
gave them **o** to a depraved mind, Ro 1:28 3860
o the sins previously committed; Ro 3:25 3929
He who was delivered **o** because of Ro 4:25
even **o** those who had not sinned in Ro 5:14 1909
death no longer is master **o** Him. Ro 6:9 2961
For sin shall not be master **o** you, Ro 6:14 2961
o a person as long as he lives? Ro 7:1 2961
but delivered Him **o** for us all, how Ro 8:32
to the flesh, who is **o** all, Ro 9:5 1909
potter have a right **o** the clay, Ro 9:21
stumbled **o** the stumbling stone, Ro 9:32 4350
ARISES TO RULE **O** THE GENTILES, Ro 15:12
therefore I am rejoicing **o** you, Ro 16:19 1909
not have authority **o** her own body, 1Co 7:4 1850
not have authority **o** his own body, 1Co 7:4 1850
but has authority **o** his own will, 1Co 7:37 4012
If others share the right **o** you, 1Co 9:12
when He hands **o** the kingdom to 1Co 15:24
I rejoice **o** the coming of 1Co 16:17 1909
Not that we lord it **o** your faith, 2Co 1:24 2961
who used to put a veil **o** his face 2Co 3:13 1909
read, a veil lies **o** their heart; 2Co 3:15 1909
o to death for Jesus' sake, 2Co 4:11 3860
and I may mourn **o** many of those 2Co 12:21
desire to be enslaved all **o** again? Ga 4:9 509
I have labored **o** you in vain. Ga 4:11 1519
head **o** all things to the church, Eph 1:22 5228
God and Father of all who is **o** all Eph 4:6 1909
given themselves **o** to sensuality for Eph 4:19 3860
the head **o** all rule and authority; Col 2:10
triumphed **o** them through Him. Col 2:15 2358
and have charge **o** you in the Lord 1Th 5:12 4291b
whom I have handed **o** to Satan, 1Tm 1:20 3860
or exercise authority **o** a man, 1Tm 2:12 831
HIM **O** THE WORKS OF YOUR HANDS; Heb 2:7 1909
o His house—whose house we are, Heb 3:6 1909
a great priest **o** the house of God, Heb 10:21 1909
for they keep watch **o** your souls as Heb 13:17 5228
"You stand **o** there, or sit down Jas 2:3 1563
mercy triumphs **o** judgment. Jas 2:13 2620
church and they are to pray **o** him, Jas 5:14 1909
o those allotted to your charge, 1Pe 5:3 2634b
of the earth will mourn **o** Him. Rv 1:7 1909
WILL GIVE AUTHORITY **O** THE NATIONS; Rv 2:26 1909
to them **o** a fourth of the earth, Rv 6:8 1909
spread His tabernacle **o** them. Rv 7:15 1909
They have as king **o** them, Rv 9:11 1909
and they have power **o** the waters Rv 11:6 1909
rejoice **o** them and celebrate; Rv 11:10 1909
and authority **o** every tribe and Rv 13:7 1909
swung His sickle **o** the earth, Rv 14:16 1909
the one who has power **o** fire, Rv 14:18 1909
and those who had been victorious **o** Rv 15:2 1537
who has the power **o** these plagues, Rv 16:9 1909
reigns **o** the kings of the earth." Rv 17:18 1909
will weep and lament **o** her when Rv 18:9 1909
of the earth weep and mourn **o** her, Rv 18:11 1909
"Rejoice **o** her, O heaven, and you Rv 18:20 1909
and shut *it* and sealed *it* **o** him, Rv 20:3 1883
o these the second death has no Rv 20:6 1909

OVERBOARD
they threw the ship's tackle **o** with Ac 27:19
jump **o** first and get to land, Ac 27:43 641

OVERCAME
as I also **o** and sat down with My Rv 3:21 3528
"And they **o** him because of the Rv 12:11 3528

OVERCOME
of it, for we will surely **o** it." Nu 13:30 3201
Ahaz, but could not **o** him. 2Ki 16:5 3898a
Jewish origin, you will not **o** him, Es 6:13 3201
my enemy will say, "I have **o** him," Ps 13:4 3201
sleep, Like a warrior **o** by wine. Ps 78:65 7320b
I suffer Your terrors; I am **o**. Ps 88:15 647a
Of those who are **o** with wine! Is 28:1 1986
you, but they will not **o** you, Jer 1:19 3201
You have **o** me and prevailed. Jer 20:7 2388
man, Even like a man **o** with wine, Jer 23:9 5674a
companions had been **o** with sleep; Lk 9:32 916
I have **o** the world." Jn 16:33 3528
he was **o** by sleep and fell down Ac 20:9 2702
Do not be **o** by evil, but overcome Ro 12:21 3528
by evil, but **o** evil with good. Ro 12:21 3528
for by what a man is **o**, 2Pe 2:19 2274
again entangled in them and are **o**, 2Pe 2:20 2274
because you have **o** the evil one. 1Jn 2:13 3528
you, and you have **o** the evil one. 1Jn 2:14 3528
little children, and have **o** them; 1Jn 4:4 3528
this is the victory that has **o** the world 1Jn 5:4 3528
has **o** so as to open the book and Rv 5:5 3528
them, and **o** them and kill them. Rv 11:7 3528
war with the saints and to **o** them, Rv 13:7 3528
Lamb, and the Lamb will **o** them, Rv 17:14 3528

OVERCOMES
is born of God **o** the world; 1Jn 5:4 3528
Who is the one who **o** the world, 1Jn 5:5 3528
To him who **o**, I will grant to eat Rv 2:7 3528
He who **o** will not be hurt by the Rv 2:11 3528
To him who **o**, to him I will give Rv 2:17 3528
'He who **o**, and he who keeps My Rv 2:26 3528
'He who **o** will thus be clothed in Rv 3:5 3528
'He who **o**, I will make him a Rv 3:12 3528
'He who **o**, I will grant to him to Rv 3:21 3528
He who **o** will inherit these things, Rv 21:7 3528

OVEREXTENDING
For we are not **o** ourselves, as if 2Co 10:14 5239b

OVERFLOW
the earth and cause it to **o**; Ps 65:9 7783
May the flood of water not **o** me Nor Ps 69:15 7857
your vats will **o** with new wine. Pr 3:10 6555
quench love, Nor will rivers **o** it; SS 8:7 7857
Judah, it will **o** and pass through, Is 8:8 7857
O your land like the Nile, O Is 23:10 5674a
waters will **o** the secret place. Is 28:17 7857
the rivers, they will not **o** you. Is 43:2 7857
o the land and all its fullness, Jer 47:2 7857
on coming and **o** and pass through, Da 11:10 7857
destroy him, and his army will **o**, Da 11:26 7857
he will enter countries, **o** *them* Da 11:40 7857
will **o** with the new wine and oil. Jl 2:24 7783
The vats **o**, for their wickedness Jl 3:13 7783
will again **o** with prosperity, Zch 1:17 6327b

OVERFLOWED
their deep poverty **o** in the wealth of 2Co 8:2 4052

OVERFLOWING
month when it was **o** all its banks 1Ch 12:15 4390, 5921
gushed out, And streams were **o**; Ps 78:20 7857
determined, **o** with righteousness. Is 10:22 7857
Like a storm of mighty **o** waters, Is 28:2 7857
His breath is like an **o** torrent, Is 30:28 7857
of the nations like an **o** stream; Is 66:12 7857
the north And become an **o** torrent, Jer 47:2 7857
"The **o** forces will be flooded Da 11:22 7858
But with an **o** flood He will make a Na 1:8 5674a
I am **o** with joy in all our affliction. 2Co 7:4 5248
but is also **o** through many 2Co 9:12 4052
instructed, *and* **o** with gratitude. Col 2:7 4052

OVERFLOWINGS
"Pour out the **o** of your anger, Jb 40:11 5678

OVERFLOWS
Jordan **o** all its banks all the days of Jos 3:15 4390, 5921
my head with oil; My cup **o**. Ps 23:5 7310
My heart **o** with a good theme; Ps 45:1 7370
deep waters, and a flood **o** me. Ps 69:2 7857
out for you a blessing until it **o**. Mal 3:10 1097, 1767

OVERGROWN
which has an **o** or stunted *member,* Lv 22:23 8311
it was completely **o** with thistles; Pr 24:31 5927

OVERHEARD
the conversation had not been **o**. Jer 38:27 8085

OVERHEARING
Jesus, **o** what was being spoken, Mk 5:36 3878

OVERLAID
pillars of acacia **o** with gold, Ex 26:32 6823
He **o** the boards with gold and Ex 36:34 6823
bars, and **o** the bars with gold. Ex 36:34 6823
for it, and **o** them with gold. Ex 36:36 6823
and he **o** their tops and their Ex 36:38 6823
and he **o** it with pure gold inside Ex 37:2 6823
acacia wood and **o** them with gold. Ex 37:4 6823
He **o** it with pure gold, and Ex 37:11 6823
acacia wood and **o** them with gold, Ex 37:15 6823
He **o** it with pure gold, its Ex 37:26 6823
acacia wood and **o** them with gold. Ex 37:28 6823
with it, and he **o** it with bronze. Ex 38:2 6823
wood and **o** them with bronze. Ex 38:6 6823
hooks for the pillars and **o** their tops Ex 38:28 6823
he **o** *the walls* on the inside with 1Ki 6:15 6823
and he **o** the floor of the house 1Ki 6:15 6823
and he **o** it with pure gold. 1Ki 6:20 6823
He also **o** the altar with cedar. 1Ki 6:20 6823
So Solomon **o** the inside of the 1Ki 6:21 6823
and he **o** it with gold. 1Ki 6:21 6823
He **o** the whole house with gold, 1Ki 6:22 6823
inner sanctuary he **o** with gold. 1Ki 6:22 6823
He also **o** the cherubim with gold. 1Ki 6:28 6823
He **o** the floor of the house 1Ki 6:30 6823
flowers, and **o** them with gold; 1Ki 6:32 6823
and he **o** *them* with gold evenly 1Ki 6:35 6823
ivory and **o** it with refined gold. 1Ki 10:18 6823
Hezekiah king of Judah had **o**, 2Ki 18:16 6823
and inside he **o** it with pure gold. 2Ch 3:4 6823
He **o** the main room with 2Ch 3:5 2645
wood and **o** it with fine gold, 2Ch 3:5 2645
He also **o** the house with gold 2Ch 3:7 2645
and he **o** it with fine gold, 2Ch 3:8 2645
also **o** the upper rooms with gold. 2Ch 3:9 2645
of holies and **o** them with gold. 2Ch 3:10 6823
and **o** their doors with bronze. 2Ch 4:9 6823
of ivory and **o** it with pure gold. 2Ch 9:17 6823
an earthen vessel **o** with silver dross Pr 26:23 6823
your graven images **o** with silver, Is 30:22 6826
it is **o** with gold and silver, Hab 2:19 8610

OVERLAPPING
"The **o** part that is left over Ex 26:12 5629

OVERLAY
"You shall **o** it with pure Ex 25:11 6823
inside and out you shall **o** it, Ex 25:11 6823
acacia wood and **o** them with gold. Ex 25:13 6823
"You shall **o** it with pure Ex 25:24 6823
acacia wood and **o** them with gold, Ex 25:28 6823
"You shall **o** the boards with Ex 26:29 6823
you shall **o** the bars with gold. Ex 26:29 6823
the screen and **o** them with gold, Ex 26:37 6823
and you shall **o** it with bronze. Ex 27:2 6823
wood, and **o** them with bronze. Ex 27:6 6823
"You shall **o** it with pure gold, Ex 30:3 6823
acacia wood and **o** them with gold. Ex 30:5 6823
to **o** the walls of the buildings; 1Ch 29:4 2902

OVERLAYING
and the **o** of their tops, of Ex 38:17 6826
and the **o** of their tops and their Ex 38:19 6826

OVERLOOK
is his glory to **o** a transgression. Pr 19:11 5674a

OVERLOOKED
o in the daily serving *of food.* Ac 6:1 3865
having **o** the times of ignorance, Ac 17:30 5237

OVERLOOKS
of Pisgah which **o** the wasteland. Nu 21:20 5921, 6440, 8259
top of Peor which **o** the wasteland. Nu 23:28 5921, 6440, 8259
border which **o** the valley of Zeboim 1Sa 13:18 8259, 5921

OVERLY
righteous and do not be **o** wise. Ec 7:16 3148

OVERNIGHT
feast to remain **o** until morning. Ex 23:18 3885a
day shall remain **o** until morning. Dt 16:4 3885a
came up **o** and perished overnight. Jon 4:10 1121, 3915
came up overnight and perished **o**. Jon 4:10 1121, 3915

OVERPOWER
how we may **o** him that we may bind Jg 16:5 3201
You forever **o** him and he departs; Jb 14:20 8630
They **o** him like a king ready for Jb 15:24 8630
And if one can **o** him who is alone, Ec 4:12 8630
you Will deceive you and **o** you. Ob 1:7 3201
the gates of Hades will not **o** it. Mt 16:18 2729

OVERPOWERED
friends Have misled and **o** you; Jer 38:22 3201
before the lions **o** them and crushed Da 6:24 7981
subdued all of them and **o** them, Ac 19:16 2480

OVERPOWERING
war with the saints and **o** them Da 7:21 3202

OVERPOWERS
than he attacks him and **o** him, Lk 11:22 3528

OVERSEE
o the work of the house of the LORD; 1Ch 23:4 5329
twenty years and older to **o** the work Ezr 3:8 5329
to **o** the workmen in the temple of Ezr 3:9 5329

OVERSEER
and he made him **o** over his house, Gn 39:4 6485
time he made him **o** in his house and Gn 39:5 6485
who was **o** of the men of war, 2Ki 25:19 6496
the son of Zichri was their **o**, Ne 11:9 6496
And their **o** was Zabdiel, the son Ne 11:14 6496
Now the **o** of the Levites in Ne 11:22 6496
to be the **o** in the house of the LORD Jer 29:26 6496

who was **o** of the men of war, Jer 52:25 6496
But Daniel said to the **o** whom the Da 1:11 4453
So the **o** continued to withhold Da 1:16 4453
man aspires to the office of **o**, 1Tm 3:1 *1984*
An **o**, then, must be above reproach, 1Tm 3:2 *1985*
For the **o** must be above reproach Ti 1:7 *1985*

OVERSEERS
appoint **o** in charge of the land, Gn 41:34 6496
made them **o** of the Reubenites, 1Ch 26:32 6485
All these were **o** of the property 1Ch 27:31 8269
and the **o** of all the property and 1Ch 28:1 8269
with the **o** over the king's work, 1Ch 29:6 8269
and Benaiah *were* **o** under the 2Ch 31:13 6496
"Let the king appoint **o** in Es 2:3 6496
And righteousness your **o**. Is 60:17 5065
the Holy Spirit has made you **o**, Ac 20:28 *1985*
including the **o** and deacons: Php 1:1 *1985*

OVERSHADOW
power of the Most High will **o** you; Lk 1:35 *1982*
cloud formed and *began* to **o** them; Lk 9:34 *1982*

OVERSHADOWED
speaking, a bright cloud **o** them Mt 17:5 *1982*

OVERSHADOWING
Then a cloud formed, **o** them, Mk 9:7 *1982*
cherubim of glory **o** the mercy seat; Heb 9:5 *2683*

OVERSIGHT
and had the **o** of those who perform Nu 3:32 6486
the **o** of the house of the LORD; 2Ki 12:11 6485
the **o** of the house of the LORD, 2Ki 22:5 6485
the **o** of the house of the LORD." 2Ki 22:9 6485
the **o** of the house of the LORD, 2Ch 34:10 6485
having **o** at the gates of the house Ezk 44:11 6486
exercising **o** not under compulsion, 1Pe 5:2 *1983*

OVERTAKE
disaster will **o** me and I will die; Gn 19:19 1692
and when you **o** them, say to them, Gn 44:4 5381
the evil that would **o** my father?" Gn 44:34 4672
'I will pursue, I will **o**, Ex 15:9 5381
the heat of his anger, and **o** him, Dt 19:6 5381
will come upon you and **o** you Dt 28:2 5381
will come upon you and **o** you: Dt 28:15 5381
and **o** you until you are destroyed, Dt 28:45 5381
quickly, for you will **o** them." Jos 2:5 5381
Shall I **o** them?" 1Sa 30:8 5381
for you will surely **o** them, 1Sa 30:8 5381
or he will **o** us quickly and bring 2Sa 15:14 5381
light, punishment will **o** us. 2Ki 7:9 4672
"Terrors **o** him like a flood; Jb 27:20 5381
the enemy pursue my soul and **o** *it;* Ps 7:5 5381
And may Your burning anger **o** them. Ps 69:24 5381
for time and chance **o** them all. Ec 9:11 7136a
And righteousness does not **o** us; Is 59:9 5381
which you are afraid of, will **o** you Jer 42:16 5381
lovers, but she will not **o** them; Hos 2:7 5381
sons of iniquity **o** them in Gibeah? Hos 10:9 5381
calamity will not **o** or confront us.' Am 9:10 5066
When the plowman will **o** the reaper Am 9:13 5066
the prophets, **o** your fathers? Zch 1:6 5381
that darkness will not **o** you; Jn 12:35 *2638*
the day would **o** you like a thief; 1Th 5:4 *2638*

OVERTAKEN
My iniquities have **o** me, Ps 40:12 5381
All her pursuers have **o** her In the La 1:3 5381
No temptation has **o** you but such 1Co 10:13 *2983*

OVERTAKES
the sword of your enemies **o** *you,* 1Ch 21:12 5381

OVERTHREW
and He **o** those cities, and all the Gn 19:25 2015
o the cities in which Lot lived. Gn 19:29 2015
then the LORD **o** the Egyptians in Ex 14:27 5287
o in His anger and in His wrath.' Dt 29:23 2015
And Joab struck Rabbah and **o** it. 1Ch 20:1 2040
But He **o** Pharaoh and his army in Ps 136:15 5287
as when God **o** Sodom and Gomorrah. Is 13:19 4114
a wilderness And **o** its cities, Is 14:17 2040
the LORD **o** without relenting, Jer 20:16 2015
when God **o** Sodom And Gomorrah Jer 50:40 4114
"I **o** you, as God overthrew Sodom Am 4:11 2015
you, as God **o** Sodom and Gomorrah, Am 4:11 4114

OVERTHROW
not to **o** the town of which you Gn 19:21 2015
Lot out of the midst of the **o**, Gn 19:29 2018
You **o** those who rise up Ex 15:7 2040
but you shall utterly **o** them and Ex 23:24 2040
like the **o** of Sodom and Gomorrah, Dt 29:23 4114
city, to spy it out and **o** it?" 2Sa 10:3 2015
the city stronger and **o** it' 2Sa 11:25 2040
to **o** and to spy out the land?" 1Ch 19:3 2015
His name to dwell there **o** any king Ezr 6:12 4049
break down, To destroy and to **o**, Jer 1:10 2040
will build them up and not **o** them, Jer 24:6 2040
to pluck up, to break down, to **o**, Jer 31:28 2040
"Like the **o** of Sodom and Gomorrah Jer 49:18 4114
of the seas On the day of your **o**. Ezk 27:27 4658
I will **o** the thrones of kingdoms Hg 2:22 2015
o the chariots and their riders, Hg 2:22 2015
you will not be able to **o** them; Ac 5:39 *2647*

OVERTHROWN
and had **o** Ziklag and burned it 1Sa 30:1 5221
The wicked are **o** and are no more, Pr 12:7 2015
is desolation, as **o** by strangers. Is 1:7 4114
But may they be **o** before You; Jer 18:23 3782
plucked up or **o** anymore forever." Jer 31:40 2040
Sodom, Which was **o** as in a moment, La 4:6 2015
days and Nineveh will be **o**." Jon 3:4 2015
is of men, it will be **o**; Ac 5:38 *2647*

OVERTHROWS
barefoot And **o** the secure ones. Jb 12:19 5557
works, And He **o** *them* in the night, Jb 34:25 2015
But He **o** the words of the Pr 22:12 5557
But a man who takes bribes **o** it. Pr 29:4 2040

OVERTOOK
and he **o** him in the hill country Gn 31:23 1692
So he **o** them and spoke these words Gn 44:6 5381
they **o** them camping by the sea, Ex 14:9 5381
assembled and **o** the sons of Dan. Jg 18:22 1692
but the battle **o** them while those Jg 20:42 1692
o them at Gidom and killed 2,000 Jg 20:45 1692
Philistines **o** Saul and his sons; 1Sa 31:2 1692
Chaldeans pursued the king and **o** him 2Ki 25:5 5381
Saul, and the archers **o** him; 1Ch 10:3 4672
I pursued my enemies and **o** them, Ps 18:37 5381
o Zedekiah in the plains of Jericho; Jer 39:5 5381
o Zedekiah in the plains of Jericho, Jer 52:8 5381

OVERTURNED
My heart is **o** within me, For I La 1:20 2015
o the tables of the moneychangers Mt 21:12 *2690*
o the tables of the moneychangers Mk 11:15 *2690*
money changers and **o** their tables; Jn 2:15 *396*

OVERTURNS
how, When He **o** them in His anger; Jb 9:5 2015
He **o** the mountains at the base. Jb 28:9 2015

OVERWHELM
"Surely the darkness will **o** me, Ps 139:11 7779
and shuddering will **o** them; Ezk 7:18 3680
done to Lebanon will **o** you, Hab 2:17 3680

OVERWHELMED
So Joshua **o** Amalek and his people Ex 17:13 2522
The torrents of destruction **o** me; 2Sa 22:5 1204
me And my humiliation has **o** me, Ps 44:15 3680
And horror has **o** me. Ps 55:5 3680
When my spirit was **o** within me, Ps 142:3 5848c
my spirit is **o** within me; Ps 143:4 5848c
a one might be **o** by excessive sorrow. 2Co 2:7 *2666*

OVERWHELMING
The **o** scourge will not reach us Is 28:15 7857
When the **o** scourge passes through, Is 28:18 7857

OVERWHELMINGLY
we **o** conquer through Him who Ro 8:37 *5245*

OVERWHELMS
My mind reels, horror **o** me; Is 21:4 1204

OWE
'Pay back what you **o**.' Mt 18:28 *3784*
'How much do you **o** my master?' Lk 16:5 *3784*
'And how much do you **o**?' Lk 16:7 *3784*
O nothing to anyone except to love Ro 13:8 *3784*
you **o** to me even your own self Phm 1:19 *4359*

OWED
who **o** him ten thousand talents was Mt 18:24 *3781*
who **o** him a hundred denarii; Mt 18:28 *3784*
he should pay back what was **o**. Mt 18:30 *3784*
should repay all that was **o** him. Mt 18:34 *3784*
one **o** five hundred denarii, and Lk 7:41 *3784*

OWES
you in any way or **o** you anything, Phm 1:18 *3784*

OWL
and the ostrich and the **o** and the Lv 11:16 8464
and the little **o** and the cormorant Lv 11:17 3563b
and the cormorant and the great **o**, Lv 11:17 3244
and the white **o** and the pelican Lv 11:18 8580
and the ostrich, the **o**, Dt 14:15 8464
the little **o**, the great owl, the Dt 14:16 3563b
the little owl, the great **o**, Dt 14:16 3244
owl, the great owl, the white **o**, Dt 14:16 8580
like an **o** of the waste places. Ps 102:6 3563b
And **o** and raven will dwell in it; Is 34:11 3244

OWLS
their houses will be full of **o**; Is 13:21 255

OWN
God created man in His **o** image, Gn 1:27
father of *a son* in his **o** likeness, Gn 5:3
will come forth from your **o** body, Gn 15:4
my **o** place and to my own country. Gn 30:25
my own place and to my **o** country. Gn 30:25
provide for my **o** household also?" Gn 30:30
and he put his **o** herds apart, and Gn 30:40
let what you have be your **o**." Gn 33:9
our **o** flesh." And his brothers Gn 37:27
each man with his **o** dream *and* Gn 40:5
dream *and* each dream with its **o** Gn 40:5
"I would make mention today of my **o** Gn 41:9
to the interpretation of his **o** Gn 41:11
he interpreted according to his **o** Gn 41:12
from its **o** surrounding fields. Gn 41:48
portions to them from his **o** table, Gn 43:34
and four-fifths shall be your **o** Gn 47:24
but it is the fault of your **o** Ex 5:16
of every beast that you **o**; Ex 13:12 1961
he went his way into his **o** land. Ex 18:27
then you shall be My **o** possession Ex 19:5
restitution from the best of his **o** field Ex 22:5
and the best of his **o** vineyard. Ex 22:5
take us as Your **o** possession." Ex 34:9
who eats of it will bear his **o** Lv 7:18
'His **o** hands are to bring Lv 7:30
to marry a virgin of his **o** people, Lv 21:14
each day's matter on its **o** day Lv 23:37
shall return to his **o** property, Lv 25:10
shall return to his **o** property. Lv 25:13
to them for his **o** redemption; Lv 25:51
of the fields of his **o** property, Lv 27:16
of the field of his **o** property, Lv 27:22
of the fields of his **o** property, Lv 27:28
camp, each man by his **o** camp, Nu 1:52
and each man by his **o** standard, Nu 1:52
camp, each by his **o** standard, Nu 2:2
but rather will go to my **o** land Nu 10:30
like grasshoppers in our **o** sight, Nu 13:33
your **o** heart and your own eyes, Nu 15:39
your own heart and your **o** eyes, Nu 15:39
So they each took his **o** censer Nu 16:18
nor **o** any portion among them; Nu 18:20 1961
good or bad, of my **o** accord. Nu 24:13
but he died in his **o** sin, Nu 27:3
nearest relative in his **o** family, Nu 27:11
called it Nobah after his **o** name. Nu 32:42
each hold to his **o** inheritance." Nu 36:9
that is, Bashan, after his **o** name, Dt 3:14
be a people for His **o** possession, Dt 4:20
to be a people for His **o** possession Dt 7:6
but your **o** eyes have seen all the Dt 11:7
whatever is right in his **o** eyes; Dt 12:8
your friend who is as your **o** soul, Dt 13:6
a people for His **o** possession out of Dt 14:2
be put to death for his **o** sin. Dt 24:16
eat the offspring of your **o** body, Dt 28:53
Nor did he regard his **o** sons, Dt 33:9
you shall return to your **o** land, Jos 1:15 3425
his blood *shall be* on his **o** head, Jos 2:19
put *them* among their **o** things. Jos 7:11
his **o** city and to his own house, Jos 20:6
his own city and to his **o** house, Jos 20:6
o eyes saw what I did in Egypt. Jos 24:7
their **o** daughters to their sons, Jg 3:6
'My **o** power has delivered me.' Jg 7:2
went and lived in his **o** house. Jg 8:29
did what was right in his **o** eyes. Jg 17:6
did what was right in his **o** eyes. Jg 21:25
I would jeopardize my **o** inheritance. Ru 4:6
And they went to their **o** home. 1Sa 2:20
and let it return to its **o** place, 1Sa 5:11
of its **o** territory to Beth-shemesh, 1Sa 6:9
Himself a man after His **o** heart, 1Sa 13:14
Philistines went to their **o** place. 1Sa 14:46
you were little in your **o** eyes, 1Sa 15:17
loved him as he loved his **o** life. 1Sa 20:17
the son of Jesse to your **o** shame 1Sa 20:30
avenging yourself by your **o** hand, 1Sa 25:26
from avenging myself by my **o** hand. 1Sa 25:33
evildoing of Nabal on his **o** head." 1Sa 25:39
buried him in Ramah, his **o** city. 1Sa 28:3
man in his **o** house on his bed, 2Sa 4:11
and will be humble in my **o** eyes, 2Sa 6:22
that they may live in their **o** place 2Sa 7:10
and according to Your **o** heart, 2Sa 7:21
Israel as Your **o** people forever, 2Sa 7:24
from his **o** flock or his own herd, 2Sa 12:4
from his own flock or his **o** herd, 2Sa 12:4
against you from your **o** household; 2Sa 12:11
Then he came to his **o** house, 2Sa 12:20
"Let him turn to his **o** house, 2Sa 14:24
So Absalom turned to his **o** house 2Sa 14:24
return to your **o** place. 2Sa 15:19
you are *taken* in your **o** evil, 2Sa 16:8
named the pillar after his **o** name, 2Sa 18:18
those who ate at your **o** table. 2Sa 19:28
has come safely to his **o** house." 2Sa 19:30
that I may die in my **o** city near 2Sa 19:37
and killed him with his **o** spear. 2Sa 23:21
my son Solomon ride on my **o** mule, 1Ki 1:33
today while my **o** eyes see *it.*' " 1Ki 1:48
this word against his **o** life. 1Ki 2:23
"Go to Anathoth to your **o** field, 1Ki 2:26
return his blood on his **o** head, 1Ki 2:32
at his **o** house in the wilderness. 1Ki 2:34
blood shall be on your **o** head." 1Ki 2:37
return your evil on your **o** head. 1Ki 2:44
he had finished building his **o** house 1Ki 3:1
Solomon was building his **o** house 1Ki 7:1
by bringing his way on his **o** head 1Ki 8:32
the affliction of his **o** heart, 1Ki 8:38
house of the LORD, his **o** house, 1Ki 9:15
report which I heard in my **o** land 1Ki 10:6
she turned and went to her **o** land 1Ki 10:13
marriage the sister of his **o** wife, 1Ki 11:19
that I may go to my **o** country." 1Ki 11:21
seeking to go to your **o** country?" 1Ki 11:22
Now look after your **o** house, 1Ki 12:16
he had devised in his **o** heart; 1Ki 12:33
He laid his body in his **o** grave, 1Ki 13:30
father and his **o** dedicated things: 1Ki 15:15
living, and laid him on his **o** bed. 1Ki 17:19
Then he took hold of his **o** clothes 2Ki 2:12
him and returned to their **o** land. 2Ki 3:27
"I live among my **o** people." 2Ki 4:13
you will see it with your **o** eyes, 2Ki 7:2
you will see it with your **o** eyes, 2Ki 7:19
and his **o** sacred things and all 2Ki 12:18
be put to death for his **o** sin." 2Ki 14:6
away into exile from their **o** land 2Ki 17:23
every nation still made gods of its **o** 2Ki 17:29
and served their **o** gods according to 2Ki 17:33
doomed to eat their **o** dung and 2Ki 18:27
drink their **o** urine with you?" 2Ki 18:27
of the waters of his **o** cistern, 2Ki 18:31
away to a land like your **o** land, 2Ki 18:32
a rumor and return to his **o** land. 2Ki 19:7
by the sword in his **o** land. 2Ki 19:7
this city to save it for My **o** sake and 2Ki 19:34
I will defend this city for My **o** sake 2Ki 20:6
in the garden of his **o** house, 2Ki 21:18

killed the king in his o house. 2Ki 21:23
and buried him in his o tomb. 2Ki 23:30
and killed him with his o spear. 1Ch 11:23
that they may dwell in their o place 1Ch 17:9
and according to Your o heart, 1Ch 17:19
You made Your o people forever, 1Ch 17:22
by bringing his way on *his* o head 2Ch 6:23
his o affliction and his own pain, 2Ch 6:29
his own affliction and his o pain, 2Ch 6:29
house of the LORD and his o house 2Ch 8:1
report which I heard in my o land 2Ch 9:5
to her o land with her servants. 2Ch 9:12
Now look after your o house, 2Ch 10:16
He set up priests of his o for the 2Ch 11:15
could not hold his o against them. 2Ch 13:7 2388
father and his o dedicated things: 2Ch 15:18
They buried him in his o tomb 2Ch 16:14
your brothers, your o family, 2Ch 21:13
his o servants conspired against 2Ch 24:25
be put to death for his o sin." 2Ch 25:4
have not delivered their o people 2Ch 25:15
not *have* transgressions of your o 2Ch 28:10 5973
as you see with your o eyes. 2Ch 29:8
returned in shame to his o land. 2Ch 32:21
some of his o children killed him 2Ch 32:21 4578
they buried him in his o house. 2Ch 33:20
put him to death in his o house. 2Ch 33:24
Stop for your o sake from 2Ch 35:21
in front of his o quarters. Ne 3:30
their reproach on their o heads Ne 4:4
inventing them in your o mind." Ne 6:8
each in front of his o house." Ne 7:3
"But they, in their o kingdom, Ne 9:35
each lived on his o property in their Ne 11:3
Judah, each on his o inheritance. Ne 11:20
gone away, each to his o field. Ne 13:10
but the language of his o people. Ne 13:24 5971a
should be the master in his o house Es 1:22
in the language of his o people. Es 1:22
took her as his o daughter. Es 2:7
Jews, should return on his o head and Es 9:25
came each one from his o place, Jb 2:11
"He captures the wise by their o Jb 5:13
And my o clothes would abhor me. Jb 9:31
"I loathe my o life; Jb 10:1
"Your o mouth condemns you, and Jb 15:6
your o lips testify against you. Jb 15:6
And his o scheme brings him down. Jb 18:7
thrown into the net by his o feet, Jb 18:8
I am loathsome to my o brothers. Jb 19:17
"Let his o eyes see his decay, Jb 21:20
he was righteous in his o eyes. Jb 32:1
your o right hand can save you. Jb 40:14
By their o devices let them fall! Ps 5:10
will return upon his o head, Ps 7:16
will descend upon his o pate. Ps 7:16
hid, their o foot has been caught. Ps 9:15
his o hands the wicked is snared. Ps 9:16
Our lips are our o; Ps 12:4
He swears to his o hurt and Ps 15:4
has chosen for His o inheritance. Ps 33:12
For it flatters him in his o eyes Ps 36:2
sword will enter their o heart, Ps 37:15
You with Your o hand drove Ps 44:2
For by their o sword they did not Ps 44:3
And their o arm did not save them, Ps 44:3
their lands after their o names. Ps 49:11
You slander your o mother's son. Ps 50:20
Their o tongue is against them; Ps 64:8
set up their o standards for signs. Ps 74:4
O God, *and* plead Your o cause; Ps 74:22
led forth His o people like sheep And Ps 78:52
heart, To walk in their o devices. Ps 81:12
His stand in His o congregation; Ps 82:1
with their o shame as with a robe. Ps 109:29
Israel for His o possession. Ps 135:4
the wicked fall into their o nets, Ps 141:10
lie in wait for their o blood; Pr 1:18
They ambush their o lives. Pr 1:18
eat of the fruit of their o way And Pr 1:31
be satiated with their o devices. Pr 1:31
not lean on your o understanding. Pr 3:5
Do not be wise in your o eyes; Pr 3:7
Drink water from your o cistern And Pr 5:15
And fresh water from your o well. Pr 5:15
His o iniquities will capture the Pr 5:22
will fall by his o wickedness. Pr 11:5
will be caught by *their* o greed. Pr 11:6
evil *will bring about* his o death. Pr 11:19
his o house will inherit wind, Pr 11:29
way of a fool is right in his o eyes, Pr 12:15
tears it down with her o hands. Pr 14:1
The heart knows its o bitterness, Pr 14:10 5315
will have his fill of his o ways, Pr 14:14
illicitly troubles his o house, Pr 15:27
of a man are clean in his o sight, Pr 16:2
made everything for its o purpose, Pr 16:4
who separates himself seeks *his* o Pr 18:1
But only in revealing his o mind. Pr 18:2
a high wall in his o imagination. Pr 18:11
who gets wisdom loves his o soul; Pr 19:8
him to anger forfeits his o life. Pr 20:2
a man proclaims his o loyalty, Pr 20:6 376
man's way is right in his o eyes, Pr 21:2
My o heart also will be glad; Pr 23:15
glory to search out one's o glory. Pr 25:27
That he not be wise in his o eyes. Pr 26:5
He cuts off *his* o feet *and* Pr 26:6
you see a man wise in his o eyes? Pr 26:12

The sluggard is wiser in his o eyes Pr 26:16
praise you, and not your o mouth; Pr 27:2
A stranger, and not your o lips. Pr 27:2
Do not forsake your o friend or Pr 27:10
Will himself fall into his o pit, Pr 28:10
rich man is wise in his o eyes, Pr 28:11
He who trusts in his o heart is a fool, Pr 28:26
But a child who gets his o way Pr 29:15
with a thief hates his o life; Pr 29:24
a kind who is pure in his o eyes, Pr 30:12
hands and consumes his o flesh. Ec 4:5
not taken care of my o vineyard. SS 1:6
very o vineyard is at my disposal; SS 8:12
"We will eat our o bread and wear Is 4:1
own bread and wear our o clothes, Is 4:1
who are wise in their o eyes And Is 5:21
eyes And clever in their o sight! Is 5:21
them eats the flesh of his o arm. Is 9:20
will each turn to his o people, Is 13:14
And each one flee to his o land. Is 13:14
and settle them in their o land, Is 14:1
lie in glory, Each in his o tomb. Is 14:18
doomed to eat their o dung and Is 36:12
drink their o urine with you?" Is 36:12
of the waters of his o cistern, Is 36:16
away to a land like your o land, Is 36:17
a rumor and return to his o land. Is 37:7
by the sword in his o land. Is 37:7
this city to save it for My o sake Is 37:35
"Lo, for *my* o welfare I had Is 38:17
your transgressions for My o sake, Is 43:25
o witnesses fail to see or know, Is 44:9
Each has wandered in his o way; Is 47:15
"For My o sake, for My own sake, Is 48:11
"For My own sake, for My o sake, Is 48:11
oppressors with their o flesh, Is 49:26
their o blood as with sweet wine; Is 49:26
For they will see with their o eyes Is 52:8 5869
of us has turned to his o way; Is 53:6
have all turned to their o way, Is 56:11
hide yourself from your o flesh? Is 58:7
turn your foot From doing your o Is 58:13
desisting from your o ways, From Is 58:13
From seeking your o pleasure Is 58:13
own pleasure And speaking *your* o Is 58:13
o arm brought salvation to Him, Is 59:16
My o arm brought salvation to Me, Is 63:5
good, following their o thoughts, Is 65:2
Both their o iniquities and the Is 65:7
As they have chosen their o ways, Is 66:3
the works of their o hands. Jer 1:16
o wickedness will correct you, Jer 2:19
you shepherds after My o heart, Jer 3:15
And the priests rule on their o Jer 5:31
after other gods to your o ruin, Jer 7:6
they spite, to their o shame?" Jer 7:19 6440
but walked in *their* o counsels Jer 7:24
the deception of their o minds. Jer 14:14
for I will pour out their o Jer 14:16
us, for Your o name's sake; Jer 14:21
stubbornness of his o evil heart, Jer 16:12
I will restore them to their o land Jer 16:15
are going to follow our o plans, Jer 18:12
he will have his o life as booty. Jer 21:9
only upon your o dishonest gain, Jer 22:17
they will live on their o soil." Jer 23:8
a vision of their o imagination, Jer 23:16
the stubbornness of his o heart, Jer 23:17
of the deception of their o heart, Jer 23:26
o word will become the oracle, Jer 23:36
work of your hands to your o harm. Jer 25:7
the time of his o land comes; Jer 27:7
you have sent letters in your o name Jer 29:25
will return to their o territory. Jer 31:17
will die for his o iniquity; Jer 31:30
fear Me always, for their o good and Jer 32:39
not plant a vineyard or o one; Jer 35:7 1961
to return to its o land of Egypt. Jer 37:7
Chaldeans will live and have his o Jer 38:2
but you will have your o life as Jer 39:18
many, as your o eyes *now* see us, Jer 42:2
and restore you to your o soil. Jer 42:12
of their wives, your o wickedness, Jer 44:9
And let us go back To our o people Jer 46:16
your o achievements and treasures, Jer 48:7
each turn back to his o people And Jer 50:16
they will each flee to his o land. Jer 50:16
let us each go to his o country, Jer 51:9
women Boiled their o children; La 4:10
will loathe themselves in their o sight Ezk 6:9
each over his o iniquity. Ezk 7:16
prophesy from their o inspiration, Ezk 13:2
who are following their o spirit Ezk 13:3
prophesying from their o inspiration Ezk 13:17
to answer him in My o person. Ezk 14:7
by their o righteousness they Ezk 14:14
conduct down on your o head," Ezk 16:43
along with them your o captivity, Ezk 16:53 7622
his blood will be on his o head. Ezk 18:13
will loathe yourselves in your o sight Ezk 20:43
moment, every man for his o life, Ezk 32:10
his blood will be on his o head. Ezk 33:4
is their o way that is not right. Ezk 33:17
and bring them to their o land; Ezk 34:13
Israel was living in their o land, Ezk 36:17
and bring you into your o land. Ezk 36:24
will loathe yourselves in your o sight Ezk 36:31
I will place you on your o land. Ezk 37:14
and bring them into their o land; Ezk 37:21

when they live securely on their o Ezk 39:26
them *again* to their o land; Ezk 39:28
inheritance from his o possession Ezk 46:18
the youths who are your o age? Da 1:10
any god except their o God. Da 3:28
king sealed it with his o signet ring Da 6:17
but not by his o power, And he Da 8:24
on account of any merits of our o, Da 9:18
For Your o sake, O my God, do not Da 9:19
though not to his o descendants, Da 11:4
but will return to his o land. Da 11:9
the fortresses of his o land, Da 11:19
action and *then* return to his o Da 11:28
will be ashamed of its o counsel. Hos 10:6
"Have we not by our o strength Am 6:13
will return on your o head. Ob 1:15
while I was still in my o country? Jon 4:2
are the men of his o household. Mi 7:6
expose your o nakedness. Hab 2:16
maker trusts in his o handiwork Hab 2:18
You pierced with his o spears Hab 3:14
everyone from his o place. Zph 2:11
each of you runs to his o house. Hg 1:9
be set there on her o pedestal." Zch 5:11
And their o shepherds have no pity Zch 11:5
on their o sites in Jerusalem. Zch 12:6
that I prepare *My* o possession, Mal 3:17
spares his o son who serves him." Mal 3:17
the magi left for their o country by Mt 2:12
day has enough trouble of its o. Mt 6:34
the log that is in your o eye? Mt 7:3
behold, the log is in your o eye? Mt 7:4
take the log out of your o eye, Mt 7:5
the dead to bury their o dead." Mt 8:22 *1438*
over *the sea* and came to His o city. Mt 9:1 *2398*
except in his hometown and in his o Mt 13:57
do what I wish with what is my o? Mt 20:15 *1699*
went their way, one to his o farm, Mt 22:5 *2398*
journey, who called his o slaves and Mt 25:14 *2398*
each according to his o ability; Mt 25:15 *2398*
off Him and put His o garments Mt 27:31
and laid it in his o new tomb, Mt 27:60
When His o people heard *of this,* Mk 3:21
privately to His o disciples. Mk 4:34 *2398*
and mother and His o companions, Mk 5:40
hometown and among his o relatives Mk 6:4
relatives and in his o household." Mk 6:4
off Him and put His o garments Mk 15:20
census, each to his o city. Lk 2:3 *1438*
a sword will pierce even your o soul Lk 2:35 *846*
to their o city of Nazareth. Lk 2:39 *1438*
the log that is in your o eye? Lk 6:41 *2398*
see the log that is in your o eye? Lk 6:42
take the log out of your o eye, Lk 6:42
each tree is known by its o fruit. Lk 6:44 *2398*
the dead to bury their o dead; Lk 9:60 *1438*
and he put him on his o beast, Lk 10:34 *2398*
armed, guards his o house, Lk 11:21 *1438*
will o what you have prepared?' Lk 12:20
your o initiative judge what is right? Lk 12:57 *1438*
took and threw into his o garden; Lk 13:19 *1438*
and does not hate his o father and Lk 14:26
sisters, yes, and even his o life, Lk 14:26 *1438*
"Whoever does not carry his o cross Lk 14:27 *1438*
not give up all his o possessions. Lk 14:33 *1438*
shrewd in relation to their o kind Lk 16:8 *1438*
give you that which is your o? Lk 16:12
"Behold, we have left our o *homes* Lk 18:28 *2398*
'By your o words I will judge you, Lk 19:22
it ourselves from His o mouth." Lk 22:71
He came to His o, and those who Jn 1:11 *2398*
were His o did not receive Him. Jn 1:11 *2398*
found first his o brother Simon and Jn 1:41 *2398*
has no honor in his o country. Jn 4:44 *2398*
also was calling God His o Father, Jn 5:18 *2398*
can do nothing on My o initiative. Jn 5:30 *1683*
because I do not seek My o will, Jn 5:30 *1699*
another comes in his o name, Jn 5:43 *2398*
from heaven, not to do My o will, Jn 6:38 *1699*
from himself seeks his o glory; Jn 7:18 *2398*
I do nothing on My o initiative, Jn 8:28 *1683*
not even come on My o initiative, Jn 8:42 *1683*
lie, he speaks from his o *nature,* Jn 8:44 *2398*
and he calls his o sheep by name and Jn 10:3 *2398*
"When he puts forth all his o, Jn 10:4 *2398*
and I know My o and My own know Jn 10:14 *1699*
I know My own and My o know Me, Jn 10:14 *1699*
I lay it down on My o initiative. Jn 10:18 *1683*
did not say this on his o initiative Jn 11:51 *1438*
did not speak on My o initiative, Jn 12:49 *1683*
loved His o who were in the world, Jn 13:1 *2398*
I do not speak on My o initiative, Jn 14:10 *1683*
world, the world would love its o; Jn 15:19 *2398*
not speak on His o initiative, Jn 16:13 *1438*
be scattered, each to his o *home,* Jn 16:32 *2398*
saying this on your o initiative, Jn 18:34 *1438*
Your o nation and the chief Jn 18:35
He went out, bearing His o cross, Jn 19:17 *1438*
took her into his o *household.* Jn 19:27 *2398*
went away again to their o homes. Jn 20:10 *1438*
has fixed by His o authority; Ac 1:7 *2398*
so that in their o language that Ac 1:19 *2398*
aside to go to his o place." Ac 1:25 *2398*
them speak in his o language. Ac 2:6 *2398*
we each hear *them* in our o language Ac 2:8 *2398*
Arabs—we hear them in our o Ac 2:11
as if by our o power or piety we Ac 3:12 *2398*
they went to their o *companions* Ac 4:23 *2398*
belonging to him was his o, Ac 4:32 *2398*

unsold, did it not remain your **o**? Ac 5:4
and nurtured him as her **o** son. Ac 7:21 1438
of God in his **o** generation, Ac 13:36 2398
the nations to go their **o** ways; Ac 14:16
some of your **o** poets have said, Ac 17:28
"Your blood *be* on your **o** heads! Ac 18:6
words and names and your **o** law, Ac 18:15
He purchased with His **o** blood. Ac 20:28 2398
your **o** selves men will arise, Ac 20:30
that these hands ministered to my **o** Ac 20:34
and bound his **o** feet and hands, Ac 21:11 1438
judge him according to our **o** Law. Ac 24:6
while Paul said in his **o** defense, Ac 25:8
about their **o** religion and about a Ac 25:19 2398
the beginning was spent among my **o** Ac 26:4
overboard with their **o** hands. Ac 27:19 849b
years in his **o** rented quarters and Ac 28:30 2398
receiving in their **o** persons the due Ro 1:27 1438
faith he contemplated his **o** body, Ro 4:19 1438
demonstrates His **o** love toward us, Ro 5:8 1438
sending His **o** Son in the likeness Ro 8:3 1438
He who did not spare His **o** Son, Ro 8:32 2398
and seeking to establish their **o**, Ro 10:3 2398
grafted into their **o** olive tree? Ro 11:24 2398
not be wise in your **o** estimation Ro 11:25 1438
not be wise in your **o** estimation. Ro 12:16 1438
Never take your **o** revenge, Ro 12:19 1438
his **o** master he stands or falls; Ro 14:4 2398
be fully convinced in his **o** mind. Ro 14:5 2398
as your **o** conviction before God. Ro 14:22 4572
for my life risked their **o** necks, Ro 16:4 1438
Christ but of their **o** appetites; Ro 16:18 1438
but each will receive his **o** reward 1Co 3:8 2398
reward according to his **o** labor. 1Co 3:8 2398
we toil, working with our **o** hands; 1Co 4:12 2398
man sins against his **o** body. 1Co 6:18 2398
God, and that you are not your **o**? 1Co 6:19 1438
each man is to have his **o** wife, 1Co 7:2 1438
each woman is to have her **o** husband. 1Co 7:2 2398
have authority over her **o** body, 1Co 7:4 2398
have authority over his **o** body, 1Co 7:4 2398
each man has his **o** gift from God, 1Co 7:7 2398
This I say for your **o** benefit; 1Co 7:35 846
but has authority over his **o** will, 1Co 7:37 2398
has decided this in his **o** heart, 1Co 7:37 2398
to keep his **o** virgin *daughter*, 1Co 7:37 1438
So then both he who gives his **o** 1Co 7:38 1438
as a soldier at his **o** expense? 1Co 9:7 2398
Let no one seek his **o** *good*, 1Co 10:24 1438
I mean not your **o** conscience, but 1Co 10:29 1438
things, not seeking my **o** profit but 1Co 10:33 1683
each one takes his **o** supper first; 1Co 11:21 2398
it does not seek its **o**, 1Co 13:5 1438
them ask their **o** husbands at home; 1Co 14:35 2398
But each in his **o** order: 1Co 15:23 2398
each of the seeds a body of its **o**. 1Co 15:38 2398
The greeting is in my **o** hand—Paul. 1Co 16:21 1699
I determined this for my **o** sake, 2Co 2:1 1683
restrained in your **o** affections. 2Co 6:12
they gave of their **o** accord, 2Co 8:3 830
has gone to you of his **o** accord. 2Co 8:17 830
on my **o** behalf I will not boast, 2Co 12:5 1683
each one must examine his **o** work, Ga 6:4 1438
each one will bear his **o** load. Ga 6:5 2398
For the one who sows to his **o** Ga 6:8 1438
am writing to you with my **o** hand. Ga 6:11 1699
a view to the redemption of *God's* **o** Eph 1:14
with his **o** hands what is good, Eph 4:28 2398
be subject to your **o** husbands, Eph 5:22 2398
their **o** wives as their own bodies. Eph 5:28 1438
their own wives as their **o** bodies. Eph 5:28 1438
loves his **o** wife loves himself; Eph 5:28 1438
for no one ever hated his **o** flesh, Eph 5:29 1438
love his **o** wife even as himself, Eph 5:33 1438
out for your **o** personal interests, Php 2:4 1438
all seek after their **o** interests, Php 2:21 1438
not having a righteousness of my **o** Php 3:9 1699
write this greeting with my **o** hand. Col 4:18 1699
tenderly cares for her **o** children. 1Th 2:7 1438
of God but also our **o** lives, 1Th 2:8 1438
as a father *would* his **o** children, 1Th 2:11 1438
you into His **o** kingdom and glory. 1Th 2:12 1438
at the hands of your **o** countrymen, 1Th 2:14 2398
know how to possess his **o** vessel 1Th 4:4 1438
attend to your **o** business and work 1Th 4:11 2398
fashion and eat their **o** bread. 2Th 3:12 1438
this greeting with my **o** hand, 2Th 3:17 1699
who manages his **o** household well, 1Tm 3:4 2398
how to manage his **o** household, 1Tm 3:5 2398
children and their **o** households. 1Tm 3:12 2398
liars seared in their **o** conscience 1Tm 4:2 2398
piety in regard to their **o** family and 1Tm 5:4 2398
anyone does not provide for his **o**, 1Tm 5:8 2398
regard their **o** masters as worthy 1Tm 6:1 2398
but according to His **o** purpose and 2Tm 1:9 2398
in accordance to their **o** desires, 2Tm 4:3 2398
themselves, a prophet of their **o**, Ti 1:12 2398
being subject to their **o** husbands, Ti 2:5 2398
to their **o** masters in everything, Ti 2:9 2398
a people for His **o** possession, Ti 2:14 1438
but of your **o** free will. Phm 1:14
am writing this with my **o** hand, Phm 1:19 1699
to me even your **o** self as well). Phm 1:19 4572
Spirit according to His **o** will. Heb 2:4
sacrifices, first for His **o** sins and Heb 7:27 2398
calves, but through His **o** blood, Heb 9:12 2398
with blood that is not his **o**. Heb 9:25 245
our **o** assembling together, Heb 10:25 1438
are seeking a country of their **o**. Heb 11:14 3968
o birthright for a *single* meal. Heb 12:16 1438
the people through His **o** blood, Heb 13:12 2398
away and enticed by his **o** lust. Jas 1:14 2398
but deceives his **o** heart, Jas 1:26
A PEOPLE FOR *God's* **O** POSSESSION, 1Pe 2:9
be submissive to your **o** husbands 1Pe 3:1 2398
submissive to their **o** husbands; 1Pe 3:5 2398
us by His **o** glory and excellence. 2Pe 1:3 2398
a matter of one's **o** interpretation, 2Pe 1:20 2398
a rebuke for his **o** transgression, 2Pe 2:16 2398
"A DOG RETURNS TO ITS **O** VOMIT," 2Pe 2:22 2398
following after their **o** lusts, 2Pe 3:3 2398
to their **o** destruction. 2Pe 3:16 2398
fall from your **o** steadfastness, 2Pe 3:17 2398
who did not keep their **o** domain, Jude 1:6 1438
casting up their **o** shame like foam; Jude 1:13 1438
following after their **o** lusts; Jude 1:16
following after their **o** ungodly lusts Jude 1:18 1438

OWNED
who had charge of all that he **o**, Gn 24:2
that he **o** he put in his charge. Gn 39:4 3426
his house and over all that he **o**, Gn 39:5 3426
blessing was upon all that he **o**, Gn 39:5 3426
everything he **o** in Joseph's charge; Gn 39:6
struck down those who **o** livestock, 2Ch 14:15 168
he was one who **o** much property. Mt 19:22 2192
he was one who **o** much property. Mk 10:22 2192
of her poverty, put in all she **o**, Mk 12:44 2192
and who **o** a tract of land, sold it Ac 4:37 5225

OWNER
o of the ox shall go unpunished. Ex 21:28 1167
goring and its **o** has been warned, Ex 21:29 1167
its **o** also shall be put to death. Ex 21:29 1167
the **o** shall give his *or her* master Ex 21:32
the **o** of the pit shall make Ex 21:34 1167
he shall give money to its **o**, Ex 21:34 1167
yet its **o** has not confined it, Ex 21:36 1167
then the **o** of the house shall Ex 22:8 1167
and its **o** shall accept *it*, and he Ex 22:11 1167
shall make restitution to its **o**. Ex 22:12 1167
dies while its **o** is not with it, Ex 22:14 1167
"If its **o** is with it, he shall Ex 22:15 1167
they spoke to the **o** of the house, Jg 19:22 1167
Then the man, the **o** of the house, Jg 19:23 1167
name of Shemer, the **o** of the hill. 1Ki 16:24 113
is a charm in the sight of its **o**; Pr 17:8 1167
hoarded by their **o** to his hurt. Ec 5:13 1167
"An ox knows its **o**, And a donkey Is 1:3 7069
the **o** of the vineyard said to his Mt 20:8 2962
when the **o** of the vineyard comes, Mt 21:40 2962
will the **o** of the vineyard do? Mk 12:9 2962
enters, say to the **o** of the house, Mk 14:14 3617
"The **o** of the vineyard said, Lk 20:13 2962
the **o** of the vineyard do to them? Lk 20:15 2962
shall say to the **o** of the house, Lk 22:11 3617
who is not the **o** of the sheep, Jn 10:12 2398
although he is **o** of everything, Ga 4:1 2962

OWNERS
caused its **o** to lose their lives, Jb 31:39 1167
So what is the advantage to their **o** Ec 5:11 1167
to others, Their fields to new **o**; Jer 8:10 3423
the colt, its **o** said to them, Lk 19:33 2962
for all who were **o** of land or Ac 4:34 2935

OWNS
the cave of Machpelah which he **o**, Gn 23:9
put all that he **o** in my charge. Gn 39:8 3426
if he **o** nothing, then he shall be Ex 22:3
then the one who **o** the house shall Lv 14:35
will bind the man who **o** this belt Ac 21:11 1510

OX
or his **o** or his donkey or anything Ex 20:17 7794
'If an **o** gores a man or a Ex 21:28 7794
the **o** shall surely be stoned and Ex 21:28 7794
owner of the **o** shall go unpunished. Ex 21:28 7794
an **o** was previously in the habit Ex 21:29 7794
the **o** shall be stoned and its Ex 21:29 7794
"If the **o** gores a male or female Ex 21:32 7794
silver, and the **o** shall be stoned. Ex 21:32 7794
an **o** or a donkey falls into it, Ex 21:33 7794
"If one man's **o** hurts Ex 21:35 7794
they shall sell the live **o** and divide Ex 21:35 7794
also they shall divide the dead **o**. Ex 21:35
the **o** was previously in the habit Ex 21:36 7794
it, he shall surely pay **o** for ox, Ex 21:36 7794
it, he shall surely pay ox for **o**, Ex 21:36 7794
"If a man steals an **o** or a sheep and Ex 22:1 7794
o and four sheep for the sheep. Ex 22:1 7794
an **o** or a donkey or a sheep, Ex 22:4 7794
of trust, *whether it is* for **o**, Ex 22:9 7794
gives his neighbor a donkey, an **o**, Ex 22:10 7794
o or his donkey wandering away, Ex 23:4 7794
your **o** and your donkey may rest, Ex 23:12 7794
just as it is removed from the **o** Lv 4:10 7794
shall not eat any fat *from* an **o**, Lv 7:23 7794
o and a ram for peace offerings, Lv 9:4 7794
he slaughtered the **o** and the ram, Lv 9:18 7794
fat from the **o** and from the ram, Lv 9:19 7794
of Israel who slaughters an **o** or Lv 17:3 7794
'In respect to an **o** or a lamb Lv 22:23 7794
an **o** or a sheep or a goat is born, Lv 22:27 7794
whether it is an **o** or a sheep, Lv 22:28 7794
whether **o** or sheep, it is the Lv 27:26 7794
the leaders and an **o** for each one, Nu 7:3 7794
'Thus it shall be done for each **o**, Nu 15:11 7794
'But the firstborn of an **o** or Nu 18:17 7794
as the **o** licks up the grass of the Nu 22:4 7794
them like the horns of the wild **o**. Nu 23:22 7214
him like the horns of the wild **o**. Nu 24:8 7214
servant or your **o** or your donkey or Dt 5:14 7794
his **o** or his donkey or anything Dt 5:21 7794
the **o**, the sheep, the goat, Dt 14:4 7794
an **o** or a sheep which has a blemish Dt 17:1 7794
sacrifice, either an **o** or a sheep, Dt 18:3 7794
o or his sheep straying away, Dt 22:1 7794
or his **o** fallen down on the way, Dt 22:4 7794
with an **o** and a donkey together. Dt 22:10 7794
You shall not muzzle the **o** while he is Dt 25:4 7794
"Your **o** shall be slaughtered Dt 28:31 7794
"As the firstborn of his **o**, Dt 33:17 7794
horns are the horns of the wild **o**; Dt 33:17 7214
old, and **o** and sheep and donkey, Jos 6:21 7794
in Israel as well as no sheep, **o**, Jg 6:4 7794
Whose **o** have I taken, or whose 1Sa 12:3 7794
you bring me his **o** or his sheep, 1Sa 14:34 7794
brought each one his **o** with him and 1Sa 14:34 7794
child and infant, **o** and sheep, 1Sa 15:3 7794
he sacrificed an **o** and a fatling. 2Sa 6:13 7794
let them choose one **o** for themselves 1Ki 18:23 6499
and I will prepare the other **o** and 1Ki 18:23 6499
"Choose one **o** for yourselves and 1Ki 18:25 6499
Then they took the **o** which was 1Ki 18:26 6499
cut the **o** in pieces and laid *it* on the 1Ki 18:33 6499
was one **o** *and* six choice sheep, Ne 5:18 7794
Or does the **o** low over his fodder? Jb 6:5 7794
"His **o** mates without fail; Jb 21:10 7794
take the widow's **o** for a pledge. Jb 24:3 7794
the wild **o** consent to serve you, Jb 39:9 7214
the wild **o** in a furrow with ropes, Jb 39:10 7214
He eats grass like an **o**. Jb 40:15 1241
And Sirion like a young wild **o**. Ps 29:6 7214
will please the LORD better than an **o** Ps 69:31 7794
my horn like *that of* the wild **o**; Ps 92:10 7214
the image of an **o** that eats grass. Ps 106:20 7794
As an **o** goes to the slaughter, Pr 7:22 7794
comes by the strength of the **o**. Pr 14:4 7794
a fattened **o** *served* with hatred. Pr 15:17 7794
"An **o** knows its owner, And a Is 1:3 7794
lion will eat straw like the **o**. Is 11:7 1241
out freely the **o** and the donkey. Is 32:20 7794
lion will eat straw like the **o**; Is 65:25 1241
an **o** is *like* one who slays a man; Is 66:3 7794
o or his donkey from the stall and Lk 13:15 1016
a son or an **o** fall into a well, Lk 14:5 1016
"YOU SHALL NOT MUZZLE THE **O** 1Co 9:9 1016
"YOU SHALL NOT MUZZLE THE **O** 1Tm 5:18 1016

OXEN
and gave him sheep and **o** and Gn 12:16 1241
o and male and female servants, Gn 20:14 1241
Abraham took sheep and **o** and Gn 21:27 1241
I have **o** and donkeys *and* Gn 32:5 7794
in their self-will they lamed **o**. Gn 49:6 7794
offerings, your sheep and your **o**; Ex 20:24 1241
he shall pay five **o** for the ox and Ex 22:1 1241
with your **o** *and* with your sheep. Ex 22:30 7794
six covered carts and twelve **o**, Nu 7:3 1241
So Moses took the carts and the **o** and Nu 7:6 1241
Two carts and four **o** he gave to Nu 7:7 1241
o he gave to the sons of Merari, Nu 7:8 1241
sacrifice of peace offerings, two **o**, Nu 7:17 1241
sacrifice of peace offerings, two **o**, Nu 7:23 1241
sacrifice of peace offerings, two **o**, Nu 7:29 1241
sacrifice of peace offerings, two **o**, Nu 7:35 1241
sacrifice of peace offerings, two **o**, Nu 7:41 1241
sacrifice of peace offerings, two **o**, Nu 7:47 1241
sacrifice of peace offerings, two **o**, Nu 7:53 1241
sacrifice of peace offerings, two **o**, Nu 7:59 1241
sacrifice of peace offerings, two **o**, Nu 7:65 1241
sacrifice of peace offerings, two **o**, Nu 7:71 1241
sacrifice of peace offerings, two **o**, Nu 7:77 1241
sacrifice of peace offerings, two **o**, Nu 7:83 1241
all the **o** for the burnt offering Nu 7:87 1241
and all the **o** for the sacrifice of Nu 7:88 1241
Balak sacrificed **o** and sheep, Nu 22:40 1241
your heart desires: for **o**, Dt 14:26 1241
his sons, his daughters, his **o**, Jos 7:24 7794
from the field behind the **o**, 1Sa 11:5 1241
yoke of **o** and cut them in pieces, 1Sa 11:7 1241
so shall it be done to his **o**." 1Sa 11:7 1241
and took sheep and **o** and calves, 1Sa 14:32 1241
and the best of the sheep, the **o**, 1Sa 15:9 1241
lowing of the **o** which I hear?" 1Sa 15:14 1241
the best of the sheep and **o**, 1Sa 15:15 1241
some of the spoil, sheep and **o**, 1Sa 15:21 1241
also **o**, donkeys, and sheep *he* 1Sa 22:19 7794
of it, for the **o** nearly upset *it*. 2Sa 6:6 1241
the **o** for the burnt offering, 2Sa 24:22 1241
the yokes of the **o** for the wood. 2Sa 24:22 1241
the **o** for fifty shekels of silver. 2Sa 24:24 1241
Adonijah sacrificed sheep and **o** 1Ki 1:9 1241
"He has sacrificed **o** and 1Ki 1:19 7794
and has sacrificed **o** and fatlings and 1Ki 1:25 7794
ten fat **o**, twenty pasture-fed 1Ki 4:23 1241
ten fat oxen, twenty pasture-fed **o** 1Ki 4:23 1241
It stood on twelve **o**, 1Ki 7:25 1241
frames *were* lions, **o** and cherubim; 1Ki 7:29 1241
o *were* wreaths of hanging work. 1Ki 7:29 1241
and the twelve **o** under the sea; 1Ki 7:44 1241
sacrificing so many sheep and **o** 1Ki 8:5 1241
LORD, 22,000 **o** and 120,000 sheep. 1Ki 8:63 1241
"Now let them give us two **o**; 1Ki 18:23 6499
was plowing with twelve pairs *of* **o** 1Ki 19:19
o and ran after Elijah and said, 1Ki 19:20 1241
and took the pair of **o** and 1Ki 19:21 1241
with the implements of the **o**, 1Ki 19:21 1241
o and male and female servants? 2Ki 5:26 1241
the bronze **o** which were under it and 2Ki 16:17 1241
donkeys, camels, mules and on **o**, 1Ch 12:40 1241

raisins, wine, oil, **o** and sheep. 1Ch 12:40 1241
because the **o** nearly upset *it.* 1Ch 13:9 1241
I will give the **o** for burnt 1Ch 21:23 1241
Now figures like **o** *were* under it 2Ch 4:3 1241
The **o** *were* in two rows, cast in 2Ch 4:3 1241
It stood on twelve **o**, 2Ch 4:4 1241
sea with the twelve **o** under it. 2Ch 4:15 1241
sacrificing so many sheep and **o** that 2Ch 5:6 1241
offered a sacrifice of 22,000 **o** and 2Ch 7:5 1241
sacrificed to the LORD that day 700 **o** 2Ch 15:11 1241
Ahab slaughtered many sheep and **o** 2Ch 18:2 1241
in the tithe of **o** and sheep, 2Ch 31:6 1241
3,000 camels, 500 yoke of **o**, Jb 1:3 1241
"The **o** were plowing and the Jb 1:14 1241
6,000 camels and 1,000 yoke of **o** Jb 42:12 1241
All sheep and **o**, And also the Ps 8:7 504
of the wild **o** You answer me. Ps 22:21 7214
Where no **o** are, the manger is Pr 14:4 504
o and for sheep to trample. Is 7:25 7794
Also the **o** and the donkeys which Is 30:24 504
Wild **o** will also fall with them Is 34:7 7214
Or does one plow them with **o**? Am 6:12 1241
my **o** and my fattened livestock are Mt 22:4 *5022*
'I have bought five yoke of **o**, Lk 14:19 *1016*
selling **o** and sheep and doves, Jn 2:14 *1016*
temple, with the sheep and the **o**; Jn 2:15 *1016*
brought **o** and garlands to the gates, Ac 14:13 *5022*
God is not concerned about **o**, 1Co 9:9 *1016*

OXGOAD
six hundred Philistines with an **o**; Jg 3:31 4451

OZEM
O the sixth, David the seventh; 1Ch 2:15 684
firstborn, then Bunah, Oren, **O** 1Ch 2:25 684

OZNI
of **O**, the family of the Oznites; Nu 26:16 244a

OZNITES
of Ozni, the family of the **O**; Nu 26:16 244b

P

PAARAI
Hezro the Carmelite, **P** the Arbite, 2Sa 23:35 6474

PACE
according to the **p** of the cattle Gn 33:14 7272
to the **p** of the children, Gn 33:14 7272
do not slow down the **p** for me 2Ki 4:24 7392

PACES
ark of the LORD had gone six **p**, 2Sa 6:13 6806

PACIFIED
I will be **p** and angry no more. Ezk 16:42 8252

PACT
And with Sheol we have made a **p**. Is 28:15 2374
your **p** with Sheol will not stand; Is 28:18 2380

PADDAN
"Now as for me, when I came from **P**, Gn 48:7 6307

PADDAN-ARAM
of Bethuel the Aramean of **P**, Gn 25:20 6307
"Arise, go to **P**, to the house of Gn 28:2 6307
away, and he went to **P** to Laban, Gn 28:5 6307
Jacob and sent him away to **P** to Gn 28:6 6307
and his mother and had gone to **P**. Gn 28:7 6307
which he had gathered in **P**, Gn 31:18 6307
of Canaan, when he came from **P**, Gn 33:18 6307
Jacob again when he came from **P**, Gn 35:9 6307
Jacob who were born to him in **P**. Gn 35:26 6307
Leah, whom she bore to Jacob in **P**, Gn 46:15 6307

PADON
the sons of Siaha, the sons of **P**, Ezr 2:44 6303
the sons of Sia, the sons of **P**, Ne 7:47 6303

PAGAN
the **p** nations that are around you. Lv 25:44

PAGANS
You know that when you were **p**, 1Co 12:2 *1484*

PAGIEL
of Asher, **P** the son of Ochran; Nu 1:13 6295
P the son of Ochran, Nu 2:27 6295
day *it was* **P** the son of Ochran, Nu 7:72 6295
offering of **P** the son of Ochran. Nu 7:77 6295
and **P** the son of Ochran over the Nu 10:26 6295

PAHATH-MOAB
the sons of **P** of the sons of Ezr 2:6 6355
of the sons of **P**, Eliehoenai the Ezr 8:4 6355
and of the sons of **P**: Ezr 10:30 6355
and Hasshub the son of **P** repaired Ne 3:11 6355
the sons of **P** of the sons of Ne 7:11 6355
Parosh, **P**, Elam, Zattu, Bani, Ne 10:14 6355

PAI
and the name of his city was **P**, 1Ch 1:50 6464

PAID
but he who **p** no regard to the word Ex 9:21 7760
answered, and no one **p** attention. 1Ki 18:29 7182
and they **p** it out to the 2Ki 12:11 3318
his servant and **p** him tribute. 2Ki 17:3 7725
The Ammonites also **p** him this 2Ch 27:5 7725
people, but they **p** no attention. 2Ch 33:10 7181
custom and toll were **p** to them. Ezr 4:20 3052
cost be **p** from the royal treasury. Ezr 6:4 3052
the full cost is to be **p** to these Ezr 6:8 3052
p attention to Your commandments Ne 9:34 7181
bowed down and **p** homage to Haman; Es 3:2 7812
neither bowed down nor **p** homage. Es 3:2 7812
bowed down nor **p** homage to him, Es 3:5 7812
"I even **p** close attention to you; Jb 32:12 995
my hand and no one **p** attention; Pr 1:24 7181
Today I have **p** my vows. Pr 7:14 7999a
burned him, but he **p** no attention. Is 42:25 7760
p attention to My commandments! Is 48:18 7181
and lead they **p** for your wares. Ezk 27:12 5414
they **p** for your merchandise. Ezk 27:13 5414
p for your wares with emeralds, Ezk 27:16 5414
balm they **p** for your merchandise. Ezk 27:17 5414
Javan **p** for your wares from Uzal; Ezk 27:19 5414
they **p** for your wares with the Ezk 27:22 5414
was going to Tarshish, **p** the fare and Jon 1:3 5414
until you have **p** up the last cent. Mt 5:26 *591*
"But they **p** no attention and went Mt 22:5 *272*
you have **p** the very last cent." Lk 12:59 *591*
and **p** their respects to Festus. Ac 25:13 *782*
IT MIGHT BE **P** BACK TO HIM AGAIN? Ro 11:35 *467*
who received tithes, **p** tithes, Heb 7:9 *1183*
"Pay her back even as she has **p**, Rv 18:6 *591*

PAILS
make its **p** for removing its ashes, Ex 27:3 5518a
the **p** and the shovels and the Ex 38:3 5518a
p and the shovels and the bowls; 1Ki 7:45 5518a
Huram also made the **p**, 2Ch 4:11 5518a
The **p**, the shovels, the forks and 2Ch 4:16 5518a

PAIN
multiply Your **p** in childbirth, Gn 3:16 6093
In **p** you will bring forth Gn 3:16 6089a
third day, when they were in **p**, Gn 34:25 3510
"Because I bore *him* with **p**." 1Ch 4:9 6090a
from harm that *it* may not **p** me!" 1Ch 4:10 6087a
his own affliction and his own **p**, 2Ch 6:29 4341
sickness and he died in great **p**. 2Ch 21:19 8463
saw that *his* **p** was very great. Jb 2:13 3511
"For He inflicts **p**, and gives relief; Jb 5:18 3510
And I rejoice in unsparing **p**, Jb 6:10 2430b
wicked man writhes in **p** all *his* days, Jb 15:20 2342a
of my lips could lessen *your* **p**. Jb 16:5
"If I speak, my **p** is not lessened, Jb 16:6 3511
also chastened with **p** on his bed, Jb 33:19 4341
And they tell of the **p** of those Ps 69:26 4341
But I am afflicted and in **p**; Ps 69:29 3510
in laughter the heart may be in **p**, Pr 14:13 3510
knowledge *results in* increasing **p**. Ec 1:18 4341
and put away **p** from your body, Ec 11:10 7463a
the LORD gives you rest from your **p** Is 14:3 6090a
day of sickliness and incurable **p**. Is 17:11 3511
Sarah who gave birth to you in **p**; Is 51:2 2342a
Before her **p** came, she gave birth Is 66:7 2256b
us, **P** as of a woman in childbirth. Jer 6:24 2427
Why has my **p** been perpetual And my Jer 15:18 3511
you, **P** like a woman in childbirth! Jer 22:23 2427
Your **p** is incurable. Jer 30:15 4341
the LORD has added sorrow to my **p**; Jer 45:3 4341
Bring balm for her **p**; Jer 51:8 4341
Look and see if there is any **p** La 1:12 4341
and see if there is any pain like my **p** La 1:12 4341
now, all peoples, And behold my **p**; La 1:18 4341
My eyes bring **p** to my soul Because La 3:51 5953a
Gaza too will writhe in great **p**; Zch 9:5 2342a
a woman is in labor she has **p**, Jn 16:21 *3077*
in labor and in **p** to give birth. Rv 12:2 *928*
gnawed their tongues because of **p**, Rv 16:10 *4192*
be *any* mourning, or crying, or **p**; Rv 21:4 *4192*

PAINED
God, And **p** the Holy One of Israel. Ps 78:41 8428

PAINFUL
"How **p** are honest words! Jb 6:25 4834
To eat the bread of **p** labors; Ps 127:2 6089a
days his task is **p** and grievous; Ec 2:23 4341
a prickling brier or a **p** thorn Ezk 28:24 3510
on destruction, A **p** destruction. Mi 2:10 4834

PAINS
birth, for her **p** came upon her. 1Sa 4:19 6735c
with great **p** I have prepared for 1Ch 22:14 6040a
Death rather than my **p**. Jb 7:15 6106
I am afraid of all my **p**, Jb 9:28 6094
"But his body **p** him, And he Jb 14:22 3510
And my gnawing **p** take no rest. Jb 30:17
They get rid of their labor **p**. Jb 39:3 2256b
For there are no **p** in their death, Ps 73:4 2784
P and anguish will take hold of Is 13:8 6735c
P have seized me like the pains of Is 21:3 6735c
me like the **p** of a woman in labor. Is 21:3 6735c
and cries out in her labor **p**, Is 26:17 2256b
The **p** of childbirth come upon him; Hos 13:13 2256b
suffering with various diseases and **p**, Mt 4:24 *931*
groans and suffers the **p** of childbirth Ro 8:22 *4944*
come upon them suddenly like labor **p** 1Th 5:3 *5604*
Take **p** with these things; 1Tm 4:15 *3191*
because of their **p** and their sores; Rv 16:11 *4192*

PAINT
you enlarge your eyes with **p**, Jer 4:30 6320

PAINTED
p her eyes and adorned her head and 2Ki 9:30 7760, 6320
whom you bathed, **p** your eyes and Ezk 23:40 3583

PAINTING
with cedar and **p** *it* bright red.' Jer 22:14 4886

PAIR
p of branches *coming* out of it, Ex 25:35 8147
p of branches *coming* out of it, Ex 25:35 8147
p of branches *coming* out of it, Ex 25:35 8147
p of branches *coming* out of it, Ex 37:21 8147
p of branches *coming* out of it, Ex 37:21 8147
p of branches *coming* out of it, Ex 37:21 8147
his servant and a **p** of donkeys. Jg 19:3 6776
with him a **p** of saddled donkeys; Jg 19:10 6776
and took the **p** of oxen and 1Ki 19:21 6776
alive a heifer and a **p** of sheep; Is 7:21 8147
And the hills in a **p** of scales? Is 40:12
And the needy for a **p** of sandals. Am 2:6
And the needy for a **p** of sandals, Am 8:6
A **P** OF TURTLEDOVES OR TWO YOUNG Lk 2:24 *2201*
it had a **p** of scales in his hand. Rv 6:5 *2218*

PAIRS
with twelve **p** *of oxen* before him, 1Ki 19:19 6776
he sees riders, horsemen in **p**, Is 21:7 6776
troop of riders, horsemen in **p**." Is 21:9 6776
and began to send them out in **p**, Mk 6:7 *1417*
and sent them in **p** ahead of Him to Lk 10:1 *1417*

PALACE
the **p** of Ahab king of Samaria. 1Ki 21:1 1964
the **p** of the king of Babylon.' " 2Ki 20:18 1964
LORD and a royal **p** for himself. 2Ch 2:1 1004
LORD and a royal **p** for himself. 2Ch 2:12 1004
house of the LORD and the king's **p**, 2Ch 7:11 1004
house of the LORD and in his **p**. 2Ch 7:11 1004
of the LORD and for the king's **p**, 2Ch 9:11 1004
and the treasures of the king's **p**. 2Ch 12:9 1004
out of the **p** of the king and of the 2Ch 28:21 1004
we are in the service of the **p**, Ezr 4:14 1965
of the garden of the king's **p**. Es 1:5 1055
a banquet for the women in the **p** Es 1:9 1004
Esther was taken to the king's **p** Es 2:8 1004
choice maids from the king's **p** and Es 2:9 1004
her from the harem to the king's **p**. Es 2:13 1004
to King Ahasuerus to his royal **p** Es 2:16 1004
that you in the king's **p** can escape Es 4:13 1004
in the inner court of the king's **p** Es 5:1 1004
opposite the entrance to the **p**. Es 5:1 1004
entered the outer court of the king's **p** Es 6:4 1004
wine *and went* into the **p** garden; Es 7:7 1055
the king returned from the **p** garden Es 7:8 1055
They will enter into the King's **p**. Ps 45:15 1964
pillars fashioned as for a **p**; Ps 144:12 1964
A **p** of strangers is a city no Is 25:2 759
Because the **p** has been abandoned, Is 32:14 759
the **p** of the king of Babylon.' " Is 39:7 1964
And the **p** will stand on its Jer 30:18 759
and in his **p** the king secretly Jer 37:17 1004
while he was in the king's **p**, Jer 38:7 1004
went out from the king's **p** Jer 38:8 1004
and went into the king's **p** to *a place* Jer 38:11 1004
women who have been left in the **p** Jer 38:22 1004
also burned with fire the king's **p** Jer 39:8 1004
of Pharaoh's **p** in Tahpanhes, Jer 43:9 1004
my house and flourishing in my **p**. Da 4:4 1965
roof of the royal **p** of Babylon. Da 4:29 1965
of the wall of the king's **p**, Da 5:5 1965
his **p** and spent the night fasting, Da 6:18 1965
"The songs of the **p** will turn to Am 8:3 1964
opened And the **p** is dissolved. Na 2:6 1964
soldiers took Him away into the **p** Mk 15:16 *833*

PALACES
Out of ivory **p** stringed Ps 45:8 1964
God, in her **p**, Has made Himself Ps 48:3 759
Go through her **p**, Ps 48:13 759
And prosperity within your **p**." Ps 122:7 759
the hands, Yet it is in kings' **p**. Pr 30:28 1964
And jackals in their luxurious **p**. Is 13:22 1964
siege towers, they stripped its **p**, Is 23:13 759
by night And destroy her **p**!" Jer 6:5 759
It has entered our **p** To cut off Jer 9:21 759
it will devour the **p** of Jerusalem Jer 17:27 759
He has swallowed up all its **p**, La 2:5 759
of the enemy The walls of her **p**. La 2:7 759
forgotten his Maker and built **p**; Hos 8:14 1964
soft *clothing* are in kings' **p**! Mt 11:8 *3624*
in luxury are *found* in royal **p**! Lk 7:25 *933*

PALAL
P the son of Uzai *made repairs* in Ne 3:25 6420

PALATE
Cannot my **p** discern calamities? Jb 6:30 2441
words, As the **p** tastes its food? Jb 12:11 2441
And their tongue stuck to their **p**. Jb 29:10 2441
tests words As the **p** tastes food. Jb 34:3 2441

PALATIAL
it may consume its **p** dwellings. Hos 8:14 759

PALE
nor shall his face now turn **p**; Is 29:22 2357
And *why* have all faces turned **p**? Jer 30:6 3420
Then the king's face grew **p** and Da 5:6 8133
alarm you or your face be **p**. Da 5:10 8133
alarming me and my face grew **p**, Da 7:28 8133
All faces turn **p**. Jl 2:6 6289
And all their faces are grown **p**! Na 2:10 6289

PALER
alarmed, his face grew *even* **p**, Da 5:9 8133

PALLET
they let down the **p** on which the Mk 2:4 *2895*
and pick up your **p** and walk'? Mk 2:9 *2895*
pick up your **p** and go home." Mk 2:11 *2895*
got up and immediately picked up the **p** Mk 2:12 *2895*
"Get up, pick up your **p** and walk." Jn 5:8 *2895*
picked up his **p** and *began* to walk. Jn 5:9 *2895*
for you to carry your **p**." Jn 5:10 *2895*
'Pick up your **p** and walk.' " Jn 5:11 *2895*
'Pick up *your* **p** and walk'?" Jn 5:12

PALLETS
to carry here and there on their **p** Mk 6:55 *2895*
and laid them on cots and **p**, Ac 5:15 *2895*

PALLOR
color turned to a deathly **p**, Da 10:8 4889

PALLU
Hanoch and **P** and Hezron and Carmi. Gn 46:9 6396
Hanoch and **P**, Hezron and Carmi; Ex 6:14 6396
of **P**, the family of the Palluites; Nu 26:5 6396
The son of **P**: Nu 26:8 6396
of Israel *were* Hanoch and **P**, 1Ch 5:3 6396

PALLUITES
of Pallu, the family of the **P**; Nu 26:5 6384a

PALM
oil, and pour *it* into his left **p**; Lv 14:15 3709
the oil that is in his left **p**, Lv 14:16 3709
remaining oil which is in his **p**, Lv 14:17 3709
the oil that is in the priest's **p**, Lv 14:18 3709
some of the oil into his left **p**; Lv 14:26 3709
some of the oil that is in his left **p** Lv 14:27 3709
oil that is in his **p** on the lobe of the Lv 14:28 3709
the oil that is in the priest's **p** he shall Lv 14:29 3709
p branches and boughs of leafy Lv 23:40 8558
of water and seventy **p** trees, Nu 33:9 8558
of Jericho, the city of **p** trees, Dt 34:3 8558
possessed the city of the **p** trees. Jg 3:13 8558
to sit under the **p** tree of Deborah Jg 4:5 8560
engravings of cherubim, **p** trees, 1Ki 6:29 8561
carvings of cherubim, **p** trees, 1Ki 6:32 8561
the cherubim and on the **p** trees. 1Ki 6:32 8561
He carved *on it* cherubim, **p** trees, 1Ki 6:35 8561
cherubim, lions and **p** trees, 1Ki 7:36 8561
and ornamented it with **p** trees and 2Ch 3:5 8561
to Jericho, the city of **p** trees, 2Ch 28:15 8558
myrtle branches, **p** branches and Ne 8:15 8558
his **p** branch will not be green. Jb 15:32 3712
man will flourish like the **p** tree, Ps 92:12 8558
"Your stature is like a **p** tree, SS 7:7 8558
'I will climb the **p** tree, SS 7:8 8558
Both **p** branch and bulrush in a Is 9:14 3712
or tail, *its* **p** branch or bulrush, Is 19:15 3712
side pillar *were* **p** tree ornaments. Ezk 40:16 8561
and its **p** tree ornaments *had* the Ezk 40:22 8561
and it had **p** tree ornaments on its Ezk 40:26 8561
and **p** tree ornaments *were* on its Ezk 40:31 8561
and **p** tree ornaments *were* on its Ezk 40:34 8561
and **p** tree ornaments *were* on its Ezk 40:37 8561
carved with cherubim and **p** trees; Ezk 41:18 8561
and a **p** tree was between cherub Ezk 41:18 8561
toward the **p** tree on one side and Ezk 41:19 8561
the **p** tree on the other side; Ezk 41:19 8561
cherubim and **p** trees were carved, Ezk 41:20 8561
cherubim and **p** trees like those Ezk 41:25 8561
were latticed windows and **p** trees Ezk 41:26 8561
The pomegranate, the **p** also, Jl 1:12 8558
took the branches of the **p** trees and Jn 12:13 *5404*
p branches *were* in their hands; Rv 7:9 *5404*

PALMS
of water and seventy date **p**, Ex 15:27 8558
city of **p** with the sons of Judah, Jg 1:16 8558
both the **p** of his hands *were* cut off 1Sa 5:4 3709
the feet and the **p** of her hands. 2Ki 9:35 3709
inscribed you on the **p** *of My hands;* Is 49:16 3709

PALTI
of Benjamin, **P** the son of Raphu; Nu 13:9 6406
wife, to **P** the son of Laish, 1Sa 25:44 6406

PALTIEL
a leader, **P** the son of Azzan. Nu 34:26 6409
husband, from **P** the son of Laish. 2Sa 3:15 6409

PALTITE
Helez the **P**, Ira the son of Ikkesh 2Sa 23:26 6407

PAMPERS
He who **p** his slave from childhood Pr 29:21 6445

PAMPHYLIA
Phrygia and **P**, Egypt and the Ac 2:10 *3828*
Paphos and came to Perga in **P**; Ac 13:13 *3828*
through Pisidia and came into **P**. Ac 14:24 *3828*
who had deserted them in **P** and had Ac 15:38 *3828*
along the coast of Cilicia and **P**, Ac 27:5 *3828*

PAN
is a grain offering *made* in a **p**, Lv 2:7 4802
prepared in a **p** or on a griddle shall Lv 7:9 4802
one gold **p** of ten *shekels,* full of Nu 7:14 3709
one gold **p** of ten *shekels,* full of Nu 7:20 3709
one gold **p** of ten *shekels,* full of Nu 7:26 3709
one gold **p** of ten *shekels,* full of Nu 7:32 3709
one gold **p** of ten *shekels,* full of Nu 7:38 3709
one gold **p** of ten *shekels,* full of Nu 7:44 3709
one gold **p** of ten *shekels,* full of Nu 7:50 3709
one gold **p** of ten *shekels,* full of Nu 7:56 3709
one gold **p** of ten *shekels,* full of Nu 7:62 3709
one gold **p** of ten *shekels,* full of Nu 7:68 3709
one gold **p** of ten *shekels,* full of Nu 7:74 3709
one gold **p** of ten *shekels,* full of Nu 7:80 3709
he would thrust it into the **p**, 1Sa 2:14 3595
She took the **p** and dished *them* 2Sa 13:9 4958
wafers, or *what is baked in* the **p** or 1Ch 23:29 4227

PANELED
It was **p** with cedar above the 1Ki 7:3 5603
and it was **p** with cedar from floor 1Ki 7:7 5603
were **p** with wood all around, Ezk 41:16 7824
to dwell in your **p** houses while this Hg 1:4 5603

PANELING
P *it* with cedar and painting *it* Jer 22:14 5603

PANGS
Will not **p** take hold of you Like Jer 13:21 2256b
will groan when **p** come upon you, Jer 22:23 2256b
Distress and **p** have taken hold of Jer 49:24 2256b
merely the beginning of birth **p**. Mt 24:8 *5604*
merely the beginning of birth **p**. Mk 13:8 *5604*

PANIC
Do not be afraid, or **p**, Dt 20:3 2648
P seized them there, Anguish, as Ps 48:6 7461b
Lord GOD of hosts has a day of **p**, Is 22:5 4103
rock will pass away because of **p**, Is 31:9 4032
to flee, And **p** has gripped her; Jer 49:24 7374
P and pitfall have befallen us, La 3:47 6343
a great **p** from the LORD will fall on Zch 14:13 4103

PANS
its **p** and its jars and its bowls with Ex 25:29 3709
its **p** and its bowls and its jars, Ex 37:16 3709
and put on it the dishes and the **p** Nu 4:7 3709
silver bowls, twelve gold **p**, Nu 7:84 3709
the twelve gold **p**, full of Nu 7:86 3709
all the gold of the **p** 120 *shekels;* Nu 7:86 3709
the things which were baked in **p**. 1Ch 9:31 2281
and **p** and utensils of gold and 2Ch 24:14 3709
things in pots, in kettles, in **p**, 2Ch 35:13 6745
the snuffers, the basins, the **p** and Jer 52:18 3709
the **p** and the drink offering bowls, Jer 52:19 3709

PANT
groan, I will both gasp and **p**. Is 42:14 7602a
They **p** for air like jackals, Their Jer 14:6 7602a
beasts of the field **p** for You; Jl 1:20 6165
"These who **p** after the *very* dust Am 2:7 7602b

PANTED
I opened my mouth wide and **p**, Ps 119:131 7602a

PANTS
"As a slave who **p** for the shade, Jb 7:2 7602a
As the deer **p** for the water brooks, Ps 42:1 6165
brooks, So my soul **p** for You, Ps 42:1 6165

PAPER
not want to *do so* with **p** and ink; 2Jn 1:12 *5489*

PAPHOS
the whole island as far as **P**, Ac 13:6 *3974*
companions put out to sea from **P** Ac 13:13 *3974*

PAPYRUS
"Can the **p** grow up without a marsh? Jb 8:11 1573
Even in **p** vessels on the surface Is 18:2 1573

PARABLE
I will open my mouth in a **p**; Ps 78:2 4912
speak a **p** to the house of Israel, Ezk 17:2 4912
Speak a **p** to the rebellious house Ezk 24:3 4912
"Hear then the **p** of the sower. Mt 13:18 *3850b*
Jesus presented another **p** to them, Mt 13:24 *3850b*
He presented another **p** to them, Mt 13:31 *3850b*
He spoke another **p** to them, Mt 13:33 *3850b*
did not speak to them without a **p**. Mt 13:34 *3850b*
the **p** of the tares of the field." Mt 13:36 *3850b*
"Explain the **p** to us." Mt 15:15 *3850b*
"Listen to another **p**. Mt 21:33 *3850b*
"Now learn the **p** from the fig tree: Mt 24:32 *3850b*
"Do you not understand this **p**? Mk 4:13 *3850b*
or by what **p** shall we present it? Mk 4:30 *3850b*
did not speak to them without a **p**; Mk 4:34 *3850b*
questioned Him about the **p**. Mk 7:17 *3850b*
that He spoke the **p** against them. Mk 12:12 *3850b*
"Now learn the **p** from the fig tree: Mk 13:28 *3850b*
And He was also telling them a **p**: Lk 5:36 *3850b*
And He also spoke a **p** to them: Lk 6:39 *3850b*
to Him, He spoke by way of a **p**: Lk 8:4 *3850b*
Him as to what this **p** meant. Lk 8:9 *3850b*
"Now the **p** is this: Lk 8:11 *3850b*
And He told them a **p**, Lk 12:16 *3850b*
are You addressing this **p** to us, Lk 12:41 *3850b*
And He *began* telling this **p**: Lk 13:6 *3850b*
And He *began* speaking a **p** to the Lk 14:7 *3850b*
So He told them this **p**, Lk 15:3 *3850b*
Now He was telling them a **p** to Lk 18:1 *3850b*
And He also told this **p** to some Lk 18:9 *3850b*
things, Jesus went on to tell a **p**, Lk 19:11 *3850b*
began to tell the people this **p**: Lk 20:9 *3850b*
that He spoke this **p** against them. Lk 20:19 *3850b*
Then He told them a **p**: Lk 21:29 *3850b*

PARABLES
'Is he not *just* speaking **p**?' " Ezk 20:49 4912
And through the prophets I gave **p**. Hos 12:10 1819
He spoke many things to them in **p**, Mt 13:3 *3850b*
"Why do You speak to them in **p**?" Mt 13:10 *3850b*
"Therefore I speak to them in **p**; Mt 13:13 *3850b*
spoke to the crowds in **p**, Mt 13:34 *3850b*
"I WILL OPEN MY MOUTH IN **P**; Mt 13:35 *3850b*
When Jesus had finished these **p**, Mt 13:53 *3850b*
and the Pharisees heard His **p**, Mt 21:45 *3850b*
Jesus spoke to them again in **p**, Mt 22:1 *3850b*
and began speaking to them in **p**, Mk 3:23 *3850b*
teaching them many things in **p**, Mk 4:2 *3850b*
began asking Him *about* the **p**. Mk 4:10 *3850b*
are outside get everything in **p**, Mk 4:11 *3850b*
How will you understand all the **p**? Mk 4:13 *3850b*
With many such **p** He was speaking Mk 4:33 *3850b*
He began to speak to them in **p**: Mk 12:1 *3850b*
God, but to the rest *it is* in **p**, Lk 8:10 *3850b*

PARADES
their tongue **p** through the earth. Ps 73:9 1980

PARADISE
today you shall be with Me in **P**." Lk 23:43 *3857*
was caught up into **P** and 2Co 12:4 *3857*
life which is in the **P** of God.' Rv 2:7 *3857*

PARAH
and Avvim and **P** and Ophrah, Jos 18:23 6511

PARALLEL
went along on the hillside **p** with him 2Sa 16:13 5980

PARALYTIC
they brought to Him a **p** Mt 9:2 *3885*
Seeing their faith, Jesus said to the **p**, Mt 9:2 *3885*
then He said to the **p**, Mt 9:6 *3885*
they came, bringing to Him a **p**, Mk 2:3 *3885*
pallet on which the **p** was lying. Mk 2:4 *3885*
seeing their faith said to the **p**, Mk 2:5 *3885*
"Which is easier, to say to the **p**, Mk 2:9 *3885*
He said to the **p**, Mk 2:10 *3885*
He said to the **p** Lk 5:24 *3886*

PARALYTICS
pains, demoniacs, epileptics, **p**; Mt 4:24 *3885*

PARALYZED
my servant is lying **p** at home, Mt 8:6 *3885*
carrying on a bed a man who was **p**; Lk 5:18 *3886*
many who had been **p** and lame Ac 8:7 *3886*
eight years, for he was **p**. Ac 9:33 *3886*

PARAMOURS
"She lusted after their **p**, Ezk 23:20 6370

PARAN
He lived in the wilderness of **P** Gn 21:21 6290
down in the wilderness of **P**. Nu 10:12 6290
and camped in the wilderness of **P**. Nu 12:16 6290
of **P** at the command of the LORD, Nu 13:3 6290
of Israel in the wilderness of **P**, Nu 13:26 6290
between **P** and Tophel and Laban and Dt 1:1 6290
He shone forth from Mount **P**, Dt 33:2 6290
went down to the wilderness of **P**. 1Sa 25:1 6290
arose from Midian and came to **P**; 1Ki 11:18 6290
they took men with them from **P** 1Ki 11:18 6290
And the Holy One from Mount **P**. Hab 3:3 6290

PARAPET
you shall make a **p** for your roof, Dt 22:8 4624

PARBAR
At the **P** on the west *there were* 1Ch 26:18 6503
at the highway and two at the **P**. 1Ch 26:18 6503

PARCEL
and will **p** out land for a price. Da 11:39 2505a
near the **p** of ground that Jacob Jn 4:5 *5564*

PARCELED
kingdom will be broken up and **p** out Da 11:4 2673
your land will be **p** up by a Am 7:17 2505a

PARCHED
unleavened cakes and **p** *grain.* Jos 5:11 7033
wheat, barley, flour, **p** *grain,* 2Sa 17:28 7039
grain, beans, lentils, **p** *seeds,* 2Sa 17:28 7039
a river becomes **p** and dried up, Jb 14:11 2717a
the rebellious dwell in a **p** land. Ps 68:6 6707
Your inheritance when it was **p**. Ps 68:9 3811
my throat is **p**; My eyes fail while I Ps 69:3 2787
My soul *longs* for You, as a **p** land. Ps 143:6 5889
their multitude is **p** with thirst. Is 5:13 6704
And the river will be **p** and dry. Is 19:5 2717a
shade of a huge rock in a **p** land. Is 32:2 5889
And their tongue is **p** with thirst; Is 41:17 5405
And like a root out of **p** ground; Is 53:2 6723
glory And sit on the **p** ground, Jer 48:18 6772
A wilderness, a **p** land and a desert. Jer 50:12 6723
of horror, A **p** land and a desert, Jer 51:43 6723
it into a **p** and desolate land, Jl 2:20 6723
desolation, **P** like the wilderness. Zph 2:13 6723

PARCHMENTS
and the books, especially the **p**. 2Tm 4:13 *3200*

PARDON
he will not **p** your transgression, Ex 23:21 5375
and **p** our iniquity and our sin, Ex 34:9 5545
"**P**, I pray, the iniquity of this Nu 14:19 5545
p my sin and return with me, 1Sa 15:25 5545
may the LORD **p** your servant: 2Ki 5:18 5545
the LORD **p** your servant in 2Ki 5:18 5545
"May the good LORD **p** 2Ch 30:18 3722a
"Why then do You not **p** my Jb 7:21 5375
name's sake, O LORD, **P** my iniquity, Ps 25:11 5545
our God, For He will abundantly **p**. Is 55:7 5545
seeks truth, Then I will **p** her. Jer 5:1 5545
"Why should I **p** you? Jer 5:7 5545
and I will **p** all their iniquities Jer 33:8 5545
for I will **p** those whom I leave Jer 50:20 5545
"Lord GOD, please **p**! Am 7:2 5545
p, and you will be pardoned. Lk 6:37 *630*

PARDONED
p *them* according to your word; Nu 14:20 5545
and rebelled, You have not **p**. La 3:42 5545
pardon, and you will be **p**. Lk 6:37 *630*

PARDONING
full price of the **p** of his sin: Is 27:9 5493

PARDONS
Who **p** all your iniquities, Ps 103:3 5545
who **p** iniquity And passes over the Mi 7:18 5375

PARENTS
children will rise up against **p** and Mt 10:21 *1118*
children will rise up against **p** Mk 13:12 *1118*
the **p** brought in the child Jesus, Lk 2:27 *1118*
Now His **p** went to Jerusalem Lk 2:41 *1118*
But His **p** were unaware of it, Lk 2:43 *1118*
Her **p** were amazed; Lk 8:56 *1118*
wife or brothers or **p** or children, Lk 18:29 *1118*
you will be betrayed even by **p** Lk 21:16 *1118*
who sinned, this man or his **p**, Jn 9:2 *1118*
that this man sinned, nor his **p**; Jn 9:3 *1118*
until they called the **p** of the Jn 9:18 *1118*
His **p** answered them and said, Jn 9:20 *1118*
His **p** said this because they were Jn 9:22 *1118*
For this reason his **p** said, Jn 9:23 *1118*
of evil, disobedient to **p**, Ro 1:30 *1118*
to save up for *their* **p**, 2Co 12:14 *1118*
parents, but **p** for *their* children. 2Co 12:14 *1118*
Children, obey your **p** in the Lord, Eph 6:1 *1118*
obedient to your **p** in all things, Col 3:20 *1118*

to make some return to their **p**; **1Tm 5:4** *4269*
reviles, disobedient to **p**, **2Tm 3:2** *1118*
hidden for three months by his **p**, **Heb 11:23** *3962*
PARKS
I made gardens and **p** for myself and **Ec 2:5** 6508
PARMASHTA
P, Arisai, Aridai and Vaizatha, **Es 9:9** 6534
PARMENAS
Nicanor, Timon, **P** and Nicolas, **Ac 6:5** *3937*
PARNACH
a leader, Elizaphan the son of **P**. **Nu 34:25** 6535
PAROSH
the sons of **P**, 2,172; **Ezr 2:3** 6551
who was of the sons of **P**, **Ezr 8:3** 6551
the sons of **P** *there were* Ramiah, **Ezr 10:25** 6551
Pedaiah the son of **P** *made repairs.* **Ne 3:25** 6551
the sons of **P**, 2,172; **Ne 7:8** 6551
P, Pahath-moab, Elam, Zattu, Bani, **Ne 10:14** 6551
PARSHANDATHA
and **P**, Dalphon, Aspatha, **Es 9:7** 6577
PART
Abel, on his **p** also brought of the **Gn 4:4** 1571
and on the smooth **p** of his neck. **Gn 27:16** 2513b
some left **p** of it until morning, **Ex 16:20**
"The overlapping **p** that is **Ex 26:12** 5629
there shall be an equal **p** of each. **Ex 30:34** 905
and put **p** of it before the **Ex 30:36**
p of its grits and its oil with **Lv 2:16**
shall add to it a fifth **p** of it and **Lv 5:16** 2549
on which **p** of their carcass may **Lv 11:35**
'If a **p** of their carcass falls **Lv 11:37**
a **p** of their carcass falls on it, **Lv 11:38**
he has to sell **p** of his property, **Lv 25:25**
he shall refund **p** of his purchase **Lv 25:51**
man consecrates to the LORD **p** of the **Lv 27:16**
which is not a **p** of the field of **Lv 27:22**
wishes to redeem **p** of his tithe, **Lv 27:31**
every tenth **p** of herd or flock, **Lv 27:32** 4643
sons of Anak are **p** of the Nephilim) **Nu 13:33**
of them, the sacred **p** from them.' **Nu 18:29** 4720
Or number the fourth **p** of Israel? **Nu 23:10** 7255
burns to the lowest **p** of Sheol, **Dt 32:22** 8482
"Then he provided the first **p** **Dt 33:21**
from the highest **p** of the land, **Jg 9:37** 2872
Levite staying in the remote **p** of the **Jg 19:1** 3411
p of the hill country of Ephraim, **Jg 19:18** 3411
come out to take **p** in the dances, **Jg 21:21** 2342a
and our **p** *shall be* to surrender **1Sa 23:20**
by the hidden **p** of the mountain, **1Sa 25:20** 5643a
(for Beeroth is also considered **p** **2Sa 4:2**
to you on the **p** of the king." **2Sa 15:3**
4480, 854
He built twenty cubits on the rear **p** **1Ki 6:16** 3411
were **p** of the stand itself. **1Ki 7:34**
and its borders *were* **p** of it. **1Ki 7:35** 4480
on your **p** to set riders on them. **2Ki 18:23**
for until now the greatest **p** of them **1Ch 12:29** 4768
They dedicated **p** of the spoil won **1Ch 26:27**
will have no **p** in unrighteousness or **2Ch 19:7**
So the priests went in to the inner **p** **2Ch 29:16** 6441
the most remote **p** of the heavens, **Ne 1:9** 7097a
also the hundredth **p** of the money **Ne 5:11**
God forgets a **p** of your iniquity. **Jb 11:6**
inward **p** is destruction *itself.* **Ps 5:9** 7130
And in the hidden **p** You will **Ps 51:6** 5640
I dwell in the remotest **p** of the sea, **Ps 139:9** 319
remotest **p** of the rivers of Egypt and **Is 7:18** 7097a
on your **p** to set riders on them. **Is 36:8**
They for their **p** may turn to you, **Jer 15:19** 1992a
the sixth **p** of a hin by measure; **Ezk 4:11** 8345
and its middle **p** has been charred, **Ezk 15:4** 8432
"But if you on your **p** warn a **Ezk 33:9** 859
"It shall be the prince's **p** **Ezk 45:17** 5921
and **p** of it will be brittle. **Da 2:42** 4481
and he on his **p** will refrain from **Da 11:8** 1931
One **p** would be rained on, While **Am 4:7** 2513a
the **p** not rained on would dry up. **Am 4:7** 2513a
in the innermost **p** of the house, **Am 6:10** 3411
the third **p** through the fire, **Zch 13:9** 7992
With such an offering on your **p**, **Mal 1:9** 3027
for Mary has chosen the good **p**, **Lk 10:42** *3310*
of light, with no dark **p** in it, **Lk 11:36** *3313*
flashes out of one **p** of the sky, **Lk 17:24**
shines to the other **p** of the sky, **Lk 17:24**
But Jesus, on His **p**, **Jn 2:24** *846*
discussion on the **p** of John's disciples **Jn 3:25**
wash you, you have no **p** with Me." **Jn 13:8** *3313*
made four parts, a **p** to every soldier **Jn 19:23** *3313*
to the remotest **p** of the earth." **Ac 1:8** *2078*
on the **p** of the Hellenistic *Jews* **Ac 6:1**
no **p** or portion in this matter, **Ac 8:21** *3310*
and we for our **p** are ready to slay **Ac 23:15**
So, for my **p**, I am eager to **Ro 1:15** *1473*
For I, on my **p**, though absent in **1Co 5:3** *1473*
and in **p** I believe it. **1Co 11:18** *3313*
I am not *a* **p** of the body," it **1Co 12:15**
for this reason any the less *a* **p** **1Co 12:15**
I am not *a* **p** of the body," it **1Co 12:16**
for this reason any the less *a* **p** **1Co 12:16**
For we know in **p** and we prophesy **1Co 13:9** *3313*
in part and we prophesy in **p**; **1Co 13:9** *3313*
now I know in **p**, but then I will **1Co 13:12** *3313*
what was lacking on your **p**. **1Co 16:17**
working of each individual **p**, **Eph 4:16** *3313*
for your **p** read my letter *that is* **Col 4:16**
a tenth **p** of all *the spoils,* **Heb 7:2** *1181*
tongue is a small **p** of the body, **Jas 3:5** *3196*
has a **p** in the first resurrection; **Rv 20:6** *3313*
their **p** *will be* in the lake that burns **Rv 21:8** *3313*
God will take away his **p** from the **Rv 22:19** *3313*
PARTAKE
for we all **p** of the one bread. **1Co 10:17** *3348*
cannot **p** of the table of the Lord **1Co 10:21** *3348*
If I **p** with thankfulness, why am I **1Co 10:30** *3348*
because those who **p** of the benefit **1Tm 6:2** *482*
PARTAKER
became **p** with them of the rich root **Ro 11:17** *4791*
I may become a fellow **p** of it. **1Co 9:23** *4791*
and a **p** also of the glory that is **1Pe 5:1** *2844*
fellow **p** in the tribulation and **Rv 1:9** *4791*
PARTAKERS
fellow **p** of the promise in Christ **Eph 3:6** *4830*
Therefore do not be **p** with them; **Eph 5:7** *4830*
you all are **p** of grace with me. **Php 1:7** *4791*
brethren, **p** of a heavenly calling, **Heb 3:1** *3353*
For we have become **p** of Christ, **Heb 3:14** *3353*
been made **p** of the Holy Spirit, **Heb 6:4** *3353*
of which all have become **p**, **Heb 12:8** *3353*
become **p** of *the* divine nature, **2Pe 1:4** *2844*
PARTAKES
For everyone who **p** *only* of milk is **Heb 5:13** *3348*
PARTED
in their death they were not **p**; **2Sa 1:23** 6504
was blessing them, He **p** from them and **Lk 24:51** *1339*
had **p** from them and had set sail, **Ac 21:1** *645*
PARTHIANS
"**P** and Medes and Elamites, and **Ac 2:9** *3934*
PARTIAL
be **p** to a poor man in his dispute. **Ex 23:3** 1921
you shall not be **p** to the poor nor **Lv 19:15**
5375, 6440
you shall not be **p**, **Dt 16:19**
5234, 6440
"Let me now be **p** to no one, **Jb 32:21**
5375, 6440
for You are not **p** to any. **Mt 22:16**
991, 4383
for You are not **p** to any, but **Mk 12:14**
991, 4383
and You are not **p** to any, **Lk 20:21**
2983, 4383
p hardening has happened to Israel **Ro 11:25** *3313*
comes, the **p** will be done away. **1Co 13:10** *3313*
PARTIALITY
'You shall not show **p** in judgment; **Dt 1:17**
5234, 6440
awesome God who does not show **p** nor **Dt 10:17**
5375, 6440
no part in unrighteousness or **p** **2Ch 19:7**
5375, 6440
"Will you show **p** for Him? **Jb 13:8**
6440, 5375
you If you secretly show **p**. **Jb 13:10**
6440, 5375
Who shows no **p** to princes Nor **Jb 34:19**
5375, 6440
And show **p** to the wicked? **Ps 82:2**
6440, 5375
show **p** to the wicked is not good, **Pr 18:5**
5375, 6440
To show **p** in judgment is not good. **Pr 24:23**
5234, 6440
To show **p** is not good, Because for **Pr 28:21**
5234, 6440
are showing **p** in the instruction. **Mal 2:9**
5375, 6440
now that God is not one to show **p**, **Ac 10:34** *4381*
For there is no **p** with God. **Ro 2:11** *4382*
God shows no **p**) **Ga 2:6** *4383*
and there is no **p** with Him. **Eph 6:9** *4382*
he has done, and that without **p**. **Col 3:25** *4382*
doing nothing in a *spirit of* **p**. **1Tm 5:21** *4346b*
But if you show **p**, you are **Jas 2:9** *4380*
PARTIALLY
as you also **p** did understand us, **2Co 1:14** *3313*
PARTICIPATE
Do not **p** in the unfruitful deeds **Eph 5:11** *4790*
that you will not **p** in her sins and **Rv 18:4** *4790*
PARTICIPATES
a greeting **p** in his evil deeds. **2Jn 1:11** *2841*
PARTICIPATION
of **p** in the support of the saints, **2Co 8:4** *2842*
in view of your **p** in the gospel **Php 1:5** *2842*
PARTICULAR
to that **p** one who was speaking, **Da 8:13** 6423
PARTICULARLY
"The man questioned **p** about us **Gn 43:7** 7592
PARTIES
the case of both **p** shall come before **Ex 22:9**
drunkenness, carousing, drinking **p** **1Pe 4:3** *4224*
PARTING
stands at the **p** of the way, **Ezk 21:21** 517
you will give **p** gifts On behalf of **Mi 1:14** 7964
leaving after Paul had spoken one **p** **Ac 28:25**
PARTITION
the veil shall serve for you as a **p** **Ex 26:33** 914
PARTLY
feet **p** of iron and partly of clay. **Da 2:33** 4481
feet partly of iron and **p** of clay. **Da 2:33** 4481
p of potter's clay and partly of **Da 2:41** 4481
of potter's clay and **p** of iron, **Da 2:41** 4481
p of iron and partly of pottery, **Da 2:42** 4481
partly of iron and **p** of pottery, **Da 2:42** 4481
p by being made a public **Heb 10:33**
3778, 3303a
and **p** by becoming sharers with **Heb 10:33** *1161*
PARTNER
He who is a **p** with a thief hates **Pr 29:24** 2505a
my **p** and fellow worker among you; **2Co 8:23** *2844*
If then you regard me a **p**, **Phm 1:17** *2844*
PARTNERS
we would not have been **p** with them **Mt 23:30** *2844*
signaled to their **p** in the other boat for **Lk 5:7** *3353*
of Zebedee, who were **p** with Simon. **Lk 5:10** *2844*
PARTNERSHIP
for what **p** have righteousness and **2Co 6:14** *3352*
PARTOOK
likewise also **p** of the same, **Heb 2:14** *3348*
PARTRIDGE
one hunts a **p** in the mountains." **1Sa 26:20** 7124
"As a **p** that hatches eggs which **Jer 17:11** 7124
PARTS
at the undefended **p** of our land." **Gn 42:9** 6172
at the undefended **p** of our land!" **Gn 42:12** 6172
and divide into three **p** the territory **Dt 19:3** 8027
anything but death **p** you and me." **Ru 1:17** 6504
"We have ten **p** in the king, **2Sa 19:43** 3027
and poured out his inward **p** on the **2Sa 20:10** 4578
was finished throughout all its **p** **1Ki 6:38** 1697
all their rear **p** *turned* inward. **1Ki 7:25** 268
of Israel were divided into two **p**: **1Ki 16:21** 2677
"Two **p** of you, *even* all who **2Ki 11:7** 3027
To the remotest **p** of Lebanon; **2Ki 19:23** 3411
p of the space behind the wall, **Ne 4:13** 8482
For You formed my inward **p**; **Ps 139:13** 3629
into the innermost **p** of the body. **Pr 18:8** 2315
all the innermost **p** of his being. **Pr 20:27** 2315
And strokes *reach* the innermost **p**. **Pr 20:30** 990
into the innermost **p** of the body. **Pr 26:22** 2315
To the remotest **p** of Lebanon; **Is 37:24** 3411
And called from its remotest **p** And **Is 41:9** 678
you lower **p** of the earth; **Is 44:23** 8482
from the remote **p** of the earth. **Jer 6:22** 3411
From the remotest **p** of the earth. **Jer 25:32** 3411
from the remote **p** of the earth, **Jer 31:8** 3411
in two and passed between its **p** **Jer 34:18** 1335
passed between the **p** of the calf **Jer 34:19** 1335
from the remote **p** of the earth. **Jer 50:41** 3411
quiver To enter into my inward **p**. **La 3:13** 3629
dwell in the lower **p** of the earth, **Ezk 26:20** 8482
set in the remotest **p** of the pit and **Ezk 32:23** 3411
to the lower **p** of the earth, **Ezk 32:24** 8482
from the remote **p** of the north **Ezk 38:6** 3411
out of the remote **p** of the north, **Ezk 38:15** 3411
from the remotest **p** of the north and **Ezk 39:2** 3411
he will enter the richest **p** of **Da 11:24**
I heard and my inward **p** trembled, **Hab 3:16** 990
"That two **p** in it will be cut off **Zch 13:8** 6310
one of the **p** of your body, **Mt 5:29** *3196*
one of the **p** of your body, **Mt 5:30** *3196*
outer garments and made four **p**, **Jn 19:23** *3313*
of the Jews who were in those **p**, **Ac 16:3** *5117*
into the lower **p** of the earth? **Eph 4:9** *3313*
great city was split into three **p**, **Rv 16:19** *3313*
PARTY
that day Israel will be the third **p** **Is 19:24**
scribes of the Pharisaic **p** stood up **Ac 23:9** *3313*
fearing the **p** of the circumcision. **Ga 2:12**
Now a mediator is not for one **p** **Ga 3:20**
PARUAH
Jehoshaphat the son of **P**, **1Ki 4:17** 6515
PARVAIM
and the gold was gold from **P**. **2Ch 3:6** 6516
PASACH
The sons of Japhlet *were* **P**, **1Ch 7:33** 6457
PASDAMMIM
He was with David at **P** when the **1Ch 11:13** 6450
PASEAH
the father of Beth-rapha and **P**, **1Ch 4:12** 6454
the sons of Uzza, the sons of **P**, **Ezr 2:49** 6454
Joiada the son of **P** and **Ne 3:6** 6454
the sons of Uzza, the sons of **P**, **Ne 7:51** 6454
PASHHUR
the son of Jeroham, the son of **P**, **1Ch 9:12** 6583
the sons of **P**, 1,247; **Ezr 2:38** 6583
and of the sons of **P**: **Ezr 10:22** 6583
the sons of **P**, 1,247; **Ne 7:41** 6583
P, Amariah, Malchijah, **Ne 10:3** 6583
son of Zechariah, the son of **P**, **Ne 11:12** 6583
When **P** the priest, the son of **Jer 20:1** 6583
P had Jeremiah the prophet beaten and **Jer 20:2** 6583
when **P** released Jeremiah from the **Jer 20:3** 6583
"**P** is not the name the LORD has **Jer 20:3** 6583
'And you, **P**, and all who live in **Jer 20:6** 6583
to him **P** the son of Malchijah, **Jer 21:1** 6583
Mattan, and Gedaliah the son of **P**, **Jer 38:1** 6583
and **P** the son of Malchijah heard **Jer 38:1** 6583
PASS
caused a wind to **p** over the earth, **Gn 8:1** 5674a
please do not **p** Your servant by. **Gn 18:3** 5674a
let me **p** through your entire flock **Gn 30:32** 5674a
will not **p** by this heap to **Gn 31:52** 5674a
and you will not **p** by this heap **Gn 31:52** 5674a
"**P** on before me, and put a space **Gn 32:16** 5674a
let my lord **p** on before his servant, **Gn 33:14** 5674a
I see the blood I will **p** over you, **Ex 12:13** 6452a
"For the LORD will **p** through to **Ex 12:23** 5674a
the LORD will **p** over the door and **Ex 12:23** 6452a

Until Your people **p** over, **Ex 15:16** 5674a
Until the people **p** over whom You **Ex 15:16** 5674a
"**P** before the people and take **Ex 17:5** 5674a
shall **p** through from end to end. **Ex 26:28** 1272
make all My goodness **p** before you, **Ex 33:19** 5674a
He made the middle bar to **p** **Ex 36:33** 1272
no sword will **p** through your land. **Lv 26:6** 5674a
to it, so that it may **p** to him. **Lv 27:19** 6965
no razor shall **p** over his head. **Nu 6:5** 5674a
'Please let us **p** through your land. **Nu 20:17** 5674a
We will not **p** through field or **Nu 20:17** 5674a
until we **p** through your territory.' **Nu 20:17** 5674a
"You shall not **p** through us, or **Nu 20:18** 5674a
Let me only **p** through on my feet, **Nu 20:19** 5674a
"You shall not **p** through." **Nu 20:20** 5674a
Israel to **p** through his territory; **Nu 20:21** 5674a
"Let me **p** through your land. **Nu 21:22** 5674a
Israel to **p** through his border. **Nu 21:23** 5674a
you shall **p** through the fire, **Nu 31:23** 5674a
you shall **p** through the water. **Nu 31:23** 5674a
"You will **p** through the territory **Dt 2:4** 5674a
and **p** through the valley of Arnon. **Dt 2:24** 5674a
'Let me **p** through your land, I **Dt 2:27** 5674a
only let me **p** through on foot, **Dt 2:28** 5674a
for us to **p** through his land; **Dt 2:30** 5674a
his daughter **p** through the fire, **Dt 18:10** 5674a
"**P** through the midst of the camp **Jos 1:11** 5674a
house of Israel failed; all came to **p**. **Jos 21:45** 935
might **p** by them along the road; **Jg 9:25** 5674a
let us **p** through your land," **Jg 11:17** 5674a
"Please let us **p** through your **Jg 11:19** 5674a
Sihon did not trust Israel to **p** **Jg 11:20** 5674a
"Now when your words come *to* **p**, **Jg 13:12**
so that when your words come *to* **p**, **Jg 13:17**
he might go ahead of us and **p** on, **1Sa 9:27** 5674a
went out to the **p** of Michmash. **1Sa 13:23** 4569a
and made him **p** before Samuel. **1Sa 16:8** 5674a
Next Jesse made Shammah **p** by. **1Sa 16:9** 5674a
seven of his sons **p** before Samuel. **1Sa 16:10** 5674a
made them **p** through the brickkiln. **2Sa 12:31** 5674a
David said to Ittai, "Go and **p** over." **2Sa 15:22** 5674a
"If you **p** over with me, then you **2Sa 15:33** 5674a
a man will **p** the night with you, **2Sa 19:7** 3885a
"For the thing shall surely come to **p** **1Ki 13:32** 1961
the Spirit of the LORD **p** from me **1Ki 22:24** 5674a
that you do not **p** this place, **2Ki 6:9** 5674a
made his son **p** through the fire, **2Ki 16:3** 5674a
daughters **p** through the fire, **2Ki 17:17** 5674a
Now I have brought it to **p**, **2Ki 19:25** 935
made his son **p** through the fire, **2Ki 21:6** 5674a
p through the fire for Molech. **2Ki 23:10** 5674a
the Spirit of the LORD **p** from me **2Ch 18:23** 5674a
He made his sons **p** through the fire **2Ch 33:6** 5674a
p through until I come to Judah, **Ne 2:7** 5674a
was no place for my mount to **p**. **Ne 2:14** 5674a
that my request might come to **p**, **Jb 6:8** 935
"Were He to **p** by me, I would not **Jb 9:11** 5674a
You have set so that he cannot **p**. **Jb 14:5** 5674a
up my way so that I cannot **p**, **Jb 19:8** 5674a
People are shaken and **p** away, **Jb 34:20** 5674a
sea and caused them to **p** through **Ps 78:13** 5674a
all who **p** *that* way pick its *fruit?* **Ps 80:12** 5674a
who **p** along the way plunder him; **Ps 89:41** 5674a
boundary that they may not **p** over, **Ps 104:9** 5674a
the time that his word came to **p**, **Ps 105:19** 935
Nor do those who **p** by say, **Ps 129:8** 5674a
Israel **p** through the midst of it, **Ps 136:14** 5674a
own nets, While I **p** by safely. **Ps 141:10** 5674a
a decree which will not **p** away. **Ps 148:6** 5674a
Avoid it, do not **p** by it; **Pr 4:15** 5674a
Turn away from it and **p** on. **Pr 4:15** 5674a
Calling to those who **p** by, **Pr 9:15** 5674a
his lips brings evil to **p**. **Pr 16:30** 3615
evil report about you will not **p** away. **Pr 25:10** 7725
fool or who hires those who **p** by. **Pr 26:10** 5674a
of Israel draw near And come to **p**, **Is 5:19** 935
not stand nor shall it come to **p**. **Is 7:7** 1961
it will overflow and **p** through, **Is 8:8** 5674a
They will **p** through the land **Is 8:21** 5674a
They have gone through the **p**, **Is 10:29** 4569b
P over to Tarshish; **Is 23:6** 5674a
Arise, **p** over to Cyprus; **Is 23:12** 5674a
after morning it will **p** through, **Is 28:19** 5674a
He will **p** over and rescue *it.* **Is 31:5** 6452a
rock will **p** away because of panic, **Is 31:9** 5674a
on which no mighty ship will **p** **Is 33:21** 5674a
None will **p** through it forever and **Is 34:10** 5674a
Now I have brought it to **p**, **Is 37:26** 935
the former things have come to **p**, **Is 42:9** 935
"When you **p** through the waters, I **Is 43:2** 5674a
truly I will bring it to **p**. **Is 46:11** 935
I acted, and they came to **p**. **Is 48:3** 935
come to **p** that before they call, **Is 65:24** 1961
P your hand again like a grape **Jer 6:9** 7725
what I have given them will **p** away **Jer 8:13** 5674a
Many nations will **p** by this city; **Jer 22:8** 5674a
word of the prophet comes to **p**, **Jer 28:9** 935
You have spoken has come to **p**; **Jer 32:24** 1961
to **p** through *the fire* to Molech, **Jer 32:35** 5674a
the flocks will again **p** under the **Jer 33:13** 5674a
has let the appointed time **p** by!' **Jer 46:17** 5674a
nothing to all you who **p** this way? **La 1:12** 5674a
All who **p** along the way Clap their **La 2:15** 5674a
who speaks and it comes to **p**, **La 3:37** 1961
So that no prayer can **p** through. **La 3:44** 5674a
you, in the sight of all who **p** by. **Ezk 5:14** 5674a
bloodshed also will **p** through you, **Ezk 5:17** 5674a
wild beasts to **p** through the land and **Ezk 14:15** 5674a
so that no one would **p** through it **Ezk 14:15** 5674a
'Let the sword **p** through the **Ezk 14:17** 5674a
causing them to **p** through *the fire.* **Ezk 16:21** 5674a
their firstborn to **p** through *the fire* **Ezk 20:26** 5674a
your sons to **p** through the fire, **Ezk 20:31** 5674a
I will make you **p** under the rod, **Ezk 20:37** 5674a
to **p** through *the fire* to them as **Ezk 23:37** 5674a
"A man's foot will not **p** through it, **Ezk 29:11** 5674a
foot of a beast will not **p** through it, **Ezk 29:11** 5674a
so that no one will **p** through. **Ezk 33:28** 5674a
"So when it comes to **p** **Ezk 33:33** 935
He caused me to **p** among them **Ezk 37:2** 5674a
of those who **p** by east of the sea, **Ezk 39:11** 5674a
it will block off those who would **p** **Ezk 39:11** 5674a
constantly **p** through the land, **Ezk 39:14** 5674a
"As those who **p** through the **Ezk 39:15** 5674a
who pass through the land **p** through **Ezk 39:15** 5674a
seven periods of time **p** over him. **Da 4:16** 2499
seven periods of time **p** over him," **Da 4:23** 2499
periods of time will **p** over you, **Da 4:25** 2499
periods of time will **p** over you until **Da 4:32** 2499
dominion Which will not **p** away; **Da 7:14** 5709
coming and overflow and **p** through, **Da 11:10** 5674a
overflow *them* and **p** through. **Da 11:40** 5674a
strangers will **p** through it no more. **Jl 3:17** 5674a
I will **p** through the midst of you," **Am 5:17** 5674a
sprawlers' banqueting will **p** away. **Am 6:7** 5493
break out, **p** through the gate and **Mi 2:13** 5674a
they will be cut off and **p** away. **Na 1:12** 5674a
will the wicked one **p** through you; **Na 1:15** 5674a
through *like* the wind and **p** on. **Hab 1:11** 5674a
And no oppressor will **p** over them **Zch 9:8** 5674a
p through the sea *of* distress **Zch 10:11** 5674a
until heaven and earth **p** away, **Mt 5:18** *3928*
stroke shall **p** from the Law **Mt 5:18** *3928*
that no one could **p** by that way. **Mt 8:28** *3928*
this generation will not **p** away **Mt 24:34** *3928*
"Heaven and earth will **p** away, **Mt 24:35** *3928*
but My words will not **p** away. **Mt 24:35** *3928*
possible, let this cup **p** from Me; **Mt 26:39** *3928*
cannot **p** away unless I drink it, **Mt 26:42** *3928*
and He intended to **p** by them. **Mk 6:48** *3928*
this generation will not **p** away **Mk 13:30** *3928*
"Heaven and earth will **p** away, **Mk 13:31** *3928*
but My words will not **p** away. **Mk 13:31** *3928*
possible, the hour might **p** Him by. **Mk 14:35** *3928*
easier for heaven and earth to **p** away **Lk 16:17** *3928*
was about to **p** through that way. **Lk 19:4** *1330*
this generation will not **p** away **Lk 21:32** *3928*
"Heaven and earth will **p** away, **Lk 21:33** *3928*
but My words will not **p** away. **Lk 21:33** *3928*
And He had to **p** through Samaria. **Jn 4:4** *1330*
telling you before *it* comes to **p**, **Jn 13:19** *1096*
For these things came to **p** to **Jn 19:36** *1096*
living oracles to **p** on to you. **Ac 7:38** *1325*
when you **p** judgment on those who **Ro 2:3** *2919*
and let the others **p** judgment. **1Co 14:29** *1252*
is, to **p** your way into Macedonia, **2Co 1:16** *1330*
and so it came to **p**, **1Th 3:4** *1096*
and He also will bring it to **p**. **1Th 5:24** *4160*
like flowering grass he will **p** away. **Jas 1:10** *3928*
in which the heavens will **p** away **2Pe 3:10** *3928*

PASSAGE

p about *the burning* bush, **Mk 12:26**
in the **p** *about the burning* bush, **Lk 20:37**
Now the **p** of Scripture which he **Ac 8:32** *4042*
what the Scripture says in *the* **p** **Ro 11:2**
and again in this **p**, "THEY **Heb 4:5**
just as He says also in another **p**, **Heb 5:6**

PASSED

Abram **p** through the land as **Gn 12:6** 5674a
which **p** between these pieces. **Gn 15:17** 5674a
So the present **p** on before him, **Gn 32:21** 5674a
But he himself **p** on ahead of them **Gn 33:3** 5674a
Then some Midianite traders **p** by, **Gn 37:28** 5674a
Seven days **p** after the LORD **Ex 7:25** 4390
to the LORD who **p** over the houses **Ex 12:27** 6452a
with My hand until I have **p** by. **Ex 33:22** 5674a
Then the LORD **p** by in front of him **Ex 34:6** 5674a
for each one who **p** over to those **Ex 38:26** 5674a
"The land which we **p** through to **Nu 14:7** 5674a
we have **p** through your border." **Nu 21:22** 5674a
and **p** through the midst of the sea **Nu 33:8** 5674a
"So we **p** beyond our brothers the **Dt 2:8** 5674a
And we turned and **p** through by the **Dt 2:8** 5674a
the nations through which you **p**; **Dt 29:16** 5674a
you have not **p** this way before." **Jos 3:4** 5674a
him **p** on from Makkedah to Libnah, **Jos 10:29** 5674a
him **p** on from Libnah to Lachish, **Jos 10:31** 5674a
him **p** on from Lachish to Eglon, **Jos 10:34** 5674a
men went and **p** through the land, **Jos 18:9** 5674a
peoples through whose midst we **p**. **Jos 24:17** 5674a
and he **p** by the idols and escaped **Jg 3:26** 5674a
he **p** through Gilead and Manasseh; **Jg 11:29** 5674a
he **p** through Mizpah of Gilead, **Jg 11:29** 5674a
They **p** from there to the hill **Jg 18:13** 5674a
they **p** along and went their way, **Jg 19:14** 5674a
He **p** through the hill country **1Sa 9:4** 5674a
p through the land of Shalishah, **1Sa 9:4** 5674a
p through the land of Shaalim, **1Sa 9:4** 5674a
Then he **p** through the land of the **1Sa 9:4** 5674a
all his servants **p** on beside him, **2Sa 15:18** 5674a
from Gath, **p** on before the king. **2Sa 15:18** 5674a
So Ittai the Gittite **p** over with **2Sa 15:22** 5674a
loud voice, all the people **p** over. **2Sa 15:23** 5674a
king also **p** over the brook Kidron, **2Sa 15:23** 5674a
and all the people **p** over toward **2Sa 15:23** 5674a
had **p** a little beyond the summit, **2Sa 16:1** 5674a
of the plain and **p** up the Cushite. **2Sa 18:23** 5674a
all the men **p** on after Joab to **2Sa 20:13** 5674a
men **p** by and saw the body thrown **1Ki 13:25** 5674a
And Elijah **p** over to him and threw **1Ki 19:19** 5674a
As the king **p** by, he cried to **1Ki 20:39** 5674a
Three years **p** without war **1Ki 22:1** 3427
Then a cry **p** throughout the army **1Ki 22:36** 5674a
day when Elisha **p** over to Shunem, **2Ki 4:8** 5674a
so it was, as often as he **p** by, **2Ki 4:8** 5674a
Then Gehazi **p** on before them and **2Ki 4:31** 5674a
But there **p** by a wild beast that **2Ki 14:9** 5674a
Riblah, and he **p** sentence on him. **2Ki 25:6** 1696
But there **p** by a wild beast that **2Ch 25:18** 5674a
So the couriers **p** from city to **2Ch 30:10** 5674a
Then I **p** on to the Fountain Gate **Ne 2:14** 5674a
So they **p** through the midst of the **Ne 9:11** 5674a
"Then a spirit **p** by my face; **Jb 4:15** 2498
trouble, As waters that have **p** by, **Jb 11:16** 5674a
given, And no alien **p** among them. **Jb 15:19** 5674a
Nor has the *fierce* lion **p** over it. **Jb 28:8** 5710a
prosperity has **p** away like a cloud. **Jb 30:15** 5674a
the wind has **p** and cleared them. **Jb 37:21** 5674a
before Him **p** His thick clouds, **Ps 18:12** 5674a
Then he **p** away, and lo, he was no **Ps 37:36** 5674a
themselves, They **p** by together. **Ps 48:4** 5674a
They **p** through the river on foot; **Ps 66:6** 5674a
Your burning anger has **p** over me; **Ps 88:16** 5674a
When the wind has **p** over it, **Ps 103:16** 5674a
I **p** by the field of the sluggard And **Pr 24:30** 5674a
been, for God seeks what has **p** by. **Ec 3:15** 7291
Aiath, He has **p** through Migron; **Is 10:28** 5674a
themselves out *and* **p** over the sea. **Is 16:8** 5674a
in two and **p** between its parts **Jer 34:18** 5674a
who **p** between the parts of the **Jer 34:19** 5674a
Hamath, and he **p** sentence on him. **Jer 39:5** 1696
and he **p** sentence on him. **Jer 52:9** 1696
"When I **p** by you and saw you **Ezk 16:6** 5674a
"Then I **p** by you and saw you, and **Ezk 16:8** 5674a
and judgment was **p** in favor of the **Da 7:22** 3052
breakers and billows **p** over me. **Jon 2:3** 5674a
has not your evil **p** continually? **Na 3:19** 5674a
As He **p** by, He saw Levi the **Mk 2:14** *3855*
And when eight days had **p**, before **Lk 2:21** *4092a*
him, he **p** by on the other side. **Lk 10:31** *492*
saw him, **p** by on the other side. **Lk 10:32** *492*
After about an hour had **p**, **Lk 22:59** *1339*
but has **p** out of death into life. **Jn 5:24** *3327*
As He **p** by, He saw a man blind **Jn 9:1** *3855*
"After forty years had **p**, **Ac 7:30** *4137*
and as he **p** through he kept **Ac 8:40** *1330*
had **p** the first and second guard, **Ac 12:10** *1330*
They **p** through Pisidia and **Ac 14:24** *1330*
They **p** through the Phrygian **Ac 16:6** *1330*
he left and **p** successively **Ac 18:23** *1330*
Paul **p** through the upper **Ac 19:1** *1330*
p through Macedonia and Achaia, **Ac 19:21** *1330*
But after two years had **p**, **Ac 24:27** *4137*
When considerable time had **p** **Ac 27:9** *1230*
He **p** over the sins previously **Ro 3:25** *3929*
cloud and all **p** through the sea; **1Co 10:1** *1330*
the old things **p** away; **2Co 5:17** *3928*
who has **p** through the heavens, **Heb 4:14** *1330*
By faith they **p** through the Red Sea **Heb 11:29** *1224*
we have **p** out of death into life, **1Jn 3:14** *3327*
and splendid have **p** away from you **Rv 18:14** *622*
heaven and the first earth **p** away, **Rv 21:1** *565*
the first things have **p** away." **Rv 21:4** *565*

PASSENGER

shipmaster and every **p** and sailor, **Rv 18:17**
1909, 5117, 4126

PASSER-BY

on every **p** who might be *willing.* **Ezk 16:15** 5674a
every **p** to multiply your harlotry. **Ezk 16:25** 5674a
a **p** coming from the country, **Mk 15:21** *3855*

PASSERS-BY

the garment From unsuspecting **p**, **Mi 2:8** 5674a

PASSES

the house that is in the walled city **p** **Lv 25:30** 6965
flock, whatever **p** under the rod, **Lv 27:32** 5674a
Between the **p** by which **1Sa 14:4** 4569b
everyone who **p** by will be **1Ki 9:8** 5674a
everyone who **p** by it will be **2Ch 7:21** 5674a
"If He **p** by or shuts up, Or calls **Jb 11:10** 2498
p through the paths of the seas. **Ps 8:8** 5674a
refuge Until destruction **p** by. **Ps 57:1** 5674a
A wind that **p** and does not return. **Ps 78:39** 1980
Are like yesterday when it **p** by, **Ps 90:4** 5674a
When the whirlwind **p**, **Pr 10:25** 5674a
he who **p** by *and* meddles with strife **Pr 26:17** 5674a
will not reach us when it **p** by, **Is 28:15** 5674a
overwhelming scourge **p** through, **Is 28:18** 5674a
"As often as it **p** through, it **Is 28:19** 5674a
waste, so that no one **p** through, **Jer 9:10** 5674a
desert, so that no one **p** through? **Jer 9:12** 5674a
Everyone who **p** by it will be **Jer 18:16** 5674a
everyone who **p** by it will be **Jer 19:8** 5674a
everyone who **p** by it will be **Jer 49:17** 5674a
Everyone who **p** by Babylon will be **Jer 50:13** 5674a
And through which no son of man **p**. **Jer 51:43** 5674a
the one who **p** through and returns. **Ezk 35:7** 5674a
in the sight of everyone who **p** by. **Ezk 36:34** 5674a
of sheep, Which, if he **p** through, **Mi 5:8** 5674a
And **p** over the rebellious act of the **Mi 7:18** 5674a
The day **p** like the chaff **Zph 2:2** 5674a
Everyone who **p** by her will hiss **Zph 2:15** 5674a
of him who **p** by and returns; **Zch 9:8** 5674a
it **p** through waterless places seeking **Mt 12:43** *1330*
into the mouth **p** into the stomach, **Mt 15:17** *5562*
it **p** through waterless places **Lk 11:24** *1330*

everyone of you who **p** judgment,	**Ro 2:1**	*2919*

PASSING

about, while My glory is **p** by,	**Ex 33:22**	5674a
"We are **p** from Bethlehem in Judah	**Jg 19:18**	5674a
of whom Boaz spoke was **p** by,	**Ru 4:1**	5674a
until all the people had finished **p**	**2Sa 15:24**	5674a
And behold, the LORD was **p** by!	**1Ki 19:11**	5674a
this is a holy man of God **p** by us	**2Ki 4:9**	5674a
As the king of Israel was **p** by	**2Ki 6:26**	5674a
now he was **p** by on the wall	**2Ki 6:30**	5674a
his life from **p** over into Sheol.	**Jb 33:18**	5674a
P through the valley of Baca they	**Ps 84:6**	5674a
I am **p** like a shadow when it	**Ps 109:23**	1980
His days are like a **p** shadow.	**Ps 144:4**	5674a
P through the street near her	**Pr 7:8**	5674a
"He pursues them, **p** on in safety,	**Is 41:3**	5674a
and hated With no one **p** through,	**Is 60:15**	5674a
Will be terrified at your **p**.' "	**Ezk 26:18**	3318
burying those who were **p** through,	**Ezk 39:14**	5674a
desolate, With no one **p** by;	**Zph 3:6**	5674a
road, hearing that Jesus was **p** by,	**Mt 20:30**	*3855*
p by were hurling abuse at Him,	**Mt 27:39**	*3899*
He was **p** through the grainfields	**Mk 2:23**	*3899*
As they were **p** by in the morning,	**Mk 11:20**	*3899*
p by were hurling abuse at Him,	**Mk 15:29**	*3899*
But **p** through their midst, He went	**Lk 4:30**	*1330*
He was **p** through *some* grainfields on	**Lk 6:1**	*1279*
And He was **p** through from one city	**Lk 13:22**	*1279*
He was **p** between Samaria and	**Lk 17:11**	*1330*
that Jesus of Nazareth was **p** by.	**Lk 18:37**	*3928*
entered Jericho and was **p** through.	**Lk 19:1**	*1330*
they were **p** through both Phoenicia	**Ac 15:3**	*1330*
they were **p** through the cities,	**Ac 16:4**	*1279*
and **p** by Mysia, they came down to	**Ac 16:8**	*3928*
"For while I was **p** through and	**Ac 17:23**	*1330*
of **p** judgment on his opinions.	**Ro 14:1**	*1253*
for I hope to see you in **p**,	**Ro 15:24**	*1279*
of this age, who are **p** away;	**1Co 2:6**	*2673*
do not go on **p** judgment before the	**1Co 4:5**	*2919*
the form of this world is **p** away.	**1Co 7:31**	*3855*
not wish to see you now *just* in **p**;	**1Co 16:7**	*3938*
to enjoy the **p** pleasures of sin,	**Heb 11:25**	*4340*
the Red Sea as though *they were* **p**	**Heb 11:29**	
because the darkness is **p** away and	**1Jn 2:8**	*3855*
The world is **p** away,	**1Jn 2:17**	*3855*

PASSION

But **p** is rottenness to the bones.	**Pr 14:30**	7068
That sniffs the wind in her **p**.	**Jer 2:24**	185, 5315
better to marry than to burn *with* **p**.	**1Co 7:9**	
dead to immorality, impurity, **p**,	**Col 3:5**	*3806*
not in lustful **p**, like the Gentiles	**1Th 4:5**	*3806*
wine of the **p** of her immorality."	**Rv 14:8**	*2372*
wine of the **p** of her immorality,	**Rv 18:3**	*2372*

PASSIONS

God gave them over to degrading **p**;	**Ro 1:26**	*3806*
were in the flesh, the sinful **p**,	**Ro 7:5**	*3804*
crucified the flesh with its **p** and	**Ga 5:24**	*3804*

PASSOVER

it is the LORD's **P**.	**Ex 12:11**	6453
families, and slay the **P** *lamb.*	**Ex 12:21**	6453
'It is a **P** sacrifice to the LORD	**Ex 12:27**	6453
"This is the ordinance of the **P**:	**Ex 12:43**	6453
and celebrates the **P** to the LORD,	**Ex 12:48**	6453
is the sacrifice of the Feast of the **P**	**Ex 34:25**	6453
month at twilight is the LORD's **P**.	**Lv 23:5**	6453
the **P** at its appointed time.	**Nu 9:2**	6453
sons of Israel to observe the **P**.	**Nu 9:4**	6453
observed the **P** in the first *month,*	**Nu 9:5**	6453
could not observe **P** on that day;	**Nu 9:6**	6453
observe the **P** to the LORD.	**Nu 9:10**	6453
of the **P** they shall observe it.	**Nu 9:12**	6453
and yet neglects to observe the **P**,	**Nu 9:13**	6453
and observes the **P** to the LORD,	**Nu 9:14**	6453
according to the statute of the **P**	**Nu 9:14**	6453
first month shall be the LORD's **P**.	**Nu 28:16**	6453
on the next day after the **P** the	**Nu 33:3**	6453
the **P** to the LORD your God,	**Dt 16:1**	6453
"You shall sacrifice the **P** to	**Dt 16:2**	6453
not allowed to sacrifice the **P** in any	**Dt 16:5**	6453
the **P** in the evening at sunset,	**Dt 16:6**	6453
they observed the **P** on the evening	**Jos 5:10**	6453
On the day after the **P**,	**Jos 5:11**	6453
"Celebrate the **P** to the LORD your	**2Ki 23:21**	6453
such a **P** had not been celebrated	**2Ki 23:22**	6453
this **P** was observed to the LORD in	**2Ki 23:23**	6453
to celebrate the **P** to the LORD God	**2Ch 30:1**	6453
the **P** in the second month,	**2Ch 30:2**	6453
come to celebrate the **P** to the LORD	**2Ch 30:5**	6453
Then they slaughtered the **P** *lambs*	**2Ch 30:15**	6453
over the slaughter of the **P** *lambs*	**2Ch 30:17**	6453
ate the **P** otherwise than prescribed.	**2Ch 30:18**	6453
Josiah celebrated the **P** to the LORD	**2Ch 35:1**	6453
and they slaughtered the **P** *animals*	**2Ch 35:1**	6453
"Now slaughter the **P** *animals,*	**2Ch 35:6**	6453
and young goats, all for the **P** offerings,	**2Ch 35:7**	6453
gave to the priests for the **P**	**2Ch 35:8**	6453
to the Levites for the **P** offerings	**2Ch 35:9**	6453
They slaughtered the **P** *animals,*	**2Ch 35:11**	6453
So they roasted the **P** *animals* on	**2Ch 35:13**	6453
on that day to celebrate the **P**,	**2Ch 35:16**	6453
celebrated the **P** at that time,	**2Ch 35:17**	6453
had not been celebrated a **P** like it	**2Ch 35:18**	6453
celebrated such a **P** as Josiah did	**2Ch 35:18**	6453
reign this **P** was celebrated.	**2Ch 35:19**	6453
The exiles observed the **P** on	**Ezr 6:19**	6453
the **P** *lamb* for all the exiles,	**Ezr 6:20**	6453
God of Israel, ate *the* **P**.	**Ezr 6:21**	
the month, you shall have the **P**,	**Ezk 45:21**	6453
after two days the **P** is coming,	**Mt 26:2**	*3957*
to prepare for You to eat the **P**?"	**Mt 26:17**	*3957*
I *am to* keep the **P** at your house	**Mt 26:18**	*3957*
and they prepared the **P**.	**Mt 26:19**	*3957*
Now the **P** and Unleavened Bread were	**Mk 14:1**	*3957*
the **P** *lamb* was being sacrificed,	**Mk 14:12**	*3957*
prepare for You to eat the **P**?"	**Mk 14:12**	*3957*
eat the **P** with My disciples?"	**Mk 14:14**	*3957*
and they prepared the **P**.	**Mk 14:16**	*3957*
every year at the Feast of the **P**.	**Lk 2:41**	*3957*
Bread, which is called the **P**,	**Lk 22:1**	*3957*
the **P** *lamb* had to be sacrificed.	**Lk 22:7**	*3957*
"Go and prepare the **P** for us,	**Lk 22:8**	*3957*
eat the **P** with My disciples?"	**Lk 22:11**	*3957*
and they prepared the **P**.	**Lk 22:13**	*3957*
have earnestly desired to eat this **P**	**Lk 22:15**	*3957*
The **P** of the Jews was near,	**Jn 2:13**	*3957*
when He was in Jerusalem at the **P**,	**Jn 2:23**	*3957*
Now the **P**, the feast of the Jews,	**Jn 6:4**	*3957*
Now the **P** of the Jews was near,	**Jn 11:55**	*3957*
out of the country before the **P** to	**Jn 11:55**	*3957*
therefore, six days before the **P**,	**Jn 12:1**	*3957*
Now before the Feast of the **P**,	**Jn 13:1**	*3957*
not be defiled, but might eat the **P**.	**Jn 18:28**	*3957*
release someone for you at the **P**;	**Jn 18:39**	*3957*
the day of preparation for the **P**;	**Jn 19:14**	*3957*
intending after the **P** to bring him	**Ac 12:4**	*3957*
our **P** also has been sacrificed.	**1Co 5:7**	*3957*
By faith he kept the **P** and the	**Heb 11:28**	*3957*

PAST

Sarah was **p** childbearing.	**Gn 18:11**	2308
days of mourning for him were **p**,	**Gn 50:4**	5674a
neither recently nor in time **p**,	**Ex 4:10**	8032a
enmity toward him in time **p**;	**Dt 4:42**	8543
the bitterness of death is **p**."	**1Sa 15:32**	5493
running, he shot an arrow **p** him.	**1Sa 20:36**	5674a
"In times **p** you were seeking for	**2Sa 3:17**	8543, 8032a
your father's servant in time **p**,	**2Sa 15:34**	3975b
When midday was **p**,	**1Ki 18:29**	5674a
"In times **p**, even when Saul was	**1Ch 11:2**	8543, 8032a
incited revolt within it in **p** days;	**Ezr 4:15**	5957
up against the kings in **p** days,	**Ezr 4:19**	5957
"Please inquire of **p** generations,	**Jb 8:8**	7223
Were He to move **p** *me,* I would not	**Jb 9:11**	2498
"For when a few years are **p**,	**Jb 16:22**	857
"My days are **p**, my plans are torn	**Jb 17:11**	5674a
'For behold, the winter is **p**,	**SS 2:11**	5674a
things, Or ponder things of the **p**.	**Is 43:18**	6931
"Remember the former things long **p**,	**Is 46:9**	5769
"Harvest is **p**, summer is ended,	**Jer 8:20**	5674a
Paul had decided to sail **p** Ephesus	**Ac 20:16**	*3896*
and with difficulty sailing **p** it	**Ac 27:8**	*3881*
been kept secret for long ages **p**,	**Ro 16:25**	
if she is **p** her youth, and if it	**1Co 7:36**	*5230*
those who have sinned in the **p**	**2Co 12:21**	*4258*
to those who have sinned in the **p**	**2Co 13:2**	*4258*
which has been hidden from the **p**	**Col 1:26**	
For the time already **p** is sufficient	**1Pe 4:3**	*3928*
The first woe is **p**;	**Rv 9:12**	*565*
The second woe is **p**;	**Rv 11:14**	*565*

PASTORS

and some *as* **p** and teachers,	**Eph 4:11**	*4166*

PASTURE

Water the sheep, and go, **p** them."	**Gn 29:7**	7462a
will again **p** *and* keep your flock:	**Gn 30:31**	7462a
went to **p** their father's flock in	**Gn 37:12**	7462a
is no **p** for your servants' flocks,	**Gn 47:4**	4829
'But **p** fields of their cities	**Lv 25:34**	4054
you shall give to the Levites **p** lands	**Nu 35:2**	4054
and their **p** lands shall be for	**Nu 35:3**	4054
"The **p** lands of the cities	**Nu 35:4**	4054
theirs as **p** lands for the cities.	**Nu 35:5**	4054
together with their **p** lands.	**Nu 35:7**	4054
with their **p** lands for their	**Jos 14:4**	4054
their **p** lands for our cattle."	**Jos 21:2**	4054
these cities with their **p** lands,	**Jos 21:3**	4054
these cities with their **p** lands,	**Jos 21:8**	4054
with its surrounding **p** lands.	**Jos 21:11**	4054
the manslayer, with its **p** lands,	**Jos 21:13**	4054
and Libnah with its **p** lands,	**Jos 21:13**	4054
and Jattir with its **p** lands and	**Jos 21:14**	4054
and Eshtemoa with its **p** lands,	**Jos 21:14**	4054
and Holon with its **p** lands and	**Jos 21:15**	4054
lands and Debir with its **p** lands,	**Jos 21:15**	4054
and Ain with its **p** lands and	**Jos 21:16**	4054
and Juttah with its **p** lands	**Jos 21:16**	4054
and Beth-shemesh with its **p** lands;	**Jos 21:16**	4054
Benjamin, Gibeon with its **p** lands,	**Jos 21:17**	4054
lands, Geba with its **p** lands,	**Jos 21:17**	4054
Anathoth with its **p** lands and	**Jos 21:18**	4054
lands and Almon with its **p** lands;	**Jos 21:18**	4054
cities with their **p** lands.	**Jos 21:19**	4054
the manslayer, with its **p** lands,	**Jos 21:21**	4054
and Gezer with its **p** lands,	**Jos 21:21**	4054
and Kibzaim with its **p** lands and	**Jos 21:22**	4054
and Beth-horon with its **p** lands;	**Jos 21:22**	4054
of Dan, Elteke with its **p** lands,	**Jos 21:23**	4054
lands, Gibbethon with its **p** lands,	**Jos 21:23**	4054
Aijalon with its **p** lands,	**Jos 21:24**	4054
Gath-rimmon with its **p** lands;	**Jos 21:24**	4054
they allotted Taanach with its **p**	**Jos 21:25**	4054
and Gath-rimmon with its **p** lands;	**Jos 21:25**	4054
All the cities with their **p** lands	**Jos 21:26**	4054
the manslayer, with its **p** lands,	**Jos 21:27**	4054
and Be-eshterah with its **p** lands;	**Jos 21:27**	4054
gave Kishion with its **p** lands,	**Jos 21:28**	4054
lands, Daberath with its **p** lands,	**Jos 21:28**	4054
Jarmuth with its **p** lands,	**Jos 21:29**	4054
lands, En-gannim with its **p** lands;	**Jos 21:29**	4054
they gave Mishal with its **p** lands,	**Jos 21:30**	4054
lands, Abdon with its **p** lands,	**Jos 21:30**	4054
Helkath with its **p** lands and Rehob	**Jos 21:31**	4054
lands and Rehob with its **p** lands;	**Jos 21:31**	4054
with its **p** lands and Hammoth-dor	**Jos 21:32**	4054
and Hammoth-dor with its **p** lands	**Jos 21:32**	4054
lands and Kartan with its **p** lands;	**Jos 21:32**	4054
cities with their **p** lands.	**Jos 21:33**	4054
Jokneam with its **p** lands and	**Jos 21:34**	4054
lands and Kartah with its **p** lands.	**Jos 21:34**	4054
Dimnah with its **p** lands, Nahalal	**Jos 21:35**	4054
lands, Nahalal with its **p** lands;	**Jos 21:35**	4054
they gave Bezer with its **p** lands	**Jos 21:36**	4054
lands and Jahaz with its **p** lands,	**Jos 21:36**	4054
Kedemoth with its **p** lands and	**Jos 21:37**	4054
and Mephaath with its **p** lands;	**Jos 21:37**	4054
with its **p** lands and Mahanaim with	**Jos 21:38**	4054
and Mahanaim with its **p** lands,	**Jos 21:38**	4054
Heshbon with its **p** lands,	**Jos 21:39**	4054
lands, Jazer with its **p** lands;	**Jos 21:39**	4054
cities with their **p** lands.	**Jos 21:41**	4054
each had its surrounding **p** lands;	**Jos 21:42**	4054
"I took you from the **p**,	**2Sa 7:8**	5116a
to seek **p** for their flocks.	**1Ch 4:39**	4829
They found rich and good **p**,	**1Ch 4:40**	4829
there was **p** there for their flocks.	**1Ch 4:41**	4829
and in all the **p** lands of Sharon,	**1Ch 5:16**	4054
Judah and its **p** lands around it;	**1Ch 6:55**	4054
Libnah also with its **p** lands,	**1Ch 6:57**	4054
Jattir, Eshtemoa with its **p** lands,	**1Ch 6:57**	4054
Hilen with its **p** lands, Debir with	**1Ch 6:58**	4054
lands, Debir with its **p** lands,	**1Ch 6:58**	4054
Ashan with its **p** lands and	**1Ch 6:59**	4054
and Beth-shemesh with its **p** lands;	**1Ch 6:59**	4054
Geba with its **p** lands, Allemeth	**1Ch 6:60**	4054
lands, Allemeth with its **p** lands,	**1Ch 6:60**	4054
and Anathoth with its **p** lands.	**1Ch 6:60**	4054
the cities with their **p** lands.	**1Ch 6:64**	4054
of Ephraim with its **p** lands,	**1Ch 6:67**	4054
Gezer also with its **p** lands,	**1Ch 6:67**	4054
Jokmeam with its **p** lands,	**1Ch 6:68**	4054
lands, Beth-horon with its **p** lands,	**1Ch 6:68**	4054
Aijalon with its **p** lands and	**1Ch 6:69**	4054
and Gath-rimmon with its **p** lands;	**1Ch 6:69**	4054
Aner with its **p** lands and Bileam	**1Ch 6:70**	4054
lands and Bileam with its **p** lands,	**1Ch 6:70**	4054
Golan in Bashan with its **p** lands	**1Ch 6:71**	4054
and Ashtaroth with its **p** lands;	**1Ch 6:71**	4054
Kedesh with its **p** lands, Daberath	**1Ch 6:72**	4054
lands, Daberath with its **p** lands	**1Ch 6:72**	4054
and Ramoth with its **p** lands,	**1Ch 6:73**	4054
lands, Anem with its **p** lands;	**1Ch 6:73**	4054
Mashal with its **p** lands, Abdon	**1Ch 6:74**	4054
lands, Abdon with its **p** lands,	**1Ch 6:74**	4054
Hukok with its **p** lands and Rehob	**1Ch 6:75**	4054
lands and Rehob with its **p** lands;	**1Ch 6:75**	4054
Kedesh in Galilee with its **p** lands,	**1Ch 6:76**	4054
lands, Hammon with its **p** lands and	**1Ch 6:76**	4054
and Kiriathaim with its **p** lands.	**1Ch 6:76**	4054
Rimmono with its **p** lands,	**1Ch 6:77**	4054
lands, Tabor with its **p** lands;	**1Ch 6:77**	4054
the wilderness with its **p** lands,	**1Ch 6:78**	4054
lands, Jahzah with its **p** lands,	**1Ch 6:78**	4054
Kedemoth with its **p** lands and	**1Ch 6:79**	4054
and Mephaath with its **p** lands;	**1Ch 6:79**	4054
Ramoth in Gilead with its **p** lands,	**1Ch 6:80**	4054
lands, Mahanaim with its **p** lands,	**1Ch 6:80**	4054
Heshbon with its **p** lands and	**1Ch 6:81**	4054
lands and Jazer with its **p** lands.	**1Ch 6:81**	4054
them in their cities with **p** lands,	**1Ch 13:2**	4054
"I took you from the **p**,	**1Ch 17:7**	5116a
For the Levites left their **p** lands	**2Ch 11:14**	4054
in the **p** lands of their cities,	**2Ch 31:19**	4054
explores the mountains for his **p** And	**Jb 39:8**	4829
smoke against the sheep of Your **p**?	**Ps 74:1**	4830
Your people and the sheep of Your **p**	**Ps 79:13**	4830
And we are the people of His **p** and	**Ps 95:7**	4830
His people and the sheep of His **p**.	**Ps 100:3**	4830
loves, Where do you **p** *your flock,*	**SS 1:7**	7462a
And **p** your young goats By the	**SS 1:8**	7462a
To **p** *his flock* in the gardens And	**SS 6:2**	7462a
lambs will graze as in their **p**,	**Is 5:17**	1699a
livestock will graze in a roomy **p**.	**Is 30:23**	3733b
for wild donkeys, a **p** for flocks;	**Is 32:14**	4829
p *will be* on all bare heights.	**Is 49:9**	4830
will stand and **p** your flocks,	**Is 61:5**	7462a
Sharon will be a **p** land for flocks,	**Is 65:10**	5116a
They will **p** each in his place.	**Jer 6:3**	7462a
scattering the sheep of My **p**!"	**Jer 23:1**	4830
and bring them back to their **p**	**Jer 23:3**	5116a
the LORD is destroying their **p**,	**Jer 25:36**	4830
against a perennially watered **p**;	**Jer 49:19**	5116a
surely He will make their **p** desolate	**Jer 49:20**	5116a
will bring Israel back to his **p**	**Jer 50:19**	5116a
Jordan to a perennially watered **p**;	**Jer 50:44**	5116a
surely He will make their **p** desolate	**Jer 50:45**	5116a
like deer That have found no **p**;	**La 1:6**	4829
I will make Rabbah a **p** for camels	**Ezk 25:5**	5116a
pilots The **p** lands will shake.	**Ezk 27:28**	4054
"I will feed them in a good **p**,	**Ezk 34:14**	4829
and feed in rich **p** on the mountains	**Ezk 34:14**	4829
you should feed in the good **p**,	**Ezk 34:18**	4829
you, My sheep, the sheep of My **p**,	**Ezk 34:31**	4830
Can the LORD now **p** them Like a	**Hos 4:16**	7462a
As *they had* their **p**,	**Hos 13:6**	4830

Because there is no **p** for them; **Jl 1:18** 4829
And the shepherds' **p** grounds mourn, **Am 1:2** 4999
Like a flock in the midst of its **p** **Mi 2:12** 1699a
house of Judah, They will **p** on it. **Zph 2:7** 7462a
"**P** the flock *doomed* to slaughter. **Zch 11:4** 7462a
"I will not **p** you. **Zch 11:9** 7462a
the ninety-nine in the open **p** and **Lk 15:4** *2048*
will go in and out and find **p**. **Jn 10:9** *3542*

PASTURED
I **p** the flock *doomed* to slaughter, **Zch 11:7** 7462a
so I **p** the flock. **Zch 11:7** 7462a

PASTURE-FED
ten fat oxen, twenty **p** oxen, **1Ki 4:23** 7471

PASTURES
He makes me lie down in green **p**; **Ps 23:2** 5116c
will be like the glory of the **p**, **Ps 37:20** 3733b
The **p** of the wilderness drip, And **Ps 65:12** 4999
possess for ourselves The **p** of God. **Ps 83:12** 4999
He **p** *his flock* among the lilies. **SS 2:16** 7462a
p *his flock* among the lilies." **SS 6:3** 7462a
for the **p** of the wilderness a dirge, **Jer 9:10** 4999
The **p** of the wilderness have dried **Jer 23:10** 4999
with your feet the rest of your **p**? **Ezk 34:18** 4829
devoured the **p** of the wilderness And **Jl 1:19** 4999
devoured the **p** of the wilderness. **Jl 1:20** 4999
For the **p** of the wilderness have **Jl 2:22** 4999
So the seacoast will be **p**, **Zph 2:6** 5116c

PASTURING
he was **p** the donkeys of his father **Gn 36:24** 7462a
was **p** the flock with his brothers **Gn 37:2** 7462a
brothers **p** *the flock* in Shechem? **Gn 37:13** 7462a
me where they are **p** *the flock*." **Gn 37:16** 7462a
Now Moses was **p** the flock of **Ex 3:1** 7462a
a place for **p** oxen and for sheep **Is 7:25** 4916a

PATARA
day to Rhodes and from there to **P**; **Ac 21:1** *3959*

PATCH
no one puts a **p** of unshrunk cloth **Mt 9:16** *1915*
the **p** pulls away from the garment, **Mt 9:16** *4138*
No one sews a **p** of unshrunk cloth **Mk 2:21** *1915*
the **p** pulls away from it, **Mk 2:21** *4138*

PATCHED
and **p** sandals on their feet, **Jos 9:5** 2921

PATE
will descend upon his own **p**. **Ps 7:16** 6936

PATH
the way, A horned snake in the **p**, **Gn 49:17** 734
in a narrow **p** of the vineyards, **Nu 22:24** 4934
And a trap for him on the **p**. **Jb 18:10** 5410a
"Will you keep to the ancient **p** **Jb 22:15** 734
"My foot has held fast to His **p**; **Jb 23:11** 804a
"The **p** no bird of prey knows, Nor **Jb 28:7** 5410a
"They break up my **p**, **Jb 30:13** 5410b
Nor stand in the **p** of sinners, **Ps 1:1** 1870
make known to me the **p** of life; **Ps 16:11** 734
O LORD, And lead me in a level **p** **Ps 27:11** 734
himself on a **p** that is not good; **Ps 36:4** 1870
He leveled a **p** for His anger; **Ps 78:50** 5410a
walk in the **p** of Your commandments, **Ps 119:35** 5410a
to my feet And a light to my **p**. **Ps 119:105** 5410b
scrutinize my **p** and my lying down, **Ps 139:3** 734
within me, You knew my **p**. **Ps 142:3** 5410b
Keep your feet from their **p**, **Pr 1:15** 5410b
Do not enter the **p** of the wicked And **Pr 4:14** 734
But the **p** of the righteous is like **Pr 4:18** 734
Watch the **p** of your feet And all **Pr 4:26** 4570
She does not ponder the **p** of life; **Pr 5:6** 734
He is *on* the **p** of life who heeds **Pr 10:17** 734
the **p** of the upright is a highway. **Pr 15:19** 734
The **p** of life *leads* upward for the **Pr 15:24** 734
you do not know the **p** of the wind **Ec 11:5** 1870
make the **p** of the righteous level. **Is 26:7** 4570
of the way, turn aside from the **p**, **Is 30:11** 734
who taught Him in the **p** of justice **Is 40:14** 734
And a **p** through the mighty waters, **Is 43:16** 5410b
On a straight **p** in which they **Jer 31:9** 1870
They march everyone in his **p**; **Jl 2:8** 4546
P OF PEACE THEY HAVE NOT KNOWN." **Ro 3:17** *3598*

PATHLESS
makes them wander in a **p** waste. **Jb 12:24** 3808, 1870
makes them wander in a **p** waste. **Ps 107:40** 3808, 1870

PATHROS
remain, From Assyria, Egypt, **P**, **Is 11:11** 6624
Memphis, and the land of **P**, **Jer 44:1** 6624
living in **P** in the land of Egypt, **Jer 44:15** 6624
make them return to the land of **P**, **Ezk 29:14** 6624
"I will make **P** desolate, Set **Ezk 30:14** 6624

PATHRUS
P, Casluh, from which the **1Ch 1:12** 6625

PATHRUSIM
and **P** and Casluhim **Gn 10:14** 6625

PATHS
"The **p** of their course wind along, **Jb 6:18** 734
are the **p** of all who forget God; **Jb 8:13** 734
stocks And watch all my **p**; **Jb 13:27** 734
And He has put darkness on my **p**. **Jb 19:8** 5410b
know its ways Nor abide in its **p**. **Jb 24:13** 5410b
He watches all my **p**.' **Jb 33:11** 734
you may discern the **p** to its home? **Jb 38:20** 5410b
passes through the **p** of the seas. **Ps 8:8** 734
kept from the **p** of the violent. **Ps 17:4** 734
My steps have held fast to Your **p**. **Ps 17:5** 4570
guides me in the **p** of righteousness **Ps 23:3** 4570
Your ways, O LORD; Teach me Your **p**. **Ps 25:4** 734
All the **p** of the LORD are **Ps 25:10** 734
And Your **p** drip *with* fatness. **Ps 65:11** 4570
And Your **p** in the mighty waters, **Ps 77:19** 7635
Guarding the **p** of justice, And He **Pr 2:8** 734
who leave the **p** of uprightness To **Pr 2:13** 734
Whose **p** are crooked, And who are **Pr 2:15** 734
Nor do they reach the **p** of life. **Pr 2:19** 734
keep to the **p** of the righteous. **Pr 2:20** 734
And He will make your **p** straight. **Pr 3:6** 734
ways And all her **p** are peace. **Pr 3:17** 5410b
I have led you in upright **p**. **Pr 4:11** 4570
LORD, And He watches all his **p**. **Pr 5:21** 4570
her ways, Do not stray into her **p**. **Pr 7:25** 5410b
beside the way, Where the **p** meet, **Pr 8:2** 5410b
In the midst of the **p** of justice, **Pr 8:20** 5410b
Who are making their **p** straight: **Pr 9:15** 734
And that we may walk in His **p**." **Is 2:3** 734
confuse the direction of your **p**. **Is 3:12** 734
In **p** they do not know I will guide **Is 42:16** 5410b
They have made their **p** crooked, **Is 59:8** 5410b
and see and ask for the ancient **p**, **Jer 6:16** 5410b
their ways, From the ancient **p**, **Jer 18:15** 7635
will be like slippery **p** to them, **Jer 23:12** 2519
He has made my **p** crooked. **La 3:9** 5410b
her so that she cannot find her **p**. **Hos 2:6** 5410b
Nor do they deviate from their **p**. **Jl 2:7** 734
And that we may walk in His **p**." **Mi 4:2** 731
THE LORD, MAKE HIS **P** STRAIGHT!' " **Mt 3:3** *5147*
THE LORD, MAKE HIS **P** STRAIGHT.' " **Mk 1:3** *5147*
OF THE LORD, MAKE HIS **P** STRAIGHT. **Lk 3:4** *5147*
AND MISERY ARE IN THEIR **P**, **Ro 3:16** *3598*
and make straight **p** for your feet, **Heb 12:13** *5163*

PATHWAY
And in *its* **p** there is no death. **Pr 12:28** 1870, 5410a
the secret place of the steep **p**, **SS 2:14** 4095
Who made the depths of the sea a **p** **Is 51:10** 1870

PATHWAYS
down, the steep **p** will collapse and **Ezk 38:20** 4095

PATIENCE
P of spirit is better than **Ec 7:8** 750
thing for you to try the **p** of men, **Is 7:13** 3811
will try the **p** of my God as well? **Is 7:13** 3811
Do not, in view of Your **p**, **Jer 15:15** 750
'Have **p** with me and I will repay **Mt 18:26** *3114*
Have **p** with me and I will repay **Mt 18:29** *3114*
kindness and tolerance and **p**, **Ro 2:4** *3115*
endured with much **p** vessels of **Ro 9:22** *3115*
in purity, in knowledge, in **p**, **2Co 6:6** *3115*
the Spirit is love, joy, peace, **p**, **Ga 5:22** *3115*
humility and gentleness, with **p**, **Eph 4:2** *3115*
of all steadfastness and **p**; **Col 1:11** *3115*
humility, gentleness and **p**; **Col 3:12** *3115*
might demonstrate His perfect **p** as **1Tm 1:16** *3115*
conduct, purpose, faith, **p**, **2Tm 3:10** *3115*
exhort, with great **p** and instruction. **2Tm 4:2** *3115*
faith and **p** inherit the promises. **Heb 6:12** *3115*
brethren, of suffering and **p**, **Jas 5:10** *3115*
treated, you endure it with **p**? **1Pe 2:20** *5278*
when the **p** of God kept waiting in **1Pe 3:20** *3115*
the **p** of our Lord *as* salvation; **2Pe 3:15** *3115*

PATIENT
Love is **p**, love is kind *and* is **1Co 13:4** *3114*
which is effective in the **p** enduring **2Co 1:6** *5281*
help the weak, be **p** with everyone. **1Th 5:14** *3114*
able to teach, **p** when wronged, **2Tm 2:24** *420*
Therefore be **p**, brethren, until **Jas 5:7** *3114*
of the soil, being **p** about it, **Jas 5:7** *3114*
You too be **p**; strengthen your hearts **Jas 5:8** *3114*
slowness, but is **p** toward you, **2Pe 3:9** *3114*

PATIENTLY
in the LORD and wait **p** for Him; **Ps 37:7** 2342a
I waited **p** for the LORD; **Ps 40:1** 6960a
I beg you to listen to me **p**. **Ac 26:3** *3116*
And so, having **p** waited, **Heb 6:15** *3114*
and suffer *for it* you **p** endure it, **1Pe 2:20** *5278*

PATMOS
Jesus, was on the island called **P** **Rv 1:9** *3963*

PATRIARCH
say to you regarding the **p** David **Ac 2:29** *3966*
to whom Abraham, the **p**, gave **Heb 7:4** *3966*

PATRIARCHS
Jacob, and Jacob *of* the twelve **p**. **Ac 7:8** *3966*
"The **p** became jealous of **Ac 7:9** *3966*

PATROBAS
Asyncritus, Phlegon, Hermes, **P**, **Ro 16:14** *3969*

PATROL
LORD has sent to **p** the earth." **Zch 1:10** 1980
were eager to go to **p** the earth." **Zch 6:7** 1980
"Go, **p** the earth." **Zch 6:7** 1980

PATROLLED
"We have **p** the earth, and behold, **Zch 1:11** 1980
So they **p** the earth. **Zch 6:7** 1980

PATTERN
as the **p** of the tabernacle and the **Ex 25:9** 8403
and the **p** of all its furniture, **Ex 25:9** 8403
make *them* after the **p** for them, **Ex 25:40** 8403
according to the **p** which the LORD **Nu 8:4** 4758
the **p** of the altar and its model, **2Ki 16:10** 1823
me, all the details of this **p**." **1Ch 28:19** 8403
to the **p** which he had seen. **Ac 7:44** *5179b*
according to the **p** you have in us. **Php 3:17** *5179b*
MAKE all things ACCORDING TO THE **P** **Heb 8:5** *5179b*

PATTERNS
and the fixed **p** of heaven and earth **Jer 33:25** 2708

PAU
and the name of his city was **P**; **Gn 36:39** 6464

PAUL
But Saul, who was also *known as* **P**, **Ac 13:9** *3972*
P and his companions put out to sea **Ac 13:13** *3972*
P stood up, and motioning with **Ac 13:16** *3972*
As **P** and Barnabas were going out, **Ac 13:42**
followed **P** and Barnabas, **Ac 13:43** *3972*
the things spoken by **P**, **Ac 13:45** *3972*
P and Barnabas spoke out **Ac 13:46** *3972*
persecution against **P** and Barnabas, **Ac 13:50** *3972*
was listening to **P** as he spoke, **Ac 14:9** *3972*
crowds saw what **P** had done, **Ac 14:11** *3972*
calling Barnabas, Zeus, and **P**, **Ac 14:12** *3972*
when the apostles Barnabas and **P** **Ac 14:14** *3972*
they stoned **P** and dragged him out **Ac 14:19** *3972*
And when **P** and Barnabas had great **Ac 15:2** *3972*
the brethren determined that **P** and **Ac 15:2** *3972*
were listening to Barnabas and **P** **Ac 15:12** *3972*
send to Antioch with **P** and Barnabas **Ac 15:22** *3972*
with our beloved Barnabas and **P**, **Ac 15:25** *3972*
But **P** and Barnabas stayed in **Ac 15:35** *3972*
some days **P** said to Barnabas, **Ac 15:36** *3972*
But **P** kept insisting that they **Ac 15:38** *3972*
But **P** chose Silas and left, **Ac 15:40** *3972*
P came also to Derbe and to Lystra. **Ac 16:1**
P wanted this man to go with him; **Ac 16:3** *3972*
vision appeared to **P** in the night: **Ac 16:9** *3972*
respond to the things spoken by **P**. **Ac 16:14** *3972*
Following after **P** and us, she kept **Ac 16:17** *3972*
But **P** was greatly annoyed, and **Ac 16:18** *3972*
they seized **P** and Silas and **Ac 16:19** *3972*
P and Silas were praying and singing **Ac 16:25** *3972*
But **P** cried out with a loud voice, **Ac 16:28** *3972*
he fell down before **P** and Silas, **Ac 16:29** *3972*
jailer reported these words to **P**, **Ac 16:36** *3972*
But **P** said to them, **Ac 16:37** *3972*
persuaded and joined **P** and Silas, **Ac 17:4** *3972*
sent **P** and Silas away by night **Ac 17:10** *3972*
proclaimed by **P** in Berea also, **Ac 17:13** *3972*
P out to go as far as the sea; **Ac 17:14** *3972*
P brought him as far as Athens; **Ac 17:15** *3972*
Now while **P** was waiting for them **Ac 17:16** *3972*
So **P** stood in the midst of the **Ac 17:22** *3972*
So **P** went out of their midst. **Ac 17:33** *3972*
P *began* devoting himself **Ac 18:5** *3972*
And the Lord said to **P** in the night **Ac 18:9** *3972*
rose up against **P** and brought him **Ac 18:12** *3972*
P was about to open his mouth, **Ac 18:14** *3972*
P, having remained many days **Ac 18:18** *3972*
P passed through the upper **Ac 19:1** *3972*
P said, "John baptized with **Ac 19:4** *3972*
P had laid his hands upon them, **Ac 19:6** *3972*
miracles by the hands of **P**, **Ac 19:11** *3972*
you by Jesus whom **P** preaches." **Ac 19:13** *3972*
Jesus, and I know about **P**, **Ac 19:15** *3972*
P purposed in the Spirit to go to **Ac 19:21** *3972*
this **P** has persuaded and turned **Ac 19:26** *3972*
And when **P** wanted to go into the **Ac 19:30** *3972*
P sent for the disciples, and when **Ac 20:1** *3972*
bread, **P** *began* talking to them, **Ac 20:7** *3972*
and as **P** kept on talking, he was **Ac 20:9** *3972*
But **P** went down and fell upon him **Ac 20:10** *3972*
from there to take **P** on board; **Ac 20:13** *3972*
For **P** had decided to sail past **Ac 20:16** *3972*
to weep aloud and embraced **P**, **Ac 20:37** *3972*
and they kept telling **P** through **Ac 21:4** *3972*
Then **P** answered, **Ac 21:13** *3972*
day **P** went in with us to James, **Ac 21:18** *3972*
Then **P** took the men, and the next **Ac 21:26** *3972*
and they supposed that **P** had **Ac 21:29** *3972*
and taking hold of **P** they **Ac 21:30** *3972*
soldiers, they stopped beating **P**. **Ac 21:32** *3972*
As **P** was about to be brought **Ac 21:37** *3972*
But **P** said, "I am a Jew of Tarsus **Ac 21:39** *3972*
he had given him permission, **P**, **Ac 21:40** *3972*
P said to the centurion who was **Ac 22:25** *3972*
P said, "But I was actually born *a* **Ac 22:28** *3972*
brought **P** down and set him before **Ac 22:30** *3972*
P, looking intently at the **Ac 23:1** *3972*
Then **P** said to him, **Ac 23:3** *3972*
P said, "I was not aware, brethren, **Ac 23:5** *3972*
P *began* crying out in the Council, **Ac 23:6** *3972*
afraid **P** would be torn to pieces by **Ac 23:10** *3972*
nor drink until they had killed **P**. **Ac 23:12** *3972*
nothing until we have killed **P**. **Ac 23:14** *3972*
entered the barracks and told **P**. **Ac 23:16** *3972*
P called one of the centurions **Ac 23:17** *3972*
"**P** the prisoner called me to him **Ac 23:18** *3972*
have agreed to ask you to bring **P** **Ac 23:20** *3972*
also to provide mounts to put **P** on **Ac 23:24** *3972*
took **P** and brought him by night to **Ac 23:31** *3972*
they also presented **P** to him. **Ac 23:33** *3972*
charges to the governor against **P**. **Ac 24:1** *3972*
After **P** had been summoned, **Ac 24:2**
for him to speak, **P** responded: **Ac 24:10** *3972*
who was a Jewess, and sent for **P** and **Ac 24:24** *3972*
money would be given him by **P**; **Ac 24:26** *3972*
a favor, Felix left **P** imprisoned. **Ac 24:27** *3972*
Jews brought charges against **P**, **Ac 25:2** *3972*
requesting a concession against **P**, **Ac 25:3**
Festus then answered that **P** was **Ac 25:4** *3972*
and ordered **P** to be brought. **Ac 25:6** *3972*
After **P** arrived, the Jews who had **Ac 25:7**
while **P** said in his own defense, **Ac 25:8** *3972*
Jews a favor, answered **P** and said, **Ac 25:9** *3972*
But **P** said, "I am standing before **Ac 25:10** *3972*
whom **P** asserted to be alive. **Ac 25:19** *3972*
P appealed to be held in custody **Ac 25:21** *3972*

of Festus, **P** was brought in. **Ac 25:23** 3972
Agrippa said to **P**, **Ac 26:1** 3972
Then **P** stretched out his hand and **Ac 26:1** 3972
While **P** was saying this in his **Ac 26:24** 3972
"**P**, you are out of your mind! **Ac 26:24** 3972
P said, "I am not out of my mind, **Ac 26:25** 3972
Agrippa *replied* to **P**, **Ac 26:28** 3972
And **P** *said,* "I would wish to God, that **Ac 26:29** 3972
they proceeded to deliver **P** and **Ac 27:1** 3972
Julius treated **P** with consideration **Ac 27:3** 3972
over, **P** *began* to admonish them, **Ac 27:9** 3972
than by what was being said by **P**. **Ac 27:11** 3972
then **P** stood up in their midst and **Ac 27:21** 3972
'Do not be afraid, **P**; **Ac 27:24** 3972
P said to the centurion and to the **Ac 27:31** 3972
P was encouraging them all to take **Ac 27:33** 3972
wanting to bring **P** safely through, **Ac 27:43** 3972
But when **P** had gathered a bundle **Ac 28:3** 3972
and **P** went in *to see* him and after **Ac 28:8** 3972
and when **P** saw them, he thanked **Ac 28:15** 3972
P was allowed to stay by himself, **Ac 28:16** 3972
After three days **P** called together **Ac 28:17** 3972
When they had set a day for **P**, they **Ac 28:23** 3972
P had spoken one *parting* word, **Ac 28:25** 3972
P, a bond-servant of Christ Jesus, **Ro 1:1** 3972
P, called *as* an apostle of Jesus **1Co 1:1** 3972
one of you is saying, "I am of **P**," **1Co 1:12** 3972
P was not crucified for you, was **1Co 1:13** 3972
you baptized in the name of **P**? **1Co 1:13** 3972
For when one says, "I am of **P**," **1Co 3:4** 3972
what is **P**? Servants through whom **1Co 3:5** 3972
whether **P** or Apollos or Cephas or **1Co 3:22** 3972
The greeting is in my own hand—**P**. **1Co 16:21** 3972
P, an apostle of Christ Jesus by **2Co 1:1** 3972
Now I, **P**, myself urge you by the **2Co 10:1** 3972
P, an apostle (not *sent* from men nor **Ga 1:1** 3972
Behold I, **P**, say to you that if **Ga 5:2** 3972
P, an apostle of Christ Jesus by **Eph 1:1** 3972
I, **P**, the prisoner of Christ Jesus **Eph 3:1** 3972
P and Timothy, bond-servants of **Php 1:1** 3972
P, an apostle of Jesus Christ by **Col 1:1** 3972
of which I, **P**, was made a minister. **Col 1:23** 3972
I, **P**, write this greeting with my **Col 4:18** 3972
P and Silvanus and Timothy, To the **1Th 1:1** 3972
I, **P**, more than once **1Th 2:18** 3972
P and Silvanus and Timothy, To the **2Th 1:1** 3972
I, **P**, write this greeting with my **2Th 3:17** 3972
P, an apostle of Christ Jesus **1Tm 1:1** 3972
P, an apostle of Christ Jesus by **2Tm 1:1** 3972
P, a bond-servant of God and an **Ti 1:1** 3972
P, a prisoner of Christ Jesus, and **Phm 1:1** 3972
since I am such a person as **P**, **Phm 1:9** 3972
I, **P**, am writing this with my own **Phm 1:19** 3972
as also our beloved brother **P**, **2Pe 3:15** 3972

PAUL'S
And according to **P** custom, **Ac 17:2** 3972
P traveling companions from **Ac 19:29** 3972
he took **P** belt and bound his own **Ac 21:11** 3972
the son of **P** sister heard of their **Ac 23:16** 3972
Festus laid **P** case before the king, **Ac 25:14** 3972

PAULUS
was with the proconsul, Sergius **P**, **Ac 13:7** 3972

PAVEMENT
appeared to be a **p** of sapphire, **Ex 24:10** 3843
it and put it on a **p** of stone. **2Ki 16:17** 4837
bowed down on the **p** with their **2Ch 7:3** 7531b
silver on a mosaic **p** of porphyry, **Es 1:6** 7531b
there were chambers and a **p** made **Ezk 40:17** 7531b
thirty chambers faced the **p**. **Ezk 40:17** 7531b
The **p** (*that is,* the lower pavement) **Ezk 40:18** 7531b
The pavement (*that is,* the lower **p**) **Ezk 40:18** 7531b
and opposite the **p** which belonged **Ezk 42:3** 7531b
seat at a place called The **P**, **Jn 19:13** 3038

PAVILION
clouds, The thundering of His **p**? **Jb 36:29** 5521
He will pitch the tents of his royal **p** **Da 11:45** 643

PAW
delivered me from the **p** of the lion **1Sa 17:37** 3027
lion and from the **p** of the bear, **1Sa 17:37** 3027

PAWS
'Also whatever walks on its **p**, **Lv 11:27** 3709
"He **p** in the valley, and rejoices **Jb 39:21** 2658

PAY
They will **p** heed to what you say; **Ex 3:18** 8085
p no attention to false words." **Ex 5:9** 8159
shall only **p** for his loss of time, **Ex 21:19** 5414
he shall **p** as the judges *decide.* **Ex 21:22** 5414
it, he shall surely **p** ox for ox, **Ex 21:36** 7999a
he shall **p** five oxen for the ox **Ex 22:1** 7999a
or a sheep, he shall **p** double. **Ex 22:4** 7999a
is caught, he shall **p** double. **Ex 22:7** 7999a
shall **p** double to his neighbor. **Ex 22:9** 7999a
he must **p** a dowry for her *to be* **Ex 22:16** 4117
he shall **p** money equal to the **Ex 22:17** 8254
"The rich shall not **p** more and **Ex 30:15** 7235a
the poor shall not **p** less than the **Ex 30:15** 4591
water, then I will **p** its price. **Nu 20:19** 5414
away, and **p** no attention to them; **Dt 22:1** 5956
way, and **p** no attention to them; **Dt 22:4** 5956
God, you shall not delay to **p** it, **Dt 23:21** 7999a
"Let the woman **p** attention to all **Jg 13:13** 8104
LORD the yearly sacrifice and **p** **1Sa 1:21**
she did not answer or **p** attention. **1Sa 4:20** 7896
do not let my lord **p** attention to **1Sa 25:25** 7760
"Please let me go and **p** my vow **2Sa 15:7** 7999a
you shall **p** a talent of silver.' **1Ki 20:39** 8254
and used to **p** the king of Israel **2Ki 3:4** 7725
"Go, sell the oil and **p** your debt, **2Ki 4:7** 7999a
but **p** it for the damages of the **2Ki 12:7** 5414
to **p** to those who did the work, **2Ki 12:15** 5414
silver to **p** the king of Assyria. **2Ki 15:20** 5414
finished, they will not **p** tribute, **Ezr 4:13** 5415
and I will **p** ten thousand talents **Es 3:9** 8254
that Haman had promised to **p** **Es 4:7** 8254
And you will **p** your vows. **Jb 22:27** 7999a
surely He would **p** attention to me. **Jb 23:6** 7760
God does not **p** attention to folly. **Jb 24:12** 7760
"**P** attention, O Job, listen to me; **Jb 33:31** 7181
I shall **p** my vows before those who **Ps 22:25** 7999a
borrows and does not **p** back, **Ps 37:21** 7999a
And **p** your vows to the Most High; **Ps 50:14** 7999a
That I may **p** my vows day by day. **Ps 61:8** 7999a
I shall **p** You my vows, **Ps 66:13** 7999a
does the God of Jacob **p** heed." **Ps 94:7** 995
P heed, you senseless among the **Ps 94:8** 995
I shall **p** my vows to the LORD, Oh **Ps 116:14** 7999a
I shall **p** my vows to the LORD, Oh **Ps 116:18** 7999a
And **p** attention to the words of my **Pr 7:24** 7181
you have nothing with which to **p**, **Pr 22:27** 7999a
naive proceed *and* **p** the penalty. **Pr 27:12** 6064
And **p** attention to your herds; **Pr 27:23** 7896
P what you vow! **Ec 5:4** 7999a
that you should vow and not **p**. **Ec 5:5** 7999a
But they do not **p** attention to the **Is 5:12** 5027
P attention, Laishah *and* wretched **Is 10:30** 7181
camels, Let him **p** close attention, **Is 21:7** 7181
to Me, O islands, And **p** attention, **Is 49:1** 7181
"**P** attention to Me, O My people, **Is 51:4** 7181
uses his neighbor's services without **p** **Jer 22:13** 2600
have to **p** for our drinking water, **La 5:4** 3701
will also no longer **p** your lovers. **Ezk 16:41** 5414
That which I have vowed I will **p**. **Jon 2:9** 7999a
your feasts, O Judah; **P** your vows. **Na 1:15** 7999a
"But they refused to **p** attention and **Zch 7:11** 7181
not **p** the two-drachma *tax?*" **Mt 17:24** 5055
'**P** back what you owe.' **Mt 18:28** 591
he should **p** back what was owed. **Mt 18:30** 591
laborers and **p** them their wages, **Mt 20:8** 591
who will **p** him the proceeds at the **Mt 21:41** 591
lawful to **p** a poll-tax to Caesar, **Mk 12:14** 1325
"Shall we **p** or shall we not pay?" **Mk 12:15** 1325
"Shall we pay or shall we not **p**?" **Mk 12:15** 1325
For you **p** tithe of mint and rue **Lk 11:42** 586b
I **p** tithes of all that I get.' **Lk 18:12** 586a
for us to **p** taxes to Caesar, **Lk 20:22** 1325
forbidding to **p** taxes to Caesar, **Lk 23:2** 1325
and **p** their expenses so that **Ac 21:24** 1159
Never **p** back evil for evil to anyone. **Ro 12:17** 591
because of this you also **p** taxes, **Ro 13:6** 5055
p the penalty of eternal destruction, **2Th 1:9** 5099
nor to **p** attention to myths and **1Tm 1:4** 4337
P close attention to yourself and **1Tm 4:16** 1907
we must **p** much closer attention to **Heb 2:1** 4337
and you **p** special attention to the **Jas 2:3** 1914
the **p** of the laborers who mowed **Jas 5:4** 3408
to which you do well to **p** attention **2Pe 1:19** 4337
and for **p** they have rushed headlong **Jude 1:11** 3408
"**P** her back even as she has paid, **Rv 18:6** 591

PAYING
"When you have finished **p** all the **Dt 26:12** 6237
to God, do not be late in **p** it; **Ec 5:4** 7999a
anyone's bread without **p** for it, **2Th 3:8** 1431
p attention to deceitful spirits **1Tm 4:1** 4337
not **p** attention to Jewish myths **Ti 1:14** 4337

PAYMENT
me ever so much bridal **p** and gift, **Gn 34:12** 4119
go out as a free man without **p**. **Ex 21:2** 2600
without **p** *of* money. **Ex 21:11**
free, Without any **p** or reward," **Is 45:13** 4242
and ebony they brought as your **p**. **Ezk 27:15** 814

PAYS
bears a grudge against us and **p** us **Gn 50:15** 7725
He **p** a man according to his work, **Jb 34:11** 7999a
A liar **p** attention to a **Pr 17:4** 238
a ruler **p** attention to falsehood, **Pr 29:12** 7181
p back what he has taken by **Ezk 33:15** 7999a
from Judah, **p** no attention to you, **Da 6:13** 7761

PEACE
you shall go to your fathers in **p**; **Gn 15:15** 7965
good and have sent you away in **p**. **Gn 26:29** 7965
and they departed from him in **p**. **Gn 26:31** 7965
you, go up in **p** to your father." **Gn 44:17** 7965
Jethro said to Moses, "Go in **p**." **Ex 4:18** 7965
will go to their place in **p**." **Ex 18:23** 7965
offerings and your **p** offerings, **Ex 20:24** 8002
bulls as **p** offerings to the LORD. **Ex 24:5** 8002
sacrifices of their **p** offerings, **Ex 29:28** 8002
and brought **p** offerings; **Ex 32:6** 8002
is a sacrifice of **p** offerings, **Lv 3:1** 8002
the sacrifice of the **p** offerings he **Lv 3:3** 8002
sacrifice of **p** offerings to the LORD **Lv 3:6** 8002
'From the sacrifice of **p** offerings **Lv 3:9** 8002
of the sacrifice of **p** offerings), **Lv 4:10** 8002
of the sacrifice of **p** offerings. **Lv 4:26** 8002
from the sacrifice of **p** offerings; **Lv 4:31** 8002
the sacrifice of the **p** offerings, **Lv 4:35** 8002
portions of the **p** offerings on it. **Lv 6:12** 8002
the law of the sacrifice of **p** offerings **Lv 7:11** 8002
his **p** offerings for thanksgiving, **Lv 7:13** 8002
the blood of the **p** offerings. **Lv 7:14** 8002
of his thanksgiving **p** offerings, **Lv 7:15** 8002
flesh of the sacrifice of his **p** offerings **Lv 7:18** 8002
p offerings which belong to the LORD, **Lv 7:20** 8002
the flesh of the sacrifice of **p** offerings **Lv 7:21** 8002
offers the sacrifice of his **p** offerings **Lv 7:29** 8002
the sacrifice of his **p** offerings. **Lv 7:29** 8002
sacrifices of your **p** offerings. **Lv 7:32** 8002
of the **p** offerings and the fat, **Lv 7:33** 8002
sacrifices of their **p** offerings, **Lv 7:34** 8002
and the sacrifice of **p** offerings, **Lv 7:37** 8002
an ox and a ram for **p** offerings, **Lv 9:4** 8002
the sacrifice of **p** offerings which **Lv 9:18** 8002
offering and the **p** offerings. **Lv 9:22** 8002
the **p** offerings of the sons of Israel. **Lv 10:14** 8002
of **p** offerings to the LORD. **Lv 17:5** 8002
of **p** offerings to the LORD, **Lv 19:5** 8002
a man offers a sacrifice of **p** offerings **Lv 22:21** 8002
for a sacrifice of **p** offerings. **Lv 23:19** 8002
'I shall also grant **p** in the land, **Lv 26:6** 7965
without defect for a **p** offering, **Nu 6:14** 8002
the ram for a sacrifice of **p** offerings **Nu 6:17** 8002
the sacrifice of **p** offerings. **Nu 6:18** 8002
on you, And give you **p**.' **Nu 6:26** 7965
for the sacrifice of **p** offerings, **Nu 7:17** 8002
for the sacrifice of **p** offerings, **Nu 7:23** 8002
for the sacrifice of **p** offerings, **Nu 7:29** 8002
for the sacrifice of **p** offerings, **Nu 7:35** 8002
for the sacrifice of **p** offerings, **Nu 7:41** 8002
for the sacrifice of **p** offerings, **Nu 7:47** 8002
for the sacrifice of **p** offerings, **Nu 7:53** 8002
for the sacrifice of **p** offerings, **Nu 7:59** 8002
for the sacrifice of **p** offerings, **Nu 7:65** 8002
for the sacrifice of **p** offerings, **Nu 7:71** 8002
for the sacrifice of **p** offerings, **Nu 7:77** 8002
for the sacrifice of **p** offerings, **Nu 7:83** 8002
sacrifice of **p** offerings 24 bulls, **Nu 7:88** 8002
sacrifices of your **p** offerings; **Nu 10:10** 8002
or for **p** offerings to the LORD, **Nu 15:8** 8002
I give him My covenant of **p**; **Nu 25:12** 7965
and for your **p** offerings.' " **Nu 29:39** 8002
king of Heshbon with words of **p**, **Dt 2:26** 7965
it, you shall offer it terms of **p**. **Dt 20:10** 7965
If it agrees to make **p** with you and **Dt 20:11** 7965
if it does not make **p** with you, **Dt 20:12** 7999b
"You shall never seek their **p** or **Dt 23:6** 7965
p offerings and eat there, **Dt 27:7** 8002
'I have **p** though I walk in the **Dt 29:19** 7965
LORD, and sacrificed **p** offerings. **Jos 8:31** 8002
Joshua made **p** with them and **Jos 9:15** 7965
Gibeon had made **p** with Israel **Jos 10:1** 7999b
for it has made **p** with Joshua and **Jos 10:4** 7999b
camp to Joshua at Makkedah in **p**. **Jos 10:21** 7965
There was not a city which made **p** **Jos 11:19** 7999b
sacrifices of **p** offerings on it, **Jos 22:23** 8002
and with our **p** offerings, **Jos 22:27** 8002
for *there was* **p** between Jabin the **Jg 4:17** 7965
"**P** to you, do not fear; **Jg 6:23** 7965
LORD and named it The LORD is **P**. **Jg 6:24** 7965
meet me when I return in **p** from **Jg 11:31** 7965
The priest said to them, "Go in **p**; **Jg 18:6** 7965
The old man said, "**P** to you. **Jg 19:20** 7965
and **p** offerings before the LORD. **Jg 20:26** 8002
burnt offerings and **p** offerings. **Jg 21:4** 8002
Rimmon, and proclaimed **p** to them. **Jg 21:13** 7965
Eli answered and said, "Go in **p**; **1Sa 1:17** 7965
So there was **p** between Israel and **1Sa 7:14** 7965
and sacrifice **p** offerings. **1Sa 10:8** 8002
of **p** offerings before the LORD; **1Sa 11:15** 8002
offering and the **p** offerings." **1Sa 13:9** 8002
"Do you come in **p**?" **1Sa 16:4** 7965
"In **p**; I have come to sacrifice to **1Sa 16:5** 7965
'Have a long life, **p** be to you, **1Sa 25:6** 7965
be to you, and **p** be to your house, **1Sa 25:6** 7965
and **p** be to all that you have. **1Sa 25:6** 7965
"Go up to your house in **p**. **1Sa 25:35** 7965
"Now therefore return and go in **p**, **1Sa 29:7** 7965
sent Abner away, and he went in **p**. **2Sa 3:21** 7965
him away, and he had gone in **p**. **2Sa 3:22** 7965
him away, and he has gone in **p**." **2Sa 3:23** 7965
and **p** offerings before the LORD. **2Sa 6:17** 8002
burnt offering and the **p** offering, **2Sa 6:18** 8002
made **p** with Israel and served them. **2Sa 10:19** 7999b
The king said to him, "Go in **p**." **2Sa 15:9** 7965
Return to the city in **p** and your two **2Sa 15:27** 7965
all the people will be at **p**." **2Sa 17:3** 7965
until the day he came *home* in **p**. **2Sa 19:24** 7965
burnt offerings and **p** offerings. **2Sa 24:25** 8002
also shed the blood of war in **p**. **1Ki 2:5** 7965
gray hair go down to Sheol in **p**. **1Ki 2:6** 7965
be **p** from the LORD forever." **1Ki 2:33** 7965
offerings and made **p** offerings, **1Ki 3:15** 8002
p on all sides around about him. **1Ki 4:24** 7965
was **p** between Hiram and Solomon, **1Ki 5:12** 7965
for the sacrifice of **p** offerings, **1Ki 8:63** 8002
and the fat of the **p** offerings; **1Ki 8:64** 8002
and the fat of the **p** offerings. **1Ki 8:64** 8002
offered burnt offerings and **p** offerings **1Ki 9:25** 8002
"If they have come out for **p**, **1Ki 20:18** 7965
them return to his house in **p**.' " **1Ki 22:17** 7965
made **p** with the king of Israel. **1Ki 22:44** 7999b
He said to him, "Go in **p**." **2Ki 5:19** 7965
and let him say, 'Is it **p**?' " **2Ki 9:17** 7965
"Thus says the king, 'Is it **p**?' " **2Ki 9:18** 7965
"What have you to do with **p**? **2Ki 9:18** 7965
"Thus says the king, 'Is it **p**?' " **2Ki 9:19** 7965
"What have you to do with **p**? **2Ki 9:19** 7965
"Is it **p**, Jehu?" **2Ki 9:22** 7965
"What **p**, so long as the **2Ki 9:22** 7965
sprinkled the blood of his **p** offerings **2Ki 16:13** 8002
Make your **p** with me and come out **2Ki 18:31** 1293
will be **p** and truth in my days?" **2Ki 20:19** 7965
be gathered to your grave in **p**, **2Ki 22:20** 7965
P, peace to you, And peace to him **1Ch 12:18** 7965
Peace, **p** to you, And peace to him **1Ch 12:18** 7965

you, And **p** to him who helps you; **1Ch 12:18** 7965
and **p** offerings before God. **1Ch 16:1** 8002
offering and the **p** offerings, **1Ch 16:2** 8002
made **p** with David and served him. **1Ch 19:19** 7999b
burnt offerings and **p** offerings. **1Ch 21:26** 8002
and I will give **p** and quiet to **1Ch 22:9** 7965
and the fat of the **p** offerings because **2Ch 7:7** 8002
there was no **p** to him who went out **2Ch 15:5** 7965
them return to his house in **p**.' " **2Ch 18:16** 7965
kingdom of Jehoshaphat was at **p**, **2Ch 20:30** 8252
with the fat of the **p** offerings and **2Ch 29:35** 8002
sacrificing **p** offerings and giving **2Ch 30:22** 8002
offerings and for **p** offerings, **2Ch 31:2** 8002
and sacrificed **p** offerings and thank **2Ch 33:16** 8002
be gathered to your grave in **p**, **2Ch 34:28** 7965
provinces beyond the River: "**P**. **Ezr 4:17** 8001
"To Darius the king, all **p**. **Ezr 5:7** 8001
God of heaven, perfect **p**. And now **Ezr 7:12**
seek their **p** or their prosperity, **Ezr 9:12** 7965
namely, words of **p** and truth, **Es 9:30** 7965
the field will be at **p** with you. **Jb 5:23** 7999b
While at **p** the destroyer comes **Jb 15:21** 7965
"Yield now and be at **p** with Him; **Jb 22:21** 7999b
Who establishes **p** in His heights. **Jb 25:2** 7965
In **p** I will both lie down and **Ps 4:8** 7965
Who speak **p** with their neighbors, **Ps 28:3** 7965
LORD will bless His people with **p**. **Ps 29:11** 7965
Seek **p** and pursue it. **Ps 34:14** 7965
For they do not speak **p**, **Ps 35:20** 7965
man of **p** will have a posterity. **Ps 37:37** 7965
He will redeem my soul in **p** from **Ps 55:18** 7965
those who were at **p** with him; **Ps 55:20** 7965
And when they are in **p**, **Ps 69:22** 7965
mountains bring **p** to the people, **Ps 72:3** 7965
abundance of **p** till the moon is no **Ps 72:7** 7965
For He will speak **p** to His people, **Ps 85:8** 7965
Righteousness and **p** have kissed **Ps 85:10** 7965
who love Your law have great **p**, **Ps 119:165** 7965
dwelling With those who hate **p**. **Ps 120:6** 7965
I am *for* **p**, but when I speak, They **Ps 120:7** 7965
Pray for the **p** of Jerusalem: **Ps 122:6** 7965
"May **p** be within your walls, And **Ps 122:7** 7965
"May **p** be within you." **Ps 122:8** 7965
P be upon Israel. **Ps 125:5** 7965
P be upon Israel! **Ps 128:6** 7965
He makes **p** in your borders; **Ps 147:14** 7965
life And **p** they will add to you. **Pr 3:2** 7965
ways And all her paths are **p**. **Pr 3:17** 7965
"I was due to offer **p** offerings; **Pr 7:14** 8002
But counselors of **p** have joy. **Pr 12:20** 7965
his enemies to be at **p** with him. **Pr 16:7** 7999b
A time for war and a time for **p**. **Ec 3:8** 7965
in his eyes as one who finds **p**. **SS 8:10** 7965
God, Eternal Father, Prince of **P**. **Is 9:6** 7965
increase of *His* government or of **p**, **Is 9:7** 7965
mind You will keep in perfect **p**, **Is 26:3** 7965
You will establish **p** for us, **Is 26:12** 7965
Let him make **p** with Me, **Is 27:5** 7965
with Me, Let him make **p** with Me." **Is 27:5** 7965
work of righteousness will be **p**, **Is 32:17** 7965
ambassadors of **p** weep bitterly. **Is 33:7** 7965
Make your **p** with me and come out **Is 36:16** 1293
will be **p** and truth in my days." **Is 39:8** 7965
blind as he that is at **p** *with Me,* **Is 42:19** 7999b
"There is no **p** for the wicked," **Is 48:22** 7965
Who announces **p** And brings good **Is 52:7** 7965
My covenant of **p** will not be shaken **Is 54:10** 7965
with joy And be led forth with **p**; **Is 55:12** 7965
He enters into **p**; **Is 57:2** 7965
P, peace to him who is far and to **Is 57:19** 7965
p to him who is far and to him who **Is 57:19** 7965
"There is no **p**," says my God, **Is 57:21** 7965
They do not know the way of **p**, **Is 59:8** 7965
treads on them does not know **p**. **Is 59:8** 7965
I will make **p** your administrators And **Is 60:17** 7965
I extend **p** to her like a river, **Is 66:12** 7965
saying, 'You will have **p**'; whereas **Jer 4:10** 7965
'**P**, peace,' But there is no peace. **Jer 6:14** 7965
'Peace, **p**,' But there is no peace. **Jer 6:14** 7965
'Peace, peace,' But there is no **p**. **Jer 6:14** 7965
'**P**, peace,' But there is no peace. **Jer 8:11** 7965
'Peace, **p**,' But there is no peace. **Jer 8:11** 7965
'Peace, peace,' But there is no **p**. **Jer 8:11** 7965
We waited for **p**, but no good *came;* **Jer 8:15** 7965
one speaks **p** to his neighbor, **Jer 9:8** 7965
If you fall down in a land of **p**, **Jer 12:5** 7965
There is no **p** for anyone. **Jer 12:12** 7965
I will give you lasting **p** in this place **Jer 14:13** 7965
We waited for **p**, but nothing good **Jer 14:19** 7965
withdrawn My **p** from this people," **Jer 16:5** 7965
"You will have **p**" **Jer 23:17** 7965
"The prophet who prophesies of **p**, **Jer 28:9** 7965
Of dread, and there is no **p**. **Jer 30:5** 7965
them an abundance of **p** and truth. **Jer 33:6** 7965
and all the **p** that I make for it.' **Jer 33:9** 7965
'You will die in **p**; **Jer 34:5** 7965
My soul has been rejected from **p**; **La 3:17** 7965
anguish comes, they will seek **p**, **Ezk 7:25** 7965
misled My people by saying, '**P**!' **Ezk 13:10** 7965
when there is no **p**. **Ezk 13:10** 7965
and who see visions of **p** for her **Ezk 13:16** 7965
peace for her when there is no **p**,' **Ezk 13:16** 7965
"I will make a covenant of **p** **Ezk 34:25** 7965
make a covenant of **p** with them; **Ezk 37:26** 7965
the altar, and your **p** offerings; **Ezk 43:27** 8002
offering and for **p** offerings, **Ezk 45:15** 8002
offering and the **p** offerings, **Ezk 45:17** 8002
offering and his **p** offerings, **Ezk 46:2** 8002
or **p** offerings *as* a freewill **Ezk 46:12** 8002
his burnt offering and his **p** offerings **Ezk 46:12** 8002
"May your **p** abound! **Da 4:1** 8001
"May your **p** abound! **Da 6:25** 8001
P be with you; take courage and be **Da 10:19** 7965
p which he will put into effect; **Da 11:17** 3477
the **p** offerings of your fatlings. **Am 5:22** 8002
And the men at **p** with you Will **Ob 1:7** 7965
with their teeth, They cry, "**P**," **Mi 3:5** 7965
This One will be *our* **p**. **Mi 5:5** 7965
brings good news, Who announces **p**! **Na 1:15** 7965
'and in this place I will give **p**,' **Hg 2:9** 7965
and the counsel of **p** will be **Zch 6:13** 7965
was no **p** because of his enemies, **Zch 8:10** 7965
'For *there will be* **p** for the seed: **Zch 8:12** 7965
and judgment for **p** in your gates. **Zch 8:16** 7965
so love truth and **p**.' **Zch 8:19** 7965
He will speak **p** to the nations; **Zch 9:10** 7965
with him was *one of* life and **p**, **Mal 2:5** 7965
with Me in **p** and uprightness, **Mal 2:6** 7965
give it your *blessing of* **p**. **Mt 10:13** *1515*
take back your *blessing of* **p**. **Mt 10:13** *1515*
I came to bring **p** on the earth; **Mt 10:34** *1515*
I did not come to bring **p**, **Mt 10:34** *1515*
go in **p** and be healed of your **Mk 5:34** *1515*
and be at **p** with one another." **Mk 9:50** *1514*
our feet into the way of **p**." **Lk 1:79** *1515*
And on earth **p** among men with whom **Lk 2:14** *1515*
rYour bond-servant to depart in **p**, **Lk 2:29** *1515*
"Your faith has saved you; go in **p**." **Lk 7:50** *1515*
faith has made you well; go in **p**." **Lk 8:48** *1515*
'**P** *be* to this house.' **Lk 10:5** *1515*
"If a man of **p** is there, your **Lk 10:6** *1515*
there, your **p** will rest on him; **Lk 10:6** *1515*
that I came to grant **p** on earth? **Lk 12:51** *1515*
a delegation and asks for terms of **p**. **Lk 14:32** *1515*
P in heaven and glory in the **Lk 19:38** *1515*
you, the things which make for **p**! **Lk 19:42** *1515*
said to them, "**P** be to you" **Lk 24:36** *1515*
"**P** I leave with you; **Jn 14:27** *1515*
My **p** I give to you; **Jn 14:27** *1515*
to you, so that in Me you may have **p**. **Jn 16:33** *1515*
and said to them, "**P** *be* with you." **Jn 20:19** *1515*
said to them again, "**P** *be* with you; **Jn 20:21** *1515*
and said, "**P** *be* with you." **Jn 20:26** *1515*
he tried to reconcile them in **p**, **Ac 7:26** *1515*
and Galilee and Samaria enjoyed **p**, **Ac 9:31** *1515*
preaching **p** through Jesus Christ **Ac 10:36** *1515*
they were asking for **p**, **Ac 12:20** *1515*
sent away from the brethren in **p** **Ac 15:33** *1515*
Therefore come out now and go in **p**." **Ac 16:36** *1515*
have through you attained much **p**, **Ac 24:2** *1515*
Grace to you and **p** from God our **Ro 1:7** *1515*
and **p** to everyone who does good, **Ro 2:10** *1515*
PATH OF **P** THEY HAVE NOT KNOWN." **Ro 3:17** *1515*
we have **p** with God through our **Ro 5:1** *1515*
mind set on the Spirit is life and **p**, **Ro 8:6** *1515*
on you, be at **p** with all men. **Ro 12:18** *1514*
and **p** and joy in the Holy Spirit. **Ro 14:17** *1515*
pursue the things which make for **p** **Ro 14:19** *1515*
with all joy and **p** in believing, **Ro 15:13** *1515*
Now the God of **p** be with you all. **Ro 15:33** *1515*
The God of **p** will soon crush **Ro 16:20** *1515*
Grace to you and **p** from God our **1Co 1:3** *1515*
cases, but God has called us to **p**. **1Co 7:15** *1515*
not *a God* of confusion but of **p**, **1Co 14:33** *1515*
But send him on his way in **p**, **1Co 16:11** *1515*
Grace to you and **p** from God our **2Co 1:2** *1515*
be like-minded, live in **p**; **2Co 13:11** *1514*
of love and **p** will be with you. **2Co 13:11** *1515*
to you and **p** from God our Father and **Ga 1:3** *1515*
the fruit of the Spirit is love, joy, **p**, **Ga 5:22** *1515*
rule, **p** and mercy *be* upon them, **Ga 6:16** *1515*
Grace to you and **p** from God our **Eph 1:2** *1515*
For He Himself is our **p**, **Eph 2:14** *1515*
one new man, *thus* establishing **p**, **Eph 2:15** *1515*
P TO YOU WHO WERE FAR AWAY, **Eph 2:17** *1515*
AND **P** TO THOSE WHO WERE NEAR; **Eph 2:17** *1515*
of the Spirit in the bond of **p**. **Eph 4:3** *1515*
PREPARATION OF THE GOSPEL OF **P**; **Eph 6:15** *1515*
P be to the brethren, and love **Eph 6:23** *1515*
Grace to you and **p** from God our **Php 1:2** *1515*
And the **p** of God, which surpasses **Php 4:7** *1515*
the God of **p** will be with you. **Php 4:9** *1515*
to you and **p** from God our Father. **Col 1:2** *1515*
having made **p** through the blood of **Col 1:20** *1517*
p of Christ rule in your hearts, **Col 3:15** *1515*
Grace to you and **p**. **1Th 1:1** *1515*
While they are saying, "**P** and safety! **1Th 5:3** *1515*
Live in **p** with one another. **1Th 5:13** *1514*
may the God of **p** Himself sanctify **1Th 5:23** *1515*
Grace to you and **p** from God the **2Th 1:2** *1515*
Now may the Lord of **p** Himself **2Th 3:16** *1515*
grant you **p** in every circumstance. **2Th 3:16** *1515*
Grace, mercy *and* **p** from God the **1Tm 1:2** *1515*
mercy *and* **p** from God the Father **2Tm 1:2** *1515*
righteousness, faith, love *and* **p**, **2Tm 2:22** *1515*
Grace and **p** from God the Father **Ti 1:4** *1515*
Grace to you and **p** from God our **Phm 1:3** *1515*
king of Salem, which is king of **p**. **Heb 7:2** *1515*
she had welcomed the spies in **p**. **Heb 11:31** *1515*
Pursue **p** with all men, and the **Heb 12:14** *1515*
Now the God of **p**, who brought up **Heb 13:20** *1515*
"Go in **p**, be warmed and be filled," **Jas 2:16** *1515*
sown in **p** by those who make peace. **Jas 3:18** *1515*
sown in peace by those who make **p**. **Jas 3:18** *1515*
and **p** be yours in the fullest measure. **1Pe 1:2** *1515*
HE MUST SEEK **P** AND PURSUE IT. **1Pe 3:11** *1515*
P be to you all who are in Christ **1Pe 5:14** *1515*
Grace and **p** be multiplied to you **2Pe 1:2** *1515*
diligent to be found by Him in **p**, **2Pe 3:14** *1515*
mercy *and* **p** will be with us, **2Jn 1:3** *1515*
P *be* to you. The friends greet you. **3Jn 1:15** *1515*
p and love be multiplied to you. **Jude 1:2** *1515*
Grace to you and **p**, **Rv 1:4** *1515*
granted to take **p** from the earth, **Rv 6:4** *1515*

PEACEABLE
who are **p** *and* faithful in Israel. **2Sa 20:19** 7999b
p, free from the love of money. **1Tm 3:3** *269*
to malign no one, to be **p**, gentle, **Ti 3:2** *269*
from above is first pure, then **p**, **Jas 3:17** *1516*

PEACEABLY
therefore, return them **p** now." **Jg 11:13** 7965

PEACEFUL
but Jacob was a **p** man, living in **Gn 25:27** 8535
land was broad and quiet and **p**; **1Ch 4:40** 7961
will live in a **p** habitation, **Is 32:18** 7965
"And the **p** folds are made silent **Jer 25:37** 7965
to carry out a **p** arrangement. **Da 11:6** 4339
all the earth is **p** and quiet." **Zch 1:11** 3427
it yields the **p** fruit of righteousness. **Heb 12:11** *1516*

PEACEFULLY
And she said, "Do you come **p**?" **1Ki 2:13** 7965
And he said, "**P**." **1Ki 2:13** 7965
"If you come **p** to me to help me, **1Ch 12:17** 7965

PEACEMAKERS
"Blessed are the **p**, for they **Mt 5:9** *1518*

PEACOCKS
and silver, ivory and apes and **p**. **1Ki 10:22** 8500
and silver, ivory and apes and **p**. **2Ch 9:21** 8500

PEAK
And I will go to its highest **p**, **Is 37:24** 7093

PEAKS
the Jordan And the **p** of Hermon, **Ps 42:6**
many **p** is the mountain of Bashan. **Ps 68:15** 1386
envy, O mountains with *many* **p**, **Ps 68:16** 1386
p of the mountains are His also. **Ps 95:4** 8443

PEALS
and sounds and **p** of thunder. **Rv 4:5** *1027*
and there followed **p** of thunder **Rv 8:5** *1027*
the seven **p** of thunder uttered **Rv 10:3** *1027*
seven **p** of thunder had spoken, **Rv 10:4** *1027*
the seven **p** of thunder have spoken **Rv 10:4** *1027*
and sounds and **p** of thunder and an **Rv 11:19** *1027*
and sounds and **p** of thunder; **Rv 16:18** *1027*
the sound of mighty **p** of thunder, **Rv 19:6** *1027*

PEARL
upon finding one **p** of great value, **Mt 13:46** *3135*
one of the gates was a single **p**. **Rv 21:21** *3135*

PEARLS
of wisdom is above *that of* **p**. **Jb 28:18** 6443
do not throw your **p** before swine, **Mt 7:6** *3135*
is like a merchant seeking fine **p**, **Mt 13:45** *3135*
and gold or **p** or costly garments, **1Tm 2:9** *3135*
gold and precious stones and **p**, **Rv 17:4** *3135*
precious stones and **p** and fine linen **Rv 18:12** *3135*
gold and precious stones and **p**; **Rv 18:16** *3135*
the twelve gates were twelve **p**; **Rv 21:21** *3135*

PEASANTRY
"The **p** ceased, they ceased in **Jg 5:7** 6520
righteous deeds for His **p** in Israel. **Jg 5:11** 6520

PECKS
took and hid in three **p** of flour **Mt 13:33** *4568*
took and hid in three **p** of flour **Lk 13:21** *4568*

PEDAHEL
a leader, **P** the son of Ammihud." **Nu 34:28** 6300

PEDAHZUR
Manasseh, Gamaliel the son of **P**; **Nu 1:10** 6301
Gamaliel the son of **P**, **Nu 2:20** 6301
day *it was* Gamaliel the son of **P**, **Nu 7:54** 6301
offering of Gamaliel the son of **P**. **Nu 7:59** 6301
and Gamaliel the son of **P** over the **Nu 10:23** 6301

PEDAIAH
the daughter of **P** of Rumah. **2Ki 23:36** 6305
and Malchiram, **P**, Shenazzar, **1Ch 3:18** 6305
of **P** *were* Zerubbabel and Shimei. **1Ch 3:19** 6305
of Manasseh, Joel the son of **P**; **1Ch 27:20** 6305
After him **P** the son of Parosh *made* **Ne 3:25** 6305
and **P**, Mishael, Malchijah, Hashum, **Ne 8:4** 6305
the son of Joed, the son of **P**, **Ne 11:7** 6305
the scribe, and **P** of the Levites, **Ne 13:13** 6305

PEDDLING
not like many, **p** the word of God, **2Co 2:17** *2585*

PEDESTAL
on the frames there *was* a **p** above, **1Ki 7:29** 3653b
was round like the design of a **p**, **1Ki 7:31** 3653b
will be set there on her own **p**." **Zch 5:11** 4350

PEDESTALS
alabaster Set on **p** of pure gold; **SS 5:15** 134

PEELED
and **p** white stripes in them, **Gn 30:37** 6478
He set the rods which he had **p** **Gn 30:38** 6478

PEERING
He is **p** through the lattice. **SS 2:9** 6692b

PEG
took a tent **p** and seized a hammer **Jg 4:21** 3489
and drove the **p** into his temple, **Jg 4:21** 3489
with the tent **p** in his temple. **Jg 4:22** 3489
out her hand for the tent **p**, **Jg 5:26** 3489
to give us a **p** in His holy place, **Ezr 9:8** 3489
drive him *like* a **p** in a firm place, **Is 22:23** 3489
"the **p** driven in a firm place **Is 22:25** 3489
or can *men* take a **p** from it on **Ezk 15:3** 3489
cornerstone, From them the tent **p**, **Zch 10:4** 3489

PEGS
in all its service, and all its **p**, **Ex 27:19** 3489

pegs, and all the **p** of the court,	**Ex 27:19**	3489
the **p** of the tabernacle and the	**Ex 35:18**	3489
the **p** of the court and their	**Ex 35:18**	3489
All the **p** of the tabernacle	**Ex 38:20**	3489
and all the **p** of the tabernacle	**Ex 38:31**	3489
all the **p** of the court all around.	**Ex 38:31**	3489
its cords and its **p** and all the	**Ex 39:40**	3489
and their **p** and their cords.	**Nu 3:37**	3489
and their **p** and their cords,	**Nu 4:32**	3489
your cords And strengthen your **p**.	**Is 54:2**	3489
PEKAH		
Then **P** son of Remaliah, his	**2Ki 15:25**	6492
P son of Remaliah became king over	**2Ki 15:27**	6492
In the days of **P** king of Israel,	**2Ki 15:29**	6492
against **P** the son of Remaliah,	**2Ki 15:30**	6492
the acts of **P** and all that he did,	**2Ki 15:31**	6492
In the second year of **P** the son of	**2Ki 15:32**	6492
P the son of Remaliah against Judah.	**2Ki 15:37**	6492
year of **P** the son of Remaliah,	**2Ki 16:1**	6492
of Aram and **P** son of Remaliah,	**2Ki 16:5**	6492
For **P** the son of Remaliah slew in	**2Ch 28:6**	6492
of Aram and **P** the son of Remaliah,	**Is 7:1**	6492
PEKAHIAH		
and **P** his son became king in his	**2Ki 15:22**	6494
P son of Menahem became king over	**2Ki 15:23**	6494
the acts of **P** and all that he did,	**2Ki 15:26**	6494
PEKOD		
And against the inhabitants of **P**.	**Jer 50:21**	6489
the Chaldeans, **P** and Shoa and Koa,	**Ezk 23:23**	6489
PELAIAH		
were Hodaviah, Eliashib, **P**,	**1Ch 3:24**	6411
Azariah, Jozabad, Hanan, **P**,	**Ne 8:7**	6384b
Shebaniah, Hodiah, Kelita, **P**,	**Ne 10:10**	6384b
PELALIAH		
the son of Jeroham, the son of **P**,	**Ne 11:12**	6421
PELATIAH		
of Hananiah *were* **P** and Jeshaiah,	**1Ch 3:21**	6410
men went to Mount Seir, with **P**,	**1Ch 4:42**	6410
P, Hanan, Anaiah,	**Ne 10:22**	6410
son of Azzur and **P** son of Benaiah,	**Ezk 11:1**	6410
that **P** son of Benaiah died.	**Ezk 11:13**	6410
PELEG		
the name of the one *was* **P**,	**Gn 10:25**	6389
years, and became the father of **P**;	**Gn 11:16**	6389
after he became the father of **P**,	**Gn 11:17**	6389
P lived thirty years, and	**Gn 11:18**	6389
and **P** lived two hundred and nine	**Gn 11:19**	6389
Eber, the name of the one was **P**,	**1Ch 1:19**	6389
Eber, **P**, Reu,	**1Ch 1:25**	6389
the son of Reu, the son of **P**,	**Lk 3:35**	*5317*
PELET		
were Regem, Jotham, Geshan, **P**,	**1Ch 2:47**	6404
and Jeziel and **P**, the sons of	**1Ch 12:3**	6404
PELETH		
of Eliab, and On the son of **P**,	**Nu 16:1**	6431
sons of Jonathan *were* **P** and Zaza.	**1Ch 2:33**	6431
PELETHITES		
over the Cherethites and the **P**;	**2Sa 8:18**	6432
all the Cherethites, all the **P** and	**2Sa 15:18**	6432
and the **P** and all the mighty men;	**2Sa 20:7**	6432
over the Cherethites and the **P**;	**2Sa 20:23**	6432
and the **P** went down and had	**1Ki 1:38**	6432
the Cherethites, and the **P**;	**1Ki 1:44**	6432
over the Cherethites and the **P**,	**1Ch 18:17**	6432
PELICAN		
and the **p** and the carrion vulture,	**Lv 11:18**	6893
the **p**, the carrion vulture, the	**Dt 14:17**	6893
I resemble a **p** of the wilderness;	**Ps 102:6**	6893
p and hedgehog will possess it,	**Is 34:11**	6893
Both the **p** and the hedgehog Will	**Zph 2:14**	6893
PELONITE		
the Harorite, Helez the **P**,	**1Ch 11:27**	6397
the Mecherathite, Ahijah the **P**,	**1Ch 11:36**	6397
the **P** of the sons of Ephraim;	**1Ch 27:10**	6397
PEN		
tongue is the **p** of a ready writer.	**Ps 45:1**	5842
the lying **p** of the scribes Has	**Jer 8:8**	5842
write *them* to you with **p** and ink;	**3Jn 1:13**	*2563*
PENALTY		
then you shall appoint *as a* **p**	**Ex 21:23**	
of great anger will bear the **p**,	**Pr 19:19**	6066
The naive proceed *and* pay the **p**.	**Pr 27:12**	6064
"You have borne *the* **p** *of* your	**Ezk 16:58**	
the **p** of *worshiping* your idols;	**Ezk 23:49**	2399
persons the due **p** of their error.	**Ro 1:27**	*489*
pay the **p** of eternal destruction,	**2Th 1:9**	*1349*
and disobedience received a just **p**,	**Heb 2:2**	*3405*
PENDANTS		
the crescent ornaments and the **p**	**Jg 8:26**	5188
PENIEL		
So Jacob named the place **P**,	**Gn 32:30**	6439
PENINNAH		
and the name of the other **P**;	**1Sa 1:2**	6444
and **P** had children, but Hannah had	**1Sa 1:2**	6444
he would give portions to **P** his wife	**1Sa 1:4**	6444
PENS		
p for all kinds of cattle and	**2Ch 32:28**	723a
PENTECOST		
When the day of **P** had come,	**Ac 2:1**	*4005*
if possible, on the day of **P**.	**Ac 20:16**	*4005*
I will remain in Ephesus until **P**;	**1Co 16:8**	*4005*
PENUEL		
him just as he crossed over **P**,	**Gn 32:31**	6439
He went up from there to **P** and	**Jg 8:8**	6439
and the men of **P** answered him just	**Jg 8:8**	6439
So he spoke also to the men of **P**,	**Jg 8:9**	6439
He tore down the tower of **P**	**Jg 8:17**	6439
went out from there and built **P**.	**1Ki 12:25**	6439
P *was* the father of Gedor, and	**1Ch 4:4**	6439
and **P** *were* the sons of Shashak.	**1Ch 8:25**	6439
PEOPLE		
"Behold, they are one **p**,	**Gn 11:6**	5971a
and also the women, and the **p**.	**Gn 14:16**	5971a
"Give the **p** to me and take the	**Gn 14:21**	5315
shall be cut off from his **p**;	**Gn 17:14**	5971b
old, all the **p** from every quarter;	**Gn 19:4**	5971a
and bowed to the **p** of the land,	**Gn 23:7**	5971a
the sons of my **p** I give it to you;	**Gn 23:11**	5971a
bowed before the **p** of the land.	**Gn 23:12**	5971a
the hearing of the **p** of the land,	**Gn 23:13**	5971a
and he was gathered to his **p**.	**Gn 25:8**	5971b
died, and was gathered to his **p**.	**Gn 25:17**	5971b
And one **p** shall be stronger than	**Gn 25:23**	3816
One of the **p** might easily have	**Gn 26:10**	5971a
So Abimelech charged all the **p**,	**Gn 26:11**	5971a
divided the **p** who were with him,	**Gn 32:7**	5971a
some of the **p** who are with me."	**Gn 33:15**	5971a
live with you and become one **p**.	**Gn 34:16**	5971a
to live with us, to become one **p**:	**Gn 34:22**	5971a
and all the **p** who were with him.	**Gn 35:6**	5971a
died and was gathered to his **p**,	**Gn 35:29**	5971b
command all my **p** shall do homage;	**Gn 41:40**	5971a
the **p** cried out to Pharaoh for	**Gn 41:55**	5971a
The **p** *of* all the earth came to	**Gn 41:57**	
who sold to all the **p** of the land.	**Gn 42:6**	5971a
As for the **p**, he removed them	**Gn 47:21**	5971a
Then Joseph said to the **p**,	**Gn 47:23**	5971a
he also will become a **p** and he	**Gn 48:19**	5971a
"Dan shall judge his **p**,	**Gn 49:16**	5971a
"I am about to be gathered to my **p**;	**Gn 49:29**	5971b
last, and was gathered to his **p**.	**Gn 49:33**	5971b
result, to preserve many **p** alive.	**Gn 50:20**	5971a
He said to his **p**,	**Ex 1:9**	5971a
the **p** of the sons of Israel are	**Ex 1:9**	5971a
midwives, and the **p** multiplied,	**Ex 1:20**	5971a
Then Pharaoh commanded all his **p**,	**Ex 1:22**	5971a
surely seen the affliction of My **p**	**Ex 3:7**	5971a
so that you may bring My **p**,	**Ex 3:10**	5971a
have brought the **p** out of Egypt,	**Ex 3:12**	5971a
"I will grant this **p** favor in	**Ex 3:21**	5971a
he shall speak for you to the **p**;	**Ex 4:16**	5971a
so that he will not let the **p** go.	**Ex 4:21**	5971a
the signs in the sight of the **p**.	**Ex 4:30**	5971a
So the **p** believed;	**Ex 4:31**	5971a
'Let My **p** go that they may	**Ex 5:1**	5971a
draw the **p** away from their work?	**Ex 5:4**	5971a
the **p** of the land are now many,	**Ex 5:5**	5971a
the taskmasters over the **p** and their	**Ex 5:6**	5971a
are no longer to give the **p** straw	**Ex 5:7**	5971a
So the taskmasters of the **p** and	**Ex 5:10**	5971a
went out and spoke to the **p**,	**Ex 5:10**	5971a
So the **p** scattered through all the	**Ex 5:12**	5971a
it is the fault of your *own* **p**."	**Ex 5:16**	5971a
have You brought harm to this **p**?	**Ex 5:22**	5971a
name, he has done harm to this **p**,	**Ex 5:23**	5971a
have not delivered Your **p** at all."	**Ex 5:23**	5971a
'Then I will take you for My **p**,	**Ex 6:7**	5971a
My hosts, My **p** the sons of Israel,	**Ex 7:4**	5971a
he refuses to let the **p** go.	**Ex 7:14**	5971a
"Let My **p** go, that they may serve	**Ex 7:16**	5971a
"Let My **p** go, that they may serve	**Ex 8:1**	5971a
of your servants and on your **p**,	**Ex 8:3**	5971a
p and all your servants.	**Ex 8:4**	5971a
the frogs from me and from my **p**;	**Ex 8:8**	5971a
and I will let the **p** go,	**Ex 8:8**	5971a
you and your servants and your **p**,	**Ex 8:9**	5971a
and your servants and your **p**;	**Ex 8:11**	5971a
"Let My **p** go, that they may serve	**Ex 8:20**	5971a
"For if you do not let My **p** go,	**Ex 8:21**	5971a
on your **p** and into your houses;	**Ex 8:21**	5971a
of Goshen, where My **p** are living,	**Ex 8:22**	5971a
between My **p** and your people.	**Ex 8:23**	5971a
between My people and your **p**.	**Ex 8:23**	5971a
servants, and from his **p** tomorrow;	**Ex 8:29**	5971a
in not letting the **p** go to sacrifice to	**Ex 8:29**	5971a
from his servants and from his **p**;	**Ex 8:31**	5971a
also, and he did not let the **p** go.	**Ex 8:32**	5971a
"Let My **p** go, that they may serve	**Ex 9:1**	5971a
and he did not let the **p** go.	**Ex 9:7**	5971a
"Let My **p** go, that they may serve	**Ex 9:13**	5971a
you and your servants and your **p**,	**Ex 9:14**	5971a
you and your **p** with pestilence,	**Ex 9:15**	5971a
"Still you exalt yourself against My **p**	**Ex 9:17**	5971a
I and my **p** are the wicked ones.	**Ex 9:27**	5971a
Let My **p** go, that they may serve	**Ex 10:3**	5971a
'For if you refuse to let My **p** go,	**Ex 10:4**	5971a
"Speak now in the hearing of the **p**	**Ex 11:2**	5971a
The LORD gave the **p** favor in	**Ex 11:3**	5971a
and in the sight of the **p**.	**Ex 11:3**	5971a
you and all the **p** who follow you,'	**Ex 11:8**	5971a
And the **p** bowed low and worshiped.	**Ex 12:27**	5971a
"Rise up, get out from among my **p**,	**Ex 12:31**	5971a
The Egyptians urged the **p**,	**Ex 12:33**	5971a
So the **p** took their dough before	**Ex 12:34**	5971a
and the LORD had given the **p** favor	**Ex 12:36**	5971a
Moses said to the **p**,	**Ex 13:3**	5971a
when Pharaoh had let the **p** go,	**Ex 13:17**	5971a
"The **p** might change their minds	**Ex 13:17**	5971a
Hence God led the **p** around by the	**Ex 13:18**	5971a
fire by night, from before the **p**.	**Ex 13:22**	5971a
was told that the **p** had fled,	**Ex 14:5**	5971a
a change of heart toward the **p**,	**Ex 14:5**	5971a
ready and took his **p** with him;	**Ex 14:6**	5971a
But Moses said to the **p**,	**Ex 14:13**	5971a
Egyptians, the **p** feared the LORD,	**Ex 14:31**	5971a
led the **p** whom You have redeemed;	**Ex 15:13**	5971a
Until Your **p** pass over, O LORD,	**Ex 15:16**	5971a
Until the **p** pass over whom You	**Ex 15:16**	5971a
So the **p** grumbled at Moses,	**Ex 15:24**	5971a
and the **p** shall go out and gather	**Ex 16:4**	5971a
some of the **p** went out to gather,	**Ex 16:27**	5971a
the **p** rested on the seventh day.	**Ex 16:30**	5971a
was no water for the **p** to drink.	**Ex 17:1**	5971a
p quarreled with Moses and said,	**Ex 17:2**	5971a
the **p** thirsted there for water;	**Ex 17:3**	5971a
"What shall I do to this **p**?	**Ex 17:4**	5971a
"Pass before the **p** and take with	**Ex 17:5**	5971a
out of it, that the **p** may drink."	**Ex 17:6**	5971a
his **p** with the edge of the sword.	**Ex 17:13**	5971a
for Moses and for Israel His **p**,	**Ex 18:1**	5971a
and who delivered the **p** from under	**Ex 18:10**	5971a
dealt proudly against the **p**."	**Ex 18:11**	
day that Moses sat to judge the **p**,	**Ex 18:13**	5971a
and the **p** stood about Moses from	**Ex 18:13**	5971a
all that he was doing for the **p**,	**Ex 18:14**	5971a
that you are doing for the **p**?	**Ex 18:14**	5971a
sit *as judge* and all the **p** stand about	**Ex 18:14**	5971a
p come to me to inquire of God.	**Ex 18:15**	5971a
and these **p** who are with you,	**Ex 18:18**	5971a
all the **p** able men who fear God,	**Ex 18:21**	5971a
Let them judge the **p** at all times;	**Ex 18:22**	5971a
and all these **p** also will go to	**Ex 18:23**	5971a
and made them heads over the **p**,	**Ex 18:25**	5971a
They judged the **p** at all times;	**Ex 18:26**	5971a
and called the elders of the **p**,	**Ex 19:7**	5971a
the **p** answered together and said,	**Ex 19:8**	5971a
brought back the words of the **p**	**Ex 19:8**	5971a
so that the **p** may hear when	**Ex 19:9**	5971a
the words of the **p** to the LORD.	**Ex 19:9**	5971a
"Go to the **p** and consecrate them	**Ex 19:10**	5971a
Sinai in the sight of all the **p**.	**Ex 19:11**	5971a
set bounds for the **p** all around,	**Ex 19:12**	5971a
down from the mountain to the **p**	**Ex 19:14**	5971a
the people and consecrated the **p**,	**Ex 19:14**	5971a
He said to the **p**,	**Ex 19:15**	5971a
p who *were* in the camp trembled.	**Ex 19:16**	5971a
And Moses brought the **p** out of the	**Ex 19:17**	5971a
"Go down, warn the **p**,	**Ex 19:21**	5971a
p cannot come up to Mount Sinai,	**Ex 19:23**	5971a
the priests and the **p** break through	**Ex 19:24**	5971a
went down to the **p** and told them.	**Ex 19:25**	5971a
All the **p** perceived the	**Ex 20:18**	5971a
and when the **p** saw *it*, they	**Ex 20:18**	5971a
Moses said to the **p**,	**Ex 20:20**	5971a
So the **p** stood at a distance,	**Ex 20:21**	5971a
authority to sell her to a foreign **p**	**Ex 21:8**	5971a
"If you lend money to My **p**,	**Ex 22:25**	5971a
God, nor curse a ruler of your **p**.	**Ex 22:28**	5971a
that the needy of your **p** may eat;	**Ex 23:11**	5971a
all the **p** among whom you come,	**Ex 23:27**	5971a
shall the **p** come up with him."	**Ex 24:2**	5971a
Moses came and recounted to the **p**	**Ex 24:3**	5971a
all the **p** answered with one voice and	**Ex 24:3**	5971a
read *it* in the hearing of the **p**;	**Ex 24:7**	5971a
blood and sprinkled *it* on the **p**,	**Ex 24:8**	5971a
shall be cut off from his **p**.' "	**Ex 30:33**	5971b
shall be cut off from his **p**.' "	**Ex 30:38**	5971b
shall be cut off from among his **p**.	**Ex 31:14**	5971b
Now when the **p** saw that Moses	**Ex 32:1**	5971a
the **p** assembled about Aaron and	**Ex 32:1**	5971a
Then all the **p** tore off the gold	**Ex 32:3**	5971a
p sat down to eat and to drink,	**Ex 32:6**	5971a
"Go down at once, for your **p**,	**Ex 32:7**	5971a
"I have seen this **p**,	**Ex 32:9**	5971a
behold, they are an obstinate **p**.	**Ex 32:9**	5971a
does Your anger burn against Your **p**	**Ex 32:11**	5971a
mind about *doing* harm to Your **p**.	**Ex 32:12**	5971a
He said He would do to His **p**.	**Ex 32:14**	5971a
sound of the **p** as they shouted,	**Ex 32:17**	5971a
"What did this **p** do to you, that	**Ex 32:21**	5971a
you know the **p** yourself, that they	**Ex 32:22**	5971a
Now when Moses saw that the **p** were	**Ex 32:25**	5971a
three thousand men of the **p** fell	**Ex 32:28**	5971a
next day Moses said to the **p**,	**Ex 32:30**	5971a
this **p** has committed a great sin,	**Ex 32:31**	5971a
now, lead the **p** where I told you.	**Ex 32:34**	5971a
Then the LORD smote the **p**,	**Ex 32:35**	5971a
you and the **p** whom you have	**Ex 33:1**	5971a
because you are an obstinate **p**,	**Ex 33:3**	5971a
When the **p** heard this sad word,	**Ex 33:4**	5971a
'You are an obstinate **p**;	**Ex 33:5**	5971a
all the **p** would arise and stand,	**Ex 33:8**	5971a
When all the **p** saw the pillar of	**Ex 33:10**	5971a
all the **p** would arise and worship,	**Ex 33:10**	5971a
'Bring up this **p**!'	**Ex 33:12**	5971a
too, that this nation is Your **p**."	**Ex 33:13**	5971a
favor in Your sight, I and Your **p**?	**Ex 33:16**	5971a
with us, so that we, I and Your **p**,	**Ex 33:16**	5971a
distinguished from all the *other* **p**	**Ex 33:16**	5971a
though the **p** are so obstinate,	**Ex 34:9**	5971a
Before all your **p** I will perform	**Ex 34:10**	5971a
and all the **p** among whom you live	**Ex 34:10**	5971a
"The **p** are bringing much more	**Ex 36:5**	5971a
Thus the **p** were restrained from	**Ex 36:6**	5971a
so as to bring guilt on the **p**,	**Lv 4:3**	5971a
'Now if anyone of the common **p**	**Lv 4:27**	5971a
shall be cut off from his **p**.	**Lv 7:20**	5971b
shall be cut off from his **p**.' "	**Lv 7:21**	5971b
eats shall be cut off from his **p**.	**Lv 7:25**	5971b
shall be cut off from his **p**.' "	**Lv 7:27**	5971b
for yourself and for the **p**;	**Lv 9:7**	5971a
then make the offering for the **p**,	**Lv 9:7**	5971a
sin offering which was for the **p**,	**Lv 9:15**	5971a

offerings which was for the **p**;	**Lv 9:18**	5971a
toward the **p** and blessed them,	**Lv 9:22**	5971a
they came out and blessed the **p**,	**Lv 9:23**	5971a
of the LORD appeared to all the **p**.	**Lv 9:23**	5971a
and when all the **p** saw *it*,	**Lv 9:24**	5971a
before all the **p** I will be honored.	**Lv 10:3**	5971a
sin offering which is for the **p**,	**Lv 16:15**	5971a
and the burnt offering of the **p** and	**Lv 16:24**	5971a
atonement for himself and for the **p**.	**Lv 16:24**	5971a
and for all the **p** of the assembly.	**Lv 16:33**	5971a
shall be cut off from among his **p**.	**Lv 17:4**	5971b
also shall be cut off from his **p**.	**Lv 17:9**	5971b
will cut him off from among his **p**.	**Lv 17:10**	5971b
be cut off from among their **p**.	**Lv 18:29**	5971b
shall be cut off from his **p**.	**Lv 19:8**	5971b
about as a slanderer among your **p**,	**Lv 19:16**	5971b
grudge against the sons of your **p**,	**Lv 19:18**	5971a
the **p** of the land shall stone him	**Lv 20:2**	5971a
will cut him off from among his **p**,	**Lv 20:3**	5971a
'If the **p** of the land, however,	**Lv 20:4**	5971a
and I will cut off from among their **p**	**Lv 20:5**	5971a
will cut him off from among his **p**.	**Lv 20:6**	5971a
the sight of the sons of their **p**.	**Lv 20:17**	5971a
be cut off from among their **p**.	**Lv 20:18**	5971a
for a *dead* person among his **p**,	**Lv 21:1**	5971b
relative by marriage among his **p**,	**Lv 21:4**	5971b
is to marry a virgin of his own **p**,	**Lv 21:14**	5971b
profane his offspring among his **p**;	**Lv 21:15**	5971b
he shall be cut off from his **p**.	**Lv 23:29**	5971b
I will destroy from among his **p**.	**Lv 23:30**	5971a
your God, and you shall be My **p**.	**Lv 26:12**	5971a
a curse and an oath among your **p**	**Nu 5:21**	5971a
will become a curse among her **p**.	**Nu 5:27**	5971a
shall then be cut off from his **p**,	**Nu 9:13**	5971b
Now the **p** became like those who	**Nu 11:1**	5971a
p therefore cried out to Moses,	**Nu 11:2**	5971a
The **p** would go about and gather *it*	**Nu 11:8**	5971a
Now Moses heard the **p** weeping	**Nu 11:10**	5971a
the burden of all this **p** on me?	**Nu 11:11**	5971a
"Was it I who conceived all this **p**?	**Nu 11:12**	5971a
to get meat to give to all this **p**?	**Nu 11:13**	5971a
am not able to carry all this **p**,	**Nu 11:14**	5971a
the elders of the **p** and their officers	**Nu 11:16**	5971a
bear the burden of the **p** with you,	**Nu 11:17**	5971a
"Say to the **p**,	**Nu 11:18**	5971a
"The **p**, among whom I am, are	**Nu 11:21**	5971a
told the **p** the words of the LORD.	**Nu 11:24**	5971a
men of the elders of the **p**,	**Nu 11:24**	5971a
all the LORD's **p** were prophets,	**Nu 11:29**	5971a
The **p** spent all day and all	**Nu 11:32**	5971a
LORD was kindled against the **p**,	**Nu 11:33**	5971a
the LORD struck the **p** with a very	**Nu 11:33**	5971a
buried the **p** who had been greedy.	**Nu 11:34**	5971a
the **p** set out for Hazeroth,	**Nu 11:35**	5971a
and the **p** did not move on until	**Nu 12:15**	5971a
the **p** moved out from Hazeroth and	**Nu 12:16**	5971a
and whether the **p** who live in it	**Nu 13:18**	5971a
the **p** who live in the land are	**Nu 13:28**	5971a
Caleb quieted the **p** before Moses and	**Nu 13:30**	5971a
not able to go up against the **p**,	**Nu 13:31**	5971a
and all the **p** whom we saw in it	**Nu 13:32**	5971a
cried, and the **p** wept that night.	**Nu 14:1**	5971a
and do not fear the **p** of the land,	**Nu 14:9**	5971a
"How long will this **p** spurn Me?	**Nu 14:11**	5971a
You brought up this **p** from	**Nu 14:13**	5971a
LORD, are in the midst of this **p**,	**Nu 14:14**	5971a
You slay this **p** as one man,	**Nu 14:15**	5971a
the LORD could not bring this **p** into	**Nu 14:16**	5971a
the iniquity of this **p** according	**Nu 14:19**	5971a
as You also have forgiven this **p**,	**Nu 14:19**	5971a
of Israel, the **p** mourned greatly.	**Nu 14:39**	5971a
happened to all the **p** through error.	**Nu 15:26**	5971a
shall be cut off from among his **p**.	**Nu 15:30**	5971a
caused the death of the LORD's **p**."	**Nu 16:41**	5971a
the plague had begun among the **p**.	**Nu 16:47**	5971a
and made atonement for the **p**.	**Nu 16:47**	5971a
and the **p** stayed at Kadesh.	**Nu 20:1**	5971a
The **p** thus contended with Moses	**Nu 20:3**	5971a
"Aaron will be gathered to his **p**;	**Nu 20:24**	5971b
So Aaron will be gathered *to his* **p**,	**Nu 20:26**	
deliver this **p** into my hand,	**Nu 21:2**	5971a
and the **p** became impatient because	**Nu 21:4**	
		5315, 5971a
The **p** spoke against God and Moses,	**Nu 21:5**	5971a
sent fiery serpents among the **p** and	**Nu 21:6**	5971a
the people and they bit the **p**,	**Nu 21:6**	5971a
so that many **p** of Israel died.	**Nu 21:6**	5971a
So the **p** came to Moses and said,	**Nu 21:7**	5971a
And Moses interceded for the **p**.	**Nu 21:7**	5971a
"Assemble the **p**, that I may give	**Nu 21:16**	5971a
Which the nobles of the **p** dug,	**Nu 21:18**	5971a
So Sihon gathered all his **p** and	**Nu 21:23**	5971a
You are ruined, O **p** of Chemosh!	**Nu 21:29**	5971a
of Bashan went out with all his **p**,	**Nu 21:33**	5971a
hand, and all his **p** and his land;	**Nu 21:34**	5971a
him and his sons and all his **p**,	**Nu 21:35**	5971a
in great fear because of the **p**,	**Nu 22:3**	5971a
in the land of the sons of his **p**,	**Nu 22:5**	5971a
"Behold, a **p** came out of Egypt;	**Nu 22:5**	5971a
curse this **p** for me since they are	**Nu 22:6**	5971a
there is a **p** who came out of Egypt	**Nu 22:11**	5971a
you shall not curse the **p**,	**Nu 22:12**	5971a
then, curse this **p** for me.' "	**Nu 22:17**	5971a
saw from there a portion of the **p**.	**Nu 22:41**	5971a
Behold, a **p** *who* dwells apart, And	**Nu 23:9**	5971a
"Behold, a **p** rises like a	**Nu 23:24**	5971a
now, behold, I am going to my **p**;	**Nu 24:14**	5971a
I will advise you what this **p** will do	**Nu 24:14**	5971a
to your **p** in the days to come."	**Nu 24:14**	5971a
the **p** began to play the harlot	**Nu 25:1**	5971a
For they invited the **p** to the	**Nu 25:2**	5971a
and the **p** ate and bowed down to	**Nu 25:2**	5971a
"Take all the leaders of the **p**	**Nu 25:4**	5971a
who was head of the **p** of a	**Nu 25:15**	523
"*Take a census of the* **p** from	**Nu 26:4**	5971a
too will be gathered to your **p**,	**Nu 27:13**	5971b
you will be gathered to your **p**."	**Nu 31:2**	5971b
Moses spoke to the **p**,	**Nu 31:3**	5971a
you will destroy all these **p**."	**Nu 32:15**	5971a
that the **p** had no water to drink.	**Nu 33:14**	5971a
p are bigger and taller than we;	**Dt 1:28**	5971a
and command the **p**, saying,	**Dt 2:4**	5971a
a **p** as great, numerous, and tall as	**Dt 2:10**	5971a
finally perished from among the **p**,	**Dt 2:16**	5971a
a **p** as great, numerous, and tall	**Dt 2:21**	5971a
"Then Sihon with all his **p** came	**Dt 2:32**	5971a
him with his sons and all his **p**.	**Dt 2:33**	5971a
with all his **p** came out to meet us	**Dt 3:1**	5971a
his **p** and his land into your hand;	**Dt 3:2**	5971a
with all his **p** into our hand,	**Dt 3:3**	5971a
go across at the head of this **p**,	**Dt 3:28**	5971a
is a wise and understanding **p**.'	**Dt 4:6**	5971a
'Assemble the **p** to Me, that I may	**Dt 4:10**	5971a
to be a **p** for His own possession,	**Dt 4:20**	5971a
"Has *any* **p** heard the voice of God	**Dt 4:33**	5971a
p which they have spoken to you.	**Dt 5:28**	5971a
are a holy **p** to the LORD your God;	**Dt 7:6**	5971a
chosen you to be a **p** for His own	**Dt 7:6**	5971a
a **p** great and tall, the sons of	**Dt 9:2**	5971a
possess, for you are a stubborn **p**.	**Dt 9:6**	5971a
for your **p** whom you brought out of	**Dt 9:12**	5971a
'I have seen this **p**,	**Dt 9:13**	5971a
and indeed, it is a stubborn **p**.	**Dt 9:13**	5971a
'O Lord GOD, do not destroy Your **p**,	**Dt 9:26**	5971a
not look at the stubbornness of this **p**	**Dt 9:27**	5971a
'Yet they are Your **p**,	**Dt 9:29**	5971a
on your journey ahead of the **p**,	**Dt 10:11**	5971a
afterwards the hand of all the **p**.	**Dt 13:9**	5971a
are a holy **p** to the LORD your God,	**Dt 14:2**	5971a
the LORD has chosen you to be a **p**	**Dt 14:2**	5971a
are a holy **p** to the LORD your God.	**Dt 14:21**	5971a
they shall judge the **p** with righteous	**Dt 16:18**	5971a
afterward the hand of all the **p**.	**Dt 17:7**	5971a
all the **p** will hear and be afraid,	**Dt 17:13**	5971a
nor shall he cause the **p** to return	**Dt 17:16**	5971a
be the priests' due from the **p**,	**Dt 18:3**	5971a
and **p** more numerous than you,	**Dt 20:1**	5971a
come near and speak to the **p**.	**Dt 20:2**	5971a
officers also shall speak to the **p**,	**Dt 20:5**	5971a
officers shall speak further to the **p** and	**Dt 20:8**	5971a
have finished speaking to the **p**,	**Dt 20:9**	5971a
of armies at the head of the **p**.	**Dt 20:9**	5971a
then all the **p**	**Dt 20:11**	5971a
'Forgive Your **p** Israel whom You	**Dt 21:8**	5971a
in the midst of Your **p** Israel.'	**Dt 21:8**	5971a
heaven, and bless Your **p** Israel,	**Dt 26:15**	5971a
today declared you to be His **p**,	**Dt 26:18**	5971a
shall be a consecrated **p** to the LORD	**Dt 26:19**	5971a
elders of Israel charged the **p**,	**Dt 27:1**	5971a
become a **p** for the LORD your God.	**Dt 27:9**	5971a
Moses also charged the **p** on that	**Dt 27:11**	5971a
on Mount Gerizim to bless the **p**:	**Dt 27:12**	5971a
all the **p** shall answer and say,	**Dt 27:15**	5971a
And all the **p** shall say,	**Dt 27:16**	5971a
And all the **p** shall say,	**Dt 27:17**	5971a
And all the **p** shall say,	**Dt 27:18**	5971a
And all the **p** shall say,	**Dt 27:19**	5971a
And all the **p** shall say,	**Dt 27:20**	5971a
And all the **p** shall say,	**Dt 27:21**	5971a
And all the **p** shall say,	**Dt 27:22**	5971a
And all the **p** shall say,	**Dt 27:23**	5971a
And all the **p** shall say,	**Dt 27:24**	5971a
And all the **p** shall say,	**Dt 27:25**	5971a
And all the **p** shall say,	**Dt 27:26**	5971a
you as a holy **p** to Himself,	**Dt 28:9**	5971a
shall be given to another **p**,	**Dt 28:32**	5971a
"A **p** whom you do not know shall	**Dt 28:33**	5971a
p where the LORD drives you.	**Dt 28:37**	5971a
may establish you today as His **p**	**Dt 29:13**	5971a
for you shall go with this **p** into	**Dt 31:7**	5971a
"Assemble the **p**, the men and the	**Dt 31:12**	5971a
and this **p** will arise and play the	**Dt 31:16**	5971a
the LORD, O foolish and unwise **p**?	**Dt 32:6**	5971a
"For the LORD's portion is His **p**;	**Dt 32:9**	5971a
with *those who* are not a **p**;	**Dt 32:21**	5971a
"For the LORD will vindicate His **p**,	**Dt 32:36**	5971a
"Rejoice, O nations, *with* His **p**;	**Dt 32:43**	5971a
atone for His land *and* His **p**."	**Dt 32:43**	5971a
this song in the hearing of the **p**,	**Dt 32:44**	5971a
ascend, and be gathered to your **p**,	**Dt 32:50**	5971b
Hor and was gathered to his **p**,	**Dt 32:50**	5971b
"Indeed, He loves the **p**;	**Dt 33:3**	5971a
the heads of the **p** were gathered,	**Dt 33:5**	5971a
of Judah, And bring him to his **p**.	**Dt 33:7**	5971a
he came *with* the leaders of the **p**;	**Dt 33:21**	5971a
like you, a **p** saved by the LORD,	**Dt 33:29**	5971a
this Jordan, you and all this **p**,	**Jos 1:2**	5971a
give this **p** possession of the land	**Jos 1:6**	5971a
commanded the officers of the **p**,	**Jos 1:10**	5971a
of the camp and command the **p**,	**Jos 1:11**	5971a
and they commanded the **p**,	**Jos 3:3**	5971a
Then Joshua said to the **p**,	**Jos 3:5**	5971a
and cross over ahead of the **p**."	**Jos 3:6**	5971a
covenant and went ahead of the **p**.	**Jos 3:6**	5971a
So when the **p** set	**Jos 3:14**	5971a
ark of the covenant before the **p**,	**Jos 3:14**	5971a
So the **p** crossed opposite Jericho.	**Jos 3:16**	5971a
yourselves twelve men from the **p**,	**Jos 4:2**	5971a
Joshua to speak to the **p**,	**Jos 4:10**	5971a
And the **p** hurried and crossed;	**Jos 4:10**	5971a
all the **p** had finished crossing,	**Jos 4:11**	5971a
the priests crossed before the **p**.	**Jos 4:11**	5971a
Now the **p** came up from the Jordan	**Jos 4:19**	5971a
all the **p** who came out of Egypt	**Jos 5:4**	5971a
For all the **p** who came out	**Jos 5:5**	5971a
but all the **p** who were born in the	**Jos 5:5**	5971a
all the **p** shall shout with a great	**Jos 6:5**	5971a
and the **p** will go up every man	**Jos 6:5**	5971a
Then he said to the **p**,	**Jos 6:7**	5971a
when Joshua had spoken to the **p**,	**Jos 6:8**	5971a
But Joshua commanded the **p**,	**Jos 6:10**	5971a
trumpets, Joshua said to the **p**,	**Jos 6:16**	5971a
So the **p** shouted, and *priests* blew	**Jos 6:20**	5971a
when the **p** heard the sound of the	**Jos 6:20**	5971a
the **p** shouted with a great	**Jos 6:20**	5971a
that the **p** went up into the city,	**Jos 6:20**	5971a
"Do not let all the **p** go up;	**Jos 7:3**	5971a
not make all the **p** toil up there,	**Jos 7:3**	5971a
men from the **p** went up there,	**Jos 7:4**	5971a
so the hearts of the **p** melted and	**Jos 7:5**	5971a
ever bring this **p** over the Jordan,	**Jos 7:7**	5971a
Consecrate the **p** and say,	**Jos 7:13**	5971a
Take all the **p** of war with you and	**Jos 8:1**	5971a
your hand the king of Ai, his **p**,	**Jos 8:1**	5971a
all the **p** of war to go up to Ai;	**Jos 8:3**	5971a
"Then I and all the **p** who are	**Jos 8:5**	5971a
spent that night among the **p**.	**Jos 8:9**	5971a
in the morning and mustered the **p**,	**Jos 8:10**	5971a
of Israel before the **p** to Ai.	**Jos 8:10**	5971a
Then all the **p** of war who *were*	**Jos 8:11**	5971a
So they stationed the **p**,	**Jos 8:13**	5971a
he and all his **p** at the appointed	**Jos 8:14**	5971a
And all the **p** who were in the city	**Jos 8:16**	5971a
for the **p** who had been fleeing to	**Jos 8:20**	5971a
all the **p** of Ai.	**Jos 8:25**	376
at first to bless the **p** of Israel.	**Jos 8:33**	5971a
he and all the **p** of war with him	**Jos 10:7**	5971a
that all the **p** returned to the	**Jos 10:21**	5971a
and Joshua defeated him and his **p**	**Jos 10:33**	5971a
as many **p** as the sand that is on	**Jos 11:4**	5971a
So Joshua and all the **p** of war	**Jos 11:7**	5971a
the heart of the **p** melt with fear;	**Jos 14:8**	5971a
since I am a numerous **p** whom the	**Jos 17:14**	5971a
"If you are a numerous **p**,	**Jos 17:15**	5971a
a numerous **p** and have great power;	**Jos 17:17**	5971a
Joshua said to all the **p**,	**Jos 24:2**	5971a
The **p** answered and said,	**Jos 24:16**	5971a
Then Joshua said to the **p**,	**Jos 24:19**	5971a
The **p** said to Joshua,	**Jos 24:21**	5971a
Joshua said to the **p**,	**Jos 24:22**	5971a
The **p** said to Joshua,	**Jos 24:24**	5971a
Joshua made a covenant with the **p**	**Jos 24:25**	5971a
Joshua said to all the **p**,	**Jos 24:27**	5971a
Then Joshua dismissed the **p**,	**Jos 24:28**	5971a
they went and lived with the **p**.	**Jg 1:16**	5971a
the **p** lifted up their voices	**Jg 2:4**	5971a
When Joshua had dismissed the **p**,	**Jg 2:6**	5971a
The **p** served the LORD all the	**Jg 2:7**	5971a
the **p** who had carried the tribute.	**Jg 3:18**	5971a
and all the **p** who *were* with him,	**Jg 4:13**	5971a
in Israel, That the **p** volunteered,	**Jg 5:2**	5971a
The volunteers among the **p**;	**Jg 5:9**	5971a
Then the **p** of the LORD went down	**Jg 5:11**	5971a
The **p** of the LORD came down to me	**Jg 5:13**	5971a
"Zebulun *was* a **p** who despised	**Jg 5:18**	5971a
and all the **p** who were with him,	**Jg 7:1**	5971a
"The **p** who are with you are too	**Jg 7:2**	5971a
proclaim in the hearing of the **p**,	**Jg 7:3**	5971a
So 22,000 **p** returned, but 10,000	**Jg 7:3**	5971a
"The **p** are still too many;	**Jg 7:4**	5971a
brought the **p** down to the water.	**Jg 7:5**	5971a
all the rest of the **p** kneeled to drink	**Jg 7:6**	5971a
so let all the *other* **p** go,	**Jg 7:7**	5971a
to the **p** who are following me,	**Jg 8:5**	5971a
this **p** were under my authority!	**Jg 9:29**	5971a
you and the **p** who are with you,	**Jg 9:32**	5971a
when he and the **p** who are with him	**Jg 9:33**	5971a
So Abimelech and all the **p** who	**Jg 9:34**	5971a
and Abimelech and the **p** who *were*	**Jg 9:35**	5971a
When Gaal saw the **p**,	**Jg 9:36**	5971a
p are coming down from the tops of	**Jg 9:36**	5971a
p are coming down from the highest	**Jg 9:37**	5971a
this not the **p** whom you despised?	**Jg 9:38**	5971a
that the **p** went out to the field,	**Jg 9:42**	5971a
So he took his **p** and divided them	**Jg 9:43**	5971a
the **p** coming out from the city,	**Jg 9:43**	5971a
and killed the **p** who *were* in it;	**Jg 9:45**	5971a
and all the **p** who *were* with him;	**Jg 9:48**	5971a
said to the **p** who *were* with him,	**Jg 9:48**	5971a
All the **p** also cut down each	**Jg 9:49**	5971a
The **p**, the leaders of Gilead,	**Jg 10:18**	5971a
and the **p** made him head and chief	**Jg 11:11**	5971a
all his **p** and camped in Jahaz and	**Jg 11:20**	5971a
gave Sihon and all his **p** into the	**Jg 11:21**	5971a
Amorites from before His **p** Israel,	**Jg 11:23**	5971a
"I and my **p** were at great strife	**Jg 12:2**	5971a
relatives, or among all our **p**,	**Jg 14:3**	5971a
a riddle to the sons of my **p**,	**Jg 14:16**	5971a
the riddle to the sons of her **p**.	**Jg 14:17**	5971a
When the **p** saw him, they praised	**Jg 16:24**	5971a
and all the **p** who were in it.	**Jg 16:30**	5971a
and came to Laish and saw the **p**	**Jg 18:7**	5971a
a secure **p** with a spacious land;	**Jg 18:10**	5971a
image and went among the **p**.	**Jg 18:20**	5971a
to Laish, to a **p** quiet and secure,	**Jg 18:27**	5971a
The chiefs of all the **p**,	**Jg 20:2**	5971a
in the assembly of the **p** of God,	**Jg 20:2**	5971a

Then all the **p** arose as one man,	Jg 20:8	5971a
10,000 to supply food for the **p**,	Jg 20:10	5971a
Out of all these **p** 700 choice men	Jg 20:16	5971a
But the **p**, the men of Israel,	Jg 20:22	5971a
sons of Israel and all the **p** went up	Jg 20:26	5971a
of Benjamin went out against the **p**	Jg 20:31	5971a
to strike and kill some of the **p** as	Jg 20:31	5971a
So the **p** came to Bethel and sat	Jg 21:2	5971a
the **p** arose early and built an altar	Jg 21:4	5971a
For when the **p** were numbered,	Jg 21:9	5971a
And the **p** were sorry for Benjamin	Jg 21:15	5971a
visited His **p** in giving them food.	Ru 1:6	5971a
return with you to your **p**."	Ru 1:10	5971a
gone back to her **p** and her gods;	Ru 1:15	5971a
Your **p** *shall be* my people, and	Ru 1:16	5971a
Your people *shall be* my **p**,	Ru 1:16	5971a
and came to a **p** that you did not	Ru 2:11	5971a
for all my **p** in the city know that	Ru 3:11	5971a
and before the elders of my **p**.	Ru 4:4	5971a
said to the elders and all the **p**,	Ru 4:9	5971a
All the **p** who were in the court,	Ru 4:11	5971a
custom of the priests with the **p**.	1Sa 2:13	5971a
that I hear from all these **p**?	1Sa 2:23	
I hear the LORD's **p** circulating.	1Sa 2:24	5971a
of every offering of My **p** Israel?'	1Sa 2:29	5971a
When the **p** came into the camp, the	1Sa 4:3	5971a
So the **p** sent to Shiloh, and from	1Sa 4:4	5971a
a great slaughter among the **p**,	1Sa 4:17	5971a
to us, to kill us and our **p**."	1Sa 5:10	5971a
it will not kill us and our **p**."	1Sa 5:11	5971a
did they not allow the **p** to go,	1Sa 6:6	
Now *the* **p** *of* Beth-shemesh were	1Sa 6:13	
He struck down of all the **p**,	1Sa 6:19	5971a
and the **p** mourned because the LORD	1Sa 6:19	5971a
the LORD had struck the **p** with a	1Sa 6:19	5971a
"Listen to the voice of the **p** in	1Sa 8:7	5971a
the **p** who had asked of him a king.	1Sa 8:10	5971a
the **p** refused to listen to the	1Sa 8:19	5971a
had heard all the words of the **p**,	1Sa 8:21	5971a
he was taller than any of the **p**.	1Sa 9:2	5971a
for the **p** have a sacrifice on the	1Sa 9:12	5971a
the **p** will not eat until he comes,	1Sa 9:13	5971a
him to be prince over My **p** Israel;	1Sa 9:16	5971a
and he will deliver My **p** from the	1Sa 9:16	5971a
For I have regarded My **p**,	1Sa 9:16	5971a
This one shall rule over My **p**."	1Sa 9:17	5971a
I said I have invited the **p**."	1Sa 9:24	5971a
that the **p** said to one another,	1Sa 10:11	5971a
Thereafter Samuel called the **p**	1Sa 10:17	5971a
and when he stood among the **p**,	1Sa 10:23	5971a
he was taller than any of the **p** from	1Sa 10:23	5971a
Samuel said to all the **p**,	1Sa 10:24	5971a
no one like him among all the **p**."	1Sa 10:24	5971a
So all the **p** shouted and said,	1Sa 10:24	5971a
Samuel told the **p** the ordinances of	1Sa 10:25	5971a
And Samuel sent all the **p** away,	1Sa 10:25	5971a
words in the hearing of the **p**,	1Sa 11:4	5971a
and all the **p** lifted up their	1Sa 11:4	5971a
"What is *the matter* with the **p** that	1Sa 11:5	5971a
dread of the LORD fell on the **p**,	1Sa 11:7	5971a
Saul put the **p** in three companies;	1Sa 11:11	5971a
Then the **p** said to Samuel,	1Sa 11:12	5971a
Then Samuel said to the **p**,	1Sa 11:14	5971a
So all the **p** went to Gilgal, and	1Sa 11:15	5971a
Then Samuel said to the **p**,	1Sa 12:6	5971a
and all the **p** greatly feared the	1Sa 12:18	5971a
Then all the **p** said to Samuel,	1Sa 12:19	5971a
Samuel said to the **p**,	1Sa 12:20	5971a
the LORD will not abandon His **p**	1Sa 12:22	5971a
to make you a **p** for Himself.	1Sa 12:22	5971a
he sent away the rest of the **p**,	1Sa 13:2	5971a
The **p** were then summoned to Saul	1Sa 13:4	5971a
and **p** like the sand which is on	1Sa 13:5	5971a
(for the **p** were hard-pressed),	1Sa 13:6	5971a
the **p** hid themselves in caves,	1Sa 13:6	5971a
all the **p** followed him trembling.	1Sa 13:7	5971a
the **p** were scattering from him.	1Sa 13:8	5971a
the **p** were scattering from me,	1Sa 13:11	5971a
appointed him as ruler over His **p**,	1Sa 13:14	5971a
And Saul numbered the **p** who were	1Sa 13:15	5971a
Saul and his son Jonathan and the	1Sa 13:16	5971a
p who *were* with Saul and Jonathan,	1Sa 13:22	5971a
And the **p** who *were* with him *were*	1Sa 14:2	5971a
And the **p** did not know that	1Sa 14:3	5971a
in the field, and among all the **p**.	1Sa 14:15	5971a
Saul said to the **p** who *were*	1Sa 14:17	5971a
Then Saul and all the **p** who *were*	1Sa 14:20	5971a
for Saul had put the **p** under oath,	1Sa 14:24	5971a
So none of the **p** tasted food.	1Sa 14:24	5971a
All *the* **p** *of* the land entered	1Sa 14:25	
When the **p** entered the forest,	1Sa 14:26	5971a
mouth, for the **p** feared the oath.	1Sa 14:26	5971a
his father put the **p** under oath;	1Sa 14:27	5971a
one of the **p** said,	1Sa 14:28	5971a
strictly put the **p** under oath,	1Sa 14:28	5971a
And the **p** were weary.	1Sa 14:28	5971a
if only the **p** had eaten freely	1Sa 14:30	5971a
And the **p** were very weary.	1Sa 14:31	5971a
The **p** rushed greedily upon the	1Sa 14:32	5971a
and the **p** ate *them* with the blood.	1Sa 14:32	5971a
the **p** are sinning against the LORD	1Sa 14:33	5971a
"Disperse yourselves among the **p**	1Sa 14:34	5971a
So all the **p** that night brought	1Sa 14:34	5971a
here, all you chiefs of the **p**,	1Sa 14:38	5971a
not one of all the **p** answered him.	1Sa 14:39	5971a
And the **p** said to Saul,	1Sa 14:40	5971a
were taken, but the **p** escaped.	1Sa 14:41	5971a
But the **p** said to Saul,	1Sa 14:45	5971a
So the **p** rescued Jonathan and he	1Sa 14:45	5971a
to anoint you as king over His **p**,	1Sa 15:1	5971a
the **p** and numbered them in Telaim,	1Sa 15:4	5971a
utterly destroyed all the **p** with the	1Sa 15:8	5971a
But Saul and the **p** spared Agag and	1Sa 15:9	5971a
for the **p** spared the best of the	1Sa 15:15	5971a
"But the **p** took *some* of the	1Sa 15:21	5971a
I feared the **p** and listened to their	1Sa 15:24	5971a
elders of my **p** and before Israel,	1Sa 15:30	5971a
The **p** answered him in accord	1Sa 17:27	5971a
and the **p** answered the same thing	1Sa 17:30	5971a
was pleasing in the sight of all the **p**	1Sa 18:5	5971a
went out and came in before the **p**.	1Sa 18:13	5971a
Saul summoned all the **p** for war,	1Sa 23:8	5971a
and the **p** were camped around him.	1Sa 26:5	5971a
Abishai came to the **p** by night,	1Sa 26:7	5971a
and the **p** were lying around him.	1Sa 26:7	5971a
David called to the **p** and to Abner	1Sa 26:14	5971a
For one of the **p** came to destroy	1Sa 26:15	5971a
himself odious among his **p** Israel;	1Sa 27:12	5971a
Then David and the **p** who were with	1Sa 30:4	5971a
the **p** spoke of stoning him,	1Sa 30:6	5971a
for all the **p** were embittered,	1Sa 30:6	5971a
sheep and the cattle *which the* **p**	1Sa 30:20	
to meet the **p** who were with him,	1Sa 30:21	5971a
approached the **p** and greeted them.	1Sa 30:21	5971a
house of their idols and to the **p**.	1Sa 31:9	5971a
"The **p** have fled from the battle,	2Sa 1:4	5971a
and also many of the **p** have fallen	2Sa 1:4	5971a
and for the **p** of the LORD	2Sa 1:12	5971a
refrain from telling the **p** to turn back	2Sa 2:26	5971a
surely then the **p** would have gone	2Sa 2:27	5971a
and all the **p** halted and pursued	2Sa 2:28	5971a
had gathered all the **p** together,	2Sa 2:30	5971a
I will save My **p** Israel from the hand	2Sa 3:18	5971a
to all the **p** who were with him,	2Sa 3:31	5971a
of Abner, and all the **p** wept.	2Sa 3:32	5971a
And all the **p** wept again over him.	2Sa 3:34	5971a
Then all the **p** came to persuade	2Sa 3:35	5971a
Now all the **p** took note *of it*, and	2Sa 3:36	5971a
the king did pleased all the **p**.	2Sa 3:36	5971a
So all the **p** and all Israel	2Sa 3:37	5971a
'You will shepherd My **p** Israel,	2Sa 5:2	5971a
for the sake of His **p** Israel.	2Sa 5:12	5971a
David arose and went with all the **p**	2Sa 6:2	5971a
he blessed the **p** in the name of	2Sa 6:18	5971a
he distributed to all the **p**,	2Sa 6:19	5971a
the **p** departed each to his house.	2Sa 6:19	5971a
me ruler over the **p** of the LORD,	2Sa 6:21	5971a
commanded to shepherd My **p** Israel,	2Sa 7:7	5971a
to be ruler over My **p** Israel.	2Sa 7:8	5971a
also appoint a place for My **p** Israel	2Sa 7:10	5971a
judges to be over My **p** Israel;	2Sa 7:11	5971a
on the earth is like Your **p** Israel,	2Sa 7:23	5971a
went to redeem for Himself as a **p**	2Sa 7:23	5971a
before Your **p** whom You have	2Sa 7:23	5971a
established for Yourself Your **p** Israel	2Sa 7:24	5971a
Israel as Your own **p** forever,	2Sa 7:24	5971a
and righteousness for all his **p**.	2Sa 8:15	5971a
But the remainder of the **p** he	2Sa 10:10	5971a
courageous for the sake of our **p**	2Sa 10:12	5971a
So Joab and the **p** who were with	2Sa 10:13	5971a
the **p** and the state of the war.	2Sa 11:7	5971a
the **p** among David's servants fell;	2Sa 11:17	5971a
gather the rest of the **p** together	2Sa 12:28	5971a
all the **p** and went to Rabbah,	2Sa 12:29	5971a
brought out the **p** who were in it,	2Sa 12:31	5971a
all the **p** returned *to* Jerusalem.	2Sa 12:31	5971a
many **p** were coming from the road	2Sa 13:34	5971a
such a thing against the **p** of God?	2Sa 14:13	5971a
that the **p** have made me afraid;	2Sa 14:15	5971a
for the **p** increased continually	2Sa 15:12	5971a
went out and all the **p** with him,	2Sa 15:17	5971a
loud voice, all the **p** passed over.	2Sa 15:23	5971a
and all the **p** passed over toward	2Sa 15:23	5971a
until all the **p** had finished passing	2Sa 15:24	5971a
Then all the **p** who were with him	2Sa 15:30	5971a
and all the **p** and all the mighty	2Sa 16:6	5971a
The king and all the **p** who	2Sa 16:14	5971a
Then Absalom and all the **p**,	2Sa 16:15	5971a
For whom the LORD, this **p**,	2Sa 16:18	5971a
the **p** who are with him will flee.	2Sa 17:2	5971a
will bring back all the **p** to you.	2Sa 17:3	5971a
all the **p** will be at peace."	2Sa 17:3	5971a
not spend the night with the **p**.	2Sa 17:8	5971a
among the **p** who follow Absalom.'	2Sa 17:9	5971a
p who are with him will be destroyed.' "	2Sa 17:16	5971a
Then David and all the **p** who *were*	2Sa 17:22	5971a
and for the **p** who *were* with him,	2Sa 17:29	5971a
"The **p** are hungry and weary and	2Sa 17:29	5971a
Then David numbered the **p** who were	2Sa 18:1	5971a
David sent the **p** out,	2Sa 18:2	5971a
And the king said to the **p**,	2Sa 18:2	5971a
the **p** said, "You should not go out;	2Sa 18:3	5971a
and all the **p** went out by hundreds	2Sa 18:4	5971a
And all the **p** heard when the king	2Sa 18:5	5971a
Then the **p** went out into the field	2Sa 18:6	5971a
The **p** of Israel were defeated	2Sa 18:7	5971a
and the forest devoured more **p**	2Sa 18:8	5971a
the **p** returned from pursuing	2Sa 18:16	5971a
Israel, for Joab restrained the **p**.	2Sa 18:16	5971a
turned to mourning for all the **p**,	2Sa 19:2	5971a
for the **p** heard *it* said that day,	2Sa 19:2	5971a
So the **p** went by stealth into the	2Sa 19:3	5971a
as **p** who are humiliated steal away	2Sa 19:3	5971a
When they told all the **p**,	2Sa 19:8	5971a
all the **p** came before the king.	2Sa 19:8	5971a
All the **p** were quarreling	2Sa 19:9	5971a
All the **p** crossed over the Jordan	2Sa 19:39	5971a
and all the **p** of Judah and also	2Sa 19:40	5971a
the **p** of Israel accompanied the king.	2Sa 19:40	5971a
saw that all the **p** stood still,	2Sa 20:12	5971a
and all the **p** who were with Joab	2Sa 20:15	5971a
woman wisely came to all the **p**.	2Sa 20:22	5971a
"And You save an afflicted **p**;	2Sa 22:28	5971a
me from the contentions of my **p**;	2Sa 22:44	5971a
A **p** whom I have not known serve me.	2Sa 22:44	5971a
and the **p** returned after him only	2Sa 23:10	5971a
the **p** fled from the Philistines.	2Sa 23:11	5971a
to Beersheba, and register the **p**,	2Sa 24:2	5971a
I may know the number of the **p**."	2Sa 24:2	5971a
may the LORD your God add to the **p**	2Sa 24:3	5971a
king to register the **p** of Israel.	2Sa 24:4	5971a
registration of the **p** to the king;	2Sa 24:9	5971a
him after he had numbered the **p**.	2Sa 24:10	5971a
the **p** from Dan to Beersheba died.	2Sa 24:15	5971a
to the angel who destroyed the **p**,	2Sa 24:16	5971a
angel who was striking down the **p**,	2Sa 24:17	5971a
may be held back from the **p**."	2Sa 24:21	5971a
the trumpet, and all the **p** said,	1Ki 1:39	5971a
All the **p** went up after him,	1Ki 1:40	5971a
and the **p** were playing on flutes	1Ki 1:40	5971a
The **p** were still sacrificing on	1Ki 3:2	5971a
Your servant is in the midst of Your **p**	1Ki 3:8	5971a
p who are too many to be numbered	1Ki 3:8	5971a
understanding heart to judge Your **p**	1Ki 3:9	5971a
to judge this great **p** of Yours?"	1Ki 3:9	5971a
a wise son over this great **p**."	1Ki 5:7	5971a
the **p** who were doing the work.	1Ki 5:16	5971a
will not forsake My **p** Israel."	1Ki 6:13	5971a
I brought My **p** Israel from Egypt,	1Ki 8:16	5971a
David to be over My **p** Israel.'	1Ki 8:16	5971a
Your servant and of Your **p** Israel,	1Ki 8:30	5971a
"When Your **p** Israel are defeated	1Ki 8:33	5971a
forgive the sin of Your **p** Israel,	1Ki 8:34	5971a
Your servants and of Your **p** Israel,	1Ki 8:36	5971a
given Your **p** for an inheritance.	1Ki 8:36	5971a
by any man *or* by all Your **p** Israel,	1Ki 8:38	5971a
who is not of Your **p** Israel,	1Ki 8:41	5971a
to fear You, as *do* Your **p** Israel,	1Ki 8:43	5971a
"When Your **p** go out to battle	1Ki 8:44	5971a
and forgive Your **p** who have sinned	1Ki 8:50	5971a
(for they are Your **p** and Your	1Ki 8:51	5971a
the supplication of Your **p** Israel,	1Ki 8:52	5971a
has given rest to His **p** Israel,	1Ki 8:56	5971a
and the cause of His **p** Israel,	1Ki 8:59	5971a
On the eighth day he sent the **p**	1Ki 8:66	5971a
His servant and to Israel His **p**.	1Ki 8:66	5971a
p who were left of the Amorites,	1Ki 9:20	5971a
ruled over the **p** doing the work.	1Ki 9:23	5971a
So the **p** departed.	1Ki 12:5	5971a
you counsel *me* to answer this **p**?"	1Ki 12:6	5971a
will be a servant to this **p** today,	1Ki 12:7	5971a
this **p** who have spoken to me,	1Ki 12:9	5971a
say to this **p** who spoke to you,	1Ki 12:10	5971a
Then Jeroboam and all the **p** came	1Ki 12:12	5971a
The king answered the **p** harshly,	1Ki 12:13	5971a
the king did not listen to the **p**;	1Ki 12:15	5971a
to them, the **p** answered the king,	1Ki 12:16	5971a
Benjamin and to the rest of the **p**,	1Ki 12:23	5971a
"If this **p** go up to offer	1Ki 12:27	5971a
this **p** will return to their lord,	1Ki 12:27	5971a
for the **p** went *to worship* before	1Ki 12:30	5971a
made priests from among all the **p**	1Ki 12:31	5971a
high places from among all the **p**;	1Ki 13:33	5971a
that I would be king over this **p**.	1Ki 14:2	5971a
I exalted you from among the **p**	1Ki 14:7	5971a
made you leader over My **p** Israel,	1Ki 14:7	5971a
made you leader over My **p** Israel,	1Ki 16:2	5971a
and have made My **p** Israel sin,	1Ki 16:2	5971a
p were camped against Gibbethon,	1Ki 16:15	5971a
p who were camped heard it said,	1Ki 16:16	5971a
Then the **p** of Israel were divided	1Ki 16:21	5971a
half of the **p** followed Tibni the	1Ki 16:21	5971a
But the **p** who followed Omri	1Ki 16:22	5971a
prevailed over the **p** who followed	1Ki 16:22	5971a
came near to all the **p** and said,	1Ki 18:21	5971a
the **p** did not answer him a word.	1Ki 18:21	5971a
Then Elijah said to the **p**,	1Ki 18:22	5971a
And all the **p** said,	1Ki 18:24	5971a
Then Elijah said to all the **p**,	1Ki 18:30	5971a
So all the **p** came near to him.	1Ki 18:30	5971a
that this **p** may know that You,	1Ki 18:37	5971a
When all the **p** saw it,	1Ki 18:39	5971a
and gave *it* to the **p** and they ate.	1Ki 19:21	5971a
elders and all the **p** said to him,	1Ki 20:8	5971a
for all the **p** who follow me."	1Ki 20:10	5971a
after them he mustered all the **p**,	1Ki 20:15	5971a
and your **p** for his people.' "	1Ki 20:42	5971a
and your people for his **p**.' "	1Ki 20:42	5971a
seat Naboth at the head of the **p**;	1Ki 21:9	5971a
Naboth at the head of the **p**.	1Ki 21:12	5971a
even against Naboth, before the **p**,	1Ki 21:13	5971a
as you are, my **p** as your people,	1Ki 22:4	5971a
as you are, my people as your **p**,	1Ki 22:4	5971a
"Listen, all you **p**."	1Ki 22:28	5971a
the **p** still sacrificed and burnt	1Ki 22:43	5971a
as you are, my **p** as your people,	2Ki 3:7	5971a
as you are, my people as your **p**,	2Ki 3:7	5971a
"I live among my own **p**."	2Ki 4:13	5971b
"Pour *it* out for the **p** that they may	2Ki 4:41	5971a
"Give *them* to the **p** that they may	2Ki 4:42	5971a
"Give *them* to the **p** that they may	2Ki 4:43	5971a
"Strike this **p** with blindness, I	2Ki 6:18	1471
and the **p** looked, and behold,	2Ki 6:30	5971a
So the **p** went out and plundered	2Ki 7:16	5971a
the **p** trampled on him at the gate,	2Ki 7:17	5971a
the **p** trampled on him at the gate and	2Ki 7:20	5971a
you king over the **p** of the LORD,	2Ki 9:6	5971a

and stood and said to all the **p**, 2Ki 10:9 5971a
Jehu gathered all the **p** and said to 2Ki 10:18 5971a
noise of the guard *and of* the **p**, 2Ki 11:13 5971a
to the **p** in the house of the LORD. 2Ki 11:13 5971a
and all the **p** of the land rejoiced 2Ki 11:14 5971a
the LORD and the king and the **p**, 2Ki 11:17 5971a
that they would be the LORD's **p**, 2Ki 11:17 5971a
also between the king and the **p**. 2Ki 11:17 5971a
All the **p** of the land went to 2Ki 11:18 5971a
guards and all the **p** of the land; 2Ki 11:19 5971a
So all the **p** of the land rejoiced 2Ki 11:20 5971a
the **p** still sacrificed and burned 2Ki 12:3 5971a
take no *more* money from the **p**, 2Ki 12:8 5971a
the **p** still sacrificed and burned 2Ki 14:4 5971a
All the **p** of Judah took Azariah, 2Ki 14:21 5971a
the **p** still sacrificed and burned 2Ki 15:4 5971a
judging the **p** of the land. 2Ki 15:5 5971a
struck him before the **p** and killed 2Ki 15:10 5971a
the **p** still sacrificed and burned 2Ki 15:35 5971a
and carried *the* **p** *of* it away into 2Ki 16:9
with the burnt offering of all the **p** 2Ki 16:15 5971a
which the **p** of Samaria had made, 2Ki 17:29 8118
in the hearing of the **p** who are on 2Ki 18:26 5971a
But the **p** were silent and answered 2Ki 18:36 5971a
to Hezekiah the leader of My **p**, 2Ki 20:5 5971a
Then the **p** of the land killed all 2Ki 21:24 5971a
and the **p** of the land made Josiah 2Ki 21:24 5971a
have gathered from the **p**. 2Ki 22:4 5971a
inquire of the LORD for me and the **p** 2Ki 22:13 5971a
and the prophets and all the **p**, 2Ki 23:2 5971a
the **p** entered into the covenant. 2Ki 23:3 5971a
on the graves of the common **p**. 2Ki 23:6 5971a
king commanded all the **p** saying, 2Ki 23:21 5971a
Then the **p** of the land took 2Ki 23:30 5971a
and gold from the **p** of the land, 2Ki 23:35 5971a
except the poorest **p** of the land. 2Ki 24:14 5971a
was no food for the **p** of the land. 2Ki 25:3 5971a
Then the rest of the **p** who were 2Ki 25:11 5971a
king of Babylon and the rest of the **p**, 2Ki 25:11 5971a
who mustered the **p** of the land; 2Ki 25:19 5971a
and sixty men of the **p** of the land 2Ki 25:19 5971a
Now *as for* the **p** who were left in 2Ki 25:22 5971a
Then all the **p**, both small and 2Ki 25:26 5971a
became the father of the **p** of Lud, 1Ch 1:11 3866
news to their idols and to the **p**. 1Ch 10:9 5971a
'You shall shepherd My **p** Israel, 1Ch 11:2 5971a
be prince over My **p** Israel.' " 1Ch 11:2 5971a
the **p** fled before the Philistines. 1Ch 11:13 5971a
right in the eyes of all the **p**. 1Ch 13:4 5971a
for the sake of His **p** Israel. 1Ch 14:2 5971a
the **p** in the name of the LORD. 1Ch 16:2 5971a
And from *one* kingdom to another **p**, 1Ch 16:20 5971a
Then all the **p** said, 1Ch 16:36 5971a
the **p** departed each to his house, 1Ch 16:43 5971a
I commanded to shepherd My **p**, 1Ch 17:6 5971a
to be leader over My **p** Israel. 1Ch 17:7 5971a
appoint a place for My **p** Israel, 1Ch 17:9 5971a
judges *to be* over My **p** Israel. 1Ch 17:10 5971a
in the earth is like Your **p** Israel, 1Ch 17:21 5971a
went to redeem for Himself *as* a **p**, 1Ch 17:21 5971a
out nations from before Your **p**, 1Ch 17:21 5971a
"For Your **p** Israel You made 1Ch 17:22 5971a
made Your own **p** forever, 1Ch 17:22 5971a
and righteousness for all his **p**. 1Ch 18:14 5971a
and the king of Maacah and his **p**, 1Ch 19:7 5971a
But the remainder of the **p** he 1Ch 19:11 5971a
courageous for the sake of our **p** 1Ch 19:13 5971a
So Joab and the **p** who were with 1Ch 19:14 5971a
brought out the **p** who *were* in it, 1Ch 20:3 5971a
all the **p** returned *to* Jerusalem. 1Ch 20:3 5971a
Joab and to the princes of the **p**, 1Ch 21:2 5971a
"May the LORD add to His **p** a 1Ch 21:3 5971a
the census of *all* the **p** to David. 1Ch 21:5 5971a
I who commanded to count the **p**? 1Ch 21:17 5971a
p that they should be plagued." 1Ch 21:17 5971a
may be restrained from the **p**." 1Ch 21:22 5971a
before the LORD and before His **p**. 1Ch 22:18 5971a
of Israel has given rest to His **p**, 1Ch 23:25 5971a
to me, my brethren and my **p**; 1Ch 28:2 5971a
The officials also and all the **p** 1Ch 28:21 5971a
Then the **p** rejoiced because they 1Ch 29:9 5971a
"But who am I and who are my **p** 1Ch 29:14 5971a
so now with joy I have seen Your **p**, 1Ch 29:17 5971a
intentions of the heart of Your **p**, 1Ch 29:18 5971a
You have made me king over a **p** 2Ch 1:9 5971a
go out and come in before this **p**, 2Ch 1:10 5971a
can rule this great **p** of Yours?" 2Ch 1:10 5971a
knowledge that you may rule My **p** 2Ch 1:11 5971a
'Because the LORD loves His **p**, 2Ch 2:11 5971a
supervisors to make the **p** work. 2Ch 2:18 5971a
My **p** from the land of Egypt, 2Ch 6:5 5971a
man for a leader over My **p** Israel; 2Ch 6:5 5971a
David to be over My **p** Israel.' 2Ch 6:6 5971a
Your servant and of Your **p** Israel when 2Ch 6:21 5971a
"If Your **p** Israel are defeated 2Ch 6:24 5971a
forgive the sin of Your **p** Israel, 2Ch 6:25 5971a
of Your servants and Your **p** Israel, 2Ch 6:27 5971a
given to Your **p** for an inheritance. 2Ch 6:27 5971a
by any man or by all Your **p** Israel, 2Ch 6:29 5971a
who is not from Your **p** Israel, 2Ch 6:32 5971a
and fear You as *do* Your **p** Israel, 2Ch 6:33 5971a
"When Your **p** go out to battle 2Ch 6:34 5971a
p who have sinned against You. 2Ch 6:39 5971a
Then the king and all the **p** 2Ch 7:4 5971a
the **p** dedicated the house of God. 2Ch 7:5 5971a
he sent the **p** to their tents, 2Ch 7:10 5971a
to Solomon and to His **p** Israel. 2Ch 7:10 5971a
if I send pestilence among My **p**, 2Ch 7:13 5971a
My **p** who are called by My name 2Ch 7:14 5971a

p who were left of the Hittites, 2Ch 8:7 5971a
and fifty who ruled over the **p**. 2Ch 8:10 5971a
So the **p** departed. 2Ch 10:5 5971a
you counsel *me* to answer this **p**?" 2Ch 10:6 5971a
"If you will be kind to this **p** 2Ch 10:7 5971a
give that we may answer this **p**, 2Ch 10:9 5971a
say to the **p** who spoke to you, 2Ch 10:10 5971a
So Jeroboam and all the **p** came to 2Ch 10:12 5971a
the king did not listen to the **p**, 2Ch 10:15 5971a
to them the **p** answered the king, 2Ch 10:16 5971a
And the **p** who came with him from 2Ch 12:3 5971a
Abijah and his **p** defeated them 2Ch 13:17 5971a
Asa and the **p** who *were* with 2Ch 14:13 5971a
Asa oppressed some of the **p** at the 2Ch 16:10 5971a
of Judah and taught among the **p**. 2Ch 17:9 5971a
him and the **p** who were with him, 2Ch 18:2 5971a
you are, and my **p** as your people, 2Ch 18:3 5971a
you are, and my people as your **p**, 2Ch 18:3 5971a
"Listen, all you **p**." 2Ch 18:27 5971a
and went out again among the **p** 2Ch 19:4 5971a
of this land before Your **p** Israel and 2Ch 20:7 5971a
When he had consulted with the **p**, 2Ch 20:21 5971a
his **p** came to take their spoil, 2Ch 20:25 5971a
the **p** had not yet directed their 2Ch 20:33 5971a
LORD is going to strike your **p**, 2Ch 21:14 5971a
And his **p** made no fire for him 2Ch 21:19 5971a
and all the **p** *shall be* in the 2Ch 23:5 5971a
the **p** keep the charge of the LORD. 2Ch 23:6 5971a
He stationed all the **p**, 2Ch 23:10 5971a
the noise of the **p** running and 2Ch 23:12 5971a
the house of the LORD to the **p**. 2Ch 23:12 5971a
And all the **p** of the land rejoiced 2Ch 23:13 5971a
and all the **p** and the king, 2Ch 23:16 5971a
that they would be the LORD's **p**. 2Ch 23:16 5971a
the **p** went to the house of Baal and 2Ch 23:17 5971a
the nobles, the rulers of the **p** and 2Ch 23:20 5971a
people and all the **p** of the land, 2Ch 23:20 5971a
So all of the **p** of the land 2Ch 23:21 5971a
All the officers and all the **p** rejoiced 2Ch 24:10 5971a
above the **p** and said to them, 2Ch 24:20 5971a
destroyed all the officials of the **p** 2Ch 24:23 5971a
of the people from among the **p**, 2Ch 24:23 5971a
himself and led his **p** forth, 2Ch 25:11 5971a
have you sought the gods of the **p** 2Ch 25:15 5971a
their own **p** from your hand?" 2Ch 25:15 5971a
all the **p** of Judah took Uzziah, 2Ch 26:1 5971a
house judging the **p** of the land. 2Ch 26:21 5971a
the **p** continued acting corruptly. 2Ch 27:2 5971a
to subjugate for yourselves the **p** of 2Ch 28:10 1121
Then Hezekiah and all the **p** 2Ch 29:36 5971a
what God had prepared for the **p**, 2Ch 29:36 5971a
the **p** been gathered to Jerusalem. 2Ch 30:3 5971a
Now many **p** were gathered at 2Ch 30:13 5971a
For a multitude of the **p**, 2Ch 30:18 5971a
heard Hezekiah and healed the **p**. 2Ch 30:20 5971a
priests arose and blessed the **p**; 2Ch 30:27 5971a
Also he commanded the **p** who lived 2Ch 31:4 5971a
blessed the LORD and His **p** Israel. 2Ch 31:8 5971a
for the LORD has blessed His **p**, 2Ch 31:10 5971a
So many **p** assembled and stopped up 2Ch 32:4 5971a
military officers over the **p** and 2Ch 32:6 5971a
And the **p** relied on the words of 2Ch 32:8 5971a
deliver his **p** out of my hand, 2Ch 32:14 5971a
able to deliver his **p** from my hand 2Ch 32:15 5971a
delivered their **p** from my hand, 2Ch 32:17 5971a
not deliver His **p** from my hand." 2Ch 32:17 5971a
p of Jerusalem who were on the wall 2Ch 32:18 5971a
LORD spoke to Manasseh and his **p**, 2Ch 33:10 5971a
Nevertheless the **p** still sacrificed in 2Ch 33:17 5971a
But the **p** of the land killed all 2Ch 33:25 5971a
and the **p** of the land made Josiah 2Ch 33:25 5971a
the Levites and all the **p**, 2Ch 34:30 5971a
LORD your God and His **p** Israel. 2Ch 35:3 5971a
of your brethren the lay **p**, 2Ch 35:5 5971a
Josiah contributed to the lay **p**, 2Ch 35:7 5971a
a freewill offering to the **p**, 2Ch 35:8 5971a
the lay **p** to present to the LORD, 2Ch 35:12 5971a
them speedily to all the lay **p**. 2Ch 35:13 5971a
Then the **p** of the land took Joahaz 2Ch 36:1 5971a
the officials of the priests and the **p** 2Ch 36:14 5971a
He had compassion on His **p** and on 2Ch 36:15 5971a
of the LORD arose against His **p**, 2Ch 36:16 5971a
there is among you of all His **p**, 2Ch 36:23 5971a
there is among you of all His **p**, Ezr 1:3 5971a
Now these are the **p** of the province Ezr 2:1 1121
of the men of the **p** of Israel: Ezr 2:2 5971a
and the Levites, some of the **p**, Ezr 2:70 5971a
the **p** gathered together as one man Ezr 3:1 5971a
And all the **p** shouted with a great Ezr 3:11 5971a
so that the **p** could not distinguish Ezr 3:13 5971a
the sound of the weeping of the **p**, Ezr 3:13 5971a
the **p** shouted with a loud shout, Ezr 3:13 5971a
p of the exile were building a temple Ezr 4:1 1121
Then the **p** of the land discouraged Ezr 4:4 5971a
land discouraged the **p** of Judah, Ezr 4:4 5971a
and deported the **p** to Babylon. Ezr 5:12 5972
the full cost is to be paid to these **p** Ezr 6:8 1400
or **p** who attempts to change *it*, Ezr 6:12 5972
a decree that any of the **p** of Israel Ezr 7:13 5972
of the **p** and of the priests, Ezr 7:16 5972
judges that they may judge all the **p** Ezr 7:25 5972
I observed the **p** and the priests, Ezr 8:15 5971a
they supported the **p** and the house Ezr 8:36 5971a
"The **p** of Israel and the priests Ezr 9:1 5971a
for the **p** wept bitterly. Ezr 10:1 5971a
and all the **p** sat in the open Ezr 10:9 5971a
"But there are many **p**; Ezr 10:13 5971a
They are Your servants and Your **p** Ne 1:10 5971a
for the **p** had a mind to work. Ne 4:6 5971a

p in families with their swords, Ne 4:13 5971a
officials and the rest of the **p**: Ne 4:14 5971a
officials and the rest of the **p**, Ne 4:19 5971a
At that time I also said to the **p**, Ne 4:22 5971a
there was a great outcry of the **p** Ne 5:1 5971a
p did according to this promise. Ne 5:13 5971a
laid burdens on the **p** and took from Ne 5:15 5971a
their servants domineered the **p**. Ne 5:15 5971a
the servitude was heavy on this **p**. Ne 5:18 5971a
all that I have done for this **p**. Ne 5:19 5971a
but the **p** in it were few and the Ne 7:4 5971a
p to be enrolled by genealogies. Ne 7:5 5971a
These are the **p** of the province Ne 7:6 1121
number of men of the **p** of Israel: Ne 7:7 5971a
That which the rest of the **p** Ne 7:72 5971a
the singers, some of the **p**, Ne 7:73 5971a
And all the **p** gathered as one man Ne 8:1 5971a
and all the **p** were attentive to Ne 8:3 5971a
the book in the sight of all the **p** Ne 8:5 5971a
he was standing above all the **p**; Ne 8:5 5971a
he opened it, all the **p** stood up. Ne 8:5 5971a
And all the **p** answered, Ne 8:6 5971a
explained the law to the **p** while Ne 8:7 5971a
the **p** *remained* in their place. Ne 8:7 5971a
the **p** said to all the people, Ne 8:9 5971a
the people said to all the **p**, Ne 8:9 5971a
For all the **p** were weeping when Ne 8:9 5971a
So the Levites calmed all the **p**, Ne 8:11 5971a
All the **p** went away to eat, to Ne 8:12 5971a
fathers' *households* of all the **p**, Ne 8:13 5971a
So the **p** went out and brought *them* Ne 8:16 5971a
and all the **p** of his land; Ne 9:10 5971a
our fathers and on all Your **p**, Ne 9:32 5971a
The leaders of the **p**: Ne 10:14 5971a
Now the rest of the **p**, Ne 10:28 5971a
the priests, the Levites and the **p** Ne 10:34 5971a
leaders of the **p** lived in Jerusalem, Ne 11:1 5971a
but the rest of the **p** cast lots to Ne 11:1 5971a
And the **p** blessed all the men who Ne 11:2 5971a
in all matters concerning the **p**. Ne 11:24 5971a
they also purified the **p**, Ne 12:30 5971a
with half of the **p** on the wall, Ne 12:38 5971a
of Moses in the hearing of the **p**; Ne 13:1 5971a
but the language of his own **p**. Ne 13:24 5971a
p who were present at the citadel Es 1:5 5971a
to display her beauty to the **p** and Es 1:11 5971a
p according to their language, Es 1:22 5971a
in the language of his own **p**. Es 1:22 5971a
make known her **p** or her kindred, Es 2:10 5971a
made known her kindred or her **p**, Es 2:20 5971a
him *who* the **p** of Mordecai *were;* Es 3:6 5971a
all the Jews, the **p** of Mordecai, Es 3:6 5971a
"There is a certain **p** scattered Es 3:8 5971a
from *those* of all *other* **p** and Es 3:8 5971a
silver is yours, and the **p** *also,* Es 3:11 5971a
and to the princes of each **p**, Es 3:12 5971a
each **p** according to its language, Es 3:12 5971a
and to plead with him for her **p**. Es 4:8 5971a
"All the king's servants and the **p** Es 4:11 5971a
petition, and my **p** as my request; Es 7:3 5971a
for we have been sold, I and my **p**, Es 7:4 5971a
calamity which will befall my **p**, Es 8:6 5971a
p according to their language as Es 8:9 5971a
annihilate the entire army of any **p** Es 8:11 5971a
one who sought the good of his **p** Es 10:3 5971a
fell on the young **p** and they died, Jb 1:19 5288
"Truly then you are the **p**, Jb 12:2 5971a
the chiefs of the earth's **p** And Jb 12:24 5971a
He has made me a byword of the **p**, Jb 17:6 5971a
or posterity among his **p**, Jb 18:19 5971a
P are shaken and pass away, Jb 34:20 5971a
not rule Nor be snares of the **p**. Jb 34:30 5971a
When **p** vanish in their place. Jb 36:20 5971a
To bring rain on a land without **p**, Jb 38:26 376
not be afraid of ten thousands of **p** Ps 3:6 5971a
LORD; Your blessing *be* upon Your **p**! Ps 3:8 5971a
Who eat up my **p** *as* they eat bread, Ps 14:4 5971a
the LORD restores His captive **p**, Ps 14:7 5971a
For You save an afflicted **p** Ps 18:27 5971a
me from the contentions of the **p**; Ps 18:43 5971a
p whom I have not known serve me. Ps 18:43 5971a
of men and despised by the **p**. Ps 22:6 5971a
To a **p** who will be born, Ps 22:31 5971a
Save Your **p** and bless Your Ps 28:9 5971a
LORD will give strength to His **p**; Ps 29:11 5971a
LORD will bless His **p** with peace. Ps 29:11 5971a
The **p** whom He has chosen for His Ps 33:12 5971a
You sell Your **p** cheaply, Ps 44:12 5971a
Forget your **p** and your father's Ps 45:10 5971a
The rich among the **p** will seek Ps 45:12 5971a
The princes of the **p** have Ps 47:9 5971a
as the **p** of the God of Abraham, Ps 47:9 5971a
And the earth, to judge His **p**: Ps 50:4 5971a
"Hear, O My **p**, and I will speak; Ps 50:7 5971a
Who eat up My **p** *as though* they ate Ps 53:4 5971a
When God restores His captive **p**, Ps 53:6 5971a
not slay them, or my **p** will forget; Ps 59:11 5971a
made Your **p** experience hardship; Ps 60:3 5971a
Trust in Him at all times, O **p**; Ps 62:8 5971a
You went forth before Your **p**, Ps 68:7 5971a
gives strength and power to the **p**. Ps 68:35 5971a
he judge Your **p** with righteousness And Ps 72:2 5971a
mountains bring peace to the **p**, Ps 72:3 5971a
vindicate the afflicted of the **p**, Ps 72:4 5971a
his **p** return to this place, Ps 73:10 5971a
a foolish **p** has spurned Your name. Ps 74:18 5971a
have by Your power redeemed Your **p**, Ps 77:15 5971a
led Your **p** like a flock Ps 77:20 5971a
Listen, O my **p**, to my instruction; Ps 78:1 5971a

Will He provide meat for His **p**?"	**Ps 78:20**	5971a
He led forth His own **p** like sheep And	**Ps 78:52**	5971a
also delivered His **p** to the sword,	**Ps 78:62**	5971a
him To shepherd Jacob His **p**,	**Ps 78:71**	5971a
So we Your **p** and the sheep of Your	**Ps 79:13**	5971a
be angry with the prayer of Your **p**?	**Ps 80:4**	5971a
"Hear, O My **p**, and I will	**Ps 81:8**	5971a
My **p** did not listen to My voice,	**Ps 81:11**	5971a
"Oh that My **p** would listen to Me,	**Ps 81:13**	5971a
make shrewd plans against Your **p**,	**Ps 83:3**	5971a
forgave the iniquity of Your **p**;	**Ps 85:2**	5971a
That Your **p** may rejoice in You?	**Ps 85:6**	5971a
For He will speak peace to His **p**,	**Ps 85:8**	5971a
the **p** who know the joyful sound!	**Ps 89:15**	5971a
exalted one chosen from the **p**.	**Ps 89:19**	5971a
They crush Your **p**, O LORD, And	**Ps 94:5**	5971a
heed, you senseless among the **p**;	**Ps 94:8**	5971a
the LORD will not abandon His **p**,	**Ps 94:14**	5971a
And we are the **p** of His pasture and	**Ps 95:7**	5971a
are a **p** who err in their heart,	**Ps 95:10**	5971a
His **p** and the sheep of His pasture.	**Ps 100:3**	5971a
That a **p** yet to be created may	**Ps 102:18**	5971a
From *one* kingdom to another **p**.	**Ps 105:13**	5971a
caused His **p** to be very fruitful,	**Ps 105:24**	5971a
turned their heart to hate His **p**,	**Ps 105:25**	5971a
He brought forth His **p** with joy,	**Ps 105:43**	5971a
O LORD, in *Your* favor toward Your **p**;	**Ps 106:4**	5971a
LORD was kindled against His **p** And	**Ps 106:40**	5971a
And let all the **p** say, "Amen."	**Ps 106:48**	5971a
also in the congregation of the **p**,	**Ps 107:32**	5971a
Your **p** will volunteer freely in the	**Ps 110:3**	5971a
to His **p** the power of His works,	**Ps 111:6**	5971a
He has sent redemption to His **p**;	**Ps 111:9**	5971a
With the princes of His **p**.	**Ps 113:8**	5971a
from a **p** of strange language,	**Ps 114:1**	5971a
be in the presence of all His **p**.	**Ps 116:14**	5971a
be in the presence of all His **p**,	**Ps 116:18**	5971a
So the LORD surrounds His **p** From	**Ps 125:2**	5971a
A heritage to Israel His **p**.	**Ps 135:12**	5971a
For the LORD will judge His **p** And	**Ps 135:14**	5971a
led His **p** through the wilderness,	**Ps 136:16**	5971a
Who subdues my **p** under me.	**Ps 144:2**	5971a
are the **p** who are so situated;	**Ps 144:15**	5971a
are the **p** whose God is the LORD!	**Ps 144:15**	5971a
He has lifted up a horn for His **p**,	**Ps 148:14**	5971a
sons of Israel, a **p** near to Him.	**Ps 148:14**	5971a
the LORD takes pleasure in His **p**;	**Ps 149:4**	5971a
there is no guidance the **p** fall,	**Pr 11:14**	5971a
grain, the **p** will curse him,	**Pr 11:26**	3816
a multitude of **p** is a king's glory,	**Pr 14:28**	5971a
the dearth of **p** is a prince's ruin.	**Pr 14:28**	3816
But sin is a disgrace to *any* **p**.	**Pr 14:34**	3816
Is a wicked ruler over a poor **p**.	**Pr 28:15**	5971a
righteous increase, the **p** rejoice,	**Pr 29:2**	5971a
when a wicked man rules, **p** groan.	**Pr 29:2**	5971a
no vision, the **p** are unrestrained,	**Pr 29:18**	5971a
The ants are not a strong **p**,	**Pr 30:25**	5971a
The shephanim are not mighty **p**,	**Pr 30:26**	5971a
There is no end to all the **p**,	**Ec 4:16**	5971a
also taught the **p** knowledge;	**Ec 12:9**	5971a
Over the chariots of my noble **p**."	**SS 6:12**	5971a
know, My **p** do not understand."	**Is 1:3**	5971a
P weighed down with iniquity,	**Is 1:4**	5971a
of our God, You **p** of Gomorrah.	**Is 1:10**	5971a
For You have abandoned Your **p**,	**Is 2:6**	5971a
And the **p** will be oppressed, Each	**Is 3:5**	5971a
not appoint me ruler of the **p**."	**Is 3:7**	5971a
O My **p**! Their oppressors are	**Is 3:12**	5971a
O My **p**! Those who guide you lead	**Is 3:12**	5971a
And stands to judge the **p**.	**Is 3:13**	5971a
the elders and princes of His **p**,	**Is 3:14**	5971a
"What do you mean by crushing My **p**	**Is 3:15**	5971a
Therefore My **p** go into exile for	**Is 5:13**	5971a
the LORD has burned against His **p**,	**Is 5:25**	5971a
I live among a **p** of unclean lips;	**Is 6:5**	5971a
"Go, and tell this **p**:	**Is 6:9**	5971a
the hearts of this **p** insensitive,	**Is 6:10**	5971a
inhabitant, Houses are without **p** And	**Is 6:11**	120
the hearts of his **p** shook as the trees	**Is 7:2**	5971a
so that it is no longer a **p**),	**Is 7:8**	
LORD will bring on you, on your **p**,	**Is 7:17**	5971a
P will come there with bows	**Is 7:24**	
"Inasmuch as these **p** have rejected	**Is 8:6**	5971a
not to walk in the way of this **p**,	**Is 8:11**	5971a
all that this **p** call a conspiracy,	**Is 8:12**	5971a
should not a **p** consult their God?	**Is 8:19**	5971a
The **p** who walk in darkness Will	**Is 9:2**	5971a
And all the **p** know *it, That is,*	**Is 9:9**	5971a
Yet the **p** do not turn back to Him	**Is 9:13**	5971a
this **p** are leading *them* astray;	**Is 9:16**	5971a
the **p** are like fuel for the fire;	**Is 9:19**	5971a
rob the poor of My **p** of *their* rights,	**Is 10:2**	5971a
And commission it against the **p**	**Is 10:6**	5971a
For though your **p**, O Israel, may	**Is 10:22**	5971a
"O My **p** who dwell in Zion, do not	**Is 10:24**	5971a
His hand The remnant of His **p**,	**Is 11:11**	5971a
remnant of His **p** who will be left,	**Is 11:16**	5971a
mountains, Like that of many **p**!	**Is 13:4**	5971a
They will each turn to his own **p**,	**Is 13:14**	5971a
country, You have slain your **p**.	**Is 14:20**	5971a
the afflicted of His **p** will seek refuge	**Is 14:32**	5971a
To a **p** feared far and wide,	**Is 18:2**	5971a
of hosts From a **p** tall and smooth,	**Is 18:7**	5971a
Even from a **p** feared far and wide,	**Is 18:7**	5971a
"Blessed is Egypt My **p**,	**Is 19:25**	5971a
O my threshed **p**, and my	**Is 21:10**	
destruction of the daughter of my **p**.	**Is 22:4**	5971a
is the **p** *which* was not;	**Is 23:13**	5971a
And the **p** will be like the priest,	**Is 24:2**	5971a
the exalted of the **p** of the earth fade	**Is 24:4**	5971a
a strong **p** will glorify You;	**Is 25:3**	5971a
will remove the reproach of His **p**	**Is 25:8**	5971a
for the **p** and are put to shame;	**Is 26:11**	5971a
Come, my **p**, enter into your rooms And	**Is 26:20**	5971a
they are not a **p** of discernment,	**Is 27:11**	5971a
diadem to the remnant of His **p**;	**Is 28:5**	5971a
He will speak to this **p** Through	**Is 28:11**	5971a
rule this **p** who are in Jerusalem,	**Is 28:14**	5971a
"Because this **p** draw near with	**Is 29:13**	5971a
deal marvelously with this **p**,	**Is 29:14**	5971a
will be ashamed because of a **p**	**Is 30:5**	5971a
To a **p** who cannot profit *them;*	**Is 30:6**	5971a
For this is a rebellious **p**,	**Is 30:9**	5971a
O **p** in Zion, inhabitant in	**Is 30:19**	5971a
LORD binds up the fracture of His **p**	**Is 30:26**	5971a
For the land of my **p** *in which*	**Is 32:13**	5971a
Then my **p** will live in a peaceful	**Is 32:18**	5971a
You will no longer see a fierce **p**,	**Is 33:19**	5971a
A **p** of unintelligible speech which	**Is 33:19**	5971a
The **p** who dwell there will be	**Is 33:24**	5971a
And upon the **p** whom I have devoted	**Is 34:5**	5971a
in the hearing of the **p** who are on	**Is 36:11**	5971a
"Comfort, O comfort My **p**,"	**Is 40:1**	5971a
Surely the **p** are grass.	**Is 40:7**	5971a
Who gives breath to the **p** on it And	**Is 42:5**	5971a
you as a covenant to the **p**,	**Is 42:6**	5971a
is a **p** plundered and despoiled;	**Is 42:22**	5971a
Bring out the **p** who are blind,	**Is 43:8**	5971a
To give drink to My chosen **p**.	**Is 43:20**	5971a
"The **p** whom I formed for Myself Will	**Is 43:21**	5971a
"I was angry with My **p**,	**Is 47:6**	5971a
give You for a covenant of the **p**,	**Is 49:8**	5971a
For the LORD has comforted His **p** And	**Is 49:13**	5971a
"Pay attention to Me, O My **p**,	**Is 51:4**	5971a
A **p** in whose heart is My law;	**Is 51:7**	5971a
'You are My **p**.' "	**Is 51:16**	5971a
your God Who contends for His **p**,	**Is 51:22**	5971a
"My **p** went down at the first into	**Is 52:4**	5971a
"seeing that My **p** have been taken	**Is 52:5**	5971a
Therefore My **p** shall know My name	**Is 52:6**	5971a
For the LORD has comforted His **p**,	**Is 52:9**	5971a
My **p**, So His appearance was	**Is 52:14**	
my **p**, to whom the stroke *was due?*	**Is 53:8**	5971a
surely separate me from His **p**."	**Is 56:3**	5971a
obstacle out of the way of My **p**."	**Is 57:14**	5971a
declare to My **p** their transgression And	**Is 58:1**	5971a
"Then all your **p** *will be* righteous;	**Is 60:21**	5971a
Clear the way for the **p**;	**Is 62:10**	5971a
"The holy **p**, The redeemed of the	**Is 62:12**	5971a
"Surely, they are My **p**,	**Is 63:8**	5971a
His **p** remembered the days of old,	**Is 63:11**	5971a
So You led Your **p**,	**Is 63:14**	5971a
Your holy **p** possessed Your sanctuary	**Is 63:18**	5971a
look now, all of us are Your **p**.	**Is 64:9**	5971a
all day long to a rebellious **p**,	**Is 65:2**	5971a
A **p** who continually provoke Me to	**Is 65:3**	5971a
for herds, For My **p** who seek Me.	**Is 65:10**	5971a
rejoicing And her **p** *for* gladness.	**Is 65:18**	5971a
in Jerusalem and be glad in My **p**;	**Is 65:19**	5971a
so will be the days of My **p**,	**Is 65:22**	5971a
priests and to the **p** of the land.	**Jer 1:18**	5971a
But My **p** have changed their glory	**Jer 2:11**	5971a
"For My **p** have committed two evils:	**Jer 2:13**	5971a
Why do My **p** say,	**Jer 2:31**	5971a
Yet My **p** have forgotten Me Days	**Jer 2:32**	5971a
deceived this **p** and Jerusalem,	**Jer 4:10**	5971a
said to this **p** and to Jerusalem,	**Jer 4:11**	5971a
direction of the daughter of My **p**	**Jer 4:11**	5971a
"For My **p** are foolish, They know	**Jer 4:22**	5971a
"Shall I not punish these **p**,"	**Jer 5:9**	
your mouth fire And this **p** wood,	**Jer 5:14**	5971a
this, O foolish and senseless **p**,	**Jer 5:21**	5971a
'But this **p** has a stubborn and	**Jer 5:23**	5971a
wicked men are found among My **p**,	**Jer 5:26**	5971a
'Shall I not punish these **p**?'	**Jer 5:29**	
And My **p** love it so!	**Jer 5:31**	5971a
have healed the brokenness of My **p**	**Jer 6:14**	5971a
I am bringing disaster on this **p**,	**Jer 6:19**	5971a
stumbling blocks before this **p**.	**Jer 6:21**	5971a
a **p** is coming from the north land,	**Jer 6:22**	5971a
O daughter of my **p**,	**Jer 6:26**	5971a
assayer *and* a tester among My **p**,	**Jer 6:27**	5971a
of the wickedness of My **p** Israel.	**Jer 7:12**	5971a
for you, do not pray for this **p**,	**Jer 7:16**	5971a
be your God, and you will be My **p**;	**Jer 7:23**	5971a
"The dead bodies of this **p**	**Jer 7:33**	5971a
"Why then has this **p**,	**Jer 8:5**	5971a
But My **p** do not know The ordinance	**Jer 8:7**	5971a
brokenness of the daughter of My **p**	**Jer 8:11**	5971a
The cry of the daughter of my **p**	**Jer 8:19**	5971a
brokenness of the daughter of my **p**	**Jer 8:21**	5971a
daughter of my **p** been restored?	**Jer 8:22**	5971a
the slain of the daughter of my **p**!	**Jer 9:1**	5971a
That I might leave my **p** And	**Jer 9:2**	5971a
because of the daughter of My **p**?	**Jer 9:7**	5971a
"behold, I will feed them, this **p**,	**Jer 9:15**	5971a
so you shall be My **p**,	**Jer 11:4**	5971a
"Therefore do not pray for this **p**,	**Jer 11:14**	5971a
which I have endowed My **p** Israel,	**Jer 12:14**	5971a
really learn the ways of My **p**,	**Jer 12:16**	5971a
they taught My **p** to swear by Baal,	**Jer 12:16**	5971a
be built up in the midst of My **p**.	**Jer 12:16**	5971a
'This wicked **p**, who refuse to	**Jer 13:10**	5971a
'that they might be for Me a **p**,	**Jer 13:11**	5971a
Thus says the LORD to this **p**,	**Jer 14:10**	5971a
pray for the welfare of this **p**.	**Jer 14:11**	5971a
"The **p** also to whom they are	**Jer 14:16**	5971a
For the virgin daughter of my **p**	**Jer 14:17**	5971a
My heart would not be with this **p**;	**Jer 15:1**	5971a
of children, I will destroy My **p**;	**Jer 15:7**	5971a
make you to this **p** A fortified wall	**Jer 15:20**	5971a
withdrawn My peace from this **p**,"	**Jer 16:5**	5971a
when you tell this **p** all these words	**Jer 16:10**	5971a
'For My **p** have forgotten Me, They	**Jer 18:15**	5971a
and *take* some of the elders of the **p**	**Jer 19:1**	5971a
I break this **p** and this city,	**Jer 19:11**	5971a
LORD's house and said to all the **p**:	**Jer 19:14**	5971a
Judah and his servants and the **p**,	**Jer 21:7**	5971a
"You shall also say to this **p**,	**Jer 21:8**	5971a
and your **p** who enter these gates.	**Jer 22:2**	5971a
and his servants and his **p**.	**Jer 22:4**	5971a
shepherds who are tending My **p**:	**Jer 23:2**	5971a
Baal and led My **p** Israel astray.	**Jer 23:13**	5971a
have announced My words to My **p**,	**Jer 23:22**	5971a
who intend to make My **p** forget My	**Jer 23:27**	5971a
and led My **p** astray by their	**Jer 23:32**	5971a
furnish this **p** the slightest benefit,"	**Jer 23:32**	5971a
"Now when this **p** or the prophet	**Jer 23:33**	5971a
or the priest or the **p** who say,	**Jer 23:34**	5971a
and they will be My **p**,	**Jer 24:7**	5971a
concerning all the **p** of Judah,	**Jer 25:1**	5971a
prophet spoke to all the **p** of Judah	**Jer 25:2**	5971a
his princes and all his **p**;	**Jer 25:19**	5971a
and all the foreign **p**,	**Jer 25:20**	6154a
foreign **p** who dwell in the desert;	**Jer 25:24**	6154a
all the **p** heard Jeremiah speaking	**Jer 26:7**	5971a
him to speak to all the **p**,	**Jer 26:8**	5971a
prophets and all the **p** seized him,	**Jer 26:8**	5971a
And all the **p** gathered about	**Jer 26:9**	5971a
to the officials and to all the **p**,	**Jer 26:11**	5971a
the officials and to all the **p**,	**Jer 26:12**	5971a
Then the officials and all the **p**	**Jer 26:16**	5971a
spoke to all the assembly of the **p**,	**Jer 26:17**	5971a
he spoke to all the **p** of Judah,	**Jer 26:18**	5971a
the burial place of the common **p**.	**Jer 26:23**	5971a
not given into the hands of the **p**	**Jer 26:24**	5971a
Babylon and serve him and his **p**,	**Jer 27:12**	5971a
"Why will you die, you and your **p**,	**Jer 27:13**	5971a
to the priests and to all this **p**,	**Jer 27:16**	5971a
of the priests and all the **p**,	**Jer 28:1**	5971a
and in the presence of all the **p**	**Jer 28:5**	5971a
and in the hearing of all the **p**!	**Jer 28:7**	5971a
spoke in the presence of all the **p**,	**Jer 28:11**	5971a
have made this **p** trust in a lie.	**Jer 28:15**	5971a
and all the **p** whom Nebuchadnezzar	**Jer 29:1**	5971a
all the **p** who dwell in this city,	**Jer 29:16**	5971a
to all the **p** who are in Jerusalem,	**Jer 29:25**	5971a
have anyone living among this **p**,	**Jer 29:32**	5971a
that I am about to do to My **p**,"	**Jer 29:32**	5971a
I will restore the fortunes of My **p**	**Jer 30:3**	5971a
'You shall be My **p**,	**Jer 30:22**	5971a
Israel, and they shall be My **p**."	**Jer 31:1**	5971a
"The **p** who survived the sword	**Jer 31:2**	5971a
'O LORD, save Your **p**,	**Jer 31:7**	5971a
And My **p** will be satisfied with	**Jer 31:14**	5971a
their God, and they shall be My **p**.	**Jer 31:33**	5971a
'You brought Your **p** Israel	**Jer 32:21**	5971a
with the houses where **p** have	**Jer 32:29**	
"They shall be My **p**,	**Jer 32:38**	5971a
all this great disaster on this **p**,	**Jer 32:42**	5971a
observed what this **p** have spoken,	**Jer 33:24**	5971a
Thus they despise My **p**,	**Jer 33:24**	5971a
had made a covenant with all the **p**	**Jer 34:8**	5971a
officials and all the **p** obeyed who	**Jer 34:10**	5971a
and all the **p** of the land who	**Jer 34:19**	5971a
but this **p** has not listened to Me.'	**Jer 35:16**	5971a
the words of the LORD to the **p**	**Jer 36:6**	5971a
you shall read them to all *the* **p** *of*	**Jer 36:6**	
has pronounced against this **p**."	**Jer 36:7**	5971a
all the **p** in Jerusalem and	**Jer 36:9**	5971a
all the **p** who came from the cities	**Jer 36:9**	5971a
of the LORD's house, to all the **p**.	**Jer 36:10**	5971a
read from the book to the **p**.	**Jer 36:13**	5971a
you have read to the **p** and come."	**Jer 36:14**	5971a
nor his servants nor the **p** of the land	**Jer 37:2**	5971a
in and going out among the **p**,	**Jer 37:4**	5971a
some property there among the **p**.	**Jer 37:12**	5971a
your servants, or against this **p**,	**Jer 37:18**	5971a
was speaking to all the **p**,	**Jer 38:1**	5971a
left in this city and all the **p**,	**Jer 38:4**	5971a
seeking the well-being of this **p** but	**Jer 38:4**	5971a
palace and the houses of the **p**,	**Jer 39:8**	5971a
the **p** who were left in the city,	**Jer 39:9**	5971a
the rest of the **p** who remained,	**Jer 39:9**	5971a
of the poorest **p** who had nothing,	**Jer 39:10**	5971a
So he stayed among the **p**.	**Jer 39:14**	5971a
Because you **p** sinned against	**Jer 40:3**	
and stay with him among the **p**;	**Jer 40:5**	5971a
the **p** who were left in the land.	**Jer 40:6**	5971a
of the **p** who were in Mizpah,	**Jer 41:10**	5971a
all the **p** who were left in Mizpah,	**Jer 41:10**	5971a
as soon as all the **p** who were with	**Jer 41:13**	5971a
So all the **p** whom Ishmael had	**Jer 41:14**	5971a
the remnant of the **p** whom he had	**Jer 41:16**	5971a
and all the **p** both small and great	**Jer 42:1**	5971a
all the **p** both small and great,	**Jer 42:8**	5971a
had finished telling all the **p** all	**Jer 43:1**	5971a
of the forces, and all the **p**,	**Jer 43:4**	5971a
including all the **p** who were	**Jer 44:15**	5971a
Then Jeremiah said to all the **p**,	**Jer 44:20**	5971a
to all the **p** who were giving him	**Jer 44:20**	5971a
princes, and the **p** of the land,	**Jer 44:21**	5971a
Then Jeremiah said to all the **p**,	**Jer 44:24**	5971a
And let us go back To our own **p**	**Jer 46:16**	5971a
the power of the **p** of the north."	**Jer 46:24**	5971a
will be destroyed from *being* a **p**	**Jer 48:42**	5971a
The **p** of Chemosh have perished;	**Jer 48:46**	5971a

And his **p** settled in its cities? **Jer 49:1** 5971a
"My **p** have become lost sheep; **Jer 50:6** 5971a
will each turn back to his own **p** And **Jer 50:16** 5971a
a **p** is coming from the north, **Jer 50:41** 5971a
"Come forth from her midst, My **p**, **Jer 51:45** 5971a
was no food for the **p** of the land. **Jer 52:6** 5971a
some of the poorest of the **p**, **Jer 52:15** 5971a
the **p** who were left in the city, **Jer 52:15** 5971a
who mustered the **p** of the land, **Jer 52:25** 5971a
and sixty men of the **p** of the land **Jer 52:25** 5971a
These are the **p** whom **Jer 52:28** 5971a
carried into exile 745 Jewish **p**; **Jer 52:30** 5315
sits the city That was full of **p**! **La 1:1** 5971a
p fell into the hand of the adversary **La 1:7** 5971a
All her **p** groan seeking bread; **La 1:11** 5971a
destruction of the daughter of my **p**, **La 2:11** 5971a
a laughingstock to all my **p**, **La 3:14** 5971a
destruction of the daughter of my **p**. **La 3:48** 5971a
But the daughter of my **p** has **La 4:3** 5971a
the iniquity of the daughter of my **p** **La 4:6** 5971a
destruction of the daughter of my **p**. **La 4:10** 5971a
p who have rebelled against Me; **Ezk 2:3** 1471
sent to a **p** of unintelligible speech **Ezk 3:5** 5971a
the exiles, to the sons of your **p**, **Ezk 3:11** 5971a
none of their **p**, none of their **Ezk 7:11** 1995
of the **p** of the land will tremble. **Ezk 7:27** 5971a
they went out and struck down *the* **p** **Ezk 9:7**
As they were striking *the* **p** and I **Ezk 9:8**
son of Benaiah, leaders of the **p**. **Ezk 11:1** 5971a
Then they will be My **p**, **Ezk 11:20** 5971a
"Then say to the **p** of the land, **Ezk 12:19** 5971a
what is this proverb you **p** have **Ezk 12:22**
no place in the council of My **p**, **Ezk 13:9** 5971a
they have misled My **p** by saying, **Ezk 13:10** 5971a
against the daughters of your **p** who **Ezk 13:17** 5971a
you hunt down the lives of My **p**, **Ezk 13:18** 5971a
you have profaned Me to My **p** to **Ezk 13:19** 5971a
by your lying to My **p** who listen to **Ezk 13:19** 5971a
and deliver My **p** from your hands, **Ezk 13:21** 5971a
deliver My **p** out of your hand. **Ezk 13:23** 5971a
will cut him off from among My **p**. **Ezk 14:8** 5971a
him from among My **p** Israel. **Ezk 14:9** 5971a
Thus they will be My **p**, **Ezk 14:11** 5971a
nor by many **p** can it be raised **Ezk 17:9** 5971a
did what was not good among his **p**, **Ezk 18:18** 5971b
for it is against My **p**, **Ezk 21:12** 5971a
over to the sword with My **p**, **Ezk 21:12** 5971a
"The **p** of the land have practiced **Ezk 22:29** 5971a
I spoke to the **p** in the morning, **Ezk 24:18** 5971a
The **p** said to me, **Ezk 24:19** 5971a
Edom by the hand of My **p** Israel. **Ezk 25:14** 5971a
will slay your **p** with the sword; **Ezk 26:11** 5971a
down to the pit, to the **p** of old, **Ezk 26:20** 5971a
and the **p** of the land that is in **Ezk 30:5** 1121
"He and his **p** with him, The most **Ezk 30:11** 5971a
man, speak to the sons of your **p** and **Ezk 33:2** 5971a
and the **p** of the land take one man **Ezk 33:2** 5971a
on the trumpet and warns the **p**, **Ezk 33:3** 5971a
trumpet and the **p** are not warned, **Ezk 33:6** 5971a
"They come to you as **p** come, **Ezk 33:31** 5971a
come, and sit before you *as* My **p** and **Ezk 33:31** 5971a
the house of Israel, are My **p**," **Ezk 34:30** 5971a
the whispering of the **p**. **Ezk 36:3** 5971a
bear your fruit for My **p** Israel; **Ezk 36:8** 5971a
I will cause men—My **p** Israel **Ezk 36:12** 5971a
'These are the **p** of the LORD; **Ezk 36:20** 5971a
so you will be My **p**, **Ezk 36:28** 5971a
come up out of your graves, My **p**; **Ezk 37:12** 5971a
come up out of your graves, My **p**. **Ezk 37:13** 5971a
the sons of your **p** speak to you **Ezk 37:18** 5971a
And they will be My **p**, **Ezk 37:23** 5971a
their God, and they will be My **p**. **Ezk 37:27** 5971a
but its **p** were brought out from **Ezk 38:8** 5971a
and against the **p** who are gathered **Ezk 38:12** 5971a
My **p** Israel are living securely, **Ezk 38:14** 5971a
and you will come up against My **p** **Ezk 38:16** 5971a
known in the midst of My **p** Israel; **Ezk 39:7** 5971a
the **p** of the land will bury *them;* **Ezk 39:13** 5971a
that which is for the **p**." **Ezk 42:14** 5971a
and the sacrifice for the **p**, **Ezk 44:11** 5971a
into the outer court to the **p**, **Ezk 44:19** 5971a
to the **p** with their garments. **Ezk 44:19** 5971a
they shall teach My **p** *the* **Ezk 44:23** 5971a
shall no longer oppress My **p**, **Ezk 45:8** 5971a
your expropriations from My **p**," **Ezk 45:9** 5971a
"All the **p** of the land shall give **Ezk 45:16** 5971a
provide for himself and all the **p** **Ezk 45:22** 5971a
'The **p** of the land shall also **Ezk 46:3** 5971a
"But when the **p** of the land come **Ezk 46:9** 5971a
that My **p** will not be scattered, **Ezk 46:18** 5971a
to transmit holiness to the **p**." **Ezk 46:20** 5971a
boil the sacrifices of the **p**." **Ezk 46:24** 5971a
will not be left for another **p**; **Da 2:44** 5972
I make a decree that any **p**, **Da 3:29** 5972
whole heaven will be given to the **p** **Da 7:27** 5972
destroy mighty men and the holy **p**. **Da 8:24** 5971a
and all the **p** of the land. **Da 9:6** 5971a
who have brought Your **p** out of the **Da 9:15** 5971a
Jerusalem and Your **p** *have become* a **Da 9:16** 5971a
Your **p** are called by Your name." **Da 9:19** 5971a
my sin and the sin of my **p** Israel, **Da 9:20** 5971a
for your **p** and your holy city, **Da 9:24** 5971a
and the **p** of the prince who is to **Da 9:26** 5971a
to your **p** in the latter days, **Da 10:14** 5971a
the violent ones among your **p** will **Da 11:14** 5971a
power with a small *force of* **p**. **Da 11:23** 1471
but the **p** who know their God will **Da 11:32** 5971a
Those who have insight among the **p** **Da 11:33** 5971a
guard over the sons of your **p**, **Da 12:1** 5971a

and at that time your **p**, **Da 12:1** 5971a
shattering the power of the holy **p**, **Da 12:7** 5971a
not My **p** and I am not your God." **Hos 1:9** 5971a
"You are not My **p**," **Hos 1:10** 5971a
say to those who were not My **p**, **Hos 2:23** 5971a
were not My people, 'You are My **p**!' **Hos 2:23** 5971a
For your **p** are like those who **Hos 4:4** 5971a
My **p** are destroyed for lack of **Hos 4:6** 5971a
They feed on the sin of My **p** And **Hos 4:8** 5971a
And it will be, like **p**, like priest; **Hos 4:9** 5971a
My **p** consult their wooden idol, **Hos 4:12** 5971a
So the **p** without understanding are **Hos 4:14** 5971a
I restore the fortunes of My **p**. **Hos 6:11** 5971a
Indeed, its **p** will mourn for it, **Hos 10:5** 5971a
a tumult will arise among your **p**, **Hos 10:14** 5971a
My **p** are bent on turning from Me. **Hos 11:7** 5971a
So there is a great and mighty **p**; **Jl 2:2** 5971a
Like a mighty **p** arranged for battle. **Jl 2:5** 5971a
Before them the **p** are in anguish; **Jl 2:6** 5971a
Gather the **p**, sanctify the **Jl 2:16** 5971a
"Spare Your **p**, O LORD, And do not **Jl 2:17** 5971a
land And will have pity on His **p**. **Jl 2:18** 5971a
LORD will answer and say to His **p**, **Jl 2:19** 5971a
My **p** will never be put to shame. **Jl 2:26** 5971a
My **p** will never be put to shame. **Jl 2:27** 5971a
behalf of My **p** and My inheritance, **Jl 3:2** 5971a
"They have also cast lots for My **p**, **Jl 3:3** 5971a
But the LORD is a refuge for His **p** **Jl 3:16** 5971a
p of Aram will go exiled to Kir," **Am 1:5** 5971a
in a city will not the **p** tremble? **Am 3:6** 5971a
line In the midst of My **p** Israel. **Am 7:8** 5971a
'Go prophesy to My **p** Israel.' **Am 7:15** 5971a
"The end has come for My **p** Israel. **Am 8:2** 5971a
"**P** will stagger from sea to sea **Am 8:12**
"All the sinners of My **p** will die by **Am 9:10** 5971a
restore the captivity of My **p** Israel, **Am 9:14** 5971a
"Do not enter the gate of My **p** **Ob 1:13** 5971a
From what **p** are you?" **Jon 1:8** 5971a
the **p** of Nineveh believed in God; **Jon 3:5** 376
It has reached the gate of my **p**, **Mi 1:9** 5971a
He exchanges the portion of my **p**; **Mi 2:4** 5971a
"Recently My **p** have arisen as an **Mi 2:8** 5971a
"The women of My **p** you evict, **Mi 2:9** 5971a
He would be spokesman to this **p**. **Mi 2:11** 5971a
Who eat the flesh of my **p**, **Mi 3:3** 5971a
the prophets who lead my **p** astray; **Mi 3:5** 5971a
the LORD has a case against His **p**; **Mi 6:2** 5971a
"My **p**, what have I done to you, **Mi 6:3** 5971a
"My **p**, remember now What Balak **Mi 6:5** 5971a
will bear the reproach of My **p**." **Mi 6:16** 5971a
Shepherd Your **p** with Your scepter, **Mi 7:14** 5971a
your **p** are women in your midst! **Na 3:13** 5971a
Your **p** are scattered on the **Na 3:18** 5971a
That fierce and impetuous **p** Who **Hab 1:6** 1471
forth for the salvation of Your **p**, **Hab 3:13** 5971a
the **p** to arise *who* will invade us. **Hab 3:16** 5971a
the **p** of Canaan will be silenced; **Zph 1:11** 5971a
With which they have taunted My **p** **Zph 2:8** 5971a
remnant of My **p** will plunder them And **Zph 2:9** 5971a
become arrogant against the **p** of **Zph 2:10** 5971a
among you A humble and lowly **p**, **Zph 3:12** 5971a
'This **p** says, "The time has not come **Hg 1:2** 5971a
with all the remnant of the **p**, **Hg 1:12** 5971a
p showed reverence for the LORD. **Hg 1:12** 5971a
commission of the LORD to the **p** **Hg 1:13** 5971a
of all the remnant of the **p**; **Hg 1:14** 5971a
to the remnant of the **p** saying, **Hg 2:2** 5971a
you **p** of the land take courage,' **Hg 2:4** 5971a
said, "'So is this **p**. **Hg 2:14** 5971a
in that day and will become My **p**. **Zch 2:11** 5971a
"Say to all the **p** of the land and **Zch 7:5** 5971a
remnant of this **p** in those days, **Zch 8:6** 5971a
I am going to save My **p** from the **Zch 8:7** 5971a
and they shall be My **p**, and I will **Zch 8:8** 5971a
of this **p** as in the former days,' **Zch 8:11** 5971a
p to inherit all these *things.* **Zch 8:12** 5971a
in that day As the flock of His **p**; **Zch 9:16** 5971a
Therefore *the* **p** wander like sheep, **Zch 10:2**
'They are My **p**,' And they will **Zch 13:9** 5971a
but the rest of the **p** will not be **Zch 14:2** 5971a
P will live in it, and there will no **Zch 14:11**
and the **p** toward whom the LORD is **Mal 1:4** 5971a
and abased before all the **p**, **Mal 2:9** 5971a
will save His **p** from their sins." **Mt 1:21** *2992*
priests and scribes of the **p**, **Mt 2:4** *2992*
WHO WILL SHEPHERD MY **P** ISRAEL.' **Mt 2:6** *2992*
P WHO WERE SITTING IN DARKNESS **Mt 4:16** *2992*
every kind of sickness among the **p**. **Mt 4:23** *2992*
"Blessed are you when **p** insult **Mt 5:11**
treat **p** the same way **Mt 7:12** *444*
"Nor do **p** put new wine into old **Mt 9:17**
Seeing the **p**, He felt compassion for **Mt 9:36** *3793*
sin and blasphemy shall be forgiven **p**, **Mt 12:31** *444*
you that every careless word that **p** **Mt 12:36** *444*
HEART OF THIS **P** HAS BECOME DULL, **Mt 13:15** *2992*
and when the **p** heard *of this,* **Mt 14:13** *3793*
Ordering the **p** to sit down on **Mt 14:19** *3793*
'THIS **P** HONORS ME WITH THEIR LIPS, **Mt 15:8** *2992*
"I feel compassion for the **p**, **Mt 15:32** *3793*
And He directed the **p** to sit down on **Mt 15:35** *3793*
the disciples *gave them* to the **p**. **Mt 15:36** *3793*
do **p** say that the Son of Man is?" **Mt 16:13** *444*
"With **p** this is impossible, but **Mt 19:26** *444*
and the elders of the **p** came to Him **Mt 21:23** *2992*
we fear the **p**; for they all regard **Mt 21:26** *3793*
taken away from you and given to a **p**, **Mt 21:43** *1484*
they feared the **p**, because they **Mt 21:46** *3793*
shut off the kingdom of heaven from **p**; **Mt 23:13** *444*
and the elders of the **p** were gathered **Mt 26:3** *2992*

a riot might occur among the **p**." **Mt 26:5** *2992*
chief priests and elders of the **p**. **Mt 26:47** *2992*
elders of the **p** conferred together **Mt 27:1** *2992*
was accustomed to release for the **p** **Mt 27:15** *3793*
So when the **p** gathered together, **Mt 27:17** *846*
And all the **p** said, **Mt 27:25** *2992*
steal Him away and say to the **p**, **Mt 27:64** *2992*
him, and all the **p** of Jerusalem; **Mk 1:5** *2415*
and all the **p** were coming to Him, **Mk 2:13** *3793*
a great number of **p** heard of all that **Mk 3:8** *4128*
When His own **p** heard *of this,* **Mk 3:21**
And *the* **p** came to see what it was **Mk 5:14**
"Go home to your **p** and report to **Mk 5:19** *4674*
and **p** loudly weeping and wailing. **Mk 5:38**
He laid His hands on a few sick **p** **Mk 6:5** *732*
oil many sick **p** and healing them. **Mk 6:13** *732*
and **p** were saying, "John **Mk 6:14**
(For there were many **p** coming **Mk 6:31**
The **p** saw them going, and many **Mk 6:33**
immediately *the* **p** recognized Him, **Mk 6:54**
'THIS **P** HONORS ME WITH THEIR LIPS, **Mk 7:6** *2992*
"I feel compassion for the **p** because **Mk 8:2** *3793*
desolate place to satisfy these **p**?" **Mk 8:4** *3778*
And He directed the **p** to sit down on **Mk 8:6** *3793*
and they served them to the **p**. **Mk 8:6** *3793*
"Who do **p** say that I am?" **Mk 8:27** *444*
"With **p** it is impossible, but not **Mk 10:27** *444*
they were afraid of the **p**, for **Mk 11:32** *3793*
and *yet* they feared the **p**, for **Mk 12:12** *3793*
and *began* observing how the **p** **Mk 12:41** *4145*
rich **p** were putting in large sums. **Mk 12:41** *4145*
there might be a riot of the **p**." **Mk 14:2** *2992*
And the whole multitude of the **p** **Lk 1:10** *2992*
ready a **p** prepared for the Lord." **Lk 1:17** *2992*
The **p** were waiting for Zacharias, **Lk 1:21** *2992*
accomplished redemption for His **p**, **Lk 1:68** *2992*
To give to His **p** *the* knowledge of **Lk 1:77** *2992*
joy which will be for all the **p**; **Lk 2:10** *2992*
And the glory of Your **p** Israel." **Lk 2:32** *2992*
Now while the **p** were in a state of **Lk 3:15** *2992*
he preached the gospel to the **p**. **Lk 3:18** *2992*
when all the **p** were baptized, **Lk 3:21** *2992*
And all *the* **p** in the synagogue **Lk 4:28**
him down in the midst *of the* **p**, **Lk 4:35**
sat down and *began* teaching the **p** **Lk 5:3** *3793*
crowd of tax collectors and other **p** **Lk 5:29**
and a great throng of **p** from all **Lk 6:17** *2992*
And all the **p** were trying to touch **Lk 6:19** *3793*
discourse in the hearing of the **p**, **Lk 7:1** *2992*
"God has visited His **p**!" **Lk 7:16** *2992*
At that very time He cured many **p** **Lk 7:21**
When all the **p** and the **Lk 7:29** *2992*
The **p** went out to see what had **Lk 8:35**
And all the **p** of the country of **Lk 8:37** *4128*
And as Jesus returned, the **p** **Lk 8:40** *3793*
the **p** are crowding and pressing in on **Lk 8:45** *3793*
declared in the presence of all the **p** **Lk 8:47** *2992*
go and buy food for all these **p**." **Lk 9:13** *2992*
to the disciples to set before the **p**. **Lk 9:16** *3793*
"Who do the **p** say that I am?" **Lk 9:18** *3793*
and the **p** who walk over *them* are **Lk 11:44** *444*
after so many thousands of **p** had **Lk 12:1** *3793*
I am removed from the management **p** **Lk 16:4**
He also told this parable to some **p** **Lk 18:9** *5100*
You that I am not like other **p**: **Lk 18:11** *3062*
"The things that are impossible with **p** **Lk 18:27** *444*
and when all the **p** saw it, **Lk 18:43** *2992*
the **p** were trying to destroy Him, **Lk 19:47** *2992*
the **p** were hanging on to every word **Lk 19:48** *2992*
the days while He was teaching the **p** **Lk 20:1** *2992*
all the **p** will stone us to death, **Lk 20:6** *2992*
began to tell the **p** this parable: **Lk 20:9** *2992*
very hour, and they feared the **p**; **Lk 20:19** *2992*
a saying in the presence of the **p**; **Lk 20:26** *2992*
while all the **p** were listening, **Lk 20:45** *2992*
the land and wrath to this **p** **Lk 21:23** *2992*
And all the **p** would get up early **Lk 21:38** *2992*
for they were afraid of the **p**. **Lk 22:2** *2992*
Council of elders of the **p** assembled, **Lk 22:66** *2992*
"He stirs up the **p**, teaching all **Lk 23:5** *2992*
priests and the rulers and the **p**, **Lk 23:13** *2992*
who incites the **p** to rebellion, **Lk 23:14** *2992*
Him was a large crowd of the **p**, **Lk 23:27** *2992*
And the **p** stood by, looking on. **Lk 23:35** *2992*
in the sight of God and all the **p**, **Lk 24:19** *2992*
and when *the* **p** have drunk freely, **Jn 2:10**
and **p** were coming and were being **Jn 3:23**
and you **p** say that in Jerusalem **Jn 4:20**
for such **p** the Father seeks to be **Jn 4:23** *5108*
"Unless you **p** see signs **Jn 4:48**
what are these for so many **p**?" **Jn 6:9** *5118*
"Have the **p** sit down." **Jn 6:10** *444*
Therefore when the **p** saw the sign **Jn 6:14** *444*
He leads the **p** astray." **Jn 7:12** *3793*
of the **p** of Jerusalem were saying, **Jn 7:25** *2415*
Some of the **p** therefore, when **Jn 7:40** *3793*
and all the **p** were coming to Him; **Jn 8:2** *2992*
because of the **p** standing around **Jn 11:42** *3793*
that one man die for the **p**, **Jn 11:50** *2992*
denarii and given to poor **p**?" **Jn 12:5**
So the **p**, who were with Him when He **Jn 12:17** *3793*
For this reason also the **p** went **Jn 12:18** *3793*
So the crowd *of* **p** who stood by **Jn 12:29**
one man to die on behalf of the **p**. **Jn 18:14** *2992*
and having favor with all the **p**. **Ac 2:47** *2992*
And all the **p** saw him walking and **Ac 3:9** *2992*
all the **p** ran together to them at **Ac 3:11** *2992*
saw *this,* he replied to the **p**, **Ac 3:12** *2992*
destroyed from among the **p**.' **Ac 3:23** *2992*

As they were speaking to the **p**,	Ac 4:1	*2992*
because they were teaching the **p**	Ac 4:2	*2992*
"Rulers and elders of the **p**,	Ac 4:8	*2992*
you and to all the **p** of Israel,	Ac 4:10	*2992*
spread any further among the **p**,	Ac 4:17	*2992*
on account of the **p**,	Ac 4:21	*2992*
were taking place among the **p**;	Ac 5:12	*2992*
the **p** held them in high esteem.	Ac 5:13	*2992*
Also the **p** from the cities in	Ac 5:16	*4128*
bringing **p** who were sick or	Ac 5:16	
stand and speak to the **p** in the	Ac 5:20	*2992*
the temple and teaching the **p**!"	Ac 5:25	*2992*
(for they were afraid of the **p**,	Ac 5:26	*2992*
the Law, respected by all the **p**,	Ac 5:34	*2992*
and drew away *some* **p** after him;	Ac 5:37	*2992*
wonders and signs among the **p**.	Ac 6:8	*2992*
And they stirred up the **p**,	Ac 6:12	*2992*
the **p** increased and multiplied in	Ac 7:17	*2992*
THE OPPRESSION OF MY **P** IN EGYPT	Ac 7:34	*2992*
and astonishing the **p** of Samaria,	Ac 8:9	*1484*
gave many alms to the *Jewish* **p** and	Ac 10:2	*2992*
and found many **p** assembled.	Ac 10:27	*4183*
not to all the **p**, but to witnesses	Ac 10:41	*2992*
He ordered us to preach to the **p**,	Ac 10:42	*2992*
to bring him out before the **p**.	Ac 12:4	*2992*
the Jewish **p** were expecting."	Ac 12:11	*2992*
angry with the **p** of Tyre and Sidon;	Ac 12:20	
The **p** kept crying out,	Ac 12:22	*1218*
any word of exhortation for the **p**,	Ac 13:15	*2992*
this **p** Israel chose our fathers and	Ac 13:17	*2992*
and made the **p** great during their	Ac 13:17	*2992*
repentance to all the **p** of Israel.	Ac 13:24	*2992*
are now His witnesses to the **p**.	Ac 13:31	*2992*
the **p** kept begging that these	Ac 13:42	
a manner that a large number of **p**	Ac 14:1	*4128*
But the **p** of the city were divided;	Ac 14:4	*4128*
All the **p** kept silent, and they were	Ac 15:12	*4128*
the Gentiles a **p** for His name.	Ac 15:14	*2992*
to bring them out to the **p**.	Ac 17:5	*1218*
since He Himself gives to all **p**	Ac 17:25	
is now declaring to men that all **p**	Ac 17:30	
for I have many **p** in this city."	Ac 18:10	*2992*
telling the **p** to believe in Him	Ac 19:4	*2992*
speaking evil of the Way before the **p**,	Ac 19:9	*4128*
away a considerable number of **p**,	Ac 19:26	*3793*
all men everywhere against our **p** and	Ac 21:28	*2992*
and the **p** rushed together,	Ac 21:30	*2992*
multitude of the **p** kept following	Ac 21:36	*2992*
you, allow me to speak to the **p**."	Ac 21:39	*2992*
motioned to the **p** with his hand;	Ac 21:40	*2992*
EVIL OF A RULER OF YOUR **P**.'	Ac 23:5	*2992*
the **p** of the Jews appealed to me,	Ac 25:24	*4128*
considered incredible among you **p**	Ac 26:8	
Jewish **p** and from the Gentiles,	Ac 26:17	*2992*
Jewish **p** and to the Gentiles."	Ac 26:23	*2992*
the rest of the **p** on the island	Ac 28:9	
I had done nothing against our **p** or	Ac 28:17	*2992*
'GO TO THIS **P** AND SAY	Ac 28:26	*2992*
HEART OF THIS **P** HAS BECOME DULL,	Ac 28:27	*2992*
CALL THOSE WHO WERE NOT MY **P**,	Ro 9:25	*2992*
WHO WERE NOT MY PEOPLE, 'MY **P**,'	Ro 9:25	*2992*
SAID TO THEM, 'YOU ARE NOT MY **P**,'	Ro 9:26	*2992*
A DISOBEDIENT AND OBSTINATE **P**."	Ro 10:21	*2992*
then, God has not rejected His **p**,	Ro 11:1	*2992*
rejected His **p** whom He foreknew.	Ro 11:2	*2992*
"REJOICE, O GENTILES, WITH HIS **P**."	Ro 15:10	*2992*
by Chloe's **p**, that there are	1Co 1:11	
not to associate with immoral **p**;	1Co 5:9	*4205*
with the immoral **p** of this world,	1Co 5:10	*4205*
THE **P** SAT DOWN TO EAT AND DRINK,	1Co 10:7	*2992*
I WILL SPEAK TO THIS **P**,	1Co 14:21	*2992*
is spreading to more and more **p**	2Co 4:15	
GOD, AND THEY SHALL BE MY **P**.	2Co 6:16	*2992*
let us do good to all **p**,	Ga 6:10	*3956*
and for all **p**, just as we also *do*	1Th 3:12	*3956*
is good for one another and for all **p**.	1Th 5:15	*3956*
purify for Himself a **p** for His own	Ti 2:14	*2992*
Our **p** must also learn to engage in	Ti 3:14	*3588*
propitiation for the sins of the **p**.	Heb 2:17	*2992*
a Sabbath rest for the **p** of God.	Heb 4:9	*2992*
sacrifices for sins, as for the **p**,	Heb 5:3	*2992*
Law to collect a tenth from the **p**,	Heb 7:5	*2992*
of it the **p** received the Law),	Heb 7:11	*2992*
and then for the *sins* of the **p**.	Heb 7:27	*2992*
GOD, AND THEY SHALL BE MY **P**.	Heb 8:10	*2992*
sins of the **p** committed in ignorance.	Heb 9:7	*2992*
been spoken by Moses to all the **p**	Heb 9:19	*2992*
the book itself and all the **p**,	Heb 9:19	*2992*
"THE LORD WILL JUDGE HIS **P**."	Heb 10:30	*2992*
that God is able to raise **p** even	Heb 11:19	
ill-treatment with the **p** of God than	Heb 11:25	*2992*
He might sanctify the **p** through His	Heb 13:12	*2992*
A **P** FOR *God's* OWN POSSESSION,	1Pe 2:9	*2992*
for you once were NOT A **P**,	1Pe 2:10	*2992*
but now you are THE **P** OF GOD;	1Pe 2:10	*2992*
Honor all **p**, love the brotherhood,	1Pe 2:17	*3956*
prophets also arose among the **p**,	2Pe 2:1	*2992*
what sort of **p** ought you to be in	2Pe 3:11	
a **p** out of the land of Egypt,	Jude 1:5	*2992*
flattering **p** for the sake of	Jude 1:16	*4383*
'But you have a few **p** in Sardis	Rv 3:4	*3686*
tribe and tongue and **p** and nation.	Rv 5:9	*2992*
p were killed in the earthquake,	Rv 11:13	*3686, 444*
and authority over every tribe and **p**	Rv 13:7	*2992*
nation and tribe and tongue and **p**;	Rv 14:6	*2992*
loathsome and malignant sore on the **p**	Rv 16:2	*444*
"Come out of her, my **p**,	Rv 18:4	*2992*
them, and they shall be His **p**,	Rv 21:3	*2992*

PEOPLE'S

the **p** representative before God,	Ex 18:19	5971a
Then he presented the **p** offering,	Lv 9:15	5971a
the 300 men took the **p** provisions	Jg 7:8	5971a
not take from the **p** inheritance,	Ezk 46:18	5971a
most **p** love will grow cold.	Mt 24:12	*4183*

PEOPLES

kings of **p** will come from her."	Gn 17:16	5971a
And two **p** will be separated from	Gn 25:23	3816
May **p** serve you, And nations bow	Gn 27:29	5971a
you may become a company of **p**.	Gn 28:3	5971a
I will make you a company of **p**,	Gn 48:4	5971a
shall be the obedience of the **p**.	Gn 49:10	5971a
"The **p** have heard, they tremble;	Ex 15:14	5971a
My own possession among all the **p**,	Ex 19:5	5971a
who has separated you from the **p**.	Lv 20:24	5971a
and I have set you apart from the **p**	Lv 20:26	5971a
p everywhere under the heavens,	Dt 2:25	5971a
the **p** who will hear all these statutes	Dt 4:6	5971a
all the **p** under the whole heaven.	Dt 4:19	5971a
LORD will scatter you among the **p**,	Dt 4:27	5971a
gods of the **p** who surround you,	Dt 6:14	5971a
His own possession out of all the **p**	Dt 7:6	5971a
more in number than any of the **p**,	Dt 7:7	5971a
for you were the fewest of all **p**,	Dt 7:7	5971a
"You shall be blessed above all **p**;	Dt 7:14	5971a
"You shall consume all the **p**	Dt 7:16	5971a
all the **p** of whom you are afraid.	Dt 7:19	5971a
after them, *even* you above all **p**,	Dt 10:15	5971a
gods of the **p** who are around you,	Dt 13:7	5971a
His own possession out of all the **p**	Dt 14:2	5971a
"Only in the cities of these **p**	Dt 20:16	5971a
"So all the **p** of the earth will	Dt 28:10	5971a
LORD will scatter you among all **p**,	Dt 28:64	5971a
will gather you again from all the **p**	Dt 30:3	5971a
He set the boundaries of the **p**	Dt 32:8	5971a
With them he will push the **p**,	Dt 33:17	5971a
"They will call **p** *to* the mountain;	Dt 33:19	5971a
that all the **p** of the earth may	Jos 4:24	5971a
p through whose midst we passed.	Jos 24:17	5971a
drove out from before us all the **p**,	Jos 24:18	5971a
of the **p** who were around them,	Jg 2:12	5971a
you, Benjamin, with your **p**;	Jg 5:14	5971b
me, And brings down **p** under me,	2Sa 22:48	5971a
Men came from all **p** to hear	1Ki 4:34	5971a
that all the **p** of the earth may know	1Ki 8:43	5971a
have separated them from all the **p**	1Ki 8:53	5971a
so that all the **p** of the earth may	1Ki 8:60	5971a
proverb and a byword among all **p**.	1Ki 9:7	5971a
the gods of the **p** of the land,	1Ch 5:25	5971a
Make known His deeds among the **p**.	1Ch 16:8	5971a
wonderful deeds among all the **p**.	1Ch 16:24	5971a
all the gods of the **p** are idols,	1Ch 16:26	5971a
to the LORD, O families of the **p**,	1Ch 16:28	5971a
that all the **p** of the earth may know	2Ch 6:33	5971a
proverb and a byword among all **p**.	2Ch 7:20	5971a
priests like the **p** of *other* lands?	2Ch 13:9	5971a
done to all the **p** of the lands?	2Ch 32:13	5971a
of the gods of the **p** of the earth,	2Ch 32:19	5971a
because of the **p** of the lands;	Ezr 3:3	5971a
from the **p** of the lands,	Ezr 9:1	5971a
intermingled with the **p** of the lands;	Ezr 9:2	5971a
uncleanness of the **p** of the lands,	Ezr 9:11	5971a
p who commit these abominations?	Ezr 9:14	5971a
women from the **p** of the land;	Ezr 10:2	5971a
and separate yourselves from the **p**	Ezr 10:11	5971a
I will scatter you among the **p**;	Ne 1:8	5971a
also gave them kingdoms and **p**,	Ne 9:22	5971a
kings and the **p** of the land,	Ne 9:24	5971a
the hand of the **p** of the lands.	Ne 9:30	5971a
had separated themselves from the **p**	Ne 10:28	5971a
will not give our daughters to the **p**	Ne 10:30	5971a
As for the **p** of the land who bring	Ne 10:31	5971a
and all the **p** who are in all the	Es 1:16	5971a
scattered and dispersed among the **p**	Es 3:8	5971a
was published to all the **p** so that	Es 3:14	5971a
was published to all the **p**,	Es 8:13	5971a
the **p** of the land became Jews,	Es 8:17	5971a
of them had fallen on all the **p**.	Es 9:2	5971a
"For by these He judges **p**;	Jb 36:31	5971a
And the **p** devising a vain thing?	Ps 2:1	3816
assembly of the **p** encompass You,	Ps 7:7	3816
The LORD judges the **p**;	Ps 7:8	5971a
judgment for the **p** with equity.	Ps 9:8	3816
Declare among the **p** His deeds.	Ps 9:11	5971a
for me, And subdues **p** under me.	Ps 18:47	5971a
He frustrates the plans of the **p**.	Ps 33:10	5971a
You afflicted the **p**,	Ps 44:2	3816
A laughingstock among the **p**.	Ps 44:14	3816
The **p** fall under You;	Ps 45:5	5971a
Therefore the **p** will give You	Ps 45:17	5971a
O clap your hands, all **p**;	Ps 47:1	5971a
He subdues **p** under us And nations	Ps 47:3	5971a
Hear this, all **p**;	Ps 49:1	5971a
forth, In anger put down the **p**,	Ps 56:7	5971a
to You, O Lord, among the **p**;	Ps 57:9	5971a
waves, And the tumult of the **p**.	Ps 65:7	3816
Bless our God, O **p**,	Ps 66:8	5971a
Let the **p** praise You, O God;	Ps 67:3	5971a
Let all the **p** praise You.	Ps 67:3	5971a
will judge the **p** with uprightness And	Ps 67:4	5971a
Let the **p** praise You, O God;	Ps 67:5	5971a
Let all the **p** praise You.	Ps 67:5	5971a
of bulls with the calves of the **p**,	Ps 68:30	5971a
He has scattered the **p** who delight	Ps 68:30	5971a
known Your strength among the **p**.	Ps 77:14	5971a
count when He registers the **p**,	Ps 87:6	5971a
the reproach of all the many **p**,	Ps 89:50	5971a
wonderful deeds among all the **p**.	Ps 96:3	5971a
all the gods of the **p** are idols,	Ps 96:5	5971a
to the LORD, O families of the **p**,	Ps 96:7	5971a
He will judge the **p** with equity."	Ps 96:10	5971a
And the **p** in His faithfulness.	Ps 96:13	5971a
And all the **p** have seen His glory.	Ps 97:6	5971a
And the **p** with equity.	Ps 98:9	5971a
LORD reigns, let the **p** tremble;	Ps 99:1	5971a
And He is exalted above all the **p**.	Ps 99:2	5971a
When the **p** are gathered together,	Ps 102:22	5971a
Make known His deeds among the **p**.	Ps 105:1	5971a
and released him, The ruler of **p**,	Ps 105:20	5971a
They did not destroy the **p**,	Ps 106:34	5971a
to You, O LORD, among the **p**,	Ps 108:3	5971a
LORD, all nations; Laud Him, all **p**!	Ps 117:1	523
Kings of the earth and all **p**;	Ps 148:11	3816
nations And punishment on the **p**	Ps 149:7	3816
P will curse him, nations will abhor	Pr 24:24	5971a
And many **p** will come and say,	Is 2:3	5971a
will render decisions for many **p**;	Is 2:4	5971a
"Be broken, O **p**, and be shattered;	Is 8:9	5971a
I removed the boundaries of the **p** And	Is 10:13	5971a
the riches of the **p** like a nest,	Is 10:14	5971a
will stand as a signal for the **p**;	Is 11:10	5971a
Make known His deeds among the **p**;	Is 12:4	5971a
The **p** will take them along and	Is 14:2	5971a
Which used to strike the **p** in fury	Is 14:6	5971a
the uproar of many **p** Who roar like	Is 17:12	5971a
midst of the earth among the **p**,	Is 24:13	5971a
prepare a lavish banquet for all **p**	Is 25:6	5971a
the covering which is over all **p**,	Is 25:7	5971a
And to *put* in the jaws of the **p**	Is 30:28	5971a
At the sound of the tumult **p** flee;	Is 33:3	5971a
"The **p** will be burned to	Is 33:12	5971a
O nations, to hear; and listen, O **p**!	Is 34:1	3816
And let the **p** gain new strength;	Is 41:1	3816
other **p** in exchange for your life.	Is 43:4	3816
So that the **p** may be assembled.	Is 43:9	3816
pay attention, you **p** from afar.	Is 49:1	3816
And set up My standard to the **p**;	Is 49:22	5971a
My justice for a light of the **p**.	Is 51:4	5971a
And My arms will judge the **p**;	Is 51:5	5971a
have made him a witness to the **p**,	Is 55:4	3816
A leader and commander for the **p**.	Is 55:4	3816
a house of prayer for all the **p**."	Is 56:7	5971a
earth And deep darkness the **p**;	Is 60:2	3816
descendants in the midst of the **p**.	Is 61:9	5971a
lift up a standard over the **p**.	Is 62:10	5971a
the **p** there was no man with Me.	Is 63:3	5971a
"I trod down the **p** in My anger And	Is 63:6	5971a
the customs of the **p** are delusion;	Jer 10:3	5971a
under his dominion and all the **p**,	Jer 34:1	5971a
So the **p** will toil for nothing,	Jer 51:58	5971a
Hear now, all **p**, And behold my	La 1:18	5971a
and refuse In the midst of the **p**.	La 3:45	5971a
nor to many **p** of unintelligible	Ezk 3:6	5971a
"I will gather you from the **p**	Ezk 11:17	5971a
"I will bring you out from the **p**	Ezk 20:34	5971a
you into the wilderness of the **p**,	Ezk 20:35	5971a
when I bring you out from the **p**	Ezk 20:41	5971a
wagons, and with a company of **p**.	Ezk 23:24	5971a
And I will cut you off from the **p**	Ezk 25:7	5971a
the gateway of the **p** is broken;	Ezk 26:2	5971a
merchant of the **p** to many	Ezk 27:3	5971a
the seas, You satisfied many **p**;	Ezk 27:33	5971a
merchants among the **p** hiss at you;	Ezk 27:36	5971a
among the **p** Are appalled at you;	Ezk 28:19	5971a
p among whom they are scattered,	Ezk 28:25	5971a
gather the Egyptians from the **p**	Ezk 29:13	5971a
And all the **p** of the earth have	Ezk 31:12	5971a
over you With a company of many **p**,	Ezk 32:3	5971a
also trouble the hearts of many **p** when	Ezk 32:9	5971a
will make many **p** appalled at you,	Ezk 32:10	5971a
"I will bring them out from the **p**	Ezk 34:13	5971a
disgrace from the **p** any longer,	Ezk 36:15	5971a
many **p** with you.	Ezk 38:6	5971a
troops, and many **p** with you."	Ezk 38:9	5971a
north, you and many **p** with you,	Ezk 38:15	5971a
on the many **p** who are with him,	Ezk 38:22	5971a
and the **p** who are with you;	Ezk 39:4	5971a
When I bring them back from the **p**	Ezk 39:27	5971a
"To you the command is given, O **p**,	Da 3:4	5972
the **p** heard the sound of the horn,	Da 3:7	5972
and all kinds of music, all the **p**,	Da 3:7	5972
the king to all the **p**,	Da 4:1	5972
He bestowed on him, all the **p**,	Da 5:19	5972
the king wrote to all the **p**,	Da 6:25	5972
and a kingdom, That all the **p**,	Da 7:14	5972
And the **p** will be gathered against	Hos 10:10	5971a
Why should they among the **p** say,	Jl 2:17	5971a
Hear, O **p**, all of you;	Mi 1:2	5971a
And the **p** will stream to it.	Mi 4:1	5971a
And He will judge between many **p**	Mi 4:3	5971a
Though all the **p** walk Each in the	Mi 4:5	5971a
That you may pulverize many **p**,	Mi 4:13	5971a
many **p** Like dew from the LORD,	Mi 5:7	5971a
Among many **p** Like a lion among the	Mi 5:8	5971a
And collects to himself all **p**.	Hab 2:5	5971a
All the remainder of the **p** will	Hab 2:8	5971a
your house By cutting off many **p**;	Hab 2:10	5971a
of hosts That **p** toil for fire,	Hab 2:13	5971a
will give to the **p** purified lips,	Zph 3:9	5971a
Among all the **p** of the earth,	Zph 3:20	5971a
'*It will* yet *be* that **p** will come,	Zch 8:20	5971a
'So many **p** and mighty nations will	Zch 8:22	5971a
"When I scatter them among the **p**,	Zch 10:9	5971a
which I had made with all the **p**.	Zch 11:10	5971a
reeling to all the **p** around;	Zch 12:2	5971a
a heavy stone for all the **p**;	Zch 12:3	5971a
horse of the **p** with blindness.	Zch 12:4	5971a

on the left all the surrounding **p**,	**Zch 12:6**	5971a
LORD will strike all the **p** who have	**Zch 14:12**	5971a
prepared in the presence of all **p**,	**Lk 2:31**	*2992*
AND THE **P** DEVISE FUTILE THINGS?	**Ac 4:25**	*2992*
the Gentiles and the **p** of Israel,	**Ac 4:27**	*2992*
AND LET ALL THE **P** PRAISE HIM."	**Ro 15:11**	*2992*
and *all* tribes and **p** and tongues,	**Rv 7:9**	*2992*
prophesy again concerning many **p**	**Rv 10:11**	*2992*
Those from the **p** and tribes	**Rv 11:9**	*2992*
are **p** and multitudes and nations	**Rv 17:15**	*2992*
PEOPLES'		
the fruit of the **p** labor,	**Ps 105:44**	3816
PEOR		
Balak took Balaam to the top of **P**	**Nu 23:28**	6465
joined themselves to Baal of **P**,	**Nu 25:3**	1187
joined themselves to Baal of **P**."	**Nu 25:5**	1187
deceived you in the affair of **P** and	**Nu 25:18**	6465
day of the plague because of **P**."	**Nu 25:18**	6465
the LORD in the matter of **P**,	**Nu 31:16**	6465
the iniquity of **P** enough for us,	**Jos 22:17**	6465
PER		
take five shekels apiece, **p** head;	**Nu 3:47**	
PERAZIM		
LORD will rise up as *at* Mount **P**,	**Is 28:21**	6559
PERCEIVE		
know and **p** that there is no evil	**1Sa 24:11**	7200
I **p** that this is a holy man of God	**2Ki 4:9**	3045
move past *me*, I would not **p** Him.	**Jb 9:11**	995
but he does not **p** it.	**Jb 14:21**	995
And **p** what He would say to me.	**Jb 23:5**	995
And backward, but I cannot **p** Him;	**Jb 23:8**	995
'Keep on listening, but do not **p**;	**Is 6:9**	995
does not **p** the majesty of the LORD.	**Is 26:10**	7200
KEEP ON SEEING, BUT WILL NOT **P**;	**Mt 13:14**	*3708*
SEEING, THEY MAY SEE AND NOT **P**	**Mk 4:12**	*3708*
them so that they would not **p** it;	**Lk 9:45**	*143*
"Sir, I **p** that You are a prophet.	**Jn 4:19**	*2334*
EYES AND **P** WITH THEIR HEART,	**Jn 12:40**	*3539*
I **p** that the voyage will certainly	**Ac 27:10**	*2334*
KEEP ON SEEING, BUT WILL NOT **P**;	**Ac 28:26**	*3708*
PERCEIVED		
All the people **p** the thunder	**Ex 20:18**	7200
David **p** that the child was dead;	**2Sa 12:19**	995
Now Joab the son of Zeruiah **p** that	**2Sa 14:1**	3045
Sheba **p** all the wisdom of Solomon,	**1Ki 10:4**	7200
Then I **p** that surely God had not	**Ne 6:12**	5234
Then I **p** their end.	**Ps 73:17**	995
they have not heard or **p** by ear,	**Is 64:4**	238
But Jesus **p** their malice, and	**Mt 22:18**	*1097*
PERCEIVING		
p in Himself that the power	**Mk 5:30**	*1921*
Jesus, **p** that they were	**Jn 6:15**	*1097*
But **p** that one group were Sadducees	**Ac 23:6**	*1097*
PERDITION		
of them perished but the son of **p**,	**Jn 17:12**	*684*
PERENNIALLY		
against a **p** watered pasture;	**Jer 49:19**	386
the Jordan to a **p** watered pasture;	**Jer 50:44**	386
PERĒS		
"'**P**'—your kingdom has been	**Da 5:28**	6537b
PERESH		
bore a son, and she named him **P**;	**1Ch 7:16**	6570
PEREZ		
So he was named **P**.	**Gn 38:29**	6557
Onan and Shelah and **P** and Zerah	**Gn 46:12**	6557
sons of **P** were Hezron and Hamul.	**Gn 46:12**	6557
of **P**, the family of the Perezites;	**Nu 26:20**	6557
The sons of **P** were:	**Nu 26:21**	6557
your house be like the house of **P**	**Ru 4:12**	6557
these are the generations of **P**:	**Ru 4:18**	6557
to **P** was born Hezron,	**Ru 4:18**	6557
bore him **P** and Zerah.	**1Ch 2:4**	6557
sons of **P** *were* Hezron and Hamul.	**1Ch 2:5**	6557
The sons of Judah *were* **P**,	**1Ch 4:1**	6557
the sons of **P** the son of Judah.	**1Ch 9:4**	6557
He was from the sons of **P**,	**1Ch 27:3**	6557
of Mahalalel, of the sons of **P**;	**Ne 11:4**	6557
All the sons of **P** who lived in	**Ne 11:6**	6557
the father of **P** and Zerah by Tamar,	**Mt 1:3**	*5329*
P was the father of Hezron,	**Mt 1:3**	*5329*
the son of Hezron, the son of **P**,	**Lk 3:33**	*5329*
PEREZITES		
of Perez, the family of the **P**;	**Nu 26:20**	6558
PEREZ-UZZA		
called that place **P** to this day.	**1Ch 13:11**	6560
PEREZ-UZZAH		
place is called **P** to this day.	**2Sa 6:8**	6560
PERFECT		
it must be **p** to be accepted;	**Lv 22:21**	8549
His work is **p**, For all His ways	**Dt 32:4**	8549
the God of Israel, "Give a **p** *lot*."	**1Sa 14:41**	8549
came to Hebron with a **p** heart to	**1Ch 12:38**	8003
give to my son Solomon a **p** heart	**1Ch 29:19**	8003
law of the God of heaven, **P** *peace*.	**Ezr 7:12**	1585
Or profit if you make your ways **p**?	**Jb 22:3**	8552
who is **p** in knowledge is with you.	**Jb 36:4**	8549
The wonders of one **p** in knowledge,	**Jb 37:16**	8549
The law of the LORD is **p**,	**Ps 19:7**	8549
my darling, My dove, my **p** one!	**SS 5:2**	8535
But my dove, my **p** one, is unique:	**SS 6:9**	8535
long ago, with **p** faithfulness.	**Is 25:1**	544
of mind You will keep in **p** peace,	**Is 26:3**	7965
for it was **p** because of My splendor	**Ezk 16:14**	3632
'I am **p** in beauty.'	**Ezk 27:3**	3632
Full of wisdom and **p** in beauty.	**Ezk 28:12**	3632
He measured the court, a **p**	**Ezk 40:47**	

"Therefore you are to be **p**,	**Mt 5:48**	*5046*
as your heavenly Father is **p**.	**Mt 5:48**	*5046*
Him has given him this **p** health	**Ac 3:16**	*3647*
is good and acceptable and **p**.	**Ro 12:2**	*5046*
but when the **p** comes, the partial	**1Co 13:10**	*5046*
who began a good work in you will **p**	**Php 1:6**	*2005*
it or have already become **p**,	**Php 3:12**	*5048*
us therefore, as many as are **p**,	**Php 3:15**	*5046*
which is the **p** bond of unity.	**Col 3:14**	*5047*
that you may stand **p** and fully	**Col 4:12**	*5046*
might demonstrate His **p** patience as	**1Tm 1:16**	*537a*
to **p** the author of their salvation	**Heb 2:10**	*5048*
And having been made **p**,	**Heb 5:9**	*5048*
(for the Law made nothing **p**),	**Heb 7:19**	*5048*
appoints a Son, made **p** forever.	**Heb 7:28**	*5048*
the worshiper **p** in conscience,	**Heb 9:9**	*5048*
the greater and more **p** tabernacle,	**Heb 9:11**	*5046*
make **p** those who draw near.	**Heb 10:1**	*5048*
from us they would not be made **p**.	**Heb 11:40**	*5048*
spirits of *the* righteous made **p**,	**Heb 12:23**	*5048*
let endurance have *its* **p** result,	**Jas 1:4**	*5046*
that you may be **p** and complete,	**Jas 1:4**	*5046*
and every **p** gift is from above,	**Jas 1:17**	*5046*
who looks intently at the **p** law,	**Jas 1:25**	*5046*
in what he says, he is a **p** man,	**Jas 3:2**	*5046*
will Himself **p**, confirm, strengthen	**1Pe 5:10**	*2675*
but **p** love casts out fear, because	**1Jn 4:18**	*5046*
PERFECTED		
Your builders have **p** your beauty.	**Ezk 27:4**	3634
they **p** your beauty.	**Ezk 27:11**	3634
Me, that they may be **p** in unity,	**Jn 17:23**	*5048*
you, for power is **p** in weakness."	**2Co 12:9**	*5055*
are you now being **p** by the flesh?	**Ga 3:3**	*2005*
For by one offering He has **p** for	**Heb 10:14**	*5048*
result of the works, faith was **p**;	**Jas 2:22**	*5048*
the love of God has truly been **p**.	**1Jn 2:5**	*5048*
in us, and His love is **p** in us.	**1Jn 4:12**	*5048*
By this, love is **p** with us,	**1Jn 4:17**	*5048*
one who fears is not **p** in love.	**1Jn 4:18**	*5048*
PERFECTER		
Jesus, the author and **p** of faith,	**Heb 12:2**	*5051*
PERFECTING		
p holiness in the fear of God.	**2Co 7:1**	*2005*
PERFECTION		
Out of Zion, the **p** of beauty,	**Ps 50:2**	4359
I have seen a limit to all **p**;	**Ps 119:96**	8502
'The **p** of beauty, A joy to all the	**La 2:15**	3632
"You had the seal of **p**,	**Ezk 28:12**	8508
Now if **p** was through the Levitical	**Heb 7:11**	*5050*
PERFECTLY		
and it became **p** calm.	**Mt 8:26**	*3173*
died down and it became **p** calm.	**Mk 4:39**	*3173*
a **p** good conscience before God	**Ac 23:1**	*3956*
PERFORM		
and **p** your duty as a	**Gn 38:8**	2992
which you shall **p** the signs."	**Ex 4:17**	6213a
p before Pharaoh all the wonders	**Ex 4:21**	6213a
that I may **p** these signs of Mine	**Ex 10:1**	7896
I will **p** miracles which have not	**Ex 34:10**	6213a
that I am going to **p** with you.	**Ex 34:10**	6213a
as to **p** in every inventive work.	**Ex 35:33**	6213a
filled them with skill to **p** every work	**Ex 35:35**	6213a
to **p** all the work in the construction	**Ex 36:1**	6213a
shall **p** in accordance with all	**Ex 36:1**	6213a
him, to come to the work to **p** it.	**Ex 36:2**	6213a
to **p** the work in the construction of	**Ex 36:3**	6213a
the LORD commanded *us* to **p**."	**Ex 36:5**	6213a
man or woman any longer **p** work	**Ex 36:6**	6213a
enough for all the work, to **p** it.	**Ex 36:7**	6213a
'You are to **p** My judgments and	**Lv 18:4**	6213a
"They shall **p** the duties for	**Nu 3:7**	8104
who **p** the duties of the sanctuary.	**Nu 3:32**	8104
all who enter to **p** the service to	**Nu 4:23**	6633
that is to be done, they shall **p**.	**Nu 4:26**	5647
to **p** the service of the LORD.	**Nu 8:11**	5647
to **p** the service of the sons of	**Nu 8:19**	5647
the Levites went in to **p** their service	**Nu 8:22**	5647
they shall enter to **p** service in the	**Nu 8:24**	6633
to **p** the service for the tent of	**Nu 18:6**	5647
veil, and you are to **p** service.	**Nu 18:7**	5647
for their service which they **p**,	**Nu 18:21**	5647
"Only the Levites shall **p** the	**Nu 18:23**	5647
which I am teaching you to **p**,	**Dt 4:1**	6213a
which He commanded you to **p**,	**Dt 4:13**	6213a
that you might **p** them in the land	**Dt 4:14**	6213a
to **p** what goes out from your lips,	**Dt 23:23**	6213a
p the duty of a husband's brother	**Dt 25:5**	2992
he is not willing to **p** the duty of	**Dt 25:7**	2992
the LORD sent him to **p** in the land	**Dt 34:11**	6213a
that we are to **p** the service of	**Jos 22:27**	5647
perhaps the king will **p** the	**2Sa 14:15**	6213a
The zeal of the LORD will **p** this.	**2Ki 19:31**	6213a
to **p** the words of the covenant	**2Ch 34:31**	6213a
Will You **p** wonders for the dead?	**Ps 88:10**	6213a
in strength, who **p** His word,	**Ps 103:20**	6213a
heart to **p** Your statutes Forever,	**Ps 119:112**	6213a
make a vow to the LORD and **p** it.	**Is 19:21**	7999a
LORD of hosts will **p** this."'	**Is 37:32**	6213a
And he will **p** all My desire.'	**Is 44:28**	7999a
watching over My word to **p** it."	**Jer 1:12**	6213a
you men will indeed **p** this thing,	**Jer 22:4**	6213a
p our vows that we have vowed,	**Jer 44:25**	6213a
vows, and certainly **p** your vows!'	**Jer 44:25**	6213a
I will speak the word and **p** it,"	**Ezk 12:25**	6213a
I have spoken, and I will **p** *it*."	**Ezk 17:24**	6213a
ground and **p** *its will* and prosper.	**Da 8:12**	6213a
degree And prosper and **p** *his will*;	**Da 8:24**	6213a
and if you will **p** My service,	**Zch 3:7**	8104

and in Your name **p** many miracles?'	**Mt 7:22**	*4160*
who will **p** a miracle in My name,	**Mk 9:39**	*4160*
was *present* for Him to **p** healing.	**Lk 5:17**	*2390*
kingdom of God and to **p** healing.	**Lk 9:2**	*2390*
and **p** cures today and tomorrow,	**Lk 13:32**	*658*
What work do You **p**?	**Jn 6:30**	*2038b*
He will not **p** more signs than	**Jn 7:31**	*4160*
who is a sinner **p** such signs?"	**Jn 9:16**	*4160*
promised, He was able also to **p**.	**Ro 4:21**	*4160*
Do you not know that those who **p**	**1Co 9:13**	*2038b*
THE BOOK OF THE LAW, TO **P** THEM."	**Ga 3:10**	*4160*
to **p** in the presence of the beast,	**Rv 13:14**	*4160*
PERFORMED		
He then **p** the signs in the sight	**Ex 4:30**	6213a
and how I **p** My signs among them,	**Ex 10:2**	7760
Moses and Aaron **p** all these	**Ex 11:10**	6213a
shall be **p** at the command of	**Nu 4:27**	
which I have **p** in their midst?	**Nu 14:11**	6213a
which I **p** in Egypt and in the	**Nu 14:22**	6213a
p in the sight of all Israel.	**Dt 34:12**	6213a
and He **p** wonders while Manoah and	**Jg 13:19**	6213a
p the request of his servant."	**2Sa 14:22**	6213a
King Solomon and **p** all his work.	**1Ki 7:14**	6213a
work which he **p** for King Solomon	**1Ki 7:40**	6213a
all the work that King Solomon **p**	**1Ki 7:51**	6213a
of those who **p** their service was:	**1Ch 25:1**	4399
work which he **p** for King Solomon	**2Ch 4:11**	6213a
Thus all the work that Solomon **p**	**2Ch 5:1**	6213a
"Then You **p** signs and wonders	**Ne 9:10**	5414
which You had **p** among them;	**Ne 9:17**	6213a
who **p** the work of the temple,	**Ne 11:12**	6213a
For they **p** the worship of their	**Ne 12:45**	8104
who **p** the service had gone away,	**Ne 13:10**	6213a
loyal deeds which I have **p** for the	**Ne 13:14**	6213a
will be born, that He has **p** *it*.	**Ps 22:31**	6213a
And to You the vow will be **p**.	**Ps 65:1**	7999a
When He **p** His signs in Egypt	**Ps 78:43**	7760
p His wondrous acts among them,	**Ps 105:27**	7760
are **p** in truth and uprightness.	**Ps 111:8**	6213a
have also **p** for us all our works.	**Is 26:12**	6466
"Who has **p** and accomplished *it*,	**Is 41:4**	6466
will not turn back Until He has **p**	**Jer 23:20**	6213a
not turn back Until He has **p**	**Jer 30:24**	6213a
the LORD has both purposed and **p**	**Jer 51:12**	6213a
whatever word I speak will be **p**.	**Ezk 12:25**	6213a
Whatever word I speak will be **p**,"	**Ezk 12:28**	6213a
labor that he had **p** against it."	**Ezk 29:18**	5647
of Egypt *for* his labor which he **p**,	**Ezk 29:20**	5647
miracles as these **p** by His hands?	**Mk 6:2**	*1096*
When they had **p** everything	**Lk 2:39**	*5055*
For if the miracles had been **p** in	**Lk 10:13**	*1096*
hoping to see some sign **p** by Him.	**Lk 23:8**	*1096*
again a second sign that Jesus **p** when	**Jn 4:54**	*4160*
saw the sign which He had **p**,	**Jn 6:14**	*4160*
"While John **p** no sign, yet	**Jn 10:41**	*4160*
heard that He had **p** this sign.	**Jn 12:18**	*4160*
had **p** so many signs before them,	**Jn 12:37**	*4160*
other signs Jesus also **p**	**Jn 20:30**	*4160*
God **p** through Him in your midst,	**Ac 2:22**	*4160*
miracle of healing had been **p**,	**Ac 4:22**	*1096*
The signs of a true apostle were **p**	**2Co 12:12**	*2716*
is **p** in the flesh by human hands	**Eph 2:11**	*5499*
kingdoms, **p** *acts of* righteousness,	**Heb 11:33**	*2038b*
who **p** the signs in his presence,	**Rv 19:20**	*4160*
PERFORMERS		
as **p** of every work and makers of	**Ex 35:35**	6213a
PERFORMING		
skillful men who were **p** all the work	**Ex 36:4**	6213a
each from the work which he was **p**,	**Ex 36:4**	6213a
among those who were **p** the work	**Ex 36:8**	6213a
p the duties of the sanctuary.	**Nu 3:28**	8104
p the duties of the sanctuary for	**Nu 3:38**	8104
p the purpose of His messengers.	**Is 44:26**	7999a
while he was **p** his priestly service	**Lk 1:8**	*2407*
He was **p** on those who were sick.	**Jn 6:2**	*4160*
For this man is **p** many signs.	**Jn 11:47**	*4160*
was **p** great wonders and signs	**Ac 6:8**	*4160*
p wonders and signs in the land of	**Ac 7:36**	*4160*
and saw the signs which he was **p**.	**Ac 8:6**	*4160*
God was **p** extraordinary miracles	**Ac 19:11**	*4160*
p deeds appropriate to repentance.	**Ac 26:20**	*4238*
p with his own hands what is good,	**Eph 4:28**	*2038b*
tabernacle **p** the divine worship,	**Heb 9:6**	*2005*
are spirits of demons, **p** signs,	**Rv 16:14**	*4160*
PERFORMS		
While Israel **p** valiantly.	**Nu 24:18**	6213a
if he resolutely **p** My commandments	**1Ch 28:7**	6213a
"For He **p** what is appointed for	**Jb 23:14**	7999a
The LORD **p** righteous deeds And	**Ps 103:6**	6213a
rescues and **p** signs and wonders	**Da 6:27**	5648
p its work in you who believe.	**1Th 2:13**	*1754*
He **p** great signs, so that he	**Rv 13:13**	*4160*
PERFUME		
a holy anointing oil, a **p** mixture,	**Ex 30:25**	7545
it you shall make incense, a **p**,	**Ex 30:35**	7545
make *any* like it, to use as **p**,	**Ex 30:38**	7381a
Oil and **p** make the heart glad, So	**Pr 27:9**	7004
My **p** gave forth its fragrance.	**SS 1:12**	5373
ankle chains, sashes, **p** boxes,	**Is 3:20**	1004, 5315
instead of sweet **p** there will be	**Is 3:24**	1314
alabaster vial of very costly **p**,	**Mt 26:7**	*3464*
"For this **p** might have been sold	**Mt 26:9**	
she poured this **p** on My body,	**Mt 26:12**	*3464*
vial of very costly **p** of pure nard;	**Mk 14:3**	*3464*
"Why has this **p** been wasted?	**Mk 14:4**	*3464*
"For this **p** might have been sold	**Mk 14:5**	*3464*
brought an alabaster vial of **p**,	**Lk 7:37**	*3464*

Context	Reference	Number
and anointing them with the **p**.	Lk 7:38	3464
but she anointed My feet with **p**.	Lk 7:46	3464
pound of very costly **p** of pure nard,	Jn 12:3	3464
with the fragrance of the **p**.	Jn 12:3	3464
"Why was this **p** not sold for	Jn 12:5	3464
and incense and **p** and frankincense	Rv 18:13	3464
PERFUMED		
P with myrrh and frankincense,	SS 3:6	6999
PERFUMER		
perfume mixture, the work of a **p**;	Ex 30:25	7543
a perfume, the work of a **p**,	Ex 30:35	7543
of spices, the work of a **p**.	Ex 37:29	7543
PERFUMER'S		
Dead flies make a **p** oil stink,	Ec 10:1	7543
PERFUMERS		
for **p** and cooks and bakers.	1Sa 8:13	7548
to him Hananiah, one of the **p**,	Ne 3:8	7546
PERFUMERS'		
various kinds blended by the **p** art;	2Ch 16:14	4842, 7543
PERFUMES		
with oil And increased your **p**;	Is 57:9	7547
and prepared spices and **p**.	Lk 23:56	3464
PERGA		
Paphos and came to **P** in Pamphylia;	Ac 13:13	4011
But going on from **P**,	Ac 13:14	4011
they had spoken the word in **P**,	Ac 14:25	4011
PERGAMUM		
to Smyrna and to **P** and to Thyatira	Rv 1:11	4010
angel of the church in **P** write:	Rv 2:12	4010
PERHAPS		
p I will obtain children through	Gn 16:2	194
"**P** my father will feel me, then I	Gn 27:12	194
p he will accept me."	Gn 32:20	194
p it was a mistake.	Gn 43:12	194
p I can make atonement for your	Ex 32:30	194
p I may be able to defeat them and	Nu 22:6	194
p I may be able to fight against	Nu 22:11	194
p the LORD will come to meet me,	Nu 23:3	194
p it will be agreeable with God	Nu 23:27	194
"**P** you are living within our land;	Jos 9:7	194
p the LORD will be with me, and I	Jos 14:12	194
p He will ease His hand from you,	1Sa 6:5	194
p he can tell us about our journey	1Sa 9:6	194
p the LORD will work for us, for	1Sa 14:6	194
p the king will perform the	2Sa 14:15	194
"**P** the LORD will look on my	2Sa 16:12	194
p we will find grass and keep the	1Ki 18:5	194
or **p** he is asleep and needs to be	1Ki 18:27	194
p he will save your life."	1Ki 20:31	194
p the Spirit of the LORD has taken	2Ki 2:16	6435
'**P** the LORD your God will hear all	2Ki 19:4	194
"**P** my sons have sinned and cursed	Jb 1:5	194
'**P** the LORD your God will hear the	Is 37:4	194
P you will be able to profit,	Is 47:12	194
profit, **P** you may cause trembling.	Is 47:12	194
"**P** he will be deceived, so that	Jer 20:10	194
p the LORD will deal with us	Jer 21:2	194
'**P** they will listen and everyone	Jer 26:3	194
"**P** the house of Judah will hear	Jer 36:3	194
"**P** their supplication will come	Jer 36:7	194
P she may be healed.	Jer 51:8	194
in the dust, **P** there is hope.	La 3:29	194
P they will understand though they	Ezk 12:3	194
P the LORD God of hosts May be	Am 5:15	194
P *your* god will be concerned about	Jon 1:6	194
P you will be hidden In the day of	Zph 2:3	194
if **p** He would find anything on it;	Mk 11:13	686
unless **p** we go and buy food for	Lk 9:13	3385
p they will respect him.'	Lk 20:13	2481
if **p** they might grope for Him and	Ac 17:27	686
if **p** now at last by the will of	Ro 1:10	4458
though **p** for the good man someone	Ro 5:7	5029
There are, **p**, a great many kinds	1Co 14:10	5177
p of wheat or of something else.	1Co 15:37	5177
and **p** I will stay with you, or	1Co 16:6	5177
For I am afraid that **p** when I come	2Co 12:20	4458
that **p** *there will be* strife,	2Co 12:20	4458
that **p** I have labored over you in	Ga 4:11	4458
if **p** God may grant them repentance	2Tm 2:25	3379
For **p** he was for this reason	Phm 1:15	5029
PERIDA		
sons of Sophereth, the sons of **P**,	Ne 7:57	6514
PERIL		
or famine, or nakedness, or **p**,	Ro 8:35	2794
who delivered us from so great a **p**	2Co 1:10	
PERIOD		
is the **p** required for embalming.	Gn 50:3	3117
the **p** of your ordination is fulfilled;	Lv 8:33	3117
the **p** of her menstrual impurity,	Lv 15:25	6256
she has a discharge beyond that **p**,	Lv 15:25	5079
was there for a **p** of four months.	Jg 19:2	3117
The **p** which he reigned over	1Ch 29:27	3117
a woman during her menstrual **p**	Ezk 18:6	5079
"But at the end of that **p**,	Da 4:34	3118
them for an appointed **p** of time.	Da 7:12	2166
at the final **p** of the indignation,	Da 8:19	319
"In the latter **p** of their rule,	Da 8:23	319
appearing to them over *a* **p** *of*	Ac 1:3	
until *the* **p** of restoration of all things	Ac 3:21	5550
"For a **p** of about forty years	Ac 13:18	5550
for a **p** of three years I did not cease	Ac 20:31	5148
PERIODS		
let seven **p** of time pass over him.	Da 4:16	
seven **p** of time pass over him,"	Da 4:23	
seven **p** of time will pass over you,	Da 4:25	
seven **p** of time will pass over you until	Da 4:32	
PERISH		
that is on the earth shall **p**.	Gn 6:17	1478
will not **p** during the famine."	Gn 41:36	3772
LORD to gaze, and many of them **p**.	Ex 19:21	5307
'But you will **p** among the nations,	Lv 26:38	6
"Behold, we **p**, we are dying, we	Nu 17:12	1478
Are we to **p** completely?"	Nu 17:13	1478
that you will surely **p** quickly	Dt 4:26	6
and hide themselves from you **p**.	Dt 7:20	6
their name **p** from under heaven;	Dt 7:24	6
you today that you will surely **p**.	Dt 8:19	6
the LORD makes to **p** before you,	Dt 8:20	6
perish before you, so you shall **p**;	Dt 8:20	6
and you will **p** quickly from the	Dt 11:17	6
destroyed and until you **p** quickly,	Dt 28:20	6
they will pursue you until you **p**.	Dt 28:22	6
until they have caused you to **p**.	Dt 28:51	6
you to make you **p** and destroy you;	Dt 28:63	6
you today that you shall surely **p**.	Dt 30:18	6
not **p** alone in his iniquity.' "	Jos 22:20	1478
until you **p** from off this good	Jos 23:13	6
and you will **p** quickly from off	Jos 23:16	6
"Thus let all Your enemies **p**,	Jg 5:31	6
he will go down into battle and **p**.	1Sa 26:10	5595
p one day by the hand of Saul.	1Sa 27:1	5595
the whole house of Ahab shall **p**,	2Ki 9:8	6
you and your father's house will **p**.	Es 4:14	6
and if I **p**, I perish."	Es 4:16	6
and if I perish, I **p**."	Es 4:16	6
day **p** on which I was to be born,	Jb 3:3	6
"By the breath of God they **p**,	Jb 4:9	6
Unobserved, they **p** forever.	Jb 4:20	6
They go up into nothing and **p**.	Jb 6:18	6
the hope of the godless will **p**,	Jb 8:13	6
"The blessing of the one ready to **p**	Jb 29:13	6
anyone **p** for lack of clothing,	Jb 31:19	6
All flesh would **p** together, And	Jb 34:15	1478
hear, they shall **p** by the sword And	Jb 36:12	5674a
But the way of the wicked will **p**.	Ps 1:6	6
angry, and you **p** *in* the way,	Ps 2:12	6
They stumble and **p** before You.	Ps 9:3	6
hope of the afflicted **p** forever.	Ps 9:18	6
But the wicked will **p**;	Ps 37:20	6
will he die, and his name **p**?"	Ps 41:5	6
stupid and the senseless alike **p** And	Ps 49:10	6
He is like the beasts that **p**.	Ps 49:12	1820
Is like the beasts that **p**.	Ps 49:20	1820
So let the wicked **p** before God.	Ps 68:2	6
who are far from You will **p**;	Ps 73:27	6
They **p** at the rebuke of Your	Ps 80:16	6
And let them be humiliated and **p**,	Ps 83:17	6
For, behold, Your enemies will **p**;	Ps 92:9	6
"Even they will **p**, but You endure	Ps 102:26	6
The desire of the wicked will **p**.	Ps 112:10	6
In that very day his thoughts **p**.	Ps 146:4	6
man dies, *his* expectation will **p**,	Pr 11:7	6
rejoices, And when the wicked **p**,	Pr 11:10	6
And he who tells lies will **p**.	Pr 19:9	6
A false witness will **p**,	Pr 21:28	6
And the rod of his fury will **p**.	Pr 22:8	3615
But when they **p**, the righteous	Pr 28:28	6
wisdom of their wise men will **p**,	Is 29:14	6
will be as nothing and will **p**.	Is 41:11	6
which will not serve you will **p**,	Is 60:12	6
Neighbor and friend will **p**."	Jer 6:21	6
cities And let us **p** there,	Jer 8:14	1826a
will **p** from the earth and from	Jer 10:11	7
of their punishment they will **p**.	Jer 10:15	6
"Flight will **p** from the	Jer 25:35	6
drive you out and you will **p**.	Jer 27:10	6
drive you out and that you may **p**,	Jer 27:15	6
and the remnant of Judah would **p**?"	Jer 40:15	6
of their punishment they will **p**.	Jer 51:18	6
and make you **p** from the lands;	Ezk 25:7	6
the remnant of the Philistines will **p**	Am 1:8	6
"Flight will **p** from the swift,	Am 2:14	6
The houses of ivory will also **p**	Am 3:15	6
about us so that we will not **p**."	Jon 1:6	6
do not let us **p** on account of this	Jon 1:14	6
anger so that we will not **p**."	Jon 3:9	6
the king will **p** from Gaza,	Zch 9:5	6
parts in it will be cut off *and* **p**;	Zch 13:8	1478
that one of these little ones **p**.	Mt 18:14	622
up the sword shall **p** by the sword.	Mt 26:52	622
repent, you will all likewise **p**.	Lk 13:3	622
repent, you will all likewise **p**."	Lk 13:5	622
would **p** outside of Jerusalem.	Lk 13:33	622
not a hair of your head will **p**.	Lk 21:18	622
believes in Him shall not **p**,	Jn 3:16	622
to them, and they will never **p**;	Jn 10:28	622
the whole nation not **p**."	Jn 11:50	622
"May your silver **p** with you,	Ac 8:20	684
YOU SCOFFERS, AND MARVEL, AND **P**;	Ac 13:41	853
the head of any of you will **p**."	Ac 27:34	622
Law will also **p** without the Law,	Ro 2:12	622
things destined to **p** with use)	Col 2:22	5356
of wickedness for those who **p**,	2Th 2:10	622
THEY WILL **P**, BUT YOU REMAIN;	Heb 1:11	622
By faith Rahab the harlot did not **p**	Heb 11:31	4881
not wishing for any to **p** but for	2Pe 3:9	622
PERISHABLE		
then *do it* to receive a **p** wreath,	1Co 9:25	5349
It is sown a **p** *body*, it is raised	1Co 15:42	5356
the **p** inherit the imperishable.	1Co 15:50	5356
p must put on the imperishable,	1Co 15:53	5349
But when this **p** will have put on	1Co 15:54	5349
precious than gold which is **p**,	1Pe 1:7	622
you were not redeemed with **p** things	1Pe 1:18	5349
born again not of seed which is **p**	1Pe 1:23	5349
PERISHED		
flesh that moved on the earth **p**,	Gn 7:21	1478
and they **p** from the midst of the	Nu 16:33	6
"If only we had **p** when our	Nu 20:3	1478
our brothers **p** before the LORD!	Nu 20:3	1478
men of war **p** from within the camp,	Dt 2:14	8552
within the camp until they all **p**.	Dt 2:15	8552
finally **p** from among the people,	Dt 2:16	8552, 4191
p because they did not listen to	Jos 5:6	8552
And the weapons of war **p**!"	2Sa 1:27	6
of Israel who have already **p**,	2Ki 7:13	8552
now, who *ever* **p** being innocent?	Jb 4:7	6
Vigor had **p** from them.	Jb 30:2	6
The very memory of them has **p**.	Ps 9:6	6
Nations have **p** from His land.	Ps 10:16	6
I would have **p** in my affliction.	Ps 119:92	6
and their zeal have already **p**,	Ec 9:6	6
truth has **p** and has been cut off	Jer 7:28	6
The people of Chemosh have **p**;	Jer 48:46	6
and my elders **p** in the city While	La 1:19	1478
"My strength has **p**, And *so has* my	La 3:18	6
'How you have **p**, O inhabited one,	Ezk 26:17	6
are dried up and our hope has **p**.	Ezk 37:11	6
came up overnight and **p** overnight.	Jon 4:10	6
you, Or has your counselor **p**,	Mi 4:9	6
godly person has **p** from the land,	Mi 7:2	6
into the sea and **p** in the waters.	Mt 8:32	599
not one of them **p** but the son of	Jn 17:12	622
some people after him; he too **p**,	Ac 5:37	622
fallen asleep in Christ have **p**.	1Co 15:18	622
and **p** in the rebellion of Korah.	Jude 1:11	622
PERISHES		
"The lion **p** for lack of prey, And	Jb 4:11	6
"Memory of him **p** from the earth,	Jb 18:17	6
He **p** forever like his refuse;	Jb 20:7	6
And their life **p** among the cult	Jb 36:14	
the expectation of the wicked **p**.	Pr 10:28	6
And the hope of strong men **p**.	Pr 11:7	6
man who **p** in his righteousness and	Ec 7:15	6
The righteous man **p**,	Is 57:1	6
"Do not work for the food which **p**,	Jn 6:27	622
PERISHING		
opposition of Your hand I am **p**.	Ps 39:10	3615
Give strong drink to him who is **p**,	Pr 31:6	6
and those who were **p** in the land	Is 27:13	6
land who will not care for the **p**,	Zch 11:16	3582
saying, "Save *us*, Lord; we are **p**!"	Mt 8:25	622
do You not care that we are **p**?"	Mk 4:38	622
"Master, Master, we are **p**!"	Lk 8:24	622
is foolishness to those who are **p**,	1Co 1:18	622
saved and among those who are **p**;	2Co 2:15	622
it is veiled to those who are **p**,	2Co 4:3	622
PERIZZITE		
Now the Canaanite and the **P** were	Gn 13:7	6522
Hittite and the **P** and the Rephaim	Gn 15:20	6522
Hittite and the Amorite and the **P**	Ex 3:8	6522
the **P** and the Hivite and the Jebusite	Ex 3:17	6522
the Amorite, the Hittite, the **P**,	Ex 33:2	6522
the Canaanite, the Hittite, the **P**,	Ex 34:11	6522
Amorite, the Canaanite and the **P**,	Dt 20:17	6522
the Hittite, the Hivite, the **P**,	Jos 3:10	6522
the Amorite, the Canaanite, the **P**,	Jos 9:1	6522
Hittite and the **P** and the Jebusite	Jos 11:3	6522
Amorite and the Canaanite, the **P**,	Jos 12:8	6522
and the Amorite and the **P** and the	Jos 24:11	6522
Hittite and the Amorite, Of the **P**,	Ne 9:8	6522
PERIZZITES		
among the Canaanites and the **P**;	Gn 34:30	6522
the Amorites, the Hittites, the **P**,	Ex 23:23	6522
Canaanites and the **P** and the Hivites	Dt 7:1	6522
land of the **P** and of the Rephaim,	Jos 17:15	6522
and the **P** into their hands,	Jg 1:4	6522
defeated the Canaanites and the **P**.	Jg 1:5	6522
the Hittites, the Amorites, the **P**,	Jg 3:5	6522
the Amorites, the Hittites, the **P**,	1Ki 9:20	6522
the Hittites, the Amorites, the **P**,	2Ch 8:7	6522
Canaanites, the Hittites, the **P**,	Ezr 9:1	6522
PERJURERS		
and kidnappers and liars and **p**,	1Tm 1:10	1965
PERJURY		
another, and do not love **p**;	Zch 8:17	7621, 8267
PERMANENT		
to celebrate it *as* a **p** ordinance.	Ex 12:14	5769
your generations as a **p** ordinance.	Ex 12:17	5769
it is a **p** ordinance throughout	Lv 6:18	5769
By a **p** ordinance it shall be	Lv 6:22	5769
This shall be a **p** statute for you:	Lv 16:29	5769
it is a **p** statute.	Lv 16:31	5769
shall have this as a **p** statute,	Lv 16:34	5769
This shall be a **p** statute to them	Lv 17:7	5769
Levites have a **p** right of redemption	Lv 25:32	5769
you can use them as **p** slaves.	Lv 25:46	5769
I *had* intended to build a **p** home	1Ch 28:2	4496
PERMANENTLY		
and he shall serve him **p**.	Ex 21:6	5769
moreover, shall not be sold **p**,	Lv 25:23	6783
passes **p** to its purchaser throughout	Lv 25:30	6783
forever, holds His priesthood **p**.	Heb 7:24	531
PERMISSIBLE		
not **p** for you to carry your pallet."	Jn 5:10	1832
PERMISSION		
yet without your **p** no one shall	Gn 41:44	
according to the **p** they had from	Ezr 3:7	7558

so he sought **p** from the commander **Da 1:8**
Jesus gave them **p**. **Mk 5:13** *2010*
told *them,* and they gave them **p**. **Mk 11:6** *863*
And He gave them **p**. **Lk 8:32** *2010*
Satan has demanded **p** to sift you **Lk 22:31**
and Pilate granted **p**. **Jn 19:38** *2010*
When he had given him **p**, **Ac 21:40** *2010*

PERMIT
of Egypt will not **p** you to go, **Ex 3:19** 5414
But Sihon would not **p** Israel to **Nu 21:23** 5414
"**P** *it* at this time; **Mt 3:15** *863*
p me first to go and bury my **Mt 8:21** *2010*
you no longer **p** him to do anything **Mk 7:12** *863*
"**P** the children to come to Me; **Mk 10:14** *863*
and He would not **p** anyone to carry **Mk 11:16** *863*
Him to **p** them to enter the swine. **Lk 8:32** *2010*
p me first to go and bury my father." **Lk 9:59** *2010*
but first **p** me to say good-bye to **Lk 9:61** *2010*
"**P** the children to come to Me, **Lk 18:16** *863*
Spirit of Jesus did not **p** them; **Ac 16:7** *1439*
wind did not **p** us *to go* farther, **Ac 27:7** *4330*
and will not **p** their dead bodies **Rv 11:9** *863*

PERMITS
"The one who **p** any of the men **2Ki 10:24**
"But when the crop **p**, **Mk 4:29** *3860*
you for some time, if the Lord **p**. **1Co 16:7** *2010*
And this we will do, if God **p**. **Heb 6:3** *2010*

PERMITTED
He **p** no man to oppress them, And **1Ch 16:21** 5117
He **p** no man to oppress them, And **Ps 105:14** 5117
"I **p** Myself to be sought by those **Is 65:1**
I **p** Myself to be found by those **Is 65:1**
Then he **p** Him. **Mt 3:15** *863*
Moses **p** you to divorce your wives; **Mt 19:8** *2010*
"Moses **p** *a man* TO WRITE A **Mk 10:4** *2010*
not **p** to put anyone to death," **Jn 18:31** *1832*
He **p** all the nations to go their own **Ac 14:16** *1439*
"You are **p** to speak for yourself." **Ac 26:1** *2010*
for they are not **p** to speak, **1Co 14:34** *2010*
which a man is not **p** to speak. **2Co 12:4** *1832*
they were not **p** to kill anyone, **Rv 9:5** *1325*

PERMITTING
He was not **p** the demons to speak, **Mk 1:34** *863*

PERPETRATED
and revolt have been **p** in it, **Ezr 4:19** 5957
treachery which they **p** against Me, **Ezk 39:26** 4603

PERPETUAL
it shall be a **p** statute throughout **Ex 27:21** 5769
the priesthood by a **p** statute. **Ex 29:9** 5769
There shall be **p** incense before **Ex 30:8** 8548
it shall be a **p** statute for them, **Ex 30:21** 5769
generations as a **p** covenant.' **Ex 31:16** 5769
will qualify them for a **p** priesthood **Ex 40:15** 5769
'It is a **p** statute throughout your **Lv 3:17** 5769
it is a **p** statute throughout your **Lv 10:9** 5769
It is to be a **p** statute throughout **Lv 23:14** 5769
It is to be a **p** statute in all **Lv 23:21** 5769
It is to be a **p** statute throughout **Lv 23:31** 5769
It *shall be* a **p** statute throughout **Lv 23:41** 5769
it shall be a **p** statute throughout **Lv 24:3** 5769
for that is their **p** possession. **Lv 25:34** 5769
and this shall be for you a **p** statute **Nu 10:8** 5769
a **p** statute throughout your **Nu 15:15** 5769
and to your sons as a **p** allotment. **Nu 18:8** 5769
with you as a **p** allotment. **Nu 18:11** 5769
with you, as a **p** allotment. **Nu 18:19** 5769
it shall be a **p** statute throughout **Nu 18:23** 5769
and it shall be a **p** statute to the **Nu 19:10** 5769
it shall be a **p** statute for them. **Nu 19:21** 5769
him, a covenant of a **p** priesthood, **Nu 25:13** 5769
has come to an end in **p** ruins, **Ps 9:6** 5331
Your footsteps toward the **p** ruins; **Ps 74:3** 5331
Why has my pain been **p** And my **Jer 15:18** 5331
An object of **p** hissing; **Jer 18:16** 5769
its cities will become **p** ruins." **Jer 49:13** 5769
sleep a **p** sleep And not wake up," **Jer 51:39** 5769
sleep a **p** sleep and not wake up," **Jer 51:57** 5769
but it will be a **p** desolation.' **Jer 51:62** 5769
LORD continually by a **p** ordinance. **Ezk 46:14** 5769
the **p** mountains were shattered, **Hab 3:6** 5703
and salt pits, And a **p** desolation. **Zph 2:9** 5769

PERPETUALLY
so it shall be a thing **p** due you **Lv 10:15** 5769
eyes and My heart will be there **p**. **1Ki 9:3**
3605, 3117
eyes and My heart will be there **p**. **2Ch 7:16**
3605, 3117
Son of God, he remains a priest **p**. **Heb 7:3**
1519, 1336

PERPETUATED
"Your name will no longer be **p**. **Na 1:14** 2232

PERPLEXED
even paler, and his nobles were **p**. **Da 5:9** 7672
when he heard him, he was very **p**; **Mk 6:20** *639*
But she was very **p** at *this* **Lk 1:29** *1298*
and he was greatly **p**, **Lk 9:7** *1280*
While they were **p** about this, **Lk 24:4** *639*
they were greatly **p** about them as **Ac 5:24** *1280*
Now while Peter was greatly **p** in **Ac 10:17** *1280*
p, but not despairing; **2Co 4:8** *639*
my tone, for I am **p** about you. **Ga 4:20** *639*

PERPLEXITY
in **p** at the roaring of the sea and **Lk 21:25** *640*
in amazement and great **p**, **Ac 2:12** *1280*

PERSECUTE
"Why do you **p** me as God *does,* And **Jb 19:22** 7291
'How shall we **p** him?' **Jb 19:28** 7291
might of Your hand You **p** me. **Jb 30:21** 7852
enemies and from those who **p** me. **Ps 31:15** 7291
judgment on those who **p** me? **Ps 119:84** 7291
Princes **p** me without cause, But my **Ps 119:161** 7291
those who **p** me be put to shame, **Jer 17:18** 7291
insult you and **p** you, **Mt 5:11** *1377*
and pray for those who **p** you **Mt 5:44** *1377*
whenever they **p** you in one city, **Mt 10:23** *1377*
and **p** from city to city, **Mt 23:34** *1377*
will kill and *some* they will **p**, **Lk 11:49** *1377*
their hands on you and will **p** you, **Lk 21:12** *1377*
Me, they will also **p** you; **Jn 15:20** *1377*
prophets did your fathers not **p**? **Ac 7:52** *1377*
Bless those who **p** you; **Ro 12:14** *1377*
how I used to **p** the church of God **Ga 1:13** *1377*

PERSECUTED
on those who hate you, who **p** you. **Dt 30:7** 7291
For they have **p** him whom You **Ps 69:26** 7291
But **p** the afflicted and needy man, **Ps 109:16** 7291
They have **p** me with a lie; **Ps 119:86** 7291
they have **p** me from my youth up," **Ps 129:1** 6887c
they have **p** me from my youth up; **Ps 129:2** 6887c
For the enemy has **p** my soul; **Ps 143:3** 7291
p for the sake of righteousness, **Mt 5:10** *1377*
same way they **p** the prophets who **Mt 5:12** *1377*
If they **p** Me, they will also **Jn 15:20** *1377*
"I **p** this Way to the death, **Ac 22:4** *1377*
when we are **p**, we endure; **1Co 4:12** *1377*
because I **p** the church of God. **1Co 15:9** *1377*
p, but not forsaken; **2Co 4:9** *1377*
"He who once **p** us is now **Ga 1:23** *1377*
p him *who was born* according to the **Ga 4:29** *1377*
circumcision, why am I still **p**? **Ga 5:11** *1377*
not be **p** for the cross of Christ. **Ga 6:12** *1377*
godly in Christ Jesus will be **p**. **2Tm 3:12** *1377*
he **p** the woman who gave birth to **Rv 12:13** *1377*

PERSECUTING
this reason the Jews were **p** Jesus, **Jn 5:16** *1377*
"Saul, Saul, why are you **p** Me?" **Ac 9:4** *1377*
"I am Jesus whom you are **p**, **Ac 9:5** *1377*
'Saul, Saul, why are you **p** Me?' **Ac 22:7** *1377*
the Nazarene, whom you are **p**.' **Ac 22:8** *1377*
'Saul, Saul, why are you **p** Me? **Ac 26:14** *1377*
'I am Jesus whom you are **p**. **Ac 26:15** *1377*

PERSECUTION
in anger with unrestrained **p**. **Is 14:6** 4783
or **p** arises because of the word, **Mt 13:21** *1375*
or **p** arises because of the word, **Mk 4:17** *1375*
And on that day a great **p** began **Ac 8:1** *1375*
who were scattered because of the **p** **Ac 11:19** *2347*
a **p** against Paul and Barnabas, **Ac 13:50** *1375*
tribulation, or distress, or **p**, **Ro 8:35** *1375*

PERSECUTIONS
children and farms, along with **p**; **Mk 10:30** *1375*
insults, with distresses, with **p**, **2Co 12:10** *1375*
and faith in the midst of all your **p** **2Th 1:4** *1375*
p, *and* sufferings, such as **2Tm 3:11** *1375*
what **p** I endured, and out of them **2Tm 3:11** *1375*

PERSECUTOR
as to zeal, a **p** of the church; **Php 3:6** *1377*
and a **p** and a violent aggressor. **1Tm 1:13** *1376*

PERSECUTORS
Many are my **p** and my adversaries, **Ps 119:157** 7291
Deliver me from my **p**, **Ps 142:6** 7291
And take vengeance for me on my **p**. **Jer 15:15** 7291
my **p** will stumble and not prevail. **Jer 20:11** 7291

PERSEVERANCE
it fast, and bear fruit with **p**. **Lk 8:15** *5281*
to those who by **p** in doing good **Ro 2:7** *5281*
that tribulation brings about **p**; **Ro 5:3** *5281*
and **p**, proven character; **Ro 5:4** *5281*
with **p** we wait eagerly for it. **Ro 8:25** *5281*
through **p** and the encouragement **Ro 15:4** *5281*
Now may the God who gives **p** and **Ro 15:5** *5281*
performed among you with all **p**, **2Co 12:12** *5281*
be on the alert with all **p** and **Eph 6:18** *4343*
your **p** and faith in the midst of all **2Th 1:4** *5281*
faith, love, **p** *and* gentleness. **1Tm 6:11** *5281*
purpose, faith, patience, love, **p**, **2Tm 3:10** *5281*
sound in faith, in love, in **p**. **Ti 2:2** *5281*
and in *your* self-control, **p**, **2Pe 1:6** *5281*
and in *your* **p**, godliness, **2Pe 1:6** *5281*
kingdom and **p** *which are* in Jesus, **Rv 1:9** *5281*
your deeds and your toil and **p**, **Rv 2:2** *5281*
and you have **p** and have endured **Rv 2:3** *5281*
love and faith and service and **p**, **Rv 2:19** *5281*
you have kept the word of My **p**, **Rv 3:10** *5281*
the **p** and the faith of the saints. **Rv 13:10** *5281*
Here is the **p** of the saints who **Rv 14:12** *5281*

PERSEVERE
p in these things, **1Tm 4:16** *1961*

PERSEVERES
Blessed is a man who **p** under trial; **Jas 1:12** *5278*

PERSEVERING
in hope, **p** in tribulation, **Ro 12:12** *5278*

PERSIA
the rule of the kingdom of **P**, **2Ch 36:20** 6539
in the first year of Cyrus king of **P** **2Ch 36:22** 6539
up the spirit of Cyrus king of **P**, **2Ch 36:22** 6539
"Thus says Cyrus king of **P**, **2Ch 36:23** 6539
the first year of Cyrus king of **P**, **Ezr 1:1** 6539
up the spirit of Cyrus king of **P**, **Ezr 1:1** 6539
"Thus says Cyrus king of **P**, **Ezr 1:2** 6539
and Cyrus, king of **P**, **Ezr 1:8** 6539
they had from Cyrus king of **P**. **Ezr 3:7** 6539
the king of **P** has commanded us." **Ezr 4:3** 6539
all the days of Cyrus king of **P**, **Ezr 4:5** 6539
the reign of Darius king of **P**. **Ezr 4:5** 6539
wrote to Artaxerxes king of **P**; **Ezr 4:7** 6539
of the reign of Darius king of **P**. **Ezr 4:24** 6540
Darius, and Artaxerxes king of **P**. **Ezr 6:14** 6540
the reign of Artaxerxes king of **P**, **Ezr 7:1** 6539
us in the sight of the kings of **P**, **Ezr 9:9** 6539
the army *officers* of **P** and Media, **Es 1:3** 6539
the seven princes of **P** and Media **Es 1:14** 6539
"This day the ladies of **P** and **Es 1:18** 6539
let it be written in the laws of **P** and **Es 1:19** 6539
of the Kings of Media and **P**? **Es 10:2** 6539
"**P** and Lud and Put were in your **Ezk 27:10** 6539
P, Ethiopia and Put with them, **Ezk 38:5** 6539
the kings of Media and **P**. **Da 8:20** 6539
In the third year of Cyrus king of **P** **Da 10:1** 6539
"But the prince of the kingdom of **P** **Da 10:13** 6539
left there with the kings of **P**. **Da 10:13** 6539
to fight against the prince of **P**; **Da 10:20** 6539
kings are going to arise in **P**. **Da 11:2** 6539

PERSIAN
in the reign of Darius the **P**. **Ne 12:22** 6542
and in the reign of Cyrus the **P**. **Da 6:28** 6543

PERSIANS
given over to the Medes and **P**." **Da 5:28** 6540
to the law of the Medes and **P**, **Da 6:8** 6540
to the law of the Medes and **P**, **Da 6:12** 6540
it is a law of the Medes and **P** that **Da 6:15** 6540

PERSIS
Greet **P** the beloved, who has **Ro 16:12** *4069*

PERSISTED
you have **p** in blessing them these **Nu 24:10** 1288
Canaanites **p** in living in that land. **Jos 17:12** 2974
Canaanites **p** in living in that land. **Jg 1:27** 2974
Amorites **p** in living in Mount Heres, **Jg 1:35** 2974
But when they **p** in asking Him, He **Jn 8:7** *1961*

PERSISTENCE
yet because of his **p** he will get **Lk 11:8** *335*

PERSISTENTLY
even to this day, warning **p**, **Jer 11:7** 7925

PERSISTS
And *if* he **p** and says, **Dt 25:8** 5975

PERSON
that **p** shall be cut off from his **Gn 17:14** 5315
p shall be cut off from Israel. **Ex 12:15** 5315
what must be eaten by every **p**, **Ex 12:16** 5315
that **p** shall be cut off from the **Ex 12:19** 5315
no uncircumcised **p** may eat of it. **Ex 12:48**
that **p** shall be cut off from among **Ex 31:14** 5315
and every skillful **p** in whom the **Ex 36:1** 376
p in whom the LORD had put skill, **Ex 36:2** 376
'If a **p** sins unintentionally in **Lv 4:2** 5315
'Now if a **p** sins after he hears a **Lv 5:1** 5315
if a **p** touches any unclean thing, **Lv 5:2** 5315
'Or if a **p** swears thoughtlessly **Lv 5:4** 5315
"If a **p** acts unfaithfully and **Lv 5:15** 5315
"Now if a **p** sins and does any of **Lv 5:17** 5315
When a **p** sins and acts unfaithfully **Lv 6:2** 5315
and the **p** who eats of it will **Lv 7:18** 5315
'But the **p** who eats the flesh of **Lv 7:20** 5315
that **p** shall be cut off from his **Lv 7:20** 5315
that **p** shall be cut off from his **Lv 7:21** 5315
even the **p** who eats shall be cut **Lv 7:25** 5315
'Any **p** who eats any blood, even **Lv 7:27** 5315
even that **p** shall be cut off from **Lv 7:27** 5315
then the priest shall isolate *the* **p** **Lv 13:31**
and the priest shall isolate *the* **p** **Lv 13:33**
'Every bed on which the **p** with the **Lv 15:4** 376
'Also whoever touches the **p** with **Lv 15:7** 1320
'Every saddle on which the **p** **Lv 15:9**
vessel which the **p** with the discharge **Lv 15:12**
against that **p** who eats blood and **Lv 17:10** 5315
'No **p** among you may eat blood, nor **Lv 17:12** 5315
any **p** eats *an animal* which dies or **Lv 17:15** 5315
and that **p** shall be cut off from **Lv 19:8** 5315
'As for the **p** who turns to mediums **Lv 20:6** 5315
will also set My face against that **p** **Lv 20:6** 5315
one shall defile himself for a *dead* **p** **Lv 21:1** 5315
nor shall he approach any dead **p**, **Lv 21:11** 5315
that **p** shall be cut off from **Lv 22:3** 5315
a **p** who touches any such shall be **Lv 22:6** 5315
"If there is any **p** who will not **Lv 23:29** 5315
"As for any **p** who does any work **Lv 23:30** 5315
that **p** I will destroy from among **Lv 23:30** 5315
is unclean because of a *dead* **p**. **Nu 5:2** 5315
the LORD, and that **p** is guilty, **Nu 5:6** 5315
he shall not go near to a dead **p**. **Nu 6:6** 5315
his sin because of the *dead* **p**. **Nu 6:11** 5315
unclean because of *the* dead **p**, **Nu 9:6** 5315
are unclean because of *the* dead **p**, **Nu 9:7** 5315
unclean because of a *dead* **p**, **Nu 9:10** 5315
that **p** shall then be cut off from **Nu 9:13** 5315
if one **p** sins unintentionally, **Nu 15:27** 5315
the **p** who goes astray when he sins **Nu 15:28** 5315
the **p** who does *anything* defiantly, **Nu 15:30** 5315
and that **p** shall be cut off from **Nu 15:30** 5315
p shall be completely cut off; **Nu 15:31** 5315
one who touches the corpse of any **p** **Nu 19:11**
5315, 120
p shall be cut off from Israel. **Nu 19:13** 5315
'Then for the unclean **p** they **Nu 19:17**
'A clean **p** shall take hyssop **Nu 19:18** 376
'Then the clean **p** shall sprinkle **Nu 19:19**
that **p** shall be cut off from the **Nu 19:20** 5315
anything that the unclean **p** **Nu 19:22**
and the **p** who touches *it* shall be **Nu 19:22** 5315
whoever has killed any **p** and **Nu 31:19** 5315
the manslayer who has killed any **p** **Nu 35:11** 5315

that anyone who kills a **p** **Nu 35:15** 5315
'If anyone kills a **p**, **Nu 35:30** 5315
but no **p** shall be put to death on **Nu 35:30** 5315
"If a slain **p** is found lying in **Dt 21:1**
'Cursed is he who misleads a blind **p** **Dt 27:18**
to strike down an innocent **p**.' **Dt 27:25** 5315
it and every **p** who was in it. **Jos 10:28** 5315
and he struck it and every **p** who **Jos 10:30** 5315
and struck it and every **p** who *was* **Jos 10:32** 5315
that day every **p** who *was* in it, **Jos 10:35** 5315
it and every **p** who *was* in it. **Jos 10:37** 5315
destroyed every **p** *who was* in it. **Jos 10:39** 5315
They struck every **p** who was in **Jos 11:11** 5315
who kills any **p** unintentionally, **Jos 20:3** 5315
that whoever kills any **p** **Jos 20:9** 5315
there was not a more handsome **p** **1Sa 9:2** 376
every **p** in your father's household. **1Sa 22:22** 5315
cut off from Jeroboam every male **p**, **1Ki 14:10**
will cut off from Ahab every male **p** **2Ki 9:8**
to the desires of each **p**. **Es 1:8** 376
And the humble **p** He will save. **Jb 22:29** 7807, 5869
A worthless **p**, a wicked man, Is **Pr 6:12** 120
for a **p** to be without knowledge, **Pr 19:2** 5315
For to a **p** who is good in His **Ec 2:26** 120
because this *applies to* every **p**. **Ec 12:13** 120
a **p** to be indicted by a word, **Is 29:21** 120
To keep the hungry **p** unsatisfied **Is 32:6** 5315
And deliver the **p** who has been **Jer 21:12**
the king's daughters and every **p** **Jer 43:6** 5315
for Him, To the **p** who seeks Him. **La 3:25** 5315
brought to answer him in My own **p**. **Ezk 14:7**
"The **p** who sins will die. **Ezk 18:20** 5315
comes and takes a **p** from them, **Ezk 33:6** 5315
to a dead **p** to defile *themselves;* **Ezk 44:25** 120
place a despicable **p** will arise, **Da 11:21**
a time the prudent **p** keeps silent, **Am 5:13**
godly **p** has perished from the land, **Mi 7:2** 2623
And there is no upright **p** among **Mi 7:2**
do not resist an evil **p**; but whoever **Mt 5:39**
and what sort of **p** this woman is **Lk 7:39** *4217*
opened the eyes of a **p** born blind. **Jn 9:32** *5185*
was not a needy **p** among them, **Ac 4:34** *5100*
who WILL RENDER TO EACH **P** ACCORDING **Ro 2:6** *1538*
law has jurisdiction over a **p** as long **Ro 7:1** *444*
for with the heart a **p** believes, **Ro 10:10**
Every **p** is to be in subjection to **Ro 13:1** *5590*
One **p** has faith that he may eat all **Ro 14:2**
One **p** regards one day above another, **Ro 14:5**
Each **p** must be fully convinced in **Ro 14:5** *1538*
if he is an immoral **p**, **1Co 5:11** *4205*
but the other **p** is not edified. **1Co 14:17** *2087*
but whenever a **p** turns to the Lord, **2Co 3:16**
is acceptable according to what *a* **p** **2Co 8:12**
Let such a **p** consider this, that **2Co 10:11** *5108*
or impure **p** or covetous man, **Eph 5:5** *169*
how you should respond to each **p**. **Col 4:6** *1520*
in **p**, not in spirit **1Th 2:17** *4383*
take special note of that **p** and do **2Th 3:14** *3778*
law is not made for a righteous **p**, **1Tm 1:9** *1342*
since I am such a **p** as Paul, **Phm 1:9** *5108*
I have sent him back to you in **p**, **Phm 1:12** *846*
no immoral or godless **p** like Esau, **Heb 12:16** *952*
forgotten what kind of **p** he was. **Jas 1:24** *3697*
seeking to know what **p** or time the **1Pe 1:11** *5101*
the sake of conscience toward God a **p** **1Pe 2:19** *5100*
it be the hidden **p** of the heart, **1Pe 3:4** *444*

PERSONAL
sight and became his **p** servant; **Gn 39:4** 8334
were to enter the king's **p** service. **Da 1:5** 6440
they entered the king's **p** service. **Da 1:19** 6440
soldier of those who were his **p** **Ac 10:7** *4342*
his **p** presence is unimpressive and **2Co 10:10** *4983*
look out for your own **p** interests, **Php 2:4** *1538*
with *an attitude of* **p** favoritism. **Jas 2:1** *4382*

PERSONALLY
And He **p** brought you from Egypt by **Dt 4:37** 6440
and that you **p** go into battle. **2Sa 17:11** 6440
"But I **p** have heard about you, **Da 5:16** 576
those who have not **p** seen my face, **Col 2:1** *4561*
you and **p** drag you into court? **Jas 2:6** *846*

PERSONS
and the **p** which they had acquired **Gn 12:5** 5315
she bore to Jacob these sixteen **p**. **Gn 46:18** 5315
there were fourteen **p** in all. **Gn 46:22** 5315
there were seven **p** in all. **Gn 46:25** 5315
All the **p** belonging to Jacob, who **Gn 46:26** 5315
sons, *were* sixty-six **p** in all, **Gn 46:26** 5315
all the **p** of the house of Jacob, **Gn 46:27** 5315
All the **p** who came from the **Ex 1:5** 5315
to the number of **p** *in them;* **Ex 12:4** 5315
according to the number of **p** **Ex 16:16** 5315
You shall speak to all the skillful **p** **Ex 28:3** 2450, 3820
those **p** who do *so* shall be cut off **Lv 18:29** 5315
according to your valuation of **p** **Lv 27:2** 5315
and on the **p** who were there, **Nu 19:18** 5315
one in five hundred of the **p** and **Nu 31:28** 120
drawn out of every fifty of the **p**, **Nu 31:30** 120
intimately, all the **p** were 32,000. **Nu 31:35** 5315
from whom the LORD's levy was 32 **p**. **Nu 31:40** 5315
down to Egypt seventy **p** *in all,* **Dt 10:22** 5315
its cities and all the **p** who *were* in it **Jos 10:37** 5315
not leave to Jeroboam any **p** alive, **1Ki 15:29** 5397
Now the king's sons, seventy **p**, **2Ki 10:6** 376
and slaughtered *them,* seventy **p**, **2Ki 10:7** 376
Then *certain* **p** went and told **1Ch 19:5**
832 **p** from Jerusalem; **Jer 52:29** 5315
there were 4,600 **p** in all. **Jer 52:30** 5315
and make veils for the heads of **p** **Ezk 13:18**
there are more than 120,000 **p** who **Jon 4:11** 120
p who need no repentance. **Lk 15:7** *1342*
and twenty **p** was there together), **Ac 1:15** *3686*
come to him, seventy-five **p** *in all.* **Ac 7:14** *5590*
were two hundred and seventy-six **p**. **Ac 27:37** *5590*
and receiving in their own **p** the due **Ro 1:27** *1438*
God who works all things in all **p**. **1Co 12:6**
that thanks may be given by many **p** **2Co 1:11** *4383*
such **p** *we are* also in deed when **2Co 10:11** *5108*
Now such **p** we command and exhort **2Th 3:12** *5108*
in which a few, that is, eight **p**, **1Pe 3:20** *5590*
certain **p** have crept in unnoticed, **Jude 1:4** *444*
ungodly **p** who turn the grace of **Jude 1:4** *765*
immoral **p** and sorcerers and idolaters **Rv 21:8** *4205*
and the sorcerers and the immoral **p** **Rv 22:15** *4205*

PERSUADE
all the people came to **p** David to **2Sa 3:35**
and trying to **p** Jews and Greeks. **Ac 18:4** *3982*
will **p** me to become a Christian." **Ac 26:28** *3982*
trying to **p** them concerning Jesus, **Ac 28:23** *3982*
the fear of the Lord, we **p** men, **2Co 5:11** *3982*

PERSUADED
she **p** him to ask her father for a **Jos 15:18** 5496
that she **p** him to ask her father **Jg 1:14** 5496
David **p** his men with *these* **1Sa 24:7** 8156
woman, and she **p** him to eat food. **2Ki 4:8** 2388
By forbearance a ruler may be **p**, **Pr 25:15** 6601b
p the crowds to ask for Barabbas **Mt 27:20** *3982*
they will not be **p** even if someone **Lk 16:31** *3982*
were **p** and joined Paul and Silas, **Ac 17:4** *3982*
this Paul has **p** and turned away a **Ac 19:26** *3982*
And since he would not be **p**, **Ac 21:14** *3982*
since I am **p** that none of these **Ac 26:26** *3982*
centurion was more **p** by the pilot **Ac 27:11** *3982*
were being **p** by the things spoken, **Ac 28:24** *3982*

PERSUADES
"This man **p** men to worship God **Ac 18:13** *374a*

PERSUADING
p *them* about the kingdom of God. **Ac 19:8** *3982*

PERSUASION
This **p** *did* not *come* from Him who **Ga 5:8** *3988*

PERSUASIONS
With her many **p** she entices him; **Pr 7:21** 3948

PERSUASIVE
were not in **p** words of wisdom, **1Co 2:4** *3981*
will delude you with **p** argument. **Col 2:4** *4086*

PERSUASIVENESS
sweetness of speech increases **p**. **Pr 16:21** 3948
his mouth And adds **p** to his lips. **Pr 16:23** 3948

PERTAINING
contribution **p** to all the holy *gifts* **Nu 5:9**
for boasting in things **p** to God. **Ro 15:17** *4314*
high priest in things **p** to God, **Heb 2:17** *4314*
behalf of men in things **p** to God, **Heb 5:1** *4314*
everything **p** to life and godliness, **2Pe 1:3** *4314*

PERTAINS
in all that **p** to the LORD, **2Ch 19:11** 1697
Judah, in all that **p** to the king. **2Ch 19:11** 1697
vision **p** to the time of the end." **Da 8:17**
for *it* **p** to the appointed time of **Da 8:19**
it **p** to many days *in the future.*" **Da 8:26**
vision **p** to the days yet *future.*" **Da 10:14**
boast of what **p** to my weakness. **2Co 11:30**

PERUDA
of Hassophereth, the sons of **P**, **Ezr 2:55** 6514

PERVERSE
are a **p** and crooked generation. **Dt 32:5** 6141
For they are a **p** generation, Sons **Dt 32:20** 8419
"You son of a **p**, rebellious woman! **1Sa 20:30** 5753a
A **p** heart shall depart from me; **Ps 101:4** 6141
From the man who speaks **p** things; **Pr 2:12** 8419
Is the one who walks with a **p** mouth, **Pr 6:12** 6143
The **p** in heart are an abomination **Pr 11:20** 6141
one of **p** mind will be despised. **Pr 12:8** 5753a
A **p** man spreads strife, And a **Pr 16:28** 8419
eyes *does so* to devise **p** things; **Pr 16:30** 8419
who is **p** in speech and is a fool. **Pr 19:1** 6141
snares are in the way of the **p**; **Pr 22:5** 6141
And your mind will utter **p** things. **Pr 23:33** 8419
"Be saved from this **p** generation!" **Ac 2:40** *4646*
men will arise, speaking **p** things, **Ac 20:30** *1294*
of a crooked and **p** generation, **Php 2:15** *1294*
be rescued from **p** and evil men; **2Th 3:2** *824*

PERVERSION
an animal to mate with it; it is a **p**. **Lv 18:23** 8397
But **p** in it crushes the spirit. **Pr 15:4** 5558
blood and the city is full of **p**; **Ezk 9:9** 4297

PERVERSITY
And rejoice in the **p** of evil; **Pr 2:14** 8419
Who *with* **p** in his heart continually **Pr 6:14** 8419

PERVERT
a multitude in order to **p** *justice;* **Ex 23:2** 5186
"You shall not **p** the justice *due* **Ex 23:6** 5186
"You shall not **p** the justice due **Dt 24:17** 5186
"Does God **p** justice? Or does the **Jb 8:3** 5791
does the Almighty **p** what is right? **Jb 8:3** 5791
the Almighty will not **p** justice. **Jb 34:12** 5791
bosom To **p** the ways of justice. **Pr 17:23** 5186
And **p** the rights of all the afflicted. **Pr 31:5** 8132

PERVERTED
and took bribes and **p** justice. **1Sa 8:3** 5186
with the **p** You show Yourself **2Sa 22:27** 6141
'I have sinned and **p** what is right, **Jb 33:27** 5753a
is nothing crooked or **p** in them. **Pr 8:8** 6141
evil way And the **p** mouth, I hate. **Pr 8:13** 8419
But the **p** tongue will be cut out. **Pr 10:31** 8419
mouth of the wicked what is **p**. **Pr 10:32** 8419
And he who is **p** in his language **Pr 17:20** 2015
Because they have **p** their way, **Jer 3:21** 5753a
p the words of the living God, **Jer 23:36** 2015
Therefore justice comes out **p**. **Hab 1:4** 6127
"You unbelieving and **p** generation, **Mt 17:17** *1294*
"You unbelieving and **p** generation, **Lk 9:41** *1294*
such a man is **p** and is sinning, **Ti 3:11** *1612*

PERVERTS
and **p** the words of the righteous. **Dt 16:19** 5557
who **p** his ways will be found out. **Pr 10:9** 6140

PEST
For we have found this man a real **p** **Ac 24:5** *3061*

PESTILENCE
otherwise He will fall upon us with **p** or **Ex 5:3** 1698
LORD will come *with* a very severe **p** **Ex 9:3** 1698
struck you and your people with **p**, **Ex 9:15** 1698
cities, I will send **p** among you, **Lv 26:25** 1698
"I will smite them with **p** and **Nu 14:12** 1698
"The LORD will make the **p** cling **Dt 28:21** 1698
be three days' **p** in your land? **2Sa 24:13** 1698
So the LORD sent a **p** upon Israel **2Sa 24:15** 1698
famine in the land, if there is **p**, **1Ki 8:37** 1698
of the LORD, even **p** in the land, **1Ch 21:12** 1698
So the LORD sent a **p** on Israel; **1Ch 21:14** 1698
famine in the land, if there is **p**, **2Ch 6:28** 1698
or if I send **p** among My people, **2Ch 7:13** 1698
us, the sword, *or* judgment, or **p**, **2Ch 20:9** 1698
trapper And from the deadly **p**. **Ps 91:3** 1698
Of the **p** that stalks in darkness, **Ps 91:6** 1698
them by the sword, famine and **p**." **Jer 14:12** 1698
they will die of a great **p**. **Jer 21:6** 1698
survive in this city from the **p**, **Jer 21:7** 1698
the sword and by famine and by **p**; **Jer 21:9** 1698
the sword, the famine and the **p** **Jer 24:10** 1698
sword, with famine and with **p**," **Jer 27:8** 1698
by the sword, famine and **p**, **Jer 27:13** 1698
of war and of calamity and of **p**. **Jer 28:8** 1698
them the sword, famine and **p**, **Jer 29:17** 1698
the sword, with famine and with **p**; **Jer 29:18** 1698
the sword, the famine and the **p**; **Jer 32:24** 1698
by sword, by famine and by **p**.' **Jer 32:36** 1698
'to the sword, to the **p** and **Jer 34:17** 1698
the sword and by famine and by **p**, **Jer 38:2** 1698
by the sword, by famine and by **p**; **Jer 42:17** 1698
by the sword, by famine and by **p**, **Jer 42:22** 1698
sword, with famine and with **p**. **Jer 44:13** 1698
the sword, the famine and the **p** **Ezk 12:16** 1698
"For I will send **p** to her And **Ezk 28:23** 1698
and in the caves will die of **p**. **Ezk 33:27** 1698
"With **p** and with blood I **Ezk 38:22** 1698
Before Him goes **p**, And plague **Hab 3:5** 1698
I will kill her children with **p**, **Rv 2:23** *2288*
sword and with famine and with **p** **Rv 6:8** *2288*
come, **p** and mourning and famine, **Rv 18:8** *2288*

PESTLE
with a **p** along with crushed grain, **Pr 27:22** 5940

PETER
brothers, Simon who was called **P**, **Mt 4:18** *4074*
The first, Simon, who is called **P**, **Mt 10:2** *4074*
P said to Him, **Mt 14:28** *4074*
And **P** got out of the boat, and **Mt 14:29** *4074*
P said to Him, **Mt 15:15** *4074*
Simon **P** answered, **Mt 16:16** *4074*
I also say to you that you are **P**, **Mt 16:18** *4074*
P took Him aside and began to **Mt 16:22** *4074*
But He turned and said to **P**, **Mt 16:23** *4074*
Jesus took with Him **P** and James **Mt 17:1** *4074*
P said to Jesus, **Mt 17:4** *4074*
the two-drachma *tax* came to **P** and **Mt 17:24** *4074*
When **P** said, "From strangers," **Mt 17:26**
Then **P** came and said to Him, **Mt 18:21** *4074*
Then **P** said to Him, **Mt 19:27** *4074*
But **P** said to Him, **Mt 26:33** *4074*
P said to Him, "Even if I have to **Mt 26:35** *4074*
He took with Him **P** and the two **Mt 26:37** *4074*
them sleeping, and said to **P**, **Mt 26:40** *4074*
But **P** was following Him at a **Mt 26:58** *4074*
Now **P** was sitting outside in the **Mt 26:69** *4074*
bystanders came up and said to **P**, **Mt 26:73** *4074*
And **P** remembered the word which **Mt 26:75** *4074*
Simon (to whom He gave the name **P**), **Mk 3:16** *4074*
except **P** and James and John the **Mk 5:37** *4074*
P answered and said to Him, **Mk 8:29** *4074*
And **P** took Him aside and began to **Mk 8:32** *4074*
His disciples, He rebuked **P** and **Mk 8:33** *4074*
with Him **P** and James and John, **Mk 9:2** *4074*
P said to Jesus, **Mk 9:5** *4074*
P began to say to Him, **Mk 10:28** *4074*
Being reminded, **P** said to Him, **Mk 11:21** *4074*
P and James and John and Andrew **Mk 13:3** *4074*
But **P** said to Him, **Mk 14:29** *4074*
But **P** kept saying insistently, **Mk 14:31**
with Him **P** and James and John, **Mk 14:33** *4074*
them sleeping, and said to **P**, **Mk 14:37** *4074*
P had followed Him at a **Mk 14:54** *4074*
As **P** was below in the courtyard, **Mk 14:66** *4074*
and seeing **P** warming himself, she **Mk 14:67** *4074*
bystanders were again saying to **P**, **Mk 14:70** *4074*
And **P** remembered how Jesus had **Mk 14:72** *4074*
"But go, tell His disciples and **P**, **Mk 16:7** *4074*
reported all these instructions to **P** **Mk 16:20**
But when Simon **P** saw *that,* he fell **Lk 5:8** *4074*
Simon, whom He also named **P**, **Lk 6:14** *4074*
they were all denying it, **P** said, **Lk 8:45** *4074*
Him, except **P** and John and James, **Lk 8:51** *4074*

And **P** answered and said,	**Lk 9:20**	*4074*
took along **P** and John and James,	**Lk 9:28**	*4074*
Now **P** and his companions had been	**Lk 9:32**	*4074*
leaving Him, **P** said to Jesus,	**Lk 9:33**	*4074*
P said, "Lord, are You addressing	**Lk 12:41**	*4074*
P said, "Behold, we have left our	**Lk 18:28**	*4074*
And Jesus sent **P** and John, saying,	**Lk 22:8**	*4074*
"I say to you, **P**, the rooster will	**Lk 22:34**	*4074*
but **P** was following at a distance.	**Lk 22:54**	*4074*
P was sitting among them.	**Lk 22:55**	*4074*
But **P** said, "Man, I am not!"	**Lk 22:58**	*4074*
P said, "Man, I do not know what	**Lk 22:60**	*4074*
The Lord turned and looked at **P**.	**Lk 22:61**	*4074*
And **P** remembered the word of the	**Lk 22:61**	*4074*
But **P** got up and ran to the tomb;	**Lk 24:12**	*4074*
Cephas" (which is translated **P**).	**Jn 1:42**	*4074*
of the city of Andrew and **P**.	**Jn 1:44**	*4074*
Simon **P** answered Him,	**Jn 6:68**	*4074*
So He came to Simon **P**.	**Jn 13:6**	*4074*
P said to Him, "Never shall You	**Jn 13:8**	*4074*
Simon **P** said to Him,	**Jn 13:9**	*4074*
Simon **P** gestured to him,	**Jn 13:24**	*4074*
Simon **P** said to Him,	**Jn 13:36**	*4074*
P said to Him, "Lord, why can I not	**Jn 13:37**	*4074*
Simon **P** then, having a sword,	**Jn 18:10**	*4074*
Jesus said to **P**,	**Jn 18:11**	*4074*
Simon **P** was following Jesus,	**Jn 18:15**	*4074*
but **P** was standing at the door	**Jn 18:16**	*4074*
the doorkeeper, and brought **P** in.	**Jn 18:16**	*4074*
who kept the door said to **P**,	**Jn 18:17**	*4074*
and **P** was also with them, standing	**Jn 18:18**	*4074*
Now Simon **P** was standing and	**Jn 18:25**	*4074*
of the one whose ear **P** cut off,	**Jn 18:26**	*4074*
P then denied *it* again	**Jn 18:27**	*4074*
So she ran and came to Simon **P**	**Jn 20:2**	*4074*
So **P** and the other disciple went forth,	**Jn 20:3**	*4074*
disciple ran ahead faster than **P** and	**Jn 20:4**	*4074*
Simon **P** also came,	**Jn 20:6**	*4074*
Simon **P**, and Thomas called Didymus,	**Jn 21:2**	*4074*
Simon **P** said to them,	**Jn 21:3**	*4074*
whom Jesus loved said to **P**,	**Jn 21:7**	*4074*
P heard that it was the Lord,	**Jn 21:7**	*4074*
Simon **P** went up and drew the net	**Jn 21:11**	*4074*
breakfast, Jesus said to Simon **P**,	**Jn 21:15**	*4074*
P was grieved because He said to	**Jn 21:17**	*4074*
P, turning around, saw the	**Jn 21:20**	*4074*
P seeing him said to	**Jn 21:21**	*4074*
P and John and James and Andrew,	**Ac 1:13**	*4074*
At this time **P** stood up in the	**Ac 1:15**	*4074*
But **P**, taking his stand with the	**Ac 2:14**	*4074*
to **P** and the rest of the apostles,	**Ac 2:37**	*4074*
P *said* to them,	**Ac 2:38**	*4074*
Now **P** and John were going up to	**Ac 3:1**	*4074*
When he saw **P** and John about	**Ac 3:3**	*4074*
But **P**, along with John, fixed his	**Ac 3:4**	*4074*
But **P** said, "I do not possess silver	**Ac 3:6**	*4074*
he was clinging to **P** and John,	**Ac 3:11**	*4074*
But when **P** saw *this,* he replied to	**Ac 3:12**	*4074*
Then **P**, filled with the Holy Spirit,	**Ac 4:8**	*4074*
the confidence of **P** and John and	**Ac 4:13**	*4074*
But **P** and John answered and said	**Ac 4:19**	*4074*
P said, "Ananias, why has Satan	**Ac 5:3**	*4074*
And **P** responded to her,	**Ac 5:8**	*4074*
Then **P** *said* to her,	**Ac 5:9**	*4074*
pallets, so that when **P** came by at	**Ac 5:15**	*4074*
But **P** and the apostles answered	**Ac 5:29**	*4074*
of God, they sent them **P** and John,	**Ac 8:14**	*4074*
But **P** said to him,	**Ac 8:20**	*4074*
as **P** was traveling through all *those*	**Ac 9:32**	*4074*
P said to him,	**Ac 9:34**	*4074*
having heard that **P** was there,	**Ac 9:38**	*4074*
So **P** arose and went with them.	**Ac 9:39**	*4074*
But **P** sent them all out and knelt	**Ac 9:40**	*4074*
her eyes, and when she saw **P**,	**Ac 9:40**	*4074*
And **P** stayed many days in Joppa with	**Ac 9:43**	*4074*
named Simon, who is also called **P**;	**Ac 10:5**	*4074*
P went up on the housetop about	**Ac 10:9**	*4074*
"Get up, **P**, kill and eat!"	**Ac 10:13**	*4074*
But **P** said, "By no means, Lord, for	**Ac 10:14**	*4074*
Now while **P** was greatly perplexed	**Ac 10:17**	*4074*
Simon, who was also called **P**,	**Ac 10:18**	*4074*
P was reflecting on the vision,	**Ac 10:19**	*4074*
P went down to the men and said,	**Ac 10:21**	*4074*
When **P** entered, Cornelius met him,	**Ac 10:25**	*4074*
But **P** raised him up, saying,	**Ac 10:26**	*4074*
Simon, who is also called **P**,	**Ac 10:32**	*4074*
Opening his mouth, **P** said:	**Ac 10:34**	*4074*
While **P** was still speaking these	**Ac 10:44**	*4074*
who came with **P** were amazed,	**Ac 10:45**	*4074*
Then **P** answered,	**Ac 10:46**	*4074*
And when **P** came up to Jerusalem,	**Ac 11:2**	*4074*
But **P** began *speaking* and *proceeded*	**Ac 11:4**	*4074*
a voice saying to me, 'Get up, **P**;	**Ac 11:7**	*4074*
have Simon, who is also called **P**,	**Ac 11:13**	*4074*
he proceeded to arrest **P** also.	**Ac 12:3**	*4074*
So **P** was kept in the prison, but	**Ac 12:5**	*4074*
P was sleeping between two soldiers	**Ac 12:6**	*4074*
When **P** came to himself, he	**Ac 12:11**	*4074*
P was standing in front of the gate.	**Ac 12:14**	*4074*
But **P** continued knocking;	**Ac 12:16**	*4074*
as to what could have become of **P**.	**Ac 12:18**	*4074*
P stood up and said to them,	**Ac 15:7**	*4074*
as **P** *had been* to the circumcised	**Ga 2:7**	*4074*
(for He who effectually worked for **P**	**Ga 2:8**	*4074*
P, an apostle of Jesus Christ, To	**1Pe 1:1**	*4074*
Simon **P**, a bond-servant and	**2Pe 1:1**	*4074*
PETER'S		
When Jesus came into **P** home,	**Mt 8:14**	*4074*
Him, was Andrew, Simon **P** brother.	**Jn 1:40**	*4074*
Andrew, Simon **P** brother,	**Jn 6:8**	*4074*
he struck **P** side and woke him	**Ac 12:7**	*4074*
When she recognized **P** voice,	**Ac 12:14**	*4074*
PETHAHIAH		
the nineteenth for **P**,	**1Ch 24:16**	6611
P, Judah and Eliezer.	**Ezr 10:23**	6611
Hodiah, Shebaniah *and* **P**,	**Ne 9:5**	6611
P the son of Meshezabel, of	**Ne 11:24**	6611
PETHOR		
to Balaam the son of Beor, at **P**,	**Nu 22:5**	6604a
son of Beor from **P** of Mesopotamia,	**Dt 23:4**	6604a
PETHUEL		
that came to Joel, the son of **P**:	**Jl 1:1**	6602
PETITION		
may the God of Israel grant your **p**	**1Sa 1:17**	7596
and the LORD has given me my **p**	**1Sa 1:27**	7596
serve them and grant them their **p**,	**1Ki 12:7**	6030a
"What is your **p**, for it shall be	**Es 5:6**	7596
"My **p** and my request is:	**Es 5:7**	7596
grant my **p** and do what I request,	**Es 5:8**	7596
"What is your **p**, Queen Esther?	**Es 7:2**	7596
let my life be given me as my **p**,	**Es 7:3**	7596
Now what is your **p**?	**Es 9:12**	7596
please let my **p** come before you and	**Jer 37:20**	8467
presenting my **p** before the king,	**Jer 38:26**	8467
"Please let our **p** come before	**Jer 42:2**	8467
me to present your **p** before Him:	**Jer 42:9**	8467
a **p** to any god or man besides you,	**Da 6:7**	1159
and found Daniel making **p** and	**Da 6:11**	1156
a **p** to any god or man besides you,	**Da 6:12**	1156
making his **p** three times a day."	**Da 6:13**	1159
for your **p** has been heard,	**Lk 1:13**	*1162*
With all prayer and **p** pray at all	**Eph 6:18**	*1162*
and **p** for all the saints,	**Eph 6:18**	*1162*
PETITIONS		
May the LORD fulfill all your **p**.	**Ps 20:5**	4862
and prayers, **p** *and* thanksgivings,	**1Tm 2:1**	*1783*
PEULLETHAI		
the seventh *and* **P** the eighth;	**1Ch 26:5**	6469
PHANTOM		
every man walks about as a **p**;	**Ps 39:6**	6754
PHANUEL		
Anna the daughter of **P**,	**Lk 2:36**	*5323*
PHARAOH		
saw her and praised her to **P**;	**Gn 12:15**	6547
But the LORD struck **P** and his	**Gn 12:17**	6547
Then **P** called Abram and said,	**Gn 12:18**	6547
P commanded *his* men concerning	**Gn 12:20**	6547
an Egyptian officer of **P**,	**Gn 39:1**	6547
P was furious with his two	**Gn 40:2**	6547
P will lift up your head and restore	**Gn 40:13**	6547
a kindness by mentioning me to **P** and	**Gn 40:14**	6547
of all sorts of baked food for **P**,	**Gn 40:17**	6547
within three more days **P** will lift	**Gn 40:19**	6547
two full years that **P** had a dream,	**Gn 41:1**	6547
sleek and fat cows. Then **P** awoke.	**Gn 41:4**	6547
Then **P** awoke, and behold, *it was* a	**Gn 41:7**	6547
And **P** told them his dreams, but	**Gn 41:8**	6547
one who could interpret them to **P**.	**Gn 41:8**	6547
the chief cupbearer spoke to **P**,	**Gn 41:9**	6547
"**P** was furious with his servants,	**Gn 41:10**	6547
Then **P** sent and called for Joseph,	**Gn 41:14**	6547
changed his clothes, he came to **P**.	**Gn 41:14**	6547
P said to Joseph,	**Gn 41:15**	6547
Joseph then answered **P**,	**Gn 41:16**	6547
God will give **P** a favorable answer.	**Gn 41:16**	6547
So **P** spoke to Joseph,	**Gn 41:17**	6547
Now Joseph said to **P**,	**Gn 41:25**	6547
told to **P** what He is about to do.	**Gn 41:25**	6547
"It is as I have spoken to **P**:	**Gn 41:28**	6547
shown to **P** what He is about to do.	**Gn 41:28**	6547
repeating of the dream to **P** twice,	**Gn 41:32**	6547
"Now let **P** look for a man	**Gn 41:33**	6547
"Let **P** take action to appoint	**Gn 41:34**	6547
good to **P** and to all his servants.	**Gn 41:37**	6547
Then **P** said to his servants,	**Gn 41:38**	6547
So **P** said to Joseph,	**Gn 41:39**	6547
P said to Joseph,	**Gn 41:41**	6547
Then **P** took off his signet ring	**Gn 41:42**	6547
Moreover, **P** said to Joseph,	**Gn 41:44**	6547
"*Though* I am **P**, yet without your	**Gn 41:44**	6547
P named Joseph Zaphenath-paneah;	**Gn 41:45**	6547
years old when he stood before **P**,	**Gn 41:46**	6547
went out from the presence of **P** and	**Gn 41:46**	6547
people cried out to **P** for bread;	**Gn 41:55**	6547
and **P** said to all the Egyptians,	**Gn 41:55**	6547
by the life of **P**, you shall not go	**Gn 42:15**	6547
But if not, by the life of **P**,	**Gn 42:16**	6547
for you are equal to **P**.	**Gn 44:18**	6547
the household of **P** heard *of it.*	**Gn 45:2**	6547
and He has made me a father to **P**	**Gn 45:8**	6547
it pleased **P** and his servants.	**Gn 45:16**	6547
Then **P** said to Joseph,	**Gn 45:17**	6547
according to the command of **P**,	**Gn 45:21**	6547
which **P** had sent to carry him.	**Gn 46:5**	6547
"I will go up and tell **P**,	**Gn 46:31**	6547
"When **P** calls you and says,	**Gn 46:33**	6547
Then Joseph went in and told **P**,	**Gn 47:1**	6547
brothers and presented them to **P**.	**Gn 47:2**	6547
Then **P** said to his brothers,	**Gn 47:3**	6547
So they said to **P**,	**Gn 47:3**	6547
They said to **P**,	**Gn 47:4**	6547
Then **P** said to Joseph,	**Gn 47:5**	6547
Jacob and presented him to **P**;	**Gn 47:7**	6547
and Jacob blessed **P**.	**Gn 47:7**	6547
P said to Jacob,	**Gn 47:8**	6547
So Jacob said to **P**,	**Gn 47:9**	6547
And Jacob blessed **P**,	**Gn 47:10**	6547
land of Rameses, as **P** had ordered.	**Gn 47:11**	6547
and our land will be slaves to **P**.	**Gn 47:19**	6547
all the land of Egypt for **P**,	**Gn 47:20**	6547
priests had an allotment from **P**,	**Gn 47:22**	6547
the allotment which **P** gave them.	**Gn 47:22**	6547
bought you and your land for **P**;	**Gn 47:23**	6547
you shall give a fifth to **P**,	**Gn 47:24**	6547
day, that **P** should have the fifth;	**Gn 47:26**	6547
spoke to the household of **P**,	**Gn 50:4**	6547
in your sight, please speak to **P**,	**Gn 50:4**	6547
P said, "Go up and bury your father,	**Gn 50:6**	6547
him went up all the servants of **P**,	**Gn 50:7**	6547
they built for **P** storage cities,	**Ex 1:11**	6547
The midwives said to **P**,	**Ex 1:19**	6547
Then **P** commanded all his people,	**Ex 1:22**	6547
The daughter of **P** came down	**Ex 2:5**	6547
When **P** heard of this matter, he	**Ex 2:15**	6547
Moses fled from the presence of **P**	**Ex 2:15**	6547
now, and I will send you to **P**,	**Ex 3:10**	6547
"Who am I, that I should go to **P**,	**Ex 3:11**	6547
perform before **P** all the wonders	**Ex 4:21**	6547
"Then you shall say to **P**,	**Ex 4:22**	6547
and Aaron came and said to **P**,	**Ex 5:1**	6547
But **P** said, "Who is the LORD that	**Ex 5:2**	6547
Again **P** said, "Look, the people of	**Ex 5:5**	6547
So the same day **P** commanded the	**Ex 5:6**	6547
Thus says **P**, 'I am not going to give	**Ex 5:10**	6547
of Israel came and cried out to **P**,	**Ex 5:15**	6547
I came to **P** to speak in Your name,	**Ex 5:23**	6547
you shall see what I will do to **P**;	**Ex 6:1**	6547
tell **P** king of Egypt to let the	**Ex 6:11**	6547
how then will **P** listen to me, for	**Ex 6:12**	6547
of Israel and to **P** king of Egypt,	**Ex 6:13**	6547
They were the ones who spoke to **P**	**Ex 6:27**	6547
speak to **P** king of Egypt all that	**Ex 6:29**	6547
how then will **P** listen to me?"	**Ex 6:30**	6547
"See, I make you *as* God to **P**,	**Ex 7:1**	6547
your brother Aaron shall speak to **P**	**Ex 7:2**	6547
"When **P** does not listen to you,	**Ex 7:4**	6547
eighty-three, when they spoke to **P**.	**Ex 7:7**	6547
"When **P** speaks to you, saying,	**Ex 7:9**	6547
staff and throw *it* down before **P**,	**Ex 7:9**	6547
So Moses and Aaron came to **P**,	**Ex 7:10**	6547
Aaron threw his staff down before **P**	**Ex 7:10**	6547
Then **P** also called for *the* wise	**Ex 7:11**	6547
"Go to **P** in the morning as he is	**Ex 7:15**	6547
in the sight of **P** and in the sight	**Ex 7:20**	6547
Then **P** turned and went into his	**Ex 7:23**	6547
"Go to **P** and say to him,	**Ex 8:1**	6547
Then **P** called for Moses and Aaron	**Ex 8:8**	6547
Moses said to **P**,	**Ex 8:9**	6547
Moses and Aaron went out from **P**,	**Ex 8:12**	6547
which He had inflicted upon **P**.	**Ex 8:12**	6547
when **P** saw that there was relief,	**Ex 8:15**	6547
Then the magicians said to **P**,	**Ex 8:19**	6547
and present yourself before **P**,	**Ex 8:20**	6547
swarms of insects into the house of **P**	**Ex 8:24**	6547
P called for Moses and Aaron	**Ex 8:25**	6547
P said, "I will let you go,	**Ex 8:28**	6547
of insects may depart from **P**,	**Ex 8:29**	6547
only do not let **P** deal deceitfully	**Ex 8:29**	6547
So Moses went out from **P** and made	**Ex 8:30**	6547
the swarms of insects from **P**,	**Ex 8:31**	6547
But **P** hardened his heart this time	**Ex 8:32**	6547
"Go to **P** and speak to him,	**Ex 9:1**	6547
P sent, and behold, there was	**Ex 9:7**	6547
But the heart of **P** was hardened,	**Ex 9:7**	6547
toward the sky in the sight of **P**.	**Ex 9:8**	6547
from a kiln, and stood before **P**;	**Ex 9:10**	6547
and stand before **P** and say to him,	**Ex 9:13**	6547
The one among the servants of **P**	**Ex 9:20**	6547
Then **P** sent for Moses and Aaron,	**Ex 9:27**	6547
Moses went out of the city from **P**,	**Ex 9:33**	6547
But when **P** saw that the rain and	**Ex 9:34**	6547
"Go to **P**, for I have hardened his	**Ex 10:1**	6547
Aaron went to **P** and said to him,	**Ex 10:3**	6547
And he turned and went out from **P**.	**Ex 10:6**	6547
and Aaron were brought back to **P**,	**Ex 10:8**	6547
Then **P** hurriedly called for Moses	**Ex 10:16**	6547
He went out from **P** and made	**Ex 10:18**	6547
Then **P** called to Moses, and said,	**Ex 10:24**	6547
Then **P** said to him,	**Ex 10:28**	6547
"One more plague I will bring on **P**	**Ex 11:1**	6547
from the firstborn of the **P** who sits	**Ex 11:5**	6547
he went out from **P** in hot anger.	**Ex 11:8**	6547
"**P** will not listen to you, so	**Ex 11:9**	6547
all these wonders before **P**;	**Ex 11:10**	6547
from the firstborn of **P** who sat	**Ex 12:29**	6547
P arose in the night, he and	**Ex 12:30**	6547
when **P** was stubborn about letting	**Ex 13:15**	6547
when **P** had let the people go,	**Ex 13:17**	6547
"For **P** will say of the sons of	**Ex 14:3**	6547
I will be honored through **P** and all	**Ex 14:4**	6547
P and his servants had a change of	**Ex 14:5**	6547
The LORD hardened the heart of **P**,	**Ex 14:8**	6547
all the horses *and* chariots of **P**,	**Ex 14:9**	6547
As **P** drew near, the sons of	**Ex 14:10**	6547
through **P** and all his army,	**Ex 14:17**	6547
LORD, when I am honored through **P**,	**Ex 14:18**	6547
For the horses of **P** with his	**Ex 15:19**	6547
delivered me from the sword of **P**."	**Ex 18:4**	6547
all that the LORD had done to **P** and	**Ex 18:8**	6547
Egyptians and from the hand of **P**,	**Ex 18:10**	6547
'We were slaves to **P** in Egypt,	**Dt 6:21**	6547
Egypt, **P** and all his household;	**Dt 6:22**	6547
from the hand of **P** king of Egypt.	**Dt 7:8**	6547
God did to **P** and to all Egypt:	**Dt 7:18**	6547
He did in the midst of Egypt to **P**	**Dt 11:3**	6547

to **P** and all his servants and all his **Dt 29:2** 6547
in the land of Egypt against **P**, **Dt 34:11** 6547
and **P** hardened their hearts? **1Sa 6:6** 6547
alliance with **P** king of Egypt, **1Ki 3:1** 6547
For **P** king of Egypt had gone up **1Ki 9:16** 6547
along with the daughter of **P**: **1Ki 11:1** 6547
came to Egypt, to **P** king of Egypt, **1Ki 11:18** 6547
Hadad found great favor before **P**, **1Ki 11:19** 6547
house among the sons of **P**. **1Ki 11:20** 6547
army was dead, Hadad said to **P**, **1Ki 11:21** 6547
Then **P** said to him, **1Ki 11:22** 6547
of Egypt from under the hand of **P**, **2Ki 17:7** 6547
So is **P** king of Egypt to all who **2Ki 18:21** 6547
In his days **P** Neco king of Egypt **2Ki 23:29** 6549
and when **P** *Neco* saw him he killed **2Ki 23:29**
P Neco imprisoned him at **2Ki 23:33** 6549
P Neco made Eliakim the son of **2Ki 23:34** 6549
gave the silver and gold to **P**, **2Ki 23:35** 6547
the money at the command of **P**. **2Ki 23:35** 6547
valuation, to give it to **P** Neco. **2Ki 23:35** 6549
sons of Bithia the daughter of **P**, **1Ch 4:17** 6547
signs and wonders against **P**, **Ne 9:10** 6547
Upon **P** and all his servants. **Ps 135:9** 6547
But He overthrew **P** and his army **Ps 136:15** 6547
My mare among the chariots of **P**. **SS 1:9** 6547
How can you *men* say to **P**, **Is 19:11** 6547
To take refuge in the safety of **P** And **Is 30:2** 6547
safety of **P** will be your shame And **Is 30:3** 6547
So is **P** king of Egypt to all who **Is 36:6** 6547
P king of Egypt, his servants, his **Jer 25:19** 6547
I am going to give over **P** Hophra **Jer 44:30** 6548
the army of **P** Neco king of Egypt, **Jer 46:2** 6549
'**P** king of Egypt *is but* a big **Jer 46:17** 6547
to punish Amon of Thebes, and **P**, **Jer 46:25** 6547
even **P** and those who trust in him. **Jer 46:25** 6547
before **P** conquered Gaza. **Jer 47:1** 6547
'**P** with *his* mighty army and **Ezk 17:17** 6547
of man, set your face against **P** king **Ezk 29:2** 6547
"Behold, I am against you, **P** king **Ezk 29:3** 6547
broken the arm of **P** king of Egypt; **Ezk 30:21** 6547
I am against **P** king of Egypt and **Ezk 30:22** 6547
and I will break the arms of **P**, **Ezk 30:24** 6547
but the arms of **P** will fall. **Ezk 30:25** 6547
of man, say to **P** king of Egypt and **Ezk 31:2** 6547
So is **P** and all his hordes!" **Ezk 31:18** 6547
lamentation over **P** king of Egypt and **Ezk 32:2** 6547
"These **P** will see, and he will be **Ezk 32:31** 6547
sword, *even* **P** and all his army," **Ezk 32:31** 6547
even **P** and all his hordes," **Ezk 32:32** 6547
and wisdom in the sight of **P**, **Ac 7:10** *5328*
Joseph's family was disclosed to **P**. **Ac 7:13** *5328*
For the Scripture says to **P**, **Ro 9:17** *5328*

PHARAOH'S

P officials saw her and **Gn 12:15** 6547
the woman was taken into **P** house. **Gn 12:15** 6547
in Egypt to Potiphar, **P** officer, **Gn 37:36** 6547
He asked **P** officials who were **Gn 40:7** 6547
"Now **P** cup was in my hand; **Gn 40:11** 6547
and squeezed them into **P** cup, **Gn 40:11** 6547
and I put the cup into **P** hand." **Gn 40:11** 6547
and you will put **P** cup into his **Gn 40:13** 6547
third day, *which was* **P** birthday, **Gn 40:20** 6547
and he put the cup into **P** hand; **Gn 40:21** 6547
"**P** dreams are one *and the same;* **Gn 41:25** 6547
in the cities under **P** authority, **Gn 41:35** 6547
the news was heard in **P** house that **Gn 45:16** 6547
brought the money into **P** house. **Gn 47:14** 6547
Thus the land became **P**. **Gn 47:20** 6547
lord, and we will be **P** slaves." **Gn 47:25** 6547
of the priests did not become **P**. **Gn 47:26** 6547
his sister said to **P** daughter, **Ex 2:7** 6547
P daughter said to her, **Ex 2:8** 6547
Then **P** daughter said to her, **Ex 2:9** 6547
and she brought him to **P** daughter and **Ex 2:10** 6547
P taskmasters had set over them, **Ex 5:14** 6547
When they left **P** presence, they **Ex 5:20** 6547
you have made us odious in **P** sight **Ex 5:21** 6547
"But I will harden **P** heart that I **Ex 7:3** 6547
Yet **P** heart was hardened, and he **Ex 7:13** 6547
"**P** heart is stubborn; **Ex 7:14** 6547
and **P** heart was hardened, and he **Ex 7:22** 6547
But **P** heart was hardened, and he **Ex 8:19** 6547
And the LORD hardened **P** heart, **Ex 9:12** 6547
P heart was hardened, and he **Ex 9:35** 6547
P servants said to him, **Ex 10:7** 6547
were driven out from **P** presence. **Ex 10:11** 6547
But the LORD hardened **P** heart, **Ex 10:20** 6547
But the LORD hardened **P** heart, **Ex 10:27** 6547
both in the sight of **P** servants **Ex 11:3** 6547
yet the LORD hardened **P** heart, **Ex 11:10** 6547
"Thus I will harden **P** heart, **Ex 14:4** 6547
up the pursuit, and all **P** horses, **Ex 14:23** 6547
even **P** entire army that had gone **Ex 14:28** 6547
"**P** chariots and his army He has **Ex 15:4** 6547
in Egypt *in bondage* to **P** house? **1Sa 2:27** 6547
and took **P** daughter and brought **1Ki 3:1** 6547
like this hall for **P** daughter, **1Ki 7:8** 6547
As soon as **P** daughter came up from **1Ki 9:24** 6547
whom Tahpenes weaned in **P** house; **1Ki 11:20** 6547
and Genubath was in **P** house among **1Ki 11:20** 6547
Then Solomon brought **P** daughter up **2Ch 8:11** 6547
The advice of **P** wisest advisers **Is 19:11** 6547
P army had set out from Egypt; **Jer 37:5** 6547
P army which has come out for your **Jer 37:7** 6547
from Jerusalem because of **P** army, **Jer 37:11** 6547
entrance of **P** palace in Tahpanhes, **Jer 43:9** 6547
outside, **P** daughter took him away **Ac 7:21** *5328*
be called the son of **P** daughter, **Heb 11:24** *5328*

PHARISAIC

some of the scribes of the **P** party **Ac 23:9** *5330*

PHARISEE

"You blind **P**, first clean the **Mt 23:26** *5330*
P who had invited Him saw this, **Lk 7:39** *5330*
a **P** asked Him to have lunch with **Lk 11:37** *5330*
When the **P** saw it, he was **Lk 11:38** *5330*
into the temple to pray, one a **P** and **Lk 18:10** *5330*
"The **P** stood and was praying this **Lk 18:11** *5330*
But a **P** named Gamaliel, a **Ac 5:34** *5330*
"Brethren, I am a **P**, **Ac 23:6** *5330*
that I lived *as* a **P** according to **Ac 26:5** *5330*
as to the Law, a **P**; **Php 3:5** *5330*

PHARISEE'S

and He entered the **P** house **Lk 7:36** *5330*
at the table in the **P** house, **Lk 7:37** *5330*

PHARISEES

But when he saw many of the **P** and **Mt 3:7** *5330*
surpasses *that* of the scribes and **P**, **Mt 5:20** *5330*
When the **P** saw *this,* they said **Mt 9:11** *5330*
"Why do we and the **P** fast, **Mt 9:14** *5330*
But the **P** were saying, **Mt 9:34** *5330*
But when the **P** saw *this,* they said **Mt 12:2** *5330*
But the **P** went out and conspired **Mt 12:14** *5330*
But when the **P** heard *this,* they **Mt 12:24** *5330*
of the scribes and **P** said to Him, **Mt 12:38** *5330*
Then some **P** and scribes came to **Mt 15:1** *5330*
"Do You know that the **P** were **Mt 15:12** *5330*
The **P** and Sadducees came up, **Mt 16:1** *5330*
leaven of the **P** and Sadducees." **Mt 16:6** *5330*
leaven of the **P** and Sadducees." **Mt 16:11** *5330*
teaching of the **P** and Sadducees. **Mt 16:12** *5330*
Some **P** came to Jesus, testing **Mt 19:3** *5330*
and the **P** heard His parables, **Mt 21:45** *5330*
Then the **P** went and plotted **Mt 22:15** *5330*
But when the **P** heard that Jesus had **Mt 22:34** *5330*
the **P** were gathered together, **Mt 22:41** *5330*
"The scribes and the **P** have **Mt 23:2** *5330*
"But woe to you, scribes and **P**, **Mt 23:13** *5330*
"Woe to you, scribes and **P**, **Mt 23:14** *5330*
"Woe to you, scribes and **P**, **Mt 23:15** *5330*
"Woe to you, scribes and **P**, **Mt 23:23** *5330*
"Woe to you, scribes and **P**, **Mt 23:25** *5330*
"Woe to you, scribes and **P**, **Mt 23:27** *5330*
"Woe to you, scribes and **P**, **Mt 23:29** *5330*
P gathered together with Pilate, **Mt 27:62** *5330*
When the scribes of the **P** saw **Mk 2:16** *5330*
disciples and the **P** were fasting; **Mk 2:18** *5330*
and the disciples of the **P** fast, **Mk 2:18** *5330*
The **P** were saying to Him, **Mk 2:24** *5330*
The **P** went out and immediately **Mk 3:6** *5330*
The **P** and some of the scribes **Mk 7:1** *5330*
(For the **P** and all the Jews do not **Mk 7:3** *5330*
The **P** and the scribes asked Him, **Mk 7:5** *5330*
The **P** came out and began to **Mk 8:11** *5330*
the **P** and the leaven of Herod." **Mk 8:15** *5330*
Some **P** came up to Jesus, testing **Mk 10:2** *5330*
sent some of the **P** and Herodians **Mk 12:13** *5330*
and there were *some* **P** and teachers **Lk 5:17** *5330*
scribes and the **P** began to reason, **Lk 5:21** *5330*
The **P** and their scribes *began* **Lk 5:30** *5330*
disciples of the **P** also do the same, **Lk 5:33** *5330*
But some of the **P** said, **Lk 6:2** *5330*
the **P** were watching Him closely **Lk 6:7** *5330*
But the **P** and the lawyers rejected **Lk 7:30** *5330*
Now one of the **P** was requesting **Lk 7:36** *5330*
"Now you **P** clean the outside of **Lk 11:39** *5330*
"But woe to you **P**! **Lk 11:42** *5330*
"Woe to you **P**! For you love the **Lk 11:43** *5330*
the scribes and the **P** began to be **Lk 11:53** *5330*
"Beware of the leaven of the **P**, **Lk 12:1** *5330*
Just at that time some **P** approached, **Lk 13:31** *5330*
house of one of the leaders of the **P** **Lk 14:1** *5330*
and spoke to the lawyers and **P**, **Lk 14:3** *5330*
Both the **P** and the scribes **Lk 15:2** *5330*
Now the **P**, who were lovers of **Lk 16:14** *5330*
having been questioned by the **P** **Lk 17:20** *5330*
P in the crowd said to Him, **Lk 19:39** *5330*
Now they had been sent from the **P**. **Jn 1:24** *5330*
Now there was a man of the **P**, **Jn 3:1** *5330*
the Lord knew that the **P** had heard **Jn 4:1** *5330*
The **P** heard the crowd **Jn 7:32** *5330*
the **P** sent officers to seize Him. **Jn 7:32** *5330*
came to the chief priests and **P**, **Jn 7:45** *5330*
The **P** then answered them, **Jn 7:47** *5330*
"No one of the rulers or **P** has **Jn 7:48** *5330*
The scribes and the **P** brought **Jn 8:3** *5330*
So the **P** said to Him, **Jn 8:13** *5330*
They brought to the **P** the man who **Jn 9:13** *5330*
the **P** also were asking him again how **Jn 9:15** *5330*
some of the **P** were saying, **Jn 9:16** *5330*
Those of the **P** who were with Him **Jn 9:40** *5330*
some of them went to the **P** **Jn 11:46** *5330*
and the **P** convened a council, **Jn 11:47** *5330*
Now the chief priests and the **P** **Jn 11:57** *5330*
P said to one another, **Jn 12:19** *5330*
because of the **P** they were not **Jn 12:42** *5330*
from the chief priests and the **P**, **Jn 18:3** *5330*
sect of the **P** who had believed stood **Ac 15:5** *5330*
were Sadducees and the other **P**, **Ac 23:6** *5330*
I am a Pharisee, a son of **P**; **Ac 23:6** *5330*
between the **P** and Sadducees, **Ac 23:7** *5330*
but the **P** acknowledge them all. **Ac 23:8** *5330*

PHARPAR

"Are not Abanah and **P**, **2Ki 5:12** 6554

PHICOL

that time that Abimelech and **P**, **Gn 21:22** 6369
and Abimelech and **P**, **Gn 21:32** 6369
and **P** the commander of his army. **Gn 26:26** 6369

PHILADELPHIA

Sardis and to **P** and to Laodicea." **Rv 1:11** *5359*
angel of the church in **P** write: **Rv 3:7** *5359*

PHILEMON

To **P** our beloved *brother* and **Phm 1:1** *5371*

PHILETUS

Among them are Hymenaeus and **P**, **2Tm 2:17** *5372*

PHILIP

P and Bartholomew; **Mt 10:3** *5376*
the wife of his brother **P**. **Mt 14:3** *5376*
and Andrew, and **P**, and **Mk 3:18** *5376*
the wife of his brother **P**, **Mk 6:17** *5376*
and his brother **P** was tetrarch of **Lk 3:1** *5376*
and **P** and Bartholomew; **Lk 6:14** *5376*
into Galilee, and He found **P**. **Jn 1:43** *5376*
Now **P** was from Bethsaida, of the **Jn 1:44** *5376*
P found Nathanael and said to him, **Jn 1:45** *5376*
P said to him, "Come and see." **Jn 1:46** *5376*
"Before **P** called you, when you **Jn 1:48** *5376*
was coming to Him, said to **P**, **Jn 6:5** *5376*
P answered Him, "Two hundred **Jn 6:7** *5376*
these then came to **P**, **Jn 12:21** *5376*
P came and told Andrew; **Jn 12:22** *5376*
Andrew and **P** came and told **Jn 12:22** *5376*
P said to Him, "Lord, show us the **Jn 14:8** *5376*
you have not come to know Me, **P**? **Jn 14:9** *5376*
James and Andrew, **P** and Thomas, **Ac 1:13** *5376*
and of the Holy Spirit, and **P**, **Ac 6:5** *5376*
P went down to the city of **Ac 8:5** *5376*
attention to what was said by **P**, **Ac 8:6** *5376*
But when they believed **P** preaching **Ac 8:12** *5376*
baptized, he continued on with **P**, **Ac 8:13** *5376*
an angel of the Lord spoke to **P** **Ac 8:26** *5376*
Then the Spirit said to **P**, **Ac 8:29** *5376*
P ran up and heard **Ac 8:30** *5376*
he invited **P** to come up and sit **Ac 8:31** *5376*
The eunuch answered **P** and said, **Ac 8:34** *5376*
Then **P** opened his mouth, and **Ac 8:35** *5376*
P said, "If you believe with all your **Ac 8:37** *5376*
water, **P** as well as the eunuch, **Ac 8:38** *5376*
Spirit of the Lord snatched **P** away; **Ac 8:39** *5376*
But **P** found himself at Azotus, **Ac 8:40** *5376*
the house of **P** the evangelist, **Ac 21:8** *5376*

PHILIPPI

into the district of Caesarea **P**, **Mt 16:13** *5376*
to the villages of Caesarea **P**; **Mk 8:27** *5376*
and from there to **P**, **Ac 16:12** *5375*
We sailed from **P** after the **Ac 20:6** *5375*
saints in Christ Jesus who are in **P**, **Php 1:1** *5375*
suffered and been mistreated in **P**, **1Th 2:2** *5375*

PHILIPPIANS

You yourselves also know, **P**, **Php 4:15** *5374*

PHILISTIA

has gripped the inhabitants of **P**. **Ex 15:14** 6429
Shout loud, O **P**, because of Me!" **Ps 60:8** 6429
P with the inhabitants of Tyre; **Ps 83:7** 6429
Behold, **P** and Tyre with Ethiopia: **Ps 87:4** 6429
Over **P** I will shout aloud." **Ps 108:9** 6429
"Do not rejoice, O **P**, **Is 14:29** 6429
Melt away, O **P**, all of you; **Is 14:31** 6429
Sidon and all the regions of **P**? **Jl 3:4** 6429

PHILISTINE

of God where the **P** garrison is; **1Sa 10:5** 6430
Am I not the **P** and you servants of **1Sa 17:8** 6430
Again the **P** said, **1Sa 17:10** 6430
Israel heard these words of the **P**, **1Sa 17:11** 6430
The **P** came forward morning and **1Sa 17:16** 6430
the **P** from Gath named Goliath, **1Sa 17:23** 6430
done for the man who kills this **P** and **1Sa 17:26** 6430
For who is this uncircumcised **P**, **1Sa 17:26** 6430
will go and fight with this **P**." **1Sa 17:32** 6430
are not able to go against this **P** **1Sa 17:33** 6430
this uncircumcised **P** will be like **1Sa 17:36** 6430
me from the hand of this **P**." **1Sa 17:37** 6430
and he approached the **P**. **1Sa 17:40** 6430
P came on and approached David, **1Sa 17:41** 6430
When the **P** looked and saw David, **1Sa 17:42** 6430
The **P** said to David, **1Sa 17:43** 6430
the **P** cursed David by his gods. **1Sa 17:43** 6430
The **P** also said to David, **1Sa 17:44** 6430
Then David said to the **P**, **1Sa 17:45** 6430
Then it happened when the **P** rose **1Sa 17:48** 6430
the battle line to meet the **P**. **1Sa 17:48** 6430
and struck the **P** on his forehead. **1Sa 17:49** 6430
David prevailed over the **P** with a **1Sa 17:50** 6430
he struck the **P** and killed him; **1Sa 17:50** 6430
David ran and stood over the **P** **1Sa 17:51** 6430
saw David going out against the **P**, **1Sa 17:55** 6430
David returned from killing the **P**, **1Sa 17:57** 6430
David returned from killing the **P**, **1Sa 18:6** 6430
life in his hand and struck the **P**, **1Sa 19:5** 6430
"The sword of Goliath the **P**, **1Sa 21:9** 6430
him the sword of Goliath the **P**." **1Sa 22:10** 6430
and struck the **P** and killed him. **2Sa 21:17** 6430
of the Shephelah the **P** *plain* **Ob 1:19** 6430

PHILISTINE'S

Then David took the **P** head and **1Sa 17:54** 6430
Saul with the **P** head in his hand. **1Sa 17:57** 6430

PHILISTINES

Casluhim (from which came the **P**) **Gn 10:14** 6430
and returned to the land of the **P**. **Gn 21:32** 6430
the land of the **P** for many days. **Gn 21:34** 6430
Gerar, to Abimelech king of the **P**. **Gn 26:1** 6430
the **P** looked out through a window, **Gn 26:8** 6430
so that the **P** envied him. **Gn 26:14** 6430
the **P** stopped up by filling them **Gn 26:15** 6430

for the **P** had stopped them up Gn 26:18 6430
by the way of the land of the **P**, Ex 13:17 6430
the Red Sea to the sea of the **P**, Ex 23:31 6430
all the regions *of* the **P** and all Jos 13:2 6430
the five lords of the **P**: Jos 13:3 6430
the five lords of the **P** and all Jg 3:3 6430
down six hundred **P** with an oxgoad; Jg 3:31 6430
of Ammon, and the gods of the **P**; Jg 10:6 6430
sold them into the hands of the **P** and Jg 10:7 6430
the sons of Ammon, and the **P**? Jg 10:11 6430
the hands of the **P** forty years. Jg 13:1 6430
Israel from the hands of the **P**." Jg 13:5 6430
one of the daughters of the **P**. Jg 14:1 6430
one of the daughters of the **P**; Jg 14:2 6430
a wife from the uncircumcised **P**?" Jg 14:3 6430
seeking an occasion against the **P**. Jg 14:4 6430
the **P** were ruling over Israel. Jg 14:4 6430
be blameless in regard to the **P** Jg 15:3 6430
into the standing grain of the **P**, Jg 15:5 6430
Then the **P** said, Jg 15:6 6430
So the **P** came up and burned her Jg 15:6 6430
the **P** went up and camped in Judah, Jg 15:9 6430
that the **P** are rulers over us? Jg 15:11 6430
you into the hands of the **P**." Jg 15:12 6430
the **P** shouted as they met him. Jg 15:14 6430
twenty years in the days of the **P**. Jg 15:20 6430
The lords of the **P** came up to her Jg 16:5 6430
Then the lords of the **P** brought up Jg 16:8 6430
"The **P** are upon you, Samson!" Jg 16:9 6430
"The **P** are upon you, Samson!" Jg 16:12 6430
"The **P** are upon you, Samson!" Jg 16:14 6430
and called the lords of the **P**, Jg 16:18 6430
the lords of the **P** came up to her and Jg 16:18 6430
"The **P** are upon you, Samson!" Jg 16:20 6430
Then the **P** seized him and gouged Jg 16:21 6430
Now the lords of the **P** assembled Jg 16:23 6430
all the lords of the **P** were there. Jg 16:27 6430
I may at once be avenged of the **P** Jg 16:28 6430
"Let me die with the **P**!" Jg 16:30 6430
Now Israel went out to meet the **P** 1Sa 4:1 6430
while the **P** camped in Aphek. 1Sa 4:1 6430
The **P** drew up in battle array 1Sa 4:2 6430
Israel was defeated before the **P** 1Sa 4:2 6430
defeated us today before the **P**? 1Sa 4:3 6430
P heard the noise of the shout, 1Sa 4:6 6430
The **P** were afraid, for they 1Sa 4:7 6430
"Take courage and be men, O **P**, 1Sa 4:9 6430
So the **P** fought and Israel was 1Sa 4:10 6430
"Israel has fled before the **P** and 1Sa 4:17 6430
Now the **P** took the ark of God and 1Sa 5:1 6430
Then the **P** took the ark of God and 1Sa 5:2 6430
and gathered all the lords of the **P** 1Sa 5:8 6430
and gathered all the lords of the **P** 1Sa 5:11 6430
the country of the **P** seven months. 1Sa 6:1 6430
And the **P** called for the priests 1Sa 6:2 6430
the number of the lords of the **P**, 1Sa 6:4 6430
And the lords of the **P** followed 1Sa 6:12 6430
the five lords of the **P** saw it, 1Sa 6:16 6430
golden tumors which the **P** returned 1Sa 6:17 6430
the number of all the cities of the **P** 1Sa 6:18 6430
"The **P** have brought back the ark 1Sa 6:21 6430
you from the hand of the **P**." 1Sa 7:3 6430
Now when the **P** heard that the sons 1Sa 7:7 6430
lords of the **P** went up against Israel. 1Sa 7:7 6430
it, they were afraid of the **P**. 1Sa 7:7 6430
save us from the hand of the **P**." 1Sa 7:8 6430
and the **P** drew near to battle 1Sa 7:10 6430
against the **P** and confused them, 1Sa 7:10 6430
out of Mizpah and pursued the **P**, 1Sa 7:11 6430
So the **P** were subdued and they did 1Sa 7:13 6430
hand of the LORD was against the **P** 1Sa 7:13 6430
The cities which the **P** had 1Sa 7:14 6430
territory from the hand of the **P**. 1Sa 7:14 6430
My people from the hand of the **P**. 1Sa 9:16 6430
and into the hand of the **P** and 1Sa 12:9 6430
smote the garrison of the **P** that was 1Sa 13:3 6430
in Geba, and the **P** heard of *it*. 1Sa 13:3 6430
had smitten the garrison of the **P**, 1Sa 13:4 6430
Israel had become odious to the **P**. 1Sa 13:4 6430
Now the **P** assembled to fight with 1Sa 13:5 6430
the **P** were assembling at Michmash, 1Sa 13:11 6430
'Now the **P** will come down against 1Sa 13:12 6430
while the **P** camped at Michmash. 1Sa 13:16 6430
came from the camp of the **P** 1Sa 13:17 6430
land of Israel, for the **P** said, 1Sa 13:19 6430
So all Israel went down to the **P**, 1Sa 13:20 6430
And the garrison of the **P** went out 1Sa 13:23 6430
to the garrison of the **P**, 1Sa 14:11 6430
of the Philistines, the **P** said, 1Sa 14:11 6430
the commotion in the camp of the **P** 1Sa 14:19 6430
who were with the **P** previously, 1Sa 14:21 6430
Ephraim heard that the **P** had fled, 1Sa 14:22 6430
slaughter among the **P** has not been 1Sa 14:30 6430
They struck among the **P** that 1Sa 14:31 6430
"Let us go down after the **P** by 1Sa 14:36 6430
"Shall I go down after the **P**? 1Sa 14:37 6430
Saul went up from pursuing the **P**, 1Sa 14:46 6430
and the **P** went to their own place. 1Sa 14:46 6430
the kings of Zobah, and the **P**; 1Sa 14:47 6430
Now the war against the **P** was 1Sa 14:52 6430
Now the **P** gathered their armies 1Sa 17:1 6430
battle array to encounter the **P**. 1Sa 17:2 6430
The **P** stood on the mountain on 1Sa 17:3 6430
the armies of the **P** named Goliath, 1Sa 17:4 6430
of Elah, fighting with the **P**." 1Sa 17:19 6430
and the **P** drew up in battle array, 1Sa 17:21 6430
coming up from the army of the **P**, 1Sa 17:23 6430
the dead bodies of the army of the **P** 1Sa 17:46 6430
When the **P** saw that their champion 1Sa 17:51 6430
pursued the **P** as far as the valley, 1Sa 17:52 6430
P lay along the way to Shaaraim, 1Sa 17:52 6430
Israel returned from chasing the **P** 1Sa 17:53 6430
hand of the **P** be against him." 1Sa 18:17 6430
hand of the **P** may be against him." 1Sa 18:21 6430
a hundred foreskins of the **P**, 1Sa 18:25 6430
David fall by the hand of the **P**. 1Sa 18:25 6430
down two hundred men among the **P**. 1Sa 18:27 6430
of the **P** went out *to battle*, 1Sa 18:30 6430
went out and fought with the **P** and 1Sa 19:8 6430
the **P** are fighting against Keilah and 1Sa 23:1 6430
"Shall I go and attack these **P**?" 1Sa 23:2 6430
"Go and attack the **P** and 1Sa 23:2 6430
against the ranks of the **P**?" 1Sa 23:3 6430
will give the **P** into your hand." 1Sa 23:4 6430
to Keilah and fought with the **P**; 1Sa 23:5 6430
P have made a raid on the land." 1Sa 23:27 6430
David and went to meet the **P**; 1Sa 23:28 6430
Saul returned from pursuing the **P**, 1Sa 24:1 6430
to escape into the land of the **P**. 1Sa 27:1 6430
David lived in the country of the **P** 1Sa 27:7 6430
lived in the country of the **P**.' " 1Sa 27:11 6430
the **P** gathered their armed camps 1Sa 28:1 6430
So the **P** gathered together and 1Sa 28:4 6430
When Saul saw the camp of the **P**, 1Sa 28:5 6430
the **P** are waging war against me, 1Sa 28:15 6430
with you into the hands of the **P**, 1Sa 28:19 6430
Israel into the hands of the **P**!" 1Sa 28:19 6430
Now the **P** gathered together all 1Sa 29:1 6430
And the lords of the **P** were 1Sa 29:2 6430
Then the commanders of the **P** said, 1Sa 29:3 6430
said to the commanders of the **P**, 1Sa 29:3 6430
commanders of the **P** were angry 1Sa 29:4 6430
commanders of the **P** said to him, 1Sa 29:4 6430
may not displease the lords of the **P**." 1Sa 29:7 6430
the commanders of the **P** have said, 1Sa 29:9 6430
to return to the land of the **P**. 1Sa 29:11 6430
And the **P** went up to Jezreel. 1Sa 29:11 6430
had taken from the land of the **P** 1Sa 30:16 6430
Now the **P** were fighting 1Sa 31:1 6430
men of Israel fled from before the **P** 1Sa 31:1 6430
The **P** overtook Saul and his sons; 1Sa 31:2 6430
and the **P** killed Jonathan and 1Sa 31:2 6430
then the **P** came and lived in them. 1Sa 31:7 6430
the **P** came to strip the slain, 1Sa 31:8 6430
them throughout the land of the **P**, 1Sa 31:9 6430
heard what the **P** had done to Saul, 1Sa 31:11 6430
the daughters of the **P** will rejoice, 2Sa 1:20 6430
a hundred foreskins of the **P**." 2Sa 3:14 6430
people Israel from the hand of the **P** 2Sa 3:18 6430
When the **P** heard that they had 2Sa 5:17 6430
the **P** went up to seek out David; 2Sa 5:17 6430
Now the **P** came and spread 2Sa 5:18 6430
"Shall I go up against the **P**? 2Sa 5:19 6430
give the **P** into your hand." 2Sa 5:19 6430
Now the **P** came up once again and 2Sa 5:22 6430
you to strike the army of the **P**." 2Sa 5:24 6430
struck down the **P** from Geba as far 2Sa 5:25 6430
defeated the **P** and subdued them; 2Sa 8:1 6430
chief city from the hand of the **P**. 2Sa 8:1 6430
of Ammon and the **P** and Amalek, 2Sa 8:12 6430
saved us from the hand of the **P**, 2Sa 19:9 6430
where the **P** had hanged them on the 2Sa 21:12 6430
the **P** struck down Saul in Gilboa. 2Sa 21:12 6430
Now when the **P** were at war 2Sa 21:15 6430
and as they fought against the **P**, 2Sa 21:15 6430
was war again with the **P** at Gob; 2Sa 21:18 6430
was war with the **P** again at Gob, 2Sa 21:19 6430
they defied the **P** who were gathered 2Sa 23:9 6430
He arose and struck the **P** until 2Sa 23:10 6430
the **P** were gathered into a troop where 2Sa 23:11 6430
and the people fled from the **P**. 2Sa 23:11 6430
defended it and struck the **P**; 2Sa 23:12 6430
while the troop of the **P** was 2Sa 23:13 6430
of the **P** was then in Bethlehem. 2Sa 23:14 6430
broke through the camp of the **P**, 2Sa 23:16 6430
from the River *to* the land of the **P** 1Ki 4:21 6430
which belonged to the **P**, 1Ki 15:27 6430
which belonged to the **P**. 1Ki 16:15 6430
in the land of the **P** seven years. 2Ki 8:2 6430
returned from the land of the **P**; 2Ki 8:3 6430
He defeated the **P** as far as Gaza 2Ki 18:8 6430
Casluh, from which the **P** came, 1Ch 1:12 6430
Now the **P** fought against Israel; 1Ch 10:1 6430
men of Israel fled before the **P** and 1Ch 10:1 6430
The **P** closely pursued Saul and 1Ch 10:2 6430
and the **P** struck down Jonathan, 1Ch 10:2 6430
and the **P** came and lived in them. 1Ch 10:7 6430
the **P** came to strip the slain, 1Ch 10:8 6430
around the land of the **P** to 1Ch 10:9 6430
all that the **P** had done to Saul, 1Ch 10:11 6430
the **P** were gathered together there 1Ch 11:13 6430
and the people fled before the **P**. 1Ch 11:13 6430
it, and struck down the **P**; 1Ch 11:14 6430
while the army of the **P** was 1Ch 11:15 6430
of the **P** *was* then in Bethlehem. 1Ch 11:16 6430
broke through the camp of the **P** and 1Ch 11:18 6430
to battle with the **P** against Saul. 1Ch 12:19 6430
for the lords of the **P** after 1Ch 12:19 6430
When the **P** heard that David had 1Ch 14:8 6430
the **P** went up in search of David; 1Ch 14:8 6430
Now the **P** had come and made a raid 1Ch 14:9 6430
"Shall I go up against the **P**? 1Ch 14:10 6430
The **P** made yet another raid in 1Ch 14:13 6430
you to strike the army of the **P**." 1Ch 14:15 6430
they struck down the army of the **P** 1Ch 14:16 6430
David defeated the **P** and subdued 1Ch 18:1 6430
its towns from the hand of the **P**. 1Ch 18:1 6430
Moab, the sons of Ammon, the **P**, 1Ch 18:11 6430
war broke out at Gezer with the **P**; 1Ch 20:4 6430
there was war with the **P** again, 1Ch 20:5 6430
River even to the land of the **P**, 2Ch 9:26 6430
Some of the **P** brought gifts 2Ch 17:11 6430
against Jehoram the spirit of the **P** 2Ch 21:16 6430
went out and warred against the **P**, 2Ch 26:6 6430
area of Ashdod and among the **P**. 2Ch 26:6 6430
God helped him against the **P**, 2Ch 26:7 6430
The **P** also had invaded the cities 2Ch 28:18 6430
they are soothsayers like the **P**, Is 2:6 6430
on the east and the **P** on the west; Is 9:12 6430
the slopes of the **P** on the west; Is 11:14 6430
the kings of the land of the **P** Jer 25:20 6430
the prophet concerning the **P**, Jer 47:1 6430
is coming To destroy all the **P**, Jer 47:4 6430
LORD is going to destroy the **P**, Jer 47:4 6430
hate you, the daughters of the **P**, Ezk 16:27 6430
of the daughters of the **P** Ezk 16:57 6430
"Because the **P** have acted in Ezk 25:15 6430
stretch out My hand against the **P**, Ezk 25:16 6430
remnant of the **P** will perish," Am 1:8 6430
Then go down to Gath of the **P**. Am 6:2 6430
And the **P** from Caphtor and the Am 9:7 6430
you, O Canaan, land of the **P**; Zph 2:5 6430
I will cut off the pride of the **P**. Zch 9:6 6430

PHILISTINES'
let us cross over to the **P** garrison 1Sa 14:1 6430
cross over to the **P** garrison, 1Sa 14:4 6430

PHILOLOGUS
Greet **P** and Julia, Nereus and his Ro 16:15 *5378*

PHILOSOPHERS
Stoic **p** were conversing with him. Ac 17:18 *5386*

PHILOSOPHY
through **p** and empty deception, Col 2:8 *5385*

PHINEHAS
of Putiel, and she bore him **P**. Ex 6:25 6372
When **P** the son of Eleazar, the son Nu 25:7 6372
"**P** the son of Eleazar, the son of Nu 25:11 6372
P the son of Eleazar the priest, Nu 31:6 6372
P the son of Eleazar the priest, Jos 22:13 6372
So when **P** the priest and the Jos 22:30 6372
And **P** the son of Eleazar the Jos 22:31 6372
Then **P** the son of Eleazar the Jos 22:32 6372
buried him at Gibeah of **P** his son, Jos 24:33 6372
and **P** the son of Eleazar, Aaron's Jg 20:28 6372
Hophni and **P**, were priests to the 1Sa 1:3 6372
your two sons, Hophni and **P**: 1Sa 2:34 6372
the two sons of Eli, Hophni and **P**, 1Sa 4:4 6372
the two sons of Eli, Hophni and **P**, 1Sa 4:11 6372
your two sons also, Hophni and **P**, 1Sa 4:17 6372
Ichabod's brother, the son of **P**, 1Sa 14:3 6372
Eleazar became the father of **P**, 1Ch 6:4 6372
P became the father of Abishua, 1Ch 6:4 6372
Eleazar his son, **P** his son, 1Ch 6:50 6372
P the son of Eleazar was ruler 1Ch 9:20 6372
son of Abishua, son of **P**, Ezr 7:5 6372
of the sons of **P**, Gershom; Ezr 8:2 6372
with him *was* Eleazar the son of **P**; Ezr 8:33 6372
Then **P** stood up and interposed, Ps 106:30 6372

PHINEHAS'S
Now his daughter-in-law, **P** wife, 1Sa 4:19 6372

PHLEGON
Greet Asyncritus, **P**, Ro 16:14 *5393*

PHOEBE
I commend to you our sister **P**, Ro 16:1 *5402*

PHOENICIA
way to **P** and Cyprus and Antioch, Ac 11:19 *5403*
through both **P** and Samaria, Ac 15:3 *5403*
found a ship crossing over to **P**, Ac 21:2 *5403*

PHOENIX
if somehow they could reach **P**, Ac 27:12 *5405*

PHRYGIA
P and Pamphylia, Egypt and the Ac 2:10 *5435*
through the Galatian region and **P**, Ac 18:23 *5435*

PHRYGIAN
through the **P** and Galatian region, Ac 16:6 *5435*

PHYGELUS
among whom are **P** and Hermogenes. 2Tm 1:15 *5436*

PHYLACTERIES
hand and as **p** on your forehead, Ex 13:16 2903
for they broaden their **p** and Mt 23:5 *5440*

PHYSICAL
basis of a law of **p** requirement, Heb 7:16 *4560*

PHYSICALLY
And he who is **p** uncircumcised, Ro 2:27 *5449*

PHYSICIAN
Is there no **p** there? Jer 8:22 7495
who are healthy who need a **p**, Mt 9:12 *2395*
who are healthy who need a **p**, Mk 2:17 *2395*
'**P**, heal yourself! Lk 4:23 *2395*
those who are well who need a **p**, Lk 5:31 *2395*
Luke, the beloved **p**, Col 4:14 *2395*

PHYSICIANS
the **p** to embalm his father. Gn 50:2 7495
So the **p** embalmed Israel. Gn 50:2 7495
did not seek the LORD, but the **p**. 2Ch 16:12 7495
You are all worthless **p**. Jb 13:4 7495
much at the hands of many **p**, Mk 5:26 *2395*

PI-BESETH
"The young men of On and of **P** Ezk 30:17 6364

PICK
all who pass *that* way **p** its *fruit*? Ps 80:12 717
of the valley will **p** it out, Pr 30:17 5365
P up your bundle from the ground, Jer 10:17 622
"**P** me up and throw me into the Jon 1:12 5375

p up your bed and go home." **Mt 9:6** *142*
to **p** the heads *of grain* and eat. **Mt 12:1** *5089*
and **p** up your pallet and walk'? **Mk 2:9** *142*
"I say to you, get up, **p** up your **Mk 2:11** *142*
of broken pieces did you **p** up?" **Mk 8:20** *142*
they will **p** up serpents, and if **Mk 16:18** *142*
and **p** up your stretcher and go home." **Lk 5:24** *142*
they **p** grapes from a briar bush. **Lk 6:44** *5166*
Jesus said to him, "Get up, **p** up **Jn 5:8** *142*
'**P** up your pallet and walk.' " **Jn 5:11** *142*
'**P** up *your pallet* and walk'?" **Jn 5:12** *142*
P up Mark and bring him with you, **2Tm 4:11** *353*

PICKED
beak was a freshly **p** olive leaf. **Gn 8:11** 2965
And Jonathan's lad **p** up the arrow **1Sa 20:38** 3950
So they **p** up Jonah, threw him into **Jon 1:15** 5375
They **p** up what was left over **Mt 14:20** *142*
and they **p** up what was left over **Mt 15:37** *142*
and how many baskets *full* you **p** **Mt 16:9** *2983*
how many large baskets *full* you **p** **Mt 16:10** *2983*
And he got up and immediately **p** up **Mk 2:12** *142*
and they **p** up twelve full baskets **Mk 6:43** *142*
and they **p** up seven large baskets **Mk 8:8** *142*
full of broken pieces you **p** up?" **Mk 8:19** *142*
and **p** up what he had been lying on, **Lk 5:25** *142*
they had left over were **p** up, **Lk 9:17** *142*
and **p** up his pallet and *began* to **Jn 5:9** *142*
they **p** up stones to throw at Him, **Jn 8:59** *142*
The Jews **p** up stones again to stone **Jn 10:31** *941*
third floor and was **p** up dead. **Ac 20:9** *142*

PICKERS
fruit **p**, like the grape gatherers. **Mi 7:1** 625

PICKING
along while **p** the heads *of grain.* **Mk 2:23** *5089*
p the heads of grain, **Lk 6:1** *5089*
He noticed how they had been **p** out **Lk 14:7** *1586*

PICKS
and whoever **p** up any of their **Lv 11:25** 5375
and the one who **p** up their **Lv 11:28** 5375
and the one who **p** up its carcass **Lv 11:40** 5375

PICTURE
"How shall we **p** the kingdom of **Mk 4:30** *3666*

PIECE
and I will bring a **p** of bread, **Gn 18:5** 6595
a **p** of land worth four hundred **Gn 23:15** 776
He bought the **p** of land where **Gn 33:19** 2513a
shall make the cherubim *of one* **p** **Ex 25:19**
and its flowers shall be *of one* **p** **Ex 25:31**
their branches *shall be of one* **p** **Ex 25:36**
p of hammered work of pure gold. **Ex 25:36**
horns shall be of one **p** with it, **Ex 27:2**
horns *shall be* of one **p** with it. **Ex 30:2**
he made the cherubim *of one* **p** **Ex 37:8**
bulbs and its flowers were *of one* **p** **Ex 37:17**
and their branches were *of one* **p** **Ex 37:22**
its horns were *of one* **p** with it. **Ex 37:25**
its horns being *of one* **p** with it, **Ex 38:2**
'Thus for every **p** of your property, **Lv 25:24** 776
in the **p** of ground which Jacob had **Jos 24:32** 2513a
"Sustain yourself with a **p** of bread, **Jg 19:5** 6595
dip your **p** of bread in the vinegar." **Ru 2:14** 6595
has to sell the **p** of land which **Ru 4:3** 2513a
a **p** of silver or a loaf of bread and **1Sa 2:36** 95
I may eat a **p** of bread. **1Sa 2:36** 6595
and let me set a **p** of bread before **1Sa 28:22** 6595
They gave him a **p** of fig cake **1Sa 30:12** 6400
bring me a **p** of bread in your hand. **1Ki 17:11** 6595
good **p** of land with stones.' " **2Ki 3:19** 2513a
a stone on every **p** of good land **2Ki 3:25** 2513a
were in two rows, cast in one **p**. **2Ch 4:3** 4166
each one gave him one **p** of money, **Jb 42:11** 7192
Because for a **p** of bread a man **Pr 28:21** 6595
Put in it the pieces, Every good **p**, **Ezk 24:4** 5409
Take out of it **p** after piece, **Ezk 24:6** 5409
Take out of it piece after **p**, **Ezk 24:6** 5409
a couple of legs or a **p** of an ear, **Am 3:12** 915
who says to a **p** *of* wood, **Hab 2:19**
tears a **p** of cloth from a new **Lk 5:36** *1915*
and the **p** from the new will not **Lk 5:36** *1915*
'I have bought a **p** of land and I **Lk 14:18** *68*
gave Him a **p** of a broiled fish; **Lk 24:42** *3313*
was seamless, woven in one **p**. **Jn 19:23** *3650*
Sapphira, sold a **p** of property, **Ac 5:1** *2933*
If the first **p** *of dough* is holy, **Ro 11:16** *536*

PIECES
which passed between these **p**. **Gn 15:17** 1506
brother a thousand **p** of silver; **Gn 20:16**
for one hundred **p** of money. **Gn 33:19** 7192
Joseph has surely been torn to **p**!" **Gn 37:33** 2963
"Surely he is torn in **p**," **Gn 44:28** 2963
to Benjamin he gave three hundred **p** **Gn 45:22**
"If it is all torn to **p**, **Ex 22:13** 2963
for what has been torn to **p**. **Ex 22:13**
any flesh torn to **p** in the field; **Ex 22:31**
break their *sacred* pillars in **p**. **Ex 23:24** 7665
shoulder **p** joined to its two ends, **Ex 28:7**
on the shoulder **p** of the ephod, **Ex 28:12**
on the shoulder **p** of the ephod, **Ex 28:25**
the two shoulder **p** of the ephod, **Ex 28:27**
you shall cut the ram into its **p**, **Ex 29:17** 5409
put *them* with its **p** and its head. **Ex 29:17** 5409
shoulder **p** for the ephod; **Ex 39:4**
on the shoulder **p** of the ephod, **Ex 39:7**
them on the shoulder **p** of the ephod **Ex 39:18**
the two shoulder **p** of the ephod, **Ex 39:20**
offering and cut it into its **p**. **Lv 1:6** 5409
the priests shall arrange the **p**, **Lv 1:8** 5409
its **p** with its head and its suet, **Lv 1:12** 5409
present the grain offering in baked **p** **Lv 6:21** 6595
he had cut the ram into its **p**, **Lv 8:20** 5409
and the **p** and the suet in smoke. **Lv 8:20** 5409
the burnt offering to him in **p**, **Lv 9:13** 5409
And will crush their bones in **p**, **Nu 24:8**
"I will cut them to **p**, **Dt 32:26** 6284
for one hundred **p** of money; **Jos 24:32** 7192
They gave him seventy **p** of silver **Jg 9:4**
will each give you eleven hundred **p** **Jg 16:5**
"The eleven hundred **p** of silver **Jg 17:2**
then returned the eleven hundred **p** **Jg 17:3**
his mother took two hundred **p** of **Jg 17:4**
and I will give you ten **p** of **Jg 17:10**
concubine and cut her in twelve **p**, **Jg 19:29** 5409
my concubine and cut her in **p** and **Jg 20:6** 5408
a yoke of oxen and cut them in **p**, **1Sa 11:7** 5408
Samuel hewed Agag to **p** **1Sa 15:33** 8158
And I would have given you ten **p** **2Sa 18:11**
if I should receive a thousand **p** *of* **2Sa 18:12**
on him and tore it into twelve **p**. **1Ki 11:30** 7168
"Take for yourself ten **p**; **1Ki 11:31** 7168
cut the ox in **p** and laid *it* on the **1Ki 18:33** 5408
breaking in **p** the rocks before the **1Ki 19:11** 7665
clothes and tore them in two **p**. **2Ki 2:12** 7168
little ones you will dash in **p**, **2Ki 8:12** 7376
images they broke in **p** thoroughly, **2Ki 11:18** 7665
He also broke in **p** the bronze **2Ki 18:4** 3807
He broke in **p** the *sacred* pillars **2Ki 23:14** 7665
and cut in **p** all the vessels of gold **2Ki 24:13** 7112
the Chaldeans broke in **p** and **2Ki 25:13** 7665
broke in **p** his altars and his images, **2Ch 23:17** 7665
so that they were all dashed to **p**. **2Ch 25:12** 1234
utensils of the house of God in **p**; **2Ch 28:24** 7112
of Judah, broke the pillars in **p**, **2Ch 31:1** 7665
and the molten images he broke in **p** **2Ch 34:4** 7665
and evening they are broken in **p**; **Jb 4:20** 3807
me by the neck and shaken me to **p**; **Jb 16:12** 6483a
in **p** mighty men without inquiry, **Jb 34:24** 7489
breaks in **p** the cedars of Lebanon. **Ps 29:5** 7665
forget God, Or I will tear *you* in **p**, **Ps 50:22** 2963
under foot the **p** of silver; **Ps 68:30** 7518
Than thousands of gold and silver **p**. **Ps 119:72**
be dashed to **p** Before their eyes; **Is 13:16** 7376
aged wine, choice **p** with marrow, **Is 25:6**
sherd will not be found among its **p** **Is 30:14** 4386
it not You who cut Rahab in **p**, **Is 51:9** 2672
out of them will be torn in **p**, **Jer 5:6** 2963
the Chaldeans broke in **p** and **Jer 52:17** 7665
aside my ways and torn me to **p**; **La 3:11** 6582
cut you to **p** with their swords. **Ezk 16:40** 1333
Put in it the **p**, Every good piece, **Ezk 24:4** 5409
death or has been torn to **p**. **Ezk 44:31** 2966
so, like iron that breaks in **p**, **Da 2:40** 7490
crush and break all these in **p**. **Da 2:40** 7490
I, will tear to **p** and go away, **Hos 5:14** 2963
hewn *them* in **p** by the prophets; **Hos 6:5** 2672
calf of Samaria will be broken to **p**. **Hos 8:6** 7616
dashed in **p** with *their* children. **Hos 10:14** 7376
little ones will be dashed in **p**, **Hos 13:16** 7376
that the great house be smashed to **p** **Am 6:11** 7447b
her small children were dashed to **p** **Na 3:10** 7376
my staff Favor and cut it in **p**, **Zch 11:10** 1438
cut in **p** my second staff Union, **Zch 11:14** 1438
like a firepot among **p** of wood **Zch 12:6**
feet, and turn and tear you to **p**. **Mt 7:6** *4486*
was left over of the broken **p**, **Mt 14:20** *2801*
was left over of the broken **p**, **Mt 15:37** *2801*
on this stone will be broken to **p**; **Mt 21:44** *4917*
and will cut him in **p** and assign **Mt 24:51** *1371*
out thirty **p** of silver to him. **Mt 26:15** *694*
and returned the thirty **p** of silver **Mt 27:3** *694*
And he threw the **p** of silver into **Mt 27:5** *694*
took the **p** of silver and said, **Mt 27:6** *694*
THEY TOOK THE THIRTY **P** OF SILVER, **Mt 27:9** *694*
him and the shackles broken in **p**, **Mk 5:4** *4937*
full baskets of the broken **p**, **Mk 6:43** *2801*
was left over of the broken **p**. **Mk 8:8** *2801*
full of broken **p** you picked up?" **Mk 8:19** *2801*
of broken **p** did you pick up?" **Mk 8:20** *2801*
and the broken **p** which they had **Lk 9:17** *2801*
not know, and will cut him in **p**, **Lk 12:46** *1371*
on that stone will be broken to **p**; **Lk 20:18** *4917*
it fifty thousand **p** of silver. **Ac 19:19** *694*
was afraid Paul would be torn to **p** **Ac 23:10** *1288*
OF THE POTTER ARE BROKEN TO **P**, **Rv 2:27** *4937*

PIERCE
shall **p** his ear with an awl; **Ex 21:6** 7527
p it through his ear into the door, **Dt 15:17** 5414
sword and **p** me through with it, **1Sa 31:4** 1856
these uncircumcised will come and **p** **1Sa 31:4** 1856
it will go into his hand and **p** it. **2Ki 18:21** 5344a
But the bronze bow will **p** him. **Jb 20:24** 2498
With barbs can anyone **p** *his* nose? **Jb 40:24** 5344a
Or **p** his jaw with a hook? **Jb 41:2** 5344a
it will go into his hand and **p** it. **Is 36:6** 5344a
who gave birth to him will **p** him **Zch 13:3** 1856
a sword will **p** even your own soul **Lk 2:35** *1330*

PIERCED
tent and **p** both of them through, **Nu 25:8** 1856
she shattered and **p** his temple. **Jg 5:26** 2498
So the young man **p** him through, **Jg 9:54** 1856
hand has **p** the fleeing serpent. **Jb 26:13** 2490a
They **p** my hands and my feet. **Ps 22:16** 3564b
embittered And I was **p** within, **Ps 73:21** 8150
the slain who are **p** with a sword, **Is 14:19** 2944
Rahab in pieces, Who **p** the dragon? **Is 51:9** 2490a
But He was **p** through for our **Is 53:5** 2490a
And **p** through in their streets." **Jer 51:4** 1856
You **p** with his own spears The head of **Hab 3:14** 5344a
will look on Me whom they have **p**; **Zch 12:10** 1856
soldiers **p** His side with a spear, **Jn 19:34** *3572*
SHALL LOOK ON HIM WHOM THEY **P**." **Jn 19:37** *1574*
this, they were **p** to the heart, **Ac 2:37** *2660*
and **p** themselves with many griefs. **1Tm 6:10** *4044*
see Him, even those who **p** Him; **Rv 1:7** *1574*

PIERCES
"At night it **p** my bones within **Jb 30:17** 5365
an arrow **p** through his liver; **Pr 7:23** 6398

PIERCING
and **p** as far as the division of **Heb 4:12** *1338*

PIETY
as if by our own power or **p** we had **Ac 3:12** *2150*
they must first learn to practice **p** in **1Tm 5:4** *2151*
and He was heard because of His **p**. **Heb 5:7** *2124*

PIG
and the **p**, for though it divides **Lv 11:7** 2386
"The **p**, because it divides **Dt 14:8** 2386

PIGEON
and a turtledove, and a young **p**." **Gn 15:9** 1469
and a young **p** or a turtledove for **Lv 12:6** 3123

PIGEONS
the turtledoves or from young **p**. **Lv 1:14** 3123
two turtledoves or two young **p**, **Lv 5:7** 3123
two turtledoves or two young **p**, **Lv 5:11** 3123
two turtledoves or two young **p**, **Lv 12:8** 3123
two turtledoves or two young **p**, **Lv 14:22** 3123
one of the turtledoves or young **p**, **Lv 14:30** 3123
two turtledoves or two young **p**, **Lv 15:14** 3123
two turtledoves or two young **p** and **Lv 15:29** 3123
two turtledoves or two young **p** **Nu 6:10** 3123
OF TURTLEDOVES OR TWO YOUNG **P**." **Lk 2:24** *4058*

PI-HAHIROTH
to turn back and camp before **P**, **Ex 14:2** 6367
them camping by the sea, beside **P**, **Ex 14:9** 6367
from Etham and turned back to **P**, **Nu 33:7** 6367

PILATE
Him to **P** the governor. **Mt 27:2** *4091*
Then **P** said to Him, **Mt 27:13** *4091*
gathered together, **P** said to them, **Mt 27:17** *4091*
P said to them, "Then what shall I **Mt 27:22** *4091*
When **P** saw that he was **Mt 27:24** *4091*
This man went to **P** and asked for **Mt 27:58** *4091*
Then **P** ordered it to be given **Mt 27:58** *4091*
gathered together with **P**, **Mt 27:62** *4091*
P said to them, "You have a guard; **Mt 27:65** *4091*
away and delivered Him to **P**. **Mk 15:1** *4091*
P questioned Him, **Mk 15:2** *4091*
Then **P** questioned Him again, **Mk 15:4** *4091*
so **P** was amazed. **Mk 15:5** *4091*
P answered them, saying, **Mk 15:9** *4091*
again, **P** said to them, **Mk 15:12** *4091*
But **P** said to them, **Mk 15:14** *4091*
P released Barabbas for them, **Mk 15:15** *4091*
up courage and went in before **P**, **Mk 15:43** *4091*
P wondered if He was dead by **Mk 15:44** *4091*
Pontius **P** was governor of Judea, **Lk 3:1** *4091*
whose blood **P** had mixed with **Lk 13:1** *4091*
up and brought Him before **P**. **Lk 23:1** *4091*
So **P** asked Him, saying, **Lk 23:3** *4091*
Then **P** said to the chief priests **Lk 23:4** *4091*
When **P** heard it, he asked **Lk 23:6** *4091*
robe and sent Him back to **P**. **Lk 23:11** *4091*
Now Herod and **P** became friends **Lk 23:12** *4091*
P summoned the chief priests **Lk 23:13** *4091*
P, wanting to release Jesus, **Lk 23:20** *4091*
And **P** pronounced sentence that **Lk 23:24** *4091*
this man went to **P** and asked for **Lk 23:52** *4091*
Therefore **P** went out to them and **Jn 18:29** *4091*
P said to them, **Jn 18:31** *4091*
P entered again into the **Jn 18:33** *4091*
P answered, "I am not a Jew, am I? **Jn 18:35** *4091*
P said to Him, **Jn 18:37** *4091*
P said to Him, "What is truth?" **Jn 18:38** *4091*
P then took Jesus and **Jn 19:1** *4091*
P came out again and said to **Jn 19:4** *4091*
P said to them, "Behold, **Jn 19:5**
P said to them, "Take Him **Jn 19:6** *4091*
Therefore when **P** heard this **Jn 19:8** *4091*
P said to Him, **Jn 19:10** *4091*
P made efforts to release Him, **Jn 19:12** *4091*
P heard these words, **Jn 19:13** *4091*
P said to them, "Shall I crucify your **Jn 19:15** *4091*
P also wrote an inscription **Jn 19:19** *4091*
of the Jews were saying to **P**, **Jn 19:21** *4091*
P answered, "What I have written I **Jn 19:22** *4091*
asked **P** that their legs might be **Jn 19:31** *4091*
asked **P** that he might take away **Jn 19:38** *4091*
and **P** granted permission. **Jn 19:38** *4091*
and disowned in the presence of **P**, **Ac 3:13** *4091*
anointed, both Herod and Pontius **P**, **Ac 4:27** *4091*
they asked **P** that He be executed. **Ac 13:28** *4091*
good confession before Pontius **P**, **1Tm 6:13** *4091*

PILDASH
and **P** and Jidlaph and Bethuel." **Gn 22:22** 6394

PILE
"His roots wrap around a rock **p**, **Jb 8:17** 1530
down in the water of a manure **p**. **Is 25:10** 4087
P her up like heaps And utterly **Jer 50:26** 5549
And also **p** wood under the pot. **Ezk 24:5** 1754
I also will make the **p** great. **Ezk 24:9** 4071
for the soil or for the manure **p**; **Lk 14:35** *2874a*

PILED
So they **p** them in heaps, and the **Ex 8:14** 6651
Your nostrils the waters were **p** up, **Ex 15:8** 6192

And **p** up silver like dust, Zch 9:3 6651
sins have **p** up as high as heaven, Rv 18:5 *2853*

PILES
"Though he **p** up silver like dust And Jb 27:16 6651

PILFER
he used to **p** what was put into it. Jn 12:6 *941*

PILFERING
not **p**, but showing all good faith Ti 2:10 *3557*

PILGRIMAGE
are my songs In the house of my **p**. Ps 119:54 4033

PILHA
Hallohesh, **P**, Shobek, Ne 10:24 6401

PILLAGE
us And the lot of those who **p** us. Is 17:14 962
jubilant, O you who **p** My heritage, Jer 50:11 8154
completely full of lies *and* **p**; Na 3:1 6563

PILLAR
and she became a **p** of salt. Gn 19:26 5333
his head and set it up as a **p** and Gn 28:18 4676
stone, which I have set up as a **p**, Gn 28:22 4676
of Bethel, where you anointed a **p**, Gn 31:13 4676
took a stone and set it up *as* a **p**. Gn 31:45 4676
p which I have set between you and Gn 31:51 4676
a witness, and the **p** is a witness, Gn 31:52 4676
by this heap and this **p** to me, Gn 31:52 4676
Jacob set up a **p** in the place Gn 35:14 4676
had spoken with him, a **p** of stone, Gn 35:14 4676
Jacob set up a **p** over her grave; Gn 35:20 4676
p of Rachel's grave to this day. Gn 35:20 4676
going before them in a **p** of cloud Ex 13:21 5982
and in a **p** of fire by night to Ex 13:21 5982
take away the **p** of cloud by day, Ex 13:22 5982
day, nor the **p** of fire by night, Ex 13:22 5982
and the **p** of cloud moved from Ex 14:19 5982
through the **p** of fire and cloud and Ex 14:24 5982
the **p** of cloud would descend and Ex 33:9 5982
all the people saw the **p** of cloud Ex 33:10 5982
yourselves an image or a *sacred* **p**, Lv 26:1 4676
LORD came down in a **p** of cloud Nu 12:5 5982
You go before them in a **p** of cloud Nu 14:14 5982
day and in a **p** of fire by night. Nu 14:14 5982
p which the LORD your God hates. Dt 16:22 4676
in the tent in a **p** of cloud, Dt 31:15 5982
and the **p** of cloud stood at the Dt 31:15 5982
oak of the **p** which was in Shechem. Jg 9:6 5324
a **p** which is in the King's Valley, 2Sa 18:18 4676
he named the **p** after his own name, 2Sa 18:18 4676
cubits was the height of one **p**, 1Ki 7:15 5982
the right **p** and named it Jachin, 1Ki 7:21 5982
up the left **p** and named it Boaz. 1Ki 7:21 5982
he put away the *sacred* **p** of Baal 2Ki 3:2 4676
They also broke down the *sacred* **p** 2Ki 10:27 4676
the king was standing by the **p**, 2Ki 11:14 5982
The king stood by the **p** and 2Ki 23:3 5982
height of the one **p** was eighteen 2Ki 25:17 5982
the second **p** was like these with 2Ki 25:17 5982
standing by his **p** at the entrance, 2Ch 23:13 5982
"And with a **p** of cloud You led Ne 9:12 5982
And with a **p** of fire by night To Ne 9:12 5982
The **p** of cloud did not leave them Ne 9:19 5982
way, Nor the **p** of fire by night, Ne 9:19 5982
spoke to them in the **p** of cloud; Ps 99:7 5982
a **p** to the LORD near its border. Is 19:19 4676
and as a **p** of iron and as walls of Jer 1:18 5982
height of each **p** *was* eighteen cubits, Jer 52:21 5982
And the second **p** was like these, Jer 52:22 5982
to the side **p** of the courtyard. Ezk 40:14 352b
on *each* side **p** *were* palm tree Ezk 40:16 352b
measured *each* side **p** of the porch, Ezk 40:48 352b
side *was* the width of the side **p**. Ezk 41:1 168
each side **p** of the doorway, Ezk 41:3 352b
without sacrifice or *sacred* **p** and Hos 3:4 4676
the **p** and support of the truth. 1Tm 3:15 *4769*
him a **p** in the temple of My God, Rv 3:12 *4769*

PILLARS
break their *sacred* **p** in pieces. Ex 23:24 4676
twelve **p** for the twelve tribes of Israel Ex 24:4 4676
p of acacia overlaid with gold, Ex 26:32 5982
five **p** of acacia for the screen and Ex 26:37 5982
and its **p** *shall be* twenty, with Ex 27:10 5982
the hooks of the **p** and their bands Ex 27:10 5982
and its twenty **p** with their twenty Ex 27:11 5982
the hooks of the **p** and their bands Ex 27:11 5982
their ten **p** and their ten sockets. Ex 27:12 5982
three **p** and their three sockets. Ex 27:14 5982
three **p** and their three sockets. Ex 27:15 5982
four **p** and their four sockets. Ex 27:16 5982
"All the **p** around the court shall Ex 27:17 5982
p and cut down their Asherim Ex 34:13 4676
and its boards, its bars, its **p**, Ex 35:11 5982
the court, its **p** and its sockets, Ex 35:17 5982
He made four **p** of acacia for it, Ex 36:36 5982
made its five **p** with their hooks, Ex 36:38 5982
their twenty **p**, and their twenty Ex 38:10 5982
the hooks of the **p** and their bands Ex 38:10 5982
their twenty **p** and their twenty Ex 38:11 5982
the hooks of the **p** and their bands Ex 38:11 5982
their ten **p** and their ten sockets; Ex 38:12 5982
the hooks of the **p** and their bands Ex 38:12 5982
three **p** and their three sockets, Ex 38:14 5982
three **p** and their three sockets. Ex 38:15 5982
sockets for the **p** *were* of bronze, Ex 38:17 5982
hooks of the **p** and their bands, Ex 38:17 5982
and all the **p** of the court were Ex 38:17 5982
Their four **p** and their four Ex 38:19 5982
he made hooks for the **p** and Ex 38:28 5982
bars, and its **p** and its sockets; Ex 39:33 5982
the court, its **p** and its sockets, Ex 39:40 5982
its bars and erected its **p**. Ex 40:18 5982
the tabernacle, its bars, its **p**, Nu 3:36 5982
and the **p** around the court with Nu 3:37 5982
bars and its **p** and its sockets, Nu 4:31 5982
and the **p** around the court and Nu 4:32 5982
altars, and smash their *sacred* **p**, Dt 7:5 4676
smash their *sacred* **p** and burn their Dt 12:3 4676
they made him stand between the **p**. Jg 16:25 5982
the **p** on which the house rests, Jg 16:26 5982
p on which the house rested, Jg 16:29 5982
the **p** of the earth are the LORD's, 1Sa 2:8 4690
on four rows of cedar **p** with cedar 1Ki 7:2 5982
pillars with cedar beams on the **p**. 1Ki 7:2 5982
chambers which were on the 45 **p**, 1Ki 7:3 5982
Then he made the hall of **p**; 1Ki 7:6 5982
a porch *was* in front of them and **p** 1Ki 7:6 5982
He fashioned the two **p** of bronze; 1Ki 7:15 5982
to set on the tops of the **p**; 1Ki 7:16 5982
which were on the top of the **p**; 1Ki 7:17 5982
So he made the **p**, and two rows 1Ki 7:18 5982
on the top of the **p** in the porch were 1Ki 7:19 5982
There were capitals on the two **p**, 1Ki 7:20 5982
up the **p** at the porch of the nave; 1Ki 7:21 5982
the top of the **p** was lily design. 1Ki 7:22 5982
So the work of the **p** was finished. 1Ki 7:22 5982
the two **p** and the *two* bowls of the 1Ki 7:41 5982
were on the top of the two **p**, 1Ki 7:41 5982
which *were* on the top of the **p**; 1Ki 7:41 5982
which *were* on the tops of the **p**; 1Ki 7:42 5982
sacred **p** and Asherim on every high 1Ki 14:23 4676
the *sacred* **p** of the house of Baal and 2Ki 10:26 4676
They set for themselves *sacred* **p** 2Ki 17:10 4676
sacred **p** and cut down the Asherah. 2Ki 18:4 4676
He broke in pieces the *sacred* **p** 2Ki 23:14 4676
Now the bronze **p** which were in the 2Ki 25:13 5982
The two **p**, the one sea, and the 2Ki 25:16 5982
and the **p** and the bronze utensils. 1Ch 18:8 5982
two **p** for the front of the house, 2Ch 3:15 5982
placed *them* on the tops of the **p**; 2Ch 3:16 5982
the **p** in front of the temple, 2Ch 3:17 5982
the two **p**, the bowls and the two 2Ch 4:12 5982
the two capitals on top of the **p**, 2Ch 4:12 5982
which were on top of the **p**, 2Ch 4:12 5982
the capitals which were on the **p**. 2Ch 4:13 5982
places, tore down the *sacred* **p**, 2Ch 14:3 4676
of Judah, broke the **p** in pieces, 2Ch 31:1 4676
of its place, And its **p** tremble; Jb 9:6 5982
"The **p** of heaven tremble And are Jb 26:11 5982
It is I who have firmly set its **p**. Ps 75:3 5982
p fashioned as for a palace; Ps 144:12
She has hewn out her seven **p**; Pr 9:1 5982
"His legs are **p** of alabaster Set SS 5:15 5982
the **p** *of Egypt* will be crushed; Is 19:10 8356
LORD of hosts concerning the **p**, Jer 27:19 5982
herself up, her **p** have fallen, Jer 50:15 806b
Now the bronze **p** which belonged to Jer 52:17 5982
The two **p**, the one sea, and the Jer 52:20 5982
As for the **p**, the height of each Jer 52:21 5982
p will come down to the ground. Ezk 26:11 4676
and its side **p**, two cubits. Ezk 40:9 352b
The side **p** also had the same Ezk 40:10 352b
made the side **p** sixty cubits *high;* Ezk 40:14 352b
side **p** within the gate all around, Ezk 40:16 352b
and its side **p** and its porches had Ezk 40:21 352b
and he measured its side **p** and its Ezk 40:24 352b
palm tree ornaments on its side **p**, Ezk 40:26 352b
Its guardrooms also, its side **p** and Ezk 40:29 352b
tree ornaments *were* on its side **p**, Ezk 40:31 352b
Its guardrooms also, its side **p** and Ezk 40:33 352b
tree ornaments *were* on its side **p**, Ezk 40:34 352b
with its guardrooms, its side **p** and Ezk 40:36 352b
Its side **p** *were* toward the Ezk 40:37 352b
were on its side **p** on each side, Ezk 40:37 352b
was by the side **p** at the gates; Ezk 40:38 352b
columns belonging to the side **p**, Ezk 40:49 352b
the nave and measured the side **p**; Ezk 41:1 352b
were in three stories and had no **p** Ezk 42:6 5982
pillars like the **p** of the courts; Ezk 42:6 5982
The better he made the *sacred* **p**. Hos 10:1 4676
altars *And* destroy their *sacred* **p**. Hos 10:2 4676
And your *sacred* **p** from among you, Mi 5:13 4676
Will lodge in the tops of her **p**; Zph 2:14 3730
John, who were reputed to be **p**, Ga 2:9 *4769*
sun, and his feet like **p** of fire; Rv 10:1 *4769*

PILOT
the **p** and the captain of the ship than Ac 27:11 *2942*
the inclination of the **p** desires. Jas 3:4 *2116*

PILOTS
they were your **p**. Ezk 27:8 2259
Your sailors and your **p**, Ezk 27:27 2259
"At the sound of the cry of your **p** Ezk 27:28 2259
and all the **p** of the sea Will come Ezk 27:29 2259

PILTAI
of Miniamin, of Moadiah, **P**; Ne 12:17 6408

PIN
the web [and fasten it with a **p**, Jg 16:13 3489
And she fastened *it* with the **p** and Jg 16:14 3489
and pulled out the **p** of the loom Jg 16:14 3489
"I will **p** David to the wall." 1Sa 18:11 5221
Saul tried to **p** David to the 1Sa 19:10 5221

PINE
eyes and cause the soul to **p** away; Lv 26:16 1727
nets on the waters will **p** away. Is 19:8 535
For they **p** away, being stricken La 4:9 2100

PINES
The land mourns *and* **p** away, Is 33:9 535
"She who bore seven *sons* **p** away; Jer 15:9 535

PINING
to me, O LORD, for I *am* **p** away; Ps 6:2 536

PINION
With the **p** and plumage of love, Jb 39:13 84

PINIONS
them, He carried them on His **p**. Dt 32:11 84
And its **p** with glistening gold. Ps 68:13 84
He will cover you with His **p**, Ps 91:4 84
long **p** and a full plumage of many Ezk 17:3 83

PINNACLE
Him stand on the **p** of the temple, Mt 4:5 *4419*
Him stand on the **p** of the temple, Lk 4:9 *4419*

PINON
Oholibamah, chief Elah, chief **P**, Gn 36:41 6373
Oholibamah, chief Elah, chief **P**, 1Ch 1:52 6373

PIPE
all those who play the lyre and **p**. Gn 4:21 5748
with stringed instruments and **p**. Ps 150:4 5748

PIPES
which are beside the two golden **p**, Zch 4:12 6804

PIPING
To hear the **p** for the flocks? Jg 5:16 8292

PIRAM
to **P** king of Jarmuth and to Japhia Jos 10:3 6502

PIRATHON
at **P** in the land of Ephraim, Jg 12:15 6552

PIRATHONITE
Now Abdon the son of Hillel the **P** Jg 12:13 6553
Abdon the son of Hillel the **P** died Jg 12:15 6553
Benaiah a **P**, Hiddai of the brooks 2Sa 23:30 6553
sons of Benjamin, Benaiah the **P**, 1Ch 11:31 6553
Benaiah the **P** of the sons of 1Ch 27:14 6553

PISGAH
P which overlooks the wasteland. Nu 21:20 6449
field of Zophim, to the top of **P**, Nu 23:14 6449
Sea, at the foot of the slopes of **P** Dt 3:17 6449
'Go up to the top of **P** and lift up Dt 3:27 6449
at the foot of the slopes of **P**. Dt 4:49 6449
to Mount Nebo, to the top of **P**, Dt 34:1 6449
at the foot of the slopes of **P**; Jos 12:3 6449
the slopes of **P** and Beth-jeshimoth, Jos 13:20 6449

PISHON
The name of the first is **P**; Gn 2:11 6376

PISIDIA
They passed through **P** and came Ac 14:24 *4099*

PISIDIAN
Perga, they arrived at **P** Antioch, Ac 13:14 *4099*

PISPA
sons of Jether *were* Jephunneh, **P** and 1Ch 7:38 6462

PISTACHIO
gum and myrrh, **p** nuts and almonds. Gn 43:11 992

PIT
this **p** that is in the wilderness, Gn 37:22 953a
took him and threw him into the **p**. Gn 37:24 953a
Now the **p** was empty, without any Gn 37:24 953a
up and lifted Joseph out of the **p**, Gn 37:28 953a
Now Reuben returned to the **p**, Gn 37:29 953a
behold, Joseph was not in the **p**; Gn 37:29 953a
"If a man opens a **p**, Ex 21:33 953a
If a man opens a pit, or digs a **p** Ex 21:33 953a
owner of the **p** shall make restitution Ex 21:34 953a
Absalom and cast him into a deep **p** 2Sa 18:17 6354
killed a lion in the middle of a **p** 2Sa 23:20 877
killed them at the **p** of Beth-eked, 2Ki 10:14 953a
killed a lion inside a **p** on a snowy 1Ch 11:22 953a
You would plunge me into the **p**, Jb 9:31 7845
If I call to the **p**, Jb 17:14 7845
He keeps back his soul from the **p**, Jb 33:18 7845
"Then his soul draws near to the **p**, Jb 33:22 7845
him from going down to the **p**, Jb 33:24 7845
my soul from going to the **p**, Jb 33:28 7845
To bring back his soul from the **p**, Jb 33:30 7845
has dug a **p** and hollowed it out, Ps 7:15 953a
in the **p** which they have made; Ps 9:15 7845
like those who go down to the **p**. Ps 28:1 953a
I would not go down to the **p**. Ps 30:3 953a
my blood, if I go down to the **p**? Ps 30:9 7845
cause they dug a **p** for my soul. Ps 35:7 7845
me up out of the **p** of destruction, Ps 40:2 953a
them down to the **p** of destruction; Ps 55:23 875
They dug a **p** before me; Ps 57:6 7882
the **p** shut its mouth on me. Ps 69:15 875
among those who go down to the **p**; Ps 88:4 953a
You have put me in the lowest **p**, Ps 88:6 953a
Until a **p** is dug for the wicked. Ps 94:13 7845
Who redeems your life from the **p**, Ps 103:4 7845
like those who go down to the **p**. Ps 143:7 953a
as those who go down to the **p**; Pr 1:12 953a
mouth of an adulteress is a deep **p**; Pr 22:14 7745
For a harlot is a deep **p** And Pr 23:27 7745
He who digs a **p** will fall into it, Pr 26:27 7845
Will himself fall into his own **p**, Pr 28:10 7816
He who digs a **p** may fall into it, Ec 10:8 1475
Sheol, To the recesses of the **p**. Is 14:15 953a
go down to the stones of the **p** Like Is 14:19 953a
and **p** and snare Confront you, Is 24:17 6354
of disaster will fall into the **p**, Is 24:18 6354
he who climbs out of the **p** will be Is 24:18 6354
my soul from the **p** of nothingness, Is 38:17 7845
Those who go down to the **p** cannot Is 38:18 953a
For they have dug a **p** for me. Jer 18:20 7745
For they have dug a **p** to capture Jer 18:22 7745
"Terror, **p** and snare are *coming* Jer 48:43 6354
the terror Will fall into the **p**, Jer 48:44 6354
the one who climbs up out of the **p** Jer 48:44 6354
They have silenced me in the **p** La 3:53 953a

name, O LORD, Out of the lowest **p**. **La 3:55** 953a
He was captured **in their p**, **Ezk 19:4** 7845
He was captured **in their p**. **Ezk 19:8** 7845
with those who go down to the **p**, **Ezk 26:20** 953a
with those who go down to the **p**, **Ezk 26:20** 953a
'They will bring you down to the **p**, **Ezk 28:8** 7845
with those who go down to the **p**." **Ezk 31:14** 953a
with those who go down to the **p**; **Ezk 31:16** 953a
with those who go down to the **p**; **Ezk 32:18** 953a
in the remotest parts of the **p** and **Ezk 32:23** 953a
with those who went down to the **p**. **Ezk 32:24** 953a
with those who go down to the **p**; **Ezk 32:25** 953a
with those who go down to the **p**. **Ezk 32:29** 953a
with those who go down to the **p**. **Ezk 32:30** 953a
brought up my life from the **p**, **Jon 2:6** 7845
free from the waterless **p**. **Zch 9:11** 953a
it falls into a **p** on the Sabbath, **Mt 12:11** *999*
man, both will fall into a **p**." **Mt 15:14** *999*
Will they not both fall into a **p**? **Lk 6:39** *999*
key of the bottomless **p** was given **Rv 9:1** *5421*
He opened the bottomless **p**, **Rv 9:2** *5421*
and smoke went up out of the **p**, **Rv 9:2** *5421*
darkened by the smoke of the **p**. **Rv 9:2** *5421*

PITCH
cover it inside and out with **p**. **Gn 6:14** 3724b
covered it over with tar and **p**. **Ex 2:3** 2203a
tent and **p** it outside the camp, **Ex 33:7** 5186
will the Arab **p** *his* tent there, **Is 13:20** 167
streams will be turned into **p**, **Is 34:9** 2203a
its land will become burning **p**. **Is 34:9** 2203a
will **p** *their* tents around her, **Jer 6:3** 8628
wall, raise up a ramp, **p** camps and **Ezk 4:2** 5414
"He will **p** the tents of his **Da 11:45** 5193

PITCHED
east of Bethel, and **p** his tent, **Gn 12:8** 5186
of the LORD, and **p** his tent there; **Gn 26:25** 5186
p his tent in the hill country, **Gn 31:25** 8628
piece of land where he had **p** his tent **Gn 33:19** 5186
p his tent beyond the tower of Eder. **Gn 35:21** 5186
the camps that are **p** on the east **Nu 10:5** 2583
the camps that are **p** on the south **Nu 10:6** 2583
and had **p** his tent as far away as **Jg 4:11** 5186
the tent which David had **p** for it; **2Sa 6:17** 5186
So they **p** a tent for Absalom on **2Sa 16:22** 5186
ark of God and **p** a tent for it. **1Ch 15:1** 5186
the tent which David had **p** for it, **1Ch 16:1** 5186
had **p** a tent for it in Jerusalem. **2Ch 1:4** 5186
The tent which He had **p** among men, **Ps 78:60** 7931
who has **p** his *tent* for the night? **Jer 14:8** 5186
true tabernacle, which the Lord **p**, **Heb 8:2** *4078*

PITCHER
the **p** by the well is shattered and **Ec 12:6** 3537
meet you carrying a **p** of water; **Mk 14:13** *2765*
meet you carrying a **p** of water; **Lk 22:10** *2765*

PITCHERS
he put trumpets and empty **p** into **Jg 7:16** 3537
them, with torches inside the **p**. **Jg 7:16** 3537
smashed the **p** that were in their **Jg 7:19** 3537
blew the trumpets and broke the **p**, **Jg 7:20** 3537
"Fill four **p** with water and pour **1Ki 18:34** 3537
basins, and the **p** of pure gold; **1Ch 28:17** 7184
of the Rechabites **p** full of wine and **Jer 35:5** 1375
of cups and **p** and copper pots.) **Mk 7:4** *3582*

PITFALL
Panic and **p** have befallen us, **La 3:47** 6354

PITHOM
storage cities, **P** and Raamses. **Ex 1:11** 6619

PITHON
The sons of Micah *were* **P**, **1Ch 8:35** 6377
The sons of Micah *were* **P**, **1Ch 9:41** 6377

PITIED
we are of all men most to be **p**. **1Co 15:19** *1652*

PITS
of Siddim was full of tar **p**; **Gn 14:10** 875
and throw him into one of the **p**; **Gn 37:20** 953a
in cliffs, in cellars, and in **p**. **1Sa 13:6** 953a
The arrogant have dug **p** for me, **Ps 119:85** 7882
p from which they cannot rise. **Ps 140:10** 4113
a land of deserts and of **p**, **Jer 2:6** 7745
reared in purple Embrace ash **p**. **La 4:5** 830
anointed, Was captured in their **p**, **La 4:20** 7825
possessed by nettles and salt **p**, **Zph 2:9** 4379
committed them to **p** of darkness, **2Pe 2:4** *4618a*

PITY
And she had **p** on him and said, **Ex 2:6** 2550
your eye shall not **p** them, **Dt 7:16** 2347
and your eye shall not **p** him, **Dt 13:8** 2347
"You shall not **p** him, but you **Dt 19:13** 2347
"Thus you shall not show **p**: **Dt 19:21** 2347
you shall not show **p**. **Dt 25:12** 2347
for the LORD was moved to **p** by **Jg 2:18** 5162
kill you, but *my eye* had **p** on you; **1Sa 24:10** 2347
"**P** me, pity me, O you my friends, **Jb 19:21** 2603a
"Pity me, **p** me, O you my friends, **Jb 19:21** 2603a
stones And feel **p** for her dust. **Ps 102:14** 2603a
Nor does He have **p** on their **Is 9:17** 7355
Nor will their eye **p** children. **Is 13:18** 2347
"I will not show **p** nor be sorry **Jer 13:14** 2550
"Indeed, who will have **p** on you, **Jer 15:5** 2550
nor have **p** nor compassion." **Jer 21:7** 2550
My eye will have no **p** and I will **Ezk 5:11** 2347
'For My eye will have no **p** on you, **Ezk 7:4** 2347
'My eye will show no **p** nor **Ezk 7:9** 2347
My eye will have no **p** nor will I **Ezk 8:18** 2347
do not let your eye have **p** and **Ezk 9:5** 2347
My eye will have no **p** nor will I **Ezk 9:10** 2347
"No eye looked with **p** on you to **Ezk 16:5** 2347
not relent, and I will not **p** **Ezk 24:14** 2347
And will have **p** on His people. **Jl 2:18** 2550
own shepherds have no **p** on them. **Zch 11:5** 2550
"For I will no longer have **p** on **Zch 11:6** 2550
take **p** on us and help us!" **Mk 9:22** *4697*

PIVOTS
leaves of the one door turned on **p**, **1Ki 6:34** 1550
leaves of the other door turned on **p**. **1Ki 6:34** 1550

PLACE
heavens be gathered into one **p**, **Gn 1:9** 4725
and closed up the flesh at that **p**. **Gn 2:21** 8478
me another offspring in **p** of Abel, **Gn 4:25** 8478
p for the sole of her foot, **Gn 8:9** 4494
to the **p** where his tent had been **Gn 13:3** 4725
to the **p** of the altar which he **Gn 13:4** 4725
and look from the **p** where you are, **Gn 13:14** 4725
sweep *it* away and not spare the **p** **Gn 18:24** 4725
I will spare the whole **p** on their **Gn 18:26** 4725
and Abraham returned to his **p**. **Gn 18:33** 4725
the city, bring *them* out of the **p**; **Gn 19:12** 4725
we are about to destroy this **p**, **Gn 19:13** 4725
"Up, get out of this **p**, **Gn 19:14** 4725
went to the **p** where he had stood **Gn 19:27** 4725
there is no fear of God in this **p**, **Gn 20:11** 4725
he called that **p** Beersheba, **Gn 21:31** 4725
the **p** of which God had told him. **Gn 22:3** 4725
and saw the **p** from a distance. **Gn 22:4** 4725
the **p** of which God had told him; **Gn 22:9** 4725
offering in the **p** of his son. **Gn 22:13** 8478
of that **p** The LORD Will Provide, **Gn 22:14** 4725
"Please **p** your hand under my thigh **Gn 24:2** 7760
house, and a **p** for the camels?" **Gn 24:31** 4725
men of the **p** asked about his wife, **Gn 26:7** 4725
"the men of the **p** might kill me **Gn 26:7** 4725
He came to a certain **p** and spent **Gn 28:11** 4725
he took one of the stones of the **p** **Gn 28:11** 4725
his head, and lay down in that **p**. **Gn 28:11** 4725
"Surely the LORD is in this **p**, **Gn 28:16** 4725
"How awesome is this **p**! **Gn 28:17** 4725
called the name of that **p** Bethel; **Gn 28:19** 4725
put the stone back in its **p** on the **Gn 29:3** 4725
gathered all the men of the **p** and **Gn 29:22** 4725
"It is not the practice in our **p** to **Gn 29:26** 4725
"Am I in the **p** of God, who has **Gn 30:2** 8478
that I may go to my own **p** and to **Gn 30:25** 4725
Jacob would **p** the rods in the **Gn 30:41** 7760
departed and returned to his **p**. **Gn 31:55** 4725
So he named that **p** Mahanaim. **Gn 32:2** 4725
So Jacob named the **p** Peniel, **Gn 32:30** 4725
therefore the **p** is named Succoth. **Gn 33:17** 4725
there, and called the **p** El-bethel, **Gn 35:7** 4725
p where He had spoken with him. **Gn 35:13** 4725
p where He had spoken with him, **Gn 35:14** 4725
p where God had spoken with him, **Gn 35:15** 4725
of Bozrah became king in his **p**. **Gn 36:33** 8478
Temanites became king in his **p**. **Gn 36:34** 8478
of Moab, became king in his **p**; **Gn 36:35** 8478
of Masrekah became king in his **p**. **Gn 36:36** 8478
River became king in his **p**. **Gn 36:37** 8478
of Achbor became king in his **p**. **Gn 36:38** 8478
and Hadar became king in his **p**; **Gn 36:39** 8478
He asked the men of her **p**, **Gn 38:21** 4725
the men of the **p** said, **Gn 38:22** 4725
took **p** while she was giving birth, **Gn 38:28** 1961
the **p** where the king's prisoners **Gn 39:20** 4725
p where Joseph was imprisoned. **Gn 40:3** 4725
and buy *some* for us from that **p**, **Gn 42:2** 8033
you shall not go from this **p** **Gn 42:15**
donkey fodder at the lodging **p**, **Gn 42:27** 4411
when we came to the lodging **p**, **Gn 43:21** 4411
and he sought *a* **p** to weep; **Gn 43:30**
p now your hand under my thigh and **Gn 47:29** 7760
and bury me in their burial **p**." **Gn 47:30** 6900
P your right hand on his head." **Gn 48:18** 7760
"When he saw that a resting **p** was **Gn 49:15** 4496
not be afraid, for am I in God's **p**? **Gn 50:19** 8478
for the **p** on which you are standing **Ex 3:5** 4725
to the **p** of the Canaanite and the **Ex 3:8** 4725
it came about at the lodging **p** on **Ex 4:24** 4411
rise from his **p** for three days, **Ex 10:23** 8478
LORD brought you out from this **p**. **Ex 13:3**
The **p**, O LORD, which You have **Ex 15:17** 4349
Remain every man in his **p**; **Ex 16:29** 8478
let no man go out of his **p** on the **Ex 16:29** 4725
in it, and **p** it before the LORD to **Ex 16:33** 5117
He named the **p** Massah and **Ex 17:7** 4725
and you shall **p** *these* over them **Ex 18:21** 7760
will go to their **p** in peace." **Ex 18:23** 4725
in every **p** where I cause My name **Ex 20:24** 4725
you a **p** to which he may flee. **Ex 21:13** 4725
into the **p** which I have prepared. **Ex 23:20** 4725
the holy **p** and the holy of holies. **Ex 26:33**
two rings of gold and shall **p** them **Ex 28:26** 7760
close to the **p** where it is joined, **Ex 28:27** 4225
heart when he enters the holy **p**, **Ex 28:29**
leaves the holy **p** before the LORD, **Ex 28:35**
altar to minister in the holy **p**, **Ex 28:43**
meeting to minister in the holy **p**. **Ex 29:30**
and boil its flesh in a holy **p**. **Ex 29:31** 4725
altar as a **p** for burning incense; **Ex 30:1** 4729a
fragrant incense for the holy **p**, **Ex 31:11**
"Behold, there is a **p** by Me, **Ex 33:21** 4725
for ministering in the holy **p**, **Ex 35:19**
for ministering in the holy **p** as **Ex 39:1**
close to the **p** where it joined, **Ex 39:20** 4225
garments for ministering in the holy **p** **Ex 39:41**
"You shall **p** the ark of the **Ex 40:3** 7760
eastward, to the **p** of the ashes. **Lv 1:16** 4725
he is to bring out to a clean **p** **Lv 4:12** 4725
he is to bring out the bull to *a* **p** **Lv 4:21**
and slay it in the **p** where they **Lv 4:24** 4725
at the **p** of the burnt offering. **Lv 4:29** 4725
p where they slay the burnt offering. **Lv 4:33** 4725
put oil on it or **p** incense on it, **Lv 5:11** 5414
and **p** them beside the altar. **Lv 6:10** 7760
outside the camp to a clean **p**. **Lv 6:11** 4725
as unleavened cakes in a holy **p**; **Lv 6:16** 4725
p among his sons shall offer it. **Lv 6:22** 8478
in the **p** where the burnt offering **Lv 6:25** 4725
It shall be eaten in a holy **p**, **Lv 6:26** 4725
in a holy **p** you shall wash what **Lv 6:27** 4725
in the holy **p** shall be eaten; **Lv 6:30**
'In the **p** where they slay the **Lv 7:2** 4725
It shall be eaten in a holy **p**; **Lv 7:6** 4725
eat it, moreover, in a holy **p**, **Lv 10:13** 4725
offering you may eat in a clean **p**, **Lv 10:14** 4725
the sin offering at the holy **p**? **Lv 10:17** 4725
and in the **p** of the boil there is **Lv 13:19** 4725
the bright spot remains in its **p** and **Lv 13:23** 8478
the bright spot remains in its **p** and **Lv 13:28** 8478
slaughter the male lamb in the **p** **Lv 14:13** 4725
at the **p** of the sanctuary **Lv 14:13** 4725
on the **p** of the blood of the guilt **Lv 14:28** 4725
at an unclean **p** outside the city. **Lv 14:40** 4725
at an unclean **p** outside the city. **Lv 14:41** 4725
outside the city to an unclean **p**. **Lv 14:45** 4725
into the holy **p** inside the veil, **Lv 16:2**
shall enter the holy **p** with this: **Lv 16:3**
make atonement for the holy **p**, **Lv 16:16**
to make atonement in the holy **p**, **Lv 16:17**
finishes atoning for the holy **p** and **Lv 16:20**
on when he went into the holy **p**, **Lv 16:23**
a holy **p** and put on his clothes, **Lv 16:24** 4725
to make atonement in the holy **p**, **Lv 16:27**
to serve as priest in his father's **p** **Lv 16:32** 8478
nor **p** a stumbling block before the **Lv 19:14** 5414
and they shall eat it in a holy **p**; **Lv 24:9** 4725
nor shall you **p** a figured stone in **Lv 26:1** 5414
p the animal before the priest. **Lv 27:11** 5975
shall set out, every man in his **p** by **Nu 2:17** 3027
and **p** the grain offering of **Nu 5:18** 5414
p where the cloud settled down, **Nu 9:17** 4725
We are setting out to the **p** of which **Nu 10:29** 4725
to seek out a resting **p** for them. **Nu 10:33** 4496
name of that **p** was called Taberah, **Nu 11:3** 4725
p was called Kibroth-hattaavah, **Nu 11:34** 4725
That **p** was called the valley of **Nu 13:24** 4725
p which the LORD has promised." **Nu 14:40** 4725
outside the camp in a clean **p**, **Nu 19:9** 4725
to bring us in to this wretched **p**? **Nu 20:5** 4725
It is not a **p** of grain or figs or **Nu 20:5** 4725
name of the **p** was called Hormah. **Nu 21:3** 4725
and stood in a narrow **p** where **Nu 22:26** 4725
p from where you may see them, **Nu 23:13** 4725
I will take you to another **p**; **Nu 23:27** 4725
"Therefore, flee to your **p** now. **Nu 24:11** 4725
"Your dwelling **p** is enduring, And **Nu 24:21** 4186
departed and returned to his **p**, **Nu 24:25** 4725
in the holy **p** you shall pour out a **Nu 28:7**
indeed a **p** suitable for livestock, **Nu 32:1** 4725
have risen up in your fathers' **p**, **Nu 32:14** 8478
we have brought them to their **p**, **Nu 32:17** 4725
walked until you came to this **p**.' **Dt 1:31** 4725
to seek out a **p** for you to encamp, **Dt 1:33** 4725
them and settled in their **p**, **Dt 2:12** 8478
them and settled in their **p**, **Dt 2:21** 8478
settled in their **p** even to this day. **Dt 2:22** 8478
them and lived in their **p**.) **Dt 2:23** 8478
Egypt until you arrived at this **p**, **Dt 9:7** 4725
son ministered as priest in his **p**. **Dt 10:6** 8478
until you came to this **p**; **Dt 11:5** 4725
"Every **p** on which the sole of **Dt 11:24** 4725
that you shall **p** the blessing on **Dt 11:29** 5414
obliterate their name from that **p**. **Dt 12:3** 4725
you shall seek *the* LORD at the **p** **Dt 12:5** 4725
have not as yet come to the resting **p** **Dt 12:9** 4496
the **p** in which the LORD your God **Dt 12:11** 4725
in every *cultic* **p** you see, **Dt 12:13** 4725
but in the **p** which the LORD **Dt 12:14** 4725
in the **p** which the LORD your God **Dt 12:18** 4725
"If the **p** which the LORD your God **Dt 12:21** 4725
to the **p** which the LORD chooses. **Dt 12:26** 4725
at the **p** where He chooses to **Dt 14:23** 4725
since the **p** where the LORD your **Dt 14:24** 4725
and go to the **p** which the LORD your **Dt 14:25** 4725
in the **p** which the LORD chooses. **Dt 15:20** 4725
in the **p** where the LORD chooses to **Dt 16:2** 4725
but at the **p** where the LORD your **Dt 16:6** 4725
You shall cook and eat *it* in the **p** **Dt 16:7** 4725
in the **p** where the LORD your God **Dt 16:11** 4725
in the **p** which the LORD chooses, **Dt 16:15** 4725
God in the **p** which He chooses, **Dt 16:16** 4725
you shall arise and go up to the **p** **Dt 17:8** 4725
that **p** which the LORD chooses; **Dt 17:10** 4725
to the **p** which the LORD chooses, **Dt 18:6** 4725
and do not **p** the guilt of innocent **Dt 21:8** 5414
"You shall also have a **p** outside **Dt 23:12** 3027
in the **p** which he shall choose in **Dt 23:16** 4725
put *it* in a basket and go to the **p** **Dt 26:2** 4725
and He has brought us to this **p** and **Dt 26:9** 4725
no resting **p** for the sole of your foot; **Dt 28:65** 4494
"When you reached this **p**, **Dt 29:7** 4725
God at the **p** which He will choose, **Dt 31:11** 4725
"Take this book of the law and **p** **Dt 31:26** 7760
you, Let them be your hiding **p**! **Dt 32:38** 5643b
"The eternal God is a dwelling **p**, **Dt 33:27** 4585
knows his burial **p** to this day. **Dt 34:6** 6900

"Every **p** on which the sole of	**Jos 1:3**	4725
then you shall set out from your **p**	**Jos 3:3**	4725
from the **p** where the priests' feet	**Jos 4:3**	4673
lay them down in the lodging **p**	**Jos 4:3**	4411
over with them to the lodging **p** and	**Jos 4:8**	4411
at the **p** where the feet of the priests	**Jos 4:9**	4673, 8478
of the Jordan returned to their **p**,	**Jos 4:18**	4725
whom He raised up in their **p**,	**Jos 5:7**	8478
p is called Gilgal to this day.	**Jos 5:9**	4725
for the **p** where you are standing	**Jos 5:15**	4725
Therefore the name of that **p** has	**Jos 7:26**	4725
and they went to the **p** of ambush	**Jos 8:9**	
p before the desert plain.	**Jos 8:14**	4150
ambush rose quickly from their **p**,	**Jos 8:19**	4725
had no **p** to flee this way or that,	**Jos 8:20**	3027
in the **p** which He would choose.	**Jos 9:27**	4725
go up to the forest and clear a **p**	**Jos 17:15**	
the city to them and give him a **p**,	**Jos 20:4**	4725
So they named that **p** Bochim;	**Jg 2:5**	4725
stood in his **p** around the camp;	**Jg 7:21**	8478
pass through your land to our **p**."	**Jg 11:19**	4725
and he named that **p** Ramath-lehi.	**Jg 15:17**	4725
But God split the hollow **p** that is	**Jg 15:19**	
they surrounded *the* **p** and lay in	**Jg 16:2**	
to stay wherever he might find *a* **p**;	**Jg 17:8**	
to stay wherever I may find *a* **p**."	**Jg 17:9**	
And what are you doing in this **p**?	**Jg 18:3**	
a **p** where there is no lack of	**Jg 18:10**	4725
that **p** Mahaneh-dan to this day;	**Jg 18:12**	4725
arose and departed and came to *a* **p**	**Jg 19:10**	
the men of the **p** were Benjamites.	**Jg 19:16**	4725
how did this wickedness take **p**?"	**Jg 20:3**	1961
that has taken **p** among you?	**Jg 20:12**	1961
p where they had arrayed themselves	**Jg 20:22**	4725
the men of Israel arose from their **p**	**Jg 20:33**	4725
in ambush broke out of their **p**,	**Jg 20:33**	4725
departed from the **p** where she was,	**Ru 1:7**	4725
shall notice the **p** where he lies,	**Ru 3:4**	4725
or from the court of his *birth* **p**;	**Ru 4:10**	4725
children from this woman in **p** of the	**1Sa 2:20**	8478
as Eli was lying down in his **p**	**1Sa 3:2**	4725
Samuel went and lay down in his **p**.	**1Sa 3:9**	4725
Dagon and set him in his **p** again.	**1Sa 5:3**	4725
and let it return to its own **p**,	**1Sa 5:11**	4725
how we shall send it to its **p**."	**1Sa 6:2**	4725
of the LORD and **p** it on the cart;	**1Sa 6:8**	5414
he will take your sons and **p** *them*	**1Sa 8:11**	7760
a sacrifice on the high **p** today.	**1Sa 9:12**	1116
he goes up to the high **p** to eat,	**1Sa 9:13**	1116
them to go up to the high **p**.	**1Sa 9:14**	1116
Go up before me to the high **p**,	**1Sa 9:19**	1116
and gave them a **p** at the head of	**1Sa 9:22**	4725
from the high **p** into the city,	**1Sa 9:25**	1116
down from the high **p** with harp,	**1Sa 10:5**	1116
he came to the high **p**.	**1Sa 10:13**	1116
Egypt and settled them in this **p**.	**1Sa 12:8**	4725
then we will stand in our **p** and not	**1Sa 14:9**	8478
Philistines went to their own **p**.	**1Sa 14:46**	4725
stay in a secret **p** and hide yourself.	**1Sa 19:2**	5643a
come to the **p** where you hid yourself	**1Sa 20:19**	4725
side, but David's **p** was empty.	**1Sa 20:25**	4725
new moon, that David's **p** was empty;	**1Sa 20:27**	4725
the lad reached the **p** of the arrow	**1Sa 20:37**	4725
the young men to a certain **p**.'	**1Sa 21:2**	4725
in order to put hot bread *in its* **p**	**1Sa 21:6**	
and see his **p** where his haunt is,	**1Sa 23:22**	4725
called that **p** the Rock of Escape.	**1Sa 23:28**	4725
to the **p** where Saul had camped.	**1Sa 26:5**	4725
David saw the **p** where Saul lay,	**1Sa 26:5**	4725
way, and Saul returned to his **p**.	**1Sa 26:25**	4725
let them give me a **p** in one of the	**1Sa 27:5**	4725
his **p** where you have assigned him,	**1Sa 29:4**	4725
that **p** was called Helkath-hazzurim,	**2Sa 2:16**	4725
p where Asahel had fallen and died,	**2Sa 2:23**	4725
sent messengers to David in his **p**,	**2Sa 3:12**	8478
he named that **p** Baal-perazim.	**2Sa 5:20**	4725
and that **p** is called Perez-uzzah	**2Sa 6:8**	4725
ark of the LORD and set it in its **p**	**2Sa 6:17**	4725
"I will also appoint a **p** for My	**2Sa 7:10**	4725
that they may live in their own **p**	**2Sa 7:10**	8478
his son became king in his **p**.	**2Sa 10:1**	8478
"**P** Uriah in the front line of the	**2Sa 11:15**	3051
that he put Uriah at the **p** where	**2Sa 11:16**	4725
return to your own **p**.	**2Sa 15:19**	4725
Saul, in whose **p** you have reigned;	**2Sa 16:8**	8478
one of the caves or in another **p**;	**2Sa 17:9**	4725
Amasa over the army in **p** of Joab.	**2Sa 17:25**	8478
took **p** in the forest of Ephraim.	**2Sa 18:6**	1961
me continually in **p** of Joab.' "	**2Sa 19:13**	8478
him, and he returned to his **p**.	**2Sa 19:39**	4725
brought me forth into a broad **p**;	**2Sa 22:20**	4800
burned with fire in *their* **p**."	**2Sa 23:7**	7675
he shall sit on my throne in my **p**	**1Ki 1:30**	8478
on my throne and be king in my **p**;	**1Ki 1:35**	8478
Jehoiada over the army in his **p**,	**1Ki 2:35**	8478
the priest in the **p** of Abiathar.	**1Ki 2:35**	8478
do not go out from there to any **p**.	**1Ki 2:36**	575
for that was the great high **p**;	**1Ki 3:4**	1116
king in **p** of my father David,	**1Ki 3:7**	8478
to the **p** where it should be,	**1Ki 4:28**	4725
him king in **p** of his father,	**1Ki 5:1**	8478
will set on your throne in your **p**,	**1Ki 5:5**	8478
sea to the **p** where you direct me,	**1Ki 5:9**	4725
even as the most holy **p**.	**1Ki 6:16**	6944
to **p** there the ark of the covenant	**1Ki 6:19**	5414
the inner house, the most holy **p**,	**1Ki 7:50**	6944
the covenant of the LORD to its **p**,	**1Ki 8:6**	4725
of the house, to the most holy **p**,	**1Ki 8:6**	6944
their wings over the **p** of the ark,	**1Ki 8:7**	4725
holy **p** before the inner sanctuary,	**1Ki 8:8**	
the priests came from the holy **p**,	**1Ki 8:10**	
A **p** for Your dwelling forever."	**1Ki 8:13**	4349
for I have risen in **p** of my father	**1Ki 8:20**	8478
There I have set a **p** for the ark,	**1Ki 8:21**	4725
the **p** of which You have said,	**1Ki 8:29**	4725
servant shall pray toward this **p**.	**1Ki 8:29**	4725
when they pray toward this **p**;	**1Ki 8:30**	4725
hear in heaven Your dwelling **p**;	**1Ki 8:30**	4725
and they pray toward this **p** and	**1Ki 8:35**	4725
hear in heaven Your dwelling **p**,	**1Ki 8:39**	4349
hear in heaven Your dwelling **p**,	**1Ki 8:43**	4349
in heaven Your dwelling **p**,	**1Ki 8:49**	4349
Then Solomon built a high **p** for	**1Ki 11:7**	1116
his son Rehoboam reigned in his **p**.	**1Ki 11:43**	8478
bread or drink water in this **p**.	**1Ki 13:8**	4725
or drink water with you in this **p**.	**1Ki 13:16**	4725
in the **p** of which He said to you,	**1Ki 13:22**	4725
Nadab his son reigned in his **p**.	**1Ki 14:20**	8478
made shields of bronze in their **p**,	**1Ki 14:27**	8478
his son became king in his **p**.	**1Ki 14:31**	8478
Asa his son became king in his **p**.	**1Ki 15:8**	8478
his son reigned in his **p**.	**1Ki 15:24**	8478
of Judah and reigned in his **p**.	**1Ki 15:28**	8478
Elah his son became king in his **p**.	**1Ki 16:6**	8478
Judah, and became king in his **p**,	**1Ki 16:10**	8478
Ahab his son became king in his **p**.	**1Ki 16:28**	8478
cut it up, and **p** it on the wood,	**1Ki 18:23**	7760
shall anoint as prophet in your **p**.	**1Ki 19:16**	8478
remove the kings, each from his **p**,	**1Ki 20:24**	4725
and put captains in their **p**,	**1Ki 20:24**	8478
better vineyard than it in its **p**;	**1Ki 21:2**	8478
give you a vineyard in its **p**.'	**1Ki 21:6**	8478
"In the **p** where the dogs licked	**1Ki 21:19**	4725
his son became king in his **p**.	**1Ki 22:40**	8478
his son became king in his **p**.	**1Ki 22:50**	8478
Jehoram became king in his **p** in	**2Ki 1:17**	8478
son who was to reign in his **p**,	**2Ki 3:27**	8478
God, and wave his hand over the **p** and	**2Ki 5:11**	4725
the **p** before you where we are	**2Ki 6:1**	4725
and let us make a **p** there for	**2Ki 6:2**	4725
And when he showed him the **p**,	**2Ki 6:6**	4725
and such a **p** shall be my camp."	**2Ki 6:8**	4725
that you do not pass this **p**,	**2Ki 6:9**	4725
The king of Israel sent to the **p**	**2Ki 6:10**	4725
And Hazael became king in his **p**.	**2Ki 8:15**	8478
his son became king in his **p**.	**2Ki 8:24**	8478
his son became king in his **p**.	**2Ki 10:35**	8478
his son became king in his **p**.	**2Ki 12:21**	8478
his son became king in his **p**.	**2Ki 13:9**	8478
his son became king in his **p**.	**2Ki 13:24**	8478
his son became king in his **p**.	**2Ki 14:16**	8478
in the **p** of his father Amaziah.	**2Ki 14:21**	8478
his son became king in his **p**.	**2Ki 14:29**	8478
his son became king in his **p**.	**2Ki 15:7**	8478
killed him, and reigned in his **p**.	**2Ki 15:10**	8478
him and became king in his **p**.	**2Ki 15:14**	8478
his son became king in his **p**.	**2Ki 15:22**	8478
him and became king in his **p**.	**2Ki 15:25**	8478
to death and became king in his **p**,	**2Ki 15:30**	8478
Ahaz his son became king in his **p**.	**2Ki 15:38**	8478
his son Hezekiah reigned in his **p**.	**2Ki 16:20**	8478
in **p** of the sons of Israel.	**2Ki 17:24**	8478
against this **p** to destroy it?	**2Ki 18:25**	4725
I entered its farthest lodging **p**,	**2Ki 19:23**	4411
his son became king in his **p**.	**2Ki 19:37**	8478
his son became king in his **p**.	**2Ki 20:21**	8478
Amon his son became king in his **p**.	**2Ki 21:18**	8478
made Josiah his son king in his **p**.	**2Ki 21:24**	8478
his son became king in his **p**.	**2Ki 21:26**	8478
on this **p** and on its inhabitants,	**2Ki 22:16**	4725
My wrath burns against this **p**,	**2Ki 22:17**	4725
you heard what I spoke against this **p**	**2Ki 22:19**	4725
the evil which I will bring on this **p**.	**2Ki 22:20**	4725
and the high **p** which Jeroboam	**2Ki 23:15**	1116
and the high **p** he broke down.	**2Ki 23:15**	1116
made him king in **p** of his father.	**2Ki 23:30**	8478
in the **p** of Josiah his father,	**2Ki 23:34**	8478
his son became king in his **p**.	**2Ki 24:6**	8478
uncle Mattaniah king in his **p**,	**2Ki 24:17**	8478
of Bozrah became king in his **p**.	**1Ch 1:44**	8478
Temanites became king in his **p**.	**1Ch 1:45**	8478
of Moab, became king in his **p**;	**1Ch 1:46**	8478
of Masrekah became king in his **p**.	**1Ch 1:47**	8478
by the River became king in his **p**.	**1Ch 1:48**	8478
of Achbor became king in his **p**.	**1Ch 1:49**	8478
died, Hadad became king in his **p**;	**1Ch 1:50**	8478
to this day, and lived in their **p**,	**1Ch 4:41**	8478
they settled in their **p** until the exile.	**1Ch 5:22**	8478
all the work of the most holy **p**,	**1Ch 6:49**	6944
called that **p** Perez-uzza to this day.	**1Ch 13:11**	4725
they named that **p** Baal-perazim.	**1Ch 14:11**	4725
prepared a **p** for the ark of God and	**1Ch 15:1**	4725
up the ark of the LORD to its **p** which	**1Ch 15:3**	4725
the LORD God of Israel to *the* **p**	**1Ch 15:12**	
Strength and joy are in His **p**.	**1Ch 16:27**	4725
in the high **p** which *was* at Gibeon,	**1Ch 16:39**	1116
from *one* dwelling **p** *to another*.	**1Ch 17:5**	4908
appoint a **p** for My people Israel,	**1Ch 17:9**	4725
their own **p** and not be moved again;	**1Ch 17:9**	8478
and his son became king in his **p**.	**1Ch 19:1**	8478
the high **p** at Gibeon at that time.	**1Ch 21:29**	1116
meeting, and charge of the holy **p**,	**1Ch 23:32**	
his son Solomon reigned in his **p**.	**1Ch 29:28**	8478
to the high **p** which was at Gibeon,	**2Ch 1:3**	1116
to the **p** he had prepared for it,	**2Ch 1:4**	
and have made me king in his **p**.	**2Ch 1:8**	8478
the high **p** which was at Gibeon,	**2Ch 1:13**	1116
at the **p** that David had prepared on	**2Ch 3:1**	4725
the covenant of the LORD to its **p**,	**2Ch 5:7**	4725
their wings over the **p** of the ark,	**2Ch 5:8**	4725
came forth from the holy **p**	**2Ch 5:11**	
a **p** for Your dwelling forever."	**2Ch 6:2**	4349
for I have risen in the **p** of my	**2Ch 6:10**	8478
toward the **p** of which You have	**2Ch 6:20**	4725
servant shall pray toward this **p**.	**2Ch 6:20**	4725
when they pray toward this **p**;	**2Ch 6:21**	4725
hear from Your dwelling **p**,	**2Ch 6:21**	4725
they pray toward this **p** and confess	**2Ch 6:26**	4725
hear from heaven Your dwelling **p**,	**2Ch 6:30**	4349
from heaven, from Your dwelling **p**,	**2Ch 6:33**	4349
from heaven, from Your dwelling **p**,	**2Ch 6:39**	4349
to the prayer *offered* in this **p**.	**2Ch 6:40**	4725
O LORD God, to Your resting **p**,	**2Ch 6:41**	4496
and have chosen this **p** for Myself	**2Ch 7:12**	4725
to the prayer *offered* in this **p**.	**2Ch 7:15**	4725
his son Rehoboam reigned in his **p**.	**2Ch 9:31**	8478
made shields of bronze in their **p** and	**2Ch 12:10**	8478
son Abijah became king in his **p**.	**2Ch 12:16**	8478
his son Asa became king in his **p**.	**2Ch 14:1**	8478
and they laid him in the resting **p**	**2Ch 16:14**	4904
his son then became king in his **p**,	**2Ch 17:1**	8478
Therefore they have named that **p**	**2Ch 20:26**	4725
his son became king in his **p**,	**2Ch 21:1**	8478
his youngest son, king in his **p**,	**2Ch 22:1**	8478
take it, and return it to its **p**.	**2Ch 24:11**	4725
his son became king in his **p**.	**2Ch 24:27**	8478
in the **p** of his father Amaziah.	**2Ch 26:1**	8478
his son became king in his **p**.	**2Ch 26:23**	8478
Ahaz his son became king in his **p**.	**2Ch 27:9**	8478
Hezekiah his son reigned in his **p**.	**2Ch 28:27**	8478
uncleanness out from the holy **p**.	**2Ch 29:5**	
from the dwelling **p** of the LORD,	**2Ch 29:6**	4908
the holy **p** to the God of Israel.	**2Ch 29:7**	
came to His holy dwelling **p**,	**2Ch 30:27**	4583
son Manasseh became king in his **p**.	**2Ch 32:33**	8478
Amon his son became king in his **p**.	**2Ch 33:20**	8478
made Josiah his son king in his **p**.	**2Ch 33:25**	8478
on this **p** and on its inhabitants,	**2Ch 34:24**	4725
will be poured out on this **p** and	**2Ch 34:25**	4725
you heard His words against this **p**	**2Ch 34:27**	4725
the evil which I will bring on this **p**	**2Ch 34:28**	4725
Then the king stood in his **p** and	**2Ch 34:31**	5977
stand in the holy **p** according to	**2Ch 35:5**	
in **p** of his father in Jerusalem.	**2Ch 36:1**	8478
his son became king in his **p**.	**2Ch 36:8**	8478
His people and on His dwelling **p**;	**2Ch 36:15**	4583
at whatever **p** he may live,	**Ezr 1:4**	4725
let the men of that **p** support him	**Ezr 1:4**	4725
of God be rebuilt in its **p**."	**Ezr 5:15**	870
p where sacrifices are offered,	**Ezr 6:3**	870
the leading man at the **p** Casiphia;	**Ezr 8:17**	4725
temple servants at the **p** Casiphia,	**Ezr 8:17**	4725
to give us a peg in His holy **p**,	**Ezr 9:8**	4725
will bring them to the **p** where I have	**Ne 1:9**	4725
city, the **p** of my fathers' tombs,	**Ne 2:3**	1004
was no **p** for my mount to pass.	**Ne 2:14**	4725
from every **p** where you may turn,"	**Ne 4:12**	4725
"At whatever **p** you hear the sound	**Ne 4:20**	4725
the people *remained* in their **p**.	**Ne 8:7**	5977
While they stood in their **p**,	**Ne 9:3**	5977
took **p** in the days of Ahasuerus,	**Es 1:1**	1961
sat in the first **p** in the kingdom	**Es 1:14**	
king be queen in **p** of Vashti."	**Es 2:4**	8478
maids to the best **p** in the harem.	**Es 2:9**	
will arise for the Jews from another **p**	**Es 4:14**	4725
p where they were drinking wine,	**Es 7:8**	1004
they came each one from his own **p**,	**Jb 2:11**	4725
hungry devour And take it to a **p** *of*	**Jb 5:5**	
And I would **p** my cause before God;	**Jb 5:8**	7760
is hot, they vanish from their **p**.	**Jb 6:17**	4725
Nor will his **p** know him anymore.	**Jb 7:10**	4725
"If he is removed from his **p**,	**Jb 8:18**	4725
Who shakes the earth out of its **p**,	**Jb 9:6**	4725
And the rock moves from its **p**;	**Jb 14:18**	4725
like you, If I were in your **p**.	**Jb 16:4**	8478
there be no *resting* **p** for my cry.	**Jb 16:18**	4725
the rock to be moved from its **p**?	**Jb 18:4**	4725
p of him who does not know God."	**Jb 18:21**	4725
And his **p** no longer beholds him.	**Jb 20:9**	4725
'Clouds are a hiding **p** for Him,	**Jb 22:14**	5643a
And **p** *your* gold in the dust, And	**Jb 22:24**	7896
For it whirls him away from his **p**.	**Jb 27:21**	4725
him And will hiss him from his **p**.	**Jb 27:23**	4725
And a **p** where they refine gold.	**Jb 28:1**	4725
where is the **p** of understanding?	**Jb 28:12**	4725
where is the **p** of understanding?	**Jb 28:20**	4725
And He knows its **p**.	**Jb 28:23**	4725
And sets others in their **p**.	**Jb 34:24**	8478
like the wicked In a public **p**,	**Jb 34:26**	4725
it, a broad **p** with no constraint;	**Jb 36:16**	7338
When people vanish in their **p**.	**Jb 36:20**	8478
trembles, And leaps from its **p**.	**Jb 37:1**	4725
And caused the dawn to know its **p**,	**Jb 38:12**	4725
And darkness, where is its **p**,	**Jb 38:19**	4725
the salt land for his dwelling **p**?	**Jb 39:6**	4908
the rocky crag, an inaccessible **p**.	**Jb 39:28**	4686b
Bind them in the hidden **p**.	**Jb 40:13**	
a hiding **p** as a lion in his lair;	**Ps 10:9**	4565
He made darkness His hiding **p**,	**Ps 18:11**	5643a
me forth also into a broad **p**;	**Ps 18:19**	4800
and majesty You **p** upon him.	**Ps 21:5**	7737b
And who may stand in His holy **p**?	**Ps 24:3**	4725
And the **p** where Your glory dwells.	**Ps 26:8**	4725
My foot stands on a level **p**;	**Ps 26:12**	4334
In the secret **p** of His tent He will	**Ps 27:5**	5643a
have set my feet in a large **p**.	**Ps 31:8**	4800

You hide them in the secret **p**	**Ps 31:20**	5643a
You are my hiding **p**;	**Ps 32:7**	5643a
From His dwelling **p** He looks out	**Ps 33:14**	4349
you will look carefully for his **p** and	**Ps 37:10**	4725
have crushed us in a **p** of jackals And	**Ps 44:19**	4725
In **p** of your fathers will be your	**Ps 45:16**	8478
"I would hasten to my **p** of refuge	**Ps 55:8**	4655
Yet You brought us out into *a* **p** *of*	**Ps 66:12**	
his people return to this **p**,	**Ps 73:10**	1988
in the midst of Your meeting **p**;	**Ps 74:4**	4150
the dwelling **p** of Your name.	**Ps 74:7**	4908
His dwelling **p** also is in Zion.	**Ps 76:2**	4585
the dwelling **p** at Shiloh,	**Ps 78:60**	4908
you in the hiding **p** of thunder;	**Ps 81:7**	5643a
our dwelling **p** in all generations.	**Ps 90:1**	4583
the Most High, your dwelling **p**.	**Ps 91:9**	4583
its **p** acknowledges it no longer.	**Ps 103:16**	4725
the valleys sank down To the **p**	**Ps 104:8**	4725
sun knows the **p** of its setting.	**Ps 104:19**	3996
me *and set me* in a large **p**.	**Ps 118:5**	4800
are my hiding **p** and my shield;	**Ps 119:114**	5643a
Until I find a **p** for the LORD, A	**Ps 132:5**	4725
A dwelling **p** for the Mighty One	**Ps 132:5**	4908
Let us go into His dwelling **p**;	**Ps 132:7**	4908
Arise, O LORD, to Your resting **p**,	**Ps 132:8**	4496
"This is My resting **p** forever;	**Ps 132:14**	4496
"She will **p** on your head a	**Pr 4:9**	5414
But the wicked takes his **p**.	**Pr 11:8**	8478
eyes of the LORD are in every **p**,	**Pr 15:3**	4725
is in the **p** of the upright.	**Pr 21:18**	8478
Do not destroy his resting **p**;	**Pr 24:15**	7258
not stand in the **p** of great men;	**Pr 25:6**	4725
to its **p** it rises there *again*.	**Ec 1:5**	4725
To the **p** where the rivers flow,	**Ec 1:7**	4725
in the **p** of justice there is wickedness	**Ec 3:16**	4725
and in the **p** of righteousness	**Ec 3:16**	4725
All go to the same **p**.	**Ec 3:20**	4725
do not all go to one **p**?"	**Ec 6:6**	4725
to go in and out from the holy **p**,	**Ec 8:10**	4725
high **p** and of terrors on the road;	**Ec 12:5**	
the secret **p** of the steep pathway,	**SS 2:14**	5643a
that every **p** where there used to	**Is 7:23**	4725
but they will become a **p** for	**Is 7:25**	4916a
"Geba will be our lodging **p**."	**Is 10:29**	4411
His resting **p** will be glorious.	**Is 11:10**	4496
the earth will be shaken from its **p**	**Is 13:13**	4725
along and bring them to their **p**,	**Is 14:2**	4725
"Prepare for his sons a **p** of	**Is 14:21**	4293
hiding **p** to them from the destroyer."	**Is 16:4**	5643a
wearies himself upon *his* high **p** And	**Is 16:12**	1116
"I will look from My dwelling **p**	**Is 18:4**	4349
To the **p** of the name of the LORD	**Is 18:7**	4725
a resting **p** for yourself in the rock?	**Is 22:16**	4908
drive him *like* a peg in a firm **p**,	**Is 22:23**	4725
driven in a firm **p** will give way;	**Is 22:25**	4725
Moab will be trodden down in his **p**	**Is 25:10**	8478
is about to come out from His **p**	**Is 26:21**	4725
vomit, without a *single clean* **p**.	**Is 28:8**	4725
will overflow the secret **p**.	**Is 28:17**	5643a
Then you become its trampling **p**.	**Is 28:18**	
wheat in rows, Barley in its **p** and	**Is 28:25**	5567
whose deeds are *done* in a dark **p**,	**Is 29:15**	4285
of the LORD comes from a remote **p**;	**Is 30:27**	4801
for us A **p** of rivers *and* wide canals On	**Is 33:21**	4725
will find herself a resting **p**.	**Is 34:14**	4494
haunt of jackals, its resting **p**,	**Is 35:7**	7258
his son became king in his **p**.	**Is 37:38**	8478
will **p** the juniper in the desert Together	**Is 41:19**	7760
to us what is going to take **p**;	**Is 41:22**	7136a
ransom, Cush and Seba in your **p**.	**Is 43:3**	8478
I will give *other* men in your **p**	**Is 43:4**	8478
events that are going to take **p**.	**Is 44:7**	935
and did not create it a waste **p**,	**Is 45:18**	8414
'Seek Me in a waste **p**';	**Is 45:19**	8414
They set it in its **p** and it stands	**Is 46:7**	8478
It does not move from its **p**.	**Is 46:7**	4725
Before they took **p** I proclaimed	**Is 48:5**	935
secret, From the time it took **p**,	**Is 48:16**	1961
'The **p** is too cramped for me;	**Is 49:20**	4725
"Enlarge the **p** of your tent;	**Is 54:2**	4725
"I dwell *on* a high and holy **p**,	**Is 57:15**	
To beautify the **p** of My sanctuary;	**Is 60:13**	4725
make the **p** of My feet glorious.	**Is 60:13**	4725
of Achor a resting **p** for herds,	**Is 65:10**	7258
And where is a **p** that I may rest?	**Is 66:1**	4725
"From this **p** also you will go	**Jer 2:37**	
He has gone out from his **p** To	**Jer 4:7**	4725
They will pasture each in his **p**.	**Jer 6:3**	3027
I will let you dwell in this **p**.	**Jer 7:3**	4725
not shed innocent blood in this **p**,	**Jer 7:6**	4725
I will let you dwell in this **p**,	**Jer 7:7**	4725
now to My **p** which was in Shiloh,	**Jer 7:12**	4725
and to the **p** which I gave you and	**Jer 7:14**	4725
will be poured out on this **p**,	**Jer 7:20**	4725
because there is no *other* **p**.	**Jer 7:32**	4725
the desert A wayfarers' lodging **p**;	**Jer 9:2**	4411
from the **p** where I had hidden it;	**Jer 13:7**	4725
you lasting peace in this **p**.' "	**Jer 14:13**	4725
sons or daughters in this **p**."	**Jer 16:2**	4725
sons and daughters born in this **p**,	**Jer 16:3**	4725
am going to eliminate from this **p**,	**Jer 16:9**	4725
Is the **p** of our sanctuary.	**Jer 17:12**	4725
to bring a calamity upon this **p**,	**Jer 19:3**	4725
have made this an alien **p** and have	**Jer 19:4**	4725
they have filled this **p** with the blood	**Jer 19:4**	4725
"when this **p** will no longer be	**Jer 19:6**	4725
of Judah and Jerusalem in this **p**,	**Jer 19:7**	4725
there is no *other* **p** for burial.	**Jer 19:11**	4725
this **p** and its inhabitants,"	**Jer 19:12**	4725

be defiled like the **p** Topheth,	**Jer 19:13**	4725
not shed innocent blood in this **p**.	**Jer 22:3**	4725
sitting in David's **p** on his throne,	**Jer 22:4**	
in the **p** of Josiah his father,	**Jer 22:11**	8478
who went forth from this **p**,	**Jer 22:11**	4725
the **p** where they led him captive,	**Jer 22:12**	4725
whom I have sent out of this **p**	**Jer 24:5**	4725
left His hiding **p** like the lion;	**Jer 25:38**	5520
the burial **p** of the common people.	**Jer 26:23**	6913
and restore them to this **p**.' "	**Jer 27:22**	4725
I am going to bring back to this **p** all	**Jer 28:3**	4725
took away from this **p** and carried	**Jer 28:3**	4725
to bring back to this **p** Jeconiah	**Jer 28:4**	4725
exiles, from Babylon to this **p**.	**Jer 28:6**	4725
you, to bring you back to this **p**.	**Jer 29:10**	4725
back to the **p** from where I sent you	**Jer 29:14**	4725
will stand on its rightful **p**.	**Jer 30:18**	4941
P for yourself guideposts;	**Jer 31:21**	7760
and I will bring them back to this **p**	**Jer 32:37**	4725
there will be heard in this **p**,	**Jer 33:10**	4725
again be in this **p** which is waste,	**Jer 33:12**	4725
reigned as king in **p** of Coniah the	**Jer 37:1**	8478
went into the king's palace to *a* **p**	**Jer 38:11**	
take **p** before you on that day.	**Jer 39:16**	1961
this calamity against this **p**;	**Jer 40:2**	4725
and you will see this **p** no more."	**Jer 42:18**	4725
in the **p** where you wish to go to	**Jer 42:22**	4725
am going to punish you in this **p**,	**Jer 44:29**	4725
one who offers *sacrifice* on the high **p**	**Jer 48:35**	1116
have forgotten their resting **p**.	**Jer 50:6**	7258
Station sentries, **P** men in ambush!	**Jer 51:12**	3559
concerning this **p** to cut it off,	**Jer 51:62**	4725
destroyed His appointed meeting **p**.	**La 2:6**	4150
the glory of the LORD in His **p**."	**Ezk 3:12**	4725
and I **p** an obstacle before him,	**Ezk 3:20**	5414
yourself a brick, **p** it before you and	**Ezk 4:1**	5414
and **p** battering rams against it	**Ezk 4:2**	7760
I will give you cow's dung in **p**	**Ezk 4:15**	8478
and they will profane My secret **p**;	**Ezk 7:22**	6845
even go into exile from your **p** to	**Ezk 12:3**	4725
place to another **p** in their sight.	**Ezk 12:3**	4725
no **p** in the council of My people,	**Ezk 13:9**	1961
yourself a high **p** in every square.	**Ezk 16:24**	7413
high **p** at the top of every street and	**Ezk 16:25**	7413
made your high **p** in every square,	**Ezk 16:31**	7413
is the high **p** to which you go?'	**Ezk 20:29**	1116
to **p** you on the necks of the wicked	**Ezk 21:29**	5414
In the **p** where you were created,	**Ezk 21:30**	4725
of Ammon a resting **p** for flocks.	**Ezk 25:5**	4769
'She will be a **p** for the spreading	**Ezk 26:5**	4894b
be a **p** for the spreading of nets.	**Ezk 26:14**	4894b
all around its planting **p**,	**Ezk 31:4**	4302
for them a renowned planting **p**,	**Ezk 34:29**	4302
and I will **p** you on your own land.	**Ezk 37:14**	5117
I will **p** them and multiply them,	**Ezk 37:26**	5414
dwelling **p** also will be with them;	**Ezk 37:27**	4908
"You will come from your **p**	**Ezk 38:15**	4725
"This is the most holy **p**."	**Ezk 41:4**	
for the **p** is holy.	**Ezk 42:13**	4725
this is the **p** of My throne and the	**Ezk 43:7**	
and the **p** of the soles of My feet,	**Ezk 43:7**	4725
in the appointed **p** of the house,	**Ezk 43:21**	4662
there shall be for the holy **p** a square	**Ezk 45:2**	
be the sanctuary, the most holy **p**.	**Ezk 45:3**	6944
and it shall be a **p** for their	**Ezk 45:4**	4725
and a holy **p** for the sanctuary.	**Ezk 45:4**	4720
there *was* a **p** at the extreme rear	**Ezk 46:19**	4725
"This is the **p** where the priests	**Ezk 46:20**	4725
in every **p** where the river goes,	**Ezk 47:9**	
be a **p** for the spreading of nets.	**Ezk 47:10**	4894a
of the land, a most holy **p**,	**Ezk 48:12**	6944
dwelling **p** is not with *mortal* flesh."	**Da 2:11**	4094b
will take **p** in the latter days.	**Da 2:28**	1934
what would take **p** in the future;	**Da 2:29**	1934
known to you what will take **p**.	**Da 2:29**	1934
what will take **p** in the future;	**Da 2:45**	1934
and your dwelling **p** be with the	**Da 4:25**	4070
and your dwelling **p** *will be* with	**Da 4:32**	4070
his dwelling **p** *was* with the wild	**Da 5:21**	4070
and in its **p** there came up four	**Da 8:8**	8478
and the **p** of His sanctuary was	**Da 8:11**	4349
holy **p** and the host to be trampled?"	**Da 8:13**	
holy **p** will be properly restored."	**Da 8:14**	
and the four *horns that* arose in its **p**	**Da 8:22**	8478
and to anoint the most holy **p**.	**Da 9:24**	
of her line will arise in his **p**,	**Da 11:7**	3653b
"Then in his **p** one will arise who	**Da 11:20**	3653b
"In his **p** a despicable person	**Da 11:21**	3653b
in the **p** Where it is said to them,	**Hos 1:10**	4725
I will go away *and* return to My **p**	**Hos 5:15**	4725
the **p** where you have sold them,	**Jl 3:7**	4725
in every **p** they will cast them	**Am 8:3**	4725
the loftiness of your dwelling **p**,	**Ob 1:3**	7675
LORD is coming forth from His **p**.	**Mi 1:3**	4725
Like water poured down a steep **p**.	**Mi 1:4**	4174
What is the high **p** of Judah?	**Mi 1:5**	1116
For this is no **p** of rest Because	**Mi 2:10**	4496
the feeding **p** of the young lions,	**Na 2:11**	4829
the **p** where they are is not known.	**Na 3:17**	4725
my bones, And in my **p** I tremble.	**Hab 3:16**	8478
the remnant of Baal from this **p**,	**Zph 1:4**	4725
A **p** possessed by nettles and salt pits,	**Zph 2:9**	4476
to Him, everyone from his *own* **p**.	**Zph 2:11**	4725
A resting **p** for beasts!	**Zph 2:15**	4769
'and in this **p** I will give	**Hg 2:9**	4725
And it will take **p** if	**Zch 6:15**	1961
with Damascus as its resting **p**	**Zch 9:1**	4496
as far as the **p** of the First Gate	**Zch 14:10**	4725
and in every **p** incense is going to	**Mal 1:11**	4725

Now all this took **p** to fulfill what was	**Mt 1:22**	*1096*
until it came and stood over *the* **p**	**Mt 2:9**	
Judea in **p** of his father Herod,	**Mt 2:22**	*473*
in that **p** there will be weeping	**Mt 8:12**	*1563*
in that **p** there will be weeping	**Mt 13:42**	*1563*
in that **p** there will be weeping	**Mt 13:50**	*1563*
a boat to a secluded **p** by Himself;	**Mt 14:13**	*5117*
"This **p** is desolate and the hour	**Mt 14:15**	*5117*
the men of that **p** recognized Him,	**Mt 14:35**	*5117*
we get so many loaves in *this* desolate **p**	**Mt 15:33**	*2047*
standing idle in the market **p**;	**Mt 20:3**	*58*
This took **p** to fulfill what was	**Mt 21:4**	*1096*
in that **p** there will be weeping	**Mt 22:13**	*1563*
love the **p** of honor at banquets and	**Mt 23:6**	*4411*
for *those things* must take **p**,	**Mt 24:6**	*1096*
prophet, standing in the holy **p**	**Mt 24:15**	*5117*
until all these things take **p**.	**Mt 24:34**	*1096*
assign him a **p** with the hypocrites;	**Mt 24:51**	*3313*
in that **p** there will be weeping	**Mt 24:51**	*3313*
in that **p** there will be weeping	**Mt 25:30**	*1563*
them to a **p** called Gethsemane,	**Mt 26:36**	*5564*
"Put your sword back into its **p**;	**Mt 26:52**	*5117*
"But all this has taken **p** to	**Mt 26:56**	*1096*
Field as a burial **p** for strangers.	**Mt 27:7**	*5027*
came to a **p** called Golgotha,	**Mt 27:33**	*5117*
which means **P** of a Skull,	**Mt 27:33**	*5117*
see the **p** where He was lying.	**Mt 28:6**	*5117*
away to a secluded **p**,	**Mk 1:35**	*5117*
"Any **p** that does not receive	**Mk 6:11**	*5117*
to a secluded **p** and rest a while."	**Mk 6:31**	*5117*
boat to a secluded **p** by themselves.	**Mk 6:32**	*5117*
"This **p** is desolate and it is	**Mk 6:35**	*5117*
sick, to the **p** they heard He was.	**Mk 6:55**	*3699*
when they come from the market **p**,	**Mk 7:4**	*58*
bread here in *this* desolate **p**	**Mk 8:4**	*2047*
those things must take **p**;	**Mk 13:7**	*1096*
until all these things take **p**.	**Mk 13:30**	*1096*
They came to a **p** named Gethsemane;	**Mk 14:32**	*5564*
but *this has taken* **p** to	**Mk 14:49**	
brought Him to the **p** Golgotha,	**Mk 15:22**	*5117*
which is translated, **P** of a Skull.	**Mk 15:22**	*5117*
here is the **p** where they laid Him.	**Mk 16:6**	*5117*
the day when these things take **p**,	**Lk 1:20**	*1096*
found the **p** where it was written,	**Lk 4:17**	*5117*
left and went to a secluded **p**;	**Lk 4:42**	*5117*
with them and stood on a level **p**;	**Lk 6:17**	*5117*
like children who sit in the market **p**	**Lk 7:32**	*58*
for here we are in a desolate **p**."	**Lk 9:12**	*5117*
ahead of Him to every city and **p**	**Lk 10:1**	*5117*
when he came to the **p** and saw him,	**Lk 10:32**	*5117*
Jesus was praying in a certain **p**,	**Lk 11:1**	*5117*
I have no **p** to store my crops?'	**Lk 12:17**	*4226*
assign him a **p** with the unbelievers.	**Lk 12:46**	*3313*
"In that **p** there will be weeping	**Lk 13:28**	*1563*
feast, do not take the **p** of honor,	**Lk 14:8**	*4411*
'Give *your* **p** to this man,'	**Lk 14:9**	*5117*
you proceed to occupy the last **p**.	**Lk 14:9**	*5117*
go and recline at the last **p**,	**Lk 14:10**	*5117*
also come to this **p** of torment.'	**Lk 16:28**	*5117*
two women grinding at the same **p**;	**Lk 17:35**	
When Jesus came to the **p**,	**Lk 19:5**	*5117*
things are about to take **p**?"	**Lk 21:7**	*1096*
these things must take **p** first,	**Lk 21:9**	*1096*
when these things begin to take **p**,	**Lk 21:28**	*1096*
pass away until all things take **p**.	**Lk 21:32**	*1096*
things that are about to take **p**,	**Lk 21:36**	*1096*
When He arrived at the **p**,	**Lk 22:40**	*5117*
Galilee even as far as this **p**."	**Lk 23:5**	*5602*
came to the **p** called The Skull,	**Lk 23:33**	*5117*
these things which had taken **p**.	**Lk 24:14**	*4819*
p in Bethany beyond the Jordan,	**Jn 1:28**	*1096*
stop making My Father's house a **p** of	**Jn 2:16**	*3624*
p where men ought to worship."	**Jn 4:20**	*5117*
while there was a crowd in *that* **p**.	**Jn 5:13**	*5117*
Now there was much grass in the **p**.	**Jn 6:10**	*5117*
to the **p** where they ate the bread	**Jn 6:23**	*5117*
because My word has no **p** in you.	**Jn 8:37**	*5562*
Dedication took **p** at Jerusalem;	**Jn 10:22**	*1096*
the **p** where John was first baptizing,	**Jn 10:40**	*5117*
days *longer* in the **p** where He was.	**Jn 11:6**	*5117*
in the **p** where Martha met Him.	**Jn 11:30**	*5117*
and take away both our **p** and our	**Jn 11:48**	*5117*
for I go to prepare a **p** for you.	**Jn 14:2**	*5117*
If I go and prepare a **p** for you,	**Jn 14:3**	*5117*
who was betraying Him, knew the **p**,	**Jn 18:2**	*5117*
seat at a **p** called The Pavement,	**Jn 19:13**	*5117*
the **p** called the Place of a Skull,	**Jn 19:17**	
the place called the **P** of a Skull,	**Jn 19:17**	*5117*
for the **p** where Jesus was	**Jn 19:20**	*5117*
Now in the **p** where He was	**Jn 19:41**	*5117*
but rolled up in a **p** by itself.	**Jn 20:7**	*5117*
my finger into the **p** of the nails,	**Jn 20:25**	*5117*
turned aside to go to his own **p**."	**Ac 1:25**	*5117*
they were all together in one **p**.	**Ac 2:1**	
taking **p** through the apostles.	**Ac 2:43**	*1096*
a noteworthy miracle has taken **p**	**Ac 4:16**	*1096*
and signs and wonders take **p**	**Ac 4:30**	*1096*
the **p** where they had gathered	**Ac 4:31**	*5117*
were taking **p** among the people;	**Ac 5:12**	*1096*
speaks against this holy **p** and	**Ac 6:13**	*5117*
will destroy this **p** and alter the	**Ac 6:14**	*5117*
COME OUT AND SERVE ME IN THIS **P**.'	**Ac 7:7**	*5117*
THE **P** ON WHICH YOU ARE STANDING	**Ac 7:33**	*5117*
a dwelling **p** for the God of Jacob.	**Ac 7:46**	*4638*
OR WHAT **P** IS THERE FOR MY REPOSE?	**Ac 7:49**	*5117*
signs and great miracles taking **p**,	**Ac 8:13**	*1096*
which took **p** throughout all Judea,	**Ac 10:37**	*1096*
took **p** in the *reign* of Claudius.	**Ac 11:28**	*1096*
he left and went to another **p**.	**Ac 12:17**	*5117*

that there would be a **p** of prayer; **Ac 16:13** 4335
we were going to the **p** of prayer, **Ac 16:16** 4335
market **p** before the authorities, **Ac 16:19** 58
some wicked men from the market **p**, **Ac 17:5** 60
and in the market **p** every day with **Ac 17:17** 58
This took **p** for two years, so **Ac 19:10** 1096
who went from **p** to place, **Ac 19:13** 4022
who went from place to **p**, **Ac 19:13** 4022
people and the Law and this **p**; **Ac 21:28** 5117
and has defiled this holy **p**." **Ac 21:28** 5117
before he comes near *the* **p**." **Ac 23:15**
the investigation has taken **p**, **Ac 25:26** 1096
Moses said was going to take **p**; **Ac 26:22** 1096
to a **p** called Fair Havens, **Ac 27:8** 5117
Now in the neighborhood of that **p** **Ac 28:7** 5117
THE **P** WHERE IT WAS SAID TO THEM, **Ro 9:26** 5117
further **p** for me in these regions, **Ro 15:23** 5117
with all who in every **p** call on **1Co 1:2** 5117
For, in the first **p**, **1Co 11:18**
the **p** of the ungifted say the **1Co 14:16** 5117
the knowledge of Him in every **p**. **2Co 2:14** 5117
to have first **p** in everything. **Col 1:18** 4409
but also in every **p** your faith **1Th 1:8** 5117
I want the men in every **p** to pray, **1Tm 2:8** 5117
resurrection has already taken **p**, **2Tm 2:18** 1096
takes **p** a change of law also. **Heb 7:12** 1096
this is called the holy **p**. **Heb 9:2** 40
the way into the holy **p** has not yet **Heb 9:8** 40
entered the holy **p** once for all, **Heb 9:12** 40
that, since a death has taken **p** for the **Heb 9:15** 1096
enter a holy **p** made with hands, **Heb 9:24** 40
high priest enters the holy **p** year by **Heb 9:25** 40
have confidence to enter the holy **p** **Heb 10:19** 40
obeyed by going out to a **p** which **Heb 11:8** 5117
for he found no **p** for repentance, **Heb 12:17** 5117
blood is brought into the holy **p** **Heb 13:11** 40
"You sit here in a good **p**," **Jas 2:3**
as to a lamp shining in a dark **p**, **2Pe 1:19** 5117
things which must soon take **p**; **Rv 1:1** 1096
will take **p** after these things. **Rv 1:19** 1096
remove your lampstand out of its **p** **Rv 2:5** 5117
I **p** no other burden on you. **Rv 2:24** 906
must take **p** after these things." **Rv 4:1** 1096
where she had a **p** prepared by God, **Rv 12:6** 5117
was no longer a **p** found for them in **Rv 12:8** 5117
fly into the wilderness to her **p**, **Rv 12:14** 5117
the **p** which in Hebrew is called **Rv 16:16** 5117
has become a dwelling **p** of demons **Rv 18:2** 2732
away, and no **p** was found for them. **Rv 20:11** 5117
things which must soon take **p**. **Rv 22:6** 1096

PLACED

God **p** them in the expanse of **Gn 1:17** 5414
He **p** the man whom He had formed. **Gn 2:8** 7760
prepared, and **p** *it* before them; **Gn 18:8** 5414
So the servant **p** his hand under **Gn 24:9** 7760
and **p** the food in the cities; **Gn 41:48** 5414
he **p** in every city the food from **Gn 41:48** 5414
and **p** in a coffin in Egypt. **Gn 50:26** 7760
Aaron **p** it before the Testimony, **Ex 16:34** 5117
And he **p** them on the shoulder **Ex 39:7** 7760
They made two gold rings and **p** *them* **Ex 39:19** 7760
p them on the bottom of the two **Ex 39:20** 5414
Then he **p** the lampstand in the **Ex 40:24** 7760
Then he **p** the gold altar in the **Ex 40:26** 7760
He **p** the laver between the **Ex 40:30** 7760
He then **p** the breastpiece on him, **Lv 8:8** 7760
He also **p** the turban on his head, **Lv 8:9** 7760
its front, he **p** the golden plate, **Lv 8:9** 7760
and **p** *them* on the portions of fat **Lv 8:26** 7760
they now **p** the portions of fat on **Lv 9:20** 7760
p incense on it and offered **Lv 10:1** 7760
he shall be **p** before the priest and **Lv 27:8** 5975
and **p** *Him* upon the seventy elders. **Nu 11:25** 5414
on which a yoke has never been **p**. **Nu 19:2** 5927
'See, I have **p** the land before you; **Dt 1:8** 5414
God has **p** the land before you; **Dt 1:21** 5414
and **p** them outside the camp of **Jos 6:23** 5117
an ephod, and **p** it in his city, **Jg 8:27** 3322
Then he **p** her on the donkey; **Jg 19:28** 3947
the book and **p** *it* before the LORD. **1Sa 10:25** 5117
They **p** the ark of God on a new **2Sa 6:3** 7392
people he **p** in the hand of Abishai **2Sa 10:10** 5414
and it was **p** on David's head. **2Sa 12:30**
and **p** them under guard and **2Sa 20:3** 5414
He **p** the cherubim in the midst **1Ki 6:27** 5414
took his garment and **p** it under him **2Ki 9:13** 7760
and **p** him and his nurse in the **2Ki 11:2** 5641
ark of God and **p** it inside the tent **1Ch 16:1** 3322
people he **p** in the hand of Abshai **1Ch 19:11** 5414
and it was **p** on David's head. **1Ch 20:2** 1961
and **p** *them* on the tops of the **2Ch 3:16** 5414
and **p** *them* on the chains. **2Ch 3:16** 5414
tables and **p** them in the temple, **2Ch 4:8** 5117
He **p** troops in all the fortified **2Ch 17:2** 5414
and **p** him and his nurse in the **2Ch 22:11** 5414
Jehoiada **p** the offices of the **2Ch 23:18** 7760
And they **p** the king upon the royal **2Ch 23:20** 3427
their God, and **p** *them* in heaps. **2Ch 31:6** 5414
We also **p** ourselves under obligation **Ne 10:32** 5975
head a royal crown has been **p**; **Es 6:8** 5414
And I **p** boundaries on it And **Jb 38:10** 7665
have **p** me as head of the nations; **Ps 18:43** 7760
them He has **p** a tent for the sun, **Ps 19:4** 7760
have **p** our iniquities before You, **Ps 90:8** 7896
have **p** Your ordinances *before me.* **Ps 119:30** 7737a
Than for you to be **p** lower in **Pr 25:7** 8213
for the foundation, firmly **p**. **Is 28:16** 3245
For I have **p** the sand as a **Jer 5:22** 7760
the pit And have **p** a stone on me. **La 3:53** 3034

He **p** *it* beside abundant waters; **Ezk 17:5** 3947
She **p** it on the bare rock; **Ezk 24:7** 7760
who covers, And I **p** you *there.* **Ezk 28:14** 5414
before one stone was **p** on another **Hg 2:15** 7760
"For I also am a man **p** under **Lk 7:8**
and **p** on him the cross to carry **Lk 23:26** 2007
already laid and fish **p** on it, **Jn 21:9** 1945
they had **p** them in the center, **Ac 4:7** 2476
'I HAVE **P** YOU AS A LIGHT FOR THE **Ac 13:47** 5087
But now God has **p** the members, **1Co 12:18** 5087
And He **p** His right hand on me, **Rv 1:17** 5087
He **p** his right foot on the sea **Rv 10:2** 5087

PLACES

in all your dwelling **p**. **Lv 23:14** 4186
bring in from your dwelling **p** two **Lv 23:17** 4186
statute in all your dwelling **p** **Lv 23:21** 4186
in all your dwelling **p**. **Lv 23:31** 4186
'I then will destroy your high **p**, **Lv 26:30** 1116
him up to the high **p** of Baal, **Nu 22:41** 1116
Moses recorded their starting **p** **Nu 33:2** 4161
according to their starting **p**. **Nu 33:2** 4161
and demolish all their high **p**; **Nu 33:52** 1116
destroy all the **p** where the nations **Dt 12:2** 4725
ride on the high **p** of the earth, **Dt 32:13** 1116
will tread upon their high **p**." **Dt 33:29** 1116
they remained in their **p** in **Jos 5:8** 8478
flocks among the watering **p**, **Jg 5:11** 4857
also, on the high **p** of the field. **Jg 5:18** 4791
let us approach one of these **p**; **Jg 19:13** 4725
he judged Israel in all these **p**. **1Sa 7:16** 4725
hiding **p** where he hides himself and **1Sa 23:23** 4224b
and to all the **p** where David **1Sa 30:31** 4725
O Israel, is slain on your high **p**! **2Sa 1:19** 1116
Jonathan is slain on your high **p**. **2Sa 1:25** 1116
one of the **p** where he can be found, **2Sa 17:12** 4725
feet, And sets me on my high **p**. **2Sa 22:34** 1116
still sacrificing on the high **p**, **1Ki 3:2** 1116
and burned incense on the high **p**. **1Ki 3:3** 1116
And he made houses on high **p**, **1Ki 12:31** 1116
priests of the high **p** which he had **1Ki 12:32** 1116
priests of the high **p** who burn **1Ki 13:2** 1116
against all the houses of the high **p** **1Ki 13:32** 1116
again he made priests of the high **p** **1Ki 13:33** 1116
to be priests of the high **p**. **1Ki 13:33** 1116
they also built for themselves high **p** **1Ki 14:23** 1116
the high **p** were not taken away; **1Ki 15:14** 1116
the high **p** were not taken away; **1Ki 22:43** 1116
and burnt incense on the high **p**. **1Ki 22:43** 1116
the high **p** were not taken away; **2Ki 12:3** 1116
and burned incense on the high **p**. **2Ki 12:3** 1116
the high **p** were not taken away; **2Ki 14:4** 1116
and burned incense on the high **p**. **2Ki 14:4** 1116
the high **p** were not taken away; **2Ki 15:4** 1116
and burned incense on the high **p**. **2Ki 15:4** 1116
the high **p** were not taken away; **2Ki 15:35** 1116
and burned incense on the high **p**. **2Ki 15:35** 1116
and burned incense on the high **p** **2Ki 16:4** 1116
high **p** in all their towns, **2Ki 17:9** 1116
they burned incense on all the high **p** **2Ki 17:11** 1116
put them in the houses of the high **p** **2Ki 17:29** 1116
themselves priests of the high **p**, **2Ki 17:32** 1116
them in the houses of the high **p**. **2Ki 17:32** 1116
He removed the high **p** and broke **2Ki 18:4** 1116
is it not He whose high **p** and **2Ki 18:22** 1116
For he rebuilt the high **p** which **2Ki 21:3** 1116
to burn incense in the high **p** **2Ki 23:5** 1116
and defiled the high **p** where the **2Ki 23:8** 1116
and he broke down the high **p** of **2Ki 23:8** 1116
priests of the high **p** did not go up **2Ki 23:9** 1116
high **p** which *were* before Jerusalem, **2Ki 23:13** 1116
filled their **p** with human bones. **2Ki 23:14** 4725
removed all the houses of the high **p** **2Ki 23:19** 1116
All the priests of the high **p** **2Ki 23:20** 1116
"In all **p** where I have walked **1Ch 17:6**
because the **p** are holy where the **2Ch 8:11** 1992a
priests of his own for the high **p**, **2Ch 11:15** 1116
the foreign altars and high **p**, **2Ch 14:3** 1116
He also removed the high **p** and the **2Ch 14:5** 1116
high **p** were not removed from Israel **2Ch 15:17** 1116
high **p** and the Asherim from Judah. **2Ch 17:6** 1116
The high **p**, however, were not **2Ch 20:33** 1116
high **p** in the mountains of Judah, **2Ch 21:11** 1116
and burned incense on the high **p**, **2Ch 28:4** 1116
he made high **p** to burn incense to **2Ch 28:25** 1116
and pulled down the high **p** and the **2Ch 31:1** 1116
away His high **p** and His altars, **2Ch 32:12** 1116
For he rebuilt the high **p** which **2Ch 33:3** 1116
still sacrificed in the high **p**, **2Ch 33:17** 1116
built high **p** and erected the Asherim **2Ch 33:19** 1116
Judah and Jerusalem of the high **p**, **2Ch 34:3** 1116
p in the temple in Jerusalem; **Ezr 6:5** 870
behind the wall, the exposed **p**, **Ne 4:13** 6706
out the Levites from all their **p**, **Ne 12:27** 4725
the dwelling **p** of the wicked?' **Jb 21:28** 4908
in the lurking **p** of the villages; **Ps 10:8** 3993
In the hiding **p** he kills the innocent; **Ps 10:8** 4565
have fallen to me in pleasant **p**; **Ps 16:6**
a young lion lurking in hiding **p**. **Ps 17:12** 4565
feet, And sets me upon my high **p**. **Ps 18:33** 1116
holy hill And to Your dwelling **p**. **Ps 43:3** 4908
holy dwelling **p** of the Most High. **Ps 46:4** 4908
dwelling **p** to all generations; **Ps 49:11** 4908
You set them in slippery **p**; **Ps 73:18** 2513b
the meeting **p** of God in the land. **Ps 74:8** 4150
For the dark **p** of the land are **Ps 74:20** 4285
provoked Him with their high **p** And **Ps 78:58** 1116
How lovely are Your dwelling **p**, **Ps 84:1** 4908
all the *other* dwelling **p** of Jacob. **Ps 87:2** 4908
me in the lowest pit, In dark **p**, **Ps 88:6** 4285
become like an owl of the waste **p**. **Ps 102:6** 2723
of His, In all **p** of His dominion; **Ps 103:22** 4725
It ran in the dry **p** *like* a river. **Ps 105:41** 6723
He has made me dwell in dark **p**, **Ps 143:3** 4285
a seat by the high **p** of the city, **Pr 9:14** 4791
folly is set in many exalted **p** **Ec 10:6** 4791
while rich men sit in humble **p**. **Ec 10:6** 8216
eat in the waste **p** of the wealthy. **Is 5:17** 2723
And the forsaken **p** are many in the **Is 6:12** 5805
bushes and on all the watering **p**. **Is 7:19** 5097
ear, all remote **p** of the earth. **Is 8:9** 4801
Dibon, *even* to the high **p** to weep. **Is 15:2** 1116
be like forsaken **p** in the forest, **Is 17:9** 5805
carry her to colonize distant **p**? **Is 23:7**
and in undisturbed resting **p**; **Is 32:18** 4496
is it not He whose high **p** and **Is 36:7** 1116
them And rugged **p** into plains. **Is 42:16** 4625
you and make the rough **p** smooth; **Is 45:2** 1921
And hidden wealth of secret **p**, **Is 45:3** 4565
"For your waste and desolate **p** and **Is 49:19**
He will comfort all her waste **p**. **Is 51:3** 2723
You waste **p** of Jerusalem; **Is 52:9** 2723
satisfy your desire in scorched **p**, **Is 58:11** 6710
and spend the night in secret **p**; **Is 65:4** 5341
have built the high **p** of Topheth, **Jer 7:31** 1116
p to which I have driven them," **Jer 8:3** 4725
Your high **p** for sin throughout **Jer 17:3** 1116
and have built the high **p** of Baal **Jer 19:5** 1116
a man hide himself in hiding **p** So **Jer 23:24** 4565
all **p** where I will scatter them. **Jer 24:9** 4725
as the high **p** of a forest." **Jer 26:18** 1116
all the **p** where I have driven you,' **Jer 29:14** 4725
have compassion on his dwelling **p**; **Jer 30:18** 4908
"They built the high **p** of Baal **Jer 32:35** 1116
the **p** to which they had been driven **Jer 40:12** 4725
in all the **p** where you may go.' " **Jer 45:5** 4725
I have uncovered his hiding **p** So **Jer 49:10** 4565
Their dwelling **p** are set on fire, **Jer 51:30** 4908
The holy **p** of the LORD's house. **Jer 51:51** 4720
In dark **p** He has made me dwell, **La 3:6** 4285
in wait, *Like* a lion in secret **p**. **La 3:10** 4565
and I will destroy your high **p**. **Ezk 6:3** 1116
and the high **p** will be desolate, **Ezk 6:6** 1116
p where they offered soothing aroma **Ezk 6:13** 4725
and their holy **p** will be profaned. **Ezk 7:24** 4720
yourself high **p** of various colors and **Ezk 16:16** 1116
shrines, demolish your high **p**, **Ezk 16:39** 7413
earth, like the ancient waste **p**, **Ezk 26:20** 2723
they who live in these waste **p** in **Ezk 33:24** 2723
waste **p** will fall by the sword, **Ezk 33:27** 2723
the **p** to which they were scattered **Ezk 34:12** 4725
all the inhabited **p** of the land. **Ezk 34:13** 4186
the **p** around My hill a blessing. **Ezk 34:26** 5439
and the waste **p** will be rebuilt. **Ezk 36:10** 2723
and the waste **p** will be rebuilt. **Ezk 36:33** 2723
have rebuilt the ruined **p** *and* **Ezk 36:36**
dwelling **p** in which they have sinned **Ezk 37:23** 4186
waste **p** which are *now* inhabited, **Ezk 38:12** 2723
from the watering **p** of Israel **Ezk 45:15** 4945b
and boiling **p** were made under the **Ezk 46:23** 4018a
"These are the boiling **p** where **Ezk 46:24** 1004
Also the high **p** of Aven, the sin **Hos 10:8** 1116
And lack of bread in all your **p**, **Am 4:6** 4725
treads on the high **p** of the earth, **Am 4:13** 1116
"The high **p** of Isaac will be **Am 7:9** 1116
tread on the high **p** of the earth. **Mi 1:3** 1116
Planting **p** for a vineyard. **Mi 1:6** 4302
will become high **p** of a forest. **Mi 3:12** 1116
dwelling **p** which are not theirs. **Hab 1:6** 4908
Sun *and* moon stood in their **p**; **Hab 3:11** 2073
And makes me walk on my high **p**. **Hab 3:19** 1116
children sitting in the market **p**, **Mt 11:16** 58
it passes through waterless **p** seeking **Mt 12:43** 5117
"Others fell on the rocky **p**, **Mt 13:5**
whom seed was sown on the rocky **p**, **Mt 13:20**
greetings in the market **p**, **Mt 23:7** 58
and in various **p** there will be **Mt 24:7** 5117
whom seed was sown on the rocky **p**, **Mk 4:16**
laying the sick in the market **p**, **Mk 6:56** 58
greetings in the market **p**, **Mk 12:38** 58
and **p** of honor at banquets, **Mk 12:39** 4411
will be earthquakes in various **p**; **Mk 13:8** 5117
through waterless **p** seeking rest, **Lk 11:24** 5117
greetings in the market **p**. **Lk 11:43** 58
out the **p** of honor *at the table,* **Lk 14:7** 4411
greetings in the market **p**, **Lk 20:46** 58
and **p** of honor at banquets, **Lk 20:46** 4411
in various **p** plagues and famines; **Lk 21:11** 5117
Father's house are many dwelling **p**; **Jn 14:2** 3438
blessing in the heavenly **p** in **Eph 1:3**
at His right hand in the heavenly **p**, **Eph 1:20**
us with Him in the heavenly **p** in **Eph 2:6**
the authorities in the heavenly **p**. **Eph 3:10**
of wickedness in the heavenly **p**. **Eph 6:12**
island were moved out of their **p**. **Rv 6:14** 5117

PLACING

by **p** upon the neck of the disciples **Ac 15:10** 2007

PLAGUE

"One more **p** I will bring on **Ex 11:1** 5061
and no **p** will befall you to **Ex 12:13** 5063
that there will be no **p** among them **Ex 30:12** 5063
I will increase the **p** on you seven **Lv 26:21** 4347
that there will be no **p** among the **Nu 8:19** 5063
the people with a very severe **p**. **Nu 11:33** 4347
land died by a **p** before the LORD. **Nu 14:37** 4046
from the LORD, the **p** has begun!" **Nu 16:46** 5063
the **p** had begun among the people. **Nu 16:47** 5063
living, so that the **p** was checked. **Nu 16:48** 4046

who died by the **p** were 14,700, **Nu 16:49** 4046
for the **p** had been checked. **Nu 16:50** 4046
So the **p** on the sons of Israel was **Nu 25:8** 4046
who died by the **p** were 24,000. **Nu 25:9** 4046
who was slain on the day of the **p** **Nu 25:18** 4046
Then it came about after the **p**, **Nu 26:1** 4046
so the **p** was among the **Nu 31:16** 4046
every sickness and every **p** which, **Dt 28:61** 4347
and consumed by **p** And bitter **Dt 32:24** 7565
although a **p** came on the **Jos 22:17** 5063
for one **p** was on all of you and on **1Sa 6:4** 4046
that the **p** may be held back from **2Sa 24:21** 4046
the **p** was held back from Israel. **2Sa 24:25** 4046
land of their cities, whatever **p**, **1Ki 8:37** 5061
that the **p** may be restrained from **1Ch 21:22** 4046
p or whatever sickness *there is,* **2Ch 6:28** 5061
will be buried because of the **p**, **Jb 27:15** 4194
my friends stand aloof from my **p**; **Ps 38:11** 5061
"Remove Your **p** from me; **Ps 39:10** 5061
But gave over their life to the **p**, **Ps 78:50** 1698
Nor will any **p** come near your tent. **Ps 91:10** 5061
And the **p** broke out among them. **Ps 106:29** 4046
And so the **p** was stayed. **Ps 106:30** 4046
'One third of you will die by **p** or **Ezk 5:12** 1698
p and bloodshed also will pass **Ezk 5:17** 1698
will fall by sword, famine and **p**! **Ezk 6:11** 1698
"He who is far off will die by the **p**, **Ezk 6:12** 1698
the **p** and the famine are within. **Ezk 7:15** 1698
famine and the **p** will also consume **Ezk 7:15** 1698
"Or *if* I should send a **p** against **Ezk 14:19** 1698
and **p** to cut off man and beast **Ezk 14:21** 1698
"I sent a **p** among you after the **Am 4:10** 1698
pestilence, And **p** comes after Him. **Hab 3:5** 7565
Now this will be the **p** with which **Zch 14:12** 4046
So also like this **p** will **Zch 14:15** 4046
will be the **p** on the horse, **Zch 14:15** 4046
it will be the **p** with which the **Zch 14:18** 4046
to strike the earth with every **p**, **Rv 11:6** *4127*
God because of the **p** of the hail, **Rv 16:21** *4127*
its **p** was extremely severe. **Rv 16:21** *4127*

PLAGUED
and I **p** Egypt by what I did in its **Jos 24:5** 5062
people that they should be **p**." **1Ch 21:17** 4046
Nor are they **p** like mankind. **Ps 73:5** 5060

PLAGUES
with great **p** because of Sarai, **Gn 12:17** 5061
this time I will send all My **p** on you **Ex 9:14** 4046
will bring extraordinary **p** on you **Dt 28:59** 4347
even severe and lasting **p**, **Dt 28:59** 4347
when they see the **p** of the land **Dt 29:22** 4347
all *kinds of* **p** in the wilderness. **1Sa 4:8** 4347
Or what **p** you that you answer? **Jb 16:3** 4834
in various places **p** and famines; **Lk 21:11** *3061*
was killed by these three **p**, **Rv 9:18** *4127*
who were not killed by these **p**, **Rv 9:20** *4127*
seven angels who had seven **p**, **Rv 15:1** *4127*
seven angels who had the seven **p** **Rv 15:6** *4127*
until the seven **p** of the seven angels **Rv 15:8** *4127*
who has the power over these **p**, **Rv 16:9** *4127*
receive of her **p**; **Rv 18:4** *4127*
reason in one day her **p** will come, **Rv 18:8** *4127*
bowls full of the seven last **p** came **Rv 21:9** *4127*
God will add to him the **p** which **Rv 22:18** *4127*

PLAIN
that they found a **p** in the land of **Gn 11:2** 1237
the **p** in the valley of Jericho, **Dt 34:3** 3603
place before the desert **p**. **Jos 8:14** 6160
valley, and all the **p** of Medeba, **Jos 13:9** 4334
valley and all the **p** by Medeba; **Jos 13:16** 4334
all its cities which are on the **p**: **Jos 13:17** 4334
even all the cities of the **p** and **Jos 13:21** 4334
on the **p** from the tribe of Reuben, **Jos 20:8** 4334
Then Ahimaaz ran by way of the **p** **2Sa 18:23** 3603
In the **p** of the Jordan the king **1Ki 7:46** 3603
us fight against them in the **p**, **1Ki 20:23** 4334
will fight against them in the **p**, **1Ki 20:25** 4334
On the **p** of the Jordan the king **2Ch 4:17** 3603
both in the lowland and in the **p**. **2Ch 26:10** 4334
to make war on the **p** of Megiddo. **2Ch 35:22** 1237
at Chephirim in the **p** of Ono." **Ne 6:2** 1237
Sharon is like a desert **p**, **Is 33:9** 6160
let the rough ground become a **p**, **Is 40:4** 4334
O valley dweller, O rocky **p**," **Jer 21:13** 4334
"Judgment has also come upon the **p**, **Jer 48:21** 4334
"Get up, go out to the **p**, **Ezk 3:22** 1237
So I got up and went out to the **p**; **Ezk 3:23** 1237
appearance which I saw in the **p**. **Ezk 8:4** 1237
he set it up on the **p** of Dura in **Da 3:1** 1236
of the Shephelah the Philistine **p**; **Ob 1:19**
Zerubbabel *you will become* a **p**; **Zch 4:7** 4334
Hadadrimmon in the **p** of Megiddo. **Zch 12:11** 1237
All the land will be changed into a **p** **Zch 14:10** 6160
This is a **p** indication of God's **2Th 1:5** *1730*
came up on the broad **p** of the earth **Rv 20:9** *4114*

PLAINLY
"We see **p** that the LORD has been **Gn 26:28** 7200
"But if the slave **p** says, **Ex 21:5** 559
"He told us **p** that the donkeys **1Sa 10:16** 5046
removed, and he *began* speaking **p**. **Mk 7:35** *3723*
And He was stating the matter **p**. **Mk 8:32** *3954*
If You are the Christ, tell us **p**." **Jn 10:24** *3954*
Jesus then said to them **p**, **Jn 11:14** *3954*
but will tell you **p** of the Father. **Jn 16:25** *3954*
"Lo, now You are speaking **p** and **Jn 16:29** *3954*

PLAINS
and camped in the **p** of Moab beyond **Nu 22:1** 6160
spoke with them in the **p** of Moab **Nu 26:3** 6160
the sons of Israel in the **p** of Moab **Nu 26:63** 6160
to the camp at the **p** of Moab, **Nu 31:12** 6160
and camped in the **p** of Moab by the **Nu 33:48** 6160
as Abel-shittim in the **p** of Moab. **Nu 33:49** 6160
spoke to Moses in the **p** of Moab **Nu 33:50** 6160
the LORD spoke to Moses in the **p** of **Nu 35:1** 6160
through Moses in the **p** of Moab by **Nu 36:13** 6160
from the **p** of Moab to Mount Nebo, **Dt 34:1** 6160
in the **p** of Moab thirty days; **Dt 34:8** 6160
LORD to the desert **p** of Jericho. **Jos 4:13** 6160
month on the desert **p** of Jericho. **Jos 5:10** 6160
an inheritance in the **p** of Moab, **Jos 13:32** 6160
and overtook him in the **p** of Jericho **2Ki 25:5** 6160
them And rugged places into **p**. **Is 42:16** 4334
Zedekiah in the **p** of Jericho; **Jer 39:5** 6160
Zedekiah in the **p** of Jericho, **Jer 52:8** 6160

PLAN
erect the tabernacle according to its **p** **Ex 26:30** 4941
as I **p** to do to them, **Nu 33:56** 1819
So the **p** pleased Absalom and all **2Sa 17:4** 1697
Shall we carry out his **p**? **2Sa 17:6** 1697
the **p** of the porch *of the temple,* **1Ch 28:11** 8403
the **p** of all that he had in mind, **1Ch 28:12** 8403
that God had frustrated their **p**, **Ne 4:15** 6098
A **p** in the heart of a man is *like* **Pr 20:5** 6098
"Devise a **p**, but it will be thwarted; **Is 8:10** 6098
Nor does it **p** so in its heart, **Is 10:7** 2803
"This is the **p** devised against **Is 14:26** 6098
"Who execute a **p**, but not Mine, **Is 30:1** 6098
you and devising a **p** against you. **Jer 18:11** 4284
which I **p** to bring on them, **Jer 36:3** 2803
Therefore hear the **p** of the LORD **Jer 49:20** 6098
king of Babylon has formed a **p** **Jer 49:30** 6098
Therefore hear the **p** of the LORD **Jer 50:45** 6098
and you will devise an evil **p**, **Ezk 38:10** 4284
and let them measure the **p**. **Ezk 43:10** 8508
consented to their **p** and action), **Lk 23:51** *1012*
delivered over by the predetermined **p** **Ac 2:23** *1012*
this **p** or action is of men, **Ac 5:38** *1012*
soldiers' **p** was to kill the prisoners, **Ac 27:42** *1012*

PLANE
of poplar and almond and **p** trees, **Gn 30:37** 6196
And the **p** trees could not match **Ezk 31:8** 6196

PLANES
He works it with **p** and **Is 44:13** 4741

PLANKS
"You shall make it hollow with **p**; **Ex 27:8** 3871
He made it hollow with **p**. **Ex 38:7** 3871
house with beams and **p** of cedar. **1Ki 6:9** 7713
barricade her with **p** of cedar." **SS 8:9** 3871
your **p** of fir trees from Senir; **Ezk 27:5** 3871
the rest *should follow,* some on **p**, **Ac 27:44** *4548*

PLANNED
Now Saul **p** to make David fall by **1Sa 18:25** 2803
"Why then have you **p** such a thing **2Sa 14:13** 2803
and who **p** to exterminate us from **2Sa 21:5** 1819
From ancient times I **p** it. **2Ki 19:25** 3335
completed all that he had **p** on doing **2Ch 7:11**
935, 5921, 3820
that God has **p** to destroy you, **2Ch 25:16** 3289
Remaliah, has **p** evil against you, **Is 7:5** 3289
just as I have **p** so it will stand, **Is 14:24** 3289
"For the LORD of hosts has **p**, **Is 14:27** 3289
Him who **p** it long ago. **Is 22:11** 3335
Who has **p** this against Tyre, the **Is 23:8** 3289
The LORD of hosts has **p** it, **Is 23:9** 3289
did it, From ancient times I **p** it. **Is 37:26** 3335
I have **p** *it, surely* I will do it. **Is 46:11** 3335
the calamity I **p** to bring on it. **Jer 18:8** 2803
LORD which He has **p** against Edom, **Jer 49:20** 3289
which He has **p** against Babylon, **Jer 50:45** 3289
and the king **p** to appoint him over **Da 6:3** 6246
p to send her away secretly. **Mt 1:19** *1014*
on they **p** together to kill Him. **Jn 11:53** *1011*
But the chief priests **p** to put **Jn 12:10** *1011*
often I have **p** to come to you **Ro 1:13** *4388*

PLANNING
himself concerning you *by* **p** to **Gn 27:42**
But they were **p** to harm me. **Ne 6:2** 2803
you and the Jews are **p** to rebel; **Ne 6:6** 2803
for there is no activity or **p** or **Ec 9:10** 2803
repent of the calamity which I am **p** **Jer 26:3** 2803
I am **p** against this family a calamity **Mi 2:3** 2803

PLANS
but **p** ways so that the banished **2Sa 14:14** 2803
parts and according to all its **p**. **1Ki 6:38** 4941
are past, my **p** are torn apart, **Jb 17:11** 2154
the **p** by which you would wrong me. **Jb 21:27** 4209
frustrates the **p** of the peoples. **Ps 33:10** 4284
The **p** of His heart from generation **Ps 33:11** 4284
He **p** wickedness upon his bed; **Ps 36:4** 2803
make shrewd **p** against Your people, **Ps 83:3** 5475
A heart that devises wicked **p**, **Pr 6:18** 4284
consultation, **p** are frustrated, **Pr 15:22** 4284
Evil **p** are an abomination to the **Pr 15:26** 4284
The **p** of the heart belong to man, **Pr 16:1** 4633
And your **p** will be established. **Pr 16:3** 4284
The mind of man **p** his way, But the **Pr 16:9** 2803
Many **p** are in a man's heart, **Pr 19:21** 4284
Prepare **p** by consultation, And **Pr 20:18** 4284
The **p** of the diligent *lead* surely **Pr 21:5** 4284
One who **p** to do evil, Men will call **Pr 24:8** 2803
worked wonders, **P** *formed* long ago, **Is 25:1** 6098
deeply hide their **p** from the LORD, **Is 29:15** 6098
But the noble man devises noble **p**; **Is 32:8** 5082
And by noble **p** he stands. **Is 32:8** 5082
this people, The fruit of their **p**, **Jer 6:19** 4284
we are going to follow our own **p**, **Jer 18:12** 4284
let us devise **p** against Jeremiah. **Jer 18:18** 4284
I know the **p** that I have for you,' **Jer 29:11** 4284
'**p** for welfare and not for calamity **Jer 29:11** 4284

PLANT
have given you every **p** yielding seed **Gn 1:29** 6212a
given every green **p** for food"; **Gn 1:30** 6212a
no **p** of the field had yet sprouted, **Gn 2:5** 6212a
all to you, as *I gave* the green **p**. **Gn 9:3** 6212a
beast and on every **p** of the field, **Ex 9:22** 6212a
hail also struck every **p** of the field **Ex 9:25** 6212a
and eat every **p** of the land, **Ex 10:12** 6212a
and they ate every **p** of the land **Ex 10:15** 6212a
nothing green was left on tree or **p** **Ex 10:15** 6212a
"You will bring them and **p** them **Ex 15:17** 5193
and **p** all kinds of trees for food, **Lv 19:23** 5193
olive trees which you did not **p**, **Dt 6:11** 5193
"You shall not **p** for yourself an **Dt 16:21** 5193
you shall **p** a vineyard, but you **Dt 28:30** 5193
shall **p** and cultivate vineyards, **Dt 28:39** 5193
olive groves which you did not **p**.' **Jos 24:13** 5193
My people Israel and will **p** them, **2Sa 7:10** 5193
third year sow, reap, **p** vineyards, **2Ki 19:29** 5193
My people Israel, and will **p** them, **1Ch 17:9** 5193
Yet it withers before any *other* **p**. **Jb 8:12** 2682
And put forth sprigs like a **p**. **Jb 14:9** 5194
And sow fields and **p** vineyards, **Ps 107:37** 5193
A time to **p** and a time to uproot **Ec 3:2** 5193
the men of Judah His delightful **p**. **Is 5:7** 5194
Therefore you **p** delightful plants **Is 17:10** 5193
p *it* you carefully fence *it* in, **Is 17:11** 5194
farmer plow continually to **p** seed? **Is 28:24** 2232
cummin And **p** wheat in rows, **Is 28:25** 7760
third year sow, reap, **p** vineyards and **Is 37:30** 5193
p vineyards and eat their fruit. **Is 65:21** 5193
They will not **p** and another eat; **Is 65:22** 5193
to overthrow, To build and to **p**." **Jer 1:10** 5193
a kingdom to build up or to **p** *it;* **Jer 18:9** 5193
will **p** them and not pluck them up. **Jer 24:6** 5193
and **p** gardens and eat their **Jer 29:5** 5193
p gardens and eat their produce. **Jer 29:28** 5193
"Again you will **p** vineyards On **Jer 31:5** 5193
will **p** And will enjoy *them.* **Jer 31:5** 5193
over them to build and to **p**," **Jer 31:28** 5193
and will faithfully **p** them in **Jer 32:41** 5193
shall not **p** a vineyard or own one; **Jer 35:7** 5193
I will **p** you and not uproot you; **Jer 42:10** 5193
and I will **p** *it* on a high and **Ezk 17:22** 8362
mountain of Israel I will **p** it, **Ezk 17:23** 8362
will build houses, **p** vineyards and **Ezk 28:26** 5193
They will also **p** vineyards and **Am 9:14** 5193
"I will also **p** them on their land, **Am 9:15** 5193
So the LORD God appointed a **p** and **Jon 4:6** 7021
was extremely happy about the **p**. **Jon 4:6** 7021
it attacked the **p** and it withered. **Jon 4:7** 7021
reason to be angry about the **p**?" **Jon 4:9** 7021
"You had compassion on the **p** for **Jon 4:10** 7021
And **p** vineyards but not drink **Zph 1:13** 5193
"Every **p** which My heavenly Father **Mt 15:13** *5451*
which My heavenly Father did not **p** **Mt 15:13** *5452*

PLANTED
God **p** a garden toward the east, **Gn 2:8** 5193
began farming and **p** a vineyard. **Gn 9:20** 5193
p a tamarisk tree at Beersheba, **Gn 21:33** 5193
river, Like aloes **p** by the LORD, **Nu 24:6** 5193
man that has **p** a vineyard and has **Dt 20:6** 5193
tree *firmly* **p** by streams of water, **Ps 1:3** 8362
Then You **p** them; You afflicted **Ps 44:2** 5193
You drove out the nations and **p** it. **Ps 80:8** 5193
shoot which Your right hand has **p**, **Ps 80:15** 5193
P in the house of the LORD, They **Ps 92:13** 8362
He who **p** the ear, does He not hear? **Ps 94:9** 5193
The cedars of Lebanon which He **p**, **Ps 104:16** 5193
myself, I **p** vineyards for myself; **Ec 2:4** 5193
and I **p** in them all kinds of fruit **Ec 2:5** 5193
and a time to uproot what is **p**. **Ec 3:2** 5193
And **p** it with the choicest vine. **Is 5:2** 5193
Scarcely have they been **p**, **Is 40:24** 5193
"Yet I **p** you a choice vine, A **Jer 2:21** 5193
The LORD of hosts, who **p** you, **Jer 11:17** 5193
You have **p** them, they have also **Jer 12:2** 5193
be like a tree **p** by the water, **Jer 17:8** 8362
I have **p** I am about to uproot, **Jer 45:4** 5193
the land and **p** it in fertile soil. **Ezk 17:5** 5414
him from the beds where it was **p**, **Ezk 17:7** 4302
"It was **p** in good soil beside **Ezk 17:8** 8362
though it is **p**, will it thrive **Ezk 17:10** 8362
in your vineyard, **P** by the waters; **Ezk 19:10** 8362
'And now it is **p** in the wilderness, **Ezk 19:13** 8362
and **p** that which was desolate; **Ezk 36:36** 5193
Is **p** in a pleasant meadow like **Hos 9:13** 8362
You have **p** pleasant vineyards, yet **Am 5:11** 5193
There was a landowner who **P** A **Mt 21:33** *5452*
"A man **P** A VINEYARD AND PUT A **Mk 12:1** *5452*
which had been **p** in his vineyard; **Lk 13:6** *5452*
'Be uprooted and be **p** in the sea'; **Lk 17:6** *5452*
"A man **p** a vineyard and rented it **Lk 20:9** *5452*
I **p**, Apollos watered, but God was **1Co 3:6** *5452*

PLANTERS
The **p** will plant And will enjoy **Jer 31:5** 5193

PLANTING
land forever, The branch of My **p**, **Is 60:21** 4302
righteousness, The **p** of the LORD, **Is 61:3** 4302
extended all around its **p** place, **Ezk 31:4** 4302
for them a renowned **p** place, **Ezk 34:29** 4302
country, **P** places for a vineyard. **Mi 1:6** 4302
they were selling, they were **p**, **Lk 17:28** *5452*

PLANTS
vegetation, **p** yielding seed, **Gn 1:11** 6212a

p yielding seed after their kind, Gn 1:12 6212a
you will eat the p of the field; Gn 3:18 6212a
"Under the lotus p he lies down, Jb 40:21 6628
"The lotus p cover him with shade; Jb 40:22 6628
like olive p Around your table. Ps 128:3 8363
in their youth be as grown-up p, Ps 144:12 5195
From her earnings she p a vineyard. Pr 31:16 5193
choice fruits, henna with nard p, SS 4:13 5373
Therefore you plant delightful p Is 17:10 5194
He p a fir, and the rain makes it Is 44:14 5193
you numerous like p of the field. Ezk 16:7 6780
it is larger than the garden p and Mt 13:32 *3001*
garden p and forms large branches; Mk 4:32 *3001*
So then neither the one who p nor 1Co 3:7 *5452*
who p and he who waters are one; 1Co 3:8 *5452*
Who p a vineyard and does not eat 1Co 9:7 *5452*

PLASTER
and they shall dump the p that Lv 14:41 6083
take other p and replaster the house. Lv 14:42 6083
and all the p of the house, Lv 14:45 6083
they p it over with whitewash; Ezk 13:10 2902
who p *it* over with whitewash, Ezk 13:11 2902
p with which you plastered *it?*'" Ezk 13:12 2915
the p of the wall of the king's palace, Da 5:5 1528

PLASTERED
plaster with which you p *it?*'" Ezk 13:12 2902
tear down the wall which you p over Ezk 13:14 2902
who have p it over with whitewash; Ezk 13:15 2902

PLASTERERS
wall is gone and its p are gone, Ezk 13:15 2902

PLATE
shall also make a p of pure gold Ex 28:36 6731b
the p of the holy crown of pure gold, Ex 39:30 6731b
its front, he placed the golden p, Lv 8:9 6731b
"Then get yourself an iron p and Ezk 4:3 4227

PLATEAU
all the cities of the p and all Dt 3:10 4334
on the p for the Reubenites, Dt 4:43
776, 4334
And the p will be destroyed, Jer 48:8 4334

PLATED
your molten images p with gold. Is 30:22 642

PLATES
He engraved on the p of its stays 1Ki 7:36 3871
it, A goldsmith p it with gold, Is 40:19 7554

PLATFORM
Now Solomon had made a bronze p, 2Ch 6:13 3595
Now on the Levites' p stood Jeshua, Ne 9:4 4608
house had a raised p all around; Ezk 41:8 1363

PLATING
sheets for a p of the altar, Nu 16:38 6826
them out as a p for the altar, Nu 16:39 6826

PLATTER
"Give me here on a p the head of Mt 14:8 *4094*
And his head was brought on a p Mt 14:11 *4094*
head of John the Baptist on a p." Mk 6:25 *4094*
and brought his head on a p, Mk 6:28 *4094*
outside of the cup and of the p; Lk 11:39 *4094*

PLAY
all those who p the lyre and pipe. Gn 4:21 8610
and to drink, and rose up to p. Ex 32:6 6711
they would p the harlot with their gods Ex 34:15 2181
p the harlot with their gods and Ex 34:16 2181
to p the harlot with their gods. Ex 34:16 2181
with which they p the harlot. Lv 17:7 2181
those who p the harlot after him, Lv 20:5 2181
to p the harlot after them, Lv 20:6 2181
the people began to p the harlot Nu 25:1 2181
p the harlot with the strange gods Dt 31:16 2181
he shall p *the harp* with his hand, 1Sa 16:16 5059
for me now a man who can p well and 1Sa 16:17 5059
the harp and p *it* with his hand; 1Sa 16:23 5059
of Jerusalem to p the harlot and led 2Ch 21:11 2181
of Jerusalem to p the harlot as the 2Ch 21:13 2181
the beasts of the field p there. Jb 40:20 7832
you p with him as with a bird, Jb 41:5 7832
P skillfully with a shout of joy. Ps 33:3 5059
those who p the flutes *shall say,* Ps 87:7 2490b
child will p by the hole of the cobra, Is 11:8 8173b
and will p the harlot with all the Is 23:17 2181
So we will p my songs on stringed Is 38:20 5059
you might p the harlot with them. Ezk 16:17 2181
p the harlot after their detestable Ezk 20:30 2181
You shall not p the harlot, nor Hos 3:3 2181
They will p the harlot, but not Hos 4:10 2181
your daughters p the harlot And Hos 4:13 2181
daughters when they p the harlot Hos 4:14 2181
Though you, Israel, p the harlot, Hos 4:15 2181
They p the harlot continually; Hos 4:18 2181
AND DRINK, AND STOOD UP TO P." 1Co 10:7 *3815*

PLAYED
Tamar has p the harlot, Gn 38:24 2181
after which you p the harlot, Nu 15:39 2181
for they p the harlot after other Jg 2:17 2181
Israel p the harlot with it there, Jg 8:27 2181
again p the harlot with the Baals, Jg 8:33 2181
his concubine p the harlot against Jg 19:2 2181
The women sang as they p, 1Sa 18:7 7832
I have p the fool and have 1Sa 26:21 5528
came about, when the minstrel p, 2Ki 3:15 5059
and p the harlot after the gods of 1Ch 5:25 2181
Asaph p loud-sounding cymbals, 1Ch 16:5
as the house of Ahab p the harlot, 2Ch 21:13 2181
And p the harlot in their deeds. Ps 106:39 2181
p the harlot after their idols; Ezk 6:9 2181
p the harlot because of your fame, Ezk 16:15 2181
colors and p the harlot on them, Ezk 16:16 2181
p the harlot with the Egyptians, Ezk 16:26 2181
you p the harlot with the Assyrians Ezk 16:28 2181
you p the harlot with them Ezk 16:28 2181
and they p the harlot in Egypt. Ezk 23:3 2181
They p the harlot in their youth; Ezk 23:3 2181
p the harlot while she was Mine; Ezk 23:5 2181
when she p the harlot in the land Ezk 23:19 2181
p the harlot with the nations, Ezk 23:30 2181
"For their mother has p the harlot; Hos 2:5 2181
And they have p the harlot, Hos 4:12 2181
O Ephraim, you have p the harlot, Hos 5:3 2181
For you have p the harlot, Hos 9:1 2181
'We p the flute for you, and you Mt 11:17 *832*
'We p the flute for you, and you Lk 7:32 *832*
is p on the flute or on the harp? 1Co 14:7 *832*

PLAYER
who is a skillful p on the harp; 1Sa 16:16 5059

PLAYING
him, by p the harlot after Molech. Lv 20:5 2181
by p the harlot in her father's Dt 22:21 2181
David was p *the harp* with his hand, 1Sa 18:10 5059
David was p *the harp* with *his* hand. 1Sa 19:9 5059
and the people were p on flutes 1Ki 1:40 2490b
will stop you from p the harlot, Ezk 16:41 2181
boys and girls p in its streets.' Zch 8:5 7832
sound of harpists p on their harps. Rv 14:2 *2789*

PLAYS
no one p the harlot as you do, Ezk 16:34 2181
voice and p well on an instrument; Ezk 33:32 5059

PLAZA
be built again, with p and moat, Da 9:25 7339

PLAZAS
"There is wailing in all the p, Am 5:16 7339

PLEA
the widow's p come before them. Is 1:23 7379

PLEAD
Whoever will p for him shall be Jg 6:31 7378
that I may p with you before the 1Sa 12:7 8199
and may He see and p my cause and 1Sa 24:15 7378
and to p with him for her people. Es 4:8 1245
"O that a man might p with God As Jb 16:21 3198
and p my case against an ungodly Ps 43:1 7378
O God, *and* p Your own cause; Ps 74:22 7378
P my cause and redeem me; Ps 119:154 7378
first to p his case *seems* right, Pr 18:17 7379
For the LORD will p their case And Pr 22:23 7378
He will p their case against you. Pr 23:11 7378
the orphan, P for the widow. Is 1:17 7378
They do not p the cause, The cause Jer 5:28 1777
that I would p *my* case with You; Jer 12:1 7378
'There is no one to p your cause; Jer 30:13 1777
He will vigorously p their case So Jer 50:34 7378
I am going to p your case And Jer 51:36 7378
p your case before the mountains, Mi 6:1 7378
to the ground and *began* to p Mt 18:29 *3870*

PLEADED
of his soul when he p with us, Gn 42:21 2603a
I also p with the LORD at that time, Dt 3:23 2603a
who has p the cause of my reproach 1Sa 25:39 7378
Elnathan and Delaiah and Gemariah p Jer 36:25 6293
O Lord, You have p my soul's cause; La 3:58 7378
you all that debt because you p with Mt 18:32 *3870*

PLEADING
his father came out and *began* p Lk 15:28 *3870*

PLEADS
righteously and no one p honestly. Is 59:4 8199
Until He p my case and executes Mi 7:9 7378
how he p with God against Israel? Ro 11:2 *1793*

PLEASANT
was good And that the land was p, Gn 49:15 5276
beloved and p in their life, 2Sa 1:23 5273a
You have been very p to me. 2Sa 1:26 5276
the situation of this city is p, 2Ki 2:19 2896a
lines have fallen to me in p places; Ps 16:6 5273a
Then they despised the p land; Ps 106:24 2532
how good and how p it is For Ps 133:1 5273a
hear my words, for they are p. Ps 141:6 5276
it is p *and* praise is becoming. Ps 147:1 5273a
knowledge will be p to your soul; Pr 2:10 5276
Her ways are p ways And all her Pr 3:17 5278
And bread *eaten* in secret is p." Pr 9:17 5276
to the LORD, But p words are pure. Pr 15:26 5278
P words are a honeycomb, Sweet to Pr 16:24 5278
be p if you keep them within you, Pr 22:18 5273a
With all precious and p riches. Pr 24:4 5273a
The sleep of the working man is p, Ec 5:12 4966
The light is p, and *it is* good for Ec 11:7 4966
and let your heart be p during the Ec 11:9 3190
you are, my beloved, *And* so p! SS 1:16 5273a
is right, Speak to us p words, Is 30:10 2513b
your breasts for the p fields, Is 32:12 2531
My sons And give you a p land, Jer 3:19 2532
My p field A desolate wilderness. Jer 12:10 2532
looked, and my sleep was p to me. Jer 31:26 6149
"Whether *it is* p or unpleasant, Jer 42:6 2896b
slain all that were p to the eye; La 2:4 4261
walls and destroy your p houses, Ezk 26:12 2532
Because their shade is p. Hos 4:13 2896a
planted in a p meadow like Tyre; Hos 9:13
You have planted p vineyards, Am 5:11 2531
evict, Each *one* from her p house. Mi 2:9 8588
they made the p land desolate." Zch 7:14 2532

PLEASE
"P say that you are my sister so Gn 12:13 4994
"P let there be no strife between Gn 13:8 4994
P separate from me; Gn 13:9 4994
P go in to my maid; Gn 16:2 4994
p do not pass Your servant by. Gn 18:3 4994
"P let a little water be brought Gn 18:4 4994
p turn aside into your servant's Gn 19:2 4994
"P, my brothers, do not act Gn 19:7 4994
p let me bring them out to you, Gn 19:8 4994
P, let me escape there Gn 19:20 4994
settle wherever you p." Gn 20:15
2896a, 5869
"If you will only p listen to me; Gn 23:13 3863
"P place your hand under my thigh, Gn 24:2 4994
Abraham, p grant me success today, Gn 24:12 4994
"P let down your jar so that I may Gn 24:14 4994
"P let me drink a little water Gn 24:17 4994
P tell me, is there room for us to Gn 24:23 4994
"P let me drink a little water Gn 24:43 4994
and I said to her, 'P let me drink.' Gn 24:45 4994
"P let me have a swallow of that Gn 25:30 4994
"Now then, p take your gear, your Gn 27:3 4994
Get up, p, sit and eat of my game, Gn 27:19 4994
"P come close, that I may feel Gn 27:21 4994
"P come close and kiss me, my son." Gn 27:26 4994
"P give me some of your son's Gn 30:14 4994
"P tell me your name." Gn 32:29 4994
"No, p, if now I have found favor Gn 33:10 4994
"P take my gift which has been Gn 33:11 4994
"P let my lord pass on before his Gn 33:14 4994
"P let me leave with you some of Gn 33:15 4994
p give her to him in marriage. Gn 34:8 4994
"P listen to this dream which I Gn 37:6 4994
p tell me where they are pasturing Gn 37:16 4994
p examine *it to see* whether it is Gn 37:32 4994
"P examine and see, whose signet Gn 38:25 4994
Tell *it* to me, p." Gn 40:8 4994
and p do me a kindness by Gn 40:14 4994
may your servant p speak a word in Gn 44:18 4994
p let your servant remain instead Gn 44:33 4994
"P come closer to me." Gn 45:4 4994
p let your servants live in the Gn 47:4 4994
"P, if I have found favor in your Gn 47:29 4994
P do not bury me in Egypt, Gn 47:29 4994
"Bring them to me, p, Gn 48:9 4994
in your sight, p speak to Pharaoh, Gn 50:4 4994
p let me go up and bury my father; Gn 50:5 4994
"P forgive, I beg you, the Gn 50:17 4994
p forgive the transgression of the Gn 50:17 4994
So now, p, let us go a three days' Ex 3:18 4994
"P, Lord, I have never been Ex 4:10 994a
"P, Lord, now send *the message* by Ex 4:13 994a
"P, let me go, that I may return Ex 4:18 4994
P, let us go a three days' journey Ex 5:3 4994
p forgive my sin only this once, Ex 10:17 4994
p blot me out from Your book which Ex 32:32 4994
"P do not leave us, inasmuch as Nu 10:31 4994
thus with me, p kill me at once, Nu 11:15 4994
"P let us pass through your land. Nu 20:17 4994
"Now, therefore, p come, curse Nu 22:6 4994
P come then, curse this people for Nu 22:17 4994
"Now p, you also stay here Nu 22:19 4994
"P come with me to another place Nu 23:13 4994
"P come, I will take you to Nu 23:27 4994
p swear to me by the LORD, Jos 2:12 4994
"P show us the entrance to the Jg 1:24 4994
"P give me a little water to Jg 4:19 4994
"P do not depart from here, until Jg 6:18 4994
p let me make a test once more Jg 6:39 4994
"P give loaves of bread to the Jg 8:5 4994
only p deliver us this day." Jg 10:15 4994
"P let us pass through your land," Jg 11:17 4994
"P let us pass through your land Jg 11:19 4994
p let the man of God whom You Jg 13:8
994a, 4994
"P let us detain you so that we Jg 13:15 4994
P let her be yours instead." Jg 15:2 4994
"P tell me where your great Jg 16:6 4994
now p tell me how you may be Jg 16:10 4994
p remember me and please Jg 16:28 4994
p strengthen me just this time, Jg 16:28 4994
"Inquire of God, p, that we may Jg 18:5 4994
"P be willing to spend the night, Jg 19:6 4994
"P sustain yourself, and wait Jg 19:8 4994
p spend the night. Jg 19:9 4994
"P come, and let us turn aside Jg 19:11 4994
fellows, p do not act so wickedly; Jg 19:23 4994
P let me bring them out that you Jg 19:24 4994
"P let me go to the field and Ru 2:2 4994
"P let me glean and gather after Ru 2:7 4994
"P assign me to one of the 1Sa 2:36 4994
P do not hide it from me. 1Sa 3:17 4994
"P tell me where the seer's house 1Sa 9:18 4994
"P tell me what Samuel said to 1Sa 10:15 4994
p pardon my sin and return with 1Sa 15:25 4994
but p honor me now before the 1Sa 15:30 4994
p be on guard in the morning, 1Sa 19:2 4994
"If it p my father *to do* you 1Sa 20:13 3190
'P let me go, since our family has 1Sa 20:29 4994
p let me get away that I may see 1Sa 20:29 4994
"P let my father and my mother 1Sa 22:3 4994
P give whatever you find at hand 1Sa 25:8 4994
And p let your maidservant speak 1Sa 25:24 4994
"P do not let my lord pay 1Sa 25:25 4994
"P forgive the transgression of 1Sa 25:28 4994
p let me strike him with the spear 1Sa 26:8 4994
but now p take the spear that is 1Sa 26:11 4994
p let my lord the king listen to 1Sa 26:19 4994
"Conjure up for me, p, 1Sa 28:8 4994
p listen to the voice of your 1Sa 28:22 4994
"P bring me the ephod." 1Sa 30:7 4994
"How did things go? P tell me." 2Sa 1:4 4994
'P stand beside me and kill me, 2Sa 1:9 4994

may it **p** You to bless the house 2Sa 7:29 2974
"**P** let my sister Tamar come and 2Sa 13:5 4994
"**P** let my sister Tamar come and 2Sa 13:6 4994
therefore, **p** speak to the king, 2Sa 13:13 4994
p let the king and his servants go 2Sa 13:24 4994
p let my brother Amnon go with us." 2Sa 13:26 4994
"**P** pretend to be a mourner, and 2Sa 14:2 4994
"**P** let the king remember the LORD 2Sa 14:11 4994
"**P** let your maidservant speak a 2Sa 14:12 4994
'**P** let the word of my lord the 2Sa 14:17 4994
"**P** do not hide anything from me 2Sa 14:18 4994
"Let my lord the king **p** speak." 2Sa 14:18 4994
"**P** let me go and pay my vow which 2Sa 15:7 4994
"**P** let me choose 12,000 men that 2Sa 17:1 4994
"**P** let me run and bring the king 2Sa 18:19 4994
p let me also run after the 2Sa 18:22 4994
"**P** let your servant return, that 2Sa 19:37 4994
P tell Joab, 'Come here that I may 2Sa 20:16 4994
p take away the iniquity of Your 2Sa 24:10 4994
P let Your hand be against me and 2Sa 24:17 4994
p let me give you counsel and save 1Ki 1:12 4994
"**P** speak to Solomon the king, for 1Ki 2:17 4994
given him, and they did not **p** him. 1Ki 9:12 3474, 5869
"**P** entreat the LORD your God, and 1Ki 13:6 4994
"**P** get me a little water in a 1Ki 17:10 4994
"**P** bring me a piece of bread in 1Ki 17:11 4994
"**P** let me kiss my father and my 1Ki 19:20 4994
"**P** observe and see how this man 1Ki 20:7 4994
p let us put sackcloth on our 1Ki 20:31 4994
'**P** let me live.' " 1Ki 20:32 4994
"**P** strike me." But the man refused 1Ki 20:35 4994
another man and said, "**P** strike me." 1Ki 20:37 4994
"**P** inquire first for the word of 1Ki 22:5 4994
P let your word be like the word 1Ki 22:13 4994
p let my life and the lives of 2Ki 1:13 4994
"Stay here **p**, for the LORD has 2Ki 2:2 4994
"Elisha, **p** stay here, for the 2Ki 2:4 4994
"**P** stay here, for the LORD has 2Ki 2:6 4994
"**P**, let a double portion of your 2Ki 2:9 4994
p let them go and search for your 2Ki 2:16 4994
"**P**, let us make a little walled 2Ki 4:10 4994
"**P** send me one of the servants 2Ki 4:22 4994
"**P** run now to meet her and say to 2Ki 4:26 4994
so **p** take a present from your 2Ki 5:15 4994
p let your servant at least be 2Ki 5:17 4994
P give them a talent of silver and 2Ki 5:22 4994
"**P** let us go to the Jordan and 2Ki 6:2 4994
"**P** be willing to go with your 2Ki 6:3 4994
"**P**, let some *men* take five of the 2Ki 7:13 4994
"**P** relate to me all the great 2Ki 8:4 4994
p take away the iniquity of Your 1Ch 21:8 4994
p let me fall into the hand of the 1Ch 21:13 4994
p let Your hand be against me and 1Ch 21:17 4994
be kind to this people and **p** them 2Ch 10:7 7521
"**P** inquire first for the word of 2Ch 18:4 4994
So **p** let your word be like one of 2Ch 18:12 4994
"If it **p** the king, and if your Ne 2:5 2895
"If it **p** the king, let letters be Ne 2:7 2895
P, let us leave off this usury. Ne 5:10 4994
"**P**, give back to them this very Ne 5:11 4994
And over our cattle as they **p**, Ne 9:37 7522
also, to do with them as you **p**." Es 3:11 2896a, 5869
"Now **p** look at me, And *see* if Jb 6:28 2974
"**P** inquire of past generations, Jb 8:8 4994
"**P** hear my argument And listen Jb 13:6 4994
"**P** receive instruction from His Jb 22:22 4994
now, Job, **p** hear my speech, Jb 33:1 4994
And it will **p** the LORD better than Ps 69:31 3190
P let them tell you, And let them Is 19:12 4994
who is literate, saying, "**P** read this," Is 29:11 4994
who is illiterate, saying, "**P** read this. Is 29:12 4994
Therefore, **p** hear this, you Is 51:21 4994
"**P** inquire of the LORD on our Jer 21:2 4994
'Buy my field, **p**, that is at Jer 32:8 4994
"Sit down, **p**, and read it to us." Jer 36:15 4994
"Tell us, **p**, how did you write all Jer 36:17 4994
"**P** pray to the LORD our God on Jer 37:3 4994
"But now, **p** listen, O my lord the Jer 37:20 4994
p let my petition come before you and Jer 37:20 4994
P obey the LORD in what I am Jer 38:20 4994
"**P** let our petition come before Jer 42:2 4994
"**P** test your servants for ten Da 1:12 4994
Their sacrifices will not **p** Him. Hos 9:4 6149
"Lord GOD, **p** pardon! Am 7:2 4994
"Lord GOD, **p** stop! Am 7:5 4994
"**P** LORD, was not this what I said Jon 4:2 577
O LORD, **p** take my life from me, Jon 4:3 4994
p come and lay Your hands on her, Mk 5:23 *2065*
p consider me excused.' Lk 14:18 *2065*
p consider me excused.' Lk 14:19 *2065*
"**P** *tell me,* of whom does the Ac 8:34 *1189a*
who are in the flesh cannot **p** God. Ro 8:8 *700*
strength and not *just* **p** ourselves. Ro 15:1 *700*
Each of us is to **p** his neighbor Ro 15:2 *700*
For even Christ did not **p** Himself; Ro 15:3 *700*
the Lord, how he may **p** the Lord; 1Co 7:32 *700*
the world, how he may **p** his wife, 1Co 7:33 *700*
world, how she may **p** her husband. 1Co 7:34 *700*
as I also **p** all men in all things, 1Co 10:33 *700*
Or am I striving to **p** men? Ga 1:10 *700*
If I were still trying to **p** men, Ga 1:10 *700*
may not do the things that you **p**. Ga 5:17 *2309*
Lord, to **p** *Him* in all respects, Col 1:10 *699*
as those who *merely* **p** men, Col 3:22 *441*
how you ought to walk and **p** God 1Th 4:1 *700*
so that he may **p** the one who 2Tm 2:4 *700*
faith it is impossible to **p** *Him,* Heb 11:6 *2100*

PLEASED

it **p** Pharaoh and his servants. Gn 45:16 3190, 5869
"If the LORD is **p** with us, then Nu 14:8 2654a
it **p** the LORD to bless Israel, Nu 24:1 2895, 5869
"The thing **p** me and I took Dt 1:23 3190, 5869
be, if you are not **p** with her, Dt 21:14 2654a
sons of Manasseh spoke, it **p** them. Jos 22:30 3190, 5869
The word **p** the sons of Israel, Jos 22:33 3190, 5869
because the LORD has been **p** to 1Sa 12:22 3190, 2974
it **p** David to become the king's 1Sa 18:26 3474, 5869
took note *of it,* and it **p** them, 2Sa 3:36 3190, 5869
the king did **p** all the people. 2Sa 3:36 2895, 5869
So the plan **p** Absalom and all the 2Sa 17:4 5869, 3474
dead today, then you would be **p**. 2Sa 19:6 3474, 5869
p Solomon to build in Jerusalem, 1Ki 9:19 2836a, 2837
"Be **p** to take two talents." 2Ki 5:23 2974
"And now it has **p** You to bless 1Ch 17:27 2974
p Solomon to build in Jerusalem, 2Ch 8:6 2836a, 2837
So it **p** the king to send me, and I Ne 2:6 3190
word **p** the king and the princes, Es 1:21 3190, 5869
And the matter **p** the king, and he Es 2:4 3190, 5869
p him and found favor with him. Es 2:9 3190, 5869
out that day glad and **p** of heart; Es 5:9 2896a
And the advice **p** Haman, so he had Es 5:14 3190
they did what they **p** to those who Es 9:5 7522
nothing When he is **p** with God.' Jb 34:9 7521
Be **p**, O LORD, to deliver me; Ps 40:13 7521
I know that You are **p** with me, Ps 41:11 2654a
see a thief, you are **p** with him, Ps 50:18 7521
are not **p** with burnt offering. Ps 51:16 7521
for my heart was **p** because of all Ec 2:10 8056
Hezekiah was **p**, Is 39:2 8055, 5921
The LORD was **p** for His Is 42:21 2654a
But the LORD was **p** To crush Him, Is 53:10 2654a
as it **p** the potter to make. Jer 18:4 5869, 3474
Then the king was very **p** and gave Da 6:23 2868
did as he **p** and magnified *himself.* Da 8:4 7522
LORD, have done as You have **p**." Jon 1:14 2654a
be **p** with it and be glorified," Hg 1:8 7521
Would he be **p** with you?" Mal 1:8 7521
I am not **p** with you," Mal 1:10 2656
danced before *them* and **p** Herod, Mt 14:6 *700*
she **p** Herod and his dinner guests; Mk 6:22 *700*
among men with whom He is **p**." Lk 2:14 *2107*
When he saw that it **p** the Jews, Ac 12:3 *701*
Macedonia and Achaia have been **p** Ro 15:26 *2106*
Yes, they were **p** *to do so,* and Ro 15:27 *2106*
me through His grace, was **p** Ga 1:15 *2106*
for with such sacrifices God is **p**. Heb 13:16 *2100*

PLEASES

"If now it **p** you, *stay with me;* Gn 30:27 4672, 2580
one of your towns where it **p** him; Dt 23:16 2896a
or else, if it **p** you, I will give 1Ki 21:6 2655
if it **p** the king, let a search be Ezr 5:17 2869
"If it **p** the king, let a royal Es 1:19 2895
"Then let the young lady who **p** Es 2:4 3190, 5869
Esther said, "If it **p** the king, Es 5:4 2895
and if it **p** the king to grant my Es 5:8 2895
and if it **p** the king, let my life be Es 7:3 2895
"If it **p** the king and if I have Es 8:5 5921, 2895
"If it **p** the king, let tomorrow Es 9:13 5921, 2895
He does whatever He **p**. Ps 115:3 2654a
Whatever the LORD **p**, Ps 135:6 2654a
for he will do whatever he **p**." Ec 8:3 2654a
or awaken *my* love Until she **p**." SS 2:7 2654a
or awaken *my* love Until she **p**." SS 3:5 2654a
or awaken *my* love Until she **p**." SS 8:4 2654a
My sabbaths, And choose what **p** Me, Is 56:4 2654a
great authority and do as he **p**. Da 11:3 7522
comes against him will do as he **p**, Da 11:16 7522
"Then the king will do as he **p**, Da 11:36 7522

PLEASING

every tree that is **p** to the sight Gn 2:9 2530
And it was **p** in the sight of all 1Sa 18:5 3190
me in the army are **p** in my sight; 1Sa 29:6 2896a
not **p** in the sight of the lords. 1Sa 29:6 2896a
"I know that you are **p** in my sight, 1Sa 29:9 2896a
It was **p** in the sight of the Lord 1Ki 3:10 3190
"If it is **p** to the king, let it Es 3:9 2895
the king and I am **p** in his sight, Es 8:5 2896a
Let my meditation be **p** to Him; Ps 104:34 6149
a man's ways are **p** to the LORD, Pr 16:7 7521
is **p** to God will escape from her, Ec 7:26 2896a
"Your oils have a **p** fragrance, SS 1:3 2896a
your sacrifices are not **p** to Me." Jer 6:20 6149
to the one who is **p** in My sight. Jer 27:5 3474

O king, may my advice be **p** to you: Da 4:27 8232
Jerusalem will be **p** to the LORD as Mal 3:4 6149
do the things that are **p** to Him." Jn 8:29 *701*
at home or absent, to be **p** to Him. 2Co 5:9 *2101*
to learn what is **p** to the Lord. Eph 5:10 *2101*
so we speak, not as **p** men, but God 1Th 2:4 *700*
They are not **p** to God, but hostile 1Th 2:15 *700*
being taken up he was **p** to God. Heb 11:5 *2100*
us that which is **p** in His sight, Heb 13:21 *2101*
things that are **p** in His sight. 1Jn 3:22 *701*

PLEASURE

I have become old, shall I have **p**, Gn 18:12 5734b
He took **p** in me to make *me* king 1Ch 28:4 7521
"Is there any **p** to the Almighty Jb 22:3 2656
a God who takes **p** in wickedness; Ps 5:4 2655
Your servants find **p** in her stones And Ps 102:14 7521
not take **p** in the legs of a man. Ps 147:10 7521
the LORD takes **p** in His people; Ps 149:4 7521
He who loves **p** *will become* a poor Pr 21:17 8057
"Come now, I will test you with **p**. Ec 2:1 8057
"It is madness," and of **p**, Ec 2:2 8057
not withhold my heart from any **p**, Ec 2:10 8057
and depriving myself of **p**?" Ec 4:8 2899b
of fools is in the house of **p**. Ec 7:4 8057
So I commended **p**, for there is Ec 8:15 8057
I take no **p** in the blood of bulls, Is 1:11 2654a
not take **p** in their young men, Is 9:17 8055
value silver or take **p** in gold. Is 13:17 2654a
I will accomplish all My good **p**'; Is 46:10 2656
carry out His good **p** on Babylon, Is 48:14 2656
And the good **p** of the LORD will Is 53:10 2656
doing your *own* **p** on My holy day, Is 58:13 2656
own ways, From seeking your *own* **p** Is 58:13 2656
your lovers with whom you took **p**, Ezk 16:37 6149
p in the death of the wicked," Ezk 18:23 2654a
"For I have no **p** in the death of Ezk 18:32 2654a
no **p** in the death of the wicked, Ezk 33:11 2654a
will and to work for *His* good **p**. Php 2:13 *2107*
For it was the *Father's* good **p** for Col 1:19 *2106*
truth, but took **p** in wickedness. 2Th 2:12 *2106*
p is dead even while she lives. 1Tm 5:6 *4684*
lovers of **p** rather than lovers of God 2Tm 3:4 *5369*
FOR SIN YOU HAVE TAKEN NO **P** Heb 10:6 *2106*
NOR HAVE YOU TAKEN **P** *in them*" Heb 10:8 *2106*
BACK, MY SOUL HAS NO **P** IN HIM. Heb 10:38 *2106*
earth and led a life of wanton **p**; Jas 5:5 *4684*
They count it a **p** to revel in the 2Pe 2:13 *2237*

PLEASURES

prosperity And their years in **p**. Jb 36:11 5273a
right hand there are **p** forever. Ps 16:11 5273a
and female singers and the **p** of men Ec 2:8 8588
and riches and **p** of *this* life, Lk 8:14 *2237*
enslaved to various lusts and **p**, Ti 3:3 *2237*
to enjoy the passing **p** of sin, Heb 11:25 *619*
p that wage war in your members? Jas 4:1 *2237*
that you may spend *it* on your **p**. Jas 4:3 *2237*

PLED

"He **p** the cause of the afflicted Jer 22:16 1777

PLEDGE

Will you give a **p** until you send *it?* Gn 38:17 6162
"What **p** shall I give you?" Gn 38:18 6162
the **p** from the woman's hand, Gn 38:20 6162
take your neighbor's cloak as a **p**, Ex 22:26 2254a
or an upper millstone in **p**, Dt 24:6 2254a
he would be taking a life in **p**. Dt 24:6 2254a
not enter his house to take his **p**. Dt 24:10 5667
loan shall bring the **p** out to you. Dt 24:11 5667
you shall not sleep with his **p**. Dt 24:12 5667
shall surely return the **p** to him, Dt 24:13 5667
nor take a widow's garment in **p**. Dt 24:17 2254a
and give me a **p** of truth, Jos 2:12 226
now, a **p** for me with Yourself; Jb 17:3 6162
They take the widow's ox for a **p**. Jb 24:3 2254a
against the poor they take a **p**. Jb 24:9 2254a
Have given a **p** for a stranger, Pr 6:1 3709
And for foreigners, hold him in **p**. Pr 20:16 2254a
an adulterous woman hold him in **p**. Pr 27:13 2254a
but restores to the debtor his **p**. Ezk 18:7 2260b
robbery, does not restore a **p**, Ezk 18:12 2258
or oppress anyone, or retain a **p**, Ezk 18:16 2258
if a wicked man restores a **p**, Ezk 33:15 2258
a **p** from Jason and the others, Ac 17:9 *2425*
the Spirit in our hearts as a **p**. 2Co 1:22 *728*
who gave to us the Spirit as a **p**. 2Co 5:5 *728*
given as a **p** of our inheritance, Eph 1:14 *728*
have set aside their previous **p**. 1Tm 5:12 *4102*

PLEDGED

p allegiance to King Solomon. 1Ch 29:24 5414
They **p** to put away their wives, Ezr 10:19 5414, 3027
and behold, he **p** his allegiance, Ezk 17:18 5414

PLEDGES

you have taken **p** of your brothers Jb 22:6 2254a
A man lacking in sense **p** And Pr 17:18 8628, 3709
Do not be among those who give **p**, Pr 22:26 8628, 3709
"On garments taken as **p** they Am 2:8 2254a

PLEIADES

makes the Bear, Orion and the **P**, Jb 9:9 3598
"Can you bind the chains of the **P**, Jb 38:31 3598
He who made the **P** and Orion And Am 5:8 3598

PLENTEOUS

ground, and it will be rich and **p**; Is 30:23 8082a

PLENTIFUL

made cedars as **p** as sycamore trees 1Ki 10:27 7230
gold as **p** in Jerusalem as stones, 2Ch 1:15 7230

he made cedars as **p** as sycamores 2Ch 1:15 7230
made cedars as **p** as sycamore trees 2Ch 9:27 7230
and the royal wine was **p** according Es 1:7 7227a
dust And prepares garments as **p** *as* Jb 27:16
You shed abroad a **p** rain, Ps 68:9 5071
is large, And their food is **p**. Hab 1:16 1277
"The harvest is **p**, but the Mt 9:37 *4183*
"The harvest is **p**, but the Lk 10:2 *4183*

PLENTY
"We have **p** of both straw and Gn 24:25 7227a
"I have **p**, my brother; Gn 33:9 7227a
with me and because I have **p**." Gn 33:11 3605
During the seven years of **p** Gn 41:47 7647
When the seven years of **p** which Gn 41:53 7647
enough to eat with **p** left over, 2Ch 31:10 7230
will be **p** of contempt and anger. Es 1:18 1767
In the fullness of his **p** he will be Jb 20:22 8231a
your barns will be filled with **p** And Pr 3:10 7647
his land will have **p** of bread, Pr 12:11 7646
his land will have **p** of food, Pr 28:19 7646
pursuits will have poverty in **p**. Pr 28:19 7646
A pyre of fire with **p** of wood; Is 30:33 7235a
for *then* we had **p** of food and Jer 44:17 7646
have **p** to eat and be satisfied And Jl 2:26 398

PLOT
was a **p** of ground full of lentils, 2Sa 23:11 2513a
his stand in the midst of the **p**, 2Sa 23:12 2513a
was a **p** of ground full of barley; 1Ch 11:13 2513a
their stand in the midst of the **p** 1Ch 11:14 2513a
the **p** became known to Mordecai and Es 2:22 1697
Now when the **p** was investigated Es 2:23 1697
Haman the Agagite and his **p** which Es 8:3 4284
against You *And* devised a **p**, Ps 21:11 4209
ready with a well-conceived **p**"; Ps 64:6 2665
but their **p** became known to Saul. Ac 9:24 *1917*
and when a **p** was formed against Ac 20:3 *1917*
more than forty who formed this **p**. Ac 23:13 *4945*
would be a **p** against the man, Ac 23:30 *1917*

PLOTS
in the **p** which they have devised. Ps 10:2 4209
wicked **p** against the righteous And Ps 37:12 2161
they had devised **p** against me, Jer 11:19 4284
upon me through the **p** of the Jews; Ac 20:19 *1917*

PLOTTED
they **p** against him to put him to Gn 37:18 5230
for evil is **p** against our master 1Sa 25:17 3615
yourself Or if you have **p** *evil*, Pr 30:32 2161
One who **p** evil against the LORD, Na 1:11 2803
Then the Pharisees went and **p** Mt 22:15 *4824*
and they **p** together to seize Jesus Mt 26:4 *4823*
the Jews **p** together to do away with Ac 9:23 *4823*

PLOTTING
that Saul was **p** evil against him; 1Sa 23:9 2790a
"He frustrates the **p** of the shrewd, Jb 5:12 4284
an oven *As* they approach their **p**; Hos 7:6 696
p against Him to catch *Him* in Lk 11:54 *1748*

PLOW
"You shall not **p** with an ox and a Dt 22:10 2790a
those who **p** iniquity And those who Jb 4:8 2790a
does not **p** after the autumn, Pr 20:4 2790a
Does the farmer **p** continually to Is 28:24 2790a
harness Ephraim, Judah will **p**, Hos 10:11 2790a
Or does one **p** them with oxen? Am 6:12 2790a
after putting his hand to the **p** and Lk 9:62 *723*
the plowman ought to **p** in hope, 1Co 9:10 *722*

PLOWED
which has not been **p** or sown, Dt 21:4 5647
"If you had not **p** with my heifer, Jg 14:18 2790a
"The plowers **p** upon my back; Ps 129:3 2790a
"Zion will be **p** *as* a field, And Jer 26:18 2790a
You have **p** wickedness, you have Hos 10:13 2790a
of you Zion will be **p** as a field, Mi 3:12 2790a

PLOWERS
"The **p** plowed upon my back; Ps 129:3 2790a

PLOWING
will be neither **p** nor harvesting. Gn 45:6 2758
even during **p** time and harvest you Ex 34:21 2758
and *some* to do his **p** and to reap 1Sa 8:12 2758
while he was **p** with twelve pairs 1Ki 19:19 2790a
"The oxen were **p** and the donkeys Jb 1:14 2790a
having a slave **p** or tending sheep, Lk 17:7 *722*

PLOWMAN
When the **p** will overtake the reaper Am 9:13 2790a
the **p** ought to plow in hope, 1Co 9:10 *722*

PLOWMEN
the land to be vinedressers and **p**. 2Ki 25:12 3009
He also had **p** and vinedressers in 2Ch 26:10 406
the land to be vinedressers and **p**. Jer 52:16 3009

PLOWS
one **p** and breaks open the earth, Ps 141:7 6398

PLOWSHARE
each to sharpen his **p**, 1Sa 13:20 4281

PLOWSHARES
two-thirds of a shekel for the **p**, 1Sa 13:21 4281
will hammer their swords into **p** and Is 2:4 855a
Beat your **p** into swords And your Jl 3:10 855a
they will hammer their swords into **p** Mi 4:3 855a

PLUCK
may **p** the heads with your hand, Dt 23:25 6998
Who **p** mallow by the bushes, And Jb 30:4 6998
He will **p** my feet out of the net. Ps 25:15 3318
P the strings skillfully, sing Is 23:16 5059
to those who **p** out the beard; Is 50:6 4803
To **p** up and to break down, Jer 1:10 5428
will plant them and not **p** them up. Jer 24:6 5428
I have watched over them to **p** up, Jer 31:28 5428
I will **p** from the topmost of its Ezk 17:22 6998
eye causes you to stumble, **p** it out and Mt 18:9 *1807*

PLUCKED
their tent-cord **p** up within them? Jb 4:21 5265
it will not be **p** up or Jer 31:40 5428
"He **p** off the topmost of its Ezk 17:4 6998
'But it was **p** up in fury; Ezk 19:12 5428
looking until its wings were **p**, Da 7:4 4804
not a brand **p** from the fire?" Zch 3:2 5337
you would have **p** out your eyes and Ga 4:15 *1846*

PLUCKED-OUT
of well-set hair, a **p** scalp; Is 3:24 7144

PLUMAGE
With the pinion and **p** of love, Jb 39:13 5133
and a full **p** of many colors came Ezk 17:3 5133
eagle with great wings and much **p**; Ezk 17:7 5133

PLUMB
And the **p** line of emptiness. Is 34:11 68
wall with a **p** line in His hand. Am 7:7 594
And I said, "A **p** line." Am 7:8 594
"Behold I am about to put a **p** line Am 7:8 594
will be glad when they see the **p** line Zch 4:10 913, 68

PLUMMET
and the **p** of the house of Ahab, 2Ki 21:13 4949

PLUMP
up on a single stalk, **p** and good. Gn 41:5 1277
up the seven **p** and full ears. Gn 41:7 1277

PLUNDER
Thus you will **p** the Egyptians." Ex 3:22 5337
and our little ones will become **p**; Nu 14:3 957
its cattle as **p** for yourselves. Jos 8:2 962
of that city as **p** for themselves, Jos 8:27 962
sons of Israel took as their **p**; Jos 11:14 962
They took no **p** in silver. Jg 5:19 1215
and they will become as **p** and 2Ki 21:14 957
And they carried away very much **p**. 2Ch 14:13 7998
for there was much **p** in them. 2Ch 14:14 961
and to **p** and to open shame, Ezr 9:7 961
up for **p** in a land of captivity. Ne 4:4 961
to seize their possessions as **p**. Es 3:13 962
and women, and to **p** their spoil, Es 8:11 962
did not lay their hands on the **p**. Es 9:10 961
did not lay their hands on the **p**. Es 9:15 961
did not lay their hands on the **p**. Es 9:16 961
All who pass along the way **p** him; Ps 89:41 8155
strangers **p** the product of his labor. Ps 109:11 962
p of the poor is in your houses. Is 3:14 1500
And that they may **p** the orphans. Is 10:2 962
To capture booty and to seize **p**, Is 10:6 957
they will **p** the sons of the east; Is 11:14 962
be the portion of those who **p** us Is 17:14 962
The lame will take the **p**. Is 33:23 957
enemies, and they will **p** them, Jer 20:5 962
who **p** you will be for plunder, Jer 30:16 8155
who plunder you will be for **p**, Jer 30:16 4933
"Their camels will become **p**, Jer 49:32 957
"Chaldea will become **p**; Jer 50:10 7998
All who **p** her will have enough," Jer 50:10 7997b
into the hands of the foreigners as **p** Ezk 7:21 957
give them over to terror and **p**. Ezk 23:46 957
capture her spoil and seize her **p**; Ezk 29:19 957
to capture spoil and to seize **p**, Ezk 38:12 957
assembled your company to seize **p**, Ezk 38:13 957
p of those who plundered them," Ezk 39:10 962
he will distribute **p**, Da 11:24 961
return to his land with much **p**; Da 11:28 7399
by flame, by captivity and by **p** for Da 11:33 961
It will **p** *his* treasury of every Hos 13:15 8154
P the silver! Plunder the gold! Na 2:9 962
Plunder the silver! **P** the gold! Na 2:9 962
you will become **p** for them. Hab 2:7 4933
their wealth will become **p** And Zph 1:13 4933
remnant of My people will **p** them And Zph 2:9 962
against the nations which **p** you, Zch 2:8 7997b
they will be **p** for their slaves. Zch 2:9 7998
And then he will **p** his house. Mt 12:29 *1283*
p his property unless he first binds Mk 3:27 *1283*
man, and then he will **p** his house. Mk 3:27 *1283*
had relied and distributes his **p**. Lk 11:22 *4661*

PLUNDERED
Thus they **p** the Egyptians. Ex 12:36 5337
and all their goods they **p**. Nu 31:9 962
spoil which the men of war had **p** Nu 31:32 962
hands of plunderers who **p** them; Jg 2:14 8155
the hands of those who **p** them. Jg 2:16 8154
the hands of those who **p** them. 1Sa 14:48 8154
the Philistines and **p** their camps. 1Sa 17:53 8155
and **p** the camp of the Arameans. 2Ki 7:16 962
3,000 of them and **p** much spoil. 2Ch 25:13 962
Or have **p** him who without cause Ps 7:4 2502a
The stouthearted were **p**, Ps 76:5 7997b
peoples And **p** their treasures, Is 10:13 8154
Their houses will be **p** And their Is 13:16 8155
this is a people **p** and despoiled; Is 42:22 962
her treasures, and they will be **p**! Jer 50:37 962
the plunder of those who **p** them," Ezk 39:10 962
will be captured, the houses **p**, Zch 14:2 8155

PLUNDERERS
the hands of **p** who plundered them; Jg 2:14 8154
and gave them into the hand of **p**, 2Ki 17:20 8154
up for spoil, and Israel to **p**? Is 42:24 962

PLUNDERING
and are **p** the threshing floors." 1Sa 23:1 8154

PLUNGE
You would **p** me into the pit, Jb 9:31 2881
p men into ruin and destruction. 1Tm 6:9 *1036*

PLUS
numbering 30,000 **p** 3,000 bulls; 2Ch 35:7

POCHERETH-HAZZEB
the sons of Hattil, the sons of **P**, Ezr 2:57 6380
the sons of Hattil, the sons of **P**, Ne 7:59 6380

PODIUM
Ezra the scribe stood at a wooden **p** Ne 8:4 4026

PODS
the **p** that the swine were eating, Lk 15:16 *2769*

POETS
even some of your own **p** have said, Ac 17:28 *4163*

POINT
p out what is yours among my Gn 31:32 5234
to **p** out *the way* before him to Gn 46:28 3384
with us to the **p** of destruction, Ezr 9:14 5704
made repairs as far as *a* **p** Ne 3:16
the glittering **p** from his gall. Jb 20:25 1300
"Shall I bring to the **p** of birth and Is 66:9 7665
With a diamond **p** it is engraved Jer 17:1 6856
border to a **p** opposite Lebo-hamath. Ezk 47:20
"At this **p** the revelation ended. Da 7:28 3542
encompassed me to the **p** of death. Jon 2:5
disciples came up to **p** out the temple Mt 24:1 *1925*
deeply grieved, to the **p** of death; Mt 26:38 *2193*
daughter is at the **p** of death; Mk 5:23 *2079*
deeply grieved to the **p** of death; Mk 14:34 *2193*
At this **p** His disciples came, Jn 4:27 *1909*
for he was at the **p** of death. Jn 4:47 *3195*
you were made sorrowful to *the* **p** *of* 2Co 7:9
obedient to the **p** of death, Php 2:8 *3360*
he was sick to the **p** of death, Php 2:27 *3897*
the main **p** in what has been said *is* Heb 8:1 *2774*
resisted to the **p** of shedding blood Heb 12:4 *3360*
whole law and yet stumbles in one **p**, Jas 2:10

POINTING
your midst, The **p** of the finger and Is 58:9 7971
In **p** out these things to the 1Tm 4:6 *5294*

POINTS
his feet, Who **p** with his fingers; Pr 6:13 3384
toward the four **p** of the compass, Da 11:4 7307
simply had some **p** of disagreement Ac 25:19 *2213*
very boldly to you on some **p** so Ro 15:15 *3313*

POISON
Their grapes are grapes of **p**, Dt 32:32 7219
And the deadly **p** of cobras. Dt 32:33 7219
Their **p** my spirit drinks; Jb 6:4 2534
"He sucks the **p** of cobras; Jb 20:16 7219
P of a viper is under their lips. Ps 140:3 2534
you have turned justice into **p** And Am 6:12 7219
and if they drink any deadly **p**, Mk 16:18
P OF ASPS IS UNDER THEIR LIPS"; Ro 3:13 *2447*
evil *and* full of deadly **p**. Jas 3:8 *2447*

POISONED
us And given us **p** water to drink, Jer 8:14 7219
and give them **p** water to drink. Jer 9:15 7219

POISONOUS
root bearing **p** fruit and wormwood. Dt 29:18 7219
And make them drink **p** water, Jer 23:15 7219
And judgment sprouts like **p** weeds Hos 10:4 7219

POLE
carried it on a **p** between two *men*, Nu 13:23 4132

POLES
You shall make **p** of acacia wood Ex 25:13 905
"You shall put the **p** into the Ex 25:14 905
"The **p** shall remain in the rings Ex 25:15 905
holders for the **p** to carry the table. Ex 25:27 905
You shall make the **p** of acacia wood Ex 25:28 905
You shall make **p** for the altar, Ex 27:6 905
for the altar, **p** of acacia wood, Ex 27:6 905
"Its **p** shall be inserted into Ex 27:7 905
so that the **p** shall be on the two Ex 27:7 905
holders for **p** with which to carry it. Ex 30:4 905
You shall make the **p** of acacia wood Ex 30:5 905
the ark and its **p**, the mercy seat, Ex 35:12 905
the table and its **p**, Ex 35:13 905
the altar of incense and its **p**, Ex 35:15 905
with its bronze grating, its **p**, Ex 35:16 905
He made **p** of acacia wood and Ex 37:4 905
He put the **p** into the rings on Ex 37:5 905
holders for the **p** to carry the table. Ex 37:14 905
He made the **p** of acacia wood Ex 37:15 905
holders for **p** with which to carry it. Ex 37:27 905
He made the **p** of acacia wood Ex 37:28 905
grating *as* holders for the **p**. Ex 38:5 905
He made the **p** of acacia wood Ex 38:6 905
He inserted the **p** into the Ex 38:7 905
and its **p** and the mercy seat; Ex 39:35 905
its **p** and all its utensils, Ex 39:39 905
and attached the **p** to the ark, Ex 40:20 905
pure blue, and shall insert its **p**. Nu 4:6 905
skin, and they shall insert its **p**. Nu 4:8 905
skin, and shall insert its **p**; Nu 4:11 905
skin over it and insert its **p**. Nu 4:14 905
over the ark and its **p** from above. 1Ki 8:7 905
But the **p** were so long that the 1Ki 8:8 905
the ends of the **p** could be seen from 1Ki 8:8 905
with the **p** thereon, as Moses had 1Ch 15:15 4133
a covering over the ark and its **p**. 2Ch 5:8 905
The **p** were so long that the 2Ch 5:9 905
ends of the **p** of the ark could be seen 2Ch 5:9 905

POLICEMEN
chief magistrates sent their **p**, Ac 16:35 *4465*
The **p** reported these words to Ac 16:38 *4465*

POLISH
P the spears, Put on the Jer 46:4 4838

POLISHED
- of the LORD *were* of **p** bronze. 1Ki 7:45 4803
- Huram-abi made of **p** bronze for 2Ch 4:16 4838
- a sword sharpened And also **p**! Ezk 21:9 4803
- **P** to flash like lightning!' Ezk 21:10 4803
- "It is given to be **p**, Ezk 21:11 4803
- the sword is sharpened and **p**, Ezk 21:11 4803
- sword is drawn, **p** for the slaughter, Ezk 21:28 4803
- feet like the gleam of **p** bronze, Da 10:6 7044

POLISHING
- Their **p** *was like* lapis lazuli. La 4:7 1508

POLL-TAX
- of the earth collect customs or **p**, Mt 17:25 *2778b*
- it lawful to give a **p** to Caesar, Mt 22:17 *2778b*
- "Show Me the coin *used* for the **p**." Mt 22:19 *2778b*
- Is it lawful to pay a **p** to Caesar, Mk 12:14 *2778b*

POLLUTE
- not **p** the land in which you are; Nu 35:33 2610
- **p** the princes of the sanctuary, Is 43:28 2490c

POLLUTED
- And the land was **p** with the blood. Ps 106:38 2610
- *Like* a trampled spring and a **p** well Pr 25:26 7843
- is also **p** by its inhabitants, Is 24:5 2610
- not that land be completely **p**? Jer 3:1 2610
- And you have **p** a land With your Jer 3:2 2610
- she **p** the land and committed Jer 3:9 2610
- sin, because they have **p** My land; Jer 16:18 2490c
- "For both prophet and priest are **p**; Jer 23:11 2610
- 'Let her be **p**, And let our eyes Mi 4:11 2610
- even the garment **p** by the flesh. Jude 1:23 *4695*

POLLUTES
- for blood **p** the land and no Nu 35:33 2610

POLLUTION
- **P** has gone forth into all the land.' Jer 23:15 2613

POMEGRANATE
- a golden bell and a **p**, Ex 28:34 7416
- a golden bell and a **p**, Ex 28:34 7416
- alternating a bell and a **p** all Ex 39:26 7416
- the **p** tree which is in Migron. 1Sa 14:2 7416
- a slice of a **p** Behind your veil. SS 4:3 7416
- a slice of a **p** Behind your veil. SS 6:7 7416
- The **p**, the palm also, and the Jl 1:12 7416
- the vine, the fig tree, the **p** and Hg 2:19 7416

POMEGRANATES
- "You shall make on its hem **p** Ex 28:33 7416
- They made **p** of blue and purple Ex 39:24 7416
- and put the bells between the **p** Ex 39:25 7416
- with some of the **p** and the figs. Nu 13:23 7416
- of grain or figs or vines or **p**, Nu 20:5 7416
- of vines and fig trees and **p**, Dt 8:8 7416
- which were on the top of the **p**; 1Ki 7:18 7416
- and the **p** *numbered* two hundred in 1Ki 7:20 7416
- hundred **p** for the two networks, 1Ki 7:42 7416
- two rows of **p** for each network to 1Ki 7:42 7416
- and **p** on the capital all around, 2Ki 25:17 7416
- and he made one hundred **p** and 2Ch 3:16 7416
- hundred **p** for the two networks, 2Ch 4:13 7416
- two rows of **p** for each network to 2Ch 4:13 7416
- orchard of **p** With choice fruits, SS 4:13 7416
- had budded *Or* the **p** had bloomed. SS 6:11 7416
- *And whether* the **p** have bloomed. SS 7:12 7416
- to drink from the juice of my **p**. SS 8:2 7416
- and **p** upon the capital all around, Jer 52:22 7416
- was like these, including **p**. Jer 52:22 7416
- There were ninety-six exposed **p**; Jer 52:23 7416
- all the **p** *numbered* a hundred on Jer 52:23 7416

POMP
- But man in *his* **p** will not endure; Ps 49:12 3366
- Man in *his* **p**, yet without Ps 49:20 3366
- and the **p** of his haughtiness." Is 10:12 8597
- 'Your **p** *and* the music of your Is 14:11 1347b
- with Bernice amid great **p**, Ac 25:23 *5325*

PONDER
- She does not **p** the path of life; Pr 5:6 6424
- gaze at you, They will **p** over you, Is 14:16 995
- things, Or **p** things of the past. Is 43:18 995

PONDERED
- While you **p** what to say. Jb 32:11 2713
- When I **p** to understand this, It Ps 73:16 2803
- and he **p**, searched out and Ec 12:9 239

PONDERING
- and kept **p** what kind of salutation Lk 1:29 *1260*
- these things, **p** them in her heart. Lk 2:19 *4820*

PONDERS
- with my heart, And my spirit **p**: Ps 77:6 2664
- The heart of the righteous **p** how to Pr 15:28 1897

PONDS
- I made **p** of water for myself from Ec 2:6 1295
- into coastlands And dry up the **p**. Is 42:15 98

PONTIUS
- **P** Pilate was governor of Judea, Lk 3:1 *4194*
- anointed, both Herod and **P** Pilate, Ac 4:27 *4194*
- good confession before **P** Pilate, 1Tm 6:13 *4194*

PONTUS
- Judea and Cappadocia, **P** and Asia, Ac 2:9 *4195*
- Jew named Aquila, a native of **P**, Ac 18:2 *4193*
- as aliens, scattered throughout **P**, 1Pe 1:1 *4195*

POOL
- and met them by the **p** of Gibeon; 2Sa 2:13 1295
- one on the one side of the **p** and 2Sa 2:13 1295
- other on the other side of the **p**. 2Sa 2:13 1295
- them up beside the **p** in Hebron. 2Sa 4:12 1295
- the chariot by the **p** of Samaria, 1Ki 22:38 1295
- by the conduit of the upper **p**, 2Ki 18:17 1295
- how he made the **p** and the conduit and 2Ki 20:20 1295
- the Fountain Gate and the King's **P**, Ne 2:14 1295
- and the wall of the **P** of Shelah at Ne 3:15 1295
- and as far as the artificial **p** and Ne 3:16 1295
- a wilderness into a **p** of water And Ps 107:35 98
- turned the rock into a **p** of water, Ps 114:8 98
- end of the conduit of the upper **p**, Is 7:3 1295
- the waters of the lower **p**. Is 22:9 1295
- walls For the waters of the old **p**. Is 22:11 1295
- The scorched land will become a **p** Is 35:7 98
- stood by the conduit of the upper **p** Is 36:2 1295
- make the wilderness a **p** of water And Is 41:18 98
- by the great **p** that is in Gibeon. Jer 41:12 4325
- Nineveh *was* like a **p** of water Na 2:8 1295
- Jerusalem by the sheep *gate* a **p**, Jn 5:2 *2861*
- at certain seasons into the **p** and Jn 5:4 *2861*
- I have no man to put me into the **p** Jn 5:7 *2861*
- "Go, wash in the **p** of Siloam" Jn 9:7 *2861*

POOLS
- their streams, and over their **p**, Ex 7:19 98
- over the streams and over the **p**, Ex 8:5 98
- Your eyes *like* the **p** in Heshbon By SS 7:4 1295

POOR
- them, **p** and very ugly and gaunt, Gn 41:19 1800b
- to My people, to the **p** among you, Ex 22:25 6041
- partial to a **p** man in his dispute. Ex 23:3 1800b
- and the **p** shall not pay less than Ex 30:15 1800b
- "But if he is **p** and his means Lv 14:21 1800b
- you shall not be partial to the **p** nor Lv 19:15 1800b
- becomes so **p** he has to sell part Lv 25:25 4134
- a countryman of yours becomes **p** Lv 25:35 4134
- a countryman of yours becomes so **p** Lv 25:39 4134
- a countryman of yours becomes so **p** Lv 25:47 4134
- there will be no **p** among you, Dt 15:4 34
- "If there is a **p** man with you, Dt 15:7 34
- your hand from your **p** brother; Dt 15:7 34
- is hostile toward your **p** brother, Dt 15:9 34
- "For the **p** will never cease *to be* Dt 15:11 34
- to your needy and **p** in your land.' Dt 15:11 6041
- "If he is a **p** man, you shall Dt 24:12 6041
- hired servant *who is* **p** and needy, Dt 24:14 6041
- he is **p** and sets his heart on it; Dt 24:15 6041
- young men, whether **p** or rich. Ru 3:10 1800b
- "The LORD makes **p** and rich; 1Sa 2:7 3423
- "He raises the **p** from the dust, 1Sa 2:8 1800b
- am a **p** man and lightly esteemed?" 1Sa 18:23 7326
- the one rich and the other **p**. 2Sa 12:1 7326
- "But the **p** man had nothing except 2Sa 12:3 7326
- Rather he took the **p** man's ewe 2Sa 12:4 7326
- to one another and gifts to the **p**. Es 9:22 34
- the **p** from the hand of the mighty. Jb 5:15 34
- "His sons favor the **p**, Jb 20:10 1800b
- has oppressed *and* forsaken the **p**; Jb 20:19 1800b
- The **p** of the land are made to hide Jb 24:4 6041
- against the **p** they take a pledge. Jb 24:9 6041
- "They cause *the* **p** to go about Jb 24:10
- He kills the **p** and the needy, And Jb 24:14 6041
- the **p** who cried for help, Jb 29:12 6041
- have kept the **p** from *their* desire, Jb 31:16 1800b
- Nor regards the rich above the **p**, Jb 34:19 1800b
- the cry of the **p** to come to Him, Jb 34:28 1800b
- This **p** man cried, and the LORD Ps 34:6 6041
- low and high, Rich and **p** together. Ps 49:2 34
- provided in Your goodness for the **p**, Ps 68:10 6041
- compassion on the **p** and needy, Ps 72:13 1800b
- He has given freely to the **p**, Ps 112:9 34
- He raises the **p** from the dust And Ps 113:7 1800b
- afflicted And justice for the **p**. Ps 140:12 34
- **P** is he who works with a negligent Pr 10:4 7326
- ruin of the **p** is their poverty. Pr 10:15 1800b
- *Another* pretends to be **p**, Pr 13:7 7326
- wealth, But the **p** hears no rebuke. Pr 13:8 7326
- *is in* the fallow ground of the **p**, Pr 13:23 7326
- **p** is hated even by his neighbor, Pr 14:20 7326
- is he who is gracious to the **p**. Pr 14:21 6035
- He who oppresses the **p** taunts Pr 14:31 1800b
- He who mocks the **p** taunts his Pr 17:5 7326
- The **p** man utters supplications, Pr 18:23 7326
- Better is a **p** man who walks in his Pr 19:1 7326
- But a **p** man is separated from his Pr 19:4 1800b
- the brothers of a **p** man hate him; Pr 19:7 7326
- One who is gracious to a **p** man lends Pr 19:17 1800b
- better to be a **p** man than a liar. Pr 19:22 7326
- not love sleep, or you will become **p**; Pr 20:13 3423
- who shuts his ear to the cry of the **p** Pr 21:13 1800b
- pleasure *will become* a **p** man; Pr 21:17 4270
- rich and the **p** have a common bond, Pr 22:2 7326
- The rich rules over the **p**, Pr 22:7 7326
- gives some of his food to the **p**. Pr 22:9 1800b
- He who oppresses the **p** to make Pr 22:16 1800b
- not rob the **p** because he is poor, Pr 22:22 1800b
- not rob the poor because he is **p**, Pr 22:22 1800b
- A **p** man who oppresses the lowly Is Pr 28:3 7326
- the **p** who walks in his integrity Than Pr 28:6 7326
- for him who is gracious to the **p**. Pr 28:8 1800b
- But the **p** who has understanding Pr 28:11 1800b
- Is a wicked ruler over a **p** people. Pr 28:15 1800b
- He who gives to the **p** will never Pr 28:27 7326
- concerned for the rights of the **p**, Pr 29:7 1800b
- The **p** man and the oppressor have Pr 29:13 7326
- If a king judges the **p** with truth, Pr 29:14 1800b
- She extends her hand to the **p**, Pr 31:20 6041
- A **p** yet wise lad is better than Ec 4:13 4542
- he was born **p** in his kingdom. Ec 4:14 7326
- If you see oppression of the **p** and Ec 5:8 7326
- *advantage* does the **p** man have, Ec 6:8 6041
- there was found in it a **p** wise man Ec 9:15 4542
- Yet no one remembered that **p** man. Ec 9:15 4542
- But the wisdom of the **p** man is Ec 9:16 4542
- plunder of the **p** is in your houses. Is 3:14 6041
- And grinding the face of the **p**?" Is 3:15 6041
- **p** of My people of *their* rights, Is 10:2 6041
- righteousness He will judge the **p**, Is 11:4 1800b
- the homeless **p** into the house; Is 58:7 6041
- The lifeblood of the innocent **p**; Jer 2:34 34
- "They are only the **p**, Jer 5:4 1800b
- do not defend the rights of the **p**. Jer 5:28 34
- she did not help the **p** and needy. Ezk 16:49 6041
- oppresses the **p** and needy, commits Ezk 18:12 6041
- he keeps his hand from the **p**, Ezk 18:17 6041
- and they have wronged the **p** and Ezk 22:29 6041
- by showing mercy to *the* **p**, Da 4:27 6040b
- of Samaria, Who oppress the **p**, Am 4:1 1800b
- you impose heavy rent on the **p** Am 5:11 1800b
- And turn aside the **p** in the gate. Am 5:12 34
- the orphan, the stranger or the **p**; Zch 7:10 6041
- "Blessed are the **p** in spirit, for Mt 5:3 *4434*
- "So when you give to the **p**, do not Mt 6:2 *4434*
- "But when you give to the **p**, do not Mt 6:3 *4434*
- *the* **P** HAVE THE GOSPEL PREACHED Mt 11:5 *4434*
- possessions and give to *the* **p**, Mt 19:21 *4434*
- and *the money* given to the **p**." Mt 26:9 *4434*
- you always have the **p** with you; Mt 26:11 *4434*
- you possess and give to the **p**, Mk 10:21 *4434*
- A **p** widow came and put in two Mk 12:42 *4434*
- this **p** widow put in more than all Mk 12:43 *4434*
- and *the money* given to the **p**." Mk 14:5 *4434*
- you always have the **p** with you, Mk 14:7 *4434*
- ME TO PREACH THE GOSPEL TO THE **P**. Lk 4:18 *4434*
- "Blessed *are you who are* **p**, Lk 6:20 *4434*
- *the* **P** HAVE THE GOSPEL PREACHED TO Lk 7:22 *4434*
- give a reception, invite *the* **p**, Lk 14:13 *4434*
- and bring in here the **p** and crippled Lk 14:21 *4434*
- a **p** man named Lazarus was Lk 16:20 *4434*
- "Now the **p** man died Lk 16:22 *4434*
- and distribute it to the **p**, Lk 18:22 *4434*
- possessions I will give to the **p**, Lk 19:8 *4434*
- And He saw a **p** widow Lk 21:2 *3998*
- this **p** widow put in more than all Lk 21:3 *4434*
- denarii and given to **p** *people?*" Jn 12:5 *4434*
- he was concerned about the **p**, Jn 12:6 *4434*
- you always have the **p** with you, Jn 12:8 *4434*
- he should give something to the **p**. Jn 13:29 *4434*
- to make a contribution for the **p** Ro 15:26 *4434*
- all my possessions to feed *the* **p**, 1Co 13:3 *4434*
- as **p** yet making many rich, 2Co 6:10 *4434*
- yet for your sake He became **p**, 2Co 8:9 *4434*
- ABROAD, HE GAVE TO THE **P**, 2Co 9:9 *3993*
- only *asked* us to remember the **p** Ga 2:10 *4434*
- comes in a **p** man in dirty clothes, Jas 2:2 *4434*
- place," and you say to the **p** man, Jas 2:3 *4434*
- did not God choose the **p** of this Jas 2:5 *4434*
- But you have dishonored the **p** man. Jas 2:6 *4434*
- and **p** and blind and naked, Rv 3:17 *4434*
- the great, and the rich and the **p**, Rv 13:16 *4434*

POORER
- if he is **p** than your valuation, Lv 27:8 4134
- freely, *then he serves* the **p** *wine;* Jn 2:10 *1640*

POOREST
- except the **p** people of the land. 2Ki 24:14 1803b
- guard left some of the **p** of the land 2Ki 25:12 1803b
- But some of the **p** people who had Jer 39:10 1800b
- those of the **p** of the land who had Jer 40:7 1803b
- exile some of the **p** of the people, Jer 52:15 1803b
- guard left some of the **p** of the land Jer 52:16 1803b

POORLY
- and thirsty, and are **p** clothed, 1Co 4:11 *1130*

POPLAR
- Then Jacob took fresh rods of **p** Gn 30:37 3839
- on the hills, Under oak, **p** and Hos 4:13 3839

POPLARS
- grass Like **p** by streams of water.' Is 44:4 6155

POPULATE
- **P** the earth abundantly and Gn 9:7 8317

POPULATED
- from these the whole earth was **p**. Gn 9:19 5310b
- abandoned, the **p** city forsaken. Is 32:14 1995

POPULATION
- along with all *his* great **p**, Is 16:14 1995
- fill you with a **p** like locusts, Jer 51:14 120
- Because they deported an entire **p** Am 1:6 1546
- they delivered up an entire **p** to Edom Am 1:9 1546

POPULOUS
- a great, mighty and **p** nation. Dt 26:5 7227a

PORATHA
- **P**, Adalia, Aridatha, Es 9:8 6334

PORCH
- The **p** in front of the nave of 1Ki 6:3 197
- and a **p** *was* in front of them and 1Ki 7:6 197
- the LORD, and the **p** of the house. 1Ki 7:12 197
- on the top of the pillars in the **p** 1Ki 7:19 197
- the pillars at the **p** of the nave; 1Ki 7:21 197
- the plan of the **p** *of the temple,* 1Ch 28:11 197
- The **p** which was in front of 2Ch 3:4 197
- which he had built before the **p**; 2Ch 8:12 197
- was in front of the **p** of the LORD. 2Ch 15:8 197
- have also shut the doors of the **p** 2Ch 29:7 197
- they entered the **p** of the LORD. 2Ch 29:17 197
- LORD, between the **p** and the altar, Ezk 8:16 197
- by the **p** of the gate facing inward Ezk 40:7 197
- the **p** of the gate facing inward, Ezk 40:8 197
- He measured the **p** of the gate, Ezk 40:9 197
- And the **p** of the gate was Ezk 40:9 197
- **p** of the gate *was* fifty cubits. Ezk 40:15 197
- and its **p** *was* in front of them. Ezk 40:22 361
- In the **p** of the gate *were* two Ezk 40:39 197
- on the other side of the **p** of the gate Ezk 40:40 197

brought me to the **p** of the temple	**Ezk 40:48**	197
each side pillar of the **p**,	**Ezk 40:48**	197
length of the **p** *was* twenty cubits	**Ezk 40:49**	197
on the front of the **p** outside.	**Ezk 41:25**	197
the other, on the sides of the **p**;	**Ezk 41:26**	197
enter by way of the **p** of the gate and	**Ezk 44:3**	197
The prince shall enter by way of the **p**	**Ezk 46:2**	197
go in by way of the **p** of the gate	**Ezk 46:8**	197
Weep between the **p** and the altar,	**Jl 2:17**	197
And he went out onto the **p**,	**Mk 14:68**	*4259*

PORCHES

around, and likewise for the **p**.	**Ezk 40:16**	361
and its side pillars and its **p** had	**Ezk 40:21**	361
Its windows and its **p**	**Ezk 40:22**	361
he measured its side pillars and its **p**	**Ezk 40:24**	361
The gate and its **p** had windows	**Ezk 40:25**	361
and its **p** *were* in front of them;	**Ezk 40:26**	361
and its **p** *were* according to those	**Ezk 40:29**	361
and its **p** had windows all around;	**Ezk 40:29**	361
There were **p** all around,	**Ezk 40:30**	361
Its **p** *were* toward the outer court;	**Ezk 40:31**	361
and its **p** *were* according to those	**Ezk 40:33**	361
and its **p** had windows all around;	**Ezk 40:33**	361
Its **p** *were* toward the outer court;	**Ezk 40:34**	361
its side pillars and its **p**.	**Ezk 40:36**	361
inner nave and the **p** of the court.	**Ezk 41:15**	197

PORCIUS

Felix was succeeded by **P** Festus,	**Ac 24:27**	*4201*

PORPHYRY

silver on a mosaic pavement of **p**,	**Es 1:6**	923

PORPOISE

rams' skins dyed red, **p** skins,	**Ex 25:5**	8476
and a covering of **p** skins above.	**Ex 26:14**	8476
rams' skins dyed red, and **p** skins,	**Ex 35:7**	8476
rams' skins dyed red and **p** skins,	**Ex 35:23**	8476
and a covering of **p** skins above.	**Ex 36:19**	8476
red, and the covering of **p** skins,	**Ex 39:34**	8476
lay a covering of **p** skin on it,	**Nu 4:6**	8476
same with a covering of **p** skin,	**Nu 4:8**	8476
utensils in a covering of **p** skin,	**Nu 4:10**	8476
it with a covering of **p** skin,	**Nu 4:11**	8476
them with a covering of **p** skin,	**Nu 4:12**	8476
shall spread a cover of **p** skin over it	**Nu 4:14**	8476
the covering of **p** skin that is on top	**Nu 4:25**	8476
sandals of **p** skin on your feet;	**Ezk 16:10**	8476

PORTICO

in the temple in the **p** of Solomon.	**Jn 10:23**	*4745*
them at the so-called **p** of Solomon,	**Ac 3:11**	*4745*
all with one accord in Solomon's **p**.	**Ac 5:12**	*4745*

PORTICOES

in Hebrew Bethesda, having five **p**.	**Jn 5:2**	*4745*

PORTION

"Do we still have any **p** or	**Gn 31:14**	2506
but Benjamin's **p** was five times as	**Gn 43:34**	4864
you one **p** more than your brothers,	**Gn 48:22**	7926
out and gather a day's **p** every day,	**Ex 16:4**	1697
and it shall be your **p**.	**Ex 29:26**	4490
be for Aaron and his sons as *their* **p**	**Ex 29:28**	2706
as its memorial **p** on the altar,	**Lv 2:2**	234
the grain offering its memorial **p**,	**Lv 2:9**	234
offer up in smoke its memorial **p**,	**Lv 2:16**	234
his handful of it as its memorial **p**	**Lv 5:12**	234
right thigh shall be his as *his* **p**.	**Lv 7:33**	4490
Moses' **p** of the ram of ordination,	**Lv 8:29**	4490
may be a memorial **p** for the bread,	**Lv 24:7**	234
by fire, *his* **p** forever."	**Lv 24:9**	2706
I have given them to you as a **p** and	**Nu 18:8**	4888a
land nor own any **p** among them;	**Nu 18:20**	2506
I am your **p** and your inheritance	**Nu 18:20**	2506
saw from there a **p** of the people.	**Nu 22:41**	7097a
p of those who went out to war,	**Nu 31:36**	2506
Levi does not have a **p** or	**Dt 10:9**	2506
has no **p** or inheritance with you.	**Dt 12:12**	2506
has no **p** or inheritance among you.	**Dt 14:27**	2506
has no **p** or inheritance among you,	**Dt 14:29**	2506
no **p** or inheritance with Israel;	**Dt 18:1**	2506
LORD's offerings by fire and His **p**.	**Dt 18:1**	5159
him a double **p** of all that he has,	**Dt 21:17**	6310
'I have removed the sacred **p**	**Dt 26:13**	
"For the LORD's **p** is His people;	**Dt 32:9**	2506
there the ruler's **p** was reserved;	**Dt 33:21**	2513a
they did not give a **p** to the Levites	**Jos 14:4**	2506
a **p** among the sons of Judah,	**Jos 15:13**	2506
lot and one **p** for an inheritance,	**Jos 17:14**	2256a
the Levites have no **p** among you,	**Jos 18:7**	2506
from the **p** of the sons of Judah,	**Jos 19:9**	2506
you have no **p** in the LORD."	**Jos 22:25**	2506
"You have no **p** in the LORD."	**Jos 22:27**	2506
the **p** of the field belonging to Boaz,	**Ru 2:3**	2513a
Hannah he would give a double **p**,	**1Sa 1:5**	4490
"Bring the **p** that I gave you,	**1Sa 9:23**	4490
"We have no **p** in David, Nor do we	**2Sa 20:1**	2506
"What **p** do we have in David?	**1Ki 12:16**	2506
let a double **p** of your spirit be upon	**2Ki 2:9**	6310
him by the king, a **p** for each day,	**2Ki 25:30**	1697
and a **p** *of meat* and a raisin cake.	**1Ch 16:3**	829
As the **p** of your inheritance."	**1Ch 16:18**	2256a
"What **p** do we have in David?	**2Ch 10:16**	2506
Ahaz took a **p** out of the house	**2Ch 28:21**	2505a
appointed the king's **p** of his goods	**2Ch 31:3**	4521
to give the **p** due to the priests and	**2Ch 31:4**	4521
you have no **p**, right or memorial	**Ne 2:20**	2506
and set apart the consecrated **p**	**Ne 12:47**	
Levites set apart the consecrated **p**	**Ne 12:47**	
is the wicked man's **p** from God,	**Jb 20:29**	2506
Their **p** is cursed on the earth.	**Jb 24:18**	2513a
is the **p** of a wicked man from God,	**Jb 27:13**	2506
"And what is the **p** of God from	**Jb 31:2**	2506
wind will be the **p** of their cup.	**Ps 11:6**	4521
p of my inheritance and my cup;	**Ps 16:5**	4521
world, whose **p** is in *this* life,	**Ps 17:14**	2506
I will **p** out Shechem and measure	**Ps 60:6**	2505a
have its **p** from *your* enemies."	**Ps 68:23**	4521
of my heart and my **p** forever.	**Ps 73:26**	2506
As the **p** of your inheritance,"	**Ps 105:11**	2256a
will exult, I will **p** out Shechem And	**Ps 108:7**	2505a
The LORD is my **p**;	**Ps 119:57**	2506
My **p** in the land of the living.	**Ps 142:5**	2506
me with the food that is my **p**,	**Pr 30:8**	2706
Divide your **p** to seven, or even to	**Ec 11:2**	2506
"Yet there will be a tenth **p** in it,	**Is 6:13**	6224
be the **p** of those who plunder us	**Is 17:14**	2506
will allot Him a **p** with the great,	**Is 53:12**	2505a
stones of the ravine Is your **p**,	**Is 57:6**	2506
shame *you will have a* double **p**,	**Is 61:7**	
will shout for joy over their **p**.	**Is 61:7**	2506
they will possess a double **p** in	**Is 61:7**	
The **p** of Jacob is not like these;	**Jer 10:16**	2506
the **p** measured to you From Me,"	**Jer 13:25**	4521
The **p** of Jacob is not like these;	**Jer 51:19**	2506
a daily **p** all the days of his life	**Jer 52:34**	1697
"The LORD is my **p**,"	**La 3:24**	2506
to the LORD, a holy **p** of the land;	**Ezk 45:1**	6944
shall be the holy **p** of the land;	**Ezk 45:4**	6944
the allotment of the holy **p**;	**Ezk 45:6**	6944
and the prescribed **p** of oil	**Ezk 45:14**	2706
west, Dan, one **p**.	**Ezk 48:1**	
side, Asher, one **p**.	**Ezk 48:2**	
side, Naphtali, one **p**.	**Ezk 48:3**	
side, Manasseh, one **p**.	**Ezk 48:4**	
side, Ephraim, one **p**.	**Ezk 48:5**	
side, Reuben, one **p**.	**Ezk 48:6**	
side, Judah, one **p**.	**Ezk 48:7**	
or alienate this choice **p** of land;	**Ezk 48:14**	
side, Benjamin, one **p**.	**Ezk 48:23**	
side, Simeon, one **p**.	**Ezk 48:24**	
side, Issachar, one **p**.	**Ezk 48:25**	
side, Zebulun, one **p**.	**Ezk 48:26**	
side, Gad, one **p**.	**Ezk 48:27**	
your allotted **p** at the end of the age	**Da 12:13**	1486
He exchanges the **p** of my people;	**Mi 2:4**	2506
Judah as His **p** in the holy land,	**Zch 2:12**	2506
knowledge, and bringing a **p** of it,	**Ac 5:2**	*3313*
have no part or **p** in this matter,	**Ac 8:21**	*2819*

PORTIONS

of his flock and of their fat **p**.	**Gn 4:4**	2459
took **p** to them from his own table,	**Gn 43:34**	4864
the fat **p** of the peace offerings on it.	**Lv 6:12**	2459
p of fat and on the right thigh.	**Lv 8:26**	2459
As for the **p** of fat from the ox	**Lv 9:19**	2459
the **p** of fat on the breasts;	**Lv 9:20**	2459
and the **p** of fat on the altar;	**Lv 9:24**	2459
offerings by fire of the **p** of fat,	**Lv 10:15**	2459
'They shall eat equal **p**,	**Dt 18:8**	2506
Thus there fell ten **p** to Manasseh,	**Jos 17:5**	2256a
They shall divide it into seven **p**;	**Jos 18:5**	2506
he would give **p** to Peninnah his	**1Sa 1:4**	4490
the LORD began to cut off **p**	**2Ki 10:32**	
to distribute faithfully *their* **p**	**2Ch 31:15**	
designated by name to distribute **p**	**2Ch 31:19**	4490
and send **p** to him who has nothing	**Ne 8:10**	4490
to send **p** and to celebrate a great	**Ne 8:12**	4490
p required by the law for the priests	**Ne 12:44**	4521
Nehemiah gave the **p** due the singers	**Ne 12:47**	4521
p of the Levites had not been given	**Ne 13:10**	4521
sending **p** *of food* to one another.	**Es 9:19**	4490
and sending **p** *of food* to one another	**Es 9:22**	4490
household And **p** to her maidens.	**Pr 31:15**	2706
length comparable to one of the **p**,	**Ezk 45:7**	2506
Joseph *shall have* two **p**.	**Ezk 47:13**	2256a
and in length like one of the **p**,	**Ezk 48:8**	2506
the west border, alongside the **p**,	**Ezk 48:21**	2506
and these are their *several* **p**,"	**Ezk 48:29**	4256
in many **p** and in many ways,	**Heb 1:1**	*4181*

PORTRAYED

And she saw men **p** on the wall,	**Ezk 23:14**	2707
of the Chaldeans **p** with vermilion,	**Ezk 23:14**	2710
Christ was publicly **p** *as* crucified?	**Ga 3:1**	*4270*

POSITION

from the **p** *of* queen mother,	**2Ch 15:16**	
and made his **p** over Israel firm.	**2Ch 17:1**	
the king give her royal **p** to another	**Es 1:19**	4438
thrust him down from his high **p**;	**Ps 62:4**	7613
not maintain his **p** before me.	**Ps 101:7**	3559
you, do not abandon your **p**,	**Ec 10:4**	4725
will not retain her **p** of power,	**Da 11:6**	2220
to glory in his high **p**;	**Jas 1:9**	*5311*

POSITIONS

horsemen took up fixed **p** at the gate.	**Is 22:7**	7896

POSSESS

to give you this land to **p** it."	**Gn 15:7**	3423
may I know that I will **p** it?"	**Gn 15:8**	3423
shall **p** the gate of their enemies.	**Gn 22:17**	3423
And may your descendants **p** The	**Gn 24:60**	3423
p the land of your sojournings,	**Gn 28:4**	3423
"You are to **p** their land, and I	**Lv 20:24**	3423
will give it to you to **p** it,	**Lv 20:24**	3423
his own family, and he shall **p** it;	**Nu 27:11**	3423
given the land to you to **p** it.	**Nu 33:53**	3423
each may **p** the inheritance of his	**Nu 36:8**	3423
go in and **p** the land which the	**Dt 1:8**	3423
it to them and they shall **p** it.	**Dt 1:39**	3423
occupy, that you may **p** his land.'	**Dt 2:31**	3423
has given you this land to **p** it;	**Dt 3:18**	3423
and they also **p** the land which the	**Dt 3:20**	3423
where you are entering to **p** it.	**Dt 4:5**	3423
where you are going over to **p** it.	**Dt 4:14**	3423
are going over the Jordan to **p** it.	**Dt 4:26**	3423
the land which I give them to **p**.'	**Dt 5:31**	3423
in the land which you will **p**.	**Dt 5:33**	3423
where you are going over to **p** it,	**Dt 6:1**	3423
you may go in and **p** the good land	**Dt 6:18**	3423
where you are entering to **p** it,	**Dt 7:1**	3423
and go in and **p** the land which the	**Dt 8:1**	3423
has brought me in to **p** this land,'	**Dt 9:4**	3423
you are going to **p** their land,	**Dt 9:5**	3423
is giving you this good land to **p**,	**Dt 9:6**	3423
'Go up and **p** the land which I have	**Dt 9:23**	3423
that they may go in and **p** the land	**Dt 10:11**	3423
be strong and go in and **p** the land	**Dt 11:8**	3423
you are about to cross to **p** it;	**Dt 11:8**	3423
which you are entering to **p** it,	**Dt 11:10**	3423
you are about to cross to **p** it,	**Dt 11:11**	3423
where you are entering to **p** it,	**Dt 11:29**	3423
go in to **p** the land which the LORD	**Dt 11:31**	3423
and you shall **p** it and live in it,	**Dt 11:31**	3423
has given you to **p** as long as you	**Dt 12:1**	3423
giving you as an inheritance to **p**,	**Dt 15:4**	3423
that you may live and **p** the land	**Dt 16:20**	3423
you, and you **p** it and live in it,	**Dt 17:14**	3423
the LORD your God gives you to **p**.	**Dt 19:2**	3423
the LORD your God gives you to **p**.	**Dt 19:14**	3423
the LORD your God gives you to **p**,	**Dt 21:1**	3423
which you are about to enter to **p**.	**Dt 23:20**	3423
gives you as an inheritance to **p**,	**Dt 25:19**	3423
and you **p** it and live in it,	**Dt 26:1**	3423
where you are entering to **p** it.	**Dt 28:21**	3423
"The cricket shall **p** all your	**Dt 28:42**	3423
where you are entering to **p** it.	**Dt 28:63**	3423
possessed, and you shall **p** it;	**Dt 30:5**	3423
where you are entering to **p** it.	**Dt 30:16**	3423
the Jordan to enter and **p** it.	**Dt 30:18**	3423
about to cross the Jordan to **p**."	**Dt 31:13**	3423
about to cross the Jordan to **p**."	**Dt 32:47**	3423
to go in to **p** the land which the	**Jos 1:11**	3423
God is giving you, to **p** it.' "	**Jos 1:11**	3423
and they also **p** the land which the	**Jos 1:15**	3423
and **p** that which Moses the servant	**Jos 1:15**	3423
and you will **p** their land, just	**Jos 23:5**	3423
Esau I gave Mount Seir to **p** it;	**Jos 24:4**	3423
to his inheritance to **p** the land.	**Jg 2:6**	3423
Israel, are you then to **p** it?	**Jg 11:23**	3423
'Do you not **p** what Chemosh your	**Jg 11:24**	3423
Chemosh your god gives you to **p**?	**Jg 11:24**	3423
out before us, we will **p** it.	**Jg 11:24**	3423
to go, to enter, to **p** the land.	**Jg 18:9**	3423
that you may **p** the good land and	**1Ch 28:8**	5157
The land which you are entering to **p**	**Ezr 9:11**	3423
enter in order to **p** The land which	**Ne 9:15**	3423
told their fathers to enter and **p**.	**Ne 9:23**	3423
own sword they did not **p** the land,	**Ps 44:3**	3423
they may dwell there and **p** it.	**Ps 69:35**	3423
"Let us **p** for ourselves The	**Ps 83:12**	3423
They will **p** Edom and Moab,	**Is 11:14**	4916b, 3027
and the house of Israel will **p**	**Is 14:2**	5157
pelican and hedgehog will **p** it,	**Is 34:11**	3423
They shall **p** it forever;	**Is 34:17**	3423
your descendants will **p** nations And	**Is 54:3**	3423
And will **p** My holy mountain."	**Is 57:13**	3423
They will **p** the land forever, The	**Is 60:21**	3423
Therefore they will **p** a double	**Is 61:7**	3423
and they shall **p** it.' "	**Jer 30:3**	3423
and they will **p** their houses.	**Ezk 7:24**	3423
Should you then **p** the land?	**Ezk 33:25**	3423
Should you then **p** the land?" '	**Ezk 33:26**	3423
will be mine, and we will **p** them,'	**Ezk 35:10**	3423
to walk on you and **p** you,	**Ezk 36:12**	3423
kingdom and **p** the kingdom forever,	**Da 7:18**	2631
that they may **p** the remnant of	**Am 9:12**	3423
of Jacob will **p** their possessions.	**Ob 1:17**	3423
Negev will **p** the mountain of Esau,	**Ob 1:19**	3423
p the territory of Ephraim	**Ob 1:19**	3423
And Benjamin *will* **p** Gilead.	**Ob 1:19**	
Will **p** the cities of the Negev.	**Ob 1:20**	3423
"The LORD will **p** Judah as His	**Zch 2:12**	5157
go and sell all you **p** and	**Mk 10:21**	*2192*
sell all that you **p** and	**Lk 18:22**	*2192*
"I do not **p** silver and gold, but	**Ac 3:6**	*5225*
who buy, as though they did not **p**;	**1Co 7:30**	*2722*
that each of you know how to **p** his	**1Th 4:4**	*2932*

POSSESSED

and they **p** his land.	**Nu 21:35**	3423
of Israel has **p** his inheritance.	**Nu 32:18**	5157
the land which your fathers **p**,	**Dt 30:5**	3423
and whose land they **p** beyond the	**Jos 12:1**	3423
much of the land remains to be **p**.	**Jos 13:1**	3423
sword and **p** it and settled in it;	**Jos 19:47**	3423
and they **p** it and lived in it.	**Jos 21:43**	3423
their possession which they had **p**,	**Jos 22:9**	270
they **p** the city of the palm trees.	**Jg 3:13**	3423
Israel **p** all the land of the Amorites,	**Jg 11:21**	3423
'So they **p** all the territory of	**Jg 11:22**	3423
So they **p** Samaria and lived in its	**2Ki 17:24**	3423
Whoever **p** *precious* stones gave	**1Ch 29:8**	4672
kings who were before you has **p** nor	**2Ch 1:12**	1961, 3651
their sons entered and **p** the land.	**Ne 9:24**	3423
"The LORD **p** me at the beginning	**Pr 8:22**	7069
Also I **p** flocks and herds larger	**Ec 2:7**	
Your holy people **p** Your sanctuary	**Is 63:18**	3423
was *only* one, yet he **p** the land;	**Ezk 33:24**	3423
he **p** an extraordinary spirit,	**Da 6:3**	
horn **p** eyes like the eyes of a man and	**Da 7:8**	

place **p** by nettles and salt pits, **Zph 2:9** 4476
"He is **p** by Beelzebul," **Mk 3:22** *2192*
p with a spirit which makes him **Mk 9:17** *2192*
there was a man **p** by the spirit **Lk 4:33** *2192*
the city who was **p** with demons; **Lk 8:27** *2192*

POSSESSES
For it is You who **p** all the nations. **Ps 82:8** 5157
who alone **p** immortality and dwells **1Tm 6:16** *2192*

POSSESSING
having nothing yet **p** all things. **2Co 6:10** *2722*

POSSESSION
of Canaan, for an everlasting **p**; **Gn 17:8** 272
to Abraham for a **p** in the presence **Gn 23:18** 4736
in the land of their **p**. **Gn 36:43** 272
whose **p** the cup has been found." **Gn 44:16** 3027
in whose **p** the cup has been found, **Gn 44:17** 3027
gave them a **p** in the land of Egypt, **Gn 47:11** 272
after you for an everlasting **p**.' **Gn 48:4** 272
and I will give it to you *for* a **p**; **Ex 6:8** 4181
be My own **p** among all the peoples, **Ex 19:5** 5459
sells him or he is found in his **p**, **Ex 21:16** 3027
is actually found alive in his **p**, **Ex 22:4** 3027
fruitful and take **p** of the land. **Ex 23:30** 5157
sin, and take us as Your own **p**." **Ex 34:9** 5157
who had in his **p** blue and purple **Ex 35:23** 854
who had in his **p** acacia wood for **Ex 35:24** 854
Canaan, which I give you for a **p**, **Lv 14:34** 272
on a house in the land of your **p**, **Lv 14:34** 272
of the cities which are their **p**. **Lv 25:32** 272
a house sale in the city of this **p** **Lv 25:33** 272
the cities of the Levites are their **p** **Lv 25:33** 272
for that is their perpetual **p**. **Lv 25:34** 272
they also may become your **p**. **Lv 25:45** 272
sons after you, to receive as a **p**; **Lv 25:46** 272
to whom the **p** of the land belongs. **Lv 27:24** 272
all means go up and take **p** of it, **Nu 13:30** 3423
descendants shall take **p** of it. **Nu 14:24** 3423
and took **p** of his land from the **Nu 21:24** 3423
"Edom shall be a **p**, **Nu 24:18** 3424
its enemies, also will be a **p**, **Nu 24:18** 3423
a **p** among our father's brothers." **Nu 27:4** 272
p among their father's brothers, **Nu 27:7** 272
be given to your servants as a **p**; **Nu 32:5** 272
be yours for a **p** before the LORD. **Nu 32:22** 272
them the land of Gilead for a **p**; **Nu 32:29** 272
and the **p** of our inheritance *shall* **Nu 32:32** 272
take **p** of the land and live in it, **Nu 33:53** 3423
apportion by lot among you as a **p**, **Nu 34:13** 5157
of Manasseh have received their **p**. **Nu 34:14** 5159
received their **p** across the Jordan **Nu 34:15** 5159
from the inheritance of their **p** cities **Nu 35:2** 272
from the **p** of the sons of Israel, **Nu 35:8** 272
to his **p** which he inherits." **Nu 35:8** 5159
shall return to the land of his **p**. **Nu 35:28** 272
who comes into **p** of an inheritance **Nu 36:8** 3423
go up, take **p**, as the LORD, the **Dt 1:21** 3423
given Mount Seir to Esau as a **p**. **Dt 2:5** 3425
give you any of their land as a **p**, **Dt 2:9** 3425
Ar to the sons of Lot as a **p**. **Dt 2:9** 3425
p which the LORD gave to them.) **Dt 2:12** 3425
land of the sons of Ammon as a **p**, **Dt 2:19** 3425
it to the sons of Lot as a **p**.' **Dt 2:19** 3425
begin to take **p** and contend with **Dt 2:24** 3423
took **p** of this land at that time. **Dt 3:12** 3423
you may return every man to his **p** **Dt 3:20** 3425
take **p** of the land which the LORD, **Dt 4:1** 3423
to be a people for His own **p**, **Dt 4:20** 5159
and take **p** of this good land. **Dt 4:22** 3423
They took **p** of his land and **Dt 4:47** 3423
you to be a people for His own **p** **Dt 7:6** 5459
you to be a people for His own **p** **Dt 14:2** 5459
your God will give you as a **p**, **Dt 19:3** 5157
to be His people, a treasured **p**, **Dt 26:18** 5459
giving to the sons of Israel for a **p**. **Dt 32:49** 272
A **p** for the assembly of Jacob. **Dt 33:4** 4181
Take **p** of the sea and the south." **Dt 33:23** 3423
shall give this people **p** of the land **Jos 1:6** 5157
ambush and take **p** of the city, **Jos 8:7** 3423
the half-tribe of Manasseh as a **p**. **Jos 12:6** 3425
gave it to the tribes of Israel as a **p** **Jos 12:7** 3425
could not take **p** of these cities, **Jos 17:12** 3423
take **p** of the land which the LORD, **Jos 18:3** 3423
the son of Jephunneh as his **p**. **Jos 21:12** 272
midst of the **p** of the sons of Israel **Jos 21:41** 272
your tents, to the land of your **p**, **Jos 22:4** 272
of Manasseh Moses had given *a* **p** **Jos 22:7**
to the other half Joshua gave *a* **p** **Jos 22:7**
their **p** which they had possessed, **Jos 22:9** 272
the land of your **p** is unclean, **Jos 22:19** 272
the land of the **p** of the LORD, **Jos 22:19** 272
stands, and take **p** among us. **Jos 22:19** 270
and you took **p** of their land when **Jos 24:8** 3423
they took **p** of the hill country; **Jg 1:19** 3423
did not take **p** of Beth-shean and its **Jg 1:27** 3423
as a **p** among the tribes of Israel. **Jg 18:1** 5159
take **p** of the vineyard of Naboth, **1Ki 21:15** 3423
the Jezreelite, to take **p** of it. **1Ki 21:16** 3423
he has gone down to take **p** of it. **1Ki 21:18** 3423
murdered and also taken **p**?"' **1Ki 21:19** 3423
coming to drive us out from Your **p** **2Ch 20:11** 3425
to their cities, each to his **p**. **2Ch 31:1** 272
as a result you will have no **p** in **Ezr 4:16** 2508
They took **p** of the land of **Ne 9:22** 3423
They took **p** of houses full of **Ne 9:25** 3423
very ends of the earth as Your **p**. **Ps 2:8** 272
That they might take **p** of *the fruit* **Ps 105:44** 3423
for Himself, Israel for His own **p**. **Ps 135:4** 5459
precious **p** of a man *is* diligence. **Pr 12:27** 1952
not arise and take **p** of the earth **Is 14:21** 3423
also make it a **p** for the hedgehog and **Is 14:23** 4180
for you have the right of **p** **Jer 32:8** 3425
'They came in and took **p** of it, **Jer 32:23** 3423
in order to take **p** of *some* property **Jer 37:12** 2505a
Why then has Malcam taken **p** of Gad **Jer 49:1** 3423
will take **p** of his possessors," **Jer 49:2** 3423
land has been given us as a **p**.' **Ezk 11:15** 4181
to the sons of the east for a **p**, **Ezk 25:4** 4181
and I will give it for a **p** along **Ezk 25:10** 4181
the land has been given as a **p**.' **Ezk 33:24** 4181
heights have become our **p**,' **Ezk 36:2** 4181
a **p** of the rest of the nations and **Ezk 36:3** 4181
My land for themselves as a **p** **Ezk 36:5** 4181
and you shall give them no **p** in **Ezk 44:28** 272
I am their **p**. **Ezk 44:28** 272
for their **p** cities to dwell in. **Ezk 45:5** 272
"You shall give the city **p** of **Ezk 45:6** 272
be his land for a **p** in Israel; **Ezk 45:8** 272
it is their **p** by inheritance. **Ezk 46:16** 272
thrusting them out of their **p**; **Ezk 46:18** 272
his sons inheritance from his own **p** **Ezk 46:18** 272
not be scattered, anyone from his **p**. **Ezk 46:18** 272
the saints took **p** of the kingdom. **Da 7:22** 2631
take **p** of the land of the Amorite. **Am 2:10** 3423
bring on you The one who takes **p**, **Mi 1:15** 3423
The flock of Your **p** Which dwells by **Mi 7:14** 5159
act of the remnant of His **p**? **Mi 7:18** 5159
the day that I prepare *My* own **p**, **Mal 3:17** 5459
HE WOULD GIVE IT TO HIM AS A **P**, **Ac 7:5** *2697*
to the redemption of *God's own* **p**, **Eph 1:14** *4047*
Himself a people for His own **p**, **Ti 2:14** *4041*
a better **p** and a lasting one. **Heb 10:34** *5223*
NATION, A PEOPLE FOR *God's* OWN **P**, **1Pe 2:9** *4047*

POSSESSIONS
p which they had accumulated, **Gn 12:5** 7399
for their **p** were so great that **Gn 13:6** 7399
Lot, Abram's nephew, and his **p** **Gn 14:12** 7399
back his relative Lot with his **p**, **Gn 14:16** 7399
they will come out with many **p**. **Gn 15:14** 7399
for he had **p** of flocks and herds **Gn 26:14** 4735
belonged to Korah with *their* **p**. **Nu 16:32** 7399
they shall have **p** among you in the **Nu 32:30** 270
Their **p** and settlements *were* **1Ch 7:28** 272
who lived in their **p** in their cities **1Ch 9:2** 272
all your **p** with a great calamity; **2Ch 21:14** 7399
and carried away all the **p** found **2Ch 21:17** 7399
these were from the king's **p**. **2Ch 35:7** 7399
our little ones, and all our **p**. **Ezr 8:21** 7399
all his **p** should be forfeited and **Ezr 10:8** 7399
man from his house and from his **p** **Ne 5:13** 3018
and to seize their **p** as plunder. **Es 3:13** 7998
His **p** also were 7,000 sheep, 3,000 **Jb 1:3** 4735
his **p** have increased in the land. **Jb 1:10** 4735
His **p** will flow away in the day **Jb 20:28**
The earth is full of Your **p**. **Ps 104:24** 7075
house And ruler over all his **p**, **Ps 105:21** 7075
plunder, booty and **p** among them, **Da 11:24** 7399
of Jacob will possess their **p**. **Ob 1:17** 4180
sell your **p** and give to *the* poor, **Mt 19:21** *5225*
put him in charge of all his **p**. **Mt 24:47** *5225*
and entrusted his **p** to them. **Mt 25:14** *5225*
house, his **p** are undisturbed **Lk 11:21** *5225*
does his life consist of his **p**." **Lk 12:15** *5225*
"Sell your **p** and give to charity; **Lk 12:33** *5225*
put him in charge of all his **p**. **Lk 12:44** *5225*
does not give up all his own **p**. **Lk 14:33** *5225*
to him as squandering his **p**. **Lk 16:1** *5225*
half of my **p** I will give to the poor, **Lk 19:8** *5225*
selling their property and **p** and **Ac 2:45** *5223*
I give all my **p** to feed *the poor,* **1Co 13:3** *5225*

POSSESSOR
Most High, **P** of heaven and earth; **Gn 14:19** 7069
Most High, **p** of heaven and earth, **Gn 14:22** 7069

POSSESSORS
It takes away the life of its **p**. **Pr 1:19** 1167
preserves the lives of its **p**. **Ec 7:12** 1167
will take possession of his **p**," **Jer 49:2** 3423

POSSIBLE
but with God all things are **p**." **Mt 19:26** *1415*
wonders, so as to mislead, if **p**, **Mt 24:24** *1415*
Father, if it is **p**, let this cup pass **Mt 26:39** *1415*
All things are **p** to him who believes **Mk 9:23** *1415*
for all things are **p** with God." **Mk 10:27** *1415*
in order to lead astray, if **p**, the elect. **Mk 13:22** *1415*
if it were **p**, the hour might pass **Mk 14:35** *1415*
All things are **p** for You; **Mk 14:36** *1415*
with people are **p** with God." **Lk 18:27** *1415*
and pray the Lord that, if **p**, **Ac 8:22** *686*
to come to him as soon as **p**, **Ac 17:15** *5035*
hurrying to be in Jerusalem, if **p**, **Ac 20:16** *1415*
If **p**, so far as it depends on you, **Ro 12:18** *1415*
if **p**, you would have plucked out **Ga 4:15** *1415*

POSSIBLY
Could we **p** know that he would say, **Gn 43:7** 3045

POST
of Jerusalem, each at his **p**, **Ne 7:3** 4929
every night at my guard **p**. **Is 21:8** 4931
P a strong guard, Station **Jer 51:12** 2388
their door **p** beside My door post, **Ezk 43:8** 4201
their door post beside My door **p**, **Ezk 43:8** 4201
and stand by the **p** of the gate. **Ezk 46:2** 4201
The day when you **p** your watchmen, **Mi 7:4**
I will stand on my guard **p** And **Hab 2:1** 4931

POSTED
when they had just **p** the watch; **Jg 7:19** 6965

POSTERITY
with my offspring or with my **p** **Gn 21:23** 5220
offspring or **p** among his people, **Jb 18:19** 5220
P will serve Him; **Ps 22:30** 2233
the man of peace will have a **p**. **Ps 37:37** 319
p of the wicked will be cut off. **Ps 37:38** 319
Let his **p** be cut off; **Ps 109:13** 319
and survivors, offspring and **p**," **Is 14:22** 5220
OF SABAOTH HAD LEFT TO US A **P**, **Ro 9:29** *4690*

POSTS
doors of the city gate and the two **p** **Jg 16:3** 4201
The priests stood at their **p** **2Ch 7:6** 4931
and restored them to their **p**. **Ne 13:11** 5977
"He made its **p** of silver, Its **SS 3:10** 5982
put *it* on the door **p** of the house, **Ezk 45:19** 4201
and on the **p** of the gate of the **Ezk 45:19** 4201

POT
boil *it* in the **p** and make cakes with **Nu 11:8** 6517
in a basket and the broth in a **p**, **Jg 6:19** 6517
pan, or kettle, or caldron, or **p**; **1Sa 2:14** 6517
"Put on the large **p** and boil stew **2Ki 4:38** 5518a
sliced them into the **p** of stew, **2Ki 4:39** 5518a
of God, there is death in the **p**." **2Ki 4:40** 5518a
He threw it into the **p** **2Ki 4:41** 5518a
Then there was no harm in the **p**. **2Ki 4:41** 5518a
a boiling **p** and *burning* rushes. **Jb 41:20** 1731
"He makes the depths boil like a **p**; **Jb 41:31** 5518a
The refining **p** is for silver and **Pr 17:3** 4715
crackling of thorn bushes under a **p**, **Ec 7:6** 5518a
"I see a boiling **p**, facing away **Jer 1:13** 5518a
This *city* is the **p** and we are the **Ezk 11:3** 5518a
the flesh and this *city* is the **p**; **Ezk 11:7** 5518a
"This *city* will not be a **p** for you, **Ezk 11:11** 5518a
"Put on the **p**, put *it* on and **Ezk 24:3** 5518a
And also pile wood under the **p**. **Ezk 24:5**
To the **p** in which there is rust **Ezk 24:6** 5518a
And chop *them* up as for the **p** **Mi 3:3** 5518a
Every cooking **p** in Jerusalem **Zch 14:21** 5518a

POTIPHAR
Midianites sold him in Egypt to **P**, **Gn 37:36** 6318
and **P**, an Egyptian officer of **Gn 39:1** 6318

POTIPHERA
the daughter of **P** priest of On, **Gn 41:45** 6319
the daughter of **P** priest of On, **Gn 41:50** 6319
whom Asenath, the daughter of **P**, **Gn 46:20** 6319

POTS
when we sat by the **p** of meat, **Ex 16:3** 5518a
They took away the **p**, **2Ki 25:14** 5518a
they boiled the holy things in **p**, **2Ch 35:13** 5518a
p can feel *the fire of* thorns He **Ps 58:9** 5518a
broth of unclean meat is *in* their **p**. **Is 65:4** 3627
They also took away the **p**, **Jer 52:18** 5518a
the firepans, the basins, the **p**, **Jer 52:19** 5518a
And the cooking **p** in the LORD's **Zch 14:20** 5518a
cups and pitchers and copper **p**.) **Mk 7:4** *5473*

POTSHERD
And he took a **p** to scrape himself **Jb 2:8** 2789
My strength is dried up like a **p**, **Ps 22:15** 2789
is by the entrance of the **p** gate, **Jer 19:2** 2777

POTSHERDS
"His underparts are *like* sharp **p**; **Jb 41:30** 2789

POTTER
Shall the **p** be considered as equal **Is 29:16** 3335
Even as the **p** treads clay." **Is 41:25** 3335
Will the clay say to the **p**, **Is 45:9** 3335
We are the clay, and You our **p**; **Is 64:8** 3335
was spoiled in the hand of the **p**; **Jer 18:4** 3335
as it pleased the **p** to make. **Jer 18:4** 3335
deal with you as this **p** *does?*" **Jer 18:6** 3335
"Throw it to the **p**, *that* **Zch 11:13** 3335
to the **p** in the house of the LORD. **Zch 11:13** 3335
the **p** have a right over the clay, **Ro 9:21** *2763*
THE VESSELS OF THE **P** ARE BROKEN **Rv 2:27** *2764*

POTTER'S
is like the smashing of a **p** jar, **Is 30:14** 3335
"Arise and go down to the **p** house, **Jer 18:2** 3335
Then I went down to the **p** house, **Jer 18:3** 3335
like the clay in the **p** hand, **Jer 18:6** 3335
"Go and buy a **p** earthenware jar, **Jer 19:1** 3335
even as one breaks a **p** vessel, **Jer 19:11** 3335
jars, The work of a **p** hands! **La 4:2** 3335
partly of **p** clay and partly of iron, **Da 2:41** 6353
bought the **P** Field as a burial place **Mt 27:7** *2763*
THEY GAVE THEM FOR THE **P** FIELD, **Mt 27:10** *2763*

POTTERS
These were the **p** and the **1Ch 4:23** 3335

POTTERY
brought beds, basins, **p**, **2Sa 17:28** 3627
partly of iron and partly of **p**, **Da 2:42** 2635
as iron does not combine with **p**. **Da 2:43** 2635

POUCH
bag which he had, even in *his* **p**, **1Sa 17:40** 3219
"My beloved is to me a **p** of myrrh **SS 1:13** 6872a

POUND
Though you **p** a fool in a mortar **Pr 27:22** 3806
took a **p** of very costly perfume **Jn 12:3** *3046*

POUNDING
surrounded the house, **p** the door; **Jg 19:22** 1849
The floods lift up their **p** waves. **Ps 93:3** 1796
My heart is **p** in me; **Jer 4:19** 1993

POUNDS
aloes, about a hundred **p** *weight* **Jn 19:39** *3046*
about one hundred **p** each, **Rv 16:21** *5006*

POUR
Nile and **p** it on the dry ground; **Ex 4:9** 8210
bowls with which to **p** drink offerings; **Ex 25:29** 5258a

p it on his head and anoint him. Ex 29:7 3332
and you shall **p** out all the blood Ex 29:12 8210
shall not **p** out a drink offering on it. Ex 30:9 5258a
with which to **p** out drink Ex 37:16 5258a
and he shall **p** oil on it and put Lv 2:1 3332
it into bits and **p** oil on it; Lv 2:6 3332
blood of the bull he shall **p** out at the Lv 4:7 8210
and all the blood he shall **p** out Lv 4:18 8210
its blood he shall **p** out at the base Lv 4:25 8210
p out at the base of the altar. Lv 4:30 8210
p out at the base of the altar. Lv 4:34 8210
oil, and **p** *it* into his left palm; Lv 14:15 3332
"The priest shall also **p** some of Lv 14:26 3332
he shall **p** out its blood and cover Lv 17:13 8210
he shall not **p** oil on it nor put Nu 5:15 3332
in the holy place you shall **p** out Nu 28:7 5258a
you are to **p** it out on the ground Dt 12:16 8210
you shall **p** it out on the ground Dt 12:24 8210
you are to **p** it out on the ground Dt 15:23 8210
this rock, and **p** out the broth." Jg 6:20 8210
water and **p** *it* on the burnt offering 1Ki 18:34 3332
p water on the hands of Elijah." 2Ki 3:11 3332
and **p** out into all these vessels, 2Ki 4:4 3332
"**P** *it* out for the people that 2Ki 4:41 3332
oil and **p** it on his head and say, 2Ki 9:3 3332
And my cries **p** out like water. Jb 3:24 5413
'Did You not **p** me out like Jb 10:10 5413
Which the clouds **p** down, Jb 36:28 5140
"**P** out the overflowings of your Jb 40:11 6327a
p out their drink offerings of blood, Ps 16:4 5258a
and I **p** out my soul within me. Ps 42:4 8210
P out your heart before Him; Ps 62:8 8210
P out Your indignation on them, Ps 69:24 8210
P out Your wrath upon the nations Ps 79:6 8210
They **p** forth *words,* they speak Ps 94:4 5042
I **p** out my complaint before Him; Ps 142:2 8210
I will **p** out my spirit on you; Pr 1:23 5042
they **p** out rain upon the earth; Ec 11:3 7385a
'For I will **p** out water on the Is 44:3 3332
I will **p** out My Spirit on your Is 44:3 3332
the clouds **p** down righteousness; Is 45:8 5140
"**P** *it* out on the children in the Jer 6:11 8210
and *they* **p** out drink offerings to other Jer 7:18 5258a
P out Your wrath on the nations Jer 10:25 8210
I will **p** out their *own* wickedness Jer 14:16 8210
and **p** out drink offerings to her." Jer 44:25 5258a
P out your heart like water Before La 2:19 8210
My eyes **p** down unceasingly, La 3:49 5064
shortly **p** out My wrath on you and Ezk 7:8 8210
and **p** out My wrath in blood on it to Ezk 14:19 8210
to **p** out My wrath on them, Ezk 20:8 8210
Then I resolved to **p** out My wrath Ezk 20:13 8210
to **p** out My wrath on them, Ezk 20:21 8210
will **p** out My indignation on you; Ezk 21:31 8210
put *it* on and also **p** water in it; Ezk 24:3 3332
She did not **p** it on the ground To Ezk 24:7 8210
"I will **p** out My wrath on Ezk 30:15 8210
I will **p** out My wrath like water. Hos 5:10 8210
They will not **p** out drink offerings of Hos 9:4 5258a
p out My Spirit on all mankind; Jl 2:28 8210
p out My Spirit in those days. Jl 2:29 8210
I will **p** her stones down into the Mi 1:6 5064
To **p** out on them My indignation, Zph 3:8 8210
"I will **p** out on the house of Zch 12:10 8210
and **p** out for you a blessing until Mal 3:10 7385a
They will **p** into your lap Lk 6:38 *1325*
'THAT I WILL **P** FORTH OF MY SPIRIT Ac 2:17 *1632a*
I WILL IN THOSE DAYS **P** FORTH OF Ac 2:18 *1632a*
"Go and **p** out on the earth the seven Rv 16:1 *1632a*

POURED

as a pillar and **p** oil on its top. Gn 28:18 3332
and he **p** out a drink offering on it; Gn 35:14 5258a
he also **p** oil on it. Gn 35:14 3332
and rain no longer **p** on the earth. Ex 9:33 5413
'It shall not be **p** on anyone's Ex 30:32 5480a
camp where the ashes are **p** out, Lv 4:12 8211
where the ashes are **p** out it shall be Lv 4:12 8211
Then he **p** some of the anointing oil Lv 8:12 3332
Then he **p** out *the rest of* the Lv 8:15 3332
and **p** out *the rest of* the blood at Lv 9:9 3332
head the anointing oil has been **p** and Lv 21:10 3332
blood of your sacrifices shall be **p** out Dt 12:27 8210
they **p** them out before the LORD. Jos 7:23 3332
p out my soul before the LORD. 1Sa 1:15 8210
and **p** it out before the LORD, 1Sa 7:6 8210
flask of oil, **p** it on his head, 1Sa 10:1 3332
p out his inward parts on the ground, 2Sa 20:10 8210
it, but **p** it out to the LORD; 2Sa 23:16 5258a
ashes which are on it shall be **p** out 1Ki 13:3 8210
ashes were **p** out from the altar, 1Ki 13:5 8210
the vessels to her and she **p**. 2Ki 4:5 3332
they **p** *it* out for the men to eat. 2Ki 4:40 3332
and he **p** the oil on his head and 2Ki 9:6 3332
and **p** his drink offering and sprinkled 2Ki 16:13 5258a
it, but **p** it out to the LORD; 1Ch 11:18 5258a
and My wrath shall not be **p** out on 2Ch 12:7 5413
the wrath of the LORD which is **p** out 2Ch 34:21 5413
wrath will be **p** out on this place and 2Ch 34:25 5413
rock **p** out for me streams of oil! Jb 29:6 6694
now my soul is **p** out within me; Jb 30:16 8210
I am **p** out like water, And all my Ps 22:14 8210
"A wicked thing is **p** out upon him, Ps 41:8 3332
Grace is **p** upon Your lips; Ps 45:2 3332
The clouds **p** out water; Ps 77:17 2229
They have **p** out their blood like Ps 79:3 8210
For the LORD has **p** over you a Is 29:10 5258a
Spirit is **p** out upon us from on high, Is 32:15 6168
So He **p** out on him the heat of His Is 42:25 8210
Because He **p** out Himself to death, Is 53:12 6168
to them you have **p** out a drink offering, Is 57:6 8210
And I **p** out their lifeblood on the Is 63:6 3381
wrath will be **p** out on this place, Jer 7:20 5413
p out drink offerings to other gods." ' " Jer 19:13 5258a
and **p** out drink offerings to other gods Jer 32:29 5258a
My anger and wrath have been **p** out Jer 42:18 5413
so My wrath will be **p** out on you Jer 42:18 5413
My wrath and My anger were **p** out Jer 44:6 5413
and **p** out drink offerings to her?" Jer 44:19 5258a
He has **p** out His wrath like fire. La 2:4 8210
My heart is **p** out on the earth Because La 2:11 8210
As their life is **p** out On their La 2:12 8210
The sacred stones are **p** out At the La 4:1 8210
He has **p** out His fierce anger; La 4:11 8210
and you **p** out your harlotries on Ezk 16:15 8210
"Because your lewdness was **p** out Ezk 16:36 8210
there they **p** out their drink offerings. Ezk 20:28 5258a
arm and with wrath **p** out, Ezk 20:33 8210
arm and with wrath **p** out; Ezk 20:34 8210
have **p** out My wrath on you.' " Ezk 22:22 8210
have **p** out My indignation on them; Ezk 22:31 8210
bosom and **p** out their lust on her. Ezk 23:8 8210
I **p** out My wrath on them for the Ezk 36:18 8210
for I will have **p** out My Spirit Ezk 39:29 8210
so the curse has been **p** out on us, Da 9:11 5413
is **p** out on the one who makes Da 9:27 5413
He has **p** down for you the rain, Jl 2:23 3381
Like water **p** down a steep place. Mi 1:4 5064
His wrath is **p** out like fire And Na 1:6 5413
blood will be **p** out like dust And Zph 1:17 8210
and she **p** it on His head as He Mt 26:7 *2708*
she **p** this perfume on My body, Mt 26:12 *906*
which is **p** out for many for Mt 26:28 *1632b*
the vial and **p** it over His head. Mk 14:3 *2708*
covenant, which is **p** out for many. Mk 14:24 *1632b*
"This cup which is **p** out for you Lk 22:20 *1632b*
and He **p** out the coins of the Jn 2:15 *1632a*
Then He **p** water into the basin, Jn 13:5 *906*
He has **p** forth this which you both Ac 2:33 *1632a*
been **p** out on the Gentiles also. Ac 10:45 *1632b*
the love of God has been **p** out Ro 5:5 *1632b*
But even if I am being **p** out as a Php 2:17 *4689*
being **p** out as a drink offering, 2Tm 4:6 *4689*
whom He **p** out upon us richly Ti 3:6 *1632a*
prayed again, and the sky **p** rain and Jas 5:18 *1325*
And the serpent **p** water like a Rv 12:15 *906*
the dragon **p** out of his mouth. Rv 12:16 *906*
and **p** out his bowl on the earth; Rv 16:2 *1632a*
angel **p** out his bowl into the sea, Rv 16:3 *1632a*
Then the third *angel* **p** out his bowl Rv 16:4 *1632a*
for they **p** out the blood of saints Rv 16:6 *1632a*
angel **p** out his bowl upon the sun, Rv 16:8 *1632a*
Then the fifth *angel* **p** out his bowl Rv 16:10 *1632a*
The sixth *angel* **p** out his bowl Rv 16:12 *1632a*
angel **p** out his bowl upon the air, Rv 16:17 *1632a*

POURING

heaven and **p** out drink offerings to her, Jer 44:17 5258a
heaven and **p** out drink offerings to her, Jer 44:18 5258a
and were **p** out drink offerings to her, Jer 44:19 5258a
by **p** out Your wrath on Jerusalem?" Ezk 9:8 8210
wounds, **p** oil and wine on *them* Lk 10:34 *2022*

POURS

"He **p** contempt on nobles And Jb 12:21 8210
He **p** out my gall on the ground. Jb 16:13 8210
Day to day **p** forth speech, And Ps 19:2 5042
well mixed, and He **p** out of this; Ps 75:8 5064
He **p** contempt upon princes And Ps 107:40 8210
the mouth of the wicked **p** out evil Pr 15:28 5042
the waters of the sea And **p** them out Am 5:8 8210
p them out on the face of the earth, Am 9:6 8210
burst, and the wine **p** out and Mt 9:17 *1632a*

POVERTY

p will come in like a vagabond And Pr 6:11 7389
The ruin of the poor is their **p**. Pr 10:15 7389
P and shame *will come* to him who Pr 13:18 7389
But mere talk *leads* only to **p**. Pr 14:23 4270
who is hasty *comes* surely to **p**. Pr 21:5 4270
to the rich, *will* only *come to* **p**. Pr 22:16 4270
and the glutton will come to **p**, Pr 23:21 3423
Then your **p** will come *as* a robber And Pr 24:34 7389
pursuits will have **p** in plenty. Pr 28:19 7389
me, Give me neither **p** nor riches; Pr 30:8 7389
Let him drink and forget his **p** And Pr 31:7 7389
but she, out of her **p**, put in all she Mk 12:44 *5304*
but she out of her **p** put in all Lk 21:4 *5303*
and their deep **p** overflowed in the 2Co 8:2 *4432*
through His **p** might become rich. 2Co 8:9 *4432*
'I know your tribulation and your **p** Rv 2:9 *4432*

POWDER

it with fire, and ground it to **p**, Ex 32:20 834, 1854
the rain of your land **p** and dust; Dt 28:24 80
he broke in pieces and ground to **p** 2Ch 34:4 1854
and the carved images into **p**, 2Ch 34:7 1854

POWDERS

all scented **p** of the merchant? SS 3:6 81

POWER

"Behold, your maid is in your **p**; Gn 16:6 3027
"It is in my **p** to do you harm, Gn 31:29 3027
in dignity and preeminent in **p**. Gn 49:3 5794
them from the **p** of the Egyptians, Ex 3:8 3027
which I have put in your **p**; Ex 4:21 3027
remain, in order to show you My **p** and Ex 9:16 3581b
When Israel saw the great **p** Ex 14:31 3027
hand, O LORD, is majestic in **p**, Ex 15:6 3581b
great **p** and with a mighty hand? Ex 32:11 3581b
also break down your pride of **p**; Lv 26:19 5797
"Is the LORD's **p** limited? Nu 11:23 3027
let the **p** of the Lord be great, Nu 14:17 3581b
you from Egypt by His great **p**, Dt 4:37 3581b
'My **p** and the strength of my hand Dt 8:17 3581b
is giving you **p** to make wealth, Dt 8:18 3581b
have brought out by Your great **p** Dt 9:29 3581b
and for all the mighty **p** and for Dt 34:12 3027
numerous people and have great **p**; Jos 17:17 3581b
the **p** of the house of Joseph grew Jg 1:35 3027
The **p** of Midian prevailed Jg 6:2 3027
'My own **p** has delivered me.' Jg 7:2 3027
us from the **p** of our enemies." 1Sa 4:3 3709
and from the **p** of all the kingdoms 1Sa 10:18 3027
p and with an outstretched arm, 2Ki 17:36 3581b
is the greatness and the **p** and the 1Ch 29:11 1369
and in Your hand is **p** and might; 1Ch 29:12 3581b
with all his reign, his **p**, 1Ch 29:30 1369
P and might are in Your hand so 2Ch 20:6 3581b
to retain the **p** of the kingdom. 2Ch 22:9 3581b
God has **p** to help and to bring 2Ch 25:8 3581b
who could wage war with great **p**, 2Ch 26:13 3581b
but His **p** and His anger are Ezr 8:22 5797
great **p** and by Your strong hand. Ne 1:10 3581b
all that he has is in your **p**, Jb 1:12 3027
"Behold, he is in your **p**, Jb 2:6 3027
in war from the **p** of the sword. Jb 5:20 3027
into the **p** of their transgression. Jb 8:4 3027
"If *it is a matter* of **p**, Jb 9:19 3581b
would show Your **p** against me. Jb 10:16 6381
Whom God brings into their **p**. Jb 12:6 3027
with me by the greatness of *His* **p**? Jb 23:6 3581b
He drags off the valiant by His **p**; Jb 24:22 3581b
"He quieted the sea with His **p**, Jb 26:12 3581b
will instruct you in the **p** of God; Jb 27:11 3027
surely try to flee from its **p**. Jb 27:22 3027
"Behold, God is exalted in His **p**; Jb 36:22 3581b
He is exalted in **p** And Jb 37:23 3581b
his **p** in the muscles of his belly. Jb 40:16 202
We will sing and praise Your **p**. Ps 21:13 1369
only *life* from the **p** of the dog. Ps 22:20 3027
my soul from the **p** of Sheol, Ps 49:15 3027
name, And vindicate me by Your **p**. Ps 54:1 1369
Scatter them by Your **p**, Ps 59:11 2428
That **p** belongs to God; Ps 62:11 5797
To see Your **p** and Your glory. Ps 63:2 5797
over to the **p** of the sword; Ps 63:10 3027
Because of the greatness of Your **p** Ps 66:3 5797
strength and **p** to the people. Ps 68:35 8592
Your **p** to all who are to come. Ps 71:18 1369
have by Your **p** redeemed Your people, Ps 77:15 2220
His **p** He directed the south wind. Ps 78:26 5797
They did not remember His **p**, Ps 78:42 3027
According to the greatness of Your **p** Ps 79:11 2220
and Manasseh, stir up Your **p** And Ps 80:2 1369
deliver his soul from the **p** of Sheol? Ps 89:48 3027
understands the **p** of Your anger Ps 90:11 5797
That He might make His **p** known. Ps 106:8 1369
they were subdued under their **p**. Ps 106:42 3027
freely in the day of Your **p**; Ps 110:3 2428
to His people the **p** of His works, Ps 111:6 3581b
of the **p** of Your awesome acts Ps 145:6 5807
of Your kingdom And talk of Your **p**; Ps 145:11 1369
When it is in your **p** to do *it*. Pr 3:27 3027
I am understanding, **p** is mine. Pr 8:14 1369
life are in the **p** of the tongue, Pr 18:21 3027
a man of knowledge increases **p**. Pr 24:5 3581b
side of their oppressors was **p**, Ec 4:1 3581b
the LORD spoke to me with mighty **p** Is 8:11 3027
"By the **p** of my hand and by my Is 10:13 3581b
His might and the strength of *His* **p** Is 40:26 3581b
who lacks might He increases **p**. Is 40:29 6109
In spite of the great **p** of your spells. Is 47:9 6109
from the **p** of the flame; Is 47:14 3027
Or have I no **p** to deliver? Is 50:2 3581b
us into the **p** of our iniquities. Is 64:7 3027
is He who made the earth by His **p**, Jer 10:12 3581b
make them know My **p** and My might; Jer 16:21 3027
them up to the **p** of the sword; Jer 18:21 3027
from the **p** of *his* oppressor, Jer 21:12 3027
from the **p** of *his* oppressor. Jer 22:3 3027
by My great **p** and by My Jer 27:5 3581b
by Your great **p** and by Your Jer 32:17 3581b
p of the people of the north." Jer 46:24 3027
I shall give them over to the **p** of Jer 46:26 3027
is He who made the earth by His **p**, Jer 51:15 3581b
Israel, each according to his **p**, Ezk 22:6 2220
My sanctuary, the pride of your **p**, Ezk 24:21 5797
the pride of her **p** will come down; Ezk 30:6 5797
pride of her **p** will cease in her; Ezk 30:18 5797
and the pride of her **p** will cease; Ezk 33:28 5797
sons of Israel to the **p** of the sword Ezk 35:5 3027
For wisdom and **p** belong to Him. Da 2:20 1370
You have given me wisdom and **p**; Da 2:23 1370
has given the kingdom, the **p**, Da 2:37 2632
by the might of my **p** and for the Da 4:30 2632
Daniel from the **p** of the lions." Da 6:27 3028
there anyone to rescue from his **p**, Da 8:4 3027
none to rescue the ram from his **p**. Da 8:7 3027
nation, although not with his **p**. Da 8:22 3581b
"His **p** will be mighty, but Da 8:24 3581b
be mighty, but not by his *own* **p**, Da 8:24 3581b
will not retain her position of **p**, Da 11:6 3581b
nor will he remain with his **p**, Da 11:6 2220
with the **p** of his whole kingdom, Da 11:17 8633
gain **p** with a small *force of* people. Da 11:23 6105a
the **p** of the holy people, Da 12:7 3027
ransom them from the **p** of Sheol? Hos 13:14 3027
will even unleash My **p** upon Ekron, Am 1:8 3027
will not strengthen his **p**, Am 2:14 3581b
For it is in the **p** of their hands. Mi 2:1 410

On the other hand I am filled with **p**	**Mi 3:8**	3581b
is slow to anger and great in **p**,	**Na 1:3**	3581b
And there is the hiding of His **p**.	**Hab 3:4**	5797
destroy the **p** of the kingdoms of the	**Hg 2:22**	2392
'Not by might nor by **p**,	**Zch 4:6**	3581b
each into another's **p** and into the	**Zch 11:6**	3027
power and into the **p** of his king;	**Zch 11:6**	3027
not deliver *them* from their **p**."	**Zch 11:6**	3027
Yours is the kingdom and the **p**	**Mt 6:13**	*1411*
the Scriptures nor the **p** of God.	**Mt 22:29**	*1411*
OF THE SKY with **p** and great glory.	**Mt 24:30**	*1411*
SITTING AT THE RIGHT HAND OF **P**,	**Mt 26:64**	*1411*
perceiving in Himself that the **p**	**Mk 5:30**	*1411*
of God after it has come with **p**."	**Mk 9:1**	*1411*
the Scriptures or the **p** of God?	**Mk 12:24**	*1411*
IN CLOUDS with great **p** and glory.	**Mk 13:26**	*1411*
SITTING AT THE RIGHT HAND OF **P**,	**Mk 14:62**	*1411*
Him in the spirit and **p** of Elijah,	**Lk 1:17**	*1411*
and the **p** of the Most High will	**Lk 1:35**	*1411*
to Galilee in the **p** of the Spirit,	**Lk 4:14**	*1411*
For with authority and **p** He	**Lk 4:36**	*1411*
and the **p** of the Lord was *present*	**Lk 5:17**	*1411*
for **p** was coming from Him and	**Lk 6:19**	*1411*
aware that **p** had gone out of Me."	**Lk 8:46**	*1411*
and gave them **p** and authority over	**Lk 9:1**	*1411*
and over all the **p** of the enemy,	**Lk 10:19**	*1411*
IN A CLOUD with **p** and great glory.	**Lk 21:27**	*1411*
and the **p** of darkness are yours."	**Lk 22:53**	*1849*
THE RIGHT HAND of the **p** OF GOD."	**Lk 22:69**	*1411*
are clothed with **p** from on high."	**Lk 24:49**	*1411*
but you will receive **p** when the	**Ac 1:8**	*1411*
for Him to be held in its **p**.	**Ac 2:24**	*5259*
p or piety we had made him walk?	**Ac 3:12**	*1411*
"By what **p**, or in what name, have	**Ac 4:7**	*1411*
And with great **p** the apostles were	**Ac 4:33**	*1411*
And Stephen, full of grace and **p**,	**Ac 6:8**	*1411*
was a man of **p** in words and deeds.	**Ac 7:22**	*1415*
is called the Great **P** of God."	**Ac 8:10**	*1411*
with the Holy Spirit and with **p**,	**Ac 10:38**	*1411*
was declared the Son of God with **p**	**Ro 1:4**	*1411*
for it is the **p** of God for	**Ro 1:16**	*1411*
His eternal **p** and divine nature,	**Ro 1:20**	*1411*
UP, TO DEMONSTRATE MY **P** IN YOU,	**Ro 9:17**	*1411*
His wrath and to make His **p** known,	**Ro 9:22**	*1415*
hope by the **p** of the Holy Spirit.	**Ro 15:13**	*1411*
in the **p** of signs and wonders, in	**Ro 15:19**	*1411*
wonders, in the **p** of the Spirit;	**Ro 15:19**	*1411*
being saved it is the **p** of God.	**1Co 1:18**	*1411*
p of God and the wisdom of God.	**1Co 1:24**	*1411*
of the Spirit and of **p**,	**1Co 2:4**	*1411*
of men, but on the **p** of God.	**1Co 2:5**	*1411*
who are arrogant but their **p**.	**1Co 4:19**	*1411*
not consist in words but in **p**.	**1Co 4:20**	*1411*
with the **p** of our Lord Jesus,	**1Co 5:4**	*1411*
also raise us up through His **p**.	**1Co 6:14**	*1411*
all rule and all authority and **p**.	**1Co 15:24**	*1411*
in weakness, it is raised in **p**;	**1Co 15:43**	*1411*
sin, and the **p** of sin is the law;	**1Co 15:56**	*1411*
greatness of the **p** will be of God	**2Co 4:7**	*1411*
word of truth, in the **p** of God;	**2Co 6:7**	*1411*
for **p** is perfected in weakness."	**2Co 12:9**	*1411*
the **p** of Christ may dwell in me.	**2Co 12:9**	*1411*
He lives because of the **p** of God.	**2Co 13:4**	*1411*
the **p** of God *directed* toward you.	**2Co 13:4**	*1411*
of His **p** toward us who believe.	**Eph 1:19**	*1411*
and authority and **p** and dominion,	**Eph 1:21**	*1411*
to the prince of the **p** of the air,	**Eph 2:2**	*1849*
according to the working of His **p**.	**Eph 3:7**	*1411*
to be strengthened with **p** through	**Eph 3:16**	*1411*
to the **p** that works within us,	**Eph 3:20**	*1411*
and the **p** of His resurrection and	**Php 3:10**	*1411*
by the exertion of the **p** that He	**Php 3:21**	*1410*
strengthened with all **p**,	**Col 1:11**	*1411*
striving according to His **p**,	**Col 1:29**	*1411*
but also in **p** and in the Holy	**1Th 1:5**	*1411*
Lord and from the glory of His **p**,	**2Th 1:9**	*2479*
and the work of faith with **p**,	**2Th 1:11**	*1411*
all **p** and signs and false wonders,	**2Th 2:9**	*1411*
but of **p** and love and discipline.	**2Tm 1:7**	*1411*
gospel according to the **p** of God,	**2Tm 1:8**	*1411*
although they have denied its **p**;	**2Tm 3:5**	*1411*
all things by the word of His **p**.	**Heb 1:3**	*1411*
him who had the **p** of death,	**Heb 2:14**	*2904*
the **p** of an indestructible life.	**Heb 7:16**	*1411*
quenched the **p** of fire, escaped	**Heb 11:34**	*1411*
who are protected by the **p** of God	**1Pe 1:5**	*1411*
seeing that His divine **p** has	**2Pe 1:3**	*1411*
the **p** and coming of our Lord Jesus	**2Pe 1:16**	*1411*
who are greater in might and **p**	**2Pe 2:11**	*1411*
that the whole world lies in *the* **p**	**1Jn 5:19**	
shut, because you have a little **p**,	**Rv 3:8**	*1411*
to receive glory and honor and **p**;	**Rv 4:11**	*1411*
the Lamb that was slain to receive **p**	**Rv 5:12**	*1411*
and honor and **p** and might,	**Rv 7:12**	*1411*
and **p** was given them, as the	**Rv 9:3**	*1849*
the scorpions of the earth have **p**.	**Rv 9:3**	*1849*
p to hurt men for five months.	**Rv 9:10**	*1849*
For the **p** of the horses is in	**Rv 9:19**	*1849*
have the **p** to shut up the sky,	**Rv 11:6**	*1849*
and they have **p** over the waters to	**Rv 11:6**	*1849*
You have taken Your great **p** and	**Rv 11:17**	*1411*
"Now the salvation, and the **p**,	**Rv 12:10**	*1411*
And the dragon gave him his **p** and	**Rv 13:2**	*1411*
the one who has **p** over fire,	**Rv 14:18**	*1849*
the glory of God and from His **p**;	**Rv 15:8**	*1411*
who has the **p** over these plagues,	**Rv 16:9**	*1849*
p and authority to the beast.	**Rv 17:13**	*1411*
and glory and **p** belong to our God;	**Rv 19:1**	*1411*
these the second death has no **p**,	**Rv 20:6**	*1849*

POWERFUL

us, for you are too **p** for us."	**Gn 26:16**	6105a
for by a **p** hand the LORD brought	**Ex 13:3**	2392
for with a **p** hand the LORD brought	**Ex 13:9**	2389
'With a **p** hand the LORD brought us	**Ex 13:14**	2392
for with a **p** hand the LORD brought	**Ex 13:16**	2392
But Abijah became **p**;	**2Ch 13:21**	2388
the battle between the **p** and those	**2Ch 14:11**	7227a
Continue on, also become very **p**?	**Jb 21:7**	2428
The voice of the LORD is **p**,	**Ps 29:4**	3581b
Those who would destroy me are **p**,	**Ps 69:4**	6105a
A **p** and oppressive nation Whose	**Is 18:2**	6978
wide, A **p** and oppressive nation,	**Is 18:7**	6978
the daughters of the **p** nations,	**Ezk 32:18**	117
but divinely **p** for the destruction	**2Co 10:4**	*1415*

POWERFULLY

he **p** refuted the Jews in public,	**Ac 18:28**	*2159*

POWERLESS

For we are **p** before this great	**2Ch 20:12**	369, 3581b
through death He might render **p**	**Heb 2:14**	*2673*

POWERS

wisdom and *these* miraculous **p**?	**Mt 13:54**	*1411*
miraculous **p** are at work in him."	**Mt 14:2**	*1411*
p of the heavens will be shaken.	**Mt 24:29**	*1411*
miraculous **p** are at work in Him."	**Mk 6:14**	*1411*
and the **p** that are in the heavens	**Mk 13:25**	*1411*
p of the heavens will be shaken.	**Lk 21:26**	*1411*
nor things to come, nor **p**,	**Ro 8:38**	*1411*
against the rulers, against the **p**,	**Eph 6:12**	*1849*
God and the **p** of the age to come,	**Heb 6:5**	*1411*
and **p** had been subjected to Him.	**1Pe 3:22**	*1411*

PRACTICE

"It is not the **p** in our place to	**Gn 29:26**	6213a, 3651
as I can indeed **p** divination?"	**Gn 44:15**	5172
that you do not **p** any of the	**Lv 18:30**	6213a
nor **p** divination or soothsaying.	**Lv 19:26**	5172
shall keep My statutes and **p** them;	**Lv 20:8**	6213a
who **p** witchcraft and to diviners,	**Dt 18:14**	6049a
has David done and so *has been* his **p**	**1Sa 27:11**	4941
the law of the LORD and to **p** *it,*	**Ezr 7:10**	6213a
Who **p** righteousness at all times!	**Ps 106:3**	6213a
To **p** deeds of wickedness With men	**Ps 141:4**	5953a
will not deliver those who **p** it.	**Ec 8:8**	1167
To **p** ungodliness and to speak	**Is 32:6**	6213a
if you truly **p** justice between a	**Jer 7:5**	6213a
has been your **p** from your youth,	**Jer 22:21**	1870
see false visions or **p** divination,	**Ezk 13:23**	7080
words but they do not **p** them.	**Ezk 33:32**	6213a
and **p** justice and righteousness.	**Ezk 45:9**	6213a
made with him he will **p** deception,	**Da 11:23**	6213a
and **p** kindness and compassion each	**Zch 7:9**	6213a
FROM ME, YOU WHO **P** LAWLESSNESS.'	**Mt 7:23**	*2038b*
that those who **p** such things are	**Ro 1:32**	*4238*
approval to those who **p** them.	**Ro 1:32**	*4238*
you who judge **p** the same things.	**Ro 2:1**	*4238*
upon those who **p** such things.	**Ro 2:2**	*4238*
pass judgment on those who **p** such	**Ro 2:3**	*4238*
is of value if you **p** the Law;	**Ro 2:25**	*4238*
but I **p** the very evil that I do	**Ro 7:19**	*4238*
contentious, we have no other **p**,	**1Co 11:16**	*4914*
forewarned you, that those who **p** such	**Ga 5:21**	*4238*
for the **p** of every kind of	**Eph 4:19**	*2039*
and seen in me, **p** these things,	**Php 4:9**	*4238*
for indeed you do **p** it toward all	**1Th 4:10**	*4160*
they must first learn to **p** piety in	**1Tm 5:4**	*2151*
who because of **p** have their senses	**Heb 5:14**	*1838*
for as long as you **p** these things,	**2Pe 1:10**	*4160*
we lie and do not **p** the truth;	**1Jn 1:6**	*4160*
not **p** righteousness is not of God,	**1Jn 3:10**	*4160*
righteous, still **p** righteousness;	**Rv 22:11**	*4160*

PRACTICED

which have been **p** before you,	**Lv 18:30**	6213a
and **p** divination and enchantments,	**2Ki 17:17**	7080
p witchcraft and used divination,	**2Ki 21:6**	6049a
and he **p** witchcraft, used	**2Ch 33:6**	6049a
used divination, **p** sorcery and	**2Ch 33:6**	3784
father, because he **p** extortion,	**Ezk 18:18**	6231
has **p** justice and righteousness and	**Ezk 18:19**	6213a
his righteousness which he has **p**,	**Ezk 18:22**	6213a
people of the land have **p** oppression	**Ezk 22:29**	6231
has **p** justice and righteousness;	**Ezk 33:16**	6213a
Because they have **p** evil deeds.	**Mi 3:4**	7489a
And many of those who **p** magic	**Ac 19:19**	*4238*
and sensuality which they have **p**.	**2Co 12:21**	*4238*

PRACTICES

divination, one who **p** witchcraft,	**Dt 18:10**	6049a
their **p** or their stubborn ways.	**Jg 2:19**	4611
according to the evil of their **p**;	**Ps 28:4**	4611
He who **p** deceit shall not dwell	**Ps 101:7**	6213a
the nations And learned their **p**,	**Ps 106:35**	4639
they became unclean in their **p**,	**Ps 106:39**	4639
to the priest Everyone **p** deceit.	**Jer 8:10**	6213a
and **p** justice and righteousness,	**Ezk 18:5**	6213a
and **p** justice and righteousness,	**Ezk 18:21**	6213a
and **p** justice and righteousness,	**Ezk 18:27**	6213a
and **p** justice and righteousness,	**Ezk 33:14**	6213a
and **p** justice and righteousness,	**Ezk 33:19**	6213a
But he who **p** the truth comes to the	**Jn 3:21**	*4160*
confessing and disclosing their **p**.	**Ac 19:18**	*4234*
For Moses writes that the man who **p**	**Ro 10:5**	*4160*
wrath on the one who **p** evil.	**Ro 13:4**	*4238*
WHO **P** THEM SHALL LIVE BY THEM."	**Ga 3:12**	*4160*
the old self with its *evil* **p**,	**Col 3:9**	*4234*
everyone also who **p** righteousness	**1Jn 2:29**	*4160*
Everyone who **p** sin also practices	**1Jn 3:4**	*4160*
practices sin also **p** lawlessness;	**1Jn 3:4**	*4160*
who **p** righteousness is righteous,	**1Jn 3:7**	*4160*
the one who **p** sin is of the devil;	**1Jn 3:8**	*4160*
No one who is born of God **p** sin,	**1Jn 3:9**	*4160*
one who **p** abomination and lying,	**Rv 21:27**	*4160*
everyone who loves and **p** lying.	**Rv 22:15**	*4160*

PRACTICING

on **p** oppression and extortion."	**Jer 22:17**	6213a
"Beware of **p** your righteousness	**Mt 6:1**	*4160*
formerly was **p** magic in the city and	**Ac 8:9**	*3096*
am not **p** what I *would* like to *do,*	**Ro 7:15**	*4238*
of the saints, **p** hospitality.	**Ro 12:13**	*1377*

PRAETORIAN

throughout the whole **p** guard and	**Php 1:13**	*4232*

PRAETORIUM

of the governor took Jesus into the **P**	**Mt 27:27**	*4232*
into the palace (that is, the **P**),	**Mk 15:16**	*4232*
from Caiaphas into the **P**,	**Jn 18:28**	*4232*
did not enter into the **P** so that	**Jn 18:28**	*4232*
entered again into the **P**,	**Jn 18:33**	*4232*
and he entered into the **P** again and	**Jn 19:9**	*4232*
for him to be kept in Herod's **P**.	**Ac 23:35**	*4232*

PRAISE

"This time I will **p** the LORD."	**Gn 29:35**	3034
"Judah, your brothers shall **p** you;	**Gn 49:8**	3034
This is my God, and I will **p** Him;	**Ex 15:2**	5115a
an offering of **p** to the LORD.	**Lv 19:24**	1974
"He is your **p** and He is your God,	**Dt 10:21**	8416
nations which He has made, for **p**,	**Dt 26:19**	8416
God of Israel, and give **p** to Him;	**Jos 7:19**	8426
sing, I will sing **p** to the LORD,	**Jg 5:3**	2167
and **p** the LORD God of Israel:	**1Ch 16:4**	1984b
holy name, And glory in Your **p**."	**1Ch 16:35**	8416
which David made for giving **p**.	**1Ch 23:5**	1984b
to thank and to **p** the LORD,	**1Ch 23:30**	1984b
You, and **p** Your glorious name.	**1Ch 29:13**	1984b
to **p** and to glorify the LORD,	**2Ch 5:13**	1984b
worshiped and gave **p** to the LORD,	**2Ch 7:3**	3034
David had made for giving **p** to the	**2Ch 7:6**	3034
he gave **p** by their means,	**2Ch 7:6**	1984b
and the Levites for their duties of **p**	**2Ch 8:14**	1984b
up to **p** the LORD God of Israel,	**2Ch 20:19**	1984b
musical instruments leading the **p**.	**2Ch 23:13**	1984b
minister and to give thanks and to **p**	**2Ch 31:2**	1984b
to **p** the LORD according to the	**Ezr 3:10**	1984b
exalted above all blessing and **p**!	**Ne 9:5**	8416
them, to **p** *and* give thanks,	**Ne 12:24**	1984b
songs of **p** and hymns of	**Ne 12:46**	8416
And will sing **p** to the name of the	**Ps 7:17**	2167
I will sing **p** to Your name, O Most	**Ps 9:2**	2167
We will sing and **p** Your power.	**Ps 21:13**	2167
of the assembly I will **p** You.	**Ps 22:22**	1984b
You who fear the LORD, **p** Him;	**Ps 22:23**	1984b
comes my **p** in the great assembly;	**Ps 22:25**	8416
who seek Him will **p** the LORD.	**Ps 22:26**	1984b
Sing **p** to the LORD, you His godly	**Ps 30:4**	2167
Will the dust **p** You?	**Ps 30:9**	3034
That *my* soul may sing **p** to You and	**Ps 30:12**	2167
P is becoming to the upright.	**Ps 33:1**	8416
His **p** shall continually be in my	**Ps 34:1**	8416
will **p** You among a mighty throng.	**Ps 35:18**	1984b
And Your **p** all day long.	**Ps 35:28**	8416
my mouth, a song of **p** to our God;	**Ps 40:3**	8416
for I shall again **p** Him *For* the	**Ps 42:5**	3034
in God, for I shall yet **p** Him,	**Ps 42:11**	3034
And upon the lyre I shall **p** You,	**Ps 43:4**	3034
in God, for I shall again **p** Him,	**Ps 43:5**	3034
is Your **p** to the ends of the earth;	**Ps 48:10**	8416
though *men* **p** you when you do well	**Ps 49:18**	3034
That my mouth may declare Your **p**.	**Ps 51:15**	8416
In God, whose word I **p**,	**Ps 56:4**	1984b
In God, *whose* word I **p**,	**Ps 56:10**	1984b
In the LORD, *whose* word I **p**,	**Ps 56:10**	1984b
I will sing **p** to Your name forever,	**Ps 61:8**	2167
than life, My lips will **p** You.	**Ps 63:3**	7623b
before You, *and* **p** in Zion,	**Ps 65:1**	8416
Make His **p** glorious.	**Ps 66:2**	8416
O peoples, And sound His **p** abroad,	**Ps 66:8**	8416
Let the peoples **p** You, O God;	**Ps 67:3**	3034
Let all the peoples **p** You.	**Ps 67:3**	3034
Let the peoples **p** You, O God;	**Ps 67:5**	3034
Let all the peoples **p** You.	**Ps 67:5**	3034
will **p** the name of God with song And	**Ps 69:30**	1984b
Let heaven and earth **p** Him,	**Ps 69:34**	1984b
My **p** is continually of You.	**Ps 71:6**	8416
My mouth is filled with Your **p** And	**Ps 71:8**	8416
And will **p** You yet more and more.	**Ps 71:14**	8416
I will also **p** You with a harp,	**Ps 71:22**	3034
afflicted and needy **p** Your name.	**Ps 74:21**	1984b
For the wrath of man shall **p** You;	**Ps 76:10**	3034
generations we will tell of Your **p**.	**Ps 79:13**	8416
departed spirits rise *and* **p** You?	**Ps 88:10**	3034
The heavens will **p** Your wonders,	**Ps 89:5**	3034
them **p** Your great and awesome name;	**Ps 99:3**	3034
And His courts with **p**.	**Ps 100:4**	8416
yet to be created may **p** the LORD.	**Ps 102:18**	1984b
in Zion And His **p** in Jerusalem	**Ps 102:21**	8416
I will sing **p** to my God while I	**Ps 104:33**	2167
O my soul. **P** the LORD!	**Ps 104:35**	1984b
And observe His laws, **P** the LORD!	**Ps 105:45**	1984b
P the LORD! Oh give thanks	**Ps 106:1**	1984b
LORD, Or can show forth all His **p**?	**Ps 106:2**	8416
They sang His **p**.	**Ps 106:12**	8416
Your holy name And glory in Your **p**.	**Ps 106:47**	8416
people say, "Amen." **P** the LORD!	**Ps 106:48**	1984b
p Him at the seat of the elders.	**Ps 107:32**	1984b
O God of my **p**, Do not be silent!	**Ps 109:1**	8416
in the midst of many I will **p** Him.	**Ps 109:30**	1984b
P the LORD! I will give thanks	**Ps 111:1**	1984b

His **p** endures forever.	**Ps 111:10**	8416
P the LORD! How blessed is the man	**Ps 112:1**	1984b
P the LORD! Praise, O servants of	**Ps 113:1**	1984b
P, O servants of the LORD,	**Ps 113:1**	1984b
P the name of the LORD.	**Ps 113:1**	1984b
mother of children. **P** the LORD!	**Ps 113:9**	1984b
The dead do not **p** the LORD, Nor *do*	**Ps 115:17**	1984b
and forever. **P** the LORD!	**Ps 115:18**	1984b
O Jerusalem. **P** the LORD!	**Ps 116:19**	1984b
P the LORD, all nations;	**Ps 117:1**	1984b
the LORD is everlasting. **P** the LORD!	**Ps 117:2**	1984b
Seven times a day I **p** You,	**Ps 119:164**	1984b
Let my lips utter **p**,	**Ps 119:171**	8416
my soul live that it may **p** You,	**Ps 119:175**	1984b
P the LORD! Praise the name of the	**Ps 135:1**	1984b
P the name of the LORD;	**Ps 135:1**	1984b
P *Him*, O servants of the LORD,	**Ps 135:1**	1984b
P the LORD, for the LORD is good;	**Ps 135:3**	1984b
dwells in Jerusalem. **P** the LORD!	**Ps 135:21**	1984b
will **p** Your name forever and ever.	**Ps 145:2**	1984b
One generation shall **p** Your works to	**Ps 145:4**	7623b
will speak the **p** of the LORD,	**Ps 145:21**	8416
P the LORD! Praise the LORD	**Ps 146:1**	1984b
P the LORD, O my soul!	**Ps 146:1**	1984b
I will **p** the LORD while I live;	**Ps 146:2**	1984b
to all generations. **P** the LORD!	**Ps 146:10**	1984b
P the LORD! For it is good to sing	**Ps 147:1**	1984b
it is pleasant *and* **p** is becoming.	**Ps 147:1**	8416
P the LORD, O Jerusalem!	**Ps 147:12**	7623b
P your God, O Zion!	**Ps 147:12**	1984b
have not known them. **P** the LORD!	**Ps 147:20**	1984b
P the LORD! Praise the LORD	**Ps 148:1**	1984b
P the LORD from the heavens;	**Ps 148:1**	1984b
P Him in the heights!	**Ps 148:1**	1984b
P Him, all His angels;	**Ps 148:2**	1984b
P Him, all His hosts!	**Ps 148:2**	1984b
P Him, sun and moon;	**Ps 148:3**	1984b
P Him, all stars of light!	**Ps 148:3**	1984b
P Him, highest heavens, And the	**Ps 148:4**	1984b
Let them **p** the name of the LORD,	**Ps 148:5**	1984b
P the LORD from the earth, Sea	**Ps 148:7**	1984b
Let them **p** the name of the LORD,	**Ps 148:13**	1984b
people, **P** for all His godly ones;	**Ps 148:14**	1984b
a people near to Him. **P** the LORD!	**Ps 148:14**	1984b
P the LORD! Sing to the LORD	**Ps 149:1**	1984b
And His **p** in the congregation of	**Ps 149:1**	8416
Let them **p** His name with dancing;	**Ps 149:3**	1984b
for all His godly ones. **P** the LORD!	**Ps 149:9**	1984b
P the LORD! Praise God in His	**Ps 150:1**	1984b
P God in His sanctuary;	**Ps 150:1**	1984b
P Him in His mighty expanse.	**Ps 150:1**	1984b
P Him for His mighty deeds;	**Ps 150:2**	1984b
P Him according to His excellent	**Ps 150:2**	1984b
P Him with trumpet sound;	**Ps 150:3**	1984b
P Him with harp and lyre.	**Ps 150:3**	1984b
P Him with timbrel and dancing;	**Ps 150:4**	1984b
P Him with stringed instruments	**Ps 150:4**	1984b
P Him with loud cymbals;	**Ps 150:5**	1984b
P Him with resounding cymbals.	**Ps 150:5**	1984b
that has breath **p** the LORD.	**Ps 150:6**	1984b
praise the LORD. **P** the LORD!	**Ps 150:6**	1984b
Let another **p** you, and not your	**Pr 27:2**	1984b
is tested by the **p** accorded him.	**Pr 27:21**	4110
who forsake the law **p** the wicked,	**Pr 28:4**	1984b
let her works **p** her in the gates.	**Pr 31:31**	1984b
P the LORD in song, for He has	**Is 12:5**	2167
thank You, Death cannot **p** You;	**Is 38:18**	1984b
Nor My **p** to graven images.	**Is 42:8**	8416
His **p** from the end of the earth!	**Is 42:10**	8416
declare His **p** in the coastlands.	**Is 42:12**	8416
for Myself Will declare My **p**.	**Is 43:21**	8416
for My **p** I restrain *it* for you,	**Is 48:9**	8416
Creating the **p** of the lips.	**Is 57:19**	5108
walls salvation, and your gates **p**.	**Is 60:18**	8416
The mantle of **p** instead of a	**Is 61:3**	8416
GOD will cause righteousness and **p**	**Is 61:11**	8416
makes Jerusalem a **p** in the earth.	**Is 62:7**	8416
it will eat it and **p** the LORD;	**Is 62:9**	1984b
Me a people, for renown, for **p** and	**Jer 13:11**	8416
will be saved, For You are my **p**.	**Jer 17:14**	8416
Sing to the LORD, **p** the LORD!	**Jer 20:13**	1984b
Proclaim, give **p** and say,	**Jer 31:7**	1984b
will be to Me a name of joy, **p**	**Jer 33:9**	8416
"There is **p** for Moab no longer;	**Jer 48:2**	8416
city of **p** has not been deserted,	**Jer 49:25**	8416
And the **p** of the whole earth been	**Jer 51:41**	8416
my fathers, I give thanks and **p**,	**Da 2:23**	7624
"Now I, Nebuchadnezzar, **p**,	**Da 4:37**	7624
p the name of the LORD your God,	**Jl 2:26**	1984b
And the earth is full of His **p**.	**Hab 3:3**	8416
p and renown In all the earth.	**Zph 3:19**	8416
I will give you renown and **p** Among	**Zph 3:20**	8416
"I **p** You, Father, Lord of	**Mt 11:25**	*1843*
HAVE PREPARED **P** FOR YOURSELF'?"	**Mt 21:16**	*136*
and he *began* to speak in **p** of God.	**Lk 1:64**	*2127*
"I **p** You, O Father, Lord of	**Lk 10:21**	*1843*
people saw it, they gave **p** to God.	**Lk 18:43**	*136*
the disciples began to **p** God joyfully	**Lk 19:37**	*134*
and singing hymns of **p** to God,	**Ac 16:25**	*5214*
and his **p** is not from men, but	**Ro 2:29**	*1868*
and you will have **p** from the same;	**Ro 13:3**	*1868*
TONGUE SHALL GIVE **P** TO GOD."	**Ro 14:11**	*1843*
GIVE **P** TO YOU AMONG THE GENTILES,	**Ro 15:9**	*1843*
"**P** THE LORD ALL YOU GENTILES, AND	**Ro 15:11**	*134*
AND LET ALL THE PEOPLES **P** HIM."	**Ro 15:11**	*1867*
man's **p** will come to him from God.	**1Co 4:5**	*1868*
Now I **p** you because you remember	**1Co 11:2**	*1867*
this instruction, I do not **p** you,	**1Co 11:17**	*1867*
Shall I **p** you?	**1Co 11:22**	*1867*
In this I will not **p** you.	**1Co 11:22**	*1867*
the **p** of the glory of His grace,	**Eph 1:6**	*1868*
would be to the **p** of His glory.	**Eph 1:12**	*1868*
possession, to the **p** of His glory.	**Eph 1:14**	*1868*
Christ, to the glory and **p** of God.	**Php 1:11**	*1868*
and if anything worthy of **p**,	**Php 4:8**	*1868*
CONGREGATION I WILL SING YOUR **P**."	**Heb 2:12**	*5214*
offer up a sacrifice of **p** to God,	**Heb 13:15**	*133*
may be found to result in **p** and	**1Pe 1:7**	*1868*
and the **p** of those who do right.	**1Pe 2:14**	*1868*
"Give **p** to our God, all you His	**Rv 19:5**	*134*

PRAISED

saw her and **p** her to Pharaoh;	**Gn 12:15**	1984b
people saw him, they **p** their god,	**Jg 16:24**	1984b
handsome as Absalom, so highly **p**;	**2Sa 14:25**	1984b
the LORD, who is worthy to be **p**,	**2Sa 22:4**	1984b
is the LORD, and greatly to be **p**;	**1Ch 16:25**	1984b
"Amen," and **p** the LORD.	**1Ch 16:36**	1984b
and when they **p** the LORD *saying,*	**2Ch 5:13**	1984b
those who **p** *Him* in holy attire,	**2Ch 20:21**	1984b
the priests **p** the LORD day after day	**2Ch 30:21**	1984b
a great shout when they **p** the LORD	**Ezr 3:11**	1984b
And they **p** the LORD.	**Ne 5:13**	1984b
the LORD, who is worthy to be **p**,	**Ps 18:3**	1984b
is the LORD, and greatly to be **p**,	**Ps 48:1**	1984b
is the LORD and greatly to be **p**;	**Ps 96:4**	1984b
The name of the LORD is to be **p**.	**Ps 113:3**	1984b
is the LORD, and highly to be **p**,	**Ps 145:3**	1984b
be **p** according to his insight,	**Pr 12:8**	1984b
fears the LORD, she shall be **p**.	**Pr 31:30**	1984b
concubines *also,* and they **p** her,	**SS 6:9**	1984b
house, Where our fathers **p** You,	**Is 64:11**	1984b
p and honored Him who lives forever;	**Da 4:34**	7624
and **p** the gods of gold and silver,	**Da 5:4**	7624
p the gods of silver and gold,	**Da 5:23**	7624
their synagogues and was **p** by all.	**Lk 4:15**	*1392*
"And his master **p** the unrighteous	**Lk 16:8**	*1867*

PRAISES

in holiness, Awesome in **p**,	**Ex 15:11**	8416
And I will sing **p** to Your name.	**2Sa 22:50**	2167
Sing to Him, sing **p** to Him;	**1Ch 16:9**	2167
officials ordered the Levites to sing **p**	**2Ch 29:30**	1984b
So they sang **p** with joy, and bowed	**2Ch 29:30**	1984b
Sing **p** to the LORD, who dwells in	**Ps 9:11**	2167
That I may tell of all Your **p**,	**Ps 9:14**	8416
And I will sing **p** to Your name.	**Ps 18:49**	2167
enthroned upon the **p** of Israel.	**Ps 22:3**	8416
yes, I will sing **p** to the LORD.	**Ps 27:6**	2167
Sing **p** to Him with a harp of ten	**Ps 33:2**	2167
Sing **p** to God, sing praises;	**Ps 47:6**	2167
Sing praises to God, sing **p**;	**Ps 47:6**	2167
Sing **p** to our King, sing praises.	**Ps 47:6**	2167
Sing praises to our King, sing **p**.	**Ps 47:6**	2167
Sing **p** with a skillful psalm.	**Ps 47:7**	2167
I will sing, yes, I will sing **p**!	**Ps 57:7**	2167
sing **p** to You among the nations.	**Ps 57:9**	2167
strength, I will sing **p** to You;	**Ps 59:17**	2167
mouth offers **p** with joyful lips.	**Ps 63:5**	1984b
You, And will sing **p** to You;	**Ps 66:4**	2167
They will sing **p** to Your name.	**Ps 66:4**	2167
Sing to God, sing **p** to His name;	**Ps 68:4**	2167
Sing **p** to the Lord,	**Ps 68:32**	2167
You I will sing **p** with the lyre,	**Ps 71:22**	2167
for joy when I sing **p** to You;	**Ps 71:23**	2167
I will sing **p** to the God of Jacob.	**Ps 75:9**	2167
to come the **p** of the LORD,	**Ps 78:4**	8416
LORD And to sing **p** to Your name,	**Ps 92:1**	2167
forth and sing for joy and sing **p**.	**Ps 98:4**	2167
Sing **p** to the LORD with the lyre,	**Ps 98:5**	2167
To You, O LORD, I will sing **p**.	**Ps 101:1**	2167
Sing to Him, sing **p** to Him;	**Ps 105:2**	2167
I will sing, I will sing **p**,	**Ps 108:1**	2167
sing **p** to You among the nations.	**Ps 108:3**	2167
Sing **p** to His name, for it is	**Ps 135:3**	2167
sing **p** to You before the gods.	**Ps 138:1**	2167
ten strings I will sing **p** to You,	**Ps 144:9**	2167
I will sing **p** to my God while I	**Ps 146:2**	2167
it is good to sing **p** to our God;	**Ps 147:1**	2167
Sing **p** to our God on the lyre,	**Ps 147:7**	2167
Let them sing **p** to Him with timbrel	**Ps 149:3**	2167
high **p** of God *be* in their mouth,	**Ps 149:6**	7318
Her husband *also,* and he **p** her,	**Pr 31:28**	1984b
good news of the **p** of the LORD.	**Is 60:6**	8416
of the LORD, the **p** of the LORD,	**Is 63:7**	8416
Is anyone cheerful? He is to sing **p**.	**Jas 5:13**	*5567*

PRAISING

and 4,000 *were* **p** the LORD with the	**1Ch 23:5**	1984b
in giving thanks and **p** the LORD.	**1Ch 25:3**	1984b
When they began singing and **p**,	**2Ch 20:22**	8416
the people running and **p** the king,	**2Ch 23:12**	1984b
p and giving thanks to the LORD,	**Ezr 3:11**	1984b
They are ever **p** You.	**Ps 84:4**	1984b
of the heavenly host **p** God and	**Lk 2:13**	*134*
glorifying and **p** God for all that	**Lk 2:20**	*134*
what had happened, he *began* **p** God,	**Lk 23:47**	*1392*
continually in the temple **p** God.	**Lk 24:53**	*2127*
p God and having favor with all	**Ac 2:47**	*134*
walking and leaping and **p** God.	**Ac 3:8**	*134*
people saw him walking and **p** God;	**Ac 3:9**	*134*

PRAY

a prophet, and he will **p** for you and	**Gn 20:7**	6419
"Deliver me, I **p**, from the hand	**Gn 32:11**	4994
"Now therefore, I **p** You,	**Ex 33:13**	4994
"I **p** You, show me Your glory!"	**Ex 33:18**	4994
O Lord, I **p**, let the Lord go along	**Ex 34:9**	4994
"O God, heal her, I **p**!"	**Nu 12:13**	4994
"But now, I **p**, let the power of	**Nu 14:17**	4994
"Pardon, I **p**, the iniquity of	**Nu 14:19**	4994
'Let me, I **p**, cross over and see	**Dt 3:25**	4994
I will **p** to the LORD for you."	**1Sa 7:5**	6419
"**P** for your servants to the LORD	**1Sa 12:19**	6419
the LORD by ceasing to **p** for you;	**1Sa 12:23**	6419
O LORD God of Israel, I **p**,	**1Sa 23:11**	4994
courage to **p** this prayer to You.	**2Sa 7:27**	6419
"O LORD, I **p**, make the counsel of	**2Sa 15:31**	4994
of Israel, let Your word, I **p**,	**1Ki 8:26**	4994
servant shall **p** toward this place.	**1Ki 8:29**	6419
when they **p** toward this place;	**1Ki 8:30**	6419
and **p** and make supplication to You	**1Ki 8:33**	6419
and they **p** toward this place and	**1Ki 8:35**	6419
and they **p** to the LORD toward the	**1Ki 8:44**	6419
and **p** to You toward their land	**1Ki 8:48**	6419
the LORD your God, and **p** for me,	**1Ki 13:6**	6419
"O LORD my God, I **p** You,	**1Ki 17:21**	4994
"O LORD, I **p**, open his eyes that	**2Ki 6:17**	4994
this people with blindness, I **p**."	**2Ki 6:18**	4994
"Now, O LORD our God, I **p**,	**2Ki 19:19**	4994
found *courage* to **p** before You.	**1Ch 17:25**	6419
servant shall **p** toward this place.	**2Ch 6:20**	6419
when they **p** toward this place;	**2Ch 6:21**	6419
and **p** and make supplication before	**2Ch 6:24**	6419
and they **p** toward this place and	**2Ch 6:26**	6419
they come and **p** toward this house,	**2Ch 6:32**	6419
and they **p** to You toward this	**2Ch 6:34**	6419
and **p** toward their land which You	**2Ch 6:38**	6419
"Now, O my God, I **p**,	**2Ch 6:40**	4994
My name humble themselves and **p** and	**2Ch 7:14**	6419
p for the life of the king and his sons.	**Ezr 6:10**	6739
"You will **p** to Him, and He will	**Jb 22:27**	6279
Then he will **p** to God, and He will	**Jb 33:26**	6279
and My servant Job will **p** for you.	**Jb 42:8**	6419
and my God, For to You I **p**.	**Ps 5:2**	6419
let everyone who is godly **p** to	**Ps 32:6**	6419
let them **p** for him continually;	**Ps 72:15**	6419
P for the peace of Jerusalem:	**Ps 122:6**	7592
And comes to his sanctuary to **p**,	**Is 16:12**	6419
And **p** to a god who cannot save.	**Is 45:20**	6419
for you, do not **p** for this people,	**Jer 7:16**	6419
do not **p** for this people,	**Jer 11:14**	6419
"Do not **p** for the welfare of this	**Jer 14:11**	6419
and **p** to the LORD on its behalf;	**Jer 29:7**	6419
call upon Me and come and **p** to Me,	**Jer 29:12**	6419
"Please **p** to the LORD our God on	**Jer 37:3**	6419
and **p** for us to the LORD your God,	**Jer 42:2**	6419
I am going to **p** to the LORD your	**Jer 42:4**	6419
'**P** for us to the LORD our God;	**Jer 42:20**	6419
"We earnestly **p**, O LORD, do not	**Jon 1:14**	577
and **p** for those who persecute you	**Mt 5:44**	*4336*
"When you **p**, you are not to	**Mt 6:5**	*4336*
for they love to stand and **p** in	**Mt 6:5**	*4336*
"But you, when you **p**,	**Mt 6:6**	*4336*
p to your Father who is in secret,	**Mt 6:6**	*4336*
"**P**, then, in this way:	**Mt 6:9**	*4336*
on the mountain by Himself to **p**;	**Mt 14:23**	*4336*
might lay His hands on them and **p**;	**Mt 19:13**	*4336*
"But **p** that your flight will not	**Mt 24:20**	*4336*
while I go over there and **p**."	**Mt 26:36**	*4336*
He left for the mountain to **p**.	**Mk 6:46**	*4336*
things for which you **p** and ask,	**Mk 11:24**	*4336*
"But **p** that it may not happen in	**Mk 13:18**	*4336*
to **p** that if it were possible,	**Mk 14:35**	*4336*
slip away to the wilderness and **p**.	**Lk 5:16**	*4336*
He went off to the mountain to **p**,	**Lk 6:12**	*4336*
you, **p** for those who mistreat you.	**Lk 6:28**	*4336*
and went up on the mountain to **p**.	**Lk 9:28**	*4336*
teach us to **p** just as John also	**Lk 11:1**	*4336*
"When you **p**, say:	**Lk 11:2**	*4336*
ought to **p** and not to lose heart,	**Lk 18:1**	*4336*
men went up into the temple to **p**,	**Lk 18:10**	*4336*
"**P** that you may not enter into	**Lk 22:40**	*4336*
and He knelt down and *began* to **p**,	**Lk 22:41**	*4336*
up and **p** that you may not enter	**Lk 22:46**	*4336*
and **p** the Lord that, if possible,	**Ac 8:22**	*1189a*
"**P** to the Lord for me yourselves,	**Ac 8:24**	*1189a*
about the sixth hour to **p**.	**Ac 10:9**	*4336*
do not know how to **p** as we should,	**Ro 8:26**	*4336*
to **p** to God *with her head* uncovered?	**1Co 11:13**	*4336*
let one who speaks in a tongue **p**	**1Co 14:13**	*4336*
For if I **p** in a tongue, my spirit	**1Co 14:14**	*4336*
I will **p** with the spirit and I	**1Co 14:15**	*4336*
and I will **p** with the mind also;	**1Co 14:15**	*4336*
we **p** to God that you do no wrong;	**2Co 13:7**	*2172*
this we also **p** for, that you be	**2Co 13:9**	*2172*
I **p** *that* the eyes of your heart	**Eph 1:18**	
p at all times in the Spirit,	**Eph 6:18**	*4336*
and **p** on my behalf, that	**Eph 6:19**	
And this I **p**, that your love may	**Php 1:9**	*4336*
we have not ceased to **p** for you	**Col 1:9**	*4336*
p without ceasing;	**1Th 5:17**	*4336*
Brethren, **p** for us.	**1Th 5:25**	*4336*
To this end also we **p** for you	**2Th 1:11**	*4336*
p for us that the word of the Lord	**2Th 3:1**	*4336*
want the men in every place to **p**,	**1Tm 2:8**	*4336*
and I **p** that the fellowship of	**Phm 1:6**	
P for us, for we are sure that we	**Heb 13:18**	*4336*
among you suffering? *Then* he must **p**.	**Jas 5:13**	*4336*
church and they are to **p** over him,	**Jas 5:14**	*4336*
another, and **p** for one another so	**Jas 5:16**	*4336*
I **p** that in all respects you may	**3Jn 1:2**	*2172*

PRAYED

Abraham **p** to God,	**Gn 20:17**	6419
Isaac **p** to the LORD on behalf	**Gn 25:21**	6279
to Moses, and Moses **p** to the LORD and	**Nu 11:2**	6419
I also **p** for Aaron at the same time.	**Dt 9:20**	6419
"I **p** to the LORD and said,	**Dt 9:26**	6419
She, greatly distressed, **p** to the LORD	**1Sa 1:10**	6419
"For this boy I **p**, and the LORD	**1Sa 1:27**	6419

Then Hannah **p** and said, **1Sa 2:1** 6419
And Samuel **p** to the LORD. **1Sa 8:6** 6419
them both and **p** to the LORD. **2Ki 4:33** 6419
Then Elisha **p** and said, **2Ki 6:17** 6419
Elisha **p** to the LORD and said, **2Ki 6:18** 6419
Hezekiah **p** before the LORD **2Ki 19:15** 6419
'Because you have **p** to Me about **2Ki 19:20** 6419
to the wall and **p** to the LORD, **2Ki 20:2** 6419
For Hezekiah **p** for them, saying, **2Ch 30:18** 6419
p about this and cried out to **2Ch 32:20** 6419
and he **p** to the LORD, and the LORD **2Ch 32:24** 6419
When he **p** to Him, He was moved by **2Ch 33:13** 6419
So I **p** to the God of heaven. **Ne 2:4** 6419
But we **p** to our God, and because **Ne 4:9** 6419
of Job when he **p** for his friends, **Jb 42:10** 6419
Hezekiah **p** to the LORD saying, **Is 37:15** 6419
'Because you have **p** to Me about **Is 37:21** 6419
to the wall and **p** to the LORD, **Is 38:2** 6419
of Neriah, then I **p** to the LORD, **Jer 32:16** 6419
I **p** to the LORD my God and **Da 9:4** 6419
Then Jonah **p** to the LORD his God **Jon 2:1** 6419
He **p** to the LORD and said, **Jon 4:2** 6419
them, and fell on His face and **p**, **Mt 26:39** *4336*
away again a second time and **p**, **Mt 26:42** *4336*
and went away and **p** a third time, **Mt 26:44** *4336*
"Sit here until I have **p**." **Mk 14:32** *4336*
Again He went away and **p**, **Mk 14:39** *4336*
but I have **p** for you, that your **Lk 22:32** *1189a*
And they **p** and said, **Ac 1:24** *4336*
And when they had **p**, **Ac 4:31** *1189a*
who came down and **p** for them that **Ac 8:15** *4336*
them all out and knelt down and **p**, **Ac 9:40** *4336*
people and **p** to God continually. **Ac 10:2** *1189a*
when they had fasted and **p** and **Ac 13:3** *4336*
church, having **p** with fasting, **Ac 14:23** *4336*
he knelt down and **p** with them all. **Ac 20:36** *4336*
in *to see* him and after he had **p**, **Ac 28:8** *4336*
he **p** earnestly that it would not rain **Jas 5:17** *4336*
Then he **p** again, and the sky poured **Jas 5:18** *4336*

PRAYER

courage to pray this **p** to You. **2Sa 7:27** 8605
and after that God was moved by **p** for **2Sa 21:14** 6279
Thus the LORD was moved by **p** for **2Sa 24:25** 6279
have regard to the **p** of Your servant **1Ki 8:28** 8605
God, to listen to the cry and to the **p** **1Ki 8:28** 8605
to listen to the **p** which Your **1Ki 8:29** 8605
whatever **p** or supplication is made **1Ki 8:38** 8605
their **p** and their supplication, **1Ki 8:45** 8605
then hear their **p** and their **1Ki 8:49** 8605
p and supplication to the LORD, **1Ki 8:54** 8605
your **p** and your supplication, **1Ki 9:3** 8605
offer a **p** for the remnant that is left. **2Ki 19:4** 8605
"I have heard your **p**, **2Ki 20:5** 8605
"Yet have regard to the **p** of Your **2Ch 6:19** 8605
God, to listen to the cry and to the **p** **2Ch 6:19** 8605
to listen to the **p** which Your **2Ch 6:20** 8605
whatever **p** or supplication is made **2Ch 6:29** 8605
their **p** and their supplication, **2Ch 6:35** 8605
place, their **p** and supplications, **2Ch 6:39** 8605
Your ears attentive to the **p** *offered* **2Ch 6:40** 8605
"I have heard your **p** and **2Ch 7:12** 8605
My ears attentive to the **p** *offered* **2Ch 7:15** 8605
and their **p** came to His holy dwelling **2Ch 30:27** 8605
of Manasseh even his **p** to his God, **2Ch 33:18** 8605
His **p** also and *how God* was **2Ch 33:19** 8605
to hear the **p** of Your servant **Ne 1:6** 8605
be attentive to the **p** of Your servant **Ne 1:11** 8605
the **p** of Your servants who delight to **Ne 1:11** 8605
beginning the thanksgiving at **p**, **Ne 11:17** 8605
in my hands, And my **p** is pure. **Jb 16:17** 8605
Be gracious to me and hear my **p**. **Ps 4:1** 8605
the morning I will order *my* **p** **Ps 5:3**
The LORD receives my **p**. **Ps 6:9** 8605
Give ear to my **p**, which is not **Ps 17:1** 8605
my **p** kept returning to my bosom. **Ps 35:13** 8605
"Hear my **p**, O LORD, and give ear **Ps 39:12** 8605
night, A **p** to the God of my life. **Ps 42:8** 8605
Hear my **p**, O God; **Ps 54:2** 8605
Give ear to my **p**, O God; **Ps 55:1** 8605
Give heed to my **p**. **Ps 61:1** 8605
O You who hear **p**, **Ps 65:2** 8605
given heed to the voice of my **p**. **Ps 66:19** 8605
God, Who has not turned away my **p** **Ps 66:20** 8605
But as for me, my **p** is to You, **Ps 69:13** 8605
be angry with the **p** of Your people? **Ps 80:4** 8605
O LORD God of hosts, hear my **p**; **Ps 84:8** 8605
Give ear, O LORD, to my **p**; **Ps 86:6** 8605
Let my **p** come before You; **Ps 88:2** 8605
morning my **p** comes before You. **Ps 88:13** 8605
Hear my **p**, O LORD! **Ps 102:1** 8605
regarded the **p** of the destitute And **Ps 102:17** 8605
And has not despised their **p**. **Ps 102:17** 8605
act as my accusers; But I am *in* **p**. **Ps 109:4** 8605
And let his **p** become sin. **Ps 109:7** 8605
May my **p** be counted as incense **Ps 141:2** 8605
my head refuse it, For still my **p** is **Ps 141:5** 8605
Hear my **p**, O LORD, Give ear to my **Ps 143:1** 8605
p of the upright is His delight. **Pr 15:8** 8605
He hears the **p** of the righteous. **Pr 15:29** 8605
law, Even his **p** is an abomination. **Pr 28:9** 8605
when you spread out your hands *in* **p**, **Is 1:15**
They could only whisper a **p**, **Is 26:16** 3908
offer a **p** for the remnant that is left **Is 37:4** 8605
"I have heard your **p**, **Is 38:5** 8605
make them joyful in My house of **p**. **Is 56:7** 8605
house of **p** for all the peoples." **Is 56:7** 8605
do not lift up cry or **p** for them, **Jer 7:16** 8605
nor lift up a cry or **p** for them; **Jer 11:14** 8605
call for help, He shuts out my **p**. **La 3:8** 8605
So that no **p** can pass through. **La 3:44** 8605
"Do not hide Your ear from my **p** **La 3:56**
seek *Him by* **p** and supplications, **Da 9:3** 8605
listen to the **p** of Your servant and **Da 9:17** 8605
while I was still speaking in **p**, **Da 9:21** 8605
And my **p** came to You, Into Your **Jon 2:7** 8605
A **p** of Habakkuk the prophet, **Hab 3:1** 8605
go out except by **p** and fasting." **Mt 17:21** *4335*
SHALL BE CALLED A HOUSE OF **P** **Mt 21:13** *4335*
"And all things you ask in **p**, **Mt 21:22** *4335*
cannot come out by anything but **p** **Mk 9:29** *4335*
A HOUSE OF **P** FOR ALL THE NATIONS'? **Mk 11:17** *4335*
multitude of the people were in **p** **Lk 1:10** *4336*
spent the whole night in **p** to God. **Lk 6:12** *4335*
MY HOUSE SHALL BE A HOUSE OF **P**,' **Lk 19:46** *4335*
When He rose from **p**, **Lk 22:45** *4335*
devoting themselves to **p**, **Ac 1:14** *4335*
to the breaking of bread and to **p**. **Ac 2:42** *4335*
at the ninth *hour,* the hour of **p**. **Ac 3:1** *4335*
"But we will devote ourselves to **p** and **Ac 6:4** *4335*
your **p** has been heard and your **Ac 10:31** *4335*
but **p** for him was being made **Ac 12:5** *4335*
that there would be a place of **p**; **Ac 16:13** *4335*
we were going to the place of **p**, **Ac 16:16** *4335*
my heart's desire and my **p** to God **Ro 10:1** *1162*
in tribulation, devoted to **p**, **Ro 12:12** *4335*
you may devote yourselves to **p**, **1Co 7:5** *4335*
they also, by **p** on your behalf, **2Co 9:14** *1162*
With all **p** and petition pray at **Eph 6:18** *4335*
always offering **p** with joy in my **Php 1:4** *1162*
joy in my every **p** for you all, **Php 1:4** *1162*
but in everything by **p** and **Php 4:6** *4335*
Devote yourselves to **p**, **Col 4:2** *4335*
by means of the word of God and **p**. **1Tm 4:5** *1783*
and the **p** offered in faith will **Jas 5:15** *2171*
The effective **p** of a righteous man **Jas 5:16** *1162*
AND HIS EARS ATTEND TO THEIR **P**, **1Pe 3:12** *1162*
sober *spirit* for the purpose of **p**. **1Pe 4:7** *4335*

PRAYERS

and He answered their **p** because they **1Ch 5:20** 6279
The **p** of David the son of Jesse **Ps 72:20** 8605
Yes, even though you multiply **p**, **Is 1:15** 8605
for a pretense you make long **p**; **Mt 23:14** *4336*
for appearance's sake offer long **p**; **Mk 12:40** *4336*
night and day with fastings and **p**. **Lk 2:37** *1162*
of John often fast and offer **p**, **Lk 5:33** *1162*
for appearance's sake offer long **p**. **Lk 20:47** *4336*
"Your **p** and alms have ascended as **Ac 10:4** *4335*
always in my **p** making request, if **Ro 1:10** *4335*
with me in your **p** to God for me, **Ro 15:30** *4335*
in helping us through your **p**, **2Co 1:11** *1162*
favor bestowed on us through *the* **p** **2Co 1:11**
making mention *of you* in my **p**; **Eph 1:16** *4335*
for my deliverance through your **p** **Php 1:19** *1162*
laboring earnestly for you in his **p**, **Col 4:12** *4335*
making mention *of you* in our **p**; **1Th 1:2** *4335*
I urge that entreaties *and* **p**, **1Tm 2:1** *4335*
in entreaties and **p** night and day. **1Tm 5:5** *4335*
you in my **p** night and day, **2Tm 1:3** *1162*
making mention of you in my **p**, **Phm 1:4** *4335*
through your **p** I will be given to **Phm 1:22** *4335*
He offered up both **p** and **Heb 5:7** *1162*
that your **p** will not be hindered. **1Pe 3:7** *4335*
which are the **p** of the saints. **Rv 5:8** *4335*
that he might add it to the **p** of **Rv 8:3** *4335*
incense, with the **p** of the saints, **Rv 8:4** *4335*

PRAYING

she continued **p** before the LORD, **1Sa 1:12** 6419
here beside you, **p** to the LORD. **1Sa 1:26** 6419
When Solomon had finished **p** **1Ki 8:54** 6419
Now when Solomon had finished **p**, **2Ch 7:1** 6419
Ezra was **p** and making confession, **Ezr 10:1** 6419
and **p** before the God of heaven. **Ne 1:4** 6419
which I am **p** before You now, **Ne 1:6** 6419
p and giving thanks before his God **Da 6:10** 6739
Now while I was speaking and **p**, **Da 9:20** 6419
"And when you are **p**, **Mt 6:7** *4336*
"Keep watching and **p** that **Mt 26:41** *4336*
a secluded place, and was **p** there. **Mk 1:35** *4336*
"Whenever you stand **p**, **Mk 11:25** *4336*
"Keep watching and **p** that **Mk 14:38** *4336*
was also baptized, and while He was **p**, **Lk 3:21** *4336*
happened that while He was **p** alone, **Lk 9:18** *4336*
And while He was **p**, **Lk 9:29** *4336*
while Jesus was **p** in a certain place, **Lk 11:1** *4336*
stood and was **p** this to himself **Lk 18:11** *4336*
p that you may have strength to escape **Lk 21:36** *1189a*
in agony He was **p** very fervently; **Lk 22:44** *4336*
and after **p**, they laid their hands **Ac 6:6** *4336*
named Saul, for he is **p**, **Ac 9:11** *4336*
I was **p** in my house during the **Ac 10:30** *4336*
"I was in the city of Joppa **p**; **Ac 11:5** *4336*
were gathered together and were **p**. **Ac 12:12** *4336*
about midnight Paul and Silas were **p** **Ac 16:25** *4336*
kneeling down on the beach and **p**, **Ac 21:5** *4336*
Jerusalem and was **p** in the temple, **Ac 22:17** *4336*
his head while **p** or prophesying **1Co 11:4** *4336*
uncovered while **p** or prophesying **1Co 11:5** *4336*
Jesus Christ, **p** always for you, **Col 1:3** *4336*
p at the same time for us as well, **Col 4:3** *4336*
as we night and day keep **p** most **1Th 3:10** *1189a*
p in the Holy Spirit, **Jude 1:20** *4336*

PRAYS

Your servant **p** before You today; **1Ki 8:28** 6419
he comes and **p** toward this house, **1Ki 8:42** 6419
which Your servant **p** before You; **2Ch 6:19** 6419
he also **p** to it and says, **Is 44:17** 6419
if I pray in a tongue, my spirit **p**, **1Co 14:14** *4336*

PREACH

time Jesus began to **p** and say, **Mt 4:17** *2784*
"And as you go, **p**, saying, **Mt 10:7** *2784*
to teach and **p** in their cities. **Mt 11:1** *2784*
so that I may **p** there also; **Mk 1:38** *2784*
that He *could* send them out to **p**, **Mk 3:14** *2784*
and **p** the gospel to all creation. **Mk 16:15** *2784*
ME TO **P** THE GOSPEL TO THE POOR. **Lk 4:18** *2097*
"I must **p** the kingdom of God to **Lk 4:43** *2097*
He ordered us to **p** to the people, **Ac 10:42** *2784*
"And we **p** to you the good news of **Ac 13:32** *2097*
they continued to **p** the gospel. **Ac 14:7** *2097*
and **p** the gospel to you **Ac 14:15** *2097*
has in every city those who **p** him, **Ac 15:21** *2784*
called us to **p** the gospel to them. **Ac 16:10** *2097*
I am eager to **p** the gospel to you **Ro 1:15** *2097*
who **p** that one shall not steal, **Ro 2:21** *2784*
will they **p** unless they are sent? **Ro 10:15** *2784*
thus I aspired to **p** the gospel, **Ro 15:20** *2097*
to baptize, but to **p** the gospel, **1Co 1:17** *2097*
but we **p** Christ crucified, to Jews **1Co 1:23** *2784*
For if I **p** the gospel, I have **1Co 9:16** *2097*
woe is me if I do not **p** the gospel. **1Co 9:16** *2097*
That, when I **p** the gospel, I may **1Co 9:18** *2097*
they, so we **p** and so you believed. **1Co 15:11** *2784*
For we do not **p** ourselves but **2Co 4:5** *2784*
so as to **p** the gospel even to the **2Co 10:16** *2097*
should **p** to you a gospel contrary **Ga 1:8** *2097*
I might **p** Him among the Gentiles, **Ga 1:16** *2097*
which I **p** among the Gentiles, **Ga 2:2** *2784*
if I still **p** circumcision, **Ga 5:11** *2784*
to **p** to the Gentiles the **Eph 3:8** *2097*
Teach and **p** these *principles.* **1Tm 6:2** *3870*
p the word; be ready in season *and* **2Tm 4:2** *2784*
having an eternal gospel to **p** to **Rv 14:6** *2097*

PREACHED

p rebellion against the LORD. **Jer 29:32** 1696
POOR HAVE THE GOSPEL **P** TO THEM. **Mt 11:5** *2097*
This gospel of the kingdom shall be **p** **Mt 24:14** *2784*
gospel is **p** in the whole world, **Mt 26:13** *2784*
out and **p** that *men* should repent. **Mk 6:12** *2784*
"The gospel must first be **p** to all **Mk 13:10** *2784*
gospel is **p** in the whole world, **Mk 14:9** *2784*
they went out and **p** everywhere, **Mk 16:20** *2784*
he **p** the gospel to the people. **Lk 3:18** *2097*
POOR HAVE THE GOSPEL **P** TO THEM. **Lk 7:22** *2097*
the kingdom of God has been **p**, **Lk 16:16** *2097*
this Scripture he **p** Jesus to him. **Ac 8:35** *2097*
After they had **p** the gospel to **Ac 14:21** *2097*
I have fully **p** the gospel of Christ. **Ro 15:19** *4137*
p to save those who believe. **1Co 1:21** *2782*
after I have **p** to others, **1Co 9:27** *2784*
the gospel which I **p** to you, **1Co 15:1** *2097*
hold fast the word which I **p** to you, **1Co 15:2** *2097*
Now if Christ is **p**, **1Co 15:12** *2784*
Jesus, who was **p** among you by us **2Co 1:19** *2784*
another Jesus whom we have not **p**, **2Co 11:4** *2784*
because I **p** the gospel of God to **2Co 11:7** *2097*
to what we have **p** to you, **Ga 1:8** *2097*
the gospel which was **p** by me is not **Ga 1:11** *2097*
p the gospel beforehand to **Ga 3:8** *4283*
I **p** the gospel to you the first time; **Ga 4:13** *2097*
AND HE CAME AND **P** PEACE TO YOU **Eph 2:17** *2097*
we have had good news **p** to us, **Heb 4:2** *2097*
those who formerly had good news **p** **Heb 4:6** *2097*
p the gospel to you by the Holy Spirit **1Pe 1:12** *2097*
is the word which was **p** to you. **1Pe 1:25** *2097*
gospel has for this purpose been **p** **1Pe 4:6** *2097*
He **p** to His servants the prophets. **Rv 10:7** *2097*

PREACHER

The words of the **P**, **Ec 1:1** 6953
"Vanity of vanities," says the **P**, **Ec 1:2** 6953
I, the **P**, have been king over **Ec 1:12** 6953
have discovered this," says the **P**, **Ec 7:27** 6953
"Vanity of vanities," says the **P**, **Ec 12:8** 6953
the **P** also taught the people **Ec 12:9** 6953
The **P** sought to find delightful **Ec 12:10** 6953
how will they hear without a **p**? **Ro 10:14** *2784*
was appointed a **p** and an apostle **1Tm 2:7** *2783*
a **p** and an apostle and a teacher. **2Tm 1:11** *2783*
Noah, a **p** of righteousness, **2Pe 2:5** *2783*

PREACHES

adjure you by Jesus whom Paul **p**." **Ac 19:13** *2784*
This is the man who **p** to all men **Ac 21:28** *1321*
if one comes and **p** another Jesus **2Co 11:4** *2784*

PREACHING

p in the wilderness of Judea, **Mt 3:1** *2784*
they repented at the **p** of Jonah; **Mt 12:41** *2782*
p a baptism of repentance for the **Mk 1:4** *2784*
And he was **p**, and saying, **Mk 1:7** *2784*
into Galilee, **p** the gospel of God, **Mk 1:14** *2784*
p and casting out the demons. **Mk 1:39** *2784*
p a baptism of repentance for the **Lk 3:3** *2784*
He kept on **p** in the synagogues of **Lk 4:44** *2784*
and **p** the kingdom of God. **Lk 8:1** *2097*
throughout the villages, **p** the gospel **Lk 9:6** *2097*
they repented at the **p** of Jonah; **Lk 11:32** *2782*
in the temple and **p** the gospel, **Lk 20:1** *2097*
and **p** Jesus *as* the Christ. **Ac 5:42** *2097*
scattered went about **p** the word. **Ac 8:4** *2097*
But when they believed Philip **p** **Ac 8:12** *2097*
and were **p** the gospel to many **Ac 8:25** *2097*
kept **p** the gospel to all the cities until **Ac 8:40** *2097*

p peace through Jesus Christ **Ac 10:36** *2097*
the Greeks also, **p** the Lord Jesus. **Ac 11:20** *2097*
stayed in Antioch, teaching and **p** with **Ac 15:35** *2097*
was **p** Jesus and the resurrection. **Ac 17:18** *2097*
whom I went about **p** the kingdom, **Ac 20:25** *2784*
p the kingdom of God and teaching **Ac 28:31** *2784*
whom I serve in my spirit in the **p** **Ro 1:9** *2098*
the word of faith which we are **p**, **Ro 10:8** *2784*
gospel and the **p** of Jesus Christ, **Ro 16:25** *2782*
and my message and my **p** were not **1Co 2:4** *2782*
been raised, then our **p** is vain, **1Co 15:14** *2782*
if any man is **p** to you a gospel **Ga 1:9** *2097*
"He who once persecuted us is now **p** **Ga 1:23** *2097*
are **p** Christ even from envy and **Php 1:15** *2784*
that at the first **p** of the gospel, **Php 4:15** *746*
that I might fully carry out the **p** **Col 1:25**
who work hard at **p** and teaching. **1Tm 5:17** *3056*

PRECAUTION
taking **p** so that no one will **2Co 8:20** *4724*

PRECEDE
not **p** those who have fallen asleep. **1Th 4:15** *5348*

PRECEDED
than all who **p** me in Jerusalem. **Ec 2:7** 6440
than all who **p** me in Jerusalem. **Ec 2:9** 6440

PRECEDING
one of the twelve, was **p** them; **Lk 22:47** *4281*

PRECEPTS
The **p** of the LORD are right, **Ps 19:8** 6490
And remember His **p** to do them. **Ps 103:18** 6490
All His **p** are sure. **Ps 111:7** 6490
You have ordained Your **p**, **Ps 119:4** 6490
I will meditate on Your **p** And **Ps 119:15** 6490
me understand the way of Your **p**, **Ps 119:27** 6490
Behold, I long for Your **p**; **Ps 119:40** 6490
walk at liberty, For I seek Your **p**. **Ps 119:45** 6490
become mine, That I observe Your **p**. **Ps 119:56** 6490
You, And of those who keep Your **p**. **Ps 119:63** 6490
all *my* heart I will observe Your **p**. **Ps 119:69** 6490
But I shall meditate on Your **p**. **Ps 119:78** 6490
for me, I did not forsake Your **p**. **Ps 119:87** 6490
I will never forget Your **p**, **Ps 119:93** 6490
For I have sought Your **p**. **Ps 119:94** 6490
Because I have observed Your **p**. **Ps 119:100** 6490
From Your **p** I get understanding; **Ps 119:104** 6490
I have not gone astray from Your **p**. **Ps 119:110** 6490
all *Your* **p** concerning everything, **Ps 119:128** 6490
of man, That I may keep Your **p**. **Ps 119:134** 6490
Yet I do not forget Your **p**. **Ps 119:141** 6490
Consider how I love Your **p**; **Ps 119:159** 6490
I keep Your **p** and Your testimonies, **Ps 119:168** 6490
help me, For I have chosen Your **p**. **Ps 119:173** 6490
I wrote for him ten thousand **p** of **Hos 8:12**
AS DOCTRINES THE **P** OF MEN.'" **Mt 15:9** *1778*
AS DOCTRINES THE **P** OF MEN.' **Mk 7:7** *1778*

PRECINCTS
the official, which *was* in the **p**; **2Ki 23:11** 6503

PRECIOUS
he also gave **p** things to her **Gn 24:53** 4030
life was **p** in your sight this day. **1Sa 26:21** 3365
of gold, and *in it was* a **p** stone; **2Sa 12:30** 3368
and very much gold and **p** stones. **1Ki 10:2** 3368
amount of spices and **p** stones. **1Ki 10:10** 3368
number of almug trees and **p** stones. **1Ki 10:11** 3368
of yours be **p** in your sight. **2Ki 1:13** 3365
let my life be **p** in your sight." **2Ki 1:14** 3365
the gold and the spices and the **p** oil **2Ki 20:13** 2896a
and there was a **p** stone in it; **1Ch 20:2** 3368
colors, and all kinds of **p** stones and **1Ch 29:2** 3368
Whoever possessed **p** stones gave **1Ch 29:8** 3368
adorned the house with **p** stones; **2Ch 3:6** 3368
large amount of gold and **p** stones; **2Ch 9:1** 3368
amount of spices and **p** stones; **2Ch 9:9** 3368
brought algum trees and **p** stones. **2Ch 9:10** 3368
gifts of silver, gold and **p** things, **2Ch 21:3** 4030
for silver, gold, **p** stones, **2Ch 32:27** 3368
of fine shiny bronze, **p** as gold. **Ezr 8:27** 2536b
mother-of-pearl and **p** stones. **Es 1:6** 5508
And his eye sees anything **p**. **Jb 28:10** 3366
in the gold of Ophir, In **p** onyx, **Jb 28:16** 3368
How **p** is Your lovingkindness, O God! **Ps 36:7** 3368
as a moth what is **p** to him; **Ps 39:11** 2530
blood will be **p** in his sight; **Ps 72:14** 3365
P in the sight of the LORD Is the **Ps 116:15** 3368
is like the **p** oil upon the head, **Ps 133:2** 2896a
How **p** also are Your thoughts to me, **Ps 139:17** 3365
will find all *kinds* of **p** wealth, **Pr 1:13** 3368
She is more **p** than jewels; **Pr 3:15** 3368
adulteress hunts for the **p** life. **Pr 6:26** 3368
But the **p** possession of a man *is* **Pr 12:27** 3368
of knowledge are a more **p** thing. **Pr 20:15** 3366
There is **p** treasure and oil in the **Pr 21:20** 2530
With all **p** and pleasant riches. **Pr 24:4** 3368
the gold and the spices and the **p** oil **Is 39:2** 2896a
"Since you are **p** in My sight, **Is 43:4** 3365
their **p** things are of no profit; **Is 44:9** 2530
And your entire wall of **p** stones. **Is 54:12** 2656
our **p** things have become a ruin. **Is 64:11** 4261
extract the **p** from the worthless, **Jer 15:19** 3368
Jerusalem remembers all her **p** things **La 1:7** 4262
his hand Over all her **p** things, **La 1:10** 4261
They have given their **p** things for **La 1:11** 4262
The **p** sons of Zion, Weighed **La 4:2** 3368
have taken treasure and **p** things; **Ezk 22:25** 3366
and with all *kinds* of **p** stones and **Ezk 27:22** 3368
Every **p** stone was your covering: **Ezk 28:13** 3368
and their **p** vessels of silver and gold **Da 11:8** 2532
over all the **p** things of Egypt; **Da 11:43** 2536b
slay the **p** ones of their womb. **Hos 9:16** 4261
his treasury of every **p** article. **Hos 13:15** 2532
My **p** treasures to your temples, **Jl 3:5** 4261
with gold, silver, **p** stones, **1Co 3:12** *5093*
for the **p** produce of the soil, **Jas 5:7** *5093*
more **p** than gold which is perishable **1Pe 1:7** *4186*
but with **p** blood, as of a lamb **1Pe 1:19** *5093*
choice and **p** in the sight of God, **1Pe 2:4** *1784*
A CHOICE STONE, A **P** CORNER *stone,* **1Pe 2:6** *1784*
This **p** value, then, is for you who **1Pe 2:7** *5092*
which is **p** in the sight of God. **1Pe 3:4** *4185*
us His **p** and magnificent promises, **2Pe 1:4** *5093*
with gold and **p** stones and pearls, **Rv 17:4** *5093*
gold and silver and **p** stones and **Rv 18:12** *5093*
with gold and **p** stones and pearls; **Rv 18:16** *5093*
with every kind of **p** stone. **Rv 21:19** *5093*

PREDATORY
as food to every kind of **p** bird and **Ezk 39:4** 5861

PREDESTINED
hand and Your purpose **p** to occur. **Ac 4:28** *4309*
He also **p** *to become* conformed to **Ro 8:29** *4309*
whom He **p**, He also called; **Ro 8:30** *4309*
God **p** before the ages to our glory; **1Co 2:7** *4309*
He **p** us to adoption as sons **Eph 1:5** *4309*
been **p** according to His purpose **Eph 1:11** *4309*

PREDETERMINED
p plan and foreknowledge of God, **Ac 2:23** *3724*

PREDICT
Those who **p** by the new moons, **Is 47:13** 3045

PREDICTED
as He **p** the sufferings of Christ **1Pe 1:11** *4303*

PREEMINENCE
as water, you shall not have **p**, **Gn 49:4** 3498

PREEMINENT
P in dignity and preeminent in **Gn 49:3** 3499a
in dignity and **p** in power. **Gn 49:3** 3499a

PREFECT
chief **p** over all the wise men of **Da 2:48** 5460

PREFECTS
with you I shatter governors and **p**. **Jer 51:23** 5461
Their governors and all their **p**, **Jer 51:28** 5461
men drunk, Her governors, her **p** and **Jer 51:57** 5461
satraps, the **p** and the governors, **Da 3:2** 5460
satraps, the **p** and the governors, **Da 3:3** 5460
The satraps, the **p**, **Da 3:27** 5460
kingdom, the **p** and the satraps, **Da 6:7** 5460

PREFER
p to come with me to Babylon, **Jer 40:4** 7489a, 5869
but if you would **p** not to come **Jer 40:4** 7489a, 5869
p rather to be absent from the body **2Co 5:8** *2106*

PREFERENCE
give **p** to one another in honor; **Ro 12:10** *4285*

PREFERRED
For you have **p** this to affliction. **Jb 36:21** 977

PREGNANCY
No birth, no **p** and no conception! **Hos 9:11** 990

PREGNANT
was **p** and about to give birth; **1Sa 4:19** 2030
and told David, and said, "I am **p**." **2Sa 11:5** 2030
formed in the womb of the **p** woman, **Ec 11:5** 4392
As the **p** woman approaches *the time* **Is 26:17** 2030
We were **p**, we writhed *in labor,* We **Is 26:18** 2029
my grave, And her womb ever **p**. **Jer 20:17** 2030
their **p** women will be ripped open. **Hos 13:16** 2034a
they ripped open the **p** women of **Am 1:13** 2030
"But woe to those who are **p** and to **Mt 24:19** *1064*
"But woe to those who are **p** and to **Mk 13:17** *1064*
days Elizabeth his wife became **p**, **Lk 1:24** *4815*
"Woe to those who are **p** and to those **Lk 21:23** *1064*

PREMATURELY
so that she gives birth **p**, **Ex 21:22** 3318

PREMEDITATION
person unintentionally, without **p**, **Jos 20:3** 1847
he struck his neighbor without **p** **Jos 20:5** 1847

PREPARATION
now I will make **p** for it." **1Ch 22:5** 3559
day, the day after the **p**, **Mt 27:62** *3904*
come, because it was the **p** day, **Mk 15:42** *3904*
It was the **p** day, and the **Lk 23:54** *3904*
was the day of **p** for the Passover; **Jn 19:14** *3904*
because it was the day of **p**, **Jn 19:31** *3904*
because of the Jewish day of **p**, **Jn 19:42** *3904*
WITH THE **P** OF THE GOSPEL OF PEACE; **Eph 6:15** *2091*

PREPARATIONS
David made ample **p** before his death. **1Ch 22:5** 3559
So I had made **p** to build *it.* **1Ch 28:2** 3559
was distracted with all her **p**; **Lk 10:40** *1248*
but while they were making **p**, **Ac 10:10** *3903*

PREPARE
p three measures of fine flour, **Gn 18:6** 4116
and he hurried to **p** it. **Gn 18:7** 6213a
and **p** a savory dish for me such as **Gn 27:4** 6213a
game and **p** a savory dish for me, **Gn 27:7** 6213a
that I may **p** them *as* a savory dish **Gn 27:9** 6213a
when they **p** what they bring in, **Ex 16:5** 3559
'The second he shall then **p** as a **Lv 5:10** 6213a
you shall **p** wine for the drink offering, **Nu 15:5** 6213a
'Or for a ram you shall **p** as a **Nu 15:6** 6213a
'When you **p** a bull as a burnt **Nu 15:8** 6213a
to the number that you **p**, **Nu 15:12** 6213a
and **p** seven bulls and seven rams **Nu 23:1** 3559
p seven bulls and seven rams for me **Nu 23:29** 3559
shall **p** the roads for yourself, **Dt 19:3** 3559
'**P** provisions for yourselves, for **Jos 1:11** 3559
so that we may **p** a young goat for you." **Jg 13:15** 6213a
but if you **p** a burnt offering, **Jg 13:16** 6213a
therefore, take and **p** a new cart and **1Sa 6:7** 6213a
To **p** for the wayfarer who had come **2Sa 12:4** 6213a
let her **p** the food in my sight, **2Sa 13:5** 6213a
house, and **p** food for him." **2Sa 13:7** 6213a
may go in and **p** for me and my son, **1Ki 17:12** 6213a
and I will **p** the other ox and lay **1Ki 18:23** 6213a
and **p** it first for you are many, **1Ki 18:25** 6213a
'**P** *your chariot* and go down, so **1Ki 18:44** 631
showbread to **p** it every sabbath. **1Ch 9:32** 3559
to **p** timber in abundance for me, **2Ch 2:9** 3559
Then Hezekiah commanded *them* to **p** **2Ch 31:11** 3559
"**P** *yourselves* by your fathers' **2Ch 35:4** 3559
and **p** for your brethren to do **2Ch 35:6** 3559
banquet which I will **p** for them, **Es 5:8** 6213a
He may **p** *it,* but the just will **Jb 27:17** 3559
You **p** a table before me in **Ps 23:5** 6186a
You **p** their grain, for thus **Ps 65:9** 3559
for thus You **p** the earth. **Ps 65:9** 3559
that did not **p** its heart And **Ps 78:8** 3559
God **p** a table in the wilderness? **Ps 78:19** 6186a
P plans by consultation, And make **Pr 20:18** 3559
P your work outside And make it **Pr 24:27** 3559
they **p** their food in the summer; **Pr 30:25** 3559
Men **p** a meal for enjoyment, and **Ec 10:19** 6213a
"**P** for his sons a place of slaughter **Is 14:21** 3559
The LORD of hosts will **p** a **Is 25:6** 6213a
To **p** an idol that will not totter. **Is 40:20** 3559
"Build up, build up, **p** the way, **Is 57:14** 6437
well you **p** your way To seek love! **Jer 2:33** 3190
"**P** war against her; **Jer 6:4** 6942
to **p** sacrifices continually.'" **Jer 33:18** 6213a
which you will **p** your bread." **Ezk 4:15** 6213a
p for yourself baggage for exile **Ezk 12:3** 6213a
"Be prepared, and **p** yourself, **Ezk 38:7** 3559
'For seven days you shall **p** daily **Ezk 43:25** 6213a
P a war; rouse the mighty men! **Jl 3:9** 6942
this to you, **P** to meet your God, **Am 4:12** 3559
I will **p** your grave, For you are **Na 1:14** 7760
day that I **p** *My* own possession, **Mal 3:17** 6213a
WHO WILL **P** YOUR WAY BEFORE YOU.' **Mt 11:10** *2680*
she did it to **p** Me for burial. **Mt 26:12** *1779*
p for You to eat the Passover?" **Mt 26:17** *2090*
YOU, WHO WILL **P** YOUR WAY; **Mk 1:2** *2680*
p for You to eat the Passover?" **Mk 14:12** *2090*
p for us there." **Mk 14:15** *2090*
ON BEFORE THE LORD TO **P** HIS WAYS; **Lk 1:76** *2090*
WHO WILL **P** YOUR WAY BEFORE YOU.' **Lk 7:27** *2680*
'**P** something for me to eat, and **Lk 17:8** *2090*
"So make up your minds not to **p** **Lk 21:14** *4304*
"Go and **p** the Passover for us, **Lk 22:8** *2090*
"Where do You want us to **p** it?" **Lk 22:9** *2090*
furnished upper room; **p** it there." **Lk 22:12** *2090*
for I go to **p** a place for you. **Jn 14:2** *2090*
"If I go and **p** a place for you, **Jn 14:3** *2090*
who will **p** himself for battle? **1Co 14:8** *3903*
the same time also **p** me a lodging, **Phm 1:22** *2090*
Therefore, **p** your minds for action, **1Pe 1:13** *328*

PREPARED
milk and the calf which he had **p**, **Gn 18:8** 6213a
and he **p** a feast for them, and **Gn 19:3** 6213a
outside since I have **p** the house, **Gn 24:31** 6437
So they **p** the present for Joseph's **Gn 43:25** 3559
Joseph **p** his chariot and went **Gn 46:29** 631
that alone may be **p** by you. **Ex 12:16** 6213a
p any provisions for themselves. **Ex 12:39** 6213a
you into the place which I have **p**. **Ex 23:20** 3559
shall be **p** with oil on a griddle. **Lv 6:21** 6213a
p in a pan or on a griddle shall **Lv 7:9** 6213a
Gideon went in and **p** a young goat **Jg 6:19** 6213a
in the morning, and he **p** to go; **Jg 19:5** 6965
jugs of wine and five sheep already **p** **1Sa 25:18** 6213a
p it for the man who had come to **2Sa 12:4** 6213a
So he **p** for himself chariots and **1Ki 1:5** 6213a
and **p** the timbers and the stones **1Ki 5:18** 3559
built of stone **p** at the quarry, **1Ki 6:7** 8003
Then he **p** an inner sanctuary **1Ki 6:19** 3559
which was given them and they **p** it **1Ki 18:26** 6213a
So he **p** a great feast for them; **2Ki 6:23** 3738b
p the mixing of the spices. **1Ch 9:30** 7543
for their kinsmen had **p** for them. **1Ch 12:39** 3559
he **p** a place for the ark of God and **1Ch 15:1** 3559
its place which he had **p** for it. **1Ch 15:3** 3559
to *the place* that I have **p** for it. **1Ch 15:12** 3559
David **p** large quantities of **1Ch 22:3** 3559
with great pains I have **p** for the **1Ch 22:14** 3559
also timber and stone I have **p**, **1Ch 22:14** 3559
to the place he had **p** for it, **2Ch 1:4** 3559
at the place that David had **p** on **2Ch 3:1** 3559
p by Jeiel the scribe and Maaseiah **2Ch 26:11** 3027
Uzziah **p** for all the army shields, **2Ch 26:14** 3559
we have **p** and consecrated; **2Ch 29:19** 3559
what God had **p** for the people, **2Ch 29:36** 3559
of the LORD, and they **p** *them.* **2Ch 31:11** 3559
So the service was **p**, **2Ch 35:10** 3559
Afterwards they **p** for **2Ch 35:14** 3559
therefore the Levites **p** for **2Ch 35:14** 3559
Levites their brethren **p** for them. **2Ch 35:15** 3559
service of the LORD was **p** on that day **2Ch 35:16** 3559
Now that which was **p** for each day **Ne 5:18** 6213a
sheep, also birds were **p** for me; **Ne 5:18** 6213a
portions to him who has nothing **p**; **Ne 8:10** 3559
had **p** a large room for him, where **Ne 13:5** 6213a
banquet that I have **p** for him." **Es 5:4** 6213a
to the banquet which Esther had **p**. **Es 5:5** 6213a
to the banquet which she had **p**; **Es 5:12** 6213a
gallows which he had **p** for him. **Es 6:4** 3559

to the banquet which Esther had **p**. **Es 6:14** 6213a
which he had **p** for Mordecai, **Es 7:10** 3559
day, Who are **p** to rouse Leviathan. **Jb 3:8** 6264
As **p** for those whose feet slip. **Jb 12:5** 3559
"Behold now, I have **p** my case; **Jb 13:18** 6186a
also **p** for Himself deadly weapons; **Ps 7:13** 3559
They have **p** a net for my steps; **Ps 57:6** 3559
You have **p** the light and the sun. **Ps 74:16** 3559
I have **p** a lamp for Mine anointed. **Ps 132:17** 6186a
She has **p** her food, she has mixed **Pr 9:2** 2873
Judgments are **p** for scoffers, And **Pr 19:29** 3559
horse is **p** for the day of battle, **Pr 21:31** 3559
it has been **p** for the king. **Is 30:33** 3559
that you were created They were **p**. **Ezk 28:13** 3559
"Be **p**, and prepare yourself, you **Ezk 38:7** 3559
without blemish, shall be **p**. **Ezk 43:25** 6213a
steel When he is **p** *to march,* **Na 2:3** 3559
For the LORD has **p** a sacrifice, **Zph 1:7** 3559
and when it is **p**, she will be set **Zch 5:11** 3559
whom it has been **p** by My Father." **Mt 20:23** *2090*
YOU HAVE **P** PRAISE FOR YOURSELF'?" **Mt 21:16** *2675*
"Behold, I have **p** my dinner; **Mt 22:4** *2090*
inherit the kingdom **p** for you from **Mt 25:34** *2090*
p for the devil and his angels; **Mt 25:41** *2090*
and they **p** the Passover. **Mt 26:19** *2090*
those for whom it has been **p**." **Mk 10:40** *2090*
and they **p** the Passover. **Mk 14:16** *2090*
ready a people **p** for the Lord." **Lk 1:17** *2680*
Which You have **p** in the presence **Lk 2:31** *2090*
now who will own what you have **p**?' **Lk 12:20** *2090*
and they **p** the Passover. **Lk 22:13** *2090*
and **p** spices and perfumes. **Lk 23:56** *2090*
the spices which they had **p**. **Lk 24:1** *2090*
of wrath **p** for destruction? **Ro 9:22** *2675*
which He **p** beforehand for glory, **Ro 9:23** *4282*
ALL THAT GOD HAS **P** FOR THOSE WHO LOVE **1Co 2:9** *2090*
Now He who **p** us for this very **2Co 5:5** *2716*
Achaia has been **p** since last year, **2Co 9:2** *3903*
as I was saying, you may be **p**; **2Co 9:3** *3903*
works, which God **p** beforehand so **Eph 2:10** *4282*
the Master, **p** for every good work. **2Tm 2:21** *2090*
For there was a tabernacle **p**, **Heb 9:2** *2680*
these things have been so **p**, **Heb 9:6** *2680*
BUT A BODY YOU HAVE **P** FOR ME; **Heb 10:5** *2675*
worlds were **p** by the word of God, **Heb 11:3** *2675*
in reverence **p** an ark for the **Heb 11:7** *2680*
for He has **p** a city for them. **Heb 11:16** *2090*
p themselves to sound them. **Rv 8:6** *2090*
was like horses **p** for battle; **Rv 9:7** *2090*
who had been **p** for the hour and **Rv 9:15** *2090*
where she had a place **p** by God, **Rv 12:6** *2090*
the way would be **p** for the kings **Rv 16:12** *2090*

PREPARES

who **p** his heart to seek God, **2Ch 30:19** 3559
And their mind **p** deception." **Jb 15:35** 3559
And **p** garments as *plentiful as* the **Jb 27:16** 3559
p for the raven its nourishment When **Jb 38:41** 3559
P her food in the summer *And* **Pr 6:8** 3559

PREPARING

by **p** a room for him in the courts **Ne 13:7** 6213a
feet on the day which I am **p**," **Mal 4:3** 6213a

PRESBYTERY

the laying on of hands by the **p**. **1Tm 4:14** *4244*

PRESCRIBE

P and teach these things. **1Tm 4:11** *3853*
P these things as well, so that **1Tm 5:7** *3853*

PRESCRIBED

lampstands in the way **p** for them and **2Ch 4:7** 4941
the inner sanctuary in the way **p**; **2Ch 4:20** 4941
it in great numbers as it was **p**. **2Ch 30:5** 3789
ate the Passover otherwise than **p**. **2Ch 30:18** 3789
as **p** by David the man of God, **Ne 12:24** 4687
wine and oil **p** for the Levites, **Ne 13:5** 4687
and the **p** portion of oil **Ezk 45:14** 2706

PRESENCE

hid themselves from the **p** of the **Gn 3:8** 6440
went out from the **p** of the LORD, **Gn 4:16** 6440
Haran died in the **p** of his **Gn 11:28** 6440
harshly, and she fled from her **p**. **Gn 16:6** 6440
from the **p** of my mistress Sarai." **Gn 16:8** 6440
let him give it to me in your **p** **Gn 23:9** 8432
In the **p** of the sons of my people **Gn 23:11** 5869
in the **p** of the sons of Heth, **Gn 23:18** 5869
bless you in the **p** of the LORD **Gn 27:7** 6440
from the **p** of Isaac his father, **Gn 27:30** 6440
in the **p** of our kinsmen point out **Gn 31:32** 5048
went out from the **p** of Pharaoh and **Gn 41:46** 6440
for they were dismayed at his **p**. **Gn 45:3** 6440
Pharaoh, and went out from his **p**. **Gn 47:10** 6440
for why should we die in your **p**? **Gn 47:15** 5048
But Moses fled from the **p** of **Ex 2:15** 6440
When they left Pharaoh's **p**, **Ex 5:20** 4480, 854
were driven out from Pharaoh's **p**. **Ex 10:11** 6440
set the bread of the **P** on the table **Ex 25:30** 6440
"My **p** shall go *with you,* and I **Ex 33:14** 6440
"If Your **p** does not go *with us,* do **Ex 33:15** 6440
utensils, and the bread of the **P**; **Ex 35:13** 6440
of Israel departed from Moses' **p**. **Ex 35:20** 6440
utensils, and the bread of the **P**; **Ex 39:36** 6440
p of the LORD and consumed them, **Lv 10:2** 6440
the **p** of the LORD and died. **Lv 16:1** 6440
"Over the table of the bread of the **P** **Nu 4:7** 6440
fell on their faces in the **p** of all the **Nu 14:5** 6440
in the **p** of the LORD tomorrow; **Nu 16:7** 6440
all the rods from the **p** of the LORD **Nu 17:9** 6440
camp and be slaughtered in his **p**. **Nu 19:3** 6440
came in from the **p** of the assembly **Nu 20:6** 6440
in the **p** of the LORD to battle, **Nu 32:27** 6440
the Jordan in the **p** of the LORD, **Nu 32:29** 6440
cross over armed in the **p** of the LORD **Nu 32:32** 6440
eat in the **p** of the LORD your God, **Dt 14:23** 6440
and there you shall eat in the **p** **Dt 14:26** 6440
in the **p** of the Levitical priests. **Dt 17:18** 6440
him lie down and be beaten in his **p** **Dt 25:2** 6440
today in the **p** of the LORD our God **Dt 29:15** 6440
in the **p** of the sons of Israel. **Jos 8:32** 6440
quaked at the **p** of the LORD, **Jg 5:5** 6440
This Sinai, at the **p** of the LORD, **Jg 5:5** 6440
David escaped from his **p** twice. **1Sa 18:11** 6440
Saul removed him from his **p** and **1Sa 18:13** 5973
and he was in his **p** as formerly. **1Sa 19:7** 6440
he slipped away out of Saul's **p**, **1Sa 19:10** 6440
no bread there but the bread of the **P** **1Sa 21:6** 6440
one to act the madman in my **p**? **1Sa 21:15** 5921
away from the **p** of the LORD; **1Sa 26:20** 6440
"Now throw this woman out of my **p**, **2Sa 13:17**
I not serve in the **p** of his son? **2Sa 16:19** 6440
I have served in your father's **p**, **2Sa 16:19** 6440
so I will be in your **p**." **2Sa 16:19** 6440
David sought the **p** of the LORD. **2Sa 21:1** 6440
went out from the **p** of the king to **2Sa 24:4** 6440
she came into the king's **p** and stood **1Ki 1:28** 6440
And they came into the king's **p**. **1Ki 1:32** 6440
on which *was* the bread of the **P**; **1Ki 7:48** 6440
in the **p** of all the assembly of Israel **1Ki 8:22** 5048
was seeking the **p** of Solomon, **1Ki 10:24** 6440
fled from the **p** of King Solomon). **1Ki 12:2** 6440
were it not that I regard the **p** of **2Ki 3:14** 6440
his **p** a leper *as white* as snow. **2Ki 5:27** 6440
the king sent a man from his **p**; **2Ki 6:32** 6440
or cast them from His **p** until now. **2Ki 13:23** 6440
Shaphan read it in the **p** of the king. **2Ki 22:10** 6440
until He cast them out from His **p**. **2Ki 24:20** 6440
and had his meals in the king's **p** **2Ki 25:29** 6440
them in the **p** of the king, **1Ch 24:6** 6440
Aaron in the **p** of David the king, **1Ch 24:31** 6440
with the bread of the **P** on them, **2Ch 4:19** 6440
in the **p** of all the assembly of Israel **2Ch 6:12** 5048
p of all the assembly of Israel and **2Ch 6:13** 5048
were seeking the **p** of Solomon, **2Ch 9:23** 6440
fled from the **p** of King Solomon), **2Ch 10:2** 6440
the altars of the Baals in his **p**, **2Ch 34:4** 6440
read from it in the **p** of the king. **2Ch 34:18** 6440
in the **p** of the king of Judah. **2Ch 34:24** 6440
Now I had not been sad in his **p**. **Ne 2:1** 6440
He spoke in the **p** of his **Ne 4:2** 6440
about his good deeds in my **p** **Ne 6:19** 6440
midday, in the **p** of men and women, **Ne 8:3** 5048
of his provinces being in his **p**. **Es 1:3** 6440
served in the **p** of King Ahasuerus, **Es 1:10** 6440
Media who had access to the king's **p** **Es 1:14** 6440
the **p** of the king and the princes, **Es 1:16** 6440
Vashti to be brought in to his **p**, **Es 1:17** 6440
come into the **p** of King Ahasuerus, **Es 1:19** 6440
of the Chronicles in the king's **p**. **Es 2:23** 6440
Then Mordecai went out from the **p** **Es 8:15** 6440
departed from the **p** of the LORD. **Jb 1:12** 6440
went out from the **p** of the LORD and **Jb 2:7** 6440
man may not come before His **p**. **Jb 13:16** 6440
in the **p** of darkness **Jb 17:12** 6440
I would be dismayed at His **p**; **Jb 23:15** 6440
"Its noise declares His **p**; **Jb 36:33** 5921
In Your **p** is fullness of joy; **Ps 16:11** 6440
my judgment come forth from Your **p**; **Ps 17:2** 6440
him joyful with gladness in Your **p**. **Ps 21:6** 6440
before me in the **p** of my enemies; **Ps 23:5** 5048
p from the conspiracies of man; **Ps 31:20** 6440
While the wicked are in my **p**." **Ps 39:1** 5048
You set me in Your **p** forever. **Ps 41:12** 6440
praise Him *For* the help of His **p**. **Ps 42:5** 6440
Your arm and the light of Your **p**, **Ps 44:3** 6440
p of the enemy and the avenger. **Ps 44:16** 6440
Do not cast me away from Your **p** And **Ps 51:11** 6440
good, in the **p** of Your godly ones. **Ps 52:9** 5048
also dropped *rain* at the **p** of God; **Ps 68:8** 6440
Sinai itself *quaked* at the **p** of God, **Ps 68:8** 6440
in Your **p** when once You are angry? **Ps 76:7** 6440
secret *sins* in the light of Your **p**. **Ps 90:8** 6440
before His **p** with thanksgiving, **Ps 95:2** 6440
like wax at the **p** of the LORD, **Ps 97:5** 6440
At the **p** of the Lord of the whole **Ps 97:5** 6440
In the **p** of all their captors. **Ps 106:46** 6440
it be in the **p** of all His people. **Ps 116:14** 5048
it be in the **p** of all His people, **Ps 116:18** 5048
Or where can I flee from Your **p**? **Ps 139:7** 6440
The upright will dwell in Your **p**. **Ps 140:13** 6440
you, To seek your **p** earnestly, **Pr 7:15** 6440
Leave the **p** of a fool, Or you will **Pr 14:7** 5048
guarantor in the **p** of his neighbor. **Pr 17:18** 6440
Wisdom is in the **p** of the one who **Pr 17:24** 6440
claim honor in the **p** of the king, **Pr 25:6** 6440
placed lower in the **p** of the prince, **Pr 25:7** 6440
bring up a matter in the **p** of God. **Ec 5:2** 6440
in the **p** of the messenger *of God* **Ec 5:6** 6440
are devouring them in your **p**; **Is 1:7** 5048
To rebel against His glorious **p**. **Is 3:8** 5869
They will be glad in Your **p** As with **Is 9:3** 6440
idols of Egypt will tremble at His **p**, **Is 19:1** 6440
who dwell in the **p** of the LORD. **Is 23:18** 6440
cut off or destroyed from My **p**." **Is 48:19** 6440
And the angel of His **p** saved them; **Is 63:9** 6440
mountains might quake at Your **p** **Is 64:1** 6440
the nations may tremble at Your **p**! **Is 64:2** 6440
the mountains quaked at Your **p**. **Is 64:3** 6440
your detested things from My **p**, **Jer 4:1** 6440
'Do you not tremble in My **p**? **Jer 5:22** 6440
send them away from My **p** **Jer 15:1** 6440
utterance of my lips Was in Your **p**. **Jer 17:16** 6440
you and cast you away from My **p**, **Jer 23:39** 6440
in the **p** of the priests and all the **Jer 28:1** 5869
Hananiah in the **p** of the priests **Jer 28:5** 5869
and in the **p** of all the people who **Jer 28:5** 5869
spoke in the **p** of all the people, **Jer 28:11** 5869
"And I commanded Baruch in their **p**, **Jer 32:13** 5869
until He cast them out from His **p**. **Jer 52:3** 6440
and had his meals in the king's **p** **Jer 52:33** 6440
water Before the **p** of the Lord; **La 2:19** 6440
justice In the **p** of the Most High, **La 3:35** 6440
The **p** of the LORD has scattered **La 4:16** 6440
words nor be dismayed at their **p**, **Ezk 2:6** 6440
am a god," In the **p** of your slayer, **Ezk 28:9** 6440
of the earth will shake at My **p**; **Ezk 38:20** 6440
appearance be observed in your **p** and **Da 1:13** 6440
Take me into the king's **p**, **Da 2:24** 6925
brought Daniel into the king's **p** **Da 2:25** 6925
I gave orders to bring into my **p** all **Da 4:6** 6925
wine in the **p** of the thousand. **Da 5:1** 6903
Tarshish from the **p** of the LORD. **Jon 1:3** 6440
Tarshish from the **p** of the LORD. **Jon 1:3** 6440
fleeing from the **p** of the LORD, **Jon 1:10** 6440
the earth is upheaved by His **p**, **Na 1:5** 6440
who stands in the **p** of God, **Lk 1:19** *1799*
prepared in the **p** of all peoples, **Lk 2:31** *4383*
and declared in the **p** of all the **Lk 8:47** *1799*
'We ate and drank in Your **p**, **Lk 13:26** *1799*
joy in the **p** of the angels of God **Lk 15:10** *1799*
them here and slay them in my **p**." **Lk 19:27** *1715*
a saying in the **p** of the people; **Lk 20:26** *1727*
in the **p** of the disciples, **Jn 20:30** *1799*
SAW THE LORD ALWAYS IN MY **P**; **Ac 2:25** *1799*
ME FULL OF GLADNESS WITH YOUR **P**.' **Ac 2:28** *4383*
and disowned in the **p** of Pilate, **Ac 3:13** *4383*
health in the **p** of you all. **Ac 3:16** *561*
may come from the **p** of the Lord; **Ac 3:19** *4383*
way from the **p** of the Council, **Ac 5:41** *4383*
thanks to God in the **p** of all, **Ac 27:35** *1799*
in the **p** of Him whom he believed, **Ro 4:17** *2713*
for your sakes in the **p** of Christ, **2Co 2:10** *4383*
his personal **p** is unimpressive and **2Co 10:10** *3952*
I said to Cephas in the **p** of all, **Ga 2:14** *1715*
obeyed, not as in my **p** only, **Php 2:12** *3952*
in the **p** of our God and Father, **1Th 1:3** *1715*
in the **p** of our Lord Jesus at His **1Th 2:19** *1715*
away from the **p** of the Lord and **2Th 1:9** *4383*
in sin, rebuke in the **p** of all, **1Tm 5:20** *1799*
solemnly charge you in the **p** of God **1Tm 5:21** *1799*
in the **p** of many witnesses. **1Tm 6:12** *1799*
I charge you in the **p** of God, **1Tm 6:13** *1799*
me in the **p** of many witnesses, **2Tm 2:2** *1223*
solemnly charge *them* in the **p** of God **2Tm 2:14** *1799*
the **p** of God and of Christ Jesus, **2Tm 4:1** *1799*
to appear in the **p** of God for us; **Heb 9:24** *4383*
yourselves in the **p** of the Lord, **Jas 4:10** *1799*
and to make you stand in the **p** of **Jude 1:24** *2714*
hide us from the **p** of Him who sits **Rv 6:16** *4383*
a time, from the **p** of the serpent. **Rv 12:14** *4383*
of the first beast in his **p**. **Rv 13:12** *1799*
to the earth in the **p** of men. **Rv 13:13** *1799*
to perform in the **p** of the beast, **Rv 13:14** *1799*
in the **p** of the holy angels and in the **Rv 14:10** *1799*
angels and in the **p** of the Lamb. **Rv 14:10** *1799*
who performed the signs in his **p**, **Rv 19:20** *1799*
from whose **p** earth and heaven fled **Rv 20:11** *4383*

PRESENT

with him a **p** for his brother Esau: **Gn 32:13** 4503
it is a **p** sent to my lord Esau. **Gn 32:18** 4503
with the **p** that goes before me. **Gn 32:20** 4503
So the **p** passed on before him, **Gn 32:21** 4503
then take my **p** from my hand, **Gn 33:10** 4503
and carry down to the man as a **p**, **Gn 43:11** 4503
So the men took this **p**, **Gn 43:15** 4503
prepared the **p** for Joseph's coming **Gn 43:25** 4503
brought into the house to him the **p** **Gn 43:26** 4503
to bring about this **p** result, **Gn 50:20** 3117
and **p** yourself before Pharaoh, **Ex 8:20** 3320
and **p** them in the basket along **Ex 29:3** 7126
and **p** yourself there to Me on the **Ex 34:2** 5324
he shall **p** an offering by fire to **Lv 3:3** 7126
'From it he shall **p** his offering **Lv 3:14** 7126
the sons of Aaron shall **p** it **Lv 6:14** 7126
which Aaron and his sons are to **p** to **Lv 6:20** 7126
You shall **p** the grain offering in **Lv 6:21** 7126
he shall **p** his offering with cakes **Lv 7:13** 7126
'Of this he shall **p** one of **Lv 7:14** 7126
sons of Israel to **p** their offerings to **Lv 7:38** 7126
to **p** as a wave offering before the **Lv 10:15** 5130
shall **p** the man to be cleansed **Lv 14:11** 5975
and **p** them as a wave offering **Lv 14:12** 5130
shall take the two goats and **p** them **Lv 16:7** 5975
to **p** *it* as an offering to the LORD **Lv 17:4** 7126
for they **p** the offerings by fire **Lv 21:6** 7126
which they **p** to the LORD for a **Lv 22:18** 7126
may **p** it for a freewill offering, **Lv 22:23** 6213a
'But for seven days you shall **p** an **Lv 23:8** 7126
then you shall **p** a new grain **Lv 23:16** 7126
you shall **p** seven one year old **Lv 23:18** 7126
but you shall **p** an offering by **Lv 23:25** 7126
and **p** an offering by fire to the LORD. **Lv 23:27** 7126
'For seven days you shall **p** an **Lv 23:36** 7126
and **p** an offering by fire to the LORD; **Lv 23:36** 7126
to **p** offerings by fire to the LORD **Lv 23:37** 7126
can **p** as an offering to the LORD, **Lv 27:9** 7126
not **p** as an offering to the LORD, **Lv 27:11** 7126
shall **p** his offering to the LORD: **Nu 6:14** 7126
'Then the priest shall **p** *them* **Nu 6:16** 7126

"Let them **p** their offering, one Nu 7:11 7126
"So you shall **p** the Levites Nu 8:9 7126
and **p** the Levites before the LORD; Nu 8:10 7126
"Aaron then shall **p** the Levites Nu 8:11 5130
so as to **p** them as a wave offering Nu 8:13 5130
and **p** them as a wave offering; Nu 8:15 5130
for he did not **p** the offering of Nu 9:13 7126
shall **p** to the LORD a grain offering Nu 15:4 7126
be **p** before the LORD tomorrow, Nu 16:16 1961
since they did **p** them before the Nu 16:38 7126
then you shall **p** an offering from Nu 18:26 7311
'So you shall also **p** an offering Nu 18:28 7311
'Out of all your gifts you shall **p** Nu 18:29 7311
shall be careful to **p** My offering, Nu 28:2 7126
p a burnt offering to the LORD: Nu 28:11 7126
You shall **p** an offering by fire, Nu 28:19 7126
'You shall **p** these besides the Nu 28:23 6213a
this manner you shall **p** daily, Nu 28:24 6213a
when you **p** a new grain offering to Nu 28:26 7126
shall **p** *them* with their drink offerings. Nu 28:31 6213a
'You shall **p** a burnt offering Nu 29:8 7126
'You shall **p** a burnt offering, Nu 29:13 7126
'But you shall **p** a burnt offering, Nu 29:36 7126
'You shall **p** these to the LORD at Nu 29:39 6213a
and **p** yourselves at the tent of Dt 31:14 3320
no **p** to bring to the man of God. 1Sa 9:7 8670
p yourselves before the LORD by 1Sa 10:19 3320
him and did not bring him any **p**. 1Sa 10:27 4503
the people who were **p** with him, 1Sa 13:15 4672
Jonathan and the people who were **p** 1Sa 13:16 4672
and a **p** from the king was sent out 2Sa 11:8 4864
days, and be **p** here yourself." 2Sa 20:4 5975
sent you a **p** of silver and gold; 1Ki 15:19 7810
take a **p** from your servant now." 2Ki 5:15 1293
sent a **p** to the king of Assyria. 2Ki 16:8 7810
sent letters and a **p** to Hezekiah, 2Ki 20:12 4503
seen Your people, who are **p** here, 1Ch 29:17 4672
priests who were **p** had sanctified 2Ch 5:11 4672
the king and all who were **p** with 2Ch 29:29 4672
The sons of Israel **p** in 2Ch 30:21 4672
all Israel who were **p** went out to 2Ch 31:1 4672
he made all who were **p** in 2Ch 34:32 4672
and made all who were **p** in Israel 2Ch 34:33 4672
the lay people, to all who were **p**, 2Ch 35:7 4672
the lay people to **p** to the LORD, 2Ch 35:12 7126
sons of Israel who were **p** celebrated 2Ch 35:17 4672
all Judah and Israel who were **p**, 2Ch 35:18 4672
princes and all Israel **p** *there* Ezr 8:25 4672
who were **p** at the citadel in Susa, Es 1:5 4672
to **p** themselves before the LORD, Jb 1:6 3320
to **p** themselves before the LORD, Jb 2:1 3320
them to **p** himself before the LORD. Jb 2:1 3320
"I would **p** *my* case before Him And Jb 23:4 6186a
A very **p** help in trouble. Ps 46:1 4672
may **p** to You a heart of wisdom. Ps 90:12 935
p you with a crown of beauty." Pr 4:9 4042
sent letters and a **p** to Hezekiah, Is 39:1 4503
"**P** your case," the LORD says. Is 41:21 7126
Let them **p** their witnesses that Is 43:9 5414
me to **p** your petition before Him: Jer 42:9 5307
you shall **p** a young bull without Ezk 43:23 7126
'You shall **p** them before the LORD, Ezk 43:24 7126
and gave orders to **p** to him an Da 2:46 5260
we may **p** the fruit of our lips. Hos 14:2 7999a
"Did you **p** Me with sacrifices and Am 5:25 5066
Shall I **p** my firstborn *for* my Mi 6:7 5414
you **p** the blind for sacrifice, Mal 1:8 5066
And when you **p** the lame and sick, Mal 1:8 5066
so that they may **p** to the LORD Mal 3:3 5066
and then come and **p** your offering. Mt 5:24 *4374*
and **p** the offering that Moses Mt 8:4 *4374*
or by what parable shall we **p** it? Mk 4:30 *5087*
times as much now in the **p** age, Mk 10:30 *3778*
to Jerusalem to **p** Him to the Lord Lk 2:22 *3936*
and the power of the Lord was **p** Lk 5:17
do you not analyze this **p** time? Lk 12:56
were some **p** who reported to Him Lk 13:1 *3918b*
"So in the **p** case, I say to Ac 5:38 *3568*
we are all here **p** before God to Ac 10:33 *3918b*
with those who happened to be **p**. Ac 17:17 *3909*
James, and all the elders were **p**. Ac 21:18 *3854*
to my nation and to **p** offerings; Ac 24:17 *4160*
ought to have been **p** before you and Ac 24:19 *3918b*
"Go away for the **p**, and when I Ac 24:25 *3568*
all you gentlemen here **p** with us, Ac 25:24 *4840*
His righteousness at the **p** time, Ro 3:26 *3568*
but **p** yourselves to God as those Ro 6:13 *3936*
Do you not know that when you **p** Ro 6:16 *3936*
so now **p** your members as slaves to Ro 6:19 *3936*
for the willing is **p** in me, Ro 7:18 *3873*
principle that evil is **p** in me, Ro 7:21 *3873*
the sufferings of this **p** time are not Ro 8:18 *3568*
nor principalities, nor things **p**, Ro 8:38 *1764*
come to be at the **p** time a remnant Ro 11:5 *3568*
to **p** your bodies a living and holy Ro 12:1 *3936*
or things **p** or things to come; 1Co 3:22 *1764*
To this **p** hour we are both hungry 1Co 4:11 *737*
absent in body but **p** in spirit, 1Co 5:3 *3918b*
this, as though I were **p**. 1Co 5:3 *3918b*
is good in view of the **p** distress, 1Co 7:26 *1764*
with Jesus and will **p** us with you. 2Co 4:14 *3936*
For if the readiness is **p**, 2Co 8:12 *4295*
at this **p** time your abundance 2Co 8:14 *3568*
I ask that when I am **p** I *need* not 2Co 10:2 *3918b*
we are also in deed when **p**. 2Co 10:11 *3918b*
I might **p** you *as* a pure virgin. 2Co 11:2 *3936*
I was **p** with you and was in need, 2Co 11:9 *3918b*
said when **p** the second time, 2Co 13:2 *3918b*
when **p** I *need* not use severity, 2Co 13:10 *3918b*
rescue us from this **p** evil age, Ga 1:4 *1764*
and not only when I am **p** with you. Ga 4:18 *3918b*
but I could wish to be **p** with you Ga 4:20 *3918b*
corresponds to the **p** Jerusalem, Ga 4:25 *3568*
that He might **p** to Himself the Eph 5:27 *3936*
in order to **p** you before Him holy Col 1:22 *3936*
p every man complete in Christ. Col 1:28 *3936*
since it holds promise for the **p** 1Tm 4:8 *3568*
those who are rich in this **p** world not 1Tm 6:17 *3568*
Be diligent to **p** yourself approved 2Tm 2:15 *3936*
Demas, having loved this **p** world, 2Tm 4:10 *3568*
and godly in the **p** age, Ti 2:12 *3568*
which *is* a symbol for the **p** time. Heb 9:9 *1764*
in the truth which is **p** with *you.* 2Pe 1:12 *3918b*
by His word the **p** heavens and earth 2Pe 3:7 *3568*

PRESENTABLE

and our less **p** members become much 1Co 12:23 *809*
members become much more **p**, 1Co 12:23 *2157*
whereas our more **p** members have no 1Co 12:24 *2158*

PRESENTED

brothers and **p** them to Pharaoh. Gn 47:2 3322, 6440
father Jacob and **p** him to Pharaoh; Gn 47:7 5975, 6440
so *did* every man who **p** an offering Ex 35:22 5130
it shall be **p** to the priest and he Lv 2:8 7126
the burnt offering which he has **p**. Lv 7:8 7126
which shall be **p** to the LORD. Lv 7:11 7126
that the breast may be **p** as a wave Lv 7:30 5130
in that day when he **p** them to Lv 7:35 7126
p the ram of the burnt offering, Lv 8:18 7126
Then he **p** the second ram, the ram Lv 8:22 7126
and **p** them as a wave offering Lv 8:27 5130
Moses also took the breast and **p** Lv 8:29 5130
Aaron's sons **p** the blood to him; Lv 9:9 7126
Then he **p** the people's offering, Lv 9:15 7126
He also **p** the burnt offering, and Lv 9:16 7126
Next he **p** the grain offering, and Lv 9:17 7126
Aaron **p** as a wave offering before Lv 9:21 5130
they **p** their sin offering and their Lv 10:19 7126
shall be **p** alive before the LORD, Lv 16:10 5975
they **p** them before the tabernacle. Nu 7:3 7126
Now the one who **p** his offering on Nu 7:12 7126
leader of Issachar, **p** *an offering;* Nu 7:18 7126
he **p** as his offering one silver Nu 7:19 7126
and Aaron **p** them as a wave Nu 8:21 5130
it shall be **p** with its drink offering in Nu 28:24 6213a
So Moses and Joshua went and **p** Dt 31:14 3320
and they **p** themselves before God. Jos 24:1 3320
He **p** the tribute to Eglon king Jg 3:17 7126
to him under the oak and **p** *them.* Jg 6:19 5066
and there they **p** the provocation Ezk 20:28 5414
p them before Nebuchadnezzar. Da 1:18 935
of Days And was **p** before Him. Da 7:13 7127
they **p** to Him gifts of gold, Mt 2:11 *4374*
Jesus **p** another parable to them, Mt 13:24 *3908*
He **p** another parable to them, Mt 13:31 *3908*
To these He also **p** Himself alive after Ac 1:3 *3936*
saints and widows, he **p** her alive. Ac 9:41 *3936*
governor, they also **p** Paul to him. Ac 23:33 *3936*
For just as you **p** your members as Ro 6:19 *3936*

PRESENTING

why are we restrained from **p** the Nu 9:7 7126
manner, in **p** an offering by fire, Nu 15:13 7126
he had finished **p** the tribute, Jg 3:18 7126
I was **p** my petition before the king, Jer 38:26 5307
the king had specified for **p** them, Da 1:18 935
for we are not **p** our supplications Da 9:18 5307
and **p** my supplication before the Da 9:20 5307
are **p** defiled food upon My altar. Mal 1:7 5066
are **p** your offering at the altar, Mt 5:23 *4374*
and do not go on **p** the members of Ro 6:13 *3936*

PRESENTS

'Now when anyone **p** a grain Lv 2:1 7126
to whom it belongs on the day *he* **p** Lv 6:5
who **p** any man's burnt offering, Lv 7:8 7126
belong to the priest who **p** it. Lv 7:9 7126
in Israel who **p** his offering, Lv 22:18 7126
'The one who **p** his offering Nu 15:4 7126
p to Hezekiah king of Judah, 2Ch 32:23 4030
and of the islands bring **p**; Ps 72:10 7725
come about when Moab **p** himself, Is 16:12 7200
or who **p** an offering to the LORD Mal 2:12 5066

PRESERVATION

some food, for this is for your **p**, Ac 27:34 *4991*

PRESERVE

p our family through our father." Gn 19:32 2421a
p our family through our father." Gn 19:34 2421a
God sent me before you to **p** life. Gn 45:5 4241
to **p** for you a remnant in the earth, Gn 45:7 7760
result, to **p** many people alive. Gn 50:20 2421a
"I have no son to **p** my name." 2Sa 18:18 2142
p this forever in the intentions 1Ch 29:18 8104
You will **p** him from this Ps 12:7 5341
P me, O God, for I take refuge in Ps 16:1 8104
integrity and uprightness **p** me, Ps 25:21 5341
You **p** me from trouble; Ps 32:7 5341
O LORD, You **p** man and beast. Ps 36:6 3467
Your truth will continually **p** me. Ps 40:11 5341
and truth that they may **p** him. Ps 61:7 5341
P my life from dread of the enemy. Ps 64:1 5341
p those who are doomed to die. Ps 79:11 3498
P my soul, for I am a godly man; O Ps 86:2 8104
P me from violent men Ps 140:1 5341
P me from violent men Who have Ps 140:4 5341
Loyalty and truth **p** the king, Pr 20:28 5341
The eyes of the LORD **p** knowledge, Pr 22:12 5341
"**P** justice and do righteousness, Is 56:1 8104
but **p** the lives *of others* for Ezk 13:18 2421a
his wicked way *and* **p** his life, Ezk 13:22 2421a
But you will not **p** *anything,* Mi 6:14 6403
And what you do **p** I will give to Mi 6:14 6403
lips of a priest should **p** knowledge, Mal 2:7 8104
whoever loses *his life* will **p** it. Lk 17:33 *2225*
diligent to **p** the unity of the Spirit Eph 4:3 *5083*

PRESERVED

to face, yet my life has been **p**." Gn 32:30 5337
p us through all the way in which we Jos 24:17 8104
And Your care has **p** my spirit. Jb 10:12 8104
They are **p** forever, Ps 37:28 8104
to restore the **p** ones of Israel; Is 49:6 5336
fresh wineskins, and both are **p**." Mt 9:17 *4933*
and soul and body be **p** complete, 1Th 5:23 *5083*
But *women* will be **p** through the 1Tm 2:15 *4982*
the ancient world, but **p** Noah, 2Pe 2:5 *5442*

PRESERVES

who **p** the covenant and Ne 1:5 8104
The LORD **p** the faithful And fully Ps 31:23 5341
Who **p** the souls of His godly ones; Ps 97:10 8104
The LORD **p** the simple; Ps 116:6 8104
He **p** the way of His godly ones. Pr 2:8 8104
one who guards his mouth **p** his life; Pr 13:3 8104
He who watches his way **p** his life. Pr 16:17 8104
wisdom **p** the lives of its possessors. Ec 7:12 2421a

PRESERVING

have faith to the **p** of the soul. Heb 10:39 *4047*

PRESIDING

Samuel standing *and* **p** over them, 1Sa 19:20 5324

PRESS

was beating out wheat in the wine **p** Jg 6:11 1660
killed Zeeb at the wine **p** of Zeeb, Jg 7:25 3342
floor, or from the wine **p**?" 2Ki 6:27 3342
Or **p** down his tongue with a cord? Jb 41:1 8257
bow And from the **p** of battle. Is 21:15 3514
the one who treads in the wine **p**? Is 63:2 1660
Lord has trodden *as in* a wine **p** La 1:15 1660
he will **p** on with a great army Da 11:13 935
let us **p** on to know the LORD. Hos 6:3 7291
and wine **p** will not feed them, Hos 9:2 3342
tread, for the wine **p** is full; Jl 3:13 1660
AROUND IT AND DUG A WINE **P** IN IT, Mt 21:33 *3025b*
AND DUG A VAT UNDER THE WINE **P** Mk 12:1 *5276*
but I **p** on so that I may lay Php 3:12 *1377*
I **p** on toward the goal for the Php 3:14 *1377*
Christ, let us **p** on to maturity, Heb 6:1 *5342*
great wine **p** of the wrath of God. Rv 14:19 *3025b*
wine **p** was trodden outside the city, Rv 14:20 *3025b*
blood came out from the wine **p**, Rv 14:20 *3025b*
wine **p** of the fierce wrath of God, Rv 19:15 *3025b*

PRESSED

So they **p** hard against Lot and Gn 19:9 6484
The taskmasters **p** them, Ex 5:13 213
she **p** herself to the wall and Nu 22:25 3905
and **p** Balaam's foot against the wall, Nu 22:25 3905
hand of the sons of Israel **p** heavier Jg 4:24 1980
her because she **p** him so hard. Jg 14:17 6693
she **p** him daily with her words and Jg 16:16 6693
but we **p** them as far as the 2Sa 11:23 1961, 5921
And Your hand has **p** down on me. Ps 38:2 5181
raw wounds, Not **p** out or bandaged, Is 1:6 2115
there their breasts were **p** and Ezk 23:3 4600
whom they **p** into service to bear Mt 27:32 *29*
those who had afflictions **p** around Him Mk 3:10 *1968*
They **p** into service a Mk 15:21 *29*
good measure—**p** down, shaken Lk 6:38 *4085*

PRESSES

treading wine **p** on the sabbath, Ne 13:15 1660
They tread wine **p** but thirst. Jb 24:11 3342
treader treads out wine in the **p**, Is 16:10 3342
the wine to cease from the wine **p**; Jer 48:33 3342
of Hananel to the king's wine **p**. Zch 14:10 3342

PRESSING

And **p** the nose brings forth blood; Pr 30:33 4330
was following Him and **p** in on Him. Mk 5:24 *4918*
"You see the crowd **p** in on You, Mk 5:31 *4918*
the crowd was **p** around Him Lk 5:1 *1945*
the crowds were **p** against Him. Lk 8:42 *4846*
are crowding and **p** in on You." Lk 8:45 *598*
in good deeds to meet **p** needs, Ti 3:14 *316*

PRESSURE

should my **p** weigh heavily on you. Jb 33:7 405
Because of the **p** of the wicked; Ps 55:3 6125
daily **p** on me *of* concern for all 2Co 11:28 *1988a*

PRESUME

is he, who would **p** to do thus?" Es 7:5 4390, 3820
For I will not **p** to speak of Ro 15:18 *5111*

PRESUMPTUOUS

keep back Your servant from **p** *sins;* Ps 19:13 2086

PRESUMPTUOUSLY

a man acts **p** toward his neighbor, Ex 21:14 2102
and acted **p** and went up into the Dt 1:43 2102
"The man who acts **p** by not Dt 17:12 2087
afraid, and will not act **p** again. Dt 17:13 2102
who speaks a word **p** in My name Dt 18:20 2102
The prophet has spoken it **p**; Dt 18:22 2087

PRETEND

down on your bed and **p** to be ill; 2Sa 13:5 2470a
"Please **p** to be a mourner, and 2Sa 14:2 56
"Foreigners **p** obedience to me; 2Sa 22:45 3584
she will **p** to be another woman." 1Ki 14:5 5235a
why do you **p** to be another woman? 1Ki 14:6 5235a
the LORD would **p** obedience to Him, Ps 81:15 3584

PRETENDED
Israel **p** to be beaten before them, **Jos 8:15** 5060
So Amnon lay down and **p** to be ill; **2Sa 13:6** 2470a
sent spies who **p** to be righteous, **Lk 20:20** *5271*

PRETENDERS
men, Nor will I go with **p**. **Ps 26:4** 5956

PRETENDS
There is one who **p** to be rich, **Pr 13:7** 6238
Another **p** to be poor, but has **Pr 13:7** 7326

PRETENSE
for a **p** you make long prayers; **Mt 23:14** *4392*
on the **p** of intending to lay out **Ac 27:30** *4392*
way, whether in **p** or in truth, **Php 1:18** *4392*

PRETEXT
'What **p** for a case against him can **Jb 19:28** 8328
nor with a **p** for greed **1Th 2:5** *4392*

PRETEXTS
'Behold, He invents **p** against me; **Jb 33:10** 8569

PRETTY
"Egypt is a **p** heifer, *But* a **Jer 46:20** 3304

PREVAIL
For not by might shall a man **p**. **1Sa 2:9** 1396
if I **p** against him and kill him, **1Sa 17:9** 3201
accomplish much and surely **p**." **1Sa 26:25** 3201
'You are to entice *him* and also **p**. **1Ki 22:22** 3201
let not man **p** against You." **2Ch 14:11** 6113
'You are to entice *him* and **p** also. **2Ch 18:21** 3201
Arise, O LORD, do not let man **p**; **Ps 9:19** 5810
"With our tongue we will **p**; **Ps 12:4** 1396
Iniquities **p** against me; **Ps 65:3** 1396
to pray, That he will not **p**. **Is 16:12** 3201
He will **p** against His enemies. **Is 42:13** 1396
the waves toss, yet they cannot **p**; **Jer 5:22** 3201
Lies and not truth **p** in the land; **Jer 9:3** 1396
you, They will not **p** over you; **Jer 15:20** 3201
so that we may **p** against him And **Jer 20:10** 3201
persecutors will stumble and not **p**. **Jer 20:11** 3201
yet he will not **p**. **Da 11:12** 5810
And their voices *began* to **p**. **Lk 23:23** *2729*
AND **P** WHEN YOU ARE JUDGED." **Ro 3:4** *3528*

PREVAILED
The water **p** and increased **Gn 7:18** 1396
The water **p** more and more upon **Gn 7:19** 1396
The water **p** fifteen cubits higher, **Gn 7:20** 1396
The water **p** upon the earth one **Gn 7:24** 1396
my sister, *and* I have indeed **p**." **Gn 30:8** 3201
saw that he had not **p** against him, **Gn 32:25** 3201
God and with men and have **p**." **Gn 32:28** 3201
held his hand up, that Israel **p**, **Ex 17:11** 1396
he let his hand down, Amalek **p**. **Ex 17:11** 1396
that he **p** over Cushan-rishathaim. **Jg 3:10** 5810, 3027
power of Midian **p** against Israel. **Jg 6:2** 5810
Thus David **p** over the Philistine **1Sa 17:50** 2388
"The men **p** against us and came **2Sa 11:23** 1396
the king's word **p** against Joab and **2Sa 24:4** 2388
the people who followed Omri **p** over **1Ki 16:22** 2388
Though Judah **p** over his brothers, **1Ch 5:2** 1396
the king's word **p** against Joab. **1Ch 21:4** 2388
the Ammonites and **p** over them **2Ch 27:5** 2388
Yet they have not **p** against me. **Ps 129:2** 3201
You have overcome me and **p**. **Jer 20:7** 3201
into my bones, And it **p** *over them.* **La 1:13** 7287a
Because the enemy has **p**." **La 1:16** 1396
prophet is **p** upon to speak a word, **Ezk 14:9** 6601b
who have **p** upon that prophet, **Ezk 14:9** 6601b
he wrestled with the angel and **p**; **Hos 12:4** 3201
And she **p** upon us. **Ac 16:15** *3849*

PREVAILING
Lord was growing mightily and **p**. **Ac 19:20** *2480*

PREVALENT
the sun and it is **p** among men **Ec 6:1** 7227a

PREVENT
in order to **p** *anyone* from going out **1Ki 15:17** 1115, 5414
in order to **p** *anyone* from going out **2Ch 16:1** 1115, 5414
But John tried to **p** Him, **Mt 3:14** *1254*
and we tried to **p** him because he was **Mk 9:38** *2967*
and we tried to **p** him because he does **Lk 9:49** *2967*
and not to **p** any of his friends **Ac 24:23** *2967*

PREVENTED
has **p** me from bearing *children.* **Gn 16:2** 6113
eyes were **p** from recognizing Him. **Lk 24:16** *2902*
and have been **p** so far **Ro 1:13** *2967*
For this reason I have often been **p** **Ro 15:22** *1465*
were **p** by death from continuing, **Heb 7:23** *2967*

PREVENTS
What **p** me from being baptized?" **Ac 8:36** *2967*

PREVIOUS
besides the **p** famine that had **Gn 26:1** 7223
he will be different from the **p** ones **Da 7:24** 6933
have set aside their **p** pledge. **1Tm 5:12** *4413*

PREVIOUSLY
p the name of the city had been **Gn 28:19** 7223
people straw to make brick as **p**; **Ex 5:7** 8543, 8032a
bricks which they were making **p**, **Ex 5:8** 8543, 8032a
or today in making brick as **p**?" **Ex 5:14** 8543, 8032a
ox was **p** in the habit of goring and **Ex 21:29** 8543, 8032a
ox was **p** in the habit of goring, **Ex 21:36** 8543, 8032a
unintentionally, not hating him **p** **Dt 19:4** 8543, 8032a
since he had not hated him **p**. **Dt 19:6** 8543, 8032a
a people that you did not **p** know. **Ru 2:11** 8543, 8032a
when all who knew him **p** saw that **1Sa 10:11** 4480, 8032a, 865a
who were with the Philistines **p**, **1Sa 14:21** 865a, 8032a
women have been kept from us as **p** **1Sa 21:5** 8543, 8032a
"**P**, when Saul was king over us, **2Sa 5:2** 1571, 865a, 8032a
of Eleazar was ruler over them **p**, **1Ch 9:20** 6440
his God, as he had been doing **p**. **Da 6:10** 6928
to the one which appeared to me **p**. **Da 8:1** 8462
whom I had seen in the vision **p**, **Da 9:21** 8462
those who **p** saw him as a beggar, **Jn 9:8** *4387*
who had **p** announced the coming **Ac 7:52** *4293*
For they had **p** seen Trophimus the **Ac 21:29** *4308*
passed over the sins **p** committed; **Ro 3:25** *4266*
that as he had **p** made a beginning, **2Co 8:6** *4278*
your **p** promised bountiful gift, **2Co 9:5** *4279*
I have **p** said when present the **2Co 13:2** *4275b*
a covenant **p** ratified by God, **Ga 3:17** *4300*
you **p** heard in the word of truth, **Col 1:5** *4257*
prophecies **p** made concerning you, **1Tm 1:18** *4254*

PREY
The birds of **p** came down upon **Gn 15:11** 5861
From the **p**, my son, you have gone **Gn 49:9** 2964
In the morning he devours the **p**, **Gn 49:27** 5706
the land, for they will be our **p**. **Nu 14:9** 3899
whom you said would become a **p** **Nu 14:31** 957
lie down until it devours the **p**, **Nu 23:24** 2964
took all the spoil and all the **p**, **Nu 31:11** 4455a
and the **p** and the spoil to Moses, **Nu 31:12** 4455a
who you said would become a **p**, **Dt 1:39** 957
"The lion perishes for lack of **p**, **Jb 4:11** 2964
an eagle that swoops on its **p**. **Jb 9:26** 400
"The path no bird of **p** knows, **Jb 28:7** 5861
And snatched the **p** from his teeth. **Jb 29:17** 2964
"Can you hunt the **p** for the lion, **Jb 38:39** 2964
They will be a **p** for foxes. **Ps 63:10** 4521
majestic than the mountains of **p**. **Ps 76:4** 2964
young lions roar after their **p** And **Ps 104:21** 2964
lazy man does not roast his **p**, **Pr 12:27** 6718a
It growls as it seizes the **p** And **Is 5:29** 2964
is the booty, speedy is the **p**. **Is 8:1** 957
together for mountain birds of **p**, **Is 18:6** 5861
And the birds of **p** will spend the **Is 18:6** 5861
the young lion growls over his **p**, **Is 31:4** 2964
Then the **p** of an abundant spoil **Is 33:23** 5706
a **p** with none to deliver *them,* **Is 42:22** 957
Calling a bird of **p** from the east, **Is 46:11** 5861
Can the **p** be taken from the mighty **Is 49:24** 4455a
p of the tyrant will be rescued; **Is 49:25** 4455a
aside from evil makes himself a **p**. **Is 59:15** 7997b
Why has he become a **p**? **Jer 2:14** 957
like a speckled bird of **p** to Me? **Jer 12:9** 5861
Are the birds of **p** against her on **Jer 12:9** 5861
And all who **p** upon you I will give for **Jer 30:16** 962
prey upon you I will give for **p**. **Jer 30:16** 957
And he learned to tear *his* **p**; **Ezk 19:3** 2964
lion, He learned to tear *his* **p**; **Ezk 19:6** 2964
like a roaring lion tearing the **p**. **Ezk 22:25** 2964
her are like wolves tearing the **p**, **Ezk 22:27** 2964
and a **p** of your merchandise, **Ezk 26:12** 962
because My flock has become a **p**, **Ezk 34:8** 957
and they will no longer be a **p**; **Ezk 34:22** 957
no longer be a **p** to the nations, **Ezk 34:28** 957
which have become a **p** and a **Ezk 36:4** 957
soul, to drive it out for a **p**." **Ezk 36:5** 957
in the forest when he has no **p**? **Am 3:4** 2964
And filled his lairs with **p** And his **Na 2:12** 2964
will cut off your **p** from the land, **Na 2:13** 2964
Her **p** never departs. **Na 3:1** 2964

PRICE
for the full **p** let him give it to **Gn 23:9** 3701
I will give the **p** of the field, **Gn 23:13** 3701
entirely consumed our purchase **p**. **Gn 31:15** 3701
live ox and divide its **p** equally; **Ex 21:35** 3701
years you shall increase its **p**, **Lv 25:16** 4736
years you shall diminish its **p** **Lv 25:16** 4736
and the **p** of his sale shall **Lv 25:50** 3701
he shall refund part of his purchase **p** **Lv 25:51** 3701
add one-fifth of your valuation **p** **Lv 27:15** 3701
the priest shall calculate the **p** for him **Lv 27:18** 3701
add one-fifth of your valuation **p** **Lv 27:19** 3701
"As to their redemption **p**, **Nu 18:16** 6299
your water, then I will pay its **p**. **Nu 20:19** 4377
surely buy *it* from you for a **p**, **2Sa 24:24** 4242
procured *them* from Kue for a **p**. **1Ki 10:28** 4242
give you the **p** of it in money." **1Ki 21:2** 4242
full **p** you shall give it to me, **1Ch 21:22** 3701
will surely buy *it* for the full **p**; **1Ch 21:24** 3701
procured them from Kue for a **p**. **2Ch 1:16** 4242
can silver be weighed as its **p**. **Jb 28:15** 4242
Why is there a **p** in the hand of a **Pr 17:16** 4242
goats *will bring* the **p** of a field, **Pr 27:26** 4242
full **p** of the pardoning of his sin: **Is 27:9** 6529
Our wood comes *to us* at a **p**. **La 5:4** 4242
and will parcel out land for a **p**. **Da 11:39** 4242
Her priests instruct for a **p** And **Mi 3:11** 4242
p at which I was valued by them." **Zch 11:13** 3366
might have been sold for a high **p** **Mt 26:9** *4183*
since it is the **p** of blood." **Mt 27:6** *5092*
THE **P** OF THE ONE WHOSE PRICE HAD **Mt 27:9** *5092*
THE PRICE OF THE ONE WHOSE **P** HAD **Mt 27:9** *5091*
with the **p** of his wickedness, **Ac 1:18** *3408*
kept back *some* of the **p** for himself, **Ac 5:2** *5092*
keep back *some* of the **p** of the land? **Ac 5:3** *5092*
the land for such and such a **p**?" **Ac 5:8** *5118*
"Yes, that was the **p**." **Ac 5:8** *5118*
and they counted up the **p** of them **Ac 19:19** *5092*
For you have been bought with a **p**: **1Co 6:20** *5092*
You were bought with a **p**; **1Co 7:23** *5092*

PRICKLING
for the house of Israel a **p** brier or **Ezk 28:24** 3992

PRICKS
will become as **p** in your eyes **Nu 33:55** 7899

PRIDE
also break down your **p** of power; **Lv 26:19** 1347b
He took great **p** in the ways of **2Ch 17:6** 1361b, 3820
Hezekiah humbled the **p** of his heart, **2Ch 32:26** 1363
his conduct, And keep man from **p**; **Jb 33:17** 1466
Because of the **p** of evil men. **Jb 35:12** 1347b
"*His* strong scales are *his* **p**, **Jb 41:15** 1346
is king over all the sons of **p**." **Jb 41:34** 7830
In **p** the wicked hotly pursue the **Ps 10:2** 1346
the righteous With **p** and contempt. **Ps 31:18** 1346
not the foot of **p** come upon me, **Ps 36:11** 1346
the mountains quake at its swelling **p**. **Ps 46:3** 1346
them even be caught in their **p**, **Ps 59:12** 1347b
Therefore **p** is their necklace; **Ps 73:6** 1346
Do not speak with insolent **p**.' " **Ps 75:5** 6677
their **p** is *but* labor and sorrow; **Ps 90:10** 7296
P and arrogance and the evil way And **Pr 8:13** 1344
When **p** comes, then comes dishonor, **Pr 11:2** 2087
P *goes* before destruction, And a **Pr 16:18** 1347b
names, Who acts with insolent **p**. **Pr 21:24** 2087
A man's **p** will bring him low, But **Pr 29:23** 1346
The **p** of man will be humbled And **Is 2:17** 1365
the fruit of the earth *will be* the **p** **Is 4:2** 1347b
in **p** and in arrogance of heart: **Is 9:9** 1346
the glory of the Chaldeans' **p**, **Is 13:19** 1347b
We have heard of the **p** of Moab, **Is 16:6** 1347b
the pride of Moab, an excessive **p**; **Is 16:6** 1343
Even of his arrogance, **p**, **Is 16:6** 1347b
it, to defile the **p** of all beauty, **Is 23:9** 1347b
But *the Lord* will lay low his **p** **Is 25:11** 1346
I will make you an everlasting **p**, **Is 60:15** 1347b
'Just so will I destroy the **p** of **Jer 13:9** 1347b
and the great **p** of Jerusalem. **Jer 13:9** 1347b
will sob in secret for *such* **p**; **Jer 13:17** 1466
"We have heard of the **p** of Moab **Jer 48:29** 1347b
Of his haughtiness, his **p**, **Jer 48:29** 1347b
beauty of His ornaments into **p**, **Ezk 7:20** 1347b
the **p** of the strong ones cease, **Ezk 7:24** 1347b
from your lips in your day of **p**, **Ezk 16:56** 1347b
My sanctuary, the **p** of your power, **Ezk 24:21** 1347b
stronghold, the joy of their **p**, **Ezk 24:25** 8597
the **p** of her power will come down; **Ezk 30:6** 1347b
Then the **p** of her power will cease **Ezk 30:18** 1347b
will devastate the **p** of Egypt, **Ezk 32:12** 1347b
and the **p** of her power will cease; **Ezk 33:28** 1347b
to humble those who walk in **p**." **Da 4:37** 1467
the **p** of Israel testifies against **Hos 5:5** 1347b
Though the **p** of Israel testifies **Hos 7:10** 1347b
LORD has sworn by the **p** of Jacob, **Am 8:7** 1347b
will have in return for their **p**, **Zph 2:10** 1347b
cut off the **p** of the Philistines. **Zch 9:6** 1347b
And the **p** of Assyria will be **Zch 10:11** 1347b
For the **p** of the Jordan is ruined. **Zch 11:3** 1347b
envy, slander, **p** *and* foolishness. **Mk 7:22** *5243*
those who take **p** in appearance and **2Co 5:12** *2744*
eyes and the boastful **p** of life, **1Jn 2:16** *212*

PRIEST
now he was a **p** of God Most High. **Gn 14:18** 3548
the daughter of Potiphera **p** of On, **Gn 41:45** 3548
the daughter of Potiphera **p** of On, **Gn 41:50** 3548
daughter of Potiphera, **p** of On, **Gn 46:20** 3548
p of Midian had seven daughters; **Ex 2:16** 3548
his father-in-law, the **p** of Midian; **Ex 3:1** 3548
Now Jethro, the **p** of Midian, **Ex 18:1** 3548
to minister as **p** to Me **Ex 28:1** 3547
that he may minister as **p** to Me. **Ex 28:3** 3547
that he may minister as **p** to Me. **Ex 28:4** 3547
one of his sons who is **p** in his stead **Ex 29:30** 3548
the holy garments for Aaron the **p**, **Ex 31:10** 3548
the holy garments for Aaron the **p** and **Ex 35:19** 3548
Ithamar the son of Aaron the **p**. **Ex 38:21** 3548
the holy garments for Aaron the **p** **Ex 39:41** 3548
that he may minister as a **p** to Me. **Ex 40:13** 3547
'The sons of Aaron the **p** shall **Lv 1:7** 3548
And the **p** shall offer up in smoke **Lv 1:9** 3548
and the **p** shall arrange them on **Lv 1:12** 3548
And the **p** shall offer all of it, **Lv 1:13** 3548
'The **p** shall bring it to the **Lv 1:15** 3548
And the **p** shall offer it up in **Lv 1:17** 3548
And the **p** shall offer *it* up in **Lv 2:2** 3548
it shall be presented to the **p** and **Lv 2:8** 3548
'The **p** then shall take up from the **Lv 2:9** 3548
'The **p** shall offer up in smoke **Lv 2:16** 3548
'Then the **p** shall offer *it* up in **Lv 3:11** 3548
'The **p** shall offer them up in **Lv 3:16** 3548
if the anointed **p** sins so as to **Lv 4:3** 3548
'Then the anointed **p** is to take **Lv 4:5** 3548
and the **p** shall dip his finger in **Lv 4:6** 3548
'The **p** shall also put some of the **Lv 4:7** 3548
and the **p** is to offer them up in **Lv 4:10** 3548
'Then the anointed **p** is to bring **Lv 4:16** 3548
and the **p** shall dip his finger in **Lv 4:17** 3548
p shall make atonement for them, **Lv 4:20** 3548
'Then the **p** is to take some of the **Lv 4:25** 3548

Thus the **p** shall make atonement	**Lv 4:26**	3548
'The **p** shall take some of its	**Lv 4:30**	3548
and the **p** shall offer it up in	**Lv 4:31**	3548
Thus the **p** shall make atonement	**Lv 4:31**	3548
'The **p** is to take some of the	**Lv 4:34**	3548
and the **p** shall offer them up in	**Lv 4:35**	3548
Thus the **p** shall make atonement	**Lv 4:35**	3548
So the **p** shall make atonement on	**Lv 5:6**	3548
'He shall bring them to the **p**,	**Lv 5:8**	3548
So the **p** shall make atonement on	**Lv 5:10**	3548
'He shall bring it to the **p**,	**Lv 5:12**	3548
and the **p** shall take his handful	**Lv 5:12**	3548
'So the **p** shall make atonement for	**Lv 5:13**	3548
part of it and give it to the **p**.	**Lv 5:16**	3548
The **p** shall then make atonement	**Lv 5:16**	3548
bring to the **p** a ram without defect	**Lv 5:18**	3548
So the **p** shall make atonement for	**Lv 5:18**	3548
shall bring to the **p** his guilt offering	**Lv 6:6**	3548
and the **p** shall make atonement for	**Lv 6:7**	3548
The **p** is to put on his linen robe,	**Lv 6:10**	3548
but the **p** shall burn wood on it	**Lv 6:12**	3548
"The anointed **p** who will be	**Lv 6:22**	3548
every grain offering of the **p** shall be	**Lv 6:23**	3548
'The **p** who offers it for sin shall	**Lv 6:26**	3548
'The **p** shall offer them up in	**Lv 7:5**	3548
the **p** who makes atonement with it	**Lv 7:7**	3548
'Also the **p** who presents any man's	**Lv 7:8**	3548
that **p** shall have for himself the	**Lv 7:8**	3548
belong to the **p** who presents it.	**Lv 7:9**	3548
it shall belong to the **p** who	**Lv 7:14**	3548
'The **p** shall offer up the fat	**Lv 7:31**	3548
You shall give the right thigh to the **p**	**Lv 7:32**	3548
and have given them to Aaron the **p**	**Lv 7:34**	3548
she shall bring to the **p** at the	**Lv 12:6**	3548
p shall make atonement for her,	**Lv 12:8**	3548
shall be brought to Aaron the **p** or	**Lv 13:2**	3548
"The **p** shall look at the mark	**Lv 13:3**	3548
when the **p** has looked at him, he	**Lv 13:3**	3548
then the **p** shall isolate *him who*	**Lv 13:4**	3548
"The **p** shall look at him on	**Lv 13:5**	3548
then the **p** shall isolate him for	**Lv 13:5**	3548
"The **p** shall look at him	**Lv 13:6**	3548
the **p** shall pronounce him clean;	**Lv 13:6**	3548
to the **p** for his cleansing,	**Lv 13:7**	3548
he shall appear again to the **p**.	**Lv 13:7**	3548
"The **p** shall look, and if the	**Lv 13:8**	3548
the **p** shall pronounce him unclean;	**Lv 13:8**	3548
then he shall be brought to the **p**.	**Lv 13:9**	3548
"The **p** shall then look, and if	**Lv 13:10**	3548
the **p** shall pronounce him unclean;	**Lv 13:11**	3548
his feet, as far as the **p** can see,	**Lv 13:12**	3548
then the **p** shall look, and behold,	**Lv 13:13**	3548
The **p** shall look at the raw flesh,	**Lv 13:15**	3548
then he shall come to the **p**,	**Lv 13:16**	3548
and the **p** shall look at him, and	**Lv 13:17**	3548
then the **p** shall pronounce clean	**Lv 13:17**	3548
then it shall be shown to the **p**;	**Lv 13:19**	3548
and the **p** shall look, and behold,	**Lv 13:20**	3548
the **p** shall pronounce him unclean;	**Lv 13:20**	3548
"But if the **p** looks at it, and	**Lv 13:21**	3548
then the **p** shall isolate him for	**Lv 13:21**	3548
the **p** shall pronounce him unclean;	**Lv 13:22**	3548
the **p** shall pronounce him clean.	**Lv 13:23**	3548
then the **p** shall look at it.	**Lv 13:25**	3548
the **p** shall pronounce him unclean;	**Lv 13:25**	3548
"But if the **p** looks at it, and	**Lv 13:26**	3548
then the **p** shall isolate him for	**Lv 13:26**	3548
and the **p** shall look at him on the	**Lv 13:27**	3548
the **p** shall pronounce him unclean;	**Lv 13:27**	3548
the **p** shall pronounce him clean,	**Lv 13:28**	3548
the **p** shall look at the infection,	**Lv 13:30**	3548
the **p** shall pronounce him unclean;	**Lv 13:30**	3548
"But if the **p** looks at the	**Lv 13:31**	3548
then the **p** shall isolate *the*	**Lv 13:31**	3548
the **p** shall look at the infection,	**Lv 13:32**	3548
and the **p** shall isolate *the person*	**Lv 13:33**	3548
day the **p** shall look at the scale,	**Lv 13:34**	3548
the **p** shall pronounce him clean;	**Lv 13:34**	3548
then the **p** shall look at him, and	**Lv 13:36**	3548
the **p** need not seek for the	**Lv 13:36**	3548
the **p** shall pronounce him clean.	**Lv 13:37**	3548
then the **p** shall look, and if the	**Lv 13:39**	3548
"Then the **p** shall look at him;	**Lv 13:43**	3548
The **p** shall surely pronounce him	**Lv 13:44**	3548
mark and shall be shown to the **p**.	**Lv 13:49**	3548
"Then the **p** shall look at the	**Lv 13:50**	3548
"But if the **p** shall look, and	**Lv 13:53**	3548
then the **p** shall order them to	**Lv 13:54**	3548
washed, the **p** shall again look,	**Lv 13:55**	3548
"Then if the **p** looks, and if	**Lv 13:56**	3548
Now he shall be brought to the **p**,	**Lv 14:2**	3548
and the **p** shall go out to the	**Lv 14:3**	3548
Thus the **p** shall look, and if the	**Lv 14:3**	3548
then the **p** shall give orders to	**Lv 14:4**	3548
"The **p** shall also give orders to	**Lv 14:5**	3548
and the **p** who pronounces him clean	**Lv 14:11**	3548
"Then the **p** shall take the one	**Lv 14:12**	3548
sin offering, belongs to the **p**;	**Lv 14:13**	3548
"The **p** shall then take some of	**Lv 14:14**	3548
and the **p** shall put *it* on the lobe	**Lv 14:14**	3548
"The **p** shall also take some of	**Lv 14:15**	3548
the **p** shall then dip his	**Lv 14:16**	3548
the **p** shall put some on the right	**Lv 14:17**	3548
So the **p** shall make atonement on	**Lv 14:18**	3548
"The **p** shall next offer the sin	**Lv 14:19**	3548
"The **p** shall offer up the	**Lv 14:20**	3548
p shall make atonement for him,	**Lv 14:20**	3548
them for his cleansing to the **p**,	**Lv 14:23**	3548
"The **p** shall take the lamb of	**Lv 14:24**	3548
and the **p** shall offer them for a	**Lv 14:24**	3548
and the **p** is to take some of the	**Lv 14:25**	3548
"The **p** shall also pour some of	**Lv 14:26**	3548
the **p** shall sprinkle some of the oil	**Lv 14:27**	3548
"The **p** shall then put some of the	**Lv 14:28**	3548
So the **p** shall make atonement	**Lv 14:31**	3548
house shall come and tell the **p**,	**Lv 14:35**	3548
"The **p** shall then command that they	**Lv 14:36**	3548
the **p** goes in to look at the mark,	**Lv 14:36**	3548
and afterward the **p** shall go in to	**Lv 14:36**	3548
the **p** shall come out of the house,	**Lv 14:38**	3548
"The **p** shall return on the	**Lv 14:39**	3548
then the **p** shall order them to	**Lv 14:40**	3548
then the **p** shall come in and make	**Lv 14:44**	3548
the **p** comes in and makes an	**Lv 14:48**	3548
then the **p** shall pronounce the	**Lv 14:48**	3548
meeting and give them to the **p**;	**Lv 15:14**	3548
and the **p** shall offer them, one	**Lv 15:15**	3548
So the **p** shall make atonement on	**Lv 15:15**	3548
and bring them in to the **p**,	**Lv 15:29**	3548
'The **p** shall offer the one for	**Lv 15:30**	3548
So the **p** shall make atonement on	**Lv 15:30**	3548
"So the **p** who is anointed and	**Lv 16:32**	3548
to serve as **p** in his father's place	**Lv 16:32**	3547
of the tent of meeting to the **p**,	**Lv 17:5**	3548
"The **p** shall sprinkle the	**Lv 17:6**	3548
'The **p** shall also make atonement	**Lv 19:22**	3548
'Also the daughter of any **p**,	**Lv 21:9**	3548
'The **p** who is the highest	**Lv 21:10**	3548
the descendants of Aaron the **p** who	**Lv 21:21**	3548
a sojourner with the **p** or a hired	**Lv 22:10**	3548
'But if a **p** buys a slave as *his*	**Lv 22:11**	3548
shall give the holy *gift* to the **p**.	**Lv 22:14**	3548
fruits of your harvest to the **p**.	**Lv 23:10**	3548
the sabbath the **p** shall wave it.	**Lv 23:11**	3548
'The **p** shall then wave them with	**Lv 23:20**	3548
to be holy to the LORD for the **p**.	**Lv 23:20**	3548
he shall be placed before the **p** and	**Lv 27:8**	3548
priest and the **p** shall value him;	**Lv 27:8**	3548
who vowed, the **p** shall value him.	**Lv 27:8**	3548
place the animal before the **p**.	**Lv 27:11**	3548
'The **p** shall value it as	**Lv 27:12**	3548
as you, the **p**, value it, so it	**Lv 27:12**	3548
then the **p** shall value it as	**Lv 27:14**	3548
as the **p** values it, so it shall	**Lv 27:14**	3548
then the **p** shall calculate the	**Lv 27:18**	3548
be for the **p** as his property.	**Lv 27:21**	3548
then the **p** shall calculate for him	**Lv 27:23**	3548
and set them before Aaron the **p**,	**Nu 3:6**	3548
and Eleazar the son of Aaron the **p**	**Nu 3:32**	3548
Eleazar the son of Aaron the **p** is the	**Nu 4:16**	3548
of Ithamar the son of Aaron the **p**.	**Nu 4:28**	3548
Ithamar the son of Aaron the **p**."	**Nu 4:33**	3548
must go to the LORD for the **p**,	**Nu 5:8**	3548
Israel, which they offer to the **p**,	**Nu 5:9**	3548
whatever any man gives to the **p**,	**Nu 5:10**	3548
then bring his wife to the **p**,	**Nu 5:15**	3548
'Then the **p** shall bring her near	**Nu 5:16**	3548
and the **p** shall take holy water in	**Nu 5:17**	3548
'The **p** shall then have the woman	**Nu 5:18**	3548
and in the hand of the **p** is to be	**Nu 5:18**	3548
'The **p** shall have her take an	**Nu 5:19**	3548
(then the **p** shall have the woman	**Nu 5:21**	3548
and the **p** shall say to the woman),	**Nu 5:21**	3548
'The **p** shall then write these	**Nu 5:23**	3548
'The **p** shall take the grain	**Nu 5:25**	3548
and the **p** shall take a handful of	**Nu 5:26**	3548
and the **p** shall apply all this law	**Nu 5:30**	3548
or two young pigeons to the **p**,	**Nu 6:10**	3548
'The **p** shall offer one for a	**Nu 6:11**	3548
'Then the **p** shall present *them*	**Nu 6:16**	3548
the **p** shall likewise offer its	**Nu 6:17**	3548
'The **p** shall take the ram's	**Nu 6:19**	3548
'Then the **p** shall wave them for a	**Nu 6:20**	3548
It is holy for the **p**,	**Nu 6:20**	3548
of Ithamar the son of Aaron the **p**.	**Nu 7:8**	3548
'Then the **p** shall make atonement	**Nu 15:25**	3548
'The **p** shall make atonement	**Nu 15:28**	3548
Eleazar, the son of Aaron the **p**,	**Nu 16:37**	3548
So Eleazar the **p** took the bronze	**Nu 16:39**	3548
the LORD's offering to Aaron the **p**.	**Nu 18:28**	3548
shall give it to Eleazar the **p**,	**Nu 19:3**	3548
'Next Eleazar the **p** shall take	**Nu 19:4**	3548
'The **p** shall take cedar wood	**Nu 19:6**	3548
'The **p** shall then wash his clothes	**Nu 19:7**	3548
but the **p** shall be unclean until	**Nu 19:7**	3548
Eleazar, the son of Aaron the **p**,	**Nu 25:7**	3548
Eleazar, the son of Aaron the **p**,	**Nu 25:11**	3548
to Eleazar the son of Aaron the **p**,	**Nu 26:1**	3548
So Moses and Eleazar the **p** spoke	**Nu 26:3**	3548
by Moses and Eleazar the **p**,	**Nu 26:63**	3548
numbered by Moses and Aaron the **p**,	**Nu 26:64**	3548
before Moses and before Eleazar the **p**	**Nu 27:2**	3548
have him stand before Eleazar the **p**	**Nu 27:19**	3548
shall stand before Eleazar the **p**,	**Nu 27:21**	3548
and set him before Eleazar the **p** and	**Nu 27:22**	3548
Phinehas the son of Eleazar the **p**,	**Nu 31:6**	3548
and to Eleazar the **p** and to the	**Nu 31:12**	3548
Moses and Eleazar the **p** and	**Nu 31:13**	3548
Then Eleazar the **p** said to the men	**Nu 31:21**	3548
"You and Eleazar the **p** and the	**Nu 31:26**	3548
half and give it to Eleazar the **p**,	**Nu 31:29**	3548
Moses and Eleazar the **p** did	**Nu 31:31**	3548
LORD's offering to Eleazar the **p**,	**Nu 31:41**	3548
the **p** took the gold from them,	**Nu 31:51**	3548
So Moses and Eleazar the **p** took	**Nu 31:54**	3548
spoke to Moses and to Eleazar the **p**	**Nu 32:2**	3548
concerning them to Eleazar the **p**,	**Nu 32:28**	3548
Then Aaron the **p** went up to Mount	**Nu 33:38**	3548
the **p** and Joshua the son of Nun.	**Nu 34:17**	3548
live in it until the death of the high **p**	**Nu 35:25**	3548
until the death of the high **p**.	**Nu 35:28**	3548
But after the death of the high **p**	**Nu 35:28**	3548
land before the death of the **p**.	**Nu 35:32**	3548
son ministered as **p** in his place.	**Dt 10:6**	3547
"So you shall come to the Levitical **p**	**Dt 17:9**	3548
not listening to the **p** who stands there	**Dt 17:12**	3548
they shall give to the **p** the shoulder	**Dt 18:3**	3548
the **p** shall come near and speak to	**Dt 20:2**	3548
p who is in office at that time and	**Dt 26:3**	3548
"Then the **p** shall take the basket	**Dt 26:4**	3548
of Canaan, which Eleazar the **p**	**Jos 14:1**	3548
They came near before Eleazar the **p**	**Jos 17:4**	3548
the inheritances which Eleazar the **p**	**Jos 19:51**	3548
one who is high **p** in those days.	**Jos 20:6**	3548
the Levites approached Eleazar the **p**	**Jos 21:1**	3548
And the sons of Aaron the **p**,	**Jos 21:4**	3548
of Aaron the **p** they gave Hebron,	**Jos 21:13**	3548
Phinehas the son of Eleazar the **p**,	**Jos 22:13**	3548
So when Phinehas the **p** and the	**Jos 22:30**	3548
Phinehas the son of Eleazar the **p** said	**Jos 22:31**	3548
Then Phinehas the son of Eleazar the **p**	**Jos 22:32**	3548
sons, that he might become his **p**.	**Jg 17:5**	3548
me and be a father and a **p** to me,	**Jg 17:10**	3548
and the young man became his **p** and	**Jg 17:12**	3548
me, seeing I have a Levite as **p**."	**Jg 17:13**	3548
me and I have become his **p**."	**Jg 18:4**	3548
The **p** said to them,	**Jg 18:6**	3548
while the **p** stood by the entrance	**Jg 18:17**	3548
molten image, the **p** said to them,	**Jg 18:18**	3548
us, and be to us a father and a **p**.	**Jg 18:19**	3548
to be a **p** to the house of one man,	**Jg 18:19**	3548
or to be **p** to a tribe and a family	**Jg 18:19**	3548
my gods which I made, and the **p**,	**Jg 18:24**	3548
and the **p** who had belonged to him,	**Jg 18:27**	3548
Now Eli the **p** was sitting on the	**1Sa 1:9**	3548
to the LORD before Eli the **p**.	**1Sa 2:11**	3548
the **p** would take for himself.	**1Sa 2:14**	3548
"Give the **p** meat for roasting, as	**1Sa 2:15**	3548
will raise up for Myself a faithful **p**	**1Sa 2:35**	3548
Eli, the **p** of the LORD at Shiloh,	**1Sa 14:3**	3548
While Saul talked to the **p**,	**1Sa 14:19**	3548
so Saul said to the **p**,	**1Sa 14:19**	3548
the **p** said, "Let us draw near to God	**1Sa 14:36**	3548
came to Nob to Ahimelech the **p**;	**1Sa 21:1**	3548
David said to Ahimelech the **p**,	**1Sa 21:2**	3548
The **p** answered David and said,	**1Sa 21:4**	3548
David answered the **p** and said	**1Sa 21:5**	3548
the **p** gave him consecrated *bread;*	**1Sa 21:6**	3548
the **p** said, "The sword of Goliath	**1Sa 21:9**	3548
someone to summon Ahimelech the **p**,	**1Sa 22:11**	3548
so he said to Abiathar the **p**,	**1Sa 23:9**	3548
Then David said to Abiathar the **p**,	**1Sa 30:7**	3548
The king said also to Zadok the **p**,	**2Sa 15:27**	3548
the Jairite was also a **p** to David.	**2Sa 20:26**	3548
Zeruiah and with Abiathar the **p**;	**1Ki 1:7**	3548
But Zadok the **p**, Benaiah the son	**1Ki 1:8**	3548
sons of the king and Abiathar the **p**	**1Ki 1:19**	3548
of the army and Abiathar the **p**,	**1Ki 1:25**	3548
and Zadok the **p** and Benaiah the	**1Ki 1:26**	3548
"Call to me Zadok the **p**,	**1Ki 1:32**	3548
"Let Zadok the **p** and Nathan	**1Ki 1:34**	3548
So Zadok the **p**, Nathan the	**1Ki 1:38**	3548
Zadok the **p** then took the horn of	**1Ki 1:39**	3548
the son of Abiathar the **p** came.	**1Ki 1:42**	3548
also sent with him Zadok the **p**,	**1Ki 1:44**	3548
"Zadok the **p** and Nathan the	**1Ki 1:45**	3548
for him, for Abiathar the **p**,	**1Ki 2:22**	3548
to Abiathar the **p** the king said,	**1Ki 2:26**	3548
Abiathar from being **p** to the LORD,	**1Ki 2:27**	3548
and the king appointed Zadok the **p**	**1Ki 2:35**	3548
Azariah the son of Zadok *was* the **p**;	**1Ki 4:2**	3548
and Zabud the son of Nathan, a **p**,	**1Ki 4:5**	3548
all that Jehoiada the **p** commanded.	**2Ki 11:9**	3548
and came to Jehoiada the **p**.	**2Ki 11:9**	3548
The **p** gave to the captains of	**2Ki 11:10**	3548
And Jehoiada the **p** commanded the	**2Ki 11:15**	3548
For the **p** said,	**2Ki 11:15**	3548
and killed Mattan the **p** of Baal	**2Ki 11:18**	3548
And the **p** appointed officers over	**2Ki 11:18**	3548
Jehoiada the **p** instructed him.	**2Ki 12:2**	3548
Jehoash called for Jehoiada the **p**,	**2Ki 12:7**	3548
But Jehoiada the **p** took a chest	**2Ki 12:9**	3548
the king's scribe and the high **p**	**2Ki 12:10**	3548
and King Ahaz sent to Urijah the **p**	**2Ki 16:10**	3548
So Urijah the **p** built an altar;	**2Ki 16:11**	3548
thus Urijah the **p** made *it*,	**2Ki 16:11**	3548
King Ahaz commanded Urijah the **p**,	**2Ki 16:15**	3548
So Urijah the **p** did according to	**2Ki 16:16**	3548
"Go up to Hilkiah the high **p** that	**2Ki 22:4**	3548
high **p** said to Shaphan the scribe,	**2Ki 22:8**	3548
Hilkiah the **p** has given me a book."	**2Ki 22:10**	3548
the king commanded Hilkiah the **p**,	**2Ki 22:12**	3548
So Hilkiah the **p**, Ahikam, Achbor,	**2Ki 22:14**	3548
king commanded Hilkiah the high **p**	**2Ki 23:4**	3548
in the book that Hilkiah the **p** found	**2Ki 23:24**	3548
of the guard took Seraiah the chief **p**	**2Ki 25:18**	3548
priest and Zephaniah the second **p**,	**2Ki 25:18**	3548
he who served as **p** in the house	**1Ch 6:10**	3547
He left Zadok the **p** and his	**1Ch 16:39**	3548
king, the princes, Zadok the **p**,	**1Ch 24:6**	3548
the son of Jehoiada the **p**,	**1Ch 27:5**	3548
ruler for the LORD and Zadok as **p**.	**1Ch 29:22**	3548
become a **p** of *what are* no gods.	**2Ch 13:9**	3548
and without a teaching **p** and	**2Ch 15:3**	3548
Amariah the chief **p** will be over	**2Ch 19:11**	3548
the wife of Jehoiada the **p**	**2Ch 22:11**	3548
all that Jehoiada the **p** commanded.	**2Ch 23:8**	3548

for Jehoiada the **p** did not dismiss **2Ch 23:8** 3548
Then Jehoiada the **p** gave to the **2Ch 23:9** 3548
Jehoiada the **p** brought out the **2Ch 23:14** 3548
For the **p** said, **2Ch 23:14** 3548
and killed Mattan the **p** of Baal **2Ch 23:17** 3548
all the days of Jehoiada the **p**. **2Ch 24:2** 3548
king summoned Jehoiada the chief **p** **2Ch 24:6**
the son of Jehoiada the **p**; **2Ch 24:20** 3548
of the son of Jehoiada the **p**, **2Ch 24:25** 3548
Then Azariah the **p** entered after **2Ch 26:17** 3548
Azariah the chief **p** and all **2Ch 26:20** 3548
the chief **p** of the house of Zadok **2Ch 31:10** 3548
They came to Hilkiah the high **p** and **2Ch 34:9** 3548
Hilkiah the **p** found the book of **2Ch 34:14** 3548
"Hilkiah the **p** gave me a book." **2Ch 34:18** 3548
until a **p** stood up with Urim **Ezr 2:63** 3548
Eleazar, son of Aaron the chief **p**. **Ezr 7:5** 3548
Artaxerxes gave to Ezra the **p**, **Ezr 7:11** 3548
king of kings, to Ezra the **p**, **Ezr 7:12** 3549
River, that whatever Ezra the **p**, **Ezr 7:21** 3549
Meremoth the son of Uriah the **p**, **Ezr 8:33** 3548
the **p** stood up and said to them, **Ezr 10:10** 3548
And Ezra the **p** selected men *who* **Ezr 10:16** 3548
Then Eliashib the high **p** arose **Ne 3:1** 3548
the house of Eliashib the high **p**. **Ne 3:20** 3548
a **p** arose with Urim and Thummim. **Ne 7:65** 3548
Then Ezra the **p** brought the law **Ne 8:2** 3548
and Ezra the **p** *and* scribe, **Ne 8:9** 3548
The **p**, the son of Aaron, shall **Ne 10:38** 3548
and of Ezra the **p** *and* scribe. **Ne 12:26** 3548
Now prior to this, Eliashib the **p**, **Ne 13:4** 3548
I appointed Shelemiah the **p**, **Ne 13:13** 3548
the son of Eliashib the high **p**, **Ne 13:28** 3548
"You are a **p** forever According **Ps 110:4** 3548
Uriah the **p** and Zechariah the son **Is 8:2** 3548
And the people will be like the **p**, **Is 24:2** 3548
The **p** and the prophet reel with **Is 28:7** 3548
from the prophet even to the **p** **Jer 6:13** 3548
From the prophet even to the **p** **Jer 8:10** 3548
For both prophet and **p** Have gone **Jer 14:18** 3548
is not going to be lost to the **p**, **Jer 18:18** 3548
When Pashhur the **p**, **Jer 20:1** 3548
of Malchijah, and Zephaniah the **p**, **Jer 21:1** 3548
both prophet and **p** are polluted; **Jer 23:11** 3548
prophet or a **p** asks you saying, **Jer 23:33** 3548
or the **p** or the people who say, **Jer 23:34** 3548
the son of Maaseiah, the **p**, **Jer 29:25** 3548
"The LORD has made you **p** instead **Jer 29:26** 3548
priest instead of Jehoiada the **p**, **Jer 29:26** 3548
Zephaniah the **p** read this **Jer 29:29** 3548
the son of Maaseiah, the **p**, **Jer 37:3** 3548
of the guard took Seraiah the chief **p** **Jer 52:24** 3548
priest and Zephaniah the second **p**, **Jer 52:24** 3548
And He has despised king and **p** In **La 2:6** 3548
Should **p** and prophet be slain In **La 2:20** 3548
came expressly to Ezekiel the **p**, **Ezk 1:3** 3548
but the law will be lost from the **p** **Ezk 7:26** 3548
near to Me to serve as a **p** to Me, **Ezk 44:13** 3547
a widow who is the widow of a **p**. **Ezk 44:22** 3548
give to the **p** the first of your dough **Ezk 44:30** 3548
"The **p** shall take some of the **Ezk 45:19** 3548
like those who contend with the **p**. **Hos 4:4** 3548
will reject you from being My **p**. **Hos 4:6** 3547
it will be, like people, like **p**; **Hos 4:9** 3548
Then Amaziah, the **p** of Bethel, **Am 7:10** 3548
of Jehozadak, the high **p**, **Hg 1:1** 3548
the son of Jehozadak, the high **p**, **Hg 1:12** 3548
the son of Jehozadak, the high **p**, **Hg 1:14** 3548
the son of Jehozadak, the high **p**, **Hg 2:2** 3548
son of Jehozadak, the high **p**, **Hg 2:4** 3548
he showed me Joshua the high **p** **Zch 3:1** 3548
'Now listen, Joshua the high **p**, **Zch 3:8** 3548
the son of Jehozadak, the high **p**. **Zch 6:11** 3548
He will be a **p** on His throne, **Zch 6:13** 3548
of a **p** should preserve knowledge, **Mal 2:7** 3548
but go, show yourself to the **p** and **Mt 8:4** *2409*
in the court of the high **p**, **Mt 26:3** *749*
struck the slave of the high **p** and **Mt 26:51** *749*
Him away to Caiaphas, the high **p**, **Mt 26:57** *749*
as the courtyard of the high **p**, **Mt 26:58** *749*
high **p** stood up and said to Him, **Mt 26:62** *749*
And the high **p** said to Him, **Mt 26:63** *749*
Then the high **p** tore his robes and **Mt 26:65** *749*
show yourself to the **p** and offer **Mk 1:44** *2409*
the time of Abiathar *the* high **p**, **Mk 2:26** *749*
struck the slave of the high **p** and **Mk 14:47** *749*
They led Jesus away to the high **p**; **Mk 14:53** *749*
into the courtyard of the high **p**; **Mk 14:54** *749*
The high **p** stood up *and came* **Mk 14:60** *749*
the high **p** was questioning Him, **Mk 14:61** *749*
his clothes, the high **p** said, **Mk 14:63** *749*
servant-girls of the high **p** came, **Mk 14:66** *749*
was a **p** named Zacharias, **Lk 1:5** *2409*
"But go and show yourself to the **p** and **Lk 5:14** *2409*
a **p** was going down on that **Lk 10:31** *2409*
struck the slave of the high **p** and **Lk 22:50** *749*
Him to the house of the high **p**; **Lk 22:54** *749*
Caiaphas, who was high **p** that year, **Jn 11:49** *749*
but being high **p** that year, he **Jn 11:51** *749*
who was high **p** that year. **Jn 18:13** *749*
disciple was known to the high **p**, **Jn 18:15** *749*
into the court of the high **p**, **Jn 18:15** *749*
who was known to the high **p**, **Jn 18:16** *749*
The high **p** then questioned **Jn 18:19** *749*
the way You answer the high **p**?" **Jn 18:22** *749*
Him bound to Caiaphas the high **p**. **Jn 18:24** *749*
One of the slaves of the high **p**, **Jn 18:26** *749*
and Annas the high **p** *was there*, **Ac 4:6** *749*
But the high **p** rose up, along with **Ac 5:17** *749*
high **p** and his associates came, **Ac 5:21** *749*
The high **p** questioned them, **Ac 5:27** *749*
The high **p** said, **Ac 7:1** *749*
of the Lord, went to the high **p**, **Ac 9:1** *749*
The **p** of Zeus, whose *temple* **Ac 14:13** *2409*
of one Sceva, a Jewish chief **p**, **Ac 19:14** *749*
as also the high **p** and all the **Ac 22:5** *749*
The high **p** Ananias commanded **Ac 23:2** *749*
"Do you revile God's high **p**?" **Ac 23:4** *749*
brethren, that he was high **p**; **Ac 23:5** *749*
the high **p** Ananias came down with **Ac 24:1** *749*
ministering as a **p** the gospel of God, **Ro 15:16** *2418*
a merciful and faithful high **p** **Heb 2:17** *749*
Jesus, the Apostle and High **P** **Heb 3:1** *749*
Therefore, since we have a great high **p** **Heb 4:14** *749*
For we do not have a high **p** who **Heb 4:15** *749*
For every high **p** taken from among **Heb 5:1** *749*
Himself so as to become a high **p**, **Heb 5:5** *749*
"YOU ARE A **P** FOREVER ACCORDING **Heb 5:6** *2409*
being designated by God as a high **p** **Heb 5:10** *749*
having become a high **p** forever **Heb 6:20** *749*
of Salem, **p** of the Most High God, **Heb 7:1** *2409*
of God, he remains a **p** perpetually. **Heb 7:3** *2409*
need *was there* for another **p** to arise **Heb 7:11** *2409*
if another **p** arises according to **Heb 7:15** *2409*
"YOU ARE A **P** FOREVER ACCORDING **Heb 7:17** *2409*
'YOU ARE A **P** FOREVER' **Heb 7:21** *2409*
for us to have such a high **p**, **Heb 7:26** *749*
we have such a high **p**, **Heb 8:1** *749*
For every high **p** is appointed to **Heb 8:3** *749*
so it is necessary that this *high* **p** **Heb 8:3**
earth, He would not be a **p** at all, **Heb 8:4** *2409*
the second, only the high **p** *enters* **Heb 9:7** *749*
high **p** of the good things to come, **Heb 9:11** *749*
as the high **p** enters the holy **Heb 9:25** *749*
Every **p** stands daily **Heb 10:11** *2409*
a great **p** over the house of God, **Heb 10:21** *2409*
into the holy place by the high **p** **Heb 13:11** *749*

PRIESTHOOD

have the **p** by a perpetual statute. **Ex 29:9** 3550
with which to carry on their **p**; **Ex 31:10** 3547
p throughout their generations." **Ex 40:15** 3550
sons that they may keep their **p**, **Nu 3:10** 3550
are you seeking for the **p** also? **Nu 16:10** 3550
guilt in connection with your **p**. **Nu 18:1** 3550
sons with you shall attend to your **p** **Nu 18:7** 3550
you the **p** as a bestowed service, **Nu 18:7** 3550
him, a covenant of a perpetual **p**, **Nu 25:13** 3550
because the **p** of the LORD is their **Jos 18:7** 3550
unclean *and excluded* from the **p**. **Ezr 2:62** 3550
unclean *and excluded* from the **p**. **Ne 7:64** 3550
because they have defiled the **p** **Ne 13:29** 3550
covenant of the **p** and the Levites. **Ne 13:29** 3550
the high **p** of Annas and Caiaphas, **Lk 3:2** *749*
was through the Levitical **p** **Heb 7:11** *2420*
For when the **p** is changed, of **Heb 7:12** *2420*
forever, holds His **p** permanently. **Heb 7:24** *2420*
as a spiritual house for a holy **p**, **1Pe 2:5** *2406*
you are A CHOSEN RACE, A royal **P**, **1Pe 2:9** *2406*

PRIESTLY

"The **p** sons of Aaron, moreover, **Nu 10:8** 3548
silver minas and 100 **p** garments. **Ezr 2:69** 3548
performing his **p** service before God **Lk 1:8** *2407*
to the custom of the **p** office, **Lk 1:9** *2405*
days of his **p** service were ended, **Lk 1:23** *3009*

PRIEST'S

then *the rest* shall become the **p**, **Lv 5:13** 3548
of the oil that is in the **p** palm, **Lv 14:18** 3548
rest of the oil that is in the **p** palm **Lv 14:29** 3548
'If a **p** daughter is married to **Lv 22:12** 3548
'But if a **p** daughter becomes a **Lv 22:13** 3548
The **p** heart was glad, and he **Jg 18:20** 3548
the **p** servant would come while the **1Sa 2:13** 3548
the **p** servant would come and say **1Sa 2:15** 3548
assign me to one of the **p** offices **1Sa 2:36** 3550
the chief **p** officer would come, **2Ch 24:11** 3548
it and struck the high **p** slave, **Jn 18:10** *749*
sons of Levi who receive the **p** office **Heb 7:5** *2405*

PRIESTS

the land of the **p** he did not buy, **Gn 47:22** 3548
p had an allotment from Pharaoh, **Gn 47:22** 3548
of the **p** did not become Pharaoh's. **Gn 47:26** 3548
a kingdom of **p** and a holy nation.' **Ex 19:6** 3548
"Also let the **p** who come near **Ex 19:22** 3548
but do not let the **p** and the **Ex 19:24** 3548
them, that they may serve Me as **p**. **Ex 28:41** 3547
them to minister as **p** to Me: **Ex 29:1** 3547
his sons to minister as **p** to Me. **Ex 29:44** 3547
that they may minister as **p** to Me. **Ex 30:30** 3547
of his sons, to minister as **p**.' " **Ex 35:19** 3547
of his sons, to minister as **p**. **Ex 39:41** 3547
that they may minister as **p** to Me; **Ex 40:15** 3547
and Aaron's sons the **p** **Lv 1:5** 3548
'Then Aaron's sons the **p** **Lv 1:8** 3548
the LORD, and Aaron's sons the **p** **Lv 1:11** 3548
bring it to Aaron's sons the **p**; **Lv 2:2** 3548
meeting, and Aaron's sons the **p** **Lv 3:2** 3548
male among the **p** may eat of it; **Lv 6:29** 3548
male among the **p** may eat of it. **Lv 7:6** 3548
them to serve as **p** to the LORD. **Lv 7:35** 3547
or to one of his sons the **p**. **Lv 13:2** 3548
shall also make atonement for the **p** **Lv 16:33** 3548
"Speak to the **p**, the sons of **Lv 21:1** 3548
the sons of Aaron, the anointed **p**, **Nu 3:3** 3548
whom he ordained to serve as **p**. **Nu 3:3** 3547
So Eleazar and Ithamar served as **p** **Nu 3:4** 3547
the presence of the Levitical **p**. **Dt 17:18** 3548
"The Levitical **p**, the whole tribe **Dt 18:1** 3548
before the **p** and the judges who **Dt 19:17** 3548
"Then the **p**, the sons of Levi, **Dt 21:5** 3548
the Levitical **p** teach you; **Dt 24:8** 3548
Levitical **p** spoke to all Israel, **Dt 27:9** 3548
this law and gave it to the **p**, **Dt 31:9** 3548
with the Levitical **p** carrying it, **Jos 3:3** 3548
And Joshua spoke to the **p**, **Jos 3:6** 3548
command the **p** who are carrying the **Jos 3:8** 3548
p who carry the ark of the LORD, **Jos 3:13** 3548
Jordan with the **p** carrying the ark of **Jos 3:14** 3548
and the feet of the **p** carrying the **Jos 3:15** 3548
And the **p** who carried the ark of **Jos 3:17** 3548
at the place where the feet of the **p** **Jos 4:9** 3548
For the **p** who carried the ark were **Jos 4:10** 3548
the **p** crossed before the people. **Jos 4:11** 3548
"Command the **p** who carry the ark **Jos 4:16** 3548
So Joshua commanded the **p**, **Jos 4:17** 3548
when the **p** who carried the ark of **Jos 4:18** 3548
"Also seven **p** shall carry seven **Jos 6:4** 3548
and the **p** shall blow the trumpets. **Jos 6:4** 3548
Joshua the son of Nun called the **p** **Jos 6:6** 3548
and let seven **p** carry seven **Jos 6:6** 3548
the seven **p** carrying the seven **Jos 6:8** 3548
the **p** who blew the trumpets, **Jos 6:9** 3548
the **p** took up the ark of the LORD. **Jos 6:12** 3548
The seven **p** carrying the seven **Jos 6:13** 3548
when the **p** blew the trumpets, **Jos 6:16** 3548
So the people shouted, and **p** **Jos 6:20**
sides of the ark before the Levitical **p** **Jos 8:33** 3548
of the sons of Aaron, the **p**, **Jos 21:19** 3548
were **p** to the tribe of the Danites **Jg 18:30** 3548
Phinehas, were **p** to the LORD there. **1Sa 1:3** 3548
custom of the **p** with the people. **1Sa 2:13** 3548
the tribes of Israel to be My **p**, **1Sa 2:28** 3548
Therefore neither the **p** of Dagon **1Sa 5:5** 3548
called for the **p** and the diviners, **1Sa 6:2** 3548
household, the **p** who were in Nob; **1Sa 22:11** 3548
put the **p** of the LORD to death, **1Sa 22:17** 3548
hands to attack the **p** of the LORD. **1Sa 22:17** 3548
turn around and attack the **p**." **1Sa 22:18** 3548
turned around and attacked the **p**, **1Sa 22:18** 3548
he struck Nob the city of the **p** **1Sa 22:19** 3548
Saul had killed the **p** of the LORD. **1Sa 22:21** 3548
the son of Abiathar *were* **p**, **2Sa 8:17** 3548
and Abiathar the **p** with you there? **2Sa 15:35** 3548
to Zadok and Abiathar the **p**. **2Sa 15:35** 3548
to Zadok and to Abiathar the **p**, **2Sa 17:15** 3548
sent to Zadok and Abiathar the **p**, **2Sa 19:11** 3548
and Zadok and Abiathar were **p**; **2Sa 20:25** 3548
and Zadok and Abiathar *were* **p**; **1Ki 4:4** 3548
came, and the **p** took up the ark. **1Ki 8:3** 3548
and the **p** and the Levites brought **1Ki 8:4** 3548
Then the **p** brought the ark of the **1Ki 8:6** 3548
the **p** came from the holy place, **1Ki 8:10** 3548
so that the **p** could not stand to **1Ki 8:11** 3548
made **p** from among all the people **1Ki 12:31** 3548
And he stationed in Bethel the **p** **1Ki 12:32** 3548
on you he shall sacrifice the **p** of the **1Ki 13:2** 3548
but again he made **p** of the high **1Ki 13:33** 3548
to be **p** of the high places. **1Ki 13:33** 3548
and his acquaintances and his **p**, **2Ki 10:11** 3548
all his worshipers and all his **p**; **2Ki 10:19** 3548
Then Jehoash said to the **p**, **2Ki 12:4** 3548
let the **p** take it for themselves, **2Ki 12:5** 3548
the **p** had not repaired the damages of **2Ki 12:6** 3548
for the *other* **p** and said to them, **2Ki 12:7** 3548
So the **p** agreed that they would **2Ki 12:8** 3548
and the **p** who guarded the **2Ki 12:9** 3548
it was for the **p**. **2Ki 12:16** 3548
"Take there one of the **p** whom you **2Ki 17:27** 3548
one of the **p** whom they had carried **2Ki 17:28** 3548
themselves **p** of the high places, **2Ki 17:32** 3548
scribe and the elders of the **p**, **2Ki 19:2** 3548
and the **p** and the prophets and all **2Ki 23:2** 3548
Hilkiah the high priest and the **p** of **2Ki 23:4** 3548
He did away with the idolatrous **p** **2Ki 23:5** 3649
the **p** from the cities of Judah, **2Ki 23:8** 3548
where the **p** had burned incense, **2Ki 23:8** 3548
Nevertheless the **p** of the high **2Ki 23:9** 3548
All the **p** of the high places **2Ki 23:20** 3548
their cities *were* Israel, the **p**, **1Ch 9:2** 3548
From the **p** *were* Jedaiah, **1Ch 9:10** 3548
Some of the sons of the **p** **1Ch 9:30** 3548
also to the **p** and Levites who are **1Ch 13:2** 3548
for Zadok and Abiathar the **p**, **1Ch 15:11** 3548
So the **p** and the Levites **1Ch 15:14** 3548
Benaiah and Eliezer, the **p**, **1Ch 15:24** 3548
and Benaiah and Jahaziel the **p** **1Ch 16:6** 3548
the priest and his relatives the **p** **1Ch 16:39** 3548
the son of Abiathar *were* **p**, **1Ch 18:16** 3548
Israel with the **p** and the Levites. **1Ch 23:2** 3548
Eleazar and Ithamar served as **p**. **1Ch 24:2** 3547
of the **p** and of the Levites; **1Ch 24:6** 3548
households of the **p** and of the Levites **1Ch 24:31** 3548
also for the divisions of the **p** **1Ch 28:13** 3548
there are the divisions of the **p** **1Ch 28:21** 3548
the sea *was* for the **p** to wash in. **2Ch 4:6** 3548
Then he made the court of the **p** **2Ch 4:9** 3548
the Levitical **p** brought them up. **2Ch 5:5** 3548
Then the **p** brought the ark of the **2Ch 5:7** 3548
When the **p** came forth from the **2Ch 5:11** 3548
the **p** who were present had sanctified **2Ch 5:11** 3548
and twenty **p** blowing trumpets **2Ch 5:12** 3548
so that the **p** could not stand to **2Ch 5:14** 3548
let Your **p**, O LORD God, be clothed **2Ch 6:41** 3548
The **p** could not enter into the **2Ch 7:2** 3548
The **p** stood at their posts, **2Ch 7:6** 3548
while the **p** on the other side blew **2Ch 7:6** 3548
he appointed the divisions of the **p** **2Ch 8:14** 3548

the **p** according to the daily rule, **2Ch 8:14** 3548
commandment of the king to the **p** **2Ch 8:15** 3548
the **p** and the Levites who were in **2Ch 11:13** 3548
from serving as **p** to the LORD. **2Ch 11:14** 3547
He set up **p** of his own for the **2Ch 11:15** 3548
not driven out the **p** of the LORD, **2Ch 13:9** 3548
and made for yourselves **p** like the **2Ch 13:9** 3548
are ministering to the LORD as **p**, **2Ch 13:10** 3548
God is with us at *our* head and His **p** **2Ch 13:12** 3548
LORD, and the **p** blew the trumpets. **2Ch 13:14** 3548
them Elishama and Jehoram, the **p**. **2Ch 17:8** 3548
some of the Levites and **p**, **2Ch 19:8** 3548
of the **p** and Levites who come in **2Ch 23:4** 3548
the **p** and the ministering Levites; **2Ch 23:6** 3548
the authority of the Levitical **p**, **2Ch 23:18** 3548
He gathered the **p** and Levites and **2Ch 24:5** 3548
and with him eighty **p** of the LORD, **2Ch 26:17** 3548
to the LORD, but for the **p**, **2Ch 26:18** 3548
while he was enraged with the **p**, **2Ch 26:19** 3548
the **p** in the house of the LORD, **2Ch 26:19** 3548
and all the **p** looked at him, **2Ch 26:20** 3548
brought in the **p** and the Levites and **2Ch 29:4** 3548
So the **p** went in to the inner part **2Ch 29:16** 3548
And he ordered the **p**, **2Ch 29:21** 3548
and the **p** took the blood and **2Ch 29:22** 3548
The **p** slaughtered them and **2Ch 29:24** 3548
and the **p** with the trumpets. **2Ch 29:26** 3548
But the **p** were too few, so that **2Ch 29:34** 3548
p had consecrated themselves. **2Ch 29:34** 3548
consecrate themselves than the **p**. **2Ch 29:34** 3548
because the **p** had not consecrated **2Ch 30:3** 3548
And the **p** and Levites were ashamed **2Ch 30:15** 3548
the **p** sprinkled the blood *which* **2Ch 30:16** 3548
Levites and the **p** praised the LORD **2Ch 30:21** 3548
a large number of **p** consecrated **2Ch 30:24** 3548
with the **p** and the Levites and **2Ch 30:25** 3548
the Levitical **p** arose and blessed **2Ch 30:27** 3548
appointed the divisions of the **p** and **2Ch 31:2** 3548
both the **p** and the Levites, **2Ch 31:2** 3548
portion due to the **p** and the Levites, **2Ch 31:4** 3548
Then Hezekiah questioned the **p** and **2Ch 31:9** 3548
Shecaniah in the cities of the **p**, **2Ch 31:15** 3548
as well as the **p** who were enrolled **2Ch 31:17** 3548
Also for the sons of Aaron the **p** **2Ch 31:19** 3548
portions to every male among the **p** **2Ch 31:19** 3548
bones of the **p** on their altars and **2Ch 34:5** 3548
inhabitants of Jerusalem, the **p**, **2Ch 34:30** 3548
He set the **p** in their offices **2Ch 35:2** 3548
offering to the people, the **p**, and **2Ch 35:8** 3548
gave to the **p** for the Passover **2Ch 35:8** 3548
and the **p** stood at their stations **2Ch 35:10** 3548
and while the **p** sprinkled the **2Ch 35:11** 3548
for themselves and for the **p**, **2Ch 35:14** 3548
for the priests, because the **p**, **2Ch 35:14** 3548
for themselves and for the **p**, **2Ch 35:14** 3548
Passover as Josiah did with the **p**, **2Ch 35:18** 3548
all the officials of the **p** and the **2Ch 36:14** 3548
and the **p** and the Levites arose, **Ezr 1:5** 3548
The **p**: the sons of Jedaiah **Ezr 2:36** 3548
Of the sons of the **p**: **Ezr 2:61** 3548
Now the **p** and the Levites, some of **Ezr 2:70** 3548
of Jozadak and his brothers the **p**, **Ezr 3:2** 3548
brothers the **p** and the Levites, **Ezr 3:8** 3548
the **p** stood in their apparel with **Ezr 3:10** 3548
Yet many of the **p** and Levites and **Ezr 3:12** 3548
as the **p** in Jerusalem request, **Ezr 6:9** 3549
And the sons of Israel, the **p**, **Ezr 6:16** 3549
Then they appointed the **p** to their **Ezr 6:18** 3549
For the **p** and the Levites had **Ezr 6:20** 3548
brothers the **p** and for themselves. **Ezr 6:20** 3548
sons of Israel and some of the **p**, **Ezr 7:7** 3548
of the people of Israel and their **p** **Ezr 7:13** 3549
offering of the people and of the **p**, **Ezr 7:16** 3549
tribute or toll *on* any of the **p**, **Ezr 7:24** 3549
I observed the people and the **p**, **Ezr 8:15** 3548
set apart twelve of the leading **p**, **Ezr 8:24** 3548
weigh *them* before the leading **p**, **Ezr 8:29** 3548
So the **p** and the Levites accepted **Ezr 8:30** 3548
"The people of Israel and the **p** **Ezr 9:1** 3548
our kings *and* our **p** have been **Ezr 9:7** 3548
Ezra rose and made the leading **p**, **Ezr 10:5** 3548
Among the sons of the **p** who **Ezr 10:18** 3548
had I as yet told the Jews, the **p**, **Ne 2:16** 3548
priest arose with his brothers the **p** **Ne 3:1** 3548
After him the **p**, **Ne 3:22** 3548
Gate the **p** carried out repairs, **Ne 3:28** 3548
So I called the **p** and took an oath **Ne 5:12** 3548
The **p**: the sons of Jedaiah **Ne 7:39** 3548
Of the **p**: the sons of Hobaiah **Ne 7:63** 3548
Now the **p**, the Levites, the **Ne 7:73** 3548
of all the people, the **p** and **Ne 8:13** 3548
us, our kings, our princes, our **p**, **Ne 9:32** 3548
"For our kings, our leaders, our **p** and **Ne 9:34** 3548
leaders, our Levites *and* our **p**." **Ne 9:38** 3548
These *were* the **p**. **Ne 10:8** 3548
Now the rest of the people, the **p**, **Ne 10:28** 3548
the supply of wood *among* the **p**, **Ne 10:34** 3548
for the **p** who are ministering in **Ne 10:36** 3548
the new wine and the oil to the **p** **Ne 10:37** 3548
the **p** who are ministering, **Ne 10:39** 3548
the Israelites, the **p**, the Levites **Ne 11:3** 3548
From the **p**: Jedaiah the son of **Ne 11:10** 3548
The rest of Israel, of the **p** **Ne 11:20** 3548
Now these are the **p** and the **Ne 12:1** 3548
These were the heads of the **p** and **Ne 12:7** 3548
Now in the days of Joiakim, the **p**, **Ne 12:12** 3548
so *were* the **p** in the reign of Darius **Ne 12:22** 3548
The **p** and the Levites purified **Ne 12:30** 3548
the sons of the **p** with trumpets; **Ne 12:35** 3548
and the **p**, Eliakim, Maaseiah, **Ne 12:41** 3548
by the law for the **p** and Levites; **Ne 12:44** 3548
over the **p** and Levites who served. **Ne 12:44** 3548
and the contributions for the **p**. **Ne 13:5** 3548
duties for the **p** and the Levites, **Ne 13:30** 3548
"He makes **p** walk barefoot And **Jb 12:19** 3548
His **p** fell by the sword, **Ps 78:64** 3548
Moses and Aaron were among His **p**, **Ps 99:6** 3548
p be clothed with righteousness, **Ps 132:9** 3548
"Her **p** also I will clothe with **Ps 132:16** 3548
scribe and the elders of the **p**, **Is 37:2** 3548
will be called the **p** of the LORD; **Is 61:6** 3548
of them for **p** *and* for Levites," **Is 66:21** 3548
of the **p** who were in Anathoth in **Jer 1:1** 3548
p and to the people of the land. **Jer 1:18** 3548
"The **p** did not say, **Jer 2:8** 3548
kings, their princes And their **p** **Jer 2:26** 3548
and the **p** will be appalled and **Jer 4:9** 3548
the **p** rule on their *own* authority; **Jer 5:31** 3548
princes, and the bones of the **p** and **Jer 8:1** 3548
for David on his throne, the **p**, **Jer 13:13** 3548
people and some of the senior **p**. **Jer 19:1** 3548
The **p** and the prophets and all **Jer 26:7** 3548
the **p** and the prophets and all the **Jer 26:8** 3548
Then the **p** and the prophets spoke **Jer 26:11** 3548
all the people said to the **p** and to **Jer 26:16** 3548
to the **p** and to all this people, **Jer 27:16** 3548
in the presence of the **p** and all the **Jer 28:1** 3548
Hananiah in the presence of the **p** **Jer 28:5** 3548
of the elders of the exile, the **p**, **Jer 29:1** 3548
the priest, and to all the **p**, **Jer 29:25** 3548
"I will fill the soul of the **p** with **Jer 31:14** 3548
kings, their leaders, their **p**, **Jer 32:32** 3548
and the Levitical **p** shall never **Jer 33:18** 3548
throne, and with the Levitical **p**, **Jer 33:21** 3548
the court officers and the **p** **Jer 34:19** 3548
with his **p** and his princes. **Jer 48:7** 3548
with his **p** and his princes. **Jer 49:3** 3548
"A sword against the oracle **p**, **Jer 50:36** 907
Her **p** are groaning, Her virgins **La 1:4** 3548
My **p** and my elders perished in the **La 1:19** 3548
And the iniquities of her **p**, **La 4:13** 3548
They did not honor the **p**, **La 4:16** 3548
"Her **p** have done violence to My **Ezk 22:26** 3548
p who keep charge of the temple; **Ezk 40:45** 3548
p who keep charge of the altar. **Ezk 40:46** 3548
p who are near to the LORD shall eat **Ezk 42:13** 3548
"When the **p** enter, then they **Ezk 42:14** 3548
'You shall give to the Levitical **p** **Ezk 43:19** 3548
the **p** shall throw salt on them, **Ezk 43:24** 3548
the **p** shall offer your burnt **Ezk 43:27** 3548
"But the Levitical **p**, **Ezk 44:15** 3548
"Nor shall any of the **p** drink **Ezk 44:21** 3548
contributions, shall be for the **p**; **Ezk 44:30** 3548
"The **p** shall not eat any bird or **Ezk 44:31** 3548
it shall be for the **p**, **Ezk 45:4** 3548
Then the **p** shall provide his burnt **Ezk 46:2** 3548
into the holy chambers for the **p**, **Ezk 46:19** 3548
"This is the place where the **p** **Ezk 46:20** 3548
be for these, *namely* for the **p**, **Ezk 48:10** 3548
shall be for the **p** who are sanctified **Ezk 48:11** 3548
"Alongside the border of the **p** **Ezk 48:13** 3548
Hear this, O **p**! Give heed, O house **Hos 5:1** 3548
a band of **p** murder on the way to **Hos 6:9** 3548
idolatrous **p** will cry out over it, **Hos 10:5** 3649
The **p** mourn, The ministers of the **Jl 1:9** 3548
with sackcloth And lament, O **p**; **Jl 1:13** 3548
Let the **p**, the LORD's ministers, **Jl 2:17** 3548
bribe, Her **p** instruct for a price And **Mi 3:11** 3548
And the names of the idolatrous **p** **Zph 1:4** 3649
idolatrous priests along with the **p**. **Zph 1:4** 3548
Her **p** have profaned the sanctuary. **Zph 3:4** 3548
'Ask now the **p** *for* a ruling: **Hg 2:11** 3548
And the **p** answered, **Hg 2:12** 3548
And the **p** answered, **Hg 2:13** 3548
speaking to the **p** who belong to **Zch 7:3** 3548
people of the land and to the **p**, **Zch 7:5** 3548
to you, O **p** who despise My name. **Mal 1:6** 3548
this commandment is for you, O **p**. **Mal 2:1** 3548
chief **p** and scribes of the people, **Mt 2:4** *749*
with him, but for the **p** alone? **Mt 12:4** *2409*
on the Sabbath the **p** in the temple **Mt 12:5** *2409*
elders and chief **p** and scribes, **Mt 16:21** *749*
to the chief **p** and scribes, **Mt 20:18** *749*
But when the chief **p** and the **Mt 21:15** *749*
the chief **p** and the elders of the **Mt 21:23** *749*
When the chief **p** and the **Mt 21:45** *749*
Then the chief **p** and the elders of **Mt 26:3** *749*
Iscariot, went to the chief **p** **Mt 26:14** *749*
chief **p** and elders of the people. **Mt 26:47** *749*
Now the chief **p** and the whole **Mt 26:59** *749*
all the chief **p** and the elders of **Mt 27:1** *749*
silver to the chief **p** and elders, **Mt 27:3** *749*
The chief **p** took the pieces of **Mt 27:6** *749*
accused by the chief **p** and elders, **Mt 27:12** *749*
But the chief **p** and the elders **Mt 27:20** *749*
In the same way the chief **p** also, **Mt 27:41** *749*
the chief **p** and the Pharisees **Mt 27:62** *749*
reported to the chief **p** all that had **Mt 28:11** *749*
for *anyone* to eat except the **p**, **Mk 2:26** *2409*
and the chief **p** and the scribes, **Mk 8:31** *749*
to the chief **p** and the scribes; **Mk 10:33** *749*
chief **p** and the scribes heard *this* **Mk 11:18** *749*
in the temple, the chief **p** and **Mk 11:27** *749*
and the chief **p** and the scribes **Mk 14:1** *749*
twelve, went off to the chief **p** in **Mk 14:10** *749*
from the chief **p** and the scribes **Mk 14:43** *749*
and all the chief **p** and the elders **Mk 14:53** *749*
Now the chief **p** and the whole **Mk 14:55** *749*
p with the elders and scribes and **Mk 15:1** *749*
p *began* to accuse Him harshly. **Mk 15:3** *749*
the chief **p** had handed Him over **Mk 15:10** *749*
But the chief **p** stirred up the **Mk 15:11** *749*
In the same way the chief **p** also, **Mk 15:31** *749*
for any to eat except the **p** alone, **Lk 6:4** *2409*
elders and chief **p** and scribes, **Lk 9:22** *749*
"Go and show yourselves to the **p**." **Lk 17:14** *2409*
but the chief **p** and the scribes **Lk 19:47** *749*
the chief **p** and the scribes **Lk 20:1** *749*
The scribes and the chief **p** **Lk 20:19** *749*
The chief **p** and the scribes **Lk 22:2** *749*
discussed with the chief **p** and officers **Lk 22:4** *749*
Then Jesus said to the chief **p** and **Lk 22:52** *749*
both chief **p** and scribes, **Lk 22:66** *749*
to the chief **p** and the crowds, **Lk 23:4** *749*
And the chief **p** and the scribes **Lk 23:10** *749*
chief **p** and the rulers and the people **Lk 23:13** *749*
and how the chief **p** and our rulers **Lk 24:20** *749*
when the Jews sent to him **p** and **Jn 1:19** *2409*
and the chief **p** and the Pharisees **Jn 7:32** *749*
came to the chief **p** and Pharisees, **Jn 7:45** *749*
chief **p** and the Pharisees convened **Jn 11:47** *749*
Now the chief **p** and the Pharisees **Jn 11:57** *749*
But the chief **p** planned to **Jn 12:10** *749*
the chief **p** and the Pharisees, **Jn 18:3** *749*
chief **p** delivered You to me; **Jn 18:35** *749*
chief **p** and the officers saw Him, **Jn 19:6** *749*
The chief **p** answered, **Jn 19:15** *749*
So the chief **p** of the Jews **Jn 19:21** *749*
the **p** and the captain of the **Ac 4:1** *2409*
and reported all that the chief **p** **Ac 4:23** *749*
and the chief **p** heard these words, **Ac 5:24** *749*
and a great many of the **p** were **Ac 6:7** *2409*
he has authority from the chief **p** **Ac 9:14** *749*
them bound before the chief **p**?" **Ac 9:21** *749*
released him and ordered the chief **p** **Ac 22:30** *749*
to the chief **p** and the elders and **Ac 23:14** *749*
And the chief **p** and the leading men **Ac 25:2** *749*
the chief **p** and the elders of the **Ac 25:15** *749*
authority from the chief **p**, **Ac 26:10** *749*
and commission of the chief **p**, **Ac 26:12** *749*
Moses spoke nothing concerning **p**. **Heb 7:14** *2409*
indeed became **p** without an oath, **Heb 7:21** *2409*
The *former* **p**, on the one hand, **Heb 7:23** *2409*
not need daily, like those high **p**, **Heb 7:27** *749*
men as high **p** who are weak, **Heb 7:28** *749*
the **p** are continually entering the **Heb 9:6** *2409*
kingdom, **p** to His God and Father **Rv 1:6** *2409*
to be a kingdom and **p** to our God; **Rv 5:10** *2409*
they will be **p** of God and of Christ **Rv 20:6** *2409*

PRIESTS'

"Now this shall be the **p** due from **Dt 18:3** 3548
from the place where the **p** feet are **Jos 4:3** 3548
and the soles of the **p** feet were **Jos 4:18** 3548
basins, 530 **p** garments. **Ne 7:70** 3548
silver minas and 67 **p** garments. **Ne 7:72** 3548

PRIME

house will die in the **p** of life. **1Sa 2:33** 376
As I was in the **p** of my days, When **Jb 29:4** 2779
and the **p** of life are fleeting. **Ec 11:10** 7839

PRINCE

lord, you are a mighty **p** among us; **Gn 23:6** 5387a
the Hivite, the **p** of the land, **Gn 34:2** 5387a
made you a **p** or a judge over us? **Ex 2:14** 8269
him to be **p** over My people Israel; **1Sa 9:16** 5057
"Do you not know that a **p** and a **2Sa 3:38** 8269
be **p** over My people Israel.' " **1Ch 11:2** 5057
to Sheshbazzar, the **p** of Judah. **Ezr 1:8** 5387a
Like a **p** I would approach Him. **Jb 31:37** 5057
Much less are lying lips to a **p**. **Pr 17:7** 5081
lower in the presence of the **p**, **Pr 25:7** 5081
God, Eternal Father, **P** of Peace. **Is 9:6** 8269
the **p** will be clothed with horror, **Ezk 7:27** 5387a
burden *concerns* the **p** in Jerusalem as **Ezk 12:10** 5387a
"The **p** who is among them will **Ezk 12:12** 5387a
wicked one, the **p** of Israel, **Ezk 21:25** 5387a
be a **p** in the land of Egypt; **Ezk 30:13** 5387a
David will be **p** among them; **Ezk 34:24** 5387a
servant will be their **p** forever. **Ezk 37:25** 5387a
the land of Magog, the **p** of Rosh, **Ezk 38:2** 5387a
am against you, O Gog, **p** of Rosh, **Ezk 38:3** 5387a
am against you, O Gog, **p** of Rosh, **Ezk 39:1** 5387a
"As for the **p**, he shall sit in it **Ezk 44:3** 5387a
he shall sit in it as **p** to eat bread **Ezk 44:3** 5387a
"The **p** shall have *land* on **Ezk 45:7** 5387a
this offering for the **p** in Israel. **Ezk 45:16** 5387a
"On that day the **p** shall **Ezk 45:22** 5387a
"The **p** shall enter by way of **Ezk 46:2** 5387a
burnt offering which the **p** shall offer **Ezk 46:4** 5387a
"When the **p** enters, he shall **Ezk 46:8** 5387a
in, the **p** shall go in among them; **Ezk 46:10** 5387a
p provides a freewill offering, **Ezk 46:12** 5387a
"If the **p** gives a gift *out of* his **Ezk 46:16** 5387a
then it shall return to the **p**. **Ezk 46:17** 5387a
"The **p** shall not take from **Ezk 46:18** 5387a
The remainder *shall be* for the **p**, **Ezk 48:21** 5387a
portions, *it shall be* for the **p**. **Ezk 48:21** 5387a
of that which belongs to the **p**, **Ezk 48:22** 5387a
of Benjamin shall be for the **p**. **Ezk 48:22** 5387a
will even oppose the **P** of princes, **Da 8:25** 8269
rebuild Jerusalem until Messiah the **P** **Da 9:25** 5057
and the people of the **p** who is to **Da 9:26** 5057
"But the **p** of the kingdom of Persia **Da 10:13** 8269
to fight against the **p** of Persia; **Da 10:20** 8269
the **p** of Greece is about to come. **Da 10:20** 8269
forces except Michael your **p**. **Da 10:21** 8269
and also the **p** of the covenant. **Da 11:22** 5057

the great **p** who stands *guard* over **Da 12:1** 8269
for many days without king or **p**, **Hos 3:4** 8269
The **p** asks, also the judge, for a **Mi 7:3** 8269
but put to death the **P** of life, **Ac 3:15** *747*
right hand as a **P** and a Savior, **Ac 5:31** *747*
to the **p** of the power of the air, **Eph 2:2** *758*

PRINCE'S

the dearth of people is a **p** ruin. **Pr 14:28** 7333
feet in sandals, O **p** daughter! **SS 7:1** 5081
"It shall be the **p** part *to* **Ezk 45:17** 5387a

PRINCES

become the father of twelve **p**, **Gn 17:20** 5387a
twelve **p** according to their tribes. **Gn 25:16** 5387a
and Hur and Reba, the **p** of Sihon, **Jos 13:21** 5257b
p of Issachar *were* with Deborah; **Jg 5:15** 8269
the **p** of Succoth and its elders, **Jg 8:14** 8269
the **p** of the Ammonites said to **2Sa 10:3** 8269
p and servants are nothing to you **2Sa 19:6** 8269
men of war, his servants, his **p**, **1Ki 9:22** 8269
men of valor, heads of the **p**. **1Ch 7:40** 5387a
But the **p** of the sons of Ammon **1Ch 19:3** 8269
Joab and to the **p** of the people, **1Ch 21:2** 8269
the presence of the king, the **p**, **1Ch 24:6** 8269
the **p** of the tribes of Israel. **1Ch 27:22** 8269
of Israel, the **p** of the tribes, **1Ch 28:1** 8269
and the **p** of the tribes of Israel, **1Ch 29:6** 8269
prophet came to Rehoboam and the **p** **2Ch 12:5** 8269
So the **p** of Israel and the king **2Ch 12:6** 8269
he found the **p** of Judah and the **2Ch 22:8** 8269
palace of the king and of the **p**, **2Ch 28:21** 8269
arose early and assembled the **p** **2Ch 29:20** 8269
For the king and his **p** and all the **2Ch 30:2** 8269
the hand of the king and his **p**, **2Ch 30:6** 8269
what the king and the **p** commanded **2Ch 30:12** 8269
and the **p** had contributed to the **2Ch 30:24** 8269
and before all the king's mighty **p**. **Ezr 7:28** 8269
whom David and the **p** had given for **Ezr 8:20** 8269
king and his counselors and his **p** and **Ezr 8:25** 8269
completed, the **p** approached me, **Ezr 9:1** 8269
the hands of the **p** and the rulers **Ezr 9:2** 8269
come upon us, our kings, our **p**, **Ne 9:32** 8269
for all his **p** and attendants, **Es 1:3** 8269
and the **p** of his provinces being **Es 1:3** 8269
beauty to the people and the **p**, **Es 1:11** 8269
the seven **p** of Persia and Media **Es 1:14** 8269
presence of the king and the **p**, **Es 1:16** 8269
not only the king but *also* all the **p** and **Es 1:16** 8269
the same way to all the king's **p**, **Es 1:18** 8269
word pleased the king and the **p**, **Es 1:21** 8269
for all his **p** and his servants; **Es 2:18** 8269
over all the **p** who *were* with him. **Es 3:1** 8269
and to the **p** of each people, **Es 3:12** 8269
he had promoted him above the **p** **Es 5:11** 8269
to one of the king's most noble **p** **Es 6:9** 8269
and the **p** of the provinces which **Es 8:9** 8269
Even all the **p** of the provinces, **Es 9:3** 8269
Or with **p** who had gold, Who were **Jb 3:15** 8269
"The **p** stopped talking And put **Jb 29:9** 8269
Who shows no partiality to **p** Nor **Jb 34:19** 8269
make them **p** in all the earth. **Ps 45:16** 8269
The **p** of the people have assembled **Ps 47:9** 5081
The **p** of Judah *in* their throng, **Ps 68:27** 8269
in their throng, The **p** of Zebulun, **Ps 68:27** 8269
of Zebulun, the **p** of Naphtali. **Ps 68:27** 8269
He will cut off the spirit of **p**; **Ps 76:12** 5057
And fall like *any* one of the **p**." **Ps 82:7** 8269
their **p** like Zebah and Zalmunna, **Ps 83:11** 5257b
To imprison his **p** at will, That he **Ps 105:22** 8269
He pours contempt upon **p** And **Ps 107:40** 5081
To make *them* sit with **p**, **Ps 113:8** 5081
princes, With the **p** of His people. **Ps 113:8** 5081
in the LORD Than to trust in **p**. **Ps 118:9** 5081
though **p** sit *and* talk against me, **Ps 119:23** 8269
P persecute me without cause, But **Ps 119:161** 8269
Do not trust in **p**, In mortal man, **Ps 146:3** 5081
P and all judges of the earth; **Ps 148:11** 8269
"By me **p** rule, and nobles, All **Pr 8:16** 8269
less for a slave to rule over **p**. **Pr 19:10** 8269
of a land many are its **p**, **Pr 28:2** 8269
and **p** walking like slaves on the land. **Ec 10:7** 8269
and whose **p** feast in the morning. **Ec 10:16** 8269
whose **p** eat at the appropriate time **Ec 10:17** 8269
And I will make mere lads their **p** **Is 3:4** 8269
the elders and **p** of His people, **Is 3:14** 8269
"Are not my **p** all kings? **Is 10:8** 8269
The **p** of Zoan are mere fools; **Is 19:11** 8269
The **p** of Zoan have acted **Is 19:13** 8269
The **p** of Memphis are deluded; **Is 19:13** 8269
of crowns, Whose merchants were **p**, **Is 23:8** 8269
"For their **p** are at Zoan And **Is 30:4** 8269
And his **p** will be terrified at the **Is 31:9** 8269
And **p** will rule justly. **Is 32:1** 8269
And all its **p** will be nothing. **Is 34:12** 8269
pollute the **p** of the sanctuary, **Is 43:28** 8269
and arise, **P** will also bow down **Is 49:7** 8269
to the kings of Judah, to its **p**, **Jer 1:18** 8269
They, their kings, their **p** And **Jer 2:26** 8269
and the heart of the **p** will fail; **Jer 4:9** 8269
of Judah and the bones of its **p**, **Jer 8:1** 8269
and **p** sitting on the throne of David **Jer 17:25** 8269
and on horses, they and their **p**, **Jer 17:25** 8269
of Judah and its kings *and* its **p**, **Jer 25:18** 8269
king of Egypt, his servants, his **p** and **Jer 25:19** 8269
the **p** of Judah and Jerusalem, **Jer 29:2** 8269
our kings and our **p** did in the **Jer 44:17** 8269
your kings and your **p**, **Jer 44:21** 8269
with his priests and his **p**. **Jer 48:7** 8269
with his priests and his **p**. **Jer 49:3** 8269
destroy out of it king and **p**,' **Jer 49:38** 8269
make her **p** and her wise men drunk, **Jer 51:57** 8269
all the **p** of Judah in Riblah. **Jer 52:10** 8269
Her **p** have become like deer That **La 1:6** 8269
profaned the kingdom and its **p**. **La 2:2** 8269
and her **p** are among the nations; **La 2:9** 8269
P were hung by their hands; **La 5:12** 8269
to Jerusalem, took its king and **p** and **Ezk 17:12** 8269
a lamentation for the **p** of Israel **Ezk 19:1** 5387a
"Her **p** within her are like wolves **Ezk 22:27** 8269
"Then all the **p** of the sea will **Ezk 26:16** 5387a
"Arabia and all the **p** of Kedar, **Ezk 27:21** 5387a
is Edom, its kings and all its **p**, **Ezk 32:29** 5387a
the blood of the **p** of the earth, **Ezk 39:18** 5387a
so My **p** shall no longer oppress My **Ezk 45:8** 5387a
"Enough, you **p** of Israel; **Ezk 45:9** 5387a
will even oppose the Prince of **p**, **Da 8:25** 8269
in Your name to our kings, our **p**, **Da 9:6** 8269
us, O Lord, to our kings, our **p** and **Da 9:8** 8269
Michael, one of the chief **p**, **Da 10:13** 8269
along with *one* of his **p** who will **Da 11:5** 8269
The **p** of Judah have become like **Hos 5:10** 8269
glad, And the **p** with their lies. **Hos 7:3** 8269
the **p** became sick with the heat of **Hos 7:5** 8269
Their **p** will fall by the sword **Hos 7:16** 8269
They have appointed **p**, **Hos 8:4** 8323
of the burden of the king of **p**. **Hos 8:10** 8269
All their **p** are rebels. **Hos 9:15** 8269
"Give me a king and **p**"? **Hos 13:10** 8269
exile, He and his **p** together," **Am 1:15** 8269
And slay all her **p** with him," **Am 2:3** 8269
That I will punish the **p**, **Zph 1:8** 8269
p within her are roaring lions, **Zph 3:3** 8269

PRINCESS

who was a **p** among the provinces **La 1:1** 8282

PRINCESSES

"Her wise **p** would answer her, **Jg 5:29** 8282
He had seven hundred wives, **p**, **1Ki 11:3** 8282
And their **p** your nurses. **Is 49:23** 8282

PRINCIPALITIES

nor life, nor angels, nor **p**, **Ro 8:38** *746*

PRINCIPLE

the **p** that evil is present in me, **Ro 7:21** *3551*

PRINCIPLES

to the elementary **p** of the world, **Col 2:8** *4747*
to the elementary **p** of the world, **Col 2:20** *4747*
to maintain these **p** without bias, **1Tm 5:21**
Teach and preach these **p**. **1Tm 6:2**
elementary **p** of the oracles of God, **Heb 5:12** *4747*

PRIOR

Now **p** to this, Eliashib the **Ne 13:4** 6440
the first-ripe fig **p** to summer, **Is 28:4** 2962
For **p** to the coming of certain men **Ga 2:12** *4253*

PRISCA

Greet **P** and Aquila, my fellow **Ro 16:3** *4251*
Aquila and **P** greet you heartily in **1Co 16:19** *4251*
Greet **P** and Aquila, and the **2Tm 4:19** *4251*

PRISCILLA

come from Italy with his wife **P**, **Ac 18:2** *4251*
and with him were **P** and Aquila. **Ac 18:18** *4251*
But when **P** and Aquila heard him, **Ac 18:26** *4251*

PRISON

all together in **p** for three days. **Gn 42:17** 4929
brothers be confined in your **p**; **Gn 42:19** 1004, 4929
and he was a grinder in the **p**. **Jg 16:21** 1004, 631
they called for Samson from the **p**, **Jg 16:25** 1004, 631
"Put this man in **p** and feed him **1Ki 22:27** 1004, 3608
shut him up and bound him in **p**. **2Ki 17:4** 1004, 3608
Jehoiachin king of Judah from **p**; **2Ki 25:27** 1004, 3608
Jehoiachin changed his **p** clothes and **2Ki 25:29** 3608
with the seer and put him in **p**, **2Ch 16:10** 1004, 4115
"Put this *man* in **p** and feed him **2Ch 18:26** 1004, 3608
"Bring my soul out of **p**, **Ps 142:7** 4525
has come out of **p** to become king, **Ec 4:14** 1004, 631
And will be confined in **p**; **Is 24:22** 4525
who dwell in darkness from the **p**. **Is 42:7** 1004, 3608
they had not *yet* put him in the **p**. **Jer 37:4** 1004, 3628
which they had made into the **p**. **Jer 37:15** 1004, 3608
people, that you have put me in **p**? **Jer 37:18** 1004, 3608
in **p** until the day of his death. **Jer 52:11** 1004, 6486
of Judah and brought him out of **p**. **Jer 52:31** 1004, 3628
Jehoiachin changed his **p** clothes, **Jer 52:33** 3608
officer, and you be thrown into **p**. **Mt 5:25** *5438*
him in **p** because of Herodias, **Mt 14:3** *5438*
and had John beheaded in the **p**. **Mt 14:10** *5438*
and went and threw him in **p** until **Mt 18:30** *5438*
I was in **p**, and you came to Me.' **Mt 25:36** *5438*
When did we see You sick, or in **p**, **Mt 25:39** *5438*
sick, and in **p**, and you did not **Mt 25:43** *5438*
or naked, or sick, or in **p**, **Mt 25:44** *5438*
bound in **p** on account of Herodias, **Mk 6:17** *5438*
and had him beheaded in the **p**, **Mk 6:27** *5438*
all: he locked John up in **p**. **Lk 3:20** *5438*
the officer throw you into **p**. **Lk 12:58** *5438*
to go both to **p** and to death!" **Lk 22:33** *5438*
one who had been thrown into **p** **Lk 23:19** *5438*
p for insurrection and murder, **Lk 23:25** *5438*
had not yet been thrown into **p**. **Jn 3:24** *5438*
Lord opened the gates of the **p**, **Ac 5:19** *5438*
p house for them to be brought. **Ac 5:21** *1201*
came did not find them in the **p**; **Ac 5:22** *5438*
"We found the **p** house locked **Ac 5:23** *1201*
The men whom you put in **p** are **Ac 5:25** *5438*
and women, he would put them in **p**. **Ac 8:3** *5438*
had seized him, he put him in **p**, **Ac 12:4** *5438*
So Peter was kept in the **p**, **Ac 12:5** *5438*
the door were watching over the **p**. **Ac 12:6** *5438*
the Lord had led him out of the **p**. **Ac 12:17** *5438*
they threw them into **p**, **Ac 16:23** *5438*
threw them into the inner **p** and **Ac 16:24** *5438*
of the **p** house were shaken; **Ac 16:26** *1201*
and saw the **p** doors opened, **Ac 16:27** *5438*
Romans, and have thrown us into **p**; **Ac 16:37** *5438*
They went out of the **p** and **Ac 16:40** *5438*
as though in **p** with them, **Heb 13:3** *4887*
to the spirits *now* in **p**, **1Pe 3:19** *5438*
about to cast some of you into **p**, **Rv 2:10** *5438*
and a **p** of every unclean spirit, **Rv 18:2** *5438*
and a **p** of every unclean **Rv 18:2** *5438*
Satan will be released from his **p**, **Rv 20:7** *5438*

PRISONER

The sons of Jeconiah, the **p**, **1Ch 3:17** 616
groaning of the **p** come before You; **Ps 79:11** 615
To hear the groaning of the **p**, **Ps 102:20** 615
release for the people *any* one **p** **Mt 27:15** *1198*
a notorious **p**, called Barabbas. **Mt 27:16** *1198*
used to release for them *any* one **p** **Mk 15:6** *1198*
to them at the feast one **p**. **Lk 23:17**
"Paul the **p** called me to him and **Ac 23:18** *1198*
who was left as a **p** by Felix; **Ac 25:14** *1198*
seems absurd to me in sending a **p**, **Ac 25:27** *1198*
yet I was delivered as a **p** from **Ac 28:17** *1198*
and making me a **p** of the law of **Ro 7:23** *163*
the **p** of Christ Jesus for the sake **Eph 3:1** *1198*
Therefore I, the **p** of the Lord, **Eph 4:1** *1198*
Aristarchus, my fellow **p**, **Col 4:10** *4869*
of our Lord or of me His **p** **2Tm 1:8** *1198*
Paul, a **p** of Christ Jesus, and **Phm 1:1** *1198*
and now also a **p** of Christ Jesus **Phm 1:9** *1198*
my fellow **p** in Christ Jesus, **Phm 1:23** *4869*

PRISONERS

where the king's **p** were confined; **Gn 39:20** 615
all the **p** who were in the jail; **Gn 39:22** 615
"The **p** are at ease together; **Jb 3:18** 615
He leads out the **p** into prosperity, **Ps 68:6** 615
does not despise His *who are* **p**. **Ps 69:33** 615
of death, **P** in misery and chains, **Ps 107:10** 615
The LORD sets the **p** free. **Ps 146:7** 631
did not allow his **p** to *go* home?' **Is 14:17** 615
together *Like* **p** in the dungeon, **Is 24:22** 616
To bring out **p** from the dungeon And **Is 42:7** 616
to captives And freedom to **p**; **Is 61:1** 631
His feet All the **p** of the land, **La 3:34** 615
p free from the waterless pit. **Zch 9:11** 615
stronghold, O **p** who have the hope; **Zch 9:12** 615
and the **p** were listening to them; **Ac 16:25** *1198*
supposing that the **p** had escaped. **Ac 16:27** *1198*
to Jerusalem as **p** to be punished. **Ac 22:5** *1210*
to deliver Paul and some other **p** to a **Ac 27:1** *1202*
soldiers' plan was to kill the **p**, **Ac 27:42** *1202*
my kinsmen and my fellow **p**, **Ro 16:7** *4869*
For you showed sympathy to the **p** and **Heb 10:34** *1198*
Remember the **p**, as though in **Heb 13:3** *1198*

PRISONS

in caves, Or are hidden away in **p**; **Is 42:22** 3608
you to the synagogues and **p**, **Lk 21:12** *5438*
putting both men and women into **p**, **Ac 22:4** *5438*
I lock up many of the saints in **p**, **Ac 26:10** *5438*

PRIVATE

go and show him his fault in **p**; **Mt 18:15** *3441*
support out of their **p** means. **Lk 8:3** *5225*
but *I did so* in **p** to those who **Ga 2:2** *2596, 2398*

PRIVATELY

of the gate to speak with him **p**, **2Sa 3:27** 7987
Then the disciples came to Jesus **p** **Mt 17:19** *2596, 2398*
the disciples came to Him **p**, **Mt 24:3** *2596, 2398*
everything **p** to His own disciples. **Mk 4:34** *2596, 2398*
disciples *began* questioning Him **p**, **Mk 9:28** *2596, 2398*
and Andrew were questioning Him **p**, **Mk 13:3** *2596, 2398*
to the disciples, He said **p**, **Lk 10:23** *2596, 2398*
aside, *began* to inquire of him **p**, **Ac 23:19** *2596, 2398*

PRIVATION

the Lord has given you bread of **p** **Is 30:20** 6862b

PRIZE

"**P** her, and she will exalt you; **Pr 4:8** 5549
run, but *only* one receives the **p**? **1Co 9:24** *1017*
I press on toward the goal for the **p** **Php 3:14** *1017*
no one keep defrauding you of your **p** **Col 2:18** *2603*
he does not win the **p** unless he **2Tm 2:5** *4737*

PROBE

Let us examine and **p** our ways, **La 3:40** 2713

PROBLEMS
p were found in this Daniel, **Da 5:12** 7001
and solve difficult **p**. **Da 5:16** 7001

PROCEDURE
tell them of the **p** of the king **1Sa 8:9** 4941
"This will be the **p** of the king **1Sa 8:11** 4941
heart knows the proper time and **p**. **Ec 8:5** 4941
time and **p** for every delight, **Ec 8:6** 4941

PROCEED
and I will **p** at my leisure, **Gn 33:14** 5095
and the border shall **p** to Ziphron, **Nu 34:9** 3318
p on your journey ahead of the **Dt 10:11** 1980
nor let a word **p** out of your mouth, **Jos 6:10** 3318
do not **p** in the way of evil men. **Pr 4:14** 833
p in the way of understanding." **Pr 9:6** 833
The naive **p** *and* pay the penalty. **Pr 27:12** 5674a
Who **p** down to Egypt Without **Is 30:2** 1980
For they **p** from evil to evil, And **Jer 9:3** 3318
'From them will **p** thanksgiving **Jer 30:19** 3318
in order to **p** into Egypt **Jer 41:17** 1980, 935
the things that **p** out of the mouth **Mt 15:18** *1607*
the things which **p** out of the man **Mk 7:15** *1607*
heart of men, **p** the evil thoughts, **Mk 7:21** *1607*
"All these evil things **p** from within **Mk 7:23** *1607*
you **p** to occupy the last place. **Lk 14:9** *757*
of the night to **p** to Caesarea, **Ac 23:23** *4198*
Let no unwholesome word **p** from **Eph 4:29** *1607*
will **p** *from bad* to worse, **2Tm 3:13** *4298*
p fire and smoke and brimstone. **Rv 9:17** *1607*

PROCEEDED
Then he **p** from there to the **Gn 12:8** 6275
they **p** to come to Moses and Aaron **Nu 13:26** 1980
Then it **p** southward to the ascent **Jos 15:3** 3318
Azmon and **p** to the brook of Egypt, **Jos 15:4** 3318
p to the cities of Mount Ephron, **Jos 15:9** 3318
The border **p** to the side of **Jos 15:11** 3318
to Mount Baalah and **p** to Jabneel, **Jos 15:11** 3318
it **p** to Daberath and up to Japhia. **Jos 19:12** 3318
and it **p** to Rimmon which stretches **Jos 19:13** 3318
then it **p** on north to Cabul, **Jos 19:27** 3318
and **p** from there to Hukkok; **Jos 19:34** 3318
The territory of the sons of Dan **p** **Jos 19:47** 3318
turned and **p** on down to Gilgal." **1Sa 15:12** 5674a
He **p** there to Naioth in Ramah; **1Sa 19:23** 1980
The second choir **p** to the left, **Ne 12:38** 1980
p to cross over to the sons of Ammon **Jer 41:10** 1980
word that has **p** from our mouths, **Jer 44:17** 3318
the eleven disciples **p** to Galilee, **Mt 28:16** *4198*
"And he **p** to send another slave; **Lk 20:11** *4369*
"And he **p** to send a third; **Lk 20:12** *4369*
And He came out and **p** as was His **Lk 22:39** *4198*
I **p** forth and have come from God, **Jn 8:42** *1831*
went along with the officers and **p** **Ac 5:26**
But Peter began *speaking* and **p** **Ac 11:4**
Jews, he **p** to arrest Peter also. **Ac 12:3** *4369*
and **p** to order *them* to be beaten **Ac 16:22**
Paul stretched out his hand and **p** **Ac 26:1**
they **p** to deliver Paul and some **Ac 27:1**
which **p** out of their mouths. **Rv 9:18** *1607*

PROCEEDING
the lords of the Philistines were **p** on **1Sa 29:2** 5674a
and David and his men were **p** on **1Sa 29:2** 5674a
the first **p** to the right on top of **Ne 12:31** 8418
in Himself that the power **p** from **Mk 5:30**
and **p** on His way to Jerusalem. **Lk 13:22** *4160*
one **p** from Mount Sinai bearing **Ga 4:24**

PROCEEDS
to all that **p** out of his mouth. **Nu 30:2** 3318
then whatever **p** out of her lips **Nu 30:12** 4161
p out of the mouth of the LORD. **Dt 8:3** 4161
P OUT OF THE MOUTH OF GOD.'" **Mt 4:4** *1607*
man, but what **p** out of the mouth, **Mt 15:11** *1607*
him the **p** at the *proper* seasons." **Mt 21:41** *2590*
"That which **p** out of the man, **Mk 7:20** *1607*
of truth who **p** from the Father, **Jn 15:26** *1607*
them and bring the **p** of the sales **Ac 4:34** *5092*

PROCESSION
them in **p** to the house of God, **Ps 42:4** 1718
They have seen Your **p**, O God, **Ps 68:24** 1979
O God, The **p** of my God, **Ps 68:24** 1979
With their kings led in **p**. **Is 60:11** 5090a

PROCHORUS
of the Holy Spirit, and Philip, **P**, **Ac 6:5** *4402*

PROCLAIM
p My name through all the earth. **Ex 9:16** 5608
and will **p** the name of the LORD **Ex 33:19** 7121
you shall **p** as holy convocations **Lv 23:2** 7121
holy convocations which you shall **p** **Lv 23:4** 7121
you shall **p** as holy convocations, **Lv 23:37** 7121
p a release through the land to all its **Lv 25:10** 7121
"For I **p** the name of the LORD; **Dt 32:3** 7121
p in the hearing of the people, **Jg 7:3** 7121
I may **p** the word of God to you." **1Sa 9:27** 8085
P it not in the streets of Ashkelon, **2Sa 1:20** 1319
"**P** a fast and seat Naboth at the **1Ki 21:9** 7121
P good tidings of His salvation **1Ch 16:23** 1319
to **p** in Jerusalem concerning you, **Ne 6:7** 7121
the city square, and **p** before him, **Es 6:9** 7121
That I may **p** with the voice of **Ps 26:7** 8085
The women who **p** the *good* tidings **Ps 68:11** 1319
P good tidings of His salvation **Ps 96:2** 1319
no one there *Whom* they may **p** king **Is 34:12** 7121
spring forth I **p** *them* to you." **Is 42:9** 8085
And **p** to us the former things? **Is 43:9** 8085
Let him **p** and declare it; **Is 44:7** 7121
I **p** to you new things from this **Is 48:6** 8085
sound of joyful shouting, **p** this, **Is 48:20** 8085
To **p** liberty to captives And **Is 61:1** 7121
To **p** the favorable year of the LORD **Is 61:2** 7121
"Go and **p** in the ears of Jerusalem, **Jer 2:2** 7121
and **p** these words toward the north **Jer 3:12** 7121
in Judah and **p** in Jerusalem, **Jer 4:5** 8085
P over Jerusalem, **Jer 4:16** 8085
house of Jacob And **p** it in Judah, **Jer 5:20** 8085
LORD's house and **p** there this word and **Jer 7:2** 7121
"**P** all these words in the cities **Jer 11:6** 7121
and **p** there the words that I tell **Jer 19:2** 7121
I **p** violence and destruction, **Jer 20:8** 7121
P, give praise and say, **Jer 31:7** 8085
in Jerusalem to **p** release to them: **Jer 34:8** 7121
"Declare in Egypt and **p** in Migdol, **Jer 46:14** 8085
P also in Memphis and Tahpanhes; **Jer 46:14** 8085
"Declare and **p** among the nations. **Jer 50:2** 8085
P it and lift up a standard. **Jer 50:2** 8085
a fast, **P** a solemn assembly; **Jl 1:14** 7121
a fast, **p** a solemn assembly, **Jl 2:15** 7121
P this among the nations: **Jl 3:9** 7121
P on the citadels in Ashdod and on **Am 3:9** 8085
And **p** freewill offerings, **Am 4:5** 7121
go to Nineveh the great city and **p** to **Jon 3:2** 7121
"**P**, saying, 'Thus says the LORD **Zch 1:14** 7121
"Again, **p**, saying, **Zch 1:17** 7121
in *your* ear, **p** upon the housetops. **Mt 10:27** *2784*
SHALL **P** JUSTICE TO THE GENTILES. **Mt 12:18** *518*
But he went out and began to **p** it **Mk 1:45** *2784*
began to **p** in Decapolis what great **Mk 5:20** *2784*
widely they continued to **p** it. **Mk 7:36** *2784*
ME TO **P** RELEASE TO THE CAPTIVES, **Lk 4:18** *2784*
TO **P** THE FAVORABLE YEAR OF THE **Lk 4:19** *2784*
them out to **p** the kingdom of God and **Lk 9:2** *2784*
p everywhere the kingdom of God." **Lk 9:60** *1229*
to **p** Jesus in the synagogues, **Ac 9:20** *2784*
they *began* to **p** the word of God in **Ac 13:5** *2605*
in ignorance, this I **p** to you. **Ac 17:23** *2605*
He would be the first to **p** light **Ac 26:23** *2605*
Lord directed those who **p** the gospel **1Co 9:14** *2605*
you **p** the Lord's death until He **1Co 11:26** *2605*
the former **p** Christ out of selfish **Php 1:17** *2605*
We **p** Him, admonishing every **Col 1:28** *2605*
"I WILL **P** YOUR NAME TO MY **Heb 2:12** *518*
that you may **p** the excellencies of **1Pe 2:9** *1804*
and **p** to you the eternal life, **1Jn 1:2** *518*
seen and heard we **p** to you also, **1Jn 1:3** *518*

PROCLAIMED
and they **p** before him, **Gn 41:43** 7121
passed by in front of him and **p**, **Ex 34:6** 7121
the LORD's remission has been **p**. **Dt 15:2** 7121
of Rimmon, and **p** peace to them. **Jg 21:13** 7121
They **p** a fast and seated Naboth at **1Ki 21:12** 7121
LORD has **p** disaster against you." **1Ki 22:23** 1696
assembly for Baal." And they **p** *it*. **2Ki 10:20** 7121
the LORD which the man of God **p**, **2Ki 23:16** 7121
proclaimed, who **p** these things. **2Ki 23:16** 7121
p these things which you have done **2Ki 23:17** 7121
LORD has **p** disaster against you." **2Ch 18:22** 1696
and **p** a fast throughout all Judah. **2Ch 20:3** 7121
Then I **p** a fast there at the river **Ezr 8:21** 7121
So they **p** and circulated a **Ne 8:15** 8085
the city square, and **p** before him, **Es 6:11** 7121
I have **p** glad tidings of **Ps 40:9** 1319
Surely there was no one who **p**, **Is 41:26** 8085
who have declared and saved and **p**, **Is 43:12** 8085
forth from My mouth, and I **p** them. **Is 48:3** 8085
they took place I **p** *them* to you, **Is 48:5** 8085
has **p** to the end of the earth, **Is 62:11** 8085
Disaster on disaster is **p**, **Jer 4:20** 7121
p a fast before the LORD. **Jer 36:9** 7121
bring the day which You have **p**, **La 1:21** 7121
Then the herald loudly **p**: **Da 3:4** 7123
to whom the former prophets **p**, **Zch 1:4** 7121
the LORD **p** by the former prophets, **Zch 7:7** 7121
will be **p** upon the housetops. **Lk 12:3** *2784*
"The Law and the Prophets *were* **p** **Lk 16:16**
forgiveness of sins would be **p** in His **Lk 24:47** *2784*
after the baptism which John **p**. **Ac 10:37** *2784*
after John had **p** before His coming **Ac 13:24** *4296*
forgiveness of sins is **p** to you, **Ac 13:38** *2605*
which we **p** the word of the Lord, **Ac 15:36** *2605*
had been **p** by Paul in Berea also, **Ac 17:13** *2605*
your faith is being **p** throughout **Ro 1:8** *2605*
MY NAME MIGHT BE **P** THROUGHOUT **Ro 9:17** *1229*
pretense or in truth, Christ is **p**; **Php 1:18** *2605*
p in all creation under heaven, **Col 1:23** *2784*
we **p** to you the gospel of God. **1Th 2:9** *2784*
by angels, **P** among the nations, **1Tm 3:16** *2784*

PROCLAIMER
He seems to be a **p** of strange deities **Ac 17:18** *2604*

PROCLAIMING
man **p** release to his neighbor, **Jer 34:15** 7121
'You have not obeyed Me in **p** **Jer 34:17** 7121
Behold, I am **p** a release to you,' **Jer 34:17** 7121
and **p** the gospel of the kingdom, **Mt 4:23** *2784*
and **p** the gospel of the kingdom, **Mt 9:35** *2784*
p and preaching the kingdom of God. **Lk 8:1** *2784*
p throughout the whole city what **Lk 8:39** *2784*
p in Jesus the resurrection from the **Ac 4:2** *2605*
and *began* **p** Christ to them. **Ac 8:5** *2784*
p to you the way of salvation." **Ac 16:17** *2605*
and are **p** customs which it is not **Ac 16:21** *2605*
"This Jesus whom I am **p** to you is **Ac 17:3** *2605*
new teaching is which you are **p**? **Ac 17:19** *2980*
p to you the testimony of God. **1Co 2:1** *2605*
that in **p** it I may speak boldly, **Eph 6:20**
strong angel **p** with a loud voice, **Rv 5:2** *2784*

PROCLAIMS
But the heart of fools **p** folly. **Pr 12:23** 7121
Many a man **p** his own loyalty, But **Pr 20:6** 7121
p wickedness from Mount Ephraim. **Jer 4:15** 8085

PROCLAMATION
and Aaron made a **p** and said, **Ex 32:5** 7121
and a **p** was circulated throughout **Ex 36:6** 6963
day you shall make a **p** as well; **Lv 23:21** 7121
Then King Asa made a **p** to all **1Ki 15:22** 8085
They made a **p** in Judah and **2Ch 24:9** 6963
established a decree to circulate a **p** **2Ch 30:5** 6963
sent a **p** throughout his kingdom, **2Ch 36:22** 6963
sent a **p** throughout all his kingdom, **Ezr 1:1** 6963
They made a **p** throughout Judah **Ezr 10:7** 6963
they proclaimed and circulated a **p** **Ne 8:15** 6963
and issued a **p** concerning him that **Da 5:29** 3745
with the **p** to their assembly. **Hos 7:12** 8088
p which I am going to tell you." **Jon 3:2** 7150
He issued a **p** and it said, **Jon 3:7** 2199
to west the sacred and imperishable **p** **Mk 16:20**
the **p** might be fully accomplished, **2Tm 4:17** *2782*
in the **p** with which I was entrusted **Ti 1:3** *2782*
p to the spirits *now* in prison, **1Pe 3:19** *2784*

PROCONSUL
who was with the **p**, Sergius Paulus, **Ac 13:7** *446*
to turn the **p** away from the faith. **Ac 13:8** *446*
Then the **p** believed when he saw **Ac 13:12** *446*
But while Gallio was **p** of Achaia, **Ac 18:12** *446*

PROCONSULS
in session and **p** are *available;* **Ac 19:38** *446*

PROCURED
p *them* from Kue for a price. **1Ki 10:28** 3947
p them from Kue for a price. **2Ch 1:16** 3947

PRODUCE
and let him exact a fifth *of the* **p** **Gn 41:34**
'Then the land will yield its **p**, **Lv 25:19** 6529
so that the land will yield its **p** **Lv 26:4** 2981
for your land will not yield its **p** **Lv 26:20** 2981
or the full **p** from the wine vat. **Nu 18:27** 4395
tithe all the **p** from what you sow, **Dt 14:22** 8393
bring out all the tithe of your **p** **Dt 14:28** 8393
your God will bless you in all your **p** **Dt 16:15** 8393
or all the **p** of the seed which **Dt 22:9** 4395
shall take some of the first of all the **p** **Dt 26:2** 6529
the first of the **p** of the ground **Dt 26:10** 6529
p of your ground and the offspring **Dt 28:4** 6529
beast and in the **p** of your ground, **Dt 28:11** 6529
body and the **p** of your ground, **Dt 28:18** 6529
shall eat up the **p** of your ground **Dt 28:33** 6529
trees and the **p** of your ground. **Dt 28:42** 6529
your herd and the **p** of your ground **Dt 28:51** 6529
and in the **p** of your ground, **Dt 30:9** 6529
And he ate the **p** of the field; **Dt 32:13** 8570
with the choice **p** of the months. **Dt 33:14** 1645
ate some of the **p** of the land, **Jos 5:11** 5669
eaten some of the **p** of the land, **Jos 5:12** 8393
the **p** of the earth as far as Gaza, **Jg 6:4** 2981
and you shall bring in *the* **p** so **2Sa 9:10**
that was hers and all the **p** of the field **2Ki 8:6** 8393
had charge of the **p** of the vineyards **1Ch 27:27**
and of all the **p** of the field; **2Ch 31:5** 8393
also for the **p** of grain, **2Ch 32:28** 8393
"Its abundant **p** is for the **Ne 9:37** 8393
"Within the walls they **p** oil; **Jb 24:11** 6671
The earth has yielded its **p**; **Ps 67:6** 2981
And our land will yield its **p**. **Ps 85:12** 2981
full, furnishing every kind of **p**, **Ps 144:13**
And from the first of all your **p**; **Pr 3:9** 8393
He expected *it* to **p** *good* grapes, **Is 5:2** 6213a
when I expected *it* to **p** *good* grapes **Is 5:4** 6213a
grapes did it **p** worthless ones? **Is 5:4** 6213a
wealth of this city, all its **p** and **Jer 20:5** 3018
plant gardens and eat their **p**. **Jer 29:5** 6529
and plant gardens and eat their **p**. **Jer 29:28** 6529
the tree and the **p** of the field, **Ezk 36:30** 8570
And its **p** shall be food for the **Ezk 48:18** 8393
fail And the fields **p** no food, **Hab 3:17** 6213a
and the earth has withheld its **p**. **Hg 1:10** 2981
fruit, the land will yield its **p** and **Zch 8:12** 2981
"A good tree cannot **p** bad fruit, **Mt 7:18** *5342*
nor can a bad tree **p** good fruit. **Mt 7:18** *5342*
the vine-growers to receive his **p**. **Mt 21:34** *2590*
receive *some* of the **p** of the vineyard **Mk 12:2** *2590*
him *some* of the **p** of the vineyard; **Lk 20:10** *2590*
not **p** a distinction in the tones, **1Co 14:7** *1325*
knowing that they **p** quarrels. **2Tm 2:23** *1080*
a fig tree, my brethren, **p** olives, **Jas 3:12** *4160*
produce olives, or a vine **p** figs? **Jas 3:12** *4160*
Nor *can* salt water **p** fresh. **Jas 3:12** *4160*
for the precious **p** of the soil, **Jas 5:7** *2590*

PRODUCED
and its clusters **p** ripe grapes. **Gn 40:10** 1310
miracles which have not been **p** in **Ex 34:10** 1254a
whether an eating away has **p** **Lv 13:55**
they will have **p** in your land; **Lv 25:45** 3205
that is **p** by the grape vine, **Nu 6:4** 6213a
and put forth buds and **p** blossoms, **Nu 17:8** 6692a
But it **p** *only* worthless ones. **Is 5:2** 6213a
of the milk **p** he will eat curds, **Is 7:22** 6213a
They grow, they have even **p** fruit. **Jer 12:2** 6213a
they have lost the abundance it **p**. **Jer 48:36** 6213a
they yielded a crop and **p** thirty, **Mk 4:8** *5342*
and **p** a crop a hundred times as **Lk 8:8** *4160*
p in me coveting of every kind; **Ro 7:8** *2716*
this godly sorrow, has **p** in you: **2Co 7:11** *2716*
rain and the earth **p** its fruit. **Jas 5:18** *985*

PRODUCES
that which p reverence for You. Ps 119:38
Good understanding p favor, Pr 13:15 5414
For the churning of milk p butter, Pr 30:33 3318
So the churning of anger p strife. Pr 30:33 3318
He p fruit for himself. Hos 10:1 7737b
on the oil, on what the ground p, Hg 1:11 3318
"The soil p crops by itself; Mk 4:28 *2592*
is no good tree which p bad fruit, Lk 6:43 *4160*
a bad tree which p good fruit. Lk 6:43 *4160*
the bugle p an indistinct sound, 1Co 14:8 *1325*
God p a repentance without regret, 2Co 7:10 *2038*
the sorrow of the world p death. 2Co 7:10 *2716*
testing of your faith p endurance. Jas 1:3 *2716*

PRODUCING
given to a people, p the fruit of it. Mt 21:43 *4160*
flute or harp, in p a sound, 1Co 14:7 *1325*
momentary, light affliction is p for us 2Co 4:17 *2716*
us is p thanksgiving to God. 2Co 9:11 *2716*

PRODUCT
as the p of the threshing floor, Nu 18:30 8393
and as the p of the wine vat. Nu 18:30 8393
p of their labor to the locust. Ps 78:46 3018
strangers plunder the p of his labor. Ps 109:11 3018
satisfied *with* the p of his lips. Pr 18:20 8393
Give her the p of her hands, And Pr 31:31 6529

PRODUCTIVE
of a rich man was very p. Lk 12:16 *2164*

PRODUCTS
best p of the land in your bags, Gn 43:11 2173
'All of you shall have the sabbath p Lv 25:6
"The p of Egypt and the Is 45:14 3018

PROFANE
your tool on it, you will p it. Ex 20:25 2490c
between the holy and the p, Lv 10:10 2455
shall you p the name of your God; Lv 18:21 2455
so as to p the name of your God; Lv 19:12 2455
'Do not p your daughter by making Lv 19:29 2455
sanctuary and to p My holy name. Lv 20:3 2455
his people, and so p himself. Lv 21:4 2490c
and not p the name of their God, Lv 21:6 2490c
nor p the sanctuary of his God, Lv 21:12 2490c
that he will not p his offspring Lv 21:15 2490c
that he will not p My sanctuaries. Lv 21:23 2490c
Me, so as not to p My holy name; Lv 22:2 2490c
and die thereby because they p it; Lv 22:9 2490c
'They shall not p the holy Lv 22:15 2490c
"You shall not p My holy name, Lv 22:32 2490c
But you shall not p the sacred gifts Nu 18:32 2490c
steal, And p the name of my God. Pr 30:9 8610
as spoil, and they will p it. Ezk 7:21 2490c
and they will p My secret place; Ezk 7:22 2490c
then robbers will enter and p it. Ezk 7:22 2490c
My holy name you will p no longer Ezk 20:39 2490c
"You will p yourself in the Ezk 22:16 2490c
between the holy and the p, Ezk 22:26 2455
sanctuary on the same day to p it; Ezk 23:39 2490c
I am about to p My sanctuary, Ezk 24:21 2490c
Therefore I have cast you as p From Ezk 28:16 2490c
divide between the holy and the p. Ezk 42:20 2455
to be in My sanctuary to p it, Ezk 44:7 2490c
between the holy and the p, Ezk 44:23 2455
girl In order to p My holy name. Am 2:7 2490c
to p the covenant of our fathers? Mal 2:10 2490c
and sinners, for the unholy and p, 1Tm 1:9 *952*

PROFANED
has p the holy thing of the LORD; Lv 19:8 2490c
take a woman who is p by harlotry, Lv 21:7 2491b
or one who is p by harlotry, Lv 21:14 2491b
You have p his crown in the dust. Ps 89:39 2490c
with My people, I p My heritage And Is 47:6 2490c
For how can *My name* be p? Is 48:11 2490c
"Yet you turned and p My name, Jer 34:16 2490c
has p the kingdom and its princes. La 2:2 2490c
and their holy places will be p. Ezk 7:24 2490c
you have p Me to My people to put Ezk 13:19 2490c
that it should not be p in the Ezk 20:9 2490c
and My sabbaths they greatly p. Ezk 20:13 2490c
be p in the sight of the nations, Ezk 20:14 2490c
they even p My sabbaths, for their Ezk 20:16 2490c
they p My sabbaths. Ezk 20:21 2490c
that it should not be p in the Ezk 20:22 2490c
statutes and had p My sabbaths, Ezk 20:24 2490c
My holy things and p My sabbaths. Ezk 22:8 2490c
My law and have p My holy things; Ezk 22:26 2490c
sabbaths, and I am p among them. Ezk 22:26 2490c
same day and have p My sabbaths. Ezk 23:38 2490c
My sanctuary when it was p, Ezk 25:3 2490c
trade You p your sanctuaries. Ezk 28:18 2490c
they went, they p My holy name, Ezk 36:20 2490c
which the house of Israel had p Ezk 36:21 2490c
which you have p among the nations Ezk 36:22 2490c
has been p among the nations, Ezk 36:23 2490c
which you have p in their midst. Ezk 36:23 2490c
not let My holy name be p anymore. Ezk 39:7 2490c
Her priests have p the sanctuary. Zph 3:4 2490c
for Judah has p the sanctuary of Mal 2:11 2490c

PROFANES
Everyone who p it shall surely be Ex 31:14 2490c
if she p herself by harlotry, Lv 21:9 2490c
by harlotry, she p her father; Lv 21:9 2490c

PROFANING
are doing, by p the sabbath day? Ne 13:17 2490c
on Israel by p the sabbath." Ne 13:18 2490c
Who keeps from p the sabbath, And Is 56:2 2490c
one who keeps from p the sabbath And Is 56:6 2490c
"But you are p it, in that you Mal 1:12 2490c

PROFESS
They p to know God, but by *their* Ti 1:16 *3670*

PROFESSED
which some have p and thus gone 1Tm 6:21 *1861*

PROFESSING
P to be wise, they became fools, Ro 1:22 *5335*

PROFESSIONAL
And p mourners to lamentation. Am 5:16 3045

PROFIT
"What p is it for us to kill our Gn 37:26 1215
things which can not p or deliver, 1Sa 12:21 3276
p if you make your ways perfect? Jb 22:3 1215
path, They p from my destruction; Jb 30:13 3276
What p will I have, more than if Jb 35:3 3276
"What p is there in my blood, if Ps 30:9 1215
For her p is better than the Pr 3:14 5504
is better than the p of silver And Pr 3:14 5504
Ill-gotten gains do not p, Pr 10:2 3276
Riches do not p in the day of wrath, Pr 11:4 3276
In all labor there is p, Pr 14:23 4195
and there was no p under the sun. Ec 2:11 3504
What p is there to the worker from Ec 3:9 3504
there is no p for the charmer. Ec 10:11 3504
of a people who cannot p them, Is 30:5 3276
them, *Who are* not for help or p, Is 30:5 3276
To a people who cannot p *them;* Is 30:6 3276
their precious things are of no p; Is 44:9 3276
a god or cast an idol to no p? Is 44:10 3276
Perhaps you will be able to p, Is 47:12 3276
your God, who teaches you to p, Is 48:17 3276
deeds, But they will not p you. Is 57:12 3276
after things that did not p. Jer 2:8 3276
glory For that which does not p. Jer 2:11 3276
have strained themselves to no p. Jer 12:13 3276
Futility and things of no p." Jer 16:19 3276
"What p is the idol when its Hab 2:18 3276
and what p is it that we have kept Mal 3:14 1215
"For what will it p a man if he Mt 16:26 *5623*
p a man to gain the whole world, Mk 8:36 *5623*
masters much p by fortune-telling. Ac 16:16 *2039*
saw that their hope of p was gone, Ac 16:19 *2039*
all things, not seeking my own p but 1Co 10:33 *4851b*
not seeking my own profit but the p 1Co 10:33
in tongues, what will I p you 1Co 14:6 *5623*
at Ephesus, what does it p me? 1Co 15:32 *3786*
but I seek for the p which Php 4:17 *2590*
bodily discipline is only of little p, 1Tm 4:8 *5624*
word they heard did not p them, Heb 4:2 *5623*
engage in business and make a p." Jas 4:13 *2770*

PROFITABLE
Or with words which are not p? Jb 15:3 3276
to you anything that was p, Ac 20:20 *4851a*
for me, but not all things are p. 1Co 6:12 *4851a*
lawful, but not all things are p. 1Co 10:23 *4851a*
is necessary, though it is not p; 2Co 12:1 *4851a*
but godliness is p for all things, 1Tm 4:8 *5624*
inspired by God and p for teaching, 2Tm 3:16 *5624*
things are good and p for men. Ti 3:8 *5624*

PROFITED
And have not p by their sale. Ps 44:12 7235a
"For what is a man p if he gains Lk 9:25 *5623*

PROFITS
'It p a man nothing When he is Jb 34:9 5532a
He who p illicitly troubles his Pr 15:27 1214
you have taken interest and p, Ezk 22:12 8636
the flesh p nothing; Jn 6:63 *5623*
do not have love, it p me nothing. 1Co 13:3 *5623*

PROFOUND
reveals the p and hidden things; Da 2:22 5994

PROFUSELY
It will blossom p And rejoice with Is 35:2 6524a

PROGRESS
for the greater p of the gospel, Php 1:12 *4297*
for your p and joy in the faith, Php 1:25 *4297*
that your p will be evident to all. 1Tm 4:15 *4297*
But they will not make further p; 2Tm 3:9 *4298*

PROGRESSED
the repair work p in their hands, 2Ch 24:13 5927

PROJECT
chief deputies who *were* over the p 1Ki 5:16 4399

PROJECTING
in front of the Angle and the tower p Ne 3:25 3318
toward the east and the p tower. Ne 3:26 3318
great p tower and as far as the wall Ne 3:27 3318

PROJECTION
p which was beside the network; 1Ki 7:20 990

PROLONG
and that you may p *your* days in Dt 5:33 748
so that you may p *your* days on the Dt 11:9 748
you and that you may p your days. Dt 22:7 748
You will not p *your* days in the Dt 30:18 748
you will p your days in the land, Dt 32:47 748
walked, then I will p your days." 1Ki 3:14 748
You will p the king's life; Ps 61:6 3254
Will You p Your anger to all Ps 85:5 4900
hates unjust gain will p *his* days. Pr 28:16 748
His offspring, He will p *His* days, Is 53:10 748

PROLONGED
that your days may be p in the Ex 20:12 748
you, that your days may be p and Dt 5:16 748
life, and that your days may be p. Dt 6:2 748
that your days may be p in the Dt 25:15 748
come And her days will not be p. Is 13:22 4900
he p his message until midnight. Ac 20:7 *3905*

PROLONGING
may be a p of your prosperity.' Da 4:27 754

PROLONGS
The fear of the LORD p life, Pr 10:27 3254
who p *his life* in his wickedness. Ec 7:15 748

PROMINENCE
Jews incited the devout women of p Ac 13:50 *2158*

PROMINENT
Shunem, where there was a p woman, 2Ki 4:8 1419
came, a p member of the Council, Mk 15:43 *2158*
a number of p Greek women and men. Ac 17:12 *2158*
and the p men of the city, Ac 25:23 *1851*

PROMISCUITY
not in sexual p and sensuality, Ro 13:13 *2845*

PROMISE
p which He spoke concerning me, 1Ki 2:4 1697
word has failed of all His good p, 1Ki 8:56 1697
Your p to my father David is 2Ch 1:9 1697
they would do according to this p. Ne 5:12 1697
who does not fulfill this p; Ne 5:13 1697
people did according to this p. Ne 5:13 1697
And You have fulfilled Your p, Ne 9:8 1697
Has *His* p come to an end forever? Ps 77:8 561
'As for the p which I made you Hg 2:5 1697
forth the p of My Father upon you; Lk 24:49 *1860*
Father the p of the Holy Spirit, Ac 2:33 *1860*
p is for you and your children and Ac 2:39 *1860*
"But as the time of the p was Ac 7:17 *1860*
according to p, God has brought to Ac 13:23 *1860*
news of the p made to the fathers, Ac 13:32 *1860*
that God has fulfilled this p to Ac 13:33
and waiting for the p from you." Ac 23:21 *1860*
standing trial for the hope of the p Ac 26:6 *1860*
the p to which our twelve tribes Ac 26:7
For the p to Abraham or to his Ro 4:13 *1860*
made void and the p is nullified; Ro 4:14 *1860*
so that the p will be guaranteed Ro 4:16 *1860*
yet, with respect to the p of God, Ro 4:20 *1860*
the children of the p are regarded as Ro 9:8 *1860*
For this is the word of p: Ro 9:9 *1860*
the p of the Spirit through faith. Ga 3:14 *1860*
by God, so as to nullify the p. Ga 3:17 *1860*
law, it is no longer based on a p; Ga 3:18 *1860*
it to Abraham by means of a p. Ga 3:18 *1860*
come to whom the p had been made. Ga 3:19 *1861*
that the p by faith in Jesus Ga 3:22 *1860*
descendants, heirs according to p. Ga 3:29 *1860*
by the free woman through the p. Ga 4:23 *1860*
like Isaac, are children of p. Ga 4:28 *1860*
in Him with the Holy Spirit of p, Eph 1:13 *1860*
strangers to the covenants of p, Eph 2:12 *1860*
and fellow partakers of the p in Eph 3:6 *1860*
the first commandment with a p), Eph 6:2 *1860*
since it holds p for the present 1Tm 4:8 *1860*
to the p of life in Christ Jesus, 2Tm 1:1 *1860*
a p remains of entering His rest, Heb 4:1 *1860*
when God made the p to Abraham, Heb 6:13 *1861*
waited, he obtained the p. Heb 6:15 *1860*
to show to the heirs of the p the Heb 6:17 *1860*
the p of the eternal inheritance. Heb 9:15 *1860*
as an alien in the land of p, Heb 11:9 *1860*
Jacob, fellow heirs of the same p; Heb 11:9 *1860*
"Where is the p of His coming? 2Pe 3:4 *1860*
The Lord is not slow about His p, 2Pe 3:9 *1860*
But according to His p we are 2Pe 3:13 *1862*
the p which He Himself made to us: 1Jn 2:25 *1860*

PROMISED
LORD did for Sarah as He had p. Gn 21:1 1696
I have done what I have p you." Gn 28:15 1696
which He p on oath to Abraham, Gn 50:24 7650
LORD will give you, as He has p, Ex 12:25 1696
has p good concerning Israel." Nu 10:29 1696
the land which He p them by oath, Nu 14:16 7650
the place which the LORD has p." Nu 14:40 559
and do what you have p." Nu 32:24 3318, 4480, 6310
bless you, just as He has p you! Dt 1:11 1696
God of your fathers, has p you, Dt 6:3 1696
into the land which He had p them Dt 9:28 1696
your border as He has p you, Dt 12:20 1696
will bless you as He has p you, Dt 15:6 1696
their inheritance, as He p them. Dt 18:2 1696
which He p to give your fathers Dt 19:8 1696
LORD your God, what you have p. Dt 23:23 1696
treasured possession, as He p you, Dt 26:18 1696
the God of your fathers, p you. Dt 27:3 1696
inheritance, as He had p to them. Jos 13:33 1696
just as the LORD your God p you. Jos 23:5 1696
fights for you, just as He p you. Jos 23:10 1696
Hebron to Caleb, as Moses had p; Jg 1:20 1696
and You have p this good thing to 2Sa 7:28 1696
who has made me a house as He p, 1Ki 2:24 1696
to Solomon, just as He p him; 1Ki 5:12 1696
throne of Israel, as the LORD p, 1Ki 8:20 1696
David, that which You have p him; 1Ki 8:24 1696
father that which You have p him, 1Ki 8:25 1696
according to all that He p; 1Ki 8:56 1696
He p through Moses His servant. 1Ki 8:56 1696
just as I p to your father David, 1Ki 9:5 1696
since He had p him to give a lamp 2Ki 8:19 559
and have p this good thing to Your 1Ch 17:26 1696
throne of Israel, as the LORD p, 2Ch 6:10 1696
that which You have p him; 2Ch 6:15 1696
that which You have p him, 2Ch 6:16 1696
and since He had p to give a lamp 2Ch 21:7 559
had p to pay to the king's treasuries Es 4:7 559
I have p to keep Your words. Ps 119:57 559
with which I had p to bless it. Jer 18:10 559
"The LORD your God p this Jer 40:2 1696
it on and done just as He p. Jer 40:3 1696

have **p** concerning this place to **Jer 51:62** 1696
that he **p** with an oath to **Mt 14:7** *3670*
this, and **p** to give him money. **Mk 14:11** *1861*
to wait for what the Father had **p**, **Ac 1:4** *1860*
He **p** that HE WOULD GIVE IT TO HIM **Ac 7:5** *1861*
which He **p** beforehand through His **Ro 1:2** *4279*
fully assured that what God had **p**, **Ro 4:21** *1861*
your previously **p** bountiful gift, **2Co 9:5** *4279*
who cannot lie, **p** long ages ago, **Ti 1:2** *1861*
for He who **p** is faithful; **Heb 10:23** *1861*
God, you may receive what was **p**. **Heb 10:36** *1860*
considered Him faithful who had **p**. **Heb 11:11** *1861*
faith, did not receive what was **p**, **Heb 11:39** *1860*
the earth then, but now He has **p**, **Heb 12:26** *1861*
Lord has **p** to those who love Him. **Jas 1:12** *1861*
which He **p** to those who love Him? **Jas 2:5** *1861*

PROMISES
Not one of the good **p** which the **Jos 21:45** 1697
and the *temple* service and the **p**, **Ro 9:4** *1860*
the **p** *given* to the fathers, **Ro 15:8** *1860*
as many as are the **p** of God, **2Co 1:20** *1860*
Therefore, having these **p**, **2Co 7:1** *1860*
Now the **p** were spoken to Abraham **Ga 3:16** *1860*
Law then contrary to the **p** of God? **Ga 3:21** *1860*
faith and patience inherit the **p**. **Heb 6:12** *1860*
and blessed the one who had the **p**. **Heb 7:6** *1860*
has been enacted on better **p**. **Heb 8:6** *1860*
died in faith, without receiving the **p** **Heb 11:13** *1860*
and he who had received the **p** was **Heb 11:17** *1860*
acts of righteousness, obtained **p**, **Heb 11:33** *1860*
us His precious and magnificent **p**, **2Pe 1:4** *1862*

PROMISING
all the good that I am **p** them. **Jer 32:42** 1696
p them freedom while they **2Pe 2:19** *1861*

PROMOTE
Do not **p** his *evil* device, *that* **Ps 140:8** 6329
upon you, but to **p** what is appropriate **1Co 7:35** *4314*

PROMOTED
events King Ahasuerus **p** Haman, **Es 3:1** 1431
and how he had **p** him above the **Es 5:11** 5375
Then the king **p** Daniel and gave **Da 2:48** 7236

PROMPT
justice And be **p** in righteousness. **Is 16:5** 4106

PROMPTED
Having been **p** by her mother, **Mt 14:8** *4264*

PROMPTLY
trees, then you shall act **p**, **2Sa 5:24** 2782
[*And they* **p** *reported all these* **Mk 16:20**

PROMPTS
money which any man's heart **p** him **2Ki 12:4**
5927, 5921

PRONE
yourself, that they are **p** to evil. **Ex 32:22**

PRONOUNCE
"By you Israel will **p** blessing, **Gn 48:20** 1288
at him, he shall **p** him unclean. **Lv 13:3** 2930
then the priest shall **p** him clean; **Lv 13:6** 2891
the priest shall **p** him unclean; **Lv 13:8** 2930
the priest shall **p** him unclean; **Lv 13:11** 2930
he shall **p** clean *him who has* the **Lv 13:13** 2891
flesh, and he shall **p** him unclean; **Lv 13:15** 2930
then the priest shall **p** clean *him* **Lv 13:17** 2891
the priest shall **p** him unclean; **Lv 13:20** 2930
the priest shall **p** him unclean; **Lv 13:22** 2930
and the priest shall **p** him clean. **Lv 13:23** 2891
the priest shall **p** him unclean; **Lv 13:25** 2930
the priest shall **p** him unclean; **Lv 13:27** 2930
and the priest shall **p** him clean, **Lv 13:28** 2891
the priest shall **p** him unclean; **Lv 13:30** 2930
the priest shall **p** him clean; **Lv 13:34** 2891
and the priest shall **p** him clean. **Lv 13:37** 2891
priest shall surely **p** him unclean; **Lv 13:44** 2930
leprosy and shall **p** him clean, **Lv 14:7** 2891
then the priest shall **p** the house **Lv 14:48** 2891
for he could not **p** it correctly. **Jg 12:6** 1696
"I will **p** My judgments on **Jer 1:16** 1696
also **p** judgments against them. **Jer 4:12** 1696
leaders **p** judgment for a bribe, **Mi 3:11** 8199
did not dare **p** against him a **Jude 1:9** *2018*

PRONOUNCED
has **p** evil against you because of **Jer 11:17** 1696
words which I have **p** against it, **Jer 25:13** 1696
which He has **p** against you. **Jer 26:13** 1696
which He had **p** against them? **Jer 26:19** 1696
disaster that I have **p** against them; **Jer 35:17** 1696
LORD has **p** against this people." **Jer 36:7** 1696
and I **p** them unclean because of **Ezk 20:26** 2930
And Pilate **p** sentence that their **Lk 23:24** *1948*
God has **p** judgment for you against **Rv 18:20** *2919*

PRONOUNCES
and the priest who **p** him clean **Lv 14:11** 2891

PRONOUNCING
for **p** it clean or unclean. **Lv 13:59** 2891

PROOF
having furnished **p** to all men by **Ac 17:31** *4102*
the **p** of your love and of our reason **2Co 8:24** *1732*
Because of the **p** given by this **2Co 9:13** *1382*
since you are seeking for **p** of the **2Co 13:3** *1382*
that the **p** of your faith, *being* **1Pe 1:7** *1383*

PROOFS
suffering, by many convincing **p**, **Ac 1:3** *5039*

PROPER
At the **p** time it shall be said to **Nu 23:23**
and the matter *seems* **p** to the king **Es 8:5** 3787
is right, And it is not **p** for me. **Jb 33:27** 7737a
and he does not even have a **p** **Ec 6:3**
knows the **p** time and procedure. **Ec 8:5**
For there is a **p** time and **Ec 8:6**
the proceeds at the **p** seasons." **Mt 21:41**
them their food at the **p** time? **Mt 24:45** *2540*
be fulfilled in their **p** time." **Lk 1:20** *2540*
them their rations at the **p** time? **Lk 12:42** *2540*
do those things which are not **p**, **Ro 1:28** *2520*
is it **p** for a woman to pray to God **1Co 11:13** *4241*
according to the **p** working of each **Eph 4:16** *3358*
among you, as is **p** among saints; **Eph 5:3** *4241*
the testimony *given* at the **p** time. **1Tm 2:6** *2398*
adorn themselves with **p** clothing, **1Tm 2:9** *2887*
as is **p** for women making a claim to **1Tm 2:10** *4241*
about things not **p** *to mention.* **1Tm 5:13** *1189b*
He will bring about at the **p** time **1Tm 6:15** *2398*
but at the **p** time manifested, *even* **Ti 1:3** *2398*
order you *to do* what is **p**, **Phm 1:8** *433*
even beyond the **p** time of life, **Heb 11:11** *2540*
He may exalt you at the **p** time, **1Pe 5:6** *2540*
but abandoned their **p** abode, **Jude 1:6** *2398*

PROPERLY
God instructs and teaches him **p**. **Is 28:26** 4941
But I will correct you **p** And by **Jer 46:28** 4941
holy place will be **p** restored." **Da 8:14** 6663
and **p** clothe yourself and serve **Lk 17:8**
Let us behave **p** as in the day, not **Ro 13:13** *2156*
done **p** and in an orderly manner. **1Co 14:40** *2156*
so that you will behave **p** toward **1Th 4:12** *2156*

PROPERTY
all his **p** which he had gathered, **Gn 31:18** 7399
in it and acquire **p** in it." **Gn 34:10** 270
p and all their animals be ours? **Gn 34:23** 7075
For their **p** had become too great **Gn 36:7** 7399
took their livestock and their **p**, **Gn 46:6** 7399
and they acquired **p** in it and were **Gn 47:27** 270
for he is his **p**. **Ex 21:21** 3701
laid his hands on his neighbor's **p**. **Ex 22:8** 4399
not laid hands on his neighbor's **p**; **Ex 22:11** 4399
a slave as *his* **p** with his money, **Lv 22:11** 7075
of you shall return to his own **p**, **Lv 25:10** 272
of you shall return to his own **p**. **Lv 25:13** 272
'Thus for every piece of your **p**, **Lv 25:24** 272
poor he has to sell part of his **p**, **Lv 25:25** 272
sold it, and so return to his **p**. **Lv 25:27** 272
that he may return to his **p**. **Lv 25:28** 272
to the **p** of his forefathers. **Lv 25:41** 272
part of the fields of his own **p**, **Lv 27:16** 272
shall be for the priest as his **p**. **Lv 27:21** 272
a part of the field of his own **p**, **Lv 27:22** 272
or of the fields of his own **p**, **Lv 27:28** 272
their livestock and for their **p**. **Jos 14:4** 7075
in the **p** of Naboth the Jezreelite. **2Ki 9:21** 2513a
"Take *him* up and cast him into the **p** **2Ki 9:25** 2513a
'and I will repay you in this **p**,' **2Ki 9:26** 2513a
take and cast him into the **p**, **2Ki 9:26** 2513a
'In the **p** of Jezreel the dogs **2Ki 9:36** 2506
of the field in the **p** of Jezreel, **2Ki 9:37** 2506
p which belonged to King David. **1Ch 27:31** 7399
and the overseers of all the **p** and **1Ch 28:1** 7399
left their pasture lands and their **p** **2Ch 11:14** 272
each lived on his own **p** in their cities **Ne 11:3** 272
of *some* **p** there among the people. **Jer 37:12** 2505a
you in hatred, take all your **p**, **Ezk 23:29** 3018
allotment and the **p** of the city, **Ezk 45:7** 272
allotment and the **p** of the city, **Ezk 45:7** 272
a square, with the **p** of the city. **Ezk 48:20** 272
and of the **p** of the city; **Ezk 48:21** 272
Exclusive of the **p** of the Levites and **Ezk 48:22** 272
the Levites and the **p** of the city, **Ezk 48:22** 272
man's house and carry off his **p**, **Mt 12:29** *4632*
for he was one who owned much **p**. **Mt 19:22** *2933*
strong man's house and plunder his **p** **Mk 3:27** *4632*
for he was one who owned much **p**. **Mk 10:22** *2933*
selling their **p** and possessions and **Ac 2:45** *2933*
all things were common **p** to them. **Ac 4:32** *2839*
wife Sapphira, sold a piece of **p**, **Ac 5:1** *2933*
joyfully the seizure of your **p**, **Heb 10:34** *5225*

PROPHECIES
in accordance with the **p** **1Tm 1:18** *4394*

PROPHECY
in the **p** of Ahijah the Shilonite, **2Ch 9:29** 5016
Asa heard these words and the **p** **2Ch 15:8** 5016
but he uttered *his* **p** against me **Ne 6:12** 5016
to seal up vision and **p** and **Da 9:24** 5030
p of Isaiah is being fulfilled, **Mt 13:14** *4394*
if **p**, according to the proportion **Ro 12:6** *4394*
of miracles, and to another **p**, **1Co 12:10** *4394*
If I have *the gift of* **p**, **1Co 13:2** *4394*
but if *there are gifts of* **p**, **1Co 13:8** *4394*
knowledge or of **p** or of teaching? **1Co 14:6** *4394*
but **p** *is for a sign,* not to **1Co 14:22** *4394*
that no **p** of Scripture is *a matter* **2Pe 1:20** *4394*
for no **p** was ever made by an act **2Pe 1:21** *4394*
those who hear the words of the **p**, **Rv 1:3** *4394*
testimony of Jesus is the spirit of **p** **Rv 19:10** *4394*
the words of the **p** of this book." **Rv 22:7** *4394*
the words of the **p** of this book, **Rv 22:10** *4394*
the words of the **p** of this book: **Rv 22:18** *4394*
the words of the book of this **p**, **Rv 22:19** *4394*

PROPHESIED
Spirit rested upon them, they **p**. **Nu 11:25** 5012
and they **p** in the camp. **Nu 11:26** 5012
mightily, so that he **p** among them. **1Sa 10:10** 5012
that he **p** now with the prophets, **1Sa 10:11** 5012
messengers of Saul; and they also **p**. **1Sa 19:20** 5012
other messengers, and they also **p**. **1Sa 19:21** 5012
the third time, and they also **p**. **1Sa 19:21** 5012
and he too **p** before Samuel and lay **1Sa 19:24** 5012
who **p** under the direction of the **1Ch 25:2** 5012
who **p** in giving thanks and **1Ch 25:3** 5012
p against Jehoshaphat saying, **2Ch 20:37** 5012
p to the Jews who were in Judah **Ezr 5:1** 5029
And the prophets **p** by Baal And **Jer 2:8** 5012
to whom you have falsely **p**.'" **Jer 20:6** 5012
They **p** by Baal and led My people **Jer 23:13** 5012
did not speak to them, But they **p**. **Jer 23:21** 5012
those who have **p** false dreams," **Jer 23:32** 5012
which Jeremiah has **p** against all the **Jer 25:13** 5012
"Why have you **p** in the name of **Jer 26:9** 5012
For he has **p** against this city as **Jer 26:11** 5012
"Micah of Moresheth **p** in the days **Jer 26:18** 5012
man who **p** in the name of the LORD, **Jer 26:20** 5012
and he **p** against this city and **Jer 26:20** 5012
confirm your words which you have **p** **Jer 28:6** 5012
from ancient times **p** against many **Jer 28:8** 5012
"Because Shemaiah has **p** to you, **Jer 29:31** 5012
are your prophets who **p** to you, **Jer 37:19** 5012
Now it came about as I **p**, **Ezk 11:13** 5012
So I **p** as I was commanded; **Ezk 37:7** 5012
and as I **p**, there was a noise, and **Ezk 37:7** 5012
So I **p** as He commanded me, and the **Ezk 37:10** 5012
who **p** in those days for *many* years **Ezk 38:17** 5012
prophets and the Law **p** until John. **Mt 11:13** *4395*
filled with the Holy Spirit, and **p**, **Lk 1:67** *4395*
he **p** that Jesus was going to die **Jn 11:51** *4395*
the prophets who **p** of the grace **1Pe 1:10** *4395*
seventh *generation* from Adam, **p**, **Jude 1:14** *4395*

PROPHESIES
for he never **p** good concerning me **2Ch 18:7** 5012
"The prophet who **p** of peace, when **Jer 28:9** 5012
the LORD over every madman who **p**, **Jer 29:26** 5012
Jeremiah of Anathoth who **p** to you? **Jer 29:27** 5012
now, and he **p** of times far off.' **Ezk 12:27** 5012
if anyone still **p**, **Zch 13:3** 5012
will pierce him through when he **p**. **Zch 13:3** 5012
ashamed of his vision when he **p**, **Zch 13:4** 5012
But one who **p** speaks to men for **1Co 14:3** *4395*
but one who **p** edifies the church. **1Co 14:4** *4395*
and greater is one who **p** than one **1Co 14:5** *4395*

PROPHESY
and you shall **p** with them and be **1Sa 10:6** 5012
he does not **p** good concerning me, **1Ki 22:8** 5012
he would not **p** good concerning me, **1Ki 22:18** 5012
who *were* to **p** with lyres, **1Ch 25:1** 5012
he would not **p** good concerning me, **2Ch 18:17** 5012
must not **p** to us what is right, **Is 30:10** 2372
to us pleasant words, **P** illusions. **Is 30:10** 2372
Those who **p** by the stars, **Is 47:13** 2372
The prophets **p** falsely, And the **Jer 5:31** 5012
"Do not **p** in the name of the **Jer 11:21** 5012
where the LORD had sent him to **p**; **Jer 19:14** 5012
said who **p** falsely in My name, **Jer 23:25** 5012
of the prophets who **p** falsehood, **Jer 23:26** 5012
p against them all these words, **Jer 25:30** 5012
"The LORD sent me to **p** against **Jer 26:12** 5012
'For they **p** a lie to you in **Jer 27:10** 5012
Babylon,' for they **p** a lie to you; **Jer 27:14** 5012
'but they **p** falsely in My name, **Jer 27:15** 5012
and the prophets who **p** to you." **Jer 27:15** 5012
of your prophets who **p** to you, **Jer 27:16** 5012
they **p** falsely to you in My name; **Jer 29:9** 5012
"Why do you **p**, saying, **Jer 32:3** 5012
your arm bared and **p** against it. **Ezk 4:7** 5012
of Israel, and **p** against them **Ezk 6:2** 5012
"Therefore, **p** against them, son **Ezk 11:4** 5012
against them, son of man, **p**!" **Ezk 11:4** 5012
p against the prophets of Israel **Ezk 13:2** 5012
the prophets of Israel who **p**, **Ezk 13:2** 5012
who **p** from their own inspiration, **Ezk 13:2** 5030
of Israel who **p** to Jerusalem, **Ezk 13:16** 5012
P against them **Ezk 13:17** 5012
and **p** against the forest land of **Ezk 20:46** 5012
and **p** against the land of Israel; **Ezk 21:2** 5012
"Son of man, **p** and say, **Ezk 21:9** 5012
"You therefore, son of man, **p** and **Ezk 21:14** 5012
"And you, son of man, **p** and say, **Ezk 21:28** 5012
sons of Ammon and **p** against them, **Ezk 25:2** 5012
face toward Sidon, **p** against her **Ezk 28:21** 5012
and **p** against him and against all **Ezk 29:2** 5012
"Son of man, **p** and say, **Ezk 30:2** 5012
p against the shepherds of Israel. **Ezk 34:2** 5012
P and say to those shepherds, **Ezk 34:2** 5012
Mount Seir, and **p** against it **Ezk 35:2** 5012
p to the mountains of Israel and **Ezk 36:1** 5012
therefore **p** and say, **Ezk 36:3** 5012
p concerning the land of Israel and **Ezk 36:6** 5012
"**P** over these bones and say to **Ezk 37:4** 5012
"**P** to the breath, prophesy, son **Ezk 37:9** 5012
"Prophesy to the breath, **p**, **Ezk 37:9** 5012
"Therefore **p** and say to them, **Ezk 37:12** 5012
and Tubal, and **p** against him **Ezk 38:2** 5012
"Therefore **p**, son of man, and **Ezk 38:14** 5012
you, son of man, **p** against Gog and **Ezk 39:1** 5012
your sons and daughters will **p**, **Jl 2:28** 5012
'You shall not **p**!' **Am 2:12** 5012
GOD has spoken! Who can but **p**? **Am 3:8** 5012
"But no longer **p** at Bethel, for **Am 7:13** 5012
'Go **p** to My people Israel.' **Am 7:15** 5012
'You shall not **p** against Israel **Am 7:16** 5012
Lord, did we not **p** in Your name, **Mt 7:22** *4395*
rightly did Isaiah **p** of you: **Mt 15:7** *4395*
"**P** to us, You Christ; **Mt 26:68** *4395*
did Isaiah **p** of you hypocrites, **Mk 7:6** *4395*
fists, and to say to Him, "**P**!" **Mk 14:65** *4395*
"**P**, who is the one who hit You?" **Lk 22:64** *4395*
SONS AND YOUR DAUGHTERS SHALL **P**, **Ac 2:17** *4395*

OF MY SPIRIT And they shall **p**.	**Ac 2:18**	*4395*
we know in part and we **p** in part;	**1Co 13:9**	*4395*
but especially that you may **p**.	**1Co 14:1**	*4395*
but *even* more that you would **p**;	**1Co 14:5**	*4395*
But if all **p**, and an unbeliever or	**1Co 14:24**	*4395*
For you can all **p** one by one, so	**1Co 14:31**	*4395*
brethren, desire earnestly to **p**,	**1Co 14:39**	*4395*
"You must **p** again concerning many	**Rv 10:11**	*4395*
and they will **p** for twelve hundred	**Rv 11:3**	*4395*

PROPHESYING

and Medad are **p** in the camp."	**Nu 11:27**	5012
before them, and they will be **p**.	**1Sa 10:5**	5012
When he had finished **p**,	**1Sa 10:13**	5012
saw the company of the prophets **p**,	**1Sa 19:20**	5012
so that he went along **p**	**1Sa 19:23**	5012
the prophets were **p** before them.	**1Ki 22:10**	5012
All the prophets were **p** thus,	**1Ki 22:12**	5012
the prophets were **p** before them.	**2Ch 18:9**	5012
All the prophets were **p** thus,	**2Ch 18:11**	5012
through the **p** of Haggai the prophet	**Ezr 6:14**	5017
are **p** falsehood in My name.	**Jer 14:14**	5012
they are **p** to you a false vision,	**Jer 14:14**	5012
the prophets who are **p** in My name,	**Jer 14:15**	5012
"The people also to whom they are **p**	**Jer 14:16**	5012
heard Jeremiah **p** these things,	**Jer 20:1**	5012
of the prophets who are **p** to you.	**Jer 23:16**	5012
for they are **p** a lie to you.	**Jer 27:16**	5012
are **p** to you falsely in My name,	**Jer 29:21**	5012
are **p** from their own inspiration.	**Ezk 13:17**	5012
eat bread and there do your **p**!	**Am 7:12**	5012
began speaking with tongues and **p**.	**Ac 19:6**	*4395*
on his head while praying or **p** disgraces	**1Co 11:4**	*4395*
while praying or **p** disgraces	**1Co 11:5**	*4395*
fall during the days of their **p**;	**Rv 11:6**	*4394*

PROPHET

the man's wife, for he is a **p**,	**Gn 20:7**	5030
brother Aaron shall be your **p**.	**Ex 7:1**	5030
If there is a **p** among you, I, the	**Nu 12:6**	5030
"If a **p** or a dreamer of dreams	**Dt 13:1**	5030
that **p** or that dreamer of dreams;	**Dt 13:3**	5030
"But that **p** or that dreamer of	**Dt 13:5**	5030
God will raise up for you a **p** like	**Dt 18:15**	5030
'I will raise up a **p** from among	**Dt 18:18**	5030
'But the **p** who speaks a word	**Dt 18:20**	5030
of other gods, that **p** shall die.'	**Dt 18:20**	5030
"When a **p** speaks in the name of	**Dt 18:22**	5030
p has spoken it presumptuously;	**Dt 18:22**	5030
Since that time no **p** has risen in	**Dt 34:10**	5030
sent a **p** to the sons of Israel,	**Jg 6:8**	5030
was confirmed as a **p** of the LORD.	**1Sa 3:20**	5030
for *he who is called* a **p** now was	**1Sa 9:9**	5030
The **p** Gad said to David,	**1Sa 22:5**	5030
the king said to Nathan the **p**,	**2Sa 7:2**	5030
sent *word* through Nathan the **p**,	**2Sa 12:25**	5030
of the LORD came to the **p** Gad,	**2Sa 24:11**	5030
the son of Jehoiada, Nathan the **p**,	**1Ki 1:8**	5030
he did not invite Nathan the **p**,	**1Ki 1:10**	5030
the king, Nathan the **p** came in.	**1Ki 1:22**	5030
"Here is Nathan the **p**."	**1Ki 1:23**	5030
me Zadok the priest, Nathan the **p**,	**1Ki 1:32**	5030
and Nathan the **p** anoint him there	**1Ki 1:34**	5030
So Zadok the priest, Nathan the **p**,	**1Ki 1:38**	5030
Zadok the priest, Nathan the **p**,	**1Ki 1:44**	5030
Nathan the **p** have anointed him king	**1Ki 1:45**	5030
that the **p** Ahijah the Shilonite	**1Ki 11:29**	5030
Now an old **p** was living in Bethel;	**1Ki 13:11**	5030
"I also am a **p** like you, and an	**1Ki 13:18**	5030
to the **p** who had brought him back;	**1Ki 13:20**	5030
the **p** whom he had brought back.	**1Ki 13:23**	5030
in the city where the old **p** lived.	**1Ki 13:25**	5030
Now when the **p** who brought him	**1Ki 13:26**	5030
So the **p** took up the body of the	**1Ki 13:29**	5030
old **p** to mourn and to bury him.	**1Ki 13:29**	5030
behold, Ahijah the **p** is there,	**1Ki 14:2**	5030
through His servant Ahijah the **p**.	**1Ki 14:18**	5030
word of the LORD through the **p** Jehu	**1Ki 16:7**	5030
against Baasha through Jehu the **p**,	**1Ki 16:12**	5030
"I alone am left a **p** of the LORD,	**1Ki 18:22**	5030
Elijah the **p** came near and said,	**1Ki 18:36**	5030
shall anoint as **p** in your place.	**1Ki 19:16**	5030
a **p** approached Ahab king of Israel	**1Ki 20:13**	5030
Then the **p** came near to the king	**1Ki 20:22**	5030
So the **p** departed and waited for	**1Ki 20:38**	5030
not yet a **p** of the LORD here that	**1Ki 22:7**	5030
"Is there not a **p** of the LORD	**2Ki 3:11**	5030
were with the **p** who is in Samaria!	**2Ki 5:3**	5030
that there is a **p** in Israel."	**2Ki 5:8**	5030
had the **p** told you *to do some*	**2Ki 5:13**	5030
Elisha, the **p** who is in Israel,	**2Ki 6:12**	5030
Now Elisha the **p** called one of the	**2Ki 9:1**	5030
young man, the servant of the **p**,	**2Ki 9:4**	5030
Jonah the son of Amittai, the **p**,	**2Ki 14:25**	5030
to Isaiah the **p** the son of Amoz.	**2Ki 19:2**	5030
And Isaiah the **p** the son of Amoz	**2Ki 20:1**	5030
Isaiah the **p** cried to the LORD,	**2Ki 20:11**	5030
Then Isaiah the **p** came to King	**2Ki 20:14**	5030
of the **p** who came from Samaria.	**2Ki 23:18**	5030
that David said to Nathan the **p**,	**1Ch 17:1**	5030
in the chronicles of Nathan the **p** and	**1Ch 29:29**	5030
in the records of Nathan the **p**,	**2Ch 9:29**	5030
Then Shemaiah the **p** came to	**2Ch 12:5**	5030
in the records of Shemaiah the **p**	**2Ch 12:15**	5030
in the treatise of the **p** Iddo.	**2Ch 13:22**	5030
the son of Oded the **p** spoke,	**2Ch 15:8**	5030
"Is there not yet a **p** of the LORD	**2Ch 18:6**	5030
to him from Elijah the **p** saying,	**2Ch 21:12**	5030
He sent him a **p** who said to him,	**2Ch 25:15**	5030
Then the **p** stopped and said,	**2Ch 25:16**	5030
first to last, the **p** Isaiah,	**2Ch 26:22**	5030
But a **p** of the LORD was there,	**2Ch 28:9**	5030
king's seer, and of Nathan the **p**;	**2Ch 29:25**	5030
King Hezekiah and Isaiah the **p**,	**2Ch 32:20**	5030
in the vision of Isaiah the **p**,	**2Ch 32:32**	5030
since the days of Samuel the **p**;	**2Ch 35:18**	5030
before Jeremiah the **p** who spoke for	**2Ch 36:12**	5030
p and Zechariah the son of Iddo,	**Ezr 5:1**	5029
the prophesying of Haggai the **p**	**Ezr 6:14**	5029
There is no longer any **p**,	**Ps 74:9**	5030
the warrior, The judge and the **p**,	**Is 3:2**	5030
And the **p** who teaches falsehood is	**Is 9:15**	5030
and the **p** reel with strong drink,	**Is 28:7**	5030
with sackcloth, to Isaiah the **p**,	**Is 37:2**	5030
And Isaiah the **p** the son of Amoz	**Is 38:1**	5030
Then Isaiah the **p** came to King	**Is 39:3**	5030
you a **p** to the nations."	**Jer 1:5**	5030
And from the **p** even to the priest	**Jer 6:13**	5030
From the **p** even to the priest	**Jer 8:10**	5030
For both **p** and priest Have gone	**Jer 14:18**	5030
nor the *divine* word to the **p**!	**Jer 18:18**	5030
Pashhur had Jeremiah the **p** beaten and	**Jer 20:2**	5030
both **p** and priest are polluted;	**Jer 23:11**	5030
"The **p** who has a dream may relate	**Jer 23:28**	5030
the **p** or a priest asks you saying,	**Jer 23:33**	5030
"Then as for the **p** or the priest	**Jer 23:34**	5030
"Thus you will say to *that* **p**,	**Jer 23:37**	5030
which Jeremiah the **p** spoke to all	**Jer 25:2**	5030
Hananiah the son of Azzur, the **p**,	**Jer 28:1**	5030
Then the **p** Jeremiah spoke to the	**Jer 28:5**	5030
Jeremiah spoke to the **p** Hananiah	**Jer 28:5**	5030
and the **p** Jeremiah said,	**Jer 28:6**	5030
"The **p** who prophesies of peace,	**Jer 28:9**	5030
word of the **p** comes to pass,	**Jer 28:9**	5030
then that **p** will be known *as* one	**Jer 28:9**	5030
Then Hananiah the **p** took the yoke	**Jer 28:10**	5030
of Jeremiah the **p** and broke it.	**Jer 28:10**	5030
Then the **p** Jeremiah went his way.	**Jer 28:11**	5030
after Hananiah the **p** had broken	**Jer 28:12**	5030
off the neck of the **p** Jeremiah,	**Jer 28:12**	5030
Jeremiah the **p** said to Hananiah	**Jer 28:15**	5030
the prophet said to Hananiah the **p**,	**Jer 28:15**	5030
So Hananiah the **p** died in the same	**Jer 28:17**	5030
the letter which Jeremiah the **p** sent	**Jer 29:1**	5030
this letter to Jeremiah the **p**.	**Jer 29:29**	5030
and Jeremiah the **p** was shut up in	**Jer 32:2**	5030
Then Jeremiah the **p** spoke all	**Jer 34:6**	5030
that Jeremiah the **p** commanded him,	**Jer 36:8**	5030
the scribe and Jeremiah the **p**,	**Jer 36:26**	5030
He spoke through Jeremiah the **p**.	**Jer 37:2**	5030
the priest, to Jeremiah the **p**,	**Jer 37:3**	5030
the LORD came to Jeremiah the **p**,	**Jer 37:6**	5030
and he arrested Jeremiah the **p**,	**Jer 37:13**	5030
that they have done to Jeremiah the **p**	**Jer 38:9**	5030
and bring up Jeremiah the **p** from	**Jer 38:10**	5030
had Jeremiah the **p** brought to him	**Jer 38:14**	5030
and said to Jeremiah the **p**,	**Jer 42:2**	5030
Then Jeremiah the **p** said to them,	**Jer 42:4**	5030
together with Jeremiah the **p** and	**Jer 43:6**	5030
message which Jeremiah the **p** spoke	**Jer 45:1**	5030
word of the LORD to Jeremiah the **p**	**Jer 46:1**	5030
the LORD spoke to Jeremiah the **p**	**Jer 46:13**	5030
word of the LORD to Jeremiah the **p**	**Jer 47:1**	5030
word of the LORD to Jeremiah the **p**	**Jer 49:34**	5030
Chaldeans, through Jeremiah the **p**:	**Jer 50:1**	5030
The message which Jeremiah the **p**	**Jer 51:59**	5030
Should priest and **p** be slain In	**La 2:20**	5030
know that a **p** has been among them.	**Ezk 2:5**	5030
they will seek a vision from a **p**,	**Ezk 7:26**	5030
iniquity, and *then* comes to the **p**,	**Ezk 14:4**	5030
p to inquire of Me for himself,	**Ezk 14:7**	5030
"But if the **p** is prevailed upon	**Ezk 14:9**	5030
who have prevailed upon that **p**,	**Ezk 14:9**	5030
so the iniquity of the **p** will be,	**Ezk 14:10**	5030
a **p** has been in their midst."	**Ezk 33:33**	5030
word of the LORD to Jeremiah the **p**	**Da 9:2**	5030
And the **p** also will stumble with	**Hos 4:5**	5030
The **p** is a fool, The inspired man	**Hos 9:7**	5030
was a watchman with my God, a **p**;	**Hos 9:8**	5030
But by a **p** the LORD brought Israel	**Hos 12:13**	5030
Egypt, And by a **p** he was kept.	**Hos 12:13**	5030
"I am not a **p**, nor am I the son	**Am 7:14**	5030
prophet, nor am I the son of a **p**;	**Am 7:14**	5030
oracle which Habakkuk the **p** saw.	**Hab 1:1**	5030
A prayer of Habakkuk the **p**,	**Hab 3:1**	5030
came by the **p** Haggai to Zerubbabel	**Hg 1:1**	5030
LORD came by Haggai the **p**,	**Hg 1:3**	5030
God and the words of Haggai the **p**,	**Hg 1:12**	5030
LORD came by Haggai the **p** saying,	**Hg 2:1**	5030
LORD came to Haggai the **p**,	**Hg 2:10**	5030
the LORD came to Zechariah the **p**,	**Zch 1:1**	5030
the LORD came to Zechariah the **p**,	**Zch 1:7**	5030
'I am not a **p**; I am a tiller of the	**Zch 13:5**	5030
I am going to send you Elijah the **p**	**Mal 4:5**	5030
spoken by the Lord through the **p**	**Mt 1:22**	*4396*
what has been written by the **p**:	**Mt 2:5**	*4396*
spoken by the Lord through the **p**	**Mt 2:15**	*4396*
been spoken through Jeremiah the **p**	**Mt 2:17**	*4396*
one referred to by Isaiah the **p** when	**Mt 3:3**	*4396*
was spoken through Isaiah the **p**:	**Mt 4:14**	*4396*
was spoken through Isaiah the **p**	**Mt 8:17**	*4396*
"He who receives a **p** in *the* name	**Mt 10:41**	*4396*
receives a prophet in *the* name of a **p**	**Mt 10:41**	*4396*
"But what did you go out to see? A **p**?	**Mt 11:9**	*4396*
you, and one who is more than a **p**.	**Mt 11:9**	*4396*
was spoken through Isaiah the **p**:	**Mt 12:17**	*4396*
to it but the sign of Jonah the **p**;	**Mt 12:39**	*4396*
what was spoken through the **p**	**Mt 13:35**	*4396*
"A **p** is not without honor except	**Mt 13:57**	*4396*
because they regarded John as a **p**.	**Mt 14:5**	*4396*
what was spoken through the **p**	**Mt 21:4**	*4396*
"This is the **p** Jesus, from	**Mt 21:11**	*4396*
they all regard John as a **p**."	**Mt 21:26**	*4396*
because they considered Him to be a **p**.	**Mt 21:46**	*4396*
spoken of through Daniel the **p**,	**Mt 24:15**	*4396*
Jeremiah the **p** was fulfilled:	**Mt 27:9**	*4396*
As it is written in Isaiah the **p**:	**Mk 1:2**	*4396*
"A **p** is not without honor except	**Mk 6:4**	*4396*
"*He is* a **p**, like one of the	**Mk 6:15**	*4396*
John to have been a real **p**.	**Mk 11:32**	*4396*
be called the **p** of the Most High;	**Lk 1:76**	*4396*
book of the words of Isaiah the **p**,	**Lk 3:4**	*4396*
of the **p** Isaiah was handed to Him.	**Lk 4:17**	*4396*
no **p** is welcome in his hometown.	**Lk 4:24**	*4396*
in the time of Elisha the **p**;	**Lk 4:27**	*4396*
"A great **p** has arisen among us!"	**Lk 7:16**	*4396*
what did you go out to see? A **p**?	**Lk 7:26**	*4396*
you, and one who is more than a **p**.	**Lk 7:26**	*4396*
"If this man were a **p** He would	**Lk 7:39**	*4396*
it cannot be that a **p** would perish	**Lk 13:33**	*4396*
are convinced that John was a **p**."	**Lk 20:6**	*4396*
who was a **p** mighty in deed and	**Lk 24:19**	*4396*
"Are you the **P**?"	**Jn 1:21**	*4396*
THE LORD,' as Isaiah the **p** said."	**Jn 1:23**	*4396*
Christ, nor Elijah, nor the **P**?"	**Jn 1:25**	*4396*
"Sir, I perceive that You are a **p**.	**Jn 4:19**	*4396*
a **p** has no honor in his own country.	**Jn 4:44**	*4396*
P who is to come into the world."	**Jn 6:14**	*4396*
"This certainly is the **P**."	**Jn 7:40**	*4396*
that no **p** arises out of Galilee."	**Jn 7:52**	*4396*
And he said, "He is a **p**."	**Jn 9:17**	*4396*
fulfill the word of Isaiah the **p**	**Jn 12:38**	*4396*
was spoken of through the **p** Joel:	**Ac 2:16**	*4396*
"And so, because he was a **p** and	**Ac 2:30**	*4396*
GOD WILL RAISE UP FOR YOU A **P**	**Ac 3:22**	*4396*
soul that does not heed that **p** shall	**Ac 3:23**	*4396*
GOD WILL RAISE UP FOR YOU A **P**	**Ac 7:37**	*4396*
made by *human* hands; as the **p** says:	**Ac 7:48**	*4396*
and was reading the **p** Isaiah.	**Ac 8:28**	*4396*
and heard him reading Isaiah the **p**,	**Ac 8:30**	*4396*
me, of whom does the **p** say this?	**Ac 8:34**	*4396*
false **p** whose name was Bar-Jesus,	**Ac 13:6**	*5578*
them judges until Samuel the **p**.	**Ac 13:20**	*4396*
a **p** named Agabus came down	**Ac 21:10**	*4396*
Isaiah the **p** to your fathers,	**Ac 28:25**	*4396*
thinks he is a **p** or spiritual,	**1Co 14:37**	*4396*
of themselves, a **p** of their own,	**Ti 1:12**	*4396*
restrained the madness of the **p**.	**2Pe 2:16**	*4396*
out of the mouth of the false **p**,	**Rv 16:13**	*5578*
and with him the false **p** who	**Rv 19:20**	*5578*
beast and the false **p** are also;	**Rv 20:10**	*5578*

PROPHETESS

Miriam the **p**, Aaron's sister,	**Ex 15:20**	5031
Now Deborah, a **p**, the wife of	**Jg 4:4**	5031
and Asaiah went to Huldah the **p**,	**2Ki 22:14**	5031
had told went to Huldah the **p**,	**2Ch 34:22**	5031
and also Noadiah the **p** and the	**Ne 6:14**	5031
So I approached the **p**,	**Is 8:3**	5031
And there was a **p**, Anna the	**Lk 2:36**	*4398*
Jezebel, who calls herself a **p**,	**Rv 2:20**	*4398*

PROPHETESSES

four virgin daughters who were **p**.	**Ac 21:9**	*4395*

PROPHETIC

do not despise **p** utterances.	**1Th 5:20**	*4394*
through **p** utterance with the laying	**1Tm 4:14**	*4394*
we have the **p** word *made* more sure,	**2Pe 1:19**	*4397*

PROPHET'S

prophet shall receive a **p** reward;	**Mt 10:41**	*4396*

PROPHETS

that all the LORD's people were **p**,	**Nu 11:29**	5030
that you will meet a group of **p**	**1Sa 10:5**	5030
behold, a group of **p** met him;	**1Sa 10:10**	5030
that he prophesied now with the **p**,	**1Sa 10:11**	5030
Is Saul also among the **p**?"	**1Sa 10:11**	5030
"Is Saul also among the **p**?"	**1Sa 10:12**	5030
the company of the **p** prophesying,	**1Sa 19:20**	5030
"Is Saul also among the **p**?"	**1Sa 19:24**	5030
by dreams or by Urim or by **p**.	**1Sa 28:6**	5030
either through **p** or by dreams;	**1Sa 28:15**	5030
Jezebel destroyed the **p** of the LORD,	**1Ki 18:4**	5030
Obadiah took a hundred **p** and	**1Ki 18:4**	5030
Jezebel killed the **p** of the LORD,	**1Ki 18:13**	5030
that I hid a hundred **p** of the LORD	**1Ki 18:13**	5030
together with 450 **p** of Baal and	**1Ki 18:19**	5030
of Baal and 400 **p** of the Asherah,	**1Ki 18:19**	5030
the **p** together at Mount Carmel.	**1Ki 18:20**	5030
the LORD, but Baal's **p** are 450 men.	**1Ki 18:22**	5030
So Elijah said to the **p** of Baal,	**1Ki 18:25**	5030
"Seize the **p** of Baal;	**1Ki 18:40**	5030
killed all the **p** with the sword.	**1Ki 19:1**	5030
and killed Your **p** with the sword.	**1Ki 19:10**	5030
and killed Your **p** with the sword.	**1Ki 19:14**	5030
a certain man of the sons of the **p**	**1Ki 20:35**	5030
him that he was of the **p**.	**1Ki 20:41**	5030
of Israel gathered the **p** together,	**1Ki 22:6**	5030
p were prophesying before them.	**1Ki 22:10**	5030
All the **p** were prophesying thus,	**1Ki 22:12**	5030
the words of the **p** are uniformly	**1Ki 22:13**	5030
spirit in the mouth of all his **p**.'	**1Ki 22:22**	5030
in the mouth of all these your **p**;	**1Ki 22:23**	5030
Then the sons of the **p** who *were at*	**2Ki 2:3**	5030
The sons of the **p** who *were* at	**2Ki 2:5**	5030
fifty men of the sons of the **p** went	**2Ki 2:7**	5030
Now when the sons of the **p** who	**2Ki 2:15**	5030
Go to the **p** of your father and to	**2Ki 3:13**	5030
and to the **p** of your mother."	**2Ki 3:13**	5030
sons of the **p** cried out to Elisha,	**2Ki 4:1**	5030

sons of the **p** were sitting before him, **2Ki 4:38** 5030
boil stew for the sons of the **p**.” **2Ki 4:38** 5030
two young men of the sons of the **p** **2Ki 5:22** 5030
the sons of the **p** said to Elisha, **2Ki 6:1** 5030
called one of the sons of the **p** and **2Ki 9:1** 5030
the blood of My servants the **p**, **2Ki 9:7** 5030
“Now, summon all the **p** of Baal, **2Ki 10:19** 5030
through all His **p** *and* every seer, **2Ki 17:13** 5030
you through My servants the **p**.” **2Ki 17:13** 5030
through all His servants the **p**. **2Ki 17:23** 5030
spoke through His servants the **p**, **2Ki 21:10** 5030
and the **p** and all the people, **2Ki 23:2** 5030
spoken through His servants the **p**. **2Ki 24:2** 5030
ones, And do My **p** no harm.” **1Ch 16:22** 5030
king of Israel assembled the **p**, **2Ch 18:5** 5030
p were prophesying before them. **2Ch 18:9** 5030
All the **p** were prophesying thus, **2Ch 18:11** 5030
the words of the **p** are uniformly **2Ch 18:12** 5030
spirit in the mouth of all his **p**.’ **2Ch 18:21** 5030
in the mouth of these your **p**, **2Ch 18:22** 5030
Put your trust in His **p** and succeed **2Ch 20:20** 5030
Yet He sent **p** to them to bring **2Ch 24:19** 5030
was from the LORD through His **p**. **2Ch 29:25** 5030
His words and scoffed at His **p**, **2Ch 36:16** 5030
When the **p**, Haggai the prophet and **Ezr 5:1** 5029
and the **p** of God were with them **Ezr 5:2** 5029
commanded by Your servants the **p**, **Ezr 9:11** 5030
“You have also appointed **p** to **Ne 6:7** 5030
the **p** who were *trying* to frighten me. **Ne 6:14** 5030
killed Your **p** who had admonished **Ne 9:26** 5030
them by Your Spirit through Your **p**, **Ne 9:30** 5030
our princes, our priests, our **p**, **Ne 9:32** 5030
ones, And do My **p** no harm.” **Ps 105:15** 5030
He has shut your eyes, the **p**; **Is 29:10** 5030
to the **p**, “You must not prophesy **Is 30:10** 2374
And the **p** prophesied by Baal And **Jer 2:8** 5030
And their priests and their **p**, **Jer 2:26** 5030
Your sword has devoured your **p** **Jer 2:30** 5030
and the **p** will be astounded.” **Jer 4:9** 5030
“The **p** are *as* wind, And the **Jer 5:13** 5030
The **p** prophesy falsely, And the **Jer 5:31** 5030
sent you all My servants the **p**, **Jer 7:25** 5030
priests and the bones of the **p**, **Jer 8:1** 5030
the **p** and all the inhabitants of **Jer 13:13** 5030
“Look, the **p** are telling them, **Jer 14:13** 5030
“The **p** are prophesying falsehood **Jer 14:14** 5030
thus says the LORD concerning the **p** **Jer 14:15** 5030
those **p** shall meet their end! **Jer 14:15** 5030
As for the **p**: My heart is broken **Jer 23:9** 5030
among the **p** of Samaria I saw an **Jer 23:13** 5030
“Also among the **p** of Jerusalem I **Jer 23:14** 5030
LORD of hosts concerning the **p**, **Jer 23:15** 5030
For from the **p** of Jerusalem **Jer 23:15** 5030
the **p** who are prophesying to you. **Jer 23:16** 5030
“I did not send *these* **p**, **Jer 23:21** 5030
“I have heard what the **p** have **Jer 23:25** 5030
of the **p** who prophesy falsehood, **Jer 23:26** 5030
even *these* **p** of the deception of **Jer 23:26** 5030
behold, I am against the **p**,” **Jer 23:30** 5030
“Behold, I am against the **p**,” **Jer 23:31** 5030
sent to you all His servants the **p** **Jer 25:4** 5030
to the words of My servants the **p**, **Jer 26:5** 5030
The priests and the **p** and all **Jer 26:7** 5030
p and all the people seized him, **Jer 26:8** 5030
Then the priests and the **p** spoke **Jer 26:11** 5030
said to the priests and to the **p**, **Jer 26:16** 5030
for you, do not listen to your **p**, **Jer 27:9** 5030
do not listen to the words of the **p** **Jer 27:14** 5030
and the **p** who prophesy to you.” **Jer 27:15** 5030
of your **p** who prophesy to you, **Jer 27:16** 5030
“But if they are **p**, and if the **Jer 27:18** 5030
“The **p** who were before me and **Jer 28:8** 5030
of the exile, the priests, the **p** and **Jer 29:1** 5030
‘Do not let your **p** who are in your **Jer 29:8** 5030
has raised up **p** for us in Babylon’ **Jer 29:15** 5030
and again by My servants the **p**; **Jer 29:19** 5030
leaders, their priests, their **p**, **Jer 32:32** 5030
sent to you all My servants the **p**, **Jer 35:15** 5030
are your **p** who prophesied to you, **Jer 37:19** 5030
I sent you all My servants the **p**, **Jer 44:4** 5030
p find No vision from the LORD. **La 2:9** 5030
Your **p** have seen for you False and **La 2:14** 5030
Because of the sins of her **p** *And* **La 4:13** 5030
prophesy against the **p** of Israel **Ezk 13:2** 5030
“Woe to the foolish **p** who are **Ezk 13:3** 5030
your **p** have been like foxes among **Ezk 13:4** 5030
“So My hand will be against the **p** **Ezk 13:9** 5030
along with the **p** of Israel who **Ezk 13:16** 5030
conspiracy of her **p** in her midst like **Ezk 22:25** 5030
“Her **p** have smeared whitewash **Ezk 22:28** 5030
My servants the **p** of Israel, **Ezk 38:17** 5030
listened to Your servants the **p**, **Da 9:6** 5030
us through His servants the **p**. **Da 9:10** 5030
have hewn *them* in pieces by the **p**; **Hos 6:5** 5030
I have also spoken to the **p**, **Hos 12:10** 5030
And through the **p** I gave parables. **Hos 12:10** 5030
I raised up some of your sons to be **p** **Am 2:11** 5030
And you commanded the **p** saying, **Am 2:12** 5030
counsel To His servants the **p**. **Am 3:7** 5030
the **p** who lead my people astray; **Mi 3:5** 5030
The sun will go down on the **p**, **Mi 3:6** 5030
price And her **p** divine for money. **Mi 3:11** 5030
Her **p** are reckless, treacherous **Zph 3:4** 5030
to whom the former **p** proclaimed, **Zch 1:4** 5030
And the **p**, do they live forever? **Zch 1:5** 5030
I commanded My servants the **p**, **Zch 1:6** 5030
of hosts, and to the **p**, **Zch 7:3** 5030
LORD proclaimed by the former **p**, **Zch 7:7** 5030
His Spirit through the former **p**; **Zch 7:12** 5030
words from the mouth of the **p**, **Zch 8:9** 5030
and I will also remove the **p** and **Zch 13:2** 5030
p will each be ashamed of his vision **Zch 13:4** 5030
what was spoken through the **p** **Mt 2:23** *4396*
the **p** who were before you. **Mt 5:12** *4396*
came to abolish the Law or the **P**; **Mt 5:17** *4396*
for this is the Law and the **P**. **Mt 7:12** *4396*
“Beware of the false **p**, **Mt 7:15** *5578*
“For all the **p** and the Law **Mt 11:13** *4396*
that many **p** and righteous men **Mt 13:17** *4396*
Jeremiah, or one of the **p**.” **Mt 16:14** *4396*
depend the whole Law and the **P**.” **Mt 22:40** *4396*
For you build the tombs of the **p** **Mt 23:29** *4396*
in *shedding* the blood of the **p**.’ **Mt 23:30** *4396*
sons of those who murdered the **p**. **Mt 23:31** *4396*
you **p** and wise men and scribes; **Mt 23:34** *4396*
who kills the **p** and stones those **Mt 23:37** *4396*
“Many false **p** will arise and **Mt 24:11** *5578*
“For false Christs and false **p** **Mt 24:24** *5578*
fulfill the Scriptures of the **p**.” **Mt 26:56** *4396*
like one of the **p** *of old*.” **Mk 6:15** *4396*
but others, one of the **p**.” **Mk 8:28** *4396*
false Christs and false **p** will arise, **Mk 13:22** *5578*
mouth of His holy **p** from of old **Lk 1:70** *4396*
their fathers used to treat the **p**. **Lk 6:23** *4396*
fathers used to treat the false **p** in **Lk 6:26** *5578*
one of the **p** of old had risen again. **Lk 9:8** *4396*
one of the **p** of old has risen again.” **Lk 9:19** *4396*
that many **p** and kings wished to **Lk 10:24** *4396*
For you build the tombs of the **p**, **Lk 11:47** *4396*
will send to them **p** and apostles, **Lk 11:49** *4396*
so that the blood of all the **p**, **Lk 11:50** *4396*
all the **p** in the kingdom of God, **Lk 13:28** *4396*
city that kills the **p** and stones those **Lk 13:34** *4396*
The Law and the **P** *were proclaimed* **Lk 16:16** *4396*
‘They have Moses and the **P**; **Lk 16:29** *4396*
do not listen to Moses and the **P**, **Lk 16:31** *4396*
written through the **p** about the Son **Lk 18:31** *4396*
in all that the **p** have spoken! **Lk 24:25** *4396*
with Moses and with all the **p**, **Lk 24:27** *4396*
in the Law of Moses and the **P** **Lk 24:44** *4396*
in the Law and *also* the **P** wrote **Jn 1:45** *4396*
“It is written in the **p**, **Jn 6:45** *4396*
Abraham died, and the **p** *also* **Jn 8:52** *4396*
The **p** died too; **Jn 8:53** *4396*
by the mouth of all the **p**, **Ac 3:18** *4396*
spoke by the mouth of His holy **p** **Ac 3:21** *4396*
all the **p** who have spoken, **Ac 3:24** *4396*
is you who are the sons of the **p** and **Ac 3:25** *4396*
is written in the book of the **p**, **Ac 7:42** *4396*
“Which one of the **p** did your **Ac 7:52** *4396*
“Of Him all the **p** bear witness **Ac 10:43** *4396*
Now at this time some **p** came down **Ac 11:27** *4396*
that was *there*, **p** and teachers: **Ac 13:1** *4396*
the reading of the Law and the **P** **Ac 13:15** *4396*
p which are read every Sabbath, **Ac 13:27** *4396*
the thing spoken of in the **P** **Ac 13:40** *4396*
this the words of the **P** agree, **Ac 15:15** *4396*
Silas, also being **p** themselves, **Ac 15:32** *4396*
Law and that is written in the **P**; **Ac 24:14** *4396*
stating nothing but what the **P** and **Ac 26:22** *4396*
Agrippa, do you believe the **P**? **Ac 26:27** *4396*
the Law of Moses and from the **P**, **Ac 28:23** *4396*
promised beforehand through His **p** **Ro 1:2** *4396*
witnessed by the Law and the **P**, **Ro 3:21** *4396*
“Lord, THEY HAVE KILLED YOUR **P**, **Ro 11:3** *4396*
and by the Scriptures of the **p**, **Ro 16:26** *4397*
church, first apostles, second **p**, **1Co 12:28** *4396*
All are not **p**, are they? **1Co 12:29** *4396*
Let two or three **p** speak, **1Co 14:29** *4396*
spirits of **p** are subject to prophets; **1Co 14:32** *4396*
spirits of prophets are subject to **p**; **1Co 14:32** *4396*
foundation of the apostles and **p**, **Eph 2:20** *4396*
holy apostles and **p** in the Spirit; **Eph 3:5** *4396*
some *as* apostles, and some *as* **p**, **Eph 4:11** *4396*
killed the Lord Jesus and the **p**, **1Th 2:15** *4396*
spoke long ago to the fathers in the **p** **Heb 1:1** *4396*
of David and Samuel and the **p**, **Heb 11:32** *4396*
take the **p** who spoke in the name **Jas 5:10** *4396*
the **p** who prophesied of the grace **1Pe 1:10** *4396*
false **p** also arose among the people, **2Pe 2:1** *5578*
spoken beforehand by the holy **p** **2Pe 3:2** *4396*
many false **p** have gone out into the **1Jn 4:1** *5578*
He preached to His servants the **p**. **Rv 10:7** *4396*
because these two **p** tormented **Rv 11:10** *4396*
reward Your bond-servants the **p** **Rv 11:18** *4396*
out the blood of saints and **p**, **Rv 16:6** *4396*
and you saints and apostles and **p**, **Rv 18:20** *4396*
“And in her was found the blood of **p** **Rv 18:24** *4396*
the God of the spirits of the **p**, **Rv 22:6** *4396*
of your brethren the **p** and of those **Rv 22:9** *4396*

PROPITIATION
as a **p** in His blood through faith. **Ro 3:25** *2435*
make **p** for the sins of the people. **Heb 2:17** *2433*
He Himself is the **p** for our sins; **1Jn 2:2** *2434*
His Son *to be* the **p** for our sins. **1Jn 4:10** *2434*

PROPORTION
‘In **p** to the extent of the years **Lv 25:16** 6310
in **p** to the fewness of the years you **Lv 25:16** 6310
refund part of his purchase price in **p** **Lv 25:51** 6310
In **p** to his years he is to refund **Lv 25:52** 6310
some of his cities to the Levites in **p** **Nu 35:8** 6310
And in the **p** that any of the **Ac 11:29** *2531a*
according to the **p** of his faith; **Ro 12:6** *356*

PROPORTIONATE
be **p** to the seed needed for it: **Lv 27:16** 6310
p to the years that are left until the **Lv 27:18** 6310

PROPORTIONS
make *any* like it in the same **p**; **Ex 30:32** 4971
make in the same **p** for yourselves; **Ex 30:37** 4971

PROPOSAL
Now the **p** seemed good to Pharaoh **Gn 41:37** 1697
Then David sent a **p** to Abigail, **1Sa 25:39** 1696
they would do according to this **p**; **Ezr 10:5** 1697
State a **p**, but it will not stand, **Is 8:10** 1697
bringing with him a **p** of peace **Da 11:17** 3477

PROPOSE
what you **p** to do with these men. **Ac 5:35** *3195*
I **p** to be courageous against some, **2Co 10:2** *3049*

PROPOSED
and the king did as Memucan **p**. **Es 1:21** 1697

PROPOSING
“Now you are **p** to subjugate **2Ch 28:10** 559
for you are **p** *to bring* upon us **2Ch 28:13** 559

PROPOUND
“Let me now **p** a riddle to you; **Jg 14:12** 2330
“**P** your riddle, that we may hear **Jg 14:13** 2330
“Son of man, **p** a riddle and **Ezk 17:2** 2330

PROPOUNDED
you have **p** a riddle to the sons of **Jg 14:16** 2330

PROPPED
and the king was **p** up in his **1Ki 22:35** 5975
and the king of Israel **p** himself **2Ch 18:34** 5975

PROSECUTE
about the man, let them **p** him.” **Ac 25:5** *2723*

PROSELYTE
on sea and land to make one **p**; **Mt 23:15** *4339*
and Nicolas, a **p** from Antioch. **Ac 6:5** *4339*

PROSELYTES
from Rome, both Jews and **p**, **Ac 2:10** *4339*
p followed Paul and Barnabas, **Ac 13:43** *4339*

PROSPER
your relatives, and I will **p** you,’ **Gn 32:9** 3190
‘I will surely **p** you and make **Gn 32:12** 3190
all that he did to **p** in his hand. **Gn 39:3** 6743b
he did, the LORD made to **p**. **Gn 39:23** 6743b
and you will not **p** in your ways; **Dt 28:29** 6743b
LORD delighted over you to **p** you, **Dt 28:63** 3190
that you may **p** in all that you do. **Dt 29:9** 7919a
and He will **p** you and multiply you **Dt 30:5** 3190
your God will **p** you abundantly **Dt 30:9** 3498
I know that the LORD will **p** me, **Jg 17:13** 3190
“Go up to Ramoth-gilead and **p**, **1Ki 22:12** 6743b
“Then you will **p**, if you are **1Ch 22:13** 6743b
of the LORD and do not **p**? **2Ch 24:20** 6743b
“The tents of the destroyers **p**, **Jb 12:6** 7951
His ways **p** at all times; **Ps 10:5** 2342b
“May they **p** who love you. **Ps 122:6** 7951
his transgressions will not **p**, **Pr 28:13** 6743b
he who trusts in the LORD will **p**. **Pr 28:25** 1878
Behold, My servant will **p**, **Is 52:13** 7919a
good pleasure of the LORD will **p** **Is 53:10** 6743b
is formed against you will **p**; **Is 54:17** 6743b
And you will not **p** with them.” **Jer 2:37** 6743b
of the orphan, that they may **p**; **Jer 5:28** 6743b
A man who will not **p** in his days; **Jer 22:30** 6743b
For no man of his descendants will **p** **Jer 22:30** 6743b
become her masters, Her enemies **p**; **La 1:5** 7951
to **p** in the province of Babylon. **Da 3:30** 6744
ground and perform *its will* and **p**. **Da 8:12** 6743b
degree And **p** and perform *his will;* **Da 8:24** 6743b
and he will **p** until the indignation **Da 11:36** 6743b
put aside and save, as he may **p**, **1Co 16:2** *2137*
you may **p** and be in good health, **3Jn 1:2** *2137*

PROSPERED
me, since the LORD has **p** my way. **Gn 24:56** 6743b
out wherever Saul sent him, *and* **p**; **1Sa 18:5** 7919a
wherever he went he **p**. **2Ki 18:7** 7919a
and he **p**, and all Israel obeyed **1Ch 29:23** 6743b
So they built and **p**. **2Ch 14:7** 6743b
as he sought the LORD, God **p** him. **2Ch 26:5** 6743b
he did with all his heart and **p**. **2Ch 31:21** 6743b
And Hezekiah **p** in all that he did. **2Ch 32:30** 6743b
Therefore they have not **p**, **Jer 10:21** 7919a
Why has the way of the wicked **p**? **Jer 12:1** 6743b

PROSPERING
David was **p** in all his ways **1Sa 18:14** 7919a
Saul saw that he was **p** greatly, **1Sa 18:15** 7919a

PROSPERITY
never seek their peace or their **p** **Dt 23:6** 2899b
LORD will make you abound in **p**, **Dt 28:11** 2899b
set before you today life and **p**, **Dt 30:15** 2896b
You exceed in wisdom and **p** **1Ki 10:7** 2896b
never seek their peace or their **p**, **Ezr 9:12** 2899b
Therefore his **p** does not endure. **Jb 20:21** 2898
“They spend their days in **p**, **Jb 21:13** 2896b
their **p** is not in their hand; **Jb 21:16** 2898
my **p** has passed away like a cloud. **Jb 30:15** 3444
They will end their days in **p** **Jb 36:11** 2896b
His soul will abide in **p**, **Ps 25:13** 2896b
Now as for me, I said in my **p**, **Ps 30:6** 7959
delights in the **p** of His servant.” **Ps 35:27** 7965
delight themselves in abundant **p**. **Ps 37:11** 7965
He leads out the prisoners into **p**, **Ps 68:6** 3574
As I saw the **p** of the wicked. **Ps 73:3** 7965
may see the **p** of Your chosen ones, **Ps 106:5** 2899b
LORD, we beseech You, do send **p**! **Ps 118:25** 6743b
And **p** within your palaces.” **Ps 122:7** 7962
And may you see the **p** of Jerusalem **Ps 128:5** 2898
righteous will be rewarded with **p**. **Pr 13:21** 2896b
In the day of **p** be happy, But in **Ec 7:14** 2899b
And will not see when **p** comes, **Jer 17:6** 2896b
“I spoke to you in your **p**; **Jer 22:21** 7962

city for disaster and not for **p**; **Jer 39:16** 2899b
may be a prolonging of your **p**.' **Da 4:27** 7963
cities will again overflow with **p**, **Zch 1:17** 2896b
our **p** depends upon this business. **Ac 19:25** *2142*
and I also know how to live in **p**; **Php 4:12** *4052*

PROSPEROUS

So the man became exceedingly **p**, **Gn 30:43** 6555
and are satisfied and become **p**, **Dt 31:20** 1878
for then you will make your way **p**, **Jos 1:8** 6743b
on which we are going will be **p**." **Jg 18:5** 6743b
All the **p** of the earth will eat **Ps 22:29** 1879
The generous man will be **p**, **Pr 11:25** 1878
when Jerusalem was inhabited and **p** **Zch 7:7** 7961

PROSPERS

or if he **p**, he may redeem himself. **Lv 25:49** 5381
And in whatever he does, he **p**. **Ps 1:3** 6743b
because of him who **p** in his way, **Ps 37:7** 6743b
Wherever he turns, he **p**. **Pr 17:8** 7919a
good health, just as your soul **p**. **3Jn 1:2** *2137*

PROSTITUTE

Where is the temple **p** who was by **Gn 38:21** 6945
"There has been no temple **p** here." **Gn 38:21** 6945
has been no temple **p** here.'" **Gn 38:22** 6945
of Israel shall be a cult **p**, **Dt 23:17** 6945
of the sons of Israel be a cult **p**. **Dt 23:17** 6945
Offspring of an adulterer and a **p**. **Is 57:3** 2181
Christ and make them members of a **p**? **1Co 6:15** *4204*
that the one who joins himself to a **p** **1Co 6:16** *4204*

PROSTITUTES

were also male cult **p** in the land. **1Ki 14:24** 6945
the male cult **p** from the land and **1Ki 15:12** 6945
the houses of the *male* cult **p** which **2Ki 23:7** 6945
life *perishes* among the cult **p**. **Jb 36:14** 6945
offer sacrifices with temple **p**; **Hos 4:14** 6945
to you that the tax collectors and **p** **Mt 21:31** *4204*
but the tax collectors and **p** did **Mt 21:32** *4204*
who has devoured your wealth with **p**, **Lk 15:30** *4204*

PROSTITUTION

The lewdness of your **p** On the hills **Jer 13:27** 2184

PROSTRATE

came near to **p** himself before him, **2Sa 15:5** 7812
And Ziba said, "I **p** myself; **2Sa 16:4** 7812
"But man dies and lies **p**. **Jb 14:10** 2522
And from the dust *where* you are **p** **Is 29:4** 7817
have your mighty ones become **p**? **Jer 46:15** 5502

PROSTRATED

face to the ground and **p** himself. **1Sa 24:8** 7812
fell to the ground and **p** himself. **2Sa 1:2** 7812
fell on his face and **p** himself. **2Sa 9:6** 7812
Again he **p** himself and said, **2Sa 9:8** 7812
the ground and **p** herself and said, **2Sa 14:4** 7812
p himself and blessed the king; **2Sa 14:22** 7812
Thus he came to the king and **p** **2Sa 14:33** 7812
And he **p** himself before the king **2Sa 18:28** 7812
and **p** herself before the king. **1Ki 1:16** 7812
he **p** himself before the king with **1Ki 1:23** 7812
and **p** herself before the king and **1Ki 1:31** 7812
and **p** himself before King Solomon, **1Ki 1:53** 7812
and **p** himself before David with **1Ch 21:21** 7812
ground and **p** himself before him, **Mt 18:26** *4352*

PROSTRATING

p himself before the house of God, **Ezr 10:1** 5307
they were **p** themselves eastward **Ezk 8:16** 7812

PROTECT

'**P** for me the young man Absalom!' **2Sa 18:12** 8104
to **p** us from the enemy on the way, **Ezr 8:22** 5826
The LORD will **p** him and keep him **Ps 41:2** 8104
The LORD will **p** you from all evil; **Ps 121:7** 8104
But the lips of the wise will **p** them. **Pr 14:3** 8104
LORD of hosts will **p** Jerusalem. **Is 31:5** 1598
He will **p** and deliver *it;* **Is 31:5** 1598
and **p** you from the evil *one.* **2Th 3:3** *5442*

PROTECTED

who are **p** by the power of God **1Pe 1:5** *5432*

PROTECTION

p has been removed from them, **Nu 14:9** 6738
For wisdom is **p** *just as* money is **Ec 7:12** 6738
is protection *just as* money is **p**, **Ec 7:12** 6738
and **p** from the storm and the rain. **Is 4:6** 4563
"Or let him rely on My **p**, **Is 27:5** 4581
hatch and gather *them* under its **p**. **Is 34:15** 6738
an encouragement and a **p** for him. **Da 11:1** 4581
'Give me legal **p** from my opponent.' **Lk 18:3** *1556*
me, I will give her legal **p**, **Lk 18:5** *1556*

PROTECTS

The LORD **p** the strangers; **Ps 146:9** 8104

PROTEST

He will **p** on that day, **Is 3:7** 5375
clings to our feet we wipe off *in* **p** **Lk 10:11**
off the dust of their feet *in* **p** **Ac 13:51**

PROUD

then your heart will become **p** **Dt 8:14** 7311
Edom, and your heart has become **p**. **2Ki 14:10** 5375
heart has become **p** in boasting. **2Ch 25:19** 5375
was so **p** that he acted corruptly, **2Ch 26:16** 1361b
received, because his heart was **p**; **2Ch 32:25** 1361b
"The **p** beasts have not trodden **Jb 28:8** 7830
And here shall your **p** waves stop'? **Jb 38:11** 1347b
And look on everyone who is **p**, **Jb 40:11** 1343
"Look on everyone who is **p**, **Jb 40:12** 1343
And fully recompenses the **p** doer. **Ps 31:23** 1346
And has not turned to the **p**, **Ps 40:4** 7295
Render recompense to the **p**. **Ps 94:2** 1343
And with the contempt of the **p**. **Ps 123:4** 1349
O Lord, my heart is not **p**, **Ps 131:1** 1361b
The **p** have hidden a trap for me, **Ps 140:5** 1343
will tear down the house of the **p**, **Pr 15:25** 1343
Everyone who is **p** in heart is an **Pr 16:5** 1364
to divide the spoil with the **p**. **Pr 16:19** 1343
Haughty eyes and a **p** heart, **Pr 21:4** 7342
"**P**," "Haughty," "Scoffer," are his **Pr 21:24** 2086
The **p** look of man will be abased And **Is 2:11** 1365
everyone who is **p** and lofty And **Is 2:12** 1343
the daughters of Zion are **p** And **Is 3:16** 1361b
eyes of the **p** also will be abased. **Is 5:15** 1364
an end to the arrogance of the **p** And **Is 13:11** 2086
Woe to the **p** crown of the **Is 28:1** 1348
The **p** crown of the drunkards of **Is 28:3** 1348
he *is* very **p** **Jer 48:29** 1343
so **p** that he behaved arrogantly, **Da 5:20** 8631
satisfied, their heart became **p**; **Hos 13:6** 7311
"Behold, as for the **p** one, **Hab 2:4** 6075a
remove from your midst Your **p**, **Zph 3:11** 1346
He has scattered *those who were* **p** **Lk 1:51** *5244a*
For our **p** confidence is this: the **2Co 1:12** *2746a*
to be **p** as you also are ours, **2Co 1:14** *2745*
you an occasion to be **p** of us, **2Co 5:12** *2745*
so that your **p** confidence in me **Php 1:26** *2745*
"GOD IS OPPOSED TO THE **P**, **Jas 4:6** *5244a*
for GOD IS OPPOSED TO THE **P**, **1Pe 5:5** *5244a*

PROUDLY

they dealt **p** against the people." **Ex 18:11** 2102
"Boast no more so very **p**, **1Sa 2:3** 1364
With their mouth they speak **p**. **Ps 17:10** 1348
are many who fight **p** against me. **Ps 56:2** 4791
warriors, My **p** exulting ones, **Is 13:3** 1346
we ourselves speak **p** of you among **2Th 1:4** *1461a*

PROVE

But what does your argument **p**? **Jb 6:25** 3198
me And **p** my disgrace to me, **Jb 19:5** 3198
it is not so, who can **p** me a liar, **Jb 24:25** 3576
and I will **p** Myself holy among **Ezk 20:41** 6942
"when I **p** Myself holy among you **Ezk 36:23** 6942
and *so* **p** to be My disciples. **Jn 15:8** *1096*
"Nor can they **p** to you *the charges* **Ac 24:13** *3936*
him which they could not **p**, **Ac 25:7** *584*
I did not **p** disobedient to the **Ac 26:19** *1096*
you may **p** what the will of God is, **Ro 12:2** *1381a*
may **p** acceptable to the saints; **Ro 15:31** *1096*
grace toward me did not **p** vain; **1Co 15:10** *1096*
I **p** myself to be a transgressor. **Ga 2:18** *4921*
that you will **p** yourselves to be **Php 2:15** *1096*
p yourselves doers of the word, **Jas 1:22** *1096*
if you **p** zealous for what is good? **1Pe 3:13** *1096*

PROVED

and He **p** Himself holy among them. **Nu 20:13** 6942
Whom You **p** at Massah, With whom **Dt 33:8** 5254
who **p** too strong for Rehoboam, **2Ch 13:7** 553
p you at the waters of Meribah. **Ps 81:7** 974
reprove you, and you will be **p** a liar. **Pr 30:6** 3576
cause, that you may be **p** right. **Is 43:26** 6663
"Faithless Israel has **p** herself **Jer 3:11** 6663
do you think **p** to be a neighbor **Lk 10:36** *1096*
life, **p** to result in death for me; **Ro 7:10** *2147*
before Titus **p** to be *the* truth. **2Co 7:14** *1096*
p to be an encouragement to me. **Col 4:11** *1096*
p to be among you for your sake. **1Th 1:5** *1096*
But we **p** to be gentle among you, **1Th 2:7** *1096*
through angels **p** unalterable, **Heb 2:2** *1096*

PROVEN

it was **p** when they dealt proudly **Ex 18:11** 1697
and perseverance, **p** character; **Ro 5:4** *1382*
and **p** character, hope; **Ro 5:4** *1382*
But you know of his **p** worth, **Php 2:22** *1382*

PROVERB

You shall become a horror, a **p**, **Dt 28:37** 4912
Therefore it became a **p**: **1Sa 10:12** 4912
"As the **p** of the ancients says, **1Sa 24:13** 4912
So Israel will become a **p** and a **1Ki 9:7** 4912
and I will make it a **p** and a **2Ch 7:20** 4912
I will incline my ear to a **p**; **Ps 49:4** 4912
To understand a **p** and a figure, **Pr 1:6** 4912
So is a **p** in the mouth of fools. **Pr 26:7** 4912
So is a **p** in the mouth of fools. **Pr 26:9** 4912
the earth, as a reproach and a **p**, **Jer 24:9** 4912
what is this **p** you *people* have **Ezk 12:22** 4912
"I will make this **p** cease so that **Ezk 12:23** 4912
will no longer use it as a **p** in Israel **Ezk 12:23** 4911b
man and make him a sign and a **p**, **Ezk 14:8** 4912
will quote *this* **p** concerning you, **Ezk 16:44** 4911b
"What do you mean by using this **p** **Ezk 18:2** 4912
not going to use this **p** in Israel **Ezk 18:3** 4912
doubt you will quote this **p** to Me, **Lk 4:23** *3850b*
to them according to the true **p**, **2Pe 2:22** *3942*

PROVERBS

Therefore those who use **p** say, **Nu 21:27** 4911b
He also spoke 3,000 **p**, **1Ki 4:32** 4912
memorable sayings are **p** of ashes, **Jb 13:12** 4912
The **p** of Solomon the son of David, **Pr 1:1** 4912
The **p** of Solomon. **Pr 10:1** 4912
These also are **p** of Solomon which **Pr 25:1** 4912
searched out and arranged many **p**. **Ec 12:9** 4912
everyone who quotes **p** will quote **Ezk 16:44** 4911b

PROVIDE

"God will **p** for Himself the lamb **Gn 22:8** 7200
of that place The LORD Will **P**, **Gn 22:14** 7200
I **p** for my own household also?" **Gn 30:30** 6213a
"There I will also **p** for you, **Gn 45:11** 3557
I will **p** for you and your little ones **Gn 50:21** 3557
you are to **p** for the redemption of **Lv 25:24** 5414
"**P** for yourselves three men from **Jos 18:4** 3051
"**P** for me now a man who can play **1Sa 16:17** 7200
had to **p** for a month in the year. **1Ki 4:7** 3557
the ravens to **p** for you there." **1Ki 17:4** 3557
a widow there to **p** for you." **1Ki 17:9** 3557
which you may have occasion to **p**, **Ezr 7:20** 5415
p *for it* from the royal treasury. **Ezr 7:20** 5415
Will He **p** meat for His people?" **Ps 78:20** 3559
"It shall be the prince's part *to* **p** **Ezk 45:17**
he shall **p** the sin offering, the **Ezk 45:17** 6213a
that day the prince shall **p** for himself **Ezk 45:22** 6213a
the feast he shall **p** as a burnt offering **Ezk 45:23** 6213a
"He shall **p** as a grain offering **Ezk 45:24** 6213a
the feast, he shall **p** like this, **Ezk 45:25** 6213a
Then the priests shall **p** his burnt **Ezk 46:2** 6213a
"And he shall **p** a grain offering, **Ezk 46:7** 6213a
And he shall **p** his burnt offering **Ezk 46:12** 6213a
"And you shall **p** a lamb a year **Ezk 46:13** 6213a
morning by morning you shall **p** it. **Ezk 46:13** 6213a
"Also you shall **p** a grain **Ezk 46:14** 6213a
"Thus they shall **p** the lamb, the **Ezk 46:15** 6213a
They were also to **p** mounts to put **Ac 23:24** *3936*
will **p** the way of escape also, **1Co 10:13** *4160*
if anyone does not **p** for his own, **1Tm 5:8** *4306*

PROVIDED

mount of the LORD it will be **p**." **Gn 22:14** 7200
Joseph **p** his father and his **Gn 47:12** 3557
he **p** the first *part* for himself, **Dt 33:21** 7200
and they **p** him water to drink. **1Sa 30:11** 8248
that Absalom **p** for himself a chariot **2Sa 15:1** 6213a
guard and **p** them with sustenance, **2Sa 20:3** 3557
who **p** for the king and his **1Ki 4:7** 3557
Those deputies **p** for King **1Ki 4:27** 3557
and **p** them with bread and water.) **1Ki 18:4** 3557
and **p** them with bread and water? **1Ki 18:13** 3557
I have **p** for the house of my God **1Ch 29:2** 3559
already **p** for the holy temple, **1Ch 29:3** 3559
all this abundance that we have **p** **1Ch 29:16** 3559
Jerusalem, whom David my father **p**. **2Ch 2:7** 3559
the sons of Israel **p** in abundance **2Ch 31:5** 7235a
"You **p** bread from heaven for them **Ne 9:15** 5414
"Indeed, forty years You **p** for them **Ne 9:21** 3557
So he quickly **p** her with her **Es 2:9** 5414
insight you have abundantly **p**! **Jb 26:3** 3045
Your creatures settled in it; You **p** **Ps 68:10** 3559
I **p** for myself male and female **Ec 2:8** 6213a
God had **p** something better for us, **Heb 11:40** *4265*

PROVIDENCE

and since by your **p** reforms are **Ac 24:2** *4307*

PROVIDES

"He **p** them with security, and **Jb 24:23** 5414
clouds, Who **p** rain for the earth, **Ps 147:8** 3559
the prince **p** a freewill offering, **Ezk 46:12** 6213a
who **p** you with the Spirit and **Ga 3:5** *2023*
and *he* **p** that no one will be able **Rv 13:17**

PROVINCE

Now these are the people of the **p** **Ezr 2:1** 4082
will have no possession in *the* **p** **Ezr 4:16**
the governor of *the* **p** beyond **Ezr 5:3**
the governor of *the* **p** beyond **Ezr 5:6**
we have gone to the **p** of Judah, **Ezr 5:8** 4083
which is in the **p** of Media, **Ezr 6:2** 4083
governor of *the* **p** beyond **Ezr 6:6**
the governor of *the* **p** beyond **Ezr 6:13**
find in the whole **p** of Babylon, **Ezr 7:16** 4083
all the people who are in *the* **p** **Ezr 7:25**
"The remnant there in the **p** who **Ne 1:3** 4082
seat of the governor *of the* **p** **Ne 3:7**
These are the people of the **p** who **Ne 7:6** 4082
to each **p** according to its script **Es 1:22** 4082
governors who were over each **p** and **Es 3:12** 4082
each **p** according to its script, **Es 3:12** 4082
edict to be issued as law in every **p** **Es 3:14** 4082
In each and every **p** where the **Es 4:3** 4082
every **p** according to its script, **Es 8:9** 4082
or **p** which might attack them, **Es 8:11** 4082
issued as law in each and every **p** was **Es 8:13** 4082
In each and every **p** and **Es 8:17** 4082
generation, every family, every **p** and **Es 9:28** 4082
and righteousness in the **p**, **Ec 5:8** 4082
he made him ruler over the whole **p** **Da 2:48** 4083
administration of the **p** of Babylon, **Da 2:49** 4083
plain of Dura in the **p** of Babylon. **Da 3:1** 4083
administration of the **p** of Babylon, **Da 3:12** 4083
to prosper in the **p** of Babylon. **Da 3:30** 4083
Susa, which is in the **p** of Elam; **Da 8:2** 4083
it, he asked from what **p** he was, **Ac 23:34** *1885a*
having arrived in the **p**, **Ac 25:1** *1885a*

PROVINCES

men of the rulers of the **p**.'" **1Ki 20:14** 4082
young men of the rulers of the **p**, **1Ki 20:15** 4082
rulers of the **p** went out first; **1Ki 20:17** 4082
young men of the rulers of the **p**, **1Ki 20:19** 4082
city and damaging to kings and **p**, **Ezr 4:15** 4083
in Samaria and in the rest of *the* **p** **Ezr 4:17**
governing all *the* **p** beyond **Ezr 4:20**
the officials of *the* **p** beyond **Ezr 6:6**
treasury out of the taxes of *the* **p** **Ezr 6:8**
all the treasurers who are *in the* **p** **Ezr 7:21**
and to the governors *in the* **p** **Ezr 8:36**
given me for the governors *of the* **p** **Ne 2:7**
I came to the governors *of the* **p** **Ne 2:9**
the heads of the **p** who lived in **Ne 11:3** 4082
from India to Ethiopia over 127 **p**, **Es 1:1** 4082
princes of his **p** being in his presence **Es 1:3** 4082
in all the **p** of King Ahasuerus. **Es 1:16** 4082
sent letters to all the king's **p**, **Es 1:22** 4082
king appoint overseers in all the **p** **Es 2:3** 4082
he also made a holiday for the **p** **Es 2:18** 4082
in all the **p** of your kingdom; **Es 3:8** 4082
sent by couriers to all the king's **p** **Es 3:13** 4082

people of the king's **p** know that for Es 4:11 4082
Jews who are in all the king's **p**. Es 8:5 4082
and the princes of the **p** which Es 8:9 4082
from India to Ethiopia, 127 **p**, Es 8:9 4082
in all the **p** of King Ahasuerus, Es 8:12 4082
in their cities throughout all the **p** of Es 9:2 4082
Even all the princes of the **p**, Es 9:3 4082
fame spread throughout all the **p**; Es 9:4 4082
done in the rest of the king's **p**! Es 9:12 4082
Jews who *were* in the king's **p** Es 9:16 4082
in all the **p** of King Ahasuerus, Es 9:20 4082
127 **p** of the kingdom of Ahasuerus, Es 9:30 4082
and the treasure of kings and **p**. Ec 2:8 4082
She who was a princess among the **p** La 1:1 4082
him On every side from *their* **p**, Ezk 19:8 4082
magistrates and all the rulers of the **p** Da 3:2 4083
magistrates and all the rulers of the **p** Da 3:3 4083

PROVING
p that this *Jesus* is the Christ. Ac 9:22 *4822*
but as **p** through the earnestness 2Co 8:8 *1381a*
but **p** to be examples to the flock. 1Pe 5:3 *1096*

PROVISION
and all the bread of their **p** was dry Jos 9:5 6718b
Solomon's **p** for one day was 1Ki 4:22 3899
temple, for which I have made **p**." 1Ch 29:19 3559
"I will abundantly bless her **p**; Ps 132:15 6718b
And gathers her **p** in the harvest. Pr 6:8 3978
and make no **p** for the flesh in Ro 13:14 *4307*
p of the Spirit of Jesus Christ, Php 1:19 *2024*

PROVISIONED
mustered and were **p** and went 1Ki 20:27 3557

PROVISIONS
to give them **p** for the journey. Gn 42:25 6720
and gave them **p** for the journey. Gn 45:21 6720
prepared any **p** for themselves. Ex 12:39 6720
'Prepare **p** for yourselves, for Jos 1:11 6720
Take **p** in your hand for the journey, Jos 9:11 6720
we took it for our **p** out of our houses Jos 9:12 6719b
men *of Israel* took some of their **p**, Jos 9:14 6718b
So the 300 men took the people's **p** Jg 7:8 6720
of the LORD for him, gave him **p**, 1Sa 22:10 6720
neglected the weightier **p** of the law: Mt 23:23 *926*

PROVOCATION
the **p** of His sons and daughters. Dt 32:19 3708a
I not feared the **p** by the enemy, Dt 32:27 3708a
out of my great concern and **p**." 1Sa 1:16 3708a
because of his **p** with which he 1Ki 15:30 3708a
p with which you have provoked *Me* 1Ki 21:22 3708a
me, And my eye gazes on their **p**. Jb 17:2 4784
But the **p** of a fool is heavier Pr 27:3 3708a
this city has been to Me *a* **p** *of* Jer 32:31 3708a
presented the **p** of their offering. Ezk 20:28 3708a

PROVOCATIONS
because of all the **p** with which 2Ki 23:26 3708a

PROVOKE
do not **p** them, for I will not give Dt 2:5 1624
harass Moab, nor **p** them to war, Dt 2:9 1624
do not harass them nor **p** them, Dt 2:19 1624
your God *so as* to **p** Him to anger, Dt 4:25 3707
of the LORD to **p** Him to anger. Dt 9:18 3707
I will **p** them to anger with a Dt 32:21 3707
p her bitterly to irritate her, 1Sa 1:6 3707
of the LORD, she would **p** her; 1Sa 1:7 3707
molten images to **p** Me to anger, 1Ki 14:9 3707
Thus Ahab did more to **p** the LORD 1Ki 16:33 3707
should you **p** trouble so that you, 2Ki 14:10 1624
that they might **p** Me to anger with 2Ki 22:17 3707
why should you **p** trouble so that you, 2Ch 25:19 1624
that they might **p** Me to anger with 2Ch 34:25 3707
And those who **p** God are secure, Jb 12:6 7264
who continually **p** Me to My face, Is 65:3 3707
which they have done to **p** Me by Jer 11:17 3707
and do not **p** Me to anger with the Jer 25:6 3707
"in order that you might **p** Me to Jer 25:7 3707
to other gods to **p** Me to anger. Jer 32:29 3707
have done to **p** Me to anger Jer 32:32 3707
which they committed so as to **p** Me Jer 44:3 3707
Or do we **p** the Lord to jealousy? 1Co 10:22 *3863*
do not **p** your children to anger, Eph 6:4 *3949*

PROVOKED
do not forget how you **p** the LORD Dt 9:7 7107
at Horeb you **p** the LORD to wrath, Dt 9:8 7107
you **p** the LORD to wrath. Dt 9:22 7107
abominations they **p** Him to anger. Dt 32:16 3707
p Me to anger with their idols. Dt 32:21 3707
thus they **p** the LORD to anger. Jg 2:12 3707
and they **p** Him to jealousy more 1Ki 14:22 7065
he **p** the LORD God of Israel to anger. 1Ki 15:30 3707
with which you have **p** *Me* to anger, 1Ki 21:22 3707
p the LORD God of Israel to anger 1Ki 22:53 3707
with which Manasseh had **p** Him. 2Ki 23:26 3707
to other gods, and **p** the LORD, 2Ch 28:25 3707
had **p** the God of heaven to wrath, Ezr 5:12 7265
they **p** Him with their high places And Ps 78:58 3707
p *Him* to anger with their deeds, Ps 106:29 3707
They also **p** *Him* to wrath at the Ps 106:32 7107
p Me with their graven images, Jer 8:19 3707
with violence and **p** Me repeatedly? Ezk 8:17 3707
Ephraim has **p** to bitter anger; Hos 12:14 3707
when your fathers **p** Me to wrath,' Zch 8:14 7107
his spirit was being **p** within him Ac 17:16 *3947*
Then all the city was **p**, Ac 21:30 *2795*
does not seek its own, is not **p**, 1Co 13:5 *3947*
YOUR HEARTS AS WHEN THEY **P** ME, Heb 3:8 *3894*
YOUR HEARTS, AS WHEN THEY **P** ME." Heb 3:15 *3894*
For who **p** *Him* when they had heard? Heb 3:16 *3893*

PROVOKES
He who **p** him to anger forfeits his Pr 20:2 5674b
of jealousy, which **p** to jealousy, Ezk 8:3 7065

PROVOKING
p Him to anger with the work of Dt 31:29 3707
Asherim, **p** the LORD to anger. 1Ki 14:15 3707
p Me to anger with their sins, 1Ki 16:2 3707
p Him to anger with the work of 1Ki 16:7 3707
p the LORD God of Israel to anger 1Ki 16:13 3707
p the LORD God of Israel with 1Ki 16:26 3707
they did evil things **p** the LORD. 2Ki 17:11 3707
in the sight of the LORD, **p** Him. 2Ki 17:17 3707
sight of the LORD **p** *Him to anger.* 2Ki 21:6 3707
and have been **p** Me to anger since 2Ki 21:15 3707
of Israel had made **p** the LORD; 2Ki 23:19 3707
sight of the LORD, **p** Him *to anger.* 2Ch 33:6 3707
p Me to anger by the work of their Jer 32:30 3707
p Me to anger with the works of Jer 44:8 3707

PROW
and the **p** stuck fast and remained Ac 27:41 *4408*

PROWL
the beasts of the forest **p** about. Ps 104:20 7430
lies desolate, Foxes **p** in it. La 5:18 1980

PROWLED
lion, lioness and lion's cub **p**, Na 2:11 1980

PROWLS
the devil, **p** around like a roaring lion, 1Pe 5:8 *4043*

PRUDENCE
To give **p** to the naive, To the Pr 1:4 6195
"O naive ones, understand **p**; Pr 8:5 6195
"I, wisdom, dwell with **p**, Pr 8:12 6195

PRUDENT
valor, a warrior, one **p** in speech, 1Sa 16:18 995
But a **p** man conceals dishonor. Pr 12:16 6175
A **p** man conceals knowledge, But Pr 12:23 6175
Every **p** man acts with knowledge, Pr 13:16 6175
closes his lips, he is *considered* **p**. Pr 17:28 995
mind of the **p** acquires knowledge, Pr 18:15 995
But a **p** wife is from the LORD. Pr 19:14 7919a
The **p** sees the evil and hides Pr 22:3 6175
A **p** man sees evil *and* hides Pr 27:12 6175
good counsel been lost to the **p**? Jer 49:7 995
a time the **p** person keeps silent, Am 5:13 7919a
were foolish, and five were **p**. Mt 25:2 *5429*
but the **p** took oil in flasks along Mt 25:4 *5429*
"The foolish said to the **p**, Mt 25:8 *5429*
"But the **p** answered, ' Mt 25:9 *5429*
sake, but you are **p** in Christ; 1Co 4:10 *5429*
husband of one wife, temperate, **p**, 1Tm 3:2 *4998*

PRUNE
six years you shall **p** your vineyard Lv 25:3 2168
your field nor **p** your vineyard. Lv 25:4 2168

PRUNED
It will not be **p** or hoed, But Is 5:6 2168

PRUNES
branch that bears fruit, He **p** it so Jn 15:2 *2508*

PRUNING
time has arrived for **p** *the vines,* SS 2:12 2159
and their spears into **p** hooks. Is 2:4 4211
will cut off the sprigs with **p** knives Is 18:5 4211
And your **p** hooks into spears; Jl 3:10 4211
And their spears into **p** hooks; Mi 4:3 4211

PSALM
Sing praises with a skillful **p**. Ps 47:7 4905b
as it is also written in the second **P**, Ac 13:33 *5568*
"Therefore He also says in another **P**, Ac 13:35
you assemble, each one has a **p**, 1Co 14:26 *5568*

PSALMIST
Jacob, And the sweet **p** of Israel, 2Sa 23:1 2158

PSALMS
Let us shout joyfully to Him with **p**. Ps 95:2 2158
David himself says in the book of **P**, Lk 20:42 *5568*
Moses and the Prophets and the **P** Lk 24:44 *5568*
it is written in the book of **P**, Ac 1:20 *5568*
p and hymns and spiritual songs, Eph 5:19 *5568*
p *and* hymns *and* spiritual songs, Col 3:16 *5568*

PSALTERY
the horn, flute, lyre, trigon, **p**, Da 3:5 6460
the horn, flute, lyre, trigon, **p**, Da 3:7 6460
the horn, flute, lyre, trigon, **p**, Da 3:10 6460
the horn, flute, lyre, trigon, **p** and Da 3:15 6460

PTOLEMAIS
voyage from Tyre, we arrived at **P**, Ac 21:7 *4424*

PUAH
and the other was named **P**; Ex 1:15 6326
Abimelech died, Tola the son of **P**, Jg 10:1 6312
Tola, **P**, Jashub and Shimron. 1Ch 7:1 6312

PUBLIC
hears a **p** adjuration *to testify* when Lv 5:1 6963
them like the wicked In a **p** place, Jb 34:26 7200
"Go and stand in the **p** gate, Jer 17:19 1121, 5971a
day of his **p** appearance to Israel. Lk 1:80 *323*
and put them in a **p** jail. Ac 5:18 *1219*
have beaten us in **p** without trial, Ac 16:37 *1219*
powerfully refuted the Jews in **p**, Ac 18:28 *1219*
He made a **p** display of them, Col 2:15 *3954*
give attention to the **p** reading 1Tm 4:13
by being made a **p** spectacle Heb 10:33 *2301*

PUBLICLY
shameful deeds and **p** defames her, Dt 22:14 3318
he **p** defamed a virgin of Israel. Dt 22:19 3318
Jesus could no longer **p** enter a city, Mk 1:45 *5320*
he himself seeks to be *known* **p**. Jn 7:4 *3954*
He Himself also went up, not **p**, Jn 7:10 *5320*
"Look, He is speaking **p**, Jn 7:26 *3954*
to walk **p** among the Jews, Jn 11:54 *3954*
teaching you **p** and from house to Ac 20:20 *1219*
whom God displayed **p** as a Ro 3:25 *4388*
Christ was **p** portrayed *as* crucified? Ga 3:1 *4270*

PUBLISHED
was **p** to all the peoples Es 3:14 1540
was **p** to all the peoples, Es 8:13 1540

PUBLIUS
man of the island, named **P**, Ac 28:7 *4196*
father of **P** was lying *in bed* afflicted Ac 28:8 *4196*

PUDENS
also **P** and Linus and Claudia and 2Tm 4:21 *4227*

PUGNACIOUS
not addicted to wine or **p**, 1Tm 3:3 *4131*
not addicted to wine, not **p**, Ti 1:7 *4131*

PUL
P, king of Assyria, came against 2Ki 15:19 6322
and Menahem gave **P** a thousand 2Ki 15:19 6322
Israel stirred up the spirit of **P**, 1Ch 5:26 6322

PULL
and **p** his sandal off his foot and Dt 25:9 2502a
and **p** down the altar of Baal which Jg 6:25 2040
"Also you shall purposely **p** Ru 2:16 7997a
You will **p** me out of the net Ps 31:4 3318
I will **p** you down from your station. Is 22:19 2040
a kingdom to uproot, to **p** down, Jer 18:7 5422
right hand, yet I would **p** you off; Jer 22:24 5423
Will he not **p** up its roots and cut Ezk 17:9 5423
Will **p** down your strength from you Am 3:11 3381
p him out on a Sabbath day?" Lk 14:5 *385*

PULLED
so they **p** *him* up and lifted Joseph Gn 37:28 4900
and which has not **p** in a yoke; Dt 21:3 4900
and **p** them up along with the bars; Jg 16:3 5265
and **p** out the pin of the loom Jg 16:14 5265
and **p** down the high places and the 2Ch 31:1 5422
and **p** some of the hair from my Ezr 9:3 4803
some of them and **p** out their hair, Ne 13:25 4803
Its stakes will never be **p** up, Nor Is 33:20 5265
my dwelling is **p** up and removed Is 38:12 5265
And all its cities were **p** down Jer 4:26 5422
So they **p** Jeremiah up with the Jer 38:13 4900
three of the first horns were **p** out Da 7:8 6132
But he **p** free of the linen sheet Mk 14:52 *2641*

PULLS
the patch **p** away from the garment, Mt 9:16 *142*
the patch **p** away from it, Mk 2:21 *142*

PULVERIZE
thresh the mountains and **p** *them,* Is 41:15 1854
That you may **p** many peoples, Mi 4:13 1854

PULVERIZED
I **p** them as the dust of the earth; 2Sa 22:43 7833
altar stones like **p** chalk stones; Is 27:9 5310a

PUNISH
nevertheless in the day when I **p**, Ex 32:34 6485
I will **p** them for their sin." Ex 32:34 6485
then I will **p** you seven times more Lv 26:18 3256
p you seven times for your sins. Lv 26:28 3256
they may **p** *them* for all the Jg 20:10 6213a
'I will **p** Amalek *for* what he did 1Sa 15:2 6485
Awake to **p** all the nations; Ps 59:5 6485
Then I will **p** their transgression Ps 89:32 6485
"I will **p** the fruit of the Is 10:12 6485
I will **p** the world for its evil And Is 13:11 6485
LORD will **p** the host of heaven on Is 24:21 6485
To **p** the inhabitants of the earth Is 26:21 6485
p Leviathan the fleeing serpent, Is 27:1 6485
"Shall I not **p** these *people,*" Jer 5:9 6485
'Shall I not **p** these *people?'* Jer 5:29 6485
At the time that I **p** them, Jer 6:15 6485
I not **p** them for these things?" Jer 9:9 6485
that I will **p** all who are circumcised Jer 9:25 6485
"Behold, I am about to **p** them! Jer 11:22 6485
"But I will **p** you according to Jer 21:14 6485
I will **p** the king of Babylon Jer 25:12 6485
will **p** that nation with the sword, Jer 27:8 6485
I am about to **p** Shemaiah the Jer 29:32 6485
And I will **p** all their oppressors. Jer 30:20 6485
"I will also **p** him and his Jer 36:31 6485
'And I will **p** those who live in Jer 44:13 6485
I am going to **p** you in this place, Jer 44:29 6485
I am going to **p** Amon of Thebes, Jer 46:25 6485
Esau upon him At the time I **p** him. Jer 49:8 6485
I am going to **p** the king of Jer 50:18 6485
come, The time when I will **p** you. Jer 50:31 6485
"I will **p** Bel in Babylon, Jer 51:44 6485
I will **p** the idols of Babylon; Jer 51:47 6485
"When I will **p** her idols, And Jer 51:52 6485
But He will **p** your iniquity, O La 4:22 6485
and I will **p** the house of Jehu for Hos 1:4 6485
"I will **p** her for the days of Hos 2:13 6485
So I will **p** them for their ways And Hos 4:9 6485
I will not **p** your daughters when Hos 4:14 6485
And **p** *them* for their sins; Hos 8:13 6485
iniquity, He will **p** their sins. Hos 9:9 6485
p Jacob according to his ways; Hos 12:2 6485
p you for all your iniquities." Am 3:2 6485
that I **p** Israel's transgressions, Am 3:14 6485
will also **p** the altars of Bethel; Am 3:14 6485
That I will **p** the princes, Zph 1:8 6485
"And I will **p** on that day all who Zph 1:9 6485
And I will **p** the men Who are Zph 1:12 6485
And I will **p** the male goats; Zch 10:3 6485
will **p** Him and release Him." Lk 23:16 *3811*
will **p** Him and release Him." Lk 23:22 *3811*
basis on which to **p** them) Ac 4:21 *2849*

are ready to **p** all disobedience, 2Co 10:6 *1556*

PUNISHABLE
it would be an iniquity **p** *by* Jb 31:11

PUNISHED
dies at his hand, he shall be **p**. Ex 21:20 5358
When the scoffer is **p**, Pr 21:11 6064
the naive go on, and are **p** for it. Pr 22:3 6064
after many days they *will be* **p**. Is 24:22 6485
You have **p** and destroyed them, Is 26:14 6485
From the LORD of hosts you will be **p** Is 29:6 6485
This is the city to be **p**, Jer 6:6 6485
of Egypt, as I have **p** Jerusalem, Jer 44:13 6485
just as I **p** the king of Assyria. Jer 50:18 6485
to Jerusalem as prisoners to be **p**. Ac 22:5 *5097*
"And as I **p** them often in all the Ac 26:11 *5097*
as **p** yet not put to death, 2Co 6:9 *3811*

PUNISHING
p the wicked by bringing his way 2Ch 6:23 7725

PUNISHMENT
"My **p** is too great to bear! Gn 4:13 5771
swept away in the **p** of the city." Gn 19:15 5771
is guilty and shall bear his **p**. Lv 5:17 5771
I have brought its **p** upon it, Lv 18:25 5771
her freedom, there shall be **p**; Lv 19:20 1244
so cause them to bear **p** for guilt Lv 22:16 5771
he turned, he inflicted **p**. 1Sa 14:47 7561
p shall come upon you for this thing." 1Sa 28:10 5771
morning light, **p** will overtake us. 2Ki 7:9 5771
wrath *brings* the **p** of the sword, Jb 19:29 5771
And their time *of* **p** would be Ps 81:15
the nations And **p** on the peoples Ps 149:7 8433a
life, The income of the wicked, **p**. Pr 10:16 2403b
Grievous **p** is for him who forsakes Pr 15:10 4148
what will you do in the day of **p**, Is 10:3 6486
And every blow of the rod of **p**, Is 30:32 4145
At the time of their **p** they shall be Jer 8:12 6486
time of their **p** they will perish. Jer 10:15 6486
the year of their **p**." Jer 11:23 6486
upon them, The year of their **p**," Jer 23:12 6486
I will bring **p** upon that man and Jer 23:34 6485
you be completely free from **p**? Jer 25:29 5352
You will not be free from **p**; Jer 25:29 5352
enemy, With the **p** of a cruel one, Jer 30:14 4148
upon them, The time of their **p**. Jer 46:21 6486
upon Moab, The year of their **p**," Jer 48:44 6486
day has come, The time of their **p**. Jer 50:27 6486
Do not be destroyed in her **p**, Jer 51:6 5771
time of their **p** they will perish. Jer 51:18 6486
The **p** of your iniquity has been La 4:22 5771
"They will bear *the* **p** *of* their Ezk 14:10
the **p** for the father's iniquity?' Ezk 18:19 5771
the **p** for the father's iniquity, Ezk 18:20 5771
bear the **p** for the son's iniquity; Ezk 18:20 5771
in the time of the **p** of the end,' Ezk 21:25 5771
in the time of the **p** of the end. Ezk 21:29 5771
bear now the **p** of your lewdness Ezk 23:35
but the **p** for their iniquity Ezk 32:27 5771
at the time of the **p** of the end, Ezk 35:5 5771
bear the **p** for their iniquity. Ezk 44:10 5771
bear *the* **p** *for* their iniquity. Ezk 44:12 5771
The days of **p** have come, The days Hos 9:7 6486
for four I will not revoke its **p**, Am 1:3
for four I will not revoke its **p**, Am 1:6
for four I will not revoke its **p**, Am 1:9
for four I will not revoke its **p**, Am 1:11
for four I will not revoke its **p**, Am 1:13
for four I will not revoke its **p**, Am 2:1
for four I will not revoke its **p**, Am 2:4
for four I will not revoke its **p**, Am 2:6
post your watchmen, Your **p** will come. Mi 7:4 6486
This will be the **p** of Egypt, Zch 14:19 2403b
and the **p** of all the nations who Zch 14:19 2403b
These will go away into eternal **p**, Mt 25:46 *2851*
Sufficient for such a one is this **p** 2Co 2:6 *2009*
How much severer **p** do you think he Heb 10:29 *5098*
sent by him for the **p** of evildoers 1Pe 2:14 *1557*
under **p** for the day of judgment, 2Pe 2:9 *2849*
out fear, because fear involves **p**, 1Jn 4:18 *2851*
undergoing the **p** of eternal fire. Jude 1:7 *1349*

PUNISHMENTS
So I will choose their **p** And Is 66:4 8586

PUNITES
of Puvah, the family of the **P**; Nu 26:23 6324

PUNON
from Zalmonah and camped at **P**. Nu 33:42 6325
They journeyed from **P** and Nu 33:43 6325

PUPIL
guarded him as the **p** of His eye. Dt 32:10 380
the teacher *as well* as the **p**. 1Ch 25:8 8527
"A **p** is not above his teacher; Lk 6:40 *3101*

PUR
twelfth year of King Ahasuerus, **P**, Es 3:7 6332
to destroy them and had cast **P**, Es 9:24 6332
days Purim after the name of **P**. Es 9:26 6332

PURAH
go with **P** your servant down to the Jg 7:10 6513
So he went with **P** his servant down Jg 7:11 6513

PURCHASE
entirely consumed our **p** price. Gn 31:15 3701
he shall refund part of his **p** price Lv 25:51 4736
and you shall also **p** water from Dt 2:6 3739
"Then I took the deeds of **p**, Jer 32:11 4736
and I gave the deed of **p** to Baruch Jer 32:12 4736
who signed the deed of **p**, Jer 32:12 4736
deeds, this sealed deed of **p** and Jer 32:14 4736
I had given the deed of **p** to Baruch Jer 32:16 4736
were going away to make the **p**, Mt 25:10 *59*

PURCHASED
Abraham **p** from the sons of Heth; Gn 25:10 7069
in it, **p** from the sons of Heth." Gn 49:32 4735
but every man's slave **p** with money, Ex 12:44 4736
people pass over whom You have **p**. Ex 15:16 7069
which You have **p** of old, Ps 74:2 7069
the tomb which Abraham had **p** Ac 7:16 *5608*
God which He **p** with His own blood. Ac 20:28 *4046*
and **p** for God with Your blood *men* Rv 5:9 *59*
who had been **p** from the earth. Rv 14:3 *59*
These have been **p** from among men Rv 14:4 *59*

PURCHASER
its **p** until the year of jubilee; Lv 25:28 7069
its **p** throughout his generations; Lv 25:30 7069
'He then with his **p** shall calculate Lv 25:50 7069

PURE
You shall overlay it with **p** gold, Ex 25:11 2889
shall make a mercy seat of **p** gold, Ex 25:17 2889
"You shall overlay it with **p** gold Ex 25:24 2889
you shall make them of **p** gold. Ex 25:29 2889
shall make a lampstand of **p** gold. Ex 25:31 2889
piece of hammered work of **p** gold. Ex 25:36 2889
their trays *shall be* of **p** gold. Ex 25:38 2889
be made from a talent of **p** gold, Ex 25:39 2889
and two chains of **p** gold; Ex 28:14 2889
of twisted cordage work in **p** gold. Ex 28:22 2889
of **p** gold and shall engrave on it, Ex 28:36 2889
You shall overlay it with **p** gold, Ex 30:3 2889
spices with **p** frankincense; Ex 30:34 2134
the work of a perfumer, salted, **p**, Ex 30:35 2889
and the **p** *gold* lampstand with all Ex 31:8 2889
he overlaid it with **p** gold inside and Ex 37:2 2889
He made a mercy seat of **p** gold, Ex 37:6 2889
He overlaid it with **p** gold, Ex 37:11 2889
to pour out drink offerings, of **p** gold. Ex 37:16 2889
he made the lampstand of **p** gold. Ex 37:17 2889
a single hammered work of **p** gold. Ex 37:22 2889
snuffers and its trays of **p** gold. Ex 37:23 2889
utensils from a talent of **p** gold. Ex 37:24 2889
He overlaid it with **p** gold, Ex 37:26 2889
the holy anointing oil and the **p**, Ex 37:29 2889
of twisted cordage work in **p** gold. Ex 39:15 2889
They also made bells of **p** gold, Ex 39:25 2889
plate of the holy crown of **p** gold, Ex 39:30 2889
the **p** *gold* lampstand, with its Ex 39:37 2889
the **p** *gold* lampstand before the LORD Lv 24:4 2889
the **p** *gold* table before the LORD. Lv 24:6 2889
put **p** frankincense on each row that Lv 24:7 2134
spread over *it* a cloth of **p** blue, Nu 4:6 3632
the **p** You show Yourself pure, 2Sa 22:27 1305
the pure You show Yourself **p**, 2Sa 22:27 1305
and he overlaid it with **p** gold. 1Ki 6:20 5462
inside of the house with **p** gold. 1Ki 6:21 5462
of the inner sanctuary, of **p** gold; 1Ki 7:49 5462
and the firepans, of **p** gold; 1Ki 7:50 5462
forest of Lebanon *were* of **p** gold. 1Ki 10:21 5462
and the pitchers of **p** gold; 1Ch 28:17 2889
inside he overlaid it with **p** gold. 2Ch 3:4 2889
with their lamps of **p** gold, 2Ch 4:20 5462
and the firepans of **p** gold; 2Ch 4:22 5462
ivory and overlaid it with **p** gold. 2Ch 9:17 2889
forest of Lebanon *were* of **p** gold; 2Ch 9:20 5462
all of them were **p**. Ezr 6:20 2889
Can a man be **p** before his Maker? Jb 4:17 2891
If you are **p** and upright, Surely Jb 8:6 2134
'My teaching is **p**, And I am Jb 11:4 2134
"What is man, that he should be **p**, Jb 15:14 2135
heavens are not **p** in His sight; Jb 15:15 2141
in my hands, And my prayer is **p**. Jb 16:17 2134
the stars are not **p** in His sight, Jb 25:5 2141
"**P** gold cannot be given in Jb 28:15 5462
Nor can it be valued in **p** gold. Jb 28:19 2889
'I am **p**, without transgression; Jb 33:9 2134
The words of the LORD are **p** words; Ps 12:6 2889
the **p** You show Yourself pure Ps 18:26 1305
the pure You show Yourself **p** Ps 18:26 1305
The commandment of the LORD is **p**, Ps 19:8 1249
who has clean hands and a **p** heart, Ps 24:4 1249
To those who are **p** in heart! Ps 73:1 1249
in vain I have kept my heart **p** And Ps 73:13 2135
can a young man keep his way **p**? Ps 119:9 2135
Your word is very **p**, Ps 119:140 6884
is better than gold, even **p** gold, Pr 8:19 6337
LORD, But pleasant words are **p**. Pr 15:26 2889
my heart, I am **p** from my sin"? Pr 20:9 2891
If his conduct is **p** and right. Pr 20:11 2134
as for the **p**, his conduct is upright. Pr 21:8 2134
a kind who is **p** in his own eyes, Pr 30:12 2889
"His head is *like* gold, **p** gold; SS 5:11 6337
Set on pedestals of **p** gold; SS 5:15 6337
p *child* of the one who bore her. SS 6:9 1249
as the full moon, As **p** as the sun, SS 6:10 1249
mortal man scarcer than **p** gold And Is 13:12 6337
How the **p** gold has changed! La 4:1 2896a
the hair of His head like **p** wool. Da 7:9 5343
with *a belt of* **p** gold of Uphaz. Da 10:5 3800
to refine, purge and make them **p** Da 11:35 3835a
eyes are too **p** to approve evil, Hab 1:13 2889
and a grain offering *that is* **p**; Mal 1:11 2889
"Blessed are the **p** in heart, for Mt 5:8 *2513*
of very costly perfume of **p** nard; Mk 14:3 *4101*
of very costly perfume of **p** nard, Jn 12:3 *4101*
I might present you *as* a **p** virgin. 2Co 11:2 *53*
rather than from **p** motives, Php 1:17 *55*
whatever is right, whatever is **p**, Php 4:8 *53*
our instruction is love from a **p** heart 1Tm 1:5 *2513*
call on the Lord from a **p** heart. 2Tm 2:22 *2513*
To the **p**, all things are pure; Ti 1:15 *2513*
To the pure, all things are **p**; Ti 1:15 *2513*
and unbelieving, nothing is **p**, Ti 1:15 *2513*
to be sensible, **p**, workers at Ti 2:5 *53*
our bodies washed with **p** water. Heb 10:22 *2513*
P and undefiled religion in the sight Jas 1:27 *2513*
the wisdom from above is first **p**, Jas 3:17 *53*
long for the **p** milk of the word, 1Pe 2:2 *97*
purifies himself, just as He is **p**. 1Jn 3:3 *53*
and the city was **p** gold, Rv 21:18 *2513*
the street of the city was **p** gold, Rv 21:21 *2513*

PURER
consecrated ones were **p** than snow, La 4:7 2141

PUREST
and the tongs of gold, of **p** gold; 2Ch 4:21 4357

PURGE
shall **p** the evil from among you. Dt 13:5 1197a
shall **p** the evil from your midst. Dt 17:7 1197a
you shall **p** the evil from Israel. Dt 17:12 1197a
but you shall **p** the blood of the Dt 19:13 1197a
shall **p** the evil from among you. Dt 19:19 1197a
shall **p** the evil from among you. Dt 21:21 1197a
you shall **p** the evil from Israel. Dt 22:22 1197a
shall **p** the evil from among you. Dt 22:24 1197a
shall **p** the evil from among you. Dt 24:7 1197a
the twelfth year he began to **p** Judah 2Ch 34:3 2891
and I will **p** from you the rebels Ezk 20:38 1305
to refine, **p** and make them pure Da 11:35 1305

PURGED
p the altar with their blood to atone 2Ch 29:24 2398
altars and **p** Judah and Jerusalem. 2Ch 34:5 2891
he had **p** the land and the house, 2Ch 34:8 2891
and **p** the bloodshed of Jerusalem Is 4:4 1740
"Many will be **p**, purified and Da 12:10 1305
everyone who steals will be **p** away Zch 5:3 5352
everyone who swears will be **p** away Zch 5:3 5352

PURIFICATION
shall remain in the blood of *her* **p** Lv 12:4 2893
the days of her **p** are completed. Lv 12:4 2892a
shall remain in the blood of *her* **p** Lv 12:5 2893
the days of her **p** are completed, Lv 12:6 2892a
it is **p** from sin. Nu 19:9 2403b
of the ashes of the burnt **p** from sin Nu 19:17 2403b
to the **p** *rules* of the sanctuary." 2Ch 30:19 2893
of their God and the service of **p**, Ne 12:45 2893
And when the days for their **p** Lk 2:22 *2512*
there for the Jewish custom of **p**, Jn 2:6 *2512*
disciples with a Jew about **p**. Jn 3:25 *2512*
the completion of the days of **p**, Ac 21:26 *49*
When He had made **p** of sins, Heb 1:3 *2512*
his **p** from his former sins. 2Pe 1:9 *2512*

PURIFIED
of the altar, and **p** the altar. Lv 8:15 2398
Levites, too, **p** themselves from sin Nu 8:21 2398
be **p** with water for impurity. Nu 31:23 2398
p herself from her uncleanness, 2Sa 11:4 6942
'I have **p** these waters; 2Ki 2:21 7495
waters have been **p** to this day, 2Ki 2:22 7495
and Zebulun, had not **p** themselves, 2Ch 30:18 2891
Levites had **p** themselves together; Ezr 6:20 2891
and the Levites **p** themselves; Ne 12:30 2891
they also **p** the people, the gates and Ne 12:30 2891
Thus I **p** them from everything Ne 13:30 2891
Your name is *like* **p** oil; SS 1:3 7385a
Many will be purged, **p** and refined, Da 12:10 3835a
I will give to the peoples **p** lips, Zph 3:9 1305
in the temple, having been **p**, Ac 24:18 *48*
in obedience to the truth **p** your souls 1Pe 1:22 *48*

PURIFIER
sit as a smelter and **p** of silver, Mal 3:3 2891

PURIFIES
this hope *fixed* on Him **p** himself, 1Jn 3:3 *48*

PURIFY
are among you, and **p** yourselves and Gn 35:2 2891
and you shall **p** the altar when you Ex 29:36 2398
'That one shall **p** himself from Nu 19:12 2398
but if he does not **p** himself on Nu 19:12 2398
has died, and does not **p** himself, Nu 19:13 2398
he shall **p** him from uncleanness, Nu 19:19 2398
not **p** himself from uncleanness, Nu 19:20 2398
touched any slain, **p** yourselves, Nu 31:19 2398
"You shall **p** for yourselves Nu 31:20 2398
Levites that they should **p** themselves Ne 13:22 2891
P me with hyssop, and I shall be Ps 51:7 2398
of the midst of her, **p** yourselves, Is 52:11 1305
who sanctify and **p** themselves Is 66:17 2891
atonement for the altar and **p** it; Ezk 43:26 2891
and He will **p** the sons of Levi and Mal 3:3 2891
the Passover to **p** themselves. Jn 11:55 *48*
and **p** yourself along with them, Ac 21:24 *48*
p for Himself a people for His own Ti 2:14 *2511*
p your hearts, you double-minded. Jas 4:8 *48*

PURIFYING
sprinkle **p** water on them, and let Nu 8:7 2891
and in the **p** of all holy things, 1Ch 23:28 2893
day, **p** himself along with them, Ac 21:26 *48*

PURIM
days **P** after the name of Pur. Es 9:26 6332
and these days of **P** were not to Es 9:28 6332
this second letter about **P**. Es 9:29 6332
to establish these days of **P** at their Es 9:31 6332
established these customs for **P**, Es 9:32 6332

PURITY
He who loves **p** of heart *And* whose Pr 22:11 2889
in **p**, in knowledge, in patience, 2Co 6:6 *54*
and **p** *of devotion* to Christ. 2Co 11:3 *54*
conduct, love, faith *and* **p**, 1Tm 4:12 *47*
women as sisters, in all **p**. 1Tm 5:2 *47*

of good deeds, *with* **p** in doctrine, Ti 2:7 *862b*
PURPLE
blue, **p** and scarlet *material,* fine Ex 25:4 713
blue and **p** and scarlet *material;* Ex 26:1 713
You shall make a veil of blue and **p** Ex 26:31 713
the doorway of the tent of blue and **p** Ex 26:36 713
of blue and **p** and scarlet *material* Ex 27:16 713
take the gold and the blue and the **p** Ex 28:5 713
of blue and **p** *and* scarlet *material* Ex 28:6 713
of blue and **p** and scarlet *material* Ex 28:8 713
of blue and **p** and scarlet *material* Ex 28:15 713
blue and **p** and scarlet *material,* Ex 28:33 713
and blue, **p** and scarlet *material,* Ex 35:6 713
blue and **p** and scarlet *material* Ex 35:23 713
in blue and **p** *and* scarlet *material* Ex 35:25 713
and in **p** *and* in scarlet *material,* Ex 35:35 713
blue and **p** and scarlet *material,* Ex 36:8 713
blue and **p** and scarlet *material,* Ex 36:35 713
blue and **p** and scarlet *material,* Ex 36:37 713
blue and **p** and scarlet *material* and Ex 38:18 713
and in **p** and in scarlet *material,* Ex 38:23 713
blue and **p** and scarlet *material,* Ex 39:1 713
blue and **p** and scarlet *material,* Ex 39:2 713
the **p** and the scarlet *material,* Ex 39:3 713
blue and **p** and scarlet *material,* Ex 39:5 713
blue and **p** and scarlet *material* Ex 39:8 713
made pomegranates of blue and **p** Ex 39:24 713
blue and **p** and scarlet *material,* Ex 39:29 713
and spread a **p** cloth over it. Nu 4:13 713
the **p** robes which *were* on the kings Jg 8:26 713
silver, brass and iron, and in **p**, 2Ch 2:7 710
iron, stone and wood, *and* in **p**, 2Ch 2:14 713
He made the veil of violet, **p**, 2Ch 3:14 713
cords of fine **p** linen on silver rings Es 1:6 713
and a garment of fine linen and **p**; Es 8:15 713
Her clothing is fine linen and **p**. Pr 31:22 713
of gold *And* its seat of **p** fabric, SS 3:10 713
of your head are like **p** threads; SS 7:5 713
Violet and **p** are their clothing; Jer 10:9 713
reared in **p** Embrace ash pits. La 4:5 8438
who were clothed in **p**, Ezk 23:6 8504
Your awning was blue and **p** from Ezk 27:7 713
for your wares with emeralds, **p**, Ezk 27:16 713
to me shall be clothed with **p** Da 5:7 711
you will be clothed with **p** and Da 5:16 711
and they clothed Daniel with **p** and Da 5:29 711
They dressed Him up in **p**, Mk 15:17 *4209*
Him, they took the **p** robe off Him Mk 15:20 *4209*
dressed in **p** and fine linen, Lk 16:19 *4209*
head, and put a **p** robe on Him; Jn 19:2 *4210*
crown of thorns and the **p** robe. Jn 19:5 *4210*
Thyatira, a seller of **p** fabrics, Ac 16:14 *4211*
woman was clothed in **p** and scarlet, Rv 17:4 *4210*
linen and **p** and silk and scarlet, Rv 18:12 *4209*
in fine linen and **p** and scarlet, Rv 18:16 *4210*
PURPOSE
and now nothing which they **p** to do Gn 11:6 2161
p for which the leather is used, Lv 13:51 4399
for the **p** of shooting arrows and 2Ch 26:15
which they had made for the **p**. Ne 8:4 1697
no **p** of Yours can be thwarted. Jb 42:2 4209
hold fast to themselves an evil **p**; Ps 64:5 1697
has made everything for its own **p**, Pr 16:4 4617
let the **p** of the Holy One of Israel Is 5:19 6098
But rather it is its **p** to destroy And Is 10:7 3824
because of the **p** of the LORD of Is 19:17 6098
performing the **p** of His messengers. Is 44:26 6098
'My **p** will be established, And I Is 46:10 6098
man of My **p** from a far country. Is 46:11 6098
"For what **p** does frankincense Jer 6:20 2088
Because His **p** is against Babylon Jer 51:11 4209
you for the **p** of shedding blood. Ezk 22:6 4616
you for the **p** of shedding blood, Ezk 22:9 4616
the **p** of making the interpretation Da 2:30 1701
what **p** *will* the day of the LORD *be* Am 5:18 2088
And they do not understand His **p**; Mi 4:12 6098
also, for I was sent for this **p**." Lk 4:43 *1012*
rejected God's **p** for themselves, Lk 7:30 *1012*
for this **p** I came to this hour. Jn 12:27
what **p** He had said this to him. Jn 13:28
and Your **p** predestined to occur. Ac 4:28 *1012*
for the **p** of bringing them bound Ac 9:21
p of God in his own generation, Ac 13:36 *1012*
declaring to you the whole **p** of God. Ac 20:27 *1012*
for this **p** I have appeared to you, Ac 26:16
that they had attained their **p**, Ac 27:13 *4286*
who are called according to *His* **p**. Ro 8:28 *4286*
God's **p** according to *His* choice Ro 9:11 *4286*
"FOR THIS VERY **P** I RAISED YOU UP, Ro 9:17
but not for *the* **p** *of* passing Ro 14:1
Or what I **p**, do I purpose according 2Co 1:17 *1011*
do I **p** according to the flesh, 2Co 1:17 *1011*
He who prepared us for this very **p** 2Co 5:5
been predestined according to His **p** Eph 1:11 *4286*
was in accordance with the eternal **p** Eph 3:11 *4286*
sent him to you for this very **p**, Eph 6:22
united in spirit, intent on one **p**. Php 2:2 *5426*
For this **p** also I labor, Col 1:29
sent him to you for this very **p**, Col 4:8
not called us for the **p** of impurity, 1Th 4:7
yourself for the **p** of godliness; 1Tm 4:7
but according to His own **p** and 2Tm 1:9 *4286*
followed my teaching, conduct, **p**, 2Tm 3:10 *4286*
the unchangeableness of His **p**, Heb 6:17 *1012*
that the Scripture speaks to no **p**: Jas 4:5 *2761*
you have been called for this **p**, 1Pe 2:21
for you were called for the very **p** 1Pe 3:9
yourselves also with the same **p**, 1Pe 4:1 *1771*
gospel has for this **p** been preached 1Pe 4:6
sober *spirit* for the **p** of prayer. 1Pe 4:7
Son of God appeared for this **p**, 1Jn 3:8
"These have one **p**, and they give Rv 17:13 *1106*
His **p** by having a common purpose, Rv 17:17 *1106*
His purpose by having a common **p**, Rv 17:17 *1106*
PURPOSED
I have **p** that my mouth will not Ps 17:3 2161
Who have **p** to trip up my feet. Ps 140:4 2803
LORD of hosts Has **p** against Egypt. Is 19:12 3289
Because I have spoken, I have **p**, Jer 4:28 2161
and His purposes which He has **p** Jer 49:20 2803
and His purposes which He has **p** Jer 50:45 2803
the LORD has both **p** and performed Jer 51:12 2161
The LORD has done what He **p**; La 2:17 2161
'As the LORD of hosts **p** to do to Zch 1:6 2161
'Just as I **p** to do harm to you Zch 8:14 2161
so I have again **p** in these days to Zch 8:15 2161
day He **p** to go into Galilee, Jn 1:43 *2309*
Paul **p** in the Spirit to go to Ac 19:21 *5087*
do just as he has **p** in his heart 2Co 9:7 *4255*
kind intention which He **p** in Him Eph 1:9 *4388*
PURPOSELY
"Also you shall **p** pull out Ru 2:16 7997a
PURPOSES
"Surely I will set you free for **p** Jer 15:11
carried out the **p** of His heart; Jer 23:20 4209
and His **p** which He has purposed Jer 49:20 4284
and His **p** which He has purposed Jer 50:45 4284
For the **p** of the LORD against Jer 51:29 4284
PURPOSING
hosts which He is **p** against them. Is 19:17 3289
PURSE
us, We shall all have one **p**," Pr 1:14 3599
"Those who lavish gold from the **p** Is 46:6 3599
wages *to put* into a **p** with holes." Hg 1:6 6872a
PURSES
outer tunics, cloaks, money **p**, Is 3:22 2754
PURSUE
they did not **p** the sons of Jacob. Gn 35:5 7291
'I will **p**, I will overtake, I will Ex 15:9 7291
and only justice, you shall **p**, Dt 16:20 7291
otherwise the avenger of blood might **p** Dt 19:6 7291
they will **p** you until you perish. Dt 28:22 7291
curses shall come on you and **p** you Dt 28:45 7291
P them quickly, for you will Jos 2:5 7291
were called together to **p** them, Jos 8:16 7291
p your enemies and attack them in Jos 10:19 7291
"**P** *them,* for the LORD has given Jg 3:28 7291
"Should anyone rise up to **p** you 1Sa 25:29 7291
"Shall I **p** this band? 1Sa 30:8 7291
"**P**, for you will surely overtake 1Sa 30:8 7291
I may arise and **p** David tonight. 2Sa 17:1 7291
your lord's servants and **p** him, 2Sa 20:6 7291
to **p** Sheba the son of Bichri. 2Sa 20:7 7291
Joab to **p** Sheba the son of Bichri. 2Sa 20:13 7291
before your foes while they **p** you? 2Sa 24:13 7291
Or will You **p** the dry chaff? Jb 13:25 7291
me; They **p** my honor as the wind, Jb 30:15 7291
Save me from all those who **p** me, Ps 7:1 7291
enemy **p** my soul and overtake *it;* Ps 7:5 7291
the wicked hotly **p** the afflicted; Ps 10:2 1814
Seek peace and **p** it. Ps 34:14 7291
battle-axe to meet those who **p** me; Ps 35:3 7291
P and seize him, for there is no Ps 71:11 7291
So **p** them with Your tempest And Ps 83:15 7291
that they may **p** strong drink, Is 5:11 7291
those who **p** you shall be swift. Is 30:16 7291
to me, you who **p** righteousness, Is 51:1 7291
'I will **p** them with the sword, Jer 29:18 7291
You will **p** them in anger and La 3:66 7291
and bloodshed will **p** you; Ezk 35:6 7291
therefore bloodshed will **p** you. Ezk 35:6 7291
"She will **p** her lovers, but Hos 2:7 7291
The enemy will **p** him. Hos 8:3 7291
will **p** His enemies into darkness. Na 1:8 7291
who did not **p** righteousness, Ro 9:30 *1377*
Why? Because *they did* not **p** *it* Ro 9:32
So then we **p** the things which Ro 14:19 *1377*
P love, yet desire earnestly 1Co 14:1 *1377*
and **p** righteousness, godliness, 1Tm 6:11 *1377*
lusts and **p** righteousness, 2Tm 2:22 *1377*
P peace with all men, and the Heb 12:14 *1377*
HE MUST SEEK PEACE AND **P** IT. 1Pe 3:11 *1377*
PURSUED
them, and **p** them as far as Hobah, Gn 14:15 7291
and **p** him *a distance of* seven Gn 31:23 7291
my sin that you have hotly **p** me? Gn 31:36 1814
So the men **p** them on the road to Jos 2:7 7291
and **p** them from the gate as far as Jos 7:5 7291
to pursue them, and they **p** Joshua and Jos 8:16 7291
the city unguarded and **p** Israel. Jos 8:17 7291
the wilderness where they **p** them, Jos 8:24 7291
and **p** them by the way of the Jos 10:10 7291
and **p** them as far as Great Sidon Jos 11:8 7291
and Egypt **p** your fathers with Jos 24:6 7291
and they **p** him and caught him and Jg 1:6 7291
But Barak **p** the chariots and the Jg 4:16 7291
And behold, as Barak **p** Sisera, Jg 4:22 7291
all Manasseh, and they **p** Midian. Jg 7:23 7291
of Zeeb, while they **p** Midian; Jg 7:25 7291
he **p** them and captured the two Jg 8:12 7291
p them without rest *and* trod them Jg 20:43 7291
of Mizpah and **p** the Philistines, 1Sa 7:11 7291
also **p** them closely in the battle. 1Sa 14:22 1692
p the Philistines as far as the valley, 1Sa 17:52 7291
he **p** David in the wilderness of 1Sa 23:25 7291
But David **p**, he and four hundred 1Sa 30:10 7291
and the horsemen **p** him closely. 2Sa 1:6 1692
Asahel **p** Abner and did not 2Sa 2:19 7291
But Joab and Abishai **p** Abner, 2Sa 2:24 7291
halted and **p** Israel no longer, 2Sa 2:28 7291
brother **p** Sheba the son of Bichri. 2Sa 20:10 7291
"I **p** my enemies and destroyed 2Sa 22:38 7291
Arameans fled and Israel **p** them, 1Ki 20:20 7291
So Gehazi **p** Naaman. 2Ki 5:21 7291
And Jehu **p** him and said, 2Ki 9:27 7291
But the army of the Chaldeans **p** 2Ki 25:5 7291
closely **p** Saul and his sons, 1Ch 10:2 1692
Abijah **p** Jeroboam and 2Ch 13:19 7291
people who *were* with him **p** them 2Ch 14:13 7291
I **p** my enemies and overtook them, Ps 18:37 7291
But the army of the Chaldeans **p** Jer 39:5 7291
But the army of the Chaldeans **p** Jer 52:8 7291
Yourself with anger And **p** us; La 3:43 7291
he **p** his brother with the sword, Am 1:11 7291
having **p** a course of sensuality, 1Pe 4:3 *4198*
PURSUER
fled without strength Before the **p**. La 1:6 7291
PURSUERS
the **p** will not happen upon you, Jos 2:16 7291
three days until the **p** return. Jos 2:16 7291
three days until the **p** returned. Jos 2:22 7291
Now the **p** had sought *them* all Jos 2:22 7291
wilderness turned against the **p**. Jos 8:20 7291
And their **p** You hurled into Ne 9:11 7291
All her **p** have overtaken her In La 1:3 7291
Our **p** were swifter Than the eagles La 4:19 7291
Our **p** are at our necks; La 5:5 7291
PURSUES
'Now if the avenger of blood **p** him, Jos 20:5 7291
And he who **p** evil *will bring about* Pr 11:19 7291
he who **p** worthless *things* lacks sense. Pr 12:11 7291
Adversity **p** sinners, But the Pr 13:21 7291
He loves one who **p** righteousness. Pr 15:9 7291
He **p** *them with* words, *but* they are Pr 19:7 7291
He who **p** righteousness and loyalty Pr 21:21 7291
"He **p** them, passing on in safety, Is 41:3 7291
And **p** the east wind continually; Hos 12:1 7291
PURSUING
will flee when no one is **p** you. Lv 26:17 7291
them, and even when no one is **p** Lv 26:36 7291
the sword, although no one is **p**; Lv 26:37 7291
engulf them while they were **p** you, Dt 11:4 7291
who were **p** them had gone out, Jos 2:7 7291
and crossed over, weary yet **p**. Jg 8:4 7291
and I am **p** Zebah and Zalmunna, Jg 8:5 7291
Saul went up from **p** the Philistines, 1Sa 14:46 310
So Saul returned from **p** David and 1Sa 23:28 7291
Saul returned from **p** the Philistines, 1Sa 24:1 310
Whom are you **p**? A dead dog, 1Sa 24:14 7291
"Why then is my lord **p** his servant? 1Sa 26:18 7291
the people returned from **p** Israel, 2Sa 18:16 7291
they turned back from **p** him. 1Ki 22:33 310
they turned back from **p** him. 2Ch 18:32 310
With the angel of the LORD **p** them. Ps 35:6 7291
The wicked flee when no one is **p**, Pr 28:1 7291
p them even to foreign cities. Ac 26:11 *1377*
Israel, **p** a law of righteousness, Ro 9:31 *1377*
PURSUIT
and went in **p** as far as Dan. Gn 14:14 7291
Then the Egyptians took up the **p**, Ex 14:23 7291
from Keilah, he gave up the **p**. 1Sa 23:13 3318
a fleeting vapor, the **p** of death. Pr 21:6 1245
PURSUITS
But he who follows empty **p** will Pr 28:19
rich man in the midst of his **p** will Jas 1:11 *4197*
PUSH
With them he will **p** the peoples, Dt 33:17 5055
Gehazi came near to **p** her away; 2Ki 4:27 1920
p the needy aside from the road; Jb 24:4 5186
we will **p** back our adversaries; Ps 44:5 5055
you **p** with side and with shoulder, Ezk 34:21 1920
PUSHED
'If he **p** him of hatred, or Nu 35:20 1920
he **p** him suddenly without enmity, Nu 35:22 1920
You **p** me violently so that I was Ps 118:13 1760
injuring his neighbor **p** him away, Ac 7:27 *683*
PUT
and **p** him into the garden of Eden Gn 2:15 5117
And I will **p** enmity Between you Gn 3:15 7896
he **p** out his hand and took her, Gn 8:9 7971
Cush and Mizraim and **P** and Canaan. Gn 10:6 6316
out, and **p** him outside the city. Gn 19:16 5117
and I **p** the ring on her nose, and Gn 24:47 7760
wife shall surely be **p** to death." Gn 26:11 4191
p them on Jacob her younger son. Gn 27:15 3847
she **p** the skins of the young goats Gn 27:16 3847
the place and **p** it under his head, Gn 28:11 7760
and took the stone that he had **p** Gn 28:18 7760
and **p** the stone back in its place Gn 29:3 7725
And he **p** *a distance of* three days' Gn 30:36 7760
and he **p** his own herds apart, and Gn 30:40 7896
did not **p** them with Laban's flock. Gn 30:40 7896
was feeble, he did not **p** *them* in; Gn 30:42 7760
p his children and his wives upon Gn 31:17 5375
and **p** them in the camel's saddle, Gn 31:34 7760
and **p** a space between droves." Gn 32:16 7760
He **p** the maids and their Gn 33:2 7760
"**P** away the foreign gods which Gn 35:2 5493
against him to **p** him to death. Gn 37:18 4191
and **p** sackcloth on his loins and Gn 37:34 7760
veil and **p** on her widow's garments. Gn 38:19 3847
giving birth, one **p** out a hand, Gn 38:28 5414

all that he owned he **p** in his charge.	**Gn 39:4**	5414
p all that he owns in my charge.	**Gn 39:8**	5414
took him and **p** him into the jail,	**Gn 39:20**	5414
So he **p** them in confinement in the	**Gn 40:3**	5414
p Joseph in charge of them,	**Gn 40:4**	6485
I **p** the cup into Pharaoh's hand."	**Gn 40:11**	5414
and you will **p** Pharaoh's cup into	**Gn 40:13**	5414
have **p** me into the dungeon."	**Gn 40:15**	7760
he **p** the cup into Pharaoh's hand;	**Gn 40:21**	5414
and he **p** me in confinement in the	**Gn 41:10**	5414
hand and **p** it on Joseph's hand,	**Gn 41:42**	5414
and **p** the gold necklace around his	**Gn 41:42**	7760
So he **p** them all together in	**Gn 42:17**	622
"You may **p** my two sons to death	**Gn 42:37**	4191
p him in my care, and I will	**Gn 42:37**	5414
who **p** our money in our sacks."	**Gn 43:22**	7760
and **p** each man's money in the	**Gn 44:1**	7760
"**P** my cup, the silver cup, in	**Gn 44:2**	7760
then **p** them in charge of my	**Gn 47:6**	7760
Thus he **p** Ephraim before Manasseh.	**Gn 48:20**	7760
then you shall **p** him to death;	**Ex 1:16**	4191
Then she **p** the child into it and	**Ex 2:3**	7760
and you will **p** them on your sons	**Ex 3:22**	7760
"Now **p** your hand into your bosom."	**Ex 4:6**	935
So he **p** his hand into his bosom,	**Ex 4:6**	935
"**P** your hand into your bosom	**Ex 4:7**	7725
p his hand into his bosom again,	**Ex 4:7**	7725
him and **p** the words in his mouth;	**Ex 4:15**	7760
which I have **p** in your power;	**Ex 4:21**	7760
him and sought to **p** him to death.	**Ex 4:24**	4191
to **p** a sword in their hand to kill	**Ex 5:21**	5414
"I will **p** a division between	**Ex 8:23**	7760
if by now I had **p** forth My hand	**Ex 9:15**	7971
blood and **p** it on the two doorposts	**Ex 12:7**	5414
I will **p** none of the diseases on	**Ex 15:26**	7760
which I have **p** on the Egyptians;	**Ex 15:26**	7760
and all that is left over **p** aside	**Ex 16:23**	5117
So they **p** it aside until morning,	**Ex 16:24**	5117
and **p** an omerful of manna in it,	**Ex 16:33**	5414
took a stone and **p** it under him,	**Ex 17:12**	7760
shall surely be **p** to death.	**Ex 19:12**	4191
dies shall surely be **p** to death.	**Ex 21:12**	4191
mother shall surely be **p** to death.	**Ex 21:15**	4191
shall surely be **p** to death.	**Ex 21:16**	4191
mother shall surely be **p** to death.	**Ex 21:17**	4191
owner also shall be **p** to death.	**Ex 21:29**	4191
animal shall surely be **p** to death.	**Ex 22:19**	4191
of the blood and **p** *it* in basins,	**Ex 24:6**	7760
"You shall **p** the poles into	**Ex 25:14**	935
"You shall **p** into the ark the	**Ex 25:16**	5414
"You shall **p** the mercy seat	**Ex 25:21**	5414
in the ark you shall **p** the testimony	**Ex 25:21**	5414
p rings on the four corners which are	**Ex 25:26**	5414
and you shall **p** the clasps into	**Ex 26:11**	935
"You shall **p** the mercy seat	**Ex 26:34**	5414
p the table on the north side.	**Ex 26:35**	5414
"You shall **p** it beneath,	**Ex 27:5**	5414
"You shall **p** the two stones	**Ex 28:12**	7760
and you shall **p** the corded chains	**Ex 28:14**	5414
and shall **p** the two rings on the	**Ex 28:23**	5414
"You shall **p** the two cords of	**Ex 28:24**	5414
"You shall **p** the *other* two	**Ex 28:25**	5414
and **p** them on the shoulder pieces	**Ex 28:25**	5414
make two rings of gold and **p** them	**Ex 28:27**	5414
You shall **p** in the breastpiece of	**Ex 28:30**	5414
"You shall **p** them on Aaron	**Ex 28:41**	3847
You shall **p** them in one basket,	**Ex 29:3**	5414
and **p** on Aaron the tunic and the	**Ex 29:5**	3847
p the holy crown on the turban.	**Ex 29:6**	5414
his sons and **p** tunics on them.	**Ex 29:8**	3847
and **p** *it* on the horns of the altar	**Ex 29:12**	5414
and **p** *them* with its pieces and its	**Ex 29:17**	5414
and take some of its blood and **p**	**Ex 29:20**	5414
and you shall **p** all these in the	**Ex 29:24**	7760
p them on when he enters the tent of	**Ex 29:30**	3847
"You shall **p** this altar in	**Ex 30:6**	5414
and you shall **p** it between the	**Ex 30:18**	5414
and you shall **p** water in it.	**Ex 30:18**	5414
and **p** part of it before the	**Ex 30:36**	5414
who are skillful I have **p** skill,	**Ex 31:6**	5414
it shall surely be **p** to death;	**Ex 31:14**	4191
day shall surely be **p** to death.	**Ex 31:15**	4191
Every man *of you* **p** his sword upon	**Ex 32:27**	7760
none of them **p** on his ornaments.	**Ex 33:4**	7896
p off your ornaments from you,	**Ex 33:5**	3381
that I will **p** you in the cleft of	**Ex 33:22**	7760
them, he **p** a veil over his face.	**Ex 34:33**	5414
work on it shall be **p** to death.	**Ex 35:2**	4191
also has **p** in his heart to teach,	**Ex 35:34**	5414
person in whom the LORD has **p** skill	**Ex 36:1**	5414
in whom the LORD had **p** skill,	**Ex 36:2**	5414
He **p** the poles into the rings	**Ex 37:5**	935
and **p** the rings on the four corners	**Ex 37:13**	5414
and **p** the two rings on the two	**Ex 39:16**	5414
Then they **p** the two gold cords in	**Ex 39:17**	5414
They **p** the *other* two ends of	**Ex 39:18**	5414
and **p** them on the shoulder pieces	**Ex 39:18**	5414
and **p** the bells between the	**Ex 39:25**	5414
and the altar and **p** water in it.	**Ex 40:7**	5414
"You shall **p** the holy garments	**Ex 40:13**	3847
his sons and **p** tunics on them;	**Ex 40:14**	3847
p the covering of the tent on top of it,	**Ex 40:19**	7760
testimony and **p** *it* into the ark,	**Ex 40:20**	5414
and **p** the mercy seat on top of the	**Ex 40:20**	5414
Then he **p** the table in the tent of	**Ex 40:22**	5414
and **p** water in it for washing.	**Ex 40:30**	5414
sons of Aaron the priest shall **p** fire	**Lv 1:7**	5414
on it and **p** frankincense on it.	**Lv 2:1**	5414
'You shall then **p** oil on it and	**Lv 2:15**	5414

'The priest shall also **p** some of	**Lv 4:7**	5414
'He shall **p** some of the blood	**Lv 4:18**	5414
and **p** it on the horns of the altar	**Lv 4:25**	5414
p it on the horns of the altar of burnt	**Lv 4:30**	5414
p it on the horns of the altar of burnt	**Lv 4:34**	5414
he shall not **p** oil on it or place	**Lv 5:11**	7760
priest is to **p** on his linen robe,	**Lv 6:10**	3847
and he shall **p** on undergarments	**Lv 6:10**	3847
garments and **p** on other garments,	**Lv 6:11**	3847
beasts may be **p** to any other use,	**Lv 7:24**	6213a
He **p** the tunic on him and	**Lv 8:7**	5414
the robe and **p** the ephod on him;	**Lv 8:7**	5414
he **p** the Urim and the Thummim.	**Lv 8:8**	5414
with his finger **p** *some of it* around on	**Lv 8:15**	5414
p it on the lobe of Aaron's right ear,	**Lv 8:23**	5414
and Moses **p** some of the blood on	**Lv 8:24**	5414
He then **p** all *these* on the hands	**Lv 8:27**	5414
and **p** *some* on the horns of the	**Lv 9:9**	5414
be **p** in the water and be unclean until	**Lv 11:32**	935
'Though if water is **p** on the seed and	**Lv 11:38**	5414
and the priest shall **p** *it* on the	**Lv 14:14**	5414
the priest shall **p** some on the	**Lv 14:17**	5414
he shall **p** on the head of the one	**Lv 14:18**	5414
blood of the guilt offering and **p** *it* on	**Lv 14:25**	5414
"The priest shall then **p** some of	**Lv 14:28**	5414
shall **p** on the head of the one to be	**Lv 14:29**	5414
and I **p** a mark of leprosy on a	**Lv 14:34**	5414
shall **p** on the holy linen tunic,	**Lv 16:4**	3847
his body in water and **p** them on.	**Lv 16:4**	3847
"He shall **p** the incense on	**Lv 16:13**	5414
and **p** it on the horns of the altar	**Lv 16:18**	5414
linen garments which he **p** on when	**Lv 16:23**	3847
a holy place and **p** on his clothes,	**Lv 16:24**	3847
thus **p** on the linen garments,	**Lv 16:32**	3847
shall not, *however,* be **p** to death,	**Lv 19:20**	4191
shall surely be **p** to death;	**Lv 20:2**	4191
so as not to **p** him to death,	**Lv 20:4**	4191
he shall surely be **p** to death;	**Lv 20:9**	4191
shall surely be **p** to death.	**Lv 20:10**	4191
them shall surely be **p** to death,	**Lv 20:11**	4191
them shall surely be **p** to death;	**Lv 20:12**	4191
they shall surely be **p** to death.	**Lv 20:13**	4191
he shall surely be **p** to death;	**Lv 20:15**	4191
they shall surely be **p** to death.	**Lv 20:16**	4191
shall surely be **p** to death.	**Lv 20:27**	4191
p pure frankincense on each row that	**Lv 24:7**	5414
They **p** him in custody so that	**Lv 24:12**	5117
LORD shall surely be **p** to death;	**Lv 24:16**	4191
the Name, shall be **p** to death.	**Lv 24:16**	4191
he shall surely be **p** to death.	**Lv 24:17**	4191
kills a man shall be **p** to death.	**Lv 24:21**	4191
he shall surely be **p** to death.	**Lv 27:29**	4191
comes near shall be **p** to death.	**Nu 1:51**	4191
comes near shall be **p** to death."	**Nu 3:10**	4191
coming near was to be **p** to death.	**Nu 3:38**	4191
also spread a cloth of blue and **p** on	**Nu 4:7**	5414
and they shall **p** it and all its	**Nu 4:10**	5414
shall **p** it on the carrying bars.	**Nu 4:10**	5414
and **p** them in a blue cloth and	**Nu 4:12**	5414
and **p** them on the carrying bars.	**Nu 4:12**	5414
"They shall also **p** on it all its	**Nu 4:14**	5414
on it nor **p** frankincense on it,	**Nu 5:15**	5414
and **p** *it* into the water.	**Nu 5:17**	5414
hair of his head and **p** *it* on the fire	**Nu 6:18**	5414
and shall **p** *them* on the hands of	**Nu 6:19**	5414
you, and will **p** *Him* upon them;	**Nu 11:17**	7760
would **p** His Spirit upon them!"	**Nu 11:29**	5414
yet have **p** Me to the test these	**Nu 14:22**	5254
and they **p** him in custody because	**Nu 15:34**	5117
man shall surely be **p** to death;	**Nu 15:35**	4191
and that they shall **p** on the	**Nu 15:38**	5414
and **p** fire in them, and lay	**Nu 16:7**	5414
you **p** out the eyes of these men?	**Nu 16:14**	5365
his firepan and **p** incense on it,	**Nu 16:17**	5414
his *own* censer and **p** fire on it,	**Nu 16:18**	5414
and **p** in it fire from the altar,	**Nu 16:46**	5414
So he **p** *on* the incense and made	**Nu 16:47**	5414
p forth buds and produced blossoms	**Nu 17:8**	3318
"**P** back the rod of Aaron before	**Nu 17:10**	7725
that you may **p** an end to their	**Nu 17:10**	3615
comes near shall be **p** to death."	**Nu 18:7**	4191
and **p** them on his son Eleazar.	**Nu 20:26**	3847
and **p** them on his son Eleazar,	**Nu 20:28**	3847
Then the LORD **p** a word in Balaam's	**Nu 23:5**	7760
p a word in his mouth and said,	**Nu 23:16**	7760
p some of your authority on him,	**Nu 27:20**	5414
shall surely be **p** to death.	**Nu 35:16**	4191
shall surely be **p** to death.	**Nu 35:17**	4191
shall surely be **p** to death.	**Nu 35:18**	4191
shall **p** the murderer to death;	**Nu 35:19**	4191
he shall **p** him to death when he	**Nu 35:19**	4191
him shall surely be **p** to death,	**Nu 35:21**	4191
shall **p** the murderer to death when	**Nu 35:21**	4191
the murderer shall be **p** to death	**Nu 35:30**	7523
but no person shall be **p** to death	**Nu 35:30**	4191
but he shall surely be **p** to death.	**Nu 35:31**	4191
I will begin to **p** the dread and fear	**Dt 2:25**	5414
p the LORD your God to the test,	**Dt 6:16**	5254
and He will not **p** on you any of	**Dt 7:15**	7760
able to **p** an end to them quickly,	**Dt 7:22**	3615
and you shall **p** them in the ark.'	**Dt 10:2**	7760
and **p** the tablets in the ark which	**Dt 10:5**	7760
your God chooses to **p** His name	**Dt 12:21**	7760
of dreams shall be **p** to death,	**Dt 13:5**	4191
against him to **p** him to death,	**Dt 13:9**	4191
from that which is **p** under the ban	**Dt 13:17**	
to **p** the sickle to the standing grain.	**Dt 16:9**	
who is to die shall be **p** to death;	**Dt 17:6**	4191
he shall not be **p** to death on the	**Dt 17:6**	4191

against him to **p** him to death,	**Dt 17:7**	4191
you may not **p** a foreigner over	**Dt 17:15**	5414
I will **p** My words in his mouth,	**Dt 18:18**	5414
of death and he is **p** to death,	**Dt 21:22**	4191
a man **p** on a woman's clothing;	**Dt 22:5**	3847
shall not **p** any in your basket.	**Dt 23:24**	5414
not be **p** to death for *their* sons,	**Dt 24:16**	4191
be **p** to death for *their* fathers;	**Dt 24:16**	4191
be **p** to death for his own sin.	**Dt 24:16**	4191
and you shall **p** *it* in a basket and	**Dt 26:2**	7760
in all that you **p** your hand to,	**Dt 28:8**	4916a
and He will **p** an iron yoke on your	**Dt 28:48**	5414
p it on their lips, so that	**Dt 31:19**	7760
And two **p** ten thousand to flight,	**Dt 32:30**	5127
is I who **p** to death and give life.	**Dt 32:39**	4191
They shall **p** incense before You,	**Dt 33:10**	7760
command him, shall be **p** to death;	**Jos 1:18**	4191
place and **p** them down there.	**Jos 4:8**	5117
they **p** into the treasury of the	**Jos 6:24**	5414
and they **p** dust on their heads.	**Jos 7:6**	5927
p *them* among their own things.	**Jos 7:11**	7760
p your feet on the necks of these	**Jos 10:24**	7760
and **p** their feet on their necks.	**Jos 10:24**	7760
struck them and **p** them to death,	**Jos 10:26**	4191
and **p** large stones over the mouth	**Jos 10:27**	7760
them down and **p** them to death.	**Jos 11:17**	4191
they **p** the Canaanites to forced	**Jos 17:13**	5414
"How long will you **p** off entering	**Jos 18:3**	7503
He **p** darkness between you and the	**Jos 24:7**	7760
and **p** away the gods which your	**Jos 24:14**	5493
p away the foreign gods which are	**Jos 24:23**	5493
that they **p** the Canaanites to	**Jg 1:28**	7760
he **p** the meat in a basket and the	**Jg 6:19**	7760
Then the angel of the LORD **p** out	**Jg 6:21**	7971
shall be **p** to death by morning.	**Jg 6:31**	4191
I will **p** a fleece of wool on the	**Jg 6:37**	3322
and he **p** trumpets and empty	**Jg 7:16**	5414
of Shechem **p** their trust in him.	**Jg 9:26**	982
and **p** *them* on the inner chamber	**Jg 9:49**	7760
So they **p** away the foreign gods	**Jg 10:16**	5493
and **p** one torch in the middle	**Jg 15:4**	7760
then he **p** them on his shoulders	**Jg 16:3**	7760
p your hand over your mouth and	**Jg 18:19**	7760
and **p** the little ones and the	**Jg 18:21**	7760
that we may **p** them to death and	**Jg 20:13**	4191
"He shall surely be **p** to death."	**Jg 21:5**	4191
and **p** on your *best* clothes,	**Ru 3:3**	7760
P away your wine from you."	**1Sa 1:14**	5493
LORD desired to **p** them to death.	**1Sa 2:25**	4191
and **p** the articles of gold which	**1Sa 6:8**	7760
They **p** the ark of the LORD on	**1Sa 6:11**	7760
and **p** them on the large stone;	**1Sa 6:15**	7760
p the people in three companies;	**1Sa 11:11**	7760
that we may **p** them to death."	**1Sa 11:12**	4191
man shall be **p** to death this day,	**1Sa 11:13**	4191
bearer **p** some to death after him.	**1Sa 14:13**	4191
Saul had **p** the people under oath,	**1Sa 14:24**	422
no man **p** his hand to his mouth,	**1Sa 14:26**	5381
father **p** the people under oath;	**1Sa 14:27**	7650
he **p** out the end of the staff that	**1Sa 14:27**	7971
and **p** his hand to his mouth,	**1Sa 14:27**	7725
strictly **p** the people under oath,	**1Sa 14:28**	7650
but **p** to death both man and woman,	**1Sa 15:3**	4191
and **p** a bronze helmet on his head,	**1Sa 17:38**	5414
and **p** them in the shepherd's bag	**1Sa 17:40**	7760
And David **p** his hand into his bag	**1Sa 17:49**	7971
but he **p** his weapons in his tent.	**1Sa 17:54**	7760
his servants to **p** David to death.	**1Sa 19:1**	4191
is seeking to **p** you to death.	**1Sa 19:2**	4191
he shall not be **p** to death."	**1Sa 19:6**	4191
to **p** him to death in the morning.	**1Sa 19:11**	4191
tomorrow you will be **p** to death."	**1Sa 19:11**	4191
and **p** a quilt of goats' *hair* at	**1Sa 19:13**	7760
bed, that I may **p** him to death."	**1Sa 19:15**	4191
Why should I **p** you to death?'"	**1Sa 19:17**	4191
in me, **p** me to death yourself;	**1Sa 20:8**	4191
"Why should he be **p** to death?	**1Sa 20:32**	4191
had decided to **p** David to death.	**1Sa 20:33**	4191
in order to **p** hot bread in *its*	**1Sa 21:6**	7760
"Turn around and **p** the priests of	**1Sa 22:17**	4191
were not willing to **p** forth their hands	**1Sa 22:17**	7971
They **p** his weapons in the	**1Sa 31:10**	7760
Who **p** ornaments of gold on your	**2Sa 1:24**	5927
had **p** their brother Asahel to death	**2Sa 3:30**	4191
bound, nor your feet **p** in fetters;	**2Sa 3:34**	5066
p Abner the son of Ner to death.	**2Sa 3:37**	4191
and he measured two lines to **p** to	**2Sa 8:2**	4191
Then David **p** garrisons among the	**2Sa 8:6**	7760
He **p** garrisons in Edom.	**2Sa 8:14**	7760
In all Edom he **p** garrisons, and	**2Sa 8:14**	7760
that he **p** Uriah at the place where	**2Sa 11:16**	5414
Tamar **p** ashes on her head and	**2Sa 13:19**	3947
and she **p** her hand on her head and	**2Sa 13:19**	7760
'Strike Amnon,' then **p** him to death.	**2Sa 13:28**	4191
have **p** to death all the young men,	**2Sa 13:32**	4191
and **p** on mourning garments now,	**2Sa 14:2**	3847
So Joab **p** the words in her mouth.	**2Sa 14:3**	7760
that we may **p** him to death for the	**2Sa 14:7**	4191
who **p** all these words in the mouth	**2Sa 14:19**	7760
in me, let him **p** me to death."	**2Sa 14:32**	4191
he would **p** out his hand and take	**2Sa 15:5**	7971
I would not **p** out my hand against	**2Sa 18:12**	7971
not Shimei be **p** to death for this,	**2Sa 19:21**	4191
man be **p** to death in Israel today?	**2Sa 19:22**	4191
he **p** the Gibeonites to death."	**2Sa 21:1**	4191
to **p** any man to death in Israel."	**2Sa 21:4**	4191
and they were **p** to death in the	**2Sa 21:9**	4191
that he will not **p** his servant to death	**1Ki 1:51**	4191
And he **p** the blood of war on his	**1Ki 2:5**	5414

p you to death with the sword.'	**1Ki 2:8**	4191
Adonijah shall be **p** to death today."	**1Ki 2:24**	4191
not **p** you to death at this time,	**1Ki 2:26**	4191
fell upon him and **p** him to death,	**1Ki 2:34**	4191
until the LORD **p** them under the	**1Ki 5:3**	5414
and he **p** them in the treasuries of	**1Ki 7:51**	5414
which Moses **p** there at Horeb,	**1Ki 8:9**	5117
and the king **p** them in the house	**1Ki 10:17**	5414
which God had **p** in his heart.	**1Ki 10:24**	5414
chosen for Myself to **p** My name.	**1Ki 11:36**	7760
therefore to **p** Jeroboam to death;	**1Ki 11:40**	4191
his heavy yoke which he **p** on us,	**1Ki 12:4**	5414
which your father **p** on us'?"	**1Ki 12:9**	5414
Bethel, and the other he **p** in Dan.	**1Ki 12:29**	5414
of Israel to **p** His name there.	**1Ki 14:21**	7760
He also **p** away the male cult	**1Ki 15:12**	5674a
and struck him and **p** him to death in	**1Ki 16:10**	4191
and to **p** my son to death!"	**1Ki 17:18**	4191
hand of Ahab to **p** me to death?	**1Ki 18:9**	4191
the wood, but **p** no fire *under it;*	**1Ki 18:23**	7760
and I will not **p** a fire *under it.*	**1Ki 18:23**	7760
god, but **p** no fire *under it."*	**1Ki 18:25**	7760
and **p** his face between his knees.	**1Ki 18:42**	7760
of Hazael, Jehu shall **p** to death,	**1Ki 19:17**	4191
of Jehu, Elisha shall **p** to death.	**1Ki 19:17**	4191
and **p** captains in their place,	**1Ki 20:24**	7760
please let us **p** sackcloth on our	**1Ki 20:31**	7760
sackcloth on their loins and **p**	**1Ki 20:32**	
and **p** on sackcloth and fasted,	**1Ki 21:27**	7760
the LORD has **p** a deceiving spirit	**1Ki 22:23**	5414
"**P** this man in prison and feed	**1Ki 22:27**	7760
battle, but you **p** on your robes."	**1Ki 22:30**	3847
me a new jar, and **p** salt in it."	**2Ki 2:20**	7760
for he **p** away the *sacred* pillar of	**2Ki 3:2**	5493
all who were able to **p** on armor	**2Ki 3:21**	2296
and **p** his mouth on his mouth and	**2Ki 4:34**	7760
"**P** on the large pot and boil stew	**2Ki 4:38**	8239
So he **p** out his hand and took it.	**2Ki 6:7**	7971
and **p** their heads in baskets,	**2Ki 10:7**	7760
"**P** them in two heaps at the	**2Ki 10:8**	7760
sons who were being **p** to death,	**2Ki 11:2**	4191
and he was not **p** to death.	**2Ki 11:2**	4191
p them under oath in the house of	**2Ki 11:4**	7650
the ranks shall be **p** to death.	**2Ki 11:8**	4191
son out and **p** the crown on him and	**2Ki 11:12**	5414
her **p** to death with the sword."	**2Ki 11:15**	4191
"Let her not be **p** to death in the	**2Ki 11:15**	4191
house, she was **p** to death there.	**2Ki 11:16**	4191
For they had **p** Athaliah to death	**2Ki 11:20**	4191
lid and **p** it beside the altar,	**2Ki 12:9**	5414
priests who guarded the threshold **p** in	**2Ki 12:9**	5414
"**P** your hand on the bow."	**2Ki 13:16**	7392
And he **p** his hand *on it,* then	**2Ki 13:16**	7392
the slayers he did not **p** to death,	**2Ki 14:6**	4191
not be **p** to death for the sons,	**2Ki 14:6**	4191
be **p** to death for the fathers;	**2Ki 14:6**	4191
be **p** to death for his own sin."	**2Ki 14:6**	4191
and struck him and **p** him to death	**2Ki 15:30**	4191
to Kir, and **p** Rezin to death.	**2Ki 16:9**	4191
and he **p** it on the north side of	**2Ki 16:14**	5414
and **p** it on a pavement of stone.	**2Ki 16:17**	5414
made gods of its own and **p** them in	**2Ki 17:29**	5117
and **p** them in Halah and on the	**2Ki 18:11**	5148
I will **p** a spirit in him so that	**2Ki 19:7**	5414
They were dismayed and **p** to shame;	**2Ki 19:26**	954
I will **p** My hook in your nose,	**2Ki 19:28**	7760
"In Jerusalem I will **p** My name."	**2Ki 21:4**	7760
Israel, I will **p** My name forever.	**2Ki 21:7**	7760
then **p** out the eyes of Zedekiah	**2Ki 25:7**	5786
p them to death at Riblah in the land	**2Ki 25:21**	4191
sons of Ham *were* Cush, Mizraim, **P**,	**1Ch 1:8**	6316
of the LORD, so He **p** him to death.	**1Ch 2:3**	4191
who **p** to flight the inhabitants of	**1Ch 8:13**	1272
They **p** his armor in the house	**1Ch 10:10**	7760
p to flight all those in the valleys,	**1Ch 12:15**	1272
p out his hand to hold the ark,	**1Ch 13:9**	7971
he **p** out his hand to the ark;	**1Ch 13:10**	7971
Then David **p** *garrisons* among the	**1Ch 18:6**	7760
Then he **p** garrisons in Edom, and	**1Ch 18:13**	7760
and **p** to death Shophach the	**1Ch 19:18**	4191
he **p** his sword back in its sheath.	**1Ch 21:27**	7725
and **p** *them* in the treasuries of	**2Ch 5:1**	5414
which Moses **p** *there* at Horeb,	**2Ch 5:10**	5414
You would **p** Your name there,	**2Ch 6:20**	7760
and the king **p** them in the house	**2Ch 9:16**	5414
which God had **p** in his heart.	**2Ch 9:23**	5414
his heavy yoke which he **p** on us,	**2Ch 10:4**	5414
which your father **p** on us'?"	**2Ch 10:9**	5414
p officers in them and stores of food,	**2Ch 11:11**	5414
He **p** shields and spears in every	**2Ch 11:12**	
of Israel, to **p** His name there.	**2Ch 12:13**	7760
of Israel should be **p** to death,	**2Ch 15:13**	4191
with the seer and **p** him in prison,	**2Ch 16:10**	5414
apart from those whom the king **p**	**2Ch 17:19**	5414
the LORD has **p** a deceiving spirit	**2Ch 18:22**	5414
"**P** this *man* in prison and feed	**2Ch 18:26**	7760
battle, but you **p** on your robes."	**2Ch 18:29**	3847
p your trust in the LORD your God and	**2Ch 20:20**	539
P your trust in His prophets and	**2Ch 20:20**	539
him to Jehu, **p** him to death and	**2Ch 22:9**	4191
sons who were being **p** to death,	**2Ch 22:11**	4191
that she would not **p** him to death.	**2Ch 22:11**	4191
king's son and **p** the crown on him,	**2Ch 23:11**	5414
her, **p** to death with the sword."	**2Ch 23:14**	4191
"Let her not be **p** to death in the	**2Ch 23:14**	4191
house, they **p** her to death there.	**2Ch 23:15**	4191
For they had **p** Athaliah to death	**2Ch 23:21**	4191
did not **p** their children to death,	**2Ch 25:4**	4191
shall not be **p** to death for sons,	**2Ch 25:4**	4191
sons be **p** to death for fathers,	**2Ch 25:4**	4191
be **p** to death for his own sin."	**2Ch 25:4**	4191
of the porch and **p** out the lamps,	**2Ch 29:7**	3518
Then he **p** the carved image of the	**2Ch 33:7**	7760
Israel, I will **p** My name forever;	**2Ch 33:7**	7760
Then he **p** army commanders in all	**2Ch 33:14**	7760
p him to death in his own house.	**2Ch 33:24**	4191
"**P** the holy ark in the house	**2Ch 35:3**	5414
p them in his temple at Babylon.	**2Ch 36:7**	5414
and also **p** *it* in writing, saying,	**2Ch 36:22**	
and also **p** *it* in writing, saying:	**Ezr 1:1**	
and **p** in the house of his gods;	**Ezr 1:7**	5414
shall **p** *them* in the house of God.'	**Ezr 6:5**	5182
who has **p** *such a thing* as this in	**Ezr 7:27**	5414
covenant with our God to **p** away	**Ezr 10:3**	3318
pledged to **p** away their wives,	**Ezr 10:19**	3318
p their hands to the good *work.*	**Ne 2:18**	2388
them and **p** a stop to the work."	**Ne 4:11**	7673a
then I **p** Hanani my brother, and	**Ne 7:2**	6680
Then my God **p** it into my heart to	**Ne 7:5**	5414
they **p** the grain offerings,	**Ne 13:5**	5414
to **p** into the king's treasuries."	**Es 3:9**	935
clothes, **p** on sackcloth and ashes,	**Es 4:1**	3847
one law, that he be **p** to death,	**Es 4:11**	4191
Esther **p** on her royal robes and stood	**Es 5:1**	3847
"But **p** forth Your hand now and	**Jb 1:11**	7971
do not **p** forth your hand on him."	**Jb 1:12**	7971
"However, **p** forth Your hand now,	**Jb 2:5**	7971
is in your hand, **p** it far away,	**Jb 11:14**	7368
teeth And **p** my life in my hands?	**Jb 13:14**	7760
"You **p** my feet in the stocks	**Jb 13:27**	7760
And **p** forth sprigs like a plant.	**Jb 14:9**	6213a
And He has **p** darkness on my paths.	**Jb 19:8**	7760
And **p** *your* hand over *your* mouth.	**Jb 21:5**	7760
is the lamp of the wicked **p** out,	**Jb 21:17**	1846
not **p** away my integrity from me.	**Jb 27:5**	5493
And **p** *their* hands on their mouths;	**Jb 29:9**	7760
"I **p** on righteousness, and it	**Jb 29:14**	3847
Whose fathers I disdained to **p** with	**Jb 30:1**	7896
"If I have **p** my confidence *in* gold,	**Jb 31:24**	7760
p wisdom in the innermost being Or	**Jb 38:36**	7896
"Can you **p** a rope in his nose Or	**Jb 41:2**	7760
You have **p** gladness in my heart,	**Ps 4:7**	5414
have **p** all things under his feet,	**Ps 8:6**	7896
name will **p** their trust in You,	**Ps 9:10**	982
P them in fear, O LORD;	**Ps 9:20**	7896
You would **p** to shame the counsel	**Ps 14:6**	954
not **p** out his money at interest,	**Ps 15:5**	5414
not **p** away His statutes from me.	**Ps 18:22**	5493
Let me not be **p** to shame, O LORD,	**Ps 31:17**	954
Let the wicked be **p** to shame,	**Ps 31:17**	954
He **p** a new song in my mouth, a	**Ps 40:3**	5414
have **p** to shame those who hate us.	**Ps 44:7**	954
You **p** *them* to shame, because God	**Ps 53:5**	954
He has **p** forth his hands against	**Ps 55:20**	7971
afraid, I will **p** my trust in You.	**Ps 56:3**	982
praise, In God I have **p** my trust;	**Ps 56:4**	982
In anger **p** down the peoples,	**Ps 56:7**	3381
P my tears in Your bottle.	**Ps 56:8**	7760
In God I have **p** my trust, I shall	**Ps 56:11**	982
Should **p** their confidence in God And	**Ps 78:7**	7760
And in their heart they **p** God to	**Ps 78:18**	5254
He **p** on them an everlasting	**Ps 78:66**	5414
You have **p** me in the lowest pit,	**Ps 88:6**	7896
in heart, to **p** *them* to death.	**Ps 109:16**	4191
O LORD, do not **p** me to shame!	**Ps 119:31**	954
p forth their hands to do wrong.	**Ps 125:3**	7971
Be **p** to shame and turned backward;	**Ps 129:5**	954
P away from you a deceitful mouth And	**Pr 4:24**	5493
And **p** devious speech far from you.	**Pr 4:24**	7368
hand will be **p** to forced labor.	**Pr 12:24**	
And **p** a knife to your throat If	**Pr 23:2**	7760
lamp of the wicked will be **p** out.	**Pr 24:20**	1846
p *your* hand on your mouth.	**Pr 30:32**	
and **p** away pain from your body,	**Ec 11:10**	5674a
my dress, How can I **p** it on *again?*	**SS 5:3**	3847
"**P** me like a seal over your	**SS 8:6**	7760
will **p** his hand on the viper's den.	**Is 11:8**	1911
I will also **p** an end to the	**Is 13:11**	7673a
for the people and are **p** to shame;	**Is 26:11**	954
And have **p** your trust in	**Is 30:12**	982
And to **p** in the jaws of	**Is 30:28**	
and **p** *sackcloth* on *your* waist,	**Is 32:11**	2296
I will **p** a spirit in him so that	**Is 37:7**	5414
They were dismayed and **p** to shame;	**Is 37:27**	954
I will **p** My hook in your nose And	**Is 37:29**	7760
p the cedar in the wilderness,	**Is 41:19**	5414
I have **p** My Spirit upon Him;	**Is 42:1**	5414
back *and* be utterly **p** to shame,	**Is 42:17**	954
"**P** Me in remembrance,	**Is 43:26**	2142
so that they will be **p** to shame.	**Is 44:9**	954
his companions will be **p** to shame,	**Is 44:11**	954
let them together be **p** to shame.	**Is 44:11**	954
be **p** to shame and even humiliated,	**Is 45:16**	954
You will not be **p** to shame or	**Is 45:17**	954
angry at Him will be **p** to shame.	**Is 45:24**	954
surely **p** on all of them as jewels and	**Is 49:18**	3847
for Me will not be **p** to shame.	**Is 49:23**	954
Awake, awake, **p** on strength, O arm	**Is 51:9**	3847
I have **p** My words in your mouth and	**Is 51:16**	7760
"I will **p** it into the hand of	**Is 51:23**	7760
for you will not be **p** to shame;	**Is 54:4**	954
He **p** on righteousness like a	**Is 59:17**	3847
And He **p** on garments of vengeance	**Is 59:17**	3847
which I have **p** in your mouth shall	**Is 59:21**	7760
Where is He who **p** His Holy Spirit	**Is 63:11**	7760
but you will be **p** to shame.	**Is 65:13**	954
But they will be **p** to shame.	**Is 66:5**	954
Tarshish, **P**, Lud, Meshech,	**Is 66:19**	6316
I have **p** My words in your mouth.	**Jer 1:9**	5414
you will be **p** to shame by Egypt	**Jer 2:36**	954
As you were **p** to shame by Assyria.	**Jer 2:36**	954
And if you will **p** away your	**Jer 4:1**	5493
"For this, **p** on sackcloth, Lament	**Jer 4:8**	2296
p on sackcloth And roll in ashes;	**Jer 6:26**	2296
"The wise men are **p** to shame,	**Jer 8:9**	954
We are **p** to great shame, For we	**Jer 9:19**	954
goldsmith is **p** to shame by his idols;	**Jer 10:14**	954
and **p** it around your waist,	**Jer 13:1**	7760
waist, but do not **p** it in water."	**Jer 13:1**	935
the LORD and **p** it around my waist.	**Jer 13:2**	7760
been **p** to shame and humiliated,	**Jer 14:3**	954
The farmers have been **p** to shame,	**Jer 14:4**	954
forsake You will be **p** to shame.	**Jer 17:13**	954
who persecute me be **p** to shame,	**Jer 17:18**	954
for me, let me not be **p** to shame;	**Jer 17:18**	954
and **p** him in the stocks that were	**Jer 20:2**	5414
"I will **p** an everlasting	**Jer 23:40**	5414
certain that if you **p** me to death,	**Jer 26:15**	4191
and all Judah **p** him to death?	**Jer 26:19**	4191
the king sought to **p** him to death;	**Jer 26:21**	4191
of the people to **p** him to death.	**Jer 26:24**	4191
and yokes and **p** them on your neck,	**Jer 27:2**	5414
and which will not **p** its neck	**Jer 27:8**	5414
"I have **p** a yoke of iron on the	**Jer 28:14**	5414
to **p** him in the stocks and in the	**Jer 29:26**	5414
"I will **p** My law within them and	**Jer 31:33**	5414
and **p** them in an earthenware jar,	**Jer 32:14**	5414
"But they **p** their detestable	**Jer 32:34**	7760
and I will **p** the fear of Me in	**Jer 32:40**	5414
had not *yet* **p** him in the prison.	**Jer 37:4**	5414
and they **p** him in jail in the	**Jer 37:15**	5414
that you have **p** me in prison?	**Jer 37:18**	5414
"Now let this man be **p** to death,	**Jer 38:4**	4191
had **p** Jeremiah into the cistern.	**Jer 38:7**	5414
"Now **p** these worn-out clothes and	**Jer 38:12**	7760
you not certainly **p** me to death?	**Jer 38:15**	4191
surely I will not **p** you to death	**Jer 38:16**	4191
and we will not **p** you to death,'	**Jer 38:25**	4191
he had **p** him in charge of the men,	**Jer 40:7**	6485
p *them* in your *storage* vessels,	**Jer 40:10**	7760
with the sword and **p** to death the	**Jer 41:2**	4191
"Do not **p** us to death;	**Jer 41:8**	4191
So he refrained and did not **p** them	**Jer 41:8**	4191
had **p** under the charge of Gedaliah	**Jer 41:10**	6485
so they will **p** us to death or exile	**Jer 43:3**	4191
the spears, **P** on the scale-armor!	**Jer 46:4**	3847
Ethiopia and **P**, that handle the	**Jer 46:9**	6316
of Egypt has been **p** to shame,	**Jer 46:24**	954
Kiriathaim has been **p** to shame,	**Jer 48:1**	954
has been **p** to shame and shattered.	**Jer 48:1**	954
"Moab has been **p** to shame, for it	**Jer 48:20**	954
"Hamath and Arpad are **p** to shame,	**Jer 49:23**	954
captured, Bel has been **p** to shame,	**Jer 50:2**	954
Her images have been **p** to shame,	**Jer 50:2**	954
P all her young bulls to the sword;	**Jer 50:27**	2717c
goldsmith is **p** to shame by his idols,	**Jer 51:17**	954
her whole land will be **p** to shame And	**Jer 51:47**	954
and **p** him in prison until the day	**Jer 52:11**	5414
and **p** them to death at Riblah	**Jer 52:27**	4191
Let him **p** his mouth in the dust,	**La 3:29**	5414
they will **p** ropes on you and bind	**Ezk 3:25**	5414
I will **p** ropes on you so that you	**Ezk 4:8**	5414
p them in one vessel and make them	**Ezk 4:9**	5414
and **p** a mark on the foreheads of	**Ezk 9:4**	8427
took *some* and **p** *it* into the hands	**Ezk 10:7**	5414
and **p** a new spirit within them.	**Ezk 11:19**	5414
p to death some who should not die	**Ezk 13:19**	4191
and have **p** right before their faces	**Ezk 14:3**	5414
has been **p** into the fire for fuel,	**Ezk 15:4**	5414
and **p** sandals of porpoise skin on	**Ezk 16:10**	5274b
p bracelets on your hands and	**Ezk 16:11**	5414
"I also **p** a ring in your nostril,	**Ezk 16:12**	5414
the king who **p** him on the throne,	**Ezk 17:16**	4427a
he will surely be **p** to death;	**Ezk 18:13**	4191
'They **p** him in a cage with	**Ezk 19:9**	5414
And they **p** bracelets on the hands	**Ezk 23:42**	5414
"**P** on the pot, put *it* on and	**Ezk 24:3**	8239
"Put on the pot, **p** *it* on and	**Ezk 24:3**	8239
P in it the pieces, Every good	**Ezk 24:4**	622
have **p** her blood on the bare rock,	**Ezk 24:8**	5414
and **p** your shoes on your feet,	**Ezk 24:17**	7760
and Lud and **P** were in your army,	**Ezk 27:10**	6316
I **p** you before kings, That they	**Ezk 28:17**	5414
"I will **p** hooks in your	**Ezk 29:4**	5414
"Ethiopia, **P**, Lud, all Arabia,	**Ezk 30:5**	6316
will **p** fear in the land of Egypt.	**Ezk 30:13**	5414
and **p** My sword in his hand;	**Ezk 30:24**	5414
when I **p** My sword into the hand of	**Ezk 30:25**	5414
were **p** in the midst of the slain.	**Ezk 32:25**	5414
you will **p** forth your branches and	**Ezk 36:8**	5414
and **p** a new spirit within you;	**Ezk 36:26**	5414
"I will **p** My Spirit within	**Ezk 36:27**	5414
'I will **p** sinews on you, make	**Ezk 37:6**	5414
and **p** breath in you that you may	**Ezk 37:6**	5414
"I will **p** My Spirit within	**Ezk 37:14**	5414
and I will **p** them with it, with	**Ezk 37:19**	5414
about and **p** hooks into your jaws,	**Ezk 38:4**	5414
Persia, Ethiopia and **P** with them,	**Ezk 38:5**	6316
They shall **p** on other garments;	**Ezk 42:14**	3847
"Now let them **p** away their harlotry	**Ezk 43:9**	7368
blood and **p** it on its four horns	**Ezk 43:20**	5414
they shall **p** off their garments in	**Ezk 44:19**	6584
then they shall **p** on other	**Ezk 44:19**	3847
p away violence and destruction,	**Ezk 45:9**	5493
blood from the sin offering and **p** *it*	**Ezk 45:19**	5414
p an end to all these kingdoms,	**Da 2:44**	5487
servants who **p** their trust in Him,	**Da 3:28**	7365

your kingdom and **p** an end to it. Da 5:26 8000
clothed Daniel with purple and **p** Da 5:29
p a stop to sacrifice and grain offering; Da 9:27 7673a
peace which he will **p** into effect; Da 11:17 6213a
But a commander will **p** a stop to Da 11:18 7673a
and I will **p** an end to the kingdom Hos 1:4 7673a
And let her **p** away her harlotry Hos 2:2 5493
also **p** an end to all her gaiety, Hos 2:11 7673a
P the trumpet to your lips! Like an Hos 8:1
people will never be **p** to shame. Jl 2:26 954
people will never be **p** to shame. Jl 2:27 954
P in the sickle, for the harvest Jl 3:13 7971
Do you **p** off the day of calamity, Am 6:3 5077
"Behold I am about to **p** a plumb Am 7:8 7760
and do not **p** innocent blood on us; Jon 1:14 5414
and they called a fast and **p** on Jon 3:5 3847
I will **p** them together like sheep Mi 2:12 7760
will **p** *their* hand on *their* mouth, Mi 7:16 7760
P and Lubim were among her helpers. Na 3:9 6316
To **p** his nest on high Hab 2:9 7760
you **p** on clothing, but no one is Hg 1:6 3847
earns wages *to* **p** into a purse Hg 1:6
p a clean turban on his head." Zch 3:5 7760
So they **p** a clean turban on his Zch 3:5 7760
on horses will be **p** to shame. Zch 10:5 954
and they will not **p** on a hairy robe Zch 13:4 3847
P THE LORD YOUR GOD TO THE TEST. Mt 4:7 *1598*
and **p** it under a basket, Mt 5:15 *5087*
do not **p** on a gloomy face as the Mt 6:16 *1096*
body, *as to* what you will **p** on. Mt 6:25 *1746a*
people **p** new wine into old wineskins; Mt 9:17 *906*
p new wine into fresh wineskins, Mt 9:17 *906*
and cause them to be **p** to death. Mt 10:21 *2289*
I WILL **P** MY SPIRIT UPON HIM, AND Mt 12:18 *5087*
WICK HE WILL NOT **P** OUT, Mt 12:20 *4570*
unoccupied, swept, and **p** in order. Mt 12:44 *2885*
and **p** him in prison because of Mt 14:3 *659*
Herod wanted to **p** him to death, Mt 14:5 *615*
OR MOTHER IS TO BE **P** TO DEATH.' Mt 15:4 *5053*
How long shall I **p** up with you? Mt 17:17 *430*
PLANTED A VINEYARD AND **P** A WALL Mt 21:33 *4060*
UNTIL I **P** YOUR ENEMIES BENEATH Mt 22:44 *5087*
master **p** in charge of his household Mt 24:45 *2525*
that he will **p** him in charge of Mt 24:47 *2525*
p you in charge of many things; Mt 25:21 *2525*
p you in charge of many things; Mt 25:23 *2525*
to have **p** my money in the bank, Mt 25:27 *906*
He will **p** the sheep on His right, Mt 25:33 *2476*
"**P** your sword back into its place; Mt 26:52 *654*
and He will at once **p** at My Mt 26:53 *3936*
that they might **p** Him to death. Mt 26:59 *2289*
against Jesus to **p** Him to death; Mt 27:1 *2289*
p them into the temple treasury, Mt 27:6 *906*
Barabbas and to **p** Jesus to death. Mt 27:20 *622*
Him and **p** a scarlet robe on Him. Mt 27:28 *4060*
of thorns, they **p** it on His head, Mt 27:29 *2007*
p His *own* garments back on Him, Mt 27:31 *1746a*
And above His head they **p** up the Mt 27:37 *2007*
sour wine and **p** it on a reed, Mt 27:48 *4060*
to be **p** under a basket, Mk 4:21 *5087*
brought to be **p** on the lampstand? Mk 4:21 *5087*
"Do not **p** on two tunics." Mk 6:9 *1746a*
him and wanted to **p** him to death Mk 6:19 *615*
OR MOTHER, IS TO BE **P** TO DEATH'; Mk 7:10 *5053*
and **p** His fingers into his ears, Mk 7:33 *906*
How long shall I **p** up with you? Mk 9:19 *430*
Jesus and **p** their coats on it; Mk 11:7 *1911*
VINEYARD AND **P** A WALL AROUND IT, Mk 12:1 *4060*
I **P** YOUR ENEMIES BENEATH YOUR FEET." ' Mk 12:36 *5087*
and **p** in two small copper coins, Mk 12:42 *906*
this poor widow **p** in more than all Mk 12:43 *906*
all **p** in out of their surplus, Mk 12:44 *906*
her poverty, **p** in all she owned, Mk 12:44 *906*
parents and have them **p** to death. Mk 13:12 *2289*
against Jesus to **p** Him to death, Mk 14:55 *2289*
crown of thorns, they **p** it on Him; Mk 15:17 *4060*
Him and **p** His *own* garments on Him. Mk 15:20 *1746a*
with sour wine, **p** it on a reed, Mk 15:36 *4060*
P THE LORD YOUR GOD TO THE TEST.' " Lk 4:12 *1598*
and asked him to **p** out a little Lk 5:3 *1877*
"**P** out into the deep water and Lk 5:4 *1877*
must be **p** into fresh wineskins. Lk 5:38 *992*
and who had not **p** on any clothing Lk 8:27 *1746a*
I be with you and **p** up with you? Lk 9:41 *430*
stood up and **p** Him to the test, Lk 10:25 *1598*
and he **p** him on his own beast, and Lk 10:34 *1913*
it finds it swept and **p** in order. Lk 11:25 *2885*
body, *as to* what you will **p** on. Lk 12:22 *1746a*
will **p** in charge of his servants, Lk 12:42 *2525*
that he will **p** him in charge of Lk 12:44 *2525*
dig around it and **p** in fertilizer; Lk 13:8 *906*
out the best robe and **p** it on him, Lk 15:22 *1746a*
and **p** a ring on his hand and Lk 15:22 *1325*
I kept **p** away in a handkerchief; Lk 19:20 *606*
you not **p** my money in the bank, Lk 19:23 *1325*
on the colt and **p** Jesus *on it.* Lk 19:35 *1913*
widow **p** in more than all *of them;* Lk 21:3 *906*
their surplus **p** into the offering; Lk 21:4 *906*
but she out of her poverty **p** in Lk 21:4 *906*
they will **p** *some* of you to death, Lk 21:16 *2289*
as soon as they **p** forth *leaves,* Lk 21:30 *4261*
how they might **p** Him to death; Lk 22:2 *337*
away to be **p** to death with Him. Lk 23:32 *337*
I have no man to **p** me into the Jn 5:7 *906*
to be **p** out of the synagogue. Jn 9:22 *656*
they **p** him out. Jn 9:34 *1544b*
heard that they had **p** him out, Jn 9:35 *1544b*
used to pilfer what was **p** into it. Jn 12:6 *906*
to **p** Lazarus to death also; Jn 12:10 *615*
would be **p** out of the synagogue; Jn 12:42 *656*
the devil having already **p** into Jn 13:2 *906*
"**P** the sword into the sheath; Jn 18:11 *906*
permitted to **p** anyone to death," Jn 18:31 *615*
of thorns and **p** it on His head, Jn 19:2 *2007*
and **p** a purple robe on Him; Jn 19:2 *2007*
and **p** it on the cross. Jn 19:19 *5087*
so they **p** a sponge full of the Jn 19:29 *4060*
and **p** my finger into the place of Jn 20:25 *906*
and **p** my hand into His side, Jn 20:25 *906*
your hand and **p** it into My side; Jn 20:27 *906*
Lord, he **p** his outer garment on Jn 21:7 *1241*
So they **p** forward two men, Joseph Ac 1:23 *2476*
of godless men and **p** *Him* to death. Ac 2:23 *337*
but **p** to death the Prince of life, Ac 3:15 *615*
and **p** them in jail until the next Ac 4:3 *5087*
to **p** the Spirit of the Lord to the test? Ac 5:9 *3985*
and **p** them in a public jail. Ac 5:18 *5087*
The men whom you **p** in prison are Ac 5:25 *5087*
whom you had **p** to death by hanging Ac 5:30 *1315a*
gave orders to **p** the men outside for Ac 5:34 *4160*
we may **p** in charge of this task. Ac 6:3 *2525*
They **p** forward false witnesses Ac 6:13 *2476*
women, he would **p** them in prison. Ac 8:3 *3860*
so that they might **p** him to death; Ac 9:24 *337*
were attempting to **p** him to death. Ac 9:29 *337*
They also **p** Him to death by Ac 10:39 *337*
of John **p** to death with a sword. Ac 12:2 *337*
seized him, he **p** him in prison, Ac 12:4 *5087*
yourself and **p** on your sandals." Ac 12:8 *5265*
having **p** on his royal apparel, Ac 12:21 *1746a*
Now Paul and his companions **p** out Ac 13:13 *321*
forty years He **p** up with them in the Ac 13:18 *5159*
why do you **p** God to the test by Ac 15:10 *3985*
reasonable for me to **p** up with you; Ac 18:14 *430*
and **p** out to sea for Syria, Ac 18:18 *1602*
since the Jews had **p** him forward; Ac 19:33 *4261*
because he had **p** him in chains. Ac 22:29 *1210*
also to provide mounts to **p** Paul on Ac 23:24 *1913*
about the Way, **p** them off, Ac 24:22 *306*
but also when they were being **p** to Ac 26:10 *337*
temple and tried to **p** me to death. Ac 26:21 *1315a*
coast of Asia, we **p** out to sea Ac 27:2 *321*
The next day we **p** in at Sidon; Ac 27:3 *2609*
From there we **p** out to sea and Ac 27:4 *321*
for Italy, and he **p** us aboard it. Ac 27:6 *1688*
to **p** out to sea from there, Ac 27:12 *321*
After we **p** in at Syracuse, we Ac 28:12 *2609*
WE ARE BEING **P** TO DEATH ALL DAY Ro 8:36 *2289*
and **p** on the armor of light. Ro 13:12 *1746a*
But **p** on the Lord Jesus Christ, Ro 13:14 *1746a*
not to **p** an obstacle or a stumbling Ro 14:13 *5087*
and have **p** my seal on this fruit Ro 15:28 *4972*
not to **p** a restraint upon you, but 1Co 7:35 *1911*
For He must reign until He has **p** 1Co 15:25 *5087*
HE HAS **P** ALL THINGS IN SUBJECTION 1Co 15:27 *5293*
"All things are **p** in subjection," 1Co 15:27 *5293*
who **p** all things in subjection to Him. 1Co 15:27 *5293*
must **p** on the imperishable, 1Co 15:53 *1746a*
this mortal must **p** on immortality. 1Co 15:53 *1746a*
will have **p** on the imperishable, 1Co 15:54 *1746a*
mortal will have **p** on immortality, 1Co 15:54 *1746a*
each one of you is to **p** aside and save, 1Co 16:2 *5087*
that I might **p** you to the test, 2Co 2:9 *1097*
who used to **p** a veil over his face 2Co 3:13 *5087*
inasmuch as we, having **p** it on, 2Co 5:3 *1746a*
as punished yet not **p** to death, 2Co 6:9 *2289*
about you, I was not **p** to shame; 2Co 7:14 *2617b*
be **p** to shame by this confidence. 2Co 9:4 *2617b*
you, I will not be **p** to shame, 2Co 10:8 *153*
And He **p** all things in subjection Eph 1:22 *5293*
it having **p** to death the enmity. Eph 2:16 *615*
and **p** on the new self, which in Eph 4:24 *1746a*
and slander be **p** away from you, Eph 4:31 *142*
P on the full armor of God, so Eph 6:11 *1746a*
HAVING **P** ON THE BREASTPLATE OF Eph 6:14 *1746a*
not be **p** to shame in anything, Php 1:20 *153*
and **p** no confidence in the flesh, Php 3:3 *3982*
mind to **p** confidence in the flesh, Php 3:4 *3982*
now you also, **p** them all aside: Col 3:8 *659*
and have **p** on the new self who is Col 3:10 *1746a*
p on a heart of compassion, Col 3:12 *1746a*
Beyond all these things **p** *on* love, Col 3:14
having **p** on the breastplate of 1Th 5:8 *1746a*
him, so that he will be **p** to shame. 2Th 3:14 *1788*
A widow is to be **p** on the list only 1Tm 5:9 *2639*
But refuse *to* **p** younger widows 1Tm 5:11
the opponent will be **p** to shame, Ti 2:8 *1788*
HAVE **P** ALL THINGS IN SUBJECTION Heb 2:8 *5293*
"I WILL **P** MY TRUST IN HIM." Heb 2:13 *3982*
of God and **p** Him to open shame. Heb 6:6 *3856*
I WILL **P** MY LAWS INTO THEIR MINDS, Heb 8:10 *1325*
He has been manifested to **p** away sin Heb 9:26 *115*
WILL **P** MY LAWS UPON THEIR HEART, Heb 10:16 *1325*
war, **p** foreign armies to flight. Heb 11:34 *2827*
were **p** to death with the sword; Heb 11:37 *599*
is lame may not be **p** out of joint, Heb 12:13 *1624*
Now if we **p** the bits into the Jas 3:3 *906*
and **p** to death the righteous *man* Jas 5:6 *5407*
in Christ will be **p** to shame. 1Pe 3:16 *2617b*
been **p** to death in the flesh, 1Pe 3:18 *2289*
and you **p** to the test those who Rv 2:2 *3985*
who kept teaching Balak to **p** a Rv 2:14 *906*
I have **p** before you an open door Rv 3:8 *1325*
"**P** in your sickle and reap, Rv 14:15 *3992*
"**P** in your sharp sickle and Rv 14:18 *3992*
"For God has **p** it in their hearts Rv 17:17 *1325*

PUTEOLI
on the second day we came to **P**. Ac 28:13 *4223*

PUTHITES
the Ithrites, the **P**, 1Ch 2:53 6336

PUTIEL
married one of the daughters of **P**, Ex 6:25 6317

PUTREFACTION
of sweet perfume there will be **p**; Is 3:24 4716

PUTS
whoever **p** any of it on a layman shall Ex 30:33 5414
The word that God **p** in my mouth, Nu 22:38 7760
what the LORD **p** in my mouth?" Nu 23:12 7760
of divorce and **p** *it* in her hand Dt 24:1 5414
of divorce and **p** *it* in her hand Dt 24:3 5414
and **p** out her hand and seizes his Dt 25:11 7971
your men **p** to flight a thousand, Jos 23:10 7291
p no trust even in His servants; Jb 4:18 539
He **p** no trust in His holy ones, Jb 15:15 539
"*Man* **p** an end to darkness, And to Jb 28:3 7760
"He **p** his hand on the flint; Jb 28:9 7971
'He **p** my feet in the stocks; Jb 33:11 7760
He **p** down one and exalts another. Ps 75:7 8213
Good news **p** fat on the bones. Pr 15:30 1878
The *cast* lot **p** an end to strife Pr 18:18 7673a
of the sluggard **p** him to death, Pr 21:25 4191
p right before his face the Ezk 14:4 7760
p right before his face the Ezk 14:7 7760
him who **p** nothing in their mouths They Mi 3:5 5414
"But no one **p** a patch of unshrunk Mt 9:16 *1911*
tender and **p** forth its leaves, Mt 24:32 *1631*
one **p** new wine into old wineskins; Mk 2:22 *906*
but *one* **p** new wine into fresh Mk 2:22
he immediately **p** in the sickle, Mk 4:29 *649*
tender and **p** forth its leaves, Mk 13:28 *1631*
and **p** it on an old garment; Lk 5:36 *1911*
one **p** new wine into old wineskins; Lk 5:37 *906*
a container, or **p** it under a bed; Lk 8:16 *5087*
but he **p** it on a lampstand, so Lk 8:16 *5087*
a lamp, **p** it away in a cellar nor Lk 11:33 *5087*
"When he **p** forth all his own, he Jn 10:4 *1544b*
who **p** the same earnestness on your 2Co 8:16 *1325*
so and **p** *them* out of the church. 3Jn 1:10 *1544b*

PUTTING
to Hagar, **p** *them* on her shoulder, Gn 21:14 7760
and after **p** fire in them, Lv 10:1 5414
p their hand to their mouth, Jg 7:6
by **p** David to death without a 1Sa 19:5 4191
himself by **p** on other clothes, 1Sa 28:8 3847
built by **p** My name there forever, 1Ki 9:3 7760
what my God was **p** into my mind Ne 2:12 5414
To crush Him, **p** *Him* to grief; Is 53:10 2470a
they are **p** the twig to their nose. Ezk 8:17 7971
with him, **p** him under oath. Ezk 17:13 935
But **p** them all out, He took along Mk 5:40 *1544b*
were **p** money into the treasury; Mk 12:41 *906*
rich people were **p** in large sums. Mk 12:41 *906*
house and **p** his slaves in charge, Mk 13:34 *1325*
after **p** his hand to the plow and Lk 9:62 *1911*
rich **p** their gifts into the treasury. Lk 21:1 *906*
widow **p** in two small copper coins. Lk 21:2 *906*
p an end to the agony of death, Ac 2:24 *3089*
agreement with **p** him to death. Ac 8:1 *336*
though they found no ground for **p** Ac 13:28
So **p** out to sea from Troas, Ac 16:11 *321*
binding and **p** both men and women Ac 22:4 *3860*
was no ground for **p** me to death. Ac 28:18
but if by the Spirit you are **p** to Ro 8:13 *2289*
me faithful, **p** me into service, 1Tm 1:12 *5087*
Therefore, **p** aside all filthiness Jas 1:21 *659*
p aside all malice and all deceit 1Pe 2:1 *659*
gold jewelry, or **p** on dresses; 1Pe 3:3 *1745*

PUVAH
of **P**, the family of the Punites; Nu 26:23 6312

PUVVAH
Tola and **P** and Iob and Shimron. Gn 46:13 6312

PYRE
A **p** of fire with plenty of wood; Is 30:33 4071

PYRRHUS
by Sopater of Berea, *the son* of **P**, Ac 20:4 *4450b*

Q

QUAIL
and it brought **q** from the sea, Nu 11:31 7958
the next day, and gathered the **q** Nu 11:32 7958
They asked, and He brought **q**, Ps 105:40 7958

QUAILS
q came up and covered the camp, Ex 16:13 7958

QUAKE
the mountains **q** at its swelling pride. Ps 46:3 7493
You have made the land **q**, Ps 60:2 7493
mountains might **q** at Your presence Is 64:1 2151a
and made all their loins **q**." Ezk 29:7 5975
"I made the nations **q** at the Ezk 31:16 7493
"Because of this will not the land **q** Am 8:8 7264
Mountains **q** because of Him And Na 1:5 7493

QUAKED
the whole mountain **q** violently. Ex 19:18 2729
The earth **q**, the heavens also dripped, Jg 5:4 7493
q at the presence of the LORD, Jg 5:5 5140
and the earth **q** so that it became 1Sa 14:15 7264
"Then the earth shook and **q**, 2Sa 22:8 7493
Then the earth shook and **q**, Ps 18:7 7493
The earth **q**; The heavens also Ps 68:8 7493
Sinai itself **q** at the presence of Ps 68:8
them down. And the mountains **q** Is 5:25 7264

the mountains **q** at Your presence. **Is 64:3** 2151a
The earth has **q** at the noise of **Jer 49:21** 7493
The mountains saw You *and* **q**; **Hab 3:10** 2342a

QUAKES
Under three things the earth **q**, **Pr 30:21** 7264
of his stallions The whole land **q**; **Jer 8:16** 7493
At His wrath the earth **q**, **Jer 10:10** 7493
So the land **q** and writhes, For the **Jer 51:29** 7493
Before them the earth **q**, **Jl 2:10** 7264

QUAKING
and behold, they were **q**, **Jer 4:24** 7493

QUALIFIED
Father, who has **q** us to share in the **Col 1:12** *2427*

QUALIFY
and their anointing will **q** them **Ex 40:15** 1961
that they may **q** to perform the **Nu 8:11** 1961

QUALITIES
For if these **q** are yours and are **2Pe 1:8**
For he who lacks these **q** is blind **2Pe 1:9**

QUALITY
will test the **q** of each man's work. **1Co 3:13** *3697*
q of a gentle and quiet spirit, **1Pe 3:4** *862a*

QUANTITIES
on oxen, great **q** of flour cakes, **1Ch 12:40** 7230
David prepared large **q** of iron **1Ch 22:3** 7230
large **q** of cedar timber to David. **1Ch 22:4** 7230
all these utensils in great **q**, **2Ch 4:18** 7230

QUANTITY
weight, for they are in great **q**; **1Ch 22:14** 7230
and this great **q** is left over." **2Ch 31:10** 1995
and the bath shall be the same **q**, **Ezk 45:11** 8506
they enclosed a great **q** of fish, **Lk 5:6** *4128*

QUARANTINE
and shall **q** the article with the mark **Lv 13:50** 5462
he shall **q** it for seven more days. **Lv 13:54** 5462
and **q** the house for seven days. **Lv 14:38** 5462

QUARANTINED
during the time that he has **q** it, **Lv 14:46** 5462

QUARREL
well, and they did not **q** over it; **Gn 26:22** 7378
"Do not **q** on the journey." **Gn 45:24** 7264
"Why do you **q** with me? **Ex 17:2** 7378
of the **q** of the sons of Israel, **Ex 17:7** 7379
"If men have a **q** and one **Ex 21:18** 7378
he is seeking a **q** against me." **2Ki 5:7** 579
abandon the **q** before it breaks out. **Pr 17:14** 7379
for a man, But any fool will **q**. **Pr 20:3** 1566
will seek those who **q** with you, **Is 41:12** 4695
"HE WILL NOT Q, NOR CRY OUT; **Mt 12:19** *2051*
so you fight and **q**. **Jas 4:2** *4170*

QUARRELED
q with the herdsmen of Isaac, **Gn 26:20** 7378
well, and they **q** over it too, **Gn 26:21** 7378
the people **q** with Moses and said, **Ex 17:2** 7378

QUARRELING
All the people were **q** **2Sa 19:9** 1777

QUARRELS
He **q** against all sound wisdom. **Pr 18:1** 1566
"Woe to *the one* who **q** with his **Is 45:9** 7378
that there are **q** among you. **1Co 1:11** *2054*
knowing that they produce **q**. **2Tm 2:23** *3163*
What is the source of **q** and conflicts **Jas 4:1** *4171*

QUARRELSOME
Lord's bond-servant must not be **q**, **2Tm 2:24** *3164*

QUARRIED
and they **q** great stones, **1Ki 5:17** 5265
and to the builders to buy **q** stone **2Ch 34:11** 4274

QUARRIES
He who **q** stones may be hurt by **Ec 10:9** 5265

QUARRY
built of stone prepared at the **q**, **1Ki 6:7** 4551a
men to **q** *stone* in the mountains and **2Ch 2:2** 2672
to **q** *stones* in the mountains and **2Ch 2:18** 2672
to the **q** from which you were dug. **Is 51:1** 953a, 4718

QUART
"A **q** of wheat for a denarius, and **Rv 6:6** *5518*

QUARTER
old, all the people from every **q**; **Gn 19:4** 7097a
in Jerusalem in the Second **Q**); **2Ki 22:14**
in Jerusalem in the Second **Q**); **2Ch 34:22**
Gate, A wail from the Second **Q**, **Zph 1:10**

QUARTERMASTER
(Now Seraiah was **q**.) **Jer 51:59** 8269, 4496

QUARTERS
out repairs in front of his own **q**. **Ne 3:30** 5393
two full years in his own rented **q** and **Ac 28:30** *3410*

QUARTS
three **q** of barley for a denarius; **Rv 6:6** *5518*

QUARTUS
city treasurer greets you, and **Q**, **Ro 16:23** *2890*

QUEEN
Now when the **q** of Sheba heard **1Ki 10:1** 4436
When the **q** of Sheba perceived all **1Ki 10:4** 4436
the **q** of Sheba gave King Solomon. **1Ki 10:10** 4436
Solomon gave to the **q** of Sheba all **1Ki 10:13** 4436
the sister of Tahpenes the **q**. **1Ki 11:19** 1377
his mother from *being* **q** mother, **1Ki 15:13** 1377
and the sons of the **q** mother." **2Ki 10:13** 1377
Now when the **q** of Sheba heard of **2Ch 9:1** 4436
When the **q** of Sheba had seen **2Ch 9:3** 4436
q of Sheba gave to King Solomon. **2Ch 9:9** 4436
Solomon gave to the **q** of Sheba all **2Ch 9:12** 4436
from the *position of* **q** mother, **2Ch 15:16** 1377
to me, the **q** sitting beside him, **Ne 2:6** 7694
Q Vashti also gave a banquet for **Es 1:9** 4436
to bring **Q** Vashti before the king **Es 1:11** 4436
But **Q** Vashti refused to come at **Es 1:12** 4436
what is to be done with **Q** Vashti, **Es 1:15** 4436
"**Q** Vashti has wronged not only **Es 1:16** 4436
Ahasuerus commanded **Q** Vashti **Es 1:17** 4436
who pleases the king be **q** in place of **Es 2:4** 4427a
and made her **q** instead of Vashti. **Es 2:17** 4427a
to Mordecai and he told **Q** Esther, **Es 2:22** 4436
the **q** writhed in great anguish. **Es 4:4** 4436
the king saw Esther the **q** standing **Es 5:2** 4436
"What is *troubling* you, **Q** Esther? **Es 5:3** 4436
"Even Esther the **q** let no one but **Es 5:12** 4436
to drink *wine* with Esther the **q**. **Es 7:1** 4436
"What is your petition, **Q** Esther? **Es 7:2** 4436
Then **Q** Esther replied, **Es 7:3** 4436
King Ahasuerus asked **Q** Esther, **Es 7:5** 4436
terrified before the king and **q**. **Es 7:6** 4436
to beg for his life from **Q** Esther, **Es 7:7** 4436
the **q** with me in the house?" **Es 7:8** 4436
enemy of the Jews, to **Q** Esther; **Es 8:1** 4436
So King Ahasuerus said to **Q** Esther **Es 8:7** 4436
The king said to **Q** Esther, **Es 9:12** 4436
Then **Q** Esther, daughter of Abihail **Es 9:29** 4436
Mordecai the Jew and **Q** Esther had **Es 9:31** 4436
stands the **q** in gold from Ophir. **Ps 45:9** 7694
longer be called The **q** of kingdoms. **Is 47:5** 1404
'I will be a **q** forever.' **Is 47:7** 1404
to make cakes for the **q** of heaven; **Jer 7:18** 4446
Say to the king and the **q** mother, **Jer 13:18** 1377
King Jeconiah and the **q** mother, **Jer 29:2** 1377
burning sacrifices to the **q** of heaven **Jer 44:17** 4446
burning sacrifices to the **q** of heaven **Jer 44:18** 4446
sacrifices to the **q** of heaven and **Jer 44:19** 4446
to burn sacrifices to the **q** of heaven **Jer 44:25** 4446
The **q** entered the banquet hall **Da 5:10** 4433
the **q** spoke and said, **Da 5:10** 4433
"*The* **Q** *of the* South will rise up **Mt 12:42** *938*
"*The* **Q** *of the* South will rise up **Lk 11:31** *938*
of Candace, **q** of the Ethiopians, **Ac 8:27** *938*
'I SIT *as* A Q AND I AM NOT A **Rv 18:7** *938*

QUEEN'S
"For the **q** conduct will become **Es 1:17** 4436
who have heard of the **q** conduct **Es 1:18** 4436

QUEENS
are sixty **q** and eighty concubines, **SS 6:8** 4436
The **q** and the concubines *also,* **SS 6:9** 4436

QUENCH
The wild donkeys **q** their thirst. **Ps 104:11** 7665
"Many waters cannot **q** love, **SS 8:7** 3518
And there will be none to **q** *them.* **Is 1:31** 3518
fire And burn with none to **q** it, **Jer 4:4** 3518
with none to **q** *it* for Bethel, **Am 5:6** 3518
Do not **q** the Spirit; **1Th 5:19** *4570*

QUENCHED
place, and it shall not be **q**." **2Ki 22:17** 3518
place and it shall not be **q**." ' **2Ch 34:25** 3518
is faint And his thirst is not **q**. **Is 29:8** 8264
It will not be **q** night or day; **Is 34:10** 3518
q *and* extinguished like a wick): **Is 43:17** 3518
And their fire will not be **q**; **Is 66:24** 3518
and it will burn and not be **q**." **Jer 7:20** 3518
of Jerusalem and not be **q**. **Jer 17:27** 3518
the blazing flame will not be **q** and **Ezk 20:47** 3518
it shall not be **q**. **Ezk 20:48** 3518
NOT DIE, AND THE FIRE IS NOT Q. **Mk 9:44** *4570*
NOT DIE, AND THE FIRE IS NOT Q. **Mk 9:46** *4570*
NOT DIE, AND THE FIRE IS NOT Q. **Mk 9:48** *4570*
q the power of fire, escaped the **Heb 11:34** *4570*

QUESTION
Was it not just a **q**?" **1Sa 17:29** 1697
asked Him *a* **q**, testing Him, **Mt 22:35**
together, Jesus asked them a **q**: **Mt 22:41** *1905*
that day on to ask Him another **q**. **Mt 22:46** *1905*
in the house, He *began* to **q** them, **Mk 9:33** *1905*
and *began* to **q** Him whether it was **Mk 10:2** *1905*
"I will ask you one **q**, **Mk 11:29** *3056*
to **q** Him closely on many subjects, **Lk 11:53** *653*
"I will also ask you a **q**, **Lk 20:3** *3056*
they did not have courage to **q** Him **Lk 20:40** *1905*
and if I ask a **q**, you will not answer **Lk 22:68** *2065*
knew that they wished to **q** Him, **Jn 16:19** *2065*
"In that day you will not **q** Me **Jn 16:23** *2065*
have no need for anyone to **q** You; **Jn 16:30** *2065*
"Why do you **q** Me? Question those **Jn 18:21** *2065*
Q those who have heard what I **Jn 18:21** *2065*
the disciples ventured to **q** Him, **Jn 21:12** *1833*

QUESTIONED
"The man **q** particularly about us **Gn 43:7** 7592
a youth from Succoth and **q** him. **Jg 8:14** 7592
Then Hezekiah **q** the priests and **2Ch 31:9** 1875
came to Jeremiah and **q** him. **Jer 38:27** 7592
And they **q** Jesus, asking, **Mt 12:10** *1905*
came to Jesus and **q** Him, **Mt 22:23** *1905*
governor, and the governor **q** Him, **Mt 27:11** *1905*
disciples **q** Him about the parable. **Mk 7:17** *1905*
and on the way He **q** His disciples, **Mk 8:27** *1905*
up *and came* forward and **q** Jesus, **Mk 14:60** *1905*
Pilate **q** Him, **Mk 15:2** *1905*
Then Pilate **q** Him again, saying, **Mk 15:4** *1905*
he **q** him as to whether He was **Mk 15:44** *1905*
were with Him, and He **q** them, **Lk 9:18** *1905*
Now having been **q** by the Pharisees **Lk 17:20** *1905*
A ruler **q** Him, **Lk 18:18** *1905*
when he came near, He **q** him, **Lk 18:40** *1905*
They **q** Him, saying, **Lk 20:21** *1905*
and they **q** Him, saying, **Lk 20:28** *1905*
They **q** Him, saying, **Lk 21:7** *1905*
And he **q** Him at some length; **Lk 23:9** *1905*
and **q** them, saying, **Jn 9:19** *2065*
q Jesus about His disciples, **Jn 18:19** *2065*
The high priest **q** them, **Ac 5:27** *1905*

QUESTIONING
And He *continued* by **q** them, **Mk 8:29** *1905*
disciples *began* **q** Him privately, **Mk 9:28** *1905*
began **q** Him about this again. **Mk 10:10** *1905*
came to Jesus, and *began* **q** Him, **Mk 12:18** *1905*
and Andrew were **q** Him privately, **Mk 13:3** *1905*
Again the high priest was **q** Him, **Mk 14:61** *1905*
And the crowds were **q** him, **Lk 3:10** *1905*
Some soldiers were **q** him, **Lk 3:14** *1905*
His disciples *began* **q** Him as **Lk 8:9** *1905*

QUESTIONS
So we answered his **q**. **Gn 43:7** 1697
came to test him with difficult **q**. **1Ki 10:1** 2420
Solomon answered all her **q**; **1Ki 10:3** 1697
to test Solomon with difficult **q**. **2Ch 9:1** 2420
Solomon answered all her **q**; **2Ch 9:2** 1697
venture to ask Him any more **q**. **Mk 12:34** *1905*
to them and asking them **q**. **Lk 2:46** *1905*
but if there are **q** about words and **Ac 18:15** *2213*
be accused over **q** about their Law, **Ac 23:29** *2213*
all customs and **q** among *the* Jews; **Ac 26:3** *2213*
asking **q** for conscience' sake; **1Co 10:25** *350*
asking **q** for conscience' sake. **1Co 10:27** *350*
a morbid interest in controversial **q** **1Tm 6:4** *2214*

QUICK
is **q** raw flesh in the swelling, **Lv 13:10** 4241
"Hurry, be **q**, do not stay!" **1Sa 20:38** 2363a
they were cut to the **q** and intended **Ac 5:33** *1282*
this, they were cut to the **q**, **Ac 7:54** *2588*
But everyone must be **q** to hear, **Jas 1:19** *5036*

QUICKLY
"**Q**, prepare three measures of **Gn 18:6** 4116
she **q** lowered her jar to her hand, **Gn 24:18** 4116
So she **q** emptied her jar into the **Gn 24:20** 4116
"She **q** lowered her jar from **Gn 24:46** 4116
"How is it that you have *it* so **q**, **Gn 27:20** 4116
and God will **q** bring it about. **Gn 41:32** 4116
"They have **q** turned aside from **Ex 32:8** 4118b
then bring it **q** to the congregation **Nu 16:46** 4120
that you will surely perish **q** **Dt 4:26** 4118b
you and He will **q** destroy you. **Dt 7:4** 4118b
able to put an end to them **q**, **Dt 7:22** 4118b
drive them out and destroy them **q**, **Dt 9:3** 4118b
'Arise, go down from here **q**, **Dt 9:12** 4118b
They have **q** turned aside from the **Dt 9:12** 4118b
you had turned aside **q** from the **Dt 9:16** 4118b
and you will perish **q** from the **Dt 11:17** 4120
destroyed and until you perish **q**, **Dt 28:20** 4118b
Pursue them **q**, for you will **Jos 2:5** 4118b
in ambush rose **q** from their place, **Jos 8:19** 4120
and they **q** set the city on fire. **Jos 8:19** 4116
come up to us **q** and save us and **Jos 10:6** 4120
and you will perish **q** from off **Jos 23:16** 4120
They turned aside **q** from the way **Jg 2:17** 4118b
to remain, not driving them out **q**; **Jg 2:23** 4118b
Then he called **q** to the young man, **Jg 9:54** 4120
woman ran **q** and told her husband, **Jg 13:10** 4116
that David ran **q** toward the battle **1Sa 17:48** 4116
you shall go down **q** and come to **1Sa 20:19** 3966
unless you had come **q** to meet me, **1Sa 25:34** 4116
Then Abigail **q** arose, and rode on **1Sa 25:42** 4116
house, and she **q** slaughtered it; **1Sa 28:24** 4116
or he will overtake us **q** and bring **2Sa 15:14** 4116
therefore, send **q** and tell David, **2Sa 17:16** 4120
so the two of them departed **q** and **2Sa 17:18** 4120
"Arise and cross over the water **q** **2Sa 17:21** 4120
and **q** catching his word said, **1Ki 20:33** 4116
"Bring **q** Micaiah son of Imlah." **1Ki 22:9** 4116
thus says the king, 'Come down **q**.' " **2Ki 1:11** 4120
"Bring **q** Micaiah, Imla's son." **2Ch 18:8** 4116
and you shall do the matter **q**." **2Ch 24:5** 4116
But the Levites did not act **q**. **2Ch 24:5** 4116
So he **q** provided her with her **Es 2:9** 926
"Bring Haman **q** that we may do as **Es 5:5** 4116
"Take **q** the robes and the horse **Es 6:10** 4116
advice of the cunning is **q** thwarted. **Jb 5:13** 4116
Your ear to me, rescue me **q**; **Ps 31:2** 4120
they will wither **q** like the grass And **Ps 37:2** 4120
Ethiopia will **q** stretch out her hands **Ps 68:31** 7323
For I am in distress; answer me **q**. **Ps 69:17** 4118b
Your compassion come **q** to meet us, **Ps 79:8** 4118b
"I would **q** subdue their enemies And **Ps 81:14** 4592
the day when I call answer me **q**. **Ps 102:2** 4118b
They **q** forgot His works; **Ps 106:13** 4116
Answer me **q**, O LORD, my spirit **Ps 143:7** 4118b
three *strands* is not **q** torn apart. **Ec 4:12** 4120
an evil deed is not executed **q**, **Ec 8:11** 4120
the LORD, Near and coming very **q**; **Zph 1:14** 4118a
"Make friends **q** with your opponent **Mt 5:25** *5035*
"Go **q** and tell His disciples **Mt 28:7** *5035*
And they left the tomb **q** **Mt 28:8** *5035*
'**Q** bring out the best robe and put **Lk 15:22** *5035*
and sit down **q** and write fifty.' **Lk 16:6** *5030*
will bring about justice for them **q**. **Lk 18:8** *5034*
when she heard it, she got up **q** **Jn 11:29** *5035*
that Mary got up **q** and went out, **Jn 11:31** *5030*
"What you do, do **q**." **Jn 13:27** *5036*
and woke him up, saying, "Get up **q**." **Ac 12:7** *5034*
haste, and get out of Jerusalem **q**, **Ac 22:18** *5034*
THE EARTH, THOROUGHLY AND Q." **Ro 9:28** *4932*
that you are so **q** deserting Him **Ga 1:6** *5030*
that you not be **q** shaken from **2Th 2:2** *5030*

or else I am coming to you **q**, **Rv 2:16** *5035*
'I am coming **q**; hold fast what you **Rv 3:11** *5035*
behold, the third woe is coming **q**. **Rv 11:14** *5035*
"And behold, I am coming **q**. **Rv 22:7** *5035*
"Behold, I am coming **q**, **Rv 22:12** *5035*
"Yes, I am coming **q**." **Rv 22:20** *5035*

QUICK-TEMPERED
A **q** man acts foolishly, And a man **Pr 14:17** 7116, 639
But he who is **q** exalts folly. **Pr 14:29** 7116, 7307
steward, not self-willed, not **q**, **Ti 1:7** *3711*

QUIET
of the Sidonians, **q** and secure; **Jg 18:7** 8252
Laish, to a people **q** and secure, **Jg 18:27** 8252
land rejoiced and the city was **q**. **2Ki 11:20** 8252
land was broad and **q** and peaceful; **1Ch 4:40** 8252
peace and **q** to Israel in his days. **1Ch 22:9** 8253
land rejoiced and the city was **q**. **2Ch 23:21** 8252
I would have lain down and been **q**; **Jb 3:13** 8252
"I am not at ease, nor am I **q**, **Jb 3:26** 8252
"Because he knew no **q** within him **Jb 20:20** 7961
When He keeps **q**, who then can **Jb 34:29** 8252
He leads me beside **q** waters. **Ps 23:2** 4496
those who are **q** in the land. **Ps 35:20** 7282
O God, do not remain **q**; **Ps 83:1** 1824
were glad because they were **q**, **Ps 107:30** 8367
whole earth is at rest *and* is **q**; **Is 14:7** 8252
tossing sea, For it cannot be **q**, **Is 57:20** 8252
Jerusalem's sake I will not keep **q**, **Is 62:1** 8252
and will be **q** and at ease, **Jer 30:10** 8252
LORD, How long will you not be **q**? **Jer 47:6** 8252
"How can it be **q**, When the LORD **Jer 47:7** 8252
Then he will answer, "Keep **q**. **Am 6:10** 2013
joy, He will be **q** in His love, **Zph 3:17** 2790b
all the earth is peaceful and **q**." **Zch 1:11** 8252
sternly told them to be **q**, **Mt 20:31** *4623*
"Be **q**, and come out of him!" **Mk 1:25** *5392*
were sternly telling him to be **q**, **Mk 10:48** *4623*
"Be **q** and come out of him!" **Lk 4:35** *5392*
were sternly telling him to be **q**; **Lk 18:39** *4601*
dialect, they became even more **q**; **Ac 22:2** *2271*
make it your ambition to lead a **q** life **1Th 4:11** *2270*
to work in **q** fashion and eat their **2Th 3:12** *2271*
we may lead a tranquil and **q** life **1Tm 2:2** *2272*
over a man, but to remain **q**. **1Tm 2:12** *2271*
quality of a gentle and **q** spirit, **1Pe 3:4** *2272*

QUIETED
Caleb **q** the people before Moses and **Nu 13:30** 2013
"He **q** the sea with His power, And **Jb 26:12** 7280a
I have composed and **q** my soul; **Ps 131:2** 1826a
When they heard this, they **q** down **Ac 11:18** *2270*

QUIETING
After **q** the crowd, the **Ac 19:35** *2687*

QUIETLY
I will look from My dwelling place **q** **Is 18:4** 8252
wait **q** for the day of distress, **Hab 3:16** 5117
A woman must **q** receive instruction **1Tm 2:11** *2271*

QUIETNESS
Better is a dry morsel and **q** with it **Pr 17:1** 7962
The words of the wise heard in **q** **Ec 9:17** 5183a
In **q** and trust is your strength." **Is 30:15** 8252
q and confidence forever. **Is 32:17** 8252

QUIETS
no whisperer, contention **q** down. **Pr 26:20** 8367

QUILT
put a **q** of goats' *hair* at its head, **1Sa 19:13** 3523
the **q** of goats' *hair* at its head. **1Sa 19:16** 3523

QUIRINIUS
while **Q** was governor of Syria. **Lk 2:2** *2958*

QUIT
on you, but after that I will **q**." **Jg 15:7** 2308

QUITE
so the governor was **q** amazed. **Mt 27:14** *3029*
When it was already **q** late, **Mk 6:35** *4183*
desolate and it is already **q** late; **Mk 6:35** *4183*
the prison house locked **q** securely **Ac 5:23** *3956*
he also used to send for him **q** often **Ac 24:26** *4437*
Q right, they were broken off for **Ro 11:20** *2573*
sins of some men are **q** evident, **1Tm 5:24** *4271*
deeds that are good are **q** evident, **1Tm 5:25** *4271*

QUIVER
your gear, your **q** and your bow, **Gn 27:3** 8522
"The **q** rattles against him, The **Jb 39:23** 827
the man whose **q** is full of them; **Ps 127:5** 827
Elam took up the **q** With the **Is 22:6** 827
He has hidden Me in His **q**. **Is 49:2** 827
"Their **q** is like an open grave, **Jer 5:16** 827
He made the arrows of His **q** To enter **La 3:13** 827

QUIVERED
trembled, At the sound my lips **q**. **Hab 3:16** 6750

QUIVERING
your water with **q** and anxiety. **Ezk 12:18** 7269

QUIVERS
Sharpen the arrows, fill the **q**! **Jer 51:11** 7982

QUOTA
"But the **q** of bricks which they **Ex 5:8** 4971
"Complete your work **q**, **Ex 5:13** 4639
must deliver the **q** of bricks." **Ex 5:18** 8506

QUOTE
everyone who quotes proverbs will **q** **Ezk 16:44** 4911b
you will **q** this proverb to Me, **Lk 4:23** *3004*

QUOTES
everyone who **q** proverbs will quote **Ezk 16:44** 4911b

R

RAAMA
Cush *were* Seba, Havilah, Sabta, **R** and **1Ch 1:9** 7484

RAAMAH
and Sabtah and **R** and Sabteca; **Gn 10:7** 7484
sons of **R** *were* Sheba and Dedan. **Gn 10:7** 7484
sons of **R** *were* Sheba and Dedan. **1Ch 1:9** 7484
"The traders of Sheba and **R**, **Ezk 27:22** 7484

RAAMIAH
Jeshua, Nehemiah, Azariah, **R**, **Ne 7:7** 7485

RAAMSES
storage cities, Pithom and **R**. **Ex 1:11** 7486

RABBAH
it is in **R** of the sons of Ammon. **Dt 3:11** 7237
as far as Aroer which is before **R**; **Jos 13:25** 7237
and **R**; two cities with their villages. **Jos 15:60** 7237
the sons of Ammon and besieged **R**. **2Sa 11:1** 7237
against **R** of the sons of Ammon and **2Sa 12:26** 7237
"I have fought against **R**, **2Sa 12:27** 7237
all the people and went to **R**, **2Sa 12:29** 7237
from **R** of the sons of Ammon, **2Sa 17:27** 7237
of Ammon, and came and besieged **R**. **1Ch 20:1** 7237
Joab struck **R** and overthrew it. **1Ch 20:1** 7237
Against **R** of the sons of Ammon; **Jer 49:2** 7237
Cry out, O daughters of **R**, **Jer 49:3** 7237
to come to **R** of the sons of Ammon, **Ezk 21:20** 7237
"I will make **R** a pasture for **Ezk 25:5** 7237
kindle a fire on the wall of **R** And **Am 1:14** 7237

RABBI
and being called **R** by men. **Mt 23:7** *4461*
"But do not be called **R**; **Mt 23:8** *4461*
"Surely it is not I, **R**?" **Mt 26:25** *4461*
Judas went to Jesus and said, "Hail, **R**!" **Mt 26:49** *4461*
"**R**, it is good for us to be here; **Mk 9:5** *4461*
"**R**, look, the fig tree which **Mk 11:21** *4461*
went to Him, saying, "**R**!" **Mk 14:45** *4461*
R (which translated means Teacher) **Jn 1:38** *4461*
"**R**, You are the Son of God; **Jn 1:49** *4461*
"**R**, we know that You have come **Jn 3:2** *4461*
"**R**, He who was with you beyond **Jn 3:26** *4461*
urging Him, saying, "**R**, eat." **Jn 4:31** *4461*
"**R**, when did You get here?" **Jn 6:25** *4461*
"**R**, who sinned, this man or his **Jn 9:2** *4461*
"**R**, the Jews were just now **Jn 11:8** *4461*

RABBIT
the **r** also, for though it chews **Lv 11:6** 768
and the **r** and the shaphan, **Dt 14:7** 768

RABBITH
and **R** and Kishion and Ebez, **Jos 19:20** 7245

RABBLE
The **r** who were among them had **Nu 11:4** 628

RABBONI
"**R**, *I want* to regain my sight!" **Mk 10:51** *4462*
and said to Him in Hebrew, "**R**!" **Jn 20:16** *4462*

RAB-MAG
the Rab-saris, Nergal-sar-ezer *the* **R**, **Jer 39:3** 7248
Rab-saris, and Nergal-sar-ezer the **R**, **Jer 39:13** 7248

RAB-SARIS
king of Assyria sent Tartan and **R** **2Ki 18:17** 7249
Samgar-nebu, Sar-sekim the **R**, **Jer 39:3** 7249
along with Nebushazban the **R**, **Jer 39:13** 7249

RABSHAKEH
sent Tartan and Rab-saris and **R** **2Ki 18:17** 7262
Then **R** said to them, **2Ki 18:19** 7262
and Shebnah and Joah, said to **R**, **2Ki 18:26** 7262
But **R** said to them, **2Ki 18:27** 7262
Then **R** stood and cried with a loud **2Ki 18:28** 7262
torn and told him the words of **R**. **2Ki 18:37** 7262
God will hear all the words of **R**, **2Ki 19:4** 7262
Then **R** returned and found the king **2Ki 19:8** 7262
And the king of Assyria sent **R** **Is 36:2** 7262
Then **R** said to them, **Is 36:4** 7262
and Shebna and Joah said to **R**, **Is 36:11** 7262
But **R** said, "Has my master sent me **Is 36:12** 7262
Then **R** stood and cried with a loud **Is 36:13** 7262
torn and told him the words of **R**. **Is 36:22** 7262
your God will hear the words of **R**, **Is 37:4** 7262
Then **R** returned and found the king **Is 37:8** 7262

RACAL
and to those who were in **R**, **1Sa 30:29** 7403

RACE
so that the holy **r** has intermingled **Ezr 9:2** 2233
that the **r** is not to the swift and **Ec 9:11** 4793
chariots **r** madly in the streets, **Na 2:4** 1984b
a mongrel **r** will dwell in Ashdod, **Zch 9:6** 4464
Gentile, of the Syrophoenician **r**. **Mk 7:26** *1085*
took shrewd advantage of our **r** and **Ac 7:19** *1085*
that those who run in a **r** all run, **1Co 9:24** *4712*
and let us run with endurance the **r** **Heb 12:1** *73*
and has been tamed by the human **r**. **Jas 3:7** *5449*
But you are A CHOSEN **R**, **1Pe 2:9** *1085*

RACES
and rage he **r** over the ground, **Jb 39:24** 1572

RACHEL
R his daughter coming with the **Gn 29:6** 7354
R came with her father's sheep, **Gn 29:9** 7354
When Jacob saw **R** the daughter of **Gn 29:10** 7354
Then Jacob kissed **R**, **Gn 29:11** 7354
Jacob told **R** that he was a **Gn 29:12** 7354
and the name of the younger was **R**. **Gn 29:16** 7354
but **R** was beautiful of form and **Gn 29:17** 7354
Now Jacob loved **R**, so he said, **Gn 29:18** 7354
for your younger daughter **R**." **Gn 29:18** 7354
So Jacob served seven years for **R** **Gn 29:20** 7354
Was it not for **R** that I served with **Gn 29:25** 7354
gave him his daughter **R** as his wife. **Gn 29:28** 7354
his maid Bilhah to his daughter **R** **Gn 29:29** 7354
So *Jacob* went in to **R** also, **Gn 29:30** 7354
indeed he loved **R** more than Leah, **Gn 29:30** 7354
opened her womb, but **R** was barren. **Gn 29:31** 7354
Now when **R** saw that she bore Jacob **Gn 30:1** 7354
Jacob's anger burned against **R**, **Gn 30:2** 7354
R said, "God has vindicated me, **Gn 30:6** 7354
So **R** said, "With mighty wrestlings **Gn 30:8** 7354
Then **R** said to Leah, **Gn 30:14** 7354
R said, "Therefore he may lie with **Gn 30:15** 7354
Then God remembered **R**, **Gn 30:22** 7354
about when **R** had borne Joseph, **Gn 30:25** 7354
So Jacob sent and called **R** and **Gn 31:4** 7354
R and Leah said **Gn 31:14** 7354
then **R** stole the household idols **Gn 31:19** 7354
not know that **R** had stolen them. **Gn 31:32** 7354
Now **R** had taken the household **Gn 31:34** 7354
Leah and **R** and the two maids. **Gn 33:1** 7354
next, and **R** and Joseph last. **Gn 33:2** 7354
afterward Joseph came near with **R**, **Gn 33:7** 7354
R began to give birth and she **Gn 35:16** 7354
So **R** died and was buried on the **Gn 35:19** 7354
the sons of **R**: Joseph and Benjamin **Gn 35:24** 7354
The sons of Jacob's wife **R**: **Gn 46:19** 7354
These are the sons of **R**, **Gn 46:22** 7354
whom Laban gave to his daughter **R**, **Gn 46:25** 7354
when I came from Paddan, **R** died, **Gn 48:7** 7354
into your home like **R** and Leah, **Ru 4:11** 7354
R is weeping for her children; **Jer 31:15** 7354
R WEEPING FOR HER CHILDREN; **Mt 2:18** *4478*

RACHEL'S
R maid Bilhah conceived again **Gn 30:7** 7354
of Leah's tent and entered **R** tent. **Gn 31:33** 7354
the pillar of **R** grave to this day. **Gn 35:20** 7354
and the sons of Bilhah, **R** maid: **Gn 35:25** 7354
will find two men close to **R** tomb **1Sa 10:2** 7354

RADDAI
Nethanel the fourth, **R** the fifth, **1Ch 2:14** 7288

RADIANCE
and *there was* a **r** around Him. **Ezk 1:27** 5051
appearance of the surrounding **r**. **Ezk 1:28** 5051
His **r** is like the sunlight; **Hab 3:4** 5051
At the **r** of Your gleaming spear. **Hab 3:11** 5051
And He is the **r** of His glory and **Heb 1:3** *541*

RADIANT
They looked to Him and were **r**, **Ps 34:5** 5102b
"Then you will see and be **r**, **Is 60:5** 5102b
And they will be **r** over the **Jer 31:12** 5102b
and His garments became **r** and **Mk 9:3** *4744*

RAFTER
And the **r** will answer it from the **Hab 2:11** 3714

RAFTERS
Through indolence the **r** sag, **Ec 10:18** 4746
houses are cedars, Our **r**, cypresses. **SS 1:17** 7351

RAFTS
and I will make them into **r** *to go* **1Ki 5:9** 1702
bring it to you on **r** by sea to Joppa, **2Ch 2:16** 7513

RAGE
So he turned and went away in a **r**. **2Ki 5:12** 2534
a **r** *which* has even reached heaven. **2Ch 28:9** 2197
to him, Haman was filled with **r**. **Es 3:5** 2534
"With shaking and **r** he races over **Jb 39:24** 7267
against the **r** of my adversaries, **Ps 7:6** 5678
embittered in the **r** of my spirit, **Ezk 3:14** 2534
Then Nebuchadnezzar in **r** and anger **Da 3:13** 7266
Did the LORD **r** against the rivers, **Hab 3:8** 2734
with **r** as they heard these things; **Lk 4:28** *2372*
themselves were filled with **r**, **Lk 6:11** *454*
'WHY DID THE GENTILES **R**, **Ac 4:25** *5433*
heard *this* and were filled with **r**, **Ac 19:28** *2372*

RAGED
The battle **r** that day, and the **1Ki 22:35** 5927
The battle **r** that day, and the **2Ch 18:34** 5927

RAGES
"If a river **r**, he is not alarmed; **Jb 40:23** 6231
And his heart **r** against the LORD. **Pr 19:3** 2196
foolish man either **r** or laughs, **Pr 29:9** 7264

RAGING
coming in, And your **r** against Me. **2Ki 19:27** 7264
'Because of your **r** against Me, And **2Ki 19:28** 7264
Like a stone into **r** waters. **Ne 9:11** 5794
"There the wicked cease from **r**, **Jb 3:17** 7267
Then the **r** waters would have swept **Ps 124:5** 2121
coming in And your **r** against Me. **Is 37:28** 7264
"Because of your **r** against Me And **Is 37:29** 7264
in anger, wrath and **r** rebukes. **Ezk 5:15** 2534
sea, and the sea stopped its **r**. **Jon 1:15** 2197

RAGS
will clothe *one* with **r**. **Pr 23:21** 7168
worn-out clothes and worn-out **r** **Jer 38:11** 4418
put these worn-out clothes and **r** **Jer 38:12** 4418

RAHAB
of a harlot whose name was **R**, **Jos 2:1** 7343
king of Jericho sent *word* to **R**, **Jos 2:3** 7343
only **R** the harlot and all who are **Jos 6:17** 7343
brought out **R** and her father and **Jos 6:23** 7343
R the harlot and her father's **Jos 6:25** 7343
Him crouch the helpers of **R**. **Jb 9:13** 7293
His understanding He shattered **R**. **Jb 26:12** 7293
"I shall mention **R** and Babylon **Ps 87:4** 7294
crushed **R** like one who is slain; **Ps 89:10** 7293
"**R** who has been exterminated." **Is 30:7** 7294
it not You who cut **R** in pieces, **Is 51:9** 7293

Salmon was the father of Boaz by R, Mt 1:5 4460
By faith R the harlot did not perish Heb 11:31 4460
was not R the harlot also justified Jas 2:25 4460

RAHAM
Shema became the father of R, 1Ch 2:44 7357

RAID
"As for Gad, raiders shall r him, Gn 49:19 1464
But he will r *at* their heels. Gn 49:19 1464
Philistines have made a r on the land 1Sa 23:27 6584
"Where have you made a r today?" 1Sa 27:10 6584
the Amalekites had made a r on the 1Sa 30:1 6584
"We made a r on the Negev of the 1Sa 30:14 6584
came from a r and brought much 2Sa 3:22 1416
made a r in the valley of Rephaim. 1Ch 14:9 6584
The Philistines made yet another r in 1Ch 14:13 6584
made a r on the camels and took Jb 1:17 6584
enters in, Bandits r outside, Hos 7:1 6584

RAIDED
David and his men went up and r 1Sa 27:8 6584
to battle, r the cities of Judah, 2Ch 25:13 6584

RAIDERS
"As for Gad, r shall raid him, Gn 49:19 1416
And the r came from the camp of 1Sa 13:17 7843
the garrison and the r trembled, 1Sa 14:15 7843
David against the band of r, 1Ch 12:21 1416
suddenly bring r upon them; Jer 18:22 1416
And as r wait for a man, *So* a band Hos 6:9 1416

RAILING
against him a r judgment, Jude 1:9 988

RAIMENT
garments, And I stained all My r. Is 63:3 4403

RAIN
God had not sent r upon the earth, Gn 2:5 4305
I will send r on the earth forty Gn 7:4 4305
The r fell upon the earth for Gn 7:12 1653
the r from the sky was restrained; Gn 8:2 1653
r no longer poured on the earth. Ex 9:33 4306
the r and the hail and the thunder Ex 9:34 4306
I will r bread from heaven for you; Ex 16:4 4305
drinks water from the r of heaven, Dt 11:11 4306
He will give the r for your land in Dt 11:14 4306
its season, the early and late r, Dt 11:14 3138, 4456
there will be no r and the ground will Dt 11:17 4306
to give r to your land in its Dt 28:12 4306
r of your land powder and dust; Dt 28:24 4306
"Let my teaching drop as the r, Dt 32:2 4306
that He may send thunder and r. 1Sa 12:17 4306
LORD sent thunder and r that day; 1Sa 12:18 4306
Let not dew or r be on you, 2Sa 1:21 4306
earth, Through sunshine after r.' 2Sa 23:4 4306
are shut up and there is no r, 1Ki 8:35 4306
And send r on Your land, which You 1Ki 8:36 4306
be neither dew nor r these years, 1Ki 17:1 4306
there was no r in the land. 1Ki 17:7 1653
r on the face of the earth.'" 1Ki 17:14 1653
send r on the face of the earth." 1Ki 18:1 4306
not see wind nor shall you see r; 2Ki 3:17 1653
there is no r because they have sinned 2Ch 6:26 4306
And send r on Your land which You 2Ch 6:27 4306
the heavens so that there is no r, 2Ch 7:13 4306
of this matter and the heavy r. Ezr 10:9 1653
"He gives r on the earth And Jb 5:10 4306
r *it* on him while he is eating. Jb 20:23 4305
When He set a limit for the r And Jb 28:26 4306
They waited for me as for the r, Jb 29:23 4306
their mouth as for the spring r. Jb 29:23 4456
They distill r from the mist, Jb 36:27 4306
And to the downpour and the r, Jb 37:6 1653, 4306
bring r on a land without people, Jb 38:26 4305
"Has the r a father? Jb 38:28 4306
Upon the wicked He will r snares; Ps 11:6 4305
The heavens also dropped r at Ps 68:8
You shed abroad a plentiful r, Ps 68:9 1653
down like r upon the mown grass, Ps 72:6 4306
early r also covers it with blessings. Ps 84:6 4175a
He gave them hail for r, Ps 105:32 1653
Who makes lightnings for the r, Ps 135:7 4306
Who provides r for the earth, Ps 147:8 4306
is like a cloud with the spring r. Pr 16:15 4456
Like clouds and wind without r Is Pr 25:14 1653
The north wind brings forth r, Pr 25:23 1653
in summer and like r in harvest, Pr 26:1 4306
dripping on a day of steady r Pr 27:15 5464
a driving r which leaves no food. Pr 28:3 4306
they pour out r upon the earth; Ec 11:3 1653
and clouds return after the r; Ec 12:2 1653
is past, The r is over *and* gone. SS 2:11 1653
protection from the storm and the r. Is 4:6 4306
charge the clouds to r no rain on it. Is 5:6 4305
charge the clouds to rain no r on it. Is 5:6 4306
breath of the ruthless Is like a r Is 25:4
Then He will give *you* r for the Is 30:23 4306
a fir, and the r makes it grow. Is 44:14 1653
"For as the r and the snow come Is 55:10 1653
And there has been no spring r. Jer 3:3 4456
God, Who gives r in its season, Jer 5:24 1653
the autumn r and the spring rain, Jer 5:24 3138
the autumn rain and the spring r, Jer 5:24 4456
He makes lightning for the r, Jer 10:13 4306
there has been no r on the land; Jer 14:4 1653
idols of the nations who give r? Jer 14:22 1652
He makes lightning for the r And Jer 51:16 4306
A flooding r will come, and you, O Ezk 13:11 1653
will also be in My anger a flooding r Ezk 13:13 1653
and I will r on him and on his Ezk 38:22 4305
who are with him, a torrential r, Ezk 38:22 1653
And He will come to us like the r, Hos 6:3 1653
the spring r watering the earth." Hos 6:3 4456
He comes to r righteousness on you. Hos 10:12 3384
the early r for *your* vindication. Jl 2:23 4175a
He has poured down for you the r, Jl 2:23 1653
The early and latter r as before. Jl 2:23 4456
I withheld the r from you While Am 4:7 1653
Then I would send r on one city Am 4:7 4305
another city I would not send r; Am 4:7 4305
Ask r from the LORD at the time of Zch 10:1 4306
the LORD at the time of the spring r Zch 10:1 4456
He will give them showers of r, Zch 10:1 1653
hosts, there will be no r on them. Zch 14:17 1653
then no r *will fall* on them; Zch 14:18
and sends r on *the* righteous and Mt 5:45 1026
"And the r fell, and the Mt 7:25 1028
"The r fell, and the Mt 7:27 1028
for because of the r that had set in Ac 28:2 5205
For ground that drinks the r which Heb 6:7 5205
earnestly that it would not r Jas 5:17 1026
and it did not r on the earth for Jas 5:17 1026
prayed again, and the sky poured r and Jas 5:18 5205
so that r will not fall Rv 11:6 5205

RAINBOW
r in the clouds on a rainy day, Ezk 1:28 7198
there was a r around the throne, Rv 4:3 2463
and the r was upon his head, and Rv 10:1 2463

RAINED
LORD r on Sodom and Gomorrah Gn 19:24 4305
LORD r hail on the land of Egypt. Ex 9:23 4305
until it r on them from the sky; 2Sa 21:10 5413
He r down manna upon them to eat Ps 78:24 4305
He r meat upon them like the dust, Ps 78:27 4305
a land that is not cleansed or r on Ezk 22:24 1652
One part would be r on, Am 4:7 4305
the part not r on would dry up. Am 4:7 4305
it r fire and brimstone from heaven Lk 17:29 1026

RAINS
shall give you r in their season, Lv 26:4 1653
"They are wet with the mountain r And Jb 24:8 2230
He did good and gave you r Ac 14:17 5205
it gets the early and late r. Jas 5:7

RAINY
many people; it is the r season Ezr 10:13 1653
rainbow in the clouds on a r day, Ezk 1:28 1653

RAISE
r up offspring for your brother." Gn 38:8 6965
no one shall r his hand or foot in all Gn 41:44 7311
Israel to r a contribution for Me; Ex 25:2 3947
him you shall r My contribution. Ex 25:2 3947
which you are to r from them: Ex 25:3 3947
"The LORD your God will r up for Dt 18:15 6965
'I will r up a prophet from among Dt 18:18 6965
certainly help him to r *them* up. Dt 22:4 6965
in order to r up the name of the Ru 4:5 6965
to be my wife in order to r up the Ru 4:10 6965
'But I will r up for Myself a 1Sa 2:35 6965
r up your descendant after you, 2Sa 7:12 6965
I will r up evil against you from 2Sa 12:11 6965
order to r him up from the ground, 2Sa 12:17 6965
the LORD will r up for Himself a 1Ki 14:14 6965
to r up his son after him and to 1Ki 15:4 6965
cymbals, to r sounds of joy. 1Ch 15:16 7311
to r up the house of our God, Ezr 9:9 7311
be gracious to me and r me up, Ps 41:10 6965
R a song, strike the timbrel, The Ps 81:2 5375
bare hill, R your voice to them. Is 13:2 7311
I will r my throne above the stars Is 14:13 7311
on the road to Horonaim they r a cry Is 15:5 5782
They r their voices, they shout Is 24:14 5375
r up battle towers against you. Is 29:3 6965
will not cry out or r *His voice,* Is 42:2 5375
a shout, yes, He will r a war cry. Is 42:13 6873
And I will r up her ruins *again.* Is 44:26 6965
To r up the tribes of Jacob and Is 49:6 6965
R your voice like a trumpet, And Is 58:1 7311
will r up the age-old foundations; Is 58:12 6965
will r up the former devastations; Is 61:4 6965
And r a signal over Beth-haccerem; Jer 6:1 5375
"I will also r up shepherds over Jer 23:4 6965
"When I will r up for David a Jer 23:5 6965
king, whom I will r up for them. Jer 30:9 6965
"R your battle cry against her on Jer 50:15 7321
and fall With no one to r him up; Jer 50:32 6965
build a siege wall, r up a ramp, Ezk 4:2 8210
"Son of man, r your eyes now Ezk 8:5 5375
r up a large shield against you. Ezk 26:8 6965
latter will r a great multitude, Da 11:11 5975
the king of the North will again r a Da 11:13 5975
He will r us up on the third day Hos 6:2 6965
in his shadow Will again r grain, Hos 14:7 2421a
There is none to r her up. Am 5:2 6965
to r up a nation against you, Am 6:14 6965
r up the fallen booth of David, Am 9:11 6965
I will also r up its ruins And Am 9:11 6965
Then we will r against him Seven Mi 5:5 6965
I am going to r up a shepherd in Zch 11:16 6965
to r up children to Abraham. Mt 3:9 1453
"Heal *the* sick, r *the* dead, Mt 10:8 1453
AND R UP CHILDREN FOR HIS Mt 22:24 450
AND R UP CHILDREN TO HIS BROTHER. Mk 12:19 1817
to r up children to Abraham. Lk 3:8 1453
AND R UP CHILDREN TO HIS BROTHER. Lk 20:28 1817
in three days I will r it up." Jn 2:19 1453
will You r it up in three days?" Jn 2:20 1453
but r it up on the last day. Jn 6:39 450
will r him up on the last day." Jn 6:40 450
I will r him up on the last day. Jn 6:44 450
I will r him up on the last day. Jn 6:54 450
GOD WILL R UP FOR YOU A PROPHET Ac 3:22 450
'GOD WILL R UP FOR YOU A PROPHET Ac 7:37 450
you *people* if God does r the dead? Ac 26:8 1453
also r us up through His power. 1Co 6:14 1825
raised Christ, whom He did not r, 1Co 15:15 1453
He who raised the Lord Jesus will r 2Co 4:14 1453
able to r *people* even from the dead Heb 11:19 1453
sick, and the Lord will r him up, Jas 5:15 1453

RAISED
Abraham r his eyes and saw the Gn 22:4 5375
Abraham r his eyes and looked, Gn 22:13 5375
as they r their eyes and looked, Gn 37:25 5375
that I r my voice and screamed, Gn 39:15 7311
as I r my voice and screamed, Gn 39:18 7311
whom He r up in their place, Jos 5:7 6965
They r over him a great heap Jos 7:26 6965
and r over it a great heap of stones Jos 8:29 6965
Then the LORD r up judges who Jg 2:16 6965
the LORD r up judges for them, Jg 2:18 6965
the LORD r up a deliverer for the Jg 3:9 6965
LORD r up a deliverer for them, Jg 3:15 6965
and they r their eyes and saw the 1Sa 6:13 5375
watchman r his eyes and looked, 2Sa 13:34 5375
wall, and r his eyes and looked, 2Sa 18:24 5375
man who was r on high declares, 2Sa 23:1 6965
LORD r up an adversary to Solomon, 1Ki 11:14 6965
r up *another* adversary to him, 1Ki 11:23 6965
against whom have you r *your* voice, 2Ki 19:22 7311
them Solomon r as forced laborers 2Ch 8:8 5927
Then the men of Judah r a war cry, 2Ch 13:15 7321
the men of Judah r the war cry, 2Ch 13:15 7321
him, they r their voices and wept. Jb 2:12 5375
He r His voice, the earth melted. Ps 46:6 5414
He spoke and r up a stormy wind, Ps 107:25 5975
his eyelids are r *in arrogance.* Pr 30:13 5375
And will be r above the hills; Is 2:2 5375
a standard is r on the mountains, Is 18:3 5375
against whom have you r *your* Is 37:23 7311
And My highways will be r up. Is 49:11 7311
'The LORD has r up prophets for us Jer 29:15 6965
to Jahaz they have r their voice, Jer 48:34 5414
So I r my eyes toward the north, Ezk 8:5 5375
can it be r from its roots *again.* Ezk 17:9 5375
And its height was r above the Ezk 19:11 1361b
the dust r *by* them will cover you; Ezk 26:10
house had a r platform all around; Ezk 41:8 1363
r my eyes toward heaven and Da 4:34 5191
And it was r up on one side, and Da 7:5 6966
as he r his right hand and his Da 12:7 7311
"Then I r up some of your sons to Am 2:11 6965
It will be r above the hills, And Mi 4:1 5375
deaf hear, *the* dead are r up, Mt 11:5 1453
and be r up on the third day. Mt 16:21 1453
He will be r on the third day." Mt 17:23 1453
the third day He will be r up." Mt 20:19 1453
"But after I have been r, Mt 26:32 1453
saints who had fallen asleep were r; Mt 27:52 1453
And He came to her and r her up, Mk 1:31 1453
took him by the hand and r him; Mk 9:27 1453
"But after I have been r, Mk 14:28 1453
And has r up a horn of salvation Lk 1:69 1453
the deaf hear, *the* dead are r up, Lk 7:22 1453
and be r up on the third day." Lk 9:22 1453
women in the crowd r her voice and Lk 11:27 1869
and they r their voices, saying, Lk 17:13 142
"But that the dead are r, Lk 20:37 1453
when He was r from the dead, Jn 2:22 1453
Then Jesus r His eyes, and said, Jn 11:41 142
whom Jesus had r from the dead. Jn 12:1 1453
Lazarus, whom He r from the dead. Jn 12:9 1453
the tomb and r him from the dead, Jn 12:17 1453
after He was r from the dead. Jn 21:14 1453
r his voice and declared to them: Ac 2:14 1869
"But God r Him up again, putting Ac 2:24 450
"This Jesus God r up again, to Ac 2:32 450
by the right hand, he r him up; Ac 3:7 1453
the one whom God r from the dead, Ac 3:15 1453
you first, God r up His Servant and Ac 3:26 450
whom God r from the dead Ac 4:10 1453
"The God of our fathers r up Jesus, Ac 5:30 1453
he gave her his hand and r her up; Ac 9:41 450
But Peter r him up, saying, Ac 10:26 1453
"God r Him up on the third day and Ac 10:40 1453
He r up David to be their king, Ac 13:22 1453
"But God r Him from the dead; Ac 13:30 1453
children in that He r up Jesus, Ac 13:33 450
that He r Him up from the dead, Ac 13:34 450
whom God r did not undergo decay. Ac 13:37 1453
Paul had done, they r their voice, Ac 14:11 1869
then they r their voices and said, Ac 22:22 1869
who r Jesus our Lord from the dead, Ro 4:24 1453
r because of our justification. Ro 4:25 1453
as Christ was r from the dead Ro 6:4 1453
Christ, having been r from the dead, Ro 6:9 1453
to Him who was r from the dead, Ro 7:4 1453
But if the Spirit of Him who r Jesus Ro 8:11 1453
He who r Christ Jesus from the Ro 8:11 1453
who died, yes, rather who was r, Ro 8:34 1453
"FOR THIS VERY PURPOSE I R YOU UP, Ro 9:17 1825
that God r Him from the dead, Ro 10:9 1453
Now God has not only r the Lord, 1Co 6:14 1453
and that He was r on the third day 1Co 15:4 1453
that He has been r from the dead, 1Co 15:12 1453
dead, not even Christ has been r; 1Co 15:13 1453
and if Christ has not been r, 1Co 15:14 1453
against God that He r Christ, 1Co 15:15 1453
if in fact the dead are not r. 1Co 15:15 1453

For if the dead are not **r**, **1Co 15:16** *1453*
not even Christ has been **r**; **1Co 15:16** *1453*
and if Christ has not been **r**, **1Co 15:17** *1453*
Christ has been **r** from the dead, **1Co 15:20** *1453*
If the dead are not **r** at all, **1Co 15:29** *1453*
If the dead are not **r**, **1Co 15:32** *1453*
"How are the dead **r**? **1Co 15:35** *1453*
it is **r** an imperishable *body;* **1Co 15:42** *1453*
it is sown in dishonor, it is **r** in glory **1Co 15:43** *1453*
is sown in weakness, it is **r** in power; **1Co 15:43** *1453*
natural body, it is **r** a spiritual body. **1Co 15:44** *1453*
the dead will be **r** imperishable, **1Co 15:52** *1453*
knowing that He who **r** the Lord **2Co 4:14** *1453*
r up against the knowledge of God, **2Co 10:5** *1869*
Father, who **r** Him from the dead), **Ga 1:1** *1453*
when He **r** Him from the dead and **Eph 1:20** *1453*
and **r** us up with Him, and seated **Eph 2:6** *4891*
in which you were also **r** up with **Col 2:12** *4891*
of God, who **r** Him from the dead. **Col 2:12** *1453*
you have been **r** up with Christ, **Col 3:1** *4891*
heaven, whom He **r** from the dead, **1Th 1:10** *1453*
who **r** Him from the dead and gave **1Pe 1:21** *1453*

RAISES
He brings down to Sheol and **r** up. **1Sa 2:6** 5927
"He **r** the poor from the dust, He **1Sa 2:8** 6965
"When he **r** himself up, the mighty **Jb 41:25** 7613
He **r** the poor from the dust And **Ps 113:7** 6965
And **r** up all who are bowed down. **Ps 145:14** 2210
r up those who are bowed down; **Ps 146:8** 2210
who **r** his door seeks destruction. **Pr 17:19** 1361b
the LORD **r** against them adversaries **Is 9:11** 7682
It **r** all the kings of the nations **Is 14:9** 6965
and **r** *it* for himself among the **Is 44:14** 553
just as the Father **r** the dead and **Jn 5:21** *1453*
but in God who **r** the dead; **2Co 1:9** *1453*

RAISIN
a portion *of meat* and a **r** cake. **1Ch 16:3** 809
"Sustain me with **r** cakes, Refresh **SS 2:5** 809
You will moan for the **r** cakes of **Is 16:7** 809
to other gods and love **r** cakes." **Hos 3:1** 809, 6025

RAISING
behold, I am **r** up the Chaldeans, **Hab 1:6** 6965
I came without even **r** any objection **Ac 10:29** *369*
all men by **r** Him from the dead." **Ac 17:31** *450*

RAISINS
r and two hundred cakes of figs, **1Sa 25:18** 6778
of fig cake and two clusters of **r**, **1Sa 30:12** 6778
of dates and one of **r** to each one. **2Sa 6:19** 809
of bread, a hundred clusters of **r**, **2Sa 16:1** 6778
cakes, fig cakes and bunches of **r**, **1Ch 12:40** 6778

RAKEM
and his sons *were* Ulam and **R**. **1Ch 7:16** 7552

RAKKATH
Zer and Hammath, **R** and Chinnereth, **Jos 19:35** 7557

RAKKON
and Me-jarkon and **R**, **Jos 19:46** 7542

RALLIED
with him **r** and came to the battle; **1Sa 14:20** 2199

RALLY
of the trumpet, **r** to us there. **Ne 4:20** 6908

RAM
goat, and a three year old **r**, **Gn 15:9** 352a
behind *him* a **r** caught in the **Gn 22:13** 352a
and Abraham went and took the **r** and **Gn 22:13** 352a
"You shall also take the one **r**, **Ex 29:15** 352a
their hands on the head of the **r**; **Ex 29:15** 352a
and you shall slaughter the **r** and **Ex 29:16** 352a
shall cut the **r** into its pieces, **Ex 29:17** 352a
shall offer up in smoke the whole **r** **Ex 29:18** 352a
"Then you shall take the other **r**, **Ex 29:19** 352a
their hands on the head of the **r**. **Ex 29:19** 352a
"You shall slaughter the **r**, **Ex 29:20** 352a
shall also take the fat from the **r** **Ex 29:22** 352a
(for it is a **r** of ordination), **Ex 29:22** 352a
breast of Aaron's **r** of ordination, **Ex 29:26** 352a
offered from the **r** of ordination, **Ex 29:27** 352a
You shall take the **r** of ordination **Ex 29:31** 352a
sons shall eat the flesh of the **r** and **Ex 29:32** 352a
a **r** without defect from the flock, **Lv 5:15** 352a
with the **r** of the guilt offering, **Lv 5:16** 352a
a **r** without defect from the flock, **Lv 5:18** 352a
a **r** without defect from the flock, **Lv 6:6** 352a
the **r** of the burnt offering, **Lv 8:18** 352a
their hands on the head of the **r**. **Lv 8:18** 352a
he had cut the **r** into its pieces, **Lv 8:20** 352a
Moses offered up the whole **r** in **Lv 8:21** 352a
Then he presented the second **r**, **Lv 8:22** 352a
second ram, the **r** of ordination, **Lv 8:22** 352a
their hands on the head of the **r**. **Lv 8:22** 352a
portion of the **r** of ordination, **Lv 8:29** 352a
and a **r** for a burnt offering, **Lv 9:2** 352a
an ox and a **r** for peace offerings, **Lv 9:4** 352a
he slaughtered the ox and the **r**, **Lv 9:18** 352a
of fat from the ox and from the **r**, **Lv 9:19** 352a
and a **r** for a burnt offering. **Lv 16:3** 352a
and one **r** for a burnt offering. **Lv 16:5** 352a
meeting, a **r** for a guilt offering. **Lv 19:21** 352a
make atonement for him with the **r** **Lv 19:22** 352a
besides the **r** of atonement, **Nu 5:8** 352c
one **r** without defect for a peace **Nu 6:14** 352a
'He shall also offer the **r** for a **Nu 6:17** 352a
one bull, one **r**, one male lamb one **Nu 7:15** 352a
one bull, one **r**, one male lamb one **Nu 7:21** 352a
one young bull, one **r**, **Nu 7:27** 352a
one bull, one **r**, one male lamb one **Nu 7:33** 352a
one bull, one **r**, one male lamb one **Nu 7:39** 352a
one bull, one **r**, one male lamb one **Nu 7:45** 352a
one bull, one **r**, one male lamb one **Nu 7:51** 352a
one bull, one **r**, one male lamb one **Nu 7:57** 352a
one bull, one **r**, one male lamb one **Nu 7:63** 352a
one bull, one **r**, one male lamb one **Nu 7:69** 352a
one bull, one **r**, one male lamb one **Nu 7:75** 352a
one bull, one **r**, one male lamb one **Nu 7:81** 352a
'Or for a **r** you shall prepare as a **Nu 15:6** 352a
done for each ox, or for each **r**, **Nu 15:11** 352a
Balaam offered up a bull and a **r** on **Nu 23:2** 352a
I have offered up a bull and a **r** on **Nu 23:4** 352a
offered a bull and a **r** on *each* altar. **Nu 23:14** 352a
offered up a bull and a **r** on *each* **Nu 23:30** 352a
two bulls and one **r**, **Nu 28:11** 352a
for a grain offering, for the one **r**; **Nu 28:12** 352a
and a third of a hin for the **r** **Nu 28:14** 352a
two bulls and one **r** and seven male **Nu 28:19** 352a
a bull and two-tenths for the **r**. **Nu 28:20** 352a
the LORD: two young bulls, one **r**, **Nu 28:27** 352a
bull, two-tenths for the one **r**, **Nu 28:28** 352a
one bull, one **r**, *and* seven male **Nu 29:2** 352a
for the bull, two-tenths for the **r**, **Nu 29:3** 352a
one bull, one **r**, seven male lambs **Nu 29:8** 352a
the bull, two-tenths for the one **r**, **Nu 29:9** 352a
one bull, one **r**, seven male lambs **Nu 29:36** 352a
bull, for the **r** and for the lambs, **Nu 29:37** 352a
and to Hezron was born **R**, **Ru 4:19** 7410
to Hezron was born Ram, and to **R**, **Ru 4:19** 7410
born to him *were* Jerahmeel, **R** and **1Ch 2:9** 7410
R became the father of Amminadab **1Ch 2:10** 7410
of Hezron *were* **R** the firstborn, **1Ch 2:25** 7410
The sons of **R**, the firstborn **1Ch 2:27** 7410
they offered a **r** of the flock for **Ezr 10:19** 352a
Buzite, of the family of **R** burned; **Jb 32:2** 7410
a **r** without blemish from the flock. **Ezk 43:23** 352a
young bull and a **r** from the flock, **Ezk 43:25** 352a
with a bull, an ephah with a **r** and **Ezk 45:24** 352a
blemish and a **r** without blemish; **Ezk 46:4** 352a
shall be an ephah with the **r**, **Ezk 46:5** 352a
blemish, also six lambs and a **r**, **Ezk 46:6** 352a
the bull and an ephah with the **r**, **Ezk 46:7** 352a
with a bull and an ephah with a **r**, **Ezk 46:11** 352a
a **r** which had two horns was **Da 8:3** 352a
I saw the **r** butting westward, **Da 8:4** 352a
to the **r** that had the two horns, **Da 8:6** 352a
I saw him come beside the **r**, **Da 8:7** 352a
the **r** and shattered his two horns, **Da 8:7** 352a
and the **r** had no strength to **Da 8:7** 352a
to rescue the **r** from his power. **Da 8:7** 352a
"The **r** which you saw with the two **Da 8:20** 352a
and Hezron the father of **R**. **Mt 1:3** *689*
R was the father of Amminadab, **Mt 1:4** *689*
the son of Admin, the son of **R**, **Lk 3:33** *689*

RAMAH
Gibeon and **R** and Beeroth, **Jos 18:25** 7414
as Baalath-beer, **R** of the Negev. **Jos 19:8** 7437b
The border turned to **R** and **Jos 19:29** 7414
and Adamah and **R** and Hazor, **Jos 19:36** 7414
palm tree of Deborah between **R** and **Jg 4:5** 7414
spend the night in Gibeah or **R**." **Jg 19:13** 7414
again to their house in **R**. **1Sa 1:19** 7414
Elkanah went to his home at **R**. **1Sa 2:11** 7414
Then his return *was* to **R**, **1Sa 7:17** 7414
together and came to Samuel at **R**; **1Sa 8:4** 7414
Then Samuel went to **R**, **1Sa 15:34** 7414
And Samuel arose and went to **R**. **1Sa 16:13** 7414
escaped and came to Samuel at **R**, **1Sa 19:18** 7414
"Behold, David is at Naioth in **R**." **1Sa 19:19** 7414
Then he himself went to **R** and **1Sa 19:22** 7414
"Behold, they are at Naioth in **R**." **1Sa 19:22** 7414
He proceeded there to Naioth in **R**; **1Sa 19:23** 7414
until he came to Naioth in **R**. **1Sa 19:23** 7414
Then David fled from Naioth in **R**, **1Sa 20:1** 7414
and buried him at his house in **R**. **1Sa 25:1** 7414
and buried him in **R**, his own city. **1Sa 28:3** 7414
went up against Judah and fortified **R** **1Ki 15:17** 7414
of it, he ceased fortifying **R** **1Ki 15:21** 7414
they carried away the stones of **R** **1Ki 15:22** 7414
had inflicted on him at **R** when **2Ki 8:29** 7414
up against Judah and fortified **R** **2Ch 16:1** 7414
he ceased fortifying **R** and stopped **2Ch 16:5** 7414
they carried away the stones of **R** **2Ch 16:6** 7414
they had inflicted on him at **R**, **2Ch 22:6** 7414
the sons of **R** and Geba, 621; **Ezr 2:26** 7414
the men of **R** and Geba, 621; **Ne 7:30** 7414
Hazor, **R**, Gittaim, **Ne 11:33** 7414
R is terrified, and Gibeah of Saul **Is 10:29** 7414
"A voice is heard in **R**, **Jer 31:15** 7414
bodyguard had released him from **R**, **Jer 40:1** 7414
horn in Gibeah, The trumpet in **R**. **Hos 5:8** 7414
"A VOICE WAS HEARD IN **R**, **Mt 2:18** *4471*

RAMATHAIM-ZOPHIM
there was a certain man from **R** **1Sa 1:1** 7436

RAMATHITE
the **R** had charge of the vineyards; **1Ch 27:27** 7435

RAMATH-LEHI
and he named that place **R**. **Jg 15:17** 7437a

RAMATH-MIZPEH
Heshbon as far as **R** and Betonim, **Jos 13:26** 7434

RAMESES
best of the land, in the land of **R**, **Gn 47:11** 7486
journeyed from **R** to Succoth, **Ex 12:37** 7486
They journeyed from **R** in the first **Nu 33:3** 7486
sons of Israel journeyed from **R** and **Nu 33:5** 7486

RAMIAH
the sons of Parosh *there were* **R**, **Ezr 10:25** 7422

RAMOTH
and **R** in Gilead for the Gadites, **Dt 4:43** 7216
and **R** in Gilead from the tribe of **Jos 20:8** 7216
of Gad, *they gave* **R** in Gilead, **Jos 21:38** 7216
those who were in **R** of the Negev, **1Sa 30:27** 7418
and **R** with its pasture lands, Anem **1Ch 6:73** 7216
R in Gilead with its pasture **1Ch 6:80** 7216

RAMOTH-GILEAD
Ben-geber, in **R** **1Ki 4:13** 7433
"Do you know that **R** belongs to us, **1Ki 22:3** 7433
you go with me to battle at **R**?" **1Ki 22:4** 7433
"Shall I go against **R** to battle or **1Ki 22:6** 7433
"Go up to **R** and prosper, for the **1Ki 22:12** 7433
shall we go to **R** to battle, **1Ki 22:15** 7433
entice Ahab to go up and fall at **R**?' **1Ki 22:20** 7433
king of Judah went up against **R**. **1Ki 22:29** 7433
against Hazael king of Aram at **R**, **2Ki 8:28** 7433
of oil in your hand and go to **R**. **2Ki 9:1** 7433
servant of the prophet, went to **R**. **2Ki 9:4** 7433
was defending **R** against Hazael **2Ki 9:14** 7433
induced him to go up against **R**. **2Ch 18:2** 7433
"Will you go with me *against* **R**?" **2Ch 18:3** 7433
"Shall we go against **R** to battle, **2Ch 18:5** 7433
"Go up to **R** and succeed, for the **2Ch 18:11** 7433
shall we go to **R** to battle, **2Ch 18:14** 7433
of Israel to go up and fall at **R**?' **2Ch 18:19** 7433
king of Judah went up against **R**. **2Ch 18:28** 7433
against Hazael king of Aram at **R**. **2Ch 22:5** 7433

RAMP
and they cast up a siege **r** against **2Sa 20:15** 5550
with a shield or throw up a siege **r** **2Ki 19:32** 5550
or throw up a siege **r** against it. **Is 37:33** 5550
build a siege wall, raise up a **r**, **Ezk 4:2** 5550
cast up a **r** against you and raise up **Ezk 26:8** 5550
cast up a siege **r** and capture a **Da 11:15** 5550

RAMPART
the city, and it stood by the **r**; **2Sa 20:15** 2426
has caused **r** and wall to lament; **La 2:8** 2426
her, Whose **r** *was* the sea, **Na 3:8** 2426
post And station myself on the **r**; **Hab 2:1** 4692

RAMPARTS
Consider her **r**; Go through her **Ps 48:13** 2426
sets up walls and **r** for security. **Is 26:1** 2426

RAMPS
'Behold, the siege **r** have reached **Jer 32:24** 5550
make a defense against the siege **r** **Jer 33:4** 5550
when they cast up **r** and build siege **Ezk 17:17** 5550
to cast up **r**, to build a siege wall. **Ezk 21:22** 5550

RAM'S
the **r** horn sounds a long blast, **Ex 19:13** 3104
'You shall then sound a **r** horn **Lv 25:9** 7782
The priest shall take the **r** shoulder **Nu 6:19** 352a
make a long blast with the **r** horn, **Jos 6:5** 3104

RAMS
have I eaten the **r** of your flocks. **Gn 31:38** 352a
two hundred ewes and twenty **r**, **Gn 32:14** 352a
bull and two **r** without blemish, **Ex 29:1** 352a
along with the bull and the two **r**. **Ex 29:3** 352a
and the two **r** and the basket of **Lv 8:2** 352a
and a bull of the herd and two **r**; **Lv 23:18** 352a
peace offerings, two oxen, five **r**, **Nu 7:17** 352a
peace offerings, two oxen, five **r**, **Nu 7:23** 352a
peace offerings, two oxen, five **r**, **Nu 7:29** 352a
peace offerings, two oxen, five **r**, **Nu 7:35** 352a
peace offerings, two oxen, five **r**, **Nu 7:41** 352a
peace offerings, two oxen, five **r**, **Nu 7:47** 352a
peace offerings, two oxen, five **r**, **Nu 7:53** 352a
peace offerings, two oxen, five **r**, **Nu 7:59** 352a
peace offerings, two oxen, five **r**, **Nu 7:65** 352a
peace offerings, two oxen, five **r**, **Nu 7:71** 352a
peace offerings, two oxen, five **r**, **Nu 7:77** 352a
peace offerings, two oxen, five **r**, **Nu 7:83** 352a
twelve bulls, *all* the **r** twelve, **Nu 7:87** 352a
offerings 24 bulls, *all* the **r** 60, **Nu 7:88** 352a
prepare seven bulls and seven **r** **Nu 23:1** 352a
prepare seven bulls and seven **r** **Nu 23:29** 352a
thirteen bulls, two **r**, **Nu 29:13** 352a
two-tenths for each of the two **r**, **Nu 29:14** 352a
twelve bulls, two **r**, **Nu 29:17** 352a
for the **r** and for the lambs, **Nu 29:18** 352a
eleven bulls, two **r**, **Nu 29:20** 352a
for the **r** and for the lambs, **Nu 29:21** 352a
ten bulls, two **r**, fourteen male **Nu 29:23** 352a
for the **r** and for the lambs, **Nu 29:24** 352a
nine bulls, two **r**, fourteen male **Nu 29:26** 352a
for the **r** and for the lambs, **Nu 29:27** 352a
eight bulls, two **r**, **Nu 29:29** 352a
for the **r** and for the lambs, **Nu 29:30** 352a
seven bulls, two **r**, **Nu 29:32** 352a
for the **r** and for the lambs, **Nu 29:33** 352a
flock, With fat of lambs, And **r**, **Dt 32:14** 352a
And to heed than the fat of **r**. **1Sa 15:22** 352a
lambs and the wool of 100,000 **r**. **2Ki 3:4** 352a
sacrificed seven bulls and seven **r**. **1Ch 15:26** 352a
bulls, 1,000 **r** *and* 1,000 lambs, **1Ch 29:21** 352a
with a young bull and seven **r**, **2Ch 13:9** 352a
7,700 **r** and 7,700 male goats. **2Ch 17:11** 352a
They brought seven bulls, seven **r**, **2Ch 29:21** 352a
They also slaughtered the **r** and **2Ch 29:22** 352a
brought was 70 bulls, 100 **r**, **2Ch 29:32** 352a
is needed, both young bulls, **r**, **Ezr 6:9** 1798
temple of God 100 bulls, 200 **r**, **Ezr 6:17** 1798
you shall diligently buy bulls, **r** and **Ezr 7:17** 1798
12 bulls for all Israel, 96 **r**, **Ezr 8:35** 352a
seven bulls and seven **r**, **Jb 42:8** 352a
fat beasts, With the smoke of **r**; **Ps 66:15** 352a
The mountains skipped like **r**, **Ps 114:4** 352a
O mountains, that you skip like **r**? **Ps 114:6** 352a
enough of burnt offerings of **r** And **Is 1:11** 352a

With the fat of the kidneys of **r**. **Is 34:6** 352a
The **r** of Nebaioth will minister to **Is 60:7** 352a
Like **r** together with male goats. **Jer 51:40** 352a
battering **r** against it all around. **Ezk 4:2** 3733c
'Jerusalem,' to set battering **r**, **Ezk 21:22** 3733c
set battering **r** against the gates, **Ezk 21:22** 3733c
"The blow of his battering **r** **Ezk 26:9** 6904
were your customers for lambs, **r** and **Ezk 27:21** 352a
between the **r** and the male goats. **Ezk 34:17** 352a
the earth, as *though they were* **r**, **Ezk 39:18** 352a
and seven **r** without blemish **Ezk 45:23** 352a
take delight in thousands of **r**, **Mi 6:7** 352a

RAMS'
r skins dyed red, porpoise skins, **Ex 25:5** 352a
covering for the tent of **r** skins **Ex 26:14** 352a
and **r** skins dyed red, and porpoise **Ex 35:7** 352a
linen and goats' *hair* and **r** skins **Ex 35:23** 352a
a covering for the tent of **r** skins **Ex 36:19** 352a
and the covering of **r** skins dyed **Ex 39:34** 352a
carry seven trumpets of **r** horns **Jos 6:4** 3104
carry seven trumpets of **r** horns **Jos 6:6** 3104
the seven trumpets of **r** horns **Jos 6:8** 3104
the seven trumpets of **r** horns **Jos 6:13** 3104

RAN
he **r** from the tent door to meet **Gn 18:2** 7323
Abraham also **r** to the herd, and **Gn 18:7** 7323
Then the servant **r** to meet her, **Gn 24:17** 7323
and **r** back to the well to draw, **Gn 24:20** 7323
Then the girl **r** and told her **Gn 24:28** 7323
and Laban **r** outside to the man at **Gn 24:29** 7323
and she **r** and told her father. **Gn 29:12** 7323
son, he **r** to meet him, **Gn 29:13** 7323
r to meet him and embraced him, **Gn 33:4** 7323
and fire **r** down to the earth. **Ex 9:23** 1980
man **r** and told Moses and said, **Nu 11:27** 7323
and **r** into the midst of the assembly **Nu 16:47** 7323
and they **r** to the tent; **Jos 7:22** 7323
they **r** and entered the city and **Jos 8:19** 7323
The border of Manasseh **r** from **Jos 17:7** 1961
r from the ascent of Akrabbim, **Jg 1:36**
and all the army **r**, **Jg 7:21** 7323
r quickly and told her husband, **Jg 13:10** 7323
Then he **r** to Eli and said, **1Sa 3:5** 7323
Now a man of Benjamin **r** from the **1Sa 4:12** 7323
So they **r** and took him from there, **1Sa 10:23** 7323
and **r** to the battle line and **1Sa 17:22** 7323
that David **r** quickly toward the **1Sa 17:48** 7323
Then David **r** and stood over the **1Sa 17:51** 7323
the Cushite bowed to Joab and **r**. **2Sa 18:21** 7323
Then Ahimaaz **r** by way of the plain **2Sa 18:23** 7323
two of the servants of Shimei **r** away **1Ki 2:39** 1272
afraid and arose and **r** for his life **1Ki 19:3** 1980
He left the oxen and **r** after Elijah **1Ki 19:20** 7323
and the blood from the wound **r** **1Ki 22:35** 3332
It **r** in the dry places *like* a river. **Ps 105:41** 1980
not send *these* prophets, But they **r**. **Jer 23:21** 7323
And the living beings **r** to and fro **Ezk 1:14** 7519
they **r** away to hide themselves. **Da 10:7** 1272
The herdsmen **r** away, **Mt 8:33** *5343*
Immediately one of them **r**, **Mt 27:48** *5143*
r to report it to His disciples. **Mt 28:8** *5143*
he **r** up and bowed down before Him; **Mk 5:6** *5143*
Their herdsmen **r** away and **Mk 5:14** *5343*
and **r** there together on foot **Mk 6:33** *4936*
and **r** about that whole country and **Mk 6:55** *4063*
a man **r** up to Him and knelt before **Mk 10:17** *4370*
Someone **r** and filled a sponge **Mk 15:36** *5143*
they **r** away and reported it in the **Lk 8:34** *5343*
for him, and **r** and embraced him and **Lk 15:20** *5143*
So he **r** on ahead and climbed up **Lk 19:4** *4390*
But Peter got up and **r** to the tomb; **Lk 24:12** *5143*
When the wine **r** out, the mother of **Jn 2:3** *5302*
So she **r** and came to Simon Peter **Jn 20:2** *5143*
other disciple **r** ahead faster than **Jn 20:4** *4390*
all the people **r** together to them **Ac 3:11** *4936*
Philip **r** up and heard him reading **Ac 8:30** *4370*
but **r** in and announced that Peter **Ac 12:14** *1532*
we **r** a straight course to **Ac 16:11** *2113*
we **r** a straight course to Cos and **Ac 21:1** *2113*
centurions and **r** down to them; **Ac 21:32** *2701*
met, they **r** the vessel aground; **Ac 27:41** *1946a*

RANDOM
a certain man drew his bow at **r** **1Ki 22:34** 8537
A certain man drew his bow at **r** **2Ch 18:33** 8537

RANGE
All beasts which **r** in herds; **Zph 2:14**
eyes of the LORD which **r** to and fro **Zch 4:10** 7751a

RANK
Of the three in the second **r** he **1Ch 11:21**
their relatives of the second **r**, **1Ch 15:18** 4932
vanity and men of **r** are a lie; **Ps 62:9** 376
after me has a higher **r** than I, **Jn 1:15** *1715*
a Man who has a higher **r** than I, **Jn 1:30** *1715*

RANKS
and shouted to the **r** of Israel and **1Sa 17:8** 4634
"I defy the **r** of Israel this day; **1Sa 17:10** 4634
the **r** of the Philistines?" **1Sa 23:3** 4634
was opposite window in three **r**. **1Ki 7:4** 6471
was opposite window in three **r**. **1Ki 7:5** 6471
whoever comes within the **r** shall be **2Ki 11:8** 7713
"Bring her out between the **r**, **2Ki 11:15** 7713
"Bring her out between the **r**, **2Ch 23:14** 7713
king, Yet all of them go out in **r**; **Pr 30:27** 2686a
there is no straggler in his **r**. **Is 14:31** 4151
the defenses, They do not break **r**. **Jl 2:8** 1214

RANSACKED
"O how Esau will be **r**, **Ob 1:6** 2664

RANSOM
"If a **r** is demanded of him, then **Ex 21:30** 3724a
give a **r** for himself to the LORD, **Ex 30:12** 3724a
For the **r** of the 273 of the firstborn **Nu 3:46** 6299
the **r** of those who are in excess **Nu 3:48** 6302b
So Moses took the **r** money from **Nu 3:49** 6302b
Then Moses gave the **r** money to **Nu 3:51** 6299
you shall not take **r** for the life **Nu 35:31** 3724a
'You shall not take **r** for him **Nu 35:32** 3724a
down to the pit, I have found a **r**'; **Jb 33:24** 3724a
greatness of the **r** turn you aside. **Jb 36:18** 3724a
Or give to God a **r** for him **Ps 49:7** 3724a
R me because of my enemies! **Ps 69:18** 6299
He will not accept any **r**, **Pr 6:35** 3724a
r of a man's life is his wealth, **Pr 13:8** 3724a
wicked is a **r** for the righteous, **Pr 21:18** 3724a
I have given Egypt as your **r**, **Is 43:3** 3724a
My hand so short that it cannot **r**? **Is 50:2** 6304
r them from the power of Sheol? **Hos 13:14** 6299
to give His life a **r** for many." **Mt 20:28** *3083*
to give His life a **r** for many." **Mk 10:45** *3083*
who gave Himself as a **r** for all, **1Tm 2:6** *487*

RANSOMED
set apart among men shall be **r**; **Lv 27:29** 6299
beyond those **r** by the Levites; **Nu 3:49** 6299
You have **r** me, O LORD, God of **Ps 31:5** 6299
And the **r** of the LORD will return And **Is 35:10** 6299
So the **r** of the LORD will return And **Is 51:11** 6299
For the LORD has **r** Jacob And **Jer 31:11** 6299
r you from the house of slavery, **Mi 6:4** 6299

RAPED
they **r** her and abused her all night **Jg 19:25** 3045

RAPHA
Nohah the fourth and **R** the fifth. **1Ch 8:2** 7498a

RAPHAH
R *was* his son, Eleasah his son, **1Ch 8:37** 7504a

RAPHU
of Benjamin, Palti the son of **R**; **Nu 13:9** 7505

RAPIDLY
plans, Feet that run **r** to evil, **Pr 6:18** 4116
saw that a crowd was **r** gathering, **Mk 9:25** *1998*
the word of the Lord will spread **r** **2Th 3:1** *5143*

RARE
word from the LORD was **r** in those **1Sa 3:1** 3368

RARELY
foot **r** be in your neighbor's house, **Pr 25:17** 3365

RASCALLY
A **r** witness makes a mockery of **Pr 19:28** 1100

RASH
vows or the **r** statement of her lips **Nu 30:6** 4008
r statement of her lips by which she **Nu 30:8** 4008
Therefore my words have been **r**. **Jb 6:3** 3886b
to keep calm and to do nothing **r**. **Ac 19:36** *4312*

RASHLY
Spirit, He spoke **r** with his lips. **Ps 106:33** 981
one who speaks **r** like the thrusts of **Pr 12:18** 981
It is a trap for a man to say **r**, **Pr 20:25** 3886b

RATHER
water, but **r** roasted with fire, **Ex 12:9** 3588, 518
"But **r**, you are to tear down **Ex 34:13**
but **r** he is to marry a virgin of **Lv 21:14** 3588, 518
but **r** will go to my *own* land and **Nu 10:30** 3588, 518
but **r** the anger of the LORD and **Dt 29:20** 3588, 227
r I indeed come now *as* captain of **Jos 5:14** 3588
r it shall be a witness between us **Jos 22:27** 3588
r it is a witness between us and **Jos 22:28** 3588
or **r** these years, and I have **1Sa 29:3**
R he took the poor man's ewe lamb **2Sa 12:4**
but **r** let us fight against them in **1Ki 20:23** 199
Death **r** than my pains. **Jb 7:15** 4480
I would **r** stand at the threshold **Ps 84:10**
knowledge **r** than choicest gold. **Pr 8:10** 4480
cubs, **R** than a fool in his folly. **Pr 17:12** 408
and draw near to listen **r** than to **Ec 5:1** 4480
there is emptiness. **R**, fear God. **Ec 5:7** 3588
r it is its purpose to destroy And **Is 10:7** 3588
R you have burdened Me with your **Is 43:24** 389
her heart, but **r** in deception," **Jer 3:10** 3588, 518
And death will be chosen **r** than life **Jer 8:3** 4480
R I am going to make an end of **Jer 14:12** 3588
but **r** the valley of Slaughter. **Jer 19:6** 3588, 518
called you, but **r** Magor-missabib. **Jer 20:3** 3588, 518
this people but **r** their harm." **Jer 38:4** 3588, 518
but **r** deal with him just as he **Jer 39:12** 3588, 518
"But **r** we will certainly carry **Jer 44:17** 3588, 518
tumult **r** than joyful shouting **Ezk 7:7** 3808
R you were thrown out into the **Ezk 16:5**
"**r** than that he should turn from **Ezk 18:23** 3808
them **r** than destroying them, **Ezk 20:17** 4480
but **r** that the wicked turn from **Ezk 33:11** 3588, 518
but **r** the shepherds fed **Ezk 34:8**
came forth a **r** small horn which grew **Da 8:9**
I delight in loyalty **r** than sacrifice, **Hos 6:6** 3808
of God **r** than burnt offerings. **Hos 6:6** 4480
But **r** for hearing the words of the **Am 8:11** 3588, 518
filled with disgrace **r** than honor. **Hab 2:16** 4480
but **r** go to the lost sheep of the **Mt 10:6** *3123*
but **r** fear Him who is able to **Mt 10:28** *3123*
but **r** that a riot was starting, **Mt 27:24** *3123*
at all, but **r** had grown worse **Mk 5:26** *3123*
I tell you, no, but **r** division; **Lk 12:51** *2228*
house justified **r** than the other; **Lk 18:14** *3844*
the darkness **r** than the Light **Jn 3:19** *3123*
of men **r** than the approval of God. **Jn 12:43** *3123*
to give heed to you **r** than to God, **Ac 4:19** *3123*
"We must obey God **r** than men. **Ac 5:29** *3123*
the creature **r** than the Creator, **Ro 1:25** *3844*
R, let God be found true, though **Ro 3:4** *1161*
R it was sin, in order that it **Ro 7:13** *235*
who died, yes, **r** who was raised, **Ro 8:34** *3123*
but **r** determine this **Ro 14:13** *3123*
Why not **r** be wronged? **1Co 6:7** *3123*
Why not **r** be defrauded? **1Co 6:7** *3123*
also to become free, **r** do that. **1Co 7:21** *3123*
r than ten thousand words in a **1Co 14:19** *2228*
should **r** forgive and comfort *him,* **2Co 2:7** *3123*
prefer **r** to be absent from the body **2Co 5:8** *3123*
will **r** boast about my weaknesses, **2Co 12:9** *3123*
but **r** to one, "And to your seed," **Ga 3:16**
know God, or **r** to be known by God, **Ga 4:9** *3123*
but **r** he must labor, performing **Eph 4:28** *3123*
fitting, but **r** giving of thanks. **Eph 5:4** *3123*
r than from pure motives, **Php 1:17** *3756*
world, **r** than according to Christ. **Col 2:8** *3756*
as for the Lord **r** than for men, **Col 3:23** *3756*
r than *furthering* the administration **1Tm 1:4** *3123*
but **r** by means of good works, as **1Tm 2:10** *235*
but **r** in speech, conduct, love, **1Tm 4:12**
but **r** appeal to *him* as a **1Tm 5:1**
of pleasure **r** than lovers of God, **2Tm 3:4** *3123*
yet for love's sake I **r** appeal *to* **Phm 1:9** *3123*
choosing **r** to endure ill-treatment **Heb 11:25** *3123*
shall we not much **r** be subject to **Heb 12:9** *3123*
put out of joint, but **r** be healed. **Heb 12:13** *3123*
r than for doing what is wrong. **1Pe 3:17** *2228*

RATIFIED
covenant, yet when it has been **r**, **Ga 3:15** *2964*
a covenant previously **r** by God, **Ga 3:17** *4300*

RATION
gave him a **r** and a gift and let him **Jer 40:5** 737
a daily **r** from the king's choice food **Da 1:5** 1697

RATIONED
bring back your bread in **r** amounts, **Lv 26:26** 4948

RATIONS
against you and diminished your **r**. **Ezk 16:27** 2706
them their **r** at the proper time? **Lk 12:42** *4620*

RATTLES
"The quiver **r** against him, The **Jb 39:23** 7439

RATTLING
He laughs at the **r** of the javelin. **Jb 41:29** 7494
was a noise, and behold, a **r**; **Ezk 37:7** 7494
The noise of the **r** of the wheel, **Na 3:2** 7494

RAVAGE
and the famine will **r** the land. **Gn 41:30** 3615
of your mice that **r** the land, **1Sa 6:5** 7843

RAVAGED
and He **r** them and smote them with **1Sa 5:6** 8074
r the land of the sons of Ammon, **1Ch 20:1** 7843

RAVAGES
Rescue my soul from their **r**, **Ps 35:17** 7722

RAVAGING
But Saul *began* **r** the church, **Ac 8:3** *3075*

RAVED
he **r** in the midst of the house, **1Sa 18:10** 5012
they **r** until the time of the **1Ki 18:29** 5012

RAVEN
and he sent out a **r**, **Gn 8:7** 6158
every **r** in its kind, **Lv 11:15** 6158
and every **r** in its kind, **Dt 14:14** 6158
prepares for the **r** its nourishment When **Jb 38:41** 6158
of dates *And* black as a **r**. **SS 5:11** 6158
And owl and **r** will dwell in it; **Is 34:11** 6158

RAVENING
at me, As a **r** and a roaring lion. **Ps 22:13** 2963

RAVENOUS
"Benjamin is a **r** wolf; **Gn 49:27** 2963
but inwardly are **r** wolves. **Mt 7:15** *727*

RAVENS
commanded the **r** to provide for you **1Ki 17:4** 6158
The **r** brought him bread and **1Ki 17:6** 6158
And to the young **r** which cry. **Ps 147:9** 6158
The **r** of the valley will pick it **Pr 30:17** 6158
"Consider the **r**, for they neither **Lk 12:24** *2876*

RAVINE
So I went up at night by the **r** and **Ne 2:15** 5158a
"Among the smooth *stones* of the **r** **Is 57:6** 5158a
myrtle trees which were in the **r**, **Zch 1:8** 4699
'EVERY **R** WILL BE FILLED, AND **Lk 3:5** *5327*
over the **r** of the Kidron, **Jn 18:1** *5493*

RAVINES
come and settle on the steep **r**, **Is 7:19** 5158a
slaughter the children in the **r**, **Is 57:5** 5158a
the hills, the **r** and the valleys: **Ezk 6:3** 650
broken in all the **r** of the land. **Ezk 31:12** 650
And the **r** will be full of you. **Ezk 32:6** 650
in all your **r** those slain by the sword **Ezk 35:8** 650
to the **r** and to the valleys, **Ezk 36:4** 650
to the **r** and to the valleys, **Ezk 36:6** 650

RAVISH
bring them out that you may **r** them **Jg 19:24** 6031a

RAVISHED
r my concubine so that she died. **Jg 20:5** 6031a
be plundered And their wives **r**. **Is 13:16** 7693
They **r** the women in Zion, The **La 5:11** 6031a
the houses plundered, the women **r** and **Zch 14:2** 7693

RAW
'Do not eat any of it **r** or boiled **Ex 12:9** 4995
is quick **r** flesh in the swelling, **Lv 13:10** 2416a
whenever **r** flesh appears on him, **Lv 13:14** 2416a
priest shall look at the **r** flesh, **Lv 13:15** 2416a
the **r** flesh is unclean, it is **Lv 13:15** 2416a
"Or if the **r** flesh turns again **Lv 13:16** 2416a
and the **r** *flesh* of the burn **Lv 13:24** 4241
boiled meat from you, only **r**." **1Sa 2:15** 2416a
Only bruises, welts and **r** wounds, **Is 1:6** 2961

RAYS
He has **r** *flashing* from His hand, **Hab 3:4** 7161
lamp illumines you with its **r**." **Lk 11:36** *796*

RAZE
"**R** it, raze it To its very foundation **Ps 137:7** 6168
"Raze it, **r** it To its very foundation **Ps 137:7** 6168

RAZED
then he **r** the city and sowed it **Jg 9:45** 5422
of Babylon will be completely **r** And **Jer 51:58** 6209

RAZOR
no **r** shall pass over his head. **Nu 6:5** 8593
use a **r** over their whole body and **Nu 8:7** 8593
and no **r** shall come upon his head, **Jg 13:5** 4177a
"A **r** has never come on my head, **Jg 16:17** 4177a
r shall never come on his head." **1Sa 1:11** 4177a
destruction, Like a sharp **r**, **Ps 52:2** 8593
day the Lord will shave with a **r**, **Is 7:20** 8593
barber's **r** on your head and beard. **Ezk 5:1** 8593

REACH
and a tower whose top *will* **r** into **Gn 11:4**
net will **r** halfway up the altar. **Ex 27:5** 1961
they shall **r** from the loins even **Ex 28:42** 1961
and it shall **r** Hazaraddar and **Nu 34:4** 3318
the border shall go down and **r** to the **Nu 34:11** 4229b
for you, nor is it out of **r**. **Dt 30:11** 7350
let him **r** the lame and the blind, **2Sa 5:8** 5060
great waters they will not **r** him. **Ps 32:6** 5060
Nor do they **r** the paths of life. **Pr 2:19** 5381
And strokes **r** the innermost parts. **Pr 20:30**
It will **r** even to the neck; **Is 8:8** 5060
will not **r** us when it passes by, **Is 28:15** 935
may **r** to the end of the earth." **Is 49:6** 1961
does not **r** the age of one hundred **Is 65:20** 2398
of the mountains will **r** to Azel; **Zch 14:5** 5060
and the third *day* I **r** My goal.' **Lk 13:32** *5048*
"**R** here with your finger, and see My **Jn 20:27** *5342*
and **r** here your hand and put it **Jn 20:27** *5342*
if somehow they could **r** Phoenix, **Ac 27:12** *2658*
measure, to **r** even as far as you. **2Co 10:13** *2185*
as if we did not **r** to you, **2Co 10:14** *2185*

REACHED
But the men **r** out their hands and **Gn 19:10** 7971
about, when Joseph **r** his brothers, **Gn 37:23** 935
"When you **r** this place, Sihon the **Dt 29:7** 935
families **r** the border of Edom, **Jos 15:1** 1961
then **r** Jericho and came out at the **Jos 16:7** 6293
and they **r** to Asher on the north **Jos 17:10** 6293
and **r** to the brook that is before **Jos 19:11** 6293
The border **r** to Tabor and **Jos 19:22** 6293
and it **r** to Carmel on the west and **Jos 19:26** 6293
to Beth-dagon and **r** to Zebulun, **Jos 19:27** 6293
and it **r** to Zebulun on the south **Jos 19:34** 6293
"She **r** out her hand for the tent peg, **Jg 5:26** 7971
so he **r** out and took it and killed **Jg 15:15** 7971, 3027
When the lad **r** the place of the **1Sa 20:37** 935
Uzzah **r** out toward the ark of God **2Sa 6:6** 7971
Now when David **r** old age, he made **1Ch 23:1** 2204
Jehoiada **r** a ripe old age he died; **2Ch 24:15** 2204
in a rage *which* has even **r** heaven. **2Ch 28:9** 5060
r to the kingdoms of the idols, **Is 10:10** 4672
And my hand **r** to the riches of the **Is 10:14** 4672
choice clusters Which **r** as far as Jazer **Is 16:8** 5060
ramps have **r** the city to take it; **Jer 32:24** 935
sea, They **r** to the sea of Jazer; **Jer 48:32** 5060
For her judgment has **r** to heaven **Jer 51:9** 5060
We have **r** *it,* we have seen *it.*" **La 2:16** 4672
and **r** the age for fine ornaments; **Ezk 16:7** 935
and it was **r** by seven steps, and **Ezk 40:22** 5927
And its height **r** to the sky, **Da 4:11** 4291
whose height **r** to the sky and was **Da 4:20** 4291
majesty has become great and **r** to **Da 4:22** 4291
and they had not **r** the bottom of **Da 6:24** 4291
the word **r** the king of Nineveh, **Jon 3:6** 5060
It has **r** the gate of my people, **Mi 1:9** 5060
one of those who were with Jesus **r** **Mt 26:51** *1614*
sound of your greeting **r** my ears, **Lk 1:44** *1096*
The news about them **r** the ears **Ac 11:22** *191*
When they **r** Salamis, they **Ac 13:5** *1096*
the majority **r** a decision to put **Ac 27:12** *5087*
of your obedience has **r** to all; **Ro 16:19** *864*
has **r** the ears of the Lord of Sabaoth. **Jas 5:4** *1525*

REACHES
even to Nophah, Which **r** to Medeba." **Nu 21:30**
his loftiness **r** the heavens, **Jb 20:6** 5927
"The sword that **r** him cannot avail, **Jb 41:26** 5381
Your faithfulness **r** to the skies. **Ps 36:5**
For Your righteousness, O God, **r** **Ps 71:19**
And Your truth **r** to the skies. **Ps 108:4**
When the report **r** Egypt, They **Is 23:5**
torrent, Which **r** to the neck, **Is 30:28** 2673

REACHING
earth with its top **r** to heaven; **Gn 28:12** 5060
under its ledge, **r** halfway up. **Ex 38:4** 5704
water **r** the ankles. **Ezk 47:3**
water **r** the knees. Again he **Ezk 47:4**
water **r** the loins. **Ezk 47:4**
and **r** forward to what *lies* ahead, **Php 3:13** *1901*
clothed in a robe **r** to the feet, **Rv 1:13** *4158*

READ
took the book of the covenant and **r** **Ex 24:7** 7121
r it all the days of his life, **Dt 17:19** 7121
you shall **r** this law in front of **Dt 31:11** 7121
he **r** all the words of the law, **Jos 8:34** 7121
which Joshua did not **r** before all the **Jos 8:35** 7121
the king of Israel **r** the letter, **2Ki 5:7** 7121
hand of the messengers and **r** it, **2Ki 19:14** 7121
gave the book to Shaphan who **r** it. **2Ki 22:8** 7121
And Shaphan **r** it in the presence **2Ki 22:10** 7121
which the king of Judah has **r**. **2Ki 22:16** 7121
and he **r** in their hearing all the **2Ki 23:2** 7121
And Shaphan **r** from it in the **2Ch 34:18** 7121
in the book which they have **r** in the **2Ch 34:24** 7121
and he **r** in their hearing all the **2Ch 34:30** 7121
been translated and **r** before me. **Ezr 4:18** 7123
King Artaxerxes' document was **r** **Ezr 4:23** 7123
He **r** from it before the square **Ne 8:3** 7121
They **r** from the book, from the **Ne 8:8** 7121
He **r** from the book of the law **Ne 8:18** 7121
they **r** from the book of the law of **Ne 9:3** 7121
On that day they **r** aloud from the **Ne 13:1** 7121
and they were **r** before the king. **Es 6:1** 7121
who is literate, saying, "Please **r** this, **Is 29:11** 7121
is illiterate, saying, "Please **r** this." **Is 29:12** 7121
And he will say, "I cannot **r**." **Is 29:12** 3045, 5612
from the book of the LORD, and **r**: **Is 34:16** 7121
hand of the messengers and **r** it, **Is 37:14** 7121
Zephaniah the priest **r** this **Jer 29:29** 7121
"So you go and **r** from the scroll **Jer 36:6** 7121
And also you shall **r** them to all **Jer 36:6** 7121
Then Baruch **r** from the book the **Jer 36:10** 7121
when Baruch **r** from the book to the **Jer 36:13** 7121
from which you have **r** to the people **Jer 36:14** 7121
"Sit down, please, and **r** it to us." **Jer 36:15** 7121
So Baruch **r** it to them. **Jer 36:15** 7121
And Jehudi **r** it to the king as **Jer 36:21** 7121
Jehudi had **r** three or four columns, **Jer 36:23** 7121
see that you **r** all these words aloud, **Jer 51:61** 7121
"Any man who can **r** this **Da 5:7** 7123
but they could not **r** the inscription **Da 5:8** 7123
that they might **r** this inscription **Da 5:15** 7123
if you are able to **r** the inscription **Da 5:16** 7123
I will **r** the inscription to the **Da 5:17** 7123
"Have you not **r** what David did when **Mt 12:3** *314*
"Or have you not **r** in the Law, **Mt 12:5** *314*
"Have you not **r** that He who **Mt 19:4** *314*
have you never **r**, **Mt 21:16** *314*
"Did you never **r** in the Scriptures, **Mt 21:42** *314*
have you not **r** what was **Mt 22:31** *314*
the charge against Him which **r**, **Mt 27:37** *1125*
"Have you never **r** what David did **Mk 2:25** *314*
"Have you not even **r** this Scripture: **Mk 12:10** *314*
you not **r** in the book of Moses, **Mk 12:26** *314*
of the charge against Him **r**, **Mk 15:26** *1924*
on the Sabbath, and stood up to **r**. **Lk 4:16** *314*
"Have you not even **r** what David **Lk 6:3** *314*
How does it **r** to you?" **Lk 10:26** *314*
Therefore many of the Jews **r** **Jn 19:20** *314*
which are **r** every Sabbath, **Ac 13:27** *314*
since he is **r** in the synagogues **Ac 15:21** *314*
When they had **r** it, **Ac 15:31** *314*
When he had **r** it, he asked **Ac 23:34** *314*
than what you **r** and understand, **2Co 1:13** *314*
hearts, known and **r** by all men; **2Co 3:2** *314*
to this day whenever Moses is **r**, **2Co 3:15** *314*
when you **r** you can understand my **Eph 3:4** *314*
When this letter is **r** among you, **Col 4:16** *314*
have it also **r** in the church of **Col 4:16** *314*
for your part **r** my letter *that is* **Col 4:16** *314*
have this letter **r** to all the brethren. **1Th 5:27** *314*

READER
(let the **r** understand), **Mt 24:15** *314*
(let the **r** understand), **Mk 13:14** *314*

READINESS
the hand of a man who *stands* in **r**. **Lv 16:21** 6261
it is wrapped up *in* **r** for **Ezk 21:15**
"Be dressed in **r**, and *keep* your **Lk 12:35** *4024*
as *there was* the **r** to desire it, **2Co 8:11** *4288*
For if the **r** is present, it is **2Co 8:12** *4288*
Lord Himself, and *to show* our **r**, **2Co 8:19** *4288*
for I know your **r**, of which I **2Co 9:2** *4288*

READING
so that they understood the **r**. **Ne 8:8** 4744
r from the book the words of the **Jer 36:8** 7121
soon as you finish **r** this scroll, **Jer 51:63** 7121
and was **r** the prophet Isaiah. **Ac 8:28** *314*
and heard him **r** Isaiah the prophet, **Ac 8:30** *314*
you understand what you are **r**?" **Ac 8:30** *314*
Scripture which he was **r** was this: **Ac 8:32** *314*
the **r** of the Law and the Prophets **Ac 13:15** *320*
at the **r** of the old covenant **2Co 3:14** *320*
to the *public* **r** *of Scripture,* **1Tm 4:13** *320*

READS
That the one who **r** it may run. **Hab 2:2** 7121
Blessed is he who **r** and those who **Rv 1:3** *314*

READY
and slay an animal and make **r**; **Gn 43:16** 3559
So he made his chariot **r** and took **Ex 14:6** 631
let them be **r** for the third day, **Ex 19:11** 3559
"Be **r** for the third day; **Ex 19:15** 3559
"So be **r** by morning, and come up **Ex 34:2** 3559
but we ourselves will be armed **r** **Nu 32:17** 2363a
the city, but all of you be **r**. **Jos 8:4** 3559
your servants *are* **r** *to do* **2Sa 15:15**
now it is better that you *be* **r** to **2Sa 18:3**
Then Joram said, "Get **r**." **2Ki 9:21** 631
And they made his chariot **r**. **2Ki 9:21** 631
who were **r** to go out with the army **1Ch 7:11**
lampstand with its lamps is **r** to **2Ch 13:11**
Uzziah had an army **r** for battle, **2Ch 26:11** 6213a
they should be **r** for this day. **Es 3:14** 6264
so that the Jews would be **r** for **Es 8:13** 6264
him like a king **r** for the attack, **Jb 15:24** 6264
The grave is **r** for me. **Jb 17:1**
And calamity is **r** at his side. **Jb 18:12** 3559
"The blessing of the one **r** to perish **Jb 29:13**
He has bent His bow and made it **r**. **Ps 7:12** 3559
They make **r** their arrow upon the **Ps 11:2** 3559
For I am **r** to fall, And my sorrow **Ps 38:17** 3559
tongue is the pen of a **r** writer. **Ps 45:1** 4106
are **r** with a well-conceived plot"; **Ps 64:6** 8552
Lord, are good, and **r** to forgive, **Ps 86:5** 5546a
Let Your hand be **r** to help me, For **Ps 119:173**
That they may be **r** on your lips. **Pr 22:18** 3559
make it **r** for yourself in the field; **Pr 24:27** 6257
For Topheth has long been **r**, **Is 30:33** 6186a
As he makes **r** to destroy? **Is 51:13** 3559
Take your stand and get yourself **r**, **Jer 46:14** 3559
"Make your baggage **r** for exile, **Jer 46:19** 6213a
the trumpet and made everything **r**, **Ezk 7:14** 3559
"Now if you are **r**, at the moment **Da 3:15** 6263
'MAKE **R** THE WAY OF THE LORD, MAKE **Mt 3:3** *2090*
all butchered and everything is **r**; **Mt 22:4** *2092*
'The wedding is **r**, but those who **Mt 22:8** *2092*
"For this reason you also must be **r**; **Mt 24:44** *2092*
and those who were **r** went in with **Mt 25:10** *2092*
'MAKE **R** THE WAY OF THE LORD, **Mk 1:3** *2090*
a boat should stand **r** for Him **Mk 3:9** *4342*
large upper room furnished *and* **r**; **Mk 14:15** *2092*
so as to make **r** a people prepared **Lk 1:17** *2090*
'MAKE **R** THE WAY OF THE LORD, **Lk 3:4** *2090*
"You too, be **r**; for the Son of Man **Lk 12:40** *2092*
and did not get **r** or act in accord **Lk 12:47** *2090*
for everything is **r** now.' **Lk 14:17** *2092*
with You I am **r** to go both to **Lk 22:33** *2092*
For I am **r** not only to be bound, **Ac 21:13** *2093*
After these days we got **r** and **Ac 21:15** *1980b*
and we for our part are **r** to slay **Ac 23:15** *2092*
and now they are **r** and waiting for **Ac 23:21** *2092*
"Get two hundred soldiers **r** by **Ac 23:23** *2090*
would be **r** as a bountiful gift **2Co 9:5** *2092*
are **r** to punish all disobedience, **2Co 10:6** *2092*
third time I am **r** to come to you, **2Co 12:14** *2093*
to be generous and **r** to share, **1Tm 6:18** *2843*
be **r** in season *and* out of season; **2Tm 4:2** *2186*
to be **r** for every good deed, **Ti 3:1** *2092*
and growing old is **r** to disappear. **Heb 8:13** *1451*
salvation **r** to be revealed in the last **1Pe 1:5** *2092*
always *being* **r** to make a defense **1Pe 3:15** *2092*
Him who is **r** to judge the living and **1Pe 4:5** *2093*
r to remind you of these things, **2Pe 1:12** *3195*
His bride has made herself **r**." **Rv 19:7** *2090*
made **r** as a bride adorned for her **Rv 21:2** *2090*

REAFFIRM
I urge you to **r** *your* love for him. **2Co 2:8** *2964*

REAIAH
R the son of Shobal became the **1Ch 4:2** 7211
Micah his son, **R** his son, Baal his **1Ch 5:5** 7211
the sons of Gahar, the sons of **R**, **Ezr 2:47** 7211
the sons of **R**, the sons of Rezin, **Ne 7:50** 7211

REAL
John to have been a **r** prophet. **Mk 11:32** *3689*
was being done by the angel was **r**, **Ac 12:9** *227*
since there is no **r** cause *for* **Ac 19:40**
we have found this man a **r** pest **Ac 24:5**
r knowledge and all discernment, **Php 1:9** *1922*

REALIZE
not **r** that Egypt is destroyed?" **Ex 10:7** 3045
They did not **r** that He had been **Jn 8:27** *1097*
"What I do you do not **r** now, **Jn 13:7** *3609a*
But I trust that you will **r** that **2Co 13:6** *1097*
But **r** this, that in the last days **2Tm 3:1** *1097*
so as to **r** the full assurance of hope **Heb 6:11**

REALIZED
And David **r** that the LORD had **2Sa 5:12** 3045
And David **r** that the LORD had **1Ch 14:2** 3045
Desire **r** is sweet to the soul, But **Pr 13:19** 1961
I **r** that this also is striving **Ec 1:17** 3045
For you also have **r** that you **Ec 7:22** 3045
r that it was the word of the LORD. **Zch 11:11** 3045
and they **r** that he had seen a **Lk 1:22** *1921*
truth were **r** through Jesus Christ. **Jn 1:17** *1096*
And when he **r** *this,* he went to the **Ac 12:12** *4894*

REALIZING
not **r** what he was saying. **Lk 9:33** *3609a*
r the fact that law is not made **1Tm 1:9** *3609a*

REALLY
whether you are **r** my son Esau or **Gn 27:21** 2088
"Are you **r** my son Esau?" **Gn 27:24** 2088
are you **r** going to rule over us?" **Gn 37:8** 4910
Am I **r** unable to honor you?" **Nu 22:37** 552
"I **r** thought that you hated her **Jg 15:2** 559
"Will you **r** annul My judgment? **Jb 40:8** 637
r learn the ways of My people, **Jer 12:16** 3925
r set your mind to enter Egypt and **Jer 42:15** 7760

"The Lord has **r** risen and has Lk 24:34 *3689*
r know that this is the Christ, Jn 7:26 *230*
which is **r** not another; only Ga 1:7
but *for* what it **r** is, the word of God 1Th 2:13 *230*
for now we **r** live, if you stand 1Th 3:8
but they were not **r** of us; for 1Jn 2:19

REALM
conjurers who *were* in all his **r**. Da 1:20 4438
is ruler over the **r** of mankind, Da 4:17 4437
is ruler over the **r** of mankind and Da 4:25 4437
is ruler over the **r** of mankind and Da 4:32 4437
is ruler over the **r** of mankind and Da 5:21 4437
empire against the **r** of Greece. Da 11:2 4438
the **r** of the king of the South, Da 11:9 4438
enter the richest *parts* of the **r**, Da 11:24 4082
is, My kingdom is not of this **r**." Jn 18:36 *1782*

REAP
you **r** the harvest of your land, Lv 19:9 7114b
you shall not **r** to the very Lv 19:9 7114b
to give to you and **r** its harvest, Lv 23:10 7114b
you **r** the harvest of your land, Lv 23:22 7114b
you shall not **r** to the very Lv 23:22 7114b
aftergrowth you shall not **r**, Lv 25:5 7114b
not sow, nor **r** its aftergrowth, Lv 25:11 7114b
"When you **r** your harvest in your Dt 24:19 7114b
eyes be on the field which they **r**, Ru 2:9 7114b
to do his plowing and to **r** his harvest 1Sa 8:12 7114b
and in the third year sow, **r**, 2Ki 19:29 7114b
Those who sow in tears shall **r** with Ps 126:5 7114b
who sows iniquity will **r** vanity, Pr 22:8 7114b
looks at the clouds will not **r**. Ec 11:4 7114b
and in the third year sow, **r**, Is 37:30 7114b
wind And they **r** the whirlwind. Hos 8:7 7114b
R in accordance with kindness; Hos 10:12 7114b
"You will sow but you will not **r**. Mi 6:15 7114b
do not sow, nor **r** Mt 6:26 *2325*
knew that I **r** where I did not sow and Mt 25:26 *2325*
for they neither sow nor **r**; Lk 12:24 *2325*
down and **r** what you did not sow.' Lk 19:21 *2325*
"I sent you to **r** that for which Jn 4:38 *2325*
we **r** material things from you? 1Co 9:11 *2325*
sparingly will also **r** sparingly 2Co 9:6 *2325*
he who sows bountifully will also **r** 2Co 9:6 *2325*
a man sows, this he will also **r**. Ga 6:7 *2325*
will from the flesh **r** corruption, Ga 6:8 *2325*
from the Spirit **r** eternal life. Ga 6:8 *2325*
will **r** if we do not grow weary. Ga 6:9 *2325*
"Put in your sickle and **r**, Rv 14:15 *2325*
for the hour to **r** has come, Rv 14:15 *2325*

REAPED
and **r** in the same year a Gn 26:12 4672
have sown wheat and have **r** thorns, Jer 12:13 7114b
wickedness, you have **r** injustice, Hos 10:13 7114b
and the earth was **r**. Rv 14:16 *2325*

REAPER
the **r** does not fill his hand, Ps 129:7 7114b
r gathering the standing grain, Is 17:5 622
And like the sheaf after the **r**, Jer 9:22 7114b
the plowman will overtake the **r** Am 9:13 7114b

REAPERS
gleaned in the field after the **r**; Ru 2:3 7114b
from Bethlehem and said to the **r**, Ru 2:4 7114b
servant who was in charge of the **r**, Ru 2:5 7114b
servant in charge of the **r** replied Ru 2:6 7114b
let me glean and gather after the **r** Ru 2:7 7114b
So she sat beside the **r**; Ru 2:14 7114b
went out to his father to the **r**. 2Ki 4:18 7114b
the harvest I will say to the **r**, Mt 13:30 *2327*
and the **r** are angels. Mt 13:39 *2327*

REAPING
people of Beth-shemesh were **r** their 1Sa 6:13 7114b
hard man, **r** where you did not sow and Mt 25:24 *2325*
down and **r** what I did not sow? Lk 19:22 *2325*

REAPPEARED
clean because the mark has not **r**. Lv 14:48 7495

REAPS
he who **r** is receiving wages and Jn 4:36 *2325*
that he who sows and he who **r** may Jn 4:36 *2325*
'One sows and another **r**.' Jn 4:37 *2325*

REAR
"For the **r** of the tabernacle, Ex 26:22 3411
corners of the tabernacle at the **r**. Ex 26:23 3411
for the **r** *side* to the west. Ex 26:27 3411
For the **r** of the tabernacle, Ex 36:27 3411
corners of the tabernacle at the **r**. Ex 36:28 3411
for the **r** *side* to the west. Ex 36:32 3411
the **r** guard for all the camps, Nu 10:25 622
r when you were faint and weary; Dt 25:18 310
the **r** guard came after the ark, Jos 6:9 622
and the **r** guard came after the ark Jos 6:13 622
and its **r** guard on the west side Jos 8:13 6119
enemies and attack them in the **r**. Jos 10:19 2179
his men were proceeding on in the **r** 1Sa 29:2 314
against him in front and in the **r**, 2Sa 10:9 268
He built twenty cubits on the **r** part 1Ki 6:16 3411
all their **r** parts *turned* inward. 1Ki 7:25 268
round top to the throne at its **r**, 1Ki 10:19 310
against him in front and in the **r**, 1Ch 19:10 268
set an ambush to come from the **r**, 2Ch 13:13 310
were attacked both front and **r**; 2Ch 13:14 268
God of Israel *will be* your **r** guard. Is 52:12 622
of the LORD will be your **r** guard. Is 58:8 622
at the extreme **r** toward the west. Ezk 46:19 3411
its **r** guard into the western sea. Jl 2:20 5490

REARED
"Sons I have **r** and brought up, Is 1:2 1431
brought up young men *nor* **r** virgins. Is 23:4 7311
And who has **r** these? Is 49:21 1431
hand among all the sons she has **r**. Is 51:18 1431
Those whom I bore and **r**, La 2:22 7235a
Those **r** in purple Embrace ash pits. La 4:5 539
among young lions, She **r** her cubs. Ezk 19:2 7235a

REARING
men of the city, *who* were **r** them. 2Ki 10:6 1431

REASON
For this **r** a man shall leave his Gn 2:24 5921, 3651
"But, indeed, for this **r** I have Ex 9:16 5668
"The **r** is so that the sons of Lv 17:5 4616
for it is the blood by **r** of the life Lv 17:11
'You will bear no sin by **r** of it Nu 18:32 5921
the **r** why Joshua circumcised them: Jos 5:4 1697
done this out of concern, for a **r**, Jos 22:24 1697
For this **r** we have now returned Jg 11:8 3651
For this **r** he has not come to the 1Sa 20:29 5921, 3651
"For this **r** You are great, O 2Sa 7:22 5921, 3651
"Now the **r** I have come to speak 2Sa 14:15 834
Now this was the **r** why he rebelled 1Ki 11:27 1697
if for any **r** he is missing, then 1Ki 20:39 6485
He was hired for this **r**, Ne 6:13 4616
whether Mordecai's **r** would stand; Es 3:4 1697
the upright would **r** with Him; Jb 23:7 3198
"Come now, and let us **r** together," Is 1:18 3198
r my loins are full of anguish; Is 21:3 5921, 3651
'For what **r** has the LORD declared Jer 16:10 5921, 4100
your wisdom by **r** of your splendor. Ezk 28:17 5921
"For good **r** they have made you Ezk 36:3 3282
"For what **r** is the decree from Da 2:15 5922, 4101
For this **r** at that time certain Da 3:8 3606, 6903
For this **r**, because the king's Da 3:22 3606, 6903
heaven and my **r** returned to me, Da 4:34 4486
"At that time my **r** returned to me. Da 4:36 4486
"Do you have good **r** to be angry?" Jon 4:4 3190
"Do you have good **r** to be angry Jon 4:9 3190
"I have good **r** to be angry, even Jon 4:9 3190
"Yet you say, 'For what **r**?' Mal 2:14 5921, 4100
except for *the* **r** of unchastity, Mt 5:32 *3056*
"For this **r** I say to you, do not Mt 6:25 *1223*
For this **r** they will be your judges. Mt 12:27 *1223, 3778*
"For this **r** the kingdom of heaven Mt 18:23 *1223*
a man to divorce his wife for any **r** Mt 19:3 *156*
and said, 'FOR THIS **R** A MAN SHALL Mt 19:5 *1752a*
"For this **r** you also must be ready; Mt 24:44 *1223*
For this **r** that field has been Mt 27:8 *1352*
"FOR THIS **R** A MAN SHALL LEAVE HIS Mk 10:7 *1752a*
this not the **r** you are mistaken, Mk 12:24 *1223*
and for that **r** the holy Child Lk 1:35 *1352*
and the Pharisees began to **r**, Lk 5:21 *1260*
so that they might find **r** to Lk 6:7
for this **r** I did not even consider Lk 7:7 *1352*
"For this **r** I say to you, her Lk 7:47 *5484*
the **r** why she had touched Him, Lk 8:47 *156*
"For this **r** also the wisdom of God Lk 11:49 *1223*
"For this **r** I say to you, do not Lk 12:22 *1223*
and for that **r** I cannot come.' Lk 14:20 *1223*
For this **r** the Jews were persecuting Jn 5:16 *1223*
For this **r** therefore the Jews were Jn 5:18 *1223*
"For this **r** I have said to you, Jn 6:65 *1223*
"For this **r** Moses has given you Jn 7:22 *1223*
for this **r** you do not hear *them*, Jn 8:47 *1223*
For this **r** his parents said, Jn 9:23 *1223*
"For this **r** the Father loves Me, Jn 10:17 *1223*
For this **r** also the people went Jn 12:18 *1223*
For this **r** they could not believe, Jn 12:39 *1223*
for this **r** He said, Jn 13:11 *1223*
for this **r** he who delivered Me to Jn 19:11 *1223*
the **r** for which you have come?" Ac 10:21 *156*
for what **r** you have sent for me." Ac 10:29 *3056*
the majority did not know for what **r** Ac 19:32 *1752a*
find out the **r** why they were shouting Ac 22:24 *156*
"For this **r** *some* Jews seized me Ac 26:21 *1752a*
and that by **r** of *His* resurrection Ac 26:23 *1537*
"For this **r**, therefore, I requested Ac 28:20 *156*
For this **r** God gave them over to Ro 1:26 *1223*
For this **r** *it is* by faith, in order that Ro 4:16 *1223*
in Christ Jesus I have found **r** for Ro 15:17 *2746a*
For this **r** I have often been Ro 15:22 *1352*
this **r** I have sent to you Timothy, 1Co 4:17 *1223*
For this **r** many among you are weak 1Co 11:30 *1223*
it is not for this **r** any the less 1Co 12:15 *3844*
it is not for this **r** any the less 1Co 12:16 *3844*
think like a child, **r** like a child; 1Co 13:11 *3049*
that we are your **r** to be proud as 2Co 1:14 *2745*
For this **r** we have been comforted. 2Co 7:13 *1223*
of our **r** for boasting about you. 2Co 8:24 *2746a*
of the revelations, for this **r**, 2Co 12:7 *1352*
For this **r** I am writing these 2Co 13:10 *1223*
and then he will have **r** *for* Ga 6:4
For this **r** I too, having heard of Eph 1:15 *1223*
For this **r** I, Paul, the prisoner Eph 3:1 *5484*
For this **r** I bow my knees before Eph 3:14 *5484*
For this **r** it says, Eph 5:14 *1352*
FOR THIS **R** A MAN SHALL LEAVE HIS Eph 5:31 *473*
For this **r** also, God highly exalted Php 2:9 *1352*
in the day of Christ I will have **r** to Php 2:16 *2745*
For this **r** also, since the day we Col 1:9 *1223*
For this **r** we also constantly thank 1Th 2:13 *1223*
For this **r**, when I could endure *it* 1Th 3:5 *1223*
for this **r**, brethren, in all our 1Th 3:7 *1223*
For this **r** God will send upon 2Th 2:11 *1223*
Yet for this **r** I found mercy, 1Tm 1:16 *1223*
For this **r** I remind you to 2Tm 1:6 *156*
this **r** I also suffer these things, 2Tm 1:12 *156*
For this **r** I endure all things for 2Tm 2:10 *1223*
For this **r** I left you in Crete, Ti 1:5 *5484*
This testimony is true. For this **r** Ti 1:13 *156*
he was for this **r** separated *from you* Phm 1:15 *1223*
For this **r** we must pay much closer Heb 2:1 *1223*
for which **r** He is not ashamed to Heb 2:11 *156*
For this **r** He is the mediator Heb 9:15 *1223*
Now for this very **r** also, 2Pe 1:5
this **r** the world does not know us, 1Jn 3:1 *1223*
And for what **r** did he slay him? 1Jn 3:12 *5484*
For this **r**, if I come, I will call 3Jn 1:10 *1223*
"For this **r**, they are before the Rv 7:15 *1223*
"For this **r**, rejoice, O heavens Rv 12:12 *1223*
"For this **r** in one day her plagues Rv 18:8 *1223*

REASONABLE
their words seemed **r** to Hamor and Gn 34:18 3190
be **r** for me to put up with you; Ac 18:14 *3056*
pure, then peaceable, gentle, **r**, Jas 3:17 *2138b*

REASONED
They **r** among themselves, Lk 20:5 *4817*
saw him, they **r** with one another, Lk 20:14 *1260*
r with them from the Scriptures, Ac 17:2 *1256*
the synagogue and **r** with the Jews. Ac 18:19 *1256*

REASONING
And they *began* **r** among themselves, Mt 21:25 *1260*
sitting there and **r** in their hearts, Mk 2:6 *1260*
were **r** that way within themselves, Mk 2:8 *1260*
"Why are you **r** about these things Mk 2:8 *1260*
They *began* **r** among themselves, Mk 11:31 *1260*
"Why are you **r** in your hearts? Lk 5:22 *1260*
"And he began **r** to himself, Lk 12:17 *1260*
So he was **r** in the synagogue with Ac 17:17 *1256*
And he was **r** in the synagogue Ac 18:4 *1256*
r and persuading *them* about the Ac 19:8 *1256*
r daily in the school of Tyrannus. Ac 19:9 *1256*

REASONINGS
your words, I listened to your **r**, Jb 32:11 8394
But Jesus, aware of their **r**, Lk 5:22 *1261*
"THE LORD KNOWS THE **R** of the wise, 1Co 3:20 *1261*

REBA
and Rekem and Zur and Hur and **R**, Nu 31:8 7254
and Rekem and Zur and Hur and **R**, Jos 13:21 7254

REBEKAH
Bethuel became the father of **R**; Gn 22:23 7259
R who was born to Bethuel the son Gn 24:15 7259
Now **R** had a brother whose name was Gn 24:29 7259
heard the words of **R** his sister, Gn 24:30 7259
R came out with her jar on her Gn 24:45 7259
"Here is **R** before you, take Gn 24:51 7259
and garments, and gave them to **R**; Gn 24:53 7259
they called **R** and said to her, Gn 24:58 7259
Thus they sent away their sister **R** Gn 24:59 7259
They blessed **R** and said to her, Gn 24:60 7259
Then **R** arose with her maids, and Gn 24:61 7259
the servant took **R** and departed. Gn 24:61 7259
R lifted up her eyes, and when Gn 24:64 7259
mother Sarah's tent, and he took **R**, Gn 24:67 7259
forty years old when he took **R**, Gn 25:20 7259
him and **R** his wife conceived. Gn 25:21 7259
but **R** loved Jacob. Gn 25:28 7259
might kill me on account of **R**, Gn 26:7 7259
Isaac was caressing his wife **R**. Gn 26:8 7259
they brought grief to Isaac and **R**. Gn 26:35 7259
R was listening while Isaac Gn 27:5 7259
R said to her son Jacob, Gn 27:6 7259
Jacob answered his mother **R**, Gn 27:11 7259
Then **R** took the best garments of Gn 27:15 7259
elder son Esau were reported to **R**, Gn 27:42 7259
R said to Isaac, Gn 27:46 7259
the Aramean, the brother of **R**, Gn 28:5 7259
they buried Isaac and his wife **R**, Gn 49:31 7259
only this, but there was **R** also, Ro 9:10 *4479*

REBEKAH'S
her father and that he was **R** son, Gn 29:12 7259
Now Deborah, **R** nurse, died, and Gn 35:8 7259

REBEL
"Only do not **r** against the LORD; Nu 14:9 4775
to **r** against the LORD this day? Jos 22:16 4775
If you **r** against the LORD today, Jos 22:18 4775
Only do not **r** against the LORD, or Jos 22:19 4775
or **r** against us by building an Jos 22:19 4775
that we should **r** against the LORD Jos 22:29 4775
and not **r** against the command of 1Sa 12:14 4784
but **r** against the command of the 1Sa 12:15 4784
and the Jews are planning to **r**; Ne 6:6 4775
those who **r** against the light; Jb 24:13 4775
To **r** against the Most High in the Ps 78:17 4784
they did not **r** against His words. Ps 105:28 4784
"But if you refuse and **r**, Is 1:20 4784
r against His glorious presence. Is 3:8 4784
have been called a **r** from birth. Is 48:8 6586

REBELLED
but the thirteenth year they **r**. Gn 14:4 4775
because you **r** against My command Nu 20:24 4784
you **r** against My command to treat Nu 27:14 4784
but **r** against the command of the Dt 1:26 4784
Instead you **r** against the command Dt 1:43 4784
then you **r** against the command of Dt 9:23 4784
a widow, also **r** against the king. 1Ki 11:26 7311, 3027

reason why he **r** against the king: **1Ki 11:27** 7311, 3027
Now Moab **r** against Israel after **2Ki 1:1** 6586
Moab **r** against the king of Israel. **2Ki 3:5** 6586
"The king of Moab has **r** against me. **2Ki 3:7** 6586
And he **r** against the king of **2Ki 18:7** 4775
rely, that you have **r** against me? **2Ki 18:20** 4775
then he turned and **r** against him. **2Ki 24:1** 4775
And Zedekiah **r** against the king of **2Ki 24:20** 4775
rose up and **r** against his master, **2Ch 13:6** 4775
He also **r** against King **2Ch 36:13** 4775
disobedient and **r** against You, **Ne 9:26** 4775
r against Him in the wilderness And **Ps 78:40** 4784
and **r** against the Most High God And **Ps 78:56** 4784
kindnesses, But **r** by the sea, **Ps 106:7** 4784
had **r** against the words of God And **Ps 107:11** 4784
rely, that you have **r** against me? **Is 36:5** 4775
r And grieved His Holy Spirit; **Is 63:10** 4784
Because she has **r** against Me,' **Jer 4:17** 4784
And Zedekiah **r** against the king of **Jer 52:3** 4775
For I have **r** against His command; **La 1:18** 4784
We have transgressed and **r**, **La 3:42** 4784
people who have **r** against Me; **Ezk 2:3** 4775
But she has **r** against My ordinances **Ezk 5:6** 4784
'But he **r** against him by sending **Ezk 17:15** 4775
"But they **r** against Me and were **Ezk 20:8** 4784
But the house of Israel **r** against Me **Ezk 20:13** 4784
"But the children **r** against Me; **Ezk 20:21** 4784
iniquity, acted wickedly and **r**, **Da 9:5** 4775
for we have **r** against Him; **Da 9:9** 4775
for they have **r** against Me! **Hos 7:13** 6586
My covenant And **r** against My law. **Hos 8:1** 6586
For she has **r** against her God. **Hos 13:16** 4784
By which you have **r** against Me; **Zph 3:11** 6586

REBELLING
Are you **r** against the king?" **Ne 2:19** 4775

REBELLION
he has counseled **r** against the LORD **Dt 13:5** 5627
know your **r** and your stubbornness; **Dt 31:27** 4805
If *it was* in **r**, or if in an **Jos 22:22** 4777
"For **r** is as the sin of divination, **1Sa 15:23** 4805
there is no evil or **r** in my hands, **1Sa 24:11** 6588
So Israel has been in **r** against **1Ki 12:19** 6586
So Israel has been in **r** against **2Ch 10:19** 6586
that **r** and revolt have been **Ezr 4:19** 4776
Make known to me my **r** and my sin. **Jb 13:23** 6588
"Even today my complaint is **r**; **Jb 23:2** 4805
'For he adds **r** to his sin; **Jb 34:37** 6588
again, *As* you continue in *your* **r**? **Is 1:5** 5627
Are you not children of **r**, **Is 57:4** 6588
counseled **r** against the LORD.'" **Jer 28:16** 5627
he has preached **r** against the LORD."'" **Jer 29:32** 5627
All this is for the **r** of Jacob And **Mi 1:5** 6588
What is the **r** of Jacob? **Mi 1:5** 6588
one who incites the people to **r**, **Lk 23:14** *654*
not accused of dissipation or **r**. **Ti 1:6** *506*
and perished in the **r** of Korah. **Jude 1:11** *485*

REBELLIOUS
do not be **r** toward him, for he **Ex 23:21** 4784
you have been **r** against the LORD. **Dt 9:7** 4784
"You have been **r** against the LORD **Dt 9:24** 4784
If any man has a stubborn and **r** son **Dt 21:18** 4784
son of ours is stubborn and **r**, **Dt 21:20** 4784
you have been **r** against the LORD; **Dt 31:27** 4784
"You son of a perverse, **r** woman! **1Sa 20:30** 4780
rebuilding the **r** and evil city and **Ezr 4:12** 4779a
and learn that that city is a **r** city **Ezr 4:15** 4779a
out, For they are **r** against You. **Ps 5:10** 4784
Let not the **r** exalt themselves. **Ps 66:7** 5637
the **r** dwell in a parched land. **Ps 68:6** 5637
among men, Even *among* the **r** also, **Ps 68:18** 5637
A stubborn and **r** generation, **Ps 78:8** 4784
they were **r** against His Spirit, **Ps 106:33** 4784
however, were **r** in their counsel, **Ps 106:43** 4784
Fools, because of their **r** way, **Ps 107:17** 6588
She is boisterous and **r**, **Pr 7:11** 5637
A **r** man seeks only evil, So a **Pr 17:11** 4805
"Woe to the **r** children," **Is 30:1** 5637
For this is a **r** people, false **Is 30:9** 4805
hands all day long to a **r** people, **Is 65:2** 5637
people has a stubborn and **r** heart; **Jer 5:23** 4784
All of them are stubbornly **r**, **Jer 6:28** 5637
within me, For I have been very **r**. **La 1:20** 4784
to a **r** people who have rebelled **Ezk 2:3** 4775
for they are a **r** house **Ezk 2:5** 4805
presence, for they are a **r** house. **Ezk 2:6** 4805
listen or not, for they are **r**. **Ezk 2:7** 4805
be **r** like that rebellious house. **Ezk 2:8** 4805
be rebellious like that **r** house. **Ezk 2:8** 4805
them, though they are a **r** house." **Ezk 3:9** 4805
them, for they are a **r** house. **Ezk 3:26** 4805
for they are a **r** house. **Ezk 3:27** 4805
live in the midst of the **r** house, **Ezk 12:2** 4805
for they are a **r** house. **Ezk 12:2** 4805
though they are a **r** house. **Ezk 12:3** 4805
the house of Israel, the **r** house, **Ezk 12:9** 4805
for in your days, O **r** house, **Ezk 12:25** 4805
"Say now to the **r** house, **Ezk 17:12** 4805
Speak a parable to the **r** house **Ezk 24:3** 4805
"You shall say to the **r** ones, **Ezk 44:6** 4805
were found The **r** acts of Israel. **Mi 1:13** 6588
To make known to Jacob his **r** act, **Mi 3:8** 6588
my firstborn *for* my **r** acts, **Mi 6:7** 6588
passes over the **r** act of the remnant **Mi 7:18** 6588
Woe to her who is **r** and defiled, **Zph 3:1** 4784
for those who are lawless and **r**, **1Tm 1:9** *506*
For there are many **r** men, **Ti 1:10** *506*

REBELS
be kept as a sign against the **r**, **Nu 17:10** 4805
"Listen now, you **r**; **Nu 20:10** 4784
who **r** against your command **Jos 1:18** 4784
Your rulers are **r** And companions **Is 1:23** 5637
and I will purge from you the **r** **Ezk 20:38** 4775
All their princes are **r**. **Hos 9:15** 5637

REBUILD
and **r** the house of the LORD, **Ezr 1:3** 1129
go up and **r** the house of the LORD **Ezr 1:5** 1129
and began to **r** the house of God **Ezr 5:2** 1124
issued you a decree to **r** this temple **Ezr 5:3** 1124
issued you a decree to **r** this temple **Ezr 5:9** 1124
a decree to **r** this house of God. **Ezr 5:13** 1124
to **r** this house of God at Jerusalem; **Ezr 5:17** 1124
r this house of God on its site. **Ezr 6:7** 1124
fathers' tombs, that I may **r** it." **Ne 2:5** 1129
let us **r** the wall of Jerusalem **Ne 2:17** 1129
are unable To **r** the wall." **Ne 4:10** 1129
But we will **r** with smooth stones; **Is 9:10** 1129
you will **r** the ancient ruins; **Is 58:12** 1129
they will **r** the ancient ruins, **Is 61:4** 1129
will **r** them as they were at first. **Jer 33:7** 1129
a decree to restore and **r** Jerusalem **Da 9:25** 1129
And **r** it as in the days of old; **Am 9:11** 1129
And they will **r** the ruined cities **Am 9:14** 1129
bring wood and **r** the temple, **Hg 1:8** 1129
God and to **r** it in three days.'" **Mt 26:61** *3618*
the temple and **r** it in three days, **Mt 27:40** *3618*
the temple and **r** it in three days, **Mk 15:29** *3618*
I WILL **R** THE TABERNACLE OF DAVID **Ac 15:16** *456*
FALLEN, AND I WILL **R** ITS RUINS, **Ac 15:16** *456*
if I **r** what I have *once* destroyed, **Ga 2:18** *3618*

REBUILDING
him and the **r** of the house of God, **2Ch 24:27** 3245
r the rebellious and evil city and **Ezr 4:12** 1124
are **r** the temple that was built many **Ezr 5:11** 1124
in the **r** of this house of God: **Ezr 6:8** 1124
heard that we were **r** the wall, **Ne 4:1** 1129
Those who were **r** the wall and **Ne 4:17** 1129
therefore you are **r** the wall. **Ne 6:6** 1129

REBUILT
It shall never be **r**. **Dt 13:16** 1129
they **r** the city and lived in it. **Jg 18:28** 1129
r the cities and lived in them. **Jg 21:23** 1129
So Solomon **r** Gezer and the lower **1Ki 9:17** 1129
For he **r** the high places which **2Ki 21:3** 7725, 1129
r all the wall that had been broken **2Ch 32:5** 1129
For he **r** the high places which **2Ch 33:3** 7725, 1129
if that city is **r** and the walls are **Ezr 4:13** 1124
city is **r** and the walls finished, **Ezr 4:16** 1124
that this city may not be **r** until a **Ezr 4:21** 1124
house of God be **r** in its place." **Ezr 5:15** 1124
be **r** and let its foundations be **Ezr 6:3** 1124
our enemies that I had **r** the wall, **Ne 6:1** 1129
when the wall was **r** and I had set **Ne 7:1** 1129
earth, Who **r** ruins for themselves; **Jb 3:14** 1129
He tears down, and it cannot be **r**; **Jb 12:14** 1129
city no more, It will never be **r**. **Is 25:2** 1129
the city will be **r** on its ruin, **Jer 30:18** 1129
build you and you will be **r**, **Jer 31:4** 1129
"when the city will be **r** for the **Jer 31:38** 1129
and the waste places will be **r**. **Ezk 36:10** 1129
and the waste places will be **r**. **Ezk 36:33** 1129
I, the LORD, have **r** the ruined places **Ezk 36:36** 1129
house of the LORD to be **r**. **Hg 1:2** 1129

REBUKE
upon you curses, confusion, and **r**, **Dt 28:20** 4045
she may glean, and do not **r** her." **Ru 2:16** 1605
themselves and he did not **r** them. **1Sa 3:13** 3543b
laid bare By the **r** of the LORD, **2Sa 22:16** 1606
'This day is a day of distress, **r**, **2Ki 19:3** 8433a
and will **r** the words which the **2Ki 19:4** 3198
And shall you scoff and none **r**? **Jb 11:3** 3637
tremble And are amazed at His **r**. **Jb 26:11** 1606
Lord, do not **r** me in Your anger, **Ps 6:1** 3198
the world were laid bare At Your **r**, **Ps 18:15** 1606
O Lord, **r** me not in Your wrath, **Ps 38:1** 3198
R the beasts in the reeds, The **Ps 68:30** 1605
At Your **r**, O God of Jacob, Both **Ps 76:6** 1606
at the **r** of Your countenance. **Ps 80:16** 1606
the nations, will He not **r**, **Ps 94:10** 3198
At Your **r** they fled, **Ps 104:7** 1606
You **r** the arrogant, the **Ps 119:21** 1605
a scoffer does not listen to **r**. **Pr 13:1** 1606
wealth, But the poor hears no **r**. **Pr 13:8** 1606
A **r** goes deeper into one who has **Pr 17:10** 1606
who **r** the *wicked* will be delight, **Pr 24:25** 3198
Better is open **r** Than love that is **Pr 27:5** 8433b
It is better to listen to the **r** of **Ec 7:5** 1606
But He will **r** them and they will **Is 17:13** 1605
'This day is a day of distress, **r** and **Is 37:3** 8433a
and will **r** the words which the **Is 37:4** 3198
I dry up the sea with My **r**, **Is 50:2** 1606
of the LORD, The **r** of your God. **Is 51:20** 1606
angry with you Nor will I **r** you. **Is 54:9** 1605
And His **r** with flames of fire. **Is 66:15** 1606
a desolation in the day of **r**; **Hos 5:9** 8433a
"The LORD **r** you, Satan! **Zch 3:2** 1605
who has chosen Jerusalem **r** you! **Zch 3:2** 1605
I am going to **r** your offspring, **Mal 2:3** 1605
I will **r** the devourer for you, **Mal 3:11** 1605
took Him aside and began to **r** Him, **Mt 16:22** *2008*
took Him aside and began to **r** Him. **Mk 8:32** *2008*
If your brother sins, **r** him; **Lk 17:3** *2008*
"Teacher, **r** Your disciples." **Lk 19:39** *2008*
Do not sharply **r** an older man, but **1Tm 5:1** *1969*
in sin, **r** in the presence of all, **1Tm 5:20** *1651*
reprove, **r**, exhort, with great **2Tm 4:2** *2008*
a **r** for his own transgression, **2Pe 2:16** *1649b*
"The Lord **r** you!" **Jude 1:9** *2008*

REBUKED
his father **r** him and said to him, **Gn 37:10** 1605
You have **r** the nations, **Ps 9:5** 1605
He **r** the Red Sea and it dried up, **Ps 106:9** 1605
why have you not **r** Jeremiah of **Jer 29:27** 1605
and **r** the winds and the sea, **Mt 8:26** *2008*
And Jesus **r** him, and the demon **Mt 17:18** *2008*
and the disciples **r** them. **Mt 19:13** *2008*
And Jesus **r** him, saying, **Mk 1:25** *2008*
and **r** the wind and said to the sea, **Mk 4:39** *2008*
seeing His disciples, He **r** Peter and **Mk 8:33** *2008*
He **r** the unclean spirit, **Mk 9:25** *2008*
but the disciples **r** them. **Mk 10:13** *2008*
But Jesus **r** him, saying, **Lk 4:35** *2008*
standing over her, He **r** the fever, **Lk 4:39** *2008*
and **r** the wind and the surging **Lk 8:24** *2008*
But Jesus **r** the unclean spirit, **Lk 9:42** *2008*
But He turned and **r** them, **Lk 9:55** *2008*

REBUKES
He who **r** a man will afterward find **Pr 28:23** 3198
and cannot be a man who **r** them, **Ezk 3:26** 3198
you in anger, wrath and raging **r**. **Ezk 5:15** 8433b
vengeance on them with wrathful **r**; **Ezk 25:17** 8433b
He **r** the sea and makes it dry; **Na 1:4** 1605

REBUKING
But **r** them, He would not allow **Lk 4:41** *2008*
saw it, they *began* **r** them. **Lk 18:15** *2008*
other answered, and **r** him said, **Lk 23:40** *2008*

RECAH
These are the men of **R**. **1Ch 4:12** 7397b

RECALL
R it to mind, you transgressors. **Is 46:8** 7725
This I **r** to my mind, Therefore I **La 3:21** 7725
For you **r**, brethren, our labor and **1Th 2:9** *3421*
see you, even as I **r** your tears, **2Tm 1:4** *3403*

RECALLS
No one **r**, nor is there **Is 44:19** 7725, 413, 3820

RECEDED
water **r** steadily from the earth, **Gn 8:3** 7725

RECEIVE
which has opened its mouth to **r** **Gn 4:11** 3947
to **r** the pledge from the woman's **Gn 38:20** 3947
after you, to **r** as a possession; **Lv 25:46** 3423
you **r** from the sons of Israel; **Nu 18:28** 3947
They shall **r** their inheritance **Nu 26:55** 5157
to **r** the tablets of stone, **Dt 9:9** 3947
except *what they* **r** from the sale **Dt 18:8**
them, that they might **r** no mercy, **Jos 11:20** 1961
"Even if I should **r** a thousand **2Sa 18:12** 8254
"Let my lord the king **r** good news, **2Sa 18:31** 1319
Is it a time to **r** money and to **2Ki 5:26** 3947
to receive money and to **r** clothes **2Ki 5:26** 3947
the Levites are they who **r** the tithes **Ne 10:37** 6237
Levites when the Levites **r** tithes, **Ne 10:38** 6237
"Why did the knees **r** me, **Jb 3:12** 6923
r instruction from His mouth And **Jb 22:22** 3947
which tyrants **r** from the Almighty. **Jb 27:13** 3947
Or what does He **r** from your hand? **Jb 35:7** 3947
He shall **r** a blessing from the **Ps 24:5** 5375
For He will **r** me. **Ps 49:15** 3947
me, And afterward **r** me to glory. **Ps 73:24** 3947
To **r** instruction in wise behavior, **Pr 1:3** 3947
My son, if you will **r** my words **Pr 2:1** 3947
The wise of heart will **r** commands, **Pr 10:8** 3947
wisdom is with those who **r** counsel. **Pr 13:10** 3289
longer knows *how* to **r** instruction. **Ec 4:13** 2094b
r his reward and rejoice in his labor; **Ec 5:19** 5375
your ear **r** the word of His mouth; **Jer 9:20** 3947
not listen and **r** instruction. **Jer 32:33** 3947
"Will you not **r** instruction by **Jer 35:13** 3947
ashamed when you **r** your sisters, **Ezk 16:61** 3947
that you will not **r** again the **Ezk 36:30** 3947
you will **r** from me gifts and a **Da 2:6** 6902
saints of the Highest One will **r** the **Da 7:18** 6902
all iniquity And **r** *us* graciously, **Hos 14:2** 3947
Or would he **r** you kindly?" **Mal 1:8** 5375, 6440
will He **r** any of you kindly?" **Mal 1:9** 5375, 6440
Should I **r** that from your hand?" **Mal 1:13** 7521
merciful, for they shall **r** mercy. **Mt 5:7** *1653*
"Whoever does not **r** you, **Mt 10:14** *1209*
prophet shall **r** a prophet's reward; **Mt 10:41** *2983*
shall **r** a righteous man's reward. **Mt 10:41** *2983*
BLIND **R** SIGHT and *the* lame walk, **Mt 11:5** *308*
sake, will **r** many times as much, **Mt 19:29** *2983*
thought that they would **r** more; **Mt 20:10** *2983*
prayer, believing, you will **r**." **Mt 21:22** *2983*
the vine-growers to **r** his produce. **Mt 21:34** *2983*
you will **r** greater condemnation. **Mt 23:14** *2983*
word, immediately **r** it with joy; **Mk 4:16** *2983*
does not **r** you or listen to you, **Mk 6:11** *1209*
whoever receives Me does not **r** Me, **Mk 9:37** *1209*
whoever does not **r** the kingdom of **Mk 10:15** *1209*
he will **r** a hundred times as much **Mk 10:30** *2983*
in order to **r** *some* of the produce **Mk 12:2** *2983*
will **r** greater condemnation." **Mk 12:40** *2983*
those from whom you expect to **r**, **Lk 6:34** *2983*
in order to **r** back the same *amount.* **Lk 6:34** *618*
the BLIND **R** SIGHT, *the* lame walk, **Lk 7:22** *308*
they hear, **r** the word with joy; **Lk 8:13** *1209*

“And as for those who do not r you, Lk 9:5 1209
But they did not r Him, Lk 9:53 1209
city you enter and they r you, Lk 10:8 1209
you enter and they do not r you, Lk 10:10 1209
his will, will r many lashes, Lk 12:47 1194
of a flogging, will r but few. Lk 12:48 1194
they will r you into the eternal Lk 16:9 1209
whoever does not r the kingdom of Lk 18:17 1209
who will not r many times as much Lk 18:30 2983
“R your sight; your faith has made Lk 18:42 308
to r a kingdom for himself, Lk 19:12 2983
will r greater condemnation.” Lk 20:47 2983
who were His own did not r Him. Jn 1:11 3880
“A man can r nothing unless it Jn 3:27 2983
testimony which I r is not from man, Jn 5:34 2983
“I do not r glory from men; Jn 5:41 2983
Father’s name, and you do not r Me; Jn 5:43 2983
in his own name, you will r him. Jn 5:43 2983
when you r glory from one another and Jn 5:44 2983
for everyone to r a little.” Jn 6:7 2983
willing to r Him into the boat Jn 6:21 2983
who believed in Him were to r; Jn 7:39 2983
Me and does not r My sayings, Jn 12:48 2983
come again and r you to Myself Jn 14:3 3880
of truth, whom the world cannot r, Jn 14:17 2983
ask and you will r, Jn 16:24 2983
“R the Holy Spirit. Jn 20:22 2983
but you will r power when the Ac 1:8 2983
r the gift of the Holy Spirit. Ac 2:38 2983
temple, he *began* asking to r alms. Ac 3:3 2983
to r something from them. Ac 3:5 2983
whom heaven must r until *the* Ac 3:21 1209
“Lord Jesus, r my spirit!” Ac 7:59 1209
that they might r the Holy Spirit. Ac 8:15 2983
my hands may r the Holy Spirit.” Ac 8:19 2983
“Did you r the Holy Spirit when Ac 19:2 2983
‘It is more blessed to give than to r.’ Ac 20:35 2983
‘Brother Saul, r your sight!’ Ac 22:13 308
that they may r forgiveness of sins Ac 26:18 2983
to go to his friends and r care. Ac 27:3 5177
much more those who r the Ro 5:17 2983
r condemnation upon themselves. Ro 13:2 2983
that you r her in the Lord in a Ro 16:2 4327
for you were not yet able *to* r *it.* 1Co 3:2
but each will r his own reward 1Co 3:8 2983
it remains, he will r a reward. 1Co 3:14 2983
do you have that you did not r? 1Co 4:7 2983
And if you did r it, why do you 1Co 4:7 2983
do it to r a perishable wreath, 1Co 9:25 2983
so that the church may r edifying. 1Co 14:5 2983
that you might twice r a blessing; 2Co 1:15 2192
not to r the grace of God in vain 2Co 6:1 1209
or you r a different spirit which 2Co 11:4 2983
if *you do,* r me even as foolish, 2Co 11:16 1209
did you r the Spirit by the works Ga 3:2 2983
so that we would r the promise of Ga 3:14 2983
we might r the adoption as sons. Ga 4:5 618
to you that if you r circumcision, Ga 5:2 4059
this he will r back from the Lord, Eph 6:8 2865
R him then in the Lord with all joy, Php 2:29 4327
r the reward of the inheritance. Col 3:24 618
For he who does wrong will r the Col 3:25 2865
they did not r the love of the truth 2Th 2:10 1209
A woman must quietly r instruction 1Tm 2:11 3129
Do not r an accusation against an 1Tm 5:19 3858
first to r his share of the crops. 2Tm 2:6 3335
that we may r mercy and find Heb 4:16 2983
sons of Levi who r the priest’s office Heb 7:5 2983
In this case mortal men r tithes, Heb 7:8 2983
those who have been called may r Heb 9:15 2983
God, you may r what was promised. Heb 10:36 2865
he was to r for an inheritance; Heb 11:8 2983
did not r what was promised, Heb 11:39 2865
since we r a kingdom which cannot Heb 12:28 3880
he will r anything from the Lord, Jas 1:7 2983
he will r the crown of life which Jas 1:12 2983
in humility r the word implanted, Jas 1:21 1209
You ask and do not r, Jas 4:3 2983
r the unfading crown of glory. 1Pe 5:4 2865
and whatever we ask we r from Him, 1Jn 3:22 2983
If we r the testimony of men, the 1Jn 5:9 2983
but that you may r a full reward. 2Jn 1:8 618
do not r him into *your* house, 2Jn 1:10 2983
he himself does not r the brethren, 3Jn 1:10 1926
r glory and honor and power; Rv 4:11 2983
to r power and riches and wisdom Rv 5:12 2983
but they r authority as kings with Rv 17:12 2983
and r of her plagues; Rv 18:4 2983

RECEIVED

God, and you have r me favorably. Gn 33:10 7521
They r from Moses all the Ex 36:3 3947
afterward she may be r again.” Nu 12:14 622
move on until Miriam was r again. Nu 12:15 622
I have r *a command* to bless; Nu 23:20 3947
the sons of Reuben have r *theirs* Nu 34:14 3947
Manasseh have r their possession. Nu 34:14 3947
“The two and a half tribes have r Nu 34:15 3947
the Reubenites and the Gadites r Jos 13:8 3947
and Ephraim, r their inheritance. Jos 16:4 5157
the daughters of Manasseh r an Jos 17:6 5157
Manasseh also have r their inheritance Jos 18:7 3947
so the sons of Simeon r *an* Jos 19:9 5157
r thirteen cities by lot from the Jos 21:4 1961
rest of the sons of Kohath r ten cities Jos 21:5
The sons of Gershon r thirteen Jos 21:6
r twelve cities from the tribe of Jos 21:7
So David r from her hand what she 1Sa 25:35 3947
Then David r them and made them 1Ch 12:18 6901
Then the Levites r *it* to carry out 2Ch 29:16 6901
sprinkled the blood *which they* r 2Ch 30:16
no return for the benefit he r, 2Ch 32:25 5921
the priests sprinkled the blood r 2Ch 35:11
And my ear r a whisper of it. Jb 4:12 3947
You have r gifts among men, Even Ps 68:18 3947
I looked, *and* r instruction. Pr 24:32 3947
That she has r of the LORD’s hand Is 40:2 3947
So Darius the Mede r the kingdom Da 5:31 6902
to me, I r strength and said, Da 10:19 2388
Freely you r, freely give. Mt 10:8 2983
hour came, each one r a denarius. Mt 20:9 2983
them also r a denarius. Mt 20:10 2983
“When they r it, they Mt 20:11 2983
“Immediately the one who had r Mt 25:16 2983
the same manner the one who *had* r Mt 25:17
“But he who r the one *talent* went Mt 25:18 2983
The one who had r the five talents Mt 25:20 2983
“Also the one who *had* r the two Mt 25:22
one also who had r the one talent Mt 25:24 2983
r my *money* back with interest. Mt 25:27 2865
they have r in order to observe, Mk 7:4 3880
ask, believe that you have r them, Mk 11:24 2983
officers r Him with slaps *in the face.* Mk 14:65 2983
to them, He was r up into heaven and Mk 16:19 353
he has r him back safe and sound.’ Lk 15:27 618
your life you r your good things, Lk 16:25 618
and came down and r Him gladly. Lk 19:6 5264
But as many as r Him, to them He Jn 1:12 2983
For of His fullness we have all r, Jn 1:16 2983
“He who has r His testimony has set Jn 3:33 2983
to Galilee, the Galileans r Him, Jn 4:45 1209
away and washed, and I r sight.” Jn 9:11 308
asking him again how he r his sight. Jn 9:15 308
had been blind and had r sight, Jn 9:18 308
the very one who had r his sight, Jn 9:18 308
commandment I r from My Father.” Jn 10:18 2983
and they r *them* and truly Jn 17:8 2983
then, having r the *Roman* cohort and Jn 18:3 2983
Jesus had r the sour wine, Jn 19:30 2983
a cloud r Him out of their sight. Ac 1:9 5274
r his share in this ministry.” Ac 1:17 2975
and having r from the Father the Ac 2:33 2983
who had r his word were baptized; Ac 2:41 588
and he r living oracles to pass on Ac 7:38 1209
“And having r it in their turn, Ac 7:45 1237
r the law as ordained by angels, Ac 7:53 2983
Samaria had r the word of God, Ac 8:14 1209
who have r the Holy Spirit just as we Ac 10:47 2983
Gentiles also had r the word of God. Ac 11:1 1209
they were r by the church and the Ac 15:4 3858
and he, having r such a command, Ac 16:24 2983
And when they had r a pledge from Ac 17:9 2983
r the word with great eagerness, Ac 17:11 1209
which I r from the Lord Jesus, Ac 20:24 2983
the brethren r us gladly. Ac 21:17 588
I also r letters to the brethren, Ac 22:5 1209
having r authority from the chief Ac 26:10 2983
they kindled a fire and r us all. Ac 28:2 4355
“We have neither r letters from Ac 28:21 1209
through whom we have r grace and Ro 1:5 2983
and he r the sign of circumcision, Ro 4:11 2983
we have now r the reconciliation. Ro 5:11 2983
you have not r a spirit of slavery Ro 8:15 2983
but you have r a spirit of adoption Ro 8:15 2983
Now we have r, not the spirit of 1Co 2:12 2983
you boast as if you had not r it? 1Co 4:7 2983
For I r from the Lord that which I 1Co 11:23 3880
preached to you, which also you r, 1Co 15:1 3880
of first importance what I also r, 1Co 15:3 3880
have this ministry, as we r mercy, 2Co 4:1 1653
you r him with fear and trembling. 2Co 7:15 1209
spirit which you have not r, 2Co 11:4 2983
Five times I r from the Jews 2Co 11:24 2983
contrary to what you r, Ga 1:9 3880
For I neither r it from man, nor Ga 1:12 3880
but *I* r *it* through a revelation Ga 1:12
but you r me as an angel of God, Ga 4:14 1209
and r and heard and seen in me, Php 4:9 3880
But I have r everything in full and Php 4:18 568
having r from Epaphroditus what Php 4:18 1209
have r Christ Jesus the Lord, Col 2:6 3880
(about whom you r instructions; Col 4:10 2983
which you have r in the Lord, Col 4:17 3880
having r the word in much 1Th 1:6 1209
r the word of God 1Th 2:13 3880
as you r from us *instruction* as to 1Th 4:1 3880
the tradition which you r from us. 2Th 3:6 3880
if it is r with gratitude; 1Tm 4:4 2983
disobedience r a just penalty, Heb 2:2 2983
Abraham even Levi, who r tithes, Heb 7:9 2983
basis of it the people r the Law), Heb 7:11 3549
Sarah herself r ability to conceive, Heb 11:11 2983
and he who had r the promises was Heb 11:17 324
he also r him back as a type. Heb 11:19 2865
Women r *back* their dead by Heb 11:35 2983
when she r the messengers and sent Jas 2:25 5264
you had NOT R MERCY, but now you 1Pe 2:10 1653
MERCY, but now you have R MERCY. 1Pe 2:10 1653
As each one has r a *special* gift, 1Pe 4:10 2983
To those who have r a faith of the 2Pe 1:1 2975
For when He r honor and glory from 2Pe 1:17 2983
but he r a rebuke for his own 2Pe 2:16 2192
you r from Him abides in you, 1Jn 2:27 2983
just as we have r commandment *to* 2Jn 1:4 2983
Demetrius has r a *good* testimony 3Jn 1:12 3140
have r *authority* from My Father; Rv 2:27 2983
what you have r and heard; Rv 3:3 2983
who have not yet r a kingdom, Rv 17:12 2983
those who had r the mark of the beast Rv 19:20 2983
and had not r the mark on their Rv 20:4 2983

RECEIVES

Everyone r of Your words. Dt 33:3 5375
The LORD r my prayer. Ps 6:9 3947
A wicked man r a bribe from the Pr 17:23 3947
is instructed, he r knowledge. Pr 21:11 3947
“For everyone who asks r, Mt 7:8 2983
“He who r you receives Me, and he Mt 10:40 1209
“He who receives you r Me, Mt 10:40 1209
who r Me receives Him who sent Me. Mt 10:40 1209
who receives Me r Him who sent Me. Mt 10:40 1209
“He who r a prophet in *the* name Mt 10:41 1209
and he who r a righteous man in Mt 10:41 1209
and immediately r it with joy; Mt 13:20 2983
“And whoever r one such child in Mt 18:5 1209
one such child in My name r Me; Mt 18:5 1209
“Whoever r one child like this in Mk 9:37 1209
child like this in My name r Me; Mk 9:37 1209
whoever r Me does not receive Me, Mk 9:37 1209
“Whoever r this child in My name Lk 9:48 1209
this child in My name r Me, Lk 9:48 1209
whoever r Me receives Him who Lk 9:48 1209
whoever receives Me r Him who Lk 9:48 1209
“For everyone who asks, r; Lk 11:10 2983
r sinners and eats with them.” Lk 15:2 4327
and no one r His testimony. Jn 3:32 2983
“If a man r circumcision on *the* Jn 7:23 2983
who r whomever I send receives Me; Jn 13:20 2983
who receives whomever I send r Me; Jn 13:20 2983
r Me receives Him who sent Me.” Jn 13:20 2983
receives Me r Him who sent Me.” Jn 13:20 2983
in Him r forgiveness of sins.” Ac 10:43 2983
all run, but *only* one r the prize? 1Co 9:24 2983
to every man who r circumcision, Ga 5:3 4059
but r *it* when he is called by God, Heb 5:4
tilled, r a blessing from God; Heb 6:7 3335
but in that case one r *them,* of Heb 7:8
HE SCOURGES EVERY SON WHOM HE R.” Heb 12:6 3858
no one knows but he who r it.’ Rv 2:17 2983
and r a mark on his forehead or Rv 14:9 2983
whoever r the mark of his name.” Rv 14:11 2983

RECEIVING

by not r from his hands what he 2Ki 5:20 3947
you are r your comfort in full. Lk 6:24 568
he returned, after r the kingdom, Lk 19:15 2983
r what we deserve for our deeds; Lk 23:41 618
“Already he who reaps is r wages and Jn 4:36 2983
So after r the morsel he went Jn 13:30 2983
and they were r the Holy Spirit. Ac 8:17 2983
and r a command for Silas and Ac 17:15 2983
r in their own persons the due penalty Ro 1:27 618
of giving and r but you alone; Php 4:15 3025a
r the knowledge of the truth, Heb 10:26 2983
in faith, without r the promises, Heb 11:13 2865

RECENTLY

neither r nor in time past, Ex 4:10 4480, 8543
“Although r you *had* turned and Jer 34:15 3117
“R My people have arisen as an Mi 2:8 865a
having r come from Italy with his Ac 18:2 4373

RECEPTION

Levi gave a big r for Him in his Lk 5:29 1403
“But when you give a r, Lk 14:13 1403
what kind of a r we had with you, 1Th 1:9 1529

RECESSES

in the inner r of the cave. 1Sa 24:3 3411
Or walked in the r of the deep? Jb 38:16 2714
of assembly In the r of the north. Is 14:13 3411
to Sheol, To the r of the pit. Is 14:15 3411

RECHAB

and the name of the other R, 2Sa 4:2 7394
the Beerothite, R and Baanah, 2Sa 4:5 7394
and R and Baanah his brother 2Sa 4:6 7394
answered R and Baanah his brother, 2Sa 4:9 7394
the son of R *coming* to meet him; 2Ki 10:15 7394
Baal with Jehonadab the son of R; 2Ki 10:23 7394
the father of the house of R. 1Ch 2:55 7394
Malchijah the son of R, Ne 3:14 7394
wine, for Jonadab the son of R, Jer 35:6 7394
the voice of Jonadab the son of R, Jer 35:8 7394
“The words of Jonadab the son of R, Jer 35:14 7394
the sons of Jonadab the son of R Jer 35:16 7394
“Jonadab the son of R shall not Jer 35:19 7394

RECHABITES

“Go to the house of the R and Jer 35:2 7397a
and the whole house of the R, Jer 35:3 7397a
of the R pitchers full of wine and Jer 35:5 7397a
Jeremiah said to the house of the R, Jer 35:18 7397a

RECITE

as a memorial and r it to Joshua, Ex 17:14 7760, 241

RECKLESS

hired worthless and r fellows, Jg 9:4 6348
their falsehoods and r boasting; Jer 23:32 6350
Her prophets are r, Zph 3:4 6348
treacherous, r, conceited, lovers 2Tm 3:4 4312

RECKONED

He r it to him as righteousness. Gn 15:6 2803
“Are we not r by him as foreigners? Gn 31:15 2803
it will not be r to his *benefit.* Lv 7:18 2803
is to be r to that man. Lv 17:4 2803
‘Your offering shall be r to Nu 18:27 2803
then *the rest* shall be r to the Nu 18:30 2803
will not be r among the nations. Nu 23:9 2803
I am r among those who go down to Ps 88:4 2803
it was r to him for righteousness, Ps 106:31 2803
It will be r a curse to him. Pr 27:14 2803

IT WAS **R** TO HIM AS RIGHTEOUSNESS. — **Ga 3:6** — *3049*
WAS **R** TO HIM AS RIGHTEOUSNESS,” — **Jas 2:23** — *3049*

RECKONING
Now comes the **r** for his blood.” — **Gn 42:22** — 1875
LORD of hosts will have a day *of* **r** — **Is 2:12**

RECLINE
Those who **r** on beds of ivory And — **Am 6:4** — 7901
and **r** *at the table* with Abraham, — **Mt 8:11** — *347*
and have them **r** *at the table,* — **Lk 12:37** — *347*
and will **r** *at the table* in the — **Lk 13:29** — *347*
go and **r** at the last place, — **Lk 14:10** — *377*

RECLINED
His head as He **r** *at the table.* — **Mt 26:7** — *345*
house and **r** *at the table.* — **Lk 7:36** — *2625*
He went in, and **r** *at the table.* — **Lk 11:37** — *377*
hour had come, He **r** *at the table,* — **Lk 22:14** — *377*
He had **r** *at the table* with them, — **Lk 24:30** — *2625*
and **r** *at the table* again, — **Jn 13:12** — *377*

RECLINES
the one who **r** *at the table* — **Lk 22:27** — *345*
it not the one who **r** *at the table?* — **Lk 22:27** — *345*

RECLINING
Jesus was **r** *at the table* in the house, — **Mt 9:10** — *345*
Jesus was **r** *at the table* with the — **Mt 26:20** — *345*
He was **r** *at the table* in his house, — **Mk 2:15** — *2621*
the leper, and **r** *at the table,* — **Mk 14:3** — *2621*
were **r** *at the table* and eating, — **Mk 14:18** — *345*
as they were **r** *at the table* — **Mk 16:14** — *345*
who were **r** *at the table* with them. — **Lk 5:29** — *2621*
she learned that He was **r** *at the table* — **Lk 7:37** — *2621*
Those who were **r** *at the table* — **Lk 7:49** — *4873*
one of those who were **r** *at the table* — **Lk 14:15** — *4873*
of those **r** *at the table* with Him. — **Jn 12:2** — *345*
There was **r** on Jesus' bosom one — **Jn 13:23** — *345*
Now no one of those **r** *at the table* — **Jn 13:28** — *345*

RECOGNIZE
He did not **r** him, because his — **Gn 27:23** — 5234
although they did not **r** him. — **Gn 42:8** — 5234
rose before one could **r** another; — **Ru 3:14** — 5234
at a distance and did not **r** him, — **Jb 2:12** — 5234
And do you not **r** their witness? — **Jb 21:29** — 5234
That they may see and **r**, — **Is 41:20** — 3045
all around, Yet he did not **r** *it;* — **Is 42:25** — 3045
All who see them will **r** them — **Is 61:9** — 5234
know us And Israel does not **r** us. — **Is 63:16** — 5234
until you **r** that the Most High is — **Da 4:25** — 3046
r that *it is* Heaven *that* rules. — **Da 4:26** — 3046
until you **r** that the Most High is — **Da 4:32** — 3046
“**R**, O king, that it is a law of — **Da 6:15** — 3046
came, and they did not **r** him, — **Mt 17:12** — *1921*
these things, **r** that He is near, — **Mt 24:33** — *1097*
happening, **r** that He is near, — **Mk 13:29** — *1097*
you did not **r** the time of your — **Lk 19:44** — *1097*
then **r** that her desolation is near. — **Lk 21:20** — *1097*
r that the kingdom of God is near. — **Lk 21:31** — *1097*
“I did not **r** Him, but so — **Jn 1:31** — *3609a*
“I did not **r** Him, but He who — **Jn 1:33** — *3609a*
and *began* to **r** them as having been — **Ac 4:13** — *1921*
“I **r** Jesus, and I know about Paul, — **Ac 19:15** — *1097*
came, they could not **r** the land; — **Ac 27:39** — *1921*
let him **r** that the things which I — **1Co 14:37** — *1921*
But if anyone does not **r** *this,* — **1Co 14:38** — *50*
r no one according to the flesh; — **2Co 5:16** — *3609a*
do you not **r** this about yourselves, — **2Co 13:5** — *1921*
But are you willing to **r**, — **Jas 2:20** — *1097*

RECOGNIZED
Judah **r** *them,* and said, — **Gn 38:26** — 5234
Joseph saw his brothers he **r** them, — **Gn 42:7** — 5234
But Joseph had **r** his brothers, — **Gn 42:8** — 5234
they **r** the voice of the young man, — **Jg 18:3** — 5234
Then Saul **r** David's voice and — **1Sa 26:17** — 5234
and he **r** him and fell on his face — **1Ki 18:7** — 5234
and the king of Israel **r** him that — **1Ki 20:41** — 5234
for they **r** that this work had been — **Ne 6:16** — 3045
They are not **r** in the streets; — **La 4:8** — 5234
until he **r** that the Most High God — **Da 5:21** — 3046
when the men of that place **r** Him, — **Mt 14:35** — *1921*
saw them going, and many **r** *them* — **Mk 6:33** — *1921*
immediately *the people* **r** Him, — **Mk 6:54** — *1921*
those who are **r** as rulers of the — **Mk 10:42** — *1380*
eyes were opened and they **r** Him; — **Lk 24:31** — *1921*
He was **r** by them in the breaking of — **Lk 24:35** — *1097*
When she **r** Peter's voice, — **Ac 12:14** — *1921*
But when they **r** that he was a Jew, — **Ac 19:34** — *1921*
not recognize *this,* he is not **r**. — **1Co 14:38** — *50*

RECOGNIZING
and **r** that He had answered them — **Mk 12:28** — *3708*
eyes were prevented from **r** Him. — **Lk 24:16** — *1921*
r neither Him nor the utterances — **Ac 13:27** — *50*
and **r** the grace that had been — **Ga 2:9** — *1097*

RECOMPENSE
“Shall He **r** on your terms, — **Jb 34:33** — 7999a
Repay them their **r**. — **Ps 28:4** — 1576
He will **r** the evil to my foes; — **Ps 54:5** — 7725
You **r** a man according to his — **Ps 62:12** — 7999a
eyes And see the **r** of the wicked. — **Ps 91:8** — 8011
Render **r** to the proud. — **Ps 94:2** — 1576
r with which you have repaid us. — **Ps 137:8** — 1576
A year of **r** for the cause of Zion. — **Is 34:8** — 7966
The **r** of God will come, But He — **Is 35:4** — 1576
is with Him And His **r** before Him. — **Is 40:10** — 6468
His adversaries, **r** to His enemies; — **Is 59:18** — 1576
To the coastlands He will make **r**. — **Is 59:18** — 1576
will faithfully give them their **r** And — **Is 61:8** — 6468
with Him, and His **r** before Him.” — **Is 62:11** — 6468
who is rendering **r** to His enemies. — **Is 66:6** — 1576
r them according to their deeds and — **Jer 25:14** — 7999a
He is going to render **r** to her. — **Jer 51:6** — 1576
For the LORD is a God of **r**, — **Jer 51:56** — 1578
You will **r** them, O LORD, — **La 3:64** — 7725, 1576
Are you rendering Me a **r**? — **Jl 3:4** — 1576
But if you do **r** Me, swiftly and — **Jl 3:4** — 1580
I will return your **r** on your head. — **Jl 3:4** — 1576
and return your **r** on your head. — **Jl 3:7** — 1576

RECOMPENSED
cleanness of my hands He has **r** me. — **2Sa 22:21** — 7725
“Therefore the LORD has **r** me — **2Sa 22:25** — 7725
cleanness of my hands He has **r** me. — **Ps 18:20** — 7725
Therefore the LORD has **r** me — **Ps 18:24** — 7725
be **r** for his deeds in the body, — **2Co 5:10** — *2865*

RECOMPENSES
And fully **r** the proud doer. — **Ps 31:23** — 7999a

RECONCILE
and he tried to **r** them in peace, — **Ac 7:26** — *4871b*
and might **r** them both in one body — **Eph 2:16** — *604*
Him to **r** all things to Himself, — **Col 1:20** — *604*

RECONCILED
first be **r** to your brother, and — **Mt 5:24** — *1259*
we were **r** to God through the death — **Ro 5:10** — *2644*
His Son, much more, having been **r**, — **Ro 5:10** — *2644*
or else be **r** to her husband), — **1Co 7:11** — *2644*
r us to Himself through Christ and — **2Co 5:18** — *2644*
on behalf of Christ, be **r** to God. — **2Co 5:20** — *2644*
yet He has now **r** you in His — **Col 1:22** — *604*

RECONCILIATION
whom we have now received the **r**. — **Ro 5:11** — *2643*
rejection is the **r** of the world, — **Ro 11:15** — *2643*
and gave us the ministry of **r**, — **2Co 5:18** — *2643*
has committed to us the word of **r**. — **2Co 5:19** — *2643*

RECONCILING
in Christ **r** the world to Himself, — **2Co 5:19** — *2644*

RECONSTRUCTING
men were who were **r** this building. — **Ezr 5:4** — 1124

RECORD
in the **r** books of your fathers. — **Ezr 4:15** — 1799b
you will discover in the **r** books and — **Ezr 4:15** — 1799b
in which I found the following **r**: — **Ne 7:5** — 3789
who constantly **r** unjust decisions, — **Is 10:1** — 3789
“**R** the vision And inscribe *it* on — **Hab 2:2** — 3789
The **r** of the genealogy of Jesus — **Mt 1:1** — *976*

RECORDED
Moses **r** their starting places — **Nu 33:2** — 3789
These, **r** by name, came in the — **1Ch 4:41** — 3789
r them in the presence of the — **1Ch 24:6** — 3789
which is **r** in the Book of the Kings — **2Ch 20:34** — 5927
all the weight was **r** at that time. — **Ezr 8:34** — 3789
Then Mordecai **r** these events, and — **Es 9:20** — 3789
may they not be **r** with the righteous. — **Ps 69:28** — 3789
who is **r** for life in Jerusalem. — **Is 4:3** — 3789
that your names are **r** in heaven.” — **Lk 10:20** — *1449*

RECORDER
the son of Ahilud *was* **r**. — **2Sa 8:16** — 2142
the son of Ahilud was the **r**; — **2Sa 20:24** — 2142
the son of Ahilud *was* the **r**; — **1Ki 4:3** — 2142
and Joah the son of Asaph the **r**, — **2Ki 18:18** — 2142
and Joah the son of Asaph, the **r**, — **2Ki 18:37** — 2142
the son of Ahilud *was* **r**; — **1Ch 18:15** — 2142
and Joah the son of Joahaz the **r**, — **2Ch 34:8** — 2142
and Joah the son of Asaph, the **r**, — **Is 36:3** — 2142
and Joah the son of Asaph, the **r**, — **Is 36:22** — 2142

RECORDS
These are *the* **r** *of* — **Gn 6:9**
Now these are *the* **r** *of* — **Gn 10:1**
These are *the* **r** *of* — **Gn 11:10**
Now these are *the* **r** *of* — **Gn 11:27**
Now these are *the* **r** *of* — **Gn 25:12**
Now these are *the* **r** *of* — **Gn 25:19**
Now these are *the* **r** *of* — **Gn 36:1**
These then are *the* **r** *of* — **Gn 36:9**
These are *the* **r** *of* — **Gn 37:2**
Now these are *the* **r** *of* — **Nu 3:1**
And the **r** are ancient. — **1Ch 4:22** — 1697
in the **r** of Nathan the prophet, — **2Ch 9:29** — 1697
in the **r** of Shemaiah the prophet — **2Ch 12:15** — 1697
the **r** of the kings of Israel. — **2Ch 33:18** — 1697
are written in the **r** of the Hozai. — **2Ch 33:19** — 1697
an order to bring the book of **r**, — **Es 6:1** — 2146

RECOUNT
they shall **r** the righteous deeds — **Jg 5:11** — 8567
Yes, let him **r** it to Me in order, — **Is 44:7** — 6186a
Come and let us **r** in Zion The work — **Jer 51:10** — 5608

RECOUNTED
Then Moses came and **r** to the — **Ex 24:3** — 5608
Then Haman **r** to them the glory of — **Es 5:11** — 5608
Haman **r** to Zeresh his wife and — **Es 6:13** — 5608

RECOVER
you not **r** them within that time? — **Jg 11:26** — 5337
I will **r** from this sickness.” — **2Ki 1:2** — 2421a
'Will I **r** from this sickness?' ” — **2Ki 8:8** — 2421a
'Will I **r** from this sickness?' ” — **2Ki 8:9** — 2421a
'You will surely **r**,' — **2Ki 8:10** — 2421a
told me that you would surely **r**.” — **2Ki 8:14** — 2421a
Jeroboam did not again **r** — **2Ch 13:20** — 6113
fell that they could not **r**, — **2Ch 14:13** — 4241
Lord Will again **r** the second time — **Is 11:11** — 7069
apply it to the boil, that he may **r**.” — **Is 38:21** — 2421a
on the sick, and they will **r**.” — **Mk 16:18** — *2192, 2573*
he has fallen asleep, he will **r**.” — **Jn 11:12** — *4982*

RECOVERED
So David **r** all that the Amalekites — **1Sa 30:18** — 5337
any of the spoil that we have **r**, — **1Sa 30:22** — 5337
him and **r** the cities of Israel. — **2Ki 13:25** — 7725
he fought and how he **r** for Israel, — **2Ki 14:28** — 7725
king of Aram **r** Elath for Aram, — **2Ki 16:6** — 7725
and laid *it* on the boil, and he **r**. — **2Ki 20:7** — 2421a
that he had been sick and had **r**. — **Is 39:1** — 2388
people whom he had **r** from Ishmael — **Jer 41:16** — 7725

RECOVERS
but so **r** his means as to find — **Lv 25:26** — 5381

RECOVERY
of Judah after his illness and **r**: — **Is 38:9** — 2421a
your **r** will speedily spring forth; — **Is 58:8** — 724
for *your* sore, No **r** for you. — **Jer 30:13** — 8585b
AND **R** OF SIGHT TO THE BLIND, — **Lk 4:18** — *309*

RECURRENT
lying *in bed* afflicted with **r** — **Ac 28:8**

RED
Now the first came forth **r**, — **Gn 25:25** — 132
a swallow of that **r** stuff there, — **Gn 25:30** — 122
and drove them into the **R** Sea; — **Ex 10:19** — 5488, 3220
of the wilderness to the **R** Sea; — **Ex 13:18** — 5488, 3220
officers are drowned in the **R** Sea. — **Ex 15:4** — 5488, 3220
Moses led Israel from the **R** Sea, — **Ex 15:22** — 5488, 3220
fix your boundary from the **R** Sea — **Ex 23:31** — 5488, 3220
rams' skins dyed **r**, porpoise — **Ex 25:5** — 119
for the tent of rams' skins dyed **r** and — **Ex 26:14** — 119
and rams' skins dyed **r**, — **Ex 35:7** — 119
goats' *hair* and rams' skins dyed **r** — **Ex 35:23** — 119
for the tent of rams' skins dyed **r**, — **Ex 36:19** — 119
the covering of rams' skins dyed **r**, — **Ex 39:34** — 119
by the way of the **R** Sea.” — **Nu 14:25** — 5488, 3220
r heifer in which is no defect — **Nu 19:2** — 122
Mount Hor by the way of the **R** Sea, — **Nu 21:4** — 5488, 3220
Elim and camped by the **R** Sea. — **Nu 33:10** — 5488, 3220
They journeyed from the **R** Sea and — **Nu 33:11** — 5488, 3220
by the way to the **R** Sea.' — **Dt 1:40** — 5488, 3220
by the way to the **R** Sea, — **Dt 2:1** — 5488, 3220
He made the water of the **R** Sea to — **Dt 11:4** — 5488, 3220
and the **r** kite, the falcon, and — **Dt 14:13**
LORD dried up the water of the **R** Sea — **Jos 2:10** — 5488, 3220
your God had done to the **R** Sea, — **Jos 4:23** — 5488, 3220
and horsemen to the **R** Sea. — **Jos 24:6** — 5488, 3220
to the **R** Sea and came to Kadesh, — **Jg 11:16** — 5488, 3220
Eloth on the shore of the **R** Sea, — **1Ki 9:26** — 5488, 3220
water opposite *them* as **r** as blood. — **2Ki 3:22** — 122
heard their cry by the **R** Sea. — **Ne 9:9** — 5488, 3220
rebelled by the sea, at the **R** Sea. — **Ps 106:7** — 5488, 3220
rebuked the **R** Sea and it dried up, — **Ps 106:9** — 5488, 3220
And awesome things by the **R** Sea. — **Ps 106:22** — 5488, 3220
Him who divided the **R** Sea asunder, — **Ps 136:13** — 5488, 3220
Pharaoh and his army in the **R** Sea, — **Ps 136:15** — 5488, 3220
not look on the wine when it is **r**, — **Pr 23:31** — 119
Though they are **r** like crimson, — **Is 1:18** — 119
he outlines it with **r** chalk. — **Is 44:13**
Why is Your apparel **r**, — **Is 63:2** — 122
cedar and painting *it* bright **r**.' — **Jer 22:14** — 8350
of it has been heard at the **R** Sea. — **Jer 49:21** — 5488, 3220
of his mighty men are *colored* **r**, — **Na 2:3** — 119
a man was riding on a **r** horse, — **Zch 1:8** — 122
which were in the ravine, with **r**, — **Zch 1:8** — 122
With the first chariot *were* **r** horses, — **Zch 6:2** — 122
fair weather, for the sky is **r**.' — **Mt 16:2** — *4449*
for the sky is **r** and threatening.' — **Mt 16:3** — *4449*
in the land of Egypt and in the **R** Sea — **Ac 7:36** — *2063*
they passed through the **R** Sea — **Heb 11:29** — *2063*
And another, a **r** horse, went out; — **Rv 6:4** — *4450a*
a great **r** dragon having seven — **Rv 12:3** — *4450a*

REDDISH
if the mark is greenish or **r** in — **Lv 13:49** — 125
has greenish or **r** depressions and — **Lv 14:37** — 125

REDDISH-WHITE
there is a white swelling or a **r**, — **Lv 13:19** — 125
the burn becomes a bright spot, **r**, — **Lv 13:24** — 125
there occurs a **r** infection, — **Lv 13:42** — 125
the infection is **r** on his bald head — **Lv 13:43** — 125

REDEEM
I will also **r** you with an — **Ex 6:6** — 1350
a donkey you shall **r** with a lamb, — **Ex 13:13** — 6299
a lamb, but if you do not **r** *it,* — **Ex 13:13** — 6299
man among your sons you shall **r**. — **Ex 13:13** — 6299
every firstborn of my sons I **r**.' — **Ex 13:15** — 6299
“You shall **r** with a lamb the — **Ex 34:20** — 6299
and if you do not **r** *it,* — **Ex 34:20** — 6299
You shall **r** all the firstborn of — **Ex 34:20** — 6299

One of his brothers may r him, Lv 25:48 1350
or his uncle's son, may r him, Lv 25:49 1350
from his family may r him; Lv 25:49 1350
if he prospers, he may r himself. Lv 25:49 1350
if he should ever *wish to* r it, Lv 27:13 1350
it should *wish to* r his house, Lv 27:15 1350
should ever wish to r the field, Lv 27:19 1350
'Yet if he will not r the field, Lv 27:20 1350
then he shall r it according to Lv 27:27 6299
man wishes to r part of his tithe, Lv 27:31 1350
firstborn of man you shall surely r, Nu 18:15 6299
of unclean animals you shall r. Nu 18:15 6299
from a month old you shall r them, Nu 18:16 6299
firstborn of a goat, you shall not r; Nu 18:17 6299
morning comes, if he will r you, Ru 3:13 1350
will redeem you, good; let him r you. Ru 3:13 1350
But if he does not wish to r you, Ru 3:13 1350
to redeem you, then I will r you, Ru 3:13 1350
If you will r *it,* redeem *it;* Ru 4:4 1350
If you will redeem *it,* r *it;* Ru 4:4 1350
there is no one but you to r *it,* Ru 4:4 1350
And he said, "I will r *it.*" Ru 4:4 1350
"I cannot r *it* for myself, because I Ru 4:6 1350
R *it* for yourself; Ru 4:6 1350
redemption, for I cannot r *it.*" Ru 4:6 1350
whom God went to r for Himself as 2Sa 7:23 6299
whom God went to r for Himself *as* 1Ch 17:21 6299
famine He will r you from death, Jb 5:20 6299
'R me from the hand of the tyrants' Jb 6:23 6299
R Israel, O God, Out of all his Ps 25:22 6299
R me, and be gracious to me. Ps 26:11 6299
And r us for the sake of Your Ps 44:26 6299
can by any means r *his* brother Or Ps 49:7 6299
But God will r my soul from the Ps 49:15 6299
He will r my soul in peace from Ps 55:18 6299
Oh draw near to my soul *and* r it; Ps 69:18 1350
R me from the oppression of man, Ps 119:134 6299
Plead my cause and r me; Ps 119:154 1350
And He will r Israel From all his Ps 130:8 6299
And I will r you from the grasp of Jer 15:21 6299
I would r them, but they speak Hos 7:13 6299
Shall I r them from death? Hos 13:14 1350
There the LORD will r you From the Mi 4:10 1350
was He who was going to r Israel. Lk 24:21 *3084*
r those who were under the Law, Ga 4:5 *1805*
to r us from every Ti 2:14 *3084*

REDEEMED

angel who has r me from all evil, Gn 48:16 1350
led the people whom You have r; Ex 15:13 1350
then he shall let her be r. Ex 21:8 6299
man, but who has in no way been r nor Lv 19:20 6299
belongs to the Levites may be r Lv 25:33 1350
if he is not r by these *means,* Lv 25:54 1350
man, it may no longer be r; Lv 27:20 1350
and if it is not r, Lv 27:27 1350
property, shall not be sold or r. Lv 27:28 1350
It shall not be r.'" Lv 27:33 1350
r you from the house of slavery, Dt 7:8 6299
You have r through Your greatness, Dt 9:26 6299
r you from the house of slavery, Dt 13:5 6299
and the LORD your God r you; Dt 15:15 6299
people Israel whom You have r, Dt 21:8 6299
LORD your God r you from there; Dt 24:18 6299
who has r my life from all distress, 2Sa 4:9 6299
whom You have r for Yourself from 2Sa 7:23 6299
has r my life from all distress, 1Ki 1:29 6299
whom You r out of Egypt? 1Ch 17:21 6299
servants and Your people whom You r Ne 1:10 6299
have r our Jewish brothers who were Ne 5:8 7069
r my soul from going to the pit, Jb 33:28 6299
And my soul, which You have r. Ps 71:23 6299
Which You have r to be the tribe Ps 74:2 1350
have by Your power r Your people, Ps 77:15 1350
when He r them from the adversary, Ps 78:42 6299
And r them from the hand of the Ps 106:10 1350
Let the r of the LORD say *so,* Whom Ps 107:2 1350
Whom He has r from the hand of the Ps 107:2 1350
Zion will be r with justice And Is 1:27 6299
thus says the LORD, who r Abraham, Is 29:22 6299
But the r will walk *there,* Is 35:9 1350
"Do not fear, for I have r you; Is 43:1 1350
Return to Me, for I have r you." Is 44:22 1350
For the LORD has r Jacob And in Is 44:23 1350
LORD has r His servant Jacob." Is 48:20 1350
a pathway For the r to cross over? Is 51:10 1350
and you will be r without money." Is 52:3 1350
His people, He has r Jerusalem. Is 52:9 1350
holy people, The r of the LORD"; Is 62:12 1350
love and in His mercy He r them, Is 63:9 1350
And r him from the hand of him who Jer 31:11 1350
You have r my life. La 3:58 1350
them together, For I have r them; Zch 10:8 6299
r us from the curse of the Law, Ga 3:13 *1805*
that you were not r with perishable 1Pe 1:18 *3084*

REDEEMER

not left you without a r today, Ru 4:14 1350
As for me, I know that my R lives, Jb 19:25 1350
sight, O LORD, my rock and my R. Ps 19:14 1350
And the Most High God their R. Ps 78:35 1350
For their R is strong; Pr 23:11 1350
your R is the Holy One of Israel. Is 41:14 1350
Thus says the LORD your R, Is 43:14 1350
And his R, the LORD of hosts: Is 44:6 1350
Thus says the LORD, your R, Is 44:24 1350
Our R, the LORD of hosts is His Is 47:4 1350
Thus says the LORD, your R, Is 48:17 1350
says the LORD, the R of Israel Is 49:7 1350
LORD, am your Savior And your R, Is 49:26 1350
your R is the Holy One of Israel, Is 54:5 1350
on you," Says the LORD your R. Is 54:8 1350
"A R will come to Zion, And Is 59:20 1350
LORD, am your Savior And your R, Is 60:16 1350
Our R from of old is Your name. Is 63:16 1350
"Their R is strong, the LORD of Jer 50:34 1350

REDEEMS

LORD r the soul of His servants, Ps 34:22 6299
Who r your life from the pit, Ps 103:4 1350

REDEMPTION

he shall give for the r of his life Ex 21:30 6306b
to provide for the r of the land. Lv 25:24 1353
as to find sufficient for its r, Lv 25:26 1353
then his r right remains valid Lv 25:29 1353
his right of r lasts a full year. Lv 25:29 1353
they have r rights and revert in Lv 25:31 1353
Levites have a permanent right of r Lv 25:32 1353
r right after he has been sold. Lv 25:48 1353
proportion to them for his own r; Lv 25:51 1353
is to refund *the amount for* his r. Lv 25:52 1353
"As to their r price, from a Nu 18:16 6299
you *may have* my right of r, Ru 4:6 1353
the r and the exchange *of land* Ru 4:7 1353
For the r of his soul is costly, Ps 49:8 6306b
He has sent r to His people; Ps 111:9 6304
And with Him is abundant r. Ps 130:7 6304
heart, And My year of r has come. Is 63:4 1347a
for you have the right of r to buy *it.* Jer 32:7 1353
of possession and the r is yours; Jer 32:8 1353
and accomplished r for His people, Lk 1:68 *3085*
looking for the r of Jerusalem. Lk 2:38 *3085*
because your r is drawing near." Lk 21:28 *629*
the r which is in Christ Jesus; Ro 3:24 *629*
as sons, the r of our body. Ro 8:23 *629*
and sanctification, and r, 1Co 1:30 *629*
Him we have r through His blood, Eph 1:7 *629*
to the r of *God's own* possession, Eph 1:14 *629*
you were sealed for the day of r. Eph 4:30 *629*
in whom we have r, the forgiveness Col 1:14 *629*
all, having obtained eternal r. Heb 9:12 *3085*
a death has taken place for the r of Heb 9:15 *629*

REDNESS

Who has r of eyes? Pr 23:29 2448

REDUCE

you are not to r any of it. Ex 5:8 1639
r *your* daily amount of bricks." Ex 5:19 1639
woman, he may not r her food, Ex 21:10 1639
destroy your cattle and r your number Lv 26:22 4591

REDUCED

none of your labor will be r.'" Ex 5:11 1639
For on account of a harlot *one is* r Pr 6:26
their houses r to a rubbish heap, Da 3:29 7739b

REDUCES

to which the fire r the burnt offering Lv 6:10 398
He *it is* who r rulers to nothing, Is 40:23 5414

REDUCING

to destruction by r *them* to ashes, 2Pe 2:6 *5077*

REED

as a r is shaken in the water; 1Ki 14:15 7070
on the staff of this crushed r, 2Ki 18:21 7070
"They slip by like r boats, Jb 9:26 16
on the staff of this crushed r, Is 36:6 7070
"A bruised r He will not break And Is 42:3 7070
it for bowing one's head like a r And Is 58:5 100
have been *only* a staff *made* of r Ezk 29:6 7070
measuring r five hundred reeds by Ezk 42:16 7070
hundred reeds by the measuring r. Ezk 42:16 7070
hundred reeds by the measuring r. Ezk 42:17 7070
reeds with the measuring r. Ezk 42:18 7070
reeds with the measuring r. Ezk 42:19 7070
A r shaken by the wind? Mt 11:7 *2563*
BATTERED R HE WILL NOT BREAK OFF, Mt 12:20 *2563*
head, and a r in His right hand; Mt 27:29 *2563*
and took the r and *began* to beat Mt 27:30 *2563*
with sour wine and put it on a r, Mt 27:48 *2563*
kept beating His head with a r, Mk 15:19 *2563*
with sour wine, put it on a r, Mk 15:36 *2563*
A r shaken by the wind? Lk 7:24 *2563*

REEDS

among the r by the bank of the Nile. Ex 2:3 5488
and she saw the basket among the r Ex 2:5 5488
the covert of the r and the marsh. Jb 40:21 7070
Rebuke the beasts in the r, Ps 68:30 7070
The r and rushes will rot away. Is 19:6 7070
place, Grass *becomes* r and rushes. Is 35:7 7070
the measuring reed five hundred r by Ezk 42:16 7070
hundred r by the measuring reed. Ezk 42:17 7070
hundred r with the measuring reed. Ezk 42:18 7070
hundred r with the measuring reed. Ezk 42:19 7070
Though he flourishes among the r, Hos 13:15 260

REEF

striking a r where two seas met, Ac 27:41 *5117*

REEFS

who are hidden r in your love feasts Jude 1:12 *4694*

REEL

And these also r with wine and Is 28:7 7686
the prophet r with strong drink, Is 28:7 7686
They r while having visions, They Is 28:7 7686

REELAIAH

Jeshua, Nehemiah, Seraiah, R, Ezr 2:2 7480

REELED

They r and staggered like a Ps 107:27 2287

REELING

The chalice of r you have drained Is 51:17 8653
out of your hand the cup of r, Is 51:22 8653
make Jerusalem a cup that causes r Zch 12:2 7478

REELS

My mind r, horror overwhelms me; Is 21:4 8582
earth r to and fro like a drunkard And Is 24:20 5128

REENTER

he may not r the camp. Dt 23:10 935, 8432
and at sundown he may r the camp. Dt 23:11 935, 8432

REESTABLISHED

so I was r in my sovereignty, and Da 4:36 8627

REFER

(which all r *to* things Col 2:22

REFERENCE

r to your former manner of life, Eph 4:22 *2596*
with r to Christ and the church. Eph 5:32 *1519*
a tribe with r to which Moses Heb 7:14 *1519*
second time for salvation without r Heb 9:28

REFERRED

one r to by Isaiah the prophet when Mt 3:3 *3004*

REFERRING

as r to many, but *rather* to Ga 3:16 *1909*
By r to this, when you read Eph 3:4 *4314*

REFERS

for that which r to Me has *its* Lk 22:37 *4012*

REFINE

And a place where they r gold. Jb 28:1 2212
I will r them and assay them; Jer 9:7 6884
insight will fall, in order to r, Da 11:35 6884
fire, R them as silver is refined, Zch 13:9 6884
and r them like gold and silver, Mal 3:3 2212

REFINED

"The man who is r and very Dt 28:54 7390
r and delicate woman among you, Dt 28:56 7390
ivory and overlaid it with r gold. 1Ki 10:18 6338
altar of incense r gold by weight; 1Ch 28:18 2212
and 7,000 talents of r silver, 1Ch 29:4 2212
on the earth, r seven times. Ps 12:6 2212
have r us as silver is refined. Ps 66:10 6884
have refined us as silver is r. Ps 66:10 6884
choice pieces with marrow, *And* r, Is 25:6 2212
"Behold, I have r you, but not as Is 48:10 6884
will be purged, purified and r, Da 12:10 6884
fire, Refine them as silver is r, Zch 13:9 6884
you to buy from Me gold r by fire so Rv 3:18 *4448*

REFINEMENT

the ground for delicateness and r, Dt 28:56 7391

REFINER'S

a r fire and like fullers' soap. Mal 3:2 6884

REFINING

The r pot is for silver and the Pr 17:3 4715
In vain the r goes on, But the Jer 6:29 6884

REFLECTED

When I saw, I r upon it; Pr 24:32 7896, 3820
"The king r and said, Da 4:30 6032

REFLECTING

While Peter was r on the vision, Ac 10:19 *1327a*

REFLECTS

As in water face r face, So Pr 27:19
So the heart of man r man. Pr 27:19

REFORM

r your ways and your deeds." Jer 18:11 3190

REFORMATION

body imposed until a time of r. Heb 9:10 *1357b*

REFORMS

r are being carried out for this Ac 24:2 *1357a*

REFRAIN

shall r from leaving it to him, Ex 23:5 2308
"However, if you r from vowing, Dt 23:22 2308
you therefore r from marrying? Ru 1:13 5702
How long will you r from telling 2Sa 2:26 3808
to battle or shall I r?" 1Ki 22:6 2308
to battle, or shall we r?" 1Ki 22:15 2308
to battle, or shall I r?" 2Ch 18:5 2308
to battle, or shall I r?" 2Ch 18:14 2308
But who can r from speaking? Jb 4:2 6113
do not r from spitting at my face. Jb 30:10 2820
and he on his part will r from Da 11:8 5975
have a right to r from working? 1Co 9:6 *3361*
but I r *from this,* so that no one 2Co 12:6 *5339*
will You r from judging and Rv 6:10 *3756*

REFRAINED

and silent, I r *even* from good, Ps 39:2 2814
So he r and did not put them to Jer 41:8 2308

REFRESH

bread, that you may r yourselves; Gn 18:5 5582
your stranger, may r themselves. Ex 23:12 5314
"Come home with me and r yourself, 1Ki 13:7 5582
raisin cakes, R me with apples, SS 2:5 7502
and r everyone who languishes." Jer 31:25 4390
r my heart in Christ. Phm 1:20 *373*

REFRESHED

He ceased *from labor,* and was r." Ex 31:17 5314
and Saul would be r and be well, 1Sa 16:23 7304
weary and he r himself there. 2Sa 16:14 5314
they have r my spirit and yours. 1Co 16:18 *373*
his spirit has been r by you all. 2Co 7:13 *373*
of Onesiphorus, for he often r me 2Tm 1:16 *404*
saints have been r through you, Phm 1:7 *373*

REFRESHES

For he r the soul of his masters. Pr 25:13 7725

REFRESHING

in order that times of r may come Ac 3:19 *403*
joy by the will of God and find r Ro 15:32

REFRESHMENT
to your body And **r** to your bones. Pr 3:8 8250
REFUGE
shall be the six cities of **r**, Nu 35:6 4733
cities to be your cities of **r**, Nu 35:11 4733
be to you as a **r** from the avenger, Nu 35:12 4733
shall be your six cities of **r**. Nu 35:13 4733
they are to be cities of **r**. Nu 35:14 4733
be for **r** for the sons of Israel, Nu 35:15 4733
restore him to his city of **r** to which Nu 35:25 4733
city of **r** to which he may flee, Nu 35:26 4733
the border of his city of **r**, Nu 35:27 4733
should have remained in his city of **r** Nu 35:28 4733
him who has fled to his city of **r**, Nu 35:32 4733
The rock in which they sought **r**? Dt 32:37 2620
'Designate the cities of **r**, Jos 20:2 4733
your **r** from the avenger of blood. Jos 20:3 4733
the city of **r** for the manslayer, Jos 21:13 4733
the city of **r** for the manslayer, Jos 21:21 4733
the city of **r** for the manslayer, Jos 21:27 4733
the city of **r** for the manslayer, Jos 21:32 4733
the city of **r** for the manslayer, Jos 21:38 4733
you, come and take **r** in my shade; Jg 9:15 2620
wings you have come to seek **r**." Ru 2:12 2620
My God, my rock, in whom I take **r**, 2Sa 22:3 2620
salvation, my stronghold and my **r**; 2Sa 22:3 4498
a shield to all who take **r** in Him. 2Sa 22:31 2620
gave the *following* cities of **r**: 1Ch 6:57 4733
to them the *following* cities of **r**: 1Ch 6:67 4733
blessed are all who take **r** in Him! Ps 2:12 2620
all who take **r** in You be glad, Ps 5:11 2620
my God, in You I have taken **r**; Ps 7:1 2620
In the LORD I take **r**; Ps 11:1 2620
afflicted, But the LORD is his **r**. Ps 14:6 4268
me, O God, for I take **r** in You. Ps 16:1 2620
O Savior of those who take **r** at Ps 17:7 2620
My God, my rock, in whom I take **r**; Ps 18:2 2620
a shield to all who take **r** in Him. Ps 18:30 2620
be ashamed, for I take **r** in You. Ps 25:20 2620
In You, O LORD, I have taken **r**; Ps 31:1 2620
for those who take **r** in You, Ps 31:19 2620
is the man who takes **r** in Him! Ps 34:8 2620
take **r** in Him will be condemned. Ps 34:22 2620
take **r** in the shadow of Your wings. Ps 36:7 2620
them, Because they take **r** in Him. Ps 37:40 2620
God is our **r** and strength, A very Ps 46:1 4268
man who would not make God his **r**, Ps 52:7 4581
"I would hasten to my place of **r** Ps 55:8 4655
me, For my soul takes **r** in You; Ps 57:1 2620
shadow of Your wings I will take **r** Until Ps 57:1 2620
And a **r** in the day of my distress. Ps 59:16 4498
For You have been a **r** for me, Ps 61:3 4268
r in the shelter of Your wings. Ps 61:4 2620
of my strength, my **r** is in God. Ps 62:7 4268
God is a **r** for us. Ps 62:8 4268
the LORD and will take **r** in Him; Ps 64:10 2620
In You, O LORD, I have taken **r**; Ps 71:1 2620
For You are my strong **r**. Ps 71:7 4268
I have made the Lord GOD my **r**, Ps 73:28 4268
"My **r** and my fortress, My God, in Ps 91:2 4268
under His wings you may seek **r**; Ps 91:4 2620
For you have made the LORD, my **r**, Ps 91:9 4268
And my God the rock of my **r**. Ps 94:22 4268
are a **r** for the shephanim. Ps 104:18 4268
It is better to take **r** in the LORD Ps 118:8 2620
It is better to take **r** in the LORD Ps 118:9 2620
In You I take **r**; Ps 141:8 2620
"You are my **r**, My portion in the Ps 142:5 4268
I take **r** in You. Ps 143:9 3680
My shield and He in whom I take **r**, Ps 144:2 2620
And his children will have **r**. Pr 14:26 4268
righteous has a **r** when he dies. Pr 14:32 2620
shield to those who take **r** in Him. Pr 30:5 2620
and **r** and protection from the storm Is 4:6 4268
inhabitants of Gebim have sought **r**. Is 10:31 5756
afflicted of His people will seek **r** Is 14:32 2620
not remembered the rock of your **r**. Is 17:10 4581
his distress, A **r** from the storm, Is 25:4 4268
For we have made falsehood our **r** Is 28:15 4268
hail will sweep away the **r** of lies Is 28:17 4268
take **r** in the safety of Pharaoh And Is 30:2 5756
will be like a **r** from the wind And Is 32:2 4224a
r will be the impregnable rock; Is 33:16 4869
he who takes **r** in Me will inherit Is 57:13 2620
Seek **r**, do not stand *still,* For I Jer 4:6 5756
And my **r** in the day of distress, Jer 16:19 4498
You are my **r** in the day of disaster. Jer 17:17 4268
And have taken **r** in flight, Jer 46:5 5127
But the LORD is a **r** for His people Jl 3:16 4268
He knows those who take **r** in Him. Na 1:7 2620
search for a **r** from the enemy. Na 3:11 4581
take **r** in the name of the LORD. Zph 3:12 2620
we who have taken **r** Heb 6:18 *2703*
REFUGEE
will flee, Or a **r** who will escape. Am 9:1 6412a
REFUGEES
no survivors or **r** from the calamity Jer 42:17 6412a
'So there will be no **r** or survivors Jer 44:14 6412a
for none will return except *a few* **r**. Jer 44:14 6412b
and **r** from the land of Babylon, Jer 50:28 6412b
the **r** from Jerusalem came to me, Ezk 33:21 6412a
in the evening, before the **r** came. Ezk 33:22 6412a
REFUND
r the balance to the man to whom he Lv 25:27 7725
he shall **r** part of his purchase Lv 25:51 7725
r *the amount for* his redemption. Lv 25:52 7725
REFUSE
none of us will **r** you his grave Gn 23:6 3607
"But if you **r** to let *them* go, Ex 8:2 3986
"For if you **r** to let *them* go and Ex 9:2 3986
will you **r** to humble yourself before Ex 10:3 3985
'For if you **r** to let My people go, Ex 10:4 3986
"How long do you **r** to keep My Ex 16:28 3985
the bull and its hide and its **r**, Ex 29:14 6569
legs and its entrails and its **r**, Lv 4:11 6569
its hide and its flesh and its **r** he Lv 8:17 6569
flesh, and their **r** in the fire. Lv 16:27 6569
flesh and its blood, with its **r**, Nu 19:5 6569
and the **r** came out. Jg 3:22 6574
one request of you; do not **r** me." 1Ki 2:16 7725
the king, for he will not **r** you, 1Ki 2:17 7725
small request of you; do not **r** me." 1Ki 2:20 7725
my mother, for I will not **r** you." 1Ki 2:20 7725
my gold, and I did not **r** him." 1Ki 20:7 4513
made a **r** heap on account of this. Ezr 6:11 5122
Dragon's Well and *on* to the **R** Gate, Ne 2:13 830
cubits of the wall to the **R** Gate. Ne 3:13 830
Beth-haccherem repaired the **R** Gate. Ne 3:14 830
top of the wall toward the **R** Gate. Ne 12:31 830
He perishes forever like his **r**; Jb 20:7 1561
Do not let my head **r** it, Ps 141:5 5106
they **r** to act with justice. Pr 21:7 3985
to death, For his hands **r** to work; Pr 21:25 3985
of You, Do not **r** me before I die: Pr 30:7 4513
my eyes desired I did not **r** them. Ec 2:10 680
"But if you **r** and rebel, You will Is 1:20 3985
their corpses lay like **r** in the middle Is 5:25 5478
He knows *enough* to **r** evil and Is 7:15 3988a
the boy will know *enough* to **r** evil Is 7:16 3988a
Sons who **r** to listen To the Is 30:9 3808, 14
And its waters toss up **r** and mud. Is 57:20 7516
fast to deceit, They **r** to return. Jer 8:5 3985
Through deceit they **r** to know Me," Jer 9:6 3985
who **r** to listen to My words, Jer 13:10 3987
if they **r** to take the cup from Jer 25:28 3985
made us mere offscouring and **r** La 3:45 3973
and he who refuses, let him **r**; Ezk 3:27 2308
And fill the valleys with your **r**. Ezk 32:5 7419
we may sell the **r** of the wheat?" Am 8:6 4651
and I will spread **r** on your faces, Mal 2:3 6569
your faces, the **r** of your feasts; Mal 2:3 6569
guests, he was unwilling to **r** her. Mk 6:26 *114*
"Surely no one can **r** the water Ac 10:47 *2967*
of death, I do not **r** to die; Ac 25:11 *3868*
But **r** *to put* younger widows *on the* 1Tm 5:11 *3868*
r foolish and ignorant speculations, 2Tm 2:23 *3868*
you do not **r** Him who is speaking. Heb 12:25 *3868*
REFUSED
him, but he **r** to be comforted. Gn 37:35 3985
he **r** and said to his master's wife, Gn 39:8 3985
But his father **r** and said, Gn 48:19 3985
but you have **r** to let him go. Ex 4:23 3985
Thus Edom **r** to allow Israel to Nu 20:21 3985
has **r** to let me go with you." Nu 22:13 3985
"Balaam **r** to come with us." Nu 22:14 3985
the people **r** to listen to the 1Sa 8:19 3985
but I **r** to stretch out my hand 1Sa 26:23 3808, 14
But he **r** and said, 1Sa 28:23 3985
However, he **r** to turn aside; 2Sa 2:23 3985
out before him, but he **r** to eat. 2Sa 13:9 3985
But the man **r** to strike him. 1Ki 20:35 3985
which he **r** to give you for money; 1Ki 21:15 3985
he urged him to take *it,* but he **r**. 2Ki 5:16 3985
"They **r** to listen, And did Ne 9:17 3985
But Queen Vashti **r** to come at the Es 1:12 3985
My soul **r** to be comforted. Ps 77:2 3985
of God And **r** to walk in His law; Ps 78:10 3985
Because I called and you **r** Pr 1:24 3985
You **r** to be ashamed. Jer 3:3 3985
But they **r** to take correction. Jer 5:3 3985
They have **r** to repent. Jer 5:3 3985
ancestors who **r** to hear My words, Jer 11:10 3985
fast, They have **r** to let them go. Jer 50:33 3985
Because they **r** to return *to Me.* Hos 11:5 3985
"But they **r** to pay attention and Zch 7:11 3985
AND SHE **R** TO BE COMFORTED, Mt 2:18 3756, 2309
seen by her, they **r** to believe it. Mk 16:11 *569*
r to be called the son of Heb 11:24 *720*
r him who warned *them* on earth, Heb 12:25 *3868*
REFUSES
he **r** to let the people go. Ex 7:14 3985
absolutely **r** to give her to him, Ex 22:17 3985
'My husband's brother **r** to Dt 25:7 3985
"My soul **r** to touch *them;* Jb 6:7 3985
She **r** to be comforted for her Jer 31:15 3985
and he who **r**, let him refuse; Ezk 3:27 2310
"If he **r** to listen to them, Mt 18:17 *3878*
he **r** to listen even to the church, Mt 18:17 *3878*
REFUSING
wound incurable, **r** to be healed? Jer 15:18 3985
"But if you keep **r** to go out, Jer 38:21 3985
REFUTE
"**R** me if you can; Array yourselves Jb 33:5 7725
opponents will be able to resist or **r**. Lk 21:15 *471*
and to **r** those who contradict. Ti 1:9 *1651*
REFUTED
there was no one who **r** Job, Jb 32:12 3198
powerfully **r** the Jews in public, Ac 18:28 *1246*
REGAIN
the seller will not **r** what he sold Ezk 7:13 7725
"Rabboni, *I want* to **r** my sight!" Mk 10:51 *308*
"Lord, *I want* to **r** my sight!" Lk 18:41 *308*
so that he might **r** his sight." Ac 9:12 *308*
me so that you may **r** your sight and Ac 9:17 *308*
REGAINED
they **r** their sight and followed Him. Mt 20:34 *308*
Immediately he **r** his sight and Mk 10:52 *308*
Immediately he **r** his sight and Lk 18:43 *308*
like scales, and he **r** his sight, Ac 9:18 *308*
REGARD
r for Abel and for his offering; Gn 4:4 8159
and for his offering He had no **r**. Gn 4:5 8159
but he who paid no **r** to the word Ex 9:21 7760, 3820
with **r** to all their holy gifts; Ex 28:38
atonement for him in **r** to his sin, Lv 4:26
atonement for him in **r** to his sin Lv 4:35 5921
and deceives his companion in **r** to Lv 6:2
so that he sins in **r** to any one of Lv 6:3 5921
in **r** to all their sins; Lv 16:16
in **r** to all their sins; Lv 16:21
his means with **r** to you falter, Lv 25:35 5973
so poor with **r** to you that he sells Lv 25:39 5973
poor with **r** to him as to sell himself Lv 25:47 5973
"Do not **r** their offering! Nu 16:15 6437
Nor did he **r** his own sons, Dt 33:9 3045
in **r** to the things under the ban, Jos 7:1
blameless in **r** to the Philistines when Jg 15:3 4480
in **r** to all that they say to you, 1Sa 8:7
you should **r** a dead dog like me?" 2Sa 9:8 6437
"Yet have **r** to the prayer of Your 1Ki 8:28 6437
were it not that I **r** the presence 2Ki 3:14 5375
without **r** to divisions), 2Ch 5:11 8104
"Yet have **r** to the prayer of Your 2Ch 6:19 6437
without **r** to their genealogical 2Ch 31:16
what they had seen in this **r** and Es 9:26 3602
And had no **r** for any of His ways; Jb 34:27 7919a
is, in **r** to both nation and man? Jb 34:29 5921
cry, Nor will the Almighty **r** it. Jb 35:13 7789
not **r** any who are wise of heart." Jb 37:24 7200
Because they do not **r** the works of Ps 28:5 995
I hate those who **r** vain idols, Ps 31:6 8104
If I **r** wickedness in my heart, The Ps 66:18 7200
on Your precepts And **r** Your ways. Ps 119:15 5027
That I may have **r** for Your statutes Ps 119:117 8159
has **r** for the life of his animal, Pr 12:10 3045
In **r** to all that this people call Is 8:12
hosts whom you should **r** as holy. Is 8:13 6942
day man will have **r** for his Maker And Is 17:7 8159
He will not have **r** for the altars, Is 17:8 8159
the cities, He has no **r** for man. Is 33:8 2803
to Jeremiah in **r** to the drought: Jer 14:1 1697
in **r** to Shallum the son of Josiah, Jer 22:11 413
Therefore thus says the LORD in **r** Jer 22:18 413
r as good the captives of Judah, Jer 24:5 5234
He will not continue to **r** them; La 4:16 5027
with **r** to an inheritance for them, Ezk 44:28
saw in **r** to these men that the fire Da 3:27
Daniel in **r** to government affairs; Da 6:4 6655
with **r** to the law of his God." Da 6:5
would be changed in **r** to Daniel. Da 6:17
so he will come back and show **r** Da 11:30 995
"He will show no **r** for the Da 11:37 995
will he show **r** for any *other* god; Da 11:37 995
"Those who **r** vain idols Forsake Jon 2:8 8104
for they all **r** John as a prophet." Mt 21:26 *2192*
with **r** to even a *single* charge, Mt 27:14 *4314*
"For He has had **r** for the humble Lk 1:48 *1914*
"In **r** to all the things of which Ac 26:2 *4012*
were free in **r** to righteousness. Ro 6:20
for the flesh in **r** to *its* lusts. Ro 13:14 *1519*
The one who eats is not to **r** with Ro 14:3 *1848*
you **r** your brother with contempt? Ro 14:10 *1848*
Let a man **r** us in this manner, as 1Co 4:1 *3049*
we have **r** for what is honorable, 2Co 8:21 *4306*
who **r** us as if we walked according 2Co 10:2 *3049*
except in **r** to *my* weaknesses. 2Co 12:5
boasting in **r** to himself alone, Ga 6:4 *1519*
alone, and not in **r** to another. Ga 6:4 *1519*
r one another as more Php 2:3 *2233*
did not **r** equality with God a Php 2:6 *2233*
and hold men like him in high **r**; Php 2:29 *1784*
I do not **r** myself as having laid Php 3:13 *3049*
one is to act as your judge in **r** to food Col 2:16
with **r** to the coming of our Lord 2Th 2:1 *5228*
Yet do not **r** him as an enemy, 2Th 3:15 *2233*
shipwreck in **r** to their faith. 1Tm 1:19 *4012*
piety in **r** to their own family and 1Tm 5:4
to **r** their own masters as worthy 1Tm 6:1 *2233*
rejected in **r** to the faith. 2Tm 3:8 *4012*
If then you **r** me a partner, accept Phm 1:17 *2192*
DO NOT **R** LIGHTLY THE DISCIPLINE OF Heb 12:5 *3643a*
faithful brother (for so I **r** *him),* 1Pe 5:12 *3049*
and **r** the patience of our Lord *as* 2Pe 3:15 *2233*
REGARDED
and **r** it as easy to go up into the Dt 1:41 1951
they are also **r** as Rephaim, Dt 2:11 2803
also **r** as the land of the Rephaim, Dt 2:20 2803
For I have **r** My people, because 1Sa 9:16 7200
was all the advice of Ahithophel **r** 2Sa 16:23
and have **r** me according to the 1Ch 17:17 7200
"Why are we **r** as beasts, As Jb 18:3 2803
"Clubs are **r** as stubble; Jb 41:29 2803
He has **r** the prayer of the destitute And Ps 102:17 6437
And are **r** as a speck of dust on Is 40:15 2803
They are **r** by Him as less than Is 40:17 2803
How they are **r** as earthen jars, La 4:2 2803
They are **r** as a strange thing. Hos 8:12 2803
because they **r** John as a prophet. Mt 14:5 *2192*
slave, who was highly **r** by him, Lk 7:2 *1784*
one of them was **r** to be greatest. Lk 22:24 *1380*
goddess Artemis be **r** as worthless Ac 19:27 *3049*

be **r** as circumcision? **Ro 2:26** *3049*
the children of the promise are **r** as **Ro 9:8** *3049*
r as deceivers and yet true; **2Co 6:8**
an opportunity to be **r** just as we are **2Co 11:12** *2147*
and has **r** as unclean the blood of **Heb 10:29** *2233*

REGARDING
This is the law **r** the animal and **Lv 11:46**
And this **r** Judah; **Dt 33:7**
"**R** the words which you have **2Ki 22:18**
and they spoke to her **r** this. **2Ch 34:22**
says the LORD God of Israel **r** **2Ch 34:26**
king of Israel sin **r** these things? **Ne 13:26** 5921
Stop **r** man, whose breath *of life* **Is 2:22** 2308, 4480
for the vision **r** all their multitude **Ezk 7:13** 413
into judgment with him there **r** **Ezk 17:20**
r the resurrection of the dead, **Mt 22:31** *4012*
"But **r** the fact that the dead **Mk 12:26** *4012*
no guilt in this man **r** the charges **Lk 23:14**
say to you **r** the patriarch David **Ac 2:29** *4012*
and Esau, even **r** things to come. **Heb 11:20** *4012*

REGARDS
And who **r** my hope? **Jb 17:15** 7789
Nor **r** the rich above the poor, **Jb 34:19** 5234
"He **r** iron as straw, Bronze as **Jb 41:27** 2803
is exalted, Yet He **r** the lowly, **Ps 138:6** 7200
For there is no one who **r** me; **Ps 142:4** 5234
he who **r** reproof will be honored. **Pr 13:18** 8104
But he who **r** reproof is sensible. **Pr 15:5** 8104
because He no longer **r** the offering **Mal 2:13** 6437
One person **r** one day above another, **Ro 14:5** *2919*
another **r** every day *alike*. **Ro 14:5** *2919*
For who **r** you as superior? **1Co 4:7** *1252*

REGATHER
And there is no one to **r** *them*. **Na 3:18** 6908

REGEM
The sons of Jahdai *were* **R**, **1Ch 2:47** 7276

REGEMMELECH
sent Sharezer and **R** and their men to **Zch 7:2** 7278

REGENERATION
in the **r** when the Son of Man will **Mt 19:28** *3824*
by the washing of **r** and renewing **Ti 3:5** *3824*

REGION
sixty cities, all the **r** of Argob, **Dt 3:4** 2256a
of Manasseh, all the **r** of Argob **Dt 3:13** 2256a
the son of Manasseh took all the **r** of **Dt 3:14** 2256a
at the sea by the **r** of Achzib. **Jos 19:29** 2256a
they came to the **r** of the Jordan **Jos 22:10** 1552
of Canaan, in the **r** of the Jordan, **Jos 22:11** 1552
the **r** of Argob, which is in **1Ki 4:13** 2256a
stream which flowed through the **r**, **2Ch 32:4** 776
rest of the **r** beyond the River. **Ezr 4:10** 5675
the men in the **r** beyond the River, **Ezr 4:11** 5675
in the wilderness in a desert **r**; **Ps 107:4** 3452
waters go out toward the eastern **r** **Ezk 47:8** 1552
in the **r** of Zebulun and Naphtali. **Mt 4:13** *3725*
Him to leave their **r**. **Mt 8:34** *3725*
woman from that **r** came out **Mt 15:22** *3725*
and came to the **r** of Magadan. **Mt 15:39** *3725*
the **r** of Judea beyond the Jordan; **Mt 19:1** *3725*
Him to leave their **r**. **Mk 5:17** *3725*
went away from there to the **r** of Tyre. **Mk 7:24** *3725*
He went out from the **r** of Tyre, **Mk 7:31** *3725*
within the **r** of Decapolis. **Mk 7:31** *3725*
went from there to the **r** of Judea and **Mk 10:1** *3725*
In the same **r** there were *some* **Lk 2:8** *5561*
the **r** of Ituraea and Trachonitis, **Lk 3:1** *5561*
the coastal **r** of Tyre and Sidon, **Lk 6:17** *3882*
being spread through the whole **r**. **Ac 13:49** *5561*
and Derbe, and the surrounding **r**; **Ac 14:6** *4066*
the Phrygian and Galatian **r**, **Ac 16:6** *5561*
the Galatian **r** and Phrygia, **Ac 18:23** *5561*
throughout all the **r** of Judea, **Ac 26:20** *5561*

REGIONS
all the **r** *of* the Philistines and **Jos 13:2** 1552
hired from **r** beyond the Euphrates **Is 7:20** 5676
Sidon and all the **r** of Philistia? **Jl 3:4** 1552
he left for the **r** of Galilee, **Mt 2:22** *3313*
the **r** of Judea and Samaria, **Ac 8:1** *5561*
was traveling through all *those* **r**, **Ac 9:32**
to the **r** along the coast of Asia, **Ac 27:2** *5117*
further place for me in these **r**, **Ro 15:23** *2824*
gospel even to the **r** beyond you, **2Co 10:16**
not be stopped in the **r** of Achaia. **2Co 11:10** *2824*
into the **r** of Syria and Cilicia. **Ga 1:21** *2824*

REGISTER
to Beersheba, and **r** the people, **2Sa 24:2** 6485
king to **r** the people of Israel. **2Sa 24:4** 6485
in the **r** of the house of Israel, **Ezk 13:9** 3791
way to **r** for the census, **Lk 2:3** *583*
in order to **r** along with Mary, **Lk 2:5** *583*

REGISTERED
they **r** by ancestry in their families, **Nu 1:18** 3205
were among those who had been **r**, **Nu 11:26** 3789
were **r** in the days of Eliashib, **Ne 12:22** 3789
were **r** in the Book of the Chronicles **Ne 12:23** 3789

REGISTERS
will count when He **r** the peoples, **Ps 87:6** 3789

REGISTRATION
genealogical **r** by their families, **Nu 1:20** 8435
genealogical **r** by their families, **Nu 1:22** 8435
genealogical **r** by their families, **Nu 1:24** 8435
genealogical **r** by their families, **Nu 1:26** 8435
genealogical **r** by their families, **Nu 1:28** 8435
genealogical **r** by their families, **Nu 1:30** 8435
genealogical **r** by their families, **Nu 1:32** 8435
genealogical **r** by their families, **Nu 1:34** 8435
genealogical **r** by their families, **Nu 1:36** 8435
genealogical **r** by their families, **Nu 1:38** 8435
genealogical **r** by their families, **Nu 1:40** 8435
genealogical **r** by their families, **Nu 1:42** 8435
the number of the **r** of the people **2Sa 24:9** 4662
searched *among* their ancestral **r**, **Ezr 2:62** 3791, 3187
searched *among* their ancestral **r**, **Ne 7:64** 3791, 3187

REGRET
"I **r** that I have made Saul king, **1Sa 15:11** 5162
and he departed with no one's **r**, **2Ch 21:20** 2532
by my letter, I do not **r** it; **2Co 7:8** *3338*
I do not regret it; though I did **r** it **2Co 7:8** *3338*
produces a repentance without **r**, **2Co 7:10** *278*

REGRETTED
And the LORD **r** that He had made **1Sa 15:35** 5162
but afterward he **r** it and went. **Mt 21:29** *3338*

REGULAR
fine flour as a **r** grain offering, **Lv 6:20** 8548
a **r** allowance was given him by the **2Ki 25:30** 8548
a **r** allowance was given him by the **Jer 52:34** 8548
removed the **r** sacrifice from Him, **Da 8:11** 8548
horn along with the **r** sacrifice; **Da 8:12** 8548
will the vision *about* the **r** sacrifice **Da 8:13** 8548
and do away with the **r** sacrifice. **Da 11:31** 8548
that the **r** sacrifice is abolished and **Da 12:11** 8548

REGULARLY
and you shall eat at my table **r**." **2Sa 9:7** 8548
shall eat at my table **r**." **2Sa 9:10** 8548
for he ate at the king's table **r**. **2Sa 9:13** 8548
r all the days of his life; **2Ki 25:29** 8548
r all the days of his life. **Jer 52:33** 8548
and those who attend **r** to the altar **1Co 9:13** *3918a*

REGULATION
He made for them a statute and **r**, **Ex 15:25** 4941
firm **r** for the song leaders day by day **Ne 11:23** 548
two days according to their **r** and **Es 9:27** 3791

REGULATIONS
end of her twelve months under the **r** **Es 2:12** 1881
first *covenant* had **r** of divine worship **Heb 9:1** *1345*
r for the body imposed until a **Heb 9:10** *1345*

REHABIAH
son of Eliezer was **R** the chief; **1Ch 23:17** 7345
but the sons of **R** were very many. **1Ch 23:17** 7345
Of **R**: of the sons of Rehabiah, **1Ch 24:21** 7345
of the sons of **R**, Isshiah the **1Ch 24:21** 7345
by Eliezer *were* **R** his son, **1Ch 26:25** 7345

REHOB
the wilderness of Zin as far as **R**, **Nu 13:21** 7340
R and Hammon and Kanah, **Jos 19:28** 7340
also *were* Ummah, and Aphek and **R**; **Jos 19:30** 7340
and **R** with its pasture lands; **Jos 21:31** 7340
of Helbah, or of Aphik, or of **R**. **Jg 1:31** 7340
the son of **R** king of Zobah, **2Sa 8:3** 7340
the spoil of Hadadezer, son of **R**, **2Sa 8:12** 7340
the Arameans of Zobah and of **R** **2Sa 10:8** 7340
and **R** with its pasture lands; **1Ch 6:75** 7340
Mica, **R**, Hashabiah, **Ne 10:11** 7340

REHOBOAM
his son **R** reigned in his place. **1Ki 11:43** 7346
Then **R** went to Shechem, for all **1Ki 12:1** 7346
of Israel came and spoke to **R**, **1Ki 12:3** 7346
King **R** consulted with the **1Ki 12:6** 7346
the people came to **R** on the third day **1Ki 12:12** 7346
Then **R** reigned over them. **1Ki 12:17** 7346
Then King **R** sent Adoram, who was **1Ki 12:18** 7346
And King **R** made haste to mount his **1Ki 12:18** 7346
Now when **R** had come to Jerusalem, **1Ki 12:21** 7346
kingdom to **R** the son of Solomon. **1Ki 12:21** 7346
"Speak to **R** the son of Solomon, **1Ki 12:23** 7346
lord, *even* to **R** king of Judah; **1Ki 12:27** 7346
and return to **R** king of Judah." **1Ki 12:27** 7346
Now **R** the son of Solomon reigned **1Ki 14:21** 7346
R was forty-one years old when he **1Ki 14:21** 7346
happened in the fifth year of King **R**, **1Ki 14:25** 7346
So King **R** made shields of bronze **1Ki 14:27** 7346
the acts of **R** and all that he did, **1Ki 14:29** 7346
R and Jeroboam continually. **1Ki 14:30** 7346
And **R** slept with his fathers and **1Ki 14:31** 7346
was war between **R** and Jeroboam **1Ki 15:6** 7346
Now Solomon's son *was* **R**, **1Ch 3:10** 7346
his son **R** reigned in his place. **2Ch 9:31** 7346
Then **R** went to Shechem, for all **2Ch 10:1** 7346
all Israel came, they spoke to **R**, **2Ch 10:3** 7346
Then King **R** consulted with the **2Ch 10:6** 7346
the people came to **R** on the third day **2Ch 10:12** 7346
and King **R** forsook the counsel of **2Ch 10:13** 7346
of Judah, **R** reigned over them. **2Ch 10:17** 7346
Then King **R** sent Hadoram, who was **2Ch 10:18** 7346
And King **R** made haste to mount his **2Ch 10:18** 7346
Now when **R** had come to Jerusalem, **2Ch 11:1** 7346
to restore the kingdom to **R**. **2Ch 11:1** 7346
"Speak to **R** the son of Solomon, **2Ch 11:3** 7346
R lived in Jerusalem and built **2Ch 11:5** 7346
and supported **R** the son of Solomon **2Ch 11:17** 7346
Then **R** took as a wife Mahalath the **2Ch 11:18** 7346
R loved Maacah the daughter of **2Ch 11:21** 7346
R appointed Abijah the son of **2Ch 11:22** 7346
When the kingdom of **R** **2Ch 12:1** 7346
Shemaiah the prophet came to **R** **2Ch 12:5** 7346
Then King **R** made shields of bronze **2Ch 12:10** 7346
So King **R** strengthened himself in **2Ch 12:13** 7346
Now **R** was forty-one years old when **2Ch 12:13** 7346
Now the acts of **R**, from first to **2Ch 12:15** 7346
were wars between **R** and Jeroboam **2Ch 12:15** 7346
And **R** slept with his fathers and **2Ch 12:16** 7346
who proved too strong for **R**, **2Ch 13:7** 7346
Solomon was the father of **R**, **Mt 1:7** *4497*
R the father of Abijah, **Mt 1:7** *4497*

REHOBOAM'S
came about in King **R** fifth year, **2Ch 12:2** 7346

REHOBOTH
so he named it **R**, for he said, **Gn 26:22** 7344
and Shaul of **R** on the *Euphrates* **Gn 36:37** 7344
Shaul of **R** by the River became **1Ch 1:48** 7344

REHOBOTH-IR
and built Nineveh and **R** and Calah, **Gn 10:11** 7344

REHUM
Bilshan, Mispar, Bigvai, **R** **Ezr 2:2** 7348a
R the commander and Shimshai the **Ezr 4:8** 7348b
then *wrote* **R** the commander and **Ezr 4:9** 7348b
sent an answer to **R** the commander, **Ezr 4:17** 7348b
document was read before **R** **Ezr 4:23** 7348b
repairs *under* **R** the son of Bani. **Ne 3:17** 7348a
R, Hashabnah, Maaseiah, **Ne 10:25** 7348a
Shecaniah, **R**, Meremoth, **Ne 12:3** 7348a

REI
Nathan the prophet, Shimei, **R**, **1Ki 1:8** 7472

REIGN
Are you actually going to **r** over us? **Gn 37:8** 4427a
LORD shall **r** forever and ever." **Ex 15:18** 4427a
said to the olive tree, '**R** over us!' **Jg 9:8** 4427a
'You come, **r** over us!' **Jg 9:10** 4427a
'You come, **r** over us!' **Jg 9:12** 4427a
'You come, **r** over us!' **Jg 9:14** 4427a
the king who will **r** over them." **1Sa 8:9** 4427a
of the king who will **r** over you: **1Sa 8:11** 4427a
'Shall Saul **r** over us?' **1Sa 11:12** 4427a
'No, but a king shall **r** over us,' **1Sa 12:12** 4427a
years old when he began to **r**, **1Sa 13:1** 4427a
year of Solomon's **r** over Israel, **1Ki 6:1** 4427a
shall **r** over whatever you desire, **1Ki 11:37** 4427a
Asa began to **r** as king of Judah. **1Ki 15:9** 4427a
"Do you now **r** over Israel? **1Ki 21:7** 6213a, 4410
son who was to **r** in his place, **2Ki 3:27** 4427a
Jehoram king of Judah began to **r**. **2Ki 8:25** 4427a
that he might not **r** in Jerusalem; **2Ki 23:33** 4427a
in the eighth year of his **r**. **2Ki 24:12** 4427a
Now in the ninth year of his **r**, **2Ki 25:1** 4427a
their cities until the **r** of David. **1Ch 4:31** 4427a
in the fortieth year of David's **r**, **1Ch 26:31** 4438
with all his **r**, his power, and the **1Ch 29:30** 4438
month of the fourth year of his **r**. **2Ch 3:2** 4438
years old when he began to **r**, **2Ch 12:13** 4427a
of the fifteenth year of Asa's **r**. **2Ch 15:10** 4438
the thirty-fifth year of Asa's **r**. **2Ch 15:19** 4438
In the thirty-sixth year of Asa's **r** **2Ch 16:1** 4438
In the thirty-ninth year of his **r** Asa **2Ch 16:12** 4438
in the forty-first year of his **r**. **2Ch 16:13** 4427a
in the third year of his **r** he sent his **2Ch 17:7** 4427a
Jehoram king of Judah began to **r**. **2Ch 22:1** 4427a
"Behold, the king's son shall **r**, **2Ch 23:3** 4427a
In the first year of his **r**, **2Ch 29:3** 4427a
Ahaz had discarded during his **r** **2Ch 29:19** 4438
in the eighth year of his **r** while he **2Ch 34:3** 4427a
in the eighteenth year of his **r**, **2Ch 34:8** 4427a
In the eighteenth year of Josiah's **r** **2Ch 35:19** 4438
the **r** of Darius king of Persia. **Ezr 4:5** 4438
Now in the **r** of Ahasuerus, in the **Ezr 4:6** 4438
in the beginning of his **r**, **Ezr 4:6** 4438
of the **r** of Darius king of Persia. **Ezr 4:24** 4437
sixth year of the **r** of King Darius. **Ezr 6:15** 4437
r of Artaxerxes king of Persia, **Ezr 7:1** 4438
in the **r** of King Artaxerxes: **Ezr 8:1** 4438
in the **r** of Darius the Persian. **Ne 12:22** 4438
in the third year of his **r** he **Es 1:3** 4427a
in the seventh year of his **r**. **Es 2:16** 4438
The LORD will **r** forever, Your God, **Ps 146:10** 4427a
"By me kings **r**, And rulers decree **Pr 8:15** 4427a
For the LORD of hosts will **r** on **Is 24:23** 4427a
Behold, a king will **r** righteously And **Is 32:1** 4427a
in the thirteenth year of his **r**. **Jer 1:2** 4427a
And He will **r** as king and act **Jer 23:5** 4427a
In the beginning of the **r** of **Jer 26:1** 4468
r of Zedekiah the son of Josiah, **Jer 27:1** 4467
the **r** of Zedekiah king of Judah, **Jer 28:1** 4467
not have a son to **r** on his throne, **Jer 33:21** 4427a
the **r** of Zedekiah king of Judah, **Jer 49:34** 4438
in the fourth year of his **r**. **Jer 51:59** 4427a
about in the ninth year of his **r**, **Jer 52:4** 4427a
in the *first* year of his **r**, **Jer 52:31** 4438
the **r** of Jehoiakim king of Judah, **Da 1:1** 4438
year of the **r** of Nebuchadnezzar, **Da 2:1** 4438
Daniel enjoyed success in the **r** of **Da 6:28** 4437
and in the **r** of Cyrus the Persian. **Da 6:28** 4437
In the third year of the **r** of **Da 8:1** 4438
in the first year of his **r**, **Da 9:2** 4427a
And the LORD will **r** over them in **Mi 4:7** 4427a
and He will **r** over the house of **Lk 1:33** *936*
year of the **r** of Tiberius Caesar, **Lk 3:1** *2231*
not want this man to **r** over us.' **Lk 19:14** *936*
did not want me to **r** over them, **Lk 19:27** *936*
And this took place in the **r** of **Ac 11:28**
will **r** in life through the One, **Ro 5:17** *936*
even so grace would **r** through **Ro 5:21** *936*
Therefore do not let sin **r** in your **Ro 6:12** *936*
so that we also might **r** with you. **1Co 4:8** *4821*
For He must **r** until He has put all **1Co 15:25** *936*
endure, we will also **r** with Him; **2Tm 2:12** *4821*
and they will **r** upon the earth." **Rv 5:10** *936*
and He will **r** forever and ever." **Rv 11:15** *936*
great power and have begun to **r**. **Rv 11:17** *936*
r with Him for a thousand years. **Rv 20:6** *936*

and they will **r** forever and ever.	**Rv 22:5**	*936*

REIGNED

Now these are the kings who **r** in	**Gn 36:31**	4427a
king **r** over the sons of Israel.	**Gn 36:31**	4427a
Bela the son of Beor **r** in Edom,	**Gn 36:32**	4427a
of the Amorites, who **r** in Heshbon,	**Jos 13:10**	4427a
who **r** in Ashtaroth and in Edrei	**Jos 13:12**	4427a
of the Amorites who **r** in Heshbon,	**Jos 13:21**	4427a
king of Canaan, who **r** in Hazor;	**Jg 4:2**	4427a
he **r** *forty* two years over Israel.	**1Sa 13:1**	4427a
became king, *and* he **r** forty years.	**2Sa 5:4**	4427a
At Hebron he **r** over Judah seven	**2Sa 5:5**	4427a
and in Jerusalem he **r** thirty-three	**2Sa 5:5**	4427a
So David **r** over all Israel;	**2Sa 8:15**	4427a
Saul, in whose place you have **r**;	**2Sa 16:8**	4427a
r over Israel *were* forty years:	**1Ki 2:11**	4427a
seven years he **r** in Hebron and	**1Ki 2:11**	4427a
years he **r** in Jerusalem.	**1Ki 2:11**	4427a
stayed there, and **r** in Damascus.	**1Ki 11:24**	4427a
abhorred Israel and **r** over Aram.	**1Ki 11:25**	4427a
Thus the time that Solomon **r** in	**1Ki 11:42**	4427a
his son Rehoboam **r** in his place.	**1Ki 11:43**	4427a
of Judah, Rehoboam **r** over them.	**1Ki 12:17**	4427a
how he made war and how he **r**,	**1Ki 14:19**	4427a
Jeroboam **r** *was* twenty-two years;	**1Ki 14:20**	4427a
and Nadab his son **r** in his place.	**1Ki 14:20**	4427a
the son of Solomon **r** in Judah.	**1Ki 14:21**	4427a
he **r** seventeen years in Jerusalem,	**1Ki 14:21**	4427a
He **r** three years in Jerusalem;	**1Ki 15:2**	4427a
He **r** forty-one years in Jerusalem;	**1Ki 15:10**	4427a
his son **r** in his place.	**1Ki 15:24**	4427a
and he **r** over Israel two years.	**1Ki 15:25**	4427a
king of Judah and **r** in his place.	**1Ki 15:28**	4427a
and **r** twenty-four years.	**1Ki 15:33**	
and **r** two years.	**1Ki 16:8**	
Zimri **r** seven days at Tirzah.	**1Ki 16:15**	4427a
Omri became king over Israel *and* **r**	**1Ki 16:23**	
he **r** six years at Tirzah.	**1Ki 16:23**	4427a
and Ahab the son of Omri **r** over	**1Ki 16:29**	4427a
and he **r** twenty-five years in	**1Ki 22:42**	4427a
and he **r** two years over Israel.	**1Ki 22:51**	4427a
king of Judah, and **r** twelve years.	**2Ki 3:1**	4427a
and he **r** eight years in Jerusalem.	**2Ki 8:17**	4427a
and he **r** one year in Jerusalem.	**2Ki 8:26**	4427a
Now the time which Jehu **r** over	**2Ki 10:36**	4427a
and he **r** forty years in Jerusalem;	**2Ki 12:1**	4427a
and he **r** seventeen years.	**2Ki 13:1**	
and **r** sixteen years.	**2Ki 13:10**	
and he **r** twenty-nine years in	**2Ki 14:2**	4427a
in Samaria, *and* **r** forty-one years.	**2Ki 14:23**	
he **r** fifty-two years in Jerusalem;	**2Ki 15:2**	4427a
killed him, and **r** in his place.	**2Ki 15:10**	4427a
and he **r** one month in Samaria.	**2Ki 15:13**	4427a
Gadi became king over Israel *and* **r**	**2Ki 15:17**	
and **r** two years.	**2Ki 15:23**	
and **r** twenty years.	**2Ki 15:27**	
he **r** sixteen years in Jerusalem;	**2Ki 15:33**	4427a
he **r** sixteen years in Jerusalem;	**2Ki 16:2**	4427a
his son Hezekiah **r** in his place.	**2Ki 16:20**	4427a
and **r** nine years.	**2Ki 17:1**	
and he **r** twenty-nine years in	**2Ki 18:2**	4427a
he **r** fifty-five years in Jerusalem;	**2Ki 21:1**	4427a
and he **r** two years in Jerusalem;	**2Ki 21:19**	4427a
he **r** thirty-one years in Jerusalem;	**2Ki 22:1**	4427a
he **r** three months in Jerusalem;	**2Ki 23:31**	4427a
he **r** eleven years in Jerusalem;	**2Ki 23:36**	4427a
he **r** three months in Jerusalem;	**2Ki 24:8**	4427a
he **r** eleven years in Jerusalem;	**2Ki 24:18**	4427a
Now these are the kings who **r** in	**1Ch 1:43**	4427a
any king of the sons of Israel **r**.	**1Ch 1:43**	4427a
he **r** seven years and six months.	**1Ch 3:4**	4427a
Jerusalem he **r** thirty-three years.	**1Ch 3:4**	4427a
So David **r** over all Israel;	**1Ch 18:14**	4427a
son of Jesse **r** over all Israel.	**1Ch 29:26**	4427a
he **r** over Israel *was* forty years;	**1Ch 29:27**	4427a
he **r** in Hebron seven years and in	**1Ch 29:27**	4427a
his son Solomon **r** in his place.	**1Ch 29:28**	4427a
Jerusalem, and he **r** over Israel.	**2Ch 1:13**	4427a
Solomon **r** forty years in	**2Ch 9:30**	4427a
his son Rehoboam **r** in his place.	**2Ch 9:31**	4427a
of Judah, Rehoboam **r** over them.	**2Ch 10:17**	4427a
himself in Jerusalem and **r**.	**2Ch 12:13**	4427a
he **r** seventeen years in Jerusalem,	**2Ch 12:13**	4427a
He **r** three years in Jerusalem;	**2Ch 13:2**	4427a
Now Jehoshaphat **r** over Judah.	**2Ch 20:31**	4427a
and he **r** in Jerusalem twenty-five	**2Ch 20:31**	4427a
and he **r** eight years in Jerusalem.	**2Ch 21:5**	4427a
and he **r** in Jerusalem eight years;	**2Ch 21:20**	4427a
and he **r** one year in Jerusalem.	**2Ch 22:2**	4427a
while Athaliah **r** over the land.	**2Ch 22:12**	4427a
and he **r** forty years in Jerusalem;	**2Ch 24:1**	4427a
and he **r** twenty-nine years in	**2Ch 25:1**	4427a
he **r** fifty-two years in Jerusalem;	**2Ch 26:3**	4427a
he **r** sixteen years in Jerusalem.	**2Ch 27:1**	4427a
he **r** sixteen years in Jerusalem.	**2Ch 27:8**	4427a
he **r** sixteen years in Jerusalem;	**2Ch 28:1**	4427a
Hezekiah his son **r** in his place.	**2Ch 28:27**	4427a
and he **r** twenty-nine years in	**2Ch 29:1**	4427a
he **r** fifty-five years in Jerusalem.	**2Ch 33:1**	4427a
and he **r** two years in Jerusalem.	**2Ch 33:21**	4427a
he **r** thirty-one years in Jerusalem.	**2Ch 34:1**	4427a
he **r** three months in Jerusalem.	**2Ch 36:2**	4427a
he **r** eleven years in Jerusalem;	**2Ch 36:5**	4427a
and he **r** three months and ten days	**2Ch 36:9**	4427a
he **r** eleven years in Jerusalem.	**2Ch 36:11**	4427a
the Ahasuerus who **r** from India to	**Es 1:1**	4427a
r as king in place of Coniah the	**Jer 37:1**	4427a
he **r** eleven years in Jerusalem;	**Jer 52:1**	4427a
death **r** from Adam until Moses,	**Ro 5:14**	*936*
the one, death **r** through the one,	**Ro 5:17**	*936*
that, as sin **r** in death, even so	**Ro 5:21**	*936*
r with Christ for a thousand years.	**Rv 20:4**	*936*

REIGNING

Athaliah was **r** over the land.	**2Ki 11:3**	4427a
that Archelaus was **r** over Judea	**Mt 2:22**	*936*

REIGNS

you and also the king who **r** over you	**1Sa 12:14**	4427a
say among the nations, "The LORD **r**.	**1Ch 16:31**	4427a
God **r** over the nations, God sits	**Ps 47:8**	4427a
The LORD **r**, He is clothed with	**Ps 93:1**	4427a
among the nations, "The LORD **r**;	**Ps 96:10**	4427a
The LORD **r**, let the earth rejoice;	**Ps 97:1**	4427a
The LORD **r**, let the peoples	**Ps 99:1**	4427a
he saw during the **r** of Uzziah,	**Is 1:1**	3117
And says to Zion, "Your God **r**!"	**Is 52:7**	4427a
r over the kings of the earth."	**Rv 17:18**	*2192, 932*
the Lord our God, the Almighty, **r**.	**Rv 19:6**	*936*

REINED

So Joram **r** about and fled and said	**2Ki 9:23**	2015, 3027

REJECT

you, and My soul will not **r** you.	**Lv 26:11**	1602
if, instead, you **r** My statutes,	**Lv 26:15**	3988a
their enemies, I will not **r** them,	**Lv 26:44**	3988a
Him, He will **r** you forever.	**1Ch 28:9**	2186a
God will not **r** *a man of* integrity,	**Jb 8:20**	3988a
To **r** the labor of Your hands,	**Jb 10:3**	3988a
Awake, do not **r** us forever.	**Ps 44:23**	2186a
Will the Lord **r** forever?	**Ps 77:7**	2186a
O LORD, why do You **r** my soul?	**Ps 88:14**	2186a
not **r** the discipline of the LORD Or	**Pr 3:11**	3988a
But He will **r** the craving of	**Pr 10:3**	1920
then I would **r** the descendants of	**Jer 33:26**	3988a
For the Lord will not **r** forever,	**La 3:31**	2186a
will **r** you from being My priest.	**Hos 4:6**	3988a
"I hate, I **r** your festivals, Nor	**Am 5:21**	3988a
R a factious man after a first and	**Ti 3:10**	*3868*
defile the flesh, and **r** authority,	**Jude 1:8**	*114*

REJECTED

because they **r** My ordinances and	**Lv 26:43**	3988a
because you have **r** the LORD who is	**Nu 11:20**	3988a
know the land which you have **r**.	**Nu 14:31**	3988a
to you, for they have not **r** you,	**1Sa 8:7**	3988a
r Me from being king over them.	**1Sa 8:7**	3988a
"But you have today **r** your God, who	**1Sa 10:19**	3988a
you have **r** the word of the LORD,	**1Sa 15:23**	3988a
has also **r** you from *being* king."	**1Sa 15:23**	3988a
you have **r** the word of the LORD,	**1Sa 15:26**	3988a
and the LORD has **r** you from being	**1Sa 15:26**	3988a
since I have **r** him from being king	**1Sa 16:1**	3988a
his stature, because I have **r** him;	**1Sa 16:7**	3988a
They **r** His statutes and His	**2Ki 17:15**	3988a
The LORD **r** all the descendants	**2Ki 17:20**	3988a
your terms, because you have **r** *it?*	**Jb 34:33**	3988a
why have You **r** me?	**Ps 43:2**	2186a
r *us* and brought us to dishonor,	**Ps 44:9**	2186a
to shame, because God had **r** them.	**Ps 53:5**	3988a
O God, You have **r** us.	**Ps 60:1**	2186a
Have not You Yourself, O God, **r** us?	**Ps 60:10**	2186a
O God, why have You **r** *us* forever?	**Ps 74:1**	2186a
He also **r** the tent of Joseph, And	**Ps 78:67**	3988a
But You have cast off and **r**,	**Ps 89:38**	3988a
Have not You Yourself, O God, **r** us?	**Ps 108:11**	2186a
The stone which the builders **r** Has	**Ps 118:22**	3988a
You have **r** all those who wander	**Ps 119:118**	5541a
r the law of the LORD of hosts And	**Is 5:24**	3988a
"Inasmuch as these people have **r**	**Is 8:6**	3988a
out of your tomb Like a **r** branch,	**Is 14:19**	8581
"Since you have **r** this word And	**Is 30:12**	3988a
I have chosen you and not **r** you.	**Is 41:9**	3988a
wife of *one's* youth when she is **r**,"	**Is 54:6**	3988a
has **r** those in whom you trust,	**Jer 2:37**	3988a
for My law, they have **r** it also.	**Jer 6:19**	3988a
They call them **r** silver, Because	**Jer 6:30**	3988a
Because the LORD has **r** them.	**Jer 6:30**	3988a
For the LORD has **r** and forsaken	**Jer 7:29**	3988a
they have **r** the word of the LORD,	**Jer 8:9**	3988a
Have You completely **r** Judah?	**Jer 14:19**	3988a
the LORD chose, He has **r** them'?	**Jer 33:24**	3988a
"The Lord has **r** all my strong men	**La 1:15**	5541a
The Lord has **r** His altar, He has	**La 2:7**	2186a
My soul has been **r** from peace;	**La 3:17**	2186a
Unless You have utterly **r** us	**La 5:22**	3988a
for they have **r** My ordinances and	**Ezk 5:6**	3988a
and they **r** My ordinances,	**Ezk 20:13**	3988a
because they **r** My ordinances, and	**Ezk 20:16**	3988a
ordinances, but had **r** My statutes and	**Ezk 20:24**	3988a
Because you have **r** knowledge,	**Hos 4:6**	3988a
Israel has **r** the good;	**Hos 8:3**	2186a
He has **r** your calf, O Samaria,	**Hos 8:5**	2186a
Because they **r** the law of the LORD	**Am 2:4**	3988a
be as though I had not **r** them,	**Zch 10:6**	2186a
'THE STONE WHICH THE BUILDERS **R**,	**Mt 21:42**	*593*
must suffer many things and be **r** by	**Mk 8:31**	*593*
'THE STONE WHICH THE BUILDERS **R**,	**Mk 12:10**	*593*
r God's purpose for themselves,	**Lk 7:30**	*114*
and be **r** by the elders and chief	**Lk 9:22**	*593*
and be **r** by this generation.	**Lk 17:25**	*593*
'THE STONE WHICH THE BUILDERS **R**,	**Lk 20:17**	*593*
is the STONE WHICH WAS **R** by you,	**Ac 4:11**	*1848*
then, God has not **r** His people,	**Ro 11:1**	*683*
not **r** His people whom He foreknew.	**Ro 11:2**	*683*
which some have **r** and suffered	**1Tm 1:19**	*683*
is good, and nothing is to be **r** if	**1Tm 4:4**	*579*
mind, **r** in regard to the faith.	**2Tm 3:8**	*96b*
to inherit the blessing, he was **r**,	**Heb 12:17**	*593*
living stone which has been **r** by men,	**1Pe 2:4**	*593*
"THE STONE WHICH THE BUILDERS **R**,	**1Pe 2:7**	*593*

REJECTING

he who rejects *this* is not **r** man	**1Th 4:8**	*114*

REJECTION

a day of distress, rebuke, and **r**;	**2Ki 19:3**	5007a
a day of distress, rebuke and **r**;	**Is 37:3**	5007a
For if their **r** is the reconciliation	**Ro 11:15**	*580*

REJECTS

A fool **r** his father's discipline,	**Pr 15:5**	5006
sincerity, He who **r** unjust gain And	**Is 33:15**	3988a
and the one who **r** you rejects Me;	**Lk 10:16**	*114*
and the one who rejects you **r** Me;	**Lk 10:16**	*114*
and he who **r** Me rejects the One	**Lk 10:16**	*114*
he who rejects Me **r** the One who	**Lk 10:16**	*114*
"He who **r** Me and does not	**Jn 12:48**	*114*
he who **r** *this* is not rejecting man	**1Th 4:8**	*114*

REJOICE

and you shall **r** before the LORD	**Lv 23:40**	8055
and **r** in all your undertakings in	**Dt 12:7**	8055
shall **r** before the LORD your God,	**Dt 12:12**	8055
and you shall **r** before the LORD	**Dt 12:18**	8055
and **r**, you and your household.	**Dt 14:26**	8055
shall **r** before the LORD your God,	**Dt 16:11**	8055
and you shall **r** in your feast, you	**Dt 16:14**	8055
the alien who is among you shall **r**	**Dt 26:11**	8055
and **r** before the LORD your God.	**Dt 27:7**	8055
LORD will again **r** over you for good,	**Dt 30:9**	7797
"**R**, O nations, *with* His people;	**Dt 32:43**	7442
"**R**, Zebulun, in your going forth,	**Dt 33:18**	8055
house this day, **r** in Abimelech,	**Jg 9:19**	8055
and let him also **r** in you.	**Jg 9:19**	8055
to Dagon their god, and to **r**,	**Jg 16:23**	8057
Because I **r** in Your salvation.	**1Sa 2:1**	8055
daughters of the Philistines will **r**,	**2Sa 1:20**	8055
be glad, and let the earth **r**;	**1Ch 16:31**	1523
Your godly ones **r** in what is good.	**2Ch 6:41**	8055
made them to **r** over their enemies.	**2Ch 20:27**	8055
for the LORD had caused them to **r**,	**Ezr 6:22**	8055
not **r** among the days of the year;	**Jb 3:6**	2302b
Who **r** greatly, *And* exult when	**Jb 3:22**	8056
And I **r** in unsparing pain,	**Jb 6:10**	5539
And **r** at the sound of the flute.	**Jb 21:12**	8055
reverence And **r** with trembling.	**Ps 2:11**	1523
of Zion I may **r** in Your salvation.	**Ps 9:14**	1523
my adversaries will **r** when I am shaken.	**Ps 13:4**	1523
My heart shall **r** in Your salvation.	**Ps 13:5**	1523
His captive people, Jacob will **r**,	**Ps 14:7**	1523
salvation how greatly he will **r**!	**Ps 21:1**	1523
have not let my enemies **r** over me.	**Ps 30:1**	8055
I will **r** and be glad in Your	**Ps 31:7**	1523
the LORD and **r**, you righteous ones	**Ps 32:11**	1523
The humble will hear it and **r**.	**Ps 34:2**	8055
And my soul shall **r** in the LORD;	**Ps 35:9**	1523
wrongfully my enemies **r** over me;	**Ps 35:19**	8055
And do not let them **r** over me.	**Ps 35:24**	8055
altogether who **r** at my distress;	**Ps 35:26**	8056
Let them shout for joy and **r**,	**Ps 35:27**	8055
"May they not **r** over me, *Who,*	**Ps 38:16**	8055
Let all who seek You **r** and be glad	**Ps 40:16**	7797
Let the daughters of Judah **r** Because	**Ps 48:11**	1523
bones which You have broken **r**.	**Ps 51:8**	1523
His captive people, Let Jacob **r**,	**Ps 53:6**	1523
will **r** when he sees the vengeance;	**Ps 58:10**	8055
But the king will **r** in God;	**Ps 63:11**	8055
There let us **r** in Him!	**Ps 66:6**	8055
Yes, let them **r** with gladness.	**Ps 68:3**	7797
Let all who seek You **r** and be glad	**Ps 70:4**	7797
That Your people may **r** in You?	**Ps 85:6**	8055
In Your name they **r** all the day,	**Ps 89:16**	1523
You have made all his enemies **r**.	**Ps 89:42**	8055
be glad, and let the earth **r**;	**Ps 96:11**	1523
The LORD reigns, let the earth **r**;	**Ps 97:1**	1523
r in the gladness of Your nation,	**Ps 106:5**	8055
Let us **r** and be glad in it.	**Ps 118:24**	1523
I **r** at Your word, As one who finds	**Ps 119:162**	7797
the sons of Zion **r** in their King.	**Ps 149:2**	1523
And **r** in the perversity of evil;	**Pr 2:14**	1523
And **r** in the wife of your youth.	**Pr 5:18**	8055
And my inmost being will **r** When	**Pr 23:16**	5937
of the righteous will greatly **r**,	**Pr 23:24**	1523
let her **r** who gave birth to you.	**Pr 23:25**	1523
Do not **r** when your enemy falls,	**Pr 24:17**	8055
righteous increase, the people **r**,	**Pr 29:2**	8055
to **r** and to do good in one's lifetime;	**Ec 3:12**	8055
his reward and **r** in his labor;	**Ec 5:19**	8055
many years, let him **r** in them all,	**Ec 11:8**	8055
R, young man, during your	**Ec 11:9**	8055
"We will **r** in you and be glad;	**SS 1:4**	1523
And **r** in Rezin and the son of	**Is 8:6**	4885
men **r** when they divide the spoil.	**Is 9:3**	1523
"Even the cypress trees **r** over you,	**Is 14:8**	8055
"Do not **r**, O Philistia, all of	**Is 14:29**	8055
r and be glad in His salvation."	**Is 25:9**	1523
will **r** in the Holy One of Israel.	**Is 29:19**	1523
And the Arabah will **r** and blossom;	**Is 35:1**	1523
It will blossom profusely And **r**	**Is 35:2**	1523
But you will **r** in the LORD, You	**Is 41:16**	1523
into the ships in which they **r**.	**Is 43:14**	7440
And **r**, O earth!	**Is 49:13**	1523
And your heart will thrill and **r**;	**Is 60:5**	7337
I will **r** greatly in the LORD, My	**Is 61:10**	7797
So your God will **r** over you.	**Is 62:5**	7797
Behold, My servants will **r**,	**Is 65:13**	8055
and **r** forever in what I create;	**Is 65:18**	1523
"I will also **r** in Jerusalem and	**Is 65:19**	1523
with Jerusalem and **r** for her,	**Is 66:10**	1523
disaster, So *that* you can **r**?"	**Jer 11:15**	5937

the virgin will **r** in the dance, Jer 31:13 8055
will **r** over them to do them good and Jer 32:41 7797
caused the enemy to **r** over you; La 2:17 8055
R and be glad, O daughter of Edom, La 4:21 7797
Let not the buyer **r** nor the seller Ezk 7:12 8055
Or shall we **r**, the rod of My son Ezk 21:10 7797
Do not **r**, O Israel, with Hos 9:1 8055
Do not fear, O land, **r** and be glad, Jl 2:21 1523
So **r**, O sons of Zion, And be glad Jl 2:23 1523
You who **r** in Lodebar, And say, Am 6:13 8056
And do not **r** over the sons of Ob 1:12 8055
Do not **r** over me, O my enemy. Mi 7:8 8055
Therefore they **r** and are glad. Hab 1:15 8055
will **r** in the God of my salvation. Hab 3:18 1523
R and exult with all *your* heart, O Zph 3:14 8055
r over you with shouts of joy. Zph 3:17 1523
R greatly, O daughter of Zion! Zch 9:9 1523
Their heart will **r** in the LORD. Zch 10:7 1523
"**R** and be glad, for your reward Mt 5:12 *5463*
and many will **r** at his birth. Lk 1:14 *5463*
"Nevertheless do not **r** in this, Lk 10:20 *5463*
but **r** that your names are recorded Lk 10:20 *5463*
'**R** with me, for I have found my Lk 15:6 *4796*
'**R** with me, for I have found the Lk 15:9 *4796*
'But we had to celebrate and **r**, Lk 15:32 *5463*
and he who reaps may **r** together. Jn 4:36 *5463*
to **r** for a while in his light. Jn 5:35 *21*
and lament, but the world will **r**; Jn 16:20 *5463*
you again, and your heart will **r**, Jn 16:22 *5463*
R with those who rejoice, and weep Ro 12:15 *5463*
Rejoice with those who **r**, Ro 12:15 *5463*
"**R**, O GENTILES, WITH HIS PEOPLE." Ro 15:10 *2165*
and those who **r**, as though they 1Co 7:30 *5463*
rejoice, as though they did not **r**; 1Co 7:30 *5463*
all the members **r** with it. 1Co 12:26 *4796*
does not **r** in unrighteousness, but 1Co 13:6 *5463*
I **r** over the coming of 1Co 16:17 *5463*
from those who ought to make me **r**; 2Co 2:3 *5463*
I now **r**, not that you were made 2Co 7:9 *5463*
I **r** that in everything I have 2Co 7:16 *5463*
we **r** when we ourselves are weak 2Co 13:9 *5463*
Finally, brethren, **r**, 2Co 13:11 *5463*
"**R**, BARREN WOMAN WHO DOES NOT Ga 4:27 *2165*
and in this I **r**. Yes, and I will Php 1:18 *5463*
and I will **r**, Php 1:18 *5463*
I **r** and share my joy with you all. Php 2:17 *5463*
r in the same way and share your Php 2:18 *5463*
when you see him again you may **r** Php 2:28 *5463*
my brethren, **r** in the Lord. Php 3:1 *5463*
R in the Lord always; Php 4:4 *5463*
again I will say, **r**! Php 4:4 *5463*
Now I **r** in my sufferings for your Col 1:24 *5463*
we **r** before our God on your account, 1Th 3:9 *5463*
R always; 1Th 5:16 *5463*
In this you greatly **r**, 1Pe 1:6 *21*
you greatly **r** with joy 1Pe 1:8 *21*
glory you may **r** with exultation. 1Pe 4:13 *5463*
will **r** over them and celebrate; Rv 11:10 *5463*
"For this reason, **r**, Rv 12:12 *2165*
"**R** over her, O heaven, and you Rv 18:20 *2165*
"Let us **r** and be glad and give Rv 19:7 *5463*

REJOICED
Jethro **r** over all the goodness Ex 18:9 2302b
just as He **r** over your fathers; Dt 30:9 7797
all the men of Israel **r** greatly. 1Sa 11:15 8055
you saw *it* and **r**. 1Sa 19:5 8055
he **r** greatly and said, 1Ki 5:7 8055
and all the people of the land **r** and 2Ki 11:14 8056
the land **r** and the city was quiet. 2Ki 11:20 8055
Then the people **r** because they had 1Ch 29:9 8055
and King David also **r** greatly. 1Ch 29:9 8055
All Judah **r** concerning the oath, 2Ch 15:15 8055
And all the people of the land **r** and 2Ch 23:13 8056
So all of the people of the land **r** 2Ch 23:21 8055
All the officers and all the people **r** 2Ch 24:10 8055
Hezekiah and all the people **r** over 2Ch 29:36 8055
All the assembly of Judah **r**, 2Ch 30:25 8055
they offered great sacrifices and **r** Ne 12:43 8055
even the women and children **r**, Ne 12:43 8055
for Judah **r** over the priests and Ne 12:44 8057
the city of Susa shouted and **r**. Es 8:15 8055
I **r** at the extinction of my enemy, Jb 31:29 8055
But at my stumbling they **r** and Ps 35:15 8055
And the daughters of Judah have **r** Ps 97:8 1523
r in the way of Your testimonies, Ps 119:14 7797
r with all the scorn of your soul Ezk 25:6 8055
"As you **r** over the inheritance of Ezk 35:15 8055
they **r** exceedingly with great joy. Mt 2:10 *5463*
my spirit has **r** in God my Savior. Lk 1:47 *21*
He **r** greatly in the Holy Spirit, Lk 10:21 *21*
father Abraham **r** to see My day, Jn 8:56 *21*
If you loved Me, you would have **r** Jn 14:28 *5463*
r when they saw the Lord. Jn 20:20 *5463*
he **r** and *began* to encourage them Ac 11:23 *5463*
r because of its encouragement. Ac 15:31 *5463*
food before them, and **r** greatly, Ac 16:34 *21*
so that I **r** even more. 2Co 7:7 *5463*
we **r** even much more for the joy of 2Co 7:13 *5463*
But I **r** in the Lord greatly, that Php 4:10 *5463*

REJOICES
the valley, and **r** in *his* strength; Jb 39:21 7797
my heart is glad and my glory **r**; Ps 16:9 1523
It **r** as a strong man to run his Ps 19:5 7797
For our heart **r** in Him, Because we Ps 33:21 8055
with the righteous, the city **r**, Pr 11:10 5970
The light of the righteous **r**, Pr 13:9 8055
He who **r** at calamity will not go Pr 17:5 8056
But the righteous sings and **r**. Pr 29:6 8055
the bridegroom **r** over the bride, Is 62:5 4885
him who **r** in doing righteousness, Is 64:5 7797
"As all the earth **r**, Ezk 35:14 8055
he **r** over it more than over the Mt 18:13 *5463*
r greatly because of the Jn 3:29 *5463*
but **r** with the truth; 1Co 13:6 *4796*

REJOICING
on flutes and **r** with great joy, 1Ki 1:40 8056
they have come up from there **r**, 1Ki 1:45 8056
were eating and drinking and **r**. 1Ki 4:20 8056
r and happy of heart because of 2Ch 7:10 8056
with **r** and singing according to the 2Ch 23:18 8057
And there was great **r**. Ne 8:17 8057
made it a day of feasting and **r**. Es 9:17 8057
made it a day of feasting and **r**. Es 9:18 8057
Adar *a* holiday for **r** and feasting Es 9:19 8057
make them days of feasting and **r** Es 9:22 8057
the LORD are right, **r** the heart; Ps 19:8 8055
be led forth with gladness and **r**; Ps 45:15 1524a
the hills gird themselves with **r**. Ps 65:12 1524a
His delight, **R** always before Him, Pr 8:30 7832
R in the world, His earth, And Pr 8:31 7832
rejoice with **r** and shout of joy. Is 35:2 1525
behold, I create Jerusalem *for* **r** And Is 65:18 1525
voice of **r** and the voice of gladness, Jer 16:9 8342
r dries up From the sons of men. Jl 1:12 8342
'and they were **r** with her. Lk 1:58 *4796*
and the entire crowd was **r** Lk 13:17 *5463*
he lays it on his shoulders, **r**. Lk 15:5 *5463*
r that they had been considered Ac 5:41 *5463*
r in the works of their hands. Ac 7:41 *2165*
So there was much **r** in that city. Ac 8:8 *5479*
but went on his way **r**. Ac 8:39 *5463*
they *began* **r** and glorifying the Ac 13:48 *5463*
r in hope, persevering in Ro 12:12 *5463*
therefore I am **r** over you, but I Ro 16:19 *5463*
as sorrowful yet always **r**, 2Co 6:10 *5463*
r to see your good discipline and Col 2:5 *5463*
sufferings of Christ, keep on **r**, 1Pe 4:13 *5463*

REKEM
and **R** and Zur and Hur and Reba, Nu 31:8 7552
and **R** and Zur and Hur and Reba, Jos 13:21 7552
and **R** and Irpeel and Taralah, Jos 18:27 7552
Korah and Tappuah and **R** and Shema. 1Ch 2:43 7552
R became the father of Shammai. 1Ch 2:44 7552

RELATE
"Please **r** to me all the great 2Ki 8:4 5608
dreams which they **r** to one another, Jer 23:27 5608
prophet who has a dream may **r** *his* Jer 23:28 5608
He gave them orders not to **r** to Mk 9:9 *1334*
They *began* to **r** their experiences Lk 24:35 *1834*
WHO WILL **R** HIS GENERATION? Ac 8:33 *1334*
he *began* to **r** one by one the Ac 21:19 *1834*
since they **r** only to food Heb 9:10

RELATED
he **r** to Laban all these things. Gn 29:13 5608
dream, and **r** it to his brothers, Gn 37:9 5608
He **r** *it* to his father and to Gn 37:10 5608
bodyguard, and we **r** *them* to him, Gn 41:12 5608
and they **r** to him all that had Jos 2:23 5608
So they **r** to him the words of the 1Sa 11:5 5608
these also they **r** to their father. 1Ki 13:11 5608
asked the woman, she **r** *it* to him. 2Ki 8:6 5608
of our God, being **r** to Tobiah, Ne 13:4 7138
and **r** Mordecai's words to Esther. Es 4:9 5046
They **r** Esther's words to Mordecai. Es 4:12 5046
"and **r** them and led My people Jer 23:32 5608
in and I **r** the dream to them Da 4:7 560
and I **r** the dream to him, *saying,* Da 4:8 560
and **r** the *following* summary of it. Da 7:1 560
"Simeon has **r** how God first Ac 15:14 *1834*

RELATING
a man was **r** a dream to his friend. Jg 7:13 5608
As he was **r** to the king how he had 2Ki 8:5 5608
Barnabas and Paul as they were **r** Ac 15:12 *1834*

RELATION
more shrewd in **r** to their own kind Lk 16:8 *1519*

RELATIONS
the man had **r** with his wife Eve, Gn 4:1 3045
Cain had **r** with his wife and Gn 4:17 3045
Adam had **r** with his wife again; Gn 4:25 3045
us that we may have **r** with them." Gn 19:5 3045
who have not had **r** with man; Gn 19:8 3045
and no man had had **r** with her; Gn 24:16 3045
he did not have **r** with her again. Gn 38:26 3045
and she had no **r** with a man. Jg 11:39 3045
that we may have **r** with him." Jg 19:22 3045
had **r** with Hannah his wife, 1Sa 1:19 3045
I speak in terms of human **r**: Ga 3:15 *444*

RELATIONSHIP
"If the **r** of the man with his wife is Mt 19:10 *156*

RELATIVE
that his **r** had been taken captive, Gn 14:14 251
also brought back his **r** Lot with his Gn 14:16 251
Jacob told Rachel that he was a **r** of Gn 29:12 251
"Because you are my **r**, Gn 29:15 251
shall approach any blood **r** of his Lv 18:6 7607
she is your father's blood **r**. Lv 18:12 7607
for she is your mother's blood **r**. Lv 18:13 7607
a one has made naked his blood **r**; Lv 20:19 7607
a **r** by marriage among his people, Lv 21:4 1167
and buy back what his **r** has sold. Lv 25:25 251
'But if the man has no **r** to whom Nu 5:8 1350
give his inheritance to his nearest **r** Nu 27:11 7607
for they said, "He is our **r**." Jg 9:3 251
of Shechem, because he is your **r** Jg 9:18 251
"The man is our **r**, he is one of Ru 2:20 7138
maid, for you are a close **r**." Ru 3:9 1350
"Now it is true I am a close **r**; Ru 3:12 1350
there is a **r** closer than I. Ru 3:12 1350
the close **r** of whom Boaz spoke was Ru 4:1 1350
Then he said to the closest **r**, Ru 4:3 1350
The closest **r** said, Ru 4:6 1350
So the closest **r** said to Boaz, Ru 4:8 1350
the king is a close **r** to us. 2Sa 19:42 7138
even your **r** Elizabeth has also Lk 1:36 *4773b*
being a **r** of the one whose ear Jn 18:26 *4773a*

RELATIVES
r And from your father's house, Gn 12:1 4138
go to my country and to my **r**, Gn 24:4 4138
to my father's house and to my **r**, Gn 24:38 4940
take a wife for my son from my **r** and Gn 24:40 4940
my oath, when you come to my **r**; Gn 24:41 4940
settled in defiance of all his **r**. Gn 25:18 251
and all his **r** I have given to him Gn 27:37 251
of your fathers and to your **r**, Gn 31:3 4138
to your country and to your **r**, Gn 32:9 4138
particularly about us and our **r**, Gn 43:7 4138
carry your **r** away from the front Lv 10:4 251
they are blood **r**. Lv 18:17 7607
for his **r** who are nearest to him, Lv 21:2 7607
or one of his blood **r** from his Lv 25:49 7607
will go to my *own* land and **r**." Nu 10:30 4138
to his **r** a Midianite woman, Nu 25:6 251
they also brought out all her **r** and Jos 6:23 4940
went to Shechem to his mother's **r**, Jg 9:1 251
And his mother's **r** spoke all these Jg 9:3 251
the son of Ebed came with his **r**, Jg 9:26 251
Gaal the son of Ebed and his **r** have Jg 9:31 251
but Zebul drove out Gaal and his **r** Jg 9:41 251
among the daughters of your **r**, Jg 14:3 251
he is one of our closest **r**." Ru 2:20 1350
against your **r** the sons of Israel; 1Ki 12:24 251
of his **r** nor of his friends. 1Ki 16:11 1350
Jehu met the **r** of Ahaziah king of 2Ki 10:13 251
"We are the **r** of Ahaziah; 2Ki 10:13 251
Their **r** among all the families 1Ch 7:5 251
and his **r** came to comfort him. 1Ch 7:22 251
And they also lived with their **r** 1Ch 8:32 251
Jerusalem opposite their *other* **r**. 1Ch 8:32 251
of Zerah *were* Jeuel and their **r**, 1Ch 9:6 251
and their **r** according to their 1Ch 9:9 251
and their **r**, heads of their 1Ch 9:13 251
and Talmon and Ahiman and their **r** 1Ch 9:17 251
the son of Korah, and his **r** of 1Ch 9:19 251
Their **r** in their villages *were* 1Ch 9:25 251
their **r** of the sons of the Kohathites 1Ch 9:32 251
And they also lived with their **r** 1Ch 9:38 251
Jerusalem opposite their *other* **r**. 1Ch 9:38 251
Uriel the chief, and 120 of his **r**; 1Ch 15:5 251
the chief, and 220 of his **r**; 1Ch 15:6 251
Joel the chief, and 130 of his **r**; 1Ch 15:7 251
the chief, and 200 of his **r**; 1Ch 15:8 251
Eliel the chief, and 80 of his **r**; 1Ch 15:9 251
the chief, and 112 of his **r**. 1Ch 15:10 251
yourselves both you and your **r**, 1Ch 15:12 251
to appoint their **r** the singers, 1Ch 15:16 251
the son of Joel, and from his **r**, 1Ch 15:17 251
from the sons of Merari their **r**, 1Ch 15:17 251
them their **r** of the second rank, 1Ch 15:18 251
his **r** to give thanks to the LORD. 1Ch 16:7 251
So he left Asaph and his **r** there 1Ch 16:37 251
and Obed-edom with his 68 **r**; 1Ch 16:38 251
Zadok the priest and his **r** the priests 1Ch 16:39 251
of the sons of Aaron their **r**, 1Ch 23:32 251
cast lots just as their **r** the sons of 1Ch 24:31 251
singing to the LORD, with their **r**, 1Ch 25:7 251
he with his **r** and sons *were* twelve; 1Ch 25:9 251
to Zaccur, his sons and his **r**, 1Ch 25:10 251
to Izri, his sons and his **r**, 1Ch 25:11 251
to Nethaniah, his sons and his **r**, 1Ch 25:12 251
to Bukkiah, his sons and his **r**, 1Ch 25:13 251
to Jesharelah, his sons and his **r**, 1Ch 25:14 251
to Jeshaiah, his sons and his **r**, 1Ch 25:15 251
to Mattaniah, his sons and his **r**, 1Ch 25:16 251
to Shimei, his sons and his **r**, 1Ch 25:17 251
to Azarel, his sons and his **r**, 1Ch 25:18 251
to Hashabiah, his sons and his **r**, 1Ch 25:19 251
Shubael, his sons and his **r**, 1Ch 25:20 251
Mattithiah, his sons and his **r**, 1Ch 25:21 251
to Jeremoth, his sons and his **r**, 1Ch 25:22 251
to Hananiah, his sons and his **r**, 1Ch 25:23 251
Joshbekashah, his sons and his **r**, 1Ch 25:24 251
to Hanani, his sons and his **r**, 1Ch 25:25 251
to Mallothi, his sons and his **r**, 1Ch 25:26 251
to Eliathah, his sons and his **r**, 1Ch 25:27 251
to Hothir, his sons and his **r**, 1Ch 25:28 251
to Giddalti, his sons and his **r**, 1Ch 25:29 251
to Mahazioth, his sons and his **r**, 1Ch 25:30 251
Romamti-ezer, his sons and his **r**, 1Ch 25:31 251
they and their sons and their **r** 1Ch 26:8 251
Meshelemiah had sons and **r**, 1Ch 26:9 251
the sons and **r** of Hosah *were* 13. 1Ch 26:11 251
were given duties like their **r** to 1Ch 26:12 251
The Levites, their **r**, had charge 1Ch 26:20 251
His **r** by Eliezer *were* Rehabiah 1Ch 26:25 251
This Shelomoth and his **r** had 1Ch 26:26 251
the care of Shelomoth and his **r**. 1Ch 26:28 251
Hebronites, Hashabiah and his **r**, 1Ch 26:30 251
and his **r**, capable men, *were* 2,700 1Ch 26:32 251
not go up or fight against your **r**; 2Ch 11:4 251
"My **r** have failed, And my Jb 19:14 7138
with his **r** And his neighbors, Jer 49:10 251
"Son of man, your brothers, your **r**, Ezk 11:15 251
his hometown and among his *own* **r** Mk 6:4 *4773a*
Her neighbors and her **r** heard Lk 1:58 *4773a*

no one among your **r** who is called Lk 1:61 4772
looking for Him among their **r** and Lk 2:44 4773a
or your **r** or rich neighbors, Lk 14:12 4773a
and brothers and **r** and friends, Lk 21:16 4773a
LEAVE YOUR COUNTRY AND YOUR **R**, Ac 7:3 4772
invited Jacob his father and all his **r** Ac 7:14 4772
and had called together his **r** and Ac 10:24 4773a

RELAX
Now **r** your hand!" 2Sa 24:16 7503
now **r** your hand." 1Ch 21:15 7503
am seething within and cannot **r**; Jb 30:27 1826a

RELAYS
to Lebanon, 10,000 a month in **r**; 1Ki 5:14 2487

RELEASE
that he will **r** to you your other Gn 43:14 7971
you shall surely **r** *it* with him. Ex 23:5 5800a
r the goat in the wilderness. Lv 16:22 7971
proclaim a **r** through the land to all Lv 25:10 1865
every creditor shall **r** what he has Dt 15:2 8058
but your hand shall **r** whatever of Dt 15:3 8058
a man, and there can be no **r**. Jb 12:14 6605a
Jerusalem to proclaim **r** to them: Jer 34:8 1865
man proclaiming **r** to his neighbor, Jer 34:15 1865
r each man to his brother and Jer 34:17 1865
I am proclaiming a **r** to you,' Jer 34:17 1865
r for the people *any* one prisoner Mt 27:15 630
"Whom do you want me to **r** for you? Mt 27:17 630
two do you want me to **r** for you?" Mt 27:21 630
Now at *the* feast he used to **r** for Mk 15:6 630
r for you the King of the Jews?" Mk 15:9 630
to **r** Barabbas for them instead. Mk 15:11 630
ME TO PROCLAIM **R** TO THE CAPTIVES, Lk 4:18 859
will punish Him and **r** Him." Lk 23:16 630
Now he was obliged to **r** to them Lk 23:17 630
this man, and **r** for us Barabbas!" Lk 23:18 630
Pilate, wanting to **r** Jesus, Lk 23:20 630
will punish Him and **r** Him." Lk 23:22 630
that I **r** someone for you at Jn 18:39 630
that I **r** for you the King Jn 18:39 630
that I have authority to **r** You, Jn 19:10 630
this Pilate made efforts to **r** Him, Jn 19:12 630
"If you **r** this Man, you are no Jn 19:12 630
when he had decided to **r** Him. Ac 3:13 630
policemen, saying, "**R** those men." Ac 16:35 630
magistrates have sent to **r** you. Ac 16:36 630
they were willing to **r** me because Ac 28:18 630
tortured, not accepting their **r**, Heb 11:35 629
"**R** the four angels who are bound Rv 9:14 3089

RELEASED
"The one who **r** the goat as Lv 16:26 7971
he **r** the foxes into the standing Jg 15:5 7971
r Jehoiachin king of Judah from 2Ki 25:27 5375, 7218
The king sent and **r** him, Ps 105:20 5425b
Pashhur **r** Jeremiah from the stocks, Jer 20:3 3318
bodyguard had **r** him from Ramah, Jer 40:1 7971
r him and forgave him the debt. Mt 18:27 630
Then he **r** Barabbas for them; Mt 27:26 630
Pilate **r** Barabbas for them, Mk 15:15 630
should she not have been **r** from Lk 13:16 3089
And he **r** the man they were asking Lk 23:25 630
When they had been **r**, Ac 4:23 630
name of Jesus, and *then* **r** them. Ac 5:40 630
Jason and the others, they **r** them. Ac 17:9 630
he **r** him and ordered the chief Ac 22:30 3089
she is **r** from the law concerning Ro 7:2 2673
now we have been **r** from the Law, Ro 7:6 2673
Do not seek to be **r**. 1Co 7:27 3080
Are you **r** from a wife? 1Co 7:27 3089
our brother Timothy has been **r**, Heb 13:23 630
r us from our sins by His blood Rv 1:5 3089
day and month and year, were **r**, Rv 9:15 3089
he must be **r** for a short time. Rv 20:3 3089
Satan will be **r** from his prison, Rv 20:7 3089

RELEASING
"Now Lord, You are **r** Your Lk 2:29 630

RELENT
Shall I **r** concerning these things? Is 57:6 5162
I will **r** concerning the calamity I Jer 18:8 5162
for I will **r** concerning the calamity Jer 42:10 5162
I will not **r**, and I will not Ezk 24:14 6544a
whether He will *not* turn and **r** And Jl 2:14 5162
"Who knows, God may turn and **r** and Jon 3:9 5162

RELENTED
it, the LORD **r** from the calamity and 2Sa 24:16 5162
And **r** according to the greatness Ps 106:45 5162
then God **r** concerning the calamity Jon 3:10 5162
'and I have not **r**, Zch 8:14 5162

RELENTING
and destroy you; I am tired of **r**! Jer 15:6 5162
the LORD overthrew without **r**, Jer 20:16 5162
in lovingkindness And **r** of evil. Jl 2:13 5162

RELENTS
and one who **r** concerning calamity. Jon 4:2 5162

RELIABLE
for they were considered **r**, Ne 13:13 539
is nothing **r** in what they say; Ps 5:9 3559

RELIANCE
there speaking boldly *with* **r** Ac 14:3

RELIED
because they **r** on the men in ambush Jg 20:36 982
"Because you have **r** on the king 2Ch 16:7 8172
have not **r** on the LORD your God, 2Ch 16:7 8172
Yet because you **r** on the LORD, 2Ch 16:8 8172
And the people **r** on the words of 2Ch 32:8 5564
and guile, and have **r** on them, Is 30:12 8172
all his armor on which he had **r** and Lk 11:22 3982

RELIEF
when Pharaoh saw that there was **r**, Ex 8:15 7309
r and deliverance will arise for Es 4:14 7305
"For He inflicts pain, and gives **r**; Jb 5:18 2280
"Let me speak that I may get **r**; Jb 32:20 7304
him **r** from the days of adversity, Ps 94:13 8252
Give yourself no **r**, La 2:18 6314
Your ear from my *prayer for* **r**, La 3:56 7309
There is no **r** for your breakdown, Na 3:19 3545
the **r** of the brethren living in Judea. Ac 11:29 1248
and *to give* **r** to you who are 2Th 1:7 425

RELIEVE
and Saul went in to **r** himself. 1Sa 24:3 5526a, 7272

RELIEVED
You have **r** me in my distress; Ps 4:1 7337
"I **r** his shoulder of the burden, Ps 81:6 5493
"Ah, I will be **r** of My adversaries And Is 1:24 5162

RELIEVING
only **r** himself in the cool room." Jg 3:24 5526a, 7272

RELIGION
r and about a dead man, Ac 25:19 1175
to the strictest sect of our **r**. Ac 26:5 2356
appearance of wisdom in self-made **r** Col 2:23 1479
heart, this man's **r** is worthless. Jas 1:26 2356
Pure and undefiled **r** in Jas 1:27 2356

RELIGIOUS
you are very **r** in all respects. Ac 17:22 1174
If anyone thinks himself to be **r**, Jas 1:26 2357

RELY
Now on whom do you **r**, 2Ki 18:20 982
you **r** on the staff of this crushed 2Ki 18:21 982
king of Egypt to all who **r** on him. 2Ki 18:21 982
and **r** on Egypt for chariots and 2Ki 18:24 982
r on the one who struck them, Is 10:20 8172
but will truly **r** on the LORD, Is 10:20 8172
"Or let him **r** on My protection, Is 27:5 2388
Egypt for help *And* **r** on horses, Is 31:1 8172
Now on whom do you **r**, Is 36:5 982
you **r** on the staff of this crushed Is 36:6 982
king of Egypt to all who **r** on him. Is 36:6 982
and **r** on Egypt for chariots and Is 36:9 982
name of the LORD and **r** on his God. Is 50:10 8172
"You **r** on your sword, you commit Ezk 33:26 5975
r upon the Law and boast in God, Ro 2:17 1879

REMADE
so he **r** it into another vessel, as Jer 18:4 7725, 6213a

REMAIN
they were not able to **r** together. Gn 13:6 3427
"**R** a widow in your father's house Gn 38:11 3427
brother, while you **r** confined, Gn 42:16
please let your servant **r** instead Gn 44:33 3427
reason I have allowed you to **r**, Ex 9:16 5975
R every man in his place; Ex 16:29 3427
the fear of Him may **r** with you, Ex 20:20 1961, 6440
to **r** overnight until morning. Ex 23:18 3885a
to Me on the mountain and **r** there, Ex 24:12 1961
shall **r** in the rings of the ark; Ex 25:15 1961
the burnt offering itself *shall* **r** Lv 6:9
r day and night for seven days and Lv 8:35 3427
'Then she shall **r** in the blood of Lv 12:4 3427
and she shall **r** in the blood of Lv 12:5 3427
"He shall **r** unclean all the days Lv 13:46 2930
and **r** unclean until evening; Lv 17:15 2930
wages of a hired man are not to **r** Lv 19:13 3885a
r seven days with its mother, Lv 22:27 1961
then what he has sold shall **r** in Lv 25:28 1961
years **r** until the year of jubilee, Lv 25:52 7604
r there in the cities of Gilead; Nu 32:26 1961
of our inheritance *shall* **r** with Nu 32:32
that those whom you let **r** of them Nu 33:55 3498
shall **r** in your cities which I Dt 3:19 3427
as long as the heavens **r** above Dt 11:21
shall **r** overnight until morning. Dt 16:4 3885a
and shall **r** in your house, Dt 21:13 3427
and it shall **r** with you until your Dt 22:2 1961
And she shall **r** his wife; Dt 22:19 1961
"You shall **r** outside, and the man Dt 24:11 5975
the rest of his children who **r**, Dt 28:54 3498
that it may **r** there as a witness Dt 31:26 1961
and your cattle shall **r** in the Jos 1:14 3427
nations which **r** as an inheritance for Jos 23:4 7604
nations, these which **r** among you, Jos 23:7 7604
nations, these which **r** among you, Jos 23:12 7604
LORD allowed those nations to **r**, Jg 2:23 5117
"I will **r** until you return." Jg 6:18 3427
that they could not **r** in Shechem Jg 9:41 3427
"**R** this night, and when morning Ru 3:13 3885a
R until you have weaned him; 1Sa 1:23 3427
God of Israel must not **r** with us, 1Sa 5:7 3427
pass on, but you **r** standing now, 1Sa 9:27
and you shall **r** by the stone Ezel. 1Sa 20:19 3427
Return and **r** with the king, for 2Sa 15:19 3427
will be, and with him I will **r**. 2Sa 16:18 3427
take five of the horses which **r**, 2Ki 7:13 7604
and did not **r** there in the land. 2Ki 15:20 5975
who **r** in all the land of Israel, 1Ch 13:2 7604
in the king's interest to let them **r**. Es 3:8 5117
"For if you **r** silent at this Es 4:14 2790b
like a shadow and does not **r**. Jb 14:2 5975
answers **r** *full of* falsehood?" Jb 21:34 7604
O God, do not **r** quiet; Ps 83:1
And the blameless will **r** in it; Pr 2:21 3498
Her feet do not **r** at home; Pr 7:11 7931
everything God does will **r** forever; Ec 3:14 1961
remnant of His people, who will **r**, Is 11:11 7604
How long will you **r** unclean?" Jer 13:27 2891
of Jerusalem who **r** in this land and Jer 24:8 7604
him, I will let **r** on its land," Jer 27:11 5117
None of them *shall* **r**, none of Ezk 7:11
nor will he **r** with his power, Da 11:6 5975
For the sons of Israel will **r** for Hos 3:4 3427
They will not **r** in the LORD's land, Hos 9:3 3427
And they will **r**, Because at that Mi 5:4 3427
all the families that **r**, Zch 12:14 7604
but Jerusalem will rise and **r** on Zch 14:10 3427
and **r** there until I tell you; Mt 2:13 1510
r here and keep watch with Me." Mt 26:38 3306
r here and keep watch." Mk 14:34 3306
does not **r** in the house forever; Jn 8:35 3306
the son does **r** forever. Jn 8:35 3306
that the Christ is to **r** forever; Jn 12:34 3306
in Me will not **r** in darkness. Jn 12:46 3306
and *that* your fruit would **r**, Jn 15:16 3306
not **r** on the cross on the Sabbath Jn 19:31 3306
"If I want him to **r** until I come, Jn 21:22 3306
"If I want him to **r** until I come, Jn 21:23 3306
unsold, did it not **r** your own? Ac 5:4 3306
heart to **r** *true* to the Lord; Ac 11:23 4357
seemed good to Silas to **r** there. Ac 15:34 1961
"Unless these men **r** in the ship, Ac 27:31 3306
good for them if they **r** even as I. 1Co 7:8 3306
does leave, she must **r** unmarried, 1Co 7:11 3306
Each man must **r** in that condition 1Co 7:20 3306
each one is to **r** with God in that 1Co 7:24 3306
is good for a man to **r** as he is. 1Co 7:26 1510
time, most of whom **r** until now, 1Co 15:6 3306
hope to **r** with you for some time, 1Co 16:7 1961
r in Ephesus until Pentecost; 1Co 16:8 1961
truth of the gospel would **r** with you. Ga 2:5 1265
yet to **r** on in the flesh is more Php 1:24 1961
I know that I will **r** and continue Php 1:25 3306
I come and see you or **r** absent, Php 1:27 548
r until the coming of the Lord, 1Th 4:15 4035
Then we who are alive and **r** will 1Th 4:17 4035
for Macedonia, **r** on at Ephesus so 1Tm 1:3 4357
over a man, but to **r** quiet. 1Tm 2:12 1510
THEY WILL PERISH, BUT YOU **R**; Heb 1:11 1265
which cannot be shaken may **r**. Heb 12:27 3306
and strengthen the things that **r**, Rv 3:2 3062
comes, he must **r** a little while. Rv 17:10 3306

REMAINDER
you shall burn the **r** with fire; Ex 29:34 3498
'The **r** of the grain offering Lv 2:3 3498
'The **r** of the grain offering Lv 2:10 3498
"The **r** of the flesh and of Lv 8:32 3498
But the **r** of the people he placed 2Sa 10:10 3499a
But the **r** of the people he placed 1Ch 19:11 3499a
and the **r** of the number of bowmen, Is 21:17 7605
"The **r**, 5,000 *cubits* in width Ezk 48:15 3498
"The **r** of the length Ezk 48:18 3498
"The **r** *shall be* for the prince, Ezk 48:21 3498
trampled down the **r** with its feet; Da 7:7 7606
trampled down the **r** with its feet, Da 7:19 7606
Then the **r** of His brethren Will Mi 5:3 3499a
All the **r** of the peoples will loot Hab 2:8 3499a
And the **r** of My nation will Zph 2:9 3499a

REMAINED
r alive here after seeing Him?" Gn 16:13 7200
But his bow **r** firm, And his arms Gn 49:24 3427
from his people; not one **r**. Ex 8:31 7604
not even one of them **r**. Ex 14:28 7604
"If in his sight the scale has **r**, Lv 13:37 5975
the tabernacle, they **r** camped. Nu 9:18 2583
If sometimes the cloud **r** a few Nu 9:20 1961
command of the LORD they **r** camped. Nu 9:20 2583
r from evening until morning, Nu 9:21 1961
or *if it* **r** in the daytime and at Nu 9:21
the sons of Israel **r** camped and did Nu 9:22 2583
But two men had **r** in the camp; Nu 11:26 7604
Hazeroth, and they **r** at Hazeroth. Nu 11:35 1961
Caleb the son of Jephunneh **r** alive Nu 14:38 2421a
While Israel **r** at Shittim, the Nu 25:1 3427
Now the booty that **r** from the spoil Nu 31:32 1961, 3499a
because he should have **r** in his Nu 35:28 3427
and their inheritance **r** with the Nu 36:12 1961
"So you **r** in Kadesh many days, Dt 1:46 3427
"So we **r** in the valley opposite Dt 3:29 3427
and have **r** long in the land, Dt 4:25 3462
then I **r** on the mountain forty Dt 9:9 3427
no courage **r** in any man any longer Jos 2:11 6965
and **r** there for three days until Jos 2:22 3427
they **r** in their places in the Jos 5:8 3427
and **r** between Bethel and Ai, Jos 8:9 3427
and the survivors *who* **r** of them Jos 10:20 8277
in Gath, and in Ashdod some **r**. Jos 11:22 7604
There **r** among the sons of Jos 18:2 3498
"Gilead **r** across the Jordan; Jg 5:17 7931
seashore, And **r** by its landings. Jg 5:17 7931
people returned, but 10,000 **r**. Jg 7:3 7604
and went to Beer and **r** there Jg 9:21 3427
Then Abimelech **r** at Arumah, but Jg 9:41 3427
So Israel **r** at Kadesh. Jg 11:17 3427
and he **r** with him three days. Jg 19:4 3427
thus they **r** there before the LORD Jg 20:26 3427
and they **r** at the rock of Rimmon Jg 20:47 3427
the land of Moab and **r** there. Ru 1:2 1961
has **r** from the morning until now; Ru 2:7 5975
So the woman **r** and nursed her son 1Sa 1:23 3427
day that the ark **r** at Kiriath-jearim 1Sa 7:2 3427
and **r** in the hill country in the 1Sa 23:14 3427

Besor, *where* those left behind r. 1Sa 30:9 5975
cross the brook Besor r *behind*. 1Sa 30:10 5975
that David r two days in Ziklag. 2Sa 1:1 3427
Thus the ark of the LORD r in the 2Sa 6:11 3427
So Uriah r in Jerusalem that day 2Sa 11:12 3427
So Tamar r and was desolate in her 2Sa 13:20 3427
of God to Jerusalem and r there. 2Sa 15:29 3427
and by dawn not even one r who had 2Sa 17:22 5737c
Judah r steadfast to their king, 2Sa 20:2 1692
fortifying Ramah and r in Tirzah. 1Ki 15:21 3427
r in the days of his father Asa, 1Ki 22:46 7604
So Jehu killed all who r of the 2Ki 10:11 7604
all who r to Ahab in Samaria, 2Ki 10:17 7604
the Asherah also r standing in Samaria. 2Ki 13:6 5975
None r except the poorest people 2Ki 24:14 7604
Thus the ark of God r with the 1Ch 13:14 3427
Jerusalem and r there three days. Ezr 8:32 3427
wall, and *that* no breach r in it, Ne 6:1 3498
to the people while the people r Ne 8:7 5975
while nine-tenths r in the Ne 11:1
and women, I would have r silent, Es 7:4 2790b
for they *alone* r as fortified cities Jer 34:7 7604
So Jeremiah r in the court of the Jer 37:21 3427
and the rest of the people who r Jer 39:9 7604
him, but its roots r under it. Ezk 17:6 1961
He r there until the death of Herod. Mt 2:15 *1510*
you, it would have r to this day. Mt 11:23 *3306*
because they have r with Me now Mt 15:32 *4357*
have r with Me now three days and Mk 8:2 *4357*
making signs to them, and r mute. Lk 1:22 *1265*
out of heaven, and He r upon Him. Jn 1:32 *3306*
"While it r *unsold*, did it not Ac 5:4 *3306*
and Silas and Timothy r there. Ac 17:14 *5278*
Paul, having r many days longer, Ac 18:18 *4357*
prow stuck fast and r immovable, Ac 27:41 *3306*
Erastus r at Corinth, but 2Tm 4:20 *3306*
of us, they would have r with us; 1Jn 2:19 *3306*

REMAINING
names of the r six on the other stone, Ex 28:10 3498
Of the r oil which is in his palm, Lv 14:17 3499a
And there is none r, bond or Dt 32:36
r within any border of Israel, 2Sa 21:5 3320
you are r in Jerusalem under siege? 2Ch 32:10 3427
against all the r cities of Judah, Jer 34:7 3498
Spirit descending and r upon Him, Jn 1:33 *3306*
The r matters I will arrange 1Co 11:34 *3062*
because of the r blasts of the Rv 8:13 *3062*

REMAINS
"While the earth r, Seedtime and Gn 8:22 5750
and he does not die but r in bed, Ex 21:18 5307
any of the bread r until morning, Ex 29:34 3498
if the bright spot r in its place and Lv 13:23 5975
if the bright spot r in its place and Lv 13:28 5975
but what r until the third day Lv 19:6 3498
then his redemption right r valid Lv 25:29 1961
heap your r on the remains of your Lv 26:30 6297
remains on the r of your idols, Lv 26:30 6297
much of the land r to be possessed. Jos 13:1 7604
"This is the land that r: Jos 13:2 7604
"There r yet the youngest, and 1Sa 16:11 7604
son of Shaphat r on him today." 2Ki 6:31 5975
"Nothing r for him to devour, Jb 20:21 8300
into its lair And r in its den. Jb 37:8 7931
she who r at home will divide the Ps 68:12 5116b
comes, But the earth r forever. Ec 1:4 5975
and r in Jerusalem will be called holy Is 4:3 3498
Whose stump r when it is felled. Is 6:13
Nothing r but to crouch among Is 10:4
enter, The one that r faithful. Is 26:2 8104
remnant that r of this evil family, Jer 8:3 7604
that r in all the places to which Jer 8:3 7604
and he who r and is besieged will Ezk 6:12 7604
r just now no strength in me, Da 10:17 5975
since you say, 'We see,' your sin r. Jn 9:41 *3306*
and dies, it r alone; Jn 12:24 *3306*
work which he has built on it r, 1Co 3:14 *3306*
she is happier if she r as she is; 1Co 7:40 *3306*
much more that which r *is* in glory. 2Co 3:11 *3306*
covenant the same veil r unlifted, 2Co 3:14 *3306*
we are faithless, He r faithful, 2Tm 2:13 *3306*
you would set in order what r Ti 1:5 *3007*
a promise r of entering His rest, Heb 4:1 *2641*
it r for some to enter it, Heb 4:6 *620*
So there r a Sabbath rest Heb 4:9 *620*
he r a priest perpetually. Heb 7:3 *3306*
no longer r a sacrifice for sins, Heb 10:26 *620*
and *all* that r of wickedness, Jas 1:21 *4050*

REMALIAH
Then Pekah son of R, 2Ki 15:25 7425
Pekah son of R became king over 2Ki 15:27 7425
against Pekah the son of R, 2Ki 15:30 7425
Pekah the son of R king of Israel, 2Ki 15:32 7425
Pekah the son of R against Judah. 2Ki 15:37 7425
year of Pekah the son of R, 2Ki 16:1 7425
king of Aram and Pekah son of R 2Ki 16:5 7425
For Pekah the son of R slew in 2Ch 28:6 7425
of Aram and Pekah the son of R, Is 7:1 7425
Rezin and Aram and the son of R, Is 7:4 7425
with Ephraim and the son of R, Is 7:5 7425
head of Samaria is the son of R. Is 7:9 7425
rejoice in Rezin and the son of R; Is 8:6 7425

REMARK
how Jesus had made the r to him, Mk 14:72 *4487*
"At this r, MOSES FLED AND Ac 7:29 *3056*

REMARKABLE
"We have seen r things today." Lk 5:26 *3861*

REMARKING
But some were indignantly r to Mk 14:4

be persuaded, we fell silent, r, Ac 21:14 *3004*

REMEDIES
In vain have you multiplied r; Jer 46:11 7499

REMEDY
His people, until there was no r. 2Ch 36:16 4832
Will suddenly be broken beyond r. Pr 29:1 4832

REMEMBER
and I will r My covenant, which is Gn 9:15 2142
to r the everlasting covenant Gn 9:16 2142
chief cupbearer did not r Joseph, Gn 40:23 2142
"R this day in which you went out Ex 13:3 2142
"R the sabbath day, to keep it holy. Ex 20:8 2142
"R Abraham, Isaac, and Israel, Ex 32:13 2142
I will r My covenant with Jacob, Lv 26:42 2142
r also My covenant with Isaac, Lv 26:42 2142
as well, and I will r the land. Lv 26:42 2142
'But I will r for them the Lv 26:45 2142
"We r the fish which we used to Nu 11:5 2142
r all the commandments of the LORD, Nu 15:39 2142
may r to do all My commandments and Nu 15:40 2142
"R the day you stood before Dt 4:10 2142
'You shall r that you were a Dt 5:15 2142
you shall well r what the LORD Dt 7:18 2142
"You shall r all the way Dt 8:2 2142
"But you shall r the LORD your God, Dt 8:18 2142
"R, do not forget how you Dt 9:7 2142
'R Your servants, Abraham, Isaac, Dt 9:27 2142
"You shall r that you were a Dt 15:15 2142
so that you may r all the Dt 16:3 2142
"You shall r that you were a Dt 16:12 2142
"R what the LORD your God did to Dt 24:9 2142
"But you shall r that you were a Dt 24:18 2142
"You shall r that you were a Dt 24:22 2142
"R what Amalek did to you along Dt 25:17 2142
"R the days of old, Consider the Dt 32:7 2142
"R the word which Moses the Jos 1:13 2142
the sons of Israel did not r the LORD Jg 8:34 2142
r that I am your bone and your Jg 9:2 2142
please r me and please strengthen Jg 16:28 2142
of Your maidservant and r me, 1Sa 1:11 2142
lord, then r your maidservant." 1Sa 25:31 2142
let the king r the LORD your God, 2Sa 14:11 2142
nor r what your servant did wrong 2Sa 19:19 2142
for r when you and I were riding 2Ki 9:25 2142
"R now, O LORD, I beseech You, 2Ki 20:3 2142
R His wonderful deeds which He has 1Ch 16:12 2142
R His covenant forever, The word 1Ch 16:15 2142
r *Your* lovingkindness to Your 2Ch 6:42 2142
Thus Joash the king did not r the 2Ch 24:22 2142
"R the word which You commanded Ne 1:8 2142
r the Lord who is great and Ne 4:14 2142
R me, O my God, for good, Ne 5:19 2142
R, O my God, Tobiah and Sanballat Ne 6:14 2142
And did not r Your wondrous deeds Ne 9:17 2142
R me for this, O my God, and do Ne 13:14 2142
For this also r me, O my God, and Ne 13:22 2142
R them, O my God, because they Ne 13:29 2142
R me, O my God, for good. Ne 13:31 2142
"R now, who *ever* perished being Jb 4:7 2142
"R that my life is *but* breath; My Jb 7:7 2142
'R now, that You have made me as Jb 10:9 2142
have passed by, you would r *it*. Jb 11:16 2142
set a limit for me and r me! Jb 14:13 2142
"Even when I r, I am disturbed, Jb 21:6 2142
"R that you should exalt His Jb 36:24 2142
R the battle; you will not do it again! Jb 41:8 2142
May He r all your meal offerings And Ps 20:3 2142
earth will r and turn to the LORD, Ps 22:27 2142
R, O LORD, Your compassion and Your Ps 25:6 2142
Do not r the sins of my youth or Ps 25:7 2142
to Your lovingkindness r me, Ps 25:7 2142
These things I r and I pour out Ps 42:4 2142
Therefore I r You from the land Ps 42:6 2142
When I r You on my bed, I Ps 63:6 2142
R Your congregation, which You Ps 74:2 2142
R this, O LORD, that the enemy has Ps 74:18 2142
R how the foolish man reproaches Ps 74:22 2142
When I r God, then I am disturbed; Ps 77:3 2142
I will r my song in the night; Ps 77:6 2142
I shall r the deeds of the LORD; Ps 77:11 2142
I will r Your wonders of old. Ps 77:11 2142
They did not r His power, The day Ps 78:42 2142
Do not r the iniquities of *our* Ps 79:8 2142
grave, Whom You r no more, Ps 88:5 2142
R what my span of life is; Ps 89:47 2142
R, O Lord, the reproach of Your Ps 89:50 2142
And r His precepts to do them. Ps 103:18 2142
R His wonders which He has done, Ps 105:5 2142
R me, O LORD, in *Your* favor toward Ps 106:4 2142
not r Your abundant kindnesses, Ps 106:7 2142
did not r to show lovingkindness, Ps 109:16 2142
He will r His covenant forever. Ps 111:5 2142
R the word to Your servant, In Ps 119:49 2142
O LORD, I r Your name in the night, Ps 119:55 2142
R, O LORD, on David's behalf, All Ps 132:1 2142
of my mouth If I do not r you, Ps 137:6 2142
R, O LORD, against the sons of Ps 137:7 2142
I r the days of old; Ps 143:5 2142
And r his trouble no more. Pr 31:7 2142
let him r the days of darkness, Ec 11:8 2142
R also your Creator in the days of Ec 12:1 2142
R *Him* before the silver cord is Ec 12:6 2142
them r that His name is exalted." Is 12:4 2142
"R now, O LORD, I beseech You, Is 38:3 2142
And I will not r your sins. Is 43:25 2142
"R these things, O Jacob, And Is 44:21 2142
"R this, and be assured; Is 46:8 2142
"R the former things long past, Is 46:9 2142

Nor r the outcome of them. Is 47:7 2142
your widowhood you will r no more. Is 54:4 2142
When you lied, and did not r Me Nor Is 57:11 2142
LORD, Nor r iniquity forever; Is 64:9 2142
"I r concerning you the devotion Jer 2:2 2142
come to mind, nor will they r it, Jer 3:16 2142
now He will r their iniquity and Jer 14:10 2142
R *and* do not annul Your covenant Jer 14:21 2142
You who know, O LORD, R me, Jer 15:15 2142
As they r their children, So they Jer 17:2 2142
So they r their altars and their Jer 17:2
R how I stood before You To speak Jer 18:20 2142
"I will not r Him Or speak Jer 20:9 2142
"For you will no longer r the oracle Jer 23:36 2142
him, I certainly *still* r him; Jer 31:20 2142
and their sin I will r no more." Jer 31:34 2142
the land, did not the LORD r them and Jer 44:21 2142
R the LORD from afar, And let Jer 51:50 2142
R my affliction and my wandering, La 3:19 2142
R, O LORD, what has befallen us; La 5:1 2142
those of you who escape will r Me Ezk 6:9 2142
did not r the days of your youth, Ezk 16:22 2142
I will r My covenant with you in Ezk 16:60 2142
"Then you will r your ways and be Ezk 16:61 2142
that you may r and be ashamed and Ezk 16:63 2142
r your ways and all your deeds with Ezk 20:43 2142
eyes to them or r Egypt anymore.' Ezk 23:27 2142
"Then you will r your evil ways Ezk 36:31 2142
That I r all their wickedness. Hos 7:2 2142
Now He will r their iniquity, And Hos 8:13 2142
He will r their iniquity, He will Hos 9:9 2142
not r *the* covenant of brotherhood. Am 1:9 2142
r now What Balak king of Moab Mi 6:5 2142
In wrath r mercy. Hab 3:2 2142
They will r Me in far countries, Zch 10:9 2142
"R the law of Moses My servant, Mal 4:4 2142
and there r that your brother has Mt 5:23 *3403*
"Do you not yet understand or r Mt 16:9 *3421*
we r that when He was still alive Mt 27:63 *3403*
And do you not r, Mk 8:18 *3421*
And to r His holy covenant, Lk 1:72 *3403*
r that during your life you Lk 16:25 *3403*
"R Lot's wife. Lk 17:32 *3421*
Jesus, r me when You come in Your Lk 23:42 *3403*
R how He spoke to you while He was Lk 24:6 *3403*
"R the word that I said to you, Jn 15:20 *3421*
you may r that I told you of them. Jn 16:4 *3421*
and r the words of the Lord Jesus, Ac 20:35 *3421*
r *that* it is not you who supports Ro 11:18
because you r me in everything and 1Co 11:2 *3403*
They only *asked* us to r the poor Ga 2:10 *3421*
Therefore r that formerly you, Eph 2:11 *3421*
r that you were at that time Eph 2:12
R my imprisonment. Col 4:18 *3421*
Do you not r that while I was 2Th 2:5 *3421*
as I constantly r you in my 2Tm 1:3
2192, 3417
R Jesus Christ, risen from the dead, 2Tm 2:8 *3421*
"WHAT IS MAN, THAT YOU R HIM? Heb 2:6 *3403*
AND I WILL R THEIR SINS NO MORE." Heb 8:12 *3403*
LAWLESS DEEDS I WILL R NO MORE." Heb 10:17 *3403*
But r the former days, when, after Heb 10:32 *363*
R the prisoners, as though in Heb 13:3 *3403*
R those who led you, who spoke the Heb 13:7 *3421*
that you should r the words spoken 2Pe 3:2 *3403*
ought to r the words that were Jude 1:17 *3403*
'Therefore r from where you have Rv 2:5 *3421*
'So r what you have received Rv 3:3 *3421*

REMEMBERED
But God r Noah and all the beasts Gn 8:1 2142
of the valley, that God r Abraham, Gn 19:29 2142
Then God r Rachel, and God gave Gn 30:22 2142
Joseph r the dreams which he Gn 42:9 2142
God r His covenant with Abraham, Ex 2:24 2142
and I have r My covenant. Ex 6:5 2142
where I cause My name to be r, Ex 20:24 2142
may be r before the LORD your God, Nu 10:9 2142
his wife, and the LORD r her. 1Sa 1:19 2142
he r Vashti and what she had done Es 2:1 2142
So these days were to be r and Es 9:28 2142
sweetly till he is no longer r. Jb 24:20 2142
Your name to be r in all generations; Ps 45:17 2142
they r that God was their rock, Ps 78:35 2142
He r that they were but flesh, Ps 78:39 2142
the name of Israel be r no more." Ps 83:4 2142
He has r His lovingkindness and Ps 98:3 2142
He has r His covenant forever, The Ps 105:8 2142
For He r His holy word *With* Ps 105:42 2142
He r His covenant for their sake, Ps 106:45 2142
his fathers be r before the LORD, Ps 109:14 2142
He has made His wonders to be r; Ps 111:4 2143
The righteous will be r forever. Ps 112:6 2143
r Your ordinances from of old, Ps 119:52 2142
Who r us in our low estate, For Ps 136:23 2142
sat down and wept, When we r Zion. Ps 137:1 2142
Yet no one r that poor man. Ec 9:15 2142
not r the rock of your refuge. Is 17:10 2142
many songs, That you may be r. Is 23:16 2142
Then His people r the days of old, Is 63:11 2142
will not be r or come to mind. Is 65:17 2142
That his name be r no more." Jer 11:19 2142
And has not r His footstool In the La 2:1 2142
which he has done shall not be r; Ezk 3:20 2142
"Because you have not r the days Ezk 16:43 2142
will not be r against him; Ezk 18:22 2142
will not be r for his treachery which Ezk 18:24 2142
have made your iniquity to be r, Ezk 21:24 2142
You will not be r, for I, the Ezk 21:32 2142
will not be r among the nations. Ezk 25:10 2142

none of his righteous deeds will be **r**; **Ezk 33:13** 2142
committed will be **r** against him. **Ezk 33:16** 2142
I was fainting away, I **r** the LORD, **Jon 2:7** 2142
and they will no longer be **r**; **Zch 13:2** 2142
r the word which Jesus had said, **Mt 26:75** *3403*
And Peter **r** how Jesus had made the **Mk 14:72** *363*
And Peter **r** the word of the Lord, **Lk 22:61** *5279*
And they **r** His words, **Lk 24:8** *3403*
disciples **r** that it was written, **Jn 2:17** *3403*
His disciples **r** that He said this; **Jn 2:22** *3403*
then they **r** that these things were **Jn 12:16** *3403*
your alms have been **r** before God. **Ac 10:31** *3403*
"And I **r** the word of the Lord, **Ac 11:16** *3403*
Babylon the great was **r** before God, **Rv 16:19** *3403*
and God has **r** her iniquities. **Rv 18:5** *3421*

REMEMBERING
r the days of her youth, **Ezk 23:19** 2142
r that night and day for a period **Ac 20:31** *3421*

REMEMBERS
For He who requires blood **r** them; **Ps 9:12** 2142
Who **r** You in Your ways. **Is 64:5** 2142
Jerusalem **r** all her precious things **La 1:7** 2142
my soul **r** And is bowed down **La 3:20** 2142
He **r** his nobles; They stumble in **Na 2:5** 2142
child, she no longer **r** the anguish **Jn 16:21** *3421*
as he **r** the obedience of you all, **2Co 7:15** *363*

REMEMBRANCE
to me to bring my iniquity to **r** and **1Ki 17:18** 2142
O LORD, is everlasting, Your **r**, **Ps 135:13** 2143
There is no **r** of earlier things; **Ec 1:11** 2146
There will be for them no **r** Among **Ec 1:11** 2146
there is no lasting **r** of the wise man **Ec 2:16** 2146
You have wiped out all **r** of them. **Is 26:14** 2143
"Put Me in **r**, let us argue our case **Is 43:26** 2142
But he brings iniquity to **r**, **Ezk 21:23** 2142
because you have come to **r**, **Ezk 21:24** 2142
and a book of **r** was written before **Mal 3:16** 2146
His servant, In **r** of His mercy, **Lk 1:54** *3403*
do this in **r** of Me." **Lk 22:19** *364*
bring to your **r** all that I said to you. **Jn 14:26** *5279*
do this in **r** of Me." **1Co 11:24** *364*
as you drink *it*, in **r** of Me." **1Co 11:25** *364*
I thank my God in all my **r** of you, **Php 1:3** *3417*

REMETH
and **R** and En-gannim and En-haddah **Jos 19:21** 7432

REMIND
To **r** a man what is right for him, **Jb 33:23** 5046
You who **r** the LORD, take no rest **Is 62:6** 2142
some points so as to **r** you again, **Ro 15:15** *1878*
and he will **r** you of my ways which **1Co 4:17** *363*
I **r** you to kindle afresh the gift of **2Tm 1:6** *363*
R *them* of these things, and **2Tm 2:14** *5279*
R them to be subject to rulers, to **Ti 3:1** *5279*
be ready to **r** you of these things, **2Pe 1:12** *5279*
Now I desire to **r** you, though you **Jude 1:5** *5279*

REMINDED
Being **r**, Peter said to Him, **Mk 11:21** *363*

REMINDER
hand, and as a **r** on your forehead, **Ex 13:9** 2146
rest, a **r** by blowing *of trumpets*, **Lv 23:24** 2146
of memorial, a **r** of iniquity. **Nu 5:15** 2142
be as a **r** of you before your God. **Nu 10:10** 2146
as a **r** to the sons of Israel that **Nu 16:40** 2146
"Now the crown will become a **r** in **Zch 6:14** 2146
there is a **r** of sins year by year. **Heb 10:3** *364*
to stir you up by way of **r**, **2Pe 1:13** *5280*
up your sincere mind by way of **r**, **2Pe 3:1** *5280*

REMISSION
you shall grant a **r** *of debts*. **Dt 15:1** 8059
"This is the manner of **r**: **Dt 15:2** 8059
the LORD's **r** has been proclaimed. **Dt 15:2** 8059
'The seventh year, the year of **r**, **Dt 15:9** 8059
time of the year of **r** of debts, **Dt 31:10** 8059

REMNANT
preserve for you a **r** in the earth, **Gn 45:7** 7611
until there was no **r** left him; **Nu 21:35** 8300
destroy the **r** from the city." **Nu 24:19** 8300
was left of the **r** of the Rephaim. **Dt 3:11** 3499a
Bashan, one of the **r** of Rephaim, **Jos 12:4** 3499a
was left of the **r** of the Rephaim); **Jos 13:12** 3499a
nor **r** on the face of the earth." **2Sa 14:7** 7611
but of the **r** of the Amorites, **2Sa 21:2** 3499a
The **r** of the sodomites who **1Ki 22:46** 3499a
offer a prayer for the **r** that is left. **2Ki 19:4** 7611
'The surviving **r** of the house **2Ki 19:30** 7604
out of Jerusalem will go forth a **r**, **2Ki 19:31** 7611
abandon the **r** of My inheritance **2Ki 21:14** 7611
r of the Amalekites who escaped, **1Ch 4:43** 7611
and from all the **r** of Israel, **2Ch 34:9** 7611
to leave us an escaped **r** and to **Ezr 9:8** 6413
given us an escaped **r** as this, **Ezr 9:13** 6413
there is no **r** nor any who escape? **Ezr 9:14** 7611
we have been left an escaped **r**, **Ezr 9:15** 6413
"The **r** there in the province who **Ne 1:3** 7604
With a **r** of wrath You will gird **Ps 76:10** 7611
in that day the **r** of Israel, **Is 10:20** 7605
A **r** will return, the remnant of **Is 10:21** 7605
will return, the **r** of Jacob, **Is 10:21** 7605
Only a **r** within them will return; **Is 10:22** 7605
with His hand The **r** of His people, **Is 11:11** 7605
a highway from Assyria For the **r** of **Is 11:16** 7605
Moab and upon the **r** of the land. **Is 15:9** 7611
and *his* **r** will be very small *and* **Is 16:14** 7605
from Damascus And the **r** of Aram; **Is 17:3** 7605
diadem to the **r** of His people; **Is 28:5** 7605
prayer for the **r** that is left.' " **Is 37:4** 7611
The surviving **r** of the house of Judah **Is 37:31** 7604
out of Jerusalem will go forth a **r** **Is 37:32** 7611
all the **r** of the house of Israel, **Is 46:3** 7611
glean as the vine the **r** of Israel; **Jer 6:9** 7611
the **r** that remains of this evil family, **Jer 8:3** 7611
and a **r** will not be left to them, **Jer 11:23** 7611
gather the **r** of My flock out of all **Jer 23:3** 7611
and the **r** of Jerusalem who remain **Jer 24:8** 7611
Gaza, Ekron and the **r** of Ashdod); **Jer 25:20** 7611
save Your people, The **r** of Israel.' **Jer 31:7** 7611
king of Babylon had left a **r** for Judah **Jer 40:11** 7611
and the **r** of Judah would perish?" **Jer 40:15** 7611
Ishmael took captive all the **r** of the **Jer 41:10** 7611
from Mizpah all the **r** of the people **Jer 41:16** 7611
your God, *that is* for all this **r**; **Jer 42:2** 7611
word of the LORD, O **r** of Judah. **Jer 42:15** 7611
has spoken to you, O **r** of Judah, **Jer 42:19** 7611
the forces took the entire **r** of Judah **Jer 43:5** 7611
leaving yourselves without **r**, **Jer 44:7** 7611
'And I will take away the **r** of Judah **Jer 44:12** 7611
no refugees or survivors for the **r** of **Jer 44:14** 7611
Then all the **r** of Judah who have **Jer 44:28** 7611
The **r** of the coastland of Caphtor. **Jer 47:4** 7611
O **r** of their valley, How long will **Jer 47:5** 7611
pardon those whom I leave as a **r**.' **Jer 50:20** 7604
scatter all your **r** to every wind. **Ezk 5:10** 7611
"However, I will leave a **r**, **Ezk 6:8** 3498
Are You destroying the whole **r** of **Ezk 9:8** 7611
r of Israel to a complete end?" **Ezk 11:13** 7611
and destroy the **r** of the seacoast. **Ezk 25:16** 7611
And the **r** of the Philistines will **Am 1:8** 7611
be gracious to the **r** of Joseph. **Am 5:15** 7611
they may possess the **r** of Edom **Am 9:12** 7611
surely gather the **r** of Israel. **Mi 2:12** 7611
"I will make the lame a **r** And **Mi 4:7** 7611
Then the **r** of Jacob Will be among **Mi 5:7** 7611
The **r** of Jacob Will be among **Mi 5:8** 7611
act of the **r** of His possession? **Mi 7:18** 7611
I will cut off the **r** of Baal from this **Zph 1:4** 7605
For the **r** of the house of Judah, **Zph 2:7** 7611
The **r** of My people will plunder **Zph 2:9** 7611
"The **r** of Israel will do no wrong **Zph 3:13** 7611
with all the **r** of the people, **Hg 1:12** 7611
spirit of all the **r** of the people; **Hg 1:14** 7611
and to the **r** of the people saying, **Hg 2:2** 7611
in the sight of the **r** of this people **Zch 8:6** 7611
I will not treat the **r** of this people **Zch 8:11** 7611
cause the **r** of this people to inherit **Zch 8:12** 7611
they also will be a **r** for our God, **Zch 9:7** 7604
done *so* who has a **r** of the Spirit. **Mal 2:15** 7605
IT IS THE **R** THAT WILL BE SAVED; **Ro 9:27** *5275a*
a **r** according to *God's* gracious choice **Ro 11:5** *3005*

REMORSE
did not even feel **r** afterward so **Mt 21:32** *3338*
he felt **r** and returned the thirty **Mt 27:3** *3338*

REMOTE
a certain Levite staying in the **r** part **Jg 19:1** 3411
Judah to the **r** part of the hill country **Jg 19:18** 3411
in the most **r** part of the heavens, **Ne 1:9** 7097a
is **r** and exceedingly mysterious. **Ec 7:24** 7350
give ear, all **r** places of the earth. **Is 8:9** 4801
of the LORD comes from a **r** place; **Is 30:27** 4801
from the **r** parts of the earth. **Jer 6:22** 3411
from the **r** parts of the earth, **Jer 31:8** 3411
from the **r** parts of the earth. **Jer 50:41** 3411
Beth-togarmah *from* the **r** parts of **Ezk 38:6** 3411
out of the **r** parts of the north, **Ezk 38:15** 3411

REMOTEST
To the **r** parts of Lebanon; **2Ki 19:23** 3411
I dwell in the **r** part of the sea, **Ps 139:9** 319
the **r** part of the rivers of Egypt and **Is 7:18** 7097a
To the **r** parts of Lebanon; **Is 37:24** 3411
And called from its **r** parts And **Is 41:9** 678
up From the **r** parts of the earth. **Jer 25:32** 3411
are set in the **r** parts of the pit and **Ezk 32:23** 3411
up from the **r** parts of the north and **Ezk 39:2** 3411
even to the **r** part of the earth." **Ac 1:8** *2078*

REMOVAL
in the **r** of the body of the flesh **Col 2:11** *555*
not the **r** of dirt from the flesh, **1Pe 3:21** *595*

REMOVE
he grasped his father's hand to **r** it **Gn 48:17** 5493
r your sandals from your feet, for **Ex 3:5** 5394
"Entreat the LORD that He **r** the **Ex 8:8** 5493
would only **r** this death from me." **Ex 10:17** 5493
shall **r** leaven from your houses; **Ex 12:15** 7673a
I will **r** sickness from your midst. **Ex 23:25** 5493
which he shall **r** with the kidneys. **Lv 3:4** 5493
he shall **r** close to the backbone, **Lv 3:9** 5493
which he shall **r** with the kidneys. **Lv 3:10** 5493
which he shall **r** with the kidneys. **Lv 3:15** 5493
'He shall **r** from it all the **Lv 4:8** 7311
which he shall **r** with the kidneys **Lv 4:9** 5493
'He shall **r** all its fat from **Lv 4:19** 7311
'Then he shall **r** all its fat, just **Lv 4:31** 5493
'Then he shall **r** all its fat, just **Lv 4:35** 5493
liver he shall **r** with the kidneys. **Lv 7:4** 5493
keep it as water to **r** impurity; **Nu 19:9**
He may **r** the serpents from us." **Nu 21:7** 5493
LORD will **r** from you all sickness; **Dt 7:15** 5493
"So you shall **r** the guilt of **Dt 21:9** 1197a
"She shall also **r** the clothes of **Dt 21:13** 5493
shall **r** the evil from your midst, **Dt 21:21** 1197a
r the memory of them from men," **Dt 32:26** 7673a
"**R** your sandals from your feet, **Jos 5:15** 5394
Then I would **r** Abimelech." **Jg 9:29** 5493
r *this* wickedness from Israel." **Jg 20:13** 1197a
r the foreign gods and the **1Sa 7:3** 5493
you down and **r** your head from you. **1Sa 17:46** 5493
that you may **r** from me and from my **1Ki 2:31** 5493
r the kings, each from his place, **1Ki 20:24** 5493
"I will **r** Judah also from My **2Ki 23:27** 5493
to **r** *them* from His sight because **2Ki 24:3** 5493
and I will not again **r** the foot of **2Ch 33:8** 5493
he might **r** his sackcloth from him, **Es 4:4** 5493
"Let Him **r** His rod from me, And **Jb 9:34** 5493
R Your hand from me, And let not **Jb 13:21** 7368
If you **r** unrighteousness far from **Jb 22:23** 7368
"Some **r** the landmarks; **Jb 24:2** 5381
"**R** Your plague from me; **Ps 39:10** 5493
R the false way from me, And **Ps 119:29** 5493
The rod of discipline will **r** it far **Pr 22:15** 7368
r grief and anger from your heart and **Ec 11:10** 5493
R the evil of your deeds from My **Is 1:16** 5493
lye And will **r** all your alloy. **Is 1:25** 5493
Lord GOD of hosts is going to **r** from **Is 3:1** 5493
I will **r** its hedge and it will be **Is 5:5** 5493
and it will also **r** the beard. **Is 7:20** 5595
And **r** *and* cut away the spreading **Is 18:5** 5493
And He will **r** the reproach of His **Is 25:8** 5493
they **r** their hearts far from Me, **Is 29:13** 7368
R your veil, strip off the skirt, **Is 47:2** 1540
R *every* obstacle out of the way of **Is 57:14** 7311
If you **r** the yoke from your midst, **Is 58:9** 5493
R the stones, lift up a standard **Is 62:10** 5619
And **r** the foreskins of your heart, **Jer 4:4** 5493
order to **r** you far from your land; **Jer 27:10** 7368
I am about to **r** you from the face **Jer 28:16** 7971
they will **r** all its detestable **Ezk 11:18** 5493
'**R** the turban and take off the **Ezk 21:26** 5493
will **r** your nose and your ears; **Ezk 23:25** 5493
from their thrones, **r** their robes and **Ezk 26:16** 5493
and I will **r** the heart of stone **Ezk 36:26** 5493
"For I will **r** the names of the **Hos 2:17** 5493
"But I will **r** the northern *army* **Jl 2:20** 7368
r them far from their territory, **Jl 3:6** 7368
which you cannot **r** your necks; **Mi 2:3** 4185
You will *try to* **r** *for safekeeping*, **Mi 6:14** 5472
"I will completely **r** all *things* **Zph 1:2** 5486
"I will **r** man and beast; **Zph 1:3** 5486
I will **r** the birds of the sky And **Zph 1:3** 5486
will **r** from your midst Your proud, **Zph 3:11** 5493
"**R** the filthy garments from him." **Zch 3:4** 5493
'and I will **r** the iniquity of that **Zch 3:9** 4185
r their blood from their mouth And **Zch 9:7** 5493
and I will also **r** the prophets and **Zch 13:2** 5674a
and I am not fit to **r** His sandals; **Mt 3:11** *941*
r this cup from Me; **Mk 14:36** *3911*
are willing, **r** this cup from Me; **Lk 22:42** *3911*
Jesus said, "**R** the stone." Martha, **Jn 11:39** *142*
I ALSO WILL **R** YOU BEYOND BABYLON.' **Ac 7:43** *3351*
WILL **R** UNGODLINESS FROM JACOB." **Ro 11:26** *654*
R THE WICKED MAN FROM AMONG **1Co 5:13** *1808*
all faith, so as to **r** mountains, **1Co 13:2** *3179*
and will **r** your lampstand out of **Rv 2:5** *2795*

REMOVED
Noah **r** the covering of the ark, **Gn 8:13** 5493
So he **r** on that day the striped **Gn 30:35** 5493
So she **r** her widow's garments and **Gn 38:14** 5493
and **r** her veil and put on her **Gn 38:19** 5493
he **r** them to the cities from one **Gn 47:21** 5674a
and **r** the swarms of insects from **Ex 8:31** 5493
they shall not be **r** from it. **Ex 25:15** 5493
(just as it is **r** from the ox of **Lv 4:10** 7311
just as the fat was **r** from the **Lv 4:31** 5493
just as the fat of the lamb is **r** **Lv 4:35** 5493
protection has been **r** from them, **Nu 14:9** 5493
house of him whose sandal is **r**.' **Dt 25:10** 2502a
'I have **r** the sacred *portion* from **Dt 26:13** 1197a
I **r** any of it while I was unclean, **Dt 26:14** 1197a
you have **r** the things under the ban **Jos 7:13** 5493
a man **r** his sandal and gave it to **Ru 4:7** 8025
And he **r** his sandal. **Ru 4:8** 8025
why His hand is not **r** from you." **1Sa 6:3** 5493
So the sons of Israel **r** the Baals **1Sa 7:4** 5493
Saul **r** him from his presence and **1Sa 18:13** 5493
which was **r** from before the LORD, **1Sa 21:6** 5493
And Saul had **r** from the land those **1Sa 28:3** 5493
Saul, whom I **r** from before you. **2Sa 7:15** 5493
he **r** Amasa from the highway into **2Sa 20:12** 5437
soon as he was **r** from the highway, **2Sa 20:13** 3014
and **r** all the idols which his **1Ki 15:12** 5493
He also **r** Maacah his mother **1Ki 15:13** 5493
stands, and **r** the laver from them; **2Ki 16:17** 5493
he **r** from the house of the LORD **2Ki 16:18** 5437
Israel and **r** them from His sight; **2Ki 17:18** 5493
the LORD **r** Israel from His sight, **2Ki 17:23** 5493
He **r** the high places and broke **2Ki 18:4** 5493
Josiah also **r** all the houses **2Ki 23:19** 5493
Josiah **r** the mediums and the **2Ki 23:24** 1197a
from My sight, as I have **r** Israel. **2Ki 23:27** 5493
for he **r** the foreign altars and **2Ch 14:3** 5493
He also **r** the high places and the **2Ch 14:5** 5493
r the abominable idols from all the **2Ch 15:8** 5674a
He also **r** Maacah, the mother **2Ch 15:16** 5493
high places were not **r** from Israel; **2Ch 15:17** 5493
r the high places and the Asherim **2Ch 17:6** 5493
for you have **r** the Asheroth from **2Ch 19:3** 1197a
high places, however, were not **r**; **2Ch 20:33** 5493
They arose and **r** the altars **2Ch 30:14** 5493
they also **r** all the incense altars **2Ch 30:14** 5493
He also **r** the foreign gods and the **2Ch 33:15** 5493
Josiah **r** all the abominations **2Ch 34:33** 5493
Then they **r** the burnt offerings **2Ch 35:12** 5493
me, none of us **r** our clothes, **Ne 4:23** 6584
"If he is **r** from his place, Then **Jb 8:18** 1104
me And **r** the crown from my head. **Jb 19:9** 5493
"He has **r** my brothers far from **Jb 19:13** 7368

You **r** a vine from Egypt; You drove Ps 80:8 5265
r my acquaintances far from me; Ps 88:8 7368
r lover and friend far from me; Ps 88:18 7368
He **r** our transgressions from us. Ps 103:12 7368
You have **r** all the wicked of the Ps 119:119 7673a
dug it all around, **r** its stones, Is 5:2 5619
"The LORD has **r** men far away, And Is 6:12 7368
I **r** the boundaries of the peoples And Is 10:13 5493
that his burden will be **r** from Is 10:27 5493
Then his yoke will be **r** from them and Is 14:25 5493
his burden **r** from their shoulder. Is 14:25 5493
about to be **r** from being a city And Is 17:1 5493
And He **r** the defense of Judah. Is 22:8 1540
my dwelling is pulled up and **r** from Is 38:12 1540
That her iniquity has been **r**, Is 40:2 7521
"For the mountains may be **r** and Is 54:10 4185
But My lovingkindness will not be **r** Is 54:10 4185
Indeed, far **r** from Me, you have Is 57:8 4480
iniquity Your skirts have been **r** And Jer 13:22 1540
should be **r** from before My face, Jer 32:31 5493
"Though I had **r** them far away Ezk 11:16 7368
Therefore I **r** them when I saw *it*. Ezk 16:50 5493
sovereignty has been **r** from you, Da 4:31 5709
and it **r** the regular sacrifice Da 8:11 7311
crowd, they **r** the roof above Him; Mk 2:4 *648*
impediment of his tongue was **r**, Mk 7:35 *3089*
when I am **r** from the management Lk 16:4 *3179*
So they **r** the stone. Jn 11:41 *142*
From there they were **r** to Shechem Ac 7:16 *3346a*
HIS LIFE IS **R** FROM THE EARTH." Ac 8:33 *142*
"After He had **r** him, Ac 13:22 *3179*
deed would be **r** from your midst. 1Co 5:2 *142*
because it is **r** in Christ. 2Co 3:14 *2673*

REMOVES
"*It is God* who **r** the mountains, Jb 9:5 6275
He **r** kings and establishes kings; Da 2:21 5709
How He **r** it from me! Mi 2:4 4185

REMOVING
r from there every speckled and Gn 30:32 5493
make its pails for **r** its ashes, Ex 27:3 1878
denotes the **r** of those things Heb 12:27 *3331*

REND
r the heavens *and* come down, Is 64:1 7167
nor did they **r** their garments. Jer 36:24 7167
And **r** your heart and not your Jl 2:13 7167

RENDER
'Do not **r** yourselves detestable Lv 11:43 8262
which they shall **r** to Me, Nu 18:9 7725
r vengeance on My adversaries, Dt 32:41 7725
r vengeance on His adversaries, Dt 32:43 7725
and forgive and act and **r** to each 1Ki 8:39 5414
and **r** to each according to all his 2Ch 6:30 5414
is with you when you **r** judgment. 2Ch 19:6 1697
I will **r** thank offerings to You. Ps 56:12 7999a
R recompense to the proud. Ps 94:2 7725
What shall I **r** to the LORD For all Ps 116:12 7725
r to man according to his work? Pr 24:12 7725
I will **r** to the man according to Pr 24:29 7725
will **r** decisions for many peoples; Is 2:4 3198
"**R** the hearts of this people Is 6:10 8080
r Himself *as* a guilt offering, Is 53:10 7760
To **r** His anger with fury, Is 66:15 7725
is going to **r** recompense to her. Jer 51:6 7999a
And **r** decisions for mighty, Mi 4:3 3198
"Then **r** to Caesar the things that Mt 22:21 *591*
"**R** to Caesar the things that are Mk 12:17 *591*
"Then **r** to Caesar the things that Lk 20:25 *591*
who WILL **R** TO EACH PERSON ACCORDING Ro 2:6 *591*
R to all what is due them: Ro 13:7 *591*
With good will **r** service, as to Eph 6:7 *1398*
For what thanks can we **r** to God 1Th 3:9 *467*
sent out to **r** service for the sake Heb 1:14
that through death He might **r** Heb 2:14 *2673*
they **r** you neither useless nor 2Pe 1:8 *2525*
to **r** to every man according to Rv 22:12 *591*

RENDERED
my service which I have **r** you." Gn 30:26 5647
so He **r** judgment last night." Gn 31:42 3198
what services he **r** at Ephesus. 2Tm 1:18 *1247*

RENDERING
They totter *when* **r** judgment. Is 28:7
is **r** recompense to His enemies. Is 66:6 7999a
Are you **r** Me a recompense? Jl 3:4 7999a

RENDING
strong wind was **r** the mountains 1Ki 19:11 6561

RENEW
Gilgal and **r** the kingdom there." 1Sa 11:14 2318
You **r** Your witnesses against me Jb 10:17 2318
r a steadfast spirit within me. Ps 51:10 2318
You **r** the face of the ground. Ps 104:30 2318
R our days as of old, La 5:21 2318
it is impossible to **r** them again to Heb 6:6 *340*

RENEWAL
a **r** in which there is no Col 3:11

RENEWED
me, And my bow is **r** in my hand.' Jb 29:20 2498
your youth is **r** like the eagle. Ps 103:5 2318
You found **r** strength, Therefore Is 57:10 2416a
inner man is being **r** day by day. 2Co 4:16 *341*
be **r** in the spirit of your mind, Eph 4:23 *365*
the new self who is being **r** to a true Col 3:10 *341*

RENEWING
transformed by the **r** of your mind, Ro 12:2 *342*
and **r** by the Holy Spirit, Ti 3:5 *342*

RENOUNCED
but we have **r** the things hidden 2Co 4:2 *550*

RENOWN
men who *were* of old, men of **r**. Gn 6:4 8034
chosen in the assembly, men of **r**. Nu 16:2 8034
might be for Me a people, for **r**, Jer 13:11 8034
of them, officers and men of **r**, Ezk 23:23 7121
and it will be to their **r** *on* the Ezk 39:13 8034
His **r** *will be* like the wine of Hos 14:7 2143
praise and **r** In all the earth. Zph 3:19 8034
I will give you **r** and praise Among Zph 3:20 8034

RENOWNED
one, From the seas, O **r** city, Ezk 26:17 1984b
establish for them a **r** planting place, Ezk 34:29 8034

RENT
because you impose heavy **r** on the Am 5:11 1318
and will **r** out the vineyard to Mt 21:41 *1554*

RENTED
and **r** it out to vine-growers and Mt 21:33 *1554*
and **r** it out to vine-growers and Mk 12:1 *1554*
and **r** it out to vine-growers, Lk 20:9 *1554*
two full years in his own **r** quarters and Ac 28:30 *3410*

REPAID
'Why have you **r** evil for good? Gn 44:4 7999a
as I have done, so God has **r** me." Jg 1:7 7999a
God **r** the wickedness of Abimelech, Jg 9:56 7725
Thus they have **r** me evil for good And Ps 109:5 7760
with which you have **r** us. Ps 137:8 1580
Should good be **r** with evil? Jer 18:20 7999a
for you will be **r** at the resurrection Lk 14:14 *467*

REPAIR
and they shall **r** the damages of 2Ki 12:5 2388
not **r** the damages of the house? 2Ki 12:7 2388
nor **r** the damages of the house. 2Ki 12:8 2388
hewn stone to **r** the damages to the 2Ki 12:12 2388
laid out for the house to **r** it. 2Ki 12:12 2388
to **r** the damages of the house, 2Ki 22:5 2388
and hewn stone to **r** the house. 2Ki 22:6 2388
to **r** the house of the LORD. 1Ch 26:27 2388
collect money from all Israel to **r** the 2Ch 24:5 2388
bronze to **r** the house of the LORD. 2Ch 24:12 2388
and the **r** work progressed in their 2Ch 24:13 724
r the house of the LORD his God. 2Ch 34:8 2388
it to restore and **r** the house. 2Ch 34:10 2388
r of the walls of Jerusalem went on, Ne 4:7 724
And they will **r** the ruined cities, Is 61:4 2318

REPAIRED
And he **r** the altar of the LORD 1Ki 18:30 7495
not **r** the damages of the house. 2Ki 12:6 2388
it they **r** the house of the LORD. 2Ki 12:14 2388
and Joab **r** the rest of the city. 1Ch 11:8 2421a
the house of the LORD and **r** them. 2Ch 29:3 2388
son of Besodeiah **r** the Old Gate; Ne 3:6 2388
son of Pahath-moab **r** another section Ne 3:11 2388
of Zanoah **r** the Valley Gate. Ne 3:13 2388
Beth-haccherem **r** the Refuse Gate. Ne 3:14 2388
of Mizpah, **r** the Fountain Gate. Ne 3:15 2388
of Mizpah, **r** another section in Ne 3:19 2388
zealously **r** another section, Ne 3:20 2388
son of Hakkoz **r** another section, Ne 3:21 2388
son of Henadad **r** another section, Ne 3:24 2388
After them the Tekoites **r** another Ne 3:27 2388
son of Zalaph, **r** another section. Ne 3:30 2388
vessel, which cannot again be **r**; Jer 19:11 7495

REPAIRER
be called the **r** of the breach, Is 58:12 1443

REPAIRERS
and your pilots, Your **r** of seams, Ezk 27:27 2388

REPAIRING
the walls and **r** the foundations. Ezr 4:12 2338
men were with you **r** your seams; Ezk 27:9 2388

REPAIRS
of Uriah the son of Hakkoz made **r**. Ne 3:4 2388
the son of Meshezabel made **r**. Ne 3:4 2388
the son of Baana *also* made **r**. Ne 3:4 2388
next to him the Tekoites made **r**, Ne 3:5 2388
also made **r** for the official seat Ne 3:7 2388
Harhaiah of the goldsmiths made **r**. Ne 3:8 2388
one of the perfumers, made **r**, Ne 3:8 2388
the district of Jerusalem, made **r**. Ne 3:9 2388
made **r** opposite his house. Ne 3:10 2388
the son of Hashabneiah made **r**. Ne 3:10 2388
the district of Jerusalem, made **r**, Ne 3:12 2388
made **r** as far as *a point* opposite Ne 3:16 2388
After him the Levites carried out **r** Ne 3:17 2388
carried out **r** for his district. Ne 3:17 2388
carried out **r** *under* Bavvai the son of Ne 3:18 2388
men of the valley, carried out **r**. Ne 3:22 2388
Benjamin and Hasshub carried out **r** Ne 3:23 2388
son of Ananiah, carried out **r** beside Ne 3:23 2388
Palal the son of Uzai *made* **r** in Ne 3:25
Pedaiah the son of Parosh *made* **r**. Ne 3:25
servants living in Ophel *made* **r** Ne 3:26
Gate the priests carried out **r**, Ne 3:28 2388
the son of Immer carried out **r** in Ne 3:29 2388
of the East Gate, carried out **r**. Ne 3:29 2388
the son of Berechiah carried out **r** in Ne 3:30 2388
carried out **r** as far as the house Ne 3:31 2388
and the merchants carried out **r**. Ne 3:32 2388

REPAY
Him, He will **r** him to his face. Dt 7:10 7999a
"Do you thus **r** the LORD, O Dt 32:6 1580
And I will **r** those who hate Me. Dt 32:41 7999a
"The LORD will **r** each man *for* 1Sa 26:23 7725
May the LORD **r** the evildoer 2Sa 3:39 7999a
'and I will **r** you in this property,' 2Ki 9:26 7999a
God **r** him so that he may know *it*. Jb 21:19 7999a
will **r** him for what he has done? Jb 21:31 7999a
given to Me that I should **r** *him*? Jb 41:11 7999a

R them their recompense. Ps 28:4 7725
They **r** me evil for good, *To* the Ps 35:12 7999a
And those who **r** evil for good, Ps 38:20 7999a
raise me up, That I may **r** them. Ps 41:10 7999a
he is found, he must **r** sevenfold; Pr 6:31 7999a
He will **r** him for his good deed. Pr 19:17 7999a
Do not say, "I will **r** evil"; Pr 20:22 7999a
to *their* deeds, so He will **r**, Is 59:18 7999a
not keep silent, but I will **r**; Is 65:6 7999a
I will even **r** into their bosom, Is 65:6 7999a
I will first doubly **r** their iniquity Jer 16:18 7999a
R her according to her work; Jer 50:29 7999a
"But I will **r** Babylon and all the Jer 51:24 7999a
of recompense, He will fully **r**. Jer 51:56 7999a
will **r** you according to your ways, Ezk 7:9 5414
he will **r** him for his scorn. Da 11:18 7725
ways And **r** them for their deeds. Hos 4:9 7725
will **r** him according to his deeds. Hos 12:2 7725
and WILL THEN **R** EVERY MAN ACCORDING Mt 16:27 *591*
he did not have *the means* to **r**, Mt 18:25 *591*
me and I will **r** you everything.' Mt 18:26 *591*
with me and I will **r** you.' Mt 18:29 *591*
he should **r** all that was owed him. Mt 18:34 *591*
"When they were unable to **r**, Lk 7:42 *591*
when I return I will **r** you.' Lk 10:35 *591*
do not have *the means* to **r** you; Lk 14:14 *467*
"VENGEANCE IS MINE, I WILL **R**," Ro 12:19 *467*
just for God to **r** with affliction those 2Th 1:6 *467*
will **r** him according to his deeds. 2Tm 4:14 *591*
with my own hand, I will **r** it Phm 1:19 *661*
"VENGEANCE IS MINE, I WILL **R**." Heb 10:30 *467*

REPAYMENT
all that he had, and **r** to be made. Mt 18:25 *591*
you in return and *that* will be your **r**. Lk 14:12 *468*

REPAYS
but **r** those who hate Him to their Dt 7:10 7999a
blessed will be the one who **r** you Ps 137:8 7999a
but **r** the iniquity of fathers into Jer 32:18 7999a
one **r** another with evil for evil, 1Th 5:15 *591*

REPEALED
and Media so that it cannot be **r**, Es 1:19 5674a

REPEATED
Balaam and **r** Balak's words to him. Nu 22:7 1696
he **r** them in the LORD's hearing. 1Sa 8:21 1696
Abner **r** again to Asahel, 2Sa 2:22 3254, 559

REPEATEDLY
"They have **r** stumbled; Jer 46:16 7235a
has turned His hand **R** all the day. La 3:3 7725
with violence and provoked Me **r**? Ezk 8:17 7725
friends of his sent to him and **r** urged Ac 19:31
embraced Paul, and **r** kissed him, Ac 20:37

REPEATING
r of the dream to Pharaoh twice, Gn 41:32 8138

REPEATS
Indeed she **r** her words to herself, Jg 5:29 7725
But he who **r** a matter separates Pr 17:9 8138
Is a fool who **r** his folly. Pr 26:11 8138

REPEL
who **r** the onslaught at the gate. Is 28:6 7725

REPENT
a son of man, that He should **r**; Nu 23:19 5162
and **r** and make supplication to 1Ki 8:47 7725
and **r** and make supplication to 2Ch 6:37 7725
And I **r** in dust and ashes." Jb 42:6 5162
If a man does not **r**, Ps 7:12 7725
They have refused to **r**. Jer 5:3 7725
Does one turn away and not **r**? Jer 8:4 7725
They did not **r** of their ways. Jer 15:7 7725
that I may **r** of the calamity which Jer 26:3 5162
"**R** and turn away from your idols and Ezk 14:6 7725
"**R** and turn away from all your Ezk 18:30 7725
"Therefore, **r** and live." Ezk 18:32 7725
"**R**, for the kingdom of heaven is Mt 3:2 *3340*
"**R**, for the kingdom of heaven is Mt 4:17 *3340*
were done, because they did not **r**. Mt 11:20 *3340*
r and believe in the gospel." Mk 1:15 *3340*
and preached that *men* should **r**. Mk 6:12 *3340*
"I tell you, no, but unless you **r**, Lk 13:3 *3340*
unless you **r**, you will all likewise perish Lk 13:5 *3340*
them from the dead, they will **r**!' Lk 16:30 *3340*
to you seven times, saying, 'I **r**,' Lk 17:4 *3340*
"**R**, and each of you be baptized Ac 2:38 *3340*
"Therefore **r** and return, so that Ac 3:19 *3340*
r of this wickedness of yours, Ac 8:22 *3340*
men that all *people* everywhere should **r**, Ac 17:30 *3340*
they should **r** and turn to God, Ac 26:20 *3340*
and **r** and do the deeds you did at Rv 2:5 *3340*
out of its place—unless you **r**. Rv 2:5 *3340*
'Therefore **r**; or else I am coming Rv 2:16 *3340*
'I gave her time to **r**, Rv 2:21 *3340*
not want to **r** of her immorality. Rv 2:21 *3340*
unless they **r** of her deeds. Rv 2:22 *3340*
and keep *it*, and **r**. Rv 3:3 *3340*
therefore be zealous and **r**. Rv 3:19 *3340*
not **r** of the works of their hands, Rv 9:20 *3340*
and they did not **r** of their murders Rv 9:21 *3340*
and they did not **r** so Rv 16:9 *3340*
and they did not **r** of their deeds. Rv 16:11 *3340*

REPENTANCE
"In **r** and rest you will be saved, Is 30:15 7729
bear fruit in keeping with **r**; Mt 3:8 *3341*
I baptize you with water for **r**, Mt 3:11 *3341*
preaching a baptism of **r** for the Mk 1:4 *3341*
preaching a baptism of **r** for the Lk 3:3 *3341*
bear fruits in keeping with **r**, Lk 3:8 *3341*
call the righteous but sinners to **r**." Lk 5:32 *3341*

righteous persons who need no **r**. Lk 15:7 *3341*
and that **r** for forgiveness of sins Lk 24:47 *3341*
a Savior, to grant **r** to Israel, Ac 5:31 *3341*
also the **r** *that leads* to life." Ac 11:18 *3341*
a baptism of **r** to all the people of Ac 13:24 *3341*
John baptized with the baptism of **r**, Ac 19:4 *3341*
r toward God and faith in our Lord Ac 20:21 *3341*
performing deeds appropriate to **r**. Ac 26:20 *3341*
kindness of God leads you to **r**? Ro 2:4 *3341*
made sorrowful to *the point of* **r**; 2Co 7:9 *3341*
God produces a **r** without regret, 2Co 7:10 *3341*
if perhaps God may grant them **r** 2Tm 2:25 *3341*
not laying again a foundation of **r** Heb 6:1 *3341*
to renew them again to **r**, Heb 6:6 *3341*
for he found no place for **r**, Heb 12:17 *3341*
perish but for all to come to **r**. 2Pe 3:9 *3341*

REPENTANT
And her **r** ones with righteousness. Is 1:27 7725

REPENTED
No man **r** of his wickedness, Jer 8:6 5162
'For after I turned back, I **r**; Jer 31:19 5162
Then they **r** and said, Zch 1:6 7725
they would have **r** long ago in Mt 11:21 *3340*
they **r** at the preaching of Jonah; Mt 12:41 *3340*
you, they would have **r** long ago, Lk 10:13 *3340*
they **r** at the preaching of Jonah; Lk 11:32 *3340*
past and not **r** of the impurity, 2Co 12:21 *3340*

REPENTS
in heaven over one sinner who **r** than Lk 15:7 *3340*
of God over one sinner who **r**." Lk 15:10 *3340*
and if he **r**, forgive him. Lk 17:3 *3340*

REPETITION
praying, do not use meaningless **r** as Mt 6:7 *945*

REPHAEL
sons of Shemaiah *were* Othni, **R**, 1Ch 26:7 7501

REPHAH
R was his son *along* with 1Ch 7:25 7506

REPHAIAH
and Jeshaiah, the sons of **R**, 1Ch 3:21 7509
Seir, with Pelatiah, Neariah, **R** and 1Ch 4:42 7509
The sons of Tola *were* Uzzi, **R**, 1Ch 7:2 7509
the father of Binea and **R** his son, 1Ch 9:43 7509
Next to them **R** the son of Hur, Ne 3:9 7509

REPHAIM
came and defeated the **R** in Gn 14:5 7497
and the Perizzite and the **R** Gn 15:20 7497
they are also regarded as **R**, Dt 2:11 7497
regarded as the land of the **R**, Dt 2:20 7497
for **R** formerly lived in it, Dt 2:20 7497
was left of the remnant of the **R**. Dt 3:11 7497
it is called the land of **R**. Dt 3:13 7497
Bashan, one of the remnant of **R**, Jos 12:4 7497
was left of the remnant of the **R**); Jos 13:12 7497
the valley of **R** toward the north. Jos 15:8 7497
of the Perizzites and of the **R**, Jos 17:15 7497
is in the valley of **R** northward; Jos 18:16 7497
themselves out in the valley of **R**. 2Sa 5:18 7497
themselves out in the valley of **R**. 2Sa 5:22 7497
was camping in the valley of **R**. 2Sa 23:13 7497
was camping in the valley of **R**. 1Ch 11:15 7497
made a raid in the valley of **R**. 1Ch 14:9 7497
ears of grain In the valley of **R**. Is 17:5 7497

REPHIDIM
of the LORD, and camped at **R**, Ex 17:1 7508
and fought against Israel at **R**. Ex 17:8 7508
When they set out from **R**, Ex 19:2 7508
from Alush and camped at **R**; Nu 33:14 7508
They journeyed from **R** and Nu 33:15 7508

REPLACE
So Moses would **r** the veil over his Ex 34:35 7725
other stones and **r** *those* stones, Lv 14:42 8478, 935
'He shall not **r** it or exchange it, Lv 27:10 2498
But we will **r** *them* with cedars." Is 9:10 2498

REPLACES
side of the second lad who **r** him. Ec 4:15 5975, 8478

REPLASTER
other plaster and **r** the house. Lv 14:42 2902

REPLASTERED
house, and after it has been **r**, Lv 14:43 2902
house after the house has been **r**, Lv 14:48 2902

REPLIED
And Abraham **r**, "Now behold, I have Gn 18:27 6030a
Then Laban and Bethuel **r**, Gn 24:50 6030a
But Isaac **r** to Esau, "Behold, I Gn 27:37 6030a
Then Jacob **r** to Laban, "Because I Gn 31:31 6030a
Then Laban **r** to Jacob, Gn 31:43 6030a
Balaam **r** to the servants of Balak, Nu 22:18 6030a
He **r**, "Must I not be careful to Nu 23:12 6030a
But Balaam **r** to Balak, "Did I not Nu 23:26 6030a
His friend **r**, "This is nothing less Jg 7:14 6030a
servant in charge of the reapers **r**, Ru 2:6 6030a
Boaz **r** to her, "All that you have Ru 2:11 6030a
But Hannah **r**, "No, my lord, I am 1Sa 1:15 6030a
Then the one who brought the news **r**, 1Sa 4:17 6030a
Saul **r**, "Am I not a Benjamite, of 1Sa 9:21 6030a
Then Abner **r**, "Who are you who 1Sa 26:14 6030a
David **r**, "Behold the spear of 1Sa 26:22 6030a
But Achish **r** to David, "I know that 1Sa 29:9 6030a
And the woman **r**, "As your soul 2Sa 14:19 6030a
Joab **r**, "Far be it, far be it from 2Sa 20:20 6030a
But Jonathan **r** to Adonijah, "No! 1Ki 1:43 6030a
The king of Israel **r**, "It is 1Ki 20:4 6030a
Then the king of Israel **r**, "Tell 1Ki 20:11 6030a
Elijah **r** to the captain of fifty, 2Ki 1:10 6030a
Elijah **r** to them, "If I am a man of 2Ki 1:12 6030a
Then all the assembly **r** with a loud Ezr 10:12 6030a
So Esther **r**, "My petition and my Es 5:7 6030a
Then Queen Esther **r**, "If I have Es 7:3 6030a
Then Job **r**, Jb 23:1 6030a, 559
The king **r** to the Chaldeans, Da 2:5 6032
The king **r**, "I know for certain Da 2:8 6032
Then Daniel **r** with discretion and Da 2:14 8421
Shadrach, Meshach and Abed-nego **r** to Da 3:16 6032
They **r** to the king, "Certainly, O Da 3:24 6032
Belteshazzar **r**, 'My lord, *if* Da 4:19 6032
The king **r**, "The statement is true, Da 6:12 6032
Then Amos **r** to Amaziah, "I am not a Am 7:14 6030a
The angel **r** to me, "These are Zch 6:5 6030a
But He **r** to them, "When it is Mt 16:2 *611*
And he **r**, "Say it, Teacher." Lk 7:40 *5346*
Jesus **r** and said, Lk 10:30 *5274*
saw *this,* he **r** to the people, Ac 3:12 *611*
Agrippa **r** to Paul, "In a short Ac 26:28

REPLY
written **r** be returned concerning it. Ezr 5:5 5407
to Hathach and ordered him *to* **r** Es 4:10
Mordecai told *them* to **r** to Esther, Es 4:13 7725
Esther told *them* to **r** to Mordecai, Es 4:15 7725
Or let me speak, then **r** to me. Jb 13:22 7725
I **r** to him with your arguments. Jb 32:14 7725
what can I **r** to You? Jb 40:4 7725
I may **r** to him who reproaches me. Pr 27:11 7725, 1697
how I may **r** when I am reproved. Hab 2:1 7725
of the lawyers said to Him in **r**, Lk 11:45 *611*
And they could make no **r** to this. Lk 14:6 *470*
they had nothing to say in **r**. Ac 4:14 *471*

REPORT
And Joseph brought back a bad **r** Gn 37:2 1681
"You shall not bear a false **r**; Ex 23:1 8088
gave out to the sons of Israel a bad **r** Nu 13:32 1681
by bringing out a bad **r** concerning Nu 14:36 1681
men who brought out the very bad **r** Nu 14:37 1681
they brought us back a **r** and said, Dt 1:25 1697
who, when they hear the **r** of you, Dt 2:25 8088
for we have heard the **r** of Him and Jos 9:9 8089
"What *do you* **r**?" Jg 18:8
for the **r** is not good which I hear 1Sa 2:24 8052
the **r** of Saul and Jonathan came 2Sa 4:4 8052
the way that the **r** came to David, 2Sa 13:30 8052
lord the king take the **r** to heart, 2Sa 13:33 1697
you shall **r** to Zadok and Abiathar 2Sa 15:35 5046
"It was a true **r** which I heard in 1Ki 10:6 1697
prosperity the **r** which I heard. 1Ki 10:7 8052
"It was a true **r** which I heard in 2Ch 9:5 1697
You surpass the **r** that I heard. 2Ch 9:6 8052
until a **r** could come to Darius, Ezr 5:5 2942
They sent a **r** to him in which it Ezr 5:7 6600
so that they might have an evil **r** Ne 6:13 8034
our ears we have heard a **r** of it.' Jb 28:22 8088
evil **r** about you will not pass away. Pr 25:10 1681
lookout, let him **r** what he sees. Is 21:6 5046
When the **r** *reaches* Egypt, They Is 23:5 8088
be in anguish at the **r** of Tyre. Is 23:5 8088
he who flees the **r** of disaster will fall Is 24:18 6963
"**R** *it* to the nations, now! Jer 4:16 2142
We have heard the **r** of it; Jer 6:24 8089
The sound of a **r**! Jer 10:22 8052
r all these words to the king." Jer 36:16 5046
Jerusalem heard the **r** about them, Jer 37:5 8088
has heard the **r** about them, Jer 50:43 8088
And you are not afraid at the **r** that Jer 51:46 8052
For the **r** will come one year, Jer 51:46 8052
that another **r** in another year, Jer 51:46 8052
We have heard a **r** from the LORD, Ob 1:1 8052
heard the **r** about You *and* I fear. Hab 3:2 8088
when you have found *Him,* **r** to me, Mt 2:8 *518*
r to John what you hear and see: Mt 11:4 *518*
and ran to **r** it to His disciples. Mt 28:8 *518*
"Go home to your people and **r** to Mk 5:19 *518*
And the **r** about Him was spreading Lk 4:37 *2279*
This **r** concerning Him went out Lk 7:17 *3056*
"Go and **r** to John what you have Lk 7:22 *518*
knew where He was, he was to **r** it, Jn 11:57 *3377*
"LORD, WHO HAS BELIEVED OUR **R**? Jn 12:38 *189*
"**R** these things to James and the Ac 12:17 *518*
they *began* to **r** all things that Ac 14:27 *312*
who themselves will also **r** the Ac 15:27 *518*
a **r** came up to the commander of Ac 21:31 *5334*
he has something to **r** to him." Ac 23:17 *518*
is it that you have to **r** to me?" Ac 23:19 *518*
"LORD, WHO HAS BELIEVED OUR **R**?" Ro 10:16 *189*
For the **r** of your obedience has Ro 16:19
by evil **r** and good report; 2Co 6:8 *1426b*
by evil report and good **r**; 2Co 6:8 *2162*
For they themselves **r** about us 1Th 1:9 *518*

REPORTED
words of her elder son Esau were **r** Gn 27:42 5046
husband has been fully **r** to me, Ru 2:11 5046
The servants of Saul **r** to him 1Sa 18:24 5046
Then Joab sent and **r** to David all 2Sa 11:18 5046
r to David all that Joab had sent him 2Sa 11:22 5046
And the watchman **r**, 2Ki 9:18 5046
The watchman **r**, 2Ki 9:20 5046
some came and **r** to Jehoshaphat, 2Ch 20:2 5046
and **r** further word to the king, 2Ch 34:16 7725
Now when it was **r** to Sanballat, Ne 6:1 8085
"It is **r** among the nations, and Ne 6:6 8085
And now it will be **r** to the king Ne 6:7 8085
my presence and **r** my words to him. Ne 6:19 3318
found written what Mordecai had **r** Es 6:2 5046
the citadel in Susa was **r** to the king. Es 9:11 935
it was **r** to the house of David, Is 7:2 5046
It is **r** to them from the land of Is 23:1 1540
they **r** all the words to the king. Jer 36:20 5046, 241
So he **r** to them in accordance with Jer 38:27 5046
loins was the writing case **r**, Ezk 9:11 7725, 1697
to the city and **r** everything, Mt 8:33 *518*
and they went and **r** to Jesus. Mt 14:12 *518*
r to their lord all that had happened. Mt 18:31 *1285*
into the city and **r** to the chief priests Mt 28:11 *518*
ran away and **r** it in the city and Mk 5:14 *518*
and they **r** to Him all that they Mk 6:30 *518*
She went and **r** to those who had Mk 16:10 *518*
went away and **r** it to the others, Mk 16:13 *518*
[*And they promptly* **r** *all these* Mk 16:20
The disciples of John **r** to him Lk 7:18 *518*
And it was **r** to Him, Lk 8:20 *518*
they ran away and **r** it in the city Lk 8:34 *518*
Those who had seen it **r** to Lk 8:36 *518*
and **r** to no one in those days any Lk 9:36 *518*
who **r** to Him about the Galileans whose Lk 13:1 *518*
back and **r** this to his master. Lk 14:21 *518*
and this *manager* was **r** to him as Lk 16:1 *1225*
and **r** all these things to the eleven Lk 24:9 *518*
and **r** all that the chief priests Ac 4:23 *518*
and they returned and **r** back, Ac 5:22 *518*
But someone came and **r** to them, Ac 5:25 *518*
"And he **r** to us how he had seen Ac 11:13 *518*
and they **r** all that God had done Ac 15:4 *312*
the jailer **r** these words to Paul, Ac 16:36 *518*
The policemen **r** these words to Ac 16:38 *518*
any of the brethren come here and **r** Ac 28:21 *518*
we are slanderously **r** and as some Ro 3:8 *987*
It is actually **r** that there is 1Co 5:1 *191*
you, as he **r** to us your longing, 2Co 7:7 *312*

REPORTS
I did not believe the **r**, 1Ki 10:7 1697
"Nevertheless I did not believe their **r** 2Ch 9:6 1697
their king, according to these **r**. Ne 6:6 1697
to the king according to these **r**. Ne 6:7 1697

REPOSE
rest to the weary," And, "Here is **r**," Is 28:12 4774
'OR WHAT PLACE IS THERE FOR MY **R**? Ac 7:49 *2663*

REPOSED
Bathed in milk, *And* **r** in *their* setting. SS 5:12 3427

REPRESENT
"Let our leaders **r** the whole Ezr 10:14 5975
horns that arose in its place **r** Da 8:22

REPRESENTATION
and the exact **r** of His nature, Heb 1:3 *5481*

REPRESENTATIVE
You be the people's **r** before God, Ex 18:19
was the king's **r** in all matters Ne 11:24 3027

REPRESENTS
r the kings of Media and Persia. Da 8:20
"The shaggy goat **r** the kingdom Da 8:21

REPRIMANDED
So I **r** the officials and said, Ne 13:11 7378
Then I **r** the nobles of Judah and Ne 13:17 7378
But when Herod the tetrarch was **r** by Lk 3:19 *1651*

REPROACH
"God has taken away my **r**." Gn 30:23 2781
I have rolled away the **r** of Egypt Jos 5:9 2781
will make it a **r** on all Israel." 1Sa 11:2 2781
and takes away the **r** from Israel? 1Sa 17:26 2781
of my **r** from the hand of Nabal and 1Sa 25:39 2781
me, where could I get rid of my **r**? 2Sa 13:13 2781
has sent to **r** the living God, 2Ki 19:4 2778a
he has sent to **r** the living God. 2Ki 19:16 2778a
are in great distress and **r**, Ne 1:3 2781
that we will no longer be a **r**." Ne 2:17 2781
Return their **r** on their own heads Ne 4:4 2781
because of the **r** of the nations, Ne 5:9 2781
in order that they could **r** me. Ne 6:13 2778a
My heart does not **r** any of my days. Jb 27:6 2778a
how long will my honor become a **r**? Ps 4:2 3639
takes up a **r** against his friend; Ps 15:3 2781
a worm and not a man, A **r** of men Ps 22:6 2781
my adversaries, I have become a **r**, Ps 31:11 2781
Make me not the **r** of the foolish. Ps 39:8 2781
You make us a **r** to our neighbors, Ps 44:13 2781
for Your sake I have borne **r**; Ps 69:7 2781
the reproaches of those who **r** You Ps 69:9 2778a
soul with fasting, It became my **r**. Ps 69:10 2781
You know my **r** and my shame Ps 69:19 2781
R has broken my heart and I am so Ps 69:20 2781
be covered with **r** and dishonor, Ps 71:13 2781
He put on them an everlasting **r**. Ps 78:66 2781
have become a **r** to our neighbors, Ps 79:4 2781
r with which they have reproached Ps 79:12 2781
has become a **r** to his neighbors. Ps 89:41 2781
O Lord, the **r** of Your servants; Ps 89:50 2781
How I bear in my bosom *the* **r** *of* Ps 89:50
I also have become a **r** to them; Ps 109:25 2781
Take away **r** and contempt from me, Ps 119:22 2781
Turn away my **r** which I dread, For Ps 119:39 2781
And his **r** will not be blotted out. Pr 6:33 2781
Or he who hears *it* will **r** you, Pr 25:10 2616b
take away our **r**!" Is 4:1 2781
He will remove the **r** of His people Is 25:8 2781
but for shame and also for **r**." Is 30:5 2781
has sent to **r** the living God, Is 37:4 2778a
who sent *them* to **r** the living God. Is 37:17 2778a
Do not fear the **r** of man, Nor Is 51:7 2781
And the **r** of your widowhood you Is 54:4 2781

the LORD has become a **r** to them; Jer 6:10 2781
Know that for Your sake I endure **r**. Jer 15:15 2781
In **r** and derision all day long. Jer 20:8 2781
"I will put an everlasting **r** Jer 23:40 2781
the earth, as a **r** and a proverb, Jer 24:9 2781
and a **r** among all the nations Jer 29:18 2781
Because I bore the **r** of my youth.' Jer 31:19 2781
horror, an imprecation and a **r**; Jer 42:18 2781
be cut off and become a curse and a **r** Jer 44:8 2781
of horror, an imprecation and a **r**. Jer 44:12 2781
become an object of horror, a **r**, Jer 49:13 2781
ashamed because we have heard **r**; Jer 51:51 2781
Let him be filled with **r**. La 3:30 2781
You have heard their **r**, La 3:61 2781
Look, and see our **r**! La 5:1 2781
I will make you a desolation and a **r** Ezk 5:14 2781
'So it will be a **r**, a reviling, a Ezk 5:15 2781
the **r** of the daughters of Edom and Ezk 16:57 2781
of Ammon and concerning their **r**,' Ezk 21:28 2781
have made you a **r** to the nations and Ezk 22:4 2781
become a **r** to all those around us. Da 9:16 2781
him And bring back his **r** to him. Hos 12:14 2781
do not make Your inheritance a **r**, Jl 2:17 2781
make you a **r** among the nations. Jl 2:19 2781
you will bear the **r** of My people." Mi 6:16 2781
r *of exile* is a burden on them. Zph 3:18 2781
children of God above **r** in the Php 2:15 *299b*
holy and blameless and beyond **r** Col 1:22 *410*
overseer, then, must be above **r**, 1Tm 3:2 *423*
into **r** and the snare of the devil. 1Tm 3:7 *3680*
as deacons if they are beyond **r**. 1Tm 3:10 *410*
well, so that they may be above **r**. 1Tm 5:7 *423*
give the enemy no occasion for **r**; 1Tm 5:14 *3059*
the commandment without stain or **r** 1Tm 6:14 *423*
namely, if any man is above **r**, Ti 1:6 *410*
For the overseer must be above **r** Ti 1:7 *410*
sound *in* speech which is beyond **r**, Ti 2:8 *176*
considering the **r** of Christ Heb 11:26 *3680*
outside the camp, bearing His **r**. Heb 13:13 *3680*
all generously and without **r**, Jas 1:5 *3679*

REPROACHED
'Whom have you **r** and blasphemed? 2Ki 19:22 2778a
messengers you have **r** the Lord, 2Ki 19:23 2778a
with which they have **r** You, Ps 79:12 2778a
With which Your enemies have **r**, Ps 89:51 2778a
With which they have **r** the Ps 89:51 2778a
My enemies have **r** me all day long; Ps 102:8 2778a
"Whom have you **r** and blasphemed? Is 37:23 2778a
your servants you have **r** the Lord, Is 37:24 2778a
and He **r** them for their unbelief Mk 16:14 *3679*
THOSE WHO **R** YOU FELL ON ME." Ro 15:3 *3679*

REPROACHES
voice of him who **r** and reviles, Ps 44:16 2778a
For it is not an enemy who **r** me, Ps 55:12 2778a
He **r** him who tramples upon me. Ps 57:3 2778a
And the **r** of those who reproach Ps 69:9 2781
foolish man **r** You all day long. Ps 74:22 2781
have an answer for him who **r** me, Ps 119:42 2778a
That I may reply to him who **r** me. Pr 27:11 2778a
things, **R** will not be turned back. Mi 2:6 3639
"THE **R** OF THOSE WHO REPROACHED Ro 15:3 *3680*
through **r** and tribulations, Heb 10:33 *3680*

REPROBATE
In whose eyes a **r** is despised, But Ps 15:4 3988a

REPROOF
I listened to the **r** which insults me, Jb 20:3 4148
"Turn to my **r**, Behold, I will Pr 1:23 8433b
my counsel And did not want my **r**; Pr 1:25 8433b
my counsel, They spurned all my **r**. Pr 1:30 8433b
of the LORD Or loathe His **r**, Pr 3:11 8433b
And my heart spurned **r**! Pr 5:12 8433b
But he who ignores **r** goes astray. Pr 10:17 8433b
But he who hates **r** is stupid. Pr 12:1 8433b
he who regards **r** will be honored. Pr 13:18 8433b
But he who regards **r** is sensible. Pr 15:5 8433b
He who hates **r** will die. Pr 15:10 8433b
r Will dwell among the wise. Pr 15:31 8433b
But he who listens to **r** acquires Pr 15:32 8433b
who hardens *his* neck after much **r** Pr 29:1 8433b
The rod and **r** give wisdom, But a Pr 29:15 8433b
find fault, and let none offer **r**; Hos 4:4 3198
profitable for teaching, for **r**, 2Tm 3:16 *1649a*

REPROOFS
"With **r** You chasten a man Ps 39:11 8433b
And **r** for discipline are the way Pr 6:23 8433b

REPROVE
you may surely **r** your neighbor, Lv 19:17 3198
"Do you intend to **r** *my* words, Jb 6:26 3198
"He will surely **r** you If you Jb 13:10 3198
"I do not **r** you for your sacrifices, Ps 50:8 3198
I will **r** you and state *the case* Ps 50:21 3198
smite me in kindness and **r** me; Ps 141:5 3198
Do not **r** a scoffer, or he will hate you, Pr 9:8 3198
R a wise man and he will love you. Pr 9:8 3198
But **r** one who has understanding Pr 19:25 3198
add to His words Or He will **r** you, Pr 30:6 3198
Seek justice, **R** the ruthless, Is 1:17 833
And your apostasies will **r** you; Jer 2:19 3198
r, rebuke, exhort, with great 2Tm 4:2 *1651*
For this reason **r** them severely Ti 1:13 *1651*
exhort and **r** with all authority. Ti 2:15 *1651*
whom I love, I **r** and discipline; Rv 3:19 *1651*

REPROVED
And He **r** kings for their sakes, 1Ch 16:21 3198
And He **r** kings for their sakes: Ps 105:14 3198
And how I may reply when I am **r**. Hab 2:1 8433b
NOR FAINT WHEN YOU ARE **R** BY HIM; Heb 12:5 *1651*

REPROVER
Is a wise **r** to a listening ear. Pr 25:12 3198

REPROVES
how happy is the man whom God **r**, Jb 5:17 3198
of your reverence that He **r** you, Jb 22:4 3198
Let him who **r** God answer it." Jb 40:2 3198
For whom the LORD loves He **r**, Pr 3:12 3198
And he who **r** a wicked man *gets* Pr 9:7 3198
scoffer does not love one who **r** him, Pr 15:12 3198
They hate him who **r** in the gate, Am 5:10 3198

REPTILE
and the lizard, and the sand **r**, Lv 11:30 2546

REPTILES
a serpent, Like **r** of the earth. Mi 7:17 2119a
of **r** and creatures of the sea, Jas 3:7 *2062*

REPUDIATE
since you **r** it and judge Ac 13:46 *683*

REPUDIATED
but **r** him and in their hearts Ac 7:39 *683*

REPULSE
"How then can you **r** one official 2Ki 18:24 7725, 6440
"How then can you **r** one official Is 36:9 7725, 6440

REPUTATION
among you seven men of good **r**, Ac 6:3 *3140*
in private to those who were of **r**, Ga 2:2 *1380*
But from those who were of high **r** Ga 2:6 *1380*
those who were of **r** contributed Ga 2:6 *1380*
he must have a good **r** with those 1Tm 3:7 *3141*
having a **r** for good works; 1Tm 5:10 *3140*

REPUTE
So you will find favor and good **r** Pr 3:4 7922
you will mock you, you of ill **r**, Ezk 22:5 8034
is lovely, whatever is of good **r**, Php 4:8 *2163*

REPUTED
John, who were **r** to be pillars, Ga 2:9 *1380*

REQUEST
"Behold, I grant you this **r** also, Gn 19:21 1697
that they let them have their **r**. Ex 12:36 7592
"I would **r** of you, that each of Jg 8:24 7596, 7592
to you and granted your **r**." 1Sa 25:35 6440
perform the **r** of his maidservant. 2Sa 14:15 1697
performed the **r** of his servant." 2Sa 14:22 1697
"Now I am making one **r** of you; 1Ki 2:16 7596
"I am making one small **r** of you; 1Ki 2:20 7596
as the priests in Jerusalem **r**, Ezr 6:9 3983
For I was ashamed to **r** from the Ezr 8:22 7592
"What would you **r**?" Ne 2:4 1245
not **r** anything except what Hegai, Es 2:15 1245
And what is your **r**? Es 5:3 1246
And what is your **r**? Es 5:6 1246
"My petition and my **r** is: Es 5:7 1246
grant my petition and do what I **r**, Es 5:8 1246
And what is your **r**? Es 7:2 1246
petition, and my people as my **r**; Es 7:3 1246
And what is your further **r**? Es 9:12 1246
"Oh that my **r** might come to pass, Jb 6:8 7596
have not withheld the **r** of his lips. Ps 21:2 782
So He gave them their **r**, Ps 106:15 7596
that they might **r** compassion from Da 2:18 1156
And Daniel made **r** of the king, and Da 2:49 1156
down and making a **r** of Him. Mt 20:20 *154*
I will **r** of the Father on your behalf; Jn 16:26 *2065*
always in my prayers making **r**, Ro 1:10 *1189a*
we **r** and exhort you in the Lord 1Th 4:1 *2065*
But we **r** of you, brethren, that 1Th 5:12 *2065*
Now we **r** you, brethren, with 2Th 2:1 *2065*
that he should make **r** for this. 1Jn 5:16 *2065*

REQUESTED
for they had **r** from the Egyptians Ex 12:35 7592
he **r** was 1,700 *shekels* of gold, Jg 8:26 7592
when he **r**, they set food before him 2Sa 12:20 7592
Sheba all her desire which she **r**, 1Ki 10:13 7592
r for himself that he might die, 1Ki 19:4 7592
And God granted him what he **r**. 1Ch 4:10 7592
of Sheba all her desire which she **r** 2Ch 9:12 7592
and the king granted him all he **r** Ezr 7:6 1246
So Daniel went in and **r** of the king Da 2:16 1156
known to me what we **r** of You, Da 2:23 1156
And your judges of whom you **r**, Hos 13:10 559
them *any* one prisoner whom they **r**. Mk 15:6 *3868*
I **r** to see you and to speak with Ac 28:20 *3870*

REQUESTING
one of the Pharisees was **r** Him to Lk 7:36 *2065*
r a concession against Paul, that Ac 25:3 *154*

REQUESTS
let your **r** be made known to God. Php 4:6 *155*
r which we have asked from Him. 1Jn 5:15 *155*

REQUIRE
Surely I will **r** your lifeblood; Gn 9:5 1875
from every beast I will **r** it. Gn 9:5 1875
brother I will **r** the life of man. Gn 9:5 1875
does the LORD your God **r** from you, Dt 10:12 7592
name, I Myself will **r** *it* of him. Dt 18:19 1875
your God will surely **r** it of you. Dt 23:21 1875
on it, may the LORD Himself **r** it. Jos 22:23 1245
"May the LORD **r** *it* at the hands 1Sa 20:16 1245
now **r** his blood from your hand and 2Sa 4:11 1245
and whatever you **r** of me, 2Sa 19:38 977
they did not **r** an accounting from 2Ki 12:15 2803
the God of heaven, may **r** of you, Ezr 7:21 7593
back and will **r** nothing from them; Ne 5:12 1245
"You will not **r** *it*." Ps 10:13 1875
his blood I will **r** at your hand. Ezk 3:18 1245
his blood I will **r** at your hand. Ezk 3:20 1245
I will **r** from the watchman's hand.' Ezk 33:6 1875
his blood I will **r** from your hand. Ezk 33:8 1245
LORD **r** of you But to do justice, Mi 6:8 1875

REQUIRED
You **r** it of my hand *whether* stolen Gn 31:39 1245
Now forty days were **r** for it, Gn 50:3 4390
is the period **r** for embalming. Gn 50:3 4390
you not completed your **r** amount Ex 5:14 2706
So the king of Assyria **r** of Hezekiah 2Ki 18:14 7760
continually, as every day's work **r**; 1Ch 16:37 1697
this *being* **r** forever in Israel. 2Ch 2:4
"Why have you not **r** the Levites 2Ch 24:6 1875
to the ordinance, as each day **r**; Ezr 3:4 1697
portions **r** by the law for the priests Ne 12:44
and the gatekeepers as each day **r**, Ne 12:47 1697
and sin offering You have not **r**. Ps 40:6 7592
very night your soul is **r** of you; Lk 12:20 *523*
been given much, much will be **r**; Lk 12:48 *523*
it is **r** of stewards that one be 1Co 4:2 *523*

REQUIREMENT
so that the **r** of the Law Ro 8:4 *1345*
the basis of a law of physical **r**, Heb 7:16 *1785*

REQUIREMENTS
commandments and **r** of the Lord. Lk 1:6 *1345*
man keeps the **r** of the Law, Ro 2:26 *1345*

REQUIRES
for yourself what the occasion **r**, 1Sa 10:7 4672
His people Israel, as each day **r**, 1Ki 8:59 1697
is cut off, When God **r** his life? Jb 27:8 7953
For He who **r** blood remembers them; Ps 9:12 1875
Who **r** of you this trampling of My Is 1:12 1245

REQUITE
R them according to their work and Ps 28:4 5414
R them according to the deeds of Ps 28:4 5414

REQUITED
since You our God have **r** *us* less Ezr 9:13 2820
Your lewdness will be **r** upon you, Ezk 23:49 5414

RESCUE
he might **r** him out of their hands, Gn 37:22 5337
and you will surely **r** *all*." 1Sa 30:8 5337
You **r** me from the violent man. 2Sa 22:49 5337
Return, O LORD, **r** my soul; Ps 6:4 2502a
You **r** me from the violent man. Ps 18:48 5337
Let Him **r** him, because He delights Ps 22:8 5337
Your ear to me, **r** me quickly; Ps 31:2 5337
R my soul from their ravages, My Ps 35:17 7725
I shall **r** you, and you will honor Ps 50:15 2502a
deliver me and **r** me; Ps 71:2 6403
R me, O my God, out of the hand of Ps 71:4 6403
He will **r** their life from Ps 72:14 1350
R the weak and needy; Ps 82:4 6403
I will **r** him and honor him. Ps 91:15 2502a
Look upon my affliction and **r** me, Ps 119:153 2502a
R me, O LORD, from evil men; Ps 140:1 2502a
R me and deliver me out of great Ps 144:7 6475
R me and deliver me out of the Ps 144:11 6475
the penalty, For if you **r** *him*, Pr 19:19 5337
shall strike him with the rod And **r** Pr 23:14 5337
He will pass over and **r** *it*. Is 31:5 4422
They could not **r** the burden, But Is 46:2 4422
"For I will certainly **r** you, Jer 39:18 4422
he kept exerting himself to **r** him. Da 6:14 5338
there anyone to **r** from his power, Da 8:4 5337
none to **r** the ram from his power. Da 8:7 5337
no one will **r** her out of My hand. Hos 2:10 5337
and tears, And there is none to **r**. Mi 5:8 5337
"HE TRUSTS IN GOD; LET GOD **R** Mt 27:43 *4506*
AND I HAVE COME DOWN TO **R** THEM; Ac 7:34 *1807*
for our sins so that He might **r** us Ga 1:4 *1807*
The Lord will **r** me from every evil 2Tm 4:18 *4506*
to **r** the godly from temptation, 2Pe 2:9 *4506*

RESCUED
But Reuben heard *this* and **r** him Gn 37:21 5337
r Jonathan and he did not die. 1Sa 14:45 6299
him, and **r** *it* from his mouth; 1Sa 17:35 5337
had taken, and **r** his two wives. 1Sa 30:18 5337
He **r** me, because He delighted in 2Sa 22:20 2502a
And many times You **r** them according Ne 9:28 5337
He **r** me, because He delighted in Ps 18:19 2502a
called in trouble and I **r** you; Ps 81:7 2502a
You have **r** my soul from death, Ps 116:8 2502a
And has **r** us from our adversaries, Ps 136:24 6561
the captives of a tyrant be **r**?" Is 49:24 4422
the prey of the tyrant will be **r**; Is 49:25 4422
these will be **r** out of his hand: Da 11:41 4422
written in the book, will be **r**. Da 12:1 4422
There you will be **r**; Mi 4:10 5337
To grant us that we, being **r** from Lk 1:74 *4506*
r him from all his afflictions, Ac 7:10 *1807*
has sent forth His angel and **r** me Ac 12:11 *1807*
them with the troops and **r** him, Ac 23:27 *1807*
that I may be **r** from those who are Ro 15:31 *4506*
For He **r** us from the domain of Col 1:13 *4506*
and that we will be **r** from perverse 2Th 3:2 *4506*
and out of them all the Lord **r** me! 2Tm 3:11 *4506*
and I was **r** out of the lion's mouth. 2Tm 4:17 *4506*
and *if* He **r** righteous Lot, 2Pe 2:7 *4506*

RESCUES
those who fear Him, And **r** them. Ps 34:7 2502a
Who gives salvation to kings, Who **r** Ps 144:10 6475
"He delivers and **r** and performs Da 6:27 5338
who **r** us from the wrath to come. 1Th 1:10 *4506*

RESCUING
r you from the *Jewish* people Ac 26:17 *1807*

RESEMBLE
I **r** a pelican of the wilderness; Ps 102:6 1819

RESEMBLED
and on that which **r** a throne, **Ezk 1:26** 1823
one who **r** a human being was **Da 10:16** 1823
AND WOULD HAVE **R** GOMORRAH." **Ro 9:29** *3666*
RESEMBLING
each one **r** the son of a king." **Jg 8:18** 8389
were figures **r** four living beings. **Ezk 1:5** 1823
there was something **r** a throne, **Ezk 1:26** 1823
stone, in appearance **r** a throne, **Ezk 10:1** 1823
beast, a second one, **r** a bear. **Da 7:5** 1821
RESEN
and **R** between Nineveh and Calah; **Gn 10:12** 7449
RESERVE
"Let the food become as a **r** **Gn 41:36** 6487
is held in **r** for his treasures, **Jb 20:26** 2934
And your lips may **r** knowledge. **Pr 5:2** 5341
RESERVED
"Have you not **r** a blessing for me?" **Gn 27:36** 680
be yours from the most holy *gifts* **r** **Nu 18:9**
there the ruler's portion was **r**; **Dt 33:21** 5603
"Here is what has been **r**! **1Sa 9:24** 7604
but **r** *enough* of them for 100 **2Sa 8:4** 3498
and You have **r** for him this great **1Ki 3:6** 8104
but **r** *enough* of them for 100 **1Ch 18:4** 3498
is **r** for the day of calamity; **Jb 21:30** 2820
I have **r** for the time of distress, **Jb 38:23** 2820
fade away, **r** in heaven for you, **1Pe 1:4** *5083*
pits of darkness, **r** for judgment; **2Pe 2:4** *5083*
the black darkness has been **r**. **2Pe 2:17** *5083*
heavens and earth are being **r** for fire, **2Pe 3:7** *2343*
black darkness has been **r** forever. **Jude 1:13** *5083*
RESERVES
And He **r** wrath for His enemies. **Na 1:2** 5201
RESERVOIR
And you made a **r** between the two **Is 22:11** 4724
RESERVOIRS
and over all their **r** of water, **Ex 7:19** 4723b
RESETTLE
And will **r** the desolate cities. **Is 54:3** 3427
RESHEPH
Rephah was his son *along* with **R**, **1Ch 7:25** 7566
RESIDE
the first into Egypt to **r** there; **Is 52:4** 1481a
enter Egypt and go in to **r** there, **Jer 42:15** 1481a
to **r** there will die by the sword, **Jer 42:17** 1481a
place where you wish to go to **r**. **Jer 42:22** 1481a
not to enter Egypt to **r** there'; **Jer 43:2** 1481a
order to **r** in the land of Judah **Jer 43:5** 1481a
where you are entering to **r**, **Jer 44:8** 1481a
the land of Egypt to **r** there, **Jer 44:12** 1481a
entered the land of Egypt to **r** there **Jer 44:14** 1481a
gone to the land of Egypt to **r** there **Jer 44:28** 1481a
nor will a son of man **r** in it. **Jer 49:18** 1481a
Nor will a son of man **r** in it." **Jer 49:33** 1481a
Nor will *any* son of man **r** in it. **Jer 50:40** 1481a
Christ, To those who **r** as aliens, **1Pe 1:1** *3927*
RESIDED
and Simeon who **r** with them, **2Ch 15:9** 1481a
RESIDENCE
which I myself have built as a royal **r** **Da 4:30** 1005
of the king and a royal **r**." **Am 7:13** 1004
RESIDENT
your hired man and your foreign **r**, **Lv 25:6** 8453
And no **r** will say, **Is 33:24** 7934
RESIDENTS
of violence, Her **r** speak lies, **Mi 6:12** 3427
Elamites, and **r** of Mesopotamia, **Ac 2:9** *2730*
we as well as the local **r** *began* **Ac 21:12** *1786*
RESIDES
stranger **r** with you in your land, **Lv 19:33** 1481a
'The stranger who **r** with you shall **Lv 19:34** 1481a
throughout Israel where he **r**, **Dt 18:6** 1481a
For anger **r** in the bosom of fools. **Ec 7:9** 5117
RESIDING
been revealed to me for any wisdom **r** **Da 2:30** 383
RESIST
"So now you intend to **r** the **2Ch 13:8** 2388
him who is alone, two can **r** him. **Ec 4:12** 5975, 5048
to you, do not **r** an evil person; **Mt 5:39** *436*
will be able to **r** or refute. **Lk 21:15** *436*
will be able to **r** in the evil day, **Eph 6:13** *436*
R the devil and he will flee from **Jas 4:7** *436*
he does not **r** you. **Jas 5:6** *498*
But **r** him, firm in *your* faith, **1Pe 5:9** *436*
RESISTED
But when they **r** and blasphemed, he **Ac 18:6** *498*
You have not yet **r** to the point of **Heb 12:4** *478*
RESISTING
ears are always **r** the Holy Spirit; **Ac 7:51** *496*
RESISTS
For who **r** His will?" **Ro 9:19** *436*
Therefore whoever **r** authority has **Ro 13:2** *436*
RESOLUTE
with **r** heart to remain *true* to the Lord **Ac 11:23** *4286*
RESOLUTELY
if he **r** performs My commandments **1Ch 28:7** 2388
Act **r**, and the LORD be with the **2Ch 19:11** 2388
RESOLVED
I **r** to pour out My wrath on them, **Ezk 20:8** 559
Then I **r** to pour out My wrath on **Ezk 20:13** 559
I **r** to pour out My wrath on them, **Ezk 20:21** 559
and they **r** to drive the ship onto **Ac 27:39** *1011*

RESOLVES
There were great **r** of heart. **Jg 5:15** 2706
RESORT
nations will **r** to the root of Jesse, **Is 11:10** 1875
So that they will **r** to idols and **Is 19:3** 1875
And a man and his father **r** to the **Am 2:7** 1980
"But do not **r** to Bethel And do **Am 5:5** 1875
RESOUNDED
great shout, so that the earth **r**. **1Sa 4:5** 1949
RESOUNDING
With **r** music upon the lyre. **Ps 92:3** 1902
Praise Him with **r** cymbals. **Ps 150:5** 8643
RESPECT
in **r** to every swarming thing that **Lv 11:42**
'In **r** to an ox or a lamb which has **Lv 22:23**
But in **r** to your countrymen, the **Lv 25:46**
who will have no **r** for the old, **Dt 28:50** 6440
is righteous with **r** to all His deeds **Da 9:14** 5921
if I am a master, where is My **r**?' **Mal 1:6** 4172
'They will **r** my son.' **Mt 21:37** *1788*
'They will **r** my son.' **Mk 12:6** *1788*
Not even in this **r** was their **Mk 14:59** *3779*
not fear God and did not **r** man. **Lk 18:2** *1788*
I do not fear God nor **r** man, **Lk 18:4** *1788*
perhaps they will **r** him.' **Lk 20:13** *1788*
honored us with many marks of **r**; **Ac 28:10** *5092*
Great in every **r**. **Ro 3:2** *5158*
yet, with **r** to the promise of God, **Ro 4:20** *1519*
R what is right in the sight of **Ro 12:17** *4306*
in whatever **r** anyone *else* is bold **2Co 11:21**
for in no **r** was I inferior to the **2Co 12:11** *3762*
For in what **r** were you treated as **2Co 12:13**
or in **r** to a festival or a new moon **Col 2:16** *3313*
of God our Savior in every **r**. **Ti 2:10** *3956*
it you may grow in **r** to salvation, **1Pe 2:2** *1519*
to your masters with all **r**, **1Pe 2:18** *5401*
RESPECTABLE
one wife, temperate, prudent, **r**, **1Tm 3:2** *2887*
RESPECTED
Now he was more **r** than all the **Gn 34:19** 3513
man with his master, and highly **r**, **2Ki 5:1** 5375, 6440
Elders were not **r**. **La 5:12** 1921
of the Law, **r** by all the people, **Ac 5:34** *5093*
to discipline us, and we **r** them; **Heb 12:9** *1788*
RESPECTFUL
and **r** greetings in the market **Mt 23:7**
and *like* **r** greetings in the market **Mk 12:38**
and the **r** greetings in the market **Lk 11:43**
and love **r** greetings in the market **Lk 20:46**
your chaste and **r** behavior. **1Pe 3:2** *5401*
RESPECTIVE
sons of Aaron, took their **r** firepans, **Lv 10:1** 376
RESPECTS
you are very religious in all **r**. **Ac 17:22** *3956*
and paid their **r** to Festus. **Ac 25:13** *782*
wife must *see to it* that she **r** **Eph 5:33** *5399*
the Lord, to please *Him* in all **r**, **Col 1:10** *3956*
I pray that in all **r** you may prosper **3Jn 1:2** *3956*
RESPLENDENT
You are **r**, More majestic than the **Ps 76:4** 215
RESPOND
my disquieting thoughts make me **r**, **Jb 20:2** 7725
"They will all **r** and say to you, **Is 14:10** 6030a
will **r** to them and will heal them. **Is 19:22** 6279
about in that day that I will **r**," **Hos 2:21** 6030a
"I will **r** to the heavens, and **Hos 2:21** 6030a
and they will **r** to the earth, **Hos 2:21** 6030a
And the earth will **r** to the grain, **Hos 2:22** 6030a
oil, And they will **r** to Jezreel. **Hos 2:22** 6030a
to **r** to the things spoken by Paul. **Ac 16:14** *4337*
how you should **r** to each person. **Col 4:6** *611*
RESPONDED
son of Shimeah, David's brother, **r**, **2Sa 13:32** 6030a, 559
Hilkiah **r** and said to Shaphan **2Ch 34:15** 6030a
Then Job **r**, **Jb 12:1** 6030a, 559
Then Eliphaz the Temanite **r**, **Jb 15:1** 6030a, 559
Then Bildad the Shuhite **r**, **Jb 18:1** 6030a, 559
Then Job **r**, **Jb 19:1** 6030a, 559
Then Eliphaz the Temanite **r**, **Jb 22:1** 6030a, 559
Then Job **r**, **Jb 26:1** 6030a, 559
"My beloved **r** and said to me, **SS 2:10** 6030a
the land of Egypt, **r** to Jeremiah, **Jer 44:15** 6030a
They **r** and said to Nebuchadnezzar **Da 3:9** 6032
Nebuchadnezzar **r** and said to them, **Da 3:14** 6032
he **r** and said, "Shadrach, Meshach **Da 3:26** 6032
Nebuchadnezzar **r** and said, **Da 3:28** 6032
The king **r** and said, **Da 4:19** 6032
And Peter **r** to her, **Ac 5:8** *611*
nodded for him to speak, Paul **r**: **Ac 24:10** *611*
RESPONSE
but there was no sound or **r**. **2Ki 4:31** 7182
understands, there will be no **r**. **Pr 29:19** 4617
I have come in **r** to your words. **Da 10:12**
saying to the crowd in **r**, **Lk 13:14** *611*
But what is the divine **r** to him? **Ro 11:4** *5538*
RESPONSIBILITY
"The **r** of Eleazar the son of **Nu 4:16** 6486
the **r** of all the tabernacle and of all **Nu 4:16** 6486

had the **r** over the things which **1Ch 9:31** 530
For this matter is your **r**, **Ezr 10:4** 5921
too hastily and thereby share **r** **1Tm 5:22**
RESPONSIBLE
was done there, he was **r** *for it.* **Gn 39:22** 6213a
you may hold me **r** for him. **Gn 43:9** 4480, 3027
r to save up for *their* parents, **2Co 12:14** *3784*
REST
one will give us **r** from our work **Gn 5:29** 5162
and **r** yourselves under the tree; **Gn 18:4** 8172
Jacob fed the **r** of Laban's flocks. **Gn 30:36** 3498
but as for *the* **r** *of* you, go, **Gn 42:19**
and *the* **r** *of* you shall be **Gn 44:10**
it was restored like *the* **r** *of* his **Ex 4:7**
They will also eat the **r** of what **Ex 10:5** 3499a
you shall let it **r** and lie fallow, **Ex 23:11** 8058
your ox and your donkey may **r**, **Ex 23:12** 5117
and sprinkle the **r** *of the* blood **Ex 29:20**
there is a sabbath of complete **r**, **Ex 31:15** 7677
with you, and I will give you **r**." **Ex 33:14** 5117
on the seventh day you shall **r**; **Ex 34:21** 7673a
time and harvest you shall **r**. **Ex 34:21** 7673a
sabbath of complete **r** to the LORD; **Ex 35:2** 7677
that is, all *the* **r** *of* the bull, **Lv 4:12**
and *the* **r** *of* its blood he shall **Lv 4:25**
and all *the* **r** *of* its blood he **Lv 4:30**
and all *the* **r** *of* its blood he **Lv 4:34**
while the **r** of the blood shall be **Lv 5:9** 7604
then *the* **r** shall become **Lv 5:13**
Then he poured out *the* **r** *of* **Lv 8:15**
Moses then sprinkled *the* **r** *of* **Lv 8:24**
and poured out *the* **r** *of* the blood **Lv 9:9**
while the **r** of the oil that is in **Lv 14:18** 3498
the **r** of the oil that is in the **Lv 14:29** 3498
be a sabbath of solemn **r** for you, **Lv 16:31** 7677
there is a sabbath of complete **r**, **Lv 23:3** 7677
of the month you shall have a **r**, **Lv 23:24** 7677
be a sabbath of complete **r** to you, **Lv 23:32** 7677
with a **r** on the first day and a **Lv 23:39** 7677
day and a **r** on the eighth day. **Lv 23:39** 7677
the land shall have a sabbath **r**, **Lv 25:4** 7677
land will **r** and enjoy its sabbaths. **Lv 26:34** 7673a
it will observe the **r** which it did not **Lv 26:35** 7673a
When it came to **r**, **Nu 10:36** 5117
Israel has separated you from the **r** **Nu 16:9**
then *the* **r** shall be reckoned to **Nu 18:30**
kings of Midian along with the **r** *of* **Nu 31:8**
"The **r** of Gilead and all **Dt 3:13** 3499a
until the LORD gives **r** to your **Dt 3:20** 5117
servant may **r** as well as you. **Dt 5:14** 5117
and He gives you **r** from all your **Dt 12:10** 5117
"The **r** will hear and be **Dt 19:20** 7604
r from all your surrounding enemies, **Dt 25:19** 5117
the **r** of his children who remain, **Dt 28:54** 3499a
those nations you shall find no **r**, **Dt 28:65** 7280b
in this book will **r** on him, **Dt 29:20** 7257
'The LORD your God gives you **r** and **Jos 1:13** 5117
the LORD gives your brothers **r**, **Jos 1:15** 5117
r in the waters of the Jordan, **Jos 3:13** 5117
Thus the land had **r** from war. **Jos 11:23** 8252
with the sword among *the* **r** *of* **Jos 13:22**
the **r** of the kingdom of Sihon king **Jos 13:27** 3499a
Then the land had **r** from war. **Jos 14:15** 8252
for the **r** of the sons of Manasseh **Jos 17:2** 3498
to the **r** of the sons of Manasseh. **Jos 17:6** 3498
The **r** of the sons of Kohath **Jos 21:5** 3498
to the **r** of the sons of Kohath. **Jos 21:20** 3498
the **r** of the sons of Kohath were ten. **Jos 21:26** 3498
of Merari, the **r** of the Levites, **Jos 21:34** 3498
the **r** of the families of the Levites; **Jos 21:40** 3498
LORD gave them **r** on every side, **Jos 21:44** 5117
God has given **r** to your brothers, **Jos 22:4** 5117
when the LORD had given **r** to **Jos 23:1** 5117
cling to the **r** of these nations, **Jos 23:12** 3499a
Then the land had **r** forty years. **Jg 3:11** 8252
but all the **r** of the people **Jg 7:6** 3499a
pursued them without **r** *and* trod **Jg 20:43** 4496
The **r** turned and fled toward the **Jg 20:45**
LORD grant that you may find **r**, **Ru 1:9** 4496
r until he has settled it today." **Ru 3:18** 8252
he sent away the **r** of the people, **1Sa 13:2** 3499a
the **r** we have utterly destroyed." **1Sa 15:15** 3498
while he was taking his midday **r**. **2Sa 4:5** 4904
and the LORD had given him **r** on **2Sa 7:1** 5117
give you **r** from all your enemies. **2Sa 7:11** 5117
gather the **r** of the people **2Sa 12:28** 3499a
neither the birds of the sky to **r** on **2Sa 21:10** 5117
God has given me **r** on every side; **1Ki 5:4** 5117
were in two rows, cast with the **r**. **1Ki 7:24** 3333
has given **r** to His people Israel, **1Ki 8:56** 4496
Now the **r** of the acts of Solomon **1Ki 11:41** 3499a
and to the **r** of the people, **1Ki 12:23** 3499a
Now the **r** of the acts of Jeroboam, **1Ki 14:19** 3499a
Now the **r** of the acts of Rehoboam **1Ki 14:29** 3499a
Now the **r** of the acts of Abijam **1Ki 15:7** 3499a
Now the **r** of all the acts of Asa **1Ki 15:23** 3499a
Now the **r** of the acts of Nadab and **1Ki 15:31** 3499a
Now the **r** of the acts of Baasha **1Ki 16:5** 3499a
Now the **r** of the acts of Elah and **1Ki 16:14** 3499a
Now the **r** of the acts of Zimri and **1Ki 16:20** 3499a
Now the **r** of the acts of Omri **1Ki 16:27** 3499a
the **r** fled to Aphek into the city, **1Ki 20:30** 3498
Now the **r** of the acts of Ahab and **1Ki 22:39** 3499a
the **r** of the acts of Jehoshaphat, **1Ki 22:45** 3499a
Now the **r** of the acts of Ahaziah **2Ki 1:18** 3499a
and your sons can live on the **r**." **2Ki 4:7** 3498
The **r** of the acts of Joram and **2Ki 8:23** 3499a

Now the **r** of the acts of Jehu and	2Ki 10:34	3499a
Now the **r** of the acts of Joash and	2Ki 12:19	3499a
Now the **r** of the acts of Jehoahaz,	2Ki 13:8	3499a
Now the **r** of the acts of Joash and	2Ki 13:12	3499a
Now the **r** of the acts of Jehoash	2Ki 14:15	3499a
Now the **r** of the acts of Amaziah,	2Ki 14:18	3499a
Now the **r** of the acts of Jeroboam	2Ki 14:28	3499a
Now the **r** of the acts of Azariah	2Ki 15:6	3499a
the **r** of the acts of Zechariah,	2Ki 15:11	3499a
Now the **r** of the acts of Shallum	2Ki 15:15	3499a
Now the **r** of the acts of Menahem	2Ki 15:21	3499a
Now the **r** of the acts of Pekahiah	2Ki 15:26	3499a
Now the **r** of the acts of Pekah and	2Ki 15:31	3499a
Now the **r** of the acts of Jotham	2Ki 15:36	3499a
Now the **r** of the acts of Ahaz	2Ki 16:19	3499a
Now the **r** of the acts of Hezekiah	2Ki 20:20	3499a
Now the **r** of the acts of Manasseh	2Ki 21:17	3499a
Now the **r** of the acts of Amon	2Ki 21:25	3499a
Now the **r** of the acts of Josiah	2Ki 23:28	3499a
Now the **r** of the acts of Jehoiakim	2Ki 24:5	3499a
Then the **r** of the people who were	2Ki 25:11	3499a
and the **r** of the people,	2Ki 25:11	3499a
Then to the **r** of the sons of Kohath	1Ch 6:61	3498
r of the family of the sons of Kohath.	1Ch 6:70	3498
To the **r** of *the Levites,* the sons	1Ch 6:77	3498
Joab repaired the **r** of the city.	1Ch 11:8	7605
and all the **r** also of Israel were	1Ch 12:38	7611
and the **r** who were chosen,	1Ch 16:41	7605
to you, who shall be a man of **r**;	1Ch 22:9	4496
and I will give him **r** from all his	1Ch 22:9	5117
He not given you **r** on every side?	1Ch 22:18	5117
Israel has given **r** to His people,	1Ch 23:25	5117
Now for the **r** of the sons of Levi:	1Ch 24:20	3498
Now the **r** of the acts of Solomon,	2Ch 9:29	7605
Now the **r** of the acts of Abijah,	2Ch 13:22	3499a
because the LORD had given him **r**.	2Ch 14:6	5117
He has given us **r** on every side."	2Ch 14:7	5117
LORD gave them **r** on every side.	2Ch 15:15	5117
his God gave him **r** on all sides.	2Ch 20:30	5117
the **r** of the acts of Jehoshaphat,	2Ch 20:34	3499a
they brought the **r** of the money	2Ch 24:14	7605
Now the **r** of the acts of Amaziah,	2Ch 25:26	3499a
Now the **r** of the acts of Uzziah,	2Ch 26:22	3499a
Now the **r** of the acts of Jotham,	2Ch 27:7	3499a
r of his acts and all his ways,	2Ch 28:26	3499a
Now the **r** of the acts of Hezekiah	2Ch 32:32	3499a
Now the **r** of the acts of Manasseh	2Ch 33:18	3499a
Now the **r** of the acts of Josiah	2Ch 35:26	3499a
Now the **r** of the acts of Jehoiakim	2Ch 36:8	3499a
and the **r** of their brothers the priests	Ezr 3:8	7605
Zerubbabel and Jeshua and the **r** of	Ezr 4:3	7605
and the **r** of his colleagues wrote	Ezr 4:7	7605
and the **r** of their colleagues,	Ezr 4:9	7606
and the **r** of the nations which the	Ezr 4:10	7606
and in the **r** of the region beyond	Ezr 4:10	7606
and to the **r** of their colleagues	Ezr 4:17	7606
Samaria and in the **r** of *the provinces*	Ezr 4:17	7606
Levites and the **r** of the exiles,	Ezr 6:16	7606
with the **r** of the silver and gold,	Ezr 7:18	7606
"The **r** of the needs for the	Ezr 7:20	7606
or the **r** who did the work.	Ne 2:16	3499a
and the **r** of the people:	Ne 4:14	3499a
and the **r** of the people,	Ne 4:19	3499a
and to the **r** of our enemies that I	Ne 6:1	3499a
Noadiah the prophetess and the **r** of	Ne 6:14	3499a
That which the **r** of the people gave	Ne 7:72	7611
"But as soon as they had **r**,	Ne 9:28	5117
Now the **r** of the people, the	Ne 10:28	7605
but the **r** of the people cast lots	Ne 11:1	7605
The **r** of Israel, of the priests	Ne 11:20	7605
in the **r** of the king's provinces!	Es 9:12	7605
Now the **r** of the Jews who *were* in	Es 9:16	7605
then, I would have been at **r**,	Jb 3:13	5117
And there the weary are at **r**.	Jb 3:17	5117
nor am I quiet, And I am not at **r**,	Jb 3:26	5117
would look around and **r** securely.	Jb 11:18	7901
Your gaze from him that he may **r**,	Jb 14:6	2308
And my gnawing *pains* take no **r**.	Jb 30:17	7901
And by night, but I have no **r**.	Ps 22:2	1747
R in the LORD and wait patiently	Ps 37:7	1826a
I would fly away and be at **r**.	Ps 55:6	7931
On God my salvation and my glory **r**;	Ps 62:7	
they shall not enter into My **r**."	Ps 95:11	4496
Return to your **r**, O my soul, For	Ps 116:7	4494
scepter of wickedness shall not **r** upon	Ps 125:3	5117
folding of the hands to **r**"	Pr 6:10	7901
may be wise the **r** of your days.	Pr 19:20	319
r in the assembly of the dead.	Pr 21:16	5117
folding of the hands to **r**,"	Pr 24:33	7901
or laughs, and there is no **r**.	Pr 29:9	5183a
even at night his mind does not **r**.	Ec 2:23	7901
One hand full of **r** is better than	Ec 4:6	5183a
government will **r** on His shoulders;	Is 9:6	1961
And the **r** of the trees of his forest	Is 10:19	7605
Spirit of the LORD will **r** on Him,	Is 11:2	5117
in the day when the LORD gives you **r**	Is 14:3	5117
whole earth is at **r** *and* is quiet;	Is 14:7	5117
even there you will find no **r**."	Is 23:12	5117
the LORD will **r** on this mountain,	Is 25:10	5117
"Here is **r**, give rest to the	Is 28:12	4496
is rest, give **r** to the weary,"	Is 28:12	5117
and **r** you will be saved,	Is 30:15	5183a
deprived of the **r** of my years."	Is 38:10	3499a
the **r** of it he makes into a god,	Is 44:17	7611
the **r** of it into an abomination,	Is 44:19	3499a
They **r** in their beds, *Each one* who	Is 57:2	5117
LORD, take no **r** for yourselves;	Is 62:6	1824
And give Him no **r** until He	Is 62:7	1824
Spirit of the LORD gave them **r**.	Is 63:14	5117
And where is a place that I may **r**?	Is 66:1	4496
you will find **r** for your souls.	Jer 6:16	4771
and concerning the **r** of the vessels	Jer 27:19	3499a
the **r** of the elders of the exile,	Jer 29:1	3499a
when it went to find its **r**."	Jer 31:2	7280b
of shepherds who **r** their flocks.	Jer 33:12	7257
and all the **r** of the officials of	Jer 39:3	7611
As for the **r** of the people who	Jer 39:9	3499a
the **r** of the people who remained,	Jer 39:9	3499a
groaning and have found no **r**."	Jer 45:3	4496
Be at **r** and stay still.	Jer 47:6	7280b
that He may bring **r** to the earth,	Jer 50:34	7280b
the **r** of the people who were left	Jer 52:15	3499a
and the **r** of the artisans.	Jer 52:15	3499a
nations, *But* she has found no **r**;	La 1:3	4494
Let your eyes have no **r**.	La 2:18	1826a
worn out, there is no **r** for us.	La 5:5	5117
flock and I will lead them to **r**,"	Ezk 34:15	7257
your feet the **r** of your pastures?	Ezk 34:18	3499a
must foul the **r** with your feet?	Ezk 34:18	3498
a possession of the **r** of the nations and	Ezk 36:3	7611
and a derision to the **r** of the nations	Ezk 36:4	7611
against the **r** of the nations,	Ezk 36:5	7611
I will go against those who are at **r**,	Ezk 38:11	8252
cause a blessing to **r** on your house.	Ezk 44:30	5117
but they shall give *the* **r** *of*	Ezk 45:8	
"As for the **r** of the tribes:	Ezk 48:23	3499a
the **r** of the wise men of Babylon.	Da 2:18	7606
"As for the **r** of the beasts,	Da 7:12	7606
then you will enter into **r** and	Da 12:13	5117
slay the **r** of them with the sword;	Am 9:1	319
For this is no place of **r** Because	Mi 2:10	4496
but the **r** of the people will not	Zch 14:2	3499a
heavy-laden, and I will give you **r**.	Mt 11:28	*373*
YOU WILL FIND **R** FOR YOUR SOULS.	Mt 11:29	*372*
waterless places seeking **r**,	Mt 12:43	*372*
and the **r** seized his slaves and	Mt 22:6	*3062*
But the **r** *of them* said,	Mt 27:49	*3062*
to a secluded place and **r** a while."	Mk 6:31	*373*
but to the **r** *it is* in parables,	Lk 8:10	*3062*
there, your peace will **r** on him;	Lk 10:6	*1879*
waterless places seeking **r**,	Lk 11:24	*372*
to the eleven and to all the **r**.	Lk 24:9	*3062*
Peter and the **r** of the apostles,	Ac 2:37	*3062*
r dared to associate with them;	Ac 5:13	*3062*
R OF MANKIND MAY SEEK THE LORD,	Ac 15:17	*2645*
and the **r** *should follow,* some on	Ac 27:44	*3062*
the **r** of the people on the island	Ac 28:9	*3062*
as among the **r** of the Gentiles.	Ro 1:13	*3062*
it, and the **r** were hardened;	Ro 11:7	*3062*
find *refreshing* **r** in your company.	Ro 15:32	*4875*
would not **r** on the wisdom of men,	1Co 2:5	*1510*
But to the **r** I say, not the Lord,	1Co 7:12	*3062*
even as the **r** of the apostles and	1Co 9:5	*3062*
I had no **r** for my spirit, not	2Co 2:13	*425*
into Macedonia our flesh had no **r**,	2Co 7:5	*425*
inferior to the **r** of the churches,	2Co 12:13	*3062*
the past and to all the **r** *as well*	2Co 13:2	*3062*
The **r** of the Jews joined him	Ga 2:13	*3062*
children of wrath, even as the **r**.	Eph 2:3	*3062*
and the **r** of my fellow workers,	Php 4:3	*3062*
as do the **r** who have no hope.	1Th 4:13	*3062*
so that the **r** also will be fearful	1Tm 5:20	*3062*
'THEY SHALL NOT ENTER MY **R**.' "	Heb 3:11	*2663*
that they would not enter His **r**,	Heb 3:18	*2663*
promise remains of entering His **r**,	Heb 4:1	*2663*
we who have believed enter that **r**,	Heb 4:3	*2663*
THEY SHALL NOT ENTER MY **R**,"	Heb 4:3	*2663*
"THEY SHALL NOT ENTER MY **R**."	Heb 4:5	*2663*
For if Joshua had given them **r**,	Heb 4:8	*2664*
a Sabbath **r** for the people of God.	Heb 4:9	*4520*
For the one who has entered His **r**	Heb 4:10	*2663*
be diligent to enter that **r**,	Heb 4:11	*2663*
so as to live the **r** of the time in	1Pe 4:2	*1954*
do also the **r** of the Scriptures,	2Pe 3:16	*3062*
to you, the **r** who are in Thyatira,	Rv 2:24	*3062*
r for a little while longer,	Rv 6:11	*373*
The **r** of mankind, who were not	Rv 9:20	*3062*
and the **r** were terrified and gave	Rv 11:13	*3062*
war with the **r** of her children,	Rv 12:17	*3062*
they have no **r** day and night,	Rv 14:11	*372*
"so that they may **r** from their labors,	Rv 14:13	*373*
And the **r** were killed with the	Rv 19:21	*3062*
The **r** of the dead did not come to	Rv 20:5	*3062*

RESTED

and He **r** on the seventh day from	Gn 2:2	7673a
because in it He **r** from all His work	Gn 2:3	7673a
ark **r** upon the mountains of Ararat.	Gn 8:4	5117
the people **r** on the seventh day.	Ex 16:30	7673a
in them, and **r** on the seventh day;	Ex 20:11	5117
glory of the LORD **r** on Mount Sinai,	Ex 24:16	7931
And when the Spirit **r** upon them,	Nu 11:25	5117
And the Spirit **r** upon them	Nu 11:26	5117
pillars on which the house **r**,	Jg 16:29	3559
in to the upper chamber and **r**.	2Ki 4:11	7901, 8033
the LORD, after the ark **r** *there.*	1Ch 6:31	4494
and on the fourteenth day they **r**	Es 9:17	5117
and they **r** on the fifteenth day	Es 9:18	5117
Your wrath has **r** upon me, And You	Ps 88:7	5564
their iniquity **r** on their bones,	Ezk 32:27	1961
r according to the commandment.	Lk 23:56	*2270*
and they **r** on each one of them.	Ac 2:3	*2523*
"AND GOD **R** ON THE SEVENTH DAY	Heb 4:4	*2664*
has himself also **r** from his works,	Heb 4:10	*2664*

RESTING

but the dove found no **r** place for	Gn 8:9	4494
he saw that a **r** place was good	Gn 49:15	4496
to seek out a **r** place for them.	Nu 10:33	4496
have not as yet come to the **r** place	Dt 12:9	4496
and there will be no **r** place for	Dt 28:65	4496
arise, O LORD God, to Your **r** place,	2Ch 6:41	5117
and they laid him in the **r** place	2Ch 16:14	4904
And let there be no **r** place for	Jb 16:18	
Arise, O LORD, to Your **r** place,	Ps 132:8	4496
"This is My **r** place forever;	Ps 132:14	4496
Do not destroy his **r** place;	Pr 24:15	7258
And His **r** place will be glorious.	Is 11:10	4496
You who carve a **r** place for	Is 22:16	4908
and in undisturbed **r** places;	Is 32:18	4496
And will find herself a **r** place.	Is 34:14	4494
the haunt of jackals, its **r** place,	Is 35:7	7258
of Achor a **r** place for herds,	Is 65:10	7258
And have forgotten their **r** place.	Jer 50:6	7258
of Ammon a **r** place for flocks.	Ezk 25:5	4769
desolation, A **r** place for beasts!	Zph 2:15	4769
with Damascus as its **r** place	Zch 9:1	4496
"Are you still sleeping and **r**?	Mt 26:45	*373*
"Are you still sleeping and **r**? It	Mk 14:41	*373*

RESTITUTION

the owner of the pit shall make **r**;	Ex 21:34	7999a
He shall surely make **r**;	Ex 22:3	7999a
he shall make **r** from the best of	Ex 22:5	7999a
the fire shall surely make **r**.	Ex 22:6	7999a
it, and he shall not make **r**.	Ex 22:11	7999a
him, he shall make **r** to its owner.	Ex 22:12	7999a
he shall not make **r** for what has	Ex 22:13	7999a
not with it, he shall make full **r**.	Ex 22:14	7999a
is with it, he shall not make **r**;	Ex 22:15	7999a
"He shall make **r** for that	Lv 5:16	7999a
he shall make **r** for it in full and	Lv 6:5	7999a
make **r** in full for his wrong and	Nu 5:7	7725
whom **r** may be made for the wrong,	Nu 5:8	7725
the **r** which is made for the wrong	Nu 5:8	7725
must make **r** for the lamb fourfold,	2Sa 12:6	7999a

RESTLESS

come about when you become **r**,	Gn 27:40	7300
I am **r** in my complaint and am	Ps 55:2	7300
it is a **r** evil *and* full of deadly	Jas 3:8	*182*

RESTORATION

until *the* period of **r** of all things	Ac 3:21	*605*

RESTORE

"Now therefore, **r** the man's wife,	Gn 20:7	7725
But if you do not **r** *her,*	Gn 20:7	7725
hands, to **r** him to his father.	Gn 37:22	7725
head and **r** you to your office;	Gn 40:13	7725
to **r** every man's money in his sack,	Gn 42:25	7725
shall **r** what he took by robbery or	Lv 6:4	7725
and the congregation shall **r** him	Nu 35:25	7725
then you shall **r** it to him.	Dt 22:2	7725
God will **r** you from captivity,	Dt 30:3	7725
I will **r** *it* to you."	1Sa 12:3	7725
went to **r** his rule at the River.	2Sa 8:3	7725
and will **r** to you all the land of	2Sa 9:7	7725
'Today the house of Israel will **r**	2Sa 16:3	7725
to **r** the kingdom to Rehoboam	1Ki 12:21	7725
took from your father I will **r**,	1Ki 20:34	7725
"**R** all that was hers and all the	2Ki 8:6	7725
to **r** the kingdom to Rehoboam.	2Ch 11:1	7725
to **r** the house of the LORD.	2Ch 24:4	2318
to **r** the house of the LORD,	2Ch 24:12	2318
used it to **r** and repair the house.	2Ch 34:10	918
of God to **r** it on its foundation.	Ezr 2:68	5975
house of our God, to **r** its ruins and	Ezr 9:9	5975
they going to **r** *it* for themselves?	Ne 4:2	5800b
you And **r** your righteous estate.	Jb 8:6	7999a
He may **r** His righteousness to man.	Jb 33:26	7725
You **r** him to health.	Ps 41:3	2015
R to me the joy of Your salvation And	Ps 51:12	2318
You have been angry; O, **r** us.	Ps 60:1	7725
I did not steal, I then have to **r**.	Ps 69:4	7725
O God, **r** us And cause Your face to	Ps 80:3	7725
O God *of* hosts, **r** us And cause	Ps 80:7	7725
O LORD God of hosts, **r** us;	Ps 80:19	7725
R us, O God of our salvation, And	Ps 85:4	7725
R our captivity, O LORD, As the	Ps 126:4	7725
r your judges as at the first,	Is 1:26	7725
O **r** me to health and let me live!	Is 38:16	2492a
to **r** the preserved ones of Israel;	Is 49:6	7725
of the people, To **r** the land,	Is 49:8	6965
I will lead him and **r** comfort to	Is 57:18	7999a
If you return, then I will **r** you	Jer 15:19	7725
For I will **r** them to their own land	Jer 16:15	7725
back and **r** them to this place.' "	Jer 27:22	7725
'and I will **r** your fortunes and	Jer 29:14	7725
'when I will **r** the fortunes of My	Jer 30:3	7725
'For I will **r** you to health And I	Jer 30:17	5927
I will **r** the fortunes of the tents	Jer 30:18	7725
cities when I **r** their fortunes,	Jer 31:23	7725
for I will **r** their fortunes,'	Jer 32:44	7725
'I will **r** the fortunes of Judah	Jer 33:7	7725
For I will **r** the fortunes of the land	Jer 33:11	7725
But I will **r** their fortunes and	Jer 33:26	7725
on you and **r** you to your own soil.	Jer 42:12	7725
"Yet I will **r** the fortunes of Moab	Jer 48:47	7725
"But afterward I will **r** The fortunes	Jer 49:6	7725
will **r** the fortunes of Elam,' "	Jer 49:39	7725
food To **r** their lives themselves.	La 1:11	7725
they sought food to **r** their strength	La 1:19	7725
So as to **r** you from captivity,	La 2:14	7725
R us to You, O LORD, that we may	La 5:21	7725
I will **r** their captivity,	Ezk 16:53	7725
robbery, does not **r** a pledge,	Ezk 18:12	7725
I will **r** the fortunes of Jacob	Ezk 39:25	7725
decree to **r** and rebuild Jerusalem	Da 9:25	7725
I **r** the fortunes of My people.	Hos 6:11	7725

When I **r** the fortunes of Judah and — Jl 3:1 — 7725
I will **r** the captivity of My people — Am 9:14 — 7725
LORD will **r** the splendor of Jacob — Na 2:2 — 7725
care for them And **r** their fortune. — Zph 2:7 — 7725
When I **r** your fortunes before your — Zph 3:20 — 7725
that I will **r** double to you. — Zch 9:12 — 7725
He will **r** the hearts of the fathers — Mal 4:6 — 7725
Elijah is coming and will **r** all things — Mt 17:11 — *600*
does first come and **r** *all* things. — Mk 9:12 — *600*
REBUILD ITS RUINS, AND I WILL **R** IT, — Ac 15:16 — *461*
r such a one in a spirit of gentleness — Ga 6:1 — *2675*
faith will **r** the one who is sick, — Jas 5:15 — *4982*

RESTORED
and **r** his wife Sarah to him. — Gn 20:14 — 7725
He **r** the chief cupbearer to — Gn 40:21 — 7725
he **r** me in my office, but he — Gn 41:13 — 7725
was **r** like *the rest of* his flesh. — Ex 4:7 — 7725
you, and will not be **r** to you; — Dt 28:31 — 7725
from Israel were **r** to Israel, — 1Sa 7:14 — 7725
me, that my hand may be **r** to me." — 1Ki 13:6 — 7725
and the king's hand was **r** to him, — 1Ki 13:6 — 7725
and your flesh will be **r** to you and — 2Ki 5:10 — 7725
and his flesh was **r** like the flesh — 2Ki 5:14 — 7725
woman whose son he had **r** to life, — 2Ki 8:1 — 2421a
he had **r** to life the one — 2Ki 8:5 — 2421a
whose son he had **r** to life appealed — 2Ki 8:5 — 2421a
whom Elisha **r** to life." — 2Ki 8:5 — 2421a
He built Elath and **r** it to Judah after — 2Ki 14:22 — 7725
He **r** the border of Israel from the — 2Ki 14:25 — 7725
He then **r** the altar of the LORD — 2Ch 15:8 — 2318
and they **r** the house of God — 2Ch 24:13 — 5975
He built Eloth and **r** it to Judah — 2Ch 26:2 — 7725
and they **r** Jerusalem as far as the — Ne 3:8 — 5800b
and **r** them to their posts. — Ne 13:11 — 5975
to the Almighty, you will be **r**; — Jb 22:23 — 1129
The LORD **r** the fortunes of Job — Jb 42:10 — 7725
You **r** the captivity of Jacob. — Ps 85:1 — 7521
the daughter of my people been **r**? — Jer 8:22 — 5927
Bring me back that I may be **r**, — Jer 31:18 — 7725
to You, O LORD, that we may be **r**; — La 5:21 — 7725
the land that is **r** from the sword, — Ezk 38:8 — 7725
my majesty and splendor were **r** to me — Da 4:36 — 8421
holy place will be properly **r**." — Da 8:14 — 6663
it out, and it was **r** to normal, — Mt 12:13 — *600*
the mute speaking, the crippled **r**, — Mt 15:31 — *5199*
it out, and his hand was **r**. — Mk 3:5 — *600*
and he looked intently and was **r**, — Mk 8:25 — *600*
and his hand was **r**. — Lk 6:10 — *600*
that I may be **r** to you the sooner. — Heb 13:19 — *600*

RESTORER
"May he also be to you a **r** of life — Ru 4:15 — 7725
The **r** of the streets in which to — Is 58:12 — 7725

RESTORES
the LORD **r** His captive people, — Ps 14:7 — 7725
He **r** my soul; He guides me in the — Ps 23:3 — 7725
When God **r** His captive people, Let — Ps 53:6 — 7725
own eyes When the LORD **r** Zion. — Is 52:8 — 7725
is a comforter, One who **r** my soul. — La 1:16 — 7725
but **r** to the debtor his pledge, — Ezk 18:7 — 7725
if a wicked man **r** a pledge, pays — Ezk 33:15 — 7725

RESTORING
the LORD is perfect, **r** the soul; — Ps 19:7 — 7725
You are **r** the kingdom to Israel?" — Ac 1:6 — *600*

RESTRAIN
"Moses, my lord, **r** them." — Nu 11:28 — 3607
"Therefore I will not **r** my mouth; — Jb 7:11 — 2820
to snatch away, who could **r** Him? — Jb 9:12 — 7725
calls an assembly, who can **r** Him? — Jb 11:10 — 7725
And He does not **r** the lightnings — Jb 37:4 — 6117
Behold, I will not **r** my lips, — Ps 40:9 — 3607
He who would **r** her restrains the — Pr 27:16 — 6845
to **r** the wind with the wind, — Ec 8:8 — 3607
And *for* My praise I **r** *it* for you, — Is 48:9 — 2413
You **r** Yourself at these things, — Is 64:12 — 662
"**R** your voice from weeping And — Jer 31:16 — 4513

RESTRAINED
and the rain from the sky was **r**; — Gn 8:2 — 3607
the people were **r** from bringing *any* — Ex 36:6 — 3607
why are we **r** from presenting the — Nu 9:7 — 1639
the LORD is not **r** to save by many — 1Sa 14:6 — 4622
LORD has **r** you from shedding blood — 1Sa 25:26 — 4513
who has **r** me from harming you, — 1Sa 25:34 — 4513
Israel, for Joab **r** the people. — 2Sa 18:16 — 2820
plague may be **r** from the people." — 1Ch 21:22 — 6113
And often He **r** His anger And did — Ps 78:38 — 7725
r my feet from every evil way, — Ps 119:101 — 3607
I have kept still and **r** Myself. — Is 42:14 — 662
Your compassion are **r** toward me. — Is 63:15 — 662
not **r** His hand from destroying, — La 2:8 — 7725
with difficulty they **r** the crowds — Ac 14:18 — *2664*
You are not **r** by us, but you are — 2Co 6:12 — *4729*
you are **r** in your own affections. — 2Co 6:12 — *4729*
man, **r** the madness of the prophet. — 2Pe 2:16 — *2967*

RESTRAINS
"Behold, He **r** the waters, and — Jb 12:15 — 6113
my destruction; No one **r** them. — Jb 30:13 — 5826
But he who **r** his lips is wise. — Pr 10:19 — 2820
He who **r** his words has knowledge, — Pr 17:27 — 2820
who would restrain her **r** the wind, — Pr 27:16 — 6845
one who **r** his sword from blood. — Jer 48:10 — 4513
And you know what **r** him now, — 2Th 2:6 — *2722*
only he who now **r** *will do so* until — 2Th 2:7 — *2722*

RESTRAINT
brought about a lack of **r** in Judah — 2Ch 28:19 — 6544a
of Tarshish, There is no more **r**. — Is 23:10 — 4206a
not to put a **r** upon you, but to — 1Co 7:35 — *1029*

RESTRICTED
while he was still **r** because of — 1Ch 12:1 — 6113
"I am **r**; I cannot go into the house — Jer 36:5 — 6113

RESTS
the pillars on which the house **r**, — Jg 16:26 — 3559
spirit of Elijah **r** on Elisha." — 2Ki 2:15 — 5117
Like a weaned child **r** against his — Ps 131:2
Wisdom **r** in the heart of one who — Pr 14:33 — 5117
of glory and of God **r** on you. — 1Pe 4:14 — *373*

RESULT
to bring about this present **r**, — Gn 50:20
and *as a* **r** he died, he is a — Nu 35:17
and *as a* **r** he died, he is a — Nu 35:18
at him lying in wait and *as a* **r** — Nu 35:20
and *as a* **r** he died, the one who — Nu 35:21
as a **r** you will have no possession — Ezr 4:16 — 6903
every skill which is done is *the* **r** — Ec 4:4
As a **r** of the anguish of His soul, — Is 53:11 — 4480
as a **r** of the vision anguish has — Da 10:16
with the **r** that all those who had — Mk 3:10 — *5620*
As a **r** of this many of His — Jn 6:66 — *1537*
As a **r** of this Pilate made efforts — Jn 19:12 — *1537*
which was to **r** in life, — Ro 7:10 — *1519*
life, proved to **r** in death for me; — Ro 7:10 — *1519*
with the **r** that even Barnabas was — Ga 2:13 — *5620*
not as a **r** of works, so that no one — Eph 2:9 — *1537*
As a **r**, we are no longer to be — Eph 4:14 — *2443*
with the **r** that they always fill — 1Th 2:16 — *1519*
the **r** of their conduct, — Heb 13:7 — *1545*
let endurance have *its* perfect **r**, — Jas 1:4 — *2041*
works, and as a **r** of the works, — Jas 2:22 — *1537*
may be found to **r** in praise and — 1Pe 1:7 — *1519*

RESULTED
word of the LORD has **r** In reproach — Jer 20:8 — 1961
there **r** condemnation to all men, — Ro 5:18 — *1519*
there **r** justification of life to all men. — Ro 5:18 — *1519*

RESULTING
of the terror **r** from their might, — Ezk 32:30
transgression **r** in condemnation, — Ro 5:16 — *1519*
transgressions **r** in justification. — Ro 5:16 — *1519*
obey, either of sin **r** in death, — Ro 6:16 — *1519*
of obedience **r** in righteousness? — Ro 6:16 — *1519*
r in *further* lawlessness, — Ro 6:19 — *1519*
r in sanctification. — Ro 6:19 — *1519*
your benefit, **r** in sanctification, — Ro 6:22 — *1519*
person believes, **r** in righteousness, — Ro 10:10 — *1519*
he confesses, **r** in salvation. — Ro 10:10 — *1519*
r in the obedience of the Gentiles — Ro 15:18 — *1519*
r in a true knowledge of God's — Col 2:2

RESULTS
and yet it **r** only in want. — Pr 11:24
and increasing knowledge **r** *in* — Ec 1:18
According to the **r** of his deeds. — Jer 17:10 — 6529
according to the **r** of your deeds," — Jer 21:14 — 6529
the garment, and a worse tear **r**. — Mt 9:16 — *1096*
from the old, and a worse tear **r**. — Mk 2:21 — *1096*

RESURRECTION
Sadducees (who say there is no **r**) — Mt 22:23 — *386*
"In the **r**, therefore, whose wife of — Mt 22:28 — *386*
"For in the **r** they neither marry nor — Mt 22:30 — *386*
"But regarding the **r** of the dead, — Mt 22:31 — *386*
after His **r** they entered the holy city — Mt 27:53 — *1454*
(who say that there is no **r**) — Mk 12:18 — *386*
"In the **r**, when they rise again, — Mk 12:23 — *386*
be repaid at the **r** of the righteous." — Lk 14:14 — *386*
(who say that there is no **r**), — Lk 20:27 — *386*
"In the **r** therefore, which one's wife — Lk 20:33 — *386*
that age and the **r** from the dead, — Lk 20:35 — *386*
sons of God, being sons of the **r**. — Lk 20:36 — *386*
did the good *deeds* to a **r** of life, — Jn 5:29 — *386*
the evil *deeds* to a **r** of judgment. — Jn 5:29 — *386*
again in the **r** on the last day." — Jn 11:24 — *386*
"I am the **r** and the life; — Jn 11:25 — *386*
a witness with us of His **r**." — Ac 1:22 — *386*
and spoke of the **r** of the Christ, — Ac 2:31 — *386*
in Jesus the **r** from the dead. — Ac 4:2 — *386*
to the **r** of the Lord Jesus, — Ac 4:33 — *386*
he was preaching Jesus and the **r**. — Ac 17:18 — *386*
they heard of the **r** of the dead, — Ac 17:32 — *386*
for the hope and **r** of the dead!" — Ac 23:6 — *386*
Sadducees say that there is no **r**, — Ac 23:8 — *386*
there shall certainly be a **r** of both — Ac 24:15 — *386*
'For the **r** of the dead I am on trial — Ac 24:21 — *386*
and that by reason of *His* **r** from — Ac 26:23 — *386*
with power by the **r** from the dead, — Ro 1:4 — *386*
be *in the likeness* of His **r**, — Ro 6:5 — *386*
that there is no **r** of the dead? — 1Co 15:12 — *386*
But if there is no **r** of the dead, — 1Co 15:13 — *386*
a man also *came* the **r** of the dead. — 1Co 15:21 — *386*
So also is the **r** of the dead. — 1Co 15:42 — *386*
and the power of His **r** and the — Php 3:10 — *386*
I may attain to the **r** from the dead. — Php 3:11 — *1815*
the **r** has already taken place, — 2Tm 2:18 — *386*
of hands, and the **r** of the dead and — Heb 6:2 — *386*
received *back* their dead by **r**; — Heb 11:35 — *386*
that they might obtain a better **r**; — Heb 11:35 — *386*
r of Jesus Christ from the dead, — 1Pe 1:3 — *386*
the **r** of Jesus Christ, — 1Pe 3:21 — *386*
This is the first **r**. — Rv 20:5 — *386*
one who has a part in the first **r**; — Rv 20:6 — *386*

RETAIN
to **r** the power of the kingdom. — 2Ch 22:9 — 6113
He does not **r** anything he desires. — Jb 20:20 — 4422
or oppress anyone, or **r** a pledge, — Ezk 18:16 — 2254a
she will not **r** her position of power, — Da 11:6 — 6113
He does not **r** His anger forever, — Mi 7:18 — 2388
if you **r** the *sins* of any, they — Jn 20:23 — *2902*
R the standard of sound words — 2Tm 1:13 — *2192*

RETAINED
to his tent, but **r** the 300 men; — Jg 7:8 — 2388
and let its foundations be **r**, — Ezr 6:3 — 5446
pallor, and I **r** no strength. — Da 10:8 — 6113
upon me, and I have **r** no strength. — Da 10:16 — 6113
sins of any, they have been **r**." — Jn 20:23 — *2902*

RETAINS
Therefore he **r** his flavor, And his — Jer 48:11 — 5975

RETINUE
to Jerusalem with a very large **r**, — 1Ki 10:2 — 2428
She had a very large **r**, — 2Ch 9:1 — 2428

RETIRE
they shall **r** from service in the work — Nu 8:25 — 7725
you to rise up early, To **r** late, — Ps 127:2 — 3427

RETRACED
So David's young men **r** their way — 1Sa 25:12 — 2015

RETRACT
Therefore I **r**, And I repent in — Jb 42:6 — 3988a
And does not **r** His words, — Is 31:2 — 5493

RETREAT
beasts And does not **r** before any, — Pr 30:30 — 7725

RETRIBUTION
'Vengeance is Mine, and **r**, — Dt 32:35 — 8005
come, The days of **r** have come; — Hos 9:7 — 7966
A STUMBLING BLOCK AND A **R** TO THEM. — Ro 11:9 — *468*
dealing out **r** to those who do not — 2Th 1:8 — *1557*

RETURN
bread, Till you **r** to the ground, — Gn 3:19 — 7725
dust, And to dust you shall **r**." — Gn 3:19 — 7725
but she did not **r** to him again. — Gn 8:12 — 7725
Then after his **r** from the defeat — Gn 14:17 — 7725
generation they will **r** here, — Gn 15:16 — 7725
"**R** to your mistress, and submit — Gn 16:9 — 7725
r to you at this time next year; — Gn 18:10 — 7725
appointed time I will **r** to you, — Gn 18:14 — 7725
we will worship and **r** to you." — Gn 22:5 — 7725
and I **r** to my father's house in — Gn 28:21 — 7725
in **r** for your son's mandrakes." — Gn 30:15 — 8478
'**R** to the land of your fathers — Gn 31:3 — 7725
r to the land of your birth.' " — Gn 31:13 — 7725
'**R** to your country and to your — Gn 32:9 — 7725
care, and I will **r** him to you." — Gn 42:37 — 7725
also, and arise, **r** to the man; — Gn 43:13 — 7725
then I will **r**.' " — Gn 50:5 — 7725
that I may **r** to my brethren who — Ex 4:18 — 7725
see war, and **r** to Egypt." — Ex 13:17 — 7725
r it to him before the sun sets, — Ex 22:26 — 7725
you shall surely **r** it to him. — Ex 23:4 — 7725
here for us until we **r** to you. — Ex 24:14 — 7725
'The priest shall **r** on the — Lv 14:39 — 7725
you shall **r** to his own property, — Lv 25:10 — 7725
each of you shall **r** to his family. — Lv 25:10 — 7725
you shall **r** to his own property. — Lv 25:13 — 7725
sold it, and so **r** to his property. — Lv 25:27 — 7725
that he may **r** to his property. — Lv 25:28 — 7725
that he may **r** to the property of — Lv 25:41 — 7725
the year of jubilee the field shall **r** to — Lv 27:24 — 7725
"**R**, O LORD, *To* the myriad — Nu 10:36 — 7725
be better for us to **r** to Egypt?" — Nu 14:3 — 7725
appoint a leader and **r** to Egypt." — Nu 14:4 — 7725
in **r** for their service which they — Nu 18:21 — 2500
for it is your compensation in **r** — Nu 18:31 — 2500
"**R** to Balak, and you shall speak — Nu 23:5 — 7725
"**R** to Balak, and thus you shall — Nu 23:16 — 7725
"We will not **r** to our homes until — Nu 32:18 — 7725
then afterward you shall **r** and be — Nu 32:22 — 7725
r to the land of his possession. — Nu 35:28 — 7725
that he may **r** to live in the land — Nu 35:32 — 7725
may **r** every man to his possession — Dt 3:20 — 7725
you will **r** to the LORD your God — Dt 4:30 — 7725
"**R** to your tents." — Dt 5:30 — 7725
you are to **r** to your tents. — Dt 16:7
6437, 1980
to **r** to Egypt to multiply horses, — Dt 17:16 — 7725
'You shall never again **r** that way.' — Dt 17:16 — 7725
Let him depart and **r** to his house, — Dt 20:5 — 7725
Let him depart and **r** to his house, — Dt 20:6 — 7725
Let him depart and **r** to his house, — Dt 20:7 — 7725
Let him depart and **r** to his house, — Dt 20:8 — 7725
shall surely **r** the pledge to him, — Dt 24:13 — 7725
and you **r** to the LORD your God and — Dt 30:2 — 7725
Then you shall **r** to your own land, — Jos 1:15 — 7725
three days until the pursuers **r**. — Jos 2:16 — 7725
then they shall **r** to me. — Jos 18:4 — 935
land and describe it, and **r** to me; — Jos 18:8 — 7725
Then the manslayer shall **r** to his — Jos 20:6
7725, 935
"**R** to your tents with great — Jos 22:8 — 7725
"I will remain until you **r**." — Jg 6:18 — 7725
r and depart from Mount Gilead — Jg 7:3 — 7725
"When I **r** safely, I will tear — Jg 8:9 — 7725
therefore, **r** them peaceably now." — Jg 11:13 — 7725
when I **r** in peace from the sons of — Jg 11:31 — 7725
therefore, I will **r** them to you." — Jg 17:3 — 7725
nor will any of us **r** to his house. — Jg 20:8 — 5493
she might **r** from the land of Moab, — Ru 1:6 — 7725
the way to **r** to the land of Judah. — Ru 1:7 — 7725
r each of you to her mother's house. — Ru 1:8 — 7725
r with you to your people." — Ru 1:10 — 7725
"**R**, my daughters. — Ru 1:11 — 7725
"**R**, my daughters! — Ru 1:12 — 7725
r after your sister-in-law." — Ru 1:15 — 7725
and let it **r** to its own place, — 1Sa 5:11 — 7725
surely **r** to Him a guilt offering. — 1Sa 6:3 — 7725
which we shall **r** to Him?" — 1Sa 6:4 — 7725
articles of gold which you **r** to Him — 1Sa 6:8 — 7725

"If you **r** to the LORD with all	1Sa 7:3	7725
Then his **r** *was* to Ramah, for his	1Sa 7:17	8666
"Come, and let us **r**,	1Sa 9:5	7725
pardon my sin and **r** with me,	1Sa 15:25	7725
"I will not **r** with you;	1Sa 15:26	7725
let him **r** to his father's house.	1Sa 18:2	7725
and **r** to me with certainty,	1Sa 23:23	7725
reward you with good in **r** for what	1Sa 24:19	8478
R, my son David, for I will not	1Sa 26:21	7725
that he may **r** to his place where	1Sa 29:4	7725
"Now therefore **r** and go in peace,	1Sa 29:7	7725
to **r** to the land of the Philistines.	1Sa 29:11	7725
the sword of Saul did not **r** empty.	2Sa 1:22	7725
Then Abner said to him, "Go, **r**."	2Sa 3:16	7725
your beards grow, and *then* **r**."	2Sa 10:5	7725
to him, but he will not **r** to me."	2Sa 12:23	7725
R and remain with the king, for	2Sa 15:19	7725
r to your own place.	2Sa 15:19	
R and take back your brothers;	2Sa 15:20	7725
"**R** the ark of God to the city.	2Sa 15:25	7725
R to the city in peace and your	2Sa 15:27	7725
"But if you **r** to the city, and	2Sa 15:34	7725
will look on my affliction and **r** good	2Sa 16:12	7725
The **r** of everyone depends on the	2Sa 17:3	7725
"**R**, you and all your servants."	2Sa 19:14	7725
"Please let your servant **r**,	2Sa 19:37	7725
I shall **r** to Him who sent me."	2Sa 24:13	7725
will **r** his blood on his own head,	1Ki 2:32	7725
"So shall their blood **r** on the	1Ki 2:33	7725
r your evil on your own head.	1Ki 2:44	7725
if they **r** to You with all their heart	1Ki 8:48	7725
for three days, then **r** to me."	1Ki 12:5	7725
"**R** to me on the third day."	1Ki 12:12	7725
r every man to his house, for this	1Ki 12:24	7725
kingdom will **r** to the house of David.	1Ki 12:26	7725
this people will **r** to their lord,	1Ki 12:27	7725
and **r** to Rehoboam king of Judah."	1Ki 12:27	7725
r by the way which you came.' "	1Ki 13:9	7725
and did not **r** by the way which he	1Ki 13:10	7725
"I cannot **r** with you, nor go with	1Ki 13:16	7725
do not **r** by going the way which	1Ki 13:17	7725
did not **r** from his evil way,	1Ki 13:33	7725
let this child's life **r** to him."	1Ki 17:21	7725
r on your way to the wilderness of	1Ki 19:15	7725
Let each of them **r** to his house in	1Ki 22:17	7725
"Take Micaiah and **r** him to Amon	1Ki 22:26	7725
with bread and water until I **r** safely	1Ki 22:27	935
"If you indeed **r** safely the LORD	1Ki 22:28	7725
r to the king who sent you and say	2Ki 1:6	7725
may run to the man of God and **r**."	2Ki 4:22	7725
came to them, but he did not **r**."	2Ki 9:18	7725
even to them, and he did not **r**;	2Ki 9:20	7725
a rumor and **r** to his own land.	2Ki 19:7	7725
he came, by the same he will **r**,	2Ki 19:33	7725
"**R** and say to Hezekiah the leader	2Ki 20:5	7725
your beards grow, and *then* **r**."	1Ch 19:5	7725
I shall **r** to Him who sent me."	1Ch 21:12	7725
r *to You* and confess Your name,	2Ch 6:24	7725
if they **r** to You with all their heart	2Ch 6:38	7725
which she requested besides *a* **r** *for*	2Ch 9:12	
"**R** to me again in three days."	2Ch 10:5	7725
"**R** to me on the third day."	2Ch 10:12	7725
r every man to his house, for this	2Ch 11:4	7725
Let each of them **r** to his house in	2Ch 18:16	7725
"Take Micaiah and **r** him to Amon	2Ch 18:25	7725
with bread and water until I **r** safely	2Ch 18:26	7725
"If you indeed **r** safely, the LORD	2Ch 18:27	7725
take it, and **r** it to its place.	2Ch 24:11	7725
listen to me and **r** the captives	2Ch 28:11	7725
r to the LORD God of Abraham,	2Ch 30:6	7725
that He may **r** to those of you who	2Ch 30:6	7725
"For if you **r** to the LORD, your	2Ch 30:9	7725
captive and will **r** to this land.	2Ch 30:9	7725
away from you if you **r** to Him."	2Ch 30:9	7725
Hezekiah gave no **r** for the benefit	2Ch 32:25	7725
but *if* you **r** to Me and keep My	Ne 1:9	7725
journey be, and when will you **r**?"	Ne 2:6	7725
R their reproach on their own heads	Ne 4:4	7725
to **r** to their slavery in Egypt.	Ne 9:17	7725
them So that they might **r** to You,	Ne 9:26	7725
she would **r** to the second harem,	Es 2:14	7725
Jews, should **r** on his own head and	Es 9:25	7725
womb, And naked I shall **r** there.	Jb 1:21	7725
"He will not **r** again to his house,	Jb 7:10	7725
Before I go—and I shall not **r**	Jb 10:21	7725
that he will **r** from darkness,	Jb 15:22	7725
past, I shall go the way of no **r**.	Jb 16:22	7725
"If you **r** to the Almighty, you	Jb 22:23	7725
Let him **r** to the days of his	Jb 33:25	7725
together, And man would **r** to dust.	Jb 34:15	7725
commands that they **r** from evil.	Jb 36:10	7725
They leave and do not **r** to them.	Jb 39:4	7725
in him that he will **r** your grain And	Jb 39:12	7725
R, O LORD, rescue my soul;	Ps 6:4	7725
And over them **r** on high.	Ps 7:7	7725
mischief will **r** upon his own head,	Ps 7:16	7725
The wicked will **r** to Sheol, *Even*	Ps 9:17	7725
They **r** at evening, they howl like	Ps 59:6	7725
They **r** at evening, they howl	Ps 59:14	7725
his people **r** to this place,	Ps 73:10	7725
Let not the oppressed **r** dishonored;	Ps 74:21	7725
A wind that passes and does not **r**.	Ps 78:39	7725
And **r** to our neighbors sevenfold	Ps 79:12	7725
"**R**, O children of men."	Ps 90:3	7725
Do **r**, O LORD; how long *will it be?*	Ps 90:13	7725
they will not **r** to cover the earth.	Ps 104:9	7725
they expire And **r** to their dust.	Ps 104:29	7725
In **r** for my love they act as my	Ps 109:4	8478
R to your rest, O my soul, For the	Ps 116:7	7725

None who go to her **r** again,	Pr 2:19	7725
deeds of a man's hands will **r** to him	Pr 12:14	7725
the dust and all **r** to the dust.	Ec 3:20	7725
have a good **r** for their labor.	Ec 4:9	7939
womb, so will he **r** as he came.	Ec 5:15	7725
and clouds **r** after the rain;	Ec 12:2	7725
the dust will **r** to the earth as it was,	Ec 12:7	7725
spirit will **r** to God who gave it.	Ec 12:7	7725
hearts, And **r** and be healed."	Is 6:10	7725
A remnant will **r**, the remnant of	Is 10:21	7725
Only a remnant within them will **r**;	Is 10:22	7725
so they will **r** to the LORD, and He	Is 19:22	7725
R to Him from whom you have	Is 31:6	7725
the ransomed of the LORD will **r** And	Is 35:10	7725
a rumor and **r** to his own land.	Is 37:7	7725
he came, by the same he will **r**,	Is 37:34	7725
R to Me, for I have redeemed you."	Is 44:22	7725
the ransomed of the LORD will **r** And	Is 51:11	7725
And let him **r** to the LORD, And He	Is 55:7	7725
And do not **r** there without	Is 55:10	7725
It will not **r** to Me empty,	Is 55:11	7725
R for the sake of Your servants,	Is 63:17	7725
man, Will he still **r** to her?	Jer 3:1	7725
these things she will **r** to Me';	Jer 3:7	7725
but she did not **r**, and her	Jer 3:7	7725
not **r** to Me with all her heart,	Jer 3:10	7725
'**R**, faithless Israel,' declares	Jer 3:12	7725
'**R**, O faithless sons,' declares	Jer 3:14	7725
"**R**, O faithless sons, I will heal	Jer 3:22	7725
"If you will **r**, O Israel,"	Jer 4:1	7725
"*Then* you should **r** to Me.	Jer 4:1	7725
fast to deceit, They refuse to **r**.	Jer 8:5	7725
"If you **r**, then I will restore	Jer 15:19	7725
he will never **r** Or see his native land.	Jer 22:10	7725
"He will never **r** there;	Jer 22:11	7725
land to which they desire to **r**,	Jer 22:27	7725
to return, they will not **r** to it.	Jer 22:27	7725
r to Me with their whole heart.	Jer 24:7	7725
And Jacob will **r** and will be	Jer 30:10	7725
great company, they will **r** here.	Jer 31:8	7725
r from the land of the enemy.	Jer 31:16	7725
children will **r** to their own territory.	Jer 31:17	7725
R, O virgin of Israel, Return to	Jer 31:21	7725
of Israel, **R** to these your cities.	Jer 31:21	7725
to **r** to its own land of Egypt.	Jer 37:7	7725
The Chaldeans will also **r** and fight	Jer 37:8	7725
and do not make me **r** to the house	Jer 37:20	7725
not to make me **r** to the house of	Jer 38:26	7725
then to **r** to the land of Judah,	Jer 44:14	7725
they are longing to **r** and live;	Jer 44:14	7725
for none will **r** except *a few* refugees	Jer 44:14	7725
Those who escape the sword will **r**	Jer 44:28	7725
Jacob will **r** and be undisturbed	Jer 46:27	7725
Who does not **r** empty-handed.	Jer 50:9	7725
ways, And let us **r** to the LORD.	La 3:40	7725
will **r** to their former state,	Ezk 16:55	7725
will *also* **r** to your former state.	Ezk 16:55	7725
not **r** *to its sheath* again."	Ezk 21:5	7725
'**R** *it* to its sheath.	Ezk 21:30	7725
make them **r** to the land of Pathros,	Ezk 29:14	7725
No one shall **r** by way of the gate	Ezk 46:9	7725
then it shall **r** to the prince.	Ezk 46:17	7725
But I shall now **r** to fight against	Da 10:20	7725
South, but will **r** to his *own* land.	Da 11:9	7725
r to his land with much plunder;	Da 11:28	7725
action and *then* **r** to his *own* land.	Da 11:28	7725
he will **r** and come into the South,	Da 11:29	7725
and will **r** and become enraged at	Da 11:30	7725
Afterward the sons of Israel will **r**	Hos 3:5	7725
not allow them To **r** to their God.	Hos 5:4	7725
I will go away *and* **r** to My place	Hos 5:15	7725
"Come, let us **r** to the LORD.	Hos 6:1	7725
They will **r** to Egypt.	Hos 8:13	7725
land, But Ephraim will **r** to Egypt,	Hos 9:3	7725
will not **r** to the land of Egypt;	Hos 11:5	7725
Because they refused to **r** *to Me.*	Hos 11:5	7725
Therefore, **r** to your God, Observe	Hos 12:6	7725
R, O Israel, to the LORD your God,	Hos 14:1	7725
words with you and **r** to the LORD.	Hos 14:2	7725
"**R** to Me with all your heart, And	Jl 2:12	7725
Now **r** to the LORD your God,	Jl 2:13	7725
r your recompense on your head.	Jl 3:4	7725
r your recompense on your head.	Jl 3:7	7725
dealings will **r** on your own head.	Ob 1:15	7725
men rowed *desperately* to **r** to land	Jon 1:13	7725
earnings of a harlot they will **r**.	Mi 1:7	7725
Will **r** to the sons of Israel.	Mi 5:3	7725
will have in **r** for their pride,	Zph 2:10	8478
says the LORD of hosts, "**R** to Me,"	Zch 1:3	7725
"that I may **r** to you,"	Zch 1:3	7725
"**R** now from your evil ways and	Zch 1:4	7725
r to Jerusalem with compassion;	Zch 1:16	7725
'I will **r** to Zion and will dwell	Zch 8:3	7725
R to the stronghold, O prisoners	Zch 9:12	7725
will **r** and build up the ruins";	Mal 1:4	7725
R to Me, and I will return to you,"	Mal 3:7	7725
to Me, and I will **r** to you,"	Mal 3:7	7725
"But you say, 'How shall we **r**?'	Mal 3:7	7725
God in a dream not to **r** to Herod,	Mt 2:12	*344*
'I will **r** to my house from which I	Mt 12:44	*1994*
UNDERSTAND WITH THEIR HEART AND **R**,	Mt 13:15	*1994*
THEY MIGHT **R** AND BE FORGIVEN."	Mk 4:12	*1994*
and lend, expecting nothing in **r**;	Lk 6:35	*560*
it will be measured to you in **r**."	Lk 6:38	*488*
"**R** to your house and describe	Lk 8:39	*5290*
but if not, it will **r** to you.	Lk 10:6	*344*
whatever more you spend, when I **r** I	Lk 10:35	*1880*
r to my house from which I came.'	Lk 11:24	*5290*
otherwise they may also invite you in **r**	Lk 14:12	*479*

a kingdom for himself, and *then* **r**.	Lk 19:12	*5290*
what had happened, *began* to **r**,	Lk 23:48	*5290*
"Therefore repent and **r**,	Ac 3:19	*1994*
the dead, no longer to **r** to decay,	Ac 13:34	*5290*
'AFTER THESE THINGS I will **r**,	Ac 15:16	*390*
"Let us **r** and visit the brethren	Ac 15:36	*1994*
r to you again if God wills,"	Ac 18:21	*344*
decided to **r** through Macedonia.	Ac 20:3	*5290*
UNDERSTAND WITH THEIR HEART AND **R**,	Ac 28:27	*1994*
in **r** for all the joy with which we	1Th 3:9	*467*
to make some **r** to their parents;	1Tm 5:4	*591*
would have had opportunity to **r**.	Heb 11:15	*344*
being reviled, He did not revile in **r**;	1Pe 2:23	*486*

RETURNED

so she **r** to him into the ark,	Gn 8:9	7725
and Abraham **r** to his place.	Gn 18:33	7725
arose and **r** to the land of the	Gn 21:32	7725
So Abraham **r** to his young men, and	Gn 22:19	7725
Laban departed and **r** to his place.	Gn 31:55	7725
The messengers **r** to Jacob,	Gn 32:6	7725
Esau **r** that day on his way to Seir.	Gn 33:16	7725
Now Reuben **r** to the pit, and	Gn 37:29	7725
He **r** to his brothers and said,	Gn 37:30	7725
So he **r** to Judah, and said,	Gn 38:22	7725
he **r** to them and spoke to them,	Gn 42:24	7725
"My money has been **r**,	Gn 42:28	7725
by now we could have **r** twice."	Gn 43:10	7725
was **r** in the mouth of your sacks;	Gn 43:12	7725
the money that was **r** in our sacks	Gn 43:18	7725
his donkey, they **r** to the city.	Gn 44:13	7725
his father, Joseph **r** to Egypt,	Gn 50:14	7725
and **r** to Jethro his father-in-law and	Ex 4:18	7725
and **r** to the land of Egypt.	Ex 4:20	7725
Then Moses **r** to the LORD and said,	Ex 5:22	7725
and the sea **r** to its normal state	Ex 14:27	7725
The waters **r** and covered the	Ex 14:28	7725
Then Moses **r** to the LORD, and	Ex 32:31	7725
When Moses **r** to the camp, his	Ex 33:11	7725
rulers in the congregation **r** to him;	Ex 34:31	7725
Then Moses **r** to the camp, *both* he	Nu 11:30	622
they **r** from spying out the land,	Nu 13:25	7725
who **r** and made all the congregation	Nu 14:36	7725
Then Aaron **r** to Moses at the	Nu 16:50	7725
So he **r** to him, and behold, he was	Nu 23:6	7725
and departed and **r** to his place,	Nu 24:25	7725
you **r** and wept before the LORD;	Dt 1:45	7725
three days until the pursuers **r**.	Jos 2:22	7725
Then the two men **r** and came down	Jos 2:23	7725
waters of the Jordan **r** to their place,	Jos 4:18	7725
the city once and **r** to the camp;	Jos 6:14	7725
They **r** to Joshua and said to him,	Jos 7:3	7725
then all Israel **r** to Ai and struck	Jos 8:24	7725
all Israel with him **r** to the camp	Jos 10:15	7725
that all the people **r** to the camp	Jos 10:21	7725
all Israel with him **r** to Debir,	Jos 10:38	7725
with him **r** to the camp at Gilgal.	Jos 10:43	7725
the half-tribe of Manasseh **r** *home*	Jos 22:9	7725
Eleazar the priest and the leaders **r**	Jos 22:32	7725
So 22,000 people **r**, but 10,000	Jg 7:3	7725
He **r** to the camp of Israel and	Jg 7:15	7725
Then Gideon the son of Joash **r**	Jg 8:13	7725
Also God **r** all the wickedness of	Jg 9:57	7725
this reason we have now **r** to you,	Jg 11:8	7725
months she **r** to her father,	Jg 11:39	7725
When he **r** later to take her, he	Jg 14:8	7725
his strength **r** and he revived.	Jg 15:19	7725
He then **r** the eleven hundred	Jg 17:3	7725
he **r** the silver to his mother,	Jg 17:4	7725
Benjamin **r** at that time, and	Jg 21:14	7725
went and **r** to their inheritance and	Jg 21:23	7725
So Naomi **r**, and with her Ruth the	Ru 1:22	7725
who **r** from the land of Moab.	Ru 1:22	7725
Moabite woman who **r** with Naomi	Ru 2:6	7725
r again to their house in Ramah.	1Sa 1:19	7725, 935
saw it, they **r** to Ekron that day.	1Sa 6:16	7725
golden tumors which the Philistines **r**	1Sa 6:17	7725
The sons of Israel **r** from	1Sa 17:53	7725
David **r** from killing the Philistine,	1Sa 17:57	7725
David **r** from killing the Philistine,	1Sa 18:6	7725
So Saul **r** from pursuing David and	1Sa 23:28	7725
Saul **r** from pursuing the Philistines,	1Sa 24:1	7725
and he has **r** me evil for good.	1Sa 25:21	7725
The LORD has also **r** the evildoing	1Sa 25:39	7725
his way, and Saul **r** to his place.	1Sa 26:25	7725
Then he **r** and came to Achish.	1Sa 27:9	7725
when David had **r** from the	2Sa 1:1	7725
Then Joab **r** from following Abner;	2Sa 2:30	7725
said to him, "Go, return." So he **r**.	2Sa 3:16	7725
So when Abner **r** to Hebron, Joab	2Sa 3:27	7725
David **r** to bless his household,	2Sa 6:20	7725
he **r** from killing 18,000 Arameans	2Sa 8:13	7725
Then Joab **r** from *fighting* against	2Sa 10:14	7725
uncleanness, she **r** to her house.	2Sa 11:4	7725
and all the people **r** *to* Jerusalem.	2Sa 12:31	7725
Therefore Zadok and Abiathar **r** the	2Sa 15:29	7725
"The LORD has **r** upon you all the	2Sa 16:8	7725
find *them,* they **r** to Jerusalem.	2Sa 17:20	7725
the people **r** from pursuing Israel,	2Sa 18:16	7725
r and came as far as the Jordan.	2Sa 19:15	7725
him, and he **r** to his place.	2Sa 19:39	7725
Joab also **r** to the king at Jerusalem.	2Sa 20:22	7725
and the people **r** after him only to	2Sa 23:10	7725
from Jerusalem to Gath, and had **r**.	1Ki 2:41	7725
Israel heard that Jeroboam had **r**,	1Ki 12:20	7725
and **r** and went *their way* according	1Ki 12:24	7725
but have **r** and eaten bread and	1Ki 13:22	7725
the child **r** to him and he revived.	1Ki 17:22	7725
So he **r** from following him, and	1Ki 19:21	7725

Then the messengers **r** and said, **1Ki 20:5** 7725
When the messengers **r** to him **2Ki 1:5** 7725
"Why have you **r**?" **2Ki 1:5** 7725
and **r** and stood by the bank of the **2Ki 2:13** 7725
They **r** to him while he was **2Ki 2:18** 7725
and from there he **r** to Samaria. **2Ki 2:25** 7725
from him and **r** to their own land. **2Ki 3:27** 7725
So he **r** to meet him and told him, **2Ki 4:31** 7725
Then he **r** and walked in the house **2Ki 4:35** 7725
When Elisha **r** to Gilgal, *there was* **2Ki 4:38** 7725
When he **r** to the man of God with **2Ki 5:15** 7725
and they **r** and entered another **2Ki 7:8** 7725
messengers **r** and told the king. **2Ki 7:15** 7725
the woman **r** from the land of **2Ki 8:3** 7725
from Elisha and **r** to his master, **2Ki 8:14** 935
So King Joram **r** to be healed in **2Ki 8:29** 7725
but King Joram had **r** to Jezreel to **2Ki 9:15** 7725
Therefore they **r** and told him. **2Ki 9:36** 7725
hostages also, and **r** to Samaria. **2Ki 14:14** 7725
So the king of Assyria **r** and did **2Ki 15:20** 7725
Then Rabshakeh **r** and found the **2Ki 19:8** 7725
of Assyria departed and **r** *home,* **2Ki 19:36** 7725
then he **r** to Jerusalem. **2Ki 23:20** 7725
David **r** to bless his household. **1Ch 16:43** 5437
and all the people **r** *to* Jerusalem. **1Ch 20:3** 7725
Jeroboam **r** from Egypt. **2Ch 10:2** 7725
and **r** from going against Jeroboam. **2Ch 11:4** 7725
Then they **r** to Jerusalem. **2Ch 14:15** 7725
Jehoshaphat the king of Judah **r** **2Ch 19:1** 7725
Every man of Judah and Jerusalem **r** **2Ch 20:27** 7725
So he **r** to be healed in Jezreel of **2Ch 22:6** 7725
and they **r** home in fierce anger. **2Ch 25:10** 7725
hostages also, and **r** to Samaria. **2Ch 25:24** 7725
then they **r** to Samaria. **2Ch 28:15** 7725
sons of Israel **r** to their cities, **2Ch 31:1** 7725
So he **r** in shame to his own land. **2Ch 32:21** 7725
Then he **r** to Jerusalem. **2Ch 34:7** 7725
and **r** to Jerusalem and Judah, **Ezr 2:1** 7725
written reply be **r** concerning it. **Ezr 5:5** 8421
be **r** and brought to their places **Ezr 6:5** 8421
The sons of Israel who **r** from exile **Ezr 6:21** 7725
entered the Valley Gate again and **r**. **Ne 2:15** 7725
then all of us **r** to the wall, **Ne 4:15** 7725
and who **r** to Jerusalem and Judah, **Ne 7:6** 7725
those who had **r** from the captivity **Ne 8:17** 7725
and I **r** there the utensils of the **Ne 13:9** 7725
Then Mordecai **r** to the king's gate. **Es 6:12** 7725
Now when the king **r** from the **Es 7:8** 7725
And **r** and searched diligently for **Ps 78:34** 7725
Then Rabshakeh **r** and found the **Is 37:8** 7725
of Assyria departed and **r** *home* **Is 37:37** 7725
have **r** with their vessels empty; **Jer 14:3** 7725
Then all the Jews **r** from all the **Jer 40:12** 7725
entire remnant of Judah who had **r** **Jer 43:5** 7725
Now when I had **r**, behold, on the **Ezk 47:7** 7725
heaven and my reason **r** to me, **Da 4:34** 8421
"At that time my reason **r** to me. **Da 4:36** 8421
not **r** to the LORD their God, **Hos 7:10** 7725
Yet you have not **r** to Me," **Am 4:6** 7725
Yet you have not **r** to Me," **Am 4:8** 7725
Yet you have not **r** to Me," **Am 4:9** 7725
Yet you have not **r** to Me," **Am 4:10** 7725
Yet you have not **r** to Me," **Am 4:11** 7725
passers-by, *From* those **r** from war. **Mi 2:8** 7725
angel who was speaking with me **r** and **Zch 4:1** 7725
he felt remorse and **r** the thirty **Mt 27:3** *4762*
months, and *then* **r** to her home. **Lk 1:56** *5290*
of the Lord, they **r** to Galilee, **Lk 2:39** *1994*
find Him, they **r** to Jerusalem looking **Lk 2:45** *5290*
Jesus, full of the Holy Spirit, **r** from **Lk 4:1** *5290*
And Jesus **r** to Galilee in the **Lk 4:14** *5290*
who had been sent **r** to the house, **Lk 7:10** *5290*
and He got into a boat and **r**. **Lk 8:37** *5290*
And as Jesus **r**, the people **Lk 8:40** *5290*
And her spirit **r**, and she got **Lk 8:55** *1994*
When the apostles **r**, **Lk 9:10** *5290*
The seventy **r** with joy, **Lk 10:17** *5290*
"Was no one found who **r** to give **Lk 17:18** *5290*
he **r**, after receiving the kingdom, **Lk 19:15** *1880*
Then they **r** and prepared spices and **Lk 23:56** *5290*
and **r** from the tomb and reported **Lk 24:9** *5290*
that very hour and **r** to Jerusalem, **Lk 24:33** *5290*
r to Jerusalem with great joy, **Lk 24:52** *5290*
Then they **r** to Jerusalem from the **Ac 1:12** *5290*
and they **r** and reported back, **Ac 5:22** *390*
And Barnabas and Saul **r** from **Ac 12:25** *5290*
John left them and **r** to Jerusalem. **Ac 13:13** *5290*
they **r** to Lystra and to Iconium **Ac 14:21** *5290*
the ship, and they **r** home again. **Ac 21:6** *5290*
I **r** to Jerusalem and was praying **Ac 22:17** *5290*
with him, they **r** to the barracks. **Ac 23:32** *5290*
and **r** once more to Damascus. **Ga 1:17** *5290*
but now you have **r** to the Shepherd **1Pe 2:25** *1994*

RETURNING
head, **r** to Jerusalem with joy, **2Ch 20:27** 7725
And my prayer kept **r** to my bosom. **Ps 35:13** 7725
Now in the morning, when He was **r** to **Mt 21:18** *1877*
and as they were **r**, **Lk 2:43** *5290*
was **r** and sitting in his chariot, **Ac 8:28** *5290*
who met Abraham as he was **r** from **Heb 7:1** *5290*
not **r** evil for evil or insult for **1Pe 3:9** *591*

RETURNS
no child and **r** to her father's house **Lv 22:13** 7725
me until Your wrath **r** *to You,* **Jb 14:13** 7725
"He **r** what he has attained And **Jb 20:18** 7725
spirit departs, he **r** to the earth; **Ps 146:4** 7725
He who **r** evil for good, Evil will **Pr 17:13** 7725
Like a dog that **r** to its vomit Is **Pr 26:11** 7725
its circular courses the wind **r**. **Ec 1:6** 7725
the one who passes through and **r**. **Ezk 35:7** 7725
Because of him who passes by and **r** **Zch 9:8** 7725
when he **r** from the wedding feast, **Lk 12:36** *360*
a day, and **r** to you seven times, **Lk 17:4** *1994*
"A DOG **R** TO ITS OWN VOMIT," **2Pe 2:22** *1994*
r to wallowing in the mire." **2Pe 2:22**

REU
years, and became the father of **R**; **Gn 11:18** 7466a
after he became the father of **R**, **Gn 11:19** 7466a
R lived thirty-two years, and **Gn 11:20** 7466a
and **R** lived two hundred and seven **Gn 11:21** 7466a
Eber, Peleg, **R**, **1Ch 1:25** 7466a
the son of Serug, the son of **R**, **Lk 3:35** *4466*

REUBEN
and bore a son and named him **R**, **Gn 29:32** 7205
R went and found mandrakes **Gn 30:14** 7205
that **R** went and lay with Bilhah **Gn 35:22** 7205
R, Jacob's firstborn, then Simeon **Gn 35:23** 7205
But **R** heard *this* and rescued him **Gn 37:21** 7205
R further said to them, **Gn 37:22** 7205
Now **R** returned to the pit, and **Gn 37:29** 7205
R answered them, saying, **Gn 42:22** 7205
Then **R** spoke to his father, **Gn 42:37** 7205
R, Jacob's firstborn. **Gn 46:8** 7205
The sons of **R**: **Gn 46:9** 7205
be mine, as **R** and Simeon are. **Gn 48:5** 7205
"**R**, you are my firstborn; **Gn 49:3** 7205
R, Simeon, Levi and Judah; **Ex 1:2** 7205
The sons of **R**, Israel's firstborn: **Ex 6:14** 7205
these are the families of **R**. **Ex 6:14** 7205
of **R**, Elizur the son of Shedeur; **Nu 1:5** 7205
Now the sons of **R**, Israel's **Nu 1:20** 7205
numbered men of the tribe of **R** **Nu 1:21** 7205
of the camp of **R** by their armies, **Nu 2:10** 7205
and the leader of the sons of **R**: **Nu 2:10** 7205
the numbered men of the camp of **R**: **Nu 2:16** 7205
Shedeur, leader of the sons of **R**; **Nu 7:30** 7205
the standard of the camp of **R**, **Nu 10:18** 7205
from the tribe of **R**, **Nu 13:4** 7205
On the son of Peleth, sons of **R**, **Nu 16:1** 7205
R, Israel's firstborn, the sons **Nu 26:5** 7205
Israel's firstborn, the sons of **R**: **Nu 26:5** 7205
Now the sons of **R** and the sons of **Nu 32:1** 7205
the sons of Gad and the sons of **R** **Nu 32:2** 7205
sons of Gad and to the sons of **R**, **Nu 32:6** 7205
and the sons of **R** spoke to Moses, **Nu 32:25** 7205
the sons of Gad and the sons of **R**, **Nu 32:29** 7205
of Gad and the sons of **R** answered, **Nu 32:31** 7205
the sons of Gad and to the sons of **R** **Nu 32:33** 7205
The sons of **R** built Heshbon **Nu 32:37** 7205
"For the tribe of the sons of **R** **Nu 34:14** 7206
the sons of Eliab, the son of **R**, **Dt 11:6** 7205
R, Gad, Asher, Zebulun, Dan, and **Dt 27:13** 7205
"May **R** live and not die, Nor his **Dt 33:6** 7205
The sons of **R** and the sons of **Jos 4:12** 7205
to the tribe of the sons of **R** **Jos 13:15** 7205
of the sons of **R** was the Jordan. **Jos 13:23** 7205
was the inheritance of the sons of **R** **Jos 13:23** 7205
the stone of Bohan the son of **R**. **Jos 15:6** 7205
Gad and **R** and the half-tribe of **Jos 18:7** 7205
the stone of Bohan the son of **R**. **Jos 18:17** 7205
on the plain from the tribe of **R**, **Jos 20:8** 7205
twelve cities from the tribe of **R** **Jos 21:7** 7205
From the tribe of **R**, **Jos 21:36** 7205
The sons of **R** and the sons of **Jos 22:9** 7205
the sons of **R** and the sons of Gad **Jos 22:10** 7205
the sons of **R** and the sons of Gad **Jos 22:11** 7205
sons of Israel sent to the sons of **R** **Jos 22:13** 7205
They came to the sons of **R** and **Jos 22:15** 7205
Then the sons of **R** and the sons of **Jos 22:21** 7205
you sons of **R** and sons of Gad; **Jos 22:25** 7205
heard the words which the sons of **R** **Jos 22:30** 7205
the priest said to the sons of **R** **Jos 22:31** 7205
leaders returned from the sons of **R** **Jos 22:32** 7205
the land in which the sons of **R** **Jos 22:33** 7205
The sons of **R** and the sons of **Jos 22:34** 7205
Among the divisions of **R** *There* **Jg 5:15** 7205
Among the divisions of **R** *There* **Jg 5:16** 7205
R, Simeon, Levi, Judah, Issachar, **1Ch 2:1** 7205
sons of **R** the firstborn of Israel **1Ch 5:1** 7205
the sons of **R** the firstborn of **1Ch 5:3** 7205
The sons of **R** and the Gadites and **1Ch 5:18** 7205
families, from the tribe of **R**, **1Ch 6:63** 7205
given them, from the tribe of **R**: **1Ch 6:78** 7205
the east side to the west side, **R**, **Ezk 48:6** 7205
"Beside the border of **R**, **Ezk 48:7** 7205
the gate of **R**, one; **Ezk 48:31** 7205
the tribe of **R** twelve thousand, **Rv 7:5** *4502*

REUBENITE
Adina the son of Shiza the **R**, **1Ch 11:42** 7206

REUBENITES
These are the families of the **R**, **Nu 26:7** 7206
gave to the **R** and to the Gadites. **Dt 3:12** 7206
"To the **R** and to the Gadites I **Dt 3:16** 7206
on the plateau for the **R**, **Dt 4:43** 7206
it as an inheritance to the **R**, **Dt 29:8** 7206
To the **R** and to the Gadites **Jos 1:12** 7206
gave it to the **R** and the Gadites and **Jos 12:6** 7206
the **R** and the Gadites received **Jos 13:8** 7206
Then Joshua summoned the **R** **Jos 22:1** 7206
and the **R** and the Manassites, **2Ki 10:33** 7206
he was leader of the **R**. **1Ch 5:6** 7206
away into exile, namely the **R**, **1Ch 5:26** 7206
the Reubenite, a chief of the **R**, **1Ch 11:42** 7206
of the **R** and the Gadites and of **1Ch 12:37** 7206
made them overseers of the **R**, **1Ch 26:32** 7206
chief officer for the **R** was Eliezer **1Ch 27:16** 7206

REUEL
to Esau, and Basemath bore **R**, **Gn 36:4** 7467
R the son of Esau's wife Basemath. **Gn 36:10** 7467
These are the sons of **R**: **Gn 36:13** 7467
These are the sons of **R**, **Gn 36:17** 7467
from **R** in the land of Edom; **Gn 36:17** 7467
When they came to **R** their father, **Ex 2:18** 7467
Hobab the son of **R** the Midianite, **Nu 10:29** 7467
The sons of Esau *were* Eliphaz, **R**, **1Ch 1:35** 7467
The sons of **R** *were* Nahath, Zerah, **1Ch 1:37** 7467
son of Shephatiah, the son of **R**, **1Ch 9:8** 7467

REUMAH
His concubine, whose name was **R**, **Gn 22:24** 7208

REVEAL
'Did I *not* indeed **r** Myself to the **1Sa 2:27** 1540
the men and **r** ourselves to them. **1Sa 14:8** 1540
fleeing and did not **r** it to me." **1Sa 22:17** 1540, 241
"The heavens will **r** his iniquity, **Jb 20:27** 1540
And the opening of my lips *will* **r** **Pr 8:6**
do not **r** the secret of another, **Pr 25:9** 1540
the earth will **r** her bloodshed And **Is 26:21** 1540
and I will **r** to them an abundance **Jer 33:6** 1540
been able to **r** this mystery." **Da 2:47** 1541
to whom the Son wills to **r** *Him.* **Mt 11:27** *601*
and blood did not **r** *this* to you, **Mt 16:17** *601*
to whom the Son wills to **r** *Him.*" **Lk 10:22** *601*
to **r** His Son in me so that I might **Ga 1:16** *601*
God will **r** that also to you; **Php 3:15** *601*

REVEALED
there God had **r** Himself to him when **Gn 35:7** 1540
but the things **r** belong to us and **Dt 29:29** 1540
word of the LORD yet been **r** to him. **1Sa 3:7** 1540
because the LORD **r** Himself to **1Sa 3:21** 1540
LORD had **r** *this* to Samuel saying, **1Sa 9:15** 1540, 241
When both of them **r** themselves **1Sa 14:11** 1540
have **r** to Your servant that You **1Ch 17:25** 1540, 241
the gates of death been **r** to you, **Jb 38:17** 1540
He has **r** His righteousness in the **Ps 98:2** 1540
His wickedness will be **r** before the **Pr 26:26** 1540
the LORD of hosts **r** Himself to me, **Is 22:14** 1540
the glory of the LORD will be **r**, **Is 40:5** 1540
has the arm of the LORD been **r**? **Is 53:1** 1540
come And My righteousness to be **r**. **Is 56:1** 1540
was **r** to Daniel in a night vision. **Da 2:19** 1541
this mystery has not been **r** to me **Da 2:30** 1541
the number of the years which was **r** **Da 9:2**
Persia a message was **r** to Daniel, **Da 10:1** 1540
concealed that will not be **r**, **Mt 10:26** *601*
the wise and intelligent and have **r** **Mt 11:25** *601*
nothing is hidden, except to be **r**; **Mk 4:22** *5319*
And it had been **r** to him by the **Lk 2:26** *5537*
from many hearts may be **r**." **Lk 2:35** *601*
the wise and intelligent and have **r** **Lk 10:21** *601*
covered up that will not be **r**, **Lk 12:2** *601*
the day that the Son of Man is **r**. **Lk 17:30** *601*
HAS THE ARM OF THE LORD BEEN **R**?" **Jn 12:38** *601*
in it *the* righteousness of God is **r** **Ro 1:17** *601*
For the wrath of God is **r** from **Ro 1:18** *601*
the glory that is to be **r** to us. **Ro 8:18** *601*
us God **r** *them* through the Spirit; **1Co 2:10** *601*
because it is *to be* **r** with fire, **1Co 3:13** *601*
the faith which was later to be **r**. **Ga 3:23** *601*
as it has now been **r** to His holy **Eph 3:5** *601*
Christ, who is our life, is **r**, **Col 3:4** *5319*
you also will be **r** with Him in glory. **Col 3:4** *5319*
Lord Jesus will be **r** from heaven **2Th 1:7** *602*
and the man of lawlessness is **r**, **2Th 2:3** *601*
so that in his time he will be **r**. **2Th 2:6** *601*
one will be **r** whom the Lord will slay **2Th 2:8** *601*
He who was **r** in the flesh, Was **1Tm 3:16** *5319*
but now has been **r** by the **2Tm 1:10** *5319*
ready to be **r** in the last time. **1Pe 1:5** *601*
It was **r** to them that they were **1Pe 1:12** *601*
also of the glory that is to be **r**, **1Pe 5:1** *601*
of your nakedness will not be **r**; **Rv 3:18** *5319*
YOUR RIGHTEOUS ACTS HAVE BEEN **R**." **Rv 15:4** *5319*

REVEALER
of kings and a **r** of mysteries, **Da 2:47** 1541

REVEALING
But only in **r** his own mind. **Pr 18:2** 1540
for the **r** of the sons of God. **Ro 8:19** *602*

REVEALS
"He **r** mysteries from the **Jb 12:22** 1540
And night to night **r** knowledge. **Ps 19:2** 2331a
about as a talebearer **r** secrets, **Pr 11:13** 1540
about as a slanderer **r** secrets, **Pr 20:19** 1540
"It is He who **r** the profound and **Da 2:22** 1541
a God in heaven who **r** mysteries, **Da 2:28** 1541
and He who **r** mysteries has made **Da 2:29** 1541
Unless He **r** His secret counsel **Am 3:7** 1540

REVEL
it a pleasure to **r** in the daytime. **2Pe 2:13** *5172*

REVELATION
have made a **r** to Your servant, **2Sa 7:27** 1540, 241
"At this point the **r** ended. **Da 7:28** 4406
A LIGHT OF **R** TO THE GENTILES, And **Lk 2:32** *602*
r of the righteous judgment of God, **Ro 2:5** *602*
according to the **r** of the mystery **Ro 16:25** *602*
the **r** of our Lord Jesus Christ, **1Co 1:7** *602*
I speak to you either by way of **r** or **1Co 14:6** *602*
a psalm, has a teaching, has a **r**, **1Co 14:26** *602*
But if a **r** is made to another who **1Co 14:30** *601*
it through a **r** of Jesus Christ. **Ga 1:12** *602*

was because of a **r** that I went up; **Ga 2:2** *602*
and of **r** in the knowledge of Him. **Eph 1:17** *602*
that by **r** there was made known to **Eph 3:3** *602*
honor at the **r** of Jesus Christ; **1Pe 1:7** *602*
to you at the **r** of Jesus Christ. **1Pe 1:13** *602*
that also at the **r** of His glory you **1Pe 4:13** *602*
The **R** of Jesus Christ, which God **Rv 1:1** *602*

REVELATIONS
go on to visions and **r** of the Lord. **2Co 12:1** *602*
the surpassing greatness of the **r**, **2Co 12:7** *602*

REVELED
fat, And **r** in Your great goodness. **Ne 9:25** 5727

REVELERS
ceases, The noise of **r** stops, **Is 24:8** 5947
And the scalps of the riotous **r**. **Jer 48:45** 1121, 7588

REVELING
blemishes, **r** in their deceptions, **2Pe 2:13** *1792*

REVELRY
her din *of* **r** and the jubilant **Is 5:14**

REVENGE
this, I will surely take **r** on you, **Jg 15:7** 5358
him And take our **r** on him." **Jer 20:10** 5360
the Philistines have acted in **r** **Ezk 25:15** 5360
Never take your own **r**, **Ro 12:19** *1556*

REVENGEFUL
To make the enemy and the **r** cease. **Ps 8:2** 5358

REVENUE
it will damage the **r** of the kings. **Ezr 4:13** 674
But much **r** *comes* by the strength **Pr 14:4** 8393
harvest of the River was her **r**; **Is 23:3** 8393

REVERE
blind, but you shall **r** your God; **Lv 19:14** 3372a
My sabbaths and **r** My sanctuary; **Lv 19:30** 3372a
aged, and you shall **r** your God; **Lv 19:32** 3372a
interest from him, but **r** your God, **Lv 25:36** 3372a
severity, but are to **r** your God. **Lv 25:43** 3372a
who delight to **r** Your name, **Ne 1:11** 3372a
You who **r** the LORD, bless the LORD. **Ps 135:20** 3372a
Cities of ruthless nations will **r** You. **Is 25:3** 3372a
no king, For we do not **r** the LORD. **Hos 10:3** 3372a
'Surely you will **r** Me, Accept **Zph 3:7** 3372a

REVERED
so that they **r** him, just as they **Jos 4:14** 3372a
just as they had **r** Moses all the **Jos 4:14** 3372a
so he **r** Me and stood in awe of My **Mal 2:5** 3372a

REVERENCE
shall **r** his mother and his father, **Lv 19:3** 3372a
My sabbaths and **r** My sanctuary; **Lv 26:2** 3372a
"Indeed, you do away with **r** And **Jb 15:4** 3374
of your **r** that He reproves you, **Jb 22:4** 3374
Worship the LORD with **r** And **Ps 2:11** 3374
temple I will bow in **r** for You. **Ps 5:7** 3374
As that which produces **r** for You. **Ps 119:38** 3374
And their **r** for Me consists of **Is 29:13** 3372a
the people showed **r** for the LORD. **Hg 1:12** 3372a
I gave them to him *as an object of* **r**; **Mal 2:5** 4172
in **r** prepared an ark for the **Heb 11:7** *2125*
acceptable service with **r** and awe; **Heb 12:28** *2124*
in you, yet with gentleness and **r**; **1Pe 3:15** *5401*

REVERENT
Older women likewise are to be **r** **Ti 2:3** *2412*

REVERSE
I act and who can **r** it?" **Is 43:13** 7725

REVERT
but at the jubilee it shall **r**, **Lv 25:28** 3318
it does not **r** in the jubilee. **Lv 25:30** 3318
rights and **r** in the jubilee. **Lv 25:31** 3318

REVERTS
this possession **r** in the jubilee, **Lv 25:33** 3318
and when it **r** in the jubilee, the **Lv 27:21** 3318

REVILE
of my bones, my adversaries **r** me, **Ps 42:10** 2778a
long, O God, will the adversary **r**, **Ps 74:10** 2778a
"Do you **r** God's high priest?" **Ac 23:4** *3058*
reviled, He did not **r** in return; **1Pe 2:23** *486*
those who **r** your good behavior in **1Pe 3:16** *1908*
when they **r** angelic majesties, **2Pe 2:10** *987*
and **r** angelic majesties. **Jude 1:8** *987*
But these men **r** the things which **Jude 1:10** *987*

REVILED
O LORD, that the enemy has **r**, **Ps 74:18** 2778a
They **r** him and said, **Jn 9:28** *3058*
when we are **r**, we bless; **1Co 4:12** *3058*
and while being **r**, He did not revile **1Pe 2:23** *3058*
you are **r** for the name of Christ, **1Pe 4:14** *3679*

REVILEMENT
Jacob to the ban and Israel to **r**. **Is 43:28** 1421

REVILER
covetous, or an idolater, or a **r**, **1Co 5:11** *3060*

REVILERS
covetous, nor drunkards, nor **r**, **1Co 6:10** *3060*
of money, boastful, arrogant, **r**, **2Tm 3:2** *989*

REVILES
voice of him who reproaches and **r**, **Ps 44:16** 1442

REVILING
'So it will be a reproach, a **r**, **Ezk 5:15** 1422
not bring a **r** judgment against them **2Pe 2:11** *989*
r where they have no knowledge, **2Pe 2:12** *987*

REVILINGS
Nor be dismayed at their **r**. **Is 51:7** 1421
have heard all your **r** which you **Ezk 35:12** 5007b
And the **r** of the sons of Ammon, **Zph 2:8** 1421

REVIVE
Can they **r** the stones from the **Ne 4:2** 2421a
who seek God, let your heart **r**. **Ps 69:32** 2421a
and distresses Will **r** me again, **Ps 71:20** 2421a
R us, and we will call upon Your **Ps 80:18** 2421a
Will You not Yourself **r** us again, **Ps 85:6** 2421a
R me according to Your word. **Ps 119:25** 2421a
at vanity, And **r** me in Your ways. **Ps 119:37** 2421a
R me through Your righteousness. **Ps 119:40** 2421a
R me according to Your **Ps 119:88** 2421a
R me, O LORD, according to Your **Ps 119:107** 2421a
R me, O LORD, according to Your **Ps 119:149** 2421a
R me according to Your word. **Ps 119:154** 2421a
R me according to Your ordinances. **Ps 119:156** 2421a
R me, O LORD, according to Your **Ps 119:159** 2421a
midst of trouble, You will **r** me; **Ps 138:7** 2421a
sake of Your name, O LORD, **r** me. **Ps 143:11** 2421a
In order to **r** the spirit of the lowly **Is 57:15** 2421a
to **r** the heart of the contrite. **Is 57:15** 2421a
"He will **r** us after two days; **Hos 6:2** 2421a
r Your work in the midst of the **Hab 3:2** 2421a

REVIVED
spirit of their father Jacob **r**. **Gn 45:27** 2421a
his strength returned and he **r**. **Jg 15:19** 2421a
then his spirit **r**. **1Sa 30:12** 7725
child returned to him and he **r**. **1Ki 17:22** 2421a
he **r** and stood up on his feet. **2Ki 13:21** 2421a
That Your word has **r** me. **Ps 119:50** 2421a
For by them You have **r** me. **Ps 119:93** 2421a
you have **r** your concern for me; **Php 4:10** *330*

REVIVING
grant us a little **r** in our bondage. **Ezr 9:8** 4241
to give us **r** to raise up the house **Ezr 9:9** 4241

REVOKE
has blessed, then I cannot **r** it. **Nu 23:20** 7725
to **r** the letters devised by Haman, **Es 8:5** 7725
for four I will not **r** its *punishment*, **Am 1:3** 7725
four I will not **r** its *punishment*, **Am 1:6** 7725
four I will not **r** its *punishment*, **Am 1:9** 7725
four I will not **r** its *punishment*, **Am 1:11** 7725
four I will not **r** its *punishment*, **Am 1:13** 7725
four I will not **r** its *punishment*, **Am 2:1** 7725
four I will not **r** its *punishment*, **Am 2:4** 7725
four I will not **r** its *punishment*, **Am 2:6** 7725

REVOKED
king's signet ring may not be **r**." **Es 8:8** 7725
Persians, which may not be **r**." **Da 6:8** 5709
Persians, which may not be **r**." **Da 6:12** 5709

REVOLT
incited **r** within it in past days; **Ezr 4:15** 849
and **r** have been perpetrated in it, **Ezr 4:19** 849
God, Speaking oppression and **r**, **Is 59:13** 5627
who some time ago stirred up a **r** **Ac 21:38** *387*

REVOLTED
r from under the hand of Judah, **2Ki 8:20** 6586
Edom **r** against Judah to this day. **2Ki 8:22** 6586
Then Libnah **r** at the same time. **2Ki 8:22** 6586
Edom **r** against the rule of Judah and **2Ch 21:8** 6586
Edom **r** against Judah to this day. **2Ch 21:10** 6586
Then Libnah **r** at the same time **2Ch 21:10** 6586
up, But they have **r** against Me. **Is 1:2** 6586

REVOLTERS
The **r** have gone deep in depravity, **Hos 5:2** 7846

REWARD
Your **r** shall be very great." **Gn 15:1** 7939
"May the LORD **r** your work, and **Ru 2:12** 7999a
May the LORD therefore **r** you with **1Sa 24:19** 7999a
was the **r** I gave him for *his* news. **2Sa 4:10** 1309
you will have no **r** for going?" **2Sa 18:22** 1309
king compensate me *with* this **r**? **2Sa 19:36** 1578
and I will give you a **r**." **1Ki 13:7** 4991
for there is **r** for your work." **2Ch 15:7** 7939
For emptiness will be his **r**. **Jb 15:31** 8545
In keeping them there is great **r**. **Ps 19:11** 6118
there is a **r** for the righteous; **Ps 58:11** 6529
r of my accusers from the LORD, **Ps 109:20** 6468
The fruit of the womb is a **r**. **Ps 127:3** 7939
sows righteousness *gets* a true **r**. **Pr 11:18** 7938
The **r** of humility *and* the fear of **Pr 22:4** 6118
his head, And the LORD will **r** you. **Pr 25:22** 7999a
this was my **r** for all my labor. **Ec 2:10** 2506
for this is his **r**. **Ec 5:18** 2506
his **r** and rejoice in his labor; **Ec 5:19** 2506
nor have they any longer a **r**, **Ec 9:5** 7939
for this is your **r** in life and **Ec 9:9** 2506
Behold, His **r** is with Him And His **Is 40:10** 7939
free, Without any payment or **r**," **Is 45:13** 7810
the LORD, And My **r** with My God." **Is 49:4** 6468
Behold His **r** is with Him, and His **Is 62:11** 7939
me gifts and a **r** and great honor; **Da 2:6** 5023
for your **r** in heaven is great; **Mt 5:12** *3408*
who love you, what **r** do you have? **Mt 5:46** *3408*
otherwise you have no **r** with your **Mt 6:1** *3408*
to you, they have their **r** in full. **Mt 6:2** *3408*
what is done in secret will **r** you. **Mt 6:4** *591*
to you, they have their **r** in full. **Mt 6:5** *3408*
what is done in secret will **r** you. **Mt 6:6** *591*
to you, they have their **r** in full. **Mt 6:16** *3408*
what is done in secret will **r** you. **Mt 6:18** *591*
shall receive a prophet's **r**; **Mt 10:41** *3408*
shall receive a righteous man's **r**. **Mt 10:41** *3408*
to you, he shall not lose his **r**." **Mt 10:42** *3408*
to you, he will not lose his **r**. **Mk 9:41** *3408*
behold, your **r** is great in heaven. **Lk 6:23** *3408*
and your **r** will be great, and you **Lk 6:35** *3408*
own **r** according to his own labor. **1Co 3:8** *3408*
it remains, he will receive a **r**. **1Co 3:14** *3408*
I do this voluntarily, I have a **r**; **1Co 9:17** *3408*
What then is my **r**? **1Co 9:18** *3408*
receive the **r** of the inheritance. **Col 3:24** *469*
confidence, which has a great **r**. **Heb 10:35** *3405*
for he was looking to the **r**. **Heb 11:26** *3405*
but that you may receive a full **r**. **2Jn 1:8** *3408*
to **r** Your bond-servants **Rv 11:18** *3408*
quickly, and My **r** *is* with Me, **Rv 22:12** *3408*

REWARDED
"The LORD has **r** me according to **2Sa 22:21** 1580
If I have **r** evil to my friend, Or **Ps 7:4** 1580
The LORD has **r** me according to my **Ps 18:20** 1580
Nor **r** us according to our iniquities. **Ps 103:10** 1580
righteous will be **r** in the earth, **Pr 11:31** 7999a
fears the commandment will be **r**. **Pr 13:13** 7999a
righteous will be **r** with prosperity. **Pr 13:21** 7999a
For your work will be **r**," **Jer 31:16** 7939

REWARDER
He is a **r** of those who seek Him. **Heb 11:6** *3406*

REWARDING
see *how* they are **r** us **2Ch 20:11** 1580

REWARDS
loves a bribe And chases after **r**. **Is 1:23** 8021
or give your **r** to someone else; **Da 5:17** 5023

REZEPH
even Gozan and Haran and **R** and the **2Ki 19:12** 7530
even Gozan and Haran and **R** and the **Is 37:12** 7530

REZIN
LORD began to send **R** king of Aram **2Ki 15:37** 7526
Then **R** king of Aram and Pekah son **2Ki 16:5** 7526
At that time **R** king of Aram **2Ki 16:6** 7526
exile to Kir, and put **R** to death. **2Ki 16:9** 7526
the sons of **R**, the sons of Nekoda, **Ezr 2:48** 7526
the sons of Reaiah, the sons of **R**, **Ne 7:50** 7526
that **R** the king of Aram and Pekah **Is 7:1** 7526
of the fierce anger of **R** and Aram and **Is 7:4** 7526
and the head of Damascus is **R** **Is 7:8** 7526
And rejoice in **R** and the son of **Is 8:6** 7526
against them adversaries from **R** And **Is 9:11** 7526

REZON
to him, **R** the son of Eliada, **1Ki 11:23** 7331

RHEGIUM
we sailed around and arrived at **R**, **Ac 28:13** *4484*

RHESA
the son of Joanan, the son of **R**, **Lk 3:27** *4488*

RHODA
a servant-girl named **R** came to **Ac 12:13** *4498*

RHODES
day to **R** and from there to Patara; **Ac 21:1** *4499*

RIB
God fashioned into a woman the **r** **Gn 2:22** 6763

RIBAI
Ittai the son of **R** of Gibeah of **2Sa 23:29** 7380
Ithai the son of **R** of Gibeah of **1Ch 11:31** 7380

RIBLAH
to **R** on the east side of Ain; **Nu 34:11** 7247
Pharaoh Neco imprisoned him at **R** **2Ki 23:33** 7247
him to the king of Babylon at **R**, **2Ki 25:6** 7247
them to the king of Babylon at **R**. **2Ki 25:20** 7247
death at **R** in the land of Hamath. **2Ki 25:21** 7247
at **R** in the land of Hamath, **Jer 39:5** 7247
of Zedekiah before his eyes at **R**; **Jer 39:6** 7247
at **R** in the land of Hamath, **Jer 52:9** 7247
all the princes of Judah in **R**. **Jer 52:10** 7247
them to the king of Babylon at **R**. **Jer 52:26** 7247
death at **R** in the land of Hamath. **Jer 52:27** 7247

RIBS
then He took one of his **r** and **Gn 2:21** 6763
and three **r** *were* in its mouth **Da 7:5** 5967

RICH
Now Abram was very **r** in livestock, **Gn 13:2** 3515
'I have made Abram **r**.' **Gn 14:23** 6238
master, so that he has become **r**; **Gn 24:35** 1431
and the man became **r**, **Gn 26:13** 1431
"As for Asher, his food shall be **r**, **Gn 49:20** 8082a
"The **r** shall not pay more and **Ex 30:15** 6223
You who sit on **r** carpets, **Jg 5:10**
young men, whether poor or **r**. **Ru 3:10** 6223
"The LORD makes poor and **r**; **1Sa 2:7** 6238
and the man was very **r**, **1Sa 25:2** 1419
the one **r** and the other poor. **2Sa 12:1** 6223
"The **r** man had a great many **2Sa 12:2** 6223
"Now a traveler came to the **r** man, **2Sa 12:4** 6223
They found **r** and good pasture, **1Ch 4:40** 8082a
With the broad and **r** land which **Ne 9:35** 8082a
"He will not become **r**, **Jb 15:29** 6238
"He lies down **r**, but never again; **Jb 27:19** 6223
Nor regards the **r** above the poor, **Jb 34:19** 7771a
The **r** among the people will **Ps 45:12** 6223
low and high, **R** and poor together. **Ps 49:2** 6223
be afraid when a man becomes **r**, **Ps 49:16** 6238
the hand of the diligent makes **r**. **Pr 10:4** 6238
The **r** man's wealth is his fortress, **Pr 10:15** 6223
blessing of the LORD that makes **r**, **Pr 10:22** 6238
There is one who pretends to be **r**, **Pr 13:7** 6238
But those who love the **r** are many. **Pr 14:20** 6223
A **r** man's wealth is his strong city, **Pr 18:11** 6223
But the **r** man answers roughly. **Pr 18:23** 6223
wine and oil will not become **r**. **Pr 21:17** 6238
The **r** and the poor have a common **Pr 22:2** 6223
The **r** rules over the poor, And the **Pr 22:7** 6223
for himself Or who gives to the **r**, **Pr 22:16** 6223
he who is crooked though he be **r**. **Pr 28:6** 6223
The **r** man is wise in his own eyes, **Pr 28:11** 6223
he who makes haste to be **r** will not **Pr 28:20** 6238
but the full stomach of the **r** man **Ec 5:12** 6223

while **r** men sit in humble places. Ec 10:6 6223
rooms do not curse a **r** man, Ec 10:20 6223
and it will be **r** and plenteous; Is 30:23 1879
He was with a **r** man in His death, Is 53:9 6223
they have become great and **r**. Jer 5:27 6238
not a **r** man boast of *his* riches; Jer 9:23 6223
and feed in **r** pasture on Ezk 34:14 8082a
"Surely I have become **r**, Hos 12:8 6238
"For the **r** men of *the* city are Mi 6:12 6223
And makes himself **r** with loans?' Hab 2:6 3513
be the LORD, for I have become **r**!' Zch 11:5 6238
it is hard for a **r** man to enter Mt 19:23 4145
than for a **r** man to enter the Mt 19:24 4145
there came a **r** man from Arimathea, Mt 27:57 4145
a **r** man to enter the kingdom of God Mk 10:25 4145
and many **r** people were putting in Mk 12:41 4145
And sent away the **r** empty-handed. Lk 1:53 4147
"But woe to you who are **r**, Lk 6:24 4145
a **r** man was very productive. Lk 12:16 4145
and is not **r** toward God." Lk 12:21 4147
or your relatives or **r** neighbors, Lk 14:12 4145
a **r** man who had a manager, Lk 16:1 4145
"Now there was a **r** man, Lk 16:19 4145
falling from the **r** man's table; Lk 16:21 4145
r man also died and was buried. Lk 16:22 4145
for he was extremely **r**. Lk 18:23 4145
than for a **r** man to enter the Lk 18:25 4145
a chief tax collector and he was **r**. Lk 19:2 4145
And He looked up and saw the **r** Lk 21:1 4145
of the **r** root of the olive tree, Ro 11:17 4096
filled, you have already become **r**, 1Co 4:8 4147
as poor yet making many **r**, 2Co 6:10 4148
Christ, that though He was **r**, 2Co 8:9 4145
His poverty might become **r**. 2Co 8:9 4147
But God, being **r** in mercy, because Eph 2:4 4145
But those who want to get **r** fall 1Tm 6:9 4147
Instruct those who are **r** in this 1Tm 6:17 4145
to do good, to be **r** in good works, 1Tm 6:18 4147
r man *is to glory* in his humiliation, Jas 1:10 4145
r man in the midst of his pursuits Jas 1:11 4145
the poor of this world *to be* **r** in faith Jas 2:5 4145
Is it not the **r** who oppress you Jas 2:6 4145
Come now, you **r**, weep and howl for Jas 5:1 4145
(but you are **r**), Rv 2:9 4145
"I am **r**, and have become wealthy, Rv 3:17 4145
by fire so that you may become **r**, Rv 3:18 4147
the **r** and the strong and every slave Rv 6:15 4145
the great, and the **r** and the poor, Rv 13:16 4145
merchants of the earth have become **r** Rv 18:3 4147
things, who became **r** from her, Rv 18:15 4147
at sea became **r** by her wealth, Rv 18:19 4147

RICHER
continued to grow **r** until he became Gn 26:13 1432
The **r** his land, The better he made Hos 10:1 2896b

RICHES
"Return to your tents with great **r** Jos 22:8 5233
the man who kills him with great **r** 1Sa 17:25 6239
nor have asked **r** for yourself, 1Ki 3:11 6239
have not asked, both **r** and honor, 1Ki 3:13 6239
of the earth in **r** and in wisdom. 1Ki 10:23 6239
"Both **r** and honor *come* from You, 1Ch 29:12 6239
age, full of days, **r** and honor; 1Ch 29:28 6239
in mind, and did not ask for **r**, 2Ch 1:11 6239
give you **r** and wealth and honor, 2Ch 1:12 6239
of the earth in **r** and wisdom. 2Ch 9:22 6239
and he had great **r** and honor. 2Ch 17:5 6239
Jehoshaphat had great **r** and honor; 2Ch 18:1 6239
Hezekiah had immense **r** and honor; 2Ch 32:27 6239
he displayed the **r** of his royal glory Es 1:4 6239
recounted to them the glory of his **r**, Es 5:11 6239
"He swallows **r**, But will vomit Jb 20:15 2428
As to the **r** of his trading, He Jb 20:18 2428
"Will your **r** keep you from distress, Jb 36:19 7770b
He amasses **r** and does not know Ps 39:6
boast in the abundance of their **r**? Ps 49:6 6239
trusted in the abundance of his **r** Ps 52:7 6239
If **r** increase, do not set *your* Ps 62:10 2428
Wealth and **r** are in his house, And Ps 112:3 6239
testimonies, As much as in all **r**. Ps 119:14 1952
In her left hand are **r** and honor. Pr 3:16 6239
"**R** and honor are with me, Pr 8:18 6239
R do not profit in the day of wrath, Pr 11:4 1952
honor, And ruthless men attain **r**. Pr 11:16 6239
He who trusts in his **r** will fall, Pr 11:28 6239
The crown of the wise is their **r**, Pr 14:24 6239
and the fear of the LORD Are **r**, Pr 22:4 6239
With all precious and pleasant **r**. Pr 24:4 1952
For **r** are not forever, Nor does a Pr 27:24 2633
me, Give me neither poverty nor **r**; Pr 30:8 6239
his eyes were not satisfied with **r** Ec 4:8 6239
r being hoarded by their owner to Ec 5:13 6239
When those **r** were lost through a Ec 5:14 6239
whom God has given **r** and wealth, Ec 5:19 6239
a man to whom God has given **r** and Ec 6:2 6239
all the **r** of his house for love, SS 8:7 1952
hand reached to the **r** of the peoples Is 10:14 2428
They carry their **r** on the backs of Is 30:6 2428
And in their **r** you will boast. Is 61:6 3519b
let not a rich man boast of his **r**; Jer 9:23 6239
Also they will make a spoil of your **r** Ezk 26:12 2428
You have acquired **r** for yourself And Ezk 28:4 2428
trade You have increased your **r** And Ezk 28:5 2428
is lifted up because of your **r** Ezk 28:5 2428
gain far more **r** than all *of them;* Da 11:2 6239
he becomes strong through his **r**, Da 11:2 6239
world, and the deceitfulness of **r**, Mk 4:19 4149
and **r** and pleasures of *this* life, Lk 8:14 4149
who will entrust the true **r** to Lk 16:11
r of His kindness and tolerance Ro 2:4 4149
make known the **r** of His Ro 9:23 4149
in **r** for all who call on Him; Ro 10:12 4147
Now if their transgression is **r** Ro 11:12 4149
failure is **r** for the Gentiles, Ro 11:12 4149
the depth of the **r** both of the Ro 11:33 4149
according to the **r** of His grace Eph 1:7 4149
what are the **r** of the glory of His Eph 1:18 4149
show the surpassing **r** of His grace Eph 2:7 4149
the unfathomable **r** of Christ, Eph 3:8 4149
according to the **r** of His glory, Eph 3:16 4149
to His **r** in glory in Christ Jesus. Php 4:19 4149
the **r** of the glory of this mystery Col 1:27 4149
hope on the uncertainty of **r**, 1Tm 6:17 4149
greater **r** than the treasures of Egypt; Heb 11:26 4149
Your **r** have rotted and your Jas 5:2 4149
that was slain to receive power and **r** Rv 5:12 4149

RICHEST
enter the **r** *parts* of the realm, Da 11:24 4924a

RICHLY
for I will indeed honor you **r**, Nu 22:17 3966
word of Christ **r** dwell within you, Col 3:16 4146
who **r** supplies us with all things 1Tm 6:17 4146
whom He poured out upon us **r** Ti 3:6 4146

RID
could I get **r** of my reproach? 2Sa 13:13 1980
and **r** themselves of their enemies, Es 9:16 5117
Jews **r** themselves of their enemies, Es 9:22 5117
They get **r** of their labor pains. Jb 39:3 7971

RIDDEN
have **r** all your life to this day? Nu 22:30 7392
the horse on which the king has **r**, Es 6:8 7392

RIDDLE
"Let me now propound a **r** to you; Jg 14:12 2420
"Propound your **r**, that we may Jg 14:13 2420
not tell the **r** in three days. Jg 14:14 2420
that he will tell us the **r**, Jg 14:15 2420
a **r** to the sons of my people, Jg 14:16 2420
told the **r** to the sons of her people. Jg 14:17 2420
would not have found out my **r**." Jg 14:18 2420
clothes to those who told the **r**. Jg 14:19 2420
I will express my **r** on the harp. Ps 49:4 2420
"Son of man, propound a **r** and Ezk 17:2 2420

RIDDLES
The words of the wise and their **r**. Pr 1:6 2420

RIDE
had him **r** in his second chariot; Gn 41:43 7392
"He made him **r** on the high places Dt 32:13 7392
"You who **r** on white donkeys, You Jg 5:10 7392
are for the king's household to **r**, 2Sa 16:2 7392
may **r** on it and go with the king,' 2Sa 19:26 7392
my son Solomon **r** on my own mule, 1Ki 1:33 7392
had Solomon **r** on King David's mule, 1Ki 1:38 7392
have made him **r** on the king's mule. 1Ki 1:44 7392
So he made him **r** in his chariot. 2Ki 10:16 7392
up to the wind *and* cause me to **r**; Jb 30:22 7392
in Your majesty **r** on victoriously, Ps 45:4 7392
made men **r** over our heads; Ps 66:12 7392
"And we will **r** on swift *horses,*" Is 30:16 7392
you **r** on the heights of the earth; Is 58:14 7392
the sea, And they **r** on horses, Jer 6:23 7392
the sea; And they **r** on horses, Jer 50:42 7392
save us, We will not **r** on horses; Hos 14:3 7392

RIDER
So that his **r** falls backward. Gn 49:17 7392
its **r** He has hurled into the sea. Ex 15:1 7392
r He has hurled into the sea." Ex 15:21 7392
She laughs at the horse and his **r**. Jb 39:18 7392
Both **r** and horse were cast into a Ps 76:6 7393
you I shatter the horse and his **r**, Jer 51:21 7392
I shatter the chariot and its **r**, Jer 51:21 7392
and his **r** with madness. Zch 12:4 7392

RIDERS
on your part to set **r** on them. 2Ki 18:23 7392
"When he sees **r**, horsemen in Is 21:7 7393
behold, here comes a troop of **r**, Is 21:9 7393
on your part to set **r** on them. Is 36:8 7392
overthrow the chariots and their **r**, Hg 2:22 7392
horses and their **r** will go down, Hg 2:22 7392
the **r** on horses will be put to shame. Zch 10:5 7392
the **r** had breastplates Rv 9:17

RIDES
the discharge **r** becomes unclean. Lv 15:9 7392
Who **r** the heavens to your help, Dt 33:26 7392
for Him who **r** through the deserts, Ps 68:4 7392
who **r** upon the highest heavens, Ps 68:33 7392
he who **r** the horse save his life. Am 2:15 7392

RIDGE
up to the **r** of the hill country, Nu 14:40 7218
to the **r** of the hill country; Nu 14:44 7218

RIDGES
You settle its **r** Ps 65:10 1417

RIDICULE
all who observe it begin to **r** him, Lk 14:29 1702

RIDING
Now he was **r** on his donkey and his Nu 22:22 7392
as she was **r** on her donkey and 1Sa 25:20 7392
For Absalom was **r** on *his* mule, and 2Sa 18:9 7392
you and I were **r** together after Ahab 2Ki 9:25 7392
the animal on which I was **r**. Ne 2:12 7392
r on steeds sired by the royal stud. Es 8:10 7392
went out, **r** on the royal steeds; Es 8:14 7392
I have seen slaves **r** on horses Ec 10:7
the LORD is **r** on a swift cloud and Is 19:1 7392
r in chariots and on horses, Jer 17:25 7392
r in chariots and on horses, Jer 22:4 7392
young men, horsemen **r** on horses. Ezk 23:6 7392
dressed, horsemen **r** on horses, Ezk 23:12 7392
renown, all of them **r** on horses. Ezk 23:23 7392
with you in saddlecloths for **r**. Ezk 27:20 7396
with you, all of them **r** on horses, Ezk 38:15 7392
a man was **r** on a red horse, Zch 1:8 7392

RIGHT
the left, then I will go to the **r**; Gn 13:9 3231
if *to* the **r**, then I will go to the left. Gn 13:9 3225
who had guided me in the **r** way to Gn 24:48 571
turn to the **r** hand or the left." Gn 24:49 3225
Ephraim with his **r** hand toward Gn 48:13 3225
his left hand toward Israel's **r**, Gn 48:13 3225
But Israel stretched out his **r** Gn 48:14 3225
laid his **r** hand on Ephraim's head, Gn 48:17 3225
Place your **r** hand on his head." Gn 48:18 3225
"It is not **r** to do so, for we Ex 8:26 3559
Moses said, "You are **r**; I shall never Ex 10:29 3653a
on their **r** hand and on their left. Ex 14:22 3225
Egyptians were fleeing **r** into it; Ex 14:27 7122
on their **r** hand and on their left. Ex 14:29 3225
"Your **r** hand, O LORD, is majestic Ex 15:6 3225
Your **r** hand, O LORD, shatters the Ex 15:6 3225
"You stretched out Your **r** hand, Ex 15:12 3225
and do what is **r** in His sight, Ex 15:26 3477
put *it* on the lobe of Aaron's **r** ear Ex 29:20
and on the lobes of his sons' **r** ears Ex 29:20 3233
and on the thumbs of their **r** hands Ex 29:20 3233
on the big toes of their **r** feet, Ex 29:20 3233
that is on them and the **r** thigh Ex 29:22 3225
'You shall give the **r** thigh to Lv 7:32 3225
the **r** thigh shall be his as *his* Lv 7:33 3225
it on the lobe of Aaron's **r** ear, Lv 8:23 3233
and on the thumb of his **r** hand and Lv 8:23 3233
and on the big toe of his **r** foot. Lv 8:23 3233
blood on the lobe of their **r** ear, Lv 8:24 3233
and on the thumb of their **r** hand and Lv 8:24 3233
on the big toe of their **r** foot. Lv 8:24 3233
and their fat and the **r** thigh. Lv 8:25 3225
of fat and on the **r** thigh. Lv 8:26 3225
But the breasts and the **r** thigh Lv 9:21 3225
r ear of the one to be cleansed, Lv 14:14 3233
and on the thumb of his **r** hand and Lv 14:14 3233
and on the big toe of his **r** foot. Lv 14:14 3233
priest shall put some on the **r** ear lobe Lv 14:17 3233
and on the thumb of his **r** hand, Lv 14:17 3233
and on the big toe of his **r** foot, Lv 14:17 3233
and put *it* on the lobe of the **r** ear Lv 14:25 3233
and on the thumb of his **r** hand and Lv 14:25 3233
and on the big toe of his **r** foot. Lv 14:25 3233
r ear of the one to be cleansed, Lv 14:28 3233
and on the thumb of his **r** hand and Lv 14:28 3233
and on the big toe of his **r** foot, Lv 14:28 3233
then his redemption **r** remains Lv 25:29 1353
his **r** of redemption lasts a full year. Lv 25:29 1353
the Levites have a permanent **r** of Lv 25:32 1353
then he shall have redemption **r** Lv 25:48 1353
offering and like the **r** thigh. Nu 18:18 3225
not turning to the **r** or left, Nu 20:17 3225
to turn to the **r** hand or the left. Nu 22:26 3225
are **r** in *their* statements. Nu 27:7 3653a
The tribe of the sons of Joseph are **r** Nu 36:5 3653a
aside to the **r** or to the left. Dt 2:27 3225
not turn aside to the **r** or to the left. Dt 5:32 3225
"You shall do what is **r** and Dt 6:18 3477
whatever is **r** in his own eyes; Dt 12:8 3477
is **r** in the sight of the LORD. Dt 12:25 3477
you will be doing what is good and **r** Dt 12:28 3477
what is **r** in the sight of the LORD Dt 13:18 3477
to you, to the **r** or the left. Dt 17:11 3225
commandment, to the **r** or the left, Dt 17:20 3225
what is **r** in the eyes of the LORD. Dt 21:9 3477
belongs the **r** of the firstborn. Dt 21:17 4941
today, to the **r** or to the left, Dt 28:14 3225
At His **r** hand there was flashing Dt 33:2 3225
from it to the **r** or to the left, Jos 1:7 3225
and **r** in your sight to do to us." Jos 9:25 3477
it to the **r** hand or to the left, Jos 23:6 3225
it on his **r** thigh under his cloak. Jg 3:16 3225
took the sword from his **r** thigh Jg 3:21 3225
r hand for the workmen's hammer. Jg 5:26 3225
trumpets in their **r** hands for blowing Jg 7:20 3225
"All **r**, when the LORD has given Jg 8:7 3651
the one with his **r** hand and the Jg 16:29 3225
did what was **r** in his own eyes. Jg 17:6 3477
did what was **r** in his own eyes. Jg 21:25 3477
you *may have* my **r** of redemption, Ru 4:6 1353
not turn aside to the **r** or to the left. 1Sa 6:12 3225
I will gouge out the **r** eye of every one 1Sa 11:2 3225
you in the good and **r** way. 1Sa 12:23 3477
did not turn to the **r** or to the left 2Sa 2:19 3225
"Turn to your **r** or to your left, 2Sa 2:21 3225
no one can turn to the **r** or to the 2Sa 14:19 3231
"See, your claims are good and **r**, 2Sa 15:3 5228
at his **r** hand and at his left. 2Sa 16:6 3225
What **r** do I have yet that I should 2Sa 19:28 6666
beard with his **r** hand to kiss him. 2Sa 20:9 3225
on the **r** side of the city that is 2Sa 24:5 3225
mother, and she sat on his **r**. 1Ki 2:19 3225
was on the **r** side of the house; 1Ki 6:8 3233
the **r** pillar and named it Jachin, 1Ki 7:21 3233
five on the **r** side of the house 1Ki 7:39 3225
set the sea *of cast metal* on the **r** side 1Ki 7:39 3233
the **r** side and five on the left, 1Ki 7:49 3225
doing what is **r** in My sight and 1Ki 11:33 3477
and do what is **r** in My sight by 1Ki 11:38 3477
only that which was **r** in My sight; 1Ki 14:8 3477
was **r** in the sight of the LORD, 1Ki 15:5 3477
was **r** in the sight of the LORD, 1Ki 15:11 3477

by Him on His **r** and on His left. **1Ki 22:19** 3225
doing **r** in the sight of the LORD. **1Ki 22:43** 3477
"We are not doing **r**. **2Ki 7:9** 3653a
"Is your heart **r**, as my heart is **2Ki 10:15** 3477
in executing what is **r** in My eyes, **2Ki 10:30** 3477
from the **r** side of the house to **2Ki 11:11** 3233
Jehoash did **r** in the sight of **2Ki 12:2** 3477
on the **r** side as one comes into **2Ki 12:9** 3225
He did **r** in the sight of the LORD, **2Ki 14:3** 3477
He did **r** in the sight of the LORD, **2Ki 15:3** 3477
was **r** in the sight of the LORD; **2Ki 15:34** 3477
and he did not do what was **r** in **2Ki 16:2** 3477
things secretly which were not **r** against **2Ki 17:9** 3653a
He did **r** in the sight of the LORD, **2Ki 18:3** 3477
He did **r** in the sight of the **2Ki 22:2** 3477
turn aside to the **r** or to the left. **2Ki 22:2** 3225
which *were* on the **r** of the mount **2Ki 23:13** 3225
brother Asaph stood at his **r** hand, **1Ch 6:39** 3225
using both the **r** hand and the left **1Ch 12:2** 3231
r in the eyes of all the people. **1Ch 13:4** 3474
the **r** and the other on the left, **2Ch 3:17** 3225
and named the one on the **r** Jachin **2Ch 3:17** 3233
he set five on the **r** side and five on **2Ch 4:6** 3225
five on the **r** side and five on the left **2Ch 4:7** 3225
five on the **r** side and five on the left **2Ch 4:8** 3225
He set the sea on the **r** side **2Ch 4:10** 3233
Asa did good and **r** in the **2Ch 14:2** 3477
standing on His **r** and on His left. **2Ch 18:18** 3225
doing **r** in the sight of the LORD. **2Ch 20:32** 3477
from the **r** side of the house to **2Ch 23:10** 3233
Joash did what was **r** in the **2Ch 24:2** 3477
He did **r** in the sight of the LORD, **2Ch 25:2** 3477
He did **r** in the sight of the **2Ch 26:4** 3477
He did **r** in the sight of the LORD, **2Ch 27:2** 3477
and he did not do **r** in the sight **2Ch 28:1** 3477
He did **r** in the sight of the LORD, **2Ch 29:2** 3477
Thus the thing was **r** in the sight **2Ch 30:4** 3474
and he did what *was* good, **r** and **2Ch 31:20** 3477
He did **r** in the sight of the LORD, **2Ch 34:2** 3477
not turn aside to the **r** or to the left. **2Ch 34:2** 3225
"That's **r**! As you have said, so it is **Ezr 10:12** 3653a
build, but you have no portion, **r** or **Ne 2:20** 6666
and Maaseiah on his **r** hand; **Ne 8:4** 3225
the first proceeding to the **r** on **Ne 12:31** 3225
were in each and every city *the* **r** **Es 8:11**
does the Almighty pervert what is **r**? **Jb 8:3** 6664
can a man be in the **r** before God? **Jb 9:2** 6663
"For though I were **r**, **Jb 9:15** 6663
'Is it **r** for You indeed to oppress, **Jb 10:3** 2896a
"If you would direct your heart **r** And **Jb 11:13** 3559
He turns on the **r**, I cannot see **Jb 23:9** 3225
lives, who has taken away my **r**, **Jb 27:2** 4941
me that I should declare you **r**; **Jb 27:5** 6663
"On the **r** hand their brood arises; **Jb 30:12** 3225
tell you, you are not **r** in this, **Jb 33:12** 6663
To remind a man what is **r** for him, **Jb 33:23** 3476
sinned and perverted what is **r**, **Jb 33:27** 3474
us choose for ourselves what is **r**; **Jb 34:4** 4941
But God has taken away my **r**; **Jb 34:5** 4941
Should I lie concerning my **r**? **Jb 34:6** 4941
That your own **r** hand can save you. **Jb 40:14** 3225
what is **r** as My servant Job has. **Jb 42:7** 3559
have not spoken of Me what is **r**, **Jb 42:8** 3559
Because He is at my **r** hand, **Ps 16:8** 3225
In Your **r** hand there are pleasures **Ps 16:11** 3225
those who take refuge at Your **r** hand **Ps 17:7** 3225
And Your **r** hand upholds me; **Ps 18:35** 3225
The precepts of the LORD are **r**, **Ps 19:8** 3477
the saving strength of His **r** hand. **Ps 20:6** 3225
Your **r** hand will find out those **Ps 21:8** 3225
whose **r** hand is full of bribes. **Ps 26:10** 3225
up Yourself, and awake to my **r** And **Ps 35:23** 4941
But Your **r** hand and Your arm and **Ps 44:3** 3225
Let Your **r** hand teach You awesome **Ps 45:4** 3225
At Your **r** hand stands the queen in **Ps 45:9** 3225
r hand is full of righteousness. **Ps 48:10** 3225
"What **r** have you to tell of My **Ps 50:16**
more than speaking what is **r**. **Ps 52:3** 6664
delivered, Save with Your **r** hand, **Ps 60:5** 3225
Your **r** hand upholds me. **Ps 63:8** 3225
You have taken hold of my **r** hand. **Ps 73:23** 3225
Your hand, even Your **r** hand? **Ps 74:11** 3225
That the **r** hand of the Most High **Ps 77:10** 3225
which His **r** hand had gained. **Ps 78:54** 3225
which Your **r** hand has planted, **Ps 80:15** 3225
be upon the man of Your **r** hand, **Ps 80:17** 3225
is mighty, Your **r** hand is exalted. **Ps 89:13** 3225
sea And his **r** hand on the rivers. **Ps 89:25** 3225
the **r** hand of his adversaries; **Ps 89:42** 3225
And ten thousand at your **r** hand, **Ps 91:7** 3225
His **r** hand and His holy arm have **Ps 98:1** 3225
delivered, Save with Your **r** hand, **Ps 108:6** 3225
an accuser stand at his **r** hand. **Ps 109:6** 3225
stands at the **r** hand of the needy, **Ps 109:31** 3225
"Sit at My **r** hand Until I make **Ps 110:1** 3225
The Lord is at Your **r** hand; **Ps 110:5** 3225
The **r** hand of the LORD does **Ps 118:15** 3225
The **r** hand of the LORD is exalted; **Ps 118:16** 3225
The **r** hand of the LORD does **Ps 118:16** 3225
Therefore I esteem **r** all *Your* **Ps 119:128** 3474
LORD is your shade on your **r** hand. **Ps 121:5** 3225
May my **r** hand forget *her skill.* **Ps 137:5** 3225
And Your **r** hand will save me. **Ps 138:7** 3225
Your **r** hand will lay hold of me. **Ps 139:10** 3225
Look to the **r** and see; **Ps 142:4** 3225
And whose **r** hand is a right hand **Ps 144:8** 3225
hand is a **r** hand of falsehood. **Ps 144:8** 3225
And whose **r** hand is a right hand **Ps 144:11** 3225
hand is a **r** hand of falsehood. **Ps 144:11** 3225

Long life is in her **r** hand; **Pr 3:16** 3225
not turn to the **r** nor to the left; **Pr 4:27** 3225
of my lips *will reveal* **r** things. **Pr 8:6** 4339
And **r** to those who find knowledge. **Pr 8:9** 3477
way of a fool is **r** in his own eyes, **Pr 12:15** 3477
He who speaks truth tells what is **r**, **Pr 12:17** 6664
is a way *which seems* **r** to a man, **Pr 14:12** 3477
And he who speaks **r** is loved. **Pr 16:13** 3477
is a way *which seems* **r** to a man, **Pr 16:25** 3477
first to plead his case *seems* **r**, **Pr 18:17** 6662
If his conduct is pure and **r**. **Pr 20:11** 3477
man's way is **r** in his own eyes, **Pr 21:2** 3477
When your lips speak what is **r**. **Pr 23:16** 4339
the lips Who gives a **r** answer. **Pr 24:26** 5228
a word spoken in **r** circumstances. **Pr 25:11**
And grasps oil with his **r** hand. **Pr 27:16** 3225
heart *directs him* toward the **r**, **Ec 10:2** 3225
head And his **r** hand embrace me." **SS 2:6** 3225
head And his **r** hand embrace me." **SS 8:3** 3225
of the ones who are in the **r**! **Is 5:23** 6662
the **r** hand but *still* are hungry, **Is 9:20** 3225
'What **r** do you have here, And whom **Is 22:16**
the **r** with meaningless arguments. **Is 29:21** 6662
must not prophesy to us what is **r**, **Is 30:10** 5228
you turn to the **r** or to the left. **Is 30:21** 3231
the needy one speaks what is **r**. **Is 32:7** 4941
you with My righteous **r** hand.' **Is 41:10** 3225
your God, who upholds your **r** hand, **Is 41:13** 3225
that we may say, "*He is* **r**!"? **Is 41:26** 6662
cause, that you may be proved **r**. **Is 43:26** 6663
"Is there not a lie in my **r** hand?" **Is 44:20** 3225
Whom I have taken by the **r** hand, **Is 45:1** 3225
My **r** hand spread out the heavens; **Is 48:13** 3225
abroad to the **r** and to the left. **Is 54:3** 3225
His **r** hand and by His strong arm, **Is 62:8** 3225
arm to go at the **r** hand of Moses, **Is 63:12** 3225
They have spoken what is not **r**; **Jer 8:6** 3653a
"What **r** has My beloved in My **Jer 11:15**
were a signet *ring* on My **r** hand, **Jer 22:24** 3225
is evil And their might is not **r**. **Jer 23:10** 3653a
me as is good and **r** in your sight. **Jer 26:14** 3477
the **r** of redemption to buy *it.*" **Jer 32:7** 4941
for you have the **r** of possession **Jer 32:8** 4941
and done what is **r** in My sight, **Jer 34:15** 3477
and he will die **r** where he is **Jer 38:9** 8478
seems good and **r** for you to go." **Jer 40:4** 3477
it seems **r** for you to go." **Jer 40:5** 3477
and I am going to set his throne **r** **Jer 43:10**
His **r** hand From before the enemy. **La 2:3** 3225
He has set His **r** hand like an **La 2:4** 3225
four had the face of a lion on the **r** **Ezk 1:10** 3225
a second time, *but* on your **r** side and **Ezk 4:6** 3233
cherubim were standing on the **r** side **Ezk 10:3** 3225
and have put **r** before their faces **Ezk 14:3** 5227
puts **r** before his face the **Ezk 14:4** 5227
puts **r** before his face the **Ezk 14:7** 5227
they are more in the **r** than you. **Ezk 16:52** 6663
'The way of the Lord is not **r**.' **Ezk 18:25** 8505
O house of Israel! Is My way not **r**? **Ezk 18:25** 8505
it not your ways that are not **r**? **Ezk 18:25** 8505
'The way of the Lord is not **r**.' **Ezk 18:29** 8505
Are My ways not **r**, O house of **Ezk 18:29** 8505
it not your ways that are not **r**? **Ezk 18:29** 8505
"Show yourself sharp, go to the **r**; **Ezk 21:16** 3231
his **r** hand came the divination, **Ezk 21:22** 3225
until He comes whose **r** it is, **Ezk 21:27** 4941
'The way of the Lord is not **r**, **Ezk 33:17** 8505
it is their own way that is not **r**. **Ezk 33:17** 8505
'The way of the Lord is not **r**.' **Ezk 33:20** 8505
down your arrows from your **r** hand. **Ezk 39:3** 3225
from the **r** side of the house, **Ezk 47:1** 3233
as he raised his **r** hand and his **Da 12:7** 3225
For the ways of the LORD are **r**, **Hos 14:9** 3477
do not know how to do what is **r**," **Am 3:10** 5228
between their **r** and left hand, **Jon 4:11** 3225
one, His soul is not **r** within him; **Hab 2:4** 3474
r hand will come around to you, **Hab 2:16** 3225
and Satan standing at his **r** hand to **Zch 3:1** 3225
one on the **r** side of the bowl and **Zch 4:3** 3225
olive trees on the **r** of the lampstand **Zch 4:11** 3225
be on his arm And on his **r** eye! **Zch 11:17** 3225
And his **r** eye will be blind." **Zch 11:17** 3225
so they will consume on the **r** hand **Zch 12:6** 3225
If your **r** eye makes you stumble, **Mt 5:29** *1188*
If your **r** hand makes you stumble, **Mt 5:30** *1188*
whoever slaps you on your **r** cheek, **Mt 5:39** *1188*
know what your **r** hand is doing **Mt 6:3** *1188*
whatever is **r** I will give you.' **Mt 20:4** *1342*
on Your **r** and one on Your left." **Mt 20:21** *1188*
but to sit on My **r** and on *My* left, **Mt 20:23** *1188*
"SIT AT MY **R** HAND, UNTIL I PUT **Mt 22:44** *1188*
He is near, **r** at the door. **Mt 24:33**
He will put the sheep on His **r**, **Mt 25:33** *1188*
King will say to those on His **r**, **Mt 25:34** *1188*
SITTING AT THE **R** HAND OF POWER, **Mt 26:64** *1188*
head, and a reed in His **r** hand; **Mt 27:29** *1188*
one on the **r** and one on the left. **Mt 27:38** *1188*
down, clothed and in his **r** mind, **Mk 5:15** *4993*
sit, one on Your **r** **Mk 10:37** *1188*
"But to sit on My **r** or on *My* left, **Mk 10:40** *1188*
"**R**, Teacher; You have truly **Mk 12:32** *2573*
"SIT AT MY **R** HAND, UNTIL I PUT **Mk 12:36** *1188*
He is near, **r** at the door. **Mk 13:29**
r into the courtyard of the high **Mk 14:54** *2193*
SITTING AT THE **R** HAND OF POWER, **Mk 14:62** *1188*
one on His **r** and one on His left. **Mk 15:27** *1188*
was standing **r** in front of Him, **Mk 15:39** *1727*
saw a young man sitting at the **r**, **Mk 16:5** *1188*
and sat down at the **r** hand of God. **Mk 16:19** *1188*

to the **r** of the altar of incense. **Lk 1:11** *1188*
there whose **r** hand was withered. **Lk 6:6** *1188*
Jesus, clothed and in his **r** mind; **Lk 8:35** *4993*
own initiative judge what is **r**? **Lk 12:57** *1342*
"SIT AT MY **R** HAND **Lk 20:42** *1188*
high priest and cut off his **r** ear. **Lk 22:50** *1188*
THE **R** HAND of the power OF GOD." **Lk 22:69** *1188*
the **r** and the other on the left. **Lk 23:33** *1188*
the **r** to become children of God, **Jn 1:12** *1849*
and you are **r**, for *so* I am. **Jn 13:13** *2573*
why can I not follow You **r** now? **Jn 13:37** *737*
slave, and cut off his **r** ear; **Jn 18:10** *1188*
FOR HE IS AT MY **R** HAND, SO THAT I WILL **Ac 2:25** *1188*
been exalted to the **r** hand of God, **Ac 2:33** *1188*
"SIT AT MY **R** HAND, **Ac 2:34** *1188*
And seizing him by the **r** hand, **Ac 3:7** *1188*
"Whether it is **r** in the sight of God **Ac 4:19** *1342*
r hand as a Prince and a Savior, **Ac 5:31** *1188*
they kept **r** on teaching and **Ac 5:42** *3756, 3973*
standing at the **r** hand of God; **Ac 7:55** *1188*
standing at the **r** hand of God." **Ac 7:56** *1188*
your heart is not **r** before God. **Ac 8:21** *2117*
who fears Him and does what is **r** **Ac 10:35** *1343*
and it came **r** down to me, **Ac 11:5** *891*
at the **r** time Christ died for the **Ro 5:6** *2540*
who is at the **r** hand of God, **Ro 8:34** *1188*
the potter have a **r** over the clay, **Ro 9:21** *1849*
Quite **r**, they were broken off for **Ro 11:20** *2573*
what is **r** in the sight of all men. **Ro 12:17** *2570*
Do we not have a **r** to eat and drink **1Co 9:4** *1849*
Do we not have a **r** to take along a **1Co 9:5** *1849*
have a **r** to refrain from working? **1Co 9:6** *1849*
If others share the **r** over you, **1Co 9:12** *1849*
we did not use this **r**, **1Co 9:12** *1849*
full use of my **r** in the gospel. **1Co 9:18** *1849*
for the **r** hand and the left, **2Co 6:7** *1188*
but that you may do what is **r**, **2Co 13:7** *2570*
Barnabas the **r** hand of fellowship, **Ga 2:9** *1188*
His **r** hand in the heavenly *places,* **Eph 1:20** *1188*
in the Lord, for this is **r**. **Eph 6:1** *1342*
For it is only **r** for me to feel **Php 1:7** *1342*
is honorable, whatever is **r**, **Php 4:8** *1342*
is, seated at the **r** hand of God. **Col 3:1** *1188*
we do not have the **r** *to this,* **2Th 3:9** *1849*
the **r** hand of the Majesty on high, **Heb 1:3** *1188*
"SIT AT MY **R** HAND, UNTIL I MAKE **Heb 1:13** *1188*
who has taken His seat at the **r** **Heb 8:1** *1188*
SAT DOWN AT THE **R** HAND OF GOD **Heb 10:12** *1188*
the **r** hand of the throne of God. **Heb 12:2** *1188*
the tabernacle have no **r** to eat. **Heb 13:10** *1849*
one who knows *the* **r** thing to do and **Jas 4:17** *2570*
Judge is standing **r** at the door. **Jas 5:9** *4253*
and the praise of those who do **r**. **1Pe 2:14** *15*
doing **r** you may silence the ignorance **1Pe 2:15** *15*
But if when you do what is **r** and **1Pe 2:20** *15*
do what is **r** without being frightened **1Pe 3:6** *15*
suffer for doing what is **r** rather than **1Pe 3:17** *15*
who is at the **r** hand of God, **1Pe 3:22** *1188*
Creator in doing what is **r**. **1Pe 4:19** *16*
I consider it **r**, **2Pe 1:13** *1342*
forsaking the **r** way, they have gone **2Pe 2:15** *2117*
In His **r** hand He held seven stars **Rv 1:16** *1188*
And He placed His **r** hand on me, **Rv 1:17** *1188*
stars which you saw in My **r** hand, **Rv 1:20** *1188*
the seven stars in His **r** hand, **Rv 2:1** *1188*
I saw in the **r** hand of Him who **Rv 5:1** *1188*
and took the book out of the **r** hand **Rv 5:7** *1188*
He placed his **r** foot on the **Rv 10:2** *1188*
lifted up his **r** hand to heaven, **Rv 10:5** *1188*
be given a mark on their **r** hand or **Rv 13:16** *1188*
have the **r** to the tree of life, **Rv 22:14** *1849*

RIGHTEOUS

Noah was a **r** man, blameless in his **Gn 6:9** 6662
to be **r** before Me in this time. **Gn 7:1** 6662
sweep away the **r** with the wicked? **Gn 18:23** 6662
there are fifty **r** within the city; **Gn 18:24** 6662
sake of the fifty **r** who are in it? **Gn 18:24** 6662
to slay the **r** with the wicked, **Gn 18:25** 6662
so that the **r** and the wicked are **Gn 18:25** 6662
in Sodom fifty **r** within the city, **Gn 18:26** 6662
"Suppose the fifty **r** are lacking five, **Gn 18:28** 6662
"She is more **r** than I, inasmuch **Gn 38:26** 6663
the LORD is the **r** one, and I and **Ex 9:27** 6662
do not kill the innocent or the **r**, **Ex 23:7** 6662
judgments as **r** as this whole law **Dt 4:8** 6662
judge the people with **r** judgment. **Dt 16:18** 6664
and perverts the words of the **r**. **Dt 16:19** 6662
the **r** and condemn the wicked, **Dt 25:1** 6662
injustice, **R** and upright is He. **Dt 32:4** 6662
they will offer **r** sacrifices; **Dt 33:19** 6664
recount the **r** deeds of the LORD, **Jg 5:11** 6666
The **r** deeds for His peasantry in **Jg 5:11** 6666
concerning all the **r** acts of the LORD **1Sa 12:7** 6666
"You are more **r** than I; **1Sa 24:17** 6662
when wicked men have killed a **r** **2Sa 4:11** 6662
because he fell upon two men more **r** **1Ki 2:32** 6662
and justifying the **r** by giving him **1Ki 8:32** 6662
and justifying the **r** by giving him **2Ch 6:23** 6662
themselves and said, "The LORD is **r**." **2Ch 12:6** 6662
"O LORD God of Israel, You are **r**, **Ezr 9:15** 6662
Your promise, For You are **r**. **Ne 9:8** 6662
for you And restore your **r** estate. **Jb 8:6** 6664
"Though I am **r**, my mouth will **Jb 9:20** 6663
And if I am **r**, I dare not lift up **Jb 10:15** 6663
of a woman, that he should be **r**? **Jb 15:14** 6663
the **r** will hold to his way, **Jb 17:9** 6662
to the Almighty if you are **r**, **Jb 22:3** 6663
"The **r** see and are glad, And the **Jb 22:19** 6662

because he was **r** in his own eyes. **Jb 32:1** 6662
'I am **r**, But God has taken away my **Jb 34:5** 6663
will you condemn the **r** mighty One, **Jb 34:17** 6662
"If you are **r**, what do you give **Jb 35:7** 6663
not withdraw His eyes from the **r**; **Jb 36:7** 6662
sinners in the assembly of the **r**. **Ps 1:5** 6662
the LORD knows the way of the **r**, **Ps 1:6** 6662
is You who blesses the **r** man, **Ps 5:12** 6662
to an end, but establish the **r**; **Ps 7:9** 6662
For the **r** God tries the hearts and **Ps 7:9** 6662
God is a **r** judge, And a God who **Ps 7:11** 6662
destroyed, What can the **r** do?" **Ps 11:3** 6662
LORD tests the **r** and the wicked, **Ps 11:5** 6662
For the LORD is **r**, **Ps 11:7** 6662
For God is with the **r** generation. **Ps 14:5** 6662
they are **r** altogether. **Ps 19:9** 6663
the **r** With pride and contempt. **Ps 31:18** 6662
the LORD and rejoice, you **r** ones **Ps 32:11** 6662
for joy in the LORD, O you **r** ones; **Ps 33:1** 6662
eyes of the LORD are toward the **r** And **Ps 34:15** 6662
The **r** cry, and the LORD **Ps 34:17**
Many are the afflictions of the **r**, **Ps 34:19** 6662
who hate the **r** will be condemned. **Ps 34:21** 6662
The wicked plots against the **r** And **Ps 37:12** 6662
Better is the little of the **r** Than **Ps 37:16** 6662
But the LORD sustains the **r**. **Ps 37:17** 6662
But the **r** is gracious and gives. **Ps 37:21** 6662
I have not seen the **r** forsaken Or **Ps 37:25** 6662
The **r** will inherit the land And **Ps 37:29** 6662
The mouth of the **r** utters wisdom, **Ps 37:30** 6662
The wicked spies upon the **r** And **Ps 37:32** 6662
salvation of the **r** is from the LORD; **Ps 37:39** 6662
You will delight in **r** sacrifices, **Ps 51:19** 6664
The **r** will see and fear, And **Ps 52:6** 6662
never allow the **r** to be shaken. **Ps 55:22** 6662
The **r** will rejoice when he sees **Ps 58:10** 6662
there is a reward for the **r**; **Ps 58:11** 6662
r man will be glad in the LORD and **Ps 64:10** 6662
But let the **r** be glad; **Ps 68:3** 6662
they not be recorded with the **r**. **Ps 69:28** 6662
In his days may the **r** flourish, **Ps 72:7** 6662
horns of the **r** will be lifted up. **Ps 75:10** 6662
The **r** man will flourish like the **Ps 92:12** 6662
For judgment will again be **r**, **Ps 94:15** 6664
against the life of the **r** And **Ps 94:21** 6662
Light is sown *like seed* for the **r** And **Ps 97:11** 6662
Be glad in the LORD, you **r** ones, **Ps 97:12** 6662
The LORD performs **r** deeds And **Ps 103:6** 6666
gracious and compassionate and **r**. **Ps 112:4** 6662
The **r** will be remembered forever. **Ps 112:6** 6662
Gracious is the LORD, and **r**; **Ps 116:5** 6662
salvation is in the tents of the **r**; **Ps 118:15** 6662
The **r** will enter through it. **Ps 118:20** 6662
When I learn Your **r** judgments. **Ps 119:7** 6664
You Because of Your **r** ordinances. **Ps 119:62** 6664
O LORD, that Your judgments are **r**, **Ps 119:75** 6664
That I will keep Your **r** ordinances. **Ps 119:106** 6664
Your salvation And for Your **r** word. **Ps 119:123** 6664
R are You, O LORD, And upright **Ps 119:137** 6662
Your testimonies are **r** forever; **Ps 119:144** 6664
every one of Your **r** ordinances is **Ps 119:160** 6664
You, Because of Your **r** ordinances. **Ps 119:164** 6664
not rest upon the land of the **r**, **Ps 125:3** 6662
that the **r** will not put forth their **Ps 125:3** 6662
The LORD is **r**; He has cut in two **Ps 129:4** 6662
r will give thanks to Your name; **Ps 140:13** 6662
Let the **r** smite me in kindness and **Ps 141:5** 6662
The **r** will surround me, For You **Ps 142:7** 6662
in Your sight no man living is **r**. **Ps 143:2** 6663
The LORD is **r** in all His ways And **Ps 145:17** 6662
The LORD loves the **r**; **Ps 146:8** 6662
And keep to the paths of the **r**. **Pr 2:20** 6662
He blesses the dwelling of the **r**. **Pr 3:33** 6662
the **r** is like the light of dawn, **Pr 4:18** 6662
be still wiser, Teach a **r** man and **Pr 9:9** 6662
will not allow the **r** to hunger, **Pr 10:3** 6662
are on the head of the **r**, **Pr 10:6** 6662
The memory of the **r** is blessed, **Pr 10:7** 6662
of the **r** is a fountain of life, **Pr 10:11** 6662
The wages of the **r** is life, **Pr 10:16** 6662
of the **r** is *as* choice silver, **Pr 10:20** 6662
The lips of the **r** feed many, But **Pr 10:21** 6662
desire of the **r** will be granted. **Pr 10:24** 6662
r *has* an everlasting foundation. **Pr 10:25** 6662
The hope of the **r** is gladness, But **Pr 10:28** 6662
The **r** will never be shaken, But **Pr 10:30** 6662
mouth of the **r** flows with wisdom, **Pr 10:31** 6662
The lips of the **r** bring forth what **Pr 10:32** 6662
The **r** is delivered from trouble, **Pr 11:8** 6662
knowledge the **r** will be delivered. **Pr 11:9** 6662
When it goes well with the **r**, **Pr 11:10** 6662
descendants of the **r** will be delivered **Pr 11:21** 6662
The desire of the **r** is only good, **Pr 11:23** 6662
the **r** will flourish like the *green* leaf. **Pr 11:28** 6662
fruit of the **r** is a tree of life, **Pr 11:30** 6662
r will be rewarded in the earth, **Pr 11:31** 6662
root of the **r** will not be moved. **Pr 12:3** 6662
The thoughts of the **r** are just, **Pr 12:5** 6662
But the house of the **r** will stand. **Pr 12:7** 6662
A **r** man has regard for the life of **Pr 12:10** 6662
the root of the **r** yields *fruit*. **Pr 12:12** 6662
the **r** will escape from trouble. **Pr 12:13** 6662
No harm befalls the **r**, **Pr 12:21** 6662
The **r** is a guide to his neighbor, **Pr 12:26** 6662
A **r** man hates falsehood, But a **Pr 13:5** 6662
The light of the **r** rejoices, **Pr 13:9** 6662
But the **r** will be rewarded with **Pr 13:21** 6662
the sinner is stored up for the **r**. **Pr 13:22** 6662
The **r** has enough to satisfy his **Pr 13:25** 6662

the wicked at the gates of the **r**. **Pr 14:19** 6662
the **r** has a refuge when he dies. **Pr 14:32** 6662
wealth is *in* the house of the **r**, **Pr 15:6** 6662
of the **r** ponders how to answer, **Pr 15:28** 6662
But He hears the prayer of the **r**. **Pr 15:29** 6662
R lips are the delight of kings, **Pr 16:13** 6664
wicked and he who condemns the **r**, **Pr 17:15** 6662
It is also not good to fine the **r**, **Pr 17:26** 6662
to thrust aside the **r** in judgment. **Pr 18:5** 6662
The **r** runs into it and is safe. **Pr 18:10** 6662
A **r** man who walks in his integrity **Pr 20:7** 6662
The **r** one considers the house of **Pr 21:12** 6662
exercise of justice is joy for the **r**, **Pr 21:15** 6662
The wicked is a ransom for the **r**, **Pr 21:18** 6662
r gives and does not hold back. **Pr 21:26** 6662
father of the **r** will greatly rejoice, **Pr 23:24** 6662
against the dwelling of the **r**; **Pr 24:15** 6662
For a **r** man falls seven times, and **Pr 24:16** 6662
who says to the wicked, "You are **r**," **Pr 24:24** 6662
Is a **r** man who gives way before the **Pr 25:26** 6662
But the **r** are bold as a lion. **Pr 28:1** 6662
When the **r** triumph, there is great **Pr 28:12** 6662
when they perish, the **r** increase. **Pr 28:28** 6662
When the **r** increase, the people **Pr 29:2** 6662
But the **r** sings and rejoices. **Pr 29:6** 6662
The **r** is concerned for the rights **Pr 29:7** 6662
But the **r** will see their fall. **Pr 29:16** 6662
unjust man is abominable to the **r**, **Pr 29:27** 6662
the **r** man and the wicked man," **Ec 3:17** 6662
there is a **r** man who perishes in **Ec 7:15** 6662
Do not be excessively **r** and **Ec 7:16** 6662
there is not a **r** man on earth who **Ec 7:20** 6662
there are **r** men to whom it happens **Ec 8:14** 6662
according to the deeds of the **r**. **Ec 8:14** 6662
heart and explain it that **r** men, **Ec 9:1** 6662
fate for the **r** and for the wicked; **Ec 9:2** 6662
Say to the **r** that *it will go* well **Is 3:10** 6662
"Glory to the **R** One," **Is 24:16** 6662
that the **r** nation may enter, **Is 26:2** 6662
The way of the **r** is smooth; **Is 26:7** 6662
One, make the path of the **r** level. **Is 26:7** 6662
uphold you with My **r** right hand.' **Is 41:10** 6664
besides Me, A **r** God and a Savior; **Is 45:21** 6662
By His knowledge the **R** One, **Is 53:11** 6662
The **r** man perishes, and no man **Is 57:1** 6662
the **r** man is taken away from evil, **Is 57:1** 6662
"Then all your people *will be* **r**; **Is 60:21** 6662
And all our **r** deeds are like a **Is 64:6** 6666
more **r** than treacherous Judah. **Jer 3:11** 6663
R are You, O LORD, that I would **Jer 12:1** 6662
hosts, You who test the **r**, **Jer 20:12** 6662
raise up for David a **r** Branch; **Jer 23:5** 6662
a **r** Branch of David to spring forth **Jer 33:15** 6666
"The LORD is **r**; For I have rebelled **La 1:18** 6662
in her midst The blood of the **r**; **La 4:13** 6662
when a **r** man turns away from his **Ezk 3:20** 6662
and his **r** deeds which he has done **Ezk 3:20** 6666
if you have warned the **r** man that **Ezk 3:21** 6662
man that the **r** should not sin and **Ezk 3:21** 6662
"Because you disheartened the **r** **Ezk 13:22** 6662
you have made your sisters appear **r** **Ezk 16:51** 6663
you made your sisters appear **r**. **Ezk 16:52** 6663
"But if a man is **r** and practices **Ezk 18:5** 6662
he is **r** *and* will surely live," **Ezk 18:9** 6662
of the **r** will be upon himself, **Ezk 18:20** 6662
"But when a **r** man turns away from **Ezk 18:24** 6662
All his **r** deeds which he has done **Ezk 18:24** 6666
"When a **r** man turns away from his **Ezk 18:26** 6662
off from you the **r** and the wicked. **Ezk 21:3** 6662
off from you the **r** and the wicked, **Ezk 21:4** 6662
"But they, **r** men, will judge them **Ezk 23:45** 6662
'The righteousness of a **r** man will **Ezk 33:12** 6662
whereas a **r** man will not be able **Ezk 33:12** 6662
say to the **r** he will surely live, **Ezk 33:13** 6662
of his **r** deeds will be remembered; **Ezk 33:13** 6666
"When the **r** turns from his **Ezk 33:18** 6662
for the LORD our God is **r** with **Da 9:14** 6662
in accordance with all Your **r** acts, **Da 9:16** 6666
And the **r** will walk in them, **Hos 14:9** 6662
Because they sell the **r** for money **Am 2:6** 6662
distress the **r** *and* accept bribes And **Am 5:12** 6662
know the **r** acts of the LORD." **Mi 6:5** 6666
For the wicked surround the **r**; **Hab 1:4** 6662
swallow up Those more **r** than they? **Hab 1:13** 6662
But the **r** will live by his faith. **Hab 2:4** 6662
The LORD is **r** within her; **Zph 3:5** 6662
between the **r** and the wicked, **Mal 3:18** 6662
Joseph her husband, being a **r** man and **Mt 1:19** *1342*
rain on *the* **r** and *the* unrighteous. **Mt 5:45** *1342*
for I did not come to call the **r**, **Mt 9:13** *1342*
and he who receives a **r** man in the **Mt 10:41** *1342*
righteous man in the name of a **r** man **Mt 10:41** *1342*
man shall receive a **r** man's reward. **Mt 10:41** *1342*
that many prophets and **r** men **Mt 13:17** *1342*
"Then THE **R** WILL SHINE FORTH AS **Mt 13:43** *1342*
out the wicked from among the **r**, **Mt 13:49** *1342*
you, too, outwardly appear **r** to men, **Mt 23:28** *1342*
and adorn the monuments of the **r**, **Mt 23:29** *1342*
of all the **r** blood shed on earth, **Mt 23:35** *1342*
from the blood of **r** Abel to the **Mt 23:35** *1342*
"Then the **r** will answer Him, **Mt 25:37** *1342*
but the **r** into eternal life." **Mt 25:46** *1342*
nothing to do with that **r** Man; **Mt 27:19** *1342*
I did not come to call the **r**, **Mk 2:17** *1342*
that he was a **r** and holy man, **Mk 6:20** *1342*
were both **r** in the sight of God, **Lk 1:6** *1342*
to the attitude of the **r**, **Lk 1:17** *1342*
and this man was **r** and devout, **Lk 2:25** *1342*
"I have not come to call the **r** but **Lk 5:32** *1342*

repaid at the resurrection of the **r**." **Lk 14:14** *1342*
than over ninety-nine **r** persons **Lk 15:7** *1342*
in themselves that they were **r**, **Lk 18:9** *1342*
sent spies who pretended to be **r**, **Lk 20:20** *1342*
of the Council, a good and **r** man **Lk 23:50** *1342*
but judge with **r** judgment." **Jn 7:24** *1342*
"O **r** Father, although the world **Jn 17:25** *1342*
you disowned the Holy and **R** One and **Ac 3:14** *1342*
announced the coming of the **R** One, **Ac 7:52** *1342*
a **r** and God-fearing man well **Ac 10:22** *1342*
His will and to see the **R** One **Ac 22:14** *1342*
of both the **r** and the wicked. **Ac 24:15** *1342*
THE **R** *MAN* SHALL LIVE BY FAITH." **Ro 1:17** *1342*
of the **r** judgment of God, **Ro 2:5** *1341*
"THERE IS NONE **R**, NOT EVEN ONE **Ro 3:10** *1342*
one will hardly die for a **r** man; **Ro 5:7** *1342*
the One the many will be made **r**. **Ro 5:19** *1342*
is holy and **r** and good. **Ro 7:12** *1342*
"THE **R** MAN SHALL LIVE BY FAITH." **Ga 3:11** *1342*
plain indication of God's **r** judgment **2Th 1:5** *1342*
that law is not made for a **r** person, **1Tm 1:9** *1342*
which the Lord, the **r** Judge, **2Tm 4:8** *1342*
AND THE **R** SCEPTER IS THE SCEPTER **Heb 1:8** *2118*
BUT MY **R** ONE SHALL LIVE BY FAITH; **Heb 10:38** *1342*
the testimony that he was **r**, **Heb 11:4** *1342*
the spirits of *the* **r** made perfect, **Heb 12:23** *1342*
and put to death the **r** *man* **Jas 5:6** *1342*
of a **r** man can accomplish much. **Jas 5:16** *1342*
EYES OF THE LORD ARE TOWARD THE **R**, **1Pe 3:12** *1342*
DIFFICULTY THAT THE **R** IS SAVED, **1Pe 4:18** *1342*
and *if* He rescued **r** Lot, **2Pe 2:7** *1342*
what he saw and heard *that* **r** man, **2Pe 2:8** *1342*
felt *his* **r** soul tormented day **2Pe 2:8** *1342*
He is faithful and **r** to forgive us **1Jn 1:9** *1342*
the Father, Jesus Christ the **r**; **1Jn 2:1** *1342*
If you know that He is **r**, **1Jn 2:29** *1342*
who practices righteousness is **r**, **1Jn 3:7** *1342*
is righteous, just as He is **r**; **1Jn 3:7** *1342*
evil, and his brother's were **r**. **1Jn 3:12** *1342*
R and true are Your ways, King **Rv 15:3** *1342*
YOUR **R** ACTS HAVE BEEN REVEALED." **Rv 15:4** *1345*
"**R** are You, who are and who **Rv 16:5** *1342*
true and **r** are Your judgments." **Rv 16:7** *1342*
HIS JUDGMENTS ARE TRUE AND **R**; **Rv 19:2** *1342*
linen is the **r** acts of the saints. **Rv 19:8** *1345*
and let the one who is **r**, **Rv 22:11** *1342*

RIGHTEOUSLY

and judge **r** between a man and his **Dt 1:16** 6664
'He who rules over men **r**, **2Sa 23:3** 6662
sat on the throne judging **r**. **Ps 9:4** 6664
Open your mouth, judge **r**, **Pr 31:9** 6664
Behold, a king will reign **r** And **Is 32:1** 6664
He who walks **r** and speaks with **Is 33:15** 6666
sues **r** and no one pleads honestly. **Is 59:4** 6664
O LORD of hosts, who judges **r**, **Jer 11:20** 6664
r and godly in the present age, **Ti 2:12** *1346*
Himself to Him who judges **r**; **1Pe 2:23** *1346*

RIGHTEOUSNESS

and He reckoned it to him as **r**. **Gn 15:6** 6666
the LORD by doing **r** and justice, **Gn 18:19** 6666
"It will be **r** for us if we **Dt 6:25** 6666
'Because of my **r** the LORD has **Dt 9:4** 6666
"It is not for your **r** or for the **Dt 9:5** 6666
it is not because of your **r** *that* **Dt 9:6** 6666
and it will be **r** for you before **Dt 24:13** 6666
LORD will repay each man *for* his **r** **1Sa 26:23** 6666
justice and **r** for all his people. **2Sa 8:15** 6666
has rewarded me according to my **r**; **2Sa 22:21** 6666
recompensed me according to my **r**, **2Sa 22:25** 6666
he walked before You in truth and **r** **1Ki 3:6** 6666
by giving him according to his **r**. **1Ki 8:32** 6666
you king, to do justice and **r**." **1Ki 10:9** 6666
justice and **r** for all his people. **1Ch 18:14** 6666
by giving him according to his **r**. **2Ch 6:23** 6666
over them, to do justice and **r**." **2Ch 9:8** 6666
Even desist, my **r** is yet in it. **Jb 6:29** 6664
I hold fast my **r** and will not let it go. **Jb 27:6** 6666
"I put on **r**, and it clothed me; **Jb 29:14** 6664
And He may restore His **r** to man. **Jb 33:26** 6666
'My **r** is more than God's'? **Jb 35:2** 6664
And your **r** is for a son of man. **Jb 35:8** 6666
And I will ascribe **r** to my Maker. **Jb 36:3** 6664
to justice and abundant **r**. **Jb 37:23** 6666
me when I call, O God of my **r**! **Ps 4:1** 6664
Offer the sacrifices of **r**, **Ps 4:5** 6664
lead me in Your **r** because of my foes **Ps 5:8** 6666
according to my **r** and my integrity **Ps 7:8** 6664
to the LORD according to His **r** And **Ps 7:17** 6664
And He will judge the world in **r**; **Ps 9:8** 6664
the LORD is righteous, He loves **r**; **Ps 11:7** 6666
walks with integrity, and works **r**, **Ps 15:2** 6664
me, I shall behold Your face in **r**; **Ps 17:15** 6664
has rewarded me according to my **r**; **Ps 18:20** 6664
recompensed me according to my **r**, **Ps 18:24** 6664
will declare His **r** To a people who **Ps 22:31** 6666
the paths of **r** For His name's sake. **Ps 23:3** 6664
r from the God of his salvation. **Ps 24:5** 6666
In Your **r** deliver me. **Ps 31:1** 6666
He loves **r** and justice; **Ps 33:5** 6666
O LORD my God, according to Your **r**, **Ps 35:24** 6664
Your **r** *And* Your praise all day long. **Ps 35:28** 6664
r is like the mountains of God; **Ps 36:6** 6666
And Your **r** to the upright in heart. **Ps 36:10** 6666
bring forth your **r** as the light And **Ps 37:6** 6664
of **r** in the great congregation; **Ps 40:9** 6664
not hidden Your **r** within my heart; **Ps 40:10** 6666
cause of truth and meekness *and* **r**; **Ps 45:4** 6664
You have loved **r** and hated **Ps 45:7** 6664

Your right hand is full of **r**. Ps 48:10 6664
And the heavens declare His **r**, Ps 50:6 6664
will joyfully sing of Your **r**. Ps 51:14 6666
Do you indeed speak **r**, Ps 58:1 6664
deeds You answer us in **r**, Ps 65:5 6664
And may they not come into Your **r**. Ps 69:27 6666
In Your **r** deliver me and rescue me; Ps 71:2 6666
My mouth shall tell of Your **r** Ps 71:15 6666
I will make mention of Your **r** Ps 71:16 6666
For Your **r**, O God, *reaches* to the Ps 71:19 6666
will utter Your **r** all day long; Ps 71:24 6666
O God, And Your **r** to the king's son. Ps 72:1 6666
May he judge Your people with **r** And Ps 72:2 6664
to the people, And the hills, in **r**. Ps 72:3 6666
R and peace have kissed each other. Ps 85:10 6664
And **r** looks down from heaven. Ps 85:11 6664
R will go before Him And will Ps 85:13 6664
r in the land of forgetfulness? Ps 88:12 6666
R and justice are the foundation Ps 89:14 6664
And by Your **r** they are exalted. Ps 89:16 6666
He will judge the world in **r** And Ps 96:13 6664
R and justice are the foundation Ps 97:2 6664
The heavens declare His **r**, Ps 97:6 6664
His **r** in the sight of the nations. Ps 98:2 6666
He will judge the world with **r** And Ps 98:9 6664
executed justice and **r** in Jacob. Ps 99:4 6666
And His **r** to children's children, Ps 103:17 6666
Who practice **r** at all times! Ps 106:3 6666
And it was reckoned to him for **r**, Ps 106:31 6666
And His **r** endures forever. Ps 111:3 6666
house, And his **r** endures forever. Ps 112:3 6666
His **r** endures forever; Ps 112:9 6666
Open to me the gates of **r**; Ps 118:19 6664
Revive me through Your **r**. Ps 119:40 6666
I have done justice and **r**; Ps 119:121 6664
in **r** And exceeding faithfulness. Ps 119:138 6664
Your **r** is an everlasting Ps 119:142 6666
righteousness is an everlasting **r**, Ps 119:142 6664
For all Your commandments are **r**. Ps 119:172 6664
Let Your priests be clothed with **r**, Ps 132:9 6664
me in Your faithfulness, in Your **r**! Ps 143:1 6666
r bring my soul out of trouble. Ps 143:11 6666
And will shout joyfully of Your **r**. Ps 145:7 6666
instruction in wise behavior, **R**, Pr 1:3 6664
Then you will discern **r** and Pr 2:9 6664
utterances of my mouth are in **r**; Pr 8:8 6664
with me, Enduring wealth and **r**. Pr 8:18 6666
"I walk in the way of **r**, Pr 8:20 6666
profit, But **r** delivers from death. Pr 10:2 6666
wrath, But **r** delivers from death. Pr 11:4 6666
The **r** of the blameless will smooth Pr 11:5 6666
The **r** of the upright will deliver Pr 11:6 6666
he who sows **r** *gets* a true reward. Pr 11:18 6666
in **r** *will attain* to life, Pr 11:19 6666
In the way of **r** is life, And in Pr 12:28 6666
R guards the one whose way is Pr 13:6 6666
R exalts a nation, But sin is a Pr 14:34 6666
But He loves one who pursues **r**. Pr 15:9 6666
Better is a little with **r** Than Pr 16:8 6666
For a throne is established on **r**. Pr 16:12 6666
It is found in the way of **r**. Pr 16:31 6666
And he upholds his throne by **r**. Pr 20:28 2617a
To do **r** and justice Is desired by Pr 21:3 6666
pursues **r** and loyalty Finds life, Pr 21:21 6666
loyalty Finds life, **r** and honor. Pr 21:21 6666
throne will be established in **r**. Pr 25:5 6664
place of **r** there is wickedness. Ec 3:16 6664
of justice and **r** in the province, Ec 5:8 6664
man who perishes in his **r** and Ec 7:15 6664
R once lodged in her, But now Is 1:21 6664
you will be called the city of **r**, Is 1:26 6664
And her repentant ones with **r**. Is 1:27 6666
For **r**, but behold, a cry of Is 5:7 6666
God will show Himself holy in **r**. Is 5:16 6666
and to uphold it with justice and **r** Is 9:7 6666
is determined, overflowing with **r**. Is 10:22 6666
But with **r** He will judge the poor, Is 11:4 6664
Also **r** will be the belt about His Is 11:5 6664
seek justice And be prompt in **r**. Is 16:5 6664
inhabitants of the world learn **r**. Is 26:9 6664
shown favor, He does not learn **r**; Is 26:10 6664
measuring line And **r** the level; Is 28:17 6666
And **r** will abide in the fertile field. Is 32:16 6666
And the work of **r** will be peace, Is 32:17 6666
be peace, And the service of **r**, Is 32:17 6666
filled Zion with justice and **r**. Is 33:5 6666
Whom He calls in **r** to His feet? Is 41:2 6664
the LORD, I have called you in **r**, Is 42:6 6664
And let the clouds pour down **r**; Is 45:8 6664
fruit, And **r** spring up with it. Is 45:8 6666
"I have aroused him in **r** And Is 45:13 6664
speak **r**, Declaring things that are Is 45:19 6664
mouth in **r** And will not turn back, Is 45:23 6666
in the LORD are **r** and strength.' Is 45:24 6666
Who are far from **r**. Is 46:12 6666
"I bring near My **r**, it is not far Is 46:13 6666
Israel, *But* not in truth nor in **r**. Is 48:1 6666
your **r** like the waves of the sea. Is 48:18 6666
"Listen to me, you who pursue **r**, Is 51:1 6664
"My **r** is near, My salvation has Is 51:5 6664
forever, And My **r** will not wane. Is 51:6 6666
"Listen to Me, you who know **r**, Is 51:7 6664
But My **r** will be forever, And My Is 51:8 6666
"In **r** you will be established; Is 54:14 6666
"Preserve justice and do **r**, Is 56:1 6666
to come And My **r** to be revealed. Is 56:1 6666
declare your **r** and your deeds, Is 57:12 6666
ways, As a nation that has done **r** And Is 58:2 6666
And your **r** will go before you; Is 58:8 6664

us, And **r** does not overtake us; Is 59:9 6666
back, And **r** stands far away; Is 59:14 6666
And His **r** upheld Him. Is 59:16 6666
He put on **r** like a breastplate, Is 59:17 6666
And **r** your overseers. Is 60:17 6666
So they will be called oaks of **r**, Is 61:3 6664
has wrapped me with a robe of **r**, Is 61:10 6666
So the Lord GOD will cause **r** and Is 61:11 6666
her **r** goes forth like brightness, Is 62:1 6664
The nations will see your **r**, Is 62:2 6664
"It is I who speak in **r**, Is 63:1 6666
meet him who rejoices in doing **r**, Is 64:5 6664
In truth, in justice and in **r**; Jer 4:2 6666
justice and **r** on earth; Jer 9:24 6666
"Do justice and **r**, and deliver Jer 22:3 6666
him who builds his house without **r** Jer 22:13 6666
and drink And do justice and **r**? Jer 22:15 6666
And do justice and **r** in the land. Jer 23:5 6666
He will be called, 'The LORD our **r**.' Jer 23:6 6664
'The LORD bless you, O abode of **r**, Jer 31:23 6664
execute justice and **r** on the earth. Jer 33:15 6666
the LORD is our **r**.' Jer 33:16 6664
LORD *who is* the habitation of **r**, Jer 50:7 6664
from his **r** and commits iniquity, Ezk 3:20 6664
by their *own* **r** they could *only* Ezk 14:14 6666
deliver only themselves by their **r**." Ezk 14:20 6666
and practices justice and **r**, Ezk 18:5 6666
son has practiced justice and **r** and Ezk 18:19 6666
the **r** of the righteous will be Ezk 18:20 6666
and practices justice and **r**, Ezk 18:21 6666
of his **r** which he has practiced, Ezk 18:22 6666
man turns away from his **r**, Ezk 18:24 6666
man turns away from his **r**, Ezk 18:26 6666
and practices justice and **r**, Ezk 18:27 6666
'The **r** of a righteous man will not Ezk 33:12 6666
man will not be able to live by his **r** Ezk 33:12
in his **r** that he commits iniquity, Ezk 33:13 6666
sin and practices justice and **r**, Ezk 33:14 6666
He has practiced justice and **r**; Ezk 33:16 6666
from his **r** and commits iniquity, Ezk 33:18 6666
and practices justice and **r**, Ezk 33:19 6666
and practice justice and **r**, Ezk 45:9 6666
now from your sins by *doing* **r** and Da 4:27 6665
"**R** belongs to You, O Lord, but Da 9:7 6666
to bring in everlasting **r**, Da 9:24 6664
and those who lead the many to **r**, Da 12:3 6663
Yes, I will betroth you to Me in **r** Hos 2:19 6664
Sow with a view to **r**, Hos 10:12 6666
Until He comes to rain **r** on you. Hos 10:12 6664
And cast **r** down to the earth." Am 5:7 6666
And **r** like an ever-flowing stream. Am 5:24 6666
And the fruit of **r** into wormwood, Am 6:12 6666
the light, *And* I will see His **r**. Mi 7:9 6666
Seek **r**, seek humility. Zph 2:3 6664
will be their God in truth and **r**.' Zch 8:8 6666
present to the LORD offerings in **r**. Mal 3:3 6666
the sun of **r** will rise with healing in Mal 4:2 6666
fitting for us to fulfill all **r**." Mt 3:15 *1343*
those who hunger and thirst for **r**, Mt 5:6 *1343*
been persecuted for the sake of **r**, Mt 5:10 *1343*
that unless your **r** surpasses *that* Mt 5:20 *1343*
"Beware of practicing your **r** Mt 6:1 *1343*
seek first His kingdom and His **r**, Mt 6:33 *1343*
of **r** and you did not believe him; Mt 21:32 *1343*
and **r** before Him all our days. Lk 1:75 *1343*
the world concerning sin and **r** Jn 16:8 *1343*
and concerning **r**, because I go to Jn 16:10 *1343*
of the devil, you enemy of all **r**, Ac 13:10 *1343*
judge the world in **r** through a Man Ac 17:31 *1343*
But as he was discussing **r**, Ac 24:25 *1343*
For in it *the* **r** of God is revealed Ro 1:17 *1343*
demonstrates the **r** of God, Ro 3:5 *1343*
the **r** of God has been manifested, Ro 3:21 *1343*
even *the* **r** of God through faith in Ro 3:22 *1343*
This was to demonstrate His **r**, Ro 3:25 *1343*
say, of His **r** at the present time, Ro 3:26 *1343*
AND IT WAS CREDITED TO HIM AS **R**." Ro 4:3 *1343*
his faith is credited as **r**, Ro 4:5 *1343*
God credits **r** apart from works: Ro 4:6 *1343*
WAS CREDITED TO ABRAHAM AS **R**." Ro 4:9 *1343*
a seal of the **r** of the faith which Ro 4:11 *1343*
that **r** might be credited to them, Ro 4:11 *1343*
Law, but through the **r** of faith. Ro 4:13 *1343*
IT WAS ALSO CREDITED TO HIM AS **R**. Ro 4:22 *1343*
of grace and of the gift of **r** will reign Ro 5:17 *1343*
even so through one act of **r** there Ro 5:18 *1345*
even so grace would reign through **r** Ro 5:21 *1343*
as instruments of **r** to God. Ro 6:13 *1343*
or of obedience resulting in **r**? Ro 6:16 *1343*
from sin, you became slaves of **r**. Ro 6:18 *1343*
present your members as slaves to **r**, Ro 6:19 *1343*
sin, you were free in regard to **r**. Ro 6:20 *1343*
the spirit is alive because of **r**. Ro 8:10 *1343*
Gentiles, who did not pursue **r**, Ro 9:30 *1343*
pursue righteousness, attained **r**, Ro 9:30 *1343*
even the **r** which is by faith; Ro 9:30 *1343*
but Israel, pursuing a law of **r**, Ro 9:31 *1343*
For not knowing about God's **r** and Ro 10:3 *1343*
subject themselves to the **r** of God. Ro 10:3 *1343*
for **r** to everyone who believes. Ro 10:4 *1343*
the man who practices the **r** which is Ro 10:5 *1343*
based on law shall live by that **r**. Ro 10:5 *846*
the **r** based on faith speaks as Ro 10:6 *1343*
person believes, resulting in **r**, Ro 10:10 *1343*
but **r** and peace and joy in the Ro 14:17 *1343*
God, and **r** and sanctification, 1Co 1:30 *1343*
the ministry of **r** abound in glory. 2Co 3:9 *1343*
might become the **r** of God in Him. 2Co 5:21 *1343*
by the weapons of **r** for the right 2Co 6:7 *1343*

for what partnership have **r** and 2Co 6:14 *1343*
THE POOR, HIS **R** ENDURES FOREVER." 2Co 9:9 *1343*
increase the harvest of your **r**; 2Co 9:10 *1343*
disguise themselves as servants of **r**, 2Co 11:15 *1343*
for if **r** *comes* through the Law, Ga 2:21 *1343*
AND IT WAS RECKONED TO HIM AS **R**. Ga 3:6 *1343*
then **r** would indeed have been Ga 3:21 *1343*
are waiting for the hope of **r**. Ga 5:5 *1343*
created in **r** and holiness of the truth. Eph 4:24 *1343*
in all goodness and **r** and truth), Eph 5:9 *1343*
PUT ON THE BREASTPLATE OF **R**, Eph 6:14 *1343*
fruit of **r** which *comes* through Jesus Php 1:11 *1343*
as to the **r** which is in the Law, Php 3:6 *1343*
not having a **r** of my own derived Php 3:9 *1343*
the **r** which *comes* from God on the Php 3:9 *1343*
and pursue **r**, godliness, faith, 1Tm 6:11 *1343*
from youthful lusts and pursue **r**, 2Tm 2:22 *1343*
for correction, for training in **r**; 2Tm 3:16 *1343*
is laid up for me the crown of **r**, 2Tm 4:8 *1343*
of deeds which we have done in **r**, Ti 3:5 *1343*
LOVED **R** AND HATED LAWLESSNESS; Heb 1:9 *1343*
not accustomed to the word of **r**, Heb 5:13 *1343*
translation *of his name,* king of **r**, Heb 7:2 *1343*
became an heir of the **r** which is Heb 11:7 *1343*
kingdoms, performed *acts of* **r**, Heb 11:33 *1343*
it yields the peaceful fruit of **r**. Heb 12:11 *1343*
man does not achieve the **r** of God. Jas 1:20 *1343*
AND IT WAS RECKONED TO HIM AS **R**," Jas 2:23 *1343*
And the seed whose fruit is **r** is Jas 3:18 *1343*
we might die to sin and live to **r**; 1Pe 2:24 *1343*
should suffer for the sake of **r**, 1Pe 3:14 *1343*
by the **r** of our God and Savior, 2Pe 1:1 *1343*
preserved Noah, a preacher of **r**, 2Pe 2:5 *1343*
not to have known the way of **r**, 2Pe 2:21 *1343*
a new earth, in which **r** dwells. 2Pe 3:13 *1343*
who practices **r** is born of Him. 1Jn 2:29 *1343*
one who practices **r** is righteous, 1Jn 3:7 *1343*
does not practice **r** is not of God, 1Jn 3:10 *1343*
and in **r** He judges and wages war. Rv 19:11 *1343*
is righteous, still practice **r**; Rv 22:11 *1343*

RIGHTEOUSNESS'
was pleased for His **r** sake Is 42:21 6664

RIGHTFUL
palace will stand on its **r** place. Jer 30:18 4941

RIGHT-HAND
the priest shall then dip his **r** finger Lv 14:16 3233
and with his **r** finger the priest Lv 14:27 3233
the net on the **r** side of the boat and Jn 21:6 *1188*

RIGHTLY
"Is he not **r** named Jacob, for he Gn 27:36
rule, and nobles, All who judge **r**. Pr 8:16 6664
R do they love you." SS 1:4 4339
r did Isaiah prophesy of you: Mt 15:7 *2573*
"**R** did Isaiah prophesy of you Mk 7:6 *2573*
"Do we not say **r** that You are a Jn 8:48 *2573*
but if **r**, why do you strike Me?" Jn 18:23 *2573*
"The Holy Spirit **r** spoke through Ac 28:25 *2573*
that the judgment of God **r** falls upon Ro 2:2 *2596, 225*
if he does not judge the body **r**. 1Co 11:29
But if we judged ourselves **r**, 1Co 11:31

RIGHTS
her clothing, or her conjugal **r**. Ex 21:10 5772b
they have redemption **r** and revert Lv 25:31 1353
concerned for the **r** of the poor, Pr 29:7 1779
And pervert the **r** of all the afflicted. Pr 31:5 1779
For the **r** of all the unfortunate. Pr 31:8 1779
the **r** of the afflicted and needy. Pr 31:9 1779
And take away the **r** of the ones Is 5:23 6666
the poor of My people of *their* **r**, Is 10:2 4941
do not defend the **r** of the poor. Jer 5:28 4941

RIGOROUSLY
the sons of Israel to labor **r**; Ex 1:13 6531
which they **r** imposed on them. Ex 1:14 6531

RIM
it a **r** of a handbreadth around *it;* Ex 25:25 4526
a gold border for the **r** around it. Ex 25:25 4526
"The rings shall be close to the **r** Ex 25:27 4526
He made a **r** for it of a Ex 37:12 4526
gold molding for its **r** all around. Ex 37:12 4526
Close by the **r** were the rings, the Ex 37:14 4526

RIMMON
Lebaoth and Shilhim and Ain and **R**; Jos 15:32 7417c
Ain, **R** and Ether and Ashan; four Jos 19:7 7417c
to **R** which stretches to Neah. Jos 19:13 7417c
the wilderness to the rock of **R**, Jg 20:45 7417c
the wilderness to the rock of **R**, Jg 20:47 7417c
at the rock of **R** four months. Jg 20:47 7417c
who were at the rock of **R**, Jg 21:13 7417c
Rechab, sons of **R** the Beerothite, 2Sa 4:2 7417b
So the sons of **R** the Beerothite, 2Sa 4:5 7417b
brother, sons of **R** the Beerothite, 2Sa 4:9 7417b
the house of **R** to worship there, 2Ki 5:18 7417a
I bow myself in the house of **R**, 2Ki 5:18 7417a
I bow myself in the house of **R**, 2Ki 5:18 7417a
Their villages *were* Etam, Ain, **R**, 1Ch 4:32 7417c
from Geba to **R** south of Jerusalem; Zch 14:10 7417c

RIMMONO
R with its pasture lands, Tabor 1Ch 6:77 7417c

RIMMON-PEREZ
from Rithmah and camped at **R**. Nu 33:19 7428
They journeyed from **R** and Nu 33:20 7428

RIMS
Their axles, their **r**, 1Ki 7:33 1354
r they were lofty and awesome, Ezk 1:18 1354
and the **r** of all four of them were Ezk 1:18 1354

RING
the man took a gold **r** Gn 24:22 5141

When he saw the **r** **Gn 24:30** 5141
and I put the **r** on her nose, and **Gn 24:47** 5141
whose signet **r** and cords and staff **Gn 38:25** 2858
off his signet **r** from his hand and **Gn 41:42** 2885
to its top to the first **r**; **Ex 26:24** 2885
to its top to the first **r**; **Ex 36:29** 2885
Then the king took his signet **r** **Es 3:10** 2885
sealed with the king's signet **r**. **Es 3:12** 2885
The king took off his signet **r** **Es 8:2** 2885
seal *it* with the king's signet **r**; **Es 8:8** 2885
and sealed with the king's signet **r** **Es 8:8** 2885
sealed it with the king's signet **r**, **Es 8:10** 2885
of money, and each a **r** of gold. **Jb 42:11** 5141
As a **r** of gold in a swine's snout **Pr 11:22** 5141
king of Judah were a signet **r** on **Jer 22:24**
"I also put a **r** in your nostril, **Ezk 16:12** 5141
king sealed it with his own signet **r** **Da 6:17** 5824
'and I will make you like a signet **r**, **Hg 2:23**
and put a **r** on his hand and **Lk 15:22** *1146*
with a gold **r** and dressed in fine **Jas 2:2** *5554*

RINGLEADER
a **r** of the sect of the Nazarenes. **Ac 24:5** *4414*

RINGS
the **r** which were in their ears, **Gn 35:4** 5141
You shall cast four gold **r** for it **Ex 25:12** 2885
and two **r** shall be on one side of **Ex 25:12** 2885
and two **r** on the other side of it. **Ex 25:12** 2885
You shall put the poles into the **r** **Ex 25:14** 2885
shall remain in the **r** of the ark; **Ex 25:15** 2885
"You shall make four gold **r** **Ex 25:26** 2885
and put **r** on the four corners **Ex 25:26** 2885
"The **r** shall be close to the rim **Ex 25:27** 2885
make their **r** of gold *as* holders **Ex 26:29** 2885
four bronze **r** at its four corners. **Ex 27:4** 2885
Its poles shall be inserted into the **r**, **Ex 27:7** 2885
on the breastpiece two **r** of gold, **Ex 28:23** 2885
and shall put the two **r** on the two **Ex 28:23** 2885
the two cords of gold on the two **r** **Ex 28:24** 2885
"You shall make two **r** of gold **Ex 28:26** 2885
"You shall make two **r** of gold **Ex 28:27** 2885
They shall bind the breastpiece by its **r** **Ex 28:28** 2885
r of the ephod with a blue cord, **Ex 28:28** 2885
You shall make two gold **r** for it **Ex 30:4** 2885
"Tear off the gold **r** which are in **Ex 32:2** 5141
gold **r** which were in their ears and **Ex 32:3** 5141
and signet **r** and bracelets, **Ex 35:22** 2885
made their **r** of gold *as* holders **Ex 36:34** 2885
He cast four **r** of gold for it **Ex 37:3** 2885
even two **r** on one side of it, and **Ex 37:3** 2885
and two **r** on the other side of it. **Ex 37:3** 2885
the **r** on the sides of the ark, **Ex 37:5** 2885
He cast four gold **r** for it and **Ex 37:13** 2885
and put the **r** on the four corners **Ex 37:13** 2885
Close by the rim were the **r**, **Ex 37:14** 2885
golden **r** for it under its molding, **Ex 37:27** 2885
He cast four **r** on the four **Ex 38:5** 2885
the **r** on the sides of the altar, **Ex 38:7** 2885
filigree *settings* and two gold **r**, **Ex 39:16** 2885
and put the two **r** on the two ends **Ex 39:16** 2885
put the two gold cords in the two **r** **Ex 39:17** 2885
They made two gold **r** and **Ex 39:19** 2885
they made two gold **r** and placed **Ex 39:20** 2885
They bound the breastpiece by its **r** **Ex 39:21** 2885
r of the ephod with a blue cord, **Ex 39:21** 2885
armlets and bracelets, signet **r**, **Nu 31:50** 2885
on silver **r** and marble columns, **Es 1:6** 1551
finger **r**, nose rings, **Is 3:21** 2885
finger rings, nose **r**, **Is 3:21** 5141
with the signet **r** of his nobles, **Da 6:17** 5824

RINNAH
sons of Shimon *were* Amnon and **R**, **1Ch 4:20** 7441

RINSE
r things for the burnt offering; **2Ch 4:6** 1740
there they **r** the burnt offering. **Ezk 40:38** 1740

RINSED
shall be scoured and **r** in water. **Lv 6:28** 7857
without having **r** his hands in water **Lv 15:11** 7857
wooden vessel shall be **r** in water. **Lv 15:12** 7857

RIOT
imaginations of *their* heart run **r**. **Ps 73:7** 5674a
a **r** might occur among the people." **Mt 26:5** *2351*
but rather that a **r** was starting, **Mt 27:24** *2351*
there might be a **r** of the people." **Mk 14:2** *2351*
are in danger of being accused of a **r** **Ac 19:40** *4714b*
with anyone or causing a **r**. **Ac 24:12** *3793, 1988a*

RIOTOUS
And the scalps of the **r** revelers. **Jer 48:45** 7588

RIP
women with child you will **r** up." **2Ki 8:12** 1234

RIPE
his last and died in a **r** old age, **Gn 25:8** 2896a
his people, an old man of **r** age; **Gn 35:29** 7649
its clusters produced **r** grapes. **Gn 40:10** 1310
the time of the first **r** grapes. **Nu 13:20** 1061
blossoms, and it bore **r** almonds. **Nu 17:8** 1580
"The first **r** fruits of all that **Nu 18:13** 1061
the son of Joash died at a **r** old age **Jg 8:32** 2896a
Then he died in a **r** old age, **1Ch 29:28** 2896a
when Jehoiada reached a **r** old age **2Ch 24:15** 7646, 3117
the sickle, for the harvest is **r**. **Jl 3:13** 1310
fortifications are fig trees with **r** fruit **Na 3:12** 1061
the harvest of the earth is **r**." **Rv 14:15** *3583*
earth, because her grapes are **r**." **Rv 14:18** *187*

RIPEN
for they **r** late.) **Ex 9:32**

RIPENED
a grain offering of early **r** things **Lv 2:14** 1061
grain offering of your early **r** things. **Lv 2:14** 1061
'The fig tree has **r** its figs, **SS 2:13** 2590

RIPENING
And the flower becomes a **r** grape, **Is 18:5** 1580

RIPHATH
were Ashkenaz and **R** and Togarmah. **Gn 10:3** 7384

RIPPED
and **r** up all its women who were **2Ki 15:16** 1234
pregnant women will be **r** open. **Hos 13:16** 1234
Because they **r** open the pregnant **Am 1:13** 1234

RISE
But a mist used to **r** from the **Gn 2:6** 5927
may **r** early and go on your way." **Gn 19:2** 7925
angry that I cannot **r** before you, **Gn 31:35** 6965
"**R** early in the morning and **Ex 8:20** 7925
"**R** up early in the morning and **Ex 9:13** 7925
r from his place for three days, **Ex 10:23** 6965
"**R** up, get out from among my **Ex 12:31** 6965
those who **r** up against You; **Ex 15:7** 6965
shall **r** up before the grayheaded and **Lv 19:32** 6965
that Moses said, "**R** up, O LORD! **Nu 10:35** 6965
call you, **r** up *and* go with them; **Nu 22:20** 6965
A scepter shall **r** from Israel, **Nu 24:17** 6965
you lie down and when you **r** up. **Dt 6:7** 6965
you lie down and when you **r** up. **Dt 11:19** 6965
"A single witness shall not **r** up **Dt 19:15** 6965
shall cause your enemies who **r** up **Dt 28:7** 6965
r above you higher and higher, **Dt 28:43** 5927
your sons who **r** up after you and **Dt 29:22** 6965
Let them **r** up and help you, Let **Dt 32:38** 6965
of those who **r** up against him, **Dt 33:11** 6965
so that they will not **r** *again*." **Dt 33:11** 6965
So the LORD said to Joshua, "**R** up! **Jos 7:10** 6965
R up! Consecrate the people and say, **Jos 7:13** 6965
"And you shall **r** from *your* ambush **Jos 8:7** 6965
"**R**, kill them." **Jg 8:20** 6965
"**R** up yourself, and fall on us; **Jg 8:21** 6965
r early and rush upon the city; **Jg 9:33** 7925
cloud of smoke **r** from the city. **Jg 20:38** 5927
But when the cloud began to **r** from **Jg 20:40** 5927
that he would **r** up against me by **1Sa 22:13** 6965
allow them to **r** up against Saul. **1Sa 24:7** 6965
"Should anyone **r** up to pursue **1Sa 25:29** 6965
Absalom used to **r** early and **2Sa 15:2** 7925
all who **r** up against you for evil, **2Sa 18:32** 6965
them, so that they did not **r**; **2Sa 22:39** 6965
above those who **r** up against me; **2Sa 22:49** 6965
So man lies down and does not **r**. **Jb 14:12** 6965
I **r** up and they speak against me. **Jb 19:18** 6965
the earth will **r** up against him. **Jb 20:27** 6965
upon whom does His light not **r**? **Jb 25:3** 6965
From those who **r** up *against them*. **Ps 17:7** 6965
so that they were not able to **r**; **Ps 18:38** 6965
above those who **r** up against me; **Ps 18:48** 6965
and shield And **r** up for my help. **Ps 35:2** 6965
Malicious witnesses **r** up; **Ps 35:11** 6965
been thrust down and cannot **r**. **Ps 36:12** 6965
down, he will not **r** up again." **Ps 41:8** 6965
down those who **r** up against us. **Ps 44:5** 6965
R up, be our help, And redeem us **Ps 44:26** 6965
from those who **r** up against me. **Ps 59:1** 6965
The uproar of those who **r** against **Ps 74:23** 6965
Will the departed spirits **r** *and* praise **Ps 88:10** 6965
When its waves **r**, You still **Ps 89:9** 5375
the evildoers who **r** up against me. **Ps 92:11** 6965
R up, O Judge of the earth, **Ps 94:2** 5375
At midnight I shall **r** to give thanks **Ps 119:62** 6965
I **r** before dawn and cry for help; **Ps 119:147** 6923
It is vain for you to **r** up early, **Ps 127:2** 6965
when I sit down and when I **r** up; **Ps 139:2** 6965
those who **r** up against You? **Ps 139:21** 6965
pits from which they cannot **r**. **Ps 140:10** 6965
their calamity will **r** suddenly, **Pr 24:22** 6965
glory, But when the wicked **r**, **Pr 28:12** 6965
When the wicked **r**, men hide **Pr 28:28** 6965
Her children **r** up and bless her; **Pr 31:28** 6965
r early *and go* to the vineyards; **SS 7:12** 7925
Woe to those who **r** early in the **Is 5:11** 7925
And it will **r** up over all its channels **Is 8:7** 5927
"I will **r** up against them," **Is 14:22** 6965
"**R** up, captains, oil the shields," **Is 21:5** 6965
it will fall, never to **r** again. **Is 24:20** 6965
the departed spirits will not **r**; **Is 26:14** 6965
Their corpses will **r**. **Is 26:19** 6965
LORD will **r** up as *at* Mount Perazim, **Is 28:21** 6965
R up, you women who are at ease, **Is 32:9** 6965
lie down together *and* not **r** again; **Is 43:17** 6965
yourself from the dust, **r** up, **Is 52:2** 6965
your light will **r** in darkness And **Is 58:10** 2224
But the LORD will **r** upon you And **Is 60:2** 2224
and **r** no more because of the sword **Jer 25:27** 6965
they would **r** up and burn this city **Jer 37:10** 6965
"I will **r** and cover *that* land; **Jer 46:8** 5927
waters are going to **r** from the **Jer 47:2** 5927
her, And **r** up for battle!" **Jer 49:14** 6965
let him **r** up in his scale-armor; **Jer 51:3** 5927
Babylon sink down and not **r** again **Jer 51:64** 6965
their wings to **r** from the ground, **Ezk 10:16** 7311
up, the wheels would **r** with them, **Ezk 10:17** 7311
"Now in those times many will **r** **Da 11:14** 5975
you will enter into rest and **r** *again* **Da 12:13** 5975
your camp **r** up in your nostrils; **Am 4:10** 5927
She has fallen, she will not **r** again **Am 5:2** 6965
Then I will **r** up against the **Am 7:9** 6965
all of it will **r** up like the Nile, **Am 8:8** 5927
They will fall and not **r** again." **Am 8:14** 6965
Though I fall I will **r**; **Mi 7:8** 6965
Distress will not **r** up twice. **Na 1:9** 6965
not your creditors **r** up suddenly, **Hab 2:7** 6965
the day when I **r** up as a witness. **Zph 3:8** 6965
but Jerusalem will **r** and remain on **Zch 14:10** 7213
will **r** with healing in its wings; **Mal 4:2** 2224
sun to **r** on *the* evil and *the* good, **Mt 5:45** *393*
children will **r** up against parents and **Mt 10:21** *1881*
"*The* Queen of *the* South will **r** **Mt 12:42** *1453*
"For nation will **r** against nation, **Mt 24:7** *1453*
'After three days I *am to* **r** again.' **Mt 27:63** *1453*
and after three days **r** again. **Mk 8:31** *450*
He will **r** three days later." **Mk 9:31** *450*
three days later He will **r** again." **Mk 10:34** *450*
resurrection, when they **r** again, **Mk 12:23** *450*
"For when they **r** from the dead, **Mk 12:25** *450*
the fact that the dead **r** again, **Mk 12:26** *1453*
"For nation will **r** up against nation, **Mk 13:8** *1453*
and children will **r** up against **Mk 13:12** *1881*
the fall and **r** of many in Israel, **Lk 2:34** *386*
"The Queen of the South will **r** **Lk 11:31** *1453*
the third day He will **r** again." **Lk 18:33** *450*
"Nation will **r** against nation and **Lk 21:10** *1453*
and the third day **r** again." **Lk 24:7** *450*
Christ would suffer and **r** again from **Lk 24:46** *450*
"Your brother will **r** again." **Jn 11:23** *450*
"I know that he will **r** again in **Jn 11:24** *450*
He must **r** again from the dead. **Jn 20:9** *450*
suffer and **r** again from the dead, **Ac 17:3** *450*
the dead in Christ will **r** first. **1Th 4:16** *450*
which give **r** to mere speculation **1Tm 1:4** *3930*

RISEN
The sun had **r** over the earth when **Gn 19:23** 3318
"*But* if the sun has **r** on him, **Ex 22:3** 2224
you have **r** up in your fathers' place, **Nu 32:14** 6965
no prophet has **r** in Israel like Moses **Dt 34:10** 6965
but you have **r** against my father's **Jg 9:18** 6965
has **r** against your maidservant, **2Sa 14:7** 6965
for I have **r** in place of my father **1Ki 8:20** 6965
attendant of the man of God had **r** **2Ki 6:15** 6965
for I have **r** in the place of my **2Ch 6:10** 6965
that city has **r** up against the kings in **Ezr 4:19** 5376
iniquities have **r** above our heads and **Ezr 9:6** 7235a
But we have **r** and stood upright. **Ps 20:8** 6965
false witnesses have **r** against me, **Ps 27:12** 6965
For strangers have **r** against me And **Ps 54:3** 6965
arrogant men have **r** up against me, **Ps 86:14** 6965
glory of the LORD has **r** upon you. **Is 60:1** 2224
not ford, for the water had **r**, **Ezk 47:5** 1342
"But when the sun had **r**, **Mt 13:6** *393*
he has **r** from the dead, **Mt 14:2** *1453*
Son of Man has **r** from the dead." **Mt 17:9** *1453*
'He has **r** from the dead,' and the **Mt 27:64** *1453*
"He is not here, for He has **r**, **Mt 28:6** *1453*
that He has **r** from the dead; **Mt 28:7** *1453*
"If Satan has **r** up against **Mk 3:26** *450*
"And after the sun had **r**, **Mk 4:6** *393*
the Baptist has **r** from the dead, **Mk 6:14** *1453*
"John, whom I beheaded, has **r**!" **Mk 6:16** *1453*
to the tomb when the sun had **r**. **Mk 16:2** *393*
He has **r**; He is not here; **Mk 16:6** *1453*
Now after He had **r** early on the **Mk 16:9** *450*
who had seen Him after He had **r**. **Mk 16:14** *1453*
that John had **r** from the dead, **Lk 9:7** *1453*
the prophets of old had **r** again. **Lk 9:8** *450*
the prophets of old has **r** again." **Lk 9:19** *450*
"He is not here, but He has **r**. **Lk 24:6** *1453*
"The Lord has really **r** and **Lk 24:34** *1453*
Jesus Christ, **r** from the dead, **2Tm 2:8** *1453*

RISES
"Behold, a people **r** like a lioness, **Nu 23:24** 6965
lies in wait for him and **r** up against **Dt 19:11** 6965
"If a malicious witness **r** up **Dt 19:16** 6965
for just as a man **r** against his **Dt 22:26** 6965
who **r** up and builds this city Jericho; **Jos 6:26** 6965
Mount Halak, that **r** toward Seir, **Jos 11:17** 5927
Mount Halak, which **r** toward Seir; **Jos 12:7** 5927
king's wrath **r** and he says to you, **2Sa 11:20** 5927
of the morning *when* the sun **r**, **2Sa 23:4** 2224
And my leanness **r** up against me, **Jb 16:8** 6965
He **r**, but no one has assurance of **Jb 24:22** 6965
My voice **r** to God, and I will **Ps 77:1**
My voice **r** to God, and He will **Ps 77:1**
When the sun **r** they withdraw And **Ps 104:22** 2224
falls seven times, and **r** again, **Pr 24:16** 6965
She **r** also while it is still night And **Pr 31:15** 6965
Also, the sun **r** and the sun sets; **Ec 1:5** 2224
to its place it **r** there *again*. **Ec 1:5** 2224
the ruler's temper **r** against you, **Ec 10:4** 5927
The sun will be dark when it **r** And **Is 13:10** 3318
Who is this that **r** like the Nile, **Jer 46:7** 5927
Egypt **r** like the Nile, Even like **Jer 46:8** 5927
And all of it **r** up like the Nile **Am 9:5** 5927
Daughter **r** up against her mother, **Mi 7:6** 6965
The sun **r** and they flee, And the **Na 3:17** 2224
if someone **r** from the dead.' " **Lk 16:31** *450*
the sun **r** with a scorching wind and **Jas 1:11** *393*
HER SMOKE **R** UP FOREVER AND EVER." **Rv 19:3** *305*

RISING
the **r** of the sun in its might." **Jg 5:31** 3318
Israel, who are **r** up against me." **2Ki 16:7** 6965
r up early in the morning and **Jb 1:5** 7925
Many are **r** up against me. **Ps 3:1** 6965
Its **r** is from one end of the heavens **Ps 19:6** 4161
the **r** of the sun to its setting. **Ps 50:1** 4217
From the **r** of the sun to its setting **Ps 113:3** 4217
From the **r** of the sun he will call **Is 41:25** 4217
That men may know from the **r** to **Is 45:6** 4217

His glory from the **r** of the sun, **Is 59:19** 4217
kings to the brightness of your **r**. **Is 60:3** 2225
to you, **r** up early and speaking, **Jer 7:13** 7925
daily **r** early and sending *them*. **Jer 7:25** 7925
Look on their sitting and their **r**; **La 3:63** 7012
fragrance of the cloud of incense **r**. **Ezk 8:11** 5927
"For from the **r** of the sun even **Mal 1:11** 4217
what **r** from the dead meant. **Mk 9:10** *450*
you see a cloud **r** in the west, **Lk 12:54** *393*
ascending from the **r** of the sun, **Rv 7:2** *395*

RISK
who went at the **r** of their lives? **1Ch 11:19**
For at the **r** of their lives they **1Ch 11:19**
to **r** his life to approach Me?' **Jer 30:21** 6148
We get our bread at the **r** of our **La 5:9**

RISKED
my father fought for you and **r** his life **Jg 9:17** 7993, 5048
men who have **r** their lives for the **Ac 15:26** *3860*
who for my life **r** their own necks, **Ro 16:4** *5294*

RISKING
r his life to complete what was **Php 2:30** *3850a*

RISSAH
from Libnah and camped at **R**. **Nu 33:21** 7446
They journeyed from **R** and **Nu 33:22** 7446

RITE
you shall observe this **r**. **Ex 12:25** 5656
'What does this **r** mean to you?' **Ex 12:26** 5656
observe this **r** in this month. **Ex 13:5** 5656

RITHMAH
from Hazeroth and camped at **R**. **Nu 33:18** 7575
They journeyed from **R** and **Nu 33:19** 7575

RIVAL
sister as a **r** while she is alive, **Lv 18:18** 6887d
Her **r**, however, would provoke her **1Sa 1:6** 6869b

RIVALRY
r between a man and his neighbor. **Ec 4:4** 7068

RIVER
Now a **r** flowed out of Eden to **Gn 2:10** 5104
The name of the second **r** is Gihon; **Gn 2:13** 5104
The name of the third **r** is Tigris; **Gn 2:14** 5104
And the fourth **r** is the Euphrates. **Gn 2:14** 5104
From the **r** of Egypt as far as the **Gn 15:18** 5104
of Egypt as far as the great **r**, **Gn 15:18** 5104
the great river, the **r** Euphrates: **Gn 15:18** 5104
arose and crossed the *Euphrates* **R**, **Gn 31:21** 5104
Rehoboth on the *Euphrates* **R** **Gn 36:37** 5104
the wilderness to the **R** *Euphrates;* **Ex 23:31** 5104
at Pethor, which is near the **R**, **Nu 22:5** 5104
out, Like gardens beside the **r**, **Nu 24:6** 5104
Lebanon, as far as the great **r**, **Dt 1:7** 5104
the great river, the **r** Euphrates. **Dt 1:7** 5104
all along the **r** Jabbok and the **Dt 2:37** 5158a
border and as far as the **r** Jabbok, **Dt 3:16** 5158a
to Lebanon, *and* from the **r**, **Dt 11:24** 5104
from the river, the **r** Euphrates, **Dt 11:24** 5104
even as far as the great **r**, **Jos 1:4** 5104
the great river, the **r** Euphrates, **Jos 1:4** 5104
your fathers lived beyond the **R**, **Jos 24:2** 5104
father Abraham from beyond the **R**, **Jos 24:3** 5104
served beyond the **R** and in Egypt, **Jos 24:14** 5104
served which were beyond the **R**, **Jos 24:15** 5104
his many *troops* to the **r** Kishon, **Jg 4:7** 5158a
Harosheth-hagoyim to the **r** Kishon. **Jg 4:13** 5158a
went to restore his rule at the **R**. **2Sa 8:3** 5104
Arameans who were beyond the **R**, **2Sa 10:16** 5104
over all the kingdoms from the **R** **1Ki 4:21** 5104
over everything west of the **R**, **1Ki 4:24** 5104
over all the kings west of the **R**; **1Ki 4:24** 5104
them beyond the *Euphrates* **R**, **1Ki 14:15** 5104
and Habor, *on* the **r** of Gozan, **2Ki 17:6** 5104
and on the Habor, the **r** of Gozan, **2Ki 18:11** 5104
of Assyria to the **r** Euphrates. **2Ki 23:29** 5104
brook of Egypt to the **r** Euphrates. **2Ki 24:7** 5104
by the **R** became king in his place. **1Ch 1:48** 5104
wilderness from the **r** Euphrates, **1Ch 5:9** 5104
Hara and to the **r** of Gozan, **1Ch 5:26** 5104
his rule to the Euphrates **R**. **1Ch 18:3** 5104
Arameans who were beyond the **R**, **1Ch 19:16** 5104
all the kings from the Euphrates **R** **2Ch 9:26** 5104
rest of the region beyond the **R**. **Ezr 4:10** 5103
men in the region beyond the **R**. **Ezr 4:11** 5103
in *the province* beyond the **R**." **Ezr 4:16** 5103
of *the provinces* beyond the **R**: **Ezr 4:17** 5103
all *the provinces* beyond the **R**, **Ezr 4:20** 5103
of *the province* beyond the **R**, **Ezr 5:3** 5103
of *the province* beyond the **R**, **Ezr 5:6** 5103
officials, who were beyond the **R**, **Ezr 5:6** 5103
of *the province* beyond the **R**, **Ezr 6:6** 5103
of *the provinces* beyond the **R**, **Ezr 6:6** 5103
of *the provinces* beyond the **R**, **Ezr 6:8** 5103
of *the province* beyond the **R**, **Ezr 6:13** 5103
are *in the provinces* beyond the **R**, **Ezr 7:21** 5103
are in *the province* beyond the **R**, **Ezr 7:25** 5103
them at the **r** that runs to Ahava, **Ezr 8:15** 5104
a fast there at the **r** of Ahava, **Ezr 8:21** 5104
Then we journeyed from the **r** Ahava **Ezr 8:31** 5104
in the provinces beyond the **R**, **Ezr 8:36** 5104
of the provinces beyond the **R**, **Ne 2:7** 5104
of the provinces beyond the **R** and **Ne 2:9** 5104
of the province beyond the **R**. **Ne 3:7** 5104
a **r** becomes parched and dried up, **Jb 14:11** 5104
were washed away by a **r**? **Jb 22:16** 5104
"If a **r** rages, he is not alarmed; **Jb 40:23** 5104
to drink of the **r** of Your delights. **Ps 36:8** 5158a
r whose streams make glad the city **Ps 46:4** 5104
They passed through the **r** on foot; **Ps 66:6** 5104
the **R** to the ends of the earth. **Ps 72:8** 5104
the sea And its shoots to the **R**. **Ps 80:11** 5104
It ran in the dry places *like* a **r**. **Ps 105:41** 5104
the **R** With His scorching wind; **Is 11:15** 5104
And the **r** will be parched and dry. **Is 19:5** 5104
harvest of the **R** was her revenue; **Is 23:3** 2975
well-being would have been like a **r**, **Is 48:18** 5104
I extend peace to her like a **r**, **Is 66:12** 5104
by the Euphrates **R** at Carchemish, **Jer 46:2** 5104
In the north beside the **r** **Jer 46:6** 5104
of the north by the **r** Euphrates. **Jer 46:10** 5104
Let *your* tears run down like a **r** **La 2:18** 5158a
by the **r** Chebar among the exiles, **Ezk 1:1** 5104
of the Chaldeans by the **r** Chebar; **Ezk 1:3** 5104
beside the **r** Chebar at Tel-abib, **Ezk 3:15** 5104
glory which I saw by the **r** Chebar, **Ezk 3:23** 5104
beings that I saw by the **r** Chebar. **Ezk 10:15** 5104
the God of Israel by the **r** Chebar; **Ezk 10:20** 5104
I had seen by the **r** Chebar. **Ezk 10:22** 5104
which I saw by the **r** Chebar; **Ezk 43:3** 5104
it was a **r** that I could not ford, **Ezk 47:5** 5158a
in, a **r** that could not be forded. **Ezk 47:5** 5158a
me back to the bank of the **r**. **Ezk 47:6** 5158a
on the bank of the **r** there *were* **Ezk 47:7** 5158a
in every place where the **r** goes, **Ezk 47:9** 5158a
will live where the **r** goes. **Ezk 47:9** 5158a
"By the **r** on its bank, on one **Ezk 47:12** 5158a
"A **r** of fire was flowing And **Da 7:10** 5103
I was by the bank of the great **r**, **Da 10:4** 5104
one on this bank of the **r** and **Da 12:5** 2975
the other on that bank of the **r**. **Da 12:5** 2975
who was above the waters of the **r**, **Da 12:6** 2975
who was above the waters of the **r**, **Da 12:7** 2975
the **R** to the ends of the earth. **Zch 9:10** 5104
baptized by him in the Jordan **R**, **Mt 3:6** *4215*
baptized by him in the Jordan **R**, **Mk 1:5** *4215*
bound at the great **r** Euphrates." **Rv 9:14** *4215*
the serpent poured water like a **r** out **Rv 12:15** *4215*
opened its mouth and drank up the **r** **Rv 12:16** *4215*
out his bowl on the great **r**, **Rv 16:12** *4215*
me a **r** of the water of life, **Rv 22:1** *4215*
of the **r** was the tree of life, **Rv 22:2** *4215*

RIVERS
it divided and became four **r**. **Gn 2:10** 7218
the waters of Egypt, over their **r**, **Ex 7:19** 5104
hand with your staff over the **r**, **Ex 8:5** 5104
water, in the seas or in the **r**, **Lv 11:9** 5158a
whatever is in the seas and in the **r** that **Lv 11:10** 5158a
and Pharpar, the **r** of Damascus, **2Ki 5:12** 5104
I dried up All the **r** of Egypt." **2Ki 19:24** 2975
r flowing with honey and curds. **Jb 20:17** 5104
And established it upon the **r**. **Ps 24:2** 5104
caused waters to run down like **r**. **Ps 78:16** 5104
And turned their **r** to blood, **Ps 78:44** 2975
sea And his right hand on the **r**. **Ps 89:25** 5104
Let the **r** clap their hands, **Ps 98:8** 5104
He changes **r** into a wilderness And **Ps 107:33** 5104
By the **r** of Babylon, There we sat **Ps 137:1** 5104
All the **r** flow into the sea, Yet **Ec 1:7** 5158a
To the place where the **r** flow, **Ec 1:7** 5158a
love, Nor will **r** overflow it; **SS 8:7** 5104
remotest part of the **r** of Egypt and **Is 7:18** 2975
Which lies beyond the **r** of Cush, **Is 18:1** 5104
nation Whose land the **r** divide. **Is 18:2** 5104
nation, Whose land the **r** divide **Is 18:7** 5104
us A place of **r** *and* wide canals On **Is 33:21** 5104
I dried up All the **r** of Egypt.' **Is 37:25** 2975
"I will open **r** on the bare **Is 41:18** 5104
I will make the **r** into coastlands And **Is 42:15** 5104
And through the **r**, they will not **Is 43:2** 5104
the wilderness, **R** in the desert. **Is 43:19** 5104
wilderness And **r** in the desert, **Is 43:20** 5104
And I will make your **r** dry. **Is 44:27** 5104
Uncover the leg, cross the **r**. **Is 47:2** 5104
rebuke, I make the **r** a wilderness; **Is 50:2** 5104
the **r** whose waters surge about? **Jer 46:7** 5104
the **r** whose waters surge about; **Jer 46:8** 5104
that lies in the midst of his **r**, **Ezk 29:3** 2975
of your **r** cling to your scales. **Ezk 29:4** 2975
you up out of the midst of your **r**, **Ezk 29:4** 2975
your **r** will cling to your scales. **Ezk 29:4** 2975
you and all the fish of your **r**; **Ezk 29:5** 2975
am against you and against your **r**, **Ezk 29:10** 2975
With its **r** it continually extended **Ezk 31:4** 5104
deep over it and held back its **r**. **Ezk 31:15** 5104
And you burst forth in your **r** And **Ezk 32:2** 5104
your feet And fouled their **r**.' " **Ezk 32:2** 5104
cause their **r** to run like oil," **Ezk 32:14** 5104
of rams, In ten thousand **r** of oil? **Mi 6:7** 5158a
He dries up all the **r**. **Na 1:4** 5104
The gates of the **r** are opened And **Na 2:6** 5104
Did the LORD rage against the **r**, **Hab 3:8** 5104
Or *was* Your anger against the **r**, **Hab 3:8** 5104
cleaved the earth with **r**. **Hab 3:9** 5104
the **r** of Ethiopia My worshipers, **Zph 3:10** 5104
will flow **r** of living water.' " **Jn 7:38** *4215*
journeys, in dangers from **r**, **2Co 11:26** *4215*
it fell on a third of the **r** and on the **Rv 8:10** *4215*
the **r** and the springs of waters; **Rv 16:4** *4215*

RIVERSIDE
we went outside the gate to a **r**, **Ac 16:13** *3844, 4215*

RIZIA
of Ulla *were* Arah, Hanniel and **R**. **1Ch 7:39** 7525

RIZPAH
had a concubine whose name was **R**, **2Sa 3:7** 7532
sons of **R** the daughter of Aiah, **2Sa 21:8** 7532
And **R** the daughter of Aiah took **2Sa 21:10** 7532
David what **R** the daughter of Aiah, **2Sa 21:11** 7532

ROAD
which is on the **r** to Timnah; **Gn 38:14** 1870
he turned aside to her by the **r**, **Gn 38:16** 1870
who was by the **r** at Enaim?" **Gn 38:21** 1870
in Seir, away from the Arabah **r**, **Dt 2:8** 1870
and went up the **r** to Bashan, **Dt 3:1** 1870
when you walk along the **r** and when **Dt 11:19** 1870
misleads a blind *person* on the **r**.' **Dt 27:18** 1870
the **r** to the Jordan to the fords; **Jos 2:7** 1870
had sought *them* all along the **r**, **Jos 2:22** 1870
And you who travel on the **r**—sing! **Jg 5:10** 1870
might pass by them along the **r**; **Jg 9:25** 1870
seat by the **r** eagerly watching, **1Sa 4:13** 1870
is before Jeshimon, beside the **r**, **1Sa 26:3** 1870
many people were coming from the **r** **2Sa 13:34** 1870
the Shilonite found him on the **r**. **1Ki 11:29** 1870
and his body was thrown on the **r**, **1Ki 13:24** 1870
and saw the body thrown on the **r**, **1Ki 13:25** 1870
and found his body thrown on the **r** **1Ki 13:28** 1870
push the needy aside from the **r**; **Jb 24:4** 1870
"There is a lion in the **r**! **Pr 26:13** 1870
along the **r**, his sense is lacking **Ec 10:3** 1870
place and of terrors on the **r**; **Ec 12:5** 1870
Surely on the **r** to Horonaim they **Is 15:5** 1870
I will make all My mountains a **r**, **Is 49:11** 1870
tired out by the length of your **r**, **Is 57:10** 1870
are you doing on the **r** to Egypt, **Jer 2:18** 1870
are you doing on the **r** to Assyria, **Jer 2:18** 1870
field And do not walk on the **r**, **Jer 6:25** 1870
"Stand by the **r** and keep watch, O **Jer 48:19** 1870
Do not stand at the fork of the **r** **Ob 1:14** 6563
Man the fortress, watch the **r**; **Na 2:1** 1870
some *seeds* fell beside the **r**, **Mt 13:4** *3598*
whom seed was sown beside the **r**. **Mt 13:19** *3598*
two blind men sitting by the **r**, **Mt 20:30** *3598*
spread their coats in the **r**, **Mt 21:8** *3598*
and spreading them in the **r**. **Mt 21:8** *3598*
Seeing a lone fig tree by the **r**, **Mt 21:19** *3598*
some *seed* fell beside the **r**, **Mk 4:4** *3598*
the **r** where the word is sown; **Mk 4:15** *3598*
They were on the **r** going **Mk 10:32** *3598*
son of Timaeus, was sitting by the **r**. **Mk 10:46** *3598*
and *began* following Him on the **r**. **Mk 10:52** *3598*
spread their coats in the **r**, **Mk 11:8** *3598*
he sowed, some fell beside the **r**, **Lk 8:5** *3598*
the **r** are those who have heard; **Lk 8:12** *3598*
As they were going along the **r**, **Lk 9:57** *3598*
priest was going down on that **r**, **Lk 10:31** *3598*
blind man was sitting by the **r** begging **Lk 18:35** *3598*
spreading their coats on the **r**. **Lk 19:36** *3598*
He was speaking to us on the **r**, **Lk 24:32** *3598*
to relate their experiences on the **r** **Lk 24:35** *3598*
"Get up and go south to the **r** that **Ac 8:26** *3598*
(This is a desert **r**.) **Ac 8:26**
the **r** they came to some water; **Ac 8:36** *3598*
on the **r** by which you were coming, **Ac 9:17** *3598*
how he had seen the Lord on the **r**, **Ac 9:27** *3598*

ROADMARKS
"Set up for yourself **r**, **Jer 31:21** 6725

ROADS
so that your **r** lie deserted. **Lv 26:22** 1870
shall prepare the **r** for yourself, **Dt 19:3** 1870
Along the **r** they will feed, And **Is 49:9** 1870
By the **r** you have sat for them **Jer 3:2** 1870
The **r** of Zion are in mourning **La 1:4** 1870
STRAIGHT, AND THE ROUGH **R** SMOOTH; **Lk 3:5** *3598*

ROADWAY
A highway will be there, a **r**, **Is 35:8** 1870
even make a **r** in the wilderness, **Is 43:19** 1870

ROAM
'We *are free to* **r**; **Jer 2:31** 7300
"**R** to and fro through the streets **Jer 5:1** 7751a

ROAMING
"From **r** about on the earth and **Jb 1:7** 7751a
"From **r** about on the earth and **Jb 2:2** 7751a

ROAR
sound of the **r** of a *heavy* shower." **1Ki 18:41** 1995
Let the sea **r**, and all it contains; **1Ch 16:32** 7481
Though its waters **r** *and* foam, **Ps 46:3** 1993
Let the sea **r**, and all it contains; **Ps 96:11** 7481
Let the sea **r** and all it contains, **Ps 98:7** 7481
young lions **r** after their prey And **Ps 104:21** 7580
r like the roaring of the seas, **Is 17:12** 1993
stirs up the sea and its waves **r** **Is 51:15** 1993
Though they **r**, yet they cannot **Jer 5:22** 1993
'The LORD will **r** from on high And **Jer 25:30** 7580
will **r** mightily against His fold. **Jer 25:30** 7580
up the sea so that its waves **r**; **Jer 31:35** 1993
will **r** together like young lions, **Jer 51:38** 7580
waves will **r** like many waters; **Jer 51:55** 1993
the LORD, He will **r** like a lion; **Hos 11:10** 7580
Indeed He will **r** And *His* sons **Hos 11:10** 7580
Does a lion **r** in the forest when **Am 3:4** 7580
is a sound of the young lions' **r**; **Zch 11:3** 7581
the heavens will pass away with a **r** **2Pe 3:10** *4500*

ROARED
Your adversaries have **r** in the **Ps 74:4** 7580
"The young lions have **r** at him, **Jer 2:15** 7580
roared at him, They have **r** loudly. **Jer 2:15** 5414, 6963
She has **r** against Me; **Jer 12:8** 5414, 6963
A lion has **r**! Who will not fear? **Am 3:8** 7580

ROARING
a young lion *came* **r** toward him. **Jg 14:5** 7580
"The **r** of the lion and the voice **Jb 4:10** 7581

at me, As a ravening and a **r** lion. Ps 22:13 7580
Who stills the **r** of the seas, Ps 65:7 7588
of the seas, The **r** of their waves, Ps 65:7 7588
wrath is like the **r** of a lion, Pr 19:12 5099
Like a **r** lion and a rushing bear Pr 28:15 5098
Its **r** is like a lioness, and it Is 5:29 7581
in that day like the **r** of the sea. Is 5:30 5100
Who roar like the **r** of the seas, Is 17:12 1993
Because of the sound of his **r**. Ezk 19:7 7581
like a **r** lion tearing the prey. Ezk 22:25 7580
princes within her are **r** lions, Zph 3:3 7580
at the **r** of the sea and the waves, Lk 21:25 *2279*
devil, prowls around like a **r** lion, 1Pe 5:8 *5612*

ROARS

"After it, a voice **r**; Jb 37:4 7580
and it **r** like young lions; Is 5:29 7580
Their voice **r** like the sea, And Jer 6:23 1993
Their voice **r** like the sea; And Jer 50:42 1993
The LORD **r** from Zion And Jl 3:16 7580
"The LORD **r** from Zion And from Am 1:2 7580
a loud voice, as when a lion **r**; Rv 10:3 *3455*

ROAST

lazy man does not **r** his prey, Pr 12:27 2760
he eats meat as he roasts a **r** and Is 44:16 6748
I **r** meat and eat *it*. Is 44:19 6740

ROASTED

that *same* night, **r** with fire, Ex 12:8 6748
water, but rather **r** with fire, Ex 12:9 6748
heads of grain **r** in the fire, Lv 2:14 7033
bread nor **r** grain nor new growth. Lv 23:14 7039
and he served her **r** grain, Ru 2:14 7039
this **r** grain and these ten loaves and 1Sa 17:17 7039
prepared and five measures of **r** grain 1Sa 25:18 7039
So they **r** the Passover *animals* on 2Ch 35:13 1310
the king of Babylon **r** in the fire, Jer 29:22 7033

ROASTING

"Give the priest meat for **r**, 1Sa 2:15 6740

ROASTS

half he eats meat as he **r** a roast and Is 44:16 6740

ROB

not oppress your neighbor, nor **r** *him*. Lv 19:13 1497
not **r** the poor because he is poor, Pr 22:22 1497
take the life of those who **r** them. Pr 22:23 6906
And **r** the poor of My people of Is 10:2 1497
They **r** a man and his house, A man Mi 2:2 6231
"Will a man **r** God? Mal 3:8 6906
who abhor idols, do you **r** temples? Ro 2:22 *2416*

ROBBED

be oppressed and **r** continually, Dt 28:29 1497
and they **r** all who might pass by Jg 9:25 1497
a bear **r** of her cubs in the field. 2Sa 17:8 7909b
And they are **r** of sleep unless Pr 4:16 1497
a man meet a bear **r** of her cubs, Pr 17:12 7909b
deliver the *person* who has been **r** Jer 21:12 1497
deliver the one who has been **r** from Jer 22:3 1497
extortion, **r** *his* brother and Ezk 18:18 1497
them like a bear **r** of her cubs, Hos 13:8 7909b
'How have we **r** You?' Mal 3:8 6906
I **r** other churches by taking wages 2Co 11:8 *4813*

ROBBER

Surely she lurks as a **r**, Pr 23:28 2863
your poverty will come *as* a **r** And Pr 24:34 1980
to arrest Me as *you would* against a **r**? Mt 26:55 *3027*
to arrest Me, as *you would* against a **r**? Mk 14:48 *3027*
clubs as you would against a **r**? Lk 22:52 *3027*
other way, he is a thief and a **r**. Jn 10:1 *3027*
Now Barabbas was a **r**. Jn 18:40 *3027*

ROBBERS

become a den of **r** in your sight? Jer 7:11 6530
then **r** will enter and profane it. Ezk 7:22 6530
"If thieves came to you, If **r** by night Ob 1:5 7703
two **r** were crucified with Him, Mt 27:38 *3027*
The **r** who had been Mt 27:44 *3027*
They crucified two **r** with Him, Mk 15:27 *3027*
and fell among **r**, Lk 10:30 *3027*
came before Me are thieves and **r**, Jn 10:8 *3027*
neither **r** of temples nor blasphemers Ac 19:37 *2417*
from rivers, dangers from **r**, 2Co 11:26 *3027*

ROBBERS'

but you are making it a **R** DEN." Mt 21:13 *3027*
But you have made it a **R** DEN." Mk 11:17 *3027*
who fell into the **r** *hands*?" Lk 10:36 *3027*
you have made it a **R** DEN." Lk 19:46 *3027*

ROBBERY

entrusted *to him*, or through **r**, Lv 6:2 1498
shall restore what he took by **r** or Lv 6:4 1497
And do not vainly hope in **r**; Ps 62:10 1498
I hate **r** in the burnt offering; Is 61:8 1498
his pledge, does not commit **r**, Ezk 18:7 1500
the poor and needy, commits **r**, Ezk 18:12 1500
or retain a pledge, or commit **r**, Ezk 18:16 1500
oppression and committed **r**, Ezk 22:29 1498
pays back what he has taken by **r**, Ezk 33:15 1500
"and you bring what was taken by **r** and Mal 1:13 1497
are full of **r** and self-indulgence. Mt 23:25 *724*
you are full of **r** and wickedness. Lk 11:39 *724*

ROBBING

Yet you are **r** Me! Mal 3:8 6906
with a curse, for you are **r** Me, Mal 3:9 6906

ROBE

a **r** and a tunic of checkered work, Ex 28:4 4598
make the **r** of the ephod all of blue. Ex 28:31 4598
all around on the hem of the **r**. Ex 28:34 4598
put on Aaron the tunic and the **r** Ex 29:5 4598
the **r** of the ephod of woven work, Ex 39:22 4598
r was *at the top* in the center, Ex 39:23 4598
twisted *linen* on the hem of the **r**. Ex 39:24 4598
all around on the hem of the **r**, Ex 39:25 7757
all around on the hem of the **r** for Ex 39:26 7757
priest is to put on his linen **r**, Lv 6:10 4055
sash, and clothed him with the **r** and Lv 8:7 4598
his mother would make him a little **r** 1Sa 2:19 4598
go, *Saul* seized the edge of his **r**, 1Sa 15:27 4598
Jonathan stripped himself of the **r** 1Sa 18:4 4598
cut off the edge of Saul's **r** secretly. 1Sa 24:4 4598
he had cut off the edge of Saul's **r**. 1Sa 24:5 4598
see the edge of your **r** in my hand! 1Sa 24:11 4598
in that I cut off the edge of your **r** 1Sa 24:11 4598
up, and he is wrapped with a **r**." 1Sa 28:14 4598
Now David was clothed with a **r** of 1Ch 15:27 4598
I tore my garment and my **r**, Ezr 9:3 4598
with my garment and my **r** torn, Ezr 9:5 4598
a royal **r** which the king has worn, Es 6:8 3830
and let the **r** and the horse be Es 6:9 3830
So Haman took the **r** and the horse, Es 6:11 3830
tore his **r** and shaved his head, Jb 1:20 4598
And each of them tore his **r** and Jb 2:12 4598
justice was like a **r** and a turban. Jb 29:14 4598
with their own shame as with a **r**. Ps 109:29 4598
train of His **r** filling the temple. Is 6:1 7757
me with a **r** of righteousness, Is 61:10 4598
throne, laid aside his **r** from him, Jon 3:6 155
You strip the **r** off the garment From Mi 2:8 145, 8008
put on a hairy **r** in order to deceive; Zch 13:4 155
Him and put a scarlet **r** on Him. Mt 27:28 *5511*
they took the *scarlet* **r** off Him Mt 27:31 *5511*
they took the purple **r** off Him Mk 15:20 *4209*
at the right, wearing a white **r**; Mk 16:5 *4749*
out the best **r** and put it on him, Lk 15:22 *4749*
dressed Him in a gorgeous **r** and Lk 23:11 *2066*
and put a purple **r** on Him; Jn 19:2 *2440*
crown of thorns and the purple **r**. Jn 19:5 *2440*
in a **r** reaching to the feet, Rv 1:13 *4158*
given to each of them a white **r**; Rv 6:11 *4749*
clothed with a **r** dipped in blood, Rv 19:13 *2440*
And on His **r** and on His thigh He Rv 19:16 *2440*

ROBES

And his **r** in the blood of grapes. Gn 49:11 5497
r which *were* on the kings of Midian Jg 8:26 899b
the king dressed themselves in **r**. 2Sa 13:18 4598
on his throne, arrayed in *their* **r**, 1Ki 22:10 899b
battle, but you put on your **r**." 1Ki 22:30 899b
on his throne, arrayed in *their* **r**, 2Ch 18:9 899b
battle, but you put on your **r**." 2Ch 18:29 899b
Esther put on her royal **r** and stood Es 5:1 4438
"Take quickly the **r** and the horse Es 6:10 3830
king in royal **r** of blue and white, Es 8:15 3830
down upon the edge of his **r**. Ps 133:2 4060a
festal **r**, outer tunics, cloaks, Is 3:22 4254
bind them in the edges of your **r**. Ezk 5:3
their thrones, remove their **r** and Ezk 26:16 4598
will clothe you with festal **r**." Zch 3:4 4254
Then the high priest tore his **r** and Mt 26:65 *2440*
who like to walk around in long **r**, Mk 12:38 *4749*
who like to walk around in long **r**, Lk 20:46 *4749*
witnesses laid aside their **r** at the feet Ac 7:58 *2440*
they tore their **r** and rushed out into Ac 14:14 *2440*
magistrates tore their **r** off them and Ac 16:22 *2440*
before the Lamb, clothed in white **r**, Rv 7:9 *4749*
who are clothed in the white **r**, Rv 7:13 *4749*
and they have washed their **r** and Rv 7:14 *4749*
Blessed are those who wash their **r**, Rv 22:14 *4749*

ROBS

the needy from him who **r** him?" Ps 35:10 1497
He who **r** his father or his mother And Pr 28:24 1497

ROBUST

Moabites, all **r** and valiant men; Jg 3:29 8082a

ROCK

you there on the **r** at Horeb; Ex 17:6 6697
and you shall strike the **r**, Ex 17:6 6697
you shall stand *there* on the **r**; Ex 33:21 6697
I will put you in the cleft of the **r** and Ex 33:22 6697
speak to the **r** before their eyes, Nu 20:8 5553
forth water for them out of the **r** and Nu 20:8 5553
gathered the assembly before the **r**. Nu 20:10 5553
water for you out of this **r**?" Nu 20:10 5553
struck the **r** twice with his rod; Nu 20:11 5553
water for you out of the **r** of flint. Dt 8:15 6697
"The **R**! His work is perfect, Dt 32:4 6697
He made him suck honey from the **r**, Dt 32:13 5553
rock, And oil from the flinty **r**, Dt 32:13 6697
scorned the **R** of his salvation. Dt 32:15 6697
"You neglected the **R** who begot you, Dt 32:18 6697
Unless their **R** had sold them, Dt 32:30 6697
their **r** is not like our Rock, Dt 32:31 6697
their rock is not like our **R**, Dt 32:31 6697
The **r** in which they sought refuge? Dt 32:37 6697
bread and lay them on this **r**, Jg 6:20 5553
and fire sprang up from the **r** and Jg 6:21 6697
they killed Oreb at the **r** of Oreb, Jg 7:25 6697
offered it on the **r** to the LORD, Jg 13:19 6697
in the cleft of the **r** of Etam. Jg 15:8 5553
the **r** of Etam and said to Samson, Jg 15:11 5553
and brought him up from the **r**. Jg 15:13 5553
the wilderness to the **r** of Rimmon, Jg 20:45 5553
the wilderness to the **r** of Rimmon, Jg 20:47 5553
at the **r** of Rimmon four months. Jg 20:47 5553
who were at the **r** of Rimmon, Jg 21:13 5553
Nor is there any **r** like our God. 1Sa 2:2 6697
and he came down to the **r** and 1Sa 23:25 5553
called that place the **R** of Escape. 1Sa 23:28 5553
spread it for herself on the **r**, 2Sa 21:10 6697
He said, "The LORD is my **r** and my 2Sa 22:2 5553
My God, my **r**, in whom I take 2Sa 22:3 6697
And who is a **r**, besides our God? 2Sa 22:32 6697
LORD lives, and blessed be my **r**; 2Sa 22:47 6697
be God, the **r** of my salvation, 2Sa 22:47 6697
said, The **R** of Israel spoke to me, 2Sa 23:3 6697
men went down to the **r** to David, 1Ch 11:15 6697
a **r** for them for their thirst, Ne 9:15 5553
"His roots wrap around a **r** pile, Jb 8:17 1530
And the **r** moves from its place; Jb 14:18 6697
the **r** to be moved from its place? Jb 18:4 6697
were engraved in the **r** forever! Jb 19:24 6697
hug the **r** for want of a shelter. Jb 24:8 6697
And copper is smelted from **r**. Jb 28:2 68
The **r** in gloom and deep shadow. Jb 28:3 68
And the **r** poured out for me Jb 29:6 6697
The LORD is my **r** and my fortress Ps 18:2 5553
and my deliverer, My God, my **r**, Ps 18:2 6697
And who is a **r**, except our God, Ps 18:31 6697
LORD lives, and blessed be my **r**; Ps 18:46 6697
O LORD, my **r** and my Redeemer. Ps 19:14 6697
He will lift me up on a **r**. Ps 27:5 6697
My **r**, do not be deaf to me, For Ps 28:1 6697
Be to me a **r** of strength, A Ps 31:2 6697
For You are my **r** and my fortress; Ps 31:3 5553
upon a **r** making my footsteps firm. Ps 40:2 5553
I will say to God my **r**, Ps 42:9 5553
Lead me to the **r** that is higher than I. Ps 61:2 6697
He only is my **r** and my salvation, Ps 62:2 6697
He only is my **r** and my salvation, Ps 62:6 6697
The **r** of my strength, my refuge is Ps 62:7 6697
Be to me a **r** of habitation Ps 71:3 6697
For You are my **r** and my fortress. Ps 71:3 5553
forth streams also from the **r** And Ps 78:16 5553
"Behold, He struck the **r** so Ps 78:20 6697
remembered that God was their **r**, Ps 78:35 6697
with honey from the **r** I would satisfy Ps 81:16 6697
God, and the **r** of my salvation.' Ps 89:26 6697
He is my **r**, and there is no Ps 92:15 6697
And my God the **r** of my refuge. Ps 94:22 6697
to the **r** of our salvation. Ps 95:1 6697
He opened the **r** and water flowed Ps 105:41 6697
turned the **r** into a pool of water, Ps 114:8 6697
your little ones Against the **r**. Ps 137:9 5553
thrown down by the sides of the **r**, Ps 141:6 5553
Blessed be the LORD, my **r**, Ps 144:1 6697
sky, The way of a serpent on a **r**, Pr 30:19 6697
"O my dove, in the clefts of the **r**, SS 2:14 5553
my bride, A **r** garden locked, SS 4:12 1530
Enter the **r** and hide in the dust Is 2:10 6697
to strike and a **r** to stumble over, Is 8:14 6697
of Midian at the **r** of Oreb; Is 10:26 6697
remembered the **r** of your refuge. Is 17:10 6697
a resting place for yourself in the **r**? Is 22:16 5553
LORD, *we have* an everlasting **R**. Is 26:4 6697
of the LORD, to the **R** of Israel. Is 30:29 6697
"His **r** will pass away because Is 31:9 5553
shade of a huge **r** in a parched land. Is 32:2 5553
refuge will be the impregnable **r**; Is 33:16 5553
Me, Or is there any *other* **R**? Is 44:8 6697
water flow out of the **r** for them; Is 48:21 6697
He split the **r** and the water Is 48:21 6697
to the **r** from which you were hewn And Is 51:1 6697
made their faces harder than **r**; Jer 5:3 5553
it there in a crevice of the **r**." Jer 13:4 5553
forsake the **r** of the open country? Jer 18:14 6697
like a hammer which shatters a **r**? Jer 23:29 5553
who live in the clefts of the **r**, Jer 49:16 5553
She placed it on the bare **r**; Ezk 24:7 5553
have put her blood on the bare **r**, Ezk 24:8 5553
from her and make her a bare **r**. Ezk 26:4 5553
"I will make you a bare **r**; Ezk 26:14 5553
who live in the clefts of the **r**, Ob 1:3 5553
And You, O **R**, have established Hab 1:12 6697
who built his house on the **r**. Mt 7:24 *4073*
it had been founded on the **r**. Mt 7:25 *4073*
upon this **r** I will build My church; Mt 16:18 *4073*
which he had hewn out in the **r**; Mt 27:60 *4073*
which had been hewn out in the **r**; Mk 15:46 *4073*
and laid a foundation on the **r**; Lk 6:48 *4073*
laid Him in a tomb cut into the **r**, Lk 23:53 *2991*
OF STUMBLING AND A **R** OF OFFENSE, Ro 9:33 *4073*
a spiritual **r** which followed them; 1Co 10:4 *4073*
and the **r** was Christ. 1Co 10:4 *4073*
OF STUMBLING AND A **R** OF OFFENSE"; 1Pe 2:8 *4073*

ROCKS

I see him from the top of the **r**, Nu 23:9 6697
front of the **R** of the Wild Goats. 1Sa 24:2 6697
in pieces the **r** before the LORD; 1Ki 19:11 5553
"Its **r** are the source of sapphires, Jb 28:6 68
hews out channels through the **r**, Jb 28:10 6697
holes of the earth and of the **r**. Jb 30:6 3710
He split the **r** in the wilderness And Ps 78:15 6697
they make their houses in the **r**; Pr 30:26 5553
Men will go into caves of the **r** Is 2:19 6697
r and the clefts of the cliffs Before Is 2:21 6697
thickets and climb among the **r**; Jer 4:29 3710
and from the clefts of the **r**. Jer 16:16 5553
Do horses run on **r**? Am 6:12 5553
And the **r** are broken up by Him. Na 1:6 6697
and the **r** were split. Mt 27:51 *4073*
run aground somewhere on the **r**, Ac 27:29 *5138*
and among the **r** of the mountains; Rv 6:15 *4073*
to the mountains and to the **r**, Rv 6:16 *4073*

ROCKY

and lodges, Upon the **r** crag, Jb 39:28 5553
O valley dweller, O **r** plain," Jer 21:13 6697
"Others fell on the **r** places, Mt 13:5 *4075*
seed was sown on the **r** places, Mt 13:20 *4075*
"Other *seed* fell on the **r** *ground* Mk 4:5 *4075*

seed was sown on the **r** *places,* **Mk 4:16** *4075*
"Other *seed* fell on **r** *soil,* **Lk 8:6** *4073*
Those on the **r** *soil are* those who, **Lk 8:13** *4073*

ROD
his male or female slave with a **r** **Ex 21:20** 7626
whatever passes under the **r**, **Lv 27:32** 7626
a **r** for each father's household: **Nu 17:2** 4294
shall write each name on his **r**, **Nu 17:2** 4294
Aaron's name on the **r** of Levi; **Nu 17:3** 4294
for there is one **r** for the head *of* **Nu 17:3** 4294
the **r** of the man whom I choose will **Nu 17:5** 4294
their leaders gave him a **r** apiece, **Nu 17:6** 4294
the **r** of Aaron among their rods. **Nu 17:6** 4294
the **r** of Aaron for the house of **Nu 17:8** 4294
looked, and each man took his **r**. **Nu 17:9** 4294
"Put back the **r** of Aaron before **Nu 17:10** 4294
"Take the **r**; and you and your **Nu 20:8** 4294
took the **r** from before the LORD, **Nu 20:9** 4294
struck the rock twice with his **r**; **Nu 20:11** 4294
I will correct him with the **r** of men **2Sa 7:14** 7626
"Let Him remove His **r** from me, **Jb 9:34** 7626
And the **r** of God is not on them. **Jb 21:9** 7626
shall break them with a **r** of iron, **Ps 2:9** 7626
Your **r** and Your staff, they comfort **Ps 23:4** 7626
their transgression with the **r** And **Ps 89:32** 7626
But a **r** is for the back of him who **Pr 10:13** 7626
He who withholds his **r** hates his son, **Pr 13:24** 7626
the foolish is a **r** for *his* back, **Pr 14:3** 2415
And the **r** of his fury will perish. **Pr 22:8** 7626
The **r** of discipline will remove it **Pr 22:15** 7626
Although you strike him with the **r**, **Pr 23:13** 7626
You shall strike him with the **r** **Pr 23:14** 7626
And a **r** for the back of fools. **Pr 26:3** 7626
The **r** and reproof give wisdom, But **Pr 29:15** 7626
The **r** of their oppressor, **Is 9:4** 7626
the **r** of My anger And the staff in **Is 10:5** 7626
a **r** lifting *him who* is not wood. **Is 10:15** 4294
Assyrian who strikes you with the **r** **Is 10:24** 7626
the earth with the **r** of His mouth, **Is 11:4** 7626
the **r** that struck you is broken; **Is 14:29** 7626
But dill is beaten out with a **r**, **Is 28:27** 4294
When He strikes with the **r**. **Is 30:31** 7626
every blow of the **r** of punishment, **Is 30:32** 4294
"I see a **r** of an almond tree." **Jer 1:11** 4731
Because of the **r** of His wrath. **La 3:1** 7626
the **r** has budded, arrogance has **Ezk 7:10** 4294
has grown into a **r** of wickedness. **Ezk 7:11** 4294
I will make you pass under the **r**, **Ezk 20:37** 7626
the **r** of My son despising every **Ezk 21:10** 7626
the **r** which despises will be no more **Ezk 21:13** 7626
and a measuring **r** in his hand; **Ezk 40:3** 7070
was a measuring **r** of six cubits, **Ezk 40:5** 7070
the thickness of the wall, one **r**; **Ezk 40:5** 7070
and the height, one **r**. **Ezk 40:5** 7070
of the gate, one **r** in width; **Ezk 40:6** 7070
threshold *was* one **r** in width. **Ezk 40:6** 7070
was one **r** long and one rod wide; **Ezk 40:7** 7070
was one rod long and one **r** wide; **Ezk 40:7** 7070
the gate facing inward *was* one **r**. **Ezk 40:7** 7070
of the gate facing inward, one **r**. **Ezk 40:8** 7070
r of six long cubits *in height.* **Ezk 41:8** 7070
With a **r** they will smite the judge **Mi 5:1** 7626
Shall I come to you with a **r**, **1Co 4:21** *4464*
manna, and Aaron's **r** which budded, **Heb 9:4** *4464*
SHALL RULE THEM WITH A **R** OF IRON, **Rv 2:27** *4464*
me a measuring **r** like a staff; **Rv 11:1** *2563*
rule all the nations with a **r** of iron; **Rv 12:5** *4464*
will rule them with a **r** of iron; **Rv 19:15** *4464*
gold measuring **r** to measure the city, **Rv 21:15** *2563*
he measured the city with the **r**, **Rv 21:16** *2563*

RODANIM
Elishah, Tarshish, Kittim and **R**. **1Ch 1:7** 7290c

RODE
sons who **r** on thirty donkeys, **Jg 10:4** 7392
who **r** on seventy donkeys; **Jg 12:14** 7392
quickly arose, and **r** on a donkey, **1Sa 25:42** 7392
men who **r** on camels and fled. **1Sa 30:17** 7392
"And He **r** on a cherub and flew; **2Sa 22:11** 7392
for him and he **r** away on it. **1Ki 13:13** 7392
And Ahab **r** and went to Jezreel. **1Ki 18:45** 7392
Then Jehu **r** in a chariot and went **2Ki 9:16** 7392
He **r** upon a cherub and flew; **Ps 18:10** 7392
That You **r** on Your horses, On Your **Hab 3:8** 7392

RODS
Then Jacob took fresh **r** of poplar **Gn 30:37** 4731
the white which *was* in the **r**. **Gn 30:37** 4731
He set the **r** which he had **Gn 30:38** 4731
So the flocks mated by the **r**, **Gn 30:39** 4731
Jacob would place the **r** in **Gn 30:41** 4731
so that they might mate by the **r**; **Gn 30:41** 4731
twelve **r**, from all their leaders **Nu 17:2** 4294
fathers' households, twelve **r**, **Nu 17:6** 4294
the rod of Aaron among their **r**. **Nu 17:6** 4294
So Moses deposited the **r** before **Nu 17:7** 4294
Moses then brought out all the **r** **Nu 17:9** 4294
are **r** of gold Set with beryl; **SS 5:14** 1551
The **r** of chastisement were sworn. **Hab 3:9** 4294
to order *them* to be beaten with **r**. **Ac 16:22** *4463*
Three times I was beaten with **r**, **2Co 11:25** *4463*

ROEBUCK
the deer, the gazelle, the **r**, **Dt 14:5** 3180

ROEBUCKS
sheep besides deer, gazelles, **r**, **1Ki 4:23** 3180

ROGELIM
Barzillai the Gileadite from **R**, **2Sa 17:27** 7274
Gileadite had come down from **R**; **2Sa 19:31** 7274

ROGUE
Or the **r** be spoken of *as* generous. **Is 32:5** 3596
As for a **r**, his weapons are evil; **Is 32:7** 3596

ROHGAH
The sons of Shemer *were* Ahi and **R**, **1Ch 7:34** 7303

ROLL
they would then **r** the stone from **Gn 29:3** 1556
and they **r** the stone from the **Gn 29:8** 1556
"**R** large stones against the mouth **Jos 10:18** 1556
r a great stone to me today." **1Sa 14:33** 1556
come, Amid the tempest they **r** on. **Jb 30:14** 1556
r upward in a column of smoke. **Is 9:18** 55
And **r** you tightly like a ball, *To* **Is 22:18** 6801
put on sackcloth And **r** in ashes; **Jer 6:26** 6428
And **r** you down from the crags, **Jer 51:25** 1556
"But let justice **r** down like waters **Am 5:24** 1556
r yourself in the dust. **Mi 1:10** 6428
"Who will **r** away the stone for us **Mk 16:3** *617*
LIKE A MANTLE YOU WILL **R** THEM UP; **Heb 1:12** *1667*

ROLLED
and **r** the stone from the mouth of **Gn 29:10** 1556
"Today I have **r** away the reproach **Jos 5:9** 1556
and Your waves have **r** over me. **Ps 42:7** 5674a
tumult, And cloak **r** in blood, **Is 9:5** 1556
sky will be **r** up like a scroll; **Is 34:4** 1556
As a weaver I **r** up my life. **Is 38:12** 7088
and he **r** a large stone against the **Mt 27:60** *4351*
and **r** away the stone and sat upon it. **Mt 28:2** *617*
and he **r** a stone against the **Mk 15:46** *4351*
that the stone had been **r** away, **Mk 16:4** *352a*
the stone **r** away from the tomb, **Lk 24:2** *617*
but **r** up in a place by itself. **Jn 20:7** *1794*
like a scroll when it is **r** up, **Rv 6:14** *1667*

ROLLING
he *began* **r** around and foaming *at* **Mk 9:20** *2947*

ROLLS
into it, And he who **r** a stone, **Pr 26:27** 1556

ROMAMTI-EZER
Hanani, Eliathah, Giddalti and **R**, **1Ch 25:4** 7320a
for the twenty-fourth to **R**, **1Ch 25:31** 7320a

ROMAN
and gathered the whole **R** cohort **Mt 27:27**
called together the whole **R** cohort. **Mk 15:16**
having received the **R** cohort **Jn 18:3**
So the **R** cohort and the commander **Jn 18:12**
a **R** colony; and we were staying **Ac 16:12**
to the commander of the **R** cohort **Ac 21:31**
man who is a **R** and uncondemned?" **Ac 22:25** *4514*
For this man is a **R**." **Ac 22:26** *4514*
"Tell me, are you a **R**?" **Ac 22:27** *4514*
when he found out that he was a **R**, **Ac 22:29** *4514*
having learned that he was a **R**. **Ac 23:27** *4514*

ROMANS
and the **R** will come and take away **Jn 11:48** *4514*
accept or to observe, being **R**." **Ac 16:21** *4514*
without trial, men who are **R**, **Ac 16:37** *4514*
when they heard that they were **R**, **Ac 16:38** *4514*
not the custom of the **R** to hand over **Ac 25:16** *4514*
Jerusalem into the hands of the **R**. **Ac 28:17** *4514*

ROME
Cyrene, and visitors from **R**, **Ac 2:10** *4514*
commanded all the Jews to leave **R**. **Ac 18:2** *4516*
been there, I must also see **R**." **Ac 19:21** *4516*
so you must witness at **R** also." **Ac 23:11** *4516*
and thus we came to **R**. **Ac 28:14** *4516*
When we entered **R**, **Ac 28:16** *4516*
all who are beloved of God in **R**, **Ro 1:7** *4516*
gospel to you also who are in **R**. **Ro 1:15** *4516*
but when he was in **R**, **2Tm 1:17** *4516*

ROMPHA
AND THE STAR OF THE GOD **R**, **Ac 7:43** *4501a*

ROOF
come under the shelter of my **r**." **Gn 19:8** 6982
shall make a parapet for your **r**, **Dt 22:8** 1406
But she had brought them up to the **r** **Jos 2:6** 1406
she had laid in order on the **r**. **Jos 2:6** 1406
she came up to them on the **r**, **Jos 2:8** 1406
alone in his cool **r** chamber. **Jg 3:20** 5944
doors of the **r** chamber behind him, **Jg 3:23** 5944
doors of the **r** chamber were locked **Jg 3:24** 5944
open the doors of the **r** chamber. **Jg 3:25** 5944
went up on the **r** of the tower. **Jg 9:51** 1406
3,000 men and women were on the **r** **Jg 16:27** 1406
Samuel spoke with Saul on the **r**. **1Sa 9:25** 1406
Samuel called to Saul on the **r**, **1Sa 9:26** 1406
on the **r** of the king's house, **2Sa 11:2** 1406
from the **r** he saw a woman bathing; **2Sa 11:2** 1406
a tent for Absalom on the **r**, **2Sa 16:22** 1406
to the **r** of the gate by the wall, **2Sa 18:24** 1406
The altars which *were* on the **r**, **2Ki 23:12** 1406
booths for themselves, each on his **r**, **Ne 8:16** 1406
tongue cling to the **r** of my mouth **Ps 137:6** 2441
better to live in a corner of a **r** Than **Pr 21:9** 1406
is better to live in a corner of the **r** **Pr 25:24** 1406
cleaves To the **r** of its mouth because **La 4:4** 2441
tongue stick to the **r** of your mouth **Ezk 3:26** 2441
from the **r** of the one guardroom to **Ezk 40:13** 1406
guardroom to the **r** of the other, **Ezk 40:13** 1406
later he was walking on the **r** *of* **Da 4:29**
in his **r** chamber he had windows **Da 6:10** 5952
worthy for You to come under my **r**, **Mt 8:8** *4721*
they removed the **r** above Him; **Mk 2:4** *4721*
they went up on the **r** and let him **Lk 5:19** *1430*
worthy for You to come under my **r**; **Lk 7:6** *4721*

ROOFS
offered incense to Baal on their **r** **Jer 32:29** 1406

ROOFTOPS
on whose **r** they burned sacrifices to **Jer 19:13** 1406

ROOM
is there **r** for us to lodge in your **Gn 24:23** 4725
and feed, and **r** to lodge in." **Gn 24:25** 4725
At last the LORD has made **r** for us, **Gn 26:22** 7337
relieving himself in the cool **r**." **Jg 3:24** 2315
will go in to my wife in *her* **r**." **Jg 15:1** 2315
men lying in wait in an inner **r**. **Jg 16:9** 2315
were lying in wait in the inner **r**. **Jg 16:12** 2315
them back into the guards' **r**. **1Ki 14:28** 8372
the upper **r** where he was living, **1Ki 17:19** 5944
brought him down from the upper **r** **1Ki 17:23** 5944
an inner **r** to hide yourself." **1Ki 22:25** 2315
and bring him to an inner **r**. **2Ki 9:2** 2315
the inner **r** of the house of Baal. **2Ki 10:25** 5892b
and the **r** for the mercy seat; **1Ch 28:11** 1004
He overlaid the main **r** with **2Ch 3:5** 1004
made the **r** of the holy of holies: **2Ch 3:8** 1004
two sculptured cherubim in the **r** of **2Ch 3:10** 1004
on their feet facing the *main* **r**. **2Ch 3:13** 1004
them back into the guards' **r**. **2Ch 12:11** 8372
an inner **r** to hide yourself." **2Ch 18:24** 2315
far as the upper **r** of the corner. **Ne 3:31** 5944
Between the upper **r** of the corner **Ne 3:32** 5944
had prepared a large **r** for him, **Ne 13:5** 3957
by preparing a **r** for him in the **Ne 13:7** 5393
household goods out of the **r**. **Ne 13:8** 3957
his royal throne in the throne **r**, **Es 5:1** 1004
A man's gift makes **r** for him And **Pr 18:16** 7337
the **r** of her who conceived me." **SS 3:4** 2315
field, Until there is no more **r**, **Is 5:8** 4725
Make **r** for me that I may live *here.*' **Is 49:20** 5066
man in the **r** of his carved images? **Ezk 8:12** 2315
Let the bridegroom come out of his **r** **Jl 2:16** 2315
of Gilead and Lebanon Until no **r** **Zch 10:10**
you pray, go into your inner **r**, **Mt 6:6** *5009*
so that there was no longer **r**, **Mk 2:2** *5562*
and entered *the* **r** where the child **Mk 5:40**
"Where is My guest **r** in which I **Mk 14:14** *2646*
large upper **r** furnished *and* ready; **Mk 14:15** *311b*
was no **r** for them in the inn. **Lk 2:7** *5117*
been done, and still there is **r**.' **Lk 14:22** *5117*
"Where is the guest **r** in which I **Lk 22:11** *2646*
you a large, furnished upper **r**; **Lk 22:12** *311b*
they went up to the upper **r** where **Ac 1:13** *5253*
body, they laid it in an upper **r**. **Ac 9:37** *5253*
they brought him into the upper **r**; **Ac 9:39** *5253*
There were many lamps in the upper **r** **Ac 20:8** *5253*
but leave **r** for the wrath *of God,* **Ro 12:19** *5117*
Make **r** for us *in your hearts* **2Co 7:2** *5562*

ROOMS
you shall make the ark with **r**, **Gn 6:14** 7064
its storehouses, its upper **r**, **1Ch 28:11** 5944
its upper rooms, its inner **r** and **1Ch 28:11** 2315
and for all the surrounding **r**, **1Ch 28:12** 3957
overlaid the upper **r** with gold. **2Ch 3:9** 5944
r in the house of the LORD, **2Ch 31:11** 3957
an order and they cleansed the **r**; **Ne 13:9** 3957
palace in front of the king's **r**, **Es 5:1** 1004
And by knowledge the **r** are filled **Pr 24:4** 2315
in your sleeping **r** do not curse a rich **Ec 10:20** 2315
my people, enter into your **r** And **Is 26:20** 2315
And his upper **r** without justice, **Jer 22:13** 5944
roomy house With spacious upper **r**, **Jer 22:14** 5944
'Behold, He is in the inner **r**,' **Mt 24:26** *5009*
have whispered in the inner **r** will be **Lk 12:3** *5009*

ROOMY
livestock will graze in a **r** pasture. **Is 30:23** 7337
'I will build myself a **r** house **Jer 22:14** 4060a

ROOSTER
The strutting **r**, the male goat also, **Pr 30:31** 4975
before a **r** crows, you will deny Me **Mt 26:34** *220*
And immediately a **r** crowed. **Mt 26:74** *220*
"Before a **r** crows, you will deny Me **Mt 26:75** *220*
the **r** crows, or in the morning **Mk 13:35** *219*
before a **r** crows twice, you yourself **Mk 14:30** *220*
Immediately a **r** crowed a second time. **Mk 14:72** *220*
"Before a **r** crows twice, you will **Mk 14:72** *220*
the **r** will not crow today until you **Lk 22:34** *220*
a **r** crowed. **Lk 22:60** *220*
"Before a **r** crows today, you will **Lk 22:61** *220*
a **r** will not crow until you deny Me **Jn 13:38** *220*
and immediately a **r** crowed. **Jn 18:27** *220*

ROOT
that there will not be among you a **r** **Dt 29:18** 8328
those whose **r** is in Amalek *came* **Jg 5:14** 8328
the house of Judah will again take **r** **2Ki 19:30** 8328
"I have seen the foolish taking **r**, **Jb 5:3** 8327
'My **r** is spread out to the waters, **Jb 29:19** 8328
food is the **r** of the broom shrub. **Jb 30:4** 8328
took deep **r** and filled the land. **Ps 80:9** 8328
But the **r** of the righteous will **Pr 12:3** 8328
r of the righteous yields *fruit.* **Pr 12:12** 8328
So their **r** will become like rot **Is 5:24** 8328
nations will resort to the **r** of Jesse, **Is 11:10** 8328
serpent's **r** a viper will come out, **Is 14:29** 8328
I will destroy your **r** with famine, **Is 14:30** 8328
days to come Jacob will take **r**, **Is 27:6** 8327
the house of Judah will again take **r** **Is 37:31** 8328
their stock taken **r** in the earth, **Is 40:24** 8327
like a **r** out of parched ground; **Is 53:2** 8328
them, they have also taken **r**; **Jer 12:2** 8327
is stricken, their **r** is dried up, **Hos 9:16** 8328
take **r** like *the cedars of* Lebanon. **Hos 14:5** 8328
his fruit above and his **r** below. **Am 2:9** 8328
"I will **r** out your Asherim from **Mi 5:14** 5428

leave them neither **r** nor branch."	Mal 4:1	8328
laid at the **r** of the trees;	Mt 3:10	*4491*
and because they had no **r**,	Mt 13:6	*4491*
yet he has no *firm* **r** in himself,	Mt 13:21	*4491*
and because it had no **r**,	Mk 4:6	*4491*
they have no *firm* **r** in themselves,	Mk 4:17	*4491*
laid at the **r** of the trees;	Lk 3:9	*4491*
and these have no *firm* **r**;	Lk 8:13	*4491*
and if the **r** is holy, the branches	Ro 11:16	*4491*
of the rich **r** of the olive tree,	Ro 11:17	*4491*
it is not you who supports the **r**,	Ro 11:18	*4491*
the root, but the **r** *supports* you.	Ro 11:18	*4491*
"THERE SHALL COME THE **R** OF JESSE,	Ro 15:12	*4491*
money is a **r** of all sorts of evil,	1Tm 6:10	*4491*
that no **r** of bitterness springing up	Heb 12:15	*4491*
tribe of Judah, the **R** of David,	Rv 5:5	*4491*
the **r** and the descendant of David,	Rv 22:16	*4491*

ROOTED

And they will not again be **r** out	Am 9:15	5428
you, being **r** and grounded in love,	Eph 3:17	*4492*
having been firmly **r** *and now* being	Col 2:7	*4492*

ROOTS

"His **r** wrap around a rock pile,	Jb 8:17	8328
its **r** grow old in the ground And	Jb 14:8	8328
"His **r** are dried below, And his	Jb 18:16	8328
branch from his **r** will bear fruit.	Is 11:1	8328
That extends its **r** by a stream And	Jer 17:8	8328
him, but its **r** remained under it.	Ezk 17:6	8328
this vine bent its **r** toward him	Ezk 17:7	8328
Will he not pull up its **r** and cut off	Ezk 17:9	8328
can it be raised from its **r** *again*.	Ezk 17:9	8328
For its **r** extended to many waters.	Ezk 31:7	8328
stump with its **r** in the ground,	Da 4:15	8330
stump with its **r** in the ground,	Da 4:23	8330
the stump with the **r** of the tree,	Da 4:26	8330
pulled out by the **r** before it;	Da 7:8	6132
to the **r** of the mountains.	Jon 2:6	7095
fig tree withered from the **r** *up*.	Mk 11:20	*4491*

ROPE

down by a **r** through the window,	Jos 2:15	2256a
"Can you put a **r** in his nose Or	Jb 41:2	100
Instead of a belt, a **r**;	Is 3:24	5364

ROPES

Then they bound him with two new **r**	Jg 15:13	5688
r that were on his arms were as flax	Jg 15:14	5688
new **r** which have not been used,	Jg 16:11	5688
So Delilah took new **r** and bound	Jg 16:12	5688
But he snapped the **r** from his arms	Jg 16:12	5688
Israel shall bring **r** to that city,	2Sa 17:13	2256a
on our loins and **r** on our heads,	1Ki 20:31	2256a
loins and *put* **r** on their heads,	1Ki 20:32	2256a
the wild ox in a furrow with **r**,	Jb 39:10	5688
And sin as if with cart **r**;	Is 5:18	5688
And all my **r** are broken;	Jer 10:20	4340
and they let Jeremiah down with **r**.	Jer 38:6	2256a
let them down by **r** into the cistern	Jer 38:11	2256a
under your armpits under the **r**";	Jer 38:12	2256a
So they pulled Jeremiah up with the **r**	Jer 38:13	2256a
they will put **r** on you and bind you	Ezk 3:25	5688
I will put **r** on you so that you	Ezk 4:8	5688
cut away the **r** of the *ship's* boat and	Ac 27:32	*4979*
loosening the **r** of the rudders;	Ac 27:40	*2202*

ROSE

that Cain **r** up against Abel his	Gn 4:8	6965
ark, so that it **r** above the earth.	Gn 7:17	7311
Then the men **r** up from there, and	Gn 18:16	6965
he **r** to meet them and bowed down	Gn 19:1	6965
So Abraham **r** early in the morning and	Gn 21:14	7925
So Abraham **r** early in the morning	Gn 22:3	7925
Abraham **r** from before his dead,	Gn 23:3	6965
So Abraham **r** and bowed to the	Gn 23:7	6965
drank, and **r** and went on his way.	Gn 25:34	6965
So Jacob **r** early in the morning,	Gn 28:18	7925
Now the sun **r** upon him just as he	Gn 32:31	2224
sheaf **r** up and also stood erect;	Gn 37:7	6965
of *their* bondage **r** up to God.	Ex 2:23	5927
So the next day they **r** early and	Ex 32:6	7965
and to drink, and **r** up to play.	Ex 32:6	6925
and Moses **r** up early in the	Ex 34:4	7925
they **r** up early and went up to the	Nu 14:40	7925
and they **r** up before Moses,	Nu 16:2	6965
Joshua **r** early in the morning;	Jos 3:1	7925
above stood *and* **r** up in one heap,	Jos 3:16	6965
Now Joshua **r** early in the morning,	Jos 6:12	7925
they **r** early at the dawning of the day	Jos 6:15	7925
So Joshua **r** with all the people of	Jos 8:3	6965
Now Joshua **r** early in the morning	Jos 8:10	7925
men of the city hurried and **r** up early	Jos 8:14	7925
men in ambush **r** quickly from	Jos 8:19	6965
r early and camped beside the	Jg 7:1	7925
"But the men of Gibeah **r** up	Jg 20:5	6965
When she **r** to glean, Boaz	Ru 2:15	6965
r before one could recognize another;	Ru 3:14	6965
Then Hannah **r** after eating and	1Sa 1:9	6965
The one crag **r** on the north	1Sa 14:5	4690
Samuel **r** early in the morning	1Sa 15:12	7925
and when he **r** up against me, I	1Sa 17:35	6965
Philistine **r** and came and drew near	1Sa 17:48	6965
David **r** up and went, he and his	1Sa 18:27	6965
then Jonathan **r** up and Abner sat	1Sa 20:25	6965
David **r** from the south side and	1Sa 20:41	6965
Then he **r** and departed, while	1Sa 20:42	6965
valiant men **r** and walked all night,	1Sa 31:12	6965
all those who **r** up against you."	2Sa 18:31	6965
me those who **r** up against me.	2Sa 22:40	6965
"When I **r** in the morning to	1Ki 3:21	6965
They **r** early in the morning,	2Ki 3:22	7925
she **r** and destroyed all the royal	2Ki 11:1	6965
when men **r** early in the morning,	2Ki 19:35	7925
King David **r** to his feet and said,	1Ch 28:2	6965
r up and rebelled against his	2Ch 13:6	6965
They **r** early in the morning	2Ch 20:20	7925
For the sons of Ammon and Moab **r**	2Ch 20:23	5975
she **r** and destroyed all the royal	2Ch 22:10	6965
Ezra **r** and made the leading priests,	Ezr 10:5	6965
Then Ezra **r** from before the house	Ezr 10:6	6965
fear, I **r** and spoke to the nobles,	Ne 4:14	6965
me those who **r** up against me.	Ps 18:39	6965
The anger of God **r** against them And	Ps 78:31	5927
The mountains **r**; the valleys sank	Ps 104:8	5927
They **r** up to the heavens, they	Ps 107:26	5927
side When men **r** up against us	Ps 124:2	6965
"I am the **r** of Sharon, The lily	SS 2:1	2261
some of the elders of the land **r** up	Jer 26:17	6965
living beings **r** from the earth,	Ezk 1:19	5375
from the earth, the wheels **r** *also*.	Ezk 1:19	5375
the wheels **r** close beside them;	Ezk 1:20	5375
whenever those **r** from the earth,	Ezk 1:21	5375
the wheels **r** close beside them;	Ezk 1:21	5375
Then the cherubim **r** up.	Ezk 10:15	7426a
and when they **r** up, the wheels	Ezk 10:17	7426a
they lifted their wings and **r** up	Ezk 10:19	7426a
But Jonah **r** up to flee to Tarshish	Jon 1:3	6965
"Then all those virgins **r** and	Mt 25:7	*1453*
until the Son of Man **r** from the dead.	Mk 9:9	*450*
When He **r** from prayer, He came	Lk 22:45	*450*
But the high priest **r** up,	Ac 5:17	*450*
"For some time ago Theudas **r** up,	Ac 5:36	*450*
r up in the days of the census and	Ac 5:37	*450*
r up and argued with Stephen.	Ac 6:9	*450*
crowd **r** up together against them,	Ac 16:22	*4911*
the Jews with one accord **r** up	Ac 18:12	*2721b*
died and **r** again on their behalf.	2Co 5:15	*1453*
believe that Jesus died and **r** again,	1Th 4:14	*450*

ROSH

Gera and Naaman, Ehi and **R**,	Gn 46:21	7220a
land of Magog, the prince of **R**,	Ezk 38:2	7220b
against you, O Gog, prince of **R**,	Ezk 38:3	7220b
against you, O Gog, prince of **R**,	Ezk 39:1	7220b

ROSTRUM

took his seat on the **r** and *began*	Ac 12:21	*968*

ROT

will **r** away because of their iniquity	Lv 26:39	4743
they will **r** away with them.	Lv 26:39	4743
But the name of the wicked will **r**.	Pr 10:7	7537
So their root will become like **r**	Is 5:24	4716
The reeds and rushes will **r** away.	Is 19:6	7060
Selects a tree that does not **r**;	Is 40:20	7537
will **r** away in your iniquities and	Ezk 24:23	4743
their flesh will **r** while they	Zch 14:12	4743
eyes will **r** in their sockets,	Zch 14:12	4743
tongue will **r** in their mouth.	Zch 14:12	4743

ROTE

consists of tradition learned *by* **r**,	Is 29:13	

ROTTED

Your riches have **r** and your	Jas 5:2	*4595*

ROTTEN

I am decaying like a **r** thing,	Jb 13:28	7538
iron as straw, Bronze as **r** wood.	Jb 41:27	7539

ROTTENNESS

shames *him* is like **r** in his bones.	Pr 12:4	7538
But passion is **r** to the bones.	Pr 14:30	7538
which could not be eaten due to **r**.	Jer 24:2	7455
which cannot be eaten due to **r**."	Jer 24:3	7455
figs which cannot be eaten due to **r**	Jer 24:8	7455
figs that cannot be eaten due to **r**	Jer 29:17	7455
And like **r** to the house of Judah.	Hos 5:12	7538

ROTTING

us, and we are **r** away in them;	Ezk 33:10	4743

ROUGH

let the **r** ground become a plain,	Is 40:4	6121b
you and make the **r** places smooth;	Is 45:2	1921
STRAIGHT, AND THE **R** ROADS SMOOTH;	Lk 3:5	*5138*

ROUGHLY

But the rich man answers **r**.	Pr 18:23	5794
poorly clothed, and are **r** treated,	1Co 4:11	*2852*

ROUND

'You shall not **r** off the	Lv 19:27	5362b
turned **r** on the west side southward,	Jos 18:14	5437
house **r** about with carved engravings	1Ki 6:29	4524
r like the design of a pedestal,	1Ki 7:31	5696
their borders were square, not **r**.	1Ki 7:31	5696
a **r** top to the throne at its rear,	1Ki 10:19	5696
set themselves against me **r** about.	Ps 3:6	5439
camp, **R** about their dwellings.	Ps 78:28	5439
poured out their blood like water **r**	Ps 79:3	5439
burns up His adversaries **r** about.	Ps 97:3	5439
the **r** shields of the mighty men.	SS 4:4	
"Your navel is *like* a **r** goblet	SS 7:2	5469
"Lift up your eyes **r** about and	Is 60:4	5439
and against all its walls **r** about and	Jer 1:15	5439
they are against her **r** about,	Jer 4:17	5439
against all these nations **r** about;	Jer 25:9	5439
That the ones **r** about him should be	La 1:17	5439
a flaming fire Consuming **r** about.	La 2:3	5439
of them were full of eyes **r** about.	Ezk 1:18	5439
or a painful thorn from any **r** about	Ezk 28:24	5439
all who scorn them **r** about them.	Ezk 28:26	5439
her graves are **r** about her.	Ezk 32:22	5439
her company is **r** about her grave.	Ezk 32:23	5439
of the nations which are **r** about,	Ezk 36:4	5439
the nations that are left **r** about you	Ezk 36:36	5439
me to pass among them **r** about,	Ezk 37:2	5439
the gate *extended* **r** about to the	Ezk 40:14	5439
galleries **r** about their three stories,	Ezk 41:16	5439
on its edge **r** about one span;	Ezk 43:13	5439
its base *shall be* a cubit **r** about;	Ezk 43:17	5439
ledge and on the border **r** about;	Ezk 43:20	5439
holy within all its boundary **r** about.	Ezk 45:1	5439
a square **r** about five hundred by	Ezk 45:2	5439
cubits for its open space **r** about.	Ezk 45:2	5439
a row *of masonry* **r** about in them,	Ezk 46:23	5439
were made under the rows **r** about.	Ezk 46:23	5439
city shall be 18,000 *cubits* **r** about;	Ezk 48:35	5439
so that from Jerusalem and **r** about	Ro 15:19	*2945*

ROUNDABOUT

And travelers went by **r** ways.	Jg 5:6	6128

ROUNDED

close to the **r** projection which	1Ki 7:20	990

ROUNDS

"The watchmen who make the **r** in	SS 3:3	5437
"The watchmen who make the **r** in	SS 5:7	5437

ROUSE

And as a lion, who dares **r** him up?	Gn 49:9	6965
And as a lion, who dares **r** him?	Nu 24:9	6965
Who are prepared to **r** Leviathan.	Jb 3:8	5782
Surely now He would **r** Himself for	Jb 8:6	5782
R yourself! Rouse yourself! Arise,	Is 51:17	5782
R yourself! Arise, O Jerusalem,	Is 51:17	5782
r the mighty men!	Jl 3:9	5782

ROUSED

and **r** me, as a man who is awakened	Zch 4:1	5782

ROUT

God will **r** him, not man.'	Jb 32:13	5086

ROUTED

The LORD **r** Sisera and all *his*	Jg 4:15	2000
Zalmunna, and **r** the whole army.	Jg 8:12	2729
so that they were **r** before Israel.	1Sa 7:10	5062
them, Lightning, and **r** them.	2Sa 22:15	2000
then it was that God **r** Jeroboam	2Ch 13:15	5062
So the LORD **r** the Ethiopians	2Ch 14:12	5062
come against Judah; so they were **r**.	2Ch 20:22	5062
flashes in abundance, and **r** them.	Ps 18:14	2000

ROVING

priest Have gone **r** about in the land	Jer 14:18	5503

ROW

first **r** *shall be* a row of ruby,	Ex 28:17	2905
first row *shall be* a **r** of ruby,	Ex 28:17	2905
and the second **r** a turquoise, a	Ex 28:18	2905
and the third **r** a jacinth, an	Ex 28:19	2905
and the fourth **r** a beryl and an	Ex 28:20	2905
The first **r** *was* a row of ruby,	Ex 39:10	2905
The first row *was* a **r** of ruby,	Ex 39:10	2905
and the second **r**, a turquoise, a	Ex 39:11	2905
and the third **r**, a jacinth, an	Ex 39:12	2905
and the fourth **r**, a beryl, an	Ex 39:13	2905
set them *in* two rows, six *to* a **r**,	Lv 24:6	4635
put pure frankincense on each **r** that	Lv 24:7	4635
cut stone and a **r** of cedar beams.	1Ki 6:36	2905
on the 45 pillars, 15 in each **r**.	1Ki 7:3	2905
cut stone and a **r** of cedar beams	1Ki 7:12	2905
There was a **r** *of masonry* round	Ezk 46:23	2905

ROWED

the men **r** *desperately* to return to	Jon 1:13	2864
had **r** about three or four miles,	Jn 6:19	*1643*

ROWERS

of Sidon and Arvad were your **r**;	Ezk 27:8	7751b
"Your **r** have brought you Into	Ezk 27:26	7751b

ROWS

mount on it four **r** of stones;	Ex 28:17	2905
mounted four **r** of stones on it.	Ex 39:10	2905
"You shall set them *in* two **r**,	Lv 24:6	4635
He built the inner court with three **r**	1Ki 6:36	2905
on four **r** of cedar pillars with	1Ki 7:2	2905
artistic window frames in three **r**,	1Ki 7:4	2905
all around *had* three **r** of cut stone	1Ki 7:12	2905
and two **r** around on the one	1Ki 7:18	2905
hundred in **r** around both capitals.	1Ki 7:20	2905
the gourds were in two **r**,	1Ki 7:24	2905
two **r** of pomegranates for each	1Ki 7:42	2905
The oxen *were* in two **r**,	2Ch 4:3	2905
two **r** of pomegranates for each	2Ch 4:13	2905
of David, Built with **r** of stones	SS 4:4	8530
cummin And plant wheat in **r**,	Is 28:25	7795a
up through her vine **r** and destroy,	Jer 5:10	7795b
were made under the **r** round about.	Ezk 46:23	2918

ROYAL

And he will yield **r** dainties.	Gn 49:20	4428
city, like one of the **r** cities,	Jos 10:2	4467
live in the **r** city with you?"	1Sa 27:5	4467
of Ammon and captured the **r** city.	2Sa 12:26	4410
her according to his **r** bounty.	1Ki 10:13	4428
he was of the **r** line in Edom.	1Ki 11:14	4428
The **r** officer on whose hand	2Ki 7:2	4428
Now the king appointed the **r** officer	2Ki 7:17	7991c
Then the **r** officer answered the	2Ki 7:19	7991c
the guard and to the **r** officers,	2Ki 10:25	7991c
and the **r** officers threw *them* out,	2Ki 10:25	7991c
and destroyed all the **r** offspring.	2Ki 11:1	4467
son of Elishama, of the **r** family,	2Ki 25:25	4410
and bestowed on him **r** majesty	1Ch 29:25	4438
LORD and a **r** palace for himself.	2Ch 2:1	4438
LORD and a **r** palace for himself.	2Ch 2:12	4438
then I will establish your **r** throne	2Ch 7:18	4438
rose and destroyed all the **r** offspring	2Ch 22:10	4467
placed the king upon the **r** throne.	2Ch 23:20	4467
we appointed you a **r** counselor?	2Ch 25:16	4428
cost be paid from the **r** treasury.	Ezr 6:4	4430
from the **r** treasury out of the taxes of	Ezr 6:8	4430
provide *for it* from the **r** treasury.	Ezr 7:20	4430

as King Ahasuerus sat on his **r** throne **Es 1:2** 4438
he displayed the riches of his **r** glory **Es 1:4** 4438
and the **r** wine was plentiful **Es 1:7** 4438
before the king with *her* **r** crown **Es 1:11** 4438
let a **r** edict be issued by him and **Es 1:19** 4438
let the king give her **r** position to **Es 1:19** 4438
to King Ahasuerus to his **r** palace **Es 2:16** 4438
so that he set the **r** crown on her **Es 2:17** 4438
Esther put on her **r** robes and stood **Es 5:1** 4438
his **r** throne in the throne room, **Es 5:1** 4438
a **r** robe which the king has worn, **Es 6:8** 4438
head a **r** crown has been placed; **Es 6:8** 4438
on steeds sired by the **r** stud. **Es 8:10** 327
went out, riding on the **r** steeds; **Es 8:14** 327
king in **r** robes of blue and white, **Es 8:15** 4438
He who keeps a **r** command **Ec 8:5**
who is in charge of the **r** **Is 22:15**
a **r** diadem in the hand of your God. **Is 62:3** 4410
of the **r** family and *one* of the **Jer 41:1** 4410
'He took one of the **r** family **Ezk 17:13** 4410
of the **r** family and of the nobles, **Da 1:3** 4410
roof of the **r** palace of Babylon. **Da 4:29** 4437
I myself have built as a **r** residence **Da 4:30** 4437
he was deposed from his **r** throne and **Da 5:20** 4437
He will pitch the tents of his **r** pavilion **Da 11:45** 643
of the king and a **r** residence." **Am 7:13** 4467
in luxury are *found* in **r** palaces! **Lk 7:25** *933*
there was a **r** official **Jn 4:46** *937*
The **r** official said to Him, **Jn 4:49** *937*
having put on his **r** apparel, **Ac 12:21** *937*
you are fulfilling the **r** law according **Jas 2:8** *937*
are A CHOSEN RACE, A **R** PRIESTHOOD, **1Pe 2:9** *934*

ROYALTY
whether you have not attained **r** for **Es 4:14** 4438
beautiful and advanced to **r**. **Ezk 16:13** 4410

RUBBED
you were not **r** with salt or even **Ezk 16:4** 4414b
and every shoulder was **r** bare. **Ezk 29:18** 4803

RUBBING
of grain, **r** them in their hands, **Lk 6:1** *5597*

RUBBISH
is failing, Yet there is much **r**; **Ne 4:10** 6083
your houses will be made a **r** heap. **Da 2:5** 5122
their houses reduced to a **r** heap, **Da 3:29** 5122
and count them but **r** so that **Php 3:8** *4657*

RUBBLE
revive the stones from the dusty **r** **Ne 4:2** 6194
And heap up **r** to capture it. **Hab 1:10** 6083

RUBIES
I will make your battlements of **r**, **Is 54:12** 3539
work, fine linen, coral and **r**. **Ezk 27:16** 3539

RUBY
the first row *shall be* a row of **r**, **Ex 28:17** 124
The first row *was* a row of **r**, **Ex 39:10** 124
The **r**, the topaz and the diamond; **Ezk 28:13** 124

RUDDER
still directed by a very small **r** wherever **Jas 3:4** *4079*

RUDDERS
were loosening the ropes of the **r**; **Ac 27:40** *4079*

RUDDY
Now he was **r**, with beautiful eyes **1Sa 16:12** 132
for he was *but* a youth, and **r**, **1Sa 17:42** 132
"My beloved is dazzling and **r**, **SS 5:10** 122
were more **r** *in* body than corals, **La 4:7** 119

RUE
For you pay tithe of mint and **r** and **Lk 11:42** *4076*

RUFFIANS
"God hands me over to **r** And **Jb 16:11** 5760

RUFUS
(the father of Alexander and **R**), **Mk 15:21** *4504*
Greet **R**, a choice man in the Lord, **Ro 16:13** *4504*

RUG
and she covered him with a **r**. **Jg 4:18** 8063

RUGGED
And the **r** terrain a broad valley; **Is 40:4** 7406
them And **r** places into plains. **Is 42:16** 4625

RUHAMAH
"Ammi," and to your sisters, "**R**." **Hos 2:1** 7355

RUIN
and it shall be a **r** forever. **Dt 13:16** 8510
kings of Judah had let go to **r**. **2Ch 34:11** 7843
him to **r** him without cause." **Jb 2:3** 1104
have brought his strongholds to **r**. **Ps 89:40** 4288
"I was almost in utter **r** In the **Pr 5:14** 7451b
of the foolish, **r** is at hand. **Pr 10:14** 4288
r of the poor is their poverty. **Pr 10:15** 4288
But **r** to the workers of iniquity. **Pr 10:29** 4288
opens wide his lips comes to **r**. **Pr 13:3** 4288
dearth of people is a prince's **r**. **Pr 14:28** 4288
A fool's mouth is his **r**, **Pr 18:7** 4288
A man of *too many* friends *comes* to **r**, **Pr 18:24** 7489b
wicked, Turning the wicked to **r**. **Pr 21:12** 7451b
r *that comes* from both of them? **Pr 24:22** 6365
And a flattering mouth works **r**. **Pr 26:28** 4072
Why should you **r** yourself? **Ec 7:16** 8074
a cry of distress over *their* **r**. **Is 15:5** 7667
And will become a fallen **r**. **Is 17:1** 4596
its palaces, they made it a **r**. **Is 23:13** 4654b
a heap, A fortified city into a **r**; **Is 25:2** 4654b
the bridle which leads to **r**. **Is 30:28** 8582
I have created the destroyer to **r**. **Is 54:16** 2254b
precious things have become a **r**. **Is 64:11** 2723
walk after other gods to your own **r**, **Jer 7:6** 7451b
for the land will become a **r**. **Jer 7:34** 2723
and its princes, to make them a **r**, **Jer 25:18** 2723
Why should this city become a **r**? **Jer 27:17** 2723
city will be rebuilt on its **r**, **Jer 30:18** 8510
so they have become a **r** and a **Jer 44:6** 2723
thus your land has become a **r**, **Jer 44:22** 2723
a reproach, a **r** and a curse; **Jer 49:13** 2721b
saw her, They mocked at her **r**. **La 1:7** 4868
For your **r** is as vast as the sea; **La 2:13** 7667
'A **r**, a ruin, a ruin, I will make **Ezk 21:27** 5754
'A ruin, a **r**, a ruin, I will make **Ezk 21:27** 5754
'A ruin, a ruin, a **r**, I will make it. **Ezk 21:27** 5754
"On its **r** all the birds of the **Ezk 31:13** 4658
him the daughter of women to **r** it. **Da 11:17** 7843
not grieved over the **r** of Joseph. **Am 6:6** 7667
the **r** of that house was great." **Lk 6:49** *4485*
plunge men into **r** and destruction. **1Tm 6:9** *3639*
and leads to the **r** of the hearers. **2Tm 2:14** *2692*

RUINED
the flax and the barley were **r**, **Ex 9:31** 5221
wheat and the spelt were not **r**, **Ex 9:32** 5221
You are **r**, O people of Chemosh! **Nu 21:29** 6
Heshbon is **r** as far as Dibon, **Nu 21:30** 6
sustenance far from their **r** homes. **Ps 109:10** 2723
But a babbling fool will be **r**. **Pr 10:8** 3832
And a babbling fool will be **r**. **Pr 10:10** 3832
"Woe is me, for I am **r**! **Is 6:5** 1820
Because you have **r** your country, **Is 14:20** 7843
Ar of Moab is devastated *and* **r**; **Is 15:1** 1820
Kir of Moab is devastated *and* **r**. **Is 15:1** 1820
And the nations will be utterly **r**. **Is 60:12** 2717b
And they will repair the **r** cities, **Is 61:4** 2721b
Woe to us, for we are **r**!" **Jer 4:13** 7703
Why is the land **r**, laid waste like **Jer 9:12** 6
'How are we **r**! We are put to great **Jer 9:19** 7703
"Many shepherds have **r** My vineyard, **Jer 12:10** 7843
and lo, the waistband was **r**, **Jer 13:7** 7843
Ashkelon has been **r**. **Jer 47:5** 1820
The valley also will be **r** And **Jer 48:8** 6
you, He has **r** your strongholds. **Jer 48:18** 7843
and **r** cities are fortified *and* **Ezk 36:35** 2040
have rebuilt the **r** places *and* **Ezk 36:36** 2040
people without understanding are **r**. **Hos 4:14** 3832
The field is **r**, The land mourns; **Jl 1:10** 7703
land mourns; For the grain is **r**, **Jl 1:10** 7703
they will rebuild the **r** cities and live **Am 9:14** 8074
O how you will be **r**! **Ob 1:5** 1820
wail, For their glory is **r**; **Zch 11:3** 7703
For the pride of the Jordan is **r**. **Zch 11:3** 7703
out and the wineskins are **r**; **Mt 9:17** *622*
out, and the skins will be **r**. **Lk 5:37** *622*
knowledge he who is weak is **r**, **1Co 8:11** *622*

RUINING
foxes that are **r** the vineyards, **SS 2:15** 2254b

RUINOUS
turn fortified cities into **r** heaps. **2Ki 19:25** 5327c
turn fortified cities into **r** heaps. **Is 37:26** 5327c

RUINS
house will become a heap of **r**; **1Ki 9:8** 5945a
Naphtali, in their surrounding **r**, **2Ch 34:6** 2723
house of our God, to restore its **r** and **Ezr 9:9** 2723
Who rebuilt **r** for themselves; **Jb 3:14** 2723
Which are destined to become **r**. **Jb 15:28** 1530
does not one in a heap of **r** stretch **Jb 30:24** 5856
has come to an end in perpetual **r**, **Ps 9:6** 2723
footsteps toward the perpetual **r**; **Ps 74:3** 4876
They have laid Jerusalem in **r**. **Ps 79:1** 5856
The foolishness of man **r** his way, **Pr 19:3** 5557
r will be under your charge," **Is 3:6** 4384
And the gate is battered to **r**. **Is 24:12** 7591
And I will raise up her **r** *again*. **Is 44:26** 2723
you will rebuild the ancient **r**; **Is 58:12** 2723
they will rebuild the ancient **r**, **Is 61:4** 2723
cities will be **r** Without inhabitant. **Jer 4:7** 5327c
I will make Jerusalem a heap of **r**, **Jer 9:11**
And Jerusalem will become **r**, **Jer 26:18** 5856
are in **r** and no one lives in them, **Jer 44:2** 2723
cities will become perpetual **r**." **Jer 49:13** 2723
"Babylon will become a heap *of* **r**, **Jer 51:37**
have been like foxes among **r**. **Ezk 13:4** 2723
I will also raise up its **r** And **Am 9:11** 2034b
For I will make Samaria a heap of **r** **Mi 1:6** 5856
Jerusalem will become a heap of **r**, **Mi 3:12** 5856
And the **r** along with the wicked; **Zph 1:3** 4384
Their corner towers are in **r**. **Zph 3:6** 8074
will return and build up the **r**"; **Mal 1:4** 2723
FALLEN, AND I WILL REBUILD ITS **R**, **Ac 15:16** *2690*

RULE
and let them **r** over the fish of **Gn 1:26** 7287a
and **r** over the fish of the sea and **Gn 1:28** 7287a
And he will **r** over you." **Gn 3:16** 4910
are you really going to **r** over us?" **Gn 37:8** 4910
to him according to the same **r**. **Ex 21:31** 4941
not **r** over him with severity, **Lv 25:43** 7287a
you shall not **r** with severity over **Lv 25:46** 7287a
he shall not **r** over him with **Lv 25:53** 7287a
who hate you will **r** over you, **Lv 26:17** 7287a
and you will **r** over many nations, **Dt 15:6** 4910
but they will not **r** over you. **Dt 15:6** 4910
"**R** over us, both you and your **Jg 8:22** 4910
"I will not **r** over you, nor shall **Jg 8:23** 4910
you, nor shall my son **r** over you; **Jg 8:23** 4910
the LORD shall **r** over you." **Jg 8:23** 4910
the sons of Jerubbaal, **r** over you, **Jg 9:2** 4910
you, or that one man **r** over you?' **Jg 9:2** 4910
This one shall **r** over My people." **1Sa 9:17** 6113
he went to restore his **r** at the River. **2Sa 8:3** 3027
and in all the land under his **r**. **1Ki 9:19** 4475
strengthen the kingdom under his **r**. **2Ki 15:19** 3027
as he went to establish his **r** to the **1Ch 18:3** 3027
You, and You **r** over all, **1Ch 29:12** 4910
who can **r** this great people of Yours?" **2Ch 1:10** 8199
that you may **r** My people over **2Ch 1:11** 8199
and in all the land under his **r**. **2Ch 8:6** 4475
did so according to the daily **r**, **2Ch 8:13** 1697
priests according to the daily **r**, **2Ch 8:14** 1697
God of Israel gave the **r** over Israel **2Ch 13:5** 4467
revolted against the **r** of Judah and **2Ch 21:8** 3027
at the same time against his **r**, **2Ch 21:10** 3027
the **r** of the kingdom of Persia, **2Ch 36:20** 4427a
They also **r** over our bodies And **Ne 9:37** 4910
"Shall one who hates justice **r**? **Jb 34:17** 2280
So that godless men would not **r** **Jb 34:30** 4427a
Or fix their **r** over the earth? **Jb 38:33** 4896
You make him to **r** over the **Ps 8:6** 4910
Let them not **r** over me; **Ps 19:13** 4910
shall **r** over them in the morning, **Ps 49:14** 7287a
May he also **r** from sea to sea And **Ps 72:8** 7287a
You **r** the swelling of the sea; **Ps 89:9** 4910
"**R** in the midst of Your enemies." **Ps 110:2** 7287a
The sun to **r** by day, For His **Ps 136:8** 4475
The moon and stars to **r** by night, **Ps 136:9** 4475
"By me princes **r**, and nobles, All **Pr 8:16** 8323
The hand of the diligent will **r**, **Pr 12:24** 4910
A servant who acts wisely will **r** **Pr 17:2** 4910
for a slave to **r** over princes. **Pr 19:10** 4910
children will **r** over them, **Is 3:4** 4910
children, And women **r** over them. **Is 3:12** 4910
and will **r** over their oppressors. **Is 14:2** 7287a
a mighty king will **r** over them," **Is 19:4** 4910
Who **r** this people who are in **Is 28:14** 4910
And princes will **r** justly. **Is 32:1** 8323
"Those who **r** over them howl, and **Is 52:5** 4910
priests **r** on their *own* authority; **Jer 5:31** 7287a
Slaves **r** over us; **La 5:8** 4910
You, O LORD, **r** forever; **La 5:19** 3427
strong branch, A scepter to **r**.' " **Ezk 19:14** 4910
they will not **r** over the nations. **Ezk 29:15** 7287a
has caused you to **r** over them all. **Da 2:38** 7981
which will **r** over all the earth. **Da 2:39** 7981
In the latter period of their **r**, **Da 8:23** 4438
and he will **r** with great authority **Da 11:3** 4910
cause them to **r** over the many, **Da 11:39** 4910
honor and sit and **r** on His throne. **Zch 6:13** 4910
so that they *could* deliver Him to the **r** **Lk 20:20** *746*
WHO ARISES TO **R** OVER THE GENTILES, **Ro 15:12** *757*
all **r** and all authority and power. **1Co 15:24** *746*
And those who will walk by this **r**, **Ga 6:16** *2583*
far above all **r** and authority and **Eph 1:21** *746*
the head over all **r** and authority; **Col 2:10** *746*
peace of Christ **r** in your hearts, **Col 3:15** *1018*
The elders who **r** well are to be **1Tm 5:17** *4291b*
SHALL **R** THEM WITH A ROD OF IRON, **Rv 2:27** *4165*
who is to **r** all the nations with a **Rv 12:5** *4165*
He will **r** them with a rod of iron; **Rv 19:15** *4165*

RULED
in Heshbon, *and* **r** from Aroer, **Jos 12:2** 4910
and **r** over Mount Hermon and **Jos 12:5** 4910
Abimelech **r** over Israel three years. **Jg 9:22** 8323
Now Solomon **r** over all the **1Ki 4:21** 4910
and who **r** over the people who were **1Ki 5:16** 7287a
who **r** over the people doing the **1Ki 9:23** 7287a
Joash, Saraph, who **r** in Moab, **1Ch 4:22** 1166
sons were born who **r** over the house **1Ch 26:6** 4474
and fifty who **r** over the people. **2Ch 8:10** 7287a
kings have **r** over Jerusalem, **Ezr 4:20** 1934
enemies, so that they **r** over them. **Ne 9:28** 7287a
those who hated them **r** over them. **Ps 106:41** 4910
masters besides You have **r** us; **Is 26:13** 1166
those over whom You have never **r**, **Is 63:19** 4910
and against our rulers who **r** us, **Da 9:12** 8199

RULER
Joseph was the **r** over the land; **Gn 42:6** 7989
and **r** over all the land of Egypt. **Gn 45:8** 4910
is **r** over all the land of Egypt." **Gn 45:26** 4910
God, nor curse a **r** of your people. **Ex 22:28** 5387a
When Zebul the **r** of the city **Jg 9:30** 8269
for there was no **r** humiliating **Jg 18:7**
3423, 6114
Has not the LORD anointed you a **r** **1Sa 10:1** 5057
him as **r** over His people, **1Sa 13:14** 5057
appoints you **r** over Israel, **1Sa 25:30** 5057
you will be a **r** over Israel.' " **2Sa 5:2** 5057
me **r** over the people of the LORD, **2Sa 6:21** 5057
to be **r** over My people Israel. **2Sa 7:8** 5057
to be **r** over Israel and Judah." **1Ki 1:35** 5057
I will make him **r** all the days of his **1Ki 11:34** 5387a
was **r** over them previously, **1Ch 9:20** 5057
and they anointed *him* as **r** for the **1Ch 29:22** 5057
not lack a man *to be* **r** in Israel.' **2Ch 7:18** 4910
He was the **r** over all the kings **2Ch 9:26** 4910
the **r** of the house of Judah, **2Ch 19:11** 5057
And are You not **r** over all the **2Ch 20:6** 4910
and Azrikam the **r** of the house and **2Ch 28:7** 5057
released him, The **r** of peoples, **Ps 105:20** 4910
And **r** over all his possessions, **Ps 105:21** 4910
having no chief, Officer or **r**, **Pr 6:7** 4910
you sit down to dine with a **r**, **Pr 23:1** 4910
forbearance a **r** may be persuaded, **Pr 25:15** 7101
Is a wicked **r** over a poor people. **Pr 28:15** 4910
a **r** pays attention to falsehood, **Pr 29:12** 4910
the shouting of a **r** among fools. **Ec 9:17** 4910
error which goes forth from the **r** **Ec 10:5** 7989
have a cloak, you shall be our **r**, **Is 3:6** 7101
not appoint me **r** of the people." **Is 3:7** 7101
tribute lamb to the **r** of the land, **Is 16:1** 4910
And their **r** shall come forth from **Jer 30:21** 4910
in the land With **r** against ruler **Jer 51:46** 4910
in the land With ruler against **r** **Jer 51:46** 4910

inasmuch as no great king or r has Da 2:10 7990
and he made him r over the whole Da 2:48 7981
the Most High is r over the realm Da 4:17 7990
the Most High is r over the realm Da 4:25 7990
the Most High is r over the realm Da 4:32 7990
and have authority as third r in Da 5:7
will have authority as the third r Da 5:16
Most High God is r over the realm Da 5:21 7990
now had authority as the third r Da 5:29
go forth for Me to be r in Israel. Mi 5:2 4910
Like creeping things without a r Hab 1:14 4910
bow of battle, From them every r, Zch 10:4 5065
OUT OF YOU SHALL COME FORTH A R Mt 2:6 *2233*
demons by the r of the demons." Mt 9:34 *758*
Beelzebul the r of the demons." Mt 12:24 *758*
demons by the r of the demons." Mk 3:22 *758*
Beelzebul, the r of the demons." Lk 11:15 *758*
A r questioned Him, Lk 18:18 *758*
named Nicodemus, a r of the Jews; Jn 3:1 *758*
now the r of this world will be Jn 12:31 *758*
for the r of the world is coming, Jn 14:30 *758*
r of this world has been judged. Jn 16:11 *758*
MADE YOU A R AND JUDGE OVER US? Ac 7:27 *758*
'WHO MADE YOU A R AND A JUDGE?' Ac 7:35 *758*
one whom God sent *to be* both a r Ac 7:35 *758*
'YOU SHALL NOT SPEAK EVIL OF A R Ac 23:5 *758*
the r of the kings of the earth. Rv 1:5 *758*

RULER'S
the r staff from between his feet, Gn 49:10 2710
there the r portion was reserved; Dt 33:21 2710
Many seek the r favor, But justice Pr 29:26 4910
If the r temper rises against you, Ec 10:4 4910

RULERS
and Aaron and all the r in the Ex 34:31 5387a
The r brought the onyx stones Ex 35:27 5387a
Hear, O kings; give ear, O r! Jg 5:3 7336
the Philistines are r over us? Jg 15:11 4910
men of the r of the provinces.'" 1Ki 20:14 8269
young men of the r of the provinces, 1Ki 20:15 8269
young men of the r of the provinces 1Ki 20:17 8269
young men of the r of the provinces, 1Ki 20:19 8269
to Samaria, to the r of Jezreel, 2Ki 10:1 8269
the r of the fathers' *households,* 1Ch 29:6 8269
and some of the r of Israel also. 2Ch 21:4 8269
the nobles, the r of the people and 2Ch 23:20 4910
and the r came and saw the heaps, 2Ch 31:8 8269
of the envoys of the r of Babylon, 2Ch 32:31 8269
hands of the princes and the r have Ezr 9:2 5461
contended with the nobles and the r Ne 5:7 5461
And the r take counsel together Ps 2:2 7336
He judges in the midst of the r. Ps 82:1 430
kings reign, And r decree justice. Pr 8:15 7336
Or for r to desire strong drink, Pr 31:4 7336
more than ten r who are in a city. Ec 7:19 7989
word of the LORD, You r of Sodom; Is 1:10 7101
Your r are rebels And companions Is 1:23 8269
of the wicked, The scepter of r Is 14:5 4910
All your r have fled together, *And* Is 22:3 7101
He *it is* who reduces r to nothing, Is 40:23 7336
will come upon r as *upon* mortar, Is 41:25 5461
the nation, To the Servant of r, Is 49:7 4910
r also transgressed against Me, Jer 2:8 7462a
not taking from his descendants r Jer 33:26 4910
branches *fit* for scepters of r, Ezk 19:11 4910
"Behold, the r of Israel, each Ezk 22:6 5387a
all the r of the provinces to come to Da 3:2 7984
and all the r of the provinces were Da 3:3 7984
us and against our r who ruled us, Da 9:12 8199
Their r dearly love shame. Hos 4:18 4043
an oven, And they consume their r; Hos 7:7 8199
And r of the house of Israel. Mi 3:1 7101
And r of the house of Israel, Mi 3:9 7101
r are a laughing matter to them. Hab 1:10 7336
r of the Gentiles lord it over them Mt 20:25 *758*
those who are recognized as r of the Mk 10:42 *757*
brought down r from *their* thrones, Lk 1:52 *1413*
and the r and the authorities, Lk 12:11 *746*
priests and the r and the people, Lk 23:13 *758*
even the r were sneering at Him, Lk 23:35 *758*
priests and our r delivered Him to Lk 24:20 *758*
The r do not really know that this Jn 7:26 *758*
"No one of the r or Pharisees has Jn 7:48 *758*
many even of the r believed in Him, Jn 12:42 *758*
just as your r did also. Ac 3:17 *758*
their r and elders and Ac 4:5 *758*
"R and elders of the people, Ac 4:8 *758*
AND THE R WERE GATHERED TOGETHER Ac 4:26 *758*
live in Jerusalem, and their r, Ac 13:27 *758*
and the Jews with their r, Ac 14:5 *758*
For r are not a cause of fear for Ro 13:3 *758*
for r are servants of God, Ro 13:6
age nor of the r of this age, 1Co 2:6 *758*
which none of the r of this age has 1Co 2:8 *758*
known through the church to the r Eph 3:10 *746*
but against the r, against the powers Eph 6:12 *746*
whether thrones or dominions or r or Col 1:16 *746*
disarmed the r and authorities, Col 2:15 *746*
Remind them to be subject to r, Ti 3:1 *746*

RULES
'He who r over men righteously, 2Sa 23:3 4910
Who r in the fear of God, 2Sa 23:3 4910
not according to the purification r 2Ch 30:19
LORD'S And He r over the nations. Ps 22:28 4910
men may know that God r in Jacob To Ps 59:13 4910
He r by His might forever; Ps 66:7 4910
And His sovereignty r over all. Ps 103:19 4910
mighty, And he who r his spirit, Pr 16:32 4910
The rich r over the poor, And the Pr 22:7 4910
when a wicked man r, people groan Pr 29:2 4910
that *it is* Heaven *that* r. Da 4:26 7990
he competes according to the r. 2Tm 2:5 *3545*

RULING
Philistines were r over Israel. Jg 14:4 4910
is Benjamin, the youngest, r them, Ps 68:27 7287a
might, With His arm r for Him. Is 40:10 4910
of David Or r again in Judah.'" Jer 22:30 4910
'Ask now the priests *for* a r: Hg 2:11 8451

RUMAH
the daughter of Pedaiah of R. 2Ki 23:36 7316

RUMBLE
The nations r on like the rumbling Is 17:13 7582

RUMBLING
r that goes out from His mouth. Jb 37:2 1899
And the r of nations Who rush on Is 17:12 7588
on like the r of mighty waters! Is 17:12 7588
on like the r of many waters, Is 17:13 7588
chariots, *and* the r of his wheels, Jer 47:3 1995
I heard a great r sound behind me, Ezk 3:12 7494
beside them, even a great r sound. Ezk 3:13 7494

RUMOR
so that he will hear a r and return 2Ki 19:7 8052
so that he will hear a r and return Is 37:7 8052
and r will be *added* to rumor; Ezk 7:26 8052
and rumor will be *added* to r; Ezk 7:26 8052

RUMORS
"But r from the East and from the Da 11:44 8052
be hearing of wars and r of wars. Mt 24:6 *189*
you hear of wars and r of wars, Mk 13:7 *189*

RUN
Its branches r over a wall. Gn 49:22 6805
they will r before his chariots. 1Sa 8:11 7323
r to the camp to your brothers. 1Sa 17:17 7323
of me to r to Bethlehem his city, 1Sa 20:6 7323
"R, find now the arrows which I 1Sa 20:36 7323
his saliva r down into his beard. 1Sa 21:13 3381
"Please let me r and bring the 2Sa 18:19 7323
let me also r after the Cushite." 2Sa 18:22 7323
"Why would you r, my son, since 2Sa 18:22 7323
whatever happens," *he said,* "I will r." 2Sa 18:23 7323
So he said to him, "R." 2Sa 18:23 7323
"For by You I can r upon a troop; 2Sa 22:30 7323
with fifty men to r before him. 1Ki 1:5 7323
r to the man of God and return." 2Ki 4:22 7323
"Please r now to meet her and say 2Ki 4:26 7323
I will r after him and take 2Ki 5:20 7323
For by You I can r upon a troop; Ps 18:29 7323
as a strong man to r his course. Ps 19:5 7323
they r and set themselves against me. Ps 59:4 7323
imaginations of *their* heart r riot. Ps 73:7 5674a
caused waters to r down like rivers. Ps 78:16 3381
r the way of Your commandments, Ps 119:32 7323
For their feet r to evil And they Pr 1:16 7323
And if you r, you will not stumble. Pr 4:12 7323
Feet that r rapidly to evil, Pr 6:18 7323
after you *and* let us r *together!* SS 1:4 7323
They will r and not get tired, Is 40:31 7323
which knows you not will r to you, Is 55:5 7323
Their feet r to evil, And they Is 59:7 7323
"If you have r with footmen and Jer 12:5 7323
I will make him r away from it, Jer 49:19 7323
"R away, flee! Dwell in the depths, Jer 49:30 5127
I will make them r away from it, Jer 50:44 7323
My eyes r down with water; La 1:16 3381
Let *your* tears r down like a river La 2:18 3381
My eyes r down with streams of La 3:48 3381
will cause their rivers to r like oil," Ezk 32:14 1980
transgressors have r *their course,* Da 8:23 8552
And like war horses, so they r. Jl 2:4 7323
They r like mighty men, Jl 2:7 7323
on the city, They r on the wall; Jl 2:9 7323
Do horses r on rocks? Am 6:12 7323
That the one who reads it may r. Hab 2:2 7323
"R, speak to that young man, Zch 2:4 7323
go away, and do not r after *them.* Lk 17:23 *1377*
fearing that they might r aground Ac 27:17 *1601b*
r aground on a certain island." Ac 27:26 *1601b*
Fearing that we might r aground Ac 27:29 *1601b*
those who r in a race all run, 1Co 9:24 *5143*
those who run in a race all r, 1Co 9:24 *5143*
R in such a way that you may win. 1Co 9:24 *5143*
Therefore I r in such a way, as 1Co 9:26 *5143*
I might be running, or had r, in vain Ga 2:2 *5143*
I did not r in vain nor toil in vain. Php 2:16 *5143*
and let us r with endurance the race Heb 12:1 *5143*
they are surprised that you do not r 1Pe 4:4 *4936*

RUNNER
"Now my days are swifter than a r; Jb 9:25 7323

RUNNERS
and fifty men as r before him. 2Sa 15:1 7323

RUNNING
earthenware vessel over r water. Lv 14:5 2416a
that was slain over the r water. Lv 14:6 2416a
earthenware vessel over r water. Lv 14:50 2416a
bird as well as in the r water, Lv 14:51 2416a
of the bird and with the r water, Lv 14:52 2416a
and bathe his body in r water and Lv 15:13 2416a
a r sore or eczema or scabs, Lv 22:22 2990
stumble over each other as if r Lv 26:37
down to a valley with r water, Dt 21:4 386
As the lad was r, he shot an arrow 1Sa 20:36 7323
and behold, a man r by himself. 2Sa 18:24 7323
the watchman saw another man r; 2Sa 18:26 7323
another man r by himself." 2Sa 18:26 7323
"I think the r of the first one 2Sa 18:27 4794
is like the r of Ahimaaz the son 2Sa 18:27 4794
When Naaman saw one r after him, 2Ki 5:21 7323
people r and praising the king, 2Ch 23:12 7323
hill there will be streams r with water Is 30:25 2988
Hamath, r from east to west, Ezk 48:1 1961
and *began* r up to greet Him. Mk 9:15 *4370*
down, shaken together, *and* r over. Lk 6:38 *5240*
The two were r together; Jn 20:4 *5143*
R under the shelter of a small island Ac 27:16 *5295*
for fear that I might be r, Ga 2:2 *5143*
You were r well; who hindered you Ga 5:7 *5143*

RUNS
them at the river that r to Ahava, Ezr 8:15 935
My skin hardens and r. Jb 7:5 3988b
He r at me like a warrior. Jb 16:14 7323
flow away like water that r off; Ps 58:7 1980
His word r very swiftly. Ps 147:15 7323
righteous r into it and is safe. Pr 18:10 7323
Until indignation r *its* course. Is 26:20 5674a
One courier r to meet another, And Jer 51:31 7323
each of you r to his own house. Hg 1:9 7323
man who wills or the man who r, Ro 9:16 *5143*

RURAL
receive the tithes in all the r towns. Ne 10:37 5656
Therefore the Jews of the r areas, Es 9:19 6521
areas, who live in the r towns, Es 9:19 6519

RUSH
rise early and r upon the city; Jg 9:33 6584
rumbling of nations Who r on like Is 17:12 7582
rushing about men r about on it. Is 33:4 8264
And r back and forth inside the Jer 49:3 7751a
They r on the city, They run on Jl 2:9 8264
They r wildly in the squares, Na 2:4 8264

RUSHED
the valley they r at his heels; Jg 5:15 7971
hurried and r against Gibeah; Jg 20:37 6584
people r greedily upon the spoil, 1Sa 14:32 5860b
but r upon the spoil and did what 1Sa 15:19 5860b
r to the Jordan before the king. 2Sa 19:17 6743a
and r at him in his mighty wrath. Da 8:6 7323
the whole herd r down the steep Mt 8:32 *3729*
and the herd r down the steep bank Mk 5:13 *3729*
and the herd r down the steep bank Lk 8:33 *3729*
r at him with one impulse. Ac 7:57 *3729*
robes and r out into the crowd, Ac 14:14 *1601a*
he called for lights and r in, Ac 16:29 *1530*
and they r with one accord into Ac 19:29 *3729*
and the people r together, Ac 21:30 *4890*
r down from the land a violent wind Ac 27:14 *906*
they have r headlong into the error Jude 1:11 *1632b*

RUSHES
Can the r grow without water? Jb 8:11 260
"He r headlong at Him With his Jb 15:26 7323
though the Jordan r to his mouth. Jb 40:23 1518
from a boiling pot and *burning* r. Jb 41:20 100
The reeds and r will rot away. Is 19:6 5488
place, Grass *becomes* reeds and r. Is 35:7 1573

RUSHING
Like a roaring lion and a r bear Pr 28:15 8264
As locusts r about men rush about Is 33:4 4944
For He will come like a r stream Which Is 59:19 6862a
a noise like a violent r wind, Ac 2:2 *5342*
of many horses r to battle. Rv 9:9 *5143*

RUST
To the pot in which there is r And Ezk 24:6 2457
whose r has not gone out of it! Ezk 24:6 2457
be melted in it, Its r consumed. Ezk 24:11 2457
her great r has not gone from her; Ezk 24:12 2457
Let her r *be* in the fire! Ezk 24:12 2457
earth, where moth and r destroy, Mt 6:19 *1035*
where neither moth nor r destroys, Mt 6:20 *1035*
and their r will be a witness Jas 5:3 *2447*

RUSTED
Your gold and your silver have r; Jas 5:3 *2728*

RUTH
Orpah and the name of the other R. Ru 1:4 7327
mother-in-law, but R clung to her. Ru 1:14 7327
R said, "Do not urge me to leave you Ru 1:16 7327
and with her R the Moabitess, Ru 1:22 7327
And R the Moabitess said to Naomi, Ru 2:2 7327
Then Boaz said to R, Ru 2:8 7327
Then R the Moabitess said, Ru 2:21 7327
Naomi said to R her daughter-in-law, Ru 2:22 7327
"I am R your maid. Ru 3:9 7327
must also acquire R the Moabitess, Ru 4:5 7327
I have acquired R the Moabitess, Ru 4:10 7327
So Boaz took R, and she became his Ru 4:13 7327
Boaz was the father of Obed by R, Mt 1:5 *4503*

RUTHLESS
are the years stored up for the r. Jb 15:20 6184
grasp of the wrongdoer and r man, Ps 71:4 2556c
And r men attain riches. Pr 11:16 6184
Seek justice, Reprove the r, Is 1:17 2541
abase the haughtiness of the r. Is 13:11 6184
Cities of r nations will revere You. Is 25:3 6184
For the breath of the r Is like a Is 25:4 6184
the song of the r is silenced. Is 25:5 6184
And the multitude of the r ones Is 29:5 6184
For the r will come to an end and Is 29:20 6184
you, The most r of the nations. Ezk 28:7 6184
him, The most r of the nations, Ezk 30:11 6184

RUTHLESSLY
struck them r with a great slaughter Jg 15:8 7785, 5921, 3409
So r shattered That a sherd will Is 30:14 3808, 2550

RYE
its place and r within its area? Is 28:25 3698

S

SABACHTHANI
"Eli, Eli, lama s?" Mt 27:46 4518
"Eloi, Eloi, lama s?" Mk 15:34 4518

SABAOTH
the Lord of S had left to us a Ro 9:29 4519
reached the ears of the Lord of S. Jas 5:4 4519

SABBATH
Tomorrow is a s observance, a holy Ex 16:23 7677
observance, a holy s to the Lord. Ex 16:23 7676
for today is a s to the Lord; Ex 16:25 7676
it, but on the seventh day, *the* s, Ex 16:26 7676
"See, the Lord has given you the s; Ex 16:29 7676
"Remember the s day, to keep it Ex 20:8 7676
the seventh day is a s of the Lord Ex 20:10 7676
therefore the Lord blessed the s day Ex 20:11 7676
you are to observe the s, Ex 31:14 7676
day there is a s of complete rest, Ex 31:15 7676
whoever does any work on the s day Ex 31:15 7676
the sons of Israel shall observe the s, Ex 31:16 7676
to celebrate the s throughout Ex 31:16 7676
a s of complete rest to the Lord; Ex 35:2 7676
of your dwellings on the s day." Ex 35:3 7676
to be a s of solemn rest for you, Lv 16:31 7676
day there is a s of complete rest, Lv 23:3 7676
it is a s to the Lord in all your Lv 23:3 7676
after the s the priest shall wave it. Lv 23:11 7676
from the day after the s, Lv 23:15 7676
to the day after the seventh s; Lv 23:16 7676
to be a s of complete rest to you, Lv 23:32 7676
evening you shall keep your s." Lv 23:32 7676
"Every s day he shall set it in Lv 24:8 7676
land shall have a s to the Lord. Lv 25:2 7676
year the land shall have a s rest, Lv 25:4 7676
a sabbath rest, a s to the Lord; Lv 25:4 7676
s *products* of the land for food; Lv 25:6 7676
a man gathering wood on the s day. Nu 15:32 7676
'Then on the s day two male lambs Nu 28:9 7676
This is the burnt offering of every s Nu 28:10 7676
'Observe the s day to keep it holy, Dt 5:12 7676
day is a s of the Lord your God; Dt 5:14 7676
you to observe the s day. Dt 5:15 7676
It is neither new moon nor s." 2Ki 4:23 7676
who come in on the s and keep 2Ki 11:5 7676
you, *even* all who go out on the s, 2Ki 11:7 7676
men who were to come in on the s, 2Ki 11:9 7676
those who were to go out on the s, 2Ki 11:9 7676
The covered way for the s 2Ki 16:18 7676
showbread to prepare it every s. 1Ch 9:32 7676
and Levites who come in on the s, 2Ch 23:4 7676
men who were to come in on the s, 2Ch 23:8 7676
those who were to go out on the s, 2Ch 23:8 7676
the days of its desolation it kept s 2Ch 36:21 7673b
made known to them Your holy s, Ne 9:14 7676
or any grain on the s day to sell, Ne 10:31 7676
we will not buy from them on the s Ne 10:31 7676
treading wine presses on the s Ne 13:15 7676
them into Jerusalem on the s day. Ne 13:15 7676
to the sons of Judah on the s, Ne 13:16 7676
are doing, by profaning the s day? Ne 13:17 7676
on Israel by profaning the s." Ne 13:18 7676
gates of Jerusalem before the s, Ne 13:19 7676
not open them until after the s. Ne 13:19 7676
no load would enter on the s day. Ne 13:19 7676
on they did not come on the s. Ne 13:21 7676
gatekeepers to sanctify the s day. Ne 13:22 7676
New moon and s, the calling of Is 1:13 7676
Who keeps from profaning the s, Is 56:2 7676
who keeps from profaning the s And Is 56:6 7676
"If because of the s, Is 58:13 7676
day, And call the s a delight, Is 58:13 7676
to new moon And from s to sabbath, Is 66:23 7676
to new moon And from sabbath to s, Is 66:23 7676
do not carry any load on the s day Jer 17:21 7676
load out of your houses on the s day Jer 17:22 7676
any work, but keep the s day holy, Jer 17:22 7676
gates of this city on the s day, Jer 17:24 7676
but to keep the s day holy by Jer 17:24 7676
keep the s day holy by not carrying Jer 17:27 7676
gates of Jerusalem on the s day, Jer 17:27 7676
The appointed feast and s in Zion, La 2:6 7676
it shall be opened on the s day and Ezk 46:1 7676
shall offer to the Lord on the s day Ezk 46:4 7676
offerings as he does on the s day. Ezk 46:12 7676
that we may sell grain, And the s, Am 8:5 7676
through the grainfields on the S, Mt 12:1 4521
what is not lawful to do on a S." Mt 12:2 4521
that on the S the priests in the Mt 12:5 4521
priests in the temple break the S and Mt 12:5 4521
the Son of Man is Lord of the S." Mt 12:8 4521
"Is it lawful to heal on the S?" Mt 12:10 4521
if it falls into a pit on the S, Mt 12:11 4521
is lawful to do good on the S." Mt 12:12 4521
not be in the winter, or on a S. Mt 24:20 4521
Now after the S, as it began to Mt 28:1 4521
on the S He entered the synagogue Mk 1:21 4521
through the grainfields on the S, Mk 2:23 4521
what is not lawful on the S?" Mk 2:24 4521
"The S was made for man, and not Mk 2:27 4521
for man, and not man for the S. Mk 2:27 4521
the Son of Man is Lord even of the S." Mk 2:28 4521
see if He would heal him on the S, Mk 3:2 4521
to do good or to do harm on the S, Mk 3:4 4521
When the S came, He began Mk 6:2 4521
that is, the day before the S, Mk 15:42 4315
When the S was over, Mary Mk 16:1 4521
He entered the synagogue on the S, Lk 4:16 4521
and He was teaching them on the S; Lk 4:31 4521
passing through *some* grainfields on a S; Lk 6:1 4521
do what is not lawful on the S?" Lk 6:2 4521
"The Son of Man is Lord of the S." Lk 6:5 4521
On another S Lk 6:6 4521
to see if He healed on the S, Lk 6:7 4521
or to do harm on the S, Lk 6:9 4521
in one of the synagogues on the S. Lk 13:10 4521
because Jesus had healed on the S, Lk 13:14 4521
healed, and not on the S day." Lk 13:14 4521
does not each of you on the S Lk 13:15 4521
from this bond on the S day?" Lk 13:16 4521
Pharisees on *the* S to eat bread, Lk 14:1 4521
"Is it lawful to heal on the S, Lk 14:3 4521
pull him out on a S day?" Lk 14:5 4521
day, and the S was about to begin. Lk 23:54 4521
And on the S they rested according Lk 23:56 4521
Now it was the S on that day. Jn 5:9 4521
"It is the S, and it is not Jn 5:10 4521
was doing these things on the S. Jn 5:16 4521
He not only was breaking the S, Jn 5:18 4521
and on *the* S you circumcise a man. Jn 7:22 4521
a man receives circumcision on *the* S Jn 7:23 4521
made an entire man well on *the* S? Jn 7:23 4521
Now it was a S on the day when Jn 9:14 4521
because He does not keep the S." Jn 9:16 4521
not remain on the cross on the S Jn 19:31 4521
(for that S was a high day), Jn 19:31 4521
Jerusalem, a S day's journey away. Ac 1:12 4521
and on the S day they went into Ac 13:14 4521
prophets which are read every S, Ac 13:27 4521
be spoken to them the next S. Ac 13:42 4521
The next S nearly the whole Ac 13:44 4521
read in the synagogues every S." Ac 15:21 4521
And on the S day we went outside Ac 16:13 4521
reasoning in the synagogue every S Ac 18:4 4521
festival or a new moon or a S day Col 2:16 4521
a S rest for the people of God. Heb 4:9 4520

SABBATHS
'You shall surely observe My s; Ex 31:13 7676
father, and you shall keep My s; Lv 19:3 7676
keep My s and revere My sanctuary; Lv 19:30 7676
there shall be seven complete s. Lv 23:15 7676
those of the s of the Lord, Lv 23:38 7676
off seven s of years for yourself, Lv 25:8 7676
the time of the seven s of years, Lv 25:8 7676
My s and reverence My sanctuary; Lv 26:2 7676
'Then the land will enjoy its s Lv 26:34 7676
land will rest and enjoy its s. Lv 26:34 7676
it did not observe on your s, Lv 26:35 7676
and will make up for its s while Lv 26:43 7676
offerings to the Lord, on the s, 1Ch 23:31 7676
on s and on new moons and on the 2Ch 2:4 7676
commandment of Moses, for the s, 2Ch 8:13 7676
and the burnt offerings for the s 2Ch 31:3 7676
until the land had enjoyed its s. 2Ch 36:21 7676
continual burnt offering, the s, Ne 10:33 7676
"To the eunuchs who keep My s, Is 56:4 7676
"Also I gave them My s to be Ezk 20:12 7676
and My s they greatly profaned. Ezk 20:13 7676
they even profaned My s, Ezk 20:16 7676
'Sanctify My s; Ezk 20:20 7676
they profaned My s. Ezk 20:21 7676
statutes and had profaned My s, Ezk 20:24 7676
My holy things and profaned My s. Ezk 22:8 7676
they hide their eyes from My s, Ezk 22:26 7676
same day and have profaned My s. Ezk 23:38 7676
feasts and sanctify My s. Ezk 44:24 7676
on the new moons and on the s, Ezk 45:17 7676
on the s and on the new moons. Ezk 46:3 7676
Her feasts, her new moons, her s And Hos 2:11 7676
and for three S reasoned with them Ac 17:2 4521

SABBATICAL
the land shall have a s year. Lv 25:5 7677

SABEANS
and the S attacked and took them. Jb 1:15 7614
the S, men of stature, Will come Is 45:14 5436
and they will sell them to the S, Jl 3:8 7615

SABTA
of Cush *were* Seba, Havilah, S, 1Ch 1:9 5454

SABTAH
and S and Raamah and Sabteca; Gn 10:7 5454

SABTECA
and Sabtah and Raamah and S; Gn 10:7 5455
Havilah, Sabta, Raama and S; 1Ch 1:9 5455

SACAR
Ahiam the son of S the Hararite, 1Ch 11:35 7940
Joah the third, S the fourth, 1Ch 26:4 7940

SACHIA
S, Mirmah. These were his sons, 1Ch 8:10 7914a

SACK
restore every man's money in his s, Gn 42:25 8242
As one *of them* opened his s to Gn 42:27 8242
it was in the mouth of his s. Gn 42:27 572
and behold, it is even in my s." Gn 42:28 572
man's bundle of money *was* in his s; Gn 42:35 8242
money was in the mouth of his s, Gn 43:21 572
man's money in the mouth of his s. Gn 44:1 572
mouth of the s of the youngest, Gn 44:2 572
man lowered his s to the ground, Gn 44:11 572
ground, and each man opened his s. Gn 44:11 572
the cup was found in Benjamin's s. Gn 44:12 572
or clothing, or a skin, or a s Lv 11:32 8242
For the bread is gone from our s 1Sa 9:7 3627
and fresh ears of grain in his s. 2Ki 4:42 6861

SACKCLOTH
clothes, and put s on his loins and Gn 37:34 8242
Tear your clothes and gird on s 2Sa 3:31 8242
Rizpah the daughter of Aiah took s 2Sa 21:10 8242
please let us put s on our loins 1Ki 20:31 8242
So they girded s on their loins 1Ki 20:32 8242
clothes and put on s and fasted, 1Ki 21:27 8242
in s and went about despondently. 1Ki 21:27 8242
he had s beneath on his body. 2Ki 6:30 8242
covered himself with s and entered 2Ki 19:1 8242
of the priests, covered with s, 2Ki 19:2 8242
and the elders, covered with s, 1Ch 21:16 8242
assembled with fasting, in s and Ne 9:1 8242
his clothes, put on s and ashes, Es 4:1 8242
enter the king's gate clothed in s. Es 4:2 8242
and many lay on s and ashes. Es 4:3 8242
he might remove his s from him, Es 4:4 8242
"I have sewed s over my skin And Jb 16:15 8242
my s and girded me with gladness, Ps 30:11 8242
they were sick, my clothing was s; Ps 35:13 8242
When I made s my clothing, I Ps 69:11 8242
of fine clothes, a donning of s; Is 3:24 8242
have girded themselves with s; Is 15:3 8242
and loosen the s from your hips and Is 20:2 8242
the head and to wearing s. Is 22:12 8242
undress and put s on *your* Is 32:11
covered himself with s and entered Is 37:1 8242
of the priests, covered with s, Is 37:2 8242
And make s their covering." Is 50:3 8242
spreading out s and ashes as a bed? Is 58:5 8242
"For this, put on s, Jer 4:8 8242
put on s And roll in ashes; Jer 6:26 8242
all the hands and s on the loins. Jer 48:37 8242
Gird yourselves with s and lament, Jer 49:3 8242
have girded themselves with s. La 2:10 8242
They will gird themselves with s Ezk 7:18 8242
you And gird themselves with s; Ezk 27:31 8242
supplications, with fasting, s and Da 9:3 8242
Wail like a virgin girded with s Jl 1:8 8242
Gird yourselves *with* s And lament, Jl 1:13
Come, spend the night in s O Jl 1:13 8242
And I will bring s on everyone's Am 8:10 8242
and they called a fast and put on s Jon 3:5 8242
from him, covered *himself* with s and Jon 3:6 8242
and beast must be covered with s; Jon 3:8 8242
repented long ago in s and ashes. Mt 11:21 4526
long ago, sitting in s and ashes. Lk 10:13 4526
sun became black as s *made* of hair, Rv 6:12 4526
and sixty days, clothed in s." Rv 11:3 4526

SACKS
as they were emptying their s, Gn 42:35 8242
returned in the mouth of your s, Gn 43:12 572
the money that was returned in our s Gn 43:18 572
place, that we opened our s, Gn 43:21 572
know who put our money in our s." Gn 43:22 572
has given you treasure in your s; Gn 43:23 572
"Fill the men's s with food, as Gn 44:1 572
we found in the mouth of our s Gn 44:8 572
took worn-out s on their donkeys, Jos 9:4 8242
and bringing in s of grain and Ne 13:15 6194

SACRED
overthrow them and break their s Ex 23:24
down their altars and smash their s Ex 34:13
up for yourselves an image or a s Lv 26:1
of them, the s part from them.' Nu 18:29 4720
the s gifts of the sons of Israel, Nu 18:32 6944
and smash their s pillars, Dt 7:5
down their altars and smash their s Dt 12:3
shall not set up for yourself a s Dt 16:22
I have removed the s *portion* from Dt 26:13 6944
for themselves high places and s 1Ki 14:23
for he put away the s pillar of 2Ki 3:2
They brought out the s pillars of 2Ki 10:26
They also broke down the s pillar 2Ki 10:27
"All the money of the s things 2Ki 12:4 6944
king of Judah took all the s things 2Ki 12:18 6944
and his own s things and all the 2Ki 12:18 6944
They set for themselves s pillars 2Ki 17:10
high places and broke down the s 2Ki 18:4
He broke in pieces the s pillars 2Ki 23:14
tore down the s pillars, cut 2Ch 14:3
and the tithe of s gifts which 2Ch 31:6 6944
The s stones are poured out At the La 4:1 6944
without sacrifice or s pillar Hos 3:4
The better he made the s pillars. Hos 10:1
And destroy their s pillars. Hos 10:2
carved images And your s pillars Mi 5:13
through them from east to west the s Mk 16:20
those who perform s services eat 1Co 9:13 2413
you have known the s writings 2Tm 3:15 2413
and the table and the s bread; Heb 9:2 4286

SACRIFICE
Jacob offered a s on the mountain, Gn 31:54 2077
we may s to the Lord our God.' Ex 3:18 2076
that we may s to the Lord our God, Ex 5:3 2076
'Let us go and s to our God.' Ex 5:8 2076
'Let us go *and* s to the Lord.' Ex 5:17 2076
go, that they may s to the Lord." Ex 8:8 2076
s to your God within the land." Ex 8:25 2076
for we will s to the Lord our God Ex 8:26 2076
If we s what is an abomination to Ex 8:26 2076
and s to the Lord our God as He Ex 8:27 2076
that you may s to the Lord your Ex 8:28 2076
the people go to s to the Lord." Ex 8:29 2076
we may s *them* to the Lord our God. Ex 10:25 6213a
'It is a Passover s to the Lord Ex 12:27 2077
I s to the Lord the males, Ex 13:15 2076
and you shall s on it your burnt Ex 20:24 2076

blood of My s with leavened bread; **Ex 23:18** 2077
by offering up in smoke a fire s **Ex 30:20**
their gods and s to their gods, **Ex 34:15** 2076
invite you to eat of his s, **Ex 34:15** 2077
blood of My s with leavened bread, **Ex 34:25** 2077
the s of the Feast of the Passover **Ex 34:25** 2077
is a s of peace offerings, **Lv 3:1** 2077
From the s of the peace offerings **Lv 3:3** 2077
his offering for a s of peace offerings **Lv 3:6** 2077
'From the s of peace offerings **Lv 3:9** 2077
ox of the s of peace offerings), **Lv 4:10** 2077
fat of the s of peace offerings. **Lv 4:26** 2077
from the s of peace offerings; **Lv 4:31** 2077
from the s of the peace offerings, **Lv 4:35** 2077
the law of the s of peace offerings **Lv 7:11** 2077
along with the s of thanksgiving **Lv 7:12** 2077
'With the s of his peace offerings **Lv 7:13** 2077
'Now *as for* the flesh of the s of **Lv 7:15** 2077
'But if the s of his offering is a **Lv 7:16** 2077
on the day that he offers his s, **Lv 7:16** 2077
left over from the flesh of the s **Lv 7:17** 2077
'So if any of the flesh of the s **Lv 7:18** 2077
the person who eats the flesh of the s **Lv 7:20** 2077
the flesh of the s of peace offerings **Lv 7:21** 2077
'He who offers the s of his peace **Lv 7:29** 2077
from the s of his peace offerings. **Lv 7:29** 2077
and the s of peace offerings, **Lv 7:37** 2077
offerings, to s before the LORD, **Lv 9:4** 2076
the s of peace offerings which was **Lv 9:18** 2077
and s them as sacrifices of peace **Lv 17:5** 2076
They shall no longer s their sacrifices **Lv 17:7** 2076
who offers a burnt offering or s, **Lv 17:8** 2077
'Now when you offer a s of peace **Lv 19:5** 2077
a man offers a s of peace offerings **Lv 22:21** 2077
to the LORD, or s in your land, **Lv 22:24** 6213a
accepted as a s of an offering by fire **Lv 22:27** 7133a
"When you s a sacrifice of **Lv 22:29** 2076
a s of thanksgiving to the LORD, **Lv 22:29** 2077
you shall s it so that you may be **Lv 22:29** 2076
old for a s of peace offerings. **Lv 23:19** 2077
'He shall also offer the ram for a s **Nu 6:17** 2077
is under the s of peace offerings. **Nu 6:18** 2077
and for the s of peace offerings, **Nu 7:17** 2077
and for the s of peace offerings, **Nu 7:23** 2077
and for the s of peace offerings, **Nu 7:29** 2077
and for the s of peace offerings, **Nu 7:35** 2077
and for the s of peace offerings, **Nu 7:41** 2077
and for the s of peace offerings, **Nu 7:47** 2077
and for the s of peace offerings, **Nu 7:53** 2077
and for the s of peace offerings, **Nu 7:59** 2077
and for the s of peace offerings, **Nu 7:65** 2077
and for the s of peace offerings, **Nu 7:71** 2077
and for the s of peace offerings, **Nu 7:77** 2077
and for the s of peace offerings, **Nu 7:83** 2077
the s of peace offerings 24 bulls, **Nu 7:88** 2077
or a s to fulfill a special vow, **Nu 15:3** 2077
the burnt offering or for the s, **Nu 15:5** 2077
a bull as a burnt offering or a s, **Nu 15:8** 2077
not s it to the LORD your God. **Dt 15:21** 2076
"You shall s the Passover to **Dt 16:2** 2076
and none of the flesh which you s **Dt 16:4** 2076
are not allowed to s the Passover **Dt 16:5** 2076
you shall s the Passover in the **Dt 16:6** 2076
"You shall not s to the LORD your **Dt 17:1** 2076
people, from those who offer a s, **Dt 18:3** 2076
s peace offerings and eat there, **Dt 27:7** 2076
not for burnt offering or for s; **Jos 22:26** 2077
not for burnt offering or for s; **Jos 22:28** 2077
for grain offering or for s, **Jos 22:29** 2077
a great s to Dagon their god, **Jg 16:23** 2077
to s to the LORD of hosts in Shiloh. **1Sa 1:3** 2076
LORD the yearly s and *pay* his vow. **1Sa 1:21** 2077
When any man was offering a s, **1Sa 2:13** 2077
her husband to offer the yearly s. **1Sa 2:19** 2077
'Why do you kick at My s and at My **1Sa 2:29** 2077
not be atoned for by s or offering **1Sa 3:14** 2077
have a s on the high place today. **1Sa 9:12** 2077
because he must bless the s; **1Sa 9:13** 2077
offerings and s peace offerings. **1Sa 10:8** 2076
oxen, to s to the LORD your God; **1Sa 15:15** 2076
to s to the LORD your God at **1Sa 15:21** 2076
Behold, to obey is better than s, **1Sa 15:22** 2077
'I have come to s to the LORD.' **1Sa 16:2** 2076
You shall invite Jesse to the s, **1Sa 16:3** 2077
I have come to s to the LORD. **1Sa 16:5** 2076
and come with me to the s." **1Sa 16:5** 2077
sons and invited them to the s. **1Sa 16:5** 2077
s there for the whole family.' **1Sa 20:6** 2077
our family has a s in the city, **1Sa 20:29** 2077
king went to Gibeon to s there, **1Ki 3:4** 2076
him offered s before the LORD. **1Ki 8:62** 2077
for the s of peace offerings, **1Ki 8:63** 2077
and on you he shall s the priests **1Ki 13:2** 2076
of the offering of the *evening* s; **1Ki 18:29** 4503
of the offering of the *evening* s, **1Ki 18:36** 4503
about the time of offering the s, **2Ki 3:20** 4503
nor will he s to other gods, **2Ki 5:17** 2077
for I have a great s for Baal; **2Ki 10:19** 2077
and all the blood of the s. **2Ki 16:15** 2077
them nor serve them nor s to them. **2Ki 17:35** 2076
down, and to Him you shall s. **2Ki 17:36** 2076
the Jebusite, he offered s there. **1Ch 21:28** 2076
people offered s before the LORD. **2Ch 7:4** 2077
Solomon offered a s of 22,000 oxen and **2Ch 7:5** 2077
place for Myself as a house of s. **2Ch 7:12** 2077
followed them to Jerusalem, to s to **2Ch 11:16** 2076
s to them that they may help me." **2Ch 28:23** 2076
S and meal offering You have not **Ps 40:6** 2077
made a covenant with Me by s." **Ps 50:5** 2077
"Offer to God a s of thanksgiving And **Ps 50:14** 2076
a s of thanksgiving honors Me; **Ps 50:23** 2076
For You do not delight in s, **Ps 51:16** 2077
Willingly I will s to You; **Ps 54:6** 2076
I shall offer a s of thanksgiving, **Ps 116:17** 2077
Bind the festival s with cords to **Ps 118:27** 2282
The s of the wicked is an **Pr 15:8** 2077
desired by the LORD more than s. **Pr 21:3** 2077
The s of the wicked is an **Pr 21:27** 2077
than to offer the s of fools; **Ec 5:1** 2077
for the man who offers a s and for **Ec 9:2** 2076
and for the one who does not s. **Ec 9:2** 2076
even worship with s and offering, **Is 19:21** 2077
For the LORD has a s in Bozrah And **Is 34:6** 2077
You also went up there to offer s. **Is 57:7** 2077
"the one who offers s on **Jer 48:35**
gather from every side to My s **Ezk 39:17** 2077
which I am going to s for you, **Ezk 39:17** 2076
great s on the mountains of Israel, **Ezk 39:17** 2077
from My s which I have sacrificed **Ezk 39:19** 2077
the burnt offering and the s. **Ezk 40:42** 2077
offering and the s for the people, **Ezk 44:11** 2077
it removed the regular s from Him, **Da 8:11** 8548
the horn along with the regular s; **Da 8:12** 8548
vision *about* the regular s apply, **Da 8:13** 8548
put a stop to s and grain offering; **Da 9:27** 2077
and do away with the regular s. **Da 11:31** 8548
that the regular s is abolished and **Da 12:11** 8548
without s or *sacred* pillar and **Hos 3:4** 2077
I delight in loyalty rather than s, **Hos 6:6** 2077
They s the flesh and eat *it*, **Hos 8:13** 2076
In Gilgal they s bulls, Yes, their **Hos 12:11** 2076
the men who s kiss the calves!" **Hos 13:2** 2076
a s to the LORD and made vows. **Jon 1:16** 2077
But I will s to You With the **Jon 2:9** 2076
they offer a s to their net And **Hab 1:16** 2076
For the LORD has prepared a s, **Zph 1:7** 2077
about on the day of the LORD's s That **Zph 1:8** 2077
and all who s will come and take **Zch 14:21** 2076
when you present the blind for s, **Mal 1:8** 2076
'I DESIRE COMPASSION, AND NOT S,' **Mt 9:13** *2378*
'I DESIRE COMPASSION, AND NOT A S,' **Mt 12:7** *2378*
and to offer a s according to what **Lk 2:24** *2378*
calf and brought a s to the idol, **Ac 7:41** *2378*
wanted to offer s with the crowds. **Ac 14:13** *2380*
crowds from offering s to them. **Ac 14:18** *2380*
until the s was offered for each **Ac 21:26** *4376*
your bodies a living and holy s, **Ro 12:1** *2378*
the things which the Gentiles s, **1Co 10:20** *2380*
sacrifice, they s to demons and **1Co 10:20** *2380*
a s to God as a fragrant aroma. **Eph 5:2** *2378*
the s and service of your faith, **Php 2:17** *2378*
a fragrant aroma, an acceptable s, **Php 4:18** *2378*
put away sin by the s of Himself. **Heb 9:26** *2378*
"S AND OFFERING YOU HAVE NOT **Heb 10:5** *2378*
one s for sins for all time, **Heb 10:12** *2378*
no longer remains a s for sins, **Heb 10:26** *2378*
to God a better s than Cain, **Heb 11:4** *2378*
offer up a s of praise to God, **Heb 13:15** *2378*

SACRIFICED

and s young bulls as peace offerings **Ex 24:5** 2076
worshiped it and have s to it **Ex 32:8** 2076
Balak s oxen and sheep, and **Nu 22:40** 2076
"They s to demons who were not **Dt 32:17** 2076
the LORD, and s peace offerings. **Jos 8:31** 2076
and there they s to the LORD. **Jg 2:5** 2076
When the day came that Elkanah s, **1Sa 1:4** 2076
and s sacrifices that day to the LORD. **1Sa 6:15** 2076
paces, he s an ox and a fatling. **2Sa 6:13** 2076
Adonijah s sheep and oxen and **1Ki 1:9** 2076
"He has s oxen and fatlings **1Ki 1:19** 2076
has s oxen and fatlings and sheep **1Ki 1:25** 2076
except he s and burned incense on **1Ki 3:3** 2076
incense and s to their gods. **1Ki 11:8** 2076
and took the pair of oxen and s **1Ki 19:21** 2076
the people still s and burnt incense **1Ki 22:43** 2076
the people still s and burned incense **2Ki 12:3** 2076
the people still s and burned incense **2Ki 14:4** 2076
the people still s and burned incense **2Ki 15:4** 2076
the people still s and burned incense **2Ki 15:35** 2076
He s and burned incense on the **2Ki 16:4** 2076
they s seven bulls and seven rams. **1Ch 15:26** 2076
They s to the LORD that day **2Ch 15:11** 2076
He s and burned incense on the **2Ch 28:4** 2076
For he s to the gods of Damascus **2Ch 28:23** 2076
s peace offerings and thank offerings **2Ch 33:16** 2076
people still s in the high places, **2Ch 33:17** 2076
and Amon s to all the carved **2Ch 33:22** 2076
graves of those who had s to them. **2Ch 34:4** 2076
They even s their sons and their **Ps 106:37** 2076
they s to the idols of Canaan; **Ps 106:38** 2076
s them to idols to be devoured. **Ezk 16:20** 2076
sacrifice which I have s for you. **Ezk 39:19** 2076
the Passover *lamb* was being s, **Mk 14:12** *2380*
the Passover *lamb* had to be s. **Lk 22:7** *2380*
you abstain from things s to idols **Ac 15:29** *1494*
should abstain from meat s to idols **Ac 21:25** *1494*
our Passover also has been s. **1Co 5:7** *2380*
Now concerning things s to idols, **1Co 8:1** *1494*
the eating of things s to idols, **1Co 8:4** *1494*
food as if it were s to an idol; **1Co 8:7** *1494*
to eat things s to idols? **1Co 8:10** *1494*
a thing s to idols is anything, **1Co 10:19** *1494*
"This is meat s to idols," **1Co 10:28** *2410b*
Israel, to eat things s to idols and **Rv 2:14** *1494*
and eat things s to idols. **Rv 2:20** *1494*

SACRIFICES

and offered s to the God of his **Gn 46:1** 2077
let us have s and burnt offerings, **Ex 10:25** 2077
a burnt offering and s for God, **Ex 18:12** 2077
"He who s to any god, other than **Ex 22:20** 2076
the s of their peace offerings, **Ex 29:28** 2077
the s of your peace offerings. **Lv 7:32** 2077
the s of their peace offerings, **Lv 7:34** 2077
s of the peace offerings of the sons **Lv 10:14** 2077
the sons of Israel may bring their s **Lv 17:5** 2077
and sacrifice them as s of peace **Lv 17:5** 2077
sacrifice their s to the goat demons **Lv 17:7** 2077
grain offerings, s and drink **Lv 23:37** 2077
the s of your peace offerings; **Nu 10:10** 2077
the people to the s of their gods, **Nu 25:2** 2077
your burnt offerings, your s, **Dt 12:6** 2077
your burnt offerings and your s, **Dt 12:11** 2077
blood of your s shall be poured out **Dt 12:27** 2077
'Who ate the fat of their s, **Dt 32:38** 2077
they will offer righteous s; **Dt 33:19** 2077
offer s of peace offerings on it, **Jos 22:23** 2077
our burnt offerings, and with our s **Jos 22:27** 2077
sacrificed s that day to the LORD. **1Sa 6:15** 2077
they also offered s of peace offerings **1Sa 11:15** 2077
much delight in burnt offerings and s **1Sa 15:22** 2077
while he was offering the s. **2Sa 15:12** 2077
"If this people go up to offer s **1Ki 12:27** 2077
in to offer s and burnt offerings. **2Ki 10:24** 2077
On the next day they made s to **1Ch 29:21** 2077
and s in abundance for all Israel. **1Ch 29:21** 2077
the burnt offering and the s, **2Ch 7:1** 2077
come near and bring s and thank **2Ch 29:31** 2077
brought s and thank offerings, **2Ch 29:31** 2077
the place where s are offered, **Ezr 6:3** 1685
that they may offer acceptable s **Ezr 6:10** 5208
Can they offer s? **Ne 4:2** 2076
they offered great s and rejoiced **Ne 12:43** 2077
Offer the s of righteousness, And **Ps 4:5** 2077
offer in His tent s with shouts of joy **Ps 27:6** 2077
"I do not reprove you for your s, **Ps 50:8** 2077
The s of God are a broken spirit; **Ps 51:17** 2077
You will delight in righteous s, **Ps 51:19** 2077
And ate s offered to the dead. **Ps 106:28** 2077
them also offer s of thanksgiving, **Ps 107:22** 2077
are your multiplied s to Me?" **Is 1:11** 2077
have you honored Me with your s. **Is 43:23** 2077
filled Me with the fat of your s; **Is 43:24** 2077
their s will be acceptable on My altar **Is 56:7** 2077
Offering s in gardens and burning **Is 65:3** 2076
He who s a lamb is *like* the one **Is 66:3** 2076
and have offered s to other gods, **Jer 1:16** 6999
your s are not pleasing to Me." **Jer 6:20** 2077
falsely, and offer s to Baal and **Jer 7:9** 6999
Add your burnt offerings to your s **Jer 7:21** 2077
concerning burnt offerings and s. **Jer 7:22** 2077
Me by offering up s to Baal. **Jer 11:17** 6999
bringing burnt offerings, s, **Jer 17:26** 2077
and bringing s of thanksgiving to **Jer 17:26** 8426
and have burned s in it to other gods **Jer 19:4** 6999
they burned s to all the heavenly host **Jer 19:13** 6999
and to prepare s continually.' " **Jer 33:18** 2077
Me to anger by continuing to burn s **Jer 44:3** 6999
so as not to burn s to other gods. **Jer 44:5** 6999
burning s to other gods in the **Jer 44:8** 6999
wives were burning s to other gods, **Jer 44:15** 6999
by burning s to the queen of heaven **Jer 44:17** 6999
"But since we stopped burning s **Jer 44:18** 6999
burning s to the queen of heaven and **Jer 44:19** 6999
"As for the smoking s that you **Jer 44:21** 7002
"Because you have burned s and **Jer 44:23** 6999
to burn s to the queen of heaven **Jer 44:25** 6999
and they offered there their s and **Ezk 20:28** 2077
"Like the flock for s, **Ezk 36:38** 6944
tables on which they slaughter s. **Ezk 40:41**
shall boil the s of the people." **Ezk 46:24** 2077
When she used to offer s to them **Hos 2:13** 6999
They offer s on the tops of the **Hos 4:13** 2076
offer s with temple prostitutes; **Hos 4:14** 2076
be ashamed because of their s. **Hos 4:19** 2077
LORD, Their s will not please Him. **Hos 9:4** 2077
Bring your s every morning, Your **Am 4:4** 2077
"Did you present Me with s and **Am 5:25** 2077
but s a blemished animal to the **Mal 1:14** 2076
than all burnt offerings and s." **Mk 12:33** *2378*
Pilate had mixed with their s. **Lk 13:1** *2378*
OFFERED VICTIMS AND S FORTY YEARS **Ac 7:42** *2378*
are not those who eat the s sharers **1Co 10:18** *2378*
offer both gifts and s for sins; **Heb 5:1** *2378*
of it he is obligated to offer s **Heb 5:3**
those high priests, to offer up s, **Heb 7:27** *2378*
to offer both gifts and s; **Heb 8:3** *2378*
both gifts and s are offered which **Heb 9:9** *2378*
with better s than these. **Heb 9:23** *2378*
never, by the same s which they offer **Heb 10:1** *2378*
But in those s there is a **Heb 10:3**
IN WHOLE BURNT OFFERINGS AND S **Heb 10:6**
"S AND OFFERINGS AND WHOLE BURNT **Heb 10:8** *2378*
AND WHOLE BURNT OFFERINGS AND S **Heb 10:8**
time after time the same s, **Heb 10:11** *2378*
for with such s God is pleased. **Heb 13:16** *2378*
to offer up spiritual s acceptable **1Pe 2:5** *2378*

SACRIFICIAL

dishes and the pans and the s bowls **Nu 4:7** 4518
Can the s flesh take away from you **Jer 11:15** 6944
our husbands that we made for her s **Jer 44:19**
As for My s gifts, They sacrifice **Hos 8:13** 2077
Who drink wine from s bowls While **Am 6:6** 4219
And they will be filled like a s **Zch 9:15**

SACRIFICING

they were s in the open field, **Lv 17:5** 2076

come and say to the man who was s, 1Sa 2:15 2076
were still s on the high places, 1Ki 3:2 2076
s so many sheep and oxen they 1Ki 8:5 2076
s to the calves which he had made. 1Ki 12:32 2076
ark, were s so many sheep and oxen 2Ch 5:6 2076
s peace offerings and giving 2Ch 30:22 2076
and we have been s to Him since Ezr 4:2 2076
They kept s to the Baals And Hos 11:2 2076

SAD
"Why are your faces so s today?" Gn 40:7 7451a
When the people heard this s word, Ex 33:4 7451a
not eat and why is your heart s? 1Sa 1:8 7489a
and her face was no longer s. 1Sa 1:18 ...
I had not been s in his presence. Ne 2:1 7451a
Why is your face s though you are Ne 2:2 7451a
Why should my face not be s when Ne 2:3 7489a
I will leave off my s countenance Jb 9:27
face, But when the heart is s, Pr 15:13 6094
For when a face is s a heart may be Ec 7:3 7455
these things, he became very s, Lk 18:23 *4036*
And they stood still, looking s. Lk 24:17 *4659*

SADDENED
But at these words he was s, and he Mk 10:22 *4768*

SADDLE
and put them in the camel's s, Gn 31:34 3733a
'Every s on which the person Lv 15:9 4817
'I will s a donkey for myself that 2Sa 19:26 2280
"S the donkey for me." 1Ki 13:13 2280
"S the donkey for me." 1Ki 13:27 2280

SADDLECLOTHS
traded with you in s for riding. Ezk 27:20
2667, 899b

SADDLED
in the morning and s his donkey, Gn 22:3 2280
in the morning, and s his donkey and Nu 22:21 2280
were with him a pair of s donkeys; Jg 19:10 2280
him with a couple of s donkeys, 2Sa 16:1 2280
he s *his* donkey and arose and went 2Sa 17:23 2280
Shimei arose and s his donkey, 1Ki 2:40 2280
So they s the donkey for him and 1Ki 13:13 2280
that he s the donkey for him, 1Ki 13:23 2280
the donkey for me." And they s *it.* 1Ki 13:27 2280
Then she s a donkey and said to 2Ki 4:24 2280

SADDUCEES
Pharisees and S coming for baptism, Mt 3:7 *4523*
The Pharisees and S came up, Mt 16:1 *4523*
leaven of the Pharisees and S." Mt 16:6 *4523*
leaven of the Pharisees and S." Mt 16:11 *4523*
teaching of the Pharisees and S. Mt 16:12 *4523*
On that day *some* S Mt 22:23 *4523*
that Jesus had silenced the S, Mt 22:34 *4523*
Some S Mk 12:18 *4523*
there came to Him some of the S Lk 20:27 *4523*
of the temple *guard* and the S Ac 4:1 *4523*
(that is the sect of the S), Ac 5:17 *4523*
perceiving that one group were S and Ac 23:6 *4523*
between the Pharisees and S, Ac 23:7 *4523*
For the S say that there is no Ac 23:8 *4523*

SADLY
like bears, And moan s like doves; Is 59:11 1897

SADNESS
This is nothing but s of heart." Ne 2:2 7455

SAFE
is good,' your servant *will be* s; 1Sa 20:7 7965
for you are s with me." 1Sa 22:23 4931
seek from Him a s journey for us, Ezr 8:21 3477
Their houses are s from fear, Jb 21:9 7965
Uphold me that I may be s, Ps 119:117 3467
righteous runs into it and is s. Pr 18:10 7682
and holy man, and he kept him s. Mk 6:20 *4933*
received him back s and sound.' Lk 15:27 *5198*

SAFEGUARD
to me, and it is a s for you. Php 3:1 *804*

SAFEKEEPING
You will *try to* remove *for* s, Mi 6:14

SAFELY
Jacob came s to the city of Shechem Gn 33:18 8003
"When I return s, I will tear Jg 8:9 7965
enemy, will he let him go away s? 1Sa 24:19
2896a, 1870
has come s to his own house." 2Sa 19:30 7965
and water until I return s. 1Ki 22:27 7965
"If you indeed return s 1Ki 22:28 7965
and water until I return s. 2Ch 18:26 7965
"If you indeed return s, 2Ch 18:27 7965
He led them s, so that they Ps 78:53 983
their own nets, While I pass by s. Ps 141:10 3162
and he will depart from there s. Jer 43:12 7965
bring him s to Felix the governor. Ac 23:24 *1295*
wanting to bring Paul s through, Ac 27:43 *1295*
they all were brought s to land. Ac 27:44 *1295*
they had been brought s through, Ac 28:1 *1295*
me s to His heavenly kingdom; 2Tm 4:18 *4982*
were brought s through *the* water. 1Pe 3:20 *1295*

SAFETY
I return to my father's house in s, Gn 28:21 7965
whatever you have in the field to s. Ex 9:19 5756
you away, that you may go in s. 1Sa 20:13 7965
there is s for you and no harm, 1Sa 20:21 7965
"Go in s, inasmuch as we have 1Sa 20:42 7965
So Judah and Israel lived in s, 1Ki 4:25 983
the king of Judah returned in s to 2Ch 19:1 7965
"His sons are far from s, Jb 5:4 3468
those who mourn are lifted to s. Jb 5:11 3468
LORD, make me to dwell in s. Ps 4:8 983
I will set him in the s for which he Ps 12:5 3468
take refuge in the s of Pharaoh And Is 30:2 4581
s of Pharaoh will be your shame And Is 30:3 4581
"He pursues them, passing on in s, Is 41:3 7965
"Flee for s, O sons of Benjamin, Jer 6:1 5756
place and make them dwell in s. Jer 32:37 983
and Jerusalem will dwell in s; Jer 33:16 983
who inhabit the coastlands in s; Ezk 39:6 983
And will make them lie down in s. Hos 2:18 983
While they are saying, "Peace and s!" 1Th 5:3 *803*

SAFFRON
Nard and s, calamus and cinnamon, SS 4:14 3750

SAG
Through indolence the rafters s, Ec 10:18 4355

SAGE
the priest, nor counsel to the s, Jer 18:18 2450

SAID
Then God s, "Let there be light"; Gn 1:3 559
God s, "Let there be an expanse Gn 1:6 559
Then God s, "Let the waters below Gn 1:9 559
Then God s, "Let the earth sprout Gn 1:11 559
Then God s, "Let there be lights Gn 1:14 559
Then God s, "Let the waters teem Gn 1:20 559
God s, "Let the earth bring forth Gn 1:24 559
God s, "Let Us make man in Our Gn 1:26 559
and God s to them, Gn 1:28 559
God s, "Behold, I have given you Gn 1:29 559
Then the LORD God s, Gn 2:18 559
The man s, "This is now bone of my Gn 2:23 559
And he s to the woman, Gn 3:1 559
"Indeed, has God s, Gn 3:1 559
The woman s to the serpent, Gn 3:2 559
middle of the garden, God has s, Gn 3:3 559
The serpent s to the woman, Gn 3:4 559
called to the man, and s to him, Gn 3:9 559
He s, "I heard the sound of You Gn 3:10 559
And He s, "Who told you that you Gn 3:11 559
The man s, "The woman whom Gn 3:12 559
Then the LORD God s to the woman, Gn 3:13 559
And the woman s, Gn 3:13 559
The LORD God s to the serpent, Gn 3:14 559
To the woman He s, Gn 3:16 559
Then to Adam He s, Gn 3:17 559
Then the LORD God s, Gn 3:22 559
and gave birth to Cain, and she s, Gn 4:1 559
Then the LORD s to Cain, Gn 4:6 559
Then the LORD s to Cain, Gn 4:9 559
And he s, "I do not know. Am I my Gn 4:9 559
He s, "What have you done? Gn 4:10 559
Cain s to the LORD, Gn 4:13 559
So the LORD s to him, Gn 4:15 559
Lamech s to his wives, Gn 4:23 559
she s, "God has appointed me Gn 4:25 559
Then the LORD s, Gn 6:3 559
The LORD s, "I will blot out man Gn 6:7 559
Then God s to Noah, Gn 6:13 559
Then the LORD s to Noah, Gn 7:1 559
and the LORD s to Himself, Gn 8:21 559
Noah and his sons and s to them, Gn 9:1 559
God s, "This is the sign of the Gn 9:12 559
And God s to Noah, Gn 9:17 559
So he s, "Cursed be Canaan; Gn 9:25 559
He also s, "Blessed be the LORD, Gn 9:26 559
therefore it is s, Gn 10:9 559
They s to one another, Gn 11:3 559
They s, "Come, let us build Gn 11:4 559
LORD s, "Behold, they are one people Gn 11:6 559
Now the LORD s to Abram, Gn 12:1 559
The LORD appeared to Abram and s, Gn 12:7 559
that he s to Sarai his wife, Gn 12:11 559
Then Pharaoh called Abram and s, Gn 12:18 559
So Abram s to Lot, Gn 13:8 559
The LORD s to Abram, after Lot Gn 13:14 559
He blessed him and s, Gn 14:19 559
The king of Sodom s to Abram, Gn 14:21 559
Abram s to the king of Sodom, Gn 14:22 559
Abram s, "O Lord GOD, what will Gn 15:2 559
Abram s, "Since You have given Gn 15:3 559
And He took him outside and s, Gn 15:5 559
And He s to him, Gn 15:5 559
And He s to him, Gn 15:7 559
He s, "O Lord GOD, how may I know Gn 15:8 559
He s to him, "Bring Me a three year Gn 15:9 559
God s to Abram, Gn 15:13 559
So Sarai s to Abram, Gn 16:2 559
And Sarai s to Abram, Gn 16:5 559
But Abram s to Sarai, Gn 16:6 559
He s, "Hagar, Sarai's maid, Gn 16:8 559
And she s, "I am fleeing from the Gn 16:8 559
the angel of the LORD s to her, Gn 16:9 559
the angel of the LORD s to her, Gn 16:10 559
of the LORD s to her further, Gn 16:11 559
she s, "Have I even remained alive Gn 16:13 559
appeared to Abram and s to him, Gn 17:1 559
God s further to Abraham, Gn 17:9 559
Then God s to Abraham, Gn 17:15 559
and laughed, and s in his heart, Gn 17:17 559
And Abraham s to God, Gn 17:18 559
God s, "No, but Sarah your wife Gn 17:19 559
same day, as God had s to him. Gn 17:23 1696
s, "My Lord, if now I have found Gn 18:3 559
they s, "So do, as you have said." Gn 18:5 559
"So do, as you have s." Gn 18:5 1696
into the tent to Sarah, and s, Gn 18:6 559
Then they s to him, Gn 18:9 559
And he s, "There, in the tent." Gn 18:9 559
He s, "I will surely return to Gn 18:10 559
And the LORD s to Abraham, Gn 18:13 559
And He s, "No, but you did laugh." Gn 18:15 559
The LORD s, "Shall I hide from Gn 18:17 559
LORD s, "The outcry of Sodom and Gn 18:20 559
Abraham came near and s, Gn 18:23 559
So the LORD s, "If I find in Sodom Gn 18:26 559
He s, "I will not destroy *it* if I find Gn 18:28 559
He spoke to Him yet again and s, Gn 18:29 559
He s, "I will not do *it* on account of Gn 18:29 559
he s, "Oh may the Lord not be angry Gn 18:30 559
He s, "I will not do *it* if I find thirty Gn 18:30 559
he s, "Now behold, I have ventured Gn 18:31 559
And He s, "I will not destroy *it* Gn 18:31 559
he s, "Oh may the Lord not be angry Gn 18:32 559
And He s, "I will not destroy *it* on Gn 18:32 559
And he s, "Now behold, my lords, Gn 19:2 559
They s however, "No, but we shall Gn 19:2 559
they called to Lot and s to him, Gn 19:5 559
s, "Please, my brothers, do not act Gn 19:7 559
But they s, "Stand aside." Gn 19:9 559
Furthermore, they s, Gn 19:9 559
Then the *two* men s to Lot, Gn 19:12 559
to marry his daughters, and s, Gn 19:14 559
brought them outside, one s, Gn 19:17 559
But Lot s to them, Gn 19:18 559
He s to him, Gn 19:21 559
the firstborn s to the younger, Gn 19:31 559
the firstborn s to the younger, Gn 19:34 559
Abraham s of Sarah his wife, Gn 20:2 559
dream of the night, and s to him, Gn 20:3 559
he s, "Lord, will You slay a nation, Gn 20:4 559
And she herself s, Gn 20:5 559
Then God s to him in the dream, Gn 20:6 559
called Abraham and s to him, Gn 20:9 559
And Abimelech s to Abraham, Gn 20:10 559
Abraham s, "Because I thought, Gn 20:11 559
my father's house, that I s to her, Gn 20:13 559
Abimelech s, Gn 20:15 559
To Sarah he s, Gn 20:16 559
took note of Sarah as He had s, Gn 21:1 559
Sarah s, "God has made laughter Gn 21:6 559
And she s, "Who would have said Gn 21:7 559
"Who would have s to Abraham that Gn 21:7 559
Therefore she s to Abraham, Gn 21:10 559
But God s to Abraham, Gn 21:12 559
about a bowshot away, for she s, Gn 21:16 559
Hagar from heaven and s to her, Gn 21:17 559
Abraham s, "I swear it." Gn 21:24 559
And Abimelech s, Gn 21:26 559
Abimelech s to Abraham, Gn 21:29 559
He s, "You shall take these seven Gn 21:30 559
God tested Abraham, and s to him, Gn 22:1 559
"Abraham!" And he s, "Here I am." Gn 22:1 559
He s, "Take now your son, Gn 22:2 559
Abraham s to his young men, Gn 22:5 559
spoke to Abraham his father and s, Gn 22:7 559
And he s, "Here I am, my son." Gn 22:7 559
he s, "Behold, the fire and the wood, Gn 22:7 559
Abraham s, "God will provide Gn 22:8 559
called to him from heaven and s, Gn 22:11 559
Abraham!" And he s, "Here I am." Gn 22:11 559
He s, "Do not stretch out your hand Gn 22:12 559
Provide, as it is s to this day, Gn 22:14 559
and s, "By Myself I have sworn, Gn 22:16 559
Abraham s to his servant, the Gn 24:2 559
The servant s to him, Gn 24:5 559
Then Abraham s to him, Gn 24:6 559
He s, "O LORD, the God of my Gn 24:12 559
servant ran to meet her, and s, Gn 24:17 559
She s, "Drink, my lord"; and Gn 24:18 559
giving him a drink, she s, Gn 24:19 559
and s, "Whose daughter are you? Gn 24:23 559
She s to him, Gn 24:24 559
Again she s to him, Gn 24:25 559
He s, "Blessed be the LORD, Gn 24:27 559
"This is what the man s to me," Gn 24:30 1696
he s, "Come in, blessed of the LORD! Gn 24:31 559
was set before him to eat, he s, Gn 24:33 559
And he s, "Speak on." Gn 24:33 559
So he s, "I am Abraham's servant. Gn 24:34 559
"I s to my master, Gn 24:39 559
"He s to me, Gn 24:40 559
I came today to the spring, and s, Gn 24:42 559
and I s to her, 'Please let me drink.' Gn 24:45 559
her jar from her *shoulder,* and s, Gn 24:46 559
"Then I asked her, and s, Gn 24:47 559
And she s, 'The daughter of Bethuel, Gn 24:47 559
they arose in the morning, he s, Gn 24:54 559
But her brother and her mother s, Gn 24:55 559
He s to them, Gn 24:56 559
And they s, "We will call the girl Gn 24:57 559
they called Rebekah and s to her, Gn 24:58 559
And she s, "I will go." Gn 24:58 559
They blessed Rebekah and s to her, Gn 24:60 559
She s to the servant, Gn 24:65 559
And the servant s, Gn 24:65 559
she s, "If it is so, why then am I *this* Gn 25:22 559
The LORD s to her, Gn 25:23 559
and Esau s to Jacob, Gn 25:30 559
But Jacob s, "First sell me your Gn 25:31 559
Esau s, "Behold, I am about to die; Gn 25:32 559
And Jacob s, "First swear to me"; Gn 25:33 559
The LORD appeared to him and s, Gn 26:2 559
place asked about his wife, he s, Gn 26:7 559
Then Abimelech called Isaac and s, Gn 26:9 559
And Isaac s to him, Gn 26:9 559
Isaac said to him, "Because I s, Gn 26:9 559
Abimelech s, Gn 26:10 559
Then Abimelech s to Isaac, Gn 26:16 559
so he named it Rehoboth, for he s, Gn 26:22 559
to him the same night and s, Gn 26:24 559

Isaac **s** to them, **Gn 26:27** 559
They **s**, "We see plainly that **Gn 26:28** 559
so we **s**, 'Let there now be an oath **Gn 26:28** 559
which they had dug, and **s** to him, **Gn 26:32** 559
his older son Esau and **s** to him, **Gn 27:1** 559
And he **s** to him, **Gn 27:1** 559
Isaac **s**, "Behold now, I am old **Gn 27:2** 559
Rebekah **s** to her son Jacob, **Gn 27:6** 559
But his mother **s** to him, **Gn 27:13** 559
Then he came to his father and **s**, **Gn 27:18** 559
"My father." And he **s**, "Here I am. **Gn 27:18** 559
Jacob **s** to his father, **Gn 27:19** 559
Isaac **s** to his son, **Gn 27:20** 559
he **s**, "Because the LORD your God **Gn 27:20** 559
Then Isaac **s** to Jacob, **Gn 27:21** 559
his father, and he felt him and **s**, **Gn 27:22** 559
he **s**, "Are you really my son Esau?" **Gn 27:24** 559
my son Esau?" And he **s**, "I am." **Gn 27:24** 559
he **s**, "Bring *it* to me, and I will eat **Gn 27:25** 559
Then his father Isaac **s** to him, **Gn 27:26** 559
garments, he blessed him and **s**, **Gn 27:27** 559
and he **s** to his father, **Gn 27:31** 559
Isaac his father **s** to him, **Gn 27:32** 559
"Who are you?" And he **s**, "I am **Gn 27:32** 559
Isaac trembled violently, and **s**, **Gn 27:33** 559
bitter cry, and **s** to his father, **Gn 27:34** 559
he **s**, "Your brother came deceitfully **Gn 27:35** 559
he **s**, "Is he not rightly named Jacob **Gn 27:36** 559
And he **s**, "Have you not reserved a **Gn 27:36** 559
Esau **s** to his father, **Gn 27:38** 559
his father answered and **s** to him, **Gn 27:39** 559
and Esau **s** to himself, **Gn 27:41** 559
younger son Jacob, and **s** to him, **Gn 27:42** 559
Rebekah **s** to Isaac, **Gn 27:46** 559
him and charged him, and **s** to him, **Gn 28:1** 559
the LORD stood above it and **s**, **Gn 28:13** 559
Jacob awoke from his sleep and **s**, **Gn 28:16** 559
He was afraid and **s**, **Gn 28:17** 559
Jacob **s** to them, **Gn 29:4** 559
And they **s**, "We are from Haran." **Gn 29:4** 559
He **s** to them, **Gn 29:5** 559
And they **s**, "We know *him.*" **Gn 29:5** 559
And he **s** to them, **Gn 29:6** 559
And they **s**, "It is well, and here **Gn 29:6** 559
He **s**, "Behold, it is still high day; **Gn 29:7** 559
But they **s**, "We cannot, until all **Gn 29:8** 559
Laban **s** to him, **Gn 29:14** 559
Then Laban **s** to Jacob, **Gn 29:15** 559
Now Jacob loved Rachel, so he **s**, **Gn 29:18** 559
Laban **s**, "It is better that I give her **Gn 29:19** 559
Then Jacob **s** to Laban, **Gn 29:21** 559
And he **s** to Laban, **Gn 29:25** 559
But Laban **s**, "It is not the practice **Gn 29:26** 559
and named him Reuben, for she **s**, **Gn 29:32** 559
again and bore a son and **s**, **Gn 29:33** 559
again and bore a son and **s**, **Gn 29:34** 559
again and bore a son and **s**, **Gn 29:35** 559
and she **s** to Jacob, **Gn 30:1** 559
burned against Rachel, and he **s**, **Gn 30:2** 559
She **s**, "Here is my maid Bilhah **Gn 30:3** 559
Rachel **s**, "God has vindicated me, **Gn 30:6** 559
Rachel **s**, "With mighty wrestlings I **Gn 30:8** 559
Then Leah **s**, "How fortunate!" **Gn 30:11** 559
Then Leah **s**, "Happy am I! For **Gn 30:13** 559
Then Rachel **s** to Leah, **Gn 30:14** 559
But she **s** to her, **Gn 30:15** 559
Rachel **s**, "Therefore he may lie with **Gn 30:15** 559
Leah went out to meet him and **s**, **Gn 30:16** 559
Then Leah **s**, "God has given me **Gn 30:18** 559
Then Leah **s**, "God has endowed me **Gn 30:20** 559
conceived and bore a son and **s**, **Gn 30:23** 559
Joseph, that Jacob **s** to Laban, **Gn 30:25** 559
But Laban **s** to him, **Gn 30:27** 559
But he **s** to him, **Gn 30:29** 559
So he **s**, "What shall I give you?" **Gn 30:31** 559
Jacob **s**, "You shall not give me **Gn 30:31** 559
Laban **s**, "Good, let it be according **Gn 30:34** 559
Then the LORD **s** to Jacob, **Gn 31:3** 559
and **s** to them, "I see your father's **Gn 31:5** 559
angel of God **s** to me in the dream, **Gn 31:11** 559
'Jacob,' and I **s**, 'Here I am.' **Gn 31:11** 559
"He **s**, 'Lift up now your eyes **Gn 31:12** 559
and Leah **s** to him, **Gn 31:14** 559
do whatever God has **s** to you." **Gn 31:16** 559
dream of the night and **s** to him, **Gn 31:24** 559
Then Laban **s** to Jacob, **Gn 31:26** 559
She **s** to her father, **Gn 31:35** 559
and Jacob **s** to Laban, **Gn 31:36** 559
Jacob **s** to his kinsmen, **Gn 31:46** 559
Laban **s**, "This heap is a witness **Gn 31:48** 559
and Mizpah, for he **s**, **Gn 31:49** 559
Laban **s** to Jacob, **Gn 31:51** 559
Jacob **s** when he saw them, **Gn 32:2** 559
for he **s**, "If Esau comes to the one **Gn 32:8** 559
Jacob **s**, "O God of my father **Gn 32:9** 559
who **s** to me, 'Return to your **Gn 32:9** 559
"For You **s**, 'I will surely prosper **Gn 32:12** 559
by itself, and **s** to his servants, **Gn 32:16** 559
Jacob also is behind us.' " For he **s**, **Gn 32:20** 559
he **s**, "Let me go, for the dawn is **Gn 32:26** 559
he **s**, "I will not let you go unless **Gn 32:26** 559
So he **s** to him, "What is your name **Gn 32:27** 559
"What is your name?" And he **s**, **Gn 32:27** 559
He **s**, "Your name shall no longer be **Gn 32:28** 559
Then Jacob asked him and **s**, **Gn 32:29** 559
But he **s**, "Why is it that you ask **Gn 32:29** 559
for *he* **s**, "I have seen God face **Gn 32:30**
the women and the children, and **s**, **Gn 33:5** 559
"Who are these with you?" So he **s**, **Gn 33:5** 559

he **s**, "What do you mean by all this **Gn 33:8** 559
And he **s**, "To find favor in the sight **Gn 33:8** 559
But Esau **s**, "I have plenty, **Gn 33:9** 559
Jacob **s**, "No, please, if now I **Gn 33:10** 559
Esau **s**, "Let us take our journey **Gn 33:12** 559
But he **s** to him, **Gn 33:13** 559
Esau **s**, "Please let me leave **Gn 33:15** 559
But he **s**, "What need is there? **Gn 33:15** 559
Shechem also **s** to her father and **Gn 34:11** 559
They **s** to them, **Gn 34:14** 559
Then Jacob **s** to Simeon and Levi, **Gn 34:30** 559
they **s**, "Should he treat our sister as **Gn 34:31** 559
Then God **s** to Jacob, **Gn 35:1** 559
So Jacob **s** to his household and to **Gn 35:2** 559
God **s** to him, **Gn 35:10** 559
God also **s** to him, **Gn 35:11** 559
labor the midwife **s** to her, **Gn 35:17** 559
He **s** to them, **Gn 37:6** 559
Then his brothers **s** to him, **Gn 37:8** 559
related it to his brothers, and **s**, **Gn 37:9** 559
father rebuked him and **s** to him, **Gn 37:10** 559
Israel **s** to Joseph, **Gn 37:13** 559
And he **s** to him, **Gn 37:13** 559
Then he **s** to him, **Gn 37:14** 559
He **s**, "I am looking for my brothers; **Gn 37:16** 559
Then the man **s**, "They have moved **Gn 37:17** 559
They **s** to one another, **Gn 37:19** 559
him out of their hands and **s**, **Gn 37:21** 559
Reuben further **s** to them, **Gn 37:22** 559
Judah **s** to his brothers, **Gn 37:26** 559
He returned to his brothers and **s**, **Gn 37:30** 559
brought it to their father and **s**, **Gn 37:32** 559
Then he examined it and **s**, **Gn 37:33** 559
refused to be comforted. And he **s**, **Gn 37:35** 559
Then Judah **s** to Onan, **Gn 38:8** 559
Then Judah **s** to his daughter-in-law **Gn 38:11** 559
aside to her by the road, and **s**, **Gn 38:16** 559
And she **s**, "What will you give me, **Gn 38:16** 559
He **s**, therefore, **Gn 38:17** 559
She **s**, moreover, **Gn 38:17** 559
He **s**, "What pledge shall I give you?" **Gn 38:18** 559
she **s**, "Your seal and your cord, **Gn 38:18** 559
But they **s**, "There has been no **Gn 38:21** 559
So he returned to Judah, and **s**, **Gn 38:22** 559
the men of the place **s**, **Gn 38:22** 559
Then Judah **s**, "Let her keep them, **Gn 38:23** 559
Then Judah **s**, "Bring her out and **Gn 38:24** 559
And she **s**, "Please examine and see, **Gn 38:25** 559
Judah recognized *them,* and **s**, **Gn 38:26** 559
his brother came out. Then she **s**, **Gn 38:29** 559
with desire at Joseph, and she **s**, **Gn 39:7** 559
refused and **s** to his master's wife, **Gn 39:8** 559
of her household and **s** to them, **Gn 39:14** 559
Then they **s** to him, **Gn 40:8** 559
Then Joseph **s** to them, **Gn 40:8** 559
his dream to Joseph, and **s** to him, **Gn 40:9** 559
Then Joseph **s** to him, **Gn 40:12** 559
favorably, he **s** to Joseph, **Gn 40:16** 559
Then Joseph answered and **s**, **Gn 40:18** 559
Pharaoh **s** to Joseph, **Gn 41:15** 559
and I have heard it **s** about you, **Gn 41:15** 559
Now Joseph **s** to Pharaoh, **Gn 41:25** 559
Then Pharaoh **s** to his servants, **Gn 41:38** 559
So Pharaoh **s** to Joseph, **Gn 41:39** 559
Pharaoh **s** to Joseph, **Gn 41:41** 559
Moreover, Pharaoh **s** to Joseph, **Gn 41:44** 559
he **s**, "God has made me forget **Gn 41:51**
he **s**, "God has made me fruitful **Gn 41:52**
to come, just as Joseph had **s**, **Gn 41:54** 559
Pharaoh **s** to all the Egyptians, **Gn 41:55** 559
in Egypt, and Jacob **s** to his sons, **Gn 42:1** 559
He **s**, "Behold, I have heard **Gn 42:2** 559
with his brothers, for he **s**, **Gn 42:4** 559
And he **s** to them, **Gn 42:7** 559
they **s**, "From the land of Canaan, **Gn 42:7** 559
he had about them, and **s** to them, **Gn 42:9** 559
Then they **s** to him, **Gn 42:10** 559
Yet he **s** to them, **Gn 42:12** 559
they **s**, "Your servants are twelve **Gn 42:13** 559
Joseph **s** to them, **Gn 42:14** 559
"It is as I **s** to you, you are spies; **Gn 42:14** 1696
Joseph **s** to them on the third day, **Gn 42:18** 559
Then they **s** to one another, **Gn 42:21** 559
Then he **s** to his brothers, **Gn 42:28** 559
"But we **s** to him, **Gn 42:31** 559
the lord of the land, **s** to us, **Gn 42:33** 559
Their father Jacob **s** to them, **Gn 42:36** 559
But Jacob **s**, "My son shall not go **Gn 42:38** 559
that their father **s** to them, **Gn 43:2** 559
for the man **s** to us, **Gn 43:5** 559
Israel **s**, "Why did you treat me so **Gn 43:6** 559
But they **s**, "The man questioned **Gn 43:7** 559
Judah **s** to his father Israel, **Gn 43:8** 559
their father Israel **s** to them, **Gn 43:11** 559
them, he **s** to his house steward, **Gn 43:16** 559
So the man did as Joseph **s**, **Gn 43:17** 559
they **s**, "*It is* because of the money **Gn 43:18** 559
and **s**, "Oh, my lord, we indeed came **Gn 43:20** 559
He **s**, "Be at ease, do not be afraid. **Gn 43:23** 559
them about their welfare, and **s**, **Gn 43:27** 559
s, "Your servant our father is well; **Gn 43:28** 559
Benjamin, his mother's son, he **s**, **Gn 43:29** 559
And he **s**, "May God be gracious to **Gn 43:29** 559
and he controlled himself and **s**, **Gn 43:31** 559
Joseph **s** to his house steward, **Gn 44:4** 559
They **s** to him, **Gn 44:7** 559
he **s**, "Now let it also be according **Gn 44:10** 559
Joseph **s** to them, **Gn 44:15** 559
So Judah **s**, "What can we say to **Gn 44:16** 559

he **s**, "Far be it from me to do this. **Gn 44:17** 559
Then Judah approached him, and **s**, **Gn 44:18** 559
"We **s** to my lord, **Gn 44:20** 559
"Then you **s** to your servants, **Gn 44:21** 559
"But we **s** to my lord, **Gn 44:22** 559
"You **s** to your servants, however, **Gn 44:23** 559
"Our father **s**, **Gn 44:25** 559
"But we **s**, 'We cannot go down. **Gn 44:26** 559
Your servant my father **s** to us, **Gn 44:27** 559
the one went out from me, and I **s**, **Gn 44:28** 559
Then Joseph **s** to his brothers, **Gn 45:3** 559
Then Joseph **s** to his brothers, **Gn 45:4** 559
he **s**, "I am your brother Joseph, **Gn 45:4** 559
Then Pharaoh **s** to Joseph, **Gn 45:17** 559
as they departed, he **s** to them, **Gn 45:24** 559
Then Israel **s**, "It is enough; my son **Gn 45:28** 559
in visions of the night and **s**, **Gn 46:2** 559
Jacob." And he **s**, "Here I am." **Gn 46:2** 559
He **s**, "I am God, the God of **Gn 46:3** 559
Then Israel **s** to Joseph, **Gn 46:30** 559
Joseph **s** to his brothers and **Gn 46:31** 559
went in and told Pharaoh, and **s**, **Gn 47:1** 559
Then Pharaoh **s** to his brothers, **Gn 47:3** 559
So they **s** to Pharaoh, **Gn 47:3** 559
They **s** to Pharaoh, **Gn 47:4** 559
Then Pharaoh **s** to Joseph, **Gn 47:5** 559
Pharaoh **s** to Jacob, **Gn 47:8** 559
So Jacob **s** to Pharaoh, **Gn 47:9** 559
Egyptians came to Joseph and **s**, **Gn 47:15** 559
Joseph **s**, "Give up your livestock, **Gn 47:16** 559
to him the next year and **s** to him, **Gn 47:18** 559
Then Joseph **s** to the people, **Gn 47:23** 559
they **s**, "You have saved our lives! **Gn 47:25** 559
his son Joseph and **s** to him, **Gn 47:29** 559
he **s**, "I will do as you have said." **Gn 47:30** 559
"I will do as you have **s**." **Gn 47:30** 1697
He **s**, "Swear to me." So he **Gn 47:31** 559
Then Jacob **s** to Joseph, **Gn 48:3** 559
and He **s** to me, 'Behold, I will **Gn 48:4** 559
Israel saw Joseph's sons, he **s**, **Gn 48:8** 559
Joseph **s** to his father, **Gn 48:9** 559
So he **s**, "Bring them to me, please, **Gn 48:9** 559
Israel **s** to Joseph, **Gn 48:11** 559
He blessed Joseph, and **s**, **Gn 48:15** 559
Joseph **s** to his father, **Gn 48:18** 559
But his father refused and **s**, **Gn 48:19** 559
Then Israel **s** to Joseph, **Gn 48:21** 559
Jacob summoned his sons and **s**, **Gn 49:1** 559
this is what their father **s** to them **Gn 49:28** 1696
he charged them and **s** to them, **Gn 49:29** 559
Pharaoh **s**, "Go up and bury your **Gn 50:6** 559
threshing floor of Atad, they **s**, **Gn 50:11** 559
their father was dead, they **s**, **Gn 50:15** 559
and fell down before him and **s**, **Gn 50:18** 559
But Joseph **s** to them, **Gn 50:19** 559
Joseph **s** to his brothers, **Gn 50:24** 559
He **s** to his people, **Ex 1:9** 559
and he **s**, "When you are helping **Ex 1:16** 559
for the midwives and **s** to them, **Ex 1:18** 559
The midwives **s** to Pharaoh, **Ex 1:19** 559
And she had pity on him and **s**, **Ex 2:6** 559
his sister **s** to Pharaoh's daughter, **Ex 2:7** 559
Pharaoh's daughter **s** to her, **Ex 2:8** 559
Then Pharaoh's daughter **s** to her, **Ex 2:9** 559
And she named him Moses, and **s**, **Ex 2:10** 559
and he **s** to the offender, **Ex 2:13** 559
But he **s**, "Who made you a prince **Ex 2:14** 559
Then Moses was afraid and **s**, **Ex 2:14** 559
came to Reuel their father, he **s**, **Ex 2:18** 559
they **s**, "An Egyptian delivered us **Ex 2:19** 559
He **s** to his daughters, **Ex 2:20** 559
he named him Gershom, for he **s**, **Ex 2:22** 559
So Moses **s**, "I must turn aside now **Ex 3:3** 559
from the midst of the bush and **s**, **Ex 3:4** 559
Moses!" And he **s**, "Here I am." **Ex 3:4** 559
Then He **s**, "Do not come near here **Ex 3:5** 559
He **s** also, "I am the God of your **Ex 3:6** 559
The LORD **s**, "I have surely seen the **Ex 3:7** 559
But Moses **s** to God, **Ex 3:11** 559
He **s**, "Certainly I will be with you, **Ex 3:12** 559
Then Moses **s** to God, **Ex 3:13** 559
God **s** to Moses, **Ex 3:14** 559
and He **s**, "Thus you shall say to **Ex 3:14** 559
God, furthermore, **s** to Moses, **Ex 3:15** 559
"So I **s**, I will bring you up out **Ex 3:17** 559
Then Moses **s**, **Ex 4:1** 559
The LORD **s** to him, **Ex 4:2** 559
in your hand?" And he **s**, "A staff." **Ex 4:2** 559
He **s**, "Throw it on the ground." **Ex 4:3** 559
But the LORD **s** to Moses, **Ex 4:4** 559
The LORD furthermore **s** to him, **Ex 4:6** 559
Then He **s**, "Put your hand into **Ex 4:7** 559
Then Moses **s** to the LORD, **Ex 4:10** 559
The LORD **s** to him, **Ex 4:11** 559
But he **s**, "Please, Lord, now send **Ex 4:13** 559
burned against Moses, and He **s**, **Ex 4:14** 559
his father-in-law and **s** to him, **Ex 4:18** 559
And Jethro **s** to Moses, **Ex 4:18** 559
Now the LORD **s** to Moses in Midian, **Ex 4:19** 559
The LORD **s** to Moses, **Ex 4:21** 559
"So I **s** to you, **Ex 4:23** 559
threw it at Moses' feet, and she **s**, **Ex 4:25** 559
At that time she **s**, **Ex 4:26** 559
Now the LORD **s** to Aaron, **Ex 4:27** 559
and Aaron came and **s** to Pharaoh, **Ex 5:1** 559
Pharaoh **s**, "Who is the LORD that **Ex 5:2** 559
they **s**, "The God of the Hebrews **Ex 5:3** 559
But the king of Egypt **s** to them, **Ex 5:4** 559
Again Pharaoh **s**, **Ex 5:5** 559

But he **s**, “You are lazy, *very* lazy; Ex 5:17 559
They **s** to them, Ex 5:21 559
Moses returned to the LORD and **s**, Ex 5:22 559
Then the LORD **s** to Moses, Ex 6:1 559
further to Moses and **s** to him, Ex 6:2 559
and Moses to whom the LORD **s**, Ex 6:26 559
But Moses **s** before the LORD, Ex 6:30 559
Then the LORD **s** to Moses, Ex 7:1 559
listen to them, as the LORD had **s**. Ex 7:13 1696
Then the LORD **s** to Moses, Ex 7:14 559
Then the LORD **s** to Moses, Ex 7:19 559
listen to them, as the LORD had **s**. Ex 7:22 1696
Then the LORD **s** to Moses, Ex 8:1 559
Then the LORD **s** to Moses, Ex 8:5 559
called for Moses and Aaron and **s**, Ex 8:8 559
Moses **s** to Pharaoh, Ex 8:9 559
Then he **s**, “Tomorrow.” Ex 8:10 559
So he **s**, “*May it be* according to Ex 8:10 559
listen to them, as the LORD had **s**. Ex 8:15 1696
Then the LORD **s** to Moses, Ex 8:16 559
Then the magicians **s** to Pharaoh, Ex 8:19 559
listen to them, as the LORD had **s**. Ex 8:19 1696
Now the LORD **s** to Moses, Ex 8:20 559
called for Moses and Aaron and **s**, Ex 8:25 559
Moses **s**, “It is not right to do so, Ex 8:26 559
Pharaoh **s**, “I will let you go, Ex 8:28 559
Then Moses **s**, “Behold, I am going Ex 8:29 559
Then the LORD **s** to Moses, Ex 9:1 559
the LORD **s** to Moses and Aaron, Ex 9:8 559
Then the LORD **s** to Moses, Ex 9:13 559
Now the LORD **s** to Moses, Ex 9:22 559
Moses and Aaron, and **s** to them, Ex 9:27 559
Moses **s** to him, Ex 9:29 559
Then the LORD **s** to Moses, Ex 10:1 559
went to Pharaoh and **s** to him, Ex 10:3 559
Pharaoh’s servants **s** to him, Ex 10:7 559
back to Pharaoh, and he **s** to them, Ex 10:8 559
Moses **s**, “We shall go with our Ex 10:9 559
Then he **s** to them, Ex 10:10 559
Then the LORD **s** to Moses, Ex 10:12 559
for Moses and Aaron, and he **s**, Ex 10:16 559
Then the LORD **s** to Moses, Ex 10:21 559
Pharaoh called to Moses, and **s**, Ex 10:24 559
But Moses **s**, “You must also let us Ex 10:25 559
Then Pharaoh **s** to him, Ex 10:28 559
Moses **s**, “You are right; Ex 10:29 559
Now the LORD **s** to Moses, Ex 11:1 559
Moses **s**, “Thus says the LORD, Ex 11:4 559
Then the LORD **s** to Moses, Ex 11:9 559
Now the LORD **s** to Moses and Aaron Ex 12:1 559
elders of Israel and **s** to them, Ex 12:21 559
Moses and Aaron at night and **s**, Ex 12:31 559
worship the LORD, as you have **s**. Ex 12:31 1696
and your herds, as you have **s**, Ex 12:32 1696
of the land in haste, for they **s**, Ex 12:33 559
The LORD **s** to Moses and Aaron, Ex 12:43 559
Moses **s** to the people, Ex 13:3 559
for God **s**, “The people might change Ex 13:17 559
toward the people, and they **s**, Ex 14:5 559
Then they **s** to Moses, Ex 14:11 559
But Moses **s** to the people, Ex 14:13 559
Then the LORD **s** to Moses, Ex 14:15 559
so the Egyptians **s**, Ex 14:25 559
Then the LORD **s** to Moses, Ex 14:26 559
sang this song to the LORD, and **s**, Ex 15:1 559
“The enemy **s**, ‘I will pursue, I will Ex 15:9 559
He **s**, “If you will give earnest heed Ex 15:26 559
The sons of Israel **s** to them, Ex 16:3 559
Then the LORD **s** to Moses, Ex 16:4 559
Aaron **s** to all the sons of Israel, Ex 16:6 559
Moses **s**, “*This will happen* when the Ex 16:8 559
Then Moses **s** to Aaron, Ex 16:9 559
saw *it*, they **s** to one another, Ex 16:15 559
And Moses **s** to them, Ex 16:15 559
Moses **s** to them, Ex 16:19 559
then he **s** to them, Ex 16:23 559
Moses **s**, “Eat it today, for today is Ex 16:25 559
Then the LORD **s** to Moses, Ex 16:28 559
Moses **s**, “This is what the LORD has Ex 16:32 559
Moses **s** to Aaron, Ex 16:33 559
people quarreled with Moses and **s**, Ex 17:2 559
And Moses **s** to them, Ex 17:2 559
they grumbled against Moses and **s**, Ex 17:3 559
Then the LORD **s** to Moses, Ex 17:5 559
So Moses **s** to Joshua, Ex 17:9 559
Then the LORD **s** to Moses, Ex 17:14 559
and he **s**, “The LORD has sworn; Ex 17:16 559
one was named Gershom, for Moses **s**, Ex 18:3 559
for *he* **s**, “The God of my father Ex 18:4
So Jethro **s**, “Blessed be the LORD Ex 18:10 559
he was doing for the people, he **s**, Ex 18:14 559
Moses **s** to his father-in-law, Ex 18:15 559
Moses’ father-in-law **s** to him, Ex 18:17 559
and did all that he had **s**. Ex 18:24 559
people answered together and **s**, Ex 19:8 559
The LORD **s** to Moses, Ex 19:9 559
The LORD also **s** to Moses, Ex 19:10 559
He **s** to the people, Ex 19:15 559
Moses **s** to the LORD, Ex 19:23 559
Then the LORD **s** to him, Ex 19:24 559
Then they **s** to Moses, Ex 20:19 559
Moses **s** to the people, Ex 20:20 559
Then the LORD **s** to Moses, Ex 20:22 559
everything which I have **s** to you, Ex 23:13 559
Then He **s** to Moses, Ex 24:1 559
answered with one voice and **s**, Ex 24:3 559
and they **s**, “All that the LORD has Ex 24:7 559
sprinkled *it* on the people, and **s**, Ex 24:8 559
Now the LORD **s** to Moses, Ex 24:12 559
But to the elders he **s**, Ex 24:14 559
Then the LORD **s** to Moses, Ex 30:34 559
about Aaron and **s** to him, Ex 32:1 559
Aaron **s** to them, Ex 32:2 559
they **s**, “This is your god, O Israel, Ex 32:4 559
Aaron made a proclamation and **s**, Ex 32:5 559
and have sacrificed to it and **s**, Ex 32:8 559
The LORD **s** to Moses, Ex 32:9 559
entreated the LORD his God, and **s**, Ex 32:11 559
and **s** to them, ‘I will multiply Ex 32:13 1696
the harm which He **s** He would do Ex 32:14 1696
as they shouted, he **s** to Moses, Ex 32:17 559
But he **s**, “It is not the sound of the Ex 32:18 559
Then Moses **s** to Aaron, Ex 32:21 559
Aaron **s**, “Do not let the anger of Ex 32:22 559
“For they **s** to me, Ex 32:23 559
“I **s** to them, Ex 32:24 559
in the gate of the camp, and **s**, Ex 32:26 559
He **s** to them, Ex 32:27 559
Then Moses **s**, “Dedicate yourselves Ex 32:29 559
day Moses **s** to the people, Ex 32:30 559
Moses returned to the LORD, and **s**, Ex 32:31 559
The LORD **s** to Moses, Ex 32:33 559
For the LORD had **s** to Moses, Ex 33:5 559
Then Moses **s** to the LORD, Ex 33:12 559
Moreover, You have **s**, Ex 33:12 559
He **s**, “My presence shall go *with you* Ex 33:14 559
Then he **s** to Him, Ex 33:15 559
The LORD **s** to Moses, Ex 33:17 559
Moses **s**, “I pray You, show me Your Ex 33:18 559
And He **s**, “I Myself will make all Ex 33:19 559
But He **s**, “You cannot see My face Ex 33:20 559
Then the LORD **s**, Ex 33:21 559
Now the LORD **s** to Moses, Ex 34:1 559
He **s**, “If now I have found favor in Ex 34:9 559
God **s**, “Behold, I am going to make Ex 34:10 559
Then the LORD **s** to Moses, Ex 34:27 559
the sons of Israel, and **s** to them, Ex 35:1 559
Moses **s** to the sons of Israel, Ex 35:30 559
and they **s** to Moses, Ex 36:5 559
Moses **s** to the congregation, Lv 8:5 559
Moses **s** to Aaron and to his sons, Lv 8:31 559
and he **s** to Aaron, Lv 9:2 559
Moses **s**, “This is the thing Lv 9:6 559
Moses then **s** to Aaron, Lv 9:7 559
Then Moses **s** to Aaron, Lv 10:3 559
uncle Uzziel, and **s** to them, Lv 10:4 559
of the camp, as Moses had **s**. Lv 10:5 1696
Then Moses **s** to Aaron and to his Lv 10:6 559
The LORD **s** to Moses: Lv 16:2 559
I **s** to the sons of Israel, Lv 17:12 559
I **s** to the sons of Israel, Lv 17:14 559
‘Hence I have **s** to you, Lv 20:24 559
Then the LORD **s** to Moses, Lv 21:1 559
Then the LORD **s** to Moses, Nu 3:40 559
Then the LORD **s** to Moses, Nu 7:11 559
Those men **s** to him, Nu 9:7 559
Moses therefore **s** to them, Nu 9:8 559
Then Moses **s** to Hobab the son of Nu 10:29 559
to the place of which the LORD **s**, Nu 10:29 559
But he **s** to him, Nu 10:30 559
Then he **s**, “Please do not leave us, Nu 10:31 559
when the ark set out that Moses **s**, Nu 10:35 559
When it came to rest, he **s**, Nu 10:36 559
sons of Israel wept again and **s**, Nu 11:4 559
So Moses **s** to the LORD, Nu 11:11 559
The LORD therefore **s** to Moses, Nu 11:16 559
But Moses **s**, “The people, among Nu 11:21 559
yet You have **s**, Nu 11:21 559
The LORD **s** to Moses, Nu 11:23 559
man ran and told Moses and **s**, Nu 11:27 559
from his youth, **s**, Nu 11:28 559
But Moses **s** to him, Nu 11:29 559
and they **s**, “Has the LORD indeed Nu 12:2 559
Suddenly the LORD **s** to Moses Nu 12:4 559
He **s**, “Hear now My words: Nu 12:6 559
Then Aaron **s** to Moses, Nu 12:11 559
But the LORD **s** to Moses, Nu 12:14 559
the land of Canaan, he **s** to them, Nu 13:17 559
Thus they told him, and **s**, Nu 13:27 559
the people before Moses and **s**, Nu 13:30 559
men who had gone up with him **s**, Nu 13:31 559
the whole congregation **s** to them, Nu 14:2 559
So they **s** to one another, Nu 14:4 559
all the congregation **s** to stone them Nu 14:10 559
The LORD **s** to Moses, Nu 14:11 559
But Moses **s** to the LORD, Nu 14:13 559
the LORD **s**, “I have pardoned *them* Nu 14:20 559
whom you **s** would become a prey Nu 14:31 559
But Moses **s**, “Why then are you Nu 14:41 559
Then the LORD **s** to Moses, Nu 15:35 559
Moses and Aaron, and **s** to them, Nu 16:3 559
Then Moses **s** to Korah, Nu 16:8 559
but they **s**, “We will not come up. Nu 16:12 559
very angry and **s** to the LORD, Nu 16:15 559
Moses **s** to Korah, Nu 16:16 559
they fell on their faces and **s**, Nu 16:22 559
Moses **s**, “By this you shall know Nu 16:28 559
fled at their outcry, for they **s**, Nu 16:34 559
Moses **s** to Aaron, Nu 16:46 559
But the LORD **s** to Moses, Nu 17:10 559
So the LORD **s** to Aaron, Nu 18:1 559
Then the LORD **s** to Aaron, Nu 18:20 559
I have **s** concerning them, Nu 18:24 559
And he **s** to them, Nu 20:10 559
But the LORD **s** to Moses and Aaron, Nu 20:12 559
“Thus your brother Israel has **s**, Nu 20:14 559
Edom, however, **s** to him, Nu 20:18 559
the sons of Israel **s** to him, Nu 20:19 559
he **s**, “You shall not pass through.” Nu 20:20 559
made a vow to the LORD and **s**, Nu 21:2 559
So the people came to Moses and **s**, Nu 21:7 559
Then the LORD **s** to Moses, Nu 21:8 559
it is **s** in the Book of the Wars Nu 21:14 559
well where the LORD **s** to Moses, Nu 21:16 559
But the LORD **s** to Moses, Nu 21:34 559
Moab **s** to the elders of Midian, Nu 22:4 559
He **s** to them, Nu 22:8 559
Then God came to Balaam and **s**, Nu 22:9 559
Balaam **s** to God, Nu 22:10 559
God **s** to Balaam, Nu 22:12 559
morning and **s** to Balak’s leaders, Nu 22:13 559
arose and went to Balak and **s**, Nu 22:14 559
They came to Balaam and **s** to him, Nu 22:16 559
to Balaam at night and **s** to him, Nu 22:20 559
the donkey, and she **s** to Balaam, Nu 22:28 559
Then Balaam **s** to the donkey, Nu 22:29 559
The donkey **s** to Balaam, Nu 22:30 559
to do so to you?” And he **s**, “No.” Nu 22:30 559
The angel of the LORD **s** to him, Nu 22:32 559
Balaam **s** to the angel of the LORD, Nu 22:34 559
the angel of the LORD **s** to Balaam, Nu 22:35 559
Then Balak **s** to Balaam, Nu 22:37 559
So Balaam **s** to Balak, Nu 22:38 559
Then Balaam **s** to Balak, Nu 23:1 559
Then Balaam **s** to Balak, Nu 23:3 559
God met Balaam, and he **s** to Him, Nu 23:4 559
put a word in Balaam’s mouth and **s**, Nu 23:5 559
He took up his discourse and **s**, Nu 23:7 559
Then Balak **s** to Balaam, Nu 23:11 559
Then Balak **s** to him, Nu 23:13 559
And he **s** to Balak, Nu 23:15 559
and put a word in his mouth and **s**, Nu 23:16 559
And Balak **s** to him, Nu 23:17 559
he took up his discourse and **s**, Nu 23:18 559
Has He **s**, and will He not do it? Nu 23:19 559
shall be **s** to Jacob And to Israel, Nu 23:23 559
Then Balak **s** to Balaam, Nu 23:25 559
Then Balak **s** to Balaam, Nu 23:27 559
Balaam **s** to Balak, Nu 23:29 559
Balak did just as Balaam had **s**, Nu 23:30 559
He took up his discourse and **s**, Nu 24:3 559
and Balak **s** to Balaam, Nu 24:10 559
I **s** I would honor you greatly, but Nu 24:11 559
Balaam **s** to Balak, Nu 24:12 559
He took up his discourse and **s**, Nu 24:15 559
and took up his discourse and **s**, Nu 24:20 559
and took up his discourse and **s**, Nu 24:21 559
he took up his discourse and **s**, Nu 24:23 559
The LORD **s** to Moses, Nu 25:4 559
Moses **s** to the judges of Israel, Nu 25:5 559
For the LORD had **s** of them, Nu 26:65 559
Then the LORD **s** to Moses, Nu 27:12 559
So the LORD **s** to Moses, Nu 27:18 559
but **s** nothing to her *and* did not Nu 30:11 2790b
because he **s** nothing to her on the Nu 30:14 2790b
And Moses **s** to them, Nu 31:15 559
Then Eleazar the priest **s** to the Nu 31:21 559
and they **s** to Moses, Nu 31:49 559
They **s**, “If we have found favor Nu 32:5 559
But Moses **s** to the sons of Gad and Nu 32:6 559
Then they came near to him and **s**, Nu 32:16 559
So Moses **s** to them, Nu 32:20 559
Moses **s** to them, Nu 32:29 559
the LORD has **s** to your servants, Nu 32:31 1696
and they **s**, “The LORD commanded Nu 36:2 559
‘You answered me and **s**, Dt 1:14 559
which you have **s** to do is good.’ Dt 1:14 1696
“I **s** to you, Dt 1:20 559
all of you approached me and **s**, Dt 1:22 559
brought us back a report and **s**, Dt 1:25 559
you grumbled in your tents and **s**, Dt 1:27 559
“Then I **s** to you, Dt 1:29 559
who you **s** would become a prey, Dt 1:39 559
“Then you **s** to me, Dt 1:41 559
“And the LORD **s** to me, Dt 1:42 559
“Then the LORD **s** to me, Dt 2:9 559
“The LORD **s** to me, Dt 2:31 559
“But the LORD **s** to me, Dt 3:2 559
and the LORD **s** to me, Dt 3:26 559
at Horeb, when the LORD **s** to me, Dt 4:10 559
all Israel and **s** to them Dt 5:1 559
did not go up the mountain. He **s**, Dt 5:5 559
You **s**, ‘Behold, the LORD our God Dt 5:24 559
spoke to me, and the LORD **s** to me, Dt 5:28 559
and of whom you have heard *it* **s**, Dt 9:2
“Then the LORD **s** to me, Dt 9:12 559
LORD had **s** He would destroy you. Dt 9:25 559
“I prayed to the LORD and **s**, Dt 9:26 559
“At that time the LORD **s** to me, Dt 10:1 559
“Then the LORD **s** to me, Dt 10:11 559
since the LORD has **s** to you, Dt 17:16 559
“The LORD **s** to me, Dt 18:17 559
summoned all Israel and **s** to them, Dt 29:2 559
And he **s** to them, Dt 31:2 559
and go, and the LORD has **s** to me, Dt 31:2 559
Then Moses called to Joshua and **s** Dt 31:7 559
Then the LORD **s** to Moses, Dt 31:14 559
The LORD **s** to Moses, Dt 31:16 559
Joshua the son of Nun, and **s**, Dt 31:23 559
“Then He **s**, ‘I will hide My face Dt 32:20 559
‘I would have **s**, Dt 32:26 559
he **s** to them, “Take to your heart Dt 32:46 559
He **s**, “The LORD came from Sinai, Dt 33:2 559
so he **s**, “Hear, O LORD, the voice Dt 33:7 559
Of Levi he **s**, Dt 33:8 559
s of his father and his mother, Dt 33:9 559
Of Benjamin he **s**, Dt 33:12 559

Of Joseph he s, Dt 33:13 559
Of Zebulun he s, Dt 33:18 559
Of Gad he s, Dt 33:20 559
Of Dan he s, Dt 33:22 559
Of Naphtali he s, Dt 33:23 559
Of Asher he s, Dt 33:24 559
the enemy from before you, And s, Dt 33:27 559
Then the LORD s to him, Dt 34:4 559
half-tribe of Manasseh, Joshua s, Jos 1:12 559
men and hidden them, and she s, Jos 2:4 559
and s to the men, Jos 2:9 559
So the men s to her, Jos 2:14 559
She s to them, Jos 2:16 559
The men s to her, Jos 2:17 559
She s, "According to your words, Jos 2:21 559
They s to Joshua, Jos 2:24 559
Then Joshua s to the people, Jos 3:5 559
Now the LORD s to Joshua, Jos 3:7 559
Joshua s to the sons of Israel, Jos 3:9 559
Joshua s, "By this you shall know Jos 3:10 559
and Joshua s to them, Jos 4:5 559
Now the LORD s to Joshua, Jos 4:15 559
He s to the sons of Israel, Jos 4:21 559
At that time the LORD s to Joshua, Jos 5:2 559
Then the LORD s to Joshua, Jos 5:9 559
Joshua went to him and s to him, Jos 5:13 559
He s, "No; rather I indeed come now Jos 5:14 559
and bowed down, and s to him, Jos 5:14 559
of the LORD's host s to Joshua, Jos 5:15 559
The LORD s to Joshua, Jos 6:2 559
called the priests and s to them, Jos 6:6 559
Then he s to the people, Jos 6:7 559
trumpets, Joshua s to the people, Jos 6:16 559
Joshua s to the two men who Jos 6:22 559
east of Bethel, and s to them, Jos 7:2 559
returned to Joshua and s to him, Jos 7:3 559
Joshua s, "Alas, O Lord GOD, Jos 7:7 559
So the LORD s to Joshua, Jos 7:10 559
LORD, the God of Israel, has s, Jos 7:13 559
Then Joshua s to Achan, Jos 7:19 559
So Achan answered Joshua and s, Jos 7:20 559
Joshua s, "Why have you Jos 7:25 559
Now the LORD s to Joshua, Jos 8:1 559
Then the LORD s to Joshua, Jos 8:18 559
and s to him and to the men of Jos 9:6 559
men of Israel s to the Hivites, Jos 9:7 559
But they s to Joshua, Jos 9:8 559
Then Joshua s to them, Jos 9:8 559
They s to him, Jos 9:9 559
s to the whole congregation, Jos 9:19 559
The leaders s to them, Jos 9:21 559
So they answered Joshua and s, Jos 9:24 559
The LORD s to Joshua, Jos 10:8 559
and he s in the sight of Israel, Jos 10:12 559
Joshua s, "Roll large stones Jos 10:18 559
Joshua s, "Open the mouth of the Jos 10:22 559
and s to the chiefs of the men of Jos 10:24 559
Joshua then s to them, Jos 10:25 559
Then the LORD s to Joshua, Jos 11:6 559
in years when the LORD s to him, Jos 13:1 559
Jephunneh the Kenizzite s to him, Jos 14:6 559
And Caleb s, "The one who attacks Jos 15:16 559
the donkey, and Caleb s to her, Jos 15:18 559
Then she s, "Give me a blessing; Jos 15:19 559
Joshua s to them, Jos 17:15 559
The sons of Joseph s, Jos 17:16 559
So Joshua s to the sons of Israel, Jos 18:3 559
and s to them, "You have kept all Jos 22:2 559
and s to them, "Return to your tents Jos 22:8 559
And the sons of Israel heard *it* s, Jos 22:11 559
"Therefore we s, Jos 22:26 559
"Therefore we s, Jos 22:28 559
the son of Eleazar the priest s to the Jos 22:31 559
they s, "it is a witness Jos 22:34 559
and their officers, and s to them, Jos 23:2 559
Joshua s to all the people, Jos 24:2 559
The people answered and s, Jos 24:16 559
Then Joshua s to the people, Jos 24:19 559
The people s to Joshua, Jos 24:21 559
Joshua s to the people, Jos 24:22 559
And they s, "We are witnesses." Jos 24:22 559
The people s to Joshua, Jos 24:24 559
Joshua s to all the people, Jos 24:27 559
The LORD s, "Judah shall go Jg 1:2 559
Judah s to Simeon his brother, Jg 1:3 559
Adoni-bezek s, Jg 1:7 559
And Caleb s, "The one who attacks Jg 1:12 559
her donkey, and Caleb s to her, Jg 1:14 559
She s to him, Jg 1:15 559
of the city and they s to him, Jg 1:24 559
And he s, "I brought you up out of Jg 2:1 559
I s, 'I will never break My covenant Jg 2:1 559
"Therefore I also s, Jg 2:3 559
burned against Israel, and He s, Jg 2:20 559
idols which were at Gilgal, and s, Jg 3:19 559
And he s, "Keep silence." Jg 3:19 559
Ehud s, "I have a message from God Jg 3:20 559
they s, "He is only relieving himself Jg 3:24 559
He s to them, Jg 3:28 559
from Kedesh-naphtali, and s to him, Jg 4:6 559
Then Barak s to her, Jg 4:8 559
She s, "I will surely go with you; Jg 4:9 559
Deborah s to Barak, Jg 4:14 559
out to meet Sisera, and s to him, Jg 4:18 559
He s to her, Jg 4:19 559
He s to her, Jg 4:20 559
came out to meet him and s to him, Jg 4:22 559
Meroz,' s the angel of the LORD, Jg 5:23 559
sons of Israel, and he s to them, Jg 6:8 559
and I s to you, "I am the LORD Jg 6:10 559
LORD appeared to him and s to him, Jg 6:12 559
Then Gideon s to him, Jg 6:13 559
The LORD looked at him and s, Jg 6:14 559
He s to Him, Jg 6:15 559
But the LORD s to him, Jg 6:16 559
So Gideon s to Him, Jg 6:17 559
He s, "I will remain until you return Jg 6:18 559
The angel of God s to him, Jg 6:20 559
was the angel of the LORD, he s, Jg 6:22 559
The LORD s to him, Jg 6:23 559
the LORD s to him, Jg 6:25 559
They s to one another, Jg 6:29 559
about and inquired, they s, Jg 6:29 559
the men of the city s to Joash, Jg 6:30 559
But Joash s to all who stood against Jg 6:31 559
Then Gideon s to God, Jg 6:36 559
Then Gideon s to God, Jg 6:39 559
The LORD s to Gideon, Jg 7:2 559
Then the LORD s to Gideon, Jg 7:4 559
And the LORD s to Gideon, Jg 7:5 559
The LORD s to Gideon, Jg 7:7 559
came about that the LORD s to him, Jg 7:9 559
And he s, "Behold, I had a dream; Jg 7:13 559
to the camp of Israel and s, Jg 7:15 559
He s to them, Jg 7:17 559
Then the men of Ephraim s to him, Jg 8:1 559
But he s to them, Jg 8:2 559
him subsided when he s that. Jg 8:3 1696
He s to the men of Succoth, Jg 8:5 559
The leaders of Succoth s, Jg 8:6 559
Gideon s, "All right, when the LORD Jg 8:7 559
came to the men of Succoth and s, Jg 8:15 559
Then he s to Zebah and Zalmunna, Jg 8:18 559
And they s, "They were like you, Jg 8:18 559
He s, "They *were* my brothers, Jg 8:19 559
So he s to Jether his firstborn, Jg 8:20 559
Then Zebah and Zalmunna s, Jg 8:21 559
the men of Israel s to Gideon, Jg 8:22 559
But Gideon s to them, Jg 8:23 559
Yet Gideon s to them, Jg 8:24 559
They s, "We will surely give Jg 8:25 559
to follow Abimelech, for they s, Jg 9:3 559
Thus he s to them, Jg 9:7 559
and they s to the olive tree, Jg 9:8 559
"But the olive tree s to them, Jg 9:9 559
"Then the trees s to the fig Jg 9:10 559
"But the fig tree s to them, Jg 9:11 559
"Then the trees s to the vine, Jg 9:12 559
"But the vine s to them, Jg 9:13 559
all the trees s to the bramble, Jg 9:14 559
"The bramble s to the trees, Jg 9:15 559
Then Gaal the son of Ebed s, Jg 9:28 559
And he s to Abimelech, Jg 9:29 559
saw the people, he s to Zebul, Jg 9:36 559
But Zebul s to him, Jg 9:36 559
Gaal spoke again and s, Jg 9:37 559
Then Zebul s to him, Jg 9:38 559
boasting now with which you s, Jg 9:38 559
Then he s to the people who *were* Jg 9:48 559
his armor bearer, and s to him, Jg 9:54 559
so that it will not be s of me, Jg 9:54 559
The LORD s to the sons of Israel, Jg 10:11 559
The sons of Israel s to the LORD, Jg 10:15 559
leaders of Gilead, s to one another, Jg 10:18 559
drove Jephthah out and s to him, Jg 11:2 559
and they s to Jephthah, Jg 11:6 559
Jephthah s to the elders of Gilead, Jg 11:7 559
elders of Gilead s to Jephthah, Jg 11:8 559
s to the elders of Gilead, Jg 11:9 559
elders of Gilead s to Jephthah, Jg 11:10 559
surely we will do as you have s." Jg 11:10 1697
s to the messengers of Jephthah, Jg 11:13 559
and they s to him, Jg 11:15 559
of Heshbon, and Israel s to him, Jg 11:19 559
made a vow to the LORD and s, Jg 11:30 559
he tore his clothes and s, Jg 11:35 559
So she s to him, Jg 11:36 559
do to me as you have s, Jg 11:36 3318, 4480, 6310
She s to her father, Jg 11:37 559
he s, "Go." So he sent her away Jg 11:38 559
to Zaphon and s to Jephthah, Jg 12:1 559
Jephthah s to them, Jg 12:2 559
defeated Ephraim, because they s, Jg 12:4 559
any of the fugitives of Ephraim s, Jg 12:5 559
you an Ephraimite?" If he s, "No," Jg 12:5 559
he s, "Sibboleth," for he could not Jg 12:6 559
to the woman and s to her, Jg 13:3 559
"But he s to me, Jg 13:7 559
Manoah entreated the LORD and s, Jg 13:8 559
he came to the man he s to him, Jg 13:11 559
spoke to the woman?" And he s, Jg 13:11 559
Manoah s, "Now when your Jg 13:12 559
the angel of the LORD s to Manoah, Jg 13:13 559
pay attention to all that I s. Jg 13:13 559
Manoah s to the angel of the LORD, Jg 13:15 559
The angel of the LORD s to Manoah, Jg 13:16 559
Manoah s to the angel of the LORD, Jg 13:17 559
the angel of the LORD s to him, Jg 13:18 559
So Manoah s to his wife, Jg 13:22 559
But his wife s to him, Jg 13:23 559
father and his mother s to him, Jg 14:3 559
But Samson s to his father, Jg 14:3 559
Then Samson s to them, Jg 14:12 559
And they s to him, Jg 14:13 559
So he s to them, Jg 14:14 559
day that they s to Samson's wife, Jg 14:15 559
wife wept before him and s, Jg 14:16 559
And he s to her, Jg 14:16 559
So the men of the city s to him on Jg 14:18 559
And he s to them, Jg 14:18 559
his wife with a young goat, and s, Jg 15:1 559
Her father s, Jg 15:2 559
Samson then s to them, Jg 15:3 559
Then the Philistines s, Jg 15:6 559
"Who did this?" And they s, Jg 15:6 559
Samson s to them, Jg 15:7 559
The men of Judah s, Jg 15:10 559
And they s, "We have come up to Jg 15:10 559
the rock of Etam and s to Samson, Jg 15:11 559
And he s to them, Jg 15:11 559
They s to him, Jg 15:12 559
And Samson s to them, Jg 15:12 559
So they s to him, Jg 15:13 559
Then Samson s, "With the jawbone Jg 15:16 559
and he called to the LORD and s, Jg 15:18 559
came up to her and s to her, Jg 16:5 559
So Delilah s to Samson, Jg 16:6 559
Samson s to her, Jg 16:7 559
And she s to him, Jg 16:9 559
Then Delilah s to Samson, Jg 16:10 559
He s to her, Jg 16:11 559
bound him with them and s to him, Jg 16:12 559
Then Delilah s to Samson, Jg 16:13 559
And he s to her, Jg 16:13 559
it with the pin and s to him, Jg 16:14 559
Then she s to him, Jg 16:15 559
was in his heart and s to her, Jg 16:17 559
She s, "The Philistines are upon you, Jg 16:20 559
And he awoke from his sleep and s, Jg 16:20 559
god, and to rejoice, for they s, Jg 16:23 559
praised their god, for they s, Jg 16:24 559
were in high spirits, that they s, Jg 16:25 559
Then Samson s to the boy who was Jg 16:26 559
Samson called to the LORD and s, Jg 16:28 559
And Samson s, "Let me die with Jg 16:30 559
He s to his mother, Jg 17:2 559
And his mother s, Jg 17:2 559
to his mother, and his mother s, Jg 17:3 559
Micah s to him, "Where do you come Jg 17:9 559
And he s to him, Jg 17:9 559
Micah then s to him, Jg 17:10 559
Then Micah s, "Now I know that Jg 17:13 559
and they s to them, Jg 18:2 559
turned aside there and s to him, Jg 18:3 559
He s to them, Jg 18:4 559
They s to him, Jg 18:5 559
The priest s to them, Jg 18:6 559
Eshtaol, their brothers s to them, Jg 18:8 559
They s, "Arise, and let us go Jg 18:9 559
s to their kinsmen, Jg 18:14 559
image, the priest s to them, Jg 18:18 559
They s to him, Jg 18:19 559
who turned around and s to Micah, Jg 18:23 559
He s, "You have taken away Jg 18:24 559
The sons of Dan s to him, Jg 18:25 559
girl's father s to his son-in-law, Jg 19:5 559
and the girl's father s to the man, Jg 19:6 559
morning, and the girl's father s, Jg 19:8 559
the girl's father, s to him, Jg 19:9 559
and the servant s to his master, Jg 19:11 559
However, his master s to him, Jg 19:12 559
He s to his servant, Jg 19:13 559
and the old man s, Jg 19:17 559
He s to him, Jg 19:18 559
The old man s, Jg 19:20 559
went out to them and s to them, Jg 19:23 559
He s to her, Jg 19:28 559
All who saw *it* s, Jg 19:30 559
And the sons of Israel s, Jg 20:3 559
who was murdered, answered and s, Jg 20:4 559
and inquired of God and s, Jg 20:18 559
Then the LORD s, Jg 20:18 559
the LORD s, "Go up against him." Jg 20:23 559
the LORD s, "Go up, for tomorrow I Jg 20:28 559
The sons of Benjamin s, Jg 20:32 559
But the sons of Israel s, Jg 20:32 559
thirty men of Israel, for they s, Jg 20:39 559
They s, "Why, O LORD, God of Jg 21:3 559
Then the sons of Israel s, Jg 21:5 559
for their brother Benjamin and s, Jg 21:6 559
And they s, "What one is there of Jg 21:8 559
the elders of the congregation s, Jg 21:16 559
They s, "*There must be* an inheritance Jg 21:17 559
So they s, "Behold, there is a feast Jg 21:19 559
Naomi s to her two daughters-in-law, Ru 1:8 559
And they s to her, Ru 1:10 559
Naomi s, "Return, my daughters. Ru 1:11 559
If I s I have hope, if I should Ru 1:12 559
she s, "Behold, your sister-in-law Ru 1:15 559
Ruth s, "Do not urge me to leave Ru 1:16 559
go with her, she s no more to her. Ru 1:18 1696
because of them, and the women s, Ru 1:19 559
She s to them, Ru 1:20 559
And Ruth the Moabitess s to Naomi, Ru 2:2 559
And she s to her, Ru 2:2 559
Bethlehem and s to the reapers, Ru 2:4 559
And they s to him, Ru 2:4 559
Then Boaz s to his servant who was Ru 2:5 559
"And she s, 'Please let me glean Ru 2:7 559
Then Boaz s to Ruth, Ru 2:8 559
bowing to the ground and s to him, Ru 2:10 559
Then she s, "I have found favor Ru 2:13 559
At mealtime Boaz s to her, Ru 2:14 559
Her mother-in-law then s to her, Ru 2:19 559
with whom she had worked and s, Ru 2:19 559
Naomi s to her daughter-in-law Ru 2:20 559

Again Naomi **s** to her,	**Ru 2:20**	559
Then Ruth the Moabitess **s**,	**Ru 2:21**	559
"Furthermore, he **s** to me,	**Ru 2:21**	559
Naomi **s** to Ruth her daughter-in-law,	**Ru 2:22**	559
Naomi her mother-in-law **s** to her,	**Ru 3:1**	559
She **s** to her,	**Ru 3:5**	559
He **s**, "Who are you?"	**Ru 3:9**	559
Then he **s**, "May you be blessed of	**Ru 3:10**	559
and he **s**, "Let it not be known that	**Ru 3:14**	559
Again he **s**, "Give me the cloak that	**Ru 3:15**	559
came to her mother-in-law, she **s**,	**Ru 3:16**	559
She **s**, "These six *measures* of barley	**Ru 3:17**	559
of barley he gave to me, for he **s**,	**Ru 3:17**	559
Then she **s**, "Wait, my daughter,	**Ru 3:18**	559
spoke was passing by, so he **s**,	**Ru 4:1**	559
of the elders of the city and **s**,	**Ru 4:2**	559
Then he **s** to the closest relative,	**Ru 4:3**	559
And he **s**, "I will redeem *it*."	**Ru 4:4**	559
Then Boaz **s**, "On the day you buy	**Ru 4:5**	559
The closest relative **s**,	**Ru 4:6**	559
So the closest relative **s** to Boaz,	**Ru 4:8**	559
Then Boaz **s** to the elders and all	**Ru 4:9**	559
in the court, and the elders, **s**,	**Ru 4:11**	559
Then the women **s** to Naomi,	**Ru 4:14**	559
Then Elkanah her husband **s** to her,	**1Sa 1:8**	559
She made a vow and **s**,	**1Sa 1:11**	559
Then Eli **s** to her,	**1Sa 1:14**	559
Then Eli answered and **s**,	**1Sa 1:17**	559
She **s**, "Let your maidservant find	**1Sa 1:18**	559
go up, for she **s** to her husband,	**1Sa 1:22**	559
Elkanah her husband **s** to her,	**1Sa 1:23**	559
She **s**, "Oh, my lord! As your soul	**1Sa 1:26**	559
Then Hannah prayed and **s**,	**1Sa 2:1**	559
If the man **s** to him,	**1Sa 2:16**	559
He **s** to them,	**1Sa 2:23**	559
of God came to Eli and **s** to him,	**1Sa 2:27**	559
the LORD called Samuel; and he **s**,	**1Sa 3:4**	559
Then he ran to Eli and **s**,	**1Sa 3:5**	559
But he **s**, "I did not call, lie down	**1Sa 3:5**	559
arose and went to Eli and **s**,	**1Sa 3:6**	559
he arose and went to Eli and **s**,	**1Sa 3:8**	559
And Eli **s** to Samuel,	**1Sa 3:9**	559
"Samuel! Samuel!" And Samuel **s**,	**1Sa 3:10**	559
The LORD **s** to Samuel,	**1Sa 3:11**	559
Then Eli called Samuel and **s**,	**1Sa 3:16**	559
my son." And he **s**, "Here I am."	**1Sa 3:16**	559
He **s**, "What is the word that	**1Sa 3:17**	559
And he **s**, "It is the LORD; let Him	**1Sa 3:18**	559
the camp, the elders of Israel **s**,	**1Sa 4:3**	559
the noise of the shout, they **s**,	**1Sa 4:6**	559
Philistines were afraid, for they **s**,	**1Sa 4:7**	559
And they **s**, "Woe to us!	**1Sa 4:7**	559
the noise of the outcry, he **s**,	**1Sa 4:14**	559
The man **s** to Eli,	**1Sa 4:16**	559
he **s**, "How did things go, my son?"	**1Sa 4:16**	559
women who stood by her **s** to her,	**1Sa 4:20**	1696
She **s**, "The glory has departed	**1Sa 4:22**	559
Ashdod saw that it was so, they **s**,	**1Sa 5:7**	559
of the Philistines to them and **s**,	**1Sa 5:8**	559
they **s**, "Let the ark of the God of	**1Sa 5:8**	559
lords of the Philistines and **s**,	**1Sa 5:11**	559
They **s**, "If you send away the ark of	**1Sa 6:3**	559
Then they **s**, "What shall be the	**1Sa 6:4**	559
And they **s**, "Five golden tumors	**1Sa 6:4**	559
The men of Beth-shemesh **s**,	**1Sa 6:20**	559
Then Samuel **s**, "Gather all Israel	**1Sa 7:5**	559
fasted on that day and **s** there,	**1Sa 7:6**	559
the sons of Israel **s** to Samuel,	**1Sa 7:8**	559
and they **s** to him,	**1Sa 8:5**	559
the sight of Samuel when they **s**,	**1Sa 8:6**	559
The LORD **s** to Samuel,	**1Sa 8:7**	559
He **s**, "This will be the procedure of	**1Sa 8:11**	559
the voice of Samuel, and they **s**,	**1Sa 8:19**	559
The LORD **s** to Samuel,	**1Sa 8:22**	559
So Samuel **s** to the men of Israel,	**1Sa 8:22**	559
So Kish **s** to his son Saul,	**1Sa 9:3**	559
Saul **s** to his servant who was with	**1Sa 9:5**	559
He **s** to him,	**1Sa 9:6**	559
Then Saul **s** to his servant,	**1Sa 9:7**	559
servant answered Saul again and **s**,	**1Sa 9:8**	559
Then Saul **s** to his servant,	**1Sa 9:10**	559
"Well **s**; come, let us go."	**1Sa 9:10**	1697
out to draw water and **s** to them,	**1Sa 9:11**	559
They answered them and **s**,	**1Sa 9:12**	559
saw Saul, the LORD **s** to him,	**1Sa 9:17**	6030a
Samuel in the gate and **s**,	**1Sa 9:18**	559
Samuel answered Saul and **s**,	**1Sa 9:19**	559
Samuel **s** to the cook,	**1Sa 9:23**	559
you, concerning which I **s** to you,	**1Sa 9:23**	559
Samuel **s**, "Here is what has been	**1Sa 9:24**	559
I s I have invited the people."	**1Sa 9:24**	559
of the city, Samuel **s** to Saul,	**1Sa 9:27**	559
it on his head, kissed him and **s**,	**1Sa 10:1**	559
that the people **s** to one another,	**1Sa 10:11**	559
A man there **s**,	**1Sa 10:12**	559
Saul's uncle **s** to him and his servant	**1Sa 10:14**	559
"Where did you go?" And he **s**,	**1Sa 10:14**	559
Saul's uncle **s**,	**1Sa 10:15**	559
tell me what Samuel **s** to you."	**1Sa 10:15**	559
So Saul **s** to his uncle,	**1Sa 10:16**	559
and he **s** to the sons of Israel,	**1Sa 10:18**	559
have **s**, 'No, but set a king over us!'	**1Sa 10:19**	559
the LORD **s**, "Behold, he is hiding	**1Sa 10:22**	559
Samuel **s** to all the people,	**1Sa 10:24**	559
So all the people shouted and **s**,	**1Sa 10:24**	559
But certain worthless men **s**,	**1Sa 10:27**	559
all the men of Jabesh **s** to Nahash,	**1Sa 11:1**	559
But Nahash the Ammonite **s** to them,	**1Sa 11:2**	559
The elders of Jabesh **s** to him,	**1Sa 11:3**	559
and he **s**, "What is *the matter* with	**1Sa 11:5**	559
They **s** to the messengers who	**1Sa 11:9**	559
Then the men of Jabesh **s**,	**1Sa 11:10**	559
Then the people **s** to Samuel,	**1Sa 11:12**	559
"Who is he that **s**,	**1Sa 11:12**	559
But Saul **s**, "Not a man shall be put	**1Sa 11:13**	559
Then Samuel **s** to the people,	**1Sa 11:14**	559
Then Samuel **s** to all Israel,	**1Sa 12:1**	559
voice in all that you **s** to me and	**1Sa 12:1**	559
They **s**, "You have not defrauded us	**1Sa 12:4**	559
He **s** to them,	**1Sa 12:5**	559
And they **s**, "*He is* witness."	**1Sa 12:5**	559
Then Samuel **s** to the people,	**1Sa 12:6**	559
They cried out to the LORD and **s**,	**1Sa 12:10**	559
came against you, you **s** to me,	**1Sa 12:12**	559
Then all the people **s** to Samuel,	**1Sa 12:19**	559
Samuel **s** to the people,	**1Sa 12:20**	559
So Saul **s**, "Bring to me the burnt	**1Sa 13:9**	559
Samuel **s**, "What have you done?"	**1Sa 13:11**	559
"What have you done?" And Saul **s**,	**1Sa 13:11**	559
I **s**, 'Now the Philistines will come	**1Sa 13:12**	559
Samuel **s** to Saul,	**1Sa 13:13**	559
of Israel, for the Philistines **s**,	**1Sa 13:19**	559
Jonathan, the son of Saul, **s** to the	**1Sa 14:1**	559
Then Jonathan **s** to the young man	**1Sa 14:6**	559
His armor bearer **s** to him,	**1Sa 14:7**	559
Then Jonathan **s**,	**1Sa 14:8**	559
Philistines, the Philistines **s**,	**1Sa 14:11**	559
and his armor bearer and **s**,	**1Sa 14:12**	559
Jonathan **s** to his armor bearer,	**1Sa 14:12**	559
Saul **s** to the people who *were*	**1Sa 14:17**	559
Then Saul **s** to Ahijah,	**1Sa 14:18**	559
so Saul **s** to the priest,	**1Sa 14:19**	559
one of the people **s**,	**1Sa 14:28**	559
Then Jonathan **s**,	**1Sa 14:29**	559
he **s**, "You have acted treacherously	**1Sa 14:33**	559
Saul **s**, "Disperse yourselves	**1Sa 14:34**	559
Then Saul **s**, "Let us go down after	**1Sa 14:36**	559
they **s**, "Do whatever seems good	**1Sa 14:36**	559
So the priest **s**,	**1Sa 14:36**	559
Saul **s**, "Draw near here,	**1Sa 14:38**	559
Then he **s** to all Israel,	**1Sa 14:40**	559
And the people **s** to Saul,	**1Sa 14:40**	559
Therefore, Saul **s** to the LORD, the	**1Sa 14:41**	559
Saul **s**, "Cast *lots* between me	**1Sa 14:42**	559
Then Saul **s** to Jonathan,	**1Sa 14:43**	559
So Jonathan told him and **s**,	**1Sa 14:43**	559
Saul **s**, "May God do this *to me*	**1Sa 14:44**	559
But the people **s** to Saul,	**1Sa 14:45**	559
Then Samuel **s** to Saul,	**1Sa 15:1**	559
Saul **s** to the Kenites,	**1Sa 15:6**	559
came to Saul, and Saul **s** to him,	**1Sa 15:13**	559
But Samuel **s**, "What then is this	**1Sa 15:14**	559
Saul **s**, "They have brought them	**1Sa 15:15**	559
Then Samuel **s** to Saul,	**1Sa 15:16**	559
the LORD **s** to me last night."	**1Sa 15:16**	1696
And he **s** to him,	**1Sa 15:16**	559
Samuel **s**, "Is it not true,	**1Sa 15:17**	559
LORD sent you on a mission, and **s**,	**1Sa 15:18**	559
Then Saul **s** to Samuel,	**1Sa 15:20**	559
Samuel **s**, "Has the LORD as	**1Sa 15:22**	559
Then Saul **s** to Samuel,	**1Sa 15:24**	559
But Samuel **s** to Saul,	**1Sa 15:26**	559
So Samuel **s** to him,	**1Sa 15:28**	559
Then he **s**, "I have sinned;	**1Sa 15:30**	559
Then Samuel **s**, "Bring me Agag,	**1Sa 15:32**	559
Agag **s**, "Surely the bitterness of	**1Sa 15:32**	559
But Samuel **s**, "As your sword has	**1Sa 15:33**	559
Now the LORD **s** to Samuel,	**1Sa 16:1**	559
But Samuel **s**, "How can I go?	**1Sa 16:2**	559
the LORD **s**, "Take a heifer with you	**1Sa 16:2**	559
So Samuel did what the LORD **s**,	**1Sa 16:4**	1696
came trembling to meet him and **s**,	**1Sa 16:4**	559
He **s**, "In peace; I have come	**1Sa 16:5**	559
But the LORD **s** to Samuel,	**1Sa 16:7**	559
he **s**, "The LORD has not chosen	**1Sa 16:8**	559
made Shammah pass by. And he **s**,	**1Sa 16:9**	559
But Samuel **s** to Jesse,	**1Sa 16:10**	559
And Samuel **s** to Jesse,	**1Sa 16:11**	559
these all the children?" And he **s**,	**1Sa 16:11**	559
Then Samuel **s** to Jesse,	**1Sa 16:11**	559
And the LORD **s**, "Arise, anoint him	**1Sa 16:12**	559
Saul's servants then **s** to him,	**1Sa 16:15**	559
So Saul **s** to his servants,	**1Sa 16:17**	559
of the young men **s**,	**1Sa 16:18**	559
sent messengers to Jesse and **s**,	**1Sa 16:19**	559
ranks of Israel and **s** to them,	**1Sa 17:8**	559
Again the Philistine **s**,	**1Sa 17:10**	559
Then Jesse **s** to David his son,	**1Sa 17:17**	559
The men of Israel **s**,	**1Sa 17:25**	559
burned against David and he **s**,	**1Sa 17:28**	559
But David **s**, "What have I done	**1Sa 17:29**	559
to another and **s** the same thing;	**1Sa 17:30**	559
David **s** to Saul,	**1Sa 17:32**	559
Then Saul **s** to David,	**1Sa 17:33**	559
But David **s** to Saul,	**1Sa 17:34**	559
David **s**, "The LORD who delivered	**1Sa 17:37**	559
And Saul **s** to David,	**1Sa 17:37**	559
So David **s** to Saul,	**1Sa 17:39**	559
The Philistine **s** to David,	**1Sa 17:43**	559
The Philistine also **s** to David,	**1Sa 17:44**	559
Then David **s** to the Philistine,	**1Sa 17:45**	559
he **s** to Abner the commander of the	**1Sa 17:55**	559
And Abner **s**, "By your life, O king,	**1Sa 17:55**	559
The king **s**, "You inquire whose son	**1Sa 17:56**	559
Saul **s** to him,	**1Sa 17:58**	559
women sang as they played, and **s**,	**1Sa 18:7**	559
this saying displeased him; and he **s**,	**1Sa 18:8**	559
Then Saul **s** to David,	**1Sa 18:17**	559
But David **s** to Saul,	**1Sa 18:18**	559
Therefore Saul **s** to David,	**1Sa 18:21**	559
David **s**, "Is it trivial in your sight	**1Sa 18:23**	559
Saul then **s**, "Thus you shall say to	**1Sa 18:25**	559
to Saul his father and **s** to him,	**1Sa 19:4**	559
messengers to take David, she **s**,	**1Sa 19:14**	559
So Saul **s** to Michal,	**1Sa 19:17**	559
And Michal **s** to Saul,	**1Sa 19:17**	559
"He **s** to me, 'Let me go!	**1Sa 19:17**	559
and he asked and **s**,	**1Sa 19:22**	559
And *someone* **s**, "Behold, they are	**1Sa 19:22**	559
Ramah, and came and **s** to Jonathan,	**1Sa 20:1**	559
He **s** to him,	**1Sa 20:2**	559
favor in your sight, and he has **s**,	**1Sa 20:3**	559
Then Jonathan **s** to David,	**1Sa 20:4**	559
So David **s** to Jonathan,	**1Sa 20:5**	559
Jonathan **s**, "Far be it from you	**1Sa 20:9**	559
Then David **s** to Jonathan,	**1Sa 20:10**	559
Jonathan **s** to David,	**1Sa 20:11**	559
Then Jonathan **s** to David,	**1Sa 20:12**	559
Then Jonathan **s** to him,	**1Sa 20:18**	559
so Saul **s** to Jonathan his son,	**1Sa 20:27**	559
for he **s**, 'Please let me go, since	**1Sa 20:29**	559
against Jonathan and he **s** to him,	**1Sa 20:30**	559
Saul his father and **s** to him,	**1Sa 20:32**	559
He **s** to his lad,	**1Sa 20:36**	559
Jonathan called after the lad and **s**,	**1Sa 20:37**	559
weapons to his lad and **s** to him,	**1Sa 20:40**	559
Jonathan **s** to David,	**1Sa 20:42**	559
to meet David and **s** to him,	**1Sa 21:1**	559
David **s** to Ahimelech the priest,	**1Sa 21:2**	559
me with a matter and has **s** to me,	**1Sa 21:2**	559
The priest answered David and **s**,	**1Sa 21:4**	559
answered the priest and **s** to him,	**1Sa 21:5**	559
David **s** to Ahimelech,	**1Sa 21:8**	559
Then the priest **s**,	**1Sa 21:9**	559
And David **s**, "There is none like it;	**1Sa 21:9**	559
the servants of Achish **s** to him,	**1Sa 21:11**	559
Then Achish **s** to his servants,	**1Sa 21:14**	559
and he **s** to the king of Moab,	**1Sa 22:3**	559
The prophet Gad **s** to David,	**1Sa 22:5**	559
Saul **s** to his servants who	**1Sa 22:7**	559
servants of Saul, **s**,	**1Sa 22:9**	559
Saul **s**, "Listen now, son of Ahitub."	**1Sa 22:12**	559
Saul then **s** to him,	**1Sa 22:13**	559
Ahimelech answered the king and **s**,	**1Sa 22:14**	559
But the king **s**, "You shall surely die,	**1Sa 22:16**	559
And the king **s** to the guards who	**1Sa 22:17**	559
Then the king **s** to Doeg,	**1Sa 22:18**	559
Then David **s** to Abiathar,	**1Sa 22:22**	559
And the LORD **s** to David,	**1Sa 23:2**	559
But David's men **s** to him,	**1Sa 23:3**	559
And the LORD answered him and **s**,	**1Sa 23:4**	559
David had come to Keilah, Saul **s**,	**1Sa 23:7**	559
so he **s** to Abiathar the priest,	**1Sa 23:9**	559
David **s**, "O LORD God of Israel,	**1Sa 23:10**	559
the LORD **s**, "He will come down."	**1Sa 23:11**	559
Then David **s**, "Will the men of	**1Sa 23:12**	559
LORD **s**, "They will surrender you."	**1Sa 23:12**	559
Thus he **s** to him,	**1Sa 23:17**	559
Saul **s**, "May you be blessed	**1Sa 23:21**	559
The men of David **s** to him,	**1Sa 24:4**	559
day of which the LORD **s** to you,	**1Sa 24:4**	559
So he **s** to his men,	**1Sa 24:6**	559
David **s** to Saul,	**1Sa 24:9**	559
the cave, and some **s** to kill you,	**1Sa 24:10**	559
but *my eye* had pity on you; and I **s**,	**1Sa 24:10**	559
these words to Saul, Saul **s**,	**1Sa 24:16**	559
He **s** to David,	**1Sa 24:17**	559
men; and David **s** to the young men,	**1Sa 25:5**	559
answered David's servants and **s**,	**1Sa 25:10**	559
David **s** to his men,	**1Sa 25:13**	559
She **s** to her young men,	**1Sa 25:19**	559
Now David had **s**,	**1Sa 25:21**	559
She fell at his feet and **s**,	**1Sa 25:24**	559
Then David **s** to Abigail,	**1Sa 25:32**	559
had brought him and **s** to her,	**1Sa 25:35**	559
heard that Nabal was dead, he **s**,	**1Sa 25:39**	559
with her face to the ground and **s**,	**1Sa 25:41**	559
Then David **s** to	**1Sa 26:6**	559
Abishai **s**, "I will go down with you.	**1Sa 26:6**	559
Then Abishai **s** to David,	**1Sa 26:8**	559
But David **s** to Abishai,	**1Sa 26:9**	559
David also **s**, "As the LORD lives,	**1Sa 26:10**	559
So David **s** to Abner,	**1Sa 26:15**	559
Saul recognized David's voice and **s**,	**1Sa 26:17**	559
David **s**, "It is my voice, my lord	**1Sa 26:17**	559
s, "Why then is my lord pursuing	**1Sa 26:18**	559
Saul **s**, "I have sinned. Return, my	**1Sa 26:21**	559
Then Saul **s** to David,	**1Sa 26:25**	559
Then David **s** to himself,	**1Sa 27:1**	559
Then David **s** to Achish,	**1Sa 27:5**	559
Achish **s**, "Where have you made a	**1Sa 27:10**	559
made a raid today?" And David **s**,	**1Sa 27:10**	559
And Achish **s** to David,	**1Sa 28:1**	559
David **s** to Achish,	**1Sa 28:2**	559
So Achish **s** to David,	**1Sa 28:2**	559
Then Saul **s** to his servants,	**1Sa 28:7**	559
And his servants **s** to him,	**1Sa 28:7**	559
he **s**, "Conjure up for me, please,	**1Sa 28:8**	559
But the woman **s** to him,	**1Sa 28:9**	559
Then the woman **s**,	**1Sa 28:11**	559
And he **s**, "Bring up Samuel for me.	**1Sa 28:11**	559
The king **s** to her,	**1Sa 28:13**	559
And the woman **s** to Saul,	**1Sa 28:13**	559
He **s** to her,	**1Sa 28:14**	559
"What is his form?" And she **s**,	**1Sa 28:14**	559
Then Samuel **s** to Saul,	**1Sa 28:15**	559
Samuel **s**, "Why then do you ask me	**1Sa 28:16**	559

he was terrified, and **s** to him, **1Sa 28:21** 559
But he refused and **s**, **1Sa 28:23** 559
commanders of the Philistines **s**, **1Sa 29:3** 559
And Achish **s** to the commanders of **1Sa 29:3** 559
the commanders of the Philistines **s**, **1Sa 29:4** 559
Achish called David and **s** to him, **1Sa 29:6** 559
David **s** to Achish, **1Sa 29:8** 559
commanders of the Philistines have **s**, **1Sa 29:9** 559
David **s** to Abiathar the priest, **1Sa 30:7** 559
And He **s** to him, **1Sa 30:8** 559
David **s** to him, **1Sa 30:13** 559
And he **s**, "I am a young man of **1Sa 30:13** 559
Then David **s** to him, **1Sa 30:15** 559
he **s**, "Swear to me by God that **1Sa 30:15** 559
the *other* livestock, and they **s**, **1Sa 30:20** 559
went with David **s**, **1Sa 30:22** 559
Then David **s**, "You must not do **1Sa 30:23** 559
Then Saul **s** to his armor bearer, **1Sa 31:4** 559
Then David **s** to him, **2Sa 1:3** 559
And he **s** to him, **2Sa 1:3** 559
David **s** to him, **2Sa 1:4** 559
And he **s**, "The people have fled **2Sa 1:4** 559
David **s** to the young man who told **2Sa 1:5** 559
The young man who told him **s**, **2Sa 1:6** 559
called to me. And I **s**, 'Here I am.' **2Sa 1:7** 559
"He **s** to me, **2Sa 1:8** 559
"Then he **s** to me, **2Sa 1:9** 559
David **s** to the young man who told **2Sa 1:13** 559
Then David **s** to him, **2Sa 1:14** 559
called one of the young men and **s**, **2Sa 1:15** 559
David **s** to him, **2Sa 1:16** 559
And the LORD **s** to him, **2Sa 2:1** 559
So David **s**, "Where shall I go up?" **2Sa 2:1** 559
"Where shall I go up?" And He **s**, **2Sa 2:1** 559
of Jabesh-gilead, and **s** to them, **2Sa 2:5** 559
Then Abner **s** to Joab, **2Sa 2:14** 559
And Joab **s**, "Let them arise." **2Sa 2:14** 559
Abner looked behind him and **s**, **2Sa 2:20** 559
So Abner **s** to him, **2Sa 2:21** 559
Then Abner called to Joab and **s**, **2Sa 2:26** 559
Joab **s**, "As God lives, if you **2Sa 2:27** 559
and Ish-bosheth **s** to Abner, **2Sa 3:7** 559
the words of Ish-bosheth and **s**, **2Sa 3:8** 559
He **s**, "Good! I will make a covenant **2Sa 3:13** 559
Then Abner **s** to him, **2Sa 3:16** 559
Abner **s** to David, **2Sa 3:21** 559
Then Joab came to the king and **s**, **2Sa 3:24** 559
when David heard it, he **s**, **2Sa 3:28** 559
Then David **s** to Joab and to all **2Sa 3:31** 559
chanted a *lament* for Abner and **s**, **2Sa 3:33** 559
Then the king **s** to his servants, **2Sa 3:38** 559
at Hebron and **s** to the king, **2Sa 4:8** 559
the Beerothite, and **s** to them, **2Sa 4:9** 559
came to David at Hebron and **s**, **2Sa 5:1** 559
And the LORD **s** to you, **2Sa 5:2** 559
of the land, and they **s** to David, **2Sa 5:6** 559
David **s** on that day, **2Sa 5:8** 559
And the LORD **s** to David, **2Sa 5:19** 559
defeated them there; and he **s**, **2Sa 5:20** 559
David inquired of the LORD, He **s**, **2Sa 5:23** 559
he **s**, "How can the ark of the LORD **2Sa 6:9** 559
Saul came out to meet David and **s**, **2Sa 6:20** 559
So David **s** to Michal, **2Sa 6:21** 559
the king **s** to Nathan the prophet, **2Sa 7:2** 559
Nathan **s** to the king, **2Sa 7:3** 559
and sat before the LORD, and he **s**, **2Sa 7:18** 559
David **s**, "Is there yet anyone left **2Sa 9:1** 559
and the king **s** to him, **2Sa 9:2** 559
And he **s**, "*I am* your servant." **2Sa 9:2** 559
The king **s**, "Is there not yet anyone **2Sa 9:3** 559
And Ziba **s** to the king, **2Sa 9:3** 559
So the king **s** to him, **2Sa 9:4** 559
And Ziba **s** to the king, **2Sa 9:4** 559
And David **s**, "Mephibosheth." **2Sa 9:6** 559
And he **s**, "Here is your servant!" **2Sa 9:6** 559
David **s** to him, **2Sa 9:7** 559
Again he prostrated himself and **s**, **2Sa 9:8** 559
Saul's servant Ziba and **s** to him, **2Sa 9:9** 559
Then Ziba **s** to the king, **2Sa 9:11** 559
Then David **s**, "I will show kindness **2Sa 10:2** 559
Ammonites **s** to Hanun their lord, **2Sa 10:3** 559
And the king **s**, "Stay at Jericho **2Sa 10:5** 559
s, "If the Arameans are too strong **2Sa 10:11** 559
And one **s**, "Is this not Bathsheba, **2Sa 11:3** 559
she sent and told David, and **s**, **2Sa 11:5** 559
Then David **s** to Uriah, **2Sa 11:8** 559
to his house," David **s** to Uriah, **2Sa 11:10** 559
Uriah **s** to David, **2Sa 11:11** 559
Then David **s** to Uriah, **2Sa 11:12** 559
The messenger **s** to David, **2Sa 11:23** 559
Then David **s** to the messenger, **2Sa 11:25** 559
And he came to him and **s**, **2Sa 12:1** 559
the man, and he **s** to Nathan, **2Sa 12:5** 559
Nathan then **s** to David, **2Sa 12:7** 559
Then David **s** to Nathan, **2Sa 12:13** 559
And Nathan **s** to David, **2Sa 12:13** 559
the child was dead, for they **s**, **2Sa 12:18** 559
so David **s** to his servants, **2Sa 12:19** 559
And they **s**, "He is dead." **2Sa 12:19** 559
Then his servants **s** to him, **2Sa 12:21** 559
He **s**, "While the child was *still* alive, **2Sa 12:22** 559
I **s**, 'Who knows, the LORD may be **2Sa 12:22** 559
Joab sent messengers to David and **s**, **2Sa 12:27** 559
He **s** to him, **2Sa 13:4** 559
Then Amnon **s** to him, **2Sa 13:4** 559
Jonadab then **s** to him, **2Sa 13:5** 559
to see him, Amnon **s** to the king, **2Sa 13:6** 559
he refused to eat. And Amnon **s**, **2Sa 13:9** 559
Then Amnon **s** to Tamar, **2Sa 13:10** 559

he took hold of her and **s** to her, **2Sa 13:11** 559
And Amnon **s** to her, **2Sa 13:15** 559
But she **s** to him, **2Sa 13:16** 559
young man who attended him and **s**, **2Sa 13:17** 559
Then Absalom her brother **s** to her, **2Sa 13:20** 559
Absalom came to the king and **s**, **2Sa 13:24** 559
But the king **s** to Absalom, **2Sa 13:25** 559
Then Absalom **s**, "If not, please let **2Sa 13:26** 559
And the king **s** to him, **2Sa 13:26** 559
Jonadab **s** to the king, **2Sa 13:35** 559
woman from there and **s** to her, **2Sa 14:2** 559
and prostrated herself and **s**, **2Sa 14:4** 559
The king **s** to her, **2Sa 14:5** 559
Then the king **s** to the woman, **2Sa 14:8** 559
The woman of Tekoa **s** to the king, **2Sa 14:9** 559
So the king **s**, "Whoever speaks to **2Sa 14:10** 559
she **s**, "Please let the king remember **2Sa 14:11** 559
they will destroy my son." And he **s**, **2Sa 14:11** 559
Then the woman **s**, **2Sa 14:12** 559
And he **s**, "Speak." **2Sa 14:12** 559
The woman **s**, **2Sa 14:13** 559
so your maidservant **s**, **2Sa 14:15** 559
"Then your maidservant **s**, **2Sa 14:17** 559
king answered and **s** to the woman, **2Sa 14:18** 559
And the woman **s**, **2Sa 14:18** 559
So the king **s**, "Is the hand of Joab **2Sa 14:19** 559
Then the king **s** to Joab, **2Sa 14:21** 559
Joab **s**, "Today your servant knows **2Sa 14:22** 559
However the king **s**, **2Sa 14:24** 559
Therefore he **s** to his servants, **2Sa 14:30** 559
Absalom at his house and **s** to him, **2Sa 14:31** 559
years that Absalom **s** to the king, **2Sa 15:7** 559
The king **s** to him, **2Sa 15:9** 559
David **s** to all his servants **2Sa 15:14** 559
the king's servants **s** to the king, **2Sa 15:15** 559
the king **s** to Ittai the Gittite, **2Sa 15:19** 559
But Ittai answered the king and **s**, **2Sa 15:21** 559
Therefore David **s** to Ittai, **2Sa 15:22** 559
The king **s** to Zadok, **2Sa 15:25** 559
king **s** also to Zadok the priest, **2Sa 15:27** 559
And David **s**, "O LORD, I pray, **2Sa 15:31** 559
David **s** to him, **2Sa 15:33** 559
The king **s** to Ziba, **2Sa 16:2** 559
Ziba **s**, "The donkeys are for the **2Sa 16:2** 559
Then the king **s**, **2Sa 16:3** 559
And Ziba **s** to the king, **2Sa 16:3** 559
is staying in Jerusalem, for he **s**, **2Sa 16:3** 559
So the king **s** to Ziba, **2Sa 16:4** 559
And Ziba **s**, "I prostrate myself; **2Sa 16:4** 559
Thus Shimei **s** when he cursed, **2Sa 16:7** 559
the son of Zeruiah **s** to the king, **2Sa 16:9** 559
But the king **s**, "What have I to do **2Sa 16:10** 559
Then David **s** to Abishai and to all **2Sa 16:11** 559
Absalom, that Hushai **s** to Absalom, **2Sa 16:16** 559
Absalom **s** to Hushai, **2Sa 16:17** 559
Then Hushai **s** to Absalom, **2Sa 16:18** 559
Then Absalom **s** to Ahithophel, **2Sa 16:20** 559
Ahithophel **s** to Absalom, **2Sa 16:21** 559
Ahithophel **s** to Absalom, **2Sa 17:1** 559
Then Absalom **s**, "Now call Hushai **2Sa 17:5** 559
come to Absalom, Absalom **s** to him, **2Sa 17:6** 559
So Hushai **s** to Absalom, **2Sa 17:7** 559
Moreover, Hushai **s**, **2Sa 17:8** 559
Absalom and all the men of Israel **s**, **2Sa 17:14** 559
Then Hushai **s** to Zadok and to **2Sa 17:15** 559
to the woman at the house and **s**, **2Sa 17:20** 559
And the woman **s** to them, **2Sa 17:20** 559
and they **s** to David, **2Sa 17:21** 559
for they **s**, "The people are hungry **2Sa 17:29** 559
And the king **s** to the people, **2Sa 18:2** 559
But the people **s**, **2Sa 18:3** 559
Then the king **s** to them, **2Sa 18:4** 559
man saw *it*, he told Joab and **s**, **2Sa 18:10** 559
Joab **s** to the man who had told him **2Sa 18:11** 559
The man **s** to Joab, **2Sa 18:12** 559
Then Joab **s**, "I will not waste time **2Sa 18:14** 559
is in the King's Valley, for he **s**, **2Sa 18:18** 559
Then Ahimaaz the son of Zadok **s**, **2Sa 18:19** 559
But Joab **s** to him, **2Sa 18:20** 559
Then Joab **s** to the Cushite, **2Sa 18:21** 559
son of Zadok **s** once more to Joab, **2Sa 18:22** 559
And Joab **s**, "Why would you run, **2Sa 18:22** 559
"But whatever happens," *he* **s**, **2Sa 18:23** 559
"I will run." So he **s** to him, "Run." **2Sa 18:23** 559
And the king **s**, "If he is by himself **2Sa 18:25** 559
called to the gatekeeper and **s**, **2Sa 18:26** 559
And the king **s**, "This one also is **2Sa 18:26** 559
The watchman **s**, "I think **2Sa 18:27** 559
And the king **s**, **2Sa 18:27** 559
Ahimaaz called and **s** to the king, **2Sa 18:28** 559
And he **s**, "Blessed is the LORD **2Sa 18:28** 559
The king **s**, "Is it well with the **2Sa 18:29** 559
Then the king **s**, **2Sa 18:30** 559
arrived, and the Cushite **s**, **2Sa 18:31** 559
Then the king **s** to the Cushite, **2Sa 18:32** 559
And thus he **s** as he walked, **2Sa 18:33** 559
the people heard *it* **s** that day, **2Sa 19:2** 559
into the house to the king and **s**, **2Sa 19:5** 559
So he **s** to the king, **2Sa 19:19** 559
the son of Zeruiah **s**, **2Sa 19:21** 559
David then **s**, "What have I to do **2Sa 19:22** 559
The king **s** to Shimei, **2Sa 19:23** 559
the king, that the king **s** to him, **2Sa 19:25** 559
for your servant **s**, **2Sa 19:26** 559
So the king **s** to him, **2Sa 19:29** 559
Mephibosheth **s** to the king, **2Sa 19:30** 559
The king **s** to Barzillai, **2Sa 19:33** 559
But Barzillai **s** to the king, **2Sa 19:34** 559
to the king and **s** to the king, **2Sa 19:41** 559

answered the men of Judah and **s**, **2Sa 19:43** 559
and he blew the trumpet and **s**, **2Sa 20:1** 559
Then the king **s** to Amasa, **2Sa 20:4** 559
And David **s** to Abishai, **2Sa 20:6** 559
Joab **s** to Amasa, **2Sa 20:9** 559
him one of Joab's young men, and **s**, **2Sa 20:11** 559
approached her, and the woman **s**, **2Sa 20:17** 559
Then she **s** to him, **2Sa 20:17** 559
And the woman **s** to Joab, **2Sa 20:21** 559
And the LORD **s**, "It is for Saul and **2Sa 21:1** 559
Thus David **s** to the Gibeonites, **2Sa 21:3** 559
Then the Gibeonites **s** to him, **2Sa 21:4** 559
he **s**, "I will do for you whatever **2Sa 21:4** 559
So they **s** to the king, **2Sa 21:5** 559
And the king **s**, "I will give *them*." **2Sa 21:6** 559
He **s**, "The LORD is my rock **2Sa 22:2** 559
"The God of Israel **s**, **2Sa 23:3** 559
David had a craving and **s**, **2Sa 23:15** 559
he **s**, "Be it far from me, O LORD, **2Sa 23:17** 559
The king **s** to Joab the **2Sa 24:2** 559
But Joab **s** to the king, **2Sa 24:3** 559
So David **s** to the LORD, **2Sa 24:10** 559
David and told him, and **s** to him, **2Sa 24:13** 559
Then David **s** to Gad, **2Sa 24:14** 559
and **s** to the angel who destroyed **2Sa 24:16** 559
striking down the people, and **s**, **2Sa 24:17** 559
Gad came to David that day and **s** **2Sa 24:18** 559
Then Araunah **s**, "Why has my lord **2Sa 24:21** 559
David **s**, "To buy the threshing floor **2Sa 24:21** 559
Araunah **s** to David, **2Sa 24:22** 559
And Araunah **s** to the king, **2Sa 24:23** 559
However, the king **s** to Araunah, **2Sa 24:24** 559
So his servants **s** to him, **1Ki 1:2** 559
And the king **s**, "What do you wish **1Ki 1:16** 559
She **s** to him, **1Ki 1:17** 559
Then Nathan **s**, "My lord the king, **1Ki 1:24** 559
"My lord the king, have you **s**, **1Ki 1:24** 559
Then King David **s**, **1Ki 1:28** 559
The king vowed and **s**, **1Ki 1:29** 559
herself before the king and **s**, **1Ki 1:31** 559
Then King David **s**, **1Ki 1:32** 559
The king **s** to them, **1Ki 1:33** 559
Jehoiada answered the king and **s**, **1Ki 1:36** 559
the trumpet, and all the people **s**, **1Ki 1:39** 559
the sound of the trumpet, he **s**, **1Ki 1:41** 559
Then Adonijah **s**, **1Ki 1:42** 559
"The king has also **s** thus, **1Ki 1:48** 559
Solomon **s**, "If he is a worthy **1Ki 1:52** 559
Solomon, and Solomon **s** to him, **1Ki 1:53** 559
she **s**, "Do you come peacefully?" **1Ki 2:13** 559
Do you come peacefully?" And he **s**, **1Ki 2:13** 559
Then he **s**, "I have something *to say* **1Ki 2:14** 559
something *to say* to you." And she **s**, **1Ki 2:14** 559
he **s**, "You know that the kingdom **1Ki 2:15** 559
And she **s** to him, **1Ki 2:16** 559
Then he **s**, "Please speak to Solomon **1Ki 2:17** 559
Bathsheba **s**, **1Ki 2:18** 559
Then she **s**, "I am making one small **1Ki 2:20** 559
And the king **s** to her, **1Ki 2:20** 559
So she **s**, "Let Abishag the **1Ki 2:21** 559
King Solomon answered and **s** **1Ki 2:22** 559
to Abiathar the priest the king **s**, **1Ki 2:26** 559
tent of the LORD and **s** to him, **1Ki 2:30** 559
"Thus the king has **s**, **1Ki 2:30** 559
But he **s**, "No, for I will die here." **1Ki 2:30** 559
The king **s** to him, **1Ki 2:31** 559
called for Shimei and **s** to him, **1Ki 2:36** 559
Shimei then **s** to the king, **1Ki 2:38** 559
As my lord the king has **s**, **1Ki 2:38** 1696
called for Shimei and **s** to him, **1Ki 2:42** 559
And you **s** to me, **1Ki 2:42** 559
The king also **s** to Shimei, **1Ki 2:44** 559
and God **s**, "Ask what *you wish* me **1Ki 3:5** 559
Then Solomon **s**, "You have shown **1Ki 3:6** 559
God **s** to him, **1Ki 3:11** 559
The one woman **s**, **1Ki 3:17** 559
Then the other woman **s**, **1Ki 3:22** 559
But the first woman **s**, **1Ki 3:22** 559
Then the king **s**, **1Ki 3:23** 559
The king **s**, "Get me a sword." **1Ki 3:24** 559
The king **s**, "Divide the living **1Ki 3:25** 559
deeply stirred over her son and **s**, **1Ki 3:26** 559
But the other **s**, **1Ki 3:26** 559
Then the king **s**, **1Ki 3:27** 559
he rejoiced greatly and **s**, **1Ki 5:7** 559
Then Solomon **s**, "The LORD has **1Ki 8:12** 559
"The LORD has **s** that He would **1Ki 8:12** 559
He **s**, "Blessed be the LORD, **1Ki 8:15** 559
"But the LORD **s** to my father **1Ki 8:18** 559
He **s**, "O LORD, the God of Israel, **1Ki 8:23** 559
the place of which You have **s**, **1Ki 8:29** 559
The LORD **s** to him, **1Ki 9:3** 559
He **s**, "What are these cities **1Ki 9:13** 559
Then she **s** to the king, **1Ki 10:6** 559
LORD had **s** to the sons of Israel, **1Ki 11:2** 559
So the LORD **s** to Solomon, **1Ki 11:11** 559
army was dead, Hadad **s** to Pharaoh, **1Ki 11:21** 559
Then Pharaoh **s** to him, **1Ki 11:22** 559
He **s** to Jeroboam, **1Ki 11:31** 559
Then he **s** to them, **1Ki 12:5** 559
So he **s** to them, **1Ki 12:9** 559
Jeroboam **s** in his heart, **1Ki 12:26** 559
golden calves, and he **s** to them, **1Ki 12:28** 559
by the word of the LORD, and **s**, **1Ki 13:2** 559
The king **s** to the man **1Ki 13:6** 559
Then the king **s** to the man of God, **1Ki 13:7** 1696
But the man of God **s** to the king, **1Ki 13:8** 559
Their father **s** to them, **1Ki 13:12** 1696
Then he **s** to his sons, **1Ki 13:13** 559

and he **s** to him,	**1Ki 13:14**	559
came from Judah?" And he **s**, "I am	**1Ki 13:14**	559
Then he **s** to him,	**1Ki 13:15**	559
He **s**, "I cannot return with you	**1Ki 13:16**	559
He **s** to him,	**1Ki 13:18**	559
in the place of which He **s** to you,	**1Ki 13:22**	1696
back from the way heard *it,* he **s**,	**1Ki 13:26**	559
Jeroboam **s** to his wife,	**1Ki 14:2**	559
Now the LORD had **s** to Ahijah,	**1Ki 14:5**	559
coming in the doorway, he **s**,	**1Ki 14:6**	559
people who were camped heard it **s**,	**1Ki 16:16**	559
the settlers of Gilead, **s** to Ahab,	**1Ki 17:1**	559
and he called to her and **s**,	**1Ki 17:10**	559
to get *it,* he called to her and **s**,	**1Ki 17:11**	559
she **s**, "As the LORD your God lives,	**1Ki 17:12**	559
Then Elijah **s** to her,	**1Ki 17:13**	559
go, do as you have **s**,	**1Ki 17:13**	1697
So she **s** to Elijah,	**1Ki 17:18**	559
He **s** to her,	**1Ki 17:19**	559
He called to the LORD and **s**,	**1Ki 17:20**	559
and called to the LORD and **s**,	**1Ki 17:21**	559
Elijah **s**, "See, your son is alive."	**1Ki 17:23**	559
Then the woman **s** to Elijah,	**1Ki 17:24**	559
Then Ahab **s** to Obadiah,	**1Ki 18:5**	559
him and fell on his face and **s**,	**1Ki 18:7**	559
He **s** to him,	**1Ki 18:8**	559
He **s**, "What sin have I committed,	**1Ki 18:9**	559
and when they **s**,	**1Ki 18:10**	559
Elijah **s**, "As the LORD of hosts	**1Ki 18:15**	559
saw Elijah, Ahab **s** to him,	**1Ki 18:17**	559
He **s**, "I have not troubled Israel,	**1Ki 18:18**	559
came near to all the people and **s**,	**1Ki 18:21**	559
Then Elijah **s** to the people,	**1Ki 18:22**	559
And all the people **s**,	**1Ki 18:24**	559
Elijah **s** to the prophets of Baal,	**1Ki 18:25**	559
that Elijah mocked them and **s**,	**1Ki 18:27**	559
Then Elijah **s** to all the people,	**1Ki 18:30**	559
And he **s**, "Fill four pitchers with	**1Ki 18:34**	559
And he **s**, "Do it a second time,"	**1Ki 18:34**	559
And he **s**, "Do it a third time,"	**1Ki 18:34**	559
the prophet came near and **s**,	**1Ki 18:36**	559
and they **s**, "The LORD, He is God;	**1Ki 18:39**	559
Then Elijah **s** to them,	**1Ki 18:40**	559
Now Elijah **s** to Ahab,	**1Ki 18:41**	559
He **s** to his servant,	**1Ki 18:43**	559
So he went up and looked and **s**,	**1Ki 18:43**	559
And he **s**, "Go back" seven times.	**1Ki 18:43**	559
at the seventh *time,* that he **s**,	**1Ki 18:44**	559
And he **s**, "Go up, say to Ahab,	**1Ki 18:44**	559
himself that he might die, and **s**,	**1Ki 19:4**	559
touching him, and he **s** to him,	**1Ki 19:5**	559
second time and touched him and **s**,	**1Ki 19:7**	559
LORD *came* to him, and He **s** to him,	**1Ki 19:9**	559
He **s**, "I have been very zealous	**1Ki 19:10**	559
So He **s**, "Go forth and stand on	**1Ki 19:11**	559
behold, a voice *came* to him and **s**,	**1Ki 19:13**	559
he **s**, "I have been very zealous for	**1Ki 19:14**	559
The LORD **s** to him,	**1Ki 19:15**	559
oxen and ran after Elijah and **s**,	**1Ki 19:20**	559
And he **s** to him,	**1Ki 19:20**	559
Ahab king of Israel and **s** to him,	**1Ki 20:2**	559
the messengers returned and **s**,	**1Ki 20:5**	559
all the elders of the land and **s**,	**1Ki 20:7**	559
and all the people **s** to him,	**1Ki 20:8**	559
So he **s** to the messengers of	**1Ki 20:9**	559
Ben-hadad sent to him and **s**,	**1Ki 20:10**	559
he **s** to his servants,	**1Ki 20:12**	559
Ahab king of Israel and **s**,	**1Ki 20:13**	559
Ahab **s**, "By whom?"	**1Ki 20:14**	559
So he **s**, "Thus says the LORD,	**1Ki 20:14**	559
he **s**, "Who shall begin the battle?"	**1Ki 20:14**	559
Then he **s**, "If they have come out	**1Ki 20:18**	559
the king of Israel and **s** to him,	**1Ki 20:22**	559
the servants of the king of Aram **s**	**1Ki 20:23**	559
spoke to the king of Israel and **s**,	**1Ki 20:28**	559
'Because the Arameans have **s**,	**1Ki 20:28**	559
His servants **s** to him,	**1Ki 20:31**	559
came to the king of Israel and **s**,	**1Ki 20:32**	559
And he **s**, "Is he still alive?	**1Ki 20:32**	559
and quickly catching his word **s**,	**1Ki 20:33**	559
Then he **s**, "Go, bring him."	**1Ki 20:33**	559
Ben-hadad **s** to him,	**1Ki 20:34**	559
Ahab **s**, "And I will let you go	**1Ki 20:34**	
s to another by the word of the LORD,	**1Ki 20:35**	559
Then he **s** to him,	**1Ki 20:36**	559
Then he found another man and **s**,	**1Ki 20:37**	559
by, he cried to the king and **s**,	**1Ki 20:39**	559
and brought a man to me and **s**,	**1Ki 20:39**	559
And the king of Israel **s** to him,	**1Ki 20:40**	559
He **s** to him,	**1Ki 20:42**	559
But Naboth **s** to Ahab,	**1Ki 21:3**	559
for he **s**, "I will not give you the	**1Ki 21:4**	559
his wife came to him and **s** to him,	**1Ki 21:5**	1696
So he **s** to her, "Because I spoke	**1Ki 21:6**	1696
the Jezreelite and **s** to him,	**1Ki 21:6**	559
But he **s**, 'I will not give you my	**1Ki 21:6**	559
Jezebel his wife **s** to him,	**1Ki 21:7**	559
was dead, Jezebel **s** to Ahab,	**1Ki 21:15**	559
Ahab **s** to Elijah,	**1Ki 21:20**	559
king of Israel **s** to his servants,	**1Ki 22:3**	559
And he **s** to Jehoshaphat,	**1Ki 22:4**	559
Jehoshaphat **s** to the king of Israel,	**1Ki 22:4**	559
Jehoshaphat **s** to the king of Israel,	**1Ki 22:5**	559
four hundred men, and **s** to them,	**1Ki 22:6**	559
they **s**, "Go up, for the Lord will give	**1Ki 22:6**	559
But Jehoshaphat **s**,	**1Ki 22:7**	559
king of Israel **s** to Jehoshaphat,	**1Ki 22:8**	559
But Jehoshaphat **s**,	**1Ki 22:8**	559
king of Israel called an officer and **s**,	**1Ki 22:9**	559
horns of iron for himself and **s**,	**1Ki 22:11**	559
But Micaiah **s**, "As the LORD lives,	**1Ki 22:14**	559
to the king, the king **s** to him,	**1Ki 22:15**	559
Then the king **s** to him,	**1Ki 22:16**	559
So he **s**, "I saw all Israel Scattered	**1Ki 22:17**	559
the LORD **s**, 'These have no master.	**1Ki 22:17**	559
king of Israel **s** to Jehoshaphat,	**1Ki 22:18**	559
Micaiah **s**, "Therefore, hear the word	**1Ki 22:19**	559
"The LORD **s**,	**1Ki 22:20**	559
one **s** this while another said that.	**1Ki 22:20**	559
one said this while another **s** that.	**1Ki 22:20**	559
and stood before the LORD and **s**,	**1Ki 22:21**	559
"The LORD **s** to him,	**1Ki 22:22**	559
LORD said to him, 'How?' And he **s**,	**1Ki 22:22**	559
Then He **s**, 'You are to entice *him*	**1Ki 22:22**	559
struck Micaiah on the cheek and **s**,	**1Ki 22:24**	559
Micaiah **s**, "Behold, you shall	**1Ki 22:25**	559
Then the king of Israel **s**,	**1Ki 22:26**	559
Micaiah **s**, "If you indeed return	**1Ki 22:28**	559
And he **s**, "Listen, all you people."	**1Ki 22:28**	559
king of Israel **s** to Jehoshaphat,	**1Ki 22:30**	559
saw Jehoshaphat, they **s**,	**1Ki 22:32**	559
he **s** to the driver of his chariot,	**1Ki 22:34**	559
the son of Ahab **s** to Jehoshaphat,	**1Ki 22:49**	559
he sent messengers and **s** to them,	**2Ki 1:2**	559
the LORD **s** to Elijah the Tishbite,	**2Ki 1:3**	1696
returned to him he **s** to them,	**2Ki 1:5**	559
They **s** to him,	**2Ki 1:6**	559
came up to meet us and **s** to us,	**2Ki 1:6**	559
He **s** to them,	**2Ki 1:7**	1696
And he **s**, "It is Elijah the Tishbite."	**2Ki 1:8**	559
And he **s** to him,	**2Ki 1:9**	1696
And he **s** to him,	**2Ki 1:11**	1696
and begged him and **s** to him,	**2Ki 1:13**	1696
The angel of the LORD **s** to Elijah,	**2Ki 1:15**	1696
Then he **s** to him,	**2Ki 1:16**	1696
Elijah **s** to Elisha,	**2Ki 2:2**	559
But Elisha **s**, "As the LORD lives	**2Ki 2:2**	559
came out to Elisha and **s** to him,	**2Ki 2:3**	559
And he **s**, "Yes, I know; be still."	**2Ki 2:3**	559
Elijah **s** to him,	**2Ki 2:4**	559
But he **s**, "As the LORD lives, and	**2Ki 2:4**	559
approached Elisha and **s** to him,	**2Ki 2:5**	559
Then Elijah **s** to him,	**2Ki 2:6**	559
And he **s**, "As the LORD lives, and	**2Ki 2:6**	559
over, Elijah **s** to Elisha,	**2Ki 2:9**	559
And Elisha **s**, "Please, let a double	**2Ki 2:9**	559
He **s**, "You have asked a hard thing.	**2Ki 2:10**	559
him and struck the waters and **s**,	**2Ki 2:14**	559
opposite *him* saw him, they **s**,	**2Ki 2:15**	559
They **s** to him,	**2Ki 2:16**	559
And he **s**, "You shall not send."	**2Ki 2:16**	559
him until he was ashamed, he **s**,	**2Ki 2:17**	559
and he **s** to them,	**2Ki 2:18**	559
the men of the city **s** to Elisha,	**2Ki 2:19**	559
He **s**, "Bring me a new jar,	**2Ki 2:20**	559
water and threw salt in it and **s**,	**2Ki 2:21**	559
city and mocked him and **s** to him,	**2Ki 2:23**	559
to fight against Moab?" And he **s**,	**2Ki 3:7**	559
He **s**, "Which way shall we go	**2Ki 3:8**	559
Then the king of Israel **s**,	**2Ki 3:10**	559
But Jehoshaphat **s**,	**2Ki 3:11**	559
Israel's servants answered and **s**,	**2Ki 3:11**	559
Jehoshaphat **s**,	**2Ki 3:12**	559
Elisha **s** to the king of Israel,	**2Ki 3:13**	559
And the king of Israel **s** to him,	**2Ki 3:13**	559
Elisha **s**, "As the LORD of hosts lives	**2Ki 3:14**	559
He **s**, "Thus says the LORD,	**2Ki 3:16**	559
Then they **s**, "This is blood;	**2Ki 3:23**	559
Elisha **s** to her,	**2Ki 4:2**	559
And she **s**, "Your maidservant has	**2Ki 4:2**	559
Then he **s**, "Go, borrow vessels	**2Ki 4:3**	559
were full, she **s** to her son,	**2Ki 4:6**	559
And he **s** to her,	**2Ki 4:6**	559
And he **s**, "Go, sell the oil and pay	**2Ki 4:7**	559
She **s** to her husband,	**2Ki 4:9**	559
Then he **s** to Gehazi his servant,	**2Ki 4:12**	559
He **s** to him,	**2Ki 4:13**	559
So he **s**, "What then is to be done	**2Ki 4:14**	559
He **s**, "Call her." When he had	**2Ki 4:15**	559
Then he **s**, "At this season next year	**2Ki 4:16**	559
she **s**, "No, my lord, O man of God,	**2Ki 4:16**	559
next year, as Elisha had **s** to her.	**2Ki 4:17**	1696
He **s** to his father, "My head, my	**2Ki 4:19**	559
And he **s** to his servant,	**2Ki 4:19**	559
she called to her husband and **s**,	**2Ki 4:22**	559
He **s**, "Why will you go to him today?	**2Ki 4:23**	559
And she **s**, "*It will be* well."	**2Ki 4:23**	559
a donkey and **s** to her servant,	**2Ki 4:24**	559
he **s** to Gehazi his servant,	**2Ki 4:25**	559
but the man of God **s**,	**2Ki 4:27**	559
Then she **s**, "Did I ask for a son	**2Ki 4:28**	559
Then he **s** to Gehazi,	**2Ki 4:29**	559
The mother of the lad **s**,	**2Ki 4:30**	559
He called Gehazi and **s**,	**2Ki 4:36**	559
And when she came in to him, he **s**,	**2Ki 4:36**	559
before him, he **s** to his servant,	**2Ki 4:38**	559
stew, they cried out and **s**,	**2Ki 4:40**	559
But he **s**, "Now bring meal."	**2Ki 4:41**	559
threw it into the pot and **s**,	**2Ki 4:41**	559
And he **s**, "Give *them* to the people	**2Ki 4:42**	559
His attendant **s**,	**2Ki 4:43**	559
But he **s**, "Give *them* to the people	**2Ki 4:43**	559
She **s** to her mistress,	**2Ki 5:3**	559
Then the king of Aram **s**,	**2Ki 5:5**	559
he tore his clothes and **s**,	**2Ki 5:7**	559
was furious and went away and **s**,	**2Ki 5:11**	559
came near and spoke to him and **s**,	**2Ki 5:13**	559
came and stood before him, he **s**,	**2Ki 5:15**	559
But he **s**, "As the LORD lives, before	**2Ki 5:16**	559
Naaman **s**, "If not, please let your	**2Ki 5:17**	559
He **s** to him,	**2Ki 5:19**	559
the chariot to meet him and **s**,	**2Ki 5:21**	559
He **s**, "All is well. My master	**2Ki 5:22**	559
Naaman **s**, "Be pleased to take	**2Ki 5:23**	559
And Elisha **s** to him,	**2Ki 5:25**	559
he **s**, "Your servant went nowhere."	**2Ki 5:25**	559
Then he **s** to him,	**2Ki 5:26**	559
sons of the prophets **s** to Elisha,	**2Ki 6:1**	559
where we may live." So he **s**, "Go."	**2Ki 6:2**	559
Then one **s**, "Please be willing to go	**2Ki 6:3**	559
and he cried out and **s**,	**2Ki 6:5**	559
Then the man of God **s**,	**2Ki 6:6**	559
He **s**, "Take it up for yourself."	**2Ki 6:7**	559
called his servants and **s** to them,	**2Ki 6:11**	559
One of his servants **s**,	**2Ki 6:12**	559
So he **s**, "Go and see where he is,	**2Ki 6:13**	559
And his servant **s** to him,	**2Ki 6:15**	559
Then Elisha prayed and **s**,	**2Ki 6:17**	559
Elisha prayed to the LORD and **s**,	**2Ki 6:18**	559
Then Elisha **s** to them,	**2Ki 6:19**	559
come into Samaria, Elisha **s**,	**2Ki 6:20**	559
when he saw them, **s** to Elisha,	**2Ki 6:21**	559
He **s**, "If the LORD does not help you,	**2Ki 6:27**	559
And the king **s** to her,	**2Ki 6:28**	559
"This woman **s** to me,	**2Ki 6:28**	559
and I **s** to her on the next day,	**2Ki 6:29**	559
Then he **s**, "May God do so to me	**2Ki 6:31**	559
came to him, he **s** to the elders,	**2Ki 6:32**	559
came down to him and he **s**,	**2Ki 6:33**	559
Elisha **s**, "Listen to the word of the	**2Ki 7:1**	559
answered the man of God and **s**,	**2Ki 7:2**	559
Then he **s**, "Behold, you will see it	**2Ki 7:2**	559
and they **s** to one another,	**2Ki 7:3**	559
so that they **s** to one another,	**2Ki 7:6**	559
Then they **s** to one another,	**2Ki 7:9**	559
the night and **s** to his servants,	**2Ki 7:12**	559
of his servants **s**,	**2Ki 7:13**	559
died just as the man of God had **s**,	**2Ki 7:17**	1696
answered the man of God and **s**,	**2Ki 7:19**	559
And he **s**, "Behold, you will see it	**2Ki 7:19**	559
And Gehazi **s**, "My lord, O king,	**2Ki 8:5**	559
The king **s** to Hazael,	**2Ki 8:8**	559
came and stood before him and **s**,	**2Ki 8:9**	559
Then Elisha **s** to him,	**2Ki 8:10**	559
Hazael **s**, "Why does my lord weep?"	**2Ki 8:12**	559
Hazael **s**, "But what is your servant,	**2Ki 8:13**	559
to his master, who **s** to him,	**2Ki 8:14**	559
of the prophets and **s** to him,	**2Ki 9:1**	559
the army were sitting, and he **s**,	**2Ki 9:5**	559
And Jehu **s**, "For which *one* of us?"	**2Ki 9:5**	559
And he **s**, "For you, O captain."	**2Ki 9:5**	559
the oil on his head and **s** to him,	**2Ki 9:6**	559
of his master, and one **s** to him,	**2Ki 9:11**	559
And he **s** to them,	**2Ki 9:11**	559
They **s**, "It is a lie, tell us now."	**2Ki 9:12**	559
"It is a lie, tell us now." And he **s**,	**2Ki 9:12**	559
"Thus and thus he **s** to me,	**2Ki 9:12**	559
So Jehu **s**, "If this is your mind,	**2Ki 9:15**	559
company of Jehu as he came, and **s**,	**2Ki 9:17**	559
And Joram **s**, "Take a horseman	**2Ki 9:17**	559
a horseman went to meet him and **s**,	**2Ki 9:18**	559
'Is it peace?' " And Jehu **s**,	**2Ki 9:18**	559
horseman, who came to them and **s**,	**2Ki 9:19**	559
Then Joram **s**, "Get ready."	**2Ki 9:21**	559
When Joram saw Jehu, he **s**,	**2Ki 9:22**	559
Joram reined about and fled and **s**	**2Ki 9:23**	559
Then *Jehu* **s** to Bidkar his officer,	**2Ki 9:25**	559
And Jehu pursued him and **s**,	**2Ki 9:27**	559
As Jehu entered the gate, she **s**,	**2Ki 9:31**	559
up his face to the window and **s**,	**2Ki 9:32**	559
He **s**, "Throw her down."	**2Ki 9:33**	559
he **s**, "See now to this cursed woman	**2Ki 9:34**	559
he **s**, "This is the word of the LORD,	**2Ki 9:36**	559
But they feared greatly and **s**,	**2Ki 10:4**	559
the heads of the king's sons," he **s**,	**2Ki 10:8**	559
stood and **s** to all the people,	**2Ki 10:9**	559
of Ahaziah king of Judah and **s**,	**2Ki 10:13**	559
He **s**, "Take them alive."	**2Ki 10:14**	559
and he greeted him and **s** to him,	**2Ki 10:15**	559
Jehu **s**, "If it is, give *me*	**2Ki 10:15**	
He **s**, "Come with me and see	**2Ki 10:16**	559
all the people and **s** to them,	**2Ki 10:18**	559
Jehu **s**, "Sanctify a solemn assembly	**2Ki 10:20**	559
He **s** to the one who *was* in	**2Ki 10:22**	559
he **s** to the worshipers of Baal,	**2Ki 10:23**	559
eighty men outside, and he had **s**,	**2Ki 10:24**	559
that Jehu **s** to the guard and to	**2Ki 10:25**	559
The LORD **s** to Jehu,	**2Ki 10:30**	559
they clapped their hands and **s**,	**2Ki 11:12**	559
over the army and **s** to them,	**2Ki 11:15**	559
For the priest **s**,	**2Ki 11:15**	559
Then Jehoash **s** to the priests,	**2Ki 12:4**	559
the *other* priests and **s** to them,	**2Ki 12:7**	559
to him and wept over him and **s**,	**2Ki 13:14**	559
Elisha **s** to him,	**2Ki 13:15**	559
Then he **s** to the king of Israel,	**2Ki 13:16**	559
He **s**, "Open the window toward	**2Ki 13:17**	559
Then Elisha **s**, "Shoot!" And he shot.	**2Ki 13:17**	559
he **s**, "The LORD's arrow of victory,	**2Ki 13:17**	559
Then he **s**, "Take the arrows,"	**2Ki 13:18**	559
And he **s** to the king of Israel,	**2Ki 13:18**	559
of God was angry with him and **s**,	**2Ki 13:19**	559
which the LORD had **s** to them,	**2Ki 17:12**	559
Then Rabshakeh **s** to them,	**2Ki 18:19**	559
has **s** to Judah and to Jerusalem,	**2Ki 18:22**	559
The LORD **s** to me,	**2Ki 18:25**	559
Shebnah and Joah, **s** to Rabshakeh,	**2Ki 18:26**	559

But Rabshakeh **s** to them, **2Ki 18:27** 559
They **s** to him, **2Ki 19:3** 559
Isaiah **s** to them, **2Ki 19:6** 559
prayed before the LORD and **s**, **2Ki 19:15** 559
the Lord, And you have **s**, **2Ki 19:23** 559
of Amoz came to him and **s** to him, **2Ki 20:1** 559
Then Isaiah **s**, "Take a cake of figs." **2Ki 20:7** 559
Now Hezekiah **s** to Isaiah, **2Ki 20:8** 559
Isaiah **s**, "This shall be the sign **2Ki 20:9** 559
to King Hezekiah and **s** to him, **2Ki 20:14** 559
Hezekiah **s**, "They have come from a **2Ki 20:14** 559
He **s**, "What have they seen in your **2Ki 20:15** 559
Then Isaiah **s** to Hezekiah, **2Ki 20:16** 559
Then Hezekiah **s** to Isaiah, **2Ki 20:19** 559
the LORD, of which the LORD had **s**, **2Ki 21:4** 559
house of which the LORD **s** to David **2Ki 21:7** 559
Hilkiah the high priest **s** to Shaphan **2Ki 22:8** 559
back word to the king and **s**, **2Ki 22:9** 559
She **s** to them, **2Ki 22:15** 559
Then he **s**, "What is this monument **2Ki 23:17** 559
He **s**, "Let him alone; let no one **2Ki 23:18** 559
The LORD **s**, "I will remove Judah **2Ki 23:27** 559
and the temple of which I **s**, **2Ki 23:27** 559
the LORD, just as the LORD had **s**. **2Ki 24:13** 1696
them and their men and **s** to them, **2Ki 25:24** 559
Then Saul **s** to his armor bearer, **1Ch 10:4** 559
gathered to David at Hebron and **s**, **1Ch 11:1** 559
and the LORD your God **s** to you, **1Ch 11:2** 559
inhabitants of Jebus **s** to David, **1Ch 11:5** 559
Now David had **s**, **1Ch 11:6** 559
David had a craving and **s**, **1Ch 11:17** 559
he **s**, "Be it far from me before my **1Ch 11:19** 559
them, and **s** to them, **1Ch 12:17** 559
and he **s**, "*We* are yours, O **1Ch 12:18** 559
David **s** to all the assembly of Israel, **1Ch 13:2** 559
assembly **s** that they would do so, **1Ch 13:4** 559
Then the LORD **s** to him, **1Ch 14:10** 559
David **s**, "God has broken through **1Ch 14:11** 559
again of God, and God **s** to him, **1Ch 14:14** 559
David **s**, "No one is to carry the ark **1Ch 15:2** 559
s to them, "You are the heads of the **1Ch 15:12** 559
Then all the people **s**, **1Ch 16:36** 559
David **s** to Nathan the prophet, **1Ch 17:1** 559
Then Nathan **s** to David, **1Ch 17:2** 559
in and sat before the LORD and **s**, **1Ch 17:16** 559
David **s**, "I will show kindness to **1Ch 19:2** 559
of the sons of Ammon **s** to Hanun, **1Ch 19:3** 559
the king **s**, "Stay at Jericho until **1Ch 19:5** 559
He **s**, "If the Arameans are too strong **1Ch 19:12** 559
So David **s** to Joab and to the **1Ch 21:2** 559
Joab **s**, "May the LORD add to His **1Ch 21:3** 559
David **s** to God, **1Ch 21:8** 559
So Gad came to David and **s** to him, **1Ch 21:11** 559
David **s** to Gad, **1Ch 21:13** 559
and **s** to the destroying angel, **1Ch 21:15** 559
David **s** to God, **1Ch 21:17** 559
Then David **s** to Ornan, **1Ch 21:22** 559
Ornan **s** to David, **1Ch 21:23** 559
But King David **s** to Ornan, **1Ch 21:24** 559
Then David **s**, "This is the house of **1Ch 22:1** 559
David **s**, "My son Solomon is young **1Ch 22:5** 559
David **s** to Solomon, **1Ch 22:7** 559
David **s**, "The LORD God of Israel **1Ch 23:25** 559
because the LORD had **s** He would **1Ch 27:23** 559
King David rose to his feet and **s**, **1Ch 28:2** 559
"But God **s** to me, **1Ch 28:3** 559
"He **s** to me, **1Ch 28:6** 559
"All *this,*" **s** *David,* **1Ch 28:19** 559
Then David **s** to his son Solomon, **1Ch 28:20** 559
David **s** to the entire assembly, **1Ch 29:1** 559
David **s**, "Blessed are You, O LORD **1Ch 29:10** 559
Then David **s** to all the assembly, **1Ch 29:20** 559
appeared to Solomon and **s** to him, **2Ch 1:7** 559
Solomon **s** to God, **2Ch 1:8** 559
God **s** to Solomon, **2Ch 1:11** 559
Solomon **s**, "The LORD has said that **2Ch 6:1** 559
"The LORD has **s** that He would **2Ch 6:1** 559
He **s**, "Blessed be the LORD, **2Ch 6:4** 559
"But the LORD **s** to my father **2Ch 6:8** 559
He **s**, "O LORD, the God of Israel, **2Ch 6:14** 559
the place of which You have **s** that **2Ch 6:20** 559
to Solomon at night and **s** to him, **2Ch 7:12** 559
for he **s**, "My wife shall not dwell in **2Ch 8:11** 559
Then she **s** to the king, **2Ch 9:5** 559
He **s** to them, **2Ch 10:5** 559
So he **s** to them, **2Ch 10:9** 559
of Shishak, and he **s** to them, **2Ch 12:5** 559
the king humbled themselves and **s**, **2Ch 12:6** 559
hill country of Ephraim, and **s**, **2Ch 13:4** 559
For he **s** to Judah, **2Ch 14:7** 559
called to the LORD his God and **s**, **2Ch 14:11** 559
went out to meet Asa and **s** to him, **2Ch 15:2** 559
to Asa king of Judah and **s** to him, **2Ch 16:7** 559
s to Jehoshaphat king of Judah, **2Ch 18:3** 559
And he **s** to him, **2Ch 18:3** 559
Jehoshaphat **s** to the king of Israel, **2Ch 18:4** 559
four hundred men, and **s** to them, **2Ch 18:5** 559
they **s**, "Go up, for God will give *it* **2Ch 18:5** 559
But Jehoshaphat **s**, **2Ch 18:6** 559
king of Israel **s** to Jehoshaphat, **2Ch 18:7** 559
But Jehoshaphat **s**, **2Ch 18:7** 559
of Israel called an officer and **s**, **2Ch 18:8** 559
horns of iron for himself and **s**, **2Ch 18:10** 559
But Micaiah **s**, "As the LORD lives, **2Ch 18:13** 559
to the king, the king **s** to him, **2Ch 18:14** 559
He **s**, "Go up and succeed, for they **2Ch 18:14** 559
Then the king **s** to him, **2Ch 18:15** 559
So he **s**, "I saw all Israel Scattered **2Ch 18:16** 559
the LORD **s**, 'These have no master. **2Ch 18:16** 559

king of Israel **s** to Jehoshaphat, **2Ch 18:17** 559
Micaiah **s**, "Therefore, hear the word **2Ch 18:18** 559
"The LORD **s**, **2Ch 18:19** 559
one **s** this while another said that. **2Ch 18:19** 559
said this while another **s** that. **2Ch 18:19** 559
and stood before the LORD and **s**, **2Ch 18:20** 559
And the LORD **s** to him, **2Ch 18:20** 559
He **s**, 'I will go and be a deceiving **2Ch 18:21** 559
Then He **s**, 'You are to entice *him* **2Ch 18:21** 559
struck Micaiah on the cheek and **s**, **2Ch 18:23** 559
Micaiah **s**, "Behold, you will see **2Ch 18:24** 559
Then the king of Israel **s**, **2Ch 18:25** 559
Micaiah **s**, "If you indeed return **2Ch 18:27** 559
And he **s**, "Listen, all you people." **2Ch 18:27** 559
king of Israel **s** to Jehoshaphat, **2Ch 18:29** 559
saw Jehoshaphat, they **s**, **2Ch 18:31** 559
he **s** to the driver of the chariot, **2Ch 18:33** 559
him and **s** to King Jehoshaphat, **2Ch 19:2** 559
He **s** to the judges, **2Ch 19:6** 559
and he **s**, "O LORD, the God of our **2Ch 20:6** 559
and he **s**, "Listen, all Judah and the **2Ch 20:15** 559
Jehoshaphat stood and **s**, "Listen **2Ch 20:20** 559
went out before the army and **s**, **2Ch 20:21** 559
they **s**, "He is the son of Jehoshaphat **2Ch 22:9** 559
And Jehoiada **s** to them, **2Ch 23:3** 559
and his sons anointed him and **s**, **2Ch 23:11** 559
Athaliah tore her clothes and **s**, **2Ch 23:13** 559
over the army and **s** to them, **2Ch 23:14** 559
For the priest **s**, **2Ch 23:14** 559
and Levites and **s** to them, **2Ch 24:5** 559
the chief *priest* and **s** to him, **2Ch 24:6** 559
above the people and **s** to them, **2Ch 24:20** 559
"Thus God has **s**, **2Ch 24:20** 559
And as he died he **s**, **2Ch 24:22** 559
Amaziah **s** to the man of God, **2Ch 25:9** 559
sent him a prophet who **s** to him, **2Ch 25:15** 559
with him, the king **s** to him, **2Ch 25:16** 559
Then the prophet stopped and **s**, **2Ch 25:16** 559
s, 'Behold, you have defeated Edom.' **2Ch 25:19** 559
Uzziah the king and **s** to him, **2Ch 26:18** 559
belonged to the kings, for they **s**, **2Ch 26:23** 559
came to Samaria and **s** to them, **2Ch 28:9** 559
and **s** to them, "You must not bring **2Ch 28:13** 559
which had defeated him, and **s**, **2Ch 28:23** 559
Then he **s** to them, **2Ch 29:5** 559
went in to King Hezekiah and **s**, **2Ch 29:18** 559
Then Hezekiah **s**, **2Ch 29:31** 559
of the house of Zadok **s** to him, **2Ch 31:10** 559
and **s** to Judah and Jerusalem, **2Ch 32:12** 559
the LORD of which the LORD had **s**, **2Ch 33:4** 559
of which God had **s** to David and to **2Ch 33:7** 559
and **s** to Shaphan the scribe, **2Ch 34:15** 559
She **s** to them, **2Ch 34:23** 559
He also **s** to the Levites who **2Ch 35:3** 559
and the king **s** to his servants, **2Ch 35:23** 559
The governor **s** to them that **Ezr 2:63** 559
fathers' *households,* and **s** to them, **Ezr 4:2** 559
households of Israel **s** to them, **Ezr 4:3** 559
those elders and **s** to them thus, **Ezr 5:9** 560
'He **s** to him, **Ezr 5:15** 560
way, because we had **s** to the king, **Ezr 8:22** 559
Then I **s** to them, **Ezr 8:28** 559
and I **s**, "O my God, I am ashamed **Ezr 9:6** 559
of Elam, **s** to Ezra, **Ezr 10:2** 559
the priest stood up and **s** to them, **Ezr 10:10** 559
As you have **s**, so it is our duty **Ezr 10:12** 1697
They **s** to me, **Ne 1:3** 559
I **s**, "I beseech You, O LORD **Ne 1:5** 559
So the king **s** to me, **Ne 2:2** 559
I **s** to the king, **Ne 2:3** 559
Then the king **s** to me, **Ne 2:4** 559
I **s** to the king, **Ne 2:5** 559
Then the king **s** to me, the queen **Ne 2:6** 559
And I **s** to the king, **Ne 2:7** 559
Then I **s** to them, **Ne 2:17** 559
Then they **s**, "Let us arise and build **Ne 2:18** 559
mocked us and despised us and **s**, **Ne 2:19** 559
So I answered them and **s** to them, **Ne 2:20** 559
the wealthy *men* of Samaria and **s**, **Ne 4:2** 559
Ammonite *was* near him and he **s**, **Ne 4:3** 559
Thus in Judah it was **s**, **Ne 4:10** 559
Our enemies **s**, **Ne 4:11** 559
I **s** to the nobles, the **Ne 4:19** 559
that time I also **s** to the people, **Ne 4:22** 559
For there were those who **s**, **Ne 5:2** 559
There were others who **s**, **Ne 5:3** 559
Also there were those who **s**, **Ne 5:4** 559
and the rulers and **s** to them, **Ne 5:7** 559
I **s** to them, **Ne 5:8** 559
I **s**, "The thing which you are doing **Ne 5:9** 559
Then they **s**, "We will give *it* back **Ne 5:12** 559
out the front of my garment and **s**, **Ne 5:13** 559
And all the assembly **s**, **Ne 5:13** 559
who was confined at home, he **s**, **Ne 6:10** 559
But I **s**, "Should a man like me flee? **Ne 6:11** 559
Then I **s** to them, **Ne 7:3** 559
The governor **s** to them that **Ne 7:65** 559
the Levites who taught the people **s** **Ne 8:9** 559
Then he **s** to them, **Ne 8:10** 559
Shebaniah *and* Pethahiah, **s**, **Ne 9:5** 559
A calf of molten metal And **s**, **Ne 9:18** 559
I reprimanded the officials and **s**, **Ne 13:11** 559
the nobles of Judah and **s** to them, **Ne 13:17** 559
Then I warned them and **s** to them, **Ne 13:21** 559
Then the king **s** to the wise men **Es 1:13** 559
king and the princes, Memucan **s**, **Es 1:16** 559
attendants, who served him, **s**, **Es 2:2** 559
at the king's gate **s** to Mordecai, **Es 3:3** 559
Then Haman **s** to King Ahasuerus, **Es 3:8** 559

The king **s** to Haman, **Es 3:11** 559
Then the king **s** to her, **Es 5:3** 559
Esther **s**, "If it pleases the king, **Es 5:4** 559
Then the king **s**, **Es 5:5** 559
the banquet, the king **s** to Esther, **Es 5:6** 559
Haman also **s**, "Even Esther the **Es 5:12** 559
wife and all his friends **s** to him, **Es 5:14** 559
The king **s**, "What honor or dignity **Es 6:3** 559
king's servants who attended him **s**, **Es 6:3** 559
So the king **s**, "Who is in the court? **Es 6:4** 559
The king's servants **s** to him, **Es 6:5** 559
And the king **s**, "Let him come in." **Es 6:5** 559
came in and the king **s** to him, **Es 6:6** 559
And Haman **s** to himself, **Es 6:6** 559
Then Haman **s** to the king, **Es 6:7** 559
Then the king **s** to Haman, **Es 6:10** 559
robes and the horse as you have **s**, **Es 6:10** 1696
anything of all that you have **s**." **Es 6:10** 1696
men and Zeresh his wife **s** to him, **Es 6:13** 559
And the king **s** to Esther on the **Es 7:2** 559
Esther **s**, "A foe and an enemy is **Es 7:6** 559
Then the king **s**, **Es 7:8** 559
eunuchs who *were* before the king **s**, **Es 7:9** 559
And the king **s**, "Hang him on it." **Es 7:9** 559
Then she **s**, "If it pleases the king **Es 8:5** 559
So King Ahasuerus **s** to Queen **Es 8:7** 559
The king **s** to Queen Esther, **Es 9:12** 559
Then **s** Esther, "If it pleases the king **Es 9:13** 559
Job **s**, "Perhaps my sons have sinned **Jb 1:5** 559
The LORD **s** to Satan, **Jb 1:7** 559
Satan answered the LORD and **s**, **Jb 1:7** 559
The LORD **s** to Satan, **Jb 1:8** 559
Then the LORD **s** to Satan, **Jb 1:12** 559
a messenger came to Job and **s**, **Jb 1:14** 559
speaking, another also came and **s**, **Jb 1:16** 559
speaking, another also came and **s**, **Jb 1:17** 559
speaking, another also came and **s**, **Jb 1:18** 559
He **s**, "Naked I came from my **Jb 1:21** 559
The LORD **s** to Satan, **Jb 2:2** 559
Satan answered the LORD and **s**, **Jb 2:2** 559
The LORD **s** to Satan, **Jb 2:3** 559
Satan answered the LORD and **s**, **Jb 2:4** 559
So the LORD **s** to Satan, **Jb 2:6** 559
Then his wife **s** to him, **Jb 2:9** 559
But he **s** to her, **Jb 2:10** 559
And Job **s**, **Jb 3:2**
6030a, 559
to be born, And the night *which* **s**, **Jb 3:3** 559
"Have I **s**, 'Give me *something,*' **Jb 6:22** 559
"For you have **s**, **Jb 11:4** 559
"They **s** to God, **Jb 22:17** 559
Job continued his discourse and **s**, **Jb 27:1** 559
"And to man He **s**, **Jb 28:28** 559
again took up his discourse and **s**, **Jb 29:1** 559
"Have the men of my tent not **s**, **Jb 31:31** 559
the Buzite spoke out and **s**, **Jb 32:6** 559
Then Elihu continued and **s**, **Jb 34:1** 559
"For Job has **s**, **Jb 34:5** 559
he has **s**, 'It profits a man nothing **Jb 34:9** 559
"For has anyone **s** to God, **Jb 34:31** 559
Then Elihu continued and **s**, **Jb 35:1** 559
Then Elihu continued and **s**, **Jb 36:1** 559
yet more to be **s** in God's behalf. **Jb 36:2** 4405
Him His way, And who has **s**, **Jb 36:23** 559
Job out of the whirlwind and **s**, **Jb 38:1** 559
And I **s**, 'Thus far you shall come, **Jb 38:11** 559
Then the LORD **s** to Job, **Jb 40:1**
6030a, 559
Then Job answered the LORD and **s**, **Jb 40:3** 559
Job out of the storm and **s**, **Jb 40:6** 559
Then Job answered the LORD and **s**, **Jb 42:1** 559
LORD **s** to Eliphaz the Temanite, **Jb 42:7** 559
He **s** to Me, 'You are My Son, **Ps 2:7** 559
He has **s** to himself, **Ps 10:13** 559
Who have **s**, "With our tongue we **Ps 12:4** 559
The fool has **s** in his heart, **Ps 14:1** 559
I **s** to the LORD, **Ps 16:2** 559
When You **s**, "Seek My face," **Ps 27:8**
"Seek My face," my heart **s** to You, **Ps 27:8** 559
as for me, I **s** in my prosperity, **Ps 30:6** 559
As for me, I **s** in my alarm, **Ps 31:22** 559
I **s**, "I will confess my transgressions **Ps 32:5** 559
They **s**, "Aha, aha, our eyes have **Ps 35:21** 559
I **s**, "May they not rejoice over me, **Ps 38:16** 559
I **s**, "I will guard my ways That **Ps 39:1** 559
Then I **s**, "Behold, I come; **Ps 40:7** 559
As for me, I **s**, "O LORD, be **Ps 41:4** 559
The fool has **s** in his heart, **Ps 53:1** 559
I **s**, "Oh, that I had wings like a **Ps 55:6** 559
The Lord **s**, "I will bring *them* back **Ps 68:22** 559
If I had **s**, "I will speak thus," **Ps 73:15** 559
They **s** in their heart, **Ps 74:8** 559
"I **s** to the boastful, **Ps 75:4** 559
Then I **s**, "It is my grief, That the **Ps 77:10** 559
They **s**, "Can God prepare a table in **Ps 78:19** 559
I **s**, "You are gods, And all of you **Ps 82:6** 559
They have **s**, "Come, and let us wipe **Ps 83:4** 559
Who **s**, "Let us possess for ourselves **Ps 83:12** 559
But of Zion it shall be **s**, **Ps 87:5** 559
For I have **s**, "Lovingkindness will **Ps 89:2** 559
And **s**, "I have given help to one **Ps 89:19** 559
They have **s**, **Ps 94:7** 559
And **s** they are a people who err in **Ps 95:10** 559
He **s** that He would destroy them, **Ps 106:23** 559

I believed when I **s**, Ps 116:10 1696
I **s** in my alarm, Ps 116:11 559
I was glad when they **s** to me, Ps 122:1 559
Then they **s** among the nations, Ps 126:2 559
Edom The day of Jerusalem, Who **s**, Ps 137:7 559
I **s** to the LORD, Ps 140:6 559
I **s**, "You are my refuge, My portion Ps 142:5 559
Then he taught me and **s** to me, Pr 4:4 559
it is better that it be **s** to you, Pr 25:7 559
I **s** to myself, "Behold, I have Ec 1:16 1696
I **s** to myself, "Come now, I will test Ec 2:1 559
I **s** of laughter, Ec 2:2 559
Then I **s** to myself, Ec 2:15 559
So I **s** to myself, Ec 2:15 1696
I **s** to myself, "God will judge both Ec 3:17 559
I **s** to myself concerning the sons Ec 3:18 559
all this with wisdom, *and* I **s**, Ec 7:23 559
I **s**, "Wisdom is better than strength. Ec 9:16 559
"My beloved responded and **s** to me, SS 2:10 559
And I **s**, 'Have you seen him SS 3:3
"I **s**, 'I will climb the palm tree, SS 7:8 559
Moreover, the LORD **s**, Is 3:16 559
one called out to another and **s**, Is 6:3 559
I **s**, "Woe is me, for I am ruined! Is 6:5 559
He touched my mouth *with it* and **s**, Is 6:7 559
Then I **s**, "Here am I. Send me!" Is 6:8 559
He **s**, "Go, and tell this people: Is 6:9 559
Then I **s**, "Lord, how long?" Is 6:11 559
Then the LORD **s** to Isaiah, Is 7:3 559
But Ahaz **s**, "I will not ask, nor will Is 7:12 559
he **s**, "Listen now, O house of David Is 7:13 559
Then the LORD **s** to me, Is 8:1 559
Then the LORD **s** to me, Is 8:3 559
he has **s**, "By the power of my hand Is 10:13 559
"But you **s** in your heart, Is 14:13 559
LORD **s**, "Even as My servant Isaiah Is 20:3 559
And one **s**, "Fallen, fallen Is 21:9 559
For thus the Lord **s** to me, Is 21:16 559
He has **s**, "You shall exult no more, Is 23:12 559
And it will be **s** in that day, Is 25:9 559
He who **s** to them, Is 28:12 559
Because you have **s**, Is 28:15 559
Then the Lord **s**, Is 29:13 559
the Holy One of Israel, has **s**, Is 30:15 559
And you **s**, "No, for we will flee on Is 30:16 559
Then Rabshakeh **s** to them, Is 36:4 559
has **s** to Judah and to Jerusalem, Is 36:7 559
The LORD **s** to me, Is 36:10 559
Shebna and Joah **s** to Rabshakeh, Is 36:11 559
But Rabshakeh **s**, Is 36:12 559
a loud voice in Judean and **s**, Is 36:13 559
They **s** to him, Is 37:3 559
Isaiah **s** to them, Is 37:6 559
the Lord, And you have **s**, Is 37:24 559
of Amoz came to him and **s** to him, Is 38:1 559
and **s**, "Remember now, O LORD, Is 38:3 559
I **s**, "In the middle of my life I am Is 38:10 559
I **s**, "I will not see the LORD, Is 38:11 559
Now Isaiah had **s**, Is 38:21 559
Then Hezekiah had **s**, Is 38:22 559
to King Hezekiah and **s** to him, Is 39:3 559
Hezekiah **s**, "They have come to me Is 39:3 559
He **s**, "What have they seen in Is 39:4 559
Then Isaiah **s** to Hezekiah, Is 39:5 559
Then Hezekiah **s** to Isaiah, Is 39:8 559
its remotest parts And **s** to you, Is 41:9 559
"Formerly *I* **s** to Zion, 'Behold, Is 41:27
you **s**, 'I will be a queen forever.' Is 47:7 559
secure in your wickedness and **s**, Is 47:10 559
For you have **s** in your heart, Is 47:10 559
He **s** to Me, "You are My Servant, Is 49:3 559
But I **s**, "I have toiled in vain, Is 49:4 559
Zion **s**, "The LORD has forsaken me, Is 49:14 559
tormentors, Who have **s** to you, Is 51:23 559
And it will be **s**, Is 57:14 559
It will no longer be **s** to you, Is 62:4 559
to your land will it any longer be **s**, Is 62:4 559
He **s**, "Surely, they are My people, Is 63:8 559
I **s**, 'Here am I, here am I,' Is 65:1 559
you for My name's sake, Have **s**, Is 66:5 559
Then I **s**, "Alas, Lord GOD! Behold, Jer 1:6 559
But the LORD **s** to me, Jer 1:7 559
my mouth, and the LORD **s** to me, Jer 1:9 559
I **s**, "I see a rod of an almond tree." Jer 1:11 559
Then the LORD **s** to me, Jer 1:12 559
And I **s**, "I see a boiling pot, Jer 1:13 559
Then the LORD **s** to me, Jer 1:14 559
But you **s**, 'I will not serve!' Jer 2:20 559
But you **s**, 'It is hopeless! Jer 2:25 559
Yet you **s**, 'I am innocent; Jer 2:35 559
Then the LORD **s** to me in the days Jer 3:6 559
And the LORD **s** to me, Jer 3:11 559
"Then I **s**, 'How I would set you Jer 3:19 559
And I **s**, 'You shall call Me, Jer 3:19 559
Then I **s**, "Ah, Lord GOD! Surely Jer 4:10 559
In that time it will be **s** to this Jer 4:11 559
Then I **s**, "They are only the poor, Jer 5:4 559
have lied about the LORD And **s**, Jer 5:12 559
But they **s**, 'We will not walk *in it*.' Jer 6:16 559
But they **s**, 'We will not listen.' Jer 6:17 559
LORD **s**, "Because they have forsaken Jer 9:13 559
But I **s**, "Truly this is a sickness, Jer 10:19 559
Then I **s**, "Amen, Jer 11:5 559
And the LORD **s** to me, Jer 11:6 559
Then the LORD **s** to me, Jer 11:9 559
snatched away, Because *men* have **s**, Jer 12:4 559
Thus the LORD **s** to me, Jer 13:1 559
many days the LORD **s** to me, Jer 13:6 559
So the LORD **s** to me, Jer 14:11 559

I **s**, "Look, the prophets are telling Jer 14:13 559
Then the LORD **s** to me, Jer 14:14 559
Then the LORD **s** to me, Jer 15:1 559
LORD **s**, "Surely I will set you free Jer 15:11 559
"when it will no longer be **s**, Jer 16:14 559
Thus the LORD **s** to me, Jer 17:19 559
they **s**, "Come and let us devise plans Jer 18:18 559
house and **s** to all the people: Jer 19:14 559
stocks, Jeremiah **s** to him, Jer 20:3 559
Then Jeremiah **s** to them, Jer 21:3 559
But you **s**, 'I will not listen!' Jer 22:21 559
'The LORD has **s**, Jer 23:17 1696
have heard what the prophets have **s** Jer 23:25 559
'Because you **s** this word, Jer 23:38 559
Then the LORD **s** to me, Jer 24:3 559
And I **s**, "Figs, the good figs, Jer 24:3 559
the officials and all the people **s** to Jer 26:16 559
'Thus the LORD of hosts has **s**, Jer 26:18 559
and the prophet Jeremiah **s**, Jer 28:6 559
prophet **s** to Hananiah the prophet, Jer 28:15 559
"Because you have **s**, Jer 29:15 559
Jeremiah **s**, "The word of the LORD Jer 32:6 559
the word of the LORD and **s** to me, Jer 32:8 559
'You have **s** to me, O Lord Jer 32:25 559
and I **s** to them, Jer 35:5 559
But they **s**, "We will not drink wine, Jer 35:6 559
up against the land, we **s**, Jer 35:11 559
Then Jeremiah **s** to the house of Jer 35:18 559
They **s** to him, Jer 36:15 559
one to another and **s** to Baruch, Jer 36:16 559
Then Baruch **s** to them, Jer 36:18 559
Then the officials **s** to Baruch, Jer 36:19 559
But Jeremiah **s**, "A lie! Jer 37:14 559
the king secretly asked him and **s**, Jer 37:17 559
And Jeremiah **s**, "There is!" Jer 37:17 559
Then he **s**, "You will be given into Jer 37:17 559
Jeremiah **s** to King Zedekiah, Jer 37:18 559
Then the officials **s** to the king, Jer 38:4 559
So King Zedekiah **s**, Jer 38:5 559
the Ethiopian **s** to Jeremiah, Jer 38:12 559
and the king **s** to Jeremiah, Jer 38:14 559
Then Jeremiah **s** to Zedekiah, Jer 38:15 559
Then Jeremiah **s** to Zedekiah, Jer 38:17 559
Then King Zedekiah **s** to Jeremiah, Jer 38:19 559
But Jeremiah **s**, "They will not give Jer 38:20 559
Then Zedekiah **s** to Jeremiah, Jer 38:24 559
us now what you **s** to the king and Jer 38:25 1696
king and what the king **s** to you; Jer 38:25 1696
had taken Jeremiah and **s** to him, Jer 40:2 559
he **s**, "Go on back then to Jer 40:5
and **s** to him, "Are you well aware Jer 40:14 559
the son of Ahikam **s** to Johanan Jer 40:16 559
as he met them, he **s** to them, Jer 41:6 559
men who were found among them **s** Jer 41:8 559
and **s** to Jeremiah the prophet, Jer 42:2 559
Jeremiah the prophet **s** to them, Jer 42:4 559
Then they **s** to Jeremiah, Jer 42:5 559
and **s** to them, "Thus says the LORD Jer 42:9 559
the arrogant men **s** to Jeremiah, Jer 43:2 559
"And," **s** *the women,* "when we Jer 44:19
Then Jeremiah **s** to all the people, Jer 44:20 559
Then Jeremiah **s** to all the people, Jer 44:24 559
'You **s**, "Ah, woe is me! Jer 45:3 559
And He has **s**, "I will rise and cover Jer 46:8 559
Then they **s**, 'Get up! And let us go Jer 46:16 559
be destroyed, As the LORD has **s**. Jer 48:8 559
And their adversaries have **s**, Jer 50:7 559
Then Jeremiah **s** to Seraiah, Jer 51:61 559
"Is this the city of which they **s**, La 2:15 559
I **s**, "I am cut off!" La 3:54 559
You **s**, "Do not fear!" La 3:57 559
Men among the nations **s**, La 4:15 559
in their pits, Of whom we had **s**, La 4:20 559
Then He **s** to me, Ezk 2:1 559
Then He **s** to me, Ezk 2:3 559
Then He **s** to me, Ezk 3:1 559
He **s** to me, "Son of man, feed Ezk 3:3 559
Then He **s** to me, Ezk 3:4 559
Moreover, He **s** to me, Ezk 3:10 559
was on me there, and He **s** to me, Ezk 3:22 559
and He spoke with me and **s** to me, Ezk 3:24 559
Then the LORD **s**, Ezk 4:13 559
But I **s**, "Ah, Lord GOD! Behold, I Ezk 4:14 559
Then He **s** to me, Ezk 4:15 559
Moreover, He **s** to me, Ezk 4:16 559
I have not **s** in vain that I would Ezk 6:10 1696
Then He **s** to me, Ezk 8:5 559
And He **s** to me, "Son of man, Ezk 8:6 559
He **s** to me, "Son of man, Ezk 8:8 559
And He **s** to me, "Go in and see the Ezk 8:9 559
Then He **s** to me, Ezk 8:12 559
He **s** to me, "Yet you will see still Ezk 8:13 559
He **s** to me, "Do you see *this,* Ezk 8:15 559
He **s** to me, "Do you see *this,* Ezk 8:17 559
The LORD **s** to him, Ezk 9:4 559
to the others He **s** in my hearing, Ezk 9:5 559
And He **s** to them, Ezk 9:7 559
Then He **s** to me, Ezk 9:9 559
to the man clothed in linen and **s**, Ezk 10:2 559
He **s** to me, "Son of man, these Ezk 11:2 559
LORD fell upon me, and He **s** to me, Ezk 11:5 559
cried out with a loud voice and **s**, Ezk 11:13 559
inhabitants of Jerusalem have **s**, Ezk 11:15 559
the rebellious house, **s** to you, Ezk 12:9 559
a lying divination when you **s**, Ezk 13:7 559
I **s** to you *while you were* in your Ezk 16:6 559
I **s** to you *while you were* in your Ezk 16:6 559
"I **s** to them, Ezk 20:7 559
"I **s** to their children in the Ezk 20:18 559

"Then I **s** to them, Ezk 20:29 559
Then I **s**, "Ah Lord GOD! Ezk 20:49 559
Moreover, the LORD **s** to me, Ezk 23:36 559
"Then I **s** concerning her who was Ezk 23:43 559
The people **s** to me, Ezk 24:19 559
Then I **s** to them, Ezk 24:20 559
"Because you **s**, Ezk 25:3 559
Tyre has **s** concerning Jerusalem, Ezk 26:2 559
'O Tyre, you have **s**, Ezk 27:3 559
heart is lifted up And you have **s**, Ezk 28:2 559
midst of his rivers, That has **s**, Ezk 29:3 559
Because you **s**, 'The Nile is mine, Ezk 29:9 559
"Because you have **s**, Ezk 35:10 559
name, because it was **s** of them, Ezk 36:20 559
He **s** to me, "Son of man, can Ezk 37:3 559
Again He **s** to me, Ezk 37:4 559
Then He **s** to me, Ezk 37:9 559
Then He **s** to me, Ezk 37:11 559
The man **s** to me, Ezk 40:4 1696
He **s** to me, "This is the chamber Ezk 40:45 1696
s to me, "This is the most holy *place.* Ezk 41:4 559
And he **s** to me, "This is the table Ezk 41:22 1696
Then he **s** to me, Ezk 42:13 559
He **s** to me, "Son of man, Ezk 43:7 559
And He **s** to me, "Son of man, Ezk 43:18 559
The LORD **s** to me, Ezk 44:2 559
The LORD **s** to me, Ezk 44:5 559
He **s** to me, "This is the place Ezk 46:20 559
Then he **s** to me, Ezk 46:24 559
He **s** to me, "Son of man, Ezk 47:6 559
Then he **s** to me, Ezk 47:8 559
of the officials **s** to Daniel, Da 1:10 559
But Daniel **s** to the overseer whom Da 1:11 559
The king **s** to them, Da 2:3 559
They answered a second time and **s**, Da 2:7 560
Chaldeans answered the king and **s**, Da 2:10 560
he **s** to Arioch, the Da 2:15 560
Daniel **s**, "Let the name of God Da 2:20 560
The king **s** to Daniel, Da 2:26 560
answered before the king and **s**, Da 2:27 560
The king answered Daniel and **s**, Da 2:47 560
and **s** to Nebuchadnezzar the king: Da 3:9 560
responded and **s** to them, Da 3:14 560
he **s** to his high officials, Da 3:24 560
He **s**, "Look! I see four men Da 3:25 560
he responded and **s**, Da 3:26 560
Nebuchadnezzar responded and **s**, Da 3:28 560
The king responded and **s**, Da 4:19 560
"The king reflected and **s**, Da 4:30 560
and **s** to the wise men of Babylon, Da 5:7 560
the queen spoke and **s**, Da 5:10 560
The king spoke and **s** to Daniel, Da 5:13 560
answered and **s** before the king, Da 5:17 560
Then these men **s**, Da 6:5 560
to the king and **s** to the king, Da 6:15 560
The king spoke and **s** to Daniel, Da 6:16 560
The king spoke and **s** to Daniel, Da 6:20 560
Daniel **s**, "I was looking in my vision Da 7:2 6032, 560
and thus they **s** to it, Da 7:5 560
"Thus he **s**: 'The fourth beast will be Da 7:23 560
and another holy one **s** to that Da 8:13 559
He **s** to me, "For 2,300 evenings Da 8:14 559
of Ulai, and he called out and **s**, Da 8:16 559
but he **s** to me, "Son of man, Da 8:17 559
He **s**, "Behold, I am going to let you Da 8:19 559
LORD my God and confessed and **s**, Da 9:4 559
and talked with me and **s**, Da 9:22 559
He **s** to me, "O Daniel, man of high Da 10:11 559
Then he **s** to me, Da 10:12 559
and **s** to him who was standing Da 10:16 559
He **s**, "O man of high esteem, Da 10:19 559
to me, I received strength and **s**, Da 10:19 559
Then he **s**, "Do you understand why Da 10:20 559
one **s** to the man dressed in linen, Da 12:6 559
so I **s**, "My lord, what *will be* the Da 12:8 559
He **s**, "Go *your way,* Daniel, Da 12:9 559
Hosea, the LORD **s** to Hosea, Hos 1:2 559
And the LORD **s** to him, Hos 1:4 559
And the LORD **s** to him, Hos 1:6 559
the LORD **s**, "Name him Lo-ammi, Hos 1:9 559
the place Where it is **s** to them, Hos 1:10 559
My people," It will be **s** to them, Hos 1:10 559
For she **s**, 'I will go after my lovers, Hos 2:5 559
and fig trees, Of which she **s**, Hos 2:12 559
Then the LORD **s** to me, Hos 3:1 559
Then I **s** to her, Hos 3:3 559
Ephraim **s**, "Surely I have become Hos 12:8 559
who escape, As the LORD has **s**, Jl 2:32 559
He **s**, "The LORD roars from Zion Am 1:2 559
be with you, Just as you have **s**! Am 5:14 559
vegetation of the land, that I **s**, Am 7:2 559
"It shall not be," **s** the LORD. Am 7:3 559
Then I **s**, "Lord GOD, please stop! Am 7:5 559
too shall not be," **s** the Lord GOD. Am 7:6 559
The LORD **s** to me, Am 7:8 559
And I **s**, "A plumb line." Am 7:8 559
Then the Lord **s**, Am 7:8 559
Then Amaziah **s** to Amos, Am 7:12 559
the flock and the LORD **s** to me, Am 7:15 559
He **s**, "What do you see, Amos?" Am 8:2 559
And I **s**, "A basket of summer fruit. Am 8:2 559
Then the LORD **s** to me, Am 8:2 559
beside the altar, and He **s**, Am 9:1 559
the captain approached him and **s**, Jon 1:6 559
Each man **s** to his mate, Jon 1:7 559
Then they **s** to him, Jon 1:8 559
He **s** to them, Jon 1:9 559
frightened and they **s** to him, Jon 1:10 559
So they **s** to him, Jon 1:11 559

He **s** to them,	**Jon 1:12**	559
they called on the LORD and **s**,	**Jon 1:14**	559
and he **s**, "I called out of my distress	**Jon 2:2**	559
"So I **s**, 'I have been expelled from	**Jon 2:4**	559
and he cried out and **s**,	**Jon 3:4**	559
He issued a proclamation and it **s**,	**Jon 3:7**	559
He prayed to the LORD and **s**,	**Jon 4:2**	559
was not this what I **s** while I was	**Jon 4:2**	1696
LORD **s**, "Do you have good reason	**Jon 4:4**	559
Then God **s** to Jonah,	**Jon 4:9**	559
And he **s**, "I have good reason to be	**Jon 4:9**	559
Then the LORD **s**,	**Jon 4:10**	559
"Is it being **s**, O house of Jacob:	**Mi 2:7**	559
and falsehood Had told lies *and* **s**,	**Mi 2:11**	559
And I **s**, "Hear now, heads of Jacob	**Mi 3:1**	559
shame will cover her who **s** to me,	**Mi 7:10**	559
Then the LORD answered me and **s**,	**Hab 2:2**	559
"I **s**, 'Surely you will revere Me,	**Zph 3:7**	559
day it will be **s** to Jerusalem:	**Zph 3:16**	559
Haggai **s**, "If one who is unclean	**Hg 2:13**	559
Then Haggai **s**,	**Hg 2:14**	559
Then they repented and **s**,	**Zch 1:6**	559
Then I **s**, "My lord, what are these?"	**Zch 1:9**	559
who was speaking with me **s** to me,	**Zch 1:9**	559
the myrtle trees answered and **s**,	**Zch 1:10**	559
among the myrtle trees and **s**,	**Zch 1:11**	559
angel of the LORD **s**,	**Zch 1:12**	559
who was speaking with me **s** to me,	**Zch 1:14**	559
So I **s** to the angel who was	**Zch 1:19**	559
I **s**, "What are these coming to do?"	**Zch 1:21**	559
And he **s**, "These are the horns	**Zch 1:21**	559
So I **s**, "Where are you going?"	**Zch 2:2**	559
he **s** to me, "To measure Jerusalem,	**Zch 2:2**	559
s to him, "Run, speak to that young	**Zch 2:4**	559
The LORD **s** to Satan,	**Zch 3:2**	559
He spoke and **s** to those who	**Zch 3:4**	559
Again he **s** to him,	**Zch 3:4**	559
I **s**, "Let them put a clean turban on	**Zch 3:5**	559
He **s** to me, "What do you see?"	**Zch 4:2**	559
I **s**, "I see, and behold, a lampstand	**Zch 4:2**	559
Then I **s** to the angel	**Zch 4:4**	559
with me answered and **s** to me,	**Zch 4:5**	559
And I **s**, "No, my lord."	**Zch 4:5**	559
Then he **s** to me,	**Zch 4:6**	559
Then I **s** to him,	**Zch 4:11**	559
the second time and **s** to him,	**Zch 4:12**	559
And I **s**, "No, my lord."	**Zch 4:13**	559
he **s**, "These are the two anointed	**Zch 4:14**	559
And he **s** to me, "What do you see?"	**Zch 5:2**	559
Then he **s** to me,	**Zch 5:3**	559
with me went out and **s** to me,	**Zch 5:5**	559
I **s**, "What is it?"	**Zch 5:6**	559
he **s**, "This is the ephah going forth."	**Zch 5:6**	559
Again he **s**, "This is their	**Zch 5:6**	559
Then he **s**, "This is Wickedness!"	**Zch 5:8**	559
I **s** to the angel who was	**Zch 5:10**	559
Then he **s** to me,	**Zch 5:11**	559
Then I spoke and **s** to the angel	**Zch 6:4**	559
And He **s**, "Go, patrol the earth."	**Zch 6:7**	559
"Thus has the LORD of hosts **s**,	**Zch 7:9**	559
Then I **s**, "I will not pasture you.	**Zch 11:9**	559
I **s** to them,	**Zch 11:12**	559
Then the LORD **s** to me,	**Zch 11:13**	559
The LORD **s** to me,	**Zch 11:15**	559
You have **s**, 'It is vain to serve God;	**Mal 3:14**	559
They **s** to him,	**Mt 2:5**	3004
he sent them to Bethlehem and **s**,	**Mt 2:8**	3004
appeared to Joseph in a dream and **s**,	**Mt 2:13**	3004
Joseph in Egypt, and **s**,	**Mt 2:19**	3004
to by Isaiah the prophet when he **s**,	**Mt 3:3**	3004
coming for baptism, he **s** to them,	**Mt 3:7**	3004
But Jesus answering **s** to him,	**Mt 3:15**	3004
a voice out of the heavens **s**, "This	**Mt 3:17**	3004
And the tempter came and **s** to Him,	**Mt 4:3**	3004
But He answered and **s**,	**Mt 4:4**	3004
and **s** to Him, "If You are the Son	**Mt 4:6**	3004
Jesus **s** to him, "On the other hand,	**Mt 4:7**	5346
and he **s** to Him,	**Mt 4:9**	3004
Then Jesus **s** to him,	**Mt 4:10**	3004
And He **s** to them,	**Mt 4:19**	3004
"You have heard that it was **s**,	**Mt 5:27**	3004
It was **s**, 'WHOEVER SENDS HIS WIFE	**Mt 5:31**	3004
"You have heard that it was **s**,	**Mt 5:38**	3004
"You have heard that it was **s**,	**Mt 5:43**	3004
and **s**, "Lord, if You are willing,	**Mt 8:2**	3004
And Jesus **s** to him,	**Mt 8:4**	3004
Jesus **s** to him,	**Mt 8:7**	3004
But the centurion **s**,	**Mt 8:8**	5346
and **s** to those who were following,	**Mt 8:10**	3004
And Jesus **s** to the centurion,	**Mt 8:13**	3004
a scribe came and **s** to Him,	**Mt 8:19**	3004
Jesus **s** to him,	**Mt 8:20**	3004
Another of the disciples **s** to Him,	**Mt 8:21**	3004
But Jesus **s** to him,	**Mt 8:22**	3004
He **s** to them,	**Mt 8:26**	3004
The men were amazed, and **s**, "What	**Mt 8:27**	3004
And He **s** to them,	**Mt 8:32**	3004
Seeing their faith, Jesus **s** to the	**Mt 9:2**	3004
some of the scribes **s** to themselves,	**Mt 9:3**	3004
Jesus knowing their thoughts **s**,	**Mt 9:4**	3004
then He **s** to the paralytic, "Get up,	**Mt 9:6**	3004
and He **s** to him,	**Mt 9:9**	3004
saw *this,* they **s** to His disciples,	**Mt 9:11**	3004
But when Jesus heard *this,* He **s**,	**Mt 9:12**	3004
And Jesus **s** to them,	**Mt 9:15**	3004
and **s**, "My daughter has just died;	**Mt 9:18**	3004
Jesus turning and seeing her **s**,	**Mt 9:22**	3004
He **s**, "Leave; for the girl has not	**Mt 9:24**	3004
up to Him, and Jesus **s** to them,	**Mt 9:28**	3004
They **s** to Him, "Yes, Lord."	**Mt 9:28**	3004
Then He **s** to His disciples,	**Mt 9:37**	3004
s to Him, "Are You the Expected	**Mt 11:3**	3004
Jesus answered and **s** to them,	**Mt 11:4**	3004
At that time Jesus **s**,	**Mt 11:25**	3004
Pharisees saw *this,* they **s** to Him,	**Mt 12:2**	3004
But He **s** to them,	**Mt 12:3**	3004
And He **s** to them,	**Mt 12:11**	3004
Then He **s** to the man,	**Mt 12:13**	3004
the Pharisees heard *this,* they **s**,	**Mt 12:24**	3004
their thoughts Jesus **s** to them,	**Mt 12:25**	3004
some of the scribes and Pharisees **s**	**Mt 12:38**	3004
But He answered and **s** to them,	**Mt 12:39**	3004
Someone **s** to Him,	**Mt 12:47**	3004
the one who was telling Him and **s**,	**Mt 12:48**	3004
hand toward His disciples, He **s**,	**Mt 12:49**	3004
the disciples came and **s** to Him,	**Mt 13:10**	3004
the landowner came and **s** to him,	**Mt 13:27**	3004
"And he **s** to them,	**Mt 13:28**	5346
The slaves **s** to him,	**Mt 13:28**	3004
"But he **s**, 'No; for while you are	**Mt 13:29**	5346
And His disciples came to Him and **s**,	**Mt 13:36**	3004
And He **s**, "The one who sows	**Mt 13:37**	3004
They **s** to Him, "Yes."	**Mt 13:51**	3004
And Jesus **s** to them,	**Mt 13:52**	3004
they were astonished, and **s**,	**Mt 13:54**	3004
But Jesus **s** to them,	**Mt 13:57**	3004
and **s** to his servants,	**Mt 14:2**	3004
prompted by her mother, she **s**,	**Mt 14:8**	5346
the disciples came to Him and **s**,	**Mt 14:15**	3004
But Jesus **s** to them,	**Mt 14:16**	3004
They **s** to Him,	**Mt 14:17**	3004
And He **s**, "Bring them here to Me."	**Mt 14:18**	3004
and **s**, "It is a ghost!" And they	**Mt 14:26**	3004
Peter **s** to Him,	**Mt 14:28**	3004
He **s**, "Come!" And Peter got out of	**Mt 14:29**	3004
took hold of him, and **s** to him,	**Mt 14:31**	3004
came to Jesus from Jerusalem and **s**,	**Mt 15:1**	3004
And He answered and **s** to them,	**Mt 15:3**	3004
"For God **s**, 'HONOR YOUR FATHER	**Mt 15:4**	3004
crowd to Him, He **s** to them,	**Mt 15:10**	3004
the disciples came and **s** to Him,	**Mt 15:12**	3004
But He answered and **s**,	**Mt 15:13**	3004
Peter **s** to Him,	**Mt 15:15**	3004
Jesus **s**, "Are you still lacking in	**Mt 15:16**	3004
But He answered and **s**,	**Mt 15:24**	3004
And He answered and **s**,	**Mt 15:26**	3004
she **s**, "Yes, Lord; but even the dogs	**Mt 15:27**	3004
Then Jesus **s** to her,	**Mt 15:28**	3004
His disciples to Him, and **s**,	**Mt 15:32**	3004
The disciples **s** to Him,	**Mt 15:33**	3004
And Jesus **s** to them,	**Mt 15:34**	3004
they **s**, "Seven, and a few small fish."	**Mt 15:34**	3004
And Jesus **s** to them,	**Mt 16:6**	3004
"*He* **s** *that* because we did not	**Mt 16:7**	
But Jesus, aware of this, **s**,	**Mt 16:8**	3004
they **s**, "Some *say* John the Baptist;	**Mt 16:14**	3004
He **s** to them, "But who do you say	**Mt 16:15**	3004
And Jesus **s** to him,	**Mt 16:17**	3004
But He turned and **s** to Peter,	**Mt 16:23**	3004
Then Jesus **s** to His disciples,	**Mt 16:24**	3004
Peter **s** to Jesus,	**Mt 17:4**	3004
a voice out of the cloud **s**, "This	**Mt 17:5**	3004
to *them* and touched them and **s**,	**Mt 17:7**	3004
And He answered and **s**,	**Mt 17:11**	3004
And Jesus answered and **s**,	**Mt 17:17**	3004
came to Jesus privately and **s**,	**Mt 17:19**	3004
And He **s** to them,	**Mt 17:20**	3004
in Galilee, Jesus **s** to them,	**Mt 17:22**	3004
tax came to Peter and **s**,	**Mt 17:24**	3004
He **s**, "Yes." And when he came into	**Mt 17:25**	3004
When Peter **s**, "From strangers,"	**Mt 17:26**	5346
"From strangers," Jesus **s** to him,	**Mt 17:26**	5346
the disciples came to Jesus and **s**,	**Mt 18:1**	3004
and **s**, "Truly I say to you, unless	**Mt 18:3**	3004
Then Peter came and **s** to Him,	**Mt 18:21**	3004
Jesus **s** to him, "I do not say to you,	**Mt 18:22**	3004
summoning him, his lord **s** to him,	**Mt 18:32**	3004
And He answered and **s**,	**Mt 19:4**	3004
and **s**, 'FOR THIS REASON A MAN SHALL	**Mt 19:5**	3004
They **s** to Him, "Why then did	**Mt 19:7**	3004
He **s** to them, "Because of your	**Mt 19:8**	3004
The disciples **s** to Him,	**Mt 19:10**	3004
But He **s** to them,	**Mt 19:11**	3004
But Jesus **s**, "Let the children alone,	**Mt 19:14**	3004
And someone came to Him and **s**,	**Mt 19:16**	3004
And He **s** to him,	**Mt 19:17**	3004
he **s** to Him, "Which ones?"	**Mt 19:18**	3004
And Jesus **s**, "YOU SHALL NOT	**Mt 19:18**	5346
The young man **s** to Him,	**Mt 19:20**	3004
Jesus **s** to him, "If you wish to be	**Mt 19:21**	5346
And Jesus **s** to His disciples,	**Mt 19:23**	3004
they were very astonished and **s**,	**Mt 19:25**	3004
looking at *them* Jesus **s** to them,	**Mt 19:26**	3004
Then Peter **s** to Him,	**Mt 19:27**	3004
And Jesus **s** to them,	**Mt 19:28**	3004
and to those he **s**,	**Mt 20:4**	3004
and he **s** to them,	**Mt 20:6**	3004
"They **s** to him,	**Mt 20:7**	3004
He **s** to them, 'You go into the	**Mt 20:7**	3004
of the vineyard **s** to his foreman,	**Mt 20:8**	3004
he answered and **s** to one of them,	**Mt 20:13**	3004
and on the way He **s** to them,	**Mt 20:17**	3004
And He **s** to her,	**Mt 20:21**	3004
She **s** to Him, "Command that in	**Mt 20:21**	3004
They **s** to Him, "We are able."	**Mt 20:22**	3004
s to them, "My cup you shall drink;	**Mt 20:23**	3004
Jesus called them to Himself and **s**,	**Mt 20:25**	3004
stopped and called them, and **s**,	**Mt 20:32**	3004
They **s** to Him, "Lord, *we want* our	**Mt 20:33**	3004
And He **s** to them,	**Mt 21:13**	3004
s to Him, "Do You hear what these	**Mt 21:16**	3004
And Jesus **s** to them,	**Mt 21:16**	3004
He **s** to it, "No longer shall there	**Mt 21:19**	3004
And Jesus answered and **s** to them,	**Mt 21:21**	3004
to Him while He was teaching, and **s**,	**Mt 21:23**	3004
Jesus **s** to them,	**Mt 21:24**	3004
And answering Jesus, they **s**,	**Mt 21:27**	3004
He also **s** to them,	**Mt 21:27**	5346
and he came to the first and **s**,	**Mt 21:28**	3004
the second and **s** the same thing;	**Mt 21:30**	3004
They **s**, "The first."	**Mt 21:31**	3004
Jesus **s** to them,	**Mt 21:31**	3004
the son, they **s** among themselves,	**Mt 21:38**	3004
They **s** to Him, "He will bring those	**Mt 21:41**	3004
Jesus **s** to them,	**Mt 21:42**	3004
"Then he **s** to his slaves,	**Mt 22:8**	3004
and he **s** to him,	**Mt 22:12**	3004
"Then the king **s** to the servants,	**Mt 22:13**	3004
they might trap Him in what He **s**.	**Mt 22:15**	3056
Jesus perceived their malice, and **s**,	**Mt 22:18**	3004
And He **s** to them,	**Mt 22:20**	3004
They **s** to Him, "Caesar's." Then He	**Mt 22:21**	3004
Then He **s** to them,	**Mt 22:21**	3004
"Teacher, Moses **s**,	**Mt 22:24**	3004
But Jesus answered and **s** to them,	**Mt 22:29**	3004
And He **s** to him,	**Mt 22:37**	5346
They **s** to Him, "*The son* of David."	**Mt 22:42**	3004
He **s** to them,	**Mt 22:43**	3004
'THE LORD **S** TO MY LORD,	**Mt 22:44**	3004
And He **s** to them,	**Mt 24:2**	3004
And Jesus answered and **s** to them,	**Mt 24:4**	3004
"The foolish **s** to the prudent,	**Mt 25:8**	3004
"His master **s** to him,	**Mt 25:21**	5346
s, 'Master, you entrusted two talents	**Mt 25:22**	3004
"His master **s** to him,	**Mt 25:23**	5346
up and **s**, 'Master, I knew you to be a	**Mt 25:24**	3004
his master answered and **s** to him,	**Mt 25:26**	3004
words, He **s** to His disciples,	**Mt 26:1**	3004
saw *this,* and **s**, "Why this waste?	**Mt 26:8**	3004
Jesus, aware of this, **s** to them,	**Mt 26:10**	3004
and **s**, "What are you willing to give	**Mt 26:15**	3004
And He **s**, "Go into the city to a	**Mt 26:18**	3004
As they were eating, He **s**,	**Mt 26:21**	3004
was betraying Him, **s**,	**Mt 26:25**	3004
s to him, "You have said *it* yourself.	**Mt 26:25**	3004
"You have **s** *it* yourself."	**Mt 26:25**	3004
gave *it* to the disciples, and **s**,	**Mt 26:26**	3004
Then Jesus **s** to them,	**Mt 26:31**	3004
But Peter **s** to Him,	**Mt 26:33**	3004
Jesus **s** to him, "Truly I say to you	**Mt 26:34**	5346
Peter **s** to Him, "Even if I have to	**Mt 26:35**	3004
disciples **s** the same thing too.	**Mt 26:35**	3004
and **s** to His disciples,	**Mt 26:36**	3004
Then He **s** to them,	**Mt 26:38**	3004
them sleeping, and **s** to Peter,	**Mt 26:40**	3004
to the disciples and **s** to them,	**Mt 26:45**	3004
Judas went to Jesus and **s**,	**Mt 26:49**	3004
And Jesus **s** to him,	**Mt 26:50**	3004
Then Jesus **s** to him,	**Mt 26:52**	3004
time Jesus **s** to the crowds,	**Mt 26:55**	3004
and **s**, "This man stated, 'I am able	**Mt 26:61**	3004
high priest stood up and **s** to Him,	**Mt 26:62**	3004
And the high priest **s** to Him,	**Mt 26:63**	3004
Jesus **s** to him, "You have said it	**Mt 26:64**	3004
"You have **s** it *yourself;*	**Mt 26:64**	3004
the high priest tore his robes and **s**,	**Mt 26:65**	3004
and **s**, "Prophesy to us, You Christ;	**Mt 26:68**	3004
servant-girl came to him and **s**,	**Mt 26:69**	3004
him and **s** to those who were there,	**Mt 26:71**	3004
bystanders came up and **s** to Peter,	**Mt 26:73**	3004
the word which Jesus had **s**,	**Mt 26:75**	3004
But they **s**, "What is that to us?	**Mt 27:4**	3004
took the pieces of silver and **s**,	**Mt 27:6**	3004
And Jesus **s** to him,	**Mt 27:11**	5346
Then Pilate **s** to Him,	**Mt 27:13**	3004
together, Pilate **s** to them,	**Mt 27:17**	3004
governor **s** to them,	**Mt 27:21**	3004
And they **s**, "Barabbas."	**Mt 27:21**	3004
Pilate **s** to them,	**Mt 27:22**	3004
They all **s**, "Crucify Him!"	**Mt 27:22**	3004
he **s**, "Why, what evil has He done?"	**Mt 27:23**	5346
And all the people **s**,	**Mt 27:25**	3004
for He **s**, 'I am the Son of God.' "	**Mt 27:43**	3004
But the rest *of them* **s**,	**Mt 27:49**	3004
became very frightened and **s**,	**Mt 27:54**	3004
and **s**, "Sir, we remember that when	**Mt 27:63**	3004
was still alive that deceiver **s**,	**Mt 27:63**	3004
Pilate **s** to them,	**Mt 27:65**	5346
angel **s** to the women,	**Mt 28:5**	3004
for He has risen, just as He **s**.	**Mt 28:6**	3004
Then Jesus **s** to them,	**Mt 28:10**	3004
and **s**, "You are to say, 'His disciples	**Mt 28:13**	3004
And Jesus **s** to them,	**Mk 1:17**	3004
they found Him, and **s** to Him,	**Mk 1:37**	3004
He **s** to them,	**Mk 1:38**	3004
and touched him, and **s** to him,	**Mk 1:41**	3004
and He **s** to him,	**Mk 1:44**	3004
And Jesus seeing their faith **s** to the	**Mk 2:5**	3004
way within themselves, **s** to them,	**Mk 2:8**	3004
He **s** to the paralytic	**Mk 2:10**	3004
the tax booth, and He **s** to him,	**Mk 2:14**	3004
they **s** to His disciples, "Why is He	**Mk 2:16**	3004
And hearing *this,* Jesus **s** to them,	**Mk 2:17**	3004
and they came and **s** to Him,	**Mk 2:18**	3004
And Jesus **s** to them,	**Mk 2:19**	3004
And He **s** to them,	**Mk 2:25**	3004
Jesus **s** to them, "The Sabbath was	**Mk 2:27**	3004

He **s** to the man with the	Mk 3:3	3004
And He **s** to them,	Mk 3:4	3004
of heart, He **s** to the man,	Mk 3:5	3004
around Him, and they **s** to Him,	Mk 3:32	3004
Answering them, He **s**,	Mk 3:33	3004
who were sitting around Him, He **s**,	Mk 3:34	3004
And He **s** to them,	Mk 4:13	3004
And He **s**, "How shall we picture	Mk 4:30	3004
evening came, He **s** to them,	Mk 4:35	3004
and they woke Him and **s** to Him,	Mk 4:38	3004
rebuked the wind and **s** to the sea,	Mk 4:39	3004
And He **s** to them,	Mk 4:40	3004
much afraid and **s** to one another,	Mk 4:41	3004
shouting with a loud voice, he **s**,	Mk 5:7	3004
And he **s** to Him,	Mk 5:9	3004
did not let him, but He **s** to him,	Mk 5:19	3004
turned around in the crowd and **s**,	Mk 5:30	3004
And His disciples **s** to Him,	Mk 5:31	3004
And He **s** to her,	Mk 5:34	3004
s to the synagogue official,	Mk 5:36	3004
And entering in, He **s** to them,	Mk 5:39	3004
child by the hand, He **s** to her,	Mk 5:41	3004
and He **s** that *something* should be	Mk 5:43	3004
Jesus **s** to them,	Mk 6:4	3004
And He **s** to them,	Mk 6:10	3004
and the king **s** to the girl,	Mk 6:22	3004
she went out and **s** to her mother,	Mk 6:24	3004
she **s**, "The head of John the Baptist.	Mk 6:24	3004
And He **s** to them,	Mk 6:31	3004
His disciples came to Him and **s**,	Mk 6:35	3004
And they **s** to Him,	Mk 6:37	3004
And He **s** to them,	Mk 6:38	3004
And when they found out, they **s**,	Mk 6:38	3004
He spoke with them and **s** to them,	Mk 6:50	3004
And He **s** to them,	Mk 7:6	3004
"For Moses **s**, 'HONOR YOUR FATHER	Mk 7:10	3004
And He **s** to them,	Mk 7:18	3004
But she answered and **s** to Him,	Mk 7:28	3004
And He **s** to her,	Mk 7:29	3004
with a deep sigh, He **s** to him,	Mk 7:34	3004
His disciples and **s** to them,	Mk 8:1	3004
And they **s**, "Seven."	Mk 8:5	3004
Sighing deeply in His spirit, He **s**,	Mk 8:12	3004
Jesus, aware of this, **s** to them,	Mk 8:17	3004
They **s** to Him, "Twelve."	Mk 8:19	3004
And they **s** to Him,	Mk 8:20	3004
And he looked up and **s**,	Mk 8:24	3004
Peter answered and **s** to Him,	Mk 8:29	3004
He rebuked Peter and **s**,	Mk 8:33	3004
with His disciples, and **s** to them,	Mk 8:34	3004
Peter **s** to Jesus,	Mk 9:5	3004
And He **s** to them,	Mk 9:12	5346
And He answered them and **s**,	Mk 9:19	3004
And he **s**, "From childhood.	Mk 9:21	3004
And Jesus **s** to him,	Mk 9:23	3004
the boy's father cried out and **s**,	Mk 9:24	3004
like a corpse that most *of them* **s**,	Mk 9:26	3004
And He **s** to them,	Mk 9:29	3004
called the twelve and **s** to them,	Mk 9:35	3004
him in His arms, He **s** to them,	Mk 9:36	3004
John **s** to Him, "Teacher, we saw	Mk 9:38	5346
But Jesus **s**, "Do not hinder him,	Mk 9:39	3004
And He answered and **s** to them,	Mk 10:3	3004
They **s**, "Moses permitted *a man*	Mk 10:4	3004
But Jesus **s** to them,	Mk 10:5	3004
And He **s** to them,	Mk 10:11	3004
He was indignant and **s** to them,	Mk 10:14	3004
And Jesus **s** to him,	Mk 10:18	3004
And he **s** to Him,	Mk 10:20	5346
felt a love for him and **s** to him,	Mk 10:21	3004
And Jesus, looking around, **s** to His	Mk 10:23	3004
Jesus answered again and **s** to them,	Mk 10:24	3004
even more astonished and **s** to Him,	Mk 10:26	3004
Looking at them, Jesus **s**,	Mk 10:27	3004
Jesus **s**, "Truly I say to you, there is	Mk 10:29	5346
And He **s** to them,	Mk 10:36	3004
They **s** to Him,	Mk 10:37	3004
But Jesus **s** to them,	Mk 10:38	3004
They **s** to Him,	Mk 10:39	3004
And Jesus **s** to them,	Mk 10:39	3004
them to Himself, Jesus **s** to them,	Mk 10:42	3004
And Jesus stopped and **s**,	Mk 10:49	3004
And answering him, Jesus **s**,	Mk 10:51	3004
And the blind man **s** to Him,	Mk 10:51	3004
And Jesus **s** to him,	Mk 10:52	3004
and **s** to them, "Go into the village	Mk 11:2	3004
He **s** to it,	Mk 11:14	3004
Being reminded, Peter **s** to Him,	Mk 11:21	3004
And Jesus **s** to them,	Mk 11:29	3004
Answering Jesus, they **s**,	Mk 11:33	3004
And Jesus **s** to them,	Mk 11:33	3004
vine-growers **s** to one another,	Mk 12:7	3004
They came and **s** to Him,	Mk 12:14	3004
He, knowing their hypocrisy, **s** to	Mk 12:15	3004
And He **s** to them,	Mk 12:16	3004
And they **s** to Him,	Mk 12:16	3004
And Jesus **s** to them,	Mk 12:17	3004
Jesus **s** to them,	Mk 12:24	5346
The scribe **s** to Him,	Mk 12:32	3004
intelligently, He **s** to him,	Mk 12:34	3004
"David himself **s** in the Holy Spirit,	Mk 12:36	3004
'THE LORD **S** TO MY LORD,	Mk 12:36	3004
disciples to Him, He **s** to them,	Mk 12:43	3004
one of His disciples **s** to Him,	Mk 13:1	3004
And Jesus **s** to him,	Mk 13:2	3004
But Jesus **s**, "Let her alone;	Mk 14:6	3004
His disciples **s** to Him,	Mk 14:12	3004
of His disciples and **s** to them,	Mk 14:13	3004
at the table and eating, Jesus **s**,	Mk 14:18	3004
And He **s** to them,	Mk 14:20	3004
and gave *it* to them, and **s**,	Mk 14:22	3004
And He **s** to them,	Mk 14:24	3004
And Jesus **s** to them,	Mk 14:27	3004
But Peter **s** to Him,	Mk 14:29	5346
And Jesus **s** to him,	Mk 14:30	3004
and He **s** to His disciples,	Mk 14:32	3004
And He **s** to them,	Mk 14:34	3004
them sleeping, and **s** to Peter,	Mk 14:37	3004
the third time, and **s** to them,	Mk 14:41	3004
And Jesus **s** to them,	Mk 14:48	3004
And Jesus **s**, "I am; and you shall	Mk 14:62	3004
Tearing his clothes, the high priest **s**,	Mk 14:63	3004
himself, she looked at him and **s**,	Mk 14:67	3004
Answering again, Pilate **s** to them,	Mk 15:12	3004
But Pilate **s** to them, "Why, what	Mk 15:14	3004
way He breathed His last, he **s**,	Mk 15:39	3004
And he **s** to them,	Mk 16:6	3004
and they **s** nothing to anyone, for	Mk 16:8	3004
And He **s** to them,	Mk 16:15	3004
But the angel **s** to him,	Lk 1:13	3004
Zacharias **s** to the angel,	Lk 1:18	3004
The angel answered and **s** to him,	Lk 1:19	3004
And coming in, he **s** to her,	Lk 1:28	3004
The angel **s** to her,	Lk 1:30	3004
Mary **s** to the angel,	Lk 1:34	3004
The angel answered and **s** to her,	Lk 1:35	3004
And Mary **s**, "Behold, the bondslave	Lk 1:38	3004
out with a loud voice and **s**,	Lk 1:42	3004
Mary **s**: "My soul exalts the Lord,	Lk 1:46	3004
But his mother answered and **s**,	Lk 1:60	3004
And they **s** to her,	Lk 1:61	3004
But the angel **s** to them,	Lk 2:10	3004
what was **s** in the Law of the Lord,	Lk 2:24	3004
his arms, and blessed God, and **s**,	Lk 2:28	3004
which were being **s** about Him.	Lk 2:33	2980
them and **s** to Mary His mother,	Lk 2:34	3004
and His mother **s** to Him,	Lk 2:48	3004
And He **s** to them,	Lk 2:49	3004
to be baptized, and they **s** to him,	Lk 3:12	3004
And he **s** to them,	Lk 3:13	3004
And he **s** to them,	Lk 3:14	3004
John answered and **s** to them all,	Lk 3:16	3004
And the devil **s** to Him,	Lk 4:3	3004
And the devil **s** to Him,	Lk 4:6	3004
of the temple, and **s** to Him,	Lk 4:9	3004
And Jesus answered and **s** to him,	Lk 4:12	3004
"It is **s**, 'YOU SHALL NOT PUT THE	Lk 4:12	3004
And He **s** to them,	Lk 4:23	3004
And He **s**, "Truly I say to you, no	Lk 4:24	3004
But He **s** to them,	Lk 4:43	3004
finished speaking, He **s** to Simon,	Lk 5:4	3004
Simon answered and **s**,	Lk 5:5	3004
And Jesus **s** to Simon,	Lk 5:10	3004
Seeing their faith, He **s**,	Lk 5:20	3004
answered and **s** to them,	Lk 5:22	3004
He **s** to the paralytic	Lk 5:24	3004
the tax booth, and He **s** to him,	Lk 5:27	3004
And Jesus answered and **s** to them,	Lk 5:31	3004
And they **s** to Him,	Lk 5:33	3004
And Jesus **s** to them,	Lk 5:34	3004
But some of the Pharisees **s**,	Lk 6:2	3004
And Jesus answering them **s**,	Lk 6:3	3004
and He **s** to the man with the	Lk 6:8	3004
And Jesus **s** to them,	Lk 6:9	3004
around at them all, He **s** to him,	Lk 6:10	3004
and turned and **s** to the crowd	Lk 7:9	3004
compassion for her, and **s** to her,	Lk 7:13	3004
And He **s**, "Young man, I say to you	Lk 7:14	3004
the men came to Him, they **s**,	Lk 7:20	3004
And He answered and **s** to them,	Lk 7:22	3004
Him saw this, he **s** to himself,	Lk 7:39	3004
Simon answered and **s**,	Lk 7:43	3004
And He **s** to him,	Lk 7:43	3004
toward the woman, He **s** to Simon,	Lk 7:44	5346
Then He **s** to her,	Lk 7:48	3004
And He **s** to the woman,	Lk 7:50	3004
As He **s** these things, He would	Lk 8:8	3004
He **s**, "To you it has been granted	Lk 8:10	3004
But He answered and **s** to them,	Lk 8:21	3004
got into a boat, and He **s** to them,	Lk 8:22	3004
And He **s** to them,	Lk 8:25	3004
before Him, and **s** in a loud voice,	Lk 8:28	3004
And he **s**, "Legion";	Lk 8:30	3004
And Jesus **s**, "Who is the one who	Lk 8:45	3004
they were all denying it, Peter **s**,	Lk 8:45	3004
But Jesus **s**, "Someone did touch Me	Lk 8:46	3004
And He **s** to her,	Lk 8:48	3004
He **s**, "Stop weeping, for she has not	Lk 8:52	3004
And He **s** to them,	Lk 9:3	3004
because it was **s** by some that John	Lk 9:7	3004
Herod **s**, "I myself had John	Lk 9:9	3004
and the twelve came and **s** to Him,	Lk 9:12	3004
But He **s** to them,	Lk 9:13	3004
And they **s**, "We have no more than	Lk 9:13	3004
And He **s** to His disciples,	Lk 9:14	3004
They answered and **s**,	Lk 9:19	3004
And He **s** to them,	Lk 9:20	3004
And Peter answered and **s**,	Lk 9:20	3004
leaving Him, Peter **s** to Jesus,	Lk 9:33	3004
And Jesus answered and **s**,	Lk 9:41	3004
was doing, He **s** to His disciples,	Lk 9:43	3004
and **s** to them, "Whoever receives	Lk 9:48	3004
John answered and **s**,	Lk 9:49	3004
But Jesus **s** to him,	Lk 9:50	3004
James and John saw *this,* they **s**,	Lk 9:54	3004
He turned and rebuked them, [and **s**,	Lk 9:55	3004
along the road, someone **s** to Him,	Lk 9:57	3004
And Jesus **s** to him,	Lk 9:58	3004
And He **s** to another,	Lk 9:59	3004
But he **s**, "Lord, permit me first to go	Lk 9:59	3004
But He **s** to him,	Lk 9:60	3004
Another also **s**,	Lk 9:61	3004
But Jesus **s** to him,	Lk 9:62	3004
And He **s** to them,	Lk 10:18	3004
greatly in the Holy Spirit, and **s**,	Lk 10:21	3004
to the disciples, He **s** privately,	Lk 10:23	3004
And He **s** to him,	Lk 10:26	3004
And He **s** to him,	Lk 10:28	3004
to justify himself, he **s** to Jesus,	Lk 10:29	3004
Jesus replied and **s**,	Lk 10:30	3004
gave them to the innkeeper and **s**,	Lk 10:35	3004
he **s**, "The one who showed mercy	Lk 10:37	3004
Then Jesus **s** to him,	Lk 10:37	3004
and she came up *to Him* and **s**,	Lk 10:40	3004
the Lord answered and **s** to her,	Lk 10:41	3004
one of His disciples **s** to Him,	Lk 11:1	3004
And He **s** to them,	Lk 11:2	3004
Then He **s** to them,	Lk 11:5	3004
But some of them **s**,	Lk 11:15	3004
their thoughts and **s** to them,	Lk 11:17	3004
raised her voice and **s** to Him,	Lk 11:27	3004
But He **s**, "On the contrary, blessed	Lk 11:28	3004
But the Lord **s** to him,	Lk 11:39	3004
of the lawyers **s** to Him in reply,	Lk 11:45	3004
He **s**, "Woe to you lawyers as well!	Lk 11:46	3004
reason also the wisdom of God **s**,	Lk 11:49	3004
whatever you have **s** in the dark	Lk 12:3	3004
Someone in the crowd **s** to Him,	Lk 12:13	3004
But He **s** to him,	Lk 12:14	3004
Then He **s** to them,	Lk 12:15	3004
"Then he **s**, 'This is what I will do:	Lk 12:18	3004
"But God **s** to him,	Lk 12:20	3004
And He **s** to His disciples,	Lk 12:22	3004
Peter **s**, "Lord, are You addressing	Lk 12:41	3004
Lord **s**, "Who then is the faithful	Lk 12:42	3004
And Jesus **s** to them,	Lk 13:2	3004
"And he **s** to the vineyard-keeper,	Lk 13:7	3004
"And he answered and **s** to him,	Lk 13:8	3004
He called her over and **s** to her,	Lk 13:12	3004
But the Lord answered him and **s**,	Lk 13:15	3004
As He **s** this, all His	Lk 13:17	3004
He **s**, "To what shall I compare the	Lk 13:20	3004
And someone **s** to Him,	Lk 13:23	3004
And He **s** to them,	Lk 13:23	3004
And He **s** to them,	Lk 13:32	3004
And He **s** to them,	Lk 14:5	3004
with Him heard this, he **s** to Him,	Lk 14:15	3004
But He **s** to him,	Lk 14:16	3004
"The first one **s** to him,	Lk 14:18	3004
"Another one **s**,	Lk 14:19	3004
"Another one **s**,	Lk 14:20	3004
became angry and **s** to his slave,	Lk 14:21	3004
"And the slave **s**,	Lk 14:22	3004
"And the master **s** to the slave,	Lk 14:23	3004
and He turned and **s** to them,	Lk 14:25	3004
He **s**, "A man had two sons	Lk 15:11	3004
younger of them **s** to his father,	Lk 15:12	3004
when he came to his senses, he **s**,	Lk 15:17	5346
"And the son **s** to him,	Lk 15:21	3004
"But the father **s** to his slaves,	Lk 15:22	3004
"And he **s** to him,	Lk 15:27	3004
he answered and **s** to his father,	Lk 15:29	3004
"And he **s** to him,	Lk 15:31	3004
"And he called him and **s** to him,	Lk 16:2	3004
"The manager **s** to himself,	Lk 16:3	3004
he **s**, 'A hundred measures of oil.'	Lk 16:6	3004
And he **s** to him,	Lk 16:6	3004
"Then he **s** to another,	Lk 16:7	3004
how much do you owe?' And he **s**,	Lk 16:7	3004
He **s** to him, 'Take your bill,	Lk 16:7	3004
And He **s** to them,	Lk 16:15	3004
"And he cried out and **s**,	Lk 16:24	3004
"But Abraham **s**,	Lk 16:25	3004
"And he **s**, 'Then I beg you, father,	Lk 16:27	3004
"But Abraham **s**,	Lk 16:29	3004
"But he **s**, 'No, father Abraham,	Lk 16:30	3004
"But he **s** to him,	Lk 16:31	3004
He **s** to His disciples,	Lk 17:1	3004
The apostles **s** to the Lord,	Lk 17:5	3004
And the Lord **s**, "If you had faith	Lk 17:6	3004
When He saw them, He **s** to them,	Lk 17:14	3004
Then Jesus answered and **s**,	Lk 17:17	3004
And He **s** to him,	Lk 17:19	3004
coming, He answered them and **s**,	Lk 17:20	3004
And He **s** to the disciples,	Lk 17:22	3004
And answering they **s** to Him,	Lk 17:37	3004
And He **s** to them,	Lk 17:37	3004
but afterward he **s** to himself,	Lk 18:4	3004
Lord **s**, "Hear what the unrighteous	Lk 18:6	3004
"Hear what the unrighteous judge **s**;	Lk 18:6	3004
And Jesus **s** to him,	Lk 18:19	3004
he **s**, "All these things I have kept	Lk 18:21	3004
Jesus heard *this,* He **s** to him,	Lk 18:22	3004
And Jesus looked at him and **s**,	Lk 18:24	3004
They who heard it **s**,	Lk 18:26	3004
He **s**, "The things that are impossible	Lk 18:27	3004
Peter **s**, "Behold, we have left	Lk 18:28	3004
And He **s** to them,	Lk 18:29	3004
the twelve aside and **s** to them,	Lk 18:31	3004
comprehend the things that were **s**.	Lk 18:34	3004
And he **s**, "Lord, *I want* to regain	Lk 18:41	3004
And Jesus **s** to him,	Lk 18:42	3004
place, He looked up and **s** to him,	Lk 19:5	3004
Zaccheus stopped and **s** to the Lord,	Lk 19:8	3004
And Jesus **s** to him,	Lk 19:9	3004
So He **s**, "A nobleman	Lk 19:12	3004
them ten minas and **s** to them,	Lk 19:13	3004

"And he **s** to him,	Lk 19:17	3004
"And he **s** to him also,	Lk 19:19	3004
"He **s** to him, 'By your own words I	Lk 19:22	3004
"Then he **s** to the bystanders,	Lk 19:24	3004
"And they **s** to him,	Lk 19:25	3004
After He had **s** these things,	Lk 19:28	3004
the colt, its owners **s** to them,	Lk 19:33	3004
They **s**, "The Lord has need of it."	Lk 19:34	3004
in the crowd **s** to Him,	Lk 19:39	3004
were hanging on to every word He **s**.	Lk 19:48	
Jesus answered and **s** to them,	Lk 20:3	3004
And Jesus **s** to them,	Lk 20:8	3004
"The owner of the vineyard **s**,	Lk 20:13	3004
When they heard it, they **s**,	Lk 20:16	3004
But Jesus looked at them and **s**,	Lk 20:17	3004
their trickery and **s** to them,	Lk 20:23	3004
They **s**, "Caesar's."	Lk 20:24	3004
And He **s** to them,	Lk 20:25	3004
Jesus **s** to them,	Lk 20:34	3004
Some of the scribes answered and **s**,	Lk 20:39	3004
Then He **s** to them,	Lk 20:41	3004
'THE LORD **S** TO MY LORD,	Lk 20:42	3004
listening, He **s** to the disciples,	Lk 20:45	3004
And He **s**, "Truly I say to you,	Lk 21:3	3004
stones and votive gifts, He **s**,	Lk 21:5	3004
And He **s**, "See to it that you are not	Lk 21:8	3004
They **s** to Him,	Lk 22:9	3004
And He **s** to them,	Lk 22:10	3004
And He **s** to them,	Lk 22:15	3004
a cup *and* given thanks, He **s**,	Lk 22:17	3004
And He **s** to them,	Lk 22:25	3004
But he **s** to Him,	Lk 22:33	3004
And He **s**, "I say to you, Peter,	Lk 22:34	3004
And He **s** to them,	Lk 22:35	3004
They **s**, "*No,* nothing."	Lk 22:35	3004
And He **s** to them,	Lk 22:36	3004
s, "Lord, look, here are two swords."	Lk 22:38	3004
And He **s** to them,	Lk 22:38	3004
at the place, He **s** to them,	Lk 22:40	3004
s to them, "Why are you sleeping?	Lk 22:46	3004
But Jesus **s** to him,	Lk 22:48	3004
what was going to happen, they **s**,	Lk 22:49	3004
But Jesus answered and **s**,	Lk 22:51	3004
Then Jesus **s** to the chief priests	Lk 22:52	3004
and looking intently at him, **s**,	Lk 22:56	3004
later, another saw him and **s**,	Lk 22:58	5346
But Peter **s**, "Man, I am not!"	Lk 22:58	5346
Peter **s**, "Man, I do not know what	Lk 22:60	3004
But He **s** to them,	Lk 22:67	3004
they all **s**, "Are You the Son of God,	Lk 22:70	3004
And He **s** to them,	Lk 22:70	5346
Then they **s**, "What further need do	Lk 22:71	3004
And He answered him and **s**,	Lk 23:3	5346
Then Pilate **s** to the chief priests	Lk 23:4	3004
and **s** to them, "You brought this	Lk 23:14	3004
And he **s** to them the third time,	Lk 23:22	3004
But Jesus turning to them **s**,	Lk 23:28	3004
answered, and rebuking him **s**,	Lk 23:40	5346
And He **s** to him,	Lk 23:43	3004
crying out with a loud voice, **s**,	Lk 23:46	3004
Having **s** this, He breathed His	Lk 23:46	3004
to the ground, *the men* **s** to them,	Lk 24:5	3004
And He **s** to them,	Lk 24:17	3004
Cleopas, answered and **s** to Him,	Lk 24:18	3004
And He **s** to them,	Lk 24:19	3004
And they **s** to Him,	Lk 24:19	3004
angels who **s** that He was alive.	Lk 24:23	3004
exactly as the women also had **s**;	Lk 24:24	3004
And He **s** to them,	Lk 24:25	3004
They **s** to one another,	Lk 24:32	3004
stood in their midst and **s**	Lk 24:36	3004
And He **s** to them,	Lk 24:38	3004
And when He had **s** this, He showed	Lk 24:40	3004
and amazement, He **s** to them,	Lk 24:41	3004
Now He **s** to them,	Lk 24:44	3004
and He **s** to them,	Lk 24:46	3004
"This was He of whom I **s**,	Jn 1:15	3004
Are you Elijah?" And he **s**,	Jn 1:21	3004
Then they **s** to him,	Jn 1:22	3004
He **s**, "I am A VOICE OF ONE CRYING	Jn 1:23	5346
LORD,' as Isaiah the prophet **s**."	Jn 1:23	3004
They asked him, and **s** to him,	Jn 1:25	3004
he saw Jesus coming to him and **s**,	Jn 1:29	3004
"This is He on behalf of whom I **s**,	Jn 1:30	3004
me to baptize in water **s** to me,	Jn 1:33	3004
at Jesus as He walked, and **s**,	Jn 1:36	3004
them following, and **s** to them,	Jn 1:38	3004
They **s** to Him,	Jn 1:38	3004
He **s** to them, "Come, and you will	Jn 1:39	3004
own brother Simon and **s** to him,	Jn 1:41	3004
Jesus looked at him and **s**,	Jn 1:42	3004
And Jesus **s** to him,	Jn 1:43	3004
found Nathanael and **s** to him,	Jn 1:45	3004
Nathanael **s** to him,	Jn 1:46	3004
Philip **s** to him,	Jn 1:46	3004
coming to Him, and **s** of him,	Jn 1:47	3004
Nathanael **s** to Him,	Jn 1:48	3004
Jesus answered and **s** to him,	Jn 1:48	3004
Jesus answered and **s** to him,	Jn 1:50	3004
"Because I **s** to you that I saw	Jn 1:50	3004
And He **s** to him,	Jn 1:51	3004
out, the mother of Jesus **s** to Him,	Jn 2:3	3004
And Jesus **s** to her,	Jn 2:4	3004
His mother **s** to the servants,	Jn 2:5	3004
Jesus **s** to them,	Jn 2:7	3004
And He **s** to them,	Jn 2:8	3004
and **s** to him, "Every man serves	Jn 2:10	3004
who were selling the doves He **s**,	Jn 2:16	3004
The Jews then **s** to Him,	Jn 2:18	3004
The Jews then **s**,	Jn 2:20	3004
remembered that He **s** this;	Jn 2:22	3004
to Jesus by night and **s** to Him,	Jn 3:2	3004
Jesus answered and **s** to him,	Jn 3:3	3004
Nicodemus **s** to Him,	Jn 3:4	3004
"Do not be amazed that I **s** to you,	Jn 3:7	3004
Nicodemus **s** to Him,	Jn 3:9	3004
Jesus answered and **s** to him,	Jn 3:10	3004
they came to John and **s** to him,	Jn 3:26	3004
John answered and **s**,	Jn 3:27	3004
are my witnesses that I **s**,	Jn 3:28	3004
Jesus **s** to her, "Give Me a drink."	Jn 4:7	3004
woman **s** to Him,	Jn 4:9	3004
Jesus answered and **s** to her,	Jn 4:10	3004
She **s** to Him, "Sir, You have	Jn 4:11	3004
Jesus answered and **s** to her,	Jn 4:13	3004
The woman **s** to Him,	Jn 4:15	3004
He **s** to her, "Go, call your husband and	Jn 4:16	3004
The woman answered and **s**,	Jn 4:17	3004
"I have no husband." Jesus **s** to her,	Jn 4:17	3004
"You have correctly **s**,	Jn 4:17	3004
this you have **s** truly."	Jn 4:18	3004
The woman **s** to Him,	Jn 4:19	3004
Jesus **s** to her, "Woman, believe Me,	Jn 4:21	3004
The woman **s** to Him,	Jn 4:25	3004
Jesus **s** to her, "I who speak to you	Jn 4:26	3004
yet no one **s**, "What do You seek?"	Jn 4:27	3004
into the city and **s** to the men,	Jn 4:28	3004
But He **s** to them,	Jn 4:32	3004
Jesus **s** to them,	Jn 4:34	3004
of what you **s** that we believe,	Jn 4:42	2981
Jesus **s** to him,	Jn 4:48	3004
The royal official **s** to Him,	Jn 4:49	3004
Jesus **s** to him, "Go;	Jn 4:50	3004
Then they **s** to him,	Jn 4:52	3004
that hour in which Jesus **s** to him,	Jn 4:53	3004
in that condition, He **s** to him,	Jn 5:6	3004
Jesus **s** to him, "Get	Jn 5:8	3004
me well was the one who **s** to me,	Jn 5:11	3004
"Who is the man who **s** to you,	Jn 5:12	3004
him in the temple and **s** to him,	Jn 5:14	3004
was coming to Him, **s** to Philip,	Jn 6:5	3004
Simon Peter's brother, **s** to Him,	Jn 6:8	3004
Jesus **s**, "Have the people sit down."	Jn 6:10	3004
filled, He **s** to His disciples,	Jn 6:12	3004
which He had performed, they **s**,	Jn 6:14	3004
But He **s** to them,	Jn 6:20	3004
side of the sea, they **s** to Him,	Jn 6:25	3004
Jesus answered them and **s**,	Jn 6:26	3004
Therefore they **s** to Him,	Jn 6:28	3004
Jesus answered and **s** to them,	Jn 6:29	3004
So they **s** to Him,	Jn 6:30	3004
Jesus then **s** to them,	Jn 6:32	3004
Then they **s** to Him,	Jn 6:34	3004
Jesus **s** to them,	Jn 6:35	3004
"But I **s** to you that you have	Jn 6:36	3004
grumbling about Him, because He **s**,	Jn 6:41	3004
Jesus answered and **s** to them,	Jn 6:43	3004
Jesus **s** to them,	Jn 6:53	3004
things He **s** in the synagogue as	Jn 6:59	3004
disciples, when they heard *this* **s**,	Jn 6:60	3004
grumbled at this, **s** to them,	Jn 6:61	3004
"For this reason I have **s** to you,	Jn 6:65	3004
Jesus **s** to the twelve,	Jn 6:67	3004
His brothers **s** to Him,	Jn 7:3	3004
Jesus **s** to them,	Jn 7:6	3004
Having **s** these things to them,	Jn 7:9	3004
So Jesus answered them and **s**,	Jn 7:16	3004
Jesus **s**,	Jn 7:33	3004
Jews then **s** to one another,	Jn 7:35	3004
"What is this statement that He **s**,	Jn 7:36	3004
in Me, as the Scripture **s**,	Jn 7:38	3004
"Has not the Scripture **s** that the	Jn 7:42	3004
and Pharisees, and they **s** to them,	Jn 7:45	3004
s to them	Jn 7:50	3004
they **s** to Him, "Teacher, this woman	Jn 8:4	3004
He straightened up, and **s** to them,	Jn 8:7	3004
Straightening up, Jesus **s** to her,	Jn 8:10	3004
She **s**, "No one, Lord."	Jn 8:11	3004
Jesus **s**, "I do not condemn you,	Jn 8:11	3004
So the Pharisees **s** to Him,	Jn 8:13	3004
Jesus answered and **s** to them,	Jn 8:14	3004
He **s** again to them,	Jn 8:21	3004
"Therefore I **s** to you that you	Jn 8:24	3004
Jesus **s** to them,	Jn 8:25	3004
Jesus **s**,	Jn 8:28	3004
They answered and **s** to Him,	Jn 8:39	3004
Jesus **s** to them,	Jn 8:39	3004
They **s** to Him, "We were not born	Jn 8:41	3004
Jesus **s** to them,	Jn 8:42	3004
The Jews answered and **s** to Him,	Jn 8:48	3004
The Jews **s** to Him,	Jn 8:52	3004
So the Jews **s** to Him,	Jn 8:57	3004
Jesus **s** to them,	Jn 8:58	3004
When He had **s** this, He spat on the	Jn 9:6	3004
and **s** to him, "Go, wash in the pool	Jn 9:7	3004
and anointed my eyes, and **s** to me,	Jn 9:11	3004
They **s** to him,	Jn 9:12	3004
He **s**, "I do not know."	Jn 9:12	3004
And he **s** to them,	Jn 9:15	3004
So they **s** to the blind man	Jn 9:17	3004
And he **s**, "He is a prophet."	Jn 9:17	3004
His parents answered them and **s**,	Jn 9:20	3004
His parents **s** this because they	Jn 9:22	3004
For this reason his parents **s**,	Jn 9:23	3004
who had been blind, and **s** to him,	Jn 9:24	3004
So they **s** to him,	Jn 9:26	3004
They reviled him and **s**,	Jn 9:28	3004
The man answered and **s** to them,	Jn 9:30	3004
and finding him, He **s**,	Jn 9:35	3004
Jesus **s** to him, "You have both seen	Jn 9:37	3004
And he **s**, "Lord, I believe."	Jn 9:38	5346
And Jesus **s**, "For judgment I came	Jn 9:39	3004
heard these things and **s** to Him,	Jn 9:40	3004
Jesus **s** to them,	Jn 9:41	3004
Jesus **s** to them again,	Jn 10:7	3004
'I **S**, YOU ARE GODS'?	Jn 10:34	3004
'You are blaspheming,' because I **s**,	Jn 10:36	3004
everything John **s** about this	Jn 10:41	3004
But when Jesus heard *this,* He **s**,	Jn 11:4	3004
after this He **s** to the disciples,	Jn 11:7	3004
The disciples **s** to Him,	Jn 11:8	3004
This He **s**, and after that He said	Jn 11:11	3004
said, and after that He **s** to them,	Jn 11:11	3004
The disciples then **s** to Him,	Jn 11:12	3004
Jesus then **s** to them plainly,	Jn 11:14	3004
s to *his* fellow disciples,	Jn 11:16	3004
Martha then **s** to Jesus,	Jn 11:21	3004
Jesus **s** to her, "Your brother will	Jn 11:23	3004
Martha **s** to Him,	Jn 11:24	3004
Jesus **s** to her, "I am the resurrection	Jn 11:25	3004
She **s** to Him, "Yes, Lord;	Jn 11:27	3004
When she had **s** this,	Jn 11:28	3004
and **s**, "Where have you laid him?"	Jn 11:34	3004
They **s** to Him, "Lord, come and see	Jn 11:34	3004
But some of them **s**,	Jn 11:37	3004
Jesus **s**, "Remove the stone."	Jn 11:39	3004
sister of the deceased, **s** to Him,	Jn 11:39	3004
Jesus **s** to her, "Did I not say to you that	Jn 11:40	3004
Then Jesus raised His eyes, and **s**,	Jn 11:41	3004
the people standing around I **s** it,	Jn 11:42	3004
When He had **s** these things, He	Jn 11:43	3004
Jesus **s** to them,	Jn 11:44	3004
high priest that year, **s** to them,	Jn 11:49	3004
was intending to betray Him, **s**,	Jn 12:4	3004
Now he **s** this, not because he was	Jn 12:6	3004
Jesus **s**,	Jn 12:7	3004
Pharisees **s** to one another,	Jn 12:19	3004
Jesus answered and **s**,	Jn 12:30	3004
Jesus **s** to them,	Jn 12:35	3004
not believe, for Isaiah **s** again,	Jn 12:39	3004
These things Isaiah **s** because	Jn 12:41	3004
And Jesus cried out and **s**,	Jn 12:44	3004
came to Simon Peter. He **s** to Him,	Jn 13:6	3004
Jesus answered and **s** to him,	Jn 13:7	3004
Peter **s** to Him, "Never shall You	Jn 13:8	3004
Simon Peter **s** to Him,	Jn 13:9	3004
Jesus **s** to him, "He who has bathed	Jn 13:10	3004
for this reason He **s**,	Jn 13:11	3004
at the table again, He **s** to them,	Jn 13:12	3004
When Jesus had **s** this, He became	Jn 13:21	3004
in spirit, and testified and **s**,	Jn 13:21	3004
gestured to him, and **s** to him,	Jn 13:24	3004
thus on Jesus' bosom, **s** to Him,	Jn 13:25	3004
Jesus **s** to him,	Jn 13:27	3004
what purpose He had **s** this to him.	Jn 13:28	3004
he had gone out, Jesus **s**,	Jn 13:31	3004
as I **s** to the Jews, now I also say	Jn 13:33	3004
Simon Peter **s** to Him,	Jn 13:36	3004
Peter **s** to Him, "Lord, why can I not	Jn 13:37	3004
Thomas **s** to Him,	Jn 14:5	3004
Jesus **s** to him, "I am the way,	Jn 14:6	3004
Philip **s** to Him,	Jn 14:8	3004
Jesus **s** to him, "Have I been so long	Jn 14:9	3004
s to Him, "Lord, what then has	Jn 14:22	3004
Jesus answered and **s** to him,	Jn 14:23	3004
remembrance all that I **s** to you.	Jn 14:26	3004
"You heard that I **s** to you,	Jn 14:28	3004
"Remember the word that I **s** to you,	Jn 15:20	3004
I have **s** these things to you,	Jn 16:6	2980
therefore I **s** that He takes of	Jn 16:15	3004
Some of His disciples then **s** to	Jn 16:17	3004
to question Him, and He **s** to them,	Jn 16:19	3004
together about this, that I **s**,	Jn 16:19	3004
His disciples **s**,	Jn 16:29	3004
up His eyes to heaven, He **s**,	Jn 17:1	3004
Him, went forth and **s** to them,	Jn 18:4	3004
He **s** to them, "I am *He.*"	Jn 18:5	3004
So when He **s** to them,	Jn 18:6	3004
"Whom do you seek?" And they **s**,	Jn 18:7	3004
Jesus **s** to Peter,	Jn 18:11	3004
who kept the door **s** to Peter,	Jn 18:17	3004
this man's disciples, are you?" He **s**,	Jn 18:17	3004
they know what I **s**."	Jn 18:21	3004
When He had **s** this, one of the	Jn 18:22	3004
So they **s** to him,	Jn 18:25	3004
He denied *it,* and **s**,	Jn 18:25	3004
one whose ear Peter cut off, **s**,	Jn 18:26	3004
Pilate went out to them and **s**,	Jn 18:29	5346
They answered and **s** to him,	Jn 18:30	3004
Pilate **s** to them,	Jn 18:31	3004
The Jews **s** to him,	Jn 18:31	3004
and summoned Jesus and **s** to Him,	Jn 18:33	3004
Pilate **s** to Him,	Jn 18:37	3004
Pilate **s** to Him,	Jn 18:38	3004
And when he had **s** this, he went	Jn 18:38	3004
again to the Jews and **s** to them,	Jn 18:38	3004
came out again and **s** to them,	Jn 19:4	3004
Pilate **s** to them,	Jn 19:5	3004
Pilate **s** to them,	Jn 19:6	3004
Praetorium again and **s** to Jesus,	Jn 19:9	3004
Pilate **s** to Him,	Jn 19:10	3004
And he **s** to the Jews,	Jn 19:14	3004
Pilate **s** to them,	Jn 19:15	3004
that He **s**, 'I am King of the Jews.	Jn 19:21	3004
So they **s** to one another,	Jn 19:24	3004
nearby, He **s** to His mother,	Jn 19:26	3004
Then He **s** to the disciple,	Jn 19:27	3004
s, "I am thirsty."	Jn 19:28	3004

had received the sour wine, He s, Jn 19:30 3004
whom Jesus loved, and s to them, Jn 20:2 3004
And they s to her, Jn 20:13 3004
why are you weeping?" She s to them, Jn 20:13 3004
When she had s this, she turned Jn 20:14 3004
Jesus s to her, "Woman, why are Jn 20:15 3004
to be the gardener, she s to Him, Jn 20:15 3004
Jesus s to her, "Mary!" She turned Jn 20:16 3004
She turned and s to Him in Hebrew, Jn 20:16 3004
Jesus s to her, "Stop clinging to Me, Jn 20:17 3004
that He had s these things to her. Jn 20:18 3004
in their midst and s to them, Jn 20:19 3004
And when He had s this, He showed Jn 20:20 3004
Jesus s to them again, Jn 20:21 3004
And when He had s this, He Jn 20:22 3004
breathed on them and s to them, Jn 20:22 3004
But he s to them, Jn 20:25 3004
and stood in their midst and s, Jn 20:26 3004
Then He s to Thomas, Jn 20:27 3004
Thomas answered and s to Him, Jn 20:28 3004
Jesus s to him, "Because you have Jn 20:29 3004
Simon Peter s to them, Jn 21:3 3004
"I am going fishing." They s to him, Jn 21:3 3004
Jesus s to them, Jn 21:5 3004
And He s to them, Jn 21:6 3004
whom Jesus loved s to Peter, Jn 21:7 3004
Jesus s to them, Jn 21:10 3004
Jesus s to them, Jn 21:12 3004
breakfast, Jesus s to Simon Peter, Jn 21:15 3004
He s to Him, "Yes, Lord; You know Jn 21:15 3004
He s to him, "Tend My lambs." Jn 21:15 3004
He s to him again a second time, Jn 21:16 3004
He s to Him, "Yes, Lord; Jn 21:16 3004
He s to him, "Shepherd My sheep. Jn 21:16 3004
He s to him the third time, Jn 21:17 3004
He s to him the third time, Jn 21:17 3004
And he s to Him, Jn 21:17 3004
Jesus s to him, "Tend My sheep. Jn 21:17 3004
Now this He s, signifying by what Jn 21:19 3004
He had spoken this, He s to him, Jn 21:19 3004
His bosom at the supper and s, Jn 21:20 3004
Peter seeing him s to Jesus, Jn 21:21 3004
Jesus s to him, "If I want him to Jn 21:22 3004
He s, "you heard of from Me; Ac 1:4
He s to them, "It is not for you to Ac 1:7 3004
And after He had s these things, Ac 1:9 3004
They also s, Ac 1:11 3004
persons was there together), and s, Ac 1:15 3004
And they prayed and s, Ac 1:24 3004
'THE LORD S TO MY LORD Ac 2:34 3004
and s to Peter and the rest of the Ac 2:37 3004
Peter s to them, "Repent, Ac 2:38
fixed his gaze on him and s, Ac 3:4 3004
But Peter s, "I do not possess silver Ac 3:6 3004
"Moses s, 'THE LORD GOD WILL Ac 3:22 3004
with the Holy Spirit, s to them, Ac 4:8 3004
and John answered and s to them, Ac 4:19 3004
and the elders had s to them. Ac 4:23 3004
to God with one accord and s, Ac 4:24 3004
s, 'WHY DID THE GENTILES RAGE, Ac 4:25 3004
Peter s, "Ananias, why has Satan Ac 5:3 3004
And she s, "Yes, that was the price. Ac 5:8 3004
Then Peter s to her, "Why is it Ac 5:9
prison, and taking them out he s, Ac 5:19 3004
And he s to them, Ac 5:35 3004
of the disciples and s, Ac 6:2 3004
put forward false witnesses who s, Ac 6:13 3004
The high priest s, Ac 7:1 3004
And he s, "Hear me, brethren Ac 7:2 5346
and s to him, 'LEAVE YOUR Ac 7:3 3004
I MYSELF WILL JUDGE,' s God, Ac 7:7 3004
"BUT THE LORD S TO HIM, Ac 7:33 3004
Moses who s to the sons of Israel, Ac 7:37 3004
and he s, "Behold, I see the heavens Ac 7:56 3004
as he called on *the Lord* and s, Ac 7:59 3004
Having s this, he fell asleep. Ac 7:60 3004
attention to what was s by Philip, Ac 8:6 3004
But Peter s to him, Ac 8:20 3004
But Simon answered and s, Ac 8:24 3004
nothing of what you have s may Ac 8:24 3004
Then the Spirit s to Philip, Ac 8:29 3004
reading Isaiah the prophet, and s, Ac 8:30 3004
And he s, "Well, how could I, Ac 8:31 3004
The eunuch answered Philip and s, Ac 8:34 3004
and the eunuch s, Ac 8:36 5346
And Philip s, "If you believe with all Ac 8:37 3004
And he answered and s, Ac 8:37 3004
And he s, "Who are You, Lord?" Ac 9:5 3004
And He s, "I am Jesus whom you Ac 9:5
and the Lord s to him in a vision, Ac 9:10 3004
And he s, "Here I am, Lord." Ac 9:10 3004
And the Lord s to him, "Get up Ac 9:11
But the Lord s to him, Ac 9:15 3004
after laying his hands on him s, Ac 9:17 3004
Peter s to him, Ac 9:34 3004
and turning to the body, he s, Ac 9:40 3004
just come in and s to him, Ac 10:3 3004
him and being much alarmed, he s, Ac 10:4 3004
And he s to him, Ac 10:4 3004
But Peter s, "By no means, Lord, Ac 10:14 3004
the vision, the Spirit s to him, Ac 10:19 3004
Peter went down to the men and s, Ac 10:21 3004
They s, "Cornelius, a centurion, Ac 10:22 3004
And he s to them, Ac 10:28 5346
Cornelius s, Ac 10:30 5346
and he s, 'Cornelius, your prayer has Ac 10:31 5346
Opening his mouth, Peter s: Ac 10:34 3004
"But I s, 'By no means, Lord, Ac 11:8 3004
And the angel s to him, Ac 12:8 3004
And he s to him, Ac 12:8 3004
When Peter came to himself, he s, Ac 12:11 3004
They s to her, Ac 12:15 3004
led him out of the prison. And he s, Ac 12:17 3004
and fasting, the Holy Spirit s, Ac 13:2 3004
and s, "You who are full of all deceit Ac 13:10 3004
and motioning with his hand s, Ac 13:16 3004
whom He also testified and s, Ac 13:22 3004
Barnabas spoke out boldly and s, Ac 13:46 3004
s with a loud voice, Ac 14:10 3004
Peter stood up and s to them, Ac 15:7 3004
some days Paul s to Barnabas, Ac 15:36 3004
and turned and s to the spirit, Ac 16:18 3004
to the chief magistrates, they s, Ac 16:20 3004
after he brought them out, he s, Ac 16:30 5346
They s, "Believe in the Lord Jesus, Ac 16:31 3004
But Paul s to them, Ac 16:37 5346
the midst of the Areopagus and s, Ac 17:22 5346
some of your own poets have s, Ac 17:28 3004
some *began* to sneer, but others s, Ac 17:32 3004
out his garments and s to them, Ac 18:6 3004
And the Lord s to Paul in the Ac 18:9 3004
his mouth, Gallio s to the Jews, Ac 18:14 3004
He s to them, Ac 19:2 3004
And they s to him, "No, we Ac 19:2
And he s, "Into what then were you Ac 19:3 3004
And they s, "Into John's baptism." Ac 19:3 3004
Paul s, "John baptized with the Ac 19:4 3004
spirit answered and s to them, Ac 19:15 3004
workmen of similar *trades,* and s, Ac 19:25 3004
the crowd, the town clerk s, Ac 19:35 5346
him, and after embracing him, he s, Ac 20:10 3004
had come to him, he s to them, Ac 20:18 3004
the Lord Jesus, that He Himself s, Ac 20:35 3004
When he had s these things, he Ac 20:36 3004
we s farewell to one another. Ac 21:5 537b
his own feet and hands, and s, Ac 21:11 3004
and they s to him, Ac 21:20 3004
barracks, he s to the commander, Ac 21:37 3004
And he s, "Do you know Greek? Ac 21:37 5346
But Paul s, "I am a Jew of Tarsus Ac 21:39 3004
became even more quiet; and he s, Ac 22:2 5346
And He s to me, 'I am Jesus the Ac 22:8 3004
"And I s, 'What shall I do, Lord?' Ac 22:10 3004
And the Lord s to me, Ac 22:10 3004
to me, and standing near s to me, Ac 22:13 3004
"And he s, 'The God of our fathers Ac 22:14 3004
"And I s, 'Lord, they themselves Ac 22:19 3004
"And He s to me, Ac 22:21 3004
they raised their voices and s, Ac 22:22 3004
Paul s to the centurion who was Ac 22:25 3004
The commander came and s to him, Ac 22:27 3004
are you a Roman?" And he s, "Yes Ac 22:27 5346
Paul s, "But I was actually born *a* Ac 22:28 5346
intently at the Council, s, Ac 23:1 3004
Then Paul s to him, Ac 23:3 3004
But the bystanders s, Ac 23:4 3004
And Paul s, "I was not aware, Ac 23:5 5346
As he s this, there occurred a Ac 23:7 2980
the Lord stood at his side and s, Ac 23:11 3004
priests and the elders and s, Ac 23:14 3004
of the centurions to him and s, Ac 23:17 5346
led him to the commander and s, Ac 23:18 5346
he s, "The Jews have agreed to ask Ac 23:20 3004
him two of the centurions and s, Ac 23:23 3004
he s, "I will give you a hearing after Ac 23:35 5346
Felix became frightened and s, Ac 24:25 611
"Therefore," he s, Ac 25:5 5346
while Paul s in his own defense, Ac 25:8 626
Jews a favor, answered Paul and s, Ac 25:9 3004
But Paul s,"I am standing before Ac 25:10 3004
Then Agrippa s to Festus, Ac 25:22
"Tomorrow," he s, Ac 25:22 5346
Festus s, "King Agrippa, and all you Ac 25:24 5346
Agrippa s to Paul, Ac 26:1 5346
"And I s, 'Who are You, Lord?' Ac 26:15 3004
Lord s, 'I am Jesus whom you are Ac 26:15 3004
Moses s was going to take place; Ac 26:22 2980
defense, Festus s in a loud voice, Ac 26:24 5346
Paul s, "I am not out of my mind, Ac 26:25 5346
And Paul s, "I would wish to Ac 26:29
And Agrippa s to Festus, Ac 26:32 5346
and s to them, "Men, I perceive that Ac 27:10 3004
than by what was being s by Paul. Ac 27:11 3004
Paul stood up in their midst and s, Ac 27:21 3004
Paul s to the centurion and to the Ac 27:31 3004
Having s this, he took bread Ac 27:35 3004
They s to him, Ac 28:21 3004
coveting if the Law had not s, Ro 7:7 3004
it was s to her, Ro 9:12 3004
THE PLACE WHERE IT WAS S TO THEM, Ro 9:26 3004
given thanks, He broke it and s, 1Co 11:24 3004
God, who s, "Light shall shine out 2Co 4:6 3004
just as God s, "I WILL DWELL IN 2Co 6:16 3004
for I have s before that you are 2Co 7:3 4275b
And He has s to me, 2Co 12:9 3004
s when present the second time, 2Co 13:2 4275b
As we have s before, so I say Ga 1:9 4275b
I s to Cephas in the presence of Ga 2:14 3004
a prophet of their own, s, Ti 1:12 3004
which of the angels has He ever s, Heb 1:13 3004
ANGRY WITH THIS GENERATION, AND S, Heb 3:10 3004
while it is s, "TODAY IF YOU HEAR Heb 3:15 3004
enter that rest, just as He has s, Heb 4:3 3004
For He has s somewhere Heb 4:4 3004
a time just as has been s before, Heb 4:7 4275b
high priest, but He who s to Him, Heb 5:5 2980
oath through the One who s to Him, Heb 7:21 3004
point in what has been s *is this:* Heb 8:1 3004
When He s, "A new *covenant,*" Heb 8:13 3004
"THEN I S, 'BEHOLD, I HAVE COME Heb 10:7 3004
then He s, "BEHOLD, I HAVE COME Heb 10:9 3004
For we know Him who s, Heb 10:30 3004
it was he to whom it was s, Heb 11:18 2980
was the sight, *that* Moses s, Heb 12:21 3004
for He Himself has s, Heb 13:5 3004
For He who s, "DO NOT COMMIT Jas 2:11 3004
"DO NOT COMMIT ADULTERY," also s, Jas 2:11 3004
him a railing judgment, but s, Jude 1:9 3004
of a trumpet speaking with me, s, Rv 4:1 3004
and one of the elders s to me, Rv 5:5 3004
and they s to the mountains and to Rv 6:16 3004
I s to him, "My lord, you know Rv 7:14 3004
And he s to me, "These are the ones Rv 7:14 3004
And he s to me, "Take it and eat it; Rv 10:9 3004
And they s to me, Rv 10:11 3004
and someone s, "Get up and measure Rv 11:1 3004
and he s with a loud voice, Rv 14:7 3004
And the angel s to me, Rv 17:7 3004
he s to me, "The waters which you Rv 17:15 3004
And a second time they s, Rv 19:3 3004
Then he s to me, "Write, 'Blessed are Rv 19:9 3004
he s to me, "These are true words of Rv 19:9 3004
But he s to me, "Do not do that; Rv 19:10 3004
And He who sits on the throne s, Rv 21:5 3004
And He s, "Write, for these words Rv 21:5 3004
He s to me, "It is done. I am the Rv 21:6 3004
he s to me, "These words are faithful Rv 22:6 3004
But he s to me, "Do not do that Rv 22:9 3004
And he s to me, "Do not seal up Rv 22:10 3004

SAIL

mast firmly, Nor spread out the s. Is 33:23 5251
"Your s was of fine embroidered Ezk 27:7 4666
God wills," he set s from Ephesus. Ac 18:21 321
he was about to set s for Syria, Ac 20:3 321
to the ship, set s for Assos, Ac 20:13 321
For Paul had decided to s past Ac 20:16 3896
parted from them and had set s, Ac 21:1 321
we went aboard and set s. Ac 21:2 321
that we would s for Italy, Ac 27:1 636
which was about to s to the Ac 27:2 4126
and not to have set s from Crete and Ac 27:21 321
and when we were setting s, Ac 28:10 321
At the end of three months we set s Ac 28:11 321

SAILED

Then they s to the country of the Lk 8:26 2668
and from there they s to Cyprus. Ac 13:4 636
From there they s to Antioch, Ac 14:26 636
with him and s away to Cyprus. Ac 15:39 1602
We s from Philippi after the Ac 20:6 1602
and s under the shelter of Cyprus Ac 27:4 5284
When we had s through the sea Ac 27:5 1277
had s slowly for a good many days, Ac 27:7 1020
we s under the shelter of Crete, Ac 27:7 5284
s around and arrived at Rhegium, Ac 28:13 4022

SAILING

they were s along He fell asleep; Lk 8:23 4126
S from there, we arrived Ac 20:15 636
s to Syria and landed at Tyre; Ac 21:3 4126
an Alexandrian ship s for Italy, Ac 27:6 4126
and with difficulty s past it we Ac 27:8 3881
anchor and *began* s along Crete, Ac 27:13 3881
you all those who are s with you.' Ac 27:24 4126

SAILOR

and every passenger and s, Rv 18:17 3492

SAILORS

the fleet, s who knew the sea, 1Ki 9:27 376, 591
All the ships of the sea and their s Ezk 27:9 4419
wares, your merchandise, Your s and Ezk 27:27 4419
"All who handle the oar, The s Ezk 27:29 4419
Then the s became afraid and Jon 1:5 4419
about midnight the s *began* to Ac 27:27 3492
But as the s were trying to escape Ac 27:30 3492

SAINT

Greet every s in Christ Jesus. Php 4:21 40

SAINTS

As for the s who are in the earth, Ps 16:3 6918
O fear the LORD, you His s; Ps 34:9 6918
'But the s of the Highest One will Da 7:18 6922
that horn was waging war with the s Da 7:21 6922
favor of the s of the Highest One, Da 7:22 6922
the s took possession of the kingdom. Da 7:22 6922
wear down the s of the Highest One, Da 7:25 6922
people of the s of the Highest One; Da 7:27 6922
and many bodies of the s who had Mt 27:52 40
harm he did to Your s at Jerusalem; Ac 9:13 40
also to the s who lived at Lydda. Ac 9:32 40
and calling the s and widows, he Ac 9:41 40
lock up many of the s in prisons, Ac 26:10 40
of God in Rome, called *as* s: Ro 1:7 40
because He intercedes for the s Ro 8:27 40
to the needs of the s, Ro 12:13 40
going to Jerusalem serving the s. Ro 15:25 40
the poor among the s in Jerusalem. Ro 15:26 40
may prove acceptable to the s; Ro 15:31 40
Lord in a manner worthy of the s, Ro 16:2 40
and all the s who are with them. Ro 16:15 40
in Christ Jesus, s by calling, 1Co 1:2 40
unrighteous and not before the s? 1Co 6:1 40
that the s will judge the world? 1Co 6:2 40
as in all the churches of the s. 1Co 14:33 40
the collection for the s, 1Co 16:1 40
themselves for ministry to the s), 1Co 16:15 40
the s who are throughout Achaia: 2Co 1:1 40
in the support of the s, 2Co 8:4 40
you about this ministry to the s; 2Co 9:1 40

supplying the needs of the **s**, 2Co 9:12 40
All the **s** greet you. 2Co 13:13 40
God, To the **s** who are at Ephesus Eph 1:1 40
you and your love for all the **s**, Eph 1:15 40
glory of His inheritance in the **s**, Eph 1:18 40
are fellow citizens with the **s**, Eph 2:19 40
To me, the very least of all **s**, Eph 3:8 40
be able to comprehend with all the **s** Eph 3:18 40
the equipping of the **s** for the work Eph 4:12 40
among you, as is proper among **s**; Eph 5:3 40
and petition for all the **s**, Eph 6:18 40
To all the **s** in Christ Jesus who Php 1:1 40
All the **s** greet you, especially Php 4:22 40
To the **s** and faithful brethren in Col 1:2 40
love which you have for all the **s**; Col 1:4 40
the inheritance of the **s** in Light. Col 1:12 40
has now been manifested to His **s**, Col 1:26 40
of our Lord Jesus with all His **s**. 1Th 3:13 40
be glorified in His **s** on that day, 2Th 1:10 40
Lord Jesus and toward all the **s**; Phm 1:5 40
hearts of the **s** have been refreshed Phm 1:7 40
and in still ministering to the **s**. Heb 6:10 40
all of your leaders and all the **s**. Heb 13:24 40
once for all handed down to the **s**. Jude 1:3 40
which are the prayers of the **s**. Rv 5:8 40
add it to the prayers of all the **s** Rv 8:3 40
with the prayers of the **s**, Rv 8:4 40
and the **s** and those who fear Rv 11:18 40
with the **s** and to overcome them, Rv 13:7 40
and the faith of the **s**. Rv 13:10 40
Here is the perseverance of the **s** Rv 14:12 40
they poured out the blood of **s** and Rv 16:6 40
drunk with the blood of the **s**, Rv 17:6 40
you **s** and apostles and prophets, Rv 18:20 40
found the blood of prophets and of **s** Rv 18:24 40
is the righteous acts of the **s**. Rv 19:8 40
of the **s** and the beloved city, Rv 20:9 40

SAINTS'
if she has washed the **s** feet, if 1Tm 5:10 40

SAKE
he treated Abram well for her **s**; Gn 12:16 5668
for the **s** of the fifty righteous who Gn 18:24 4616
For the **s** of My servant Abraham." Gn 26:24 5668
to the Egyptians for Israel's **s**, Ex 18:8 5921, 182
"Are you jealous for my **s**? Nu 11:29
forehead for the **s** of the dead. Dt 14:1
for the **s** of His people Israel. 2Sa 5:12 5668
"For the **s** of Your word, and 2Sa 7:21 5668
him kindness for Jonathan's **s**?" 2Sa 9:1 5668
for the **s** of your father Jonathan, 2Sa 9:7 5668
courageous for the **s** of our people 2Sa 10:12 1157
him Jedidiah for the LORD's **s**. 2Sa 12:25 5668
Deal gently for my **s** with the young 2Sa 18:5
a far country for Your name's **s** 1Ki 8:41 4616
for the **s** of your father David, 1Ki 11:12 4616
for the **s** of My servant David and 1Ki 11:13 4616
for the **s** of Jerusalem which I have 1Ki 11:13 4616
for the **s** of My servant David and 1Ki 11:32 4616
David and for the **s** of Jerusalem, 1Ki 11:32 4616
for the **s** of My servant David whom 1Ki 11:34 4616
But for David's **s** the LORD his God 1Ki 15:4 4616
for the **s** of David His servant, 2Ki 8:19 4616
this city to save it for My own **s** and 2Ki 19:34 4616
and for My servant David's **s**.' " 2Ki 19:34 4616
I will defend this city for My own **s** 2Ki 20:6 4616
for My servant David's **s**." 2Ki 20:6 4616
for the **s** of His people Israel. 1Ch 14:2 5668
"O LORD, for Your servant's **s**, 1Ch 17:19 5668
courageous for the **s** of our people 1Ch 19:13 1157
a far country for Your great name's **s** 2Ch 6:32 4616
Stop for your own **s** from 2Ch 35:21
For your **s** is the earth to be Jb 18:4 4616
of righteousness For His name's **s**. Ps 23:3 4616
remember me, For Your goodness' **s**, Ps 25:7 4616
For Your name's **s**, O LORD, Pardon Ps 25:11 4616
For Your name's **s** You will lead me Ps 31:3 4616
for Your **s** we are killed all day long; Ps 44:22 5921
for the **s** of Your lovingkindness. Ps 44:26 4616
for Your **s** I have borne reproach; Ps 69:7 5921
forgive our sins for Your name's **s**. Ps 79:9 4616
saved them for the **s** of His name, Ps 106:8 4616
His covenant for their **s**, Ps 106:45
kindly with me for Your name's **s**; Ps 109:21 4616
For the **s** of my brothers and my Ps 122:8 4616
For the **s** of the house of the LORD Ps 122:9 4616
For the **s** of David Your servant, Do Ps 132:10 5668
For the **s** of Your name, O LORD, Ps 143:11 4616
this city to save it for My own **s** and Is 37:35 4616
and for My servant David's **s**.' " Is 37:35 4616
was pleased for His righteousness' **s** Is 42:21 4616
"For your **s** I have sent to Is 43:14 4616
your transgressions for My own **s**, Is 43:25 4616
"For the **s** of Jacob My servant, Is 45:4 4616
the **s** of My name I delay My wrath, Is 48:9 4616
"For My own **s**, for My own sake, I Is 48:11 4616
"For My own sake, for My own **s**, Is 48:11 4616
Zion's **s** I will not keep silent, Is 62:1 4616
for Jerusalem's **s** I will not keep Is 62:1 4616
Return for the **s** of Your servants, Is 63:17 4616
who exclude you for My name's **s**, Is 66:5 4616
us, O LORD, act for Your name's **s**! Jer 14:7 4616
despise *us*, for Your own name's **s**; Jer 14:21 4616
that for Your **s** I endure reproach. Jer 15:15 5921
"But I acted for the **s** of My name, Ezk 20:9 4616
"But I acted for the **s** of My name, Ezk 20:14 4616
and acted for the **s** of My name, Ezk 20:22 4616
dealt with you for My name's **s**, Ezk 20:44 4616
"It is not for your **s**, Ezk 36:22 4616
"I am not doing *this* for your **s**," Ezk 36:32 4616
for Your **s**, O Lord, let Your face Da 9:17 4616
For Your own **s**, O my God, do not Da 9:19 4616
For the **s** of grain and new wine Hos 7:14 5921
persecuted for the **s** of righteousness, Mt 5:10 1752a
governors and kings for My **s**, Mt 10:18 1752a
he who has lost his life for My **s** Mt 10:39 1752a
God for the **s** of your tradition? Mt 15:3 1223
God for the **s** of your tradition. Mt 15:6 1223
whoever loses his life for My **s** will Mt 16:25 1752a
for the **s** of the kingdom of heaven. Mt 19:12 1223
children or farms for My name's **s**, Mt 19:29 1752a
but for the **s** of the elect those Mt 24:22 1223
but whoever loses his life for My **s** Mk 8:35 1752a
for My **s** and for the gospel's sake, Mk 10:29 1752a
for My sake and for the gospel's **s**, Mk 10:29 1752a
for appearance's **s** offer long prayers Mk 12:40 4392
governors and kings for My **s**, Mk 13:9 1752a
for the **s** of the elect, whom He chose Mk 13:20 1223
evil, for the **s** of the Son of Man. Lk 6:22 1752a
whoever loses his life for My **s**, Lk 9:24 1752a
for the **s** of the kingdom of God, Lk 18:29 1752a
for appearance's **s** offer long prayers Lk 20:47 4392
and governors for My name's **s**. Lk 21:12 1752a
they came, not for Jesus' **s** only, Jn 12:9 1223
"This voice has not come for My **s**, Jn 12:30 1223
will do to you for My name's **s**, Jn 15:21 1223
he must suffer for My name's **s**." Ac 9:16 5228
for the **s** of the hope of Israel." Ac 28:20 1752a
all the Gentiles for His name's **s**, Ro 1:5 5228
not for his **s** only was it written that Ro 4:23 1223
but for our **s** also, to whom it Ro 4:24 1223
"FOR YOUR **S** WE ARE BEING PUT TO Ro 8:36 1752a
Christ for the **s** of my brethren, Ro 9:3 5228
they are enemies for your **s**, Ro 11:28 1223
beloved for the **s** of the fathers; Ro 11:28 1223
wrath, but also for conscience' **s**. Ro 13:5 1223
the work of God for the **s** of food. Ro 14:20 1752a
We are fools for Christ's **s**, 1Co 4:10 1223
brother for whose **s** Christ died. 1Co 8:11 1223
He speaking altogether for our **s**? 1Co 9:10 1223
Yes, for our **s** it was written, 1Co 9:10 1223
things for the **s** of the gospel, 1Co 9:23 1223
questions for conscience' **s**; 1Co 10:25 1223
questions for conscience' **s**. 1Co 10:27 1223
for the **s** of the one who informed 1Co 10:28 1223
you, and for conscience' **s**; 1Co 10:28
was not created for the woman's **s**, 1Co 11:9 1223
sake, but woman for the man's **s**. 1Co 11:9 1223
I determined this for my own **s**, 2Co 2:1 1683
as your bond-servants for Jesus' **s**. 2Co 4:5 1223
over to death for Jesus' **s**, 2Co 4:11 1223
was not for the **s** of the offender 2Co 7:12 1752a
nor for the **s** of the one offended, 2Co 7:12 1752a
yet for your **s** He became poor, 2Co 8:9 1223
with difficulties, for Christ's **s**; 2Co 12:10 5228
Jesus for the **s** of you Gentiles Eph 3:1 5228
is more necessary for your **s**. Php 1:24 1223
it has been granted for Christ's **s**, Php 1:29 5228
Him, but also to suffer for His **s**, Php 1:29 5228
as loss for the **s** of Christ. Php 3:7 1223
in my sufferings for your **s**, Col 1:24 5228
proved to be among you for your **s**. 1Th 1:5 1223
little wine for the **s** of your stomach 1Tm 5:23 1223
for the **s** of those who are chosen, 2Tm 2:10 1223
teach for the **s** of sordid gain. Ti 1:11 5484
which is in you for Christ's **s**. Phm 1:6 1519
yet for love's **s** I rather appeal Phm 1:9 1223
for the **s** of those who will inherit Heb 1:14 1223
for whose **s** it is also tilled, Heb 6:7 1223
these last times for the **s** of you 1Pe 1:20 1223
Submit yourselves for the Lord's **s** 1Pe 2:13 1223
if for the **s** of conscience toward God 1Pe 2:19 1223
suffer for the **s** of righteousness, 1Pe 3:14 1223
been forgiven you for His name's **s**. 1Jn 2:12 1223
for the **s** of the truth which 2Jn 1:2 1223
went out for the **s** of the Name, 3Jn 1:7 5228
for the **s** of *gaining an* advantage. Jude 1:16 5484
and have endured for My name's **s**, Rv 2:3 1223

SAKES
And He reproved kings for their **s**, 1Ch 16:21 5921
And He reproved kings for their **s**: Ps 105:14 5921
I am glad for your **s** that I was not Jn 11:15 1223
come for My sake, but for your **s**. Jn 12:30 1223
"For their **s** I sanctify Myself, Jn 17:19 5228
to myself and Apollos for your **s**, 1Co 4:6 1223
for your **s** in the presence of Christ, 2Co 2:10 1223
For all things *are* for your **s**, 2Co 4:15 1223

SALAMIS
When they reached **S**, Ac 13:5 4529

SALE
'If you make a **s**, moreover, to Lv 25:14 4465
shall calculate the years since its **s** Lv 25:27 4465
until a full year from its **s**; Lv 25:29 4465
house **s** in the city of this possession Lv 25:33 4465
are not to be sold *in* a slave **s**. Lv 25:42 4466
and the price of his **s** shall Lv 25:50 4465
the **s** of their fathers' *estates*. Dt 18:8 4465
offer yourselves for **s** to your enemies Dt 28:68 4376
And have not profited by their **s**. Ps 44:12 4242

SALECAH
all Bashan, as far as **S** and Edrei, Dt 3:10 5548
Mount Hermon and **S** and all Bashan, Jos 12:5 5548
and all Bashan as far as **S**; Jos 13:11 5548
in the land of Bashan as far as **S**. 1Ch 5:11 5548

SALEM
Melchizedek king of **S** brought out Gn 14:18 8004
His tabernacle is in **S**; Ps 76:2 8004
For this Melchizedek, king of **S**, Heb 7:1 4532
and then also king of **S**, Heb 7:2 4532

SALES
and bring the proceeds of the **s** Ac 4:34 4097

SALIM
was baptizing in Aenon near **S**, Jn 3:23 4530

SALIVA
let his **s** run down into his beard. 1Sa 21:13 7388b
He touched his tongue *with the* **s**; Mk 7:33

SALLAI
and after him Gabbai *and* **S**, Ne 11:8 5546b
of **S**, Kallai; of Amok, Eber; Ne 12:20 5546b

SALLU
were **S** the son of Meshullam, 1Ch 9:7 5543b
S the son of Meshullam, the son of Ne 11:7 5543b
S, Amok, Hilkiah and Jedaiah. Ne 12:7 5543a

SALMA
Nahshon became the father of **S**, 1Ch 2:11 8007
S became the father of Boaz, 1Ch 2:11 8007
S the father of Bethlehem *and* 1Ch 2:51 8007
The sons of **S** *were* Bethlehem and 1Ch 2:54 8007

SALMON
born Nahshon, and to Nahshon, **S**, Ru 4:20 8009
and to **S** was born Boaz, and to Ru 4:21 8012
and Nahshon the father of **S**. Mt 1:4 4533
S was the father of Boaz by Rahab, Mt 1:5 4533
the son of Boaz, the son of **S**, Lk 3:32 4533

SALMONE
under the shelter of Crete, off **S**; Ac 27:7 4534

SALOME
James the Less and Joses, and **S**. Mk 15:40 4539
Mary the *mother* of James, and **S**, Mk 16:1 4539

SALT
of Siddim (that is, the **S** Sea). Gn 14:3 4417
and she became a pillar of **s**. Gn 19:26 4417
moreover, you shall season with **s**, Lv 2:13 4417
the **s** of the covenant of your God Lv 2:13 4417
your offerings you shall offer **s**. Lv 2:13 4417
covenant of **s** before the LORD Nu 18:19 4417
the end of the **S** Sea eastward. Nu 34:3 4417
termination shall be at the **S** Sea. Nu 34:12 4417
the sea of the Arabah, the **S** Sea, Dt 3:17 4417
'All its land is brimstone and **s**, Dt 29:23 4417
the sea of the Arabah, the **S** Sea, Jos 3:16 4417
sea of the Arabah, *even* the **S** Sea, Jos 12:3 4417
from the lower end of the **S** Sea, Jos 15:2 4417
The east border *was* the **S** Sea, Jos 15:5 4417
and the City of **S** and Engedi; Jos 15:62 5898
at the north bay of the **S** Sea, Jos 18:19 4417
the city and sowed it with **s**. Jg 9:45 4417
Arameans in the Valley of **S**. 2Sa 8:13 4417
me a new jar, and put **s** in it." 2Ki 2:20 4417
water and threw **s** in it and said, 2Ki 2:21 4417
killed *of* Edom in the Valley of **S** 2Ki 14:7 4417
Edomites in the Valley of **S**. 1Ch 18:12 4417
and his sons by a covenant of **s**? 2Ch 13:5 4417
and went to the Valley of **S** and 2Ch 25:11 4417
wheat, **s**, wine and anointing oil, Ezr 6:9 4416
100 baths of oil, and **s** as needed. Ezr 7:22 4416
tasteless be eaten without **s**, Jb 6:6 4417
the **s** land for his dwelling place? Jb 39:6 4420
A fruitful land into a **s** waste, Ps 107:34 4420
A land of **s** without inhabitant. Jer 17:6 4420
with **s** or even wrapped in cloths. Ezk 16:4 4414b
the priests shall throw **s** on them, Ezk 43:24 4417
they will be left for **s**. Ezk 47:11 4417
possessed by nettles and **s** pits, Zph 2:9 4417
"You are the **s** of the earth; Mt 5:13 217
but if the **s** has become tasteless, Mt 5:13 217
"**S** is good; but if the salt becomes Mk 9:50 217
but if the **s** becomes unsalty, with Mk 9:50 217
Have **s** in yourselves, and be at Mk 9:50 217
"Therefore, **s** is good; Lk 14:34 217
if even **s** has become tasteless, Lk 14:34 217
as though seasoned with **s**, Col 4:6 217
Nor *can* **s** water produce fresh. Jas 3:12 252

SALTED
the work of a perfumer, **s**, Ex 30:35 4414b
work the ground will eat **s** fodder, Is 30:24 2548
"For everyone will be **s** with fire. Mk 9:49 233

SALTY
how can it be made **s** *again?* Mt 5:13 233
with what will you make it **s** *again?* Mk 9:50 741

SALU
woman, was Zimri the son of **S**, Nu 25:14 5543c

SALUTATION
what kind of **s** this was. Lk 1:29 783

SALUTE
if you meet any man, do not **s** him, 2Ki 4:29 1288

SALUTES
if anyone **s** you, do not answer him; 2Ki 4:29 1288

SALVATION
"For Your **s** I wait, O LORD. Gn 49:18 3444
Stand by and see the **s** of the LORD Ex 14:13 3444
and song, And He has become my **s**; Ex 15:2 3444
And scorned the Rock of his **s**. Dt 32:15 3444
Because I rejoice in Your **s**. 1Sa 2:1 3444
My shield and the horn of my **s**, 2Sa 22:3 3468
also given me the shield of Your **s**, 2Sa 22:36 3468
exalted be God, the rock of my **s**, 2Sa 22:47 3468
For all my **s** and all *my* desire, 2Sa 23:5 3468
tidings of His **s** from day to day. 1Ch 16:23 3444
"Save us, O God of our **s**, 1Ch 16:35 3468
O LORD God, be clothed with **s** and 2Ch 6:41 8668
the **s** of the LORD on your behalf, 2Ch 20:17 3444

"This also will be my **s**, **Jb 13:16** 3444
S belongs to the LORD; **Ps 3:8** 3444
of Zion I may rejoice in Your **s**. **Ps 9:14** 3444
My heart shall rejoice in Your **s**. **Ps 13:5** 3444
that the **s** of Israel would come **Ps 14:7** 3444
My shield and the horn of my **s**, **Ps 18:2** 3468
also given me the shield of Your **s**, **Ps 18:35** 3468
And exalted be the God of my **s**, **Ps 18:46** 3468
Your **s** how greatly he will rejoice! **Ps 21:1** 3444
His glory is great through Your **s**, **Ps 21:5** 3444
from the God of his **s**. **Ps 24:5** 3468
me, For You are the God of my **s**; **Ps 25:5** 3468
The LORD is my light and my **s**; **Ps 27:1** 3468
me nor forsake me, O God of my **s**! **Ps 27:9** 3468
Say to my soul, "I am your **s**." **Ps 35:3** 3444
It shall exult in His **s**. **Ps 35:9** 3444
But the **s** of the righteous is from **Ps 37:39** 8668
haste to help me, O Lord, my **s**! **Ps 38:22** 8668
of Your faithfulness and Your **s**; **Ps 40:10** 8668
Let those who love Your **s** say **Ps 40:16** 8668
I shall show the **s** of God." **Ps 50:23** 3468
Restore to me the joy of Your **s** And **Ps 51:12** 3468
O God, the God of my **s**; **Ps 51:14** 8668
that the **s** of Israel would come **Ps 53:6** 3444
From Him is my **s**. **Ps 62:1** 3444
He only is my rock and my **s**, **Ps 62:2** 3444
He only is my rock and my **s**, **Ps 62:6** 3444
On God my **s** and my glory *rest;* **Ps 62:7** 3468
in righteousness, O God of our **s**, **Ps 65:5** 3468
earth, Your **s** among all nations. **Ps 67:2** 3444
The God *who* is our **s** **Ps 68:19** 3444
May Your **s**, O God, set me *securely* **Ps 69:29** 3444
who love Your **s** say continually, **Ps 70:4** 3444
And of Your **s** all day long; **Ps 71:15** 8668
God And did not trust in His **s**. **Ps 78:22** 3444
Help us, O God of our **s**, **Ps 79:9** 3468
Restore us, O God of our **s**, **Ps 85:4** 3468
O LORD, And grant us Your **s**. **Ps 85:7** 3468
s is near to those who fear Him, **Ps 85:9** 3468
O Lord, the God of my **s**, **Ps 88:1** 3444
My God, and the rock of my **s**.' **Ps 89:26** 3444
him And let him see My **s**." **Ps 91:16** 3444
shout joyfully to the rock of our **s**. **Ps 95:1** 3468
Proclaim good tidings of His **s** from **Ps 96:2** 3444
The LORD has made known His **s**; **Ps 98:2** 3444
earth have seen the **s** of our God. **Ps 98:3** 3444
Visit me with Your **s**, **Ps 106:4** 3444
I shall lift up the cup of **s** And **Ps 116:13** 3444
and song, And He has become my **s**. **Ps 118:14** 3444
and **s** is in the tents of the righteous; **Ps 118:15** 3444
And You have become my **s**. **Ps 118:21** 3444
LORD, Your **s** according to Your word; **Ps 119:41** 8668
My soul languishes for Your **s**; **Ps 119:81** 8668
eyes fail *with longing* for Your **s** And **Ps 119:123** 3444
S is far from the wicked, For they **Ps 119:155** 3444
I hope for Your **s**, O LORD, And do **Ps 119:166** 3444
I long for Your **s**, O LORD, And Your **Ps 119:174** 3444
priests also I will clothe with **s**, **Ps 132:16** 3468
the Lord, the strength of my **s**, **Ps 140:7** 3444
Who gives **s** to kings, **Ps 144:10** 8668
mortal man, in whom there is no **s**. **Ps 146:3** 8668
beautify the afflicted ones with **s**. **Ps 149:4** 3444
"Behold, God is my **s**, **Is 12:2** 3444
song, And He has become my **s**." **Is 12:2** 3444
draw water From the springs of **s**. **Is 12:3** 3444
you have forgotten the God of your **s** **Is 17:10** 3468
us rejoice and be glad in His **s**." **Is 25:9** 3444
s also in the time of distress. **Is 33:2** 3444
of your times, A wealth of **s**, **Is 33:6** 3444
earth open up and **s** bear fruit, **Is 45:8** 3468
by the LORD With an everlasting **s**; **Is 45:17** 8668
And My **s** will not delay. **Is 46:13** 8668
And I will grant **s** in Zion, **Is 46:13** 8668
So that My **s** may reach to the end of **Is 49:6** 3444
in a day of **s** I have helped You; **Is 49:8** 3444
is near, My **s** has gone forth, **Is 51:5** 3468
manner; But My **s** will be forever, **Is 51:6** 3444
And My **s** to all generations." **Is 51:8** 3444
of happiness, Who announces **s**, **Is 52:7** 3444
earth may see The **s** of our God. **Is 52:10** 3444
For My **s** is about to come And My **Is 56:1** 3444
justice, but there is none, For **s**, **Is 59:11** 3444
Then His own arm brought **s** to Him, **Is 59:16** 3467
And a helmet of **s** on His head; **Is 59:17** 3444
But you will call your walls **s**, **Is 60:18** 3444
has clothed me with garments of **s**, **Is 61:10** 3468
s like a torch that is burning. **Is 62:1** 3444
"Lo, your **s** comes; **Is 62:11** 3468
So My own arm brought **s** to Me, **Is 63:5** 3467
LORD our God Is the **s** of Israel. **Jer 3:23** 8668
waits silently For the **s** of the LORD. **La 3:26** 8668
S is from the LORD." **Jon 2:9** 3444
I will wait for the God of my **s**. **Mi 7:7** 3468
Your horses, On Your chariots of **s**? **Hab 3:8** 3444
went forth for the **s** of Your people, **Hab 3:13** 3468
For the **s** of Your anointed. **Hab 3:13** 3468
I will rejoice in the God of my **s**. **Hab 3:18** 3468
He is just and endowed with **s**, **Zch 9:9** 3467
proclamation of eternal **s**.] **Mk 16:20**
And has raised up a horn of **s** for **Lk 1:69** *4991*
S FROM OUR ENEMIES, And FROM THE **Lk 1:71** *4991*
give to His people *the* knowledge of **s** **Lk 1:77** *4991*
For my eyes have seen Your **s**, **Lk 2:30** *4992*
FLESH WILL SEE THE **S** OF GOD.' " **Lk 3:6** *4992*
"Today **s** has come to this house, **Lk 19:9** *4991*
we know, for **s** is from the Jews. **Jn 4:22** *4991*
"And there is **s** in no one else; **Ac 4:12** *4991*
us the message of this **s** has been sent. **Ac 13:26** *4991*
S TO THE END OF THE EARTH.' " **Ac 13:47** *4991*
proclaiming to you the way of **s**." **Ac 16:17** *4991*
that this **s** of God has been sent **Ac 28:28** *4992*
for it is the power of God for **s** to **Ro 1:16** *4991*
prayer to God for them is for *their* **s**. **Ro 10:1** *4991*
he confesses, resulting in **s**. **Ro 10:10** *4991*
s *has come* to the Gentiles, **Ro 11:11** *4991*
for now **s** is nearer to us than **Ro 13:11** *4991*
it is for your comfort and **s**; **2Co 1:6** *4991*
ON THE DAY OF **S** I HELPED YOU." **2Co 6:2** *4991*
behold, now is "THE DAY OF **S**" **2Co 6:2** *4991*
without regret, *leading* to **s**, **2Co 7:10** *4991*
message of truth, the gospel of your **s** **Eph 1:13** *4991*
And take THE HELMET OF **S**, **Eph 6:17** *4992*
for them, but of **s** for you, **Php 1:28** *4991*
work out your **s** with fear and **Php 2:12** *4991*
and as a helmet, the hope of **s**. **1Th 5:8** *4991*
s through our Lord Jesus Christ, **1Th 5:9** *4991*
chosen you from the beginning for **s** **2Th 2:13** *4991*
for as you do this you will ensure **s** **1Tm 4:16** *4982*
that they also may obtain the **s** **2Tm 2:10** *4991*
give you the wisdom that leads to **s** **2Tm 3:15** *4991*
appeared, bringing **s** to all men, **Ti 2:11** *4992*
sake of those who will inherit **s**? **Heb 1:14** *4991*
escape if we neglect so great a **s**? **Heb 2:3** *4991*
of their **s** through sufferings. **Heb 2:10** *4991*
obey Him the source of eternal **s**, **Heb 5:9** *4991*
you, and things that accompany **s**, **Heb 6:9** *4991*
for **s** without *reference to* sin, **Heb 9:28** *4991*
an ark for the **s** of his household, **Heb 11:7** *4991*
power of God through faith for a **s** **1Pe 1:5** *4991*
of your faith the **s** of your souls. **1Pe 1:9** *4991*
As to this **s**, the prophets who **1Pe 1:10** *4991*
it you may grow in respect to **s**, **1Pe 2:2** *4991*
the patience of our Lord *as* **s**; **2Pe 3:15** *4991*
to write you about our common **s**, **Jude 1:3** *4991*
"**S** to our God who sits on the **Rv 7:10** *4991*
"Now the **s**, and the power, and **Rv 12:10** *4991*
S and glory and power belong to **Rv 19:1** *4991*

SALVE

and eye **s** to anoint your eyes so that **Rv 3:18** *2854*

SAMARIA

which are in the cities of **S**." **1Ki 13:32** 8111
He bought the hill **S** from **1Ki 16:24** 8111
named the city which he built **S**, **1Ki 16:24** 8111
his fathers and was buried in **S**; **1Ki 16:28** 8111
son of Omri reigned over Israel in **S** **1Ki 16:29** 8111
of Baal which he built in **S**. **1Ki 16:32** 8111
Now the famine *was* severe in **S**. **1Ki 18:2** 8111
And he went up and besieged **S** and **1Ki 20:1** 8111
if the dust of **S** will suffice for **1Ki 20:10** 8111
"Men have come out from **S**." **1Ki 20:17** 8111
as my father made in **S**." **1Ki 20:34** 8111
sullen and vexed, and came to **S**. **1Ki 20:43** 8111
the palace of Ahab king of **S**. **1Ki 21:1** 8111
Ahab king of Israel, who is in **S**; **1Ki 21:18** 8111
at the entrance of the gate of **S**; **1Ki 22:10** 8111
king died and was brought to **S**, **1Ki 22:37** 8111
and they buried the king in **S**. **1Ki 22:37** 8111
the chariot by the pool of **S**, **1Ki 22:38** 8111
Ahab became king over Israel in **S** **1Ki 22:51** 8111
his upper chamber which *was* in **S**, **2Ki 1:2** 8111
of the king of **S** and say to them, **2Ki 1:3** 8111
and from there he returned to **S**. **2Ki 2:25** 8111
Ahab became king over Israel at **S** **2Ki 3:1** 8111
And King Jehoram went out of **S** at **2Ki 3:6** 8111
were with the prophet who is in **S**! **2Ki 5:3** 8111
And he brought them to **S**. **2Ki 6:19** 8111
When they had come into **S**, **2Ki 6:20** 8111
they were in the midst of **S**. **2Ki 6:20** 8111
army and went up and besieged **S**. **2Ki 6:24** 8111
There was a great famine in **S**; **2Ki 6:25** 8111
a shekel, in the gate of **S**.' " **2Ki 7:1** 8111
this time at the gate of **S**." **2Ki 7:18** 8111
Now Ahab had seventy sons in **S**. **2Ki 10:1** 8111
wrote letters and sent *them* to **S**, **2Ki 10:1** 8111
arose and departed and went to **S**. **2Ki 10:12** 8111
When he came to **S**, **2Ki 10:17** 8111
all who remained to Ahab in **S**, **2Ki 10:17** 8111
fathers, and they buried him in **S**. **2Ki 10:35** 8111
which Jehu reigned over Israel in **S** **2Ki 10:36** 8111
Jehu became king over Israel at **S**, **2Ki 13:1** 8111
also remained standing in **S**. **2Ki 13:6** 8111
fathers, and they buried him in **S**; **2Ki 13:9** 8111
became king over Israel in **S**, **2Ki 13:10** 8111
and Joash was buried in **S** with the **2Ki 13:13** 8111
hostages also, and returned to **S**. **2Ki 14:14** 8111
was buried in **S** with the kings of **2Ki 14:16** 8111
king of Israel became king in **S**, **2Ki 14:23** 8111
over Israel in **S** *for* six months. **2Ki 15:8** 8111
and he reigned one month in **S**. **2Ki 15:13** 8111
went up from Tirzah and came to **S**, **2Ki 15:14** 8111
struck Shallum son of Jabesh in **S**, **2Ki 15:14** 8111
Israel *and reigned* ten years in **S**. **2Ki 15:17** 8111
became king over Israel in **S**, **2Ki 15:23** 8111
against him and struck him in **S**, **2Ki 15:25** 8111
became king over Israel in **S**, **2Ki 15:27** 8111
Elah became king over Israel in **S**, **2Ki 17:1** 8111
to **S** and besieged it three years. **2Ki 17:5** 8111
the king of Assyria captured **S** and **2Ki 17:6** 8111
and settled *them* in the cities of **S** in **2Ki 17:24** 8111
So they possessed **S** and lived in its **2Ki 17:24** 8111
away into exile in the cities of **S** **2Ki 17:26** 8111
from **S** came and lived at Bethel, **2Ki 17:28** 8111
which the people of **S** had made, **2Ki 17:29** 8118
came up against **S** and besieged it. **2Ki 18:9** 8111
king of Israel, **S** was captured. **2Ki 18:10** 8111
they delivered **S** from my hand? **2Ki 18:34** 8111
stretch over Jerusalem the line of **S** **2Ki 21:13** 8111
of the prophet who came from **S**. **2Ki 23:18** 8111
which *were* in the cities of **S**, **2Ki 23:19** 8111
he went down to *visit* Ahab at **S**. **2Ch 18:2** 8111
at the entrance of the gate of **S**; **2Ch 18:9** 8111
him while he was hiding in **S**; **2Ch 22:9** 8111
of Judah, from **S** to Beth-horon, **2Ch 25:13** 8111
hostages also, and returned to **S**. **2Ch 25:24** 8111
and brought the spoil to **S**. **2Ch 28:8** 8111
which came to **S** and said to them, **2Ch 28:9** 8111
then they returned to **S**. **2Ch 28:15** 8111
and settled in the city of **S**, **Ezr 4:10** 8115
rest of their colleagues who live in **S** **Ezr 4:17** 8115
and the wealthy *men* of **S** and said, **Ne 4:2** *8111*
and the head of Ephraim is **S** and **Is 7:9** 8111
head of **S** is the son of Remaliah. **Is 7:9** 8111
the spoil of **S** will be carried away **Is 8:4** 8111
Ephraim and the inhabitants of **S**, **Is 9:9** 8111
like Arpad, Or **S** like Damascus? **Is 10:9** 8111
than those of Jerusalem and **S**, **Is 10:10** 8111
I have done to **S** and her idols?" **Is 10:11** 8111
they delivered **S** from my hand? **Is 36:19** 8111
of **S** I saw an offensive thing: **Jer 23:13** 8111
plant vineyards On the hills of **S**; **Jer 31:5** 8111
and from **S** with their beards **Jer 41:5** 8111
"Now your older sister is **S**, **Ezk 16:46** 8111
S did not commit half of your **Ezk 16:51** 8111
captivity of **S** and her daughters, **Ezk 16:53** 8111
and **S** with her daughters, **Ezk 16:55** 8111
as for their names, **S** is Oholah and **Ezk 23:4** 8111
The cup of your sister **S**. **Ezk 23:33** 8111
And the evil deeds of **S**, **Hos 7:1** 8111
He has rejected your calf, O **S**, **Hos 8:5** 8111
Surely the calf of **S** will be broken **Hos 8:6** 8111
The inhabitants of **S** will fear For **Hos 10:5** 8111
S will be cut off *with* her king Like **Hos 10:7** 8111
S will be held guilty, For she has **Hos 13:16** 8111
of **S** and see *the* great tumults within **Am 3:9** 8111
will the sons of Israel dwelling in **S** **Am 3:12** 8111
who are on the mountain of **S**, **Am 4:1** 8111
feel secure in the mountain of **S**, **Am 6:1** 8111
those who swear by the guilt of **S**, **Am 8:14** 8111
of Ephraim and the territory of **S**, **Ob 1:19** 8111
he saw concerning **S** and Jerusalem. **Mi 1:1** 8111
the rebellion of Jacob? Is it not **S**? **Mi 1:5** 8111
For I will make **S** a heap of ruins **Mi 1:6** 8111
was passing between **S** and Galilee. **Lk 17:11** *4540*
And He had to pass through **S**. **Jn 4:4** *4540*
So He came to a city of **S** called **Jn 4:5** *4540*
came a woman of **S** to draw water. **Jn 4:7** *4540*
Jerusalem, and in all Judea and **S**, **Ac 1:8** *4540*
the regions of Judea and **S**, **Ac 8:1** *4540*
Philip went down to the city of **S** **Ac 8:5** *4540*
and astonishing the people of **S**, **Ac 8:9** *4540*
S had received the word of God, **Ac 8:14** *4540*
and Galilee and **S** enjoyed peace, **Ac 9:31** *4540*
through both Phoenicia and **S**, **Ac 15:3** *4540*

SAMARITAN

"But a **S**, who was on a **Lk 10:33** *4541*
thanks to Him. And he was a **S**. **Lk 17:16** *4541*
Therefore the **S** woman said to Him, **Jn 4:9** *4542*
a drink since I am a **S** woman?" **Jn 4:9** *4542*
You are a **S** and have a demon?" **Jn 8:48** *4541*

SAMARITANS

do not enter *any* city of the **S**; **Mt 10:5** *4541*
and entered a village of the **S** to **Lk 9:52** *4541*
(For Jews have no dealings with **S**.) **Jn 4:9** *4541*
many of the **S** believed in Him **Jn 4:39** *4541*
So when the **S** came to Jesus, they **Jn 4:40** *4541*
gospel to many villages of the **S**. **Ac 8:25** *4541*

SAME

on the **s** day all the fountains of **Gn 7:11** 2088
On the very **s** day Noah and Shem **Gn 7:13** 6106
the **s** language and the same words. **Gn 11:1** 259
the same language and the **s** words. **Gn 11:1** 259
and they all have the **s** language. **Gn 11:6** 259
their foreskin in the very **s** day, **Gn 17:23** 6106
s day Abraham was circumcised, **Gn 17:26** 6106
in the **s** year a hundredfold. **Gn 26:12** 1931
and he gave them the **s** names which **Gn 26:18** 8034
LORD appeared to him the **s** night **Gn 26:24** 1931
Now it came about on the **s** day, **Gn 26:32** 1931
Now he arose that **s** night and took **Gn 32:22** 1931
the **s** place where Joseph was **Gn 40:3**
both had a dream the **s** night, **Gn 40:5** 259
"We had a dream on the **s** night, **Gn 41:11** 259
"Pharaoh's dreams are one *and the* **s**; **Gn 41:25**
the dreams are one *and the* **s**. **Gn 41:26**
So the **s** day Pharaoh commanded the **Ex 5:6** 1931
It was *the* **s** Aaron and Moses to **Ex 6:26**
it was *the* **s** Moses and Aaron. **Ex 6:27**
the magicians of Egypt, did the **s** **Ex 7:11** 3651
the magicians of Egypt did the **s** **Ex 7:22** 3651
The magicians did the **s** with their **Ex 8:7** 3651
the fourteenth day of the **s** month, **Ex 12:6** 2088
'They shall eat the flesh that **s** **Ex 12:8**
"The **s** law shall apply to the **Ex 12:49** 259
And on that **s** day the LORD brought **Ex 12:51** 6106
to him according to the **s** rule. **Ex 21:31** 2088
"You shall do the **s** with your **Ex 22:30** 3651
You are to do the **s** with your **Ex 23:11** 3651
shall have the **s** measurements. **Ex 26:2** 259
shall have the **s** measurements. **Ex 26:8** 259
workmanship, of the **s** material: **Ex 28:8** 4480
and shall offer with it the **s** **Ex 29:41**
grain offering and the **s** drink **Ex 29:41**
any like it in the **s** proportions; **Ex 30:32**
shall not make in the **s** proportions **Ex 30:37**
curtains had the **s** measurements. **Ex 36:9** 259

curtains had the **s** measurements.	**Ex 36:15**	259
workmanship, of the **s** material:	**Ex 39:5**	4480
be eaten the **s** day you offer *it,*	**Lv 19:6**	
"It shall be eaten on the **s** day,	**Lv 22:30**	1931
on the fifteenth day of the **s** month	**Lv 23:6**	2088
'Until this **s** day, until you have	**Lv 23:14**	6106
'On this **s** day you shall make a	**Lv 23:21**	6106
not do any work on this **s** day,	**Lv 23:28**	6106
not humble himself on this **s** day,	**Lv 23:29**	6106
who does any work on this **s** day,	**Lv 23:30**	6106
and cover the **s** with a covering of	**Nu 4:8**	853
And that **s** day he shall consecrate	**Nu 6:11**	1931
prayed for Aaron at the **s** time.	**Dt 9:20**	1931
surely bury him on the **s** day	**Dt 21:23**	1931
shall do the **s** with his garment,	**Dt 22:3**	3651
Moses wrote this song the **s** day,	**Dt 31:22**	1931
spoke to Moses that very **s** day,	**Dt 32:48**	6106
city in the **s** manner seven times;	**Jos 6:15**	2088
Now on the **s** night the LORD	**Jg 6:25**	1931
Now the **s** night it came about that	**Jg 7:9**	1931
the **s** day both of them will die.	**1Sa 2:34**	259
and came to Shiloh the **s** day with his	**1Sa 4:12**	1931
and he spoke these **s** words;	**1Sa 17:23**	428
to another and said the **s** thing;	**1Sa 17:30**	2088
answered the **s** thing as before.	**1Sa 17:30**	1697
But in the **s** night the word	**2Sa 7:4**	1931
woman and I live in the **s** house;	**1Ki 3:17**	259
the **s** measure and the same form.	**1Ki 6:25**	259
the same measure and the **s** form.	**1Ki 6:25**	259
hall, was of the **s** workmanship.	**1Ki 7:8**	2088
On the **s** day the king consecrated	**1Ki 8:64**	1931
and by the **s** means they exported	**1Ki 10:29**	3651
Then he gave a sign the **s** day,	**1Ki 13:3**	1931
Libnah revolted at the **s** time.	**2Ki 8:22**	1931
year what springs from the **s**,	**2Ki 19:29**	
he came, by the **s** he will return,	**2Ki 19:33**	
the **s** cities as far as Baal.	**1Ch 4:33**	428
It came about the **s** night that	**1Ch 17:3**	1931
and by the **s** means they exported	**2Ch 1:17**	3651
some of the people at the **s** time.	**2Ch 16:10**	1931
Then Libnah revolted at the **s** time	**2Ch 21:10**	1931
time of his distress this **s** King Ahaz	**2Ch 28:22**	1931
'Has not the **s** Hezekiah taken away	**2Ch 32:12**	1931
and I answered them in the **s** way.	**Ne 6:4**	2088
sent his servant to me in the **s** manner	**Ne 6:5**	2088
"Did not your fathers do the **s**	**Ne 13:18**	3541
queen's conduct will speak in *the* **s**	**Es 1:18**	
also will fast in the **s** way.	**Es 4:16**	3651
and the fourteenth of the **s** month,	**Es 9:18**	
the fifteenth day of the **s** month,	**Es 9:21**	
is the **s** to him as thick darkness,	**Jb 24:17**	3164a
the **s** one fashion us in the womb?	**Jb 31:15**	259
"But You are the **s**,	**Ps 102:27**	1931
and the fate of beasts is the **s**.	**Ec 3:19**	259
they all have the **s** breath and	**Ec 3:19**	259
All go to the **s** place.	**Ec 3:20**	259
It is the **s** for all.	**Ec 9:2**	3512c
year what springs from the **s**,	**Is 37:30**	
he came, by the **s** he will return,	**Is 37:34**	
to *your* old age I will be the **s**,	**Is 46:4**	1931
Now in the **s** year,	**Jer 28:1**	1931
the **s** year in the seventh month.	**Jer 28:17**	1931
all four of them had the **s** form,	**Ezk 1:16**	259
four of them had the **s** likeness,	**Ezk 10:10**	259
they were the **s** faces whose	**Ezk 10:22**	1992a
this *will* no longer *be* the **s**.	**Ezk 21:26**	2088
they both took the **s** way.	**Ezk 23:13**	259
defiled My sanctuary on the **s** day	**Ezk 23:38**	1931
on the **s** day to profane it;	**Ezk 23:39**	1931
but in that **s** iniquity of his	**Ezk 33:13**	
on that **s** day the hand of the LORD	**Ezk 40:1**	6106
of them had the **s** measurement.	**Ezk 40:10**	259
the **s** measurement on each side.	**Ezk 40:10**	259
s measurement as the first gate.	**Ezk 40:21**	
ornaments *had* the **s** measurements	**Ezk 40:22**	
according to those **s** measurements.	**Ezk 40:24**	
according to those **s** measurements.	**Ezk 40:28**	
according to those **s** measurements.	**Ezk 40:29**	
according to those **s** measurements.	**Ezk 40:32**	
according to those **s** measurements.	**Ezk 40:33**	
according to those **s** measurements,	**Ezk 40:35**	
and shall go out by the **s** way."	**Ezk 44:3**	
the bath shall be the **s** quantity,	**Ezk 45:11**	259
the gate and go out by the **s** way.	**Ezk 46:8**	
in the corners *were* the **s** size.	**Ezk 46:22**	259
were crushed all at the **s** time and	**Da 2:35**	2298
That **s** night Belshazzar the	**Da 5:30**	
lies *to each other* at the **s** table;	**Da 11:27**	259
man and his father resort to the **s** girl	**Am 2:7**	
and you go the **s** day and enter the	**Zch 6:10**	1931
for in the **s** way they persecuted	**Mt 5:12**	*3779*
and teaches others *to do* the **s**,	**Mt 5:19**	*3779*
even the tax collectors do the **s**?	**Mt 5:46**	*846*
Do not even the Gentiles do the **s**?	**Mt 5:47**	*846*
treat people the **s** way you want them	**Mt 7:12**	*3779*
in the **s** way that I had mercy on you?'	**Mt 18:33**	*5613*
"My heavenly Father will also do the **s**	**Mt 18:35**	*3779*
ninth hour, and did the **s** thing.	**Mt 20:5**	*5615*
to this last man the **s** as to you.	**Mt 20:14**	*2532*
the second and said the **s** thing;	**Mt 21:30**	*5615*
and they did the **s** thing to them.	**Mt 21:36**	*5615*
the **s** manner the one who *had received*	**Mt 25:17**	*5615*
disciples said the **s** thing too.	**Mt 26:35**	*3668*
saying the **s** thing once more.	**Mt 26:44**	*846*
the **s** way the chief priests also,	**Mt 27:41**	*3668*
were also insulting Him with the **s** words.	**Mt 27:44**	*846*
they all were saying the **s** thing also	**Mk 14:31**	*5615*
and prayed, saying the **s** words.	**Mk 14:39**	*846*
the **s** way the chief priests also,	**Mk 15:31**	*3668*
In the **s** region there were	**Lk 2:8**	*846*
of the Pharisees also do the **s**,	**Lk 5:33**	*3668*
For in the **s** way their fathers	**Lk 6:23**	*846*
treat the false prophets in the **s** way.	**Lk 6:26**	*846*
the **s** way you want them to treat you.	**Lk 6:31**	*3668*
For even sinners do the **s**.	**Lk 6:33**	*846*
to receive back the **s** *amount.*	**Lk 6:34**	*2470*
"Go and do the **s**."	**Lk 10:37**	*3668*
Now on the **s** occasion there were	**Lk 13:1**	*846*
"I tell you that in the **s** way,	**Lk 15:7**	*3779*
"In the **s** way, I tell you, there	**Lk 15:10**	*3779*
"It was the **s** as happened in the	**Lk 17:28**	*3668*
"It will be just the **s** on the day	**Lk 17:30**	*846*
two women grinding at the **s** place;	**Lk 17:35**	*846*
and in the **s** way all seven died,	**Lk 20:31**	*5615*
And in the **s** way *He took* the cup	**Lk 22:20**	*5615*
the **s** sentence of condemnation?	**Lk 23:40**	*846*
will come in just the **s** way as you	**Ac 1:11**	*5158*
God gave to them the **s** gift	**Ac 11:17**	*2470*
also men of the **s** nature as you,	**Ac 14:15**	*3663*
in the **s** way as they also are."	**Ac 15:11**	*3739*
the **s** things by word *of mouth.*	**Ac 15:27**	*846*
and because he was of the **s** trade,	**Ac 18:3**	*3673*
At the **s** time too, he was hoping	**Ac 24:26**	*260*
him brought to Jerusalem (*at the* **s**	**Ac 25:3**	
at the **s** time they were loosening the	**Ac 27:40**	*260*
and in the **s** way also the men	**Ro 1:27**	*3668*
of death, they not only do the **s**,	**Ro 1:32**	*846*
you who judge practice the **s** things.	**Ro 2:1**	*846*
such things and do the **s** *yourself,*	**Ro 2:3**	*846*
In the **s** way the Spirit also	**Ro 8:26**	*5615*
to make from the **s** lump one vessel	**Ro 9:21**	*846*
for the **s** *Lord* is Lord of all,	**Ro 10:12**	*846*
In the **s** way then, there has also	**Ro 11:5**	*3779*
do not have the **s** function,	**Ro 12:4**	*846*
of the **s** mind toward one another;	**Ro 12:16**	*846*
you will have praise from the **s**;	**Ro 13:3**	*846*
to be of the **s** mind with one another	**Ro 15:5**	*846*
s mind and in the same judgment.	**1Co 1:10**	*846*
same mind and in the **s** judgment.	**1Co 1:10**	*846*
and all ate the **s** spiritual food;	**1Co 10:3**	*846*
all drank the **s** spiritual drink,	**1Co 10:4**	*846*
s as the woman whose head is shaved.	**1Co 11:5**	*846*
In the **s** way *He took* the cup also after	**1Co 11:25**	*5615*
of gifts, but the **s** Spirit.	**1Co 12:4**	*846*
of ministries, and the **s** Lord.	**1Co 12:5**	*846*
but the **s** God who works all things	**1Co 12:6**	*846*
according to the **s** Spirit;	**1Co 12:8**	*846*
to another faith by the **s** Spirit,	**1Co 12:9**	*846*
s Spirit works all these things,	**1Co 12:11**	*846*
have the **s** care for one another.	**1Co 12:25**	*846*
All flesh is not the **s** flesh,	**1Co 15:39**	*846*
patient enduring of the **s** sufferings	**2Co 1:6**	*846*
no *at the* **s** *time?*	**2Co 1:17**	
the **s** veil remains unlifted,	**2Co 3:14**	*846*
the **s** image from glory to glory,	**2Co 3:18**	*846*
But having the **s** spirit of faith,	**2Co 4:13**	*846*
who puts the **s** earnestness on your	**2Co 8:16**	*846*
that the **s** would be ready as a	**2Co 9:5**	*3778*
not conduct ourselves in the **s** spirit	**2Co 12:18**	*846*
spirit *and walk* in the **s** steps?	**2Co 12:18**	*846*
masters, do the **s** things to them,	**Eph 6:9**	*846*
s conflict which you saw in me,	**Php 1:30**	*846*
complete by being of the **s** mind,	**Php 2:2**	*846*
same mind, maintaining the **s** love,	**Php 2:2**	*846*
rejoice in the **s** way and share	**Php 2:18**	*846*
To write the **s** things *again* is no	**Php 3:1**	*846*
let us keep living by that **s** *standard*	**Php 3:16**	*846*
at the **s** time for us as well,	**Col 4:3**	*260*
for you also endured the **s** sufferings	**1Th 2:14**	*846*
At the **s** time they also learn	**1Tm 5:13**	*260*
At the **s** time also prepare me	**Phm 1:22**	*260*
BUT YOU ARE THE **S**,	**Heb 1:12**	*846*
likewise also partook of the **s**,	**Heb 2:14**	*846*
the **s** example of disobedience.	**Heb 4:11**	*846*
each one of you show the **s** diligence	**Heb 6:11**	*846*
In the **s** way God, desiring even	**Heb 6:17**	*3739*
And in the **s** way he sprinkled both	**Heb 9:21**	*3668*
by the **s** sacrifices which they offer	**Heb 10:1**	*846*
time after time the **s** sacrifices,	**Heb 10:11**	*846*
fellow heirs of the **s** promise;	**Heb 11:9**	*846*
is the **s** yesterday and today and	**Heb 13:8**	*846*
In the **s** way, was not Rahab the	**Jas 2:25**	*3668*
from the **s** mouth come *both*	**Jas 3:10**	*846*
fountain send out from the **s** opening	**Jas 3:11**	*846*
In the **s** way, you wives, be	**1Pe 3:1**	*3668*
You husbands in the **s** way, live with	**1Pe 3:7**	*3668*
also with the **s** purpose,	**1Pe 4:1**	*846*
into the **s** excesses of dissipation,	**1Pe 4:4**	*846*
knowing that the **s** experiences of	**1Pe 5:9**	*846*
a faith of the **s** kind as ours,	**2Pe 1:1**	*2472*
walk in the **s** manner as He walked.	**1Jn 2:6**	*3779*
since they in the **s** way as these	**Jude 1:7**	*3664*
Yet in the **s** way these men,	**Jude 1:8**	*3668*
who in the **s** way hold the teaching	**Rv 2:15**	*3668*
of it, and the night in the **s** way.	**Rv 8:12**	*3668*
to the **s** degree give her torment	**Rv 18:7**	*5118*

SAMGAR-NEBU

Nergal-sar-ezer, **S**, Sar-sekim the	**Jer 39:3**	5562

SAMLAH

and **S** of Masrekah became king in	**Gn 36:36**	8072
Then **S** died, and Shaul of Rehoboth	**Gn 36:37**	8072
S of Masrekah became king in his	**1Ch 1:47**	8072
When **S** died, Shaul of Rehoboth by	**1Ch 1:48**	8072

SAMOS

the next day we crossed over to **S**;	**Ac 20:15**	*4544*

SAMOTHRACE

we ran a straight course to **S**,	**Ac 16:11**	*4543*

SAMSON

birth to a son and named him **S**;	**Jg 13:24**	8123
S went down to Timnah and saw	**Jg 14:1**	8123
But **S** said to his father,	**Jg 14:3**	8123
Then **S** went down to Timnah with	**Jg 14:5**	8123
and she looked good to **S**.	**Jg 14:7**	8123
and **S** made a feast there, for the	**Jg 14:10**	8123
Then **S** said to them,	**Jg 14:12**	8123
S visited his wife with a young goat,	**Jg 15:1**	8123
S then said to them,	**Jg 15:3**	8123
S went and caught three	**Jg 15:4**	8123
"**S**, the son-in-law of the	**Jg 15:6**	8123
S said to them,	**Jg 15:7**	8123
"We have come up to bind **S** in	**Jg 15:10**	8123
of the rock of Etam and said to **S**,	**Jg 15:11**	8123
And **S** said to them,	**Jg 15:12**	8123
Then **S** said, "With the jawbone of	**Jg 15:16**	8123
Now **S** went to Gaza and saw a	**Jg 16:1**	8123
"**S** has come here,"	**Jg 16:2**	8123
Now **S** lay until midnight, and at	**Jg 16:3**	8123
So Delilah said to **S**,	**Jg 16:6**	8123
S said to her,	**Jg 16:7**	8123
"The Philistines are upon you, **S**!"	**Jg 16:9**	8123
Then Delilah said to **S**,	**Jg 16:10**	8123
"The Philistines are upon you, **S**!"	**Jg 16:12**	8123
Then Delilah said to **S**,	**Jg 16:13**	8123
"The Philistines are upon you, **S**!"	**Jg 16:14**	8123
"The Philistines are upon you, **S**!"	**Jg 16:20**	8123
"Our god has given **S** our enemy	**Jg 16:23**	8123
"Call for **S**, that he may amuse us."	**Jg 16:25**	8123
they called for **S** from the prison,	**Jg 16:25**	8123
Then **S** said to the boy who was	**Jg 16:26**	8123
on while **S** was amusing *them.*	**Jg 16:27**	8123
S called to the LORD and said,	**Jg 16:28**	8123
S grasped the two middle	**Jg 16:29**	8123
And **S** said, "Let me die with the	**Jg 16:30**	8123
me if I tell of Gideon, Barak, **S**,	**Heb 11:32**	*4546*

SAMSON'S

day that they said to **S** wife,	**Jg 14:15**	8123
S wife wept before him and said,	**Jg 14:16**	8123
But **S** wife was *given* to his	**Jg 14:20**	8123

SAMUEL

of Simeon, **S** the son of Ammihud.	**Nu 34:20**	8050
and she named him **S**,	**1Sa 1:20**	8050
Now **S** was ministering before the	**1Sa 2:18**	8050
the boy **S** grew before the LORD.	**1Sa 2:21**	8050
Now the boy **S** was growing in	**1Sa 2:26**	8050
Now the boy **S** was ministering to	**1Sa 3:1**	8050
and **S** was lying down in the temple	**1Sa 3:3**	8050
that the LORD called **S**;	**1Sa 3:4**	8050
The LORD called yet again, "**S**!"	**1Sa 3:6**	8050
So **S** arose and went to Eli and	**1Sa 3:6**	8050
Now **S** did not yet know the LORD,	**1Sa 3:7**	8050
So the LORD called **S** again for the	**1Sa 3:8**	8050
And Eli said to **S**,	**1Sa 3:9**	8050
So **S** went and lay down in his	**1Sa 3:9**	8050
and called as at other times, "**S**!	**1Sa 3:10**	8050
called as at other times, "Samuel! **S**!	**1Sa 3:10**	8050
And **S** said, "Speak, for Your servant	**1Sa 3:10**	8050
The LORD said to **S**,	**1Sa 3:11**	8050
So **S** lay down until morning.	**1Sa 3:15**	8050
But **S** was afraid to tell the	**1Sa 3:15**	8050
Then Eli called **S** and said,	**1Sa 3:16**	8050
called Samuel and said, "**S**, my son."	**1Sa 3:16**	8050
So **S** told him everything and hid	**1Sa 3:18**	8050
Thus **S** grew and the LORD was with	**1Sa 3:19**	8050
that **S** was confirmed as a prophet	**1Sa 3:20**	8050
LORD revealed Himself to **S** at Shiloh	**1Sa 3:21**	8050
the word of **S** came to all Israel.	**1Sa 4:1**	8050
Then **S** spoke to all the house of	**1Sa 7:3**	8050
S said, "Gather all Israel to Mizpah and	**1Sa 7:5**	8050
And **S** judged the sons of Israel at	**1Sa 7:6**	8050
Then the sons of Israel said to **S**,	**1Sa 7:8**	8050
S took a suckling lamb and	**1Sa 7:9**	8050
and **S** cried to the LORD for Israel	**1Sa 7:9**	8050
Now **S** was offering up the burnt	**1Sa 7:10**	8050
Then **S** took a stone and set it	**1Sa 7:12**	8050
the Philistines all the days of **S**.	**1Sa 7:13**	8050
Now **S** judged Israel all the days	**1Sa 7:15**	8050
And it came about when **S** was old	**1Sa 8:1**	8050
together and came to **S** at Ramah;	**1Sa 8:4**	8050
was displeasing in the sight of **S**	**1Sa 8:6**	8050
And **S** prayed to the LORD.	**1Sa 8:6**	8050
The LORD said to **S**,	**1Sa 8:7**	8050
So **S** spoke all the words of the	**1Sa 8:10**	8050
refused to listen to the voice of **S**,	**1Sa 8:19**	8050
Now after **S** had heard all the	**1Sa 8:21**	8050
The LORD said to **S**,	**1Sa 8:22**	8050
So **S** said to the men of Israel,	**1Sa 8:22**	8050
S was coming out toward them to go	**1Sa 9:14**	8050
had revealed *this* to **S** saying,	**1Sa 9:15**	8050
When **S** saw Saul, the LORD said to	**1Sa 9:17**	8050
Saul approached **S** in the gate and	**1Sa 9:18**	8050
S answered Saul and said,	**1Sa 9:19**	8050
Then **S** took Saul and his servant	**1Sa 9:22**	8050
S said to the cook,	**1Sa 9:23**	8050
And **S** said, "Here is what has	**1Sa 9:24**	
So Saul ate with **S** that day.	**1Sa 9:24**	8050
S spoke with Saul on the roof.	**1Sa 9:25**	8050
daybreak **S** called to Saul on the roof,	**1Sa 9:26**	8050
he and **S** went out into the street.	**1Sa 9:26**	8050
edge of the city, **S** said to Saul,	**1Sa 9:27**	8050
Then **S** took the flask of oil,	**1Sa 10:1**	8050
he turned his back to leave **S**,	**1Sa 10:9**	8050
not be found, we went to **S**."	**1Sa 10:14**	8050
tell me what **S** said to you."	**1Sa 10:15**	8050
the kingdom which **S** had mentioned.	**1Sa 10:16**	8050
Thereafter **S** called the people	**1Sa 10:17**	8050

Context	Reference	Number
Thus **S** brought all the tribes of	1Sa 10:20	8050
S said to all the people,	1Sa 10:24	8050
Then **S** told the people the	1Sa 10:25	8050
And **S** sent all the people away,	1Sa 10:25	8050
come out after Saul and after **S**,	1Sa 11:7	8050
Then the people said to **S**,	1Sa 11:12	8050
Then **S** said to the people,	1Sa 11:14	8050
Then **S** said to all Israel,	1Sa 12:1	8050
Then **S** said to the people,	1Sa 12:6	8050
and Bedan and Jephthah and **S**,	1Sa 12:11	8050
So **S** called to the LORD, and the	1Sa 12:18	8050
greatly feared the LORD and **S**.	1Sa 12:18	8050
Then all the people said to **S**,	1Sa 12:19	8050
S said to the people,	1Sa 12:20	8050
to the appointed time set by **S**,	1Sa 13:8	8050
but **S** did not come to Gilgal;	1Sa 13:8	8050
offering, behold, **S** came;	1Sa 13:10	8050
But **S** said, "What have you done?"	1Sa 13:11	8050
S said to Saul,	1Sa 13:13	8050
Then **S** arose and went up from	1Sa 13:15	8050
Then **S** said to Saul,	1Sa 15:1	8050
the word of the LORD came to **S**,	1Sa 15:10	8050
And **S** was distressed and cried out	1Sa 15:11	8050
S rose early in the morning to	1Sa 15:12	8050
and it was told **S**, saying,	1Sa 15:12	8050
S came to Saul, and Saul said	1Sa 15:13	8050
S said, "What then is this bleating	1Sa 15:14	8050
Then **S** said to Saul,	1Sa 15:16	8050
S said, "Is it not true, though	1Sa 15:17	8050
Then Saul said to **S**,	1Sa 15:20	8050
S said, "Has the LORD as much	1Sa 15:22	8050
Then Saul said to **S**,	1Sa 15:24	8050
But **S** said to Saul,	1Sa 15:26	8050
As **S** turned to go, *Saul* seized	1Sa 15:27	8050
So **S** said to him,	1Sa 15:28	8050
So **S** went back following Saul, and	1Sa 15:31	8050
S said, "Bring me Agag, the king of	1Sa 15:32	8050
But **S** said, "As your sword has	1Sa 15:33	8050
And **S** hewed Agag to pieces before	1Sa 15:33	8050
Then **S** went to Ramah, but Saul	1Sa 15:34	8050
S did not see Saul again until	1Sa 15:35	8050
for **S** grieved over Saul.	1Sa 15:35	8050
Now the LORD said to **S**,	1Sa 16:1	8050
S said, "How can I go? When Saul	1Sa 16:2	8050
So **S** did what the LORD said, and	1Sa 16:4	8050
But the LORD said to **S**,	1Sa 16:7	8050
and made him pass before **S**.	1Sa 16:8	8050
seven of his sons pass before **S**.	1Sa 16:10	8050
But **S** said to Jesse,	1Sa 16:10	8050
And **S** said to Jesse,	1Sa 16:11	8050
Then **S** said to Jesse,	1Sa 16:11	8050
Then **S** took the horn of oil and	1Sa 16:13	8050
And **S** arose and went to Ramah.	1Sa 16:13	8050
escaped and came to **S** at Ramah,	1Sa 19:18	8050
he and **S** went and stayed in Naioth.	1Sa 19:18	8050
with **S** standing *and* presiding over	1Sa 19:20	8050
"Where are **S** and David?"	1Sa 19:22	8050
and he too prophesied before **S** and	1Sa 19:24	8050
Then **S** died; and all Israel gathered	1Sa 25:1	8050
Now **S** was dead, and all Israel had	1Sa 28:3	8050
"Bring up **S** for me."	1Sa 28:11	8050
When the woman saw **S**,	1Sa 28:12	8050
And Saul knew that it was **S**,	1Sa 28:14	8050
Then **S** said to Saul,	1Sa 28:15	8050
S said, "Why then do you ask me,	1Sa 28:16	8050
afraid because of the words of **S**;	1Sa 28:20	8050
The sons of **S** *were* Joel the	1Ch 6:28	8050
the son of Joel, the son of **S**,	1Ch 6:33	8050
Jeriel, Jahmai, Ibsam and **S**,	1Ch 7:2	8050
whom David and **S** the seer	1Ch 9:22	8050
to the word of the LORD through **S**.	1Ch 11:3	8050
And all that **S** the seer had	1Ch 26:28	8050
in the chronicles of **S** the seer,	1Ch 29:29	8050
since the days of **S** the prophet;	2Ch 35:18	8050
And **S** was among those who called	Ps 99:6	8050
though Moses and **S** were to stand	Jer 15:1	8050
from **S** and *his* successors onward,	Ac 3:24	*4545*
them judges until **S** the prophet.	Ac 13:20	*4545*
of David and **S** and the prophets,	Heb 11:32	*4545*

SANBALLAT

Context	Reference	Number
When **S** the Horonite and Tobiah	Ne 2:10	5571
But when **S** the Horonite and	Ne 2:19	5571
S heard that we were rebuilding the	Ne 4:1	5571
when **S**, Tobiah, the Arabs,	Ne 4:7	5571
Now when it was reported to **S**,	Ne 6:1	5571
then **S** and Geshem sent *a message*	Ne 6:2	5571
Then **S** sent his servant to me in	Ne 6:5	5571
Tobiah and **S** had hired him.	Ne 6:12	5571
Tobiah and **S** according to these	Ne 6:14	5571
was a son-in-law of **S** the Horonite.	Ne 13:28	5571

SANCTIFICATION

Context	Reference	Number
to righteousness, resulting in **s**.	Ro 6:19	*38*
your benefit, resulting in **s**,	Ro 6:22	*38*
from God, and righteousness and **s**,	1Co 1:30	*38*
this is the will of God, your **s**;	1Th 4:3	*38*
his own vessel in **s** and honor,	1Th 4:4	*38*
the purpose of impurity, but in **s**.	1Th 4:7	*38*
salvation through **s** by the Spirit	2Th 2:13	*38*
and the **s** without which no one	Heb 12:14	*38*

SANCTIFIED

Context	Reference	Number
God blessed the seventh day and **s** it	Gn 2:3	6942
I will be **s** among the sons of Israel;	Lv 22:32	6942
I **s** to Myself all the firstborn	Nu 3:13	6942
land of Egypt I **s** them for Myself.	Nu 8:17	6942
the priests who were present had **s**	2Ch 5:11	6942
LORD which He had **s** in Jerusalem.	2Ch 36:14	6942
when I am **s** through you	Ezk 38:16	6942
then I shall be **s** through them in	Ezk 39:27	6942
who are **s** of the sons of Zadok,	Ezk 48:11	6942
or the temple that **s** the gold?	Mt 23:17	*37*
you say of Him, whom the Father **s**	Jn 10:36	*37*
themselves also may be **s** in truth.	Jn 17:19	*37*
among all those who are **s**.	Ac 20:32	*37*
who have been **s** by faith in Me.'	Ac 26:18	*37*
acceptable, **s** by the Holy Spirit.	Ro 15:16	*37*
who have been **s** in Christ Jesus,	1Co 1:2	*37*
you were washed, but you were **s**,	1Co 6:11	*37*
husband is **s** through his wife,	1Co 7:14	*37*
unbelieving wife is **s** through	1Co 7:14	*37*
for it is **s** by means of the word	1Tm 4:5	*37*
he will be a vessel for honor, **s**,	2Tm 2:21	*37*
who are **s** are all from one *Father;*	Heb 2:11	*37*
By this will we have been **s**	Heb 10:10	*37*
for all time those who are **s**.	Heb 10:14	*37*
of the covenant by which he was **s**,	Heb 10:29	*37*

SANCTIFIES

Context	Reference	Number
know that I am the LORD who **s** you.	Ex 31:13	6942
I am the LORD who **s** you.	Lv 20:8	6942
for I the LORD, who **s** you, am holy.	Lv 21:8	6942
for I am the LORD who **s** him.'	Lv 21:15	6942
For I am the LORD who **s** them.' "	Lv 21:23	6942
I am the LORD who **s** them.	Lv 22:9	6942
for I am the LORD who **s** them.' "	Lv 22:16	6942
I am the LORD who **s** you,	Lv 22:32	6942
that I am the LORD who **s** them.	Ezk 20:12	6942
that I am the LORD who **s** Israel,	Ezk 37:28	6942
or the altar that **s** the offering?	Mt 23:19	*37*
For both He who **s** and those who	Heb 2:11	*37*

SANCTIFY

Context	Reference	Number
"**S** to Me every firstborn, the	Ex 13:2	6942
"**S** a solemn assembly for Baal."	2Ki 10:20	6942
And Aaron was set apart to **s** him	1Ch 23:13	6942
Passover *animals,* **s** yourselves and	2Ch 35:6	6942
gatekeepers to **s** the sabbath day.	Ne 13:22	6942
in his midst, They will **s** My name;	Is 29:23	6942
they will **s** the Holy One of Jacob And	Is 29:23	6942
"Those who **s** and purify	Is 66:17	6942
'**S** My sabbaths; and they shall be a	Ezk 20:20	6942
I will magnify Myself, **s** Myself,	Ezk 38:23	6942
feasts and **s** My sabbaths.	Ezk 44:24	6942
the people, **s** the congregation,	Jl 2:16	6942
"**S** them in the truth;	Jn 17:17	*37*
"For their sakes I **s** Myself,	Jn 17:19	*37*
that He might **s** her, having	Eph 5:26	*37*
may the God of peace Himself **s** you	1Th 5:23	*37*
s for the cleansing of the flesh,	Heb 9:13	*37*
that He might **s** the people through	Heb 13:12	*37*
s Christ as Lord in your hearts,	1Pe 3:15	*37*

SANCTIFYING

Context	Reference	Number
by the **s** work of the Spirit,	1Pe 1:2	*38*

SANCTITY

Context	Reference	Number
continue in faith and love and **s**	1Tm 2:15	*38*

SANCTUARIES

Context	Reference	Number
that he will not profane My **s**.	Lv 21:23	4720
and will make your **s** desolate,	Lv 26:31	4720
inner and outer **s**.	1Ki 6:29	
inner and outer **s**.	1Ki 6:30	
and speak against the **s** and	Ezk 21:2	4720
your trade You profaned your **s**.	Ezk 28:18	4720
And the **s** of Israel laid waste.	Am 7:9	4720

SANCTUARY

Context	Reference	Number
have made for Your dwelling, The **s**,	Ex 15:17	4720
"Let them construct a **s** for Me,	Ex 25:8	4720
according to the shekel of the **s**	Ex 30:13	6944
according to the shekel of the **s**,	Ex 30:24	6944
work in the construction of the **s**,	Ex 36:1	6944
work in the construction of the **s**.	Ex 36:3	6944
performing all the work of the **s**	Ex 36:4	6944
for the contributions of the **s**."	Ex 36:6	6944
work, in all the work of the **s**,	Ex 38:24	6944
according to the shekel of the **s**.	Ex 38:24	6944
according to the shekel of the **s**;	Ex 38:25	6944
according to the shekel of the **s**),	Ex 38:26	6944
were for casting the sockets of the **s**	Ex 38:27	6944
in front of the veil of the **s**	Lv 4:6	6944
in *terms of* the shekel of the **s**,	Lv 5:15	6944
away from the front of the **s**	Lv 10:4	6944
been brought inside, into the **s**,	Lv 10:18	6944
certainly have eaten it in the **s**,	Lv 10:18	6944
thing, nor enter the **s** until	Lv 12:4	4720
burnt offering, at the place of the **s**	Lv 14:13	6944
and make atonement for the holy **s**,	Lv 16:33	4720
keep My sabbaths and revere My **s**;	Lv 19:30	4720
so as to defile My **s** and to profane	Lv 20:3	4720
nor shall he go out of the **s** nor	Lv 21:12	4720
nor profane the **s** of his God,	Lv 21:12	4720
My sabbaths and reverence My **s**;	Lv 26:2	4720
silver, after the shekel of the **s**.	Lv 27:3	6944
be after the shekel of the **s**.	Lv 27:25	6944
performing the duties of the **s**.	Nu 3:28	6944
of the **s** with which they minister,	Nu 3:31	6944
who perform the duties of the **s**.	Nu 3:32	6944
performing the duties of the **s** for	Nu 3:38	4720
in terms of the shekel of the **s**	Nu 3:47	6944
in terms of the shekel of the **s**,	Nu 3:50	6944
with which they serve in the **s**,	Nu 4:12	6944
and all the furnishings of the **s**,	Nu 4:15	6944
with the **s** and its furnishings."	Nu 4:16	6944
according to the shekel of the **s**,	Nu 7:13	6944
according to the shekel of the **s**,	Nu 7:19	6944
according to the shekel of the **s**,	Nu 7:25	6944
according to the shekel of the **s**,	Nu 7:31	6944
according to the shekel of the **s**,	Nu 7:37	6944
according to the shekel of the **s**,	Nu 7:43	6944
according to the shekel of the **s**,	Nu 7:49	6944
according to the shekel of the **s**,	Nu 7:55	6944
according to the shekel of the **s**,	Nu 7:61	6944
according to the shekel of the **s**,	Nu 7:67	6944
according to the shekel of the **s**,	Nu 7:73	6944
according to the shekel of the **s**,	Nu 7:79	6944
according to the shekel of the **s**;	Nu 7:85	6944
according to the shekel of the **s**,	Nu 7:86	6944
by their coming near to the **s**."	Nu 8:19	6944
guilt in connection with the **s**,	Nu 18:1	4720
come near to the furnishings of the **s**	Nu 18:3	6944
attend to the obligations of the **s**	Nu 18:5	6944
according to the shekel of the **s**,	Nu 18:16	6944
he has defiled the **s** of the LORD;	Nu 19:20	4720
oak that was by the **s** of the LORD.	Jos 24:26	4720
both the nave and the inner **s**;	1Ki 6:5	1687
it on the inside as an inner **s**,	1Ki 6:16	1687
the nave in front of *the inner* **s**,	1Ki 6:17	
Then he prepared an inner **s** within	1Ki 6:19	1687
s *was* twenty cubits in length,	1Ki 6:20	1687
across the front of the inner **s**,	1Ki 6:21	1687
the inner **s** he overlaid with gold.	1Ki 6:22	1687
Also in the inner **s** he made two	1Ki 6:23	1687
s he made doors of olive wood,	1Ki 6:31	1687
the left, in front of the inner **s**,	1Ki 7:49	1687
into the inner **s** of the house,	1Ki 8:6	1687
the holy place before the inner **s**,	1Ki 8:8	1687
and over all the utensils of the **s**	1Ch 9:29	6944
and build the **s** of the LORD God,	1Ch 22:19	4720
officers of the **s** and officers of God,	1Ch 24:5	6944
you to build a house for the **s**;	1Ch 28:10	4720
He made chains in the inner **s** and	2Ch 3:16	1687
to burn in front of the inner **s** in the	2Ch 4:20	1687
into the inner **s** of the house,	2Ch 5:7	1687
be seen in front of the inner **s**,	2Ch 5:9	1687
built You a **s** there for Your name,	2Ch 20:8	4720
Get out of the **s**, for you have	2Ch 26:18	4720
offering for the kingdom, the **s**,	2Ch 29:21	4720
but yield to the LORD and enter His **s**	2Ch 30:8	4720
the purification *rules* of the **s**."	2Ch 30:19	6944
the sword in the house of their **s**,	2Ch 36:17	4720
there are the utensils of the **s**,	Ne 10:39	4720
May He send you help from the **s** And	Ps 20:2	6944
up my hands toward Your holy **s**.	Ps 28:2	1687
Thus I have seen You in the **s**,	Ps 63:2	6944
of my God, my King, into the **s**.	Ps 68:24	6944
God, *You are* awesome from Your **s**.	Ps 68:35	4720
Until I came into the **s** of God;	Ps 73:17	4720
damaged everything within the **s**.	Ps 74:3	6944
have burned Your **s** to the ground;	Ps 74:7	4720
He built His **s** like the heights,	Ps 78:69	4720
Strength and beauty are in His **s**.	Ps 96:6	4720
Judah became His **s**,	Ps 114:2	6944
Lift up your hands to the **s** And	Ps 134:2	6944
Praise God in His **s**;	Ps 150:1	6944
"Then He shall become a **s**;	Is 8:14	4720
place And comes to his **s** to pray,	Is 16:12	4720
will pollute the princes of the **s**,	Is 43:28	6944
To beautify the place of My **s**;	Is 60:13	4720
drink it in the courts of My **s**.	Is 62:9	6944
Your holy people possessed Your **s** for	Is 63:18	4720
beginning Is the place of our **s**.	Jer 17:12	4720
has seen the nations enter her **s**,	La 1:10	4720
His altar, He has abandoned His **s**;	La 2:7	4720
be slain In the **s** of the Lord?	La 2:20	4720
because you have defiled My **s** with	Ezk 5:11	4720
that I would be far from My **s**?	Ezk 8:6	4720
and you shall start from My **s**."	Ezk 9:6	4720
yet I was a **s** for them a little	Ezk 11:16	4720
they have defiled My **s** on the same	Ezk 23:38	4720
they entered My **s** on the same day	Ezk 23:39	4720
I am about to profane My **s**,	Ezk 24:21	4720
you said, 'Aha!' against My **s** when	Ezk 25:3	4720
set My **s** in their midst forever.	Ezk 37:26	4720
when My **s** is in their midst forever.	Ezk 37:28	4720
as for the front of the **s**,	Ezk 41:21	6944
and the **s** each had a double door.	Ezk 41:23	6944
go out into the outer court from the **s**	Ezk 42:14	6944
place of the house, outside the **s**.	Ezk 43:21	4720
way of the outer gate of the **s**,	Ezk 44:1	4720
house, with all exits of the **s**.	Ezk 44:5	4720
to be in My **s** to profane it,	Ezk 44:7	4720
to keep charge of My **s**."	Ezk 44:8	4720
sons of Israel, shall enter My **s**.	Ezk 44:9	4720
they shall be ministers in My **s**,	Ezk 44:11	4720
who kept charge of My **s** when the	Ezk 44:15	4720
"They shall enter My **s**;	Ezk 44:16	4720
the day that he goes into the **s**,	Ezk 44:27	6944
inner court to minister in the **s**,	Ezk 44:27	6944
and in it shall be the **s**,	Ezk 45:3	4720
priests, the ministers of the **s**,	Ezk 45:4	4720
houses and a holy place for the **s**.	Ezk 45:4	4720
without blemish and cleanse the **s**.	Ezk 45:18	4720
their water flows from the **s**,	Ezk 47:12	4720
s shall be in the middle of it.	Ezk 48:8	4720
and the **s** of the LORD shall be in	Ezk 48:10	4720
And the holy allotment and the **s**	Ezk 48:21	4720
place of His **s** was thrown down.	Da 8:11	4720
Your face shine on Your desolate **s**.	Da 9:17	4720
will destroy the city and the **s**.	Da 9:26	6944
arise, desecrate the **s** fortress,	Da 11:31	4720
for it is a **s** of the king and a	Am 7:13	4720
Her priests have profaned the **s**.	Zph 3:4	6944
the **s** of the LORD which He loves and	Mal 2:11	6944
pieces of silver into the temple **s**	Mt 27:5	*3485*
a minister in the **s** and	Heb 8:2	*40*
divine worship and the earthly **s**.	Heb 9:1	*40*

SAND

Context	Reference	Number
as the **s** which is on the seashore;	Gn 22:17	2344
descendants as the **s** of the sea,	Gn 32:12	2344
abundance like the **s** of the sea,	Gn 41:49	2344

the Egyptian and hid him in the s. Ex 2:12 2344
and the lizard, and the s reptile, Lv 11:30 2546
the hidden treasures of the s." Dt 33:19 2344
as the s that is on the seashore, Jos 11:4 2344
numerous as the s on the seashore. Jg 7:12 2344
like the s which is on the seashore 1Sa 13:5 2344
as the s that is by the sea in 2Sa 17:11 2344
as the s that is on the seashore 1Ki 4:20 2344
like the s that is on the seashore. 1Ki 4:29 2344
be heavier than the s of the seas; Jb 6:3 2344
I shall multiply *my* days as the s. Jb 29:18 2344
fowl like the s of the seas, Ps 78:27 2344
them, they would outnumber the s. Ps 139:18 2344
stone is heavy and the s weighty, Pr 27:3 2344
may be like the s of the sea, Is 10:22 2344
would have been like the s, Is 48:19 2344
the s as a boundary for the sea, Jer 5:22 2344
before Me Than the s of the seas; Jer 15:8 2344
s of the sea cannot be measured, Jer 33:22 2344
Will be like the s of the sea, Hos 1:10 2344
They collect captives like s. Hab 1:9 2344
who built his house on the s. Mt 7:26 *285*
OF ISRAEL BE LIKE THE S OF THE SEA, Ro 9:27 *285*
AS THE S WHICH IS BY THE SEASHORE. Heb 11:12 *285*
dragon stood on the s of the seashore. Rv 13:1 *285*
is like the s of the seashore. Rv 20:8 *285*

SANDAL
I will not take a thread or a s thong Gn 14:23 5275
and pull his s off his foot and Dt 25:9 5275
house of him whose s is removed.' Dt 25:10 5275
s has not worn out on your foot. Dt 29:5 5275
his s and gave it to another; Ru 4:7 5275
And he removed his s. Ru 4:8 5275
undone, Nor its s strap broken. Is 5:27 5275
s I am not worthy to untie." Jn 1:27 *5266*

SANDALS
remove your s from your feet, for Ex 3:5 5275
loins girded, your s on your feet, Ex 12:11 5275
"Remove your s from your feet, Jos 5:15 5275
and patched s on their feet, Jos 9:5 5275
and these our clothes and our s Jos 9:13 5275
waist, and on his s on his feet. 1Ki 2:5 5275
and they gave them clothes and s, 2Ch 28:15 5274b
"How beautiful are your feet in s, SS 7:1 5275
s of porpoise skin on your feet; Ezk 16:10 5274b
And the needy for a pair of s. Am 2:6 5275
And the needy for a pair of s, Am 8:6 5275
and I am not fit to remove His s; Mt 3:11 *5266*
journey, or even two coats, or s, Mt 10:10 *5266*
down and untie the thong of His s. Mk 1:7 *5266*
to wear s; and *He added,* "Do not put Mk 6:9 *4547*
fit to untie the thong of His s; Lk 3:16 *5266*
on his hand and s on his feet; Lk 15:22 *5266*
out without money belt and bag and s, Lk 22:35 *5266*
'TAKE OFF THE S FROM YOUR FEET, Ac 7:33 *5266*
"Gird yourself and put on your s." Ac 12:8 *4547*
the s of whose feet I am not worthy Ac 13:25 *5266*

SANG
Moses and the sons of Israel s this song Ex 15:1 7891
Then Israel s this song: Nu 21:17 7891
the son of Abinoam s on that day, Jg 5:1 7891
The women s as they played, 1Sa 18:7 6031b
appointed those who s to the LORD 2Ch 20:21 7891
also s and the trumpets sounded; 2Ch 29:28 7891
So they s praises with joy, and 2Ch 29:30 1984b
They s, praising and giving Ezr 3:11 6031b
And the singers s, with Jezrahiah Ne 12:42 8085
When the morning stars s together And Jb 38:7 7442
They s His praise. Ps 106:12 7891
we s a dirge, and you did not Mt 11:17 *2354*
we s a dirge, and you did not weep.' Lk 7:32 *2354*
And they s a new song, saying, Rv 5:9 *103*
And they s a new song before the Rv 14:3 *103*
And they s the song of Moses, Rv 15:3 *103*

SANITY
So he disguised his s before them, 1Sa 21:13 2940

SANK
And their hearts s, and they Gn 42:28 3318
They s like lead in the mighty Ex 15:10 6749
"The well, which the leaders s, Nu 21:18 2658
And the stone s into his forehead, 1Sa 17:49 2883
heart and he s in his chariot. 2Ki 9:24 3766
They s into sleep; Ps 76:5 5123
the valleys s down To the place Ps 104:8 3381
And *so* s down in their iniquity. Ps 106:43 4355
mud, and Jeremiah s into the mud. Jer 38:6 2883
I s into a deep sleep with my face Da 8:18 7290a

SANSANNAH
and Ziklag and Madmannah and S, Jos 15:31 5578

SAP
shall be full of s and very green, Ps 92:14 1879

SAPH
the Hushathite struck down S, 2Sa 21:18 5593

SAPPHIRA
named Ananias, with his wife S, Ac 5:1 *4551*

SAPPHIRE
appeared to be a pavement of s, Ex 24:10 5601
a turquoise, a s and a diamond; Ex 28:18 5601
a turquoise, a s and a diamond; Ex 39:11 5601
of Ophir, In precious onyx, or s. Jb 28:16 5601
cherubim something like a s stone, Ezk 10:1 5601
the second, s; the third, chalcedony; Rv 21:19 *4552*

SAPPHIRES
"Its rocks are the source of s, Jb 28:6 5601
is carved ivory Inlaid with s. SS 5:14 5601
your foundations I will lay in s. Is 54:11 5601

SARAH
Sarai, but S *shall be* her name. Gn 17:15 8283
will S, who is ninety years old, bear Gn 17:17 8283
but S your wife will bear you a Gn 17:19 8283
whom S will bear to you at this Gn 17:21 8283
Abraham hurried into the tent to S, Gn 18:6 8283
"Where is S your wife?" Gn 18:9 8283
S your wife will have a son." Gn 18:10 8283
And S was listening at the tent Gn 18:10 8283
Now Abraham and S were old, Gn 18:11 8283
S was past childbearing. Gn 18:11 8283
S laughed to herself, saying, Gn 18:12 8283
"Why did S laugh, saying, Gn 18:13 8283
year, and S will have a son." Gn 18:14 8283
S denied *it* however, saying, Gn 18:15 8283
Abraham said of S his wife, Gn 20:2 8283
king of Gerar sent and took S. Gn 20:2 8283
and restored his wife S to him. Gn 20:14 8283
To S he said, Gn 20:16 8283
of Abimelech because of S, Gn 20:18 8283
LORD took note of S as He had said, Gn 21:1 8283
LORD did for S as He had promised. Gn 21:1 8283
So S conceived and bore a son to Gn 21:2 8283
born to him, whom S bore to him, Gn 21:3 8283
S said, "God has made laughter Gn 21:6 8283
that S would nurse children? Gn 21:7 8283
Now S saw the son of Hagar the Gn 21:9 8283
whatever S tells you, listen to Gn 21:12 8283
Now S lived one hundred and Gn 23:1 8283
were the years of the life of S. Gn 23:1 8283
S died in Kiriath-arba Gn 23:2 8283
mourn for S and to weep for her. Gn 23:2 8283
Abraham buried S his wife in the Gn 23:19 8283
"Now S my master's wife bore a Gn 24:36 8283
there Abraham was buried with S Gn 25:10 8283
buried Abraham and his wife S, Gn 49:31 8283
S who gave birth to you in pain; Is 51:2 8283
COME, AND S SHALL HAVE A SON." Ro 9:9 *4564*
By faith even S herself received Heb 11:11 *4564*
as S obeyed Abraham, calling him 1Pe 3:6 *4564*

SARAH'S
her into his mother S tent, Gn 24:67 8283
whom Hagar the Egyptian, S maid, Gn 25:12 8283
old, and the deadness of S womb; Ro 4:19 *4564*

SARAI
The name of Abram's wife was S; Gn 11:29 8297
S was barren; Gn 11:30 8297
grandson, and S his daughter-in-law, Gn 11:31 8297
S his wife and Lot his nephew, Gn 12:5 8297
Egypt, that he said to S his wife, Gn 12:11 8297
with great plagues because of S, Gn 12:17 8297
Now S, Abram's wife had borne him Gn 16:1 8297
So S said to Abram, Gn 16:2 8297
Abram listened to the voice of S. Gn 16:2 8297
wife S took Hagar the Egyptian, Gn 16:3 8297
And S said to Abram, Gn 16:5 8297
But Abram said to S, Gn 16:6 8297
So S treated her harshly, and she Gn 16:6 8297
the presence of my mistress S." Gn 16:8 8297
"As for S your wife, you shall Gn 17:15 8297
you shall not call her name S, Gn 17:15 8297

SARAI'S
"Hagar, S maid, where have you Gn 16:8 8297

SARAPH
the men of Cozeba, Joash, S, 1Ch 4:22 8315

SARDIS
Pergamum and to Thyatira and to S Rv 1:11 *4554*
angel of the church in S write: Rv 3:1 *4554*
'But you have a few people in S Rv 3:4 *4554*

SARDIUS
stone and a s in appearance; Rv 4:3 *4556*
the fifth, sardonyx; the sixth, s; Rv 21:20 *4556*

SARDONYX
the fifth, s; the sixth, sardius; Rv 21:20 *4557*

SARGON
when S the king of Assyria sent Is 20:1 5623

SARID
their inheritance was as far as S. Jos 19:10 8301a
Then it turned from S to the east Jos 19:12 8301a

SAR-SEKIM
Samgar-nebu, S the Rab-saris, Jer 39:3 8310

SASH
checkered work, a turban and a s, Ex 28:4 73
linen, and you shall make a s, Ex 28:39 73
and the s of fine twisted linen, Ex 39:29 73
on him and girded him with the s, Lv 8:7 73
shall be girded with the linen s and Lv 16:4 73
And tie your s securely about him. Is 22:21 73
across His chest with a golden s. Rv 1:13 *2223*

SASHES
you shall also make s for them, Ex 28:40 73
"You shall gird them with s, Ex 29:9 73
tunics, and girded them with s and Lv 8:13 73
headdresses, ankle chains, s, Is 3:20 7196
around their chests with golden s. Rv 15:6 *2223*

SAT
she went and s down opposite him, Gn 21:16 3427
And she s opposite him, and lifted Gn 21:16 3427
camel's saddle, and she s on them. Gn 31:34 3427
Then they s down to eat a meal. Gn 37:25 3427
and s in the gateway of Enaim, Gn 38:14 3427
his strength and s up in the bed. Gn 48:2 3427
and he s down by a well. Ex 2:15 3427
firstborn of Pharaoh who s on his Ex 12:29 3427
when we s by the pots of meat, Ex 16:3 3427
put it under him, and he s on it; Ex 17:12 3427
that Moses s to judge the people, Ex 18:13 3427
people s down to eat and to drink, Ex 32:6 3427
Asher s at the seashore, And Jg 5:17 3427
the angel of the LORD came and s under Jg 6:11 3427
So both of them s down and ate and Jg 19:6 3427
they s down in the open square of Jg 19:15 3427
and s there before God until evening, Jg 21:2 3427
So she s beside the reapers; Ru 2:14 3427
up to the gate and s down there, Ru 4:1 3427
And he turned aside and s down. Ru 4:1 3427
"Sit down here." So they s down. Ru 4:2 3427
came, the king s down to eat food. 1Sa 20:24 3427
The king s on his seat as usual, 1Sa 20:25 3427
up and Abner s down by Saul's side, 1Sa 20:25 3427
from the ground and s on the bed. 1Sa 28:23 3427
and they s down, one on the one 2Sa 2:13 3427
went in and s before the LORD, 2Sa 7:18 3427
the king arose and s in the gate. 2Sa 19:8 3427
And Solomon s on the throne of 1Ki 2:12 3427
before her, and s on his throne; 1Ki 2:19 3427
mother, and she s on his right. 1Ki 2:19 3427
as soon as he s on his throne, 1Ki 16:11 3427
and s down under a juniper tree; 1Ki 19:4 3427
men came in and s before him; 1Ki 21:13 3427
he s on her lap until noon, 2Ki 4:20 3427
he s on the throne of the kings. 2Ki 11:19 3427
and Jeroboam s on his throne; 2Ki 13:13 3427
in and s before the LORD and said, 1Ch 17:16 3427
Then Solomon s on the throne of 1Ch 29:23 3427
and my beard, and s down appalled. Ezr 9:3 3427
and I s appalled until the evening Ezr 9:4 3427
and all the people s in the open Ezr 10:9 3427
I s down and wept and mourned for Ne 1:4 3427
in those days as King Ahasuerus s Es 1:2 3427
access to the king's presence and s in Es 1:14 3427
king and Haman s down to drink, Es 3:15 3427
Then they s down on the ground Jb 2:13 3427
a way for them and s as chief, Jb 29:25 3427
You have s on the throne judging Ps 9:4 3427
The LORD s *as King* at the flood; Ps 29:10 3427
Babylon, There we s down and wept, Ps 137:1 3427
I took great delight and s down, SS 2:3 3427
By the roads you have s for them Jer 3:2 3427
of Your hand *upon me* I s alone, Jer 15:17 3427
s in the entrance of the New Gate Jer 26:10 3427
in and s down at the Middle Gate: Jer 39:3 3427
and I s there seven days where Ezk 3:15 3427
came to me and s down before me. Ezk 14:1 3427
of the LORD, and s before me. Ezk 20:1 3427
and you s on a splendid couch with Ezk 23:41 3427
The court s, And the books were Da 7:10 3488
sackcloth and s on the ashes. Jon 3:6 3427
from the city and s east of it. Jon 4:5 3427
he made a shelter for himself and s Jon 4:5 3427
and after He s down, His disciples Mt 5:1 *2523*
He got into a boat and s down, Mt 13:2 *2521*
and they s down and gathered the Mt 13:48 *2523*
He s on the coats. Mt 21:7 *1940*
and s down with the officers to Mt 26:58 *2521*
rolled away the stone and s upon it. Mt 28:2 *2521*
into a boat in the sea and s down; Mk 4:1 *2521*
They s down in groups of hundreds Mk 6:40 *377*
on which no one yet has ever s; Mk 11:2 *2523*
and He s on it. Mk 11:7 *2523*
He s down opposite the treasury, Mk 12:41 *2523*
s down at the right hand of God. Mk 16:19 *2523*
back to the attendant and s down; Lk 4:20 *2523*
And He s down and *began* teaching Lk 5:3 *2523*
The dead man s up and Lk 7:15 *339*
on which no one yet has ever s; Lk 19:30 *2523*
courtyard and had s down together, Lk 22:55 *4776*
him as he s in the firelight and Lk 22:56 *2521*
and there He s down with His disciples. Jn 6:3 *2521*
So the men s down, in number about Jn 6:10 *377*
He s down and *began* to teach them. Jn 8:2 *2523*
finding a young donkey, s on it; Jn 12:14 *2523*
and s down on the judgment seat at Jn 19:13 *2523*
and when she saw Peter, she s up. Ac 9:40 *339*
into the synagogue and s down. Ac 13:14 *2523*
and we s down and began speaking Ac 16:13 *2523*
PEOPLE S DOWN TO EAT AND DRINK, 1Co 10:7 *2523*
He s down at the right hand of the Heb 1:3 *2523*
S DOWN AT THE RIGHT HAND OF GOD Heb 10:12 *2523*
and has s down at the right hand Heb 12:2 *2523*
as I also overcame and s down with Rv 3:21 *2523*
in the right hand of Him who s on Rv 5:1 *2521*
hand of Him who s on the throne. Rv 5:7 *2521*
and he who s on it had a bow; Rv 6:2 *2521*
and to him who s on it, it was Rv 6:4 *2521*
and he who s on it had a pair of Rv 6:5 *2521*
he who s on it had the name Death; Rv 6:8 *2521*
horses and those who s on them: Rv 9:17 *2521*
voice to Him who s on the cloud, Rv 14:15 *2521*
Then He who s on the cloud swung Rv 14:16 *2521*
and He who s on it *is* called Rv 19:11 *2521*
against Him who s on the horse Rv 19:19 *2521*
mouth of Him who s on the horse, Rv 19:21 *2521*
saw thrones, and they s on them, Rv 20:4 *2523*
throne and Him who s upon it, Rv 20:11 *2521*

SATAN
Then S stood up against Israel and 1Ch 21:1 7854
LORD, and S also came among them. Jb 1:6 7854
The LORD said to S, Jb 1:7 7854
Then S answered the LORD and said, Jb 1:7 7854
The LORD said to S, Jb 1:8 7854
Then S answered the LORD, Jb 1:9 7854
Then the LORD said to S, Jb 1:12 7854
So S departed from the presence of Jb 1:12 7854
and S also came among them to Jb 2:1 7854

The LORD said to **S**, Jb 2:2 7854
Then **S** answered the LORD and said, Jb 2:2 7854
The LORD said to **S**, Jb 2:3 7854
S answered the LORD and said, Jb 2:4 7854
So the LORD said to **S**, Jb 2:6 7854
Then **S** went out from the presence Jb 2:7 7854
and **S** standing at his right hand Zch 3:1 7854
The LORD said to **S**, Zch 3:2 7854
"The LORD rebuke you, **S**! Zch 3:2 7854
Then Jesus said to him, "Go, **S**! Mt 4:10 *4567*
"If **S** casts out Satan, he is Mt 12:26 *4567*
"If Satan casts out **S**, he is Mt 12:26 *4567*
"Get behind Me, **S**! Mt 16:23 *4567*
forty days being tempted by **S**; Mk 1:13 *4567*
"How can **S** cast out Satan? Mk 3:23 *4567*
"How can Satan cast out **S**? Mk 3:23 *4567*
"If **S** has risen up against Mk 3:26 *4567*
immediately **S** comes and takes away Mk 4:15 *4567*
"Get behind Me, **S**; Mk 8:33 *4567*
"I was watching **S** fall from Lk 10:18 *4567*
"If **S** also is divided against Lk 11:18 *4567*
whom **S** has bound for eighteen long Lk 13:16 *4567*
And **S** entered into Judas who was Lk 22:3 *4567*
S has demanded *permission* to sift Lk 22:31 *4567*
morsel, **S** then entered into him. Jn 13:27 *4567*
why has **S** filled your heart to lie Ac 5:3 *4567*
and from the dominion of **S** to God, Ac 26:18 *4567*
The God of peace will soon crush **S** Ro 16:20 *4567*
decided to deliver such a one to **S** 1Co 5:5 *4567*
and come together again so that **S** 1Co 7:5 *4567*
no advantage would be taken of us by **S** 2Co 2:11 *4567*
for even **S** disguises himself as an 2Co 11:14 *4567*
thorn in the flesh, a messenger of **S** 2Co 12:7 *4567*
and *yet* **S** hindered us. 1Th 2:18 *4567*
in accord with the activity of **S**, 2Th 2:9 *4567*
whom I have handed over to **S**, 1Tm 1:20 *4567*
already turned aside to follow **S**. 1Tm 5:15 *4567*
are not, but are a synagogue of **S**. Rv 2:9 *4567*
killed among you, where **S** dwells. Rv 2:13 *4567*
not known the deep things of **S**, Rv 2:24 *4567*
cause *those* of the synagogue of **S**, Rv 3:9 *4567*
old who is called the devil and **S**, Rv 12:9 *4567*
of old, who is the devil and **S**, Rv 20:2 *4567*
S will be released from his prison Rv 20:7 *4567*

SATAN'S
you dwell, where **S** throne is; Rv 2:13 *4567*

SATED
I am **s** with disgrace and conscious Jb 10:15 7649
A **s** man loathes honey, But to a Pr 27:7 7649
with blood, It is **s** with fat, Is 34:6 1878

SATELLITES
And guide the Bear with her **s**? Jb 38:32 1121

SATIATED
And be **s** with their own devices. Pr 1:31 7646
For My sword is **s** in heaven, Is 34:5 7301
And the sword will devour and be **s** Jer 46:10 7646

SATISFACTION
And my eye has looked *with* **s** upon Ps 54:7
Until he looks *with* **s** on his Ps 112:8
Therefore I will look *with* **s** on Ps 118:7

SATISFIED
age, an old man and **s** *with life;* Gn 25:8 7649
so that you will eat and not be **s**. Lv 26:26 7646
plant, and you eat and are **s**, Dt 6:11 7646
"When you have eaten and are **s**, Dt 8:10 7646
when you have eaten and are **s**, Dt 8:12 7646
and you will eat and be **s**. Dt 11:15 7646
town, shall come and eat and be **s**, Dt 14:29 7646
eat grapes until you are fully **s**, Dt 23:24 7648
may eat in your towns and be **s**. Dt 26:12 7646
and are **s** and become prosperous, Dt 31:20 7646
"O Naphtali, **s** with favor, And Dt 33:23 7649
ate and was **s** and had some left. Ru 2:14 7646
what she had left after she was **s**. Ru 2:18 7648
does, And are not **s** with my flesh? Jb 19:22 7646
Being wholly at ease and **s**; Jb 21:23 7961
descendants will not be **s** with bread Jb 27:14 7646
who has not been **s** with his meat'? Jb 31:31 7646
They are **s** with children, And Ps 17:14 7646
I will be **s** with Your likeness when Ps 17:15 7646
The afflicted will eat and be **s**; Ps 22:26 7646
food And growl if they are not **s**. Ps 59:15 7646
My soul is **s** as with marrow and Ps 63:5 7646
We will be **s** with the goodness of Ps 65:4 7646
Before they had **s** their desire, Ps 78:30 2114a
is **s** with the fruit of His works. Ps 104:13 7646
Your hand, they are **s** with good. Ps 104:28 7646
s them with the bread of heaven. Ps 105:40 7646
For He has **s** the thirsty soul, And Ps 107:9 7646
Nor will he be **s** though you give many Pr 6:35 14
A man will be **s** with good by the Pr 12:14 7646
But a good man will *be* **s** with his. Pr 14:14
man's mouth his stomach will be **s**; Pr 18:20 7646
be **s** *with* the product of his lips. Pr 18:20 7646
to life, So that one may sleep **s**, Pr 19:23 7649
eyes, *and* you will be **s** with food. Pr 20:13 7646
Sheol and Abaddon are never **s**, Pr 27:20 7646
Nor are the eyes of man ever **s**. Pr 27:20 7646
three things that will not be **s**, Pr 30:15 7646
Earth that is never **s** with water, Pr 30:16 7646
And a fool when he is **s** with food, Pr 30:22 7646
The eye is not **s** with seeing, Nor Ec 1:8 7646
his eyes were not **s** with riches Ec 4:8 7646
money will not be **s** with money, Ec 5:10 7646
soul is not **s** with good things and Ec 6:3 7646
and yet the appetite is not **s**. Ec 6:7 4390
the left hand but they are not **s**; Is 9:20 7646
he awakens, his hunger is not **s**, Is 29:8 7386
as he roasts a roast and is **s**. Is 44:16 7646
His soul, He will see *it and* be **s**; Is 53:11 7646
dogs are greedy, they are not **s**. Is 56:11 3045, 7654
be **s** with her comforting breasts, Is 66:11 7646
will be **s** with My goodness," Jer 31:14 7646
and his desire will be **s** in the Jer 50:19 7646
Assyrians because you were not **s**; Ezk 16:28 7654
with them and still were not **s**. Ezk 16:28 7646
with this you were not **s**. Ezk 16:29 7646
from the seas, You **s** many peoples; Ezk 27:33 7646
had their pasture, they became **s**, Hos 13:6 7646
being **s**, their heart became proud Hos 13:6 7646
you will be **s** *in full* with them; Jl 2:19 7646
will have plenty to eat and be **s** Jl 2:26 7646
drink water, But would not be **s**; Am 4:8 7646
will eat, but you will not be **s**, Mi 6:14 7646
And he is like death, never **s**. Hab 2:5 7646
but *there is* not *enough* to be **s**; Hg 1:6 7654
for they shall be **s**. Mt 5:6 *5526*
and they all ate and were **s**. Mt 14:20 *5526*
And they all ate and were **s**, Mt 15:37 *5526*
They all ate and were **s**, Mk 6:42 *5526*
"Let the children be **s** first, Mk 7:27 *5526*
And they ate and were **s**; Mk 8:8 *5526*
hunger now, for you shall be **s**. Lk 6:21 *5526*
And they all ate and were **s**; Lk 9:17 *5526*
and not **s** with this, 3Jn 1:10 *714*

SATISFIES
Who **s** your years with good things, Ps 103:5 7646
He **s** you with the finest of the Ps 147:14 7646

SATISFY
"Yet all of this does not **s** me Es 5:13 7737a
To **s** the waste and desolate land And Jb 38:27 7646
Or **s** the appetite of the young Jb 38:39 4390
with honey from the rock I would **s** Ps 81:16 7646
O **s** us in the morning with Your Ps 90:14 7646
"With a long life I will **s** him And Ps 91:16 7646
I will **s** her needy with bread. Ps 132:15 7646
And **s** the desire of every Ps 145:16 7646
her breasts **s** you at all times; Pr 5:19 7301
To **s** himself when he is hungry; Pr 6:30 4390
has enough to **s** his appetite, Pr 13:25 7648
your wages for what does not **s**? Is 55:2 7654
And **s** the desire of the afflicted, Is 58:10 7646
And **s** your desire in scorched Is 58:11 7646
"For I **s** the weary ones and Jer 31:25 7301
and I will **s** My wrath on them, Ezk 5:13 5117
They cannot **s** their appetite nor Ezk 7:19 7646
And I will **s** the beasts of the Ezk 32:4 7646
to **s** such a large crowd?" Mt 15:33 *5526*
in *this* desolate place to **s** these people?" Mk 8:4 *5526*
Wishing to **s** the crowd, Mk 15:15 *4160, 2425*

SATISFYING
s your hearts with food and Ac 14:17 *1705a*

SATRAPS
the king's edicts to the king's **s** and Ezr 8:36 323
as Haman commanded to the king's **s**, Es 3:12 323
commanded to the Jews, the **s**, Es 8:9 323
princes of the provinces, the **s**, Es 9:3 323
king sent *word* to assemble the **s**, Da 3:2 324
Then the **s**, the prefects and the Da 3:3 324
The **s**, the prefects, the Da 3:27 324
to appoint 120 **s** over the kingdom, Da 6:1 324
s might be accountable to them, Da 6:2 324
among the commissioners and **s** Da 6:3 324
Then the commissioners and **s** began Da 6:4 324
Then these commissioners and **s** Da 6:6 324
kingdom, the prefects and the **s**, Da 6:7 324

SATURATES
breath, But **s** me with bitterness. Jb 9:18 7646

SATYRS
for the high places, for the **s** and 2Ch 11:15 8163c

SAUL
He had a son whose name was **S**, 1Sa 9:2 7586
So Kish said to his son **S**, 1Sa 9:3 7586
S said to his servant who was with 1Sa 9:5 7586
Then **S** said to his servant, 1Sa 9:7 7586
servant answered **S** again and said, 1Sa 9:8 7586
Then **S** said to his servant, 1Sa 9:10 7586
When Samuel saw **S**, the LORD said 1Sa 9:17 7586
S approached Samuel in the gate and 1Sa 9:18 7586
Samuel answered **S** and said, 1Sa 9:19 7586
S replied, "Am I not a Benjamite, 1Sa 9:21 7586
Then Samuel took **S** and his servant 1Sa 9:22 7586
was on it and set *it* before **S**. 1Sa 9:24 7586
So **S** ate with Samuel that day. 1Sa 9:24 7586
Samuel spoke with **S** on the roof. 1Sa 9:25 7586
Samuel called to **S** on the roof, 1Sa 9:26 7586
So **S** arose, and both he and Samuel 1Sa 9:26 7586
of the city, Samuel said to **S**, 1Sa 9:27 7586
Is **S** also among the prophets?" 1Sa 10:11 7586
"Is **S** also among the prophets?" 1Sa 10:12 7586
So **S** said to his uncle, 1Sa 10:16 7586
And **S** the son of Kish was taken; 1Sa 10:21 7586
S also went to his house at 1Sa 10:26 7586
the messengers came to Gibeah of **S** 1Sa 11:4 7586
S was coming from the field behind 1Sa 11:5 7586
Then the Spirit of God came upon **S** 1Sa 11:6 7586
come out after **S** and after Samuel, 1Sa 11:7 7586
The next morning **S** put the people 1Sa 11:11 7586
'Shall **S** reign over us?' 1Sa 11:12 7586
S said, "Not a man shall be put to 1Sa 11:13 7586
and there they made **S** king before 1Sa 11:15 7586
S and all the men of Israel rejoiced 1Sa 11:15 7586
S was *thirty* years old when he 1Sa 13:1 7586
Now **S** chose for himself 3,000 men 1Sa 13:2 7586
of which 2,000 were with **S** in 1Sa 13:2 7586
Then **S** blew the trumpet throughout 1Sa 13:3 7586
news that **S** had smitten the garrison 1Sa 13:4 7586
were then summoned to **S** at Gilgal. 1Sa 13:4 7586
But as for **S**, he *was* still in 1Sa 13:7 7586
So **S** said, "Bring to me the burnt 1Sa 13:9 7586
and **S** went out to meet him *and* to 1Sa 13:10 7586
"What have you done?" And **S** said, 1Sa 13:11 7586
Samuel said to **S**, 1Sa 13:13 7586
And **S** numbered the people who were 1Sa 13:15 7586
Now **S** and his son Jonathan and the 1Sa 13:16 7586
who *were* with **S** and Jonathan, 1Sa 13:22 7586
found with **S** and his son Jonathan. 1Sa 13:22 7586
came that Jonathan, the son of **S**, 1Sa 14:1 7586
S was staying in the outskirts 1Sa 14:2 7586
S said to the people who *were* 1Sa 14:17 7586
Then **S** said to Ahijah, 1Sa 14:18 7586
While **S** talked to the priest, 1Sa 14:19 7586
so **S** said to the priest, 1Sa 14:19 7586
Then **S** and all the people who *were* 1Sa 14:20 7586
who *were* with **S** and Jonathan. 1Sa 14:21 7586
S had put the people under oath, 1Sa 14:24 7586
Then they told **S**, saying, 1Sa 14:33 7586
S said, "Disperse yourselves among the 1Sa 14:34 7586
And **S** built an altar to the LORD; 1Sa 14:35 7586
Then **S** said, "Let us go down after 1Sa 14:36 7586
S inquired of God, 1Sa 14:37 7586
S said, "Draw near here, 1Sa 14:38 7586
And the people said to **S**, 1Sa 14:40 7586
Therefore, **S** said to the LORD, the 1Sa 14:41 7586
And Jonathan and **S** were taken, but 1Sa 14:41 7586
S said, "Cast *lots* between me 1Sa 14:42 7586
Then **S** said to Jonathan, 1Sa 14:43 7586
S said, "May God do this *to me* 1Sa 14:44 7586
But the people said to **S**, 1Sa 14:45 7586
Then **S** went up from pursuing the 1Sa 14:46 7586
Now when **S** had taken the kingdom 1Sa 14:47 7586
Now the sons of **S** were Jonathan 1Sa 14:49 7586
Kish *was* the father of **S**, 1Sa 14:51 7586
was severe all the days of **S**; 1Sa 14:52 7586
and when **S** saw any mighty man or 1Sa 14:52 7586
Then Samuel said to **S**, 1Sa 15:1 7586
Then **S** summoned the people and 1Sa 15:4 7586
S came to the city of Amalek and 1Sa 15:5 7586
S said to the Kenites, 1Sa 15:6 7586
So **S** defeated the Amalekites, from 1Sa 15:7 7586
But **S** and the people spared Agag 1Sa 15:9 7586
"I regret that I have made **S** king, 1Sa 15:11 7586
early in the morning to meet **S**; 1Sa 15:12 7586
"**S** came to Carmel, and behold, he 1Sa 15:12 7586
Samuel came to **S**, 1Sa 15:13 7586
came to Saul, and **S** said to him, 1Sa 15:13 7586
S said, "They have brought them 1Sa 15:15 7586
Then Samuel said to **S**, 1Sa 15:16 7586
Then **S** said to Samuel, 1Sa 15:20 7586
Then **S** said to Samuel, 1Sa 15:24 7586
But Samuel said to **S**, 1Sa 15:26 7586
As Samuel turned to go, **S** seized 1Sa 15:27 7586
So Samuel went back following **S**, 1Sa 15:31 7586
Saul, and **S** worshiped the LORD. 1Sa 15:31 7586
but **S** went up to his house at 1Sa 15:34 7586
up to his house at Gibeah of **S**. 1Sa 15:34 7586
Samuel did not see **S** again 1Sa 15:35 7586
for Samuel grieved over **S**. 1Sa 15:35 7586
He had made **S** king over Israel. 1Sa 15:35 7586
"How long will you grieve over **S**, 1Sa 16:1 7586
When **S** hears *of it,* he will kill 1Sa 16:2 7586
Spirit of the LORD departed from **S**, 1Sa 16:14 7586
So **S** said to his servants, 1Sa 16:17 7586
So **S** sent messengers to Jesse and 1Sa 16:19 7586
sent *them* to **S** by David his son. 1Sa 16:20 7586
David came to **S** and attended him; 1Sa 16:21 7586
him; and **S** loved him greatly 1Sa 16:21 7586
S sent to Jesse, saying, 1Sa 16:22 7586
evil spirit from God came to **S**, 1Sa 16:23 7586
and **S** would be refreshed and be 1Sa 16:23 7586
S and the men of Israel were 1Sa 17:2 7586
Philistine and you servants of **S**? 1Sa 17:8 7586
When **S** and all Israel heard these 1Sa 17:11 7586
Jesse was old in the days of **S**, 1Sa 17:12 7586
had gone after **S** to the battle. 1Sa 17:13 7586
Now the three oldest followed **S**, 1Sa 17:14 7586
David went back and forth from **S** to 1Sa 17:15 7586
"For **S** and they and all the men 1Sa 17:19 7586
were heard, they told *them* to **S**, 1Sa 17:31 7586
David said to **S**, 1Sa 17:32 7586
Then **S** said to David, 1Sa 17:33 7586
But David said to **S**, 1Sa 17:34 7586
And **S** said to David, 1Sa 17:37 7586
Then **S** clothed David with his 1Sa 17:38 7586
So David said to **S**, 1Sa 17:39 7586
Now when **S** saw David going out 1Sa 17:55 7586
took him and brought him before **S** 1Sa 17:57 7586
S said to him, 1Sa 17:58 7586
he had finished speaking to **S**, 1Sa 18:1 7586
S took him that day and did 1Sa 18:2 7586
went out wherever **S** sent him, 1Sa 18:5 7586
and **S** set him over the men of war. 1Sa 18:5 7586
and dancing, to meet King **S**, 1Sa 18:6 7586
"**S** has slain his thousands, And 1Sa 18:7 7586
Then **S** became very angry, for this 1Sa 18:8 7586
S looked at David with 1Sa 18:9 7586
from God came mightily upon **S**, 1Sa 18:10 7586
S hurled the spear for he 1Sa 18:11 7586
Now **S** was afraid of David, for the 1Sa 18:12 7586
with him but had departed from **S**. 1Sa 18:12 7586
S removed him from his presence and 1Sa 18:13 7586
When **S** saw that he was prospering 1Sa 18:15 7586

Then **S** said to David, **1Sa 18:17** 7586
For **S** thought, "My hand shall not **1Sa 18:17** 7586
But David said to **S**, **1Sa 18:18** 7586
When they told **S**, the thing was **1Sa 18:20** 7586
S thought, "I will give her to him **1Sa 18:21** 7586
Therefore **S** *said to David,* **1Sa 18:21** 7586
Then **S** commanded his servants, **1Sa 18:22** 7586
The servants of **S** reported to **1Sa 18:24** 7586
S then said, "Thus you shall say to **1Sa 18:25** 7586
Now **S** planned to make David fall **1Sa 18:25** 7586
So **S** gave him Michal his daughter **1Sa 18:27** 7586
When **S** saw and knew that the LORD **1Sa 18:28** 7586
S was even more afraid of David. **1Sa 18:29** 7586
S was David's enemy continually. **1Sa 18:29** 7586
wisely than all the servants of **S**. **1Sa 18:30** 7586
Now **S** told Jonathan his son and **1Sa 19:1** 7586
"**S** my father is seeking to put **1Sa 19:2** 7586
Jonathan spoke well of David to **S** **1Sa 19:4** 7586
S listened to the voice of **1Sa 19:6** 7586
voice of Jonathan, and **S** vowed, **1Sa 19:6** 7586
And Jonathan brought David to **S**, **1Sa 19:7** 7586
an evil spirit from the LORD on **S** as **1Sa 19:9** 7586
S tried to pin David to the **1Sa 19:10** 7586
Then **S** sent messengers to David's **1Sa 19:11** 7586
S sent messengers to take David, **1Sa 19:14** 7586
S sent messengers to see David, **1Sa 19:15** 7586
So **S** said to Michal, **1Sa 19:17** 7586
And Michal said to **S**, **1Sa 19:17** 7586
him all that **S** had done to him. **1Sa 19:18** 7586
It was told **S**, saying, **1Sa 19:19** 7586
S sent messengers to take David, **1Sa 19:20** 7586
God came upon the messengers of **S**; **1Sa 19:20** 7586
When it was told **S**, **1Sa 19:21** 7586
So **S** sent messengers again the **1Sa 19:21** 7586
"Is **S** also among the prophets?" **1Sa 19:24** 7586
Nevertheless **S** did not speak **1Sa 20:26** 7586
so **S** said to Jonathan his son, **1Sa 20:27** 7586
Jonathan then answered **S**, **1Sa 20:28** 7586
But Jonathan answered **S** his father **1Sa 20:32** 7586
Then **S** hurled his spear at him to **1Sa 20:33** 7586
servants of **S** was there that day, **1Sa 21:7** 7586
arose and fled that day from **S**, **1Sa 21:10** 7586
'**S** has slain his thousands, And **1Sa 21:11** 7586
Then **S** heard that David and the **1Sa 22:6** 7586
Now **S** was sitting in Gibeah, under **1Sa 22:6** 7586
S said to his servants who **1Sa 22:7** 7586
was standing by the servants of **S**, **1Sa 22:9** 7586
S said, "Listen now, son of Ahitub. **1Sa 22:12** 7586
S then said to him, **1Sa 22:13** 7586
Abiathar told David that **S** had **1Sa 22:21** 7586
that he would surely tell **S**. **1Sa 22:22** 7586
S that David had come to Keilah, **1Sa 23:7** 7586
David had come to Keilah, **S** said, **1Sa 23:7** 7586
So **S** summoned all the people for **1Sa 23:8** 7586
S was plotting evil against him; **1Sa 23:9** 7586
that **S** is seeking to come to Keilah **1Sa 23:10** 7586
Will **S** come down just as Your **1Sa 23:11** 7586
and my men into the hand of **S**?" **1Sa 23:12** 7586
When it was told **S** that David had **1Sa 23:13** 7586
And **S** sought him every day, but **1Sa 23:14** 7586
Now David became aware that **S** had **1Sa 23:15** 7586
of **S** my father will not find you, **1Sa 23:17** 7586
and **S** my father knows that also." **1Sa 23:17** 7586
Ziphites came up to **S** at Gibeah, **1Sa 23:19** 7586
S said, "May you be blessed **1Sa 23:21** 7586
arose and went to Ziph before **S**. **1Sa 23:24** 7586
S and his men went to seek *him,* **1Sa 23:25** 7586
And when **S** heard *it,* he pursued **1Sa 23:25** 7586
S went on one side of the **1Sa 23:26** 7586
was hurrying to get away from **S**, **1Sa 23:26** 7586
for **S** and his men were surrounding **1Sa 23:26** 7586
But a messenger came to **S**, **1Sa 23:27** 7586
So **S** returned from pursuing David and **1Sa 23:28** 7586
when **S** returned from pursuing the **1Sa 24:1** 7586
Then **S** took three thousand chosen **1Sa 24:2** 7586
and **S** went in to relieve himself. **1Sa 24:3** 7586
allow them to rise up against **S**. **1Sa 24:7** 7586
And **S** arose, left the cave, and **1Sa 24:7** 7586
of the cave and called after **S**, **1Sa 24:8** 7586
And when **S** looked behind him, **1Sa 24:8** 7586
David said to **S**, **1Sa 24:9** 7586
speaking these words to **S**, **1Sa 24:16** 7586
these words to Saul, **S** said, **1Sa 24:16** 7586
S lifted up his voice and wept. **1Sa 24:16** 7586
David swore to **S**. **1Sa 24:22** 7586
And **S** went to his home, but David **1Sa 24:22** 7586
S had given Michal his daughter, **1Sa 25:44** 7586
the Ziphites came to **S** at Gibeah, **1Sa 26:1** 7586
So **S** arose and went down to the **1Sa 26:2** 7586
S camped in the hill of **1Sa 26:3** 7586
When he saw that **S** came after him **1Sa 26:3** 7586
knew that **S** was definitely coming. **1Sa 26:4** 7586
to the place where **S** had camped. **1Sa 26:5** 7586
David saw the place where **S** lay, **1Sa 26:5** 7586
and **S** was lying in the circle of **1Sa 26:5** 7586
"Who will go down with me to **S** in **1Sa 26:6** 7586
S lay sleeping inside the circle **1Sa 26:7** 7586
Then **S** recognized David's voice **1Sa 26:17** 7586
Then **S** said, "I have sinned. Return, **1Sa 26:21** 7586
Then **S** said to David, **1Sa 26:25** 7586
way, and **S** returned to his place. **1Sa 26:25** 7586
perish one day by the hand of **S**. **1Sa 27:1** 7586
S then will despair of searching **1Sa 27:1** 7586
S that David had fled to Gath, **1Sa 27:4** 7586
And **S** had removed from the land **1Sa 28:3** 7586
and **S** gathered all Israel together **1Sa 28:4** 7586
When **S** saw the camp of the **1Sa 28:5** 7586
When **S** inquired of the LORD, the **1Sa 28:6** 7586
Then **S** said to his servants, **1Sa 28:7** 7586
Then **S** disguised himself by **1Sa 28:8** 7586
"Behold, you know what **S** has done, **1Sa 28:9** 7586
S vowed to her by the LORD, **1Sa 28:10** 7586
and the woman spoke to **S**, **1Sa 28:12** 7586
you deceived me? For you are **S**." **1Sa 28:12** 7586
And the woman said to **S**, **1Sa 28:13** 7586
And **S** knew that it was Samuel, and **1Sa 28:14** 7586
Then Samuel said to **S**, **1Sa 28:15** 7586
S answered, "I am greatly distressed; **1Sa 28:15** 7586
Then **S** immediately fell full **1Sa 28:20** 7586
The woman came to **S** and saw that **1Sa 28:21** 7586
it before **S** and his servants, **1Sa 28:25** 7586
servant of **S** the king of Israel, **1Sa 29:3** 7586
'**S** has slain his thousands, And **1Sa 29:5** 7586
Philistines overtook **S** and his sons; **1Sa 31:2** 7586
and Malchi-shua the sons of **S**. **1Sa 31:2** 7586
The battle went heavily against **S**, **1Sa 31:3** 7586
Then **S** said to his armor bearer, **1Sa 31:4** 7586
S took his sword and fell on it. **1Sa 31:4** 7586
armor bearer saw that **S** was dead, **1Sa 31:5** 7586
Thus **S** died with his three sons, **1Sa 31:6** 7586
and that **S** and his sons were dead, **1Sa 31:7** 7586
that they found **S** and his three **1Sa 31:8** 7586
the Philistines had done to **S**, **1Sa 31:11** 7586
and took the body of **S** and the **1Sa 31:12** 7586
came about after the death of **S**, **2Sa 1:1** 7586
a man came out of the camp from **S**, **2Sa 1:2** 7586
and **S** and Jonathan his son are **2Sa 1:4** 7586
S and his son Jonathan are dead?" **2Sa 1:5** 7586
S was leaning on his spear. **2Sa 1:6** 7586
wept and fasted until evening for **S** **2Sa 1:12** 7586
chanted with this lament over **S** and **2Sa 1:17** 7586
was defiled, The shield of **S**, **2Sa 1:21** 7586
sword of **S** did not return empty. **2Sa 1:22** 7586
"**S** and Jonathan, beloved and **2Sa 1:23** 7586
daughters of Israel, weep over **S**, **2Sa 1:24** 7586
men of Jabesh-gilead who buried **S**. **2Sa 2:4** 7586
shown this kindness to **S** your lord, **2Sa 2:5** 7586
for **S** your lord is dead, and also **2Sa 2:7** 7586
had taken Ish-bosheth the son of **S** and **2Sa 2:8** 7586
servants of Ish-bosheth the son of **S**, **2Sa 2:12** 7586
and Ish-bosheth the son of **S**, **2Sa 2:15** 7586
house of **S** and the house of David; **2Sa 3:1** 7586
house of **S** grew weaker continually. **2Sa 3:1** 7586
was war between the house of **S** and **2Sa 3:6** 7586
himself strong in the house of **S**. **2Sa 3:6** 7586
Now **S** had a concubine whose name **2Sa 3:7** 7586
I show kindness to the house of **S** **2Sa 3:8** 7586
the kingdom from the house of **S** and **2Sa 3:10** 7586
when the report of **S** and Jonathan **2Sa 4:4** 7586
head of Ish-bosheth the son of **S**, **2Sa 4:8** 7586
day on **S** and his descendants." **2Sa 4:8** 7586
'Behold, **S** is dead,' and thought **2Sa 4:10** 7586
when **S** was king over us, **2Sa 5:2** 7586
Michal the daughter of **S** looked out **2Sa 6:16** 7586
Michal the daughter of **S** came out **2Sa 6:20** 7586
Michal the daughter of **S** had **2Sa 6:23** 7586
him, as I took *it* away from **S**, **2Sa 7:15** 7586
yet anyone left of the house of **S**, **2Sa 9:1** 7586
house of **S** whose name was Ziba, **2Sa 9:2** 7586
not yet anyone of the house of **S** to **2Sa 9:3** 7586
the son of Jonathan the son of **S**, **2Sa 9:6** 7586
the land of your grandfather **S**; **2Sa 9:7** 7586
"All that belonged to **S** and to **2Sa 9:9** 7586
delivered you from the hand of **S**. **2Sa 12:7** 7586
house of **S** whose name was Shimei, **2Sa 16:5** 7586
the bloodshed of the house of **S**, **2Sa 16:8** 7586
the servant of the house of **S**, **2Sa 19:17** 7586
Mephibosheth the son of **S** came **2Sa 19:24** 7586
"It is for **S** and his bloody **2Sa 21:1** 7586
but **S** had sought to kill them in **2Sa 21:2** 7586
or gold with **S** or his house, **2Sa 21:4** 7586
before the LORD in Gibeah of **S**, **2Sa 21:6** 7586
the son of Jonathan the son of **S**, **2Sa 21:7** 7586
whom she had borne to **S**, **2Sa 21:8** 7586
sons of Merab the daughter of **S**, **2Sa 21:8** 7586
of Aiah, the concubine of **S**, **2Sa 21:11** 7586
David went and took the bones of **S** **2Sa 21:12** 7586
Philistines struck down **S** in Gilboa. **2Sa 21:12** 7586
He brought up the bones of **S** **2Sa 21:13** 7586
They buried the bones of **S** and **2Sa 21:14** 7586
enemies and from the hand of **S**. **2Sa 22:1** 7586
In the days of **S** they made war **1Ch 5:10** 7586
and Kish became the father of **S**, **1Ch 8:33** 7586
S became the father of Jonathan, **1Ch 8:33** 7586
and Kish became the father of **S**, **1Ch 9:39** 7586
S became the father of Jonathan, **1Ch 9:39** 7586
The Philistines closely pursued **S** and **1Ch 10:2** 7586
and Malchi-shua, the sons of **S**. **1Ch 10:2** 7586
The battle became heavy against **S**, **1Ch 10:3** 7586
Then **S** said to his armor bearer, **1Ch 10:4** 7586
S took his sword and fell on it. **1Ch 10:4** 7586
armor bearer saw that **S** was dead, **1Ch 10:5** 7586
Thus **S** died with his three sons, **1Ch 10:6** 7586
and that **S** and his sons were dead, **1Ch 10:7** 7586
that they found **S** and his sons **1Ch 10:8** 7586
the Philistines had done to **S**, **1Ch 10:11** 7586
arose and took away the body of **S** **1Ch 10:12** 7586
So **S** died for his trespass which **1Ch 10:13** 7586
times past, even when **S** was king, **1Ch 11:2** 7586
because of **S** the son of Kish; **1Ch 12:1** 7586
battle with the Philistines against **S**. **1Ch 12:19** 7586
he may defect to his master **S**." **1Ch 12:19** 7586
to turn the kingdom of **S** to him, **1Ch 12:23** 7586
allegiance to the house of **S**. **1Ch 12:29** 7586
not seek it in the days of **S**." **1Ch 13:3** 7586
Michal the daughter of **S** looked out **1Ch 15:29** 7586
dedicated and **S** the son of Kish, **1Ch 26:28** 7586
and Gibeah of **S** has fled away. **Is 10:29** 7586
the feet of a young man named **S**. **Ac 7:58** *4569*
S was in hearty agreement with **Ac 8:1** *4569*
But **S** *began* ravaging the church, **Ac 8:3** *4569*
Now **S**, still breathing threats and **Ac 9:1** *4569*
"**S**, Saul, why are you persecuting **Ac 9:4** *4549*
"Saul, **S**, why are you persecuting **Ac 9:4** *4549*
S got up from the ground, and **Ac 9:8** *4569*
for a man from Tarsus named **S**, **Ac 9:11** *4569*
"Brother **S**, the Lord Jesus, who **Ac 9:17** *4549*
But **S** kept increasing in strength **Ac 9:22** *4569*
but their plot became known to **S**. **Ac 9:24** *4569*
he left for Tarsus to look for **S**; **Ac 11:25** *4569*
in charge of Barnabas and **S** to the **Ac 11:30** *4569*
And Barnabas and **S** returned from **Ac 12:25** *4569*
up with Herod the tetrarch, and **S**. **Ac 13:1** *4569*
"Set apart for Me Barnabas and **S** **Ac 13:2** *4569*
This man summoned Barnabas and **S** **Ac 13:7** *4569*
But **S**, who was also *known as* Paul, **Ac 13:9** *4569*
God gave them **S** the son of Kish, **Ac 13:21** *4549*
'**S**, Saul, why are you persecuting **Ac 22:7** *4549*
'Saul, **S**, why are you persecuting **Ac 22:7** *4549*
'Brother **S**, receive your sight!' **Ac 22:13** *4549*
'**S**, Saul, why are you persecuting **Ac 26:14** *4549*
'Saul, **S**, why are you persecuting **Ac 26:14** *4549*

SAUL'S

Now the donkeys of Kish, **S** father, **1Sa 9:3** 7586
Now a day before **S** coming, **1Sa 9:15** 7586
Now **S** uncle said to him and his **1Sa 10:14** 7586
S uncle said, **1Sa 10:15** 7586
Now **S** watchmen in Gibeah of **1Sa 14:16** 7586
The name of **S** wife was Ahinoam **1Sa 14:50** 7586
was Abner the son of Ner, **S** uncle. **1Sa 14:50** 7586
S servants then said to him, **1Sa 16:15** 7586
also in the sight of **S** servants. **1Sa 18:5** 7586
and a spear *was* in **S** hand. **1Sa 18:10** 7586
the time when Merab, **S** daughter, **1Sa 18:19** 7586
Now Michal, **S** daughter, loved **1Sa 18:20** 7586
So **S** servants spoke these words to **1Sa 18:23** 7586
and *that* Michal, **S** daughter, **1Sa 18:28** 7586
But Jonathan, **S** son, greatly **1Sa 19:1** 7586
he slipped away out of **S** presence, **1Sa 19:10** 7586
up and Abner sat down by **S** side, **1Sa 20:25** 7586
Then **S** anger burned against **1Sa 20:30** 7586
Edomite, the chief of **S** shepherds. **1Sa 21:7** 7586
And Jonathan, **S** son, arose and **1Sa 23:16** 7586
off the edge of **S** robe secretly. **1Sa 24:4** 7586
he had cut off the edge of **S** *robe.* **1Sa 24:5** 7586
jug of water from *beside* **S** head, **1Sa 26:12** 7586
son of Ner, commander of **S** army, **2Sa 2:8** 7586
Ish-bosheth, **S** son, was forty **2Sa 2:10** 7586
first bring Michal, **S** daughter, **2Sa 3:13** 7586
messengers to Ish-bosheth, **S** son, **2Sa 3:14** 7586
Now when Ish-bosheth, **S** son, **2Sa 4:1** 7586
S son *had* two men who were **2Sa 4:2** 7586
Now Jonathan, **S** son, had a son **2Sa 4:4** 7586
the king called **S** servant Ziba and **2Sa 9:9** 7586
between David and **S** son Jonathan. **2Sa 21:7** 7586
they were **S** kinsmen from Benjamin. **1Ch 12:2** 7586
the sons of Benjamin, **S** kinsmen, **1Ch 12:29** 7586

SAVAGE

s wolves will come in among you, **Ac 20:29** *926*

SAVE

against your enemies, to **s** you.' **Dt 20:4** 3467
but there was no one to **s** her. **Dt 22:27** 3467
continually, with none to **s** you. **Dt 28:29** 3467
and you will have none to **s** you. **Dt 28:31** 3467
us quickly and **s** us and help us, **Jos 10:6** 3467
LORD do not **s** us this day! **Jos 22:22** 3467
order to **s** *it* from the Midianites. **Jg 6:11** 5127
of Issachar, arose to **s** Israel; **Jg 10:1** 3467
that He may **s** us from the hand of **1Sa 7:8** 3467
to **s** by many or by few." **1Sa 14:6** 3467
"If you do not **s** your life **1Sa 19:11** 4422
I will **s** My people Israel from the **2Sa 3:18** 3467
You **s** me from violence. **2Sa 22:3** 3467
You **s** an afflicted people; **2Sa 22:28** 3467
looked, but there was none to **s**; **2Sa 22:42** 3467
me give you counsel and **s** your life **1Ki 1:12** 4422
perhaps he will **s** your life." **1Ki 20:31** 2421a
'For I will defend this city to **s** it **2Ki 19:34** 3467
"**S** us, O God of our salvation, **1Ch 16:35** 3467
go into the temple to **s** his life? **Ne 6:11** 2421a
And the humble person He will **s**. **Jb 22:29** 3467
your own right hand can **s** you. **Jb 40:14** 3467
Arise, O LORD; **s** me, O my God! **Ps 3:7** 3467
S me because of Your lovingkindness. **Ps 6:4** 3467
S me from all those who pursue me, **Ps 7:1** 3467
You **s** an afflicted people **Ps 18:27** 3467
for help, but there was none to **s**, **Ps 18:41** 3467
S, O LORD; May the King answer **Ps 20:9** 3467
S me from the lion's mouth; **Ps 22:21** 3467
S Your people and bless Your **Ps 28:9** 3467
of strength, A stronghold to **s** me. **Ps 31:2** 3467
S me in Your lovingkindness. **Ps 31:16** 3467
And their own arm did not **s** them, **Ps 44:3** 3467
in my bow, Nor will my sword **s** me. **Ps 44:6** 3467
S me, O God, by Your name, And **Ps 54:1** 3467
upon God, And the LORD will **s** me. **Ps 55:16** 3467
He will send from heaven and **s** me; **Ps 57:3** 3467
And **s** me from men of bloodshed. **Ps 59:2** 3467
delivered, **S** with Your right hand, **Ps 60:5** 3467
S me, O God, For the waters have **Ps 69:1** 3467
For God will **s** Zion and build the **Ps 69:35** 3467
Incline Your ear to me and **s** me. **Ps 71:2** 3467
have given commandment to **s** me, **Ps 71:3** 3467
S the children of the needy And **Ps 72:4** 3467
the lives of the needy he will **s**. **Ps 72:13** 3467
To **s** all the humble of the earth. **Ps 76:9** 3467

up Your power And come to **s** us!	**Ps 80:2**	3444
s Your servant who trusts in You.	**Ps 86:2**	3467
And **s** the son of Your handmaid.	**Ps 86:16**	3467
S us, O LORD our God, And gather	**Ps 106:47**	3467
delivered, **S** with Your right hand,	**Ps 108:6**	3467
S me according to Your	**Ps 109:26**	3467
To **s** him from those who judge his	**Ps 109:31**	3467
LORD, I beseech You, **s** my life!"	**Ps 116:4**	4422
O LORD, do **s**, we beseech You;	**Ps 118:25**	3467
I am Yours, **s** me;	**Ps 119:94**	3467
s me And I shall keep Your	**Ps 119:146**	3467
And Your right hand will **s** me.	**Ps 138:7**	3467
hear their cry and will **s** them.	**Ps 145:19**	3467
for the LORD, and He will **s** you.	**Pr 20:22**	3467
we have waited that He might **s** us.	**Is 25:9**	3467
The LORD is our king; He will **s** us	**Is 33:22**	3467
will come, But He will **s** you."	**Is 35:4**	3467
'For I will defend this city to **s** it	**Is 37:35**	3467
"The LORD will surely **s** me;	**Is 38:20**	3467
And pray to a god who cannot **s**.	**Is 45:20**	3467
Stand up and **s** you from what will	**Is 47:13**	3467
There is none to **s** you.	**Is 47:15**	3467
with you, And I will **s** your sons.	**Is 49:25**	3467
is not so short That it cannot **s**;	**Is 59:1**	3467
in righteousness, mighty to **s**."	**Is 63:1**	3467
they will say, 'Arise and **s** us.'	**Jer 2:27**	3467
if they can **s** you In the time of	**Jer 2:28**	3467
but they surely will not **s** them in	**Jer 11:12**	3467
Like a mighty man who cannot **s**?	**Jer 14:9**	3467
I am with you to **s** you And deliver	**Jer 15:20**	3467
S me and I will be saved, For You	**Jer 17:14**	3467
behold, I will **s** you from afar And	**Jer 30:10**	3467
'to **s** you; For I will destroy	**Jer 30:11**	3467
'O LORD, **s** Your people, The remnant	**Jer 31:7**	3467
'for I am with you to **s** you and	**Jer 42:11**	3467
I am going to **s** you from afar,	**Jer 46:27**	3467
"Flee, **s** your lives, That you may	**Jer 48:6**	4422
And each of you **s** his life!	**Jer 51:6**	4422
And each of you **s** yourselves From	**Jer 51:45**	4422
For a nation that could not **s**.	**La 4:17**	3467
righteousness, he will **s** his life.	**Ezk 18:27**	2421a
s you from all your uncleanness;	**Ezk 36:29**	3467
he may **s** you in all your cities,	**Hos 13:10**	3467
"Assyria will not **s** us,	**Hos 14:3**	3467
Nor the mighty man **s** his life.	**Am 2:14**	4422
he who rides the horse **s** his life.	**Am 2:15**	4422
Yet You do not **s**.	**Hab 1:2**	3467
I will **s** the lame And gather the	**Zph 3:19**	3467
I am going to **s** My people from the	**Zch 8:7**	3467
so I will **s** you that you may	**Zch 8:13**	3467
And the LORD their God will **s** them	**Zch 9:16**	3467
And I will **s** the house of Joseph,	**Zch 10:6**	3467
"The LORD also will **s** the tents	**Zch 12:7**	3467
s His people from their sins."	**Mt 1:21**	*4982*
woke Him, saying, "**S** *us*, Lord;	**Mt 8:25**	*4982*
he cried out, "Lord, **s** me!"	**Mt 14:30**	*4982*
whoever wishes to **s** his life will	**Mt 16:25**	*4982*
come to **s** that which was lost.]	**Mt 18:11**	*4982*
it in three days, **s** Yourself!	**Mt 27:40**	*4982*
He cannot **s** Himself.	**Mt 27:42**	*4982*
whether Elijah will come to **s** Him."	**Mt 27:49**	*4982*
do harm on the Sabbath, to **s** a life or	**Mk 3:4**	*4982*
whoever wishes to **s** his life will	**Mk 8:35**	*4982*
sake and the gospel's will **s** it.	**Mk 8:35**	*4982*
s Yourself, and come down from the	**Mk 15:30**	*4982*
He cannot **s** Himself.	**Mk 15:31**	*4982*
to **s** a life or to destroy it?	**Lk 6:9**	*4982*
come and **s** the life of his slave.	**Lk 7:3**	*1295*
whoever wishes to **s** his life will	**Lk 9:24**	*4982*
sake, he is the one who will **s** it.	**Lk 9:24**	*4982*
men's lives, but to **s** them."]	**Lk 9:56**	*4982*
and to **s** that which was lost."	**Lk 19:10**	*4982*
let Him **s** Himself if this is the	**Lk 23:35**	*4982*
King of the Jews, **s** Yourself!"	**Lk 23:37**	*4982*
S Yourself and us!"	**Lk 23:39**	*4982*
'Father, **s** Me from this hour'?	**Jn 12:27**	*4982*
the world, but to **s** the world.	**Jn 12:47**	*4982*
countrymen and **s** some of them.	**Ro 11:14**	*4982*
preached to **s** those who believe.	**1Co 1:21**	*4982*
whether you will **s** your husband?	**1Co 7:16**	*4982*
whether you will **s** your wife?	**1Co 7:16**	*4982*
that I may by all means **s** some.	**1Co 9:22**	*4982*
each one of you is to put aside and **s**,	**1Co 16:2**	*2343*
to **s** up for *their* parents,	**2Co 12:14**	*2343*
came into the world to **s** sinners,	**1Tm 1:15**	*4982*
the One able to **s** Him from death,	**Heb 5:7**	*4982*
He is able also to **s** forever those who	**Heb 7:25**	*4982*
which is able to **s** your souls.	**Jas 1:21**	*4982*
Can that faith **s** him?	**Jas 2:14**	*4982*
who is able to **s** and to destroy;	**Jas 4:12**	*4982*
way will **s** his soul from death and	**Jas 5:20**	*4982*
s others, snatching them out of	**Jude 1:23**	*4982*

SAVED

that my life may be **s**."	**Gn 19:20**	2421a
"You have **s** our lives!	**Gn 47:25**	2421a
Thus the LORD **s** Israel that day	**Ex 14:30**	3467
God, and be **s** from your enemies.	**Nu 10:9**	3467
like you, a people **s** by the LORD,	**Dt 33:29**	3467
and he also **s** Israel.	**Jg 3:31**	3467
who today have **s** your life and the	**2Sa 19:5**	4422
s us from the hand of the Philistines,	**2Sa 19:9**	4422
And I am **s** from my enemies.	**2Sa 22:4**	3467
but He **s** them by the hand of	**2Ki 14:27**	3467
LORD **s** them by a great victory.	**1Ch 11:14**	3467
So the LORD **s** Hezekiah and the	**2Ch 32:22**	3467
have **s** the arm without strength!	**Jb 26:2**	3467
And I am **s** from my enemies.	**Ps 18:3**	3467
king is not **s** by a mighty army;	**Ps 33:16**	3467
And **s** him out of all his troubles.	**Ps 34:6**	3467
have **s** us from our adversaries,	**Ps 44:7**	3467
shine *upon us,* and we will be **s**.	**Ps 80:3**	3467
shine *upon us,* and we will be **s**.	**Ps 80:7**	3467
shine *upon us,* and we will be **s**.	**Ps 80:19**	3467
He **s** them for the sake of His name,	**Ps 106:8**	3467
So He **s** them from the hand of the	**Ps 106:10**	3467
He **s** them out of their distresses.	**Ps 107:13**	3467
He **s** them out of their distresses.	**Ps 107:19**	3467
I was brought low, and He **s** me.	**Ps 116:6**	3467
old, Which I have **s** up for you,	**SS 7:13**	6845
and rest you will be **s**,	**Is 30:15**	3467
declared and **s** and proclaimed,	**Is 43:12**	3467
Israel has been **s** by the LORD With	**Is 45:17**	3467
"Turn to Me and be **s**,	**Is 45:22**	3467
the angel of His presence **s** them;	**Is 63:9**	3467
And shall we be **s**?	**Is 64:5**	3467
O Jerusalem, That you may be **s**.	**Jer 4:14**	3467
is ended, And we are not **s**."	**Jer 8:20**	3467
Save me and I will be **s**,	**Jer 17:14**	3467
"In His days Judah will be **s**,	**Jer 23:6**	3467
But he will be **s** from it.	**Jer 30:7**	3467
"In those days Judah will be **s**	**Jer 33:16**	3467
endured to the end who will be **s**.	**Mt 10:22**	*4982*
"Then who can be **s**?"	**Mt 19:25**	*4982*
endures to the end, he will be **s**.	**Mt 24:13**	*4982*
short, no life would have been **s**;	**Mt 24:22**	*4982*
"He **s** others; He cannot save Himself.	**Mt 27:42**	*4982*
"Then who can be **s**?"	**Mk 10:26**	*4982*
endures to the end, he will be **s**.	**Mk 13:13**	*4982*
days, no life would have been **s**;	**Mk 13:20**	*4982*
"He **s** others; He cannot save Himself.	**Mk 15:31**	*4982*
and has been baptized shall be **s**;	**Mk 16:16**	*4982*
"Your faith has **s** you;	**Lk 7:50**	*4982*
they will not believe and be **s**.	**Lk 8:12**	*4982*
just a few who are being **s**?"	**Lk 13:23**	*4982*
"Then who can be **s**?"	**Lk 18:26**	*4982*
"He **s** others; let Him save Himself	**Lk 23:35**	*4982*
the world might be **s** through Him.	**Jn 3:17**	*4982*
these things so that you may be **s**.	**Jn 5:34**	*4982*
enters through Me, he will be **s**.	**Jn 10:9**	*4982*
THE NAME OF THE LORD WILL BE **S**.'	**Ac 2:21**	*4982*
Be **s** from this perverse generation!"	**Ac 2:40**	*4982*
day by day those who were being **s**.	**Ac 2:47**	*4982*
men by which we must be **s**."	**Ac 4:12**	*4982*
to you by which you will be **s**,	**Ac 11:14**	*4982*
of Moses, you cannot be **s**."	**Ac 15:1**	*4982*
that we are **s** through the grace of	**Ac 15:11**	*4982*
"Sirs, what must I do to be **s**?"	**Ac 16:30**	*4982*
Lord Jesus, and you will be **s**,	**Ac 16:31**	*4982*
being **s** was gradually abandoned.	**Ac 27:20**	*4982*
you yourselves cannot be **s**."	**Ac 27:31**	*4982*
though he has been **s** from the sea,	**Ac 28:4**	*1295*
we shall be **s** from the wrath *of*	**Ro 5:9**	*4982*
we shall be **s** by His life.	**Ro 5:10**	*4982*
For in hope we have been **s**,	**Ro 8:24**	*4982*
IT IS THE REMNANT THAT WILL BE **S**;	**Ro 9:27**	*4982*
Him from the dead, you will be **s**;	**Ro 10:9**	*4982*
THE NAME OF THE LORD WILL BE **S**."	**Ro 10:13**	*4982*
and so all Israel will be **s**;	**Ro 11:26**	*4982*
to us who are being **s** it is the power	**1Co 1:18**	*4982*
but he himself will be **s**,	**1Co 3:15**	*4982*
that his spirit may be **s** in the day	**1Co 5:5**	*4982*
of the many, so that they may be **s**.	**1Co 10:33**	*4982*
by which also you are **s**,	**1Co 15:2**	*4982*
to God among those who are being **s**	**2Co 2:15**	*4982*
(by grace you have been **s**),	**Eph 2:5**	*4982*
you have been **s** through faith;	**Eph 2:8**	*4982*
the Gentiles so that they may be **s**;	**1Th 2:16**	*4982*
love of the truth so as to be **s**.	**2Th 2:10**	*4982*
who desires all men to be **s** and to	**1Tm 2:4**	*4982*
who has **s** us and called us with a	**2Tm 1:9**	*4982*
He **s** us, not on the basis of deeds	**Ti 3:5**	*4982*
THAT THE RIGHTEOUS IS **S**,	**1Pe 4:18**	*4982*

SAVES

He **s** from the sword of their mouth,	**Jb 5:15**	3467
God, Who **s** the upright in heart.	**Ps 7:10**	3467
know that the LORD **s** His anointed;	**Ps 20:6**	3467
And **s** those who are crushed in	**Ps 34:18**	3467
them from the wicked and **s** them,	**Ps 37:40**	3467
A truthful witness **s** lives,	**Pr 14:25**	5337
baptism now **s** you—not the removal	**1Pe 3:21**	*4982*

SAVING

you have shown me by **s** my life;	**Gn 19:19**	2421a
the **s** strength of His right hand.	**Ps 20:6**	3468
He is a **s** defense to His anointed.	**Ps 28:8**	3444
Answer me with Your **s** truth.	**Ps 69:13**	3468
after **s** a people out of the land	**Jude 1:5**	*4982*

SAVIOR

My **s**, You save me from	**2Sa 22:3**	3467
O **S** of those who take refuge at	**Ps 17:7**	3467
They forgot God their **S**,	**Ps 106:21**	3467
will send them a **S** and a Champion,	**Is 19:20**	3467
The Holy One of Israel, your **S**;	**Is 43:3**	3467
And there is no **s** besides Me.	**Is 43:11**	3467
hides Himself, O God of Israel, **S**!	**Is 45:15**	3467
Me, A righteous God and a **S**;	**Is 45:21**	3467
know that I, the LORD, am your **S** And	**Is 49:26**	3467
know that I, the LORD, am your **S** And	**Is 60:16**	3467
So He became their **S**.	**Is 63:8**	3467
Israel, Its **S** in time of distress,	**Jer 14:8**	3467
Me, For there is no **s** besides Me.	**Hos 13:4**	3467
spirit has rejoiced in God my **S**.	**Lk 1:47**	*4990*
there has been born for you a **S**,	**Lk 2:11**	*4990*
is indeed the **S** of the world."	**Jn 4:42**	*4990*
right hand as a Prince and a **S**,	**Ac 5:31**	*4990*
God has brought to Israel a **S**,	**Ac 13:23**	*4990*
Himself *being* the **S** of the body.	**Eph 5:23**	*4990*
also we eagerly wait for a **S**,	**Php 3:20**	*4990*
to the commandment of God our **S**,	**1Tm 1:1**	*4990*
in the sight of God our **S**,	**1Tm 2:3**	*4990*
God, who is the **S** of all men,	**1Tm 4:10**	*4990*
appearing of our **S** Christ Jesus,	**2Tm 1:10**	*4990*
to the commandment of God our **S**,	**Ti 1:3**	*4990*
the Father and Christ Jesus our **S**.	**Ti 1:4**	*4990*
adorn the doctrine of God our **S**	**Ti 2:10**	*4990*
the glory of our great God and **S**,	**Ti 2:13**	*4990*
But when the kindness of God our **S**	**Ti 3:4**	*4990*
richly through Jesus Christ our **S**,	**Ti 3:6**	*4990*
righteousness of our God and **S**,	**2Pe 1:1**	*4990*
eternal kingdom of our Lord and **S**	**2Pe 1:11**	*4990*
of the Lord and **S** Jesus Christ,	**2Pe 2:20**	*4990*
commandment of the Lord and **S**	**2Pe 3:2**	*4990*
of our Lord and **S** Jesus Christ.	**2Pe 3:18**	*4990*
the Son *to be* the **S** of the world.	**1Jn 4:14**	*4990*
to the only God our **S**,	**Jude 1:25**	*4990*

SAVORY

a **s** dish for me such as I love,	**Gn 27:4**	4303
game and prepare a **s** dish for me,	**Gn 27:7**	4303
them *as* a **s** dish for your father,	**Gn 27:9**	4303
his mother made **s** food such as his	**Gn 27:14**	4303
gave the **s** food and the bread,	**Gn 27:17**	4303
Then he also made **s** food,	**Gn 27:31**	4303

SAW

God **s** that the light was good;	**Gn 1:4**	7200
and God **s** that it was good.	**Gn 1:10**	7200
and God **s** that it was good.	**Gn 1:12**	7200
and God **s** that it was good.	**Gn 1:18**	7200
and God **s** that it was good.	**Gn 1:21**	7200
and God **s** that it was good.	**Gn 1:25**	7200
God **s** all that He had made,	**Gn 1:31**	7200
When the woman **s** that the tree was	**Gn 3:6**	7200
that the sons of God **s** that the	**Gn 6:2**	7200
Then the LORD **s** that the	**Gn 6:5**	7200
s the nakedness of his father,	**Gn 9:22**	7200
the Egyptians **s** that the woman was	**Gn 12:14**	7200
Pharaoh's officials **s** her and	**Gn 12:15**	7200
s all the valley of the Jordan,	**Gn 13:10**	7200
when she **s** that she had conceived,	**Gn 16:4**	7200
when she **s** that she had conceived,	**Gn 16:5**	7200
and when he **s** *them*, he ran from	**Gn 18:2**	7200
When Lot **s** *them*, he rose to meet	**Gn 19:1**	7200
he **s**, and behold, the smoke of the	**Gn 19:28**	7200
Now Sarah **s** the son of Hagar	**Gn 21:9**	7200
eyes and she **s** a well of water;	**Gn 21:19**	7200
and **s** the place from a distance.	**Gn 22:4**	7200
When he **s** the ring	**Gn 24:30**	7200
and when she **s** Isaac she	**Gn 24:64**	7200
out through a window, and **s**,	**Gn 26:8**	7200
Now Esau **s** that Isaac had blessed	**Gn 28:6**	7200
So Esau **s** that the daughters of	**Gn 28:8**	7200
looked, and **s** a well in the field,	**Gn 29:2**	7200
When Jacob **s** Rachel the daughter	**Gn 29:10**	7200
the LORD **s** that Leah was unloved,	**Gn 29:31**	7200
Now when Rachel **s** that she bore	**Gn 30:1**	7200
Leah **s** that she had stopped bearing,	**Gn 30:9**	7200
Jacob **s** the attitude of Laban,	**Gn 31:2**	7200
up my eyes and **s** in a dream,	**Gn 31:10**	7200
Jacob said when he **s** them,	**Gn 32:2**	7200
When he **s** that he had not	**Gn 32:25**	7200
and **s** the women and the children,	**Gn 33:5**	7200
the prince of the land, **s** her,	**Gn 34:2**	7200
His brothers **s** that their	**Gn 37:4**	7200
When they **s** him from a distance	**Gn 37:18**	7200
Judah **s** there a daughter of a	**Gn 38:2**	7200
she **s** that Shelah had grown up,	**Gn 38:14**	7200
When Judah **s** her, he thought she	**Gn 38:15**	7200
Now his master **s** that the LORD was	**Gn 39:3**	7200
When she **s** that he had left his	**Gn 39:13**	7200
When the chief baker **s** that he had	**Gn 40:16**	7200
"I also **s** in my dream,	**Gn 40:16**	
"I **s** also in my dream, and	**Gn 41:22**	7200
Now Jacob **s** that there was grain in	**Gn 42:1**	7200
When Joseph **s** his brothers he	**Gn 42:7**	7200
because we **s** the distress of his	**Gn 42:21**	7200
the lodging place, he **s** his money;	**Gn 42:27**	7200
father **s** their bundles of money,	**Gn 42:35**	7200
When Joseph **s** Benjamin with them,	**Gn 43:16**	7200
eyes and **s** his brother Benjamin,	**Gn 43:29**	7200
and when he **s** the wagons that	**Gn 45:27**	7200
When Israel **s** Joseph's sons, he	**Gn 48:8**	7200
When Joseph **s** that his father laid	**Gn 48:17**	7200
"When he **s** that a resting place	**Gn 49:15**	7200
s the mourning at the threshing	**Gn 50:11**	7200
Joseph's brothers **s** that their father	**Gn 50:15**	7200
Joseph **s** the third generation	**Gn 50:23**	7200
when she **s** that he was beautiful,	**Ex 2:2**	7200
and she **s** the basket among the	**Ex 2:5**	7200
she opened *it*, she **s** the child,	**Ex 2:6**	7200
he **s** an Egyptian beating a Hebrew,	**Ex 2:11**	7200
when he **s** there was no one *around*,	**Ex 2:12**	7200
God **s** the sons of Israel, and	**Ex 2:25**	7200
the LORD **s** that he turned aside to	**Ex 3:4**	7200
The foremen of the sons of Israel **s**	**Ex 5:19**	7200
Pharaoh **s** that there was relief,	**Ex 8:15**	7200
But when Pharaoh **s** that the rain	**Ex 9:34**	7200
and Israel **s** the Egyptians dead on	**Ex 14:30**	7200
When Israel **s** the great power	**Ex 14:31**	7200
When the sons of Israel **s** *it*,	**Ex 16:15**	7200
Now when Moses' father-in-law **s**	**Ex 18:14**	7200
and when the people **s** *it*,	**Ex 20:18**	7200
and they **s** the God of Israel;	**Ex 24:10**	7200
and they **s** God, and they ate	**Ex 24:11**	2372
Now when the people **s** that Moses	**Ex 32:1**	7200
Now when Aaron **s** *this*, he built an	**Ex 32:5**	7200
he **s** the calf and *the* dancing;	**Ex 32:19**	7200
Now when Moses **s** that the people	**Ex 32:25**	7200

When all the people **s** the pillar	**Ex 33:10**	7200
all the sons of Israel **s** Moses,	**Ex 34:30**	7200
and when all the people **s** *it,*	**Lv 9:24**	7200
we **s** the descendants of Anak there.	**Nu 13:28**	7200
we **s** in it are men of *great* size.	**Nu 13:32**	7200
"There also we **s** the Nephilim	**Nu 13:33**	7200
all the congregation **s** that Aaron	**Nu 20:29**	7200
Now Balak the son of Zippor **s** all	**Nu 22:2**	7200
When the donkey **s** the angel of the	**Nu 22:23**	7200
donkey **s** the angel of the LORD,	**Nu 22:25**	7200
donkey **s** the angel of the LORD,	**Nu 22:27**	7200
and he **s** the angel of the LORD	**Nu 22:31**	7200
"But the donkey **s** me and turned	**Nu 22:33**	7200
and he **s** from there a portion of	**Nu 22:41**	7200
When Balaam **s** that it pleased the	**Nu 24:1**	7200
s Israel camping tribe by tribe;	**Nu 24:2**	7200
the son of Aaron the priest, **s** it,	**Nu 25:7**	7200
So when they **s** the land of Jazer	**Nu 32:1**	7200
valley of Eshcol and **s** the land,	**Nu 32:9**	7200
terrible wilderness which you **s** on	**Dt 1:19**	7200
we **s** the sons of the Anakim there."	**Dt 1:28**	7200
and in the wilderness where you **s**	**Dt 1:31**	7200
sound of words, but you **s** no form	**Dt 4:12**	7200
the great trials which your eyes **s**	**Dt 7:19**	7200
"And I **s** that you had indeed	**Dt 9:16**	7200
heard our voice and **s** our affliction	**Dt 26:7**	7200
"The LORD **s** *this,* and spurned	**Dt 32:19**	7200
when I **s** among the spoil a	**Jos 7:21**	7200
about when the king of Ai **s** *it,*	**Jos 8:14**	7200
When Joshua and all Israel **s** that	**Jos 8:21**	7200
own eyes **s** what I did in Egypt.	**Jos 24:7**	7200
spies **s** a man coming out of the city and	**Jg 1:24**	7200
When Gideon **s** that he was the	**Jg 6:22**	7200
When Gaal **s** the people, he	**Jg 9:36**	7200
when he looked and **s** the people	**Jg 9:43**	7200
Israel **s** that Abimelech was dead,	**Jg 9:55**	7200
When he **s** her, he tore his clothes	**Jg 11:35**	7200
I **s** that you would not deliver *me,*	**Jg 12:3**	7200
When Manoah and his wife **s** *this,*	**Jg 13:20**	7200
to Timnah and **s** a woman in Timnah,	**Jg 14:1**	7200
"I **s** a woman in Timnah, *one* of	**Jg 14:2**	7200
When they **s** him, they brought	**Jg 14:11**	7200
went to Gaza and **s** a harlot there,	**Jg 16:1**	7200
When Delilah **s** that he had told	**Jg 16:18**	7200
When the people **s** him, they	**Jg 16:24**	7200
came to Laish and **s** the people who	**Jg 18:7**	7200
and when Micah **s** that they were	**Jg 18:26**	7200
and when the girl's father **s** him,	**Jg 19:3**	7200
s the traveler in the open square of	**Jg 19:17**	7200
All who **s** *it* said,	**Jg 19:30**	7200
the sons of Benjamin **s** that they	**Jg 20:36**	7200
for they **s** that disaster was close	**Jg 20:41**	7200
When she **s** that she was determined	**Ru 1:18**	7200
her mother-in-law **s** what she had	**Ru 2:18**	7200
men of Ashdod **s** that it was so,	**1Sa 5:7**	7200
they raised their eyes and **s** the ark	**1Sa 6:13**	7200
lords of the Philistines **s** it,	**1Sa 6:16**	7200
When Samuel **s** Saul, the LORD said	**1Sa 9:17**	7200
when all who knew him previously **s**	**1Sa 10:11**	7200
we **s** that they could not be found,	**1Sa 10:14**	7200
"When you **s** that Nahash the king	**1Sa 12:12**	7200
the men of Israel **s** that they were in	**1Sa 13:6**	7200
"Because I **s** that the people were	**1Sa 13:11**	7200
and when Saul **s** any mighty man or	**1Sa 14:52**	7200
all the men of Israel **s** the man,	**1Sa 17:24**	7200
the Philistine looked and **s** David,	**1Sa 17:42**	7200
the Philistines **s** that their champion	**1Sa 17:51**	7200
Now when Saul **s** David going out	**1Sa 17:55**	7200
When Saul **s** that he was prospering	**1Sa 18:15**	7200
When Saul **s** and knew that the LORD	**1Sa 18:28**	7200
you **s** *it* and rejoiced.	**1Sa 19:5**	7200
but when they **s** the company of the	**1Sa 19:20**	7200
"I **s** the son of Jesse coming to	**1Sa 22:9**	7200
When Abigail **s** David, she hurried	**1Sa 25:23**	7200
When he **s** that Saul came after him	**1Sa 26:3**	7200
David **s** the place where Saul lay,	**1Sa 26:5**	7200
away, but no one **s** or knew *it,*	**1Sa 26:12**	7200
Saul **s** the camp of the Philistines,	**1Sa 28:5**	7200
When the woman **s** Samuel, she cried	**1Sa 28:12**	7200
Saul and **s** that he was terrified,	**1Sa 28:21**	7200
armor bearer **s** that Saul was dead,	**1Sa 31:5**	7200
s that the men of Israel had fled	**1Sa 31:7**	7200
him, he **s** me and called to me.	**2Sa 1:7**	7200
s King David leaping and dancing	**2Sa 6:16**	7200
Now when the sons of Ammon **s** that	**2Sa 10:6**	7200
Now when Joab **s** that the battle	**2Sa 10:9**	7200
of Ammon **s** that the Arameans fled,	**2Sa 10:14**	7200
When the Arameans **s** that they had	**2Sa 10:15**	7200
s that they were defeated by	**2Sa 10:19**	7200
from the roof he **s** a woman bathing;	**2Sa 11:2**	7200
But when David **s** that his servants	**2Sa 12:19**	7200
Now when Ahithophel **s** that his	**2Sa 17:23**	7200
When a certain man **s** *it,*	**2Sa 18:10**	7200
I **s** Absalom hanging in an oak."	**2Sa 18:10**	7200
"Now behold, you **s** *him!*	**2Sa 18:11**	7200
watchman **s** another man running;	**2Sa 18:26**	7200
your servant, I **s** a great tumult,	**2Sa 18:29**	7200
And when the man **s** that all the	**2Sa 20:12**	7200
threw a garment over him when he **s**	**2Sa 20:12**	7200
David spoke to the LORD when he **s**	**2Sa 24:17**	7200
s the king and his servants crossing	**2Sa 24:20**	7200
for they **s** that the wisdom of God	**1Ki 3:28**	7200
and when Solomon **s** that the young	**1Ki 11:28**	7200
When all Israel **s** that the king	**1Ki 12:16**	7200
and **s** the body thrown on the road,	**1Ki 13:25**	7200
Zimri **s** that the city was taken,	**1Ki 16:18**	7200
Ahab **s** Elijah, Ahab said to him	**1Ki 18:17**	7200
When all the people **s** it,	**1Ki 18:39**	7200
"I **s** all Israel Scattered on the	**1Ki 22:17**	7200

I **s** the LORD sitting on His	**1Ki 22:19**	7200
of the chariots **s** Jehoshaphat,	**1Ki 22:32**	7200
When the captains of the chariots **s**	**1Ki 22:33**	7200
Elisha **s** *it* and cried out,	**2Ki 2:12**	7200
And he **s** Elijah no more.	**2Ki 2:12**	7200
at Jericho opposite *him* **s** him,	**2Ki 2:15**	7200
he looked behind him and **s** them,	**2Ki 2:24**	7200
and the Moabites **s** the water	**2Ki 3:22**	7200
When the king of Moab **s** that the	**2Ki 3:26**	7200
man of God **s** her at a distance,	**2Ki 4:25**	7200
Naaman **s** one running after him,	**2Ki 5:21**	7200
the servant's eyes and he **s**;	**2Ki 6:17**	7200
opened their eyes and they **s**;	**2Ki 6:20**	7200
the king of Israel when he **s** them,	**2Ki 6:21**	7200
he **s** the company of Jehu as he came,	**2Ki 9:17**	7200
When Joram **s** Jehu,	**2Ki 9:22**	7200
Ahaziah the king of Judah **s** *this,*	**2Ki 9:27**	7200
mother of Ahaziah **s** that her son	**2Ki 11:1**	7200
When they **s** that there was	**2Ki 12:10**	7200
for He **s** the oppression of Israel,	**2Ki 13:4**	7200
behold, they **s** a marauding band;	**2Ki 13:21**	7200
LORD **s** the affliction of Israel,	**2Ki 14:26**	7200
and **s** the altar which *was* at	**2Ki 16:10**	7200
Damascus, the king **s** the altar;	**2Ki 16:12**	7200
he **s** the graves that *were* there on	**2Ki 23:16**	7200
when *Pharaoh Neco* **s** him he killed	**2Ki 23:29**	7200
armor bearer **s** that Saul was dead,	**1Ch 10:5**	7200
the valley **s** that they had fled,	**1Ch 10:7**	7200
and **s** King David leaping and	**1Ch 15:29**	7200
When the sons of Ammon **s** that they	**1Ch 19:6**	7200
Now when Joab **s** that the battle	**1Ch 19:10**	7200
of Ammon **s** that the Arameans fled,	**1Ch 19:15**	7200
When the Arameans **s** that they had	**1Ch 19:16**	7200
when the servants of Hadadezer **s**	**1Ch 19:19**	7200
the LORD **s** and was sorry over the	**1Ch 21:15**	7200
David lifted up his eyes and **s** the	**1Ch 21:16**	7200
Ornan turned back and **s** the angel,	**1Ch 21:20**	7200
Ornan, Ornan looked and **s** David,	**1Ch 21:21**	7200
when David **s** that the LORD had	**1Ch 21:28**	7200
When all Israel **s** that the king	**2Ch 10:16**	7200
When the LORD **s** that they humbled	**2Ch 12:7**	7200
when they **s** that the LORD his God	**2Ch 15:9**	7200
"I **s** all Israel Scattered on the	**2Ch 18:16**	7200
I **s** the LORD sitting on His	**2Ch 18:18**	7200
of the chariots **s** Jehoshaphat,	**2Ch 18:31**	7200
s that it was not the king of Israel,	**2Ch 18:32**	7200
Ahaziah **s** that her son was dead,	**2Ch 22:10**	7200
they **s** that there was much money,	**2Ch 24:11**	7200
the rulers came and **s** the heaps,	**2Ch 31:8**	7200
s that Sennacherib had come and	**2Ch 32:2**	7200
When I **s** *their fear,* I rose and	**Ne 4:14**	7200
the nations surrounding us **s** *it,*	**Ne 6:16**	7200
"You **s** the affliction of our fathers	**Ne 9:9**	7200
In those days I **s** in Judah some	**Ne 13:15**	7200
In those days I also **s** that the	**Ne 13:23**	7200
in the eyes of all who **s** her.	**Es 2:15**	7200
When Haman **s** that Mordecai neither	**Es 3:5**	7200
When the king **s** Esther the queen	**Es 5:2**	7200
when Haman **s** Mordecai in the	**Es 5:9**	7200
for he **s** that harm had been	**Es 7:7**	7200
they **s** that *his* pain was very great.	**Jb 2:13**	7200
be, As infants that never **s** light.	**Jb 3:16**	7200
will deny him, *saying,* 'I never **s** you	**Jb 8:18**	7200
eye which **s** him sees him no longer,	**Jb 20:9**	7805
Then He **s** it and declared it;	**Jb 28:27**	7200
young men **s** me and hid themselves,	**Jb 29:8**	7200
And when the eye **s**,	**Jb 29:11**	7200
I **s** I had support in the gate,	**Jb 31:21**	7200
And when Elihu **s** that there was no	**Jb 32:5**	7200
Job lived 140 years, and **s** his sons and	**Jb 42:16**	7200
They **s** *it,* then they were amazed;	**Ps 48:5**	7200
I **s** the prosperity of the wicked.	**Ps 73:3**	7200
The waters **s** You, O God;	**Ps 77:16**	7200
The waters **s** You, they were in	**Ps 77:16**	7200
The earth **s** and trembled.	**Ps 97:4**	7200
And I **s** among the naive,	**Pr 7:7**	7200
When I **s**, I reflected upon it;	**Pr 24:32**	2372
And I **s** that wisdom excels folly	**Ec 2:13**	7200
And behold *I* **s** the tears of	**Ec 4:1**	7200
and I **s** every work of God, *I*	**Ec 8:17**	7200
I again **s** under the sun that the	**Ec 9:11**	7200
maidens **s** her and called her blessed	**SS 6:9**	7200
he **s** during the reigns of Uzziah,	**Is 1:1**	2372
word which Isaiah the son of Amoz **s**	**Is 2:1**	2372
I **s** the Lord sitting on a throne,	**Is 6:1**	7200
Is the **s** to exalt itself over the	**Is 10:15**	4883
which Isaiah the son of Amoz **s**.	**Is 13:1**	2372
And you **s** that the breaches In the	**Is 22:9**	7200
Now the LORD **s**, And it was	**Is 59:15**	7200
And He **s** that there was no man,	**Is 59:16**	7200
her treacherous sister Judah **s** it.	**Jer 3:7**	7200
"And I **s** that for all the	**Jer 3:8**	7200
of Samaria I **s** an offensive thing:	**Jer 23:13**	7200
and all the men of war **s** them,	**Jer 39:4**	7200
the people who were with Ishmael **s**	**Jer 41:13**	7200
well off and **s** no misfortune.	**Jer 44:17**	7200
The adversaries **s** her, They mocked	**La 1:7**	7200
opened and I **s** visions of God.	**Ezk 1:1**	7200
downward I **s** something like fire;	**Ezk 1:27**	7200
And when I **s** *it,* I fell on my face	**Ezk 1:28**	7200
which I **s** by the river Chebar,	**Ezk 3:23**	7200
appearance which I **s** in the plain.	**Ezk 8:4**	7200
that I **s** by the river Chebar.	**Ezk 10:15**	7200
These are the living beings that I **s**	**Ezk 10:20**	7200
and among them I **s** Jaazaniah son	**Ezk 11:1**	7200
and **s** you squirming in your blood,	**Ezk 16:6**	7200
"Then I passed by you and **s** you,	**Ezk 16:8**	7200
I removed them when I **s** *it.*	**Ezk 16:50**	7200
'When she **s**, as she waited, *That*	**Ezk 19:5**	7200

then they **s** every high hill and	**Ezk 20:28**	7200
"Now her sister Oholibah **s** *this,*	**Ezk 23:11**	7200
I **s** that she had defiled herself;	**Ezk 23:13**	7200
she **s** men portrayed on the wall,	**Ezk 23:14**	7200
"When she **s** them she lusted	**Ezk 23:16**	4758, 5869
I **s** also that the house had a	**Ezk 41:8**	7200
of the vision which I **s**,	**Ezk 43:3**	7200
like the vision which I **s** when He	**Ezk 43:3**	7200
which I **s** by the river Chebar;	**Ezk 43:3**	7200
In that you **s** the feet and toes,	**Da 2:41**	2370
inasmuch as you **s** the iron mixed	**Da 2:41**	2370
"And in that you **s** the iron mixed	**Da 2:43**	2370
"Inasmuch as you **s** that a stone	**Da 2:45**	2370
high officials gathered around *and* **s**	**Da 3:27**	2370
"I **s** a dream and it made me	**Da 4:5**	2370
'The tree that you **s**,	**Da 4:20**	2370
the king **s** an *angelic* watcher,	**Da 4:23**	2370
and the king **s** the back of the	**Da 5:5**	2370
Daniel **s** a dream and visions in his	**Da 7:1**	2370
I **s** the ram butting westward,	**Da 8:4**	7200
I **s** him come beside the ram,	**Da 8:7**	7200
"The ram which you **s** with the two	**Da 8:20**	7200
Now I, Daniel, alone **s** the vision,	**Da 10:7**	7200
alone and **s** this great vision;	**Da 10:8**	7200
When Ephraim **s** his sickness, And	**Hos 5:13**	7200
I **s** your forefathers as the	**Hos 9:10**	7200
I **s** the Lord standing beside the	**Am 9:1**	7200
When God **s** their deeds, that they	**Jon 3:10**	7200
which he **s** concerning Samaria and	**Mi 1:1**	2372
which Habakkuk the prophet **s**.	**Hab 1:1**	2372
I **s** the tents of Cushan under	**Hab 3:7**	7200
The mountains **s** You *and* quaked;	**Hab 3:10**	7200
'Who is left among you who **s** this	**Hg 2:3**	7200
I **s** at night, and behold, a man	**Zch 1:8**	7200
For we **s** His star in the east and	**Mt 2:2**	3708
When they **s** the star, they	**Mt 2:10**	3708
s the Child with Mary His mother;	**Mt 2:11**	3708
Then when Herod **s** that he had been	**Mt 2:16**	3708
But when he **s** many of the	**Mt 3:7**	3708
and he **s** the Spirit of God	**Mt 3:16**	3708
IN DARKNESS **S** A GREAT LIGHT,	**Mt 4:16**	3708
Sea of Galilee, He **s** two brothers,	**Mt 4:18**	3708
there He **s** two other brothers,	**Mt 4:21**	3708
When Jesus **s** the crowds, He	**Mt 5:1**	3708
He **s** his mother-in-law lying sick	**Mt 8:14**	3708
when Jesus **s** a crowd around Him,	**Mt 8:18**	3708
and when they **s** Him, they	**Mt 8:34**	3708
But when the crowds **s** *this,*	**Mt 9:8**	3708
went on from there, He **s** a man	**Mt 9:9**	3708
When the Pharisees **s** *this,*	**Mt 9:11**	3708
house, and **s** the flute-players and	**Mt 9:23**	3708
But when the Pharisees **s**	**Mt 12:2**	3708
so that the mute man spoke and **s**.	**Mt 12:22**	991
ashore, He **s** a large crowd,	**Mt 14:14**	3708
disciples **s** Him walking on the sea,	**Mt 14:26**	3708
as they **s** the mute speaking,	**Mt 15:31**	991
up their eyes, they **s** no one except	**Mt 17:8**	3708
fellow slaves **s** what had happened,	**Mt 18:31**	3708
third hour and **s** others standing idle	**Mt 20:3**	3708
and the scribes **s** the wonderful things	**Mt 21:15**	3708
when the vine-growers **s** the son,	**Mt 21:38**	3708
s a man there who was not dressed in	**Mt 22:11**	3708
were indignant when they **s** *this,*	**Mt 26:8**	3708
another *servant-girl* **s** him and	**Mt 26:71**	3708
Him, **s** that He had been condemned,	**Mt 27:3**	3708
When Pilate **s** that he was	**Mt 27:24**	3708
when they **s** the earthquake and the	**Mt 27:54**	3708
When they **s** Him, they	**Mt 28:17**	3708
water, He **s** the heavens opening,	**Mk 1:10**	3708
of Galilee, He **s** Simon and Andrew,	**Mk 1:16**	3708
He **s** James the son of Zebedee,	**Mk 1:19**	3708
He **s** Levi the *son* of Alphaeus	**Mk 2:14**	3708
s that He was eating with the sinners	**Mk 2:16**	3708
Whenever the unclean spirits **s** Him,	**Mk 3:11**	2334
and He **s** a commotion, and *people*	**Mk 5:38**	2335
The people **s** them going, and	**Mk 6:33**	3708
ashore, He **s** a large crowd,	**Mk 6:34**	3708
they **s** Him walking on the sea,	**Mk 6:49**	3708
all **s** Him and were terrified.	**Mk 6:50**	3708
and **s** no one with them anymore,	**Mk 9:8**	3708
they **s** a large crowd around them,	**Mk 9:14**	3708
when the entire crowd **s** Him,	**Mk 9:15**	3708
When he **s** Him, immediately the	**Mk 9:20**	3708
When Jesus **s** that a crowd was	**Mk 9:25**	3708
we **s** someone casting out demons in	**Mk 9:38**	3708
But when Jesus **s** this, He was	**Mk 10:14**	3708
they **s** the fig tree withered from	**Mk 11:20**	3708
When Jesus **s** that he had	**Mk 12:34**	3708
The servant-girl **s** him, and began once	**Mk 14:69**	3708
s the way He breathed His last,	**Mk 15:39**	3708
they **s** that the stone had been	**Mk 16:4**	2334
they **s** a young man sitting at the	**Mk 16:5**	3708
was troubled when he **s** *the*	**Lk 1:12**	3708
When they **s** Him, they were	**Lk 2:48**	3708
and He **s** two boats lying at the	**Lk 5:2**	3708
But when Simon Peter **s** *that,*	**Lk 5:8**	3708
and when he **s** Jesus, he fell on	**Lk 5:12**	3708
When the Lord **s** her,	**Lk 7:13**	3708
Pharisee who had invited Him **s** this,	**Lk 7:39**	3708
the herdsmen **s** what had happened,	**Lk 8:34**	3708
When the woman **s** that she had	**Lk 8:47**	3708
they **s** His glory and the two men	**Lk 9:32**	3708
we **s** someone casting out demons in	**Lk 9:49**	3708
disciples James and John **s** *this,*	**Lk 9:54**	3708
on that road, and when he **s** him,	**Lk 10:31**	3708
he came to the place and **s** him,	**Lk 10:32**	3708
and when he **s** him, he felt	**Lk 10:33**	3708
When the Pharisee **s** it,	**Lk 11:38**	3708

When Jesus **s** her, He called	Lk 13:12	*3708*
a long way off, his father **s** him and	Lk 15:20	*3708*
torment, and **s** Abraham far away and	Lk 16:23	*3708*
When He **s** them, He said to	Lk 17:14	*3708*
when he **s** that he had been healed,	Lk 17:15	*3708*
them, but when the disciples **s** it,	Lk 18:15	*3708*
and when all the people **s** it,	Lk 18:43	*3708*
When they **s** it, they all *began*	Lk 19:7	*3708*
He **s** the city and wept over it,	Lk 19:41	*3708*
"But when the vine-growers **s** him,	Lk 20:14	*3708*
And He looked up and **s** the rich	Lk 21:1	*3708*
And He **s** a poor widow	Lk 21:2	*3708*
Him **s** what was going to happen,	Lk 22:49	*3708*
later, another **s** him and said,	Lk 22:58	*3708*
was very glad when he **s** Jesus;	Lk 23:8	*3708*
the centurion **s** what had happened,	Lk 23:47	*3708*
and **s** the tomb and how His body	Lk 23:55	*2300*
in, he **s** the linen wrappings only;	Lk 24:12	*991*
and we **s** His glory, glory as of	Jn 1:14	*2300*
next day he **s** Jesus coming to him and	Jn 1:29	*991*
And Jesus turned and **s** them following,	Jn 1:38	*2300*
and **s** where He was staying;	Jn 1:39	*3708*
Jesus **s** Nathanael coming to Him,	Jn 1:47	*3708*
under the fig tree, I **s** you."	Jn 1:48	*3708*
that I **s** you under the fig tree,	Jn 1:50	*3708*
When Jesus **s** him lying *there,* and	Jn 5:6	*3708*
because they **s** the signs which He was	Jn 6:2	*3708*
Therefore when the people **s** the	Jn 6:14	*3708*
they **s** Jesus walking on the sea	Jn 6:19	*2334*
s that there was no other small boat	Jn 6:22	*3708*
s that Jesus was not there,	Jn 6:24	*3708*
seek Me, not because you **s** signs,	Jn 6:26	*3708*
day, and he **s** *it* and was glad."	Jn 8:56	*3708*
by, He **s** a man blind from birth.	Jn 9:1	*3708*
who previously **s** him as a beggar,	Jn 9:8	*2334*
when they **s** that Mary got up	Jn 11:31	*3708*
came where Jesus was, she **s** Him,	Jn 11:32	*3708*
Jesus therefore **s** her weeping,	Jn 11:33	*3708*
and **s** what He had done, believed in	Jn 11:45	*2300*
said because he **s** His glory,	Jn 12:41	*3708*
priests and the officers **s** Him,	Jn 19:6	*3708*
When Jesus then **s** His mother,	Jn 19:26	*3708*
they **s** that He was already dead,	Jn 19:33	*3708*
and **s** the stone *already* taken away	Jn 20:1	*991*
he **s** the linen wrappings lying	Jn 20:5	*991*
and he **s** the linen wrappings lying	Jn 20:6	*2334*
then also entered, and he **s** and believed.	Jn 20:8	*3708*
and she **s** two angels in white sitting,	Jn 20:12	*2334*
she turned around and **s** Jesus	Jn 20:14	*2334*
rejoiced when they **s** the Lord.	Jn 20:20	*3708*
s a charcoal fire *already* laid and	Jn 21:9	*991*
s the disciple whom Jesus loved	Jn 21:20	*991*
"For David says of Him, 'I **S**	Ac 2:25	*4308*
When he **s** Peter and John about	Ac 3:3	*3708*
s him walking and praising God;	Ac 3:9	*3708*
But when Peter **s** *this,* he replied	Ac 3:12	*3708*
all who were sitting in the Council **s**	Ac 6:15	*3708*
"And when he **s** one *of them* being	Ac 7:24	*3708*
"When Moses **s** it, he marveled	Ac 7:31	*3708*
heaven and **s** the glory of God,	Ac 7:55	*3708*
as they heard and **s** the signs	Ac 8:6	*991*
Now when Simon **s** that the Spirit	Ac 8:18	*3708*
and the eunuch no longer **s** him, but	Ac 8:39	*3708*
lived at Lydda and Sharon **s** him,	Ac 9:35	*3708*
her eyes, and when she **s** Peter,	Ac 9:40	*3708*
clearly **s** in a vision an angel of God	Ac 10:3	*3708*
and he **s** the sky opened up, and an	Ac 10:11	*2334*
and in a trance I **s** a vision,	Ac 11:5	*3708*
I **s** the four-footed animals of the	Ac 11:6	*3708*
he **s** that it pleased the Jews,	Ac 12:3	*3708*
door, they **s** him and were amazed.	Ac 12:16	*3708*
when he **s** what had happened,	Ac 13:12	*3708*
But when the Jews **s** the crowds,	Ac 13:45	*3708*
crowds **s** what Paul had done,	Ac 14:11	*3708*
But when her masters **s** that their	Ac 16:19	*3708*
When the jailer awoke and **s**	Ac 16:27	*3708*
and when they **s** the brethren,	Ac 16:40	*3708*
and when they **s** the commander and	Ac 21:32	*3708*
"And those who were with me **s**	Ac 22:9	*2300*
and I **s** Him saying to me,	Ac 22:18	*3708*
I **s** on the way a light from	Ac 26:13	*3708*
When the natives **s** the	Ac 28:4	*3708*
and when Paul **s** them, he thanked	Ac 28:15	*3708*
But when I **s** that they were not	Ga 2:14	*3708*
same conflict which you **s** in me,	Php 1:30	*3708*
AND **S** MY WORKS FOR FORTY YEARS	Heb 3:9	*3708*
they **s** he was a beautiful child;	Heb 11:23	*3708*
he **s** and heard *that* righteous man,	2Pe 2:8	*990*
Christ, *even* to all that he **s**.	Rv 1:2	*3708*
I **s** seven golden lampstands;	Rv 1:12	*3708*
in the middle of the lampstands *I* **s**	Rv 1:13	
When I **s** Him, I fell at His	Rv 1:17	*3708*
which you **s** in My right hand,	Rv 1:20	*3708*
and upon the thrones *I* **s**	Rv 4:4	
I **s** in the right hand of Him	Rv 5:1	*3708*
And I **s** a strong angel proclaiming	Rv 5:2	*3708*
And I **s** between the throne	Rv 5:6	*3708*
Then I **s** when the Lamb broke one of	Rv 6:1	*3708*
I **s** underneath the altar the souls	Rv 6:9	*3708*
After this I **s** four angels	Rv 7:1	*3708*
And I **s** another angel ascending	Rv 7:2	*3708*
And I **s** the seven angels who stand	Rv 8:2	*3708*
and I **s** a star from heaven which	Rv 9:1	*3708*
And this is how I **s** in the vision	Rv 9:17	*3708*
I **s** another strong angel	Rv 10:1	*3708*
Then the angel whom I **s** standing on	Rv 10:5	*3708*
And when the dragon **s** that he was	Rv 12:13	*3708*
Then I **s** a beast coming up out of	Rv 13:1	*3708*
which I **s** was like a leopard,	Rv 13:2	*3708*
I **s** one of his heads as if it had	Rv 13:3	
Then I **s** another beast coming up	Rv 13:11	*3708*
And I **s** another angel flying in	Rv 14:6	*3708*
Then I **s** another sign in heaven,	Rv 15:1	*3708*
And I **s** something like a sea of	Rv 15:2	*3708*
And I **s** *coming* out of the mouth of	Rv 16:13	*3708*
and I **s** a woman sitting on a	Rv 17:3	*3708*
And I **s** the woman drunk with the	Rv 17:6	*3708*
When I **s** her, I wondered	Rv 17:6	*3708*
beast that you **s** was, and is not,	Rv 17:8	*3708*
horns which you **s** are ten kings who	Rv 17:12	*3708*
waters which you **s** where the harlot	Rv 17:15	*3708*
"And the ten horns which you **s**,	Rv 17:16	*3708*
whom you **s** is the great city,	Rv 17:18	*3708*
I **s** another angel coming down from	Rv 18:1	*3708*
they **s** the smoke of her burning,	Rv 18:18	*991*
And I **s** heaven opened,	Rv 19:11	*3708*
I **s** an angel standing in the sun,	Rv 19:17	*3708*
And I **s** the beast and the kings of	Rv 19:19	*3708*
Then I **s** an angel coming down from	Rv 20:1	*3708*
Then I **s** thrones, and they sat on	Rv 20:4	*3708*
And I **s** the souls of those who	Rv 20:4	
Then I **s** a great white throne and	Rv 20:11	*3708*
And I **s** the dead, the great and	Rv 20:12	*3708*
I **s** a new heaven and a new earth;	Rv 21:1	*3708*
And I **s** the holy city, new	Rv 21:2	*3708*
I **s** no temple in it, for the	Rv 21:22	*3708*
one who heard and **s** these things.	Rv 22:8	*991*
And when I heard and **s**,	Rv 22:8	*991*
SAWED		
according to measure, **s** with saws,	1Ki 7:9	1641
SAWN		
were stoned, they were **s** in two,	Heb 11:37	*4249*
SAWS		
were in it, and set *them* under **s**,	2Sa 12:31	4050
to measure, sawed with **s**,	1Ki 7:9	4050
and cut *them* with **s** and with sharp	1Ch 20:3	4050
SAY		
see you, they will **s**,	Gn 12:12	559
"Please **s** that you are my sister	Gn 12:13	559
"Why did you **s**,	Gn 12:19	559
that is yours, for fear you would **s**,	Gn 14:23	559
"Did he not himself **s** to me,	Gn 20:5	559
everywhere we go, **s** of me,	Gn 20:13	559
it be that the girl to whom I **s**,	Gn 24:14	559
out to draw, and to whom I **s**,	Gn 24:43	559
and she will **s** to me,	Gn 24:44	559
stay with us *a few* days, **s** ten;	Gn 24:55	176
my sister," for he was afraid to **s**,	Gn 26:7	559
How then did you **s**,	Gn 26:9	559
"Thus you shall **s** to my lord Esau:	Gn 32:4	559
then you shall **s**,	Gn 32:18	559
and you shall **s**,	Gn 32:20	559
I will give whatever you **s** to me.	Gn 34:11	559
give according as you **s** to me;	Gn 34:12	559
for I heard *them* **s**,	Gn 37:17	559
we will **s**, 'A wild beast devoured him	Gn 37:20	559
we possibly know that he would **s**,	Gn 43:7	559
when you overtake them, **s** to them,	Gn 44:4	559
"What can we **s** to my lord?	Gn 44:16	559
go up to my father, and **s** to him,	Gn 45:9	559
"**S** to your brothers,	Gn 45:17	559
tell Pharaoh, and will **s** to him,	Gn 46:31	559
you shall **s**,	Gn 46:34	559
'Thus you shall **s** to Joseph,	Gn 50:17	559
of Israel, and I will **s** to them,	Ex 3:13	559
Now they may **s** to me,	Ex 3:13	559
What shall I **s** to them?"	Ex 3:13	559
you shall **s** to the sons of Israel,	Ex 3:14	559
you shall **s** to the sons of Israel,	Ex 3:15	559
of Israel together and **s** to them,	Ex 3:16	559
They will pay heed to what you **s**;	Ex 3:18	6963
of Egypt and you will **s** to him,	Ex 3:18	559
believe me or listen to what I **s**?	Ex 4:1	6963
For they may **s**, 'The LORD has not	Ex 4:1	559
two signs or heed what you **s**,	Ex 4:9	6963
and teach you what you are to **s**."	Ex 4:12	1696
"Then you shall **s** to Pharaoh,	Ex 4:22	559
therefore you **s**,	Ex 5:17	559
"**S**, therefore, to the sons of Israel,	Ex 6:6	559
then you shall **s** to Aaron,	Ex 7:9	559
"You shall **s** to him,	Ex 7:16	559
"**S** to Aaron, 'Take your staff and	Ex 7:19	559
"Go to Pharaoh and **s** to him,	Ex 8:1	559
"**S** to Aaron, 'Stretch out your hand	Ex 8:5	559
"**S** to Aaron, 'Stretch out your staff	Ex 8:16	559
out to the water, and **s** to him,	Ex 8:20	559
stand before Pharaoh and **s** to him,	Ex 9:13	559
when your children **s** to you,	Ex 12:26	559
you shall **s**,	Ex 12:27	559
then you shall **s** to him,	Ex 13:14	559
Pharaoh will **s** of the sons of Israel,	Ex 14:3	559
"**S** to all the congregation of the	Ex 16:9	559
"Thus you shall **s** to the house of	Ex 19:3	559
you shall **s** to the sons of Israel,	Ex 20:22	559
his voice and do all that I **s**,	Ex 23:22	1696
"**S** to the sons of Israel,	Ex 33:5	559
"See, You **s** to me,	Ex 33:12	559
the sons of Israel, and **s** to them,	Lv 1:2	559
the sons of Israel, and **s** to them,	Lv 15:2	559
the sons of Israel and **s** to them,	Lv 17:2	559
"Then you shall **s** to them,	Lv 17:8	559
the sons of Israel and **s** to them,	Lv 18:2	559
the sons of Israel and **s** to them,	Lv 19:2	559
also **s** to the sons of Israel:	Lv 20:2	559
the sons of Aaron, and **s** to them:	Lv 21:1	559
"**S** to them, 'If any man among all	Lv 22:3	559
the sons of Israel and **s** to them,	Lv 22:18	559
the sons of Israel and **s** to them,	Lv 23:2	559
the sons of Israel and **s** to them,	Lv 23:10	559
the sons of Israel and **s** to them,	Lv 25:2	559
if you **s**, "What are we going to eat	Lv 25:20	559
the sons of Israel and **s** to them,	Lv 27:2	559
the sons of Israel and **s** to them,	Nu 5:12	559
an oath and shall **s** to the woman,	Nu 5:19	559
the priest shall **s** to the woman),	Nu 5:21	559
And the woman shall **s**,	Nu 5:22	559
the sons of Israel and **s** to them,	Nu 6:2	559
You shall **s** to them:	Nu 6:23	559
"Speak to Aaron and **s** to him,	Nu 8:2	559
that You should **s** to me,	Nu 11:12	559
"**S** to the people, 'Consecrate	Nu 11:18	559
who have heard of Your fame will **s**,	Nu 14:15	559
"**S** to them, 'As I live,' says the	Nu 14:28	559
the sons of Israel and **s** to them,	Nu 15:2	559
the sons of Israel and **s** to them,	Nu 15:18	559
"**S** to Eleazar, the son of Aaron	Nu 16:37	559
to the Levites and **s** to them,	Nu 18:26	559
"You shall **s** to them,	Nu 18:30	559
those who use proverbs **s**,	Nu 21:27	559
I will do whatever you **s** to me.	Nu 22:17	559
s, 'Behold, I give him My covenant	Nu 25:12	559
the sons of Israel and **s** to them,	Nu 28:2	559
"You shall **s** to them,	Nu 28:3	559
the sons of Israel and **s** to them,	Nu 33:51	559
the sons of Israel and **s** to them,	Nu 34:2	559
the sons of Israel and **s** to them,	Nu 35:10	559
the LORD said to me, '**S** to them,	Dt 1:42	559
hear all these statutes and **s**,	Dt 4:6	559
'Go, **s** to them, "Return to your	Dt 5:30	559
then you shall **s** to your son,	Dt 6:21	559
"If you should **s** in your heart,	Dt 7:17	559
you may **s** in your heart,	Dt 8:17	559
"Do not **s** in your heart when the	Dt 9:4	559
which You brought us may **s**,	Dt 9:28	559
as He has promised you, and you **s**,	Dt 12:20	559
it and live in it, and you **s**,	Dt 17:14	559
"You may **s** in your heart,	Dt 18:21	559
"He shall **s** to them,	Dt 20:3	559
to the people and **s**,	Dt 20:8	559
and they shall answer and **s**,	Dt 21:7	559
They shall **s** to the elders of his city,	Dt 21:20	559
father shall **s** to the elders,	Dt 22:16	559
to the gate to the elders and **s**,	Dt 25:7	559
office at that time and **s** to him,	Dt 26:3	559
and **s** before the LORD your God,	Dt 26:5	559
shall **s** before the LORD your God,	Dt 26:13	559
Levites shall then answer and **s** to all	Dt 27:14	559
all the people shall answer and **s**,	Dt 27:15	559
And all the people shall **s**,	Dt 27:16	559
And all the people shall **s**,	Dt 27:17	559
And all the people shall **s**,	Dt 27:18	559
And all the people shall **s**,	Dt 27:19	559
And all the people shall **s**,	Dt 27:20	559
And all the people shall **s**,	Dt 27:21	559
And all the people shall **s**,	Dt 27:22	559
And all the people shall **s**,	Dt 27:23	559
And all the people shall **s**,	Dt 27:24	559
And all the people shall **s**,	Dt 27:25	559
And all the people shall **s**,	Dt 27:26	559
"In the morning you shall **s**,	Dt 28:67	559
And at evening you shall **s**,	Dt 28:67	559
the LORD has afflicted it, will **s**,	Dt 29:22	559
"All the nations will **s**,	Dt 29:24	559
"Then *men* will **s**,	Dt 29:25	559
not in heaven, that you should **s**,	Dt 30:12	559
beyond the sea, that you should **s**,	Dt 30:13	559
so that they will **s** in that day,	Dt 31:17	559
misjudge, That they would **s**,	Dt 32:27	559
"And He will **s**,	Dt 32:37	559
lift up My hand to heaven, And **s**,	Dt 32:40	559
then you shall **s** to them,	Jos 4:7	559
has my lord to **s** to his servant?"	Jos 5:14	1696
what can I **s** since Israel has	Jos 7:8	559
Consecrate the people and **s**,	Jos 7:13	559
from the city, for they will **s**,	Jos 8:6	559
and go to meet them and **s** to them,	Jos 9:11	559
come your sons may **s** to our sons,	Jos 22:24	559
not **s** to our sons in time to come,	Jos 22:27	559
It shall also come about if they **s** *this*	Jos 22:28	559
in time to come, then we shall **s**,	Jos 22:28	559
that you shall **s**,	Jg 4:20	559
named him Jerubbaal, that is to **s**,	Jg 6:32	559
be that he of whom I **s** to you,	Jg 7:4	559
but everyone of whom I **s** to you,	Jg 7:4	559
and you will hear what they **s**;	Jg 7:11	1696
all around the camp and **s**,	Jg 7:18	559
the men of Gilead would **s** to him,	Jg 12:5	559
then they would **s** to him,	Jg 12:6	559
say to him, "**S** now, 'Shibboleth.	Jg 12:6	559
"How can you **s**,	Jg 16:15	559
So how can you **s** to me,	Jg 18:24	559
to us, that we shall **s** to them,	Jg 21:22	559
"All that you **s** I will do."	Ru 3:5	559
the priest's servant would come and **s**	1Sa 2:15	559
as you desire," then he would **s**,	1Sa 2:16	559
bless Elkanah and his wife and **s**,	1Sa 2:20	559
'I did indeed **s** that your house	1Sa 2:30	559
silver or a loaf of bread and **s**,	1Sa 2:36	559
if He calls you, that you shall **s**,	1Sa 3:9	559
regard to all that they **s** to you,	1Sa 8:7	559
to inquire of God, he used to **s**,	1Sa 9:9	559
"**S** to the servant that he might	1Sa 9:27	559
and they will **s** to you,	1Sa 10:2	559
s to the men of Jabesh-gilead,	1Sa 11:9	559
"If they **s** to us,	1Sa 14:9	559
"But if they **s**,	1Sa 14:10	559

among the people and **s** to them,	**1Sa 14:34**	559
"Take a heifer with you and **s**,	**1Sa 16:2**	559
"Thus you shall **s** to David,	**1Sa 18:25**	559
Therefore they **s**,	**1Sa 19:24**	559
"Whatever you **s**, I will do for	**1Sa 20:4**	559
father misses me at all, then **s**,	**1Sa 20:6**	559
If I specifically **s** to the lad,	**1Sa 20:21**	559
"But if I **s** to the youth,	**1Sa 20:22**	559
and thus you shall **s**,	**1Sa 25:6**	559
Therefore they **s**,	**2Sa 5:8**	559
"Go and **s** to My servant David,	**2Sa 7:5**	559
you shall **s** to My servant David,	**2Sa 7:8**	559
what more can David **s** to You?	**2Sa 7:20**	1696
you shall **s**, 'Your servant Uriah the	**2Sa 11:21**	559
"Thus you shall **s** to Joab,	**2Sa 11:25**	559
father comes to see you, **s** to him,	**2Sa 13:5**	559
with wine, and when I **s** to you,	**2Sa 13:28**	559
your maidservant, and they **s**,	**2Sa 14:7**	559
I may send you to the king, to **s**,	**2Sa 14:32**	559
Absalom would call to him and **s**,	**2Sa 15:2**	559
And he would **s**, "Your servant is	**2Sa 15:2**	559
Then Absalom would **s** to him,	**2Sa 15:3**	559
Moreover, Absalom would **s**,	**2Sa 15:4**	559
of the trumpet, then you shall **s**,	**2Sa 15:10**	559
"But if He should **s** thus,	**2Sa 15:26**	559
to the city, and **s** to Absalom,	**2Sa 15:34**	559
'Curse David,' then who shall **s**,	**2Sa 16:10**	559
let us hear what he has to **s**."	**2Sa 17:5**	6310
that whoever hears *it* will **s**,	**2Sa 17:9**	559
"**S** to Amasa, 'Are you not my bone	**2Sa 19:13**	559
"Formerly they used to **s**,	**2Sa 20:18**	559
will do for you whatever you **s**."	**2Sa 21:4**	559
incited David against them to **s**,	**2Sa 24:1**	559
once to King David and **s** to him,	**1Ki 1:13**	559
and they **s**, '*Long* live King Adonijah	**1Ki 1:25**	559
and blow the trumpet and **s**,	**1Ki 1:34**	559
the God of my lord the king, **s**.	**1Ki 1:36**	559
"I have something *to* **s** to you."	**1Ki 2:14**	
according to all that you **s**,	**1Ki 5:6**	559
will be astonished and hiss and **s**,	**1Ki 9:8**	559
"And they will **s**,	**1Ki 9:9**	559
"Thus you shall **s** to this people	**1Ki 12:10**	559
You shall **s** thus and thus to her,	**1Ki 14:5**	1696
"Go, **s** to Jeroboam,	**1Ki 14:7**	559
Go, **s** to your master,	**1Ki 18:8**	559
'Go, **s** to your master,	**1Ki 18:11**	559
'Go, **s** to your master,	**1Ki 18:14**	559
"Go up, **s** to Ahab,	**1Ki 18:44**	559
"Let not the king **s** so."	**1Ki 22:8**	559
s, 'Thus says the king, "Put this man	**1Ki 22:27**	559
the king of Samaria and **s** to them,	**2Ki 1:3**	1696
king who sent you and **s** to him,	**2Ki 1:6**	1696
"Did I not **s** to you,	**2Ki 2:18**	559
He said to him, "**S** now to her,	**2Ki 4:13**	559
run now to meet her and **s** to her,	**2Ki 4:26**	559
Did I not **s**, 'Do not deceive me'?"	**2Ki 4:28**	559
"If we **s**, 'We will enter the city,'	**2Ki 7:4**	559
Elisha said to him, "Go, **s** to him,	**2Ki 8:10**	559
"What did Elisha **s** to you?"	**2Ki 8:14**	559
oil and pour it on his head and **s**,	**2Ki 9:3**	559
him to meet them and let him **s**,	**2Ki 9:17**	559
of Jezreel, so they cannot **s**,	**2Ki 9:37**	559
all that you **s** to us we will do,	**2Ki 10:5**	559
The LORD did not **s** that He	**2Ki 14:27**	1696
"**S** now to Hezekiah,	**2Ki 18:19**	559
s (but *they are* only empty words),	**2Ki 18:20**	559
"But if you **s** to me,	**2Ki 18:22**	559
"Thus you shall **s** to your master,	**2Ki 19:6**	559
When he heard *them* **s** concerning	**2Ki 19:9**	559
shall **s** to Hezekiah king of Judah,	**2Ki 19:10**	559
"Return and **s** to Hezekiah the	**2Ki 20:5**	559
"What did these men **s**,	**2Ki 20:14**	559
the LORD thus shall you **s** to him,	**2Ki 22:18**	559
And let them **s** among the nations,	**1Ch 16:31**	559
s, "Save us, O God of our salvation,	**1Ch 16:35**	559
shall you **s** to My servant David,	**1Ch 17:7**	559
"What more can David still **s** to	**1Ch 17:18**	
LORD commanded Gad to **s** to David,	**1Ch 21:18**	559
by it will be astonished and **s**,	**2Ch 7:21**	559
"And they will **s**,	**2Ch 7:22**	559
"Thus you shall **s** to the people	**2Ch 10:10**	559
Thus you shall **s** to them,	**2Ch 10:10**	559
"Let not the king **s** so."	**2Ch 18:7**	559
s, 'Thus says the king, "Put this *man*	**2Ch 18:26**	559
the LORD, thus you will **s** to him,	**2Ch 34:26**	559
I told them what to **s** to Iddo *and*	**Ezr 8:17**	1696
God, what shall we **s** after this?	**Ezr 9:10**	559
and could not find a word *to* **s**.	**Ne 5:8**	
we will do exactly as you **s**."	**Ne 5:12**	559
"When I lie down I **s**,	**Jb 7:4**	559
"If I **s**, 'My bed will comfort me,	**Jb 7:13**	559
"How long will you **s** these things,	**Jb 8:2**	4448a
Who could **s** to Him,	**Jb 9:12**	559
I **s**, 'He destroys the guiltless and	**Jb 9:22**	559
"Though I **s**, 'I will forget my	**Jb 9:27**	559
"I will **s** to God,	**Jb 10:2**	559
"If you **s**, 'How shall we persecute	**Jb 19:28**	559
Those who have seen him will **s**,	**Jb 20:7**	559
"They **s** to God,	**Jb 21:14**	559
"*You* **s**, 'God stores away a	**Jb 21:19**	
"For you **s**, 'Where is the house of	**Jb 21:28**	559
"You **s**, 'What does God know?	**Jb 22:13**	559
perceive what He would **s** to me.	**Jb 23:5**	559
"Abaddon and Death **s**,	**Jb 28:22**	559
"So I **s**, 'Listen to me, I too will tell	**Jb 32:10**	559
While you pondered what to **s**.	**Jb 32:11**	4405
"Do not **s**, 'We have found wisdom;	**Jb 32:13**	559
let him be gracious to him, and **s**,	**Jb 33:24**	559
"He will sing to men and **s**,	**Jb 33:27**	559
"*Then* if you have anything to **s**,	**Jb 33:32**	4405
"Men of understanding will **s** to me,	**Jb 34:34**	559
Do you **s**, 'My righteousness is more	**Jb 35:2**	559
For you **s**, 'What advantage will it be	**Jb 35:3**	559
when you **s** you do not behold Him,	**Jb 35:14**	559
"Teach us what we shall **s** to Him;	**Jb 37:19**	559
s that he would be swallowed up?	**Jb 37:20**	559
that they may go And **s** to you,	**Jb 38:35**	559
nothing reliable in what they **s**;	**Ps 5:9**	6310
How can you **s** to my soul,	**Ps 11:1**	559
And my enemy will **s**,	**Ps 13:4**	559
me, I trust in You, O LORD, I **s**,	**Ps 31:14**	559
S to my soul, "I am your salvation."	**Ps 35:3**	559
All my bones will **s**,	**Ps 35:10**	559
Do not let them **s** in their heart,	**Ps 35:25**	559
Do not let them **s**,	**Ps 35:25**	559
And let them **s** continually,	**Ps 35:27**	559
of their shame Who **s** to me,	**Ps 40:15**	559
love Your salvation **s** continually,	**Ps 40:16**	559
While *they* **s** to me all day long,	**Ps 42:3**	559
I will **s** to God my rock,	**Ps 42:9**	559
While they **s** to me all day long,	**Ps 42:10**	559
men will **s**, "Surely there is a reward	**Ps 58:11**	559
they **s**, "Who hears?"	**Ps 59:7**	
They **s**, "Who can see them?"	**Ps 64:5**	559
S to God, "How awesome are Your	**Ps 66:3**	559
back because of their shame Who **s**,	**Ps 70:3**	559
love Your salvation **s** continually,	**Ps 70:4**	559
They **s**, "How does God know?	**Ps 73:11**	559
Why should the nations **s**,	**Ps 79:10**	559
hear what God the LORD will **s**;	**Ps 85:8**	1696
those who play the flutes *shall* **s**,	**Ps 87:7**	
man back into dust And **s**,	**Ps 90:3**	559
I will **s** to the LORD,	**Ps 91:2**	559
If I should **s**, "My foot has slipped,"	**Ps 94:18**	559
S among the nations,	**Ps 96:10**	559
I **s**, "O my God, do not take me	**Ps 102:24**	559
And let all the people **s**, "Amen."	**Ps 106:48**	559
Let the redeemed of the LORD **s** *so,*	**Ps 107:2**	559
Why should the nations **s**,	**Ps 115:2**	559
Oh let Israel **s**,	**Ps 118:2**	559
Oh let the house of Aaron **s**,	**Ps 118:3**	559
Oh let those who fear the LORD **s**,	**Ps 118:4**	559
longing for Your word, While I **s**,	**Ps 119:82**	559
and my friends, I will now **s**,	**Ps 122:8**	1696
was on our side," Let Israel now **s**,	**Ps 124:1**	559
my youth up," Let Israel now **s**,	**Ps 129:1**	559
Nor do those who pass by **s**,	**Ps 129:8**	559
If I **s**, "Surely the darkness will	**Ps 139:11**	559
If they **s**, "Come with us, Let us lie	**Pr 1:11**	559
Do not **s** to your neighbor,	**Pr 3:28**	559
you **s**, "How I have hated instruction	**Pr 5:12**	559
S to wisdom, "You are my sister,"	**Pr 7:4**	559
Who can **s**, "I have cleansed my	**Pr 20:9**	559
Do not **s**, "I will repay evil";	**Pr 20:22**	559
is a trap for a man to **s** rashly,	**Pr 20:25**	3886b
If you **s**, "See, we did not know this,	**Pr 24:12**	559
Do not **s**, "Thus I shall do to him	**Pr 24:29**	559
I not be full and deny *You* and **s**,	**Pr 30:9**	559
satisfied, Four that will not **s**,	**Pr 30:15**	559
anything of which one might **s**,	**Ec 1:10**	559
speech cause you to sin and do not **s**	**Ec 5:6**	559
have a *proper* burial, *then* I **s**,	**Ec 6:3**	559
Do not **s**, "Why is it that the former	**Ec 7:10**	559
I **s**, "Keep the command of the king	**Ec 8:2**	
authoritative, who will **s** to him,	**Ec 8:4**	559
I **s** that this too is futility.	**Ec 8:14**	559
and though the wise man should **s**,	**Ec 8:17**	559
years draw near when you will **s**,	**Ec 12:1**	559
And many peoples will come and **s**,	**Is 2:3**	559
S to the righteous that *it will go*	**Is 3:10**	559
Who **s**, "Let Him make speed,	**Is 5:19**	559
s to him, 'Take care and be calm,	**Is 7:4**	559
"You are not to **s**,	**Is 8:12**	559
When they **s** to you,	**Is 8:19**	559
He will **s**, "I will punish	**Is 10:12**	
Then you will **s** on that day,	**Is 12:1**	559
And in that day you will **s**,	**Is 12:4**	559
the king of Babylon, and **s**,	**Is 14:4**	559
will all respond and **s** to you,	**Is 14:10**	559
How can you *men* **s** to Pharaoh,	**Is 19:11**	559
this coastland will **s** in that day,	**Is 20:6**	559
Therefore I **s**, "Turn your eyes away	**Is 22:4**	559
But I **s**, "Woe to me! Woe to me!	**Is 24:16**	559
he will **s**, "I cannot, for it is sealed."	**Is 29:11**	559
And he will **s**, "I cannot read."	**Is 29:12**	559
And they **s**, "Who sees us?" or	**Is 29:15**	559
what is made would **s** to its maker,	**Is 29:16**	559
is formed **s** to him who formed it,	**Is 29:16**	559
Who **s** to the seers,	**Is 30:10**	559
and **s** to them, "Be gone!"	**Is 30:22**	559
And no resident will **s**,	**Is 33:24**	559
S to those with anxious heart,	**Is 35:4**	559
"**S** now to Hezekiah,	**Is 36:4**	559
"I **s**, 'Your counsel and strength for	**Is 36:5**	559
"But if you **s** to me,	**Is 36:7**	559
"Thus you shall **s** to your master,	**Is 37:6**	559
When he heard *them* **s** concerning	**Is 37:9**	559
shall **s** to Hezekiah king of Judah,	**Is 37:10**	559
"Go and **s** to Hezekiah,	**Is 38:5**	559
"What shall I **s**? For He has spoken	**Is 38:15**	1696
"What did these men **s**,	**Is 39:3**	559
S to the cities of Judah,	**Is 40:9**	559
Why do you **s**, O Jacob, and assert,	**Is 40:27**	559
from former times, that we may **s**,	**Is 41:26**	559
in idols, Who **s** to molten images,	**Is 42:17**	559
them, And a spoil, with none to **s**,	**Is 42:22**	559
"I will **s** to the north,	**Is 43:6**	559
justified, Or let them hear and **s**,	**Is 43:9**	559
"This one will **s**,	**Is 44:5**	559
knowledge or understanding to **s**,	**Is 44:19**	559
he cannot deliver himself, nor **s**,	**Is 44:20**	559
Will the clay **s** to the potter,	**Is 45:9**	559
Or the thing you are making **s**,	**Is 45:9**	
I did not **s** to the offspring of Jacob,	**Is 45:19**	559
"They will **s** of Me,	**Is 45:24**	559
So that you would not **s**,	**Is 48:5**	559
not heard them, So that you will not **s**,	**Is 48:7**	559
S, "The LORD has redeemed His	**Is 48:20**	559
bereaved will yet **s** in your ears,	**Is 49:20**	559
"Then you will **s** in your heart,	**Is 49:21**	559
found the earth, and to **s** to Zion,	**Is 51:16**	559
has joined himself to the LORD **s**,	**Is 56:3**	559
Nor let the eunuch **s**,	**Is 56:3**	559
"Come," *they* **s**, "let us get	**Is 56:12**	
of your road, *Yet* you did not **s**,	**Is 57:10**	559
You will cry, and He will **s**,	**Is 58:9**	559
earth, **S** to the daughter of Zion,	**Is 62:11**	559
"Who **s**, 'Keep to yourself, do not	**Is 65:5**	559
But the LORD said to me, "Do not **s**,	**Jer 1:7**	559
"They did not **s**,	**Jer 2:6**	559
"The priests did not **s**,	**Jer 2:8**	559
"How can you **s**,	**Jer 2:23**	559
Who **s** to a tree,	**Jer 2:27**	559
time of their trouble they will **s**,	**Jer 2:27**	559
Why do My people **s**,	**Jer 2:31**	559
judgment with you Because you **s**,	**Jer 2:35**	559
words toward the north and **s**,	**Jer 3:12**	559
"they will no longer **s**,	**Jer 3:16**	559
and proclaim in Jerusalem, and **s**,	**Jer 4:5**	559
Cry aloud and **s**,	**Jer 4:5**	559
"And although they **s**,	**Jer 5:2**	559
can you understand what they **s**.	**Jer 5:15**	1696
It shall come about when they **s**,	**Jer 5:19**	559
then you shall **s** to them,	**Jer 5:19**	559
'They do not **s** in their heart,	**Jer 5:24**	559
proclaim there this word and **s**,	**Jer 7:2**	559
which is called by My name, and **s**,	**Jer 7:10**	559
"You shall **s** to them,	**Jer 7:28**	559
"You shall **s** to them,	**Jer 8:4**	559
"How can you **s**,	**Jer 8:8**	559
Thus you shall **s** to them,	**Jer 10:11**	560
and **s** to them, 'Thus says the LORD,	**Jer 11:3**	559
they may **s** nice things to you."	**Jer 12:6**	1696
And when they **s** to you,	**Jer 13:12**	559
then **s** to them, 'Thus says the LORD,	**Jer 13:13**	559
S to the king and the queen	**Jer 13:18**	559
"What will you **s** when He appoints	**Jer 13:21**	559
"If you **s** in your heart,	**Jer 13:22**	559
"You will **s** this word to	**Jer 14:17**	559
shall be that when they **s** to you,	**Jer 15:2**	559
words, they will **s** to you,	**Jer 16:10**	559
"Then you are to **s** to them,	**Jer 16:11**	559
From the ends of the earth and **s**,	**Jer 16:19**	559
and **s** to them, 'Listen to the word	**Jer 17:20**	559
"But they will **s**,	**Jer 18:12**	559
and **s**, 'Hear the word of the LORD,	**Jer 19:3**	559
and **s** to them, 'Thus says the LORD	**Jer 19:11**	559
But if I **s**, "I will not remember Him	**Jer 20:9**	559
friends, Watching for my fall, **s**:	**Jer 20:10**	
shall **s** to Zedekiah as follows:	**Jer 21:3**	559
"You shall also **s** to this people,	**Jer 21:8**	559
"Then **s** to the household of	**Jer 21:11**	
"You men who **s**,	**Jer 21:13**	559
and **s**, 'Hear the word of the LORD,	**Jer 22:2**	559
and they will **s** to one another,	**Jer 22:8**	559
"when they will no longer **s**,	**Jer 23:7**	559
of his own heart, They **s**,	**Jer 23:17**	559
then you shall **s** to them,	**Jer 23:33**	559
or the priest or the people who **s**,	**Jer 23:34**	559
"Thus will each of you **s** to his	**Jer 23:35**	559
"Thus you will **s** to *that* prophet,	**Jer 23:37**	559
if you **s**, 'The oracle of the LORD!'	**Jer 23:38**	559
"You shall not **s**,	**Jer 23:38**	559
"You shall **s** to them,	**Jer 25:27**	559
to drink, then you will **s** to them,	**Jer 25:28**	559
words, and you shall **s** to them,	**Jer 25:30**	559
"And you will **s** to them,	**Jer 26:4**	559
thus you shall **s** to your masters,	**Jer 27:4**	559
Proclaim, give praise and **s**,	**Jer 31:7**	559
in the coastlands afar off, And **s**,	**Jer 31:10**	559
those days they will not **s** again,	**Jer 31:29**	559
this city of which you **s**,	**Jer 32:36**	559
in this land of which you **s**,	**Jer 32:43**	559
in this place, of which you **s**,	**Jer 33:10**	559
bride, the voice of those who **s**,	**Jer 33:11**	559
king of Judah and **s** to him:	**Jer 34:2**	559
'Go and **s** to the men of Judah and	**Jer 35:13**	559
king of Judah you shall **s**,	**Jer 36:29**	559
you are to **s** to the king of Judah,	**Jer 37:7**	559
and those women will **s**,	**Jer 38:22**	559
you and come to you and **s** to you,	**Jer 38:25**	559
then you are to **s** to them,	**Jer 38:26**	559
'But if you are going to **s**,	**Jer 42:13**	559
our God has not sent you to **s**,	**Jer 43:2**	559
and **s** to them, 'Thus says the LORD	**Jer 43:10**	559
"Thus you are to **s** to him,	**Jer 45:4**	559
S, 'Take your stand and get	**Jer 46:14**	559
"How can you **s**,	**Jer 48:14**	559
S, 'How has the mighty scepter	**Jer 48:17**	559
flees and her who escapes *And* **s**,	**Jer 48:19**	559
Do not conceal *it but* **s**,	**Jer 50:2**	559
The inhabitant of Zion will **s**;	**Jer 51:35**	559
of Chaldea," Jerusalem will **s**.	**Jer 51:35**	559
and **s**, 'You, O LORD, have promised	**Jer 51:62**	559
and **s**, 'Just so shall Babylon sink	**Jer 51:64**	559
They **s** to their mothers,	**La 2:12**	559
They **s**, "We have swallowed *her* up!	**La 2:16**	559

So I **s**, "My strength has perished,	**La 3:18**	559
and you shall **s** to them,	**Ezk 2:4**	559
"When I **s** to the wicked,	**Ezk 3:18**	559
mouth and you will **s** to them,	**Ezk 3:27**	559
and **s**, 'Mountains of Israel, listen to	**Ezk 6:3**	559
your hand, stamp your foot and **s**,	**Ezk 6:11**	559
they **s**, 'The LORD does not see us;	**Ezk 8:12**	559
for they **s**, 'The LORD has forsaken	**Ezk 9:9**	559
who **s**, '*The time* is not near to build	**Ezk 11:3**	559
"**S**, 'Thus says the LORD,	**Ezk 11:5**	559
"Therefore **s**, 'Thus says the Lord	**Ezk 11:16**	559
"Therefore **s**, 'Thus says the Lord	**Ezk 11:17**	559
"**S** to them, 'Thus says the Lord	**Ezk 12:10**	559
"**S**, 'I am a sign to you.	**Ezk 12:11**	559
"Then **s** to the people of the	**Ezk 12:19**	559
"Therefore **s** to them,	**Ezk 12:23**	559
"Therefore **s** to them,	**Ezk 12:28**	559
and **s** to those who prophesy from	**Ezk 13:2**	559
and I will **s** to you,	**Ezk 13:15**	559
and **s**, 'Thus says the Lord GOD,	**Ezk 13:18**	559
s to the house of Israel,	**Ezk 14:6**	559
a sword on that country and **s**,	**Ezk 14:17**	559
and **s**, 'Thus says the Lord GOD to	**Ezk 16:3**	559
"**S**, 'Thus says the Lord GOD,	**Ezk 17:9**	559
"**S** now to the rebellious house,	**Ezk 17:12**	559
S, 'Behold, the king of Babylon	**Ezk 17:12**	559
"Yet you **s**, 'Why should the son not	**Ezk 18:19**	559
"Yet you **s**, 'The way of the Lord is	**Ezk 18:25**	559
and **s**, 'What was your mother?	**Ezk 19:2**	559
elders of Israel and **s** to them,	**Ezk 20:3**	559
s to them, 'Thus says the Lord GOD,	**Ezk 20:5**	559
house of Israel and **s** to them,	**Ezk 20:27**	559
s to the house of Israel,	**Ezk 20:30**	559
will not come about, when you **s**:	**Ezk 20:32**	559
and **s** to the forest of the Negev,	**Ezk 20:47**	559
and **s** to the land of Israel,	**Ezk 21:3**	559
when they **s** to you,	**Ezk 21:7**	559
you shall **s**,	**Ezk 21:7**	559
"Son of man, prophesy and **s**,	**Ezk 21:9**	559
S, 'A sword, a sword sharpened	**Ezk 21:9**	559
you, son of man, prophesy and **s**,	**Ezk 21:28**	559
concerning their reproach,' and **s**:	**Ezk 21:28**	559
"You shall **s**,	**Ezk 22:3**	559
"Son of man, **s** to her,	**Ezk 22:24**	559
rebellious house and **s** to them,	**Ezk 24:3**	559
and **s** to the sons of Ammon,	**Ezk 25:3**	559
"Because Moab and Seir **s**,	**Ezk 25:8**	559
lamentation over you and **s** to you,	**Ezk 26:17**	559
and **s** to Tyre, who dwells at the	**Ezk 27:3**	559
of man, **s** to the leader of Tyre,	**Ezk 28:2**	559
'Will you still **s**,	**Ezk 28:9**	559
the king of Tyre and **s** to him,	**Ezk 28:12**	559
and **s**, 'Thus says the Lord GOD,	**Ezk 28:22**	559
"Speak and **s**, 'Thus says the Lord	**Ezk 29:3**	559
"Son of man, prophesy and **s**,	**Ezk 30:2**	559
man, **s** to Pharaoh king of Egypt and	**Ezk 31:2**	559
king of Egypt and **s** to him,	**Ezk 32:2**	559
of your people and **s** to them,	**Ezk 33:2**	559
"When I **s** to the wicked,	**Ezk 33:8**	559
of man, **s** to the house of Israel,	**Ezk 33:10**	559
"**S** to them, 'As I live!' declares the	**Ezk 33:11**	559
of man, **s** to your fellow citizens,	**Ezk 33:12**	559
"When I **s** to the righteous he	**Ezk 33:13**	559
"But when I **s** to the wicked,	**Ezk 33:14**	559
"Yet your fellow citizens **s**,	**Ezk 33:17**	559
"Yet you **s**, 'The way of the Lord is	**Ezk 33:20**	559
"Therefore **s** to them,	**Ezk 33:25**	559
"Thus you shall **s** to them,	**Ezk 33:27**	559
Prophesy and **s** to those shepherds,	**Ezk 34:2**	559
and **s** to it, 'Thus says the Lord GOD	**Ezk 35:3**	559
to the mountains of Israel and **s**,	**Ezk 36:1**	559
therefore prophesy and **s**,	**Ezk 36:3**	559
and **s** to the mountains and to the	**Ezk 36:6**	559
'Because they **s** to you,	**Ezk 36:13**	559
s to the house of Israel,	**Ezk 36:22**	559
"They will **s**,	**Ezk 36:35**	559
over these bones and **s** to them,	**Ezk 37:4**	559
son of man, and **s** to the breath,	**Ezk 37:9**	559
they **s**, 'Our bones are dried up and	**Ezk 37:11**	559
"Therefore prophesy and **s** to them,	**Ezk 37:12**	559
s to them, 'Thus says the Lord GOD,	**Ezk 37:19**	1696
"**S** to them, 'Thus says the Lord	**Ezk 37:21**	1696
and **s**, 'Thus says the Lord GOD,	**Ezk 38:3**	559
and you will **s**, 'I will go up against	**Ezk 38:11**	559
all its villages will **s** to you,	**Ezk 38:13**	559
son of man, and **s** to Gog,	**Ezk 38:14**	559
man, prophesy against Gog and **s**,	**Ezk 39:1**	559
hear with your ears all that I **s** to you	**Ezk 44:5**	1696
You shall **s** to the rebellious ones,	**Ezk 44:6**	559
can ward off His hand Or **s** to Him,	**Da 4:35**	560
S to your brothers,	**Hos 2:1**	559
Then she will **s**,	**Hos 2:7**	559
And I will **s** to those who were not	**Hos 2:23**	559
And they will **s**,	**Hos 2:23**	559
Surely now they will **s**,	**Hos 10:3**	559
Then they will **s** to the mountains,	**Hos 10:8**	559
They **s** of them, "Let the men who	**Hos 13:2**	559
S to Him, "Take away all iniquity And	**Hos 14:2**	559
Nor will we **s** again,	**Hos 14:3**	559
and the altar, And let them **s**,	**Jl 2:17**	559
should they among the peoples **s**,	**Jl 2:17**	559
will answer and **s** to His people,	**Jl 2:19**	559
Let the weak **s**, "I am a mighty man.	**Jl 3:10**	559
in the land of Egypt and **s**,	**Am 3:9**	559
the needy, Who **s** to your husbands,	**Am 4:1**	559
And in all the streets they **s**,	**Am 5:16**	559
and he will **s** to the one who is in	**Am 6:10**	559
And that one will **s**,	**Am 6:10**	559
You who rejoice in Lodebar, And **s**,	**Am 6:13**	559
by the guilt of Samaria, Who **s**,	**Am 8:14**	559
die by the sword, Those who **s**,	**Am 9:10**	559
place, Who **s** in your heart,	**Ob 1:3**	559
utter a bitter lamentation *and* **s**,	**Mi 2:4**	559
Many nations will come and **s**,	**Mi 4:2**	559
been assembled against you Who **s**,	**Mi 4:11**	559
you Will shrink from you and **s**,	**Na 3:7**	559
insinuations against him And **s**,	**Hab 2:6**	559
in spirit, Who **s** in their hearts,	**Zph 1:12**	559
"Therefore **s** to them,	**Zch 1:3**	559
"Then **s** to him,	**Zch 6:12**	559
"**S** to all the people of the land	**Zch 7:5**	559
clans of Judah will **s** in their hearts,	**Zch 12:5**	559
gave birth to him will **s** to him,	**Zch 13:3**	559
but he will **s**, 'I am not a prophet;	**Zch 13:5**	559
"And one will **s** to him,	**Zch 13:6**	559
Then he will **s**, '*Those* with which I	**Zch 13:6**	559
I will **s**, 'They are My people,'	**Zch 13:9**	559
are My people,' And they will **s**,	**Zch 13:9**	559
But you **s**, "How have You loved	**Mal 1:2**	559
eyes will see this and you will **s**,	**Mal 1:5**	559
But you **s**, 'How have we despised	**Mal 1:6**	559
you **s**, 'How have we defiled You?'	**Mal 1:7**	559
In that you **s**, 'The table of the LORD	**Mal 1:7**	559
are profaning it, in that you **s**,	**Mal 1:12**	559
You also **s**, 'My, how tiresome it is!'	**Mal 1:13**	559
"Yet you **s**, 'For what reason?'	**Mal 2:14**	559
you **s**, "How have we wearied *Him?*"	**Mal 2:17**	559
you **s**, "Everyone who does evil is	**Mal 2:17**	559
"But you **s**, 'How shall we return?'	**Mal 3:7**	559
you **s**, 'How have we robbed You?'	**Mal 3:8**	559
"Yet you **s**, 'What have we spoken	**Mal 3:13**	559
that you can **s** to yourselves,	**Mt 3:9**	*3004*
for I **s** to you that from these stones	**Mt 3:9**	*3004*
time Jesus began to preach and **s**,	**Mt 4:17**	*3004*
and falsely **s** all kinds of evil against	**Mt 5:11**	*3004*
"For truly I **s** to you, until	**Mt 5:18**	*3004*
"For I **s** to you that unless your	**Mt 5:20**	*3004*
"But I **s** to you that everyone who	**Mt 5:22**	*3004*
"Truly I **s** to you, you will not	**Mt 5:26**	*3004*
but I **s** to you that everyone who	**Mt 5:28**	*3004*
but I **s** to you that everyone who	**Mt 5:32**	*3004*
"But I **s** to you, make no oath at	**Mt 5:34**	*3004*
"But I **s** to you, do not resist	**Mt 5:39**	*3004*
"But I **s** to you, love your	**Mt 5:44**	*3004*
Truly I **s** to you, they have their	**Mt 6:2**	*3004*
Truly I **s** to you, they have their	**Mt 6:5**	*3004*
Truly I **s** to you, they have their	**Mt 6:16**	*3004*
"For this reason I **s** to you,	**Mt 6:25**	*3004*
yet I **s** to you that not even Solomon	**Mt 6:29**	*3004*
"Or how can you **s** to your	**Mt 7:4**	*3004*
"Many will **s** to Me on that day,	**Mt 7:22**	*3004*
my roof, but just **s** the word,	**Mt 8:8**	*3004*
and I **s** to this one,	**Mt 8:9**	*3004*
"Truly I **s** to you, I have not	**Mt 8:10**	*3004*
"I **s** to you that many will	**Mt 8:11**	*3004*
"Which is easier, to **s**,	**Mt 9:5**	*3004*
or to **s**, 'Get up, and walk'?	**Mt 9:5**	*3004*
"Truly I **s** to you, it will be	**Mt 10:15**	*3004*
worry about how or what you are to **s**;	**Mt 10:19**	*2980*
you in that hour what you are to **s**.	**Mt 10:19**	*2980*
for truly I **s** to you, you will	**Mt 10:23**	*3004*
truly I **s** to you, he shall not lose	**Mt 10:42**	*3004*
"Truly I **s** to you, among those	**Mt 11:11**	*3004*
and **s**, 'We played the flute for you,	**Mt 11:17**	*3004*
eating nor drinking, and they **s**,	**Mt 11:18**	*3004*
eating and drinking, and they **s**,	**Mt 11:19**	*3004*
"Nevertheless I **s** to you, it	**Mt 11:22**	*3004*
"Nevertheless I **s** to you that it	**Mt 11:24**	*3004*
"But I **s** to you that something	**Mt 12:6**	*3004*
"Therefore I **s** to you, any sin	**Mt 12:31**	*3004*
"For truly I **s** to you that many	**Mt 13:17**	*3004*
harvest I will **s** to the reapers,	**Mt 13:30**	*3004*
"But you **s**, 'Whoever says to *his*	**Mt 15:5**	*3004*
"When it is evening, you **s**,	**Mt 16:2**	*3004*
they understood that He did not **s** to	**Mt 16:12**	*3004*
people **s** that the Son of Man is?"	**Mt 16:13**	*3004*
And they said, "Some **s** John	**Mt 16:14**	
"But who do you **s** that I am?"	**Mt 16:15**	*3004*
also **s** to you that you are Peter,	**Mt 16:18**	*3004*
"Truly I **s** to you, there are some	**Mt 16:28**	*3004*
s that Elijah must come first?"	**Mt 17:10**	*3004*
but I **s** to you that Elijah	**Mt 17:12**	*3004*
for truly I **s** to you, if you have	**Mt 17:20**	*3004*
you will **s** to this mountain,	**Mt 17:20**	*3004*
"Truly I **s** to you, unless you are	**Mt 18:3**	*3004*
these little ones, for I **s** to you that	**Mt 18:10**	*3004*
he finds it, truly I **s** to you,	**Mt 18:13**	*3004*
"Truly I **s** to you, whatever you	**Mt 18:18**	*3004*
"Again I **s** to you, that if two of	**Mt 18:19**	*3004*
"I do not **s** to you, up to seven	**Mt 18:22**	*3004*
"And I **s** to you, whoever divorces	**Mt 19:9**	*3004*
"Truly I **s** to you, it is hard for	**Mt 19:23**	*3004*
"Again I **s** to you, it is	**Mt 19:24**	*3004*
"Truly I **s** to you, that you who	**Mt 19:28**	*3004*
anything to you, you shall **s**,	**Mt 21:3**	*3004*
"**S** TO THE DAUGHTER OF ZION	**Mt 21:5**	*3004*
"Truly I **s** to you, if you have	**Mt 21:21**	*3004*
even if you **s** to this mountain,	**Mt 21:21**	*3004*
"If we **s**, 'From heaven,' He will say	**Mt 21:25**	*3004*
'From heaven,' He will **s** to us,	**Mt 21:25**	*3004*
"But if we **s**, 'From men,' we fear	**Mt 21:26**	*3004*
"Truly I **s** to you that the	**Mt 21:31**	*3004*
"Therefore I **s** to you, the	**Mt 21:43**	*3004*
(who **s** there is no resurrection)	**Mt 22:23**	*3004*
for they **s** *things* and do not do	**Mt 23:3**	*3004*
"Woe to you, blind guides, who **s**,	**Mt 23:16**	*3004*
s, 'If we had been *living* in the days	**Mt 23:30**	*3004*
"Truly I **s** to you, all these	**Mt 23:36**	*3004*
"For I **s** to you, from now on you	**Mt 23:39**	*3004*
you will not see Me until you **s**,	**Mt 23:39**	*3004*
Truly I **s** to you, not one stone	**Mt 24:2**	*3004*
"So if they **s** to you,	**Mt 24:26**	*3004*
"Truly I **s** to you, this	**Mt 24:34**	*3004*
"Truly I **s** to you that he will	**Mt 24:47**	*3004*
"Truly I **s** to you, I do not know	**Mt 25:12**	*3004*
King will **s** to those on His right,	**Mt 25:34**	*3004*
King will answer and **s** to them,	**Mt 25:40**	*3004*
'Truly I **s** to you, to the extent	**Mt 25:40**	*3004*
will also **s** to those on His left,	**Mt 25:41**	*3004*
'Truly I **s** to you, to the extent	**Mt 25:45**	*3004*
"Truly I **s** to you, wherever this	**Mt 26:13**	*3004*
to a certain man, and **s** to him,	**Mt 26:18**	*3004*
"Truly I **s** to you that one of you	**Mt 26:21**	*3004*
they each one began to **s** to Him,	**Mt 26:22**	*3004*
"But I **s** to you, I will not drink	**Mt 26:29**	*3004*
I **s** to you that this *very* night,	**Mt 26:34**	*3004*
which **s** that it must happen this	**Mt 26:54**	
"*It is as* you **s**."	**Mt 27:11**	*3004*
Him away and **s** to the people,	**Mt 27:64**	*3004*
"You are to **s**, 'His disciples came by	**Mt 28:13**	*3004*
"See that you **s** nothing to anyone;	**Mk 1:44**	*3004*
is easier, to **s** to the paralytic,	**Mk 2:9**	*3004*
'Your sins are forgiven'; or to **s**,	**Mk 2:9**	*3004*
"I **s** to you, get up, pick up your	**Mk 2:11**	*3004*
"Truly I **s** to you, all sins shall	**Mk 3:28**	*3004*
pressing in on You, and You **s**,	**Mk 5:31**	*3004*
"Little girl, I **s** to you, get up!")	**Mk 5:41**	*3004*
you **s**, 'If a man says to *his* father	**Mk 7:11**	*3004*
(that is to **s**, given *to God*)	**Mk 7:11**	
Truly I **s** to you, no sign will be	**Mk 8:12**	*3004*
"Who do people **s** that I am?"	**Mk 8:27**	*3004*
and others **s** Elijah; but others,	**Mk 8:28**	
"But who do you **s** that I am?"	**Mk 8:29**	*3004*
"Truly I **s** to you, there are some	**Mk 9:1**	*3004*
scribes **s** that Elijah must come first	**Mk 9:11**	*3004*
"But I **s** to you that Elijah has	**Mk 9:13**	*3004*
of Christ, truly I **s** to you,	**Mk 9:41**	*3004*
"Truly I **s** to you, whoever does	**Mk 10:15**	*3004*
Peter began to **s** to Him,	**Mk 10:28**	*3004*
"Truly I **s** to you, there is no	**Mk 10:29**	*3004*
he began to cry out and **s**,	**Mk 10:47**	*3004*
you **s**, 'The Lord has need of it';	**Mk 11:3**	*3004*
He *began* to teach and **s** to them,	**Mk 11:17**	*3004*
"Truly I **s** to you, whoever says	**Mk 11:23**	*3004*
"Therefore I **s** to you, all things	**Mk 11:24**	*3004*
"If we **s**, 'From heaven,' He will say,	**Mk 11:31**	*3004*
He will **s**, 'Then why did you not	**Mk 11:31**	*3004*
"But shall we **s**, 'From men'?"	**Mk 11:32**	*3004*
who **s** that there is no resurrection	**Mk 12:18**	*3004*
And Jesus *began* to **s**,	**Mk 12:35**	*3004*
"How *is it that* the scribes **s**	**Mk 12:35**	*3004*
"Truly I **s** to you, this poor	**Mk 12:43**	*3004*
And Jesus began to **s** to them,	**Mk 13:5**	*3004*
about what you are to **s**,	**Mk 13:11**	*2980*
but **s** whatever is given you in	**Mk 13:11**	*2980*
"Truly I **s** to you, this	**Mk 13:30**	*3004*
"What I **s** to you I say to	**Mk 13:37**	*3004*
"What I say to you I **s** to all,	**Mk 13:37**	*3004*
"Truly I **s** to you, wherever	**Mk 14:9**	*3004*
s to the owner of the house,	**Mk 14:14**	*3004*
"Truly I **s** to you that one of you	**Mk 14:18**	*3004*
and to **s** to Him one by one,	**Mk 14:19**	*3004*
"Truly I **s** to you, I will never	**Mk 14:25**	*3004*
"Truly I **s** to you, that this	**Mk 14:30**	*3004*
"We heard Him **s**,	**Mk 14:58**	*3004*
with their fists, and to **s** to Him,	**Mk 14:65**	*3004*
once more to **s** to the bystanders,	**Mk 14:69**	*3004*
"*It is as* you **s**."	**Mk 15:2**	*3004*
do not begin to **s** to yourselves,	**Lk 3:8**	*3004*
for I **s** to you that from these stones	**Lk 3:8**	*3004*
And he would answer and **s** to them,	**Lk 3:11**	*3004*
And He began to **s** to them,	**Lk 4:21**	*3004*
"Truly I **s** to you, no prophet is	**Lk 4:24**	*3004*
"But I **s** to you in truth, there	**Lk 4:25**	*3004*
but I will do as You **s** *and* let	**Lk 5:5**	*4487*
"Which is easier, to **s**,	**Lk 5:23**	*3004*
or to **s**, 'Get up and walk'?	**Lk 5:23**	*3004*
"I **s** to you, get up, and pick up	**Lk 5:24**	*3004*
toward His disciples, He *began* to **s**,	**Lk 6:20**	*3004*
"But I **s** to you who hear, love	**Lk 6:27**	*3004*
"Or how can you **s** to your	**Lk 6:42**	*3004*
Lord,' and do not do what I **s**?	**Lk 6:46**	*3004*
come to You, but *just* **s** the word,	**Lk 7:7**	*3004*
and I **s** to this one,	**Lk 7:8**	*3004*
"I **s** to you, not even in Israel	**Lk 7:9**	*3004*
"Young man, I **s** to you, arise!"	**Lk 7:14**	*3004*
Yes, I **s** to you, and one who is	**Lk 7:26**	*3004*
"I **s** to you, among those born of	**Lk 7:28**	*3004*
they **s**, 'We played the flute for you,	**Lk 7:32**	*3004*
and you **s**, 'He has a demon!'	**Lk 7:33**	*3004*
you **s**, 'Behold, a gluttonous man and	**Lk 7:34**	*3004*
I have something to **s** to you."	**Lk 7:40**	*3004*
"**S** it, Teacher."	**Lk 7:40**	*3004*
"For this reason I **s** to you,	**Lk 7:47**	*3004*
with Him began to **s** to themselves,	**Lk 7:49**	*3004*
do the people **s** that I am?"	**Lk 9:18**	*3004*
and others **s** Elijah; but others,	**Lk 9:19**	
"But who do you **s** that I am?"	**Lk 9:20**	*3004*
"But I **s** to you truthfully, there	**Lk 9:27**	*3004*
to **s** good-bye to those at home."	**Lk 9:61**	*657*
Whatever house you enter, first **s**,	**Lk 10:5**	*3004*
in it who are sick, and **s** to them,	**Lk 10:9**	*3004*
go out into its streets and **s**,	**Lk 10:10**	*3004*
"I **s** to you, it will be more	**Lk 10:12**	*3004*
for I **s** to you, that many prophets	**Lk 10:24**	*3004*
"When you pray, **s**:	**Lk 11:2**	*3004*
"So I **s** to you, ask, and it	**Lk 11:9**	*3004*

For you s that I cast out demons Lk 11:18 3004
were increasing, He began to s, Lk 11:29 3004
"Teacher, when You s this, Lk 11:45 3004
catch *Him* in something He might s. Lk 11:54
1537, 4750
"I s to you, My friends, do Lk 12:4 3004
"And I s to you, everyone who Lk 12:8 3004
defense, or what you are to s; Lk 12:11 3004
very hour what you ought to s." Lk 12:12 3004
'And I will s to my soul, Lk 12:19 3004
"For this reason I s to you, Lk 12:22 3004
truly I s to you, that he will Lk 12:37 3004
"Truly I s to you that he will Lk 12:44 3004
in the west, immediately you s, Lk 12:54 3004
see a south wind blowing, you s, Lk 12:55 3004
"I s to you, you will not get Lk 12:59 3004
then He will answer and s to you, Lk 13:25 3004
"Then you will begin to s, Lk 13:26 3004
He will s, 'I tell you, I do not know Lk 13:27 3004
and I s to you, you will not see Lk 13:35 3004
until *the time* comes when you s, Lk 13:35 3004
you both will come and s to you, Lk 14:9 3004
you comes, he may s to you, Lk 14:10 3004
And He also went on to s to the Lk 14:12 3004
s to those who had been invited, Lk 14:17 3004
to my father, and will s to him, Lk 15:18 3004
"And I s to you, make friends for Lk 16:9 3004
you would s to this mulberry tree, Lk 17:6 3004
will s to him when he has come in Lk 17:7 3004
"But will he not s to him, Lk 17:8 3004
things which are commanded you, s, Lk 17:10 3004
nor will they s, Lk 17:21 3004
"They will s to you, Lk 17:23 3004
"Truly I s to you, whoever does Lk 18:17 3004
"Truly I s to you, there is no Lk 18:29 3004
you shall s, 'The Lord has need Lk 19:31 3004
"If we s, 'From heaven,' He will say Lk 20:5 3004
'From heaven,' He will s, Lk 20:5 3004
if we s, 'From men,' all the people Lk 20:6 3004
s that there is no resurrection), Lk 20:27 483
they s the Christ is David's son? Lk 20:41 3004
"Truly I s to you, this poor Lk 21:3 3004
"Truly I s to you, this Lk 21:32 3004
shall s to the owner of the house, Lk 22:11 3004
for I s to you, I shall never Lk 22:16 3004
for I s to you, I will not drink Lk 22:18 3004
"I s to you, Peter, the rooster will Lk 22:34 3004
"*It is as* you s." Lk 23:3 3004
days are coming when they will s, Lk 23:29 3004
will begin TO S TO THE MOUNTAINS, Lk 23:30 3004
"Truly I s to you, today you Lk 23:43 3004
What do you s about yourself?" Jn 1:22 3004
"Truly, truly, I s to you, you Jn 1:51 3004
"Truly, truly, I s to you, unless Jn 3:3 3004
"Truly, truly, I s to you, unless Jn 3:5 3004
"Truly, truly, I s to you, we Jn 3:11 3004
and you *people* s that in Jerusalem Jn 4:20 3004
"Do you not s, 'There are yet four Jn 4:35 3004
Behold, I s to you, lift up your Jn 4:35 3004
"Truly, truly, I s to you, the Jn 5:19 3004
"Truly, truly, I s to you, he who Jn 5:24 3004
"Truly, truly, I s to you, an Jn 5:25 3004
but I s these things so that you may Jn 5:34 3004
"Truly, truly, I s to you, you Jn 6:26 3004
"Truly, truly, I s to you, it is Jn 6:32 3004
How does He now s, Jn 6:42 3004
"Truly, truly, I s to you, he who Jn 6:47 3004
"Truly, truly, I s to you, unless Jn 6:53 3004
what then do You s?" Jn 8:5 3004
how is it that You s, Jn 8:33 3004
"Truly, truly, I s to you, Jn 8:34 3004
"Do we not s rightly that You are Jn 8:48 3004
"Truly, truly, I s to you, if Jn 8:51 3004
You s, 'If anyone keeps My word, Jn 8:52 3004
who glorifies Me, of whom you s, Jn 8:54 3004
and if I s that I do not know Him, Jn 8:55 3004
"Truly, truly, I s to you, before Jn 8:58 3004
"What do you s about Him, since Jn 9:17 3004
son, who you s was born blind? Jn 9:19 3004
but since you s, Jn 9:41 3004
"Truly, truly, I s to you, he who Jn 10:1 3004
"Truly, truly, I s to you, I am Jn 10:7 3004
do you s of Him, whom the Father Jn 10:36 3004
"Did I not s to you that if you Jn 11:40 3004
did not s this on his own initiative Jn 11:51 3004
"Truly, truly, I s to you, unless Jn 12:24 3004
and what shall I s, Jn 12:27 3004
and how can You s, Jn 12:34 3004
a commandment *as to* what to s Jn 12:49 3004
"Truly, truly, I s to you, a Jn 13:16 3004
"Truly, truly, I s to you, he who Jn 13:20 3004
"Truly, truly, I s to you, that Jn 13:21 3004
to the Jews, now I also s to you, Jn 13:33 3004
Truly, truly, I s to you, a rooster Jn 13:38 3004
how *can* you s, 'Show us the Father'? Jn 14:9 3004
The words that I s to you I do not Jn 14:10 3004
"Truly, truly, I s to you, he who Jn 14:12 3004
did not s to you at the beginning, Jn 16:4 3004
have many more things to s to you, Jn 16:12 3004
"Truly, truly, I s to you, that Jn 16:20 3004
Truly, truly, I s to you, if you Jn 16:23 3004
and I do not s to you that I will Jn 16:26 3004
"You s *correctly* that I am a king. Jn 18:37 3004
began to come up to Him and s, Jn 19:3 3004
go to My brethren and s to them, Jn 20:17 3004
"Truly, truly, I s to you, when Jn 21:18 3004
s to him that he would not die, Jn 21:23 3004
I may confidently s to you Ac 2:29 3004
they had nothing to s in reply. Ac 4:14 471
in the present case, I s to you, Ac 5:38 3004
they secretly induced men to s, Ac 6:11 3004
heard him s that this Nazarene, Ac 6:14 3004
of whom does the prophet s this? Ac 8:34 3004
of the Lord, how He used to s, Ac 11:16 3004
for the people, s it." Ac 13:15 3004
this idle babbler wish to s?" Ac 17:18 3004
"May I s something to you?" Ac 21:37 3004
s that there is no resurrection, Ac 23:8 3004
and *began* to s that he was a god. Ac 28:6
'GO TO THIS PEOPLE AND S Ac 28:26 3004
You who s that one should not Ro 2:22 3004
of God, what shall we s? Ro 3:5 3004
And why not s (as we are Ro 3:8
and as some claim that we s), Ro 3:8 3004
for the demonstration, *I s*, of Ro 3:26
What then shall we s that Abraham, Ro 4:1 3004
For what does the Scripture s? Ro 4:3 3004
For we s, "FAITH WAS CREDITED Ro 4:9 3004
What shall we s then? Ro 6:1 3004
What shall we s then? Ro 7:7 3004
then shall we s to these things? Ro 8:31 3004
What shall we s then? Ro 9:14 3004
You will s to me then, Ro 9:19 3004
molded will not s to the molder, Ro 9:20 3004
What shall we s then? Ro 9:30 3004
"DO NOT S IN YOUR HEART, Ro 10:6 3004
But what does it s? Ro 10:8 3004
But I s, surely they have never Ro 10:18 3004
But I s, surely Israel did not Ro 10:19 3004
I s then, God has not rejected His Ro 11:1 3004
I s then, they did not stumble so Ro 11:11 3004
You will s then, Ro 11:19 3004
through the grace given to me I s to Ro 12:3 3004
For I s that Christ has become a Ro 15:8 3004
s you were baptized in my name. 1Co 1:15 3004
I s *this* to your shame. 1Co 6:5 3004
But this I s by way of concession, 1Co 7:6 3004
But I s to the unmarried and to 1Co 7:8 3004
But to the rest I s, 1Co 7:12 3004
But this I s, brethren, the time 1Co 7:29 5346
This I s for your own benefit; 1Co 7:35 3004
not the Law also s these things? 1Co 9:8 3004
you judge what I s. 1Co 10:15 5346
No, but *I* s that the things 1Co 10:20
What shall I s to you? 1Co 11:22 3004
and no one can s, 1Co 12:3 3004
And the eye cannot s to the hand, 1Co 12:21 3004
who fills the place of the ungifted s 1Co 14:16 3004
will they not s that you are mad? 1Co 14:23 3004
how do some among you s that there 1Co 15:12 3004
But someone will s, 1Co 15:35 3004
Now I s this, brethren, that flesh 1Co 15:50 5346
in order not to s too much 2Co 2:5 1912
we are of good courage, I s, 2Co 5:8
Now this *I s*, he who sows 2Co 9:6
For they s, "His letters are weighty 2Co 10:10 5346
Again I s, let no one think me 2Co 11:16 3004
To *my* shame I *must* s that we have 2Co 11:21 3004
though now absent I s in advance 2Co 13:2 4302
said before, so I s again now, Ga 1:9 3004
He does not s, "And to seeds," Ga 3:16 3004
Now I s, as long as the heir is a Ga 4:1 3004
But what does the Scripture s? Ga 4:30 3004
s to you that if you receive Ga 5:2 3004
But I s, walk by the Spirit, and Ga 5:16 3004
So this I s, and affirm Eph 4:17 3004
again I will s, rejoice! Php 4:4 3004
I s, whether things on earth or Col 1:20
I s this so that no one will Col 2:4 3004
S to Archippus, "Take heed to Col 4:17 3004
we have no need to s anything. 1Th 1:8 2980
For this we s to you by the word 1Th 4:15 3004
Consider what I s, for the Lord 2Tm 2:7 3004
having nothing bad to s about us. Ti 2:8 3004
will do even more than what I s. Phm 1:21 3004
to which of the angels did He ever s, Heb 1:5 3004
Concerning him we have much to s, Heb 5:11 3056
not made with hands, that is to s, Heb 9:11
one may almost s, all things Heb 9:22
For those who s such things make Heb 11:14 3004
And what more shall I s? Heb 11:32 3004
so that we confidently s, Heb 13:6 3004
Let no one s when he is tempted, Jas 1:13 3004
wearing the fine clothes, and s, Jas 2:3 3004
place," and you s to the poor man, Jas 2:3 3004
But someone may *well* s, Jas 2:18 3004
Come now, you who s, Jas 4:13 3004
Instead, *you ought* to s, Jas 4:15 3004
If we s that we have fellowship 1Jn 1:6 3004
If we s that we have no sin, we 1Jn 1:8 3004
If we s that we have not sinned, 1Jn 1:10 3004
I do not s that he should make 1Jn 5:16 3004
them, does not accept what we s. 3Jn 1:9 1473
who s they are Jews and are not, Rv 2:9 3004
'But I s to you, the rest who are Rv 2:24 3004
Satan, who s that they are Jews and Rv 3:9 3004
'Because you s, "I am rich, Rv 3:17 3004
and night they do not cease to s, Rv 4:8 3004
The Spirit and the bride s, Rv 22:17 3004
And let the one who hears s, Rv 22:17 3004

SAYING

God blessed them, s, Gn 1:22 559
The LORD God commanded the man, s, Gn 2:16 559
about which I commanded you, s, Gn 3:17 559
Now he called his name Noah, s, Gn 5:29 559
Then God spoke to Noah, s, Gn 8:15 559
Noah and to his sons with him, s, Gn 9:8 559
LORD came to Abram in a vision, s, Gn 15:1 559
word of the LORD came to him, s, Gn 15:4 559
made a covenant with Abram, s, Gn 15:18 559
face, and God talked with him, s, Gn 17:3 559
Sarah laughed to herself, s, Gn 18:12 559
"Why did Sarah laugh, s, Gn 18:13 559
Sarah denied *it* however, s, Gn 18:15 559
dawned, the angels urged Lot, s, Gn 19:15 559
of his army, spoke to Abraham, s, Gn 21:22 559
that it was told Abraham, s, Gn 22:20 559
and spoke to the sons of Heth, s, Gn 23:3 559
Heth answered Abraham, s to him, Gn 23:5 559
And he spoke with them, s, Gn 23:8 559
in at the gate of his city, s, Gn 23:10 559
of the people of the land, s, Gn 23:13 559
Ephron answered Abraham, s to him, Gn 23:14 559
to me and who swore to me, s, Gn 24:7 559
words of Rebekah his sister, s, Gn 24:30 559
"My master made me swear, s, Gn 24:37 559
charged all the people, s, Gn 26:11 559
with the herdsmen of Isaac, s, Gn 26:20 559
speak to your brother Esau, s, Gn 27:6 559
he blessed him he charged him, s, Gn 28:6 559
Then Jacob made a vow, s, Gn 28:20 559
She named him Joseph, s, Gn 30:24 559
heard the words of Laban's sons, s, Gn 31:1 559
father spoke to me last night, s, Gn 31:29 559
He also commanded them s, Gn 32:4 559
messengers returned to Jacob, s, Gn 32:6 559
He commanded the one in front, s, Gn 32:17 559
Esau meets you and asks you, s, Gn 32:17 559
those who followed the droves, s, Gn 32:19 559
spoke to his father Hamor, s, Gn 34:4 559
But Hamor spoke with them, s, Gn 34:8 559
spoke to the men of their city, s, Gn 34:20 559
but his father kept the s *in mind.* Gn 37:11 1697
He asked the men of her place, s, Gn 38:21 559
she sent to her father-in-law, s, Gn 38:25 559
a scarlet *thread* on his hand, s, Gn 38:28 559
She caught him by his garment, s, Gn 39:12 559
wife, which she spoke to him, s, Gn 39:19 559
cupbearer spoke to Pharaoh, s, Gn 41:9 559
Joseph then answered Pharaoh, s, Gn 41:16 559
Reuben answered them, s, Gn 42:22 559
trembling to one another, s, Gn 42:28 559
all that had happened to them, s, Gn 42:29 559
Reuben spoke to his father, s, Gn 42:37 559
Judah spoke to him, however, s, Gn 43:3 559
about us and our relatives, s, Gn 43:7 559
he commanded his house steward, s, Gn 44:1 559
"My lord asked his servants, s, Gn 44:19 559
for the lad to my father, s, Gn 44:32 559
They told him, s, Gn 45:26 559
He blessed them that day, s, Gn 48:20 559
will pronounce blessing, s, Gn 48:20 559
to the household of Pharaoh, s, Gn 50:4 559
sight, please speak to Pharaoh, s, Gn 50:4 559
'My father made me swear, s, Gn 50:5 559
they sent *a message* to Joseph, s, Gn 50:16 559
father charged before he died, s, Gn 50:16 559
made the sons of Israel swear, s, Gn 50:25 559
commanded all his people, s, Ex 1:22 559
and Jacob, has appeared to me, s, Ex 3:16 559
the people and their foremen, s, Ex 5:6 559
out and spoke to the people, s, Ex 5:10 559
The taskmasters pressed them, s, Ex 5:13 559
came and cried out to Pharaoh, s, Ex 5:15 559
servants, yet they keep s to us, Ex 5:16 559
Now the LORD spoke to Moses, s, Ex 6:10 559
Moses spoke before the LORD, s, Ex 6:12 559
that the LORD spoke to Moses, s, Ex 6:29 559
LORD spoke to Moses and Aaron, s, Ex 7:8 559
"When Pharaoh speaks to you, s, Ex 7:9 559
of the Hebrews, sent me to you, s, Ex 7:16 559
The LORD set a definite time, s, Ex 9:5 559
and bow themselves before me, s, Ex 11:8 559
all the congregation of Israel, s, Ex 12:3 559
Then the LORD spoke to Moses, s, Ex 13:1 559
tell your son on that day, s, Ex 13:8 559
son asks you in time to come, s, Ex 13:14 559
sons of Israel solemnly swear, s, Ex 13:19 559
Now the LORD spoke to Moses, s, Ex 14:1 559
that we spoke to you in Egypt, s, Ex 14:12 559
the people grumbled at Moses, s, Ex 15:24 559
And the LORD spoke to Moses, s, Ex 16:11 559
speak to them, s, Ex 16:12 559
So Moses cried out to the LORD, s, Ex 17:4 559
because they tested the LORD, s, Ex 17:7 559
to him from the mountain, s, Ex 19:3 559
for the people all around, s, Ex 19:12 559
Sinai, for You warned us, s, Ex 19:23 559
Then God spoke all these words, s, Ex 20:1 559
Then the LORD spoke to Moses, s, Ex 25:1 559
The LORD also spoke to Moses, s, Ex 30:11 559
The LORD spoke to Moses, s, Ex 30:17 559
the LORD spoke to Moses, s, Ex 30:22 559
speak to the sons of Israel, s, Ex 30:31 559
Now the LORD spoke to Moses, s, Ex 31:1 559
The LORD spoke to Moses, s, Ex 31:12 559
speak to the sons of Israel, s, Ex 31:13 559
"Why should the Egyptians speak, s, Ex 32:12 559
to Abraham, Isaac, and Jacob, s, Ex 33:1 559
of the sons of Israel, s, Ex 35:4 559
which the LORD has commanded, s, Ex 35:4 559
circulated throughout the camp, s, Ex 36:6 559
Then the LORD spoke to Moses, s, Ex 40:1 559
him from the tent of meeting, s, Lv 1:1 559
Then the LORD spoke to Moses, s, Lv 4:1 559
"Speak to the sons of Israel, s, Lv 4:2 559
Then the LORD spoke to Moses, s, Lv 5:14 559

Then the LORD spoke to Moses, **s**,	**Lv 6:1**	559
Then the LORD spoke to Moses, **s**,	**Lv 6:8**	559
“Command Aaron and his sons, **s**,	**Lv 6:9**	559
Then the LORD spoke to Moses, **s**,	**Lv 6:19**	559
Then the LORD spoke to Moses, **s**,	**Lv 6:24**	559
“Speak to Aaron and to his sons, **s**,	**Lv 6:25**	559
Then the LORD spoke to Moses, **s**,	**Lv 7:22**	559
“Speak to the sons of Israel, **s**,	**Lv 7:23**	559
Then the LORD spoke to Moses, **s**,	**Lv 7:28**	559
“Speak to the sons of Israel, **s**,	**Lv 7:29**	559
Then the LORD spoke to Moses, **s**,	**Lv 8:1**	559
offering, just as I commanded, **s**,	**Lv 8:31**	559
sons of Israel you shall speak, **s**,	**Lv 9:3**	559
“It is what the LORD spoke, **s**,	**Lv 10:3**	559
The LORD then spoke to Aaron, **s**,	**Lv 10:8**	559
sons Eleazar and Ithamar, **s**,	**Lv 10:16**	559
to Moses and to Aaron, **s** to them,	**Lv 11:1**	559
“Speak to the sons of Israel, **s**,	**Lv 11:2**	559
Then the LORD spoke to Moses, **s**,	**Lv 12:1**	559
“Speak to the sons of Israel, **s**:	**Lv 12:2**	559
spoke to Moses and to Aaron, **s**,	**Lv 13:1**	559
Then the LORD spoke to Moses, **s**,	**Lv 14:1**	559
spoke to Moses and to Aaron, **s**:	**Lv 14:33**	559
shall come and tell the priest, **s**,	**Lv 14:35**	559
spoke to Moses and to Aaron, **s**,	**Lv 15:1**	559
Then the LORD spoke to Moses, **s**,	**Lv 17:1**	559
is what the LORD has commanded, **s**,	**Lv 17:2**	559
Then the LORD spoke to Moses, **s**,	**Lv 18:1**	559
Then the LORD spoke to Moses, **s**:	**Lv 19:1**	559
Then the LORD spoke to Moses, **s**,	**Lv 20:1**	559
Then the LORD spoke to Moses, **s**,	**Lv 21:16**	559
“Speak to Aaron, **s**,	**Lv 21:17**	559
Then the LORD spoke to Moses, **s**,	**Lv 22:1**	559
Then the LORD spoke to Moses, **s**,	**Lv 22:17**	559
Then the LORD spoke to Moses, **s**,	**Lv 22:26**	559
The LORD spoke again to Moses, **s**,	**Lv 23:1**	559
Then the LORD spoke to Moses, **s**,	**Lv 23:9**	559
Again the LORD spoke to Moses, **s**,	**Lv 23:23**	559
“Speak to the sons of Israel, **s**,	**Lv 23:24**	559
The LORD spoke to Moses, **s**,	**Lv 23:26**	559
Again the LORD spoke to Moses, **s**,	**Lv 23:33**	559
“Speak to the sons of Israel, **s**,	**Lv 23:34**	559
Then the LORD spoke to Moses, **s**,	**Lv 24:1**	559
Then the LORD spoke to Moses, **s**,	**Lv 24:13**	559
speak to the sons of Israel, **s**,	**Lv 24:15**	559
spoke to Moses at Mount Sinai, **s**,	**Lv 25:1**	559
Again, the LORD spoke to Moses, **s**,	**Lv 27:1**	559
come out of the land of Egypt, **s**,	**Nu 1:1**	559
the LORD had spoken to Moses, **s**,	**Nu 1:48**	559
spoke to Moses and to Aaron, **s**,	**Nu 2:1**	559
Then the LORD spoke to Moses, **s**,	**Nu 3:5**	559
Again the LORD spoke to Moses, **s**,	**Nu 3:11**	559
in the wilderness of Sinai, **s**,	**Nu 3:14**	559
Then the LORD spoke to Moses, **s**,	**Nu 3:44**	559
spoke to Moses and to Aaron, **s**,	**Nu 4:1**	559
spoke to Moses and to Aaron, **s**,	**Nu 4:17**	559
Then the LORD spoke to Moses, **s**,	**Nu 4:21**	559
Then the LORD spoke to Moses, **s**,	**Nu 5:1**	559
Then the LORD spoke to Moses, **s**,	**Nu 5:5**	559
Then the LORD spoke to Moses, **s**,	**Nu 5:11**	559
Again the LORD spoke to Moses, **s**,	**Nu 6:1**	559
Then the LORD spoke to Moses, **s**,	**Nu 6:22**	559
“Speak to Aaron and to his sons, **s**,	**Nu 6:23**	559
Then the LORD spoke to Moses, **s**,	**Nu 7:4**	559
Then the LORD spoke to Moses, **s**,	**Nu 8:1**	559
Again the LORD spoke to Moses, **s**,	**Nu 8:5**	559
Now the LORD spoke to Moses, **s**,	**Nu 8:23**	559
come out of the land of Egypt, **s**,	**Nu 9:1**	559
Then the LORD spoke to Moses, **s**,	**Nu 9:9**	559
“Speak to the sons of Israel, **s**,	**Nu 9:10**	559
LORD spoke further to Moses, **s**,	**Nu 10:1**	559
For they weep before me, **s**,	**Nu 11:13**	559
wept in the ears of the LORD, **s**,	**Nu 11:18**	559
you and have wept before Him, **s**,	**Nu 11:20**	559
Moses cried out to the LORD, **s**,	**Nu 12:13**	559
Then the LORD spoke to Moses **s**,	**Nu 13:1**	559
land which they had spied out, **s**,	**Nu 13:32**	559
of the sons of Israel, **s**,	**Nu 14:7**	559
LORD spoke to Moses and Aaron, **s**,	**Nu 14:26**	559
the ridge of the hill country, **s**,	**Nu 14:40**	559
Now the LORD spoke to Moses, **s**,	**Nu 15:1**	559
Then the LORD spoke to Moses, **s**,	**Nu 15:17**	559
The LORD also spoke to Moses, **s**,	**Nu 15:37**	559
to Korah and all his company, **s**,	**Nu 16:5**	559
LORD spoke to Moses and Aaron, **s**,	**Nu 16:20**	559
Then the LORD spoke to Moses, **s**,	**Nu 16:23**	559
“Speak to the congregation, **s**,	**Nu 16:24**	559
he spoke to the congregation, **s**,	**Nu 16:26**	559
Then the LORD spoke to Moses, **s**,	**Nu 16:36**	559
against Moses and Aaron, **s**,	**Nu 16:41**	559
and the LORD spoke to Moses, **s**,	**Nu 16:44**	559
Then the LORD spoke to Moses, **s**,	**Nu 17:1**	559
sons of Israel spoke to Moses, **s**,	**Nu 17:12**	559
Then the LORD spoke to Moses, **s**,	**Nu 18:25**	559
LORD spoke to Moses and Aaron, **s**,	**Nu 19:1**	559
which the LORD has commanded, **s**,	**Nu 19:2**	559
contended with Moses and spoke, **s**,	**Nu 20:3**	559
and the LORD spoke to Moses, **s**,	**Nu 20:7**	559
the border of the land of Edom, **s**,	**Nu 20:23**	559
to Sihon, king of the Amorites, **s**,	**Nu 21:21**	559
of his people, to call him, **s**,	**Nu 22:5**	559
whom you had sent to me, **s**,	**Nu 24:12**	559
Then the LORD spoke to Moses, **s**,	**Nu 25:10**	559
Then the LORD spoke to Moses, **s**,	**Nu 25:16**	559
the son of Aaron the priest, **s**,	**Nu 26:1**	559
Moab by the Jordan at Jericho, **s**,	**Nu 26:3**	559
Then the LORD spoke to Moses, **s**,	**Nu 26:52**	559
doorway of the tent of meeting, **s**,	**Nu 27:2**	559
Then the LORD spoke to Moses, **s**,	**Nu 27:6**	559
speak to the sons of Israel, **s**,	**Nu 27:8**	559
Then Moses spoke to the LORD, **s**,	**Nu 27:15**	559
Then the LORD spoke to Moses, **s**,	**Nu 28:1**	559
tribes of the sons of Israel, **s**,	**Nu 30:1**	559
Then the LORD spoke to Moses, **s**,	**Nu 31:1**	559
Moses spoke to the people, **s**,	**Nu 31:3**	559
Then the LORD spoke to Moses, **s**,	**Nu 31:25**	559
leaders of the congregation, **s**,	**Nu 32:2**	559
in that day, and He swore, **s**,	**Nu 32:10**	559
sons of Reuben spoke to Moses, **s**,	**Nu 32:25**	559
the sons of Reuben answered, **s**,	**Nu 32:31**	559
by the Jordan *opposite* Jericho, **s**,	**Nu 33:50**	559
Then the LORD spoke to Moses, **s**,	**Nu 34:1**	559
commanded the sons of Israel, **s**,	**Nu 34:13**	559
Then the LORD spoke to Moses, **s**,	**Nu 34:16**	559
by the Jordan *opposite* Jericho, **s**,	**Nu 35:1**	559
Then the LORD spoke to Moses, **s**,	**Nu 35:9**	559
to the word of the LORD, **s**,	**Nu 36:5**	559
the daughters of Zelophehad, **s**,	**Nu 36:6**	559
undertook to expound this law, **s**,	**Dt 1:5**	559
our God spoke to us at Horeb, **s**,	**Dt 1:6**	559
I spoke to you at that time, **s**,	**Dt 1:9**	559
your judges at that time, **s**,	**Dt 1:16**	559
have made our hearts melt, **s**,	**Dt 1:28**	559
He was angry and took an oath, **s**,	**Dt 1:34**	559
with me also on your account, **s**,	**Dt 1:37**	559
“And the LORD spoke to me, **s**,	**Dt 2:2**	559
and command the people, **s**,	**Dt 2:4**	559
that the LORD spoke to me, **s**,	**Dt 2:17**	559
of Heshbon with words of peace, **s**,	**Dt 2:26**	559
I commanded you at that time, **s**,	**Dt 3:18**	559
commanded Joshua at that time, **s**,	**Dt 3:21**	559
with the LORD at that time, **s**,	**Dt 3:23**	559
son asks you in time to come, **s**,	**Dt 6:20**	559
“The LORD spoke further to me, **s**,	**Dt 9:13**	559
sent you from Kadesh-barnea, **s**,	**Dt 9:23**	559
not inquire after their gods, **s**,	**Dt 12:30**	559
which he spoke to you, **s**,	**Dt 13:2**	559
own soul, entice you secretly, **s**,	**Dt 13:6**	559
you to live in, *anyone* **s** *that*	**Dt 13:12**	559
the inhabitants of their city, **s**,	**Dt 13:13**	559
no base thought in your heart, **s**,	**Dt 15:9**	559
therefore I command you, **s**,	**Dt 15:11**	559
on the day of the assembly, **s**,	**Dt 18:16**	559
“Therefore, I command you, **s**,	**Dt 19:7**	559
also shall speak to the people, **s**,	**Dt 20:5**	559
her with shameful deeds, **s**,	**Dt 22:17**	559
of Israel charged the people, **s**,	**Dt 27:1**	559
priests spoke to all Israel, **s**,	**Dt 27:9**	559
charged the people on that day, **s**,	**Dt 27:11**	559
this curse, that he will boast, **s**,	**Dt 29:19**	559
Then Moses commanded them, **s**,	**Dt 31:10**	559
of the covenant of the LORD, **s**,	**Dt 31:25**	559
to Moses that very same day, **s**,	**Dt 32:48**	559
to Abraham, Isaac, and Jacob, **s**,	**Dt 34:4**	559
the son of Nun, Moses' servant, **s**,	**Jos 1:1**	559
the officers of the people, **s**,	**Jos 1:10**	559
camp and command the people, **s**,	**Jos 1:11**	559
of the LORD commanded you, **s**,	**Jos 1:13**	559
They answered Joshua, **s**,	**Jos 1:16**	559
as spies secretly from Shittim, **s**,	**Jos 2:1**	559
was told the king of Jericho, **s**,	**Jos 2:2**	559
of Jericho sent *word* to Rahab, **s**,	**Jos 2:3**	559
and they commanded the people, **s**,	**Jos 3:3**	559
Joshua spoke to the priests, **s**,	**Jos 3:6**	559
the ark of the covenant, **s**,	**Jos 3:8**	559
the LORD spoke to Joshua, **s**,	**Jos 4:1**	559
and command them, **s**,	**Jos 4:3**	559
when your children ask later, **s**,	**Jos 4:6**	559
Joshua commanded the priests, **s**,	**Jos 4:17**	559
their fathers in time to come, **s**,	**Jos 4:21**	559
you shall inform your children, **s**,	**Jos 4:22**	559
Joshua commanded the people, **s**,	**Jos 6:10**	559
them take an oath at that time, **s**,	**Jos 6:26**	559
He commanded them, **s**,	**Jos 8:4**	559
of our country spoke to us, **s**,	**Jos 9:11**	559
for them and spoke to them, **s**,	**Jos 9:22**	559
“Why have you deceived us, **s**,	**Jos 9:22**	559
and to Debir king of Eglon, **s**,	**Jos 10:3**	559
Joshua to the camp at Gilgal, **s**,	**Jos 10:6**	559
It was told Joshua, **s**,	**Jos 10:17**	559
“So Moses swore on that day, **s**,	**Jos 14:9**	559
of Nun and before the leaders, **s**,	**Jos 17:4**	559
sons of Joseph spoke to Joshua, **s**,	**Jos 17:14**	559
to Ephraim and Manasseh, **s**,	**Jos 17:17**	559
who went to describe the land, **s**,	**Jos 18:8**	559
Then the LORD spoke to Joshua, **s**,	**Jos 20:1**	559
“Speak to the sons of Israel, **s**,	**Jos 20:2**	559
Shiloh in the land of Canaan, **s**,	**Jos 21:2**	559
and they spoke with them **s**,	**Jos 22:15**	559
out of concern, for a reason, **s**,	**Jos 22:24**	559
of Israel inquired of the LORD, **s**,	**Jg 1:1**	559
of Abinoam sang on that day, **s**,	**Jg 5:1**	559
our fathers told us about, **s**,	**Jg 6:13**	559
for Israel would become boastful, **s**,	**Jg 7:2**	559
in the hearing of the people, **s**,	**Jg 7:3**	559
the hill country of Ephraim, **s**,	**Jg 7:24**	559
also to the men of Penuel, **s**,	**Jg 8:9**	559
concerning whom you taunted me, **s**,	**Jg 8:15**	559
of his mother's father, **s**,	**Jg 9:1**	559
to Abimelech deceitfully, **s**,	**Jg 9:31**	559
Israel cried out to the LORD, **s**,	**Jg 10:10**	559
the king of the sons of Ammon, **s**,	**Jg 11:12**	559
messengers to the king of Edom, **s**,	**Jg 11:17**	559
came and told her husband, **s**,	**Jg 13:6**	559
it was told to the Gazites, **s**,	**Jg 16:2**	559
And they kept silent all night, **s**,	**Jg 16:2**	559
the lords of the Philistines, **s**,	**Jg 16:18**	559
of the house, the old man, **s**,	**Jg 19:22**	559
the people arose as one man, **s**,	**Jg 20:8**	559
the entire tribe of Benjamin, **s**,	**Jg 20:12**	559
and inquired of the LORD, **s**,	**Jg 20:23**	559
s, “Shall I yet again go out to	**Jg 20:28**	559
of Israel had sworn in Mizpah, **s**,	**Jg 21:1**	559
come up to the LORD at Mizpah, **s**,	**Jg 21:5**	559
there, and commanded them, **s**,	**Jg 21:10**	559
the sons of Israel had sworn, **s**,	**Jg 21:18**	559
commanded the sons of Benjamin, **s**,	**Jg 21:20**	559
Boaz commanded his servants, **s**,	**Ru 2:15**	559
“So I thought to inform you, **s**,	**Ru 4:4**	559
neighbor women gave him a name, **s**,	**Ru 4:17**	559
s, “Because I have asked him of	**1Sa 1:20**	
And she called the boy Ichabod, **s**,	**1Sa 4:21**	559
Ekron the Ekronites cried out, **s**,	**1Sa 5:10**	559
the priests and the diviners, **s**,	**1Sa 6:2**	559
inhabitants of Kiriath-jearim, **s**,	**1Sa 6:21**	559
to all the house of Israel, **s**,	**1Sa 7:3**	559
Shen, and named it Ebenezer, **s**,	**1Sa 7:12**	559
had revealed *this* to Samuel **s**,	**1Sa 9:15**	559
called to Saul on the roof, **s**,	**1Sa 9:26**	559
donkeys and is anxious for you, **s**,	**1Sa 10:2**	559
by the hand of messengers, **s**,	**1Sa 11:7**	559
trumpet throughout the land, **s**,	**1Sa 13:3**	559
had put the people under oath, **s**,	**1Sa 14:24**	559
put the people under oath, **s**,	**1Sa 14:28**	559
Then they told Saul, **s**,	**1Sa 14:33**	559
of the LORD came to Samuel, **s**,	**1Sa 15:10**	559
and it was told Samuel, **s**,	**1Sa 15:12**	559
Saul sent to Jesse, **s**,	**1Sa 16:22**	559
men who were standing by him, **s**,	**1Sa 17:26**	559
him in accord with this word, **s**,	**1Sa 17:27**	559
angry, for this **s** displeased him;	**1Sa 18:8**	1697
“Speak to David secretly, **s**,	**1Sa 18:22**	559
So Jonathan told David **s**,	**1Sa 19:2**	559
Michal, David's wife, told him, **s**,	**1Sa 19:11**	559
sent messengers to see David, **s**,	**1Sa 19:15**	559
It was told Saul, **s**,	**1Sa 19:19**	559
Yet David vowed again, **s**,	**1Sa 20:3**	559
s, “May the LORD require	**1Sa 20:16**	
s, 'Go, find the arrows.' If	**1Sa 20:21**	
other in the name of the LORD, **s**,	**1Sa 20:42**	559
of this one as they danced, **s**,	**1Sa 21:11**	559
Then they told David, **s**,	**1Sa 23:1**	559
So David inquired of the LORD, **s**,	**1Sa 23:2**	559
came up to Saul at Gibeah, **s**,	**1Sa 23:19**	559
But a messenger came to Saul, **s**,	**1Sa 23:27**	559
the Philistines, he was told, **s**,	**1Sa 24:1**	559
the cave and called after Saul, **s**,	**1Sa 24:8**	559
you listen to the words of men, **s**,	**1Sa 24:9**	559
men told Abigail, Nabal's wife, **s**,	**1Sa 25:14**	559
at Carmel, they spoke to her, **s**,	**1Sa 25:40**	559
came to Saul at Gibeah, **s**,	**1Sa 26:1**	559
son of Zeruiah, Joab's brother, **s**,	**1Sa 26:6**	559
and to Abner the son of Ner, **s**,	**1Sa 26:14**	559
the inheritance of the LORD, **s**,	**1Sa 26:19**	559
woman alive to bring to Gath, **s**,	**1Sa 27:11**	559
“Otherwise they will tell about us, **s**,	**1Sa 27:11**	559
So Achish believed David, **s**,	**1Sa 27:12**	559
Saul vowed to her by the LORD, **s**,	**1Sa 28:10**	559
and the woman spoke to Saul, **s**,	**1Sa 28:12**	559
whom they sing in the dances, **s**,	**1Sa 29:5**	559
David inquired of the LORD, **s**,	**1Sa 30:8**	559
of Judah, to his friends, **s**,	**1Sa 30:26**	559
has testified against you, **s**,	**2Sa 1:16**	559
David inquired of the LORD, **s**,	**2Sa 2:1**	559
And they told David, **s**,	**2Sa 2:4**	559
to David in his place, **s**,	**2Sa 3:12**	559
to Ish-bosheth, Saul's son, **s**,	**2Sa 3:14**	559
with the elders of Israel, **s**,	**2Sa 3:17**	559
the LORD has spoken of David, **s**,	**2Sa 3:18**	559
him arrived, they told Joab, **s**,	**2Sa 3:23**	559
but David vowed, **s**,	**2Sa 3:35**	559
when one told me, **s**,	**2Sa 4:10**	559
David inquired of the LORD, **s**,	**2Sa 5:19**	559
Now it was told King David, **s**,	**2Sa 6:12**	559
of the LORD came to Nathan, **s**,	**2Sa 7:4**	559
to shepherd My people Israel, **s**,	**2Sa 7:7**	559
may be magnified forever, by **s**,	**2Sa 7:26**	559
a revelation to Your servant, **s**,	**2Sa 7:27**	559
Then David sent to Joab, **s**,	**2Sa 11:6**	559
Now when they told David, **s**,	**2Sa 11:10**	559
He had written in the letter, **s**,	**2Sa 11:15**	559
He charged the messenger, **s**,	**2Sa 11:19**	559
sent to the house for Tamar, **s**,	**2Sa 13:7**	559
Absalom commanded his servants, **s**,	**2Sa 13:28**	559
that the report came to David, **s**,	**2Sa 13:30**	559
“Behold, I sent for you, **s**,	**2Sa 14:32**	559
I was living at Geshur in Aram, **s**,	**2Sa 15:8**	559
all the tribes of Israel, **s**,	**2Sa 15:10**	559
Then a messenger came to David, **s**,	**2Sa 15:13**	559
Now someone told David, **s**,	**2Sa 15:31**	559
send quickly and tell David, **s**,	**2Sa 17:16**	559
Joab and Abishai and Ittai, **s**,	**2Sa 18:5**	559
you and Abishai and Ittai, **s**,	**2Sa 18:12**	559
When they told all the people, **s**,	**2Sa 19:8**	559
all the tribes of Israel, **s**,	**2Sa 19:9**	559
Zadok and Abiathar the priests, **s**,	**2Sa 19:11**	559
“Speak to the elders of Judah, **s**,	**2Sa 19:11**	559
to the king, **s**, “Return, you and all your	**2Sa 19:14**	
Then she spoke, **s**,	**2Sa 20:18**	559
the men of David swore to him, **s**,	**2Sa 21:17**	559
the prophet Gad, David's seer, **s**,	**2Sa 24:11**	559
son of Haggith exalted himself, **s**,	**1Ki 1:5**	559
the mother of Solomon, **s**,	**1Ki 1:11**	559
sworn to your maidservant, **s**,	**1Ki 1:13**	559
s, 'Surely your son Solomon	**1Ki 1:17**	
They told the king, **s**,	**1Ki 1:23**	559
by the LORD the God of Israel, **s**,	**1Ki 1:30**	559

to bless our lord King David, s, **1Ki 1:47** 559
Now it was told Solomon, s, **1Ki 1:51** 559
hold of the horns of the altar, s, **1Ki 1:51** 559
he charged Solomon his son, s, **1Ki 2:1** 559
which He spoke concerning me, s, **1Ki 2:4** 559
I swore to him by the LORD, s, **1Ki 2:8** 559
King Solomon swore by the LORD, s, **1Ki 2:23** 559
Benaiah the son of Jehoiada, s, **1Ki 2:29** 559
brought the king word again, s, **1Ki 2:30** 559
And they told Shimei, s, **1Ki 2:39** 559
the LORD and solemnly warn you, s, **1Ki 2:42** 559
Solomon sent *word* to Hiram, s, **1Ki 5:2** 559
LORD spoke to David my father, s, **1Ki 5:5** 559
So Hiram sent *word* to Solomon, s, **1Ki 5:8** 559
of the LORD came to Solomon s, **1Ki 6:11** 559
has fulfilled *it* with His hand, s, **1Ki 8:15** 559
which You have promised him, s, **1Ki 8:25** 559
who have taken them captive, s, **1Ki 8:47** 559
of Israel with a loud voice, s: **1Ki 8:55** 559
promised to your father David, s, **1Ki 9:5** 559
came and spoke to Rehoboam, s, **1Ki 12:3** 559
while he was still alive, s, **1Ki 12:6** 559
Then they spoke to him, s, **1Ki 12:7** 559
people who have spoken to me, s, **1Ki 12:9** 559
grew up with him spoke to him, s, **1Ki 12:10** 559
this people who spoke to you, s, **1Ki 12:10** 559
day as the king had directed, s, **1Ki 12:12** 559
to the advice of the young men, s, **1Ki 12:14** 559
the people answered the king, s, **1Ki 12:16** 559
to Shemaiah the man of God, s, **1Ki 12:22** 559
and to the rest of the people, s, **1Ki 12:23** 559
he gave a sign the same day, s, **1Ki 13:3** 559
heard the s of the man of God, **1Ki 13:4** 1697
out his hand from the altar, s, **1Ki 13:4** 559
me by the word of the LORD, s, **1Ki 13:9** 559
to me by the word of the LORD, s, **1Ki 13:18** 559
man of God who came from Judah, s, **1Ki 13:21** 559
Then he spoke to his sons, s, **1Ki 13:27** 559
s, "Alas, my brother!" **1Ki 13:30** 559
him, he spoke to his sons, s, **1Ki 13:31** 559
of Aram, who lived in Damascus, s, **1Ki 15:18** 559
son of Hanani against Baasha, s, **1Ki 16:1** 559
word of the LORD came to him, s, **1Ki 17:2** 559
word of the LORD came to him, s, **1Ki 17:8** 559
to Elijah in the third year, s, **1Ki 18:1** 559
"And now you are s, **1Ki 18:11** 559
"And now you are s, **1Ki 18:14** 559
of Baal from morning until noon s, **1Ki 18:26** 559
the word of the LORD had come, s, **1Ki 18:31** 559
sent a messenger to Elijah, s, **1Ki 19:2** 559
'Surely, I sent to you s, **1Ki 20:5** 559
sent out and they told him, s, **1Ki 20:17** 559
Ahab spoke to Naboth, s, **1Ki 21:2** 559
Now she wrote in the letters, s, **1Ki 21:9** 559
let them testify against him, s, **1Ki 21:10** 559
Naboth, before the people, s, **1Ki 21:13** 559
Then they sent *word* to Jezebel, s, **1Ki 21:14** 559
came to Elijah the Tishbite, s, **1Ki 21:17** 559
"You shall speak to him, s, **1Ki 21:19** 559
And you shall speak to him, s, **1Ki 21:19** 559
also has the LORD spoken, s, **1Ki 21:23** 559
came to Elijah the Tishbite, s, **1Ki 21:28** 559
prophets were prophesying thus, s, **1Ki 22:12** 559
to summon Micaiah spoke to him s, **1Ki 22:13** 559
captains of his chariots, s, **1Ki 22:31** 559
the army close to sunset, s, **1Ki 22:36** 559
Jehoshaphat the king of Judah, s, **2Ki 3:7** 559
went in and told his master, s, **2Ki 5:4** 559
letter to the king of Israel, s, **2Ki 5:6** 559
that he sent *word* to the king, s, **2Ki 5:8** 559
Elisha sent a messenger to him, s, **2Ki 5:10** 559
My master has sent me, s, **2Ki 5:22** 559
he counseled with his servants s, **2Ki 6:8** 559
sent *word* to the king of Israel s, **2Ki 6:9** 559
And it was told him, s, **2Ki 6:13** 559
wall a woman cried out to him, s, **2Ki 6:26** 559
the city, and they told them, s, **2Ki 7:10** 559
hide themselves in the field, s, **2Ki 7:12** 559
after the army of the Arameans, s, **2Ki 7:14** 559
of God had spoken to the king, s, **2Ki 7:18** 559
son he had restored to life, s, **2Ki 8:1** 559
the servant of the man of God, s, **2Ki 8:4** 559
for her a certain officer, s, **2Ki 8:6** 559
was sick, and it was told him, s, **2Ki 8:7** 559
and inquire of the LORD by him, s, **2Ki 8:8** 559
of Aram has sent me to you, s, **2Ki 8:9** 559
steps, and blew the trumpet, s, **2Ki 9:13** 559
servant Elijah the Tishbite, s, **2Ki 9:36** 559
of *the children of* Ahab, s, **2Ki 10:1** 559
children, sent *word* to Jehu, s, **2Ki 10:5** 559
a letter to them a second time s, **2Ki 10:6** 559
messenger came and told him, s, **2Ki 10:8** 559
He commanded them, s, **2Ki 11:5** 559
Moses, as the LORD commanded, s, **2Ki 14:6** 559
son of Jehu, king of Israel, s, **2Ki 14:8** 559
sent to Amaziah king of Judah, s, **2Ki 14:9** 559
the cedar which was in Lebanon, s, **2Ki 14:9** 559
LORD which He spoke to Jehu, s, **2Ki 15:12** 559
Tiglath-pileser king of Assyria, s, **2Ki 16:7** 559
commanded Urijah the priest, s, **2Ki 16:15** 559
His prophets *and* every seer, s, **2Ki 17:13** 559
spoke to the king of Assyria, s, **2Ki 17:26** 559
the king of Assyria commanded, s, **2Ki 17:27** 559
a covenant and commanded them, s, **2Ki 17:35** 559
the king of Assyria at Lachish, s, **2Ki 18:14** 559
with a loud voice in Judean, s, **2Ki 18:28**
1696, 559
make you trust in the LORD, s, **2Ki 18:30** 559
Hezekiah when he misleads you, s, **2Ki 18:32** 559

messengers again to Hezekiah s, **2Ki 19:9** 559
in whom you trust deceive you s, **2Ki 19:10** 559
son of Amoz sent to Hezekiah s, **2Ki 19:20** 559
wall and prayed to the LORD, s, **2Ki 20:2** 559
word of the LORD came to him, s, **2Ki 20:4** 559
His servants the prophets, s, **2Ki 21:10** 559
to the house of the LORD s, **2Ki 22:3** 559
the scribe told the king s, **2Ki 22:10** 559
and Asaiah the king's servant s, **2Ki 22:12** 559
king commanded all the people s, **2Ki 23:21** 559
and his mother named him Jabez s, **1Ch 4:9** 559
called on the God of Israel, s, **1Ch 4:10** 559
consultation sent him away, s, **1Ch 12:19** 559
was afraid of God that day, s, **1Ch 13:12** 559
David inquired of God, s, **1Ch 14:10** 559
S, "To you I will give the land **1Ch 16:18** 559
for their sakes, s, **1Ch 16:21** 559
the word of God came to Nathan, s, **1Ch 17:3** 559
to shepherd My people, s, **1Ch 17:6** 559
and magnified forever, s, **1Ch 17:24** 559
LORD spoke to Gad, David's seer, s, **1Ch 21:9** 559
"Go and speak to David, s, **1Ch 21:10** 559
word of the LORD came to me, s, **1Ch 22:8** 559
his son Solomon, s, **1Ch 22:17**
word to Huram the king of Tyre, s, **2Ch 2:3** 559
when they praised the LORD s, **2Ch 5:13**
fulfilled *it* with His hands, s, **2Ch 6:4** 559
which You have promised him, s, **2Ch 6:16** 559
in the land of their captivity, s, **2Ch 6:37** 559
s, "Truly He is good, truly **2Ch 7:3**
with your father David, s, **2Ch 7:18** 559
came, they spoke to Rehoboam, s, **2Ch 10:3** 559
while he was still alive, s, **2Ch 10:6** 559
They spoke to him, s, **2Ch 10:7** 559
people, who have spoken to me, s, **2Ch 10:9** 559
grew up with him spoke to him, s, **2Ch 10:10** 559
to the people who spoke to you, s, **2Ch 10:10** 559
day as the king had directed, s, **2Ch 10:12** 559
to the advice of the young men, s, **2Ch 10:14** 559
the people answered the king, s, **2Ch 10:16** 559
to Shemaiah the man of God, s, **2Ch 11:2** 559
Israel in Judah and Benjamin, s, **2Ch 11:3** 559
of the LORD came to Shemaiah, s, **2Ch 12:7** 559
of Aram, who lived in Damascus, s, **2Ch 16:2** 559
prophets were prophesying thus, s, **2Ch 18:11** 559
to summon Micaiah spoke to him s, **2Ch 18:12** 559
the captains of his chariots, s, **2Ch 18:30** 559
Then he charged them s, **2Ch 19:9** 559
and reported to Jehoshaphat, s, **2Ch 20:2** 559
a sanctuary there for Your name, s, **2Ch 20:8** 559
prophesied against Jehoshaphat s, **2Ch 20:37** 559
to him from Elijah the prophet s, **2Ch 21:12** 559
which the LORD commanded, s, **2Ch 25:4** 559
But a man of God came to him s, **2Ch 25:7** 559
of Jehu, the king of Israel, s, **2Ch 25:17** 559
sent to Amaziah king of Judah, s, **2Ch 25:18** 559
the cedar which was in Lebanon, s, **2Ch 25:18** 559
to the command of the king, s, **2Ch 30:6** 559
For Hezekiah prayed for them, s, **2Ch 30:18** 559
flowed through the region, s, **2Ch 32:4** 559
spoke encouragingly to them, s, **2Ch 32:6** 559
Judah who *were* at Jerusalem, s, **2Ch 32:9** 559
to die by hunger and by thirst, s, **2Ch 32:11** 559
and to speak against Him, s, **2Ch 32:17** 559
further word to the king, s, **2Ch 34:16** 559
the scribe told the king s, **2Ch 34:18** 559
and Asaiah the king's servant, s, **2Ch 34:20** 559
Neco sent messengers to him, s, **2Ch 35:21** 559
and also *put it* in writing, s, **2Ch 36:22** 559
and also *put it* in writing, s: **Ezr 1:1** 559
s, "For He is good, for His **Ezr 3:11**
"Thus they answered us, s, **Ezr 5:11** 560
the princes approached me, s, **Ezr 9:1** 559
by Your servants the prophets, s, **Ezr 9:11** 559
commanded Your servant Moses, s, **Ne 1:8** 559
Geshem sent *a message* to me, s, **Ne 6:2** 559
So I sent messengers to them, s, **Ne 6:3** 559
Then I sent *a message* to him s, **Ne 6:8** 559
Such things as you are s have not **Ne 6:8** 559
Levites calmed all the people, s, **Ne 8:11** 559
their cities and in Jerusalem, s, **Ne 8:15** 559
contempt on their husbands by s, **Es 1:17** 559
s, 'I never saw you.' **Jb 8:18**
"He wanders about for food, s, **Jb 15:23**
"They make night into day, s, **Jb 17:12**
S, 'Truly our adversaries are **Jb 22:20**
waits for the twilight, S, **Jb 24:15** 559
against His Anointed, s, **Ps 2:2**
in His fury, s, **Ps 2:5**
Many are s of my soul, **Ps 3:2** 559
Many are s, "Who will show us *any* **Ps 4:6** 559
wag the head, s, **Ps 22:7**
devise my hurt, s, **Ps 41:7**
laugh at him, s, **Ps 52:6**
They devise injustices, s, **Ps 64:6**
S, "God has forsaken him; **Ps 71:11** 559
S, "To you I will give the land **Ps 105:11** 559
s, "Rule in the midst of Your **Ps 110:2**
s, "Sing us one of the songs of **Ps 137:3**
he praises her, s: **Pr 31:28**
they praised her, s, **SS 6:9**
s, "You have a cloak, you **Is 3:6**
He will protest on that day, s, **Is 3:7** 559
hold of one man in that day, s, **Is 4:1** 559
I heard the voice of the Lord, s, **Is 6:8** 559
reported to the house of David, s, **Is 7:2** 559
has planned evil against you, s, **Is 7:5** 559
the LORD spoke again to Ahaz, s, **Is 7:10** 559
the LORD spoke to me further, s, **Is 8:5** 559

walk in the way of this people, s, **Is 8:11** 559
They have gone through the pass, s, **Is 10:29**
s, 'Since you were laid low, **Is 14:8**
s, 'Is this the man who made **Is 14:16**
The LORD of hosts has sworn s, **Is 14:24** 559
But now the LORD speaks, s, **Is 16:14** 559
the LORD of hosts has blessed, s, **Is 19:25** 559
through Isaiah the son of Amoz, s, **Is 20:2** 559
the stronghold of the sea, s, **Is 23:4** 559
it to the one who is literate, s, **Is 29:11** 559
to the one who is illiterate, s, **Is 29:12** 559
make you trust in the LORD, s, **Is 36:15** 559
that Hezekiah does not mislead you, s, **Is 36:18** 559
he sent messengers to Hezekiah, s, **Is 37:9** 559
in whom you trust deceive you, s, **Is 37:10** 559
Hezekiah prayed to the LORD s, **Is 37:15** 559
of Amoz sent *word* to Hezekiah, s, **Is 37:21** 559
of the LORD came to Isaiah, s, **Is 38:4** 559
the anvil, S of the soldering, **Is 41:7** 559
which have not been done, S, **Is 46:10** 559
S to those who are bound, **Is 49:9** 559
the word of the LORD came to me s, **Jer 1:4** 559
The word of the LORD came to me s, **Jer 1:11** 559
LORD came to me a second time s, **Jer 1:13** 559
the word of the LORD came to me s, **Jer 2:1** 559
in the ears of Jerusalem, s, **Jer 2:2** 559
this people and Jerusalem, s, **Jer 4:10** 559
s, "Ah, woe is me, for I **Jer 4:31**
Jacob And proclaim it in Judah, s, **Jer 5:20** 559
of My people superficially, S, **Jer 6:14** 559
"And I set watchmen over you, s, **Jer 6:17**
came to Jeremiah from the LORD, s, **Jer 7:1** 559
not trust in deceptive words, s, **Jer 7:4** 559
this is what I commanded them, s, **Jer 7:23** 559
man repented of his wickedness, S, **Jer 8:6** 559
of My people superficially, S, **Jer 8:11** 559
came to Jeremiah from the LORD, s, **Jer 11:1** 559
Egypt, from the iron furnace, s, **Jer 11:4** 559
in the streets of Jerusalem, s, **Jer 11:6** 559
this day, warning persistently, s, **Jer 11:7** 559
s, "Let us destroy the tree **Jer 11:19**
Anathoth, who seek your life, s, **Jer 11:21** 559
LORD came to me a second time, s, **Jer 13:3** 559
word of the LORD came to me, s, **Jer 13:8** 559
they keep s, 'There will be no sword **Jer 14:15** 559
of the LORD also came to me s, **Jer 16:1** 559
Look, they keep s to me, **Jer 17:15** 559
came to Jeremiah from the LORD s, **Jer 18:1** 559
the word of the LORD came to me s, **Jer 18:5** 559
the inhabitants of Jerusalem s, **Jer 18:11** 559
listen to what my opponents are s! **Jer 18:19** 6963
brought the news To my father, s, **Jer 20:15** 559
priest, the son of Maaseiah, s, **Jer 21:1** 559
keep s to those who despise Me, **Jer 23:17** 559
prophesy falsely in My name, s, **Jer 23:25** 559
prophet or a priest asks you s, **Jer 23:33** 559
I have also sent to you, s, **Jer 23:38** 559
word of the LORD came to me, s, **Jer 24:4** 559
the inhabitants of Jerusalem, s, **Jer 25:2** 559
s, 'Turn now everyone from his **Jer 25:5** 559
this word came from the LORD, s, **Jer 26:1** 559
and all the people seized him, s, **Jer 26:8** 559
in the name of the LORD s, **Jer 26:9** 559
and to all the people, s, **Jer 26:11** 559
and to all the people, s, **Jer 26:12** 559
all the assembly of the people, s, **Jer 26:17** 559
to all the people of Judah, s, **Jer 26:18** 559
came to Jeremiah from the LORD, s **Jer 27:1** 559
them *to go* to their masters, s, **Jer 27:4** 559
sorcerers who speak to you, s, **Jer 27:9** 559
to Zedekiah king of Judah, s, **Jer 27:12** 559
the prophets who speak to you, s, **Jer 27:14** 559
priests and to all this people, s, **Jer 27:16** 559
prophets who prophesy to you, s, **Jer 27:16** 559
the priests and all the people, s, **Jer 28:1** 559
the presence of all the people, s, **Jer 28:11** 559
neck of the prophet Jeremiah, s, **Jer 28:12** 559
"Go and speak to Hananiah, s, **Jer 28:13** 559
Nebuchadnezzar king of Babylon, s, **Jer 29:3** 559
from Judah who are in Babylon, s, **Jer 29:22** 559
the Nehelamite you shall speak, s, **Jer 29:24** 559
priest, and to all the priests, s, **Jer 29:25** 559
he has sent to us in Babylon, s, **Jer 29:28** 559
word of the LORD to Jeremiah, s, **Jer 29:30** 559
"Send to all the exiles, s, **Jer 29:31** 559
came to Jeremiah from the LORD, s, **Jer 30:1** 559
have called you an outcast, s: **Jer 30:17**
s, "I have loved you with an **Jer 31:3**
and each man his brother, s, **Jer 31:34** 559
king of Judah had shut him up, s, **Jer 32:3** 559
"Why do you prophesy, s, **Jer 32:3** 559
word of the LORD came to me, s, **Jer 32:6** 559
your uncle is coming to you, s, **Jer 32:7** 559
Baruch in their presence, s, **Jer 32:13** 559
then I prayed to the LORD, s, **Jer 32:16** 559
of the LORD came to Jeremiah, s, **Jer 32:26** 559
in the court of the guard, s, **Jer 33:1** 559
of the LORD came to Jeremiah, s, **Jer 33:19** 559
of the LORD came to Jeremiah, s, **Jer 33:23** 559
what this people have spoken, s, **Jer 33:24** 559
and against all its cities, s, **Jer 34:1** 559
came to Jeremiah from the LORD, s, **Jer 34:12** 559
from the house of bondage, s, **Jer 34:13** 559
son of Josiah, king of Judah, s, **Jer 35:1** 559
our father, commanded us, s, **Jer 35:6** 559
of the LORD came to Jeremiah, s, **Jer 35:12** 559
sending *them* again and again, s: **Jer 35:15** 559
came to Jeremiah from the LORD, s, **Jer 36:1** 559
Jeremiah commanded Baruch, s, **Jer 36:5** 559

the son of Cushi, to Baruch, **s**, | Jer 36:14 | 559
And they asked Baruch, **s**, | Jer 36:17 | 559
at the dictation of Jeremiah, **s**, | Jer 36:27 | 559
"You have burned this scroll, **s**, | Jer 36:29 | 559
to Jeremiah the prophet, **s**, | Jer 37:3 | 559
came to Jeremiah the prophet, **s**, | Jer 37:6 | 559
'Do not deceive yourselves, **s**, | Jer 37:9 | 559
arrested Jeremiah the prophet, **s**, | Jer 37:13 | 559
prophets who prophesied to you, **s**, | Jer 37:19 | 559
was speaking to all the people, **s**, | Jer 38:1 | 559
palace and spoke to the king, **s**, | Jer 38:8 | 559
Ebed-melech the Ethiopian, **s**, | Jer 38:10 | 559
swore to Jeremiah in secret **s**, | Jer 38:16 | 559
the LORD in what I am **s** to you, | Jer 38:20 | 1696
the captain of the bodyguard, **s**, | Jer 39:11 | 559
in the court of the guardhouse, **s**, | Jer 39:15 | 559
to Ebed-melech the Ethiopian, **s**, | Jer 39:16 | 559
swore to them and to their men, **s**, | Jer 40:9 | 559
secretly to Gedaliah in Mizpah, **s**, | Jer 40:15 | 559
s, "No, but we will go to the | Jer 42:14 | 559
sent me to the LORD your God, **s**, | Jer 42:20 | 559
came to Jeremiah in Tahpanhes, **s**, | Jer 43:8 | 559
and the land of Pathros, **s**, | Jer 44:1 | 559
the prophets, again and again, **s**, | Jer 44:4 | 559
Egypt, responded to Jeremiah, **s**, | Jer 44:15 | 559
were giving him *such* an answer—**s**, | Jer 44:20 | 559
fulfilled *it* with your hands, **s**, | Jer 44:25 | 559
Judah in all the land of Egypt, **s**, | Jer 44:26 | 559
son of Josiah, king of Judah, **s**: | Jer 45:1 | 559
s, 'Who will come against me?' | Jer 49:4
s, "Gather yourselves together | Jer 49:14
of Zedekiah king of Judah, **s**: | Jer 49:34 | 559
word of the LORD came to me, **s**, | Ezk 3:16 | 559
the word of the LORD came to me **s**, | Ezk 6:1 | 559
the word of the LORD came to me **s**, | Ezk 7:1 | 559
in my hearing with a loud voice **s**, | Ezk 9:1 | 559
I fell on my face and cried out **s**, | Ezk 9:8 | 559
was the writing case reported, **s**, | Ezk 9:11 | 559
the man clothed in linen, **s**, | Ezk 10:6 | 559
word of the LORD came to me, **s**, | Ezk 11:14 | 559
came to me, **s**, | Ezk 12:1 | 559
word of the LORD came to me, **s**, | Ezk 12:8 | 559
the word of the LORD came to me **s**, | Ezk 12:17 | 559
came to me, **s**, | Ezk 12:21 | 559
concerning the land of Israel, **s**, | Ezk 12:22 | 559
came to me, **s**, | Ezk 12:26 | 559
behold, the house of Israel is **s**, | Ezk 12:27 | 559
the word of the LORD came to me **s**, | Ezk 13:1 | 559
and lying divination who are **s**, | Ezk 13:6 | 559
they have misled My people by **s**, | Ezk 13:10 | 559
came to me, **s**, | Ezk 14:2 | 559
the word of the LORD came to me **s**, | Ezk 14:12 | 559
came to me, **s**, | Ezk 15:1 | 559
came to me, **s**, | Ezk 16:1 | 559
this proverb concerning you, **s**, | Ezk 16:44 | 559
the word of the LORD came to me **s**, | Ezk 17:1 | 559
s, 'Thus says the Lord GOD, | Ezk 17:3 | 559
came to me, **s**, | Ezk 17:11 | 559
came to me, **s**, | Ezk 18:1 | 559
s, 'The fathers eat the sour grapes, | Ezk 18:2 | 559
the word of the LORD came to me **s**, | Ezk 20:2 | 559
of Egypt, when I swore to them, **s**, | Ezk 20:5 | 559
came to me, **s**, | Ezk 20:45 | 559
They are **s** of me, | Ezk 20:49 | 559
the word of the LORD came to me **s**, | Ezk 21:1 | 559
came to me, **s**, | Ezk 21:8 | 559
The word of the LORD came to me **s**, | Ezk 21:18 | 559
came to me, **s**, | Ezk 22:1 | 559
came to me, **s**, | Ezk 22:17 | 559
came to me, **s**, | Ezk 22:23 | 559
and divining lies for them, **s**, | Ezk 22:28 | 559
to me again, **s**, | Ezk 23:1 | 559
on the tenth of the month, **s**, | Ezk 24:1 | 559
the word of the LORD came to me **s**, | Ezk 24:15 | 559
"The word of the LORD came to me **s**, | Ezk 24:20 | 559
the word of the LORD came to me **s**, | Ezk 25:1 | 559
the word of the LORD came to me **s**, | Ezk 26:1 | 559
the word of the LORD came to me **s**, | Ezk 27:1 | 559
again to me, **s**, | Ezk 28:1 | 559
the word of the LORD came to me **s**, | Ezk 28:11 | 559
the word of the LORD came to me **s**, | Ezk 28:20 | 559
the word of the LORD came to me **s**, | Ezk 29:1 | 559
the word of the LORD came to me **s**, | Ezk 29:17 | 559
of the LORD came again to me **s**, | Ezk 30:1 | 559
the word of the LORD came to me **s**, | Ezk 30:20 | 559
the word of the LORD came to me **s**, | Ezk 31:1 | 559
the word of the LORD came to me **s**, | Ezk 32:1 | 559
the word of the LORD came to me **s**, | Ezk 32:17 | 559
came to me, **s**, | Ezk 33:1 | 559
'Thus you have spoken, **s**, | Ezk 33:10 | 559
from Jerusalem came to me, **s**, | Ezk 33:21 | 559
the word of the LORD came to me **s**, | Ezk 33:23 | 559
in the land of Israel are **s**, | Ezk 33:24 | 559
another, each to his brother, **s**, | Ezk 33:30 | 559
the word of the LORD came to me **s**, | Ezk 34:1 | 559
the word of the LORD came to me **s**, | Ezk 35:1 | 559
against the mountains of Israel **s**, | Ezk 35:12 | 559
the word of the LORD came to me **s**, | Ezk 36:16 | 559
of the LORD came again to me **s**, | Ezk 37:15 | 559
of your people speak to you **s**, | Ezk 37:18 | 559
the word of the LORD came to me **s**, | Ezk 38:1 | 559
dream to him, **s**, | Da 4:8
one, descending from heaven and **s**, | Da 4:23 | 560
s, 'King Nebuchadnezzar, to | Da 4:31
rejected your calf, O Samaria, **s**, | Hos 8:5
And you commanded the prophets **s**, | Am 2:12 | 559
to Jeroboam king of Israel, **s**, | Am 7:10 | 559
you are **s**, 'You shall not prophesy | Am 7:16 | 559
s, "When will the new moon be | Am 8:5 | 559

has been sent among the nations **s**, | Ob 1:1
to Jonah the son of Amittai **s**, | Jon 1:1 | 559
came to Jonah the second time, **s**, | Jon 3:1 | 559
with *all* his soul to die, **s**, | Jon 4:8 | 559
Yet they lean on the LORD **s**, | Mi 3:11 | 559
Hear now what the LORD is **s**, | Mi 6:1 | 559
the high priest, **s**, | Hg 1:1 | 559
Haggai the prophet, **s**, | Hg 1:3 | 559
of the LORD to the people **s**, | Hg 1:13 | 559
LORD came by Haggai the prophet **s**, | Hg 2:1 | 559
to the remnant of the people **s**, | Hg 2:2 | 559
Haggai the prophet, **s**, | Hg 2:10 | 559
of the month, **s**, | Hg 2:20 | 559
s, 'I am going to shake the heavens | Hg 2:21 | 559
of Berechiah, the son of Iddo **s**, | Zch 1:1 | 559
the former prophets proclaimed, **s**, | Zch 1:4 | 559
"Proclaim, **s**, 'Thus says the LORD | Zch 1:14 | 559
"Again, proclaim, **s**, | Zch 1:17 | 559
"Run, speak to that young man, **s**, | Zch 2:4 | 559
s, "Remove the filthy garments from | Zch 3:4 | 559
admonished Joshua , **s**, | Zch 3:6 | 559
angel who was speaking with me **s**, | Zch 4:4 | 559
word of the LORD to Zerubbabel **s**, | Zch 4:6 | 559
came to me, **s**, | Zch 4:8 | 559
So he answered me, **s**, "Do you not | Zch 4:13 | 559
cried out to me and spoke to me **s**, | Zch 6:8 | 559
came to me, **s**, | Zch 6:9 | 559
s, "Shall I weep in the fifth month | Zch 7:3 | 559
came to me, **s**, | Zch 7:4 | 559
of the LORD came to Zechariah **s**, | Zch 7:8 | 559
of hosts came, **s**, | Zch 8:1 | 559
came to me, **s**, | Zch 8:18 | 559
s, "Let us go at once to entreat | Zch 8:21 | 559
s, "Let us go with you, for we | Zch 8:23 | 559
Lord appeared to him in a dream, **s**, | Mt 1:20 | *3004*
the east arrived in Jerusalem, **s**, | Mt 2:1 | *3004*
in the wilderness of Judea, **s**, | Mt 3:1 | *3004*
But John tried to prevent Him, **s**, | Mt 3:14 | *3004*
mouth and *began* to teach them, **s**, | Mt 5:2 | *3004*
"Do not worry then, **s**, | Mt 6:31 | *3004*
out His hand and touched him, **s**, | Mt 8:3 | *3004*
and **s**, "Lord, my servant is lying | Mt 8:6 | *3004*
came to *Him* and woke Him, **s**, | Mt 8:25 | *3004*
And they cried out, **s**, | Mt 8:29 | *3004*
demons *began* to entreat Him, **s**, | Mt 8:31 | *3004*
He was **s** these things to them, | Mt 9:18 | *2980*
for she was **s** to herself, | Mt 9:21 | *3004*
Then He touched their eyes, **s**, | Mt 9:29 | *3004*
crowds were amazed, *and were* **s**, | Mt 9:33 | *3004*
But the Pharisees were **s**, | Mt 9:34 | *3004*
"And as you go, preach, **s**, | Mt 10:7 | *3004*
and were **s**, "This man cannot be | Mt 12:23 | *3004*
things to them in parables, **s**, | Mt 13:3 | *3004*
another parable to them, **s**, | Mt 13:24 | *3004*
another parable to them, **s**, | Mt 13:31 | *3004*
For John had been **s** to him, | Mt 14:4 | *3004*
Jesus spoke to them, **s**, | Mt 14:27 | *3004*
were in the boat worshiped Him, **s**, | Mt 14:33 | *3004*
region came out and *began* to cry out, **s**, | Mt 15:22 | *3004*
and implored Him, **s**, | Mt 15:23 | *3004*
began to bow down before Him, **s**, | Mt 15:25 | *3004*
to discuss *this* among themselves, **s**, | Mt 16:7 | *3004*
aside and began to rebuke Him, **s**, | Mt 16:22 | *3004*
mountain, Jesus commanded them, **s**, | Mt 17:9 | *3004*
on his knees before Him and **s**, | Mt 17:14 | *3004*
Jesus spoke to him first, **s**, | Mt 17:25 | *3004*
prostrated himself before him, **s**, | Mt 18:26 | *3004*
him and *began* to choke *him*, **s**, | Mt 18:28 | *3004*
and *began* to plead with him, **s**, | Mt 18:29 | *3004*
s, 'These last men have worked | Mt 20:12 | *3004*
s to them, "Go into the village | Mt 21:2 | *3004*
all the city was stirred, **s**, | Mt 21:10 | *3004*
And the crowds were **s**, | Mt 21:11 | *3004*
hear what these *children* are **s**?" | Mt 21:16 | *3004*
reasoning among themselves, **s**, | Mt 21:25 | *3004*
he sent his son to them, **s**, | Mt 21:37 | *3004*
to them again in parables, **s**, | Mt 22:1 | *3004*
"Again he sent out other slaves **s**, | Mt 22:4 | *3004*
Him, along with the Herodians, **s**, | Mt 22:16 | *3004*
David in the Spirit call Him 'Lord,' **s**, | Mt 22:43 | *3004*
s: "The scribes and the Pharisees | Mt 23:2 | *3004*
came to Him privately, **s**, | Mt 24:3 | *3004*
"For many will come in My name, **s**, | Mt 24:5 | *3004*
the other virgins also came, **s**, | Mt 25:11 | *3004*
and brought five more talents, **s**, | Mt 25:20 | *3004*
But they were **s**, | Mt 26:5 | *3004*
thanks, He gave *it* to them, **s**, | Mt 26:27 | *3004*
fell on His face and prayed, **s**, | Mt 26:39 | *3004*
again a second time and prayed, **s**, | Mt 26:42 | *3004*
time, **s** the same thing once more. | Mt 26:44 | *3004*
betraying Him gave them a sign, **s**, | Mt 26:48 | *3004*
he denied *it* before them all, **s**, | Mt 26:70 | *3004*
s, "I have sinned by betraying | Mt 27:4 | *3004*
the governor questioned Him, **s**, | Mt 27:11 | *3004*
seat, his wife sent him *a message*, **s**, | Mt 27:19 | *3004*
kept shouting all the more, **s**, | Mt 27:23 | *3004*
in front of the crowd, **s**, | Mt 27:24 | *3004*
down before Him and mocked Him, **s**, | Mt 27:29 | *3004*
s, "You who *are going to* destroy | Mt 27:40 | *3004*
elders, were mocking *Him* and **s**, | Mt 27:41 | *3004*
cried out with a loud voice, **s**, | Mt 27:46 | *3004*
when they heard it, *began* **s**, | Mt 27:47 | *3004*
came up and spoke to them, **s**, | Mt 28:18 | *3004*
And he was preaching, and **s**, | Mk 1:7 | *3004*
and **s**, "The time is fulfilled, | Mk 1:15 | *3004*
s, "What business do we have with | Mk 1:24 | *3004*
And Jesus rebuked him, **s**, | Mk 1:25 | *3004*
they debated among themselves, **s**, | Mk 1:27 | *3004*
knees before Him, and **s**, | Mk 1:40 | *3004*

amazed and were glorifying God, **s**, | Mk 2:12 | *3004*
The Pharisees were **s** to Him, | Mk 2:24 | *3004*
for they were **s**, | Mk 3:21 | *3004*
came down from Jerusalem were **s**, | Mk 3:22 | *3004*
because they were **s**, | Mk 3:30 | *3004*
and was **s** to them in His teaching, | Mk 4:2 | *3004*
He was **s**, "He who has ears to hear, | Mk 4:9 | *3004*
And He was **s** to them, | Mk 4:11 | *3004*
And He was **s** to them, | Mk 4:21 | *3004*
And He was **s** to them, | Mk 4:24 | *3004*
He was **s**, "The kingdom of God is | Mk 4:26 | *3004*
For He had been **s** to him, | Mk 5:8 | *3004*
The demons implored Him, **s**, | Mk 5:12 | *3004*
and implored Him earnestly, **s**, | Mk 5:23 | *3004*
of the synagogue official, **s**, | Mk 5:35 | *3004*
many listeners were astonished, **s**, | Mk 6:2 | *3004*
and *people* were **s**, | Mk 6:14 | *3004*
But others were **s**, | Mk 6:15 | *3004*
And others were **s**, | Mk 6:15 | *3004*
when Herod heard *of it*, he kept **s**, | Mk 6:16 | *3004*
For John had been **s** to Herod, | Mk 6:18 | *3004*
to the king and asked, **s**, | Mk 6:25 | *3004*
He was also **s** to them, | Mk 7:9
to Him again, He *began* **s** to them, | Mk 7:14 | *3004*
He was **s**, "That which proceeds out | Mk 7:20 | *3004*
And He was **s** to her, | Mk 7:27 | *3004*
They were utterly astonished, **s**, | Mk 7:37 | *3004*
He was giving orders to them, **s**, | Mk 8:15 | *3004*
And He was **s** to them, | Mk 8:21 | *3004*
And He sent him to his home, **s**, | Mk 8:26 | *3004*
His disciples, **s** to them, | Mk 8:27 | *3004*
They told Him, **s**, | Mk 8:28 | *3004*
And Jesus was **s** to them, | Mk 9:1 | *3004*
They asked Him, **s**, | Mk 9:11 | *3004*
the unclean spirit, **s** to it, | Mk 9:25 | *3004*
s, "Behold, we are going up to | Mk 10:33
Zebedee, came up to Jesus, **s**, | Mk 10:35 | *3004*
called the blind man, **s** to him, | Mk 10:49 | *3004*
of the bystanders were **s** to them, | Mk 11:5 | *3004*
And Jesus answered **s** to them, | Mk 11:22 | *3004*
and *began* **s** to Him, | Mk 11:28 | *3004*
reasoning among themselves, **s**, | Mk 11:31 | *3004*
sent him last *of all* to them, **s**, | Mk 12:6 | *3004*
Jesus, and *began* questioning Him, **s**, | Mk 12:18 | *3004*
bush, how God spoke to him, **s**, | Mk 12:26 | *3004*
In His teaching He was **s**: | Mk 12:38 | *3004*
"Many will come in My name, **s**, | Mk 13:6 | *3004*
for they were **s**, | Mk 14:2 | *3004*
But *Peter* kept **s** insistently, | Mk 14:31 | *2980*
they all were **s** the same thing also | Mk 14:31 | *3004*
And He was **s**, "Abba! Father! | Mk 14:36 | *3004*
away and prayed, **s** the same words. | Mk 14:39 | *3004*
Him had given them a signal, **s**, | Mk 14:44 | *3004*
Judas immediately went to Him, **s**, | Mk 14:45 | *3004*
false testimony against Him, **s**, | Mk 14:57 | *3004*
forward and questioned Jesus, **s**, | Mk 14:60 | *3004*
was questioning Him, and **s** to Him, | Mk 14:61 | *3004*
But he denied *it*, **s**, | Mk 14:68 | *3004*
bystanders were again **s** to Peter, | Mk 14:70 | *3004*
Pilate questioned Him again, **s**, | Mk 15:4 | *3004*
Pilate answered them, **s**, | Mk 15:9 | *3004*
Him, wagging their heads, and **s**, | Mk 15:29 | *3004*
Him among themselves and **s**, | Mk 15:31 | *3004*
bystanders heard it, they *began* **s**, | Mk 15:35 | *3004*
a reed, and gave Him a drink, **s**, | Mk 15:36 | *3004*
They were **s** to one another, | Mk 16:3 | *3004*
in seclusion for five months, **s**, | Lk 1:24 | *3004*
heard them kept them in mind, **s**, | Lk 1:66 | *3004*
Holy Spirit, and prophesied, **s**: | Lk 1:67 | *3004*
heavenly host praising God and **s**, | Lk 2:13 | *3004*
shepherds *began* **s** to one another, | Lk 2:15 | *2980*
So he *began* **s** to the | Lk 3:7 | *3004*
were questioning him, **s**, | Lk 3:10 | *3004*
soldiers were questioning him, **s**, | Lk 3:14 | *3004*
and they were **s**, | Lk 4:22 | *3004*
But Jesus rebuked him, **s**, | Lk 4:35 | *3004*
talking with one another **s**, | Lk 4:36 | *3004*
he fell down at Jesus' feet, **s**, | Lk 5:8 | *3004*
on his face and implored Him, **s**, | Lk 5:12 | *3004*
out His hand and touched him, **s**, | Lk 5:13 | *3004*
the Pharisees began to reason, **s**, | Lk 5:21 | *3004*
and they were filled with fear, **s**, | Lk 5:26 | *3004*
grumbling at His disciples, **s**, | Lk 5:30 | *3004*
And He was **s** to them, | Lk 6:5 | *3004*
they earnestly implored Him, **s**, | Lk 7:4 | *3004*
centurion sent friends, **s** to Him, | Lk 7:6 | *3004*
and they *began* glorifying God, **s**, | Lk 7:16 | *3004*
John sent them to the Lord, **s**, | Lk 7:19 | *3004*
came to Jesus and woke Him up, **s**, | Lk 8:24 | *3004*
and amazed, **s** to one another, | Lk 8:25 | *3004*
but He sent him away, **s**, | Lk 8:38 | *3004*
of the synagogue official, **s**, | Lk 8:49 | *3004*
her by the hand and called, **s**, | Lk 8:54 | *3004*
Him, and He questioned them, **s**, | Lk 9:18 | *3004*
s, "The Son of Man must suffer | Lk 9:22 | *3004*
And He was **s** to *them* all, | Lk 9:23 | *3004*
not realizing what he was **s**. | Lk 9:33 | *3004*
While he was **s** this, | Lk 9:34 | *3004*
a voice came out of the cloud, **s**, | Lk 9:35 | *3004*
from the crowd shouted, **s**, | Lk 9:38 | *3004*
And He was **s** to them, | Lk 10:2 | *3004*
The seventy returned with joy, **s**, | Lk 10:17 | *3004*
up and put Him to the test, **s**, | Lk 10:25 | *3004*
While Jesus was **s** these things, one | Lk 11:27 | *3004*
s to His disciples first *of all*, | Lk 12:1 | *3004*
And He told them a parable, **s**, | Lk 12:16 | *3004*
he began reasoning to himself, **s**, | Lk 12:17 | *3004*
He was also **s** to the crowds, | Lk 12:54 | *3004*
s to the crowd in response, | Lk 13:14 | *3004*

So He was **s**,	**Lk 13:18**	*3004*
outside and knock on the door, **s**,	**Lk 13:25**	*3004*
some Pharisees approached, **s** to Him,	**Lk 13:31**	*3004*
to the lawyers and Pharisees, **s**,	**Lk 14:3**	*3004*
at the table, **s** to them,	**Lk 14:7**	*3004*
s, 'This man began to build and	**Lk 14:30**	*3004*
the scribes *began* to grumble, **s**,	**Lk 15:2**	*3004*
So He told them this parable, **s**,	**Lk 15:3**	*3004*
and his neighbors, **s** to them,	**Lk 15:6**	*3004*
her friends and neighbors, **s**,	**Lk 15:9**	*3004*
He was also **s** to the disciples,	**Lk 16:1**	*3004*
and he *began* **s** to the first,	**Lk 16:5**	*3004*
and returns to you seven times, **s**,	**Lk 17:4**	*3004*
and they raised their voices, **s**,	**Lk 17:13**	*3004*
s, "In a certain city there was a	**Lk 18:2**	*3004*
and she kept coming to him, **s**,	**Lk 18:3**	*3004*
but was beating his breast, **s**,	**Lk 18:13**	*3004*
But Jesus called for them, **s**,	**Lk 18:16**	*3004*
A ruler questioned Him, **s**,	**Lk 18:18**	*3004*
And he called out, **s**,	**Lk 18:38**	*3004*
it, they all *began* to grumble, **s**,	**Lk 19:7**	*3004*
sent a delegation after him, **s**,	**Lk 19:14**	*3004*
"The first appeared, **s**,	**Lk 19:16**	*3004*
"The second came, **s**,	**Lk 19:18**	*3004*
"Another came, **s**,	**Lk 19:20**	*3004*
s, "Go into the village ahead	**Lk 19:30**	*3004*
s, "If you had known in this day,	**Lk 19:42**	*3004*
s to them, "It is written,	**Lk 19:46**	*3004*
and they spoke, **s** to Him,	**Lk 20:2**	*3004*
They reasoned among themselves, **s**,	**Lk 20:5**	*3004*
they reasoned with one another, **s**,	**Lk 20:14**	*3004*
They questioned Him, **s**,	**Lk 20:21**	*3004*
a **s** in the presence of the people;	**Lk 20:26**	*4487*
and they questioned Him, **s**,	**Lk 20:28**	*3004*
They questioned Him, **s**,	**Lk 21:7**	*3004*
for many will come in My name, **s**,	**Lk 21:8**	*3004*
Then He continued by **s** to them,	**Lk 21:10**	*3004*
And Jesus sent Peter and John, **s**,	**Lk 22:8**	*3004*
broke it and gave it to them, **s**,	**Lk 22:19**	*3004*
the cup after they had eaten, **s**,	**Lk 22:20**	*3004*
s, "Father, if You are willing,	**Lk 22:42**	*3004*
But he denied *it,* **s**,	**Lk 22:57**	*3004*
another man *began* to insist, **s**,	**Lk 22:59**	*3004*
Him and were asking Him, **s**,	**Lk 22:64**	*3004*
s many other things against Him,	**Lk 22:65**	*3004*
away to their council *chamber,* **s**,	**Lk 22:66**	*3004*
And they began to accuse Him, **s**,	**Lk 23:2**	*3004*
and **s** that He Himself is Christ,	**Lk 23:2**	*3004*
So Pilate asked Him, **s**,	**Lk 23:3**	*3004*
But they kept on insisting, **s**,	**Lk 23:5**	*3004*
they cried out all together, **s**,	**Lk 23:18**	*3004*
but they kept on calling out, **s**,	**Lk 23:21**	*3004*
But Jesus was **s**,	**Lk 23:34**	*3004*
rulers were sneering at Him, **s**,	**Lk 23:35**	*3004*
s, "If You are the King of the Jews,	**Lk 23:37**	*3004*
there was hurling abuse at Him, **s**,	**Lk 23:39**	*3004*
And he was **s**, "Jesus, remember me	**Lk 23:42**	*3004*
he *began* praising God, **s**,	**Lk 23:47**	*3004*
s that the Son of Man must be	**Lk 24:7**	*3004*
s that they had also seen a vision	**Lk 24:23**	*3004*
But they urged Him, **s**,	**Lk 24:29**	*3004*
s, "The Lord has really risen and	**Lk 24:34**	*3004*
testified about Him and cried out, **s**,	**Jn 1:15**	*3004*
John answered them **s**,	**Jn 1:26**	*3004*
John testified **s**,	**Jn 1:32**	*3004*
disciples were urging Him, **s**,	**Jn 4:31**	*3004*
disciples were **s** to one another,	**Jn 4:33**	*3004*
"For in this *case* the **s** is true,	**Jn 4:37**	*3056*
and they were **s** to the woman,	**Jn 4:42**	*3004*
him, **s** that his son was living.	**Jn 4:51**	*3004*
were **s** to the man who was cured,	**Jn 5:10**	*3004*
answered and was **s** to them,	**Jn 5:19**	*3004*
This He was **s** to test him,	**Jn 6:6**	*3004*
They were **s**,	**Jn 6:42**	*3004*
to argue with one another, **s**,	**Jn 6:52**	*3004*
He was **s**, "For this reason I have	**Jn 6:65**	*3004*
Him at the feast and were **s**,	**Jn 7:11**	*3004*
some were **s**, "He is a good man";	**Jn 7:12**	*3004*
others were **s**, "No, on the contrary,	**Jn 7:12**	*3004*
Jews then were astonished, **s**,	**Jn 7:15**	*3004*
of the people of Jerusalem were **s**,	**Jn 7:25**	*3004*
and they are **s** nothing to Him.	**Jn 7:26**	*3004*
out in the temple, teaching and **s**,	**Jn 7:28**	*3004*
and they were **s**,	**Jn 7:31**	*3004*
Jesus stood and cried out, **s**,	**Jn 7:37**	*3004*
they heard these words, were **s**,	**Jn 7:40**	*3004*
Others were **s**, "This is the Christ."	**Jn 7:41**	*3004*
Still others were **s**,	**Jn 7:41**	*3004*
They were **s** this, testing Him,	**Jn 8:6**	*3004*
Then Jesus again spoke to them, **s**,	**Jn 8:12**	*3004*
So they were **s** to Him,	**Jn 8:19**	*3004*
So the Jews were **s**,	**Jn 8:22**	*3004*
And He was **s** to them,	**Jn 8:23**	*3004*
So they were **s** to Him,	**Jn 8:25**	*3004*
"What have I been **s** to you *from*	**Jn 8:25**	*2980*
Jesus was **s** to those	**Jn 8:31**	*3004*
do you not understand what I am **s**?	**Jn 8:43**	*2981*
saw him as a beggar, were **s**,	**Jn 9:8**	*3004*
Others were **s**, "This is he,"	**Jn 9:9**	*3004*
"This is he," *still* others were **s**,	**Jn 9:9**	*3004*
He kept **s**, "I am the one."	**Jn 9:9**	*3004*
So they were **s** to him,	**Jn 9:10**	*3004*
some of the Pharisees were **s**,	**Jn 9:16**	*3004*
But others were **s**,	**Jn 9:16**	*3004*
and questioned them, **s**,	**Jn 9:19**	*3004*
were which He had been **s** to them.	**Jn 10:6**	*2980*
Many of them were **s**,	**Jn 10:20**	*3004*
Others were **s**, "These are not the	**Jn 10:21**	*3004*
around Him, and were **s** to Him,	**Jn 10:24**	*3004*
Many came to Him and were **s**,	**Jn 10:41**	*3004*
sisters sent *word* to Him, **s**,	**Jn 11:3**	*3004*
Mary her sister, **s** secretly,	**Jn 11:28**	*3004*
and fell at His feet, **s** to Him,	**Jn 11:32**	*3004*
So the Jews were **s**,	**Jn 11:36**	*3004*
convened a council, and were **s**,	**Jn 11:47**	*3004*
Jesus, and were **s** to one another as	**Jn 11:56**	*3004*
Galilee, and *began to* ask him, **s**,	**Jn 12:21**	*3004*
And Jesus answered them, **s**,	**Jn 12:23**	*3004*
it were **s** that it had thundered;	**Jn 12:29**	*3004*
others were **s**, "An angel has spoken	**Jn 12:29**	*3004*
But He was **s** this to indicate the	**Jn 12:33**	*3004*
box, that Jesus was **s** to him,	**Jn 13:29**	*3004*
So they were **s**,	**Jn 16:18**	*3004*
standing nearby struck Jesus, **s**,	**Jn 18:22**	*3004*
you **s** this on your own initiative,	**Jn 18:34**	*3004*
So they cried out again, **s**,	**Jn 18:40**	*3004*
saw Him, they cried out **s**,	**Jn 19:6**	*3004*
Him, but the Jews cried out **s**,	**Jn 19:12**	*3004*
the chief priests of the Jews were **s**	**Jn 19:21**	*3004*
disciples were **s** to him,	**Jn 20:25**	*3004*
Therefore this **s** went out among	**Jn 21:23**	*3056*
together, they were asking Him, **s**,	**Ac 1:6**	*3004*
They were amazed and astonished, **s**,	**Ac 2:7**	*3004*
perplexity, **s** to one another,	**Ac 2:12**	*3004*
But others were mocking and **s**,	**Ac 2:13**	*3004*
and kept on exhorting them, **s**,	**Ac 2:40**	*3004*
with your fathers, **s** to Abraham,	**Ac 3:25**	*3004*
s, "What shall we do with these	**Ac 4:16**	*3004*
s, "We found the prison house	**Ac 5:23**	*3004*
s, "We gave you strict orders not	**Ac 5:28**	*3004*
to reconcile them in peace, **s**,	**Ac 7:26**	*3004*
his neighbor pushed him away, **s**,	**Ac 7:27**	*3004*
"This Moses whom they disowned, **s**,	**Ac 7:35**	*3004*
S TO AARON, 'MAKE FOR US GODS	**Ac 7:40**	*3004*
were giving attention to him, **s**,	**Ac 8:10**	*3004*
s, "Give this authority to me as	**Ac 8:19**	*3004*
of the Lord spoke to Philip **s**,	**Ac 8:26**	*3004*
and heard a voice **s** to him,	**Ac 9:4**	*3004*
Jesus in the synagogues, **s**,	**Ac 9:20**	*3754*
to be amazed, and were **s**,	**Ac 9:21**	*3004*
But Peter raised him up, **s**,	**Ac 10:26**	*3004*
s, "You went to uncircumcised men	**Ac 11:3**	*3004*
to them in orderly sequence, **s**,	**Ac 11:4**	*3004*
"I also heard a voice **s** to me,	**Ac 11:7**	*3004*
standing in his house, and **s**,	**Ac 11:13**	*3004*
down and glorified God, **s**,	**Ac 11:18**	*3004*
Peter's side and woke him up, **s**,	**Ac 12:7**	*3004*
They kept **s**,	**Ac 12:15**	*3004*
officials sent to them, **s**,	**Ac 13:15**	*3004*
completing his course, he kept **s**,	**Ac 13:25**	*3004*
s in the Lycaonian language,	**Ac 14:11**	*3004*
s, "Men, why are you doing these	**Ac 14:15**	*3004*
Even **s** these things, with	**Ac 14:18**	*3004*
and **s**, "Through many	**Ac 14:22**	
who had believed stood up, **s**,	**Ac 15:5**	*3004*
speaking, James answered, **s**,	**Ac 15:13**	*3004*
and appealing to him, and **s**,	**Ac 16:9**	*3004*
been baptized, she urged us, **s**,	**Ac 16:15**	*3004*
and us, she kept crying out, **s**,	**Ac 16:17**	*3004*
cried out with a loud voice, **s**,	**Ac 16:28**	*3004*
magistrates sent their policemen, **s**,	**Ac 16:35**	*3004*
s, "The chief magistrates have	**Ac 16:36**	
and **s**, "This Jesus whom I am	**Ac 17:3**	
s that there is another king,	**Ac 17:7**	*3004*
Some were **s**,	**Ac 17:18**	*3004*
brought him to the Areopagus, **s**,	**Ac 17:19**	*3004*
s, "This man persuades men to	**Ac 18:13**	*3004*
but taking leave of them and **s**,	**Ac 18:21**	*3004*
the name of the Lord Jesus, **s**,	**Ac 19:13**	*3004*
through Macedonia and Achaia, **s**,	**Ac 19:21**	*3004*
s that gods made with hands are no	**Ac 19:26**	*3004*
rage, they *began* crying out, **s**,	**Ac 19:28**	*3004*
After **s** this he dismissed the	**Ac 19:41**	*3004*
s that bonds and afflictions await	**Ac 20:23**	*3004*
to them in the Hebrew dialect, **s**,	**Ac 21:40**	*3004*
ground and heard a voice **s** to me,	**Ac 22:7**	*3004*
and I saw Him **s** to me,	**Ac 22:18**	*3004*
to the commander and told him, **s**,	**Ac 22:26**	*3004*
up and *began* to argue heatedly, **s**,	**Ac 23:9**	*3004*
s that they would neither eat nor	**Ac 23:12**	*3004*
to accuse him, **s** *to the governor,*	**Ac 24:2**	*3004*
about the Way, put them off, **s**,	**Ac 24:22**	*3004*
Paul's case before the king, **s**,	**Ac 25:14**	*3004*
s to me in the Hebrew dialect,	**Ac 26:14**	*3004*
Paul was **s** this in his defense,	**Ac 26:24**	*626*
began talking to one another, **s**,	**Ac 26:31**	*3004*
s, 'Do not be afraid, Paul;	**Ac 27:24**	*3004*
them all to take some food, **s**,	**Ac 27:33**	*3004*
hand, they *began* **s** to one another,	**Ac 28:4**	*3004*
came together, he *began* **s** to them,	**Ac 28:17**	*3004*
s, 'GO TO THIS PEOPLE AND SAY	**Ac 28:26**	*3004*
it is summed up in this **s**,	**Ro 13:9**	*3056*
this, that each one of you is **s**,	**1Co 1:12**	*3004*
the cup also after supper, **s**,	**1Co 11:25**	*3004*
he does not know what you are **s**?	**1Co 14:16**	*3004*
come about the **s** that is written,	**1Co 15:54**	*3056*
that, as I was **s**, you may be	**2Co 9:3**	*3004*
What I am **s**, I am not saying as	**2Co 11:17**	*2980*
What I am saying, I am not **s** as	**2Co 11:17**	*2980*
s, "ALL THE NATIONS WILL BE	**Ga 3:8**	
What I am **s** is this:	**Ga 3:17**	*3004*
While they are **s**, "Peace and safety!	**1Th 5:3**	*3004*
not understand either what they are **s**	**1Tm 1:7**	*3004*
s that the resurrection has already	**2Tm 2:18**	*3004*
one has testified somewhere, **s**,	**Heb 2:6**	*3004*
s, "I WILL PROCLAIM YOUR NAME TO	**Heb 2:12**	*3004*
s through David after so long a	**Heb 4:7**	*3004*
s, "I WILL SURELY BLESS YOU AND	**Heb 6:14**	*3004*
AND EVERYONE HIS BROTHER, **S**,	**Heb 8:11**	*3004*
s, "THIS IS THE BLOOD OF THE	**Heb 9:20**	*3004*
s above, "SACRIFICES AND OFFERINGS	**Heb 10:8**	*3004*
also testifies to us; for after **s**,	**Heb 10:15**	*3004*
then, but now He has promised, **s**,	**Heb 12:26**	*3004*
and **s**, "Where is the promise of His	**2Pe 3:4**	*3004*
from Adam, prophesied, **s**,	**Jude 1:14**	*3004*
that they were **s** to you,	**Jude 1:18**	*3004*
s, "Write in a book what you see,	**Rv 1:11**	*3004*
He placed His right hand on me, **s**,	**Rv 1:17**	*3004*
their crowns before the throne, **s**,	**Rv 4:10**	*3004*
And they sang a new song, **s**,	**Rv 5:9**	*3004*
s with a loud voice,	**Rv 5:12**	*3004*
and all things in them, I heard **s**,	**Rv 5:13**	*3004*
the four living creatures kept **s**,	**Rv 5:14**	*3004*
s as with a voice of thunder,	**Rv 6:1**	*3004*
the second living creature **s**,	**Rv 6:3**	*3004*
heard the third living creature **s**,	**Rv 6:5**	*3004*
of the four living creatures **s**,	**Rv 6:6**	*3004*
of the fourth living creature **s**,	**Rv 6:7**	*3004*
cried out with a loud voice, **s**,	**Rv 6:10**	*3004*
s, "Do not harm the earth or the	**Rv 7:3**	*3004*
they cry out with a loud voice, **s**,	**Rv 7:10**	*3004*
s, "Amen, blessing and glory and	**Rv 7:12**	*3004*
of the elders answered, **s** to me,	**Rv 7:13**	*3004*
in midheaven, **s** with a loud voice,	**Rv 8:13**	*3004*
one **s** to the sixth angel who had	**Rv 9:14**	*3004*
and I heard a voice from heaven **s**,	**Rv 10:4**	*3004*
again speaking with me, and **s**,	**Rv 10:8**	*3004*
loud voice from heaven **s** to them,	**Rv 11:12**	*3004*
were loud voices in heaven, **s**,	**Rv 11:15**	*3004*
s, "We give You thanks, O Lord	**Rv 11:17**	*3004*
I heard a loud voice in heaven, **s**,	**Rv 12:10**	*3004*
and they worshiped the beast, **s**,	**Rv 13:4**	*3004*
angel, a second one, followed, **s**,	**Rv 14:8**	*3004*
them, **s** with a loud voice,	**Rv 14:9**	*3004*
I heard a voice from heaven, **s**,	**Rv 14:13**	*3004*
him who had the sharp sickle, **s**,	**Rv 14:18**	*3004*
God, and the song of the Lamb, **s**,	**Rv 15:3**	*3004*
the temple, **s** to the seven angels,	**Rv 16:1**	*3004*
I heard the angel of the waters **s**,	**Rv 16:5**	*3004*
And I heard the altar **s**,	**Rv 16:7**	*3004*
of the temple from the throne, **s**,	**Rv 16:17**	*3004*
bowls came and spoke with me, **s**,	**Rv 17:1**	*3004*
cried out with a mighty voice, **s**,	**Rv 18:2**	*3004*
another voice from heaven, **s**,	**Rv 18:4**	*3004*
of the fear of her torment, **s**,	**Rv 18:10**	*3004*
s, 'Woe, woe, the great city, she	**Rv 18:16**	*3004*
saw the smoke of her burning, **s**,	**Rv 18:18**	*3004*
out, weeping and mourning, **s**,	**Rv 18:19**	*3004*
and threw it into the sea, **s**,	**Rv 18:21**	*3004*
of a great multitude in heaven, **s**,	**Rv 19:1**	*3004*
God who sits on the throne **s**,	**Rv 19:4**	*3004*
a voice came from the throne, **s**,	**Rv 19:5**	*3004*
of mighty peals of thunder, **s**,	**Rv 19:6**	*3004*
s to all the birds which fly in	**Rv 19:17**	*3004*
a loud voice from the throne, **s**,	**Rv 21:3**	*3004*
came and spoke with me, **s**,	**Rv 21:9**	*3004*

SAYINGS

Even openly, and not in dark **s**,	**Nu 12:8**	2420
memorable **s** are proverbs of ashes,	**Jb 13:12**	2146
I will utter dark **s** of old,	**Ps 78:2**	2420
To discern the **s** of understanding,	**Pr 1:2**	561
in the city she utters her **s**:	**Pr 1:21**	561
Hear, my son, and accept my **s** And	**Pr 4:10**	561
Incline your ear to my **s**.	**Pr 4:20**	561
These also are **s** of the wise.	**Pr 24:23**	
Some eight days after these **s**,	**Lk 9:28**	*3056*
not the **s** of one demon-possessed.	**Jn 10:21**	*4487*
"If anyone hears My **s** and	**Jn 12:47**	*4487*
Me and does not receive My **s**,	**Jn 12:48**	*4487*

SAYS

'Thus **s** your servant Jacob,	**Gn 32:4**	559
whatever he **s** to you, you shall do."	**Gn 41:55**	559
'Thus **s** your son Joseph,	**Gn 45:9**	559
When Pharaoh calls you and **s**,	**Gn 46:33**	559
'Thus **s** the LORD,	**Ex 4:22**	559
'Thus **s** the LORD, the God of	**Ex 5:1**	559
"Thus **s** Pharaoh,	**Ex 5:10**	559
'Thus **s** the LORD,	**Ex 7:17**	559
'Thus **s** the LORD,	**Ex 8:1**	559
'Thus **s** the LORD,	**Ex 8:20**	559
'Thus **s** the LORD, the God of the	**Ex 9:1**	559
'Thus **s** the LORD, the God of the	**Ex 9:13**	559
"Thus **s** the LORD, the God of the	**Ex 10:3**	559
"Thus **s** the LORD,	**Ex 11:4**	559
"But if the slave plainly **s**,	**Ex 21:5**	559
any lost thing about which one **s**,	**Ex 22:9**	559
"Thus **s** the LORD, the God of	**Ex 32:27**	1696
'As I live,' **s** the LORD,	**Nu 14:28**	5002
"Thus **s** Balak the son of Zippor,	**Nu 22:16**	559
and her father **s** nothing to her,	**Nu 30:4**	2790b
s nothing to her on the day he hears	**Nu 30:7**	2790b
her husband indeed **s** nothing to her	**Nu 30:14**	2790b
to battle, just as my lord **s**."	**Nu 32:27**	1696
hear all that the LORD our God **s**;	**Dt 5:27**	559
shall come about if he **s** to you,	**Dt 15:16**	559
and publicly defames her, and **s**,	**Dt 22:14**	559
And *if* he persists and **s**,	**Dt 25:8**	559
"Thus **s** the whole congregation of	**Jos 22:16**	559
"Thus **s** the LORD, the God of	**Jos 24:2**	559
comes and inquires of you, and **s**,	**Jg 4:20**	559
"Thus **s** the LORD, the God of	**Jg 6:8**	559
"Thus **s** Jephthah,	**Jg 11:15**	559
"Thus **s** the LORD,	**1Sa 2:27**	559
all that he **s** surely comes true.	**1Sa 9:6**	1696
"Thus **s** the LORD, the God of	**1Sa 10:18**	559
"Thus **s** the LORD of hosts,	**1Sa 15:2**	559

Context	Reference	No.
“If he **s**, ‘It is good,’ your servant	**1Sa 20:7**	559
“As the proverb of the ancients **s**,	**1Sa 24:13**	559
‘Thus **s** the LORD,	**2Sa 7:5**	559
‘Thus **s** the LORD of hosts,	**2Sa 7:8**	559
king’s wrath rises and he **s** to you,	**2Sa 11:20**	559
Thus **s** the LORD God of Israel,	**2Sa 12:7**	559
“Thus **s** the LORD,	**2Sa 12:11**	559
‘Thus the LORD **s**,	**2Sa 24:12**	559
one **s**, ‘This is my son who is living,	**1Ki 3:23**	559
and the other **s**,	**1Ki 3:23**	559
for thus **s** the LORD, the God of	**1Ki 11:31**	559
‘Thus **s** the LORD,	**1Ki 12:24**	559
“O altar, altar, thus **s** the LORD,	**1Ki 13:2**	559
“Thus **s** the LORD,	**1Ki 13:21**	559
‘Thus **s** the LORD God of Israel,	**1Ki 14:7**	559
“For thus **s** the LORD God of	**1Ki 17:14**	559
“Thus **s** Ben-hadad,	**1Ki 20:2**	559
“Thus **s** Ben-hadad,	**1Ki 20:5**	559
‘Thus **s** the LORD,	**1Ki 20:13**	559
‘Thus **s** the LORD,	**1Ki 20:14**	559
‘Thus **s** the LORD,	**1Ki 20:28**	559
“Your servant Ben-hadad **s**,	**1Ki 20:32**	559
‘Thus **s** the LORD,	**1Ki 20:42**	559
‘Thus **s** the LORD,	**1Ki 21:19**	559
‘Thus **s** the LORD,	**1Ki 21:19**	559
‘Thus **s** the LORD,	**1Ki 22:11**	559
LORD lives, what the LORD **s** to me,	**1Ki 22:14**	559
‘Thus **s** the king,	**1Ki 22:27**	559
“Now therefore thus **s** the LORD,	**2Ki 1:4**	559
‘Thus **s** the LORD,	**2Ki 1:6**	559
“O man of God, the king **s**,	**2Ki 1:9**	1696
“O man of God, thus **s** the king,	**2Ki 1:11**	559
‘Thus **s** the LORD,	**2Ki 1:16**	559
‘Thus **s** the LORD,	**2Ki 2:21**	559
‘Thus **s** the LORD,	**2Ki 3:16**	559
“For thus **s** the LORD,	**2Ki 3:17**	559
they may eat, for thus **s** the LORD,	**2Ki 4:43**	559
much more *then*, when he **s** to you,	**2Ki 5:13**	559
thus **s** the LORD,	**2Ki 7:1**	559
‘Thus **s** the LORD,	**2Ki 9:3**	559
‘Thus **s** the LORD, the God of	**2Ki 9:6**	559
‘Thus **s** the LORD,	**2Ki 9:12**	559
‘Thus **s** the king,	**2Ki 9:18**	559
‘Thus **s** the king,	**2Ki 9:19**	559
the blood of his sons,’ **s** the LORD,	**2Ki 9:26**	5002
you in this property,’ **s** the LORD.	**2Ki 9:26**	5002
‘Thus **s** the great king, the king	**2Ki 18:19**	559
‘Thus **s** the king,	**2Ki 18:29**	559
for thus **s** the king of Assyria,	**2Ki 18:31**	559
‘Thus **s** Hezekiah,	**2Ki 19:3**	559
‘Thus **s** the LORD,	**2Ki 19:6**	559
‘Thus **s** the LORD, the God of	**2Ki 19:20**	559
‘Therefore thus **s** the LORD	**2Ki 19:32**	559
‘Thus **s** the LORD,	**2Ki 20:1**	559
‘Thus **s** the LORD, the God of your	**2Ki 20:5**	559
nothing shall be left,’ **s** the LORD.	**2Ki 20:17**	559
therefore thus **s** the LORD, the God	**2Ki 21:12**	559
“Thus **s** the LORD God of Israel,	**2Ki 22:15**	559
thus **s** the LORD,	**2Ki 22:16**	559
‘Thus **s** the LORD God of Israel,	**2Ki 22:18**	559
‘Thus **s** the LORD,	**1Ch 17:4**	559
‘Thus **s** the LORD of hosts,	**1Ch 17:7**	559
‘Thus **s** the LORD,	**1Ch 21:10**	559
‘Thus **s** the LORD,	**1Ch 21:11**	559
‘Thus **s** the LORD,	**2Ch 11:4**	559
‘Thus **s** the LORD,	**2Ch 12:5**	559
‘Thus **s** the LORD,	**2Ch 18:10**	559
“As the LORD lives, what my God **s**,	**2Ch 18:13**	559
‘Thus **s** the king,	**2Ch 18:26**	559
thus **s** the LORD to you,	**2Ch 20:15**	559
“Thus **s** the LORD God of your	**2Ch 21:12**	559
s Sennacherib king of Assyria,	**2Ch 32:10**	559
‘Thus **s** the LORD, the God of	**2Ch 34:23**	559
thus **s** the LORD,	**2Ch 34:24**	559
‘Thus **s** the LORD God of Israel	**2Ch 34:26**	559
“Thus **s** Cyrus king of Persia,	**2Ch 36:23**	559
“Thus **s** Cyrus king of Persia,	**Ezr 1:2**	559
among the nations, and Gashmu **s**,	**Ne 6:6**	559
I will do as the king **s**.”	**Es 5:8**	1697
“The deep **s**, ‘It is not in me’;	**Jb 28:14**	559
And the sea **s**, ‘It is not with me.’	**Jb 28:14**	559
Who **s** to a king,	**Jb 34:18**	559
no one **s**, ‘Where is God my Maker,	**Jb 35:10**	559
“For to the snow He **s**,	**Jb 37:6**	559
often as the trumpet *sounds* he **s**,	**Jb 39:25**	559
He **s** to himself,	**Ps 10:6**	559
He **s** to himself,	**Ps 10:11**	559
Now I will arise,” **s** the LORD;	**Ps 12:5**	559
And in His temple everything **s**,	**Ps 29:9**	559
But to the wicked God **s**,	**Ps 50:16**	559
The LORD **s** to my Lord:	**Ps 110:1**	5002
with a brazen face she **s** to him:	**Pr 7:13**	559
him who lacks understanding she **s**,	**Pr 9:4**	559
him who lacks understanding she **s**,	**Pr 9:16**	559
“Bad, bad,” **s** the buyer,	**Pr 20:14**	559
The sluggard **s**, “There is a lion	**Pr 22:13**	559
He **s** to you, “Eat and drink!”	**Pr 23:7**	559
He who **s** to the wicked,	**Pr 24:24**	559
The sluggard **s**, “There is a lion in	**Pr 26:13**	559
who deceives his neighbor, And **s**,	**Pr 26:19**	559
his father or his mother And **s**,	**Pr 28:24**	559
with water, And fire that never **s**,	**Pr 30:16**	559
eats and wipes her mouth, And **s**,	**Pr 30:20**	559
of vanities,” **s** the Preacher,	**Ec 1:2**	559
discovered this,” **s** the Preacher,	**Ec 7:27**	559
“Vanity of vanities,” **s** the Preacher,	**Ec 12:8**	559
S the LORD. “I have had enough of	**Is 1:11**	559
us reason together,” **S** the LORD,	**Is 1:18**	559
thus **s** the Lord GOD:	**Is 7:7**	559
it **s**, “Are not my princes all kings?	**Is 10:8**	559
thus **s** the Lord GOD of hosts,	**Is 10:24**	559
For thus the Lord **s** to me,	**Is 21:6**	559
The watchman **s**, “Morning comes	**Is 21:12**	559
you die,” **s** the Lord GOD of hosts.	**Is 22:14**	559
Thus **s** the Lord GOD of hosts,	**Is 22:15**	559
“For *He* **s**, ‘Order on order,	**Is 28:10**	
Therefore thus **s** the Lord GOD,	**Is 28:16**	559
Therefore thus **s** the LORD, who	**Is 29:22**	559
thus **s** the Holy One of Israel,	**Is 30:12**	559
For thus **s** the LORD to me,	**Is 31:4**	559
“Now I will arise,” **s** the LORD,	**Is 33:10**	559
“Thus **s** the great king, the king	**Is 36:4**	559
“Thus **s** the king,	**Is 36:14**	559
for thus **s** the king of Assyria,	**Is 36:16**	559
“Thus **s** Hezekiah,	**Is 37:3**	559
‘Thus **s** the LORD,	**Is 37:6**	559
“Thus **s** the LORD, the God of	**Is 37:21**	559
thus **s** the LORD concerning the	**Is 37:33**	559
“Thus **s** the LORD,	**Is 38:1**	559
“Thus **s** the LORD, the God of your	**Is 38:5**	559
nothing will be left,’ **s** the LORD.	**Is 39:6**	559
O comfort My people,” **s** your God.	**Is 40:1**	559
A voice **s**, “Call out.”	**Is 40:6**	559
be *his* equal?” **s** the Holy One.	**Is 40:25**	559
neighbor And **s** to his brother,	**Is 41:6**	559
your right hand, Who **s** to you,	**Is 41:13**	559
“Present your case,” the LORD **s**.	**Is 41:21**	559
arguments,” The King of Jacob **s**.	**Is 41:21**	559
Thus **s** God the LORD, Who created	**Is 42:5**	559
But now, thus **s** the LORD, your	**Is 43:1**	559
Thus **s** the LORD your Redeemer, the	**Is 43:14**	559
Thus **s** the LORD, Who makes a way	**Is 43:16**	559
Thus **s** the LORD who made you And	**Is 44:2**	559
“Thus **s** the LORD, the King of	**Is 44:6**	559
He also warms himself and **s**,	**Is 44:16**	559
he also prays to it and **s**,	**Is 44:17**	559
Thus **s** the LORD, your Redeemer,	**Is 44:24**	559
It is I who **s** of Jerusalem,	**Is 44:26**	559
I who **s** to the depth of the sea,	**Is 44:27**	559
“*It is I* who **s** of Cyrus,	**Is 44:28**	559
Thus **s** the LORD to Cyrus His	**Is 45:1**	559
“Woe to him who **s** to a father,	**Is 45:10**	559
Thus **s** the LORD, the Holy One of	**Is 45:11**	559
or reward,” **s** the LORD of hosts.	**Is 45:13**	559
Thus **s** the LORD,	**Is 45:14**	559
For thus **s** the LORD, who created	**Is 45:18**	559
securely, Who **s** in your heart,	**Is 47:8**	559
Thus **s** the LORD, your Redeemer,	**Is 48:17**	559
peace for the wicked,” **s** the LORD.	**Is 48:22**	559
And now **s** the LORD, who formed Me	**Is 49:5**	559
He **s**, “It is too small a thing that	**Is 49:6**	559
Thus **s** the LORD, the Redeemer of	**Is 49:7**	559
Thus **s** the LORD,	**Is 49:8**	559
Thus **s** the Lord GOD,	**Is 49:22**	559
Surely, thus **s** the LORD,	**Is 49:25**	559
Thus **s** the LORD,	**Is 50:1**	559
Thus **s** your Lord, the LORD, even	**Is 51:22**	559
For thus **s** the LORD,	**Is 52:3**	559
For thus **s** the Lord GOD,	**Is 52:4**	559
salvation, *And* **s** to Zion,	**Is 52:7**	559
of the married woman,” **s** the LORD.	**Is 54:1**	559
when she is rejected,” **S** your God.	**Is 54:6**	559
on you,” **S** the LORD your Redeemer.	**Is 54:8**	559
S the LORD who has compassion on	**Is 54:10**	559
Thus **s** the LORD,	**Is 56:1**	559
For thus **s** the LORD,	**Is 56:4**	559
For thus **s** the high and exalted	**Is 57:15**	559
to him who is near,” **S** the LORD,	**Is 57:19**	559
“There is no peace,” **s** my God,	**Is 57:21**	559
My covenant with them,” **s** the LORD:	**Is 59:21**	559
offspring’s offspring,” **s** the LORD,	**Is 59:21**	559
fathers together,” **s** the LORD.	**Is 65:7**	559
Thus **s** the LORD,	**Is 65:8**	559
found in the cluster, And one **s**,	**Is 65:8**	559
Therefore, thus **s** the Lord GOD,	**Is 65:13**	559
all My holy mountain,” **s** the LORD.	**Is 65:25**	559
Thus **s** the LORD,	**Is 66:1**	559
and not give delivery?” **s** the LORD.	**Is 66:9**	559
shut *the womb?*” **s** your God.	**Is 66:9**	559
For thus **s** the LORD,	**Is 66:12**	559
mountain Jerusalem,” **s** the LORD,	**Is 66:20**	559
and for Levites,” **s** the LORD.	**Is 66:21**	559
to bow down before Me,” **s** the LORD.	**Is 66:23**	559
‘Thus **s** the LORD,	**Jer 2:2**	559
Thus **s** the LORD,	**Jer 2:5**	559
God **s**, “If a husband divorces his	**Jer 3:1**	559
For thus **s** the LORD to the men of	**Jer 4:3**	559
For thus **s** the LORD,	**Jer 4:27**	559
Therefore, thus **s** the LORD, the	**Jer 5:14**	559
For thus **s** the LORD of hosts,	**Jer 6:6**	559
Thus **s** the LORD of hosts,	**Jer 6:9**	559
shall be cast down,” **s** the LORD.	**Jer 6:15**	559
Thus **s** the LORD,	**Jer 6:16**	559
Therefore, thus **s** the LORD,	**Jer 6:21**	559
Thus **s** the LORD,	**Jer 6:22**	559
Thus **s** the LORD of hosts, the God	**Jer 7:3**	559
Therefore thus **s** the Lord GOD,	**Jer 7:20**	559
Thus **s** the LORD of hosts, the God	**Jer 7:21**	559
‘Thus **s** the LORD,	**Jer 8:4**	559
brought down,” **S** the LORD.	**Jer 8:12**	559
thus **s** the LORD of hosts,	**Jer 9:7**	559
thus **s** the LORD of hosts,	**Jer 9:15**	559
Thus **s** the LORD of hosts,	**Jer 9:17**	559
Speak, “Thus **s** the LORD,	**Jer 9:22**	5002
Thus **s** the LORD,	**Jer 9:23**	559
Thus **s** the LORD,	**Jer 10:2**	559
For thus **s** the LORD,	**Jer 10:18**	559
‘Thus **s** the LORD, the God of	**Jer 11:3**	559
Therefore thus **s** the LORD,	**Jer 11:11**	559
Therefore thus **s** the LORD	**Jer 11:21**	559
thus **s** the LORD of hosts,	**Jer 11:22**	559
Thus **s** the LORD concerning all My	**Jer 12:14**	559
‘Thus **s** the LORD,	**Jer 13:9**	559
‘Thus **s** the LORD, the God of	**Jer 13:12**	559
‘Thus **s** the LORD,	**Jer 13:13**	559
Thus **s** the LORD to this people,	**Jer 14:10**	559
“Therefore thus **s** the LORD	**Jer 14:15**	559
‘Thus **s** the LORD: “Those *destined*	**Jer 15:2**	559
Therefore, thus **s** the LORD,	**Jer 15:19**	559
For thus **s** the LORD concerning the	**Jer 16:3**	559
For thus **s** the LORD,	**Jer 16:5**	559
For thus **s** the LORD of hosts, the	**Jer 16:9**	559
Thus **s** the LORD,	**Jer 17:5**	559
‘Thus **s** the LORD,	**Jer 17:21**	559
‘Thus **s** the LORD,	**Jer 18:11**	559
‘Therefore thus **s** the LORD,	**Jer 18:13**	559
Thus **s** the LORD,	**Jer 19:1**	559
thus **s** the LORD of hosts, the God	**Jer 19:3**	559
‘Thus **s** the LORD of hosts,	**Jer 19:11**	559
“Thus **s** the LORD of hosts, the	**Jer 19:15**	559
“For thus **s** the LORD,	**Jer 20:4**	559
‘Thus **s** the LORD God of Israel,	**Jer 21:4**	559
‘Thus **s** the LORD,	**Jer 21:8**	559
O house of David, thus **s** the LORD:	**Jer 21:12**	559
Thus **s** the LORD,	**Jer 22:1**	559
‘Thus **s** the LORD,	**Jer 22:3**	559
For thus **s** the LORD concerning the	**Jer 22:6**	559
For thus **s** the LORD in regard to	**Jer 22:11**	559
s, ‘I will build myself a roomy house	**Jer 22:14**	559
Therefore thus **s** the LORD in	**Jer 22:18**	559
“Thus **s** the LORD,	**Jer 22:30**	559
Therefore thus **s** the LORD God of	**Jer 23:2**	559
“Therefore thus **s** the LORD of	**Jer 23:15**	559
Thus **s** the LORD of hosts,	**Jer 23:16**	559
surely thus **s** the LORD,	**Jer 23:38**	559
“Thus **s** the LORD God of Israel,	**Jer 24:5**	559
indeed, thus **s** the LORD	**Jer 24:8**	559
thus **s** the LORD of hosts,	**Jer 25:8**	559
LORD, the God of Israel, **s** to me,	**Jer 25:15**	559
‘Thus **s** the LORD of hosts, the God	**Jer 25:27**	559
‘Thus **s** the LORD of hosts:	**Jer 25:28**	559
Thus **s** the LORD of hosts,	**Jer 25:32**	559
‘Thus **s** the LORD,	**Jer 26:2**	559
‘Thus **s** the LORD,	**Jer 26:4**	559
thus **s** the LORD to	**Jer 27:2**	559
‘Thus **s** the LORD of hosts, the God	**Jer 27:4**	559
‘Thus **s** the LORD: Do not listen to	**Jer 27:16**	559
‘For thus **s** the LORD of hosts	**Jer 27:19**	559
‘Yes, thus **s** the LORD of hosts,	**Jer 27:21**	559
‘Thus **s** the LORD of hosts, the	**Jer 28:2**	559
‘Thus **s** the LORD,	**Jer 28:11**	559
‘Thus **s** the LORD,	**Jer 28:13**	559
‘For thus **s** the LORD of hosts, the	**Jer 28:14**	559
‘Therefore thus **s** the LORD,	**Jer 28:16**	559
‘Thus **s** the LORD of hosts, the	**Jer 29:4**	559
‘For thus **s** the LORD of hosts,	**Jer 29:8**	559
‘For thus **s** the LORD,	**Jer 29:10**	559
for thus **s** the LORD concerning the	**Jer 29:16**	559
thus **s** the LORD of hosts,	**Jer 29:17**	559
‘Thus **s** the LORD of hosts, the	**Jer 29:21**	559
‘Thus **s** the LORD of hosts, the	**Jer 29:25**	559
‘Thus **s** the LORD concerning	**Jer 29:31**	559
therefore thus **s** the LORD,	**Jer 29:32**	559
‘Thus **s** the LORD, the God of	**Jer 30:2**	559
LORD **s**, ‘I will also bring them back	**Jer 30:3**	559
‘For thus **s** the LORD,	**Jer 30:5**	559
‘For thus **s** the LORD,	**Jer 30:12**	559
‘Thus **s** the LORD,	**Jer 30:18**	559
Thus **s** the LORD,	**Jer 31:2**	559
For thus **s** the LORD,	**Jer 31:7**	559
Thus **s** the LORD,	**Jer 31:15**	559
Thus **s** the LORD,	**Jer 31:16**	559
Thus **s** the LORD of hosts, the God	**Jer 31:23**	559
Thus **s** the LORD, Who gives the sun	**Jer 31:35**	559
Thus **s** the LORD,	**Jer 31:37**	559
‘Thus **s** the LORD,	**Jer 32:3**	559
‘Thus **s** the LORD of hosts, the God	**Jer 32:14**	559
‘For thus **s** the LORD of hosts, the	**Jer 32:15**	559
Therefore thus **s** the LORD,	**Jer 32:28**	559
“Now therefore thus **s** the LORD	**Jer 32:36**	559
“For thus **s** the LORD,	**Jer 32:42**	559
s the LORD who made *the earth*,	**Jer 33:2**	559
“For thus **s** the LORD God of	**Jer 33:4**	559
“Thus **s** the LORD,	**Jer 33:10**	559
as they were at first,’ **s** the LORD.	**Jer 33:11**	559
“Thus **s** the LORD of hosts,	**Jer 33:12**	559
one who numbers them,’ **s** the LORD.	**Jer 33:13**	559
“For thus **s** the LORD,	**Jer 33:17**	559
“Thus **s** the LORD,	**Jer 33:20**	559
“Thus **s** the LORD,	**Jer 33:25**	559
“Thus **s** the LORD God of Israel,	**Jer 34:2**	559
‘Thus **s** the LORD, ‘Behold, I	**Jer 34:2**	559
Thus **s** the LORD concerning you,	**Jer 34:4**	559
“Thus **s** the LORD God of Israel,	**Jer 34:13**	559
“Therefore thus **s** the LORD,	**Jer 34:17**	559
“Thus **s** the LORD of hosts, the	**Jer 35:13**	559
“Therefore thus **s** the LORD, the	**Jer 35:17**	559
“Thus **s** the LORD of hosts, the	**Jer 35:18**	559
thus **s** the LORD of hosts,	**Jer 35:19**	559
‘Thus **s** the LORD,	**Jer 36:29**	559
‘Therefore thus **s** the LORD	**Jer 36:30**	559
“Thus **s** the LORD God of Israel,	**Jer 37:7**	559
“Thus **s** the LORD,	**Jer 37:9**	559
“Thus **s** the LORD,	**Jer 38:2**	559
“Thus **s** the LORD,	**Jer 38:3**	559
“Thus **s** the LORD God of hosts,	**Jer 38:17**	559
‘Thus **s** the LORD of hosts, the God	**Jer 39:16**	559

“Thus **s** the LORD the God of	**Jer 42:9**	559
Thus **s** the LORD of hosts, the God	**Jer 42:15**	559
For thus **s** the LORD of hosts, the	**Jer 42:18**	559
and whatever the LORD our God **s**,	**Jer 42:20**	559
‘Thus **s** the LORD of hosts, the God	**Jer 43:10**	559
“Thus **s** the LORD of hosts, the	**Jer 44:2**	559
then thus **s** the LORD God of hosts,	**Jer 44:7**	559
thus **s** the LORD of hosts,	**Jer 44:11**	559
thus **s** the LORD of hosts, the God	**Jer 44:25**	559
by My great name,’ **s** the LORD,	**Jer 44:26**	559
‘Thus **s** the LORD,	**Jer 44:30**	559
“Thus **s** the LORD the God of	**Jer 45:2**	559
‘Thus **s** the LORD,	**Jer 45:4**	559
of hosts, the God of Israel, **s**,	**Jer 46:25**	559
Thus **s** the LORD: “Behold, waters	**Jer 47:2**	559
Thus **s** the LORD of hosts, the God	**Jer 48:1**	559
For thus **s** the LORD:	**Jer 48:40**	559
s the LORD: “Does Israel have no	**Jer 49:1**	559
of his possessors,” **S** the LORD.	**Jer 49:2**	559
Thus **s** the LORD of hosts,	**Jer 49:7**	559
For thus **s** the LORD,	**Jer 49:12**	559
with its neighbors,” **s** the LORD,	**Jer 49:18**	559
Thus **s** the LORD,	**Jer 49:28**	559
“Thus **s** the LORD of hosts,	**Jer 49:35**	559
thus **s** the LORD of hosts,	**Jer 50:18**	559
Thus **s** the LORD of hosts,	**Jer 50:33**	559
Thus **s** the LORD: “Behold, I am	**Jer 51:1**	559
He **s**, “You are My war-club,	**Jer 51:20**	559
For thus **s** the LORD of hosts, the	**Jer 51:33**	559
Therefore thus **s** the LORD,	**Jer 51:36**	559
Thus **s** the LORD of hosts,	**Jer 51:58**	559
“The LORD is my portion,” **s** my soul,	**La 3:24**	559
‘Thus **s** the Lord GOD.’	**Ezk 2:4**	559
‘Thus **s** the Lord GOD.’ ”	**Ezk 3:11**	559
‘Thus **s** the Lord GOD.’	**Ezk 3:27**	559
‘Thus **s** the Lord GOD,	**Ezk 5:5**	559
‘Therefore, thus **s** the Lord GOD,	**Ezk 5:7**	559
therefore, thus **s** the Lord GOD,	**Ezk 5:8**	559
s the Lord GOD to the mountains,	**Ezk 6:3**	559
‘Thus **s** the Lord GOD,	**Ezk 6:11**	559
thus **s** the Lord GOD to the land of	**Ezk 7:2**	559
‘Thus **s** the Lord GOD,	**Ezk 7:5**	559
‘Thus **s** the LORD,	**Ezk 11:5**	559
‘Therefore, thus **s** the Lord GOD,	**Ezk 11:7**	559
‘Thus **s** the Lord GOD,	**Ezk 11:16**	559
‘Thus **s** the Lord GOD,	**Ezk 11:17**	559
‘Thus **s** the Lord GOD,	**Ezk 12:10**	559
‘Thus **s** the Lord GOD concerning	**Ezk 12:19**	559
‘Thus **s** the Lord GOD,	**Ezk 12:23**	559
‘Thus **s** the Lord GOD,	**Ezk 12:28**	559
‘Thus **s** the Lord GOD,	**Ezk 13:3**	559
Therefore, thus **s** the Lord GOD,	**Ezk 13:8**	559
Therefore, thus **s** the Lord GOD,	**Ezk 13:13**	559
‘Thus **s** the Lord GOD,	**Ezk 13:18**	559
Therefore, thus **s** the Lord GOD,	**Ezk 13:20**	559
‘Thus **s** the Lord GOD,	**Ezk 14:4**	559
‘Thus **s** the Lord GOD,	**Ezk 14:6**	559
For thus **s** the Lord GOD,	**Ezk 14:21**	559
‘Therefore, thus **s** the Lord GOD,	**Ezk 15:6**	559
‘Thus **s** the Lord GOD to Jerusalem,	**Ezk 16:3**	559
Thus **s** the Lord GOD,	**Ezk 16:36**	559
For thus **s** the Lord GOD,	**Ezk 16:59**	559
‘Thus **s** the Lord GOD,	**Ezk 17:3**	559
‘Thus **s** the Lord GOD,	**Ezk 17:9**	559
Therefore, thus **s** the Lord GOD,	**Ezk 17:19**	559
Thus **s** the Lord GOD,	**Ezk 17:22**	559
“But the house of Israel **s**,	**Ezk 18:29**	559
‘Thus **s** the Lord GOD,	**Ezk 20:3**	559
‘Thus **s** the Lord GOD,	**Ezk 20:5**	559
‘Thus **s** the Lord GOD,	**Ezk 20:27**	559
‘Thus **s** the Lord GOD,	**Ezk 20:30**	559
of Israel,” thus **s** the Lord GOD,	**Ezk 20:39**	559
thus **s** the Lord GOD,	**Ezk 20:47**	559
‘Thus **s** the LORD,	**Ezk 21:3**	559
‘Thus **s** the LORD.’	**Ezk 21:9**	559
“Therefore, thus **s** the Lord GOD,	**Ezk 21:24**	559
thus **s** the Lord GOD,	**Ezk 21:26**	559
‘Thus **s** the Lord GOD concerning	**Ezk 21:28**	559
‘Thus **s** the Lord GOD,	**Ezk 22:3**	559
“Therefore, thus **s** the Lord GOD,	**Ezk 22:19**	559
‘Thus **s** the Lord GOD,’ when the	**Ezk 22:28**	559
O Oholibah, thus **s** the Lord GOD,	**Ezk 23:22**	559
“For thus **s** the Lord GOD,	**Ezk 23:28**	559
‘Thus **s** the Lord GOD,	**Ezk 23:32**	559
“Therefore, thus **s** the Lord GOD,	**Ezk 23:35**	559
“For thus **s** the Lord GOD,	**Ezk 23:46**	559
‘Thus **s** the Lord GOD,	**Ezk 24:3**	559
‘Therefore, thus **s** the Lord GOD,	**Ezk 24:6**	559
‘Therefore, thus **s** the Lord GOD,	**Ezk 24:9**	559
‘Thus **s** the Lord GOD,	**Ezk 24:21**	559
Thus **s** the Lord GOD,	**Ezk 25:3**	559
‘For thus **s** the Lord GOD,	**Ezk 25:6**	559
‘Thus **s** the Lord GOD,	**Ezk 25:8**	559
‘Thus **s** the Lord GOD,	**Ezk 25:12**	559
therefore thus **s** the Lord GOD,	**Ezk 25:13**	559
‘Thus **s** the Lord GOD,	**Ezk 25:15**	559
therefore thus **s** the Lord GOD,	**Ezk 25:16**	559
therefore thus **s** the Lord GOD,	**Ezk 26:3**	559
For thus **s** the Lord GOD,	**Ezk 26:7**	559
Thus **s** the Lord GOD to Tyre,	**Ezk 26:15**	559
For thus **s** the Lord GOD,	**Ezk 26:19**	559
‘Thus **s** the Lord GOD,	**Ezk 27:3**	559
‘Thus **s** the Lord GOD,	**Ezk 28:2**	559
Therefore thus **s** the Lord GOD,	**Ezk 28:6**	559
‘Thus **s** the Lord GOD,	**Ezk 28:12**	559
‘Thus **s** the Lord GOD,	**Ezk 28:22**	559
‘Thus **s** the Lord GOD,	**Ezk 28:25**	559
‘Thus **s** the Lord GOD,	**Ezk 29:3**	559
‘Therefore thus **s** the Lord GOD,	**Ezk 29:8**	559
‘For thus **s** the Lord GOD,	**Ezk 29:13**	559
Therefore thus **s** the Lord GOD,	**Ezk 29:19**	559
‘Thus **s** the Lord GOD,	**Ezk 30:2**	559
‘Thus **s** the LORD,	**Ezk 30:6**	559
‘Thus **s** the Lord GOD,	**Ezk 30:10**	559
‘Thus **s** the Lord GOD,	**Ezk 30:13**	559
“Therefore thus **s** the Lord GOD,	**Ezk 30:22**	559
‘Therefore thus **s** the Lord GOD,	**Ezk 31:10**	559
‘Thus **s** the Lord GOD,	**Ezk 31:15**	559
Thus **s** the Lord GOD,	**Ezk 32:3**	559
For thus **s** the Lord GOD,	**Ezk 32:11**	559
‘Thus **s** the Lord GOD,	**Ezk 33:25**	559
‘Thus **s** the Lord GOD,	**Ezk 33:27**	559
‘Thus **s** the Lord GOD,	**Ezk 34:2**	559
‘Thus **s** the Lord GOD,	**Ezk 34:10**	559
For thus **s** the Lord GOD,	**Ezk 34:11**	559
My flock, thus **s** the Lord GOD,	**Ezk 34:17**	559
thus **s** the Lord GOD to them,	**Ezk 34:20**	559
‘Thus **s** the Lord GOD,	**Ezk 35:3**	559
‘Thus **s** the Lord GOD,	**Ezk 35:14**	559
‘Thus **s** the Lord GOD,	**Ezk 36:2**	559
‘Thus **s** the Lord GOD,	**Ezk 36:3**	559
Thus **s** the Lord GOD to the	**Ezk 36:4**	559
therefore thus **s** the Lord GOD,	**Ezk 36:5**	559
“Thus **s** the Lord GOD,	**Ezk 36:6**	559
“Therefore thus **s** the Lord GOD,	**Ezk 36:7**	559
“Thus **s** the Lord GOD,	**Ezk 36:13**	559
‘Thus **s** the Lord GOD,	**Ezk 36:22**	559
‘Thus **s** the Lord GOD,	**Ezk 36:33**	559
‘Thus **s** the Lord GOD,	**Ezk 36:37**	559
s the Lord GOD to these bones,	**Ezk 37:5**	559
‘Thus **s** the Lord GOD,	**Ezk 37:9**	559
‘Thus **s** the Lord GOD,	**Ezk 37:12**	559
‘Thus **s** the Lord GOD,	**Ezk 37:19**	559
‘Thus **s** the Lord GOD,	**Ezk 37:21**	559
‘Thus **s** the Lord GOD,	**Ezk 38:3**	559
‘Thus **s** the Lord GOD,	**Ezk 38:10**	559
‘Thus **s** the Lord GOD,	**Ezk 38:14**	559
‘Thus **s** the Lord GOD,	**Ezk 38:17**	559
‘Thus **s** the Lord GOD,	**Ezk 39:1**	559
son of man, thus **s** the Lord GOD,	**Ezk 39:17**	559
Therefore thus **s** the Lord GOD,	**Ezk 39:25**	559
“Son of man, thus **s** the Lord GOD,	**Ezk 43:18**	559
‘Thus **s** the Lord GOD,	**Ezk 44:6**	559
‘Thus **s** the Lord GOD,	**Ezk 44:9**	559
‘Thus **s** the Lord GOD,	**Ezk 45:9**	559
‘Thus **s** the Lord GOD,	**Ezk 45:18**	559
‘Thus **s** the Lord GOD,	**Ezk 46:1**	559
‘Thus **s** the Lord GOD,	**Ezk 46:16**	559
Thus **s** the Lord GOD,	**Ezk 47:13**	559
Thus **s** the LORD,	**Am 1:3**	559
will go exiled to Kir,” **S** the LORD.	**Am 1:5**	559
Thus **s** the LORD,	**Am 1:6**	559
will perish,” **S** the Lord GOD.	**Am 1:8**	559
Thus **s** the LORD,	**Am 1:9**	559
Thus **s** the LORD,	**Am 1:11**	559
Thus **s** the LORD,	**Am 1:13**	559
his princes together,” **s** the LORD.	**Am 1:15**	559
Thus **s** the LORD,	**Am 2:1**	559
her princes with him,” **s** the LORD.	**Am 2:3**	559
Thus **s** the LORD,	**Am 2:4**	559
Thus **s** the LORD,	**Am 2:6**	559
Therefore, thus **s** the Lord GOD,	**Am 3:11**	559
Thus **s** the LORD,	**Am 3:12**	559
For thus **s** the Lord GOD,	**Am 5:3**	559
For thus **s** the LORD to the house	**Am 5:4**	559
thus **s** the LORD God of hosts,	**Am 5:16**	559
the midst of you,” **s** the LORD.	**Am 5:17**	559
exile beyond Damascus,” **s** the LORD,	**Am 5:27**	559
“For thus Amos **s**,	**Am 7:11**	559
“Therefore, thus **s** the LORD,	**Am 7:17**	559
given them,” **S** the LORD your God.	**Am 9:15**	559
The vision of Obadiah. Thus **s**	**Ob 1:1**	559
Therefore thus **s** the LORD,	**Mi 2:3**	559
Thus **s** the LORD concerning the	**Mi 3:5**	559
Thus **s** the LORD,	**Na 1:12**	559
to him who **s** to a *piece of* wood,	**Hab 2:19**	559
securely, Who **s** in her heart,	**Zph 2:15**	559
before your eyes,” **S** the LORD.	**Zph 3:20**	559
“Thus **s** the LORD of hosts,	**Hg 1:2**	559
people **s**, “The time has not come,	**Hg 1:2**	559
thus **s** the LORD of hosts,	**Hg 1:5**	559
Thus **s** the LORD of hosts,	**Hg 1:7**	559
it and be glorified,” **s** the LORD.	**Hg 1:8**	559
“For thus **s** the LORD of hosts,	**Hg 2:6**	559
with glory,’ **s** the LORD of hosts.	**Hg 2:7**	559
the former,’ **s** the LORD of hosts,	**Hg 2:9**	559
“Thus **s** the LORD of hosts,	**Hg 2:11**	559
‘Thus **s** the LORD of hosts,	**Zch 1:3**	559
to you,” **s** the LORD of hosts.	**Zch 1:3**	559
‘Thus **s** the LORD of hosts,	**Zch 1:4**	559
‘Thus **s** the LORD of hosts,	**Zch 1:14**	559
‘Therefore thus **s** the LORD,	**Zch 1:16**	559
‘Thus **s** the LORD of hosts,	**Zch 1:17**	559
For thus **s** the LORD of hosts,	**Zch 2:8**	559
‘Thus **s** the LORD of hosts,	**Zch 3:7**	559
by My Spirit,’ **s** the LORD of hosts.	**Zch 4:6**	559
‘Thus **s** the LORD of hosts,	**Zch 6:12**	559
not listen,” **s** the LORD of hosts;	**Zch 7:13**	559
‘Thus **s** the LORD of hosts,	**Zch 8:2**	559
‘Thus **s** the LORD,	**Zch 8:3**	559
‘Thus **s** the LORD of hosts,	**Zch 8:4**	559
‘Thus **s** the LORD of hosts,	**Zch 8:6**	559
‘Thus **s** the LORD of hosts,	**Zch 8:7**	559
‘Thus **s** the LORD of hosts,	**Zch 8:9**	559
“For thus **s** the LORD of hosts,	**Zch 8:14**	559
Me to wrath,’ **s** the LORD of hosts,	**Zch 8:14**	559
‘Thus **s** the LORD of hosts,	**Zch 8:19**	559
‘Thus **s** the LORD of hosts,	**Zch 8:20**	559
“Thus **s** the LORD of hosts,	**Zch 8:23**	559
Thus **s** the LORD my God,	**Zch 11:4**	559
and *each of* those who sell them **s**,	**Zch 11:5**	559
“I have loved you,” **s** the LORD.	**Mal 1:2**	559
Edom **s**, “We have been beaten down	**Mal 1:4**	559
thus **s** the LORD of hosts,	**Mal 1:4**	559
s the LORD of hosts to you,	**Mal 1:6**	559
s the LORD of hosts.	**Mal 1:8**	559
s the LORD of hosts.	**Mal 1:9**	559
with you,” **s** the LORD of hosts,	**Mal 1:10**	559
the nations,” **s** the LORD of hosts.	**Mal 1:11**	559
sniff at it,” **s** the LORD of hosts,	**Mal 1:13**	559
that from your hand?” **s** the LORD.	**Mal 1:13**	559
a great King,” **s** the LORD of hosts,	**Mal 1:14**	559
to My name,” **s** the LORD of hosts,	**Mal 2:2**	559
with Levi,” **s** the LORD of hosts.	**Mal 2:4**	559
of Levi,” **s** the LORD of hosts.	**Mal 2:8**	559
“For I hate divorce,” **s** the LORD,	**Mal 2:16**	559
with wrong,” **s** the LORD of hosts.	**Mal 2:16**	559
He is coming,” **s** the LORD of hosts.	**Mal 3:1**	559
not fear Me,” **s** the LORD of hosts.	**Mal 3:5**	559
to you,” **s** the LORD of hosts.	**Mal 3:7**	559
now in this,” **s** the LORD of hosts,	**Mal 3:10**	559
its grapes,” **s** the LORD of hosts.	**Mal 3:11**	559
land,” **s** the LORD of hosts.	**Mal 3:12**	559
arrogant against Me,” **s** the LORD.	**Mal 3:13**	559
will be Mine,” **s** the LORD of hosts,	**Mal 3:17**	559
them ablaze,” **s** the LORD of hosts,	**Mal 4:1**	559
am preparing,” **s** the LORD of hosts.	**Mal 4:3**	559
and whoever **s** to his brother, ‘You	**Mt 5:22**	3004
and whoever **s**, ‘You fool,’ shall	**Mt 5:22**	3004
“Not everyone who **s** to Me,	**Mt 7:21**	3004
Then it **s**, ‘I will return to my house	**Mt 12:44**	3004
is being fulfilled, which **s**,	**Mt 13:14**	3004
“But you say, ‘Whoever **s** to *his*	**Mt 15:5**	3004
“If anyone **s** anything to	**Mt 21:3**	3004
“Then if anyone **s** to you,	**Mt 24:23**	3004
if that evil slave **s** in his heart,	**Mt 24:48**	3004
‘The Teacher **s**, “My time is near;	**Mt 26:18**	3004
man **s** to *his* father or *his* mother,	**Mk 7:11**	3004
“If anyone **s** to you,	**Mk 11:3**	3004
you, whoever **s** to this mountain,	**Mk 11:23**	3004
that what he **s** is going to happen,	**Mk 11:23**	2980
“And then if anyone **s** to you,	**Mk 13:21**	3004
Teacher **s**, “Where is My guest room	**Mk 14:14**	3004
Scripture was fulfilled which **s**,	**Mk 15:28**	3004
for he **s**, ‘The old is good *enough*.’ ”	**Lk 5:39**	3004
and goes to him at midnight and **s** to	**Lk 11:5**	3004
and from inside he answers and **s**,	**Lk 11:7**	3004
rest, and not finding any, it **s**,	**Lk 11:24**	3004
“But if that slave **s** in his heart,	**Lk 12:45**	3004
himself **s** in the book of Psalms,	**Lk 20:42**	3004
‘The Teacher **s** to you,	**Lk 22:11**	3004
“Whatever He **s** to you, do it.”	**Jn 2:5**	3004
God, and who it is who **s** to you,	**Jn 4:10**	3004
kill Himself, will He, since He **s**,	**Jn 8:22**	3004
“What is this that He **s**,	**Jn 16:18**	3004
And again another Scripture **s**,	**Jn 19:37**	3004
SHALL BE IN THE LAST DAYS,’ God **s**,	**Ac 2:17**	3004
“For David **s** of Him,	**Ac 2:25**	3004
into heaven, but he himself **s**:	**Ac 2:34**	3004
HEED to everything He **s** to you.	**Ac 3:22**	2980
as the prophet **s**:	**Ac 7:48**	3004
YOU BUILD FOR ME?’ **s** the Lord	**Ac 7:49**	3004
He also **s** in another *Psalm*,	**Ac 13:35**	3004
S THE LORD, WHO MAKES THESE	**Ac 15:18**	3004
“This is what the Holy Spirit **s**:	**Ac 21:11**	3004
we know that whatever the Law **s**,	**Ro 3:19**	3004
For He **s** to Moses,	**Ro 9:15**	3004
For the Scripture **s** to Pharaoh,	**Ro 9:17**	3004
As He **s** also in Hosea,	**Ro 9:25**	3004
For the Scripture **s**,	**Ro 10:11**	3004
Isaiah **s**, “LORD, WHO HAS BELIEVED	**Ro 10:16**	3004
First Moses **s**,	**Ro 10:19**	3004
And Isaiah is very bold and **s**,	**Ro 10:20**	3004
But as for Israel He **s**,	**Ro 10:21**	3004
s *in the passage about* Elijah,	**Ro 11:2**	3004
David **s**, “LET THEIR TABLE BECOME	**Ro 11:9**	3004
IS MINE, I WILL REPAY,” **s** the Lord.	**Ro 12:19**	3004
“AS I LIVE, **S** THE LORD, EVERY	**Ro 14:11**	3004
Again he **s**, “REJOICE, O GENTILES,	**Ro 15:10**	3004
Again Isaiah **s**,	**Ro 15:12**	3004
For when one **s**, “I am of Paul,”	**1Co 3:4**	3004
He **s**, “THE TWO SHALL BECOME ONE	**1Co 6:16**	5346
But if anyone **s** to you, “This is	**1Co 10:28**	3004
speaking by the Spirit of God **s**,	**1Co 12:3**	3004
If the foot **s**, “Because I am not a	**1Co 12:15**	3004
And if the ear **s**, “Because I am not	**1Co 12:16**	3004
WILL NOT LISTEN TO ME,” **s** the Lord.	**1Co 14:21**	3004
just as the Law also **s**.	**1Co 14:34**	3004
when He **s**, “All things are put in	**1Co 15:27**	3004
for He **s**, “AT THE ACCEPTABLE TIME	**2Co 6:2**	3004
MIDST AND BE SEPARATE,” **s** the Lord.	**2Co 6:17**	3004
to Me,” **S** the Lord Almighty.	**2Co 6:18**	3004
it **s**, “WHEN HE ASCENDED ON HIGH,	**Eph 4:8**	3004
For this reason it **s**,	**Eph 5:14**	3004
But the Spirit explicitly **s** that	**1Tm 4:1**	3004
For the Scripture **s**,	**1Tm 5:18**	3004
firstborn into the world, He **s**,	**Heb 1:6**	3004
And of the angels He **s**,	**Heb 1:7**	3004
But of the Son *He* **s**, “YOUR	**Heb 1:8**	3004
just as the Holy Spirit **s**,	**Heb 3:7**	3004
as He **s** also in another *passage*,	**Heb 5:6**	3004
“SEE,” He **s**, “THAT YOU MAKE all	**Heb 8:5**	5346
For finding fault with them, He **s**,	**Heb 8:8**	3004
DAYS ARE COMING, **S** THE LORD,	**Heb 8:8**	3004
DID NOT CARE FOR THEM, **S** THE LORD.	**Heb 8:9**	3004
AFTER THOSE DAYS, **S** THE LORD:	**Heb 8:10**	3004
He comes into the world, He **s**,	**Heb 10:5**	3004

AFTER THOSE DAYS, S THE LORD: Heb 10:16 3004
WRITE THEM," He then s, Heb 10:16 3004
brethren, if someone s he has faith Jas 2:14 3004
and one of you s to them, Jas 2:16 3004
Scripture was fulfilled which s, Jas 2:23 3004
does not stumble in what he s, Jas 3:2 3056
s, "GOD IS OPPOSED TO THE PROUD, Jas 4:6 3004
who s, "I have come to know Him," 1Jn 2:4 3004
the one who s he abides in Him 1Jn 2:6 3004
The one who s he is in the Light 1Jn 2:9 3004
If someone s, "I love God," and 1Jn 4:20 3004
and the Omega," s the Lord God, Rv 1:8 3004
seven golden lampstands, s this: Rv 2:1 3004
what the Spirit s to the churches. Rv 2:7 3004
and has come to life, s this: Rv 2:8 3004
what the Spirit s to the churches. Rv 2:11 3004
the sharp two-edged sword s this: Rv 2:12 3004
what the Spirit s to the churches. Rv 2:17 3004
are like burnished bronze, s this: Rv 2:18 3004
the Spirit s to the churches.' Rv 2:29 3004
God and the seven stars, s this: Rv 3:1 3004
the Spirit s to the churches.' Rv 3:6 3004
shuts and no one opens, s this: Rv 3:7 3004
the Spirit s to the churches.' Rv 3:13 3004
of the creation of God, s this: Rv 3:14 3004
the Spirit s to the churches.'" Rv 3:22 3004
"Yes," s the Spirit, "so that they may Rv 14:13 3004
for she s in her heart, Rv 18:7 3004
who testifies to these things s, Rv 22:20 3004

SCAB
swelling or a s or a bright spot, Lv 13:2 5597
pronounce him clean; it is *only* a s. Lv 13:6 4556
the s spreads farther on the skin after Lv 13:7 4556
if the s has spread on the skin, Lv 13:8 4556
and for a swelling, and for a s, Lv 14:56 5597
and with the s and with the itch, Dt 28:27 1618

SCABS
eczema or s or crushed testicles. Lv 21:20 3217
a running sore or eczema or s, Lv 22:22 3217
of the daughters of Zion with s, Is 3:17 8197c

SCALE
it is a s, it is leprosy of the head or Lv 13:30 5424
looks at the infection of the s, Lv 13:31 5424
and if the s has not spread and Lv 13:32 5424
the s is no deeper than the skin, Lv 13:32 5424
but he shall not shave the s; Lv 13:33 5424
person with the s seven more days. Lv 13:33 5424
the priest shall look at the s, Lv 13:34 5424
the s has not spread in the skin and Lv 13:34 5424
"But if the s spreads farther in Lv 13:35 5424
if the s has spread in the skin, Lv 13:36 5424
in his sight the s has remained, Lv 13:37 5424
has grown in it, the s has healed, Lv 13:37 5424
any mark of leprosy—even for a s, Lv 14:54 5424
LORD, And a false s is not good. Pr 20:23 3976
silver on the s Hire a goldsmith, Is 46:6 7070

SCALE-ARMOR
and he was clothed with s which 1Sa 17:5 7193
Polish the spears, Put on the s! Jer 46:4 5630
it, Nor let him rise up in his s; Jer 51:3 5630

SCALES
all that have fins and s, Lv 11:9 7193
that does not have fins and s among Lv 11:10 7193
fins and s is abhorrent to you. Lv 11:12 7193
that has fins and s you may eat, Dt 14:9 7193
have fins and s you shall not eat; Dt 14:10 7193
Let Him weigh me with accurate s, Jb 31:6 3976
"*His* strong s are *his* pride, Shut Jb 41:15 4043
balance and s belong to the LORD; Pr 16:11 3976
A wise man s the city of the mighty Pr 21:22 5927
And the hills in a pair of s? Is 40:12 3976
as a speck of dust on the s; Is 40:15 3976
weighed out the silver on the s. Jer 32:10 3976
Then take s for weighing and Ezk 5:1 3976
of your rivers cling to your s. Ezk 29:4 7193
your rivers will cling to your s. Ezk 29:4 7193
you have been weighed on the s Da 5:27 3977
And to cheat with dishonest s, Am 8:5 3976
"Can I justify wicked s And a bag Mi 6:11 3976
from his eyes something like s, Ac 9:18 3013
on it had a pair of s in his hand. Rv 6:5 2218

SCALP
Lord will afflict the s of the daughters Is 3:17 6936
of well-set hair, a plucked-out s; Is 3:24 7144

SCALPS
And the s of the riotous revelers. Jer 48:45 6936

SCALY
isolate *the person* with the s infection Lv 13:31 5424

SCAPEGOAT
LORD and the other lot for the s. Lv 16:8 5799
on which the lot for the s fell shall Lv 16:10 5799
it into the wilderness as the s. Lv 16:10 5799
one who released the goat as the s Lv 16:26 5799

SCAR
it is *only* the s of the boil; Lv 13:23 6867
for it is *only* the s of the burn. Lv 13:28 6867

SCARCE
because bread and water will be s; Ezk 4:17 2637

SCARCELY
"S had I left them When I found SS 3:4 4592
S have they been planted, Scarcely Is 40:24 1077, 637
planted, S have they been sown, Is 40:24 1077, 637
S has their stock taken root Is 40:24 1077, 637
WITH THEIR EARS THEY S HEAR, Mt 13:15 917
we were s able to get the *ship's* Ac 27:16 3433
AND WITH THEIR EARS THEY S HEAR, Ac 28:27 917

SCARCER
make mortal man s than pure gold And Is 13:12 3365

SCARCITY
you will eat food without s, Dt 8:9 4544

SCARECROW
Like a s in a cucumber field are they Jer 10:5 8560

SCARLET
and tied a s *thread* on his hand, Gn 38:28 8144
who had the s *thread* on his hand; Gn 38:30 8144
blue, purple and s *material,* Ex 25:4 8144
blue and purple and s *material;* Ex 26:1 8144
make a veil of blue and purple and s Ex 26:31 8144
tent of blue and purple and s *material* Ex 26:36 8144
of blue and purple and s *material* Ex 27:16 8144
the s *material* and the fine linen. Ex 28:5 8144
of blue and purple *and* s *material* Ex 28:6 8144
of blue and purple and s *material* Ex 28:8 8144
of blue and purple and s *material* Ex 28:15 8144
of blue and purple and s *material,* Ex 28:33 8144
and blue, purple and s *material,* Ex 35:6 8144
purple and s *material* and fine linen Ex 35:23 8144
and s *material* and *in* fine linen. Ex 35:25 8144
and in purple *and* in s *material,* Ex 35:35 8144
blue and purple and s *material,* Ex 36:8 8144
of blue and purple and s *material,* Ex 36:35 8144
of blue and purple and s *material,* Ex 36:37 8144
of blue and purple and s *material* and Ex 38:18 8144
and in purple and in s *material,* Ex 38:23 8144
blue and purple and s *material,* Ex 39:1 8144
of blue and purple and s *material,* Ex 39:2 8144
and the purple and the s *material,* Ex 39:3 8144
of blue and purple and s *material,* Ex 39:5 8144
blue and purple and s *material* and Ex 39:8 8144
blue and purple and s *material and* Ex 39:24 8144
blue and purple and s *material,* Ex 39:29 8144
cedar wood and a s string and hyssop Lv 14:4 8144
and the s string and the hyssop, Lv 14:6 8144
wood and a s string and hyssop, Lv 14:49 8144
and the hyssop and the s string, Lv 14:51 8144
the hyssop and with the s string. Lv 14:52 8144
over them a cloth of s *material,* Nu 4:8 8144
wood and hyssop and s *material* Nu 19:6 8144
you tie this cord of s thread in Jos 2:18 8144
she tied the s cord in the window. Jos 2:21 8144
Who clothed you luxuriously in s, 2Sa 1:24 8144
her household are clothed with s. Pr 31:21 8144
"Your lips are like a s thread, SS 4:3 8144
"Though your sins are as s, Is 1:18 8144
Although you dress in s, Jer 4:30 8144
The warriors are dressed in s, Na 2:3 8529
Him and put a s robe on Him. Mt 27:28 2847
they took the s robe off Him Mt 27:31
with water and s wool and hyssop, Heb 9:19 2847
saw a woman sitting on a s beast, Rv 17:3 2847
woman was clothed in purple and s, Rv 17:4 2847
linen and purple and silk and s, Rv 18:12 2847
in fine linen and purple and s, Rv 18:16 2847

SCATTER
in Jacob, And s them in Israel. Gn 49:7 6327a
I will s among the nations and Lv 26:33 2219
you s the burning coals abroad. Nu 16:37 2219
LORD will s you among the peoples, Dt 4:27 6327a
LORD will s you among all peoples, Dt 28:64 6327a
and will s them beyond the 1Ki 14:15 2219
I will s you among the peoples; Ne 1:8 6327a
S them by Your power, and bring Ps 59:11 5128
nations And s them in the lands. Ps 106:27 2219
Flash forth lightning and s them; Ps 144:6 6327a
And sow dill and s cummin And Is 28:25 2236b
will s them as an impure thing, Is 30:22 2219
away, And the storm will s them; Is 41:16 6327a
I will s them among the nations, Jer 9:16 6327a
"Therefore I will s them like Jer 13:24 6327a
I will s them Before the enemy; Jer 18:17 6327a
all places where I will s them. Jer 24:9 5080
And I will s to all the winds Jer 49:32 2219
will s them to all these winds; Jer 49:36 2219
one third you shall s to the wind; Ezk 5:2 2219
and s all your remnant to every Ezk 5:10 2219
one third I will s to every wind, Ezk 5:12 2219
s your bones around your altars. Ezk 6:5 2219
and s *them* over the city." Ezk 10:2 2236b
"I will s to every wind all Ezk 12:14 2219
when I s them among the nations and Ezk 12:15 6327a
I would s them among the nations Ezk 20:23 6327a
I will s you among the nations Ezk 22:15 6327a
and I will s the Egyptians among Ezk 29:12 6327a
'I will s the Egyptians among Ezk 30:23 6327a
'When I s the Egyptians among the Ezk 30:26 6327a
off its foliage and s its fruit; Da 4:14 921
They stormed in to s us; Hab 3:14 6327a
land of Judah in order to s it." Zch 1:21 2219
"When I s them among the peoples, Zch 10:9 2232
falls, it will s him like dust." Mt 21:44 3039
falls, it will s him like dust." Lk 20:18 3039

SCATTERED
we will be s abroad over the face Gn 11:4 6327a
So the LORD s them abroad from Gn 11:8 6327a
and from there the LORD s them Gn 11:9 6327a
So the people s through all the Ex 5:12 6327a
and s it over the surface of the Ex 32:20 2219
And let Your enemies be s, Nu 10:35 6327a
where the LORD your God has s you. Dt 30:3 6327a
Those who survived were s, 1Sa 11:11 6327a
the well's mouth and s grain on it, 2Sa 17:19 7849
He sent out arrows, and s them, 2Sa 22:15 6327a
saw all Israel S on the mountains, 1Ki 22:17 6327a
and all his army was s from him. 2Ki 25:5 6327a
saw all Israel S on the mountains, 2Ch 18:16 6327a
s *it* on the graves of those who had 2Ch 34:4 2236b
those of you who have been s were Ne 1:9 5080
"There is a certain people s and Es 3:8 6340
the whelps of the lioness are s. Jb 4:11 6504
Brimstone is s on his habitation. Jb 18:15 2219
Or the east wind s on the earth? Jb 38:24 6327a
sent out His arrows, and s them, Ps 18:14 6327a
And have s us among the nations. Ps 44:11 2219
For God s the bones of him who Ps 53:5 6340
God arise, let His enemies be s, Ps 68:1 6327a
the Almighty s the kings there, Ps 68:14 6566
He has s the peoples who delight Ps 68:30 967
You s Your enemies with Your mighty Ps 89:10 6340
All who do iniquity will be s. Ps 92:9 6504
Our bones have been s at the mouth Ps 141:7 6340
like fleeing birds *or* s nestlings, Is 16:2 7971
who were s in the land of Egypt will Is 27:13 5080
have s your favors to the strangers Jer 3:13 6340
And all their flock is s. Jer 10:21 6327a
s My flock and driven them away, Jer 23:2 6327a
the nations where I have s you, Jer 30:11 6327a
"He who s Israel will gather him And Jer 31:10 2219
who are gathered to you would be s Jer 40:15 6327a
"Israel is a s flock, the lions Jer 50:17 6340
and all his army was s from him. Jer 52:8 6327a
presence of the LORD has s them, La 4:16 2505a
you are s among the countries. Ezk 6:8 2219
I had s them among the countries, Ezk 11:16 6327a
among which you have been s, Ezk 11:17 6327a
survivors will be s to every wind; Ezk 17:21 6566
from the lands where you are s, Ezk 20:34 6327a
from the lands where you are s; Ezk 20:41 6327a
the peoples among whom they are s, Ezk 28:25 6327a
peoples among whom they were s. Ezk 29:13 6327a
the s you have not brought back, Ezk 34:4 5080
They were s for lack of a shepherd, Ezk 34:5 6327a
beast of the field and were s. Ezk 34:5 6327a
My flock was s over all the Ezk 34:6 6327a
day when he is among his s sheep, Ezk 34:12 6567a
were s on a cloudy and gloomy day. Ezk 34:12 6327a
seek the lost, bring back the s, Ezk 34:16 5080
until you have s them abroad, Ezk 34:21 6327a
"Also I s them among the nations and Ezk 36:19 6327a
so that My people will not be s, Ezk 46:18 6327a
they have s among the nations; Jl 3:2 6340
people are s on the mountains And Na 3:18 6335b
are the horns which have s Judah, Zch 1:19 2219
are the horns which have s Judah so Zch 1:21 2219
"but I s them with a storm wind Zch 7:14 5590
for the perishing, seek the s, Zch 11:16 5289
Shepherd that the sheep may be s; Zch 13:7 6327a
and gathering where you s no *seed.* Mt 25:24 1287
sow and gather where I s no *seed.* Mt 25:26 1287
SHEEP OF THE FLOCK SHALL BE S.' Mt 26:31 1287
AND THE SHEEP SHALL BE S.' Mk 14:27 1287
He has s *those who were* proud in Lk 1:51 1287
children of God who are s abroad. Jn 11:52 1287
has *already* come, for you to be s, Jn 16:32 4650
all those who followed him were s. Ac 5:37 1287
and they were all s throughout the Ac 8:1 1289
those who had been s went about Ac 8:4 1289
So then those who were s because Ac 11:19 1289
"HE S ABROAD, HE GAVE TO THE 2Co 9:9 4650
as aliens, s throughout Pontus, 1Pe 1:1 1290

SCATTERING
and the people were s from him. 1Sa 13:8 6327a
that the people were s from me, 1Sa 13:11 5310b
and s the sheep of My pasture!" Jer 23:1 6327a

SCATTERS
He s the frost like ashes. Ps 147:16 6340
There is one who s, Pr 11:24 6340
surface and s its inhabitants. Is 24:1 6327a
one who s has come up against you. Na 2:1 4650
he who does not gather with Me s. Mt 12:30 4650
he who does not gather with Me, s. Lk 11:23 4650
wolf snatches them and s *them.* Jn 10:12 4650

SCENT
At the s of water it will flourish Jb 14:9 7381b

SCENTED
all s powders of the merchant? SS 3:6 81

SCENTS
And he s the battle from afar, And Jb 39:25 7381a

SCEPTER
"The s shall not depart from Judah, Gn 49:10 7626
With the s *and* with their staffs." Nu 21:18 2710
A s shall rise from Israel, Nu 24:17 7626
the golden s so that he may live. Es 4:11 8275
golden s which *was* in his hand. Es 5:2 8275
near and touched the top of the s. Es 5:2 8275
extended the golden s to Esther. Es 8:4 8275
A s of uprightness is the scepter Ps 45:6 7626
is the s of Your kingdom. Ps 45:6 7626
helmet of My head; Judah is My s. Ps 60:7 2710
helmet of My head; Judah is My s. Ps 108:8 2710
LORD will stretch forth Your strong s Ps 110:2 4294
For the s of wickedness shall not Ps 125:3 7626
of the wicked, The s of rulers Is 14:5 7626
'How has the mighty s been broken, Jer 48:17 4294
a strong branch, A s to rule.'" Ezk 19:14 7626
of Aven, And him who holds the s, Am 1:5 7626
Ashdod, And him who holds the s, Am 1:8 7626
Shepherd Your people with Your s, Mi 7:14 7626
And the s of Egypt will depart. Zch 10:11 7626
S IS THE SCEPTER OF HIS KINGDOM. Heb 1:8 4464
SCEPTER IS THE S OF HIS KINGDOM. Heb 1:8 4464

SCEPTERS
branches *fit* for **s** of rulers, Ezk 19:11 7626
SCEVA
Seven sons of one **S**, Ac 19:14 *4630*
SCHEDULE
to year, observe *your* feasts on **s**. Is 29:1 5362b
SCHEME
implored him to avert the evil **s** Es 8:3
his wicked **s** which he had devised Es 9:25 4284
And his own **s** brings him down. Jb 18:7 6098
In whose hands is a wicked **s**, Ps 26:10 2154
you And devised a **s** against you. Jer 49:30 4284
Woe to those who **s** iniquity, Mi 2:1 2803
SCHEMED
had **s** against the Jews to destroy Es 9:24 2803
me, They **s** to take away my life. Ps 31:13 2161
SCHEMER
the **s** is eager for their wealth. Jb 5:5 6782
to do evil, Men will call a **s**. Pr 24:8 1167, 4209
SCHEMES
favorably on the **s** of the wicked? Jb 10:3 6098
the man who carries out wicked **s**. Ps 37:7 4209
He devises wicked **s** To destroy *the* Is 32:7 2154
vengeance, All their **s** against me. La 3:60 4284
O LORD, All their **s** against me. La 3:61 4284
devise his **s** against strongholds, Da 11:24 4284
for **s** will be devised against him. Da 11:25 4284
for we are not ignorant of his **s**. 2Co 2:11 *3540*
firm against the **s** of the devil. Eph 6:11 *3180*
SCHEMING
men, by craftiness in deceitful **s**; Eph 4:14 *3180*
SCHOOL
daily in the **s** of Tyrannus. Ac 19:9 *4981*
SCOFF
And shall you **s** and none rebuke? Jb 11:3 3932
You **s** at all the nations. Ps 59:8 3932
And if you **s**, you alone will bear it. Pr 9:12 3917b
SCOFFED
His words and **s** at His prophets, 2Ch 36:16 8591a
SCOFFER
a **s** gets dishonor for himself, Pr 9:7 3917b
Do not reprove a **s**, Pr 9:8 3917b
But a **s** does not listen to rebuke. Pr 13:1 3917b
A **s** seeks wisdom and *finds* none, Pr 14:6 3917b
A **s** does not love one who reproves Pr 15:12 3917b
Strike a **s** and the naive may Pr 19:25 3917b
When the **s** is punished, the naive Pr 21:11 3917b
"Proud," "Haughty," "**S**," Pr 21:24 3917b
Drive out the **s**, and contention Pr 22:10 3917b
the **s** is an abomination to men. Pr 24:9 3917b
SCOFFERS
"My friends are my **s**; Jb 16:20 3917b
sinners, Nor sit in the seat of **s**! Ps 1:1 3917b
And **s** delight themselves in Pr 1:22 3917b
Though He scoffs at the **s**, Pr 3:34 3917b
Judgments are prepared for **s**, Pr 19:29 3917b
hear the word of the LORD, O **s**, Is 28:14 582, 3944
And now do not carry on as **s**, Is 28:22 3917b
He stretched out his hand with **s**, Hos 7:5 3917b
'BEHOLD, YOU **S**, AND MARVEL, AND Ac 13:41 *2707*
SCOFFING
that wrath does not entice you to **s**; Jb 36:18 5607
A **s** and a derision to those around Ps 44:13 3933
A **s** and derision to those around Ps 79:4 3933
the **s** of those who are at ease, Ps 123:4 3933
scoffers delight themselves in **s** And Pr 1:22 3944
things and were **s** at Him. Lk 16:14 *1592*
SCOFFS
laughs, The Lord **s** at them. Ps 2:4 3932
Though He **s** at the scoffers, Yet Pr 3:34 3917b
SCOLDING
And they were **s** her. Mk 14:5 *1690*
SCOOP
Or to **s** water from a cistern." Is 30:14 2834
SCORCH
given to it to **s** men with fire. Rv 16:8 *2739*
SCORCHED
ears, thin and **s** by the east wind, Gn 41:6 7710
thin, *and* **s** by the east wind, Gn 41:23 7710
seven thin ears **s** by the east wind Gn 41:27 7710
is **s** before it is grown up. 2Ki 19:26 7711a
bones have been **s** like a hearth. Ps 102:3 2787
hot coals And his feet not be **s**? Pr 6:28 3554
The **s** land will become a pool And Is 35:7 8273
is **s** before it is grown up. Is 37:27 7711a
the fire, you will not be **s**, Is 43:2 3554
satisfy your desire in **s** places, Is 58:11 6710
the sun had risen, they were **s**; Mt 13:6 *2739*
after the sun had risen, it was **s**; Mk 4:6 *2739*
Men were **s** with fierce heat; Rv 16:9 *2739*
SCORCHING
While his words are like **s** fire. Pr 16:27 6866b
over the River With His **s** wind; Is 11:15 5868
s heat or sun strike them down; Is 49:10 8273
"A **s** wind from the bare heights Jer 4:11 6703
smote you with **s** *wind* and mildew; Am 4:9 7711b
up God appointed a **s** east wind, Jon 4:8 2759
burden and the **s** heat of the day.' Mt 20:12 *2742*
For the sun rises with a **s** wind and Jas 1:11 *2742*
SCORN
but they laughed them to **s** and 2Ch 30:10 7832
And with dishonor *comes* **s**. Pr 18:3 2781
about him you shake *your head in* **s**. Jer 48:27
rejoiced with all the **s** of your soul Ezk 25:6 7589
have taken vengeance with **s** of soul Ezk 25:15 7589
all who **s** them round about them. Ezk 28:26 7751c
joy *and* with **s** of soul, Ezk 36:5 7589
put a stop to his **s** against him; Da 11:18 2781
he will repay him for his **s**. Da 11:18 2781
and **s** your name as evil, for Lk 6:22 *1544b*
SCORNED
And **s** the Rock of his salvation. Dt 32:15 5034a
greet our master, and he **s** them. 1Sa 25:14 5860a
mountains And **s** Me on the hills, Is 65:7 2778a
any round about them who **s** them; Ezk 28:24 7751c
SCORNER
end and the **s** will be finished, Is 29:20 3917b
SCORNERS
S set a city aflame, But wise men Pr 29:8 582, 3944
SCORNS
"He **s** the tumult of the city, The Jb 39:7 7832
mocks a father And **s** a mother, Pr 30:17 936, 3349
SCORPION
he will not give him a **s**, will he? Lk 11:12 *4651*
like the torment of a **s** when it stings Rv 9:5 *4651*
SCORPIONS
with its fiery serpents and **s** and Dt 8:15 6137
I will discipline you with **s**.'" 1Ki 12:11 6137
I will discipline you with **s**." 1Ki 12:14 6137
I *will discipline you* with **s**.'" 2Ch 10:11 6137
I *will discipline you* with **s**." 2Ch 10:14 6137
are with you and you sit on **s**; Ezk 2:6 6137
to tread on serpents and **s**, Lk 10:19 *4651*
as the **s** of the earth have power. Rv 9:3 *4651*
They have tails like **s**, Rv 9:10 *4651*
SCOUNDRELS
men gathered about him, **s**, 2Ch 13:7 1121, 1100
SCOUR
Stripes that wound **s** away evil, Pr 20:30 4838
SCOURED
it shall be **s** and rinsed in water. Lv 6:28 4838
SCOURGE
hidden from the **s** of the tongue, Jb 5:21 7752
"If the **s** kills suddenly, He Jb 9:23 7752
LORD of hosts will arouse a **s** against Is 10:26 7752
The overwhelming **s** will not reach Is 28:15 7752
the overwhelming **s** passes through, Is 28:18 7752
and **s** you in their synagogues; Mt 10:17 *3146*
to mock and **s** and crucify *Him*, Mt 20:19 *3146*
you will **s** in your synagogues, Mt 23:34 *3146*
Him and spit on Him, and **s** Him Mk 10:34 *3146*
And He made a **s** of cords, and Jn 2:15 *5416*
"Is it lawful for you to **s** a man Ac 22:25 *3147*
SCOURGED
a name, They were **s** from the land. Jb 30:8 5217
but after having Jesus **s**, Mt 27:26 *5417*
them, and after having Jesus **s**, Mk 15:15 *5417*
and after they have **s** Him, Lk 18:33 *3146*
took Jesus and **s** Him. Jn 19:1 *3146*
SCOURGES
HE **S** EVERY SON WHOM HE RECEIVES." Heb 12:6 *3146*
SCOURGING
Him, And by His **s** we are healed. Is 53:5 2250
be examined by **s** so that he might Ac 22:24 *3148*
SCOURGINGS
others experienced mockings and **s**, Heb 11:36 *3148*
SCRAPE
shall dump the plaster that they **s** off Lv 14:41 7096
And he took a potsherd to **s** Jb 2:8 1623
and I will **s** her debris from her Ezk 26:4 5500
SCRAPED
the house **s** all around inside, Lv 14:41 7106a
out the stones and **s** the house, Lv 14:43 7096
So he **s** the honey into his hands Jg 14:9 7287b
he had **s** the honey out of the body Jg 14:9 7287b
SCRAPS
toes cut off used to gather up **s** Jg 1:7
SCREAMED
in to me to lie with me, and I **s**. Gn 39:14 7121, 6963, 1419
that I raised my voice and **s**, Gn 39:15 7121
as I raised my voice and **s**, Gn 39:18 7121
SCREAMING
Constantly, night and day, he was **s** Mk 5:5 *2896*
SCREAMS
seizes him, and he suddenly **s**, Lk 9:39 *2896*
SCREEN
"You shall make a **s** for the Ex 26:36 4539
five pillars of acacia for the **s** and Ex 26:37 4539
shall be a **s** of twenty cubits, Ex 27:16 4539
seat, and the curtain of the **s**; Ex 35:12 4539
and the **s** for the doorway at the Ex 35:15 4539
the **s** for the gate of the court; Ex 35:17 4539
a **s** for the doorway of the tent, Ex 36:37 4539
The **s** of the gate of the court Ex 38:18 4539
the **s** for the gate of the court, Ex 39:40 4539
you shall **s** the ark with the veil. Ex 40:3 5526a
and set up a veil for the **s**, Ex 40:21 4539
the **s** for the doorway of the tent Nu 3:25 4539
s for the doorway of the court which Nu 3:26 4539
the **s**, and all the service concerning Nu 3:31 4539
take down the veil of the **s** and cover Nu 4:5 4539
and the **s** for the doorway of the Nu 4:25 4539
and the **s** for the doorway of the Nu 4:26 4539
SCREENED
s off the ark of the testimony, Ex 40:21 5526a
SCREENING
of porpoise skins, and the **s** veil; Ex 39:34 4539
SCRIBBLED
and **s** on the doors of the gate, 1Sa 21:13 8427
SCRIBE
and Sheva was **s**, and Zadok and 2Sa 20:25 5613b
the king's **s** and the high priest 2Ki 12:10 5613b
and Shebnah the **s** and Joah the son 2Ki 18:18 5613b
the **s** and Joah the son of Asaph, 2Ki 18:37 5613b
s and the elders of the priests, 2Ki 19:2 5613b
the son of Meshullam the **s**, 2Ki 22:3 5613b
high priest said to Shaphan the **s**, 2Ki 22:8 5613b
Shaphan the **s** came to the king 2Ki 22:9 5613b
Shaphan the **s** told the king saying, 2Ki 22:10 5613b
the son of Micaiah, Shaphan the **s**, 2Ki 22:12 5613b
the **s** of the captain of the army who 2Ki 25:19 5613b
the son of Nethanel the **s**, 1Ch 24:6 5613b
a man of understanding, and a **s**; 1Ch 27:32 5613b
then the king's **s** and the chief 2Ch 24:11 5613b
the **s** and Maaseiah the official, 2Ch 26:11 5613b
and said to Shaphan the **s**, 2Ch 34:15 5613b
the **s** told the king saying, 2Ch 34:18 5613b
the son of Micah, Shaphan the **s**, 2Ch 34:20 5613b
Shimshai the **s** wrote a letter against Ezr 4:8 5613a
the **s** and the rest of their colleagues, Ezr 4:9 5613a
the commander, to Shimshai the **s**, Ezr 4:17 5613a
the **s** and their colleagues, Ezr 4:23 5613a
a **s** skilled in the law of Moses, Ezr 7:6 5613b
gave to Ezra the priest, the **s**, Ezr 7:11 5613b
s of the law of the God of heaven, Ezr 7:12 5613a
s of the law of the God of heaven, Ezr 7:21 5613a
and they asked Ezra the **s** to bring Ne 8:1 5613b
Ezra the **s** stood at a wooden Ne 8:4 5613b
and Ezra the priest *and* **s**, Ne 8:9 5613b
Levites were gathered to Ezra the **s** Ne 8:13 5613b
and of Ezra the priest *and* **s**. Ne 12:26 5613b
And Ezra the **s** went before them. Ne 12:36 5613b
Shelemiah the priest, Zadok the **s**, Ne 13:13 5613b
the household, and Shebna the **s**, Is 36:3 5613b
the **s** and Joah the son of Asaph, Is 36:22 5613b
s and the elders of the priests, Is 37:2 5613b
Gemariah the son of Shaphan the **s**, Jer 36:10 5613b
Elishama the **s**, and Delaiah the son Jer 36:12 5613b
in the chamber of Elishama the **s**, Jer 36:20 5613b
of the chamber of Elishama the **s**. Jer 36:21 5613b
the **s** and Jeremiah the prophet, Jer 36:26 5613b
Baruch the son of Neraiah, the **s**, Jer 36:32 5613b
in the house of Jonathan the **s**, Jer 37:15 5613b
to the house of Jonathan the **s**, Jer 37:20 5613b
and the **s** of the commander of the Jer 52:25 5613b
a **s** came and said to Him, Mt 8:19 *1122*
"Therefore every **s** who has become Mt 13:52 *1122*
The **s** said to Him, Mk 12:32 *1122*
Where is the **s**? Where is the debater 1Co 1:20 *1122*
SCRIBE'S
king's house, into the **s** chamber. Jer 36:12 5613b
the king cut it with a **s** knife and Jer 36:23 5613b
SCRIBES
The families of **s** who lived at 1Ch 2:55 5613b
s and officials and gatekeepers. 2Ch 34:13 5613b
Then the king's **s** were summoned on Es 3:12 5613b
So the king's **s** were called at Es 8:9 5613b
lying pen of the **s** Has made *it* into Jer 8:8 5613b
chief priests and **s** of the people, Mt 2:4 *1122*
that of the **s** and Pharisees, Mt 5:20 *1122*
authority, and not as their **s**. Mt 7:29 *1122*
some of the **s** said to themselves, Mt 9:3 *1122*
the **s** and Pharisees said to Him, Mt 12:38 *1122*
s came to Jesus from Jerusalem and Mt 15:1 *1122*
elders and chief priests and **s**, Mt 16:21 *1122*
"Why then do the **s** say that Mt 17:10 *1122*
to the chief priests and **s**, Mt 20:18 *1122*
when the chief priests and the **s** saw Mt 21:15 *1122*
"The **s** and the Pharisees have Mt 23:2 *1122*
"But woe to you, **s** and Pharisees, Mt 23:13 *1122*
["Woe to you, **s** and Pharisees, Mt 23:14 *1122*
"Woe to you, **s** and Pharisees, Mt 23:15 *1122*
"Woe to you, **s** and Pharisees, Mt 23:23 *1122*
"Woe to you, **s** and Pharisees, Mt 23:25 *1122*
"Woe to you, **s** and Pharisees, Mt 23:27 *1122*
"Woe to you, **s** and Pharisees, Mt 23:29 *1122*
you prophets and wise men and **s**; Mt 23:34 *1122*
where the **s** and the elders were Mt 26:57 *1122*
also, along with the **s** and elders, Mt 27:41 *1122*
authority, and not as the **s**. Mk 1:22 *1122*
But some of the **s** Mk 2:6 *1122*
When the **s** of the Pharisees Mk 2:16 *1122*
The **s** who came down from Mk 3:22 *1122*
Pharisees and some of the **s** gathered Mk 7:1 *1122*
The Pharisees and the **s** asked Him, Mk 7:5 *1122*
and the chief priests and the **s**, Mk 8:31 *1122*
"*Why is it* that the **s** say that Mk 9:11 *1122*
and *some* **s** arguing with them. Mk 9:14 *1122*
to the chief priests and the **s**; Mk 10:33 *1122*
The chief priests and the **s** heard *this* Mk 11:18 *1122*
temple, the chief priests and the **s** Mk 11:27 *1122*
the **s** came and heard them arguing, Mk 12:28 *1122*
"How *is it that* the **s** say that Mk 12:35 *1122*
"Beware of the **s** who like to walk Mk 12:38 *1122*
and the chief priests and the **s** Mk 14:1 *1122*
chief priests and the **s** and the elders Mk 14:43 *1122*
chief priests and the elders and the **s** Mk 14:53 *1122*
chief priests with the elders and **s** and Mk 15:1 *1122*
chief priests also, along with the **s**, Mk 15:31 *1122*
The **s** and the Pharisees began Lk 5:21 *1122*
The Pharisees and their **s** Lk 5:30 *1122*

The **s** and the Pharisees were Lk 6:7 *1122*
elders and chief priests and **s**, Lk 9:22 *1122*
the **s** and the Pharisees began to Lk 11:53 *1122*
Pharisees and the **s** *began* to grumble Lk 15:2 *1122*
but the chief priests and the **s** Lk 19:47 *1122*
the chief priests and the **s** Lk 20:1 *1122*
The **s** and the chief priests Lk 20:19 *1122*
Some of the **s** answered and said, Lk 20:39 *1122*
"Beware of the **s**, who like to Lk 20:46 *1122*
The chief priests and the **s** Lk 22:2 *1122*
both chief priests and **s**, Lk 22:66 *1122*
chief priests and the **s** were standing Lk 23:10 *1122*
The **s** and the Pharisees Jn 8:3 *1122*
rulers and elders and **s** were gathered Ac 4:5 *1122*
the people, the elders and the **s**, Ac 6:12 *1122*
some of the **s** of the Pharisaic party Ac 23:9 *1122*

SCRIPT
to each province according to its **s** Es 1:22 3791
each province according to its **s**, Es 3:12 3791
every province according to its **s**, Es 8:9 3791
to their **s** and their language. Es 8:9 3791

SCRIPTURE
"Have you not even read this **S**: Mk 12:10 *1124*
the **S** was fulfilled which says, Mk 15:28 *1124*
"Today this **S** has been fulfilled Lk 4:21 *1124*
and they believed the **S** and Jn 2:22 *1124*
who believes in Me, as the **S** said, Jn 7:38 *1124*
"Has not the **S** said that the Jn 7:42 *1124*
came (and the **S** cannot be broken), Jn 10:35 *1124*
it is that the **S** may be fulfilled, Jn 13:18 *1124*
that the **S** would be fulfilled. Jn 17:12 *1124*
this was to fulfill the **S**: Jn 19:24 *1124*
to fulfill the **S**, Jn 19:28 *1124*
to fulfill the **S**, Jn 19:36 *1124*
And again another **S** says, Jn 19:37 *1124*
yet they did not understand the **S**, Jn 20:9 *1124*
the **S** had to be fulfilled, Ac 1:16 *1124*
S which he was reading was this: Ac 8:32 *1124*
this **S** he preached Jesus to him. Ac 8:35 *1124*
For what does the **S** say? Ro 4:3 *1124*
For the **S** says to Pharaoh, Ro 9:17 *1124*
S says, "Whoever believes in Him Ro 10:11 *1124*
Or do you not know what the **S** says Ro 11:2 *1124*
The **S**, foreseeing that God Ga 3:8 *1124*
S has shut up everyone under sin, Ga 3:22 *1124*
But what does the **S** say? Ga 4:30 *1124*
to the *public* reading *of* **S**, 1Tm 4:13
the **S** says, "You shall not muzzle 1Tm 5:18 *1124*
All **S** is inspired by God and 2Tm 3:16 *1124*
the royal law according to the **S**, Jas 2:8 *1124*
the **S** was fulfilled which says, Jas 2:23 *1124*
that the **S** speaks to no purpose: Jas 4:5 *1124*
For *this* is contained in **S**: 1Pe 2:6 *1124*
that no prophecy of **S** is *a matter* 2Pe 1:20 *1124*

SCRIPTURES
"Did you never read in the **S**, Mt 21:42 *1124*
mistaken, not understanding the **S** nor Mt 22:29 *1124*
"How then will the **S** be fulfilled, Mt 26:54 *1124*
to fulfill the **S** of the prophets." Mt 26:56 *1124*
that you do not understand the **S** or Mk 12:24 *1124*
to fulfill the **S**." Mk 14:49 *1124*
concerning Himself in all the **S**. Lk 24:27 *1124*
He was explaining the **S** to us?" Lk 24:32 *1124*
their minds to understand the **S**, Lk 24:45 *1124*
"You search the **S** because you Jn 5:39 *1124*
reasoned with them from the **S**, Ac 17:2 *1124*
eagerness, examining the **S** daily Ac 17:11 *1124*
and he was mighty in the **S**. Ac 18:24 *1124*
the **S** that Jesus was the Christ. Ac 18:28 *1124*
through His prophets in the holy **S**, Ro 1:2 *1124*
of the **S** we might have hope. Ro 15:4 *1124*
and by the **S** of the prophets, Ro 16:26 *1124*
died for our sins according to the **S**, 1Co 15:3 *1124*
the third day according to the **S**, 1Co 15:4 *1124*
as *they do* also the rest of the **S**, 2Pe 3:16 *1124*

SCROLL
then write these curses on a **s**, Nu 5:23 5612
for himself a copy of this law on a **s** Dt 17:18 5612
a **s** was found and there was Ezr 6:2 4040
In the **s** of the book it is written Ps 40:7 4039
them And inscribe it on a **s**, Is 30:8 5612
sky will be rolled up like a **s**; Is 34:4 5612
"Take a **s** and write on it all the Jer 36:2 4039, 5612
wrote on a **s** at the dictation Jer 36:4 4039, 5612
"So you go and read from the **s** Jer 36:6 4039
"Take in your hand the **s** from Jer 36:14 4039
Baruch the son of Neriah took the **s** Jer 36:14 4039
but they had deposited the **s** in Jer 36:20 4039
the king sent Jehudi to get the **s**, Jer 36:21 4039
until all the **s** was consumed in Jer 36:23 4039
with the king not to burn the **s**, Jer 36:25 4039
after the king had burned the **s** and Jer 36:27 4039
"Take again another **s** and write Jer 36:28 4039
former words that were on the first **s** Jer 36:28 4039
"You have burned this **s**, Jer 36:29 4039
Then Jeremiah took another **s** and Jer 36:32 4039
So Jeremiah wrote in a single **s** Jer 51:60 5612
as soon as you finish reading this **s**, Jer 51:63 5612
and lo, a **s** *was* in it. Ezk 2:9 4039, 5612
eat this **s**, and go, speak to the Ezk 3:1 4039
my mouth, and He fed me this **s**. Ezk 3:2 4039
this **s** which I am giving you." Ezk 3:3 4039
and behold, *there was* a flying **s**. Zch 5:1 4039
"I see a flying **s**; Zch 5:2 4039
I have come (In the **s** of Heb 10:7 *2777*

like a **s** when it is rolled up, Rv 6:14 *975*

SCRUTINIZE
You **s** my path and my lying down, Ps 139:3 2219

SCULPTURED
Then he made two **s** cherubim in the 2Ch 3:10 4639, 6816

SCUM
have become as the **s** of the world, 1Co 4:13 *4027*

SCYTHIAN
and uncircumcised, barbarian, **S**, Col 3:11 *4658*

SEA
God created the great **s** monsters and Gn 1:21 8577
let them rule over the fish of the **s** Gn 1:26 3220
and rule over the fish of the **s** and Gn 1:28 3220
ground, and all the fish of the **s**, Gn 9:2 3220
valley of Siddim (that is, the Salt **S**). Gn 14:3 3220
descendants as the sand of the **s**, Gn 32:12 3220
abundance like the sand of the **s**, Gn 41:49 3220
and drove them into the Red **S**; Ex 10:19 3220
way of the wilderness to the Red **S**; Ex 13:18 3220
between Migdol and the **s**; Ex 14:2 3220
Baal-zephon, opposite it, by the **s**. Ex 14:2 3220
overtook them camping by the **s**, Ex 14:9 3220
stretch out your hand over the **s** Ex 14:16 3220
the midst of the **s** on dry land. Ex 14:16 3220
stretched out his hand over the **s**; Ex 14:21 3220
and the Lord swept the **s** *back* by a Ex 14:21 3220
and turned the **s** into dry land, Ex 14:21 3220
midst of the **s** on the dry land, Ex 14:22 3220
them into the midst of the **s**. Ex 14:23 3220
"Stretch out your hand over the **s** Ex 14:26 3220
stretched out his hand over the **s**, Ex 14:27 3220
and the **s** returned to its normal Ex 14:27 3220
Egyptians in the midst of the **s**. Ex 14:27 3220
had gone into the **s** after them; Ex 14:28 3220
land through the midst of the **s**, Ex 14:29 3220
rider He has hurled into the **s**. Ex 15:1 3220
his army He has cast into the **s**; Ex 15:4 3220
officers are drowned in the Red **S**. Ex 15:4 3220
congealed in the heart of the **s**. Ex 15:8 3220
with Your wind, the **s** covered them; Ex 15:10 3220
and his horsemen went into the **s**, Ex 15:19 3220
back the waters of the **s** on them, Ex 15:19 3220
land through the midst of the **s**. Ex 15:19 3220
rider He has hurled into the **s**." Ex 15:21 3220
Moses led Israel from the Red **S**, Ex 15:22 3220
the **s** and all that is in them, Ex 20:11 3220
fix your boundary from the Red **S** Ex 23:31 3220
Red Sea to the **s** of the Philistines, Ex 23:31 3220
s gull and the hawk in its kind, Lv 11:16 7828
s be gathered together for them, Nu 11:22 3220
and it brought quail from the **s**, Nu 11:31 3220
s and by the side of the Jordan." Nu 13:29 3220
wilderness by the way of the Red **S**. Nu 14:25 3220
Mount Hor by the way of the Red **S**, Nu 21:4 3220
passed through the midst of the **s** Nu 33:8 3220
Elim and camped by the Red **S**. Nu 33:10 3220
They journeyed from the Red **S** and Nu 33:11 3220
from the end of the Salt **S** eastward. Nu 34:3 3220
its termination shall be at the **s**. Nu 34:5 3220
you shall have the Great **S**, Nu 34:6 3220
from the Great **S** to Mount Hor. Nu 34:7 3220
east side of the **S** of Chinnereth. Nu 34:11 3220
termination shall be at the Salt **S**. Nu 34:12 3220
by the way to the Red **S**.' Dt 1:40 3220
by the way to the Red **S**, Dt 2:1 3220
as far as the **s** of the Arabah, Dt 3:17 3220
the sea of the Arabah, the Salt **S**, Dt 3:17 3220
as far as the **s** of the Arabah, Dt 4:49 3220
He made the water of the Red **S** to Dt 11:4 3220
as far as the western **s**. Dt 11:24 3220
the ostrich, the owl, the **s** gull, Dt 14:15 7828
"Nor is it beyond the **s**, Dt 30:13 3220
'Who will cross the **s** for us to Dt 30:13 3220
Take possession of the **s** and the Dt 33:23 3220
of Judah as far as the western **s**, Dt 34:2 3220
as far as the Great **S** toward the Jos 1:4 3220
dried up the water of the Red **S** Jos 2:10 3220
down toward the **s** of the Arabah, Jos 3:16 3220
the sea of the Arabah, the Salt **S**, Jos 3:16 3220
your God had done to the Red **S**, Jos 4:23 3220
the Canaanites who *were* by the **s**, Jos 5:1 3220
of the Great **S** toward Lebanon, Jos 9:1 3220
as the **S** of Chinneroth toward the east, Jos 12:3 3220
and as far as the **s** of the Arabah, Jos 12:3 3220
sea of the Arabah, *even* the Salt **S**, Jos 12:3 3220
as far as the *lower* end of the **S** Jos 13:27 3220
from the lower end of the Salt **S**, Jos 15:2 3220
and the border ended at the **s**. Jos 15:4 3220
The east border *was* the Salt **S**, Jos 15:5 3220
the **s** at the mouth of the Jordan. Jos 15:5 3220
and the border ended at the **s**. Jos 15:11 3220
west border *was* at the Great **S**, Jos 15:12 3220
from Ekron even to the **s**, Jos 15:46 3220
brook of Egypt and the Great **S**, Jos 15:47 3220
to Gezer, and it ended at the **s**. Jos 16:3 3220
of Kanah, and it ended at the **s**. Jos 16:8 3220
the brook and it ended at the **s**. Jos 17:9 3220
and the **s** was their border; Jos 17:10 3220
at the north bay of the Salt **S**, Jos 18:19 3220
at the **s** by the region of Achzib. Jos 19:29 3220
from the Jordan even to the Great **S** Jos 23:4 3220
of Egypt, and you came to the **s**; Jos 24:6 3220
and horsemen to the Red **S**. Jos 24:6 3220
the **s** upon them and covered them; Jos 24:7 3220
to the Red **S** and came to Kadesh, Jg 11:16 3220
that is by the **s** in abundance, 1Sa 17:11 3220
the channels of the **s** appeared, 2Sa 22:16 3220

them down from Lebanon to the **s**; 1Ki 5:9 3220
will make them into rafts *to go* by **s** 1Ki 5:9 3220
Now he made the **s** of cast *metal* 1Ki 7:23 3220
completely surrounding the **s**; 1Ki 7:24 3220
and the **s** *was set* on top of them, 1Ki 7:25 3220
and he set the **s** *of cast metal* on 1Ki 7:39 3220
and the one **s** and the twelve oxen 1Ki 7:44 3220
and the twelve oxen under the **s**; 1Ki 7:44 3220
Eloth on the shore of the Red **S**, 1Ki 9:26 3220
the fleet, sailors who knew the **s**, 1Ki 9:27 3220
For the king had at **s** the ships of 1Ki 10:22 3220
"Go up now, look toward the **s**." 1Ki 18:43 3220
hand is coming up from the **s**." 1Ki 18:44 3220
as far as the **S** of the Arabah, 2Ki 14:25 3220
he also took down the **s** from the 2Ki 16:17 3220
and the stands and the bronze **s** 2Ki 25:13 3220
The two pillars, the one **s**, 2Ki 25:16 3220
Let the **s** roar, and all it contains; 1Ch 16:32 3220
Solomon made the bronze **s** and the 1Ch 18:8 3220
it to you on rafts by **s** to Joppa, 2Ch 2:16 3220
Also he made the cast *metal* **s**, 2Ch 4:2 3220
cubits, entirely encircling the **s**. 2Ch 4:3 3220
and the **s** *was set* on top of them and 2Ch 4:4 3220
but the **s** *was* for the priests to 2Ch 4:6 3220
He set the **s** on the right side 2Ch 4:10 3220
one **s** with the twelve oxen under it. 2Ch 4:15 3220
ships and servants who knew the **s**; 2Ch 8:18 3220
against you from beyond the **s**, 2Ch 20:2 3220
from Lebanon to the **s** at Joppa, Ezr 3:7 3220
heard their cry by the Red **S**. Ne 9:9 3220
"You divided the **s** before them, Ne 9:11 3220
the midst of the **s** on dry ground; Ne 9:11 3220
and on the coastlands of the **s**. Es 10:1 3220
"Am I the **s**, or the sea monster, Jb 7:12 3220
"Am I the sea, or the **s** monster, Jb 7:12 8577
tramples down the waves of the **s**; Jb 9:8 3220
the earth And broader than the **s**. Jb 11:9 3220
the fish of the **s** declare to you. Jb 12:8 3220
"*As* water evaporates from the **s**, Jb 14:11 3220
"He quieted the **s** with His power, Jb 26:12 3220
And the **s** says, 'It is not with me.' Jb 28:14 3220
And He covers the depths of the **s**. Jb 36:30 3220
"Or *who* enclosed the **s** with Jb 38:8 3220
entered into the springs of the **s** Or Jb 38:16 3220
the **s** like a jar of ointment. Jb 41:31 3220
heavens and the fish of the **s**, Ps 8:8 3220
He gathers the waters of the **s** Ps 33:7 3220
slip into the heart of the **s**; Ps 46:2 3220
the earth and of the farthest **s**; Ps 65:5 3220
He turned the **s** into dry land; Ps 66:6 3220
back from the depths of the **s**; Ps 68:22 3220
May he also rule from **s** to sea And Ps 72:8 3220
May he also rule from sea to **s** And Ps 72:8 3220
divided the **s** by Your strength; Ps 74:13 3220
broke the heads of the **s** monsters Ps 74:13 8577
Your way was in the **s** And Ps 77:19 3220
He divided the **s** and caused them Ps 78:13 3220
But the **s** engulfed their enemies. Ps 78:53 3220
sending out its branches to the **s** And Ps 80:11 3220
You rule the swelling of the **s**; Ps 89:9 3220
"I shall also set his hand on the **s** And Ps 89:25 3220
Than the mighty breakers of the **s**, Ps 93:4 3220
The **s** is His, for it was He who Ps 95:5 3220
Let the **s** roar, and all it contains; Ps 96:11 3220
Let the **s** roar and all it contains, Ps 98:7 3220
There is the **s**, great and broad, Ps 104:25 3220
kindnesses, But rebelled by the **s**, Ps 106:7 3220
rebelled by the sea, at the Red **S**. Ps 106:7 3220
rebuked the Red **S** and it dried up, Ps 106:9 3220
And awesome things by the Red **S**. Ps 106:22 3220
who go down to the **s** in ships, Ps 107:23 3220
lifted up the waves of the **s**. Ps 107:25
the waves of the **s** were hushed. Ps 107:29
The **s** looked and fled; Ps 114:3 3220
What ails you, O **s**, Ps 114:5 3220
Him who divided the Red **S** asunder, Ps 136:13 3220
Pharaoh and his army in the Red **S**, Ps 136:15 3220
dwell in the remotest part of the **s**, Ps 139:9 3220
The **s** and all that is in them; Ps 146:6 3220
earth, **S** monsters and all deeps; Ps 148:7 8577
He set for the **s** its boundary So Pr 8:29 3220
lies down in the middle of the **s**, Pr 23:34 3220
of a ship in the middle of the **s**, Pr 30:19 3220
All the rivers flow into the **s**, Ec 1:7 3220
the sea, Yet the **s** is not full. Ec 1:7 3220
day like the roaring of the **s**. Is 5:30 3220
it glorious, by the way of the **s**, Is 9:1 3220
may be like the sand of the **s**, Is 10:22 3220
and His staff will be over the **s** and Is 10:26 3220
Lord As the waters cover the **s**. Is 11:9 3220
And from the islands of the **s**. Is 11:11 3220
The tongue of the **S** of Egypt; Is 11:15 3220
out *and* passed over the **s**. Is 16:8 3220
Which sends envoys by the **s**, Is 18:2 3220
The waters from the **s** will dry up, Is 19:5 3220
the wilderness of the **s**. Is 21:1 3220
Your messengers crossed the **s** Is 23:2 3220
For the **s** speaks, the stronghold Is 23:4 3220
speaks, the stronghold of the **s**, Is 23:4 3220
stretched His hand out over the **s**, Is 23:11 3220
Israel, In the coastlands of the **s**. Is 24:15 3220
the dragon who *lives* in the **s**. Is 27:1 3220
You who go down to the **s**, Is 42:10 3220
Who makes a way through the **s** And Is 43:16 3220
I who says to the depth of the **s**, Is 44:27 6683
like the waves of the **s**. Is 48:18 3220
I dry up the **s** with My rebuke, Is 50:2 3220
it not You who dried up the **s**, Is 51:10 3220
Who made the depths of the **s** a Is 51:10 3220

who stirs up the s and its waves roar	Is 51:15	3220
the wicked are like the tossing s,	Is 57:20	3220
of the s will be turned to you,	Is 60:5	3220
He who brought them up out of the s	Is 63:11	3220
the sand as a boundary for the s,	Jer 5:22	3220
Their voice roars like the s,	Jer 6:23	3220
coastlands which are beyond the s;	Jer 25:22	3220
the pillars, *concerning the* s,	Jer 27:19	3220
Who stirs up the s so that its waves	Jer 31:35	3220
sand of the s cannot be measured,	Jer 33:22	3220
Or like Carmel by the s.	Jer 46:18	3220
tendrils stretched across the s,	Jer 48:32	3220
They reached to the s of Jazer;	Jer 48:32	3220
of it has been heard at the Red S.	Jer 49:21	3220
There is anxiety by the s,	Jer 49:23	3220
Their voice roars like the s;	Jer 50:42	3220
her s And make her fountain dry.	Jer 51:36	3220
"The s has come up over Babylon;	Jer 51:42	3220
and the stands and the bronze s,	Jer 52:17	3220
The two pillars, the one s,	Jer 52:20	3220
bulls that were under the s,	Jer 52:20	3220
For your ruin is as vast as the s;	La 2:13	3220
you, as the s brings up its waves.	Ezk 26:3	3220
of nets in the midst of the s,	Ezk 26:5	3220
"Then all the princes of the s	Ezk 26:16	3220
city, Which was mighty on the s,	Ezk 26:17	3220
the coastlands which are by the s	Ezk 26:18	3220
dwells at the entrance to the s,	Ezk 27:3	3220
All the ships of the s and their	Ezk 27:9	3220
and all the pilots of the s Will	Ezk 27:29	3220
is silent in the midst of the s?	Ezk 27:32	3220
"The fish of the s,	Ezk 38:20	3220
those who pass by east of the s,	Ezk 39:11	3220
then they go toward the s,	Ezk 47:8	3220
being made to flow into the s,	Ezk 47:8	3220
and the waters *of the* s become	Ezk 47:8	
like the fish of the Great S,	Ezk 47:10	3220
the Great S *by* the way of Hethlon,	Ezk 47:15	3220
The boundary shall extend from the s	Ezk 47:17	3220
the eastern s you shall measure.	Ezk 47:18	3220
of Egypt and to the Great S.	Ezk 47:19	3220
west side *shall be* the Great S,	Ezk 47:20	3220
brook *of Egypt,* to the Great S.	Ezk 48:28	3220
were stirring up the great s.	Da 7:2	3221
beasts were coming up from the s,	Da 7:3	3221
Israel Will be like the sand of the s,	Hos 1:10	3220
also the fish of the s disappear.	Hos 4:3	3220
its vanguard into the eastern s,	Jl 2:20	3220
its rear guard into the western s.	Jl 2:20	3220
Who calls for the waters of the s	Am 5:8	3220
People will stagger from s to sea	Am 8:12	3220
People will stagger from sea to s	Am 8:12	3220
My sight on the floor of the s,	Am 9:3	3220
He who calls for the waters of the s	Am 9:6	3220
LORD hurled a great wind on the s	Jon 1:4	3220
there was a great storm on the s so	Jon 1:4	3220
into the s to lighten *it for them.*	Jon 1:5	3220
who made the s and the dry land."	Jon 1:9	3220
that the s may become calm for us?"	Jon 1:11	3220
the s was becoming increasingly	Jon 1:11	3220
me up and throw me into the s.	Jon 1:12	3220
the s will become calm for you,	Jon 1:12	3220
the s was becoming *even* stormier	Jon 1:13	3220
up Jonah, threw him into the s,	Jon 1:15	3220
sea, and the s stopped its raging.	Jon 1:15	3220
Even from s to sea and mountain to	Mi 7:12	3220
sea to s and mountain to mountain.	Mi 7:12	3220
sins Into the depths of the s.	Mi 7:19	3220
He rebukes the s and makes it dry;	Na 1:4	3220
her, Whose rampart *was* the s,	Na 3:8	3220
Whose wall *consisted* of the s?	Na 3:8	3220
made men like the fish of the s,	Hab 1:14	3220
LORD, As the waters cover the s.	Hab 2:14	3220
Or *was* Your wrath against the s,	Hab 3:8	3220
trampled on the s with Your horses,	Hab 3:15	3220
of the sky And the fish of the s,	Zph 1:3	3220
the s also and the dry land.	Hg 2:6	3220
And cast her wealth into the s;	Zch 9:4	3220
His dominion will be from s to sea,	Zch 9:10	3220
dominion will be from sea to s,	Zch 9:10	3220
pass through the s *of* distress	Zch 10:11	3220
And He will strike the waves in the s,	Zch 10:11	3220
half of them toward the eastern s and	Zch 14:8	3220
other half toward the western s;	Zch 14:8	3220
in Capernaum, which is by the s,	Mt 4:13	3864
OF NAPHTALI, BY THE WAY OF THE S,	Mt 4:15	2281
was walking by the S of Galilee,	Mt 4:18	2281
brother, casting a net into the s;	Mt 4:18	2281
depart to the other side *of the* s.	Mt 8:18	
arose a great storm on the s,	Mt 8:24	2281
and rebuked the winds and the s,	Mt 8:26	2281
the winds and the s obey Him?"	Mt 8:27	2281
down the steep bank into the s	Mt 8:32	2281
Jesus crossed over *the* s and came	Mt 9:1	
IN THE BELLY OF THE S MONSTER,	Mt 12:40	2785
house and was sitting by the s.	Mt 13:1	2281
is like a dragnet cast into the s,	Mt 13:47	2281
He came to them, walking on the s.	Mt 14:25	2281
disciples saw Him walking on the s,	Mt 14:26	2281
Jesus went along by the S of Galilee	Mt 15:29	2281
came to the other side *of the* s,	Mt 16:5	
we do not offend them, go to the s	Mt 17:27	2281
to be drowned in the depth of the s.	Mt 18:6	2281
'Be taken up and cast into the s,'	Mt 21:21	2281
because you travel around on s and	Mt 23:15	2281
going along by the S of Galilee,	Mk 1:16	2281
of Simon, casting a net in the s;	Mk 1:16	2281
Jesus withdrew to the s with His	Mk 3:7	2281
He began to teach again by the s.	Mk 4:1	2281
into a boat in the s and sat down;	Mk 4:1	2281
crowd was by the s on the land.	Mk 4:1	2281
rebuked the wind and said to the s,	Mk 4:39	2281
the wind and the s obey Him?"	Mk 4:41	2281
came to the other side of the s,	Mk 5:1	2281
down the steep bank into the s,	Mk 5:13	2281
and they were drowned in the s.	Mk 5:13	2281
boat was in the middle of the s,	Mk 6:47	2281
He came to them, walking on the s;	Mk 6:48	2281
they saw Him walking on the s,	Mk 6:49	2281
through Sidon to the S of Galilee,	Mk 7:31	2281
neck, he had been cast into the s.	Mk 9:42	2281
'Be taken up and cast into the s,'	Mk 11:23	2281
and he were thrown into the s,	Lk 17:2	2281
Be uprooted and be planted in the s';	Lk 17:6	2281
roaring of the s and the waves,	Lk 21:25	2281
other side of the S of Galilee	Jn 6:1	2281
His disciples went down to the s,	Jn 6:16	2281
to cross the s to Capernaum.	Jn 6:17	2281
The s *began* to be stirred up	Jn 6:18	2281
they saw Jesus walking on the s	Jn 6:19	2281
that stood on the other side of the s	Jn 6:22	2281
Him on the other side of the s,	Jn 6:25	2281
disciples at the S of Tiberias,	Jn 21:1	2281
and threw himself into the s.	Jn 21:7	2281
HEAVEN AND THE EARTH AND THE S,	Ac 4:24	2281
the land of Egypt and in the Red S	Ac 7:36	2281
Simon, whose house is by the s."	Ac 10:6	2281
of Simon *the* tanner by the s.'	Ac 10:32	2281
Paul and his companions put out to s	Ac 13:13	321
HEAVEN AND THE EARTH AND THE S	Ac 14:15	2281
putting out to s from Troas,	Ac 16:11	321
sent Paul out to go as far as the s;	Ac 17:14	2281
and put out to s for Syria,	Ac 18:18	1602
coast of Asia, we put out to s	Ac 27:2	321
From there we put out to s and	Ac 27:4	321
When we had sailed through the s	Ac 27:5	3989
to put out to s from there,	Ac 27:12	321
they let down the s anchor and	Ac 27:17	4632
driven about in the Adriatic S,	Ac 27:27	
let down the *ship's* boat into the s,	Ac 27:30	2281
throwing out the wheat into the s.	Ac 27:38	2281
they left them in the s while at	Ac 27:40	2281
he has been saved from the s,	Ac 28:4	2281
OF ISRAEL BE LIKE THE SAND OF THE S,	Ro 9:27	2281
and all passed through the s;	1Co 10:1	2281
Moses in the cloud and in the s;	1Co 10:2	2281
the wilderness, dangers on the s,	2Co 11:26	2281
they passed through the Red S as	Heb 11:29	2281
s, driven and tossed by the wind.	Jas 1:6	2281
reptiles and creatures of the s,	Jas 3:7	1724
wild waves of the s,	Jude 1:13	2281
like a s of glass, like crystal;	Rv 4:6	2281
and under the earth and on the s,	Rv 5:13	2281
earth or on the s or on any tree.	Rv 7:1	2281
to harm the earth and the s,	Rv 7:2	2281
the earth or the s or the trees until	Rv 7:3	2281
with fire was thrown into the s;	Rv 8:8	2281
and a third of the s became blood,	Rv 8:8	2281
which were in the s and had life,	Rv 8:9	2281
He placed his right foot on the s and	Rv 10:2	2281
angel whom I saw standing on the s	Rv 10:5	2281
AND THE S AND THE THINGS IN IT,	Rv 10:6	2281
stands on the s and on the land."	Rv 10:8	2281
Woe to the earth and the s,	Rv 12:12	2281
a beast coming up out of the s,	Rv 13:1	2281
and s and springs of waters."	Rv 14:7	2281
a s of glass mixed with fire,	Rv 15:2	2281
name, standing on the s of glass,	Rv 15:2	2281
poured out his bowl into the s,	Rv 16:3	2281
every living thing in the s died.	Rv 16:3	2281
as make their living by the s,	Rv 18:17	2281
all who had ships at s became rich	Rv 18:19	2281
millstone and threw it into the s,	Rv 18:21	2281
And the s gave up the dead which	Rv 20:13	2281
and there is no longer *any* s.	Rv 21:1	2281

SEACOAST

and in the Negev and by the s,	Dt 1:7	3220, 2348
Against Ashkelon and against the s	Jer 47:7	3220, 2348
and destroy the remnant of the s.	Ezk 25:16	3220, 2348
Woe to the inhabitants of the s,	Zph 2:5	3220, 2256a
So the s will be pastures, *With*	Zph 2:6	3220, 2256a

SEAL

"Your s and your cord, and your	Gn 38:18	2368
be *like* the engravings of a s,	Ex 28:21	2368
on it, like the engravings of a s,	Ex 28:36	2368
name and sealed them with his s,	1Ki 21:8	2368
and s *it* with the king's signet	Es 8:8	2856
And sets a s upon the stars;	Jb 9:7	2856
is changed like clay *under* the s;	Jb 38:14	2368
pride, Shut up *as with* a tight s.	Jb 41:15	2368
"Put me like a s over your heart,	SS 8:6	2368
your heart, Like a s on your arm.	SS 8:6	2368
S the law among my disciples.	Is 8:16	2856
for money, sign and s deeds,	Jer 32:44	2856
"You had the s of perfection,	Ezk 28:12	2856
to s up vision and prophecy and	Da 9:24	2856
conceal these words and s up the	Da 12:4	2856
guard they set a s on the stone.	Mt 27:66	4972
His testimony has set his s to *this,*	Jn 3:33	4972
Father, God, has set His s."	Jn 6:27	4972
a s of the righteousness of the faith	Ro 4:11	4973
put my s on this fruit of theirs,	Ro 15:28	4972
s of my apostleship in the Lord.	1Co 9:2	4973
of God stands, having this s,	2Tm 2:19	4973
When He broke the second s,	Rv 6:3	4973
When He broke the third s,	Rv 6:5	4973
When the Lamb broke the fourth s,	Rv 6:7	4973
When the Lamb broke the fifth s,	Rv 6:9	4973
looked when He broke the sixth s,	Rv 6:12	4973
having the s of the living God;	Rv 7:2	4973
When the Lamb broke the seventh s,	Rv 8:1	4973
the s of God on their foreheads.	Rv 9:4	4973
"S up the things which the seven	Rv 10:4	4972
"Do not s up the words of the	Rv 22:10	4972

SEALED

with Me, S up in My treasuries?	Dt 32:34	2856
name and s them with his seal,	1Ki 21:8	2856
And on the s document *are the*	Ne 9:38	2856
on the s document *were the names of*	Ne 10:1	2856
and s with the king's signet ring.	Es 3:12	2856
s with the king's signet ring may not	Es 8:8	2856
and s it with the king's signet	Es 8:10	2856
"My transgression is s up in a bag,	Jb 14:17	2856
rock garden locked, a spring s up.	SS 4:12	2856
to you like the words of a s book,	Is 29:11	2856
"I cannot, for it is s."	Is 29:11	2856
"I signed and s the deed,	Jer 32:10	2856
both the s *copy containing* the terms	Jer 32:11	2856
deeds, this s deed of purchase and	Jer 32:14	2856
and the king s it with his own	Da 6:17	2857
and s up until the end time.	Da 12:9	2856
who also s us and gave *us* the	2Co 1:22	4972
you were s in Him with the Holy	Eph 1:13	4972
were s for the day of redemption.	Eph 4:30	4972
the back, s up with seven seals.	Rv 5:1	2696
until we have s the bond-servants	Rv 7:3	4972
the number of those who were s,	Rv 7:4	4972
s from every tribe of the sons of Israel	Rv 7:4	4972
of Judah, twelve thousand *were* s,	Rv 7:5	4972
Benjamin, twelve thousand *were* s.	Rv 7:8	4972
and shut *it* and s *it* over him,	Rv 20:3	4972

SEALS

of men, And s their instruction,	Jb 33:16	2856
"He s the hand of every man, That	Jb 37:7	2856
the back, sealed up with seven s.	Rv 5:1	4973
the book and to break its s?"	Rv 5:2	4973
open the book and its seven s."	Rv 5:5	4973
take the book and to break its s;	Rv 5:9	4973
the Lamb broke one of the seven s,	Rv 6:1	4973

SEAMLESS

now the tunic was s,	Jn 19:23	690a

SEAMS

were with you repairing your s;	Ezk 27:9	919
your pilots, Your repairers of s,	Ezk 27:27	919

SEARCH

they may s out the land for us,	Dt 1:22	2658
and you will find *Him* if you s for	Dt 4:29	1875
and s out and inquire thoroughly.	Dt 13:14	2713
here tonight to s out the land."	Jos 2:2	2658
have come to s out all the land."	Jos 2:3	2658
to spy out the land and to s it;	Jg 18:2	2713
"Go, s the land."	Jg 18:2	2713
and arise, go s for the donkeys."	1Sa 9:3	1245
I will s him out among all the	1Sa 23:23	2664
to s for David in the wilderness	1Sa 26:2	1245
come out to s for a single flea,	1Sa 26:20	1245
to you in order to s the city,	2Sa 10:3	2713
master has not sent to s for you;	1Ki 18:10	1245
and they will s your house and the	1Ki 20:6	2664
let them go and s for your master;	2Ki 2:16	1245
s out Jehu the son of Jehoshaphat	2Ki 9:2	7200
"S and see that there is here	2Ki 10:23	2664
Philistines went up in s of David;	1Ch 14:8	1245
his servants come to you to s and to	1Ch 19:3	2713
so that a s may be made in the	Ezr 4:15	1240
and a s has been made and it has	Ezr 4:19	1240
if it pleases the king, let a s be	Ezr 5:17	1240
and s was made in the archives,	Ezr 6:1	1240
for my guilt And s after my sin?	Jb 10:6	1875
S me, O God, and know my heart;	Ps 139:23	2713
And s for her as for hidden	Pr 2:4	2664
glory of kings is to s out a matter.	Pr 25:2	2713
it glory to s out one's own glory.	Pr 25:27	2714
A time to s and a time to give up	Ec 3:6	1245
"I, the LORD, s the heart, I test	Jer 17:10	2713
you s for Me with all your heart.	Jer 29:13	1875
's will be made for the iniquity	Jer 50:20	1245
was no one to s or seek *for them.*	Ezk 34:6	1875
shepherds did not s for My flock,	Ezk 34:8	1875
I Myself will s for My sheep and	Ezk 34:11	1875
seven months they will make a s.	Ezk 39:14	2713
I will s them out and take them	Am 9:3	2664
s for a refuge from the enemy.	Na 3:11	1245
I will s Jerusalem with lamps,	Zph 1:12	2664
and s carefully for the Child;	Mt 2:8	1833
s for the Child to destroy Him."	Mt 2:13	2212
s for the one that is straying?	Mt 18:12	2212
s carefully until she finds it?	Lk 15:8	2212
"You s the Scriptures because	Jn 5:39	2045
S, and see that no prophet arises	Jn 7:52	2045
signs and Greeks s for wisdom;	1Co 1:22	2212

SEARCHED

So he s but did not find the	Gn 31:35	2664
He s, beginning with the	Gn 44:12	2664
But Moses s carefully for the goat	Lv 10:16	1875
when they s about and inquired,	Jg 6:29	1875
Gath, so he no longer s for him.	1Sa 27:4	1245
they s and could not find *them,*	2Sa 17:20	1245
So they s for a beautiful girl	1Ki 1:3	1245
and they s three days but did not	2Ki 2:17	1245

These s among their ancestral Ezr 2:62 1245
These s among their ancestral Ne 7:64 1245
the things s out by their fathers. Jb 8:8 2714
He established it and also s it out. Jb 28:27 2713
returned and s diligently for God; Ps 78:34 7836
Lord, You have s me and known me. Ps 139:1 2713
s out and arranged many proverbs. Ec 12:9 2713
I s for him but I did not find SS 5:6 1245
foundations of the earth s out below, Jer 31:37 2713
"I s for a man among them who Ezk 22:30 1245
And his hidden treasures s out! Ob 1:6 1158
Simon and his companions s for Him; Mk 1:36 2614
s for him and had not found him, Ac 12:19 1934
was in Rome, he eagerly s for me and 2Tm 1:17 2212

SEARCHES
for the LORD s all hearts, and 1Ch 28:9 1875
And to the farthest limit he s out Jb 28:3 2713
And s after every green thing. Jb 39:8 1875
and He who s the hearts knows what Ro 8:27 2045
for the Spirit s all things, even 1Co 2:10 2045
would come to you made careful s 1Pe 1:10 1567a
am He who s the minds and hearts; Rv 2:23 2045

SEARCHING
Saul then will despair of s for me 1Sa 27:1 1245
S all the innermost parts of his being Pr 20:27 2664
and the crowds were s for Him, Lk 4:42 1934

SEARCHINGS
There were great s of heart. Jg 5:16 2714

SEARED
the hypocrisy of liars s in their own 1Tm 4:2 2741b

SEAS
gathering of the waters He called s; Gn 1:10 3220
and fill the waters in the s, Gn 1:22 3220
water, in the s or in the rivers, Lv 11:9 3220
is in the s and in the rivers that Lv 11:10 3220
draw out the abundance of the s, Dt 33:19 3220
it, The s and all that is in them. Ne 9:6 3220
be heavier than the sand of the s; Jb 6:3 3220
passes through the paths of the s. Ps 8:8 3220
For He has founded it upon the s And Ps 24:2 3220
stills the roaring of the s, Ps 65:7 3220
The s and everything that moves in Ps 69:34 3220
fowl like the sand of the s, Ps 78:27 3220
earth, in the s and in all deeps. Ps 135:6 3220
roar like the roaring of the s, Is 17:12 3220
before Me Than the sand of the s; Jer 15:8 3220
O inhabited one, From the s, Ezk 26:17 3220
borders are in the heart of the s; Ezk 27:4 3220
glorious In the heart of the s. Ezk 27:25 3220
broken you In the heart of the s. Ezk 27:26 3220
Will fall into the heart of the s Ezk 27:27 3220
your wares went out from the s, Ezk 27:33 3220
the s In the depths of the waters, Ezk 27:34 3220
of gods In the heart of the s'; Ezk 28:2 3220
are slain In the heart of the s. Ezk 28:8 3220
you are like the monster in the s; Ezk 32:2 3220
his royal pavilion between the s and Da 11:45 3220
the deep, Into the heart of the s, Jon 2:3 3220
striking a reef where two s met, Ac 27:41 1337

SEASHORE
and as the sand which is on the s; Gn 22:17 3220, 8193
"Zebulun will dwell at the s; Gn 49:13 3220, 2348
saw the Egyptians dead on the s. Ex 14:30 3220, 8193
as the sand that is on the s, Jos 11:4 3220, 8193
Asher sat at the s, Jg 5:17 3220, 2348
as numerous as the sand on the s. Jg 7:12 3220, 8193
sand which is on the s in abundance 1Sa 13:5 3220, 8193
sand that is on the s in abundance; 1Ki 4:20 3220
like the sand that is on the s. 1Ki 4:29 3220, 8193
on the s in the land of Edom. 2Ch 8:17 3220, 8193
And He went out again by the s; Mk 2:13 2281
and so He stayed by the s. Mk 5:21 2281
AS THE SAND WHICH IS BY THE S. Heb 11:12 2281
the dragon stood on the sand of the s. Rv 13:1 2281
of them is like the sand of the s. Rv 20:8 2281

SEASON
bear to you at this s next year." Gn 17:21 4150
moreover, you shall s with salt, Lv 2:13 4414b
I shall give you rains in their s, Lv 26:4 6256
the rain for your land in its s, Dt 11:14 6256
to give rain to your land in its s and Dt 28:12 6256
"At this s next year you will 2Ki 4:16 4150
bore a son at that s the next year, 2Ki 4:17 4150
many people; it is the rainy s Ezr 10:13 6256
the stacking of grain in its s. Jb 5:26 6256
lead forth a constellation in its s, Jb 38:32 6256
Which yields its fruit in its s And Ps 1:3 6256
To give them their food in due s. Ps 104:27 6256
our God, Who gives rain in its s, Jer 5:24 6256
showers to come down in their s; Ezk 34:26 6256
time And My new wine in its s. Hos 2:9 4150
on the fig tree in its first s. Hos 9:10
for it was not the s for figs. Mk 11:13 2540
be ready in s and out of season; 2Tm 4:2 2122
be ready in season and out of s; 2Tm 4:2 171

SEASONED
tasteless, with what will it be s? Lk 14:34 741
as though s with salt, so that Col 4:6 741

SEASONS
let them be for signs and for s Gn 1:14 4150
He made the moon for the s; Ps 104:19 4150
the stork in the sky Knows her s; Jer 8:7 4150
pay him the proceeds at the proper s. Mt 21:41 2540
went down at certain s into the pool and Jn 5:4 2540
rains from heaven and fruitful s, Ac 14:17 2540
days and months and s and years. Ga 4:10 2540

SEAT
shall make a mercy s of pure gold, Ex 25:17 3727
at the two ends of the mercy s. Ex 25:18 3727
with the mercy s at its two ends. Ex 25:19 3727
covering the mercy s with their Ex 25:20 3727
to be turned toward the mercy s. Ex 25:20 3727
put the mercy s on top of the ark, Ex 25:21 3727
and from above the mercy s, Ex 25:22 3727
"You shall put the mercy s on Ex 26:34 3727
in front of the mercy s that is Ex 30:6 3727
and the mercy s upon it, Ex 31:7 3727
ark and its poles, the mercy s, Ex 35:12 3727
He made a mercy s of pure gold, Ex 37:6 3727
at the two ends of the mercy s; Ex 37:7 3727
with the mercy s at the two ends. Ex 37:8 3727
covering the mercy s with their Ex 37:9 3727
cherubim were toward the mercy s. Ex 37:9 3727
and its poles and the mercy s; Ex 39:35 3727
put the mercy s on top of the ark. Ex 40:20 3727
the mercy s which is on the ark, Lv 16:2 3727
in the cloud over the mercy s. Lv 16:2 3727
the mercy s that is on the ark of the Lv 16:13 3727
on the mercy s on the east side; Lv 16:14 3727
also in front of the mercy s he Lv 16:14 3727
and sprinkle it on the mercy s and Lv 16:15 3727
seat and in front of the mercy s. Lv 16:15 3727
mercy s that was on the ark of the Nu 7:89 3727
And he arose from his s. Jg 3:20 3678
Eli the priest was sitting on the s by 1Sa 1:9 3678
nobles, And inherit a s of honor; 1Sa 2:8 3678
Eli was sitting on his s by the road 1Sa 4:13 3678
Eli fell off the s backward beside 1Sa 4:18 3678
because your s will be empty. 1Sa 20:18 4186
The king sat on his s as usual, 1Sa 20:25 4186
seat as usual, the s by the wall; 1Sa 20:25 4186
s on the throne of the kingdom. 1Ki 1:46 3427
and arms on each side of the s, 1Ki 10:19 4725, 7675
and s Naboth at the head of the 1Ki 21:9 3427
s two worthless men before him, 1Ki 21:10 3427
and the room for the mercy s; 1Ch 28:11 3727
and arms on each side of the s, 2Ch 9:18 4725, 7675
also made repairs for the official s of Ne 3:7 3678
Him, That I might come to His s! Jb 23:3 8499
When I took my s in the square, Jb 29:7 4186
Nor sit in the s of scoffers! Ps 1:1 4186
praise Him at the s of the elders. Ps 107:32 4186
On a s by the high places of the city Pr 9:14 3678
gold And its s of purple fabric, SS 3:10 4817
"Take a lowly s, For your Jer 13:18 3427
the s of the idol of jealousy, Ezk 8:3 4186
am a god, I sit in the s of gods In Ezk 28:2 4186
the Ancient of Days took His s; Da 7:9 3488
you bring near the s of violence? Am 6:3 7675
he was sitting on the judgment s, Mt 27:19 968
and sat down on the judgment s at Jn 19:13 968
OATH TO S ONE OF HIS DESCENDANTS Ac 2:30 2523
took his s on the rostrum and Ac 12:21 2523
brought him before the judgment s, Ac 18:12 968
them away from the judgment s. Ac 18:16 968
him in front of the judgment s. Ac 18:17 968
next day he took his s on the tribunal Ac 25:6 2523
took my s on the tribunal and Ac 25:17 2523
stand before the judgment s of God. Ro 14:10 968
before the judgment s of Christ, 2Co 5:10 968
takes his s in the temple of God, 2Th 2:4 2523
who has taken His s at the right Heb 8:1 2523
glory overshadowing the mercy s; Heb 9:5 2435

SEATED
Now they were s before him, the Gn 43:33 3427
s Naboth at the head of the people. 1Ki 21:12 3427
the throne He has s them forever, Jb 36:7 3427
s themselves in the chair of Moses; Mt 23:2 2523
s at the Lord's feet, listening Lk 10:39 3869a
SON OF MAN WILL BE S AT THE RIGHT Lk 22:69 2521
doves, and the money changers s Jn 2:14 2521
distributed to those who were s; Jn 6:11 345
IS COMING, S ON A DONKEY'S COLT." Jn 12:15 2521
is made to another who is s, 1Co 14:30 2521
and s Him at His right hand in the Eph 1:20 2523
and s us with Him in the heavenly Eph 2:6 4776
Christ is, s at the right hand of God. Col 3:1 2521

SEATING
his table, the s of his servants, 1Ki 10:5 4186
his table, the s of his servants, 2Ch 9:4 4186

SEATS
the s of those who were selling doves. Mt 21:12 2515
and the chief s in the synagogues, Mt 23:6 4410
s of those who were selling doves; Mk 11:15 2515
and chief s in the synagogues and Mk 12:39 4410
the chief s in the synagogues Lk 11:43 4410
and chief s in the synagogues and Lk 20:46 4410

SEBA
The sons of Cush were S and Gn 10:7 5434
The sons of Cush were S, 1Ch 1:9 5434
kings of Sheba and S offer gifts. Ps 72:10 5434
ransom, Cush and S in your place. Is 43:3 5434

SEBAM
Nimrah, Heshbon, Elealeh, S, Nu 32:3 7643

SECACAH
Beth-arabah, Middin and S, Jos 15:61 5527b

SECLUDED
security, The fountain of Jacob s, Dt 33:28 910
withdrew from there in a boat to a s Mt 14:13 2048
and went away to a s place, and was Mk 1:35 2048
"Come away by yourselves to a s Mk 6:31 2048
They went away in the boat to a s Mk 6:32 2048
Jesus left and went to a s place; Lk 4:42 2048

SECLUSION
kept herself in s for five months, Lk 1:24 4032

SECOND
and there was morning, a s day. Gn 1:8 8145
The name of the s river is Gihon; Gn 2:13 8145
you shall make it with lower, s, Gn 6:16 8145
of Noah's life, in the s month, Gn 7:11 8145
In the s month, on the Gn 8:14 8145
to Abraham a s time from heaven, Gn 22:15 8145
again and bore Jacob a s son. Gn 30:7 8145
maid Zilpah bore Jacob a s son. Gn 30:12 8145
Then he commanded also the s and Gn 32:19 8145
fell asleep and dreamed a s time; Gn 41:5 8145
He had him ride in his s chariot; Gn 41:43 4932
He named the s Ephraim, Gn 41:52 8145
on the fifteenth day of the s month Ex 16:1 8145
and a bulb under the s pair of Ex 25:35
that is outermost in the s set. Ex 26:4 8145
the curtain that is in the s set; Ex 26:5 8145
that is outermost in the s set. Ex 26:10 8145
for the s side of the tabernacle, Ex 26:20 8145
and the s row a turquoise, a Ex 28:18 8145
that was outermost in the s set. Ex 36:11 8145
the curtain that was in the s set; Ex 36:12 8145
that was outermost in the s set. Ex 36:17 8145
for the s side of the tabernacle, Ex 36:25 8145
and a bulb under the s pair of Ex 37:21
and the s row, a turquoise, a Ex 39:11 8145
in the first month of the s year, Ex 40:17 8145
'The s he shall then prepare as a Lv 5:10 8145
Then he presented the s ram, Lv 8:22 8145
a s time and will be clean." Lv 13:58 8145
on the first of the s month, Nu 1:1 8145
in the s year after they had come Nu 1:1 8145
on the first of the s month. Nu 1:18 8145
And they shall set out s. Nu 2:16 8145
On the s day Nethanel the son of Nu 7:18 8145
and a s bull you shall take for a Nu 8:8 8145
in the first month of the s year Nu 9:1 8145
'In the s month on the fourteenth Nu 9:11 8145
When you blow an alarm the s time, Nu 10:6 8145
Now in the s year, Nu 10:11 8145
the second year, in the s month, Nu 10:11 8145
'Then on the s day: Nu 29:17 8145
the sons of Israel the s time." Jos 5:2 8145
Thus the s day they marched around Jos 6:14 8145
and he captured it on the s day, Jos 10:32 8145
Then the s lot fell to Simeon, to Jos 19:1 8145
bull and a s bull seven years old, Jg 6:25 8145
and take a s bull and offer a Jg 6:26 8145
and the s bull was offered on the Jg 6:28 8145
the sons of Benjamin the s day. Jg 20:24 8145
against them from Gibeah the s day Jg 20:25 8145
and the name of his s, Abijah; 1Sa 8:2 4932
and the s to him Abinadab, 1Sa 17:13 4932
"For a s time you may be my 1Sa 18:21 8147
day, the s day of the new moon, 1Sa 20:27 8145
food on the s day of the new moon, 1Sa 20:34 8145
I will not strike him the s time." 1Sa 26:8 8138
and his s, Chileab, by Abigail the 2Sa 3:3 4932
So he sent again a s time, 2Sa 14:29 8145
month of Ziv which is the s month, 1Ki 6:1 8145
LORD appeared to Solomon a s time, 1Ki 9:2 8145
the s year of Asa king of Judah, 1Ki 15:25 8147
"Do it a s time," 1Ki 18:34 8138
time," and they did it a s time. 1Ki 18:34 8138
a s time and touched him and said, 1Ki 19:7 8145
in the s year of Jehoram the son of 2Ki 1:17 8147
Then he sent out a s horseman, 2Ki 9:19 8145
a letter to them a s time saying, 2Ki 10:6 8145
In the s year of Joash son of 2Ki 14:1 8147
In the s year of Pekah the son of 2Ki 15:32 8147
in the s year what springs from 2Ki 19:29 8145
in Jerusalem in the S Quarter); 2Ki 22:14 4932
the s order and the doorkeepers, 2Ki 23:4 4932
And the s pillar was like these 2Ki 25:17 8145
priest and Zephaniah the s priest, 2Ki 25:18 4932
firstborn, then Abinadab the s, 1Ch 2:13 8145
the s was Daniel, by Abigail the 1Ch 3:1 8145
and the s was Jehoiakim, 1Ch 3:15 8145
was the chief and Shapham the s, 1Ch 5:12 4932
the firstborn, and Abijah the s. 1Ch 6:28 8145
the name of the s was Zelophehad, 1Ch 7:15 8145
Bela his firstborn, Ashbel the s, 1Ch 8:1 8145
Ulam his firstborn, Jeush the s and 1Ch 8:39 8145
s rank he was the most honored and 1Ch 11:21 8147
Ezer was the first, Obadiah the s, 1Ch 12:9 8145
their relatives of the s rank, 1Ch 15:18 4932
the chief, and s to him Zechariah, 1Ch 16:5 4932
was the first and Zizah the s; 1Ch 23:11 8145
Jeriah the first, Amariah the s, 1Ch 23:19 8145
Micah the first and Isshiah the s. 1Ch 23:20 8145
for Jehoiarib, the s for Jedaiah, 1Ch 24:7 8145
Jeriah the first, Amariah the s, 1Ch 24:23 8145
to Joseph, the s for Gedaliah, 1Ch 25:9 8145
the firstborn, Jediael the s, 1Ch 26:2 8145
the firstborn, Jehozabad the s, 1Ch 26:4 8145
Hilkiah the s, Tebaliah the third, 1Ch 26:11 8145
of the division for the s month, 1Ch 27:4 8145

the son of David king a s time, 1Ch 29:22 8145
He began to build on the s *day* 2Ch 3:2 8145
in the s month of the fourth year of 2Ch 3:2 8145
in the s and in the third year. 2Ch 27:5 8145
and Elkanah the s to the king. 2Ch 28:7 4932
the Passover in the s month, 2Ch 30:2 8145
Unleavened Bread in the s month, 2Ch 30:13 8145
on the fourteenth of the s month. 2Ch 30:15 8145
them and his brother Shimei *was* s. 2Ch 31:12 4932
in Jerusalem in the S Quarter); 2Ch 34:22 4932
him in the s chariot which he had, 2Ch 35:24 4932
410 silver bowls of a s *kind and* Ezr 1:10 4932
Now in the s year of their coming Ezr 3:8 8145
God at Jerusalem in the s month, Ezr 3:8 8145
the s year of the reign of Darius Ezr 4:24 8648
Then on the s day the heads of Ne 8:13 8145
was s in command of the city. Ne 11:9 4932
the s among his brethren; Ne 11:17 4932
The s choir proceeded to the left, Ne 12:38 8145
she would return to the s harem, Es 2:14 8145
were gathered together the s time, Es 2:19 8145
the king said to Esther on the s day Es 7:2 8145
confirm this s letter about Purim. Es 9:29 8145
For Mordecai the Jew was s *only* to Es 10:3 4932
first Jemimah, and the s Keziah, Jb 42:14 8145
throng to the side of the s lad who Ec 4:15 8145
Lord Will again recover the s time Is 11:11 8145
in the s year what springs from Is 37:30 8145
LORD came to me a s time saying, Jer 1:13 8145
of the LORD came to me a s time, Jer 13:3 8145
LORD came to Jeremiah the s time, Jer 33:1 8145
And the s pillar was like these, Jer 52:22 8145
priest and Zephaniah the s priest, Jer 52:24 4932
you shall lie down a s time, Ezk 4:6 8145
the s face *was* the face of a man, Ezk 10:14 8145
the highest by way of the s *story*. Ezk 41:7 8484
'On the s day you shall offer Ezk 43:22 8145
Now in the s year of the reign of Da 2:1 8147
They answered a s time and said, Da 2:7 8579
behold, another beast, a s one, Da 7:5 8578
the LORD came to Jonah the s time, Jon 3:1 8145
Gate, A wail from the S Quarter, Zph 1:10 4932
In the s year of Darius the king, Hg 1:1 8147
in the s year of Darius the king. Hg 1:15 8147
month, in the s year of Darius, Hg 2:10 8147
word of the LORD came a s time to Hg 2:20 8145
eighth month of the s year of Darius, Zch 1:1 8147
Shebat, in the s year of Darius, Zch 1:7 8147
the s time and said to him, Zch 4:12 8145
with the s chariot black horses, Zch 6:2 8145
I cut in pieces my s staff Union, Zch 11:14 8145
to the s and said the same thing; Mt 21:30 *1208*
so also the s, and the third, down Mt 22:26 *1208*
"The s is like it, Mt 22:39 *1208*
He went away again a s time and Mt 26:42 *1208*
"The s one married her, and Mk 12:21 *1208*
"The s is this, Mk 12:31 *1208*
a rooster crowed a s time. Mk 14:72 *1208*
"Whether he comes in the s watch, Lk 12:38 *1208*
"The s came, saying, Lk 19:18 *1208*
and the s Lk 20:30 *1208*
He cannot enter a s time into his Jn 3:4 *1208*
a s sign that Jesus performed when Jn 4:54 *1208*
So a s time they called the man Jn 9:24 *1208*
He said to him again a s time, Jn 21:16 *1208*
"On the s *visit* Joseph made Ac 7:13 *1208*
a voice *came* to him a s time, Ac 10:15 *1208*
voice from heaven answered a s time, Ac 11:9 *1208*
had passed the first and s guard, Ac 12:10 *1208*
it is also written in the s Psalm, Ac 13:33 *1208*
on the s day we came to Puteoli. Ac 28:13 *1206*
first apostles, s prophets, 1Co 12:28 *1208*
the s man is from heaven. 1Co 15:47 *1208*
said when present the s time, 2Co 13:2 *1208*
man after a first and s warning, Ti 3:10 *1208*
been no occasion sought for a s. Heb 8:7 *1208*
Behind the s veil there was a Heb 9:3 *1208*
into the s, only the high priest *enters* Heb 9:7 *1208*
will appear a s time for salvation Heb 9:28 *1208*
first in order to establish the s. Heb 10:9 *1208*
the s letter I am writing to you 2Pe 3:1 *1208*
will not be hurt by the s death.' Rv 2:11 *1208*
and the s creature like a calf, Rv 4:7 *1208*
When He broke the s seal, Rv 6:3 *1208*
I heard the s living creature saying, Rv 6:3 *1208*
The s angel sounded, and Rv 8:8 *1208*
The s woe is past; Rv 11:14 *1208*
And another angel, a s one, Rv 14:8 *1208*
The s *angel* poured out his bowl Rv 16:3 *1208*
And a s time they said, Rv 19:3 *1208*
these the s death has no power, Rv 20:6 *1208*
This is the s death, the lake of Rv 20:14 *1208*
brimstone, which is the s death." Rv 21:8 *1208*
the s, sapphire; the third, chalcedony Rv 21:19 *1208*

SECRET
did the same with their s arts. Ex 7:11 3909
did the same with their s arts; Ex 7:22 3909
did the same with their s arts; Ex 8:7 3909
their s arts to bring forth gnats, Ex 8:18 3909
craftsman, and sets *it* up in s.' Dt 27:15 5643a
he who strikes his neighbor in s.' Dt 27:24 5643a
"The s things belong to the LORD Dt 29:29 5641
"I have a s message for you, O Jg 3:19 5643a
stay in a s place and hide yourself. 1Sa 19:2 5643a
"Do you hear the s counsel of Jb 15:8 5475
The s of the LORD is for those who Ps 25:14 5475
In the s place of His tent He will Ps 27:5 5643a
You hide them in the s place Ps 31:20 5643a
from the s counsel of evildoers, Ps 64:2 5475
Our s *sins* in the light of Your Ps 90:8 5956
from You, When I was made in s, Ps 139:15 5643a
bread *eaten* in s is pleasant." Pr 9:17 5643a
A gift in s subdues anger, And a Pr 21:14 5643a
do not reveal the s of another, Pr 25:9 5475
the s place of the steep pathway, SS 2:14 5643a
waters will overflow the s place. Is 28:17 5643a
And hidden wealth of s places, Is 45:3 4565
"I have not spoken in s, Is 45:19 5643a
the first I have not spoken in s, Is 48:16 5643a
and spend the night in s places; Is 65:4 5341
soul will sob in s for *such* pride; Jer 13:17 4565
swore to Jeremiah in s saying, Jer 38:16 5643a
in wait, *Like* a lion in s places. La 3:10 4565
and they will profane My s place; Ezk 7:22 6845
is no s that is a match for you. Ezk 28:3 5640
But keep the vision s, Da 8:26 5640
Unless He reveals His s counsel To Am 3:7 5475
Who devour the oppressed in s. Hab 3:14 4565
so that your giving will be in s; Mt 6:4 *2927*
Father who sees *what is done* in s Mt 6:4 *2927*
pray to your Father who is in s, Mt 6:6 *2927*
Father who sees *what is done* in s Mt 6:6 *2927*
Father who is in s; Mt 6:18 *2931a*
Father who sees *what is done* in s Mt 6:18 *2931a*
nor has *anything* been s, Mk 4:22 *614*
nor *anything* s that will not be Lk 8:17 *614*
"For no one does anything in s when Jn 7:4 *2927*
publicly, but as if, in s. Jn 7:10 *2927*
and I spoke nothing in s. Jn 18:20 *2927*
a disciple of Jesus, but a s *one* Jn 19:38 *2928*
the mystery which has been kept s Ro 16:25 *4601*
which are done by them in s. Eph 5:12 *2931b*
I have learned the s of being filled Php 4:12 *3453*

SECRETARIES
Ahijah, the sons of Shisha *were* s; 1Ki 4:3 5613b
governors, the officials, the s, Ezr 4:9 670

SECRETARY
were priests, and Seraiah *was* s. 2Sa 8:17 5613b
were priests, and Shavsha *was* s; 1Ch 18:16 5613b

SECRETLY
"Why did you flee s and deceive me, Gn 31:27 2244
is as your own soul, entice you s, Dt 13:6 5643a
for she will eat them s for lack of Dt 28:57 5643a
son of Nun sent two men as spies s Jos 2:1 2791a
and went s to him and drove the Jg 4:21 3909
and she came s, and uncovered his Ru 3:7 3909
"Speak to David s, saying, 1Sa 18:22 3909
cut off the edge of Saul's robe s. 1Sa 24:4 3909
'Indeed you did it s, 2Sa 12:12 5643a
did things s which were not right against 2Ki 17:9 2644
you If you s show partiality. Jb 13:10 5643a
And my heart became s enticed, Jb 31:27 5643a
net which they have s laid for me, Ps 31:4 2934
You keep them s in a shelter Ps 31:20 6845
They talk of laying snares s; Ps 64:5 2934
Whoever s slanders his neighbor, Ps 101:5 5643a
the king s asked him and said, Jer 37:17 5643a
spoke s to Gedaliah in Mizpah, Jer 40:15 5643a
her, planned to send her away s. Mt 1:19 *2977*
Then Herod s called the magi and Mt 2:7 *2977*
called Mary her sister, saying s, Jn 11:28 *2977*
Then they s induced men to say, Ac 6:11 *5260*
now are they sending us away s? Ac 16:37 *2977*
was because of the false brethren s Ga 2:4 *3920*
who will s introduce destructive 2Pe 2:1 *3919*

SECRETS
And show you the s of wisdom! Jb 11:6 8587
For He knows the s of the heart. Ps 44:21 8587
about as a talebearer reveals s, Pr 11:13 5475
about as a slanderer reveals s, Pr 20:19 5475
God will judge the s of men through Ro 2:16 *2927*
the s of his heart are disclosed; 1Co 14:25 *2927*

SECT
(that is the s of the Sadducees), Ac 5:17 *139*
some of the s of the Pharisees Ac 15:5 *139*
of the s of the Nazarenes. Ac 24:5 *139*
the Way which they call a s Ac 24:14 *139*
the strictest s of our religion. Ac 26:5 *139*
for concerning this s, Ac 28:22 *139*

SECTION
and they buried him in the upper s of 2Ch 32:33 4608
repaired another s and the Tower Ne 3:11 4060a
of Mizpah, repaired another s in Ne 3:19 4060a
zealously repaired another s, Ne 3:20 4060a
son of Hakkoz repaired another s, Ne 3:21 4060a
son of Henadad repaired another s, Ne 3:24 4060a
the Tekoites repaired another s in Ne 3:27 4060a
son of Zalaph, repaired another s. Ne 3:30 4060a

SECTIONS
the s of the fathers' households 2Ch 35:5 6391
give them to the s of the fathers' 2Ch 35:12 4653

SECTOR
'Your southern s shall extend from Nu 34:3 6285

SECU
as the large well that is in S; 1Sa 19:22 7906

SECUNDUS
and S of the Thessalonians, Ac 20:4 *4580*

SECURE
of the Sidonians, quiet and s; Jg 18:7 982
a s people with a spacious land; Jg 18:10 982
to Laish, to a people quiet and s, Jg 18:27 982
of his father and made himself s, 2Ch 21:4 2388
You will know that your tent is s, Jb 5:24 7965
And those who provoke God are s, Jb 12:6 987
And overthrows the s ones. Jb 12:19 386
he who hates being a guarantor is s. Pr 11:15 982
And in s dwellings and in Is 32:18 4009
"You felt s in your wickedness Is 47:10 982
return and be undisturbed And s, Jer 46:27 7599
in ships to frighten s Ethiopia; Ezk 30:9 983
and they will be s on their land. Ezk 34:27 983
feel s in the mountain of Samaria, Am 6:1 982
to be made s until the third day, Mt 27:64 *805*
make it *as* s as you know how." Mt 27:65 *805*
they went and made the grave s, Mt 27:66 *805*
what is appropriate and *to* s 1Co 7:35

SECURED
me, Ordered in all things, and s; 2Sa 23:5 8104
And because my hand had s *so* much; Jb 31:25 4672

SECURELY
that you may live s on the land. Lv 25:18 983
eat your fill and live s on it. Lv 25:19 983
the full and live s in your land. Lv 26:5 983
son of David established himself s 2Ch 1:1 2388
you would look around and rest s. Jb 11:18 983
My flesh also will dwell s. Ps 16:9 983
name of the God of Jacob set you s Ps 20:1
Set me s on high away from those Ps 59:1
set me s on high. Ps 69:29
I will set him s on high, Ps 91:14
But He sets the needy s on high Ps 107:41 7682
he who listens to me shall live s And Pr 1:33 983
Then you will walk in your way s And Pr 3:23 983
While he lives s beside you. Pr 3:29 983
He who walks in integrity walks s, Pr 10:9 983
And tie your sash s about him. Is 22:21 2388
you sensual one, Who dwells s, Is 47:8 983
be saved, And Israel will dwell s; Jer 23:6 983
which is at ease, Which lives s," Jer 49:31 983
"They will live in it s; Ezk 28:26 983
plant vineyards and live s Ezk 28:26 983
so that they may live s in the Ezk 34:25 983
but they will live s, Ezk 34:28 983
nations, and they are living s, Ezk 38:8 983
who are at rest, that live s, Ezk 38:11 983
My people Israel are living s, Ezk 38:14 983
when they live s on their *own* land Ezk 39:26 983
the exultant city Which dwells s, Zph 2:15 983
found the prison house locked quite s Ac 5:23 *803*
the jailer to guard them s; Ac 16:23 *806*

SECURITY
a deposit or a s entrusted *to him,* Lv 6:2 8667
around *you* so that you live in s, Dt 12:10 983
the beloved of the LORD dwell in s Dt 33:12 983
"So Israel dwells in s, Dt 33:28 983
people who were in it living in s, Jg 18:7 983
shall I not seek s for you, Ru 3:1 4494
around, so that you lived in s. 1Sa 12:11 983
"He is torn from the s of his tent, Jb 18:14 4009
"He provides them with s, Jb 24:23 983
And the needy will lie down in s; Is 14:30 983
sets up walls and ramparts for s. Is 26:1 3444
O Lord, I am oppressed, be my s. Is 38:14 6148
for Jerusalem will dwell in s. Zch 14:11 983

SEDAN
has made for himself a s chair From SS 3:9 668

SEDUCE
to s you from the way in which the Dt 13:5 5080
sought to s you from the LORD your Dt 13:10 5080

SEDUCED
s the inhabitants of their city, Dt 13:13 5080
and Manasseh s them to do evil 2Ki 21:9 8582

SEDUCES
man s a virgin who is not engaged, Ex 22:16 6601b
With her flattering lips she s him. Pr 7:21 5080

SEDUCTIVE
with heads held high and s eyes, Is 3:16 8265

SEE
man to s what he would call them; Gn 2:19 7200
to s if the water was abated from Gn 8:8 7200
did not s their father's nakedness. Gn 9:23 7200
The LORD came down to s the city Gn 11:5 7200
"S now, I know that you are a Gn 12:11 2009
and when the Egyptians s you, Gn 12:12 7200
for all the land which you s, Gn 13:15 7200
and s if they have done entirely Gn 18:21 7200
"Do not let me s the boy die." Gn 21:16 7200
"We s plainly that the LORD has Gn 26:28 7200
and his eyes were too dim to s, Gn 27:1 7200
"S, the smell of my son Is like Gn 27:27 7200
"I s your father's attitude, that Gn 31:5 7200
your eyes and s *that* all the male Gn 31:12 7200
and all that you s is mine. Gn 31:43 7200
s, God is witness between you and Gn 31:50 7200
Then afterward I will s his face; Gn 32:20 7200
for I s your face as one sees the Gn 33:10 7200
"Go now and s about the welfare Gn 37:14 7200
Then let us s what will become of Gn 37:20 7200
please examine *it* to s Gn 37:32
"Please examine and s, Gn 38:25 5234
"S, he has brought in a Hebrew to Gn 39:14 7200
"S, I have set you over all the Gn 41:41 7200
'You shall not s my face unless Gn 43:3 7200
'You will not s my face unless Gn 43:5 7200
you will not s my face again.' Gn 44:23 7200
for we cannot s the man's face Gn 44:26 7200
that I s the evil that would Gn 44:34 7200
"Behold, your eyes s, Gn 45:12 7200
the eyes of my brother Benjamin s, Gn 45:12
will go and s him before I die." Gn 45:28 7200
dim from age *that* he could not s. Gn 48:10 7200
"I never expected to s your face, Gn 48:11 7200
God has let me s your children Gn 48:11 7200

and **s** *them* upon the birthstool,	**Ex 1:16**	7200
now and **s** this marvelous sight,	**Ex 3:3**	7200
and **s** if they are still alive."	**Ex 4:18**	7200
s that you perform before Pharaoh	**Ex 4:21**	7200
shall **s** what I will do to Pharaoh;	**Ex 6:1**	7200
"**S**, I make you *as* God to Pharaoh,	**Ex 7:1**	7200
one will be able to **s** the land.	**Ex 10:5**	7200
They did not **s** one another, nor	**Ex 10:23**	7200
Beware, do not **s** my face again,	**Ex 10:28**	7200
day you **s** my face you shall die!"	**Ex 10:28**	7200
I shall never **s** your face again!"	**Ex 10:29**	7200
and when I **s** the blood I will pass	**Ex 12:13**	7200
their minds when they **s** war,	**Ex 13:17**	7200
and **s** the salvation of the LORD	**Ex 14:13**	7200
will never **s** them again forever.	**Ex 14:13**	7200
you will **s** the glory of the LORD,	**Ex 16:7**	7200
"**S**, the LORD has given you the	**Ex 16:29**	7200
that they may **s** the bread that I	**Ex 16:32**	7200
"If you **s** the donkey of one who	**Ex 23:5**	7200
"**S** that you make *them* after	**Ex 25:40**	7200
"**S**, I have called by name	**Ex 31:2**	7200
"**S**, You say to me,	**Ex 33:12**	7200
"You cannot **s** My face, for no man	**Ex 33:20**	7200
for no man can **s** Me and live!"	**Ex 33:20**	7200
hand away and you shall **s** My back,	**Ex 33:23**	7200
will **s** the working of the LORD,	**Ex 34:10**	7200
Israel would **s** the face of Moses,	**Ex 34:35**	7200
"**S**, the LORD has called by name	**Ex 35:30**	7200
feet, as far as the priest can **s**,	**Lv 13:12**	
		4758, 5869
shall not go in to **s** the holy *objects*	**Nu 4:20**	7200
do not let me **s** my wretchedness."	**Nu 11:15**	7200
Now you shall **s** whether My word	**Nu 11:23**	7200
"**S** what the land is like,	**Nu 13:18**	7200
shall by no means **s** the land which	**Nu 14:23**	7200
any of those who spurned Me **s** it.	**Nu 14:23**	7200
I **s** him from the top of the rocks,	**Nu 23:9**	7200
place from where you may **s** them,	**Nu 23:13**	7200
only **s** the extreme end of them and	**Nu 23:13**	7200
them and will not **s** all of them;	**Nu 23:13**	7200
"I **s** him, but not now;	**Nu 24:17**	7200
and **s** the land which I have given	**Nu 27:12**	7200
from Kadesh-barnea to **s** the land.	**Nu 32:8**	7200
shall **s** the land which I swore to	**Nu 32:11**	7200
'**S**, I have placed the land before	**Dt 1:8**	7200
'**S**, the LORD your God has placed	**Dt 1:21**	7200
shall **s** the good land which I	**Dt 1:35**	7200
he shall **s** it, and to him and to	**Dt 1:36**	7200
'**S**, I have begun to deliver Sihon	**Dt 2:31**	7200
cross over and **s** the fair land	**Dt 3:25**	7200
and east, and **s** *it* with your eyes,	**Dt 3:27**	7200
the land which you will **s**.'	**Dt 3:28**	7200
"**S**, I have taught you statutes	**Dt 4:5**	7200
since you did not **s** any form on	**Dt 4:15**	7200
lift up your eyes to heaven and **s** the	**Dt 4:19**	7200
s nor hear nor eat nor smell.	**Dt 4:28**	7200
earth He let you **s** His great fire,	**Dt 4:36**	7200
"**S**, I am setting before you today	**Dt 11:26**	7200
in every *cultic* place you **s**,	**Dt 12:13**	7200
me not **s** this great fire anymore,	**Dt 18:16**	7200
and **s** horses and chariots *and* people	**Dt 20:1**	7200
this blood, nor did our eyes **s** *it*.	**Dt 21:7**	7200
and **s** among the captives a	**Dt 21:11**	7200
"You shall not **s** your	**Dt 22:1**	7200
"You shall not **s** your	**Dt 22:4**	7200
and He must not **s** anything	**Dt 23:14**	7200
all the peoples of the earth will **s**	**Dt 28:10**	7200
mad by the sight of what you **s**.	**Dt 28:34**	7200
of your eyes which you will **s**.	**Dt 28:67**	7200
'You will never **s** it again!'	**Dt 28:68**	7200
a heart to know, nor eyes to **s**,	**Dt 29:4**	7200
when they **s** the plagues of the	**Dt 29:22**	7200
"**S**, I have set before you today	**Dt 30:15**	7200
I will **s** what their end *shall be;*	**Dt 32:20**	7200
'**S** now that I, I am He, And there	**Dt 32:39**	7200
shall **s** the land at a distance,	**Dt 32:52**	7200
have let you **s** *it* with your eyes,	**Dt 34:4**	7200
"When you **s** the ark of the	**Jos 3:3**	7200
that He would not let them **s** the land	**Jos 5:6**	7200
"**S**, I have given Jericho into	**Jos 6:2**	7200
s, I have given into your hand the	**Jos 8:1**	7200
"**S**, you are going to ambush the	**Jos 8:4**	7200
S, I have commanded you."	**Jos 8:8**	7200
'**S** the copy of the altar of the LORD	**Jos 22:28**	7200
"**S**, I have apportioned to you	**Jos 23:4**	7200
and **s** where his great strength *lies*	**Jg 16:5**	7200
s the distress of *My* dwelling,	**1Sa 2:32**	5027
grow dim *and* he could not **s** *well*),	**1Sa 3:2**	7200
were set so that he could not **s**.	**1Sa 4:15**	7200
saw the ark and were glad to **s** *it*.	**1Sa 6:13**	7200
s, *he is* ahead of you.	**1Sa 9:12**	2009
s him whom the LORD has chosen?	**1Sa 10:24**	7200
take your stand and **s** this great	**1Sa 12:16**	7200
Then you will know and **s** that your	**1Sa 12:17**	7200
now and **s** who has gone from us."	**1Sa 14:17**	7200
S now, how my eyes have brightened	**1Sa 14:29**	7200
s how this sin has happened today.	**1Sa 14:38**	7200
Samuel did not **s** Saul again	**1Sa 15:35**	7200
down in order to **s** the battle."	**1Sa 17:28**	7200
Saul sent messengers to **s** David,	**1Sa 19:15**	7200
away that I may **s** my brothers.'	**1Sa 20:29**	7200
s the man behaving as a madman.	**1Sa 21:14**	7200
s his place where his haunt is,	**1Sa 23:22**	7200
"Now, my father, **s**!	**1Sa 24:11**	7200
Indeed, **s** the edge of your robe	**1Sa 24:11**	7200
and may He **s** and plead my cause and	**1Sa 24:15**	7200
but I your maidservant did not **s**	**1Sa 25:25**	7200
S, I have listened to you and	**1Sa 25:35**	7200
now, **s** where the king's spear is and	**1Sa 26:16**	7200
but what do you **s**?"	**1Sa 28:13**	7200
"I **s** a divine being coming up out	**1Sa 28:13**	7200
you shall not **s** my face unless you	**2Sa 3:13**	7200
daughter, when you come to **s** me."	**2Sa 3:13**	7200
"**S** now, I dwell in a house of	**2Sa 7:2**	7200
when your father comes to **s** you,	**2Sa 13:5**	7200
I may **s** *it* and eat from her hand.	**2Sa 13:5**	7200
when the king came to **s** him,	**2Sa 13:6**	7200
"**S** now, when Amnon's heart is	**2Sa 13:28**	7200
and let him not **s** my face."	**2Sa 14:24**	7200
and did not **s** the king's face.	**2Sa 14:24**	7200
and did not **s** the king's face.	**2Sa 14:28**	7200
"**S**, Joab's field is next to mine,	**2Sa 14:30**	7200
let me **s** the king's face,	**2Sa 14:32**	7200
"**S**, your claims are good and	**2Sa 15:3**	7200
"**S**, I am going to wait at the	**2Sa 15:28**	7200
But a lad did **s** them and told	**2Sa 17:18**	7200
eyes of my lord the king *still* **s**;	**2Sa 24:3**	7200
Now consider and **s** what answer I	**2Sa 24:13**	7200
today while my own eyes **s** *it*.' "	**1Ki 1:48**	7200
So Hiram came out from Tyre to **s**	**1Ki 9:12**	7200
Now Ahijah could not **s**,	**1Ki 14:4**	7200
"**S**, your son is alive."	**1Ki 17:23**	7200
"Please observe and **s** how this	**1Ki 20:7**	7200
observe and **s** what you have to do;	**1Ki 20:22**	7200
"Do you **s** how Ahab has humbled	**1Ki 21:29**	7200
you shall **s** on that day when you	**1Ki 22:25**	7200
you **s** me when I am taken from you,	**2Ki 2:10**	7200
I would not look at you nor **s** you.	**2Ki 3:14**	7200
not **s** wind nor shall you see rain;	**2Ki 3:17**	7200
not see wind nor shall you **s** rain;	**2Ki 3:17**	7200
and **s** how he is seeking a quarrel	**2Ki 5:7**	7200
"Go and **s** where he is, that I may	**2Ki 6:13**	7200
open his eyes that he may **s**."	**2Ki 6:17**	7200
of these *men*, that they may **s**."	**2Ki 6:20**	7200
"Do you **s** how this son of a	**2Ki 6:32**	7200
you will **s** it with your own eyes,	**2Ki 7:2**	7200
perished, so let us send and **s**."	**2Ki 7:13**	7200
of the Arameans, saying, "Go and **s**	**2Ki 7:14**	7200
you will **s** it with your own eyes,	**2Ki 7:19**	7200
king of Judah went down to **s** Joram	**2Ki 8:29**	7200
of Judah had come down to **s** Joram.	**2Ki 9:16**	7200
"I **s** a company." And Joram said,	**2Ki 9:17**	7200
"**S** now to this cursed woman and	**2Ki 9:34**	6485
me and **s** my zeal for the LORD."	**2Ki 10:16**	7200
"Search and **s** that there is	**2Ki 10:23**	7200
open Your eyes, O LORD, and **s**;	**2Ki 19:16**	7200
and your eyes will not **s** all the evil	**2Ki 22:20**	7200
"What is this monument that I **s**?"	**2Ki 23:17**	7200
S, I will give the oxen for burnt	**1Ch 21:23**	7200
"Behold, you will **s** on that day	**2Ch 18:24**	7200
s *how* they are rewarding us by	**2Ch 20:11**	2009
stand and **s** the salvation of the	**2Ch 20:17**	7200
went down to **s** Jehoram the son of	**2Ch 22:6**	7200
"May the LORD **s** and avenge!"	**2Ch 24:22**	7200
as you **s** with your own eyes.	**2Ch 29:8**	7200
He made them a horror, as you **s**.	**2Ch 30:7**	7200
so your eyes will not **s** all the evil	**2Ch 34:28**	7200
for us to **s** the king's dishonor,	**Ezr 4:14**	2370
"You **s** the bad situation we are	**Ne 2:17**	7200
or **s** until we come among them,	**Ne 4:11**	7200
that they told Haman to **s** whether	**Es 3:4**	7200
every time I **s** Mordecai the Jew	**Es 5:13**	7200
"For how can I endure to **s** the	**Es 8:6**	7200
and how can I endure to **s** the	**Es 8:6**	7200
write to the Jews as you **s** fit,	**Es 8:8**	5869
let it not **s** the breaking dawn;	**Jb 3:9**	7200
You **s** a terror and are afraid.	**Jb 6:21**	7200
"Now please look at me, And **s**	**Jb 6:28**	
My eye will not again **s** good.	**Jb 7:7**	7200
to pass by me, I would not **s** Him;	**Jb 9:11**	7200
They flee away, they **s** no good.	**Jb 9:25**	7200
Or do You **s** as a man sees?	**Jb 10:4**	7200
Yet from my flesh I shall **s** God;	**Jb 19:26**	2372
my eyes will **s** and not another.	**Jb 19:27**	7200
"Let his own eyes **s** his decay,	**Jb 21:20**	7200
Or darkness, so that you cannot **s**,	**Jb 22:11**	7200
for Him, so that He cannot **s**;	**Jb 22:14**	7200
"The righteous **s** and are glad,	**Jb 22:19**	7200
on the right, I cannot **s** Him.	**Jb 23:9**	7200
those who know Him not **s** His days?	**Jb 24:1**	2372
'No eye will **s** me.'	**Jb 24:15**	7789
"Does He not **s** my ways And	**Jb 31:4**	7200
That he may **s** His face with joy,	**Jb 33:26**	7200
And my life shall **s** the light.'	**Jb 33:28**	7200
Teach me what I do not **s**;	**Jb 34:32**	2372
"Look at the heavens and **s**;	**Jb 35:5**	7200
"Now men do not **s** the light	**Jb 37:21**	7200
His eyes **s** *it* from afar.	**Jb 39:29**	5027
Be gracious to me, O LORD; **S** my	**Ps 9:13**	7200
He will never **s** it."	**Ps 10:11**	7200
To **s** if there are any who	**Ps 14:2**	7200
All who **s** me sneer at me;	**Ps 22:7**	7200
I would **s** the goodness of the LORD	**Ps 27:13**	7200
Those who **s** me in the street flee	**Ps 31:11**	7200
taste and **s** that the LORD is good;	**Ps 34:8**	7200
length of days that he may **s** good?	**Ps 34:12**	7200
In Your light we **s** light.	**Ps 36:9**	7200
wicked are cut off, you will **s** it.	**Ps 37:34**	7200
Many will **s** and fear And will	**Ps 40:3**	7200
me, so that I am not able to **s**;	**Ps 40:12**	7200
And when he comes to **s** *me*,	**Ps 41:6**	7200
They will never **s** the light.	**Ps 49:19**	7200
"When you **s** a thief, you are	**Ps 50:18**	7200
The righteous will **s** and fear,	**Ps 52:6**	7200
To **s** if there is anyone who	**Ps 53:2**	7200
of a woman which never **s** the sun.	**Ps 58:8**	2372
Arouse Yourself to help me, and **s**!	**Ps 59:4**	7200
To **s** Your power and Your glory.	**Ps 63:2**	7200
"Who can **s** them?"	**Ps 64:5**	7200
All who **s** them will shake the head.	**Ps 64:8**	7200
Come and **s** the works of God, *Who*	**Ps 66:5**	7200
grow dim so that they cannot **s**,	**Ps 69:23**	7200
We do not **s** our signs;	**Ps 74:9**	7200
Look down from heaven and **s**,	**Ps 80:14**	7200
That those who hate me may **s** *it* and	**Ps 86:17**	7200
What man can live and not **s** death?	**Ps 89:48**	7200
s the recompense of the wicked.	**Ps 91:8**	7200
life I will satisfy him And let him **s**	**Ps 91:16**	7200
"The LORD does not **s**,	**Ps 94:7**	7200
who formed the eye, does He not **s**?	**Ps 94:9**	5027
That I may **s** the prosperity of Your	**Ps 106:5**	7200
The upright **s** it and are glad;	**Ps 107:42**	7200
When they **s** me, they wag their	**Ps 109:25**	7200
The wicked will **s** it and be vexed,	**Ps 112:10**	7200
They have eyes, but they cannot **s**;	**Ps 115:5**	7200
who fear You **s** me and be glad,	**Ps 119:74**	7200
And may you **s** the prosperity of	**Ps 128:5**	7200
may you **s** your children's children.	**Ps 128:6**	7200
They have eyes, but they do not **s**;	**Ps 135:16**	7200
And **s** if there be any hurtful way	**Ps 139:24**	7200
Look to the right and **s**;	**Ps 142:4**	7200
you **s** a man skilled in his work?	**Pr 22:29**	2372
Your eyes will **s** strange things And	**Pr 23:33**	7200
"**S**, we did not know this,"	**Pr 24:12**	2005
the LORD will **s** *it* and be displeased,	**Pr 24:18**	7200
you **s** a man wise in his own eyes?	**Pr 26:12**	7200
the righteous will **s** their fall.	**Pr 29:16**	7200
Do you **s** a man who is hasty in his	**Pr 29:20**	2372
"**S** this, it is new"?	**Ec 1:10**	7200
until I could **s** what good there is	**Ec 2:3**	7200
to **s** that they are but beasts."	**Ec 3:18**	7200
to **s** what will occur after him?	**Ec 3:22**	7200
If you **s** oppression of the poor	**Ec 5:8**	7200
What the eyes **s** is better than	**Ec 6:9**	4758
advantage to those who **s** the sun.	**Ec 7:11**	7200
to know wisdom and to **s** the task	**Ec 8:16**	7200
came to **s** as wisdom under the sun,	**Ec 9:13**	7200
is good for the eyes to **s** the sun.	**Ec 11:7**	7200
steep pathway, Let me **s** your form,	**SS 2:14**	7200
To **s** the blossoms of the valley,	**SS 6:11**	7200
To **s** whether the vine had budded	**SS 6:11**	7200
Let us **s** whether the vine has	**SS 7:12**	7200
hasten His work, that we may **s** *it;*	**Is 5:19**	7200
they might **s** with their eyes,	**Is 6:10**	7200
in darkness Will **s** a great light;	**Is 9:2**	7200
will not judge by what His eyes **s**,	**Is 11:3**	4758
"Those who **s** you will gaze at	**Is 14:16**	7200
on the mountains, you will **s** *it*,	**Is 18:3**	7200
hear, so terrified I cannot **s**.	**Is 21:3**	7200
is lifted up *yet* they do not **s** it.	**Is 26:11**	2372
They **s** *Your* zeal for the people and	**Is 26:11**	2372
the eyes of the blind will **s**.	**Is 29:18**	7200
"You must not **s** *visions*";	**Is 30:10**	7200
those who **s** will not be blinded,	**Is 32:3**	7200
eyes will **s** the King in His beauty;	**Is 33:17**	2372
will no longer **s** a fierce people,	**Is 33:19**	7200
Your eyes will **s** Jerusalem, an	**Is 33:20**	7200
They will **s** the glory of the LORD,	**Is 35:2**	7200
open Your eyes, O LORD, and **s**;	**Is 37:17**	7200
"I will not **s** the LORD, The LORD	**Is 38:11**	7200
And all flesh will **s** *it* together;	**Is 40:5**	7200
And **s** who has created these *stars*,	**Is 40:26**	7200
That they may **s** and recognize, And	**Is 41:20**	7200
look, you blind, that you may **s**.	**Is 42:18**	7200
own witnesses fail to **s** or know,	**Is 44:9**	7200
over their eyes so that they cannot **s**	**Is 44:18**	7200
"Kings will **s** and arise, Princes	**Is 49:7**	7200
For they will **s** with their own	**Is 52:8**	7200
may **s** The salvation of our God.	**Is 52:10**	7200
not been told them they will **s**,	**Is 52:15**	7200
offering, He will **s** *His* offspring,	**Is 53:10**	7200
He will **s** *it and* be satisfied;	**Is 53:11**	7200
we fasted and You do not **s**?	**Is 58:3**	7200
When you **s** the naked, to cover him;	**Is 58:7**	7200
up your eyes round about and **s**;	**Is 60:4**	7200
"Then you will **s** and be radiant,	**Is 60:5**	7200
All who **s** them will recognize them	**Is 61:9**	7200
nations will **s** your righteousness,	**Is 62:2**	7200
and **s** from Your holy and glorious	**Is 63:15**	7200
that we may **s** your joy.'	**Is 66:5**	7200
Then you will **s** *this*, and your	**Is 66:14**	7200
they shall come and **s** My glory.	**Is 66:18**	7200
"**S**, I have appointed you this day	**Jer 1:10**	7200
"What do you **s**, Jeremiah?"	**Jer 1:11**	7200
"I **s** a rod of an almond tree."	**Jer 1:11**	7200
"What do you **s**?" And I said,	**Jer 1:13**	7200
"I **s** a boiling pot, facing away	**Jer 1:13**	7200
to the coastlands of Kittim and **s**,	**Jer 2:10**	7200
And **s** if there has been such *a*	**Jer 2:10**	7200
Know therefore and **s** that it is	**Jer 2:19**	7200
eyes to the bare heights and **s**;	**Jer 3:2**	7200
How long must I **s** the standard And	**Jer 4:21**	7200
And we will not **s** sword or famine.	**Jer 5:12**	7200
people, Who have eyes but do not **s**;	**Jer 5:21**	7200
s and ask for the ancient paths,	**Jer 6:16**	7200
and **s** what I did to it because of	**Jer 7:12**	7200
"Do you not **s** what they are doing	**Jer 7:17**	7200
Let me **s** Your vengeance on them,	**Jer 11:20**	7200
You **s** me; And You examine	**Jer 12:3**	7200
"He will not **s** our latter ending."	**Jer 12:4**	7200
and **s** Those coming from the north.	**Jer 13:20**	7200
'You will not **s** the sword nor will	**Jer 14:13**	7200
will not **s** when prosperity comes,	**Jer 17:6**	7200
Who **s** the mind and the heart;	**Jer 20:12**	7200
Let me **s** Your vengeance on them;	**Jer 20:12**	7200
never return Or **s** his native land.	**Jer 22:10**	7200
die and not **s** this land again.	**Jer 22:12**	7200

he should **s** and hear His word? Jer 23:18 7200
places So I do not **s** him?" Jer 23:24 7200
"What do you **s**, Jeremiah?" Jer 24:3 7200
and he will not **s** the good that I Jer 29:32 7200
'Ask now, and **s** If a male can Jer 30:6 7200
Why do I **s** every man *With* his Jer 30:6 7200
to face and **s** him eye to eye; Jer 32:4 7200
and behold, You **s** *it*. Jer 32:24 7200
and you will **s** the king of Babylon Jer 34:3 7200
many, as your own eyes *now* **s** us, Jer 42:2 7200
where we will not **s** war or hear Jer 42:14 7200
you will **s** this place no more." Jer 42:18 7200
For, **s**, I am going to save you Jer 46:27 2009
then **s** that you read all these Jer 51:61 7200
"**S**, O LORD, my affliction, For La 1:9 7200
"**S**, O LORD, and look, For I am La 1:11 7200
Look and **s** if there is any pain La 1:12 7200
"**S**, O LORD, for I am in distress; La 1:20 7200
S, O LORD, and look! La 2:20 7200
Look, and **s** our reproach! La 5:1 7200
"**S**, I will give you cow's dung Ezk 4:15 7200
man, do you **s** what they are doing, Ezk 8:6 7200
s still greater abominations." Ezk 8:6 7200
"Go in and **s** the wicked Ezk 8:9 7200
do you **s** what the elders of the Ezk 8:12 7200
'The LORD does not **s** us; Ezk 8:12 7200
"Yet you will **s** still greater Ezk 8:13 7200
"Do you **s** *this*, son of man? Ezk 8:15 7200
Yet you will **s** still greater Ezk 8:15 7200
"Do you **s** *this*, son of man? Ezk 8:17 7200
land, and the LORD does not **s**!' Ezk 9:9 7200
who have eyes to **s** but do not see, Ezk 12:2 7200
who have eyes to see but do not **s**, Ezk 12:2 7200
so that you cannot **s** the land, Ezk 12:6 7200
can not **s** the land with *his* eyes. Ezk 12:12 7200
yet he will not **s** it, though he Ezk 12:13 7200
"They **s** falsehood and lying Ezk 13:6 2372
"Did you not **s** a false vision and Ezk 13:7 7200
prophets who **s** false visions and utter Ezk 13:9 7200
and who **s** visions of peace for her Ezk 13:16 7200
women will no longer **s** false visions Ezk 13:23 7200
will **s** their conduct and actions; Ezk 14:22 7200
you **s** their conduct and actions, Ezk 14:23 7200
they may **s** all your nakedness. Ezk 16:37 7200
"All flesh will **s** that I, Ezk 20:48 7200
they **s** for you false visions, Ezk 21:29 2372
before kings, That they may **s** you. Ezk 28:17 7200
In the eyes of all who **s** you. Ezk 28:18 7200
"These Pharaoh will **s**, Ezk 32:31 7200
and all the nations will **s** My Ezk 39:21 7200
"Son of man, **s** with your eyes, Ezk 40:4 7200
house of Israel all that you **s**." Ezk 40:4 7200
man, mark well, **s** with your eyes and Ezk 44:5 7200
for why should he **s** your faces Da 1:10 7200
according to what you **s**." Da 1:13 7200
I **s** four men loosed *and* walking Da 3:25 2370
wood and stone, which do not **s**, Da 5:23 7200
Open Your eyes and **s** our Da 9:18 7200
were with me did not **s** the vision; Da 10:7 7200
Your young men will **s** visions. Jl 2:28 7200
and **s** *the* great tumults within her Am 3:9 7200
"What do you **s**, Amos?" Am 7:8 7200
"What do you **s**, Amos?" Am 8:2 7200
s what would happen in the city. Jon 4:5 7200
And I will **s** His righteousness. Mi 7:9 7200
Then my enemy will **s**, Mi 7:10 7200
Nations will **s** and be ashamed Of Mi 7:16 7200
all who **s** you Will shrink from you Na 3:7 7200
Why do You make me **s** iniquity, Hab 1:3 7200
to **s** what He will speak to me, Hab 2:1 7200
And how do you **s** it now? Hg 2:3 7200
to **s** how wide it is and how long Zch 2:2 7200
"**S**, I have taken your iniquity Zch 3:4 7200
He said to me, "What do you **s**?" Zch 4:2 7200
"I **s**, and behold, a lampstand all Zch 4:2 7200
these seven will be glad when they **s** Zch 4:10 7200
he said to me, "What do you **s**?" Zch 5:2 7200
"I **s** a flying scroll; Zch 5:2 7200
now your eyes and **s** what this is Zch 5:5 7200
"**S**, those who are going to the Zch 6:8 7200
Ashkelon will **s** *it* and be afraid. Zch 9:5 7200
And the diviners **s** lying visions And Zch 10:2 2372
children will **s** *it* and be glad, Zch 10:7 7200
eyes will **s** this and you will say, Mal 1:5 7200
in heart, for they shall **s** God. Mt 5:8 3708
that they may **s** your good works, Mt 5:16 3708
and then you will **s** clearly to Mt 7:5 1227
"**S** that you tell no one; Mt 8:4 3708
"**S** that no one knows *about* Mt 9:30 3708
to John what you hear and **s**: Mt 11:4 991
you go out into the wilderness to **s**? Mt 11:7 2300
"But what did you go out to **s**? Mt 11:8 3708
what did you go out to **s**? A prophet? Mt 11:9 3708
we want to **s** a sign from You." Mt 12:38 3708
while seeing they do not **s**, Mt 13:13 991
THEY WOULD **S** WITH THEIR EYES, Mt 13:15 3708
are your eyes, because they **s**; Mt 13:16 991
men desired to **s** what you see, Mt 13:17 3708
men desired to see what you **s**, Mt 13:17 991
what you see, and did not **s** *it*, Mt 13:17 3708
who will not taste death until they **s** Mt 16:28 3708
"**S** that you do not despise one of Mt 18:10 3708
their angels in heaven continually **s** Mt 18:10 3708
you will not **s** Me until you say, Mt 23:39 3708
"Do you not **s** all these things? Mt 24:2 991
"**S** to it that no one misleads you. Mt 24:4 991
S that you are not frightened, for Mt 24:6 3708
when you **s** the ABOMINATION Mt 24:15 3708
and they will **s** the SON OF MAN Mt 24:30 3708

too, when you **s** all these things, Mt 24:33 3708
S, I have gained five more talents.' Mt 25:20 2396
S, I have gained two more talents.' Mt 25:22 2396
S, you have what is yours.' Mt 25:25 2396
'Lord, when did we **s** You hungry, Mt 25:37 3708
'And when did we **s** You a stranger, Mt 25:38 3708
'When did we **s** You sick, or in Mt 25:39 3708
'Lord, when did we **s** You hungry, Mt 25:44 3708
the officers to **s** the outcome. Mt 26:58 3708
hereafter you will **s** THE SON OF Mt 26:64 3708
S *to that* yourself!" Mt 27:4 3708
s *to that* yourselves." Mt 27:24 3708
"Let us **s** whether Elijah will Mt 27:49 3708
s the place where He was lying. Mt 28:6 3708
Galilee, there you will **s** Him; Mt 28:7 3708
and there they will **s** Me." Mt 28:10 3708
"**S** that you say nothing to anyone; Mk 1:44 3708
They were watching Him *to* **s** if He Mk 3:2
THEY MAY **S** AND NOT PERCEIVE Mk 4:12 991
s what it was that had happened. Mk 5:14 3708
"You **s** the crowd pressing in Mk 5:31 991
to **s** the woman who had done this. Mk 5:32 3708
Do you not yet **s** or understand? Mk 8:17 3539
"HAVING EYES, DO YOU NOT **S**? Mk 8:18 991
"Do you **s** anything?" Mk 8:23 991
And he looked up and said, "I **s** men, Mk 8:24 991
for I **s** *them* like trees, walking Mk 8:24 3708
and *began* to **s** everything clearly. Mk 8:25 1227
who will not taste death until they **s** Mk 9:1 3708
He went *to* **s** if perhaps He would Mk 11:13
"Do you **s** these great buildings? Mk 13:2 991
"**S** to it that no one misleads you. Mk 13:5 991
"But when you **s** the ABOMINATION Mk 13:14 3708
"Then they will **s** THE SON OF Mk 13:26 3708
when you **s** these things happening, Mk 13:29 3708
and you shall **s** THE SON OF MAN Mk 14:62 3708
S how many charges they bring Mk 15:4 2396
so that we may **s** and believe!" Mk 15:32 3708
"Let us **s** whether Elijah will Mk 15:36 3708
of Joses were looking on *to* **s** Mk 15:47
there you will **s** Him, just as He Mk 16:7 3708
and **s** this thing that has happened Lk 2:15 3708
he would not **s** death before he had Lk 2:26 3708
ALL FLESH WILL **S** THE SALVATION Lk 3:6 3708
were watching Him closely *to* **s** if Lk 6:7
when you yourself do not **s** the log Lk 6:42 991
and then you will **s** clearly to Lk 6:42 1227
you go out into the wilderness to **s**? Lk 7:24 2300
"But what did you go out to **s**? Lk 7:25 3708
"But what did you go out to **s**? Lk 7:26 3708
"Do you **s** this woman? Lk 7:44 991
so that SEEING THEY MAY NOT **S**, Lk 8:10 991
those who come in may **s** the light. Lk 8:16 991
outside, wishing to **s** You." Lk 8:20 3708
went out to **s** what had happened; Lk 8:35 3708
And he kept trying to **s** Him. Lk 9:9 3708
until they **s** the kingdom of God." Lk 9:27 3708
eyes which **s** the things you see, Lk 10:23 991
eyes which see the things you **s**, Lk 10:23 991
to **s** the things which you see, Lk 10:24 3708
to see the things which you **s**, Lk 10:24 991
which you see, and did not **s** *them*, Lk 10:24 3708
those who enter may **s** the light. Lk 11:33 991
you **s** a cloud rising in the west, Lk 12:54 3708
"And when *you* **s** a south wind Lk 12:55
when you **s** Abraham and Isaac and Lk 13:28 3708
you will not **s** Me until *the time* Lk 13:35 3708
to **s** if he has enough to complete Lk 14:28
you will long to **s** one of the days Lk 17:22 3708
Son of Man, and you will not **s** it. Lk 17:22 3708
Zaccheus was trying to **s** who Jesus was, Lk 19:3 3708
a sycamore tree in order to **s** Him, Lk 19:4 3708
"**S** to it that you are not misled; Lk 21:8 991
"But when you **s** Jerusalem Lk 21:20 3708
"Then they will **s** THE SON OF Lk 21:27 3708
you **s** it and know for yourselves Lk 21:30 991
when you **s** these things happening, Lk 21:31 3708
wanted to **s** Him for a long time, Lk 23:8 3708
to **s** some sign performed by Him. Lk 23:8 3708
but Him they did not **s**." Lk 24:24 3708
"**S** My hands and My feet, that it Lk 24:39 3708
touch Me and **s**, for a spirit does Lk 24:39 3708
and bones as you **s** that I have." Lk 24:39 2334
'He upon whom you **s** the Spirit Jn 1:33 3708
"Come, and you will **s**." Jn 1:39 3708
Philip said to him, "Come and **s**." Jn 1:46 3708
s greater things than these." Jn 1:50 3708
you will **s** the heavens opened Jn 1:51 3708
he cannot **s** the kingdom of God." Jn 3:3 3708
not obey the Son will not **s** life, Jn 3:36 3708
s a man who told me all the things Jn 4:29 3708
you *people* **s** signs and wonders, Jn 4:48 3708
You do for a sign, so that we may **s**, Jn 6:30 3708
"*What* then if you **s** the Son of Jn 6:62 2334
so that Your disciples also may **s** Jn 7:3 2334
and **s** that no prophet arises out Jn 7:52 3708
My word he will never **s** death." Jn 8:51 2334
Abraham rejoiced to **s** My day, Jn 8:56 3708
my eyes, and I washed, and I **s**." Jn 9:15 991
Then how does he now **s**?" Jn 9:19 991
though I was blind, now I **s**." Jn 9:25 991
that those who do not **s** may see, Jn 9:39 991
that those who do not see may **s**, Jn 9:39 991
those who **s** may become blind." Jn 9:39 991
'We **s**,' your sin remains. Jn 9:41 991
"Lord, come and **s**." Jn 11:34 3708
So the Jews were saying, "**S** how He Jn 11:36 2396
you will **s** the glory of God?" Jn 11:40 3708
that they might also **s** Lazarus, Jn 12:9 3708

"You **s** that you are not doing any Jn 12:19 2334
"Sir, we wish to **s** Jesus." Jn 12:21 3708
THEY WOULD NOT **S** WITH THEIR EYES Jn 12:40 3708
because it does not **s** Him or know Jn 14:17 2334
while the world will no longer **s** Me, Jn 14:19 2334
but you *will* **s** Me; because I Jn 14:19 2334
go to the Father and you no longer **s** Jn 16:10 2334
and you will no longer **s** Me; Jn 16:16 3708
little while, and you will **s** Me." Jn 16:16 3708
and you will not **s** Me; and again a Jn 16:17 3708
little while, and you will **s** Me'; Jn 16:17 3708
and you will not **s** Me, and again a Jn 16:19 3708
little while, and you will **s** Me'? Jn 16:19 3708
but I will **s** you again, and your Jn 16:22 3708
so that they may **s** My glory which Jn 17:24 2334
s you in the garden with Him?" Jn 18:26 3708
"Unless I **s** in His hands Jn 20:25 3708
here with your finger, and **s** My hands; Jn 20:27 3708
Blessed *are* they who did not **s**, Jn 20:29 3708
YOUR YOUNG MEN SHALL **S** VISIONS, Ac 2:17 3708
this which you both **s** and hear. Ac 2:33 991
this man whom you **s** and know; Ac 3:16 2334
I **s** the heavens opened up and the Ac 7:56 2334
"For I **s** that you are in the gall Ac 8:23 3708
were open, he could **s** nothing; Ac 9:8 991
and not **s** the sun for a time." Ac 13:11 991
and **s** how they are." Ac 15:36
examining the Scriptures daily *to* **s** Ac 17:11
been there, I must also **s** Rome." Ac 19:21 3708
"You **s** and hear that not only Ac 19:26 2334
kingdom, will no longer **s** my face. Ac 20:25 3708
they would not **s** his face again. Ac 20:38 2334
"You **s**, brother, how many Ac 21:20 2334
"But since I could not **s** because Ac 22:11 1689
will and to **s** the Righteous One Ac 22:14 3708
you **s** this man about whom all Ac 25:24 2334
and Paul went in *to* **s** him Ac 28:8
I requested to **s** you and to speak Ac 28:20 3708
THEY MIGHT **S** WITH THEIR EYES, Ac 28:27 3708
For I long to **s** you so that Ro 1:11 3708
And just as they did not **s** fit to Ro 1:28 1381a
but I **s** a different law in the Ro 7:23 991
if we hope for what we do not **s**, Ro 8:25 991
TO **S** NOT AND EARS TO HEAR NOT, Ro 11:8 991
THEIR EYES BE DARKENED TO **S** NOT, Ro 11:10 991
WHO HAD NO NEWS OF HIM SHALL **S**, Ro 15:21 3708
I hope to **s** you in passing, Ro 15:24 2300
For now we **s** in a mirror dimly, 1Co 13:12 991
wish to **s** you now *just* in passing; 1Co 16:7 3708
s that he is with you without 1Co 16:10 991
that they might not **s** the light of 2Co 4:4 826
I **s** that that letter caused you sorrow, 2Co 7:8 991
s that you abound in this 2Co 8:7
Test yourselves *to* **s** if you are 2Co 13:5
But I did not **s** any other of the Ga 1:19 3708
S with what large letters I am Ga 6:11 3708
and the wife must **s** *to it* that Eph 5:33
I come and **s** you or remain absent, Php 1:27 3708
soon as I **s** how things *go* with me; Php 2:23 872
you **s** him again you may rejoice and Php 2:28 3708
beloved brethren whom I long *to* **s**, Php 4:1
rejoicing to **s** your good Col 2:5 991
S to it that no one takes you Col 2:8 991
with great desire to **s** your face. 1Th 2:17 3708
longing to **s** us just as we also 1Th 3:6 3708
us just as we also long to **s** you, 1Th 3:6
earnestly that we may **s** your face, 1Th 3:10 3708
S that no one repays another with 1Th 5:15 3708
whom no man has seen or can **s**. 1Tm 6:16 3708
longing to **s** you, even as I recall 2Tm 1:4 3708
we do not yet **s** all things subjected Heb 2:8 3708
But we do **s** Him who was made Heb 2:9 991
So we **s** that they were not Heb 3:19 991
for, "**S**," He says, "THAT YOU MAKE Heb 8:5 3708
as you **s** the day drawing near. Heb 10:25 991
up so that he would not **s** death; Heb 11:5 3708
which no one will **s** the Lord. Heb 12:14 3708
S to it that no one comes short of Heb 12:15 1983
S to it that you do not refuse Him Heb 12:25 991
if he comes soon, I will **s** you. Heb 13:23 3708
You **s** that faith was working with Jas 2:22 991
You **s** that a man is justified by Jas 2:24 3708
S how great a forest is set aflame by Jas 3:5 2400
and though you do not **s** Him now, 1Pe 1:8 3708
TO LOVE AND **S** GOOD DAYS, 1Pe 3:10 3708
S how great a love the Father has 1Jn 3:1 3708
we will **s** Him just as He is. 1Jn 3:2 3708
to **s** whether they are from God, 1Jn 4:1
but I hope to **s** you shortly, and 3Jn 1:14 3708
CLOUDS, and every eye will **s** Him, Rv 1:7 3708
"Write in a book what you **s**, Rv 1:11 991
Then I turned to **s** the voice that Rv 1:12 991
anoint your eyes so that you may **s**. Rv 3:18 991
can neither **s** nor hear nor walk; Rv 9:20 991
naked and men will not **s** his shame.") Rv 16:15 991
will wonder when they **s** the beast, Rv 17:8 991
and will never **s** mourning.' Rv 18:7 3708
they **s** the smoke of her burning, Rv 18:9 991
they will **s** His face, and His Rv 22:4 3708

SEED

vegetation, plants yielding **s**, Gn 1:11 2233
after their kind with **s** in them Gn 1:11 2233
yielding **s** after their kind, Gn 1:12 2233
bearing fruit with **s** in them, Gn 1:12 2233
given you every plant yielding **s** that Gn 1:29 2233
tree which has fruit yielding **s**; Gn 1:29 2233
And between your **s** and her seed; Gn 3:15 2233
And between your seed and her **s**; Gn 3:15 2233
I will greatly multiply your **s** as the Gn 22:17 2233

and your **s** shall possess the gate	Gn 22:17	2233
"In your **s** all the nations of	Gn 22:18	2233
he wasted his **s** on the ground in	Gn 38:9	2233
So give us **s**, that we may live and	Gn 47:19	2233
now, *here* is **s** for you, and you	Gn 47:23	2233
shall be your own for **s** of the field	Gn 47:24	2233
and it was like coriander **s**,	Ex 16:31	2233
part of their carcass falls on any **s** for	Lv 11:37	2233
'Though if water is put on the **s** and	Lv 11:38	2233
your field with two kinds of **s**,	Lv 19:19	2233
you will sow your **s** uselessly,	Lv 26:16	2233
proportionate to the **s** needed for it:	Lv 27:16	2233
a homer of barley **s** at fifty shekels	Lv 27:16	2233
tithe of the land, of the **s** of the land	Lv 27:30	2233
the manna was like coriander **s**,	Nu 11:7	2233
And his **s** *will be* by many waters,	Nu 24:7	2233
where you used to sow your **s** and	Dt 11:10	2233
your vineyard with two kinds of **s**,	Dt 22:9	
or all the produce of the **s** which	Dt 22:9	2233
"You shall bring out much **s** to	Dt 28:38	2233
He will take a tenth of your **s** and	1Sa 8:15	2233
enough to hold two measures of **s**.	1Ki 18:32	2233
O **s** of Israel His servant, Sons of	1Ch 16:13	2233
I will establish your **s** forever And	Ps 89:4	2233
Light is sown *like* **s** for	Ps 97:11	
O **s** of Abraham, His servant, O	Ps 105:6	2233
cast their **s** among the nations And	Ps 106:27	2233
weeping, carrying *his* bag of **s**,	Ps 126:6	2233
Sow your **s** in the morning and do	Ec 11:6	2233
And a homer of **s** will yield *but* an	Is 5:10	2233
The holy **s** is its stump."	Is 6:13	2233
you bring your **s** to blossom;	Is 17:11	2233
plow continually to plant **s**?	Is 28:24	2232
Then He will give *you* rain for the **s**	Is 30:23	2233
And furnishing **s** to the sower and	Is 55:10	2233
vine, A completely faithful **s**.	Jer 2:21	2233
the house of Judah with the **s** of man	Jer 31:27	2233
of man and with the **s** of beast.	Jer 31:27	2233
a house, and you shall not sow **s** and	Jer 35:7	2233
not have vineyard or field or **s**.	Jer 35:9	2233
"He also took some of the **s** of	Ezk 17:5	2233
with one another in the **s** of men;	Da 2:43	2234
treader of grapes him who sows **s**;	Am 9:13	2233
'Is the **s** still in the barn?	Hg 2:19	2233
'For *there will be* peace for the **s**:	Zch 8:12	2233
whom **s** was sown beside the road.	Mt 13:19	
s was sown on the rocky places,	Mt 13:20	
whom **s** was sown among the thorns,	Mt 13:22	
whom **s** was sown on the good soil,	Mt 13:23	
man who sowed good **s** in his field.	Mt 13:24	*4690*
you not sow good **s** in your field?	Mt 13:27	*4690*
of heaven is like a mustard **s**,	Mt 13:31	*2848*
sows the good **s** is the Son of Man,	Mt 13:37	*4690*
and *as for* the good **s**,	Mt 13:38	*4690*
faith the size of a mustard **s**,	Mt 17:20	*2848*
gathering where you scattered no **s**.	Mt 25:24	
and gather where I scattered no **s**.	Mt 25:26	
as he was sowing, some **s** fell	Mk 4:4	
"Other **s** fell on the rocky	Mk 4:5	
"Other **s** fell among the thorns,	Mk 4:7	
s was sown on the rocky *places*,	Mk 4:16	
whom **s** was sown among the thorns;	Mk 4:18	
whom **s** was sown on the good soil;	Mk 4:20	
a man who casts **s** upon the soil;	Mk 4:26	*4703*
and the **s** sprouts and grows	Mk 4:27	*4703*
"*It is* like a mustard **s**,	Mk 4:31	*2848*
"The sower went out to sow his **s**;	Lk 8:5	*4703*
"Other **s** fell on rocky *soil*,	Lk 8:6	
"Other **s** fell among the thorns;	Lk 8:7	
"Other **s** fell into the good soil,	Lk 8:8	
the **s** is the word of God.	Lk 8:11	*4703*
"The **s** which fell among	Lk 8:14	
"But the **s** in the good soil,	Lk 8:15	
"It is like a mustard **s**,	Lk 13:19	*2848*
"If you had faith like a mustard **s**,	Lk 17:6	*2848*
'AND IN YOUR **S** ALL THE FAMILIES OF	Ac 3:25	*4690*
Now He who supplies **s** to the sower	2Co 9:10	*4690*
will supply and multiply your **s**	2Co 9:10	*4703*
spoken to Abraham and to his **s**.	Ga 3:16	*4690*
"And to your **s**," that is, Christ.	Ga 3:16	*4690*
until the **s** would come to whom	Ga 3:19	*4690*
And the **s** whose fruit is	Jas 3:18	
not of **s** which is perishable but	1Pe 1:23	*4701*
sin, because His **s** abides in him;	1Jn 3:9	*4690*

SEEDS

vine, from *the* **s** even to *the* skin.	Nu 6:4	2785
beans, lentils, parched **s**,	2Sa 17:28	
to make the **s** of grass to sprout?	Jb 38:27	4161
The **s** shrivel under their clods;	Jl 1:17	6507
and as he sowed, some **s** fell	Mt 13:4	
this is smaller than all *other* **s**,	Mt 13:32	*4690*
"Other **s** fell into the good soil,	Mk 4:8	
all the **s** that are upon the soil,	Mk 4:31	*4690*
each of the **s** a body of its own.	1Co 15:38	*4690*
"And to **s**," as *referring* to many,	Ga 3:16	*4690*

SEEDTIME

the earth remains, **S** and harvest,	Gn 8:22	2233

SEEING

remained alive here after **s** Him?"	Gn 16:13	7210
him mute or deaf, or **s** or blind?	Ex 4:11	6493
and without **s** it dropped on him so	Nu 35:23	7200
"You are **s** the shadow of the	Jg 9:36	7200
ask my name, **s** it is wonderful?"	Jg 13:18	
me, **s** I have a Levite as priest."	Jg 17:13	3588
s the fire come down and the glory	2Ch 7:3	7200
The hearing ear and the **s** eye,	Pr 20:12	7200
The eye is not satisfied with **s**,	Ec 1:8	7200
"**s** that My people have been taken	Is 52:5	
s false visions and divining lies	Ezk 22:28	2372
S their faith, Jesus said to	Mt 9:2	*3708*
But Jesus turning and **s** her said,	Mt 9:22	*3708*
S the people, He felt compassion for	Mt 9:36	*3708*
because while **s** they do not see,	Mt 13:13	*991*
YOU WILL KEEP ON **S**, BUT WILL NOT	Mt 13:14	*991*
But **s** the wind, he became frightened,	Mt 14:30	*991*
the lame walking, and the blind **s**;	Mt 15:31	*991*
S a lone fig tree by the road,	Mt 21:19	*3708*
S *this*, the disciples were	Mt 21:20	*3708*
and you, **s** *this*, did not even feel	Mt 21:32	*3708*
And Jesus **s** their faith said to	Mk 2:5	*3708*
WHILE **S**, THEY MAY SEE AND NOT	Mk 4:12	*991*
S Jesus from a distance, he ran up	Mk 5:6	*3708*
Jairus came up, and on **s** Him,	Mk 5:22	*3708*
S them straining at the oars, for	Mk 6:48	*3708*
around and **s** His disciples,	Mk 8:33	*3708*
S at a distance a fig tree in leaf,	Mk 11:13	*3708*
and **s** Peter warming himself, she	Mk 14:67	*3708*
S their faith, He said, "Friend,	Lk 5:20	*3708*
so that **S** THEY MAY NOT SEE,	Lk 8:10	*991*
S Jesus, he cried out and fell	Lk 8:28	*3708*
s him as he sat in the firelight and	Lk 22:56	*3708*
at a distance, **s** these things.	Lk 23:49	*3708*
thought that they were **s** a spirit.	Lk 24:37	*2334*
and **s** that a large crowd was	Jn 6:5	*2300*
away and washed, and came *back* **s**.	Jn 9:7	*991*
Peter **s** him said to Jesus,	Jn 21:21	*3708*
And **s** the man who had been healed	Ac 4:14	*991*
hearing the voice but **s** no one.	Ac 9:7	*2334*
but thought he was **s** a vision.	Ac 12:9	*991*
Asia, upon **s** him in the temple,	Ac 21:27	*2300*
AND YOU WILL KEEP ON **S**,	Ac 28:26	*991*
s that I had been entrusted with	Ga 2:7	*3708*
endured, as **s** Him who is unseen.	Heb 11:27	*3708*
s that His divine power has	2Pe 1:3	*5613*

SEEK

that he may **s** occasion against us	Gn 43:18	1556
priest need not **s** for the yellowish	Lv 13:36	1239
do not **s** them out to be defiled by	Lv 19:31	1245
to **s** out a resting place for them.	Nu 10:33	8446
not go as at other times to **s** omens	Nu 24:1	7122
s out a place for you to encamp,	Dt 1:33	8446
you will **s** the LORD your God,	Dt 4:29	1245
"But you shall **s** *the* LORD at	Dt 12:5	1875
"You shall never **s** their peace or	Dt 23:6	1875
wings you have come to **s** refuge."	Ru 2:12	2620
shall I not **s** security for you,	Ru 3:1	1245
Let them **s** a man who is a skillful	1Sa 16:16	1245
that Saul had come out to **s** his life	1Sa 23:15	1245
Saul and his men went to **s** *him*,	1Sa 23:25	1245
and went to **s** David and his men in	1Sa 24:2	1245
those who **s** evil against my lord,	1Sa 25:26	1245
to pursue you and to **s** your life,	1Sa 25:29	1245
"**S** for me a woman who is a	1Sa 28:7	1875
went up to **s** out David;	2Sa 5:17	1245
everyone depends on the man you **s**;	2Sa 17:3	1245
"Let them **s** a young virgin for my	1Ki 1:2	1245
and they **s** my life, to take it	1Ki 19:10	1245
and they **s** my life, to take it	1Ki 19:14	1245
bring you to the man whom you **s**."	2Ki 6:19	1245
to **s** pasture for their flocks.	1Ch 4:39	1245
we did not **s** it in the days of Saul."	1Ch 13:3	1875
for we did not **s** Him according to	1Ch 15:13	1875
of those who **s** the LORD be glad.	1Ch 16:10	1245
S the LORD and His strength;	1Ch 16:11	1875
S His face continually.	1Ch 16:11	1245
Why does my lord **s** this thing?	1Ch 21:3	1245
your soul to **s** the LORD your God;	1Ch 22:19	1875
observe and **s** after all the	1Ch 28:8	1875
If you **s** Him, He will let you find	1Ch 28:9	1875
and **s** My face and turn from their	2Ch 7:14	1245
not set his heart to **s** the LORD.	2Ch 12:14	1875
and commanded Judah to **s** the LORD	2Ch 14:4	1875
And if you **s** Him, He will let you	2Ch 15:2	1875
into the covenant to **s** the LORD God	2Ch 15:12	1875
and whoever would not **s** the LORD	2Ch 15:13	1875
his disease he did not **s** the LORD,	2Ch 16:12	1875
days and did not **s** the Baals,	2Ch 17:3	1875
have set your heart to **s** God."	2Ch 19:3	1875
his attention to **s** the LORD,	2Ch 20:3	1875
together to **s** help from the LORD;	2Ch 20:4	1245
the cities of Judah to **s** the LORD.	2Ch 20:4	1245
to **s** God in the days of Zechariah,	2Ch 26:5	1875
who prepares his heart to **s** God,	2Ch 30:19	1875
to **s** the God of his father David;	2Ch 34:3	1875
you, for we, like you, **s** your God;	Ezr 4:2	1875
them, to **s** the LORD God of Israel,	Ezr 6:21	1875
to **s** from Him a safe journey for us,	Ezr 8:21	1245
disposed to all those who **s** Him,	Ezr 8:22	1245
and never **s** their peace or their	Ezr 9:12	1875
to **s** the welfare of the sons of Israel.	Ne 2:10	1245
"But as for me, I would **s** God,	Jb 5:8	1875
And You will **s** me, but I will not	Jb 7:21	7836
"If you would **s** God And implore	Jb 8:5	7836
That You should **s** for my guilt And	Jb 10:6	1245
not forsaken those who **s** You.	Ps 9:10	1875
his countenance, does not **s** *Him*.	Ps 10:4	1875
S out his wickedness until You	Ps 10:15	1875
who understand, Who **s** after God.	Ps 14:2	1875
Those who **s** Him will praise the	Ps 22:26	1875
the generation of those who **s** Him,	Ps 24:6	1875
those who seek Him, Who **s** Your face	Ps 24:6	1245
from the LORD, that I shall **s**:	Ps 27:4	1245
When You said, "**S** My face,"	Ps 27:8	1245
"Your face, O LORD, I shall **s**."	Ps 27:8	1245
But they who **s** the LORD shall not	Ps 34:10	1875
S peace and pursue it.	Ps 34:14	1245
and dishonored who **s** my life;	Ps 35:4	1245
who **s** my life lay snares *for me;*	Ps 38:12	1245
And those who **s** to injure me have	Ps 38:12	1875
Who **s** my life to destroy it;	Ps 40:14	1245
Let all who **s** You rejoice and be	Ps 40:16	1245
The rich among the people will **s** your	Ps 45:12	2470b
I shall **s** You earnestly;	Ps 63:1	7836
But those who **s** my life to	Ps 63:9	1245
May those who **s** You not be	Ps 69:6	1245
You who **s** God, let your heart	Ps 69:32	1875
and humiliated Who **s** my life;	Ps 70:2	1245
Let all who **s** You rejoice and be	Ps 70:4	1245
and dishonor, who **s** to injure me.	Ps 71:13	1245
they are humiliated who **s** my hurt.	Ps 71:24	1245
That they may **s** Your name,	Ps 83:16	1245
under His wings you may **s** refuge;	Ps 91:4	2620
prey And **s** their food from God.	Ps 104:21	1245
the heart of those who **s** the LORD	Ps 105:3	1245
S the LORD and His strength;	Ps 105:4	1875
S His face continually.	Ps 105:4	1245
And let them **s** *sustenance* far from	Ps 109:10	1875
Who **s** Him with all *their* heart.	Ps 119:2	1875
at liberty, For I **s** Your precepts.	Ps 119:45	1875
For they do not **s** Your statutes.	Ps 119:155	1875
s Your servant, For I do not forget	Ps 119:176	1245
LORD our God, I will **s** your good.	Ps 122:9	1245
They will **s** me diligently but	Pr 1:28	7836
If you **s** her as silver And search	Pr 2:4	1245
you, To **s** your presence earnestly,	Pr 7:15	7836
those who diligently **s** me will find	Pr 8:17	7836
Many will **s** the favor of a generous	Pr 19:6	2470b
I will **s** another drink."	Pr 23:35	1245
But those who **s** the LORD	Pr 28:5	1245
Many **s** the ruler's favor, But	Pr 29:26	1245
And I set my mind to **s** and explore	Ec 1:13	1875
to **s** wisdom and an explanation,	Ec 7:25	1245
though man should **s** laboriously,	Ec 8:17	1245
I must **s** him whom my soul loves.'	SS 3:2	1245
That we may **s** him with you?"	SS 6:1	1245
S justice, Reprove the ruthless,	Is 1:17	1875
Nor do they **s** the LORD of hosts.	Is 9:13	1875
His people will **s** refuge in it."	Is 14:32	2620
he will **s** justice And be prompt in	Is 16:5	1875
And to **s** shelter in the shadow of	Is 30:2	2620
One of Israel, nor **s** the LORD!	Is 31:1	1875
S from the book of the LORD, and	Is 34:16	1875
"You will **s** those who quarrel with	Is 41:12	1245
'**S** Me in a waste place';	Is 45:19	1245
righteousness, Who **s** the LORD:	Is 51:1	1245
S the LORD while He may be found;	Is 55:6	1875
"Yet they **s** Me day by day and	Is 58:2	1875
found by those who did not **s** Me.	Is 65:1	1245
for herds, For My people who **s** Me.	Is 65:10	1875
who **s** her will not become weary;	Jer 2:24	1245
you prepare your way To **s** love!	Jer 2:33	1245
S refuge, do not stand *still*, For	Jer 4:6	5756
lovers despise you; They **s** your life.	Jer 4:30	1245
And **s** in her open squares, If you	Jer 5:1	1245
men of Anathoth, who **s** your life,	Jer 11:21	1245
hand of those who **s** their life;	Jer 19:7	1245
those who **s** their life will distress	Jer 19:9	1245
hand of those who **s** their lives;	Jer 21:7	1245
'**S** the welfare of the city where I	Jer 29:7	1875
'You will **s** Me and find *Me*	Jer 29:13	1245
forgotten you, They do not **s** you;	Jer 30:14	1875
hand of those who **s** their life.	Jer 34:20	1245
hand of those who **s** their life,	Jer 34:21	1245
the hand of those who **s** his life,	Jer 44:30	1245
things for yourself? Do not **s** *them;*	Jer 45:5	1245
before those who **s** their lives;	Jer 49:37	1245
be the LORD their God they will **s**.	Jer 50:4	1245
anguish comes, they will **s** peace,	Ezk 7:25	1245
will **s** a vision from a prophet,	Ezk 7:26	1245
there I will **s** your contributions	Ezk 20:40	1875
was no one to search or **s** *for them.*"	Ezk 34:6	1245
search for My sheep and **s** them out.	Ezk 34:11	1239
"I will **s** the lost, bring back	Ezk 34:16	1245
to **s** *Him* by prayer and supplications,	Da 9:3	1245
And she will **s** them, but will not	Hos 2:7	1245
and **s** the LORD their God and David	Hos 3:5	1245
flocks and herds To **s** the LORD,	Hos 5:6	1245
their guilt and **s** My face;	Hos 5:15	1245
they will earnestly **s** Me.	Hos 5:15	7836
For it is time to **s** the LORD Until	Hos 10:12	1875
"**S** Me that you may live.	Am 5:4	1875
"**S** the LORD that you may live,	Am 5:6	1875
S good and not evil, that you may	Am 5:14	1875
and fro to **s** the word of the LORD,	Am 8:12	1245
will I **s** comforters for you?"	Na 3:7	1245
S the LORD, All you humble of the	Zph 2:3	1245
S righteousness, seek humility.	Zph 2:3	1245
Seek righteousness, **s** humility.	Zph 2:3	1245
men to **s** the favor of the LORD,	Zch 7:2	2470b
LORD, and to **s** the LORD of hosts;	Zch 8:21	1245
nations will come to **s** the LORD	Zch 8:22	1245
the perishing, **s** the scattered,	Zch 11:16	1245
s instruction from his mouth;	Mal 2:7	1245
And the Lord, whom you **s**,	Mal 3:1	1245
For the Gentiles eagerly **s**	Mt 6:32	*1934*
"But **s** first His kingdom and His	Mt 6:33	*2212*
s, and you will find;	Mt 7:7	*2212*
does this generation **s** for a sign?	Mk 8:12	*2212*
s, and you will find;	Lk 11:9	*2212*
"And do not **s** what you will eat	Lk 12:29	*2212*
nations of the world eagerly **s**;	Lk 12:30	*1934*
"But **s** His kingdom, and these	Lk 12:31	*2212*
s to enter and will not be able.	Lk 13:24	*2212*
"For the Son of Man has come to **s**	Lk 19:10	*2212*
s the living One among the dead?	Lk 24:5	*2212*
and said to them, "What do you **s**?"	Jn 1:38	*2212*

yet no one said, "What do You s?"	Jn 4:27	*2212*
because I do not s My own will,	Jn 5:30	*2212*
and you do not s the glory that is	Jn 5:44	*2212*
truly, I say to you, you s Me,	Jn 6:26	*2212*
Why do you s to kill Me?"	Jn 7:19	*2212*
"You will s Me, and will not	Jn 7:34	*2212*
'You will s Me, and will not find	Jn 7:36	*2212*
"I go away, and you will s Me,	Jn 8:21	*2212*
yet you s to kill Me, because My	Jn 8:37	*2212*
"But I do not s My glory;	Jn 8:50	*2212*
a little while longer. You will s Me;	Jn 13:33	*2212*
and said to them, "Whom do you s?"	Jn 18:4	*2212*
asked them, "Whom do you s?"	Jn 18:7	*2212*
if you s Me,	Jn 18:8	*2212*
REST OF MANKIND MAY S THE LORD,	Ac 15:17	*1567a*
that they would s God,	Ac 17:27	*2212*
in doing good s for glory and honor	Ro 2:7	*2212*
"I WAS FOUND BY THOSE WHO DID NOT S	Ro 10:20	*2212*
Do not s to be released.	1Co 7:27	*2212*
Do not s a wife.	1Co 7:27	*2212*
Let no one s his own *good,* but	1Co 10:24	*2212*
it does not s its own, is not	1Co 13:5	*2212*
s to abound for the edification of	1Co 14:12	*2212*
for I do not s what is yours, but	2Co 12:14	*2212*
They eagerly s you, not	Ga 4:17	*2206*
out so that you will s them.	Ga 4:17	*2206*
all s after their own interests,	Php 2:21	*2212*
Not that I s the gift itself, but	Php 4:17	*1934*
but I s for the profit which	Php 4:17	*1934*
nor did we s glory from men,	1Th 2:6	*2212*
always s after that which is good	1Th 5:15	*1377*
is a rewarder of those who s Him.	Heb 11:6	*1567a*
HE MUST S PEACE AND PURSUE IT.	1Pe 3:11	*2212*
will s death and will not find it;	Rv 9:6	*2212*

SEEKING

who were s your life are dead."	Ex 4:19	1245
are you s for the priesthood also?	Nu 16:10	1245
not his enemy nor s his injury,	Nu 35:23	1245
show you the man whom you are s."	Jg 4:22	1245
for He was s an occasion against	Jg 14:4	1245
of the Danites was s an inheritance	Jg 18:1	1245
father is s to put you to death.	1Sa 19:2	1245
father, that he is s my life?"	1Sa 20:1	1245
Saul is s to come to Keilah to destroy	1Sa 23:10	1245
s for David to be king over you.	2Sa 3:17	1245
You are s to destroy a city, even a	2Sa 20:19	1245
was s the presence of Solomon,	1Ki 10:24	1245
are s to go to your own country?"	1Ki 11:22	1245
he is s a quarrel against me."	2Ki 5:7	579
were s the presence of Solomon,	2Ch 9:23	1245
on s the LORD God of Israel followed	2Ch 11:16	1245
s his God, he did with all his heart	2Ch 31:21	1875
go forth s food in their activity,	Jb 24:5	7836
I am still s but have not found.	Ec 7:28	1245
afflicted and needy are s water,	Is 41:17	1245
ways, From s your *own* pleasure And	Is 58:13	4672
hand of those who are s your life,	Jer 22:25	1245
not s the well-being of this people but	Jer 38:4	1875
these men who are s your life."	Jer 38:16	1245
his enemy and was s his life.' "	Jer 44:30	1245
are you s great things for yourself?	Jer 45:5	1245
of those who are s their lives,	Jer 46:26	1245
All her people groan s bread;	La 1:11	1245
and my nobles began s me out;	Da 4:36	1156
while he was s a godly offspring?	Mal 2:15	1245
through waterless places s rest,	Mt 12:43	*2212*
outside, s to speak to Him.	Mt 12:46	*2212*
outside s to speak to You."	Mt 12:47	*2212*
is like a merchant s fine pearls,	Mt 13:45	*2212*
s from Him a sign from heaven,	Mk 8:11	*2212*
and *began* s how to destroy Him;	Mk 11:18	*2212*
And they were s to seize Him,	Mk 12:12	*2212*
s how to seize Him by stealth and	Mk 14:1	*2212*
And he *began* s how to betray Him	Mk 14:11	*2212*
through waterless places s rest,	Lk 11:24	*2212*
s how they might put Him to death;	Lk 22:2	*2212*
and *began* s a good opportunity to	Lk 22:6	*2212*
were s all the more to kill Him,	Jn 5:18	*2212*
and came to Capernaum s Jesus.	Jn 6:24	*2212*
the Jews were s to kill Him.	Jn 7:1	*2212*
Jews were s Him at the feast	Jn 7:11	*2212*
but He who is s the glory of the	Jn 7:18	*2212*
the man whom they are s to kill?	Jn 7:25	*2212*
were s to seize Him;	Jn 7:30	*2212*
as it is, you are s to kill Me,	Jn 8:40	*2212*
they were s again to seize Him,	Jn 10:39	*2212*
Jews were just now s to stone You,	Jn 11:8	*2212*
So they were s for Jesus,	Jn 11:56	*2212*
Whom are you s?"	Jn 20:15	*2212*
s to turn the proconsul away from	Ac 13:8	*2212*
and he went about s those who	Ac 13:11	*2212*
they were s to bring them out to	Ac 17:5	*2212*
While they were s to kill him,	Ac 21:31	*2212*
and s to establish their own,	Ro 10:3	*2212*
AM LEFT, AND THEY ARE S MY LIFE."	Ro 11:3	*2212*
What Israel is s,	Ro 11:7	*1934*
all things, not s my own profit but	1Co 10:33	*2212*
since you are s for proof of the	2Co 13:3	*2212*
For am I now s the favor of men,	Ga 1:10	*3982*
while s to be justified in Christ,	Ga 2:17	*2212*
who are s to be justified by law;	Ga 5:4	
Christ, keep s the things above,	Col 3:1	*2212*
they are s a country of their own.	Heb 11:14	*1934*
are s *the city* which is to come.	Heb 13:14	*1934*
s to know what person or time the	1Pe 1:11	*2045*
roaring lion, s someone to devour.	1Pe 5:8	*2212*

SEEKS

he who s my life seeks your life,	1Sa 22:23	1245
he who seeks my life s your life,	1Sa 22:23	1245
'Behold, David s to harm you'?	1Sa 24:9	1245
who came out from me s my life;	2Sa 16:11	1245
the righteous And s to kill him.	Ps 37:32	1245
who understands, Who s after God.	Ps 53:2	1875
who diligently s good seeks favor,	Pr 11:27	7836
who diligently seeks good s favor,	Pr 11:27	1245
But he who s evil, evil will come to	Pr 11:27	1875
A scoffer s wisdom and *finds* none,	Pr 14:6	1245
mind of the intelligent s knowledge,	Pr 15:14	1245
who conceals a transgression s love,	Pr 17:9	1245
A rebellious man s only evil,	Pr 17:11	1245
who raises his door s destruction.	Pr 17:19	1245
He who separates himself s *his own*	Pr 18:1	1245
the ear of the wise s knowledge.	Pr 18:15	1245
for God s what has passed by.	Ec 3:15	1245
spirit within me s You diligently;	Is 26:9	7836
He s out for himself a skillful	Is 40:20	1245
one who does justice, who s truth,	Jer 5:1	1245
for Him, To the person who s Him.	La 3:25	1875
asks receives, and he who s finds,	Mt 7:8	*2212*
adulterous generation s after a sign;	Mt 16:4	*1934*
and he who s, finds;	Lk 11:10	*2212*
it s for a sign, and *yet* no sign	Lk 11:29	*2212*
"Whoever s to keep his life will	Lk 17:33	*2212*
the Father s to be His worshipers.	Jn 4:23	*2212*
he himself s to be *known* publicly.	Jn 7:4	*2212*
"He who speaks from himself s his	Jn 7:18	*2212*
Who s to kill You?"	Jn 7:20	*2212*
there is One who s and judges.	Jn 8:50	*2212*
THERE IS NONE WHO S FOR GOD;	Ro 3:11	*1567a*

SEEM

"It shall not s hard to you when	Dt 15:18	7185
s insignificant before You,	Ne 9:32	4591
hoofs of its horses s like flint and	Is 5:28	2803
Does it not s to you like nothing	Hg 2:3	5869
how does it s to you?"	Mk 14:64	*5316*
which s to be weaker are necessary;	1Co 12:22	*1380*
for I do not wish to s as if I	2Co 10:9	*1380*
may s to have come short of it.	Heb 4:1	*1380*

SEEMED

seven years for Rachel and they s to	Gn 29:20	1961, 5869
Now their words s reasonable to	Gn 34:18	3190
Now the proposal s good to Pharaoh	Gn 41:37	3190
that, it s good in his sight.	Lv 10:20	3190
in Hebron all that s good to Israel	2Sa 3:19	
and it s hard to Amnon to do	2Sa 13:2	6381
ten days their appearance s better	Da 1:15	7200
"It has s good to me to declare	Da 4:2	8232
It s good to Darius to appoint 120	Da 6:1	8232
it s fitting for me as well,	Lk 1:3	*1380*
Then it s good to the apostles and	Ac 15:22	*1380*
it s good to us, having become of	Ac 15:25	*1380*
"For it s good to the Holy Spirit	Ac 15:28	*1380*
"s good to Silas to remain there.]	Ac 15:34	*1380*
a short time as s best to them,	Heb 12:10	*1380*

SEEMS

do as it s good and right in your	Jos 9:25	
do to us whatever s good to You;	Jg 10:15	
"Do what s best to you.	1Sa 1:23	
let Him do what s good to Him."	1Sa 3:18	
do to us whatever s good to you."	1Sa 11:10	
"Do whatever s good to you."	1Sa 14:36	
"Do what s good to you."	1Sa 14:40	
do to him as it s good to you.' "	1Sa 24:4	3190
Him do to me as s good to Him."	2Sa 15:26	
"Whatever s best to you I will do."	2Sa 18:4	3190
"If it s good to you, and if it	1Ch 13:2	
"Whatever s good to you and	Ezr 7:18	3190
favor before him and the matter s	Es 8:5	
It s as if one had lifted up *His*	Ps 74:5	3045
There is a way *which* s right to a	Pr 14:12	
There is a way *which* s right to a	Pr 16:25	
The first to plead his case s	Pr 18:17	
as it s, *only* to wind. We could	Is 26:18	
go wherever it s good and right	Jer 40:4	
or else go anywhere it s right	Jer 40:5	
"He s to be a proclaimer of	Ac 17:18	*1380*
"For it s absurd to me in sending	Ac 25:27	*1380*
for the moment s not to be joyful,	Heb 12:11	*1380*

SEEN

you *alone* I have s *to be* righteous	Gn 7:1	7200
the bow will be s in the cloud,	Gn 9:14	7200
the LORD has s my affliction;	Gn 29:32	7200
for I have s all that Laban has	Gn 31:12	7200
God has s my affliction and the	Gn 31:42	7200
"I have s God face to face, yet	Gn 32:30	7200
such as I had never s for ugliness	Gn 41:19	7200
and I have not s him since.	Gn 44:28	7200
in Egypt, and all that you have s;	Gn 45:13	7200
me die, since I have s your face,	Gn 46:30	7200
"I have surely s the affliction	Ex 3:7	7200
I have s the oppression with which	Ex 3:9	7200
that He had s their affliction,	Ex 4:31	7200
such as has not been s in Egypt	Ex 9:18	7200
nor your grandfathers have s,	Ex 10:6	7200
nothing leavened shall be s among	Ex 13:7	7200
nor shall any leaven be s among you	Ex 13:7	7200
Egyptians whom you have s today,	Ex 14:13	7200
's what I did to the Egyptians,	Ex 19:4	7200
'You yourselves have s that I have	Ex 20:22	7200
"I have s this people, and	Ex 32:9	7200
but My face shall not be s."	Ex 33:23	7200
man be s anywhere on the mountain;	Ex 34:3	7200
he has s or *otherwise* known,	Lv 5:1	7200
You, O LORD, are s eye to eye,	Nu 14:14	7200
have s My glory and My signs which	Nu 14:22	7200
Nor has He s trouble in Israel;	Nu 23:21	7200
"When you have s it,	Nu 27:13	7200
'Your eyes have s all that the	Dt 3:21	7200
"Your eyes have s what the LORD	Dt 4:3	7200
the things which your eyes have s and	Dt 4:9	7200
we have s today that God speaks	Dt 5:24	7200
'I have s this people, and indeed,	Dt 9:13	7200
for you which your eyes have s.	Dt 10:21	7200
have not s the discipline of the LORD	Dt 11:2	7200
but your own eyes have s all the	Dt 11:7	7200
"For seven days no leaven shall be s	Dt 16:4	7200
"You have s all that the LORD did	Dt 29:2	7200
trials which your eyes have s,	Dt 29:3	7200
you have s their abominations and	Dt 29:17	7200
"And you have s all that the LORD	Jos 23:3	7200
who had s all the great work of	Jg 2:7	7200
Not a shield or a spear was s	Jg 5:8	7200
now I have s the angel of the LORD	Jg 6:22	7200
"What you have s me do, hurry *and*	Jg 9:48	7200
surely die, for we have s God."	Jg 13:22	7200
for we have s the land, and	Jg 18:9	7200
ever happened or been s from the day	Jg 19:30	7200
I have s a son of Jesse the	1Sa 16:18	7200
Have you s this man who is coming	1Sa 17:25	7200
haunt is, *and* who has s him there;	1Sa 23:22	7200
this day your eyes have s that the	1Sa 24:10	7200
could not be s entering the city.	2Sa 17:17	7200
tell the king what you have s."	2Sa 18:21	7200
was cedar, there was no stone s.	1Ki 6:18	7200
poles could be s from the holy place	1Ki 8:8	7200
but they could not be s outside;	1Ki 8:8	7200
until I came and my eyes had s it.	1Ki 10:7	7200
nor have they been s to this day.	1Ki 10:12	7200
Now his sons had s the way which	1Ki 13:12	7200
you s all this great multitude?	1Ki 20:13	7200
'Surely I have s yesterday the	2Ki 9:26	7200
your prayer, I have s your tears;	2Ki 20:5	7200
"What have they s in your house?"	2Ki 20:15	7200
have s all that is in my house;	2Ki 20:15	7200
abominations that were s in the land	2Ki 23:24	7200
now with joy I have s Your people,	1Ch 29:17	7200
poles of the ark could be s in front of	2Ch 5:9	7200
but they could not be s outside;	2Ch 5:9	7200
Sheba had s the wisdom of Solomon,	2Ch 9:3	7200
until I came and my eyes had s it.	2Ch 9:6	7200
was s before in the land of Judah.	2Ch 9:11	7200
men who had s the first temple,	Ezr 3:12	7200
both what they had s in this	Es 9:26	7200
"According to what I have s,	Jb 4:8	7200
"I have s the foolish taking	Jb 5:3	7200
I had died and no eye had s me!	Jb 10:18	7200
"Behold, my eye has s all *this,*	Jb 13:1	7200
what I have s I will also declare;	Jb 15:17	2372
Those who have s him will say,	Jb 20:7	7200
"Behold, all of you have s *it;*	Jb 27:12	2372
If I have s anyone perish for lack	Jb 31:19	7200
bones which were not s stick out.	Jb 33:21	7210
"All men have s it;	Jb 36:25	2372
you s the gates of deep darkness?	Jb 38:17	7200
you s the storehouses of the hail,	Jb 38:22	7200
You have s *it,* for You have	Ps 10:14	7200
Because You have s my affliction;	Ps 31:7	7200
"Aha, aha, our eyes have s it!"	Ps 35:21	7200
You have s it, O LORD, do not	Ps 35:22	7200
have not s the righteous forsaken Or	Ps 37:25	7200
I have s a wicked, violent man	Ps 37:35	7200
so have we s In the city of the	Ps 48:8	7200
For I have s violence and strife	Ps 55:9	7200
Thus I have s You in the sanctuary,	Ps 63:2	2372
They have s Your procession, O God,	Ps 68:24	7200
The humble have s *it and* are glad;	Ps 69:32	7200
us, *And* the years we have s evil.	Ps 90:15	7200
Me, though they had s My work.	Ps 95:9	7200
all the peoples have s His glory.	Ps 97:6	7200
have s the salvation of our God.	Ps 98:3	7200
They have s the works of the LORD,	Ps 107:24	7200
have s a limit to all perfection;	Ps 119:96	7200
eyes have s my unformed substance;	Ps 139:16	7200
the prince, Whom your eyes have s.	Pr 25:7	7200
disappears, the new growth is s,	Pr 27:25	7200
I have s all the works which have	Ec 1:14	7200
This also I have s that	Ec 2:24	7200
I have s the task which God has	Ec 3:10	7200
I have s under the sun *that* in the	Ec 3:16	7200
I have s that nothing is	Ec 3:22	7200
who has never s the evil activity	Ec 4:3	7200
I have s that every labor and	Ec 4:4	7200
I have s all the living under the	Ec 4:15	7200
evil *which* I have s under the sun:	Ec 5:13	7200
I have s to be good and fitting:	Ec 5:18	7200
There is an evil which I have s	Ec 6:1	7200
I have s everything during my	Ec 7:15	7200
All this I have s and applied my	Ec 8:9	7200
then, I have s the wicked buried,	Ec 8:10	7200
is an evil I have s under the sun,	Ec 10:5	7200
I have s slaves *riding* on horses	Ec 10:7	7200
you s him whom my soul loves?'	SS 3:3	7200
For my eyes have s the King,	Is 6:5	7200
His arm to be s in fierce anger,	Is 30:30	7200
your prayer, I have s your tears;	Is 38:5	7200
"What have they s in your house?"	Is 39:4	7200
have s all that is in my house;	Is 39:4	7200
coastlands have s and are afraid;	Is 41:5	7200
You have s many things, but you do	Is 42:20	7200
I am warm, I have s the fire."	Is 44:16	7200
"I have s his ways, but I will	Is 57:18	7200
has the eye s a God besides You,	Is 64:4	7200
Who has s such things?	Is 66:8	7200
heard My fame nor s My glory.	Is 66:19	7200

"You have **s** well, for I am	**Jer 1:12**	7200
you **s** what faithless Israel did?	**Jer 3:6**	7200
Behold, I, even I, have **s** *it,*"	**Jer 7:11**	7200
face, That your shame may be **s**.	**Jer 13:26**	7200
field, I have **s** your abominations.	**Jer 13:27**	7200
I have **s** a horrible thing:	**Jer 23:14**	7200
'You yourselves have **s** all the	**Jer 44:2**	7200
"Why have I **s** *it?* They are terrified,	**Jer 46:5**	7200
Because they have **s** her nakedness;	**La 1:8**	7200
For she has **s** the nations enter	**La 1:10**	7200
Your prophets have **s** for you False	**La 2:14**	2372
But they have **s** for you false and	**La 2:14**	2372
have reached *it,* we have **s** *it.*"	**La 2:16**	7200
I am the man who has **s** affliction	**La 3:1**	7200
O LORD, You have **s** my oppression;	**La 3:59**	7200
You have **s** all their vengeance,	**La 3:60**	7200
I had **s** by the river Chebar.	**Ezk 10:22**	7200
the vision that I had **s** left me.	**Ezk 11:24**	7200
own spirit and have **s** nothing.	**Ezk 13:3**	7200
have spoken falsehood and **s** a lie,	**Ezk 13:8**	2372
above the clouds So that it was **s**	**Ezk 19:11**	7200
"Son of man, have you **s** *this?*"	**Ezk 47:6**	7200
inasmuch as you have **s** that the	**Da 2:8**	2370
I have **s** and its interpretation?"	**Da 2:26**	2370
of my dream which I have **s**,	**Da 4:9**	2370
I, King Nebuchadnezzar, have **s**.	**Da 4:18**	2370
which I had **s** standing in front of	**Da 8:6**	7200
When I, Daniel, had **s** the vision,	**Da 8:15**	7200
I had **s** in the vision previously,	**Da 9:21**	7200
Israel I have **s** a horrible thing;	**Hos 6:10**	7200
Ephraim, as I have **s**,	**Hos 9:13**	7200
For now I have **s** with My eyes.	**Zch 9:8**	7200
which they had **s** in the east,	**Mt 2:9**	*3708*
corners so that they may be **s** by men.	**Mt 6:5**	*5316*
this has ever been **s** in Israel."	**Mt 9:33**	*5316*
We have never **s** anything like this."	**Mk 2:12**	*3708*
Those who had **s** it described	**Mk 5:16**	*3708*
and had **s** that some of His	**Mk 7:2**	*3708*
relate to anyone what they had **s**,	**Mk 9:9**	*3708*
was alive and had been **s** by her,	**Mk 16:11**	*2300*
who had **s** Him after He had risen.	**Mk 16:14**	*2300*
he had **s** a vision in the temple;	**Lk 1:22**	*3708*
When they had **s** this,	**Lk 2:17**	*3708*
for all that they had heard and **s**,	**Lk 2:20**	*3708*
before he had **s** the Lord's Christ.	**Lk 2:26**	*3708*
For my eyes have **s** Your salvation,	**Lk 2:30**	*3708*
have **s** remarkable things today."	**Lk 5:26**	*3708*
to John what you have **s** and heard:	**Lk 7:22**	*3708*
Those who had **s** it reported to	**Lk 8:36**	*3708*
of the things which they had **s**.	**Lk 9:36**	*3708*
all the miracles which they had **s**,	**Lk 19:37**	*3708*
had also **s** a vision of angels who	**Lk 24:23**	*3708*
No one has **s** God at any time;	**Jn 1:18**	*3708*
John testified saying, "I have **s**	**Jn 1:32**	*2300*
"I myself have **s**, and have testified	**Jn 1:34**	*3708*
testify of what we have **s**,	**Jn 3:11**	*3708*
"What He has **s** and heard, of that	**Jn 3:32**	*3708*
having **s** all the things that He	**Jn 4:45**	*3708*
voice at any time nor **s** His form.	**Jn 5:37**	*3708*
I said to you that you have **s** Me,	**Jn 6:36**	*3708*
"Not that anyone has **s** the Father,	**Jn 6:46**	*3708*
He has **s** the Father.	**Jn 6:46**	*3708*
which I have **s** with *My* Father;	**Jn 8:38**	*3708*
old, and have You **s** Abraham?"	**Jn 8:57**	*3708*
"You have both **s** Him, and He is	**Jn 9:37**	*3708*
on you know Him, and have **s** Him."	**Jn 14:7**	*3708*
who has **s** Me has seen the Father;	**Jn 14:9**	*3708*
who has seen Me has **s** the Father;	**Jn 14:9**	*3708*
but now they have both **s** and hated	**Jn 15:24**	*3708*
he who has **s** has testified,	**Jn 19:35**	*3708*
"I have **s** the Lord,"	**Jn 20:18**	*3708*
"We have **s** the Lord!"	**Jn 20:25**	*3708*
"Because you have **s** Me,	**Jn 20:29**	*3708*
what we have **s** and heard."	**Ac 4:20**	*3708*
'I HAVE CERTAINLY **S** THE OPPRESSION	**Ac 7:34**	*3708*
to the pattern which he had **s**.	**Ac 7:44**	*3708*
and he has **s** in a vision a man	**Ac 9:12**	*3708*
how he had **s** the Lord on the road,	**Ac 9:27**	*3708*
vision which he had **s** might be,	**Ac 10:17**	*3708*
how he had **s** the angel standing in	**Ac 11:13**	*3708*
and had **s** that he had faith to be	**Ac 14:9**	*3708*
When he had **s** the vision,	**Ac 16:10**	*3708*
For they had previously **s**	**Ac 21:29**	*4308*
men of what you have **s** and heard.	**Ac 22:15**	*3708*
to the things which you have **s**,	**Ac 26:16**	*3708*
s nothing unusual happen to him,	**Ac 28:6**	*2334*
nature, have been clearly **s**,	**Ro 1:20**	*2529*
but hope that is **s** is not hope;	**Ro 8:24**	*991*
"THINGS WHICH EYE HAS NOT **S** AND	**1Co 2:9**	*3708*
Have I not **s** Jesus our Lord?	**1Co 9:1**	*3708*
not at the things which are **s**,	**2Co 4:18**	*991*
but at the things which are not **s**;	**2Co 4:18**	*991*
things which are **s** are temporal,	**2Co 4:18**	*991*
things which are not **s** are eternal.	**2Co 4:18**	*991*
received and heard and **s** in me,	**Php 4:9**	*3708*
who have not personally **s** my face,	**Col 2:1**	*3708*
his stand on *visions* he has **s**,	**Col 2:18**	*3708*
S by angels, Proclaimed among	**1Tm 3:16**	*3708*
whom no man has **s** or can see.	**1Tm 6:16**	*3708*
the conviction of things not **s**.	**Heb 11:1**	*991*
so that what is **s** was not made out	**Heb 11:3**	*991*
by God about things not yet **s**,	**Heb 11:7**	*991*
but having **s** them and having	**Heb 11:13**	*3708*
s the outcome of the Lord's dealings,	**Jas 5:11**	*3708*
and though you have not **s** Him,	**1Pe 1:8**	*3708*
what we have **s** with our eyes,	**1Jn 1:1**	*3708*
and we have **s** and testify and	**1Jn 1:2**	*3708*
what we have **s** and heard we	**1Jn 1:3**	*3708*
no one who sins has **s** Him or	**1Jn 3:6**	*3708*
No one has **s** God at any time; if we	**1Jn 4:12**	*2300*
We have **s** and testify that the Father	**1Jn 4:14**	*2300*
love his brother whom he has **s**,	**1Jn 4:20**	*3708*
cannot love God whom he has not **s**.	**1Jn 4:20**	*3708*
one who does evil has not **s** God.	**3Jn 1:11**	*3708*
the things which you have **s**,	**Rv 1:19**	*3708*

SEER

"Come, and let us go to the **s**";	**1Sa 9:9**	7203a
now was formerly called a **s**.)	**1Sa 9:9**	7203a
and said to them, "Is the **s** here?"	**1Sa 9:11**	7203a
answered Saul and said, "I am the **s**.	**1Sa 9:19**	7203a
Zadok the priest, "Are you *not* a **s**?	**2Sa 15:27**	7203a
came to the prophet Gad, David's **s**,	**2Sa 24:11**	2374
all His prophets *and* every **s**,	**2Ki 17:13**	2374
whom David and Samuel the **s**	**1Ch 9:22**	7203a
The LORD spoke to Gad, David's **s**,	**1Ch 21:9**	2374
were the sons of Heman the king's **s**	**1Ch 25:5**	2374
And all that Samuel the **s** had	**1Ch 26:28**	7203a
in the chronicles of Samuel the **s**,	**1Ch 29:29**	7203a
in the chronicles of Gad the **s**,	**1Ch 29:29**	2374
and in the visions of Iddo the **s**	**2Ch 9:29**	2374
the prophet and of Iddo the **s**,	**2Ch 12:15**	2374
At that time Hanani the **s** came to	**2Ch 16:7**	7203a
Then Asa was angry with the **s** and	**2Ch 16:10**	7203a
Jehu the son of Hanani the **s**	**2Ch 19:2**	2374
of David and of Gad the king's **s**,	**2Ch 29:25**	2374
words of David and Asaph the **s**.	**2Ch 29:30**	2374
Heman, and Jeduthun the king's **s**;	**2Ch 35:15**	2374
"Go, you **s**, flee away to the land	**Am 7:12**	2374

SEER'S

tell me where the **s** house is."	**1Sa 9:18**	7203a

SEERS

and the words of the **s** who spoke	**2Ch 33:18**	2374
He has covered your heads, the **s**.	**Is 29:10**	2374
Who say to the **s**,	**Is 30:10**	7203a
The **s** will be ashamed And the	**Mi 3:7**	2374

SEES

"You are a God who **s**";	**Gn 16:13**	7200
face as one **s** the face of God,	**Gn 33:10**	7200
he **s** that the lad is not *with us,*	**Gn 44:31**	7200
when he **s** you, he will be glad in	**Ex 4:14**	7200
and when He **s** the blood on the	**Ex 12:23**	7200
If he **s** that the mark has indeed	**Lv 14:44**	2009
so that he **s** her nakedness and she	**Lv 20:17**	7200
nakedness and she **s** his nakedness,	**Lv 20:17**	7200
Who **s** the vision of the Almighty,	**Nu 24:4**	2372
Who **s** the vision of the Almighty,	**Nu 24:16**	2372
He **s** that *their* strength is gone,	**Dt 32:36**	7200
for God **s** not as man sees, for	**1Sa 16:7**	
for God *sees* not as man **s**,	**1Sa 16:7**	7200
city is pleasant, as my lord **s**;	**2Ki 2:19**	7200
eye of him who **s** me will behold me	**Jb 7:8**	7210
Or do You see as a man **s**?	**Jb 10:4**	7200
And He **s** iniquity without	**Jb 11:11**	7200
eye which saw him **s** him no longer,	**Jb 20:9**	
And his eye **s** anything precious.	**Jb 28:10**	7200
s everything under the heavens.	**Jb 28:24**	7200
of a man, And He **s** all his steps.	**Jb 34:21**	7200
But now my eye **s** You;	**Jb 42:5**	7200
He **s** all the sons of men;	**Ps 33:13**	7200
For He **s** his day is coming.	**Ps 37:13**	7200
For he **s** *that even* wise men die;	**Ps 49:10**	7200
rejoice when he **s** the vengeance;	**Ps 58:10**	2372
prudent **s** the evil and hides himself,	**Pr 22:3**	7200
man **s** evil *and* hides himself,	**Pr 27:12**	7200
the poor who has understanding **s**	**Pr 28:11**	2713
man who eats and drinks **s** good	**Ec 3:13**	7200
"It never **s** the sun and it never	**Ec 6:5**	7200
lookout, let him report what he **s**.	**Is 21:6**	7200
"When he **s** riders, horsemen in	**Is 21:7**	7200
Which one **s**, *And* as soon as it is	**Is 28:4**	7200
And they say, "Who **s** us?"	**Is 29:15**	7200
But when he **s** his children, the	**Is 29:23**	7200
'No one **s** me,' Your wisdom and	**Is 47:10**	7200
LORD looks down And **s** from heaven.	**La 3:50**	7200
vision that he **s** is for many years	**Ezk 12:27**	2372
and he **s** the sword coming upon the	**Ezk 33:3**	7200
'But if the watchman **s** the sword	**Ezk 33:6**	7200
through and anyone **s** a man's bone,	**Ezk 39:15**	7200
who **s** *what is done* in secret	**Mt 6:4**	*991*
who **s** *what is done* in secret	**Mt 6:6**	*991*
who **s** *what is done* in secret	**Mt 6:18**	*991*
something He **s** the Father doing;	**Jn 5:19**	*991*
but how he now **s**, we do not know;	**Jn 9:21**	*991*
s the wolf coming, and leaves	**Jn 10:12**	*2334*
he **s** the light of this world.	**Jn 11:9**	*991*
"He who **s** Me sees the One who sent	**Jn 12:45**	*2334*
"He who sees Me **s** the One who sent	**Jn 12:45**	*2334*
who hopes for what he *already* **s**?	**Ro 8:24**	*991*
For if someone **s** you, who have	**1Co 8:10**	*3708*
than he **s** *in* me or hears from me.	**2Co 12:6**	*991*
and **s** his brother in need and closes	**1Jn 3:17**	*2334*
If anyone **s** his brother committing	**1Jn 5:16**	*3708*

SEETHE

Also **s** its bones in it."	**Ezk 24:5**	1310

SEETHING

"I am **s** within and cannot relax;	**Jb 30:27**	7570

SEGUB

the *loss of* his youngest son **S**,	**1Ki 16:34**	7687
and she bore him **S**.	**1Ch 2:21**	7687
S became the father of Jair,	**1Ch 2:22**	7687

SEIR

and the Horites in their Mount **S**,	**Gn 14:6**	8165
his brother Esau in the land of **S**,	**Gn 32:3**	8165
until I come to my lord at **S**."	**Gn 33:14**	8165
returned that day on his way to **S**.	**Gn 33:16**	8165
lived in the hill country of **S**;	**Gn 36:8**	8165
Edomites in the hill country of **S**.	**Gn 36:9**	8165
are the sons of **S** the Horite,	**Gn 36:20**	8165
the sons of **S** in the land of Edom.	**Gn 36:21**	8165
various chiefs in the land of **S**.	**Gn 36:30**	8165
S, its enemies, also will be a	**Nu 24:18**	8165
from Horeb by the way of Mount **S**	**Dt 1:2**	8165
and crushed you from **S** to Hormah.	**Dt 1:44**	8165
and circled Mount **S** for many days.	**Dt 2:1**	8165
the sons of Esau who live in **S**;	**Dt 2:4**	8165
Mount **S** to Esau as a possession.	**Dt 2:5**	8165
the sons of Esau, who live in **S**,	**Dt 2:8**	8165
The Horites formerly lived in **S**,	**Dt 2:12**	8165
the sons of Esau, who live in **S**,	**Dt 2:22**	8165
as the sons of Esau who live in **S**	**Dt 2:29**	8165
Sinai, And dawned on them from **S**;	**Dt 33:2**	8165
Mount Halak, that rises toward **S**,	**Jos 11:17**	8165
Mount Halak, which rises toward **S**;	**Jos 12:7**	8165
from Baalah westward to Mount **S**,	**Jos 15:10**	8165
Esau, and to Esau I gave Mount **S** to	**Jos 24:4**	8165
when You went out from **S**,	**Jg 5:4**	8165
The sons of **S** *were* Lotan,	**1Ch 1:38**	8165
five hundred men went to Mount **S**,	**1Ch 4:42**	8165
of Ammon and Moab and Mount **S**,	**2Ch 20:10**	8165
sons of Ammon, Moab and Mount **S**,	**2Ch 20:22**	8165
against the inhabitants of Mount **S**	**2Ch 20:23**	8165
with the inhabitants of **S**,	**2Ch 20:23**	8165
down 10,000 of the sons of **S**.	**2Ch 25:11**	8165
brought the gods of the sons of **S**,	**2Ch 25:14**	8165
One keeps calling to me from **S**,	**Is 21:11**	8165
"Because Moab and **S** say,	**Ezk 25:8**	8165
set your face against Mount **S**,	**Ezk 35:2**	8165
"Behold, I am against you, Mount **S**,	**Ezk 35:3**	8165
Mount **S** a waste and a desolation and	**Ezk 35:7**	8165
will be a desolation, O Mount **S**,	**Ezk 35:15**	8165

SEIRAH

by the idols and escaped to **S**.	**Jg 3:26**	8167

SEIZE

his father and mother shall **s** him,	**Dt 21:19**	8610
David and his men to **s** them.	**1Sa 23:26**	8610
from the altar, saying, "**S** him."	**1Ki 13:4**	8610
"**S** the prophets of Baal;	**1Ki 18:40**	8610
to **s** their possessions as plunder.	**Es 3:13**	962
for that night, let darkness **s** it;	**Jb 3:6**	3947
They **s** and devour flocks.	**Jb 24:2**	1497
Pursue and **s** him, for there is no	**Ps 71:11**	8610
the creditor **s** all that he has,	**Ps 109:11**	5367
To capture booty and to **s** plunder,	**Is 10:6**	962
it passes through, it will **s** you;	**Is 28:19**	3947
"They **s** bow and spear;	**Jer 6:23**	2388
to **s** Baruch the scribe and Jeremiah	**Jer 36:26**	3947
"They **s** *their* bow and javelin;	**Jer 50:42**	2388
her spoil and **s** her plunder;	**Ezk 29:19**	962
to capture spoil and to **s** plunder,	**Ezk 38:12**	962
your company to **s** plunder,	**Ezk 38:13**	962
and **s** the plunder of those who	**Ezk 39:10**	962
and **s** the kingdom by intrigue.	**Da 11:21**	2388
They covet fields and then **s** *them,*	**Mi 2:2**	1497
To **s** dwelling places which are not	**Hab 1:6**	3423
and they will **s** one another's hand,	**Zch 14:13**	2388
kill him and **s** his inheritance.'	**Mt 21:38**	*2192*
When they sought to **s** Him,	**Mt 21:46**	*2902*
together to **s** Jesus by stealth and	**Mt 26:4**	*2902*
I kiss, He is the one; **s** Him."	**Mt 26:48**	*2902*
teaching and you did not **s** Me.	**Mt 26:55**	*2902*
And they were seeking to **s** Him,	**Mk 12:12**	*2902*
seeking how to **s** Him by stealth and	**Mk 14:1**	*2902*
s Him and lead Him away under	**Mk 14:44**	*2902*
teaching, and you did not **s** Me;	**Mk 14:49**	*2902*
were seeking to **s** Him;	**Jn 7:30**	*4084*
Pharisees sent officers to **s** Him.	**Jn 7:32**	*4084*
Some of them wanted to **s** Him,	**Jn 7:44**	*4084*
they were seeking again to **s** Him,	**Jn 10:39**	*4084*
report it, so that they might **s** Him.	**Jn 11:57**	*4084*
the Damascenes in order to **s** me,	**2Co 11:32**	*4084*

SEIZED

So the men **s** his hand and the hand	**Gn 19:16**	2388
the servants of Abimelech had **s**.	**Gn 21:25**	1497
will be when you have **s** the city,	**Jos 8:8**	8610
went down after him and **s** the fords	**Jg 3:28**	3920
peg and **s** a hammer in her hand,	**Jg 4:21**	7760
Then they **s** him and slew him at	**Jg 12:6**	270
s him and gouged out his eyes;	**Jg 16:21**	270
So the man **s** his concubine and	**Jg 19:25**	2388
go, *Saul* **s** the edge of his robe,	**1Sa 15:27**	2388
I **s** *him* by his beard and struck	**1Sa 17:35**	2388
for agony has **s** me because my life	**2Sa 1:9**	270
Each one of them **s** his opponent	**2Sa 2:16**	2388
I **s** him and killed him in Ziklag,	**2Sa 4:10**	270
So they **s** them; and Elijah brought	**1Ki 18:40**	8610
So they **s** her, and when she	**2Ki 11:16**	7760, 3027
cities of Judah and **s** them.	**2Ki 18:13**	8610
So they **s** her, and when she	**2Ch 23:15**	7760, 3027
in the east are **s** with horror.	**Jb 18:20**	270
He has **s** a house which he has not	**Jb 20:19**	1497
Days of affliction have **s** me.	**Jb 30:16**	270
Panic **s** them there, Anguish, as of	**Ps 48:6**	270
has **s** me because of the wicked,	**Ps 119:53**	270
Pains have **s** me like the pains of	**Is 21:3**	270
Trembling has **s** the godless.	**Is 33:14**	270
cities of Judah and **s** them.	**Is 36:1**	8610
Anguish has **s** us, Pain as of a	**Jer 6:24**	2388
prophets and all the people **s** him,	**Jer 26:8**	8610
but will be **s** by the hand of the	**Jer 38:23**	8610
and they **s** him and brought him up	**Jer 39:5**	3947
And the strongholds have been **s**,	**Jer 48:41**	8610
You have been found and also **s**	**Jer 50:24**	8610

“Babylon has been **s**!” **Jer 50:46** 8610
The fords also have been **s**, **Jer 51:32** 8610
praise of the whole earth been **s**! **Jer 51:41** 8610
remembrance, that they may be **s**. **Ezk 21:23** 8610
you will be **s** with the hand. **Ezk 21:24** 8610
Ephraim will be **s** with shame And **Hos 10:6** 3947
he **s** him and *began* to choke *him,* **Mt 18:28** *2902*
and the rest **s** his slaves and **Mt 22:6** *2902*
and laid hands on Jesus and **s** Him. **Mt 26:50** *2902*
Those who had **s** Jesus led Him **Mt 26:57** *2902*
They **s** upon that statement, **Mk 9:10** *2902*
They laid hands on Him and **s** Him. **Mk 14:46** *2902*
over *his* naked *body;* and they **s** him. **Mk 14:51** *2902*
For amazement had **s** him and all **Lk 5:9** *4023*
For it had **s** him many times; **Lk 8:29** *4884*
When they led Him away, they **s** a man, **Lk 23:26** *1949*
and no one **s** Him, because His hour **Jn 8:20** *4084*
When he had **s** him, he put him **Ac 12:4** *4084*
they **s** Paul and Silas and dragged **Ac 16:19** *1949*
“For this reason *some* Jews **s** me **Ac 26:21** *4815*
And the beast was **s**, **Rv 19:20** *4084*

SEIZES
and **s** her and lies with her and **Dt 22:28** 8610
out her hand and **s** his genitals, **Dt 25:11** 2388
“A snare **s** *him* by the heel, *And* a **Jb 18:9** 270
How blessed will be the one who **s** **Ps 137:9** 270
So she **s** him and kisses him And **Pr 7:13** 2388
It growls as it **s** the prey And **Is 5:29** 270
and whenever it **s** him, it slams **Mk 9:18** *2638*
and a spirit **s** him, **Lk 9:39** *2983*

SEIZING
And **s** him by the right hand, he **Ac 3:7** *4084*

SEIZURE
joyfully the **s** of your property, **Heb 10:34** *724*

SELA
of Akrabbim, from **S** and upward. **Jg 1:36** 5554
of Salt 10,000 and took **S** by war, **2Ki 14:7** 5554
From **S** by way of the wilderness to **Is 16:1** 5554
the inhabitants of **S** sing aloud, **Is 42:11** 5553

SELAH
deliverance for him in God.” **S**. **Ps 3:2** 5542
from His holy mountain. **S**. **Ps 3:4** 5542
Your blessing *be* upon Your people! **S**. **Ps 3:8** 5542
worthless and aim at deception? **S**. **Ps 4:2** 5542
upon your bed, and be still. **S**. **Ps 4:4** 5542
And lay my glory in the dust. **S**. **Ps 7:5** 5542
the wicked is snared. Higgaion **S**. **Ps 9:16** 5542
know that they are but men. **S**. **Ps 9:20** 5542
your burnt offering acceptable! **S**. **Ps 20:3** 5542
not withheld the request of his lips. **S**. **Ps 21:2** 5542
Who seek Your face—*even* Jacob. **S**. **Ps 24:6** 5542
He is the King of glory. **S**. **Ps 24:10** 5542
with the fever heat of summer. **S**. **Ps 32:4** 5542
forgave the guilt of my sin. **S**. **Ps 32:5** 5542
me with songs of deliverance. **S**. **Ps 32:7** 5542
man at his best is a mere breath. **S**. **Ps 39:5** 5542
every man is a mere breath. **S**. **Ps 39:11** 5542
thanks to Your name forever. **S**. **Ps 44:8** 5542
quake at its swelling pride. **S**. **Ps 46:3** 5542
God of Jacob is our stronghold. **S**. **Ps 46:7** 5542
God of Jacob is our stronghold. **S**. **Ps 46:11** 5542
glory of Jacob whom He loves. **S**. **Ps 47:4** 5542
God will establish her forever. **S**. **Ps 48:8** 5542
them who approve their words. **S**. **Ps 49:13** 5542
For He will receive me. **S**. **Ps 49:15** 5542
For God Himself is judge. **S**. **Ps 50:6** 5542
more than speaking what is right. **S**. **Ps 52:3** 5542
from the land of the living. **S**. **Ps 52:5** 5542
They have not set God before them. **S**. **Ps 54:3** 5542
I would lodge in the wilderness. **S**. **Ps 55:7** 5542
who sits enthroned from of old—**S**. **Ps 55:19** 5542
him who tramples upon me. **S**. **Ps 57:3** 5542
have fallen into the midst of it. **S**. **Ps 57:6** 5542
who are treacherous in iniquity. **S**. **Ps 59:5** 5542
Jacob To the ends of the earth. **S**. **Ps 59:13** 5542
displayed because of the truth. **S**. **Ps 60:4** 5542
in the shelter of Your wings. **S**. **Ps 61:4** 5542
mouth, But inwardly they curse. **S**. **Ps 62:4** 5542
God is a refuge for us. **S**. **Ps 62:8** 5542
will sing praises to Your name.” **S**. **Ps 66:4** 5542
not the rebellious exalt themselves. **S**. **Ps 66:7** 5542
offering of bulls with male goats. **S**. **Ps 66:15** 5542
cause His face to shine upon us—**S**. **Ps 67:1** 5542
guide the nations on the earth. **S**. **Ps 67:4** 5542
marched through the wilderness, **S**. **Ps 68:7** 5542
The God *who* is our salvation. **S**. **Ps 68:19** 5542
Sing praises to the Lord, **S**. **Ps 68:32** 5542
is I who have firmly set its pillars. **S**. **Ps 75:3** 5542
sword and the weapons of war. **S**. **Ps 76:3** 5542
To save all the humble of the earth. **S**. **Ps 76:9** 5542
I sigh, then my spirit grows faint. **S**. **Ps 77:3** 5542
anger withdrawn His compassion? **S**. **Ps 77:9** 5542
The sons of Jacob and Joseph. **S**. **Ps 77:15** 5542
you at the waters of Meribah. **S**. **Ps 81:7** 5542
show partiality to the wicked? **S**. **Ps 82:2** 5542
a help to the children of Lot. **S**. **Ps 83:8** 5542
They are ever praising You. **S**. **Ps 84:4** 5542
Give ear, O God of Jacob! **S**. **Ps 84:8** 5542
You covered all their sin. **S**. **Ps 85:2** 5542
spoken of you, O city of God. **S**. **Ps 87:3** 5542
“This one was born there.” **S**. **Ps 87:6** 5542
afflicted me with all Your waves. **S**. **Ps 88:7** 5542
spirits rise *and* praise You? **S**. **Ps 88:10** 5542
throne to all generations.” **S**. **Ps 89:4** 5542
the witness in the sky is faithful.” **S**. **Ps 89:37** 5542
have covered him with shame. **S**. **Ps 89:45** 5542
his soul from the power of Sheol? **S**. **Ps 89:48** 5542
Poison of a viper is under their lips. **S**. **Ps 140:3** 5542
They have set snares for me. **S**. **Ps 140:5** 5542
that they *not* be exalted. **S**. **Ps 140:8** 5542
longs for You, as a parched land. **S**. **Ps 143:6** 5542
the Holy One from Mount Paran. **S**. **Hab 3:3** 5542
rods of chastisement were sworn. **S**. **Hab 3:9** 5542
lay him open from thigh to neck. **S**. **Hab 3:13** 5542

SELECT
he took six hundred **s** chariots, **Ex 14:7** 977
you shall **s** out of all the people **Ex 18:21** 2372
then you shall **s** for yourselves **Nu 35:11** 7136a
s the best and fittest of your **2Ki 10:3** 7200
“When I **s** an appointed time, It **Ps 75:2** 3947
And He has also made Me a **s** arrow, **Is 49:2** 1305
“Therefore, brethren, **s** from among you **Ac 6:3** *1980a*
to **s** men to send to you with our **Ac 15:25** *1586*

SELECTED
Then he **s** from what he had with **Gn 32:13** 3947
for I have **s** a king for Myself **1Sa 16:1** 7200
he **s** from all the choice men of **2Sa 10:9** 977
he **s** from all the choice men of **1Ch 19:10** 977
And Ezra the priest **s** men *who were* **Ezr 10:16** 914
into a land that I had **s** for them, **Ezk 20:6** 8446

SELECTION
“According to the **s** by lot, **Nu 26:56**

SELECTS
S a tree that does not rot; **Is 40:20** 977

SELED
sons of Nadab *were* **S** and Appaim, **1Ch 2:30** 5540
Appaim, and **S** died without sons. **1Ch 2:30** 5540

SELEUCIA
they went down to **S** and from there **Ac 13:4** *4581*

SELF
our old **s** was crucified with *Him,* **Ro 6:6** *444*
of life, you lay aside the old **s**, **Eph 4:22** *444*
and put on the new **s**, **Eph 4:24** *444*
the old **s** with its *evil* practices, **Col 3:9** *444*
and have put on the new **s** who is **Col 3:10** *3501b*
For men will be lovers of **s**, **2Tm 3:2** *5367*
owe to me even your own **s** as well). **Phm 1:19** *4572*

SELF-ABASEMENT
delighting in **s** and the worship of **Col 2:18** *5012a*
s and severe treatment of the body, **Col 2:23** *5012a*

SELF-CONDEMNED
perverted and is sinning, being **s**. **Ti 3:11** *843*

SELF-CONTROL
s and the judgment to come, **Ac 24:25** *1466*
you because of your lack of **s**. **1Co 7:5** *192*
But if they do not have **s**, **1Co 7:9** *1467*
games exercises **s** in all things. **1Co 9:25** *1467*
gentleness, **s**; against such things **Ga 5:23** *1466*
malicious gossips, without **s**, **2Tm 3:3** *193*
and in *your* knowledge, **s**, **2Pe 1:6** *1466*
and in *your* **s**, perseverance, **2Pe 1:6** *1466*

SELF-CONTROLLED
good, sensible, just, devout, **s**, **Ti 1:8** *1468*

SELF-EXALTATION
pride, his arrogance and his **s**. **Jer 48:29** 3820, 7312

SELF-INDULGENCE
they are full of robbery and **s**. **Mt 23:25** *192*

SELFISH
Do not eat the bread of a **s** man, **Pr 23:6** 7451a, 5869
proclaim Christ out of **s** ambition rather **Php 1:17** *2052*
and **s** ambition in your heart, **Jas 3:14** *2052*
jealousy and **s** ambition exist, **Jas 3:16** *2052*

SELFISHLY
but to those who are **s** ambitious **Ro 2:8** *2052*

SELFISHNESS
nothing from **s** or empty conceit, **Php 2:3** *2052*

SELF-MADE
appearance of wisdom in **s** religion **Col 2:23** *1479*

SELF-RESTRAINT
and love and sanctity with **s**. **1Tm 2:15** *4997*

SELF-WILL
And in their **s** they lamed oxen. **Gn 49:6** 7522

SELF-WILLED
reproach as God’s steward, not **s**, **Ti 1:7** *829*
Daring, **s**, they do not tremble **2Pe 2:10** *829*

SELL
“First **s** me your birthright.” **Gn 25:31** 4376
let us **s** him to the Ishmaelites and **Gn 37:27** 4376
they did not **s** their land. **Gn 47:22** 4376
He does not have authority to **s** **Ex 21:8** 4376
then they shall **s** the live ox and **Ex 21:35** 4376
he is to **s** to you according to the **Lv 25:15** 4376
he has to **s** part of his property, **Lv 25:25** 4376
as to **s** himself to a stranger **Lv 25:47** 4376
‘You will **s** me food for money so **Dt 2:28** 7666
or you may **s** it to a foreigner, **Dt 14:21** 4376
certainly not **s** her for money, **Dt 21:14** 4376
for the LORD will **s** Sisera into **Jg 4:9** 4376
has to **s** the piece of land which **Ru 4:3** 4376
“Go, **s** the oil and pay your debt, **2Ki 4:7** 4376
now would you even **s** your brothers **Ne 5:8** 4376
any grain on the sabbath day to **s**, **Ne 10:31** 4376
You **s** Your people cheaply, **Ps 44:12** 4376
Buy truth, and do not **s** *it,* **Pr 23:23** 4376
to whom of My creditors did I **s** you **Is 50:1** 4376
s the land into the hands of evil men **Ezk 30:12** 4376
shall not **s** or exchange any of it, **Ezk 48:14** 4376
“Also I will **s** your sons and your **Jl 3:8** 4376
they will **s** them to the Sabeans, **Jl 3:8** 4376
Because they **s** the righteous for **Am 2:6** 4376
So that we may **s** grain **Am 8:5** 7666
may **s** the refuse of the wheat?” **Am 8:6** 7666
and *each of* those who **s** them says, **Zch 11:5** 4376
go *and* **s** your possessions and give **Mt 19:21** *4453*
go and **s** all you possess and give **Mk 10:21** *4453*
“**S** your possessions and give to **Lk 12:33** *4453*
s all that you possess and **Lk 18:22** *4453*
and whoever has no sword is to **s** his **Lk 22:36** *4453*
owners of land or houses would **s** **Ac 4:34** *4453*
one will be able to buy or to **s**, **Rv 13:17** *4453*

SELLER
mistress, the buyer like the **s**, **Is 24:2** 4376
the buyer rejoice nor the **s** mourn; **Ezk 7:12** 4376
the **s** will not regain what he sold **Ezk 7:13** 4376
Thyatira, a **s** of purple fabrics, **Ac 16:14** *4211*

SELLING
a number of crops he is **s** to you. **Lv 25:16** 4376
were buying and **s** in the temple, **Mt 21:12** *4453*
seats of those who were **s** doves. **Mt 21:12** *4453*
were buying and **s** in the temple, **Mk 11:15** *4453*
seats of those who were **s** doves; **Mk 11:15** *4453*
they were buying, they were **s**, **Lk 17:28** *4453*
to drive out those who were **s**, **Lk 19:45** *4453*
were **s** oxen and sheep and the doves, **Jn 2:14** *4453*
and to those who were **s** the doves **Jn 2:16** *4453*
and they *began* **s** their property **Ac 2:45** *4097*

SELLS
“If a man **s** his daughter as a **Ex 21:7** 4376
whether he **s** him or he is found in **Ex 21:16** 4376
sheep and slaughters it or **s** it, **Ex 22:1** 4376
if a man **s** a dwelling house in a **Lv 25:29** 4376
to you that he **s** himself to you, **Lv 25:39** 4376
with him violently or **s** him, **Dt 24:7** 4376
be on the head of him who **s** *it.* **Pr 11:26** 7666
makes linen garments and **s** *them,* **Pr 31:24** 4376
Who **s** nations by her harlotries **Na 3:4** 4376
it he goes and **s** all that he has and **Mt 13:44** *4453*

SELVES
among your own **s** men will arise, **Ac 20:30** *846*

SEMACHIAH
whose brothers, Elihu and **S**, **1Ch 26:7** 5565

SEMEIN
son of Mattathias, the son of **S**, **Lk 3:26** *4584*

SEMINAL
‘Now if a man has a **s** emission, **Lv 15:16** 2233
on which there is **s** emission, **Lv 15:17** 2233
so that there is a **s** emission, **Lv 15:18** 2233
for the man who has a **s** emission **Lv 15:32** 2233
or if a man has a **s** emission, **Lv 22:4** 7902, 2233

SENAAH
the sons of **S**, 3,630. **Ezr 2:35** 5570
the sons of **S**, 3,930. **Ne 7:38** 5570

SENATE
all the **S** of the sons of Israel, **Ac 5:21** *1087*

SEND
I will **s** rain on the earth forty **Gn 7:4** 4305
walking with them to **s** them off. **Gn 18:16** 7971
He will **s** His angel before you, **Gn 24:7** 7971
will **s** His angel with you to make **Gn 24:40** 7971
“**S** me away to my master.” **Gn 24:54** 7971
S me away that I may go to my **Gn 24:56** 7971
I will **s** and get you from there. **Gn 27:45** 7971
“**S** me away, that I may go to my **Gn 30:25** 7971
Come, and I will **s** you to them.” **Gn 37:13** 7971
will **s** you a young goat from the flock.” **Gn 38:17** 7971
give a pledge until you **s** *it?”* **Gn 38:17** 7971
But Jacob did not **s** Joseph’s **Gn 42:4** 7971
“**S** one of you that he may get **Gn 42:16** 7971
“If you **s** our brother with us, we **Gn 43:4** 7971
“But if you do not **s** *him,* **Gn 43:5** 7971
“**S** the lad with me and we will **Gn 43:8** 7971
now, and I will **s** you to Pharaoh, **Ex 3:10** 7971
now **s** *the message* by whomever You **Ex 4:13** 7971
Why did You ever **s** me? **Ex 5:22** 7971
I will **s** swarms of insects on you **Ex 8:21** 7971
“For this time I will **s** all My **Ex 9:14** 7971
I will **s** a very heavy hail, **Ex 9:18** 4305
“Now therefore **s**, bring your **Ex 9:19** 7971
s them out of the land in haste, **Ex 12:33** 7971
You **s** forth Your burning anger, **Ex 15:7** 7971
I am going to **s** an angel before **Ex 23:20** 7971
“I will **s** My terror ahead of you, **Ex 23:27** 7971
“I will **s** hornets ahead of **Ex 23:28** 7971
“I will **s** an angel before you **Ex 33:2** 7971
me know whom You will **s** with me. **Ex 33:12** 7971
to **s** it into the wilderness as the **Lv 16:10** 7971
on the head of the goat and **s** *it* away **Lv 16:21** 7971
I will **s** pestilence among you, **Lv 26:25** 7971
s away from the camp every leper **Nu 5:2** 7971
shall **s** away both male and female; **Nu 5:3** 7971
you shall **s** them outside the camp **Nu 5:3** 7971
“**S** out for yourself men so that **Nu 13:2** 7971
you shall **s** a man from each of **Nu 13:2** 7971
not urgently **s** to you to call you? **Nu 22:37** 7971
Israel you shall **s** to the war.” **Nu 31:4** 7971
‘Let us **s** men before us, that they **Dt 1:22** 7971
will **s** the hornet against them, **Dt 7:20** 7971
shall not **s** him away empty-handed. **Dt 15:13** 7971
elders of his city shall **s** and take him **Dt 19:12** 7971
“The LORD will **s** upon you curses, **Dt 28:20** 7971
whom the LORD will **s** against you, **Dt 28:48** 7971
of beasts I will **s** upon them, **Dt 32:24** 7971
and wherever you **s** us we will go. **Jos 1:16** 7971
from each tribe that I may **s** them, **Jos 18:4** 7971
“**S** away the ark of the God of **1Sa 5:11** 7971
how we shall **s** it to its place.” **1Sa 6:2** 7971
“If you **s** away the ark of the God **1Sa 6:3** 7971

God of Israel, do not s it empty; 1Sa 6:3 7971
Then s it away that it may go. 1Sa 6:8 7971
I will s you a man from the land of 1Sa 9:16 7971
"Get up, that I may s you away." 1Sa 9:26 7971
that we may s messengers 1Sa 11:3 7971
that He may s thunder and rain. 1Sa 12:17 5414
s you to Jesse the Bethlehemite, 1Sa 16:1 7971
Samuel said to Jesse, "S and bring 1Sa 16:11 7971
"S me your son David who is with 1Sa 16:19 7971
shall I not then s to you and make 1Sa 20:12 7971
it known to you and s you away, 1Sa 20:13 7971
"And behold, I will s the lad, 1Sa 20:21 7971
now, s and bring him to me, 1Sa 20:31 7971
"S me Uriah the Hittite." 2Sa 11:6 7971
for Joab, to s him to the king, 2Sa 14:29 7971
that I may s you to the king, 2Sa 14:32 7971
s me everything that you hear." 2Sa 15:36 7971
s quickly and tell David, 2Sa 17:16 7971
And s rain on Your land, which You 1Ki 8:36 5414
by whatever way You shall s them, 1Ki 8:44 7971
"S me away, that I may go to my 1Ki 11:21 7971
s rain on the face of the earth." 1Ki 18:1 5414
"Now then s *and* gather to me all 1Ki 18:19 7971
I will s my servants to you, 1Ki 20:6 7971
"You shall not s." 2Ki 2:16 7971
he was ashamed, he said, "S." 2Ki 2:17 7971
"Please s me one of the servants 2Ki 4:22 7971
and I will s a letter to the king 2Ki 5:5 7971
is, that I may s and take him." 2Ki 6:13 7971
perished, so let us s and see." 2Ki 7:13 7971
"Take a horseman and s him to 2Ki 9:17 7971
In those days the LORD began to s 2Ki 15:37 7971
let us s everywhere to our kinsmen 1Ch 13:2 7971
"Now s me a skilled man to 2Ch 2:7 7971
"S me also cedar, cypress and 2Ch 2:8 7971
let my lord s to his servants 2Ch 2:15 7971
And s rain on Your land which You 2Ch 6:27 5414
by whatever way You shall s them, 2Ch 6:34 7971
if I s pestilence among My people, 2Ch 7:13 7971
and let the king s to us his Ezr 5:17 7972
favor before you, s me to Judah, Ne 2:5 7971
So it pleased the king to s me, Ne 2:6 7971
and s portions to him who has Ne 8:10 7971
to s portions and to celebrate a Ne 8:12 7971
and they would s and invite their Jb 1:4 7971
Job would s and consecrate them, Jb 1:5 7971
his appearance and s him away. Jb 14:20 7971
God will s His fierce anger on him Jb 20:23 7971
"They s forth their little ones Jb 21:11 7971
"Can you s forth lightnings that Jb 38:35 7971
He s you help from the sanctuary And Ps 20:2 7971
O s out Your light and Your truth, Ps 43:3 7971
He will s from heaven and save me; Ps 57:3 7971
God will s forth His lovingkindness Ps 57:3 7971
You s forth Your Spirit, they Ps 104:30 7971
we beseech You, do s prosperity! Ps 118:25 6743b
S out Your arrows and confuse Ps 144:6 7971
the lazy one to those who s him. Pr 10:26 7971
messenger to those who s him, Pr 25:13 7971
"Whom shall I s, and who will go Is 6:8 7971
Then I said, "Here am I. S me!" Is 6:8 7971
I s it against a godless nation Is 10:6 7971
will s a wasting disease among his Is 10:16 7971
S the *tribute* lamb to the ruler of Is 16:1 7971
s them a Savior and a Champion, Is 19:20 7971
so deaf as My messenger whom I s? Is 42:19 7971
S it out to the end of the earth; Is 48:20 3318
s survivors from them to the nations: Is 66:19 7971
youth,' Because everywhere I s you, Jer 1:7 7971
s to Kedar and observe closely And Jer 2:10 7971
and I will s the sword after them Jer 9:16 7971
And s for the wailing women, that Jer 9:17 7971
s them away from My presence and Jer 15:1 7971
going to s for many fishermen," Jer 16:16 7971
I will s for many hunters, Jer 16:16 7971
"I did not s *these* prophets, But Jer 23:21 7971
I did not s them or command them, Jer 23:32 7971
'I will s the sword, the Jer 24:10 7971
I will s and take all the families Jer 25:9 7971
'and *I will* s to Jer 25:9
all the nations to whom I s you Jer 25:15 7971
sword that I will s among them." Jer 25:16 7971
which I will s among you." Jer 25:27 7971
and s word to the king of Edom, to Jer 27:3 7971
"S to all the exiles, saying, Jer 29:31 7971
to you, although I did not s him, Jer 29:31 7971
you shall s him out free from you; Jer 34:14 7971
LORD your God will s you to us. Jer 42:5 7971
I am going to s and get Jer 43:10 7971
s to him those who tip *vessels,* Jer 48:12 7971
'And I will s out the sword after Jer 49:37 7971
'When I s against them the deadly Ezk 5:16 7971
whom I will s to destroy you, Ezk 5:16 7971
s on you famine and wild beasts, Ezk 5:17 7971
I will s My anger against you; Ezk 7:3 7971
of bread, s famine against it and Ezk 14:13 7971
"Or *if* I should s a plague Ezk 14:19 7971
when I s My four severe judgments Ezk 14:21 7971
"For I will s pestilence to her Ezk 28:23 7971
"And I will s fire upon Magog Ezk 39:6 7971
one will arise who will s an oppressor Da 11:20 5674a
But I will s a fire on its cities Hos 8:14 7971
"Behold, I am going to s you grain, Jl 2:19 7971
s fire upon the house of Hazael And Am 1:4 7971
will s fire upon the wall of Gaza And Am 1:7 7971
will s fire upon the wall of Tyre And Am 1:10 7971
"So I will s fire upon Teman And Am 1:12 7971
"So I will s fire upon Moab And Am 2:2 7971
"So I will s fire upon Judah And Am 2:5 7971
Then I would s rain on one city Am 4:7 4305
another city I would not s rain; Am 4:7 4305
I will s a famine on the land, Am 8:11 7971
Will s you forth to the border, Ob 1:7 7971
"then I will s the curse upon Mal 2:2 7971
I am going to s My messenger, Mal 3:1 7971
I am going to s you Elijah the Mal 4:5 7971
planned to s her away secretly. Mt 1:19 *630*
s us into the herd of swine." Mt 8:31 *649*
s out workers into His harvest." Mt 9:38 *1544b*
I s you out as sheep in the midst Mt 10:16 *649*
'BEHOLD, I S MY MESSENGER AHEAD Mt 11:10 *649*
Son of Man will s forth His angels, Mt 13:41 *649*
so s the crowds away, that Mt 14:15 *630*
"S her away, because she keeps shouting Mt 15:23 *630*
do not want to s them away hungry, Mt 15:32 *630*
OF DIVORCE AND S *her* AWAY?" Mt 19:7 *630*
and immediately he will s them." Mt 21:3 *649*
"And He will s forth His angels Mt 24:31 *649*
"BEHOLD, I S MY MESSENGER AHEAD Mk 1:2 *649*
He *could* s them out to preach, Mk 3:14 *649*
not to s them out of the country. Mk 5:10 *649*
"S us into the swine so that we Mk 5:12 *3992*
and began to s them out in pairs, Mk 6:7 *649*
s them away so that they may go Mk 6:36 *630*
"If I s them away hungry to Mk 8:3 *630*
OF DIVORCE AND S *her* AWAY." Mk 10:4 *630*
he will s it back here." Mk 11:3 *649*
"He had one more *to* s, a Mk 12:6
then He will s forth the angels, Mk 13:27 *649*
I S MY MESSENGER AHEAD OF YOU, Lk 7:27 *649*
"S the crowd away, that they Lk 9:12 *630*
s out laborers into His harvest. Lk 10:2 *1544b*
I s you out as lambs in the midst Lk 10:3 *649*
s to them prophets and apostles, Lk 11:49 *649*
have mercy on me, and s Lazarus so Lk 16:24 *3992*
you s him to my father's house Lk 16:27 *3992*
he proceeded to s another slave; Lk 20:11 *3992*
"And he proceeded to s a third; Lk 20:12 *3992*
I will s my beloved son; Lk 20:13 *3992*
"For God did not s the Son into Jn 3:17 *649*
receives whomever I s receives Me; Jn 13:20 *3992*
whom the Father will s in My name, Jn 14:26 *3992*
I will s to you from the Father, Jn 15:26 *3992*
but if I go, I will s Him to you. Jn 16:7 *3992*
has sent Me, I also s you." Jn 20:21 *3992*
and that He may s Jesus, the Ac 3:20 *649*
NOW, AND I WILL S YOU TO EGYPT.' Ac 7:34 *649*
and s for a man *named* Simon, Ac 10:5 *3343*
directed by a holy angel to s for you Ac 10:22 *3343*
'Therefore s to Joppa and invite Ac 10:32 *3992*
'S to Joppa and have Simon, who Ac 11:13 *649*
each of them determined to s *a* Ac 11:29 *3992*
s to Antioch with Paul and Barnabas Ac 15:22 *3992*
to select men to s to you with our Ac 15:25 *3992*
I will s you far away to the Gentiles. Ac 22:21 *1821*
he also used to s for him quite often Ac 24:26 *3343*
custody until I s him to Caesar." Ac 25:21 *375*
the Emperor, I decided to s him. Ac 25:25 *3992*
Christ did not s me to baptize, 1Co 1:17 *649*
she must not s her husband away. 1Co 7:13 *863*
I will s them with letters to 1Co 16:3 *3992*
that you may s me on my way 1Co 16:6 *4311*
But s him on his way in peace, so 1Co 16:11 *4311*
Jesus to s Timothy to you shortly, Php 2:19 *3992*
I hope to s him immediately, Php 2:23 *3992*
to s to you Epaphroditus, Php 2:25 *3992*
For this reason God will s 2Th 2:11 *3992*
I s Artemas or Tychicus to you, Ti 3:12 *3992*
Does a fountain s out from the Jas 3:11 *1032*
You will do well to s them on 3Jn 1:6 *4311*
and s *it* to the seven churches: Rv 1:11 *3992*
they will s gifts to one another, Rv 11:10 *3992*

SENDING
the matter on which I am s you 1Sa 21:2 7971
because this wrong in s me away is 2Sa 13:16 7971
you are s to inquire of Baal-zebub, 2Ki 1:6 7971
that this man is s *word* to me to 2Ki 5:7 7971
"Now I am s Huram-abi, 2Ch 2:13 7971
and s portions *of food* to one another. Es 9:19 4916b
and s portions *of food* to one another Es 9:22 4916b
was s out its branches to the sea And Ps 80:11 7971
daily rising early and s *them.* Jer 7:25 7971
I am s serpents against you, Jer 8:17 7971
I have been s to you again and Jer 26:5 7971
I am s upon them the sword, Jer 29:17 7971
prophets, s *them* again and again, Jer 35:15 7971
LORD our God to whom we are s you, Jer 42:6 7971
I am s you to the sons of Israel, Ezk 2:3 7971
"I am s you to them who are Ezk 2:4 7971
rebelled against him by s his envoys Ezk 17:15 7971
And s away the crowds, Jesus got Mt 15:39 *630*
I am s you prophets and wise men Mt 23:34 *649*
Himself was s the crowd away. Mk 6:45 *630*
I am s forth the promise of My Lk 24:49 *1821*
s it in charge of Barnabas and Ac 11:30 *649*
now are they s us away secretly? Ac 16:37 *1544b*
absurd to me in s a prisoner, Ac 25:27 *3992*
the Gentiles, to whom I am s you, Ac 26:17 *649*
s His own Son in the likeness of Ro 8:3 *3992*
s my very heart, Phm 1:12

SENDS
hand and s her out from his house, Dt 24:1 7971
hand and s her out of his house, Dt 24:3 7971
s rain on the face of the earth.' " 1Ki 17:14 5414
earth And s water on the fields, Jb 5:10 7971
And He s them out, and they Jb 12:15 7971
He s forth springs in the valleys; Ps 104:10 7971
He s forth His command to the Ps 147:15 7971
s forth His word and melts them; Ps 147:18 7971
Who s a message by the hand of a Pr 26:6 7971
Lord s a message against Jacob, Is 9:8 7971
Which s envoys by the sea, Even in Is 18:2 7971
'WHOEVER S HIS WIFE AWAY, Mt 5:31 *630*
and s rain on *the* righteous and Mt 5:45 *1026*
he s a delegation and asks for Lk 14:32 *649*
prisoner, s you his greetings; Col 4:10 *782*
Jesus Christ, s you his greetings, Col 4:12 *782*
physician, s you his greetings, Col 4:14 *782*
with you, s you greetings, 1Pe 5:13 *782*

SENEH
and the name of the other S. 1Sa 14:4 5573

SENIOR
people and some of the s priests. Jer 19:1 2205

SENIR
and the Amorites call it S): Dt 3:9 8149
from Bashan to Baal-hermon and S 1Ch 5:23 8149
From the summit of S and Hermon, SS 4:8 8149
your planks of fir trees from S; Ezk 27:5 8149

SENNACHERIB
S king of Assyria came up against 2Ki 18:13 5576
and listen to the words of S, 2Ki 19:16 5576
to Me about S king of Assyria, 2Ki 19:20 5576
So S king of Assyria departed and 2Ki 19:36 5576
S king of Assyria came and invaded 2Ch 32:1 5576
Hezekiah saw that S had come 2Ch 32:2 5576
After this S king of Assyria sent 2Ch 32:9 5576
"Thus says S king of Assyria, 2Ch 32:10 5576
the hand of S the king of Assyria and 2Ch 32:22 5576
S king of Assyria came up against Is 36:1 5576
and listen to all the words of S, Is 37:17 5576
to Me about S king of Assyria, Is 37:21 5576
So S king of Assyria departed Is 37:37 5576

SENSE
translating to give the s so that Ne 8:8 7922
with a woman is lacking s; Pr 6:32 3820
the youths A young man lacking s, Pr 7:7 3820
who despises his neighbor lacks s, Pr 11:12 3820
who pursues worthless *things* lacks s. Pr 12:11 3820
Folly is joy to him who lacks s, Pr 15:21 3820
to buy wisdom, When he has no s? Pr 17:16 3820
A man lacking in s pledges And Pr 17:18 3820
the vineyard of the man lacking s, Pr 24:30 3820
along the road, his s is lacking Ec 10:3 3820
like a silly dove, without s; Hos 7:11 3820
so in what s is He his son?" Mk 12:37 *4159*
Everyone kept feeling a s of awe; Ac 2:43 *5401*
where would the s of smell be? 1Co 12:17 *3750*
is that s of blessing you had? Ga 4:15 *3108*

SENSELESS
The stupid and the s alike perish And Ps 49:10 1198
Then I was s and ignorant; Ps 73:22 1198
A s man has no knowledge, Ps 92:6 1198
Pay heed, you s among the people; Ps 94:8 1197b
hear this, O foolish and s people, Jer 5:21
369, 3820

SENSES
She s that her gain is good; Pr 31:18 2938
"He has lost His s." Mk 3:21 *1839*
"But when he came to his s, Lk 15:17 *1438*
and they may come to their s *and* 2Tm 2:26 *366*
s trained to discern good and evil. Heb 5:14 *145*

SENSIBLE
The wisdom of the s is to understand Pr 14:8 6175
But the s man considers his steps. Pr 14:15 6175
But the s are crowned with knowledge. Pr 14:18 6175
But he who regards reproof is s. Pr 15:5 6191
Who then is the faithful and s slave Mt 24:45 *5429*
is the faithful and s steward, Lk 12:42 *5429*
loving what is good, s, Ti 1:8 *4998*
are to be temperate, dignified, s, Ti 2:2 *4998*
to be s, pure, workers at home, Ti 2:5 *4998*
urge the young men to be s; Ti 2:6 *4993*

SENSIBLY
to live s, righteously and godly in Ti 2:12 *4996*

SENSUAL
"Now, then, hear this, you s one, Is 47:8 5719
you are to them like a s song by Ezk 33:32 5690
for when they feel s desires in 1Tm 5:11 *2691*
the s conduct of unprincipled men 2Pe 2:7 *766*

SENSUALITY
wickedness, *as well as* deceit, s, Mk 7:22 *766*
not in sexual promiscuity and s, Ro 13:13 *766*
and s which they have practiced. 2Co 12:21 *766*
immorality, impurity, s, Ga 5:19 *766*
have given themselves over to s for Eph 4:19 *766*
having pursued a course of s, 1Pe 4:3 *766*
Many will follow their s, 2Pe 2:2 *766*
entice by fleshly desires, by s, 2Pe 2:18 *766*
rich by the wealth of her s." Rv 18:3 *4764*

SENSUOUSLY
she glorified herself and lived s, Rv 18:7 *4763*
immorality and lived s with her, Rv 18:9 *4763*

SENT
God had not s rain upon the earth, Gn 2:5 4305
therefore the LORD God s him out Gn 3:[illegible] 7971
and he s out a raven, and it flew Gn 8:7 7971
Then he s out a dove from him, to Gn 8:8 7971
he s out the dove from the ark. Gn 8:10 7971
seven days, and s out the dove; Gn 8:12 7971
the LORD has s us to destroy it." Gn 19:13 7971
and s Lot out of the midst of the Gn 19:29 7971
king of Gerar s and took Sarah. Gn 20:2 7971
gave her the boy, and s her away. Gn 21:14 7971

Thus they **s** away their sister **Gn 24:59** 7971
and **s** them away from his son Isaac **Gn 25:6** 7971
me and have **s** me away from you?" **Gn 26:27** 7971
and have **s** you away in peace. **Gn 26:29** 7971
then Isaac **s** them away and they **Gn 26:31** 7971
she **s** and called her younger son **Gn 27:42** 7971
Then Isaac **s** Jacob away, and he **Gn 28:5** 7971
and **s** him away to Paddan-aram to **Gn 28:6** 7971
So Jacob **s** and called Rachel and **Gn 31:4** 7971
so that I might have **s** you away **Gn 31:27** 7971
would have **s** me away empty-handed. **Gn 31:42** 7971
Then Jacob **s** messengers before him **Gn 32:3** 7971
and I have **s** to tell my lord, that **Gn 32:5** 7971
it is a present **s** to my lord Esau. **Gn 32:18** 7971
them and **s** them across the stream. **Gn 32:23** 5674a
And he **s** across whatever he had. **Gn 32:23** 5674a
he **s** him from the valley of Hebron, **Gn 37:14** 7971
and they **s** the varicolored tunic **Gn 37:32** 7971
When Judah **s** the young goat by his **Gn 38:20** 7971
After all, I **s** this young goat, but you **Gn 38:23** 7971
out that she **s** to her father-in-law, **Gn 38:25** 7971
so he **s** and called for all the **Gn 41:8** 7971
Pharaoh **s** and called for Joseph, **Gn 41:14** 7971
it was light, the men were **s** away, **Gn 44:3** 7971
for God **s** me before you to **Gn 45:5** 7971
"God **s** me before you to **Gn 45:7** 7971
it was not you who **s** me here, **Gn 45:8** 7971
To his father he **s** as follows: **Gn 45:23** 7971
So he **s** his brothers away, and as **Gn 45:24** 7971
that Joseph had **s** to carry him, **Gn 45:27** 7971
which Pharaoh had **s** to carry him. **Gn 46:5** 7971
he **s** Judah before him to Joseph, **Gn 46:28** 7971
So they **s** *a message* to Joseph, **Gn 50:16** 6680
among the reeds and **s** her maid, **Ex 2:5** 7971
you that it is I who have **s** you: **Ex 3:12** 7971
of your fathers has **s** me to you.' **Ex 3:13** 7971
'I AM has **s** me to you.' " **Ex 3:14** 7971
God of Jacob, has **s** me to you.' **Ex 3:15** 7971
the LORD with which He had **s** him, **Ex 4:28** 7971
God of the Hebrews, **s** me to you, **Ex 7:16** 7971
Pharaoh **s**, and behold, there **Ex 9:7** 7971
and the LORD **s** thunder and hail, **Ex 9:23** 5414
Pharaoh **s** for Moses and Aaron, **Ex 9:27** 7971
Zipporah, after he had **s** her away, **Ex 18:2** 7971
He **s** word to Moses, **Ex 18:6** 559
He **s** young men of the sons of **Ex 24:5** 7971
so and **s** them outside the camp; **Nu 5:4** 7971
So Moses **s** them from the **Nu 13:3** 7971
whom Moses **s** to spy out the land; **Nu 13:16** 7971
When Moses **s** them to spy out the **Nu 13:17** 7971
in to the land where you **s** us; **Nu 13:27** 7971
As for the men whom Moses **s** to spy **Nu 14:36** 7971
Then Moses **s** a summons to Dathan **Nu 16:12** 7971
has **s** me to do all these deeds; **Nu 16:28** 7971
men, *then* the LORD has not **s** me. **Nu 16:29** 7971
From Kadesh Moses then **s** **Nu 20:14** 7971
He heard our voice and **s** an angel **Nu 20:16** 7971
The LORD **s** fiery serpents **Nu 21:6** 7971
Then Israel **s** messengers to Sihon, **Nu 21:21** 7971
Moses **s** to spy out Jazer, and **Nu 21:32** 7971
So he **s** messengers to Balaam the **Nu 22:5** 7971
king of Moab, has **s** *word* to me, **Nu 22:10** 7971
Then Balak again **s** leaders, **Nu 22:15** 7971
and **s** *some* to Balaam and the **Nu 22:40** 7971
messengers whom you had **s** to me, **Nu 24:12** 7971
Moses **s** them, a thousand from **Nu 31:6** 7971
when I **s** them from Kadesh-barnea **Nu 32:8** 7971
"So I **s** messengers from the **Dt 2:26** 7971
the LORD **s** you from Kadesh-barnea, **Dt 9:23** 7971
her former husband who **s** her away **Dt 24:4** 7971
which the LORD **s** him to perform **Dt 34:11** 7971
Then Joshua the son of Nun **s** two **Jos 2:1** 7971
king of Jericho **s** *word* to Rahab, **Jos 2:3** 7971
So she **s** them away, and they **Jos 2:21** 7971
she hid the messengers whom we **s**. **Jos 6:17** 7971
whom Joshua **s** to spy out Jericho. **Jos 6:25** 7971
Joshua **s** men from Jericho to Ai, **Jos 7:2** 7971
So Joshua **s** messengers, and they **Jos 7:22** 7971
warriors, and **s** them out at night. **Jos 8:3** 7971
So Joshua **s** them away, and they **Jos 8:9** 7971
king of Jerusalem **s** *word* **Jos 10:3** 7971
Then the men of Gibeon **s** *word* to **Jos 10:6** 7971
that he **s** to Jobab king of Madon **Jos 11:1** 7971
Moses the servant of the LORD **s** me **Jos 14:7** 7971
as I was in the day Moses **s** me; **Jos 14:11** 7971
blessed them and **s** them away, **Jos 22:6** 7971
Joshua **s** them away to their tents, **Jos 22:7** 7971
Then the sons of Israel **s** to the **Jos 22:13** 7971
'Then I **s** Moses and Aaron, and I **Jos 24:5** 7971
and he **s** and summoned Balaam the **Jos 24:9** 7971
'Then I **s** the hornet before you **Jos 24:12** 7971
And the sons of Israel **s** tribute **Jg 3:15** 7971
that he **s** away the people who had **Jg 3:18** 7971
Now she **s** and summoned Barak the **Jg 4:6** 7971
that the LORD **s** a prophet to the **Jg 6:8** 7971
Have I not **s** you?" **Jg 6:14** 7971
He **s** messengers throughout **Jg 6:35** 7971
and he **s** messengers to Asher, **Jg 6:35** 7971
s all the *other* men of Israel, **Jg 7:8** 7971
Gideon **s** messengers throughout **Jg 7:24** 7971
Then God **s** an evil spirit between **Jg 9:23** 7971
He **s** messengers to Abimelech **Jg 9:31** 7971
Now Jephthah **s** messengers to the **Jg 11:12** 7971
But Jephthah **s** messengers again to **Jg 11:14** 7971
then Israel **s** messengers to the **Jg 11:17** 7971
they also **s** to the king of Moab, **Jg 11:17** 7971
'And Israel **s** messengers to Sihon **Jg 11:19** 7971
the message which Jephthah **s** him. **Jg 11:28** 7971
So he **s** her away for two months; **Jg 11:38** 7971

the man of God whom You have **s** **Jg 13:8** 7971
she **s** and called the lords of the **Jg 16:18** 7971
So the sons of Dan **s** from their **Jg 18:2** 7971
and **s** her throughout the territory **Jg 19:29** 7971
cut her in pieces and **s** her throughout **Jg 20:6** 7971
Then the tribes of Israel **s** men **Jg 20:12** 7971
And the congregation **s** 12,000 of **Jg 21:10** 7971
Then the whole congregation **s** *word* **Jg 21:13** 7971
So the people **s** to Shiloh, and **1Sa 4:4** 7971
So they **s** and gathered all the **1Sa 5:8** 7971
So they **s** the ark of God to Ekron. **1Sa 5:10** 7971
They **s** therefore and gathered all **1Sa 5:11** 7971
So they **s** messengers to the **1Sa 6:21** 7971
And Samuel **s** all the people away, **1Sa 10:25** 7971
and **s** *them* throughout the territory **1Sa 11:7** 7971
then the LORD **s** Moses and Aaron **1Sa 12:8** 7971
"Then the LORD **s** Jerubbaal and **1Sa 12:11** 7971
LORD **s** thunder and rain that day; **1Sa 12:18** 5414
he **s** away the rest of the people, **1Sa 13:2** 7971
"The LORD **s** me to anoint you as **1Sa 15:1** 7971
and the LORD **s** you on a mission, **1Sa 15:18** 7971
mission on which the LORD **s** me, **1Sa 15:20** 7971
So he **s** and brought him in. **1Sa 16:12** 7971
So Saul **s** messengers to Jesse and **1Sa 16:19** 7971
s *them* to Saul by David his son. **1Sa 16:20** 7971
Saul **s** to Jesse, saying, **1Sa 16:22** 7971
them to Saul, and he **s** for him. **1Sa 17:31** 3947
went out wherever Saul **s** him, **1Sa 18:5** 7971
Then Saul **s** messengers to David's **1Sa 19:11** 7971
Saul **s** messengers to take David, **1Sa 19:14** 7971
Saul **s** messengers to see David, **1Sa 19:15** 7971
Saul **s** messengers to take David, **1Sa 19:20** 7971
told Saul, he **s** other messengers, **1Sa 19:21** 7971
So Saul **s** messengers again the **1Sa 19:21** 7971
go, for the LORD has **s** you away. **1Sa 20:22** 7971
Then the king **s** someone to summon **1Sa 22:11** 7971
So David **s** ten young men; and **1Sa 25:5** 7971
David **s** messengers from the **1Sa 25:14** 7971
young men of my lord whom you **s**. **1Sa 25:25** 7971
who **s** you this day to meet me, **1Sa 25:32** 7971
David **s** a proposal to Abigail, **1Sa 25:39** 7971
"David has **s** us to you to take **1Sa 25:40** 7971
David **s** out spies, and he knew **1Sa 26:4** 7971
he **s** *some* of the spoil to the **1Sa 30:26** 7971
and **s** *them* throughout the land of **1Sa 31:9** 7971
David **s** messengers to the men **2Sa 2:5** 7971
Then Abner **s** messengers to David **2Sa 3:12** 7971
David **s** messengers to Ish-bosheth, **2Sa 3:14** 7971
s and took her from *her* husband, **2Sa 3:15** 7971
So David **s** Abner away, and he went **2Sa 3:21** 7971
in Hebron, for he had **s** him away, **2Sa 3:22** 7971
the king, and he has **s** him away, **2Sa 3:23** 7971
why then have you **s** him away and **2Sa 3:24** 7971
he **s** messengers after Abner, **2Sa 3:26** 7971
Then Hiram king of Tyre **s** **2Sa 5:11** 7971
Toi **s** Joram his son to King David **2Sa 8:10** 7971
Then King David **s** and brought him **2Sa 9:5** 7971
So David **s** some of his servants to **2Sa 10:2** 7971
because he has **s** consolers to you? **2Sa 10:3** 7971
Has David not **s** his servants to **2Sa 10:3** 7971
as their hips, and **s** them away. **2Sa 10:4** 7971
it to David, he **s** to meet them, **2Sa 10:5** 7971
the sons of Ammon **s** and hired the **2Sa 10:6** 7971
of it, he **s** Joab and all the army, **2Sa 10:7** 7971
And Hadadezer **s** and brought out **2Sa 10:16** 7971
that David **s** Joab and his servants **2Sa 11:1** 7971
s and inquired about the woman. **2Sa 11:3** 7971
David **s** messengers and took her, **2Sa 11:4** 7971
and she **s** and told David, and **2Sa 11:5** 7971
Then David **s** to Joab, *saying,* **2Sa 11:6** 7971
So Joab **s** Uriah to David. **2Sa 11:6** 7971
from the king was **s** out after him. **2Sa 11:8** 3318
and **s** *it* by the hand of Uriah. **2Sa 11:14** 7971
Then Joab **s** and reported to David **2Sa 11:18** 7971
all that Joab had **s** him *to tell.* **2Sa 11:22** 7971
David **s** and brought her to his **2Sa 11:27** 7971
Then the LORD **s** Nathan to David. **2Sa 12:1** 7971
and **s** *word* through Nathan the **2Sa 12:25** 7971
s messengers to David and said, **2Sa 12:27** 7971
David **s** to the house for Tamar, **2Sa 13:7** 7971
So Joab **s** to Tekoa and brought a **2Sa 14:2** 7971
Then Absalom **s** for Joab, to send **2Sa 14:29** 7971
So he **s** again a second time, but **2Sa 14:29** 7971
"Behold, I **s** for you, saying, **2Sa 14:32** 7971
But Absalom **s** spies throughout all **2Sa 15:10** 7971
s for Ahithophel the Gilonite, **2Sa 15:12** 7971
David **s** the people out, one **2Sa 18:2** 7971
"When Joab **s** the king's servant, **2Sa 18:29** 7971
Then King David **s** to Zadok and **2Sa 19:11** 7971
so that they **s** *word* to the king, **2Sa 19:14** 7971
"And He **s** out arrows, and **2Sa 22:15** 7971
"He **s** from on high, He took me; **2Sa 22:17** 7971
I shall return to Him who **s** me." **2Sa 24:13** 7971
So the LORD **s** a pestilence upon **2Sa 24:15** 5414
The king has also **s** with him Zadok **1Ki 1:44** 7971
So King Solomon **s**, and they **1Ki 1:53** 7971
So King Solomon **s** Benaiah the son **1Ki 2:25** 7971
Then Solomon **s** Benaiah the son of **1Ki 2:29** 7971
Now the king **s** and called for **1Ki 2:36** 7971
So the king **s** and called for **1Ki 2:42** 7971
Hiram king of Tyre **s** his servants to **1Ki 5:1** 7971
Then Solomon **s** *word* to Hiram, **1Ki 5:2** 7971
So Hiram **s** *word* to Solomon, **1Ki 5:8** 7971
the message which you have **s** me; **1Ki 5:8** 7971
He **s** them to Lebanon, 10,000 a **1Ki 5:14** 7971
s and brought Hiram from Tyre. **1Ki 7:13** 7971
On the eighth day he **s** the people **1Ki 8:66** 7971
And Hiram **s** to the king 120 **1Ki 9:14** 7971
Hiram **s** his servants with the fleet, **1Ki 9:27** 7971

Then they **s** and called him, and **1Ki 12:3** 7971
Then King Rehoboam **s** Adoram, **1Ki 12:18** 7971
that they **s** and called him to the **1Ki 12:20** 7971
am **s** to you *with* a harsh *message.* **1Ki 14:6** 7971
And King Asa **s** them to Ben-hadad **1Ki 15:18** 7971
I have **s** you a present of silver **1Ki 15:19** 7971
and **s** the commanders of his armies **1Ki 15:20** 7971
has not **s** to search for you; **1Ki 18:10** 7971
So Ahab **s** *a message* among all the **1Ki 18:20** 7971
Jezebel **s** a messenger to Elijah, **1Ki 19:2** 7971
Then he **s** messengers to the city **1Ki 20:2** 7971
'Surely, I **s** to you saying, **1Ki 20:5** 7971
for he **s** to me for my wives and my **1Ki 20:7** 7971
'All that you **s** for to your **1Ki 20:9** 7971
Ben-hadad **s** to him and said, **1Ki 20:10** 7971
Ben-hadad **s** out and they told him, **1Ki 20:17** 7971
and **s** letters to the elders and to **1Ki 21:8** 7971
did as Jezebel had **s** *word* to them, **1Ki 21:11** 7971
the letters which she had **s** them. **1Ki 21:11** 7971
Then they **s** *word* to Jezebel, **1Ki 21:14** 7971
he **s** messengers and said to them, **2Ki 1:2** 7971
'Go, return to the king who **s** you **2Ki 1:6** 7971
Then *the king* **s** to him a captain **2Ki 1:9** 7971
So he again **s** to him another **2Ki 1:11** 7971
So he again **s** the captain of a **2Ki 1:13** 7971
'Because you have **s** messengers to **2Ki 1:16** 7971
LORD has **s** me as far as Bethel." **2Ki 2:2** 7971
the LORD has **s** me to Jericho." **2Ki 2:4** 7971
the LORD has **s** me to the Jordan." **2Ki 2:6** 7971
They **s** therefore fifty men; **2Ki 2:17** 7971
Then he went and **s** *word* to **2Ki 3:7** 7971
I have **s** Naaman my servant to you, **2Ki 5:6** 7971
that he **s** *word* to the king, **2Ki 5:8** 7971
Elisha **s** a messenger to him, **2Ki 5:10** 7971
My master has **s** me, saying, **2Ki 5:22** 7971
the house, and he **s** the men away, **2Ki 5:24** 7971
The man of God **s** *word* to the **2Ki 6:9** 7971
The king of Israel **s** to the **2Ki 6:10** 7971
He **s** horses and chariots and a **2Ki 6:14** 7971
eaten and drunk he **s** them away, **2Ki 6:23** 7971
king **s** a man from his presence; **2Ki 6:32** 7971
has **s** to take away my head? **2Ki 6:32** 7971
and the king **s** after the army of **2Ki 7:14** 7971
king of Aram has **s** me to you, **2Ki 8:9** 7971
Then he **s** out a second horseman, **2Ki 9:19** 7971
letters and **s** *them* to Samaria, **2Ki 10:1** 7971
of *the children,* **s** *word* to Jehu, **2Ki 10:5** 7971
and **s** *them* to him at Jezreel. **2Ki 10:7** 7971
Then Jehu **s** throughout Israel and **2Ki 10:21** 7971
Jehoiada **s** and brought the captains **2Ki 11:4** 7971
and **s** *them* to Hazael king of Aram. **2Ki 12:18** 7971
Amaziah **s** messengers to Jehoash, **2Ki 14:8** 7971
Israel **s** to Amaziah king of Judah, **2Ki 14:9** 7971
thorn bush which was in Lebanon **s** **2Ki 14:9** 7971
but they **s** after him to Lachish **2Ki 14:19** 7971
So Ahaz **s** messengers to **2Ki 16:7** 7971
and **s** a present to the king of **2Ki 16:8** 7971
and King Ahaz **s** to Urijah the **2Ki 16:10** 7971
King Ahaz had **s** from Damascus, **2Ki 16:11** 7971
who had **s** messengers to So king of **2Ki 17:4** 7971
and which I **s** to you through My **2Ki 17:13** 7971
therefore the LORD **s** lions among **2Ki 17:25** 7971
so he has **s** lions among them, and **2Ki 17:26** 7971
Then Hezekiah king of Judah **s** to **2Ki 18:14** 7971
Then the king of Assyria **s** Tartan **2Ki 18:17** 7971
"Has my master **s** me only to your **2Ki 18:27** 7971
Then he **s** Eliakim who was over the **2Ki 19:2** 7971
has **s** to reproach the living God, **2Ki 19:4** 7971
he **s** messengers again to Hezekiah **2Ki 19:9** 7971
has **s** to reproach the living God. **2Ki 19:16** 7971
son of Amoz **s** to Hezekiah saying, **2Ki 19:20** 7971
s letters and a present to **2Ki 20:12** 7971
Josiah, the king **s** Shaphan, **2Ki 22:3** 7971
'Tell the man who **s** you to me, **2Ki 22:15** 7971
who **s** you to inquire of the LORD **2Ki 22:18** 7971
Then the king **s**, and they gathered **2Ki 23:1** 7971
and he **s** and took the bones from **2Ki 23:16** 7971
The LORD **s** against him bands **2Ki 24:2** 7971
So He **s** them against Judah to **2Ki 24:2** 7971
after he had **s** away Hushim and **1Ch 8:8** 7971
and **s** *messengers* around the land **1Ch 10:9** 7971
after consultation **s** him away, **1Ch 12:19** 7971
Now Hiram king of Tyre **s** **1Ch 14:1** 7971
s Hadoram his son to King David to **1Ch 18:10** 7971
So David **s** messengers to console **1Ch 19:2** 7971
that he has **s** comforters to you? **1Ch 19:3** 7971
as their hips, and **s** them away. **1Ch 19:4** 7971
And he **s** to meet them, for the men **1Ch 19:5** 7971
Hanun and the sons of Ammon **s** **1Ch 19:6** 7971
of it, he **s** Joab and all the army, **1Ch 19:8** 7971
by Israel, they **s** messengers and **1Ch 19:16** 7971
I shall return to Him who **s** me." **1Ch 21:12** 7971
the LORD **s** a pestilence on Israel; **1Ch 21:14** 5414
And God **s** an angel to Jerusalem to **1Ch 21:15** 7971
Then Solomon **s** *word* to Huram the **2Ch 2:3** 7971
and **s** him cedars to build him a **2Ch 2:3** 7971
answered in a letter **s** to Solomon: **2Ch 2:11** 7971
he **s** the people to their tents, **2Ch 7:10** 7971
And Huram by his servants **s** him **2Ch 8:18** 7971
So they **s** and summoned him. **2Ch 10:3** 7971
Then King Rehoboam **s** Hadoram, **2Ch 10:18** 7971
and **s** them to Ben-hadad king of **2Ch 16:2** 7971
I have **s** you silver and gold; **2Ch 16:3** 7971
and **s** the commanders of his armies **2Ch 16:4** 7971
of his reign he **s** his officials, **2Ch 17:7** 7971
Yet He **s** prophets to them to bring **2Ch 24:19** 7971
and **s** all their spoil to the king **2Ch 24:23** 7971
But the troops whom Amaziah **s** back **2Ch 25:13** 7725
s him a prophet who said to him, **2Ch 25:15** 7971

and s to Joash the son of Jehoahaz 2Ch 25:17 7971
Joash the king of Israel s to 2Ch 25:18 7971
thorn bush which was in Lebanon s 2Ch 25:18 7971
but they s after him to Lachish 2Ch 25:27 7971
At that time King Ahaz s to the 2Ch 28:16 7971
Now Hezekiah s to all Israel and 2Ch 30:1 7971
Sennacherib king of Assyria s his 2Ch 32:9 7971
And the LORD s an angel who 2Ch 32:21 7971
who s to him to inquire of the 2Ch 32:31 7971
he s Shaphan the son of Azaliah, 2Ch 34:8 7971
'Tell the man who s you to Me, 2Ch 34:23 7971
who s you to inquire of the LORD, 2Ch 34:26 7971
Then the king s and gathered all 2Ch 34:29 7971
But Neco s messengers to him, 2Ch 35:21 7971
Nebuchadnezzar s and brought him 2Ch 36:10 7971
God of their fathers, s *word* to them 2Ch 36:15 7971
so that he s a proclamation 2Ch 36:22 5674a
so that he s a proclamation Ezr 1:1 5674a
of the letter which they s to him: Ezr 4:11 7972
we have s and informed the king, Ezr 4:14 7972
Then the king s an answer to Rehum Ezr 4:17 7972
the document which you s to us has Ezr 4:18 7972
the River, s to Darius the king. Ezr 5:6 7972
They s a report to him in which it Ezr 5:7 7972
just as King Darius had s. Ezr 6:13 7972
Forasmuch as you are s by the king Ezr 7:14 7972
So I s for Eliezer, Ariel, Ezr 8:16 7971
I s them to Iddo the leading Ezr 8:17 3318
Now the king had s with me Ne 2:9 7971
and Geshem s *a message* to me, Ne 6:2 7971
So I s messengers to them, saying, Ne 6:3 7971
They s *messages* to me four Ne 6:4 7971
Then Sanballat s his servant to me Ne 6:5 7971
Then I s *a message* to him saying, Ne 6:8 7971
that surely God had not s him, Ne 6:12 7971
Tobiah s letters to frighten me. Ne 6:19 7971
So he s letters to all the king's Es 1:22 7971
Letters were s by couriers to Es 3:13 7971
And she s garments to clothe Es 4:4 7971
and s for his friends and his wife Es 5:10 7971
s letters by couriers on horses, Es 8:10 7971
and he s letters to all the Jews Es 9:20 7971
He s letters to all the Jews, Es 9:30 7971
"You have s widows away empty, Jb 22:9 7971
"Who s out the wild donkey free? Jb 39:5 7971
He s out His arrows, and Ps 18:14 7971
He s from on high, He took me; Ps 18:16 7971
He s them food in abundance. Ps 78:25 7971
He s among them swarms of flies which Ps 78:45 7971
He s upon them His burning anger, Ps 78:49 7971
He s a man before them, Joseph, Ps 105:17 7971
The king s and released him, The Ps 105:20 7971
He s Moses His servant, *And* Aaron Ps 105:26 7971
He s darkness and made *it* dark; Ps 105:28 7971
s a wasting disease among them. Ps 106:15 7971
He s His word and healed them, And Ps 107:20 7971
He has s redemption to His people; Ps 111:9 7971
He s signs and wonders into your Ps 135:9 7971
She has s out her maidens, she Pr 9:3 7971
messenger will be s against him. Pr 17:11 7971
correctly answer him who s you? Pr 22:21 7971
Sargon the king of Assyria s him Is 20:1 7971
And the king of Assyria s Is 36:2 7971
"Has my master s me only to your Is 36:12 7971
Then he s Eliakim who was over the Is 37:2 7971
has s to reproach the living God, Is 37:4 7971
it he s messengers to Hezekiah, Is 37:9 7971
who s *them* to reproach the living Is 37:17 7971
son of Amoz s *word* to Hezekiah, Is 37:21 7971
s letters and a present to Is 39:1 7971
"For your sake I have s to Babylon, Is 43:14 7971
And now the Lord GOD has s Me, Is 48:16 7971
which I have s your mother away? Is 50:1 7971
your mother was s away. Is 50:1 7971
in the matter for which I s it. Is 55:11 7971
s your envoys a great distance And Is 57:9 7971
He has s me to bind up the Is 61:1 7971
I had s her away and given her a Jer 3:8 7971
I have s you all My servants the Jer 7:25 7971
Their nobles have s their servants for Jer 14:3 7971
I have neither s them nor Jer 14:14 7971
although it was not I who s them Jer 14:15 7971
the LORD had s him to prophesy; Jer 19:14 7971
King Zedekiah s to him Pashhur Jer 21:1 7971
I have also s to you, saying, Jer 23:38 7971
whom I have s out of this place Jer 24:5 7971
"And the LORD has s to you all Jer 25:4 7971
to whom the LORD s me drink it: Jer 25:17 7971
"The LORD s me to prophesy Jer 26:12 7971
for truly the LORD has s me to you Jer 26:15 7971
King Jehoiakim s men to Egypt: Jer 26:22 7971
for I have not s them," Jer 27:15 7971
one whom the LORD has truly s." Jer 28:9 7971
Hananiah, the LORD has not s you, Jer 28:15 7971
letter which Jeremiah the prophet s Jer 29:1 7971
The letter was s by the hand of Jer 29:3
whom Zedekiah king of Judah s to Jer 29:3 7971
to all the exiles whom I have s Jer 29:4 1540
where I have s you into exile, Jer 29:7 1540
I have not s them,' declares the Jer 29:9 7971
from where I s you into exile.' Jer 29:14 1540
'which I s to them again and again Jer 29:19 7971
whom I have s away from Jerusalem Jer 29:20 7971
'Because you have s letters in Jer 29:25 7971
"For he has s to us in Babylon, Jer 29:28 7971
"Also I have s to you all My Jer 35:15 7971
all the officials s Jehudi the son of Jer 36:14 7971
king s Jehudi to get the scroll, Jer 36:21 7971
King Zedekiah s Jehucal the son of Jer 37:3 7971

who s you to Me to inquire of Me: Jer 37:7 7971
King Zedekiah s and took him *out;* Jer 37:17 7971
Then King Zedekiah s and had Jer 38:14 7971
captain of the bodyguard s *word,* Jer 39:13 7971
they even s and took Jeremiah out Jer 39:14 7971
the king of the sons of Ammon has s Jer 40:14 7971
to whom you s me to present your Jer 42:9 7971
you who s me to the LORD your God, Jer 42:20 7971
whatever He has s me to *tell* you. Jer 42:21 7971
whom the LORD their God had s, Jer 43:1 7971
LORD our God has not s you to say, Jer 43:2 7971
'Yet I s you all My servants the Jer 44:4 7971
an envoy is s among the nations, Jer 49:14 7971
on high He s fire into my bones, La 1:13 7971
"For you are not being s to a Ezk 3:5 7971
But I have s you to them who Ezk 3:6 7971
when the LORD has not s them; Ezk 13:6 7971
yielded shoots and s out branches. Ezk 17:6 7971
and s out its branches toward him Ezk 17:7 7971
s messengers to them in Chaldea. Ezk 23:16 7971
they have even s for men who come Ezk 23:40 7971
afar, to whom a messenger was s; Ezk 23:40 7971
And s out its channels to all Ezk 31:4 7971
Nebuchadnezzar the king s *word* to Da 3:2 7972
who has s His angel and delivered Da 3:28 7972
"Then the hand was s from Him and Da 5:24 7972
"My God s His angel and shut the Da 6:22 7972
for I have now been s to you." Da 10:11 7971
to Assyria And s to King Jareb. Hos 5:13 7971
My great army which I s among you. Jl 2:25 7971
"I s a plague among you after the Am 4:10 7971
Amaziah, the priest of Bethel, s Am 7:10 7971
envoy has been s among the nations Ob 1:1 7971
slavery, And I s before you Moses, Mi 6:4 7971
as the LORD their God had s him. Hg 1:12 7971
LORD has s to patrol the earth." Zch 1:10 7971
"After glory He has s Me against Zch 2:8 7971
that the LORD of hosts has s Me. Zch 2:9 7971
the LORD of hosts has s Me to you. Zch 2:11 7971
the LORD of hosts has s me to you. Zch 4:9 7971
the LORD of hosts has s me to you. Zch 6:15 7971
Now *the town of* Bethel had s Zch 7:2 7971
words which the LORD of hosts had s Zch 7:12 7971
I have s this commandment to you, Mal 2:4 7971
And he s them to Bethlehem and Mt 2:8 3992
and s and slew all the male children Mt 2:16 649
But when the crowd had been s out, Mt 9:25 1544b
These twelve Jesus s out after Mt 10:5 649
receives Me receives Him who s Me. Mt 10:40 649
he s *word* by his disciples Mt 11:2 3992
He s and had John beheaded in Mt 14:10 3992
while He s the crowds away. Mt 14:22 630
He had s the crowds away, Mt 14:23 630
they s *word* into all that surrounding Mt 14:35 649
"I was s only to the lost sheep Mt 15:24 649
day, he s them into his vineyard. Mt 20:2 649
then Jesus s two disciples, Mt 21:1 649
he s his slaves to the Mt 21:34 649
"Again he s another group of Mt 21:36 649
afterward he s his son to them, Mt 21:37 649
"And he s out his slaves to call Mt 22:3 649
he s out other slaves saying, Mt 22:4 649
king was enraged, and he s his armies Mt 22:7 3992
And they s their disciples to Him, Mt 22:16 649
and stones those who are s to her! Mt 23:37 649
judgment seat, his wife s him Mt 27:19 649
him and immediately s him away, Mk 1:43 1544b
outside they s *word* to Him and Mk 3:31 649
For Herod himself had s and had Mk 6:17 649
Immediately the king s an Mk 6:27 649
And He s them away. Mk 8:9 630
And He s him to his home, saying, Mk 8:26 649
receive Me, but Him who s Me." Mk 9:37 649
Olives, He s two of His disciples, Mk 11:1 649
he s a slave to the vine-growers, Mk 12:2 649
him and s him away empty-handed. Mk 12:3 649
"Again he s them another Mk 12:4 649
"And he s another, and that one Mk 12:5 649
he s him last *of all* to them, Mk 12:6 649
Then they s some of the Pharisees Mk 12:13 649
And He s two of His disciples and Mk 14:13 649
Jesus Himself s *out through them from* Mk 16:20
and I have been s to speak to you and Lk 1:19 649
s from God to a city in Galilee called Lk 1:26 649
And s away the rich empty-handed. Lk 1:53 1821
HE HAS S ME TO PROCLAIM RELEASE Lk 4:18 649
yet Elijah was s to none of them, Lk 4:26 3992
for I was s for this purpose." Lk 4:43 649
he s some Jewish elders asking Him Lk 7:3 649
house, the centurion s friends, Lk 7:6 3992
had been s returned to the house, Lk 7:10 3992
John s them to the Lord, Lk 7:19 3992
"John the Baptist has s us to You, Lk 7:20 649
but He s him away, saying, Lk 8:38 630
And He s them out to proclaim the Lk 9:2 649
receives Me receives Him who s Me; Lk 9:48 649
He s messengers on ahead of Him, Lk 9:52 649
and s them in pairs ahead of Lk 10:1 649
Me rejects the One who s Me." Lk 10:16 649
and stones those s to her! Lk 13:34 649
and healed him, and s him away. Lk 14:4 630
at the dinner hour he s his slave to Lk 14:17 649
and he s him into his fields to Lk 15:15 3992
him and s a delegation after him, Lk 19:14 649
Olivet, He s two of the disciples, Lk 19:29 649
So those who were s went away and Lk 19:32 649
he s a slave to the vine-growers, Lk 20:10 649
him and s him away empty-handed. Lk 20:10 1821
and s him away empty-handed. Lk 20:11 1821

and s spies who pretended to be Lk 20:20 649
And Jesus s Peter and John, saying, Lk 22:8 649
"When I s you out without money Lk 22:35 649
jurisdiction, he s Him to Herod, Lk 23:7 375
robe and s Him back to Pilate. Lk 23:11 375
Herod, for he s Him back to us; Lk 23:15 375
There came a man s from God, Jn 1:6 649
when the Jews s to him priests and Jn 1:19 649
give an answer to those who s us? Jn 1:22 3992
had been s from the Pharisees. Jn 1:24 649
but He who s me to baptize in Jn 1:33 3992
'I have been s ahead of Him.' Jn 3:28 649
For He whom God has s speaks the Jn 3:34 649
is to do the will of Him who s Me and Jn 4:34 3992
"I s you to reap that for which Jn 4:38 649
not honor the Father who s Him. Jn 5:23 3992
word, and believes Him who s Me, Jn 5:24 3992
but the will of Him who s Me. Jn 5:30 3992
"You have s to John, and he has Jn 5:33 649
about Me, that the Father has s Me. Jn 5:36 649
"And the Father who s Me, Jn 5:37 3992
you do not believe Him whom He s. Jn 5:38 649
believe in Him whom He has s." Jn 6:29 649
but the will of Him who s Me. Jn 6:38 3992
This is the will of Him who s Me, Jn 6:39 3992
the Father who s Me draws him; Jn 6:44 3992
"As the living Father s Me, Jn 6:57 649
is not Mine, but His who s Me. Jn 7:16 3992
the glory of the One who s Him, Jn 7:18 3992
Myself, but He who s Me is true, Jn 7:28 3992
I am from Him, and He s Me." Jn 7:29 649
Pharisees s officers to seize Him. Jn 7:32 649
you, then I go to Him who s Me. Jn 7:33 3992
but I and the Father who s Me. Jn 8:16 3992
who s Me testifies about Me." Jn 8:18 3992
you, but He who s Me is true; Jn 8:26 3992
"And He who s Me is with Me; Jn 8:29 3992
on My own initiative, but He s Me. Jn 8:42 649
work the works of Him who s Me as Jn 9:4 3992
Siloam" (which is translated, S). Jn 9:7 649
sanctified and s into the world, Jn 10:36 649
So the sisters s *word* to Him, Jn 11:3 649
so that they may believe that You s Jn 11:42 649
in Me but in Him who s Me. Jn 12:44 3992
Me sees the One who s Me. Jn 12:45 3992
Father Himself who s Me has given Jn 12:49 3992
nor *is* one who is s greater Jn 13:16 652
greater than the one who s him. Jn 13:16 3992
Me receives Him who s Me." Jn 13:20 3992
Mine, but the Father's who s Me. Jn 14:24 3992
they do not know the One who s Me. Jn 15:21 3992
now I am going to Him who s Me; Jn 16:5 3992
and Jesus Christ whom You have s. Jn 17:3 649
and they believed that You s Me. Jn 17:8 649
"As You s Me into the world, I also Jn 17:18 649
I also have s them into the world. Jn 17:18 649
that the world may believe that You s Jn 17:21 649
so that the world may know that You s Jn 17:23 649
and these have known that You s Me; Jn 17:25 649
Annas s Him bound to Jn 18:24 649
as the Father has s Me, Jn 20:21 649
and s Him to bless you by turning Ac 3:26 649
and s *orders* to the prison house Ac 5:21 649
he s our fathers *there* the first Ac 7:12 1821
"Then Joseph s *word* and invited Ac 7:14 649
whom God s *to be* both a ruler and Ac 7:35 649
God, they s them Peter and John, Ac 8:14 649
has s me so that you may regain Ac 9:17 649
Caesarea and s him away to Tarsus. Ac 9:30 1821
Peter was there, s two men to him, Ac 9:38 649
But Peter s them all out and knelt Ac 9:40 1544b
to them, he s them to Joppa. Ac 10:8 649
men who had been s by Cornelius, Ac 10:17 649
for I have s them Myself." Ac 10:20 649
any objection when I was s for. Ac 10:29 3343
what reason you have s for me." Ac 10:29 3343
"So I s for you immediately, Ac 10:33 3992
which He s to the sons of Israel, Ac 10:36 649
having been s to me from Caesarea. Ac 11:11 649
they s Barnabas off to Antioch. Ac 11:22 1821
the Lord has s forth His angel Ac 12:11 1821
hands on them, they s them away. Ac 13:3 630
being s out by the Holy Spirit, Ac 13:4 1599
the synagogue officials s to them, Ac 13:15 649
message of this salvation has been s. Ac 13:26 1821
s on their way by the church, Ac 15:3 4311
and they s this letter by them, Ac 15:23 1125
we have s Judas and Silas, Ac 15:27 649
So when they were s away, Ac 15:30 630
they were s away from the brethren Ac 15:33 630
peace to those who had s them out. Ac 15:33 649
magistrates s their policemen, Ac 16:35 649
magistrates have s to release you. Ac 16:36 649
The brethren immediately s Paul and Ac 17:10 1599
brethren s Paul out to go as far as Ac 17:14 1821
And having s into Macedonia two of Ac 19:22 649
Asiarchs who were friends of his s to Ac 19:31 3992
Paul s for the disciples, and when Ac 20:1 3343
From Miletus he s to Ephesus Ac 20:17 3992
the man, I s him to you at once, Ac 23:30 3992
who was a Jewess, and s for Paul and Ac 24:24 3343
of God has been s to the Gentiles; Ac 28:28 649
they preach unless they are s? Ro 10:15 649
reason I have s to you Timothy, 1Co 4:17 3992
We have s along with him the 2Co 8:18 4842
We have s with them our brother, 2Co 8:22 4842
But I have s the brethren, in 2Co 9:3 3992
any of those whom I have s to you, 2Co 12:17 649
to go, and I s the brother with him. 2Co 12:18 4882

Paul, an apostle (not s from Ga 1:1
time came, God s forth His Son, Ga 4:4 *1821*
God has s forth the Spirit of His Ga 4:6 *1821*
I have s him to you for this Eph 6:22 *3992*
Therefore I have s him all the Php 2:28 *3992*
you s *a gift* more than once for my Php 4:16 *3992*
from Epaphroditus what you have s, Php 4:18 *3844*
For I have s him to you for this Col 4:8 *3992*
and we s Timothy, our brother and 1Th 3:2 *3992*
s to find out about your faith, 1Th 3:5 *3992*
But Tychicus I have s to Ephesus. 2Tm 4:12 *649*
have s him back to you in person, Phm 1:12 *375*
s out to render service for the Heb 1:14 *649*
and s them out by another way? Jas 2:25 *1544b*
by the Holy Spirit s from heaven 1Pe 1:12 *649*
or to governors as s by him for 1Pe 2:14 *3992*
that God has s His only begotten 1Jn 4:9 *649*
but that He loved us and s His Son 1Jn 4:10 *649*
Father has s the Son *to be* the Savior 1Jn 4:14 *649*
and He s and communicated *it* by Rv 1:1 *649*
of God, s out into all the earth. Rv 5:6 *649*
s His angel to show to His Rv 22:6 *649*
have s My angel to testify to you Rv 22:16 *3992*

SENTENCE
at Riblah, and he passed s on him. 2Ki 25:6 1696
Because the s against an evil deed Ec 8:11 6599
"A death s for this man! Jer 26:11 4941
"No death s for this man! Jer 26:16 4941
of Hamath, and he passed s on him. Jer 39:5 1696
and he passed s on him. Jer 52:9 1696
"This s is by the decree of the Da 4:17 6600
will you escape the s of hell? Mt 23:33 *2920*
And Pilate pronounced s that their Lk 23:24 *1948*
under the same s of condemnation? Lk 23:40 *2917*
Him to the s of death, Lk 24:20 *2917*
for a s of condemnation against him. Ac 25:15 *2613b*
we had the s of death within 2Co 1:9 *610*

SENTENCED
those who were not s to drink the Jer 49:12 4941

SENTRIES
Post a strong guard, Station s, Jer 51:12 8104

SEORIM
third for Harim, the fourth for S, 1Ch 24:8 8188

SEPARATE
it s the waters from the waters." Gn 1:6 914
to s the day from the night, Gn 1:14 914
to s the light from the darkness; Gn 1:18 914
Please s from me; Gn 13:9 6504
"Thus you shall s the Levites Nu 8:14 914
"S yourselves from among this Nu 16:21 914
"You shall s everyone who laps Jg 7:5 905
and there was no one to s them, 2Sa 14:6 5337
And he lived in a s house, 2Ki 15:5 2669
and he lived in a s house, 2Ch 26:21 2669
and s yourselves from the peoples Ezr 10:11 914
They s with the lip, they wag the Ps 22:7 6362
surely s me from His people." Is 56:3 914
building that *was* in front of the s area Ezk 41:12 1508
the s area with the building and Ezk 41:13 1508
that of the s areas along the east *side* Ezk 41:14 1508
the front of the s area behind it, Ezk 41:15 1508
opposite the s area and opposite the Ezk 42:1 1508
facing the s area and facing the Ezk 42:10 1508
which are opposite the s area, Ezk 42:13 1508
joined together, let no man s." Mt 19:6 *5563*
He will s them from one another, Mt 25:32 *873*
joined together, let no man s." Mk 10:9 *5563*
s us from the love of Christ? Ro 8:35 *5563*
able to s us from the love of God, Ro 8:39 *5563*
OUT FROM THEIR MIDST AND BE S," 2Co 6:17 *873*
were at that time s from Christ, Eph 2:12 *5565*

SEPARATED
God s the light from the darkness. Gn 1:4 914
and s the waters which were below Gn 1:7 914
nations were s into their lands, Gn 10:5 6504
s on the earth after the flood. Gn 10:32 6504
Thus they s from each other. Gn 13:11 6504
Abram, after Lot had s from him, Gn 13:14 6504
peoples will be s from your body; Gn 25:23 6504
Jacob s the lambs, and made Gn 30:40 6504
Israel s from their uncleanness, Lv 15:31 5144a
who has s you from the peoples. Lv 20:24 914
which I have s for you as unclean. Lv 20:25 914
which he s himself to the LORD; Nu 6:5 5144b
God of Israel has s you from the *rest* Nu 16:9 914
which Moses s from the men who had Nu 31:42 2673
When He s the sons of man, Dt 32:8 6504
had s himself from the Kenites, Jg 4:11 6504
"For You have s them from all 1Ki 8:53 914
of fire which s the two of them. 2Ki 2:11 6504
and all those who had s themselves Ezr 6:21 914
the Levites have not s themselves Ezr 9:1 914
and we are s on the wall far from Ne 4:19 6504
The descendants of Israel s Ne 9:2 914
and all those who had s themselves Ne 10:28 914
clasp each other and cannot be s. Jb 41:17 6504
a poor man is s from his friend. Pr 19:4 6504
the day that Ephraim s from Judah, Is 7:17 5493
goes on, But the wicked are not s. Jer 6:29 5423
that they s from one another, Ac 15:39 *673*
s from Christ for the sake of my Ro 9:3
For perhaps he was for this reason s Phm 1:15 *5563*
s from sinners and exalted above Heb 7:26 *5563*

SEPARATES
a slanderer s intimate friends. Pr 16:28 6504
a matter s intimate friends. Pr 17:9 6504
s himself seeks *his own* desire, Pr 18:1 6504
in Israel who s himself from Me, Ezk 14:7 5144a
shepherd s the sheep from the goats; Mt 25:32 *873*

SEPARATION
'All the days of his s he shall Nu 6:4 5145
'All the days of his vow of s no Nu 6:5 5145
'All the days of his s to the LORD Nu 6:6 5144b
his s to God is on his head. Nu 6:7 5145
'All the days of his s he is holy to Nu 6:8 5145
be void because his s was defiled. Nu 6:12 5145
the days of his s are fulfilled, Nu 6:13 5145
to the LORD according to his s, Nu 6:21 5145
according to the law of his s." Nu 6:21 5145
made a s between you and your God, Is 59:2 914

SEPHAR
from Mesha as you go toward S, Gn 10:30 5611

SEPHARAD
the exiles of Jerusalem who are in S Ob 1:20 5614

SEPHAR-VAIM
from Avva and from Hamath and S, 2Ki 17:24 5617
and Anammelech the gods of S. 2Ki 17:31 5617
Where are the gods of S, 2Ki 18:34 5617
Arpad, the king of the city of S, 2Ki 19:13 5617
Where are the gods of S? Is 36:19 5617
Arpad, the king of the city of S, Is 37:13 5617

SEPHARVITES
and the S burned their children in 2Ki 17:31 5616

SEQUENCE
to explain to them in orderly s, Ac 11:4 *2517*

SERAH
and Beriah and their sister S. Gn 46:17 8294
of the daughter of Asher *was* S. Nu 26:46 8294
and Beriah, and S their sister. 1Ch 7:30 8294

SERAIAH
were priests, and S *was* secretary. 2Sa 8:17 8304
captain of the guard took S the chief 2Ki 25:18 8304
and S the son of Tanhumeth the 2Ki 25:23 8304
sons of Kenaz *were* Othniel and S. 1Ch 4:13 8304
and S became the father of Joab 1Ch 4:14 8304
son of Joshibiah, the son of S, 1Ch 4:35 8304
Azariah became the father of S, 1Ch 6:14 8304
and S became the father of 1Ch 6:14 8304
Zerubbabel, Jeshua, Nehemiah, S, Ezr 2:2 8304
there went up Ezra son of S, Ezr 7:1 8304
S, Azariah, Jeremiah, Ne 10:2 8304
S the son of Hilkiah, the son of Ne 11:11 8304
S, Jeremiah, Ezra, Ne 12:1 8304
of S, Meraiah; of Jeremiah, Ne 12:12 8304
king's son, S the son of Azriel, Jer 36:26 8304
and S the son of Tanhumeth, Jer 40:8 8304
commanded S the son of Neriah, Jer 51:59 8304
(Now S was quartermaster.) Jer 51:59 8304
Then Jeremiah said to S, Jer 51:61 8304
the captain of the guard took S Jer 52:24 8304

SERAPHIM
S stood above Him, each having six Is 6:2 8314b
Then one of the s flew to me with Is 6:6 8314b

SERED
S and Elon and Jahleel. Gn 46:14 5624
of S, the family of the Seredites; Nu 26:26 5624

SEREDITES
of Sered, the family of the S; Nu 26:26 5625

SERGIUS
was with the proconsul, S Paulus, Ac 13:7 *4588a*

SERIOUS
or blindness, *or* any s defect, Dt 15:21 7451a
and have committed a s error." 1Sa 26:21 7235a, 3966
incurable And your injury is s. Jer 30:12 2470a
bringing many and s charges Ac 25:7 926

SERIOUSLY
take s all words which are spoken, Ec 7:21 3820

SERPENT
Now the s was more crafty than any Gn 3:1 5175
The woman said to the s, Gn 3:2 5175
The s said to the woman, Gn 3:4 5175
"The s deceived me, and I ate." Gn 3:13 5175
The LORD God said to the s, Gn 3:14 5175
"Dan shall be a s in the way, A Gn 49:17 5175
on the ground, and it became a s; Ex 4:3 5175
that it may become a s.'" Ex 7:9 8577
his servants, and it became a s. Ex 7:10 8577
staff that was turned into a s. Ex 7:15 5175
"Make a fiery s, and set it on Nu 21:8
Moses made a bronze s and set it on Nu 21:9 5175
about, that if a s bit any man, Nu 21:9 5175
when he looked to the bronze s, Nu 21:9 5175
the bronze s that Moses had made, 2Ki 18:4 5175
hand has pierced the fleeing s. Jb 26:13 5175
have venom like the venom of a s; Ps 58:4 5175
and the s you will trample down. Ps 91:13 8577
They sharpen their tongues as a s; Ps 140:3 5175
At the last it bites like a s And Pr 23:32 5175
the sky, The way of a s on a rock, Pr 30:19 5175
and a s may bite him who breaks Ec 10:8 5175
the s bites before being charmed, Ec 10:11 5175
And its fruit will be a flying s. Is 14:29 8314a
punish Leviathan the fleeing s, Is 27:1 5175
Even Leviathan the twisted s; Is 27:1 5175
and lion, viper and flying s, Is 30:6 8314a
"Its sound moves along like a s; Jer 46:22 5175
the s and it will bite them. Am 9:3 5175
They will lick the dust like a s, Mi 7:17 5175
lifted up the s in the wilderness, Jn 3:14 *3789*
as the s deceived Eve by his 2Co 11:3 *3789*
the s of old who is called the Rv 12:9 *3789*
time, from the presence of the s. Rv 12:14 *3789*
And the s poured water like a Rv 12:15 *3789*
hold of the dragon, the s of old, Rv 20:2 *3789*

SERPENT'S
the s root a viper will come out, Is 14:29 5175
and dust will be the s food. Is 65:25 5175

SERPENTS
his staff and they turned into s. Ex 7:12 8577
The LORD sent fiery s among Nu 21:6 8314a
He may remove the s from us." Nu 21:7 5175
with its fiery s and scorpions and Dt 8:15 8314a
"Their wine is the venom of s, Dt 32:33 8577
I am sending s against you, Jer 8:17 5175
so be shrewd as s Mt 10:16 *3789*
"You s, you brood of vipers, how Mt 23:33 *3789*
they will pick up s, Mk 16:18 *3789*
to tread on s and scorpions, Lk 10:19 *3789*
did, and were destroyed by the s. 1Co 10:9 *3789*
tails are like s and have heads, Rv 9:19 *3789*

SERUG
years, and became the father of S; Gn 11:20 8286
after he became the father of S, Gn 11:21 8286
S lived thirty years, and Gn 11:22 8286
and S lived two hundred years Gn 11:23 8286
S, Nahor, Terah, 1Ch 1:26 8286
the son of S, the son of Reu, the Lk 3:35 *4588b*

SERVANT
A s of servants He shall be to his Gn 9:25 5650
And let Canaan be his s. Gn 9:26 5650
And let Canaan be his s." Gn 9:27 5650
a s who is born in the house or Gn 17:12
"A s who is born in your house Gn 17:13
please do not pass Your s by. Gn 18:3 5650
since you have visited your s." Gn 18:5 5650
choice calf and gave *it* to the s Gn 18:7 5288
s has found favor in your sight, Gn 19:19 5650
Abraham said to his s, Gn 24:2 5650
The s said to him, Gn 24:5 5650
So the s placed his hand under the Gn 24:9 5650
Then the s took ten camels from Gn 24:10 5650
have appointed for Your s Isaac; Gn 24:14 5650
Then the s ran to meet her, and Gn 24:17 5650
So he said, "I am Abraham's s. Gn 24:34 5650
When Abraham's s heard their words, Gn 24:52 5650
The s brought out articles of Gn 24:53 5650
nurse with Abraham's s and his men. Gn 24:59 5650
the s took Rebekah and departed. Gn 24:61 5650
She said to the s, Gn 24:65 5650
And the s said, "He is my master." Gn 24:65 5650
The s told Isaac all the Gn 24:66 5650
For the sake of My s Abraham." Gn 26:24 5650
'Thus says your s Jacob, Gn 32:4 5650
which You have shown to Your s; Gn 32:10 5650
'*These* belong to your s Jacob; Gn 32:18 5650
your s Jacob also is behind us.' Gn 32:20 5650
God has graciously given your s." Gn 33:5 5650
let my lord pass on before his s, Gn 33:14 5650
sight and became his personal s; Gn 39:4 8334
a s of the captain of the Gn 41:12 5650
"Your s our father is well; Gn 43:28 5650
may your s please speak a word in Gn 44:18 5650
and do not be angry with your s; Gn 44:18 5650
we went up to your s my father, Gn 44:24 5650
"Your s my father said to us, Gn 44:27 5650
when I come to your s my father, Gn 44:30 5650
will bring the gray hair of your s Gn 44:31 5650
"For your s became surety for the Gn 44:32 5650
please let your s remain instead Gn 44:33 5650
since You have spoken to Your s; Ex 4:10 5650
or a hired s shall not eat of it. Ex 12:45 7916
in the LORD and in His s Moses. Ex 14:31 5650
your male or your female s or your Ex 20:10 5650, 519
or his male s or his female servant Ex 20:17 5650
his female s or his ox or his donkey Ex 20:17 519
So Moses arose with Joshua his s, Ex 24:13 8334
his s Joshua, the son of Nun, Ex 33:11 8334
have You been so hard on Your s? Nu 11:11 5650
"Not so, with My s Moses, He is Nu 12:7 5650
not afraid To speak against My s, Nu 12:8 5650
"But My s Caleb, because he has Nu 14:24 5650
You have begun to show Your s Your Dt 3:24 5650
son or your daughter or your male s Dt 5:14 5650
or your female s or your ox or your Dt 5:14 519
so that your male s and your Dt 5:14 5650
female s may rest as well as you. Dt 5:14 519
his male s or his female servant, Dt 5:21 5650
his male servant or his female s, Dt 5:21 519
and he shall be your s forever. Dt 15:17 5650
a hired s *who is* poor and needy, Dt 24:14 7916
So Moses the s of the LORD died Dt 34:5 5650
the death of Moses the s of the LORD, Jos 1:1 5650
to Joshua the son of Nun, Moses' s, Jos 1:1 8334
"Moses My s is dead; Jos 1:2 5650
which Moses My s commanded you; Jos 1:7 5650
the s of the LORD commanded you, Jos 1:13 5650
Moses the s of the LORD gave you Jos 1:15 5650
"What has my lord to say to his s?" Jos 5:14 5650
just as Moses the s of the LORD Jos 8:31 5650
just as Moses the s of the LORD Jos 8:33 5650
God had commanded His s Moses Jos 9:24 5650
the s of the LORD had commanded. Jos 11:12 5650
LORD had commanded Moses his s, Jos 11:15 5650
Moses the s of the LORD and the Jos 12:6 5650
and Moses the s of the LORD gave Jos 12:6 5650
the s of the LORD gave to them; Jos 13:8 5650
Moses the s of the LORD sent me Jos 14:7 5650
the s of the LORD gave them." Jos 18:7 5650
the s of the LORD commanded you, Jos 22:2 5650

which Moses the s of the LORD gave	Jos 22:4	5650
the s of the LORD commanded you,	Jos 22:5	5650
the son of Nun, the s of the LORD,	Jos 24:29	5650
the son of Nun, the s of the LORD,	Jg 2:8	5650
Purah your s down to the camp,	Jg 7:10	5288
So he went with Purah his s down	Jg 7:11	5288
deliverance by the hand of Your s,	Jg 15:18	5650
him his s and a pair of donkeys.	Jg 19:3	5288
go along with his concubine and s,	Jg 19:9	5288
and the s said to his master,	Jg 19:11	5288
He said to his s,	Jg 19:13	5288
Then Boaz said to his s who was in	Ru 2:5	5288
The s in charge of the reapers	Ru 2:6	5288
the priest's s would come while	1Sa 2:13	5288
the priest's s would come and say	1Sa 2:15	5288
LORD, for Your s is listening.'"	1Sa 3:9	5650
"Speak, for Your s is listening."	1Sa 3:10	5650
Saul said to his s who was with him,	1Sa 9:5	5288
Then Saul said to his s,	1Sa 9:7	5288
s answered Saul again and said,	1Sa 9:8	5288
Then Saul said to his s,	1Sa 9:10	5288
Then Samuel took Saul and his s	1Sa 9:22	5288
"Say to the s that he might go	1Sa 9:27	5288
Saul's uncle said to him and his s,	1Sa 10:14	5288
your s will go and fight with this	1Sa 17:32	5650
"Your s was tending his father's	1Sa 17:34	5650
"Your s has killed both the lion	1Sa 17:36	5650
your s Jesse the Bethlehemite."	1Sa 17:58	5650
the king sin against his s David,	1Sa 19:4	5650
'It is good,' your s *will be* safe;	1Sa 20:7	5650
"Therefore deal kindly with your s,	1Sa 20:8	5650
for you have brought your s into a	1Sa 20:8	5650
my son has stirred up my s against	1Sa 22:8	5650
let the king impute anything to his s	1Sa 22:15	5650
for your s knows nothing at all of	1Sa 22:15	5650
Your s has heard for certain that	1Sa 23:10	5650
come down just as Your s has heard?	1Sa 23:11	5650
of Israel, I pray, tell Your s."	1Sa 23:11	5650
and has kept back His s from evil.	1Sa 25:39	5650
then is my lord pursuing his s?	1Sa 26:18	5650
king listen to the words of his s.	1Sa 26:19	5650
for why should your s live in the	1Sa 27:5	5650
he will become my s forever."	1Sa 27:12	5650
shall know what your s can do."	1Sa 28:2	5650
the s of Saul the king of Israel,	1Sa 29:3	5650
And what have you found in your s	1Sa 29:8	5650
man of Egypt, a s of an Amalekite;	1Sa 30:13	5650
'By the hand of My s David I will	2Sa 3:18	5650
"Go and say to My s David,	2Sa 7:5	5650
thus you shall say to My s David,	2Sa 7:8	5650
s concerning the distant future.	2Sa 7:19	5650
For You know Your s,	2Sa 7:20	5650
this greatness to let Your s know.	2Sa 7:21	5650
concerning Your s and his house,	2Sa 7:25	5650
and may the house of Your s David	2Sa 7:26	5650
have made a revelation to Your s,	2Sa 7:27	5650
therefore Your s has found courage	2Sa 7:27	5650
promised this good thing to Your s.	2Sa 7:28	5650
You to bless the house of Your s,	2Sa 7:29	5650
house of Your s be blessed forever."	2Sa 7:29	5650
there was a s of the house of Saul	2Sa 9:2	5650
Ziba?" And he said, "*I am* your s."	2Sa 9:2	5650
"Here is your s!"	2Sa 9:6	5650
"What is your s, that you should	2Sa 9:8	5650
Then the king called Saul's s Ziba and	2Sa 9:9	5288
my lord the king commands his s	2Sa 9:11	5650
his servant so your s will do."	2Sa 9:11	5650
'Your s Uriah the Hittite is dead	2Sa 11:21	5650
and your s Uriah the Hittite is	2Sa 11:24	5650
now, your s has sheepshearers;	2Sa 13:24	5650
and his servants go with your s."	2Sa 13:24	5650
was your s Joab who commanded me,	2Sa 14:19	5650
your s Joab has done this thing.	2Sa 14:20	5650
"Today your s knows that I have	2Sa 14:22	5650
performed the request of his s."	2Sa 14:22	5650
"Your s is from one of the tribes	2Sa 15:2	5650
"For your s vowed a vow while I	2Sa 15:8	5650
life, there also your s will be."	2Sa 15:21	5650
'I will be your s, O king;	2Sa 15:34	5650
been your father's s in time past,	2Sa 15:34	5650
past, so I will now be your s,'	2Sa 15:34	5650
Ziba the s of Mephibosheth met him	2Sa 16:1	5288
"When Joab sent the king's s,	2Sa 18:29	5650
the king's servant, and your s,	2Sa 18:29	5650
Ziba the s of the house of Saul,	2Sa 19:17	5288
nor remember what your s did wrong	2Sa 19:19	5650
your s knows that I have sinned;	2Sa 19:20	5650
lord, the king, my s deceived me;	2Sa 19:26	5650
for your s said,	2Sa 19:26	5650
the king,' because your s is lame.	2Sa 19:26	5650
he has slandered your s to my lord	2Sa 19:27	5650
yet you set your s among those who	2Sa 19:28	5650
Or can your s taste what I eat or	2Sa 19:35	5650
Why then should your s be an added	2Sa 19:35	5650
"Your s would merely cross over	2Sa 19:36	5650
"Please let your s return, that I	2Sa 19:37	5650
However, here is your s Chimham,	2Sa 19:37	5650
take away the iniquity of Your s,	2Sa 24:10	5650
my lord the king come to his s?"	2Sa 24:21	5650
he has not invited Solomon your s.	1Ki 1:19	5650
"But me, *even* me your s,	1Ki 1:26	5650
of Jehoiada and your s Solomon,	1Ki 1:26	5650
his s to death with the sword.'"	1Ki 1:51	5650
has said, so your s will do."	1Ki 2:38	5650
to Your s David my father,	1Ki 3:6	5650
You have made Your s king in place	1Ki 3:7	5650
"Your s is in the midst of Your	1Ki 3:8	5650
"So give Your s an understanding	1Ki 3:9	5650
who have kept with Your s,	1Ki 8:24	5650
keep with Your s David my father	1Ki 8:25	5650
which You have spoken to Your s,	1Ki 8:26	5650
of Your s and to his supplication,	1Ki 8:28	5650
Your s prays before You today;	1Ki 8:28	5650
Your s shall pray toward this place.	1Ki 8:29	5650
of Your s and of Your people Israel,	1Ki 8:30	5650
be open to the supplication of Your s	1Ki 8:52	5650
spoke through Moses Your s,	1Ki 8:53	5650
He promised through Moses His s.	1Ki 8:56	5650
He may maintain the cause of His s	1Ki 8:59	5650
the LORD had shown to David His s	1Ki 8:66	5650
you, and will give it to your s.	1Ki 11:11	5650
your son for the sake of My s David	1Ki 11:13	5650
Ephraimite of Zeredah, Solomon's s,	1Ki 11:26	5650
for the sake of My s David and for	1Ki 11:32	5650
sake of My s David whom I chose,	1Ki 11:34	5650
that My s David may have a lamp	1Ki 11:36	5650
commandments, as My s David did,	1Ki 11:38	5650
will be a s to this people today,	1Ki 12:7	5650
you have not been like My s David,	1Ki 14:8	5650
through His s Ahijah the prophet.	1Ki 14:18	5650
by His s Ahijah the Shilonite,	1Ki 15:29	5650
His s Zimri, commander of half	1Ki 16:9	5650
your s into the hand of Ahab to	1Ki 18:9	5650
although *I* your s have feared the	1Ki 18:12	5650
in Israel and that I am Your s	1Ki 18:36	5650
He said to his s,	1Ki 18:43	5288
to Judah, and left his s there.	1Ki 19:3	5288
to your s at the first I will do,	1Ki 20:9	5650
"Your s Ben-hadad says,	1Ki 20:32	5650
"Your s went out into the midst	1Ki 20:39	5650
your s was busy here and there,	1Ki 20:40	5650
"Your s my husband is dead, and	2Ki 4:1	5650
know that your s feared the LORD;	2Ki 4:1	5650
Then he said to Gehazi his s,	2Ki 4:12	5288
And he said to his s,	2Ki 4:19	5288
a donkey and said to her s,	2Ki 4:24	5288
he said to Gehazi his s,	2Ki 4:25	5288
before him, he said to his s,	2Ki 4:38	5288
I have sent Naaman my s to you,	2Ki 5:6	5650
take a present from your s now."	2Ki 5:15	5650
please let your s at least be	2Ki 5:17	5650
for your s will no longer offer	2Ki 5:17	5650
matter may the LORD pardon your s:	2Ki 5:18	5650
LORD pardon your s in this matter."	2Ki 5:18	5650
the s of Elisha the man of God,	2Ki 5:20	5288
"Your s went nowhere."	2Ki 5:25	5650
And his s said to him,	2Ki 6:15	5288
Gehazi, the s of the man of God,	2Ki 8:4	5288
"But what is your s,	2Ki 8:13	5650
for the sake of David His s,	2Ki 8:19	5650
young man, the s of the prophet,	2Ki 9:4	5288
by His s Elijah the Tishbite,	2Ki 9:36	5650
He spoke through His s Elijah."	2Ki 10:10	5650
His s Jonah the son of Amittai,	2Ki 14:25	5650
"I am your s and your son;	2Ki 16:7	5650
Hoshea became his s and paid him	2Ki 17:3	5650
Moses the s of the LORD commanded;	2Ki 18:12	5650
sake and for My s David's sake.'"	2Ki 19:34	5650
and for My s David's sake.	2Ki 20:6	5650
that My s Moses commanded them."	2Ki 21:8	5650
and Asaiah the king's s saying,	2Ki 22:12	5650
Jehoiakim became his s *for* three	2Ki 24:1	5650
guard, a s of the king of Babylon,	2Ki 25:8	5650
Egyptian s whose name was Jarha.	1Ch 2:34	5650
gave his daughter to Jarha his s in	1Ch 2:35	5650
Moses the s of God had commanded.	1Ch 6:49	5650
O seed of Israel His s,	1Ch 16:13	5650
"Go and tell David My s,	1Ch 17:4	5650
thus shall you say to My s David,	1Ch 17:7	5650
the honor *bestowed* on Your s?	1Ch 17:18	5650
For You know Your s.	1Ch 17:18	5650
Your s and concerning his house be	1Ch 17:23	5650
Your s is established before You.'	1Ch 17:24	5650
have revealed to Your s that You	1Ch 17:25	5650
therefore Your s has found *courage*	1Ch 17:25	5650
promised this good thing to Your s.	1Ch 17:26	5650
You to bless the house of Your s,	1Ch 17:27	5650
take away the iniquity of Your s,	1Ch 21:8	5650
which Moses the s of the LORD had	2Ch 1:3	5650
who has kept with Your s David,	2Ch 6:15	5650
of Israel, keep with Your s David,	2Ch 6:16	5650
You have spoken to Your s David.	2Ch 6:17	5650
have regard to the prayer of Your s	2Ch 6:19	5650
which Your s prays before You;	2Ch 6:19	5650
s shall pray toward this place.	2Ch 6:20	5650
Listen to the supplications of Your s	2Ch 6:21	5650
lovingkindness to Your s David."	2Ch 6:42	5650
the s of Solomon the son of David,	2Ch 13:6	5650
levy *fixed by* Moses the s of the LORD	2Ch 24:6	5650
the levy *fixed by* Moses the s of God	2Ch 24:9	5650
God and against His s Hezekiah.	2Ch 32:16	5650
scribe, and Asaiah the king's s,	2Ch 34:20	5650
hear the prayer of Your s which I am	Ne 1:6	5650
You commanded Your s Moses.	Ne 1:7	5650
You commanded Your s Moses,	Ne 1:8	5650
be attentive to the prayer of Your s	Ne 1:11	5650
and make Your s successful today and	Ne 1:11	5650
your s has found favor before you,	Ne 2:5	5650
"Let each man with his s spend	Ne 4:22	5288
Then Sanballat sent his s to me in	Ne 6:5	5288
and law, Through Your s Moses.	Ne 9:14	5650
was given through Moses, God's s,	Ne 10:29	5650
"Have you considered My s Job?	Jb 1:8	5650
"Have you considered My s Job?	Jb 2:3	5650
"I call to my s, but he does not	Jb 19:16	5650
Will you take him for a s forever?	Jb 41:4	5650
Me what is right as My s Job has.	Jb 42:7	5650
seven rams, and go to My s Job,	Jb 42:8	5650
and My s Job will pray for you.	Jb 42:8	5650
what is right, as My s Job has."	Jb 42:8	5650
Moreover, by them Your s is warned;	Ps 19:11	5650
back Your s from presumptuous *sins;*	Ps 19:13	5650
Do not turn Your s away in anger;	Ps 27:9	5650
Make Your face to shine upon Your s;	Ps 31:16	5650
in the prosperity of His s."	Ps 35:27	5650
do not hide Your face from Your s,	Ps 69:17	5650
He also chose David His s And	Ps 78:70	5650
save Your s who trusts in You.	Ps 86:2	5650
Make glad the soul of Your s,	Ps 86:4	5650
Oh grant Your strength to Your s,	Ps 86:16	5650
I have sworn to David My s,	Ps 89:3	5650
"I have found David My s;	Ps 89:20	5650
spurned the covenant of Your s;	Ps 89:39	5650
O seed of Abraham, His s,	Ps 105:6	5650
He sent Moses His s,	Ps 105:26	5650
His holy word *With* Abraham His s;	Ps 105:42	5650
ashamed, But Your s shall be glad.	Ps 109:28	5650
O LORD, surely I am Your s,	Ps 116:16	5650
I am Your servant, I am Your s,	Ps 116:16	5650
Deal bountifully with Your s,	Ps 119:17	5650
Your s meditates on Your statutes.	Ps 119:23	5650
Establish Your word to Your s,	Ps 119:38	5650
Remember the word to Your s,	Ps 119:49	5650
You have dealt well with Your s,	Ps 119:65	5650
According to Your word to Your s.	Ps 119:76	5650
How many are the days of Your s?	Ps 119:84	5650
Be surety for Your s for good;	Ps 119:122	5650
Deal with Your s according to Your	Ps 119:124	5650
I am Your s; give me understanding,	Ps 119:125	5650
Make Your face shine upon Your s,	Ps 119:135	5650
pure, Therefore Your s loves it.	Ps 119:140	5650
seek Your s, For I do not forget	Ps 119:176	5650
For the sake of David Your s,	Ps 132:10	5650
Even a heritage to Israel His s,	Ps 136:22	5650
enter into judgment with Your s,	Ps 143:2	5650
who afflict my soul, For I am Your s.	Ps 143:12	5650
Who rescues David His s from	Ps 144:10	5650
foolish will be s to the wisehearted.	Pr 11:29	5650
is lightly esteemed and has a s Than	Pr 12:9	5650
is toward a s who acts wisely,	Pr 14:35	5650
A s who acts wisely will rule over	Pr 17:2	5650
you will not hear your s cursing you.	Ec 7:21	5650
"Even as My s Isaiah has gone	Is 20:3	5650
My s Eliakim the son of Hilkiah	Is 22:20	5650
the priest, the s like his master,	Is 24:2	5650
sake and for My s David's sake.'"	Is 37:35	5650
"But you, Israel, My s,	Is 41:8	5650
'You are My s, I have chosen you	Is 41:9	5650
"Behold, My S, whom I uphold;	Is 42:1	5650
Who is blind but My s,	Is 42:19	5650
Or so blind as the s of the LORD?	Is 42:19	5650
"And My s whom I have chosen, So	Is 43:10	5650
"But now listen, O Jacob, My s,	Is 44:1	5650
'Do not fear, O Jacob My s;	Is 44:2	5650
And Israel, for you are My s;	Is 44:21	5650
I have formed you, you are My s,	Is 44:21	5650
Confirming the word of His s And	Is 44:26	5650
"For the sake of Jacob My s,	Is 45:4	5650
LORD has redeemed His s Jacob."	Is 48:20	5650
"You are My S, Israel, In Whom I	Is 49:3	5650
Me from the womb to be His S,	Is 49:5	5650
You should be My S To raise up the	Is 49:6	5650
by the nation, To the S of rulers,	Is 49:7	5650
That obeys the voice of His s,	Is 50:10	5650
Behold, My s will prosper, He will	Is 52:13	5650
knowledge the Righteous One, My S,	Is 53:11	5650
Or is he a homeborn s?	Jer 2:14	5650
king of Babylon, My s,	Jer 25:9	5650
king of Babylon, My s,	Jer 27:6	5650
great kings will make him their s.	Jer 27:7	5647
'Fear not, O Jacob My s,'	Jer 30:10	5650
may also be broken with David My s	Jer 33:21	5650
the descendants of David My s	Jer 33:22	5650
of Jacob and David My s,	Jer 33:26	5650
each man should set free his male s	Jer 34:9	5650
servant and each man his female s,	Jer 34:9	8198
each man should set free his male s	Jer 34:10	5650
servant and each man his female s,	Jer 34:10	8198
and each man took back his male s	Jer 34:16	5650
servant and each man his female s whom	Jer 34:16	8198
the king of Babylon, My s,	Jer 43:10	5650
"But as for you, O Jacob My s,	Jer 46:27	5650
"O Jacob My s, do not fear,"	Jer 46:28	5650
land which I gave to My s Jacob.	Ezk 28:25	5650
them one shepherd, My s David,	Ezk 34:23	5650
and My s David will be prince	Ezk 34:24	5650
My s David will be king over them,	Ezk 37:24	5650
land that I gave to Jacob My s,	Ezk 37:25	5650
David My s will be their prince	Ezk 37:25	5650
"Daniel, s of the living God, has	Da 6:20	5649
in the law of Moses the s of God,	Da 9:11	5650
God, listen to the prayer of Your s	Da 9:17	5650
"For how can such a s of my lord	Da 10:17	5650
Zerubbabel, son of Shealtiel, My s,'	Hg 2:23	5650
going to bring in My s the Branch.	Zch 3:8	5650
his father, and a s his master.	Mal 1:6	5650
"Remember the law of Moses My s,	Mal 4:4	5650
my s is lying paralyzed at home,	Mt 8:6	*3816*
the word, and my s will be healed.	Mt 8:8	*3816*
the s was healed that *very* moment.	Mt 8:13	*3816*
"BEHOLD, MY S WHOM I HAVE CHOSEN;	Mt 12:18	*3816*
great among you shall be your s,	Mt 20:26	*1249*
among you shall be your s.	Mt 23:11	*1249*
be last of all and s of all."	Mk 9:35	*1249*
great among you shall be your s;	Mk 10:43	*1249*
"He has given help to Israel His s,	Lk 1:54	*3816*
us In the house of David His s	Lk 1:69	*3816*

the word, and my s will be healed. Lk 7:7 *3816*
"No s can serve two masters; Lk 16:13 *3610b*
youngest, and the leader like the s. Lk 22:26 *1247*
I am, there My s will be also; Jn 12:26 *1249*
has glorified His s Jesus, Ac 3:13 *3816*
you first, God raised up His S and Ac 3:26 *3816*
mouth of our father David Your s, Ac 4:25 *3816*
together against Your holy s Jesus, Ac 4:27 *3816*
the name of Your holy s Jesus." Ac 4:30 *3816*
are you to judge the s of another? Ro 14:4 *3610b*
For I say that Christ has become a s Ro 15:8 *1249*
who is a s of the church which is Ro 16:1 *1249*
s of Christ on our behalf, Col 1:7 *1249*
our beloved brother and faithful s Col 4:7 *1249*
will be a good s of Christ Jesus, 1Tm 4:6 *1249*
faithful in all His house as a s, Heb 3:5 *2324*
I am a fellow s of yours and your Rv 19:10 *4889*
I am a fellow s of yours and of Rv 22:9 *4889*

SERVANT-GIRL
a s came to him and said, Mt 26:69 *3814*
another s saw him and said to Mt 26:71
The s saw him, and began once more Mk 14:69 *3814*
And a s, seeing him as he Lk 22:56 *3814*
a s named Rhoda came to answer. Ac 12:13 *3814*

SERVANT-GIRLS
of the s of the high priest came, Mk 14:66 *3814*

SERVANT'S
turn aside into your s house, Gn 19:2 5650
according to your s word, 2Sa 13:35 5650
And the LORD opened the s eyes and 2Ki 6:17 5288
You have spoken of Your s house 1Ch 17:17 5650
"O LORD, for Your s sake, and 1Ch 17:19 5650

SERVANTS
A servant of s He shall be to his Gn 9:25 5650
s and female donkeys and camels. Gn 12:16 8198
them by night, he and his s, Gn 14:15 5650
and all *the* s who were born in Gn 17:23
and called all his s and told all these Gn 20:8 5650
and oxen and male and female s, Gn 20:14 5650, 8198
the s of Abimelech had seized. Gn 21:25 5650
silver and gold, and s and maids, Gn 24:35 5650
wells which his father's s had dug Gn 26:15 5650
But when Isaac's s dug in the Gn 26:19 5650
and there Isaac's s dug a well. Gn 26:25 5650
that Isaac's s came in and told Gn 26:32 5650
I have given to him as s; Gn 27:37 5650
and male s and camels and donkeys. Gn 30:43 5650, 8198
and flocks and male and female s; Gn 32:5 5650, 8198
them into the hand of his s, Gn 32:16 5650
by itself, and said to his s, Gn 32:16 5650
he made a feast for all his s; Gn 40:20 5650
of the chief baker among his s. Gn 40:20 5650
"Pharaoh was furious with his s, Gn 41:10 5650
good to Pharaoh and to all his s. Gn 41:37 5650
Then Pharaoh said to his s, Gn 41:38 5650
but your s have come to buy food. Gn 42:10 5650
men, your s are not spies." Gn 42:11 5650
"Your s are twelve brothers *in* Gn 42:13 5650
Far be it from your s to do such a Gn 44:7 5650
whomever of your s it is found, Gn 44:9 5650
found out the iniquity of your s; Gn 44:16 5650
"My lord asked his s, Gn 44:19 5650
"Then you said to your s, Gn 44:21 5650
"You said to your s, Gn 44:23 5650
Thus your s will bring the gray Gn 44:31 5650
it pleased Pharaoh and his s. Gn 45:16 5650
'Your s have been keepers of Gn 46:34 5650
"Your s are shepherds, both we Gn 47:3 5650
s live in the land of Goshen." Gn 47:4 5650
Joseph commanded his s the Gn 50:2 5650
him went up all the s of Pharaoh, Gn 50:7 5650
the s of the God of your father." Gn 50:17 5650
"Behold, we are your s." Gn 50:18 5650
do you deal this way with your s? Ex 5:15 5650
"There is no straw given to your s, Ex 5:16 5650
behold, your s are being beaten; Ex 5:16 5650
sight and in the sight of his s, Ex 5:21 5650
down before Pharaoh and his s, Ex 7:10 5650
Pharaoh and in the sight of his s, Ex 7:20 5650
of your s and on your people, Ex 8:3 5650
your people and all your s. Ex 8:4 5650
you and your s and your people, Ex 8:9 5650
houses and your s and your people; Ex 8:11 5650
insects on you and on your s Ex 8:21 5650
Pharaoh and the houses of his s Ex 8:24 5650
depart from Pharaoh, from his s, Ex 8:29 5650
from his s and from his people; Ex 8:31 5650
on you and your s and your people, Ex 9:14 5650
The one among the s of Pharaoh who Ex 9:20 5650
made his s and his livestock flee Ex 9:20 5650
left his s and his livestock in the field. Ex 9:21 5650
"But as for you and your s, Ex 9:30 5650
hardened his heart, he and his s. Ex 9:34 5650
his heart and the heart of his s, Ex 10:1 5650
and the houses of all your s and Ex 10:6 5650
Pharaoh's s said to him, Ex 10:7 5650
both in the sight of Pharaoh's s Ex 11:3 5650
"All these your s will come Ex 11:8 5650
all his s and all the Egyptians, Ex 12:30 5650
Pharaoh and his s had a change of Ex 14:5 5650
Your s to whom You swore by Ex 32:13 5650
'For they are My s whom I brought Lv 25:42 5650
'For the sons of Israel are My s; Lv 25:55 5650
they are My s whom I brought out Lv 25:55 5650
replied to the s of Balak, Nu 22:18 5650

and his two s were with him. Nu 22:22 5288
"Your s have taken a census of Nu 31:49 5650
and your s have livestock." Nu 32:4 5650
let this land be given to your s as a Nu 32:5 5650
"Your s will do just as my lord Nu 32:25 5650
while your s, everyone who is Nu 32:27 5650
"As the LORD has said to your s, Nu 32:31 5650
'Remember Your s, Abraham, Isaac, Dt 9:27 5650
daughters, your male and female s, Dt 12:12 5650, 519
and your male and female s, Dt 12:18 5650, 519
daughter and your male and female s Dt 16:11 5650, 519
male and female s and the Levite Dt 16:14 5650, 519
and all his s and all his land; Dt 29:2 5650
And will have compassion on His s, Dt 32:36 5650
He will avenge the blood of His s, Dt 32:43 5650
Egypt against Pharaoh, all his s, Dt 34:11 5650
they said to Joshua, "We are your s." Jos 9:8 5650
"Your s have come from a very far Jos 9:9 5650
and say to them, "We are your s; Jos 9:11 5650
certainly told your s that the LORD Jos 9:24 5650
"Do not abandon your s; Jos 10:6 5650
gone out, his s came and looked, Jg 3:24 5650
Then Gideon took ten men of his s Jg 6:27 5650
the young man who is with your s; Jg 19:19 5650
commanded the s not to touch you. Ru 2:9 5288
and drink from what the s draw." Ru 2:9 5288
to glean, Boaz commanded his s, Ru 2:15 5288
'You should stay close to my s Ru 2:21 5288
groves and give *them* to his s. 1Sa 8:14 5650
give to his officers and to his s. 1Sa 8:15 5650
"He will also take your male s 1Sa 8:16 5650
female s and your best young men 1Sa 8:16 8198
you yourselves will become his s. 1Sa 8:17 5650
"Take now with you one of the s, 1Sa 9:3 5288
"Pray for your s to the LORD your 1Sa 12:19 5650
Saul's s then said to him, 1Sa 16:15 5650
command your s who are before you. 1Sa 16:16 5650
So Saul said to his s, 1Sa 16:17 5650
the Philistine and you s of Saul? 1Sa 17:8 5650
me, then we will become your s; 1Sa 17:9 5650
shall become our s and serve us." 1Sa 17:9 5650
and also in the sight of Saul's s. 1Sa 18:5 5650
Then Saul commanded his s, 1Sa 18:22 5650
in you, and all his s love you; 1Sa 18:22 5650
Saul's s spoke these words to David. 1Sa 18:23 5650
The s of Saul reported to him 1Sa 18:24 5650
When his s told David these words, 1Sa 18:26 5650
wisely than all the s of Saul. 1Sa 18:30 5650
all his s to put David to death. 1Sa 19:1 5650
the s of Saul was there that day, 1Sa 21:7 5650
But the s of Achish said to him, 1Sa 21:11 5650
Then Achish said to his s, 1Sa 21:14 5650
his s were standing around him. 1Sa 22:6 5650
Saul said to his s who stood around 1Sa 22:7 5650
who was standing by the s of Saul, 1Sa 22:9 5650
your s is as faithful as David, 1Sa 22:14 5650
But the s of the king were not 1Sa 22:17 5650
your s and to your son David.' " 1Sa 25:8 5650
But Nabal answered David's s and 1Sa 25:10 5650
There are many s today who are 1Sa 25:10 5650
When the s of David came to 1Sa 25:40 5650
to wash the feet of my lord's s." 1Sa 25:41 5650
Then Saul said to his s, 1Sa 28:7 5650
And his s said to him, 1Sa 28:7 5650
his s together with the woman 1Sa 28:23 5650
brought *it* before Saul and his s, 1Sa 28:25 5650
arise early in the morning with the s 1Sa 29:10 5650
the s of Ish-bosheth the son of Saul. 2Sa 2:12 5650
s of David went out and met them 2Sa 2:13 5650
and twelve of the s of David. 2Sa 2:15 5650
were beaten before the s of David. 2Sa 2:17 5650
nineteen of David's s besides Asahel 2Sa 2:30 5650
But the s of David had struck down 2Sa 2:31 5650
the s of David and Joab came from 2Sa 3:22 5650
Then the king said to his s, 2Sa 3:38 5650
the Moabites became s to David, 2Sa 8:2 5650
the Arameans became s to David, 2Sa 8:6 5650
carried by the s of Hadadezer and 2Sa 8:7 5650
the Edomites became s to David. 2Sa 8:14 5650
"You and your sons and your s 2Sa 9:10 5650
had fifteen sons and twenty s. 2Sa 9:10 5650
of Ziba were s to Mephibosheth. 2Sa 9:12 5650
So David sent some of his s to 2Sa 10:2 5650
But when David's s came to the 2Sa 10:2 5650
Has David not sent his s to you in 2Sa 10:3 5650
So Hanun took David's s and shaved 2Sa 10:4 5650
all the kings, s of Hadadezer, 2Sa 10:19 5650
and his s with him and all Israel, 2Sa 11:1 5650
house with all the s of his lord, 2Sa 11:9 5650
and my lord Joab and the s of my 2Sa 11:11 5650
lie on his bed with his lord's s, 2Sa 11:13 5650
of the people among David's s fell; 2Sa 11:17 5650
shot at your s from the wall; 2Sa 11:24 5650
so some of the king's s are dead, 2Sa 11:24 5650
And the s of David were afraid to 2Sa 12:18 5650
his s were whispering together, 2Sa 12:19 5650
so David said to his s, 2Sa 12:19 5650
Then his s said to him, 2Sa 12:21 5650
and his s go with your servant." 2Sa 13:24 5650
Absalom commanded his s, 2Sa 13:28 5288
The s of Absalom did to Amnon 2Sa 13:29 5288
and all his s were standing by 2Sa 13:31 5650
and all his s wept very bitterly. 2Sa 13:36 5650
Therefore he said to his s, 2Sa 14:30 5650
Absalom's s set the field on fire. 2Sa 14:30 5650

Why have your s set my field on fire 2Sa 14:31 5650
David said to all his s who 2Sa 15:14 5650
Then the king's s said to the king, 2Sa 15:15 5650
your s *are ready to do* whatever my 2Sa 15:15 5650
all his s passed on beside him, 2Sa 15:18 5650
and at all the s of King David; 2Sa 16:6 5650
said to Abishai and to all his s, 2Sa 16:11 5650
Then Absalom's s came to the woman 2Sa 17:20 5650
there before the s of David, 2Sa 18:7 5650
happened to meet the s of David. 2Sa 18:9 5650
shame the faces of all your s, 2Sa 19:5 5650
princes and s are nothing to you; 2Sa 19:6 5650
go out and speak kindly to your s, 2Sa 19:7 5650
"Return, you and all your s." 2Sa 19:14 5650
sons and his twenty s with him; 2Sa 19:17 5650
take your lord's s and pursue him, 2Sa 20:6 5650
went down and his s with him; 2Sa 21:15 5650
of David and by the hand of his s. 2Sa 21:22 5650
his s crossing over toward him; 2Sa 24:20 5650
So his s said to him, 1Ki 1:2 5650
all the men of Judah, the king's s. 1Ki 1:9 5650
and you have not shown to your s 1Ki 1:27 5650
"Take with you the s of your lord, 1Ki 1:33 5650
the king's s came to bless our 1Ki 1:47 5650
that two of the s of Shimei ran 1Ki 2:39 5650
"Behold, your s are in Gath." 1Ki 2:39 5650
Gath to Achish to look for his s. 1Ki 2:40 5650
went and brought his s from Gath. 1Ki 2:40 5650
and made a feast for all his s. 1Ki 3:15 5650
of Tyre sent his s to Solomon, 1Ki 5:1 5650
my s will be with your servants; 1Ki 5:6 5650
my servants will be with your s; 1Ki 5:6 5650
I will give you wages for your s 1Ki 5:6 5650
"My s will bring *them* down from 1Ki 5:9 5650
showing lovingkindness to Your s 1Ki 8:23 5650
in heaven and act and judge Your s, 1Ki 8:32 5650
of Your s and of Your people Israel, 1Ki 8:36 5650
for they were men of war, his s, 1Ki 9:22 5650
Hiram sent his s with the fleet, 1Ki 9:27 5650
sea, along with the s of Solomon. 1Ki 9:27 5650
his table, the seating of his s, 1Ki 10:5 5650
how blessed are these your s who 1Ki 10:8 5650
her own land together with her s. 1Ki 10:13 5650
of his father's s with him, 1Ki 11:17 5650
they will be your s forever." 1Ki 12:7 5650
them into the hand of his s. 1Ki 15:18 5650
tomorrow I will send my s to you, 1Ki 20:6 5650
house and the houses of your s; 1Ki 20:6 5650
shelters, he said to his s, 1Ki 20:12 5650
Now the s of the king of Aram said 1Ki 20:23 5650
His s said to him, 1Ki 20:31 5650
the king of Israel said to his s, 1Ki 22:3 5650
"Let my s go with your servants 1Ki 22:49 5650
go with your s in the ships." 1Ki 22:49 5650
and the lives of these fifty s of yours 2Ki 1:13 5650
are with your s fifty strong men, 2Ki 2:16 5650
of Israel's s answered and said, 2Ki 3:11 5650
of the s and one of the donkeys, 2Ki 4:22 5288
Then his s came near and spoke to 2Ki 5:13 5650
and gave them to two of his s; 2Ki 5:23 5288
and oxen and male and female s? 2Ki 5:26 5650, 8198
be willing to go with your s." 2Ki 6:3 5650
he counseled with his s saying, 2Ki 6:8 5650
he called his s and said to them, 2Ki 6:11 5650
One of his s said, 2Ki 6:12 5650
in the night and said to his s, 2Ki 7:12 5650
One of his s said, 2Ki 7:13 5650
the blood of My s the prophets, 2Ki 9:7 5650
blood of all the s of the LORD, 2Ki 9:7 5650
came out to the s of his master, 2Ki 9:11 5650
Then his s carried him in a 2Ki 9:28 5650
"We are your s, all that you say 2Ki 10:5 5650
you none of the s of the LORD, 2Ki 10:23 5650
His s arose and made a conspiracy 2Ki 12:20 5650
the son of Shomer, his s, 2Ki 12:21 5650
that he killed his s who had slain 2Ki 14:5 5650
you through My s the prophets." 2Ki 17:13 5650
through all His s the prophets. 2Ki 17:23 5650
of the least of my master's s, 2Ki 18:24 5650
"Speak now to your s in Aramaic, 2Ki 18:26 5650
So the s of King Hezekiah came to 2Ki 19:5 5650
with which the s of the king of 2Ki 19:6 5288
spoke through His s the prophets, 2Ki 21:10 5650
The s of Amon conspired 2Ki 21:23 5650
"Your s have emptied out the 2Ki 22:9 5650
His s drove his body in a 2Ki 23:30 5650
spoken through His s the prophets. 2Ki 24:2 5650
the s of Nebuchadnezzar king of 2Ki 24:10 5650
while his s were besieging it. 2Ki 24:11 5650
he and his mother and his s and 2Ki 24:12 5650
afraid of the s of the Chaldeans; 2Ki 25:24 5650
the Levites and the temple s. 1Ch 9:2 5411
the Moabites became s to David, 1Ch 18:2 5650
the Arameans became s to David, 1Ch 18:6 5650
carried by the s of Hadadezer and 1Ch 18:7 5650
the Edomites became s to David. 1Ch 18:13 5650
And David's s came into the land 1Ch 19:2 5650
Have not his s come to you to 1Ch 19:3 5650
took David's s and shaved them and 1Ch 19:4 5650
So when the s of Hadadezer saw 1Ch 19:19 5650
of David and by the hand of his s. 1Ch 20:8 5650
king, are they not all my lord's s? 1Ch 21:3 5650
for I know that your s know how to 2Ch 2:8 5650
my s *will work* with your servants, 2Ch 2:8 5650
my servants *will work* with your s, 2Ch 2:8 5650
"Now behold, I will give to your s, 2Ch 2:10 5650
send to his s wheat and barley, 2Ch 2:15 5650
and *showing* lovingkindness to Your s 2Ch 6:14 5650

heaven and act and judge Your **s**,	**2Ch 6:23**	5650
of Your **s** and Your people Israel,	**2Ch 6:27**	5650
And Huram by his **s** sent him ships	**2Ch 8:18**	5650
him ships and **s** who knew the sea;	**2Ch 8:18**	5650
went with Solomon's **s** to Ophir,	**2Ch 8:18**	5650
his table, the seating of his **s**,	**2Ch 9:4**	5650
how blessed are these your **s** who	**2Ch 9:7**	5650
The **s** of Huram and the	**2Ch 9:10**	5650
the **s** of Solomon who brought gold	**2Ch 9:10**	5650
went to her own land with her **s**.	**2Ch 9:12**	5650
to Tarshish with the **s** of Huram;	**2Ch 9:21**	5650
they will be your **s** forever."	**2Ch 10:7**	5650
his own **s** conspired against him	**2Ch 24:25**	5650
that he killed his **s** who had slain	**2Ch 25:3**	5650
king of Assyria sent his **s** to Jerusalem	**2Ch 32:9**	5650
His **s** spoke further against	**2Ch 32:16**	5650
Finally his **s** conspired against	**2Ch 33:24**	5650
to your **s** they are doing.	**2Ch 34:16**	5650
and the king said to his **s**,	**2Ch 35:23**	5650
So his **s** took him out of the	**2Ch 35:24**	5650
and they were **s** to him and to his	**2Ch 36:20**	5650
The temple **s**: the sons of Ziha,	**Ezr 2:43**	5411
The sons of Solomon's **s**:	**Ezr 2:55**	5650
All the temple **s** and the sons of	**Ezr 2:58**	5411
and the sons of Solomon's **s** were	**Ezr 2:58**	5650
besides their male and female **s** who	**Ezr 2:65**	5650, 519
temple **s** lived in their cities,	**Ezr 2:70**	5411
Your **s**, the men in the region	**Ezr 4:11**	5649
'We are the **s** of the God of heaven	**Ezr 5:11**	5649
and the temple **s** went up to	**Ezr 7:7**	5411
or **s** of this house of God.	**Ezr 7:24**	6399
temple **s** at the place Casiphia,	**Ezr 8:17**	5411
and 220 of the temple **s**,	**Ezr 8:20**	5411
commanded by Your **s** the prophets,	**Ezr 9:11**	5650
of the sons of Israel Your **s**,	**Ne 1:6**	5650
"They are Your **s** and Your	**Ne 1:10**	5650
prayer of Your **s** who delight to revere	**Ne 1:11**	5650
we His **s** will arise and build,	**Ne 2:20**	5650
The temple **s** living in Ophel	**Ne 3:26**	5411
the temple **s** and of the merchants,	**Ne 3:31**	5411
half of my **s** carried on the	**Ne 4:16**	5288
So neither I, my brothers, my **s**,	**Ne 4:23**	5288
likewise I, my brothers and my **s** are	**Ne 5:10**	5288
their **s** domineered the people.	**Ne 5:15**	5288
and all my **s** were gathered there	**Ne 5:16**	5288
The temple **s**: the sons of Ziha,	**Ne 7:46**	5411
The sons of Solomon's **s**:	**Ne 7:57**	5650
All the temple **s** and the sons of	**Ne 7:60**	5411
the sons of Solomon's **s** *were* 392.	**Ne 7:60**	5650
their male and their female **s**,	**Ne 7:67**	5650, 519
some of the people, the temple **s** and	**Ne 7:73**	5411
Against all his **s** and all the	**Ne 9:10**	5650
the singers, the temple **s** and	**Ne 10:28**	5411
the temple **s** and the descendants	**Ne 11:3**	5411
and the descendants of Solomon's **s**.	**Ne 11:3**	5650
the temple **s** were living in Ophel,	**Ne 11:21**	5411
were in charge of the temple **s**.	**Ne 11:21**	5411
Then I stationed some of my **s** at	**Ne 13:19**	5288
for all his princes and his **s**;	**Es 2:18**	5650
All the king's **s** who were at	**Es 3:2**	5650
Then the king's **s** who were at the	**Es 3:3**	5650
"All the king's **s** and the people	**Es 4:11**	5650
the princes and **s** of the king.	**Es 5:11**	5650
the king's **s** who attended him said,	**Es 6:3**	5288
The king's **s** said to him,	**Es 6:5**	5288
female donkeys, and very many **s**;	**Jb 1:3**	5657
the **s** with the edge of the sword,	**Jb 1:15**	5288
sheep and the **s** and consumed them,	**Jb 1:16**	5288
the **s** with the edge of the sword,	**Jb 1:17**	5288
'He puts no trust even in His **s**;	**Jb 4:18**	5650
LORD redeems the soul of His **s**,	**Ps 34:22**	5650
descendants of His **s** will inherit it,	**Ps 69:36**	5650
bodies of Your **s** for food to the birds	**Ps 79:2**	5650
Vengeance for the blood of Your **s** which	**Ps 79:10**	5650
O Lord, the reproach of Your **s**;	**Ps 89:50**	5650
And be sorry for Your **s**.	**Ps 90:13**	5650
Let Your work appear to Your **s**	**Ps 90:16**	5650
Your **s** find pleasure in her stones And	**Ps 102:14**	5650
children of Your **s** will continue,	**Ps 102:28**	5650
To deal craftily with His **s**.	**Ps 105:25**	5650
Praise, O **s** of the LORD,	**Ps 113:1**	5650
For all things are Your **s**.	**Ps 119:91**	5650
as the eyes of **s** *look* to the hand	**Ps 123:2**	5650
bless the LORD, all **s** of the LORD,	**Ps 134:1**	5650
Praise *Him*, O **s** of the LORD,	**Ps 135:1**	5650
Egypt, Upon Pharaoh and all his **s**.	**Ps 135:9**	5650
And will have compassion on His **s**.	**Ps 135:14**	5650
as male **s** and female servants;	**Is 14:2**	5650
as male servants and female **s**;	**Is 14:2**	5650, 8198
of the least of my master's **s** and	**Is 36:9**	5650
"Speak now to your **s** in Aramaic,	**Is 36:11**	5650
So the **s** of King Hezekiah came to	**Is 37:5**	5650
with which the **s** of the king of	**Is 37:6**	5288
s you have reproached the Lord,	**Is 37:24**	5650
the heritage of the **s** of the LORD,	**Is 54:17**	5650
the name of the LORD, To be His **s**,	**Is 56:6**	5650
Return for the sake of Your **s**,	**Is 63:17**	5650
So I will act on behalf of My **s** In	**Is 65:8**	5650
it, And My **s** will dwell there.	**Is 65:9**	5650
"Behold, My **s** will eat, but you	**Is 65:13**	5650
Behold, My **s** will drink, but you	**Is 65:13**	5650
Behold, My **s** will rejoice, but	**Is 65:13**	5650
My **s** will shout joyfully with a	**Is 65:14**	5650
But My **s** will be called by another	**Is 65:15**	5650
LORD will be made known to His **s**,	**Is 66:14**	5650
sent you all My **s** the prophets,	**Jer 7:25**	5650

have sent their **s** for water;	**Jer 14:3**	6810
of Judah and his **s** and the people,	**Jer 21:7**	5650
you and your **s** and your people who	**Jer 22:2**	5650
himself and his **s** and his people.	**Jer 22:4**	5650
the LORD has sent to you all His **s**	**Jer 25:4**	5650
Pharaoh king of Egypt, his **s**,	**Jer 25:19**	5650
to the words of My **s** the prophets,	**Jer 26:5**	5650
and again by My **s** the prophets;	**Jer 29:19**	5650
male **s** and the female servants whom	**Jer 34:11**	5650
male servants and the female **s** whom	**Jer 34:11**	8198
male **s** and for female servants.	**Jer 34:11**	5650
male servants and for female **s**.	**Jer 34:11**	8198
male **s** and female servants."	**Jer 34:16**	5650
male servants and female **s**."	**Jer 34:16**	8198
sent to you all My **s** the prophets,	**Jer 35:15**	5650
Yet the king and all his **s** who	**Jer 36:24**	5650
and his **s** for their iniquity,	**Jer 36:31**	5650
But neither he nor his **s** nor the	**Jer 37:2**	5650
against you, or against your **s**,	**Jer 37:18**	5650
I sent you all My **s** the prophets,	**Jer 44:4**	5650
My **s** the prophets of Israel,	**Ezk 38:17**	5650
his inheritance to one of his **s**,	**Ezk 46:17**	5650
"Please test your **s** for ten days,	**Da 1:12**	5650
deal with your **s** according to what	**Da 1:13**	5650
Tell the dream to your **s**,	**Da 2:4**	5649
the king tell the dream to his **s**,	**Da 2:7**	5649
out, you **s** of the Most High God,	**Da 3:26**	5649
His **s** who put their trust in Him,	**Da 3:28**	5649
listened to Your **s** the prophets,	**Da 9:6**	5650
us through His **s** the prophets.	**Da 9:10**	5650
on the male and female **s** I will pour	**Jl 2:29**	5650, 8198
counsel To His **s** the prophets.	**Am 3:7**	5650
I commanded My **s** the prophets,	**Zch 1:6**	5650
and said to his **s**,	**Mt 14:2**	3816
"Then the king said to the **s**,	**Mt 22:13**	1249
in the boat with the hired **s**,	**Mk 1:20**	3411
were eyewitnesses and **s** of the word	**Lk 1:2**	5257
will put in charge of his **s**,	**Lk 12:42**	2322
"And he summoned one of the **s** and	**Lk 15:26**	3816
His mother said to the **s**,	**Jn 2:5**	1249
s who had drawn the water knew),	**Jn 2:9**	1249
then My **s** would be fighting so	**Jn 18:36**	5257
he summoned two of his **s** and a	**Ac 10:7**	3610b
taxes, for *rulers* are **s** of God,	**Ro 13:6**	3011
S through whom you believed, even	**1Co 3:5**	1249
us in this manner, as **s** of Christ and	**1Co 4:1**	5257
adequate *as* **s** of a new covenant,	**2Co 3:6**	1249
commending ourselves as **s** of God,	**2Co 6:4**	1249
is not surprising if his **s** also disguise	**2Co 11:15**	1249
themselves as **s** of righteousness,	**2Co 11:15**	1249
Are they **s** of Christ?	**2Co 11:23**	1249
S, be submissive to your masters	**1Pe 2:18**	3610b
until *the number of* their fellow **s** and	**Rv 6:11**	4889
He preached to His **s** the prophets.	**Rv 10:7**	1401

SERVANTS'

is no pasture for your **s** flocks,	**Gn 47:4**	5650
today in the eyes of his **s** maids	**2Sa 6:20**	5650

SERVE

judge the nation whom they will **s**,	**Gn 15:14**	5647
the older shall **s** the younger."	**Gn 25:23**	5647
May peoples **s** you, And nations bow	**Gn 27:29**	5647
And your brother you shall **s**;	**Gn 27:40**	5647
you therefore **s** me for nothing?	**Gn 29:15**	5647
"I will **s** you seven years for	**Gn 29:18**	5647
you shall **s** with me for another seven	**Gn 29:27**	5647
and said, "**S** the meal."	**Gn 43:31**	7760
'Let My son go that he may **s** Me';	**Ex 4:23**	5647
they may **s** Me in the wilderness.	**Ex 7:16**	5647
My people go, that they may **s** Me.	**Ex 8:1**	5647
My people go, that they may **s** Me.	**Ex 8:20**	5647
My people go, that they may **s** Me.	**Ex 9:1**	5647
My people go, that they may **s** Me.	**Ex 9:13**	5647
My people go, that they may **s** Me.	**Ex 10:3**	5647
they may **s** the LORD their God.	**Ex 10:7**	5647
"Go, **s** the LORD your God!	**Ex 10:8**	5647
the men *among you*, and **s** the LORD,	**Ex 10:11**	5647
to Moses, and said, "Go, **s** the LORD;	**Ex 10:24**	5647
of them to **s** the LORD our God.	**Ex 10:26**	5647
with what we shall **s** the LORD."	**Ex 10:26**	5647
s as a sign to you on your hand,	**Ex 13:9**	1961
it shall **s** as a sign on your hand and	**Ex 13:16**	1961
that we may **s** the Egyptians'?	**Ex 14:12**	5647
been better for us to **s** the Egyptians	**Ex 14:12**	5647
shall not worship them or **s** them;	**Ex 20:5**	5647
slave, he shall **s** for six years;	**Ex 21:2**	5647
and he shall **s** him permanently.	**Ex 21:6**	5647
worship their gods, nor **s** them,	**Ex 23:24**	5647
"But you shall **s** the LORD your	**Ex 23:25**	5647
for *if* you **s** their gods, it will	**Ex 23:33**	5647
and the veil shall **s** for you as a	**Ex 26:33**	914
that they may **s** Me as priests.	**Ex 28:41**	3547
them to **s** as priests to the LORD.	**Lv 7:35**	3547
anointed and ordained to **s** as priest	**Lv 16:32**	3547
he shall **s** with you until the year	**Lv 25:40**	5647
whom he ordained to **s** as priests.	**Nu 3:3**	3547
the priest, that they may **s** him.	**Nu 3:6**	8334
oil vessels, by which they **s** it;	**Nu 4:9**	8334
which they **s** in the sanctuary,	**Nu 4:12**	8334
they **s** in connection with it:	**Nu 4:14**	8334
go in to **s** the tent of meeting.	**Nu 8:15**	5647
may be joined with you and **s** you,	**Nu 18:2**	8334
away and worship them and **s** them,	**Dt 4:19**	5647
"There you will **s** gods,	**Dt 4:28**	5647
shall not worship them or **s** them;	**Dt 5:9**	5647
from following Me to **s** other gods;	**Dt 7:4**	5647
nor shall you **s** their gods,	**Dt 7:16**	5647
gods and **s** them and worship them,	**Dt 8:19**	5647

to stand before the LORD to **s** Him	**Dt 10:8**	8334
and to **s** the LORD your God with	**Dt 10:12**	5647
you shall **s** Him and cling to Him,	**Dt 10:20**	5647
to **s** Him with all your heart and all	**Dt 11:13**	5647
and **s** other gods and worship them.	**Dt 11:16**	5647
nations whom you shall dispossess **s**	**Dt 12:2**	5647
'How do these nations **s** their gods,	**Dt 12:30**	5647
and let us **s** them,'	**Dt 13:2**	5647
listen to His voice, **s** Him,	**Dt 13:4**	5647
'Let us go and **s** other gods'	**Dt 13:6**	5647
'Let us go and **s** other gods'	**Dt 13:13**	5647
then he shall **s** you six years,	**Dt 15:12**	5647
there to **s** the LORD your God,	**Dt 17:12**	8334
to stand and **s** in the name of the	**Dt 18:5**	8334
then he shall **s** in the name of the	**Dt 18:7**	8334
your forced labor and shall **s** you.	**Dt 20:11**	5647
your God has chosen them to **s** Him	**Dt 21:5**	8334
to go after other gods to **s** them.	**Dt 28:14**	5647
and there you shall **s** other gods,	**Dt 28:36**	5647
"Because you did not **s** the LORD	**Dt 28:47**	5647
therefore you shall **s** your enemies	**Dt 28:48**	5647
and there you shall **s** other gods,	**Dt 28:64**	5647
and **s** the gods of those nations;	**Dt 29:18**	5647
and worship other gods and **s** them,	**Dt 30:17**	5647
turn to other gods and **s** them,	**Dt 31:20**	5647
s Him with all your heart and with	**Jos 22:5**	5647
anyone swear by them, or **s** them,	**Jos 23:7**	5647
you, and go and **s** other gods and	**Jos 23:16**	5647
and **s** Him in sincerity and truth;	**Jos 24:14**	5647
and in Egypt, and **s** the LORD.	**Jos 24:14**	5647
in your sight to **s** the LORD,	**Jos 24:15**	5647
yourselves today whom you will **s**:	**Jos 24:15**	5647
my house, we will **s** the LORD."	**Jos 24:15**	5647
forsake the LORD to **s** other gods;	**Jos 24:16**	5647
We also will **s** the LORD, for He is	**Jos 24:18**	5647
will not be able to **s** the LORD,	**Jos 24:19**	5647
the LORD and **s** foreign gods,	**Jos 24:20**	5647
"No, but we will **s** the LORD."	**Jos 24:21**	5647
yourselves the LORD, to **s** Him."	**Jos 24:22**	5647
"We will **s** the LORD our God and	**Jos 24:24**	5647
to **s** them and bow down to them;	**Jg 2:19**	5647
is Shechem, that we should **s** him?	**Jg 9:28**	5647
S the men of Hamor the father of	**Jg 9:28**	5647
but why should we **s** him?	**Jg 9:28**	5647
Abimelech that we should **s** him?'	**Jg 9:38**	5647
forsook the LORD and did not **s** Him	**Jg 10:6**	5647
to the LORD and **s** Him alone;	**1Sa 7:3**	5647
with us and we will **s** you."	**1Sa 11:1**	5647
our enemies, and we will **s** You.'	**1Sa 12:10**	5647
you will fear the LORD and **s** Him,	**1Sa 12:14**	5647
s the LORD with all your heart.	**1Sa 12:20**	5647
"Only fear the LORD and **s** Him in	**1Sa 12:24**	5647
become our servants and **s** us."	**1Sa 17:9**	5647
'Go, **s** other gods.'	**1Sa 26:19**	5647
then I will **s** the LORD.' "	**2Sa 15:8**	5647
"Besides, whom should I **s**?	**2Sa 16:19**	5647
Should I not **s** in	**2Sa 16:19**	
people whom I have not known **s** me.	**2Sa 22:44**	5647
and **s** other gods and worship them,	**1Ki 9:6**	5647
he put on us, and we will **s** you."	**1Ki 12:4**	5647
to this people today, and will **s** them	**1Ki 12:7**	5647
went to **s** Baal and worshiped him.	**1Ki 16:31**	5647
Jehu will **s** him much.	**2Ki 10:18**	5647
nor **s** them nor sacrifice to them.	**2Ki 17:35**	5647
king of Assyria and did not **s** him.	**2Ki 18:7**	5647
land and **s** the king of Babylon,	**2Ki 25:24**	5647
and **s** Him with a whole heart and a	**1Ch 28:9**	5647
and **s** other gods and worship them,	**2Ch 7:19**	5647
he put on us, and we will **s** you."	**2Ch 10:4**	5647
forever, and **s** the LORD your God,	**2Ch 30:8**	5647
Judah to **s** the LORD God of Israel.	**2Ch 33:16**	5647
in Israel to **s** the LORD their God.	**2Ch 34:33**	5647
Now **s** the LORD your God and His	**2Ch 35:3**	5647
Did not **s** You or turn from their	**Ne 9:35**	5647
Almighty, that we should **s** Him,	**Jb 21:15**	5647
"If they hear and **s** *Him*,	**Jb 36:11**	5647
"Will the wild ox consent to **s** you,	**Jb 39:9**	5647
people whom I have not known **s** me.	**Ps 18:43**	5647
Posterity will **s** Him;	**Ps 22:30**	5647
before him, All nations **s** him.	**Ps 72:11**	5647
be ashamed who **s** graven images,	**Ps 97:7**	5647
S the LORD with gladness;	**Ps 100:2**	5647
And the kingdoms, to **s** the LORD.	**Ps 102:22**	5647
all you His hosts, You who **s** Him,	**Ps 103:21**	8334
Who **s** by night in the house of the	**Ps 134:1**	5975
That it may **s** in the time to come	**Is 30:8**	1961
which will not **s** you will perish,	**Is 60:12**	5647
But you said, 'I will not **s**!'	**Jer 2:20**	5647
so you will **s** strangers in a land	**Jer 5:19**	5647
gone after other gods to **s** them;	**Jer 11:10**	5647
to **s** them and to bow down to them,	**Jer 13:10**	5647
will **s** other gods day and night,	**Jer 16:13**	5647
And I will make you **s** your enemies	**Jer 17:4**	5647
to **s** them and to worship them,	**Jer 25:6**	5647
and these nations will **s** the king	**Jer 25:11**	5647
animals of the field to **s** him.	**Jer 27:6**	5647
"All the nations shall **s** him and	**Jer 27:7**	5647
the kingdom which will not **s** him,	**Jer 27:8**	5647
will not **s** the king of Babylon.'	**Jer 27:9**	5647
of the king of Babylon and **s** him,	**Jer 27:11**	5647
Babylon and **s** him and his people,	**Jer 27:12**	5647
will not **s** the king of Babylon?	**Jer 27:13**	5647
will not **s** the king of Babylon,'	**Jer 27:14**	5647
s the king of Babylon, and live!	**Jer 27:17**	5647
that they may **s** Nebuchadnezzar	**Jer 28:14**	5647
and they will **s** him.	**Jer 28:14**	5647
they shall **s** the LORD their God and	**Jer 30:9**	5647
land and **s** the king of Babylon,	**Jer 40:9**	5647
to burn sacrifices *and* to **s** other gods	**Jer 44:3**	5647

I will **s** *them* their banquet And Jer 51:39 7896
"Go, **s** everyone his idols; Ezk 20:39 5647
of them, will **s** Me in the land; Ezk 20:40 5647
near to Me to **s** as a priest to Me, Ezk 44:13 3547
they do not **s** your gods or worship Da 3:12 6399
that you do not **s** my gods or Da 3:14 6399
our God whom we **s** is able to Da 3:17 6399
that we are not going to **s** your Da 3:18 6399
not to **s** or worship any god except Da 3:28 6399
"Your God whom you constantly **s** Da 6:16 6399
your God, whom you constantly **s**, Da 6:20 6399
men of every language Might **s** Him. Da 7:14 6399
dominions will **s** and obey Him.' Da 7:27 6399
To **s** Him shoulder to shoulder. Zph 3:9 5647
'It is vain to **s** God; Mal 3:14 5647
God and one who does not **s** Him. Mal 3:18 5647
LORD YOUR GOD, AND **S** HIM ONLY.'" Mt 4:10 *3000*
"No one can **s** two masters; Mt 6:24 *1398*
You cannot **s** God and wealth. Mt 6:24 *1398*
not come to be served, but to **s**, Mt 20:28 *1247*
to His disciples to **s** to them, Mk 8:6 *3908*
not come to be served, but to **s**, Mk 10:45 *1247*
enemies, Might **s** Him without fear, Lk 1:74 *3000*
LORD YOUR GOD AND **S** HIM ONLY.'" Lk 4:8 *3000*
that he will gird himself *to* **s**, Lk 12:37
"No servant can **s** two masters; Lk 16:13 *1398*
You cannot **s** God and wealth." Lk 16:13 *1398*
s me while I eat and drink; Lk 17:8 *1247*
word of God in order to **s** tables. Ac 6:2 *1247*
COME OUT AND **S** ME IN THIS PLACE.' Ac 7:7 *3000*
them up to **s** the host of heaven; Ac 7:42 *3000*
I do **s** the God of our fathers, Ac 24:14 *3000*
earnestly **s** *God* night and day. Ac 26:7 *3000*
and whom I **s** stood before me, Ac 27:23 *3000*
whom I **s** in my spirit in the Ro 1:9 *3000*
so that we **s** in newness of the Spirit Ro 7:6 *1398*
"THE OLDER WILL **S** THE YOUNGER." Ro 9:12 *1398*
taking wages *from them* to **s** you; 2Co 11:8 *1248*
but through love **s** one another. Ga 5:13 *1398*
It is the Lord Christ whom you **s**. Col 3:24 *1398*
idols to **s** a living and true God, 1Th 1:9 *1398*
then let them **s** as deacons if they 1Tm 3:10 *1247*
but must **s** them all the more, 1Tm 6:2 *1398*
whom I **s** with a clear conscience 2Tm 1:3 *3000*
who **s** a copy and shadow of the Heb 8:5 *3000*
dead works to **s** the living God? Heb 9:14 *3000*
from which those who **s** the Heb 13:10 *3000*
and they **s** Him day and night in Rv 7:15 *3000*
and His bond-servants will **s** Him; Rv 22:3 *3000*

SERVED
years they had **s** Chedorlaomer, Gn 14:4 5647
So Jacob **s** seven years for Rachel Gn 29:20 5647
not for Rachel that I **s** with you? Gn 29:25 5647
and he **s** with Laban for another Gn 29:30 5647
my children for whom I have **s** you, Gn 30:26 5647
"You yourself know how I have **s** Gn 30:29 5647
"You know that I have **s** your Gn 31:6 5647
I **s** you fourteen years for your Gn 31:41 5647
So they **s** him by himself, and them Gn 43:32 7760
serving women who **s** at the doorway Ex 38:8 6633
So Eleazar and Ithamar **s** as priests Nu 3:4 3547
s other gods and worshiped them, Dt 17:3 5647
s other gods and worshiped them, Dt 29:26 5647
of Nahor, and they **s** other gods. Jos 24:2 5647
s beyond the River and in Egypt, Jos 24:14 5647
s which were beyond the River, Jos 24:15 5647
Israel **s** the LORD all the days Jos 24:31 5647
The people **s** the LORD all the Jg 2:7 5647
of the LORD and **s** the Baals, Jg 2:11 5647
LORD and **s** Baal and the Ashtaroth. Jg 2:13 5647
to their sons, and **s** their gods. Jg 3:6 5647
and **s** the Baals and the Asheroth. Jg 3:7 5647
sons of Israel **s** Cushan-rishathaim Jg 3:8 5647
The sons of Israel **s** Eglon the Jg 3:14 5647
s the Baals and the Ashtaroth the Jg 10:6 5647
our God and **s** the Baals." Jg 10:10 5647
have forsaken Me and **s** other gods; Jg 10:13 5647
from among them and **s** the LORD; Jg 10:16 5647
and he **s** her roasted grain, and Ru 2:14 6642
they lay with the women who **s** at the 1Sa 2:22 6633
Ashtaroth and **s** the LORD alone. 1Sa 7:4 5647
have forsaken Me and **s** other gods 1Sa 8:8 5647
s the Baals and the Ashtaroth; 1Sa 12:10 5647
made peace with Israel and **s** them. 2Sa 10:19 5647
I have **s** in your father's presence, 2Sa 16:19 5647
became the king's nurse and **s** him, 1Ki 1:4 8334
they brought tribute and **s** Solomon 1Ki 4:21 5647
and worshiped them and **s** them, 1Ki 9:9 5647
elders who had **s** his father Solomon 1Ki 12:6 5975, 6440
who grew up with him and **s** him. 1Ki 12:8 5975, 6440
So he **s** Baal and worshiped him and 1Ki 22:53 5647
"Ahab **s** Baal a little; 2Ki 10:18 5647
They **s** idols, concerning which 2Ki 17:12 5647
all the host of heaven and **s** Baal. 2Ki 17:16 5647
They feared the LORD and **s** their 2Ki 17:33 5647
the LORD, they also **s** their idols; 2Ki 17:41 5647
all the host of heaven and **s** them. 2Ki 21:3 5647
and **s** the idols that his father 2Ki 21:21 5647
father had **s** and worshiped them. 2Ki 21:21 5647
he who **s** as the priest in the house 1Ch 6:10 3547
and they **s** in their office 1Ch 6:32 5975
are those who **s** with their sons: 1Ch 6:33 5975
made peace with David and **s** him. 1Ch 19:19 5647
Eleazar and Ithamar **s** as priests. 1Ch 24:2 3547
and their officers who **s** the king 1Ch 27:1 8334
of the divisions that **s** the king, 1Ch 28:1 8334
and worshiped them and **s** them; 2Ch 7:22 5647
elders who had **s** his father Solomon 2Ch 10:6 5975, 6440
who grew up with him and **s** him. 2Ch 10:8 5975, 6440
These are they who **s** the king, 2Ch 17:19 8334
and **s** the Asherim and the idols; 2Ch 24:18 5647
all the host of heaven and **s** them. 2Ch 33:3 5647
Manasseh had made, and he **s** them. 2Ch 33:22 5647
These **s** in the days of Joiakim Ne 12:26
the priests and Levites who **s**. Ne 12:44 5975
Drinks were **s** in golden vessels of Es 1:7 8248
the seven eunuchs who **s** in the Es 1:10 8334
the king's attendants, who **s** him, Es 2:2 8334
And **s** their idols, Which became a Ps 106:36 5647
where love is Than a fattened ox **s** Pr 15:17
forsaken Me and **s** foreign gods Jer 5:19 5647
have loved and which they have **s**, Jer 8:2 5647
followed other gods and **s** them Jer 16:11 5647
down to other gods and **s** them.'" Jer 22:9 5647
to you and has **s** you six years, Jer 34:14 5647
Son of Man did not come to be **s**, Mt 20:28 *1247*
and they **s** them to the people. Mk 8:6 *3908*
He ordered these to be **s** as well. Mk 8:7 *3908*
Son of Man did not come to be **s**, Mk 10:45 *1247*
after he had **s** the purpose of God Ac 13:36 *5256*
nor is He **s** by human hands, as Ac 17:25 *2323*
and worshiped and **s** the creature Ro 1:25 *3000*
he **s** with me in the furtherance of Php 2:22 *1398*
those who have **s** well as deacons 1Tm 3:13 *1247*

SERVES
spares his own son who **s** him." Mal 3:17 5647
between one who **s** God and one who Mal 3:18 5647
at the table or the one who **s**? Lk 22:27 *1247*
I am among you as the one who **s**. Lk 22:27 *1247*
"Every man **s** the good wine first, Jn 2:10 *5087*
then he **s** the poorer *wine;* Jn 2:10
"If anyone **s** Me, he must follow Jn 12:26 *1247*
if anyone **s** Me, the Father will Jn 12:26 *1247*
For he who in this *way* **s** Christ is Ro 14:18 *1398*
Who at any time **s** as a soldier at 1Co 9:7 *4754*
whoever **s** *is to do so* as one 1Pe 4:11 *1247*

SERVICE
the **s** which you shall serve with me Gn 29:27 5656
my **s** which I have rendered you." Gn 30:26 5656
the tabernacle *used* in all its **s**, Ex 27:19 5656
for the **s** of the tent of meeting, Ex 30:16 5656
its **s** and for the holy garments. Ex 35:21 5656
for any work of the **s** brought Ex 35:24 5656
Moses, for the **s** of the Levites, Ex 38:21 5656
on the hem of the robe for the **s**, Ex 39:26 8334
for the **s** of the tabernacle, Ex 39:40 5656
not subject him to a slave's **s**. Lv 25:39 5656
to do the **s** of the tabernacle. Nu 3:7 5656
to do the **s** of the tabernacle. Nu 3:8 5656
to all the **s** concerning them. Nu 3:26 5656
and all the **s** concerning them; Nu 3:31 5656
and the **s** concerning them, Nu 3:36 5656
all who enter the **s** to do the work Nu 4:3 6635
shall take all the utensils of **s**, Nu 4:12 8335
all who enter to perform the **s** to Nu 4:23 6635
"This is the **s** of the families of Nu 4:24 5656
and all the equipment for their **s**; Nu 4:26 5656
the **s** of the sons of the Gershonites, Nu 4:27 5656
"This is the **s** of the families of Nu 4:28 5656
everyone who enters the **s** to do Nu 4:30 6635
their **s** in the tent of meeting: Nu 4:31 5656
equipment and with all their **s**; Nu 4:32 5656
"This is the **s** of the families of Nu 4:33 5656
their **s** in the tent of meeting, Nu 4:33 5656
everyone who entered the **s** for Nu 4:35 6635
everyone who entered the **s** for Nu 4:39 6635
everyone who entered the **s** for Nu 4:43 6635
who could enter to do the work of **s** Nu 4:47 5656
in the **s** of the tent of meeting, Nu 7:5 5656
to each man according to his **s**." Nu 7:5 5656
of Gershon, according to their **s**, Nu 7:7 5656
of Merari, according to their **s**, Nu 7:8 5656
was the **s** of the holy *objects,* Nu 7:9 5656
to perform the **s** of the LORD. Nu 8:11 5656
to perform the **s** of the sons of Israel Nu 8:19 5656
Levites went in to perform their **s** Nu 8:22 5656
they shall enter to perform **s** in the Nu 8:24 6635
they shall retire from **s** in the work Nu 8:25 6635
s of the tabernacle of the LORD, Nu 16:9 5656
for all the **s** of the tent; Nu 18:4 5656
the **s** for the tent of meeting. Nu 18:6 5656
veil, and you are to perform **s**. Nu 18:7 5656
the priesthood as a bestowed **s**, Nu 18:7 5656
for their **s** which they perform, Nu 18:21 5656
the **s** of the tent of meeting. Nu 18:21 5656
the **s** of the tent of meeting, Nu 18:23 5656
for your **s** in the tent of meeting. Nu 18:31 5656
who had come from **s** in the war. Nu 31:14 6635
with double the **s** of a hired man; Dt 15:18 7939
that we are to perform the **s** of Jos 22:27 5656
therefore lighten the hard **s** of 1Ki 12:4 5656
which were used in *temple* **s**. 2Ki 25:14 8334
David appointed over the **s** of song 1Ch 6:31 3027
Levites were appointed for all the **s** 1Ch 6:48 5656
for **s** in war was 26,000 men. 1Ch 7:40 6635
work of the **s** of the house of God. 1Ch 9:13 5656
were over the work of the **s**, 1Ch 9:19 5656
had charge of the utensils of **s**, 1Ch 9:28 5656
of the temple free *from other* **s**; 1Ch 9:33
the **s** of the house of the LORD, 1Ch 23:24 5656
and all its utensils for its **s**." 1Ch 23:26 5656
the **s** of the house of the LORD, 1Ch 23:28 5656
work of the **s** of the house of God, 1Ch 23:28 5656
the **s** of the house of the LORD. 1Ch 23:32 5656
set apart for the **s** *some* of the sons of 1Ch 25:1 5656
those who performed their **s** was: 1Ch 25:1 5656
for the **s** of the house of God. 1Ch 25:6 5656
able men with strength for the **s**, 1Ch 26:8 5656
of the LORD and the **s** of the king. 1Ch 26:30 5656
the **s** of the house of the LORD 1Ch 28:13 5656
of **s** in the house of the LORD; 1Ch 28:13 5656
all utensils for every kind of **s**; 1Ch 28:14 5656
all utensils for every kind of **s**; 1Ch 28:14 5656
all the work for the **s** of the house of 1Ch 28:20 5656
for all the **s** of the house of God, 1Ch 28:21 5656
all the work for all kinds of **s**. 1Ch 28:21 5656
and for the **s** for the house of God 1Ch 29:7 5656
of the priests for their **s**, 2Ch 8:14 5656
now therefore lighten the hard **s** 2Ch 10:4 5656
learn *the difference between* My **s** and 2Ch 12:8 5656
the **s** of the kingdoms of the countries 2Ch 12:8 5656
of the **s** of the house of the LORD; 2Ch 24:12 5656
for the **s** and the burnt offering, 2Ch 24:14 8335
Thus the **s** of the house of the LORD 2Ch 29:35 5656
each according to his **s**, 2Ch 31:2 5656
work which he began in the **s** of the 2Ch 31:21 5656
in the **s** of the house of the LORD. 2Ch 35:2 5656
So the **s** was prepared, and the 2Ch 35:10 5656
not have to depart from their **s**, 2Ch 35:15 5656
So all the **s** of the LORD was 2Ch 35:16 5656
we are in the **s** of the palace, Ezr 4:14 4415
for the **s** of God in Jerusalem, Ezr 6:18 5673
the **s** of the house of your God, Ezr 7:19 6402
given for the **s** of the Levites, Ezr 8:20 5656
for the **s** of the house of our God: Ne 10:32 5656
for the **s** of the house of God. Ne 11:22 4399
them in *their* **s** divisions. Ne 12:9 4931
God and the **s** of purification, Ne 12:45 4931
who performed the **s** had gone away, Ne 13:10 4399
s in which you have been enslaved, Is 14:3 5656
And honor Me with their lip **s**, Is 29:13 8193
peace, And the **s** of righteousness, Is 32:17 5656
in the **s** of the king of Babylon, Jer 52:12 5975, 6440
which were used in *temple* **s**. Jer 52:18 8334
charge of the house, of all its **s** and Ezk 44:14 5656
to enter the king's personal **s**. Da 1:5 5975, 6440
they entered the king's personal **s**. Da 1:19 5975, 6440
and if you will perform My **s**, Zch 3:7 4931
pressed into **s** to bear His cross. Mt 27:32 *29*
They pressed into **s** a Mk 15:21 *29*
performing his priestly **s** before God Lk 1:8 *2407*
days of his priestly **s** were ended, Lk 1:23 *3009*
that he is offering **s** to God. Jn 16:2 *2999*
and the *temple* **s** and the promises, Ro 9:4 *2999*
is your spiritual **s** of worship. Ro 12:1 *2999*
if **s**, in his serving; Ro 12:7 *1248*
and *that* my **s** for Jerusalem may Ro 15:31 *1248*
for a wide door for effective **s** 1Co 16:9
For the ministry of this **s** is not 2Co 9:12 *3009*
of the saints for the work of **s**, Eph 4:12 *1248*
With good will render **s**, Eph 6:7 *1398*
the sacrifice and **s** of your faith, Php 2:17 *3009*
was deficient in your **s** to me. Php 2:30 *3009*
on earth, not with external **s**, Col 3:22 *3787*
me faithful, putting me into **s**, 1Tm 1:12 *1248*
No soldier in active **s** entangles 2Tm 2:4 *4754*
you, for he is useful to me for **s**. 2Tm 4:11 *1248*
sent out to render **s** for the sake Heb 1:14 *1248*
s with reverence and awe; Heb 12:28 *3000*
and faith and **s** and perseverance, Rv 2:19 *1248*

SERVICES
for the house of my God and its **s**. Ne 13:14 4929
Who uses his neighbor's **s** without Jer 22:13 5647
those who perform sacred **s** eat the 1Co 9:13 *2413*
what **s** he rendered at Ephesus. 2Tm 1:18 *1247*

SERVING
we have let Israel go from **s** us?" Ex 14:5 5647
from the mirrors of the **s** women Ex 38:8 6633
Gershonites, in **s** and in carrying: Nu 4:24 5647
who was **s** in the tent of meeting, Nu 4:37 5647
who was **s** in the tent of meeting, Nu 4:41 5647
everyone by his **s** or carrying; Nu 4:49 5656
had excluded them from **s** as priests 2Ch 11:14 3547
not be afraid of **s** the Chaldeans; Jer 40:9 5647
of the lands, **s** wood and stone.' Ezk 20:32 8334
ability for **s** in the king's court; Da 1:4 5975
s night and day with fastings and Lk 2:37 *3000*
has left me to do all the **s** alone? Lk 10:40 *1247*
so many years I have been **s** you and Lk 15:29 *1398*
a supper there, and Martha was **s**; Jn 12:2 *1247*
overlooked in the daily **s** *of food.* Ac 6:1 *1248*
s the Lord with all humility and Ac 20:19 *1398*
with my mind am **s** the law of God, Ro 7:25 *1398*
if service, in his **s**; Ro 12:7 *1248*
fervent in spirit, **s** the Lord; Ro 12:11 *1398*
I am going to Jerusalem **s** the saints. Ro 15:25 *1247*
of the gospel like a child **s** his Php 2:22
that they were not **s** themselves, 1Pe 1:12 *1247*
gift, employ it in **s** one another as 1Pe 4:10 *1247*
is to do so as one who is **s** 1Pe 4:11 *1247*

SERVITUDE
the **s** was heavy on this people. Ne 5:18 5656
affliction And under harsh **s**; La 1:3 5656

SESSION
the courts are in **s** and proconsuls Ac 19:38 *71*

SET
and **s** the door of the ark in the Gn 6:16 7760
I **s** My bow in the cloud, and it Gn 9:13 5414

they s out for the land of Canaan; Gn 12:5 3318, 1980
It came about when the sun had s, Gn 15:17 935
Then Abraham s seven ewe lambs of Gn 21:28 5324
which you have s by themselves?" Gn 21:29 5324
and s out with a variety of good Gn 24:10 1980
when *food* was s before him to eat, Gn 24:33 7760
there, because the sun had s; Gn 28:11 935
a ladder was s on the earth with Gn 28:12 5324
his head and s it up as a pillar and Gn 28:18 7760
which I have s up as a pillar, Gn 28:22 7760
He s the rods which he had Gn 30:38 3322
and s his face toward the hill Gn 31:21 7760
S *it* here before my kinsmen and Gn 31:37 7760
a stone and s it up *as* a pillar. Gn 31:45 7311
which I have s between you and me. Gn 31:51 3384
Jacob s up a pillar in the Gn 35:14 5324
Jacob s up a pillar over her grave; Gn 35:20 5324
and s him over the land of Egypt. Gn 41:33 7896
"See, I have s you over all the Gn 41:41 5414
And he s him over all the land of Gn 41:43 5414
back to you and s him before you, Gn 43:9 3322
me that I may s my eyes on him.' Gn 44:21 7760
Israel s out with all that he had, Gn 46:1 5265
and s *it* among the reeds by the Ex 2:3 7760
taskmasters had s over them, Ex 5:14 7760
I will s apart the land of Goshen, Ex 8:22 6395
The LORD s a definite time, Ex 9:5 7760
Then they s out from Succoth and Ex 13:20 5265
Then they s out from Elim, and all Ex 16:1 5265
hands were steady until the sun s. Ex 17:12 935
When they s out from Rephidim, Ex 19:2 5265
and s before them all these words Ex 19:7 7760
"You shall s bounds for the Ex 19:12 1379
'S bounds about the mountain and Ex 19:23 1379
which you are to s before them: Ex 21:1 7760
"You shall s the bread of the Ex 25:30 5414
outermost curtain in the *first* s, Ex 26:4 2279
that is outermost in the second s. Ex 26:4 4225
curtain that is in the second s; Ex 26:5 4225
that is outermost in the *first* s, Ex 26:10 2279
that is outermost in the second s. Ex 26:10 2279
s the table outside the veil, Ex 26:35 7760
you shall s them in filigree Ex 28:11 6213a, 5437
they shall be s in gold filigree. Ex 28:20 7660
shall s the turban on his head and Ex 29:6 7660
of unleavened bread which is s Ex 29:23
outermost curtain in the first s; Ex 36:11 4225
was outermost in the second s. Ex 36:11 4225
curtain that was in the second s; Ex 36:12 4225
that was outermost in the *first* s, Ex 36:17 4225
was outermost in the second s. Ex 36:17 2279
s in gold filigree *settings;* Ex 39:6 5437
They were s in gold filigree Ex 39:13 5437
you shall s up the tabernacle of the Ex 40:2 6965
you shall s the gold altar of Ex 40:5 5414
and s up the veil for the doorway Ex 40:5 7760
"You shall s the altar of Ex 40:6 5414
"You shall s the laver Ex 40:7 5414
"You shall s up the court all Ex 40:8 7760
its sockets, and s up its boards, Ex 40:18 7760
and s up a veil for the screen, Ex 40:21 7760
He s the arrangement of bread Ex 40:23 6186a
Then he s up the veil for the Ex 40:28 7760
He s the altar of burnt Ex 40:29 7760
the sons of Israel would s out; Ex 40:36 5265
then they did not s out until the Ex 40:37 5265
I will s My face against that Lv 17:10 5414
'I will also s My face against Lv 20:3 5414
then I Myself will s My face Lv 20:5 7760
I will also s My face against that Lv 20:6 5414
and I have s you apart from the Lv 20:26 914
"You shall s them *in* two Lv 24:6 7760
"Every sabbath day he shall s it Lv 24:8 6186a
nor shall you s up for yourselves Lv 26:1 6965
'I will s My face against you Lv 26:17 5414
to the LORD, like a field s apart; Lv 27:21 2764a
'No one who may have been s apart Lv 27:29 2763a
when the tabernacle is to s out, Nu 1:51 5265
the Levites shall s it up. Nu 1:51 6965
They shall s out first. Nu 2:9 5265
And they shall s out second. Nu 2:16 5265
"Then the tent of meeting shall s Nu 2:17 5265
as they camp, so they shall s out, Nu 2:17 5265
And they shall s out third. Nu 2:24 5265
s out last by their standards." Nu 2:31 5265
standards, and so they s out, Nu 2:34 5265
s them before Aaron the priest, Nu 3:6 5975
when the camp is to s out, Nu 4:15 5265
sons of Israel would then s out; Nu 9:17 5265
the sons of Israel would s out, Nu 9:18 5265
the LORD's charge and not s out. Nu 9:19 5265
command of the LORD they s out. Nu 9:20 5265
was lifted, they would s out. Nu 9:21 5265
remained camped and did not s out; Nu 9:22 5265
it was lifted, they did s out. Nu 9:22 5265
command of the LORD they s out; Nu 9:23 5265
and for having the camps s out. Nu 10:2 4550
on the east side shall s out. Nu 10:5 5265
on the south side shall s out; Nu 10:6 5265
is to be blown for them to s out. Nu 10:6 4550
and the sons of Israel s out on Nu 10:12 5265
to their armies, s out first, Nu 10:14 5265
carrying the tabernacle, s out. Nu 10:17 5265
s out with Elizur the son of Nu 10:18 5265
Then the Kohathites s out, Nu 10:21 5265
the tabernacle was s up before their Nu 10:21 6965
to their armies, was s out, Nu 10:22 5265
guard for all the camps, s out, Nu 10:25 5265
by their armies as they s out. Nu 10:28 5265
Thus they s out from the mount of Nu 10:33 5265
when they s out from the camp. Nu 10:34 5265
when the ark s out that Moses said, Nu 10:35 5265
the people s out for Hazeroth, Nu 11:35 5265
turn tomorrow and s out to the Nu 14:25 5265
Now when they s out from Kadesh, Nu 20:22 5265
Then they s out from Mount Hor by Nu 21:4 5265
serpent, and s it on a standard; Nu 21:8 7760
serpent and s it on the standard; Nu 21:9 7760
s out and camped in Wadi Zered. Nu 21:12 5265
"I have s up the seven altars, Nu 23:4 6186a
he s his face toward the wilderness. Nu 24:1 7896
And your nest is s in the cliff. Nu 24:21 7760
s him before Eleazar the priest and Nu 27:22 5975
'Turn and s your journey, and go Dt 1:7 5265
"Then we s out from Horeb, and Dt 1:19 5265
the land on which he has s foot, Dt 1:36 1869
turn around and s out for the Dt 1:40 5265
"Then we turned and s out for the Dt 2:1 5265
'Arise, s out, and pass through Dt 2:24 5265
Then Moses s apart three cities Dt 4:41 914
Moses s before the sons of Israel; Dt 4:44 7760
"The LORD did not s His love on Dt 7:7 2836a
(Now the sons of Israel s out from Dt 10:6 5265
From there they s out to Gudgodah, Dt 10:7 5265
At that time the LORD s apart the Dt 10:8 914
LORD s His affection to love them, Dt 10:15 2836a
all the land on which you s foot, Dt 11:25 1869
chooses to s His name is too far away Dt 14:24 7760
seventh year you shall s him free. Dt 15:12 7971
"When you s him free, you Dt 15:13 7971
hard to you when you s him free, Dt 15:18 7971
"You shall not s up for Dt 16:22 6965
'I will s a king over me like all Dt 17:14 7760
you shall surely s a king over you Dt 17:15 7760
shall s as king over yourselves; Dt 17:15 7760
you shall s aside three cities for Dt 19:2 914
'You shall s aside three cities Dt 19:7 914
mark, which the ancestors have s, Dt 19:14 1379
basket from your hand and s it down Dt 26:4 5117
And you shall s it down before the Dt 26:10 5117
and that He will s you high above Dt 26:19 5414
s up for yourself large stones and Dt 27:2 6965
you shall s up on Mount Ebal, Dt 27:4 6965
the LORD your God will s you high Dt 28:1 5414
king, whom you s over you, Dt 28:36 6965
not venture to s the sole of her foot Dt 28:56 3322
curse which I have s before you, Dt 30:1 5414
I have s before you today life and Dt 30:15 5414
have s before you life and death, Dt 30:19 5414
He s the boundaries of the peoples Dt 32:8 5324
he and all the sons of Israel s out Jos 3:1 5265
then you shall s out from your Jos 3:3 5265
the people s out from their tents to Jos 3:14 5265
Then Joshua s up twelve stones in Jos 4:9 6965
the Jordan, Joshua s up at Gilgal. Jos 4:20 6965
son he shall s up its gates." Jos 6:26 5324
S an ambush for the city behind it." Jos 8:2 7760
that you shall s the city on fire. Jos 8:8 3341
5,000 men and s them in ambush Jos 8:12 7760
they quickly s the city on fire. Jos 8:19 3341
craftily and s out as envoys, Jos 9:4 1980
Then the sons of Israel s out and Jos 9:17 5265
with the cities which were s apart for Jos 16:9 3995
s up the tent of meeting there; Jos 18:1 7931
So they s apart Kedesh in Galilee Jos 20:7 6942
and he took a large stone and s it Jos 24:26 6965
the sword and s the city on fire. Jg 1:8 7971
the LORD s the sword of one Jg 7:22 7760
men of Shechem s men in ambush Jg 9:25 7760
and s the inner chamber on fire over Jg 9:49 3341
When he had s fire to the torches, Jg 15:5 1197a
armed with weapons of war s out. Jg 18:11 5265
The sons of Dan s up for Jg 18:30 6965
So they s up for themselves Jg 18:31 7760
and the sun s on them near Gibeah Jg 19:14 935
s men in ambush around Gibeah. Jg 20:29 7760
whom they had s against Gibeah, Jg 20:36 7760
they also s on fire all the cities Jg 20:48 7971
LORD's, And He s the world on them. 1Sa 2:8 7896
eyes were s so that he could not see. 1Sa 4:15 6965
house of Dagon and s it by Dagon. 1Sa 5:2 3322
and s him in his place again. 1Sa 5:3 7725
on which they s the ark of the LORD 1Sa 6:18 5117
and s it between Mizpah and Shen, 1Sa 7:12 7760
journey on which we have s out." 1Sa 9:6 1980
ago, do not s your mind on them, 1Sa 9:20 7760
which I said to you, 'S it aside.' 1Sa 9:23 7760
was on it and s *it* before Saul. 1Sa 9:24 7760
S *it* before you *and* eat, because 1Sa 9:24 7760
'No, but s a king over us!' 1Sa 10:19 7760
the LORD has s a king over you. 1Sa 12:13 5414
to the appointed time s by Samuel, 1Sa 13:8 834
how he s himself against him on 1Sa 15:2 7760
and s an ambush in the valley. 1Sa 15:5 693
he s up a monument for himself, 1Sa 15:12 5324
Saul s him over the men of war. 1Sa 18:5 7760
when I s out and the vessels of the 1Sa 21:5 3318
and let me s a piece of bread 1Sa 28:22 7760
ark of the LORD and s it in its place 2Sa 6:17 3322
Joab saw that the battle was s against 2Sa 10:9
they s food before him and he ate. 2Sa 12:20 7760
were in it, and s *them* under saws, 2Sa 12:31 7760
go and s it on fire." 2Sa 14:30 3341
servants s the field on fire. 2Sa 14:30 3341
servants s my field on fire?" 2Sa 14:31 3341
And they s down the ark of God, 2Sa 15:24 3332
city, and s his house in order, 2Sa 17:23 6680
Absalom s Amasa over the army 2Sa 17:25 7760
and s over them commanders of 2Sa 18:1 7760
taken and s up for himself a pillar 2Sa 18:18 5324
yet you s your servant among those 2Sa 19:28 7896
he delayed longer than the s time 2Sa 20:5 4150
a throne s for the king's mother, 1Ki 2:19 7760
s me on the throne of David my 1Ki 2:24 3427
son, whom I will s on your throne 1Ki 5:5 5414
to s on the tops of the pillars; 1Ki 7:16 5414
Thus he s up the pillars at the 1Ki 7:21 6965
and he s up the right pillar and 1Ki 7:21 6965
and he s up the left pillar and 1Ki 7:21 6965
and the sea *was* s on top of them, 1Ki 7:25
Then he s the stands, five on the 1Ki 7:39 5414
and he s the sea *of cast metal* on 1Ki 7:39 5414
I have s a place for the ark, 1Ki 8:21 7760
My statutes which I have s before you 1Ki 9:6 5414
to s you on the throne of Israel; 1Ki 10:9 5414
He s one in Bethel, and the 1Ki 12:29 7760
and s up its gates with the *loss* 1Ki 16:34 5324
you shall s aside what is full." 2Ki 4:4 5265
and let us s a bed for him there, 2Ki 4:10 7760
I s this before a hundred men?" 2Ki 4:43 5414
So he s *it* before them, and they 2Ki 4:44 5414
S bread and water before them, 2Ki 6:22 7760
strongholds you will s on fire, 2Ki 8:12 7971
and s *him* on his father's throne, 2Ki 10:3 7760
and Hazael s his face to go up to 2Ki 12:17 7760
They s for themselves *sacred* 2Ki 17:10 5324
on your part to s riders on them. 2Ki 18:23 5414
'S your house in order, for you 2Ki 20:1 6680
Then he s the carved image of 2Ki 21:7 7760
s his throne above the throne of the 2Ki 25:28 5414
I will s up *one of* your descendants 1Ch 17:11 6965
Joab saw that the battle was s against 1Ch 19:10
and he s stonecutters to hew out 1Ch 22:2 5975
"Now s your heart and your soul 1Ch 22:19 5414
And Aaron was s apart to sanctify 1Ch 23:13 914
the fixed festivals in the number s 1Ch 23:31
the commanders of the army s apart 1Ch 25:1 914
incense before Him and *to* s *out* 2Ch 2:4
and the sea *was* s on top of them 2Ch 4:4
and he s five on the right side 2Ch 4:6 5414
them and he s them in the temple, 2Ch 4:7 5414
He s the sea on the right side 2Ch 4:10 5414
"There I have s the ark in 2Ch 6:11 7760
s it in the midst of the court; 2Ch 6:13 5414
My commandments which I have s 2Ch 7:19 5414
He s up priests of his own for 2Ch 11:15 5975
s their hearts on seeking the LORD 2Ch 11:16 5414
not s his heart to seek the LORD. 2Ch 12:14 3559
and the showbread is s on 2Ch 13:11
But Jeroboam had s an ambush to 2Ch 13:13 5437
and s garrisons in the land of 2Ch 17:2 5414
have s your heart to seek God." 2Ch 19:3 3559
the LORD s ambushes against the 2Ch 20:22 5414
and s up a king over themselves. 2Ch 21:8 4427a
s it outside by the gate of the house 2Ch 24:8 5414
of Seir, s them up as his gods, 2Ch 25:14 5975
He s up the altar of the LORD 2Ch 33:16 3559
He s the priests in their 2Ch 35:2 5975
Josiah had s the temple in order, 2Ch 35:20 3559
So they s up the altar on its Ezr 3:3 3559
For Ezra had s his heart to study Ezr 7:10 3559
Then I s apart twelve of the Ezr 8:24 914
we s up a guard against them day Ne 4:9 5975
not s up the doors in the gates, Ne 6:1 5975
rebuilt and I had s up the doors, Ne 7:1 5975
which You s before them, Ne 9:35 5414
s over us because of our sins; Ne 9:37 5414
and s apart the consecrated *portion* Ne 12:47 6942
and the Levites s apart the Ne 12:47 6942
so that he s the royal crown on Es 2:17 7760
And Esther s Mordecai over the Es 8:2 7760
That You s a guard over me? Jb 7:12 7760
Why have You s me as Your target, Jb 7:20 7760
You s a limit for the soles Jb 13:27 2707
have s so that he cannot pass. Jb 14:5 6213a
That You would s a limit for me Jb 14:13 7896
He has also s me up as His target. Jb 16:12 6965
When He s a limit for the rain And Jb 28:26 6213a
And that which was s on your table Jb 36:16 5183a
Who s its measurements? Since you Jb 38:5 7760
on it And s a bolt and doors, Jb 38:10 7760
Who have s themselves against me Ps 3:6 7896
But know that the LORD has s apart Ps 4:3 6395
"I will s him in the safety for Ps 12:5 7896
I have s the LORD continually Ps 16:8 7737b
They s their eyes to cast *us* down Ps 17:11 7896
of Jacob s you *securely* on high! Ps 20:1 7682
our God we will s up our banners. Ps 20:5 1713b
You s a crown of fine gold Ps 21:3 7896
have s my feet in a large place. Ps 31:8 5975
And He s my feet upon a rock Ps 40:2 6965
You s me in Your presence forever. Ps 41:12 5324
They have not s God before them. Ps 54:3 7760
S me *securely* on high away from Ps 59:1 7682
they have s an ambush for my life; Ps 59:3 693
run and s themselves against me. Ps 59:4 3559
do not s *your heart upon them.* Ps 62:10 7896
O God, s me *securely* on high. Ps 69:29 7682
They have s their mouth against Ps 73:9 7896
You s them in slippery places; Ps 73:18 7896
They have s up their own standards Ps 74:4 7760
It is I who have firmly s its pillars. Ps 75:3 8505
And they have not s You before them. Ps 86:14 7760
"I shall also s his hand on the sea And Ps 89:25 7760
I will s him *securely* on high, Ps 91:14 7682

I will **s** no worthless thing before Ps 101:3 7896
To **s** free those who were doomed to Ps 102:20 6605a
You **s** a boundary that they Ps 104:9 7760
ruler of peoples, and **s** him free. Ps 105:20 6605a
The LORD answered me *and* **s** Ps 118:5
there thrones were **s** for judgment, Ps 122:5 3427
body I will **s** upon your *throne.* Ps 132:11 7896
They have **s** snares for me. Ps 140:5 7896
S a guard, O LORD, over my mouth; Ps 141:3 7896
the trap which they have **s** for me, Ps 141:9 3369
He **s** for the sea its boundary So Pr 8:29 7760
She has also **s** her table; Pr 9:2 6186a
Which your fathers have **s**. Pr 22:28 6213a
When you **s** your eyes on it, it is Pr 23:5 5774a
Scorners **s** a city aflame, But wise Pr 29:8 6315
And I **s** my mind to seek and Ec 1:13 5414
And I **s** my mind to know wisdom Ec 1:17 5414
He has also **s** eternity in their heart, Ec 3:11 5414
folly is **s** in many exalted places Ec 10:6 5414
are rods of gold **S** with beryl; SS 5:14 4390
S on pedestals of pure gold; SS 5:15 3245
my soul **s** me *Over* the chariots of SS 6:12 7760
and **s** up the son of Tabeel as king Is 7:6 4427a
plant delightful plants And **s** them Is 17:10 2232
They **s** the table, they spread out Is 21:5 6186a
"Then I will **s** the key of the Is 22:22 5414
wages will be **s** apart to the LORD; Is 23:18 6944
I will **s** siegeworks against you, Is 29:3 6696a
on your part to **s** riders on them. Is 36:8 5414
'**S** your house in order, for you Is 38:1 6680
And it **s** him aflame all around, Is 42:25 3857
"Declare and **s** forth *your case;* Is 45:21 5066
They **s** it in its place and it Is 46:7 5117
s up My standard to the peoples; Is 49:22 7311
I have **s** My face like flint, Is 50:7 7760
the brands you have **s** ablaze. Is 50:11 1197a
And I will **s** My justice for a Is 51:4 7280b
"The exile will soon be **s** free, Is 51:14 6605a
I will **s** your stones in antimony, Is 54:11 7257
doorpost You have **s** up your sign; Is 57:8 7760
"Your sun will no longer **s**, Nor Is 60:20 935
Who **s** a table for Fortune, Is 65:11 6186a
"I will **s** a sign among them Is 66:19 7760
and they will **s** each one his throne Jer 1:15 5414
'How I would **s** you among My sons Jer 3:19 7896
a destroyer of nations has **s** out; Jer 4:7 5265
They **s** a trap, They catch men. Jer 5:26 7843
"And I **s** watchmen over you, Jer 6:17 6965
"they have **s** their detestable things Jer 7:30 7760
My law which I **s** before them, Jer 9:13 5414
tent again Or to **s** up my curtains. Jer 10:20 6965
have **s** up to the shameful thing, Jer 11:13 7760
s them apart for a day of carnage! Jer 12:3 6942
sun has **s** while it was yet day; Jer 15:9 935
s you free for *purposes of* good; Jer 15:11 8281
to You I have **s** forth my cause. Jer 20:12 1540
I **s** before you the way of life and Jer 21:8 5414
"For I have **s** My face against Jer 21:10 7760
s apart destroyers against you, Jer 22:7 6942
behold, two baskets of figs **s** before Jer 24:1 3259
I will **s** My eyes on them for good, Jer 24:6 7760
My law which I have **s** before you, Jer 26:4 5414
"**S** up for yourself roadmarks, Jer 31:21 5324
teeth are **s** on edge.' Jer 31:29 6949a
his teeth will be **s** on edge. Jer 31:30 6949a
who has **s** signs and wonders in Jer 32:20 7760
s this city on fire and burn it, Jer 32:29 3341
that each man should **s** free his Jer 34:9 7971
covenant that each man should **s** free Jer 34:10 7971
they obeyed, and **s** *them free.* Jer 34:10 7971
servants whom they had **s** free, Jer 34:11 7971
shall **s** free his Hebrew brother who Jer 34:14 7971
whom you had **s** free according to Jer 34:16 7971
Then I **s** before the men of the Jer 35:5 5414
army had **s** out from Egypt; Jer 37:5 3318
really **s** your mind to enter Egypt and Jer 42:15 7760
"So all the men who **s** their mind Jer 42:17 7760
and I am going to **s** his throne Jer 43:10 7760
"And I shall **s** fire to the Jer 43:12 3341
which I have **s** before you and Jer 44:10 5414
to **s** My face against you for woe, Jer 44:11 7760
remnant of Judah who have **s** their Jer 44:12 7760
And her towns will be **s** on fire. Jer 49:2 3341
s fire to the wall of Damascus, Jer 49:27 3341
'Then I will **s** My throne in Elam Jer 49:38 7760
"I **s** a snare for you and you Jer 50:24 3369
And I will **s** fire to his cities Jer 50:32 3341
dwelling places are **s** on fire, Jer 51:30 3341
s me down *like* an empty vessel; Jer 51:34 3322
her high gates will be **s** on fire; Jer 51:58 3341
s his throne above the thrones of Jer 52:32 5414
He has **s** His right hand like an La 2:4 5324
s me as a target for the arrow. La 3:12 5324
entered me and **s** me on my feet; Ezk 2:2 5975
iron plate and **s** it up as an iron Ezk 4:3 3559
and **s** your face toward it so that Ezk 4:3 3559
"Then you shall **s** your face Ezk 4:7 3559
I have **s** her at the center of the Ezk 5:5 7760
s your face toward the mountains Ezk 6:2 7760
for I have **s** you as a sign to the Ezk 12:6 5414
s your face against the daughters Ezk 13:17 7760
these men have **s** up their idols in Ezk 14:3 5927
"I will **s** My face against Ezk 14:8 5414
and I **s** My face against them. Ezk 15:7 5414
when I **s** My face against them. Ezk 15:7 7760
he **s** it in a city of traders. Ezk 17:4 7760
he **s** it *like* a willow. Ezk 17:5 7760
top of the cedar and **s** *it* out; Ezk 17:22 5414
children's teeth are **s** on edge'? Ezk 18:2 6949a
'Then nations **s** against him On Ezk 19:8 5414
of man, **s** your face toward Teman, Ezk 20:46 7760
man, **s** your face toward Jerusalem, Ezk 21:2 7760
s yourself; go to the left, wherever Ezk 21:16 7760
'Jerusalem,' to **s** battering rams, Ezk 21:22 7760
to **s** battering rams against the Ezk 21:22 7760
They will **s** themselves against you Ezk 23:24 7760
I will **s** My jealousy against you, Ezk 23:25 5414
you had **s** My incense and My oil. Ezk 23:41 7760
"Then **s** it empty on its coals So Ezk 24:11 5975
s your face toward the sons of Ezk 25:2 7760
and they will **s** their encampments Ezk 25:4 3427
but I will **s** glory in the land of Ezk 26:20 5414
they **s** forth your splendor. Ezk 27:10 5414
of man, **s** your face toward Sidon, Ezk 28:21 7760
man, **s** your face against Pharaoh king Ezk 29:2 7760
When I **s** a fire in Egypt And all Ezk 30:8 5414
desolate, **S** a fire in Zoan And Ezk 30:14 5414
"I will **s** a fire in Egypt; Ezk 30:16 5414
and has **s** its top among the clouds, Ezk 31:10 5414
nor **s** their top among the clouds," Ezk 31:14 5414
will **s** darkness on your land," Ezk 32:8 5414
whose graves are **s** in the remotest Ezk 32:23 5414
I will **s** over them one shepherd, Ezk 34:23 6965
s your face against Mount Seir, Ezk 35:2 7760
s me down in the middle of the valley Ezk 37:1 5117
and will **s** My sanctuary in their Ezk 37:26 5414
s your face toward Gog of the land Ezk 38:2 7760
"They will **s** apart men who Ezk 39:14 914
then he will **s** up a marker by it Ezk 39:15 1129
s My glory among the nations; Ezk 39:21 5414
and **s** me on a very high mountain, Ezk 40:2 5117
the upper chambers were **s** back from Ezk 42:6 680
but you have **s** *foreigners* to keep Ezk 44:8 7760
allotment which you shall **s** apart, Ezk 48:8 7311
that you shall **s** apart to the LORD Ezk 48:9 7311
shall **s** apart the holy allotment, Ezk 48:20 7311
God of heaven will **s** up a kingdom Da 2:44 6966
he **s** it up on the plain of Dura in Da 3:1 6966
Nebuchadnezzar the king had **s** up. Da 3:2 6966
Nebuchadnezzar the king had **s** up; Da 3:3 6966
that Nebuchadnezzar had **s** up. Da 3:3 6966
Nebuchadnezzar the king has **s** up. Da 3:5 6966
Nebuchadnezzar the king had **s** up. Da 3:7 6966
golden image which you have **s** up." Da 3:12 6966
the golden image that I have **s** up? Da 3:14 6966
golden image that you have **s** up." Da 3:18 6966
s *his* mind on delivering Daniel; Da 6:14 7761
looking Until thrones were **s** up, Da 7:9 7412
to walk in His teachings which He **s** Da 9:10 5414
s me trembling on my hands and Da 10:10 5128
the first day that you **s** your heart on Da 10:12 5414
"He will **s** his face to come Da 11:17 7760
but his heart will be **s** against Da 11:28
And they will **s** up the abomination Da 11:31 5414
abomination of desolation is **s** up, Da 12:11 5414
They have **s** up kings, but not by Hos 8:4 4427a
And I will **s** My eyes against them Am 9:4 7760
you **s** your nest among the stars, Ob 1:4 7760
bread Will **s** an ambush for you. Ob 1:7 7760
s them on fire and consume them, Ob 1:18 1814
wall, And the mantelet is **s** up. Na 2:5 3559
vile, And **s** you up as a spectacle. Na 3:6 7760
stone that I have **s** before Joshua; Zch 3:9 5414
be **s** there on her own pedestal." Zch 5:11 5117
and **s** *it* on the head of Joshua the Zch 6:11 7760
I **s** all men one against another. Zch 8:10 7971
I have **s** your prisoners free from Zch 9:11 7971
in that day I will **s** about to Zch 12:9 1245
is coming will **s** them ablaze," Mal 4:1 3857
city **s** on a hill cannot be hidden; Mt 5:14 2749
to **S** A MAN AGAINST HIS FATHER, Mt 10:35 1369
to Himself and **s** him before them, Mt 18:2 2476
and **s** their city on fire. Mt 22:7 1705b
THE ONE WHOSE PRICE HAD BEEN **S** Mt 27:9 5091
guard they **s** a seal on the stone. Mt 27:66 4972
came, after the sun had **s**, Mk 1:32 1416
to the disciples to **s** before them; Mk 6:41 3908
a child, He **s** him before them, Mk 9:36 2476
TO **S** FREE THOSE WHO ARE Lk 4:18 649
to **s** him down in front of Him. Lk 5:18 5087
to **s** before the people. Lk 9:16 3908
you, eat what is **s** before you; Lk 10:8 3908
I have nothing to **s** before him'; Lk 11:6 3908
stone waterpots **s** there for the Jewish Jn 2:6 2749
testimony has **s** his seal to *this,* Jn 3:33 4972
in whom you have **s** your hope. Jn 5:45 1679
God, has **s** His seal." Jn 6:27 4972
and having **s** her in the center Jn 8:3 2476
whom they used to **s** down every day Ac 3:2 5087
"And after he had been **s** outside, Ac 7:21 1620
"**S** apart for Me Barnabas and Saul Ac 13:2 873
his house and **s** food before them, Ac 16:34 3908
a mob and **s** the city in an uproar; Ac 17:5 2350b
God wills," he **s** sail from Ephesus. Ac 18:21 321
he was about to **s** sail for Syria, Ac 20:3 321
to the ship, **s** sail for Assos, Ac 20:13 321
first day that I **s** foot in Asia, Ac 20:18 1910
parted from them and had **s** sail, Ac 21:1 321
we went aboard and **s** sail. Ac 21:2 321
Spirit not to **s** foot in Jerusalem. Ac 21:4 1910
Paul down and **s** him before them. Ac 22:30 2476
"This man might have been **s** free Ac 26:32 630
and not to have **s** sail from Crete and Ac 27:21 321
because of the rain that had **s** in Ac 28:2 2186
At the end of three months we **s** sail Ac 28:11 321
When they had **s** a day for Paul, Ac 28:23 5021
s apart for the gospel of God, Ro 1:1 873
Who will **s** me free from the body Ro 7:24 4506
has **s** you free from the law of sin Ro 8:2 1659
s their minds on the things of the Ro 8:5 5426
the mind **s** on the flesh is death, Ro 8:6 5427
mind **s** on the Spirit is life and peace Ro 8:6 5427
mind **s** on the flesh is hostile toward Ro 8:7 5427
the creation itself also will be **s** free Ro 8:21 1659
OF THE CLEVER I WILL **S** ASIDE." 1Co 1:19 114
eat anything that is **s** before you 1Co 10:27 3908
us, He on whom we have **s** our hope. 2Co 1:10 1679
But when God, who had **s** me apart Ga 1:15 873
until the date **s** by the father. Ga 4:2 4287
for freedom that Christ **s** us free; Ga 5:1 1659
s their minds on earthly things. Php 3:19 5426
S your mind on the things above, Col 3:2 5426
s aside their previous pledge. 1Tm 5:12 114
you would **s** in order what remains Ti 1:5 1930
take hold of the hope **s** before us. Heb 6:18 4295
Anyone who has **s** aside the Law of Heb 10:28 114
the race that is **s** before us, Heb 12:1 4295
who for the joy **s** before Him Heb 12:2 4295
how great a forest is **s** aflame by Jas 3:5 381
the tongue is **s** among our members Jas 3:6 2525
life, and is **s** on fire by hell. Jas 3:6 5394

SETH

birth to a son, and named him **S**, Gn 4:25 8352
To **S**, to him also a son was born; Gn 4:26 8352
to his image, and named him **S**. Gn 5:3 8352
of **S** were eight hundred years, Gn 5:4 8352
S lived one hundred and five Gn 5:6 8352
Then **S** lived eight hundred and Gn 5:7 8352
So all the days of **S** were nine Gn 5:8 8352
Adam, **S**, Enosh, 1Ch 1:1 8352
the son of Enosh, the son of **S**, Lk 3:38 4589

SETHUR

of Asher, **S** the son of Michael; Nu 13:13 5639

SETS

return it to him before the sun **s**, Ex 22:26 935
'But when the sun **s**, Lv 22:7 935
anything which a man **s** apart to Lv 27:28 2763a
"When the camp **s** out, Aaron and Nu 4:5 5265
wages on his day before the sun **s**, Dt 24:15 935
he is poor and **s** his heart on it; Dt 24:15 5375
craftsman, and **s** *it up* in secret.' Dt 27:15 7760
And **s** on fire the foundations of Dt 32:22 3857
And He **s** the blameless in His way. 2Sa 22:33 5425b
feet, And **s** me on my high places. 2Sa 22:34 5975
He **s** on high those who are lowly, Jb 5:11 7760
And **s** a seal upon the stars; Jb 9:7 2856
And **s** others in their place. Jb 34:24 5975
And **s** me upon my high places. Ps 18:33 5975
He **s** himself on a path that is not Ps 36:4 3320
flame that **s** the mountains on fire, Ps 83:14 3857
But He **s** the needy securely on high Ps 107:41 7682
The LORD **s** the prisoners free. Ps 146:7 5425b
Also, the sun rises and the sun **s**; Ec 1:5 935
s the thickets of the forest aflame Is 9:18 3341
He **s** up walls and ramparts for Is 26:1 7896
torrent of brimstone, **s** it afire. Is 30:33 1197a
inwardly he **s** an ambush for him. Jer 9:8 7760
who **s** up his idols in his heart, Ezk 14:4 5927
Me, **s** up his idols in his heart, Ezk 14:7 5927
s over it the lowliest of men." Da 4:17 6966
He **s** over it whomever He wishes. Da 5:21 6966
when he **s** out to meet another king Lk 14:31 4198
no one **s** it aside or adds Ga 3:15 114
flesh **s** its desire against the Spirit, Ga 5:17 1937
and **s** on fire the course of *our* Jas 3:6 5394

SETTING

onyx stones and **s** stones for the Ex 25:7 4394
and onyx stones and **s** stones for Ex 35:9 4394
and the stones for **s** for the ephod Ex 35:27 4394
had finished **s** up the tabernacle, Nu 7:1 6965
"We are **s** out to the place of Nu 10:29 5265
law which I am **s** before you today? Dt 4:8 5414
I am **s** before you today a blessing Dt 11:26 5414
which I am **s** before you today. Dt 11:32 5414
Great Sea toward the **s** of the sun will Jos 1:4 3996
Great Sea toward the **s** of the sun. Jos 23:4 3996
s you on His throne as king for 2Ch 9:8 5414
the rising of the sun to its **s**. Ps 50:1 3996
The sun knows the place of its **s**. Ps 104:19 3996
From the rising of the sun to its **s** Ps 113:3 3996
in milk, *And* reposed in *their* **s**. SS 5:12 4402
from the rising to the **s** of the sun Is 45:6 4628
by **s** their threshold by My threshold Ezk 43:8 5414
rising of the sun even to its **s**, Mal 1:11 3996
not **s** your mind on God's interests, Mt 16:23 5426
"You are experts at **s** aside Mk 7:9 114
not **s** your mind on God's interests, Mk 8:33 5426
As He was **s** out on a journey, Mk 10:17 1607
While the sun was **s**, Lk 4:40 1416
s an ambush to kill him on the way). Ac 25:3 4160
and when we were **s** sail, Ac 28:10 321
a **s** aside of a former commandment Heb 7:18 115

SETTINGS

you shall set them in filigree **s** Ex 28:11
"You shall make filigree **s** of Ex 28:13
the corded chains on the filigree **s**. Ex 28:14
the two cords on the two filigree **s**, Ex 28:25
in the cutting of stones for **s**, Ex 31:5 4390
in the cutting of stones for **s** and Ex 35:33 4390
set in gold filigree **s**; they Ex 39:6
They were set in gold filigree **s** Ex 39:13
They made two gold filigree **s** Ex 39:16
the two cords on the two filigree **s**, Ex 39:18
Like apples of gold in **s** of silver Pr 25:11 4906
workmanship of your **s** and sockets, Ezk 28:13 8596

SETTLE
s wherever you please." Gn 20:15 3427
s your father and your brothers in Gn 47:6 3427
enemies who s in it will be appalled Lv 26:32 3427
land in which I swore to s you, Nu 14:30 7931
s in their cities and in their houses, Dt 19:1 3427
"But I will s him in My house and 1Ch 17:14 3427
Let a cloud s on it; Jb 3:5 7931
You s its ridges Ps 65:10 5181
come and s on the steep ravines, Is 7:19 5117
and s them in their own land, Is 14:1 5117
the night monster will s there Is 34:14 7280b
"Then I will make their waters s And Ezk 32:14 8257
And I will s them in their houses, Hos 11:11 3427
to s accounts with his slaves. Mt 18:23 *4868*
"When he had begun to s *them,* Mt 18:24 *4868*
make an effort to s with him, Lk 12:58 *525*

SETTLED
LORD, and s in the land of Nod, Gn 4:16 3427
in the land of Shinar and s there. Gn 11:2 3427
went as far as Haran, and s there. Gn 11:31 3427
Abram s in the land of Canaan, Gn 13:12 3427
Lot s in the cities of the valley, Gn 13:12 3427
and s between Kadesh and Shur; Gn 20:1 3427
They s from Havilah to Shur Gn 25:18 7931
he s in defiance of all his relatives. Gn 25:18 5307
the valley of Gerar, and s there. Gn 26:17 3427
s his father and his brothers and Gn 47:11 3427
and s in the land of Midian, Ex 2:15 3427
s in all the territory of Egypt; Ex 10:14 5117
because the cloud had s on it, Ex 40:35 7931
the place where the cloud s down, Nu 9:17 7931
the cloud s over the tabernacle, Nu 9:18 7931
Then the cloud s down in the Nu 10:12 7931
before them and s in their place, Dt 2:12 3427
them and s in their place, Dt 2:21 3427
and s in their place even to this Dt 2:22 3427
every assault shall be s by them. Dt 21:5 5921, 6310
and possessed it and s in it; Jos 19:47 3427
So he built the city and s in it. Jos 19:50 3427
rest until he has s it today." Ru 3:18 3615
of Egypt and s them in this place. 1Sa 12:8 3427
and s them in Halah and Habor, 2Ki 17:6 3427
and s *them* in the cities of Samaria 2Ki 17:24 3427
To the east he s as far as the 1Ch 5:9 3427
And they s in their place until 1Ch 5:22 3427
and s the sons of Israel there. 2Ch 8:2 3427
its villages, and they s there. 2Ch 28:18 3427
and s in the city of Samaria, Ezr 4:10 3488
Your creatures s in it; Ps 68:10 3427
O LORD, Your word is s in heaven. Ps 119:89 5324
"Before the mountains were s, Pr 8:25 2883
And his people s in its cities? Jer 49:1 3427
He came and s in Capernaum, Mt 4:13 *2730*
came and s accounts with them. Mt 25:19 *4868*
of the Chaldeans and s in Haran. Ac 7:4 *2730*
he s *there* a year and six months, Ac 18:11 *2523*
shall be s in the lawful assembly. Ac 19:39 *1956*

SETTLEMENT
Now their s extended from Mesha as Gn 10:30 4186

SETTLEMENTS
These *were* their s, 1Ch 4:33 4186
Now these are their s according to 1Ch 6:54 4186
and s *were* Bethel with its towns, 1Ch 7:28 4186
The s where Kedar inhabits. Is 42:11 2691b

SETTLERS
who was of the s of Gilead, 1Ki 17:1 8453

SETTLING
are like hordes of grasshoppers S in Na 3:17 2583

SEVEN
Seth lived eight hundred and s years Gn 5:7 7651
Then Methuselah lived s hundred Gn 5:26 7651
So all the days of Lamech were s Gn 5:31 7651
"For after s more days, I will Gn 7:4 7651
It came about after the s days, Gn 7:10 7651
So he waited yet another s days; Gn 8:10 7651
Then he waited yet another s days, Gn 8:12 7651
Reu lived two hundred and s years Gn 11:21 7651
Then Abraham set s ewe lambs of Gn 21:28 7651
"What do these s ewe lambs mean, Gn 21:29 7651
"You shall take these s ewe lambs Gn 21:30 7651
"I will serve you s years for Gn 29:18 7651
So Jacob served s years for Rachel Gn 29:20 7651
serve with me for another s years." Gn 29:27 7651
with Laban for another s years. Gn 29:30 7651
him *a distance of* s days' journey, Gn 31:23 7651
bowed down to the ground s times, Gn 33:3 7651
from the Nile there came up s cows, Gn 41:2 7651
s other cows came up after them Gn 41:3 7651
ate up the s sleek and fat cows. Gn 41:4 7651
s ears of grain came up on a Gn 41:5 7651
Then behold, s ears, thin and Gn 41:6 7651
up the s plump and full ears. Gn 41:7 7651
and behold, s cows, fat and sleek Gn 41:18 7651
s other cows came up after them, Gn 41:19 7651
cows ate up the first s fat cows. Gn 41:20 7651
s ears, full and good, came up on a Gn 41:22 7651
s ears, withered, thin, *and* scorched Gn 41:23 7651
thin ears swallowed the s good ears. Gn 41:24 7651
"The s good cows are seven years; Gn 41:26 7651
"The seven good cows are s years; Gn 41:26 7651
the s good ears are seven years; Gn 41:26 7651
the seven good ears are s years; Gn 41:26 7651
"The s lean and ugly cows Gn 41:27 7651
came up after them are s years, Gn 41:27 7651
and the s thin ears scorched by Gn 41:27 7651
wind will be s years of famine. Gn 41:27 7651
s years of great abundance are Gn 41:29 7651
them s years of famine will come, Gn 41:30 7651
Egypt in the s years of abundance. Gn 41:34 7651
the s years of famine which will occur Gn 41:36 7651
During the s years of plenty Gn 41:47 7651
gathered all the food of *these* s years Gn 41:48 7651
When the s years of plenty which Gn 41:53 7651
s years of famine began to come, Gn 41:54 7651
there were s persons in all. Gn 46:25 7651
s days mourning for his father. Gn 50:10 7651
priest of Midian had s daughters; Ex 2:16 7651
S days passed after the LORD had Ex 7:25 7651
'S days you shall eat unleavened Ex 12:15 7651
'S days there shall be no leaven Ex 12:19 7651
"For s days you shall eat Ex 13:6 7651
be eaten throughout the s days; Ex 13:7 7651
shall be with its mother s days; Ex 22:30 7651
for s days you are to eat Ex 23:15 7651
shall make its lamps s *in number;* Ex 25:37 7651
"For s days the one of his sons Ex 29:30 7651
shall ordain them through s days. Ex 29:35 7651
For s days you shall make Ex 29:37 7651
For s days you are to eat Ex 34:18 7651
He made its s lamps with its Ex 37:23 7651
sprinkle some of the blood s times Lv 4:6 7651
it s times before the LORD, Lv 4:17 7651
some of it on the altar s times and Lv 8:11 7651
of the tent of meeting for s days, Lv 8:33 7651
he will ordain you through s days. Lv 8:33 7651
remain day and night for s days and Lv 8:35 7651
she shall be unclean for s days, Lv 12:2 7651
who has the infection for s days. Lv 13:4 7651
shall isolate him for s more days. Lv 13:5 7651
priest shall isolate him for s days; Lv 13:21 7651
shall isolate him for s days; Lv 13:26 7651
the scaly infection for s days. Lv 13:31 7651
person with the scale s more days. Lv 13:33 7651
article with the mark for s days. Lv 13:50 7651
quarantine it for s more days. Lv 13:54 7651
"He shall then sprinkle s times Lv 14:7 7651
stay outside his tent for s days. Lv 14:8 7651
the oil s times before the LORD. Lv 14:16 7651
left palm s times before the LORD. Lv 14:27 7651
quarantine the house for s days. Lv 14:38 7651
and sprinkle the house s times. Lv 14:51 7651
himself s days for his cleansing; Lv 15:13 7651
her menstrual impurity for s days; Lv 15:19 7651
him, he shall be unclean s days, Lv 15:24 7651
count off for herself s days; Lv 15:28 7651
the blood with his finger s times. Lv 16:14 7651
some of the blood on it s times and Lv 16:19 7651
remain s days with its mother, Lv 22:27 7651
for s days you shall eat Lv 23:6 7651
'But for s days you shall present Lv 23:8 7651
shall be s complete sabbaths. Lv 23:15 7651
present s one year old male lambs Lv 23:18 7651
is the Feast of Booths for s days to Lv 23:34 7651
'For s days you shall present an Lv 23:36 7651
the feast of the LORD for s days, Lv 23:39 7651
the LORD your God for s days. Lv 23:40 7651
as a feast to the LORD for s days in Lv 23:41 7651
shall live in booths for s days; Lv 23:42 7651
also to count off s sabbaths of years Lv 25:8 7651
for yourself, s times seven years, Lv 25:8 7651
for yourself, seven times s years, Lv 25:8 7651
time of the s sabbaths of years, Lv 25:8 7651
then I will punish you s times more Lv 26:18 7651
increase the plague on you s times Lv 26:21 7651
strike you s times for your sins. Lv 26:24 7651
punish you s times for your sins. Lv 26:28 7651
the s lamps will give light in the Nu 8:2 7651
she not bear her shame for s days? Nu 12:14 7651
Let her be shut up for s days Nu 12:14 7651
shut up outside the camp for s days, Nu 12:15 7651
Hebron was built s years before Nu 13:22 7651
of the tent of meeting s times. Nu 19:4 7651
shall be unclean for s days. Nu 19:11 7651
tent shall be unclean for s days. Nu 19:14 7651
shall be unclean for s days. Nu 19:16 7651
"Build s altars for me here, and Nu 23:1 7651
and prepare s bulls and seven rams Nu 23:1 7651
bulls and s rams for me here." Nu 23:1 7651
"I have set up the s altars, Nu 23:4 7651
and built s altars and offered a Nu 23:14 7651
"Build s altars for me here and Nu 23:29 7651
and prepare s bulls and seven rams Nu 23:29 7651
bulls and s rams for me here." Nu 23:29 7651
s male lambs one year old without Nu 28:11 7651
bread *shall be* eaten for s days. Nu 28:17 7651
ram and s male lambs one year old, Nu 28:19 7651
offer for each of the s lambs; Nu 28:21 7651
shall present daily, for s days, Nu 28:24 7651
ram, s male lambs one year old; Nu 28:27 7651
a tenth for each of the s lambs; Nu 28:29 7651
and s male lambs one year old Nu 29:2 7651
one-tenth for each of the s lambs. Nu 29:4 7651
ram, s male lambs one year old, Nu 29:8 7651
a tenth for each of the s lambs; Nu 29:10 7651
a feast to the LORD for s days. Nu 29:12 7651
s bulls, two rams, fourteen male Nu 29:32 7651
s male lambs one year old without Nu 29:36 7651
you, camp outside the camp s days; Nu 31:19 7651
s nations greater and stronger Dt 7:1 7651
"At the end of *every* s years you Dt 15:1 7651
s days you shall eat with it Dt 16:3 7651
"For s days no leaven shall be Dt 16:4 7651
shall count s weeks for yourself; Dt 16:9 7651
you shall begin to count s weeks Dt 16:9 7651
celebrate the Feast of Booths s days Dt 16:13 7651
"S days you shall celebrate a Dt 16:15 7651
and will flee before you s ways. Dt 28:7 7651
you will flee s ways before them, Dt 28:25 7651
"At the end of *every* s years, Dt 31:10 7651
"Also s priests shall carry seven Jos 6:4 7651
"Also seven priests shall carry s Jos 6:4 7651
march around the city s times, Jos 6:4 7651
and let s priests carry seven Jos 6:6 7651
and let seven priests carry s Jos 6:6 7651
the s priests carrying the seven Jos 6:8 7651
the seven priests carrying the s Jos 6:8 7651
The s priests carrying the Jos 6:13 7651
seven priests carrying the s trumpets Jos 6:13 7651
city in the same manner s times; Jos 6:15 7651
marched around the city s times. Jos 6:15 7651
of Israel s tribes who had not divided Jos 18:2 7651
shall divide it into s portions; Jos 18:5 7651
describe the land in s divisions, Jos 18:6 7651
cities in s divisions in a book; Jos 18:9 7651
into the hands of Midian s years. Jg 6:1 7651
and a second bull s years old, Jg 6:25 7651
And he judged Israel s years. Jg 12:9 7651
me within the s days of the feast, Jg 14:12 7651
s days while their feast lasted. Jg 14:17 7651
"If they bind me with s fresh cords Jg 16:7 7651
brought up to her s fresh cords that Jg 16:8 7651
If you weave the s locks of my hair Jg 16:13 7651
Delilah took the s locks of his hair Jg 16:14 7651
shave off the s locks of his hair. Jg 16:19 7651
and is better to you than s sons, Ru 4:15 7651
Even the barren gives birth to s, 1Sa 2:5 7651
country of the Philistines s months. 1Sa 6:1 7651
You shall wait s days until I come 1Sa 10:8 7651
"Let us alone for s days, 1Sa 11:3 7651
Now he waited s days, according to 1Sa 13:8 7651
Thus Jesse made s of his sons pass 1Sa 16:10 7651
tree at Jabesh, and fasted s days. 1Sa 31:13 7651
Judah was s years and six months. 2Sa 2:11 7651
over Judah s years and six months, 2Sa 5:5 7651
let s men from his sons be given 2Sa 21:6 7651
that the s of them fell together; 2Sa 21:9 7651
"Shall s years of famine come to 2Sa 24:13 7651
s years he reigned in Hebron and 1Ki 2:11 7651
and the third *was* s cubits wide; 1Ki 6:6 7651
So he was s years in building it. 1Ki 6:38 7651
s for the one capital and seven 1Ki 7:17 7651
and s for the other capital. 1Ki 7:17 7651
for s days and seven *more* days, 1Ki 8:65 7651
for seven days and s *more* days, 1Ki 8:65 7651
He had s hundred wives, 1Ki 11:3 7651
Zimri reigned s days at Tirzah. 1Ki 16:15 7651
And he said, "Go back" s times. 1Ki 18:43 7651
one over against the other s days. 1Ki 20:29 7651
made a circuit of s days' journey, 2Ki 3:9 7651
and the lad sneezed s times and 2Ki 4:35 7651
"Go and wash in the Jordan s times, 2Ki 5:10 7651
dipped *himself* s times in the Jordan, 2Ki 5:14 7651
come on the land for s years." 2Ki 8:1 7651
land of the Philistines s years. 2Ki 8:2 7651
At the end of s years, 2Ki 8:3 7651
s years old when he became king. 2Ki 11:21 7651
All the men of valor, s thousand, 2Ki 24:16 7651
he reigned s years and six months. 1Ch 3:4 7651
Johanan, Delaiah and Anani, s. 1Ch 3:24 7651
Jorai, Jacan, Zia and Eber, s. 1Ch 5:13 7651
to come in every s days from time to 1Ch 9:25 7651
oak in Jabesh, and fasted s days. 1Ch 10:12 7651
sacrificed s bulls and seven rams. 1Ch 15:26 7651
sacrificed seven bulls and s rams. 1Ch 15:26 7651
he reigned in Hebron s years and 1Ch 29:27 7651
the feast at that time for s days, 2Ch 7:8 7651
of the altar they observed s days and 2Ch 7:9 7651
seven days and the feast s days. 2Ch 7:9 7651
with a young bull and s rams, 2Ch 13:9 7651
s years old when he became king, 2Ch 24:1 7651
They brought s bulls, 2Ch 29:21 7651
They brought seven bulls, s rams, 2Ch 29:21 7651
seven bulls, seven rams, s lambs and 2Ch 29:21 7651
and s male goats for a sin offering 2Ch 29:21 7651
Bread *for* s days with great joy, 2Ch 30:21 7651
they ate for the appointed s days, 2Ch 30:22 7651
the feast another s days, 2Ch 30:23 7651
celebrated the s days with joy. 2Ch 30:23 7651
Feast of Unleavened Bread s days. 2Ch 35:17 7651
Unleavened Bread s days with joy, Ezr 6:22 7651
sent by the king and his s counselors Ezr 7:14 7655
they celebrated the feast s days, Ne 8:18 7651
king gave a banquet lasting s days Es 1:5 7651
the s eunuchs who served in the Es 1:10 7651
the s princes of Persia and Media Es 1:14 7651
gave her s choice maids from the Es 2:9 7651
S sons and three daughters were born Jb 1:2 7651
on the ground with him for s days Jb 2:13 7651
with him for seven days and s nights Jb 2:13 7651
Even in s evil will not touch you. Jb 5:19 7651
yourselves s bulls and seven rams, Jb 42:8 7651
yourselves seven bulls and s rams, Jb 42:8 7651
He had s sons and three daughters. Jb 42:13 7658
on the earth, refined s times. Ps 12:6 7659
S times a day I praise You, Ps 119:164 7651
s which are an abomination to Him: Pr 6:16 7651
She has hewn out her s pillars; Pr 9:1 7651
For a righteous man falls s times, Pr 24:16 7651
is wiser in his own eyes Than s men Pr 26:16 7651
are s abominations in his heart. Pr 26:25 7651
Divide your portion to s, Ec 11:2 7651
For s women will take hold of one Is 4:1 7651
He will strike it into s streams And Is 11:15 7651
the sun will be s times *brighter,* Is 30:26 7659

like the light of **s** days,	**Is 30:26**	7651
"She who bore **s** *sons* pines away;	**Jer 15:9**	7651
"At the end of **s** years each of	**Jer 34:14**	7651
and **s** of the king's advisers who	**Jer 52:25**	7651
s days where they were living,	**Ezk 3:15**	7651
At the end of **s** days	**Ezk 3:16**	7651
for **s** years they will make fires of	**Ezk 39:9**	7651
"For **s** months the house of Israel	**Ezk 39:12**	7651
At the end of **s** months they will	**Ezk 39:14**	7651
and it was reached by **s** steps,	**Ezk 40:22**	7651
There were **s** steps going up to it,	**Ezk 40:26**	7651
width of the doorway, **s** cubits.	**Ezk 41:3**	7651
'For **s** days you shall prepare	**Ezk 43:25**	7651
'For **s** days they shall make	**Ezk 43:26**	7651
s days shall elapse for him.	**Ezk 44:26**	7651
the Passover, a feast of **s** days;	**Ezk 45:21**	7620
"*During* the **s** days of the feast	**Ezk 45:23**	7651
a burnt offering to the LORD **s** bulls	**Ezk 45:23**	7651
bulls and **s** rams without blemish	**Ezk 45:23**	7651
on every day of the **s** days,	**Ezk 45:23**	7651
this, **s** days for the sin offering,	**Ezk 45:25**	7651
orders to heat the furnace **s** times	**Da 3:19**	7655
s periods of time pass over him.	**Da 4:16**	7655
s periods of time pass over him,"	**Da 4:23**	7655
and **s** periods of time will pass	**Da 4:25**	7655
and **s** periods of time will pass	**Da 4:32**	7655
be **s** weeks and sixty-two weeks;	**Da 9:25**	7655
raise against him **S** shepherds and	**Mi 5:5**	7651
on one stone are **s** eyes.	**Zch 3:9**	7651
and its **s** lamps on it with seven	**Zch 4:2**	7651
its seven lamps on it with **s** spouts	**Zch 4:2**	7651
But these **s** will be glad when they	**Zch 4:10**	7651
takes along with it **s** other spirits	**Mt 12:45**	2033
"**S**, and a few small fish."	**Mt 15:34**	2033
He took the **s** loaves and the fish;	**Mt 15:36**	2033
pieces, **s** large baskets full.	**Mt 15:37**	2033
the **s** loaves of the four thousand,	**Mt 16:10**	2033
and I forgive him? Up to **s** times?"	**Mt 18:21**	2034
do not say to you, up to **s** times,	**Mt 18:22**	2034
times, but up to seventy times **s**.	**Mt 18:22**	2033
"Now there were **s** brothers with us;	**Mt 22:25**	2033
whose wife of the **s** will she be?	**Mt 22:28**	2033
And they said, "**S**."	**Mk 8:5**	2033
and taking the **s** loaves, He gave	**Mk 8:6**	2033
and they picked up **s** large baskets	**Mk 8:8**	2033
broke the **s** for the four thousand,	**Mk 8:20**	2033
And they said to Him, "**S**."	**Mk 8:20**	2033
"There were **s** brothers;	**Mk 12:20**	2033
and *so* all **s** left no children.	**Mk 12:22**	2033
For all **s** had married her."	**Mk 12:23**	2033
whom He had cast out **s** demons.	**Mk 16:9**	2033
s years after her marriage,	**Lk 2:36**	2033
from whom **s** demons had gone out,	**Lk 8:2**	2033
takes *along* **s** other spirits more evil	**Lk 11:26**	2033
he sins against you **s** times a day,	**Lk 17:4**	2034
a day, and returns to you **s** times,	**Lk 17:4**	2034
"Now there were **s** brothers;	**Lk 20:29**	2033
and in the *same* way all **s** died,	**Lk 20:31**	2033
For all **s** had married her."	**Lk 20:33**	2033
was about **s** miles from Jerusalem.	**Lk 24:13**	1835
s men of good reputation,	**Ac 6:3**	2033
s nations in the land of Canaan,	**Ac 13:19**	2033
S sons of one Sceva, a Jewish chief	**Ac 19:14**	2033
and there we stayed **s** days.	**Ac 20:6**	2033
disciples, we stayed there **s** days;	**Ac 21:4**	2033
evangelist, who was one of the **s**,	**Ac 21:8**	2033
When the **s** days were almost over,	**Ac 21:27**	2033
to stay with them for **s** days;	**Ac 28:14**	2033
KEPT for Myself **S** THOUSAND MEN	**Ro 11:4**	2035
had been encircled for **s** days.	**Heb 11:30**	2033
of righteousness, with **s** others,	**2Pe 2:5**	3590
the **s** churches that are in Asia:	**Rv 1:4**	2033
and from the **s** Spirits who are	**Rv 1:4**	2033
and send *it* to the **s** churches:	**Rv 1:11**	2033
turned I saw **s** golden lampstands;	**Rv 1:12**	2033
In His right hand He held **s** stars	**Rv 1:16**	2033
mystery of the **s** stars which you saw	**Rv 1:20**	2033
hand, and the **s** golden lampstands:	**Rv 1:20**	2033
the **s** stars are the angels of the	**Rv 1:20**	2033
are the angels of the **s** churches,	**Rv 1:20**	2033
and the **s** lampstands are the seven	**Rv 1:20**	2033
lampstands are the **s** churches.	**Rv 1:20**	2033
the **s** stars in His right hand,	**Rv 2:1**	2033
among the **s** golden lampstands,	**Rv 2:1**	2033
He who has the **s** Spirits of God and	**Rv 3:1**	2033
Spirits of God and the **s** stars,	**Rv 3:1**	2033
And *there were* **s** lamps of fire	**Rv 4:5**	2033
which are the **s** Spirits of God;	**Rv 4:5**	2033
the back, sealed up with **s** seals.	**Rv 5:1**	2033
open the book and its **s** seals."	**Rv 5:5**	2033
having **s** horns and seven eyes,	**Rv 5:6**	2033
having seven horns and **s** eyes,	**Rv 5:6**	2033
which are the **s** Spirits of God,	**Rv 5:6**	2033
the Lamb broke one of the **s** seals,	**Rv 6:1**	2033
the **s** angels who stand before God,	**Rv 8:2**	2033
and **s** trumpets were given to them.	**Rv 8:2**	2033
And the **s** angels who had the seven	**Rv 8:6**	2033
seven angels who had the **s** trumpets	**Rv 8:6**	2033
the **s** peals of thunder uttered	**Rv 10:3**	2033
the **s** peals of thunder had spoken,	**Rv 10:4**	2033
the **s** peals of thunder have spoken	**Rv 10:4**	2033
s thousand people were killed	**Rv 11:13**	2033
having **s** heads and ten horns,	**Rv 12:3**	2033
and on his heads *were* **s** diadems.	**Rv 12:3**	2033
sea, having ten horns and **s** heads,	**Rv 13:1**	2033
s angels who had seven plagues,	**Rv 15:1**	2033
seven angels who had **s** plagues,	**Rv 15:1**	2033
and the **s** angels who had the seven	**Rv 15:6**	2033
seven angels who had the **s** plagues	**Rv 15:6**	2033
gave to the **s** angels seven golden	**Rv 15:7**	2033
gave to the seven angels **s** golden	**Rv 15:7**	2033
until the **s** plagues of the seven angels	**Rv 15:8**	2033
of the **s** angels were finished.	**Rv 15:8**	2033
temple, saying to the **s** angels,	**Rv 16:1**	2033
pour out on the earth the **s** bowls of	**Rv 16:1**	2033
Then one of the **s** angels who had	**Rv 17:1**	2033
s bowls came and spoke with me,	**Rv 17:1**	2033
having **s** heads and ten horns.	**Rv 17:3**	2033
has the **s** heads and the ten horns.	**Rv 17:7**	2033
The **s** heads are seven mountains on	**Rv 17:9**	2033
The seven heads are **s** mountains on	**Rv 17:9**	2033
and they are **s** kings;	**Rv 17:10**	2033
an eighth and is *one* of the **s**,	**Rv 17:11**	2033
Then one of the **s** angels who had	**Rv 21:9**	2033
the seven angels who had the **s** bowls	**Rv 21:9**	2033
bowls full of the **s** last plagues came	**Rv 21:9**	2033

SEVENFOLD

will be taken on him **s**."	**Gn 4:15**	7659
If Cain is avenged **s**,	**Gn 4:24**	7659
And return to our neighbors **s** into	**Ps 79:12**	7659
when he is found, he must repay **s**;	**Pr 6:31**	7659

SEVENS

you of every clean animal by **s**,	**Gn 7:2**	7651
of the birds of the sky, by **s**,	**Gn 7:3**	7651

SEVENTEEN

Joseph, when **s** years of age, was	**Gn 37:2**	7651, 6240
in the land of Egypt **s** years;	**Gn 47:28**	7651, 6240
he reigned **s** years in Jerusalem,	**1Ki 14:21**	7651, 6240
Samaria, *and he reigned* **s** years.	**2Ki 13:1**	7651, 6240
he reigned **s** years in Jerusalem,	**2Ch 12:13**	7651, 6240
for him, **s** shekels of silver.	**Jer 32:9**	7651, 6235

SEVENTEENTH

month, on the **s** day of the month,	**Gn 7:11**	7651, 6240
month, on the **s** day of the month,	**Gn 8:4**	7651, 6240
in the **s** year of Jehoshaphat king of	**1Ki 22:51**	7651, 6240
In the **s** year of Pekah the son of	**2Ki 16:1**	7651, 6240
the **s** for Hezir, the eighteenth	**1Ch 24:15**	7651, 6240
for the **s** to Joshbekashah, his	**1Ch 25:24**	7651, 6240

SEVENTH

By the **s** day God completed His	**Gn 2:2**	7637
and He rested on the **s** day from	**Gn 2:2**	7637
the **s** day and sanctified it,	**Gn 2:3**	7637
In the **s** month, on the	**Gn 8:4**	7637
the first day until the **s** day,	**Ex 12:15**	7637
holy assembly on the **s** day;	**Ex 12:16**	7637
and on the **s** day there shall be a	**Ex 13:6**	7637
shall gather it, but on the **s** day,	**Ex 16:26**	7637
It came about on the **s** day	**Ex 16:27**	7637
out of his place on the **s** day."	**Ex 16:29**	7637
So the people rested on the **s** day.	**Ex 16:30**	7637
but the **s** day is a sabbath of the	**Ex 20:10**	7637
in them, and rested on the **s** day;	**Ex 20:11**	7637
but on the **s** he shall go out as a	**Ex 21:2**	7637
but *on* the **s** year you shall let it	**Ex 23:11**	7637
but on the **s** day you shall cease	**Ex 23:12**	7637
and on the **s** day He called to	**Ex 24:16**	7637
but on the **s** day there is a sabbath	**Ex 31:15**	7637
on the **s** day He ceased *from labor,*	**Ex 31:17**	7637
but on the **s** day you shall rest;	**Ex 34:21**	7637
s day you shall have a holy *day,*	**Ex 35:2**	7637
shall look at him on the **s** day,	**Lv 13:5**	7637
look at him again on the **s** day,	**Lv 13:6**	7637
shall look at him on the **s** day.	**Lv 13:27**	7637
"On the **s** day the priest	**Lv 13:32**	7637
"Then on the **s** day the priest	**Lv 13:34**	7637
look at the mark on the **s** day;	**Lv 13:51**	7637
"It will be on the **s** day that	**Lv 14:9**	7637
the **s** day and make an inspection.	**Lv 14:39**	7637
in the **s** month, on the tenth day	**Lv 16:29**	7637
but on the **s** day there is a	**Lv 23:3**	7637
the **s** day is a holy convocation;	**Lv 23:8**	7637
to the day after the **s** sabbath;	**Lv 23:16**	7637
'In the **s** month on the first of	**Lv 23:24**	7637
s month is the day of atonement;	**Lv 23:27**	7637
'On the fifteenth of this **s** month	**Lv 23:34**	7637
the fifteenth day of the **s** month,	**Lv 23:39**	7637
shall celebrate it in the **s** month.	**Lv 23:41**	7637
but during the **s** year the land	**Lv 25:4**	7637
on the tenth day of the **s** month;	**Lv 25:9**	7637
going to eat on the **s** year if we do	**Lv 25:20**	7637
he shall shave it on the **s** day.	**Nu 6:9**	7637
On the **s** day *it was* Elishama the	**Nu 7:48**	7637
on the third day and on the **s** day,	**Nu 19:12**	7637
on the third day and on the **s** day,	**Nu 19:12**	7637
on the third day and on the **s** day;	**Nu 19:19**	7637
and on the **s** day he shall purify	**Nu 19:19**	7637
'On the **s** day you shall have a	**Nu 28:25**	7637
'Now in the **s** month, on the first	**Nu 29:1**	7637
on the tenth day of this **s** month	**Nu 29:7**	7637
on the fifteenth day of the **s** month	**Nu 29:12**	7637
'Then on the **s** day:	**Nu 29:32**	7637
on the third day and on the **s** day.	**Nu 31:19**	7637
clothes on the **s** day and be clean,	**Nu 31:24**	7637
but the **s** day is a sabbath of the	**Dt 5:14**	7637
'The **s** year, the year of remission,	**Dt 15:9**	7651
the **s** year you shall set him free.	**Dt 15:12**	7637
and on the **s** day there shall be a	**Dt 16:8**	7637
then on the **s** day you shall march	**Jos 6:4**	7637
Then on the **s** day	**Jos 6:15**	7637
At the **s** time,	**Jos 6:16**	7637
The **s** lot fell to the tribe of the	**Jos 19:40**	7637
And on the **s** day	**Jg 14:17**	7637
s day before the sun went down,	**Jg 14:18**	7637
on the **s** day that the child died.	**2Sa 12:18**	7637
Ethanim, which is the **s** month.	**1Ki 8:2**	7637
It came about at the **s** *time,*	**1Ki 18:44**	7637
on the **s** day the battle was joined,	**1Ki 20:29**	7637
Now in the **s** year Jehoiada sent	**2Ki 11:4**	7637
In the **s** year of Jehu, Jehoash	**2Ki 12:1**	7651
which was the **s** year of Hoshea son	**2Ki 18:9**	7637
on the **s** day of the fifth month,	**2Ki 25:8**	7651
But it came about in the **s** month,	**2Ki 25:25**	7637
Ozem the sixth, David the **s**;	**1Ch 2:15**	7637
Attai the sixth, Eliel the **s**,	**1Ch 12:11**	7637
the **s** for Hakkoz, the eighth for	**1Ch 24:10**	7637
the **s** to Jesharelah, his sons and	**1Ch 25:14**	7637
the sixth, Eliehoenai the **s**.	**1Ch 26:3**	7637
Ammiel the sixth, Issachar the **s**	**1Ch 26:5**	7637
The **s** for the seventh month *was*	**1Ch 27:10**	7637
The seventh for the **s** month *was*	**1Ch 27:10**	7637
the feast, that is *in* the **s** month.	**2Ch 5:3**	7637
the twenty-third day of the **s** month	**2Ch 7:10**	7637
Now in the **s** year Jehoiada	**2Ch 23:1**	7637
and finished *them* by the **s** month.	**2Ch 31:7**	7637
Now when the **s** month came, and the	**Ezr 3:1**	7637
From the first day of the **s** month	**Ezr 3:6**	7637
in the **s** year of King Artaxerxes.	**Ezr 7:7**	7651
was in the **s** year of the king.	**Ezr 7:8**	7637
And when the **s** month came, the	**Ne 7:73**	7637
on the first day of the **s** month.	**Ne 8:2**	7637
during the feast of the **s** month.	**Ne 8:14**	7637
we will forego *the crops* the **s** year	**Ne 10:31**	7637
On the **s** day, when the heart of	**Es 1:10**	7637
in the **s** year of his reign.	**Es 2:16**	7651
in the same year in the **s** month.	**Jer 28:17**	7637
In the **s** month Ishmael	**Jer 41:1**	7637
in the **s** year 3,023 Jews;	**Jer 52:28**	7651
Now in the **s** year,	**Ezk 20:1**	7637
month, on the **s** of the month,	**Ezk 30:20**	7651
"Thus you shall do on the **s**	**Ezk 45:20**	7651
"In the **s** *month,* on the fifteenth	**Ezk 45:25**	7637
On the twenty-first of the **s** month,	**Hg 2:1**	7637
mourned in the fifth and **s** months	**Zch 7:5**	7637
of the fifth, the fast of the **s** and	**Zch 8:19**	7637
and the third, down to the **s**.	**Mt 22:26**	2033
the **s** hour the fever left him."	**Jn 4:52**	1442
somewhere concerning the **s** *day:*	**Heb 4:4**	1442
AND GOD RESTED ON THE **S** DAY	**Heb 4:4**	1442
in the **s** *generation* from Adam,	**Jude 1:14**	1442
When the Lamb broke the **s** seal,	**Rv 8:1**	1442
days of the voice of the **s** angel,	**Rv 10:7**	1442
Then the **s** angel sounded;	**Rv 11:15**	1442
Then the **s** *angel* poured out his	**Rv 16:17**	1442
the **s**, chrysolite; the eighth, beryl;	**Rv 21:20**	1442

SEVENTY

Kenan lived **s** years, and	**Gn 5:12**	7657
Terah lived **s** years, and	**Gn 11:26**	7657
Jacob, who came to Egypt, *were* **s**.	**Gn 46:27**	7657
the Egyptians wept for him **s** days.	**Gn 50:3**	7657
loins of Jacob were **s** in number,	**Ex 1:5**	7657
springs of water and **s** date palms,	**Ex 15:27**	7657
and **s** of the elders of Israel,	**Ex 24:1**	7657
and **s** of the elders of Israel,	**Ex 24:9**	7657
one silver bowl of **s** shekels,	**Nu 7:13**	7657
one silver bowl of **s** shekels,	**Nu 7:19**	7657
one silver bowl of **s** shekels,	**Nu 7:25**	7657
one silver bowl of **s** shekels,	**Nu 7:31**	7657
one silver bowl of **s** shekels,	**Nu 7:37**	7657
one silver bowl of **s** shekels,	**Nu 7:43**	7657
one silver bowl of **s** shekels,	**Nu 7:49**	7657
one silver bowl of **s** shekels,	**Nu 7:55**	7657
one silver bowl of **s** shekels,	**Nu 7:61**	7657
one silver bowl of **s** shekels,	**Nu 7:67**	7657
one silver bowl of **s** shekels,	**Nu 7:73**	7657
one silver bowl of **s** shekels,	**Nu 7:79**	7657
thirty *shekels* and each bowl **s**;	**Nu 7:85**	7657
s men from the elders of Israel,	**Nu 11:16**	7657
he gathered **s** men of the elders of	**Nu 11:24**	7657
and placed *Him* upon the **s** elders.	**Nu 11:25**	7657
springs of water and **s** palm trees,	**Nu 33:9**	7657
down to Egypt **s** persons *in all,*	**Dt 10:22**	7657
"**S** kings with their thumbs and	**Jg 1:7**	7657
Now Gideon had **s** sons who were his	**Jg 8:30**	7657
that **s** men, all the sons of Jerubbaal	**Jg 9:2**	7657
They gave him **s** *pieces* of silver	**Jg 9:4**	7657
the sons of Jerubbaal, **s** men,	**Jg 9:5**	7657
and have killed his sons, **s** men,	**Jg 9:18**	7657
s sons of Jerubbaal might come,	**Jg 9:24**	7657
father in killing his **s** brothers.	**Jg 9:56**	7657
grandsons who rode on **s** donkeys;	**Jg 12:14**	7657
and **s** thousand men of the people	**2Sa 24:15**	7657
Now Ahab had **s** sons in Samaria.	**2Ki 10:1**	7657
Now the king's sons, **s** persons,	**2Ki 10:6**	7657
and slaughtered *them,* **s** persons,	**2Ki 10:7**	7657
until **s** years were complete.	**2Ch 36:21**	7657
of our life, they contain **s** years,	**Ps 90:10**	7657
Tyre will be forgotten for **s** years like	**Is 23:15**	7657
At the end of **s** years it will	**Is 23:15**	7657
end of **s** years that the LORD will visit	**Is 23:17**	7657
serve the king of Babylon **s** years.	**Jer 25:11**	7657
when **s** years are completed I will	**Jer 25:12**	7657
'When **s** years have been completed	**Jer 29:10**	7657
s elders of the house of Israel,	**Ezk 8:11**	7657
toward the west *was* **s** cubits wide;	**Ezk 41:12**	7657

of Jerusalem, *namely,* **s** years. Da 9:2 7657
"**S** weeks have been decreed for Da 9:24 7657
been indignant these **s** years?" Zch 1:12 7657
and seventh months these **s** years, Zch 7:5 7657
times, but up to **s** times seven. Mt 18:22 *1441*
this the Lord appointed **s** others, Lk 10:1 *1440*
The **s** returned with joy, Lk 10:17 *1440*
with **s** horsemen and two hundred Ac 23:23 *1440*

SEVENTY-FIVE
Now Abram was **s** years old when he Gn 12:4 7657
he lived, one hundred and **s** years. Gn 25:7 7657
to come to him, **s** persons *in all.* Ac 7:14 *1440, 4002*

SEVENTY-SEVEN
were seven hundred and **s** years, Gn 5:31 7657
of Succoth and its elders, **s** men. Jg 8:14 7657

SEVENTY-SEVENFOLD
sevenfold, Then Lamech **s**." Gn 4:24 7657

SEVENTY-SIX
were two hundred and **s** persons. Ac 27:37 *1440, 1803*

SEVENTY-TWO
And he measured its wall, **s** yards, Rv 21:17

SEVER
by its wings, *but* shall not **s** *it.* Lv 1:17 914
its neck, but he shall not **s** *it.* Lv 5:8 914

SEVERAL
Jeroboam and captured from him **s** 2Ch 13:19
and these are their **s** portions," Ezk 48:29
to Capernaum **s** days afterward, Mk 2:1
Now for **s** days he was with the Ac 9:19 *5100*
"Now after **s** years I came to Ac 24:17 *4183*
Now when **s** days had elapsed, King Ac 25:13 *5100*

SEVERE
for the famine was **s** in the land. Gn 12:10 3515
birth and she suffered **s** labor. Gn 35:16 7185
When she was in **s** labor Gn 35:17 7185
for it *will be* very **s**. Gn 41:31 3515
famine was **s** in the land of Egypt. Gn 41:56 2388
the famine was **s** in all the earth. Gn 41:57 2388
Now the famine was **s** in the land. Gn 43:1 3515
famine is **s** in the land of Canaan. Gn 47:4 3515
because the famine was very **s**, Gn 47:13 3515
the famine was **s** upon them. Gn 47:20 2388
will come *with* a very **s** pestilence on Ex 9:3 3515
in the midst of the hail, very **s**, Ex 9:24 3515
the people with a very **s** plague. Nu 11:33 7227a
even **s** and lasting plagues, Dt 28:59 1419
is **s** on us and on Dagon our god." 1Sa 5:7 7185
was **s** all the days of Saul; 1Sa 14:52 2389
That day the battle was very **s**, 2Sa 2:17 7186
and his sickness was so **s** that 1Ki 17:17 2389
Now the famine *was* **s** in Samaria. 1Ki 18:2 2389
the *fourth* month the famine was so **s** 2Ki 25:3 2388
His disease was **s**, yet even in his 2Ch 16:12 4605
and you will suffer **s** sickness, 2Ch 21:15 7227a
This is vanity and a **s** affliction. Ec 6:2 7451a
death, Jealousy is as **s** as Sheol; SS 8:6 7186
the fourth month the famine was so **s** Jer 52:6 2388
s judgments against Jerusalem: Ezk 14:21 7451a
a **s** earthquake had occurred, Mt 28:2 *3173*
a **s** famine occurred in that country, Lk 15:14 *2478*
and **s** treatment of the body, Col 2:23 *857*
its plague was extremely **s**. Rv 16:21 *3173*

SEVERED
You have been **s** from Christ, you Ga 5:4 *2673*

SEVERELY
so that they were **s** distressed. Jg 2:15 3966
he oppressed the sons of Israel **s** for Jg 4:3 2394
When He had **s** dealt with them, did 1Sa 6:6 5953a
for I am **s** wounded." 1Ki 22:34 2470a
for I am **s** wounded." 2Ch 18:33 2470a
The Lord has disciplined me **s**, Ps 118:18 3256
pain Which was **s** dealt out to me, La 1:12 5953a
all who lift it will be **s** injured. Zch 12:3 8295
For this reason reprove them **s** so that Ti 1:13 *664*

SEVERER
How much **s** punishment do you think Heb 10:29 *5501*

SEVERITY
shall not rule over him with **s**, Lv 25:43 6531
not rule with **s** over one another. Lv 25:46 6531
he shall not rule over him with **s** in Lv 25:53 6531
with **s** you have dominated them. Ezk 34:4 6531
then the kindness and **s** of God; Ro 11:22 *663*
to those who fell, **s**, Ro 11:22 *663*
that when present I *need* not use **s**, 2Co 13:10 *664*

SEW
apart and a time to **s** together; Ec 3:7 8609
who **s** *magic* bands on all wrists and Ezk 13:18 8609

SEWED
and they **s** fig leaves together and Gn 3:7 8609
"I have **s** sackcloth over my skin And Jb 16:15 8609

SEWS
No one **s** a patch of unshrunk cloth Mk 2:21 *1976*

SEXUAL
in **s** promiscuity and sensuality, Ro 13:13 *2845*
you abstain from **s** immorality; 1Th 4:3 *4202*

SHAALABBIN
and **S** and Aijalon and Ithlah, Jos 19:42 8169

SHAALBIM
Mount Heres, in Aijalon and in **S**; Jg 1:35 8169
Ben-deker in Makaz and **S** and 1Ki 4:9 8169

SHAALBONITE
Eliahba the **S**, the sons of Jashen, 2Sa 23:32 8170
the Baharumite, Eliahba the **S**, 1Ch 11:33 8170

SHAALIM
they passed through the land of **S**, 1Sa 9:4 8171

SHAAPH
Geshan, Pelet, Ephah and **S**. 1Ch 2:47 8174a
bore **S** the father of Madmannah, 1Ch 2:49 8174a

SHAARAIM
and **S** and Adithaim and Gederah and Jos 15:36 8189
lay along the way to **S**, 1Sa 17:52 8189
Hazar-susim, Beth-biri and **S**. 1Ch 4:31 8189

SHAASHGAZ
second harem, to the custody of **S**, Es 2:14 8190

SHABBETHAI
and **S** the Levite supporting them. Ezr 10:15 7678
Bani, Sherebiah, Jamin, Akkub, **S**, Ne 8:7 7678
and **S** and Jozabad, from the Ne 11:16 7678

SHACK
drunkard And it totters like a **s**, Is 24:20 4412

SHACKLES
you, And I will tear off your **s**." Na 1:13 4147
been bound with **s** and chains, Mk 5:4 *3976*
him and the **s** broken in pieces, Mk 5:4 *3976*
chains and **s** and kept under guard, Lk 8:29 *3976*

SHADE
you, come and take refuge in my **s**; Jg 9:15 6738
"As a slave who pants for the **s**, Jb 7:2 6738
"The lotus plants cover him with **s**; Jb 40:22 6738
Lord is your **s** on your right hand. Ps 121:5 6738
In his **s** I took great delight and SS 2:3 6738
to *give* **s** from the heat by day, Is 4:6 6738
from the storm, a **s** from the heat; Is 25:4 6738
Like the **s** of a huge rock in a Is 32:2 6738
nest in the **s** of its branches. Ezk 17:23 6738
beautiful branches and forest **s**, Ezk 31:3 6751
great nations lived under its **s**. Ezk 31:6 6738
gone down from its **s** and left it. Ezk 31:12 6738
under its **s** among the nations. Ezk 31:17 6738
beasts of the field found **s** under it, Da 4:12 2927
Because their **s** is pleasant. Hos 4:13 6738
sat under it in the **s** until he could see Jon 4:5 6738
it grew up over Jonah to be a **s** over Jon 4:6 6738
OF THE AIR CAN NEST UNDER ITS **S**." Mk 4:32 *4639*

SHADOW
are seeing the **s** of the mountains as Jg 9:36 6738
shall the **s** go forward ten steps 2Ki 20:9 6738
for the **s** to decline ten steps; 2Ki 20:10 6738
the **s** turn backward ten steps." 2Ki 20:10 6738
and He brought the **s** on the 2Ki 20:11 6738
days on the earth are like a **s**, 1Ch 29:15 6738
our days on earth are as a **s**. Jb 8:9 6738
the land of darkness and deep **s**, Jb 10:21 6757
itself, Of deep **s** without order, Jb 10:22 6757
He also flees like a **s** and does not Jb 14:2 6738
And all my members are as a **s**. Jb 17:7 6738
out The rock in gloom and deep **s**. Jb 28:3 6757
"There is no darkness or deep **s** Jb 34:22 6757
Hide me in the **s** of Your wings Ps 17:8 6738
the valley of the **s** of death, Ps 23:4 6757
take refuge in the **s** of Your wings. Ps 36:7 6738
covered us with the **s** of death. Ps 44:19 6757
And in the **s** of Your wings I will Ps 57:1 6738
the **s** of Your wings I sing for joy. Ps 63:7 6738
mountains were covered with its **s**, Ps 80:10 6738
abide in the **s** of the Almighty. Ps 91:1 6738
My days are like a lengthened **s**, Ps 102:11 6738
in darkness and in the **s** of death, Ps 107:10 6757
of darkness and the **s** of death And Ps 107:14 6757
like a **s** when it lengthens; Ps 109:23 6738
His days are like a passing **s**. Ps 144:4 6738
He will spend them like a **s**. Ec 6:12 6738
not lengthen his days like a **s**, Ec 8:13 6738
Cast your **s** like night at high noon; Is 16:3 6738
Like heat by the **s** of a cloud, Is 25:5 6738
to seek shelter in the **s** of Egypt! Is 30:2 6738
And the shelter in the **s** of Egypt, Is 30:3 6738
will cause the **s** on the stairway, Is 38:8 6738
So the sun's **s** went back ten Is 38:8 6738
In the **s** of His hand He has Is 49:2 6738
covered you with the **s** of My hand, Is 51:16 6738
"In the **s** of Heshbon The Jer 48:45 6738
"Under his **s** We shall live among La 4:20 6738
Those who live in his **s** Will again Hos 14:7 6738
IN THE LAND AND **S** OF DEATH, Mt 4:16 *4639*
IN DARKNESS AND THE **S** OF DEATH, Lk 1:79 *4639*
s might fall on any one of them. Ac 5:15 *4639*
are a *mere* **s** of what is to come; Col 2:17 *4639*
copy and **s** of the heavenly things, Heb 8:5 *4639*
since it has *only* a **s** of the good Heb 10:1 *4639*
is no variation or shifting **s**. Jas 1:17 *644*

SHADOWS
of the day when the **s** flee away, SS 2:17 6738
of the day When the **s** flee away, SS 4:6 6738
For the **s** of the evening lengthen! Jer 6:4 6738

SHADRACH
name Belteshazzar, to Hananiah **S**, Da 1:7 7714
of the king, and he appointed **S**, Da 2:49 7715
the province of Babylon, *namely* **S**, Da 3:12 7715
and anger gave orders to bring **S**, Da 3:13 7715
"Is it true, **S**, Meshach and Da 3:14 7715
S, Meshach and Abed-nego replied Da 3:16 7715
expression was altered toward **S**, Da 3:19 7715
who *were* in his army to tie up **S**, Da 3:20 7715
slew those men who carried up **S**, Da 3:22 7715
S, Meshach and Abed-nego, fell Da 3:23 7715
"**S**, Meshach and Abed-nego, come Da 3:26 7715
S, Meshach and Abed-nego came Da 3:26 7715
"Blessed be the God of **S**, Da 3:28 7715
offensive against the God of **S**, Da 3:29 7715
Then the king caused **S**, Da 3:30 7715

SHAFT
its base and its **s** are to be made of Ex 25:31 7070
hammered work, its base and its **s**; Ex 37:17 7070
The **s** of his spear was like a 1Sa 17:7 2671
the **s** of whose spear was like a 2Sa 21:19 6086
with iron and the **s** of a spear, 2Sa 23:7 6086
the **s** of whose spear *was* like a 1Ch 20:5 6086
"He sinks a **s** far from habitation, Jb 28:4 5158a

SHAFTS
He makes His arrows fiery **s**. Ps 7:13 1814
arrows, let them be as headless **s**. Ps 58:7 4135

SHAGEE
the son of **S** the Hararite, 1Ch 11:34 7681

SHAGGY
and **s** goats will frolic there. Is 13:21 8163a
"The **s** goat *represents* the Da 8:21 8163a

SHAHARAIM
S became the father of 1Ch 8:8 7842

SHAHAZUMAH
to Tabor and **S** and Beth-shemesh, Jos 19:22 7831

SHAKE
other times and **s** myself free." Jg 16:20 5287
"Thus may God **s** out every man Ne 5:13 5287
And made all my bones **s**. Jb 4:14 6342
against you And **s** my head at you. Jb 16:4 5128
All who see them will **s** the head. Ps 64:8 5074
make their loins **s** continually. Ps 69:23 4571
the cherubim, let the earth **s**! Ps 99:1 5120
trees of the forest **s** with the wind. Is 7:2 5128
the foundations of the earth **s**. Is 24:18 7493
To **s** the nations back and forth in Is 30:28 5130
S yourself from the dust, rise up, Is 52:2 5287
be removed and the hills may **s**, Is 54:10 4131
will be astonished And **s** his head. Jer 18:16 5110
him you **s** *your head in scorn.* Jer 48:27 5110
They hiss and **s** their heads At the La 2:15 5128
your walls will **s** at the noise of Ezk 26:10 7493
"Shall not the coastlands **s** at Ezk 26:15 7493
pilots The pasture lands will **s**. Ezk 27:28 7493
the earth will **s** at My presence; Ezk 38:20 7493
so that the thresholds will **s**, Am 9:1 7493
And I will **s** the house of Israel Am 9:9 5128
to **s** the heavens and the earth, Hg 2:6 7493
'I will **s** all the nations; Hg 2:7 7493
to **s** the heavens and the earth. Hg 2:21 7493
city, **s** the dust off your feet. Mt 10:14 *1621*
s the dust off the soles of Mk 6:11 *1621*
that house and could not **s** it, Lk 6:48 *4531*
s the dust off your feet as a Lk 9:5 *660*
MORE I WILL **S** NOT ONLY THE EARTH, Heb 12:26 *4579*

SHAKEN
heaven were trembling And were **s**, 2Sa 22:8 1607
as a reed is **s** in the water; 1Ki 14:15 5110
She has **s** *her* head behind you, The 2Ki 19:21 5128
may he be **s** out and emptied." Ne 5:13 5287
me by the neck and **s** me to pieces; Jb 16:12 6483a
People are **s** and pass away, Jb 34:20 1607
And the wicked be **s** out of it? Jb 38:13 5287
adversaries will rejoice when I am **s**. Ps 13:4 4131
does these things will never be **s**. Ps 15:5 4131
at my right hand, I will not be **s**. Ps 16:8 4131
were trembling And were **s**, Ps 18:7 1607
of the Most High he will not be **s**. Ps 21:7 4131
never allow the righteous to be **s**. Ps 55:22 4131
I shall not be greatly **s**. Ps 62:2 4131
I shall not be **s**. Ps 62:6 4131
foundations of the earth are **s**. Ps 82:5 4131
I am **s** off like the locust. Ps 109:23 5287
For he will never be **s**; Ps 112:6 4131
The righteous will never be **s**, Pr 10:30 4131
And the earth will be **s** from its Is 13:13 7493
through, The earth is **s** violently. Is 24:19 4131
She has **s** *her* head behind you, The Is 37:22 5128
covenant of peace will not be **s**," Is 54:10 4131
the earth is **s**, and an outcry is Jer 50:46 7493
nations As *grain* is **s** in a sieve, Am 9:9 5128
When **s**, they fall into the eater's Na 3:12 5128
A reed **s** by the wind? Mt 11:7 *4531*
powers of the heavens will be **s**. Mt 24:29 *4531*
that are in the heavens will be **s**. Mk 13:25 *4531*
measure—pressed down, **s** together, Lk 6:38 *4531*
A reed **s** by the wind? Lk 7:24 *4531*
powers of the heavens will be **s**. Lk 21:26 *4531*
RIGHT HAND, SO THAT I WILL NOT BE **S**. Ac 2:25 *4531*
they had gathered together was **s**, Ac 4:31 *4531*
of the prison house were **s**; Ac 16:26 *4531*
that you not be quickly **s** from 2Th 2:2 *4531*
of those things which can be **s**, Heb 12:27 *4531*
which cannot be **s** may remain. Heb 12:27 *4531*
a kingdom which cannot be **s**, Heb 12:28 *761*
figs when **s** by a great wind. Rv 6:13 *4579*

SHAKES
Who **s** the earth out of its place, Jb 9:6 7264
of the Lord **s** the wilderness; Ps 29:8 2342a
Lord **s** the wilderness of Kadesh. Ps 29:8 2342a
He **s** his fist at the mountain of Is 10:32 5130
And **s** his hands so that they hold Is 33:15 5287
he **s** the arrows, he consults the Ezk 21:21 7043

SHAKING
"With **s** and rage he races over Jb 39:24 7494
in it like the **s** of an olive tree, Is 17:6 5363
As the **s** of an olive tree, Is 24:13 5363

SHALISHAH
and passed through the land of **S**, 1Sa 9:4 8031

SHALLECHETH
was to the west, by the gate of **S**, 1Ch 26:16 7996

SHALLOWS
they might run aground on *the* s Ac 27:17
SHALLUM
Then S the son of Jabesh conspired 2Ki 15:10 7967
S son of Jabesh became king in the 2Ki 15:13 7967
struck S son of Jabesh in Samaria, 2Ki 15:14 7967
Now the rest of the acts of S and 2Ki 15:15 7967
the wife of S the son of Tikvah, 2Ki 22:14 7967
and Sismai became the father of S, 1Ch 2:40 7967
S became the father of Jekamiah, 1Ch 2:41 7967
the third Zedekiah, the fourth S. 1Ch 3:15 7967
S his son, Mibsam his son, Mishma 1Ch 4:25 7967
and Zadok became the father of S, 1Ch 6:12 7967
S became the father of Hilkiah, 1Ch 6:13 7967
were Jahziel, Guni, Jezer, and S, 1Ch 7:13 7967
Now the gatekeepers *were* S and 1Ch 9:17 7967
and their relatives (S the chief 1Ch 9:17 7967
S the son of Kore, the son of 1Ch 9:19 7967
the firstborn of S the Korahite, 1Ch 9:31 7967
Jehizkiah the son of S, 2Ch 28:12 7967
the wife of S the son of Tokhath, 2Ch 34:22 7967
the sons of S, the sons of Ater, Ezr 2:42 7967
son of S, son of Zadok, son of Ezr 7:2 7967
S, Telem and Uri. Ezr 10:24 7967
S, Amariah *and* Joseph. Ezr 10:42 7967
to him S the son of Hallohesh, Ne 3:12 7967
S the son of Col-hozeh, the Ne 3:15 7968
the sons of S, the sons of Ater, Ne 7:45 7967
in regard to S the son of Josiah, Jer 22:11 7967
of S your uncle is coming to you, Jer 32:7 7967
chamber of Maaseiah the son of S, Jer 35:4 7967
SHALMAI
the sons of Hagab, the sons of S, Ezr 2:46 8014
the sons of Hagaba, the sons of S, Ne 7:48 8014
SHALMAN
As S destroyed Beth-arbel on the Hos 10:14 8020
SHALMANESER
S king of Assyria came up against 2Ki 17:3 8022
S king of Assyria came up 2Ki 18:9 8022
SHAMA
S and Jeiel the sons of Hotham the 1Ch 11:44 8091
SHAME
she not bear her s for seven days? Nu 12:14 3637
the son of Jesse to your own s and to 1Sa 20:30 1322
the s of your mother's nakedness? 1Sa 20:30 1322
"Today you have covered with s 2Sa 19:5 954
They were dismayed and put to s; 2Ki 19:26 954
he returned in s to his own land. 2Ch 32:21 1322, 6440
and to plunder and to open s, Ezr 9:7 1322
hate you will be clothed with s, Jb 8:22 1322
to s the counsel of the afflicted, Ps 14:6 954
Let me not be put to s, Ps 31:17 954
Let the wicked be put to s, Ps 31:17 954
Let those be clothed with s and Ps 35:26 1322
because of their s Who say to me, Ps 40:15 1322
have put to s those who hate us. Ps 44:7 954
You put *them* to s, because God had Ps 53:5 954
reproach and my s and my dishonor; Ps 69:19 1322
be turned back because of their s Ps 70:3 1322
You have covered him with s. Ps 89:45 955
with their own s as with a robe. Ps 109:29 1322
O LORD, do not put me to s! Ps 119:31 954
Be put to s and turned backward; Ps 129:5 954
"His enemies I will clothe with s, Ps 132:18 1322
Poverty and s *will come* to him who Pr 13:18 7036
hears, It is folly and s to him. Pr 18:13 3639
own way brings s to his mother. Pr 29:15 954
uncovered, to the s of Egypt. Is 20:4 6172
be, You s of your master's house.' Is 22:18 7036
for the people and are put to s; Is 26:11 954
safety of Pharaoh will be your s And Is 30:3 1322
but for s and also for reproach." Is 30:5 1322
They were dismayed and put to s; Is 37:27 954
back *and* be utterly put to s, Is 42:17 954
so that they will be put to s. Is 44:9 954
his companions will be put to s, Is 44:11 954
let them together be put to s. Is 44:11 954
be put to s and even humiliated, Is 45:16 954
s or humiliated To all eternity. Is 45:17 954
angry at Him will be put to s. Is 45:24 954
Your s also will be exposed; Is 47:3 2781
wait for Me will not be put to s. Is 49:23 954
not, for you will not be put to s; Is 54:4 954
will forget the s of your youth, Is 54:4 1322
Instead of your s *you will have a* Is 61:7 1322
but you will be put to s. Is 65:13 954
But they will be put to s. Is 66:5 954
you will be put to s by Egypt As Jer 2:36 954
As you were put to s by Assyria. Jer 2:36 954
"Let us lie down in our s, Jer 3:25 1322
they spite, to their own s?" Jer 7:19 1322, 6440
"The wise men are put to s, Jer 8:9 954
We are put to great s, Jer 9:19 954
goldsmith is put to s by his idols; Jer 10:14 954
face, That your s may be seen. Jer 13:26 7036
have been put to s and humiliated, Jer 14:3 954
The farmers have been put to s, Jer 14:4 954
who forsake You will be put to s. Jer 17:13 954
who persecute me be put to s, Jer 17:18 954
as for me, let me not be put to s; Jer 17:18 954
that my days have been spent in s? Jer 20:18 1322
The nations have heard of your s, Jer 46:12 7036
of Egypt has been put to s, Jer 46:24 954
Kiriathaim has been put to s, Jer 48:1 954
has been put to s and shattered. Jer 48:1 954
"Moab has been put to s, Jer 48:20 954
"Hamath and Arpad are put to s, Jer 49:23 954
captured, Bel has been put to s, Jer 50:2 954
Her images have been put to s, Jer 50:2 954
is put to s by his idols, Jer 51:17 954
her whole land will be put to s And Jer 51:47 954
and s *will be* on all faces and Ezk 7:18 955
in s went down with the slain. Ezk 32:30 954
but they will bear their s and Ezk 44:13 3639
to You, O Lord, but to us open s, Da 9:7 1322
"Open s belongs to us, O Lord, to Da 9:8 1322
I will change their glory into s. Hos 4:7 7036
Their rulers dearly love s. Hos 4:18 7036
and devoted themselves to s, Hos 9:10 1322
Ephraim will be seized with s And Hos 10:6 1317
My people will never be put to s. Jl 2:26 954
My people will never be put to s. Jl 2:27 954
Jacob, You will be covered *with* s, Ob 1:10 955
s will cover her who said to me, Mi 7:10 955
yes, gather, O nation without s, Zph 2:1 3700
But the unjust knows no s. Zph 3:5 1322
"In that day you will feel no s Zph 3:11 954
And I will turn their s into Zph 3:19 1322
riders on horses will be put to s. Zch 10:5 954
worthy to suffer s for *His* name. Ac 5:41 *818*
things of the world to s the wise, 1Co 1:27 *2617b*
to s the things which are strong, 1Co 1:27 *2617b*
not write these things to s you, 1Co 4:14 *1788*
I say *this* to your s. 1Co 6:5 *1791*
God and s those who have nothing? 1Co 11:22 *2617b*
I speak *this* to your s. 1Co 15:34 *1791*
the things hidden because of s, 2Co 4:2 *152*
him about you, I was not put to s; 2Co 7:14 *2617b*
be put to s by this confidence. 2Co 9:4 *2617b*
you, I will not be put to s, 2Co 10:8 *153*
To *my* s I *must* say that we have 2Co 11:21 *819*
will not be put to s in anything, Php 1:20 *153*
and *whose* glory is in their s, Php 3:19 *152*
him, so that he will be put to s. 2Th 3:14 *1788*
that the opponent will be put to s, Ti 2:8 *1788*
Son of God and put Him to open s. Heb 6:6 *3856*
endured the cross, despising the s, Heb 12:2 *152*
behavior in Christ will be put to s. 1Pe 3:16 *2617b*
away from Him in s at His coming. 1Jn 2:28 *153*
casting up their own s like foam; Jude 1:13 *152*
and *that* the s of your nakedness Rv 3:18 *152*
naked and men will not see his s.") Rv 16:15 *808*
SHAMED
away, Lebanon is s *and* withers; Is 33:9 2659
at you will be s and dishonored; Is 41:11 954
thief is s when he is discovered, Jer 2:26 954
So the house of Israel is s; Jer 2:26 954
She has been s and humiliated. Jer 15:9 954
SHAMEFUL
and charges her with s deeds and Dt 22:14 5949
he has charged her with s deeds, Dt 22:17 5949
away Is a s and disgraceful son. Pr 19:26 954
"But the s thing has consumed the Jer 3:24 1322
you have set up to the s thing, Jer 11:13 1322
of Shaphir, in s nakedness. Mi 1:11 1322
"You have devised a s thing for Hab 2:10 1322
SHAMEFULLY
in harvest is a son who acts s. Pr 10:5 954
man acts disgustingly and s. Pr 13:5 2659
anger is toward him who acts s. Pr 14:35 954
will rule over a son who acts s, Pr 17:2 954
who conceived them has acted s. Hos 2:5 954
in the head, and treated him s. Mk 12:4 *818*
beat him also and treated him s and Lk 20:11 *818*
SHAMELESSLY
ones s uncovers himself!" 2Sa 6:20 1540
SHAMES
But she who s *him* is like rottenness Pr 12:4 954
SHAMGAR
After him came S the son of Anath, Jg 3:31 8044
"In the days of S the son of Anath, Jg 5:6 8044
SHAMHUTH
was the commander S the Izrahite; 1Ch 27:8 8049
SHAMIR
S and Jattir and Socoh, Jos 15:48 8069a
and he lived in S in the hill Jg 10:1 8069a
Then he died and was buried in S. Jg 10:2 8069a
of the sons of Micah, S. 1Ch 24:24 8069b
SHAMMA
Bezer, Hod, S, Shilshah, Ithran and 1Ch 7:37 8037
SHAMMAH
Nahath and Zerah, S and Mizzah. Gn 36:13 8048
Nahath, chief Zerah, chief S, Gn 36:17 8048
Next Jesse made S pass by. 1Sa 16:9 8048
to him Abinadab, and the third S. 1Sa 17:13 8048
was S the son of Agee a Hararite. 2Sa 23:11 8048
S the Harodite, Elika the 2Sa 23:25 8048
S the Hararite, Ahiam the son of 2Sa 23:33 8048
of Reuel *were* Nahath, Zerah, S and 1Ch 1:37 8048
SHAMMAI
The sons of Onam were S and Jada. 1Ch 2:28 8060
sons of S *were* Nadab and Abishur. 1Ch 2:28 8060
The sons of Jada the brother of S 1Ch 2:32 8060
and Rekem became the father of S. 1Ch 2:44 8060
The son of S was Maon, and 1Ch 2:45 8060
she conceived *and bore* Miriam, S and 1Ch 4:17 8060
SHAMMOTH
S the Harorite, Helez the 1Ch 11:27 8054
SHAMMUA
of Reuben, S the son of Zaccur; Nu 13:4 8051
S, Shobab, Nathan, Solomon, 2Sa 5:14 8051
S, Shobab, Nathan, Solomon, 1Ch 14:4 8051
and Abda the son of S, Ne 11:17 8051
of Bilgah, S; of Shemaiah, Ne 12:18 8051
SHAMSHERAI
S, SheharIah, Athaliah, 1Ch 8:26 8125
SHAPE
carved *in the* s of gourds 1Ki 6:18
SHAPED
"Three cups *shall be* s like Ex 25:33 8246
and three cups s like almond Ex 25:33 8246
four cups s like almond *blossoms,* Ex 25:34 8246
three cups s like almond *blossoms,* Ex 37:19 8246
three cups s like almond *blossoms,* Ex 37:19 8246
four cups s like almond *blossoms,* Ex 37:20 8246
SHAPES
man s iron into a cutting tool and Is 44:12 2796
Another s wood, he extends a Is 44:13 2796
SHAPHAM
was the chief and S the second, 1Ch 5:12 8223
SHAPHAN
'Likewise, the s, for though it Lv 11:5 8227a
the camel and the rabbit and the s, Dt 14:7 8227a
King Josiah, the king sent S, 2Ki 22:3 8227b
high priest said to S the scribe, 2Ki 22:8 8227b
gave the book to S who read it. 2Ki 22:8 8227b
S the scribe came to the king 2Ki 22:9 8227b
S the scribe told the king saying, 2Ki 22:10 8227b
And S read it in the presence of 2Ki 22:10 8227b
the priest, Ahikam the son of S, 2Ki 22:12 8227b
the son of Micaiah, S the scribe, 2Ki 22:12 8227b
the priest, Ahikam, Achbor, S, 2Ki 22:14 8227b
of Ahikam, the son of S over them. 2Ki 25:22 8227b
he sent S the son of Azaliah, 2Ch 34:8 8227b
and said to S the scribe, 2Ch 34:15 8227b
And Hilkiah gave the book to S. 2Ch 34:15 8227b
Then S brought the book to the 2Ch 34:16 8227b
S the scribe told the king saying, 2Ch 34:18 8227b
And S read from it in the presence 2Ch 34:18 8227b
Hilkiah, Ahikam the son of S, 2Ch 34:20 8227b
the son of Micah, S the scribe, 2Ch 34:20 8227b
the son of S was with Jeremiah, Jer 26:24 8227b
the hand of Elasah the son of S, Jer 29:3 8227b
Gemariah the son of S the scribe, Jer 36:10 8227b
the son of Gemariah, the son of S, Jer 36:11 8227b
Achbor, and Gemariah the son of S, Jer 36:12 8227b
the son of Ahikam, the son of S, Jer 39:14 8227b
the son of Ahikam, the son of S, Jer 40:5 8227b
the son of Ahikam, the son of S, Jer 40:9 8227b
the son of Ahikam, the son of S. Jer 40:11 8227b
the son of Ahikam, the son of S, Jer 41:2 8227b
son of Ahikam and grandson of S, Jer 43:6 8227b
the son of S standing among them, Ezk 8:11 8227b
SHAPHAT
of Simeon, S the son of Hori; Nu 13:5 8202
and Elisha the son of S of 1Ki 19:16 8202
and found Elisha the son of S, 1Ki 19:19 8202
"Elisha the son of S is here, 2Ki 3:11 8202
son of S remains on him today." 2Ki 6:31 8202
Igal, Bariah, Neariah and S, 1Ch 3:22 8202
then Janai and S in Bashan. 1Ch 5:12 8202
and S the son of Adlai had charge 1Ch 27:29 8202
SHAPHIR
Go on your way, inhabitant of S, Mi 1:11 8208
SHARAI
Machnadebai, Shashai, S, Ezr 10:40 8298
SHARAR
Ahiam the son of S the Ararite, 2Sa 23:33 8325
SHARE
the s of the men who went with me, Gn 14:24 2506
let them take their s." Gn 14:24 2506
their s from My offerings by fire; Lv 6:17 2506
for the s of the sons of Judah was Jos 19:9 2506
For as his s is who goes down to 1Sa 30:24 2506
his s be who stays by the baggage; 1Sa 30:24 2506
they shall s alike." 1Sa 30:24 2505a
friends for a s *of the spoil,* Jb 17:5 2506
"I too will answer my s, Jb 32:17 2506
given her a s of understanding. Jb 39:17 2505a
And a stranger does not s its joy. Pr 14:10 6148
And will s in the inheritance Pr 17:2 2505a
and they will no longer have a s Ec 9:6 2506
And let him s with the beasts in Da 4:15 2508
and let him s with the beasts of Da 4:23 2508
"The man who has two tunics is to s Lk 3:11 *3330*
give me the s of the estate that Lk 15:12 *3313*
Take this and s it among yourselves; Lk 22:17 *1266*
counted among us and received his s Ac 1:17 *2819*
If others s the right over you, do 1Co 9:12 *3348*
altar have their s from the altar? 1Co 9:13 *4829*
one who is taught the word is to s Ga 6:6 *2841*
to s with one who has need. Eph 4:28 *3330*
rejoice and s my joy with you all. Php 2:17 *4796*
same way and s your joy with me. Php 2:18 *4796*
to s *with me* in my affliction. Php 4:14 *4790*
who has qualified us to s in the Col 1:12 *3310*
I do my s on behalf of His body Col 1:24 *466*
thereby s *responsibility for* the sins of 1Tm 5:22 *2841*
to be generous and ready to s, 1Tm 6:18 *2843*
to receive his s of the crops. 2Tm 2:6 *3335*
the children s in flesh and blood, Heb 2:14 *2841*
good, so that we may s His holiness. Heb 12:10 *3335*
you s the sufferings of Christ, 1Pe 4:13 *2841*
SHARED
And the orphan has not s it Jb 31:17 398, 4480
house s with a contentious woman. Pr 21:9 2267
house s with a contentious woman. Pr 25:24 2267
have s in their spiritual things, Ro 15:27 *2841*

these women who have **s** my struggle Php 4:3 *4866*
no church **s** with me in the matter Php 4:15 *2841*
God has created to be gratefully **s** in 1Tm 4:3 *3336*

SHARERS
eat the sacrifices **s** in the altar? 1Co 10:18 *2844*
want you to become **s** in demons. 1Co 10:20 *2844*
as you are **s** of our sufferings, 2Co 1:7 *2844*
so also you are **s** of our comfort. 2Co 1:7
and partly by becoming **s** with Heb 10:33 *2844*

SHAREZER
and **S** killed him with the sword; 2Ki 19:37 8272
that Adrammelech and **S** his sons Is 37:38 8272
Now *the town of* Bethel had sent **S** Zch 7:2 8272

SHARING
and were **s** them with all, Ac 2:45 *1266*
to thresh in hope of **s** *the crops.* 1Co 9:10 *3348*
bless a **s** in the blood of Christ? 1Co 10:16 *2842*
break a **s** in the body of Christ? 1Co 10:16 *2842*
do not neglect doing good and **s**, Heb 13:16 *2842*

SHARON
and in all the pasture lands of **S**, 1Ch 5:16 8289
cattle which were grazing in **S**; 1Ch 27:29 8289
"I am the rose of **S**, SS 2:1 8289
S is like a desert plain, And Is 33:9 8289
it, The majesty of Carmel and **S**. Is 35:2 8289
"**S** will be a pasture land Is 65:10 8289
who lived at Lydda and **S** saw him, Ac 9:35 *4565*

SHARONITE
Shitrai the **S** had charge of 1Ch 27:29 8290

SHARP
was a **s** crag on the one side and 1Sa 14:4 8127
and a **s** crag on the other side, 1Sa 14:4 8127
under saws, **s** iron instruments, 2Sa 12:31 2757
with **s** instruments and with axes. 1Ch 20:3 2757
underparts are *like* **s** potsherds; Jb 41:30 2303
Your arrows are **s**; Ps 45:5 8150
destruction, Like a **s** razor, Ps 52:2 3913
And their tongue a **s** sword. Ps 57:4 2299
S arrows of the warrior, With the Ps 120:4 8150
wormwood, **S** as a two-edged sword. Pr 5:4 2299
Like a club and a sword and a **s** Pr 25:18 8150
Its arrows are **s** and all its bows Is 5:28 8150
s threshing sledge with double Is 41:15 2742a
has made My mouth like a **s** sword, Is 49:2 2299
you, son of man, take a **s** sword; Ezk 5:1 2299
"Show yourself **s**, go to the right; Ezk 21:16 2300
Gilead with *implements* of **s** iron. Am 1:3 2742a
there occurred such a **s** disagreement Ac 15:39 *3948*
His mouth came a **s** two-edged sword; Rv 1:16 *3691*
the **s** two-edged sword says this: Rv 2:12 *3691*
head and a **s** sickle in His hand. Rv 14:14 *3691*
and he also had a **s** sickle. Rv 14:17 *3691*
voice to him who had the **s** sickle, Rv 14:18 *3691*
"Put in your **s** sickle and gather Rv 14:18 *3691*
From His mouth comes a **s** sword, Rv 19:15 *3691*

SHARPEN
If I **s** My flashing sword, And My Dt 32:41 8150
each to **s** his plowshare, 1Sa 13:20 3913
not repent, He will **s** His sword; Ps 7:12 3913
They **s** their tongues as a serpent; Ps 140:3 8150
dull and he does not **s** *its* edge, Ec 10:10 7043
S the arrows, fill the quivers! Jer 51:11 1305

SHARPENED
have **s** their tongue like a sword. Ps 64:3 8150
a sword **s** And also polished! Ezk 21:9 2300
'**S** to make a slaughter, Polished Ezk 21:10 2300
the sword is **s** and polished, to Ezk 21:11 2300

SHARPENS
Iron **s** iron, So one man sharpens Pr 27:17 2302a
iron, So one man **s** another. Pr 27:17 2302a

SHARPER
and **s** than any two-edged sword, Heb 4:12 *5114*

SHARPLY
Do not **s** rebuke an older man, but 1Tm 5:1 *1969*

SHARUHEN
and Beth-lebaoth and **S**; Jos 19:6 8287

SHASHAI
Machnadebai, **S**, Sharai, Ezr 10:40 8343

SHASHAK
and Ahio, **S** and Jeremoth. 1Ch 8:14 8349
and Penuel *were* the sons of **S**. 1Ch 8:25 8349

SHATTER
And **s** *them* with his arrows. Nu 24:8 4272
S the loins of those who rise up Dt 33:11 4272
You shall **s** them like earthenware. Ps 2:9 5310a
God, **s** their teeth in their mouth; Ps 58:6 2040
God will **s** the head of His enemies, Ps 68:21 4272
your foot may **s** *them* in blood, Ps 68:23 4272
s kings in the day of His wrath. Ps 110:5 4272
He will **s** the chief men over a Ps 110:6 4272
I will **s** the doors of bronze and Is 45:2 7665
also **s** the obelisks of Heliopolis, Jer 43:13 7665
empty his vessels and **s** his jars. Jer 48:12 5310a
'So I will **s** Elam before their Jer 49:37 2865
And with you I **s** nations, And with Jer 51:20 5310a
you I **s** the horse and his rider, Jer 51:21 5310a
you I **s** the chariot and its rider, Jer 51:21 5310a
And with you I **s** man and woman, Jer 51:22 5310a
with you I **s** old man and youth, Jer 51:22 5310a
with you I **s** young man and virgin, Jer 51:22 5310a
I **s** the shepherd and his flock, Jer 51:23 5310a
you I **s** the farmer and his team, Jer 51:23 5310a
you I **s** governors and prefects. Jer 51:23 5310a

SHATTERED
and **s** every tree of the field. Ex 9:25 7665
the tablets from his hands and **s** them Ex 32:19 7665
on the former tablets which you **s**. Ex 34:1 7665
on the former tablets which you **s**, Dt 10:2 7665
And she **s** and pierced his temple. Jg 5:26 4272
"The bows of the mighty are **s**, 1Sa 2:4 2844b
contend with the LORD will be **s**; 1Sa 2:10 2865
I have devoured them and **s** them, 2Sa 22:39 4272
for they were **s** before the LORD and 2Ch 14:13 7665
"I was at ease, but He **s** me, Jb 16:12 6565a
by His understanding He **s** Rahab. Jb 26:12 4272
have **s** the teeth of the wicked. Ps 3:7 7665
I **s** them, so that they were not Ps 18:38 4272
s the trees of their territory. Ps 105:33 7665
For He has **s** gates of bronze And Ps 107:16 7665
the pitcher by the well is **s** and Ec 12:6 7665
65 years Ephraim will be **s**, Is 7:8 2865
"Be broken, O peoples, and be **s**; Is 8:9 2865
Gird yourselves, yet be **s**; Is 8:9 2865
Gird yourselves, yet be **s**. Is 8:9 2865
of her gods are **s** on the ground." Is 21:9 7665
So ruthlessly **s** That a sherd will Is 30:14 3807
this man Coniah a despised, **s** jar? Jer 22:28 5310a
has been put to shame and **s**. Jer 48:1 2865
put to shame, for it has been **s**. Jer 48:20 2865
"How **s** it is! *How* they have wailed! Jer 48:39 2865
put to shame, Marduk has been **s**; Jer 50:2 2865
to shame, her idols have been **s**.' Jer 50:2 2865
mighty men, and they will be **s**! Jer 50:36 2865
be captured, Their bows are **s**; Jer 51:56 2865
the ram and **s** his two horns, Da 8:7 7665
within a few days he will be **s**, Da 11:20 7665
be flooded away before him and **s**, Da 11:22 7665
the perpetual mountains were **s**, Hab 3:6 6483a

SHATTERING
As a **s** of my bones, my adversaries Ps 42:10 7524
with his **s** weapon in his hand; Ezk 9:2 4660
s the power of the holy people, Da 12:7 5310a

SHATTERS
right hand, O LORD, **s** the enemy. Ex 15:6 7492
"and like a hammer which **s** a rock? Jer 23:29 6483a
as iron crushes and **s** all things, Da 2:40 2827

SHAUL
and **S** of Rehoboth on the *Euphrates* Gn 36:37 7586
Then **S** died, and Baal-hanan the Gn 36:38 7586
S the son of a Canaanite woman. Gn 46:10 7586
S the son of a Canaanite woman; Ex 6:15 7586
of **S**, the family of the Shaulites. Nu 26:13 7586
S of Rehoboth by the River became 1Ch 1:48 7586
When **S** died, Baal-hanan the son of 1Ch 1:49 7586
Nemuel and Jamin, Jarib, Zerah, **S**; 1Ch 4:24 7586
Uzziah his son and **S** his son. 1Ch 6:24 7586

SHAULITES
of Shaul, the family of the **S**. Nu 26:13 7587

SHAVE
then he shall **s** himself, but he Lv 13:33 1548
but he shall not **s** the scale; Lv 13:33 1548
clothes and **s** off all his hair and Lv 14:8 1548
that he shall **s** off all his hair: Lv 14:9 1548
he shall **s** his head and his beard Lv 14:9 1548
s off the edges of their beards, Lv 21:5 1548
then he shall **s** his head on the Nu 6:9 1548
he shall **s** it on the seventh day. Nu 6:9 1548
'The Nazirite shall then **s** his Nu 6:18 1548
not cut yourselves nor **s** your forehead Dt 14:1 7760, 7144
s her head and trim her nails. Dt 21:12 1548
s off the seven locks of his hair. Jg 16:19 1548
day the Lord will **s** with a razor, Is 7:20 1548
himself or **s** his head for them. Jer 16:6 7139
"Also they shall not **s** their heads, Ezk 44:20 1548
so that they may **s** their heads; Ac 21:24 *3587b*

SHAVED
and when he had **s** himself and Gn 41:14 1548
after he has **s** his dedicated *hair.* Nu 6:19 1548
If I am **s**, then my strength will Jg 16:17 1548
to grow again after it was **s** off. Jg 16:22 1548
and **s** off half of their beards, 2Sa 10:4 1548
took David's servants and **s** them and 1Ch 19:4 1548
and tore his robe and **s** his head, Jb 1:20 1494
Have **s** the crown of your head. Jer 2:16 7462a
from Samaria with their beards **s** off Jer 41:5 1548
same as the woman whose head is **s**. 1Co 11:5 *3587b*
her hair cut off or her head **s**, 1Co 11:6 *3587a*

SHAVEH
to meet him at the valley of **S** Gn 14:17 7740

SHAVEH-KIRIATHAIM
Zuzim in Ham and the Emim in **S**, Gn 14:5 7741

SHAVING
to wailing, To **s** the head and Is 22:12 7144

SHAVSHA
were priests, and **S** *was* secretary; 1Ch 18:16 7798

SHAWL
the walls took away my **s** from me. SS 5:7 7289

SHEAF
my **s** rose up and also stood erect; Gn 37:7 485
around and bowed down to my **s**." Gn 37:7 485
s of the first fruits of your harvest Lv 23:10 6016a
'He shall wave the **s** before Lv 23:11 6016a
on the day when you wave the **s**, Lv 23:12 6016a
in the **s** of the wave offering; Lv 23:15 6016a
have forgotten a **s** in the field, Dt 24:19 6016a
And like the **s** after the reaper, Jer 9:22 5995

SHEAL
Malluch and Adaiah, Jashub, **S** Ezr 10:29 7594

SHEALTIEL
the prisoner, *were* **S** his son, 1Ch 3:17 7597
and Zerubbabel the son of **S** and Ezr 3:2 7597
Zerubbabel the son of **S** and Jeshua Ezr 3:8 7597
then Zerubbabel the son of **S** and Ezr 5:2 7598
up with Zerubbabel the son of **S**, Ne 12:1 7597
Haggai to Zerubbabel the son of **S**, Hg 1:1 7597
Then Zerubbabel the son of **S**, Hg 1:12 8032b
spirit of Zerubbabel the son of **S**, Hg 1:14 8032b
now to Zerubbabel the son of **S**, Hg 2:2 8032b
take you, Zerubbabel, son of **S**, Hg 2:23 7597
Jeconiah became the father of **S**, Mt 1:12 *4528*
and **S** the father of Zerubbabel. Mt 1:12 *4528*
son of Zerubbabel, the son of **S**, Lk 3:27 *4528*

SHEAR
Laban had gone to **s** his flock, Gn 31:19 1494
up to Timnah to **s** his sheep." Gn 38:13 1494
nor **s** the firstborn of your flock. Dt 15:19 1494

SHEARER
AS A LAMB BEFORE ITS **S** IS SILENT, Ac 8:32 *2751*

SHEARERS
Now I have heard that you have **s**; 1Sa 25:7 1494
that I have slaughtered for my **s**, 1Sa 25:11 1494
sheep that is silent before its **s**, Is 53:7 1494

SHEARIAH
Azrikam, Bocheru, Ishmael, **S**, 1Ch 8:38 8187
and **S** and Obadiah and Hanan. 1Ch 9:44 8187

SHEARING
and the first **s** of your sheep. Dt 18:4 1488
he was **s** his sheep in Carmel 1Sa 25:2 1494
that Nabal was **s** his sheep. 1Sa 25:4 1494

SHEAR-JASHUB
to meet Ahaz, you and your son **S**, Is 7:3 7610

SHEATH
it out of its **s** and killed him, 1Sa 17:51 8593
in its **s** fastened at his waist; 2Sa 20:8 8593
he put his sword back in its **s**. 1Ch 21:27 5084
Withdraw into your **s**; Jer 47:6 8593
I will draw My sword out of its **s** Ezk 21:3 8593
My sword will go forth from its **s** Ezk 21:4 8593
have drawn My sword out of its **s**. Ezk 21:5 8593
It will not return *to its* **s** again."' Ezk 21:5
'Return *it* to its **s**. Ezk 21:30 8593
"Put the sword into the **s**; Jn 18:11 *2336*

SHEAVES
we were binding **s** in the field, Gn 37:7 485
your **s** gathered around and bowed Gn 37:7 485
after the reapers among the **s**.' Ru 2:7 6016a
"Let her glean even among the **s**, Ru 2:15 6016a
take away the **s** from the hungry. Jb 24:10 6016a
of joy, bringing his **s** *with him.* Ps 126:6 485
Or the binder of **s** his bosom; Ps 129:7 6014a
weighted down when filled with **s**. Am 2:13 5995
like **s** to the threshing floor. Mi 4:12 5995
wood and a flaming torch among **s**, Zch 12:6 5995

SHEBA
sons of Raamah *were* **S** and Dedan. Gn 10:7 7614
and Obal and Abimael and **S** Gn 10:28 7614
became the father of **S** and Dedan. Gn 25:3 7614
Beersheba or **S** and Moladah, Jos 19:2 7652b
to be there whose name was **S**, 2Sa 20:1 7652a
and followed **S** the son of Bichri; 2Sa 20:2 7652a
"Now **S** the son of Bichri will do 2Sa 20:6 7652a
to pursue **S** the son of Bichri. 2Sa 20:7 7652a
pursued **S** the son of Bichri. 2Sa 20:10 7652a
to pursue **S** the son of Bichri. 2Sa 20:13 7652a
S the son of Bichri by name, 2Sa 20:21 7652a
And they cut off the head of **S** the 2Sa 20:22 7652a
Now when the queen of **S** heard 1Ki 10:1 7614
When the queen of **S** perceived all 1Ki 10:4 7614
the queen of **S** gave King Solomon. 1Ki 10:10 7614
King Solomon gave to the queen of **S** 1Ki 10:13 7614
sons of Raamah *were* **S** and Dedan. 1Ch 1:9 7614
Ebal, Abimael, **S**, 1Ch 1:22 7614
sons of Jokshan *were* **S** and Dedan. 1Ch 1:32 7614
were Michael, Meshullam, **S**, 1Ch 5:13 7652a
the queen of **S** heard of the fame 2Ch 9:1 7614
When the queen of **S** had seen 2Ch 9:3 7614
queen of **S** gave to King Solomon. 2Ch 9:9 7614
King Solomon gave to the queen of **S** 2Ch 9:12 7614
The travelers of **S** hoped for them. Jb 6:19 7614
kings of **S** and Seba offer gifts. Ps 72:10 7614
may the gold of **S** be given to him; Ps 72:15 7614
All those from **S** will come; Is 60:6 7614
frankincense come to Me from **S** And Jer 6:20 7614
"The traders of **S** and Raamah, Ezk 27:22 7614
Canneh, Eden, the traders of **S**, Ezk 27:23 7614
"**S** and Dedan and the merchants Ezk 38:13 7614

SHEBANIAH
S, Joshaphat, Nethanel, 1Ch 15:24 7645
stood Jeshua, Bani, Kadmiel, **S**, Ne 9:4 7645
Hashabneiah, Sherebiah, Hodiah, **S** Ne 9:5 7645
Hattush, **S**, Malluch, Ne 10:4 7645
also their brothers **S**, Ne 10:10 7645
Zaccur, Sherebiah, **S**, Ne 10:12 7645
of Malluchi, Jonathan; of **S**, Joseph; Ne 12:14 7645

SHEBARIM
them from the gate as far as **S** and Jos 7:5 7671

SHEBAT
month, which is the month **S**, Zch 1:7 7627

SHEBER
concubine, bore **S** and Tirhanah. 1Ch 2:48 7669

SHEBNA
and **S** the scribe and Joah the son 2Ki 18:37 7644
over the household with **S** the scribe 2Ki 19:2 7644
"Come, go to this steward, To **S**, Is 22:15 7644
the household, and **S** the scribe, Is 36:3 7644
and **S** and Joah said to Rabshakeh, Is 36:11 7644
and **S** the scribe and Joah the son Is 36:22 7644

over the household with **S** the scribe **Is 37:2** 7644

SHEBNAH
and **S** the scribe and Joah the son **2Ki 18:18** 7644
son of Hilkiah, and **S** and Joah, **2Ki 18:26** 7644

SHEBUEL
son of Gershom *was* **S** the chief. **1Ch 23:16** 7619
Mattaniah, Uzziel, **S** and Jerimoth, **1Ch 25:4** 7619
S the son of Gershom, the son of **1Ch 26:24** 7619

SHECANIAH
sons of Obadiah, the sons of **S**. **1Ch 3:21** 7935
The descendants of **S** *were* Shemaiah, **1Ch 3:22** 7935
ninth for Jeshua, the tenth for **S**, **1Ch 24:11** 7935
S in the cities of the priests, **2Ch 31:15** 7935
S *who was* of the sons of Parosh, **Ezr 8:3** 7935
the sons of Zattu, **S**, the son of **Ezr 8:5** 7935
S the son of Jehiel, one of **Ezr 10:2** 7935
after him Shemaiah the son of **S**, **Ne 3:29** 7935
the son-in-law of **S** the son of Arah, **Ne 6:18** 7935
S, Rehum, Meremoth, **Ne 12:3** 7935

SHECHEM
the land as far as the site of **S**, **Gn 12:6** 7927
came safely to the city of **S**, **Gn 33:18** 7927
S the son of Hamor the Hivite, **Gn 34:2** 7927
So **S** spoke to his father Hamor, **Gn 34:4** 7927
Then Hamor the father of **S** went **Gn 34:6** 7927
my son **S** longs for your daughter; **Gn 34:8** 7927
S also said to her father and to **Gn 34:11** 7927
answered **S** and his father Hamor with **Gn 34:13** 7927
seemed reasonable to Hamor and **S**, **Gn 34:18** 7927
So Hamor and his son **S** came to the **Gn 34:20** 7927
to Hamor and to his son **S**, **Gn 34:24** 7927
son **S** with the edge of the sword, **Gn 34:26** 7927
under the oak which was near **S**. **Gn 35:4** 7927
pasture their father's flock in **S**. **Gn 37:12** 7927
brothers pasturing *the flock* in **S**? **Gn 37:13** 7927
of Hebron, and he came to **S**. **Gn 37:14** 7927
of **S**, the family of the Shechemites; **Nu 26:31** 7928
sons of Asriel and for the sons of **S** **Jos 17:2** 7928
Michmethath which was east of **S**; **Jos 17:7** 7927
and **S** in the hill country of Ephraim, **Jos 20:7** 7927
They gave them **S**, **Jos 21:21** 7927
all the tribes of Israel to **S**, **Jos 24:1** 7927
a statute and an ordinance in **S**. **Jos 24:25** 7927
brought up from Egypt, at **S**, **Jos 24:32** 7927
the sons of Hamor the father of **S** **Jos 24:32** 7927
His concubine who was in **S** also **Jg 8:31** 7927
the son of Jerubbaal went to **S** **Jg 9:1** 7927
hearing of all the leaders of **S**, **Jg 9:2** 7927
hearing of all the leaders of **S**; **Jg 9:3** 7927
All the men of **S** and all **Jg 9:6** 7927
oak of the pillar which was in **S**. **Jg 9:6** 7927
"Listen to me, O men of **S**, **Jg 9:7** 7927
king over the men of **S**, **Jg 9:18** 7927
the men of **S** and Beth-millo; **Jg 9:20** 7927
the men of **S** and from Beth-millo, **Jg 9:20** 7927
Abimelech and the men of **S**; **Jg 9:23** 7927
the men of **S** dealt treacherously **Jg 9:23** 7927
killed them, and on the men of **S**, **Jg 9:24** 7927
The men of **S** set men in ambush **Jg 9:25** 7927
and crossed over into **S**; **Jg 9:26** 7927
men of **S** put their trust in him. **Jg 9:26** 7927
"Who is Abimelech, and who is **S**, **Jg 9:28** 7927
the men of Hamor the father of **S**; **Jg 9:28** 7927
and his relatives have come to **S**; **Jg 9:31** 7927
wait against **S** in four companies. **Jg 9:34** 7927
of **S** and fought with Abimelech. **Jg 9:39** 7927
that they could not remain in **S** **Jg 9:41** 7927
of the tower of **S** heard of *it*, **Jg 9:46** 7927
tower of **S** were gathered together. **Jg 9:47** 7927
men of the tower of **S** also died, **Jg 9:49** 7927
all the wickedness of the men of **S** **Jg 9:57** 7927
that goes up from Bethel to **S**, **Jg 21:19** 7927
Then Rehoboam went to **S**, **1Ki 12:1** 7927
had come to **S** to make him king. **1Ki 12:1** 7927
Then Jeroboam built **S** in the hill **1Ki 12:25** 7927
S in the hill country of Ephraim **1Ch 6:67** 7927
Ahian and **S** and Likhi and Aniam. **1Ch 7:19** 7928
and **S** with its towns as far as **1Ch 7:28** 7927
Then Rehoboam went to **S**, **2Ch 10:1** 7927
had come to **S** to make him king. **2Ch 10:1** 7927
I will portion out **S** and measure **Ps 60:6** 7927
will exult, I will portion out **S** And **Ps 108:7** 7927
that eighty men came from **S**, **Jer 41:5** 7927
of priests murder on the way to **S**; **Hos 6:9** 7927
From there they were removed to **S** **Ac 7:16** *4966*
money from the sons of Hamor in **S**. **Ac 7:16** *4966*

SHECHEMITES
of Shechem, the family of the **S**; **Nu 26:31** 7930

SHECHEM'S
of the sons of Hamor, **S** father, **Gn 33:19** 7927
and took Dinah from **S** house, **Gn 34:26** 7927

SHED
By man his blood shall be **s**, **Gn 9:6** 8210
"**S** no blood. Throw him into this pit **Gn 37:22** 8210
to **s** light on the space in front of it. **Ex 25:37** 215
He has **s** blood and that man shall **Lv 17:4** 8210
for the blood that is **s** on it, **Nu 35:33** 8210
by the blood of him who **s** it. **Nu 35:33** 8210
"So innocent blood will not be **s** **Dt 19:10** 8210
'Our hands did not **s** this blood, **Dt 21:7** 8210
both by having **s** blood without **1Sa 25:31** 8210
also **s** the blood of war in peace. **1Ki 2:5** 7760
blood which Joab **s** without cause. **1Ki 2:31** 8210
Manasseh **s** very much innocent **2Ki 21:16** 8210
for the innocent blood which he **s**, **2Ki 24:4** 8210
'You have **s** much blood and have **1Ch 22:8** 8210
because you have **s** *so* much blood **1Ch 22:8** 8210
a man of war and have **s** blood.' **1Ch 28:3** 8210
You **s** abroad a plentiful rain, **Ps 68:9** 5130
of Your servants which has been **s**. **Ps 79:10** 8210
And **s** innocent blood, The blood of **Ps 106:38** 8210
My eyes **s** streams of water, **Ps 119:136** 3381
evil And they hasten to **s** blood. **Pr 1:16** 8210
And hands that **s** innocent blood, **Pr 6:17** 8210
And the moon will not **s** its light. **Is 13:10** 5050
they hasten to **s** innocent blood; **Is 59:7** 8210
s innocent blood in this place, **Jer 7:6** 8210
for us, That our eyes may **s** tears And **Jer 9:18** 3381
s innocent blood in this place. **Jer 22:3** 8210
Who have **s** in her midst The blood **La 4:13** 8210
adultery or **s** blood are judged; **Ezk 16:38** 8210
by the blood which you have **s**, **Ezk 22:4** 8210
they have taken bribes to **s** blood; **Ezk 22:12** 8210
the judgment of women who **s** blood, **Ezk 23:45** 8210
eyes to your idols as you **s** blood. **Ezk 33:25** 8210
which they had **s** on the land, **Ezk 36:18** 8210
land they have **s** innocent blood. **Jl 3:19** 8210
the righteous blood **s** on earth, **Mt 23:35** *1632b*
s since the foundation of the **Lk 11:50** *1632b*
Your witness Stephen was being **s**, **Ac 22:20** *1632b*
"THEIR FEET ARE SWIFT TO **S** BLOOD, **Ro 3:15** *1632a*

SHEDDING
has restrained you from **s** blood, **1Sa 25:26** 935
And on **s** innocent blood And on **Jer 22:17** 8210
"A city **s** blood in her midst, so **Ezk 22:3** 8210
in you for the purpose of **s** blood. **Ezk 22:6** 8210
in you for the purpose of **s** blood, **Ezk 22:9** 8210
by **s** blood *and* destroying lives in **Ezk 22:27** 8210
have been partners with them in **s** **Mt 23:30**
and without **s** of blood there is no **Heb 9:22** *130*
not yet resisted to the point of **s** blood **Heb 12:4**

SHEDEUR
of Reuben, Elizur the son of **S**; **Nu 1:5** 7707
Elizur the son of **S**, **Nu 2:10** 7707
day *it was* Elizur the son of **S**, **Nu 7:30** 7707
offering of Elizur the son of **S**, **Nu 7:35** 7707
set out with Elizur the son of **S**, **Nu 10:18** 7707

SHEDS
"Whoever **s** man's blood, By man **Gn 9:6** 8210
have a violent son who **s** blood and **Ezk 18:10** 8210

SHEEP
and gave him **s** and oxen and **Gn 12:16** 6629
Abimelech then took **s** and oxen and **Gn 20:14** 6629
Abraham took **s** and oxen and **Gn 21:27** 6629
three flocks of **s** were lying there **Gn 29:2** 6629
of the well and water the **s**, **Gn 29:3** 6629
daughter coming with the **s**." **Gn 29:6** 6629
Water the **s**, and go, pasture them." **Gn 29:7** 6629
then we water the **s**." **Gn 29:8** 6629
Rachel came with her father's **s**, **Gn 29:9** 6629
s of Laban his mother's brother, **Gn 29:10** 6629
every speckled and spotted **s** and **Gn 30:32** 7716
all the black ones among the **s**, **Gn 30:35** 3775
up to Timnah to shear his **s**." **Gn 38:13** 6629
it from the **s** or from the goats. **Ex 12:5** 3532
offerings, your **s** and your oxen; **Ex 20:24** 6629
"If a man steals an ox or a **s** and **Ex 22:1** 7716
the ox and four **s** for the sheep. **Ex 22:1** 6629
the ox and four sheep for the **s**. **Ex 22:1** 7716
whether an ox or a donkey or a **s**, **Ex 22:4** 7716
it is for ox, for donkey, for **s**, **Ex 22:9** 7716
his neighbor a donkey, an ox, a **s**, **Ex 22:10** 7716
with your oxen *and* with your **s**. **Ex 22:30** 6629
first offspring from cattle and **s**. **Ex 34:19** 7716
flock, of the **s** or of the goats, **Lv 1:10** 3775
not eat any fat *from* an ox, a **s** or **Lv 7:23** 3775
defect from the cattle, the **s**, **Lv 22:19** 3775
an ox or a **s** or a goat is born, **Lv 22:27** 3775
"But, *whether* it is an ox or a **s**, **Lv 22:28** 7716
whether ox or **s**, it is the LORD's. **Lv 27:26** 7716
of a **s** or the firstborn of a goat, **Nu 18:17** 3775
Balak sacrificed oxen and **s**, **Nu 22:40** 6629
like **s** which have no shepherd." **Nu 27:17** 6629
and of the donkeys and of the **s**; **Nu 31:28** 6629
of the donkeys and of the **s**, **Nu 31:30** 6629
war had plundered was 675,000 **s**, **Nu 31:32** 6629
the number of **s** was 337,500, **Nu 31:36** 6629
the LORD's levy of the **s** was 675; **Nu 31:37** 6629
congregation's half was 337,500 **s**, **Nu 31:43** 6629
ones, and sheepfolds for your **s**, **Nu 32:24** 6792
cities, and sheepfolds for **s**. **Nu 32:36** 6629
the ox, the **s**, the goat, **Dt 14:4** 3775, 7716
the antelope and the mountain **s**. **Dt 14:5** 2169
heart desires: for oxen, or **s**, **Dt 14:26** 6629
to the LORD your God an ox or a **s** **Dt 17:1** 7716
a sacrifice, either an ox or a **s**, **Dt 18:3** 7716
and the first shearing of your **s**. **Dt 18:4** 6629
ox or his **s** straying away, **Dt 22:1** 7716
your **s** shall be given to your **Dt 28:31** 6629
and old, and ox and **s** and donkey, **Jos 6:21** 7716
his oxen, his donkeys, his **s**, **Jos 7:24** 7716
in Israel as well as no **s**, **Jg 6:4** 7716
and took **s** and oxen and calves, **1Sa 14:32** 6629
of you bring me his ox or his **s**, **1Sa 14:34** 7716
woman, child and infant, ox and **s**, **1Sa 15:3** 7716
spared Agag and the best of the **s**, **1Sa 15:9** 6629
this bleating of the **s** in my ears, **1Sa 15:14** 6629
spared the best of the **s** and oxen, **1Sa 15:15** 6629
some of the spoil, **s** and oxen, **1Sa 15:21** 6629
and behold, he is tending the **s**." **1Sa 16:11** 6629
you left those few **s** in the wilderness **1Sa 17:28** 6629
servant was tending his father's **s**. **1Sa 17:34** 6629
also oxen, donkeys, and **s** **1Sa 22:19** 7716
thousand **s** and a thousand goats. **1Sa 25:2** 6629
he was shearing his **s** in Carmel **1Sa 25:2** 6629
that Nabal was shearing his **s**. **1Sa 25:4** 6629
we were with them tending the **s**. **1Sa 25:16** 6629
and two jugs of wine and five **s** **1Sa 25:18** 6629
alive, and he took away the **s**, **1Sa 27:9** 6629
So David had captured all the **s** **1Sa 30:20** 6629
the pasture, from following the **s**, **2Sa 7:8** 6629
honey, curds, **s**, and cheese of the **2Sa 17:29** 6629
but these **s**, what have they done? **2Sa 24:17** 6629
Adonijah sacrificed **s** and oxen **1Ki 1:9** 6629
and fatlings and **s** in abundance, **1Ki 1:19** 6629
and fatlings and **s** in abundance, **1Ki 1:25** 6629
oxen, a hundred **s** besides deer, **1Ki 4:23** 6629
sacrificing so many **s** and oxen **1Ki 8:5** 6629
LORD, 22,000 oxen and 120,000 **s**. **1Ki 8:63** 6629
Like **s** which have no shepherd. **1Ki 22:17** 6629
king of Moab was a **s** breeder, **2Ki 3:4** 5349
and olive groves and vineyards and **s** **2Ki 5:26** 6629
their 50,000 camels, 250,000 **s**, **1Ch 5:21** 6629
of raisins, wine, oil, oxen and **s**. **1Ch 12:40** 6629
the pasture, from following the **s**, **1Ch 17:7** 6629
done very wickedly, but these **s**, **1Ch 21:17** 6629
sacrificing so many **s** and oxen that **2Ch 5:6** 6629
of 22,000 oxen and 120,000 **s**. **2Ch 7:5** 6629
large numbers of **s** and camels. **2Ch 14:15** 6629
700 oxen and 7,000 **s** from the spoil **2Ch 15:11** 6629
And Ahab slaughtered many **s** and **2Ch 18:2** 6629
Like **s** which have no shepherd; **2Ch 18:16** 6629
things were 600 bulls and 3,000 **s**. **2Ch 29:33** 6629
assembly 1,000 bulls and 7,000 **s**, **2Ch 30:24** 6629
assembly 1,000 bulls and 10,000 **s**; **2Ch 30:24** 6629
in the tithe of oxen and **s**, **2Ch 31:6** 6629
the priests and built the **S** Gate; **Ne 3:1** 6629
room of the corner and the **S** Gate **Ne 3:32** 6629
day was one ox *and* six choice **s**, **Ne 5:18** 6629
the Hundred, as far as the **S** Gate; **Ne 12:39** 6629
His possessions also were 7,000 **s**, **Jb 1:3** 6629
fell from heaven and burned up the **s** **Jb 1:16** 6629
warmed with the fleece of my **s**, **Jb 31:20** 3532
beginning; and he had 14,000 **s** **Jb 42:12** 6629
All **s** and oxen, And also the **Ps 8:7** 6792
You give us as **s** to be eaten **Ps 44:11** 6629
considered as **s** to be slaughtered. **Ps 44:22** 6629
As **s** they are appointed for Sheol; **Ps 49:14** 6629
against the **s** of Your pasture? **Ps 74:1** 6629
led forth His own people like **s** And **Ps 78:52** 6629
So we Your people and the **s** of Your **Ps 79:13** 6629
pasture and the **s** of His hand. **Ps 95:7** 6629
His people and the **s** of His pasture. **Ps 100:3** 6629
I have gone astray like a lost **s**; **Ps 119:176** 7716
keep alive a heifer and a pair of **s**; **Is 7:21** 6629
oxen and for **s** to trample. **Is 7:25** 7716
like **s** with none to gather *them*, **Is 13:14** 6629
of cattle and slaughtering of **s**, **Is 22:13** 6629
Me the **s** of your burnt offerings, **Is 43:23** 7716
All of us like **s** have gone astray, **Is 53:6** 6629
And like a **s** that is silent before **Is 53:7** 7353
Drag them off like **s** for the **Jer 12:3** 6629
was given you, Your beautiful **s**? **Jer 13:20** 6629
scattering the **s** of My pasture!" **Jer 23:1** 6629
"My people have become lost **s**; **Jer 50:6** 6629
you slaughter the fat **s** without **Ezk 34:3**
and I will demand My **s** from them **Ezk 34:10** 6629
make them cease from feeding **s**. **Ezk 34:10** 6629
search for My **s** and seek them out. **Ezk 34:11** 6629
when he is among his scattered **s**, **Ezk 34:12** 6629
so I will care for My **s** and will **Ezk 34:12** 6629
judge between one **s** and another, **Ezk 34:17** 7716
the fat **s** and the lean sheep. **Ezk 34:20** 7716
the fat sheep and the lean **s**. **Ezk 34:20** 7716
judge between one **s** and another. **Ezk 34:22** 7716
"As for you, My **s**, the sheep of **Ezk 34:31** 6629
My sheep, the **s** of My pasture, **Ezk 34:31** 6629
and one **s** from *each* flock of two **Ezk 45:15** 7716
And for a wife he kept **s**. **Hos 12:12**
Even the flocks of **s** suffer. **Jl 1:18** 6629
put them together like **s** in the fold; **Mi 2:12** 6629
a young lion among flocks of **s**, **Mi 5:8** 6629
the people wander like **s**, **Zch 10:2** 6629
will devour the flesh of the fat **s** **Zch 11:16**
that the **s** may be scattered; **Zch 13:7** 6629
like **s** without a shepherd. **Mt 9:36** *4263b*
the lost **s** of the house of Israel. **Mt 10:6** *4263b*
out as **s** in the midst of wolves; **Mt 10:16** *4263b*
among you who has a **s**, **Mt 12:11** *4263b*
more valuable then is a man than a **s**! **Mt 12:12** *4263b*
lost **s** of the house of Israel." **Mt 15:24** *4263b*
If any man has a hundred **s**, **Mt 18:12** *4263b*
separates the **s** from the goats; **Mt 25:32** *4263b*
He will put the **s** on His right, **Mt 25:33** *4263b*
AND THE **S** OF THE FLOCK SHALL BE **Mt 26:31** *4263b*
were like **s** without a shepherd; **Mk 6:34** *4263b*
AND THE **S** SHALL BE SCATTERED.' **Mk 14:27** *4263b*
if he has a hundred **s** and has lost **Lk 15:4** *4263b*
I have found my **s** which was lost!' **Lk 15:6** *4263b*
a slave plowing or tending **s**, **Lk 17:7** *4165*
were selling oxen and **s** and doves, **Jn 2:14** *4263b*
temple, with the **s** and the oxen; **Jn 2:15** *4263b*
in Jerusalem by the **s** *gate* a pool, **Jn 5:2** *4262*
the door into the fold of the **s**, **Jn 10:1** *4263b*
the door is a shepherd of the **s**. **Jn 10:2** *4263b*
opens, and the **s** hear his voice, **Jn 10:3** *4263b*
and he calls his own **s** by name and **Jn 10:3** *4263b*
and the **s** follow him because they **Jn 10:4** *4263b*
to you, I am the door of the **s**. **Jn 10:7** *4263b*
but the **s** did not hear them. **Jn 10:8** *4263b*
lays down His life for the **s**. **Jn 10:11** *4263b*
who is not the owner of the **s**, **Jn 10:12** *4263b*
the wolf coming, and leaves the **s** and **Jn 10:12** *4263b*

and is not concerned about the **s**. **Jn 10:13** *4263b*
and I lay down My life for the **s**. **Jn 10:15** *4263b*
other **s**, which are not of this fold; **Jn 10:16** *4263b*
because you are not of My **s**. **Jn 10:26** *4263b*
"My **s** hear My voice, and I know **Jn 10:27** *4263b*
He said to him, "Shepherd My **s**." **Jn 21:16** *4263a*
Jesus said to him, "Tend My **s**. **Jn 21:17** *4263a*
"HE WAS LED AS A **S** TO SLAUGHTER; **Ac 8:32** *4263b*
AS **S** TO BE SLAUGHTERED." **Ro 8:36** *4263b*
Shepherd of the **s** through the blood **Heb 13:20** *4263b*
were continually straying like **s**, **1Pe 2:25** *4263b*
flour and wheat and cattle and **s**, **Rv 18:13** *4263b*

SHEEPFOLDS
donkey, Lying down between the **s**. **Gn 49:14** 4942
"We will build here **s** for our **Nu 32:16**
6629, 1448
little ones, and **s** for your sheep, **Nu 32:24** 1448
fortified cities, and **s** for sheep. **Nu 32:36** 1448
"Why did you sit among the **s**, **Jg 5:16** 4942
He came to the **s** on the way, **1Sa 24:3**
6629, 1448
of cattle and **s** for the flocks. **2Ch 32:28** 723a
When you lie down among the **s**, **Ps 68:13** 8240a
servant And took him from the **s**; **Ps 78:70**
6629, 4356

SHEEPHERDERS
who was among the **s** from Tekoa, **Am 1:1** 5349

SHEEP'S
who come to you in **s** clothing, **Mt 7:15** *4263b*

SHEEPSHEARERS
Judah went up to his **s** at Timnah, **Gn 38:12**
6629, 1494
that Absalom had **s** in Baal-hazor, **2Sa 13:23** 1494
"Behold now, your servant has **s**; **2Sa 13:24** 1494

SHEEPSKINS
they went about in **s**, **Heb 11:37** *3374*

SHEER
And it will be **s** terror to **Is 28:19** 7534

SHEERAH
His daughter was **S**, **1Ch 7:24** 7609

SHEET
but a linen **s** over *his* naked *body* **Mk 14:51** *4616*
But he pulled free of the linen **s** **Mk 14:52** *4616*
object like a great **s** coming down, **Ac 10:11** *3607*
object coming down like a great **s** **Ac 11:5** *3607*

SHEETS
Then they hammered out gold **s** and **Ex 39:3** 6341b
let them be made into hammered **s** **Nu 16:38** 6341b

SHEHARIAH
Shamsherai, **S**, Athaliah, **1Ch 8:26** 7841

SHEKEL
half a **s** according to the shekel **Ex 30:13** 8255
to the **s** of the sanctuary **Ex 30:13** 8255
(the **s** is twenty gerahs), **Ex 30:13** 8255
a **s** as a contribution to the LORD. **Ex 30:13** 8255
not pay less than the half **s**, **Ex 30:15** 8255
to the **s** of the sanctuary, **Ex 30:24** 8255
to the **s** of the sanctuary. **Ex 38:24** 8255
to the **s** of the sanctuary; **Ex 38:25** 8255
half a **s** according to the shekel **Ex 38:26** 8255
to the **s** of the sanctuary), **Ex 38:26** 8255
terms of the **s** of the sanctuary, **Lv 5:15** 8255
after the **s** of the sanctuary. **Lv 27:3** 8255
be after the **s** of the sanctuary. **Lv 27:25** 8255
The **s** shall be twenty gerahs. **Lv 27:25** 8255
terms of the **s** of the sanctuary **Nu 3:47** 8255
(the **s** is twenty gerahs), **Nu 3:47** 8255
terms of the **s** of the sanctuary, **Nu 3:50** 8255
to the **s** of the sanctuary, **Nu 7:13** 8255
to the **s** of the sanctuary, **Nu 7:19** 8255
to the **s** of the sanctuary, **Nu 7:25** 8255
to the **s** of the sanctuary, **Nu 7:31** 8255
to the **s** of the sanctuary, **Nu 7:37** 8255
to the **s** of the sanctuary, **Nu 7:43** 8255
to the **s** of the sanctuary, **Nu 7:49** 8255
to the **s** of the sanctuary, **Nu 7:55** 8255
to the **s** of the sanctuary, **Nu 7:61** 8255
to the **s** of the sanctuary, **Nu 7:67** 8255
to the **s** of the sanctuary, **Nu 7:73** 8255
to the **s** of the sanctuary, **Nu 7:79** 8255
to the **s** of the sanctuary; **Nu 7:85** 8255
to the **s** of the sanctuary, **Nu 7:86** 8255
to the **s** of the sanctuary, **Nu 18:16** 8255
my hand a fourth of a **s** of silver; **1Sa 9:8** 8255
The charge was two-thirds of a **s** for **1Sa 13:21**
fine flour will be *sold* for a **s**, **2Ki 7:1** 8255
two measures of barley for a **s**, **2Ki 7:1** 8255
measure of fine flour *was sold* for a **s** **2Ki 7:16** 8255
two measures of barley for a **s**, **2Ki 7:16** 8255
"Two measures of barley for a **s** **2Ki 7:18** 8255
a measure of fine flour for a **s**, **2Ki 7:18** 8255
to contribute yearly one third of a **s** **Ne 10:32** 8255
"The **s** shall be twenty gerahs; **Ezk 45:12** 8255
bushel smaller and the **s** bigger, **Am 8:5** 8255
you will find a **s**. Take that **Mt 17:27** *4715*

SHEKELS
worth four hundred **s** of silver, **Gn 23:15** 8255
of Heth, four hundred **s** of silver, **Gn 23:16** 8255
her wrists weighing ten **s** in gold, **Gn 24:22**
him to the Ishmaelites for twenty **s** **Gn 37:28**
or her master thirty **s** of silver, **Ex 21:32** 8255
of flowing myrrh five hundred **s**, **Ex 30:23**
was 29 talents and 730 **s**, **Ex 38:24** 8255
was 100 talents and 1,775 **s**, **Ex 38:25** 8255
Of the 1,775 **s**, he made hooks **Ex 38:28**
was 70 talents and 2,400 **s**. **Ex 38:29** 8255
to your valuation in silver by **s**, **Lv 5:15** 8255
shall be fifty **s** of silver, **Lv 27:3** 8255
your valuation shall be thirty **s**. **Lv 27:4** 8255
for the male shall be twenty **s** and **Lv 27:5** 8255
shekels and for the female ten **s**. **Lv 27:5** 8255
be five **s** of silver for the male, **Lv 27:6** 8255
valuation shall be three **s** of silver. **Lv 27:6** 8255
your valuation shall be fifteen **s**, **Lv 27:7** 8255
shekels, and for the female ten **s**. **Lv 27:7** 8255
barley seed at fifty **s** of silver. **Lv 27:16** 8255
you shall take five **s** apiece, **Nu 3:47** 8255
was one hundred and thirty **s**, **Nu 7:13**
one silver bowl of seventy **s**, **Nu 7:13** 8255
one gold pan of ten **s**, full of **Nu 7:14**
was one hundred and thirty **s**, **Nu 7:19**
one silver bowl of seventy **s**, **Nu 7:19** 8255
one gold pan of ten **s**, full of **Nu 7:20**
was one hundred and thirty **s**, **Nu 7:25**
one silver bowl of seventy **s**, **Nu 7:25** 8255
one gold pan of ten **s**, full of **Nu 7:26**
was one hundred and thirty **s**, **Nu 7:31**
one silver bowl of seventy **s**, **Nu 7:31** 8255
one gold pan of ten **s**, full of **Nu 7:32**
was one hundred and thirty **s**, **Nu 7:37**
one silver bowl of seventy **s**, **Nu 7:37** 8255
one gold pan of ten **s**, full of **Nu 7:38**
was one hundred and thirty **s**, **Nu 7:43**
one silver bowl of seventy **s**, **Nu 7:43** 8255
one gold pan of ten **s**, full of **Nu 7:44**
was one hundred and thirty **s**, **Nu 7:49**
one silver bowl of seventy **s**, **Nu 7:49** 8255
one gold pan of ten **s**, full of **Nu 7:50**
was one hundred and thirty **s**, **Nu 7:55**
one silver bowl of seventy **s**, **Nu 7:55** 8255
one gold pan of ten **s**, full of **Nu 7:56**
was one hundred and thirty **s**, **Nu 7:61**
one silver bowl of seventy **s**, **Nu 7:61** 8255
one gold pan of ten **s**, full of **Nu 7:62**
was one hundred and thirty **s**, **Nu 7:67**
one silver bowl of seventy **s**, **Nu 7:67** 8255
one gold pan of ten **s**, full of **Nu 7:68**
was one hundred and thirty **s**, **Nu 7:73**
one silver bowl of seventy **s**, **Nu 7:73** 8255
one gold pan of ten **s**, full of **Nu 7:74**
was one hundred and thirty **s**, **Nu 7:79**
one silver bowl of seventy **s**, **Nu 7:79** 8255
one gold pan of ten **s**, full of **Nu 7:80**
weighing one hundred and thirty **s** **Nu 7:85**
2,400 **s**, according to the shekel **Nu 7:85**
weighing ten **s** apiece, **Nu 7:86**
all the gold of the pans 120 **s**; **Nu 7:86**
your valuation, five **s** in silver, **Nu 18:16** 8255
of hundreds, was 16,750 **s**. **Nu 31:52** 8255
and they shall fine him a hundred **s** **Dt 22:19**
give to the girl's father fifty **s** **Dt 22:29**
two hundred **s** of silver and a bar of **Jos 7:21** 8255
a bar of gold fifty **s** in weight, **Jos 7:21** 8255
1,700 **s** of gold, besides **Jg 8:26**
weighed five thousand **s** of bronze. **1Sa 17:5** 8255
weighed six hundred **s** of iron; **1Sa 17:7** 8255
head at 200 **s** by the king's weight. **2Sa 14:26** 8255
of whose spear was three hundred **s** **2Sa 21:16**
the oxen for fifty **s** of silver. **2Sa 24:24** 8255
using 600 **s** *of* gold on each large **1Ki 10:16**
was imported from Egypt for 600 **s** **1Ki 10:29**
of silver and six thousand **s** of **2Ki 5:5**
donkey's head was sold for eighty **s** **2Ki 6:25**
of a kab of dove's dung for five **s** **2Ki 6:25**
from each man fifty **s** of silver to **2Ki 15:20** 8255
So David gave Ornan 600 **s** of gold **1Ch 21:25** 8255
chariots from Egypt for 600 **s** of **2Ch 1:17**
of the nails was fifty **s** of gold. **2Ch 3:9** 8255
using 600 **s** *of* beaten gold on **2Ch 9:15**
hundred **s** of gold on each shield, **2Ch 9:16**
wine besides forty **s** of silver; **Ne 5:15** 8255
Each one was to bring a thousand **s** **SS 8:11**
The thousand **s** are for you, **SS 8:12**
valued at a thousand **s** of **Is 7:23**
for him, seventeen **s** of silver. **Jer 32:9** 8255
shall be twenty **s** a day by weight; **Ezk 4:10** 8255
twenty **s**, twenty-five shekels, *and* **Ezk 45:12** 8255
twenty shekels, twenty-five **s**, **Ezk 45:12** 8255
and fifteen **s** shall be your maneh. **Ezk 45:12** 8255
bought her for myself for fifteen **s** **Hos 3:2**
So they weighed out thirty **s** of **Zch 11:12**
So I took the thirty **s** of silver **Zch 11:13**

SHELAH
Arpachshad became the father of **S**; **Gn 10:24** 7974
and **S** became the father of Eber. **Gn 10:24** 7974
years, and became the father of **S**; **Gn 11:12** 7974
after he became the father of **S**, **Gn 11:13** 7974
S lived thirty years, and **Gn 11:14** 7974
and **S** lived four hundred and three **Gn 11:15** 7974
still another son and named him **S**; **Gn 38:5** 7956
house until my son **S** grows up"; **Gn 38:11** 7956
for she saw that **S** had grown up, **Gn 38:14** 7956
I did not give her to my son **S**." **Gn 38:26** 7956
Onan and **S** and Perez and Zerah **Gn 46:12** 7956
of **S**, the family of the Shelanites; **Nu 26:20** 7956
Arpachshad became the father of **S** **1Ch 1:18** 7974
and **S** became the father of Eber. **1Ch 1:18** 7974
Shem, Arpachshad, **S**, **1Ch 1:24** 7974
sons of Judah *were* Er, Onan and **S** **1Ch 2:3** 7956
The sons of **S** the son of Judah **1Ch 4:21** 7956
and the wall of the Pool of **S** at **Ne 3:15** 7975a
the son of Heber, the son of **S**, **Lk 3:35** *4527*

SHELANITES
of Shelah, the family of the **S**; **Nu 26:20** 8024

SHELEMIAH
The lot to the east fell to **S**. **1Ch 26:14** 8018
S, Nathan, Adaiah, **Ezr 10:39** 8018
Azarel, **S**, Shemariah, **Ezr 10:41** 8018
After him Hananiah the son of **S**, **Ne 3:30** 8018
I appointed **S** the priest, **Ne 13:13** 8018
son of Nethaniah, the son of **S**, **Jer 36:14** 8018
and **S** the son of Abdeel to seize **Jer 36:26** 8018
sent Jehucal the son of **S**, **Jer 37:3** 8018
S the son of Hananiah was there; **Jer 37:13** 8018
Pashhur, and Jucal the son of **S**, **Jer 38:1** 8018

SHELEPH
and **S** and Hazarmaveth and Jerah **Gn 10:26** *8026a*
became the father of Almodad, **S**, **1Ch 1:20** 8026a

SHELESH
Helem *were* Zophah, Imna, **S** and **1Ch 7:35** 8028

SHELOMI
a leader, Ahihud the son of **S**. **Nu 34:27** 8015

SHELOMITH
(Now his mother's name was **S**, **Lv 24:11** 8019b
Hananiah, and **S** *was* their sister; **1Ch 3:19** 8019b
The son of Izhar was **S** the chief. **1Ch 23:18** 8019a
him Abijah, Attai, Ziza and **S**. **2Ch 11:20** 8019a
and of the sons of Bani, **S**, the son **Ezr 8:10** 8019a

SHELOMOTH
were **S** and Haziel and Haran, **1Ch 23:9** 8013
Of the Izharites, **S**; **1Ch 24:22** 8013
of the sons of **S**, Jahath. **1Ch 24:22** 8013
Zichri his son and **S** his son. **1Ch 26:25** 8013
This **S** and his relatives had **1Ch 26:26** 8013
the care of **S** and his relatives. **1Ch 26:28** 8019a

SHELTER
come under the **s** of my roof." **Gn 19:8** 6738
And hug the rock for want of a **s**. **Jb 24:8** 4268
And may You **s** them, That those **Ps 5:11** 5526a
in a **s** from the strife of tongues. **Ps 31:20** 5521
take refuge in the **s** of Your wings. **Ps 61:4** 5643a
He who dwells in the **s** of the Most **Ps 91:1** 5643a
is left like a **s** in a vineyard, **Is 1:8** 5521
There will be a **s** to *give* **Is 4:6** 5521
to seek **s** in the shadow of Egypt! **Is 30:2** 2620
And the **s** in the shadow of Egypt, **Is 30:3** 2622
the wind And a **s** from the storm, **Is 32:2** 5643a
There he made a **s** for himself and **Jon 4:5** 5521
and sailed under the **s** of Cyprus **Ac 27:4** *5284*
we sailed under the **s** of Crete, **Ac 27:7** *5284*
Running under the **s** of a small island **Ac 27:16** *5295*

SHELTERS
Judah are staying in temporary **s**, **2Sa 11:11** 5521
with the kings in the temporary **s**, **1Ki 20:12** 5521
himself drunk in the temporary **s** **1Ki 20:16** 5521

SHELUMIEL
Simeon, **S** the son of Zurishaddai; **Nu 1:6** 8017
S the son of Zurishaddai, **Nu 2:12** 8017
it was **S** the son of Zurishaddai, **Nu 7:36** 8017
offering of **S** the son of Zurishaddai. **Nu 7:41** 8017
and **S** the son of Zurishaddai over **Nu 10:19** 8017

SHEM
and Noah became the father of **S**, **Gn 5:32** 8035
S, Ham, and Japheth. **Gn 6:10** 8035
Noah and **S** and Ham and Japheth, **Gn 7:13** 8035
ark were **S** and Ham and Japheth; **Gn 9:18** 8035
But **S** and Japheth took a garment **Gn 9:23** 8035
"Blessed be the LORD, The God of **S**; **Gn 9:26** 8035
let him dwell in the tents of **S**; **Gn 9:27** 8035
records of the generations of **S**, **Gn 10:1** 8035
Also to **S**, the father of all **Gn 10:21** 8035
The sons of **S** *were* Elam and Asshur **Gn 10:22** 8035
These are the sons of **S**, **Gn 10:31** 8035
records of the generations of **S**. **Gn 11:10** 8035
S was one hundred years old, and **Gn 11:10** 8035
and **S** lived five hundred years **Gn 11:11** 8035
Noah, **S**, Ham and Japheth. **1Ch 1:4** 8035
The sons of **S** *were* Elam, Asshur, **1Ch 1:17** 8035
S, Arpachshad, Shelah, **1Ch 1:24** 8035
the son of Arphaxad, the son of **S**, **Lk 3:36** *4590*

SHEMA
Amam and **S** and Moladah, **Jos 15:26** 8090
and Tappuah and Rekem and **S**. **1Ch 2:43** 8087b
S became the father of Raham, **1Ch 2:44** 8087b
the son of Azaz, the son of **S**, **1Ch 5:8** 8087b
and Beriah and **S**, who were heads **1Ch 8:13** 8087b
beside him stood Mattithiah, **S**, **Ne 8:4** 8087b

SHEMAAH
the sons of **S** the Gibeathite; **1Ch 12:3** 8094

SHEMAIAH
of God came to **S** the man of God, **1Ki 12:22** 8098
The descendants of Shecaniah *were* **S**, **1Ch 3:22** 8098
and the sons of **S**: Hattush, **1Ch 3:22** 8098
the son of Shimri, the son of **S**; **1Ch 4:37** 8098
The sons of Joel *were* **S** his son, **1Ch 5:4** 8098
Levites *were* **S** the son of Hasshub, **1Ch 9:14** 8098
and Obadiah the son of **S**, **1Ch 9:16** 8098
sons of Elizaphan, **S** the chief, **1Ch 15:8** 8098
for Uriel, Asaiah, Joel, **S**, **1Ch 15:11** 8098
S, the son of Nethanel the **1Ch 24:6** 8098
S the firstborn, Jehozabad the **1Ch 26:4** 8098
Also to his son **S** sons were born **1Ch 26:6** 8098
The sons of **S** *were* Othni, Rephael, **1Ch 26:7** 8098
the LORD came to **S** the man of God, **2Ch 11:2** 8098
Then **S** the prophet came to **2Ch 12:5** 8098
the word of the LORD came to **S**, **2Ch 12:7** 8098
not written in the records of **S** **2Ch 12:15** 8098
and with them the Levites, **S**, **2Ch 17:8** 8098
sons of Jeduthun, **S** and Uzziel. **2Ch 29:14** 8098
were Eden, Miniamin, Jeshua, **S**, **2Ch 31:15** 8098
Conaniah also, and **S** and Nethanel, **2Ch 35:9** 8098

and **S**, and 60 males with them; Ezr 8:13 8098
So I sent for Eliezer, Ariel, **S**, Ezr 8:16 8098
Maaseiah, Elijah, **S**, Ezr 10:21 8098
Eliezer, Isshijah, Malchijah, **S**, Ezr 10:31 8098
after him **S** the son of Shecaniah, Ne 3:29 8098
the house of **S** the son of Delaiah, Ne 6:10 8098
Maaziah, Bilgai, **S**. Ne 10:8 8098
S the son of Hasshub, the son of Ne 11:15 8098
S and Joiarib, Jedaiah, Ne 12:6 8098
of **S**, Jehonathan; Ne 12:18 8098
Judah, Benjamin, **S**, Ne 12:34 8098
the son of Jonathan, the son of **S**, Ne 12:35 8098
and his kinsmen, **S**, Ne 12:36 8098
and Maaseiah, **S**, Eleazar, Uzzi, Ne 12:42 8098
the son of **S** from Kiriath-jearim; Jer 26:20 8098
To **S** the Nehelamite you shall Jer 29:24 8098
LORD concerning **S** the Nehelamite, Jer 29:31 8098
"Because **S** has prophesied to you, Jer 29:31 8098
I am about to punish **S** the Jer 29:32 8098
scribe, and Delaiah the son of **S**, Jer 36:12 8098

SHEMARIAH
Eluzai, Jerimoth, Bealiah, **S**, 1Ch 12:5 8114
Jeush, **S** and Zaham. 2Ch 11:19 8114
Benjamin, Malluch *and* **S**; Ezr 10:32 8114
Azarel, Shelemiah, **S**, Ezr 10:41 8114

SHEMEBER
of Admah, and **S** king of Zeboiim, Gn 14:2 8038

SHEMED
Elpaal *were* Eber, Misham, and **S**, 1Ch 8:12 8046b

SHEMER
He bought the hill Samaria from **S** 1Ki 16:24 8106
Samaria, after the name of **S**, 1Ki 16:24 8106
the son of Bani, the son of **S**, 1Ch 6:46 8106
The sons of **S** *were* Ahi and Rohgah, 1Ch 7:34 8106

SHEMIDA
of **S**, the family of the Shemidaites; Nu 26:32 8061
of Hepher and for the sons of **S**; Jos 17:2 8061
The sons of **S** were Ahian and 1Ch 7:19 8061

SHEMIDAITES
of Shemida, the family of the **S**; Nu 26:32 8062

SHEMINITH
to lead with lyres tuned to the **s**. 1Ch 15:21 8066

SHEMIRAMOTH
rank, Zechariah, Ben, Jaaziel, **S**, 1Ch 15:18 8070
and Zechariah, Aziel, **S**, 1Ch 15:20 8070
to him Zechariah, *then* Jeiel, **S**, 1Ch 16:5 8070
Nethaniah, Zebadiah, Asahel, **S**, 2Ch 17:8 8070

SHEN
and set it between Mizpah and **S**, 1Sa 7:12 8129

SHENAZZAR
and Malchiram, Pedaiah, **S**, 1Ch 3:18 8137

SHEOL
I will go down to **S** in mourning Gn 37:35 7585
gray hair down to **S** in sorrow." Gn 42:38 7585
my gray hair down to **S** in sorrow.' Gn 44:29 7585
our father down to **S** in sorrow. Gn 44:31 7585
and they descend alive into **S**, Nu 16:30 7585
to them went down alive to **S**; Nu 16:33 7585
And burns to the lowest part of **S**, Dt 32:22 7585
He brings down to **S** and raises up. 1Sa 2:6 7585
The cords of **S** surrounded me; 2Sa 22:6 7585
gray hair go down to **S** in peace. 1Ki 2:6 7585
gray hair down to **S** with blood." 1Ki 2:9 7585
goes down to **S** does not come up. Jb 7:9 7585
Deeper than **S**, what can you know? Jb 11:8 7585
"Oh that You would hide me in **S**, Jb 14:13 7585
"If I look for **S** as my home, I Jb 17:13 7585
"Will it go down with me to **S**? Jb 17:16 7585
And suddenly they go down to **S**. Jb 21:13 7585
So does **S** *those who* have sinned. Jb 24:19 7585
"Naked is **S** before Him, Jb 26:6 7585
his life from passing over into **S**. Jb 33:18 7973
In **S** who will give You thanks? Ps 6:5 7585
The wicked will return to **S**, Ps 9:17 7585
will not abandon my soul to **S**; Ps 16:10 7585
The cords of **S** surrounded me; Ps 18:5 7585
have brought up my soul from **S**; Ps 30:3 7585
to shame, let them be silent in **S**. Ps 31:17 7585
As sheep they are appointed for **S**; Ps 49:14 7585
form shall be for **S** to consume So Ps 49:14 7585
my soul from the power of **S**, Ps 49:15 7585
Let them go down alive to **S**, Ps 55:15 7585
my soul from the depths of **S**. Ps 86:13 7585
And my life has drawn near to **S**. Ps 88:3 7585
deliver his soul from the power of **S**? Ps 89:48 7585
And the terrors of **S** came upon me; Ps 116:3 7585
If I make my bed in **S**, Ps 139:8 7585
been scattered at the mouth of **S**. Ps 141:7 7585
Let us swallow them alive like **S**, Pr 1:12 7585
to death, Her steps take hold of **S**. Pr 5:5 7585
Her house is the way to **S**, Pr 7:27 7585
her guests are in the depths of **S**. Pr 9:18 7585
S and Abaddon *lie open* before the Pr 15:11 7585
he may keep away from **S** below. Pr 15:24 7585
rod And rescue his soul from **S**. Pr 23:14 7585
S and Abaddon are never satisfied, Pr 27:20 7585
S, and the barren womb, Earth that Pr 30:16 7585
wisdom in **S** where you are going. Ec 9:10 7585
death, Jealousy is as severe as **S**; SS 8:6 7585
Therefore **S** has enlarged its throat Is 5:14 7585
it deep as **S** or high as heaven." Is 7:11 7585
"**S** from beneath is excited over Is 14:9 7585
harps Have been brought down to **S**; Is 14:11 7585
you will be thrust down to **S**, Is 14:15 7585
And with **S** we have made a pact. Is 28:15 7585
your pact with **S** will not stand; Is 28:18 7585
life I am to enter the gates of **S**; Is 38:10 7585
"For **S** cannot thank You, Death Is 38:18 7585
And made *them* go down to **S**. Is 57:9 7585
On the day when it went down to **S** Ezk 31:15 7585
when I made it go down to **S** Ezk 31:16 7585
"They also went down with it to **S** Ezk 31:17 7585
his helpers from the midst of **S**, Ezk 32:21 7585
to **S** with their weapons of war and Ezk 32:27 7585
ransom them from the power of **S**? Hos 13:14 7585
O **S**, where is your sting? Hos 13:14 7585
"Though they dig into **S**, Am 9:2 7585
I cried for help from the depth of **S**; Jon 2:2 7585
He enlarges his appetite like **S**, Hab 2:5 7585

SHEPHAM
draw a line from Hazar-enan to **S**, Nu 34:10 8221
the border shall go down from **S** to Nu 34:11 8221

SHEPHANIM
The cliffs are a refuge for the **s**. Ps 104:18 8227a
The **s** are not mighty people, Pr 30:26 8227a

SHEPHATIAH
the fifth, **S** the son of Abital; 2Sa 3:4 8203
the fifth *was* **S**, by Abital; 1Ch 3:3 8203
and Meshullam the son of **S**, 1Ch 9:8 8203
Shemariah, **S** the Haruphite, 1Ch 12:5 8203
Simeonites, **S** the son of Maacah; 1Ch 27:16 8203
Azaryahu, Michael and **S**. 2Ch 21:2 8203
the sons of **S**, 372; Ezr 2:4 8203
the sons of **S**, the sons of Hattil, Ezr 2:57 8203
and of the sons of **S**, Ezr 8:8 8203
the sons of **S**, 372; Ne 7:9 8203
the sons of **S**, the sons of Hattil, Ne 7:59 8203
the son of Amariah, the son of **S**, Ne 11:4 8203
Now **S** the son of Mattan, and Jer 38:1 8203

SHEPHELAH
olive and sycamore trees in the **S**; 1Ch 27:28 8219
those of the **S** the Philistine *plain;* Ob 1:19 8219

SHEPHER
Kehelathah and camped at Mount **S**. Nu 33:23 8234
They journeyed from Mount **S** and Nu 33:24 8234

SHEPHERD
s is loathsome to the Egyptians." Gn 46:34 7462a
God who has been my **s** all my life Gn 48:15 7462a
there is the **S**, the Stone of Israel Gn 49:24 7462a
be like sheep which have no **s**." Nu 27:17 7462a
'You will **s** My people Israel, and 2Sa 5:2 7462a
I commanded to **s** My people Israel, 2Sa 7:7 7462a
Like sheep which have no **s**. 1Ki 22:17 7462a
'You shall **s** My people Israel, and 1Ch 11:2 7462a
whom I commanded to **s** My people, 1Ch 17:6 7462a
Like sheep which have no **s**; 2Ch 18:16 7462a
The LORD is my **s**, I shall not want. Ps 23:1 7462a
Be their **s** also, and carry them Ps 28:9 7462a
Death shall be their **s**; Ps 49:14 7462a
him To **s** Jacob His people, Ps 78:71 7462a
Oh, give ear, **S** of Israel, You Ps 80:1 7462a
they are given by one **S**. Ec 12:11 7462a
Like a **s** He will tend His flock, Is 40:11 7462a
is I who says of Cyrus, '*He is* My **s**! Is 44:28 7462a
away from *being* a **s** after You, Jer 17:16 7462a
keep him as a **s** keeps his flock." Jer 31:10 7462a
as a **s** wraps himself with his garment Jer 43:12 7462a
the **s** who can stand against Me?" Jer 49:19 7462a
the **s** who can stand before Me?" Jer 50:44 7462a
with you I shatter the **s** and his flock Jer 51:23 7462a
were scattered for lack of a **s**, Ezk 34:5 7462a
of the field for lack of a **s**, Ezk 34:8 7462a
"As a **s** cares for his herd in the Ezk 34:12 7462a
"Then I will set over them one **s**, Ezk 34:23 7462a
feed them himself and be their **s**. Ezk 34:23 7462a
and they will all have one **s**; Ezk 37:24 7462a
"Just as the **s** snatches from the Am 3:12 7462a
And He will arise and **s** *His flock* Mi 5:4 7462a
They will **s** the land of Mi 5:6 7462a
S Your people with Your scepter, The Mi 7:14 7462a
afflicted, because there is no **s**. Zch 10:2 7462a
the equipment of a foolish **s**. Zch 11:15 7462a
I am going to raise up a **s** in the Zch 11:16 7462a
worthless **s** Who leaves the flock! Zch 11:17 7473
"Awake, O sword, against My **S**, Zch 13:7 7462a
"Strike the **S** that the sheep may Zch 13:7 7462a
WHO WILL **S** MY PEOPLE ISRAEL.'" Mt 2:6 *4165*
dispirited like sheep without a **s**. Mt 9:36 *4166*
as the **s** separates the sheep from Mt 25:32 *4166*
'I WILL STRIKE DOWN THE **S**, Mt 26:31 *4166*
they were like sheep without a **s**; Mk 6:34 *4166*
'I WILL STRIKE DOWN THE **S**, Mk 14:27 *4166*
by the door is a **s** of the sheep. Jn 10:2 *4166*
"I am the good **s**; Jn 10:11 *4166*
the good **s** lays down His life for Jn 10:11 *4166*
who is a hired hand, and not a **s**, Jn 10:12 *4166*
I am the good **s**, and I know My own Jn 10:14 *4166*
will become one flock *with* one **s**. Jn 10:16 *4166*
He said to him, "**S** My sheep." Jn 21:16 *4165*
to **s** the church of God which He Ac 20:28 *4165*
brought up from the dead the great **S** Heb 13:20 *4166*
the **S** and Guardian of your souls. 1Pe 2:25 *4166*
s the flock of God among you, 1Pe 5:2 *4165*
And when the Chief **S** appears, 1Pe 5:4 *750*
of the throne will be their **s**, Rv 7:17 *4165*

SHEPHERD'S
put them in the **s** bag which he had, 1Sa 17:40 7462a
"Like a **s** tent my dwelling is Is 38:12 7473

SHEPHERDED
So he **s** them according to the Ps 78:72 7462a

SHEPHERDESS
father's sheep, for she was a **s**. Gn 29:9 7462a

SHEPHERDS
and the men are **s**, for they have Gn 46:32 7462a
"Your servants are **s**, Gn 47:3 7462a
the **s** came and drove them away, Ex 2:17 7462a
us from the hand of the **s**, Ex 2:19 7462a
Your sons shall be **s** for forty years Nu 14:33 7462a
the Edomite, the chief of Saul's **s**. 1Sa 21:7 7462a
now your **s** have been with us and 1Sa 25:7 7462a
while he was at Beth-eked of the **s**, 2Ki 10:12 7462a
young goats By the tents of the **s**. SS 1:8 7462a
Nor will **s** make *their flocks* lie Is 13:20 7462a
which a band of **s** is called out, Is 31:4 7462a
are **s** who have no understanding; Is 56:11 7462a
the sea with the **s** of His flock? Is 63:11 7462a
give you **s** after My own heart, Jer 3:15 7462a
"**S** and their flocks will come to Jer 6:3 7462a
For the **s** have become stupid And Jer 10:21 7462a
"Many **s** have ruined My vineyard, Jer 12:10 7462a
wind will sweep away all your **s**, Jer 22:22 7462a
"Woe to the **s** who are destroying Jer 23:1 7462a
the **s** who are tending My people: Jer 23:2 7462a
"I will also raise up **s** over them Jer 23:4 7462a
"Wail, you **s**, and cry; Jer 25:34 7462a
"Flight will perish from the **s**, Jer 25:35 7462a
the sound of the cry of the **s**, Jer 25:36 7462a
habitation of **s** who rest their flocks. Jer 33:12 7462a
Their **s** have led them astray. Jer 50:6 7462a
prophesy against the **s** of Israel. Ezk 34:2 7462a
Prophesy and say to those **s**, Ezk 34:2 7462a
s of Israel who have been feeding Ezk 34:2 7462a
Should not the **s** feed the flock? Ezk 34:2 7462a
Therefore, you **s**, hear the word of Ezk 34:7 7462a
My **s** did not search for My flock, Ezk 34:8 7462a
but *rather* the **s** fed themselves Ezk 34:8 7462a
therefore, you **s**, hear the word of Ezk 34:9 7462a
"Behold, I am against the **s**, Ezk 34:10 7462a
So the **s** will not feed themselves Ezk 34:10 7462a
Seven **s** and eight leaders of men. Mi 5:5 7462a
Your **s** are sleeping, O king of Na 3:18 7462a
caves for **s** and folds for flocks. Zph 2:6 7462a
"My anger is kindled against the **s**, Zch 10:3 7462a
their own **s** have no pity on them. Zch 11:5 7462a
I annihilated the three **s** in one Zch 11:8 7462a
some **s** staying out in the fields and Lk 2:8 *4166*
the **s** *began* saying to one another, Lk 2:15 *4166*
which were told them by the **s**. Lk 2:18 *4166*
The **s** went back, glorifying Lk 2:20 *4166*

SHEPHERDS'
And the **s** pasture grounds mourn, Am 1:2 7462a
There is a sound of the **s** wail, Zch 11:3 7462a

SHEPHI
were Alian, Manahath, Ebal, **S** and 1Ch 1:40 8195

SHEPHO
and Manahath and Ebal, **S** and Onam. Gn 36:23 8195

SHEPHUPHAM
of **S**, the family of the Shuphamites Nu 26:39 8197a

SHEPHUPHAN
Gera, **S** and Huram. 1Ch 8:5 8197b

SHERD
s will not be found among its pieces Is 30:14 2789

SHEREBIAH
Levi, the son of Israel, namely **S**, Ezr 8:18 8274
twelve of the leading priests, **S**, Ezr 8:24 8274
Also Jeshua, Bani, **S**, Ne 8:7 8274
Kadmiel, Shebaniah, Bunni, **S**, Ne 9:4 8274
Kadmiel, Bani, Hashabneiah, **S**, Ne 9:5 8274
Zaccur, **S**, Shebaniah, Ne 10:12 8274
were Jeshua, Binnui, Kadmiel, **S**, Ne 12:8 8274
of the Levites *were* Hashabiah, **S** and Ne 12:24 8274

SHERESH
and the name of his brother *was* **S**, 1Ch 7:16 8329

SHESHACH
king of **S** shall drink after them. Jer 25:26 8347

SHESHAI
Hebron where Ahiman, **S** and Talmai, Nu 13:22 8344
S and Ahiman and Talmai, the Jos 15:14 8344
struck **S** and Ahiman and Talmai. Jg 1:10 8344

SHESHAK
"How **S** has been captured, And the Jer 51:41 8347

SHESHAN
And the son of Ishi *was* **S**. 1Ch 2:31 8348
And the son of **S** *was* Ahlai. 1Ch 2:31 8348
Now **S** had no sons, only daughters. 1Ch 2:34 8348
And **S** had an Egyptian servant 1Ch 2:34 8348
S gave his daughter to Jarha 1Ch 2:35 8348

SHESHBAZZAR
and he counted them out to **S**, Ezr 1:8 8339
S brought them all up with the Ezr 1:11 8339
given to one whose name was **S**, Ezr 5:14 8340
'Then that **S** came *and* laid the Ezr 5:16 8340

SHETH
And tear down all the sons of **S**. Nu 24:17 8352

SHETHAR
Carshena, **S**, Admatha, Tarshish, Es 1:14 8369

SHETHAR-BOZENAI
and **S** and their colleagues came to Ezr 5:3 8370
and **S** and his colleagues the Ezr 5:6 8370
the province beyond the River, **S** and Ezr 6:6 8370
the province beyond the River, **S** and Ezr 6:13 8370

SHEVA
and **S** was scribe, and Zadok and 2Sa 20:25 7724a
S the father of Machbena and the 1Ch 2:49 7724a

SHIBAH
So he called it **S**; Gn 26:33 7656

SHIBBOLETH
would say to him, "Say now, '**S**.'" Jg 12:6 7642b

SHIELD
not fear, Abram, I am a s to you; Gn 15:1 4043
LORD, Who is the s of your help And Dt 33:29 4043
Not a s or a spear was seen Among Jg 5:8 4043
the s of the mighty was defiled, 2Sa 1:21 4043
The s of Saul, not anointed with oil. 2Sa 1:21 4043
My s and the horn of my salvation, 2Sa 22:3 4043
a s to all who take refuge in Him. 2Sa 22:31 4043
given me the s of Your salvation, 2Sa 22:36 4043
shekels of gold on each large s. 1Ki 10:16 6793c
three minas of gold on each s, 1Ki 10:17 4043
he will not come before it with a s 2Ki 19:32 4043
s and sword and shot with bow and 1Ch 5:18 4043
war, who could handle s and spear, 1Ch 12:8 6793c
who bore s and spear *were* 6,800, 1Ch 12:24 6793c
with them 37,000 with s and spear. 1Ch 12:34 6793c
of beaten gold on each large s. 2Ch 9:15 6793c
hundred shekels of gold on each s, 2Ch 9:16 4043
him 200,000 armed with bow and s; 2Ch 17:17 4043
go to war *and* handle spear and s. 2Ch 25:5 6793c
at Him With his massive s. Jb 15:26 4043
You, O LORD, are a s about me, Ps 3:3 4043
surround him with favor as with a s. Ps 5:12 6793c
My s is with God, Who saves the Ps 7:10 4043
My s and the horn of my salvation, Ps 18:2 4043
a s to all who take refuge in Him. Ps 18:30 4043
given me the s of Your salvation, Ps 18:35 4043
The LORD is my strength and my s; Ps 28:7 4043
He is our help and our s. Ps 33:20 4043
Take hold of buckler and s And Ps 35:2 6793c
bring them down, O Lord, our s. Ps 59:11 4043
broke the flaming arrows, The s and Ps 76:3 4043
Behold our s, O God, And look upon Ps 84:9 4043
For the LORD God is a sun and s; Ps 84:11 4043
For our s belongs to the LORD, And Ps 89:18 4043
faithfulness is a s and bulwark. Ps 91:4 6793c
He is their help and their s. Ps 115:9 4043
He is their help and their s. Ps 115:10 4043
He is their help and their s. Ps 115:11 4043
You are my hiding place and my s; Ps 119:114 4043
My s and He in whom I take refuge, Ps 144:2 4043
He is a s to those who walk in Pr 2:7 4043
He is a s to those who take refuge Pr 30:5 4043
And Kir uncovered the s. Is 22:6 4043
he will not come before it with a s, Is 37:33 4043
"Line up the s and buckler, And Jer 46:3 4043
Ethiopia and Put, that handle the s, Jer 46:9 4043
with buckler and s and helmet; Ezk 23:24 4043
raise up a large s against you. Ezk 26:8 6793c
They hung s and helmet in you; Ezk 27:10 4043
great company *with* buckler and s, Ezk 38:4 4043
all of them *with* s and helmet; Ezk 38:5 4043
taking up the s of faith with Eph 6:16 *2375*

SHIELD-BEARER
David, with the s in front of him. 1Sa 17:41 6793c, 5375

SHIELD-CARRIER
his s also walked before him. 1Sa 17:7 6793c, 5375

SHIELDS
by Him, Who s him all the day, Dt 33:12 2653
David took the s of gold which 2Sa 8:7 7982
made 200 large s of beaten gold, 1Ki 10:16 6793c
He made 300 s of beaten gold, 1Ki 10:17 4043
even taking all the s of gold 1Ki 14:26 4043
made s of bronze in their place, 1Ki 14:27 4043
and s that *had been* King David's, 2Ki 11:10 7982
David took the s of gold which 1Ch 18:7 7982
made 200 large s of beaten gold, 2Ch 9:15 6793c
He made 300 s of beaten gold, 2Ch 9:16 4043
He put s and spears in every 2Ch 11:12 6793c
golden s which Solomon had made. 2Ch 12:9 4043
made s of bronze in their place and 2Ch 12:10 4043
Judah, bearing large s and spears, 2Ch 14:8 6793c
bearing s and wielding bows; 2Ch 14:8 4043
s which had been King David's, 2Ch 23:9 7982
prepared for all the army s, 2Ch 26:14 4043
weapons and s in great number. 2Ch 32:5 4043
s and all kinds of valuable articles, 2Ch 32:27 4043
half of them held the spears, the s, Ne 4:16 4043
the s of the earth belong to God; Ps 47:9 4043
On which are hung a thousand s, SS 4:4 4043
All the round s of the mighty men. SS 4:4 7982
"Rise up, captains, oil the s," Is 21:5 4043
They hung their s on your walls Ezk 27:11 7982
burn *them,* both s and bucklers, Ezk 39:9 4043
The s of his mighty men are Na 2:3 4043

SHIFTED
So the LORD s *the wind* to a very Ex 10:19 2015

SHIFTING
there is no variation or s shadow. Jas 1:17 *5157*

SHIGIONOTH
the prophet, according to S. Hab 3:1 7692

SHIHOR
from the S which is east of Egypt, Jos 13:3 7883
from the S of Egypt even to the 1Ch 13:5 7883

SHIHOR-LIBNATH
to Carmel on the west and to S. Jos 19:26 7884

SHIKKERON
Then the border curved to S and Jos 15:11 7942

SHILHI
name was Azubah the daughter of S. 1Ki 22:42 7977
name *was* Azubah the daughter of S. 2Ch 20:31 7977

SHILHIM
Lebaoth and S and Ain and Rimmon; Jos 15:32 7978

SHILLEM
Jahzeel and Guni and Jezer and S. Gn 46:24 8006
of S, the family of the Shillemites. Nu 26:49 8006

SHILLEMITES
of Shillem, the family of the S. Nu 26:49 8016

SHILOAH
the gently flowing waters of S And Is 8:6 7975b

SHILOH
between his feet, Until S comes, Gn 49:10 7886
Israel assembled themselves at S, Jos 18:1 7887
you here before the LORD in S." Jos 18:8 7887
came to Joshua to the camp at S. Jos 18:9 7887
Joshua cast lots for them in S Jos 18:10 7887
by lot in S before the LORD at Jos 19:51 7887
them at S in the land of Canaan, Jos 21:2 7887
departed from the sons of Israel at S Jos 22:9 7887
Israel gathered themselves at S to Jos 22:12 7887
that the house of God was at S. Jg 18:31 7887
brought them to the camp at S, Jg 21:12 7887
the LORD from year to year in S, Jg 21:19 7887
if the daughters of S come out to Jg 21:21 7887
his wife from the daughters of S, Jg 21:21 7887
to the LORD of hosts in S. 1Sa 1:3 7887
after eating and drinking in S, 1Sa 1:9 7887
him to the house of the LORD in S, 1Sa 1:24 7887
Thus they did in S to all the 1Sa 2:14 7887
And the LORD appeared again at S, 1Sa 3:21 7887
at S by the word of the LORD. 1Sa 3:21 7887
Let us take to ourselves from S 1Sa 4:3 7887
So the people sent to S, 1Sa 4:4 7887
and came to S the same day with his 1Sa 4:12 7887
Eli, the priest of the LORD at S, 1Sa 14:3 7887
concerning the house of Eli in S. 1Ki 2:27 7887
the wife of Jeroboam, and go to S; 1Ki 14:2 7887
did so, and arose and went to S, 1Ki 14:4 7887
abandoned the dwelling place at S, Ps 78:60 7887
go now to My place which was in S, Jer 7:12 7887
and your fathers, as I did to S. Jer 7:14 7887
I will make this house like S, Jer 26:6 7887
'This house will be like S and Jer 26:9 7887
men came from Shechem, from S, Jer 41:5 7887

SHILONITE
the S found him on the road. 1Ki 11:29 7888
LORD spoke through Ahijah the S 1Ki 12:15 7888
spoke by His servant Ahijah the S, 1Ki 15:29 7888
in the prophecy of Ahijah the S, 2Ch 9:29 7888
He spoke through Ahijah the S 2Ch 10:15 7888
of Zechariah, the son of the S. Ne 11:5 7888

SHILONITES
From the S *were* Asaiah the 1Ch 9:5 7888

SHILSHAH
Bezer, Hod, Shamma, S, 1Ch 7:37 8030

SHIMEA
Abinadab the second, S the third, 1Ch 2:13 8092
S, Shobab, Nathan and Solomon, 1Ch 3:5 8092
S his son, Haggiah his son, Asaiah 1Ch 6:30 8092
son of Berechiah, the son of S, 1Ch 6:39 8092
Israel, Jonathan the son of S, 1Ch 20:7 8092

SHIMEAH
name was Jonadab, the son of S, 2Sa 13:3 8093
Jonadab, the son of S, 2Sa 13:32 8093
Mikloth became the father of S. 1Ch 8:32 8039

SHIMEAM
Mikloth became the father of S. 1Ch 9:38 8043

SHIMEATH
For Jozacar the son of S and 2Ki 12:21 8100
Zabad the son of S the Ammonitess, 2Ch 24:26 8100

SHIMEATHITES
Jabez *were* the Tirathites, the S 1Ch 2:55 8101

SHIMEI
Libni and S, according to their Ex 6:17 8096
by their families: Libni and S; Nu 3:18 8096
house of Saul whose name was S, 2Sa 16:5 8096
Thus S said when he cursed, 2Sa 16:7 8096
and S went along on the hillside 2Sa 16:13 8096
Then S the son of Gera, the 2Sa 19:16 8096
And S the son of Gera fell down 2Sa 19:18 8096
"Should not S be put to death for 2Sa 19:21 8096
The king said to S, 2Sa 19:23 8096
Israel, Jonathan the son of S, 2Sa 21:21 8096
Jehoiada, Nathan the prophet, S, 1Ki 1:8 8096
S the son of Gera the Benjamite, 1Ki 2:8 8096
Now the king sent and called for S 1Ki 2:36 8096
S then said to the king, 1Ki 2:38 8096
So S lived in Jerusalem many days. 1Ki 2:38 8096
that two of the servants of S ran 1Ki 2:39 8096
And they told S, saying, 1Ki 2:39 8096
S arose and saddled his donkey, 1Ki 2:40 8096
And S went and brought his 1Ki 2:40 8096
It was told Solomon that S had 1Ki 2:41 8096
So the king sent and called for S 1Ki 2:42 8096
The king also said to S, 1Ki 2:44 8096
S the son of Ela, in Benjamin; 1Ki 4:18 8096
of Pedaiah *were* Zerubbabel and S. 1Ch 3:19 8096
son, Zaccur his son, S his son. 1Ch 4:26 8096
Now S had sixteen sons and six 1Ch 4:27 8096
his son, Gog his son, S his son, 1Ch 5:4 8096
the sons of Gershom: Libni and S. 1Ch 6:17 8096
Mahli, Libni his son, S his son, 1Ch 6:29 8096
the son of Zimmah, the son of S, 1Ch 6:42 8096
and Shimrath *were* the sons of S. 1Ch 8:21 8096
the Gershonites *were* Ladan and S. 1Ch 23:7 8096
The sons of S *were* Shelomoth and 1Ch 23:9 8096
The sons of S *were* Jahath, 1Ch 23:10 8096
These four *were* the sons of S. 1Ch 23:10 8096
Gedaliah, Zeri, Jeshaiah, S, 1Ch 25:3
the tenth to S, his sons and his 1Ch 25:17 8096
S the Ramathite had charge of 1Ch 27:27 8096
the sons of Heman, Jehiel and S; 2Ch 29:14 8096
them and his brother S *was* second. 2Ch 31:12 8096
the authority of Conaniah and S 2Ch 31:13 8096
Of Levites *there were* Jozabad, S, Ezr 10:23 8096
Jeremai, Manasseh *and* S; Ezr 10:33 8096
Bani, Binnui, S, Ezr 10:38 8096
the son of Jair, the son of S, Es 2:5 8096

SHIMEITES
Libnites and the family of the S; Nu 3:21 8097
the family of the S by itself and Zch 12:13 8097

SHIMEON
Isshijah, Malchijah, Shemaiah, S, Ezr 10:31 8095

SHIMON
sons of S *were* Amnon and Rinnah, 1Ch 4:20 7889

SHIMRATH
and S *were* the sons of Shimei. 1Ch 8:21 8119

SHIMRI
the son of Jedaiah, the son of S, 1Ch 4:37 8113
the son of S and Joha his brother, 1Ch 11:45 8113
sons of Merari had sons: S the first 1Ch 26:10 8113
sons of Elizaphan, S and Jeiel; 2Ch 29:13 8113

SHIMRITH
the son of S the Moabitess. 2Ch 24:26 8116

SHIMRON
Tola and Puvvah and Iob and S. Gn 46:13 8110b
of S, the family of the Shimronites. Nu 26:24 8110b
to the king of S and to the king of Jos 11:1 8110a
and S and Idalah and Bethlehem; Jos 19:15 8110a
Tola, Puah, Jashub and S. 1Ch 7:1 8110b

SHIMRONITES
of Shimron, the family of the S. Nu 26:24 8117

SHIMRON-MERON
the king of S, one; Jos 12:20 8112

SHIMSHAI
S the scribe wrote a letter against Ezr 4:8 8124
wrote Rehum the commander and S Ezr 4:9 8124
the commander, to S the scribe, Ezr 4:17 8124
read before Rehum and S the scribe Ezr 4:23 8124

SHINAB
king of Gomorrah, S king of Admah, Gn 14:2 8134

SHINAR
and Calneh, in the land of S. Gn 10:10 8152
they found a plain in the land of S Gn 11:2 8152
in the days of Amraphel king of S, Gn 14:1 8152
Amraphel king of S and Arioch king Gn 14:9 8152
a beautiful mantle from S and two Jos 7:21 8152
Egypt, Pathros, Cush, Elam, S, Is 11:11 8152
he brought them to the land of S, Da 1:2 8152
a temple for her in the land of S; Zch 5:11 8152

SHINE
The LORD make His face s on you, Nu 6:25 215
care for it, Nor light s on it. Jb 3:4 3313
Who commands the sun not to s, Jb 9:7 2224
And light will s on your ways. Jb 22:28 5050
the lightning of His cloud to s? Jb 37:15 3313
"Behind him he makes a wake to s; Jb 41:32 215
Your face to s upon Your servant; Ps 31:16 215
And cause His face to s upon us Ps 67:1 215
above the cherubim, s forth! Ps 80:1 3313
And cause Your face to s *upon us,* Ps 80:3 215
And cause Your face to s *upon us,* Ps 80:7 215
Cause Your face to s *upon us,* Ps 80:19 215
God of vengeance, s forth! Ps 94:1 3313
Make Your face s upon Your servant, Ps 119:135 215
upon himself his crown shall s." Ps 132:18 6692a
land, The light will s on them. Is 9:2 5050
"Arise, s; for your light has come, Is 60:1 215
let Your face s on Your desolate Da 9:17 215
"Those who have insight will s Da 12:3 2094a
"Let your light s before men in Mt 5:16 *2989*
"Then THE RIGHTEOUS WILL S FORTH Mt 13:43 *1584*
TO S UPON THOSE WHO SIT IN Lk 1:79 *2014*
"Light shall s out of darkness," 2Co 4:6 *2989*
And Christ will s on you." Eph 5:14 *2017*
day would not s for a third of it, Rv 8:12 *5316*
the light of a lamp will not s in you Rv 18:23 *5316*
need of the sun or of the moon to s Rv 21:23 *5316*

SHINES
And which s as the darkness." Jb 10:22 3313
name increase as long as the sun s; Ps 72:17
That s brighter and brighter until Pr 4:18 215
s to the other part of the sky, Lk 17:24 *2989*
The Light s in the darkness, Jn 1:5 *5316*

SHINING
"All the s lights in the heavens Ezk 32:8 3974
the lamp that was burning and was s Jn 5:35 *5316*
man stood before me in s garments, Ac 10:30 *2986*
s all around me and those who were Ac 26:13 *4034*
as to a lamp s in a dark place, 2Pe 1:19 *5316*
and the true Light is already s. 1Jn 2:8 *5316*
like the sun s in its strength. Rv 1:16 *5316*

SHINY
and two utensils of fine s bronze, Ezr 8:27 6668

SHION
and Hapharaim and S and Anaharath, Jos 19:19 7866

SHIP
way of a s in the middle of the sea, Pr 30:19 591
on which no mighty s will pass Is 33:21 6716a
a s which was going to Tarshish, Jon 1:3 591
that the s was about to break up. Jon 1:4 591
threw the cargo which was in the s Jon 1:5 591
gone below into the hold of the s, Jon 1:5 5600
But we, going ahead to the s, Ac 20:13 *4143*
were accompanying him to the s. Ac 20:38 *4143*
a s crossing over to Phoenicia, Ac 21:2 *4143*
the s was to unload its cargo. Ac 21:3 *4143*

Then we went on board the **s**, Ac 21:6 *4143*
And embarking in an Adramyttian **s**, Ac 27:2 *4143*
Alexandrian **s** sailing for Italy, Ac 27:6 *4143*
not only of the cargo and the **s**, Ac 27:10 *4143*
pilot and the captain of the **s** than Ac 27:11 *3490*
and when the **s** was caught *in it* Ac 27:15 *4143*
cables in undergirding the **s**; Ac 27:17 *4143*
life among you, but *only* of the **s**. Ac 27:22 *4143*
were trying to escape from the **s** and Ac 27:30 *4143*
"Unless these men remain in the **s**, Ac 27:31 *4143*
All of us in the **s** were two Ac 27:37 *4143*
they *began* to lighten the **s** by Ac 27:38 *4143*
drive the **s** onto it if they could. Ac 27:39 *4143*
on various things from the **s**. Ac 27:44 *4143*
we set sail on an Alexandrian **s** Ac 28:11 *4143*

SHIPHI
Ziza the son of **S**, the son of 1Ch 4:37 8230a

SHIPHMITE
and Zabdi the **S** had charge of the 1Ch 27:27 8225

SHIPHRAH
one of whom was named **S** and Ex 1:15 8236

SHIPHTAN
a leader, Kemuel the son of **S**. Nu 34:24 8204

SHIPMASTER
And every **s** and every passenger Rv 18:17 *2942*

SHIP'S
scarcely able to get the **s** boat Ac 27:16
they threw the **s** tackle overboard Ac 27:19 *4143*
and had let down the **s** boat Ac 27:30
cut away the ropes of the **s** boat Ac 27:32

SHIPS
And he *shall be* a haven for **s**, Gn 49:13 591
"But **s** *shall come* from the coast Nu 24:24 6716a
will bring you back to Egypt in **s**, Dt 28:68 591
And why did Dan stay in **s**? Jg 5:17 591
built a fleet of **s** in Ezion-geber, 1Ki 9:26 590
Also the **s** of Hiram, which 1Ki 10:11 590
For the king had at sea the **s** of 1Ki 10:22 590
of Tarshish with the **s** of Hiram; 1Ki 10:22 590
the **s** of Tarshish came bringing gold 1Ki 10:22 590
Jehoshaphat made **s** of Tarshish to 1Ki 22:48 591
the **s** were broken at Ezion-geber. 1Ki 22:48 591
go with your servants in the **s**." 1Ki 22:49 591
s and servants who knew the sea; 2Ch 8:18 591
For the king had **s** which went to 2Ch 9:21 591
the **s** of Tarshish came bringing gold 2Ch 9:21 591
him to make **s** to go to Tarshish, 2Ch 20:36 591
and they made the **s** in Ezion-geber. 2Ch 20:36 591
So the **s** were broken and could not 2Ch 20:37 591
You break the **s** of Tarshish. Ps 48:7 591
There the **s** move along, *And* Ps 104:26 591
Those who go down to the sea in **s**, Ps 107:23 591
She is like merchant **s**; Pr 31:14 591
Against all the **s** of Tarshish And Is 2:16 591
Wail, O **s** of Tarshish, For *Tyre* is Is 23:1 591
Wail, O **s** of Tarshish, For your Is 23:14 591
into the **s** in which they rejoice. Is 43:14 591
the **s** of Tarshish *will come* first, Is 60:9 591
All the **s** of the sea and their Ezk 27:9 591
"The **s** of Tarshish were the Ezk 27:25 591
sea Will come down from their **s**; Ezk 27:29 591
go forth from Me in **s** to frighten Ezk 30:9 6716a
"For **s** of Kittim will come Da 11:30 6716a
with horsemen and with many **s**; Da 11:40 591
Look at the **s** also, though they Jas 3:4 *4143*
a third of the **s** were destroyed. Rv 8:9 *4143*
all who had **s** at sea became rich by Rv 18:19 *4143*

SHIPWRECK
suffered **s** in regard to their faith. 1Tm 1:19 *3489*

SHIPWRECKED
I was stoned, three times I was **s**, 2Co 11:25 *3489*

SHIRT
wants to sue you and take your **s**, Mt 5:40 *5509*
not withhold your **s** from him either. Lk 6:29 *5509*

SHISHA
the sons of **S** *were* secretaries; 1Ki 4:3 7894

SHISHAK
fled to Egypt to **S** king of Egypt, 1Ki 11:40 7895
that **S** the king of Egypt came up 1Ki 14:25 7895
that **S** king of Egypt came up 2Ch 12:2 7895
gathered at Jerusalem because of **S**, 2Ch 12:5 7895
I also have forsaken you to **S**.' " 2Ch 12:5 7895
out on Jerusalem by means of **S**. 2Ch 12:7 7895
So **S** king of Egypt came up against 2Ch 12:9 7895

SHITRAI
S the Sharonite had charge of 1Ch 27:29 7861

SHITTIM
While Israel remained at **S**, Nu 25:1 7851
two men as spies secretly from **S**, Jos 2:1 7851
all the sons of Israel set out from **S** Jos 3:1 7851
LORD To water the valley of **S**. Jl 3:18 7851
him, *And* from **S** to Gilgal, Mi 6:5 7851

SHIZA
Adina the son of **S** the Reubenite, 1Ch 11:42 7877

SHOA
Chaldeans, Pekod and **S** and Koa, Ezk 23:23 7772

SHOBAB
Shammua, **S**, Nathan, Solomon, 2Sa 5:14 7727
Jesher, **S**, and Ardon. 1Ch 2:18 7727
Shimea, **S**, Nathan and Solomon, 1Ch 3:5 7727
Shammua, **S**, Nathan, Solomon, 1Ch 14:4 7727

SHOBACH
and **S** the commander of the army of 2Sa 10:16 7731
S the commander of their army, 2Sa 10:18 7731

SHOBAI
the sons of Hatita, the sons of **S**, Ezr 2:42 7630
the sons of Hatita, the sons of **S**, Ne 7:45 7630

SHOBAL
Lotan and **S** and Zibeon and Anah, Gn 36:20 7732
These are the sons of **S**: Gn 36:23 7732
chief Lotan, chief **S**, Gn 36:29 7732
The sons of Seir *were* Lotan, **S**, 1Ch 1:38 7732
The sons of **S** *were* Alian, 1Ch 1:40 7732
S the father of Kiriath-jearim, 1Ch 2:50 7732
S the father of Kiriath-jearim 1Ch 2:52 7732
Perez, Hezron, Carmi, Hur and **S**. 1Ch 4:1 7732
Reaiah the son of **S** became 1Ch 4:2 7732

SHOBEK
Hallohesh, Pilha, **S**, Ne 10:24 7733

SHOBI
S the son of Nahash from Rabbah of 2Sa 17:27 7629

SHOCKED
'Do not be **s**, nor fear them. Dt 1:29 6206
do not be **s** at the sight; Ec 5:8 8539

SHOCKS
both the **s** and the standing grain, Jg 15:5 1430a

SHOD
and having **s** YOUR FEET WITH THE Eph 6:15 *5265*

SHOE
Over Edom I shall throw My **s**; Ps 60:8 5275
Over Edom I shall throw My **s**; Ps 108:9 5275

SHOES
and take your **s** off your feet." Is 20:2 5275
and put your **s** on your feet, Ezk 24:17 5275
heads and your **s** on your feet. Ezk 24:23 5275
"Carry no money belt, no bag, no **s**; Lk 10:4 *5266*

SHOHAM
by Jaaziah *were* Beno, **S**, 1Ch 24:27 7719

SHOMER
and Jehozabad the son of **S**, 2Ki 12:21 7763
father of Japhlet, **S** and Hotham, 1Ch 7:32 7763

SHONE
the skin of his face **s** because of his Ex 34:29 7160
behold, the skin of his face **s**, Ex 34:30 7160
that the skin of Moses' face **s**. Ex 34:35 7160
He **s** forth from Mount Paran, And Dt 33:2 3313
and the sun **s** on the water, 2Ki 3:22 2224
When His lamp **s** over my head, *And* Jb 29:3 1984a
have looked at the sun when it **s** Or Jb 31:26 1984a
of beauty, God has **s** forth. Ps 50:2 3313
and the earth **s** with His glory. Ezk 43:2 215
and His face **s** like the sun, and Mt 17:2 *2989*
glory of the Lord **s** around them; Lk 2:9 *4034*
and a light **s** in the cell; Ac 12:7 *2989*
is the One who has **s** in our hearts 2Co 4:6 *2989*

SHOOK
"Then the earth **s** and quaked, The 2Sa 22:8 1607
that the earth **s** at their noise. 1Ki 1:40 1234
I also **s** out the front of my garment Ne 5:13 5287
Then the earth **s** and quaked; Ps 18:7 1607
The earth trembled and **s**. Ps 77:18 7493
the hearts of his people **s** as the trees Is 7:2 5128
the earth tremble, Who **s** kingdoms, Is 14:16 7493
top to bottom; and the earth **s** Mt 27:51 *4579*
The guards **s** for fear of him Mt 28:4 *4579*
Moses **s** with fear and would Ac 7:32 *1790*
But they **s** off the dust of their Ac 13:51 *1621*
he **s** out his garments and said to Ac 18:6 *1621*
However he **s** the creature off into Ac 28:5 *660*
And His voice **s** the earth then, Heb 12:26 *4531*

SHOOT
I will **s** three arrows to the side, 1Sa 20:20 3384
arrows which I am about to **s**." 1Sa 20:36 3384
that they would **s** from the wall? 2Sa 11:20 3384
"**S** him too, in the chariot." 2Ki 9:27 5221
Then Elisha said, "**S**!" 2Ki 13:17 3384
to this city or **s** an arrow there; 2Ki 19:32 3384
left *to sling* stones and *to* **s** 1Ch 12:2
To **s** in darkness at the upright in Ps 11:2 3384
To **s** from concealment at the Ps 64:4 3384
Suddenly they **s** at him, and do not Ps 64:4 3384
God will **s** at them with an arrow; Ps 64:7 3384
s which Your right hand has planted, Ps 80:15 3657
Then a **s** will spring from the stem Is 11:1 2415
to this city or **s** an arrow there; Is 37:33 3384
up before Him like a tender **s**, Is 53:2 3126
S at her, do not be sparing with Jer 50:14 3034

SHOOTING
for the purpose of **s** arrows and 2Ch 26:15 3372b

SHOOTS
his **s** spread out over his garden. Jb 8:16 3127
again, And its **s** will not fail. Jb 14:7 3127
The flame will wither his **s**, Jb 15:30 3127
the sea And its **s** to the River. Ps 80:11 3127
"Your **s** are an orchard of SS 4:13 7973
degenerate **s** of a foreign vine? Jer 2:21
yielded **s** and sent out branches. Ezk 17:6 909
It has consumed its **s** *and* fruit, Ezk 19:14 909
His **s** will sprout, And his beauty Hos 14:6 3127

SHOPHACH
with **S** the commander of the army 1Ch 19:16 7780
put to death **S** the commander of 1Ch 19:18 7780

SHORE
Eloth on the **s** of the Red Sea, 1Ki 9:26 8193
Gennesaret, and moored to the **s**. Mk 6:53

SHORN
teeth are like a flock of *newly* **s** ewes SS 4:2 7094

SHORT
inhabitants were **s** of strength, 2Ki 19:26 7116
do not fall **s** in anything of all Es 6:10
the triumphing of the wicked is **s**, Jb 20:5 7138
bed is too **s** on which to stretch out, Is 28:20 7114a
inhabitants were **s** of strength, Is 37:27 7116
Is My hand so **s** that it cannot Is 50:2 7114a
the LORD's hand is not so **s** That it Is 59:1 7114a
is bald and every beard cut **s**; Jer 48:37 1639
And a **s** measure *that is* cursed? Mi 6:10 7332
Unless those days had been cut **s**, Mt 24:22 *2856*
elect those days will be cut **s**. Mt 24:22 *2856*
put the men outside for a **s** time. Ac 5:34 *1024*
"In a **s** time you will persuade me Ac 26:28 *3641*
that whether in a **s** or long time, Ac 26:29 *3641*
and fall **s** of the glory of God, Ro 3:23 *5302*
taken away from you for a **s** while 1Th 2:17 *2540, 5610*
may seem to have come **s** of it. Heb 4:1 *5302*
For they disciplined us for a **s** time Heb 12:10 *3641*
no one comes **s** of the grace of God; Heb 12:15 *5302*
knowing that he has *only* a **s** time." Rv 12:12 *3641*
he must be released for a **s** time. Rv 20:3 *3398*

SHORTENED
"His vigorous stride is **s**, Jb 18:7 6887a
You have **s** the days of his youth; Ps 89:45 7114a
He has **s** my days. Ps 102:23 7114a
the years of the wicked will be **s**. Pr 10:27 7114a
Unless the Lord had **s** *those* days, Mk 13:20 *2856*
whom He chose, He **s** the days. Mk 13:20 *2856*
brethren, the time has been **s**, 1Co 7:29 *4958*

SHORT-LIVED
"Man, who is born of woman, Is **s** Jb 14:1 7116, 3117

SHORTLY
s be brought again from Babylon Jer 27:16 4120
I will **s** pour out My wrath on you and Ezk 7:8 7138
he himself was about to leave **s**. Ac 25:4 *5034*
Jesus to send Timothy to you **s**, Php 2:19 *5030*
I myself also will be coming **s**. Php 2:24 *5030*
but I hope to see you **s**, 3Jn 1:14 *2112*

SHORT-SIGHTED
these *qualities* is blind *or* **s**, 2Pe 1:9 *3467*

SHOT
And **s** *at him* and harassed him; Gn 49:23 7232b
surely be stoned or **s** through; Ex 19:13 3384
side, as though I **s** at a target. 1Sa 20:20 7971
running, he **s** an arrow past him. 1Sa 20:36 3384
of the arrow which Jonathan had **s**, 1Sa 20:37 3384
the archers **s** at your servants 2Sa 11:24 3372b
and **s** Joram between his arms; 2Ki 9:24 5221
So they **s** *him* at the ascent of 2Ki 9:27
Then Elisha said, "Shoot!" And he **s**. 2Ki 13:17 3384
shield and sword and **s** with bow and 1Ch 5:18 1869
The archers **s** King Josiah, and 2Ch 35:23 3384

SHOULD
s I take your son back to the land Gn 24:5
Why **s** I be bereaved of you both in Gn 27:45
s you therefore serve me for Gn 29:15
"**S** he treat our sister as a Gn 34:31
s have put me into the dungeon." Gn 40:15
If harm **s** befall him on the Gn 42:38
for if he **s** leave his father, Gn 44:22
for why **s** we die in your presence? Gn 47:15
"Why **s** we die before your eyes, Gn 47:19
that Pharaoh **s** have the fifth; Gn 47:26
"Who am I, that I **s** go to Pharaoh, Ex 3:11
and that I **s** bring the sons of Ex 3:11
"Who is the LORD that I **s** obey Ex 5:2
according to what each man **s** eat, Ex 12:4
it every man as much as he **s** eat; Ex 16:16
man gathered as much as he **s** eat. Ex 16:18
every man as much as he **s** eat; Ex 16:21
"Why **s** the Egyptians speak, Ex 32:12
s I go up in your midst for one Ex 33:5
his peace offerings **s** *ever* be eaten Lv 7:18
you **s** certainly have eaten it in Lv 10:18
not spew you out, **s** you defile it, Lv 18:28
s ever disregard that man when he Lv 20:4
if he **s** ever *wish to* redeem it, Lv 27:13
it **s** *wish to* redeem his house, Lv 27:15
s ever wish to redeem the field, Lv 27:19
where we **s** camp in the wilderness, Nu 10:31
them forth, that You **s**ay to me, Nu 11:12
"**S** flocks and herds be slaughtered Nu 11:22
Or **s** all the fish of the sea be Nu 11:22
"We **s** by all means go up and take Nu 13:30
declared what **s** be done to him. Nu 15:34
descendants of Aaron **s** come near Nu 16:40
"God is not a man, that He **s** lie, Nu 23:19
a son of man, that He **s** repent; Nu 23:19
"Why **s** the name of our father be Nu 27:4
"But if her father **s** forbid her Nu 30:5
if she **s** marry while under her Nu 30:6
because he **s** have remained in his Nu 35:28
time all the things that you **s** do. Dt 1:18
of the way by which we **s** go up and Dt 1:22
you the way in which you **s** go. Dt 1:33
that you **s** do thus in the land Dt 4:5
'Now then why **s** we die? Dt 5:25
you **s** listen and be careful to do Dt 6:3
"You **s** diligently keep the Dt 6:17
"If you **s** say in your heart, Dt 7:17
man, that it **s** be besieged by you? Dt 20:19
you **s** keep all His commandments; Dt 26:18
is not in heaven, that you **s** say, Dt 30:12
it beyond the sea, that you **s** say, Dt 30:13
that we **s** rebel against the LORD Jos 22:29
that we **s** forsake the LORD to serve Jos 24:16
we **s** give bread to your army?" Jg 8:6

that we **s** give bread to your men Jg 8:15
is Shechem, that we **s** serve him? Jg 9:28
but why **s** we serve him? Jg 9:28
is Abimelech that we **s** serve him?' Jg 9:38
"She **s** not eat anything that Jg 13:14
so **s** I tell you?" Jg 14:16
consider what you **s** do." Jg 18:14
s be *missing* today in Israel?" Jg 21:3
Why **s** you go with me? Ru 1:11
if I **s** even have a husband tonight Ru 1:12
that you **s** take notice of me, Ru 2:10
'You **s** stay close to my servants Ru 2:21
father **s** walk before Me forever'; 1Sa 2:30
you and show you what you **s** do." 1Sa 10:8
far be it from me that I **s** sin 1Sa 12:23
a man that He **s** change His mind." 1Sa 15:29
that he **s** taunt the armies of the 1Sa 17:26
that I **s** be the king's son-in-law?" 1Sa 18:18
s have been given to David, 1Sa 18:19
Why **s** I put you to death?'" 1Sa 19:17
So why **s** my father hide this thing 1Sa 20:2
s you bring me to your father?" 1Sa 20:8
For if I **s** indeed learn that evil 1Sa 20:9
"Why **s** he be put to death? 1Sa 20:32
that I **s** do this thing to my lord, 1Sa 24:6
know and consider what you **s** do, 1Sa 25:17
"**S** anyone rise up to pursue you 1Sa 25:29
"The LORD forbid that I **s** stretch 1Sa 26:11
for why **s** your servant live in the 1Sa 27:5
make known to me what I **s** do." 1Sa 28:15
Why **s** I strike you to the ground? 2Sa 2:22
"**S** Abner die as a fool dies? 2Sa 3:33
s build Me a house to dwell in? 2Sa 7:5
you **s** regard a dead dog like me?" 2Sa 9:8
"But now he has died; why **s** I fast? 2Sa 12:23
"No, my son, we **s** not all go, 2Sa 13:25
"Why **s** he go with you?" 2Sa 13:26
"But if He **s** say thus, 2Sa 15:26
"Why **s** this dead dog curse my 2Sa 16:9
"Besides, whom **s** I serve? 2Sa 16:19
"Besides, whom should I serve? **S** 2Sa 16:19
"You **s** not go out; 2Sa 18:3
"Even if I **s** receive a thousand 2Sa 18:12
Why then **s** you be the last to 2Sa 19:12
"**S** not Shimei be put to death for 2Sa 19:21
that you **s** this day be an adversary 2Sa 19:22
S any man be put to death in 2Sa 19:22
I **s** complain anymore to the king?" 2Sa 19:28
that I **s** go up with the king to 2Sa 19:34
Why then **s** your servant be an 2Sa 19:35
Why **s** the king compensate me *with* 2Sa 19:36
me that I **s** swallow up or destroy! 2Sa 20:20
"What **s** I do for you? 2Sa 21:3
from me, O LORD, that I **s** do this. 2Sa 23:17
who **s** sit on the throne of my lord 1Ki 1:27
steeds to the place where it **s** be, 1Ki 4:28
the good way in which they **s** walk. 1Ki 8:36
that he **s** not go after other gods; 1Ki 11:10
"The LORD forbid me that I **s** give 1Ki 21:3
why **s** I wait for the LORD any 2Ki 6:33
the LORD **s** make windows in heaven, 2Ki 7:2
the LORD **s** make windows in heaven, 2Ki 7:19
that he **s** do this great thing?" 2Ki 8:13
s have struck five or six times, 2Ki 13:19
for why **s** you provoke trouble so 2Ki 14:10
them how they **s** fear the LORD. 2Ki 17:28
that the LORD **s** deliver Jerusalem 2Ki 18:35
That you **s** turn fortified cities 2Ki 19:25
that they **s** become a desolation and 2Ki 22:19
me before my God that I **s** do this. 1Ch 11:19
knowledge of what Israel **s** do, 1Ch 12:32
for those who **s** sound aloud, 1Ch 16:42
Why **s** he be a cause of guilt to 1Ch 21:3
people that they **s** be plagued." 1Ch 21:17
that David **s** go up and build an 1Ch 21:18
we **s** be able to offer as generously as 1Ch 29:14
I, that I **s** build a house for Him, 2Ch 2:6
the good way in which they **s** walk. 2Ch 6:27
God of Israel **s** be put to death, 2Ch 15:13
"**S** you help the wicked and love 2Ch 19:2
'**S** evil come upon us, the sword, 2Ch 20:9 518
Why **s** you be struck down?" 2Ch 25:16
s you provoke trouble so that you, 2Ch 25:19
that they **s** come to the house of 2Ch 30:1
that they **s** come to celebrate the 2Ch 30:5
"Why **s** the kings of Assyria come 2Ch 32:4
that your God **s** be able to deliver 2Ch 32:14
they **s** not eat from the most holy Ezr 2:63
why **s** damage increase to the Ezr 4:22
that they **s** assemble at Jerusalem, Ezr 10:7
all his possessions **s** be forfeited Ezr 10:8
Why **s** my face not be sad when the Ne 2:3
if a fox **s** jump on *it,* he would break Ne 4:3
s you not walk in the fear of our Ne 5:9
Why **s** the work stop while I leave Ne 6:3
"**S** a man like me flee? Ne 6:11
they **s** not eat from the most holy Ne 7:65
the sons of Israel **s** live in booths Ne 8:14
no Ammonite or Moabite **s** ever enter Ne 13:1
I commanded that the doors **s** be Ne 13:19
they **s** not open them until after the Ne 13:19
Levites that they **s** purify themselves Ne 13:22
that he **s** do according to the desires Es 1:8
that every man **s** be the master in Es 1:22
that she **s** not make *them* known. Es 2:10
that they **s** be ready for this day. Es 3:14
commanded that it **s** be done so; Es 9:14
that they **s** make them days of Es 9:22
Jews, **s** return on his own head and Es 9:25
sons **s** be hanged on the gallows. Es 9:25
why the breasts, that I **s** suck? Jb 3:12
is my strength, that I **s** wait? Jb 6:11
what is my end, that I **s** endure? Jb 6:11
"For the despairing man *there* **s** *be* Jb 6:14
wicked, Why then **s** I toil in vain? Jb 9:29
"If I **s** wash myself with snow And Jb 9:30
That You **s** seek for my guilt And Jb 10:6
'**S** *my head* be lifted up, You Jb 10:16
'I **s** have been as though I had not Jb 10:19
"Why **s** I take my flesh in my Jb 13:14
"**S** a wise man answer with windy Jb 15:2
"**S** he argue with useless talk, Or Jb 15:3
s turn your spirit against God And Jb 15:13
"What is man, that he **s** be pure, Jb 15:14
a woman, that he **s** be righteous? Jb 15:14
And why **s** I not be impatient? Jb 21:4
the Almighty, that we **s** serve Him, Jb 21:15
me that I **s** declare you right; Jb 27:5
"I thought age **s** speak, And Jb 32:7
increased years **s** teach wisdom. Jb 32:7
no fear of me **s** terrify you, Jb 33:7
Nor **s** my pressure weigh heavily on Jb 33:7
S I lie concerning my right? Jb 34:6
"If He **s** determine to do so, If Jb 34:14
If He **s** gather to Himself His Jb 34:14
he **s** go before God in judgment. Jb 34:23
that you **s** exalt His work, Jb 36:24
Or **s** a man say that he would be Jb 37:20
given to Me that I **s** repay *him?* Jb 41:11
him in the way he **s** choose. Ps 25:12
you in the way which you **s** go; Ps 32:8
fear, though the earth **s** change And Ps 46:2
Why **s** I fear in days of adversity, Ps 49:5
And he **s** cease *trying* forever Ps 49:8
That he **s** live on eternally, Ps 49:9
That he **s** not undergo decay. Ps 49:9
s teach them to their children, Ps 78:5
s put their confidence in God And Ps 78:7
Why **s** the nations say, Ps 79:10
If I **s** say, "My foot has slipped," Ps 94:18
Why **s** the nations say, Ps 115:2
That we **s** keep *them* diligently. Ps 119:4
If You, LORD, **s** mark iniquities, Ps 130:3
If I **s** count them, they would Ps 139:18
me the way in which I **s** walk; Ps 143:8
S your springs be dispersed Pr 5:16
why **s** you, my son, be exhilarated Pr 5:20
His mouth **s** not err in judgment. Pr 16:10
Train up a child in the way he **s** go, Pr 22:6
Why **s** he take your bed from under Pr 22:27
has *so* worked that men **s** fear Him. Ec 3:14
man **s** be happy in his activities, Ec 3:22
It is better that you **s** not vow Ec 5:5
than that you **s** vow and not pay. Ec 5:5
Why **s** God be angry on account of Ec 5:6
Why **s** you ruin yourself? Ec 7:16
Why **s** you die before your time? Ec 7:17
one **s** never sleep day or night), Ec 8:16
though man **s** seek laboriously, Ec 8:17
and though the wise man **s** say, Ec 8:17
if a man **s** live many years, Ec 11:8
For why **s** I be like one who veils SS 1:7
"Why **s** you gaze at the SS 6:13
For why **s** he be esteemed? Is 2:22
You **s** not appoint me ruler of the Is 3:7
hosts whom you **s** regard as holy. Is 8:13
s not a people consult their God? Is 8:19
S *they consult* the dead on Is 8:19
S someone give Me briars *and* Is 27:4
That you **s** turn fortified cities Is 37:26
Who leads you in the way you **s** go. Is 48:17
You **s** be My Servant To raise up the Is 49:6
majesty That we **s** look upon Him, Is 53:2
that we **s** be attracted to Him. Is 53:2
"*Then* you **s** return to Me. Jer 4:1
"Why **s** I pardon you? Jer 5:7
they say to you, 'Where **s** we go?' Jer 15:2
S good be repaid with evil? Jer 18:20
That he **s** see and hear His word? Jer 23:18
Why **s** this city become a ruin? Jer 27:17
that it **s** be removed from before Jer 32:31
that they **s** do this abomination, Jer 32:35
that each man **s** set free his male Jer 34:9
so that no one **s** keep them, a Jew Jer 34:9
each man **s** set free his male servant Jer 34:10
so that no one **s** keep them any Jer 34:10
Why **s** he take your life, so that Jer 40:15
tell us the way in which we **s** walk Jer 42:3
walk and the thing that we **s** do." Jer 42:3
You **s** clearly understand that Jer 42:19
you **s** now clearly understand that Jer 42:22
Babylon **s** ascend to the heavens, Jer 51:53
s fortify her lofty stronghold, Jer 51:53
they **s** not enter into Your congregation La 1:10
about him **s** be his adversaries; La 1:17
S women eat their offspring, The La 2:20
S priest and prophet be slain In La 2:20
he **s** bear The yoke in his youth. La 3:27
Why **s** *any* living mortal, or *any* La 3:39
you to them who **s** listen to you; Ezk 3:6
man that the righteous **s** not sin and Ezk 3:21
to put to death some who **s** not die Ezk 13:19
keep others alive who **s** not live, Ezk 13:19
S I be consulted by them at all? Ezk 14:3
"Or *if* I **s** bring a sword on that Ezk 14:17
"Or *if* I **s** send a plague against Ezk 14:19
s never come about nor happen. Ezk 16:16
'Why **s** the son not bear the Ezk 18:19
he **s** turn from his ways and live? Ezk 18:23
that it **s** not be profaned in the Ezk 20:9
that it **s** not be profaned in the Ezk 20:14
that it **s** not be profaned in the Ezk 20:22
S you then possess the land? Ezk 33:25
S you then possess the land?"' Ezk 33:26
S not the shepherds feed the flock? Ezk 34:2
you **s** feed in the good pasture, Ezk 34:18
you **s** drink of the clear waters, Ezk 34:18
they **s** be educated three years, Da 1:5
for why **s** he see your faces Da 1:10
that the wise men **s** be slain; Da 2:13
king **s** establish a statute and enforce Da 6:7
S it yield, strangers would Hos 8:7 194
it is not the time that he **s** delay at Hos 13:13
Why **s** they among the peoples say, Jl 2:17
"What **s** we do to you that the sea Jon 1:11
"**S** I not have compassion on Nineveh, Jon 4:11
Though the fig tree **s** not blossom And Hab 3:17
the yield of the olive **s** fail And Hab 3:17
flock **s** be cut off from the fold And Hab 3:17
are the things which you **s** do: Zch 8:16
S I receive that from your hand?" Mal 1:13
of a priest **s** preserve knowledge, Mal 2:7
and men **s** seek instruction from Mal 2:7
they **s** tell no one that He was the Mt 16:20
until he **s** pay back what was owed. Mt 18:30
'**S** you not also have had mercy on Mt 18:33 1163
he **s** repay all that was owed him. Mt 18:34
these are the things you **s** have done Mt 23:23 1163
this **s** come to the governor's ears, Mt 28:14
a boat **s** stand ready for Him Mk 3:9
that no one **s** know about this, Mk 5:43
something **s** be given her to eat. Mk 5:43
they **s** take nothing for *their* journey, Mk 6:8
and preached that *men* **s** repent. Mk 6:12
HIS BROTHER **S** MARRY THE WIFE Mk 12:19
standing where it **s** not be Mk 13:14 1163
in case he **s** come suddenly and find Mk 13:36
them *to decide* what each man **s** take. Mk 15:24
these are the things you **s** have done Lk 11:42 1163
six days in which work **s** be done; Lk 13:14 1163
s she not have been released from Lk 13:16 1163
HIS BROTHER **S** MARRY THE WIFE AND Lk 20:28
you also **s** do as I did to you. Jn 13:15
he **s** give something to the poor. Jn 13:29
that I **s** not call any man unholy Ac 10:28
SOMEONE **S** DESCRIBE IT TO YOU.' Ac 13:41
you **s** turn from these vain things Ac 14:15
others of them **s** go up to Jerusalem Ac 15:2
Paul kept insisting that they **s** not take Ac 15:38
men that all *people* everywhere **s** repent, Ac 17:30
having decided that they **s** abstain Ac 21:25
for he **s** not be allowed to live!" Ac 22:22 2520
stating that he **s** be examined by Ac 22:24
they **s** have anything against me. Ac 24:19
they **s** repent and turn to God, Ac 26:20
who could swim **s** jump overboard Ac 27:43
and the rest **s** *follow,* some on Ac 27:44
that one **s** not commit adultery, Ro 2:22
do not know how to pray as we **s**, Ro 8:26 1163
the wife **s** not leave her husband 1Co 7:10
husband **s** not divorce his wife. 1Co 7:11
s be as though they had none; 1Co 7:29
If anyone speaks in a tongue, *it* **s** 1Co 14:27
you **s** rather forgive and comfort *him* 2Co 2:7
I **s** have been commended by you, 2Co 12:11 3784
s preach to you a gospel contrary Ga 1:8
Lord forgave you, so also **s** you. Col 3:13
how you **s** respond to each person. Col 4:6 1163
But we **s** always give thanks to God 2Th 2:13 3784
teaching things they **s** not *teach* for Ti 1:11 1163
But even if you **s** suffer for the 1Pe 3:14
it is better, if God **s** will it so, 1Pe 3:17
that you **s** remember the words 2Pe 3:2
that we **s** love one another; 1Jn 3:11
loves God **s** love his brother also. 1Jn 4:21
that he **s** make request for this. 1Jn 5:16
beginning, that you **s** walk in it. 2Jn 1:6
that they **s** rest for a little while Rv 6:11

SHOULDER

to Hagar, putting *them* on her **s**, Gn 21:14 7926
came out with her jar on her **s**, Gn 24:15 7926
came out with her jar on her **s**, Gn 24:45 7926
quickly lowered her jar from her **s**, Gn 24:46
He bowed his **s** to bear *burdens,* Gn 49:15 7926
s pieces joined to its two ends, Ex 28:7 3802
on the **s** pieces of the ephod, Ex 28:12 3802
them on the **s** pieces of the ephod, Ex 28:25 3802
of the two **s** pieces of the ephod, Ex 28:27 3802
attaching **s** pieces for the ephod; Ex 39:4 3802
them on the **s** pieces of the ephod, Ex 39:7 3802
and put them on the **s** pieces of Ex 39:18 3802
of the two **s** pieces of the ephod, Ex 39:20 3802
ram's **s** *when it has been* boiled, Nu 6:19 2220
which they carried on the **s**. Nu 7:9 3802
they shall give to the priest the **s** and Dt 18:3 2220
of you take up a stone on his **s**, Jos 4:5 7926
lifted it and laid *it* on his **s**. Jg 9:48 7926
they turned a stubborn **s** and Ne 9:29 3802
Let my **s** fall from the socket, And Jb 31:22 3802
Surely I would carry it on my **s**, Jb 31:36 7926
"I relieved his **s** of the burden, Ps 81:6 7926
his burden removed from their **s**. Is 14:25 7926
of the house of David on his **s**, Is 22:22 7926
lift it upon the **s** *and* carry it; Is 46:7 3802
baggage on *your* **s** in their sight Ezk 12:6 3802
baggage on *my* **s** in their sight. Ezk 12:7 3802
on *his* **s** in the dark and go out. Ezk 12:12 3802

good piece, the thigh and the **s**;	**Ezk 24:4**	3802
bald and every **s** was rubbed bare.	**Ezk 29:18**	3802
you push with side and with **s**,	**Ezk 34:21**	3802
LORD, To serve Him **s** to shoulder.	**Zph 3:9**	7926
LORD, To serve Him shoulder to **s**.	**Zph 3:9**	7926
and turned a stubborn **s** and	**Zch 7:11**	3802

SHOULDERS

garment and laid it upon both their **s**	**Gn 9:23**	7926
bound up in the clothes on their **s**.	**Ex 12:34**	7926
LORD on his two **s** for a memorial.	**Ex 28:12**	3802
And he dwells between His **s**."	**Dt 33:12**	3802
then he put them on his **s** and	**Jg 16:3**	3802
from his **s** and up he was taller	**1Sa 9:2**	7926
of the people from his **s** upward.	**1Sa 10:23**	7926
javelin *slung* between his **s**.	**1Sa 17:6**	3802
carried the ark of God on their **s** with	**1Ch 15:15**	3802
be a burden on *your* **s** no longer.	**2Ch 35:3**	3802
burden and the staff on their **s**,	**Is 9:4**	7926
the government will rest on His **s**;	**Is 9:6**	7926
burden will be removed from your **s**	**Is 10:27**	7926
will be carried on *their* **s**.	**Is 49:22**	3802
burdens and lay them on men's **s**,	**Mt 23:4**	*5606*
has found it, he lays it on his **s**,	**Lk 15:5**	*5606*

SHOUT

And the **s** of a king is among them.	**Nu 23:21**	8643
people shall **s** with a great shout;	**Jos 6:5**	7321
people shall shout with a great **s**;	**Jos 6:5**	8643
not **s** nor let your voice be heard nor	**Jos 6:10**	7321
until the day I tell you, '**S**!'	**Jos 6:10**	7321
Then you shall **s**!"	**Jos 6:10**	7321
Joshua said to the people, "**S**!	**Jos 6:16**	7321
s and the wall fell down flat,	**Jos 6:20**	8643
all Israel shouted with a great **s**,	**1Sa 4:5**	8643
Philistines heard the noise of the **s**,	**1Sa 4:6**	8643
s in the camp of the Hebrews *mean?*	**1Sa 4:6**	8643
all the people shouted with a great **s**	**Ezr 3:11**	8643
distinguish the sound of the **s** of joy	**Ezr 3:13**	8643
the people shouted with a loud **s**,	**Ezr 3:13**	8643
Let no joyful **s** enter it.	**Jb 3:7**	7445
I **s** for help, but there is no	**Jb 19:7**	7768
They **s** against them as *against* a	**Jb 30:5**	7321
a **s** of joy *comes* in the morning.	**Ps 30:5**	7440
And **s** for joy, all you who are	**Ps 32:11**	7442
Play skillfully with a **s** of joy.	**Ps 33:3**	8643
Let them **s** for joy and rejoice,	**Ps 35:27**	7442
does not **s** in triumph over me.	**Ps 41:11**	7321
S to God with the voice of joy.	**Ps 47:1**	7321
God has ascended with a **s**,	**Ps 47:5**	8643
S loud, O Philistia, because of Me!"	**Ps 60:8**	7321
the dawn and the sunset **s** for joy.	**Ps 65:8**	7442
They **s** for joy, yes, they sing.	**Ps 65:13**	7321
S joyfully to God, all the earth;	**Ps 66:1**	7321
My lips will **s** for joy when I sing	**Ps 71:23**	7442
S joyfully to the God of Jacob.	**Ps 81:1**	7321
and Hermon **s** for joy at Your name.	**Ps 89:12**	7442
Let us **s** joyfully to the rock of	**Ps 95:1**	7321
us **s** joyfully to Him with psalms.	**Ps 95:2**	7321
S joyfully to the LORD, all the	**Ps 98:4**	7321
horn **S** joyfully before the King,	**Ps 98:6**	7321
S joyfully to the LORD, all the	**Ps 100:1**	7321
His chosen ones with a joyful **s**.	**Ps 105:43**	7440
Over Philistia I will **s** aloud."	**Ps 108:9**	7321
indeed come again with a **s** of joy,	**Ps 126:6**	7440
s joyfully of Your righteousness.	**Ps 145:7**	7442
Cry aloud and **s** for joy, O	**Is 12:6**	7442
their voices, they **s** for joy;	**Is 24:14**	7442
in the dust, awake and **s** for joy,	**Is 26:19**	7442
with rejoicing and **s** of joy.	**Is 35:2**	7442
tongue of the mute will **s** for joy.	**Is 35:6**	7442
Let them **s** for joy from the tops	**Is 42:11**	6681
He will utter a **s**, yes, He will	**Is 42:13**	7321
S for joy, O heavens, for the LORD	**Is 44:23**	7442
S joyfully, you lower parts of the	**Is 44:23**	7321
Break forth into a **s** of joy,	**Is 44:23**	7440
S for joy, O heavens!	**Is 49:13**	7442
voices, They **s** joyfully together;	**Is 52:8**	7442
Break forth, **s** joyfully together,	**Is 52:9**	7442
"**S** for joy, O barren one, you who	**Is 54:1**	7442
will **s** for joy over their portion.	**Is 61:7**	7442
s joyfully with a glad heart,	**Is 65:14**	7442
morning And a **s** of alarm at noon;	**Jer 20:16**	8643
He will **s** like those who tread *the*	**Jer 25:30**	1959
And **s** among the chief of the	**Jer 31:7**	6670a
s for joy on the height of Zion,	**Jer 31:12**	7442
At the **s**, "Babylon has been seized!"	**Jer 50:46**	6963
them Will **s** for joy over Babylon,	**Jer 51:48**	7442
S for joy, O daughter of Zion!	**Zph 3:14**	7442
S *in triumph,* O Israel!	**Zph 3:14**	7321
S *in triumph,* O daughter of	**Zch 9:9**	7321
"But at midnight there was a **s**,	**Mt 25:6**	*2906*
they would fall down before Him and **s**,	**Mk 3:11**	*2896*
and *began* to **s**, "Hosanna!	**Jn 12:13**	*2905*
BREAK FORTH AND **S**, YOU WHO ARE NOT	**Ga 4:27**	*994*
will descend from heaven with a **s**,	**1Th 4:16**	*2752*

SHOUTED

the sound of the people as they **s**,	**Ex 32:17**	7452
they **s** and fell on their faces.	**Lv 9:24**	7442
So the people **s**, and *priests* blew	**Jos 6:20**	7321
the people **s** with a great shout	**Jos 6:20**	7321
the Philistines **s** as they met him.	**Jg 15:14**	7321
all Israel **s** with a great shout,	**1Sa 4:5**	7321
So all the people **s** and said,	**1Sa 10:24**	7321
and **s** to the ranks of Israel and	**1Sa 17:8**	7121
men of Israel and Judah arose and **s**	**1Sa 17:52**	7321
all the people **s** with a great shout	**Ezr 3:11**	7321
eyes, while many **s** aloud for joy,	**Ezr 3:12**	8643
the people **s** with a loud shout,	**Ezr 3:13**	7321
the city of Susa **s** and rejoiced.	**Es 8:15**	6670a
And all the sons of God **s** for joy?	**Jb 38:7**	7321
'He **s** out and spoke as follows:	**Da 4:14**	7123
They **s** back, "Crucify Him!"	**Mk 15:13**	*2896*
But they **s** all the more,	**Mk 15:14**	*2896*
a man from the crowd **s**,	**Lk 9:38**	*994*
all as they **s** for about two hours,	**Ac 19:34**	*2896*
I **s** out while standing among them,	**Ac 24:21**	*2896*

SHOUTING

out in battle array **s** the war cry.	**1Sa 17:20**	7321
s and the sound of the trumpet.	**2Sa 6:15**	8643
the covenant of the LORD with **s**,	**1Ch 15:28**	8643
LORD with a loud voice, with **s**,	**2Ch 15:14**	8643
laughter And your lips with **s**.	**Jb 8:21**	8643
The sound of joyful **s** and salvation	**Ps 118:15**	7440
And our tongue with joyful **s**;	**Ps 126:2**	7440
in tears shall reap with joyful **s**.	**Ps 126:5**	7440
wicked perish, there is joyful **s**.	**Pr 11:10**	7440
than the **s** of a ruler among fools.	**Ec 9:17**	2199
For the **s** over your summer fruits	**Is 16:9**	1959
be no cries of joy or jubilant **s**,	**Is 16:10**	7321
For I have made the **s** to cease.	**Is 16:10**	1959
And come with joyful **s** to Zion,	**Is 35:10**	7440
with the sound of joyful **s**,	**Is 48:20**	7440
Break forth into joyful **s**,	**Is 49:13**	7440
And come with joyful **s** to Zion,	**Is 51:11**	7440
forth into joyful **s** and cry aloud,	**Is 54:1**	7440
No one will tread *them* with **s**,	**Jer 48:33**	1959
The **s** will not be shouts *of joy.*	**Jer 48:33**	1959
than joyful **s** on the mountains.	**Ezk 7:7**	1906
away, because she keeps **s** at us."	**Mt 15:23**	*2896*
were **s**, "Hosanna to the Son of	**Mt 21:9**	*2896*
and the children who were **s** in	**Mt 21:15**	*2896*
But they kept **s** all the more,	**Mt 27:23**	*2896*
and **s** with a loud voice, he said,	**Mk 5:7**	*2896*
front and those who followed were **s**:	**Mk 11:9**	*2896*
s, "You are the Son of God!"	**Lk 4:41**	*2905*
s: "BLESSED IS THE KING WHO COMES	**Lk 19:38**	*3004*
out *of them* **s** with a loud voice;	**Ac 8:7**	*994*
before the city authorities, **s**,	**Ac 17:6**	*994*
were **s** one thing and some another,	**Ac 19:32**	*2896*
were **s** one thing *and* some another,	**Ac 21:34**	*2019*
s, "Away with him!"	**Ac 21:36**	*2896*
they were **s** against him that way.	**Ac 22:24**	*2019*

SHOUTINGS

The **s** of the driver he does not	**Jb 39:7**	8663

SHOUTS

His tent sacrifices with **s** of joy;	**Ps 27:6**	8643
Wisdom **s** in the street, She lifts	**Pr 1:20**	7442
They break forth into **s** of joy.	**Is 14:7**	7440
forth into **s** of joy before you,	**Is 55:12**	7440
The shouting will not be **s** *of joy.*	**Jer 48:33**	1959
out with **s** of victory over you."	**Jer 51:14**	1959
rejoice over you with **s** of joy.	**Zph 3:17**	7440
with **s** of "Grace, grace to it!"	**Zch 4:7**	8663

SHOVEL

has been winnowed with **s** and fork.	**Is 30:24**	7371

SHOVELS

and its **s** and its basins and its	**Ex 27:3**	3257
pails and the **s** and the basins,	**Ex 38:3**	3257
the forks and **s** and the basins,	**Nu 4:14**	3257
basins and the **s** and the bowls.	**1Ki 7:40**	3257
the pails and the **s** and the bowls;	**1Ki 7:45**	3257
They took away the pots, the **s**,	**2Ki 25:14**	3257
Huram also made the pails, the **s** and	**2Ch 4:11**	3257
The pails, the **s**,	**2Ch 4:16**	3257
also took away the pots, the **s**,	**Jer 52:18**	3257

SHOW

To the land which I will **s** you;	**Gn 12:1**	7200
kindness which you will **s** to me:	**Gn 20:13**	6213a
shown to you, you shall **s** to me and	**Gn 21:23**	6213a
and **s** lovingkindness to my master	**Gn 24:12**	6213a
in order to **s** you My power and	**Ex 9:16**	7200
to all that I am going to **s** you,	**Ex 25:9**	7200
"I pray You, **s** me Your glory!"	**Ex 33:18**	7200
and will **s** compassion on whom I	**Ex 33:19**	7355
on whom I will **s** compassion."	**Ex 33:19**	7355
the LORD will **s** who is His,	**Nu 16:5**	3045
not **s** partiality in judgment;	**Dt 1:17**	5234
to **s** you the way in which you	**Dt 1:33**	7200
You have begun to **s** Your servant	**Dt 3:24**	7200
with them and **s** no favor to them.	**Dt 7:2**	2603a
God who does not **s** partiality nor	**Dt 10:17**	5375
"So **s** your love for the alien,	**Dt 10:19**	157
burning anger and **s** mercy to you,	**Dt 13:17**	5414
"Thus you shall not **s** pity:	**Dt 19:21**	2347
you shall not **s** pity.	**Dt 25:12**	2347
the old, nor **s** favor to the young.	**Dt 28:50**	2603a
"Please **s** us the entrance to the	**Jg 1:24**	7200
and I will **s** you the man whom you	**Jg 4:22**	7200
then **s** me a sign that it is You	**Jg 6:17**	6213a
nor did they **s** kindness to the	**Jg 8:35**	6213a
and **s** you what you should do."	**1Sa 10:8**	3045
I will **s** you what you shall do;	**1Sa 16:3**	3045
will you not **s** me the lovingkindness	**1Sa 20:14**	6213a
may the LORD **s** lovingkindness and	**2Sa 2:6**	6213a
also will **s** this goodness to you,	**2Sa 2:6**	6213a
Today I **s** kindness to the house of	**2Sa 3:8**	6213a
that I may **s** him kindness for	**2Sa 9:1**	6213a
I may **s** the kindness of God?"	**2Sa 9:3**	6213a
for I will surely **s** kindness to	**2Sa 9:7**	6213a
"I will **s** kindness to Hanun the	**2Sa 10:2**	6213a
and let us **s** ourselves courageous	**2Sa 10:12**	2388
s me both it and His habitation.	**2Sa 15:25**	7200
the kind You **s** Yourself kind,	**2Sa 22:26**	2616a
You **s** Yourself blameless;	**2Sa 22:26**	8552
the pure You **s** Yourself pure,	**2Sa 22:27**	1305
You **s** Yourself astute.	**2Sa 22:27**	6617
therefore, and **s** yourself a man.	**1Ki 2:2**	1961
"But **s** kindness to the sons of	**1Ki 2:7**	6213a
"Go, **s** yourself to Ahab, and I	**1Ki 18:1**	7200
Elijah went to **s** himself to Ahab.	**1Ki 18:2**	7200
surely **s** myself to him today."	**1Ki 18:15**	7200
that Hezekiah did not **s** them.	**2Ki 20:13**	7200
"I will **s** kindness to Hanun the	**1Ch 19:2**	6213a
and let us **s** ourselves courageous	**1Ch 19:13**	2388
but they could not **s** their	**Ne 7:61**	5046
he might **s** Esther and inform her,	**Es 4:8**	7200
And **s** me how I have erred.	**Jb 6:24**	995
would **s** Your power against me.	**Jb 10:16**	6381
And **s** you the secrets of wisdom!	**Jb 11:6**	5046
"Will you **s** partiality for Him?	**Jb 13:8**	5375
you If you secretly **s** partiality.	**Jb 13:10**	5375
S understanding and then we can	**Jb 18:2**	995
and I will **s** you That there is yet	**Jb 36:2**	2331a
therefore, O kings, **s** discernment;	**Ps 2:10**	7919a
"Who will **s** us *any* good?"	**Ps 4:6**	7200
Wondrously **s** Your lovingkindness, O	**Ps 17:7**	6395
the kind You **s** Yourself kind;	**Ps 18:25**	2616a
You **s** Yourself blameless;	**Ps 18:25**	8552
the pure You **s** Yourself pure	**Ps 18:26**	1305
You **s** Yourself astute.	**Ps 18:26**	6617
I shall **s** the salvation of God."	**Ps 50:23**	7200
S Yourself strong, O God, who have	**Ps 68:28**	5810
And **s** partiality to the wicked?	**Ps 82:2**	5375
S us Your lovingkindness, O LORD,	**Ps 85:7**	7200
S me a sign for good, That those	**Ps 86:17**	6213a
Or can **s** forth all His praise?	**Ps 106:2**	8085
not remember to **s** lovingkindness,	**Ps 109:16**	6213a
To **s** partiality to the wicked is	**Pr 18:5**	5375
To **s** partiality in judgment is not	**Pr 24:23**	5234
To **s** partiality is not good,	**Pr 28:21**	5234
the holy God will **s** Himself holy in	**Is 5:16**	6942
that Hezekiah did not **s** them.	**Is 39:2**	7200
You did not **s** mercy to them, On	**Is 47:6**	7760
In Whom I will **s** My glory."	**Is 49:3**	6286
who are in darkness, '**S** yourselves.'	**Is 49:9**	1540
"I will not **s** pity nor be sorry	**Jer 13:14**	2550
I will **s** them My back and not *My*	**Jer 18:17**	7200
'I will also **s** you compassion, so	**Jer 42:12**	5414
'My eye will **s** no pity nor	**Ezk 7:9**	2347
"**S** yourself sharp, go to the	**Ezk 21:16**	2300
to all that I am going to **s** you;	**Ezk 40:4**	7200
here in order to **s** *it* to you.	**Ezk 40:4**	7200
so he will come back and **s** regard	**Da 11:30**	995
"He will **s** no regard for the	**Da 11:37**	995
he **s** regard for any *other* god;	**Da 11:37**	995
of Egypt, I will **s** you miracles."	**Mi 7:15**	7200
And **s** to the nations your nakedness	**Na 3:5**	7200
"I will **s** you what these are."	**Zch 1:9**	7200
but go, **s** yourself to the priest and	**Mt 8:4**	*1166*
Him to **s** them a sign from heaven.	**Mt 16:1**	*1925*
Jesus began to **s** His disciples	**Mt 16:21**	*1166*
"If your brother sins, go and **s** him	**Mt 18:15**	*1651*
"**S** Me the coin *used* for the	**Mt 22:19**	*1925*
will **s** great signs and wonders,	**Mt 24:24**	*1325*
s yourself to the priest and offer	**Mk 1:44**	*1166*
and will **s** signs and wonders,	**Mk 13:22**	*4160*
"And he himself will **s** you a	**Mk 14:15**	*1166*
To **s** mercy toward our fathers, And	**Lk 1:72**	*4160*
go and **s** yourself to the priest and	**Lk 5:14**	*1166*
I will **s** you whom he is like:	**Lk 6:47**	*5263*
and **s** yourselves to the priests."	**Lk 17:14**	*1925*
a parable to **s** that at all times they	**Lk 18:1**	
"**S** Me a denarius. Whose likeness	**Lk 20:24**	*1166*
"And he will **s** you a large,	**Lk 22:12**	*1166*
"What sign do You **s** us	**Jn 2:18**	*1166*
will **s** Him greater works than these,	**Jn 5:20**	*1166*
things, **s** Yourself to the world."	**Jn 7:4**	*5319*
"Lord, **s** us the Father, and it is	**Jn 14:8**	*1166*
how *can* you say, '**S** us the Father'?	**Jn 14:9**	*1166*
s which one of these two You have	**Ac 1:24**	*322*
INTO THE LAND THAT I WILL **S** YOU.'	**Ac 7:3**	*1166*
for I will **s** him how much he must	**Ac 9:16**	*5263*
God is not one to **s** partiality,	**Ac 10:34**	*4381*
in that they **s** the work of the Law	**Ro 2:15**	*1731*
that He may **s** mercy to all.	**Ro 11:32**	*1653*
for the day will **s** it because	**1Co 3:13**	*1213*
And I **s** you a still more excellent	**1Co 12:31**	*1166*
and *to* **s** our readiness,	**2Co 8:19**	
s them the proof of your love	**2Co 8:24**	*1731*
He might **s** the surpassing riches of	**Eph 2:7**	*1731*
s yourself an example of those who	**1Tm 4:12**	*1096*
in all things **s** yourself to be an	**Ti 2:7**	*3930*
each one of you **s** the same diligence	**Heb 6:11**	*1731*
to **s** to the heirs of the promise the	**Heb 6:17**	*1925*
be shaken, let us **s** gratitude,	**Heb 12:28**	*2192*
to **s** hospitality to strangers,	**Heb 13:2**	
But if you **s** partiality, you are	**Jas 2:9**	*4380*
s me your faith without the works,	**Jas 2:18**	*1166*
will **s** you my faith by my works."	**Jas 2:18**	*1166*
Let him **s** by his good behavior his	**Jas 3:13**	*1166*
and **s** her honor as a fellow heir of	**1Pe 3:7**	*632*
gave Him to **s** to His bond-servants,	**Rv 1:1**	*1166*
and I will **s** you what must take	**Rv 4:1**	*1166*
I will **s** you the judgment of the	**Rv 17:1**	*1166*
here, I will **s** you the bride,	**Rv 21:9**	*1166*
His angel to **s** to His bond-servants	**Rv 22:6**	*1166*

SHOWBREAD

the **s** to prepare it every sabbath.	**1Ch 9:32**	3899, 4635
and with the **s**, and the fine flour	**1Ch 23:29**	3899, 4635
by weight for the tables of **s**,	**1Ch 28:16**	4635
and *to set out* the **s** continually,	**2Ch 2:4**	4635
the **s** is *set* on the clean table,	**2Ch 13:11**	3899, 4635
the table of **s** with all of its utensils.	**2Ch 29:18**	4635

for the s, for the continual grain Ne 10:33
3899, 4635

SHOWED
LORD, and the LORD s him a tree; Ex 15:25 3384
and s them the fruit of the land. Nu 13:26 7200
the LORD s great and distressing Dt 6:22 5414
And the LORD s him all the land, Dt 34:1 7200
s them the entrance to the city, Jg 1:25 7200
for you s kindness to all the sons 1Sa 15:6 6213a
as his father s kindness to me." 2Sa 10:2 6213a
he did and his might which he s, 1Ki 16:27 6213a
which he s and how he warred, 1Ki 22:45 6213a
And when he s him the place, he 2Ki 6:6 7200
LORD, and s them the king's son. 2Ki 11:4 7200
and s them all his treasure house, 2Ki 20:13 7200
his father s kindness to me." 1Ch 19:2 6213a
to all the Levites who s good insight 2Ch 30:22 7919a
O Lord, You s favor to Your land; Ps 85:1 7521
and s them *all* his treasure house, Is 39:2 7200
Then You s me their deeds. Jer 11:18 7200
them to Babylon, the LORD s me: Jer 24:1 7200
s favor to Jehoiachin king of Jer 52:31 5375
envy which you s because of your Ezk 35:11 6213a
Thus the Lord GOD s me, Am 7:1 7200
Thus the Lord GOD s me, Am 7:4 7200
Thus He s me, and behold, the Lord Am 7:7 7200
Thus the Lord GOD s me, Am 8:1 7200
people s reverence for the LORD. Hg 1:12 3372a
Then the LORD s me four craftsmen. Zch 1:20 7200
Then he s me Joshua the high Zch 3:1 7200
and s Him all the kingdoms of the Mt 4:8 *1166*
And he led Him up and s Him all Lk 4:5 *1166*
"The one who s mercy toward him." Lk 10:37 *4160*
the dead are raised, even Moses s, Lk 20:37 *3377*
He s them His hands and His feet. Lk 24:40 *1166*
"I s you many good works from the Jn 10:32 *1166*
He s them both His hands and His Jn 20:20 *1166*
"In everything I s you that by Ac 20:35 *5263*
natives s us extraordinary kindness; Ac 28:2 *3930*
you s sympathy to the prisoners and Heb 10:34 *4834*
mountain, and s me the holy city, Rv 21:10 *1166*
Then he s me a river of the water Rv 22:1 *1166*
the angel who s me these things. Rv 22:8 *1166*

SHOWER
sound of the roar of a *heavy* s." 1Ki 18:41 1653
the *heavy* s does not stop you.'" 1Ki 18:44 1653
and wind, and there was a heavy s. 1Ki 18:45 1653
immediately you say, 'A s is coming, Lk 12:54 *3655a*

SHOWERS
grass And as the s on the herb. Dt 32:2 7241
You soften it with s Ps 65:10 7241
Like s that water the earth. Ps 72:6 7241
the s have been withheld, Jer 3:3 7241
Or can the heavens grant s? Jer 14:22 7241
s to come down in their season; Ezk 34:26 1653
they will be s of blessing. Ezk 34:26 1653
Like s on vegetation Which do not Mi 5:7 7241
And He will give them s of rain, Zch 10:1 1653

SHOWING
but s lovingkindness to thousands, Ex 20:6 6213a
but s lovingkindness to thousands, Dt 5:10 6213a
keeping covenant and s 1Ki 8:23
keeping covenant and s 2Ch 6:14
s intelligence in every *branch of* Da 1:4 7919a
iniquities by s mercy to *the* poor, Da 4:27 2604
s partiality in the instruction. Mal 2:9 5375
and s all the tunics and garments Ac 9:39 *1925*
Those who desire to make a good s Ga 6:12 *2146a*
s tolerance for one another in love, Eph 4:2 *430*
s all good faith so that they will Ti 2:10 *1731*
s every consideration for all men. Ti 3:2 *1731*

SHOWN
you have s me by saving my life; Gn 19:19 6213a
the kindness that I have s to you, Gn 21:23 6213a
s lovingkindness to my master." Gn 24:14 6213a
which You have s to Your servant; Gn 32:10 6213a
God has s to Pharaoh what He is Gn 41:28 7200
was s to you on the mountain. Ex 25:40 7200
you have been s in the mountain. Ex 26:30 7200
it was s to you in the mountain, Ex 27:8 7200
after he has s himself to the Lv 13:7 7200
then it shall be s to the priest; Lv 13:19 7200
mark and shall be s to the priest. Lv 13:49 7200
which the LORD had s Moses, Nu 8:4 7200
"To you it was s that you might Dt 4:35 7200
the LORD our God has s us His Dt 5:24 7200
nor would He have s us all these Jg 13:23 7200
You have s your last kindness to Ru 3:10 3190
you have s this kindness to Saul 2Sa 2:5 6213a
For you have s today that princes 2Sa 19:6 5046
and you have not s to your 1Ki 1:27 3045
"You have s great lovingkindness 1Ki 3:6 6213a
that the LORD had s to David 1Ki 8:66 6213a
s me that he will certainly die." 2Ki 8:10 7200
LORD has s me that you will be king 2Ki 8:13 7200
that I have not s them." 2Ki 20:15 7200
the goodness that the LORD had s to 2Ch 7:10 6213a
his father Jehoiada had s him, 2Ch 24:22 6213a
for a brief moment grace has been s Ezr 9:8
who have s me many troubles and Ps 71:20 7200
His miracles that He had s them. Ps 78:11 7200
A harsh vision has been s to me; Is 21:2 5046
Though the wicked is s favor, Is 26:10 2603a
that I have not s them." Is 39:4 7200
the faithful mercies s to David. Is 55:3
the word which the LORD has s me: Jer 38:21 7200
the things that the LORD had s me. Ezk 11:25 7200
and *yet* God has s me that I should Ac 10:28 *1166*
in order that it might be s to be Ro 7:13 *5316*
but now have been s mercy because Ro 11:30 *1653*
because of the mercy s to you they Ro 11:31
you they also may now be s mercy. Ro 11:31 *1653*
Yet I was s mercy because I 1Tm 1:13 *1653*
has s hospitality to strangers, 1Tm 5:10 *3580*
which you have s toward His name, Heb 6:10 *1731*
WHICH WAS S YOU ON THE MOUNTAIN." Heb 8:5 *1166*
to one who has s no mercy; Jas 2:13 *4160*
be s that they all are not of us. 1Jn 2:19 *5319*

SHOWS
whatever He s me I will tell you." Nu 23:3 7200
and s His love for the alien by Dt 10:18 157
And s lovingkindness to His 2Sa 22:51 6213a
Who s no partiality to princes Nor Jb 34:19 5375
And s lovingkindness to His Ps 18:50 6213a
the God who s me lovingkindness. Ps 59:17
in Israel He s forth His glory. Is 44:23 6286
who s lovingkindness to thousands, Jer 32:18 6213a
and s Him all things that He Jn 5:20 *1166*
he who s mercy, with cheerfulness. Ro 12:8 *1653*
difference to me; God s no partiality Ga 2:6 *2983*

SHREWD
and Jonadab was a very s man. 2Sa 13:3 2450
frustrates the plotting of the s, Jb 5:12 6175
make s plans against Your people, Ps 83:3 6191
and the naive may become s, Pr 19:25 6191
They are s to do evil, But to do Jer 4:22 2450
so be s as serpents and Mt 10:16 *5429*
sons of this age are more s in relation Lk 16:8 *5429*
who took s advantage of our race and Ac 7:19 *2686*

SHREWDLY
manager because he had acted s; Lk 16:8 *5430*

SHREWDNESS
He captures the wise by their own s Jb 5:13 6193
"And through his s He will cause Da 8:25 7922

SHRINE
And the man Micah had a s and he Jg 17:5
1004, 430
that you built yourself a s and Ezk 16:24 1354
"When you built your s at the Ezk 16:31 1354

SHRINES
and they will tear down your s, Ezk 16:39 1354
and does not eat at the mountain s Ezk 18:6
he even eats at the mountain s, Ezk 18:11
"He does not eat at the mountain s Ezk 18:15
they have eaten at the mountain s. Ezk 22:9
who made silver s of Artemis, Ac 19:24 *3485*

SHRINK
all who see you Will s from you Na 3:7 5074
how I did not s from declaring to Ac 20:20 *5288*
"For I did not s from declaring Ac 20:27 *5288*
those who s back to destruction, Heb 10:39 *5289*
not s away from Him in shame at 1Jn 2:28 *153*

SHRINKS
AND IF HE S BACK, MY SOUL HAS NO Heb 10:38 *5288*

SHRIVEL
The seeds s under their clods; Jl 1:17 5685

SHRIVELED
"You have s me up, It has Jb 16:8 7059
Their skin is s on their bones, It La 4:8 6821

SHRUB
Now no s of the field was yet in Gn 2:5 7880
food is the root of the broom s. Jb 30:4 7574

SHUA
Canaanite whose name was S; Gn 38:2 7770a
and Hotham, and S their sister. 1Ch 7:32 7774

SHUAH
Medan and Midian and Ishbak and S. Gn 25:2 7774
Medan, Midian, Ishbak and S. 1Ch 1:32 7774

SHUAL
toward Ophrah, to the land of S, 1Sa 13:17 7777a
of Zophah *were* Suah, Harnepher, S, 1Ch 7:36 7777b

SHUA'S
S daughter, the wife of Judah, died; Gn 38:12 7770a

SHUBAEL
of the sons of Amram, S; 1Ch 24:20 7619
of the sons of S, Jehdeiah. 1Ch 24:20 7619
for the thirteenth, S, 1Ch 25:20 7619

SHUDDER
And s, be very desolate," Jer 2:12 8175c
the demons also believe, and s. Jas 2:19 *5425*

SHUDDERING
and s will overwhelm them; Ezk 7:18 6427

SHUHAH
Chelub the brother of S became the 1Ch 4:11 7746

SHUHAM
of S, the family of the Shuhamites. Nu 26:42 7748

SHUHAMITES
of Shuham, the family of the S. Nu 26:42 7749
All the families of the S, Nu 26:43 7749

SHUHITE
the Temanite, Bildad the S and Jb 2:11 7747
Then Bildad the S answered, Jb 8:1 7747
Then Bildad the S responded, Jb 18:1 7747
Then Bildad the S answered, Jb 25:1 7747
Bildad the S *and* Zophar the Jb 42:9 7747

SHULAMMITE
"Come back, come back, O S; SS 6:13 7759
"Why should you gaze at the S, SS 6:13 7759

SHUMATHITES
the Ithrites, the Puthites, the S and 1Ch 2:53 8126

SHUN
and a time to s embracing. Ec 3:5 7368

SHUNAMMITE
Israel, and found Abishag the S, 1Ki 1:3 7767
Abishag the S was ministering to 1Ki 1:15 7767
give me Abishag the S as a wife." 1Ki 2:17 7767
"Let Abishag the S be given to 1Ki 2:21 7767
asking Abishag the S for Adonijah? 1Ki 2:22 7767
to Gehazi his servant, "Call this S." 2Ki 4:12 7767
"Behold, there is the S. 2Ki 4:25 7767
called Gehazi and said, "Call this S." 2Ki 4:36 7767

SHUNEM
and *included* Chesulloth and S, Jos 19:18 7766
together and came and camped in S; 1Sa 28:4 7766
day when Elisha passed over to S, 2Ki 4:8 7766

SHUNI
Ziphion and Haggi, S and Ezbon, Gn 46:16 7764
of S, the family of the Shunites; Nu 26:15 7764

SHUNITES
of Shuni, the family of the S; Nu 26:15 7765

SHUPHAMITES
Shephupham, the family of the S; Nu 26:39 7781

SHUPPIM
S and Huppim *were* the sons of 1Ch 7:12 8206
took a wife for Huppim and S, 1Ch 7:15 8206
For S and Hosah *it was* to the west, 1Ch 26:16 8206

SHUR
by the spring on the way to S. Gn 16:7 7793
and settled between Kadesh and S; Gn 20:1 7793
They settled from Havilah to S Gn 25:18 7793
went out into the wilderness of S; Ex 15:22 7793
from Havilah as you go to S, 1Sa 15:7 7793
as you come to S even as far as 1Sa 27:8 7793

SHUT
and s the door behind him, Gn 19:6 5462
house with them, and s the door. Gn 19:10 5462
the wilderness has s them in.' Ex 14:3 5462
Let her be s up for seven days Nu 12:14 5462
So Miriam was s up outside the Nu 12:15 5462
and He will s up the heavens so Dt 11:17 6113
when *it was time* to s the gate at Jos 2:5 5462
had gone out, they s the gate. Jos 2:7 5462
s because of the sons of Israel; Jos 6:1 5462
and s the doors of the roof chamber Jg 3:23 5462
fled there and s themselves in; Jg 9:51 5462
and s up their calves at home. 1Sa 6:10 3607
for he s himself in by entering a 1Sa 23:7 5462
So they were s up until the day of 2Sa 20:3 6887a
the heavens are s up and there is no 1Ki 8:35 6113
"And you shall go in and s the 2Ki 4:4 5462
So she went from him and s the 2Ki 4:5 5462
of God, and s *the door* behind him and 2Ki 4:21 5462
and s the door behind them both and 2Ki 4:33 5462
s the door and hold the door shut 2Ki 6:32 5462
and hold the door s against him. 2Ki 6:32 3905
so the king of Assyria s him up 2Ki 17:4 6113
"When the heavens are s up and 2Ch 6:26 6113
"If I s up the heavens so that 2Ch 7:13 6113
"They have also s the doors of 2Ch 29:7 5462
let them s and bolt the doors. Ne 7:3 1479
that the doors should be s and that Ne 13:19 5462
Because it did not s the opening Jb 3:10 5462
unrighteousness must s its mouth. Jb 5:16 7092
heel, *And* a trap snaps s on him. Jb 18:9 2388
They s themselves up by day; Jb 24:16 2856
pride, S up *as with* a tight seal. Jb 41:15 5462
Nor the pit s its mouth on me. Ps 69:15 332
I am s up and cannot go out. Ps 88:8 3607
and the doors on the street are s Ec 12:4 5462
When he opens no one will s, Is 22:22 5462
Every house is s up so that none Is 24:10 5462
of deep sleep, He has s your eyes, Is 29:10 6105b
him so that gates will not be s: Is 45:1 5462
Kings will s their mouths on Is 52:15 7092
who gives delivery s *the womb?"* Is 66:9 6113
a burning fire S up in my bones; Jer 20:9 6113
Jeremiah the prophet was s up in Jer 32:2 3607
king of Judah had s him up, Jer 32:3 3607
"Go, s yourself up in your house. Ezk 3:24 5462
which faces the east; and it was s. Ezk 44:1 5462
"This gate shall be s; Ezk 44:2 5462
therefore it shall be s. Ezk 44:2 5462
shall be s the six working days; Ezk 46:1 5462
shall not be s until the evening. Ezk 46:2 5462
gate shall be s after he goes out. Ezk 46:12 5462
His angel and s the lions' mouths and Da 6:22 5463
among you who would s the gates, Mal 1:10 5462
because you s off the kingdom of Mt 23:13 *2808*
and the door was s. Mt 25:10 *2808*
when the sky was s up for three Lk 4:25 *2808*
the door has already been s and my Lk 11:7 *2808*
the doors were s where the disciples Jn 20:19 *2808*
came, the doors having been s, Jn 20:26 *2808*
and immediately the doors were s. Ac 21:30 *2808*
God has s up all in disobedience Ro 11:32 *4788*
Scripture has s up everyone under sin, Ga 3:22 *4788*
being s up to the faith which was Ga 3:23 *4788*
but they wish to s you out so Ga 4:17 *1576*
promises, s the mouths of lions, Heb 11:33 *5420*
who opens and no one will s, Rv 3:7 *2808*
an open door which no one can s, Rv 3:8 *2808*
have the power to s up the sky, Rv 11:6 *2808*
threw him into the abyss, and s *it* Rv 20:3 *2808*

SHUTHELAH
of S, the family of the Shuthelahites Nu 26:35 7803
These are the sons of S: Nu 26:36 7803
Ephraim *were* S and Bered his son, 1Ch 7:20 7803
Zabad his son, S his son, and Ezer 1Ch 7:21 7803

SHUTHELAHITES
of Shuthelah, the family of the **S**; Nu 26:35 8364

SHUTS
"If He passes by or **s** up, Jb 11:10 5462
all unrighteousness **s** its mouth. Ps 107:42 7092
He who **s** *his* ear to the cry of the Pr 21:13 331
But he who **s** his eyes will have Pr 28:27 5956
shut, When he **s** no one will open. Is 22:22 5462
And **s** his eyes from looking upon Is 33:15 6105b
call for help, He **s** out my prayer. La 3:8 8365a
the house gets up and **s** the door, Lk 13:25 *608*
shut, and who **s** and no one opens, Rv 3:7 *2808*

SHUTTERED
There were **s** windows *looking* Ezk 40:16 331

SHUTTLE
days are swifter than a weaver's **s**, Jb 7:6 708

SHY
Therefore I was **s** and afraid to Jb 32:6 2119b

SIA
the sons of Keros, the sons of **S**, Ne 7:47 5517

SIAHA
the sons of Keros, the sons of **S**, Ezr 2:44 5517

SIBBECAI
then **S** the Hushathite struck down 2Sa 21:18 5444
S the Hushathite, Ilai the 1Ch 11:29 5444
S the Hushathite killed Sippai, 1Ch 20:4 5444
eighth month *was* **S** the Hushathite 1Ch 27:11 5444

SIBBOLETH
'Shibboleth.' " But he said, "**S**," Jg 12:6 5451

SIBMAH
names being changed—and **S**, Nu 32:38 7643
and Kiriathaim and **S** and Jos 13:19 7643
withered, the vines of **S** *as well;* Is 16:8 7643
for Jazer, for the vine of **S**; Is 16:9 7643
I will weep for you, O vine of **S**! Jer 48:32 7643

SIBRAIM
Hamath, Berothah, **S**, Ezk 47:16 5453

SICK
"Behold, your father is **s**." Gn 48:1 2470a
to take David, she said, "He is **s**." 1Sa 19:14 2470a
when I fell **s** three days ago. 1Sa 30:13 2470a
to David, so that he was *very* **s**. 2Sa 12:15 605
the son of Jeroboam became **s**. 1Ki 14:1 2470a
concerning her son, for he is **s**. 1Ki 14:5 2470a
mistress of the house, became **s**; 1Ki 17:17 2470a
Now Ben-hadad king of Aram was **s**, 2Ki 8:7 2470a
Ahab in Jezreel because he was **s**. 2Ki 8:29 2470a
When Elisha became **s** with the 2Ki 13:14 2470a
he heard that Hezekiah had been **s**. 2Ki 20:12 2470a
Ahab in Jezreel, because he was **s**. 2Ch 22:6 2470a
(for they left him very **s**), 2Ch 24:25 4251
face sad though you are not **s**? Ne 2:2 2470a
But as for me, when they were **s**, Ps 35:13 2470a
broken my heart and I am so **s**. Ps 69:20 5136
Hope deferred makes the heart **s**, Pr 13:12 2470a
The whole head is **s** And Is 1:5 2483
be as when a **s** man wastes away. Is 10:18 5263
And no resident will say, "I am **s**"; Is 33:24 2470a
he had been **s** and had recovered. Is 39:1 2470a
all else And is desperately **s**; Jer 17:9 605
the broken and strengthen the **s**; Ezk 34:16 2470a
was exhausted and **s** for days. Da 8:27 2470a
became **s** with the heat of wine; Hos 7:5 2470a
"So also I will make *you* **s**, Mi 6:13 2470a
when you present the lame and **s**, Mal 1:8 2470a
by robbery and *what is* lame or **s**; Mal 1:13 2470a
lying **s** in bed with a fever. Mt 8:14 *906*
a physician, but those who are **s**. Mt 9:12 *2560*
"Heal *the* **s**, raise *the* dead, Mt 10:8 *770*
for them and healed their **s**. Mt 14:14 *732*
and brought to Him all who were **s**; Mt 14:35 *2560*
I was **s**, and you visited Me; Mt 25:36 *770*
'When did we see You **s**, Mt 25:39 *770*
s, and in prison, and you did not Mt 25:43 *772*
or a stranger, or naked, or **s**, Mt 25:44 *772*
was lying **s** with a fever; Mk 1:30 *2621*
a physician, but those who are **s**; Mk 2:17 *2560*
a few **s** people and healed them. Mk 6:5 *732*
many **s** people and healing them. Mk 6:13 *732*
on their pallets those who were **s**, Mk 6:55 *2560*
laying the **s** in the market places, Mk 6:56 *770*
they will lay hands on the **s**, Mk 16:18 *732*
any *who were* **s** with various diseases Lk 4:40 *770*
a physician, but those who are **s**. Lk 5:31 *2560*
by him, was **s** and about to die. Lk 7:2 *2560*
and heal those in it who are **s**, Lk 10:9 *772*
whose son was **s** at Capernaum. Jn 4:46 *770*
a multitude of those who were **s**, Jn 5:3 *770*
The **s** man answered Him, Jn 5:7 *770*
performing on those who were **s**. Jn 6:2 *770*
Now a certain man was **s**, Jn 11:1 *770*
hair, whose brother Lazarus was **s**. Jn 11:2 *770*
behold, he whom You love is **s**." Jn 11:3 *770*
when He heard that he was **s**, Jn 11:6 *770*
for a benefit done to a **s** man, Ac 4:9 *772*
carried the **s** out into the streets and Ac 5:15 *772*
bringing people who were **s** or Ac 5:16 *772*
time that she fell **s** and died; Ac 9:37 *770*
carried from his body to the **s**, Ac 19:12 *770*
many among you are weak and **s**, 1Co 11:30 *732*
you had heard that he was **s**. Php 2:26 *770*
he was **s** to the point of death, Php 2:27 *770*
but Trophimus I left **s** at Miletus. 2Tm 4:20 *770*
Is anyone among you **s**? Jas 5:14 *770*
will restore the one who is **s**, Jas 5:15 *2577*

SICKBED
LORD will sustain him upon his **s**; Ps 41:3
1741, 6210

SICKLE
put the **s** to the standing grain. Dt 16:9 2770
but you shall not wield a **s** in Dt 23:25 2770
the **s** at the time of harvest; Jer 50:16 4038
Put in the **s**, for the harvest is Jl 3:13 4038
he immediately puts in the **s**, Mk 4:29 *1407*
head and a sharp **s** in His hand. Rv 14:14 *1407*
"Put in your **s** and reap, for Rv 14:15 *1407*
who sat on the cloud swung His **s** Rv 14:16 *1407*
heaven, and he also had a sharp **s**. Rv 14:17 *1407*
voice to him who had the sharp **s**, Rv 14:18 *1407*
"Put in your sharp **s** and Rv 14:18 *1407*
angel swung his **s** to the earth and Rv 14:19 *1407*

SICKLINESS
In a day of **s** and incurable pain. Is 17:11 2470a

SICKLY
"Those who are **s** you have not Ezk 34:4 2470a

SICKNESS
I will remove **s** from your midst. Ex 23:25 4245a
LORD will remove from you all **s**; Dt 7:15 2483
every **s** and every plague which, Dt 28:61 2483
plague, whatever **s** *there is,* 1Ki 8:37 4245a
and his **s** was so severe that 1Ki 17:17 2483
I will recover from this **s**." 2Ki 1:2 2483
'Will I recover from this **s**?' " 2Ki 8:8 2483
'Will I recover from this **s**?' " 2Ki 8:9 2483
plague or whatever **s** *there is,* 2Ch 6:28 4245a
and you will suffer severe **s**, 2Ch 21:15 2483
bowels come out because of the **s**, 2Ch 21:15 2483
in his bowels with an incurable **s**. 2Ch 21:18 2483
his **s** and he died in great pain. 2Ch 21:19 2483
spirit of a man can endure his **s**, Pr 18:14 4245b
with great vexation, **s** and anger. Ec 5:17 2483
S and wounds are ever before Me. Jer 6:7 2483
"Truly this is a **s**, And I must Jer 10:19 2483
When Ephraim saw his **s**, Hos 5:13 2483
every kind of **s** among the people. Mt 4:23 *3119*
of disease and every kind of **s**. Mt 9:35 *3119*
of disease and every kind of **s**. Mt 10:1 *3119*
had had a **s** caused by a spirit; Lk 13:11 *769*
you are freed from your **s**." Lk 13:12 *769*
"This **s** is not to end in death, Jn 11:4 *769*
I will throw her on a bed *of* **s**, Rv 2:22

SICKNESSES
and miserable and chronic **s**. Dt 28:59 2483
Him and to be healed of their **s**. Lk 5:15 *769*
been healed of evil spirits and **s**: Lk 8:2 *769*

SIDDIM
came as allies to the valley of **S** Gn 14:3 7708
against them in the valley of **S**, Gn 14:8 7708
valley of **S** was full of tar pits; Gn 14:10 7708

SIDE
door of the ark in the **s** of it; Gn 6:16 6654
to the west **s** of the wilderness and Ex 3:1 310
one on one **s** and one on the other. Ex 17:12 2088
and two rings shall be on one **s** of Ex 25:12 6763
two rings on the other **s** of it. Ex 25:12 6763
of the lampstand from its one **s** and Ex 25:32 6654
of the lampstand from its other **s**. Ex 25:32 6654
one **s** and the cubit on the other, Ex 26:13 2088
on one **s** and on the other, Ex 26:13 2088
twenty boards for the south **s**. Ex 26:18 6285
the second **s** of the tabernacle, Ex 26:20 6763
of the tabernacle, on the north **s**, Ex 26:20 6285
boards of one **s** of the tabernacle, Ex 26:26 6763
of the other **s** of the tabernacle, Ex 26:27 6763
the boards of the **s** of the tabernacle Ex 26:27 6763
of the tabernacle for the rear **s** Ex 26:27
the table on the **s** of the tabernacle Ex 26:35 6763
put the table on the north **s**. Ex 26:35 6763
On the south **s** *there shall be* Ex 27:9 6285
one hundred cubits long for one **s**; Ex 27:9 6285
"Likewise for the north **s** in Ex 27:11 6285
the width of the court on the west **s** Ex 27:12 6285
the east **s** *shall be* fifty cubits. Ex 27:13 6285
"The hangings for the *one* **s** *of* Ex 27:14 3802
"And for the other **s** *shall be* Ex 27:15 3802
toward the inner **s** of the ephod. Ex 28:26 5676
shall make *them* on its two **s** walls Ex 30:4 6654
they were written on one **s** Ex 32:15
twenty boards for the south **s**; Ex 36:23 6285
the second **s** of the tabernacle, Ex 36:25 6763
of the tabernacle, on the north **s**, Ex 36:25 6285
boards of one **s** of the tabernacle, Ex 36:31 6763
of the other **s** of the tabernacle, Ex 36:32 6763
of the tabernacle for the rear **s** Ex 36:32
even two rings on one **s** of it, Ex 37:3 6763
two rings on the other **s** of it. Ex 37:3 6763
lampstand from the one **s** of it and Ex 37:18 6654
lampstand from the other **s** of it; Ex 37:18 6654
for the south **s** the hangings of Ex 38:9 6285
s *there were* one hundred cubits; Ex 38:11 6285
For the west **s** *there were* Ex 38:12 6285
For the east **s** fifty cubits. Ex 38:13 6285
The hangings for the *one* **s** *of the* Ex 38:14 3802
and so for the other **s**. Ex 38:15 3802
on the north **s** of the tabernacle, Ex 40:22 3409
on the south **s** of the tabernacle. Ex 40:24 3409
He shall slay it on the **s** of the altar Lv 1:11 3409
drained out on the **s** of the altar. Lv 1:15 7023
offering on the **s** of the altar, Lv 5:9 7023
on the mercy seat on the east **s**; Lv 16:14
"Now those who camp on the east **s** Nu 2:3 6924b
"On the south **s** *shall be* the Nu 2:10 8486
"On the west **s** *shall be* the Nu 2:18 3220
"On the north **s** *shall be* the Nu 2:25 6828
the southward **s** of the tabernacle, Nu 3:29 3409
the northward **s** of the tabernacle. Nu 3:35 3409
on the east **s** shall set out. Nu 10:5 6924b
on the south **s** shall set out; Nu 10:6 8486
about a day's journey on this **s** Nu 11:31 3541
and a day's journey on the other **s**, Nu 11:31 3541
sea and by the **s** of the Jordan." Nu 13:29 3027
on the other **s** of the Arnon, Nu 21:13 5676
a wall on this **s** and a wall on that Nu 22:24 2088
on this side and a wall on that **s**. Nu 22:24 2088
other **s** of the Jordan and beyond, Nu 32:19 5676
s of the Jordan toward the east." Nu 32:19 5676
of Zin along the **s** of Edom, Nu 34:3 3027
to Riblah on the east **s** of Ain; Nu 34:11 6924a
east **s** of the Sea of Chinnereth. Nu 34:11 6924b
on the east **s** two thousand cubits, Nu 35:5 6285
the south **s** two thousand cubits, Nu 35:5 6285
on the west **s** two thousand cubits, Nu 35:5 6285
the north **s** two thousand cubits, Nu 35:5 6285
and Ai, on the west **s** of Ai; Jos 8:9 3220
and camped on the north **s** of Ai. Jos 8:11 6828
and Ai, on the west **s** of the city. Jos 8:12 3220
was on the north **s** of the city, Jos 8:13 6828
guard on the west **s** of the city, Jos 8:13 3220
on this **s** and some on that side; Jos 8:22 2088
on this side and some on that **s**; Jos 8:22 2088
And the border of the north **s** was Jos 15:5 6285
to the **s** of Ekron northward. Jos 15:11 3802
all that were by the **s** of Ashdod, Jos 15:46 3027
was on the north **s** of the brook and Jos 17:9 6828
The south **s** *belonged* to Ephraim Jos 17:10 5045
and the north **s** to Manasseh, Jos 17:10 6828
the north **s** was from the Jordan, Jos 18:12 6285
to the **s** of Jericho on the north, Jos 18:12 3802
continued to Luz, to the **s** of Luz Jos 18:13 3802
round on the west **s** southward, Jos 18:14 6285
This *was* the west **s**. Jos 18:14 6285
Then the south **s** *was* from the edge Jos 18:15 6285
It continued to the **s** in front Jos 18:18 3802
to the **s** of Beth-hoglah northward; Jos 18:19 3802
was its border on the east **s**. Jos 18:20 6285
LORD gave them rest on every **s**, Jos 21:44 5439
on the **s** *belonging to* the sons of Jos 22:11 5676
from all their enemies on every **s**, Jos 23:1 5439
camp of Midian was on the north **s** Jg 7:1 6828
of all their enemies on every **s**; Jg 8:34 5439
to the east **s** of the land of Moab, Jg 11:18
4217, 8121
which is on the north **s** of Bethel, Jg 21:19 6828
on the east **s** of the highway that Jg 21:19
4217, 8121
and on the south **s** of Lebonah." Jg 21:19 5045
guilt offering in a box by its **s**. 1Sa 6:8 6654
garrison that is on the other **s**." 1Sa 14:1 5676
was a sharp crag on the one **s** and 1Sa 14:4 5676
and a sharp crag on the other **s**, 1Sa 14:4 5676
"You shall be on one **s** and I and 1Sa 14:40 5676
my son will be on the other **s**." 1Sa 14:40 5676
all his enemies on every **s**, 1Sa 14:47 5439
stood on the mountain on one **s** 1Sa 17:3 2088
on the mountain on the other **s**, 1Sa 17:3 2088
will shoot three arrows to the **s**, 1Sa 20:20 6654
the arrows are on this **s** of you, 1Sa 20:21 2008
up and Abner sat down by Saul's **s**, 1Sa 20:25 6654
David rose from the south **s** and 1Sa 20:41 681a
went on one **s** of the mountain, 1Sa 23:26 6654
on the other **s** of the mountain; 1Sa 23:26 6654
David crossed over to the other **s** and 1Sa 26:13 5676
were on the other **s** of the valley, 1Sa 31:7 5676
one on the one **s** of the pool and 2Sa 2:13 2088
other on the other **s** of the pool. 2Sa 2:13 2088
his sword in his opponent's **s**; 2Sa 2:16 6654
on every **s** from all his enemies, 2Sa 7:1 5439
him by the **s** of the mountain. 2Sa 13:34 6654
on the right **s** of the city that is 2Sa 24:5 3225
as far as the other **s** of Jokmeam; 1Ki 4:12 5676
God has given me rest on every **s**; 1Ki 5:4 5439
he made **s** chambers all around. 1Ki 6:5 6763
doorway for the lowest **s** chamber 1Ki 6:8 6763
was on the right **s** of the house; 1Ki 6:8 3802
with cedar above the **s** chambers 1Ki 7:3 6763
supports with wreaths at each **s**. 1Ki 7:30 5676
five on the right **s** of the house 1Ki 7:39 3802
five on the left **s** of the house; 1Ki 7:39 3802
sea *of cast metal* on the right **s** of the 1Ki 7:39 3802
five on the right **s** and five on the 1Ki 7:49 3225
and arms on each **s** of the seat, 1Ki 10:19 2088
on the one **s** and on the other; 1Ki 10:20 2088
and said, "Who is on my **s**? Who?" 2Ki 9:32 854
"If you are on my **s**, 2Ki 10:6
from the right **s** of the house to 2Ki 11:11 3802
house to the left **s** of the house, 2Ki 11:11 3802
on the right **s** as one comes into 2Ki 12:9 3225
it on the north **s** of *his* altar. 2Ki 16:14 3409
even to the east **s** of the valley, 1Ch 4:39 4217
on the east **s** of the Jordan, 1Ch 6:78 4217
From the other **s** of the Jordan, 1Ch 12:37 5676
David *were* chiefs at the king's **s**. 1Ch 18:17 3027
from all his enemies on every **s**; 1Ch 22:9 5439
He not given you rest on every **s**? 1Ch 22:18 5439
he set five on the right **s** and five on 2Ch 4:6 3225
five on the right **s** and five on the 2Ch 4:7 3225
five on the right **s** and five on the 2Ch 4:8 3225
He set the sea on the right **s** 2Ch 4:10 3802
priests on the other **s** blew trumpets; 2Ch 7:6 5048
and arms on each **s** of the seat, 2Ch 9:18 2088
on the one **s** and on the other; 2Ch 9:19 2088

He has given us rest on every s." 2Ch 14:7 5439
LORD gave them rest on every s. 2Ch 15:15 5439
from the right s of the house to 2Ch 23:10 3802
house to the left s of the house, 2Ch 23:10 3802
and guided them on every s. 2Ch 32:22 5439
the west s of the city of David. 2Ch 32:30 4628
of David on the west s of Gihon, 2Ch 33:14 4628
sword girded at his s as he built, Ne 4:18 4975
and all that he has, on every s? Jb 1:10 5439
And calamity is ready at his s. Jb 18:12 6763
"He breaks me down on every s, Jb 19:10 5439
The wicked strut about on every s Ps 12:8 5439
of many, Terror is on every s; Ps 31:13 5439
A thousand may fall at your s And Ps 91:7 6654
been the LORD who was on our s," Ps 124:1 5973
been the LORD who was on our s Ps 124:2 5973
s of their oppressors was power, Ec 4:1 3027
throng to the s of the second lad Ec 4:15 5973
Each man has his sword at his s, SS 3:8 3409
the sea, on the other s of Jordan, Is 9:1 5676
has a sword, Terror is on every s. Jer 6:25 5439
of prey against her on every s? Jer 12:9 5439
"Terror on every s! Jer 20:10 5439
Terror is on every s!" Jer 46:5 5439
'Terror on every s!' Jer 49:29 5439
their disaster from every s," Jer 49:32 5676
lines against Babylon on every s, Jer 50:14 5439
battle cry against her on every s! Jer 50:15 5439
Encamp against her on every s, Jer 50:29 5439
For on every s they will be Jer 51:2 5439
feast My terrors on every s; La 2:22 5439
on the one s and on the other. Ezk 1:23 2008
for you, lie down on your left s and Ezk 4:4 6654
second time, *but* on your right s and Ezk 4:6 6654
turn from one s to the other until Ezk 4:8 6654
the days that you lie on your s, Ezk 4:9 6654
standing on the right s of the temple Ezk 10:3 3225
On every s from *their* provinces, Ezk 19:8 5439
them against you from every s: Ezk 23:22 5439
set themselves against you on every s Ezk 23:24 5439
By the sword upon her on every s; Ezk 28:23 5439
you push with s and with shoulder, Ezk 34:21 6654
and crushed you from every s, Ezk 36:3 5439
and I will gather them from every s Ezk 37:21 5439
gather from every s to My Ezk 39:17 5439
and its s pillars, two cubits. Ezk 40:9 352b
the east *numbered* three on each s; Ezk 40:10 6311
The s pillars also had the same Ezk 40:10 352b
the same measurement on each s. Ezk 40:10 6311
front of the guardrooms on each s; Ezk 40:12 6311
were six cubits *square* on each s. Ezk 40:12 6311
the s pillars sixty cubits *high;* Ezk 40:14 352b
to the s pillar of the courtyard. Ezk 40:14 352b
and toward their s pillars within Ezk 40:16 352b
and on *each* s pillar *were* palm Ezk 40:16 352b
was by the s of the gates, Ezk 40:18 3802
It had three guardrooms on each s; Ezk 40:21 6311
and its s pillars and its porches Ezk 40:21 352b
and he measured its s pillars and Ezk 40:24 352b
tree ornaments on its s pillars, Ezk 40:26 352b
its side pillars, one on each s. Ezk 40:26 6311
guardrooms also, its s pillars and Ezk 40:29 352b
ornaments *were* on its s pillars, Ezk 40:31 352b
guardrooms also, its s pillars and Ezk 40:33 352b
ornaments *were* on its s pillars, Ezk 40:34 352b
on its side pillars, on each s, Ezk 40:34 6311
its guardrooms, its s pillars and Ezk 40:36 352b
Its s pillars *were* toward the Ezk 40:37 352b
on its s pillars on each side, Ezk 40:37 352b
on its side pillars on each s, Ezk 40:37 6311
was by the s pillars at the gates; Ezk 40:38 352b
gate *were* two tables on each s, Ezk 40:39 6311
On the outer s, Ezk 40:40 3802
and on the other s of the porch of Ezk 40:40 3802
were on each s next to the gate; Ezk 40:41 6311
was at the s of the north gate, Ezk 40:44 3802
and one at the s of the south gate Ezk 40:44 3802
each s pillar of the porch, Ezk 40:48 352b
the porch, five cubits on each s; Ezk 40:48 6311
gate was three cubits on each s. Ezk 40:48 6311
belonging to the s pillars, Ezk 40:49 352b
the side pillars, one on each s. Ezk 40:49 6311
nave and measured the s pillars; Ezk 41:1 352b
six cubits wide on each s *was* the Ezk 41:1 6311
was the width of the s pillar. Ezk 41:1 168
were five cubits on each s. Ezk 41:2 6311
each s pillar of the doorway, Ezk 41:3 352b
and the width of the s chambers, Ezk 41:5 6763
around about the house on every s. Ezk 41:5 5439
The s chambers were in three Ezk 41:6 6763
and the s chambers extended to the Ezk 41:6
wall which *stood* on their inward s Ezk 41:6 6763
The s chambers surrounding the Ezk 41:7 6763
the foundations of the s chambers Ezk 41:8 6763
of the s chambers *was* five cubits. Ezk 41:9 6763
free space between the s chambers Ezk 41:9 6763
all around the temple on every s. Ezk 41:10 5439
The doorways of the s chambers Ezk 41:11 6763
separate area at the s toward the west Ezk 41:12 6285
the separate areas along the east s Ezk 41:14 6285
it, with a gallery on each s, Ezk 41:15 6311
toward the palm tree on one s and Ezk 41:19 6311
the palm tree on the other s; Ezk 41:19 6311
trees on one s and on the other, Ezk 41:26 6311
were the s chambers of the house Ezk 41:26 6763
wall by the s of the chambers, Ezk 42:7 5980
was the entrance on the east s, Ezk 42:9 6921
He measured on the east s with the Ezk 42:16 7307
He measured on the north s five Ezk 42:17 7307
On the south s he measured five Ezk 42:18 7307
He turned to the west s Ezk 42:19 7307
land on either s of the holy allotment Ezk 45:7 2088
on the west s toward the west and Ezk 45:7 6285
and on the east s toward the east, Ezk 45:7 6285
which *was* at the s of the gate, Ezk 46:19 3802
from the right s of the house, Ezk 47:1 3802
was trickling from the south s. Ezk 47:2 3802
on the one s and on the other. Ezk 47:7 2088
bank, on one s and on the other, Ezk 47:12 2088
on the north s, from the Great Sea Ezk 47:15 6285
This is the north s. Ezk 47:17 6285
"The east s, from between Ezk 47:18 6285
This is the east s. Ezk 47:18 6285
"The south s toward the south Ezk 47:19 6285
is the south s toward the south. Ezk 47:19 6285
The west s *shall be* the Great Sea, Ezk 47:20 6285
This is the west s. Ezk 47:20 6285
from the east s to the west side, Ezk 48:2 6285
from the east side to the west s, Ezk 48:2 6285
from the east s to the west side, Ezk 48:3 6285
from the east side to the west s, Ezk 48:3 6285
from the east s to the west side, Ezk 48:4 6285
from the east side to the west s, Ezk 48:4 6285
from the east s to the west side, Ezk 48:5 6285
from the east side to the west s, Ezk 48:5 6285
from the east s to the west side, Ezk 48:6 6285
from the east side to the west s, Ezk 48:6 6285
from the east s to the west side, Ezk 48:7 6285
from the east side to the west s, Ezk 48:7 6285
from the east s to the west side, Ezk 48:8 6285
from the east side to the west s, Ezk 48:8 6285
from the east side to the west side; Ezk 48:8 6285
from the east side to the west s; Ezk 48:8 6285
the north s 4,500 *virgin cubits,* the Ezk 48:16 6285
cubits, the south s 4,500 *cubits,* Ezk 48:16 6285
cubits, the east s 4,500 *cubits,* Ezk 48:16 6285
and the west s 4,500 *cubits.* Ezk 48:16 6285
on the one s and on the other of Ezk 48:21 2088
from the east s to the west side, Ezk 48:23 6285
from the east side to the west s, Ezk 48:23 6285
from the east s to the west side, Ezk 48:24 6285
from the east side to the west s, Ezk 48:24 6285
from the east s to the west side, Ezk 48:25 6285
from the east side to the west s, Ezk 48:25 6285
from the east s to the west side, Ezk 48:26 6285
from the east side to the west s, Ezk 48:26 6285
from the east s to the west side, Ezk 48:27 6285
from the east side to the west s, Ezk 48:27 6285
at the south s toward the south, Ezk 48:28 6285
on the north s, 4,500 cubits by Ezk 48:30 6285
"On the east s, 4,500 *cubits,* Ezk 48:32 6285
"On the south s, Ezk 48:33 6285
"On the west s, 4,500 *cubits,* Ezk 48:34 6285
And it was raised up on one s, Da 7:5 7859
a stand *for him* or be on his s. Da 11:17
one on the right s of the bowl and Zch 4:3 3225
and the other on its left s." Zch 4:3 8040
according to the writing on one s, Zch 5:3 2088
to the writing on the other s. Zch 5:3 2088
orders to depart to the other s Mt 8:18 *4008*
When He came to the other s Mt 8:28 *4008*
go ahead of Him to the other s, Mt 14:22 *4008*
And the disciples came to the other s Mt 16:5 *4008*
"Let us go over to the other s." Mk 4:35 *4008*
came to the other s of the sea, Mk 5:1 *4008*
again in the boat to the other s, Mk 5:21 *4008*
Him to the other s to Bethsaida, Mk 6:45 *4008*
and went away to the other s. Mk 8:13 *4008*
over to the other s of the lake." Lk 8:22 *4008*
a child and stood him by His s, Lk 9:47 *3844*
him, he passed by on the other s. Lk 10:31 *492*
saw him, passed by on the other s. Lk 10:32 *492*
you and hem you in on every s, Lk 19:43 *3840*
the other s of the Sea of Galilee Jn 6:1 *4008*
crowd that stood on the other s Jn 6:22 *4008*
Him on the other s of the sea, Jn 6:25 *4008*
two other men, one on either s, Jn 19:18 *1782*
pierced His s with a spear, Jn 19:34 *4125*
them both His hands and His s. Jn 20:20 *4125*
nails, and put my hand into His s, Jn 20:25 *4125*
your hand and put it into My s; Jn 20:27 *4125*
on the right-hand s of the boat and Jn 21:6 *3313*
he struck Peter's s and woke him Ac 12:7 *4125*
the Lord stood at his s and said, Ac 23:11
but we were afflicted on every s: 2Co 7:5
On either s of the river was Rv 22:2 *1782*

SIDED

and some s with the Jews, and some Ac 14:4 *1510*

SIDE-GROWTH

not round off the s of your heads nor Lv 19:27 6285

SIDES

the rings on the s of the ark, Ex 25:14 6763
branches shall go out from its s; Ex 25:32 6654
shall lap over the s of the tabernacle Ex 26:13 6654
poles shall be on the two s of the altar Ex 27:7 6763
its top and its s all around, Ex 30:3 7023
on its two side walls—on opposite s Ex 30:4 6654
which were written on both s; Ex 32:15 5676
the rings on the s of the ark, Ex 37:5 6763
six branches going out of its s; Ex 37:18 6654
its top and its s all around, Ex 37:26 7023
for it under its molding, on its two s Ex 37:27 6763
on its two sides—on opposite s Ex 37:27 6654
the rings on the s of the altar, Ex 38:7 6763
On both s of the gate of the court Ex 38:15 3802
becomes bald at the front and s, Lv 13:41 6285
the horns of the altar on all s. Lv 16:18 5439
your eyes and as thorns in your s, Nu 33:55 6654
their judges were standing on both s Jos 8:33 4480, 2088
on your s and thorns in your eyes, Jos 23:13 6654
will become *as thorns* in your s Jg 2:3 6654
peace on all s around about him. 1Ki 4:24 5676
gatekeepers were on the four s, 1Ch 9:24 7307
his God gave him rest on all s. 2Ch 20:30 5439
For sound wisdom has two s. Jb 11:6 3718
His s are filled out with fat, And Jb 21:24 5845
thrown down by the s of the rock, Ps 141:6 3027
on their four s *were* human hands. Ezk 1:8 7253
and the s of the entrance Ezk 41:2 3802
by stages on all s of the temple, Ezk 41:7 5439
its base and its s *were* of wood. Ezk 41:22 7023
the other, on the s of the porch; Ezk 41:26 3802
He measured it on the four s; Ezk 42:20 7307
twelve wide, square in its four s. Ezk 43:16 7253
by fourteen wide in its four s, Ezk 43:17 7253
covered on all s with gold, Heb 9:4 *3840*

SIDON

Canaan became the father of S, Gn 10:15 6721
from S as you go toward Gerar, Gn 10:19 6721
And his flank *shall be* toward S. Gn 49:13 6721
and pursued them as far as Great S Jos 11:8 6721
and Kanah, as far as Great S. Jos 19:28 6721
of Acco, or the inhabitants of S, Jg 1:31 6721
the gods of Aram, the gods of S, Jg 10:6 6721
because it was far from S and they Jg 18:28 6721
came to Dan-jaan and around to S, 2Sa 24:6 6721
to Zarephath, which belongs to S, 1Ki 17:9 6721
Canaan became the father of S, 1Ch 1:13 6721
the coastland, You merchants of S; Is 23:2 6721
Be ashamed, O S; For the sea speaks Is 23:4 6721
O crushed virgin daughter of S. Is 23:12 6721
kings of Tyre, all the kings of S and Jer 25:22 6721
and to the king of S by the Jer 27:3 6721
cut off from Tyre and S Every ally Jer 47:4 6721
inhabitants of S and Arvad were Ezk 27:8 6721
of man, set your face toward S, Ezk 28:21 6721
"Behold, I am against you, O S, Ezk 28:22 6721
what are you to Me, O Tyre, S and Jl 3:4 6721
Tyre and S, though they are very Zch 9:2 6721
miracles had occurred in Tyre and S Mt 11:21 *4605*
Tyre and S in *the* day of judgment than Mt 11:22 *4605*
into the district of Tyre and S. Mt 15:21 *4605*
and the vicinity of Tyre and S, Mk 3:8 *4605*
through S to the Sea of Galilee, Mk 7:31 *4605*
to Zarephath, *in the land* of S, Lk 4:26 *4606*
the coastal region of Tyre and S, Lk 6:17 *4605*
had been performed in Tyre and S Lk 10:13 *4605*
be more tolerable for Tyre and S Lk 10:14 *4605*
with the people of Tyre and S; Ac 12:20 *4606*
The next day we put in at S; Ac 27:3 *4605*

SIDONIAN

Moabite, Ammonite, Edomite, S, 1Ki 11:1 6722

SIDONIANS

(S call Hermon Sirion, and the Dt 3:9 6722
and Mearah that belongs to the S, Jos 13:4 6722
far as Misrephoth-maim, all the S, Jos 13:6 6722
and all the Canaanites and the S Jg 3:3 6722
"Also when the S, the Amalekites Jg 10:12 6722
after the manner of the S, Jg 18:7 6722
and they were far from the S and Jg 18:7 6722
how to cut timber like the S." 1Ki 5:6 6722
after Ashtoreth the goddess of the S 1Ki 11:5 6722
Ashtoreth the goddess of the S, 1Ki 11:33 6722
daughter of Ethbaal king of the S, 1Ki 16:31 6722
the abomination of the S, 2Ki 23:13 6722
for the S and Tyrians brought 1Ch 22:4 6722
oil to the S and to the Tyrians, Ezr 3:7 6722
north, all of them, and all the S, Ezk 32:30 6722

SIEGE

during the s and the distress by Dt 28:53 4692
during the s and the distress by Dt 28:55 4692
during the s and the distress by Dt 28:57 4692
and they cast up a s ramp against 2Sa 20:15 5550
Israel were laying s to Gibbethon. 1Ki 15:27 6696a
it with a shield or throw up a s ramp 2Ki 19:32 5550
and the city came under s. 2Ki 24:10 4692
and built a s wall all around it. 2Ki 25:1 1785
So the city was under s until the 2Ki 25:2 4692
remaining in Jerusalem under s? 2Ch 32:10 4692
Go up, Elam, lay s, Media; Is 21:2 6696a
erected their s towers, Is 23:13 969a
or throw up a s ramp against it. Is 37:33 5550
And cast up a s against Jerusalem. Jer 6:6 8210
the ground, You who dwell under s! Jer 10:17 4692
will eat one another's flesh in the s Jer 19:9 4692
the s ramps have reached the city Jer 32:24 5550
make a defense against the s ramps Jer 33:4 5550
they lifted the s from Jerusalem. Jer 37:5
of the Chaldeans had lifted *the* s Jer 37:11
to Jerusalem and laid s to it; Jer 39:1 6696a
and built a s wall all around it. Jer 52:4 1785
So the city was under s until the Jer 52:5 4692
"Then lay s against it, build a Ezk 4:2 4692
siege against it, build a s wall, Ezk 4:2 1785
toward it so that it is under s, Ezk 4:3 4692
your face toward the s of Jerusalem Ezk 4:7 4692
have completed the days of your s. Ezk 4:8 4692
the days of the s are completed. Ezk 5:2 4692
build s walls to cut off many lives. Ezk 17:17 1785
cast up ramps, to build a s wall. Ezk 21:22 1785
laid s to Jerusalem this very day. Ezk 24:2 5564
he will make s walls against you, Ezk 26:8 1785
will come, cast up a s ramp Da 11:15 5550
They have laid s against us; Mi 5:1 4692

Draw for yourself water for the **s**! **Na 3:14** 4692
when the **s** is against Jerusalem, **Zch 12:2** 4692

SIEGEWORKS
that you may construct **s** against **Dt 20:20** 4692
constructed large **s** against it. **Ec 9:14** 4685a
you, And I will set **s** against you, **Is 29:3** 4674

SIEVE
the nations back and forth in a **s**, **Is 30:28** 5299a
nations As *grain* is shaken in a **s**, **Am 9:9** 3531

SIFT
permission to **s** you like wheat; **Lk 22:31** *4617a*

SIGH
When I **s**, then my spirit grows **Ps 77:3** 7878
have finished our years like a **s**. **Ps 90:9** 1899
decays, All the merry-hearted **s**. **Is 24:7** 584
on the foreheads of the men who **s** **Ezk 9:4** 584
up to heaven with a deep **s**, **Mk 7:34** *4727*

SIGHED
Israel **s** because of the bondage, **Ex 2:23** 584

SIGHING
I am weary with my **s**; **Ps 6:6** 585
with sorrow And my years with **s**; **Ps 31:10** 585
And my **s** is not hidden from You. **Ps 38:9** 585
And sorrow and **s** will flee away. **Is 35:10** 585
And sorrow and **s** will flee away. **Is 51:11** 585
S deeply in His spirit, He said, **Mk 8:12** *389*

SIGHT
every tree that is pleasing to the **s** **Gn 2:9** 4758
earth was corrupt in the **s** of God, **Gn 6:11** 6440
mistress was despised in her **s**. **Gn 16:4** 5869
I was despised in her **s**. **Gn 16:5** 5869
to her what is good in your **s**." **Gn 16:6** 5869
now I have found favor in Your **s**, **Gn 18:3** 5869
servant has found favor in your **s**, **Gn 19:19** 5869
I may bury my dead out of my **s**." **Gn 23:4** 6440
me to bury my dead out of my **s**, **Gn 23:8** 6440
I will be as a deceiver in his **s** **Gn 27:12** 5869
place the rods in the **s** of the flock **Gn 30:41** 5869
I may find favor in your **s**. **Gn 32:5** 5869
find favor in the **s** of my lord." **Gn 33:8** 5869
now I have found favor in your **s**, **Gn 33:10** 5869
find favor in the **s** of my lord." **Gn 33:15** 5869
"If I find favor in your **s**, **Gn 34:11** 5869
was evil in the **s** of the LORD, **Gn 38:7** 5869
displeasing in the **s** of the LORD; **Gn 38:10** 5869
So Joseph found favor in his **s** and **Gn 39:4** 5869
in the **s** of the chief jailer. **Gn 39:21** 5869
compassion in the **s** of the man, **Gn 43:14** 6440
Let us find favor in the **s** of my lord, **Gn 47:25** 5869
if I have found favor in your **s**, **Gn 47:29** 5869
now I have found favor in your **s**, **Gn 50:4** 5869
now and see this marvelous **s**, **Ex 3:3** 4758
favor in the **s** of the Egyptians; **Ex 3:21** 5869
the signs in the **s** of the people. **Ex 4:30** 5869
have made us odious in Pharaoh's **s** **Ex 5:21** 5869
and in the **s** of his servants, **Ex 5:21** 5869
in the **s** of Pharaoh and in the **Ex 7:20** 5869
and in the **s** of his servants, **Ex 7:20** 5869
the sky in the **s** of Pharaoh. **Ex 9:8** 5869
favor in the **s** of the Egyptians. **Ex 11:3** 5869
both in the **s** of Pharaoh's servants **Ex 11:3** 5869
and in the **s** of the people. **Ex 11:3** 5869
favor in the **s** of the Egyptians, **Ex 12:36** 5869
and do what is right in His **s**, **Ex 15:26** 5869
in the **s** of the elders of Israel. **Ex 17:6** 5869
Sinai in the **s** of all the people. **Ex 19:11** 5869
have also found favor in My **s**.' **Ex 33:12** 5869
if I have found favor in Your **s**, **Ex 33:13** 5869
so that I may find favor in Your **s**. **Ex 33:13** 5869
that I have found favor in Your **s**, **Ex 33:16** 5869
for you have found favor in My **s** and **Ex 33:17** 5869
now I have found favor in Your **s**, **Ex 34:9** 5869
the **s** of all the house of Israel. **Ex 40:38** 5869
been good in the **s** of the LORD?" **Lv 10:19** 5869
that, it seemed good in his **s**. **Lv 10:20** 5869
in his **s** the scale has remained, **Lv 13:37** 5869
in the **s** of the sons of their people. **Lv 20:17** 5869
over him with severity in your **s**. **Lv 25:53** 5869
of Egypt in the **s** of the nations, **Lv 26:45** 5869
have I not found favor in Your **s**, **Nu 11:11** 5869
if I have found favor in Your **s**, **Nu 11:15** 5869
like grasshoppers in our own **s**, **Nu 13:33** 5869
and so we were in their **s**." **Nu 13:33** 5869
heifer shall be burned in his **s**; **Nu 19:5** 5869
in the **s** of the sons of Israel, **Nu 20:12** 5869
in the **s** of all the congregation. **Nu 20:27** 5869
in the **s** of Moses and in the sight **Nu 25:6** 5869
and in the **s** of all the congregation **Nu 25:6** 5869
and commission him in their **s**. **Nu 27:19** 5869
"If we have found favor in your **s**, **Nu 32:5** 5869
had done evil in the **s** of the LORD **Nu 32:13** 5869
in the **s** of all the Egyptians, **Nu 33:3** 5869
understanding in the **s** of the peoples **Dt 4:6** 5869
which is evil in the **s** of the LORD **Dt 4:25** 5869
and good in the **s** of the LORD, **Dt 6:18** 5869
what was evil in the **s** of the LORD **Dt 9:18** 5869
is right in the **s** of the LORD. **Dt 12:25** 5869
right in the **s** of the LORD your God. **Dt 12:28** 5869
right in the **s** of the LORD your God. **Dt 13:18** 5869
evil in the **s** of the LORD your God, **Dt 17:2** 5869
to him in the **s** of the elders, **Dt 25:9** 5869
mad by the **s** of what you see. **Dt 28:34** 4758
and for the **s** of your eyes which **Dt 28:67** 4758
to him in the **s** of all Israel, **Dt 31:7** 5869
is evil in the **s** of the LORD, **Dt 31:29** 5869
performed in the **s** of all Israel. **Dt 34:12** 5869
exalt you in the **s** of all Israel, **Jos 3:7** 5869
Joshua in the **s** of all Israel; **Jos 4:14** 5869
and right in your **s** to do to us." **Jos 9:25** 5869
and he said in the **s** of Israel, **Jos 10:12** 5869
it is disagreeable in your **s** to serve **Jos 24:15** 5869
who did these great signs in our **s** **Jos 24:17** 5869
did evil in the **s** of the LORD and **Jg 2:11** 5869
was evil in the **s** of the LORD, **Jg 3:7** 5869
did evil in the **s** of the LORD. **Jg 3:12** 5869
done evil in the **s** of the LORD. **Jg 3:12** 5869
did evil in the **s** of the LORD, **Jg 4:1** 5869
was evil in the **s** of the LORD; **Jg 6:1** 5869
now I have found favor in Your **s**, **Jg 6:17** 5869
of the LORD vanished from his **s**. **Jg 6:21** 5869
did evil in the **s** of the LORD, **Jg 10:6** 5869
did evil in the **s** of the LORD, **Jg 13:1** 5869
one in whose **s** I may find favor." **Ru 2:2** 5869
"Why have I found favor in your **s** **Ru 2:10** 5869
"I have found favor in your **s**, **Ru 2:13** 5869
find favor in your **s**." **1Sa 1:18** 5869
was displeasing in the **s** of Samuel **1Sa 8:6** 5869
you have done in the **s** of the LORD **1Sa 12:17** 5869
was evil in the **s** of the LORD?" **1Sa 15:19** 5869
for he has found favor in my **s**." **1Sa 16:22** 5869
pleasing in the **s** of all the people **1Sa 18:5** 5869
also in the **s** of Saul's servants. **1Sa 18:5** 5869
"Is it trivial in your **s** to **1Sa 18:23** 5869
that I have found favor in your **s**, **1Sa 20:3** 5869
if I have found favor in your **s**, **1Sa 20:29** 5869
was precious in your **s** this day. **1Sa 26:21** 5869
highly valued in my **s** this day, **1Sa 26:24** 5869
valued in the **s** of the LORD, **1Sa 26:24** 5869
now I have found favor in your **s**, **1Sa 27:5** 5869
in the army are pleasing in my **s**; **1Sa 29:6** 5869
pleasing in the **s** of the lords. **1Sa 29:6** 5869
that you are pleasing in my **s**, **1Sa 29:9** 5869
LORD do what is good in His **s**." **2Sa 10:12** 5869
was evil in the **s** of the LORD. **2Sa 11:27** 5869
the LORD by doing evil in His **s**? **2Sa 12:9** 5869
let her prepare the food in my **s**, **2Sa 13:5** 5869
make me a couple of cakes in my **s**, **2Sa 13:6** 5869
kneaded *it,* made cakes in his **s**, **2Sa 13:8** 5869
that I have found favor in your **s**, **2Sa 14:22** 5869
I find favor in the **s** of the LORD, **2Sa 15:25** 5869
let me find favor in your **s**, **2Sa 16:4** 5869
concubines in the **s** of all Israel. **2Sa 16:22** 5869
and to do what was good in his **s**. **2Sa 19:18** 5869
do what is good in your **s**. **2Sa 19:27** 5869
for him what is good in your **s**." **2Sa 19:37** 5869
do for him what is good in your **s**; **2Sa 19:38** 5869
cities and escape from our **s**." **2Sa 20:6** 5869
offer up what is good in his **s**. **2Sa 24:22** 5869
It was pleasing in the **s** of the Lord **1Ki 3:10** 5869
My name, I will cast out of My **s**. **1Ki 9:7** 6440
was evil in the **s** of the LORD, **1Ki 11:6** 5869
doing what is right in My **s** and **1Ki 11:33** 5869
and do what is right in My **s** by **1Ki 11:38** 5869
only that which was right in My **s**; **1Ki 14:8** 5869
did evil in the **s** of the LORD, **1Ki 14:22** 5869
was right in the **s** of the LORD, **1Ki 15:5** 5869
was right in the **s** of the LORD, **1Ki 15:11** 5869
He did evil in the **s** of the LORD, **1Ki 15:26** 5869
He did evil in the **s** of the LORD, **1Ki 15:34** 5869
which he did in the **s** of the LORD, **1Ki 16:7** 5869
doing evil in the **s** of the LORD, **1Ki 16:19** 5869
did evil in the **s** of the LORD, **1Ki 16:25** 5869
did evil in the **s** of the LORD more **1Ki 16:30** 5869
to do evil in the **s** of the LORD. **1Ki 21:20** 5869
to do evil in the **s** of the LORD, **1Ki 21:25** 5869
doing right in the **s** of the LORD. **1Ki 22:43** 5869
He did evil in the **s** of the LORD **1Ki 22:52** 5869
of yours be precious in your **s**. **2Ki 1:13** 5869
my life be precious in your **s**." **2Ki 1:14** 5869
He did evil in the **s** of the LORD, **2Ki 3:2** 5869
slight thing in the **s** of the LORD; **2Ki 3:18** 5869
he did evil in the **s** of the LORD. **2Ki 8:18** 5869
and did evil in the **s** of the LORD, **2Ki 8:27** 5869
do what is good in your **s**." **2Ki 10:5** 5869
did right in the **s** of the LORD **2Ki 12:2** 5869
He did evil in the **s** of the LORD, **2Ki 13:2** 5869
He did evil in the **s** of the LORD; **2Ki 13:11** 5869
He did right in the **s** of the LORD, **2Ki 14:3** 5869
He did evil in the **s** of the LORD; **2Ki 14:24** 5869
He did right in the **s** of the LORD, **2Ki 15:3** 5869
He did evil in the **s** of the LORD, **2Ki 15:9** 5869
He did evil in the **s** of the LORD; **2Ki 15:18** 5869
He did evil in the **s** of the LORD; **2Ki 15:24** 5869
He did evil in the **s** of the LORD; **2Ki 15:28** 5869
was right in the **s** of the LORD; **2Ki 15:34** 5869
right in the **s** of the LORD his God, **2Ki 16:2** 5869
He did evil in the **s** of the LORD, **2Ki 17:2** 5869
to do evil in the **s** of the LORD, **2Ki 17:17** 5869
and removed them from His **s**; **2Ki 17:18** 6440
He has cast them out of His **s**. **2Ki 17:20** 6440
LORD removed Israel from His **s**, **2Ki 17:23** 6440
He did right in the **s** of the LORD, **2Ki 18:3** 5869
have done what is good in Your **s**." **2Ki 20:3** 5869
He did evil in the **s** of the LORD, **2Ki 21:2** 5869
did much evil in the **s** of the LORD **2Ki 21:6** 5869
they have done evil in My **s**, **2Ki 21:15** 5869
doing evil in the **s** of the LORD. **2Ki 21:16** 5869
He did evil in the **s** of the LORD, **2Ki 21:20** 5869
He did right in the **s** of the LORD **2Ki 22:2** 5869
will remove Judah also from My **s**, **2Ki 23:27** 6440
He did evil in the **s** of the LORD, **2Ki 23:32** 5869
He did evil in the **s** of the LORD, **2Ki 23:37** 5869
to remove *them* from His **s** because **2Ki 24:3** 6440
He did evil in the **s** of the LORD, **2Ki 24:9** 5869
He did evil in the **s** of the LORD, **2Ki 24:19** 5869
was wicked in the **s** of the LORD, **1Ch 2:3** 5869
LORD do what is good in His **s**." **1Ch 19:13** 5869
the king do what is good in his **s**. **1Ch 21:23** 5869
"So now, in the **s** of all Israel, **1Ch 28:8** 5869
LORD in the **s** of all the assembly; **1Ch 29:10** 5869
Solomon in the **s** of all Israel, **1Ch 29:25** 5869
My name I will cast out of My **s** and **2Ch 7:20** 6440
right in the **s** of the LORD his God, **2Ch 14:2** 5869
doing right in the **s** of the LORD. **2Ch 20:32** 5869
he did evil in the **s** of the LORD. **2Ch 21:6** 5869
He did evil in the **s** of the LORD **2Ch 22:4** 5869
what was right in the **s** of the LORD **2Ch 24:2** 5869
He did right in the **s** of the LORD, **2Ch 25:2** 5869
He did right in the **s** of the LORD **2Ch 26:4** 5869
He did right in the **s** of the LORD, **2Ch 27:2** 5869
not do right in the **s** of the LORD **2Ch 28:1** 5869
He did right in the **s** of the LORD, **2Ch 29:2** 5869
evil in the **s** of the LORD our God, **2Ch 29:6** 5869
thing was right in the **s** of the king **2Ch 30:4** 5869
he was exalted in the **s** of all nations **2Ch 32:23** 5869
He did evil in the **s** of the LORD **2Ch 33:2** 5869
much evil in the **s** of the LORD, **2Ch 33:6** 5869
He did evil in the **s** of the LORD **2Ch 33:22** 5869
He did right in the **s** of the LORD, **2Ch 34:2** 5869
evil in the **s** of the LORD his God. **2Ch 36:5** 5869
he did evil in the **s** of the LORD. **2Ch 36:9** 5869
evil in the **s** of the LORD his God; **2Ch 36:12** 5869
in the **s** of the kings of Persia, **Ezr 9:9** 6440
the book in the **s** of all the people **Ne 8:5** 5869
she obtained favor in his **s**; **Es 5:2** 5869
found favor in the **s** of the king, **Es 5:8** 5869
"If I have found favor in your **s**, **Es 7:3** 5869
king and I am pleasing in his **s**, **Es 8:5** 5869
comes at the **s** of my food, **Jb 3:24** 6440
the heavens are not pure in His **s**; **Jb 15:15** 5869
I am a foreigner in their **s**. **Jb 19:15** 5869
established with them in their **s**, **Jb 21:8** 6440
the stars are not pure in His **s**, **Jb 25:5** 5869
the falcon's eye caught **s** of it. **Jb 28:7** 7805
"His flesh wastes away from **s**, **Jb 33:21** 7210
be laid low even at the **s** of him? **Jb 41:9** 4758
are on high, out of his **s**; **Ps 10:5** 5048
my heart Be acceptable in Your **s**, **Ps 19:14** 6440
my lifetime as nothing in Your **s**; **Ps 39:5** 5048
And done what is evil in Your **s**, **Ps 51:4** 5869
blood will be precious in his **s**; **Ps 72:14** 5869
this, It was troublesome in my **s** **Ps 73:16** 5869
known among the nations in our **s**, **Ps 79:10** 5869
For a thousand years in Your **s** Are **Ps 90:4** 5869
in the **s** of the nations. **Ps 98:2** 5869
Precious in the **s** of the LORD Is **Ps 116:15** 5869
in Your **s** no man living is righteous. **Ps 143:2** 6440
to spread the *baited* net In the **s** **Pr 1:17** 5869
repute In the **s** of God and man. **Pr 3:4** 5869
let them not vanish from your **s**; **Pr 3:21** 5869
only son in the **s** of my mother, **Pr 4:3** 6440
not let them depart from your **s**; **Pr 4:21** 5869
of a man are clean in his own **s**, **Pr 16:2** 5869
is a charm in the **s** of its owner; **Pr 17:8** 5869
to a person who is good in His **s** He **Ec 2:26** 6440
give to one who is good in God's **s**. **Ec 2:26** 6440
do not be shocked at the **s**; **Ec 5:8** 2656
the evil of your deeds from My **s**. **Is 1:16** 5048, 5869
eyes And clever in their own **s**! **Is 5:21** 5048, 6440
have done what is good in Your **s**." **Is 38:3** 5869
"Since you are precious in My **s**, **Is 43:4** 5869
I am honored in the **s** of the LORD, **Is 49:5** 5869
arm In the **s** of all the nations, **Is 52:10** 5869
And it was displeasing in His **s** that **Is 59:15** 5869
And you did evil in My **s** And **Is 65:12** 5869
because they are hidden from My **s**! **Is 65:16** 5869
And they did evil in My **s** And **Is 66:4** 5869
become a den of robbers in your **s**? **Jer 7:11** 5869
"I will cast you out of My **s**, **Jer 7:15** 6440
done that which is evil in My **s**," **Jer 7:30** 5869
does evil in My **s** by not obeying **Jer 18:10** 5869
Or blot out their sin from Your **s**. **Jer 18:23** 6440
to break the jar in the **s** of the men **Jer 19:10** 5869
me as is good and right in your **s**. **Jer 26:14** 5869
the one who is pleasing in My **s**. **Jer 27:5** 5869
in the **s** of Hanamel my uncle's *son* **Jer 32:12** 5869
and in the **s** of the witnesses who **Jer 32:12** 5869
evil in My **s** from their youth; **Jer 32:30** 5869
are they as a nation in their **s**. **Jer 33:24** 6440
and done what is right in My **s**, **Jer 34:15** 5869
in the **s** of some *of the* Jews; **Jer 43:9** 5869
He did evil in the **s** of the LORD **Jer 52:2** 5869
having baked *it* in their **s** over **Ezk 4:12** 5869
among you in the **s** of the nations. **Ezk 5:8** 5869
you, in the **s** of all who pass by. **Ezk 5:14** 5869
loathe themselves in their own **s** for **Ezk 6:9** 6440
And he entered in my **s**. **Ezk 10:2** 5869
and rose up from the earth in my **s** **Ezk 10:19** 5869
go into exile by day in their **s**; **Ezk 12:3** 5869
place to another place in their **s**. **Ezk 12:3** 5869
baggage out by day in their **s**, **Ezk 12:4** 5869
will go out at evening in their **s**, **Ezk 12:4** 5869
a hole through the wall in their **s** **Ezk 12:5** 5869
baggage on *your* shoulder in their **s** **Ezk 12:6** 5869
baggage on *my* shoulder in their **s**. **Ezk 12:7** 5869
on you in the **s** of many women. **Ezk 16:41** 5869
not be profaned in the **s** of the nations **Ezk 20:9** 5869
in whose **s** I made Myself known to **Ezk 20:9** 5869
profaned in the **s** of the nations, **Ezk 20:14** 5869
before whose **s** I had brought them **Ezk 20:14** 5869
be profaned in the **s** of the nations **Ezk 20:22** 5869
in whose **s** I had brought them out. **Ezk 20:22** 5869
among you in the **s** of the nations. **Ezk 20:41** 5869

will loathe yourselves in your own **s**	**Ezk 20:43**	6440
bitter grief, groan in their **s**.	**Ezk 21:6**	5869
yourself in the **s** of the nations,	**Ezk 22:16**	5869
in them in the **s** of the nations,	**Ezk 28:25**	5869
Myself holy among you in their **s**.	**Ezk 36:23**	5869
will loathe yourselves in your own **s**	**Ezk 36:31**	6440
in the **s** of everyone who passes by.	**Ezk 36:34**	5869
known in the **s** of many nations;	**Ezk 38:23**	5869
them in the **s** of the many nations.	**Ezk 39:27**	5869
And write *it* in their **s**,	**Ezk 43:11**	5869
in the **s** of the commander of the	**Da 1:9**	6440
lewdness In the **s** of her lovers,	**Hos 2:10**	5869
will be hidden from My **s**.	**Hos 13:14**	5869
from My **s** on the floor of the sea,	**Am 9:3**	5869
'I have been expelled from Your **s**.	**Jon 2:4**	5869
'If it is too difficult in the **s**	**Zch 8:6**	5869
it also be too difficult in My **s**?'	**Zch 8:6**	5869
"If it is good in your **s**,	**Zch 11:12**	5869
is good in the **s** of the LORD,	**Mal 2:17**	5869
BLIND RECEIVE **S** and *the* lame walk,	**Mt 11:5**	*308*
this way was well-pleasing in Your **s**.	**Mt 11:26**	*1715*
regained their **s** and followed Him.	**Mt 20:34**	*308*
and went out in the **s** of everyone	**Mk 2:12**	*1715*
"Rabboni, *I want* to regain my **s**!"	**Mk 10:51**	*308*
Immediately he regained his **s**	**Mk 10:52**	*308*
both righteous in the **s** of God,	**Lk 1:6**	*1727*
be great in the **s** of the Lord;	**Lk 1:15**	*1799*
AND RECOVERY OF **S** TO THE BLIND,	**Lk 4:18**	*309*
gave **s** to many *who were* blind.	**Lk 7:21**	*991*
the BLIND RECEIVE **S**, *the* lame walk,	**Lk 7:22**	*308*
this way was well-pleasing in Your **s**.	**Lk 10:21**	*1715*
you will have honor in the **s** of all	**Lk 14:10**	*1799*
against heaven, and in your **s**;	**Lk 15:18**	*1799*
against heaven and in your **s**;	**Lk 15:21**	*1799*
yourselves in the **s** of men,	**Lk 16:15**	*1799*
men is detestable in the **s** of God.	**Lk 16:15**	*1799*
"Lord, *I want* to regain my **s**!"	**Lk 18:41**	*308*
Jesus said to him, "Receive your **s**;	**Lk 18:42**	*308*
Immediately he regained his **s** and	**Lk 18:43**	*308*
in deed and word in the **s** of God	**Lk 24:19**	*1727*
and He vanished from their **s**.	**Lk 24:31**	*846*
and washed, and I received **s**."	**Jn 9:11**	*308*
asking him again how he received his **s**.	**Jn 9:15**	*308*
been blind and had received **s**,	**Jn 9:18**	*308*
very one who had received his **s**,	**Jn 9:18**	*308*
cloud received Him out of their **s**.	**Ac 1:9**	*3788*
"Whether it is right in the **s** of God	**Ac 4:19**	*1799*
and wisdom in the **s** of Pharaoh,	**Ac 7:10**	*1727*
and he was lovely in the **s** of God,	**Ac 7:20**	*3588*
it, he marveled at the **s**;	**Ac 7:31**	*3705*
"*David* found favor in God's **s**,	**Ac 7:46**	*1799*
And he was three days without **s**,	**Ac 9:9**	*991*
so that he might regain his **s**."	**Ac 9:12**	*308*
me so that you may regain your **s** and	**Ac 9:17**	*308*
scales, and he regained his **s**,	**Ac 9:18**	*308*
burning them in the **s** of everyone;	**Ac 19:19**	*1799*
When we came in **s** of Cyprus,	**Ac 21:3**	*398*
'Brother Saul, receive your **s**!'	**Ac 22:13**	*308*
flesh will be justified in His **s**;	**Ro 3:20**	*1799*
what is right in the **s** of all men.	**Ro 12:17**	*1799*
speak in Christ in the **s** of God.	**2Co 2:17**	*2713*
man's conscience in the **s** of God.	**2Co 4:2**	*1799*
for we walk by faith, not by **s**	**2Co 5:7**	*1491b*
made known to you in the **s** of God.	**2Co 7:12**	*1799*
not only in the **s** of the Lord,	**2Co 8:21**	*1799*
Lord, but also in the **s** of men.	**2Co 8:21**	*1799*
it is in the **s** of God that we have	**2Co 12:19**	*2713*
I was *still* unknown by **s** to	**Ga 1:22**	*4383*
in the **s** of God our Savior,	**1Tm 2:3**	*1799*
is acceptable in the **s** of God.	**1Tm 5:4**	*1799*
is no creature hidden from His **s**,	**Heb 4:13**	*1799*
And so terrible was the **s**,	**Heb 12:21**	*5324*
that which is pleasing in His **s**,	**Heb 13:21**	*1799*
in the **s** of *our* God and Father is	**Jas 1:27**	*3844*
and precious in the **s** of God,	**1Pe 2:4**	*3844*
which is precious in the **s** of God.	**1Pe 3:4**	*1799*
things that are pleasing in His **s**.	**1Jn 3:22**	*1799*
completed in the **s** of My God.	**Rv 3:2**	*1799*

SIGN

the LORD appointed a **s** for Cain,	**Gn 4:15**	226
"This is the **s** of the covenant	**Gn 9:12**	226
a **s** of a covenant between Me and	**Gn 9:13**	226
"This is the **s** of the covenant	**Gn 9:17**	226
s of the covenant between Me and	**Gn 17:11**	226
and this shall be the **s** to you	**Ex 3:12**	226
heed the witness of the first **s**,	**Ex 4:8**	226
believe the witness of the last **s**.	**Ex 4:8**	226
Tomorrow this **s** will occur."	**Ex 8:23**	226
'The blood shall be a **s** for	**Ex 12:13**	226
serve as a **s** to you on your hand,	**Ex 13:9**	226
shall serve as a **s** on your hand and	**Ex 13:16**	226
for *this* is a **s** between Me and you	**Ex 31:13**	226
"It is a **s** between Me and the	**Ex 31:17**	226
for a **s** to the sons of Israel."	**Nu 16:38**	226
be kept as a **s** against the rebels,	**Nu 17:10**	226
"You shall bind them as a **s**	**Dt 6:8**	226
bind them as a **s** on your hand,	**Dt 11:18**	226
you and gives you a **s** or a wonder,	**Dt 13:1**	226
the **s** or the wonder comes true,	**Dt 13:2**	226
"They shall become a **s** and a	**Dt 28:46**	226
"Let this be a **s** among you, so	**Jos 4:6**	226
then show me a **s** that it is You	**Jg 6:17**	226
Now the appointed **s** between the	**Jg 20:38**	4150
'This will be the **s** to you	**1Sa 2:34**	226
and this shall be the **s** to us."	**1Sa 14:10**	226
Then he gave a **s** the same day,	**1Ki 13:3**	4159
the **s** which the LORD has spoken,	**1Ki 13:3**	4159
according to the **s** which the man	**1Ki 13:5**	4159
'Then this shall be the **s** for you:	**2Ki 19:29**	226
the **s** that the LORD will heal me,	**2Ki 20:8**	226
be the **s** to you from the LORD,	**2Ki 20:9**	226
spoke to him and gave him a **s**.	**2Ch 32:24**	4159
Show me a **s** for good, That those	**Ps 86:17**	226
"Ask a **s** for yourself from the	**Is 7:11**	226
Lord Himself will give you a **s**:	**Is 7:14**	226
It will become a **s** and a	**Is 19:20**	226
s and token against Egypt and Cush,	**Is 20:3**	226
"Then this shall be the **s** for you:	**Is 37:30**	226
be the **s** to you from the LORD,	**Is 38:7**	226
"What is the **s** that I shall go up	**Is 38:22**	226
s which will not be cut off."	**Is 55:13**	226
doorpost You have set up your **s**;	**Is 57:8**	2146
"I will set a **s** among them	**Is 66:19**	226
for money, **s** and seal deeds,	**Jer 32:44**	3789
'This will be the **s** to you,'	**Jer 44:29**	226
is a **s** to the house of Israel.	**Ezk 4:3**	226
as a **s** to the house of Israel."	**Ezk 12:6**	4159
'I am a **s** to you. As I have done,	**Ezk 12:11**	4159
and make him a **s** and a proverb,	**Ezk 14:8**	226
to be a **s** between Me and them,	**Ezk 20:12**	226
shall be a **s** between Me and you,	**Ezk 20:20**	226
'Thus Ezekiel will be a **s** to you;	**Ezk 24:24**	4159
Thus you will be a **s** to them,	**Ezk 24:27**	4159
s the document so that it may not	**Da 6:8**	7560
"Did you not **s** an injunction that	**Da 6:12**	7560
we want to see a **s** from You."	**Mt 12:38**	*4592*
generation craves for a **s**;	**Mt 12:39**	*4592*
and *yet* no **s** will be given to it	**Mt 12:39**	*4592*
it but the **s** of Jonah the prophet;	**Mt 12:39**	*4592*
Him to show them a **s** from heaven.	**Mt 16:1**	*4592*
generation seeks after a **s**;	**Mt 16:4**	*4592*
and a **s** will not be given it,	**Mt 16:4**	*4592*
given it, except the **s** of Jonah."	**Mt 16:4**	*4592*
what *will be* the **s** of Your coming,	**Mt 24:3**	*4592*
"And then the **s** of the Son of Man	**Mt 24:30**	*4592*
was betraying Him gave them a **s**,	**Mt 26:48**	*4592*
seeking from Him a **s** from heaven,	**Mk 8:11**	*4592*
does this generation seek for a **s**?	**Mk 8:12**	*4592*
no **s** will be given to this	**Mk 8:12**	*4592*
and what *will be* the **s** when all	**Mk 13:4**	*4592*
"This *will be* the **s** for you:	**Lk 2:12**	*4592*
Israel, and for a **s** to be opposed	**Lk 2:34**	*4592*
demanding of Him a **s** from heaven.	**Lk 11:16**	*4592*
it seeks for a **s**, and *yet* no sign	**Lk 11:29**	*4592*
and *yet* no **s** will be given to it	**Lk 11:29**	*4592*
be given to it but the **s** of Jonah.	**Lk 11:29**	*4592*
Jonah became a **s** to the Ninevites,	**Lk 11:30**	*4592*
And what *will be* the **s** when these	**Lk 21:7**	*4592*
to see some **s** performed by Him.	**Lk 23:8**	*4592*
"What **s** do You show us	**Jn 2:18**	*4592*
a second **s** that Jesus performed when	**Jn 4:54**	*4592*
saw the **s** which He had performed,	**Jn 6:14**	*4592*
"What then do You do for a **s**,	**Jn 6:30**	*4592*
"While John performed no **s**,	**Jn 10:41**	*4592*
that He had performed this **s**.	**Jn 12:18**	*4592*
he received the **s** of circumcision,	**Ro 4:11**	*4592*
So then tongues are for a **s**,	**1Co 14:22**	*4592*
but prophecy *is for a* **s**, not to	**1Co 14:22**	
is a **s** of destruction for them,	**Php 1:28**	*1732*
A great **s** appeared in heaven:	**Rv 12:1**	*4592*
Then another **s** appeared in heaven:	**Rv 12:3**	*4592*
Then I saw another **s** in heaven,	**Rv 15:1**	*4592*

SIGNAL

and His priests with the **s** trumpets	**2Ch 13:12**	8643
will stand as a **s** for the peoples;	**Is 11:10**	5251
top And as a **s** on a hill.	**Is 30:17**	5251
And raise a **s** over Beth-haccerem;	**Jer 6:1**	4864
a **s** against the walls of Babylon;	**Jer 51:12**	5251
Lift up a **s** in the land, Blow a	**Jer 51:27**	5251
betraying Him had given them a **s**,	**Mk 14:44**	*4953*

SIGNALED

so they **s** to their partners in	**Lk 5:7**	*2656*

SIGNALS

his eyes, who **s** with his feet,	**Pr 6:13**	4448b

SIGNATURE

Behold, here is my **s**;	**Jb 31:35**	8420a

SIGNED

"I **s** and sealed the deed, and	**Jer 32:10**	3789
who **s** the deed of purchase,	**Jer 32:12**	3789
King Darius **s** the document,	**Da 6:9**	7560
knew that the document was **s**,	**Da 6:10**	7560
or to the injunction which you **s**,	**Da 6:13**	7560

SIGNET

whose **s** ring and cords and staff	**Gn 38:25**	2368
took off his **s** ring from his hand and	**Gn 41:42**	2885
"As a jeweler engraves a **s**,	**Ex 28:11**	2368
and **s** rings and bracelets,	**Ex 35:22**	2885
engraved *like* the engravings of a **s**,	**Ex 39:6**	2368
engraved with the engravings of a **s**,	**Ex 39:14**	2368
it like the engravings of a **s**,	**Ex 39:30**	2368
armlets and bracelets, **s** rings,	**Nu 31:50**	2885
Then the king took his **s** ring from	**Es 3:10**	2885
and sealed with the king's **s** ring.	**Es 3:12**	2885
The king took off his **s** ring	**Es 8:2**	2885
and seal *it* with the king's **s** ring;	**Es 8:8**	2885
and sealed with the king's **s** ring	**Es 8:8**	2885
sealed it with the king's **s** ring,	**Es 8:10**	2885
were a **s** *ring* on My right hand,	**Jer 22:24**	2368
the king sealed it with his own **s** ring	**Da 6:17**	5824
with the **s** rings of his nobles,	**Da 6:17**	5824
'and I will make you like a **s** *ring*,	**Hg 2:23**	2368

SIGNIFYING

s by what kind of death He was	**Jn 18:32**	*4591*
s by what kind of death he would	**Jn 21:19**	*4591*
The Holy Spirit *is* **s** this, that the	**Heb 9:8**	*1213*

SIGNPOST

And make a **s**; make it at the head	**Ezk 21:19**	3027

SIGNS

the night, and let them be for **s** and	**Gn 1:14**	226
will not believe even these two **s**	**Ex 4:9**	226
which you shall perform the **s**."	**Ex 4:17**	226
and all the **s** that He had	**Ex 4:28**	226
the **s** in the sight of the people.	**Ex 4:30**	226
that I may multiply My **s** and My	**Ex 7:3**	226
that I may perform these **s** of Mine	**Ex 10:1**	226
how I performed My **s** among them,	**Ex 10:2**	226
despite all the **s** which I have	**Nu 14:11**	226
who have seen My glory and My **s**	**Nu 14:22**	226
by **s** and wonders and by war and by	**Dt 4:34**	226
LORD showed great and distressing **s**	**Dt 6:22**	226
trials which your eyes saw and the **s**	**Dt 7:19**	226
and His **s** and His works which He	**Dt 11:3**	226
terror and with **s** and wonders;	**Dt 26:8**	226
seen, those great **s** and wonders.	**Dt 29:3**	226
for all the **s** and wonders which	**Dt 34:11**	226
and who did these great **s** in our	**Jos 24:17**	226
shall be when these **s** come to you,	**1Sa 10:7**	226
those **s** came about on that day.	**1Sa 10:9**	226
s and wonders against Pharaoh,	**Ne 9:10**	226
the earth stand in awe of Your **s**;	**Ps 65:8**	226
set up their own standards for **s**.	**Ps 74:4**	226
We do not see our **s**;	**Ps 74:9**	226
When He performed His **s** in Egypt	**Ps 78:43**	226
s and wonders into your midst,	**Ps 135:9**	226
are for **s** and wonders in Israel	**Is 8:18**	226
And do not be terrified by the **s**	**Jer 10:2**	226
who has set **s** and wonders in the	**Jer 32:20**	226
of Egypt with **s** and with wonders,	**Jer 32:21**	226
seemed good to me to declare the **s**	**Da 4:2**	852
"How great are His **s** And	**Da 4:3**	852
rescues and performs **s** and wonders	**Da 6:27**	852
cannot *discern* the **s** of the times?	**Mt 16:3**	*4592*
and will show great **s** and wonders,	**Mt 24:24**	*4592*
and will show **s** and wonders,	**Mk 13:22**	*4592*
"These **s** will accompany those	**Mk 16:17**	*4592*
the word by the **s** that followed.]	**Mk 16:20**	*4592*
and he kept making **s** to them,	**Lk 1:22**	*1269*
And they made **s** to his father, as	**Lk 1:62**	*1770*
not coming with **s** to be observed;	**Lk 17:20**	*3907*
terrors and great **s** from heaven.	**Lk 21:11**	*4592*
be **s** in sun and moon and stars,	**Lk 21:25**	*4592*
This beginning of *His* **s** Jesus did in	**Jn 2:11**	*4592*
His **s** which He was doing.	**Jn 2:23**	*4592*
for no one can do these **s** that You	**Jn 3:2**	*4592*
you *people* see **s** and wonders,	**Jn 4:48**	*4592*
because they saw the **s**	**Jn 6:2**	*4592*
seek Me, not because you saw **s**,	**Jn 6:26**	*4592*
He will not perform more **s** than	**Jn 7:31**	*4592*
who is a sinner perform such **s**?"	**Jn 9:16**	*4592*
For this man is performing many **s**.	**Jn 11:47**	*4592*
performed so many **s** before them,	**Jn 12:37**	*4592*
Therefore many other **s** Jesus also	**Jn 20:30**	*4592*
ABOVE AND **S** ON THE EARTH BELOW,	**Ac 2:19**	*4592*
s which God performed through Him	**Ac 2:22**	*4592*
and many wonders and **s** were taking	**Ac 2:43**	*4592*
and **s** and wonders take place	**Ac 4:30**	*4592*
s and wonders were taking place	**Ac 5:12**	*4592*
wonders and **s** among the people.	**Ac 6:8**	*4592*
performing wonders and **s** in the	**Ac 7:36**	*4592*
saw the **s** which he was performing.	**Ac 8:6**	*4592*
as he observed **s** and great miracles	**Ac 8:13**	*4592*
granting that **s** and wonders be	**Ac 14:3**	*4592*
what **s** and wonders God had done	**Ac 15:12**	*4592*
in the power of **s** and wonders, in	**Ro 15:19**	*4592*
For indeed Jews ask for **s** and	**1Co 1:22**	*4592*
The **s** of a true apostle were	**2Co 12:12**	*4592*
by **s** and wonders and miracles.	**2Co 12:12**	*4592*
all power and **s** and false wonders,	**2Th 2:9**	*4592*
both by **s** and wonders and by	**Heb 2:4**	*4592*
He performs great **s**,	**Rv 13:13**	*4592*
because of the **s** which it was given	**Rv 13:14**	*4592*
spirits of demons, performing **s**,	**Rv 16:14**	*4592*
performed the **s** in his presence,	**Rv 19:20**	*4592*

SIHON

Then Israel sent messengers to **S**,	**Nu 21:21**	5511
But **S** would not permit Israel to	**Nu 21:23**	5511
So **S** gathered all his people and	**Nu 21:23**	5511
For Heshbon was the city of **S**,	**Nu 21:26**	5511
let the city of **S** be established.	**Nu 21:27**	5511
A flame from the town of **S**;	**Nu 21:28**	5511
captivity, To an Amorite king, **S**.	**Nu 21:29**	5511
shall do to him as you did to **S**,	**Nu 21:34**	5511
son Manasseh, the kingdom of **S**,	**Nu 32:33**	5511
S the king of the Amorites,	**Dt 1:4**	5511
I have given **S** the Amorite, king	**Dt 2:24**	5511
to **S** king of Heshbon with words of	**Dt 2:26**	5511
"But **S** king of Heshbon was not	**Dt 2:30**	5511
I have begun to deliver **S** and his	**Dt 2:31**	5511
"Then **S** with all his people came	**Dt 2:32**	5511
you did to **S** king of the Amorites,	**Dt 3:2**	5511
as we did to **S** king of Heshbon,	**Dt 3:6**	5511
the land of **S** king of the Amorites	**Dt 4:46**	5511
S the king of Heshbon and Og the	**Dt 29:7**	5511
them just as He did to **S** and Og,	**Dt 31:4**	5511
beyond the Jordan, to **S** and Og,	**Jos 2:10**	5511
to **S** king of Heshbon and to Og	**Jos 9:10**	5511
S king of the Amorites, who lived	**Jos 12:2**	5511
the border of **S** king of Heshbon.	**Jos 12:5**	5511
cities of **S** king of the Amorites,	**Jos 13:10**	5511
kingdom of **S** king of the Amorites	**Jos 13:21**	5511
Hur and Reba, the princes of **S**,	**Jos 13:21**	5511
the kingdom of **S** king of Heshbon,	**Jos 13:27**	5511
to **S** king of the Amorites,	**Jg 11:19**	5511

‘But **S** did not trust Israel to **Jg 11:20** 5511
so **S** gathered all his people and **Jg 11:20** 5511
gave **S** and all his people into the **Jg 11:21** 5511
country of **S** king of the Amorites **1Ki 4:19** 5511
the land of **S** the king of Heshbon And **Ne 9:22** 5511
S, king of the Amorites, And Og, **Ps 135:11** 5511
S, king of the Amorites, For His **Ps 136:19** 5511
And a flame from the midst of **S**, **Jer 48:45** 5511

SIKKUTH

along **S** your king and Kiyyun, **Am 5:26** 5522

SILAS

Judas called Barsabbas, and **S**, **Ac 15:22** *4609*
we have sent Judas and **S**, **Ac 15:27** *4609*
Judas and **S**, also being **Ac 15:32** *4609*
seemed good to **S** to remain there.] **Ac 15:34** *4609*
But Paul chose **S** and left, **Ac 15:40** *4609*
they seized Paul and **S** and dragged **Ac 16:19** *4609*
But about midnight Paul and **S** were **Ac 16:25** *4609*
he fell down before Paul and **S**, **Ac 16:29** *4609*
persuaded and joined Paul and **S**, **Ac 17:4** *4609*
immediately sent Paul and **S** away **Ac 17:10** *4609*
and **S** and Timothy remained there. **Ac 17:14** *4609*
a command for **S** and Timothy to **Ac 17:15** *4609*
But when **S** and Timothy came down **Ac 18:5** *4609*

SILENCE

the man was gazing at her in **s**, **Gn 24:21** 2790b
And he said, “Keep **s**.” **Jg 3:19** 2013
There was **s**, then I heard a voice: **Jb 4:16** 1827
“Shall your boasts **s** men? **Jb 11:3** 2790b
not keep **s** concerning his limbs, **Jb 41:12** 2790b
May our God come and not keep **s**; **Ps 50:3** 2790b
you have done and I kept **s**; **Ps 50:21** 2790b
My soul *waits* in **s** for God only; **Ps 62:1** 1747
My soul, wait in **s** for God only, **Ps 62:5** 1826a
There will be **s** before You, *and* **Ps 65:1** 1747
soon have dwelt in *the abode of* **s**. **Ps 94:17** 1745
Nor *do* any who go down into **s**; **Ps 115:17** 1745
“Coastlands, listen to Me in **s**, **Is 41:1** 2790b
I will **s** the sound of your songs, **Ezk 26:13** 7673a
they will cast them forth in **s**.” **Am 8:3** 2013
s the ignorance of foolish men. **1Pe 2:15** *5392*
there was **s** in heaven for about **Rv 8:1** *4602*

SILENCED

the wicked ones are **s** in darkness; **1Sa 2:9** 1826a
But I am not **s** by the darkness, **Jb 23:17** 6789
the song of the ruthless is **s**. **Is 25:5** 6031a
You too, Madmen, will be **s**; **Jer 48:2** 1826a
men of war will be **s** in that day,” **Jer 49:26** 1826a
men of war will be **s** in that day,” **Jer 50:30** 1826a
They have **s** me in the pit And have **La 3:53** 6789
the people of Canaan will be **s**; **Zph 1:11** 1820
the Pharisees heard that Jesus had **s** **Mt 22:34** *5392*
who must be **s** because they are **Ti 1:11** *1993*

SILENT

Jacob kept **s** until they came in. **Gn 34:5** 2790b
fight for you while you keep **s**.” **Ex 14:14** 2790b
So Aaron, therefore, kept **s**. **Lv 10:3** 1826a
“Be **s** and listen, O Israel! **Dt 27:9** 5535
And they kept **s** all night, saying, **Jg 16:2** 2790b
“Be **s**, put your hand over your **Jg 18:19** 2790b
But he kept **s**. **1Sa 10:27** 2790b
But now keep **s**, my sister, he is **2Sa 13:20** 2790b
s about bringing the king back?” **2Sa 19:10** 2790b
good news, but we are keeping **s**; **2Ki 7:9** 2814
But the people were **s** and answered **2Ki 18:36** 2790b
Then they were **s** and could not **Ne 5:8** 2790b
“For if you remain **s** at this time, **Es 4:14** 2790b
women, I would have remained **s**, **Es 7:4** 2790b
they become waterless, they are **s**, **Jb 6:17** 6789
“Teach me, and I will be **s**; **Jb 6:24** 2790b
“O that you would be completely **s**, **Jb 13:5** 2790b
Be **s** before me so that I may speak; **Jb 13:13** 2790b
For then I would be **s** and die. **Jb 13:19** 2790b
waited, And kept **s** for my counsel. **Jb 29:21** 1826a
kept **s** and did not go out of doors? **Jb 31:34** 1826a
Keep **s**, and let me speak. **Jb 33:31** 2790b
Keep **s**, and I will teach you **Jb 33:33** 2790b
to me, For if You are **s** to me, **Ps 28:1** 2814
sing praise to You and not be **s**. **Ps 30:12** 1826a
to shame, let them be **s** in Sheol. **Ps 31:17** 1826a
When I kept **s** *about my sin,* my **Ps 32:3** 2790b
seen it, O LORD, do not keep **s**; **Ps 35:22** 2790b
I was mute and **s**, I refrained *even* **Ps 39:2** 1747
Do not be **s** at my tears; **Ps 39:12** 2790b
Do not be **s** and, O God, do not be **Ps 83:1** 2790b
O God of my praise, Do not be **s**! **Ps 109:1** 2790b
a man of understanding keeps **s**. **Pr 11:12** 2790b
Even a fool, when he keeps **s**, **Pr 17:28** 2790b
A time to be **s** and a time to **Ec 3:7** 2814
Be **s**, you inhabitants of the **Is 23:2** 1826a
But they were **s** and answered him **Is 36:21** 2790b
“I have kept **s** for a long time, I **Is 42:14** 2814
a sheep that is **s** before its shearers, **Is 53:7** 481
Was I not **s** even for a long time **Is 57:11** 2814
For Zion’s sake I will not keep **s**, **Is 62:1** 2814
all night they will never keep **s**. **Is 62:6** 2814
Will You keep **s** and afflict us **Is 64:12** 2814
before Me, I will not keep **s**, **Is 65:6** 2814
I cannot be **s**, Because you have **Jer 4:19** 2790b
peaceful folds are made **s** Because of **Jer 25:37** 1826a
Sit on the ground, they are **s**. **La 2:10** 1826a
Let him sit alone and be **s** Since He **La 3:28** 1826a
who is **s** in the midst of the sea? **Ezk 27:32** 1822
a time the prudent person keeps **s**, **Am 5:13** 1826a
Why are You **s** when the wicked **Hab 1:13** 2790b
Let all the earth be **s** before Him.” **Hab 2:20** 2013
Be **s** before the Lord GOD! **Zph 1:7** 2013
“Be **s**, all flesh, before the LORD; **Zch 2:13** 2013
But Jesus kept **s**. **Mt 26:63** *4623*
But they kept **s**. **Mk 3:4** *4623*
But they kept **s**, for on the way **Mk 9:34** *4623*
But He kept **s** and did not answer. **Mk 14:61** *4623*
you shall be **s** and unable to speak **Lk 1:20** *4623*
And they kept **s**, and reported to **Lk 9:36** *4601*
But they kept **s**. And He took hold **Lk 14:4** *2270*
“I tell you, if these become **s**, **Lk 19:40** *4623*
at His answer, they became **s**. **Lk 20:26** *4601*
AS A LAMB BEFORE ITS SHEARER IS **S**, **Ac 8:32** *880*
to them with his hand to be **s**, **Ac 12:17** *4601*
All the people kept **s**, **Ac 15:12** *4601*
go on speaking and do not be **s**; **Ac 18:9** *4623*
would not be persuaded, we fell **s**, **Ac 21:14** *2270*
he must keep **s** in the church; **1Co 14:28** *4601*
is seated, the first one must keep **s**. **1Co 14:30** *4601*
women are to keep **s** in the churches; **1Co 14:34** *4601*

SILENTLY

“Sit **s**, and go into darkness, O **Is 47:5** 1748
that he waits **s** For the salvation of **La 3:26** 1748
“Groan **s**; make no mourning for **Ezk 24:17** 1826a

SILK

fine linen and covered you with **s**. **Ezk 16:10** 4897
your dress was of fine linen, **s** and **Ezk 16:13** 4897
and purple and **s** and scarlet, **Rv 18:12** *4596*

SILL

Eutychus sitting on the window **s**, **Ac 20:9** *2376*

SILLA

Millo *as he was* going down to **S**. **2Ki 12:20** 5538

SILLY

Ephraim has become like a **s** dove, **Hos 7:11** 6601b
must be no filthiness and **s** talk, **Eph 5:4** *3473*

SILOAM

tower in **S** fell and killed them were **Lk 13:4** *4611*
“Go, wash in the pool of **S**” **Jn 9:7** *4611*
‘Go to **S** and wash’; **Jn 9:11** *4611*

SILVANUS

by me and **S** and Timothy **2Co 1:19** *4610*
Paul and **S** and Timothy, To the **1Th 1:1** *4610*
Paul and **S** and Timothy, To the **2Th 1:1** *4610*
Through **S**, our faithful brother **1Pe 5:12** *4610*

SILVER

rich in livestock, in **s** and in gold. **Gn 13:2** 3701
brother a thousand pieces of **s**; **Gn 20:16** 3701
worth four hundred shekels of **s**, **Gn 23:15** 3701
weighed out for Ephron the **s** **Gn 23:16** 3701
Heth, four hundred shekels of **s**, **Gn 23:16** 3701
flocks and herds, and **s** and gold, **Gn 24:35** 3701
articles of **s** and articles of gold, **Gn 24:53** 3701
for twenty *shekels* of **s**. **Gn 37:28** 3701
“Put my cup, the **s** cup, **Gn 44:2** 3701
How then could we steal **s** or gold **Gn 44:8** 3701
he gave three hundred *pieces of* **s** **Gn 45:22** 3701
articles of **s** and articles of gold, **Ex 3:22** 3701
articles of **s** and articles of gold.” **Ex 11:2** 3701
articles of **s** and articles of gold, **Ex 12:35** 3701
gods of **s** or gods of gold, you **Ex 20:23** 3701
or her master thirty shekels of **s**, **Ex 21:32** 3701
gold, **s** and bronze, **Ex 25:3** 3701
You shall make forty sockets of **s** **Ex 26:19** 3701
and their forty sockets of **s**; **Ex 26:21** 3701
boards with their sockets of **s**, **Ex 26:25** 3701
of gold, on four sockets of **s**. **Ex 26:32** 3701
and their bands *shall be* of **s**. **Ex 27:10** 3701
and their bands *shall be* of **s**. **Ex 27:11** 3701
shall be furnished with **s** bands **Ex 27:17** 3701
silver bands *with* their hooks of **s** **Ex 27:17** 3701
designs for work in gold, in **s**, **Ex 31:4** 3701
gold, **s**, and bronze, **Ex 35:5** 3701
who could make a contribution of **s** **Ex 35:24** 3701
in gold and in **s** and in bronze, **Ex 35:32** 3701
and he made forty sockets of **s** **Ex 36:24** 3701
and their forty sockets of **s**; **Ex 36:26** 3701
boards with their sockets of **s**, **Ex 36:30** 3701
cast four sockets of **s** for them. **Ex 36:36** 3701
pillars and their bands *were* of **s**. **Ex 38:10** 3701
pillars and their bands *were* of **s**. **Ex 38:11** 3701
pillars and their bands *were* of **s**. **Ex 38:12** 3701
the pillars and their bands, of **s**; **Ex 38:17** 3701
overlaying of their tops, of **s**, **Ex 38:17** 3701
court were furnished with **s** bands. **Ex 38:17** 3701
their hooks *were* of **s**, **Ex 38:19** 3701
tops and their bands *were* of **s**. **Ex 38:19** 3701
The **s** of those of the congregation **Ex 38:25** 3701
The hundred talents of **s** were **Ex 38:27** 3701
to your valuation in **s** by shekels, **Lv 5:15** 3701
not give him your **s** at interest, **Lv 25:37** 3701
shall be fifty shekels of **s**, **Lv 27:3** 3701
be five shekels of **s** for the male, **Lv 27:6** 3701
shall be three shekels of **s**. **Lv 27:6** 3701
barley seed at fifty shekels of **s**. **Lv 27:16** 3701
and his offering *was* one **s** dish **Nu 7:13** 3701
one **s** bowl of seventy shekels, **Nu 7:13** 3701
he presented as his offering one **s** dish **Nu 7:19** 3701
one **s** bowl of seventy shekels, **Nu 7:19** 3701
his offering *was* one **s** dish whose **Nu 7:25** 3701
one **s** bowl of seventy shekels, **Nu 7:25** 3701
his offering *was* one **s** dish whose **Nu 7:31** 3701
one **s** bowl of seventy shekels, **Nu 7:31** 3701
his offering *was* one **s** dish whose **Nu 7:37** 3701
one **s** bowl of seventy shekels, **Nu 7:37** 3701
his offering *was* one **s** dish whose **Nu 7:43** 3701
one **s** bowl of seventy shekels, **Nu 7:43** 3701
his offering *was* one **s** dish whose **Nu 7:49** 3701
one **s** bowl of seventy shekels, **Nu 7:49** 3701
his offering *was* one **s** dish whose **Nu 7:55** 3701
one **s** bowl of seventy shekels, **Nu 7:55** 3701
his offering *was* one **s** dish whose **Nu 7:61** 3701
one **s** bowl of seventy shekels, **Nu 7:61** 3701
his offering *was* one **s** dish whose **Nu 7:67** 3701
one **s** bowl of seventy shekels, **Nu 7:67** 3701
his offering *was* one **s** dish whose **Nu 7:73** 3701
one **s** bowl of seventy shekels, **Nu 7:73** 3701
his offering *was* one **s** dish whose **Nu 7:79** 3701
one **s** bowl of seventy shekels, **Nu 7:79** 3701
twelve **s** dishes, twelve silver **Nu 7:84** 3701
silver dishes, twelve **s** bowls, **Nu 7:84** 3701
each **s** dish *weighing* one hundred **Nu 7:85** 3701
all the **s** of the utensils *was* **Nu 7:85** 3701
“Make yourself two trumpets of **s**, **Nu 10:2** 3701
your valuation, five shekels in **s**, **Nu 18:16** 3701
me his house full of **s** and gold, **Nu 22:18** 3701
me his house full of **s** and gold, **Nu 24:13** 3701
only the gold and the **s**, **Nu 31:22** 3701
the **s** or the gold that is on them, **Dt 7:25** 3701
and your **s** and gold multiply, **Dt 8:13** 3701
increase **s** and gold for himself. **Dt 17:17** 3701
shall fine him a hundred *shekels* of **s** **Dt 22:19** 3701
girl’s father fifty *shekels* of **s**, **Dt 22:29** 3701
and their idols of wood, stone, **s**, **Dt 29:17** 3701
“But all the **s** and gold and **Jos 6:19** 3701
Only the **s** and gold, and articles **Jos 6:24** 3701
two hundred shekels of **s** and a bar **Jos 7:21** 3701
tent with the **s** underneath it.” **Jos 7:21** 3701
his tent with the **s** underneath it. **Jos 7:22** 3701
Achan the son of Zerah, the **s**, **Jos 7:24** 3701
with very much livestock, with **s**, **Jos 22:8** 3701
They took no plunder in **s**. **Jg 5:19** 3701
They gave him seventy *pieces* of **s** **Jg 9:4** 3701
you eleven hundred *pieces* of **s**.” **Jg 16:5** 3701
“The eleven hundred *pieces* of **s** **Jg 17:2** 3701
hearing, behold, the **s** is with me; **Jg 17:2** 3701
hundred *pieces* of **s** to his mother, **Jg 17:3** 3701
“I wholly dedicate the **s** from my **Jg 17:3** 3701
he returned the **s** to his mother, **Jg 17:4** 3701
mother took two hundred *pieces* of **s** **Jg 17:4** 3701
give you ten *pieces* of **s** a year, **Jg 17:10** 3701
a piece of **s** or a loaf of bread and **1Sa 2:36** 3701
my hand a fourth of a shekel of **s**; **1Sa 9:8** 3701
brought with him articles of **s**, **2Sa 8:10** 3701
with the **s** and gold that he had **2Sa 8:11** 3701
you ten *pieces* of **s** and a belt.” **2Sa 18:11** 3701
a thousand *pieces of* **s** in my hand, **2Sa 18:12** 3701
“We have no *concern* of **s** or gold **2Sa 21:4** 3701
the oxen for fifty shekels of **s**. **2Sa 24:24** 3701
s and the gold and the utensils. **1Ki 7:51** 3701
None was of **s**; it was not considered **1Ki 10:21** 3701
Tarshish came bringing gold and **s**, **1Ki 10:22** 3701
his gift, articles of **s** and gold, **1Ki 10:25** 3701
The king made **s** *as common* as **1Ki 10:27** 3701
from Egypt for 600 *shekels* of **s**, **1Ki 10:29** 3701
s and gold and utensils. **1Ki 15:15** 3701
Asa took all the **s** and the gold **1Ki 15:18** 3701
sent you a present of **s** and gold; **1Ki 15:19** 3701
from Shemer for two talents of **s**; **1Ki 16:24** 3701
‘Your **s** and your gold are mine; **1Ki 20:3** 3701
‘You shall give me your **s** and **1Ki 20:5** 3701
my children and my **s** and my gold, **1Ki 20:7** 3701
else you shall pay a talent of **s**.’ **1Ki 20:39** 3701
took with him ten talents of **s** **2Ki 5:5** 3701
Please give them a talent of **s** and **2Ki 5:22** 3701
and bound two talents of **s** in two **2Ki 5:23** 3701
was sold for eighty *shekels* of **s**, **2Ki 6:25** 3701
dove’s dung for five *shekels* of **s**. **2Ki 6:25** 3701
from there **s** and gold and clothes, **2Ki 7:8** 3701
for the house of the LORD **s** cups, **2Ki 12:13** 3701
or vessels of **s** from the money **2Ki 12:13** 3701
He took all the gold and **s** and **2Ki 14:14** 3701
gave Pul a thousand talents of **s** **2Ki 15:19** 3701
from each man fifty shekels of **s** **2Ki 15:20** 3701
Ahaz took the **s** and gold that **2Ki 16:8** 3701
three hundred talents of **s** and **2Ki 18:14** 3701
Hezekiah gave *him* all the **s** **2Ki 18:15** 3701
the **s** and the gold and the spices **2Ki 20:13** 3701
talents of **s** and a talent of gold. **2Ki 23:33** 3701
gave the **s** and gold to Pharaoh, **2Ki 23:35** 3701
He exacted the **s** and gold from the **2Ki 23:35** 3701
was fine gold and what was fine **s**. **2Ki 25:15** 3701
articles of gold and **s** and bronze. **1Ch 18:10** 3701
with the **s** and the gold which he had **1Ch 18:11** 3701
sons of Ammon sent 1,000 talents of **s** **1Ch 19:6** 3701
gold and 1,000,000 talents of **s**, **1Ch 22:14** 3701
the **s** and the bronze and the iron there **1Ch 22:16** 3701
for the **s** utensils, the weight of **1Ch 28:14** 3701
the weight *of* **s** for all utensils **1Ch 28:14**
and *the weight of* **s** for **1Ch 28:15**
of silver for the **s** lampstands, **1Ch 28:15** 3701
and **s** for the silver tables; **1Ch 28:16** 3701
and silver for the **s** tables; **1Ch 28:16** 3701
and for the **s** bowls with the **1Ch 28:17** 3701
the **s** for the *things of* silver, **1Ch 29:2** 3701
the silver for the *things of* **s**, **1Ch 29:2** 3701
the treasure I have of gold and **s**, **1Ch 29:3** 3701
and 7,000 talents of refined **s**, **1Ch 29:4** 3701
and of **s** for the *things of* silver, **1Ch 29:5** 3701
and of silver for the *things of* **s**, **1Ch 29:5** 3701
of gold, and 10,000 talents of **s**, **1Ch 29:7** 3701
The king made **s** and gold as **2Ch 1:15** 3701
Egypt for 600 *shekels* of **s** apiece and **2Ch 1:17** 3701
a skilled man to work in gold, **s**, **2Ch 2:7** 3701
who knows how to work in gold, **s**, **2Ch 2:14** 3701
even the **s** and the gold and all **2Ch 5:1** 3701
brought gold and **s** to Solomon. **2Ch 9:14** 3701
s was not considered valuable in **2Ch 9:20** 3701
Tarshish came bringing gold and **s**, **2Ch 9:21** 3701
his gift, articles of **s** and gold, **2Ch 9:24** 3701

The king made s *as common* as 2Ch 9:27 3701
s and gold and utensils. 2Ch 15:18 3701
Then Asa brought out s and gold 2Ch 16:2 3701
I have sent you s and gold; 2Ch 16:3 3701
and s as tribute to Jehoshaphat; 2Ch 17:11 3701
father gave them many gifts of s, 2Ch 21:3 3701
pans and utensils of gold and s. 2Ch 24:14 3701
for one hundred talents of s. 2Ch 25:6 3701
He took all the gold and s 2Ch 25:24 3701
year one hundred talents of s, 2Ch 27:5 3701
made for himself treasuries for s, 2Ch 32:27 3701
a fine of one hundred talents of s 2Ch 36:3 3701
place support him with s and gold, Ezr 1:4 3701
them with articles of s, Ezr 1:6 3701
30 gold dishes, 1,000 s dishes, Ezr 1:9 3701
410 s bowls of a second *kind and* Ezr 1:10 3701
of gold and s *numbered* 5,400. Ezr 1:11 3701
gold drachmas and 5,000 s minas Ezr 2:69 3701
'Also the gold and s utensils Ezr 5:14 3702
s utensils of the house of God, Ezr 6:5 3702
and to bring the s and gold, Ezr 7:15 3702
with all the s and gold which you Ezr 7:16 3702
with the rest of the s and gold, Ezr 7:18 3702
even up to 100 talents of s, Ezr 7:22 3702
and I weighed out to them the s, Ezr 8:25 3701
into their hands 650 talents of s, Ezr 8:26 3701
and s utensils *worth* 100 talents, Ezr 8:26 3701
and the s and the gold are a Ezr 8:28 3701
out s and gold and the utensils, Ezr 8:30 3701
the s and the gold and the utensils Ezr 8:33 3701
wine besides forty shekels of s; Ne 5:15 3701
gold drachmas and 2,200 s minas. Ne 7:71 3701
gold drachmas and 2,000 s minas and Ne 7:72 3701
on s rings and marble columns, Es 1:6 3701
and couches of gold and s on a Es 1:6 3701
I will pay ten thousand talents of s Es 3:9 3701
"The s is yours, and the people Es 3:11 3701
were filling their houses *with* s. Jb 3:15 3701
be your gold And choice s to you. Jb 22:25 3701
"Though he piles up s like dust And Jb 27:16 3701
the innocent will divide the s. Jb 27:17 3701
"Surely there is a mine for s And Jb 28:1 3701
Nor can s be weighed as its price. Jb 28:15 3701
As s tried in a furnace on the Ps 12:6 3701
have refined us as s is refined. Ps 66:10 3701
wings of a dove covered with s, Ps 68:13 3701
under foot the pieces of s; Ps 68:30 3701
brought them out with s and gold, Ps 105:37 3701
Their idols are s and gold, The Ps 115:4 3701
thousands of gold and s *pieces.* Ps 119:72 3701
of the nations are *but* s and gold, Ps 135:15 3701
If you seek her as s And Pr 2:4 3701
is better than the profit of s And Pr 3:14 3701
"Take my instruction and not s, Pr 8:10 3701
And my yield *better* than choicest s. Pr 8:19 3701
of the righteous is *as* choice s, Pr 10:20 3701
is to be chosen above s. Pr 16:16 3701
The refining pot is for s and the Pr 17:3 3701
Favor is better than s and gold. Pr 22:1 3701
Take away the dross from the s, Pr 25:4 3701
Like apples of gold in settings of s Pr 25:11 3701
earthen vessel overlaid with s dross Pr 26:23 3701
The crucible is for s and the furnace Pr 27:21 3701
I collected for myself s and gold and Ec 2:8 3701
Remember Him before the s cord is Ec 12:6 3701
of gold With beads of s." SS 1:11 3701
"He made its posts of s, SS 3:10 3701
build on her a battlement of s; SS 8:9 3701
shekels of s for its fruit. SS 8:11 3701
Your s has become dross, Your Is 1:22 3701
also been filled with s and gold Is 2:7 3701
idols of s and their idols of gold, Is 2:20 3701
valued at a thousand *shekels* of s, Is 7:23 3701
value s or take pleasure in gold. Is 13:17 3701
graven images overlaid with s, Is 30:22 3701
his s idols and his gold idols, Is 31:7 3701
the s and the gold and the spices Is 39:2 3701
silversmith *fashions* chains of s. Is 40:19 3701
And weigh s on the scale Hire a Is 46:6 3701
I have refined you, but not as s; Is 48:10 3701
Their s and their gold with them, Is 60:9 3701
instead of iron I will bring s, Is 60:17 3701
They call them rejected s, Jer 6:30 3701
decorate *it* with s and with gold; Jer 10:4 3701
Beaten s is brought from Tarshish, Jer 10:9 3701
and I weighed out the s for him, Jer 32:9 3701
for him, seventeen shekels of s. Jer 32:9 3701
weighed out the s on the scales. Jer 32:10 3701
was fine gold and what was fine s. Jer 52:19 3701
fling their s into the streets and Ezk 7:19 3701
their s and their gold will not Ezk 7:19 3701
you were adorned with gold and s, Ezk 16:13 3701
made of My gold and of My s, Ezk 16:17 3701
they are the dross of s. Ezk 22:18 3701
'As they gather s and bronze and Ezk 22:20 3701
'As s is melted in the furnace, so Ezk 22:22 3701
with s, iron, tin and lead they Ezk 27:12 3701
gold and s for your treasuries. Ezk 28:4 3701
plunder, to carry away s and gold, Ezk 38:13 3701
its breast and its arms of s, Da 2:32 3702
the s and the gold were crushed Da 2:35 3702
iron, the bronze, the clay, the s and Da 2:45 3702
orders to bring the gold and s vessels Da 5:2 3702
praised the gods of gold and s, Da 5:4 3702
praised the gods of s and gold, Da 5:23 3702
vessels of s and gold he will take Da 11:8 3701
he will honor *him* with gold, s, Da 11:38 3701
hidden treasures of gold and s and Da 11:43 3701
And lavished on her s and gold, Hos 2:8 3701
her for myself for fifteen *shekels* of s Hos 3:2 3701
With their s and gold they have Hos 8:4 3701
take over their treasures of s; Hos 9:6 3701
skillfully made from their s, Hos 13:2 3701
you have taken My s and My gold, Jl 3:5 3701
Plunder the s! Plunder the gold! Na 2:9 3701
it is overlaid with gold and s, Hab 2:19 3701
who weigh out s will be cut off. Zph 1:11 3701
Neither their s nor their gold Zph 1:18 3701
'The s is Mine and the gold is Hg 2:8 3701
'Take s and gold, make an Zch 6:11 3701
fortress And piled up s like dust, Zch 9:3 3701
thirty *shekels* of s as my wages. Zch 11:12 3701
So I took the thirty *shekels* of s Zch 11:13 3701
fire, Refine them as s is refined, Zch 13:9 3701
gold and s and garments in great Zch 14:14 3701
as a smelter and purifier of s, Mal 3:3 3701
and refine them like gold and s, Mal 3:3 3701
"Do not acquire gold, or s, Mt 10:9 *696*
out thirty pieces of s to him. Mt 26:15 *694*
and returned the thirty pieces of s Mt 27:3 *694*
And he threw the pieces of s into Mt 27:5 *694*
The chief priests took the pieces of s Mt 27:6 *694*
THEY TOOK THE THIRTY PIECES OF S, Mt 27:9 *694*
if she has ten s coins and loses one Lk 15:8 *1406*
"I do not possess s and gold, Ac 3:6 *694*
"May your s perish with you, Ac 8:20 *694*
Nature is like gold or s or stone, Ac 17:29 *696*
it fifty thousand pieces of s. Ac 19:19 *694*
who made s shrines of Artemis, Ac 19:24 *693*
no one's s or gold or clothes. Ac 20:33 *694*
gold, s, precious stones, wood, hay, 1Co 3:12 *694*
are not only gold and s vessels, 2Tm 2:20 *693*
Your gold and your s have rusted; Jas 5:3 *696*
with perishable things like s or gold 1Pe 1:18 *694*
and the idols of gold and of s and Rv 9:20 *693*
cargoes of gold and s and precious Rv 18:12 *696*

SILVERSMITH
s who made them into a graven image Jg 17:4 6884
And a s *fashions* chains of silver. Is 40:19 6884
a man named Demetrius, a s, Ac 19:24 *695*

SIMEON
So she named him S. Gn 29:33 8095
two of Jacob's sons, S and Levi, Gn 34:25 8095
Then Jacob said to S and Levi, Gn 34:30 8095
then S and Levi and Judah and Gn 35:23 8095
he took S from them and bound him Gn 42:24 8095
is no more, and S is no more, Gn 42:36 8095
Then he brought S out to them. Gn 43:23 8095
The sons of S: Gn 46:10 8095
be mine, as Reuben and S are. Gn 48:5 8095
"S and Levi are brothers; Gn 49:5 8095
Reuben, S, Levi and Judah; Ex 1:2 8095
The sons of S: Ex 6:15 8095
these are the families of S. Ex 6:15 8095
of S, Shelumiel the son of Nu 1:6 8095
Of the sons of S, their Nu 1:22 8095
numbered men of the tribe of S Nu 1:23 8095
to him *shall be* the tribe of S, Nu 2:12 8095
and the leader of the sons of S: Nu 2:12 8095
leader of the children of S; Nu 7:36 8095
the tribal army of the sons of S, Nu 10:19 8095
from the tribe of S, Nu 13:5 8095
sons of S according to their families: Nu 26:12 8095
"Of the tribe of the sons of S, Nu 34:20 8095
S, Levi, Judah, Issachar, Joseph, Dt 27:12 8095
Then the second lot fell to S, Jos 19:1 8095
Simeon, to the tribe of the sons of S Jos 19:1 8095
the tribe of the sons of S according Jos 19:8 8095
The inheritance of the sons of S Jos 19:9 8095
so the sons of S received *an* Jos 19:9 8095
from the tribe of the sons of S; Jos 21:9 8095
Then Judah said to S his brother, Jg 1:3 8095
So S went with him. Jg 1:3 8095
Judah went with S his brother, Jg 1:17 8095
Reuben, S, Levi, Judah, Issachar, 1Ch 2:1 8095
sons of S *were* Nemuel and Jamin, 1Ch 4:24 8095
From them, from the sons of S, 1Ch 4:42 8095
Judah, the tribe of the sons of S and 1Ch 6:65 8095
Of the sons of S, mighty men of 1Ch 12:25 8095
and S who resided with them, 2Ch 15:9 8095
cities of Manasseh, Ephraim, S, 2Ch 34:6 8095
the east side to the west side, S, Ezk 48:24 8095
"Beside the border of S, Ezk 48:25 8095
the gate of S, one; Ezk 48:33 8095
man in Jerusalem whose name was S; Lk 2:25 *4826*
And S blessed them and said to Lk 2:34 *4826*
the son of S, the son of Judah, Lk 3:30 *4826*
and S who was called Niger, Ac 13:1 *4826*
"S has related how God first Ac 15:14 *4826*
the tribe of S twelve thousand, Rv 7:7 *4826*

SIMEONITES
a father's household among the S. Nu 25:14 8099
These are the families of the S, Nu 26:14 8099
from the tribe of the S and from the Jos 21:4 8099
for the S, Shephatiah the son of 1Ch 27:16 8099

SIMILAR
words s to all those of Jeremiah. Jer 26:20
many s words were added to them. Jer 36:32
"In a s way these are the Mk 4:16 *3668*
with the workmen of s *trades,* Ac 19:25 *5108*

SIMILARLY
to Penuel and spoke s to them; Jg 8:8 2088

SIMON
brothers, S who was called Peter, Mt 4:18 *4613*
The first, S, who is called Peter, Mt 10:2 *4613*
S the Zealot, and Judas Iscariot, Mt 10:4 *4613*
James and Joseph and S and Judas? Mt 13:55 *4613*
S Peter answered, Mt 16:16 *4613*
"Blessed are you, S Barjona, Mt 16:17 *4613*
"What do you think, S? Mt 17:25 *4613*
at the home of S the leper, Mt 26:6 *4613*
found a man of Cyrene named S, Mt 27:32 *4613*
of Galilee, He saw S and Andrew, Mk 1:16 *4613*
and Andrew, the brother of S, Mk 1:16 *4613*
into the house of S and Andrew, Mk 1:29 *4613*
S and his companions searched Mk 1:36 *4613*
S (to whom He gave the name Peter), Mk 3:16 *4613*
and Thaddaeus, and S the Zealot; Mk 3:18 *4613*
and Joses and Judas and S? Mk 6:3 *4613*
at the home of S the leper, Mk 14:3 *4613*
"S, are you asleep? Mk 14:37 *4613*
from the country, S of Cyrene Mk 15:21 *4613*
finished speaking, He said to S, Lk 5:4 *4613*
S answered and said, Lk 5:5 *4613*
But when S Peter saw *that,* he fell Lk 5:8 *4613*
Zebedee, who were partners with S. Lk 5:10 *4613*
And Jesus said to S, Lk 5:10 *4613*
S, whom He also named Peter, and Lk 6:14 *4613*
and S who was called the Zealot; Lk 6:15 *4613*
"S, I have something to say to Lk 7:40 *4613*
S answered and said, Lk 7:43 *4613*
toward the woman, He said to S, Lk 7:44 *4613*
"S, Simon, behold, Satan has Lk 22:31 *4613*
"Simon, S, behold, Satan has Lk 22:31 *4613*
they seized a man, S of Cyrene, Lk 23:26 *4613*
risen and has appeared to S." Lk 24:34 *4613*
Him, was Andrew, S Peter's brother. Jn 1:40 *4613*
He found first his own brother S and Jn 1:41 *4613*
"You are S the son of John; Jn 1:42 *4613*
Andrew, S Peter's brother, Jn 6:8 *4613*
S Peter answered Him, Jn 6:68 *4613*
meant Judas *the son* of S Iscariot, Jn 6:71 *4613*
of Judas Iscariot, *the son* of S, Jn 13:2 *4613*
So He came to S Peter. Jn 13:6 *4613*
S Peter said to Him, Jn 13:9 *4613*
S Peter gestured to him, Jn 13:24 *4613*
to Judas, *the son* of S Iscariot. Jn 13:26 *4613*
S Peter said to Him, Jn 13:36 *4613*
S Peter then, having a sword, Jn 18:10 *4613*
S Peter was following Jesus, Jn 18:15 *4613*
Now S Peter was standing and Jn 18:25 *4613*
So she ran and came to S Peter Jn 20:2 *4613*
S Peter also came, Jn 20:6 *4613*
S Peter, and Thomas called Didymus, Jn 21:2 *4613*
S Peter said to them, Jn 21:3 *4613*
So when S Peter heard that it Jn 21:7 *4613*
S Peter went up and drew the net Jn 21:11 *4613*
breakfast, Jesus said to S Peter, Jn 21:15 *4613*
"S, *son* of John, do you love Me Jn 21:15 *4613*
"S, *son* of John, do you love Me?" Jn 21:16 *4613*
"S, *son* of John, do you love Me?" Jn 21:17 *4613*
son of Alphaeus, and S the Zealot, Ac 1:13 *4613*
there was a man named S, Ac 8:9 *4613*
Even S himself believed; Ac 8:13 *4613*
Now when S saw that the Spirit was Ac 8:18 *4613*
But S answered and said, Ac 8:24 *4613*
in Joppa with a tanner *named* S. Ac 9:43 *4613*
Joppa and send for a man *named* S, Ac 10:5 *4613*
with a tanner *named* S, Ac 10:6 *4613*
out, they were asking whether S, Ac 10:18 *4613*
send to Joppa and invite S, Ac 10:32 *4613*
house of S *the* tanner by the sea.' Ac 10:32 *4613*
have S, who is also called Peter, Ac 11:13 *4613*
S Peter, a bond-servant and 2Pe 1:1 *4613*

SIMON'S
Now S mother-in-law was lying sick Mk 1:30 *4613*
the synagogue, and entered S home. Lk 4:38 *4613*
Now S mother-in-law was suffering Lk 4:38 *4613*
one of the boats, which was S, Lk 5:3 *4613*
asked directions for S house, Ac 10:17 *4613*

SIMPLE
man, And jealousy kills the s. Jb 5:2 6601b
LORD is sure, making wise the s. Ps 19:7 6612a
The LORD preserves the s; Ps 116:6 6612a
It gives understanding to the s. Ps 119:130 6612a

SIMPLE-MINDED
will you love being s? Pr 1:22 6612b

SIMPLICITY
the s and purity *of devotion* to Christ. 2Co 11:3 *572*

SIMPLY
you s will not believe." Jn 4:48
A stranger they s will not follow, Jn 10:5
they had s been baptized in the Ac 8:16 *3440*
but they s had some points of Ac 25:19
s so that they will not be persecuted Ga 6:12 *3440*

SIN
well, s is crouching at the door; Gn 4:7 2403b
and their s is exceedingly grave. Gn 18:20 2403b
on me and on my kingdom a great s? Gn 20:9 2401
What is my s that you have hotly Gn 31:36 2403b
great evil and s against God?" Gn 39:9 2398
'Do not s against the boy'; Gn 42:22 2398
of your brothers and their s, Gn 50:17 2403b
forgive my s only this once, Ex 10:17 2403b
came to the wilderness of S, Ex 16:1 5512b
stages from the wilderness of S, Ex 17:1 5512b
with you, so that you may not s." Ex 20:20 2398
they will make you s against Me; Ex 23:33 2398
it is a s offering. Ex 29:14 2403b
as a s offering for atonement, Ex 29:36 2403b
blood of the s offering of atonement Ex 30:10 2403b
brought *such* great s upon them?" Ex 32:21 2401
have committed a great s; Ex 32:30 2401
I can make atonement for your s." Ex 32:30 2403b
people has committed a great s, Ex 32:31 2401

But now, if You will, forgive their **s**	**Ex 32:32**	2403b
I will punish them for their **s**."	**Ex 32:34**	2403b
iniquity, transgression and **s**;	**Ex 34:7**	2403a
pardon our iniquity and our **s**,	**Ex 34:9**	2403b
a bull without defect as a **s** offering	**Lv 4:3**	2403b
for the **s** he has committed.	**Lv 4:3**	2403b
fat of the bull of the **s** offering:	**Lv 4:8**	2403b
when the **s** which they have	**Lv 4:14**	2403b
bull of the herd for a **s** offering and	**Lv 4:14**	2403b
with the bull of the **s** offering;	**Lv 4:20**	2403b
the **s** offering for the assembly.	**Lv 4:21**	2403b
if his **s** which he has committed is	**Lv 4:23**	2403b
it is a **s** offering.	**Lv 4:24**	2403b
some of the blood of the **s** offering	**Lv 4:25**	2403b
for him in regard to his **s**,	**Lv 4:26**	2403b
if his **s** which he has committed	**Lv 4:28**	2403b
for his **s** which he has committed.	**Lv 4:28**	2403b
on the head of the **s** offering and	**Lv 4:29**	2403b
and slay the **s** offering at the	**Lv 4:29**	2403b
as his offering for a **s** offering,	**Lv 4:32**	2403b
on the head of the **s** offering and	**Lv 4:33**	2403b
and slay it for a **s** offering in	**Lv 4:33**	2403b
some of the blood of the **s** offering	**Lv 4:34**	2403b
to his **s** which he has committed,	**Lv 4:35**	2403b
for his **s** which he has committed,	**Lv 5:6**	2403b
a lamb or a goat as a **s** offering.	**Lv 5:6**	2403b
atonement on his behalf for his **s**.	**Lv 5:6**	2403b
one for a **s** offering and the other	**Lv 5:7**	2403b
first that which is for the **s** offering	**Lv 5:8**	2403b
some of the blood of the **s** offering	**Lv 5:9**	2403b
it is a **s** offering.	**Lv 5:9**	2403b
for his **s** which he has committed,	**Lv 5:10**	2403b
of fine flour for a **s** offering;	**Lv 5:11**	2403b
on it, for it is a **s** offering.	**Lv 5:11**	2403b
it is a **s** offering.	**Lv 5:12**	2403b
atonement for him concerning his **s**	**Lv 5:13**	2403b
like the **s** offering and the guilt	**Lv 6:17**	2403b
'This is the law of the **s** offering:	**Lv 6:25**	2403b
the **s** offering shall be slain before the	**Lv 6:25**	2403b
who offers it for **s** shall eat it.	**Lv 6:26**	2398
'But no **s** offering of which any of	**Lv 6:30**	2403b
guilt offering is like the **s** offering,	**Lv 7:7**	2403b
the grain offering and the **s** offering	**Lv 7:37**	2403b
and the bull of the **s** offering,	**Lv 8:2**	2403b
the bull of the **s** offering,	**Lv 8:14**	2403b
of the bull of the **s** offering.	**Lv 8:14**	2403b
for a **s** offering and a ram for a	**Lv 9:2**	2403b
'Take a male goat for a **s** offering,	**Lv 9:3**	2403b
to the altar and offer your **s** offering	**Lv 9:7**	2403b
slaughtered the calf of the **s** offering	**Lv 9:8**	2403b
of the liver of the **s** offering,	**Lv 9:10**	2403b
and took the goat of the **s** offering	**Lv 9:15**	2403b
it and offered it for **s**,	**Lv 9:15**	2398
after making the **s** offering and the	**Lv 9:22**	2403b
for the goat of the **s** offering,	**Lv 10:16**	2403b
the **s** offering at the holy place?	**Lv 10:17**	2403b
they presented their **s** offering	**Lv 10:19**	2403b
if I had eaten a **s** offering today,	**Lv 10:19**	2403b
or a turtledove for a **s** offering.	**Lv 12:6**	2403b
and the other for a **s** offering;	**Lv 12:8**	2403b
where they slaughter the **s** offering	**Lv 14:13**	2403b
the guilt offering, like the **s** offering,	**Lv 14:13**	2403b
priest shall next offer the **s** offering	**Lv 14:19**	2403b
the one shall be a **s** offering and	**Lv 14:22**	2403b
afford, the one for a **s** offering and	**Lv 14:31**	2403b
offer them, one for a **s** offering and	**Lv 15:15**	2403b
shall offer the one for a **s** offering	**Lv 15:30**	2403b
with a bull for a **s** offering and a	**Lv 16:3**	2403b
two male goats for a **s** offering	**Lv 16:5**	2403b
s offering which is for himself,	**Lv 16:6**	2403b
fell, and make it a **s** offering.	**Lv 16:9**	2403b
s offering which is for himself and	**Lv 16:11**	2403b
s offering which is for himself.	**Lv 16:11**	2403b
slaughter the goat of the **s** offering	**Lv 16:15**	2403b
the fat of the **s** offering on the altar.	**Lv 16:25**	2403b
"But the bull of the **s** offering	**Lv 16:27**	2403b
and the goat of the **s** offering,	**Lv 16:27**	2403b
shall not incur **s** because of him.	**Lv 19:17**	2399
for his **s** which he has committed,	**Lv 19:22**	2403b
and the **s** which he has committed	**Lv 19:22**	2403b
they will bear their **s**.	**Lv 20:20**	2399
they will not bear **s** because of it	**Lv 22:9**	2399
offer one male goat for a **s** offering	**Lv 23:19**	2403b
his God, then he will bear his **s**.	**Lv 24:15**	2399
priest shall offer one for a **s** offering	**Nu 6:11**	2403b
atonement for him concerning his **s**	**Nu 6:11**	2398
without defect for a **s** offering	**Nu 6:14**	2403b
shall offer his **s** offering and his burnt	**Nu 6:16**	2403b
one male goat for a **s** offering;	**Nu 7:16**	2403b
one male goat for a **s** offering;	**Nu 7:22**	2403b
one male goat for a **s** offering;	**Nu 7:28**	2403b
one male goat for a **s** offering;	**Nu 7:34**	2403b
one male goat for a **s** offering;	**Nu 7:40**	2403b
one male goat for a **s** offering;	**Nu 7:46**	2403b
one male goat for a **s** offering;	**Nu 7:52**	2403b
one male goat for a **s** offering;	**Nu 7:58**	2403b
one male goat for a **s** offering;	**Nu 7:64**	2403b
one male goat for a **s** offering;	**Nu 7:70**	2403b
one male goat for a **s** offering;	**Nu 7:76**	2403b
one male goat for a **s** offering;	**Nu 7:82**	2403b
goats for a **s** offering twelve;	**Nu 7:87**	2403b
you shall take for a **s** offering.	**Nu 8:8**	2403b
then offer the one for a **s** offering	**Nu 8:12**	2403b
purified themselves from **s** and	**Nu 8:21**	2398
That man will bear his **s**.	**Nu 9:13**	2399
you, do not account *this* **s** to us,	**Nu 12:11**	2403b
one male goat for a **s** offering.	**Nu 15:24**	2403b
their **s** offering before the LORD,	**Nu 15:25**	2403b
year old female goat for a **s** offering.	**Nu 15:27**	2403b
be swept away in all their **s**."	**Nu 16:26**	2403b
every grain offering and every **s** offering	**Nu 18:9**	2403b
again, or they will bear **s** and die.	**Nu 18:22**	2399
will bear no **s** by reason of it	**Nu 18:32**	2399
it is purification from **s**.	**Nu 19:9**	2403b
ashes of the burnt purification from **s**	**Nu 19:17**	2403b
but he died in his own **s**,	**Nu 27:3**	2399
goat for a **s** offering to the LORD;	**Nu 28:15**	2403b
one male goat for a **s** offering to	**Nu 28:22**	2403b
one male goat for a **s** offering,	**Nu 29:5**	2403b
one male goat for a **s** offering,	**Nu 29:11**	2403b
besides the **s** offering of atonement	**Nu 29:11**	2403b
one male goat for a **s** offering,	**Nu 29:16**	2403b
one male goat for a **s** offering,	**Nu 29:19**	2403b
one male goat for a **s** offering,	**Nu 29:22**	2403b
one male goat for a **s** offering,	**Nu 29:25**	2403b
one male goat for a **s** offering,	**Nu 29:28**	2403b
one male goat for a **s** offering,	**Nu 29:31**	2403b
one male goat for a **s** offering,	**Nu 29:34**	2403b
one male goat for a **s** offering,	**Nu 29:38**	2403b
be sure your **s** will find you out.	**Nu 32:23**	2403b
and camped in the wilderness of **S**.	**Nu 33:11**	5512b
from the wilderness of **S** and	**Nu 33:12**	5512b
because of all your **s** which you	**Dt 9:18**	2403b
or at their wickedness or their **s**.	**Dt 9:27**	2403b
you, and it will be a **s** in you.	**Dt 15:9**	2399
or any **s** which he has committed;	**Dt 19:15**	2399
would **s** against the LORD your God.	**Dt 20:18**	2398
has committed a **s** worthy of death and	**Dt 21:22**	2399
no **s** in the girl worthy of death,	**Dt 22:26**	2399
pay it, for it would be **s** in you,	**Dt 23:21**	2399
vowing, it would not be **s** in you.	**Dt 23:22**	2399
and you shall not bring **s** on the	**Dt 24:4**	2398
the LORD and it become **s** in you.	**Dt 24:15**	2399
be put to death for his own **s**.	**Dt 24:16**	2399
Thus the **s** of the young men was	**1Sa 2:17**	2403b
s against the LORD by ceasing to pray	**1Sa 12:23**	2398
and do not **s** against the LORD by	**1Sa 14:34**	2398
see how this **s** has happened today.	**1Sa 14:38**	2403b
rebellion is as the **s** of divination,	**1Sa 15:23**	2403b
pardon my **s** and return with me,	**1Sa 15:25**	2403b
king **s** against his servant David,	**1Sa 19:4**	2398
will you **s** against innocent blood by	**1Sa 19:5**	2398
what is my **s** before your father,	**1Sa 20:1**	2403b
LORD also has taken away your **s**;	**2Sa 12:13**	2403b
the **s** of Your people Israel,	**1Ki 8:34**	2403b
turn from their **s** when You afflict	**1Ki 8:35**	2403b
and forgive the **s** of Your servants	**1Ki 8:36**	2403b
"When they **s** against You	**1Ki 8:46**	2398
there is no man who does not **s**)	**1Ki 8:46**	2398
Now this thing became a **s**,	**1Ki 12:30**	2403b
became **s** to the house of Jeroboam,	**1Ki 13:34**	2403b
with which he made Israel to **s**."	**1Ki 14:16**	2398
in his **s** which he made Israel sin.	**1Ki 15:26**	2403b
in his sin which he made Israel **s**.	**1Ki 15:26**	2398
and which he made Israel **s**,	**1Ki 15:30**	2398
in his **s** which he made Israel sin.	**1Ki 15:34**	2403b
in his sin which he made Israel **s**.	**1Ki 15:34**	2398
and have made My people Israel **s**,	**1Ki 16:2**	2398
and which they made Israel **s**,	**1Ki 16:13**	2398
and in his **s** which he did,	**1Ki 16:19**	2403b
sin which he did, making Israel **s**.	**1Ki 16:19**	2398
his sins which he made Israel **s**,	**1Ki 16:26**	2398
"What **s** have I committed, that	**1Ki 18:9**	2398
because you have made Israel **s**.	**1Ki 21:22**	2398
of Nebat, who caused Israel to **s**.	**1Ki 22:52**	2398
of Nebat, which he made Israel **s**;	**2Ki 3:3**	2398
of Nebat, which he made Israel **s**,	**2Ki 10:29**	2398
Jeroboam, which he made Israel **s**.	**2Ki 10:31**	2398
the money from the **s** offerings was	**2Ki 12:16**	2403b
with which he made Israel **s**;	**2Ki 13:2**	2398
with which he made Israel **s**,	**2Ki 13:6**	2398
with which he made Israel **s**,	**2Ki 13:11**	2398
be put to death for his own **s**."	**2Ki 14:6**	2399
of Nebat, which he made Israel **s**.	**2Ki 14:24**	2398
of Nebat, which he made Israel **s**.	**2Ki 15:9**	2398
of Nebat, which he made Israel **s**.	**2Ki 15:18**	2398
of Nebat, which he made Israel **s**.	**2Ki 15:24**	2398
of Nebat, which he made Israel **s**.	**2Ki 15:28**	2398
and made them commit a great **s**.	**2Ki 17:21**	2401
also made Judah **s** with his idols;	**2Ki 21:11**	2398
s with which he made Judah sin,	**2Ki 21:16**	2403b
sin with which he made Judah **s**,	**2Ki 21:16**	2398
did and his **s** which he committed,	**2Ki 21:17**	2403b
son of Nebat, who made Israel **s**,	**2Ki 23:15**	2398
the **s** of Your people Israel,	**2Ch 6:25**	2403b
s when You afflict them;	**2Ch 6:26**	2403b
and forgive the **s** of Your servants	**2Ch 6:27**	2403b
"When they **s** against You	**2Ch 6:36**	2398
there is no man who does not **s**)	**2Ch 6:36**	2398
from heaven, will forgive their **s** and	**2Ch 7:14**	2403b
be put to death for his own **s**."	**2Ch 25:4**	2399
for a **s** offering for the kingdom,	**2Ch 29:21**	2403b
the male goats of the **s** offering	**2Ch 29:23**	2403b
and the **s** offering for all Israel.	**2Ch 29:24**	2403b
entreated by him, and all his **s**,	**2Ch 33:19**	2403b
and as a **s** offering for all Israel	**Ezr 6:17**	2409
12 male goats for a **s** offering,	**Ezr 8:35**	2403b
s be blotted out before You,	**Ne 4:5**	2403b
and act accordingly and **s**,	**Ne 6:13**	2398
the **s** offerings to make atonement	**Ne 10:33**	2403b
"Did not Solomon king of Israel **s**	**Ne 13:26**	2398
women caused even him to **s**.	**Ne 13:26**	2403b
Through all this Job did not **s** nor	**Jb 1:22**	2398
In all this Job did not **s** with his lips.	**Jb 2:10**	2398
my guilt And search after my **s**?	**Jb 10:6**	2403b
If I **s**, then You would take	**Jb 10:14**	2398
known to me my rebellion and my **s**.	**Jb 13:23**	2403b
steps, You do not observe my **s**.	**Jb 14:16**	2403b
I have not allowed my mouth to **s**	**Jb 31:30**	2398
'For he adds rebellion to his **s**;	**Jb 34:37**	2403b
Tremble, and do not **s**;	**Ps 4:4**	2398
is forgiven, Whose **s** is covered!	**Ps 32:1**	2401
When I kept silent *about my* **s**,	**Ps 32:3**	
I acknowledged my **s** to You,	**Ps 32:5**	2403b
forgave the guilt of my **s**.	**Ps 32:5**	2403b
in my bones because of my **s**.	**Ps 38:3**	2403b
full of anxiety because of my **s**.	**Ps 38:18**	2403b
That I may not **s** with my tongue;	**Ps 39:1**	2398
Burnt offering and **s** offering You	**Ps 40:6**	2401
And cleanse me from my **s**.	**Ps 51:2**	2403b
And my **s** is ever before me.	**Ps 51:3**	2403b
And in **s** my mother conceived me.	**Ps 51:5**	2399
for my transgression nor for my **s**,	**Ps 59:3**	2403b
On account of the **s** of their mouth	**Ps 59:12**	2403b
still continued to **s** against Him,	**Ps 78:17**	2398
You covered all their **s**.	**Ps 85:2**	2403b
And let his prayer become **s**.	**Ps 109:7**	2401
s of his mother be blotted out.	**Ps 109:14**	2403b
That I may not **s** against You.	**Ps 119:11**	2398
be held with the cords of his **s**.	**Pr 5:22**	2403b
Fools mock at **s**, But among the	**Pr 14:9**	817
But **s** is a disgrace to *any* people.	**Pr 14:34**	2403b
my heart, I am pure from my **s**"?	**Pr 20:9**	2403b
The lamp of the wicked, is **s**.	**Pr 21:4**	2403b
The devising of folly is **s**,	**Pr 24:9**	2403b
Do not let your speech cause you to **s**	**Ec 5:6**	2398
they display their **s** like Sodom;	**Is 3:9**	2403b
And **s** as if with cart ropes;	**Is 5:18**	2403a
away and your **s** is forgiven."	**Is 6:7**	2403b
price of the pardoning of his **s**:	**Is 27:9**	2403b
Spirit, In order to add **s** to sin;	**Is 30:1**	2403b
Spirit, In order to add sin to **s**;	**Is 30:1**	2403b
sinful hands have made for you as a **s**.	**Is 31:7**	2399
Yet He Himself bore the **s** of many,	**Is 53:12**	2399
or what is our **s** which we have	**Jer 16:10**	2403b
repay their iniquity and their **s**,	**Jer 16:18**	2403b
The **s** of Judah is written down	**Jer 17:1**	2403b
for **s** throughout your borders.	**Jer 17:3**	2403b
blot out their **s** from Your sight.	**Jer 18:23**	2403b
their **s** I will remember no more."	**Jer 31:34**	2403b
abomination, to cause Judah to **s**.	**Jer 32:35**	2398
their iniquity and their **s**."	**Jer 36:3**	2403b
Is greater than the **s** of Sodom,	**La 4:6**	2403b
warned him, he shall die in his **s**,	**Ezk 3:20**	2403b
that the righteous should not **s** and	**Ezk 3:21**	2398
should not sin and he does not **s**,	**Ezk 3:21**	2398
and his **s** which he has committed;	**Ezk 18:24**	2403b
"I will pour out My wrath on **S**,	**Ezk 30:15**	5512a
S will writhe in anguish, Thebes	**Ezk 30:16**	5512a
on the day when he commits **s**.'	**Ezk 33:12**	2398
and he turns from his **s** and	**Ezk 33:14**	2403b
burnt offering, the **s** offering and	**Ezk 40:39**	2403b
grain offering, the **s** offering and	**Ezk 42:13**	2403b
'a young bull for a **s** offering.	**Ezk 43:19**	2403b
take the bull for the **s** offering,	**Ezk 43:21**	2403b
without blemish for a **s** offering,	**Ezk 43:22**	2403b
daily a goat for a **s** offering;	**Ezk 43:25**	2403b
he shall offer his **s** offering,"	**Ezk 44:27**	2403b
grain offering, the **s** offering and	**Ezk 44:29**	2403b
he shall provide the **s** offering,	**Ezk 45:17**	2403b
some of the blood from the **s** offering	**Ezk 45:19**	2403b
the land a bull for a **s** offering.	**Ezk 45:22**	2403b
male goat daily for a **s** offering.	**Ezk 45:23**	2403b
seven days for the **s** offering,	**Ezk 45:25**	2403b
guilt offering and the **s** offering	**Ezk 46:20**	2403b
and confessing my **s** and the sin of	**Da 9:20**	2403b
sin and the **s** of my people Israel,	**Da 9:20**	2403b
to make an end of **s**,	**Da 9:24**	2403b
They feed on the **s** of My people And	**Hos 4:8**	2403b
has multiplied altars for **s**,	**Hos 8:11**	2398
places of Aven, the **s** of Israel,	**Hos 10:8**	2398
No iniquity, which *would be* **s**."	**Hos 12:8**	2399
And now they **s** more and more, And	**Hos 13:2**	2398
His **s** is stored up.	**Hos 13:12**	2403b
She was the beginning of **s**	**Mi 1:13**	2403b
act, Even to Israel his **s**.	**Mi 3:8**	2403b
of my body for the **s** of my soul?	**Mi 6:7**	2403b
Jerusalem, for **s** and for impurity.	**Zch 13:1**	2403b
any **s** and blasphemy shall be	**Mt 12:31**	*266*
"Lord, how often shall my brother **s**	**Mt 18:21**	*264*
but is guilty of an eternal **s**"	**Mk 3:29**	*265*
who takes away the **s** of the world!	**Jn 1:29**	*266*
do not **s** anymore, so that nothing	**Jn 5:14**	*264*
"He who is without **s** among you,	**Jn 8:7**	*361*
From now on **s** no more."]	**Jn 8:11**	*264*
seek Me, and will die in your **s**;	**Jn 8:21**	*266*
everyone who commits **s** is the slave	**Jn 8:34**	*266*
who commits sin is the slave of **s**.	**Jn 8:34**	*266*
"Which one of you convicts Me of **s**?	**Jn 8:46**	*266*
were blind, you would have no **s**;	**Jn 9:41**	*266*
'We see,' your **s** remains.	**Jn 9:41**	*266*
to them, they would not have **s**,	**Jn 15:22**	*266*
they have no excuse for their **s**.	**Jn 15:22**	*266*
else did, they would not have **s**;	**Jn 15:24**	*266*
convict the world concerning **s** and	**Jn 16:8**	*266*
concerning **s**, because they do not	**Jn 16:9**	*266*
Me to you has *the* greater **s**."	**Jn 19:11**	*266*
do not hold this **s** against them!"	**Ac 7:60**	*266*
Jews and Greeks are all under **s**;	**Ro 3:9**	*266*
the Law *comes* the knowledge of **s**.	**Ro 3:20**	*266*
"BLESSED IS THE MAN WHOSE **S** THE	**Ro 4:8**	*266*
one man **s** entered into the world,	**Ro 5:12**	*266*

the world, and death through **s**,	**Ro 5:12**	*266*
until the Law **s** was in the world,	**Ro 5:13**	*266*
but **s** is not imputed when there is	**Ro 5:13**	*266*
but where **s** increased, grace	**Ro 5:20**	*266*
that, as **s** reigned in death, even	**Ro 5:21**	*266*
Are we to continue in **s** so that grace	**Ro 6:1**	*266*
How shall we who died to **s** still live	**Ro 6:2**	*266*
body of **s** might be done away with,	**Ro 6:6**	*266*
we would no longer be slaves to **s**;	**Ro 6:6**	*266*
he who has died is freed from **s**.	**Ro 6:7**	*266*
death that He died, He died to **s** once	**Ro 6:10**	*266*
consider yourselves to be dead to **s**,	**Ro 6:11**	*266*
Therefore do not let **s** reign in	**Ro 6:12**	*266*
the members of your body to **s** *as*	**Ro 6:13**	*266*
s shall not be master over you,	**Ro 6:14**	*266*
Shall we **s** because we are not	**Ro 6:15**	*264*
either of **s** resulting in death,	**Ro 6:16**	*266*
that though you were slaves of **s**,	**Ro 6:17**	*266*
and having been freed from **s**,	**Ro 6:18**	*266*
For when you were slaves of **s**,	**Ro 6:20**	*266*
freed from **s** and enslaved to God,	**Ro 6:22**	*266*
For the wages of **s** is death,	**Ro 6:23**	*266*
Is the Law **s**? May it never be!	**Ro 7:7**	*266*
I would not have come to know **s**	**Ro 7:7**	*266*
But **s**, taking opportunity through	**Ro 7:8**	*266*
for apart from the Law **s** *is* dead.	**Ro 7:8**	*266*
commandment came, **s** became alive	**Ro 7:9**	*266*
for **s**, taking an opportunity through	**Ro 7:11**	*266*
Rather it was **s**, in order that it	**Ro 7:13**	*266*
shown to be **s** by effecting my death	**Ro 7:13**	*266*
s would become utterly sinful.	**Ro 7:13**	*266*
of flesh, sold into bondage to **s**.	**Ro 7:14**	*266*
doing it, but **s** which dwells in me.	**Ro 7:17**	*266*
it, but **s** which dwells in me.	**Ro 7:20**	*266*
law of **s** which is in my members.	**Ro 7:23**	*266*
other, with my flesh the law of **s**.	**Ro 7:25**	*266*
from the law of **s** and of death.	**Ro 8:2**	*266*
flesh and *as an offering* for **s**,	**Ro 8:3**	*266*
sin, He condemned **s** in the flesh,	**Ro 8:3**	*266*
the body is dead because of **s**,	**Ro 8:10**	*266*
whatever is not from faith is **s**.	**Ro 14:23**	*266*
Every *other* **s** that a man commits	**1Co 6:18**	*265*
do what he wishes, he does not **s**;	**1Co 7:36**	*264*
it is weak, you **s** against Christ.	**1Co 8:12**	*264*
The sting of death is **s**,	**1Co 15:56**	*266*
and the power of **s** is the law;	**1Co 15:56**	*266*
He made Him who knew no **s** *to be*	**2Co 5:21**	*266*
knew no sin *to be* **s** on our behalf,	**2Co 5:21**	*266*
Or did I commit a **s** in humbling	**2Co 11:7**	*266*
Who is led into **s** without my	**2Co 11:29**	*4624*
is Christ then a minister of **s**?	**Ga 2:17**	*266*
has shut up everyone under **s**,	**Ga 3:22**	*266*
BE ANGRY, AND *yet* DO NOT **S**;	**Eph 4:26**	*264*
Those who continue in **s**, rebuke in	**1Tm 5:20**	*264*
keep yourself free from **s**.	**1Tm 5:22**	*53*
hardened by the deceitfulness of **s**.	**Heb 3:13**	*266*
things as *we are, yet* without **s**.	**Heb 4:15**	*266*
has been manifested to put away **s**	**Heb 9:26**	*266*
salvation without *reference to* **s**,	**Heb 9:28**	*266*
OFFERINGS AND *sacrifices* FOR **S**	**Heb 10:6**	*266*
OFFERINGS AND *sacrifices* FOR **S**	**Heb 10:8**	*266*
is no longer *any* offering for **s**.	**Heb 10:18**	*266*
enjoy the passing pleasures of **s**,	**Heb 11:25**	*266*
s which so easily entangles us,	**Heb 12:1**	*266*
blood in your striving against **s**;	**Heb 12:4**	*266*
high priest *as an offering* for **s**,	**Heb 13:11**	*266*
conceived, it gives birth to **s**;	**Jas 1:15**	*266*
and when **s** is accomplished, it	**Jas 1:15**	*266*
you are committing **s** *and* are	**Jas 2:9**	*266*
does not do it, to him it is **s**.	**Jas 4:17**	*266*
you **s** and are harshly treated,	**1Pe 2:20**	*264*
WHO COMMITTED NO **S**,	**1Pe 2:22**	*266*
that we might die to **s** and live to	**1Pe 2:24**	*266*
in the flesh has ceased from **s**,	**1Pe 4:1**	*266*
adultery that never cease from **s**,	**2Pe 2:14**	*266*
His Son cleanses us from all **s**.	**1Jn 1:7**	*266*
If we say that we have no **s**,	**1Jn 1:8**	*266*
things to you so that you may not **s**.	**1Jn 2:1**	*264*
Everyone who practices **s** also	**1Jn 3:4**	*266*
and **s** is lawlessness.	**1Jn 3:4**	*266*
and in Him there is no **s**.	**1Jn 3:5**	*266*
one who practices **s** is of the devil;	**1Jn 3:8**	*266*
one who is born of God practices **s**,	**1Jn 3:9**	*266*
and he cannot **s**, because he is	**1Jn 3:9**	*264*
sees his brother committing a **s**	**1Jn 5:16**	*266*
who commit **s** not *leading* to death.	**1Jn 5:16**	*264*
There is a **s** *leading* to death;	**1Jn 5:16**	*266*
All unrighteousness is **s**,	**1Jn 5:17**	*266*
there is a **s** not *leading* to death.	**1Jn 5:17**	*266*

SINAI

Sin, which is between Elim and **S**,	**Ex 16:1**	5514
came into the wilderness of **S**.	**Ex 19:1**	5514
they came to the wilderness of **S** and	**Ex 19:2**	5514
LORD will come down on Mount **S**	**Ex 19:11**	5514
Now Mount **S** *was* all in smoke	**Ex 19:18**	5514
The LORD came down on Mount **S**,	**Ex 19:20**	5514
people cannot come up to Mount **S**,	**Ex 19:23**	5514
of the LORD rested on Mount **S**,	**Ex 24:16**	5514
speaking with him upon Mount **S**,	**Ex 31:18**	5514
come up in the morning to Mount **S**,	**Ex 34:2**	5514
morning and went up to Mount **S**,	**Ex 34:4**	5514
was coming down from Mount **S**	**Ex 34:29**	5514
LORD had spoken to him on Mount **S**.	**Ex 34:32**	5514
LORD commanded Moses at Mount **S**	**Lv 7:38**	5514
the LORD in the wilderness of **S**.	**Lv 7:38**	5514
then spoke to Moses at Mount **S**,	**Lv 25:1**	5514
Israel through Moses at Mount **S**.	**Lv 26:46**	5514
for the sons of Israel at Mount **S**.	**Lv 27:34**	5514
to Moses in the wilderness of **S**,	**Nu 1:1**	5514
them in the wilderness of **S**.	**Nu 1:19**	5514
LORD spoke with Moses on Mount **S**.	**Nu 3:1**	5514
the LORD in the wilderness of **S**;	**Nu 3:4**	5514
to Moses in the wilderness of **S**,	**Nu 3:14**	5514
to Moses in the wilderness of **S**,	**Nu 9:1**	5514
twilight, in the wilderness of **S**;	**Nu 9:5**	5514
journeys from the wilderness of **S**.	**Nu 10:12**	5514
of Israel in the wilderness of **S**.	**Nu 26:64**	5514
which was ordained in Mount **S**	**Nu 28:6**	5514
and camped in the wilderness of **S**.	**Nu 33:15**	5514
from the wilderness of **S** and	**Nu 33:16**	5514
"The LORD came from **S**,	**Dt 33:2**	5514
the presence of the LORD, This **S**,	**Jg 5:5**	5514
"Then You came down on Mount **S**,	**Ne 9:13**	5514
S itself *quaked* at the presence of	**Ps 68:8**	5514
The Lord is among them *as at* **S**,	**Ps 68:17**	5514
HIM IN THE WILDERNESS OF MOUNT **S**,	**Ac 7:30**	*4614*
was speaking to him on Mount **S**,	**Ac 7:38**	*4614*
one *proceeding* from Mount **S**	**Ga 4:24**	*4614*
this Hagar is Mount **S** in Arabia and	**Ga 4:25**	*4614*

SINCE

You give me, **s** I am childless,	**Gn 15:2**	
"**S** You have given no offspring	**Gn 15:3**	2005
s you have visited your servant."	**Gn 18:5**	
		3588, 5921, 3651
s Abraham will surely become a	**Gn 18:18**	
s you have not withheld your son,	**Gn 22:12**	
s I have prepared the house,	**Gn 24:31**	
s the LORD has prospered my way.	**Gn 24:56**	
you come to me, **s** you hate me and	**Gn 26:27**	
"**S** God has informed you of all	**Gn 41:39**	310
pieces," and I have not seen him **s**.	**Gn 44:28**	
		5704, 2008
s his life is bound up in the	**Gn 44:30**	
me die, **s** I have seen your face,	**Gn 46:30**	310
livestock, **s** *your* money is gone."	**Gn 47:16**	518
nor **s** You have spoken to Your	**Ex 4:10**	3975b
"Ever **s** I came to Pharaoh to	**Ex 5:23**	3975b
of Egypt **s** it became a nation.	**Ex 9:24**	3975b
s they were driven out of Egypt	**Ex 12:39**	3588
s you yourselves know the feelings	**Ex 23:9**	
s My name is in him.	**Ex 23:21**	3588
s its blood had not been brought	**Lv 10:18**	
s he has a defect, he shall not	**Lv 21:21**	
he shall calculate the years **s** its sale	**Lv 25:27**	
s they did present them before the	**Nu 16:38**	3588
me **s** they are too mighty for me;	**Nu 22:6**	3588
s no inheritance was given to them	**Nu 26:62**	3588
s you did not see any form on the	**Dt 4:15**	3588
s the day that God created man on	**Dt 4:32**	4480
s he has no portion or inheritance	**Dt 12:12**	3588
s the place where the LORD your	**Dt 14:24**	3588
s the LORD will surely bless you	**Dt 15:4**	3588
s he fares well with you;	**Dt 15:16**	3588
s the LORD has said to you,	**Dt 17:16**	
s he had not hated him previously.	**Dt 19:6**	3588
"**S** the LORD your God walks in the	**Dt 23:14**	3588
his wife, **s** she has been defiled;	**Dt 24:4**	310, 834
eat, **s** he has nothing *else* left,	**Dt 28:55**	4480
S that time no prophet has risen in	**Dt 34:10**	5750
s I have dealt kindly with you,	**Jos 2:12**	3588
what can I say **s** Israel has turned	**Jos 7:8**	310
s you have given me the land of	**Jos 15:19**	3588
s I am a numerous people whom the	**Jos 17:14**	
s the hill country of Ephraim is	**Jos 17:15**	3588
s you have given me the land of	**Jg 1:15**	3588
'**S** now the LORD, the God of	**Jg 11:23**	
s the LORD has avenged you of your	**Jg 11:36**	
		310, 834
"**S** you act like this, I will	**Jg 15:7**	518
s this man has come into my house,	**Jg 19:23**	
		310, 834
s we have sworn by the LORD not to	**Jg 21:7**	
s the women are destroyed out of	**Jg 21:16**	3588
s the LORD has witnessed against	**Ru 1:21**	
of me, **s** I am a foreigner?"	**Ru 2:10**	
s the day that I brought them up	**1Sa 8:8**	4480
s I said I have invited the people."	**1Sa 9:24**	
s I have rejected him from being	**1Sa 16:1**	
s he has taunted the armies of the	**1Sa 17:36**	3588
s I am a poor man and lightly	**1Sa 18:23**	
s he has not sinned against you,	**1Sa 19:4**	3588
and **s** his deeds *have been* very	**1Sa 19:4**	3588
s our family has a sacrifice in	**1Sa 20:29**	3588
him, **s** he is the LORD's anointed."	**1Sa 24:6**	3588
s the LORD has restrained you from	**1Sa 25:26**	834
s the LORD has departed from you	**1Sa 28:16**	
not dwelt in a house **s** the day I	**2Sa 7:6**	4480
s he might do *himself* harm!"	**2Sa 12:18**	
s he was stronger than she, he	**2Sa 13:14**	
s the day that he violated his sister	**2Sa 13:32**	4480
concerning Amnon, **s** he was dead.	**2Sa 13:39**	3588
s you will have no reward for	**2Sa 18:22**	
s the word of all Israel has come	**2Sa 19:11**	
s my lord the king has come safely	**2Sa 19:30**	
		310, 834
'**S** the day that I brought My	**1Ki 8:16**	4480
s He had promised him to give a	**2Ki 8:19**	3512c
s your master's sons are with you,	**2Ki 10:2**	
s the day their fathers came from	**2Ki 21:15**	4480
s there is no wrong in my hands,	**1Ch 12:17**	
s the day that I brought up Israel	**1Ch 17:5**	4480
S more chief men were found from	**1Ch 24:4**	
"**S** I know, O my God, that You	**1Ch 29:17**	
'**S** the day that I brought My	**2Ch 6:5**	4480
Judah, **s** the land was undisturbed,	**2Ch 14:6**	3588
and **s** He had promised to give a	**2Ch 21:7**	3512c
s they could not celebrate it at	**2Ch 30:3**	3588
in Jerusalem **s** the days of Solomon	**2Ch 30:26**	3588
"**S** the contributions began to be	**2Ch 31:10**	4480
s the days of Samuel the prophet;	**2Ch 35:18**	4480
we have been sacrificing to Him **s** the	**Ezr 4:2**	4480
"**S** the days of our fathers to	**Ezr 9:7**	4480
s You our God have requited *us*	**Ezr 9:13**	3588
"**S** his days are determined, The	**Jb 14:5**	518
Who set its measurements? **S** you know.	**Jb 38:5**	3588
S I am afflicted and needy, Let	**Ps 40:17**	
S you have come into the hand of	**Pr 6:3**	3588
S the word of the king is	**Ec 8:4**	834
s the day that Ephraim separated	**Is 7:17**	4480
'**S** you were laid low, no *tree*	**Is 14:8**	3975b
S You have also performed for us	**Is 26:12**	3588
"**S** you have rejected this word And	**Is 30:12**	3282
"**S** you are precious in My sight,	**Is 43:4**	
		4480, 834
S you are honored and I love you,	**Is 43:4**	
Have I not long **s** announced *it* to	**Is 44:8**	3975b
Who has long **s** declared it?	**Is 45:21**	3975b
S I have been bereaved of my	**Is 49:21**	
labor of our fathers **s** our youth,	**Jer 3:24**	4480
"**S** the day that your fathers came	**Jer 7:25**	4480
s the conversation had not been	**Jer 38:27**	3588
s Ishmael the son of Nethaniah had	**Jer 41:18**	3588
"But **s** we stopped burning sacrifices	**Jer 44:18**	
		4480, 227
"Moab has been at ease **s** his youth;	**Jer 48:11**	4480
be silent **S** He has laid *it* on him.	**La 3:28**	3588
s they are not willing to listen	**Ezk 3:7**	3588
s you have not warned him, he	**Ezk 3:20**	3588
s you have not hated bloodshed,	**Ezk 35:6**	518
s you have been able to reveal	**Da 2:47**	1768
s I know that a spirit of the holy	**Da 4:9**	1768
s there was a nation until that time;	**Da 12:1**	4480
S you have forgotten the law of	**Hos 4:6**	
S Israel is stubborn Like a	**Hos 4:16**	3588
S Ephraim has multiplied altars	**Hos 8:11**	3588
glory, **s** it has departed from it.	**Hos 10:5**	3588
LORD your God **s** the land of Egypt;	**Hos 12:9**	4480
LORD your God **S** the land of Egypt;	**Hos 13:4**	4480
"**S** you have taken My silver and	**Jl 3:5**	834
S THE FOUNDATION OF THE WORLD."	**Mt 13:35**	*575*
"But **s** he did not have *the means*	**Mt 18:25**	
s the beginning of the world until	**Mt 24:21**	*575*
s it is the price of blood."	**Mt 27:6**	*1893*
the twelve, **s** it was already late.	**Mk 11:11**	
s the beginning of the creation	**Mk 13:19**	*575*
can this be, **s** I am a virgin?"	**Lk 1:34**	*1893*
but she, **s** the time I came in, has	**Lk 7:45**	*575*
s the foundation of the world,	**Lk 11:50**	*575*
s I have no place to store my	**Lk 12:17**	*3754*
s they do not have *the means* to	**Lk 14:14**	*3754*
s my master is taking the	**Lk 16:3**	*3754*
s that time the gospel of the kingdom	**Lk 16:16**	*575*
s you are under the same sentence	**Lk 23:40**	*3754*
third day **s** these things happened.	**Lk 24:21**	
		575, 3739
drink **s** I am a Samaritan woman?"	**Jn 4:9**	
kill Himself, will He, **s** He says,	**Jn 8:22**	*3754*
Him, **s** He opened your eyes?"	**Jn 9:17**	*3754*
"**S** the beginning of time it has	**Jn 9:32**	*1537*
but **s** you say, 'We see,' your sin	**Jn 9:41**	*3568*
s the tomb was nearby, they laid	**Jn 19:42**	*3754*
s it was impossible for Him to be	**Ac 2:24**	*2530*
S Lydda was near Joppa,	**Ac 9:38**	
s you repudiate it and judge	**Ac 13:46**	*1894*
s he is read in the synagogues	**Ac 15:21**	
"**S** we have heard that some of our	**Ac 15:24**	*1894*
s He is Lord of heaven and earth,	**Ac 17:24**	
s He Himself gives to all *people* life	**Ac 17:25**	
s the Jews had put him forward;	**Ac 19:33**	
"So, **s** these are undeniable facts,	**Ac 19:36**	
s there is no *real* cause *for it*,	**Ac 19:40**	
And **s** he would not be persuaded,	**Ac 21:14**	
"But **s** I could not see because of	**Ac 22:11**	*5613*
s he has something to tell you."	**Ac 23:18**	
"**S** we have through you attained	**Ac 24:2**	
and **s** by your providence reforms	**Ac 24:2**	
s you can take note of the fact	**Ac 24:11**	
and **s** he himself appealed to the	**Ac 25:25**	
s they have known about me for a	**Ac 26:5**	
s I am persuaded that none of	**Ac 26:26**	*1063*
s the wind did not permit us *to go*	**Ac 27:7**	
s even the fast was already over,	**Ac 27:9**	*1223*
S neither sun nor stars appeared for	**Ac 27:20**	
For **s** the creation of the world	**Ro 1:20**	*575*
s indeed God who will justify the	**Ro 3:30**	*1512*
s he was about a hundred years old,	**Ro 4:19**	
S we have gifts that differ according	**Ro 12:6**	
and **s** I have had for many years a	**Ro 15:23**	
For **s** in the wisdom of God the	**1Co 1:21**	*1894*
For **s** there is jealousy and strife	**1Co 3:3**	*3699*
S there is one bread, we who are	**1Co 10:17**	*3754*
s he is the image and glory of God;	**1Co 11:7**	
s you are zealous of spiritual *gifts*,	**1Co 14:12**	*1893*
s he does not know what you are	**1Co 14:16**	*1894*
For **s** by a man *came* death, by a	**1Co 15:21**	*1894*
s we have this ministry,	**2Co 4:1**	
has been prepared **s** last year,	**2Co 9:2**	*575*
S many boast according to the	**2Co 11:18**	*1893*
s you are seeking for proof of the	**2Co 13:3**	*1893*
s by the works of the Law no	**Ga 2:16**	*3754*
s both in my imprisonment and in	**Php 1:7**	
s we heard of your faith in Christ	**Col 1:4**	
s the day you heard *of it* and	**Col 1:6**	*575*
also, **s** the day we heard *of it*,	**Col 1:9**	*575*
s you laid aside the old self with	**Col 3:9**	
But **s** we are of *the* day, let us be	**1Th 5:8**	
s it holds promise for the present	**1Tm 4:8**	

s I am such a person as Paul, Phm 1:9
s I know that you will do even Phm 1:21
Therefore, s the children share in Heb 2:14 1893
For s He Himself was tempted in Heb 2:18
Therefore, s it remains for some to Heb 4:6 1893
Therefore, s we have a great high Heb 4:14
s he himself also is beset with Heb 5:2 1893
s you have become dull of hearing. Heb 5:11 1893
s they again crucify to themselves Heb 6:6
s He could swear by no one greater, Heb 6:13 1893
s He always lives to make Heb 7:25
s there are those who offer the Heb 8:4
s they *relate* only to food and Heb 9:10
s a death has taken place for the Heb 9:15
s the foundation of the world; Heb 9:26 575
s it has *only* a shadow of the good Heb 10:1
Therefore, brethren, s we have Heb 10:19
and s *we have* a great priest over Heb 10:21
s she considered Him faithful who Heb 11:11 1893
s we have so great a cloud of Heb 12:1
s we receive a kingdom which Heb 12:28
s you yourselves also are in the Heb 13:3 5613
S you have in obedience to the 1Pe 1:22
s Christ also suffered for you, 1Pe 2:21 3754
someone weaker, s she is a woman; 1Pe 3:7
s Christ has suffered in the 1Pe 4:1
ever s the fathers fell asleep, 2Pe 3:4 575, 3739
S all these things are to be 2Pe 3:11
s you look for these things, 2Pe 3:14
s they in the same way as these Jude 1:7
s man came to be upon the earth, Rv 16:18 575, 3739

SINCERE
in order to be s and blameless Php 1:10 1506
a good conscience and a s faith. 1Tm 1:5 505
mindful of the s faith within you, 2Tm 1:5 505
let us draw near with a s heart in Heb 10:22 228
for a s love of the brethren, 1Pe 1:22 505
I am stirring up your s mind by way 2Pe 3:1 1506

SINCERELY
And my lips speak knowledge s. Jb 33:3 1305

SINCERITY
LORD and serve Him in s and truth; Jos 24:14 8549
righteously and speaks with s, Is 33:15 4339
with gladness and s of heart, Ac 2:46 858
unleavened bread of s and truth. 1Co 5:8 1505
that in holiness and godly s, 2Co 1:12 1505
the word of God, but as from s, 2Co 2:17 1505
of others the s of your love also. 2Co 8:8 1103
trembling, in the s of your heart, Eph 6:5 572
please men, but with s of heart, Col 3:22 572

SINEW
Israel do not eat the s of the hip Gn 32:32 1517
Jacob's thigh in the s of the hip. Gn 32:32 1517
And your neck is an iron s And Is 48:4 1517

SINEWS
knit me together with bones and s? Jb 10:11 1517
The s of his thighs are knit Jb 40:17 1517
'I will put s on you, make Ezk 37:6 1517
and behold, s were on them, Ezk 37:8 1517

SINFUL
fathers' place, a brood of s men, Nu 32:14 2400
"I took your s *thing,* the Dt 9:21 2403b
Alas, s nation, People weighed Is 1:4 2398
which your s hands have made for you Is 31:7
the Lord GOD are on the s kingdom, Am 9:8 2400
this adulterous and s generation, Mk 8:38 268
away from me Lord, for I am a s man, Lk 5:8 268
delivered into the hands of s men, Lk 24:7 268
were in the flesh, the s passions, Ro 7:5 266
sin would become utterly s. Ro 7:13 266
His own Son in the likeness of s flesh Ro 8:3 266

SING
"I will s to the LORD, for He is Ex 15:1 7891
"S to the LORD, for He is highly Ex 15:21 7891
this song: "Spring up, O well! S to it! Nu 21:17 6031b
to the LORD, I will s, I will sing Jg 5:3 7891
sing, I will s praise to the LORD, Jg 5:3 2167
And you who travel on the road—s! Jg 5:10 7878
Awake, awake, s a song! Jg 5:12 1696
not s of this one as they danced, 1Sa 21:11 6031b
of whom they s in the dances, 1Sa 29:5 6031b
And I will s praises to Your name. 2Sa 22:50 2167
S to Him, sing praises to Him; 1Ch 16:9 7891
Sing to Him, s praises to Him; 1Ch 16:9 2167
S to the LORD, all the earth; 1Ch 16:23 7891
will s for joy before the LORD; 1Ch 16:33 7442
to s in the house of the LORD, 1Ch 25:6 7892a
ordered the Levites to s praises 2Ch 29:30 1984b
"They s to the timbrel and harp Jb 21:12 5375
I made the widow's heart s for joy. Jb 29:13 7442
"He will s to men and say, Jb 33:27 7891
be glad, Let them ever s for joy; Ps 5:11 7442
And will s praise to the name of Ps 7:17 2167
I will s praise to Your name, O Ps 9:2 2167
S praises to the LORD, who dwells Ps 9:11 2167
I will s to the LORD, Because He Ps 13:6 7891
And I will s praises to Your name. Ps 18:49 2167
will s for joy over your victory, Ps 20:5 7442
We will s and praise Your power. Ps 21:13 7891
I will s, yes, I will sing praises Ps 27:6 7891
yes, I will s praises to the LORD. Ps 27:6 2167
S praise to the LORD, you His Ps 30:4 2167
That *my* soul may s praise to You and Ps 30:12 2167
S for joy in the LORD, O you Ps 33:1 7442
S praises to Him with a harp of Ps 33:2 2167
S to Him a new song; Ps 33:3 7891
S praises to God, sing praises; Ps 47:6 2167
Sing praises to God, s praises; Ps 47:6 2167
S praises to our King, sing Ps 47:6 2167
praises to our King, s praises. Ps 47:6 2167
S praises with a skillful psalm. Ps 47:7 2167
joyfully s of Your righteousness. Ps 51:14 7442
I will s, yes, I will sing praises! Ps 57:7 7891
will sing, yes, I will s praises! Ps 57:7 2167
I will s praises to You among the Ps 57:9 2167
for me, I shall s of Your strength; Ps 59:16 7891
I shall joyfully s of Your Ps 59:16 7442
I will s praises to You; Ps 59:17 2167
will s praise to Your name forever, Ps 61:8 2167
shadow of Your wings I s for joy. Ps 63:7 7442
They shout for joy, yes, they s. Ps 65:13 7891
S the glory of His name; Ps 66:2 2167
You, And will s praises to You; Ps 66:4 2167
They will s praises to Your name." Ps 66:4 2167
the nations be glad and s for joy; Ps 67:4 7442
S to God, sing praises to His name; Ps 68:4 7891
to God, s praises to His name; Ps 68:4 2167
S to God, O kingdoms of the earth, Ps 68:32 7891
S praises to the Lord, Selah. Ps 68:32 2167
I will s praises with the lyre, Ps 71:22 2167
for joy when I s praises to You; Ps 71:23 2167
s praises to the God of Jacob. Ps 75:9 2167
S for joy to God our strength; Ps 81:1 7442
flesh s for joy to the living God. Ps 84:2 7442
Then those who s as well as those Ps 87:7 7891
I will s of the lovingkindness of Ps 89:1 7891
That we may s for joy and be glad Ps 90:14 7442
And to s praises to Your name, Ps 92:1 2167
I will s for joy at the works of Ps 92:4 7442
let us s for joy to the LORD, Ps 95:1 7442
S to the LORD a new song; Ps 96:1 7891
S to the LORD, all the earth. Ps 96:1 7891
S to the LORD, bless His name; Ps 96:2 7891
of the forest will s for joy Ps 96:12 7442
O s to the LORD a new song, For He Ps 98:1 7891
and s for joy and sing praises. Ps 98:4 7442
and sing for joy and s praises. Ps 98:4 2167
S praises to the LORD with the Ps 98:5 2167
the mountains s together for joy Ps 98:8 7442
I will s of lovingkindness and Ps 101:1 2167
To You, O LORD, I will s praises. Ps 101:1 2167
I will s to the LORD as long Ps 104:33 2167
I will s praise to my God while I Ps 104:33 2167
S to Him, sing praises to Him; Ps 105:2 7891
Sing to Him, s praises to Him; Ps 105:2 2167
I will s, I will sing praises, Ps 108:1 7891
I will sing, I will s praises, Ps 108:1 2167
And I will s praises to You among Ps 108:3 2167
Let my tongue s of Your word, For Ps 119:172 6031b
And let Your godly ones s for joy. Ps 132:9 7442
godly ones will s aloud for joy. Ps 132:16 7442
S praises to His name, for it is Ps 135:3 2167
"S us one of the songs of Zion." Ps 137:3 7891
How can we s the LORD's song In a Ps 137:4 7891
I will s praises to You before Ps 138:1 2167
will s of the ways of the LORD, Ps 138:5 7891
I will s a new song to You, O God; Ps 144:9 7891
strings I will s praises to You, Ps 144:9 2167
I will s praises to my God while I Ps 146:2 2167
is good to s praises to our God; Ps 147:1 2167
S to the LORD with thanksgiving; Ps 147:7 6031b
S praises to our God on the lyre, Ps 147:7 2167
S to the LORD a new song, *And* His Ps 149:1 7891
Let them s praises to Him with Ps 149:3 2167
Let them s for joy on their beds. Ps 149:5 7442
daughters of song will s softly. Ec 12:4 7817
Let me s now for my well-beloved A Is 5:1 7891
strings skillfully, s many songs, Is 23:16
"A vineyard of wine, s of it! Is 27:2 6031b
S to the LORD a new song, *Sing* His Is 42:10 7891
Sing to the LORD a new song, S Is 42:10
the inhabitants of Sela s aloud, Is 42:11 7442
S to the LORD, praise the LORD! Jer 20:13 7891
"S aloud with gladness for Jacob, Jer 31:7 7442
And she will s there as in the Hos 2:15 6031b
Birds will s in the window, Zph 2:14 7891
"S for joy and be glad, O Zch 2:10 7442
AND I WILL S TO YOUR NAME." Ro 15:9 5567
I will s with the spirit and I 1Co 14:15 5567
and I will s with the mind also. 1Co 14:15 5567
I WILL S YOUR PRAISE." Heb 2:12 5214
He is to s praises. Jas 5:13 5567

SINGED
nor was the hair of their head s, Da 3:27 2761

SINGER
the Kohathites *were* Heman the s, 1Ch 6:33 7891

SINGERS
also lyres and harps for the s; 1Ki 10:12 7891
Now these are the s, 1Ch 9:33 7891
to appoint their relatives the s, 1Ch 15:16 7891
So the s, Heman, Asaph and Ethan 1Ch 15:19 7891
and the s and Chenaniah the leader 1Ch 15:27 7891
leader of the singing *with* the s. 1Ch 15:27 7891
and all the Levitical s, 2Ch 5:12 7891
the s were to make themselves heard 2Ch 5:13 7891
and lyres and harps for the s; 2Ch 9:11 7891
the s with *their* musical instruments 2Ch 23:13 7891
the s also sang and the trumpets 2Ch 29:28 7892a
The s, the sons of Asaph, *were* 2Ch 35:15 7891
And all the male and female s 2Ch 35:25 7891
The s: the sons of Asaph, 128. Ezr 2:41 7891
some of the people, the s, Ezr 2:70 7891
the priests, the Levites, the s, Ezr 7:7 7891
on any of the priests, Levites, s, Ezr 7:24 2171
Of the s *there was* Eliashib; Ezr 10:24 7891
and the gatekeepers and the s and Ne 7:1 7891
The s: the sons of Asaph, 148. Ne 7:44 7891
they had 245 male and female s. Ne 7:67 7891
Levites, the gatekeepers, the s, Ne 7:73 7891
Levites, the gatekeepers, the s, Ne 10:28 7891
the gatekeepers and the s. Ne 10:39 7891
who were the s for the service of Ne 11:22 7891
So the sons of the s were Ne 12:28 7891
for the s had built themselves Ne 12:29 7891
And the s sang, with Jezrahiah Ne 12:42 7891
together with the s and the Ne 12:45 7891
there were leaders of the s, Ne 12:46 7891
Nehemiah gave the portions due the s Ne 12:47 7891
the s and the gatekeepers, Ne 13:5 7891
so that the Levites and the s who Ne 13:10 7891
The s went on, the musicians after Ps 68:25 7891
provided for myself male and female s Ec 2:8 7891
for the s in the inner court, Ezk 40:44 7891

SINGING
But the sound of s I hear." Ex 32:18 6031b
cities of Israel, s and dancing, 1Sa 18:6 7891
the voice of s men and women? 2Sa 19:35 7891
Levites, was *in charge of* the s; 1Ch 15:22 4853a
he gave instruction in s because he 1Ch 15:22 4853a
leader of the s *with* the singers. 1Ch 15:27 4853a
who were trained in s to the LORD, 1Ch 25:7 7892a
When they began s and praising, 2Ch 20:22 7440
with rejoicing and s according to the 2Ch 23:18 7892a
and they had 200 s men and women. Ezr 2:65 7891
Come before Him with joyful s. Ps 100:2 7445
tell of His works with joyful s. Ps 107:22 7440
After s a hymn, they went out Mt 26:30 5214
After s a hymn, they went out Mk 14:26 5214
and s hymns of praise to God, Ac 16:25 5214
s and making melody with your Eph 5:19 103
s with thankfulness in your hearts Col 3:16 103

SINGLE
of grain came up on a s stalk, Gn 41:5 259
and good, came up on a s stalk; Gn 41:22 259
"It is to be eaten in a s house; Ex 12:46 259
them out before you in a s year, Ex 23:29 259
a s hammered work of pure gold. Ex 37:22 259
branch with a s cluster of grapes; Nu 13:23 259
not taken a s donkey from them, Nu 16:15 259
"A s witness shall not rise up Dt 19:15 259
"Then the LORD will s him out for Dt 29:21 914
A dead dog, a s flea? 1Sa 24:14 259
come out to search for a s flea, 1Sa 26:20 259
he did not leave a s male, 1Ki 16:11
with a s *glance* of your eyes, SS 4:9 259
With a s strand of your necklace. SS 4:9 259
branch and bulrush in a s day. Is 9:14 259
thorns and his briars in a s day. Is 10:17 259
without a s *clean* place. Is 28:8
So Jeremiah wrote in a s scroll Jer 51:60 259
there was a s great statue; Da 2:31 2298
of you by being worried can add a s Mt 6:27
answer him with regard to even a s Mt 27:14
by worrying can add a s hour Lk 12:25
a s outcry arose from them all as Ac 19:34
who sold his own birthright for a s Heb 12:16
one of the gates was a s pearl. Rv 21:21 1520

SINGS
who s songs to a troubled heart. Pr 25:20 7891
But the righteous s and rejoices. Pr 29:6 7442

SINIM
And these from the land of S." Is 49:12 5515

SINITE
Hivite and the Arkite and the S Gn 10:17 5513

SINITES
the Hivites, the Arkites, the S, 1Ch 1:15 5513

SINK
the mire and do not let me s; Ps 69:14 2883
Babylon s down and not rise again Jer 51:64 8257
became frightened, and beginning to s, Mt 14:30 2670
boats, so that they began to s. Lk 5:7 1036
"Let these words s into your ears; Lk 9:44 5087

SINKING
window sill, s into a deep sleep; Ac 20:9 2702

SINKS
"He s a shaft far from Jb 28:4 6555
For her house s down to death And Pr 2:18 7743

SINNED
And how have I s against you, that Gn 20:9 2398
"I have s this time; Ex 9:27 2398
he s again and hardened his heart, Ex 9:34 2398
"I have s against the LORD your Ex 10:16 2398
"Whoever has s against Me, I will Ex 32:33 2398
confess that in which he has s. Lv 5:5 2398
for that in which he has s, Lv 5:7 2398
offering for that which he has s, Lv 5:11 2398
he has s against the holy thing, Lv 5:16 2398
he s unintentionally and did not know Lv 5:18 7683
foolishly and in which we have s. Nu 12:11 2398
we have indeed s, but we will go Nu 14:40 2398
have s at the cost of their lives, Nu 16:38 2400
"We have s, because we have Nu 21:7 2398
"I have s, for I did not know Nu 22:34 2398
you have s against the LORD, Nu 32:23 2398
'We have s against the LORD; Dt 1:41 2398
s against the LORD your God. Dt 9:16 2398
"Israel has s, and they have also Jos 7:11 2398
"Truly, I have s against the Jos 7:20 2398
"We have s against You, for Jg 10:10 2398
"We have s, do to us whatever Jg 10:15 2398
'I therefore have not s against you, Jg 11:27 2398

"We have **s** against the LORD." 1Sa 7:6 2398
'We have **s** because we have 1Sa 12:10 2398
Then Saul said to Samuel, "I have **s**; 1Sa 15:24 2398
he said, "I have **s**; *but* please honor 1Sa 15:30 2398
since he has not **s** against you, 1Sa 19:4 2398
and I have not **s** against you, 1Sa 24:11 2398
Saul said, "I have **s**. Return, my son 1Sa 26:21 2398
"I have **s** against the LORD." 2Sa 12:13 2398
your servant knows that I have **s**; 2Sa 19:20 2398
s greatly in what I have done. 2Sa 24:10 2398
"Behold, it is I who have **s**, 2Sa 24:17 2398
because they have **s** against You, 1Ki 8:33 2398
because they have **s** against You, 1Ki 8:35 2398
have **s** and have committed iniquity, 1Ki 8:47 2398
and forgive Your people who have **s** 1Ki 8:50 2398
the sins of Jeroboam which he **s**, 1Ki 15:30 2398
which they **s** and which they made 1Ki 16:13 2398
because of his sins which he **s**, 1Ki 16:19 2398
had **s** against the LORD their God, 2Ki 17:7 2398
"I have **s** greatly, in that I have 1Ch 21:8 2398
who has **s** and done very wickedly, 1Ch 21:17 2398
because they have **s** against You, 2Ch 6:24 2398
because they have **s** against You, 2Ch 6:26 2398
'We have **s**, we have committed 2Ch 6:37 2398
people who have **s** against You. 2Ch 6:39 2398
which we have **s** against You; Ne 1:6 2398
I and my father's house have **s**. Ne 1:6 2398
but **s** against Your ordinances, Ne 9:29 2398
"Perhaps my sons have **s** and Jb 1:5 2398
Have I **s**? What have I done to You Jb 7:20 2398
"If your sons **s** against Him, Then Jb 8:4 2398
So does Sheol *those who* have **s**. Jb 24:19 2398
I have **s** and perverted what is right, Jb 33:27 2398
I have, more than if I had **s**?' Jb 35:3 2403b
"If you have **s**, what do you Jb 35:6 2398
soul, for I have **s** against You." Ps 41:4 2398
Against You, You only, I have **s** And Ps 51:4 2398
In spite of all this they still **s** And Ps 78:32 2398
We have **s** like our fathers, We Ps 106:6 2398
the LORD, against whom we have **s**, Is 42:24 2398
"Your first forefather **s**, Is 43:27 2398
Behold, You were angry, for we **s**, Is 64:5 2398
Because you say, 'I have not **s**.' Jer 2:35 2398
have **s** against the LORD our God, Jer 3:25 2398
For we have **s** against the LORD. Jer 8:14 2398
been many, We have **s** against You. Jer 14:7 2398
for we have **s** against You. Jer 14:20 2398
by which they have **s** against Me, Jer 33:8 2398
by which they have **s** against Me Jer 33:8 2398
"*In* what *way* have I **s** against you, Jer 37:18 2398
Because you *people* **s** against the Jer 40:3 2398
and have **s** against the LORD and not Jer 44:23 2398
Inasmuch as they have **s** against Jer 50:7 2398
For she has **s** against the LORD. Jer 50:14 2398
Jerusalem **s** greatly, Therefore she La 1:8 2398
Our fathers **s**, *and* are no more; La 5:7 2398
Woe to us, for we have **s**! La 5:16 2398
filled with violence, And you **s**; Ezk 28:16 2398
places in which they have **s**, Ezk 37:23 2398
we have **s**, committed iniquity, Da 9:5 2398
because we have **s** against You. Da 9:8 2398
of God, for we have **s** against Him. Da 9:11 2398
we have **s**, we have been wicked. Da 9:15 2398
the more they **s** against Me; Hos 4:7 2398
the days of Gibeah you have **s**, Hos 10:9 2398
LORD Because I have **s** against Him, Mi 7:9 2398
they have **s** against the LORD; Zph 1:17 2398
I have **s** by betraying innocent blood Mt 27:4 264
"Father, I have **s** against heaven, Lk 15:18 264
I have **s** against heaven and in Lk 15:21 264
"Rabbi, who **s**, this man or his Jn 9:2 264
"*It was* neither *that* this man **s**, Jn 9:3 264
For all who have **s** without the Law Ro 2:12 264
and all who have **s** under the Law Ro 2:12 264
for all have **s** and fall short of Ro 3:23 264
spread to all men, because all **s** Ro 5:12 264
even over those who had not **s** in Ro 5:14 264
which came through the one who **s**; Ro 5:16 264
you marry, you have not **s**; 1Co 7:28 264
marries, she has not **s**. 1Co 7:28 264
those who have **s** in the past and not 2Co 12:21 4258
I say in advance to those who have **s** 2Co 13:2 4258
Was it not with those who **s**, Heb 3:17 264
did not spare angels when they **s**, 2Pe 2:4 264
If we say that we have not **s**, 1Jn 1:10 264
devil has **s** from the beginning. 1Jn 3:8 264

SINNER

much more the wicked and the **s**! Pr 11:31 2398
But wickedness subverts the **s**. Pr 13:6 2403b
And the wealth of the **s** is stored Pr 13:22 2398
while to the **s** He has given the Ec 2:26 2398
but the **s** will be captured by her. Ec 7:26 2398
Although a **s** does evil a hundred Ec 8:12 2398
As the good man is, so is the **s**; Ec 9:2 2398
war, but one **s** destroys much good. Ec 9:18 2398
a woman in the city who was a **s**; Lk 7:37 268
touching Him, that she is a **s**." Lk 7:39 268
in heaven over one **s** who repents than Lk 15:7 268
of God over one **s** who repents." Lk 15:10 268
'God, be merciful to me, the **s**!' Lk 18:13 268
the guest of a man who is a **s**." Lk 19:7 268
How can a man who is a **s** perform Jn 9:16 268
we know that this man is a **s**." Jn 9:24 268
"Whether He is a **s**, I do not know; Jn 9:25 268
I also still being judged as a **s**? Ro 3:7 268
he who turns a **s** from the error of his Jas 5:20 268
OF THE GODLESS MAN AND THE **S**? 1Pe 4:18 268

SINNERS

and **s** against the LORD. Gn 13:13 2400
'Go and utterly destroy the **s**, 1Sa 15:18 2400
Nor stand in the path of **s**, Ps 1:1 2400
Nor **s** in the assembly of the Ps 1:5 2400
He instructs **s** in the way. Ps 25:8 2400
take my soul away *along* with **s**, Ps 26:9 2400
And **s** will be converted to You. Ps 51:13 2400
Let **s** be consumed from the earth And Ps 104:35 2400
My son, if **s** entice you, Do not Pr 1:10 2400
Adversity pursues **s**, Pr 13:21 2400
Do not let your heart envy **s**, Pr 23:17 2400
and **s** will be crushed together, Is 1:28 2400
He will exterminate its **s** from it. Is 13:9 2400
S in Zion are terrified; Is 33:14 2400
"All the **s** of My people will die Am 9:10 2400
behold, many tax collectors and **s** Mt 9:10 268
with the tax collectors and **s**?" Mt 9:11 268
not come to call the righteous, but **s** Mt 9:13 268
a friend of tax collectors and **s**!' Mt 11:19 268
betrayed into the hands of **s**. Mt 26:45 268
and many tax collectors and **s** were Mk 2:15 268
with the **s** and tax collectors, Mk 2:16 268
with tax collectors and **s**?" Mk 2:16 268
to call the righteous, but **s**." Mk 2:17 268
betrayed into the hands of **s**. Mk 14:41 268
with the tax collectors and **s**?" Lk 5:30 268
not come to call the righteous but **s** Lk 5:32 268
even **s** love those who love them. Lk 6:32 268
For even **s** do the same. Lk 6:33 268
Even **s** lend to sinners in order Lk 6:34 268
Even sinners lend to **s** in Lk 6:34 268
a friend of tax collectors and **s**!' Lk 7:34 268
greater **s** than all *other* Galileans Lk 13:2 268
the **s** were coming near Him to listen Lk 15:1 268
man receives **s** and eats with them." Lk 15:2 268
"We know that God does not hear **s**; Jn 9:31 268
us, in that while we were yet **s**, Ro 5:8 268
disobedience the many were made **s**, Ro 5:19 268
and not **s** from among the Gentiles; Ga 2:15 268
ourselves have also been found **s**, Ga 2:17 268
rebellious, for the ungodly and **s**, 1Tm 1:9 268
Jesus came into the world to save **s**, 1Tm 1:15 268
undefiled, separated from **s** and Heb 7:26 268
who has endured such hostility by **s** Heb 12:3 268
Cleanse your hands, you **s**; Jas 4:8 268
ungodly **s** have spoken against Him. Jude 1:15 268

SINNING

I also kept you from **s** against Me; Gn 20:6 2398
the people are **s** against the LORD 1Sa 14:33 2398
have become altars of **s** for him. Hos 8:11 2398
So you are **s** against yourself. Hab 2:10 2398
by **s** against the brethren and 1Co 8:12 264
as you ought, and stop **s**; 1Co 15:34 264
the rest also will be fearful *of* **s**. 1Tm 5:20
such a man is perverted and is **s**, Ti 3:11 264
For if we go on **s** willfully after Heb 10:26 264

SINS

'If a person **s** unintentionally in Lv 4:2 2398
if the anointed priest **s** so as to Lv 4:3 2398
'When a leader **s** and Lv 4:22 2398
if anyone of the common people **s** Lv 4:27 2398
'Now if a person **s** after he hears Lv 5:1 2398
s unintentionally against the LORD's Lv 5:15 2398
"Now if a person **s** and does any Lv 5:17 2398
"When a person **s** and acts Lv 6:2 2398
so that he **s** in regard to any one Lv 6:3 2398
be, when he **s** and becomes guilty, Lv 6:4 2398
in regard to all their **s**; Lv 16:16 2403b
in regard to all their **s**; Lv 16:21 2403b
from all your **s** before the LORD. Lv 16:30 2403b
for all their **s** once every year." Lv 16:34 2403b
you seven times more for your **s**. Lv 26:18 2403b
seven times according to your **s**. Lv 26:21 2403b
strike you seven times for your **s**. Lv 26:24 2403b
punish you seven times for your **s**. Lv 26:28 2403b
commits any of the **s** of mankind, Nu 5:6 2403b
his **s** which he has committed, Nu 5:7 2403b
if one person **s** unintentionally, Nu 15:27 2398
astray when he **s** unintentionally, Nu 15:28 2398
of all flesh, when one man **s**, Nu 16:22 2398
your transgression or your **s**. Jos 24:19 2403b
"If one man **s** against another, 1Sa 2:25 2398
but if a man **s** against the LORD, 1Sa 2:25 2398
for we have added to all our **s** 1Sa 12:19 2403b
"If a man **s** against his neighbor 1Ki 8:31 2398
on account of the **s** of Jeroboam, 1Ki 14:16 2403b
with the **s** which they committed. 1Ki 14:22 2403b
He walked in all the **s** of his father 1Ki 15:3 2403b
the **s** of Jeroboam which he sinned, 1Ki 15:30 2403b
Me to anger with their **s**, 1Ki 16:2 2403b
for all the **s** of Baasha and the 1Ki 16:13 2403b
Baasha and the **s** of Elah his son, 1Ki 16:13 2403b
because of his **s** which he sinned, 1Ki 16:19 2403b
in his **s** which he made Israel sin, 1Ki 16:26 2403b
s of Jeroboam the son of Nebat, 1Ki 16:31 2403b
s of Jeroboam the son of Nebat, 2Ki 3:3 2403b
s of Jeroboam the son of Nebat, 2Ki 10:29 2399
not depart from the **s** of Jeroboam, 2Ki 10:31 2403b
s of Jeroboam the son of Nebat, 2Ki 13:2 2403b
the **s** of the house of Jeroboam, 2Ki 13:6 2403b
s of Jeroboam the son of Nebat, 2Ki 13:11 2403b
s of Jeroboam the son of Nebat, 2Ki 14:24 2403b
s of Jeroboam the son of Nebat, 2Ki 15:9 2403b
s of Jeroboam the son of Nebat, 2Ki 15:18 2403b
the **s** of Jeroboam the son of Nebat, 2Ki 15:24 2403b
the **s** of Jeroboam son of Nebat, 2Ki 15:28 2403b
the **s** of Jeroboam which he did; 2Ki 17:22 2403b
because of the **s** of Manasseh, 2Ki 24:3 2403b
"If a man **s** against his neighbor and 2Ch 6:22 2398
adding to our **s** and our guilt; 2Ch 28:13 2403b
confessing the **s** of the sons of Israel Ne 1:6 2403b
and stood and confessed their **s** Ne 9:2 2403b
have set over us because of our **s**; Ne 9:37 2403b
"How many are my iniquities and **s**? Jb 13:23 2403b
Your servant from presumptuous **s**; Ps 19:13
Do not remember the **s** of my youth Ps 25:7 2403b
my trouble, And forgive all my **s**. Ps 25:18 2403b
Hide Your face from my **s** And Ps 51:9 2399
And deliver us and forgive our **s** Ps 79:9 2403b
Our secret **s** in the light of Your Ps 90:8
dealt with us according to our **s**, Ps 103:10 2399
he who **s** against me injures himself; Pr 8:36 2398
He who despises his neighbor **s**, Pr 14:21 2398
does good and who never **s**. Ec 7:20 2398
"Though your **s** are as scarlet, Is 1:18 2399
cast all my **s** behind Your back. Is 38:17 2399
LORD's hand Double for all her **s**." Is 40:2 2403b
you have burdened Me with your **s**, Is 43:24 2403b
And I will not remember your **s**. Is 43:25 2403b
And your **s** like a heavy mist. Is 44:22 2403b
And to the house of Jacob their **s**. Is 58:1 2403b
s have hidden *His* face from you so Is 59:2 2403b
And our **s** testify against us; Is 59:12 2403b
s have withheld good from you. Jer 5:25 2403b
and call their **s** to account." Jer 14:10 2403b
Even for all your **s** And within all Jer 15:13 2403b
is great *And* your **s** are numerous. Jer 30:14 2403b
is great *And* your **s** are numerous, Jer 30:15 2403b
and for the **s** of Judah, but they Jer 50:20 2403b
Offer complaint in view of his **s**? La 3:39 2399
Because of the **s** of her prophets La 4:13 2403b
He will expose your **s**! La 4:22 2403b
if a country **s** against Me by Ezk 14:13 2398
did not commit half of your **s**, Ezk 16:51 2403b
Because of your **s** in which you Ezk 16:52 2403b
The soul who **s** will die. Ezk 18:4 2398
his father's **s** which he committed, Ezk 18:14 2403b
"The person who **s** will die. Ezk 18:20 2398
if the wicked man turns from all his **s** Ezk 18:21 2403b
that in all your deeds your **s** appear Ezk 21:24 2403b
and our **s** are upon us, Ezk 33:10 2403b
"None of his **s** that he has Ezk 33:16 2403b
break away now from your **s** by Da 4:27 2408
for because of our **s** and the Da 9:16 2399
And punish *them* for their **s**; Hos 8:13 2403b
iniquity, He will punish their **s**. Hos 9:9 2403b
are many and your **s** are great, Am 5:12 2403b
for the **s** of the house of Israel. Mi 1:5 2403b
Desolating *you* because of your **s**. Mi 6:13 2403b
You will cast all their **s** Into the Mi 7:19 2403b
save His people from their **s**." Mt 1:21 266
River, as they confessed their **s**. Mt 3:6 266
son; your **s** are forgiven." Mt 9:2 266
'Your **s** are forgiven,' or to say, Mt 9:5 266
has authority on earth to forgive **s** Mt 9:6 266
"If your brother **s**, Mt 18:15 264
out for many for forgiveness of **s**. Mt 26:28 266
for the forgiveness of **s**. Mk 1:4 266
Jordan River, confessing their **s**. Mk 1:5 266
"Son, your **s** are forgiven." Mk 2:5 266
who can forgive **s** but God alone?" Mk 2:7 266
'Your **s** are forgiven'; Mk 2:9 266
has authority on earth to forgive **s** Mk 2:10 266
all **s** shall be forgiven the sons Mk 3:28 265
By the forgiveness of their **s**, Lk 1:77 266
for the forgiveness of **s**; Lk 3:3 266
"Friend, your **s** are forgiven you." Lk 5:20 266
Who can forgive **s**, but God alone?" Lk 5:21 266
'Your **s** have been forgiven you,' Lk 5:23 266
has authority on earth to forgive **s** Lk 5:24 266
this reason I say to you, her **s**, Lk 7:47 266
"Your **s** have been forgiven." Lk 7:48 266
is this *man* who even forgives **s**?" Lk 7:49 266
'And forgive us our **s**, Lk 11:4 266
If your brother **s**, rebuke him; Lk 17:3 264
s against you seven times a day, Lk 17:4 264
repentance for forgiveness of **s** would Lk 24:47 266
you that you will die in your **s**; Jn 8:24 266
am *He*, you will die in your **s**." Jn 8:24 266
"You were born entirely in **s**, Jn 9:34 266
"If you forgive the **s** of any, Jn 20:23 266
their **s** have been forgiven them; Jn 20:23
if you retain the **s** of any, they Jn 20:23
for the forgiveness of your **s**; Ac 2:38 266
that your **s** may be wiped away, Ac 3:19 266
to Israel, and forgiveness of **s**. Ac 5:31 266
Him receives forgiveness of **s**." Ac 10:43 266
forgiveness of **s** is proclaimed to you Ac 13:38 266
be baptized, and wash away your **s**, Ac 22:16 266
that they may receive forgiveness of **s** Ac 26:18 266
over the **s** previously committed; Ro 3:25 265
AND WHOSE **S** HAVE BEEN COVERED. Ro 4:7 266
THEM, WHEN I TAKE AWAY THEIR **S**." Ro 11:27 266
man **s** against his own body. 1Co 6:18 264
Christ died for our **s** according to 1Co 15:3 266
you are still in your **s**. 1Co 15:17 266
who gave Himself for our **s** so Ga 1:4 266
dead in your trespasses and **s**, Eph 2:1 266
redemption, the forgiveness of **s**. Col 1:14 266
fill up the measure of their **s**. 1Th 2:16 266
responsibility for the **s** of others; 1Tm 5:22 266
s of some men are quite evident, 1Tm 5:24 266
for others, their **s** follow after. 1Tm 5:24
weak women weighed down with **s**, 2Tm 3:6 266
He had made purification of **s**, Heb 1:3 266
propitiation for the **s** of the people. Heb 2:17 266

both gifts and sacrifices for **s**; Heb 5:1 *266*
to offer *sacrifices* for **s**, Heb 5:3 *266*
sacrifices, first for His own **s** and Heb 7:27 *266*
for His own sins and then for the **s** Heb 7:27 *266*
I WILL REMEMBER THEIR **S** NO MORE." Heb 8:12 *266*
he offers for himself and for the **s** of Heb 9:7 *51*
once to bear the **s** of many, Heb 9:28 *266*
have had consciousness of **s**? Heb 10:2 *266*
is a reminder of **s** year by year. Heb 10:3 *266*
of bulls and goats to take away **s**. Heb 10:4 *266*
which can never take away **s**; Heb 10:11 *266*
one sacrifice for **s** for all time, Heb 10:12 *266*
"AND THEIR **S** AND THEIR LAWLESS Heb 10:17 *266*
longer remains a sacrifice for **s**, Heb 10:26 *266*
him up, and if he has committed **s**, Jas 5:15 *266*
confess your **s** to one another, Jas 5:16 *266*
and will cover a multitude of **s**. Jas 5:20 *266*
He Himself bore our **s** in His body 1Pe 2:24 *266*
Christ also died for **s** once for all, 1Pe 3:18 *266*
love covers a multitude of **s**. 1Pe 4:8 *266*
purification from his former **s**. 2Pe 1:9 *266*
If we confess our **s**, He is faithful 1Jn 1:9 *266*
and righteous to forgive us our **s** 1Jn 1:9 *266*
And if anyone **s**, we have an 1Jn 2:1 *264*
is the propitiation for our **s**; 1Jn 2:2 *266*
because your **s** have been forgiven you 1Jn 2:12 *266*
appeared in order to take away **s**; 1Jn 3:5 *266*
No one who abides in Him **s**; 1Jn 3:6 *264*
no one who **s** has seen Him or 1Jn 3:6 *264*
to be the propitiation for our **s**. 1Jn 4:10 *266*
that no one who is born of God **s**; 1Jn 5:18 *264*
released us from our **s** by His blood Rv 1:5 *266*
that you will not participate in her **s** Rv 18:4 *266*
for her **s** have piled up as high as Rv 18:5 *266*

SION
of Arnon, even as far as Mount **S** Dt 4:48 7865

SIPHMOTH
Aroer, and to those who were in **S**, 1Sa 30:28 8224

SIPPAI
Sibbecai the Hushathite killed **S**, 1Ch 20:4 5598

SIR
'**S**, did you not sow good seed in Mt 13:27 *2962*
s'; but he did not go. Mt 21:30 *2962*
"**S**, we remember that when He was Mt 27:63 *2962*
'Let it alone, **s**, for this year Lk 13:8 *2962*
"**S**, You have nothing to draw with Jn 4:11 *2962*
"**S**, give me this water, so I will Jn 4:15 *2962*
"**S**, I perceive that You are a Jn 4:19 *2962*
"**S**, come down before my child Jn 4:49 *2962*
"**S**, I have no man to put me into Jn 5:7 *2962*
"**S**, we wish to see Jesus." Jn 12:21 *2962*
"**S**, if you have carried Him away, Jn 20:15 *2962*

SIRAH
him back from the well of **S**; 2Sa 3:26 5626

SIRED
on steeds **s** by the royal stud. Es 8:10 1121
her in and the one who **s** her Da 11:6 3205

SIRES
He who **s** a fool *does so* to his Pr 17:21 3205
And he who **s** a wise son will be glad Pr 23:24 3205

SIRION
(Sidonians call Hermon **S**, Dt 3:9 8303
calf, And **S** like a young wild ox. Ps 29:6 8303

SIRS
"**S**, what must I do to be saved?" Ac 16:30 *2962*

SISERA
the commander of his army was **S**, Jg 4:2 5516
'I will draw out to you **S**, Jg 4:7 5516
the LORD will sell **S** into the hands Jg 4:9 5516
Then they told **S** that Barak the Jg 4:12 5516
S called together all his Jg 4:13 5516
LORD has given **S** into your hands; Jg 4:14 5516
The LORD routed **S** and all *his* Jg 4:15 5516
and **S** alighted from *his* chariot Jg 4:15 5516
S fell by the edge of the sword; Jg 4:16 5516
Now **S** fled away on foot to the Jg 4:17 5516
Jael went out to meet **S**, Jg 4:18 5516
And behold, as Barak pursued **S**, Jg 4:22 5516
and behold **S** was lying dead with Jg 4:22 5516
courses they fought against **S**. Jg 5:20 5516
Then she struck **S**, she smashed his Jg 5:26 5516
mother of **S** through the lattice, Jg 5:28 5516
To **S** a spoil of dyed work, A spoil Jg 5:30 5516
He sold them into the hand of **S**, 1Sa 12:9 5516
the sons of Barkos, the sons of **S**, Ezr 2:53 5516
the sons of Barkos, the sons of **S**, Ne 7:55 5516
with Midian, As with **S** *and* Jabin at Ps 83:9 5516

SISMAI
Eleasah became the father of **S**, 1Ch 2:40 5581
S became the father of Shallum, 1Ch 2:40 5581

SISTER
and the **s** of Tubal-cain was Naamah. Gn 4:22 269
"Please say that you are my **s** so Gn 12:13 269
'She is my **s**,' so that I took her Gn 12:19 269
said of Sarah his wife, "She is my **s**." Gn 20:2 269
not himself say to me, 'She is my **s**'? Gn 20:5 269
"Besides, she actually is my **s**, Gn 20:12 269
heard the words of Rebekah his **s**, Gn 24:30 269
Thus they sent away their **s** Gn 24:59 269
"May you, our **s**, Become thousands Gn 24:60 269
the **s** of Laban the Aramean, Gn 25:20 269
about his wife, he said, "She is my **s**," Gn 26:7 269
How then did you say, 'She is my **s**'? Gn 26:9 269
Abraham's son, the **s** of Nebaioth. Gn 28:9 269
she became jealous of her **s**; Gn 30:1 269
I have wrestled with my **s**, Gn 30:8 269
he had defiled Dinah their **s**. Gn 34:13 269
cannot do this thing, to give our **s** Gn 34:14 269
because they had defiled their **s**. Gn 34:27 269
he treat our **s** as a harlot?" Gn 34:31 269
daughter, the **s** of Nebaioth. Gn 36:3 269
and Lotan's **s** was Timna. Gn 36:22 269
and Beriah and their **s** Serah. Gn 46:17 269
His **s** stood at a distance to Ex 2:4 269
his **s** said to Pharaoh's daughter, Ex 2:7 269
married his father's **s** Jochebed, Ex 6:20 1733
of Amminadab, the **s** of Nahshon, Ex 6:23 269
Miriam the prophetess, Aaron's **s**, Ex 15:20 269
'The nakedness of your **s**, Lv 18:9 269
born to your father, she is your **s**, Lv 18:11 269
the nakedness of your father's **s**; Lv 18:12 269
the nakedness of your mother's **s**, Lv 18:13 269
marry a woman in addition to her **s** Lv 18:18 269
'If *there is* a man who takes his **s**, Lv 20:17 269
the nakedness of your mother's **s** Lv 20:19 269
mother's sister or of your father's **s**, Lv 20:19 269
also for his virgin **s**, Lv 21:3 269
for his brother or for his **s**, Nu 6:7 269
their **s** who was slain on the day Nu 25:18 269
and Moses and their **s** Miriam. Nu 26:59 269
'Cursed is he who lies with his **s**, Dt 27:22 269
younger **s** more beautiful than she? Jg 15:2 269
beautiful **s** whose name was Tamar, 2Sa 13:1 269
so frustrated because of his **s** Tamar 2Sa 13:2 269
the **s** of my brother Absalom." 2Sa 13:4 269
'Please let my **s** Tamar come and 2Sa 13:5 269
"Please let my **s** Tamar come and 2Sa 13:6 269
"Come, lie with me, my **s**." 2Sa 13:11 269
But now keep silent, my **s**, 2Sa 13:20 269
he had violated his **s** Tamar. 2Sa 13:22 269
day that he violated his **s** Tamar. 2Sa 13:32 269
daughter of Nahash, **s** of Zeruiah, 2Sa 17:25 269
in marriage the **s** of his own wife, 1Ki 11:19 269
wife, the **s** of Tahpenes the queen. 1Ki 11:19 269
The **s** of Tahpenes bore his son 1Ki 11:20 269
of King Joram, **s** of Ahaziah, 2Ki 11:2 269
and Lotan's **s** *was* Timna. 1Ch 1:39 269
and Tamar *was* their **s**. 1Ch 3:9 269
and Shelomith *was* their **s**; 1Ch 3:19 269
name of their **s** *was* Hazzelelponi. 1Ch 4:3 269
wife of Hodiah, the **s** of Naham, 1Ch 4:19 269
His **s** Hammolecheth bore Ishhod 1Ch 7:18 269
and Beriah, and Serah their **s**. 1Ch 7:30 269
and Hotham, and Shua their **s**. 1Ch 7:32 269
(for she was the **s** of Ahaziah), 2Ch 22:11 269
To the worm, 'my mother and my **s**'; Jb 17:14 269
Say to wisdom, "You are my **s**," Pr 7:4 269
made my heart beat faster, my **s**, SS 4:9 269
"How beautiful is your love, my **s**, SS 4:10 269
"A garden locked is my **s**, SS 4:12 269
"I have come into my garden, my **s**, SS 5:1 269
'Open to me, my **s**, my darling, My SS 5:2 269
"We have a little **s**, SS 8:8 269
What shall we do for our **s** On the SS 8:8 269
her treacherous **s** Judah saw it. Jer 3:7 269
treacherous **s** Judah did not fear; Jer 3:8 269
treacherous **s** Judah did not return Jer 3:10 269
'Alas, my brother!' or, 'Alas, **s**!' Jer 22:18 269
are also the **s** of your sisters, Ezk 16:45 269
"Now your older **s** is Samaria, who Ezk 16:46 269
and your younger **s**, Ezk 16:46 269
"Sodom, your **s** and her Ezk 16:48 269
was the guilt of your **s** Sodom: Ezk 16:49 269
"As *the name of* your **s** Sodom was Ezk 16:56 269
another in you has humbled his **s**, Ezk 22:11 269
the elder and Oholibah her **s**. Ezk 23:4 269
"Now her **s** Oholibah saw *this,* yet Ezk 23:11 269
more than the harlotries of her **s**. Ezk 23:11 269
I had become disgusted with her **s**. Ezk 23:18 269
have walked in the way of your **s**; Ezk 23:31 269
The cup of your **s** Samaria. Ezk 23:33 269
for a **s** who has not had a husband, Ezk 44:25 269
he is My brother and **s** and mother. Mt 12:50 *79*
he is My brother and **s** and mother. Mk 3:35 *79*
She had a **s** called Mary, who Lk 10:39 *79*
do You not care that my **s** has left Lk 10:40 *79*
village of Mary and her **s** Martha. Jn 11:1 *79*
Now Jesus loved Martha and her **s** Jn 11:5 *79*
went away and called Mary her **s**, Jn 11:28 *79*
Martha, the **s** of the deceased, Jn 11:39 *79*
His mother, and His mother's **s**, Jn 19:25 *79*
the son of Paul's **s** heard of their Ac 23:16 *79*
I commend to you our **s** Phoebe, Ro 16:1 *79*
and Julia, Nereus and his **s**, Ro 16:15 *79*
the brother or the **s** is not under 1Co 7:15 *79*
and to Apphia our **s**, Phm 1:2 *79*
If a brother or **s** is without clothing Jas 2:15 *79*
children of your chosen **s** greet you. 2Jn 1:13 *79*

SISTER-IN-LAW
your **s** has gone back to her people Ru 1:15 2994
return after your **s**." Ru 1:15 2994

SISTER'S
and the bracelets on his **s** wrists, Gn 24:30 269
heard the news of Jacob his **s** son, Gn 29:13 269
He has uncovered his **s** nakedness; Lv 20:17 269
Shuppim, whose **s** name was Maacah. 1Ch 7:15 269
'You will drink your **s** cup, Ezk 23:32 269

SISTERS
mother and my brothers and my **s**, Jos 2:13 269
their **s** *were* Zeruiah and Abigail. 1Ch 2:16 269
invite their three **s** to eat and drink Jb 1:4 269
all his brothers and all his **s** Jb 42:11 269
You are also the sister of your **s**, Ezk 16:45 269
Thus you have made your **s** appear Ezk 16:51 269
judgment favorable for your **s**. Ezk 16:52 269
you made your **s** appear righteous. Ezk 16:52 269
"Your **s**, Sodom with her Ezk 16:55 269
ashamed when you receive your **s**, Ezk 16:61 269
and to your **s**, "Ruhamah." Hos 2:1 269
"And His **s**, are they not all with Mt 13:56 *79*
who has left houses or brothers or **s** Mt 19:29 *79*
Are not His **s** here with us?" Mk 6:3 *79*
who has left house or brothers or **s** Mk 10:29 *79*
houses and brothers and **s** and Mk 10:30 *79*
and children and brothers and **s**, Lk 14:26 *79*
So the **s** sent *word* to Him, Jn 11:3 *79*
and the younger women as **s**, 1Tm 5:2 *79*

SIT
up, please, **s** and eat of my game, Gn 27:19 3427
Why do you alone **s** *as judge* and Ex 18:14 3427
war while you yourselves **s** here? Nu 32:6 3427
when you **s** in your house and when Dt 6:7 3427
when you **s** in your house and when Dt 11:19 3427
shall be when you **s** down outside, Dt 23:13 3427
She used to **s** under the palm Jg 4:5 3427
You who **s** on *rich* carpets, Jg 5:10 3427
did you **s** among the sheepfolds, Jg 5:16 3427
And will you **s** still? Jg 18:9 2814
"Turn aside, friend, **s** down here." Ru 4:1 3427
elders of the city and said, "**S** down Ru 4:2 3427
heap To make them **s** with nobles, 1Sa 2:8 3427
not **s** down until he comes here." 1Sa 16:11 5437
to **s** down to eat with the king. 1Sa 20:5 3427
me, and he shall **s** on my throne"? 1Ki 1:13 3427
me and he shall **s** on my throne.' 1Ki 1:17 3427
who shall **s** on the throne of my lord 1Ki 1:20 3427
me, and he shall **s** on my throne'? 1Ki 1:24 3427
who should **s** on the throne of my 1Ki 1:27 3427
shall **s** on my throne in my place'; 1Ki 1:30 3427
he shall come and **s** on my throne 1Ki 1:35 3427
who has granted one to **s** on my 1Ki 1:48 3427
him a son to **s** on his throne, 1Ki 3:6 3427
and **s** on the throne of Israel, 1Ki 8:20 3427
man to **s** on the throne of Israel, 1Ki 8:25 3427
"Why do we **s** here until we die? 2Ki 7:3 3427
and if we **s** here, we die also. 2Ki 7:4 3427
shall **s** on the throne of Israel." 2Ki 10:30 3427
shall **s** on the throne of Israel." 2Ki 15:12 3427
not to the men who **s** on the wall, 2Ki 18:27 3427
to **s** on the throne of the kingdom 1Ch 28:5 3427
and **s** on the throne of Israel, 2Ch 6:10 3427
man to **s** on the throne of Israel, 2Ch 6:16 3427
Nor **s** in the seat of scoffers! Ps 1:1 3427
I do not **s** with deceitful men, Nor Ps 26:4 3427
And I will not **s** with the wicked. Ps 26:5 3427
"You **s** and speak against your Ps 50:20 3427
Those who **s** in the gate talk about Ps 69:12 3427
"**S** at My right hand Until I make Ps 110:1 3427
To make *them* **s** with princes, With Ps 113:8 3427
princes **s** *and* talk against me, Ps 119:23 3427
Their sons also shall **s** upon your Ps 132:12 3427
when I **s** down and when I rise up; Ps 139:2 3427
you **s** down to dine with a ruler, Pr 23:1 3427
while rich men **s** in humble places. Ec 10:6 3427
"O you who **s** in the gardens, *My* SS 8:13 3427
deserted she will **s** on the ground. Is 3:26 3427
And I will **s** on the mount of Is 14:13 3427
And a judge will **s** on it in Is 16:5 3427
not to the men who **s** on the wall, Is 36:12 3427
man, so that it may **s** in a house. Is 44:13 3427
"Come down and **s** in the dust, O Is 47:1 3427
S on the ground without a throne, Is 47:1 3427
"**S** silently, and go into Is 47:5 3427
I will not **s** as a widow, Nor Is 47:8 3427
warm by *Nor* a fire to **s** before! Is 47:14 3427
Who **s** among graves and spend the Is 65:4 3427
that **s** for David on his throne, Jer 13:13 3427
They **s** on the ground in mourning, Jer 14:2 6937
s in the circle of merrymakers, Jer 15:17 3427
to **s** with them to eat and drink." Jer 16:8 3427
'David shall never lack a man to **s** Jer 33:17 3427
"**S** down, please, and read it to us." Jer 36:15 3427
one to **s** on the throne of David, Jer 36:30 3427
glory And **s** on the parched ground, Jer 48:18 3427
daughter of Zion **S** on the ground, La 2:10 3427
Let him **s** alone and be silent La 3:28 3427
with you and you **s** on scorpions; Ezk 2:6 3427
they will **s** on the ground, tremble Ezk 26:16 3427
am a god, I **s** in the seat of gods In Ezk 28:2 3427
and **s** before you *as* My people and Ezk 33:31 3427
he shall **s** in it as prince to eat Ezk 44:3 3427
'But the court will **s** *for judgment,* Da 7:26 3488
For there I will **s** to judge All Jl 3:12 3427
Each of them will **s** under his Mi 4:4 3427
you will invite his neighbor to **s** Zch 3:10 3427
and **s** and rule on His throne. Zch 6:13 3427
old women will again **s** in the streets Zch 8:4 3427
"He will **s** as a smelter and Mal 3:3 3427
Ordering the people to **s** down on Mt 14:19 *347*
people to **s** down on the ground; Mt 15:35 *377*
Son of Man will **s** on His glorious Mt 19:28 *2523*
also shall **s** upon twelve thrones, Mt 19:28 *2521*
these two sons of mine may **s** one Mt 20:21 *2523*
to **s** on My right and on *My* left, Mt 20:23 *2523*
'**S** AT MY RIGHT HAND, UNTIL I PUT Mt 22:44 *2521*
He will **s** on His glorious throne. Mt 25:31 *2523*
"**S** here while I go over there and Mt 26:36 *2523*
Every day I used to **s** in the Mt 26:55 *2516*
And He commanded them all to **s** down Mk 6:39 *347*
people to **s** down on the ground; Mk 8:6 *377*
"Grant that we may **s**, Mk 10:37 *2523*
to **s** on My right or on *My* left, Mk 10:40 *2523*
"**S** AT MY RIGHT HAND, UNTIL I PUT Mk 12:36 *2521*
"**S** here until I have prayed." Mk 14:32 *2523*

UPON THOSE WHO **s** IN DARKNESS **Lk 1:79** *2521*
children who **s** in the market place **Lk 7:32** *2521*
"Have them **s** down *to eat* in **Lk 9:14** *2625*
They did so, and had them all **s** down. **Lk 9:15** *2625*
s down and calculate the cost to **Lk 14:28** *2523*
will not first **s** down and consider **Lk 14:31** *2523*
s down quickly and write fifty.' **Lk 16:6** *2523*
immediately and **s** down to eat'? **Lk 17:7** *377*
"**S** AT MY RIGHT HAND **Lk 20:42** *2521*
and you will **s** on thrones judging **Lk 22:30** *2521*
"Have the people **s** down." **Jn 6:10** *377*
the one who used to **s** and beg?" **Jn 9:8** *2521*
"**S** AT MY RIGHT HAND, **Ac 2:34** *2521*
who used to **s** at the Beautiful Gate **Ac 3:10** *2521*
Philip to come up and **s** with him. **Ac 8:31** *2523*
Do you **s** to try me according **Ac 23:3** *2521*
"**S** AT MY RIGHT HAND, UNTIL I MAKE **Heb 1:13** *2521*
"You **s** here in a good place," **Jas 2:3** *2521*
or **s** down by my footstool," **Jas 2:3** *2521*
to **s** down with Me on My throne, **Rv 3:21** *2523*
who **s** on their thrones before God, **Rv 11:16** *2521*
'I **S** *as* A QUEEN AND I AM **Rv 18:7** *2521*
horses and of those who **s** on them **Rv 19:18** *2521*

SITE
land as far as the **s** of Shechem, **Gn 12:6** 4725
give me a burial **s** among you that **Gn 23:4** 272
in your presence for a burial **s**." **Gn 23:9** 272
a burial **s** by the sons of Heth. **Gn 23:20** 272
Ephron the Hittite for a burial **s**. **Gn 49:30** 272
burial **s** from Ephron the Hittite. **Gn 50:13** 272
wadis That extends to the **s** of Ar, **Nu 21:15** 7675
Give me the **s** of *this* threshing floor, **1Ch 21:22** 4725
of gold by weight for the **s**. **1Ch 21:25** 4725
this house of God on its **s**. **Ezr 6:7** 870
will make a complete end of its **s**, **Na 1:8** 4725
Jerusalem will rise and remain on its **s** **Zch 14:10** 8478

SITES
and the **s** on which he built high **2Ch 33:19** 4725
dwell on their own **s** in Jerusalem. **Zch 12:6** 8478

SITHRI
Mishael and Elzaphan and **S**. **Ex 6:22** 5644

SITNAH
over it too, so he named it **S**. **Gn 26:21** 7856

SITS
the Pharaoh who **s** on his throne, **Ex 11:5** 3427
on which he **s** becomes unclean. **Lv 15:4** 3427
and whoever **s** on the thing on **Lv 15:6** 3427
on which she **s** shall be unclean. **Lv 15:20** 3427
touches any thing on which she **s** **Lv 15:22** 3427
on which she **s** shall be unclean, **Lv 15:26** 3427
he **s** on the throne of his kingdom, **Dt 17:18** 3427
of hosts who **s** *above* the cherubim; **1Sa 4:4** 3427
He who **s** in the heavens laughs, **Ps 2:4** 3427
He **s** in the lurking places of the **Ps 10:8** 3427
Yes, the LORD **s** as King forever. **Ps 29:10** 3427
nations, God **s** on His holy throne. **Ps 47:8** 3427
the one who **s** enthroned from of old **Ps 55:19** 3427
She **s** at the doorway of her house, **Pr 9:14** 3427
A king who **s** on the throne of **Pr 20:8** 3427
he **s** among the elders of the land. **Pr 31:23** 3427
justice for him who **s** in judgment, **Is 28:6** 3427
s above the circle of the earth, **Is 40:22** 3427
of Judah, who **s** on David's throne, **Jer 22:2** 3427
king who **s** on the throne of David, **Jer 29:16** 3427
How lonely **s** the city That was **La 1:1** 3427
of God and by Him who **s** upon it. **Mt 23:22** *2521*
thanks to Him who **s** on the throne, **Rv 4:9** *2521*
before Him who **s** on the throne, **Rv 4:10** *2521*
"To Him who **s** on the throne, and **Rv 5:13** *2521*
of Him who **s** on the throne, **Rv 6:16** *2521*
to our God who **s** on the throne, **Rv 7:10** *2521*
and He who **s** on the throne will **Rv 7:15** *2521*
great harlot who **s** on many waters, **Rv 17:1** *2521*
mountains on which the woman **s**, **Rv 17:9** *2521*
which you saw where the harlot **s**, **Rv 17:15** *2521*
God who **s** on the throne saying, **Rv 19:4** *2521*
And He who **s** on the throne said, **Rv 21:5** *2521*

SITTING
while he was **s** at the tent door in **Gn 18:1** 3427
as Lot was **s** in the gate of Sodom. **Gn 19:1** 3427
Now Ephron was **s** among the sons **Gn 23:10** 3427
man with the discharge has been **s**, **Lv 15:6** 3427
or on the thing on which she is **s**, **Lv 15:23** 3427
the mother **s** on the young or on the **Dt 22:6** 7257
Ehud came to him while he was **s** **Jg 3:20** 3427
woman as she was **s** in the field, **Jg 13:9** 3427
she has been **s** in the house for a **Ru 2:7** 3427
it before those who are **s** *here*, **Ru 4:4** 3427
Now Eli the priest was **s** on the **1Sa 1:9** 3427
Eli was **s** on *his* seat by the road **1Sa 4:13** 3427
on Saul as he was **s** in his house **1Sa 19:9** 3427
Now Saul was **s** in Gibeah, under **1Sa 22:6** 3427
Now David and his men were **s** in **1Sa 24:3** 3427
David was **s** between the two gates; **2Sa 18:24** 3427
the king is **s** in the gate," **2Sa 19:8** 3427
God and found him **s** under an oak; **1Ki 13:14** 3427
as they were **s** down at the table, **1Ki 13:20** 3427
Judah were **s** each on his throne, **1Ki 22:10** 3427
I saw the LORD **s** on His throne, **1Ki 22:19** 3427
he was **s** on the top of the hill. **2Ki 1:9** 3427
of the prophets were **s** before him, **2Ki 4:38** 3427
Now Elisha was **s** in his house, and **2Ki 6:32** 3427
and the elders were **s** with him. **2Ki 6:32** 3427
the captains of the army were **s**, **2Ki 9:5** 3427
'But I know your **s** down, And your **2Ki 19:27** 3427
Judah were **s** each on his throne, **2Ch 18:9** 3427
and *they* were **s** at the threshing **2Ch 18:9** 3427
I saw the LORD **s** on His throne, **2Ch 18:18** 3427
to me, the queen **s** beside him, **Ne 2:6** 3427
Mordecai was **s** at the king's gate. **Es 2:19** 3427
Mordecai was **s** at the king's gate, **Es 2:21** 3427
and the king was **s** on his royal **Es 5:1** 3427
the Jew **s** at the king's gate." **Es 5:13** 3427
Jew, who is **s** at the king's gate; **Es 6:10** 3427
while he was **s** among the ashes. **Jb 2:8** 3427
I saw the Lord **s** on a throne, **Is 6:1** 3427
"But I know your **s** down And your **Is 37:28** 3427
Why are we **s** still? **Jer 8:14** 3427
princes **s** on the throne of David, **Jer 17:25** 3427
s in David's place on his throne, **Jer 22:4** 3427
will prosper **S** on the throne of David **Jer 22:30** 3427
were **s** in the court of the guard. **Jer 32:12** 3427
behold, all the officials were **s** there **Jer 36:12** 3427
Now the king was **s** in the winter **Jer 36:22** 3427
king was **s** in the Gate of Benjamin; **Jer 38:7** 3427
Look on their **s** and their rising; **La 3:63** 3427
as I was **s** in my house with the **Ezk 8:1** 3427
the elders of Judah **s** before me, **Ezk 8:1** 3427
women were **s** there weeping for **Ezk 8:14** 3427
you and your friends who are **s** in **Zch 3:8** 3427
this is a woman **s** inside the ephah." **Zch 5:7** 3427
PEOPLE WHO WERE **S** IN DARKNESS **Mt 4:16** *2521*
THOSE WHO WERE **S** IN THE LAND **Mt 4:16** *2521*
Matthew, **s** in the tax collector's **Mt 9:9** *2521*
children **s** in the market places, **Mt 11:16** *2521*
the house and was **s** by the sea. **Mt 13:1** *2521*
on the mountain, He was **s** there. **Mt 15:29** *2521*
two blind men **s** by the road, **Mt 20:30** *2521*
He was **s** on the Mount of Olives, **Mt 24:3** *2521*
MAN **S** AT THE RIGHT HAND OF POWER, **Mt 26:64** *2521*
was **s** outside in the courtyard, **Mt 26:69** *2521*
he was **s** on the judgment seat, **Mt 27:19** *2521*
And **s** down, they *began* to keep **Mt 27:36** *2521*
other Mary, **s** opposite the grave. **Mt 27:61** *2521*
some of the scribes were **s** there **Mk 2:6** *2521*
son of Alphaeus **s** in the tax booth, **Mk 2:14** *2521*
A crowd was **s** around Him, **Mk 3:32** *2521*
at those who were **s** around Him, **Mk 3:34** *2521*
had been demon-possessed **s** down, **Mk 5:15** *2521*
S down, He called the twelve **Mk 9:35** *2523*
son of Timaeus, was **s** by the road. **Mk 10:46** *2521*
As He was **s** on the Mount of Olives **Mk 13:3** *2521*
and he was **s** with the officers and **Mk 14:54** *4775*
SON OF MAN **S** AT THE RIGHT HAND **Mk 14:62** *2521*
saw a young man **s** at the right, **Mk 16:5** *2521*
s in the midst of the teachers, **Lk 2:46** *2516*
and teachers of the law **s** *there*, **Lk 5:17** *2521*
named Levi **s** in the tax booth, **Lk 5:27** *2521*
out, **s** down at the feet of Jesus, **Lk 8:35** *2521*
ago, **s** in sackcloth and ashes. **Lk 10:13** *2521*
blind man was **s** by the road begging **Lk 18:35** *2521*
together, Peter was **s** among them. **Lk 22:55** *2521*
journey, was **s** thus by the well. **Jn 4:6** *2516*
she saw two angels in white **s**, **Jn 20:12** *2516*
the whole house where they were **s**. **Ac 2:2** *2521*
all who were **s** in the Council saw **Ac 6:15** *2516*
returning and **s** in his chariot, **Ac 8:28** *2521*
Lystra a man was **s** **Ac 14:8** *2521*
Eutychus **s** on the window sill, **Ac 20:9** *2516*
and those who were **s** with them, **Ac 26:30** *4775*
heaven, and One **s** on the throne. **Rv 4:2** *2521*
And He who was **s** *was* like a jasper **Rv 4:3** *2521*
thrones *I saw* twenty-four elders **s**, **Rv 4:4** *2521*
and **s** on the cloud *was* one like a **Rv 14:14** *2521*
I saw a woman **s** on a scarlet beast, **Rv 17:3** *2521*

SITUATED
are the people who are so **s**; **Ps 144:15**
was **s** by the waters of the Nile, **Na 3:8** 3427

SITUATION
the **s** of this city is pleasant, **2Ki 2:19** 4186
"You see the bad **s** we are in, **Ne 2:17** 7463a
before me until the **s** is changed; **Da 2:9** 5732
inform you about the whole **s** here. **Col 4:9**

SIVAN
third month (that is, the month **S**), **Es 8:9** 5510

SIX
Now Noah was **s** hundred years old **Gn 7:6** 8337a
s hundredth year of Noah's life, **Gn 7:11** 8337a
in the **s** hundred and first year, **Gn 8:13** 8337a
because I have borne him **s** sons." **Gn 30:20** 8337a
and **s** years for your flock, **Gn 31:41** 8337a
s hundred thousand men on foot, **Ex 12:37** 8337a
he took **s** hundred select chariots, **Ex 14:7** 8337a
"**S** days you shall gather it, but **Ex 16:26** 8337a
"**S** days you shall labor and do **Ex 20:9** 8337a
"For in **s** days the LORD made the **Ex 20:11** 8337a
slave, he shall serve for **s** years; **Ex 21:2** 8337a
You shall sow your land for **s** years **Ex 23:10** 8337a
"**S** days you are to do your work, **Ex 23:12** 8337a
the cloud covered it for **s** days; **Ex 24:16** 8337a
"**S** branches shall go out from its **Ex 25:32** 8337a
so for **s** branches going out from the **Ex 25:33** 8337a
for the **s** branches coming out of the **Ex 25:35** 8337a
other **s** curtains by themselves, **Ex 26:9** 8337a
the west, you shall make **s** boards. **Ex 26:22** 8337a
s of their names on the one stone and **Ex 28:10** 8337a
and the names of the remaining **s** **Ex 28:10** 8337a
'For **s** days work may be done, but **Ex 31:15** 8337a
for in **s** days the LORD made heaven **Ex 31:17** 8337a
"You shall work **s** days, but on **Ex 34:21** 8337a
"For **s** days work may be done, but **Ex 35:2** 8337a
other **s** curtains by themselves. **Ex 36:16** 8337a
to the west, he made **s** boards. **Ex 36:27** 8337a
There were **s** branches going **Ex 37:18** 8337a
s branches going out of the lampstand **Ex 37:19** 8337a
for the **s** branches coming out of **Ex 37:21** 8337a
'For **s** days work may be done, **Lv 23:3** 8337a
set them *in* two rows, **s** *to* a row, **Lv 24:6** 8337a
'**S** years you shall sow your field, **Lv 25:3** 8337a
and **s** years you shall prune your **Lv 25:3** 8337a
s covered carts and twelve oxen, **Nu 7:3** 8337a
shall be the **s** cities of refuge, **Nu 35:6** 8337a
shall be your **s** cities of refuge. **Nu 35:13** 8337a
'These **s** cities shall be for **Nu 35:15** 8337a
'**S** days you shall labor and do all **Dt 5:13** 8337a
then he shall serve you **s** years, **Dt 15:12** 8337a
for he has given you **s** years *with* **Dt 15:18** 8337a
"**S** days you shall eat unleavened **Dt 16:8** 8337a
You shall do so for **s** days. **Jos 6:3** 8337a
they did so for **s** days. **Jos 6:14** 8337a
s cities with their villages. **Jos 15:59** 8337a
s cities with their villages. **Jos 15:62** 8337a
who struck down **s** hundred **Jg 3:31** 8337a
Jephthah judged Israel **s** years. **Jg 12:7** 8337a
s hundred men armed with weapons **Jg 18:11** 8337a
The **s** hundred men armed with **Jg 18:16** 8337a
s hundred men armed with weapons **Jg 18:17** 8337a
he measured **s** *measures* of barley **Ru 3:15** 8337a
"These **s** *measures* of barley he **Ru 3:17** 8337a
with him, about **s** hundred men. **1Sa 13:15** 8337a
with him *were* about **s** hundred men, **1Sa 14:2** 8337a
height was **s** cubits and a span. **1Sa 17:4** 8337a
weighed **s** hundred shekels of iron; **1Sa 17:7** 8337a
and his men, about **s** hundred, **1Sa 23:13** 8337a
s hundred men who were with him, **1Sa 27:2** 8337a
s hundred men who were with him, **1Sa 30:9** 8337a
was seven years and **s** months. **2Sa 2:11** 8337a
Judah seven years and **s** months, **2Sa 5:5** 8337a
ark of the LORD had gone **s** paces, **2Sa 6:13** 8337a
s hundred men who had come with **2Sa 15:18** 8337a
who had **s** fingers on each hand and **2Sa 21:20** 8337a
each hand and **s** toes on each foot, **2Sa 21:20** 8337a
and the middle *was* **s** cubits wide, **1Ki 6:6** 8337a
There were **s** steps to the throne **1Ki 10:19** 8337a
on the **s** steps on the one side and on **1Ki 10:20** 8337a
all Israel stayed there **s** months, **1Ki 11:16** 8337a
he reigned **s** years at Tirzah. **1Ki 16:23** 8337a
silver and **s** thousand *shekels* of gold **2Ki 5:5** 8337a
in the house of the LORD **s** years, **2Ki 11:3** 8337a
have struck five or **s** times, **2Ki 13:19** 8337a
Israel in Samaria *for* **s** months. **2Ki 15:8** 8337a
S were born to him in Hebron, and **1Ch 3:4** 8337a
reigned seven years and **s** months. **1Ch 3:4** 8337a
Bariah, Neariah and Shaphat, **s**. **1Ch 3:22** 8337a
had sixteen sons and **s** daughters; **1Ch 4:27** 8337a
Azel had **s** sons, and these **1Ch 8:38** 8337a
had **s** sons whose names are these: **1Ch 9:44** 8337a
s *fingers on each hand* and six **1Ch 20:6** 8337a
each hand and **s** *toes on each foot;* **1Ch 20:6** 8337a
Hashabiah and Mattithiah, **s**, **1Ch 25:3** 8337a
On the east there were **s** Levites, **1Ch 26:17** 8337a
There were **s** steps to the throne **2Ch 9:18** 8337a
were standing there on the **s** steps **2Ch 9:19** 8337a
with them in the house of God **s** years **2Ch 22:12** 8337a
day was one ox *and* **s** choice sheep, **Ne 5:18** 8337a
s months with oil of myrrh and six **Es 2:12** 8337a
oil of myrrh and **s** months with spices **Es 2:12** 8337a
From **s** troubles He will deliver you, **Jb 5:19** 8337a
are **s** things which the LORD hates, **Pr 6:16** 8337a
above Him, each having **s** wings: **Is 6:2** 8337a
to you and has served you **s** years, **Jer 34:14** 8337a
s men came from the direction of **Ezk 9:2** 8337a
was a measuring rod of **s** cubits, **Ezk 40:5** 8337a
were **s** cubits *square* on each side. **Ezk 40:12** 8337a
s cubits wide on each side *was* the **Ezk 41:1** 8337a
and the doorway, **s** cubits *high;* **Ezk 41:3** 8337a
the wall of the temple, **s** cubits; **Ezk 41:5** 8337a
rod of **s** long cubits *in height.* **Ezk 41:8** 8337a
shall be shut the **s** working days; **Ezk 46:1** 8337a
shall be **s** lambs without blemish **Ezk 46:4** 8337a
blemish, also **s** lambs and a ram, **Ezk 46:6** 8337a
cubits *and* its width **s** cubits; **Da 3:1** 8353
S days later Jesus took with Him **Mt 17:1** *1803*
S days later, Jesus took with Him **Mk 9:2** *1803*
up for three years and **s** months, **Lk 4:25** *1803*
"There are **s** days in which work **Lk 13:14** *1803*
Now there were **s** stone waterpots **Jn 2:6** *1803*
s days before the Passover, **Jn 12:1** *1803*
s brethren also went with me and **Ac 11:12** *1803*
settled *there* a year and **s** months, **Ac 18:11** *1803*
for three years and **s** months. **Jas 5:17** *1803*
each one of them having **s** wings, **Rv 4:8** *1803*
number is **s** hundred and sixty-six. **Rv 13:18** *1812*

SIXTEEN
she bore to Jacob these **s** persons. **Gn 46:18** 8337a, 6240
sockets of silver, **s** sockets; **Ex 26:25** 8337a, 6240
sockets of silver, **s** sockets, **Ex 36:30** 8337a, 6240
s cities with their villages. **Jos 15:41** 8337a, 6240
s cities with their villages. **Jos 19:22** 8337a, 6240
in Samaria, *and reigned* **s** years. **2Ki 13:10** 8337a, 6240
took Azariah, who *was* **s** years old, **2Ki 14:21** 8337a, 6240
s years old when he became king, **2Ki 15:2** 8337a, 6240
he reigned **s** years in Jerusalem; **2Ki 15:33** 8337a, 6240
he reigned **s** years in Jerusalem; **2Ki 16:2** 8337a, 6240

had **s** sons and six daughters; **1Ch 4:27** 8337a, 6240
there were **s** heads of fathers' **1Ch 24:4** 8337a, 6240
of twenty-two sons and **s** daughters. **2Ch 13:21** 8337a, 6240
took Uzziah, who *was* **s** years old, **2Ch 26:1** 8337a, 6240
s years old when he became king, **2Ch 26:3** 8337a, 6240
he reigned **s** years in Jerusalem. **2Ch 27:1** 8337a, 6240
he reigned **s** years in Jerusalem. **2Ch 27:8** 8337a, 6240
he reigned **s** years in Jerusalem; **2Ch 28:1** 8337a, 6240

SIXTEENTH
for Bilgah, the **s** for Immer, **1Ch 24:14** 8337a, 6240
for the **s** to Hananiah, his sons **1Ch 25:23** 8337a, 6240
on the **s** day of the first month. **2Ch 29:17** 8337a, 6240

SIXTH
and there was morning, the **s** day. **Gn 1:31** 8345
again and bore a **s** son to Jacob. **Gn 30:19** 8345
"On the **s** day, **Ex 16:5** 8345
Now on the **s** day **Ex 16:22** 8345
bread for two days on the **s** day. **Ex 16:29** 8345
you shall double over the **s** curtain **Ex 26:9** 8345
My blessing for you in the **s** year that **Lv 25:21** 8345
On the **s** day *it was* Eliasaph the **Nu 7:42** 8345
'Then on the **s** day: **Nu 29:29** 8345
The **s** lot fell to the sons of **Jos 19:32** 8345
and the **s**, Ithream, by David's **2Sa 3:5** 8345
in the **s** year of Hezekiah, which **2Ki 18:10** 8337a
Ozem the **s**, David the seventh; **1Ch 2:15** 8345
the **s** *was* Ithream, by his wife **1Ch 3:3** 8345
Attai the **s**, Eliel the seventh, **1Ch 12:11** 8345
for Malchijah, the **s** for Mijamin, **1Ch 24:9** 8345
the **s** to Bukkiah, his sons and his **1Ch 25:13** 8345
Elam the fifth, Johanan the **s**, **1Ch 26:3** 8345
Ammiel the **s**, Issachar the **1Ch 26:5** 8345
The **s** for the sixth month *was* Ira **1Ch 27:9** 8345
The sixth for the **s** month *was* Ira **1Ch 27:9** 8345
it was the **s** year of the reign of **Ezr 6:15** 8353
and Hanun the **s** son of Zalaph, **Ne 3:30** 8345
be the **s** part of a hin by measure; **Ezk 4:11** 8345
It came about in the **s** year, **Ezk 8:1** 8345
on the fifth *day* of the **s** month, **Ezk 8:1** 8345
a **s** of an ephah from a homer of **Ezk 45:13** 8345
a **s** of an ephah from a homer of **Ezk 45:13** 8341
by morning, a **s** of an ephah and **Ezk 46:14** 8345
on the first day of the **s** month, **Hg 1:1** 8345
twenty-fourth day of the **s** month **Hg 1:15** 8345
about the **s** and the ninth hour, **Mt 20:5** *1623*
Now from the **s** hour darkness fell **Mt 27:45** *1623*
When the **s** hour came, **Mk 15:33** *1623*
Now in the **s** month the angel **Lk 1:26** *1623*
barren is now in her **s** month. **Lk 1:36** *1623*
It was now about the **s** hour, **Lk 23:44** *1623*
It was about the **s** hour. **Jn 4:6** *1623*
it was about the **s** hour. **Jn 19:14** *1623*
housetop about the **s** hour to pray. **Ac 10:9** *1623*
I looked when He broke the **s** seal, **Rv 6:12** *1623*
Then the **s** angel sounded, and I **Rv 9:13** *1623*
the **s** angel who had the trumpet, **Rv 9:14** *1623*
The **s** *angel* poured out his **Rv 16:12** *1623*
the fifth, sardonyx; the **s**, sardius; **Rv 21:20** *1623*

SIXTY
and Isaac was **s** years old when she **Gn 25:26** 8346
twenty years even to **s** years old, **Lv 27:3** 8346
are from **s** years old and upward, **Lv 27:7** 8346
s cities, all the region of Argob, **Dt 3:4** 8346
which are in Bashan, **s** cities; **Jos 13:30** 8346
that three hundred and **s** men died. **2Sa 2:31** 8346
s great cities with walls and **1Ki 4:13** 8346
of fine flour and **s** kors of meal, **1Ki 4:22** 8346
its length *was* **s** cubits and its **1Ki 6:2** 8346
and **s** men of the people of the **2Ki 25:19** 8346
married when he was **s** years old; **1Ch 2:21** 8346
and its villages, *even* **s** cities. **1Ch 2:23** 8346
to the old standard *was* **s** cubits, **2Ch 3:3** 8346
taken eighteen wives and **s** concubines **2Ch 11:21** 8346
twenty-eight sons and **s** daughters. **2Ch 11:21** 8346
S mighty men around it, Of the **SS 3:7** 8346
s queens and eighty concubines, **SS 6:8** 8346
and **s** men of the people of the **Jer 52:25** 8346
the side pillars **s** cubits *high;* **Ezk 40:14** 8346
the height of which *was* **s** cubits **Da 3:1** 8361
crop, some a hundredfold, some **s**, **Mt 13:8** *1835*
forth, some a hundredfold, some **s**, **Mt 13:23** *1835*
a crop and produced thirty, **s**, **Mk 4:8** *1835*
it and bear fruit, thirty, **s**, **Mk 4:20** *1835*
she is not less than **s** years old, **1Tm 5:9** *1835*
for twelve hundred and **s** days, **Rv 11:3** *1835*
thousand two hundred and **s** days. **Rv 12:6** *1835*

SIXTY-FIVE
Mahalalel lived **s** years, **Gn 5:15** 8346, 2568
Enoch lived **s** years, and **Gn 5:21** 8346, 2568
were three hundred and **s** years. **Gn 5:23** 8346, 2568

SIXTY-NINE
were nine hundred and **s** years, **Gn 5:27** 8346, 8672

SIXTY-SIX
sons, *were* **s** persons in all, **Gn 46:26** 8346, 8337a
of *her* purification for **s** days. **Lv 12:5** 8346, 8337a
his number is six hundred and **s**. **Rv 13:18** *1835, 1803*

SIXTY-TWO
lived one hundred and **s** years, **Gn 5:18** 8346, 8147
were nine hundred and **s** years, **Gn 5:20** 8346, 8147
the kingdom at about the age of **s**. **Da 5:31** 8361, 8648
will be seven weeks and **s** weeks; **Da 9:25** 8346, 8147
after the **s** weeks the Messiah will **Da 9:26** 8346, 8147

SIZE
we saw in it are men of *great* **s**. **Nu 13:32** 4060a
and all measures of volume and **s**. **1Ch 23:29** 4060a
in the corners *were* the same **s**. **Ezk 46:22** 4060a
if you have faith the **s** of a mustard **Mt 17:20** *5613*

SIZEABLE
and a **s** crowd from the city was **Lk 7:12** *2425*

SKIES
And through the **s** in His majesty. **Dt 33:26** 7834
you, with Him, spread out the **s**, **Jb 37:18** 7834
light which is bright in the **s**; **Jb 37:21** 7834
of waters, thick clouds of the **s**. **Ps 18:11** 7834
Your faithfulness *reaches* to the **s**. **Ps 36:5** 7834
And His strength is in the **s**. **Ps 68:34** 7834
The **s** gave forth a sound; **Ps 77:17** 7834
who in the **s** is comparable to the **Ps 89:6** 7834
And Your truth *reaches* to the **s**. **Ps 108:4** 7834
up And the **s** drip with dew. **Pr 3:20** 7834
When He made firm the **s** above, **Pr 8:28** 7834
And towers up to the very **s**. **Jer 51:9** 7834

SKILL
all who are skillful I have put **s**, **Ex 31:6** 2451
women whose heart stirred with a **s** **Ex 35:26** 2451
"He has filled them with **s** to **Ex 35:35** 2451, 3820
person in whom the LORD has put **s** **Ex 36:1** 2451
person in whom the LORD had put **s**, **Ex 36:2** 2451
s for doing any work in bronze. **1Ki 7:14** 1847
and every willing man of any **s** **1Ch 28:21** 2451
Him who made the heavens with **s**, **Ps 136:5** 8394
May my right hand forget *her* **s**. **Ps 137:5**
with wisdom, knowledge and **s**, **Ec 2:21** 3788
every **s** which is done is *the result of* **Ec 4:4** 3788

SKILLED
the **s** women spun with their hands, **Ex 35:25** 2450, 3820
send me a **s** man to work in gold, **2Ch 2:7** 2450
to *work* with the **s** men whom I have **2Ch 2:7** 2450
I am sending Huram-abi, a **s** man, **2Ch 2:13** 2450
to him, *to work* with your **s** men and **2Ch 2:14** 2450
a scribe **s** in the law of Moses, **Ezr 7:6** 4106
Do you see a man **s** in his work? **Pr 22:29** 4106
They are all the work of **s** men. **Jer 10:9** 2450
of brutal men, **s** in destruction. **Ezk 21:31** 2796
arise, Insolent and **s** in intrigue. **Da 8:23** 995

SKILLFUL
grew up, Esau became a **s** hunter, **Gn 25:27** 3045
cherubim, the work of a **s** workman. **Ex 26:1** 2803
cherubim, the work of a **s** workman. **Ex 26:31** 2803
You shall speak to all the **s** persons **Ex 28:3** 2450, 3820
linen, the work of the **s** workman. **Ex 28:6** 2803
judgment, the work of a **s** workman; **Ex 28:15** 2803
in the hearts of all who are **s** I have **Ex 31:6** 2450, 3820
Let every **s** man among you come, **Ex 35:10** 2450, 3820
and every **s** person in whom the **Ex 36:1** 2450, 3820
every **s** person in whom the LORD **Ex 36:2** 2450, 3820
And all the **s** men who were **Ex 36:4** 2450
All the **s** men among those who **Ex 36:8** 2450, 3820
cherubim, the work of a **s** workman, **Ex 36:8** 2803
cherubim, the work of a **s** workman. **Ex 36:35** 2803
an engraver and a **s** workman and a **Ex 38:23** 2803
linen, the work of a **s** workman. **Ex 39:3** 2803
the work of a **s** workman, **Ex 39:8** 2803
man who is a **s** player on the harp; **1Sa 16:16** 3045
Bethlehemite who is a **s** musician, **1Sa 16:18** 3045
with bow and *were* **s** in battle, **1Ch 5:18** 3925
in singing because he was **s**. **1Ch 15:22** 995
who are **s** in every kind of work. **1Ch 22:15** 2450
their relatives, all who were **s**, **1Ch 25:7** 995
engines *of war* invented by **s** men to **2Ch 26:15** 2803
were **s** with musical instruments. **2Ch 34:12** 995
Sing praises with a **s** psalm. **Ps 47:7** 4905b
charmers, *Or* a **s** caster of spells. **Ps 58:5** 2449
And guided them with his **s** hands. **Ps 78:72** 8394
artisan, And the **s** enchanter. **Is 3:3** 995
seeks out for himself a **s** craftsman **Is 40:20** 2450

SKILLFULLY
"The **s** woven band, which is **Ex 28:8** 2805
the **s** woven band of the ephod. **Ex 28:27** 2805
on the **s** woven band of the ephod, **Ex 28:28** 2805
the **s** woven band of the ephod; **Ex 29:5** 2805
The **s** woven band which was on **Ex 39:5** 2805
Play **s** with a shout of joy. **Ps 33:3** 3190
And **s** wrought in the depths of the **Ps 139:15** 7551
Pluck the strings **s**, **Is 23:16** 3190
Idols **s** made from their silver, **Hos 13:2** 8394

SKIN
God made garments of **s** for Adam **Gn 3:21** 5785
and took bread and a **s** of water and **Gn 21:14** 2573
the water in the **s** was used up, **Gn 21:15** 2573
went and filled the **s** with water and **Gn 21:19** 2573
not know that the **s** of his face shone **Ex 34:29** 5785
behold, the **s** of his face shone, **Ex 34:30** 5785
that the **s** of Moses' face shone. **Ex 34:35** 5785
'He shall then **s** the burnt offering **Lv 1:6** 6584
for himself the **s** of the burnt offering **Lv 7:8** 5785
The flesh and the **s**, **Lv 9:11** 5785
article, or clothing, or a **s**, **Lv 11:32** 5785
has on the **s** of his body a swelling **Lv 13:2** 5785
of leprosy on the **s** of his body, **Lv 13:2** 5785
at the mark on the **s** of the body, **Lv 13:3** 5785
be deeper than the **s** of his body, **Lv 13:3** 5785
is white on the **s** of his body, **Lv 13:4** 5785
appear to be deeper than the **s**, **Lv 13:4** 5785
infection has not spread on the **s**, **Lv 13:5** 5785
the mark has not spread on the **s**, **Lv 13:6** 5785
the scab spreads farther on the **s** after **Lv 13:7** 5785
if the scab has spread on the **s**, **Lv 13:8** 5785
is a white swelling in the **s**, **Lv 13:10** 5785
leprosy on the **s** of his body, **Lv 13:11** 5785
breaks out farther on the **s**, **Lv 13:12** 5785
and the leprosy covers all the **s** **Lv 13:12** 5785
When the body has a boil on its **s** **Lv 13:18** 5785
it appears to be lower than the **s**, **Lv 13:20** 5785
not lower than the **s** and is faded, **Lv 13:21** 5785
if it spreads farther on the **s**, **Lv 13:22** 5785
sustains in its **s** a burn by fire, **Lv 13:24** 5785
appears to be deeper than the **s**, **Lv 13:25** 5785
and it is no deeper than the **s**, **Lv 13:26** 5785
If it spreads farther in the **s**, **Lv 13:27** 5785
and has not spread in the **s**, **Lv 13:28** 5785
appears to be deeper than the **s** and **Lv 13:30** 5785
to be no deeper than the **s** and **Lv 13:31** 5785
the scale is no deeper than the **s**, **Lv 13:32** 5785
the scale has not spread in the **s** and **Lv 13:34** 5785
to be no deeper than the **s**, **Lv 13:34** 5785
if the scale spreads farther in the **s** **Lv 13:35** 5785
if the scale has spread in the **s**, **Lv 13:36** 5785
bright spots on the **s** of the body, **Lv 13:38** 5785
and if the bright spots on the **s** **Lv 13:39** 5785
that has broken out on the **s**; **Lv 13:39** 5785
of leprosy in the **s** of the body, **Lv 13:43** 5785
a covering of porpoise **s** on it, **Nu 4:6** 5785
with a covering of porpoise **s**, **Nu 4:8** 5785
in a covering of porpoise **s**, **Nu 4:10** 5785
it with a covering of porpoise **s**, **Nu 4:11** 5785
with a covering of porpoise **s**, **Nu 4:12** 5785
spread a cover of porpoise **s** over it **Nu 4:14** 5785
porpoise **s** that is on top of it, **Nu 4:25** 8476
from *the* seeds even to *the* **s**. **Nu 6:4** 2085
to **s** all the burnt offerings; **2Ch 29:34** 6584
and said, "**S** for skin! **Jb 2:4** 5785
"Skin for **s**! Yes, all that a man has **Jb 2:4** 5785
My **s** hardens and runs. **Jb 7:5** 5785
Clothe me with **s** and flesh, And **Jb 10:11** 5785
"I have sewed sackcloth over my **s** And **Jb 16:15** 1539
"His **s** is devoured by disease, **Jb 18:13** 5785
bone clings to my **s** and my flesh, **Jb 19:20** 5785
escaped *only* by the **s** of my teeth. **Jb 19:20** 5785
"Even after my **s** is destroyed, **Jb 19:26** 5785
"My **s** turns black on me, And my **Jb 30:30** 5785
"Can you fill his **s** with harpoons, **Jb 41:7** 5785
"Can the Ethiopian change his **s** Or **Jer 13:23** 5785
caused my flesh and my **s** to waste **La 3:4** 5785
s is shriveled on their bones, **La 4:8** 5785
s has become as hot as an oven, **La 5:10** 5785
sandals of porpoise **s** on your feet; **Ezk 16:10** 8476
back on you, cover you with **s** and **Ezk 37:6** 5785
flesh grew and **s** covered them; **Ezk 37:8** 5785
Who tear off their **s** from them And **Mi 3:2** 5785
Strip off their **s** from them, **Mi 3:3** 5785

SKINNED
their hand, the Levites **s** *them.* **2Ch 35:11** 6584

SKINS
And she put the **s** of the young goats on **Gn 27:16** 5785
rams' **s** dyed red, porpoise skins, **Ex 25:5** 5785
rams' skins dyed red, porpoise **s**, **Ex 25:5** 5785
for the tent of rams' **s** dyed red and **Ex 26:14** 5785
a covering of porpoise **s** above. **Ex 26:14** 5785
and rams' **s** dyed red, and porpoise **Ex 35:7** 5785
skins dyed red, and porpoise **s**, **Ex 35:7** 5785
rams' **s** dyed red and porpoise skins, **Ex 35:23** 5785
skins dyed red and porpoise **s**, **Ex 35:23** 5785
a covering for the tent of rams' **s** **Ex 36:19** 5785
a covering of porpoise **s** above. **Ex 36:19** 5785
the covering of rams' **s** dyed red, **Ex 39:34** 5785
and the covering of porpoise **s**, **Ex 39:34** 5785
the wine will burst the **s**, **Mk 2:22** *779*
wine is lost and the **s** *as well* **Mk 2:22** *779*
the new wine will burst the **s** and **Lk 5:37** *779*
out, and the **s** will be ruined. **Lk 5:37** *779*

SKIP
flock, And their children **s** about. **Jb 21:11** 7540
He makes Lebanon **s** like a calf, **Ps 29:6** 7540
O mountains, that you **s** like rams? **Ps 114:6** 7540
Because you **s** about like a **Jer 50:11** 6335a
s about like calves from the stall. **Mal 4:2** 6335a

SKIPPED
The mountains **s** like rams, The **Ps 114:4** 7540

SKIRT
will not uncover his father's **s**. **Dt 22:30** 3671

he has uncovered his father's **s**.' **Dt 27:20** 3671
Remove your veil, strip off the **s**, **Is 47:2** 7640
so I spread My **s** over you and **Ezk 16:8** 3671

SKIRTS
on your **s** is found The lifeblood of **Jer 2:34** 3671
iniquity Your **s** have been removed And **Jer 13:22** 7757
stripped your **s** off over your face, **Jer 13:26** 7757
Her uncleanness was in her **s**; **La 1:9** 7757
lift up your **s** over your face, **Na 3:5** 7757

SKULL
Abimelech's head, crushing his **s**. **Jg 9:53** 1538
found nothing more of her than the **s** **2Ki 9:35** 1538
which means Place of a **S**, **Mt 27:33** *2898*
which is translated, Place of a **S**. **Mk 15:22** *2898*
came to the place called The **S**, **Lk 23:33** *2898*
the place called the Place of a **S**, **Jn 19:17** *2898*

SKY
over the birds of the **s** and over the **Gn 1:26** 8064
sea and over the birds of the **s** and **Gn 1:28** 8064
every bird of the **s** and to every thing **Gn 1:30** 8064
the field and every bird of the **s**, **Gn 2:19** 8064
cattle, and to the birds of the **s**, **Gn 2:20** 8064
things and to birds of the **s**; **Gn 6:7** 8064
also of the birds of the **s**, **Gn 7:3** 8064
floodgates of the **s** were opened. **Gn 7:11** 8064
things and to birds of the **s**, **Gn 7:23** 8064
floodgates of the **s** were closed, **Gn 8:2** 8064
rain from the **s** was restrained; **Gn 8:2** 8064
earth and on every bird of the **s**; **Gn 9:2** 8064
and let Moses throw it toward the **s** **Ex 9:8** 8064
and Moses threw it toward the **s**, **Ex 9:10** 8064
Stretch out your hand toward the **s**, **Ex 9:22** 8064
stretched out his staff toward the **s**, **Ex 9:23** 8064
Stretch out your hand toward the **s**, **Ex 10:21** 8064
stretched out his hand toward the **s**, **Ex 10:22** 8064
as clear as the **s** itself. **Ex 24:10** 8064
I will also make your **s** like iron **Lv 26:19** 8064
winged bird that flies in the **s**, **Dt 4:17** 8064
will be food to all birds of the **s** and **Dt 28:26** 8064
smoke of the city ascended to the **s**, **Jos 8:20** 8064
sun stopped in the middle of the **s** and **Jos 10:13** 8064
give your flesh to the birds of the **s** **1Sa 17:44** 8064
this day to the birds of the **s** and the **1Sa 17:46** 8064
it rained on them from the **s**; **2Sa 21:10** 8064
she allowed neither the birds of the **s** **2Sa 21:10** 8064
of waters, thick clouds of the **s**. **2Sa 22:12** 7834
while the **s** grew black with clouds **1Ki 18:45** 8064
over their heads toward the **s**. **Jb 2:12** 8064
concealed from the birds of the **s**. **Jb 28:21** 8064
And the witness in the **s** is faithful. **Ps 89:37** 7834
The way of an eagle in the **s**, **Pr 30:19** 8064
And the **s** will be rolled up like a **Is 34:4** 8064
"Lift up your eyes to the **s**, **Is 51:6** 8064
For the **s** will vanish like smoke, **Is 51:6** 8064
be food for the birds of the **s** and **Jer 7:33** 8064
stork in the **s** Knows her seasons; **Jer 8:7** 8064
the birds of the **s** and the beasts **Jer 9:10** 8064
and the birds of the **s** and the **Jer 15:3** 8064
will become food for the birds of the **s** **Jer 16:4** 8064
as food for the birds of the **s** and **Jer 19:7** 8064
will be food for the birds of the **s** **Jer 34:20** 8064
swifter Than the eagles of the **s**; **La 4:19** 8064
earth and to the birds of the **s**. **Ezk 29:5** 8064
the field, or the birds of the **s**, **Da 2:38** 8065
And its height reached to the **s**, **Da 4:11** 8065
birds of the **s** dwelt in its branches, **Da 4:12** 8065
whose height reached to the **s** and **Da 4:20** 8065
the birds of the **s** lodged **Da 4:21** 8065
become great and reached to the **s** **Da 4:22** 8065
of the field, The birds of the **s** And **Hos 2:18** 8064
the field and the birds of the **s**, **Hos 4:3** 8064
them down like the birds of the **s**. **Hos 7:12** 8064
wonders in the **s** and on the earth, **Jl 2:30** 8064
I will remove the birds of the **s** **Zph 1:3** 8064
of you the **s** has withheld its dew and **Hg 1:10** 8064
fair weather, for the **s** is red.' **Mt 16:2** *3772*
for the **s** is red and threatening.' **Mt 16:3** *3772*
discern the appearance of the **s**, **Mt 16:3** *3772*
THE STARS WILL FALL from the **s**, **Mt 24:29** *3772*
Son of Man will appear in the **s**, **Mt 24:30** *3772*
COMING ON THE CLOUDS OF THE **S** **Mt 24:30** *3772*
one end of the **s** to the other. **Mt 24:31** *3772*
when the **s** was shut up for three **Lk 4:25** *3772*
appearance of the earth and the **s**, **Lk 12:56** *3772*
flashes out of one part of the **s**, **Lk 17:24** *3772*
shines to the other part of the **s**, **Lk 17:24** *3772*
they were gazing intently into the **s** **Ac 1:10** *3772*
why do you stand looking into the **s**? **Ac 1:11** *3772*
WILL GRANT WONDERS IN THE **S** ABOVE AND **Ac 2:19** *3772*
and he saw the **s** opened up, **Ac 10:11** *3772*
object was taken up into the **s**. **Ac 10:16** *3772*
by four corners from the **s**; **Ac 11:5** *3772*
was drawn back up into the **s**. **Ac 11:10** *3772*
again, and the **s** poured rain and **Jas 5:18** *3772*
stars of the **s** fell to the earth, **Rv 6:13** *3772*
The **s** was split apart like a **Rv 6:14** *3772*
have the power to shut up the **s**, **Rv 11:6** *3772*

SLACK
But the **s** *hand* will be put to **Pr 12:24** 7423b
He also who is **s** in his work Is **Pr 18:9** 7503
you are **s** in the day of distress, **Pr 24:10** 7503
Your tackle hangs **s**; **Is 33:23** 5203
and his hip joints went **s** and **Da 5:6** 8271

SLACKNESS
and through **s** the house leaks. **Ec 10:18** 8220, 3027

SLAIN
Jacob's sons came upon the **s** and **Gn 34:27** 2491a
bull shall be **s** before the LORD. **Lv 4:15** 7819
the place where the burnt offering is **s** **Lv 6:25** 7819
shall be **s** before the LORD; **Lv 6:25** 7819
that was **s** over the running water. **Lv 14:6** 7819
them in the blood of the **s** bird as **Lv 14:51** 7819
one who has been **s** with a sword or **Nu 19:16** 2491a
the one **s** or the one dying *naturally* **Nu 19:18** 2491a
And drinks the blood of the **s**." **Nu 23:24** 2491a
the name of the **s** man of Israel who **Nu 25:14** 5221
was **s** with the Midianite woman, **Nu 25:14** 5221
the Midianite woman who was **s** **Nu 25:15** 5221
their sister who was **s** on the day **Nu 25:18** 5221
along with the *rest of* their **s**: **Nu 31:8** 2491a
and whoever has touched any **s**, **Nu 31:19** 2491a
"If a **s** person is found lying in **Dt 21:1** 2491a
cities which are around the **s** one. **Dt 21:2** 2491a
which is nearest to the **s** man, **Dt 21:3** 2491a
that city which is nearest to the **s** man **Dt 21:6** 2491a
blood of the **s** and the captives, **Dt 32:42** 2491a
all of them **s** before Israel; **Jos 11:6** 2491a
sword among *the rest of* their **s**. **Jos 13:22** 2491a
country, Who has **s** many of us." **Jg 16:24** 2491a
And the **s** Philistines lay along **1Sa 17:52** 2491a
"Saul has **s** his thousands, And **1Sa 18:7** 5221
'Saul has **s** his thousands, And **1Sa 21:11** 5221
'Saul has **s** his thousands, And **1Sa 29:5** 5221
and fell **s** on Mount Gilboa. **1Sa 31:1** 2491a
Philistines came to strip the **s**, **1Sa 31:8** 2491a
"Your beauty, O Israel, is **s** on your **2Sa 1:19** 2491a
"From the blood of the **s**, **2Sa 1:22** 2491a
Jonathan is **s** on your high places. **2Sa 1:25** 2491a
eight hundred **s** *by him* at one time; **2Sa 23:8** 2491a
after him only to strip *the* **s**. **2Sa 23:10**
army had gone up to bury the **s**, **1Ki 11:15** 2491a
and they have **s** one another. **2Ki 3:23** 5221
who had **s** the king his father. **2Ki 14:5** 5221
For many fell **s**, because the war **1Ch 5:22** 2491a
and fell **s** on Mount Gilboa. **1Ch 10:1** 2491a
Philistines came to strip the **s**, **1Ch 10:8** 2491a
chosen men of Israel fell **s**. **2Ch 13:17** 2491a
the camp had **s** all the older *sons*. **2Ch 22:1** 2026
who had **s** his father the king. **2Ch 25:3** 5221
and you have **s** them in a rage **2Ch 28:9** 2026
And where the **s** are, there is he." **Jb 39:30** 2491a
Like the **s** who lie in the grave, **Ps 88:5** 2491a
crushed Rahab like one who is **s**; **Ps 89:10** 2491a
down, And numerous are all her **s**. **Pr 7:26** 2026
the captives Or fall among the **s**. **Is 10:4** 2026
s who are pierced with a sword, **Is 14:19** 2026
country, You have **s** your people. **Is 14:20** 2026
s were not slain with the sword, **Is 22:2** 2491a
slain were not **s** with the sword, **Is 22:2** 2491a
And will no longer cover her **s**. **Is 26:21** 2026
Or like the slaughter of His **s**, **Is 27:7** 2026
of His slain, have they been **s**? **Is 27:7** 2026
So their **s** will be thrown out, And **Is 34:3** 2491a
those **s** by the LORD will be many. **Is 66:16** 2491a
s of the daughter of my people! **Jer 9:1** 2491a
Behold, those **s** with the sword! **Jer 14:18** 2491a
"Those **s** by the LORD on that **Jer 25:33** 2491a
s in My anger and in My wrath, **Jer 33:5** 5221
of Nethaniah filled it with the **s**. **Jer 41:9** 2491a
s in the land of the Chaldeans, **Jer 51:4** 2491a
all her **s** will fall in her midst. **Jer 51:47** 2491a
is to fall *for* the **s** of Israel, **Jer 51:49** 2491a
s of all the earth have fallen. **Jer 51:49** 2491a
s all that were pleasant to the eye; **La 2:4** 2026
Should priest and prophet be **s** In **La 2:20** 2026
You have **s** *them* in the day of **La 2:21** 2026
You have **s** *and* have not spared. **La 3:43** 2026
Better are those **s** with the sword **La 4:9** 2491a
sword Than those **s** with hunger; **La 4:9** 2491a
I will make your **s** fall in front of **Ezk 6:4** 2491a
"The **s** will fall among you, **Ezk 6:7** 2491a
when their **s** are among their idols **Ezk 6:13** 2491a
and fill the courts with the **s**. **Ezk 9:7** 2491a
multiplied your **s** in this city, **Ezk 11:6** 2491a
"Your **s** whom you have laid in the **Ezk 11:7** 2491a
third time, the sword for the **s**. **Ezk 21:14** 2491a
is the sword for the great one **s**, **Ezk 21:14** 2491a
'And you, O **s**, wicked one, the **Ezk 21:25** 2491a
the necks of the wicked who are **s**, **Ezk 21:29** 2491a
mainland will be **s** by the sword, **Ezk 26:6** 2026
are **s** In the heart of the seas. **Ezk 28:8** 2491a
When the **s** fall in Egypt, **Ezk 30:4** 2491a
And fill the land with the **s**. **Ezk 30:11** 2491a
to those who were **s** by the sword; **Ezk 31:17** 2491a
those who were **s** by the sword. **Ezk 31:18** 2491a
of those who are **s** by the sword. **Ezk 32:20** 2491a
uncircumcised, **s** by the sword.' **Ezk 32:21** 2491a
All of them are **s**, fallen by the **Ezk 32:22** 2491a
All of them are **s**, fallen by the **Ezk 32:23** 2491a
all of them **s**, fallen by the **Ezk 32:24** 2491a
made a bed for her among the **s** **Ezk 32:25** 2491a
all uncircumcised, **s** by the sword **Ezk 32:25** 2491a
were put in the midst of the **s**. **Ezk 32:25** 2491a
All of them were **s** by the sword **Ezk 32:26** 2490a
and lie with those **s** by the sword. **Ezk 32:28** 2491a
laid with those **s** by the sword; **Ezk 32:29** 2491a
in shame went down with the **s**. **Ezk 32:30** 2491a
with those **s** by the sword and **Ezk 32:30** 2491a
all his hordes **s** by the sword, **Ezk 32:31** 2491a
along with those **s** by the sword, **Ezk 32:32** 2491a
fill its mountains with its **s**; **Ezk 35:8** 2491a
those **s** by the sword will fall. **Ezk 35:8** 2491a
O breath, and breathe on these **s**, **Ezk 37:9** 2026
that the wise men should be **s**; **Da 2:13** 6992
the Chaldean king was **s**. **Da 5:30** 6992
looking until the beast was **s**, **Da 7:11** 6992
but many will fall down **s**. **Da 11:26** 2491a
s them by the words of My mouth; **Hos 6:5** 2026
flashing, spears gleaming, Many **s**, **Na 3:3** 2491a
will be **s** by My sword." **Zph 2:12** 2491a
and was about to be **s** by them, **Ac 23:27** *337*
elders a Lamb standing, as if **s**, **Rv 5:6** *4969*
for You were **s**, and purchased **Rv 5:9** *4969*
"Worthy is the Lamb that was **s** to **Rv 5:12** *4969*
the souls of those who had been **s** **Rv 6:9** *4969*
of his heads as if it had been **s**, **Rv 13:3** *4969*
life of the Lamb who has been **s**. **Rv 13:8** *4969*
who have been **s** on the earth." **Rv 18:24** *4969*

SLAMMED
and the winds blew and **s** against that **Mt 7:25** *4363*
and the winds blew and **s** against that **Mt 7:27** *4350*
the demon **s** him *to the ground* **Lk 9:42** *4486*

SLAMS
and whenever it seizes him, it **s** him **Mk 9:18** *4486*

SLANDER
He does not **s** with his tongue, Nor **Ps 15:3** 7270
For I have heard the **s** of many, **Ps 31:13** 1681
You **s** your own mother's son. **Ps 50:20** 5414, 1848
And he who spreads **s** is a fool. **Pr 10:18** 1681
Do not **s** a slave to his master, **Pr 30:10** 3960
To destroy *the* afflicted with **s**, **Is 32:7** 561, 8267
as deceit, sensuality, envy, **s**, **Mk 7:22** *988*
clamor and **s** be put away from you, **Eph 4:31** *988*
anger, wrath, malice, **s**, **Col 3:8** *988*
and hypocrisy and envy and all **s**, **1Pe 2:1** *2636*
in which they **s** you as evildoers, **1Pe 2:12** *2635*

SLANDERED
he has **s** your servant to my lord **2Sa 19:27** 7270
me, They **s** me without ceasing. **Ps 35:15** 7167
when we are **s**, we try to **1Co 4:13** *1426a*
why am I **s** concerning that for **1Co 10:30** *987*
in the thing in which you are **s**, **1Pe 3:16** *2635*

SLANDERER
go about as a **s** among your people, **Lv 19:16** 7400
"May a **s** not be established in **Ps 140:11** 376, 3956
a **s** separates intimate friends. **Pr 16:28** 7279
goes about as a **s** reveals secrets, **Pr 20:19** 7400
every neighbor goes about as a **s**. **Jer 9:4** 7400

SLANDERERS
s, haters of God, insolent, **Ro 1:30** *2637*

SLANDEROUS
"**S** men have been in you for the **Ezk 22:9** 7400

SLANDEROUSLY
as we are **s** reported and as some **Ro 3:8** *987*

SLANDERS
Whoever secretly **s** his neighbor, **Ps 101:5** 3960
thefts, false witness, **s**. **Mt 15:19** *988*
angry tempers, disputes, **s**, **2Co 12:20** *2636*

SLAPPED
s me on the cheek with contempt; **Jb 16:10** 5221
and others **s** Him, **Mt 26:67** *4474*

SLAPS
whoever **s** you on your right cheek, **Mt 5:39** *4474*
received Him with **s** *in the face*. **Mk 14:65** *4475*
and to give Him **s** *in the face*. **Jn 19:3** *4475*

SLAUGHTER
"You shall **s** the bull before **Ex 29:11** 7819
and you shall **s** the ram and shall **Ex 29:16** 7819
"You shall **s** the ram, and **Ex 29:20** 7819
"Next he shall **s** the male lamb in **Lv 14:13** 7819
the place where they **s** the sin offering **Lv 14:13** 7819
he shall **s** the burnt offering. **Lv 14:19** 7819
"Next he shall **s** the lamb of the **Lv 14:25** 7819
and he shall **s** the one bird in an **Lv 14:50** 7819
and he shall **s** the bull of the sin **Lv 16:11** 7819
"Then he shall **s** the goat of the **Lv 16:15** 7819
you may **s** and eat meat within any **Dt 12:15** 2076
then you may **s** of your herd and **Dt 12:21** 2076
and He slew them with a great **s** at **Jos 10:10** 4347
slaying them with a very great **s**, **Jos 10:20** 4347
He struck them with a very great **s** **Jg 11:33** 4347
them ruthlessly with a great **s**; **Jg 15:8** 4347
tent; and the **s** was very great **1Sa 4:10** 4347
been a great **s** among the people, **1Sa 4:17** 4046
struck the people with a great **s**. **1Sa 6:19** 4347
That first **s** which Jonathan **1Sa 14:14** 4347
For now the **s** among the Philistines **1Sa 14:30** 4347
his sheep, and **s** *it* here and eat; **1Sa 14:34** 7819
and defeated them with great **s**, **1Sa 19:8** 4347
and struck them with a great **s**. **1Sa 23:5** 4347
from the **s** of the Amalekites, **2Sa 1:1** 5221
'There has been a **s** among the **2Sa 17:9** 4046
the **s** there that day was great, **2Sa 18:7** 4046
the Arameans with a great **s**. **1Ki 20:21** 4347
defeated them with a great **s**, **2Ch 13:17** 4347
over the **s** of the Passover *lambs* **2Ch 30:17** 7821b
"Now **s** the Passover *animals*, **2Ch 35:6** 7819
her As an ox goes to the **s**, **Pr 7:22** 2874
And those who are staggering to **s**, **Pr 24:11** 2027
s of Midian at the rock of Oreb; **Is 10:26** 4347
"Prepare for his sons a place of **s** **Is 14:21** 4293
Or like the **s** of His slain, have **Is 27:7** 4347
water on the day of the great **s**, **Is 30:25** 2027
them, He has given them over to **s**. **Is 34:2** 2874
And a great **s** in the land of Edom. **Is 34:6** 2874
Like a lamb that is led to **s**, **Is 53:7** 2874
Who **s** the children in the ravines, **Is 57:5** 7819
all of you will bow down to the **s**. **Is 65:12** 2874
Hinnom, but the valley of the **S**; **Jer 7:32** 2028
like a gentle lamb led to the **s**; **Jer 11:19** 2873

Drag them off like sheep for the **s** **Jer 12:3** 2878
but rather the valley of **S**. **Jer 19:6** 2028
For the days of your **s** and your **Jer 25:34** 2873
be a **s** for the Lord GOD of hosts, **Jer 46:10** 2077
have also gone down to the **s**," **Jer 48:15** 2874
Let them go down to the **s**! **Jer 50:27** 2874
them down like lambs to the **s**, **Jer 51:40** 2873
'Sharpened to make a **s**, **Ezk 21:10** 2874
is wrapped up *in readiness* for **s**. **Ezk 21:15** 2874
rams, to open the mouth for **s**, **Ezk 21:22** 7524
is drawn, polished for the **s**, **Ezk 21:28** 2874
when the **s** occurs in your midst? **Ezk 26:15** 2027
you **s** the fat *sheep* without **Ezk 34:3** 2076
on which to **s** the burnt offering, **Ezk 40:39** 7819
tables on which they **s** *sacrifices*. **Ezk 40:41** 7819
with which they **s** the burnt offering **Ezk 40:42** 7819
they shall **s** the burnt offering **Ezk 44:11** 7819
will bring out his children for **s**. **Hos 9:13** 2026
from the mountain of Esau by **s**. **Ob 1:9** 6993
"Pasture the flock *doomed* to **s**. **Zch 11:4** 2028
I pastured the flock *doomed* to **s**, **Zch 11:7** 2028
"HE WAS LED AS A SHEEP TO **S**; **Ac 8:32** *4967*
returning from the **s** of the kings **Heb 7:1** *2871*
your hearts in a day of **s**. **Jas 5:5** *4967*

SLAUGHTERED

Joseph's tunic, and **s** a male goat and **Gn 37:31** 7819
Next Moses **s** *it* and took the blood **Lv 8:15** 7819
Moses **s** *it* and sprinkled the **Lv 8:19** 7819
Moses **s** *it* and took some of **Lv 8:23** 7819
and **s** the calf of the sin offering **Lv 9:8** 7819
Then he **s** the burnt offering; **Lv 9:12** 7819
and **s** it and offered it for sin, **Lv 9:15** 7819
Then he **s** the ox and the ram, the **Lv 9:18** 7819
flocks and herds be **s** for them, **Nu 11:22** 7819
He **s** them in the wilderness.' **Nu 14:16** 7819
the camp and be **s** in his presence. **Nu 19:3** 7819
ox shall be **s** before your eyes, **Dt 28:31** 2873
Then they **s** the bull, and brought **1Sa 1:25** 7819
his ox with him and **s** *it* there. **1Sa 14:34** 7819
meat that I have **s** for my shearers, **1Sa 25:11** 2873
the house, and she quickly **s** it; **1Sa 28:24** 2076
David **s** them from the twilight **1Sa 30:17** 5221
took the king's sons and **s** *them*, **2Ki 10:7** 7819
he **s** on the altars and burned human **2Ki 23:20** 2076
They **s** the sons of Zedekiah **2Ki 25:7** 7819
And Ahab **s** many sheep and oxen for **2Ch 18:2** 2076
So they **s** the bulls, and the **2Ch 29:22** 7819
They also **s** the rams and sprinkled **2Ch 29:22** 7819
they **s** the lambs also and **2Ch 29:22** 7819
The priests **s** them and purged **2Ch 29:24** 7819
Then they **s** the Passover *lambs* on **2Ch 30:15** 7819
and they **s** the Passover *animals* on **2Ch 35:1** 7819
They **s** the Passover *animals*, **2Ch 35:11** 7819
Then they **s** the Passover *lamb* for **Ezr 6:20** 7819
are considered as sheep to be **s**. **Ps 44:22** 2878
the men that were with him **s** them **Jer 41:7** 7819
The king of Babylon **s** the sons **Jer 52:10** 7819
and he also **s** all the princes of **Jer 52:10** 7819
day of Your anger, You have **s**, **La 2:21** 2873
"You **s** My children and offered **Ezk 16:21** 7819
"For when they had **s** their children **Ezk 23:39** 7819
CONSIDERED AS SHEEP TO BE **S**." **Ro 8:36** *4967*

SLAUGHTERING

into the land, **s** the Moabites. **2Ki 3:24** 5221
Amaziah came from **s** the Edomites **2Ch 25:14** 5221
Killing of cattle and **s** of sheep, **Is 22:13** 7819

SLAUGHTERS

or a sheep and **s** it or sells it, **Ex 22:1** 2873
the house of Israel who **s** an ox or **Lv 17:3** 7819
or who **s** it outside the camp, **Lv 17:3** 7819

SLAVE

"The Hebrew **s**, whom you brought **Gn 39:17** 5650
"This is what your **s** did to me," **Gn 39:19** 5650
whom it is found shall be my **s**," **Gn 44:10** 5650
has been found, he shall be my **s**; **Gn 44:17** 5650
instead of the lad a **s** to my lord, **Gn 44:33** 5650
And became a **s** at forced labor. **Gn 49:15** 5647
even to the firstborn of the **s** girl **Ex 11:5** 8198
every man's **s** purchased with money, **Ex 12:44** 5650
"If you buy a Hebrew **s**, **Ex 21:2** 5650
"But if the **s** plainly says, **Ex 21:5** 5650
sells his daughter as a female **s**, **Ex 21:7** 519
If a man strikes his male or female **s** **Ex 21:20** 519, 5650
the eye of his male or female **s**, **Ex 21:26** 519, 5650
a tooth of his male or female **s**, **Ex 21:27** 519, 5650
the ox gores a male or female **s**, **Ex 21:32** 519, 5650
and the son of your female **s**, **Ex 23:12** 519
carnally with a woman who is a **s** **Lv 19:20** 8198
'But if a priest buys a **s** as *his* **Lv 22:11** 5315
are not to be sold *in* a **s** sale. **Lv 25:42** 5650
you were a **s** in the land of Egypt, **Dt 5:15** 5650
you were a **s** in the land of Egypt, **Dt 15:15** 5650
that you were a **s** in Egypt, **Dt 16:12** 5650
a **s** who has escaped from his master **Dt 23:15** 5650
that you were a **s** in Egypt, **Dt 24:18** 5650
you were a **s** in the land of Egypt; **Dt 24:22** 5650
And the **s** is free from his master. **Jb 3:19** 5650
"As a **s** who pants for the shade, **Jb 7:2** 5650
them, Joseph, *who* was sold as a **s**. **Ps 105:17** 5650
less for a **s** to rule over princes. **Pr 19:10** 5650
borrower *becomes* the lender's **s**. **Pr 22:7** 5650
A **s** will not be instructed by **Pr 29:19** 5650
He who pampers his **s** from **Pr 29:21** 5650
Do not slander a **s** to his master, **Pr 30:10** 5650
Under a **s** when he becomes king, **Pr 30:22** 5650
"Is Israel a **s**? Or is he a homeborn **Jer 2:14** 5650
a man sold me as a **s** in my youth.' **Zch 13:5**
to my **s**, 'Do this!' and he does *it*." **Mt 8:9** *1401*
teacher, nor a **s** above his master. **Mt 10:24** *1401*
teacher, and the **s** like his master. **Mt 10:25** *1401*
"So the **s** fell *to the ground* **Mt 18:26** *1401*
the lord of that **s** felt compassion **Mt 18:27** *1401*
"But that **s** went out and found **Mt 18:28** *1401*
"So his fellow **s** fell *to the ground* **Mt 18:29** *4889*
'You wicked **s**, I forgave you all **Mt 18:32** *1401*
have had mercy on your fellow **s**, **Mt 18:33** *4889*
first among you shall be your **s**; **Mt 20:27** *1401*
Who then is the faithful and sensible **s** **Mt 24:45** *1401*
"Blessed is that **s** whom his **Mt 24:46** *1401*
if that evil **s** says in his heart, **Mt 24:48** *1401*
the master of that **s** will come on **Mt 24:50** *1401*
'Well done, good and faithful **s**. **Mt 25:21** *1401*
'Well done, good and faithful **s**. **Mt 25:23** *1401*
'You wicked, lazy **s**, **Mt 25:26** *1401*
Throw out the worthless **s** into the **Mt 25:30** *1401*
struck the **s** of the high priest and **Mt 26:51** *1401*
first among you shall be **s** of all. **Mk 10:44** *1401*
he sent a **s** to the vine-growers, **Mk 12:2** *1401*
"Again he sent them another **s**, **Mk 12:4** *1401*
struck the **s** of the high priest and **Mk 14:47** *1401*
And a centurion's **s**, **Lk 7:2** *1401*
come and save the life of his **s**. **Lk 7:3** *1401*
to my **s**, 'Do this!' and he does it." **Lk 7:8** *1401*
they found the **s** in good health. **Lk 7:10** *1401*
"Blessed is that **s** whom his **Lk 12:43** *1401*
"But if that **s** says in his heart, **Lk 12:45** *1401*
the master of that **s** will come on **Lk 12:46** *1401*
"And that **s** who knew his master's **Lk 12:47** *1401*
at the dinner hour he sent his **s** to say **Lk 14:17** *1401*
"And the **s** came *back* and reported **Lk 14:21** *1401*
became angry and said to his **s**, **Lk 14:21** *1401*
"And the **s** said, **Lk 14:22** *1401*
"And the master said to the **s**, **Lk 14:23** *1401*
a **s** plowing or tending sheep, **Lk 17:7** *1401*
"He does not thank the **s** because **Lk 17:9** *1401*
'Well done, good **s**, because you **Lk 19:17** *1401*
I will judge you, you worthless **s**. **Lk 19:22** *1401*
he sent a **s** to the vine-growers, **Lk 20:10** *1401*
he proceeded to send another **s**; **Lk 20:11** *1401*
struck the **s** of the high priest and **Lk 22:50** *1401*
who commits sin is the **s** of sin. **Jn 8:34** *1401*
"The **s** does not remain in the **Jn 8:35** *1401*
a **s** is not greater than his master, **Jn 13:16** *1401*
for the **s** does not know what his **Jn 15:15** *1401*
'A **s** is not greater than his **Jn 15:20** *1401*
it and struck the high priest's **s**, **Jn 18:10** *1401*
Were you called while a **s**? **1Co 7:21** *1401*
was called in the Lord while a **s**, **1Co 7:22** *1401*
called while free, is Christ's **s**. **1Co 7:22** *1401*
I have made myself a **s** to all, **1Co 9:19** *1402*
I discipline my body and make it my **s**, **1Co 9:27** *1396*
there is neither **s** nor free man, **Ga 3:28** *1401*
he does not differ at all from a **s** **Ga 4:1** *1401*
Therefore you are no longer a **s**, **Ga 4:7** *1401*
from the Lord, whether **s** or free. **Eph 6:8** *1401*
Scythian, **s** and freeman, **Col 3:11** *1401*
no longer as a **s**, but more than a **Phm 1:16** *1401*
as a slave, but more than a **s**, **Phm 1:16** *1401*
strong and every **s** and free man hid **Rv 6:15** *1401*

SLAVERY

from Egypt, from the house of **s**; **Ex 13:3** 5650
out of Egypt, from the house of **s**. **Ex 13:14** 5650
of Egypt, out of the house of **s**. **Ex 20:2** 5650
of Egypt, out of the house of **s**. **Dt 5:6** 5650
of Egypt, out of the house of **s**. **Dt 6:12** 5650
redeemed you from the house of **s**, **Dt 7:8** 5650
of Egypt, out of the house of **s**, **Dt 8:14** 5650
redeemed you from the house of **s**, **Dt 13:5** 5650
of Egypt, out of the house of **s**. **Dt 13:10** 5650
you out from the house of **s**. **Jg 6:8** 5650
to return to their **s** in Egypt. **Ne 9:17** 5659
ransomed you from the house of **s**, **Mi 6:4** 5650
spirit of **s** leading to fear again, **Ro 8:15** *1397*
be set free from its **s** to corruption **Ro 8:21** *1397*
for she is in **s** with her children. **Ga 4:25** *1398*
be subject again to a yoke of **s**. **Ga 5:1** *1397*
were subject to **s** all their lives. **Heb 2:15** *1397*

SLAVE-GIRL

Then the **s** who kept the door **Jn 18:17** *3814*
a **s** having a spirit of **Ac 16:16** *3814*

SLAVE'S

not subject him to a **s** service. **Lv 25:39** 5650
and the **s** name was Malchus. **Jn 18:10** *1401*

SLAVES

take us for **s** with our donkeys." **Gn 43:18** 5650
and we also will be my lord's **s**." **Gn 44:9** 5650
behold, we are my lord's **s**, **Gn 44:16** 5650
and our land will be **s** to Pharaoh. **Gn 47:19** 5650
lord, and we will be Pharaoh's **s**." **Gn 47:25** 5650
not to go free as the male **s** do. **Ex 21:7** 5650
and your male and female **s**, **Lv 25:6** 519, 5650
'As for your male and female **s** **Lv 25:44** 519, 5650
you may acquire male and female **s** **Lv 25:44** 519, 5650
you can use them as permanent **s**. **Lv 25:46** 5647
so that *you* would not be their **s**, **Lv 26:13** 5650
'We were **s** to Pharaoh in Egypt, **Dt 6:21** 5650
your enemies as male and female **s**, **Dt 28:68** 8198, 5650
and you shall never cease being **s**, **Jos 9:23** 5650
or you will become **s** to the Hebrews, **1Sa 4:9** 5647
as they have been **s** to you; **1Sa 4:9** 5647
not make **s** of the sons of Israel; **1Ki 9:22** 5650
my two children to be his **s**." **2Ki 4:1** 5650
But Solomon did not make **s** for his **2Ch 8:9** 5650
"But they will become his **s** so **2Ch 12:8** 5650
Jerusalem for male and female **s**. **2Ch 28:10** 8198, 5650
"For we are **s**; yet in our bondage our **Ezr 9:9** 5650
sons and our daughters to be **s**, **Ne 5:5** 5650
"Behold, we are **s** today, And as **Ne 9:36** 5650
bounty, Behold, we are **s** in it. **Ne 9:36** 5650
Now if we had only been sold as **s**, **Es 7:4** 8198, 5650
the claim of my male or female **s** **Jb 31:13** 519, 5650
I bought male and female **s** and **Ec 2:7** 8198, 5650
slaves and I had homeborn **s**. **Ec 2:7** 1121
I have seen **s** *riding* on horses and **Ec 10:7** 5650
walking like **s** on the land. **Ec 10:7** 5650
great kings will make **s** of them, **Jer 25:14** 5647
will no longer make them their **s**. **Jer 30:8** 5647
S rule over us; There is no one to **La 5:8** 5650
they will be plunder for their **s**. **Zch 2:9** 5647
"The **s** of the landowner came **Mt 13:27** *1401*
The **s** said to him, **Mt 13:28** *1401*
to settle accounts with his **s**. **Mt 18:23** *1401*
found one of his fellow **s** who owed **Mt 18:28** *4889*
fellow **s** saw what had happened, **Mt 18:31** *4889*
he sent his **s** to the vine-growers **Mt 21:34** *1401*
"The vine-growers took his **s** and **Mt 21:35** *1401*
group of **s** larger than the first; **Mt 21:36** *1401*
"And he sent out his **s** to call **Mt 22:3** *1401*
"Again he sent out other **s** saying, **Mt 22:4** *1401*
and the rest seized his **s** and **Mt 22:6** *1401*
"Then he said to his **s**, **Mt 22:8** *1401*
Those **s** went out into the streets **Mt 22:10** *1401*
and begins to beat his fellow **s** **Mt 24:49** *4889*
a journey, who called his own **s** and **Mt 25:14** *1401*
the master of those **s** came and settled **Mt 25:19** *1401*
house and putting his **s** in charge, **Mk 13:34** *1401*
"Blessed are those **s** whom the **Lk 12:37** *1401*
blessed are those **s**. **Lk 12:38**
coming,' and begins to beat the **s**, **Lk 12:45** *3814, 3816*
"But the father said to his **s**, **Lk 15:22** *1401*
'We are unworthy **s**; **Lk 17:10** *1401*
"And he called ten of his **s**, **Lk 19:13** *1401*
kingdom, he ordered that these **s**, **Lk 19:15** *1401*
was now going down, *his* **s** met him, **Jn 4:51** *1401*
"No longer do I call you **s**, **Jn 15:15** *1401*
Now the **s** and the officers were **Jn 18:18** *1401*
One of the **s** of the high priest, **Jn 18:26** *1401*
we would no longer be **s** to sin; **Ro 6:6** *1398*
to someone *as* **s** for obedience, **Ro 6:16** *1401*
are **s** of the one whom you obey, **Ro 6:16** *1401*
God that though you were **s** of sin, **Ro 6:17** *1401*
you became **s** of righteousness. **Ro 6:18** *1402*
as **s** to impurity and to lawlessness, **Ro 6:19** *1401*
members as **s** to righteousness, **Ro 6:19** *1401*
For when you were **s** of sin, **Ro 6:20** *1401*
For such men are **s**, **Ro 16:18** *1398*
do not become **s** of men. **1Co 7:23** *1401*
Jews or Greeks, whether **s** or free, **1Co 12:13** *1401*
you were **s** to those which by **Ga 4:8** *1398*
bearing children who are to be **s**; **Ga 4:24** *1397*
S, be obedient to those who are **Eph 6:5** *1401*
men-pleasers, but as **s** of Christ, **Eph 6:6** *1401*
S, in all things obey those who **Col 3:22** *1401*
grant to your **s** justice and fairness, **Col 4:1** *1401*
All who are under the yoke as **s** **1Tm 6:1** *1401*
themselves are **s** of corruption; **2Pe 2:19** *1401*
poor, and the free men and the **s**, **Rv 13:16** *1401*
chariots and **s** and human lives. **Rv 18:13** *4983*
of all men, both free men and **s**, **Rv 19:18** *1401*

SLAY

no one finding him would **s** him. **Gn 4:15** 5221
s the righteous with the wicked, **Gn 18:25** 4191
"Lord, will You **s** a nation, even **Gn 20:4** 2026
and took the knife to **s** his son. **Gn 22:10** 7819
and **s** an animal and make ready; **Gn 43:16** 2873
families, and **s** the Passover *lamb*. **Ex 12:21** 7819
'He shall **s** the young bull **Lv 1:5** 7819
'He shall **s** it on the side of **Lv 1:11** 7819
and **s** it at the doorway of the tent **Lv 3:2** 7819
s it before the tent of meeting, **Lv 3:8** 7819
s it before the tent of meeting, **Lv 3:13** 7819
and **s** the bull before the LORD. **Lv 4:4** 7819
and **s** it in the place where they **Lv 4:24** 7819
place where they **s** the burnt offering **Lv 4:24** 7819
and **s** the sin offering at the **Lv 4:29** 7819
and **s** it for a sin offering in the **Lv 4:33** 7819
where they **s** the burnt offering. **Lv 4:33** 7819
place where they **s** the burnt offering **Lv 7:2** 7819
they are to **s** the guilt offering, **Lv 7:2** 7819
also give orders to **s** the one bird **Lv 14:5** 7819
You **s** this people as one man, **Nu 14:15** 5221
"Each of you **s** his men who have **Nu 25:5** 2026
out to **s** them in the wilderness." **Dt 9:28** 4191
"Though He **s** me, I will hope in **Jb 13:15** 6991
Evil shall **s** the wicked, **Ps 34:21** 4191
To **s** those who are upright in **Ps 37:14** 2873
Do not **s** them, or my people **Ps 59:11** 2026
They **s** the widow and the stranger And **Ps 94:6** 2026
O that You would **s** the wicked, **Ps 139:19** 6991
of His lips He will **s** the wicked. **Is 11:4** 4191
ones, And the Lord GOD will **s** you. **Is 65:15** 4191
lion from the forest will **s** them, **Jer 5:6** 5221

“the sword to **s**, the dogs to drag **Jer 15:3** 2026
and will **s** them with the sword. **Jer 20:4** 5221
he will **s** them before your eyes. **Jer 29:21** 5221
S and utterly destroy them,” **Jer 50:21** 2717c
“Utterly **s** old men, young men, **Ezk 9:6** 2026
they will **s** their sons and their **Ezk 23:47** 2026
“He will **s** your daughters on the **Ezk 26:8** 2026
will **s** your people with the sword; **Ezk 26:11** 2026
to **s** the wise men of Babylon; **Da 2:14** 6992
land And **s** her with thirst. **Hos 2:3** 4191
I will **s** the precious ones of **Hos 9:16** 4191
And **s** all her princes with him,” **Am 2:3** 2026
Then I will **s** the rest of them **Am 9:1** 2026
command the sword that it **s** them, **Am 9:4** 2026
s nations without sparing? **Hab 1:17** 2026
“Those who buy them **s** them and **Zch 11:5** 2026
here and **s** them in my presence.” **Lk 19:27** *2695*
we for our part are ready to **s** him **Ac 23:15** *337*
to eat or drink until they **s** him; **Ac 23:21** *337*
will be revealed whom the Lord will **s** **2Th 2:8** *337*
And for what reason did he **s** him? **1Jn 3:12** *4969*
and that *men* would **s** one another; **Rv 6:4** *4969*

SLAYER
between the **s** and the blood avenger **Nu 35:24** 5221
to give it into the hand of the **s**. **Ezk 21:11** 2026
a god,” In the presence of your **s**, **Ezk 28:9** 2026

SLAYERS
sons of the **s** he did not put to death, **2Ki 14:6** 5221

SLAYING
the sons of Israel had finished **s** them **Jos 10:20** 5221
coats of those who were **s** him.’ **Ac 22:20** *337*

SLAYS
“For anger **s** the foolish man, **Jb 5:2** 2026
The viper’s tongue **s** him. **Jb 20:16** 2026
an ox is *like* one who **s** a man; **Is 66:3** 5221
In the street the sword **s**; **La 1:20** 7921

SLEDGE
like a threshing **s** on the mire. **Jb 41:30** 2742a
not threshed with a threshing **s**, **Is 28:27** 2742a
threshing **s** with double edges; **Is 41:15** 4173

SLEDGES
the threshing **s** and the yokes of **2Sa 24:22** 4173
threshing **s** for wood and the wheat **1Ch 21:23** 4173

SLEEK
came up seven cows, **s** and fat; **Gn 41:2** 3303
ate up the seven **s** and fat cows. **Gn 41:4** 3303
fat and **s** came up out of the Nile, **Gn 41:18** 3303
You are grown fat, thick, and **s** **Dt 32:15** 3780
‘They are fat, they are **s**, **Jer 5:28** 6245a

SLEEP
LORD God caused a deep **s** to fall **Gn 2:21** 8639
down, a deep **s** fell upon Abram; **Gn 15:12** 8639
Jacob awoke from his **s** and said, **Gn 28:16** 8142
night, and my **s** fled from my eyes. **Gn 31:40** 8142
What else shall he **s** in? **Ex 22:27** 7901
you shall not **s** with his pledge. **Dt 24:12** 7901
may **s** in his cloak and bless you; **Dt 24:13** 7901
But he awoke from his **s** and pulled **Jg 16:14** 8142
She made him **s** on her knees, **Jg 16:19** 3462
And he awoke from his **s** and said, **Jg 16:20** 8142
because a sound **s** from the LORD **1Sa 26:12** 8639
During that night the king could not **s** **Es 6:1** 8142
night, When deep **s** falls on men, **Jb 4:13** 8639
awake nor be aroused out of his **s**. **Jb 14:12** 8142
night, When sound **s** falls on men, **Jb 33:15** 8639
peace I will both lie down and **s**, **Ps 4:8** 3462
or I will **s** the *sleep of* death, **Ps 13:3** 3462
or I will sleep the **s** *of* death, **Ps 13:3**
Arouse Yourself, why do You **s**, **Ps 44:23** 3462
They sank into **s**; **Ps 76:5** 8142
and horse were cast into a dead **s**. **Ps 76:6** 7290a
Then the Lord awoke as *if from* **s**, **Ps 78:65** 3463
Israel Will neither slumber nor **s**. **Ps 121:4** 3462
to His beloved *even in his* **s**. **Ps 127:2** 8142
I will not give **s** to my eyes Or **Ps 132:4** 8142
lie down, your **s** will be sweet. **Pr 3:24** 8142
they cannot **s** unless they do evil; **Pr 4:16** 3462
And they are robbed of **s** unless **Pr 4:16** 8142
Give no **s** to your eyes, Nor **Pr 6:4** 8142
When will you arise from your **s**? **Pr 6:9** 8142
“A little **s**, a little slumber, A **Pr 6:10** 8142
When you **s**, they will watch over **Pr 6:22** 7901
Laziness casts into a deep **s**, **Pr 19:15** 8639
life, So that one may **s** satisfied, **Pr 19:23** 3885a
Do not love **s**, or you will become **Pr 20:13** 8142
“A little **s**, a little slumber, A **Pr 24:33** 8142
The **s** of the working man is **Ec 5:12** 8142
rich man does not allow him to **s**. **Ec 5:12** 3462
one should never **s** day or night), **Ec 8:16**
7200, 8142, 5869
over you a spirit of deep **s**, **Is 29:10** 8639
and my **s** was pleasant to me. **Jer 31:26** 8142
And may **s** a perpetual **s**leep **Jer 51:39** 3462
may sleep a perpetual **s** And not **Jer 51:39** 8142
That they may **s** a perpetual sleep **Jer 51:57** 3462
a perpetual **s** and not wake up,” **Jer 51:57** 8142
the wilderness and **s** in the woods. **Ezk 34:25** 3462
was troubled and his **s** left him. **Da 2:1** 8142
and his **s** fled from him. **Da 6:18** 8139
I sank into a deep **s** with my face to **Da 8:18** 7290a
I fell into a deep **s** on my face, **Da 10:9** 7290a
who **s** in the dust of the ground **Da 12:2** 3463
a man who is awakened from his **s**. **Zch 4:1** 8142
And Joseph awoke from his **s** **Mt 1:24** *5258*
all got drowsy and *began* to **s**. **Mt 25:5** *2518*
had been overcome with **s**; **Lk 9:32** *5258*
that I may awaken him out of **s**.” **Jn 11:11** *1852*
that He was speaking of literal **s**. **Jn 11:13** *5258*
sill, sinking into a deep **s**; **Ac 20:9** *5258*
he was overcome by **s** and fell down **Ac 20:9** *5258*
the hour for you to awaken from **s**; **Ro 13:11** *5258*
are weak and sick, and a number **s**. **1Co 11:30** *2837*
we will not all **s**, **1Co 15:51** *2837*
so then let us not **s** as others do, **1Th 5:6** *2518*
For those who **s** do their sleeping at **1Th 5:7** *2518*

SLEEPER
“Awake, **s**, And arise from the **Eph 5:14** *2518*

SLEEPING
Saul lay **s** inside the circle of the **1Sa 26:7** 3463
in your **s** rooms do not curse a rich **Ec 10:20** 4904
“How is it that you are **s**? **Jon 1:6** 7290a
Your shepherds are **s**, **Na 3:18** 5123
“But while his men were **s**, **Mt 13:25** *2518*
to the disciples and found them **s**, **Mt 26:40** *2518*
Again He came and found them **s**, **Mt 26:43** *2518*
“Are you still **s** and resting? **Mt 26:45** *2518*
And He came and found them **s**, **Mk 14:37** *2518*
again He came and found them **s**, **Mk 14:40** *2518*
“Are you still **s** and resting? **Mk 14:41** *2518*
and found them **s** from sorrow, **Lk 22:45** *2837*
“Why are you **s**? Get up and pray **Lk 22:46** *2518*
Peter was **s** between two soldiers, **Ac 12:6** *2837*
who sleep do their **s** at night, **1Th 5:7** *2518*

SLEEPLESS
hardship, through many **s** nights, **2Co 11:27** *70*

SLEEPLESSNESS
in tumults, in labors, in **s**, **2Co 6:5** *70*

SLEEPS
lord the king **s** with his fathers, **1Ki 1:21** 7901
But he who **s** in harvest is a son **Pr 10:5** 7290a
or stumbles, None slumbers or **s**; **Is 5:27** 3462

SLEPT
to fall upon the man, and he **s**; **Gn 2:21** 3462
So while he **s**, Delilah took the **Jg 16:14** 3462
But Uriah **s** at the door of the **2Sa 11:9** 7901
Then David **s** with his fathers and **1Ki 2:10** 7901
me while your maidservant **s**, **1Ki 3:20** 3463
that David **s** with his fathers and **1Ki 11:21** 7901
And Solomon **s** with his fathers and **1Ki 11:43** 7901
and he **s** with his fathers, and **1Ki 14:20** 7901
And Rehoboam **s** with his fathers and **1Ki 14:31** 7901
And Abijam **s** with his fathers and **1Ki 15:8** 7901
And Asa **s** with his fathers and was **1Ki 15:24** 7901
And Baasha **s** with his fathers and **1Ki 16:6** 7901
So Omri **s** with his fathers and **1Ki 16:28** 7901
down and **s** under a juniper tree; **1Ki 19:5** 3462
So Ahab **s** with his fathers, and **1Ki 22:40** 7901
And Jehoshaphat **s** with his fathers **1Ki 22:50** 7901
So Joram **s** with his fathers and **2Ki 8:24** 7901
And Jehu **s** with his fathers, and **2Ki 10:35** 7901
And Jehoahaz **s** with his fathers, **2Ki 13:9** 7901
So Joash **s** with his fathers, and **2Ki 13:13** 7901
So Jehoash **s** with his fathers and **2Ki 14:16** 7901
after the king **s** with his fathers. **2Ki 14:22** 7901
And Jeroboam **s** with his fathers, **2Ki 14:29** 7901
And Azariah **s** with his fathers, **2Ki 15:7** 7901
And Menahem **s** with his fathers, **2Ki 15:22** 7901
And Jotham **s** with his fathers, and **2Ki 15:38** 7901
So Ahaz **s** with his fathers, and **2Ki 16:20** 7901
So Hezekiah **s** with his fathers, **2Ki 20:21** 7901
And Manasseh **s** with his fathers **2Ki 21:18** 7901
So Jehoiakim **s** with his fathers, **2Ki 24:6** 7901
And Solomon **s** with his fathers and **2Ch 9:31** 7901
And Rehoboam **s** with his fathers and **2Ch 12:16** 7901
So Abijah **s** with his fathers, and **2Ch 14:1** 7901
So Asa **s** with his fathers, having **2Ch 16:13** 7901
Then Jehoshaphat **s** with his **2Ch 21:1** 7901
after the king **s** with his fathers. **2Ch 26:2** 7901
So Uzziah **s** with his fathers, and **2Ch 26:23** 7901
And Jotham **s** with his fathers, and **2Ch 27:9** 7901
So Ahaz **s** with his fathers, and **2Ch 28:27** 7901
So Hezekiah **s** with his fathers, **2Ch 32:33** 7901
So Manasseh **s** with his fathers, **2Ch 33:20** 7901
I would have **s** then, I would have **Jb 3:13** 3462
I lay down and **s**; **Ps 3:5** 3462

SLEW
Because in their anger they **s** men, **Gn 49:6** 2026
who unintentionally **s** his neighbor **Dt 4:42** 7523
turned back and **s** the men of Ai. **Jos 8:21** 5221
and they **s** them until no one was **Jos 8:22** 5221
and He **s** them with a great **Jos 10:10** 5221
he arose against them and **s** them. **Jg 9:43** 5221
who *were* in the field and **s** them. **Jg 9:44** 5221
‘A woman **s** him.’ ” **Jg 9:54** 2026
Then they seized him and **s** him at **Jg 12:6** 7819
calves, and **s** *them* on the ground; **1Sa 14:32** 7819
band, after David **s** them of *Zobah;* **1Ki 11:24** 2026
brook Kishon, and **s** them there. **1Ki 18:40** 7819
to Ahaziah, and **s** them. **2Ch 22:8** 2026
Pekah the son of Remaliah **s** in **2Ch 28:6** 2026
Ephraim, **s** Maaseiah the king’s son and **2Ch 28:7** 2026
who **s** their young men with the **2Ch 36:17** 2026
They also **s** the servants with the **Jb 1:15** 5221
and **s** the servants with the edge of **Jb 1:17** 5221
many nations And **s** mighty kings, **Ps 135:10** 2026
And **s** mighty kings, For His **Ps 136:18** 2026
Jehoiakim, who **s** him with a sword and **Jer 26:23** 5221
Then the king of Babylon **s** the **Jer 39:6** 7819
king of Babylon also **s** all the nobles **Jer 39:6** 7819
but they **s** her with the sword. **Ezk 23:10** 2026
the flame of the fire **s** those men **Da 3:22** 6992
I **s** your young men by the sword **Am 4:10** 2026
and sent and **s** all the male children **Mt 2:16** *337*
the evil one and **s** his brother. **1Jn 3:12** *4969*

SLICE
like a **s** of a pomegranate Behind **SS 4:3** 6400
like a **s** of a pomegranate Behind **SS 6:7** 6400
They **s** off *what is* on the **Is 9:20** 1504

SLICED
and **s** them into the pot of stew, **2Ki 4:39** 6398

SLIGHT
‘This is but a **s** thing in the **2Ki 3:18** 7043
Is it too **s** a thing for you to try **Is 7:13** 4592
‘Is it too **s** a thing for you that **Ezk 34:18** 4592

SLIGHTEST
furnish this people the **s** benefit,” **Jer 23:32** 3276

SLING
each one could **s** a stone at a hair **Jg 20:16** 7049a
pouch, and his **s** was in his hand; **1Sa 17:40** 7050a
Philistine with a **s** and a stone, **1Sa 17:50** 7050a
lives of your enemies He will **s** out **1Sa 25:29** 7049a
out as from the hollow of a **s**. **1Sa 25:29** 7050a
the right hand and the left *to* **s** **1Ch 12:2**
body armor, bows and **s** stones. **2Ch 26:14** 7050a
Like one who binds a stone in a **s**, **Pr 26:8** 4773
and trample on the **s** stones; **Zch 9:15** 7050a

SLINGERS
the **s** went about *it* and struck it. **2Ki 3:25** 7051

SLINGING
I am **s** out the inhabitants of the **Jer 10:18** 7049a

SLINGSTONES
S are turned into stubble for him. **Jb 41:28**
7050a, 68

SLIP
In due time their foot will **s**; **Dt 32:35** 4131
“They **s** by like reed boats, Like **Jb 9:26** 2498
prepared for those whose feet **s**. **Jb 12:5** 4571
His steps do not **s**. **Ps 37:31** 4571
the mountains **s** into the heart of the **Ps 46:2** 4131
And does not allow our feet to **s**. **Ps 66:9** 4131
He will not allow your foot to **s**; **Ps 121:3** 4131
But Jesus Himself would *often* **s** away **Lk 5:16** *5298*

SLIPPED
he **s** away out of Saul’s presence, **1Sa 19:10** 6362
under me, And my feet have not **s**. **2Sa 22:37** 4571
My feet have not **s**. **Ps 17:5** 4131
under me, And my feet have not **s**. **Ps 18:36** 4571
My steps had almost **s**. **Ps 73:2** 8210
If I should say, “My foot has **s**,” **Ps 94:18** 4131
for Jesus had **s** away while there **Jn 5:13** *1593*

SLIPPERY
Let their way be dark and **s**, **Ps 35:6** 2519
You set them in **s** places; **Ps 73:18** 2513b
way will be like **s** paths to them, **Jer 23:12** 2519

SLIPS
and the iron *head* **s** off the handle **Dt 19:5** 5394
over me, *Who,* when my foot **s**, **Ps 38:16** 4131
them with vine **s** of a strange *god.* **Is 17:10** 2156

SLOPE
And the **s** of the wadis That **Nu 21:15** 793
shall go down and reach to the **s** on **Nu 34:11** 3802
s of the Jebusite on the south **Jos 15:8** 3802
s of Mount Jearim on the north **Jos 15:10** 3802
the **s** of the Jebusite southward, **Jos 18:16** 3802
As they went up the **s** to the city, **1Sa 9:11** 4608

SLOPES
foot of the **s** of Pisgah on the east. **Dt 3:17** 794
at the foot of the **s** of Pisgah. **Dt 4:49** 794
and the **s** and all their kings. **Jos 10:40** 794
at the foot of the **s** of Pisgah; **Jos 12:3** 794
lowland, in the Arabah, on the **s**, **Jos 12:8** 794
the **s** of Pisgah and Beth-jeshimoth, **Jos 13:20** 794
They will swoop down on the **s** **Is 11:14** 3802

SLOW
s of speech and slow of tongue.” **Ex 4:10** 3515
slow of speech and **s** of tongue.” **Ex 4:10** 3515
and gracious, **s** to anger, **Ex 34:6** 750
‘The LORD is **s** to anger and **Nu 14:18** 750
do not **s** down the pace for me **2Ki 4:24** 6113
and compassionate, **S** to anger and **Ne 9:17** 750
S to anger and abundant in **Ps 86:15** 750
S to anger and abounding in **Ps 103:8** 750
S to anger and great in **Ps 145:8** 750
He who is **s** to anger has great **Pr 14:29** 750
the **s** to anger calms a dispute. **Pr 15:18** 750
He who is **s** to anger is better **Pr 16:32** 750
discretion makes him **s** to anger, **Pr 19:11** 748
and compassionate, **S** to anger, **Jl 2:13** 750
s to anger and abundant in **Jon 4:2** 750
The LORD is **s** to anger and great in **Na 1:3** 750
“O foolish men and **s** of heart to **Lk 24:25** *1021*
s to speak *and* slow to anger; **Jas 1:19** *1021*
slow to speak *and* **s** to anger; **Jas 1:19** *1021*
Lord is not **s** about His promise, **2Pe 3:9** *1019*

SLOWLY
had sailed **s** for a good many days, **Ac 27:7** *1020*

SLOWNESS
His promise, as some count **s**, **2Pe 3:9** *1022*

SLUGGARD
Go to the ant, O **s**, **Pr 6:6** 6102
How long will you lie down, O **s**? **Pr 6:9** 6102
The soul of the **s** craves and *gets* **Pr 13:4** 6102
The **s** buries his hand in the dish, **Pr 19:24** 6102
The **s** does not plow after the **Pr 20:4** 6102
desire of the **s** puts him to death, **Pr 21:25** 6102
The **s** says, “There is a lion outside; **Pr 22:13** 6102
I passed by the field of the **s** And **Pr 24:30** 6102
s says, “There is a lion in the road! **Pr 26:13** 6102
hinges, So *does* the **s** on his bed. **Pr 26:14** 6102
The **s** buries his hand in the dish; **Pr 26:15** 6102

The **s** is wiser in his own eyes Pr 26:16 6102

SLUGGISH
that you will not be **s**, Heb 6:12 *3576*

SLUMBER
men, While they **s** in their beds, Jb 33:15 8572
He who keeps you will not **s**. Ps 121:3 5123
Israel Will neither **s** nor sleep. Ps 121:4 5123
to my eyes Or **s** to my eyelids Ps 132:4 8572
your eyes, Nor **s** to your eyelids; Pr 6:4 8572
"A little sleep, a little **s**, Pr 6:10 8572
"A little sleep, a little **s**, Pr 24:33 8572
lying down, who love to **s**; Is 56:10 5123

SLUMBERS
or stumbles, None **s** or sleeps; Is 5:27 5123

SLUNG
on his legs and a bronze javelin **s** 1Sa 17:6
and took from it a stone and **s** *it*, 1Sa 17:49 7049a

SMALL
with blindness, both **s** and great, Gn 19:11 6996b
enough to flee to, and it is **s**. Gn 19:20 4705
let me escape there (is it not **s**?) Gn 19:20 4705
"Is it a **s** matter for you to take Gn 30:15 4592
the household is too **s** for a lamb, Ex 12:4 4591
do anything, either **s** or great, Nu 22:18 6996a
hear the **s** and the great alike. Dt 1:17 6996a
grinding it very **s** until it was as fine Dt 9:21 3190
weights, a large and a **s**. Dt 25:13 6996a
measures, a large and a **s**. Dt 25:14 6996a
father does nothing either great or **s** 1Sa 20:2 6996b
who were in it, both **s** and great, 1Sa 30:2 6996b
was missing, whether **s** or great, 1Sa 30:19 6996b
not even a **s** stone is found there." 2Sa 17:13 6872b
"I am making one **s** request of you; 1Ki 2:20 6996b
was too **s** to hold the burnt offering 1Ki 8:64 6996b
a cloud as **s** as a man's hand is 1Ki 18:44 6996a
"Do not fight with **s** or great, 1Ki 22:31 6996b
all the people, both **s** and great; 2Ki 23:2 6996b
all the people, both **s** and great, 2Ki 25:26 6996b
"This was a **s** thing in Your eyes, 1Ch 17:17 6994
alike, the **s** as well as the great, 1Ch 25:8 6996b
lots, the **s** and the great alike, 1Ch 26:13 6996b
put to death, whether **s** or great, 2Ch 15:13 6996b
"Do not fight with **s** or great, 2Ch 18:30 6996b
the spears and the large and **s** shields 2Ch 23:9 7982
came with a **s** number of men; 2Ch 24:24 4705
by divisions, whether great or **s**, 2Ch 31:15 6996a
of the house of God, great and **s**, 2Ch 36:18 6996a
to their husbands, great and **s**." Es 1:20 6996a
"The **s** and the great are there, Jb 3:19 6996b
consolations of God too **s** for you, Jb 15:11 4592
number, Animals both **s** and great. Ps 104:25 6996a
The **s** together with the great. Ps 115:13 6996a
I am **s** and despised, *Yet* I do not Ps 119:141 6810
Four things are **s** on the earth, Pr 30:24 6996a
There was a **s** city with few men in Ec 9:14 6996a
the trees of his forest will be so **s** in Is 10:19
will be very **s** *and* impotent." Is 16:14 4592
is too **s** to wrap oneself in. Is 28:20 6887a
"It is too **s** a thing that You Is 49:6 7043
"Both great men and **s** will die in Jer 16:6 6996a
people both **s** and great approached Jer 42:1 6996b
all the people both **s** and great, Jer 42:8 6996b
Both **s** and great will die by the Jer 44:12 6996b
have made you **s** among the nations, Jer 49:15 6996b
Were your harlotries so **s** a matter? Ezk 16:20 4592
And I will make them so **s** that Ezk 29:15 4591
of the court *there was* a **s** Ezk 46:21
came forth a rather **s** horn which Da 8:9 6810
power with a **s** *force of* people. Da 11:23 4592
and the **s** house to fragments. Am 6:11 6996b
can Jacob stand, For he is **s**?" Am 7:2 6996b
can Jacob stand, for he is **s**?" Am 7:5 6996b
will make you **s** among the nations; Ob 1:2 6996b
Also her **s** children were dashed to Na 3:10
has despised the day of **s** things? Zch 4:10 6996a
"For the gate is **s** and the way Mt 7:14 *4728*
"Seven, and a few **s** fish." Mt 15:34 *2485*
They also had a few **s** fish; Mk 8:7 *2485*
and put in two **s** copper coins, Mk 12:42 *3016*
crowd, for he was **s** in stature. Lk 19:3 *3398*
putting in two **s** copper coins. Lk 21:2 *3016*
there was no other **s** boat there, Jn 6:22 *4142*
There came other **s** boats from Jn 6:23 *4142*
themselves got into the **s** boats, Jn 6:24 *4142*
there was no **s** disturbance among Ac 12:18 *3641*
that time there occurred no **s** disturbance Ac 19:23 *3641*
testifying both to **s** and great, Ac 26:22 *3398*
shelter of a **s** island called Clauda, Ac 27:16 *3519*
and no **s** storm was assailing *us*, Ac 27:20 *3641*
But to me it is a very **s** thing 1Co 4:3 *1646*
still directed by a very **s** rudder wherever Jas 3:4 *1646*
tongue is a **s** part of the body, Jas 3:5 *3398*
is set aflame by such a **s** fire! Jas 3:5 *2245*
fear Your name, the **s** and the great, Rv 11:18 *3398*
causes all, the **s** and the great, Rv 13:16 *3398*
fear Him, the **s** and the great." Rv 19:5 *3398*
men and slaves, and **s** and great." Rv 19:18 *3398*
saw the dead, the great and the **s**, Rv 20:12 *3398*

SMALLER
and to the **s** *group* you shall Nu 26:54 4592
the larger and the **s** *groups*." Nu 26:56 4592
and to the **s** you shall give less Nu 33:54 4592
you shall take less from the **s**; Nu 35:8 4592
Now the upper chambers *were* **s** Ezk 42:5 7114a
and from the **s** ledge to the larger Ezk 43:14 6996a
To make the bushel **s** and the shekel Am 8:5 6994
this is **s** than all *other* seeds, Mt 13:32 *3398*
though it is **s** than all the seeds Mk 4:31 *3398*

SMALLEST
of the **s** of the tribes of Israel, 1Sa 9:21 6996a
"The **s** one will become a clan, Is 60:22 6996b
not the **s** letter or stroke shall Mt 5:18 *1520*
and they all, from **s** to greatest, Ac 8:10 *3398*
to constitute the **s** law courts? 1Co 6:2 *1646*

SMASH
s their *sacred* pillars and cut down Ex 34:13 7665
and **s** their *sacred* pillars, Dt 7:5 7665
s their *sacred* pillars and burn their Dt 12:3 7665
They **s** with hatchet and hammers. Ps 74:6 1986
"Can anyone **s** iron, Iron from the Jer 15:12 7489b

SMASHED
an oven or a stove shall be **s**; Lv 11:35 5422
and **s** them before your eyes. Dt 9:17 7665
she struck Sisera, she **s** his head; Jg 5:26 4277
blew the trumpets and **s** the pitchers Jg 7:19 5310a
and he **s** them there and threw 2Ki 23:12 7323
and your incense altars will be **s**; Ezk 6:4 7665
that the great house be **s** to pieces Am 6:11 5221
All of her idols will be **s**, Mi 1:7 3807

SMASHING
is like the **s** of a potter's jar, Is 30:14 7667

SMEAR
"But you **s** with lies; Jb 13:4 2950

SMEARED
for He has **s** over their eyes so Is 44:18 2911b
prophets have **s** whitewash for them, Ezk 22:28 2902

SMELL
he smelled the **s** of his garments, Gn 27:27 7381b
the **s** of my son Is like the smell Gn 27:27 7381b
smell of my son Is like the **s** of a field Gn 27:27 7381b
I will not **s** your soothing aromas. Lv 26:31 7381a
see nor hear nor eat nor **s**. Dt 4:28 7381a
have noses, but they cannot **s**; Ps 115:6 7381a
the **s** of fire *even* come upon them. Da 3:27 7382
arise and its foul **s** will come up, Jl 2:20 6709
where would the sense of **s** be? 1Co 12:17 *3750*

SMELLED
The LORD **s** the soothing aroma; Gn 8:21 7381a
he **s** the smell of his garments, Gn 27:27 7381a

SMELT
s away your dross as with lye And Is 1:25 6884

SMELTED
dust, And copper is **s** from rock. Jb 28:2 6694

SMELTER
So the craftsman encourages the **s**, Is 41:7 6884
sit as a **s** and purifier of silver, Mal 3:3 6884

SMILE
from me, that I may **s** *again* Before Ps 39:13 1082

SMILED
"I **s** on them when they did not Jb 29:24 7832

SMILES
clothing, And she **s** at the future. Pr 31:25 7832

SMITE
I will **s** your whole territory with Ex 8:2 5062
pass through to **s** the Egyptians; Ex 12:23 5062
come in to your houses to **s** *you*. Ex 12:23 5062
"I will **s** them with pestilence Nu 14:12 5221
"The LORD will **s** you with Dt 28:22 5221
"The LORD will **s** you with the Dt 28:27 5221
"The LORD will **s** you with madness Dt 28:28 5221
The sun will not **s** you by day, Ps 121:6 5221
Let the righteous **s** me in kindness Ps 141:5 1986
of Babylon to **s** the land of Egypt: Jer 46:13 5221
I **s** My hand at your dishonest gain Ezk 22:13 5221
When I **s** all those who live in it, Ezk 32:15 5221
"I will also **s** the winter house Am 3:15 5221
"**S** the capitals so that the Am 9:1 5221
With a rod they will **s** the judge Mi 5:1 5221
and **s** the land with a curse." Mal 4:6 5221

SMITER
Let him give his cheek to the **s**, La 3:30 5221

SMITERS
The **s** whom I did not know gathered Ps 35:15 5222

SMITES
with which the LORD **s** the nations Zch 14:18 5062

SMITH
comes out a vessel for the **s**; Pr 25:4 6884
the **s** who blows the fire of coals And Is 54:16 2796

SMITHS
and all the craftsmen and the **s**. 2Ki 24:14 4525
and the craftsmen and the **s**, 2Ki 24:16 4525
the craftsmen and **s** from Jerusalem Jer 24:1 4525
craftsmen and the **s** had departed Jer 29:2 4525

SMITING
know that I, the LORD, do the **s**. Ezk 7:9 5221

SMITTEN
the men who did not die were **s** 1Sa 5:12 5221
the news that Saul had **s** the garrison 1Sa 13:4 5221
out because the LORD had **s** him. 2Ch 26:20 5060
For You have **s** all my enemies on Ps 3:7 5221
him whom You Yourself have **s**, Ps 69:26 5221
My heart has been **s** like grass and Ps 102:4 5221
esteemed Him stricken, **S** of God, Is 53:4 5221
You have **s** them, *But* they did not Jer 5:3 5221
Let their men also be **s** to death, Jer 18:21 2026

SMOKE
the **s** of the land ascended like Gn 19:28 7008
ascended like the **s** of a furnace. Gn 19:28 7008
Now Mount Sinai *was* all in **s** Ex 19:18 6225
and its **s** ascended like the smoke Ex 19:18 6227
ascended like the **s** of a furnace, Ex 19:18 6227
offer them up in **s** on the altar. Ex 29:13 6999
shall offer up in **s** the whole ram Ex 29:18 6999
and offer them up in **s** on the Ex 29:25 6999
by offering up in **s** a fire *sacrifice* to Ex 30:20 6999
the priest shall offer up in **s** all of it Lv 1:9 6999
and offer it up in **s** on the altar; Lv 1:13 6999
and offer it up in **s** on the altar; Lv 1:15 6999
priest shall offer it up in **s** on the altar Lv 1:17 6999
the priest shall offer *it* up in **s** *as* its Lv 2:2 6999
and shall offer *it* up in **s** on the Lv 2:9 6999
for you shall not offer up in **s** Lv 2:11 6999
'The priest shall offer up in **s** Lv 2:16 6999
Aaron's sons shall offer *it* up in **s** on Lv 3:5 6999
offer *it* up in **s** on the altar Lv 3:11 6999
The priest shall offer them up in **s** Lv 3:16 6999
the priest is to offer them up in **s** on Lv 4:10 6999
and offer it up in **s** on the altar. Lv 4:19 6999
All its fat he shall offer up in **s** on the Lv 4:26 6999
priest shall offer it up in **s** on the altar Lv 4:31 6999
offer them up in **s** on the altar, Lv 4:35 6999
and offer *it* up in **s** on the altar, Lv 5:12 6999
and offer up in **s** the fat portions Lv 6:12 6999
offer *it* up in **s** on the altar, Lv 6:15 6999
offered up in **s** to the LORD. Lv 6:22 6999
The priest shall offer them up in **s** on Lv 7:5 6999
The priest shall offer up the fat in **s** Lv 7:31 6999
Moses offered it up in **s** on the altar. Lv 8:16 6999
and the pieces and the suet in **s**. Lv 8:20 6999
Moses offered up the whole ram in **s** Lv 8:21 6999
offered them up in **s** on the altar with Lv 8:28 6999
he then offered up in **s** on the Lv 9:10 6999
offered *them* up in **s** on the altar. Lv 9:13 6999
and offered *them* up in **s** with the Lv 9:14 6999
offered *it* up in **s** on the altar, Lv 9:17 6999
offered them up in **s** on the altar. Lv 9:20 6999
"Then he shall offer up in **s** the Lv 16:25 6999
and offer up the fat in **s** as a Lv 17:6 6999
and offer it up in **s** on the altar, Nu 5:26 6999
offer up their fat in **s** *as* an offering Nu 18:17 6999
the **s** of the city ascended to the Jos 8:20 6227
that the **s** of the city ascended, Jos 8:21 6227
cloud of **s** rise from the city. Jg 20:38 6227
from the city in a column of **s**, Jg 20:40 6227
the whole city was going up *in* **s** Jg 20:40
"**S** went up out of His nostrils, 2Sa 22:9 6227
"Out of his nostrils **s** goes forth As Jb 41:20 6227
S went up out of His nostrils, And Ps 18:8 6227
like **s** they vanish away. Ps 37:20 6227
of fat beasts, With the **s** of rams; Ps 66:15 7004
As **s** is driven away, *so* drive *them* Ps 68:2 6227
Why does Your anger **s** against the Ps 74:1 6225
my days have been consumed in **s**, Ps 102:3 6227
touches the mountains, and they **s**. Ps 104:32 6225
become like a wineskin in the **s**, Ps 119:83 7008
the mountains, that they may **s**. Ps 144:5 6225
to the teeth and **s** to the eyes, Pr 10:26 6227
the wilderness Like columns of **s**, SS 3:6 6227
assemblies a cloud by day, even **s**, Is 4:5 6227
the temple was filling with **s**. Is 6:4 6227
they roll upward in a column of **s**. Is 9:18 6227
For **s** comes from the north, And Is 14:31 6227
is His anger and dense is *His* **s**; Is 30:27 4858
Its **s** will go up forever Is 34:10 6227
For the sky will vanish like **s**, Is 51:6 6227
These are **s** in My nostrils, A fire Is 65:5 6227
floor And like **s** from a chimney. Hos 13:3 6227
Blood, fire and columns of **s**. Jl 2:30 6227
"I will burn up her chariots in **s**, Na 2:13 6227
BLOOD, AND FIRE, AND VAPOR OF **S**. Ac 2:19 *2586*
And the **s** of the incense, with the Rv 8:4 *2586*
and **s** went up out of the pit, like Rv 9:2 *2586*
like the **s** of a great furnace; Rv 9:2 *2586*
were darkened by the **s** of the pit. Rv 9:2 *2586*
Then out of the **s** came locusts Rv 9:3 *2586*
proceed fire and **s** and brimstone. Rv 9:17 *2586*
fire and the **s** and the brimstone which Rv 9:18 *2586*
"And the **s** of their torment goes Rv 14:11 *2586*
And the temple was filled with **s** Rv 15:8 *2586*
they see the **s** of her burning, Rv 18:9 *2586*
as they saw the **s** of her burning, Rv 18:18 *2586*
HER **S** RISES UP FOREVER AND EVER." Rv 19:3 *2586*

SMOKING
there appeared a **s** oven and a Gn 15:17 6227
of the trumpet and the mountain **s**; Ex 20:18 6226
"As for the **s** sacrifices that you Jer 44:21 7002

SMOLDERING
these two stubs of **s** firebrands, Is 7:4 6226
AND A **S** WICK HE WILL NOT PUT OUT, Mt 12:20 *5188*

SMOLDERS
Their anger **s** all night, In the Hos 7:6 3463

SMOOTH
is a hairy man and I am a **s** man. Gn 27:11 2509
and on the **s** part of his neck. Gn 27:16 2513b
five **s** stones from the brook, 1Sa 17:40 2512
the **s** tongue of the adulteress. Pr 6:24 2513b
righteousness of the blameless will **s** Pr 11:5 3474
But we will rebuild with **s** stones; Is 9:10 1496
to a nation tall and **s**, Is 18:2 4803
of hosts From a people tall and **s**, Is 18:7 4803
The way of the righteous is **s**; Is 26:7 4339
Make **s** in the desert a highway for Is 40:3 3474
you and make the rough places **s**; Is 45:2 3474
And I will make all his ways **s**; Is 45:13 3474
"Among the **s** *stones* of the ravine Is 57:6 2509
"By **s** *words* he will turn to Da 11:32 2514
STRAIGHT, AND THE ROUGH ROADS **S**; Lk 3:5 *3006*
and by their **s** and flattering speech Ro 16:18 *5542*

SMOOTHER
His speech was **s** than butter, But Ps 55:21 2505b
And **s** than oil is her speech; Pr 5:3 2509

SMOOTHLY
in the cup, When it goes down **s**; Pr 23:31 4339
"It goes *down* **s** for my beloved, SS 7:9 4339

SMOOTHS
And he who **s** *metal* with the hammer Is 41:7 2505b

SMOTE
in Egypt when He **s** the Egyptians, Ex 12:27 5062
Then the LORD **s** the people, Ex 32:35 5062
and we **s** them until no survivor Dt 3:3 5221
gods who **s** the Egyptians with all 1Sa 4:8 5221
them and **s** them with tumors, 1Sa 5:6 5221
and He **s** the men of the city, both 1Sa 5:9 5221
Jonathan **s** the garrison of the 1Sa 13:3 5221
So after all this the LORD **s** him 2Ch 21:18 5062
and **s** Job with sore boils from the Jb 2:7 5221
And **s** all the firstborn in Egypt, Ps 78:51 5221
He **s** the firstborn of Egypt, Both Ps 135:8 5221
He **s** many nations And slew mighty Ps 135:10 5221
To Him who **s** the Egyptians in Ps 136:10 5221
To Him who **s** great kings, For His Ps 136:17 5221
I was instructed, I **s** on *my* thigh; Jer 31:19 5606
"I **s** you with scorching *wind* and Am 4:9 5221
'I **s** you *and* every work of your Hg 2:17 5221

SMYRNA
to Ephesus and to **S** and to Rv 1:11 *4667*
to the angel of the church in **S** write Rv 2:8 *4667*

SNAIL
as a **s** which melts away as it goes Ps 58:8 7642a

SNAKE
the way, A horned **s** in the path, Gn 49:17 8207
The tree **s** will make its nest and Is 34:15 7091
which is crushed a **s** breaks forth. Is 59:5 660
the wall And a **s** bites him. Am 5:19 5175
a fish, he will not give him a **s**, Mt 7:10 *3789*
give him a **s** instead of a fish, Lk 11:11 *3789*

SNAPPED
But he **s** the cords as a string of Jg 16:9 5423
But he **s** the ropes from his arms Jg 16:12 5423

SNAPS
as a string of tow **s** when it touches Jg 16:9 5423
heel, *And* a trap **s** shut on him. Jb 18:9 2388

SNARE
How long will this man be a **s** to us? Ex 10:7 4170
it will surely be a **s** to you." Ex 23:33 4170
or it will become a **s** in your midst. Ex 34:12 4170
for that *would be* a **s** to you. Dt 7:16 4170
will be a **s** and a trap to you, Jos 23:13 6341a
gods will be a **s** to you.'" Jg 2:3 4170
a **s** to Gideon and his household. Jg 8:27 4170
that she may become a **s** to him, 1Sa 18:21 4170
are you then laying a **s** for my life 1Sa 28:9 5367
"A **s** seizes *him* by the heel, *And* Jb 18:9 6341a
table before them become a **s**; Ps 69:22 4170
you from the **s** of the trapper And Ps 91:3 6341a
idols, Which became a **s** to them. Ps 106:36 4170
The wicked have laid a **s** for me, Ps 119:110 6341a
bird out of the **s** of the trapper; Ps 124:7 6341a
s is broken and we have escaped. Ps 124:7 6341a
As a bird hastens to the **s**, Pr 7:23 6341a
his lips are the **s** of his soul. Pr 18:7 4170
ways And find a **s** for yourself. Pr 22:25 4170
The fear of man brings a **s**, Pr 29:25 4170
net and birds trapped in a **s**, Ec 9:12 6341a
And a **s** and a trap for the Is 8:14 6341a
Terror and pit and **s** Confront you, Is 24:17 6341a
the pit will be caught in the **s**; Is 24:18 6341a
pit and **s** are *coming* upon you, Jer 48:43 6341a
the pit Will be caught in the **s**; Jer 48:44 6341a
"I set a **s** for you and you were Jer 50:24 3369
and he will be caught in My **s**. Ezk 12:13 4686a
and he will be caught in My **s**. Ezk 17:20 4686a
For you have been a **s** at Mizpah And Hos 5:1 6341a
Yet the **s** of a bird catcher is in Hos 9:8 6341a
THEIR TABLE BECOME A **S** AND A TRAP, Ro 11:9 *3803*
reproach and the **s** of the devil. 1Tm 3:7 *3803*
get rich fall into temptation and a **s** 1Tm 6:9 *3803*
escape from the **s** of the devil, 2Tm 2:26 *3803*

SNARED
yourselves, or you will be **s** by it, Dt 7:25 3369
of his own hands the wicked is **s**. Ps 9:16 5367
s with the words of your mouth, Pr 6:2 3369
They will even be **s** and caught." Is 8:15 3369
stumble backward, be broken, **s** and Is 28:13 3369

SNARES
The **s** of death confronted me. 2Sa 22:6 4170
"Therefore **s** surround you, And Jb 22:10 6341a
not rule Nor be **s** of the people. Jb 34:30 4170
Upon the wicked He will rain **s**; Ps 11:6 6341a
The **s** of death confronted me. Ps 18:5 4170
who seek my life lay **s** *for me;* Ps 38:12 5367
They talk of laying **s** secretly; Ps 64:5 4170
They have set **s** for me. Ps 140:5 4170
the **s** of those who do iniquity. Ps 141:9 4170
To turn aside from the **s** of death. Pr 13:14 4170
That one may avoid the **s** of death. Pr 14:27 4170
Thorns *and* **s** are in the way of the Pr 22:5 6341a
woman whose heart is **s** and nets, Ec 7:26 4685b
me And hidden **s** for my feet. Jer 18:22 6341a

SNATCH
"Were He to **s** away, who could Jb 9:12 2862
Others **s** the orphan from the breast, Jb 24:9 1497
He will **s** you up and tear you Ps 52:5 2846
"I will surely **s** them away," Jer 8:13 5486
no one will **s** them out of My hand. Jn 10:28 *726*
to **s** *them* out of the Father's hand. Jn 10:29 *726*

SNATCHED
s the spear from the Egyptian's hand 2Sa 23:21 1497
s the spear from the Egyptian's hand 1Ch 11:23 1497
Who were **s** away before their time, Jb 22:16 7059
And **s** the prey from his teeth. Jb 29:17 7993
and birds have been **s** away, Jer 12:4 5595
from a foreign *land* ever **s** away? Jer 18:14 5428
Israel dwelling in Samaria be **s** away Am 3:12 5337
like a firebrand **s** from a blaze; Am 4:11 5337
Spirit of the Lord **s** Philip away; Ac 8:39 *726*

SNATCHES
"Just as the shepherd **s** from the Am 3:12 5337
the evil *one* comes and **s** away what Mt 13:19 *726*
and flees, and the wolf **s** them and Jn 10:12 *726*

SNATCHING
others, **s** them out of the fire; Jude 1:23 *726*

SNEAKED
who had **s** in to spy out our liberty Ga 2:4 *3920*

SNEER
All who see me **s** at me; Ps 22:7 3932
of the dead, some *began* to **s**, Ac 17:32 *5512*

SNEERING
And even the rulers were **s** at Him, Lk 23:35 *1592*

SNEEZED
and the lad **s** seven times and the 2Ki 4:35 2237

SNEEZES
"His **s** flash forth light, And his Jb 41:18 5846

SNIFF
And you disdainfully **s** at it," Mal 1:13 5301

SNIFFS
That **s** the wind in her passion. Jer 2:24 7602a

SNORTING
His majestic **s** is terrible. Jb 39:20 5170a
Dan is heard the **s** of his horses; Jer 8:16 5170b

SNORTS
all his adversaries, he **s** at them. Ps 10:5 6315

SNOUT
As a ring of gold in a swine's **s** Pr 11:22 639

SNOW
his hand was leprous like **s**. Ex 4:6 7950
Miriam *was* leprous, as *white as* **s**. Nu 12:10 7950
presence a leper *as white* as **s**. 2Ki 5:27 7950
ice *And* into which the **s** melts. Jb 6:16 7950
"If I should wash myself with **s** Jb 9:30 7950
and heat consume the **s** waters, Jb 24:19 7950
"For to the **s** He says, Jb 37:6 7950
entered the storehouses of the **s**, Jb 38:22 7950
me, and I shall be whiter than **s**. Ps 51:7 7950
He gives **s** like wool; Ps 147:16 7950
Fire and hail, **s** and clouds; Ps 148:8 7950
Like the cold of **s** in the time of Pr 25:13 7950
Like **s** in summer and like rain in Pr 26:1 7950
afraid of the **s** for her household, Pr 31:21 7950
They will be as white as **s**; Is 1:18 7950
and the **s** come down from heaven, Is 55:10 7950
'Does the **s** of Lebanon forsake the Jer 18:14 7950
ones were purer than **s**, La 4:7 7950
His vesture *was* like white **s** And Da 7:9 8517
and his clothing as white as **s** Mt 28:3 *5510*
white like white wool, like **s**; Rv 1:14 *5510*

SNOWING
kings there, It was **s** in Zalmon. Ps 68:14 7949

SNOWY
in the middle of a pit on a **s** day. 2Sa 23:20 7950
a lion inside a pit on a **s** day. 1Ch 11:22 7950

SNUFFERS
"Its **s** and their trays *shall* Ex 25:38 4457
its **s** and its trays of pure gold. Ex 37:23 4457
along with its lamps and its **s**, Nu 4:9 4457
and the cups and the **s** and the 1Ki 7:50 4212
house of the LORD silver cups, **s**, 2Ki 12:13 4212
away the pots, the shovels, the **s**, 2Ki 25:14 4212
and the **s**, the bowls, the spoons and 2Ch 4:22 4212
away the pots, the shovels, the **s**, Jer 52:18 4212

SO
were above the expanse; and it was **s**. Gn 1:7 3651
the dry land appear"; and it was **s**. Gn 1:9 3651
with seed in them"; and it was **s**. Gn 1:11 3651
give light on the earth"; and it was **s**. Gn 1:15 3651
earth after their kind"; and it was **s**. Gn 1:24 3651
green plant for food"; and it was **s**. Gn 1:30 3651
S the LORD God caused a deep sleep Gn 2:21
s I hid myself." Gn 3:10
S He drove the man out; Gn 3:24
S it came about in the course of Gn 4:3
S Cain became very angry and his Gn 4:5
S the LORD said to him, Gn 4:15
s that no one finding him would slay Gn 4:15
S all the days that Adam lived Gn 5:5
S all the days of Seth were nine Gn 5:8
S all the days of Enosh were nine Gn 5:11
S all the days of Kenan were nine Gn 5:14
S all the days of Mahalalel were Gn 5:17
S all the days of Jared were nine Gn 5:20
S all the days of Enoch were three Gn 5:23
S all the days of Methuselah were Gn 5:27
S all the days of Lamech were Gn 5:31
God had commanded him, **s** he did. Gn 6:22 3651
S they went into the ark to Noah, Gn 7:15
s that it rose above the earth. Gn 7:17
s that all the high mountains Gn 7:19
s she returned to him into the ark, Gn 8:9
S he waited yet another seven days; Gn 8:10
S Noah knew that the water was Gn 8:11
S Noah went out, and his sons and Gn 8:18
s that they did not see their Gn 9:23
S he said, "Cursed be Canaan; Gn 9:25
S all the days of Noah were nine Gn 9:29
s that they will not understand one Gn 11:7 834
S the LORD scattered them abroad Gn 11:8
And **s** you shall be a blessing; Gn 12:2
S Abram went forth as the LORD had Gn 12:4
S he built an altar there to the Gn 12:7
s Abram went down to Egypt to Gn 12:10
say that you are my sister **s** that it Gn 12:13 4616
s that I took her for my wife? Gn 12:19
S Abram went up from Egypt to the Gn 13:1
for their possessions were **s** great Gn 13:6
S Abram said to Lot, "Please let Gn 13:8
S Lot chose for himself all the Gn 13:11
s that if anyone can number the Gn 13:16 *834*
"**S** shall your descendants be." Gn 15:5 3541
S He said to him, Gn 15:9
S Sarai said to Abram, Gn 16:2
S Sarai treated her harshly, Gn 16:6
s that they will be too many to Gn 16:10
S Hagar bore Abram a son; Gn 16:15
"**S** do, as you have said." Gn 18:5 3651
S Abraham hurried into the tent to Gn 18:6
when I am **s** old?' Gn 18:13
"For I have chosen him, **s** that he Gn 18:19 4616
s that the LORD may bring upon Gn 18:19 4616
s that the righteous and the Gn 18:25
S the LORD said, Gn 18:26
s they turned aside to him and Gn 19:3
S they pressed hard against Lot Gn 19:9
s that they wearied *themselves* Gn 19:11
their outcry has become **s** great before Gn 19:13 3588
S the men seized his hand and the Gn 19:16
S they made their father drink Gn 19:33
S they made their father drink Gn 19:35
S Abimelech king of Gerar sent and Gn 20:2
S Abimelech arose early in the Gn 20:8
maids, **s** that they bore *children.* Gn 20:17
S Sarah conceived and bore a son Gn 21:2
S Abraham rose early in the Gn 21:14
seven ewe lambs from my hand **s** that Gn 21:30 5668
S they made a covenant at Gn 21:32
S Abraham rose early in the Gn 22:3
S the two of them walked on Gn 22:6
S the two of them walked on Gn 22:8
S Abraham returned to his young Gn 22:19
S Abraham rose and bowed to the Gn 23:7
S bury your dead." Gn 23:15
S Ephron's field, which was in Gn 23:17
S the field and the cave that is Gn 23:20
S the servant placed his hand Gn 24:9
down your jar **s** that I may drink,' Gn 24:14
S she quickly emptied her jar into Gn 24:20
S the man entered the house. Gn 24:32
S he said, "I am Abraham's servant. Gn 24:34
master, **s** that he has become rich; Gn 24:35
"**S** I came today to the spring, Gn 24:42
s I drank, and she watered the Gn 24:46
"**S** now if you are going to deal Gn 24:49
s we cannot speak to you bad or Gn 24:50
S the servant took Rebekah and Gn 24:61
"If it is **s**, why then am I *this* Gn 25:22 3651
S she went to inquire of the LORD. Gn 25:22
heel, **s** his name was called Jacob; Gn 25:26
s of what *use* then is the Gn 25:32
s he swore to him, and sold his Gn 25:33
S Isaac went to Gerar, to Gn 26:1
S Isaac lived in Gerar. Gn 26:6
S Abimelech charged all the Gn 26:11
s that the Philistines envied him. Gn 26:14
S he named the well Esek, Gn 26:20
over it too, **s** he named it Sitnah. Gn 26:21
s he named it Rehoboth, for he Gn 26:22
S he built an altar there and Gn 26:25
s we said, 'Let there now be an oath Gn 26:28
S he called it Shibah; Gn 26:33
s that my soul may bless you Gn 27:4 5668
S when Esau went to the field to Gn 27:5
s that he may bless you before his Gn 27:10 5668
S he went and got *them,* and Gn 27:14
is it that you have *it* **s** quickly, Gn 27:20
S Jacob came close to Isaac his Gn 27:22
s he blessed him. Gn 27:23
S he said, "Bring *it* to me, Gn 27:25
S he came close and kissed him; Gn 27:27
s that I ate of all *of it* before Gn 27:33
S Esau lifted his voice and wept. Gn 27:38
S Esau bore a grudge against Jacob Gn 27:41
S Isaac called Jacob and blessed Gn 28:1
S Esau saw that the daughters of Gn 28:8
S Jacob rose early in the morning, Gn 28:18
S when Laban heard Gn 29:13
Now Jacob loved Rachel, **s** he said, Gn 29:18
S Jacob served seven years for Gn 29:20
S it came about in the morning Gn 29:25
did **s** and completed her week, Gn 29:28 3651
S *Jacob* went in to Rachel also, Gn 29:30
s she named him Simeon. Gn 29:33
S she gave him her maid Bilhah as Gn 30:4
S Rachel said, "With mighty Gn 30:8
S she named him Gad. Gn 30:11
S she named him Asher. Gn 30:13
S Rachel said, "Therefore he may lie Gn 30:15
S he lay with her that night. Gn 30:16
S she named him Issachar. Gn 30:18
S she named him Zebulun. Gn 30:20
S she conceived and bore a son and Gn 30:23
S he said, "What shall I give you?" Gn 30:31
"**S** my honesty will answer for me Gn 30:33
S he removed on that day the Gn 30:35
S the flocks mated by the rods, Gn 30:39

s that they might mate by the rods;	Gn 30:41	
s the feebler were Laban's and the	Gn 30:42	
S the man became exceedingly	Gn 30:43	
S Jacob sent and called Rachel and	Gn 31:4	
S he fled with all that he had;	Gn 31:21	
s that I might have sent you away	Gn 31:27	
S Laban went into Jacob's tent and	Gn 31:33	
S he searched but did not find the	Gn 31:35	
s He rendered judgment last night."	Gn 31:42	
"S now come, let us make a	Gn 31:44	
S they took stones and made a	Gn 31:46	
S Jacob swore by the fear of his	Gn 31:53	
S he named that place Mahanaim.	Gn 32:2	
S he spent the night there.	Gn 32:13	
S the present passed on before	Gn 32:21	
s the socket of Jacob's thigh was	Gn 32:25	
S he said to him,	Gn 32:27	
S Jacob named the place Peniel,	Gn 32:30	
S he divided the children among	Gn 33:1	
S he said, "The children whom God	Gn 33:5	
S Esau returned that day on his	Gn 33:16	
S Shechem spoke to his father	Gn 34:4	
s Jacob kept silent until they	Gn 34:5	
Ask me ever s much bridal payment	Gn 34:12	3966
S Hamor and his son Shechem came	Gn 34:20	
S Jacob said to his household and	Gn 35:2	
S they gave to Jacob all the	Gn 35:4	
S Jacob came to Luz	Gn 35:6	
S Jacob named the place where God	Gn 35:15	
S Rachel died and was buried on	Gn 35:19	
S Esau lived in the hill country	Gn 36:8	
and s they hated him and could	Gn 37:4	
S they hated him even more for his	Gn 37:8	
S he sent him from the valley of	Gn 37:14	
S Joseph went after his brothers	Gn 37:17	
S it came about, when Joseph	Gn 37:23	
s they pulled *him* up and lifted	Gn 37:28	
s he tore his garments.	Gn 37:29	
S they took Joseph's tunic, and	Gn 37:31	
S Jacob tore his clothes, and put	Gn 37:34	
S his father wept for him.	Gn 37:35	
S she conceived and bore a son and	Gn 38:3	
LORD, s the LORD took his life.	Gn 38:7	
s when he went in to	Gn 38:9	
S He took his life also.	Gn 38:10	
S Tamar went and lived in her	Gn 38:11	
S she removed her widow's garments	Gn 38:14	
S he turned aside to her by the	Gn 38:16	
S he gave *them* to her and	Gn 38:18	
S he returned to Judah, and said,	Gn 38:22	
S he was named Perez.	Gn 38:29	
s he became a successful man.	Gn 39:2	
S Joseph found favor in his sight and	Gn 39:4	
S he left everything he owned in	Gn 39:6	
S she left his garment beside her	Gn 39:16	
S Joseph's master took him and put	Gn 39:20	
s that whatever was done there, he	Gn 39:22	
S he put them in confinement in	Gn 40:3	
"Why are your faces s sad today?"	Gn 40:7	
S the chief cupbearer told his	Gn 40:9	
s I took the grapes and squeezed	Gn 40:11	
s he sent and called for all the	Gn 41:8	
interpreted for us, s it happened;	Gn 41:13	3651
S Pharaoh spoke to Joseph,	Gn 41:17	
"S the abundance will be unknown	Gn 41:31	
s that the land will not perish	Gn 41:36	
S Pharaoh said to Joseph,	Gn 41:39	
there is no one s discerning and	Gn 41:39	
S he gathered all the food of	Gn 41:48	
S when all the land of Egypt was	Gn 41:55	
s that we may live and not die."	Gn 42:2	
S the sons of Israel came to buy	Gn 42:5	
S he put them all together in	Gn 42:17	
me, s your words may be verified,	Gn 42:20	
you will not die." And they did s.	Gn 42:20	3651
S they loaded their donkeys with	Gn 42:26	
S it came about when they had	Gn 43:2	
"Why did you treat me s badly by	Gn 43:6	
S we answered his questions.	Gn 43:7	
"If *it must be* s, then do this:	Gn 43:11	3651
s that he will release to you your	Gn 43:14	
S the men took this present, and	Gn 43:15	
S the man did as Joseph said, and	Gn 43:17	
S they came near to Joseph's house	Gn 43:19	
S we have brought it back in our	Gn 43:21	
S they prepared the present for	Gn 43:25	
S they served him by himself, and	Gn 43:32	
S they feasted and drank freely	Gn 43:34	
S he overtook them and spoke these	Gn 44:6	
S he said, "Now let it also be	Gn 44:10	
S Judah said, "What can we say to	Gn 44:16	
s he alone is left of his mother,	Gn 44:20	
S there was no man with him when	Gn 45:1	
He wept s loudly that the	Gn 45:2	
Then the sons of Israel did s;	Gn 45:21	3651
S he sent his brothers away, and	Gn 45:24	
S Israel set out with all that he	Gn 46:1	
S they said to Pharaoh,	Gn 47:3	
S Jacob said to Pharaoh,	Gn 47:9	
S Joseph settled his father and	Gn 47:11	
s that the land of Egypt and the	Gn 47:13	
S they brought their livestock to	Gn 47:17	
S give us seed, that we may live	Gn 47:19	
S Joseph bought all the land of	Gn 47:20	
S they said, "You have saved our	Gn 47:25	
s the length of Jacob's life was	Gn 47:28	
"Swear to me." S he swore to him.	Gn 47:31	
S he took his two sons Manasseh	Gn 48:1	
S he said, "Bring them to me, please,	Gn 48:9	
Now the eyes of Israel were s dim	Gn 48:10	
"Not s, my father, for this one	Gn 48:18	3651
S that his rider falls backward.	Gn 49:17	
S the physicians embalmed Israel.	Gn 50:2	
S Joseph went up to bury his	Gn 50:7	
S they sent *a message* to Joseph,	Gn 50:16	
"S therefore, do not be afraid;	Gn 50:21	6258
S he comforted them and spoke	Gn 50:21	
S Joseph died at the age of one	Gn 50:26	
s that the land was filled with	Ex 1:7	
S they appointed taskmasters over	Ex 1:11	
s that they were in dread of the	Ex 1:12	
S the king of Egypt called for the	Ex 1:18	
S God was good to the midwives,	Ex 1:20	
S the girl went and called the	Ex 2:8	
S the woman took the child and	Ex 2:9	
S he looked this way and that, and	Ex 2:12	
have you come *back* s soon today?"	Ex 2:18	
S they said, "An Egyptian delivered	Ex 2:19	
S God heard their groaning;	Ex 2:24	
S Moses said, "I must turn aside	Ex 3:3	
"S I have come down to deliver	Ex 3:8	
s that you may bring My people,	Ex 3:10	
"S I said, I will bring you up	Ex 3:17	
S now, please, let us go a three	Ex 3:18	
"S I will stretch out My hand and	Ex 3:20	
S he threw it on the ground,	Ex 4:3	
s he stretched out his hand and	Ex 4:4	
S he put his hand into his bosom,	Ex 4:6	
S he put his hand into his bosom	Ex 4:7	
S Moses took his wife and his sons	Ex 4:20	
but I will harden his heart s that	Ex 4:21	
"S I said to you,	Ex 4:23	
S He let him alone.	Ex 4:26	
S he went and met him at the	Ex 4:27	
S the people believed;	Ex 4:31	
S the same day Pharaoh commanded	Ex 5:6	
and let them work at it s that they	Ex 5:9	
S the taskmasters of the people	Ex 5:10	
S the people scattered through all	Ex 5:12	
"S go now *and* work;	Ex 5:18	
S Moses spoke thus to the sons of	Ex 6:9	
S Moses and Aaron did *it;*	Ex 7:6	
S Moses and Aaron came to Pharaoh,	Ex 7:10	
S Moses and Aaron did even as the	Ex 7:20	
s that the Egyptians could not	Ex 7:21	
S all the Egyptians dug around the	Ex 7:24	
"S the frogs will come up on you	Ex 8:4	
S Aaron stretched out his hand	Ex 8:6	
S he said, "*May it be* according to	Ex 8:10	
S they piled them in heaps, and	Ex 8:14	
They did s; and Aaron stretched out	Ex 8:17	3651
s there were gnats on man and	Ex 8:18	
s that no swarms of insects will	Ex 8:22	
Then the LORD did s.	Ex 8:24	3651
"It is not right to do s,	Ex 8:26	3651
S Moses went out from Pharaoh and	Ex 8:30	
s that nothing will die of all	Ex 9:4	
S the LORD did this thing on the	Ex 9:6	
S they took soot from a kiln, and	Ex 9:10	
s that you may know that there is	Ex 9:14	5668
S there was hail, and fire	Ex 9:24	
S Moses went out of the city from	Ex 9:33	
s that no one will be able to see	Ex 10:5	
S Moses and Aaron were brought	Ex 10:8	
"Not s! Go now, the men *among you,*	Ex 10:11	3651
S they were driven out from	Ex 10:11	
S Moses stretched out his staff	Ex 10:13	
had never been s *many* locusts,	Ex 10:14	3651
nor would there be s *many* again.	Ex 10:14	3651
s that the land was darkened;	Ex 10:15	
S the LORD shifted *the wind* to a	Ex 10:19	
S Moses stretched out his hand	Ex 10:22	
s that My wonders will be	Ex 11:9	4616
the sons of Israel went and did s;	Ex 12:28	
Moses and Aaron, s they did.	Ex 12:28	3651
S the people took their dough	Ex 12:34	
s that they let them have their	Ex 12:36	
Then all the sons of Israel did s;	Ex 12:50	
"S it shall serve as a sign on	Ex 13:16	
I am the LORD." And they did s.	Ex 14:4	3651
S he made his chariot ready and	Ex 14:6	
s the sons of Israel cried out to	Ex 14:10	
s that they will go in after them;	Ex 14:17	
S it came between the camp of	Ex 14:20	
land, s the waters were divided.	Ex 14:21	
s the Egyptians said,	Ex 14:25	
s that the waters may come back over	Ex 14:26	
S Moses stretched out his hand	Ex 14:27	
S the people grumbled at Moses,	Ex 15:24	
S Moses and Aaron said to all the	Ex 16:6	
S it came about at evening that	Ex 16:13	
The sons of Israel did s,	Ex 16:17	3651
S they put it aside until morning,	Ex 16:24	
S the people rested on the seventh	Ex 16:30	
s Aaron placed it before the	Ex 16:34	
S Moses cried out to the LORD,	Ex 17:4	
And Moses did s in the sight of	Ex 17:6	3651
S Moses said to Joshua,	Ex 17:9	
S it came about when Moses held	Ex 17:11	
S Joshua overwhelmed Amalek and	Ex 17:13	
S Jethro said, "Blessed be the LORD	Ex 18:10	
S it will be easier for you, and	Ex 18:22	
"If you do this thing and God s	Ex 18:23	
S Moses listened to his	Ex 18:24	
S Moses came and called the elders	Ex 19:7	
s that the people may hear when I	Ex 19:9	5668
S Moses went down from the	Ex 19:14	
S it came about on the third day,	Ex 19:16	
s that all the people who *were* in	Ex 19:16	
s that they do not break through to	Ex 19:21	6435
S Moses went down to the people	Ex 19:25	
you, s that you may not sin."	Ex 20:20	
S the people stood at a distance,	Ex 20:21	
s that your nakedness will not be	Ex 20:26	834
"He who strikes a man s that he	Ex 21:12	
s as to kill him craftily,	Ex 21:14	
s that she gives birth prematurely,	Ex 21:22	
ox hurts another's s that it dies,	Ex 21:35	
in and is struck s that he dies,	Ex 22:2	
lets his animal loose s that it grazes in	Ex 22:5	
s that stacked grain or the	Ex 22:6	
testify in a dispute s as to turn aside	Ex 23:2	
s that the needy of your people	Ex 23:11	
shall cease *from labor* s that	Ex 23:12	4616
send hornets ahead of you s that	Ex 23:28	
S Moses took the blood and	Ex 24:8	
S Moses arose with Joshua his	Ex 24:13	
just s you shall construct *it.*	Ex 25:9	3651
s that with them the table may be	Ex 25:28	
s for six branches going out from the	Ex 25:33	3651
s as to shed light on the space in	Ex 25:37	
to one another with the clasps s that	Ex 26:6	
and join the tent together s that	Ex 26:11	
s that the net will reach halfway up	Ex 27:5	
s that the poles shall be on the	Ex 27:7	
mountain, s they shall make *it.*	Ex 27:8	3651
s that it will be on the skillfully	Ex 28:28	
s that it will not be torn.	Ex 28:32	
s that he will not die.	Ex 28:35	
s that they do not incur guilt and	Ex 28:43	
S you shall ordain Aaron and his	Ex 29:9	
s he and his garments shall be	Ex 29:21	
s that there will be no plague among	Ex 30:12	
s that they will not die; or when	Ex 30:20	
"S they shall wash their hands	Ex 30:21	
s that they will not die; and it	Ex 30:21	
'S the sons of Israel shall	Ex 31:16	
S the next day they rose early and	Ex 32:6	
S the LORD changed His mind about	Ex 32:14	
S they gave *it* to me,	Ex 32:24	
S the sons of Levi did as Moses	Ex 32:28	
S the sons of Israel stripped	Ex 33:6	
s that I may find favor in Your	Ex 33:13	4616
s that we, I and Your people, may be	Ex 33:16	
"S be ready by morning, and come	Ex 34:2	
S he cut out two stone tablets	Ex 34:4	
though the people are s obstinate,	Ex 34:9	
S he was there with the LORD forty	Ex 34:28	
S when Aaron and all the sons of	Ex 34:30	
S Moses would replace the veil	Ex 34:35	
s *did* every man who presented an	Ex 35:22	
s as to perform in every inventive	Ex 35:33	
S Moses issued a command, and a	Ex 36:6	
s the tabernacle was a unit.	Ex 36:13	
to join the tent together s that	Ex 36:18	
s for the six branches going out of the	Ex 37:19	3651
and s for the other side.	Ex 38:15	
s that it would be on the woven band	Ex 39:21	
s that it would not be torn.	Ex 39:23	
had commanded Moses; s they did.	Ex 39:32	3651
S the sons of Israel did all the	Ex 39:42	
S Moses blessed them.	Ex 39:43	
LORD had commanded him, s he did.	Ex 40:16	3651
s that the salt of the covenant of	Lv 2:13	
s as to bring guilt on the people,	Lv 4:3	
S the priest shall make atonement	Lv 4:20	
'S it shall be when he becomes	Lv 5:5	
S the priest shall make atonement	Lv 5:6	
S the priest shall make atonement	Lv 5:10	
'S the priest shall make atonement	Lv 5:13	
S the priest shall make atonement	Lv 5:18	
s that he sins in regard to any	Lv 6:3	
"S every grain offering of the	Lv 6:23	
'S if any of the flesh of the	Lv 7:18	
S Moses did just as the LORD	Lv 8:4	
S Moses took some of the anointing	Lv 8:30	
s that you will not die, for so I	Lv 8:35	
for s I have been commanded."	Lv 8:35	3651
S they took what Moses had	Lv 9:5	
S Aaron came near to the altar and	Lv 9:8	
S Aaron, therefore, kept silent.	Lv 10:3	
S they came forward and carried	Lv 10:5	
clothes, s that you will not die	Lv 10:6	
S they did according to the word	Lv 10:7	
s that you will not die	Lv 10:9	
and s as to make a distinction	Lv 10:10	
and s as to teach the sons of	Lv 10:11	
s it shall be a thing perpetually	Lv 10:15	
S he was angry with Aaron's	Lv 10:16	
them s that you become unclean.	Lv 11:43	
"S he shall burn the garment,	Lv 13:52	
S the priest shall make atonement	Lv 14:18	
S the priest shall make atonement	Lv 14:31	
s that everything in the house	Lv 14:36	
"S he shall look at the mark, and	Lv 14:37	
S he shall make atonement for the	Lv 14:53	
S the priest shall make atonement	Lv 15:15	
'If a man lies with a woman s *that*	Lv 15:18	
s that her menstrual impurity is	Lv 15:24	
S the priest shall make atonement	Lv 15:30	
s that they will not die in their	Lv 15:31	3808
s that he is unclean by it,	Lv 15:32	
"S the priest who is anointed and	Lv 16:32	
had commanded Moses, s he did.	Lv 16:34	
s that the sons of Israel may bring	Lv 17:5	4616
"S when any man from the sons of	Lv 17:13	
'S you shall keep My statutes and	Lv 18:5	

Context	Reference	No.
s the land has spewed out its	**Lv 18:25**	
s that the land will not spew you	**Lv 18:28**	
those persons who do **s** shall be	**Lv 18:29**	
s as not to defile yourselves with	**Lv 18:30**	
it **s** that you may be accepted.	**Lv 19:5**	
'**S** if it is eaten at all on the	**Lv 19:7**	
s as to profane the name of your	**Lv 19:12**	
s that the land will not fall to	**Lv 19:29**	
s as to defile My sanctuary and to	**Lv 20:3**	4616
s as not to put him to death,	**Lv 20:4**	
s that there will be no immorality in	**Lv 20:14**	
s that he sees her nakedness and	**Lv 20:17**	
s that the land to which I am	**Lv 20:22**	
his people, and **s** profane himself.	**Lv 21:4**	
s they shall be holy.	**Lv 21:6**	
s that he will not profane his	**Lv 21:15**	
s that he will not profane My	**Lv 21:23**	
S Moses spoke to Aaron and to his	**Lv 21:24**	
s as not to profane My holy name;	**Lv 22:2**	
s that they will not bear sin	**Lv 22:9**	
and **s** cause them to bear	**Lv 22:16**	
it **s** that you may be accepted.	**Lv 22:29**	
"**S** you shall keep My	**Lv 22:31**	
s that your generations may know	**Lv 23:43**	4616
S Moses declared to the sons of	**Lv 23:44**	
S they brought him to Moses.	**Lv 24:11**	
They put him in custody **s** that	**Lv 24:12**	
done, **s** it shall be done to him:	**Lv 24:19**	3651
s it shall be inflicted on him.	**Lv 24:20**	3651
s that you have the time of the	**Lv 25:8**	
'**S** you shall not wrong one	**Lv 25:17**	
judgments, **s** as to carry them out,	**Lv 25:18**	
s that you can eat your fill and	**Lv 25:19**	
then I will **s** order My blessing	**Lv 25:21**	
countryman of yours becomes **s** poor	**Lv 25:25**	
but **s** recovers his means as to	**Lv 25:26**	
it, and **s** return to his property.	**Lv 25:27**	
countryman of yours becomes **s** poor	**Lv 25:39**	
countryman of yours becomes **s** poor	**Lv 25:47**	
he shall **s** calculate with him.	**Lv 25:52**	
s as to carry them out,	**Lv 26:3**	
s that the land will yield its	**Lv 26:4**	
s that you may lie down with no	**Lv 26:6**	
'**S** I will turn toward you and make	**Lv 26:9**	
s that *you* would not be their slaves,	**Lv 26:13**	4480
s as not to carry out all My	**Lv 26:15**	
and **s** break My covenant,	**Lv 26:15**	
s that you will be struck down	**Lv 26:17**	
s that your roads lie deserted.	**Lv 26:22**	
s that you shall be delivered into	**Lv 26:25**	
s that you will eat and not be	**Lv 26:26**	
s that your enemies who settle in it	**Lv 26:32**	
'**S** those of you who may be left	**Lv 26:39**	
s that they then make amends for	**Lv 26:41**	
I **s** abhor them as to destroy them,	**Lv 26:44**	
priest, value it, **s** it shall be.	**Lv 27:12**	3651
values it, **s** it shall stand.	**Lv 27:14**	3651
price to it, **s** that it may be his.	**Lv 27:15**	
to it, **s** that it may pass to him.	**Lv 27:19**	
S Moses and Aaron took these men	**Nu 1:17**	
S he numbered them in the	**Nu 1:19**	
S all the numbered men of the sons	**Nu 1:45**	
"**S** when the tabernacle is to set	**Nu 1:51**	
s that there will be no wrath on	**Nu 1:53**	
S the Levites shall keep charge of	**Nu 1:53**	
had commanded Moses, **s** they did.	**Nu 1:54**	3651
they camp, **s** they shall set out,	**Nu 2:17**	3651
s they camped by their standards,	**Nu 2:34**	3651
standards, and **s** they set out,	**Nu 2:34**	3651
S Eleazar and Ithamar served as	**Nu 3:4**	
"**S** you shall appoint Aaron and	**Nu 3:10**	
S the Levites shall be Mine.	**Nu 3:12**	
S Moses numbered them according to	**Nu 3:16**	
S Moses numbered all the	**Nu 3:42**	
S Moses took the ransom money from	**Nu 3:49**	
s that they will not touch the holy	**Nu 4:15**	
S Moses and Aaron and the leaders	**Nu 4:34**	
s that they will not defile their camp	**Nu 5:3**	
The sons of Israel did **s** and	**Nu 5:4**	3651
'**S** every man's holy *gifts* shall be	**Nu 5:10**	
s that the water which brings a	**Nu 5:24**	
s he shall do according to the law	**Nu 6:21**	3651
"**S** they shall invoke My name on	**Nu 6:27**	
S Moses took the carts and the	**Nu 7:6**	
s the leaders offered their	**Nu 7:10**	
two cherubim, **s** He spoke to him.	**Nu 7:89**	
Aaron therefore did **s**;	**Nu 8:3**	3651
Moses, **s** he made the lampstand.	**Nu 8:4**	3651
"**S** you shall present the Levites	**Nu 8:9**	
s as to present them as a wave	**Nu 8:13**	
s that there will be no plague among	**Nu 8:19**	
s the sons of Israel did to them.	**Nu 8:20**	3651
the Levites, **s** they did to them.	**Nu 8:22**	3651
S Moses told the sons of Israel to	**Nu 9:4**	
Moses, **s** the sons of Israel did.	**Nu 9:5**	3651
s that they could not observe	**Nu 9:6**	
s they came before Moses and Aaron	**Nu 9:6**	
to its ordinance, **s** he shall do;	**Nu 9:14**	3651
S it was continuously;	**Nu 9:16**	3651
S they moved out for the first	**Nu 10:13**	
"**S** it will be, if you go with us,	**Nu 10:32**	
S the name of that place was	**Nu 11:3**	
S Moses said to the LORD,	**Nu 11:11**	
Why have You been **s** hard on Your	**Nu 11:11**	
"**S** if You are going to deal thus	**Nu 11:15**	
s that you will not bear *it* all	**Nu 11:17**	
s that they may eat for a whole month.'	**Nu 11:21**	
S Moses went out and told the	**Nu 11:24**	
S a young man ran and told Moses	**Nu 11:27**	
S the name of that place was	**Nu 11:34**	
S the three of them came out.	**Nu 12:4**	
"Not **s**, with My servant Moses, He	**Nu 12:7**	3651
S the anger of the LORD burned	**Nu 12:9**	
S Miriam was shut up outside the	**Nu 12:15**	
s that they may spy out the land of	**Nu 13:2**	
S Moses sent them from the	**Nu 13:3**	
S they went up and spied out the	**Nu 13:21**	
S they gave out to the sons of	**Nu 13:32**	
and **s** we were in their sight."	**Nu 13:33**	3651
S they said to one another,	**Nu 14:4**	
S the LORD said,	**Nu 14:20**	
s I will surely do to you;	**Nu 14:28**	3651
s you shall do for everyone	**Nu 15:12**	3602
just as you do **s** he shall do.	**Nu 15:14**	3651
s shall the alien be before the	**Nu 15:15**	
floor, **s** you shall lift it up.	**Nu 15:20**	3651
'**S** all the congregation of the	**Nu 15:26**	
S all the congregation brought him	**Nu 15:36**	
s as to do them and not follow	**Nu 15:39**	
s that you may remember to do all My	**Nu 15:40**	4616
s why do you exalt yourselves	**Nu 16:3**	
S they each took his *own* censer	**Nu 16:18**	
S they got back from around the	**Nu 16:27**	
S they and all that belonged to	**Nu 16:33**	
S Eleazar the priest took the	**Nu 16:39**	
s that he will not become like	**Nu 16:40**	
S he put *on* the incense and made	**Nu 16:47**	
s that the plague was checked.	**Nu 16:48**	
S Moses deposited the rods before	**Nu 17:7**	
Me, **s** that they will not die."	**Nu 17:10**	
LORD had commanded him, **s** he did.	**Nu 17:11**	3651
S the LORD said to Aaron,	**Nu 18:1**	
"**S** you shall attend to the	**Nu 18:5**	
s that there will no longer be wrath	**Nu 18:5**	
'**S** you shall also present an	**Nu 18:28**	3651
'**S** it shall be a perpetual statute	**Nu 19:21**	
S Moses took the rod from before	**Nu 20:9**	
s Israel turned away from him.	**Nu 20:21**	
S Aaron will be gathered *to his*	**Nu 20:26**	
S Moses did just as the LORD had	**Nu 20:27**	
S Israel made a vow to the LORD and	**Nu 21:2**	
s that many people of Israel died.	**Nu 21:6**	
S the people came to Moses and	**Nu 21:7**	
S Sihon gathered all his people	**Nu 21:23**	
S let the city of Sihon be	**Nu 21:27**	
S they killed him and his sons and	**Nu 21:35**	
S Moab was in great fear because	**Nu 22:3**	
S he sent messengers to Balaam the	**Nu 22:5**	
S the elders of Moab and the	**Nu 22:7**	
S Balaam arose in the morning and	**Nu 22:13**	
S Balaam arose in the morning, and	**Nu 22:21**	
the wall, **s** he struck her again.	**Nu 22:25**	
s Balaam was angry and struck the	**Nu 22:27**	
been accustomed to do **s** to you?"	**Nu 22:30**	3541
S Balaam went along with the	**Nu 22:35**	
S Balaam said to Balak,	**Nu 22:38**	
S he went to a bare hill.	**Nu 23:3**	
S he returned to him, and behold,	**Nu 23:6**	
S he took him to the field of	**Nu 23:14**	
S Balak took Balaam to the top of	**Nu 23:28**	
S they also *will come* to	**Nu 24:24**	
S Israel joined themselves to Baal	**Nu 25:3**	
s that the fierce anger of the	**Nu 25:4**	
S Moses said to the judges of	**Nu 25:5**	
S the plague on the sons of Israel	**Nu 25:8**	
s that I did not destroy the sons	**Nu 25:11**	
S Moses and Eleazar the priest	**Nu 26:3**	
men, **s** that they became a warning.	**Nu 26:10**	
S Moses brought their case before	**Nu 27:5**	
s that the congregation of the LORD	**Nu 27:17**	
S the LORD said to Moses,	**Nu 27:18**	
S there were furnished from the	**Nu 31:5**	
S they made war against Midian,	**Nu 31:7**	
s the plague was among the	**Nu 31:16**	
"**S** we have brought as an offering	**Nu 31:50**	
S Moses and Eleazar the priest	**Nu 31:54**	
S when they saw the land of Jazer	**Nu 32:1**	
s that they did not go into the land	**Nu 32:9**	
"**S** the LORD's anger burned in	**Nu 32:10**	
"**S** the LORD's anger burned	**Nu 32:13**	
S Moses said to them,	**Nu 32:20**	
"But if you will not do **s**,	**Nu 32:23**	3651
S Moses gave command concerning	**Nu 32:28**	
to your servants, **s** we will do.	**Nu 32:31**	3651
S Moses gave to them, to the sons	**Nu 32:33**	
S Moses gave Gilead to Machir the	**Nu 32:40**	
to them, **s** I will do to you.' "	**Nu 33:56**	
S Moses commanded the sons of	**Nu 34:13**	
s that the manslayer will not die	**Nu 35:12**	
an iron object, **s** that he died,	**Nu 35:16**	
it dropped on him **s** that he died,	**Nu 35:23**	
'**S** you shall not pollute the land	**Nu 35:33**	
s their inheritance will be withdrawn	**Nu 36:4**	
s that the sons of Israel each may	**Nu 36:8**	4616
s the daughters of Zelophehad did:	**Nu 36:10**	3651
"**S** I took the heads of your	**Dt 1:15**	
"**S** I spoke to you, but you would	**Dt 1:43**	
"**S** you remained in Kadesh many	**Dt 1:46**	
S be very careful;	**Dt 2:4**	
with money **s** that you may eat,	**Dt 2:6**	
with money **s** that you may drink.	**Dt 2:6**	
"**S** we passed beyond our brothers	**Dt 2:8**	
S we crossed over the brook Zered.	**Dt 2:13**	
"**S** it came about when all the men	**Dt 2:16**	
"**S** I sent messengers from the	**Dt 2:26**	
food for money **s** that I may eat,	**Dt 2:28**	
for money **s** that I may drink,	**Dt 2:28**	
"**S** we captured all his cities at	**Dt 2:34**	
"**S** the LORD our God delivered Og	**Dt 3:3**	
"**S** we took possession of this	**Dt 3:12**	
s the LORD shall do to all the	**Dt 3:21**	3651
"**S** we remained in the valley	**Dt 3:29**	
s that you may live and go in	**Dt 4:1**	4616
"**S** keep and do *them*, for that is	**Dt 4:6**	
a god **s** near to it as is the LORD our	**Dt 4:7**	
s that you do not forget the things	**Dt 4:9**	6435
s they may learn to fear Me all the	**Dt 4:10**	834
"**S** He declared to you His	**Dt 4:13**	
"**S** watch yourselves carefully,	**Dt 4:15**	
s that you do not act corruptly	**Dt 4:16**	6435
"**S** watch yourselves, that you	**Dt 4:23**	
sight of the LORD your God **s** *as*	**Dt 4:25**	
"**S** you shall keep His statutes	**Dt 4:40**	
s that your male servant and your	**Dt 5:14**	4616
"**S** you shall observe to do just	**Dt 5:32**	
s that you and your son and your	**Dt 6:2**	4616
"**S** the LORD commanded us to	**Dt 6:24**	
S shall the LORD your God do to	**Dt 7:19**	3651
s that you will make their name	**Dt 7:24**	
before you, **s** you shall perish;	**Dt 8:20**	3651
s that you may drive them out and	**Dt 9:3**	
and the LORD was **s** angry with you	**Dt 9:8**	
"**S** I turned and came down from	**Dt 9:15**	
s I also prayed for Aaron at the	**Dt 9:20**	
"**S** I fell down before the LORD	**Dt 9:25**	
"**S** I made an ark of acacia wood	**Dt 10:3**	
"**S** circumcise your heart,	**Dt 10:16**	
"**S** show your love for the alien,	**Dt 10:19**	
s that you may be strong and go in	**Dt 11:8**	4616
s that you may prolong *your* days	**Dt 11:9**	
s that there will be no rain and the	**Dt 11:17**	
s that your days and the days of	**Dt 11:21**	4616
you **s** that you live in security,	**Dt 12:10**	
deer is eaten, **s** you will eat it;	**Dt 12:22**	3651
"You shall not eat it, **s** that it	**Dt 12:25**	4616
s that it may be well with you	**Dt 12:28**	4616
S you shall purge the evil from	**Dt 13:5**	
"**S** you shall stone him to death	**Dt 13:10**	
your town, **s** that he may eat it,	**Dt 14:21**	
s that you may learn to fear the	**Dt 14:23**	4616
"If the distance is **s** great	**Dt 14:24**	
s the LORD your God will bless you	**Dt 15:18**	
s that you may remember all the days	**Dt 16:3**	4616
s that you will be altogether	**Dt 16:15**	
S you shall purge the evil from	**Dt 17:7**	
"**S** you shall come to the	**Dt 17:9**	
s that he and his sons may continue	**Dt 17:20**	4616
God has not allowed you *to do* **s**.	**Dt 18:14**	3651
s that any manslayer may flee	**Dt 19:3**	
and strikes his friend **s** that he dies	**Dt 19:5**	
"**S** innocent blood will not be	**Dt 19:10**	
and strikes him **s** that he dies,	**Dt 19:11**	
s that he might not make his	**Dt 20:8**	
s that they may not teach you to do	**Dt 20:18**	4616
s that you would sin against the	**Dt 20:18**	
"**S** you shall remove the guilt of	**Dt 21:9**	
s you shall remove the evil from	**Dt 21:21**	
s that you do not defile your land	**Dt 21:23**	
s that you will not bring bloodguilt	**Dt 22:8**	
"**S** the elders of that city shall	**Dt 22:18**	
and murders him, **s** is this case.	**Dt 22:26**	3651
s that he will not uncover his	**Dt 22:30**	
s that the LORD your God may bless	**Dt 23:20**	4616
s you shall purge the evil from	**Dt 24:7**	
s you shall be careful to do.	**Dt 24:8**	
s that he will not cry against you	**Dt 24:15**	
s that he does not beat him with many	**Dt 25:3**	6435
s that his name will not be blotted	**Dt 25:6**	
"**S** it shall be on the day when	**Dt 27:2**	
s that you may enter the land which	**Dt 27:3**	4616
"**S** it shall be when you cross the	**Dt 27:4**	
"**S** all the peoples of the earth	**Dt 28:10**	
"**S** all these curses shall come on	**Dt 28:45**	
s that he will not give *even* one	**Dt 28:55**	4480
s the LORD will delight over you	**Dt 28:63**	3651
"**S** your life shall hang in doubt	**Dt 28:66**	
"**S** keep the words of this	**Dt 29:9**	
s that there will not be among you a	**Dt 29:18**	6435
"**S** it shall be when all of these	**Dt 30:1**	
s that you may live.	**Dt 30:6**	4616
S choose life in order that you	**Dt 30:19**	
S Moses went and spoke these words	**Dt 31:1**	
S Moses wrote this law and gave it	**Dt 31:9**	
s that they may hear and learn	**Dt 31:12**	4616
S Moses and Joshua went and	**Dt 31:14**	
s that they will say in that day,	**Dt 31:17**	
s that this song may be a witness for	**Dt 31:19**	4616
S Moses wrote this song the same	**Dt 31:22**	
S I will make them jealous with	**Dt 32:21**	
s he said, "Hear, O LORD, the voice	**Dt 33:7**	
s that they will not rise *again*."	**Dt 33:11**	4480
s will your leisurely walk be.	**Dt 33:25**	
"**S** Israel dwells in security, The	**Dt 33:28**	
S your enemies will cringe before	**Dt 33:29**	
S Moses the servant of the LORD	**Dt 34:5**	
S the sons of Israel wept for	**Dt 34:8**	
s that you may have success	**Jos 1:7**	4616
s that you may be careful to do	**Jos 1:8**	4616
in all things, **s** we will obey you;	**Jos 1:17**	3651
S they went and came into the	**Jos 2:1**	
S the men pursued them on the road	**Jos 2:7**	
S the men said to her,	**Jos 2:14**	
s that she was living on the wall.	**Jos 2:15**	
s that the pursuers will not happen	**Jos 2:16**	6435
to your words, **s** be it."	**Jos 2:21**	3651
S she sent them away,	**Jos 2:21**	
S they took up the ark of the	**Jos 3:6**	

S when the people set out	Jos 3:14	
S the people crossed opposite	Jos 3:16	
S Joshua called the twelve men	Jos 4:4	
s that when your children ask	Jos 4:6	
S these stones shall become a	Jos 4:7	
s that they revered him, just as	Jos 4:14	
S Joshua commanded the priests,	Jos 4:17	
s that you may fear the LORD your	Jos 4:24	4616
S Joshua made himself flint knives	Jos 5:3	
S the name of that place is called	Jos 5:9	
s that the sons of Israel no	Jos 5:12	
standing is holy." And Joshua did s.	Jos 5:15	3651
You shall do s for six days.	Jos 6:3	3541
S Joshua the son of Nun called the	Jos 6:6	
And it was s, that when Joshua	Jos 6:8	
S he had the ark of the LORD taken	Jos 6:11	
they did s for six days.	Jos 6:14	3541
s that you do not covet *them*	Jos 6:18	6435
S the people shouted, and *priests*	Jos 6:20	
s that the people went up into the	Jos 6:20	
S the young men who were spies	Jos 6:23	
S the LORD was with Joshua, and	Jos 6:27	
S the men went up and spied out Ai.	Jos 7:2	
S about three thousand men from	Jos 7:4	
s the hearts of the people melted	Jos 7:5	
S the LORD said to Joshua,	Jos 7:10	
S Joshua arose early in the	Jos 7:16	
S Achan answered Joshua and said,	Jos 7:20	
S Joshua sent messengers, and they	Jos 7:22	
S Joshua rose with all the people	Jos 8:3	
S we will flee before them.	Jos 8:6	
S Joshua sent them away, and they	Jos 8:9	
S they stationed the people, all	Jos 8:13	
S not a man was left in Ai or	Jos 8:17	
S Joshua stretched out the javelin	Jos 8:18	
s that they were *trapped* in the	Jos 8:22	
S Joshua burned Ai and made it a	Jos 8:28	
"S our elders and all the	Jos 9:11	
S the men *of Israel* took some of	Jos 9:14	
s that wrath will not be upon us for	Jos 9:20	3808
S they became hewers of wood and	Jos 9:21	
S they answered Joshua and said,	Jos 9:24	
s he had done to Ai and its king),	Jos 10:1	3651
S the five kings of the Amorites,	Jos 10:5	
S Joshua went up from Gilgal, he	Jos 10:7	
S Joshua came upon them suddenly	Jos 10:9	
S the sun stood still, and the	Jos 10:13	
They did s, and brought these	Jos 10:23	3651
S they came near and put their	Jos 10:24	
S afterward Joshua struck them and	Jos 10:26	
s he did to Debir and its king,	Jos 10:39	3651
S Joshua and all Israel with him	Jos 10:43	
S all of these kings having agreed	Jos 11:5	
S Joshua and all the people of war	Jos 11:7	
Israel, s that they defeated them,	Jos 11:8	
servant, s Moses commanded Joshua,	Jos 11:15	3651
Joshua, and s Joshua did;	Jos 11:15	3651
S Joshua took the whole land,	Jos 11:23	
S Moses gave *an inheritance* to the	Jos 13:15	
"S Moses swore on that day,	Jos 14:9	
was then, s my strength is now,	Jos 14:11	
S Joshua blessed him and gave	Jos 14:13	
s he gave him Achsah his daughter	Jos 15:17	
S she alighted from the donkey,	Jos 15:18	
S he gave her the upper springs	Jos 15:19	
s the Jebusites live with the sons	Jos 15:63	
s the Canaanites live in the midst	Jos 16:10	
S *the lot* was *made* for the rest of	Jos 17:2	
S according to the command of the	Jos 17:4	
S Joshua said to the sons of	Jos 18:3	
S the men went and passed through	Jos 18:9	
S they had as their inheritance	Jos 19:2	
s the sons of Simeon received *an*	Jos 19:9	
S he built the city and settled in	Jos 19:50	
S they finished dividing the land.	Jos 19:51	
s that he may dwell among them.	Jos 20:4	
S they set apart Kedesh in Galilee	Jos 20:7	
S the sons of Israel gave the	Jos 21:3	
S to the sons of Aaron the priest	Jos 21:13	
S the LORD gave Israel all the	Jos 21:43	
S Joshua blessed them and sent	Jos 22:6	
S when Joshua sent them away to	Jos 22:7	
S your sons may make our sons stop	Jos 22:25	
s that your sons will not say to our	Jos 22:27	3808
S when Phinehas the priest and the	Jos 22:30	
s that you may not turn aside from	Jos 23:6	
s that you will not associate with	Jos 23:7	1115
"S take diligent heed to	Jos 23:11	
s that you associate with them and	Jos 23:12	
s the LORD will bring upon you all	Jos 23:15	3651
S he had to bless you, and I	Jos 24:10	
S Joshua made a covenant with the	Jos 24:25	
s that you do not deny your God."	Jos 24:27	6435
S Simeon went with him.	Jg 1:3	
have done, s God has repaid me."	Jg 1:7	3651
S they brought him to Jerusalem	Jg 1:7	
S Judah went against the	Jg 1:10	
s he gave him his daughter Achsah	Jg 1:13	
S Caleb gave her the upper springs	Jg 1:15	
S the name of the city was called	Jg 1:17	
s the Jebusites have lived with	Jg 1:21	
S he showed them the entrance to	Jg 1:25	
s the Canaanites persisted in	Jg 1:27	
s the Canaanites lived in Gezer	Jg 1:29	
s the Canaanites lived among them	Jg 1:30	
S the Asherites lived among the	Jg 1:32	
S they named that place Bochim;	Jg 2:5	
S they forsook the LORD and served	Jg 2:13	
s that they could no longer stand	Jg 2:14	
s that they were severely	Jg 2:15	
S the anger of the LORD burned	Jg 2:20	
S the LORD allowed those nations	Jg 2:23	
s that He sold them into the hands	Jg 3:8	
s that he prevailed over	Jg 3:10	
S the LORD strengthened Eglon the	Jg 3:12	
S they went down after him and	Jg 3:28	
S Moab was subdued that day under	Jg 3:30	
S Barak went down from Mount Tabor	Jg 4:14	
S she opened a bottle of milk and	Jg 4:19	
asleep and exhausted. S he died.	Jg 4:21	
S God subdued on that day Jabin	Jg 4:23	
As *was* Issachar, s *was* Barak;	Jg 5:15	3651
S they would camp against them and	Jg 6:4	
S Israel was brought very low	Jg 6:6	
S Gideon said to Him,	Jg 6:17	
pour out the broth." And he did s.	Jg 6:20	3651
S the Spirit of the LORD came upon	Jg 6:34	
And it was s. When he arose early	Jg 6:38	3651
God did s that night;	Jg 6:40	3651
S 22,000 people returned,	Jg 7:3	
S he brought the people down to	Jg 7:5	
s let all the *other* people go,	Jg 7:7	
S the 300 men took the people's	Jg 7:8	
S he went with Purah his servant	Jg 7:11	
tent and struck it s that it fell,	Jg 7:13	
down s that the tent lay flat."	Jg 7:13	
S Gideon and the hundred men who	Jg 7:19	
S all the men of Ephraim were	Jg 7:24	
S he spoke also to the men of	Jg 8:9	
S he said to Jether his	Jg 8:20	
as the man, s is his strength."	Jg 8:21	
S Gideon arose and killed Zebah	Jg 8:21	
S they spread out a garment,	Jg 8:25	
s that it became a snare to Gideon	Jg 8:27	
S Midian was subdued before the	Jg 8:28	
s that the violence done to	Jg 9:24	
S Abimelech and all the people who	Jg 9:34	
S Gaal went out before the leaders	Jg 9:39	
s that they could not remain in	Jg 9:41	4480
S he took his people and divided	Jg 9:43	
S Abimelech went up to Mount	Jg 9:48	
s that all the men of the tower of	Jg 9:49	
S Abimelech came to the tower and	Jg 9:52	
s that it will not be said of me,	Jg 9:54	6435
S the young man pierced him	Jg 9:54	
s that Israel was greatly	Jg 10:9	
S they put away the foreign gods	Jg 10:16	
S Jephthah fled from his brothers	Jg 11:3	
S why have you come to me now when	Jg 11:7	
S Jephthah said to the elders of	Jg 11:9	
S Israel remained at Kadesh.	Jg 11:17	
s Sihon gathered all his people	Jg 11:20	
s Israel possessed all the land of	Jg 11:21	
'S they possessed all the	Jg 11:22	
S whatever the LORD our God has	Jg 11:24	
s that he passed through Gilead	Jg 11:29	
S Jephthah crossed over to the	Jg 11:32	
S the sons of Ammon were subdued	Jg 11:33	
S she said to him,	Jg 11:36	
S he sent her away for two months;	Jg 11:38	
s that the LORD gave them into the	Jg 13:1	
S the woman ran quickly and told	Jg 13:10	
S the angel of the LORD said to	Jg 13:13	
"Please let us detain you s that	Jg 13:15	
s that when your words come *to*	Jg 13:17	
S Manoah took the young goat with the	Jg 13:19	
S Manoah said to his wife,	Jg 13:22	
S he came back and told his father	Jg 14:2	
s that he tore him as one tears a	Jg 14:6	
S he went down and talked to the	Jg 14:7	
S he scraped the honey into his	Jg 14:9	
S he said to them,	Jg 14:14	
s that he will tell us the riddle,	Jg 14:15	
Is this not s?"	Jg 14:15	
s should I tell you?"	Jg 14:16	
because she pressed him s hard.	Jg 14:17	
S the men of the city said to him	Jg 14:18	
s I gave her to your companion.	Jg 15:2	
S the Philistines came up and	Jg 15:6	
to me, s I have done to them."	Jg 15:11	3651
s that we may give you into the	Jg 15:12	
S they said to him,	Jg 15:13	
s that the ropes that were on his	Jg 15:14	
s he reached out and took it and	Jg 15:15	
Lehi s that water came out of it.	Jg 15:19	
S he judged Israel twenty years in	Jg 15:20	
S Delilah said to Samson,	Jg 16:6	
S his strength was not discovered.	Jg 16:9	
S Delilah took new ropes and bound	Jg 16:12	
S while he slept, Delilah took the	Jg 16:14	
S he told her all *that was* in his	Jg 16:17	
It s happened when they were in	Jg 16:25	
S they called for Samson from the	Jg 16:25	
s that the house fell on the lords	Jg 16:30	
S the dead whom he killed at his	Jg 16:30	
S when he returned the silver to	Jg 17:4	
S the Levite went *in*.	Jg 17:10	
S Micah consecrated the Levite,	Jg 17:12	
S the sons of Dan sent from their	Jg 18:2	
"Thus and s has Micah done to me,	Jg 18:4	2088
S how can you say to me,	Jg 18:24	
S the sons of Dan went on their	Jg 18:26	
S they set up for themselves	Jg 18:31	
S she brought him into her	Jg 19:3	
S they ate and drank and lodged	Jg 19:4	
S both of them sat down and ate	Jg 19:6	
s that he spent the night there again	Jg 19:7	
s both of them ate.	Jg 19:8	
journey s that you may go home."	Jg 19:9	
s he arose and departed and came	Jg 19:10	
S they passed along and went their	Jg 19:14	
S he took him into his house and	Jg 19:21	
please do not act s wickedly;	Jg 19:23	
S the man seized his concubine	Jg 19:25	
S the Levite, the husband of the	Jg 20:4	
my concubine s that she died.	Jg 20:5	
S the sons of Israel arose in the	Jg 20:19	
S Israel set men in ambush around	Jg 20:29	
s that the sons of Israel	Jg 20:35	
S the sons of Benjamin saw that	Jg 20:36	
S all of Benjamin who fell that	Jg 20:46	
S the people came to Bethel and	Jg 21:2	
s that one tribe should be *missing*	Jg 21:3	
s that a tribe will not be blotted	Jg 21:17	3808
S they said, "Behold, there is a feast	Jg 21:19	
The sons of Benjamin did s,	Jg 21:23	3651
S she departed from the place	Ru 1:7	
S they both went until they came	Ru 1:19	
S Naomi returned, and with her	Ru 1:22	
S she departed and went and	Ru 2:3	
S she sat beside the reapers;	Ru 2:14	
S she gleaned in the field until	Ru 2:17	
S she told her mother-in-law with	Ru 2:19	
s that *others* do not fall upon	Ru 2:22	3808
S she stayed close by the maids of	Ru 2:23	
S she went down to the threshing	Ru 3:6	
S spread your covering over your	Ru 3:9	
S she lay at his feet until	Ru 3:14	
S she held it, and he measured six	Ru 3:15	
spoke was passing by, s he said,	Ru 4:1	
"Sit down here." S they sat down.	Ru 4:2	
"S I thought to inform you,	Ru 4:4	
S the closest relative said to	Ru 4:8	
s that the name of the deceased	Ru 4:10	
S Boaz took Ruth, and she became	Ru 4:13	
S they named him Obed.	Ru 4:17	
her; s she wept and would not eat.	1Sa 1:7	
S Eli thought she was drunk.	1Sa 1:13	
S the woman went her way and ate,	1Sa 1:18	
S the woman remained and nursed	1Sa 1:23	
"S I have also dedicated him to	1Sa 1:28	
"Boast no more s very proudly, Do	1Sa 2:3	
s that there will not be an old man in	1Sa 2:31	4480
man of yours from My altar s that	1Sa 2:33	
s that I may eat a piece of bread.	1Sa 2:36	
S he went and lay down.	1Sa 3:5	
S Samuel arose and went to Eli and	1Sa 3:6	
S the LORD called Samuel again for	1Sa 3:8	
S Samuel went and lay down in his	1Sa 3:9	
S Samuel lay down until morning.	1Sa 3:15	
May God do s to you, and more	1Sa 3:17	3541
S Samuel told him everything and	1Sa 3:18	
S the people sent to Shiloh, and	1Sa 4:4	
shout, s that the earth resounded.	1Sa 4:5	
S the Philistines fought and	1Sa 4:10	
S the man came to tell *it* in the	1Sa 4:13	
were set s that he could not see.	1Sa 4:15	
S they took Dagon and set him in	1Sa 5:3	
men of Ashdod saw that it was s,	1Sa 5:7	3651
S they sent and gathered all the	1Sa 5:8	
s that tumors broke out on them.	1Sa 5:9	
S they sent the ark of God to	1Sa 5:10	
s that it will not kill us and our	1Sa 5:11	3808
"S you shall make likenesses of	1Sa 6:5	
Then the men did s,	1Sa 6:10	3651
S they sent messengers to the	1Sa 6:21	
S the sons of Israel removed the	1Sa 7:4	
s that they were routed before	1Sa 7:10	
S the Philistines were subdued and	1Sa 7:13	
S there was peace between Israel	1Sa 7:14	
s they are doing to you also.	1Sa 8:8	3651
S Samuel spoke all the words of	1Sa 8:10	
S Samuel said to the men of	1Sa 8:22	
S Kish said to his son Saul,	1Sa 9:3	
S they went to the city where the	1Sa 9:10	
S they went up to the city.	1Sa 9:14	
S Saul ate with Samuel that day.	1Sa 9:24	
S Saul arose, and both he and	1Sa 9:26	
s that he prophesied among them.	1Sa 10:10	
S Saul said to his uncle,	1Sa 10:16	
S the LORD said, "Behold, he is	1Sa 10:22	
S they ran and took him from	1Sa 10:23	
S all the people shouted and said,	1Sa 10:24	
S they related to him the words of	1Sa 11:5	
s shall it be done to his oxen."	1Sa 11:7	3541
S the messengers went and told the	1Sa 11:9	
s that no two of them were left	1Sa 11:11	
S all the people went to Gilgal,	1Sa 11:15	
"S now, take your stand, that I	1Sa 12:7	
s He sold them into the hand of	1Sa 12:9	
s that you lived in security.	1Sa 12:11	
S Samuel called to the LORD, and	1Sa 12:18	
your God, s that we may not die,	1Sa 12:19	
S Saul said, "Bring to me the burnt	1Sa 13:9	
S I forced myself and offered the	1Sa 13:12	
S all Israel went down to the	1Sa 13:20	
S it came about on the day of	1Sa 13:22	
S the men of the garrison hailed	1Sa 14:12	
s that it became a great trembling.	1Sa 14:15	
s Saul said to the priest,	1Sa 14:19	
S the LORD delivered Israel that	1Sa 14:23	
S none of the people tasted food.	1Sa 14:24	
S all the people that night	1Sa 14:34	
S the priest said, "Let us draw near	1Sa 14:36	
S Jonathan told him and said,	1Sa 14:43	
S the people rescued Jonathan and	1Sa 14:45	
s that I do not destroy you with them;	1Sa 15:6	

S the Kenites departed from among	**1Sa 15:6**	
S Saul defeated the Amalekites,	**1Sa 15:7**	
S Samuel said to him,	**1Sa 15:28**	
S Samuel went back following Saul,	**1Sa 15:31**	
s shall your mother be childless	**1Sa 15:33**	3651
S Samuel did what the LORD said,	**1Sa 16:4**	
S he sent and brought him in.	**1Sa 16:12**	
S Saul said to his servants,	**1Sa 16:17**	
S Saul sent messengers to Jesse and	**1Sa 16:19**	
S it came about whenever the *evil*	**1Sa 16:23**	
S David arose early in the morning	**1Sa 17:20**	
S David said to Saul,	**1Sa 17:39**	
s that he fell on his face to the	**1Sa 17:49**	
S when David returned from killing	**1Sa 17:57**	
S David went out wherever Saul	**1Sa 18:5**	
S it came about at the time when	**1Sa 18:19**	
S Saul's servants spoke these	**1Sa 18:23**	
S Saul gave him Michal his	**1Sa 18:27**	
S his name was highly esteemed.	**1Sa 18:30**	
S Jonathan told David saying,	**1Sa 19:2**	
s that they fled before him.	**1Sa 19:8**	
s that he stuck the spear into	**1Sa 19:10**	
S Michal let David down through a	**1Sa 19:12**	
S Saul said to Michal,	**1Sa 19:17**	
enemy go, **s** that he has escaped?"	**1Sa 19:17**	
S Saul sent messengers again the	**1Sa 19:21**	
s that he went along prophesying	**1Sa 19:23**	
S why should my father hide this	**1Sa 20:2**	
hide this thing from me? It is not **s**!"	**1Sa 20:2**	2088
S David said to Jonathan,	**1Sa 20:5**	
S both of them went out to the	**1Sa 20:11**	
may the LORD do **s** to Jonathan and	**1Sa 20:13**	3541
S Jonathan made a *covenant* with	**1Sa 20:16**	
S David hid in the field;	**1Sa 20:24**	
s Saul said to Jonathan his son,	**1Sa 20:27**	
s Jonathan knew that his father	**1Sa 20:33**	
S the priest gave him consecrated	**1Sa 21:6**	
S he disguised his sanity before	**1Sa 21:13**	
S David departed from there and	**1Sa 22:1**	
S David departed and went into the	**1Sa 22:5**	
s that there is no one who discloses	**1Sa 22:8**	
s that he would rise up against me by	**1Sa 22:13**	
S David inquired of the LORD,	**1Sa 23:2**	
S David and his men went to Keilah	**1Sa 23:5**	
S Saul summoned all the people for	**1Sa 23:8**	
s he said to Abiathar the priest,	**1Sa 23:9**	
S the two of them made a covenant	**1Sa 23:18**	
the desire of your soul to do **s**;	**1Sa 23:20**	3381
"**S** look, and learn about all the	**1Sa 23:23**	
S Saul returned from pursuing	**1Sa 23:28**	
S he said to his men,	**1Sa 24:6**	
"**S** now swear to me by the LORD	**1Sa 24:21**	
S David sent ten young men; and	**1Sa 25:5**	
S David's young men retraced their	**1Sa 25:12**	
S each man girded on his sword.	**1Sa 25:13**	
down toward her; **s** she met them.	**1Sa 25:20**	
s that nothing was missed of all	**1Sa 25:21**	
God do **s** to the enemies of David,	**1Sa 25:22**	3541
for as his name is, **s** is he.	**1Sa 25:25**	3651
S David received from her hand	**1Sa 25:35**	
s she did not tell him anything at	**1Sa 25:36**	
him **s** that he became *as* a stone.	**1Sa 25:37**	
S Saul arose and went down to the	**1Sa 26:2**	
S David and Abishai came to the	**1Sa 26:7**	
S David took the spear and the jug	**1Sa 26:12**	
S David said to Abner,	**1Sa 26:15**	
they have driven me out today **s** that	**1Sa 26:19**	4480
s may my life be highly valued in	**1Sa 26:24**	3651
S David went on his way,	**1Sa 26:25**	
S David arose and crossed over, he	**1Sa 27:2**	
s he no longer searched for him.	**1Sa 27:4**	
S Achish gave him Ziklag that day;	**1Sa 27:6**	
'**S** has David done and so *has been*	**1Sa 27:11**	3541
s *has been* his practice all the time	**1Sa 27:11**	3541
S Achish believed David, saying,	**1Sa 27:12**	
S Achish said to David,	**1Sa 28:2**	
S the Philistines gathered	**1Sa 28:4**	
s the LORD has done this thing to	**1Sa 28:18**	5921, 3651
"**S** now also, please listen to the	**1Sa 28:22**	
S he arose from the ground and sat	**1Sa 28:23**	
S David arose early, he and his	**1Sa 29:11**	
S Abiathar brought the ephod to	**1Sa 30:7**	
S David went, he and the six	**1Sa 30:9**	
S David recovered all that the	**1Sa 30:18**	
S David had captured all the sheep	**1Sa 30:20**	
"You must not do **s**, my brothers,	**1Sa 30:23**	3651
s shall his share be who stays by	**1Sa 30:24**	
S it has been from that day forward,	**1Sa 30:25**	
S Saul took his sword and fell on	**1Sa 31:4**	
S David said to the young man who	**2Sa 1:5**	
"**S** I stood beside him and killed	**2Sa 1:10**	
and **s** also *did* all the men	**2Sa 1:11**	
S he struck him and he died.	**2Sa 1:15**	
S David said, "Where shall I go up?	**2Sa 2:1**	
S David went up there, and his two	**2Sa 2:2**	
S they arose and went over by	**2Sa 2:15**	
s they fell down together.	**2Sa 2:16**	
S Abner said to him,	**2Sa 2:21**	
s that the spear came out at his	**2Sa 2:23**	
S Joab blew the trumpet;	**2Sa 2:28**	
s they crossed the Jordan, walked	**2Sa 2:29**	
s *that* three hundred and sixty	**2Sa 2:31**	
"May God do **s** to Abner, and more	**2Sa 3:9**	3541
S David sent messengers to	**2Sa 3:14**	
"Go, return." **S** he returned.	**2Sa 3:16**	
S David sent Abner away,	**2Sa 3:21**	
S when Abner returned to Hebron,	**2Sa 3:27**	
struck him in the belly **s** that he died	**2Sa 3:27**	

S Joab and Abishai his brother	**2Sa 3:30**	
"May God do **s** to me, and more	**2Sa 3:35**	3541
S all the people and all Israel	**2Sa 3:37**	
S the sons of Rimmon the	**2Sa 4:5**	
S all the elders of Israel came to	**2Sa 5:3**	
S David lived in the stronghold and	**2Sa 5:9**	
S David came to Baal-perazim and	**2Sa 5:20**	
s David and his men carried them	**2Sa 5:21**	
Then David did **s**, just as the LORD	**2Sa 5:25**	3651
S they brought it with the ark of	**2Sa 6:4**	
S David was afraid of the LORD	**2Sa 6:9**	
And **s** it was, that when the	**2Sa 6:13**	
S David and all the house of	**2Sa 6:15**	
S they brought in the ark of the	**2Sa 6:17**	
S David said to Michal,	**2Sa 6:21**	
vision, **s** Nathan spoke to David.	**2Sa 7:17**	3651
S David made a name *for himself*	**2Sa 8:13**	
S David reigned over all Israel;	**2Sa 8:15**	
S the king said to him,	**2Sa 9:4**	
s that your master's grandson may	**2Sa 9:10**	
servant **s** your servant will do."	**2Sa 9:11**	3651
S Mephibosheth ate at David's	**2Sa 9:11**	
S Mephibosheth lived in Jerusalem,	**2Sa 9:13**	
S David sent some of his servants	**2Sa 10:2**	
S Hanun took David's servants and	**2Sa 10:4**	
S Joab and the people who were	**2Sa 10:13**	
S the Arameans feared to help the	**2Sa 10:19**	
S David sent and inquired about	**2Sa 11:3**	
S Joab sent Uriah to David.	**2Sa 11:6**	
S Uriah remained in Jerusalem that	**2Sa 11:12**	
s that he may be struck down and	**2Sa 11:15**	
S it was as Joab kept watch on the	**2Sa 11:16**	
Why did you go **s** near to the city	**2Sa 11:20**	
the wall **s** that he died at Thebez?	**2Sa 11:21**	
Why did you go **s** near the wall?	**2Sa 11:21**	
S the messenger departed and came	**2Sa 11:22**	
s some of the king's servants are	**2Sa 11:24**	
and **s** encourage him."	**2Sa 11:25**	
S Nathan went to his house.	**2Sa 12:15**	
to David, **s** that he was *very* sick.	**2Sa 12:15**	
s David said to his servants,	**2Sa 12:19**	
S David arose from the ground,	**2Sa 12:20**	
S David gathered all the people	**2Sa 12:29**	
Amnon was **s** frustrated because	**2Sa 13:2**	
why are you **s** depressed morning	**2Sa 13:4**	3602
S Amnon lay down and pretended to	**2Sa 13:6**	
S Tamar went to her brother	**2Sa 13:8**	
S everyone went out from him.	**2Sa 13:9**	
S Tamar took the cakes which she	**2Sa 13:10**	
S Tamar remained and was desolate	**2Sa 13:20**	
servant's word, **s** it happened."	**2Sa 13:35**	3651
S Absalom had fled and gone to	**2Sa 13:38**	
S Joab sent to Tekoa and brought a	**2Sa 14:2**	
S Joab put the words in her mouth.	**2Sa 14:3**	
s one struck the other and killed	**2Sa 14:6**	
s as to leave my husband neither	**2Sa 14:7**	
S the king said,	**2Sa 14:10**	
s *that* the avenger of blood will	**2Sa 14:11**	
but plans ways **s** that the banished	**2Sa 14:14**	
s your maidservant said,	**2Sa 14:15**	
s is my lord the king to discern	**2Sa 14:17**	3651
S the king said,	**2Sa 14:19**	
S Joab arose and went to Geshur and	**2Sa 14:23**	
S Absalom turned to his own house	**2Sa 14:24**	
as Absalom, **s** highly praised;	**2Sa 14:25**	
it was heavy on him **s** he cut it),	**2Sa 14:26**	
S he sent again a second time, but	**2Sa 14:29**	
S Absalom's servants set the field	**2Sa 14:30**	
S when Joab came to the king and	**2Sa 14:33**	
s Absalom stole away the hearts of	**2Sa 15:6**	
S he arose and went to Hebron.	**2Sa 15:9**	
S the king went out and all his	**2Sa 15:16**	
S Ittai the Gittite passed over	**2Sa 15:22**	
s I will now be your servant,'	**2Sa 15:34**	
S it shall be that whatever you	**2Sa 15:35**	
S Hushai, David's friend, came	**2Sa 15:37**	
S the king said to Ziba,	**2Sa 16:4**	
'Why have you done **s**?' "	**2Sa 16:10**	3651
S David and his men went on the	**2Sa 16:13**	
s I will be in your presence."	**2Sa 16:19**	3651
S they pitched a tent for Absalom	**2Sa 16:22**	
s was all the advice of Ahithophel	**2Sa 16:23**	3651
terrify him, **s** that all the people	**2Sa 17:2**	
S the plan pleased Absalom and all	**2Sa 17:4**	
S Hushai said to Absalom,	**2Sa 17:7**	
"**S** we shall come to him in one of	**2Sa 17:12**	
s that the LORD might bring	**2Sa 17:14**	5668
s the two of them departed quickly	**2Sa 17:18**	
on it, **s** that nothing was known.	**2Sa 17:19**	
S the king stood beside the gate,	**2Sa 18:4**	
s he was left hanging between	**2Sa 18:9**	
S he took three spears in his hand	**2Sa 18:14**	
S he named the pillar after his	**2Sa 18:18**	
S the Cushite bowed to Joab and	**2Sa 18:21**	
S he said to him, "Run."	**2Sa 18:23**	
S he turned aside and stood still.	**2Sa 18:30**	
S the people went by stealth into	**2Sa 19:3**	
S the king arose and sat in the	**2Sa 19:8**	
May God do **s** to me, and more also,	**2Sa 19:13**	3541
s that they sent *word* to the king,	**2Sa 19:14**	
S he said to the king,	**2Sa 19:19**	
s that the king would take *it* to	**2Sa 19:19**	
S he answered, "O my lord, the king,	**2Sa 19:26**	
S the king said to him,	**2Sa 19:29**	
S all the men of Israel withdrew	**2Sa 20:2**	
S they were shut up until the day	**2Sa 20:3**	
S Amasa went to call out *the men*	**2Sa 20:5**	
s that he does not find for himself	**2Sa 20:6**	6435
S Joab's men went out after him,	**2Sa 20:7**	

s he struck him in the belly with it	**2Sa 20:10**	
S he approached her, and the woman	**2Sa 20:17**	
S he blew the trumpet, and they	**2Sa 20:22**	
S the king called the Gibeonites	**2Sa 21:2**	
S they said to the king,	**2Sa 21:5**	
S the king took the two sons of	**2Sa 21:8**	
s that the seven of them fell	**2Sa 21:9**	
s that you do not extinguish the lamp	**2Sa 21:17**	3808
S that my arms can bend a bow of	**2Sa 22:35**	
them, **s** that they did not rise;	**2Sa 22:39**	
"Truly is not my house **s** with God?	**2Sa 23:5**	3651
S the three mighty men broke	**2Sa 23:16**	
S Joab and the commanders of the	**2Sa 24:4**	
S when they had gone about through	**2Sa 24:8**	
S David said to the LORD,	**2Sa 24:10**	
S Gad came to David and told him,	**2Sa 24:13**	
S the LORD sent a pestilence upon	**2Sa 24:15**	
S Gad came to David that day and	**2Sa 24:18**	
S David bought the threshing floor	**2Sa 24:24**	
S his servants said to him,	**1Ki 1:2**	
S they searched for a beautiful	**1Ki 1:3**	
S he prepared for himself chariots	**1Ki 1:5**	
"Why have you done **s**?"	**1Ki 1:6**	3602
"**S** now come, please let me give	**1Ki 1:12**	
S Bathsheba went in to the king in	**1Ki 1:15**	
I will indeed do **s** this day."	**1Ki 1:30**	3651
king, **s** may He be with Solomon,	**1Ki 1:37**	3651
S Zadok the priest, Nathan the	**1Ki 1:38**	
s that the earth shook at their	**1Ki 1:40**	
s that the city is in an uproar.	**1Ki 1:45**	
S King Solomon sent, and they	**1Ki 1:53**	
s that the LORD may carry out His	**1Ki 2:4**	4616
"**S** act according to your wisdom,	**1Ki 2:6**	
S he said, "You know that	**1Ki 2:15**	
S Bathsheba went to King Solomon	**1Ki 2:19**	
S she said, "Let Abishag	**1Ki 2:21**	
"May God do **s** to me and more	**1Ki 2:23**	3541
S King Solomon sent Benaiah the	**1Ki 2:25**	
he fell upon him **s** that he died.	**1Ki 2:25**	
S Solomon dismissed Abiathar from	**1Ki 2:27**	
S Benaiah came to the tent of the	**1Ki 2:30**	
"**S** shall their blood return on	**1Ki 2:33**	
said, **s** your servant will do."	**1Ki 2:38**	3651
S Shimei lived in Jerusalem many	**1Ki 2:38**	
S the king sent and called for	**1Ki 2:42**	
S the king commanded Benaiah the	**1Ki 2:46**	
and fell upon him **s** that he died.	**1Ki 2:46**	
"**S** give Your servant an	**1Ki 3:9**	
s that there has been no one like	**1Ki 3:12**	834
s that there will not be any among	**1Ki 3:13**	834
"**S** she arose in the middle of the	**1Ki 3:20**	
S they brought a sword before the	**1Ki 3:24**	
S Judah and Israel lived in	**1Ki 4:25**	
S Hiram sent *word* to Solomon,	**1Ki 5:8**	
S Hiram gave Solomon as much as he	**1Ki 5:10**	
S Solomon's builders and Hiram's	**1Ki 5:18**	
S he built the house and finished	**1Ki 6:9**	
S Solomon built the house and	**1Ki 6:14**	
S Solomon overlaid the inside of	**1Ki 6:21**	
and **s** *was* the other cherub.	**1Ki 6:26**	3651
s that the wing of the one was	**1Ki 6:27**	
S their wings were touching each	**1Ki 6:27**	
S *he made* two doors of olive wood,	**1Ki 6:32**	
S also he made for the entrance of	**1Ki 6:33**	3651
S he was seven years in building	**1Ki 6:38**	
and **s** on the outside to the great	**1Ki 7:9**	
S the great court all around *had*	**1Ki 7:12**	
S he came to King Solomon and	**1Ki 7:14**	
S he made the pillars, and two	**1Ki 7:18**	
s he did for the other capital.	**1Ki 7:18**	3651
S the work of the pillars was	**1Ki 7:22**	
S Hiram finished doing all the	**1Ki 7:40**	
sacrificing **s** many sheep and oxen	**1Ki 8:5**	7230
But the poles were **s** long that the	**1Ki 8:8**	
s that the priests could not stand	**1Ki 8:11**	
s that they take them away captive	**1Ki 8:46**	
s that all the peoples of the	**1Ki 8:60**	4616
S the king and all the sons of	**1Ki 8:63**	
S Solomon observed the feast at	**1Ki 8:65**	
S Israel will become a proverb and	**1Ki 9:7**	
S Hiram came out from Tyre to see	**1Ki 9:12**	
S they were called the land of	**1Ki 9:13**	
S Solomon rebuilt Gezer and the	**1Ki 9:17**	
S he finished the house.	**1Ki 9:25**	
S she came to Jerusalem with a	**1Ki 10:2**	
S King Solomon became greater than	**1Ki 10:23**	
and mules, **s** much year by year.	**1Ki 10:25**	1697
S the LORD said to Solomon,	**1Ki 11:11**	
s that he gave him in marriage the	**1Ki 11:19**	
S he was an adversary to Israel	**1Ki 11:25**	
S the people departed.	**1Ki 12:5**	
S he said to them,	**1Ki 12:9**	
S the king did not listen to the	**1Ki 12:15**	
S Israel departed to their tents.	**1Ki 12:16**	
S Israel has been in rebellion	**1Ki 12:19**	
S they listened to the word of the	**1Ki 12:24**	
S the king consulted, and made two	**1Ki 12:28**	
s that he could not draw it back	**1Ki 13:4**	
S the man of God entreated the	**1Ki 13:6**	
"For **s** it was commanded me by the	**1Ki 13:9**	3651
S he went another way and did not	**1Ki 13:10**	
S they saddled the donkey for him	**1Ki 13:13**	
S he went after the man of God and	**1Ki 13:14**	
S he went back with him, and ate	**1Ki 13:19**	
S they came and told *it* in the	**1Ki 13:25**	
S the prophet took up the body of	**1Ki 13:29**	
and disguise yourself **s** that they	**1Ki 14:2**	
Jeroboam's wife did **s**,	**1Ki 14:4**	3651
S King Rehoboam made shields of	**1Ki 14:27**	

S in the twentieth year of **1Ki 15:9**
s that he will withdraw from me." **1Ki 15:19**
S Ben-hadad listened to King Asa **1Ki 15:20**
S Baasha killed him in the third **1Ki 15:28**
S Omri slept with his fathers and **1Ki 16:28**
S he erected an altar for Baal in **1Ki 16:32**
S he went and did according to the **1Ki 17:5**
S he arose and went to Zarephath, **1Ki 17:10**
S she went and did according to **1Ki 17:15**
and his sickness was **s** severe that **1Ki 17:17** 3966
S she said to Elijah, **1Ki 17:18**
S Elijah went to show himself to **1Ki 18:2**
S they divided the land between **1Ki 18:6**
s when I come and tell Ahab and he **1Ki 18:12**
S Obadiah went to meet Ahab and **1Ki 18:16**
S Ahab sent *a message* among all **1Ki 18:20**
S Elijah said to the prophets of **1Ki 18:25**
S they cried with a loud voice and **1Ki 18:28**
S all the people came near to him. **1Ki 18:30**
S with the stones he built an **1Ki 18:32**
S they seized them; **1Ki 18:40**
S Ahab went up to eat and drink. **1Ki 18:42**
S he went up and looked and said, **1Ki 18:43**
s that the *heavy* shower does not **1Ki 18:44**
"**S** may the gods do to me and even **1Ki 19:2** 3541
S he ate and drank and lay down **1Ki 19:6**
S he arose and ate and drank, and **1Ki 19:8**
S He said, "Go forth and stand on **1Ki 19:11**
S he departed from there and found **1Ki 19:19**
S he returned from following him, **1Ki 19:21**
S he said to the messengers of **1Ki 20:9**
the gods do **s** to me and more also, **1Ki 20:10** 3541
S they stationed *themselves* **1Ki 20:12**
S he said, "Thus says the LORD, **1Ki 20:14**
S these went out from the city, **1Ki 20:19**
listened to their voice and did **s**. **1Ki 20:25** 3651
S they camped one over against the **1Ki 20:29**
S they girded sackcloth on their **1Ki 20:32**
S he made a covenant with him and **1Ki 20:34**
S the prophet departed and waited **1Ki 20:38**
"**S** shall your judgment be; **1Ki 20:40** 3651
S the king of Israel went to his **1Ki 20:43**
S Ahab came into his house sullen **1Ki 21:4**
"How is it that your spirit is **s** sullen **1Ki 21:5**
S he said to her, **1Ki 21:6**
S she wrote letters in Ahab's name **1Ki 21:8**
S the men of his city, the elders **1Ki 21:11**
S they took him outside the city **1Ki 21:13**
"Let not the king say **s**." **1Ki 22:8** 3651
S he said, "I saw all Israel Scattered **1Ki 22:17**
and also prevail. Go and do **s**.' **1Ki 22:22** 3651
S the king of Israel and **1Ki 22:29**
S the king of Israel disguised **1Ki 22:30**
S when the captains of the chariots **1Ki 22:32**
S he said to the driver of his **1Ki 22:34**
S the king died and was brought to **1Ki 22:37**
S Ahab slept with his fathers, and **1Ki 22:40**
S he served Baal and worshiped him **1Ki 22:53**
S he sent messengers and said to **2Ki 1:2**
S he again sent to him another **2Ki 1:11**
S he again sent the captain of a **2Ki 1:13**
S he arose and went down with him **2Ki 1:15**
S Ahaziah died according to the **2Ki 1:17**
S they went down to Bethel. **2Ki 2:2**
S they came to Jericho. **2Ki 2:4**
S the two of them went on. **2Ki 2:6**
s that the two of them crossed **2Ki 2:8**
from you, it shall be **s** for you; **2Ki 2:10** 3651
it shall not be **s**." **2Ki 2:10**
S they brought *it* to him. **2Ki 2:20**
S the waters have been purified to **2Ki 2:22**
S the king of Israel went with the **2Ki 3:9**
S the king of Israel and **2Ki 3:12**
water, **s** that you shall drink, **2Ki 3:17**
s that they fled before them; **2Ki 3:24**
S they stopped all the springs of **2Ki 3:25**
S she went from him and shut the **2Ki 4:5**
And **s** it was, as often as he **2Ki 4:8**
S he said, "What then is to be done **2Ki 4:14**
S she went and came to the man of **2Ki 4:25**
S he returned to meet him and told **2Ki 4:31**
S he entered and shut the door **2Ki 4:33**
Shunammite." **S** he called her. **2Ki 4:36**
S they poured *it* out for the men **2Ki 4:40**
S he set *it* before them, and they **2Ki 4:44**
S Naaman came with his horses and **2Ki 5:9**
S he turned and went away in a **2Ki 5:12**
S he went down and dipped *himself* **2Ki 5:14**
s please take a present from your **2Ki 5:15**
S he departed from him some **2Ki 5:19**
S Gehazi pursued Naaman. **2Ki 5:21**
S he went out from his presence a **2Ki 5:27**
where we may live." **S** he said, "Go." **2Ki 6:2**
S he went with them; **2Ki 6:4**
S he put out his hand and took it. **2Ki 6:7**
s that he guarded himself there, **2Ki 6:10**
S he said, "Go and see where he is, **2Ki 6:13**
S he answered, "Do not fear, **2Ki 6:16**
S He struck them with blindness **2Ki 6:18**
S the LORD opened their eyes and **2Ki 6:20**
S he prepared a great feast for **2Ki 6:23**
"**S** we boiled my son and ate him; **2Ki 6:29**
"May God do **s** to me and more **2Ki 6:31** 3541
s that they said to one another, **2Ki 7:6**
S they came and called to the **2Ki 7:10**
perished, **s** let us send and see." **2Ki 7:13**
S the people went out and **2Ki 7:16**
And **s** it happened to him, for the **2Ki 7:20** 3651
S the woman arose and did **2Ki 8:2**

S the king appointed for her a **2Ki 8:6**
S Hazael went to meet him and took **2Ki 8:9**
S he departed from Elisha and **2Ki 8:14**
it on his face, **s** that he died. **2Ki 8:15**
S Edom revolted against Judah to **2Ki 8:22**
S Joram slept with his fathers and **2Ki 8:24**
S King Joram returned to be healed **2Ki 8:29**
S the young man, the servant of **2Ki 9:4**
S Jehu the son of Jehoshaphat the **2Ki 9:14**
S Jehu said, "If this is your mind, **2Ki 9:15**
S a horseman went to meet him and **2Ki 9:18**
s long as the harlotries of your **2Ki 9:22** 5704
and her witchcrafts are **s** many?" **2Ki 9:22**
S Joram reined about and fled and **2Ki 9:23**
S *they shot him* at the ascent of **2Ki 9:27**
S they threw her down, **2Ki 9:33**
of Jezreel, **s** they cannot say, **2Ki 9:37** 834
S Jehu killed all who remained of **2Ki 10:11**
S they took them alive and **2Ki 10:14**
S he made him ride in his chariot. **2Ki 10:16**
s that he might destroy **2Ki 10:19** 4616
s that there was not a man left **2Ki 10:21**
S he brought out garments for them. **2Ki 10:22**
S they hid him from Athaliah, and **2Ki 11:2**
S he was hidden with her in the **2Ki 11:3**
S the captains of hundreds did **2Ki 11:9**
S they seized her, and when she **2Ki 11:16**
S all the people of the land **2Ki 11:20**
S the priests agreed that they **2Ki 12:8**
S the anger of the LORD was **2Ki 13:3**
s that they escaped from under the **2Ki 13:5**
S Joash slept with his fathers, **2Ki 13:13**
S he took a bow and arrows. **2Ki 13:15**
S the man of God was angry with **2Ki 13:19**
s that you, even you, would fall, **2Ki 14:10**
S Jehoash king of Israel went up; **2Ki 14:11**
S Jehoash slept with his fathers **2Ki 14:16**
s that he was a leper to the day **2Ki 15:5**
on the throne of Israel." And **s** it was. **2Ki 15:12** 3651
s that his hand might be with him **2Ki 15:19**
S the king of Assyria returned and **2Ki 15:20**
S Ahaz sent messengers to **2Ki 16:7**
S the king of Assyria listened to **2Ki 16:9**
S Urijah the priest built an altar; **2Ki 16:11**
S Urijah the priest did according **2Ki 16:16**
S Ahaz slept with his fathers, and **2Ki 16:20**
sent messengers to **S** king of Egypt **2Ki 17:4** 5471
s the king of Assyria shut him up **2Ki 17:4**
S the LORD was very angry with **2Ki 17:18**
S Israel was carried away into **2Ki 17:23**
S they possessed Samaria and lived **2Ki 17:24**
S they spoke to the king of **2Ki 17:26**
s he has sent lions among them, **2Ki 17:26**
S one of the priests whom they had **2Ki 17:28**
S while these nations feared the **2Ki 17:41**
did, **s** they do to this day. **2Ki 17:41**
s that after him there was none **2Ki 18:5**
S the king of Assyria required of **2Ki 18:14**
S they went up and came to **2Ki 18:17**
S is Pharaoh king of Egypt to all **2Ki 18:21** 3651
S the servants of King Hezekiah **2Ki 19:5**
s that he will hear a rumor and **2Ki 19:7**
S will you be spared? **2Ki 19:11**
S they have destroyed them. **2Ki 19:18**
S Sennacherib king of Assyria **2Ki 19:36**
S Hezekiah answered, **2Ki 20:10**
S Hezekiah answered, **2Ki 20:15**
"Is it not **s**, if there will be **2Ki 20:19**
S Hezekiah slept with his fathers, **2Ki 20:21**
S he forsook the LORD, the God of **2Ki 21:22**
S Hilkiah the priest, Ahikam, **2Ki 22:14**
S they brought back word to the **2Ki 22:20**
S they left his bones undisturbed **2Ki 23:18**
S Jehoiakim gave the silver and **2Ki 23:35**
S He sent them against Judah to **2Ki 24:2**
S Jehoiakim slept with his **2Ki 24:6**
S the king of Babylon took him **2Ki 24:12**
S he led Jehoiachin away into **2Ki 24:15**
S the city was under siege until **2Ki 25:2**
the famine was **s** severe in the city **2Ki 25:3**
S all the army of the Chaldeans **2Ki 25:10**
S Judah was led away into exile **2Ki 25:21**
struck Gedaliah down **s** that he died **2Ki 25:25**
the LORD, **s** He put him to death. **1Ch 2:3**
s that he is not enrolled in the **1Ch 5:1**
s that they occupied their tents **1Ch 5:10**
S the God of Israel stirred up the **1Ch 5:26**
S the sons of Israel gave to the **1Ch 6:64**
S all Israel was enrolled by **1Ch 9:1**
S they and their sons had charge **1Ch 9:23**
S they stripped him and took his **1Ch 10:9**
S Saul died for his trespass which **1Ch 10:13**
S all the elders of Israel came to **1Ch 11:3**
went up first, **s** he became chief. **1Ch 11:6**
S the three broke through the camp **1Ch 11:18**
said that they would do **s**, **1Ch 13:4** 3651
S David assembled all Israel **1Ch 13:5**
s He struck him down because he **1Ch 13:10**
S David did not take the ark with **1Ch 13:13**
S they came up to Baal-perazim, **1Ch 14:11**
s David gave the order and they **1Ch 14:12**
S the priests and the Levites **1Ch 15:14**
S the Levites appointed Heman the **1Ch 15:17**
S the singers, Heman, Asaph and **1Ch 15:19**
S *it was* David, with the elders of **1Ch 15:25**
S he left Asaph and his relatives **1Ch 16:37**
s that they may dwell in their own **1Ch 17:9**
vision, **s** Nathan spoke to David. **1Ch 17:15** 3651
S David reigned over all Israel; **1Ch 18:14**

S David sent messengers to console **1Ch 19:2**
S Hanun took David's servants and **1Ch 19:4**
S they hired for themselves 32,000 **1Ch 19:7**
S Joab and the people who were **1Ch 19:14**
S when the servants of Hadadezer **1Ch 19:19**
S David said to Joab and to the **1Ch 21:2**
this thing, **s** He struck Israel. **1Ch 21:7**
S Gad came to David and said to **1Ch 21:11**
S the LORD sent a pestilence on **1Ch 21:14**
S David went up at the word of **1Ch 21:19**
S David gave Ornan 600 shekels of **1Ch 21:25**
S David gave orders to gather the **1Ch 22:2**
S David made ample preparations **1Ch 22:5**
because you have shed **s** much **1Ch 22:8**
s that you may keep the law of the **1Ch 22:12**
s that you may bring the ark of **1Ch 22:19**
s they became a father's **1Ch 23:11**
s their brothers, the sons of Kish, **1Ch 23:22**
S Eleazar and Ithamar served as **1Ch 24:2**
S I had made preparations to build **1Ch 28:2**
"**S** now, in the sight of all **1Ch 28:8**
of the LORD your God **s** that you **1Ch 28:8** 4616
they had offered **s** willingly, **1Ch 29:9**
S David blessed the LORD in the **1Ch 29:10**
s now with joy I have seen Your **1Ch 29:17**
S they ate and drank that day **1Ch 29:22**
S Solomon went from the high place **2Ch 1:13**
S Solomon assigned 70,000 men to **2Ch 2:2**
a house to dwell in, **s** do for me. **2Ch 2:3**
S who am I, that I should build a **2Ch 2:6**
s that you may carry it up to **2Ch 2:16**
S Huram finished doing the work **2Ch 4:11**
sacrificing **s** many sheep and oxen that **2Ch 5:6**
s that the cherubim made a **2Ch 5:8**
The poles were **s** long that the **2Ch 5:9**
s that the priests could not stand **2Ch 5:14**
s that they take them away captive **2Ch 6:36**
S Solomon observed the feast at **2Ch 7:8**
heavens **s** that there is no rain, **2Ch 7:13**
and *did* **s** according to the daily **2Ch 8:13**
the man of God had **s** commanded. **2Ch 8:14** 3651
S the house of the LORD was **2Ch 8:16**
S King Solomon became greater than **2Ch 9:22**
and mules, **s** much year by year. **2Ch 9:24** 1697
S they sent and summoned him. **2Ch 10:3**
S the people departed. **2Ch 10:5**
S he said to them, **2Ch 10:9**
S Jeroboam and all the people came **2Ch 10:12**
S the king did not listen to the **2Ch 10:15**
S all Israel departed to their **2Ch 10:16**
S Israel has been in rebellion **2Ch 10:19**
S they listened to the words of **2Ch 11:4**
S he held Judah and Benjamin. **2Ch 11:12**
s I also have forsaken you to **2Ch 12:5**
S the princes of Israel and the **2Ch 12:6**
s I will not destroy them, **2Ch 12:7**
s that they may learn *the difference* **2Ch 12:8**
S Shishak king of Egypt came up **2Ch 12:9**
s as not to destroy *him* completely; **2Ch 12:12**
S King Rehoboam strengthened **2Ch 12:13**
"**S** now you intend to resist the **2Ch 13:8**
s that *Israel* was in front of **2Ch 13:13**
s they cried to the LORD, and the **2Ch 13:14**
s that 500,000 chosen men of **2Ch 13:17**
S Abijah slept with his fathers, **2Ch 14:1**
S they built and prospered. **2Ch 14:7**
S Asa went out to meet him, and **2Ch 14:10**
s help us, O LORD our God, for we **2Ch 14:11**
S the LORD routed the Ethiopians **2Ch 14:12**
and **s** many Ethiopians fell that **2Ch 14:13**
S they assembled at Jerusalem in **2Ch 15:10**
S the LORD gave them rest on every **2Ch 15:15**
s that he will withdraw from me." **2Ch 16:3**
S Ben-hadad listened to King Asa **2Ch 16:4**
S Asa slept with his fathers, **2Ch 16:13**
S the LORD established the kingdom **2Ch 17:5**
s that they did not make war **2Ch 17:10**
S Jehoshaphat grew greater and **2Ch 17:12**
"Let not the king say **s**." **2Ch 18:7** 3651
S please let your word be like one **2Ch 18:12**
S he said, "I saw all Israel Scattered **2Ch 18:16**
him and prevail also. Go and do **s**.' **2Ch 18:21** 3651
S the king of Israel and **2Ch 18:28**
S the king of Israel disguised **2Ch 18:29**
S when the captains of the chariots **2Ch 18:31**
S he said to the driver of the **2Ch 18:33**
s *bring* wrath on yourself from the **2Ch 19:2** 2088
S Jehoshaphat lived in Jerusalem **2Ch 19:4**
you shall warn them **s** that they may **2Ch 19:10** 3808
S Judah gathered together to seek **2Ch 20:4**
s that no one can stand against You. **2Ch 20:6**
s they were routed. **2Ch 20:22**
spoil because there was **s** much. **2Ch 20:25**
S the kingdom of Jehoshaphat was **2Ch 20:30**
He acted wickedly in **s** doing. **2Ch 20:35**
S he allied himself with him to **2Ch 20:36**
S the ships were broken and could **2Ch 20:37**
S Edom revolted against Judah to **2Ch 21:10**
s that no son was left to him **2Ch 21:17**
S after all this the LORD smote **2Ch 21:18**
S Ahaziah the son of Jehoram king **2Ch 22:1**
S he returned to be healed in **2Ch 22:6**
S there was no one of the house of **2Ch 22:9**
S Jehoshabeath, the daughter of **2Ch 22:11**
s that she would not put him to **2Ch 22:11**
S the Levites and all Judah did **2Ch 23:8**
S they seized her, and when she **2Ch 23:15**
s that no one would enter *who was* **2Ch 23:19**
S all of the people of the land **2Ch 23:21**

S the king summoned Jehoiada the	2Ch 24:6	
S the king commanded, and they	2Ch 24:8	
S the workmen labored, and the	2Ch 24:13	
s wrath came upon Judah and	2Ch 24:18	
S they conspired against him and	2Ch 24:21	
S he died, and they buried him in	2Ch 24:25	
s their anger burned against Judah	2Ch 25:10	
s that they were all dashed to pieces.	2Ch 25:12	
should you provoke trouble **s** that	2Ch 25:19	
S Joash king of Israel went up,	2Ch 25:21	
s proud that he acted corruptly,	2Ch 26:16	
S Uzziah slept with his fathers,	2Ch 26:23	
s that the Ammonites gave him	2Ch 27:5	
S Jotham became mighty because he	2Ch 27:6	
s that *His* burning anger is against	2Ch 28:13	
S the armed men left the captives	2Ch 28:14	
S Tilgath-pilneser king of Assyria	2Ch 28:20	
S Ahaz slept with his fathers, and	2Ch 28:27	
S the priests went in to the inner	2Ch 29:16	
S they slaughtered the bulls, and	2Ch 29:22	
S they sang praises with joy, and	2Ch 29:30	
s that they were unable to skin	2Ch 29:34	
S they established a decree to	2Ch 30:5	
s that He made them a horror,	2Ch 30:7	
S the couriers passed from city to	2Ch 30:10	
S the LORD heard Hezekiah and	2Ch 30:20	
S they ate for the appointed seven	2Ch 30:22	
s they celebrated the seven days	2Ch 30:23	
S there was great joy in	2Ch 30:26	
S many people assembled and	2Ch 32:4	
s the God of Hezekiah will not	2Ch 32:17	3651
s that they might take the city.	2Ch 32:18	4616
S he returned in shame to his own	2Ch 32:21	
S the LORD saved Hezekiah and the	2Ch 32:22	
s that he was exalted in the sight	2Ch 32:23	
s that the wrath of the LORD did	2Ch 32:26	
S Hezekiah slept with his fathers,	2Ch 32:33	
S Manasseh slept with his fathers,	2Ch 33:20	
S Hilkiah and *those* whom the king	2Ch 34:22	
s your eyes will not see all the	2Ch 34:28	
S the inhabitants of Jerusalem did	2Ch 34:32	
S the service was prepared, and	2Ch 35:10	
S they roasted the Passover	2Ch 35:13	
S all the service of the LORD was	2Ch 35:16	
s that He will not destroy you."	2Ch 35:21	408
S his servants took him out of the	2Ch 35:24	
s that he sent a proclamation	2Ch 36:22	
s that he sent a proclamation	Ezr 1:1	
S they set up the altar on its	Ezr 3:3	
s that the people could not	Ezr 3:13	
s that a search may be made in the	Ezr 4:15	1768
"**S**, now issue a decree to make	Ezr 4:21	
their names **s** as to inform you,	Ezr 5:10	
s as to destroy this house of God	Ezr 6:12	
s that there will not be wrath	Ezr 7:23	1768
S I sent for Eliezer, Ariel,	Ezr 8:16	
S we fasted and sought our God	Ezr 8:23	
S the priests and the Levites	Ezr 8:30	
s that the holy race has	Ezr 9:2	
'**S** now do not give your daughters	Ezr 9:12	
"**S** now let us make a covenant	Ezr 10:3	
s they took the oath.	Ezr 10:5	
S all the men of Judah and	Ezr 10:9	
have said, **s** it is our duty to do.	Ezr 10:12	
But the exiles did **s**.	Ezr 10:16	3651
S they convened on the first day	Ezr 10:16	
S the king said to me,	Ne 2:2	
S I prayed to the God of heaven.	Ne 2:4	
S it pleased the king to send me,	Ne 2:6	
S I came to Jerusalem and was	Ne 2:11	
S I went out at night by the	Ne 2:13	
S I went up at night by the ravine	Ne 2:15	
the wall of Jerusalem **s** that	Ne 2:17	3808
S they put their hands to the good	Ne 2:18	
S I answered them and said to	Ne 2:20	
S we built the wall and the whole	Ne 4:6	
S we carried on the work with half	Ne 4:21	
s that they may be a guard for us	Ne 4:22	
S neither I, my brothers, my	Ne 4:23	
S I called the priests and took an	Ne 5:12	
do **s** because of the fear of God.	Ne 5:15	3651
S I sent messengers to them,	Ne 6:3	
S come now, let us take counsel	Ne 6:7	
s that they might have an evil	Ne 6:13	
S the wall was completed on the	Ne 6:15	
s that they understood the reading.	Ne 8:8	
S the Levites calmed all the	Ne 8:11	
S they proclaimed and circulated a	Ne 8:15	
S the people went out and brought	Ne 8:16	
sons of Israel had indeed not done **s**	Ne 8:17	3651
S they passed through the midst of	Ne 9:11	
"**S** You made known to them	Ne 9:14	
S they became stubborn and	Ne 9:17	
"**S** their sons entered and	Ne 9:24	
S they ate, were filled and grew	Ne 9:25	
s that they might return to You,	Ne 9:26	
s that they ruled over them.	Ne 9:28	
S we are in great distress.	Ne 9:37	
the Levites and the people **s** that	Ne 10:34	
S they encamped from Beersheba as	Ne 11:30	
s *were* the priests in the reign of	Ne 12:22	
s that they might celebrate the	Ne 12:27	
S the sons of the singers were	Ne 12:28	
S did I and half of the officials	Ne 12:40	
s that the joy of Jerusalem was	Ne 12:43	
S all Israel in the days of	Ne 12:47	
S when they heard the law,	Ne 13:3	
s I threw all of Tobiah's	Ne 13:8	
s that the Levites and the singers	Ne 13:10	
S I reprimanded the officials and	Ne 13:11	
S I admonished *them* on the day	Ne 13:15	
same, **s** that our God brought on us	Ne 13:18	
of my servants at the gates **s** *that*	Ne 13:19	
If you do **s** again, I will use	Ne 13:21	
S I contended with them and cursed	Ne 13:25	
s I drove him away from me.	Ne 13:28	
for **s** the king had given orders to	Es 1:8	3651
custom of the king **s** *to speak* before	Es 1:13	3651
s that it cannot be repealed,	Es 1:19	
S he sent letters to all the	Es 1:22	
S it came about when the command	Es 2:8	
S he quickly provided her with her	Es 2:9	
S Esther was taken to King	Es 2:16	
s that he set the royal crown on	Es 2:17	
was investigated and found *to be* **s**,	Es 2:23	
for **s** the king had commanded	Es 3:2	3651
s it is not in the king's interest	Es 3:8	
s that they should be ready for this	Es 3:14	
S Hathach went out to Mordecai to	Es 4:6	
golden scepter **s** that he may live.	Es 4:11	
S Mordecai went away and did just	Es 4:17	
S Esther came near and touched the	Es 5:2	
S the king and Haman came to the	Es 5:5	
S Esther replied,	Es 5:7	
Haman, **s** he had the gallows made.	Es 5:14	
s he gave an order to bring the book	Es 6:1	
S the king said,	Es 6:4	
S Haman came in and the king said	Es 6:6	
and do **s** for Mordecai the Jew,	Es 6:10	3651
S Haman took the robe and the	Es 6:11	
S they hanged Haman on the gallows	Es 7:10	
S Esther arose and stood before	Es 8:4	
S King Ahasuerus said to Queen	Es 8:7	
S the king's scribes were called	Es 8:9	
s that the Jews would be ready	Es 8:13	
s that the Jews themselves gained	Es 9:1	
S the king commanded that it	Es 9:14	
that it should be done **s**;	Es 9:14	3651
s that they would not fail to	Es 9:27	
S these days were to be remembered	Es 9:28	
S Satan departed from the presence	Jb 1:12	
S the LORD said to Satan,	Jb 2:6	
S that He sets on high those who	Jb 5:11	
S that their hands cannot attain	Jb 5:12	
"**S** the helpless has hope, And	Jb 5:16	
S do not despise the discipline of	Jb 5:17	
and **s** it is. Hear it, and know	Jb 5:27	3651
S that he does not forsake the fear	Jb 6:14	
S am I allotted months of vanity,	Jb 7:3	3651
S he who goes down to Sheol does	Jb 7:9	3651
S that my soul would choose	Jb 7:15	
S that I am a burden to myself?	Jb 7:20	
"**S** are the paths of all who	Jb 8:13	3651
"In truth I know that this is **s**;	Jb 9:2	3651
before me **s** that I may speak;	Jb 13:13	
have set **s** that he cannot pass.	Jb 14:5	
S man lies down and does not rise.	Jb 14:12	
S You destroy man's hope.	Jb 14:19	
up my way **s** that I cannot pass,	Jb 19:8	
S that you may know there is	Jb 19:29	4616
repay him **s** that he may know *it.*	Jb 21:19	
darkness, **s** that you cannot see,	Jb 22:11	
for Him, **s** that He cannot see;	Jb 22:14	
S *does* Sheol *those who* have	Jb 24:19	
"Now if it is not **s**,	Jb 24:25	645
S that they dwell in dreadful	Jb 30:6	
And because my hand had secured **s**	Jb 31:25	
S Elihu the son of Barachel the	Jb 32:6	
"**S** I say, 'Listen to me, I too will tell	Jb 32:10	3651
S that his life loathes bread, And	Jb 33:20	
"If He should determine to do **s**,	Jb 34:14	
S that they caused the cry of the	Jb 34:28	
S that godless men would not	Jb 34:30	4480
S Job opens his mouth emptily;	Jb 35:16	
S that an abundance of water will	Jb 38:34	
"No one is **s** fierce that he dares	Jb 41:10	
"One is **s** near to another That	Jb 41:16	
s that I may not do with you	Jb 42:8	1115
S Eliphaz the Temanite and Bildad	Jb 42:9	
found **s** fair as Job's daughters;	Jb 42:15	
The wicked are not **s**,	Ps 1:4	3651
S that man who is of the earth will	Ps 10:18	
S that my arms can bend a bow of	Ps 18:34	
s that they were not able to rise;	Ps 18:38	
do good, **S** you will abide forever.	Ps 37:27	
me, **s** that I am not able to see;	Ps 40:12	
brooks, **S** my soul pants for You,	Ps 42:1	3651
s have we seen In the city of the	Ps 48:8	3651
S is Your praise to the ends of the	Ps 48:10	3651
S that they have no habitation.	Ps 49:14	4480
S that You are justified when	Ps 51:4	4616
S that I may walk before God In	Ps 56:13	
S that it does not hear the voice	Ps 58:5	834
S I will sing praise to Your name	Ps 61:8	3651
S I will bless You as long as I	Ps 63:4	3651
S they will make him stumble;	Ps 64:8	
As smoke is driven away, **s** drive	Ps 68:2	
S let the wicked perish before	Ps 68:2	
broken my heart and I am **s** sick.	Ps 69:20	
grow dim **s** that they cannot see,	Ps 69:23	4480
S may he live, and may the gold of	Ps 72:15	
am **s** troubled that I cannot speak.	Ps 77:4	
rock **s** that waters gushed out,	Ps 78:20	
S they ate and were well filled,	Ps 78:29	
S He brought their days to an end	Ps 78:33	
safely, **s** that they did not fear;	Ps 78:53	
S He brought them to His holy	Ps 78:54	
S that He abandoned the dwelling	Ps 78:60	
S he shepherded them according to	Ps 78:72	
S we Your people and the sheep of	Ps 79:13	
S that all who pass *that* way pick	Ps 80:12	
"**S** I gave them over to the	Ps 81:12	
S pursue them with Your tempest And	Ps 83:15	3651
"**S** I will establish his	Ps 89:29	
S teach us to number our days,	Ps 90:12	3651
S as to cut off from the city of	Ps 101:8	
S the nations will fear the name	Ps 102:15	
S *that* your youth is renewed like	Ps 103:5	
S great is His lovingkindness	Ps 103:11	
S far has He removed our	Ps 103:12	
S the LORD has compassion on those	Ps 103:13	
of the field, **s** he flourishes.	Ps 103:15	3651
S that it will not totter forever	Ps 104:5	
S that they will not return to cover	Ps 104:9	
S that he may bring forth food	Ps 104:14	
S that he may make *his* face	Ps 104:15	
S that they might keep His	Ps 105:45	5668
S He saved them from the hand of	Ps 106:10	
S He gave them their request, But	Ps 106:15	
And **s** the plague was stayed.	Ps 106:30	
S that it went hard with Moses on	Ps 106:32	
And **s** sank down in their iniquity.	Ps 106:43	
the redeemed of the LORD say **s**,	Ps 107:2	
S that the waves of the sea were	Ps 107:29	
S He guided them to their desired	Ps 107:30	
S that they may establish an	Ps 107:36	
loved cursing, **s** it came to him;	Ps 109:17	
blessing, **s** it was far from him.	Ps 109:17	
me violently **s** that I was falling,	Ps 118:13	
S I will meditate on Your wonders.	Ps 119:27	
S I will have an answer for him	Ps 119:42	
S I will keep Your law continually,	Ps 119:44	
S that I will not be ashamed.	Ps 119:80	
S that I may keep the testimony of	Ps 119:88	
S our eyes *look* to the LORD our	Ps 123:2	3651
S the LORD surrounds His people	Ps 125:2	
S that the righteous will not put	Ps 125:3	
S are the children of one's youth.	Ps 127:4	3651
S that I may give thanks to Your	Ps 142:7	
are the people who are **s** situated;	Ps 144:15	3602
S are the ways of everyone who	Pr 1:19	3651
"**S** they shall eat of the fruit of	Pr 1:31	
S you will walk in the way of good	Pr 2:20	4616
S you will find favor and good	Pr 3:4	
S your barns will be filled with	Pr 3:10	
S they will be life to your soul And	Pr 3:22	
S is the one who goes in to his	Pr 6:29	3651
S she seizes him and kisses him And	Pr 7:13	
S he does not know that it *will*	Pr 7:23	
S that the water would not	Pr 8:29	
And **s** *is* wisdom to a man of	Pr 10:23	
S is the lazy one to those who	Pr 10:26	3651
a ring of gold in a swine's snout **S**	Pr 11:22	
But the hearts of fools are not **s**.	Pr 15:7	3651
He who winks his eyes *does* **s** to	Pr 16:30	
S a cruel messenger will be sent	Pr 17:11	
S abandon the quarrel before it	Pr 17:14	
He who sires a fool *does* **s** to his	Pr 17:21	
S that one may sleep satisfied,	Pr 19:23	
S he begs during the harvest and	Pr 20:4	
S that your trust may be in the	Pr 22:19	
he thinks within himself, **s** he is.	Pr 23:7	3651
S the heart of kings is	Pr 25:3	
S is good news from a distant land.	Pr 25:25	
S honor is not fitting for a fool.	Pr 26:1	3651
S a curse without cause does not	Pr 26:2	3651
S is a proverb in the mouth of	Pr 26:7	
S is he who gives honor to a fool.	Pr 26:8	3651
S is a proverb in the mouth of	Pr 26:9	
S is he who hires a fool or who	Pr 26:10	
S *does* the sluggard on his bed.	Pr 26:14	
S is the man who deceives his	Pr 26:19	3651
S is a contentious man to kindle	Pr 26:21	
S is a man who wanders from his	Pr 27:8	3651
S a man's counsel is sweet to his	Pr 27:9	
iron, **S** one man sharpens another.	Pr 27:17	
S the heart of man *reflects* man.	Pr 27:19	3651
and knowledge, **s** it endures.	Pr 28:2	3651
S the churning of anger produces	Pr 30:33	
S there is nothing new under the	Ec 1:9	
S enjoy yourself."	Ec 2:1	
S I turned to consider wisdom,	Ec 2:12	
S I said to myself,	Ec 2:15	
S I hated life, for the work which	Ec 2:17	
collecting **s** that he may give to one	Ec 2:26	
yet **s** that man will not find out	Ec 3:11	1097
for God has **s** worked that men	Ec 3:14	
As one dies **s** dies the other;	Ec 3:19	3651
S I congratulated the dead who are	Ec 4:2	
S what is the advantage to their	Ec 5:11	
womb, **s** will he return as he came.	Ec 5:15	
S what is the advantage to him	Ec 5:16	
honor **s** that his soul lacks nothing	Ec 6:2	
S is the laughter of the fool;	Ec 7:6	3651
S that man will not discover	Ec 7:14	5921, 1700
s that you will not hear your servant	Ec 7:21	3808
S then, I have seen the wicked	Ec 8:10	3651
S I commended pleasure, for there	Ec 8:15	
the good man is, **s** is the sinner;	Ec 9:2	
as the swearer is, **s** is the one who	Ec 9:2	
s the sons of men are ensnared at	Ec 9:12	
S I said, "Wisdom is better than	Ec 9:16	
s a little foolishness is	Ec 10:1	
The toil of a fool **s** wearies him	Ec 10:15	
s you do not know the activity of	Ec 11:5	3602
S, remove grief and anger	Ec 11:10	

are, my beloved, *And* **s** pleasant! SS 1:16 637
S is my darling among the maidens." SS 2:2 3651
S is my beloved among the young SS 2:3 3651
"**S** when you spread out your hands Is 1:15
S the *common* man has been humbled Is 2:9
"**S** now let Me tell you what I am Is 5:5
S that you have to *live* alone in Is 5:8
S the *common* man will be humbled and Is 5:15
S their root will become like rot Is 5:24
s *that it is* no longer a people), Is 7:8
S I approached the prophetess, and Is 8:3
S the LORD cuts off head and tail Is 9:14
S as to deprive the needy of Is 10:2
S that widows may be their spoil And Is 10:2
Yet it does not **s** intend, Nor does Is 10:7 3651
Nor does it plan **s** in its heart, Is 10:7 3651
S it will be that when the Lord Is 10:12
his forest will be **s** small in number Is 10:19
S it will be in that day, that his Is 10:27
I have intended **s** it has happened, Is 14:24 3651
as I have planned **s** it will stand, Is 14:24
S it will come about when Moab Is 16:12
"**S** I will incite Egyptians Is 19:2
S that they will resort to idols Is 19:3
s they will return to the LORD, Is 19:22
And he did **s**, going naked and Is 20:2 3651
s the king of Assyria will lead Is 20:4 3651
"**S** the inhabitants of this Is 20:6
I am **s** bewildered I cannot hear, Is 21:3 4480
hear, **s** terrified I cannot see. Is 21:3 4480
"**S** they will hang on him all the Is 22:24
is shut up **s** that none may enter. Is 24:10 4480
S it will happen in that day, That Is 24:21
S that no one will damage it, I Is 27:3
S the word of the LORD to them Is 28:13
S ruthlessly shattered That a Is 30:14
S the LORD will stretch out His Is 31:3
S will the LORD of hosts come down Is 31:4 3651
s the LORD of hosts will protect Is 31:5 3651
S he will not escape the sword, Is 31:8
hands **s** that they hold no bribe; Is 33:15 4480
S their slain will be thrown out, Is 34:3
S is Pharaoh king of Egypt to all Is 36:6 3651
S the servants of King Hezekiah Is 37:5
S that he will hear a rumor and Is 37:7
S will you be spared? Is 37:11
S they have destroyed them. Is 37:19
S Sennacherib king of Assyria Is 37:37
S the sun's *shadow* went back ten Is 38:8
s He breaks all my bones, Is 38:13 3651
like a crane, **s** I twitter; Is 38:14 3651
S we will play my songs on Is 38:20
S Hezekiah answered, Is 39:4
S the craftsman encourages the Is 41:7
S *that* it will not totter. Is 41:7
Or **s** deaf as My messenger whom I Is 42:19
Who is **s** blind as he that is at Is 42:19
Or **s** blind as the servant of the Is 42:19
S He poured out on him the heat of Is 42:25
the nations have gathered together **S** Is 43:9
S that you may know and believe Me Is 43:10
S you are My witnesses," Is 43:12
"**S** I will pollute the princes of Is 43:28
s that they will be put to shame. Is 44:9 4616
man, **s** that it may sit in a house. Is 44:13
s he takes one of them and warms Is 44:15
over their eyes **s** that they cannot see Is 44:18 4480
s that they cannot comprehend. Is 44:18 4480
him **s** that gates will not be shut: Is 45:1
S that you may know that it is I, Is 45:3
"**S** have those become to you with Is 47:15 3651
S that you would not say, 'My idol Is 48:5
S that you will not say, 'Behold, Is 48:7
s that Israel might be gathered to Is 49:5
S that My salvation may reach to Is 49:6
s short that it cannot ransom? Is 50:2 4480
S the ransomed of the LORD will Is 51:11
S His appearance was marred more Is 52:14 3651
S He did not open His mouth. Is 53:7
S I have sworn that I will not be Is 54:9 3651
S are My ways higher than your Is 55:9 3651
S will My word be which goes Is 55:11 3651
will be like today, only more **s**." Is 56:12
a long time **S** you do not fear Me? Is 57:11
not **s** short That it cannot save; Is 59:1 4480
ear **s** dull That it cannot hear. Is 59:1 4480
from you **s** that He does not hear. Is 59:2 4480
to *their* deeds, **s** He will repay, Is 59:18 5921
S they will fear the name of the Is 59:19
S that *men* may bring to you the Is 60:11
S they will be called oaks of Is 61:3
S the Lord GOD will cause Is 61:11 3651
S your sons will marry you; Is 62:5
S your God will rejoice over you. Is 62:5
S My own arm brought salvation to Is 63:5
S He became their Savior. Is 63:8
S You led Your people, To Is 63:14 3651
S I will act on behalf of My Is 65:8 3651
s *will be* the days of My people, Is 65:22
S I will choose their punishments And Is 66:4 1571
comforts, **s** I will comfort you; Is 66:13 3651
"**S** your offspring and your name Is 66:22 3651
S the house of Israel is shamed; Jer 2:26 3651
"Why do you go around **s** much Jer 2:36 3966
S you have dealt treacherously Jer 3:20 3651
s you will serve strangers in a Jer 5:19 3651
decree, **s** it cannot cross over it. Jer 5:22
S their houses are full of deceit; Jer 5:27 3651
And My people love it **s**! Jer 5:31 3651

S she keeps fresh her wickedness. Jer 6:7 3651
s that no one passes through, Jer 9:10
4480, 1097
s that no one passes through? Jer 9:12
4480, 1097
hammers **S** that it will not totter. Jer 10:4
s you shall be My people, and I Jer 11:4
S *that* you can rejoice?" Jer 11:15 227
s that you will not die at our hand"; Jer 11:21 3808
S I bought the waistband in Jer 13:2
S I went and hid it by the Jer 13:5
'Just **s** will I destroy the pride Jer 13:9 3602
s I made the whole household of Jer 13:11 3651
nor be sorry nor have compassion **s** as Jer 13:14
"**S** I Myself have also stripped Jer 13:26
"Even **s** they have loved to wander; Jer 14:10 3651
S the LORD said to me, Jer 14:11
us **s** that we are beyond healing? Jer 14:19
S I will stretch out My hand Jer 15:6
S I will give over their Jer 15:9
"**S** I will deliver you from the Jer 15:21
'**S** I will hurl you out of this Jer 16:13
S they *remember* their altars and Jer 17:2
S is he who makes a fortune, but Jer 17:11
s he remade it into another Jer 18:4
hand, **s** are you in My hand, Jer 18:6 3651
"**S** now then, speak to the men of Jer 18:11
S as to turn away Your wrath from Jer 18:20
"Just **s** will I break this people Jer 19:11 3602
"**s** as to make this city like Jer 19:12
s as not to heed My words.' " Jer 19:15
S I will give over all Judah to Jer 20:4
s that we may prevail against him Jer 20:10
S that my mother would have been Jer 20:17
S that my days have been spent in Jer 20:18
s that *the enemy* will withdraw Jer 21:2
S that no one has turned back from Jer 23:14
places **S** I do not see him?" Jer 23:24
s I will regard as good the Jer 24:5 3651
s I will abandon Zedekiah king of Jer 24:8 3651
s that he was not given into the Jer 26:24
"**S** do not listen to the words of Jer 27:14
May the LORD do **s**; Jer 28:6 3651
'Even **s** will I break within two Jer 28:11 3602
S Hananiah the prophet died in the Jer 28:17
s I will watch over them to build Jer 31:28 3651
up the sea **s** that its waves roar; Jer 31:35
s that it should be removed from Jer 32:31
s that they will not turn away from Jer 32:40
s I am going to bring on them all Jer 32:42 3651
s that day and night will not be Jer 33:20
with David My servant **s** that Jer 33:21
s I will multiply the descendants Jer 33:22 3651
s they will burn *spices* for you; Jer 34:5 3651
s that no one should keep them, a Jer 34:9
s that no one should keep them any Jer 34:10
S we have dwelt in Jerusalem." Jer 35:11
S they do not drink *wine* to this Jer 35:14
"**S** you go and read from the Jer 36:6
S Baruch the son of Neriah took Jer 36:14
S Baruch read it to them. Jer 36:15
S they went to the king in the Jer 36:20
S Irijah arrested Jeremiah and Jer 37:14
S Jeremiah remained in the court Jer 37:21
S King Zedekiah said, Jer 38:5
S Ebed-melech took the men under Jer 38:11
and Jeremiah did **s**. Jer 38:12 3651
S they pulled Jeremiah up with the Jer 38:13
S he reported to them in Jer 38:27
S Jeremiah stayed in the court of Jer 38:28
S Nebuzaradan the captain of the Jer 39:13
S he stayed among the people. Jer 39:14
S the captain of the bodyguard Jer 40:5
S they came to Gedaliah at Mizpah, Jer 40:8
s that all the Jews who are Jer 40:15
S he refrained and did not put Jer 41:8
S they took all the men and went Jer 41:12
S all the people whom Ishmael had Jer 41:14
s that it may go well with us when we Jer 42:6 4616
s that he will have compassion on Jer 42:12
s as not to listen to the voice of Jer 42:13
"**S** all the men who set their mind Jer 42:17
s My wrath will be poured out on Jer 42:18 3651
the LORD our God says, tell us **s**, Jer 42:20 3651
S I have told you today, but you Jer 42:21
s they will put us to death or Jer 43:3
S Johanan the son of Kareah and Jer 43:4
S he will wrap himself with the Jer 43:12
they committed **s** as to provoke Me Jer 44:3
s as not to burn sacrifices to Jer 44:5
s they have become a ruin and a Jer 44:6
s as to cut off from you man and Jer 44:7
s that you might be cut off and Jer 44:8 4616
'**S** there will be no refugees or Jer 44:14
"**S** the LORD was no longer able to Jer 44:22
s that you may know that My words Jer 44:29 4616
s as to avenge Himself on His foes; Jer 46:10
city, **S** that no city will escape; Jer 48:8
s Moab will wallow in his vomit, Jer 48:26
"**S** gladness and joy are taken Jer 48:33
S Moab will become a laughingstock Jer 48:39
S the hearts of the mighty men of Jer 48:41
S that he will not be able to conceal Jer 49:10
'**S** I will shatter Elam before Jer 49:37
to others, **s** do to her. Jer 50:15
s do to her; For she has become Jer 50:29
S that He may bring rest to the Jer 50:34 4616
S do not spare her young men; Jer 51:3
S the land quakes and writhes, For Jer 51:29

"Now **s** that your heart does not grow Jer 51:46 6435
S the peoples will toil for Jer 51:58
S Jeremiah wrote in a single Jer 51:60
s that there will be nothing Jer 51:62
'Just **s** shall Babylon sink down Jer 51:64 3602
S the city was under siege until Jer 52:5
famine was **s** severe in the city that Jer 52:6
S all the army of the Chaldeans Jer 52:14
S Judah was led away into exile Jer 52:27
S Jehoiachin changed his prison Jer 52:33
S as to restore you from captivity, La 2:14
me in **s** that I cannot go out; La 3:7
S I say, "My strength has perished, La 3:18
And **s** *has* my hope from the LORD." La 3:18
S that no prayer can pass through. La 3:44 4480
S that no one could touch their La 4:14
S they fled and wandered; La 4:15 3588
S that we could not walk in our La 4:18 4480
Why do You forsake us **s** long? La 5:20
753, 3117
s *was* the appearance of the Ezk 1:28 3651
S I opened my mouth, and He fed me Ezk 3:2
S the Spirit lifted me up and took Ezk 3:14
S I got up and went out to the Ezk 3:23
s that you cannot go out among Ezk 3:25
mouth **s** that you will be mute and Ezk 3:26
it **s** that it is under siege, Ezk 4:3
s that you cannot turn from one Ezk 4:8
'**S** as I live,' declares the Lord Ezk 5:11 3651
'**S** it will be a reproach, a Ezk 5:15
"**S** your altars will become Ezk 6:4
"**S** throughout all their Ezk 6:14
S I raised my eyes toward the Ezk 8:5
s that I would be far from My Ezk 8:6
S I dug through the wall, Ezk 8:8
S I entered and looked, and Ezk 8:10
S they started with the elders who Ezk 9:6
s I knew that they *were* cherubim. Ezk 10:20
"**S** you think, house of Israel, Ezk 11:5 3651
s I will bring a sword upon you," Ezk 11:8
s you shall know that I am the Ezk 11:10
S the vision that I had seen left Ezk 11:24
s that you cannot see the land, Ezk 12:6
I did **s**, as I had been Ezk 12:7 3651
done, **s** it will be done to them; Ezk 12:11 3651
s that he can not see the land with Ezk 12:12
3282, 834
"**S** they will know that I am the Ezk 12:15
S you will know that I am the LORD. Ezk 12:20
s that they will no longer use it as a Ezk 12:23
"**S** My hand will be against the Ezk 13:9
s tell those who plaster *it* Ezk 13:11
"**S** I will tear down the wall Ezk 13:14
s that its foundation is laid bare; Ezk 13:14
S you will know that I am the LORD. Ezk 14:8
s the iniquity of the prophet will Ezk 14:10
s that no one would pass through it Ezk 14:15
4480, 1097
s have I given up the inhabitants Ezk 15:6 3651
S I spread My skirt over you and Ezk 16:8
with you **s** that you became Mine," Ezk 16:8
s you were exceedingly beautiful Ezk 16:13
s it happened," declares the Lord Ezk 16:19
your harlotries **s** small a matter? Ezk 16:20 4592
S I will gather them against you Ezk 16:37
"**S** I will calm My fury against Ezk 16:42
"**s** that you will not commit this Ezk 16:43
s now you have become the reproach Ezk 16:57 3644
s that you may remember and be Ezk 16:63
S it became a vine and yielded Ezk 17:6
s that it withers—so that all its Ezk 17:9
s that all its sprouting leaves wither? Ezk 17:9
My ordinances **s** as to deal faithfully Ezk 18:9
s that iniquity may not become a Ezk 18:30
S that his voice would be heard no Ezk 19:9 4616
S that it was seen in its height with Ezk 19:11
was torn off **S** that it withered; Ezk 19:12
S that there is not in it a strong Ezk 19:14
"**S** I took them out of the land of Ezk 20:10
S I resolved to pour out My wrath Ezk 20:21
s that I might make them desolate, Ezk 20:26 4616
S its name is called Bamah to this Ezk 20:29
s I will enter into judgment with Ezk 20:36 3651
s that in all your deeds your sins Ezk 21:24
midst, **s** that her time will come, Ezk 22:3
s I will gather *you* in My anger Ezk 22:20 3651
s you will be melted in the midst Ezk 22:22 3651
s that I would not destroy it; but I Ezk 22:30 1115
"**S** she increased her harlotries. Ezk 23:14
s that you will not lift up your Ezk 23:27
its coals **S** that it may be hot Ezk 24:11 4616
S I spoke to the people in the Ezk 24:18
s that the sons of Ammon will not be Ezk 25:10 4616
"**S** I will silence the sound of Ezk 26:13
s that you will not be inhabited; Ezk 26:20 4616
S that it became your distinguishing Ezk 27:7
"**S** I will make the land of Egypt Ezk 29:12
And I will make them **s** small that Ezk 29:15
s that he will groan before him Ezk 30:24
'**S** it was beautiful in its Ezk 31:7
s that all the trees by the waters Ezk 31:14 4616
S is Pharaoh and all his hordes!" ' Ezk 31:18
S they lay down uncircumcised with Ezk 32:30
s you will hear a message from My Ezk 33:7
and he **s** trusts in his Ezk 33:13
s my mouth was opened and I was Ezk 33:22
s to us who are many the land has Ezk 33:24
s that no one will pass through. Ezk 33:28 4480
"**S** when it comes to pass Ezk 33:33

S the shepherds will not feed	**Ezk 34:10**	
s that they will not be food for them."' "	**Ezk 34:10**	
s I will care for My sheep and	**Ezk 34:12**	3651
s that they may live securely in	**Ezk 34:25**	
s I will make Myself known among	**Ezk 35:11**	
was desolate, **s** I will do to you.	**Ezk 35:15**	3651
s that you will become their	**Ezk 36:12**	
s you will be My people, and I	**Ezk 36:28**	
s that you will not receive again	**Ezk 36:30**	4616
s will the waste cities be filled	**Ezk 36:38**	3651
S I prophesied as I was commanded;	**Ezk 37:7**	
S I prophesied as He commanded me,	**Ezk 37:10**	
s that the nations may know Me when I	**Ezk 38:16**	4616
S they will bury Gog there with	**Ezk 39:11**	
S they will cleanse the land."	**Ezk 39:16**	
"**S** you will eat fat until you are	**Ezk 39:19**	
S I gave them into the hand of	**Ezk 39:23**	
S He brought me there;	**Ezk 40:3**	
S he measured the thickness of the	**Ezk 40:5**	
to their length **s** was their width,	**Ezk 42:11**	3651
S I have consumed them in My anger.	**Ezk 43:8**	
s that they may observe its whole	**Ezk 43:11**	
s shall they consecrate it.	**Ezk 43:26**	
shall put on other garments **s** that	**Ezk 44:19**	3808
s My princes shall no longer	**Ezk 45:8**	
s that the bath will contain a	**Ezk 45:11**	
s you shall make atonement for the	**Ezk 45:20**	
s that My people will not be	**Ezk 46:18**	4616
s everything will live where the	**Ezk 47:9**	
"**S** you shall divide this land	**Ezk 47:21**	
s he sought *permission* from the	**Da 1:8**	
S he listened to them in this	**Da 1:14**	
S the overseer continued to	**Da 1:16**	
s they entered the king's personal	**Da 1:19**	
S they came in and stood before	**Da 2:2**	
S the decree went forth that the	**Da 2:13**	
is the decree from the king **s**	**Da 2:15**	
S Daniel went in and requested of	**Da 2:16**	
s that they might request compassion	**Da 2:18**	
s that Daniel and his friends	**Da 2:18**	1768
s that not a trace of them was found	**Da 2:35**	
s, like iron that breaks in pieces, it	**Da 2:40**	
s some of the kingdom will be	**Da 2:42**	
s the dream is true and its	**Da 2:45**	
"If it be **s**, our God whom we	**Da 3:17**	
s as not to serve or worship any god	**Da 3:28**	1768
"**S** I gave orders to bring into my	**Da 4:6**	
s I was reestablished in my	**Da 4:36**	
s that the king and his nobles, his	**Da 5:2**	
his spirit became **s** proud that he	**Da 5:20**	
S Darius the Mede received the	**Da 5:31**	
s that it may not be changed,	**Da 6:8**	1768
s that nothing would be changed in	**Da 6:17**	1768
S Daniel was taken up out of the	**Da 6:23**	
S this Daniel enjoyed success in	**Da 6:28**	
S he told me and made known to me	**Da 7:16**	
S he hurled him to the ground and	**Da 8:7**	
s as to allow both the holy place	**Da 8:13**	
S he came near to where I was	**Da 8:17**	
S I gave my attention to the Lord	**Da 9:3**	
s the curse has been poured out on	**Da 9:11**	
"**S** now, our God, listen to the	**Da 9:17**	
s give heed to the message and	**Da 9:23**	
"**S** you are to know and discern	**Da 9:25**	
S I was left alone and saw this	**Da 10:8**	
s I am going forth, and behold,	**Da 10:20**	
"**S** he will turn his face toward	**Da 11:19**	
s the king of the South will	**Da 11:25**	
s he will come back and show	**Da 11:30**	
not understand; **s** I said, "My lord,	**Da 12:8**	
S he went and took Gomer the	**Hos 1:3**	
s that she cannot find her paths.	**Hos 2:6**	
lovers, **s** that she forgot Me,"	**Hos 2:13**	
s that they will be mentioned by	**Hos 2:17**	
S I bought her for myself for	**Hos 3:2**	
s I will also be toward you."	**Hos 3:3**	
s that bloodshed follows bloodshed.	**Hos 4:2**	
S you will stumble by day, And the	**Hos 4:5**	
S I will punish them for their	**Hos 4:9**	
S the people without understanding	**Hos 4:14**	
"**S** let us know, let us press on	**Hos 6:3**	
And as raiders wait for a man, **S**	**Hos 6:9**	
S Ephraim has become like a silly	**Hos 7:11**	
made it, **s** it is not God;	**Hos 8:6**	
because your hostility is **s** great.	**Hos 9:7**	
S My people are bent on turning	**Hos 11:7**	
S his Lord will leave his	**Hos 12:14**	
S I will be like a lion to them;	**Hos 13:7**	
S there is a great and mighty	**Jl 2:2**	
And like war horses, **s** they run.	**Jl 2:4**	3651
S rejoice, O sons of Zion, And be	**Jl 2:23**	
S Jerusalem will be holy, And	**Jl 3:17**	
"**S** I will send fire upon the	**Am 1:4**	
S the people of Aram will go	**Am 1:5**	
"**S** I will send fire upon the wall	**Am 1:7**	
"**S** I will send fire upon the wall	**Am 1:10**	
"**S** I will send fire upon Teman And	**Am 1:12**	
"**S** I will kindle a fire on the	**Am 1:14**	
"**S** I will send fire upon Moab And	**Am 2:2**	
"**S** I will send fire upon Judah And	**Am 2:5**	
Is this not **s**, O sons of Israel?"	**Am 2:11**	637
S will the sons of Israel dwelling	**Am 3:12**	3651
For **s** you love *to do*, you sons of	**Am 4:5**	3651
"**S** two or three cities would	**Am 4:8**	
S that destruction comes upon the	**Am 5:9**	
be over, **S** that we may sell grain,	**Am 8:5**	
S as to buy the helpless for money	**Am 8:6**	
s that the thresholds will shake,	**Am 9:1**	
touches the land **s** that it melts,	**Am 9:5**	
S that everyone may be cut off from	**Ob 1:9**	
s that there will be no survivor	**Ob 1:18**	
S he went down to Joppa, found a	**Jon 1:3**	
s that the ship was about to break up.	**Jon 1:4**	
S the captain approached him and	**Jon 1:6**	
us **s** that we will not perish."	**Jon 1:6**	
let us cast lots **s** we may learn on	**Jon 1:7**	
S they cast lots and the lot fell	**Jon 1:7**	
S they said to him,	**Jon 1:11**	
S they picked up Jonah, threw him	**Jon 1:15**	
"**S** I said, 'I have been expelled from	**Jon 2:4**	
S Jonah arose and went to Nineveh	**Jon 3:3**	
s that we will not perish."	**Jon 3:9**	
S the LORD God appointed a plant	**Jon 4:6**	
Jonah's head **s** that he became faint	**Jon 4:8**	
'Do not speak out,' **s** they	**Mi 2:6**	
S their king goes on before them,	**Mi 2:13**	
S that you will no longer bow down	**Mi 5:13**	
S that you might know the righteous	**Mi 6:5**	4616
"**S** also I will make *you* sick,	**Mi 6:13**	
S they weave it together.	**Mi 7:3**	
Even **s**, they will be cut off and pass	**Na 1:12**	3651
"**S** now, I will break his yoke bar	**Na 1:13**	
S that he does not stay at home.	**Hab 2:5**	
S you are sinning against yourself.	**Hab 2:10**	
S as to look on their nakedness!	**Hab 2:15**	4616
"**S** I will stretch out My hand	**Zph 1:4**	
S that they will walk like the	**Zph 1:17**	
S that there will be no inhabitant.	**Zph 2:5**	4480
S the seacoast will be pastures,	**Zph 2:6**	
S her dwelling will not be cut off	**Zph 3:7**	
S the LORD stirred up the spirit	**Hg 1:14**	
"'**S** is this people.	**Hg 2:14**	3651
And **s** is this nation before Me,'	**Hg 2:14**	3651
s is every work of their hands;	**Hg 2:14**	3651
s He has dealt with us.	**Zch 1:6**	3651
S they answered the angel of the	**Zch 1:11**	
S the angel who was speaking with	**Zch 1:14**	
S I said to the angel who was	**Zch 1:19**	
s that no man lifts up his head;	**Zch 1:21**	6310
S I said, "Where are you going?"	**Zch 2:2**	
s that they will be plunder for	**Zch 2:9**	
S they put a clean turban on his	**Zch 3:5**	
S the angel who was speaking with	**Zch 4:5**	
S he answered me,	**Zch 4:13**	
S they patrolled the earth.	**Zch 6:7**	
s that they could not hear the law and	**Zch 7:12**	4480
s they called and I would not	**Zch 7:13**	3651
s that no one went back and forth,	**Zch 7:14**	4480
s I will save you that you may	**Zch 8:13**	3651
s I have again purposed in these	**Zch 8:15**	3651
s love truth and peace.'	**Zch 8:19**	
'**S** many peoples and mighty nations	**Zch 8:22**	
S that all the depths of the Nile	**Zch 10:11**	
S I pastured the flock *doomed* to	**Zch 11:7**	
s I pastured the flock.	**Zch 11:7**	
S it was broken on that day, and	**Zch 11:11**	
S they weighed out thirty *shekels*	**Zch 11:12**	
S I took the thirty *shekels* of	**Zch 11:13**	
s they will consume on the right	**Zch 12:6**	
s that the glory of the house of	**Zch 12:7**	4616
s that they will look on Me whom	**Zch 12:10**	
s that half of the mountain will	**Zch 14:4**	
S also like this plague will be	**Zch 14:15**	3651
s you bring the offering!	**Mal 1:13**	
s he revered Me and stood in awe	**Mal 2:5**	
"**S** I also have made you despised	**Mal 2:9**	
s as to profane the covenant of our	**Mal 2:10**	
"But not one has done **s** who has	**Mal 2:15**	
"**S** take heed to your spirit, that	**Mal 2:16**	
s that they may present to the	**Mal 3:3**	
s that there may be food in My	**Mal 3:10**	
s that it will not destroy the	**Mal 3:11**	
'**S** now we call the arrogant	**Mal 3:15**	
S you will again distinguish	**Mal 3:18**	
"**s** that it will leave them	**Mal 4:1**	834
s that I will not come and smite	**Mal 4:6**	6435
S all the generations from Abraham to	**Mt 1:17**	*3767*
s that I too may come and worship	**Mt 2:8**	*3704*
S Joseph got up and took the Child	**Mt 2:14**	*1161*
S Joseph got up, took the Child	**Mt 2:21**	*1161*
S THAT YOU WILL NOT STRIKE YOUR FOOT	**Mt 4:6**	*3379*
s that your opponent may not hand you	**Mt 5:25**	*3379*
s that you may be sons of your Father	**Mt 5:45**	*3704*
"**S** when you give to the poor, do	**Mt 6:2**	*3767*
s that they may be honored by men.	**Mt 6:2**	*3767*
s that your giving will be in secret;	**Mt 6:4**	*3704*
and on the street corners **s** that they	**Mt 6:5**	*3704*
"**S** do not be like them; for your	**Mt 6:8**	*3767*
they neglect their appearance **s** that	**Mt 6:16**	*3704*
s that your fasting will not be noticed	**Mt 6:18**	*3704*
eye is the lamp of the body; **s** then	**Mt 6:22**	*3767*
s clothes the grass of the field,	**Mt 6:30**	*3779*
"**S** do not worry about tomorrow;	**Mt 6:34**	*3767*
"Do not judge **s** that you will not be	**Mt 7:1**	*2443*
"**S** every good tree bears good fruit,	**Mt 7:17**	*3779*
"**S** then, you will know them by	**Mt 7:20**	*1065*
s that the boat was being covered with	**Mt 8:24**	*5620*
They were **s** extremely violent	**Mt 8:28**	
"But **s** that you may know that	**Mt 9:6**	*2443*
and **s** *did* His disciples.	**Mt 9:19**	
s be shrewd as serpents and innocent	**Mt 10:16**	*3767*
"**S** do not fear; you are more	**Mt 10:31**	*3767*
s that they might accuse Him.	**Mt 12:10**	*2443*
S then, it is lawful to do good on	**Mt 12:12**	*5620*
s that the mute man spoke and saw.	**Mt 12:22**	*5620*
s will the Son of Man be three	**Mt 12:40**	*3779*
S He got into a boat and sat	**Mt 13:2**	*5620*
s that THE BIRDS OF THE AIR come	**Mt 13:32**	*5620*
"**S** just as the tares are gathered up	**Mt 13:40**	*3779*
s shall it be at the end of the	**Mt 13:40**	*3779*
"**S** it will be at the end of the	**Mt 13:49**	*3779*
s that they were astonished,	**Mt 13:54**	*5620*
s *much* that he promised with an	**Mt 14:7**	*3606*
s send the crowds away, that	**Mt 14:15**	*3767*
S the crowd marveled as they saw	**Mt 15:31**	*5620*
"Where would we get **s** many loaves	**Mt 15:33**	*5118*
S also the Son of Man is going to	**Mt 17:12**	*3779*
"However, **s** that we do not offend	**Mt 17:27**	*2443, 3361*
"**S** it is not *the* will of your	**Mt 18:14**	*3379*
s that BY THE MOUTH OF TWO OR	**Mt 18:16**	*2443*
"**S** the slave fell *to the ground*	**Mt 18:26**	*3767*
"**S** his fellow slave fell *to the ground*	**Mt 18:29**	*3767*
"**S** when his fellow slaves saw	**Mt 18:31**	*3767*
"**S** they are no longer two, but one	**Mt 19:6**	*5620*
s that He might lay His hands on	**Mt 19:13**	*2443*
will give you.' And **s** they went.	**Mt 20:4**	
"**S** the last shall be first,	**Mt 20:16**	*3779*
afterward **s** as to believe him.	**Mt 21:32**	
s also the second, and the third,	**Mt 22:26**	*3668*
to move them with **s** *much*	**Mt 23:4**	
s that the outside of it may	**Mt 23:26**	*2443*
"**S** you, too, outwardly appear	**Mt 23:28**	*3779*
"**S** you testify against yourselves,	**Mt 23:31**	*5620*
s that upon you may fall *the guilt*	**Mt 23:35**	*3704*
s as to mislead, if possible, even the	**Mt 24:24**	*5620*
"**S** if they say to you, 'Behold,	**Mt 24:26**	*3767*
s will the coming of the Son of	**Mt 24:27**	*3779*
S, you too, when you see all these	**Mt 24:33**	*3779*
s will the coming of the Son of	**Mt 24:39**	*3779*
finds **s** doing when he comes.	**Mt 24:46**	*3779*
"**S**, you *men* could not keep watch	**Mt 26:40**	*3779*
s that they might put Him to death.	**Mt 26:59**	*3704*
s the governor was quite	**Mt 27:14**	*5620*
S when the people gathered together,	**Mt 27:17**	*3767*
s that they debated among	**Mk 1:27**	*5620*
s that I may preach there also; for	**Mk 1:38**	*2443*
s that there was no longer room,	**Mk 2:2**	*5620*
"But **s** that you may know that	**Mk 2:10**	*2443*
s that they were all amazed and	**Mk 2:12**	*5620*
S long as they have the bridegroom	**Mk 2:19**	*3745*
"**S** the Son of Man is Lord even of	**Mk 2:28**	*5620*
s that they might accuse Him.	**Mk 3:2**	*2443*
s that they would not crowd Him;	**Mk 3:9**	*2443*
And He appointed twelve, **s** that they	**Mk 3:14**	*2443*
s that WHILE SEEING, THEY MAY SEE	**Mk 4:12**	*2443*
s that THE BIRDS OF THE AIR can	**Mk 4:32**	*5620*
s far as they were able to hear it;	**Mk 4:33**	*2531a*
breaking over the boat **s** much that	**Mk 4:37**	*5620*
swine **s** that we may enter them."	**Mk 5:12**	*2443*
and **s** He stayed by the seashore.	**Mk 5:21**	
s that she will get well and live."	**Mk 5:23**	*2443*
put him to death and could not *do* **s**;	**Mk 6:19**	
send them away **s** that they may go	**Mk 6:36**	*2443*
s lacking in understanding also?	**Mk 7:18**	*3779*
and *the boy* became **s** much like a	**Mk 9:26**	
s they are no longer two, but one	**Mk 10:8**	*5620*
to Him **s** that He might touch them;	**Mk 10:13**	*2443*
S they called the blind man, saying	**Mk 10:49**	*2532*
s that your Father who is in	**Mk 11:25**	*2443*
and **s** *with* many others, beating	**Mk 12:5**	
And **s** they left Him and went away.	**Mk 12:12**	
and **s** all seven left no children.	**Mk 12:22**	
s in what sense is He his son?"	**Mk 12:37**	*2532*
"Even **s**, you too, when you see	**Mk 13:29**	*3779*
s Pilate was amazed.	**Mk 15:5**	*5620*
s that we may see and believe!"	**Mk 15:32**	*2443*
s that they might come and anoint Him.	**Mk 16:1**	*2443*
S then, when the Lord Jesus had	**Mk 16:19**	*3767*
s that you may know the exact	**Lk 1:4**	*2443*
s as to make ready a people	**Lk 1:17**	
S they came in a hurry and found	**Lk 2:16**	*2532*
S he *began* saying to the crowds	**Lk 3:7**	*3767*
s every tree that does not bear good	**Lk 3:9**	*3767*
S with many other exhortations	**Lk 3:18**	*3767*
S THAT YOU WILL NOT STRIKE YOUR FOOT	**Lk 4:11**	*3379*
S He kept on preaching in	**Lk 4:44**	*2532*
s they signaled to their partners in	**Lk 5:7**	*5620*
boats, **s** that they began to sink.	**Lk 5:7**	*5620*
and **s** also *were* James and John,	**Lk 5:10**	*3668*
"But, **s** that you may know that	**Lk 5:24**	*2443*
s that they might find *reason* to	**Lk 6:7**	*2443*
And he did **s**; and his hand was	**Lk 6:10**	
S which of them will love him more?"	**Lk 7:42**	*3767*
s that SEEING THEY MAY NOT SEE,	**Lk 8:10**	*2443*
s that they will not believe and be	**Lk 8:12**	*2443*
s that those who come in may see	**Lk 8:16**	*2443*
"**S** take care how you listen; for	**Lk 8:18**	*3767*
S they launched out.	**Lk 8:22**	*2532*
S he went away, proclaiming	**Lk 8:39**	*2532*
They did **s**, and had them all	**Lk 9:15**	*3779*
s that they would not perceive it;	**Lk 9:45**	*2443*
and bothered about **s** many things;	**Lk 10:41**	
"**S** I say to you, ask, and it will	**Lk 11:9**	*2532*
S they will be your judges.	**Lk 11:19**	*1223, 3778*
s will the Son of Man be to this	**Lk 11:30**	*3779*
s that those who enter may see	**Lk 11:33**	*2443*
"**S** you are witnesses and approve	**Lk 11:48**	*686*
s that the blood of all the prophets,	**Lk 11:50**	*2443*
after **s** many thousands of people	**Lk 12:1**	
"**S** is the man who stores up	**Lk 12:21**	*3779*
God **s** clothes the grass in the field,	**Lk 12:28**	*3779*
s that they may immediately open	**Lk 12:36**	*2443*
in the third, and finds *them* **s**,	**Lk 12:38**	*3779*
finds **s** doing when he comes.	**Lk 12:43**	*3779*
is coming,' and **s** it turns out.	**Lk 12:54**	*3779*

s that he may not drag you before Lk 12:58 *3379*
s come during them and get healed, Lk 13:14 *3767*
S He was saying, "What is Lk 13:18 *3767*
s that when the one who has Lk 14:10 *2443*
s that my house may be filled. Lk 14:23 *2443*
"**S** *then, none* of you can Lk 14:33 *3779*
S He told them this parable, saying, Lk 15:3 *1161*
S he divided his wealth between Lk 15:12 *1161*
"**S** he went and hired himself out to Lk 15:15 *2532*
"**S** he got up and came to his father. Lk 15:20 *2532*
For **s** many years I have been Lk 15:29 *5118*
s that I might celebrate with my Lk 15:29 *5118*
s that when I am removed from the Lk 16:4 *2443*
s that when it fails, they will Lk 16:9 *2443*
and send Lazarus **s** that he may dip Lk 16:24 *2443*
s that those who wish to come over Lk 16:26 *3704*
s that they will not also come to Lk 16:28 *2443*
"**S** you too, when you do all the Lk 17:10 *3779*
s will the Son of Man be in His Lk 17:24 *3779*
s it will be also in the days of Lk 17:26 *3779*
to Him **s** that He would touch them, Lk 18:15 *2443*
S he ran on ahead and climbed up into Lk 19:4 *2532*
S He said, "A nobleman went to a Lk 19:12 *3767*
be called to him **s** that he might know Lk 19:15 *2443*
S those who were sent went away Lk 19:32 *1161*
S they answered that they did not Lk 20:7 *2532*
s that they would give him *some* Lk 20:10 *2443*
let us kill him **s** that Lk 20:14 *2443*
"**S** they threw him out of Lk 20:15 *2532*
S they watched Him, and sent spies Lk 20:20 *5620*
s that they *could* deliver Him to the rule Lk 20:20 *5620*
"**S** make up your minds not to Lk 21:14 *3767*
s that all things which are written Lk 21:22
"**S** you also, when you see these Lk 21:31 *3779*
"Be on guard, **s** that your hearts Lk 21:34 *3379*
S he consented, and *began* Lk 22:6 *2532*
s that we may eat it." Lk 22:8 *2443*
S Pilate asked Him, saying, "Are Lk 23:3 *1161*
S He went in to stay with them. Lk 24:29 *2532*
s that all might believe through him. Jn 1:7 *2443*
s that we may give an answer to Jn 1:22 *2443*
not recognize Him, but **s** that Jn 1:31 *2443*
S they came and saw where He was Jn 1:39 *3767*
S they filled them up to the brim. Jn 2:7 *2532*
S they took it *to him.* Jn 2:8 *1161*
S when He was raised from the dead, Jn 2:22 *3767*
s is everyone who is born of the Jn 3:8 *3779*
even **s** must the Son of Man be Jn 3:14 *3779*
s that whoever believes will in Him Jn 3:15 *2443*
"For God **s** loved the world, that Jn 3:16 *3779*
s that his deeds may be manifested as Jn 3:21 *2443*
S this joy of mine has been made full. Jn 3:29 *3767*
S He came to a city of Samaria called Jn 4:5 *3767*
and Jacob's well was there. **S** Jesus, Jn 4:6 *3767*
water, **s** I will not be thirsty nor Jn 4:15 *2443*
S the woman left her waterpot, and Jn 4:28 *3767*
S the disciples were saying to one Jn 4:33 *3767*
s that he who sows and he who reaps Jn 4:36 *2443*
S when the Samaritans came to Jesus, Jn 4:40 *3767*
S when He came to Galilee, the Jn 4:45 *3767*
S Jesus said to him, "Unless you Jn 4:48 *3767*
S he inquired of them the hour Jn 4:52 *3767*
S the father knew that *it was* at Jn 4:53 *3767*
S the Jews were saying to the man who Jn 5:10 *3767*
s that nothing worse happens Jn 5:14 *2443*
s that you will marvel. Jn 5:20 *2443*
even **s** the Son also gives life to Jn 5:21 *3779*
s that all will honor the Son even as Jn 5:23 *2443*
even **s** He gave to the Son also to Jn 5:26 *3779*
but I say these things **s** that you may Jn 5:34 *2443*
are unwilling to come to Me **s** that Jn 5:40 *2443*
s that these may eat?" Jn 6:5 *2443*
are these for **s** many people?" Jn 6:9 *5118*
S the men sat down, in number Jn 6:10 *3767*
up the leftover fragments **s** that Jn 6:12 *2443*
S they gathered them up, and filled Jn 6:13 *3767*
S Jesus, perceiving that they were Jn 6:15 *3767*
S they were willing to receive Him Jn 6:21 *3767*
S when the crowd saw that Jesus was Jn 6:24 *3767*
s that we may work the works of God?" Jn 6:28 *2443*
S they said to Him, "What then do Jn 6:30 *3767*
s that we may see, and believe You? Jn 6:30 *2443*
s that one may eat of it and not Jn 6:50 *2443*
S Jesus said to them, "Truly, Jn 6:53 *3767*
of the Father, **s** he who eats Me, Jn 6:57 *2532*
S Jesus said to the twelve, "You do Jn 6:67 *3767*
s that Your disciples also may see Jn 7:3 *2443*
S Jesus said to them, "My time is Jn 7:6 *3767*
S the Jews were seeking Him at Jn 7:11 *3767*
S Jesus answered them and said, "My Jn 7:16 *3767*
on *the* Sabbath **s** that Jn 7:23 *2443*
S some of the people of Jerusalem Jn 7:25 *3767*
S they were seeking to seize Him; Jn 7:30 *3767*
S a division occurred in the Jn 7:43 *3767*
s that they might have grounds for Jn 8:6 *2443*
S the Pharisees said to Him, "You Jn 8:13 *3767*
S they were saying to Him, "Where Jn 8:19 *3767*
S the Jews were saying, "Surely He Jn 8:22 *3767*
S they were saying to Him, "Who are Jn 8:25 *3767*
S Jesus said, "When you lift up Jn 8:28 *3767*
S Jesus was saying to those Jews who Jn 8:31 *3767*
"**S** if the Son makes you free, you Jn 8:36 *3767*
S the Jews said to Him, "You are Jn 8:57 *3767*
but *it was* **s** that the works of Jn 9:3 *2443*
S he went away and washed, and came Jn 9:7 *3767*
S they were saying to him, "How Jn 9:10 *3767*
S I went away and washed, and I Jn 9:11 *3767*
S they said to the blind man again, Jn 9:17 *3767*
S a second time they called the Jn 9:24 *3767*
S they said to him, "What did He do Jn 9:26 *3767*
S they put him out. Jn 9:34 *2532*
s that those who do not see may see, Jn 9:39 *2443*
S Jesus said to them again, "Truly, Jn 10:7 *3767*
because I lay down My life **s** that I Jn 10:17 *2443*
s that you may know and understand Jn 10:38 *2443*
S the sisters sent *word* to Him, Jn 11:3 *3767*
s that the Son of God may be Jn 11:4 *2443*
S when He heard that he was sick, He Jn 11:6 *3767*
s that I may awaken him out of sleep." Jn 11:11 *2443*
S Jesus then said to them plainly, Jn 11:14 *3767*
not there, **s** that you may believe; Jn 11:15 *2443*
s that we may die with Him." Jn 11:16 *2443*
S when Jesus came, He found that Jn 11:17 *3767*
S the Jews were saying, "See how He Jn 11:36 *3767*
S Jesus, again being deeply moved Jn 11:38 *3767*
S they removed the stone. Then Jesus Jn 11:41 *3767*
s that they may believe that You sent Jn 11:42 *2443*
S from that day on they planned Jn 11:53 *3767*
S they were seeking for Jesus, Jn 11:56 *3767*
s that they might seize Him. Jn 11:57 *3704*
S they made Him a supper there, Jn 12:2 *3767*
s that she may keep it for the day of Jn 12:7 *2443*
S the people, who were with Him when Jn 12:17 *3767*
S the Pharisees said to one another, Jn 12:19 *3767*
S the crowd *of people* who stood Jn 12:29 *3767*
S Jesus said to them, "For a little Jn 12:35 *3767*
s that darkness will not overtake you; Jn 12:35 *2443*
s that you may become sons of Light." Jn 12:36 *2443*
He had performed **s** many signs Jn 12:37 *5118*
S THAT THEY WOULD NOT SEE WITH THEIR Jn 12:40 *2443, 3361*
s that everyone who believes in Me Jn 12:46 *2443*
S He came to Simon Peter. He said to Jn 13:6 *3767*
S when He had washed their feet, Jn 13:12 *3767*
you are right, for **s** I am. Jn 13:13
pass, **s** that when it does occur, Jn 13:19 *2443*
S Simon Peter gestured to him, Jn 13:24 *3767*
S when He had dipped the morsel, Jn 13:26 *3767*
S after receiving the morsel he went Jn 13:30 *3767*
if it were not **s**, I would have Jn 14:2
"Have I been **s** long with you, and Jn 14:9 *5118*
s that the Father may be glorified in Jn 14:13 *2443*
s that when it happens, you may Jn 14:29 *2443*
but **s** that the world may know that I Jn 14:31 *3779*
He prunes it **s** that it may bear more Jn 15:2 *2443*
in the vine, **s** neither *can* you unless Jn 15:4 *3779*
and **s** prove to be My disciples. Jn 15:8
things I have spoken to you **s** that Jn 15:11 *2443*
s that whatever you ask of the Father Jn 15:16 *2443*
things I have spoken to you **s** that Jn 16:1 *2443*
s that when their hour comes, you Jn 16:4 *2443*
S they were saying, "What is this Jn 16:18 *3767*
s that your joy may be made full. Jn 16:24 *2443*
s that in Me you may have peace. In Jn 16:33 *2443*
s that the Scripture would be Jn 17:12 *2443*
things I speak in the world **s** that Jn 17:13 *2443*
s that the world may believe that You Jn 17:21 *2443*
s that the world may know that You Jn 17:23 *2443*
s that they may see My glory which Jn 17:24 *2443*
s that the love with which You loved Jn 17:26 *2443*
S Jesus, knowing all the things that Jn 18:4 *3767*
S when He said to them, "I am *He* Jn 18:6 *3767*
S if you seek Me, let these go their Jn 18:8 *3767*
S Jesus said to Peter, "Put Jn 18:11 *3767*
S the *Roman* cohort and the Jn 18:12 *3767*
and **s** *was* another disciple. Jn 18:15
S the other disciple, who was Jn 18:16 *3767*
S Annas sent Him bound to Caiaphas Jn 18:24 *3767*
S they said to him, "You are not Jn 18:25 *3767*
enter into the Praetorium **s** that Jn 18:28 *2443*
S Pilate said to them, "Take Him Jn 18:31 *3767*
My servants would be fighting **s** that Jn 18:36 *2443*
"**S** You are a king?" Jn 18:37 *3766*
S they cried out again, saying, Jn 18:40 *3767*
I am bringing Him out to you **s** that Jn 19:4 *2443*
S when the chief priests Jn 19:6 *3767*
S Pilate said to Him, "You do not Jn 19:10 *3767*
S they cried out, "Away with *Him,* Jn 19:15 *3767*
S he then handed Him over to them Jn 19:16 *3767*
S the chief priests of the Jews were Jn 19:21 *3767*
S they said to one another, "Let us Jn 19:24 *3767*
S they put a sponge full of the Jn 19:29 *3767*
s that the bodies would not Jn 19:31 *2443*
S the soldiers came, and broke Jn 19:32 *3767*
s that you also may believe. Jn 19:35 *2443*
S he came and took away His body. Jn 19:38 *3767*
S they took the body of Jesus Jn 19:40 *3767*
S she ran and came to Simon Peter Jn 20:2 *3767*
S Peter and the other disciple went Jn 20:3 *3767*
And **s** Simon Peter also came, Jn 20:6 *3767*
S the other disciple who had first Jn 20:8 *3767*
S the disciples went away again to Jn 20:10 *3767*
and **s**, as she wept, she stooped Jn 20:11 *3767*
S when it was evening on that day, Jn 20:19 *3767*
S Jesus said to them again, "Peace Jn 20:21 *3767*
S the other disciples were saying to Jn 20:25 *3767*
but these have been written **s** that Jn 20:31 *2443*
S Jesus said to them, "Children, Jn 21:5 *3767*
S they cast, and then they were not Jn 21:6 *3767*
S when Simon Peter heard that it was Jn 21:7 *3767*
S when they got out on the land, Jn 21:9 *3767*
and although there were **s** many, Jn 21:11 *5118*
S when they had finished Jn 21:15 *3767*
S Peter seeing him said to Jesus, Jn 21:21 *3767*
S when they had come together, they Ac 1:6 *3767*
s that in their own language that Ac 1:19 *5620*
S they put forward two men, Joseph Ac 1:23 *2532*
S THAT I WILL NOT BE SHAKEN. Ac 2:25 *2443*
"And **s**, because he was a prophet and Ac 2:30 *3767*
S then, those who had received his Ac 2:41 *3767*
repent and return, **s** that Ac 3:19 *1519*
"But **s** that it will not spread any Ac 4:17 *2443*
s that when Peter came by at Ac 5:15 *2443*
and **s** *is* the Holy Spirit, whom Ac 5:32
"**S** in the present case, I say to Ac 5:38 *2532*
S they went on their way from the Ac 5:41 *3767*
S the twelve summoned Ac 6:2 *1161*
"Are these things **s**?" Ac 7:1 *3779*
and **s** *Abraham* became the father of Ac 7:8 *3779*
s that they would expose their Ac 7:19
S there was much rejoicing in that Ac 8:8 *1161*
s that everyone on whom I lay my Ac 8:19 *2443*
s that nothing of what you have Ac 8:24 *3704*
S, when they had solemnly testified Ac 8:25 *3767*
S he got up and went; and there was Ac 8:27 *2532*
S HE DOES NOT OPEN HIS MOUTH. Ac 8:32 *3779*
s that if he found any belonging Ac 9:2 *3704*
s that he might regain his sight." Ac 9:12 *3704*
S Ananias departed and entered Ac 9:17 *3704*
s that you may regain your sight and Ac 9:17 *3704*
s that they might put him to death; Ac 9:24 *3704*
S the church throughout all Judea Ac 9:31 *3767*
S Peter arose and went with them. Ac 9:39 *1161*
S he invited them in and gave them Ac 10:23 *3767*
S I ask for what reason you have sent Ac 10:29 *3767*
"**S** I sent for you immediately, Ac 10:33 *3767*
S then those who were scattered Ac 11:19 *3767*
S Peter was kept in the prison, Ac 12:5 *3767*
put on your sandals." And he did **s**. Ac 12:8 *3779*
she kept insisting that it was **s**. Ac 12:15 *3779*
S, being sent out by the Holy Ac 13:4 *3767*
But Elymas the magician (for **s** his Ac 13:8 *3779*
s that the thing spoken of in the Ac 13:40 *3361*
"For **s** the Lord has commanded us, Ac 13:47 *3779*
S THAT THE REST OF MANKIND MAY SEEK Ac 15:17 *3704*
S when they were sent away, they Ac 15:30 *3767*
S the churches were being Ac 16:5 *3767*
S putting out to sea from Troas, we Ac 16:11 *3767*
s that the foundations of the Ac 16:26 *5620*
see whether these things were **s**. Ac 17:11 *3779*
S he was reasoning in the Ac 17:17 *3767*
s we want to know what these things Ac 17:20 *3767*
S Paul stood in the midst of Ac 17:22 *1161*
S Paul went out of their midst. Ac 17:33 *3779*
s that all who lived in Asia heard Ac 19:10 *5620*
s that handkerchiefs or aprons Ac 19:12 *5620*
s that they fled out of that house Ac 19:16 *5620*
S the word of the Lord was growing Ac 19:20 *3779*
S then, some were shouting one Ac 19:32 *3767*
"**S**, since these are undeniable Ac 19:36 *3767*
"**S** then, if Demetrius and the Ac 19:38 *3767*
for **s** he had arranged it, intending Ac 20:13 *3779*
to sail past Ephesus **s** that Ac 20:16 *3704*
s that I may finish my course Ac 20:24 *5613*
and pay their expenses **s** that they Ac 21:24 *2443*
s that he might find out the reason Ac 22:24 *2443*
s you must witness at Rome also." Ac 23:11 *3779*
S he took him and led him to the Ac 23:18 *3767*
"**S** do not listen to them, for Ac 23:21 *3767*
S the commander let the young man go, Ac 23:22 *3767*
S the soldiers, in accordance with Ac 23:31 *3767*
that these things were **s**. Ac 24:9 *3779*
"**S** after they had assembled here, I Ac 25:17 *3767*
S, on the next day when Agrippa came Ac 25:23 *3767*
s that after the investigation has Ac 25:26 *3704*
"**S** then, all Jews know my manner Ac 26:4 *3767*
"**S** then, I thought to myself that Ac 26:9 *3767*
"While **s** engaged as I was journeying Ac 26:12 *3739*
s that they may turn from darkness Ac 26:18
"**S**, King Agrippa, I did not prove Ac 26:19 *3606*
"**S**, having obtained help from God, Ac 26:22 *3767*
s that none *of them* would swim Ac 27:42
And **s** it happened that they all were Ac 27:44 *3779*
For I long to see you **s** that I may Ro 1:11 *2443*
to you (and have been prevented **s** Ro 1:13 *2443*
have been prevented so far) **s** that Ro 1:13 *2443*
S, for my part, I am eager to Ro 1:15 *3779*
s that they are without excuse. Ro 1:20 *1519*
s that their bodies would be Ro 1:24 *1519*
S if the uncircumcised man keeps Ro 2:26 *3767*
s that every mouth may be closed Ro 3:19 *2443*
s that He would be just Ro 3:26 *1519*
s that he might be the father of all Ro 4:11 *1519*
s that the promise will be guaranteed Ro 4:16 *1519*
against hope he believed, **s** that Ro 4:18 *3779*
"**S** SHALL YOUR DESCENDANTS BE." Ro 4:18 *3779*
and **s** death spread to all men, Ro 5:12 *3779*
S then as through one transgression Ro 5:18 *686*
even **s** through one act of Ro 5:18 *3779*
even **s** through the obedience of Ro 5:19 *3779*
The Law came in **s** that Ro 5:20 *2443*
s that, as sin reigned in death, Ro 5:21 *3779*
even **s** grace would reign through Ro 5:21 *3779*
Are we to continue in sin **s** that Ro 6:1 *2443*
s that as Christ was raised from Ro 6:4 *3779*
s we too might walk in newness of Ro 6:4 *3779*
s that we would no longer be slaves Ro 6:6
Even **s** consider yourselves to be Ro 6:11 *3779*
reign in your mortal body **s** that Ro 6:12 *1519*
s now present your members as Ro 6:19 *3779*
S then, if while her husband is Ro 7:3 *686*
s that she is not an adulteress though Ro 7:3
s that you might be joined to another, Ro 7:4 *1519*
s that we serve in newness of the Ro 7:6 *5620*
S then, the Law is holy, and the Ro 7:12 *5620*
s that through the commandment sin Ro 7:13 *2443*
S now, no longer am I the one Ro 7:17 *1161*

S then, on the one hand I myself	**Ro 7:25**	*686*
s that the requirement of the Law	**Ro 8:4**	*2443*
for it is not even able *to do* **s**,	**Ro 8:7**	
S then, brethren, we are under	**Ro 8:12**	*686*
we suffer with *Him* **s** that	**Ro 8:17**	*2443*
s that He would be the firstborn	**Ro 8:29**	*1519*
s that God's purpose according to	**Ro 9:11**	*2443*
S then it *does* not *depend* on the	**Ro 9:16**	*686*
S then He has mercy on whom He	**Ro 9:18**	*686*
And *He did* **s** to make known	**Ro 9:23**	
S faith *comes* from hearing, and	**Ro 10:17**	*686*
they did not stumble **s** as to fall,	**Ro 11:11**	*2443*
s that I might be grafted in."	**Ro 11:19**	*2443*
of this mystery—**s** that	**Ro 11:25**	
		2443, 3361
and **s** all Israel will be saved; just	**Ro 11:26**	*3779*
s these also now have been	**Ro 11:31**	*3779*
shut up all in disobedience **s** that	**Ro 11:32**	*2443*
s that you may prove what the will of	**Ro 12:2**	*1519*
think **s** as to have sound judgment,	**Ro 12:3**	*1519*
s we, who are many, are one body	**Ro 12:5**	*3779*
s far as it depends on you,	**Ro 12:18**	
FOR IN **S** DOING YOU WILL HEAP	**Ro 12:20**	*3778*
he who eats, does **s** for the Lord,	**Ro 14:6**	*2068*
S then each one of us will give	**Ro 14:12**	*686*
S then we pursue the things	**Ro 14:19**	*686*
s that through perseverance	**Ro 15:4**	*2443*
s that with one accord you may with	**Ro 15:6**	*2443*
s that you will abound in hope by	**Ro 15:13**	*1519*
points **s** as to remind you again,	**Ro 15:15**	*5613*
s that *my* offering of	**Ro 15:16**	*2443*
s that from Jerusalem and round	**Ro 15:19**	*5620*
s that I would not build on another	**Ro 15:20**	*2443*
Yes, they were pleased *to do* **s**,	**Ro 15:27**	
s that I may come to you in joy by	**Ro 15:32**	*2443*
and **s** *do* Lucius and Jason	**Ro 16:21**	
s that you are not lacking in any	**1Co 1:7**	*5620*
s that no one would say you were	**1Co 1:15**	*2443*
s that the cross of Christ would not	**1Co 1:17**	*2443*
s that He may nullify the things that	**1Co 1:28**	*2443*
s that no man may boast before God.	**1Co 1:29**	*3704*
s that, just as it is written,	**1Co 1:31**	*2443*
s that your faith would not rest on	**1Co 2:5**	*2443*
Even **s** the *thoughts* of God no one	**1Co 2:11**	*3779*
s that we may know the things freely	**1Co 2:12**	*2443*
S then neither the one who plants	**1Co 3:7**	*5620*
be saved, yet **s** as through fire.	**1Co 3:15**	*3779*
s that he may become wise.	**1Co 3:18**	*2443*
S then let no one boast in men.	**1Co 3:21**	*5620*
s that in us you may learn not to	**1Co 4:6**	*2443*
s that no one of you will become	**1Co 4:6**	*2443*
s that we also might reign with you.	**1Co 4:8**	*2443*
s that the one who had done this deed	**1Co 5:2**	*2443*
him who has **s** committed this,	**1Co 5:3**	*3779*
s that his spirit may be saved in	**1Co 5:5**	*2443*
Clean out the old leaven **s** that you	**1Co 5:7**	*2443*
S if you have law courts dealing with	**1Co 6:4**	*3767*
Is it **s**, *that* there is not among	**1Co 6:5**	*3779*
s that you may devote yourselves to	**1Co 7:5**	
		2443, 3361
and come together again **s** that Satan	**1Co 7:5**	
		2443, 3361
And **s** I direct in all the churches.	**1Co 7:17**	*3779*
s that from now on those who have	**1Co 7:29**	*2443*
past her youth, and if it must be **s**,	**1Co 7:36**	*3779*
S then both he who gives his own	**1Co 7:38**	*5620*
And **s**, by sinning against	**1Co 8:12**	*3779*
s that I will not cause my brother to	**1Co 8:13**	*2443*
but we endure all things **s** that we	**1Co 9:12**	*2443*
S also the Lord directed those who	**1Co 9:14**	*3779*
am not writing these things **s** that	**1Co 9:15**	*3779*
that it will be done **s** in my case;	**1Co 9:15**	*3779*
s as not to make full use of my	**1Co 9:18**	*1519*
s that I may win more.	**1Co 9:19**	*2443*
Jews I became as a Jew, **s** that	**1Co 9:20**	*2443*
s that I might win those who are	**1Co 9:20**	*2443*
s that I might win those who are	**1Co 9:21**	*2443*
s that I may by all means save some.	**1Co 9:22**	*2443*
s that I may become a fellow partaker	**1Co 9:23**	*2443*
s that, after I have preached to	**1Co 9:27**	
s that we would not crave evil things	**1Co 10:6**	*1519*
s that you will be able to endure it.	**1Co 10:13**	
s that they may be saved.	**1Co 10:33**	*2443*
s also the man *has his birth*	**1Co 11:12**	*3779*
s that those who are approved may	**1Co 11:19**	*2443*
in **s** doing he is to eat of the bread	**1Co 11:28**	*3779*
we are disciplined by the Lord **s** that	**1Co 11:32**	*2443*
S then, my brethren, when you come	**1Co 11:33**	*5620*
s that you will not come together	**1Co 11:34**	*2443*
are one body, **s** also is Christ.	**1Co 12:12**	*3779*
But God has **s** composed the body,	**1Co 12:24**	
s that there may be no division in	**1Co 12:25**	*2443*
faith, **s** as to remove mountains,	**1Co 13:2**	*5620*
s that the church may receive	**1Co 14:5**	*2443*
S also you, unless you utter by	**1Co 14:9**	*3779*
S also you, since you are zealous	**1Co 14:12**	*3779*
five words with my mind **s** that	**1Co 14:19**	*2443*
S THEY WILL NOT LISTEN TO ME,"	**1Co 14:21**	*3779*
S then tongues are for a sign, not	**1Co 14:22**	*5620*
and **s** he will fall on his face and	**1Co 14:25**	*3779*
s that all may learn and all may	**1Co 14:31**	*2443*
s we preach and so you believed.	**1Co 15:11**	*3779*
so we preach and **s** you believed.	**1Co 15:11**	*3779*
s also in Christ all will be made	**1Co 15:22**	*3779*
s that God may be all in all.	**1Co 15:28**	*2443*
S also is the resurrection of the	**1Co 15:42**	*3779*
S also it is written,	**1Co 15:45**	*3779*
s also are those who are earthy;	**1Co 15:48**	*5108*
s also are those who are heavenly.	**1Co 15:48**	*5108*

of Galatia, **s** do you also.	**1Co 16:1**	*3779*
s that no collections be made when I	**1Co 16:2**	*2443*
s that you may send me on my way	**1Co 16:6**	*2443*
S let no one despise him. But send	**1Co 16:11**	*2443*
peace, **s** that he may come to me;	**1Co 16:11**	*2443*
s that we will be able to comfort	**2Co 1:4**	*1519*
s also our comfort is abundant	**2Co 1:5**	*3779*
s also you are *sharers* of our	**2Co 1:7**	*3779*
s that we despaired even of life;	**2Co 1:8**	*5620*
of death within ourselves **s** that	**2Co 1:9**	*2443*
us from **s** great a *peril of* death,	**2Co 1:10**	*5082*
s that thanks may be given by many	**2Co 1:11**	*2443*
s that you might twice receive a	**2Co 1:15**	*2443*
s that with me there will be yes,	**2Co 1:17**	*2443*
s that when I came, I would not have	**2Co 2:3**	
		2443, 3361
not **s** that you would be made	**2Co 2:4**	*2443*
s that on the contrary you should	**2Co 2:7**	*5620*
For to this end also I wrote, **s** that	**2Co 2:9**	*2443*
s that no advantage would be taken of	**2Co 2:11**	*2443*
s that the sons of Israel could	**2Co 3:7**	*5620*
to put a veil over his face **s** that	**2Co 3:13**	*4314*
the minds of the unbelieving **s** that	**2Co 4:4**	*1519*
s that the surpassing greatness of	**2Co 4:7**	*2443*
s that the life of Jesus also may be	**2Co 4:10**	*2443*
s that the life of Jesus also may be	**2Co 4:11**	*2443*
S death works in us, but life in	**2Co 4:12**	*5620*
s that the grace which is spreading	**2Co 4:15**	*2443*
s that what is mortal will be	**2Co 5:4**	*2443*
s that each one may be recompensed	**2Co 5:10**	*2443*
s that you will have *an answer*	**2Co 5:12**	*2443*
and He died for all, **s** that they who	**2Co 5:15**	*2443*
s that we might become	**2Co 5:21**	*2443*
s that the ministry will not be	**2Co 6:3**	*2443*
s that I rejoiced even more.	**2Co 7:7**	*5620*
s that you might not suffer loss in	**2Co 7:9**	*2443*
S although I wrote to you, *it was*	**2Co 7:12**	*686*
s also our boasting before Titus	**2Co 7:14**	*3779*
S we urged Titus that as he had	**2Co 8:6**	*3779*
s he would also complete in you	**2Co 8:6**	*3779*
s that you through His poverty might	**2Co 8:9**	*2443*
But now finish doing it also, **s** that	**2Co 8:11**	*3779*
s *there may be* also the completion	**2Co 8:11**	*3779*
s that their abundance also may	**2Co 8:14**	*2443*
taking precaution **s** that no one will	**2Co 8:20**	
s that, as I was saying, you may be	**2Co 9:3**	*2443*
S I thought it necessary to urge	**2Co 9:5**	*3767*
s that the same would be ready as a	**2Co 9:5**	*3767*
s that always having all sufficiency	**2Co 9:8**	*2443*
as he is Christ's, **s** also are we.	**2Co 10:7**	*3779*
s as to preach the gospel even to	**2Co 10:16**	*1519*
s that to Christ I might present you	**2Co 11:2**	
yet I am not **s** in knowledge;	**2Co 11:6**	
a sin in humbling myself **s** that	**2Co 11:7**	*2443*
to you, and will continue to do **s**.	**2Co 11:9**	
s that I may cut off opportunity from	**2Co 11:12**	*2443*
s that I also may boast a little.	**2Co 11:16**	*2443*
For you, being **s** wise, tolerate	**2Co 11:19**	*2443*
Are they Hebrews? **S** am I.	**2Co 11:22**	*2532*
Are they Israelites? **S** am I.	**2Co 11:22**	*2532*
descendants of Abraham? **S** am I.	**2Co 11:22**	*2532*
I more **s**; in far more labors,	**2Co 11:23**	*5228*
and **s** escaped his hands.	**2Co 11:33**	
s that no one will credit me with	**2Co 12:6**	*3361*
s that the power of Christ may dwell	**2Co 12:9**	*2443*
s that when present I *need* not	**2Co 13:10**	*2443*
who gave Himself for our sins **s** that	**Ga 1:4**	*3704*
that you are **s** quickly deserting Him	**Ga 1:6**	*3779*
said before, **s** I say again now,	**Ga 1:9**	*2532*
to reveal His Son in me **s** that I	**Ga 1:16**	*2443*
but *I did* **s** in private to those	**Ga 2:2**	
s that the truth of the gospel	**Ga 2:5**	*2443*
s that we *might go* to	**Ga 2:9**	*2443*
s that we may be justified by faith	**Ga 2:16**	*2443*
s that I might live to God.	**Ga 2:19**	*2443*
Are you **s** foolish?	**Ga 3:3**	*3779*
Did you suffer **s** many things in	**Ga 3:4**	*5118*
S then, does He who provides you	**Ga 3:5**	*3767*
Even **s** Abraham BELIEVED GOD, AND	**Ga 3:6**	*2531a*
S then those who are of faith are	**Ga 3:9**	*5620*
s that we would receive the	**Ga 3:14**	*2443*
God, **s** as to nullify the promise.	**Ga 3:17**	*1519*
s that the promise by faith in Jesus	**Ga 3:22**	*2443*
s that we may be justified by faith.	**Ga 3:24**	*2443*
S also we, while we were children,	**Ga 4:3**	*3779*
s that He might redeem those who were	**Ga 4:5**	*2443*
S have I become your enemy by telling	**Ga 4:16**	*5620*
but they wish to shut you out **s** that	**Ga 4:17**	*2443*
to the Spirit, **s** it is now also.	**Ga 4:29**	*3779*
S then, brethren, we are not	**Ga 4:31**	*1352*
s that you may not do the things	**Ga 5:17**	*2443*
s that you too will not be tempted.	**Ga 6:1**	*3361*
S then, while we have opportunity,	**Ga 6:10**	*686*
simply **s** that they will not be	**Ga 6:12**	*2443*
desire to have you circumcised **s** that	**Ga 6:13**	*2443*
s that you will know what is the	**Eph 1:18**	*1519*
s that in the ages to come He might	**Eph 2:7**	*2443*
not as a result of works, **s** that no	**Eph 2:9**	*2443*
which God prepared beforehand **s** that	**Eph 2:10**	*2443*
s that in Himself He might make	**Eph 2:15**	*2443*
S then you are no longer strangers	**Eph 2:19**	*686*
s that the manifold wisdom of God	**Eph 3:10**	*2443*
s that Christ may dwell in your	**Eph 3:17**	
s that He might fill all things.)	**Eph 4:10**	*2443*
S this I say, and affirm together	**Eph 4:17**	*3767*
s that he will have *something* to	**Eph 4:28**	*2443*
s that it will give grace to those	**Eph 4:29**	*2443*
S then do not be foolish, but	**Eph 5:17**	
		1223, 3778

s also the wives *ought to be* to	**Eph 5:24**	*3779*
s that He might sanctify her, having	**Eph 5:26**	*2443*
S husbands ought also to love	**Eph 5:28**	*3779*
S THAT IT MAY BE WELL WITH YOU,	**Eph 6:3**	*2443*
Put on the full armor of God, **s** that	**Eph 6:11**	*4314*
s that you will be able to resist in	**Eph 6:13**	*2443*
s that you may know about us,	**Eph 6:22**	*2443*
s that you may approve the things	**Php 1:10**	*1519*
s that my imprisonment in *the*	**Php 1:13**	*5620*
s that your proud confidence in me	**Php 1:26**	*2443*
s that whether I come and see you	**Php 1:27**	*2443*
s that at the name of Jesus EVERY	**Php 2:10**	*2443*
S then, my beloved, just as you	**Php 2:12**	*5620*
s that you will prove yourselves to	**Php 2:15**	*2443*
s that in the day of Christ I will	**Php 2:16**	*1519*
s that I also may be encouraged	**Php 2:19**	*2443*
s that I would not have sorrow upon	**Php 2:27**	
		2443, 3361
sent him all the more eagerly **s** that	**Php 2:28**	*2443*
and count them but rubbish **s** that I	**Php 3:8**	*2443*
but I press on **s** that I may lay hold	**Php 3:12**	*2532*
s that you will walk in a manner	**Col 1:10**	
s that He Himself will come to	**Col 1:18**	*2443*
s that I might fully carry out the	**Col 1:25**	
s that we may present every man	**Col 1:28**	*2443*
I say this **s** that no one will delude	**Col 2:4**	*2443*
s walk in Him,	**Col 2:6**	
S, as those who have been chosen of	**Col 3:12**	*3767*
forgave you, **s** also should you.	**Col 3:13**	*3779*
s that they will not lose heart.	**Col 3:21**	*2443*
s that we may speak forth the	**Col 4:3**	
s that you will know how you should	**Col 4:6**	
s that you became an example to	**1Th 1:7**	*5620*
s that we have no need to say	**1Th 1:8**	*5620*
with the gospel, **s** we speak,	**1Th 2:4**	*3779*
Having **s** fond an affection for you,	**1Th 2:8**	*3779*
s as not to be a burden to any of	**1Th 2:9**	*4314*
You are witnesses, and **s** *is* God,	**1Th 2:10**	
s that you would walk in a manner	**1Th 2:12**	*1519*
speaking to the Gentiles **s** that	**1Th 2:16**	*2443*
s that no one would be disturbed by	**1Th 3:3**	
and **s** it came to pass, as you know.	**1Th 3:4**	*2531a*
s that He may establish your	**1Th 3:13**	*1519*
S, he who rejects *this* is not	**1Th 4:8**	*5105*
s that you will behave properly	**1Th 4:12**	*2443*
s that you will not grieve as do	**1Th 4:13**	*2443*
even **s** God will bring with Him	**1Th 4:14**	*3779*
and **s** we shall always be with	**1Th 4:17**	*3779*
s then let us not sleep as others	**1Th 5:6**	*686*
who died for us, **s** that whether we	**1Th 5:10**	*2443*
s that you will be considered worthy	**2Th 1:5**	*1519*
s that the name of our Lord Jesus	**2Th 1:12**	*3704*
s that he takes his seat in the	**2Th 2:4**	*5620*
s that in his time he will be	**2Th 2:6**	*1519*
only he who now restrains *will do* **s**	**2Th 2:7**	
of the truth **s** as to be saved.	**2Th 2:10**	*1519*
s that they will believe what is	**2Th 2:11**	*1519*
S then, brethren, stand firm and	**2Th 2:15**	*686*
s that we would not be a burden to	**2Th 3:8**	*4314*
s that you would follow our example.	**2Th 3:9**	*1519*
s that he will be put to shame.	**2Th 3:14**	*2443*
remain on at Ephesus **s** that you may	**1Tm 1:3**	*2443*
this reason I found mercy, **s** that	**1Tm 1:16**	*2443*
s that they will be taught not to	**1Tm 1:20**	*2443*
s that we may lead a tranquil	**1Tm 2:2**	*2443*
and not a new convert, **s** that he	**1Tm 3:6**	
		2443, 3361
s that he will not fall into	**1Tm 3:7**	*2443*
I write **s** that you will know how	**1Tm 3:15**	*2443*
s that your progress will be	**1Tm 4:15**	*2443*
s that they may be above reproach.	**1Tm 5:7**	*2443*
s that it may assist those who are	**1Tm 5:16**	*2443*
s that the rest also will be	**1Tm 5:20**	*2443*
s that the name of God and *our*	**1Tm 6:1**	*2443*
s we cannot take anything out of	**1Tm 6:7**	*3754*
s that they may take hold of that	**1Tm 6:19**	*2443*
s that I may be filled with joy.	**2Tm 1:4**	*2443*
s that he may please the one who	**2Tm 2:4**	*2443*
s that they also may obtain	**2Tm 2:10**	*2443*
s these *men* also oppose the truth,	**2Tm 3:8**	*3779*
s that the man of God may be adequate,	**2Tm 3:17**	*2443*
s that through me the proclamation	**2Tm 4:17**	*2443*
s that he will be able both to exhort	**Ti 1:9**	*2443*
reason reprove them severely **s** that	**Ti 1:13**	*2443*
s that they may encourage the young	**Ti 2:4**	*2443*
s that the word of God will not be	**Ti 2:5**	*2443*
s that the opponent will be put to	**Ti 2:8**	*2443*
but showing all good faith **s** that	**Ti 2:10**	*2443*
s that being justified by His grace	**Ti 3:7**	*2443*
s that those who have believed God	**Ti 3:8**	*2443*
s that nothing is lacking for them.	**Ti 3:13**	*2443*
s that they will not be unfruitful.	**Ti 3:14**	*2443*
I wished to keep with me, **s** that	**Phm 1:13**	*2443*
s that your goodness would not be,	**Phm 1:14**	*2443*
s that we do not drift away *from it.*	**Heb 2:1**	*3379*
if we neglect **s** great a salvation?	**Heb 2:3**	*5082*
s that by the grace of God He might	**Heb 2:9**	*3704*
s that He might become a merciful	**Heb 2:17**	*2443*
by just **s** much as the builder of	**Heb 3:3**	*3745*
s that none of you will be hardened	**Heb 3:13**	
		2443, 3361
S we see that they were not able	**Heb 3:19**	
saying through David after **s** long	**Heb 4:7**	*5118*
S there remains a Sabbath rest for	**Heb 4:9**	*686*
s that no one will fall, through	**Heb 4:11**	
		2443, 3361
s that we may receive mercy and find	**Heb 4:16**	*2443*
the people, **s** also for himself.	**Heb 5:3**	*3779*
S also Christ did not glorify	**Heb 5:5**	*3779*

s as to become a high priest, Heb 5:5 2443
s as to forget your work and the Heb 6:10 2443
s as to realize the full assurance of Heb 6:11 *4314*
s that you will not be sluggish, but Heb 6:12 2443
And s, having patiently waited, he Heb 6:15 3779
s that by two unchangeable things in Heb 6:18 2443
And, s to speak, through Abraham Heb 7:9 *5613, 2031*
s much the more also Jesus has Heb 7:22 *5118*
s it is necessary that this *high* Heb 8:3 *3606*
Now when these things have been s Heb 9:6 3779
s that, since a death has taken Heb 9:15 3704
s Christ also, having been offered Heb 9:28 3779
with those who were s treated. Heb 10:33 3779
s that when you have done the will Heb 10:36 2443
s that what is seen was not made Heb 11:3 *1519*
up s that he would not see death; Heb 11:5
s that he who destroyed the Heb 11:28 2443
s that they might obtain a better Heb 11:35 2443
s that apart from us they would Heb 11:40 2443
we have s great a cloud of witnesses Heb 12:1 *5118*
sin which s easily entangles us, Heb 12:1
s that you will not grow weary and Heb 12:3 2443
s that we may share His holiness. Heb 12:10 *1519*
s that *the limb* which is lame may Heb 12:13 2443
And s terrible was the sight, *that* Heb 12:21 3779
s that those things which cannot be Heb 12:27 2443
s that we confidently say, Heb 13:6 *5620*
those who were s occupied Heb 13:9 *4043*
S, let us go out to Him outside Heb 13:13 *5106*
S that I may be restored to you Heb 13:19 2443
s that you may be perfect Jas 1:4 2443
s too the rich man in the midst of Jas 1:11 3779
word of truth, s that we would be Jas 1:18 *1519*
S speak and so act as those who Jas 2:12 3779
So speak and s act as those who Jas 2:12 3779
Even s faith, if it has no works, Jas 2:17 3779
s also faith without works is dead. Jas 2:26 3779
mouths s that they will obey us, Jas 3:3 *1519*
though they are s great and are Jas 3:4 5082
S also the tongue is a small part Jas 3:5 3779
do not be arrogant and s lie Jas 3:14
You lust and do not have; s you Jas 4:2
s you fight and quarrel. You do Jas 4:2
s that you may spend *it* on your Jas 4:3 2443
s that you yourselves may not be Jas 5:9 2443
s that you may not fall under Jas 5:12 2443
another s that you may be healed. Jas 5:16 3704
s that the proof of your faith, 1Pe 1:7 2443
s that your faith and hope are in 1Pe 1:21 5620
s that by it you may grow in respect 1Pe 2:2 2443
S that you may proclaim 1Pe 2:9 3704
s that in the thing in which they 1Pe 2:12 2443
s that we might die to sin and live 1Pe 2:24 2443
husbands s that even if any *of them* 1Pe 3:1 2443
s that your prayers will not be 1Pe 3:7 *1519*
and keep a good conscience s that 1Pe 3:16 2443
better, if God should will it s, 1Pe 3:17
s that He might bring us to God, 1Pe 3:18 2443
s as to live the rest of the time 1Pe 4:2 *1519*
Whoever speaks, *is to do* s as 1Pe 4:11
whoever serves *is to do* s as 1Pe 4:11
s that in all things God may be 1Pe 4:11 2443
s that also at the revelation of 1Pe 4:13 2443
brother (for s I regard *him*), 1Pe 5:12 *5613*
and s *does* my son, Mark. 1Pe 5:13
s that by them you may become 2Pe 1:4 2443
S we have the prophetic word 2Pe 1:19
be on your guard s that you are not 2Pe 3:17 *2443, 3361*
s that you too may have fellowship 1Jn 1:3 2443
s that our joy may be made 1Jn 1:4 2443
writing these things to you s that 1Jn 2:1 2443
s that it would be shown that they 1Jn 2:19 2443
in Him, s that when He appears, 1Jn 2:28 2443
s that we might live through Him. 1Jn 4:9 2443
Beloved, if God s loved us, we 1Jn 4:11 3779
s that we may have confidence in 1Jn 4:17 2443
is, s also are we in this world. 1Jn 4:17
s that you may know that you have 1Jn 5:13 2443
and has given us understanding s that 1Jn 5:20 2443
I do not want to *do* s with paper 2Jn 1:12
s that your joy may be made full. 2Jn 1:12 2443
s that we may be fellow workers with 3Jn 1:8 2443
he forbids those who desire *to do* s 3Jn 1:10
S it is to be. Amen. Rv 1:7 *3483a*
s that you will be tested, and you Rv 2:10 2443
'S you also have some who in Rv 2:15 3779
s that they commit *acts of* Rv 2:20
'S remember what you have received Rv 3:3 3767
s that no one will take your crown. Rv 3:11 2443
'S because you are lukewarm, and Rv 3:16 3779
from Me gold refined by fire s that Rv 3:18 2443
and white garments s that you may Rv 3:18 2443
salve to anoint your eyes s that Rv 3:18 2443
has overcome s as to open the book Rv 5:5
s that no wind would blow on the Rv 7:1 2443
s that he might add it to the prayers Rv 8:3 2443
s that a third of them would be Rv 8:12 2443
s that they would kill a third of Rv 9:15 2443
hands, s as not to worship demons, Rv 9:20 2443
S I went to the angel, telling him Rv 10:9 2532
s if anyone wants to harm them, he Rv 11:5 2532
s that rain will not fall during Rv 11:6 2443
s that when she gave birth he Rv 12:4 2443
s that there she would be Rv 12:6 2443
s that she could fly into Rv 12:14 2443
s that he might cause her to be Rv 12:15 2443
S the dragon was enraged with Rv 12:17 2532
s that he even makes fire come Rv 13:13 2443
s that the image of the beast would Rv 13:15 2443
"s that they may rest from their Rv 14:13 2443
S the angel swung his sickle to Rv 14:19 2532
S the first *angel* went and poured Rv 16:2 2532
repent s as to give Him glory. Rv 16:9
s that the way would be prepared for Rv 16:12 2443
s that he will not walk about naked Rv 16:15 *2443, 3361*
s great an earthquake *was it,* Rv 16:18 5082
earthquake *was it, and* s mighty. Rv 16:18 3779
s that you will not participate in Rv 18:4 2443
"S will Babylon, the great city, Rv 18:21 3779
s that with it He may strike down Rv 19:15 2443
s that you may eat the flesh of kings Rv 19:18 2443
s that he would not deceive the Rv 20:3 2443
s that they may have the right to Rv 22:14 2443

SOAKED
their land will be s with blood, Is 34:7 7301

SOAP
yourself with lye And use much s, Jer 2:22 1287
refiner's fire and like fullers' s. Mal 3:2 1287

SOARS
understanding that the hawk s, Jb 39:26 82

SOB
My soul will s in secret for *such* Jer 13:17 1058

SOBER
but I utter words of s truth. Ac 26:25 *4997*
do, but let us be alert and s. 1Th 5:6 *3525*
we are of *the* day, let us be s, 1Th 5:8 *3525*
But you, be s in all things, 2Tm 4:5 *3525*
for action, keep s *in spirit,* 1Pe 1:13 *3525*
be of sound judgment and s *spirit* 1Pe 4:7 *3525*
Be of s *spirit,* be on the alert. 1Pe 5:8 *3525*

SOBER-MINDED
Become s as you ought, and stop 1Co 15:34 *1594*

SO-CALLED
them at the s portico of Solomon, Ac 3:11 *2564*
not to associate with any s brother 1Co 5:11 *3687*
For even if there are s gods 1Co 8:5 *3004*
by the s "Circumcision," *which is* Eph 2:11 *3004*
exalts himself above every s god 2Th 2:4 *3004*

SOCKET
he touched the s of his thigh; Gn 32:25 3709
so the s of Jacob's thigh was Gn 32:25 3709
which is on the s of the thigh, Gn 32:32 3709
he touched the s of Jacob's thigh Gn 32:32 3709
hundred talents, a talent for a s. Ex 38:27 134
Let my shoulder fall from the s, Jb 31:22 7926

SOCKETS
"You shall make forty s of silver Ex 26:19 134
two s under one board for its two Ex 26:19 134
two tenons and two s under another Ex 26:19 134
and their forty s of silver; Ex 26:21 134
two s under one board and two Ex 26:21 134
and two s under another board. Ex 26:21 134
boards with their s of silver, Ex 26:25 134
sockets of silver, sixteen s; Ex 26:25 134
two s under one board and two Ex 26:25 134
and two s under another board. Ex 26:25 134
of gold, on four s of silver. Ex 26:32 134
cast five s of bronze for them. Ex 26:37 134
with their twenty s of bronze; Ex 27:10 134
with their twenty s of bronze; Ex 27:11 134
their ten pillars and their ten s. Ex 27:12 134
three pillars and their three s. Ex 27:14 134
three pillars and their three s. Ex 27:15 134
four pillars and their four s. Ex 27:16 134
of silver and their s of bronze. Ex 27:17 134
linen, and their s of bronze. Ex 27:18 134
its bars, its pillars, and its s; Ex 35:11 134
the court, its pillars and its s, Ex 35:17 134
and he made forty s of silver Ex 36:24 134
two s under one board for its two Ex 36:24 134
two s under another board for its Ex 36:24 134
and their forty s of silver; Ex 36:26 134
two s under one board and two Ex 36:26 134
and two s under another board. Ex 36:26 134
boards with their s of silver, Ex 36:30 134
sockets of silver, sixteen s, Ex 36:30 134
he cast four s of silver for them. Ex 36:36 134
but their five s were of bronze. Ex 36:38 134
pillars, and their twenty s, Ex 38:10 134
and their twenty s *were* of bronze, Ex 38:11 134
their ten pillars and their ten s; Ex 38:12 134
three pillars and their three s, Ex 38:14 134
three pillars and their three s. Ex 38:15 134
The s for the pillars *were* of Ex 38:17 134
and their four s *were* of bronze; Ex 38:19 134
for casting the s of the sanctuary Ex 38:27 134
sanctuary and the s of the veil; Ex 38:27 134
hundred s for the hundred talents, Ex 38:27 134
With it he made the s to the Ex 38:30 134
and the s of the court all around Ex 38:31 134
the s of the gate of the court, Ex 38:31 134
bars, and its pillars and its s; Ex 39:33 134
the court, its pillars and its s, Ex 39:40 134
the tabernacle and laid its s, Ex 40:18 134
its bars, its pillars, its s, Nu 3:36 134
the court with their s and their pegs Nu 3:37 134
bars and its pillars and its s, Nu 4:31 134
the court and their s and their pegs Nu 4:32 134
workmanship of your settings and s, Ezk 28:13 5345
their eyes will rot in their s, Zch 14:12 2356

SOCO
Gedor, and Heber the father of S, 1Ch 4:18 7755
Beth-zur, S, Adullam, 2Ch 11:7 7755
Gederoth, and S with its villages, 2Ch 28:18 7755

SOCOH
Jarmuth and Adullam, S and Azekah, Jos 15:35 7755
Shamir and Jattir and S, Jos 15:48 7755
at S which belongs to Judah, 1Sa 17:1 7755
they camped between S and Azekah, 1Sa 17:1 7755
S *was* his and all the land of Hepher 1Ki 4:10 7755

SODA
a cold day, *or like* vinegar on s, Pr 25:20 5427

SODI
of Zebulun, Gaddiel the son of S; Nu 13:10 5476

SODOM
as you go toward S and Gomorrah Gn 10:19 5467
LORD destroyed S and Gomorrah Gn 13:10 5467
and moved his tents as far as S. Gn 13:12 5467
Now the men of S were wicked Gn 13:13 5467
they made war with Bera king of S, Gn 14:2 5467
And the king of S and the king of Gn 14:8 5467
the kings of S and Gomorrah fled, Gn 14:10 5467
all the goods of S and Gomorrah Gn 14:11 5467
departed, for he was living in S. Gn 14:12 5467
the king of S went out to meet him Gn 14:17 5467
The king of S said to Abram, Gn 14:21 5467
Abram said to the king of S, Gn 14:22 5467
there, and looked down toward S; Gn 18:16 5467
outcry of S and Gomorrah is indeed Gn 18:20 5467
away from there and went toward S, Gn 18:22 5467
"If I find in S fifty righteous Gn 18:26 5467
Now the two angels came to S in Gn 19:1 5467
Lot was sitting in the gate of S. Gn 19:1 5467
the men of the city, the men of S, Gn 19:4 5467
LORD rained on S and Gomorrah Gn 19:24 5467
looked down toward S and Gomorrah, Gn 19:28 5467
the overthrow of S and Gomorrah, Dt 29:23 5467
their vine is from the vine of S, Dt 32:32 5467
few survivors, We would be like S, Is 1:9 5467
word of the LORD, You rulers of S; Is 1:10 5467
And they display their sin like S; Is 3:9 5467
when God overthrew S and Gomorrah. Is 13:19 5467
of them have become to Me like S, Jer 23:14 5467
the overthrow of S and Gomorrah Jer 49:18 5467
God overthrew S And Gomorrah Jer 50:40 5467
Is greater than the sin of S, La 4:6 5467
of you, is S with her daughters, Ezk 16:46 5467
"S, your sister and her Ezk 16:48 5467
was the guilt of your sister S: Ezk 16:49 5467
captivity of S and her daughters, Ezk 16:53 5467
S with her daughters and Samaria Ezk 16:55 5467
"As *the name of* your sister S was Ezk 16:56 5467
as God overthrew S and Gomorrah, Am 4:11 5467
"Surely Moab will be like S And Zph 2:9 5467
for *the* land of S and Gomorrah Mt 10:15 *4670*
if the miracles had occurred in S Mt 11:23 *4670*
be more tolerable for the land of S Mt 11:24 *4670*
more tolerable in that day for S than Lk 10:12 *4670*
on the day that Lot went out from S Lk 17:29 *4670*
WE WOULD HAVE BECOME LIKE S, Ro 9:29 *4670*
the cities of S and Gomorrah 2Pe 2:6 *4670*
just as S and Gomorrah and the Jude 1:7 *4670*
mystically is called S and Egypt, Rv 11:8 *4670*

SODOMITES
The remnant of the s who 1Ki 22:46 6945

SOFT
Or will he speak to you s words? Jb 41:3 7390
And a s tongue breaks the bone. Pr 25:15 7390
A man dressed in s *clothing?* Mt 11:8 *3120*
Those who wear s *clothing* are in Mt 11:8 *3120*
A man dressed in s clothing? Lk 7:25 *3120*

SOFTEN
You s it with showers Ps 65:10 4127

SOFTENED
out or bandaged, Nor s with oil. Is 1:6 7401

SOFTER
His words were s than oil, Yet Ps 55:21 7401

SOFTLY
the daughters of song will sing s. Ec 12:4 7817

SOIL
first fruits of your s into the house of Ex 23:19 127
first fruits of your s into the house of Ex 34:26 127
workers who tilled the s. 1Ch 27:26 127
fields, for he loved the s. 2Ch 26:10 127
And its stump dies in the dry s, Jb 14:8 6083
a luxuriant tree in its native s. Ps 37:35
they will live on their own s." Jer 23:8 127
you and restore you to your own s. Jer 42:12 127
land and planted it in fertile s. Ezk 17:5 7704
in good s beside abundant waters, Ezk 17:8 7704
yourself will die upon unclean s. Am 7:17 127
where they did not have much s; Mt 13:5 *1093*
because they had no depth of s. Mt 13:5 *1093*
"And others fell on the good s and Mt 13:8 *1093*
whom seed was sown on the good s, Mt 13:23 *1093*
where it did not have much s; Mk 4:5 *1093*
up because it had no depth of s. Mk 4:5 *1093*
"Other *seeds* fell into the good s Mk 4:8 *1093*
whom seed was sown on the good s, Mk 4:20 *1093*
a man who casts seed upon the s; Mk 4:26 *1093*
"The s produces crops by itself; Mk 4:28 *1093*
seed, which, when sown upon the s, Mk 4:31 *1093*
all the seeds that are upon the s, Mk 4:31 *1093*
"Other *seed* fell on rocky s, Lk 8:6
Other *seed* fell into the good s, Lk 8:8 *1093*
"Those on the rocky s *are* those Lk 8:13
"But the *seed* in the good s, Lk 8:15 *1093*
"It is useless either for the s or for Lk 14:35 *1093*
for the precious produce of the s, Jas 5:7 *1093*

SOILED
who have not s their garments; Rv 3:4 3435
SOJOURN
went down to Egypt to s there, Gn 12:10 1481a
"S in this land and I will be Gn 26:3 1481a
"We have come to s in the land, Gn 47:4 1481a
from the aliens who s among them, Lv 17:8 1481a
from the aliens who s among them, Lv 17:10 1481a
from the aliens who s among them, Lv 17:13 1481a
Judah went to s in the land of Moab Ru 1:1 1481a
and s wherever you can sojourn; 2Ki 8:1 1481a
and sojourn wherever you can s; 2Ki 8:1 1481a
Woe is me, for I s in Meshech, Ps 120:5 1481a
days in the land where you s.' Jer 35:7 1481a
them out of the land where they s, Ezk 20:38 4033
SOJOURNED
then he s in Gerar. Gn 20:1 1481a
to the land in which you have s." Gn 21:23 1481a
And Abraham s in the land of the Gn 21:34 1481a
"I have s with Laban, and stayed Gn 32:4 1481a
where Abraham and Isaac had s. Gn 35:27 1481a
and the land where they s could Gn 36:7 4033
the land where his father had s, Gn 37:1 4033
Canaan, the land in which they s. Ex 6:4 1481a
he went down to Egypt and s there, Dt 26:5 1481a
s in the land of the Philistines seven 2Ki 8:2 1481a
Nor any survivor where he s. Jb 18:19 4033
Thus Jacob s in the land of Ham. Ps 105:23 1481a
SOJOURNER
"I am a stranger and a s among you; Gn 23:4 8453
"I have been a s in a foreign land." Ex 2:22 1616
"A s or a hired servant shall not Ex 12:45 8453
have been a s in a foreign land." Ex 18:3 1616
or your s who stays with you. Ex 20:10 1616
a s with the priest or a hired man Lv 22:10 8453
him, like a stranger or a s, Lv 25:35 8453
as a hired man, as if he were a s; Lv 25:40 8453
a s with you becomes sufficient, Lv 25:47 8453
alien and for the s among them; Nu 35:15 8453
or your s who stays with you, Dt 5:14 1616
You, A s like all my fathers. Ps 39:12 8453
oppressed the s without justice. Ezk 22:29 1616
SOJOURNERS
you are *but* aliens and s with Me. Lv 25:23 8453
it is out of the sons of the s who Lv 25:45 8453
"For we are s before You, and 1Ch 29:15 1616
both the s who came from the land 2Ch 30:25 1616
SOJOURNING
The years of my s are one hundred Gn 47:9 4033
during the days of their s." Gn 47:9 4033
or from the aliens s in Israel who Lv 20:2 1481a
to a stranger who is s with you, Lv 25:47 8453
SOJOURNINGS
after you, the land of your s, Gn 17:8 4033
may possess the land of your s, Gn 28:4 4033
SOJOURNS
"But if a stranger s with you, Ex 12:48 1481a
to the stranger who s among you." Ex 12:49 1481a
or the alien who s among you; Lv 16:29 1481a
alien who s among you eat blood.' Lv 17:12 1481a
nor the alien who s among you Lv 18:26 1481a
'If an alien s among you and Nu 9:14 1481a
'If an alien s with you, or Nu 15:14 1481a
and for the alien who s *with you,* Nu 15:15 1481a
for the alien who s with you.'" Nu 15:16 1481a
with the alien who s among them, Nu 15:26 1481a
for the alien who s among them. Nu 15:29 1481a
and to the alien who s among them. Nu 19:10 1481a
for the stranger who s among them, Jos 20:9 1481a
SOLACE
And the s of my lips could lessen Jb 16:5 5205
SOLD
and s his birthright to Jacob. Gn 25:33 4376
For he has s us, and has also Gn 31:15 4376
and s him to the Ishmaelites for Gn 37:28 4376
the Midianites s him in Egypt to Gn 37:36 4376
and s to the Egyptians; Gn 41:56 7666
s to all the people of the land. Gn 42:6 7666
Joseph, whom you s into Egypt. Gn 45:4 4376
yourselves, because you s me here, Gn 45:5 4376
for every Egyptian s his field, Gn 47:20 4376
then he shall be s for his theft. Ex 22:3 4376
'The land, moreover, shall not be s Lv 25:23 4376
buy back what his relative has s. Lv 25:25 4465
to the man to whom he s it, Lv 25:27 4376
then what he has s shall remain in Lv 25:28 4465
of their cities shall not be s, Lv 25:34 4376
are not to be s *in* a slave sale. Lv 25:42 4376
right after he has been s. Lv 25:48 4376
from the year when he s himself to Lv 25:50 4376
has s the field to another man, Lv 27:20 4376
be s according to your valuation. Lv 27:27 4376
shall not be s or redeemed. Lv 27:28 4376
Hebrew man or woman, is s to you, Dt 15:12 4376
Unless their Rock had s them, Dt 32:30 4376
and He s them into the hands of Jg 2:14 4376
so that He s them into the hands Jg 3:8 4376
And the LORD s them into the hand Jg 4:2 4376
and He s them into the hands of Jg 10:7 4376
He s them into the hand of Sisera, 1Sa 12:9 4376
because you have s yourself to do 1Ki 21:20 4376
like Ahab who s himself to do evil in 1Ki 21:25 4376
a donkey's head was s for eighty 2Ki 6:25 1961
a measure of fine flour will be s 2Ki 7:1
Then a measure of fine flour *was* s 2Ki 7:16
will be s tomorrow about this 2Ki 7:18
and s themselves to do evil in the 2Ki 17:17 4376
who were s to the nations; Ne 5:8 4376
that they may be s to us?" Ne 5:8 4376
them on the day they s food. Ne 13:15 4376
and s *them* to the sons of Judah on Ne 13:16 4376
for we have been s, Es 7:4 4376
if we had only been s as slaves, Es 7:4 4376
Joseph, *who* was s as a slave. Ps 105:17 4376
you were s for your iniquities, Is 50:1 4376
"You were s for nothing and you Is 52:3 4376
who has been s to you and has Jer 34:14 4376
the seller will not regain what he s Ezk 7:13 4465
And s a girl for wine that they Jl 3:3 4376
and s the sons of Judah and Jl 3:6 4376
the place where you have s them, Jl 3:7 4376
man s me as a slave in my youth.' Zch 13:5 7069
"Are not two sparrows s for a cent? Mt 10:29 4453
he went and s all that he had and Mt 13:46 4097
his lord commanded him to be s, Mt 18:25 4097
perfume might have been s for a high Mt 26:9 4097
this perfume might have been s for Mk 14:5 4097
not five sparrows s for two cents? Lk 12:6 4453
"Why was this perfume not s for Jn 12:5 4097
s it and brought the money and Ac 4:37 4453
Sapphira, s a piece of property, Ac 5:1 4453
And after it was s, Ac 5:4 4097
"Tell me whether you s the land Ac 5:8 591
of Joseph and s him into Egypt. Ac 7:9 591
I am of flesh, s into bondage to sin. Ro 7:14 4097
that is s in the meat market without 1Co 10:25 4453
who s his own birthright for a Heb 12:16 591
SOLDERING
beats the anvil, Saying of the s, Is 41:7 1694
SOLDIER
a part to every s and *also* the tunic; Jn 19:23 4757
two of his servants and a devout s Ac 10:7 4757
with the s who was guarding him. Ac 28:16 4757
serves as a s at his own expense? 1Co 9:7 4754
and fellow worker and fellow s, Php 2:25 4961
me, as a good s of Christ Jesus. 2Tm 2:3 4757
No s in active service entangles 2Tm 2:4 4754
the one who enlisted him as a s. 2Tm 2:4 4758
and to Archippus our fellow s, Phm 1:2 4961
SOLDIERS
400,000 foot s who drew the sword. Jg 20:2 376
of Israel thirty thousand foot s. 1Sa 4:10 7273
200,000 foot s and 10,000 men of 1Sa 15:4 7273
1,700 horsemen and 20,000 foot s; 2Sa 8:4 376, 7273
Arameans of Zobah, 20,000 foot s, 2Sa 10:6 7273
100,000 foot s in one day. 1Ki 20:29 7273
7,000 horsemen and 20,000 foot s, 1Ch 18:4 376, 7273
charioteers and 40,000 foot s, 1Ch 19:18 376, 7273
that is, the men who were s, Jer 41:16 582, 4421
They climb the wall like s; Jl 2:7 582, 4421
Let all the s draw near, let them Jl 3:9 582, 4421
under authority, with s under me; Mt 8:9 4757
Then the s of the governor took Mt 27:27 4757
a large sum of money to the s, Mt 28:12 4757
The s took Him away into the Mk 15:16 4757
Some s were questioning him, Lk 3:14 4754
under authority, with s under me; Lk 7:8 4757
And Herod with his s, Lk 23:11 4753
The s also mocked Him, coming Lk 23:36 4757
s twisted together a crown of thorns Jn 19:2 4757
Then the s, when they had Jn 19:23 4757
Therefore the s did these things. Jn 19:25 4757
So the s came, and broke Jn 19:32 4757
s pierced His side with a spear, Jn 19:34 4757
to four squads of s to guard him, Ac 12:4 4757
Peter was sleeping between two s, Ac 12:6 4757
no small disturbance among the s *as* Ac 12:18 4757
took along *some* s and centurions and Ac 21:32 4757
they saw the commander and the s, Ac 21:32 4757
he was carried by the s because of the Ac 21:35 4757
"Get two hundred s ready by the Ac 23:23 4757
So the s, in accordance with their Ac 23:31 4757
to the centurion and to the s, Ac 27:31 4757
Then the s cut away the ropes of Ac 27:32 4757
SOLDIERS'
The s plan was to kill Ac 27:42 4757
SOLE
resting place for the s of her foot, Gn 8:9 3709
place on which the s of your foot Dt 11:24 3709
from the s of your foot to the Dt 28:35 3709
not venture to set the s of her foot Dt 28:56 3709
resting place for the s of your foot; Dt 28:65 3709
which the s of your foot treads, Jos 1:3 3709
from the s of his foot to the 2Sa 14:25 3709
And with the s of my feet I dried 2Ki 19:24 3709
sore boils from the s of his foot to Jb 2:7 3709
From the s of the foot even to the Is 1:6 3709
And with the s of my feet I dried Is 37:25 3709
SOLEMN
to be a sabbath of s rest for you, Lv 16:31 7677
day you shall have a s assembly; Nu 29:35 6116
a s assembly to the LORD your God; Dt 16:8 6116
"Sanctify a s assembly for Baal." 2Ki 10:20 6116
eighth day they held a s assembly, 2Ch 7:9 6116
eighth day *there was* a s assembly Ne 8:18 6116
iniquity and the s assembly. Is 1:13 6116
they have *sworn* s oaths. Ezk 21:23 7650
a fast, Proclaim a s assembly; Jl 1:14 6116
a fast, proclaim a s assembly, Jl 2:15 6116
do I delight in your s assemblies. Am 5:21 6116
have bound ourselves under a s oath Ac 23:14 331
SOLEMNLY
"The man s warned us, Gn 43:3 5749b
made the sons of Israel s swear, Ex 13:19 7650
you shall s warn them and tell 1Sa 8:9 5749b
swear by the LORD and s warn you, 1Ki 2:42 5749b
'For I s warned your fathers in Jer 11:7 5749b
with many other words he s testified Ac 2:40 1263
when they had s testified and Ac 8:25 1263
and s to testify that this is the Ac 10:42 1263
s testifying to the Jews that Ac 18:5 1263
s testifying to both Jews and Ac 20:21 1263
that the Holy Spirit s testifies to me Ac 20:23 1263
to testify s of the gospel of the Ac 20:24 1263
for as you have s witnessed to My Ac 23:11 1263
explaining to them by s testifying Ac 28:23 1263
told you before and s warned *you.* 1Th 4:6 1263
I s charge you in the presence of 1Tm 5:21 1263
and s charge *them* in the presence 2Tm 2:14 1263
I s charge *you* in the presence of 2Tm 4:1 1263
SOLES
when the s of the feet of the priests Jos 3:13 3709
and the s of the priests' feet Jos 4:18 3709
put them under the s of his feet. 1Ki 5:3 3709
set a limit for the s of my feet, Jb 13:27 8328
themselves at the s of your feet; Is 60:14 3709
and the place of the s of My feet, Ezk 43:7 3709
be ashes under the s of your feet on Mal 4:3 3709
shake the dust off the s of Mk 6:11 5270
SOLID
you milk to drink, not s food; 1Co 3:2
come to need milk and not s food. Heb 5:12 4731
But s food is for the mature, who Heb 5:14 4731
SOLITARY
all their iniquities to a s land; Lv 16:22 1509
SOLOMON
Shammua, Shobab, Nathan, S, 2Sa 5:14 8010
to a son, and he named him S. 2Sa 12:24 8010
the mighty men, and S his brother. 1Ki 1:10 8010
to Bathsheba the mother of S, 1Ki 1:11 8010
life and the life of your son S. 1Ki 1:12 8010
"Surely S your son shall be king 1Ki 1:13 8010
'Surely your son S shall be king 1Ki 1:17 8010
he has not invited S your servant. 1Ki 1:19 8010
I and my son S will be considered 1Ki 1:21 8010
of Jehoiada and your servant S, 1Ki 1:26 8010
'Your son S shall be king after 1Ki 1:30 8010
have my son S ride on my own mule, 1Ki 1:33 8010
'*Long* live King S!' 1Ki 1:34 8010
the king, so may He be with S, 1Ki 1:37 8010
had S ride on King David's mule, 1Ki 1:38 8010
oil from the tent and anointed S. 1Ki 1:39 8010
"*Long* live King S!" 1Ki 1:39 8010
lord King David has made S king. 1Ki 1:43 8010
S has even taken his seat on the 1Ki 1:46 8010
'May your God make the name of S 1Ki 1:47 8010
And Adonijah was afraid of S, 1Ki 1:50 8010
Now it was told S, saying, 1Ki 1:51 8010
Adonijah is afraid of King S, 1Ki 1:51 8010
'Let King S swear to me today that 1Ki 1:51 8010
S said, "If he is a worthy man, 1Ki 1:52 8010
So King S sent, and they brought 1Ki 1:53 8010
prostrated himself before King S, 1Ki 1:53 8010
King Solomon, and S said to him, 1Ki 1:53 8010
drew near, he charged S his son, 1Ki 2:1 8010
And S sat on the throne of David 1Ki 2:12 8010
came to Bathsheba the mother of S. 1Ki 2:13 8010
"Please speak to S the king, for 1Ki 2:17 8010
Bathsheba went to King S to speak 1Ki 2:19 8010
King S answered and said to 1Ki 2:22 8010
Then King S swore by the LORD, 1Ki 2:23 8010
So King S sent Benaiah the son of 1Ki 2:25 8010
So S dismissed Abiathar from being 1Ki 2:27 8010
It was told King S that Joab 1Ki 2:29 8010
Then S sent Benaiah the son of 1Ki 2:29 8010
It was told S that Shimei had 1Ki 2:41 8010
"But King S shall be blessed, and 1Ki 2:45 8010
was established in the hands of S. 1Ki 2:46 8010
Then S formed a marriage alliance 1Ki 3:1 8010
Now S loved the LORD, walking in 1Ki 3:3 8010
S offered a thousand burnt 1Ki 3:4 8010
the LORD appeared to S in a dream 1Ki 3:5 8010
Then S said, "You have shown great 1Ki 3:6 8010
Lord that S had asked this thing. 1Ki 3:10 8010
Then S awoke, and behold, it was a 1Ki 3:15 8010
King S was king over all Israel. 1Ki 4:1 8010
S had twelve deputies over all 1Ki 4:7 8010
the daughter of S was his wife); 1Ki 4:11 8010
Basemath the daughter of S); 1Ki 4:15 8010
Now S ruled over all the kingdoms 1Ki 4:21 8010
served S all the days of his life. 1Ki 4:21 8010
to Beersheba, all the days of S. 1Ki 4:25 8010
S had 40,000 stalls of horses 1Ki 4:26 8010
deputies provided for King S and all 1Ki 4:27 8010
Now God gave S wisdom and very 1Ki 4:29 8010
peoples to hear the wisdom of S, 1Ki 4:34 8010
of Tyre sent his servants to S, 1Ki 5:1 8010
Then S sent *word* to Hiram, saying, 1Ki 5:2 8010
When Hiram heard the words of S, 1Ki 5:7 8010
So Hiram sent *word* to S, 1Ki 5:8 8010
So Hiram gave S as much as he 1Ki 5:10 8010
S then gave Hiram 20,000 kors of 1Ki 5:11 8010
S would give Hiram year by year. 1Ki 5:11 8010
The LORD gave wisdom to S, 1Ki 5:12 8010
was peace between Hiram and S, 1Ki 5:12 8010
Now King S levied forced laborers 1Ki 5:13 8010
Now S had 70,000 transporters, and 1Ki 5:15 8010
which King S built for the LORD, 1Ki 6:2 8010
word of the LORD came to S saying, 1Ki 6:11 8010

So **S** built the house and finished	**1Ki 6:14**	8010
So **S** overlaid the inside of the	**1Ki 6:21**	8010
Now **S** was building his own house	**1Ki 7:1**	8010
daughter, whom **S** had married.	**1Ki 7:8**	8010
Now King **S** sent and brought Hiram	**1Ki 7:13**	8010
he came to King **S** and performed	**1Ki 7:14**	8010
which he performed for King **S** *in*	**1Ki 7:40**	8010
Hiram made for King **S** *in* the house	**1Ki 7:45**	8010
S left all the utensils	**1Ki 7:47**	8010
S made all the furniture which	**1Ki 7:48**	8010
all the work that King **S** performed	**1Ki 7:51**	8010
And **S** brought in the things	**1Ki 7:51**	8010
Then **S** assembled the elders of	**1Ki 8:1**	8010
of Israel, to King **S** in Jerusalem,	**1Ki 8:1**	8010
themselves to King **S** at the feast,	**1Ki 8:2**	8010
And King **S** and all the	**1Ki 8:5**	8010
Then **S** said, "The LORD has said	**1Ki 8:12**	8010
Then **S** stood before the altar of	**1Ki 8:22**	8010
When **S** had finished praying this	**1Ki 8:54**	8010
S offered for the sacrifice of	**1Ki 8:63**	8010
So **S** observed the feast at that	**1Ki 8:65**	8010
when **S** had finished building the	**1Ki 9:1**	8010
and all that **S** desired to do,	**1Ki 9:1**	8010
LORD appeared to **S** a second time,	**1Ki 9:2**	8010
in which **S** had built the two houses,	**1Ki 9:10**	8010
(Hiram king of Tyre had supplied **S**	**1Ki 9:11**	8010
then King **S** gave Hiram twenty	**1Ki 9:11**	8010
the cities which **S** had given him,	**1Ki 9:12**	8010
forced labor which King **S** levied to	**1Ki 9:15**	8010
So **S** rebuilt Gezer and the lower	**1Ki 9:17**	8010
the storage cities which **S** had,	**1Ki 9:19**	8010
pleased **S** to build in Jerusalem,	**1Ki 9:19**	8010
from them **S** levied forced laborers,	**1Ki 9:21**	8010
But **S** did not make slaves of the	**1Ki 9:22**	8010
city of David to her house which **S**	**1Ki 9:24**	8010
S offered burnt offerings and peace	**1Ki 9:25**	8010
King **S** also built a fleet of ships	**1Ki 9:26**	8010
sea, along with the servants of **S**.	**1Ki 9:27**	8010
there, and brought *it* to King **S**.	**1Ki 9:28**	8010
of Sheba heard about the fame of **S**	**1Ki 10:1**	8010
When she came to **S**,	**1Ki 10:2**	8010
S answered all her questions;	**1Ki 10:3**	8010
perceived all the wisdom of **S**,	**1Ki 10:4**	8010
the queen of Sheba gave King **S**.	**1Ki 10:10**	8010
King **S** gave to the queen of	**1Ki 10:13**	8010
gold which came in to **S** in one year	**1Ki 10:14**	8010
King **S** made 200 large shields	**1Ki 10:16**	8010
valuable in the days of **S**.	**1Ki 10:21**	8010
So King **S** became greater than all	**1Ki 10:23**	8010
was seeking the presence of **S**,	**1Ki 10:24**	8010
Now **S** gathered chariots and	**1Ki 10:26**	8010
Now King **S** loved many foreign	**1Ki 11:1**	8010
S held fast to these in love.	**1Ki 11:2**	8010
For when **S** was old,	**1Ki 11:4**	8010
For **S** went after Ashtoreth the	**1Ki 11:5**	8010
S did what was evil in the	**1Ki 11:6**	8010
Then **S** built a high place for	**1Ki 11:7**	8010
Now the LORD was angry with **S**	**1Ki 11:9**	8010
So the LORD said to **S**,	**1Ki 11:11**	8010
LORD raised up an adversary to **S**,	**1Ki 11:14**	8010
to Israel all the days of **S**,	**1Ki 11:25**	8010
S built the Millo, *and* closed up	**1Ki 11:27**	8010
and when **S** saw that the young man	**1Ki 11:28**	8010
the kingdom out of the hand of **S**	**1Ki 11:31**	8010
S sought therefore to put Jeroboam	**1Ki 11:40**	8010
was in Egypt until the death of **S**.	**1Ki 11:40**	8010
the acts of **S** and whatever he did,	**1Ki 11:41**	8010
in the book of the acts of **S**?	**1Ki 11:41**	8010
time that **S** reigned in Jerusalem	**1Ki 11:42**	8010
And **S** slept with his fathers and	**1Ki 11:43**	8010
fled from the presence of King **S**).	**1Ki 12:2**	8010
elders who had served his father **S**	**1Ki 12:6**	8010
kingdom to Rehoboam the son of **S**.	**1Ki 12:21**	8010
"Speak to Rehoboam the son of **S**,	**1Ki 12:23**	8010
the son of **S** reigned in Judah.	**1Ki 14:21**	8010
shields of gold which **S** had made.	**1Ki 14:26**	8010
said to David and to his son **S**,	**2Ki 21:7**	8010
which **S** the king of Israel had built	**2Ki 23:13**	8010
which **S** king of Israel had made in	**2Ki 24:13**	8010
and the stands which **S** had made	**2Ki 25:16**	8010
Shimea, Shobab, Nathan and **S**,	**1Ch 3:5**	8010
house which **S** built in Jerusalem),	**1Ch 6:10**	8010
until **S** had built the house of the	**1Ch 6:32**	8010
Shammua, Shobab, Nathan, **S**,	**1Ch 14:4**	8010
with which **S** made the bronze sea	**1Ch 18:8**	8010
son **S** is young and inexperienced,	**1Ch 22:5**	8010
Then he called for his son **S**,	**1Ch 22:6**	8010
David said to **S**,	**1Ch 22:7**	8010
for his name shall be **S**,	**1Ch 22:9**	8010
of Israel to help his son **S**,	**1Ch 22:17**	8010
made his son **S** king over Israel.	**1Ch 23:1**	8010
He has chosen my son **S** to sit on	**1Ch 28:5**	8010
'Your son **S** is the one who shall	**1Ch 28:6**	8010
"As for you, my son **S**,	**1Ch 28:9**	8010
Then David gave to his son **S** the	**1Ch 28:11**	8010
Then David said to his son **S**,	**1Ch 28:20**	8010
"My son **S**, whom alone God has	**1Ch 29:1**	8010
and give to my son **S** a perfect	**1Ch 29:19**	8010
And they made **S** the son of David	**1Ch 29:22**	8010
Then **S** sat on the throne of the	**1Ch 29:23**	8010
David pledged allegiance to King **S**.	**1Ch 29:24**	8010
The LORD highly exalted **S** in the	**1Ch 29:25**	8010
his son **S** reigned in his place.	**1Ch 29:28**	8010
Now **S** the son of David established	**2Ch 1:1**	8010
S spoke to all Israel, to the	**2Ch 1:2**	8010
Then **S** and all the assembly with	**2Ch 1:3**	8010
and **S** and the assembly sought it	**2Ch 1:5**	8010
S went up there before the	**2Ch 1:6**	8010
God appeared to **S** and said to him,	**2Ch 1:7**	8010
S said to God,	**2Ch 1:8**	8010
God said to **S**,	**2Ch 1:11**	8010
So **S** went from the high place	**2Ch 1:13**	8010
S amassed chariots and horsemen.	**2Ch 1:14**	8010
Now **S** decided to build a house for	**2Ch 2:1**	8010
So **S** assigned 70,000 men to carry	**2Ch 2:2**	8010
Then **S** sent *word* to Huram the king	**2Ch 2:3**	8010
answered in a letter sent to **S**:	**2Ch 2:11**	8010
S numbered all the aliens who	**2Ch 2:17**	8010
Then **S** began to build the house of	**2Ch 3:1**	8010
foundations which **S** laid for building	**2Ch 3:3**	8010
which he performed for King **S** in	**2Ch 4:11**	8010
made of polished bronze for King **S**	**2Ch 4:16**	8010
Thus **S** made all these utensils in	**2Ch 4:18**	8010
S also made all the things that	**2Ch 4:19**	8010
Thus all the work that **S** performed	**2Ch 5:1**	8010
And **S** brought in the things that	**2Ch 5:1**	8010
Then **S** assembled to Jerusalem the	**2Ch 5:2**	8010
And King **S** and all the	**2Ch 5:6**	8010
Then **S** said, "The LORD has said	**2Ch 6:1**	8010
Now **S** had made a bronze platform,	**2Ch 6:13**	8010
Now when **S** had finished praying,	**2Ch 7:1**	8010
King **S** offered a sacrifice of	**2Ch 7:5**	8010
Then **S** consecrated the middle of	**2Ch 7:7**	8010
the bronze altar which **S** had made	**2Ch 7:7**	8010
So **S** observed the feast at that	**2Ch 7:8**	8010
and to **S** and to His people Israel.	**2Ch 7:10**	8010
Thus **S** finished the house of the	**2Ch 7:11**	8010
the LORD appeared to **S** at night	**2Ch 7:12**	8010
years in which **S** had built the house	**2Ch 8:1**	8010
Then **S** went to Hamath-zobah and	**2Ch 8:3**	8010
all the storage cities that **S** had,	**2Ch 8:6**	8010
pleased **S** to build in Jerusalem,	**2Ch 8:6**	8010
them **S** raised as forced laborers	**2Ch 8:8**	8010
But **S** did not make slaves for his	**2Ch 8:9**	8010
were the chief officers of King **S**,	**2Ch 8:10**	8010
Then **S** brought Pharaoh's daughter	**2Ch 8:11**	8010
Then **S** offered burnt offerings to	**2Ch 8:12**	8010
Thus all the work of **S** was carried	**2Ch 8:16**	8010
Then **S** went to Ezion-geber and to	**2Ch 8:17**	8010
gold and brought them to King **S**.	**2Ch 8:18**	8010
of Sheba heard of the fame of **S**,	**2Ch 9:1**	8010
test **S** with difficult questions.	**2Ch 9:1**	8010
and when she came to **S**,	**2Ch 9:1**	8010
S answered all her questions;	**2Ch 9:2**	8010
nothing was hidden from **S** which he	**2Ch 9:2**	8010
of Sheba had seen the wisdom of **S**,	**2Ch 9:3**	8010
the queen of Sheba gave to King **S**.	**2Ch 9:9**	8010
the servants of **S** who brought gold	**2Ch 9:10**	8010
King **S** gave to the queen of	**2Ch 9:12**	8010
gold which came to **S** in one year	**2Ch 9:13**	8010
brought gold and silver to **S**.	**2Ch 9:14**	8010
King **S** made 200 large shields	**2Ch 9:15**	8010
valuable in the days of **S**.	**2Ch 9:20**	8010
So King **S** became greater than all	**2Ch 9:22**	8010
were seeking the presence of **S**,	**2Ch 9:23**	8010
Now **S** had 4,000 stalls for horses	**2Ch 9:25**	8010
bringing horses for **S** from Egypt	**2Ch 9:28**	8010
Now the rest of the acts of **S**,	**2Ch 9:29**	8010
S reigned forty years in	**2Ch 9:30**	8010
And **S** slept with his fathers and	**2Ch 9:31**	8010
fled from the presence of King **S**),	**2Ch 10:2**	8010
elders who had served his father **S**	**2Ch 10:6**	8010
"Speak to Rehoboam the son of **S**,	**2Ch 11:3**	8010
supported Rehoboam the son of **S**	**2Ch 11:17**	8010
walked in the way of David and **S**	**2Ch 11:17**	8010
golden shields which **S** had made.	**2Ch 12:9**	8010
the servant of **S** the son of David,	**2Ch 13:6**	8010
strong for Rehoboam, the son of **S**,	**2Ch 13:7**	8010
the days of **S** the son of David,	**2Ch 30:26**	8010
said to David and to **S** his son,	**2Ch 33:7**	8010
the holy ark in the house which **S**	**2Ch 35:3**	8010
to the writing of his son **S**.	**2Ch 35:4**	8010
command of David *and* of his son **S**.	**Ne 12:45**	8010
"Did not **S** king of Israel sin	**Ne 13:26**	8010
proverbs of **S** the son of David,	**Pr 1:1**	8010
The proverbs of **S**.	**Pr 10:1**	8010
These also are proverbs of **S** which	**Pr 25:1**	8010
of Kedar, Like the curtains of **S**.	**SS 1:5**	8010
it is the *traveling* couch of **S**;	**SS 3:7**	8010
"King **S** has made for himself a	**SS 3:9**	8010
And gaze on King **S** with the crown	**SS 3:11**	8010
"**S** had a vineyard at Baal-hamon;	**SS 8:11**	8010
thousand *shekels* are for you, **S**,	**SS 8:12**	8010
which King **S** had made for the	**Jer 52:20**	8010
David was the father of **S** by Bathsheba	**Mt 1:6**	*4672*
S was the father of Rehoboam,	**Mt 1:7**	*4672*
not even **S** in all his glory clothed	**Mt 6:29**	*4672*
the earth to hear the wisdom of **S**;	**Mt 12:42**	*4672*
something greater than **S** is here.	**Mt 12:42**	*4672*
the earth to hear the wisdom of **S**;	**Lk 11:31**	*4672*
something greater than **S** is here.	**Lk 11:31**	*4672*
not even **S** in all his glory	**Lk 12:27**	*4672*
in the temple in the portico of **S**.	**Jn 10:23**	*4672*
them at the so-called portico of **S**,	**Ac 3:11**	*4672*
was **S** who built a house for Him.	**Ac 7:47**	*4672*

SOLOMON'S

S provision for one day was	**1Ki 4:22**	8010
and all who came to King **S** table,	**1Ki 4:27**	8010
S wisdom surpassed the wisdom	**1Ki 4:30**	8010
besides **S** 3,300 chief deputies who	**1Ki 5:16**	8010
So **S** builders and Hiram's builders	**1Ki 5:18**	8010
year of **S** reign over Israel,	**1Ki 6:1**	8010
a dowry to his daughter, **S** wife.	**1Ki 9:16**	8010
officers who *were* over **S** work,	**1Ki 9:23**	8010
S drinking vessels *were* of gold,	**1Ki 10:21**	8010
Also **S** import of horses was from	**1Ki 10:28**	8010
Ephraimite of Zeredah, **S** servant,	**1Ki 11:26**	8010
Now **S** son *was* Rehoboam, Abijah *was*	**1Ch 3:10**	8010
S horses were imported from	**2Ch 1:16**	8010
went with **S** servants to Ophir,	**2Ch 8:18**	8010
S drinking vessels *were* of gold,	**2Ch 9:20**	8010
The sons of **S** servants:	**Ezr 2:55**	8010
and the sons of **S** servants were	**Ezr 2:58**	8010
The sons of **S** servants:	**Ne 7:57**	8010
the sons of **S** servants *were* 392.	**Ne 7:60**	8010
and the descendants of **S** servants.	**Ne 11:3**	8010
The Song of Songs, which is **S**.	**SS 1:1**	8010
all with one accord in **S** portico.	**Ac 5:12**	*4672*

SOLVE

and **s** difficult problems.	**Da 5:16**	8271

SOLVING

and **s** of difficult problems were	**Da 5:12**	8271

SOME

s of all food which is edible,	**Gn 6:21**	4480
'Bring me **s** game and prepare a	**Gn 27:7**	
me **s** of your son's mandrakes."	**Gn 30:14**	4480
s of the people who are with me."	**Gn 33:15**	4480
still **s** distance to go to Ephrath,	**Gn 35:16**	3530
s Midianite traders passed by,	**Gn 37:28**	376
were in confinement for **s** time.	**Gn 40:4**	3117
were **s** of all sorts of baked food for	**Gn 40:17**	4480
go down there and buy **s** for us	**Gn 42:2**	
take **s** of the best products of the	**Gn 43:11**	4480
still **s** distance to go to Ephrath;	**Gn 48:7**	3530
then you shall take **s** water from	**Ex 4:9**	4480
for we shall take **s** of them to	**Ex 10:26**	4480
they shall take **s** of the blood and	**Ex 12:7**	4480
and apply **s** of the blood that is	**Ex 12:22**	4480
The sons of Israel did so, and **s**	**Ex 16:17**	
and *some* gathered much and **s**	**Ex 16:17**	
s left part of it until morning,	**Ex 16:20**	376
s of the people went out to gather,	**Ex 16:27**	4480
you **s** of the elders of Israel;	**Ex 17:5**	4480
take **s** of the blood of the bull	**Ex 29:12**	4480
and take **s** of its blood and put *it*	**Ex 29:20**	4480
"Then you shall take **s** of the blood	**Ex 29:21**	4480
altar and **s** of the anointing oil,	**Ex 29:21**	4480
You shall beat **s** of it very fine,	**Ex 30:36**	4480
and you might take **s** of his daughters	**Ex 34:16**	4480
is to take **s** of the blood of the bull	**Lv 4:5**	4480
and sprinkle **s** of the blood seven	**Lv 4:6**	4480
priest shall also put **s** of the blood	**Lv 4:7**	4480
is to bring **s** of the blood of the bull	**Lv 4:16**	4480
'He shall put **s** of the blood	**Lv 4:18**	4480
s of the blood of the sin offering	**Lv 4:25**	4480
The priest shall take **s** of its blood	**Lv 4:30**	4480
s of the blood of the sin offering	**Lv 4:34**	4480
s of the blood of the sin offering	**Lv 5:9**	4480
He sprinkled **s** of it on the altar	**Lv 8:11**	4480
he poured **s** of the anointing oil on	**Lv 8:12**	4480
the blood and with his finger put **s**	**Lv 8:15**	
slaughtered *it* and took **s** of its blood	**Lv 8:23**	4480
and Moses put **s** of the blood on	**Lv 8:24**	4480
So Moses took **s** of the anointing oil	**Lv 8:30**	4480
the anointing oil and **s** of the blood	**Lv 8:30**	4480
his finger in the blood and put **s**	**Lv 9:9**	
and filled his hand with **s** of it	**Lv 9:17**	4480
who eats **s** of its carcass shall	**Lv 11:40**	4480
s of the blood of the guilt offering,	**Lv 14:14**	4480
also take **s** of the log of oil,	**Lv 14:15**	4480
with his finger sprinkle **s** of the oil	**Lv 14:16**	4480
the priest shall put **s** on the	**Lv 14:17**	
s of the blood of the guilt offering	**Lv 14:25**	4480
priest shall also pour **s** of the oil	**Lv 14:26**	4480
the priest shall sprinkle **s** of the oil	**Lv 14:27**	4480
The priest shall then put **s** of the oil	**Lv 14:28**	4480
shall take **s** of the blood of the bull	**Lv 16:14**	4480
he shall sprinkle **s** of the blood with	**Lv 16:14**	4480
shall take **s** of the blood of the bull	**Lv 16:18**	4480
he shall sprinkle **s** of the blood on it	**Lv 16:19**	4480
given **s** of his offspring to Molech,	**Lv 20:3**	4480
and he shall take **s** of the dust	**Nu 5:17**	4480
But there were **s** men who were	**Nu 9:6**	
burned among them and consumed **s**	**Nu 11:1**	
get **s** of the fruit of the land."	**Nu 13:20**	4480
with **s** of the pomegranates and the	**Nu 13:23**	4480
with **s** of the sons of Israel,	**Nu 16:2**	376
the priest shall take **s** of its blood	**Nu 19:4**	4480
and sprinkle **s** of its blood toward	**Nu 19:4**	4480
they shall take **s** of the ashes	**Nu 19:17**	4480
and took **s** of them captive.	**Nu 21:1**	4480
and sent **s** to Balaam	**Nu 22:40**	
put **s** of your authority on him,	**Nu 27:20**	4480
each shall give **s** of his cities to	**Nu 35:8**	4480
"Then they took **s** of the fruit	**Dt 1:25**	
s worthless men have gone out from	**Dt 13:13**	
he has found **s** indecency in her,	**Dt 24:1**	1697
take **s** of the first of all the produce	**Dt 26:2**	4480
ate **s** of the produce of the land,	**Jos 5:11**	4480
s of the produce of the land,	**Jos 5:12**	4480
s of the yield of the land of Canaan	**Jos 5:12**	4480
s of the things under the ban,	**Jos 6:18**	4480
s of the things under the ban,	**Jos 7:1**	4480
taken **s** of the things under the ban	**Jos 7:11**	4480
s on this side and some on that	**Jos 8:22**	428
on this side and **s** on that side;	**Jos 8:22**	428
Israel took **s** of their provisions,	**Jos 9:14**	4480
in Gath, and in Ashdod **s** remained.	**Jos 11:22**	
he gave **s** to them and they ate	**Jg 14:9**	
When they had gone **s** distance from	**Jg 18:22**	7368
strike and kill **s** of the people as	**Jg 20:31**	4480
and was satisfied and had **s** left.	**Ru 2:14**	
shall purposely pull out for her **s**	**Ru 2:16**	
s of the men of Beth-shemesh	**1Sa 6:19**	
and **s** to do his plowing	**1Sa 8:12**	
Also **s** *of* the Hebrews crossed	**1Sa 13:7**	

bearer put **s** to death after him. **1Sa 14:13**
"But the people took **s** of **1Sa 15:21**
the cave, and **s** said to kill you, **1Sa 24:10**
he sent **s** of the spoil to **1Sa 30:26**
So David sent **s** of his servants to **2Sa 10:2** 3027
and **s** of the people among David's **2Sa 11:17** 4480
so **s** of the king's servants are **2Sa 11:24** 4480
my sister Tamar come and give me **s** **2Sa 13:5**
"Take ten loaves with you, **s** **1Ki 14:3**
have to kill **s** of the cattle." **1Ki 18:5** 4480
s mountain or into some valley." **2Ki 2:16** 259
some mountain or into **s** valley." **2Ki 2:16** 259
'They shall eat and have **s** **2Ki 4:43**
and they ate and had **s** left over, **2Ki 4:44**
had the prophet told you *to do* **s** **2Ki 5:13**
he departed from him **s** distance. **2Ki 5:19** 3530
let **s** *men* take five of the horses **2Ki 7:13**
and **s** of her blood was sprinkled **2Ki 9:33** 4480
among them which killed **s** of them. **2Ki 17:25**
'**S** of your sons who shall issue from **2Ki 20:18** 4480
the guard left **s** of the poorest of the **2Ki 25:12** 4480
Now **s** of the families of the sons **1Ch 6:66** 4480
S of the sons of Judah, of the sons **1Ch 9:3** 4480
Now **s** of them had charge of the **1Ch 9:28** 4480
S of them also were appointed over **1Ch 9:29** 4480
S of the sons of the priests prepared **1Ch 9:30** 4480
S of their relatives of the sons of **1Ch 9:32** 4480
Then **s** of the sons of Benjamin and **1Ch 12:16** 4480
Manasseh also **s** defected to David when **1Ch 12:19** 4480
He appointed **s** of the Levites **1Ch 16:4** 4480
army set apart for the service **s** **1Ch 25:1**
distributed **s** of his sons through all **2Ch 11:23** 4480
them **s** *measure* of deliverance, **2Ch 12:7** 4592
And Asa oppressed **s** of the people **2Ch 16:10** 4480
S of the Philistines brought gifts **2Ch 17:11** 4480
S years later he went down to *visit* **2Ch 18:2**
"But there is **s** good in you, **2Ch 19:3**
s of the Levites and priests, **2Ch 19:8** 4480
and **s** of the heads of the fathers' **2Ch 19:8** 4480
together with **s** of the Meunites, **2Ch 20:1** 4480
Then **s** came and reported to **2Ch 20:2**
s of the rulers of Israel also. **2Ch 21:4** 4480
Then **s** of the heads of the sons of **2Ch 28:12** 376
Nevertheless **s** men of Asher, **2Ch 30:11** 4480
s of his own children killed him **2Ch 32:21** 4480
and **s** of the Levites *were* **2Ch 34:13** 4480
Nebuchadnezzar also brought **s** of **2Ch 36:7** 4480
S of the heads of fathers' **Ezr 2:68** 4480
and the Levites, **s** of the people, **Ezr 2:70** 4480
S of the sons of Israel and some of **Ezr 7:7** 4480
of Israel and **s** of the priests, **Ezr 7:7** 4480
taken **s** of their daughters *as wives* **Ezr 9:2** 4480
and pulled **s** of the hair from my **Ezr 9:3** 4480
and **s** of them had wives *by whom* **Ezr 10:44** 4480
and **s** men from Judah came; **Ne 1:2**
and **s** of our daughters are forced **Ne 5:5** 4480
S from among the heads of fathers' **Ne 7:70** 4480
S of the heads of fathers' **Ne 7:71** 4480
the singers, **s** of the people, **Ne 7:73** 4480
S of the sons of Judah and some of **Ne 11:4** 4480
Judah and **s** of the sons of Benjamin **Ne 11:4** 4480
s of the sons of Judah lived in **Ne 11:25** 4480
From the Levites, **s** divisions in **Ne 11:36**
and **s** of the sons of the priests **Ne 12:35** 4480
After **s** time, however, I asked **Ne 13:6**
In those days I saw in Judah **s** who **Ne 13:15**
Then I stationed **s** of my servants **Ne 13:19**
struck **s** of them and pulled out their **Ne 13:25** 376
"**S** remove the landmarks; **Jb 24:2**
S *boast* in chariots and some in **Ps 20:7** 428
in chariots and **s** in horses **Ps 20:7** 428
killed **s** of their stoutest ones, **Ps 78:31**
gives **s** of his food to the poor. **Pr 22:9** 4480
'And **s** of your sons who will **Is 39:7**
spoken in secret, In **s** dark land; **Is 45:19** 4725
"I will also take **s** of them for **Is 66:21** 4480
take **s** of the elders of the people **Jer 19:1** 4480
and **s** of the senior priests. **Jer 19:1** 4480
Then **s** of the elders of the land **Jer 26:17** 376
in order to take possession of **s** **Jer 37:12**
But **s** of the poorest people who **Jer 39:10** 4480
"Take **s** large stones in your **Jer 43:9**
in the sight of **s** *of the* Jews; **Jer 43:9** 376
s of the poorest of the people, **Jer 52:15** 4480
left **s** of the poorest of the land to be **Jer 52:16** 4480
"Take again **s** of them and **Ezk 5:4** 4480
took **s** and put *it* into the hands **Ezk 10:7**
put to death **s** who should not die **Ezk 13:19** 5315
Then **s** elders of Israel came to me **Ezk 14:1** 376
"You took **s** of your clothes, **Ezk 16:16** 4480
also took **s** of the seed of the land **Ezk 17:5** 4480
'You shall take **s** of its blood and **Ezk 43:20** 4480
s of the blood from the sin offering **Ezk 45:19** 4480
s of the vessels of the house of God; **Da 1:2**
4480, 7117
bring in **s** of the sons of Israel, **Da 1:3** 4480
including **s** of the royal family **Da 1:3** 4480
and let us be given **s** vegetables **Da 1:12** 4480
so **s** of the kingdom will be strong **Da 2:42**
4481, 7118
heaven and caused **s** of the host and **Da 8:10** 4480
some of the host and **s** of the stars **Da 8:10** 4480
"After **s** years they will form **Da 11:6**
king of the North for **s** years. **Da 11:8**
and after an interval of **s** years **Da 11:13** 6256
"**S** of those who have insight will **Da 11:35** 4480
"Then I raised up **s** of your sons **Am 2:11** 4480
prophets And **s** of your young men **Am 2:11** 4480
Would they not leave **s** gleanings? **Ob 1:5**

s of the scribes said to **Mt 9:3** *5100*
Then **s** of the scribes and Pharisees **Mt 12:38** *5100*
s *seeds* fell beside the road, **Mt 13:4**
3739, 3303a
yielded a crop, **s** a hundredfold, **Mt 13:8**
3739, 3303a
crop, some a hundredfold, **s** sixty, **Mt 13:8** *3739*
some sixty, and **s** thirty. **Mt 13:8** *3739*
and brings forth, **s** a hundredfold, **Mt 13:23**
3739, 3303a
some a hundredfold, **s** sixty, **Mt 13:23** *3739*
some sixty, and **s** thirty." **Mt 13:23** *3739*
Then **s** Pharisees and scribes came **Mt 15:1**
"**S** *say* John the Baptist; **Mt 16:14**
3588, 3303a
s of those who are standing here **Mt 16:28** *5100*
S Pharisees came to Jesus, **Mt 19:3**
Then **s** children were brought to **Mt 19:13**
On that day **s** Sadducees (who say **Mt 22:23**
s of them you will kill and **Mt 23:34** *1537*
and **s** of them you will scourge in **Mt 23:34** *1537*
'Give us **s** of your oil, for our **Mt 25:8** *1537*
go instead to the dealers and buy **s** **Mt 25:9**
Jesus took **s** bread, and after a **Mt 26:26**
And **s** of those who were standing **Mt 27:47** *5100*
s of the guard came into the city **Mt 28:11** *5100*
but **s** were doubtful. **Mt 28:17** *3588*
But **s** of the scribes were sitting **Mk 2:6** *5100*
s *seed* fell beside the road, **Mk 4:4**
3739, 3303a
s of the scribes gathered around **Mk 7:1** *5100*
s of His disciples were eating their **Mk 7:2** *5100*
and **s** of them have come from a **Mk 8:3** *5100*
there are **s** of those who are **Mk 9:1** *5100*
and **s** scribes arguing with them. **Mk 9:14**
S Pharisees came up to Jesus, **Mk 10:2**
S of the bystanders were saying to **Mk 11:5** *5100*
in order to receive **s** of **Mk 12:2**
so with many others, beating **s** and **Mk 12:5**
3739, 3303a
Then they sent **s** of the Pharisees **Mk 12:13** *5100*
S Sadducees (who say that there **Mk 12:18**
But **s** were indignantly *remarking* **Mk 14:4** *5100*
While they were eating, He took **s** **Mk 14:22**
S stood up and *began* to give **Mk 14:57** *5100*
S began to spit at Him, and to **Mk 14:65** *5100*
When **s** of the bystanders heard it, **Mk 15:35** *5100*
There were also **s** women looking **Mk 15:40**
region there were **s** shepherds **Lk 2:8**
And **s** tax collectors also came to **Lk 3:12**
S soldiers were questioning him, **Lk 3:14**
and there were **s** Pharisees **Lk 5:17**
And **s** men *were* carrying on a **Lk 5:18**
passing through **s** grainfields **Lk 6:1**
But **s** of the Pharisees said, **Lk 6:2** *5100*
he sent **s** Jewish elders asking Him **Lk 7:3**
and *also* **s** women who had been **Lk 8:2** *5100*
he sowed, **s** fell beside the road, **Lk 8:5**
3739, 3303a
because it was said by **s** that John **Lk 9:7** *5100*
and by **s** that Elijah had appeared, **Lk 9:8** *5100*
there are **s** of those standing here **Lk 9:27** *5100*
S eight days after these sayings, He **Lk 9:28** *5616*
But **s** of them said, **Lk 11:15** *5100*
and **s** of them they will kill **Lk 11:49**
some of them they will kill and **s** **Lk 11:49**
were **s** present who reported to Him **Lk 13:1** *5100*
"And behold, **s** are last who **Lk 13:30**
are last who will be first and **s** **Lk 13:30**
at that time **s** Pharisees approached, **Lk 13:31** *5100*
And He also told this parable to **s** **Lk 18:9** *5100*
standing **s** distance away, **Lk 18:13** *3113*
S of the Pharisees in the crowd said **Lk 19:39** *5100*
so that they would give him **s** of **Lk 20:10**
might catch Him in **s** statement, **Lk 20:20**
came to Him **s** of the Sadducees **Lk 20:27** *5100*
S of the scribes answered and said, **Lk 20:39** *5100*
s were talking about the temple, **Lk 21:5** *5100*
and they will put **s** of you to **Lk 21:16**
And when He had taken **s** bread **Lk 22:19**
to see **s** sign performed by Him. **Lk 23:8** *5100*
And he questioned Him at **s** length; **Lk 23:9** *2425*
also **s** women among us amazed us. **Lk 24:22** *5100*
"**S** of those who were with us went to **Lk 24:24** *5100*
And He said to them, "Draw **s** **Jn 2:8**
are **s** of you who do not believe." **Jn 6:64** *5100*
s were saying, "He is a good man"; **Jn 7:12**
3588, 3303a
s of the people of Jerusalem were **Jn 7:25** *5100*
S of the people therefore, when **Jn 7:40**
S of them wanted to seize Him, but **Jn 7:44** *5100*
s of the Pharisees were saying, **Jn 9:16** *5100*
sheep, but climbs up **s** other way, **Jn 10:1** *237a*
But **s** of them said, **Jn 11:37** *5100*
But **s** of them went to the **Jn 11:46** *5100*
Now there were **s** Greeks among those **Jn 12:20** *5100*
For **s** were supposing, because **Jn 13:29** *5100*
S of His disciples then said to **Jn 16:17**
"Bring **s** of the fish which you **Jn 21:10** *575*
and kept back **s** of the price for **Ac 5:2**
the Holy Spirit and to keep back **s** **Ac 5:3**
"For **s** time ago Theudas rose up, **Ac 5:36** *3778*
days of the census and drew away **s** **Ac 5:37**
But **s** men from what was called the **Ac 6:9** *5100*
and **s** from Cilicia and Asia, **Ac 6:9** *3588*
S devout men buried Stephen, **Ac 8:2**
the road they came to **s** water; **Ac 8:36** *5100*
"Now dispatch **s** men to Joppa **Ac 10:5**
and **s** of the brethren from Joppa **Ac 10:23** *5100*

But there were **s** of them, men of **Ac 11:20** *5100*
Now at this time **s** prophets came **Ac 11:27**
on **s** who belonged to the church in **Ac 12:1** *5100*
and **s** sided with the Jews, and **Ac 14:4**
3588, 3303a
the Jews, and **s** with the apostles. **Ac 14:4** *3588*
S men came down from Judea and **Ac 15:1** *5100*
that Paul and Barnabas and **s** others **Ac 15:2** *5100*
But **s** of the sect of the Pharisees **Ac 15:5** *5100*
s of our number to whom we gave **Ac 15:24** *5100*
After **s** days Paul said to Barnabas, **Ac 15:36** *5100*
staying in this city for **s** days. **Ac 16:12** *5100*
And **s** of them were persuaded and **Ac 17:4** *5100*
taking along **s** wicked men from the **Ac 17:5** *5100*
began dragging Jason and **s** brethren **Ac 17:6** *5100*
also **s** of the Epicurean and Stoic **Ac 17:18** *5100*
S were saying, **Ac 17:18** *5100*
bringing **s** strange things to our ears; **Ac 17:20** *5100*
s of your own poets have said, **Ac 17:28** *5100*
of the dead, **s** *began* to sneer, **Ac 17:32**
3588, 3303a
But **s** men joined him and believed, **Ac 17:34** *5100*
And having spent **s** time *there,* **Ac 18:23** *5100*
to Ephesus, and found **s** disciples. **Ac 19:1** *5100*
But when **s** were becoming hardened **Ac 19:9** *5100*
also **s** of the Jewish exorcists, **Ac 19:13** *5100*
Also **s** of the Asiarchs who **Ac 19:31** *5100*
s were shouting one thing and some **Ac 19:32** *243*
shouting one thing and **s** another, **Ac 19:32** *243*
S of the crowd concluded *it was* **Ac 19:33**
we were staying there for **s** days, **Ac 21:10** *4183*
S of the disciples from Caesarea **Ac 21:16**
At once he took along **s** soldiers **Ac 21:32**
s were shouting one thing *and* some **Ac 21:34** *243*
shouting one thing *and* **s** another, **Ac 21:34** *243*
not the Egyptian who **s** time ago stirred **Ac 21:38** *3778*
and **s** of the scribes of the Pharisaic **Ac 23:9** *5100*
Ananias came down with **s** elders, **Ac 24:1** *5100*
there were **s** Jews from Asia **Ac 24:18** *5100*
kept in custody and *yet* have **s** **Ac 24:23**
But **s** days later Felix arrived **Ac 24:24** *5100*
simply had **s** points of disagreement **Ac 25:19** *5100*
"For this reason **s** Jews seized **Ac 26:21**
to deliver Paul and **s** other prisoners **Ac 27:1** *5100*
that they were approaching **s** land. **Ac 27:27** *5100*
them all to take **s** food, **Ac 27:33**
I encourage you to take **s** food, **Ac 27:34**
rest *should follow,* **s** on planks, **Ac 27:44**
3739, 3303a
There we found **s** brethren, **Ac 28:14**
S were being persuaded by the things **Ac 28:24** *3588*
impart **s** spiritual gift to you, **Ro 1:11** *5100*
obtain **s** fruit among you also, **Ro 1:13** *5100*
If **s** did not believe, their **Ro 3:3** *5100*
and as **s** claim that we say), **Ro 3:8** *5100*
countrymen and save **s** of them. **Ro 11:14** *5100*
if **s** of the branches were broken off, **Ro 11:17** *5100*
very boldly to you on **s** points so **Ro 15:15** *3313*
Now **s** have become arrogant, as **1Co 4:18** *5100*
Such were **s** of you; **1Co 6:11** *5100*
but **s**, being accustomed to the idol **1Co 8:7** *5100*
that I may by all means save **s**. **1Co 9:22** *5100*
be idolaters, as **s** of them were; **1Co 10:7** *5100*
act immorally, as **s** of them did, **1Co 10:8** *5100*
us try the Lord, as **s** of them did, **1Co 10:9** *5100*
Nor grumble, as **s** of them did, and **1Co 10:10** *5100*
now, but **s** have fallen asleep; **1Co 15:6** *5100*
how do **s** among you say that there **1Co 15:12** *5100*
for **s** have no knowledge of God. **1Co 15:34** *5100*
to remain with you for **s** time, **1Co 16:7** *5100*
sorrow not to me, but in **s** degree **2Co 2:5** *3313*
Or do we need, as **s**, **2Co 3:1** *5100*
to be courageous against **s**, **2Co 10:2** *5100*
compare ourselves with **s** of those **2Co 10:12** *5100*
are **s** who are disturbing you and **Ga 1:7** *5100*
And He gave **s** *as* apostles, and **Eph 4:11**
3588, 3303a
as apostles, and **s** *as* prophets, **Eph 4:11** *3588*
as prophets, and **s** *as* evangelists, **Eph 4:11** *3588*
and **s** *as* pastors and teachers, **Eph 4:11** *3588*
S, to be sure, are preaching Christ **Php 1:15** *5100*
strife, but **s** also from good will; **Php 1:15** *5100*
For we hear that **s** among you are **2Th 3:11** *5100*
For **s** men, straying from these **1Tm 1:6** *5100*
which **s** have rejected and suffered **1Tm 1:19** *5100*
s will fall away from the faith, **1Tm 4:1** *5100*
to make **s** return to their parents; **1Tm 5:4**
for **s** have already turned aside to **1Tm 5:15** *5100*
sins of **s** men are quite evident, **1Tm 5:24** *5100*
and **s** by longing for it have **1Tm 6:10** *5100*
which **s** have professed and thus **1Tm 6:21** *5100*
and they upset the faith of **s**. **2Tm 2:18** *5100*
s to honor and some to dishonor. **2Tm 2:20** *3739*
some to honor and **s** to dishonor. **2Tm 2:20** *3739*
it remains for **s** to enter it, **Heb 4:6** *5100*
together, as is the habit of **s**, **Heb 10:25** *5100*
for by this **s** have entertained angels **Heb 13:2** *5100*
as though **s** strange thing were **1Pe 4:12**
His promise, as **s** count slowness, **2Pe 3:9** *5100*
are **s** things hard to understand, **2Pe 3:16** *5100*
I was very glad to find **s** of your **2Jn 1:4**
And have mercy on **s**, **Jude 1:22**
3739, 3303a
and on **s** have mercy with fear, **Jude 1:23** *3739*
to cast **s** of you into prison, **Rv 2:10**
because you have there **s** who hold **Rv 2:14**
'So you also have **s** who in the **Rv 2:15**
to him I will give **s** of **Rv 2:17**

SOMEBODY
Theudas rose up, claiming to be s, Ac 5:36 5100
SOMEHOW
if s they could reach Phoenix, Ac 27:12 4458
if s I might move to jealousy my Ro 11:14 4458
this liberty of yours does not s become 1Co 8:9 4458
SOMEONE
home where there was not s dead. Ex 12:30
and s might invite you to eat of his Ex 34:15
that s would give us meat to eat! Nu 11:18 4310
s has torn down his altar." Jg 6:31
And s said, "Behold, they are 1Sa 19:22
Then the king sent s to summon 1Sa 22:11
Now s told David, saying, 2Sa 15:31
"Oh that s would give me water to 2Sa 23:15 4310
"Oh that s would give me water to 1Ch 11:17 4310
s had come to seek the welfare of Ne 2:10 120
robbed of sleep unless they make s Pr 4:16
Should s give Me briars *and* thorns Is 27:4 4310
or give your rewards to s else; Da 5:17 321
or shall we look for s else?" Mt 11:3 2087
S said to Him, "Behold, Your Mt 12:47 5100
And s came to Him and said, Mt 19:16 1520
we saw s casting out demons in Mk 9:38 5100
S ran and filled a sponge with sour Mk 15:36 5100
One, or do we look for s else?" Lk 7:19 243
One, or do we look for s else?' " Lk 7:20 243
"S did touch Me, for I was aware Lk 8:46 5100
s came from *the house of the* Lk 8:49 5100
we saw s casting out demons in Lk 9:49 5100
along the road, s said to Him, Lk 9:57 5100
"But when s stronger than he Lk 11:22
S in the crowd said to Him, Lk 12:13 5100
And s said to Him, Lk 13:23 5100
invited by s to a wedding feast, Lk 14:8 5100
for s more distinguished than you Lk 14:8
if s goes to them from the dead, Lk 16:30 5100
if s rises from the dead.' " Lk 16:31 5100
release s for you at the Passover; Jn 18:39 1520
hands and s else will gird you, Jn 21:18 243
But s came and reported to them, Ac 5:25 5100
Samaria, claiming to be s great; Ac 8:9 5100
how could I, unless s guides me?" Ac 8:31 5100
Of himself or of s else?" Ac 8:34 5100
S SHOULD DESCRIBE IT TO YOU.' " Ac 13:41 5100
good man s would dare even to die. Ro 5:7 5100
when you present yourselves to s *as* Ro 6:16 3739
that s has his father's wife. 1Co 5:1 5100
For if s sees you, who have 1Co 8:10 5100
s will say, "How are the dead raised? 1Co 15:35 5100
For every house is built by s, Heb 3:4 5100
you have need again for s to teach Heb 5:12 5100
What use is it, my brethren, if s Jas 2:14 5100
But s may *well* say, Jas 2:18 5100
as with s weaker, since she is a 1Pe 3:7 4632
roaring lion, seeking s to devour. 1Pe 5:8 5100
If s says, "I love God," and hates 1Jn 4:20 5100
s said, "Get up and measure the temple Rv 11:1
SOMETHING
Invite him to have s to eat." Ex 2:20 3899
s which neither your fathers nor Ex 10:6
'S like a mark *of leprosy* Lv 14:35
or threw s at him lying in wait Nu 35:20
threw s at him without lying in wait, Nu 35:22
3605, 3627
abhor it, for it is s banned. Dt 7:26 2764a
"Out of the eater came s to eat, Jg 14:14 3978
out of the strong came s sweet." Jg 14:14 4966
up to us and we will tell you s." 1Sa 14:12 1697
"I have s *to say* to you." 1Ki 2:14 1697
because in him s good was found 1Ki 14:13 1697
after him and take s from him." 2Ki 5:20 3972
Can s tasteless be eaten without salt Jb 6:6 8602a
"Have I said, 'Give me s,' Jb 6:22
"Behold, I will do s new, Is 43:19 2319
Then it becomes s for a man to Is 44:15
he was, making s on the wheel. Jer 18:3 4399
"I am going to ask you s; Jer 38:14 1697
and in its midst s like glowing metal Ezk 1:4
s that looked like burning coals of Ezk 1:13
there was s like an expanse, Ezk 1:22
there was s resembling a throne, Ezk 1:26 1823
s like glowing metal that looked like Ezk 1:27 4758
and downward I saw s like fire; Ezk 1:27 4758
cherubim s like a sapphire stone, Ezk 10:1
his den unless he has captured s? Am 3:4
When they have s to bite with Mi 3:5
Because *I am* doing s in your days Hab 1:5 6467
your brother has s against you, Mt 5:23 5100
s greater than the temple is here. Mt 12:6
s greater than Jonah is here. Mt 12:41
s greater than Solomon is here. Mt 12:42
you give them s to eat!" Mt 14:16
and you gave Me s to eat; I was Mt 25:35
and you gave Me s to drink; Mt 25:35
and give You s to drink? Mt 25:37
and He said that s should be Mk 5:43
and buy themselves s to eat." Mk 6:36 5101
"You give them s to eat!" Mk 6:37
denarii on bread and give them s Mk 6:37
"Simon, I have s to say to you." Lk 7:40 5100
and He gave orders for s to be Lk 8:55
and find lodging and get s to eat; Lk 9:12 1979
"You give them s to eat!" Lk 9:13
s greater than Solomon is here. Lk 11:31 4183
s greater than Jonah is here. Lk 11:32 4183
to catch *Him* in s He might say. Lk 11:54 5100
'Prepare s for me to eat, and Lk 17:8 5101
it is s He sees the Father doing; Jn 5:19 5100
that he should give s to the poor. Jn 13:29 5100
expecting to receive s from them. Ac 3:5 5100
fell from his eyes s like scales, Ac 9:18
than telling or hearing s new.) Ac 17:21 5100
"May I say s to you?" Ac 21:37 5100
for he has s to report to him." Ac 23:17 5100
you since he has s to tell you." Ac 23:18 5100
place, I may have s to write. Ac 25:26 5101
by works, he has s to boast about, Ro 4:2 2745
Every man who has s on his head 1Co 11:4
perhaps of wheat or of s else. 1Co 15:37 5100
thinks he is s when he is nothing, Ga 6:3 5100
so that he will have s to share Eph 4:28
high priest also have s to offer. Heb 8:3 5100
God had provided s better for us, Heb 11:40 5100
I wrote s to the church; 3Jn 1:9 5100
and before the throne *there was* s Rv 4:6
And I heard s like a voice in Rv 6:6
The second angel sounded, and s Rv 8:8
And I saw s like a sea of glass mixed Rv 15:2
After these things I heard s like a Rv 19:1
Then I heard s like the voice of Rv 19:6
SOMETIMES
If s the cloud remained a few days Nu 9:20 3426
If s the cloud remained from Nu 9:21 3426
SOMEWHAT
they were going to inquire s more Ac 23:20 5100
For even if I boast s further 2Co 10:8 5100
SOMEWHERE
us go s else to the towns nearby, Mk 1:38 237b
might run aground s on the rocks, Ac 27:29 4225
But one has testified s, Heb 2:6 4225
said s concerning the seventh *day:* Heb 4:4 4225
SON
Enoch, after the name of his s. Gn 4:17 1121
and she gave birth to a s, Gn 4:25 1121
To Seth, to him also a s was born; Gn 4:26 1121
he became the father of *a* s in Gn 5:3
and became the father of a s. Gn 5:28 1121
his youngest s had done to him. Gn 9:24 1121
Terah took Abram his s, Gn 11:31 1121
his son, and Lot the s of Haran, Gn 11:31 1121
daughter-in-law, his s Abram's wife; Gn 11:31 1121
child, And you will bear a s; Gn 16:11 1121
So Hagar bore Abram a s; Gn 16:15 1121
Abram called the name of his s, Gn 16:15 1121
indeed I will give you a s by her. Gn 17:16 1121
your wife will bear you a s, Gn 17:19 1121
Then Abraham took Ishmael his s, Gn 17:23 1121
And Ishmael his s was thirteen Gn 17:25 1121
circumcised, and Ishmael his s. Gn 17:26 1121
Sarah your wife will have a s." Gn 18:10 1121
year, and Sarah will have a s." Gn 18:14 1121
The firstborn bore a s, Gn 19:37 1121
the younger, she also bore a s, Gn 19:38 1121
a s to Abraham in his old age, Gn 21:2 1121
name of his s who was born to him, Gn 21:3 1121
Then Abraham circumcised his s Gn 21:4 1121
when his s Isaac was born to him. Gn 21:5 1121
borne him a s in his old age." Gn 21:7 1121
saw the s of Hagar the Egyptian, Gn 21:9 1121
"Drive out this maid and her s, Gn 21:10 1121
for the s of this maid shall not Gn 21:10 1121
not be an heir with my s Isaac." Gn 21:10 1121
Abraham greatly because of his s. Gn 21:11 1121
"And of the s of the maid I will Gn 21:13 1121
"Take now your s, your only son, Gn 22:2 1121
"Take now your son, your only s, Gn 22:2 1121
men with him and Isaac his s; Gn 22:3 1121
and laid it on Isaac his s, Gn 22:6 1121
"Here I am, my s." Gn 22:7 1121
lamb for the burnt offering, my s." Gn 22:8 1121
the wood, and bound his s Isaac and Gn 22:9 1121
and took the knife to slay his s. Gn 22:10 1121
you have not withheld your s, Gn 22:12 1121
withheld your son, your only s, Gn 22:12 1121
burnt offering in the place of his s. Gn 22:13 1121
and have not withheld your s, Gn 22:16 1121
withheld your son, your only s, Gn 22:16 1121
Ephron the s of Zohar for me, Gn 23:8 1121
you shall not take a wife for my s Gn 24:3 1121
and take a wife for my s Isaac." Gn 24:4 1121
should I take your s back to the Gn 24:5 1121
that you do not take my s back there! Gn 24:6 1121
take a wife for my s from there. Gn 24:7 1121
do not take my s back there." Gn 24:8 1121
born to Bethuel the s of Milcah, Gn 24:15 1121
of Bethuel, the s of Milcah, Gn 24:24 1121
a s to my master in her old age, Gn 24:36 1121
'You shall not take a wife for my s Gn 24:37 1121
and take a wife for my s.' Gn 24:38 1121
a wife for my s from my relatives and Gn 24:40 1121
has appointed for my master's s.' Gn 24:44 1121
'The daughter of Bethuel, Nahor's s, Gn 24:47 1121
of my master's kinsman for his s. Gn 24:48 1121
her be the wife of your master's s, Gn 24:51 1121
away from his s Isaac eastward, Gn 25:6 1121
Ephron the s of Zohar the Hittite, Gn 25:9 1121
that God blessed his s Isaac; Gn 25:11 1121
of Ishmael, Abraham's s, Gn 25:12 1121
generations of Isaac, Abraham's s: Gn 25:19 1121
his older s Esau and said to him, Gn 27:1 1121
Esau and said to him, "My s." Gn 27:1 1121
while Isaac spoke to his s Esau. Gn 27:5 1121
Rebekah said to her s Jacob, Gn 27:6 1121
"Now therefore, my s, listen to me Gn 27:8 1121
"Your curse be on me, my s; Gn 27:13 1121
best garments of Esau her elder s, Gn 27:15 1121
put them on Jacob her younger s. Gn 27:15 1121
she had made, to her s Jacob. Gn 27:17 1121
Who are you, my s?" Gn 27:18 1121
Isaac said to his s, Gn 27:20 1121
you have *it* so quickly, my s?" Gn 27:20 1121
close, that I may feel you, my s, Gn 27:21 1121
you are really my s Esau or not." Gn 27:21 1121
"Are you really my s Esau?" Gn 27:24 1121
come close and kiss me, my s." Gn 27:26 1121
the smell of my s Is like the Gn 27:27 1121
"I am your s, your firstborn, Gn 27:32 1121
you then, what can I do, my s?" Gn 27:37 1121
the words of her elder s Esau were Gn 27:42 1121
and called her younger s Jacob, Gn 27:42 1121
my s, obey my voice, and arise, flee Gn 27:43 1121
Laban, s of Bethuel the Aramean, Gn 28:5 1121
daughter of Ishmael, Abraham's s, Gn 28:9 1121
you know Laban the s of Nahor?" Gn 29:5 1121
father and that he was Rebekah's s, Gn 29:12 1121
the news of Jacob his sister's s, Gn 29:13 1121
and bore a s and named him Reuben, Gn 29:32 1121
again and bore a s and said, Gn 29:33 1121
He has therefore given me this s Gn 29:33 1121
again and bore a s and said, Gn 29:34 1121
again and bore a s and said, Gn 29:35 1121
conceived and bore Jacob a s. Gn 30:5 1121
my voice and has given me a s." Gn 30:6 1121
again and bore Jacob a second s. Gn 30:7 1121
Leah's maid Zilpah bore Jacob a s. Gn 30:10 1121
maid Zilpah bore Jacob a second s. Gn 30:12 1121
and bore Jacob a fifth s. Gn 30:17 1121
again and bore a sixth s to Jacob. Gn 30:19 1121
conceived and bore a s and said, Gn 30:23 1121
"May the LORD give me another s." Gn 30:24 1121
Shechem the s of Hamor the Hivite, Gn 34:2 1121
"The soul of my s Shechem longs Gn 34:8 1121
to Hamor and Shechem, Hamor's s. Gn 34:18 1121
So Hamor and his s Shechem came to Gn 34:20 1121
to Hamor and to his s Shechem, Gn 34:24 1121
They killed Hamor and his s Gn 34:26 1121
for now you have another s." Gn 35:17 1121
Eliphaz the s of Esau's wife Adah, Gn 36:10 1121
the s of Esau's wife Basemath. Gn 36:10 1121
Timna was a concubine of Esau's s Gn 36:12 1121
are the sons of Reuel, Esau's s: Gn 36:17 1121
the s of Beor reigned in Edom, Gn 36:32 1121
and Jobab the s of Zerah of Bozrah Gn 36:33 1121
died, and Hadad the s of Bedad, Gn 36:35 1121
and Baal-hanan the s of Achbor Gn 36:38 1121
Baal-hanan the s of Achbor died, Gn 36:39 1121
he was the s of his old age; Gn 37:3 1121
and mourned for his s many days. Gn 37:34 1121
to Sheol in mourning for my s." Gn 37:35 1121
and bore a s and he named him Er. Gn 38:3 1121
and bore a s and named him Onan. Gn 38:4 1121
another s and named him Shelah; Gn 38:5 1121
until my s Shelah grows up"; Gn 38:11 1121
did not give her to my s Shelah." Gn 38:26 1121
"My s shall not go down with you; Gn 42:38 1121
brother Benjamin, his mother's s, Gn 43:29 1121
God be gracious to you, my s." Gn 43:29 1121
'Thus says your s Joseph, Gn 45:9 1121
my s Joseph is still alive. Gn 45:28 1121
Shaul the s of a Canaanite woman. Gn 46:10 1121
he called his s Joseph and said to Gn 47:29 1121
your s Joseph has come to you," Gn 48:2 1121
"I know, my s, I know; Gn 48:19 1121
From the prey, my s, Gn 49:9 1121
sons of Machir, the s of Manasseh, Gn 50:23 1121
if it is a s, then you shall put him to Ex 1:16 1121
"Every s who is born you are to Ex 1:22 1121
The woman conceived and bore a s; Ex 2:2 1121
daughter and he became her s. Ex 2:10 1121
Then she gave birth to a s, Ex 2:22 1121
'Israel is My s, My firstborn. Ex 4:22 1121
'Let My s go that he may serve Ex 4:23 1121
Behold, I will kill your s, Ex 4:23 1121
Shaul the s of a Canaanite woman; Ex 6:15 1121
Aaron's s Eleazar married one Ex 6:25 1121
may tell in the hearing of your s, Ex 10:2 1121
You shall tell your s on that day, Ex 13:8 1121
your s asks you in time to come, Ex 13:14 1121
you or your s or your daughter, Ex 20:10 1121
If he designates her for his s, Ex 21:9 1121
it gores a s or a daughter, Ex 21:31 1121
and the s of your female slave, Ex 23:12 1121
by name Bezalel, the s of Uri, Ex 31:2 1121
the son of Uri, the s of Hur, Ex 31:2 1121
him Oholiab, the s of Ahisamach, Ex 31:6 1121
for every man has been against his s Ex 32:29 1121
his servant Joshua, the s of Nun, Ex 33:11 1121
by name Bezalel the s of Uri, Ex 35:30 1121
the son of Uri, the s of Hur, Ex 35:30 1121
and Oholiab, the s of Ahisamach, Ex 35:34 1121
the s of Aaron the priest. Ex 38:21 1121
the s of Uri, the son of Hur, Ex 38:22 1121
the son of Uri, the s of Hur, Ex 38:22 1121
was Oholiab the s of Ahisamach, Ex 38:23 1121
for a s or for a daughter, Lv 12:6 1121
his mother and his father and his s Lv 21:2 1121
Now the s of an Israelite woman, Lv 24:10 1121
and the Israelite woman's s and a Lv 24:10 1121
The s of the Israelite woman Lv 24:11 1121
or his uncle, or his uncle's s, Lv 25:49 1121
Reuben, Elizur the s of Shedeur; Nu 1:5 1121
Shelumiel the s of Zurishaddai; Nu 1:6 1121
Judah, Nahshon the s of Amminadab; Nu 1:7 1121
Issachar, Nethanel the s of Zuar; Nu 1:8 1121

of Zebulun, Eliab the **s** of Helon;	**Nu 1:9**	1121
Elishama the **s** of Ammihud;	**Nu 1:10**	1121
Gamaliel the **s** of Pedahzur;	**Nu 1:10**	1121
Benjamin, Abidan the **s** of Gideoni;	**Nu 1:11**	1121
Dan, Ahiezer the **s** of Ammishaddai;	**Nu 1:12**	1121
of Asher, Pagiel the **s** of Ochran;	**Nu 1:13**	1121
of Gad, Eliasaph the **s** of Deuel;	**Nu 1:14**	1121
of Naphtali, Ahira the **s** of Enan.	**Nu 1:15**	1121
Nahshon the **s** of Amminadab,	**Nu 2:3**	1121
Nethanel the **s** of Zuar,	**Nu 2:5**	1121
Eliab the **s** of Helon,	**Nu 2:7**	1121
Elizur the **s** of Shedeur,	**Nu 2:10**	1121
Shelumiel the **s** of Zurishaddai,	**Nu 2:12**	1121
Eliasaph the **s** of Deuel,	**Nu 2:14**	1121
be Elishama the **s** of Ammihud,	**Nu 2:18**	1121
Gamaliel the **s** of Pedahzur,	**Nu 2:20**	1121
Abidan the **s** of Gideoni,	**Nu 2:22**	1121
Ahiezer the **s** of Ammishaddai,	**Nu 2:25**	1121
Pagiel the **s** of Ochran,	**Nu 2:27**	1121
Ahira the **s** of Enan,	**Nu 2:29**	1121
was Eliasaph the **s** of Lael.	**Nu 3:24**	1121
was Elizaphan the **s** of Uzziel.	**Nu 3:30**	1121
and Eleazar the **s** of Aaron the	**Nu 3:32**	1121
was Zuriel the **s** of Abihail.	**Nu 3:35**	1121
The responsibility of Eleazar the **s** of	**Nu 4:16**	1121
Ithamar the **s** of Aaron the priest.	**Nu 4:28**	1121
Ithamar the **s** of Aaron the priest."	**Nu 4:33**	1121
Ithamar the **s** of Aaron the priest.	**Nu 7:8**	1121
was Nahshon the **s** of Amminadab,	**Nu 7:12**	1121
of Nahshon the **s** of Amminadab.	**Nu 7:17**	1121
second day Nethanel the **s** of Zuar,	**Nu 7:18**	1121
of Nethanel the **s** of Zuar.	**Nu 7:23**	1121
day *it was* Eliab the **s** of Helon,	**Nu 7:24**	1121
offering of Eliab the **s** of Helon.	**Nu 7:29**	1121
it was Elizur the **s** of Shedeur,	**Nu 7:30**	1121
of Elizur the **s** of Shedeur.	**Nu 7:35**	1121
Shelumiel the **s** of Zurishaddai,	**Nu 7:36**	1121
of Shelumiel the **s** of Zurishaddai.	**Nu 7:41**	1121
it was Eliasaph the **s** of Deuel,	**Nu 7:42**	1121
of Eliasaph the **s** of Deuel.	**Nu 7:47**	1121
it was Elishama the **s** of Ammihud,	**Nu 7:48**	1121
of Elishama the **s** of Ammihud.	**Nu 7:53**	1121
it was Gamaliel the **s** of Pedahzur,	**Nu 7:54**	1121
of Gamaliel the **s** of Pedahzur.	**Nu 7:59**	1121
it was Abidan the **s** of Gideoni,	**Nu 7:60**	1121
of Abidan the **s** of Gideoni.	**Nu 7:65**	1121
was Ahiezer the **s** of Ammishaddai,	**Nu 7:66**	1121
of Ahiezer the **s** of Ammishaddai.	**Nu 7:71**	1121
day *it was* Pagiel the **s** of Ochran,	**Nu 7:72**	1121
of Pagiel the **s** of Ochran.	**Nu 7:77**	1121
day *it was* Ahira the **s** of Enan,	**Nu 7:78**	1121
offering of Ahira the **s** of Enan.	**Nu 7:83**	1121
with Nahshon the **s** of Amminadab.	**Nu 10:14**	1121
and Nethanel the **s** of Zuar,	**Nu 10:15**	1121
and Eliab the **s** of Helon over the	**Nu 10:16**	1121
out with Elizur the **s** of Shedeur,	**Nu 10:18**	1121
and Shelumiel the **s** of Zurishaddai	**Nu 10:19**	1121
and Eliasaph the **s** of Deuel was	**Nu 10:20**	1121
the **s** of Ammihud over its army,	**Nu 10:22**	1121
and Gamaliel the **s** of Pedahzur	**Nu 10:23**	1121
and Abidan the **s** of Gideoni over	**Nu 10:24**	1121
s of Ammishaddai over its army,	**Nu 10:25**	1121
and Pagiel the **s** of Ochran over	**Nu 10:26**	1121
and Ahira the **s** of Enan over the	**Nu 10:27**	1121
the **s** of Reuel the Midianite,	**Nu 10:29**	1121
Then Joshua the **s** of Nun, the	**Nu 11:28**	1121
Reuben, Shammua the **s** of Zaccur;	**Nu 13:4**	1121
of Simeon, Shaphat the **s** of Hori;	**Nu 13:5**	1121
Judah, Caleb the **s** of Jephunneh;	**Nu 13:6**	1121
of Issachar, Igal the **s** of Joseph;	**Nu 13:7**	1121
of Ephraim, Hoshea the **s** of Nun;	**Nu 13:8**	1121
of Benjamin, Palti the **s** of Raphu;	**Nu 13:9**	1121
of Zebulun, Gaddiel the **s** of Sodi;	**Nu 13:10**	1121
of Manasseh, Gaddi the **s** of Susi;	**Nu 13:11**	1121
of Dan, Ammiel the **s** of Gemalli;	**Nu 13:12**	1121
of Asher, Sethur the **s** of Michael;	**Nu 13:13**	1121
Naphtali, Nahbi the **s** of Vophsi;	**Nu 13:14**	1121
of Gad, Geuel the **s** of Machi.	**Nu 13:15**	1121
Moses called Hoshea the **s** of Nun,	**Nu 13:16**	1121
Joshua the **s** of Nun and Caleb	**Nu 14:6**	1121
Nun and Caleb the **s** of Jephunneh,	**Nu 14:6**	1121
except Caleb the **s** of Jephunneh	**Nu 14:30**	1121
Jephunneh and Joshua the **s** of Nun.	**Nu 14:30**	1121
But Joshua the **s** of Nun and Caleb	**Nu 14:38**	1121
Caleb the **s** of Jephunneh remained	**Nu 14:38**	1121
Now Korah the **s** of Izhar, the son	**Nu 16:1**	1121
the son of Izhar, the **s** of Kohath,	**Nu 16:1**	1121
the son of Kohath, the **s** of Levi,	**Nu 16:1**	1121
of Eliab, and On the **s** of Peleth,	**Nu 16:1**	1121
the **s** of Aaron the priest,	**Nu 16:37**	1121
"Take Aaron and his **s** Eleazar and	**Nu 20:25**	1121
and put them on his **s** Eleazar.	**Nu 20:26**	1121
and put them on his **s** Eleazar,	**Nu 20:28**	1121
Now Balak the **s** of Zippor saw all	**Nu 22:2**	1121
And Balak the **s** of Zippor was king	**Nu 22:4**	1121
to Balaam the **s** of Beor,	**Nu 22:5**	1121
"Balak the **s** of Zippor, king of	**Nu 22:10**	1121
"Thus says Balak the **s** of Zippor,	**Nu 22:16**	1121
Give ear to me, O **s** of Zippor!	**Nu 23:18**	1121
Nor a **s** of man, that He should	**Nu 23:19**	1121
oracle of Balaam the **s** of Beor,	**Nu 24:3**	1121
oracle of Balaam the **s** of Beor,	**Nu 24:15**	1121
When Phinehas the **s** of Eleazar,	**Nu 25:7**	1121
the **s** of Aaron the priest,	**Nu 25:7**	1121
"Phinehas the **s** of Eleazar, the	**Nu 25:11**	1121
the **s** of Aaron the priest,	**Nu 25:11**	1121
woman, was Zimri the **s** of Salu,	**Nu 25:14**	1121
Eleazar the **s** of Aaron the priest,	**Nu 26:1**	1121
The **s** of Pallu:	**Nu 26:8**	1121
the **s** of Hepher had no sons,	**Nu 26:33**	1121
except Caleb the **s** of Jephunneh and	**Nu 26:65**	1121
and Joshua the **s** of Nun.	**Nu 26:65**	1121
of Zelophehad, the **s** of Hepher,	**Nu 27:1**	1121
son of Hepher, the **s** of Gilead,	**Nu 27:1**	1121
son of Gilead, the **s** of Machir,	**Nu 27:1**	1121
son of Machir, the **s** of Manasseh,	**Nu 27:1**	1121
of Manasseh the **s** of Joseph,	**Nu 27:1**	1121
his family because he had no **s**?	**Nu 27:4**	1121
'If a man dies and has no **s**,	**Nu 27:8**	1121
"Take Joshua the **s** of Nun, a man	**Nu 27:18**	1121
the **s** of Eleazar the priest,	**Nu 31:6**	1121
the **s** of Beor with the sword.	**Nu 31:8**	1121
except Caleb the **s** of Jephunneh	**Nu 32:12**	1121
Kenizzite and Joshua the **s** of Nun,	**Nu 32:12**	1121
and to Joshua the **s** of Nun,	**Nu 32:28**	1121
half-tribe of Joseph's **s** Manasseh,	**Nu 32:33**	1121
sons of Machir the **s** of Manasseh	**Nu 32:39**	1121
to Machir the **s** of Manasseh,	**Nu 32:40**	1121
Jair the **s** of Manasseh went	**Nu 32:41**	1121
priest and Joshua the **s** of Nun.	**Nu 34:17**	1121
Judah, Caleb the **s** of Jephunneh.	**Nu 34:19**	1121
Simeon, Samuel the **s** of Ammihud.	**Nu 34:20**	1121
Benjamin, Elidad the **s** of Chislon.	**Nu 34:21**	1121
a leader, Bukki the **s** of Jogli.	**Nu 34:22**	1121
a leader, Hanniel the **s** of Ephod.	**Nu 34:23**	1121
leader, Kemuel the **s** of Shiphtan.	**Nu 34:24**	1121
Elizaphan the **s** of Parnach.	**Nu 34:25**	1121
a leader, Paltiel the **s** of Azzan.	**Nu 34:26**	1121
a leader, Ahihud the **s** of Shelomi.	**Nu 34:27**	1121
Pedahel the **s** of Ammihud."	**Nu 34:28**	1121
sons of Gilead, the **s** of Machir,	**Nu 36:1**	1121
son of Machir, the **s** of Manasseh,	**Nu 36:1**	1121
sons of Manasseh the **s** of Joseph,	**Nu 36:12**	1121
you, just as a man carries his **s**,	**Dt 1:31**	1121
except Caleb the **s** of Jephunneh;	**Dt 1:36**	1121
'Joshua the **s** of Nun, who stands	**Dt 1:38**	1121
Jair the **s** of Manasseh took all	**Dt 3:14**	1121
you or your **s** or your daughter or	**Dt 5:14**	1121
so that you and your **s** and your	**Dt 6:2**	1121
your **s** asks you in time to come,	**Dt 6:20**	1121
then you shall say to your **s**,	**Dt 6:21**	1121
just as a man disciplines his **s**.	**Dt 8:5**	1121
and Eleazar his **s** ministered as priest	**Dt 10:6**	1121
sons of Eliab, the **s** of Reuben,	**Dt 11:6**	1121
you and your **s** and daughter,	**Dt 12:18**	1121
"If your brother, your mother's **s**,	**Dt 13:6**	1121
son, or your **s** or daughter,	**Dt 13:6**	1121
you and your **s** and your daughter	**Dt 16:11**	1121
you and your **s** and your daughter	**Dt 16:14**	1121
who makes his **s** or his daughter pass	**Dt 18:10**	1121
firstborn **s** belongs to the unloved,	**Dt 21:15**	1121
he cannot make the **s** of the loved	**Dt 21:16**	1121
before the **s** of the unloved,	**Dt 21:16**	1121
firstborn, the **s** of the unloved,	**Dt 21:17**	1121
and rebellious **s** who will not obey his	**Dt 21:18**	1121
'This **s** of ours is stubborn and	**Dt 21:20**	1121
hired against you Balaam the **s** of	**Dt 23:4**	1121
and one of them dies and has no **s**,	**Dt 25:5**	1121
and toward her **s** and daughter,	**Dt 28:56**	1121
commissioned Joshua the **s** of Nun,	**Dt 31:23**	1121
he, with Joshua the **s** of Nun.	**Dt 32:44**	1121
Now Joshua the **s** of Nun was filled	**Dt 34:9**	1121
LORD spoke to Joshua the **s** of Nun,	**Jos 1:1**	1121
Then Joshua the **s** of Nun sent two	**Jos 2:1**	1121
and came to Joshua the **s** of Nun,	**Jos 2:23**	1121
So Joshua the **s** of Nun called the	**Jos 6:6**	1121
and with *the loss of* his youngest **s**	**Jos 6:26**	6810
ban, for Achan, the **s** of Carmi,	**Jos 7:1**	1121
the son of Carmi, the **s** of Zabdi,	**Jos 7:1**	1121
the son of Zabdi, the **s** of Zerah,	**Jos 7:1**	1121
and Achan, **s** of Carmi, son of	**Jos 7:18**	1121
Achan, son of Carmi, **s** of Zabdi,	**Jos 7:18**	1121
Carmi, son of Zabdi, **s** of Zerah,	**Jos 7:18**	1121
"My **s**, I implore you, give glory	**Jos 7:19**	1121
him, took Achan the **s** of Zerah,	**Jos 7:24**	1121
also killed Balaam the **s** of Beor,	**Jos 13:22**	1121
sons of Machir the **s** of Manasseh,	**Jos 13:31**	1121
priest, and Joshua the **s** of Nun,	**Jos 14:1**	1121
and Caleb the **s** of Jephunneh the	**Jos 14:6**	1121
Hebron to Caleb the **s** of Jephunneh	**Jos 14:13**	1121
became the inheritance of Caleb the **s**	**Jos 14:14**	1121
stone of Bohan the **s** of Reuben.	**Jos 15:6**	1121
he gave to Caleb the **s** of Jephunneh	**Jos 15:13**	1121
Othniel the **s** of Kenaz, the	**Jos 15:17**	1121
male descendants of Manasseh the **s** of	**Jos 17:2**	1121
Zelophehad, the **s** of Hepher,	**Jos 17:3**	1121
son of Hepher, the **s** of Gilead,	**Jos 17:3**	1121
son of Gilead, the **s** of Machir,	**Jos 17:3**	1121
son of Machir, the **s** of Manasseh,	**Jos 17:3**	1121
and before Joshua the **s** of Nun and	**Jos 17:4**	1121
stone of Bohan the **s** of Reuben.	**Jos 18:17**	1121
midst to Joshua the **s** of Nun.	**Jos 19:49**	1121
Eleazar the priest, and Joshua the **s** of	**Jos 19:51**	1121
Eleazar the priest, and Joshua the **s** of	**Jos 21:1**	1121
gave to Caleb the **s** of Jephunneh	**Jos 21:12**	1121
the **s** of Eleazar the priest,	**Jos 22:13**	1121
'Did not Achan the **s** of Zerah act	**Jos 22:20**	1121
And Phinehas the **s** of Eleazar the	**Jos 22:31**	1121
Then Phinehas the **s** of Eleazar the	**Jos 22:32**	1121
'Then Balak the **s** of Zippor, king	**Jos 24:9**	1121
Balaam the **s** of Beor to curse you.	**Jos 24:9**	1121
things that Joshua the **s** of Nun,	**Jos 24:29**	1121
And Eleazar the **s** of Aaron died;	**Jos 24:33**	1121
him at Gibeah of Phinehas his **s**,	**Jos 24:33**	1121
Othniel the **s** of Kenaz,	**Jg 1:13**	1121
Then Joshua the **s** of Nun, the	**Jg 2:8**	1121
them, Othniel the **s** of Kenaz,	**Jg 3:9**	1121
And Othniel the **s** of Kenaz died.	**Jg 3:11**	1121
for them, Ehud the **s** of Gera,	**Jg 3:15**	1121
him came Shamgar the **s** of Anath,	**Jg 3:31**	1121
she sent and summoned Barak the **s**	**Jg 4:6**	1121
they told Sisera that Barak the **s** of	**Jg 4:12**	1121
the **s** of Abinoam sang on that day,	**Jg 5:1**	1121
days of Shamgar the **s** of Anath,	**Jg 5:6**	1121
your captives, O **s** of Abinoam.	**Jg 5:12**	1121
as his **s** Gideon was beating out wheat	**Jg 6:11**	1121
the **s** of Joash did this thing."	**Jg 6:29**	1121
"Bring out your **s**, that he may	**Jg 6:30**	1121
sword of Gideon the **s** of Joash,	**Jg 7:14**	1121
Then Gideon the **s** of Joash	**Jg 8:13**	1121
one resembling the **s** of a king."	**Jg 8:18**	1121
"Rule over us, both you and your **s**,	**Jg 8:22**	1121
and your son, also your son's **s**,	**Jg 8:22**	1121
you, nor shall my **s** rule over you;	**Jg 8:23**	1121
Then Jerubbaal the **s** of Joash went	**Jg 8:29**	1121
was in Shechem also bore him a **s**,	**Jg 8:31**	1121
And Gideon the **s** of Joash died at	**Jg 8:32**	1121
And Abimelech the **s** of Jerubbaal	**Jg 9:1**	1121
youngest **s** of Jerubbaal was left,	**Jg 9:5**	1121
Abimelech, the **s** of his maidservant,	**Jg 9:18**	1121
Now Gaal the **s** of Ebed came with	**Jg 9:26**	1121
Then Gaal the **s** of Ebed said,	**Jg 9:28**	1121
Is he not the **s** of Jerubbaal, and	**Jg 9:28**	1121
the words of Gaal the **s** of Ebed,	**Jg 9:30**	1121
Gaal the **s** of Ebed and his	**Jg 9:31**	1121
Now Gaal the **s** of Ebed went out	**Jg 9:35**	1121
the **s** of Jerubbaal came upon them.	**Jg 9:57**	1121
died, Tola the **s** of Puah,	**Jg 10:1**	1121
the son of Puah, the **s** of Dodo,	**Jg 10:1**	1121
but he was the **s** of a harlot.	**Jg 11:1**	1121
you are the **s** of another woman."	**Jg 11:2**	1121
better than Balak the **s** of Zippor,	**Jg 11:25**	1121
her he had no **s** or daughter.	**Jg 11:34**	1121
Now Abdon the **s** of Hillel the	**Jg 12:13**	1121
Then Abdon the **s** of Hillel the	**Jg 12:15**	1121
conceive and give birth to a **s**.	**Jg 13:3**	1121
conceive and give birth to a **s**,	**Jg 13:5**	1121
conceive and give birth to a **s**,	**Jg 13:7**	1121
birth to a **s** and named him Samson;	**Jg 13:24**	1121
"Blessed be my **s** by the LORD."	**Jg 17:2**	1121
for my **s** to make a graven image and	**Jg 17:3**	1121
and Jonathan, the **s** of Gershom,	**Jg 18:30**	1121
son of Gershom, the **s** of Manasseh,	**Jg 18:30**	1121
and Phinehas the **s** of Eleazar,	**Jg 20:28**	1121
the son of Eleazar, Aaron's **s**,	**Jg 20:28**	1121
and she gave birth to a **s**.	**Ru 4:13**	1121
"A **s** has been born to Naomi!"	**Ru 4:17**	1121
name was Elkanah the **s** of Jeroham,	**1Sa 1:1**	1121
son of Jeroham, the **s** of Elihu,	**1Sa 1:1**	1121
the son of Elihu, the **s** of Tohu,	**1Sa 1:1**	1121
the son of Tohu, the **s** of Zuph,	**1Sa 1:1**	1121
but will give Your maidservant a **s**,	**1Sa 1:11**	2233, 376
that she gave birth to a **s**;	**1Sa 1:20**	1121
nursed her **s** until she weaned him.	**1Sa 1:23**	1121
"I did not call, my **s**,	**1Sa 3:6**	1121
"Samuel, my **s**." And he said, "Here	**1Sa 3:16**	1121
"How did things go, my **s**?"	**1Sa 4:16**	1121
for you have given birth to a **s**."	**1Sa 4:20**	1121
consecrated Eleazar his **s** to keep	**1Sa 7:1**	1121
name was Kish the **s** of Abiel,	**1Sa 9:1**	1121
the son of Abiel, the **s** of Zeror,	**1Sa 9:1**	1121
son of Zeror, the **s** of Becorath,	**1Sa 9:1**	1121
son of Becorath, the **s** of Aphiah,	**1Sa 9:1**	1121
of Aphiah, the **s** of a Benjamite,	**1Sa 9:1**	1121
He had a **s** whose name was Saul,	**1Sa 9:2**	1121
So Kish said to his **s** Saul,	**1Sa 9:3**	1121
"What shall I do about my **s**?" '	**1Sa 10:2**	1121
has happened to the **s** of Kish?	**1Sa 10:11**	1121
And Saul the **s** of Kish was taken;	**1Sa 10:21**	1121
Now Saul and his **s** Jonathan and	**1Sa 13:16**	1121
with Saul and his **s** Jonathan.	**1Sa 13:22**	1121
came that Jonathan, the **s** of Saul,	**1Sa 14:1**	1121
and Ahijah, the **s** of Ahitub,	**1Sa 14:3**	1121
brother, the **s** of Phinehas,	**1Sa 14:3**	1121
the son of Phinehas, the **s** of Eli,	**1Sa 14:3**	1121
though it is in Jonathan my **s**,	**1Sa 14:39**	1121
my **s** will be on the other side."	**1Sa 14:40**	1121
between me and Jonathan my **s**."	**1Sa 14:42**	1121
his army was Abner the **s** of Ner,	**1Sa 14:50**	1121
of Abner *was* the **s** of Abiel.	**1Sa 14:51**	1121
I have seen a **s** of Jesse the	**1Sa 16:18**	1121
"Send me your **s** David who is with	**1Sa 16:19**	1121
sent *them* to Saul by David his **s**.	**1Sa 16:20**	1121
Now David was the **s** of the	**1Sa 17:12**	1121
Then Jesse said to David his **s**,	**1Sa 17:17**	1121
whose **s** is this young man?"	**1Sa 17:55**	1121
inquire whose **s** the youth is."	**1Sa 17:56**	1121
"Whose **s** are you, young man?"	**1Sa 17:58**	1121
"*I am* the **s** of your servant	**1Sa 17:58**	1121
Now Saul told Jonathan his **s** and	**1Sa 19:1**	1121
But Jonathan, Saul's **s**,	**1Sa 19:1**	1121
so Saul said to Jonathan his **s**,	**1Sa 20:27**	1121
s of Jesse not come to the meal,	**1Sa 20:27**	1121
"You **s** of a perverse, rebellious	**1Sa 20:30**	1121
that you are choosing the **s** of Jesse	**1Sa 20:30**	1121
the **s** of Jesse lives on the earth,	**1Sa 20:31**	1121
Will the **s** of Jesse also give to	**1Sa 22:7**	1121
who discloses to me when my **s** makes	**1Sa 22:8**	1121
a covenant with the **s** of Jesse,	**1Sa 22:8**	1121
that my **s** has stirred up my servant	**1Sa 22:8**	1121
saw the **s** of Jesse coming to Nob,	**1Sa 22:9**	1121
Nob, to Ahimelech the **s** of Ahitub.	**1Sa 22:9**	1121
the priest, the **s** of Ahitub,	**1Sa 22:11**	1121
"Listen now, **s** of Ahitub."	**1Sa 22:12**	1121
s of Jesse conspired against me,	**1Sa 22:13**	1121
But one **s** of Ahimelech the son of	**1Sa 22:20**	1121

son of Ahimelech the **s** of Ahitub,	**1Sa 22:20**	1121
when Abiathar the **s** of Ahimelech	**1Sa 23:6**	1121
And Jonathan, Saul's **s**,	**1Sa 23:16**	1121
"Is this your voice, my **s** David?"	**1Sa 24:16**	1121
servants and to your **s** David.' "	**1Sa 25:8**	1121
And who is the **s** of Jesse?	**1Sa 25:10**	1121
wife, to Palti the **s** of Laish,	**1Sa 25:44**	1121
Saul lay, and Abner the **s** of Ner,	**1Sa 26:5**	1121
and to Abishai the **s** of Zeruiah,	**1Sa 26:6**	1121
people and to Abner the **s** of Ner,	**1Sa 26:14**	1121
"Is this your voice, my **s** David?"	**1Sa 26:17**	1121
Return, my **s** David, for I will not	**1Sa 26:21**	1121
"Blessed are you, my **s** David;	**1Sa 26:25**	1121
him, to Achish the **s** of Maoch,	**1Sa 27:2**	1121
the priest, the **s** of Ahimelech,	**1Sa 30:7**	1121
Jonathan his **s** are dead also."	**2Sa 1:4**	1121
and his **s** Jonathan are dead?"	**2Sa 1:5**	1121
fasted until evening for Saul and his **s**	**2Sa 1:12**	1121
"I am the **s** of an alien, an	**2Sa 1:13**	1121
over Saul and Jonathan his **s**,	**2Sa 1:17**	1121
But Abner the **s** of Ner, commander	**2Sa 2:8**	1121
taken Ish-bosheth the **s** of Saul and	**2Sa 2:8**	1121
Ish-bosheth, Saul's **s**,	**2Sa 2:10**	1121
Now Abner the **s** of Ner, went out	**2Sa 2:12**	1121
of Ish-bosheth the **s** of Saul.	**2Sa 2:12**	1121
And Joab the **s** of Zeruiah and the	**2Sa 2:13**	1121
and Ish-bosheth the **s** of Saul,	**2Sa 2:15**	1121
third, Absalom the **s** of Maacah,	**2Sa 3:3**	1121
fourth, Adonijah the **s** of Haggith;	**2Sa 3:4**	1121
fifth, Shephatiah the **s** of Abital;	**2Sa 3:4**	1121
messengers to Ish-bosheth, Saul's **s**,	**2Sa 3:14**	1121
from Paltiel the **s** of Laish.	**2Sa 3:15**	1121
the **s** of Ner came to the king,	**2Sa 3:23**	1121
"You know Abner the **s** of Ner,	**2Sa 3:25**	1121
the blood of Abner the **s** of Ner.	**2Sa 3:28**	1121
put Abner the **s** of Ner to death.	**2Sa 3:37**	1121
Now when Ish-bosheth, Saul's **s**,	**2Sa 4:1**	1121
Saul's **s** *had* two men who were	**2Sa 4:2**	1121
Now Jonathan, Saul's **s**,	**2Sa 4:4**	1121
Saul's son, had a **s** crippled in his	**2Sa 4:4**	1121
head of Ish-bosheth the **s** of Saul,	**2Sa 4:8**	1121
to him and he will be a **s** to Me;	**2Sa 7:14**	1121
the **s** of Rehob king of Zobah,	**2Sa 8:3**	1121
Toi sent Joram his **s** to King David	**2Sa 8:10**	1121
spoil of Hadadezer, **s** of Rehob,	**2Sa 8:12**	1121
Joab the **s** of Zeruiah *was*	**2Sa 8:16**	1121
the **s** of Ahilud *was* recorder.	**2Sa 8:16**	1121
Zadok the **s** of Ahitub and	**2Sa 8:17**	1121
the **s** of Abiathar *were* priests,	**2Sa 8:17**	1121
Benaiah the **s** of Jehoiada was	**2Sa 8:18**	1121
"There is still a **s** of Jonathan	**2Sa 9:3**	1121
the **s** of Ammiel in Lo-debar."	**2Sa 9:4**	1121
house of Machir the **s** of Ammiel,	**2Sa 9:5**	1121
Mephibosheth, the **s** of Jonathan	**2Sa 9:6**	1121
the son of Jonathan the **s** of Saul,	**2Sa 9:6**	1121
Mephibosheth had a young **s** whose	**2Sa 9:12**	1121
his **s** became king in his place.	**2Sa 10:1**	1121
kindness to Hanun the **s** of Nahash,	**2Sa 10:2**	1121
Abimelech the **s** of Jerubbesheth?	**2Sa 11:21**	1121
then she bore him a **s**.	**2Sa 11:27**	1121
and she gave birth to a **s**,	**2Sa 12:24**	1121
the **s** of David had a beautiful sister	**2Sa 13:1**	1121
Amnon the **s** of David loved her.	**2Sa 13:1**	1121
was Jonadab, the **s** of Shimeah,	**2Sa 13:3**	1121
"O **s** of the king, why are you so	**2Sa 13:4**	1121
"No, my **s**, we should not all go,	**2Sa 13:25**	1121
Jonadab, the **s** of Shimeah,	**2Sa 13:32**	1121
went to Talmai the **s** of Ammihud,	**2Sa 13:37**	1121
David mourned for his **s** every day.	**2Sa 13:37**	1121
Now Joab the **s** of Zeruiah	**2Sa 14:1**	1121
otherwise they will destroy my **s**."	**2Sa 14:11**	1121
not one hair of your **s** shall fall to	**2Sa 14:11**	1121
my **s** from the inheritance of God.'	**2Sa 14:16**	1121
your **s** Ahimaaz and Jonathan the	**2Sa 15:27**	1121
and Jonathan the **s** of Abiathar.	**2Sa 15:27**	1121
Ahimaaz, Zadok's **s** and Jonathan,	**2Sa 15:36**	
son and Jonathan, Abiathar's **s**;	**2Sa 15:36**	
"And where is your master's **s**?"	**2Sa 16:3**	1121
name was Shimei, the **s** of Gera;	**2Sa 16:5**	1121
into the hand of your **s** Absalom.	**2Sa 16:8**	1121
the **s** of Zeruiah said to the king,	**2Sa 16:9**	1121
my **s** who came out from me seeks my	**2Sa 16:11**	1121
serve in the presence of his **s**?	**2Sa 16:19**	1121
Now Amasa was the **s** of a man whose	**2Sa 17:25**	1121
Shobi the **s** of Nahash from Rabbah	**2Sa 17:27**	1121
the **s** of Ammiel from Lo-debar,	**2Sa 17:27**	1121
of Abishai the **s** of Zeruiah,	**2Sa 18:2**	1121
out my hand against the king's **s**;	**2Sa 18:12**	1121
"I have no **s** to preserve my name."	**2Sa 18:18**	1121
Then Ahimaaz the **s** of Zadok said,	**2Sa 18:19**	1121
because the king's **s** is dead."	**2Sa 18:20**	1121
Now Ahimaaz the **s** of Zadok said	**2Sa 18:22**	1121
"Why would you run, my **s**,	**2Sa 18:22**	1121
of Ahimaaz the **s** of Zadok."	**2Sa 18:27**	1121
"O my **s** Absalom, my son, my son	**2Sa 18:33**	1121
"O my son Absalom, my **s**,	**2Sa 18:33**	1121
son Absalom, my son, my **s** Absalom!	**2Sa 18:33**	1121
instead of you, O Absalom, my **s**,	**2Sa 18:33**	1121
of you, O Absalom, my son, my **s**!"	**2Sa 18:33**	1121
"The king is grieved for his **s**."	**2Sa 19:2**	1121
"O my **s** Absalom, O Absalom, my	**2Sa 19:4**	1121
"O my son Absalom, O Absalom, my **s**,	**2Sa 19:4**	1121
O Absalom, my son, my **s**!"	**2Sa 19:4**	1121
Then Shimei the **s** of Gera, the	**2Sa 19:16**	1121
And Shimei the **s** of Gera fell down	**2Sa 19:18**	1121
Abishai the **s** of Zeruiah said,	**2Sa 19:21**	1121
Then Mephibosheth the **s** of Saul	**2Sa 19:24**	1121
name was Sheba, the **s** of Bichri,	**2Sa 20:1**	1121
inheritance in the **s** of Jesse;	**2Sa 20:1**	1121
followed Sheba the **s** of Bichri;	**2Sa 20:2**	1121
"Now Sheba the **s** of Bichri will	**2Sa 20:6**	1121
to pursue Sheba the **s** of Bichri.	**2Sa 20:7**	1121
pursued Sheba the **s** of Bichri.	**2Sa 20:10**	1121
to pursue Sheba the **s** of Bichri.	**2Sa 20:13**	1121
Sheba the **s** of Bichri by name,	**2Sa 20:21**	1121
they cut off the head of Sheba the **s** of	**2Sa 20:22**	1121
and Benaiah the **s** of Jehoiada was	**2Sa 20:23**	1121
the **s** of Ahilud was the recorder;	**2Sa 20:24**	1121
the **s** of Jonathan the son of Saul,	**2Sa 21:7**	1121
the son of Jonathan the **s** of Saul,	**2Sa 21:7**	1121
David and Saul's **s** Jonathan.	**2Sa 21:7**	1121
s of Barzillai the Meholathite.	**2Sa 21:8**	1121
and the bones of Jonathan his **s**	**2Sa 21:12**	1121
of Jonathan his **s** from there,	**2Sa 21:13**	1121
the bones of Saul and Jonathan his **s**	**2Sa 21:14**	1121
the **s** of Zeruiah helped him,	**2Sa 21:17**	1121
and Elhanan the **s** of Jaare-oregim	**2Sa 21:19**	1121
Israel, Jonathan the **s** of Shimei,	**2Sa 21:21**	1121
David the **s** of Jesse declares, The	**2Sa 23:1**	1121
Eleazar the **s** of Dodo the Ahohite,	**2Sa 23:9**	1121
Shammah the **s** of Agee a Hararite.	**2Sa 23:11**	1121
brother of Joab, the **s** of Zeruiah,	**2Sa 23:18**	1121
Then Benaiah the **s** of Jehoiada,	**2Sa 23:20**	1121
the **s** of a valiant man of Kabzeel,	**2Sa 23:20**	1121
Benaiah the **s** of Jehoiada did,	**2Sa 23:22**	1121
the **s** of Dodo of Bethlehem,	**2Sa 23:24**	1121
Ira the **s** of Ikkesh the Tekoite,	**2Sa 23:26**	1121
the **s** of Baanah the Netophathite,	**2Sa 23:29**	1121
Ittai the **s** of Ribai of Gibeah of	**2Sa 23:29**	1121
Ahiam the **s** of Sharar the Ararite,	**2Sa 23:33**	1121
Eliphelet the **s** of Ahasbai, the	**2Sa 23:34**	1121
Ahasbai, the **s** of the Maacathite,	**2Sa 23:34**	1121
the **s** of Ahithophel the Gilonite,	**2Sa 23:34**	1121
Igal the **s** of Nathan of Zobah,	**2Sa 23:36**	1121
bearers of Joab the **s** of Zeruiah,	**2Sa 23:37**	1121
the **s** of Haggith exalted himself,	**1Ki 1:5**	1121
conferred with Joab the **s** of Zeruiah	**1Ki 1:7**	1121
priest, Benaiah the **s** of Jehoiada,	**1Ki 1:8**	1121
the **s** of Haggith has become king,	**1Ki 1:11**	1121
and the life of your **s** Solomon.	**1Ki 1:12**	1121
your **s** shall be king after me,	**1Ki 1:13**	1121
'Surely your **s** Solomon shall be	**1Ki 1:17**	1121
that I and my **s** Solomon will be	**1Ki 1:21**	1121
priest and Benaiah the **s** of Jehoiada	**1Ki 1:26**	1121
'Your **s** Solomon shall be king	**1Ki 1:30**	1121
and Benaiah the **s** of Jehoiada."	**1Ki 1:32**	1121
my **s** Solomon ride on my own mule,	**1Ki 1:33**	1121
Benaiah the **s** of Jehoiada	**1Ki 1:36**	1121
Benaiah the **s** of Jehoiada,	**1Ki 1:38**	1121
the **s** of Abiathar the priest came.	**1Ki 1:42**	1121
Benaiah the **s** of Jehoiada,	**1Ki 1:44**	1121
near, he charged Solomon his **s**,	**1Ki 2:1**	1121
Joab the **s** of Zeruiah did to me,	**1Ki 2:5**	1121
of Israel, to Abner the **s** of Ner,	**1Ki 2:5**	1121
Ner, and to Amasa the **s** of Jether,	**1Ki 2:5**	1121
the **s** of Gera the Benjamite,	**1Ki 2:8**	1121
Now Adonijah the **s** of Haggith came	**1Ki 2:13**	1121
and for Joab the **s** of Zeruiah!"	**1Ki 2:22**	1121
sent Benaiah the **s** of Jehoiada;	**1Ki 2:25**	1121
sent Benaiah the **s** of Jehoiada,	**1Ki 2:29**	1121
Abner the **s** of Ner, commander of	**1Ki 2:32**	1121
Israel, and Amasa the **s** of Jether,	**1Ki 2:32**	1121
Then Benaiah the **s** of Jehoiada	**1Ki 2:34**	1121
The king appointed Benaiah the **s** of	**1Ki 2:35**	1121
ran away to Achish **s** of Maacah,	**1Ki 2:39**	1121
Benaiah the **s** of Jehoiada,	**1Ki 2:46**	1121
You have given him a **s** to sit on	**1Ki 3:6**	1121
This woman's **s** died in the night,	**1Ki 3:19**	1121
and took my **s** from beside me while	**1Ki 3:20**	1121
and laid her dead **s** in my bosom.	**1Ki 3:20**	1121
rose in the morning to nurse my **s**,	**1Ki 3:21**	1121
morning, behold, he was not my **s**,	**1Ki 3:21**	1121
For the living one is my **s**,	**1Ki 3:22**	1121
son, and the dead one is your **s**."	**1Ki 3:22**	1121
For the dead one is your **s**,	**1Ki 3:22**	1121
son, and the living one is my **s**."	**1Ki 3:22**	1121
'This is my **s** who is living, and	**1Ki 3:23**	1121
and your **s** is the dead one';	**1Ki 3:23**	1121
For your **s** is the dead one, and my	**1Ki 3:23**	1121
and my **s** is the living one.' "	**1Ki 3:23**	1121
stirred over her **s** and said,	**1Ki 3:26**	1121
the **s** of Zadok *was* the priest;	**1Ki 4:2**	1121
the **s** of Ahilud *was* the recorder;	**1Ki 4:3**	1121
s of Jehoiada *was* over the army;	**1Ki 4:4**	1121
and Azariah the **s** of Nathan *was*	**1Ki 4:5**	1121
and Zabud the **s** of Nathan, a	**1Ki 4:5**	1121
and Adoniram the **s** of Abda *was*	**1Ki 4:6**	1121
Baana the **s** of Ahilud, *in* Taanach	**1Ki 4:12**	1121
towns of Jair, the **s** of Manasseh,	**1Ki 4:13**	1121
Ahinadab the **s** of Iddo, *in*	**1Ki 4:14**	1121
Baana the **s** of Hushai, in Asher	**1Ki 4:16**	1121
Jehoshaphat the **s** of Paruah, in	**1Ki 4:17**	1121
Shimei the **s** of Ela, in Benjamin;	**1Ki 4:18**	1121
Geber the **s** of Uri, in the land of	**1Ki 4:19**	1121
'Your **s**, whom I will set on your	**1Ki 5:5**	1121
a wise **s** over this great people."	**1Ki 5:7**	1121
He was a widow's **s** from the tribe	**1Ki 7:14**	1121
your **s** who will be born to you,	**1Ki 8:19**	1121
tear it out of the hand of your **s**.	**1Ki 11:12**	1121
I will give one tribe to your **s** for	**1Ki 11:13**	1121
of Tahpenes bore his **s** Genubath,	**1Ki 11:20**	1121
to him, Rezon the **s** of Eliada,	**1Ki 11:23**	1121
Then Jeroboam the **s** of Nebat,	**1Ki 11:26**	1121
to his **s** I will give one tribe,	**1Ki 11:36**	1121
his **s** Rehoboam reigned in his place	**1Ki 11:43**	1121
the **s** of Nebat heard *of it*,	**1Ki 12:2**	1121
to Jeroboam the **s** of Nebat.	**1Ki 12:15**	1121
no inheritance in the **s** of Jesse;	**1Ki 12:16**	1121
to Rehoboam the **s** of Solomon.	**1Ki 12:21**	1121
to Rehoboam the **s** of Solomon,	**1Ki 12:23**	1121
a **s** shall be born to the house of	**1Ki 13:2**	1121
the **s** of Jeroboam became sick.	**1Ki 14:1**	1121
inquire of you concerning her **s**,	**1Ki 14:5**	1121
Nadab his **s** reigned in his place.	**1Ki 14:20**	1121
the **s** of Solomon reigned in Judah.	**1Ki 14:21**	1121
his **s** became king in his place.	**1Ki 14:31**	1121
of King Jeroboam, the **s** of Nebat,	**1Ki 15:1**	1121
to raise up his **s** after him and to	**1Ki 15:4**	1121
his **s** became king in his place.	**1Ki 15:8**	1121
to Ben-hadad the **s** of Tabrimmon,	**1Ki 15:18**	1121
son of Tabrimmon, the **s** of Hezion,	**1Ki 15:18**	1121
his **s** reigned in his place.	**1Ki 15:24**	1121
Now Nadab the **s** of Jeroboam became	**1Ki 15:25**	1121
Then Baasha the **s** of Ahijah of the	**1Ki 15:27**	1121
Baasha the **s** of Ahijah became king	**1Ki 15:33**	1121
the **s** of Hanani against Baasha,	**1Ki 16:1**	1121
house of Jeroboam the **s** of Nebat.	**1Ki 16:3**	1121
his **s** became king in his place.	**1Ki 16:6**	1121
the prophet Jehu the **s** of Hanani also	**1Ki 16:7**	1121
Elah the **s** of Baasha became king	**1Ki 16:8**	1121
Baasha and the sins of Elah his **s**,	**1Ki 16:13**	1121
followed Tibni the **s** of Ginath,	**1Ki 16:21**	1121
followed Tibni the **s** of Ginath.	**1Ki 16:22**	1121
the way of Jeroboam the **s** of Nebat	**1Ki 16:26**	1121
his **s** became king in his place.	**1Ki 16:28**	1121
Now Ahab the **s** of Omri became king	**1Ki 16:29**	1121
and Ahab the **s** of Omri reigned	**1Ki 16:29**	1121
Ahab the **s** of Omri did evil in	**1Ki 16:30**	1121
sins of Jeroboam the **s** of Nebat,	**1Ki 16:31**	1121
the *loss of* his youngest **s** Segub,	**1Ki 16:34**	
He spoke by Joshua the **s** of Nun.	**1Ki 16:34**	1121
go in and prepare for me and my **s**,	**1Ki 17:12**	1121
one for yourself and for your **s**.	**1Ki 17:13**	1121
things that the **s** of the woman,	**1Ki 17:17**	1121
and to put my **s** to death!"	**1Ki 17:18**	1121
"Give me your **s**."	**1Ki 17:19**	1121
by causing her **s** to die?"	**1Ki 17:20**	1121
"See, your **s** is alive."	**1Ki 17:23**	1121
and Jehu the **s** of Nimshi you shall	**1Ki 19:16**	1121
and Elisha the **s** of Shaphat of	**1Ki 19:16**	1121
and found Elisha the **s** of Shaphat,	**1Ki 19:19**	1121
house of Jeroboam the **s** of Nebat,	**1Ki 21:22**	1121
house of Baasha the **s** of Ahijah,	**1Ki 21:22**	1121
He is Micaiah **s** of Imlah."	**1Ki 22:8**	1121
quickly Micaiah **s** of Imlah."	**1Ki 22:9**	1121
Then Zedekiah the **s** of Chenaanah	**1Ki 22:11**	1121
Then Zedekiah the **s** of Chenaanah	**1Ki 22:24**	1121
the city and to Joash the king's **s**;	**1Ki 22:26**	1121
his **s** became king in his place.	**1Ki 22:40**	1121
Now Jehoshaphat the **s** of Asa	**1Ki 22:41**	1121
the **s** of Ahab said to Jehoshaphat,	**1Ki 22:49**	1121
his **s** became king in his place.	**1Ki 22:50**	1121
Ahaziah the **s** of Ahab became king	**1Ki 22:51**	1121
way of Jeroboam the **s** of Nebat,	**1Ki 22:52**	1121
And because he had no **s**,	**2Ki 1:17**	1121
of Jehoram the **s** of Jehoshaphat,	**2Ki 1:17**	1121
Now Jehoram the **s** of Ahab became	**2Ki 3:1**	1121
sins of Jeroboam the **s** of Nebat,	**2Ki 3:3**	1121
"Elisha the **s** of Shaphat is here,	**2Ki 3:11**	1121
s who was to reign in his place,	**2Ki 3:27**	1121
were full, she said to her **s**,	**2Ki 4:6**	1121
she has no **s** and her husband is old.	**2Ki 4:14**	1121
next year you will embrace a **s**."	**2Ki 4:16**	1121
bore a **s** at that season the next year	**2Ki 4:17**	1121
"Did I ask for a **s** from my lord?	**2Ki 4:28**	1121
"Take up your **s**."	**2Ki 4:36**	1121
she took up her **s** and went out.	**2Ki 4:37**	1121
'Give your **s** that we may eat him	**2Ki 6:28**	1121
and we will eat my **s** tomorrow.'	**2Ki 6:28**	1121
"So we boiled my **s** and ate him;	**2Ki 6:29**	1121
'Give your **s**, that we may eat him';	**2Ki 6:29**	1121
but she has hidden her **s**."	**2Ki 6:29**	1121
if the head of Elisha the **s** of	**2Ki 6:31**	1121
"Do you see how this **s** of a	**2Ki 6:32**	1121
whose **s** he had restored to life,	**2Ki 8:1**	1121
whose **s** he had restored to life	**2Ki 8:5**	1121
is the woman and this is her **s**,	**2Ki 8:5**	1121
"Your **s** Ben-hadad king of Aram	**2Ki 8:9**	1121
the **s** of Ahab king of Israel,	**2Ki 8:16**	1121
Jehoram the **s** of Jehoshaphat king	**2Ki 8:16**	1121
his **s** became king in his place.	**2Ki 8:24**	1121
the **s** of Ahab king of Israel,	**2Ki 8:25**	1121
Ahaziah the **s** of Jehoram king of	**2Ki 8:25**	1121
Then he went with Joram the **s** of	**2Ki 8:28**	1121
Then Ahaziah the **s** of Jehoram king	**2Ki 8:29**	1121
Judah went down to see Joram the **s**	**2Ki 8:29**	1121
search out Jehu the **s** of	**2Ki 9:2**	1121
of Jehoshaphat the **s** of Nimshi,	**2Ki 9:2**	1121
house of Jeroboam the **s** of Nebat,	**2Ki 9:9**	1121
house of Baasha the **s** of Ahijah.	**2Ki 9:9**	1121
So Jehu the **s** of Jehoshaphat the	**2Ki 9:14**	1121
Jehoshaphat the **s** of Nimshi	**2Ki 9:14**	1121
driving of Jehu the **s** of Nimshi,	**2Ki 9:20**	1121
year of Joram, the **s** of Ahab,	**2Ki 9:29**	1121
s of Rechab *coming* to meet him;	**2Ki 10:15**	1121
with Jehonadab the **s** of Rechab;	**2Ki 10:23**	1121
sins of Jeroboam the **s** of Nebat,	**2Ki 10:29**	1121
his **s** became king in his place.	**2Ki 10:35**	1121
Ahaziah saw that her **s** was dead,	**2Ki 11:1**	1121
took Joash the **s** of Ahaziah and	**2Ki 11:2**	1121
Lord, and showed them the king's **s**.	**2Ki 11:4**	1121
Then he brought the king's **s** out	**2Ki 11:12**	1121
For Jozacar the **s** of Shimeath and	**2Ki 12:21**	1121
and Jehozabad the **s** of Shomer,	**2Ki 12:21**	1121
his **s** became king in his place.	**2Ki 12:21**	1121
year of Joash the **s** of Ahaziah,	**2Ki 13:1**	1121
Jehoahaz the **s** of Jehu became king	**2Ki 13:1**	1121

Context	Reference	No.
sins of Jeroboam the **s** of Nebat,	**2Ki 13:2**	1121
hand of Ben-hadad the **s** of Hazael.	**2Ki 13:3**	1121
his **s** became king in his place.	**2Ki 13:9**	1121
Jehoash the **s** of Jehoahaz became	**2Ki 13:10**	1121
sins of Jeroboam the **s** of Nebat,	**2Ki 13:11**	1121
his **s** became king in his place.	**2Ki 13:24**	1121
Then Jehoash the **s** of Jehoahaz	**2Ki 13:25**	1121
from the hand of Ben-hadad the **s** of	**2Ki 13:25**	1121
Joash **s** of Joahaz king of Israel,	**2Ki 14:1**	1121
Amaziah the **s** of Joash king of	**2Ki 14:1**	1121
the **s** of Jehoahaz son of Jehu,	**2Ki 14:8**	1121
the son of Jehoahaz **s** of Jehu,	**2Ki 14:8**	1121
daughter to my **s** in marriage.'	**2Ki 14:9**	1121
the **s** of Jehoash the son of	**2Ki 14:13**	1121
son of Jehoash the **s** of Ahaziah,	**2Ki 14:13**	1121
his **s** became king in his place.	**2Ki 14:16**	1121
Amaziah the **s** of Joash king of	**2Ki 14:17**	1121
s of Jehoahaz king of Israel.	**2Ki 14:17**	1121
the **s** of Joash king of Judah,	**2Ki 14:23**	1121
Jeroboam the **s** of Joash king of	**2Ki 14:23**	1121
sins of Jeroboam the **s** of Nebat,	**2Ki 14:24**	1121
servant Jonah the **s** of Amittai,	**2Ki 14:25**	1121
hand of Jeroboam the **s** of Joash.	**2Ki 14:27**	1121
his **s** became king in his place.	**2Ki 14:29**	1121
Azariah **s** of Amaziah king of Judah	**2Ki 15:1**	1121
king's **s** was over the household,	**2Ki 15:5**	1121
his **s** became king in his place.	**2Ki 15:7**	1121
Zechariah the **s** of Jeroboam became	**2Ki 15:8**	1121
sins of Jeroboam the **s** of Nebat,	**2Ki 15:9**	1121
Then Shallum the **s** of Jabesh	**2Ki 15:10**	1121
Shallum **s** of Jabesh became king in	**2Ki 15:13**	1121
Then Menahem **s** of Gadi went up	**2Ki 15:14**	1121
and struck Shallum **s** of Jabesh in	**2Ki 15:14**	1121
Menahem **s** of Gadi became king over	**2Ki 15:17**	1121
sins of Jeroboam the **s** of Nebat,	**2Ki 15:18**	1121
his **s** became king in his place.	**2Ki 15:22**	1121
Pekahiah **s** of Menahem became king	**2Ki 15:23**	1121
the sins of Jeroboam **s** of Nebat,	**2Ki 15:24**	1121
Then Pekah **s** of Remaliah, his	**2Ki 15:25**	1121
Pekah **s** of Remaliah became king	**2Ki 15:27**	1121
the sins of Jeroboam **s** of Nebat,	**2Ki 15:28**	1121
And Hoshea the **s** of Elah made a	**2Ki 15:30**	1121
against Pekah the **s** of Remaliah,	**2Ki 15:30**	1121
year of Jotham the **s** of Uzziah.	**2Ki 15:30**	1121
the **s** of Remaliah king of Israel,	**2Ki 15:32**	1121
Jotham the **s** of Uzziah king of	**2Ki 15:32**	1121
the **s** of Remaliah against Judah.	**2Ki 15:37**	1121
his **s** became king in his place.	**2Ki 15:38**	1121
year of Pekah the **s** of Remaliah,	**2Ki 16:1**	1121
of Remaliah, Ahaz the **s** of Jotham,	**2Ki 16:1**	1121
made his **s** pass through the fire,	**2Ki 16:3**	1121
of Aram and Pekah **s** of Remaliah,	**2Ki 16:5**	1121
"I am your servant and your **s**;	**2Ki 16:7**	1121
s Hezekiah reigned in his place.	**2Ki 16:20**	1121
Hoshea the **s** of Elah became king	**2Ki 17:1**	1121
made Jeroboam the **s** of Nebat king.	**2Ki 17:21**	1121
the **s** of Elah king of Israel,	**2Ki 18:1**	1121
that Hezekiah the **s** of Ahaz king	**2Ki 18:1**	1121
Hoshea **s** of Elah king of Israel,	**2Ki 18:9**	1121
king, Eliakim the **s** of Hilkiah,	**2Ki 18:18**	1121
Joah the **s** of Asaph the recorder,	**2Ki 18:18**	1121
Then Eliakim the **s** of Hilkiah,	**2Ki 18:26**	1121
Then Eliakim the **s** of Hilkiah,	**2Ki 18:37**	1121
scribe and Joah the **s** of Asaph,	**2Ki 18:37**	1121
Isaiah the prophet the **s** of Amoz.	**2Ki 19:2**	1121
Then Isaiah the **s** of Amoz sent to	**2Ki 19:20**	1121
his **s** became king in his place.	**2Ki 19:37**	1121
And Isaiah the prophet the **s** of	**2Ki 20:1**	1121
Berodach-baladan a **s** of Baladan,	**2Ki 20:12**	1121
his **s** became king in his place.	**2Ki 20:21**	1121
made his **s** pass through the fire,	**2Ki 21:6**	1121
to David and to his **s** Solomon,	**2Ki 21:7**	1121
his **s** became king in his place.	**2Ki 21:18**	1121
Josiah his **s** king in his place.	**2Ki 21:24**	1121
his **s** became king in his place.	**2Ki 21:26**	1121
the **s** of Azaliah the son of	**2Ki 22:3**	1121
the **s** of Meshullam the scribe,	**2Ki 22:3**	1121
priest, Ahikam the **s** of Shaphan,	**2Ki 22:12**	1121
Shaphan, Achbor the **s** of Micaiah,	**2Ki 22:12**	1121
wife of Shallum the **s** of Tikvah,	**2Ki 22:14**	1121
son of Tikvah, the **s** of Harhas,	**2Ki 22:14**	1121
in the valley of the **s** of Hinnom,	**2Ki 23:10**	1121
that no man might make his **s** or	**2Ki 23:10**	1121
which Jeroboam the **s** of Nebat,	**2Ki 23:15**	1121
took Jehoahaz the **s** of Josiah and	**2Ki 23:30**	1121
Pharaoh Neco made Eliakim the **s** of	**2Ki 23:34**	1121
his **s** became king in his place.	**2Ki 24:6**	1121
Gedaliah the **s** of Ahikam,	**2Ki 25:22**	1121
the **s** of Shaphan over them.	**2Ki 25:22**	1121
Ishmael the **s** of Nethaniah,	**2Ki 25:23**	1121
and Johanan the **s** of Kareah,	**2Ki 25:23**	1121
s of Tanhumeth the Netophathite,	**2Ki 25:23**	1121
Jaazaniah the **s** of the Maacathite,	**2Ki 25:23**	1121
that Ishmael the **s** of Nethaniah,	**2Ki 25:25**	1121
of Nethaniah, the **s** of Elishama,	**2Ki 25:25**	1121
The **s** of Anah *was* Dishon.	**1Ch 1:41**	1121
Bela was the **s** of Beor, and the	**1Ch 1:43**	1121
Jobab the **s** of Zerah of Bozrah	**1Ch 1:44**	1121
Husham died, Hadad the **s** of Bedad,	**1Ch 1:46**	1121
Baal-hanan the **s** of Achbor became	**1Ch 1:49**	1121
The **s** of Carmi *was* Achar, the	**1Ch 2:7**	1121
The **s** of Ethan *was* Azariah.	**1Ch 2:8**	1121
Now Caleb the **s** of Hezron had sons	**1Ch 2:18**	1121
The **s** of Appaim *was* Ishi.	**1Ch 2:31**	1121
And the **s** of Ishi *was* Sheshan.	**1Ch 2:31**	1121
And the **s** of Sheshan *was* Ahlai.	**1Ch 2:31**	1121
and his **s** was Mareshah, the father	**1Ch 2:42**	1121
The **s** of Shammai was Maon, and	**1Ch 2:45**	1121
third *was* Absalom the **s** of Maacah,	**1Ch 3:2**	1121
was Adonijah the **s** of Haggith;	**1Ch 3:2**	1121
Now Solomon's **s** *was* Rehoboam,	**1Ch 3:10**	1121
was Rehoboam, Abijah *was* his **s**,	**1Ch 3:10**	1121
Abijah *was* his son, Asa his **s**,	**1Ch 3:10**	1121
Asa his son, Jehoshaphat his **s**,	**1Ch 3:10**	1121
Joram his **s**, Ahaziah his son,	**1Ch 3:11**	1121
Joram his son, Ahaziah his **s**,	**1Ch 3:11**	1121
son, Ahaziah his son, Joash his **s**,	**1Ch 3:11**	1121
Amaziah his **s**, Azariah his son,	**1Ch 3:12**	1121
Amaziah his son, Azariah his **s**,	**1Ch 3:12**	1121
Azariah his son, Jotham his **s**,	**1Ch 3:12**	1121
Ahaz his **s**, Hezekiah his son,	**1Ch 3:13**	1121
Ahaz his son, Hezekiah his **s**,	**1Ch 3:13**	1121
Hezekiah his son, Manasseh his **s**,	**1Ch 3:13**	1121
Amon his **s**, Josiah his son.	**1Ch 3:14**	1121
Amon his son, Josiah his **s**.	**1Ch 3:14**	1121
of Jehoiakim *were* Jeconiah his **s**,	**1Ch 3:16**	1121
Jeconiah his son, Zedekiah his **s**.	**1Ch 3:16**	1121
prisoner, *were* Shealtiel his **s**,	**1Ch 3:17**	1121
Reaiah the **s** of Shobal became	**1Ch 4:2**	1121
of Aharhel the **s** of Harum.	**1Ch 4:8**	1121
Caleb the **s** of Jephunneh *were* Iru,	**1Ch 4:15**	1121
and the **s** of Elah *was* Kenaz.	**1Ch 4:15**	1121
The sons of Shelah the **s** of Judah	**1Ch 4:21**	1121
Shallum his **s**, Mibsam his son,	**1Ch 4:25**	1121
Shallum his son, Mibsam his **s**,	**1Ch 4:25**	1121
son, Mibsam his son, Mishma his **s**.	**1Ch 4:25**	1121
sons of Mishma *were* Hammuel his **s**,	**1Ch 4:26**	1121
Hammuel his son, Zaccur his **s**,	**1Ch 4:26**	1121
son, Zaccur his son, Shimei his **s**.	**1Ch 4:26**	1121
and Joshah the **s** of Amaziah,	**1Ch 4:34**	1121
Joel and Jehu the **s** of Joshibiah,	**1Ch 4:35**	1121
of Joshibiah, the **s** of Seraiah,	**1Ch 4:35**	1121
son of Seraiah, the **s** of Asiel,	**1Ch 4:35**	1121
Ziza the **s** of Shiphi, the son of	**1Ch 4:37**	1121
the son of Shiphi, the **s** of Allon,	**1Ch 4:37**	1121
son of Allon, the **s** of Jedaiah,	**1Ch 4:37**	1121
son of Jedaiah, the **s** of Shimri,	**1Ch 4:37**	1121
son of Shimri, the **s** of Shemaiah;	**1Ch 4:37**	1121
sons of Joseph the **s** of Israel;	**1Ch 5:1**	1121
sons of Joel *were* Shemaiah his **s**,	**1Ch 5:4**	1121
were Shemaiah his son, Gog his **s**,	**1Ch 5:4**	1121
son, Gog his son, Shimei his **s**,	**1Ch 5:4**	1121
Micah his **s**, Reaiah his son, Baal	**1Ch 5:5**	1121
Micah his son, Reaiah his **s**,	**1Ch 5:5**	1121
son, Reaiah his son, Baal his **s**,	**1Ch 5:5**	1121
Beerah his **s**, whom	**1Ch 5:6**	1121
and Bela the **s** of Azaz, the son of	**1Ch 5:8**	1121
the son of Azaz, the **s** of Shema,	**1Ch 5:8**	1121
the son of Shema, the **s** of Joel,	**1Ch 5:8**	1121
sons of Abihail, the **s** of Huri,	**1Ch 5:14**	1121
the son of Huri, the **s** of Jaroah,	**1Ch 5:14**	1121
son of Jaroah, the **s** of Gilead,	**1Ch 5:14**	1121
son of Gilead, the **s** of Michael,	**1Ch 5:14**	1121
of Michael, the **s** of Jeshishai,	**1Ch 5:14**	1121
son of Jeshishai, the **s** of Jahdo,	**1Ch 5:14**	1121
the son of Jahdo, the **s** of Buz;	**1Ch 5:14**	1121
Ahi the **s** of Abdiel, the son of	**1Ch 5:15**	1121
the son of Abdiel, the **s** of Guni,	**1Ch 5:15**	1121
Libni his **s**, Jahath his son,	**1Ch 6:20**	1121
Libni his son, Jahath his **s**,	**1Ch 6:20**	1121
son, Jahath his son, Zimmah his **s**,	**1Ch 6:20**	1121
Joah his **s**, Iddo his son, Zerah	**1Ch 6:21**	1121
Joah his son, Iddo his **s**,	**1Ch 6:21**	1121
son, Iddo his son, Zerah his **s**,	**1Ch 6:21**	1121
Zerah his son, Jeatherai his **s**.	**1Ch 6:21**	1121
of Kohath *were* Amminadab his **s**,	**1Ch 6:22**	1121
Amminadab his son, Korah his **s**,	**1Ch 6:22**	1121
son, Korah his son, Assir his **s**,	**1Ch 6:22**	1121
Elkanah his **s**, Ebiasaph his son and	**1Ch 6:23**	1121
Elkanah his son, Ebiasaph his **s** and	**1Ch 6:23**	1121
Ebiasaph his son and Assir his **s**,	**1Ch 6:23**	1121
Tahath his **s**, Uriel his son,	**1Ch 6:24**	1121
Tahath his son, Uriel his **s**,	**1Ch 6:24**	1121
son, Uriel his son, Uzziah his **s** and	**1Ch 6:24**	1121
Uzziah his son and Shaul his **s**.	**1Ch 6:24**	1121
Zophai his **s** and Nahath his son,	**1Ch 6:26**	1121
Zophai his son and Nahath his **s**,	**1Ch 6:26**	1121
Eliab his **s**, Jeroham his son,	**1Ch 6:27**	1121
Eliab his son, Jeroham his **s**,	**1Ch 6:27**	1121
Jeroham his son, Elkanah his **s**.	**1Ch 6:27**	1121
of Merari *were* Mahli, Libni his **s**,	**1Ch 6:29**	1121
Libni his son, Shimei his **s**,	**1Ch 6:29**	1121
son, Shimei his son, Uzzah his **s**,	**1Ch 6:29**	1121
Shimea his **s**, Haggiah his son,	**1Ch 6:30**	1121
Shimea his son, Haggiah his **s**,	**1Ch 6:30**	1121
Haggiah his son, Asaiah his **s**.	**1Ch 6:30**	1121
Heman the singer, the **s** of Joel,	**1Ch 6:33**	1121
the son of Joel, the **s** of Samuel,	**1Ch 6:33**	1121
the **s** of Elkanah, the son of	**1Ch 6:34**	1121
son of Elkanah, the **s** of Jeroham,	**1Ch 6:34**	1121
son of Jeroham, the **s** of Eliel,	**1Ch 6:34**	1121
the son of Eliel, the **s** of Toah,	**1Ch 6:34**	1121
the **s** of Zuph, the son of Elkanah,	**1Ch 6:35**	1121
the son of Zuph, the **s** of Elkanah,	**1Ch 6:35**	1121
son of Elkanah, the **s** of Mahath,	**1Ch 6:35**	1121
son of Mahath, the **s** of Amasai,	**1Ch 6:35**	1121
the **s** of Elkanah, the son of Joel,	**1Ch 6:36**	1121
the son of Elkanah, the **s** of Joel,	**1Ch 6:36**	1121
the son of Joel, the **s** of Azariah,	**1Ch 6:36**	1121
of Azariah, the **s** of Zephaniah,	**1Ch 6:36**	1121
the **s** of Tahath, the son of Assir,	**1Ch 6:37**	1121
the son of Tahath, the **s** of Assir,	**1Ch 6:37**	1121
son of Assir, the **s** of Ebiasaph,	**1Ch 6:37**	1121
son of Ebiasaph, the **s** of Korah,	**1Ch 6:37**	1121
the **s** of Izhar, the son of Kohath,	**1Ch 6:38**	1121
the son of Izhar, the **s** of Kohath,	**1Ch 6:38**	1121
the son of Kohath, the **s** of Levi,	**1Ch 6:38**	1121
the son of Levi, the **s** of Israel.	**1Ch 6:38**	1121
even Asaph the **s** of Berechiah,	**1Ch 6:39**	1121
son of Berechiah, the **s** of Shimea,	**1Ch 6:39**	1121
the **s** of Michael, the son of	**1Ch 6:40**	1121
son of Michael, the **s** of Baaseiah,	**1Ch 6:40**	1121
of Baaseiah, the **s** of Malchijah,	**1Ch 6:40**	1121
the **s** of Ethni, the son of Zerah,	**1Ch 6:41**	1121
the son of Ethni, the **s** of Zerah,	**1Ch 6:41**	1121
the son of Zerah, the **s** of Adaiah,	**1Ch 6:41**	1121
the **s** of Ethan, the son of Zimmah,	**1Ch 6:42**	1121
the son of Ethan, the **s** of Zimmah,	**1Ch 6:42**	1121
son of Zimmah, the **s** of Shimei,	**1Ch 6:42**	1121
the **s** of Jahath, the son of	**1Ch 6:43**	1121
son of Jahath, the **s** of Gershom,	**1Ch 6:43**	1121
the son of Gershom, the **s** of Levi.	**1Ch 6:43**	1121
Ethan the **s** of Kishi, the son of	**1Ch 6:44**	1121
the son of Kishi, the **s** of Abdi,	**1Ch 6:44**	1121
the son of Abdi, the **s** of Malluch,	**1Ch 6:44**	1121
the **s** of Hashabiah, the son of	**1Ch 6:45**	1121
of Hashabiah, the **s** of Amaziah,	**1Ch 6:45**	1121
son of Amaziah, the **s** of Hilkiah,	**1Ch 6:45**	1121
the **s** of Amzi, the son of Bani,	**1Ch 6:46**	1121
the son of Amzi, the **s** of Bani,	**1Ch 6:46**	1121
the son of Bani, the **s** of Shemer,	**1Ch 6:46**	1121
the **s** of Mahli, the son of Mushi,	**1Ch 6:47**	1121
the son of Mahli, the **s** of Mushi,	**1Ch 6:47**	1121
the son of Mushi, the **s** of Merari,	**1Ch 6:47**	1121
the son of Merari, the **s** of Levi.	**1Ch 6:47**	1121
Eleazar his **s**, Phinehas his son,	**1Ch 6:50**	1121
Eleazar his son, Phinehas his **s**,	**1Ch 6:50**	1121
Phinehas his son, Abishua his **s**,	**1Ch 6:50**	1121
Bukki his **s**, Uzzi his son,	**1Ch 6:51**	1121
Bukki his son, Uzzi his **s**,	**1Ch 6:51**	1121
son, Uzzi his son, Zerahiah his **s**,	**1Ch 6:51**	1121
Meraioth his **s**, Amariah his son,	**1Ch 6:52**	1121
Meraioth his son, Amariah his **s**,	**1Ch 6:52**	1121
Amariah his son, Ahitub his **s**,	**1Ch 6:52**	1121
Zadok his **s**, Ahimaaz his son.	**1Ch 6:53**	1121
Zadok his son, Ahimaaz his **s**.	**1Ch 6:53**	1121
gave to Caleb the **s** of Jephunneh.	**1Ch 6:56**	1121
The **s** of Uzzi *was* Izrahiah.	**1Ch 7:3**	1121
The **s** of Jediael *was* Bilhan.	**1Ch 7:10**	1121
Hushim *was* the **s** of Aher.	**1Ch 7:12**	1121
the wife of Machir bore a **s**,	**1Ch 7:16**	1121
The **s** of Ulam *was* Bedan.	**1Ch 7:17**	1121
sons of Gilead the **s** of Machir,	**1Ch 7:17**	1121
son of Machir, the **s** of Manasseh.	**1Ch 7:17**	1121
were Shuthelah and Bered his **s**,	**1Ch 7:20**	1121
and Bered his son, Tahath his **s**,	**1Ch 7:20**	1121
Tahath his son, Eleadah his **s**,	**1Ch 7:20**	1121
Eleadah his son, Tahath his **s**,	**1Ch 7:20**	1121
Zabad his **s**, Shuthelah his son,	**1Ch 7:21**	1121
Zabad his son, Shuthelah his **s**,	**1Ch 7:21**	1121
and she conceived and bore a **s**,	**1Ch 7:23**	1121
Rephah was his **s** *along* with	**1Ch 7:25**	1121
along with Resheph, Telah his **s**,	**1Ch 7:25**	1121
Telah his son, Tahan his **s**,	**1Ch 7:25**	1121
Ladan his **s**, Ammihud his son,	**1Ch 7:26**	1121
Ladan his son, Ammihud his **s**,	**1Ch 7:26**	1121
Ammihud his son, Elishama his **s**,	**1Ch 7:26**	1121
Non his **s** and Joshua his son.	**1Ch 7:27**	1121
Non his son and Joshua his **s**.	**1Ch 7:27**	1121
sons of Joseph the **s** of Israel.	**1Ch 7:29**	1121
and his firstborn **s** *was* Abdon,	**1Ch 8:30**	1121
The **s** of Jonathan *was* Merib-baal,	**1Ch 8:34**	1121
Raphah *was* his **s**, Eleasah his son,	**1Ch 8:37**	1121
Raphah *was* his son, Eleasah his **s**,	**1Ch 8:37**	1121
son, Eleasah his son, Azel his **s**.	**1Ch 8:37**	1121
Uthai the **s** of Ammihud, the son of	**1Ch 9:4**	1121
the son of Ammihud, the **s** of Omri,	**1Ch 9:4**	1121
the son of Omri, the **s** of Imri,	**1Ch 9:4**	1121
the son of Imri, the **s** of Bani,	**1Ch 9:4**	1121
the sons of Perez the **s** of Judah.	**1Ch 9:4**	1121
were Sallu the **s** of Meshullam,	**1Ch 9:7**	1121
of Meshullam, the **s** of Hodaviah,	**1Ch 9:7**	1121
of Hodaviah, the **s** of Hassenuah,	**1Ch 9:7**	1121
and Ibneiah the **s** of Jeroham, and	**1Ch 9:8**	1121
Jeroham, and Elah the **s** of Uzzi,	**1Ch 9:8**	1121
the son of Uzzi, the **s** of Michri,	**1Ch 9:8**	1121
and Meshullam the **s** of Shephatiah,	**1Ch 9:8**	1121
son of Shephatiah, the **s** of Reuel,	**1Ch 9:8**	1121
son of Reuel, the **s** of Ibnijah;	**1Ch 9:8**	1121
and Azariah the **s** of Hilkiah, the	**1Ch 9:11**	1121
of Hilkiah, the **s** of Meshullam,	**1Ch 9:11**	1121
son of Meshullam, the **s** of Zadok,	**1Ch 9:11**	1121
son of Zadok, the **s** of Meraioth,	**1Ch 9:11**	1121
son of Meraioth, the **s** of Ahitub,	**1Ch 9:11**	1121
and Adaiah the **s** of Jeroham, the	**1Ch 9:12**	1121
son of Jeroham, the **s** of Pashhur,	**1Ch 9:12**	1121
of Pashhur, the **s** of Malchijah,	**1Ch 9:12**	1121
and Maasai the **s** of Adiel,	**1Ch 9:12**	1121
son of Adiel, the **s** of Jahzerah,	**1Ch 9:12**	1121
of Jahzerah, the **s** of Meshullam,	**1Ch 9:12**	1121
Meshullam, the **s** of Meshillemith,	**1Ch 9:12**	1121
of Meshillemith, the **s** of Immer;	**1Ch 9:12**	1121
were Shemaiah the **s** of Hasshub,	**1Ch 9:14**	1121
son of Hasshub, the **s** of Azrikam,	**1Ch 9:14**	1121
of Azrikam, the **s** of Hashabiah,	**1Ch 9:14**	1121
Galal and Mattaniah the **s** of Mica,	**1Ch 9:15**	1121
the son of Mica, the **s** of Zichri,	**1Ch 9:15**	1121
the son of Zichri, the **s** of Asaph,	**1Ch 9:15**	1121
and Obadiah the **s** of Shemaiah, the	**1Ch 9:16**	1121
son of Shemaiah, the **s** of Galal,	**1Ch 9:16**	1121
son of Galal, the **s** of Jeduthun,	**1Ch 9:16**	1121
and Berechiah the **s** of Asa,	**1Ch 9:16**	1121
the son of Asa, the **s** of Elkanah,	**1Ch 9:16**	1121
Shallum the **s** of Kore, the son	**1Ch 9:19**	1121
son of Kore, the **s** of Ebiasaph,	**1Ch 9:19**	1121
son of Ebiasaph, the **s** of Korah,	**1Ch 9:19**	1121
Phinehas the **s** of Eleazar was	**1Ch 9:20**	1121

Zechariah the **s** of Meshelemiah was 1Ch 9:21 1121
and his firstborn **s** *was* Abdon, 1Ch 9:36 1121
The **s** of Jonathan *was* Merib-baal; 1Ch 9:40 1121
of Binea and Rephaiah his **s**, 1Ch 9:43 1121
Rephaiah his son, Eleasah his **s**, 1Ch 9:43 1121
son, Eleasah his son, Azel his **s**. 1Ch 9:43 1121
kingdom to David the **s** of Jesse. 1Ch 10:14 1121
the **s** of Zeruiah went up first, 1Ch 11:6 1121
Jashobeam, the **s** of a Hachmonite, 1Ch 11:11 1121
him was Eleazar the **s** of Dodo, 1Ch 11:12 1121
Benaiah the **s** of Jehoiada, the son 1Ch 11:22 1121
the **s** of a valiant man of Kabzeel, 1Ch 11:22 1121
Benaiah the **s** of Jehoiada did, 1Ch 11:24 1121
Elhanan the **s** of Dodo of Bethlehem, 1Ch 11:26 1121
Ira the **s** of Ikkesh the Tekoite, 1Ch 11:28 1121
Heled the **s** of Baanah the 1Ch 11:30 1121
Ithai the **s** of Ribai of Gibeah of 1Ch 11:31 1121
Jonathan the **s** of Shagee the 1Ch 11:34 1121
Ahiam the **s** of Sacar the Hararite, 1Ch 11:35 1121
the Hararite, Eliphal the **s** of Ur, 1Ch 11:35 1121
Carmelite, Naarai the **s** of Ezbai, 1Ch 11:37 1121
of Nathan, Mibhar the **s** of Hagri, 1Ch 11:38 1121
bearer of Joab the **s** of Zeruiah, 1Ch 11:39 1121
the Hittite, Zabad the **s** of Ahlai, 1Ch 11:41 1121
the **s** of Shiza the Reubenite, 1Ch 11:42 1121
Hanan the **s** of Maacah and 1Ch 11:43 1121
Jediael the **s** of Shimri and Joha 1Ch 11:45 1121
because of Saul the **s** of Kish; 1Ch 12:1 1121
David, And with you, O **s** of Jesse! 1Ch 12:18 1121
appointed Heman the **s** of Joel, 1Ch 15:17 1121
Asaph the **s** of Berechiah; 1Ch 15:17 1121
Ethan the **s** of Kushaiah, 1Ch 15:17 1121
Obed-edom, also the **s** of Jeduthun, 1Ch 16:38 1121
his father and he shall be My **s**; 1Ch 17:13 1121
sent Hadoram his **s** to King David to 1Ch 18:10 1121
Moreover Abishai the **s** of Zeruiah 1Ch 18:12 1121
Joab the **s** of Zeruiah *was* 1Ch 18:15 1121
the **s** of Ahilud *was* recorder; 1Ch 18:15 1121
and Zadok the **s** of Ahitub and 1Ch 18:16 1121
the **s** of Abiathar *were* priests, 1Ch 18:16 1121
and Benaiah the **s** of Jehoiada *was* 1Ch 18:17 1121
his **s** became king in his place. 1Ch 19:1 1121
kindness to Hanun the **s** of Nahash, 1Ch 19:2 1121
and Elhanan the **s** of Jair killed 1Ch 20:5 1121
Israel, Jonathan the **s** of Shimea, 1Ch 20:7 1121
"My **s** Solomon is young and 1Ch 22:5 1121
Then he called for his **s** Solomon, 1Ch 22:6 1121
"My **s**, I had intended to build a 1Ch 22:7 1121
'Behold, a **s** will be born to you, 1Ch 22:9 1121
for My name, and he shall be My **s** and 1Ch 22:10 1121
"Now, my **s**, the LORD be with you 1Ch 22:11 1121
of Israel to help his **s** Solomon, 1Ch 22:17 1121
his **s** Solomon king over Israel. 1Ch 23:1 1121
The **s** of Gershom *was* Shebuel the 1Ch 23:16 1121
The **s** of Eliezer was Rehabiah 1Ch 23:17 1121
The **s** of Izhar was Shelomith the 1Ch 23:18 1121
the **s** of Nethanel the scribe, 1Ch 24:6 1121
Ahimelech the **s** of Abiathar, 1Ch 24:6 1121
Meshelemiah the **s** of Kore, 1Ch 26:1 1121
Also to his **s** Shemaiah sons were 1Ch 26:6 1121
cast lots *for* his **s** Zechariah, 1Ch 26:14 1121
Shebuel the **s** of Gershom, the son 1Ch 26:24 1121
son of Gershom, the **s** of Moses, 1Ch 26:24 1121
by Eliezer *were* Rehabiah his **s**, 1Ch 26:25 1121
Rehabiah his son, Jeshaiah his **s**, 1Ch 26:25 1121
Jeshaiah his son, Joram his **s**, 1Ch 26:25 1121
son, Joram his son, Zichri his **s** and 1Ch 26:25 1121
his son and Shelomoth his **s**. 1Ch 26:25 1121
dedicated and Saul the **s** of Kish, 1Ch 26:28 1121
Abner the **s** of Ner and Joab the 1Ch 26:28 1121
of Ner and Joab the **s** of Zeruiah, 1Ch 26:28 1121
Jashobeam the **s** of Zabdiel had 1Ch 27:2 1121
the **s** of Jehoiada the priest, 1Ch 27:5 1121
his division was Ammizabad his **s**. 1Ch 27:6 1121
and Zebadiah his **s** after him; 1Ch 27:7 1121
Ira the **s** of Ikkesh the Tekoite; 1Ch 27:9 1121
was Eliezer the **s** of Zichri; 1Ch 27:16 1121
Shephatiah the **s** of Maacah; 1Ch 27:16 1121
Levi, Hashabiah the **s** of Kemuel; 1Ch 27:17 1121
Issachar, Omri the **s** of Michael; 1Ch 27:18 1121
Ishmaiah the **s** of Obadiah; 1Ch 27:19 1121
Jeremoth the **s** of Azriel; 1Ch 27:19 1121
Ephraim, Hoshea the **s** of Azaziah; 1Ch 27:20 1121
Manasseh, Joel the **s** of Pedaiah; 1Ch 27:20 1121
Gilead, Iddo the **s** of Zechariah; 1Ch 27:21 1121
Benjamin, Jaasiel the **s** of Abner; 1Ch 27:21 1121
for Dan, Azarel the **s** of Jeroham. 1Ch 27:22 1121
Joab the **s** of Zeruiah had begun to 1Ch 27:24 1121
Now Azmaveth the **s** of Adiel had 1Ch 27:25 1121
And Jonathan the **s** of Uzziah had 1Ch 27:25 1121
Ezri the **s** of Chelub had 1Ch 27:26 1121
and Shaphat the **s** of Adlai had 1Ch 27:29 1121
and Jehiel the **s** of Hachmoni 1Ch 27:32 1121
Jehoiada the **s** of Benaiah, 1Ch 27:34 1121
He has chosen my **s** Solomon to sit 1Ch 28:5 1121
'Your **s** Solomon is the one who 1Ch 28:6 1121
I have chosen him to be a **s** to Me, 1Ch 28:6 1121
"As for you, my **s** Solomon, know 1Ch 28:9 1121
Then David gave to his **s** Solomon 1Ch 28:11 1121
Then David said to his **s** Solomon, 1Ch 28:20 1121
"My **s** Solomon, whom alone God has 1Ch 29:1 1121
and give to my **s** Solomon a 1Ch 29:19 1121
made Solomon the **s** of David king 1Ch 29:22 1121
Now David the **s** of Jesse reigned 1Ch 29:26 1121
his **s** Solomon reigned in his place. 1Ch 29:28 1121
Now Solomon the **s** of David 2Ch 1:1 1121
altar, which Bezalel the **s** of Uri, 2Ch 1:5 1121
the son of Uri, the **s** of Hur, 2Ch 1:5 1121
who has given King David a wise **s**, 2Ch 2:12 1121
the **s** of a Danite woman and a 2Ch 2:14 1121
your **s** who will be born to you, 2Ch 6:9 1121
Jeroboam the **s** of Nebat? 2Ch 9:29 1121
s Rehoboam reigned in his place. 2Ch 9:31 1121
the **s** of Nebat heard *of it* 2Ch 10:2 1121
to Jeroboam the **s** of Nebat. 2Ch 10:15 1121
no inheritance in the **s** of Jesse. 2Ch 10:16 1121
to Rehoboam the **s** of Solomon, 2Ch 11:3 1121
the **s** of Solomon for three years, 2Ch 11:17 1121
daughter of Jerimoth the **s** of David 2Ch 11:18 1121
daughter of Eliab the **s** of Jesse, 2Ch 11:18 1121
Rehoboam appointed Abijah the **s** of 2Ch 11:22 1121
and his **s** Abijah became king in 2Ch 12:16 1121
"Yet Jeroboam the **s** of Nebat, 2Ch 13:6 1121
servant of Solomon the **s** of David, 2Ch 13:6 1121
for Rehoboam, the **s** of Solomon, 2Ch 13:7 1121
s Asa became king in his place. 2Ch 14:1 1121
God came on Azariah the **s** of Oded, 2Ch 15:1 1121
the **s** of Oded the prophet spoke, 2Ch 15:8 1121
his **s** then became king in his place, 2Ch 17:1 1121
to him Amasiah the **s** of Zichri, 2Ch 17:16 1121
He is Micaiah, **s** of Imla." 2Ch 18:7 1121
"Bring quickly Micaiah, Imla's **s**." 2Ch 18:8 1121
Zedekiah the **s** of Chenaanah 2Ch 18:10 1121
Then Zedekiah the **s** of Chenaanah 2Ch 18:23 1121
city and to Joash the king's **s**; 2Ch 18:25 1121
Jehu the **s** of Hanani the seer 2Ch 19:2 1121
and Zebadiah the **s** of Ishmael, 2Ch 19:11 1121
upon Jahaziel the **s** of Zechariah, 2Ch 20:14 1121
of Zechariah, the **s** of Benaiah, 2Ch 20:14 1121
son of Benaiah, the **s** of Jeiel, 2Ch 20:14 1121
son of Jeiel, the **s** of Mattaniah, 2Ch 20:14 1121
annals of Jehu the **s** of Hanani, 2Ch 20:34 1121
Then Eliezer the **s** of Dodavahu of 2Ch 20:37 1121
his **s** became king in his place. 2Ch 21:1 1121
so that no **s** was left to him 2Ch 21:17 1121
made Ahaziah, his youngest **s**, 2Ch 22:1 1121
So Ahaziah the **s** of Jehoram king 2Ch 22:1 1121
and went with Jehoram the **s** of 2Ch 22:5 1121
the **s** of Jehoram king of Judah, 2Ch 22:6 1121
Jehoram the **s** of Ahab in Jezreel, 2Ch 22:6 1121
against Jehu the **s** of Nimshi, 2Ch 22:7 1121
"He is the **s** of Jehoshaphat, who 2Ch 22:9 1121
Ahaziah saw that her **s** was dead, 2Ch 22:10 1121
took Joash the **s** of Ahaziah, 2Ch 22:11 1121
Azariah the **s** of Jeroham, Ishmael 2Ch 23:1 1121
Jeroham, Ishmael the **s** of Johanan, 2Ch 23:1 1121
of Johanan, Azariah the **s** of Obed, 2Ch 23:1 1121
of Obed, Maaseiah the **s** of Adaiah, 2Ch 23:1 1121
and Elishaphat the **s** of Zichri, 2Ch 23:1 1121
"Behold, the king's **s** shall reign, 2Ch 23:3 1121
king's **s** and put the crown on him, 2Ch 23:11 1121
came on Zechariah the **s** of Jehoiada 2Ch 24:20 1121
shown him, but he murdered his **s**. 2Ch 24:22 1121
blood of the **s** of Jehoiada the priest 2Ch 24:25 1121
Zabad the **s** of Shimeath the 2Ch 24:26 1121
Jehozabad the **s** of Shimrith the 2Ch 24:26 1121
his **s** became king in his place. 2Ch 24:27 1121
the **s** of Jehoahaz the son of Jehu, 2Ch 25:17 1121
the son of Jehoahaz the **s** of Jehu, 2Ch 25:17 1121
'Give your daughter to my **s** in 2Ch 25:18 1121
the **s** of Joash the son of 2Ch 25:23 1121
son of Joash the **s** of Jehoahaz, 2Ch 25:23 1121
the **s** of Joash king of Judah, 2Ch 25:25 1121
the death of Joash, **s** of Jehoahaz, 2Ch 25:25 1121
And Jotham his **s** *was* over the 2Ch 26:21 1121
prophet Isaiah, the **s** of Amoz, 2Ch 26:22 1121
his **s** became king in his place. 2Ch 26:23 1121
his **s** became king in his place. 2Ch 27:9 1121
For Pekah the **s** of Remaliah slew 2Ch 28:6 1121
slew Maaseiah the king's **s** and 2Ch 28:7 1121
Azariah the **s** of Johanan, 2Ch 28:12 1121
Berechiah the **s** of Meshillemoth, 2Ch 28:12 1121
Jehizkiah the **s** of Shallum, 2Ch 28:12 1121
and Amasa the **s** of Hadlai 2Ch 28:12 1121
his **s** reigned in his place. 2Ch 28:27 1121
Mahath, the **s** of Amasai and Joel 2Ch 29:12 1121
Amasai and Joel the **s** of Azariah, 2Ch 29:12 1121
Kish the **s** of Abdi and Azariah the 2Ch 29:12 1121
and Azariah the **s** of Jehallelel; 2Ch 29:12 1121
Joah the **s** of Zimmah and Eden the 2Ch 29:12 1121
of Zimmah and Eden the **s** of Joah; 2Ch 29:12 1121
days of Solomon the **s** of David, 2Ch 30:26 1121
Kore the **s** of Imnah the Levite, 2Ch 31:14 1121
Isaiah the prophet, the **s** of Amoz, 2Ch 32:20 1121
Isaiah the prophet, the **s** of Amoz, 2Ch 32:32 1121
And his **s** Manasseh became king in 2Ch 32:33 1121
to David and to Solomon his **s**, 2Ch 33:7 1121
his **s** became king in his place. 2Ch 33:20 1121
Josiah his **s** king in his place. 2Ch 33:25 1121
he sent Shaphan the **s** of Azaliah, 2Ch 34:8 1121
Joah the **s** of Joahaz the recorder, 2Ch 34:8 1121
Hilkiah, Ahikam the **s** of Shaphan, 2Ch 34:20 1121
of Shaphan, Abdon the **s** of Micah, 2Ch 34:20 1121
wife of Shallum the **s** of Tokhath, 2Ch 34:22 1121
son of Tokhath, the **s** of Hasrah, 2Ch 34:22 1121
s of David king of Israel built; 2Ch 35:3 1121
to the writing of his **s** Solomon. 2Ch 35:4 1121
land took Joahaz the **s** of Josiah, 2Ch 36:1 1121
his **s** became king in his place. 2Ch 36:8 1121
Then Jeshua the **s** of Jozadak and Ezr 3:2 1121
and Zerubbabel the **s** of Shealtiel and Ezr 3:2 1121
Zerubbabel the **s** of Shealtiel and Ezr 3:8 1121
Shealtiel and Jeshua the **s** of Jozadak Ezr 3:8 1121
and Zechariah the **s** of Iddo, Ezr 5:1 1247
then Zerubbabel the **s** of Shealtiel Ezr 5:2 1247
and Jeshua the **s** of Jozadak arose Ezr 5:2 1247
and Zechariah the **s** of Iddo. Ezr 6:14 1247
there went up Ezra **s** of Seraiah, Ezr 7:1 1121
Ezra son of Seraiah, **s** of Azariah, Ezr 7:1 1121
son of Azariah, **s** of Hilkiah, Ezr 7:1 1121
s of Shallum, son of Zadok, son of Ezr 7:2 1121
son of Shallum, son of Zadok, **s** of Ezr 7:2 1121
son of Zadok, **s** of Ahitub, Ezr 7:2 1121
s of Amariah, son of Azariah, son Ezr 7:3 1121
son of Amariah, **s** of Azariah, son Ezr 7:3 1121
son of Azariah, **s** of Meraioth, Ezr 7:3 1121
s of Zerahiah, son of Uzzi, son of Ezr 7:4 1121
son of Zerahiah, **s** of Uzzi, Ezr 7:4 1121
Zerahiah, son of Uzzi, **s** of Bukki, Ezr 7:4 1121
s of Abishua, son of Phinehas, son Ezr 7:5 1121
son of Abishua, **s** of Phinehas, son Ezr 7:5 1121
son of Phinehas, **s** of Eleazar, Ezr 7:5 1121
s of Aaron the chief priest. Ezr 7:5 1121
Eliehoenai the **s** of Zerahiah and Ezr 8:4 1121
the **s** of Jahaziel and 300 males Ezr 8:5 1121
Ebed the **s** of Jonathan and 50 Ezr 8:6 1121
Jeshaiah the **s** of Athaliah and 70 Ezr 8:7 1121
Zebadiah the **s** of Michael and 80 Ezr 8:8 1121
Obadiah the **s** of Jehiel and 218 Ezr 8:9 1121
the **s** of Josiphiah and 160 males Ezr 8:10 1121
Zechariah the **s** of Bebai and 28 Ezr 8:11 1121
Johanan the **s** of Hakkatan and 110 Ezr 8:12 1121
the sons of Mahli, the **s** of Levi, Ezr 8:18 1121
the son of Levi, the **s** of Israel, Ezr 8:18 1121
the **s** of Uriah the priest, Ezr 8:33 1121
him *was* Eleazar the **s** of Phinehas; Ezr 8:33 1121
Jozabad the **s** of Jeshua and Ezr 8:33 1121
and Noadiah the **s** of Binnui. Ezr 8:33 1121
Shecaniah the **s** of Jehiel, Ezr 10:2 1121
of Jehohanan the **s** of Eliashib. Ezr 10:6 1121
Only Jonathan the **s** of Asahel and Ezr 10:15 1121
the **s** of Tikvah opposed this, Ezr 10:15 1121
sons of Jeshua the **s** of Jozadak, Ezr 10:18 1121
of Nehemiah the **s** of Hacaliah. Ne 1:1 1121
them Zaccur the **s** of Imri built. Ne 3:2 1121
Next to them Meremoth the **s** of Ne 3:4 1121
the **s** of Hakkoz made repairs. Ne 3:4 1121
And next to him Meshullam the **s** of Ne 3:4 1121
the **s** of Meshezabel made repairs. Ne 3:4 1121
the **s** of Baana *also* made repairs. Ne 3:4 1121
Joiada the **s** of Paseah and Ne 3:6 1121
and Meshullam the **s** of Besodeiah Ne 3:6 1121
Next to him Uzziel the **s** of Ne 3:8 1121
to them Rephaiah the **s** of Hur, Ne 3:9 1121
Next to them Jedaiah the **s** of Ne 3:10 1121
the **s** of Hashabneiah made repairs. Ne 3:10 1121
Malchijah the **s** of Harim and Ne 3:11 1121
and Hasshub the **s** of Pahath-moab Ne 3:11 1121
to him Shallum the **s** of Hallohesh, Ne 3:12 1121
Malchijah the **s** of Rechab, Ne 3:14 1121
Shallum the **s** of Col-hozeh, the Ne 3:15 1121
After him Nehemiah the **s** of Azbuk, Ne 3:16 1121
repairs *under* Rehum the **s** of Bani. Ne 3:17 1121
under Bavvai the **s** of Henadad, Ne 3:18 1121
Next to him Ezer the **s** of Jeshua, Ne 3:19 1121
After him Baruch the **s** of Zabbai Ne 3:20 1121
After him Meremoth the **s** of Uriah Ne 3:21 1121
the son of Uriah the **s** of Hakkoz Ne 3:21 1121
them Azariah the **s** of Maaseiah, Ne 3:23 1121
s of Ananiah, carried out repairs Ne 3:23 1121
After him Binnui the **s** of Henadad Ne 3:24 1121
Palal the **s** of Uzai *made repairs* Ne 3:25 1121
the **s** of Parosh *made repairs.* Ne 3:25 1121
After them Zadok the **s** of Immer Ne 3:29 1121
him Shemaiah the **s** of Shecaniah, Ne 3:29 1121
him Hananiah the **s** of Shelemiah, Ne 3:30 1121
and Hanun the sixth **s** of Zalaph, Ne 3:30 1121
After him Meshullam the **s** of Ne 3:30 1121
of Shemaiah the **s** of Delaiah, Ne 6:10 1121
son of Delaiah, **s** of Mehetabel, Ne 6:10 1121
of Shecaniah the **s** of Arah, Ne 6:18 1121
and his **s** Jehohanan had married Ne 6:18 1121
of Meshullam the **s** of Berechiah. Ne 6:18 1121
Joshua the **s** of Nun to that day. Ne 8:17 1121
the governor, the **s** of Hacaliah, Ne 10:1 1121
Jeshua the **s** of Azaniah, Binnui of Ne 10:9 1121
The priest, the **s** of Aaron, Ne 10:38 1121
Athaiah the **s** of Uzziah, the son Ne 11:4 1121
son of Uzziah, the **s** of Zechariah, Ne 11:4 1121
of Zechariah, the **s** of Amariah, Ne 11:4 1121
of Amariah, the **s** of Shephatiah, Ne 11:4 1121
of Shephatiah, the **s** of Mahalalel, Ne 11:4 1121
and Maaseiah the **s** of Baruch, Ne 11:5 1121
son of Baruch, the **s** of Col-hozeh, Ne 11:5 1121
son of Col-hozeh, the **s** of Hazaiah, Ne 11:5 1121
son of Hazaiah, the **s** of Adaiah, Ne 11:5 1121
son of Adaiah, the **s** of Joiarib, Ne 11:5 1121
of Joiarib, the **s** of Zechariah, Ne 11:5 1121
Zechariah, the **s** of the Shilonite. Ne 11:5 1121
Sallu the **s** of Meshullam, the son Ne 11:7 1121
son of Meshullam, the **s** of Joed, Ne 11:7 1121
the son of Joed, the **s** of Pedaiah, Ne 11:7 1121
son of Pedaiah, the **s** of Kolaiah, Ne 11:7 1121
son of Kolaiah, the **s** of Maaseiah, Ne 11:7 1121
son of Maaseiah, the **s** of Ithiel, Ne 11:7 1121
son of Ithiel, the **s** of Jeshaiah; Ne 11:7 1121
Joel the **s** of Zichri was their Ne 11:9 1121
and Judah the **s** of Hassenuah was Ne 11:9 1121
Jedaiah the **s** of Joiarib, Jachin, Ne 11:10 1121
Seraiah the **s** of Hilkiah, the son Ne 11:11 1121
of Hilkiah, the **s** of Meshullam, Ne 11:11 1121
son of Meshullam, the **s** of Zadok, Ne 11:11 1121
son of Zadok, the **s** of Meraioth, Ne 11:11 1121
son of Meraioth, the **s** of Ahitub, Ne 11:11 1121
and Adaiah the **s** of Jeroham, the Ne 11:12 1121
son of Jeroham, the **s** of Pelaliah, Ne 11:12 1121
son of Pelaliah, the **s** of Amzi, Ne 11:12 1121

son of Amzi, the s of Zechariah,	Ne 11:12	1121
of Zechariah, the s of Pashhur,	Ne 11:12	1121
of Pashhur, the s of Malchijah,	Ne 11:12	1121
and Amashsai the s of Azarel,	Ne 11:13	1121
the son of Azarel, the s of Ahzai,	Ne 11:13	1121
of Ahzai, the s of Meshillemoth,	Ne 11:13	1121
of Meshillemoth, the s of Immer,	Ne 11:13	1121
was Zabdiel, the s of Haggedolim.	Ne 11:14	1121
Shemaiah the s of Hasshub, the son	Ne 11:15	1121
son of Hasshub, the s of Azrikam,	Ne 11:15	1121
of Azrikam, the s of Hashabiah,	Ne 11:15	1121
son of Hashabiah, the s of Bunni;	Ne 11:15	1121
and Mattaniah the s of Mica,	Ne 11:17	1121
the son of Mica, the s of Zabdi,	Ne 11:17	1121
the son of Zabdi, the s of Asaph,	Ne 11:17	1121
and Abda the s of Shammua, the son	Ne 11:17	1121
son of Shammua, the s of Galal,	Ne 11:17	1121
son of Galal, the s of Jeduthun.	Ne 11:17	1121
Jerusalem was Uzzi the s of Bani,	Ne 11:22	1121
son of Bani, the s of Hashabiah,	Ne 11:22	1121
of Hashabiah, the s of Mattaniah,	Ne 11:22	1121
son of Mattaniah, the s of Mica,	Ne 11:22	1121
Pethahiah the s of Meshezabel,	Ne 11:24	1121
the sons of Zerah the s of Judah,	Ne 11:24	1121
Zerubbabel the s of Shealtiel,	Ne 12:1	1121
days of Johanan the s of Eliashib.	Ne 12:23	1121
and Jeshua the s of Kadmiel,	Ne 12:24	1121
days of Joiakim the s of Jeshua,	Ne 12:26	1121
son of Jeshua, the s of Jozadak,	Ne 12:26	1121
and Zechariah the s of Jonathan,	Ne 12:35	1121
of Jonathan, the s of Shemaiah,	Ne 12:35	1121
of Shemaiah, the s of Mattaniah,	Ne 12:35	1121
of Mattaniah, the s of Micaiah,	Ne 12:35	1121
son of Micaiah, the s of Zaccur,	Ne 12:35	1121
the son of Zaccur, the s of Asaph,	Ne 12:35	1121
of David *and* of his s Solomon.	Ne 12:45	1121
to them was Hanan the s of Zaccur,	Ne 13:13	1121
son of Zaccur, the s of Mattaniah;	Ne 13:13	1121
the s of Eliashib the high priest,	Ne 13:28	1121
name was Mordecai, the s of Jair,	Es 2:5	1121
the son of Jair, the s of Shimei,	Es 2:5	1121
the son of Shimei, the s of Kish,	Es 2:5	1121
the s of Hammedatha the Agagite,	Es 3:1	1121
the s of Hammedatha the Agagite,	Es 3:10	1121
the s of Hammedatha the Agagite,	Es 8:5	1121
sons of Haman the s of Hammedatha,	Es 9:10	1121
For Haman the s of Hammedatha, the	Es 9:24	1121
that maggot, And the s of man,	Jb 25:6	1121
the s of Barachel the Buzite,	Jb 32:2	1121
So Elihu the s of Barachel the	Jb 32:6	1121
righteousness is for a s of man.	Jb 35:8	1121
'You are My S, Today I have	Ps 2:7	1121
Do homage to the S,	Ps 2:12	1248
And the s of man that You	Ps 8:4	1121
You slander your own mother's s.	Ps 50:20	1121
Your righteousness to the king's s.	Ps 72:1	1121
prayers of David the s of Jesse	Ps 72:20	1121
And on the s whom You have	Ps 80:15	1121
Upon the s of man whom You made	Ps 80:17	1121
And save the s of Your handmaid.	Ps 86:16	1121
the s of wickedness afflict him.	Ps 89:22	1121
servant, the s of Your handmaid,	Ps 116:16	1121
Or the s of man, that You think	Ps 144:3	1121
of Solomon the s of David,	Pr 1:1	1121
Hear, my s, your father's	Pr 1:8	1121
My s, if sinners entice you, Do	Pr 1:10	1121
My s, do not walk in the way with	Pr 1:15	1121
My s, if you will receive my	Pr 2:1	1121
My s, do not forget my teaching,	Pr 3:1	1121
My s, do not reject the discipline	Pr 3:11	1121
corrects the s in whom he delights.	Pr 3:12	1121
My s, let them not vanish from	Pr 3:21	1121
When I was a s to my father,	Pr 4:3	1121
only s in the sight of my mother,	Pr 4:3	3173
Hear, my s, and accept my sayings And	Pr 4:10	1121
My s, give attention to my words;	Pr 4:20	1121
My s, give attention to my wisdom,	Pr 5:1	1121
For why should you, my s,	Pr 5:20	1121
My s, if you have become surety	Pr 6:1	1121
Do this then, my s,	Pr 6:3	1121
My s, observe the commandment of	Pr 6:20	1121
My s, keep my words And treasure	Pr 7:1	1121
A wise s makes a father glad, But	Pr 10:1	1121
a foolish s is a grief to his mother.	Pr 10:1	1121
in summer is a s who acts wisely,	Pr 10:5	1121
is a s who acts shamefully.	Pr 10:5	1121
A wise s *accepts his* father's	Pr 13:1	1121
He who withholds his rod hates his s,	Pr 13:24	1121
A wise s makes a father glad, But	Pr 15:20	1121
rule over a s who acts shamefully,	Pr 17:2	1121
A foolish s is a grief to his father And	Pr 17:25	1121
foolish s is destruction to his father,	Pr 19:13	1121
Discipline your s while there is hope	Pr 19:18	1121
Is a shameful and disgraceful s.	Pr 19:26	1121
Cease listening, my s, to discipline,	Pr 19:27	1121
My s, if your heart is wise, My	Pr 23:15	1121
Listen, my s, and be wise, And	Pr 23:19	1121
he who sires a wise s will be glad	Pr 23:24	2450
Give me your heart, my s,	Pr 23:26	1121
My s, eat honey, for it is good,	Pr 24:13	1121
My s, fear the LORD and the king;	Pr 24:21	1121
Be wise, my s, and make my heart	Pr 27:11	1121
keeps the law is a discerning s,	Pr 28:7	1121
Correct your s, and he will give	Pr 29:17	1121
in the end find him to be a s.	Pr 29:21	4497
The words of Agur the s of Jakeh,	Pr 30:1	1121
What, O my s? And what, O son of	Pr 31:2	1248
And what, O s of my womb?	Pr 31:2	1248
And what, O s of my vows?	Pr 31:2	1248
of the Preacher, the s of David,	Ec 1:1	1121
having neither a s nor a brother,	Ec 4:8	1121
and he had fathered a s,	Ec 5:14	1121
But beyond this, my s,	Ec 12:12	1121
vision of Isaiah the s of Amoz	Is 1:1	1121
The word which Isaiah the s of	Is 2:1	1121
the days of Ahaz, the s of Jotham,	Is 7:1	1121
son of Jotham, the s of Uzziah,	Is 7:1	1121
Aram and Pekah the s of Remaliah,	Is 7:1	1121
Ahaz, you and your s Shear-jashub,	Is 7:3	1121
and Aram and the s of Remaliah.	Is 7:4	1121
Ephraim and the s of Remaliah,	Is 7:5	1121
and set up the s of Tabeel as king	Is 7:6	1121
of Samaria is the s of Remaliah.	Is 7:9	1121
will be with child and bear a s,	Is 7:14	1121
Zechariah the s of Jeberechiah."	Is 8:2	1121
conceived and gave birth to a s.	Is 8:3	1121
in Rezin and the s of Remaliah;	Is 8:6	1121
to us, a s will be given to us;	Is 9:6	1121
which Isaiah the s of Amoz saw.	Is 13:1	1121
of the morning, s of the dawn!	Is 14:12	1121
"I am a s of the wise, a son of	Is 19:11	1121
the wise, a s of ancient kings"?	Is 19:11	1121
through Isaiah the s of Amoz,	Is 20:2	1121
servant Eliakim the s of Hilkiah	Is 22:20	1121
Then Eliakim the s of Hilkiah,	Is 36:3	1121
scribe, and Joah the s of Asaph,	Is 36:3	1121
Then Eliakim the s of Hilkiah,	Is 36:22	1121
scribe and Joah the s of Asaph,	Is 36:22	1121
Isaiah the prophet, the s of Amoz.	Is 37:2	1121
s of Amoz sent *word* to Hezekiah,	Is 37:21	1121
his s became king in his place.	Is 37:38	1121
And Isaiah the prophet the s of	Is 38:1	1121
time Merodach-baladan s of Baladan,	Is 39:1	1121
compassion on the s of her womb?	Is 49:15	1121
s of man who is made like grass,	Is 51:12	1121
the s of man who takes hold of it;	Is 56:2	1121
of Jeremiah the s of Hilkiah,	Jer 1:1	1121
the days of Josiah the s of Amon,	Jer 1:2	1121
of Jehoiakim the s of Josiah,	Jer 1:3	1121
year of Zedekiah the s of Josiah,	Jer 1:3	1121
Mourn as for an only s,	Jer 6:26	3173
in the valley of the s of Hinnom,	Jer 7:31	1121
or the valley of the s of Hinnom,	Jer 7:32	1121
of Manasseh, the s of Hezekiah,	Jer 15:4	1121
the priest, the s of Immer,	Jer 20:1	1121
to him Pashhur the s of Malchijah,	Jer 21:1	1121
the priest, the s of Maaseiah,	Jer 21:1	1121
regard to Shallum the s of Josiah,	Jer 22:11	1121
to Jehoiakim the s of Josiah,	Jer 22:18	1121
"even though Coniah the s of	Jer 22:24	1121
Jeconiah the s of Jehoiakim,	Jer 24:1	1121
year of Jehoiakim the s of Josiah,	Jer 25:1	1121
year of Josiah the s of Amon,	Jer 25:3	1121
of Jehoiakim the s of Josiah,	Jer 26:1	1121
Uriah the s of Shemaiah from	Jer 26:20	1121
Elnathan the s of Achbor and	Jer 26:22	1121
hand of Ahikam the s of Shaphan	Jer 26:24	1121
reign of Zedekiah the s of Josiah,	Jer 27:1	1121
shall serve him and his s	Jer 27:7	1121
exile Jeconiah the s of Jehoiakim,	Jer 27:20	1121
Hananiah the s of Azzur,	Jer 28:1	1121
place Jeconiah the s of Jehoiakim,	Jer 28:4	1121
hand of Elasah the s of Shaphan,	Jer 29:3	1121
and Gemariah the s of Hilkiah,	Jer 29:3	1121
concerning Ahab the s of Kolaiah	Jer 29:21	1121
Zedekiah the s of Maaseiah,	Jer 29:21	1121
to Zephaniah the s of Maaseiah,	Jer 29:25	1121
"Is Ephraim My dear s?	Jer 31:20	1121
Hanamel the s of Shallum your	Jer 32:7	1121
"Then Hanamel my uncle's s came	Jer 32:8	1121
Anathoth from Hanamel my uncle's s,	Jer 32:9	1121
to Baruch the s of Neriah,	Jer 32:12	1121
son of Neriah, the s of Mahseiah,	Jer 32:12	1121
the sight of Hanamel my uncle's s	Jer 32:12	1121
to Baruch the s of Neriah,	Jer 32:16	1121
have a s to reign on his throne,	Jer 33:21	1121
days of Jehoiakim the s of Josiah,	Jer 35:1	1121
took Jaazaniah the s of Jeremiah,	Jer 35:3	1121
son of Jeremiah, s of Habazziniah,	Jer 35:3	1121
sons of Hanan the s of Igdaliah,	Jer 35:4	1121
of Maaseiah the s of Shallum,	Jer 35:4	1121
wine, for Jonadab the s of Rechab,	Jer 35:6	1121
voice of Jonadab the s of Rechab,	Jer 35:8	1121
words of Jonadab the s of Rechab,	Jer 35:14	1121
the sons of Jonadab the s of Rechab	Jer 35:16	1121
"Jonadab the s of Rechab shall	Jer 35:19	1121
year of Jehoiakim the s of Josiah,	Jer 36:1	1121
called Baruch the s of Neriah,	Jer 36:4	1121
Baruch the s of Neriah did	Jer 36:8	1121
year of Jehoiakim the s of Josiah,	Jer 36:9	1121
the s of Shaphan the scribe,	Jer 36:10	1121
when Micaiah the s of Gemariah,	Jer 36:11	1121
son of Gemariah, the s of Shaphan,	Jer 36:11	1121
and Delaiah the s of Shemaiah,	Jer 36:12	1121
and Elnathan the s of Achbor,	Jer 36:12	1121
and Gemariah the s of Shaphan,	Jer 36:12	1121
and Zedekiah the s of Hananiah,	Jer 36:12	1121
sent Jehudi the s of Nethaniah,	Jer 36:14	1121
of Nethaniah, the s of Shelemiah,	Jer 36:14	1121
son of Shelemiah, the s of Cushi,	Jer 36:14	1121
So Baruch the s of Neriah took the	Jer 36:14	1121
commanded Jerahmeel the king's s,	Jer 36:26	1121
son, Seraiah the s of Azriel,	Jer 36:26	1121
and Shelemiah the s of Abdeel to	Jer 36:26	1121
it to Baruch the s of Neraiah,	Jer 36:32	1121
Now Zedekiah the s of Josiah whom	Jer 37:1	1121
of Coniah the s of Jehoiakim.	Jer 37:1	1121
sent Jehucal the s of Shelemiah,	Jer 37:3	1121
and Zephaniah the s of Maaseiah,	Jer 37:3	1121
the s of Shelemiah the son of	Jer 37:13	1121
the s of Hananiah was there;	Jer 37:13	1121
Now Shephatiah the s of Mattan,	Jer 38:1	1121
and Gedaliah the s of Pashhur,	Jer 38:1	1121
and Jucal the s of Shelemiah,	Jer 38:1	1121
and Pashhur the s of Malchijah	Jer 38:1	1121
cistern *of* Malchijah the king's s,	Jer 38:6	1121
him to Gedaliah, the s of Ahikam,	Jer 39:14	1121
son of Ahikam, the s of Shaphan,	Jer 39:14	1121
then to Gedaliah the s of Ahikam,	Jer 40:5	1121
son of Ahikam, the s of Shaphan,	Jer 40:5	1121
went to Mizpah to Gedaliah the s of	Jer 40:6	1121
appointed Gedaliah the s of Ahikam	Jer 40:7	1121
with Ishmael the s of Nethaniah,	Jer 40:8	1121
and Seraiah the s of Tanhumeth,	Jer 40:8	1121
Jezaniah the s of the Maacathite,	Jer 40:8	1121
Then Gedaliah the s of Ahikam,	Jer 40:9	1121
son of Ahikam, the s of Shaphan,	Jer 40:9	1121
them Gedaliah the s of Ahikam,	Jer 40:11	1121
son of Ahikam, the s of Shaphan.	Jer 40:11	1121
Now Johanan the s of Kareah and	Jer 40:13	1121
has sent Ishmael the s of Nethaniah	Jer 40:14	1121
But Gedaliah the s of Ahikam did	Jer 40:14	1121
Then Johanan the s of Kareah spoke	Jer 40:15	1121
kill Ishmael the s of Nethaniah,	Jer 40:15	1121
But Gedaliah the s of Ahikam said	Jer 40:16	1121
said to Johanan the s of Kareah,	Jer 40:16	1121
month Ishmael the s of Nethaniah,	Jer 41:1	1121
of Nethaniah, the s of Elishama,	Jer 41:1	1121
to Gedaliah the s of Ahikam.	Jer 41:1	1121
Ishmael the s of Nethaniah and the	Jer 41:2	1121
down Gedaliah the s of Ahikam,	Jer 41:2	1121
son of Ahikam, the s of Shaphan,	Jer 41:2	1121
Then Ishmael the s of Nethaniah	Jer 41:6	1121
to Gedaliah the s of Ahikam!"	Jer 41:6	1121
Ishmael the s of Nethaniah and the	Jer 41:7	1121
Ishmael the s of Nethaniah filled	Jer 41:9	1121
of Gedaliah the s of Ahikam;	Jer 41:10	1121
thus Ishmael the s of Nethaniah	Jer 41:10	1121
But Johanan the s of Kareah and	Jer 41:11	1121
the s of Nethaniah had done.	Jer 41:11	1121
fight with Ishmael the s of Nethaniah	Jer 41:12	1121
saw Johanan the s of Kareah and the	Jer 41:13	1121
went to Johanan the s of Kareah.	Jer 41:14	1121
But Ishmael the s of Nethaniah	Jer 41:15	1121
Then Johanan the s of Kareah and	Jer 41:16	1121
from Ishmael the s of Nethaniah,	Jer 41:16	1121
down Gedaliah the s of Ahikam,	Jer 41:16	1121
since Ishmael the s of Nethaniah	Jer 41:18	1121
down Gedaliah the s of Ahikam,	Jer 41:18	1121
forces, Johanan the s of Kareah,	Jer 42:1	1121
Jezaniah the s of Hoshaiah,	Jer 42:1	1121
for Johanan the s of Kareah and	Jer 42:8	1121
Azariah the s of Hoshaiah,	Jer 43:2	1121
and Johanan the s of Kareah,	Jer 43:2	1121
but Baruch the s of Neriah is	Jer 43:3	1121
So Johanan the s of Kareah and all	Jer 43:4	1121
But Johanan the s of Kareah and	Jer 43:5	1121
left with Gedaliah the s of Ahikam	Jer 43:6	1121
and Baruch the s of Neriah	Jer 43:6	1121
spoke to Baruch the s of Neriah,	Jer 45:1	1121
year of Jehoiakim the s of Josiah,	Jer 45:1	1121
year of Jehoiakim the s of Josiah,	Jer 46:2	1121
nor will a s of man reside in it.	Jer 49:18	1121
Nor will a s of man reside in it."	Jer 49:33	1121
Nor will *any* s of man reside in it.	Jer 50:40	1121
through which no s of man passes.	Jer 51:43	1121
commanded Seraiah the s of Neriah,	Jer 51:59	1121
to Ezekiel the priest, s of Buzi,	Ezk 1:3	1121
"S of man, stand on your feet	Ezk 2:1	1121
"S of man, I am sending you to	Ezk 2:3	1121
"And you, s of man, neither fear	Ezk 2:6	1121
"Now you, s of man, listen to	Ezk 2:8	1121
"S of man, eat what you find;	Ezk 3:1	1121
"S of man, feed your stomach and	Ezk 3:3	1121
"S of man, go to the house of	Ezk 3:4	1121
"S of man, take into your heart	Ezk 3:10	1121
"S of man, I have appointed you a	Ezk 3:17	1121
"As for you, s of man, they will	Ezk 3:25	1121
"Now you s of man, get yourself a	Ezk 4:1	1121
"S of man, behold, I am going to	Ezk 4:16	1121
"As for you, s of man, take a	Ezk 5:1	1121
"S of man, set your face toward	Ezk 6:2	1121
"And you, s of man, thus says the	Ezk 7:2	1121
"S of man, raise your eyes now	Ezk 8:5	1121
"S of man, do you see what they	Ezk 8:6	1121
"S of man, now dig through the	Ezk 8:8	1121
with Jaazaniah the s of Shaphan	Ezk 8:11	1121
"S of man, do you see what the	Ezk 8:12	1121
"Do you see *this*, s of man?	Ezk 8:15	1121
"Do you see *this*, s of man?	Ezk 8:17	1121
I saw Jaazaniah s of Azzur and	Ezk 11:1	1121
Azzur and Pelatiah s of Benaiah,	Ezk 11:1	1121
"S of man, these are the men who	Ezk 11:2	1121
prophesy against them, s of man,	Ezk 11:4	1121
that Pelatiah s of Benaiah died.	Ezk 11:13	1121
"S of man, your brothers, your	Ezk 11:15	1121
"S of man, you live in the midst	Ezk 12:2	1121
"Therefore, s of man, prepare for	Ezk 12:3	1121
"S of man, has not the house of	Ezk 12:9	1121
"S of man, eat your bread with	Ezk 12:18	1121
"S of man, what is this proverb	Ezk 12:22	1121
"S of man, behold, the house of	Ezk 12:27	1121
"S of man, prophesy against the	Ezk 13:2	1121
"Now you, s of man, set your face	Ezk 13:17	1121
"S of man, these men have set up	Ezk 14:3	1121
"S of man, if a country sins	Ezk 14:13	1121
either *their* s or *their* daughter.	Ezk 14:20	1121

"**S** of man, how is the wood of the	**Ezk 15:2**	1121
"**S** of man, make known to	**Ezk 16:2**	1121
"**S** of man, propound a riddle and	**Ezk 17:2**	1121
father as well as the soul of the **s**	**Ezk 18:4**	1121
have a violent **s** who sheds blood and	**Ezk 18:10**	1121
he has a **s** who has observed all	**Ezk 18:14**	1121
'Why should the **s** not bear the	**Ezk 18:19**	1121
When the **s** has practiced justice	**Ezk 18:19**	1121
The **s** will not bear the punishment	**Ezk 18:20**	1121
"**S** of man, speak to the elders of	**Ezk 20:3**	1121
will you judge them, **s** of man?	**Ezk 20:4**	1121
"Therefore, **s** of man, speak to	**Ezk 20:27**	1121
"**S** of man, set your face toward	**Ezk 20:46**	1121
"**S** of man, set your face toward	**Ezk 21:2**	1121
"As for you, **s** of man, groan with	**Ezk 21:6**	1121
"**S** of man, prophesy and say,	**Ezk 21:9**	1121
rod of My **s** despising every tree?	**Ezk 21:10**	1121
"Cry out and wail, **s** of man;	**Ezk 21:12**	1121
"You therefore, **s** of man, prophesy and	**Ezk 21:14**	1121
"As for you, **s** of man, make two	**Ezk 21:19**	1121
"And you, **s** of man, prophesy and	**Ezk 21:28**	1121
"And you, **s** of man, will you judge,	**Ezk 22:2**	1121
"**S** of man, the house of Israel	**Ezk 22:18**	1121
"**S** of man, say to her,	**Ezk 22:24**	1121
"**S** of man, there were two women,	**Ezk 23:2**	1121
"**S** of man, will you judge Oholah	**Ezk 23:36**	1121
"**S** of man, write the name of the	**Ezk 24:2**	1121
"**S** of man, behold, I am about to	**Ezk 24:16**	1121
'As for you, **s** of man, will *it* not	**Ezk 24:25**	1121
"**S** of man, set your face toward	**Ezk 25:2**	1121
"**S** of man, because Tyre has said	**Ezk 26:2**	1121
"And you, **s** of man, take up a	**Ezk 27:2**	1121
"**S** of man, say to the leader of	**Ezk 28:2**	1121
"**S** of man, take up a lamentation	**Ezk 28:12**	1121
"**S** of man, set your face toward	**Ezk 28:21**	1121
"**S** of man, set your face against	**Ezk 29:2**	1121
"**S** of man, Nebuchadnezzar king of	**Ezk 29:18**	1121
"**S** of man, prophesy and say,	**Ezk 30:2**	1121
"**S** of man, I have broken the arm	**Ezk 30:21**	1121
"**S** of man, say to Pharaoh king of	**Ezk 31:2**	1121
"**S** of man, take up a lamentation	**Ezk 32:2**	1121
"**S** of man, wail for the hordes	**Ezk 32:18**	1121
"**S** of man, speak to the sons of	**Ezk 33:2**	1121
"Now as for you, **s** of man, I have	**Ezk 33:7**	1121
"Now as for you, **s** of man, say to	**Ezk 33:10**	1121
"And you, **s** of man, say to your	**Ezk 33:12**	1121
"**S** of man, they who live in these	**Ezk 33:24**	1121
"But as for you, **s** of man, your	**Ezk 33:30**	1121
"**S** of man, prophesy against the	**Ezk 34:2**	1121
"**S** of man, set your face against	**Ezk 35:2**	1121
"And you, **s** of man, prophesy to	**Ezk 36:1**	1121
"**S** of man, when the house of	**Ezk 36:17**	1121
"**S** of man, can these bones live?"	**Ezk 37:3**	1121
to the breath, prophesy, **s** of man,	**Ezk 37:9**	1121
"**S** of man, these bones are the	**Ezk 37:11**	1121
"And you, **s** of man, take for	**Ezk 37:16**	1121
"**S** of man, set your face toward	**Ezk 38:2**	1121
"Therefore prophesy, **s** of man,	**Ezk 38:14**	1121
"And you, **s** of man, prophesy	**Ezk 39:1**	1121
"As for you, **s** of man, thus	**Ezk 39:17**	1121
"**S** of man, see with your eyes,	**Ezk 40:4**	1121
"**S** of man, *this is* the place of	**Ezk 43:7**	1121
"As for you, **s** of man, describe	**Ezk 43:10**	1121
"**S** of man, thus says the Lord	**Ezk 43:18**	1121
"**S** of man, mark well, see with	**Ezk 44:5**	1121
for father, for mother, for **s**,	**Ezk 44:25**	1121
"**S** of man, have you seen *this?*"	**Ezk 47:6**	1121
fourth is like a **s** of *the* gods!"	**Da 3:25**	1247
"Yet you, his **s**, Belshazzar, have	**Da 5:22**	1247
One like a **S** of Man was coming,	**Da 7:13**	1247
"**S** of man, understand that the	**Da 8:17**	1121
year of Darius the **s** of Ahasuerus,	**Da 9:1**	1121
came to Hosea the **s** of Beeri,	**Hos 1:1**	1121
days of Jeroboam the **s** of Joash,	**Hos 1:1**	1121
she conceived and bore him a **s**.	**Hos 1:3**	1121
conceived and gave birth to a **s**.	**Hos 1:8**	1121
And out of Egypt I called My **s**.	**Hos 11:1**	1121
He is not a wise **s**,	**Hos 13:13**	1121
came to Joel, the **s** of Pethuel:	**Jl 1:1**	1121
the days of Jeroboam **s** of Joash,	**Am 1:1**	1121
nor am I the **s** of a prophet;	**Am 7:14**	1121
a time of mourning for an only **s**,	**Am 8:10**	3173
to Jonah the **s** of Amittai saying,	**Jon 1:1**	1121
Balaam **s** of Beor answered him,	**Mi 6:5**	1121
s treats father contemptuously,	**Mi 7:6**	1121
came to Zephaniah **s** of Cushi,	**Zph 1:1**	1121
son of Cushi, **s** of Gedaliah,	**Zph 1:1**	1121
son of Gedaliah, **s** of Amariah,	**Zph 1:1**	1121
son of Amariah, **s** of Hezekiah,	**Zph 1:1**	1121
in the days of Josiah **s** of Amon,	**Zph 1:1**	1121
to Zerubbabel the **s** of Shealtiel,	**Hg 1:1**	1121
and to Joshua the **s** of Jehozadak,	**Hg 1:1**	1121
Zerubbabel the **s** of Shealtiel,	**Hg 1:12**	1121
and Joshua the **s** of Jehozadak,	**Hg 1:12**	1121
of Zerubbabel the **s** of Shealtiel,	**Hg 1:14**	1121
of Joshua the **s** of Jehozadak,	**Hg 1:14**	1121
to Zerubbabel the **s** of Shealtiel,	**Hg 2:2**	1121
and to Joshua the **s** of Jehozadak,	**Hg 2:2**	1121
also, Joshua **s** of Jehozadak,	**Hg 2:4**	1121
you, Zerubbabel, **s** of Shealtiel,	**Hg 2:23**	1121
the prophet, the **s** of Berechiah,	**Zch 1:1**	1121
Berechiah, the **s** of Iddo saying,	**Zch 1:1**	1121
the prophet, the **s** of Berechiah,	**Zch 1:7**	1121
son of Berechiah, the **s** of Iddo,	**Zch 1:7**	1121
of Josiah the **s** of Zephaniah,	**Zch 6:10**	1121
head of Joshua the **s** of Jehozadak,	**Zch 6:11**	1121
and Hen the **s** of Zephaniah.	**Zch 6:14**	1121
Him, as one mourns for an only **s**,	**Zch 12:10**	3173
"'A **s** honors *his* father, and a	**Mal 1:6**	1121
spares his own **s** who serves him."	**Mal 3:17**	1121
of Jesus the Messiah, the **s** of David,	**Mt 1:1**	*5207*
son of David, the **s** of Abraham:	**Mt 1:1**	*5207*
"Joseph, **s** of David, do not be	**Mt 1:20**	*5207*
"She will bear a **S**;	**Mt 1:21**	*5207*
BE WITH CHILD AND SHALL BEAR A **S**,	**Mt 1:23**	*5207*
until she gave birth to a **S**;	**Mt 1:25**	*5207*
"OUT OF EGYPT I CALLED MY **S**."	**Mt 2:15**	*5207*
"This is My beloved **S**,	**Mt 3:17**	*5207*
"If You are the **S** of God, command	**Mt 4:3**	*5207*
the **S** of God, throw Yourself down;	**Mt 4:6**	*5207*
James the **s** of Zebedee, and John	**Mt 4:21**	
his **s** asks for a loaf,	**Mt 7:9**	*5207*
but the **S** of Man has nowhere to	**Mt 8:20**	*5207*
do we have with each other, **S** of God?	**Mt 8:29**	*5207*
"Take courage, **s**	**Mt 9:2**	*5043*
the **S** of Man has authority on earth	**Mt 9:6**	*5207*
"Have mercy on us, **S** of David!"	**Mt 9:27**	*5207*
and James the **s** of Zebedee, and John	**Mt 10:2**	
James the **s** of Alphaeus,	**Mt 10:3**	
Israel until the **S** of Man comes.	**Mt 10:23**	*5207*
and he who loves **s** or daughter	**Mt 10:37**	*5207*
"The **S** of Man came eating and	**Mt 11:19**	*5207*
and no one knows the **S** except	**Mt 11:27**	*5207*
know the Father except the **S**,	**Mt 11:27**	*5207*
to whom the **S** wills to reveal *Him*.	**Mt 11:27**	*5207*
S of Man is Lord of the Sabbath."	**Mt 12:8**	*5207*
"This man cannot be the **S** of David,	**Mt 12:23**	*5207*
speaks a word against the **S** of Man,	**Mt 12:32**	*5207*
so will the **S** of Man be three	**Mt 12:40**	*5207*
the good seed is the **S** of Man,	**Mt 13:37**	*5207*
"The **S** of Man will send forth His	**Mt 13:41**	*5207*
"Is not this the carpenter's **s**?	**Mt 13:55**	*5207*
"You are certainly God's **S**!"	**Mt 14:33**	*5207*
mercy on me, Lord, **S** of David;	**Mt 15:22**	*5207*
people say that the **S** of Man is?"	**Mt 16:13**	*5207*
Christ, the **S** of the living God."	**Mt 16:16**	*5207*
"For the **S** of Man is going to	**Mt 16:27**	*5207*
S of Man coming in His kingdom."	**Mt 16:28**	*5207*
"This is My beloved **S**,	**Mt 17:5**	*5207*
until the **S** of Man has risen from the	**Mt 17:9**	*5207*
So also the **S** of Man is going to	**Mt 17:12**	*5207*
"Lord, have mercy on my **s**,	**Mt 17:15**	*5207*
"The **S** of Man is going to be	**Mt 17:22**	*5207*
the **S** of Man has come to save that	**Mt 18:11**	*5207*
when the **S** of Man will sit on His	**Mt 19:28**	*5207*
and the **S** of Man will be delivered	**Mt 20:18**	*5207*
just as the **S** of Man did not come	**Mt 20:28**	*5207*
have mercy on us, **S** of David!"	**Mt 20:30**	*5207*
S of David, have mercy on us!"	**Mt 20:31**	*5207*
"Hosanna to the **S** of David;	**Mt 21:9**	*5207*
"Hosanna to the **S** of David,"	**Mt 21:15**	*5207*
'**S**, go work today in the vineyard.'	**Mt 21:28**	*5043*
afterward he sent his **s** to them,	**Mt 21:37**	*5207*
'They will respect my **s**.'	**Mt 21:37**	*5207*
when the vine-growers saw the **s**,	**Mt 21:38**	*5207*
gave a wedding feast for his **s**.	**Mt 22:2**	*5207*
about the Christ, whose **s** is He?"	**Mt 22:42**	*5207*
"*The* **s** of David."	**Mt 22:42**	
'Lord,' how is He his **s**?"	**Mt 22:45**	*5207*
as much a **s** of hell as yourselves.	**Mt 23:15**	*5207*
of Zechariah, the **s** of Berechiah,	**Mt 23:35**	*5207*
the coming of the **S** of Man be.	**Mt 24:27**	*5207*
S of Man will appear in the sky,	**Mt 24:30**	*5207*
S OF MAN COMING ON THE CLOUDS	**Mt 24:30**	*5207*
the angels of heaven, nor the **S**,	**Mt 24:36**	*5207*
"For the coming of the **S** of Man	**Mt 24:37**	*5207*
the coming of the **S** of Man be.	**Mt 24:39**	*5207*
for the **S** of Man is coming at an	**Mt 24:44**	*5207*
the **S** of Man comes in His glory,	**Mt 25:31**	*5207*
the **S** of Man is *to be* handed over	**Mt 26:2**	*5207*
"The **S** of Man *is to* go, just as	**Mt 26:24**	*5207*
by whom the **S** of Man is betrayed!	**Mt 26:24**	*5207*
the **S** of Man is being betrayed into	**Mt 26:45**	*5207*
You are the Christ, the **S** of God."	**Mt 26:63**	*5207*
S OF MAN SITTING AT THE RIGHT	**Mt 26:64**	*5207*
If You are the **S** of God, come down	**Mt 27:40**	*5207*
'I am the **S** of God.'"	**Mt 27:43**	*5207*
"Truly this was the **S** of God!"	**Mt 27:54**	*5207*
Father and the **S** and the Holy Spirit	**Mt 28:19**	*5207*
of Jesus Christ, the **S** of God.	**Mk 1:1**	*5207*
"You are My beloved **S**,	**Mk 1:11**	*5207*
He saw James the **s** of Zebedee,	**Mk 1:19**	
"**S**, your sins are forgiven."	**Mk 2:5**	*5043*
the **S** of Man has authority on earth	**Mk 2:10**	*5207*
As He passed by, He saw Levi the **s**	**Mk 2:14**	
the **S** of Man is Lord even of the	**Mk 2:28**	*5207*
"You are the **S** of God!"	**Mk 3:11**	*5207*
and James, the **s** of Zebedee,	**Mk 3:17**	
and James the **s** of Alphaeus,	**Mk 3:18**	
Jesus, **S** of the Most High God?	**Mk 5:7**	*5207*
this the carpenter, the **s** of Mary,	**Mk 6:3**	*5207*
that the **S** of Man must suffer many	**Mk 8:31**	*5207*
the **S** of Man will also be ashamed	**Mk 8:38**	*5207*
"This is My beloved **S**,	**Mk 9:7**	*5207*
until the **S** of Man rose	**Mk 9:9**	*5207*
yet how is it written of the **S** of Man	**Mk 9:12**	*5207*
"Teacher, I brought You my **s**,	**Mk 9:17**	*5207*
"The **S** of Man is to be delivered	**Mk 9:31**	*5207*
and the **S** of Man will be delivered	**Mk 10:33**	*5207*
"For even the **S** of Man did not	**Mk 10:45**	*5207*
Bartimaeus, the **s** of Timaeus,	**Mk 10:46**	*5207*
"Jesus, **S** of David, have mercy on	**Mk 10:47**	*5207*
"**S** of David, have mercy on me!"	**Mk 10:48**	*5207*
had one more *to send,* a beloved **s**;	**Mk 12:6**	*5207*
'They will respect my **s**.'	**Mk 12:6**	*5207*
that the Christ is the **s** of David?	**Mk 12:35**	*5207*
so in what sense is He his **s**?"	**Mk 12:37**	*5207*
THE **S** OF MAN COMING IN CLOUDS	**Mk 13:26**	*5207*
the angels in heaven, nor the **S**,	**Mk 13:32**	*5207*
"For the **S** of Man *is to* go just	**Mk 14:21**	*5207*
by whom the **S** of Man is betrayed!	**Mk 14:21**	*5207*
the **S** of Man is being betrayed	**Mk 14:41**	*5207*
the Christ, the **S** of the Blessed *One?*"	**Mk 14:61**	*5207*
and you shall see THE **S** OF MAN	**Mk 14:62**	*5207*
"Truly this man was the **S** of God!"	**Mk 15:39**	*5207*
wife Elizabeth will bear you a **s**,	**Lk 1:13**	*5207*
in your womb and bear a **s**,	**Lk 1:31**	*5207*
be called the **S** of the Most High;	**Lk 1:32**	*5207*
shall be called the **S** of God.	**Lk 1:35**	*5207*
also conceived a **s** in her old age;	**Lk 1:36**	*5207*
birth, and she gave birth to a **s**.	**Lk 1:57**	*5207*
she gave birth to her firstborn **s**;	**Lk 2:7**	*5207*
"**S**, why have You treated us this	**Lk 2:48**	*5043*
came to John, the **s** of Zacharias,	**Lk 3:2**	*5207*
"You are My beloved **S**,	**Lk 3:22**	*5207*
being, as was supposed, the **s** of Joseph,	**Lk 3:23**	*5207*
the **s** of Eli,	**Lk 3:23**	*5207*
the **s** of Matthat, the son of Levi,	**Lk 3:24**	
the son of Matthat, the **s** of Levi,	**Lk 3:24**	
the **s** of Melchi, the son of Jannai,	**Lk 3:24**	
the **s** of Jannai, the son of Joseph,	**Lk 3:24**	
the **s** of Joseph,	**Lk 3:24**	
the **s** of Mattathias, the son of Amos,	**Lk 3:25**	
the son of Mattathias, the **s** of Amos,	**Lk 3:25**	
the **s** of Nahum, the son of Hesli,	**Lk 3:25**	
the **s** of Hesli, the son of Naggai,	**Lk 3:25**	
the **s** of Naggai,	**Lk 3:25**	
the **s** of Maath, the son of	**Lk 3:26**	
the son of Maath, the **s** of	**Lk 3:26**	
the **s** of Semein, the son of Josech,	**Lk 3:26**	
the **s** of Josech, the son of Joda,	**Lk 3:26**	
the **s** of Joda,	**Lk 3:26**	
the **s** of Joanan, the son of Rhesa,	**Lk 3:27**	
the son of Joanan, the **s** of Rhesa,	**Lk 3:27**	
the **s** of Zerubbabel, the son of	**Lk 3:27**	
the **s** of Shealtiel, the son of Neri,	**Lk 3:27**	
the **s** of Neri,	**Lk 3:27**	
the **s** of Melchi, the son of Addi,	**Lk 3:28**	
the son of Melchi, the **s** of Addi,	**Lk 3:28**	
the **s** of Cosam, the son of Elmadam,	**Lk 3:28**	
the **s** of Elmadam, the son of Er,	**Lk 3:28**	
the **s** of Er,	**Lk 3:28**	
the **s** of Joshua, the son of Eliezer,	**Lk 3:29**	
the son of Joshua, the **s** of Eliezer,	**Lk 3:29**	
the **s** of Jorim, the son of Matthat,	**Lk 3:29**	
the **s** of Matthat, the son of Levi,	**Lk 3:29**	
the **s** of Levi,	**Lk 3:29**	
the **s** of Simeon, the son of Judah,	**Lk 3:30**	
the son of Simeon, the **s** of Judah,	**Lk 3:30**	
the **s** of Joseph, the son of Jonam,	**Lk 3:30**	
the **s** of Jonam, the son of Eliakim,	**Lk 3:30**	
the **s** of Eliakim,	**Lk 3:30**	
the **s** of Melea, the son of Menna,	**Lk 3:31**	
the son of Melea, the **s** of Menna,	**Lk 3:31**	
the **s** of Mattatha, the son of Nathan,	**Lk 3:31**	
the **s** of Nathan, the son of David,	**Lk 3:31**	
the **s** of David,	**Lk 3:31**	
the **s** of Jesse, the son of Obed,	**Lk 3:32**	
the son of Jesse, the **s** of Obed,	**Lk 3:32**	
the **s** of Boaz, the son of Salmon,	**Lk 3:32**	
the **s** of Salmon, the son of Nahshon,	**Lk 3:32**	
the **s** of Nahshon,	**Lk 3:32**	
the **s** of Amminadab, the son of Admin,	**Lk 3:33**	
the son of Amminadab, the **s** of Admin,	**Lk 3:33**	
the **s** of Ram, the son of Hezron,	**Lk 3:33**	
the **s** of Hezron, the son of Perez,	**Lk 3:33**	
the **s** of Perez, the son of Judah,	**Lk 3:33**	
the **s** of Judah,	**Lk 3:33**	
the **s** of Jacob, the son of Isaac,	**Lk 3:34**	
the son of Jacob, the **s** of Isaac,	**Lk 3:34**	
the **s** of Abraham, the son of Terah,	**Lk 3:34**	
the **s** of Terah, the son of Nahor,	**Lk 3:34**	
the **s** of Nahor,	**Lk 3:34**	
the **s** of Serug, the son of Reu,	**Lk 3:35**	
the son of Serug, the **s** of Reu,	**Lk 3:35**	
the **s** of Peleg, the son of Heber,	**Lk 3:35**	
the **s** of Heber, the son of Shelah,	**Lk 3:35**	
the **s** of Shelah,	**Lk 3:35**	
the **s** of Cainan, the son of Arphaxad,	**Lk 3:36**	
the son of Cainan, the **s** of Arphaxad,	**Lk 3:36**	
the **s** of Shem, the son of Noah,	**Lk 3:36**	
the **s** of Noah, the son of Lamech,	**Lk 3:36**	
the **s** of Lamech,	**Lk 3:36**	
the **s** of Methuselah, the son of	**Lk 3:37**	
the son of Methuselah, the **s** of	**Lk 3:37**	
the **s** of Jared, the son of	**Lk 3:37**	
the **s** of Mahalaleel, the son of	**Lk 3:37**	
the **s** of Cainan,	**Lk 3:37**	
the **s** of Enosh, the son of Seth,	**Lk 3:38**	
the son of Enosh, the **s** of Seth,	**Lk 3:38**	
the **s** of Adam, the son of God.	**Lk 3:38**	
the **s** of God.	**Lk 3:38**	
"If You are the **S** of God, tell	**Lk 4:3**	*5207*
"If You are the **S** of God, throw	**Lk 4:9**	*5207*
"Is this not Joseph's **s**?"	**Lk 4:22**	*5207*
"You are the **S** of God!"	**Lk 4:41**	*5207*
that the **S** of Man has authority on	**Lk 5:24**	*5207*
S of Man is Lord of the Sabbath."	**Lk 6:5**	*5207*
James *the* **s** of Alphaeus,	**Lk 6:15**	
Judas *the* **s** of James, and Judas	**Lk 6:16**	
for the sake of the **S** of Man.	**Lk 6:22**	*5207*
out, the only **s** of his mother,	**Lk 7:12**	*5207*
"The **S** of Man has come eating and	**Lk 7:34**	*5207*
Jesus, **S** of the Most High God?	**Lk 8:28**	*5207*
"The **S** of Man must suffer many	**Lk 9:22**	*5207*
S of Man will be ashamed of him	**Lk 9:26**	*5207*
"This is My **S**, *My* Chosen One;	**Lk 9:35**	*5207*

I beg You to look at my **s**, Lk 9:38 *5207*
Bring your **s** here." Lk 9:41 *5207*
S of Man is going to be delivered Lk 9:44 *5207*
for the **S** of Man did not come to Lk 9:56 *5207*
but the **S** of Man has nowhere to Lk 9:58 *5207*
no one knows who the **S** is except Lk 10:22 *5207*
who the Father is except the **S**, Lk 10:22 *5207*
whom the **S** wills to reveal *Him*." Lk 10:22 *5207*
is asked by his **s** for a fish; Lk 11:11 *5207*
S of Man be to this generation. Lk 11:30 *5207*
the **S** of Man will confess him Lk 12:8 *5207*
speaks a word against the **S** of Man, Lk 12:10 *5207*
for the **S** of Man is coming at an Lk 12:40 *5207*
will be divided, father against **s** and Lk 12:53 *5207*
against son and **s** against father Lk 12:53 *5207*
a **s** or an ox fall into a well, Lk 14:5 *5207*
the younger **s** gathered everything Lk 15:13 *5207*
longer worthy to be called your **s**; Lk 15:19 *5207*
"And the **s** said to him, Lk 15:21 *5207*
worthy to be called your **s**.' Lk 15:21 *5207*
for this **s** of mine was dead and Lk 15:24 *5207*
"Now his older **s** was in the field, Lk 15:25 *5207*
but when this **s** of yours came, who Lk 15:30 *5207*
"And he said to him, '**S**, you have Lk 15:31 *5043*
one of the days of the **S** of Man, Lk 17:22 *5207*
so will the **S** of Man be in His day. Lk 17:24 *5207*
also in the days of the **S** of Man: Lk 17:26 *5207*
day that the **S** of Man is revealed. Lk 17:30 *5207*
However, when the **S** of Man comes, Lk 18:8 *5207*
the **S** of Man will be accomplished. Lk 18:31 *5207*
"Jesus, **S** of David, have mercy on Lk 18:38 *5207*
"**S** of David, have mercy on me!" Lk 18:39 *5207*
he, too, is a **s** of Abraham. Lk 19:9 *5207*
For the **S** of Man has come to seek Lk 19:10 *5207*
I will send my beloved **s**; Lk 20:13 *5207*
they say the Christ is David's **s**? Lk 20:41 *5207*
'Lord,' and how is He his **s**?" Lk 20:44 *5207*
THE **S** OF MAN COMING IN A CLOUD Lk 21:27 *5207*
to stand before the **S** of Man." Lk 21:36 *5207*
the **S** of Man is going as it has Lk 22:22 *5207*
the **S** of Man with a kiss?" Lk 22:48 *5207*
"But from now on THE **S** OF MAN Lk 22:69 *5207*
"Are You the **S** of God, then?" Lk 22:70 *5207*
the **S** of Man must be delivered into Lk 24:7 *5207*
testified that this is the **S** of God." Jn 1:34 *5207*
"You are Simon the **s** of John; Jn 1:42 *5207*
Jesus of Nazareth, the **s** of Joseph." Jn 1:45 *5207*
"Rabbi, You are the **S** of God; Jn 1:49 *5207*
and descending on the **S** of Man." Jn 1:51 *5207*
from heaven: the **S** of Man. Jn 3:13 *5207*
so must the **S** of Man be lifted up; Jn 3:14 *5207*
that He gave His only begotten **S**, Jn 3:16 *5207*
"For God did not send the **S** into Jn 3:17 *5207*
of the only begotten **S** of God. Jn 3:18 *5207*
"The Father loves the **S** and Jn 3:35 *5207*
He who believes in the **S** has eternal Jn 3:36 *5207*
not obey the **S** will not see life, Jn 3:36 *5207*
that Jacob gave to his **s** Joseph; Jn 4:5 *5207*
whose **s** was sick at Capernaum. Jn 4:46 *5207*
Him to come down and heal his **s**; Jn 4:47 *5207*
"Go; your **s** lives." Jn 4:50 *5207*
him, saying that his **s** was living. Jn 4:51 *3816*
Jesus said to him, "Your **s** lives"; Jn 4:53 *5207*
the **S** can do nothing of Himself, Jn 5:19 *5207*
the **S** also does in like manner. Jn 5:19 *5207*
"For the Father loves the **S**, Jn 5:20 *5207*
even so the **S** also gives life to Jn 5:21 *5207*
has given all judgment to the **S**, Jn 5:22 *5207*
so that all will honor the **S** Jn 5:23 *5207*
He who does not honor the **S** does Jn 5:23 *5207*
hear the voice of the **S** of God, Jn 5:25 *5207*
S also to have life in Himself; Jn 5:26 *5207*
because He is *the* **S** of Man. Jn 5:27 *5207*
the **S** of Man will give to you, Jn 6:27 *5207*
beholds the **S** and believes in Him will Jn 6:40 *5207*
"Is not this Jesus, the **s** of Joseph, Jn 6:42 *5207*
the **S** of Man and drink His blood, Jn 6:53 *5207*
if you see the **S** of Man Jn 6:62 *5207*
Now He meant Judas *the* **s** of Simon Jn 6:71
"When you lift up the **S** of Man, Jn 8:28 *5207*
the **s** does remain forever. Jn 8:35 *5207*
the **S** makes you free, Jn 8:36 *5207*
"Is this your **s**, who you say was Jn 9:19 *5207*
"We know that this is our **s**, Jn 9:20 *5207*
"Do you believe in the **S** of Man?" Jn 9:35 *5207*
'I am the **S** of God'? Jn 10:36 *5207*
S of God may be glorified by it." Jn 11:4 *5207*
You are the Christ, the **S** of God, Jn 11:27 *5207*
for the **S** of Man to be glorified. Jn 12:23 *5207*
'The **S** of Man must be lifted up'? Jn 12:34 *5207*
Who is this **S** of Man?" Jn 12:34 *5207*
the **s** of Simon, to betray Him, Jn 13:2
the **s** of Simon Iscariot. Jn 13:26
"Now is the **S** of Man glorified, Jn 13:31 *5207*
Father may be glorified in the **S**. Jn 14:13 *5207*
glorify Your **S**, that the Son may Jn 17:1 *5207*
Son, that the **S** may glorify You, Jn 17:1 *5207*
perished but the **s** of perdition, Jn 17:12 *5207*
Himself out *to be* the **S** of God." Jn 19:7 *5207*
"Woman, behold, your **s**!" Jn 19:26 *5207*
Jesus is the Christ, the **S** of God; Jn 20:31 *5207*
s of John, do you love Me more Jn 21:15
s of John, do you love Me?" Jn 21:16
s of John, do you love Me?" Jn 21:17
James *the* **s** of Alphaeus, Ac 1:13
and Judas *the* **s** of James. Ac 1:13
means **S** of Encouragement), Ac 4:36 *5207*
and nurtured him as her own **s**. Ac 7:21 *5207*
S of Man standing at the right hand Ac 7:56 *5207*

Jesus Christ is the **S** of God."] Ac 8:37 *5207*
"He is the **S** of God." Ac 9:20 *5207*
and fraud, you **s** of the devil, Ac 13:10 *5207*
God gave them Saul the **s** of Kish, Ac 13:21 *5207*
'I HAVE FOUND DAVID the **s** of Jesse, Ac 13:22
'YOU ARE MY **S**; TODAY I HAVE Ac 13:33 *5207*
the **s** of a Jewish woman who was a Ac 16:1 *5207*
the **s** of Pyrrhus, and by Ac 20:4
I am a Pharisee, a **s** of Pharisees; Ac 23:6 *5207*
But the **s** of Paul's sister heard Ac 23:16 *5207*
concerning His **S**, who was born of Ro 1:3 *5207*
declared the **S** of God with power Ro 1:4 *5207*
preaching of the gospel of His **S**, Ro 1:9 *5207*
to God through the death of His **S**, Ro 5:10 *5207*
sending His own **S** in the likeness Ro 8:3 *5207*
conformed to the image of His **S**, Ro 8:29 *5207*
He who did not spare His own **S**, Ro 8:32 *5207*
COME, AND SARAH SHALL HAVE A **S**." Ro 9:9 *5207*
called into fellowship with His **S**, 1Co 1:9 *5207*
the **S** Himself also will be subjected 1Co 15:28 *5207*
For the **S** of God, Christ Jesus, 2Co 1:19 *5207*
to reveal His **S** in me so that I Ga 1:16 *5207*
I live by faith in the **S** of God, Ga 2:20 *5207*
time came, God sent forth His **S**, Ga 4:4 *5207*
Spirit of His **S** into our hearts, Ga 4:6 *5207*
are no longer a slave, but a **s**; Ga 4:7 *5207*
and if a **s**, then an heir through Ga 4:7 *5207*
But the **s** by the bondwoman was Ga 4:23
and the **s** by the free woman Ga 4:23
CAST OUT THE BONDWOMAN AND HER **S**, Ga 4:30 *5207*
FOR THE **S** OF THE BONDWOMAN SHALL Ga 4:30 *5207*
WITH THE **S** OF THE FREE WOMAN." Ga 4:30 *5207*
of the knowledge of the **S** of God, Eph 4:13 *5207*
to the kingdom of His beloved **S**, Col 1:13 *5207*
and to wait for His **S** from heaven, 1Th 1:10 *5207*
is revealed, the **s** of destruction, 2Th 2:3 *5207*
I entrust to you, Timothy, *my* **s**, 1Tm 1:18 *5043*
To Timothy, my beloved **s**: 2Tm 1:2 *5043*
You therefore, my **s**, 2Tm 2:1 *5043*
days has spoken to us in His **S**, Heb 1:2 *5207*
"YOU ARE MY **S**, TODAY I HAVE Heb 1:5 *5207*
HIM AND HE SHALL BE A **S** TO ME"? Heb 1:5 *5207*
But of the **S** *He says,* Heb 1:8 *5207*
OR THE **S** OF MAN, THAT YOU ARE Heb 2:6 *5207*
but Christ *was faithful* as a **S** Heb 3:6 *5207*
the heavens, Jesus the **S** of God, Heb 4:14 *5207*
"YOU ARE MY **S**, TODAY I HAVE Heb 5:5 *5207*
Although He was a **S**, Heb 5:8 *5207*
to themselves the **S** of God and Heb 6:6 *5207*
life, but made like the **S** of God, Heb 7:3 *5207*
came after the Law, *appoints* a **S**, Heb 7:28 *5207*
trampled under foot the **S** of God, Heb 10:29 *5207*
was offering up his only begotten **s**; Heb 11:17
called the **s** of Pharaoh's daughter, Heb 11:24 *5207*
"MY **S**, DO NOT REGARD LIGHTLY THE Heb 12:5 *5207*
EVERY **S** WHOM HE RECEIVES." Heb 12:6 *5207*
for what **s** is there whom *his* Heb 12:7 *5207*
offered up Isaac his **s** on the altar? Jas 2:21 *5207*
greetings, and *so does* my **s**, Mark. 1Pe 5:13 *5207*
This is My beloved **S** with whom I 2Pe 1:17 *5207*
the **s** of Beor, who loved 2Pe 2:15
and with His **S** Jesus Christ. 1Jn 1:3 *5207*
the blood of Jesus His **S** cleanses us 1Jn 1:7 *5207*
who denies the Father and the **S**. 1Jn 2:22 *5207*
Whoever denies the **S** does not have 1Jn 2:23 *5207*
the one who confesses the **S** has the 1Jn 2:23 *5207*
abide in the **S** and in the Father. 1Jn 2:24 *5207*
The **S** of God appeared for this 1Jn 3:8 *5207*
in the name of His **S** Jesus Christ, 1Jn 3:23 *5207*
God has sent His only begotten **S** 1Jn 4:9 *5207*
sent His **S** *to be* the propitiation for 1Jn 4:10 *5207*
the Father has sent the **S** *to be* the 1Jn 4:14 *5207*
that Jesus is the **S** of God, 1Jn 4:15 *5207*
believes that Jesus is the **S** of God? 1Jn 5:5 *5207*
testified concerning His **S**. 1Jn 5:9 *5207*
one who believes in the **S** of God 1Jn 5:10 *5207*
God has given concerning His **S**. 1Jn 5:10 *5207*
life, and this life is in His **S**. 1Jn 5:11 *5207*
He who has the **S** has the life; 1Jn 5:12 *5207*
he who does not have the **S** of God 1Jn 5:12 *5207*
in the name of the **S** of God, 1Jn 5:13 *5207*
know that the **S** of God has come, 1Jn 5:20 *5207*
is true, in His **S** Jesus Christ. 1Jn 5:20 *5207*
Jesus Christ, the **S** of the Father, 2Jn 1:3 *5207*
he has both the Father and the **S**. 2Jn 1:9 *5207*
one like a **s** of man, clothed in a Rv 1:13 *5207*
The **S** of God, who has eyes like a Rv 2:18 *5207*
And she gave birth to a **s**, Rv 12:5 *5207*
one like a **s** of man, having a golden Rv 14:14 *5207*
be his God and he will be My **s**. Rv 21:7 *5207*

SONG

of Israel sang this **s** to the LORD, Ex 15:1 7892b
"The LORD is my strength and **s**, Ex 15:2 2172
Then Israel sang this **s**: Nu 21:17 7892b
write this **s** for yourselves, Dt 31:19 7892b
that this **s** may be a witness for Me Dt 31:19 7892b
that this **s** will testify before Dt 31:21 7892b
Moses wrote this **s** the same day, Dt 31:22 7892b
of Israel the words of this **s**, Dt 31:30 7892b
spoke all the words of this **s** in the Dt 32:44 7892b
Awake, awake, sing a **s**! Jg 5:12 7892b
to teach the sons of Judah *the* **s** 2Sa 1:18
David spoke the words of this **s** to the 2Sa 22:1 7892b
of **s** in the house of the LORD, 1Ch 6:31 7892a
They ministered with **s** before 1Ch 6:32 7892a
the **s** to the LORD also began with 2Ch 29:27 7892a
for the **s** leaders day by day. Ne 11:23 7891
And with my **s** I shall thank Him. Ps 28:7 7892a
Sing to Him a new **s**; Ps 33:3 7892a

He put a new **s** in my mouth, Ps 40:3 7892a
mouth, a **s** of praise to our God; Ps 40:3 8416
His **s** will be with me in the night, Ps 42:8 7892a
Lift up *a* **s** for Him who rides Ps 68:4
And I *am* the **s** of the drunkards. Ps 69:12 5058
praise the name of God with **s** And Ps 69:30 7892a
I will remember my **s** in the night; Ps 77:6 5058
Raise a **s**, strike the timbrel, The Ps 81:2 2172
Sing to the LORD a new **s**; Ps 96:1 7892a
O sing to the LORD a new **s**, Ps 98:1 7892a
The LORD is my strength and **s**, Ps 118:14 2172
How can we sing the LORD'S **s** In a Ps 137:4 7892a
I will sing a new **s** to You, Ps 144:9 7892a
Sing to the LORD a new **s**, Ps *149:1* 7892a
one to listen to the **s** of fools. Ec 7:5 7892a
daughters of **s** will sing softly. Ec 12:4 7892a
The **S** of Songs, which is Solomon's. SS 1:1 7892a
A **s** of my beloved concerning His Is 5:1 7892b
the LORD GOD is my strength and **s**, Is 12:2 2176
Praise the LORD in **s**, Is 12:5 2167
to Tyre as *in* the **s** of the harlot: Is 23:15 7892b
They do not drink wine with **s**; Is 24:9 7892a
the **s** of the ruthless is silenced. Is 25:5 2158
In that day this **s** will be sung in Is 26:1 7892a
Sing to the LORD a new **s**, Is 42:10 7892a
Their *mocking* **s** all the day. La 3:14 5058
I am their mocking **s**. La 3:63 4485
you are to them like a sensual **s** Ezk 33:32 7892a
And they sang a new **s**, Rv 5:9 *5603*
And they sang a new **s** before the Rv 14:3 *5603*
and no one could learn the **s** Rv 14:3 *5603*
And they sang the **s** of Moses, Rv 15:3 *5603*
of God, and the **s** of the Lamb, Rv 15:3 *5603*

SONGS

sent you away with joy and with **s**, Gn 31:27 7892a
proverbs, and his **s** were 1,005. 1Ki 4:32 7892a
might, even with **s** and with lyres, 1Ch 13:8 7892a
with instruments *for* the **s** of God, 1Ch 16:42 7892a
charge of the **s** of thanksgiving, Ne 12:8 1960
hymns of thanksgiving and with **s** Ne 12:27 7892a
s of praise and hymns of Ne 12:46 7892a
Maker, Who gives **s** in the night, Jb 35:10 2158
surround me with **s** of deliverance. Ps 32:7 7438
And His virgins had no wedding **s**. Ps 78:63 1984b
Your statutes are my **s** In the house Ps 119:54 2158
our captors demanded of us **s**, Ps 137:3 1697, 7892a
"Sing us one of the **s** of Zion." Ps 137:3 7892a
who sings **s** to a troubled heart. Pr 25:20 7892a
The Song of **S**, which is Solomon's. SS 1:1 7892a
strings skillfully, sing many **s**, Is 23:16 7892a
the ends of the earth we hear **s**, Is 24:16 2158
You will have **s** as in the night Is 30:29 7892a
So we will play my **s** on stringed Is 38:20 5058
will silence the sound of your **s**, Ezk 26:13 7892a
away from Me the noise of your **s**; Am 5:23 7892a
have composed **s** for themselves, Am 6:5 7892a
"The **s** of the palace will turn to Am 8:3 7892b
And all your **s** into lamentation; Am 8:10 7892a
psalms and hymns and spiritual **s**, Eph 5:19 *5603*
psalms *and* hymns *and* spiritual **s**, Col 3:16 *5603*

SON-IN-LAW

A **s**, and your sons, and your Gn 19:12 2860a
"Samson, the **s** of the Timnite, Jg 15:6 2860a
the girl's father said to his **s**, Jg 19:5 2860a
that I should be the king's **s**?" 1Sa 18:18 2860a
time you may be my **s** today." 1Sa 18:21 2859
therefore, become the king's **s**.' " 1Sa 18:22 2859
your sight to become the king's **s**, 1Sa 18:23 2859
David to become the king's **s**. 1Sa 18:26 2859
that he might become the king's **s**. 1Sa 18:27 2859
as David, even the king's **s**, 1Sa 22:14 2860a
he was a **s** of the house of Ahab. 2Ki 8:27 2860a
s of Shecaniah the son of Arah, Ne 6:18 2860a
was a **s** of Sanballat the Horonite, Ne 13:28 2860a

SONS-IN-LAW

Lot went out and spoke to his **s**, Gn 19:14 2860a
he appeared to his **s** to be jesting. Gn 19:14 2860a

SON'S

me, and I will eat of my **s** game, Gn 27:25 1121
arise and eat of his **s** game, Gn 27:31 1121
me some of your **s** mandrakes." Gn 30:14 1121
you take my **s** mandrakes also?" Gn 30:15 1121
in return for your **s** mandrakes." Gn 30:15 1121
hired you with my **s** mandrakes." Gn 30:16 1121
whether it is your **s** tunic or not." Gn 37:32 1121
"It is my **s** tunic. Gn 37:33 1121
took a flint and cut off her **s** foreskin Ex 4:25 1121
'The nakedness of your **s** daughter Lv 18:10 1121
she is your **s** wife, you shall not Lv 18:15 1121
nor shall you take her **s** daughter Lv 18:17 1121
you and your son, also your **s** son, Jg 8:22 1121
his **s** hand and give it to you, 1Ki 11:35 1121
upon his house in his **s** days." 1Ki 21:29 1121
What is His name or His **s** name? Pr 30:4 1121
the punishment for the **s** iniquity; Ezk 18:20 1121

SONS

and he had *other* **s** and daughters. Gn 5:4 1121
and he had *other* **s** and daughters. Gn 5:7 1121
and he had *other* **s** and daughters. Gn 5:10 1121
and he had *other* **s** and daughters. Gn 5:13 1121
and he had *other* **s** and daughters. Gn 5:16 1121
and he had *other* **s** and daughters. Gn 5:19 1121
and he had *other* **s** and daughters. Gn 5:22 1121
and he had *other* **s** and daughters. Gn 5:26 1121
and he had *other* **s** and daughters. Gn 5:30 1121
that the **s** of God saw that the Gn 6:2 1121
when the **s** of God came in to the Gn 6:4 1121

Noah became the father of three **s**:	**Gn 6:10**	1121
you and your **s** and your wife,	**Gn 6:18**	1121
Then Noah and his **s** and his wife	**Gn 7:7**	1121
Ham and Japheth, the **s** of Noah,	**Gn 7:13**	1121
three wives of his **s** with them,	**Gn 7:13**	1121
s and your sons' wives with you.	**Gn 8:16**	1121
and his **s** and his wife and his	**Gn 8:18**	1121
Noah and his **s** and said to them,	**Gn 9:1**	1121
to Noah and to his **s** with him,	**Gn 9:8**	1121
Now the **s** of Noah who came out of	**Gn 9:18**	1121
These three *were* the **s** of Noah,	**Gn 9:19**	1121
Ham, and Japheth, the **s** of Noah;	**Gn 10:1**	1121
s were born to them after the flood.	**Gn 10:1**	1121
The **s** of Japheth *were* Gomer and	**Gn 10:2**	1121
The **s** of Gomer *were* Ashkenaz	**Gn 10:3**	1121
The **s** of Javan *were* Elishah	**Gn 10:4**	1121
The **s** of Ham *were* Cush and	**Gn 10:6**	1121
The **s** of Cush *were* Seba and	**Gn 10:7**	1121
and the **s** of Raamah *were* Sheba and	**Gn 10:7**	1121
These are the **s** of Ham, according	**Gn 10:20**	1121
The **s** of Shem *were* Elam and Asshur	**Gn 10:22**	1121
The **s** of Aram *were* Uz and Hul	**Gn 10:23**	1121
Two **s** were born to Eber;	**Gn 10:25**	1121
all these were the **s** of Joktan.	**Gn 10:29**	1121
These are the **s** of Shem, according	**Gn 10:31**	1121
are the families of the **s** of Noah,	**Gn 10:32**	1121
which the **s** of men had built.	**Gn 11:5**	1121
and he had *other* **s** and daughters.	**Gn 11:11**	1121
and he had *other* **s** and daughters.	**Gn 11:13**	1121
and he had *other* **s** and daughters.	**Gn 11:15**	1121
and he had *other* **s** and daughters.	**Gn 11:17**	1121
and he had *other* **s** and daughters.	**Gn 11:19**	1121
and he had *other* **s** and daughters.	**Gn 11:21**	1121
and he had *other* **s** and daughters.	**Gn 11:23**	1121
and he had *other* **s** and daughters.	**Gn 11:25**	1121
A son-in-law, and your **s**,	**Gn 19:12**	1121
of the **s** of Ammon to this day.	**Gn 19:38**	1121
dead, and spoke to the **s** of Heth,	**Gn 23:3**	1121
The **s** of Heth answered Abraham,	**Gn 23:5**	1121
people of the land, the **s** of Heth.	**Gn 23:7**	1121
was sitting among the **s** of Heth;	**Gn 23:10**	1121
in the hearing of the **s** of Heth;	**Gn 23:10**	1121
the presence of the **s** of my people	**Gn 23:11**	1121
in the hearing of the **s** of Heth,	**Gn 23:16**	1121
in the presence of the **s** of Heth,	**Gn 23:18**	1121
a burial site by the **s** of Heth.	**Gn 23:20**	1121
And the **s** of Dedan were Asshurim	**Gn 25:3**	1121
The **s** of Midian *were* Ephah and	**Gn 25:4**	1121
All these *were* the **s** of Keturah.	**Gn 25:4**	1121
but to the **s** of his concubines,	**Gn 25:6**	1121
his **s** Isaac and Ishmael buried him	**Gn 25:9**	1121
purchased from the **s** of Heth;	**Gn 25:10**	1121
are the names of the **s** of Ishmael,	**Gn 25:13**	1121
These are the **s** of Ishmael and	**Gn 25:16**	1121
your mother's **s** bow down to you.	**Gn 27:29**	1121
to the land of the **s** of the east.	**Gn 29:1**	1121
I have borne him three **s**."	**Gn 29:34**	1121
because I have borne him six **s**."	**Gn 30:20**	1121
gave them into the care of his **s**.	**Gn 30:35**	1121
Jacob heard the words of Laban's **s**,	**Gn 31:1**	1121
me to kiss my **s** and my daughters?	**Gn 31:28**	1121
and kissed his **s** and his daughters	**Gn 31:55**	1121
the **s** of Israel do not eat the sinew	**Gn 32:32**	1121
from the hand of the **s** of Hamor,	**Gn 33:19**	1121
but his **s** were with his livestock	**Gn 34:5**	1121
Now the **s** of Jacob came in from	**Gn 34:7**	1121
But Jacob's **s** answered Shechem and	**Gn 34:13**	1121
two of Jacob's **s**, Simeon and Levi,	**Gn 34:25**	1121
Jacob's **s** came upon the slain and	**Gn 34:27**	1121
did not pursue the **s** of Jacob.	**Gn 35:5**	1121
Now there were twelve **s** of Jacob	**Gn 35:22**	1121
the **s** of Leah: Reuben, Jacob's	**Gn 35:23**	1121
the **s** of Rachel: Joseph and	**Gn 35:24**	1121
and the **s** of Bilhah, Rachel's maid:	**Gn 35:25**	1121
and the **s** of Zilpah, Leah's maid:	**Gn 35:26**	1121
These are the **s** of Jacob who were	**Gn 35:26**	1121
his **s** Esau and Jacob buried him.	**Gn 35:29**	1121
These are the **s** of Esau who were	**Gn 36:5**	1121
Esau took his wives and his **s** and	**Gn 36:6**	1121
These are the names of Esau's **s**:	**Gn 36:10**	1121
The **s** of Eliphaz were Teman,	**Gn 36:11**	1121
are the **s** of Esau's wife Adah.	**Gn 36:12**	1121
These are the **s** of Reuel:	**Gn 36:13**	1121
were the **s** of Esau's wife Basemath.	**Gn 36:13**	1121
the **s** of Esau's wife Oholibamah,	**Gn 36:14**	1121
are the chiefs of the **s** of Esau.	**Gn 36:15**	1121
The **s** of Eliphaz, the firstborn	**Gn 36:15**	1121
these are the **s** of Adah.	**Gn 36:16**	1121
These are the **s** of Reuel,	**Gn 36:17**	1121
are the **s** of Esau's wife Basemath.	**Gn 36:17**	1121
the **s** of Esau's wife Oholibamah:	**Gn 36:18**	1121
These are the **s** of Esau	**Gn 36:19**	1121
are the **s** of Seir the Horite,	**Gn 36:20**	1121
the **s** of Seir in the land of Edom.	**Gn 36:21**	1121
s of Lotan were Hori and Hemam;	**Gn 36:22**	1121
These are the **s** of Shobal:	**Gn 36:23**	1121
These are the **s** of Zibeon:	**Gn 36:24**	1121
These are the **s** of Dishon:	**Gn 36:26**	1121
These are the **s** of Ezer:	**Gn 36:27**	1121
These are the **s** of Dishan:	**Gn 36:28**	1121
king reigned over the **s** of Israel.	**Gn 36:31**	1121
along with the **s** of Bilhah and the	**Gn 37:2**	1121
of Bilhah and the **s** of Zilpah,	**Gn 37:2**	1121
loved Joseph more than all his **s**,	**Gn 37:3**	1121
Then all his **s** and all his	**Gn 37:35**	1121
came, two **s** were born to Joseph,	**Gn 41:50**	1121
in Egypt, and Jacob said to his **s**,	**Gn 42:1**	1121
So the **s** of Israel came to buy	**Gn 42:5**	1121
"We are all **s** of one man;	**Gn 42:11**	1121
the **s** of one man in the land of	**Gn 42:13**	1121
twelve brothers, **s** of our father;	**Gn 42:32**	1121
"You may put my two **s** to death if	**Gn 42:37**	1121
know that my wife bore me two **s**;	**Gn 44:27**	1121
Then the **s** of Israel did so;	**Gn 45:21**	1121
s of Israel carried their father Jacob	**Gn 46:5**	1121
his **s** and his grandsons with him,	**Gn 46:7**	1121
are the names of the **s** of Israel,	**Gn 46:8**	1121
sons of Israel, Jacob and his **s**,	**Gn 46:8**	1121
The **s** of Reuben:	**Gn 46:9**	1121
The **s** of Simeon:	**Gn 46:10**	1121
The **s** of Levi:	**Gn 46:11**	1121
The **s** of Judah:	**Gn 46:12**	1121
And the **s** of Perez were Hezron and	**Gn 46:12**	1121
The **s** of Issachar:	**Gn 46:13**	1121
The **s** of Zebulun:	**Gn 46:14**	1121
These are the **s** of Leah, whom she	**Gn 46:15**	1121
all his **s** and his daughters	**Gn 46:15**	1121
The **s** of Gad:	**Gn 46:16**	1121
The **s** of Asher: Imnah and Ishvah	**Gn 46:17**	1121
And the **s** of Beriah:	**Gn 46:17**	1121
These are the **s** of Zilpah, whom	**Gn 46:18**	1121
The **s** of Jacob's wife Rachel:	**Gn 46:19**	1121
The **s** of Benjamin:	**Gn 46:21**	1121
These are the **s** of Rachel, who	**Gn 46:22**	1121
The **s** of Dan:	**Gn 46:23**	1121
The **s** of Naphtali:	**Gn 46:24**	1121
These are the **s** of Bilhah, whom	**Gn 46:25**	1121
including the wives of Jacob's **s**,	**Gn 46:26**	1121
and the **s** of Joseph, who were born	**Gn 46:27**	1121
s Manasseh and Ephraim with him.	**Gn 48:1**	1121
"Now your two **s**,	**Gn 48:5**	1121
When Israel saw Joseph's **s**,	**Gn 48:8**	1121
"They are my **s**, whom God has	**Gn 48:9**	1121
Jacob summoned his **s** and said,	**Gn 49:1**	1121
together and hear, O **s** of Jacob;	**Gn 49:2**	1121
father's **s** shall bow down to you.	**Gn 49:8**	1121
purchased from the **s** of Heth."	**Gn 49:32**	1121
Jacob finished charging his **s**,	**Gn 49:33**	1121
Thus his **s** did for him as he	**Gn 50:12**	1121
for his **s** carried him to the land	**Gn 50:13**	1121
third generation of Ephraim's **s**;	**Gn 50:23**	1121
also the **s** of Machir, the son of	**Gn 50:23**	1121
Joseph made the **s** of Israel swear,	**Gn 50:25**	1121
these are the names of the **s** of Israel	**Ex 1:1**	1121
But the **s** of Israel were fruitful	**Ex 1:7**	1121
the people of the **s** of Israel are	**Ex 1:9**	1121
were in dread of the **s** of Israel.	**Ex 1:12**	1121
s of Israel to labor rigorously;	**Ex 1:13**	1121
And the **s** of Israel sighed because	**Ex 2:23**	1121
God saw the **s** of Israel, and	**Ex 2:25**	1121
of the **s** of Israel has come to Me;	**Ex 3:9**	1121
bring My people, the **s** of Israel,	**Ex 3:10**	1121
the **s** of Israel out of Egypt?"	**Ex 3:11**	1121
I am going to the **s** of Israel,	**Ex 3:13**	1121
you shall say to the **s** of Israel,	**Ex 3:14**	1121
you shall say to the **s** of Israel,	**Ex 3:15**	1121
put them on your **s** and daughters.	**Ex 3:22**	1121
So Moses took his wife and his **s**	**Ex 4:20**	1121
all the elders of the **s** of Israel;	**Ex 4:29**	1121
was concerned about the **s** of Israel	**Ex 4:31**	1121
the foremen of the **s** of Israel,	**Ex 5:14**	1121
the foremen of the **s** of Israel came	**Ex 5:15**	1121
The foremen of the **s** of Israel saw	**Ex 5:19**	1121
the groaning of the **s** of Israel,	**Ex 6:5**	1121
therefore, to the **s** of Israel,	**Ex 6:6**	1121
spoke thus to the **s** of Israel,	**Ex 6:9**	1121
s of Israel go out of his land."	**Ex 6:11**	1121
the **s** of Israel have not listened	**Ex 6:12**	1121
gave them a charge to the **s** of Israel	**Ex 6:13**	1121
to bring the **s** of Israel out of	**Ex 6:13**	1121
The **s** of Reuben, Israel's firstborn:	**Ex 6:14**	1121
The **s** of Simeon:	**Ex 6:15**	1121
These are the names of the **s** of Levi	**Ex 6:16**	1121
The **s** of Gershon:	**Ex 6:17**	1121
The **s** of Kohath:	**Ex 6:18**	1121
The **s** of Merari:	**Ex 6:19**	1121
The **s** of Izhar:	**Ex 6:21**	1121
The **s** of Uzziel:	**Ex 6:22**	1121
The **s** of Korah:	**Ex 6:24**	1121
"Bring out the **s** of Israel from	**Ex 6:26**	1121
out the **s** of Israel from Egypt;	**Ex 6:27**	1121
s of Israel go out of his land.	**Ex 7:2**	1121
hosts, My people the **s** of Israel,	**Ex 7:4**	1121
bring out the **s** of Israel from their	**Ex 7:5**	1121
belongs to the **s** of Israel.	**Ex 9:4**	1121
the livestock of the **s** of Israel,	**Ex 9:6**	1121
where the **s** of Israel *were*,	**Ex 9:26**	1121
he did not let the **s** of Israel go,	**Ex 9:35**	1121
with our **s** and our daughters, with	**Ex 10:9**	1121
he did not let the **s** of Israel go.	**Ex 10:20**	1121
but all the **s** of Israel had light	**Ex 10:23**	1121
'But against any of the **s** of Israel	**Ex 11:7**	1121
s of Israel go out of his land.	**Ex 11:10**	1121
the houses of the **s** of Israel in Egypt	**Ex 12:27**	1121
the **s** of Israel went and did *so;*	**Ex 12:28**	1121
both you and the **s** of Israel;	**Ex 12:31**	1121
Now the **s** of Israel had done	**Ex 12:35**	1121
Now the **s** of Israel journeyed from	**Ex 12:37**	1121
that the **s** of Israel lived in Egypt	**Ex 12:40**	1121
to be observed by all the **s** of	**Ex 12:42**	1121
Then all the **s** of Israel did *so;*	**Ex 12:50**	1121
LORD brought the **s** of Israel out of	**Ex 12:51**	1121
every womb among the **s** of Israel,	**Ex 13:2**	1121
man among your **s** you shall redeem.	**Ex 13:13**	1121
every firstborn of my **s** I redeem.'	**Ex 13:15**	1121
and the **s** of Israel went up in	**Ex 13:18**	1121
the **s** of Israel solemnly swear,	**Ex 13:19**	1121
"Tell the **s** of Israel to turn	**Ex 14:2**	1121
Pharaoh will say of the **s** of Israel,	**Ex 14:3**	1121
and he chased after the **s** of Israel	**Ex 14:8**	1121
as the **s** of Israel were going out	**Ex 14:8**	1121
drew near, the **s** of Israel looked,	**Ex 14:10**	1121
so the **s** of Israel cried out to	**Ex 14:10**	1121
Tell the **s** of Israel to go forward.	**Ex 14:15**	1121
and the **s** of Israel shall go	**Ex 14:16**	1121
The **s** of Israel went through	**Ex 14:22**	1121
But the **s** of Israel walked on dry	**Ex 14:29**	1121
Then Moses and the **s** of Israel	**Ex 15:1**	1121
but the **s** of Israel walked on dry	**Ex 15:19**	1121
all the congregation of the **s** of Israel	**Ex 16:1**	1121
s of Israel grumbled against Moses	**Ex 16:2**	1121
The **s** of Israel said to them,	**Ex 16:3**	1121
Aaron said to all the **s** of Israel,	**Ex 16:6**	1121
congregation of the **s** of Israel,	**Ex 16:9**	1121
congregation of the **s** of Israel,	**Ex 16:10**	1121
the grumblings of the **s** of Israel;	**Ex 16:12**	1121
When the **s** of Israel saw *it*, they	**Ex 16:15**	1121
The **s** of Israel did so, and	**Ex 16:17**	1121
The **s** of Israel ate the manna	**Ex 16:35**	1121
the **s** of Israel journeyed by stages	**Ex 17:1**	1121
of the quarrel of the **s** of Israel,	**Ex 17:7**	1121
and her two **s**, of whom one was	**Ex 18:3**	1121
came with his **s** and his wife to	**Ex 18:5**	1121
wife and her two **s** with her."	**Ex 18:6**	1121
after the **s** of Israel had gone out of	**Ex 19:1**	1121
of Jacob and tell the **s** of Israel:	**Ex 19:3**	1121
shall speak to the **s** of Israel."	**Ex 19:6**	1121
you shall say to the **s** of Israel,	**Ex 20:22**	1121
and she bears him **s** or daughters,	**Ex 21:4**	1121
of your **s** you shall give to Me.	**Ex 22:29**	1121
sent young men of the **s** of Israel,	**Ex 24:5**	1121
the nobles of the **s** of Israel;	**Ex 24:11**	1121
And to the eyes of the **s** of Israel	**Ex 24:17**	1121
"Tell the **s** of Israel to raise a	**Ex 25:2**	1121
commandment for the **s** of Israel.	**Ex 25:22**	1121
You shall charge the **s** of Israel	**Ex 27:20**	1121
Aaron and his **s** shall keep it in	**Ex 27:21**	1121
generations for the **s** of Israel.	**Ex 27:21**	1121
your brother, and his **s** with him,	**Ex 28:1**	1121
him, from among the **s** of Israel,	**Ex 28:1**	1121
Eleazar and Ithamar, Aaron's **s**.	**Ex 28:1**	1121
for Aaron your brother and his **s**,	**Ex 28:4**	1121
them the names of the **s** of Israel,	**Ex 28:9**	1121
to the names of the **s** of Israel;	**Ex 28:11**	1121
of memorial for the **s** of Israel,	**Ex 28:12**	1121
to the names of the **s** of Israel:	**Ex 28:21**	1121
Aaron shall carry the names of the **s**	**Ex 28:29**	1121
carry the judgment of the **s** of Israel	**Ex 28:30**	1121
which the **s** of Israel consecrate,	**Ex 28:38**	1121
Aaron's **s** you shall make tunics;	**Ex 28:40**	1121
brother and on his **s** with him;	**Ex 28:41**	1121
They shall be on Aaron and on his **s**	**Ex 28:43**	1121
bring Aaron and his **s** to the doorway	**Ex 29:4**	1121
You shall bring his **s** and put tunics	**Ex 29:8**	1121
them with sashes, Aaron and his **s**,	**Ex 29:9**	1121
you shall ordain Aaron and his **s**.	**Ex 29:9**	1121
and Aaron and his **s** shall lay	**Ex 29:10**	1121
and Aaron and his **s** shall lay	**Ex 29:15**	1121
and Aaron and his **s** shall lay	**Ex 29:19**	1121
and on his **s** and on his sons'	**Ex 29:21**	1121
as well as his **s** and his sons'	**Ex 29:21**	1121
Aaron and in the hands of his **s**,	**Ex 29:24**	1121
from the one which was for his **s**.	**Ex 29:27**	1121
"It shall be for Aaron and his **s**	**Ex 29:28**	1121
forever from the **s** of Israel,	**Ex 29:28**	1121
a heave offering from the **s** of Israel	**Ex 29:28**	1121
shall be for his **s** after him,	**Ex 29:29**	1121
one of his **s** who is priest in his stead	**Ex 29:30**	1121
"Aaron and his **s** shall eat	**Ex 29:32**	1121
shall do to Aaron and to his **s**,	**Ex 29:35**	1121
meet there with the **s** of Israel,	**Ex 29:43**	1121
s to minister as priests to Me.	**Ex 29:44**	1121
I will dwell among the **s** of Israel	**Ex 29:45**	1121
of the **s** of Israel to number them,	**Ex 30:12**	1121
money from the **s** of Israel and	**Ex 30:16**	1121
the **s** of Israel before the LORD,	**Ex 30:16**	1121
"Aaron and his **s** shall wash	**Ex 30:19**	1121
You shall anoint Aaron and his **s**,	**Ex 30:30**	1121
shall speak to the **s** of Israel,	**Ex 30:31**	1121
priest, and the garments of his **s**,	**Ex 31:10**	1121
for you, speak to the **s** of Israel,	**Ex 31:13**	1121
'So the **s** of Israel shall observe	**Ex 31:16**	1121
Me and the **s** of Israel forever;	**Ex 31:17**	1121
in the ears of your wives, your **s**,	**Ex 32:2**	1121
and made the **s** of Israel drink *it*.	**Ex 32:20**	1121
And all the **s** of Levi gathered	**Ex 32:26**	1121
So the **s** of Levi did as Moses	**Ex 32:28**	1121
"Say to the **s** of Israel,	**Ex 33:5**	1121
So the **s** of Israel stripped	**Ex 33:6**	1121
some of his daughters for your **s**,	**Ex 34:16**	1121
and cause your **s** *also* to play the	**Ex 34:16**	1121
all the firstborn of your **s**.	**Ex 34:20**	1121
and all the **s** of Israel saw Moses,	**Ex 34:30**	1121
all the **s** of Israel came near,	**Ex 34:32**	1121
came out and spoke to the **s** of Israel	**Ex 34:34**	1121
the **s** of Israel would see the face	**Ex 34:35**	1121
congregation of the **s** of Israel,	**Ex 35:1**	1121
congregation of the **s** of Israel,	**Ex 35:4**	1121
priest and the garments of his **s**,	**Ex 35:19**	1121
all the congregation of the **s** of Israel	**Ex 35:20**	1121
Moses said to the **s** of Israel,	**Ex 35:30**	1121
the contributions which the **s** of Israel	**Ex 36:3**	1121
to the names of the **s** of Israel.	**Ex 39:6**	1121
stones for the **s** of Israel,	**Ex 39:7**	1121
to the names of the **s** of Israel;	**Ex 39:14**	1121
woven linen for Aaron and his **s**,	**Ex 39:27**	1121
and the **s** of Israel did according	**Ex 39:32**	1121

priest and the garments of his **s**,	**Ex 39:41**	1121
So the **s** of Israel did all the	**Ex 39:42**	1121
bring Aaron and his **s** to the doorway	**Ex 40:12**	1121
You shall bring his **s** and put tunics	**Ex 40:14**	1121
Aaron and his **s** washed their hands	**Ex 40:31**	1121
the **s** of Israel would set out;	**Ex 40:36**	1121
"Speak to the **s** of Israel and say to	**Lv 1:2**	1121
and Aaron's **s** the priests shall	**Lv 1:5**	1121
'The **s** of Aaron the priest	**Lv 1:7**	1121
'Then Aaron's **s** the priests	**Lv 1:8**	1121
Aaron's **s** the priests shall sprinkle	**Lv 1:11**	1121
'He shall then bring it to Aaron's **s** the	**Lv 2:2**	1121
belongs to Aaron and his **s**:	**Lv 2:3**	1121
belongs to Aaron and his **s**:	**Lv 2:10**	1121
Aaron's **s** the priests shall sprinkle	**Lv 3:2**	1121
'Then Aaron's **s** shall offer *it* up	**Lv 3:5**	1121
and Aaron's **s** shall sprinkle its	**Lv 3:8**	1121
and the **s** of Aaron shall sprinkle	**Lv 3:13**	1121
"Speak to the **s** of Israel,	**Lv 4:2**	1121
"Command Aaron and his **s**,	**Lv 6:9**	1121
the **s** of Aaron shall present it	**Lv 6:14**	1121
of it Aaron and his **s** are to eat.	**Lv 6:16**	1121
among the **s** of Aaron may eat it;	**Lv 6:18**	1121
which Aaron and his **s** are to present	**Lv 6:20**	1121
place among his **s** shall offer it.	**Lv 6:22**	1121
"Speak to Aaron and to his **s**,	**Lv 6:25**	1121
belong to all the **s** of Aaron,	**Lv 7:10**	1121
"Speak to the **s** of Israel,	**Lv 7:23**	1121
"Speak to the **s** of Israel,	**Lv 7:29**	1121
shall belong to Aaron and his **s**.	**Lv 7:31**	1121
'The one among the **s** of Aaron who	**Lv 7:33**	1121
contribution from the **s** of Israel from	**Lv 7:34**	1121
and to his **s** as *their* due forever from	**Lv 7:34**	1121
due forever from the **s** of Israel.	**Lv 7:34**	1121
consecrated to his **s** from the offerings	**Lv 7:35**	1121
to be given them from the **s** of Israel	**Lv 7:36**	1121
commanded the **s** of Israel to present	**Lv 7:38**	1121
"Take Aaron and his **s** with him,	**Lv 8:2**	1121
had Aaron and his **s** come near and	**Lv 8:6**	1121
Next Moses had Aaron's **s** come near	**Lv 8:13**	1121
and Aaron and his **s** laid their	**Lv 8:14**	1121
and Aaron and his **s** laid their	**Lv 8:18**	1121
and Aaron and his **s** laid their	**Lv 8:22**	1121
He also had Aaron's **s** come near;	**Lv 8:24**	1121
Aaron and on the hands of his **s** and	**Lv 8:27**	1121
Aaron, on his garments, on his **s**,	**Lv 8:30**	1121
on the garments of his **s** with him;	**Lv 8:30**	1121
Aaron, his garments, and his **s**,	**Lv 8:30**	1121
the garments of his **s** with him.	**Lv 8:30**	1121
Moses said to Aaron and to his **s**,	**Lv 8:31**	1121
'Aaron and his **s** shall eat it.'	**Lv 8:31**	1121
Thus Aaron and his **s** did all the	**Lv 8:36**	1121
Moses called Aaron and his **s** and	**Lv 9:1**	1121
the **s** of Israel you shall speak,	**Lv 9:3**	1121
Aaron's **s** presented the blood to him	**Lv 9:9**	1121
and Aaron's **s** handed the blood to	**Lv 9:12**	1121
and Aaron's **s** handed the blood to	**Lv 9:18**	1121
Nadab and Abihu, the **s** of Aaron,	**Lv 10:1**	1121
the **s** of Aaron's uncle Uzziel,	**Lv 10:4**	1121
and to his **s** Eleazar and Ithamar,	**Lv 10:6**	1121
neither you nor your **s** with you,	**Lv 10:9**	1121
and so as to teach the **s** of Israel	**Lv 10:11**	1121
to Aaron, and to his surviving **s**,	**Lv 10:12**	1121
s and your daughters with you;	**Lv 10:14**	1121
offerings of the **s** of Israel.	**Lv 10:14**	1121
due you and your **s** with you,	**Lv 10:15**	1121
surviving **s** Eleazar and Ithamar,	**Lv 10:16**	1121
"Speak to the **s** of Israel,	**Lv 11:2**	1121
"Speak to the **s** of Israel,	**Lv 12:2**	1121
or to one of his **s** the priests.	**Lv 13:2**	1121
"Speak to the **s** of Israel, and	**Lv 15:2**	1121
"Thus you shall keep the **s** of Israel	**Lv 15:31**	1121
the death of the two **s** of Aaron,	**Lv 16:1**	1121
of the **s** of Israel two male goats for	**Lv 16:5**	1121
the impurities of the **s** of Israel and	**Lv 16:16**	1121
from the impurities of the **s** of Israel	**Lv 16:19**	1121
the iniquities of the **s** of Israel and	**Lv 16:21**	1121
to make atonement for the **s** of	**Lv 16:34**	1121
"Speak to Aaron and to his **s** and	**Lv 17:2**	1121
sons and to all the **s** of Israel	**Lv 17:2**	1121
"The reason is so that the **s** of	**Lv 17:5**	1121
I said to the **s** of Israel,	**Lv 17:12**	1121
when any man from the **s** of Israel,	**Lv 17:13**	1121
I said to the **s** of Israel,	**Lv 17:14**	1121
the **s** of Israel and say to them,	**Lv 18:2**	1121
the **s** of Israel and say to them,	**Lv 19:2**	1121
against the **s** of your people,	**Lv 19:18**	1121
shall also say to the **s** of Israel:	**Lv 20:2**	1121
'Any man from the **s** of Israel or	**Lv 20:2**	1121
sight of the **s** of their people.	**Lv 20:17**	1121
to the priests, the **s** of Aaron,	**Lv 21:1**	1121
Moses spoke to Aaron and to his **s**	**Lv 21:24**	1121
sons and to all the **s** of Israel.	**Lv 21:24**	1121
"Tell Aaron and his **s** to be	**Lv 22:2**	1121
the holy *gifts* of the **s** of Israel,	**Lv 22:2**	1121
the holy *gifts* which the **s** of Israel	**Lv 22:3**	1121
not profane the holy *gifts* of the **s** of	**Lv 22:15**	1121
"Speak to Aaron and to his **s** and to	**Lv 22:18**	1121
sons and to all the **s** of Israel and	**Lv 22:18**	1121
sanctified among the **s** of Israel;	**Lv 22:32**	1121
"Speak to the **s** of Israel and	**Lv 23:2**	1121
"Speak to the **s** of Israel and	**Lv 23:10**	1121
"Speak to the **s** of Israel,	**Lv 23:24**	1121
"Speak to the **s** of Israel,	**Lv 23:34**	1121
know that I had the **s** of Israel live in	**Lv 23:43**	1121
So Moses declared to the **s** of Israel	**Lv 23:44**	1121
"Command the **s** of Israel that	**Lv 24:2**	1121
covenant for the **s** of Israel.	**Lv 24:8**	1121
It shall be for Aaron and his **s**,	**Lv 24:9**	1121
went out among the **s** of Israel;	**Lv 24:10**	1121
shall speak to the **s** of Israel,	**Lv 24:15**	1121
Moses spoke to the **s** of Israel,	**Lv 24:23**	1121
Thus the **s** of Israel did, just as	**Lv 24:23**	1121
"Speak to the **s** of Israel and	**Lv 25:2**	1121
possession among the **s** of Israel.	**Lv 25:33**	1121
from you, he and his **s** with him,	**Lv 25:41**	1121
it is out of the **s** of the sojourners	**Lv 25:45**	1121
bequeath them to your **s** after you,	**Lv 25:46**	1121
your countrymen, the **s** of Israel,	**Lv 25:46**	1121
of jubilee, he and his **s** with him.	**Lv 25:54**	1121
the **s** of Israel are My servants;	**Lv 25:55**	1121
you will eat the flesh of your **s** and	**Lv 26:29**	1121
between Himself and the **s** of Israel	**Lv 26:46**	1121
"Speak to the **s** of Israel and	**Lv 27:2**	1121
the **s** of Israel at Mount Sinai.	**Lv 27:34**	1121
congregation of the **s** of Israel,	**Nu 1:2**	1121
of the **s** of Joseph:	**Nu 1:10**	1121
Now the **s** of Reuben, Israel's	**Nu 1:20**	1121
Of the **s** of Simeon, their	**Nu 1:22**	1121
Of the **s** of Gad, their	**Nu 1:24**	1121
Of the **s** of Judah, their	**Nu 1:26**	1121
Of the **s** of Issachar, their	**Nu 1:28**	1121
Of the **s** of Zebulun, their	**Nu 1:30**	1121
Of the **s** of Joseph, *namely*, of the	**Nu 1:32**	1121
namely, of the **s** of Ephraim,	**Nu 1:32**	1121
Of the **s** of Manasseh, their	**Nu 1:34**	1121
Of the **s** of Benjamin, their	**Nu 1:36**	1121
Of the **s** of Dan, their	**Nu 1:38**	1121
Of the **s** of Asher, their	**Nu 1:40**	1121
Of the **s** of Naphtali, their	**Nu 1:42**	1121
the numbered men of the **s** of Israel	**Nu 1:45**	1121
census among the **s** of Israel.	**Nu 1:49**	1121
"The **s** of Israel shall camp,	**Nu 1:52**	1121
congregation of the **s** of Israel.	**Nu 1:53**	1121
Thus the **s** of Israel did;	**Nu 1:54**	1121
"The **s** of Israel shall camp, each	**Nu 2:2**	1121
and the leader of the **s** of Judah:	**Nu 2:3**	1121
the leader of the **s** of Issachar:	**Nu 2:5**	1121
the leader of the **s** of Zebulun:	**Nu 2:7**	1121
and the leader of the **s** of Reuben:	**Nu 2:10**	1121
the leader of the **s** of Simeon:	**Nu 2:12**	1121
and the leader of the **s** of Gad:	**Nu 2:14**	1121
and the leader of the **s** of Ephraim	**Nu 2:18**	1121
the leader of the **s** of Manasseh:	**Nu 2:20**	1121
the leader of the **s** of Benjamin:	**Nu 2:22**	1121
and the leader of the **s** of Dan:	**Nu 2:25**	1121
and the leader of the **s** of Asher:	**Nu 2:27**	1121
the leader of the **s** of Naphtali:	**Nu 2:29**	1121
the numbered men of the **s** of Israel	**Nu 2:32**	1121
numbered among the **s** of Israel,	**Nu 2:33**	1121
Thus the **s** of Israel did;	**Nu 2:34**	1121
are the names of the **s** of Aaron:	**Nu 3:2**	1121
are the names of the **s** of Aaron,	**Nu 3:3**	1121
the duties of the **s** of Israel,	**Nu 3:8**	1121
the Levites to Aaron and to his **s**;	**Nu 3:9**	1121
to him from among the **s** of Israel.	**Nu 3:9**	1121
"So you shall appoint Aaron and his **s**	**Nu 3:10**	1121
Levites from among the **s** of Israel	**Nu 3:12**	1121
of the womb among the **s** of Israel.	**Nu 3:12**	1121
"Number the **s** of Levi by their	**Nu 3:15**	1121
are the **s** of Levi by their names:	**Nu 3:17**	1121
are the names of the **s** of Gershon	**Nu 3:18**	1121
the **s** of Kohath by their families:	**Nu 3:19**	1121
the **s** of Merari by their families:	**Nu 3:20**	1121
Now the duties of the **s** of Gershon	**Nu 3:25**	1121
The families of the **s** of Kohath	**Nu 3:29**	1121
appointed duties of the **s** of Merari	**Nu 3:36**	1121
are Moses and Aaron and his **s**,	**Nu 3:38**	1121
the obligation of the **s** of Israel;	**Nu 3:38**	1121
every firstborn male of the **s** of Israel	**Nu 3:40**	1121
all the firstborn among the **s** of Israel,	**Nu 3:41**	1121
the cattle of the **s** of Israel."	**Nu 3:41**	1121
firstborn among the **s** of Israel,	**Nu 3:42**	1121
all the firstborn among the **s** of Israel	**Nu 3:45**	1121
273 of the firstborn of the **s** of Israel	**Nu 3:46**	1121
them, to Aaron and to his **s**."	**Nu 3:48**	1121
from the firstborn of the **s** of Israel	**Nu 3:50**	1121
money to Aaron and to his **s**,	**Nu 3:51**	1121
Kohath from among the **s** of Levi,	**Nu 4:2**	1121
Aaron and his **s** shall go in and	**Nu 4:5**	1121
"When Aaron and his **s** have	**Nu 4:15**	1121
after that the **s** of Kohath shall	**Nu 4:15**	1121
the **s** of Kohath are to carry.	**Nu 4:15**	1121
Aaron and his **s** shall go in and	**Nu 4:19**	1121
a census of the **s** of Gershon also,	**Nu 4:22**	1121
of the **s** of the Gershonites,	**Nu 4:27**	1121
at the command of Aaron and his **s**;	**Nu 4:27**	1121
families of the **s** of the Gershonites	**Nu 4:28**	1121
"*As for* the **s** of Merari, you	**Nu 4:29**	1121
the families of the **s** of Merari,	**Nu 4:33**	1121
numbered the **s** of the Kohathites by	**Nu 4:34**	1121
s of Gershon by their families and	**Nu 4:38**	1121
the families of the **s** of Gershon,	**Nu 4:41**	1121
the **s** of Merari by their families,	**Nu 4:42**	1121
the families of the **s** of Merari,	**Nu 4:45**	1121
"Command the **s** of Israel that	**Nu 5:2**	1121
The **s** of Israel did so and	**Nu 5:4**	1121
Moses, thus the **s** of Israel did.	**Nu 5:4**	1121
"Speak to the **s** of Israel,	**Nu 5:6**	1121
the holy *gifts* of the **s** of Israel,	**Nu 5:9**	1121
"Speak to the **s** of Israel and	**Nu 5:12**	1121
"Speak to the **s** of Israel and	**Nu 6:2**	1121
"Speak to Aaron and to his **s**,	**Nu 6:23**	1121
you shall bless the **s** of Israel.	**Nu 6:23**	1121
invoke My name on the **s** of Israel,	**Nu 6:27**	1121
oxen he gave to the **s** of Gershon,	**Nu 7:7**	1121
oxen he gave to the **s** of Merari,	**Nu 7:8**	1121
did not give *any* to the **s** of Kohath	**Nu 7:9**	1121
Helon, leader of the **s** of Zebulun;	**Nu 7:24**	1121
leader of the **s** of Reuben;	**Nu 7:30**	1121
of Deuel, leader of the **s** of Gad;	**Nu 7:42**	1121
leader of the **s** of Ephraim;	**Nu 7:48**	1121
leader of the **s** of Manasseh;	**Nu 7:54**	1121
leader of the **s** of Benjamin;	**Nu 7:60**	1121
leader of the **s** of Dan;	**Nu 7:66**	1121
Ochran, leader of the **s** of Asher;	**Nu 7:72**	1121
Enan, leader of the **s** of Naphtali;	**Nu 7:78**	1121
Levites from among the **s** of Israel	**Nu 8:6**	1121
congregation of the **s** of Israel,	**Nu 8:9**	1121
and the **s** of Israel shall lay	**Nu 8:10**	1121
offering from the **s** of Israel,	**Nu 8:11**	1121
stand before Aaron and before his **s**	**Nu 8:13**	1121
from among the **s** of Israel,	**Nu 8:14**	1121
to Me from among the **s** of Israel.	**Nu 8:16**	1121
firstborn of all the **s** of Israel.	**Nu 8:16**	1121
firstborn among the **s** of Israel is	**Nu 8:17**	1121
firstborn among the **s** of Israel.	**Nu 8:18**	1121
as a gift to Aaron and to his **s** from	**Nu 8:19**	1121
sons from among the **s** of Israel,	**Nu 8:19**	1121
to perform the service of the **s** of	**Nu 8:19**	1121
on behalf of the **s** of Israel,	**Nu 8:19**	1121
no plague among the **s** of Israel by	**Nu 8:19**	1121
of the **s** of Israel to the Levites;	**Nu 8:20**	1121
so the **s** of Israel did to them.	**Nu 8:20**	1121
before Aaron and before his **s**;	**Nu 8:22**	1121
let the **s** of Israel observe the	**Nu 9:2**	1121
So Moses told the **s** of Israel to	**Nu 9:4**	1121
Moses, so the **s** of Israel did.	**Nu 9:5**	1121
time among the **s** of Israel?"	**Nu 9:7**	1121
"Speak to the **s** of Israel,	**Nu 9:10**	1121
the **s** of Israel would then set	**Nu 9:17**	1121
there the **s** of Israel would camp.	**Nu 9:17**	1121
the **s** of Israel would set out,	**Nu 9:18**	1121
the **s** of Israel would keep the	**Nu 9:19**	1121
the **s** of Israel remained camped	**Nu 9:22**	1121
"The priestly **s** of Aaron,	**Nu 10:8**	1121
and the **s** of Israel set out on	**Nu 10:12**	1121
of the camp of the **s** of Judah,	**Nu 10:14**	1121
tribal army of the **s** of Issachar;	**Nu 10:15**	1121
tribal army of the **s** of Zebulun.	**Nu 10:16**	1121
and the **s** of Gershon and the sons	**Nu 10:17**	1121
of Gershon and the **s** of Merari,	**Nu 10:17**	1121
tribal army of the **s** of Simeon,	**Nu 10:19**	1121
the tribal army of the **s** of Gad.	**Nu 10:20**	1121
of the camp of the **s** of Ephraim,	**Nu 10:22**	1121
tribal army of the **s** of Manasseh;	**Nu 10:23**	1121
tribal army of the **s** of Benjamin.	**Nu 10:24**	1121
of the camp of the **s** of Dan,	**Nu 10:25**	1121
the tribal army of the **s** of Asher;	**Nu 10:26**	1121
tribal army of the **s** of Naphtali.	**Nu 10:27**	1121
the order of march of the **s** of Israel	**Nu 10:28**	1121
s of Israel wept again and said,	**Nu 11:4**	1121
going to give to the **s** of Israel;	**Nu 13:2**	1121
who were heads of the **s** of Israel.	**Nu 13:3**	1121
the cluster which the **s** of Israel cut	**Nu 13:24**	1121
all the congregation of the **s** of Israel	**Nu 13:26**	1121
So they gave out to the **s** of Israel	**Nu 13:32**	1121
s of Anak are part of the Nephilim	**Nu 13:33**	1121
All the **s** of Israel grumbled	**Nu 14:2**	1121
congregation of the **s** of Israel.	**Nu 14:5**	1121
congregation of the **s** of Israel,	**Nu 14:7**	1121
of meeting to all the **s** of Israel.	**Nu 14:10**	1121
the complaints of the **s** of Israel,	**Nu 14:27**	1121
'Your **s** shall be shepherds for	**Nu 14:33**	1121
words to all the **s** of Israel,	**Nu 14:39**	1121
"Speak to the **s** of Israel and	**Nu 15:2**	1121
"Speak to the **s** of Israel and	**Nu 15:18**	1121
congregation of the **s** of Israel,	**Nu 15:25**	1121
the **s** of Israel will be forgiven,	**Nu 15:26**	1121
who is native among the **s** of Israel	**Nu 15:29**	1121
Now while the **s** of Israel were in	**Nu 15:32**	1121
"Speak to the **s** of Israel, and	**Nu 15:38**	1121
Dathan and Abiram, the **s** of Eliab,	**Nu 16:1**	1121
On the son of Peleth, **s** of Reuben,	**Nu 16:1**	1121
with some of the **s** of Israel,	**Nu 16:2**	1121
gone far enough, you **s** of Levi!"	**Nu 16:7**	1121
"Hear now, you **s** of Levi,	**Nu 16:8**	1121
and all your brothers, **s** of Levi,	**Nu 16:10**	1121
Dathan and Abiram, the **s** of Eliab;	**Nu 16:12**	1121
and their **s** and their little ones.	**Nu 16:27**	1121
for a sign to the **s** of Israel."	**Nu 16:38**	1121
as a reminder to the **s** of Israel	**Nu 16:40**	1121
s of Israel grumbled against Moses	**Nu 16:41**	1121
"Speak to the **s** of Israel, and	**Nu 17:2**	1121
the grumblings of the **s** of Israel,	**Nu 17:5**	1121
spoke to the **s** of Israel,	**Nu 17:6**	1121
the LORD to all the **s** of Israel;	**Nu 17:9**	1121
the **s** of Israel spoke to Moses,	**Nu 17:12**	1121
"You and your **s** and your father's	**Nu 18:1**	1121
and you and your **s** with you shall	**Nu 18:1**	1121
while you and your **s** with you are	**Nu 18:2**	1121
no longer be wrath on the **s** of Israel.	**Nu 18:5**	1121
from among the **s** of Israel;	**Nu 18:6**	1121
"But you and your **s** with you	**Nu 18:7**	1121
the holy gifts of the **s** of Israel I	**Nu 18:8**	1121
your **s** as a perpetual allotment.	**Nu 18:8**	1121
most holy for you and for your **s**.	**Nu 18:9**	1121
wave offerings of the **s** of Israel;	**Nu 18:11**	1121
to your **s** and daughters with you as	**Nu 18:11**	1121
the **s** of Israel offer to the LORD,	**Nu 18:19**	1121
I have given to you and your **s** and	**Nu 18:19**	1121
inheritance among the **s** of Israel.	**Nu 18:20**	1121
"To the **s** of Levi, behold, I	**Nu 18:21**	1121
"The **s** of Israel shall not	**Nu 18:22**	1121
and among the **s** of Israel they	**Nu 18:23**	1121
"For the tithe of the **s** of Israel,	**Nu 18:24**	1121
no inheritance among the **s** of Israel	**Nu 18:24**	1121

'When you take from the **s** of Israel **Nu 18:26** 1121
you receive from the **s** of Israel; **Nu 18:28** 1121
sacred gifts of the **s** of Israel, **Nu 18:32** 1121
'Speak to the **s** of Israel that **Nu 19:2** 1121
the congregation of the **s** of Israel **Nu 19:9** 1121
a perpetual statute to the **s** of Israel **Nu 19:10** 1121
Then the **s** of Israel, the whole **Nu 20:1** 1121
in the sight of the **s** of Israel, **Nu 20:12** 1121
because the **s** of Israel contended **Nu 20:13** 1121
the **s** of Israel said to him, **Nu 20:19** 1121
out from Kadesh, the **s** of Israel, **Nu 20:22** 1121
I have given to the **s** of Israel, **Nu 20:24** 1121
Now the **s** of Israel moved out and **Nu 21:10** 1121
Jabbok, as far as the **s** of Ammon; **Nu 21:24** 1121
border of the **s** of Ammon *was* Jazer. **Nu 21:24** 1121
He has given his **s** as fugitives, **Nu 21:29** 1121
they killed him and his **s** and all his **Nu 21:35** 1121
Then the **s** of Israel journeyed, **Nu 22:1** 1121
Moab was in dread of the **s** of Israel **Nu 22:3** 1121
the land of the **s** of his people, **Nu 22:5** 1121
And tear down all the **s** of Sheth. **Nu 24:17** 1121
one of the **s** of Israel came and **Nu 25:6** 1121
congregation of the **s** of Israel, **Nu 25:6** 1121
So the plague on the **s** of Israel was **Nu 25:8** 1121
My wrath from the **s** of Israel in **Nu 25:11** 1121
the **s** of Israel in My jealousy. **Nu 25:11** 1121
atonement for the **s** of Israel.' " **Nu 25:13** 1121
all the congregation of the **s** of Israel **Nu 26:2** 1121
Now the **s** of Israel who came out **Nu 26:4** 1121
firstborn, the **s** of Reuben: **Nu 26:5** 1121
The **s** of Eliab: **Nu 26:9** 1121
The **s** of Korah, however, did not **Nu 26:11** 1121
The **s** of Simeon according to their **Nu 26:12** 1121
The **s** of Gad according to their **Nu 26:15** 1121
These are the families of the **s** of **Nu 26:18** 1121
The **s** of Judah *were* Er and Onan, **Nu 26:19** 1121
The **s** of Judah according to **Nu 26:20** 1121
The **s** of Perez were: **Nu 26:21** 1121
The **s** of Issachar according to **Nu 26:23** 1121
The **s** of Zebulun according to **Nu 26:26** 1121
The **s** of Joseph according to their **Nu 26:28** 1121
The **s** of Manasseh: **Nu 26:29** 1121
These are the **s** of Gilead: **Nu 26:30** 1121
the son of Hepher had no **s**, **Nu 26:33** 1121
These are the **s** of Ephraim **Nu 26:35** 1121
These are the **s** of Shuthelah: **Nu 26:36** 1121
These are the families of the **s** of **Nu 26:37** 1121
These are the **s** of Joseph **Nu 26:37** 1121
The **s** of Benjamin according to **Nu 26:38** 1121
The **s** of Bela were Ard and Naaman: **Nu 26:40** 1121
These are the **s** of Benjamin **Nu 26:41** 1121
These are the **s** of Dan according **Nu 26:42** 1121
The **s** of Asher according to their **Nu 26:44** 1121
Of the **s** of Beriah: **Nu 26:45** 1121
are the families of the **s** of Asher **Nu 26:47** 1121
The **s** of Naphtali according to **Nu 26:48** 1121
were numbered of the **s** of Israel, **Nu 26:51** 1121
not numbered among the **s** of Israel **Nu 26:62** 1121
to them among the **s** of Israel. **Nu 26:62** 1121
who numbered the **s** of Israel in **Nu 26:63** 1121
who numbered the **s** of Israel in **Nu 26:64** 1121
in his own sin, and he had no **s**. **Nu 27:3** 1121
shall speak to the **s** of Israel, **Nu 27:8** 1121
ordinance to the **s** of Israel, **Nu 27:11** 1121
I have given to the **s** of Israel. **Nu 27:12** 1121
of the **s** of Israel may obey *him.* **Nu 27:20** 1121
he and the **s** of Israel with him, **Nu 27:21** 1121
the **s** of Israel and say to them, **Nu 28:2** 1121
Moses spoke to the **s** of Israel **Nu 29:40** 1121
of the tribes of the **s** of Israel, **Nu 30:1** 1121
the **s** of Israel on the Midianites; **Nu 31:2** 1121
The **s** of Israel captured the **Nu 31:9** 1121
congregation of the **s** of Israel, **Nu 31:12** 1121
these caused the **s** of Israel, **Nu 31:16** 1121
"From the **s** of Israel's half, **Nu 31:30** 1121
As for the **s** of Israel's half, **Nu 31:42** 1121
and from the **s** of Israel's half, **Nu 31:47** 1121
the **s** of Israel before the LORD. **Nu 31:54** 1121
Now the **s** of Reuben and the sons **Nu 32:1** 1121
Now the sons of Reuben and the **s** **Nu 32:1** 1121
the **s** of Gad and the sons of **Nu 32:2** 1121
the **s** of Reuben came and spoke to **Nu 32:2** 1121
But Moses said to the **s** of Gad and **Nu 32:6** 1121
of Gad and to the **s** of Reuben, **Nu 32:6** 1121
discouraging the **s** of Israel from **Nu 32:7** 1121
they discouraged the **s** of Israel **Nu 32:9** 1121
to go before the **s** of Israel, **Nu 32:17** 1121
until every one of the **s** of Israel has **Nu 32:18** 1121
The **s** of Gad and the sons of **Nu 32:25** 1121
the **s** of Reuben spoke to Moses, **Nu 32:25** 1121
of the tribes of the **s** of Israel. **Nu 32:28** 1121
s of Gad and the sons of Reuben, **Nu 32:29** 1121
sons of Gad and the **s** of Reuben, **Nu 32:29** 1121
The **s** of Gad and the sons of **Nu 32:31** 1121
Gad and the **s** of Reuben answered, **Nu 32:31** 1121
to the **s** of Gad and to the sons of **Nu 32:33** 1121
sons of Gad and to the **s** of Reuben **Nu 32:33** 1121
The **s** of Gad built Dibon and **Nu 32:34** 1121
The **s** of Reuben built Heshbon **Nu 32:37** 1121
The **s** of Machir the son of **Nu 32:39** 1121
the journeys of the **s** of Israel, **Nu 33:1** 1121
the **s** of Israel started out boldly in **Nu 33:3** 1121
Then the **s** of Israel journeyed **Nu 33:5** 1121
after the **s** of Israel had come from **Nu 33:38** 1121
of the coming of the **s** of Israel. **Nu 33:40** 1121
"Speak to the **s** of Israel and say to **Nu 33:51** 1121
"Command the **s** of Israel and say **Nu 34:2** 1121
Moses commanded the **s** of Israel, **Nu 34:13** 1121
"For the tribe of the **s** of Reuben **Nu 34:14** 1121
and the tribe of the **s** of Gad **Nu 34:14** 1121
Of the tribe of the **s** of Simeon, **Nu 34:20** 1121
tribe of the **s** of Dan a leader, **Nu 34:22** 1121
"Of the **s** of Joseph: **Nu 34:23** 1121
of the **s** of Manasseh a leader, **Nu 34:23** 1121
of the **s** of Ephraim a leader, **Nu 34:24** 1121
of the **s** of Zebulun a leader, **Nu 34:25** 1121
of the **s** of Issachar a leader, **Nu 34:26** 1121
tribe of the **s** of Asher a leader, **Nu 34:27** 1121
of the **s** of Naphtali a leader, **Nu 34:28** 1121
the inheritance to the **s** of Israel in **Nu 34:29** 1121
"Command the **s** of Israel that **Nu 35:2** 1121
the possession of the **s** of Israel, **Nu 35:8** 1121
"Speak to the **s** of Israel and say to **Nu 35:10** 1121
be for refuge for the **s** of Israel, **Nu 35:15** 1121
the midst of the **s** of Israel.' " **Nu 35:34** 1121
of the family of the **s** of Gilead, **Nu 36:1** 1121
the families of the **s** of Joseph, **Nu 36:1** 1121
households of the **s** of Israel, **Nu 36:1** 1121
give the land by lot to the **s** of Israel **Nu 36:2** 1121
"But if they marry one of the **s** **Nu 36:3** 1121
other tribes of the **s** of Israel, **Nu 36:3** 1121
jubilee of the **s** of Israel comes, **Nu 36:4** 1121
Moses commanded the **s** of Israel **Nu 36:5** 1121
"The tribe of the **s** of Joseph are **Nu 36:5** 1121
no inheritance of the **s** of Israel shall **Nu 36:7** 1121
for the **s** of Israel shall each **Nu 36:7** 1121
of any tribe of the **s** of Israel shall **Nu 36:8** 1121
so that the **s** of Israel each may **Nu 36:8** 1121
for the tribes of the **s** of Israel **Nu 36:9** 1121
married their uncles' **s**. **Nu 36:11** 1121
s of Manasseh the son of Joseph, **Nu 36:12** 1121
LORD commanded to the **s** of Israel **Nu 36:13** 1121
saw the **s** of the Anakim there." **Dt 1:28** 1121
and to him and to his **s** I will **Dt 1:36** 1121
your **s**, who this day have no **Dt 1:39** 1121
the **s** of Esau who live in Seir; **Dt 2:4** 1121
beyond our brothers the **s** of Esau, **Dt 2:8** 1121
to the **s** of Lot as a possession. **Dt 2:9** 1121
but the **s** of Esau dispossessed **Dt 2:12** 1121
you come opposite the **s** of Ammon, **Dt 2:19** 1121
of the **s** of Ammon as a possession, **Dt 2:19** 1121
to the **s** of Lot as a possession.' **Dt 2:19** 1121
just as He did for the **s** of Esau, **Dt 2:22** 1121
just as the **s** of Esau who live in **Dt 2:29** 1121
him with his **s** and all his people. **Dt 2:33** 1121
to the land of the **s** of Ammon, **Dt 2:37** 1121
it is in Rabbah of the **s** of Ammon. **Dt 3:11** 1121
the border of the **s** of Ammon; **Dt 3:16** 1121
your brothers, the **s** of Israel. **Dt 3:18** 1121
to your **s** and your grandsons. **Dt 4:9** 1121
Moses set before the **s** of Israel; **Dt 4:44** 1121
Moses spoke to the **s** of Israel, **Dt 4:45** 1121
whom Moses and the **s** of Israel **Dt 4:46** 1121
them and with their **s** forever! **Dt 5:29** 1121
shall teach them diligently to your **s** **Dt 6:7** 1121
give your daughters to their **s**, **Dt 7:3** 1121
take their daughters for your **s**. **Dt 7:3** 1121
"For they will turn your **s** away **Dt 7:4** 1121
and tall, the **s** of the Anakim, **Dt 9:2** 1121
can stand before the **s** of Anak?' **Dt 9:2** 1121
(Now the **s** of Israel set out from **Dt 10:6** 1121
I *am* not *speaking* with your **s** who **Dt 11:2** 1121
Dathan and Abiram, the **s** of Eliab, **Dt 11:6** 1121
You shall teach them to your **s**, **Dt 11:19** 1121
the days of your **s** may be multiplied **Dt 11:21** 1121
God, you and your **s** and daughters, **Dt 12:12** 1121
with you and your **s** after you, **Dt 12:25** 1121
you and your **s** after you forever, **Dt 12:28** 1121
for they even burn their **s** and **Dt 12:31** 1121
are the **s** of the LORD your God; **Dt 14:1** 1121
so that he and his **s** may **Dt 17:20** 1121
and his **s** from all your tribes, **Dt 18:5** 1121
"Then the priests, the **s** of Levi, **Dt 21:5** 1121
and the unloved have borne him **s**, **Dt 21:15** 1121
day he wills what he has to his **s**, **Dt 21:16** 1121
"The **s** of the third generation **Dt 23:8** 1121
nor shall any of the **s** of Israel **Dt 23:17** 1121
his countrymen of the **s** of Israel, **Dt 24:7** 1121
not be put to death for *their* **s**, **Dt 24:16** 1121
nor shall **s** be put to death for **Dt 24:16** 1121
"Your **s** and your daughters shall **Dt 28:32** 1121
"You shall have **s** and daughters **Dt 28:41** 1121
the flesh of your **s** and of your **Dt 28:53** 1121
s of Israel in the land of Moab, **Dt 29:1** 1121
your **s** who rise up after you and **Dt 29:22** 1121
belong to us and to our **s** forever, **Dt 29:29** 1121
command you today, you and your **s**, **Dt 30:2** 1121
the **s** of Levi who carried the ark **Dt 31:9** 1121
and teach it to the **s** of Israel; **Dt 31:19** 1121
for Me against the **s** of Israel. **Dt 31:19** 1121
and taught it to the **s** of Israel. **Dt 31:22** 1121
for you shall bring the **s** of Israel **Dt 31:23** 1121
When He separated the **s** of man, **Dt 32:8** 1121
to the number of the **s** of Israel. **Dt 32:8** 1121
Because of the provocation of His **s** **Dt 32:19** 1121
S in whom is no faithfulness. **Dt 32:20** 1121
command your **s** to observe carefully **Dt 32:46** 1121
which I am giving to the **s** of Israel **Dt 32:49** 1121
in the midst of the **s** of Israel at the **Dt 32:51** 1121
in the midst of the **s** of Israel. **Dt 32:51** 1121
I am giving the **s** of Israel." **Dt 32:52** 1121
man of God blessed the **s** of Israel **Dt 33:1** 1121
Nor did he regard his own **s**, **Dt 33:9** 1121
"More blessed than **s** is Asher; **Dt 33:24** 1121
So the **s** of Israel wept for Moses **Dt 34:8** 1121
and the **s** of Israel listened to **Dt 34:9** 1121
to them, to the **s** of Israel. **Jos 1:2** 1121
men from the **s** of Israel have come **Jos 2:2** 1121
and he and all the **s** of Israel set **Jos 3:1** 1121
Joshua said to the **s** of Israel, **Jos 3:9** 1121
appointed from the **s** of Israel, **Jos 4:4** 1121
of the tribes of the **s** of Israel. **Jos 4:5** 1121
become a memorial to the **s** of Israel **Jos 4:7** 1121
Thus the **s** of Israel did as **Jos 4:8** 1121
of the tribes of the **s** of Israel; **Jos 4:8** 1121
The **s** of Reuben and the sons **Jos 4:12** 1121
sons of Reuben and the **s** of Gad **Jos 4:12** 1121
array before the **s** of Israel, **Jos 4:12** 1121
He said to the **s** of Israel, **Jos 4:21** 1121
the Jordan before the **s** of Israel **Jos 5:1** 1121
because of the **s** of Israel. **Jos 5:1** 1121
and circumcise again the **s** of Israel **Jos 5:2** 1121
and circumcised the **s** of Israel at **Jos 5:3** 1121
For the **s** of Israel walked forty **Jos 5:6** 1121
the **s** of Israel camped at Gilgal they **Jos 5:10** 1121
s of Israel no longer had manna, **Jos 5:12** 1121
shut because of the **s** of Israel; **Jos 6:1** 1121
But the **s** of Israel acted unfaithfully **Jos 7:1** 1121
burned against the **s** of Israel. **Jos 7:1** 1121
"Therefore the **s** of Israel cannot **Jos 7:12** 1121
Joshua and to all the **s** of Israel, **Jos 7:23** 1121
mantle, the bar of gold, his **s**, **Jos 7:24** 1121
had commanded the **s** of Israel, **Jos 8:31** 1121
the presence of the **s** of Israel. **Jos 8:32** 1121
Then the **s** of Israel set out and **Jos 9:17** 1121
The **s** of Israel did not strike **Jos 9:18** 1121
from the hands of the **s** of Israel, **Jos 9:26** 1121
Joshua and with the **s** of Israel." **Jos 10:4** 1121
than those whom the **s** of Israel killed **Jos 10:11** 1121
Amorites before the **s** of Israel, **Jos 10:12** 1121
when Joshua and the **s** of Israel had **Jos 10:20** 1121
against any of the **s** of Israel. **Jos 10:21** 1121
the **s** of Israel took as their **Jos 11:14** 1121
made peace with the **s** of Israel **Jos 11:19** 1121
in the land of the **s** of Israel; **Jos 11:22** 1121
whom the **s** of Israel defeated, **Jos 12:1** 1121
the border of the **s** of Ammon; **Jos 12:2** 1121
and the **s** of Israel defeated them; **Jos 12:6** 1121
Joshua and the **s** of Israel defeated **Jos 12:7** 1121
out from before the **s** of Israel; **Jos 13:6** 1121
as the border of the **s** of Ammon; **Jos 13:10** 1121
But the **s** of Israel did not **Jos 13:13** 1121
to the tribe of the **s** of Reuben **Jos 13:15** 1121
The **s** of Israel also killed Balaam **Jos 13:22** 1121
The border of the **s** of Reuben was **Jos 13:23** 1121
the inheritance of the **s** of Reuben **Jos 13:23** 1121
the tribe of Gad, to the **s** of Gad, **Jos 13:24** 1121
half the land of the **s** of Ammon, **Jos 13:25** 1121
This is the inheritance of the **s** **Jos 13:28** 1121
for the half-tribe of the **s** of Manasseh **Jos 13:29** 1121
the **s** of Machir the son of Manasseh, **Jos 13:31** 1121
for half of the **s** of Machir **Jos 13:31** 1121
which the **s** of Israel inherited in the **Jos 14:1** 1121
tribes of the **s** of Israel apportioned to **Jos 14:1** 1121
the **s** of Joseph were two tribes, **Jos 14:4** 1121
Thus the **s** of Israel did just as **Jos 14:5** 1121
Then the **s** of Judah drew near to **Jos 14:6** 1121
the lot for the tribe of the **s** of Judah **Jos 15:1** 1121
is the border around the **s** of Judah **Jos 15:12** 1121
a portion among the **s** of Judah, **Jos 15:13** 1121
from there the three **s** of Anak: **Jos 15:14** 1121
the tribe of the **s** of Judah according **Jos 15:20** 1121
of the tribe of the **s** of Judah toward **Jos 15:21** 1121
the **s** of Judah could not drive **Jos 15:63** 1121
the Jebusites live with the **s** of Judah **Jos 15:63** 1121
Then the lot for the **s** of Joseph **Jos 16:1** 1121
The **s** of Joseph, Manasseh and **Jos 16:4** 1121
was the territory of the **s** of Ephraim **Jos 16:5** 1121
tribe of the **s** of Ephraim according **Jos 16:8** 1121
were set apart for the **s** of Ephraim **Jos 16:9** 1121
inheritance of the **s** of Manasseh, **Jos 16:9** 1121
the rest of the **s** of Manasseh according **Jos 17:2** 1121
for the **s** of Abiezer and for the **Jos 17:2** 1121
for the **s** of Helek and for the sons of **Jos 17:2** 1121
sons of Helek and for the **s** of Asriel **Jos 17:2** 1121
of Asriel and for the **s** of Shechem **Jos 17:2** 1121
of Shechem and for the **s** of Hepher **Jos 17:2** 1121
Hepher and for the **s** of Shemida; **Jos 17:2** 1121
the son of Manasseh, had no **s**, **Jos 17:3** 1121
an inheritance among his **s**. **Jos 17:6** 1121
to the rest of the **s** of Manasseh. **Jos 17:6** 1121
belonged to the **s** of Ephraim. **Jos 17:8** 1121
But the **s** of Manasseh could not **Jos 17:12** 1121
the **s** of Israel became strong, **Jos 17:13** 1121
the **s** of Joseph spoke to Joshua, **Jos 17:14** 1121
The **s** of Joseph said, **Jos 17:16** 1121
s of Israel assembled themselves at **Jos 18:1** 1121
There remained among the **s** of Israel **Jos 18:2** 1121
So Joshua said to the **s** of Israel, **Jos 18:3** 1121
divided the land to the **s** of Israel **Jos 18:10** 1121
lot of the tribe of the **s** of Benjamin **Jos 18:11** 1121
their lot lay between the **s** of Judah **Jos 18:11** 1121
sons of Judah and the **s** of Joseph. **Jos 18:11** 1121
a city of the **s** of Judah. **Jos 18:14** 1121
inheritance of the **s** of Benjamin, **Jos 18:20** 1121
cities of the tribe of the **s** of Benjamin **Jos 18:21** 1121
the inheritance of the **s** of Benjamin **Jos 18:28** 1121
to the tribe of the **s** of Simeon **Jos 19:1** 1121
the inheritance of the **s** of Judah. **Jos 19:1** 1121
of the tribe of the **s** of Simeon **Jos 19:8** 1121
The inheritance of the **s** of Simeon **Jos 19:9** 1121
the portion of the **s** of Judah, **Jos 19:9** 1121
for the share of the **s** of Judah **Jos 19:9** 1121
so the **s** of Simeon received *an* **Jos 19:9** 1121
third lot came up for the **s** of Zebulun **Jos 19:10** 1121
the inheritance of the **s** of Zebulun **Jos 19:16** 1121
to the **s** of Issachar according to **Jos 19:17** 1121

of the tribe of the **s** of Issachar	**Jos 19:23**	1121
lot fell to the tribe of the **s** of Asher	**Jos 19:24**	1121
of the tribe of the **s** of Asher	**Jos 19:31**	1121
lot fell to the **s** of Naphtali;	**Jos 19:32**	1121
to the **s** of Naphtali according to	**Jos 19:32**	1121
of the tribe of the **s** of Naphtali	**Jos 19:39**	1121
lot fell to the tribe of the **s** of Dan	**Jos 19:40**	1121
s of Dan proceeded beyond them;	**Jos 19:47**	1121
for the **s** of Dan went up and	**Jos 19:47**	1121
of the tribe of the **s** of Dan according	**Jos 19:48**	1121
the **s** of Israel gave an	**Jos 19:49**	1121
of the **s** of Israel distributed by lot in	**Jos 19:51**	1121
"Speak to the **s** of Israel,	**Jos 20:2**	1121
appointed cities for all the **s** of Israel	**Jos 20:9**	1121
of the tribes of the **s** of Israel.	**Jos 21:1**	1121
So the **s** of Israel gave the	**Jos 21:3**	1121
And the **s** of Aaron the priest, who	**Jos 21:4**	1121
The rest of the **s** of Kohath	**Jos 21:5**	1121
The **s** of Gershon received	**Jos 21:6**	1121
The **s** of Merari according to their	**Jos 21:7**	1121
Now the **s** of Israel gave by lot to	**Jos 21:8**	1121
from the tribe of the **s** of Judah and	**Jos 21:9**	1121
from the tribe of the **s** of Simeon;	**Jos 21:9**	1121
and they were for the **s** of Aaron,	**Jos 21:10**	1121
the Kohathites, of the **s** of Levi,	**Jos 21:10**	1121
So to the **s** of Aaron the priest	**Jos 21:13**	1121
All the cities of the **s** of Aaron,	**Jos 21:19**	1121
the families of the **s** of Kohath,	**Jos 21:20**	1121
to the rest of the **s** of Kohath.	**Jos 21:20**	1121
rest of the **s** of Kohath were ten.	**Jos 21:26**	1121
To the **s** of Gershon, one of	**Jos 21:27**	1121
the families of the **s** of Merari,	**Jos 21:34**	1121
these were the cities of the **s** of Merari	**Jos 21:40**	1121
of the possession of the **s** of Israel	**Jos 21:41**	1121
The **s** of Reuben and the sons	**Jos 22:9**	1121
sons of Reuben and the **s** of Gad	**Jos 22:9**	1121
departed from the **s** of Israel at Shiloh	**Jos 22:9**	1121
the **s** of Reuben and the sons of	**Jos 22:10**	1121
sons of Reuben and the **s** of Gad	**Jos 22:10**	1121
And the **s** of Israel heard *it* said,	**Jos 22:11**	1121
the **s** of Reuben and the sons of	**Jos 22:11**	1121
sons of Reuben and the **s** of Gad	**Jos 22:11**	1121
belonging to the **s** of Israel."	**Jos 22:11**	1121
When the **s** of Israel heard *of it*,	**Jos 22:12**	1121
whole congregation of the **s** of Israel	**Jos 22:12**	1121
Then the **s** of Israel sent to the	**Jos 22:13**	1121
sons of Israel sent to the **s** of Reuben	**Jos 22:13**	1121
sons of Reuben and to the **s** of Gad	**Jos 22:13**	1121
They came to the **s** of Reuben	**Jos 22:15**	1121
sons of Reuben and to the **s** of Gad	**Jos 22:15**	1121
Then the **s** of Reuben and the sons	**Jos 22:21**	1121
sons of Reuben and the **s** of Gad	**Jos 22:21**	1121
come your **s** may say to our sons,	**Jos 22:24**	1121
come your sons may say to our **s**,	**Jos 22:24**	1121
you **s** of Reuben and sons of Gad;	**Jos 22:25**	1121
you sons of Reuben and **s** of Gad;	**Jos 22:25**	1121
So your **s** may make our sons stop	**Jos 22:25**	1121
make our **s** stop fearing the LORD.'	**Jos 22:25**	1121
that your **s** will not say to our	**Jos 22:27**	1121
not say to our **s** in time to come,	**Jos 22:27**	1121
words which the **s** of Reuben and	**Jos 22:30**	1121
the sons of Reuben and the **s** of Gad	**Jos 22:30**	1121
Gad and the **s** of Manasseh spoke,	**Jos 22:30**	1121
the priest said to the **s** of Reuben	**Jos 22:31**	1121
sons of Reuben and to the **s** of Gad	**Jos 22:31**	1121
of Gad and to the **s** of Manasseh,	**Jos 22:31**	1121
you have delivered the **s** of Israel	**Jos 22:31**	1121
leaders returned from the **s** of Reuben	**Jos 22:32**	1121
of Reuben and from the **s** of Gad,	**Jos 22:32**	1121
of Canaan, to the **s** of Israel,	**Jos 22:32**	1121
The word pleased the **s** of Israel,	**Jos 22:33**	1121
and the **s** of Israel blessed God;	**Jos 22:33**	1121
the land in which the **s** of Reuben	**Jos 22:33**	1121
and the **s** of Gad were living.	**Jos 22:33**	1121
The **s** of Reuben and the sons	**Jos 22:34**	1121
sons of Reuben and the **s** of Gad	**Jos 22:34**	1121
and his **s** went down to Egypt.	**Jos 24:4**	1121
which the **s** of Israel brought up	**Jos 24:32**	1121
had bought from the **s** of Hamor	**Jos 24:32**	1121
the inheritance of Joseph's **s**.	**Jos 24:32**	1121
the **s** of Israel inquired of the LORD,	**Jg 1:1**	1121
Then the **s** of Judah fought against	**Jg 1:8**	1121
Afterward the **s** of Judah went	**Jg 1:9**	1121
city of palms with the **s** of Judah,	**Jg 1:16**	1121
from there the three **s** of Anak.	**Jg 1:20**	1121
But the **s** of Benjamin did not	**Jg 1:21**	1121
have lived with the **s** of Benjamin in	**Jg 1:21**	1121
the Amorites forced the **s** of Dan	**Jg 1:34**	1121
words to all the **s** of Israel,	**Jg 2:4**	1121
the **s** of Israel went each to his	**Jg 2:6**	1121
Then the **s** of Israel did evil in	**Jg 2:11**	1121
s of Israel might be taught war,	**Jg 3:2**	1121
The **s** of Israel lived among	**Jg 3:5**	1121
their own daughters to their **s**,	**Jg 3:6**	1121
The **s** of Israel did what was	**Jg 3:7**	1121
and the **s** of Israel served	**Jg 3:8**	1121
the **s** of Israel cried to the LORD,	**Jg 3:9**	1121
the **s** of Israel to deliver them,	**Jg 3:9**	1121
Now the **s** of Israel again did evil	**Jg 3:12**	1121
himself the **s** of Ammon and Amalek;	**Jg 3:13**	1121
The **s** of Israel served Eglon	**Jg 3:14**	1121
the **s** of Israel cried to the LORD,	**Jg 3:15**	1121
And the **s** of Israel sent tribute	**Jg 3:15**	1121
and the **s** of Israel went down with	**Jg 3:27**	1121
Then the **s** of Israel again did	**Jg 4:1**	1121
The **s** of Israel cried to the LORD;	**Jg 4:3**	1121
and he oppressed the **s** of Israel	**Jg 4:3**	1121
and the **s** of Israel came up to her	**Jg 4:5**	1121
thousand men from the **s** of Naphtali	**Jg 4:6**	1121
and from the **s** of Zebulun.	**Jg 4:6**	1121
from the **s** of Hobab the	**Jg 4:11**	1121
of Canaan before the **s** of Israel.	**Jg 4:23**	1121
The hand of the **s** of Israel	**Jg 4:24**	1121
Then the **s** of Israel did what was	**Jg 6:1**	1121
Because of Midian the **s** of Israel	**Jg 6:2**	1121
the Amalekites and the **s** of the east	**Jg 6:3**	1121
the **s** of Israel cried to the LORD.	**Jg 6:6**	1121
the **s** of Israel cried to the LORD	**Jg 6:7**	1121
sent a prophet to the **s** of Israel,	**Jg 6:8**	1121
the **s** of the east assembled themselves	**Jg 6:33**	1121
all the **s** of the east were lying in the	**Jg 7:12**	1121
entire army of the **s** of the east;	**Jg 8:10**	1121
my brothers, the **s** of my mother.	**Jg 8:19**	1121
subdued before the **s** of Israel,	**Jg 8:28**	1121
Now Gideon had seventy **s** who were	**Jg 8:30**	1121
that the **s** of Israel again played	**Jg 8:33**	1121
Thus the **s** of Israel did not	**Jg 8:34**	1121
men, all the **s** of Jerubbaal,	**Jg 9:2**	1121
his brothers the **s** of Jerubbaal,	**Jg 9:5**	1121
house today and have killed his **s**,	**Jg 9:18**	1121
seventy **s** of Jerubbaal might come,	**Jg 9:24**	1121
thirty **s** who rode on thirty donkeys,	**Jg 10:4**	1121
Then the **s** of Israel again did	**Jg 10:6**	1121
Moab, the gods of the **s** of Ammon,	**Jg 10:6**	1121
into the hands of the **s** of Ammon.	**Jg 10:7**	1121
crushed the **s** of Israel that year;	**Jg 10:8**	1121
years they *afflicted* all the **s** of Israel	**Jg 10:8**	1121
The **s** of Ammon crossed the	**Jg 10:9**	1121
Then the **s** of Israel cried out to	**Jg 10:10**	1121
The LORD said to the **s** of Israel,	**Jg 10:11**	1121
the Amorites, the **s** of Ammon,	**Jg 10:11**	1121
The **s** of Israel said to the LORD,	**Jg 10:15**	1121
Then the **s** of Ammon were summoned	**Jg 10:17**	1121
the **s** of Israel gathered together and	**Jg 10:17**	1121
to fight against the **s** of Ammon?	**Jg 10:18**	1121
Gilead's wife bore him **s**;	**Jg 11:2**	1121
and when his wife's **s** grew up,	**Jg 11:2**	1121
the **s** of Ammon fought against Israel.	**Jg 11:4**	1121
s of Ammon fought against Israel	**Jg 11:5**	1121
fight against the **s** of Ammon."	**Jg 11:6**	1121
and fight with the **s** of Ammon and	**Jg 11:8**	1121
to fight against the **s** of Ammon and	**Jg 11:9**	1121
to the king of the **s** of Ammon,	**Jg 11:12**	1121
The king of the **s** of Ammon	**Jg 11:13**	1121
to the king of the **s** of Ammon,	**Jg 11:14**	1121
nor the land of the **s** of Ammon.	**Jg 11:15**	1121
judge today between the **s** of Israel	**Jg 11:27**	1121
of Israel and the **s** of Ammon.' "	**Jg 11:27**	1121
But the king of the **s** of Ammon	**Jg 11:28**	1121
he went on to the **s** of Ammon.	**Jg 11:29**	1121
give the **s** of Ammon into my hand,	**Jg 11:30**	1121
in peace from the **s** of Ammon,	**Jg 11:31**	1121
crossed over to the **s** of Ammon to	**Jg 11:32**	1121
So the **s** of Ammon were subdued	**Jg 11:33**	1121
subdued before the **s** of Israel.	**Jg 11:33**	1121
of your enemies, the **s** of Ammon."	**Jg 11:36**	1121
over to fight against the **s** of Ammon	**Jg 12:1**	1121
great strife with the **s** of Ammon;	**Jg 12:2**	1121
over against the **s** of Ammon,	**Jg 12:3**	1121
He had thirty **s**,	**Jg 12:9**	1121
daughters from outside for his **s**.	**Jg 12:9**	1121
He had forty **s** and thirty	**Jg 12:14**	1121
Now the **s** of Israel again did evil	**Jg 13:1**	1121
a riddle to the **s** of my people,	**Jg 14:16**	1121
the riddle to the **s** of her people.	**Jg 14:17**	1121
and consecrated one of his **s**,	**Jg 17:5**	1121
became to him like one of his **s**.	**Jg 17:11**	1121
So the **s** of Dan sent from their	**Jg 18:2**	1121
of war, who were of the **s** of Dan,	**Jg 18:16**	1121
and overtook the **s** of Dan.	**Jg 18:22**	1121
They cried to the **s** of Dan,	**Jg 18:23**	1121
The **s** of Dan said to him,	**Jg 18:25**	1121
So the **s** of Dan went on their way;	**Jg 18:26**	1121
The **s** of Dan set up for	**Jg 18:30**	1121
he and his **s** were priests to the	**Jg 18:30**	1121
who are not of the **s** of Israel;	**Jg 19:12**	1121
from the day when the **s** of Israel	**Jg 19:30**	1121
Then all the **s** of Israel from Dan	**Jg 20:1**	1121
(Now the **s** of Benjamin heard that	**Jg 20:3**	1121
the **s** of Israel had gone up to Mizpah	**Jg 20:3**	1121
And the **s** of Israel said,	**Jg 20:3**	1121
"Behold, all you **s** of Israel,	**Jg 20:7**	1121
But the **s** of Benjamin would not	**Jg 20:13**	1121
their brothers, the **s** of Israel.	**Jg 20:13**	1121
The **s** of Benjamin gathered	**Jg 20:14**	1121
to battle against the **s** of Israel.	**Jg 20:14**	1121
the **s** of Benjamin were numbered,	**Jg 20:15**	1121
Now the **s** of Israel arose, went up	**Jg 20:18**	1121
against the **s** of Benjamin?"	**Jg 20:18**	1121
So the **s** of Israel arose in the	**Jg 20:19**	1121
Then the **s** of Benjamin came out of	**Jg 20:21**	1121
The **s** of Israel went up and	**Jg 20:23**	1121
the **s** of my brother Benjamin?"	**Jg 20:23**	1121
Then the **s** of Israel came against	**Jg 20:24**	1121
the **s** of Benjamin the second day.	**Jg 20:24**	1121
18,000 men of the **s** of Israel;	**Jg 20:25**	1121
Then all the **s** of Israel and all	**Jg 20:26**	1121
The **s** of Israel inquired of	**Jg 20:27**	1121
the **s** of my brother Benjamin,	**Jg 20:28**	1121
The **s** of Israel went up	**Jg 20:30**	1121
went up against the **s** of Benjamin on	**Jg 20:30**	1121
The **s** of Benjamin went out	**Jg 20:31**	1121
The **s** of Benjamin said,	**Jg 20:32**	1121
But the **s** of Israel said,	**Jg 20:32**	1121
so that the **s** of Israel destroyed	**Jg 20:35**	1121
So the **s** of Benjamin saw that they	**Jg 20:36**	1121
turned back against the **s** of Benjamin	**Jg 20:48**	1121
Then the **s** of Israel said,	**Jg 21:5**	1121
And the **s** of Israel were sorry for	**Jg 21:6**	1121
spoke to the **s** of Benjamin who were	**Jg 21:13**	1121
For the **s** of Israel had sworn,	**Jg 21:18**	1121
they commanded the **s** of Benjamin,	**Jg 21:20**	1121
The **s** of Benjamin did so, and	**Jg 21:23**	1121
The **s** of Israel departed from	**Jg 21:24**	1121
Moab with his wife and his two **s**.	**Ru 1:1**	1121
names of his two **s** *were* Mahlon and	**Ru 1:2**	1121
and she was left with her two **s**.	**Ru 1:3**	1121
Have I yet **s** in my womb, that they	**Ru 1:11**	1121
a husband tonight and also bear **s**,	**Ru 1:12**	1121
and is better to you than seven **s**,	**Ru 4:15**	1121
And the two **s** of Eli, Hophni and	**1Sa 1:3**	1121
to all her **s** and her daughters;	**1Sa 1:4**	1121
I not better to you than ten **s**?"	**1Sa 1:8**	1121
the **s** of Eli were worthless men;	**1Sa 2:12**	1121
to three **s** and two daughters.	**1Sa 2:21**	1121
his **s** were doing to all Israel,	**1Sa 2:22**	1121
"No, my **s**; for the report is not good	**1Sa 2:24**	1121
fire *offerings* of the **s** of Israel?	**1Sa 2:28**	1121
and honor your **s** above Me,	**1Sa 2:29**	1121
will come concerning your two **s**,	**1Sa 2:34**	1121
because his **s** brought a curse on	**1Sa 3:13**	1121
and the two **s** of Eli, Hophni and	**1Sa 4:4**	1121
and the two **s** of Eli, Hophni and	**1Sa 4:11**	1121
the people, and your two **s** also,	**1Sa 4:17**	1121
So the **s** of Israel removed the	**1Sa 7:4**	1121
judged the **s** of Israel at Mizpah.	**1Sa 7:6**	1121
Philistines heard that the **s** of Israel	**1Sa 7:7**	1121
And when the **s** of Israel heard it,	**1Sa 7:7**	1121
the **s** of Israel said to Samuel,	**1Sa 7:8**	1121
appointed his **s** judges over Israel.	**1Sa 8:1**	1121
His **s**, however, did not walk in	**1Sa 8:3**	1121
your **s** do not walk in your ways.	**1Sa 8:5**	1121
he will take your **s** and place *them*	**1Sa 8:11**	1121
than he among the **s** of Israel;	**1Sa 9:2**	1121
and he said to the **s** of Israel,	**1Sa 10:18**	1121
and the **s** of Israel were 300,000,	**1Sa 11:8**	1121
and behold my **s** are with you.	**1Sa 12:2**	1121
the **s** of Ammon came against you,	**1Sa 12:12**	1121
at that time with the **s** of Israel.	**1Sa 14:18**	1121
against Moab, the **s** of Ammon,	**1Sa 14:47**	1121
Now the **s** of Saul were Jonathan	**1Sa 14:49**	1121
showed kindness to all the **s** of Israel	**1Sa 15:6**	1121
a king for Myself among his **s**."	**1Sa 16:1**	1121
also consecrated Jesse and his **s** and	**1Sa 16:5**	1121
seven of his **s** pass before Samuel.	**1Sa 16:10**	1121
was Jesse, and he had eight **s**.	**1Sa 17:12**	1121
The three older **s** of Jesse had	**1Sa 17:13**	1121
And the names of his three **s** who	**1Sa 17:13**	1121
The **s** of Israel returned from	**1Sa 17:53**	1121
you and your **s** will be with me.	**1Sa 28:19**	1121
and their wives and their **s** and	**1Sa 30:3**	1121
each one because of his **s** and his	**1Sa 30:6**	1121
small or great, **s** or daughters,	**1Sa 30:19**	1121
overtook Saul and his **s**;	**1Sa 31:2**	1121
and Malchi-shua the **s** of Saul.	**1Sa 31:2**	1121
Thus Saul died with his three **s**,	**1Sa 31:6**	1121
and that Saul and his **s** were dead,	**1Sa 31:7**	1121
three **s** fallen on Mount Gilboa.	**1Sa 31:8**	1121
his **s** from the wall of Beth-shan,	**1Sa 31:12**	1121
s of Judah *the song of* the bow;	**2Sa 1:18**	1121
the three **s** of Zeruiah were there,	**2Sa 2:18**	1121
The **s** of Benjamin gathered	**2Sa 2:25**	1121
S were born to David at Hebron:	**2Sa 3:2**	1121
and these men the **s** of Zeruiah are	**2Sa 3:39**	1121
s of Rimmon the Beerothite,	**2Sa 4:2**	1121
Beerothite, of the **s** of Benjamin	**2Sa 4:2**	1121
So the **s** of Rimmon the Beerothite,	**2Sa 4:5**	1121
s of Rimmon the Beerothite,	**2Sa 4:9**	1121
and more **s** and daughters were born	**2Sa 5:13**	1121
Uzzah and Ahio, the **s** of Abinadab,	**2Sa 6:3**	1121
I brought up the **s** of Israel from	**2Sa 7:6**	1121
gone with all the **s** of Israel,	**2Sa 7:7**	1121
and the strokes of the **s** of men,	**2Sa 7:14**	1121
the **s** of Ammon and the Philistines	**2Sa 8:12**	1121
and David's **s** were chief ministers.	**2Sa 8:18**	1121
"You and your **s** and your	**2Sa 9:10**	1121
had fifteen **s** and twenty servants.	**2Sa 9:10**	1121
table as one of the king's **s**.	**2Sa 9:11**	1121
Now when the **s** of Ammon saw that	**2Sa 10:6**	1121
the **s** of Ammon sent and hired the	**2Sa 10:6**	1121
The **s** of Ammon came out and	**2Sa 10:8**	1121
them against the **s** of Ammon.	**2Sa 10:10**	1121
but if the **s** of Ammon are too	**2Sa 10:11**	1121
When the **s** of Ammon saw that the	**2Sa 10:14**	1121
from *fighting* against the **s** of Ammon	**2Sa 10:14**	1121
to help the **s** of Ammon anymore.	**2Sa 10:19**	1121
they destroyed the **s** of Ammon and	**2Sa 11:1**	1121
with the sword of the **s** of Ammon.	**2Sa 12:9**	1121
against Rabbah of the **s** of Ammon and	**2Sa 12:26**	1121
all the cities of the **s** of Ammon.	**2Sa 12:31**	1121
Absalom invited all the king's **s**.	**2Sa 13:23**	1121
and all the king's **s** go with him.	**2Sa 13:27**	1121
Then all the king's **s** arose and	**2Sa 13:29**	1121
has struck down all the king's **s**,	**2Sa 13:30**	1121
all the young men, the king's **s**,	**2Sa 13:32**	1121
'all the king's **s** are dead,' for	**2Sa 13:33**	1121
"Behold, the king's **s** have come;	**2Sa 13:35**	1121
the king's **s** came and lifted their	**2Sa 13:36**	1121
"Your maidservant had two **s**,	**2Sa 14:6**	1121
Absalom there were born three **s**,	**2Sa 14:27**	1121
in peace and your two **s** with you,	**2Sa 15:27**	1121
their two **s** are with them there,	**2Sa 15:36**	1121
I to do with you, O **s** of Zeruiah?	**2Sa 16:10**	1121
from Rabbah of the **s** of Ammon,	**2Sa 17:27**	1121
the lives of your **s** and daughters,	**2Sa 19:5**	1121
and his fifteen **s** and his twenty	**2Sa 19:17**	1121
I to do with you, O **s** of Zeruiah,	**2Sa 19:22**	1121

Gibeonites were not of the **s** of Israel	**2Sa 21:2**	1121
and the **s** of Israel made a covenant	**2Sa 21:2**	1121
for the **s** of Israel and Judah).	**2Sa 21:2**	1121
men from his **s** be given to us,	**2Sa 21:6**	1121
So the king took the two **s** of Rizpah	**2Sa 21:8**	1121
s of Merab the daughter of Saul,	**2Sa 21:8**	1121
killed the two **s** *of* Ariel of Moab.	**2Sa 23:20**	1121
of Gibeah of the **s** of Benjamin,	**2Sa 23:29**	1121
the Shaalbonite, the **s** of Jashen,	**2Sa 23:32**	1121
all his brothers, the king's **s**,	**1Ki 1:9**	1121
and has invited all the **s** of the	**1Ki 1:19**	1121
and has invited all the king's **s**	**1Ki 1:25**	1121
your **s** are careful of their way,	**1Ki 2:4**	1121
the **s** of Barzillai the Gileadite,	**1Ki 2:7**	1121
the **s** of Shisha *were* secretaries;	**1Ki 4:3**	1121
surpassed the wisdom of all the **s** of	**1Ki 4:30**	1121
Calcol and Darda, the **s** of Mahol;	**1Ki 4:31**	1121
after the **s** of Israel came out of the	**1Ki 6:1**	1121
will dwell among the **s** of Israel,	**1Ki 6:13**	1121
households of the **s** of Israel,	**1Ki 8:1**	1121
a covenant with the **s** of Israel,	**1Ki 8:9**	1121
if only your **s** take heed to their	**1Ki 8:25**	1121
the hearts of all the **s** of men,	**1Ki 8:39**	1121
So the king and all the **s** of Israel	**1Ki 8:63**	1121
"But if you or your **s** indeed	**1Ki 9:6**	1121
who were not of the **s** of Israel,	**1Ki 9:20**	1121
whom the **s** of Israel were unable to	**1Ki 9:21**	1121
make slaves of the **s** of Israel;	**1Ki 9:22**	1121
LORD had said to the **s** of Israel,	**1Ki 11:2**	1121
detestable idol of the **s** of Ammon.	**1Ki 11:7**	1121
house among the **s** of Pharaoh.	**1Ki 11:20**	1121
Milcom the god of the **s** of Ammon;	**1Ki 11:33**	1121
But as for the **s** of Israel who	**1Ki 12:17**	1121
your relatives the **s** of Israel;	**1Ki 12:24**	1121
who were not of the **s** of Levi.	**1Ki 12:31**	1121
a feast for the **s** of Israel and	**1Ki 12:33**	1121
and his **s** came and told him all	**1Ki 13:11**	1121
Now his **s** had seen the way which	**1Ki 13:12**	1121
Then he said to his **s**,	**1Ki 13:13**	1121
Then he spoke to his **s**,	**1Ki 13:27**	1121
him, he spoke to his **s**,	**1Ki 13:31**	1121
dispossessed before the **s** of Israel.	**1Ki 14:24**	1121
message among all the **s** of Israel	**1Ki 18:20**	1121
of the tribes of the **s** of Jacob,	**1Ki 18:31**	1121
for the **s** of Israel have forsaken	**1Ki 19:10**	1121
for the **s** of Israel have forsaken	**1Ki 19:14**	1121
people, *even* all the **s** of Israel,	**1Ki 20:15**	1121
The **s** of Israel were mustered	**1Ki 20:27**	1121
and the **s** of Israel camped before	**1Ki 20:27**	1121
and the **s** of Israel killed *of* the	**1Ki 20:29**	1121
certain man of the **s** of the prophets	**1Ki 20:35**	1121
LORD cast out before the **s** of Israel.	**1Ki 21:26**	1121
Then the **s** of the prophets who	**2Ki 2:3**	1121
The **s** of the prophets who *were*	**2Ki 2:5**	1121
fifty men of the **s** of the prophets	**2Ki 2:7**	1121
Now when the **s** of the prophets who	**2Ki 2:15**	1121
of the wives of the **s** of the prophets	**2Ki 4:1**	1121
the door behind you and your **s**,	**2Ki 4:4**	1121
the door behind her and her **s**;	**2Ki 4:5**	1121
and your **s** can live on the rest."	**2Ki 4:7**	1121
As the **s** of the prophets were	**2Ki 4:38**	1121
stew for the **s** of the prophets."	**2Ki 4:38**	1121
young men of the **s** of the prophets	**2Ki 5:22**	1121
Now the **s** of the prophets said to	**2Ki 6:1**	1121
you will do to the **s** of Israel:	**2Ki 8:12**	1121
lamp to him through his **s** always.	**2Ki 8:19**	1121
one of the **s** of the prophets and	**2Ki 9:1**	1121
of Naboth and the blood of his **s**,'	**2Ki 9:26**	1121
Now Ahab had seventy **s** in Samaria.	**2Ki 10:1**	1121
since your master's **s** are with you,	**2Ki 10:2**	1121
and fittest of your master's **s**,	**2Ki 10:3**	1121
heads of the men, your master's **s**,	**2Ki 10:6**	1121
Now the king's **s**, seventy persons,	**2Ki 10:6**	1121
them, they took the king's **s**	**2Ki 10:7**	1121
the heads of the king's **s**,"	**2Ki 10:8**	1121
come down to greet the **s** of the king	**2Ki 10:13**	1121
and the **s** of the queen mother."	**2Ki 10:13**	1121
your **s** of the fourth generation	**2Ki 10:30**	1121
s who were being put to death,	**2Ki 11:2**	1121
and the **s** of Israel lived in their	**2Ki 13:5**	1121
But the **s** of the slayers he did	**2Ki 14:6**	1121
not be put to death for the **s**,	**2Ki 14:6**	1121
nor the **s** be put to death for the	**2Ki 14:6**	1121
"Your **s** to the fourth generation	**2Ki 15:12**	1121
out from before the **s** of Israel.	**2Ki 16:3**	1121
because the **s** of Israel had sinned	**2Ki 17:7**	1121
driven out before the **s** of Israel,	**2Ki 17:8**	1121
The **s** of Israel did things	**2Ki 17:9**	1121
Then they made their **s** and their	**2Ki 17:17**	1121
The **s** of Israel walked in all	**2Ki 17:22**	1121
in place of the **s** of Israel.	**2Ki 17:24**	1121
the LORD commanded the **s** of Jacob,	**2Ki 17:34**	1121
the **s** of Israel burned incense to it;	**2Ki 18:4**	1121
s of Eden who *were* in Telassar?	**2Ki 19:12**	1121
your **s** who shall issue from you,	**2Ki 20:18**	1121
before the **s** of Israel.	**2Ki 21:2**	1121
destroyed before the **s** of Israel.	**2Ki 21:9**	1121
the abomination of the **s** of Ammon,	**2Ki 23:13**	1121
the **s** of Zedekiah before his eyes,	**2Ki 25:7**	1121
The **s** of Japheth *were* Gomer,	**1Ch 1:5**	1121
The **s** of Gomer *were* Ashkenaz,	**1Ch 1:6**	1121
The **s** of Javan *were* Elishah,	**1Ch 1:7**	1121
The **s** of Ham *were* Cush, Mizraim,	**1Ch 1:8**	1121
The **s** of Cush *were* Seba,	**1Ch 1:9**	1121
and the **s** of Raamah *were* Sheba and	**1Ch 1:9**	1121
The **s** of Shem *were* Elam, Asshur,	**1Ch 1:17**	1121
Two **s** were born to Eber, the	**1Ch 1:19**	1121
all these *were* the **s** of Joktan.	**1Ch 1:23**	1121
The **s** of Abraham *were* Isaac and	**1Ch 1:28**	1121
these *were* the **s** of Ishmael.	**1Ch 1:31**	1121
The **s** of Keturah, Abraham's	**1Ch 1:32**	1121
And the **s** of Jokshan *were* Sheba	**1Ch 1:32**	1121
The **s** of Midian were Ephah,	**1Ch 1:33**	1121
All these were the **s** of Keturah.	**1Ch 1:33**	1121
s of Isaac *were* Esau and Israel.	**1Ch 1:34**	1121
The **s** of Esau *were* Eliphaz, Reuel,	**1Ch 1:35**	1121
The **s** of Eliphaz *were* Teman, Omar,	**1Ch 1:36**	1121
The **s** of Reuel *were* Nahath, Zerah,	**1Ch 1:37**	1121
The **s** of Seir *were* Lotan,	**1Ch 1:38**	1121
s of Lotan *were* Hori and Homam;	**1Ch 1:39**	1121
The **s** of Shobal *were* Alian,	**1Ch 1:40**	1121
s of Zibeon *were* Aiah and Anah.	**1Ch 1:40**	1121
And the **s** of Dishon *were* Hamran,	**1Ch 1:41**	1121
The **s** of Ezer *were* Bilhan, Zaavan	**1Ch 1:42**	1121
The **s** of Dishan *were* Uz and Aran.	**1Ch 1:42**	1121
king of the **s** of Israel reigned.	**1Ch 1:43**	1121
These are the **s** of Israel:	**1Ch 2:1**	1121
The **s** of Judah *were* Er, Onan and	**1Ch 2:3**	1121
Judah had five **s** in all.	**1Ch 2:4**	1121
The **s** of Perez *were* Hezron and	**1Ch 2:5**	1121
The **s** of Zerah *were* Zimri,	**1Ch 2:6**	1121
Now the **s** of Hezron, who were born	**1Ch 2:9**	1121
Nahshon, leader of the **s** of Judah;	**1Ch 2:10**	1121
three **s** of Zeruiah *were* Abshai,	**1Ch 2:16**	1121
Hezron had **s** by Azubah *his* wife,	**1Ch 2:18**	3205
and these were her **s**:	**1Ch 2:18**	1121
All these were the **s** of Machir,	**1Ch 2:23**	1121
Now the **s** of Jerahmeel the	**1Ch 2:25**	1121
The **s** of Ram, the firstborn	**1Ch 2:27**	1121
s of Onam were Shammai and Jada.	**1Ch 2:28**	1121
And the **s** of Shammai *were* Nadab	**1Ch 2:28**	1121
The **s** of Nadab *were* Seled and	**1Ch 2:30**	1121
Appaim, and Seled died without **s**.	**1Ch 2:30**	1121
The **s** of Jada the brother of	**1Ch 2:32**	1121
and Jether died without **s**.	**1Ch 2:32**	1121
The **s** of Jonathan *were* Peleth	**1Ch 2:33**	1121
These were the **s** of Jerahmeel.	**1Ch 2:33**	1121
Now Sheshan had no **s**,	**1Ch 2:34**	1121
Now the **s** of Caleb, the brother of	**1Ch 2:42**	1121
The **s** of Hebron *were* Korah and	**1Ch 2:43**	1121
The **s** of Jahdai *were* Regem,	**1Ch 2:47**	1121
These were the **s** of Caleb.	**1Ch 2:50**	1121
The **s** of Hur, the firstborn of	**1Ch 2:50**	1121
the father of Kiriath-jearim had **s**:	**1Ch 2:52**	1121
The **s** of Salma *were* Bethlehem and	**1Ch 2:54**	1121
Now these were the **s** of David who	**1Ch 3:1**	1121
All *these were* the **s** of David,	**1Ch 3:9**	1121
besides the **s** of the concubines;	**1Ch 3:9**	1121
The **s** of Josiah *were* Johanan	**1Ch 3:15**	1121
The **s** of Jehoiakim *were*	**1Ch 3:16**	1121
The **s** of Jeconiah, the	**1Ch 3:17**	1121
The **s** of Pedaiah *were* Zerubbabel	**1Ch 3:19**	1121
And the **s** of Zerubbabel *were*	**1Ch 3:19**	1121
The **s** of Hananiah *were*	**1Ch 3:21**	1121
and Jeshaiah, the **s** of Rephaiah,	**1Ch 3:21**	1121
sons of Rephaiah, the **s** of Arnan,	**1Ch 3:21**	1121
sons of Arnan, the **s** of Obadiah,	**1Ch 3:21**	1121
of Obadiah, the **s** of Shecaniah.	**1Ch 3:21**	1121
the **s** of Shemaiah: Hattush,	**1Ch 3:22**	1121
The **s** of Neariah *were* Elioenai,	**1Ch 3:23**	1121
The **s** of Elioenai *were* Hodaviah,	**1Ch 3:24**	1121
The **s** of Judah *were* Perez, Hezron,	**1Ch 4:1**	1121
These *were* the **s** of Etam:	**1Ch 4:3**	1
These *were* the **s** of Hur, the	**1Ch 4:4**	1121
These were the **s** of Naarah.	**1Ch 4:6**	1121
The **s** of Helah *were* Zereth,	**1Ch 4:7**	1121
Now the **s** of Kenaz *were* Othniel	**1Ch 4:13**	1121
And the **s** of Othniel *were* Hathath	**1Ch 4:13**	1121
The **s** of Caleb the son of	**1Ch 4:15**	1121
The **s** of Jehallelel *were* Ziph	**1Ch 4:16**	1121
The **s** of Ezrah *were* Jether,	**1Ch 4:17**	1121
(And these are the **s** of Bithia the	**1Ch 4:17**	1121
The **s** of the wife of Hodiah,	**1Ch 4:19**	1121
The **s** of Shimon *were* Amnon and	**1Ch 4:20**	1121
And the **s** of Ishi *were* Zoheth and	**1Ch 4:20**	1121
The **s** of Shelah the son of Judah	**1Ch 4:21**	1121
The **s** of Simeon *were* Nemuel and	**1Ch 4:24**	1121
The **s** of Mishma *were* Hammuel	**1Ch 4:26**	1121
had sixteen **s** and six daughters;	**1Ch 4:27**	1121
his brothers did not have many **s**,	**1Ch 4:27**	1121
multiply like the **s** of Judah.	**1Ch 4:27**	1121
From them, from the **s** of Simeon,	**1Ch 4:42**	1121
and Uzziel, the **s** of Ishi,	**1Ch 4:42**	1121
Now the **s** of Reuben the firstborn	**1Ch 5:1**	1121
the **s** of Joseph the son of Israel;	**1Ch 5:1**	1121
the **s** of Reuben the firstborn of	**1Ch 5:3**	1121
s of Joel *were* Shemaiah his son,	**1Ch 5:4**	1121
Now the **s** of Gad lived opposite	**1Ch 5:11**	1121
These *were* the **s** of Abihail, the	**1Ch 5:14**	1121
The **s** of Reuben and the Gadites	**1Ch 5:18**	1121
s of the half-tribe of Manasseh lived	**1Ch 5:23**	1121
The **s** of Levi *were* Gershon, Kohath	**1Ch 6:1**	1121
The **s** of Kohath *were* Amram,	**1Ch 6:2**	1121
And the **s** of Aaron *were* Nadab,	**1Ch 6:3**	1121
The **s** of Levi *were* Gershom,	**1Ch 6:16**	1121
are the names of the **s** of Gershom:	**1Ch 6:17**	1121
The **s** of Kohath *were* Amram,	**1Ch 6:18**	1121
The **s** of Merari *were* Mahli and	**1Ch 6:19**	1121
The **s** of Kohath *were* Amminadab his	**1Ch 6:22**	1121
The **s** of Elkanah *were* Amasai	**1Ch 6:25**	1121
the **s** of Elkanah *were* Zophai his	**1Ch 6:26**	1121
The **s** of Samuel *were* Joel the	**1Ch 6:28**	1121
The **s** of Merari *were* Mahli, Libni	**1Ch 6:29**	1121
are those who served with their **s**:	**1Ch 6:33**	1121
From the **s** of the Kohathites *were*	**1Ch 6:33**	1121
their kinsmen the **s** of Merari:	**1Ch 6:44**	1121
But Aaron and his **s** offered on the	**1Ch 6:49**	1121
These are the **s** of Aaron:	**1Ch 6:50**	1121
To the **s** of Aaron of the families	**1Ch 6:54**	1121
To the **s** of Aaron they gave	**1Ch 6:57**	1121
the **s** of Kohath *were given* by lot,	**1Ch 6:61**	1121
To the **s** of Gershom, according	**1Ch 6:62**	1121
the **s** of Merari *were given* by lot,	**1Ch 6:63**	1121
So the **s** of Israel gave to the	**1Ch 6:64**	1121
from the tribe of the **s** of Judah,	**1Ch 6:65**	1121
the tribe of the **s** of Simeon	**1Ch 6:65**	1121
the tribe of the **s** of Benjamin,	**1Ch 6:65**	1121
the families of the **s** of Kohath had	**1Ch 6:66**	1121
rest of the family of the **s** of Kohath.	**1Ch 6:70**	1121
To the **s** of Gershom *were given*,	**1Ch 6:71**	1121
of *the Levites*, the **s** of Merari,	**1Ch 6:77**	1121
Now the **s** of Issachar *were* four:	**1Ch 7:1**	1121
The **s** of Tola *were* Uzzi,	**1Ch 7:2**	1121
The **s** of Tola *were* mighty men	**1Ch 7:2**	
the **s** of Izrahiah *were* Michael,	**1Ch 7:3**	1121
for they had many wives and **s**.	**1Ch 7:4**	1121
The **s** *of* Benjamin *were* three:	**1Ch 7:6**	
The **s** of Bela were five:	**1Ch 7:7**	1121
The **s** of Becher *were* Zemirah,	**1Ch 7:8**	1121
All these *were* the **s** of Becher.	**1Ch 7:8**	1121
And the **s** of Bilhan *were* Jeush,	**1Ch 7:10**	1121
All these *were* **s** of Jediael,	**1Ch 7:11**	1121
and Huppim *were* the **s** of Ir;	**1Ch 7:12**	1121
The **s** of Naphtali *were* Jahziel,	**1Ch 7:13**	1121
and Shallum, the **s** of Bilhah.	**1Ch 7:13**	1121
The **s** of Manasseh *were* Asriel,	**1Ch 7:14**	1121
and his **s** *were* Ulam and Rakem.	**1Ch 7:16**	1121
the **s** of Gilead the son of Machir,	**1Ch 7:17**	1121
The **s** of Shemida were Ahian	**1Ch 7:19**	1121
The **s** of Ephraim *were*	**1Ch 7:20**	1121
the borders of the **s** of Manasseh,	**1Ch 7:29**	1121
the **s** of Joseph the son of Israel.	**1Ch 7:29**	1121
The **s** of Asher *were* Imnah, Ishvah,	**1Ch 7:30**	1121
The **s** of Beriah *were* Heber and	**1Ch 7:31**	1121
The **s** of Japhlet *were* Pasach,	**1Ch 7:33**	1121
These were the **s** of Japhlet.	**1Ch 7:33**	1121
s of Shemer *were* Ahi and Rohgah,	**1Ch 7:34**	1121
The **s** of his brother Helem	**1Ch 7:35**	1121
The **s** of Zophah *were* Suah,	**1Ch 7:36**	1121
The **s** of Jether *were* Jephunneh,	**1Ch 7:38**	1121
The **s** of Ulla *were* Arah,	**1Ch 7:39**	1121
All these *were* the **s** of Asher,	**1Ch 7:40**	1121
Bela had **s**: Addar, Gera,	**1Ch 8:3**	1121
These are the **s** of Ehud:	**1Ch 8:6**	1121
These were his **s**, heads of	**1Ch 8:10**	1121
The **s** of Elpaal *were* Eber,	**1Ch 8:12**	1121
and Joha *were* the **s** of Beriah.	**1Ch 8:16**	1121
and Jobab *were* the **s** of Elpaal.	**1Ch 8:18**	1121
and Shimrath *were* the **s** of Shimei.	**1Ch 8:21**	1121
and Penuel *were* the **s** of Shashak.	**1Ch 8:25**	1121
and Zichri *were* the **s** of Jeroham.	**1Ch 8:27**	1121
The **s** of Micah *were* Pithon,	**1Ch 8:35**	1121
Azel had six **s**,	**1Ch 8:38**	1121
All these *were* the **s** of Azel.	**1Ch 8:38**	1121
The **s** of Eshek his brother	**1Ch 8:39**	1121
The **s** of Ulam were mighty men	**1Ch 8:40**	1121
and had many **s** and grandsons,	**1Ch 8:40**	1121
these *were* of the **s** of Benjamin.	**1Ch 8:40**	1121
Some of the **s** of Judah, of the	**1Ch 9:3**	1121
of Judah, of the **s** of Benjamin and	**1Ch 9:3**	1121
and of the **s** of Ephraim and	**1Ch 9:3**	1121
the **s** of Perez the son of Judah.	**1Ch 9:4**	1121
Asaiah the firstborn and his **s**.	**1Ch 9:5**	1121
From the **s** of Zerah *were* Jeuel	**1Ch 9:6**	1121
From the **s** of Benjamin *were*	**1Ch 9:7**	1121
of Hashabiah, of the **s** of Merari;	**1Ch 9:14**	1121
for the camp of the **s** of Levi.	**1Ch 9:18**	1121
So they and their **s** had charge of	**1Ch 9:23**	1121
Some of the **s** of the priests	**1Ch 9:30**	1121
relatives of the **s** of the Kohathites	**1Ch 9:32**	1121
The **s** of Micah *were* Pithon,	**1Ch 9:41**	1121
had six **s** whose names are these:	**1Ch 9:44**	1121
These were the **s** of Azel.	**1Ch 9:44**	1121
closely pursued Saul and his **s**,	**1Ch 10:2**	1121
and Malchi-shua, the **s** of Saul.	**1Ch 10:2**	1121
Thus Saul died with his three **s**,	**1Ch 10:6**	1121
and that Saul and his **s** were dead,	**1Ch 10:7**	1121
and his **s** fallen on Mount Gilboa.	**1Ch 10:8**	1121
of Saul and the bodies of his **s** and	**1Ch 10:12**	1121
struck down the two **s** *of* Ariel of	**1Ch 11:22**	
of Gibeah of the **s** of Benjamin,	**1Ch 11:31**	1121
the **s** of Hashem the Gizonite,	**1Ch 11:34**	1121
the **s** of Hotham the Aroerite,	**1Ch 11:44**	1121
and Joshaviah, the **s** of Elnaam,	**1Ch 11:46**	1121
the **s** of Shemaah the Gibeathite;	**1Ch 12:3**	1121
and Pelet, the **s** of Azmaveth,	**1Ch 12:3**	1121
the **s** of Jeroham of Gedor.	**1Ch 12:7**	1121
These of the **s** of Gad were	**1Ch 12:14**	1121
Then some of the **s** of Benjamin and	**1Ch 12:16**	1121
the **s** of Judah who bore shield and	**1Ch 12:24**	1121
Of the **s** of Simeon, mighty men of	**1Ch 12:25**	1121
Of the **s** of Levi 4,600.	**1Ch 12:26**	1121
Of the **s** of Benjamin, Saul's	**1Ch 12:29**	1121
Of the **s** of Ephraim 20,800,	**1Ch 12:30**	1121
Of the **s** of Issachar, men who	**1Ch 12:32**	1121
father of more **s** and daughters.	**1Ch 14:3**	1121
gathered together the **s** of Aaron and	**1Ch 15:4**	1121
of the **s** of Kohath, Uriel the	**1Ch 15:5**	1121
of the **s** of Merari, Asaiah the	**1Ch 15:6**	1121
of the **s** of Gershom, Joel the	**1Ch 15:7**	1121
of the **s** of Elizaphan, Shemaiah	**1Ch 15:8**	1121
of the **s** of Hebron, Eliel the	**1Ch 15:9**	1121
of the **s** of Uzziel, Amminadab the	**1Ch 15:10**	1121
The **s** of the Levites carried	**1Ch 15:15**	1121
the **s** of Merari their relatives,	**1Ch 15:17**	1121
of Israel His servant, **S** of Jacob,	**1Ch 16:13**	1121
the **s** of Jeduthun for the gate.	**1Ch 16:42**	1121

after you, who will be of your **s**; **1Ch 17:11** 1121
from Edom, Moab, the **s** of Ammon, **1Ch 18:11** 1121
and the **s** of David *were* chiefs at **1Ch 18:17** 1121
the king of the **s** of Ammon died, **1Ch 19:1** 1121
land of the **s** of Ammon to Hanun to **1Ch 19:2** 1121
princes of the **s** of Ammon said **1Ch 19:3** 1121
When the **s** of Ammon saw that they **1Ch 19:6** 1121
Hanun and the **s** of Ammon sent **1Ch 19:6** 1121
And the **s** of Ammon gathered **1Ch 19:7** 1121
The **s** of Ammon came out and **1Ch 19:9** 1121
themselves against the **s** of Ammon. **1Ch 19:11** 1121
but if the **s** of Ammon are too **1Ch 19:12** 1121
When the **s** of Ammon saw that the **1Ch 19:15** 1121
to help the **s** of Ammon anymore. **1Ch 19:19** 1121
the land of the **s** of Ammon, **1Ch 20:1** 1121
all the cities of the **s** of Ammon. **1Ch 20:3** 1121
and his four **s** *who were* with him **1Ch 21:20** 1121
according to the **s** of Levi: **1Ch 23:6** 1121
The **s** of Ladan *were* Jehiel the **1Ch 23:8** 1121
The **s** of Shimei *were* Shelomoth and **1Ch 23:9** 1121
The **s** of Shimei *were* Jahath, **1Ch 23:10** 1121
These four *were* the **s** of Shimei. **1Ch 23:10** 1121
and Beriah did not have many **s**, **1Ch 23:11** 1121
The **s** of Kohath were four: **1Ch 23:12** 1121
s of Amram were Aaron and Moses. **1Ch 23:13** 1121
most holy, he and his **s** forever, **1Ch 23:13** 1121
his **s** were named among the tribe **1Ch 23:14** 1121
The **s** of Moses *were* Gershom and **1Ch 23:15** 1121
and Eliezer had no other **s**, **1Ch 23:17** 1121
the **s** of Rehabiah were very many. **1Ch 23:17** 1121
The **s** of Hebron *were* Jeriah the **1Ch 23:19** 1121
The **s** of Uzziel *were* Micah the **1Ch 23:20** 1121
The **s** of Merari were Mahli and **1Ch 23:21** 1121
The **s** of Mahli *were* Eleazar and **1Ch 23:21** 1121
Eleazar died and had no **s**, **1Ch 23:22** 1121
so their brothers, the **s** of Kish, **1Ch 23:22** 1121
The **s** of Mushi *were* three: **1Ch 23:23** 1121
These were the **s** of Levi according **1Ch 23:24** 1121
David the **s** of Levi *were* numbered **1Ch 23:27** 1121
their office is to assist the **s** of Aaron **1Ch 23:28** 1121
of the **s** of Aaron their relatives, **1Ch 23:32** 1121
the **s** of Aaron *were* Nadab, Abihu, **1Ch 24:1** 1121
before their father and had no **s**. **1Ch 24:2** 1121
with Zadok of the **s** of Eleazar and **1Ch 24:3** 1121
and Ahimelech of the **s** of Ithamar, **1Ch 24:3** 1121
Now for the rest of the **s** of Levi: **1Ch 24:20** 1121
of the **s** of Amram, Shubael; **1Ch 24:20** 1121
of the **s** of Shubael, Jehdeiah. **1Ch 24:20** 1121
of the **s** of Rehabiah, Isshiah the **1Ch 24:21** 1121
of the **s** of Shelomoth, Jahath. **1Ch 24:22** 1121
The **s** *of Hebron:* **1Ch 24:23** 1121
Of the **s** of Uzziel, Micah; **1Ch 24:24** 1121
of the **s** of Micah, Shamir. **1Ch 24:24** 1121
of the **s** of Isshiah, Zechariah. **1Ch 24:25** 1121
The **s** of Merari, Mahli and Mushi; **1Ch 24:26** 1121
the **s** of Jaaziah, Beno. **1Ch 24:26** 1121
s of Merari: by Jaaziah *were* Beno, **1Ch 24:27** 1121
Eleazar, who had no **s**. **1Ch 24:28** 1121
the **s** of Kish, Jerahmeel. **1Ch 24:29** 1121
The **s** of Mushi: **1Ch 24:30** 1121
These *were* the **s** of the Levites **1Ch 24:30** 1121
just as their relatives the **s** of **1Ch 24:31** 1121
for the service *some* of the **s** of Asaph **1Ch 25:1** 1121
Of the **s** of Asaph: **1Ch 25:2** 1121
the **s** of Asaph *were* under the **1Ch 25:2** 1121
Of Jeduthun, the **s** of Jeduthun: **1Ch 25:3** 1121
Of Heman, the **s** of Heman: **1Ch 25:4** 1121
All these *were* the **s** of Heman the **1Ch 25:5** 1121
for God gave fourteen **s** and three **1Ch 25:5** 1121
his relatives and **s** *were* twelve; **1Ch 25:9** 1121
Zaccur, his **s** and his relatives, **1Ch 25:10** 1121
to Izri, his **s** and his relatives, **1Ch 25:11** 1121
Nethaniah, his **s** and his relatives, **1Ch 25:12** 1121
Bukkiah, his **s** and his relatives, **1Ch 25:13** 1121
Jesharelah, his **s** and his relatives, **1Ch 25:14** 1121
Jeshaiah, his **s** and his relatives, **1Ch 25:15** 1121
Mattaniah, his **s** and his relatives, **1Ch 25:16** 1121
Shimei, his **s** and his relatives, **1Ch 25:17** 1121
Azarel, his **s** and his relatives, **1Ch 25:18** 1121
Hashabiah, his **s** and his relatives, **1Ch 25:19** 1121
Shubael, his **s** and his relatives, **1Ch 25:20** 1121
Mattithiah, his **s** and his relatives, **1Ch 25:21** 1121
Jeremoth, his **s** and his relatives, **1Ch 25:22** 1121
Hananiah, his **s** and his relatives, **1Ch 25:23** 1121
Joshbekashah, his **s** and his relatives, **1Ch 25:24** 1121
Hanani, his **s** and his relatives, **1Ch 25:25** 1121
Mallothi, his **s** and his relatives, **1Ch 25:26** 1121
Eliathah, his **s** and his relatives, **1Ch 25:27** 1121
Hothir, his **s** and his relatives, **1Ch 25:28** 1121
Giddalti, his **s** and his relatives, **1Ch 25:29** 1121
Mahazioth, his **s** and his relatives, **1Ch 25:30** 1121
Romamti-ezer, his **s** and his relatives **1Ch 25:31** 1121
son of Kore, of the **s** of Asaph. **1Ch 26:1** 1121
Meshelemiah had **s**: **1Ch 26:2** 1121
Obed-edom had **s**: **1Ch 26:4** 1121
Also to his son Shemaiah **s** were **1Ch 26:6** 1121
The **s** of Shemaiah *were* Othni, **1Ch 26:7** 1121
these *were* of the **s** of Obed-edom; **1Ch 26:8** 1121
they and their **s** and their **1Ch 26:8** 1121
Meshelemiah had **s** and relatives, **1Ch 26:9** 1121
one of the **s** of Merari had sons: **1Ch 26:10** 1121
one of the sons of Merari had **s**: **1Ch 26:10** 1121
all the **s** and relatives of Hosah **1Ch 26:11** 1121
and to his **s** went the storehouse. **1Ch 26:15** 1121
of the gatekeepers of the **s** of Korah **1Ch 26:19** 1121
of Korah and of the **s** of Merari. **1Ch 26:19** 1121
The **s** of Ladan, the sons of the **1Ch 26:21** 1121
the **s** of the Gershonites belonging **1Ch 26:21** 1121
The **s** of Jehieli, Zetham and Joel **1Ch 26:22** 1121
Chenaniah and his **s** were *assigned* **1Ch 26:29** 1121
enumeration of the **s** of Israel, **1Ch 27:1** 1121
He was from the **s** of Perez, *and* **1Ch 27:3** 1121
the Pelonite of the **s** of Ephraim; **1Ch 27:10** 1121
Pirathonite of the **s** of Ephraim; **1Ch 27:14** 1121
for the **s** of Ephraim, Hoshea the **1Ch 27:20** 1121
of Hachmoni tutored the king's **s**. **1Ch 27:32** 1121
belonging to the king and his **s**, **1Ch 28:1** 1121
and among the **s** of my father He **1Ch 28:4** 1121
"Of all my **s** **1Ch 28:5** 1121
(for the LORD has given me many **s**), **1Ch 28:5** 1121
it to your **s** after you forever. **1Ch 28:8** 1121
and also all the **s** of King David **1Ch 29:24** 1121
households of the **s** of Israel, **2Ch 5:2** 1121
a covenant with the **s** of Israel, **2Ch 5:10** 1121
Jeduthun, and their **s** and kinsmen, **2Ch 5:12** 1121
He made with the **s** of Israel." **2Ch 6:11** 1121
your **s** take heed to their way, **2Ch 6:16** 1121
know the hearts of the **s** of men, **2Ch 6:30** 1121
All the **s** of Israel, seeing **2Ch 7:3** 1121
and settled the **s** of Israel there. **2Ch 8:2** 1121
the **s** of Israel had not destroyed, **2Ch 8:8** 1121
for his work from the **s** of Israel; **2Ch 8:9** 1121
But as for the **s** of Israel who **2Ch 10:17** 1121
s of Israel stoned him to death. **2Ch 10:18** 1121
for Jeroboam and his **s** had **2Ch 11:14** 1121
and she bore him **s**: **2Ch 11:19** 1121
twenty-eight **s** and sixty daughters. **2Ch 11:21** 1121
distributed some of his **s** through all **2Ch 11:23** 1121
and his **s** by a covenant of salt? **2Ch 13:5** 1121
the LORD through the **s** of David, **2Ch 13:8** 1121
the **s** of Aaron and the Levites, **2Ch 13:9** 1121
and the **s** of Aaron are ministering **2Ch 13:10** 1121
O **s** of Israel, do not fight **2Ch 13:12** 1121
the **s** of Israel fled before Judah, **2Ch 13:16** 1121
Thus the **s** of Israel were subdued **2Ch 13:18** 1121
and the **s** of Judah conquered **2Ch 13:18** 1121
twenty-two **s** and sixteen daughters. **2Ch 13:21** 1121
s of Moab and the sons of Ammon, **2Ch 20:1** 1121
sons of Moab and the **s** of Ammon, **2Ch 20:1** 1121
the **s** of Ammon and Moab and Mount **2Ch 20:10** 1121
the Levite of the **s** of Asaph; **2Ch 20:14** 1121
from the **s** of the Kohathites and **2Ch 20:19** 1121
and of the **s** of the Korahites, **2Ch 20:19** 1121
ambushes against the **s** of Ammon, **2Ch 20:22** 1121
For the **s** of Ammon and Moab rose **2Ch 20:23** 1121
brothers, the **s** of Jehoshaphat: **2Ch 21:2** 1121
these *were* the **s** of Jehoshaphat **2Ch 21:2** 1121
a lamp to him and his **s** forever. **2Ch 21:7** 1121
to strike your people, your **s**, **2Ch 21:14** 1121
together with his **s** and his wives, **2Ch 21:17** 1121
Jehoahaz, the youngest of his **s**. **2Ch 21:17** 1121
the camp had slain all the older **s**. **2Ch 22:1** 1121
the **s** of Ahaziah's brothers ministering **2Ch 22:8** 1121
s who were being put to death, **2Ch 22:11** 1121
spoken concerning the **s** of David. **2Ch 23:3** 1121
and his **s** anointed him and said, **2Ch 23:11** 1121
the father of **s** and daughters. **2Ch 24:3** 1121
For the **s** of the wicked Athaliah **2Ch 24:7** 1121
As to his **s** and the many oracles **2Ch 24:27** 1121
shall not be put to death for **s**, **2Ch 25:4** 1121
nor **s** be put to death for fathers, **2Ch 25:4** 1121
nor with any of the **s** of Ephraim. **2Ch 25:7** 1121
struck down 10,000 of the **s** of Seir. **2Ch 25:11** 1121
The **s** of Judah also captured **2Ch 25:12** 1121
brought the gods of the **s** of Seir, **2Ch 25:14** 1121
the **s** of Aaron who are consecrated **2Ch 26:18** 1121
and burned his **s** in fire, **2Ch 28:3** 1121
driven out before the **s** of Israel. **2Ch 28:3** 1121
The **s** of Israel carried away **2Ch 28:8** 1121
their brethren 200,000 women, **s** and **2Ch 28:8** 1121
the heads of the **s** of Ephraim **2Ch 28:12** 1121
and our **s** and our daughters and **2Ch 29:9** 1121
"My **s**, do not be negligent now, **2Ch 29:11** 1121
from the **s** of the Kohathites; **2Ch 29:12** 1121
and from the **s** of Merari, Kish the **2Ch 29:12** 1121
and from the **s** of Elizaphan, **2Ch 29:13** 1121
and from the **s** of Asaph, Zechariah **2Ch 29:13** 1121
and from the **s** of Heman, Jehiel **2Ch 29:14** 1121
and from the **s** of Jeduthun, **2Ch 29:14** 1121
the priests, the **s** of Aaron, **2Ch 29:21** 1121
"O **s** of Israel, return to the **2Ch 30:6** 1121
your brothers and your **s** *will find* **2Ch 30:9** 1121
The **s** of Israel present in **2Ch 30:21** 1121
Then all the **s** of Israel returned **2Ch 31:1** 1121
the **s** of Israel provided in **2Ch 31:5** 1121
The **s** of Israel and Judah who **2Ch 31:6** 1121
children, their wives, their **s** and **2Ch 31:18** 1121
Also for the **s** of Aaron the **2Ch 31:19** 1121
of the tombs of the **s** of David; **2Ch 32:33** 1121
before the **s** of Israel. **2Ch 33:2** 1121
He made his **s** pass through the **2Ch 33:6** 1121
destroyed before the **s** of Israel. **2Ch 33:9** 1121
the Levites of the **s** of Merari, **2Ch 34:12** 1121
of the **s** of the Kohathites, **2Ch 34:12** 1121
belonging to the **s** of Israel, **2Ch 34:33** 1121
the priests, the **s** of Aaron, **2Ch 35:14** 1121
for the priests, the **s** of Aaron. **2Ch 35:14** 1121
The singers, the **s** of Asaph, **2Ch 35:15** 1121
Thus the **s** of Israel who were **2Ch 35:17** 1121
they were servants to him and to his **s** **2Ch 36:20** 1121
the **s** of Parosh, 2,172; **Ezr 2:3** 1121
the **s** of Shephatiah, 372; **Ezr 2:4** 1121
the **s** of Arah, 775; **Ezr 2:5** 1121
the **s** of Pahath-moab of the sons **Ezr 2:6** 1121
of the **s** of Jeshua *and* Joab, **Ezr 2:6** 1121
the **s** of Elam, 1,254; **Ezr 2:7** 1121
the **s** of Zattu, 945; **Ezr 2:8** 1121
the **s** of Zaccai, 760; **Ezr 2:9** 1121
the **s** of Bani, 642; **Ezr 2:10** 1121
the **s** of Bebai, 623; **Ezr 2:11** 1121
the **s** of Azgad, 1,222; **Ezr 2:12** 1121
the **s** of Adonikam, 666; **Ezr 2:13** 1121
the **s** of Bigvai, 2,056; **Ezr 2:14** 1121
the **s** of Adin, 454; **Ezr 2:15** 1121
the **s** of Ater of Hezekiah, 98; **Ezr 2:16** 1121
the **s** of Bezai, 323; **Ezr 2:17** 1121
the **s** of Jorah, 112; **Ezr 2:18** 1121
the **s** of Hashum, 223; **Ezr 2:19** 1121
the **s** of Gibbar, 95; **Ezr 2:20** 1121
the **s** of Azmaveth, 42; **Ezr 2:24** 1121
the **s** of Kiriath-arim, Chephirah and **Ezr 2:25** 1121
the **s** of Ramah and Geba, 621; **Ezr 2:26** 1121
the **s** of Nebo, 52; **Ezr 2:29** 1121
the **s** of Magbish, 156; **Ezr 2:30** 1121
the **s** of the other Elam, 1,254; **Ezr 2:31** 1121
the **s** of Harim, 320; **Ezr 2:32** 1121
the **s** of Lod, Hadid and Ono, 725; **Ezr 2:33** 1121
the **s** of Senaah, 3,630. **Ezr 2:35** 1121
the **s** of Jedaiah of the house of **Ezr 2:36** 1121
the **s** of Immer, 1,052; **Ezr 2:37** 1121
the **s** of Pashhur, 1,247; **Ezr 2:38** 1121
the **s** of Harim, 1,017. **Ezr 2:39** 1121
the **s** of Jeshua and Kadmiel, of **Ezr 2:40** 1121
and Kadmiel, of the **s** of Hodaviah, **Ezr 2:40** 1121
the **s** of Asaph, 128. **Ezr 2:41** 1121
The **s** of the gatekeepers: **Ezr 2:42** 1121
the **s** of Shallum, the sons of **Ezr 2:42** 1121
sons of Shallum, the **s** of Ater, **Ezr 2:42** 1121
the sons of Ater, the **s** of Talmon, **Ezr 2:42** 1121
sons of Talmon, the **s** of Akkub, **Ezr 2:42** 1121
sons of Akkub, the **s** of Hatita, **Ezr 2:42** 1121
sons of Hatita, the **s** of Shobai, **Ezr 2:42** 1121
the **s** of Ziha, the sons of **Ezr 2:43** 1121
sons of Ziha, the **s** of Hasupha, **Ezr 2:43** 1121
of Hasupha, the **s** of Tabbaoth, **Ezr 2:43** 1121
the **s** of Keros, the sons of Siaha, **Ezr 2:44** 1121
the sons of Keros, the **s** of Siaha, **Ezr 2:44** 1121
the sons of Siaha, the **s** of Padon, **Ezr 2:44** 1121
the **s** of Lebanah, the sons of **Ezr 2:45** 1121
sons of Lebanah, the **s** of Hagabah, **Ezr 2:45** 1121
sons of Hagabah, the **s** of Akkub, **Ezr 2:45** 1121
the **s** of Hagab, the sons of **Ezr 2:46** 1121
sons of Hagab, the **s** of Shalmai, **Ezr 2:46** 1121
sons of Shalmai, the **s** of Hanan, **Ezr 2:46** 1121
the **s** of Giddel, the sons of **Ezr 2:47** 1121
sons of Giddel, the **s** of Gahar, **Ezr 2:47** 1121
sons of Gahar, the **s** of Reaiah, **Ezr 2:47** 1121
the **s** of Rezin, the sons of **Ezr 2:48** 1121
sons of Rezin, the **s** of Nekoda, **Ezr 2:48** 1121
sons of Nekoda, the **s** of Gazzam, **Ezr 2:48** 1121
the **s** of Uzza, the sons of Paseah, **Ezr 2:49** 1121
the sons of Uzza, the **s** of Paseah, **Ezr 2:49** 1121
sons of Paseah, the **s** of Besai, **Ezr 2:49** 1121
the **s** of Asnah, the sons of **Ezr 2:50** 1121
sons of Asnah, the **s** of Meunim, **Ezr 2:50** 1121
sons of Meunim, the **s** of Nephisim, **Ezr 2:50** 1121
the **s** of Bakbuk, the sons of **Ezr 2:51** 1121
sons of Bakbuk, the **s** of Hakupha, **Ezr 2:51** 1121
sons of Hakupha, the **s** of Harhur, **Ezr 2:51** 1121
the **s** of Bazluth, the sons of **Ezr 2:52** 1121
sons of Bazluth, the **s** of Mehida, **Ezr 2:52** 1121
sons of Mehida, the **s** of Harsha, **Ezr 2:52** 1121
the **s** of Barkos, the sons of **Ezr 2:53** 1121
sons of Barkos, the **s** of Sisera, **Ezr 2:53** 1121
sons of Sisera, the **s** of Temah, **Ezr 2:53** 1121
the **s** of Neziah, the sons of **Ezr 2:54** 1121
sons of Neziah, the **s** of Hatipha. **Ezr 2:54** 1121
The **s** of Solomon's servants: **Ezr 2:55** 1121
the **s** of Sotai, the sons of **Ezr 2:55** 1121
of Sotai, the **s** of Hassophereth, **Ezr 2:55** 1121
of Hassophereth, the **s** of Peruda, **Ezr 2:55** 1121
the **s** of Jaalah, the sons of **Ezr 2:56** 1121
sons of Jaalah, the **s** of Darkon, **Ezr 2:56** 1121
sons of Darkon, the **s** of Giddel, **Ezr 2:56** 1121
the **s** of Shephatiah, the sons of **Ezr 2:57** 1121
of Shephatiah, the **s** of Hattil, **Ezr 2:57** 1121
the **s** of Pochereth-hazzebaim, **Ezr 2:57** 1121
Pochereth-hazzebaim, the **s** of Ami. **Ezr 2:57** 1121
and the **s** of Solomon's servants were **Ezr 2:58** 1121
the **s** of Delaiah, the sons of **Ezr 2:60** 1121
sons of Delaiah, the **s** of Tobiah, **Ezr 2:60** 1121
sons of Tobiah, the **s** of Nekoda, **Ezr 2:60** 1121
Of the **s** of the priests: **Ezr 2:61** 1121
the **s** of Habaiah, the sons of **Ezr 2:61** 1121
sons of Habaiah, the **s** of Hakkoz, **Ezr 2:61** 1121
of Hakkoz, the **s** of Barzillai, **Ezr 2:61** 1121
s of Israel *were* in the cities, **Ezr 3:1** 1121
Then Jeshua *with* his **s** and **Ezr 3:9** 1121
united *with* Kadmiel and his **s**, **Ezr 3:9** 1121
the **s** of Judah *and* the sons of **Ezr 3:9** 1121
sons of Judah *and* the **s** of Henadad **Ezr 3:9** 1121
their **s** and brothers the Levites, **Ezr 3:9** 1121
and the Levites, the **s** of Asaph, **Ezr 3:10** 1121
the life of the king and his **s**. **Ezr 6:10** 1123
And the **s** of Israel, the priests, **Ezr 6:16** 1123
The **s** of Israel who returned **Ezr 6:21** 1121
Some of the **s** of Israel and **Ezr 7:7** 1121
the kingdom of the king and his **s**. **Ezr 7:23** 1123
of the **s** of Phinehas, Gershom; **Ezr 8:2** 1121
of the **s** of Ithamar, Daniel; **Ezr 8:2** 1121
of the **s** of David, Hattush; **Ezr 8:2** 1121
of the **s** of Shecaniah *who was* of **Ezr 8:3** 1121
who was of the **s** of Parosh, **Ezr 8:3** 1121
of the **s** of Pahath-moab, **Ezr 8:4** 1121
of the **s** of Zattu, Shecaniah, the son **Ezr 8:5** 1121
and of the **s** of Adin, Ebed the son **Ezr 8:6** 1121
and of the **s** of Elam, Jeshaiah the **Ezr 8:7** 1121

and of the s of Shephatiah,	Ezr 8:8	1121
of the s of Joab, Obadiah the son	Ezr 8:9	1121
of the s of Bani, Shelomith the son	Ezr 8:10	1121
and of the s of Bebai, Zechariah	Ezr 8:11	1121
and of the s of Azgad, Johanan the	Ezr 8:12	1121
and of the s of Adonikam, the last	Ezr 8:13	1121
and of the s of Bigvai, Uthai and	Ezr 8:14	1121
man of insight of the s of Mahli,	Ezr 8:18	1121
Sherebiah, and his s and brothers,	Ezr 8:18	1121
and Jeshaiah of the s of Merari,	Ezr 8:19	1121
with his brothers and their s,	Ezr 8:19	1121
for themselves and for their s,	Ezr 9:2	1121
do not give your daughters to their s	Ezr 9:12	1121
take their daughters to your s,	Ezr 9:12	1121
an inheritance to your s forever.'	Ezr 9:12	1121
of Jehiel, one of the s of Elam,	Ezr 10:2	1121
Among the s of the priests who	Ezr 10:18	1121
Among the s of the priests who	Ezr 10:18	1121
Of the s of Immer *there were*	Ezr 10:20	1121
and of the s of Harim:	Ezr 10:21	1121
and of the s of Pashhur:	Ezr 10:22	1121
the s of Parosh *there were* Ramiah,	Ezr 10:25	1121
and of the s of Elam:	Ezr 10:26	1121
and of the s of Zattu:	Ezr 10:27	1121
and of the s of Bebai:	Ezr 10:28	1121
and of the s of Bani:	Ezr 10:29	1121
and of the s of Pahath-moab:	Ezr 10:30	1121
and *of* the s of Harim:	Ezr 10:31	1121
of the s of Hashum:	Ezr 10:33	1121
of the s of Bani:	Ezr 10:34	1121
Of the s of Nebo *there were* Jeiel,	Ezr 10:43	1121
of the s of Israel Your servants,	Ne 1:6	1121
confessing the sins of the s of Israel	Ne 1:6	1121
the welfare of the s of Israel.	Ne 2:10	1121
Now the s of Hassenaah built the	Ne 3:3	1121
fight for your brothers, your s,	Ne 4:14	1121
"We, our s and our daughters are	Ne 5:2	1121
we are forcing our s and our	Ne 5:5	1121
the s of Parosh, 2,172;	Ne 7:8	1121
the s of Shephatiah, 372;	Ne 7:9	1121
the s of Arah, 652;	Ne 7:10	1121
the s of Pahath-moab of the sons	Ne 7:11	1121
of the s of Jeshua and Joab,	Ne 7:11	1121
the s of Elam, 1,254;	Ne 7:12	1121
the s of Zattu, 845;	Ne 7:13	1121
the s of Zaccai, 760;	Ne 7:14	1121
the s of Binnui, 648;	Ne 7:15	1121
the s of Bebai, 628;	Ne 7:16	1121
the s of Azgad, 2,322;	Ne 7:17	1121
the s of Adonikam, 667;	Ne 7:18	1121
the s of Bigvai, 2,067;	Ne 7:19	1121
the s of Adin, 655;	Ne 7:20	1121
the s of Ater, of Hezekiah, 98;	Ne 7:21	1121
the s of Hashum, 328;	Ne 7:22	1121
the s of Bezai, 324;	Ne 7:23	1121
the s of Hariph, 112;	Ne 7:24	1121
the s of Gibeon, 95;	Ne 7:25	1121
the s of the other Elam, 1,254;	Ne 7:34	1121
the s of Harim, 320;	Ne 7:35	1121
the s of Lod, Hadid and Ono, 721;	Ne 7:37	1121
the s of Senaah, 3,930.	Ne 7:38	1121
the s of Jedaiah of the house of	Ne 7:39	1121
the s of Immer, 1,052;	Ne 7:40	1121
the s of Pashhur, 1,247;	Ne 7:41	1121
the s of Harim, 1,017.	Ne 7:42	1121
the s of Jeshua, of Kadmiel, of	Ne 7:43	1121
of Kadmiel, of the s of Hodevah,	Ne 7:43	1121
the s of Asaph, 148.	Ne 7:44	1121
the s of Shallum, the sons of	Ne 7:45	1121
sons of Shallum, the s of Ater,	Ne 7:45	1121
the sons of Ater, the s of Talmon,	Ne 7:45	1121
sons of Talmon, the s of Akkub,	Ne 7:45	1121
sons of Akkub, the s of Hatita,	Ne 7:45	1121
sons of Hatita, the s of Shobai,	Ne 7:45	1121
the s of Ziha, the sons of	Ne 7:46	1121
sons of Ziha, the s of Hasupha,	Ne 7:46	1121
of Hasupha, the s of Tabbaoth,	Ne 7:46	1121
the s of Keros, the sons of Sia,	Ne 7:47	1121
the sons of Keros, the s of Sia,	Ne 7:47	1121
the sons of Sia, the s of Padon,	Ne 7:47	1121
the s of Lebana, the sons of	Ne 7:48	1121
sons of Lebana, the s of Hagaba,	Ne 7:48	1121
sons of Hagaba, the s of Shalmai,	Ne 7:48	1121
the s of Hanan, the sons of	Ne 7:49	1121
sons of Hanan, the s of Giddel,	Ne 7:49	1121
sons of Giddel, the s of Gahar,	Ne 7:49	1121
the s of Reaiah, the sons of	Ne 7:50	1121
sons of Reaiah, the s of Rezin,	Ne 7:50	1121
sons of Rezin, the s of Nekoda,	Ne 7:50	1121
the s of Gazzam, the sons of Uzza,	Ne 7:51	1121
the sons of Gazzam, the s of Uzza,	Ne 7:51	1121
the sons of Uzza, the s of Paseah,	Ne 7:51	1121
the s of Besai, the sons of	Ne 7:52	1121
sons of Besai, the s of Meunim,	Ne 7:52	1121
of Meunim, the s of Nephushesim,	Ne 7:52	1121
the s of Bakbuk, the sons of	Ne 7:53	1121
sons of Bakbuk, the s of Hakupha,	Ne 7:53	1121
sons of Hakupha, the s of Harhur,	Ne 7:53	1121
the s of Bazlith, the sons of	Ne 7:54	1121
sons of Bazlith, the s of Mehida,	Ne 7:54	1121
sons of Mehida, the s of Harsha,	Ne 7:54	1121
the s of Barkos, the sons of	Ne 7:55	1121
sons of Barkos, the s of Sisera,	Ne 7:55	1121
sons of Sisera, the s of Temah,	Ne 7:55	1121
the s of Neziah, the sons of	Ne 7:56	1121
sons of Neziah, the s of Hatipha.	Ne 7:56	1121
The s of Solomon's servants:	Ne 7:57	1121
the s of Sotai, the sons of	Ne 7:57	1121
sons of Sotai, the s of Sophereth,	Ne 7:57	1121

of Sophereth, the s of Perida,	Ne 7:57	1121
the s of Jaala, the sons of	Ne 7:58	1121
sons of Jaala, the s of Darkon,	Ne 7:58	1121
sons of Darkon, the s of Giddel,	Ne 7:58	1121
the s of Shephatiah, the sons of	Ne 7:59	1121
of Shephatiah, the s of Hattil,	Ne 7:59	1121
the s of Pochereth-hazzebaim,	Ne 7:59	1121
Pochereth-hazzebaim, the s of Amon.	Ne 7:59	1121
the s of Solomon's servants *were* 392	Ne 7:60	1121
the s of Delaiah, the sons of	Ne 7:62	1121
sons of Delaiah, the s of Tobiah,	Ne 7:62	1121
sons of Tobiah, the s of Nekoda,	Ne 7:62	1121
the s of Hobaiah, the sons of	Ne 7:63	1121
sons of Hobaiah, the s of Hakkoz,	Ne 7:63	1121
of Hakkoz, the s of Barzillai,	Ne 7:63	1121
the s of Israel *were* in their	Ne 7:73	1121
the s of Israel should live in booths	Ne 8:14	1121
The s of Israel had indeed not	Ne 8:17	1121
the s of Israel assembled with fasting,	Ne 9:1	1121
"You made their s numerous as	Ne 9:23	1121
"So their s entered and possessed	Ne 9:24	1121
Binnui of the s of Henadad,	Ne 10:9	1121
their s and their daughters,	Ne 10:28	1121
or take their daughters for our s.	Ne 10:30	1121
of our s and of our cattle,	Ne 10:36	1121
For the s of Israel and the sons	Ne 10:39	1121
For the sons of Israel and the s	Ne 10:39	1121
Some of the s of Judah and	Ne 11:4	1121
the s of Benjamin lived in Jerusalem.	Ne 11:4	1121
From the s of Judah:	Ne 11:4	1121
of Mahalalel, of the s of Perez;	Ne 11:4	1121
All the s of Perez who lived in	Ne 11:6	1121
Now these are the s of Benjamin:	Ne 11:7	1121
son of Mica, from the s of Asaph,	Ne 11:22	1121
the s of Zerah the son of Judah,	Ne 11:24	1121
some of the s of Judah lived in	Ne 11:25	1121
The s of Benjamin also *lived* from	Ne 11:31	1121
The s of Levi, the heads of	Ne 12:23	1121
So the s of the singers were	Ne 12:28	1121
s of the priests with trumpets;	Ne 12:35	1121
portion for the s of Aaron.	Ne 12:47	1121
they did not meet the s of Israel	Ne 13:2	1121
to the s of Judah on the sabbath,	Ne 13:16	1121
give your daughters to their s,	Ne 13:25	1121
for your s or for yourselves.	Ne 13:25	1121
Even one of the s of Joiada, the	Ne 13:28	1121
riches, and the number of his s,	Es 5:11	1121
the ten s of Haman the son of	Es 9:10	1121
s of Haman at the citadel in Susa.	Es 9:12	1121
ten s be hanged on the gallows."	Es 9:13	1121
and Haman's ten s were hanged.	Es 9:14	1121
and that he and his s should be	Es 9:25	1121
Seven s and three daughters	Jb 1:2	1121
His s used to go and hold a	Jb 1:4	1121
"Perhaps my s have sinned and	Jb 1:5	1121
s of God came to present themselves	Jb 1:6	1121
his s and his daughters were eating	Jb 1:13	1121
"Your s and your daughters were	Jb 1:18	1121
s of God came to present themselves	Jb 2:1	1121
"His s are far from safety, They	Jb 5:4	1121
"If your s sinned against Him,	Jb 8:4	1121
"His s achieve honor, but he does	Jb 14:21	1121
"His s favor the poor, And his	Jb 20:10	1121
away a man's iniquity for his s.'	Jb 21:19	1121
"Though his s are many, they are	Jb 27:14	1121
all the s of God shouted for joy?	Jb 38:7	1121
is king over all the s of pride."	Jb 41:34	1121
had seven s and three daughters.	Jb 42:13	1121
lived 140 years, and saw his s and	Jb 42:16	1121
O s of men, how long will my honor	Ps 4:2	1121
His eyelids test the s of men.	Ps 11:4	1121
disappear from among the s of men.	Ps 12:1	1121
is exalted among the s of men.	Ps 12:8	1121
from heaven upon the s of men To	Ps 14:2	1121
from among the s of men.	Ps 21:10	1121
to the LORD, O s of the mighty,	Ps 29:1	1121
in You, Before the s of men!	Ps 31:19	1121
He sees all the s of men;	Ps 33:13	1121
You are fairer than the s of men;	Ps 45:2	1121
of your fathers will be your s;	Ps 45:16	1121
from heaven upon the s of men To	Ps 53:2	1121
forth fire, *Even* the s of men,	Ps 57:4	1121
you judge uprightly, O s of men?	Ps 58:1	1121
in *His* deeds toward the s of men.	Ps 66:5	1121
And an alien to my mother's s.	Ps 69:8	1121
The s of Jacob and Joseph	Ps 77:15	1121
The s of Ephraim were archers	Ps 78:9	1121
all of you are s of the Most High.	Ps 82:6	1121
Who among the s of the mighty is	Ps 89:6	1121
"If his s forsake My law And do	Ps 89:30	1121
You have created all the s of men!	Ps 89:47	1121
His acts to the s of Israel.	Ps 103:7	1121
His servant, O s of Jacob,	Ps 105:6	1121
They even sacrificed their s and	Ps 106:37	1121
blood of their s and their daughters,	Ps 106:38	1121
for His wonders to the s of men!	Ps 107:8	1121
for His wonders to the s of men!	Ps 107:15	1121
for His wonders to the s of men!	Ps 107:21	1121
for His wonders to the s of men!	Ps 107:31	1121
He has given to the s of men.	Ps 115:16	1121
"If your s will keep My covenant And	Ps 132:12	1121
Their s also shall sit upon your	Ps 132:12	1121
O LORD, against the s of Edom	Ps 137:7	1121
Let our s in their youth be as	Ps 144:12	1121
To make known to the s of men	Ps 145:12	1121
He has blessed your s within you.	Ps 147:13	1121
Even for the s of Israel, a people	Ps 148:14	1121
s of Zion rejoice in their King.	Ps 149:2	1121
Hear, *O* s, the instruction of a father	Pr 4:1	1121

Now then, *my* s, listen to me And	Pr 5:7	1121
Now therefore, *my* s, listen to me,	Pr 7:24	1121
And my voice *is* to the s of men.	Pr 8:4	1121
having my delight in the s of men.	Pr 8:31	1121
"Now therefore, *O* s, listen to me,	Pr 8:32	1121
the glory of s is their fathers.	Pr 17:6	1121
How blessed are his s after him.	Pr 20:7	1121
the s of men to be afflicted with.	Ec 1:13	1121
good there is for the s of men to do	Ec 2:3	1121
which God has given the s of men	Ec 3:10	1121
to myself concerning the s of men,	Ec 3:18	1121
For the fate of the s of men and	Ec 3:19	1121
therefore the hearts of the s of	Ec 8:11	1121
hearts of the s of men are full of evil	Ec 9:3	1121
so the s of men are ensnared at an	Ec 9:12	1121
My mother's s were angry with me;	SS 1:6	1121
"S I have reared and brought up,	Is 1:2	1121
of evildoers, S who act corruptly!	Is 1:4	1121
will plunder the s of the east;	Is 11:14	1121
And the s of Ammon will be subject	Is 11:14	1121
"Prepare for his s a place of	Is 14:21	1121
the glory of the s of Israel,"	Is 17:3	1121
abandoned before the s of Israel;	Is 17:9	1121
the mighty men of the s of Kedar,	Is 21:17	1121
up one by one, O s of Israel.	Is 27:12	1121
is a rebellious people, false s,	Is 30:9	1121
S who refuse to listen To the	Is 30:9	1121
deeply defected, O s of Israel.	Is 31:6	1121
s of Eden who *were* in Telassar?	Is 37:12	1121
his s killed him with the sword;	Is 37:38	1121
A father tells his s about Your	Is 38:19	1121
your s who will issue from you,	Is 39:7	1121
Bring My s from afar And My	Is 43:6	1121
things to come concerning My s,	Is 45:11	1121
will bring your s in *their* bosom,	Is 49:22	1121
with you, And I will save your s.	Is 49:25	1121
her among all the s she has borne,	Is 51:18	1121
among all the s she has reared.	Is 51:18	1121
Your s have fainted, They lie	Is 51:20	1121
His form more than the s of men.	Is 52:14	1121
For the s of the desolate one *will*	Is 54:1	1121
Than the s of the married woman,"	Is 54:1	1121
your s will be taught of the LORD;	Is 54:13	1121
well-being of your s will be great.	Is 54:13	1121
than that of s and daughters;	Is 56:5	1121
come here, you s of a sorceress,	Is 57:3	1121
Your s will come from afar, And	Is 60:4	1121
first, To bring your s from afar,	Is 60:9	1121
"The s of those who afflicted	Is 60:14	1121
virgin, *So* your s will marry you;	Is 62:5	1121
S who will not deal falsely."	Is 63:8	1121
she also brought forth her s.	Is 66:8	1121
"just as the s of Israel bring	Is 66:20	1121
with your sons' s I will contend.	Jer 2:9	1121
"In vain I have struck your s;	Jer 2:30	1121
'Return, O faithless s,'	Jer 3:14	1121
'How I would set you among My s	Jer 3:19	1121
supplications of the s of Israel;	Jer 3:21	1121
"Return, O faithless s,	Jer 3:22	1121
their s and their daughters.	Jer 3:24	1121
Your s have forsaken Me And sworn	Jer 5:7	1121
devour your s and your daughters;	Jer 5:17	1121
"Flee for safety, O s of Benjamin,	Jer 6:1	1121
them, Fathers and s together;	Jer 6:21	1121
"For the s of Judah have done	Jer 7:30	1121
to burn their s and their	Jer 7:31	1121
and Edom and the s of Ammon,	Jer 9:26	1121
My s have gone from me and are no	Jer 10:20	1121
their s and daughters will die by	Jer 11:22	1121
the fathers and the s together,"	Jer 13:14	1121
nor their wives, nor their s,	Jer 14:16	1121
"She who bore seven s pines away;	Jer 15:9	1121
nor have s or daughters in this place	Jer 16:2	1121
s and daughters born in this place,	Jer 16:3	1121
who brought up the s of Israel out	Jer 16:14	1121
who brought up the s of Israel	Jer 16:15	1121
to burn their s in the fire as burnt	Jer 19:5	1121
make them eat the flesh of their s	Jer 19:9	1121
who brought up the s of Israel	Jer 23:7	1121
Edom, Moab and the s of Ammon;	Jer 25:21	1121
to the king of the s of Ammon,	Jer 27:3	1121
the fathers of s and daughters,	Jer 29:6	1121
and take wives for your s and give	Jer 29:6	1121
they may bear s and daughters;	Jer 29:6	1121
to all the ways of the s of men,	Jer 32:19	1121
"Indeed the s of Israel and the	Jer 32:30	1121
s of Judah have been doing only evil	Jer 32:30	1121
for the s of Israel have been only	Jer 32:30	1121
all the evil of the s of Israel and the	Jer 32:32	1121
sons of Israel and the s of Judah which	Jer 32:32	1121
cause their s and their daughters to	Jer 32:35	1121
and his brothers and all his s	Jer 35:3	1121
s of Hanan the son of Igdaliah,	Jer 35:4	1121
not drink wine, you or your s,	Jer 35:6	1121
our days, we, our wives, our s or	Jer 35:8	1121
commanded his s not to drink wine,	Jer 35:14	1121
the s of Jonadab the son of Rechab	Jer 35:16	1121
wives and your s to the Chaldeans,	Jer 38:23	1121
king of Babylon slew the s of Zedekiah	Jer 39:6	1121
and Jonathan the s of Kareah,	Jer 40:8	1121
the s of Ephai the Netophathite,	Jer 40:8	1121
among the s of Ammon and in Edom	Jer 40:11	1121
Baalis the king of the s of Ammon	Jer 40:14	1121
to cross over to the s of Ammon.	Jer 41:10	1121
men and went to the s of Ammon.	Jer 41:15	1121
s have been taken away captive And	Jer 48:46	1121
Concerning the s of Ammon.	Jer 49:1	1121
"Does Israel have no s?	Jer 49:1	1121
Against Rabbah of the s of Ammon;	Jer 49:2	1121

The fortunes of the **s** of Ammon,"	**Jer 49:6**	1121
"the **s** of Israel will come, *both*	**Jer 50:4**	1121
they and the **s** of Judah as well;	**Jer 50:4**	1121
"The **s** of Israel are oppressed,	**Jer 50:33**	1121
And the **s** of Judah as well;	**Jer 50:33**	1121
slaughtered the **s** of Zedekiah before	**Jer 52:10**	1121
willingly Or grieve the **s** of men.	**La 3:33**	1121
The precious **s** of Zion, Weighed	**La 4:2**	1121
I am sending you to the **s** of Israel,	**Ezk 2:3**	1121
exiles, to the **s** of your people,	**Ezk 3:11**	1121
"Thus will the **s** of Israel eat	**Ezk 4:13**	1121
will eat *their* **s** among you,	**Ezk 5:10**	1121
you, and **s** will eat their fathers;	**Ezk 5:10**	1121
lay the dead bodies of the **s** of Israel	**Ezk 6:5**	1121
either *their* **s** or *their* daughters.	**Ezk 14:16**	1121
either *their* **s** or *their* daughters,	**Ezk 14:18**	1121
brought out, *both* **s** and daughters.	**Ezk 14:22**	1121
you took your **s** and daughters whom	**Ezk 16:20**	1121
because of the blood of your **s**	**Ezk 16:36**	1121
cause your **s** to pass through the fire,	**Ezk 20:31**	1121
come to Rabbah of the **s** of Ammon,	**Ezk 21:20**	1121
GOD concerning the **s** of Ammon	**Ezk 21:28**	1121
and they bore **s** and daughters.	**Ezk 23:4**	1121
they took her **s** and her daughters,	**Ezk 23:10**	1121
take your **s** and your daughters;	**Ezk 23:25**	1121
idols and even caused their **s**,	**Ezk 23:37**	1121
they will slay their **s** and their	**Ezk 23:47**	1121
and your **s** and your daughters whom	**Ezk 24:21**	1121
their **s** and their daughters,	**Ezk 24:25**	1121
your face toward the **s** of Ammon and	**Ezk 25:2**	1121
and say to the **s** of Ammon,	**Ezk 25:3**	1121
going to give you to the **s** of the east	**Ezk 25:4**	1121
s of Ammon a resting place for flocks.	**Ezk 25:5**	1121
along with the **s** of Ammon to	**Ezk 25:10**	1121
of Ammon to the **s** of the east,	**Ezk 25:10**	1121
that the **s** of Ammon will not be	**Ezk 25:10**	1121
"The **s** of Arvad and your army	**Ezk 27:11**	1121
"The **s** of Dedan were your traders.	**Ezk 27:15**	1121
earth beneath, among the **s** of men,	**Ezk 31:14**	1121
speak to the **s** of your people and	**Ezk 33:2**	1121
delivered the **s** of Israel to the power	**Ezk 35:5**	1121
'For Judah and for the **s** of Israel,	**Ezk 37:16**	1121
"When the **s** of your people	**Ezk 37:18**	1121
I will take the **s** of Israel from	**Ezk 37:21**	1121
live on it, they, and their **s** and	**Ezk 37:25**	1121
and their sons and their sons' **s**,	**Ezk 37:25**	1121
These are the **s** of Zadok, who from	**Ezk 40:46**	1121
who from the **s** of Levi come near	**Ezk 40:46**	1121
dwell among the **s** of Israel forever.	**Ezk 43:7**	1121
who are among the **s** of Israel.	**Ezk 44:9**	1121
Levitical priests, the **s** of Zadok,	**Ezk 44:15**	1121
the **s** of Israel went astray from	**Ezk 44:15**	1121
his inheritance to any of his **s**,	**Ezk 46:16**	1121
sons, it shall belong to his **s**;	**Ezk 46:16**	1121
he shall give his **s** inheritance	**Ezk 46:18**	1121
who bring forth **s** in your midst.	**Ezk 47:22**	1121
native-born among the **s** of Israel;	**Ezk 47:22**	1121
are sanctified of the **s** of Zadok,	**Ezk 48:11**	1121
when the **s** of Israel went astray as	**Ezk 48:11**	1121
bring in some of the **s** of Israel,	**Da 1:3**	1121
from the **s** of Judah were Daniel,	**Da 1:6**	1121
and wherever the **s** of men dwell,	**Da 2:38**	1123
"His **s** will mobilize and	**Da 11:10**	1121
the foremost of the **s** of Ammon.	**Da 11:41**	1121
guard over the **s** of your people,	**Da 12:1**	1121
Yet the number of the **s** of Israel	**Hos 1:10**	1121
"*You are* the **s** of the living God."	**Hos 1:10**	1121
the **s** of Judah and the sons of	**Hos 1:11**	1121
And the sons of Judah and the **s** of	**Hos 1:11**	1121
as the LORD loves the **s** of Israel,	**Hos 3:1**	1121
For the **s** of Israel will remain	**Hos 3:4**	1121
Afterward the **s** of Israel will	**Hos 3:5**	1121
word of the LORD, O **s** of Israel,	**Hos 4:1**	1121
the battle against the **s** of iniquity	**Hos 10:9**	1121
And *His* **s** will come trembling from	**Hos 11:10**	1121
Tell your **s** about it, And *let* your	**Jl 1:3**	1121
And *let* your **s** *tell* their sons,	**Jl 1:3**	1121
And *let* your sons *tell* their **s**,	**Jl 1:3**	1121
And their **s** the next generation.	**Jl 1:3**	1121
dries up From the **s** of men.	**Jl 1:12**	1121
So rejoice, O **s** of Zion, And be	**Jl 2:23**	1121
s and daughters will prophesy,	**Jl 2:28**	1121
and sold the **s** of Judah and	**Jl 3:6**	1121
"Also I will sell your **s** and your	**Jl 3:8**	1121
into the hand of the **s** of Judah,	**Jl 3:8**	1121
a stronghold to the **s** of Israel.	**Jl 3:16**	1121
violence done to the **s** of Judah,	**Jl 3:19**	1121
transgressions of the **s** of Ammon	**Am 1:13**	1121
"Then I raised up some of your **s**	**Am 2:11**	1121
Is this not so, O **s** of Israel?"	**Am 2:11**	1121
spoken against you, **s** of Israel,	**Am 3:1**	1121
So will the **s** of Israel dwelling	**Am 3:12**	1121
you love *to do*, you **s** of Israel,"	**Am 4:5**	1121
your **s** and your daughters will	**Am 7:17**	1121
not as the **s** of Ethiopia to Me,	**Am 9:7**	1121
Ethiopia to Me, O **s** of Israel?"	**Am 9:7**	1121
do not rejoice over the **s** of Judah	**Ob 1:12**	1121
of this host of the **s** of Israel,	**Ob 1:20**	1121
Will return to the **s** of Israel.	**Mi 5:3**	1121
for man Or delay for the **s** of men.	**Mi 5:7**	1121
punish the princes, the king's **s** And	**Zph 1:8**	1121
the revilings of the **s** of Ammon,	**Zph 2:8**	1121
And the **s** of Ammon like Gomorrah	**Zph 2:9**	1121
And I will stir up your **s**,	**Zch 9:13**	1121
your sons, O Zion, against your **s**,	**Zch 9:13**	1121
and He will purify the **s** of Levi	**Mal 3:3**	1121
therefore you, O **s** of Jacob,	**Mal 3:6**	1121
for they shall be called **s** of God.	**Mt 5:9**	*5207*
that you may be **s** of your Father	**Mt 5:45**	*5207*
but the **s** of the kingdom will be	**Mt 8:12**	*5207*
by whom do your **s** cast *them* out?	**Mt 12:27**	*5207*
these are the **s** of the kingdom;	**Mt 13:38**	*5207*
tares are the **s** of the evil *one;*	**Mt 13:38**	*5207*
from their **s** or from strangers?"	**Mt 17:25**	*5207*
"Then the **s** are exempt.	**Mt 17:26**	*5207*
mother of the **s** of Zebedee came to	**Mt 20:20**	*5207*
of Zebedee came to Jesus with her **s**,	**Mt 20:20**	*5207*
these two **s** of mine may sit one	**Mt 20:21**	*5207*
A man had two **s**, and he came to	**Mt 21:28**	*5043*
that you are **s** of those who	**Mt 23:31**	*5207*
Peter and the two **s** of Zebedee,	**Mt 26:37**	*5207*
HAD BEEN SET by the **s** of Israel;	**Mt 27:9**	*5207*
the mother of the **s** of Zebedee.	**Mt 27:56**	*5207*
which means, "**S** of Thunder");	**Mk 3:17**	*5207*
shall be forgiven the **s** of men,	**Mk 3:28**	*5207*
and John, the two **s** of Zebedee,	**Mk 10:35**	*5207*
will turn many of the **s** of Israel	**Lk 1:16**	*5207*
James and John, **s** of Zebedee,	**Lk 5:10**	*5207*
you will be **s** of the Most High;	**Lk 6:35**	*5207*
by whom do your **s** cast them out?	**Lk 11:19**	*5207*
"A man had two **s**	**Lk 15:11**	*5207*
the **s** of this age are more shrewd	**Lk 16:8**	*5207*
own kind than the **s** of light.	**Lk 16:8**	*5207*
"The **s** of this age marry and are	**Lk 20:34**	*5207*
are like angels, and are **s** of God,	**Lk 20:36**	*5207*
God, being **s** of the resurrection.	**Lk 20:36**	*5207*
drank of it himself and his **s**	**Jn 4:12**	*5207*
that you may become **s** of Light."	**Jn 12:36**	*5207*
and the **s** of Zebedee, and two	**Jn 21:2**	
AND YOUR **S** AND YOUR DAUGHTERS	**Ac 2:17**	*5207*
you who are the **s** of the prophets and	**Ac 3:25**	*5207*
all the Senate of the **s** of Israel,	**Ac 5:21**	*5207*
from the **s** of Hamor in Shechem.	**Ac 7:16**	*5207*
his brethren, the **s** of Israel.	**Ac 7:23**	*5207*
he became the father of two **s**.	**Ac 7:29**	*5207*
Moses who said to the **s** of Israel,	**Ac 7:37**	*5207*
and kings and the **s** of Israel;	**Ac 9:15**	*5207*
which He sent to the **s** of Israel,	**Ac 10:36**	*5207*
"Brethren, **s** of Abraham's family,	**Ac 13:26**	*5207*
Seven **s** of one Sceva, a Jewish	**Ac 19:14**	*5207*
Spirit of God, these are **s** of God.	**Ro 8:14**	*5207*
adoption as **s** by which we cry out,	**Ro 8:15**	*5206*
for the revealing of the **s** of God.	**Ro 8:19**	*5207*
eagerly for *our* adoption as **s**,	**Ro 8:23**	*5206*
to whom belongs the adoption as **s**	**Ro 9:4**	*5206*
BE CALLED **S** OF THE LIVING GOD."	**Ro 9:26**	*5207*
THE NUMBER OF THE **S** OF ISRAEL BE	**Ro 9:27**	*5207*
so that the **s** of Israel could not	**2Co 3:7**	*5207*
that the **s** of Israel would not look	**2Co 3:13**	*5207*
shall be **s** and daughters to Me,"	**2Co 6:18**	*5207*
are of faith who are **s** of Abraham.	**Ga 3:7**	*5207*
For you are all **s** of God through	**Ga 3:26**	*5207*
might receive the adoption as **s**.	**Ga 4:5**	*5206*
Because you are **s**,	**Ga 4:6**	*5207*
is written that Abraham had two **s**,	**Ga 4:22**	*5207*
He predestined us to adoption as **s**	**Eph 1:5**	*5206*
working in the **s** of disobedience.	**Eph 2:2**	*5207*
not made known to the **s** of men,	**Eph 3:5**	*5207*
comes upon the **s** of disobedience.	**Eph 5:6**	*5207*
the wrath of God will come upon the **s**	**Col 3:6**	*5207*
all **s** of light and sons of day.	**1Th 5:5**	*5207*
all sons of light and **s** of day.	**1Th 5:5**	*5207*
in bringing many **s** to glory,	**Heb 2:10**	*5207*
And those indeed of the **s** of Levi	**Heb 7:5**	*5207*
blessed each of the **s** of Joseph,	**Heb 11:21**	*5207*
of the exodus of the **s** of Israel,	**Heb 11:22**	*5207*
which is addressed to you as **s**,	**Heb 12:5**	*5207*
God deals with you as with **s**;	**Heb 12:7**	*5207*
illegitimate children and not **s**.	**Heb 12:8**	*5207*
block before the **s** of Israel,	**Rv 2:14**	*5207*
every tribe of the **s** of Israel:	**Rv 7:4**	*5207*
twelve tribes of the **s** of Israel.	**Rv 21:12**	*5207*

SONS'

and your **s** wives with you.	**Gn 6:18**	1121
sons and his wife and his **s** wives	**Gn 7:7**	1121
wife and your sons and your **s** wives	**Gn 8:16**	1121
sons and his wife and his **s** wives	**Gn 8:18**	1121
on the lobes of his **s** right ears	**Ex 29:20**	1121
and on his sons and on his **s** garments	**Ex 29:21**	1121
and his **s** garments	**Ex 29:21**	1121
it is your due and your **s** due	**Lv 10:13**	1121
given as your due and your **s** due	**Lv 10:14**	1121
"And with your **s** sons I will	**Jer 2:9**	1121
and their sons and their **s** sons,	**Ezk 37:25**	1121
inheritance *shall be* only his **s**;	**Ezk 46:17**	1121

SOON

As **s** as He had finished	**Gn 18:33**	3512c
as **s** as Isaac had finished	**Gn 27:30**	3512c
As **s** as it was light, the men were	**Gn 44:3**	1242
as **s** as he appeared before him, he	**Gn 46:29**	
have you come *back* so **s** today?"	**Ex 2:18**	4116
"As **s** as I go out of the city, I	**Ex 9:29**	
as **s** as Moses came near the camp,	**Ex 32:19**	3512c
as **s** as those who were pursuing	**Jos 2:7**	3512c
about, as **s** as Gideon was dead,	**Jg 8:33**	3512c
morning, as **s** as the sun is up,	**Jg 9:33**	
"As **s** as you enter the city you	**1Sa 9:13**	
as **s** as you have come there to the	**1Sa 10:5**	
As **s** as he finished offering the burnt	**1Sa 13:10**	
and as **s** as you have arisen early	**1Sa 29:10**	
As **s** as he had finished speaking,	**2Sa 13:36**	
"As **s** as you hear the sound of	**2Sa 15:10**	
As **s** as he was removed from the	**2Sa 20:13**	3512c
As **s** as they hear, they obey me.	**2Sa 22:45**	
as **s** as my lord the king sleeps	**1Ki 1:21**	
As **s** as Pharaoh's daughter came up	**1Ki 9:24**	389
came about as **s** as he was king,	**1Ki 15:29**	
as **s** as he sat on his throne,	**1Ki 16:11**	
as **s** as you have departed from me,	**1Ki 20:36**	
And as **s** as he had departed from	**1Ki 20:36**	
as **s** as he had finished offering	**2Ki 10:25**	
as **s** as the kingdom was firmly in	**2Ki 14:5**	3512c
as **s** as the kingdom was firmly in	**2Ch 25:3**	3512c
As **s** as the order spread, the	**2Ch 31:5**	
Then as **s** as the copy of King	**Ezr 4:23**	
		4481, 1768
"But as **s** as they had rest, they	**Ne 9:28**	
my Maker would **s** take me away.	**Jb 32:22**	4592
For His wrath may **s** be kindled.	**Ps 2:12**	4592
As **s** as they hear, they obey me;	**Ps 18:44**	
For **s** it is gone and we fly away.	**Ps 90:10**	2440
My soul would **s** have dwelt in *the*	**Ps 94:17**	4592
and they are **s** forgotten in	**Ec 8:10**	
Her *fateful* time also will **s** come	**Is 13:22**	7138
As **s** as a standard is raised on	**Is 18:3**	
And as **s** as the trumpet is blown,	**Is 18:3**	
as **s** as the bud blossoms And the	**Is 18:5**	
And as **s** as it is in his hand,	**Is 28:4**	5750
As **s** as you finish	**Is 33:1**	
As **s** as you cease to deal	**Is 33:1**	
"The exile will **s** be set free,	**Is 51:14**	4116
As **s** as Zion travailed, she also	**Is 66:8**	3588
as **s** as they came inside the city,	**Jer 41:7**	
as **s** as all the people who were	**Jer 41:13**	
as **s** as Jeremiah, whom the LORD	**Jer 43:1**	
"The disaster of Moab will **s** come,	**Jer 48:16**	7138
"As **s** as you come to Babylon,	**Jer 51:61**	
as **s** as you finish reading this scroll,	**Jer 51:63**	
wither as **s** as the east wind strikes it	**Ezk 17:10**	
for they will **s** come.	**Ezk 36:8**	7126
as **s** as the king heard this	**Da 6:14**	1768
But as **s** as he was mighty, the	**Da 8:8**	
and as **s** as I heard the sound of	**Da 10:9**	
Now as **s** as he spoke to me, I	**Da 10:19**	
as **s** as he becomes strong through	**Da 11:2**	
"But as **s** as he has arisen, his	**Da 11:4**	
and as **s** as they finish shattering	**Da 12:7**	
And like dew which **s** disappears,	**Hos 13:3**	7925
As **s** as He was alone, His	**Mk 4:10**	*3753*
s afterward to speak evil of Me.	**Mk 9:39**	*5035*
S afterwards He went to a city called	**Lk 7:11**	*1836*
S afterwards, He *began* going	**Lk 8:1**	
soil, and as **s** as it grew up,	**Lk 8:6**	
As **s** as He was approaching, near	**Lk 19:37**	*1448*
as **s** as they put forth *leaves,* you	**Lk 21:30**	
		3752, 2235
to come to him as **s** as possible,	**Ac 17:15**	*5036*
s crush Satan under your feet.	**Ro 16:20**	*5034*
But I will come to you **s**,	**1Co 4:19**	*5030*
as **s** as I see how things *go* with	**Php 2:23**	
Make every effort to come to me **s**;	**2Tm 4:9**	*5030*
with whom, if he comes **s**,	**Heb 13:23**	*5036*
the things which must **s** take place;	**Rv 1:1**	*5034*
bond-servants the things which must **s**	**Rv 22:6**	*5034*

SOONER

I may be restored to you the **s**.	**Heb 13:19**	*5036*

SOOT

handfuls of **s** from a kiln,	**Ex 9:8**	6368
So they took **s** from a kiln, and	**Ex 9:10**	6368
appearance is blacker than **s**,	**La 4:8**	7815

SOOTHING

The LORD smelled the **s** aroma;	**Gn 8:21**	5207
it is a **s** aroma, an offering by	**Ex 29:18**	5207
for a **s** aroma before the LORD;	**Ex 29:25**	5207
in the morning, for a **s** aroma,	**Ex 29:41**	5207
by fire of a **s** aroma to the LORD.	**Lv 1:9**	5207
by fire of a **s** aroma to the LORD.	**Lv 1:13**	5207
by fire of a **s** aroma to the LORD.	**Lv 1:17**	5207
by fire of a **s** aroma to the LORD.	**Lv 2:2**	5207
by fire of a **s** aroma to the LORD.	**Lv 2:9**	5207
ascend for a **s** aroma on the altar.	**Lv 2:12**	5207
by fire of a **s** aroma to the LORD.	**Lv 3:5**	5207
an offering by fire for a **s** aroma;	**Lv 3:16**	5207
altar for a **s** aroma to the LORD.	**Lv 4:31**	5207
in smoke on the altar, a **s** aroma,	**Lv 6:15**	5207
pieces as a **s** aroma to the LORD.	**Lv 6:21**	5207
a burnt offering for a **s** aroma;	**Lv 8:21**	5207
ordination offering for a **s** aroma;	**Lv 8:28**	5207
in smoke as a **s** aroma to the LORD.	**Lv 17:6**	5207
by fire to the LORD *for* a **s** aroma,	**Lv 23:13**	5207
by fire of a **s** aroma to the LORD	**Lv 23:18**	5207
I will not smell your **s** aromas.	**Lv 26:31**	5207
to make a **s** aroma to the LORD,	**Nu 15:3**	5207
of wine as a **s** aroma to the LORD.	**Nu 15:7**	5207
by fire, as a **s** aroma to the LORD.	**Nu 15:10**	5207
by fire, as a **s** aroma to the LORD.	**Nu 15:13**	5207
by fire, as a **s** aroma to the LORD,	**Nu 15:14**	5207
as a **s** aroma to the LORD,	**Nu 15:24**	5207
fire, for a **s** aroma to the LORD.	**Nu 18:17**	5207
by fire, of a **s** aroma to Me,	**Nu 28:2**	5207
in Mount Sinai as a **s** aroma,	**Nu 28:6**	5207
by fire, a **s** aroma to the LORD.	**Nu 28:8**	5207
for a burnt offering of a **s** aroma,	**Nu 28:13**	5207
by fire, of a **s** aroma to the LORD;	**Nu 28:24**	5207
for a **s** aroma to the LORD:	**Nu 28:27**	5207
offering as a **s** aroma to the LORD:	**Nu 29:2**	5207
to their ordinance, for a **s** aroma,	**Nu 29:6**	5207
offering to the LORD *as* a **s** aroma:	**Nu 29:8**	5207
by fire as a **s** aroma to the LORD:	**Nu 29:13**	5207
by fire, as a **s** aroma to the LORD:	**Nu 29:36**	5207
A **s** tongue is a tree of life, But	**Pr 15:4**	4832
they offered **s** aroma to all their	**Ezk 6:13**	5207
offer before them for a **s** aroma;	**Ezk 16:19**	5207
also they made their **s** aroma and	**Ezk 20:28**	5207
"As a **s** aroma I will accept you	**Ezk 20:41**	5207

SOOTHSAYERS
they are s like the Philistines, Is 2:6 6049a
diviners, your dreamers, your s or Jer 27:9 6049a
SOOTHSAYING
nor practice divination or s. Lv 19:26 6049a
SOPATER
he was accompanied by S of Berea, Ac 20:4 4986
SOPHERETH
the sons of Sotai, the sons of S, Ne 7:57 5618
SORCERER
one who interprets omens, or a s, Dt 18:10 3784
SORCERERS
called for the wise men and the s, Ex 7:11 3784
your soothsayers or your s Jer 27:9 3786
the s and the Chaldeans to Da 2:2 3784
will be a swift witness against the s Mal 3:5 3784
and s and idolaters and all liars, Rv 21:8 5333
Outside are the dogs and the s and Rv 22:15 5333
SORCERESS
"You shall not allow a s to live. Ex 22:18 3784
"But come here, you sons of a s, Is 57:3 6049a
SORCERIES
measure In spite of your many s, Is 47:9 3785
in your spells And in your many s Is 47:12 3785
"I will cut off s from your hand, Mi 5:12 3785
charming one, the mistress of s, Na 3:4 3785
harlotries And families by her s. Na 3:4 3785
repent of their murders nor of their s Rv 9:21 5331
SORCERY
used divination, practiced s and 2Ch 33:6 3784
idolatry, s, enmities, strife, Ga 5:20 5331
nations were deceived by your s. Rv 18:23 5331
SORDID
to much wine or fond of s gain, 1Tm 3:8 146
pugnacious, not fond of s gain, Ti 1:7 146
not teach for the sake of s gain. Ti 1:11 150
and not for s gain, but with 1Pe 5:2 147
SORE
a running s or eczema or scabs, Lv 22:22 2990
the knees and legs with s boils, Dt 28:35 7451a
and smote Job with s boils from Jb 2:7 7451a
No healing for your s, Jer 30:13 4205
became a loathsome and malignant s Rv 16:2 1668
SOREK
loved a woman in the valley of S, Jg 16:4 7796a
SORELY
blow, With a s infected wound. Jer 14:17 3966
SORES
boils breaking out with s on man Ex 9:9 76
boils breaking out with s on man Ex 9:10 76
laid at his gate, covered with s, Lk 16:20 1669
dogs were coming and licking his s. Lk 16:21 1668
because of their pains and their s; Rv 16:11 1668
SORREL
were in the ravine, with red, s and Zch 1:8 8320
SORROW
my gray hair down to Sheol in s." Gn 42:38 3015
my gray hair down to Sheol in s.' Gn 44:29 7463a
our father down to Sheol in s. Gn 44:31 3015
from Paddan, Rachel died, to my s, Gn 48:7 5921
turned for them from s into gladness Es 9:22 3015
Having s in my heart all the day? Ps 13:2 3015
For my life is spent with s And Ps 31:10 3015
And my s is continually before me. Ps 38:17 4341
And my s grew worse. Ps 39:2 3511
their pride is but labor and s; Ps 90:10 205
Through oppression, misery and s, Ps 107:39 3015
I found distress and s. Ps 116:3 3015
rich, And He adds no s to it. Pr 10:22 6089a
sires a fool does so to his s, Pr 17:21 8424
Who has s? Who has contentions? Pr 23:29 17
S is better than laughter, For Ec 7:3 3708a
And s and sighing will flee away. Is 35:10 3015
And s and sighing will flee away. Is 51:11 3015
My s is beyond healing, My heart Jer 8:18 3015
the womb To look on trouble and s, Jer 20:18 3015
and give them joy for their s. Jer 31:13 3015
the LORD has added s to my pain; Jer 45:3 3015
be filled with drunkenness and s, Ezk 23:33 3015
and found them sleeping from s, Lk 22:45 3077
to you, s has filled your heart. Jn 16:6 3077
that I have great s and unceasing Ro 9:2 3077
would not come to you in s again. 2Co 2:1 3077
For if I cause you s, 2Co 2:2 3076
I would not have s from those who 2Co 2:3 3077
But if any has caused s, 2Co 2:5 3076
sorrow, he has caused s not to me, 2Co 2:5 3076
might be overwhelmed by excessive s. 2Co 2:7 3077
I caused you s by my letter, 2Co 7:8 3076
see that that letter caused you s, 2Co 7:8 3076
For the s that is according to the 2Co 7:10 3077
the s of the world produces death. 2Co 7:10 3077
this very thing, this godly s, 2Co 7:11 3076
so that I would not have s upon Php 2:27 3077
that I would not have sorrow upon s. Php 2:27 3077
SORROWFUL
a very great and s lamentation; Gn 50:10 3515
me glad but the one whom I made s? 2Co 2:2 3076
not so that you would be made s, 2Co 2:4 3076
as s yet always rejoicing, as poor 2Co 6:10 3076
rejoice, not that you were made s, 2Co 7:9 3076
made s to the point of repentance; 2Co 7:9 3076
made s according to the will of God, 2Co 7:9 3076
seems not to be joyful, but s; Heb 12:11 3077
SORROWS
The s of those who have bartered Ps 16:4 6094
Many are the s of the wicked, Ps 32:10 4341
as one who s for a mother. Ps 35:14 57
man of s and acquainted with grief; Is 53:3 4341
bore, And our s He carried; Is 53:4 4341
person bears up under s when suffering 1Pe 2:19 3077
SORRY
The LORD was s that He had Gn 6:6 5162
I am s that I have made them." Gn 6:7 5162
And the sons of Israel were s for Jg 21:6 5162
And the people were s for Benjamin Jg 21:15 5162
there is none of you who is s for me 1Sa 22:8 2470a
saw and was s over the calamity, 1Ch 21:15 5162
S comforters are you all. Jb 16:2 5999
And be s for Your servants. Ps 90:13 5162
"I will not show pity nor be s Jer 13:14 2347
not pity and I will not be s; Ezk 24:14 5162
And although the king was very s, Mk 6:26 4036
SORT
of whatever s his uncleanness Lv 5:3
your neighbor a loan of any s, Dt 24:10 3972
with men of the common s. Ezk 23:42
7230, 120
and what s of person this woman is Lk 7:39 4217
what s of people ought you to be 2Pe 3:11 4217
SORTS
after its kind, all s of birds. Gn 7:14 3671
all s of baked food for Pharaoh, Gn 40:17
and once in ten days all s of wine Ne 5:18
money is a root of all s of evil, 1Tm 6:10
SOSIPATER
and so do Lucius and Jason and S, Ro 16:21 4989
SOSTHENES
And they all took hold of S, Ac 18:17 4988
will of God, and S our brother, 1Co 1:1 4988
SOTAI
the sons of S, the sons of Ezr 2:55 5479
the sons of S, the sons of Ne 7:57 5479
SOUGHT
brother, and he s a place to weep; Gn 43:30 1245
met him and s to put him to death. Ex 4:24 1245
And everyone who s the LORD would Ex 33:7 1245
he has s to seduce you from the LORD Dt 13:10 1245
The rock in which they s refuge? Dt 32:37 2620
had s them all along the road, Jos 2:22 1245
The LORD has s out for Himself a 1Sa 13:14 1245
passes by which Jonathan s to cross 1Sa 14:4 1245
And Saul s him every day, but God 1Sa 23:14 1245
Saul, your enemy, who s your life; 2Sa 4:8 1245
David s the presence of the LORD. 2Sa 21:1 1245
but Saul had s to kill them in his 2Sa 21:2 1245
Solomon s therefore to put 1Ki 11:40 1245
Solomon and the assembly s it out. 2Ch 1:5 1875
And he s many wives for them. 2Ch 11:23 7592
we have s the LORD our God; 2Ch 14:7 1875
we have s Him, and He has given us 2Ch 14:7 1875
God of Israel, and they s Him, 2Ch 15:4 1245
heart and had s Him earnestly, 2Ch 15:15 1245
but s the God of his father, 2Ch 17:4 1875
He also s Ahaziah, and they caught 2Ch 22:9 1245
who s the LORD with all his heart." 2Ch 22:9 1875
"Why have you s the gods of the 2Ch 25:15 1875
they had s the gods of Edom. 2Ch 25:20 1875
and as long as he s the LORD, 2Ch 26:5 1875
So we fasted and s our God Ezr 8:23 1245
they s out the Levites from all their Ne 12:27 1245
young virgins be s for the king. Es 2:2 1245
became angry and s to lay hands on Es 2:21 1245
Haman s to destroy all the Jews, Es 3:6 1245
that they had s to lay hands on Es 6:2 1245
hands on those who s their harm; Es 9:2 1245
one who s the good of his people Es 10:3 1875
I s the LORD, and He answered me, Ps 34:4 1875
I s for him, but he could not be Ps 37:36 1245
And violent men have s my life; Ps 54:3 1245
day of my trouble I s the Lord; Ps 77:2 1875
He killed them, then they s Him, Ps 78:34 1875
band of violent men have s my life, Ps 86:14 1245
With all my heart I have s You; Ps 119:10 1875
I s Your favor with all my heart; Ps 119:58 2470b
For I have s Your precepts. Ps 119:94 1875
they have s out many devices." Ec 7:29 1245
The Preacher s to find delightful Ec 12:10 1245
night I s him Whom my soul loves; SS 3:1 1245
I s him but did not find him. SS 3:1 1245
I s him but did not find him. SS 3:2 1245
inhabitants of Gebim have s refuge. Is 10:31 5756
O LORD, they s You in distress; Is 26:16 6485
"S out, a city not forsaken." Is 62:12 1875
"I permitted Myself to be s by Is 65:1 1875
gone after and which they have s, Jer 8:2 1875
stupid And have not s the LORD; Jer 10:21 1875
the king s to put him to death; Jer 26:21 1245
While they s food to restore their La 1:19 1245
though you will be s, Ezk 26:21 1245
back, nor have you s for the lost; Ezk 34:4 1245
so he s permission from the Da 1:8 1245
vision, I s to understand it; Da 8:15 1245
yet we have not s the favor of the Da 9:13 2470b
their God, Nor have they s Him, Hos 7:10 1245
He wept and s His favor. Hos 12:4 2603a
those who have not s the LORD or Zph 1:6 1245
those who s the Child's life are dead Mt 2:20 2212
When they s to seize Him, they Mt 21:46 2212
and s to hear the word of God. Ac 13:7 1934
we s to go into Macedonia, Ac 16:10 2212
But it is good always to be eagerly s Ga 4:18 2206
there would have been no occasion s Heb 8:7 2212
though he s for it with tears. Heb 12:17 1567a
SOUL
my s may bless you before I die." Gn 27:4 5315
"The s of my son Shechem longs Gn 34:8 5315
came about as her s was departing Gn 35:18 5315
because we saw the distress of his s Gn 42:21 5315
my s not enter into their council; Gn 49:6 5315
you, and My s will not reject you. Lv 26:11 5315
and if your s abhors My ordinances Lv 26:15 5315
eyes and cause the s to pine away; Lv 26:16 5315
for My s shall abhor you. Lv 26:30 5315
and their s abhorred My statutes. Lv 26:43 5315
and keep your s diligently, Dt 4:9 5315
all your heart and all your s. Dt 4:29 5315
all your heart and with all your s Dt 6:5 5315
your heart and with all your s, Dt 10:12 5315
all your heart and all your s, Dt 11:13 5315
mine on your heart and on your s; Dt 11:18 5315
your heart and with all your s. Dt 13:3 5315
your friend who is as your own s, Dt 13:6 5315
your heart and with all your s. Dt 26:16 5315
failing of eyes, and despair of s. Dt 28:65 5315
obey Him with all your heart and s Dt 30:2 5315
your heart and with all your s, Dt 30:6 5315
God with all your heart and s. Dt 30:10 5315
your heart and with all your s." Jos 22:5 5315
O my s, march on with strength. Jg 5:21 5315
that his s was annoyed to death. Jg 16:16 5315
poured out my s before the LORD. 1Sa 1:15 5315
As your s lives, my lord, I am the 1Sa 1:26 5315
from weeping and your s grieve, 1Sa 2:33 5315
what is in My heart and in My s; 1Sa 2:35 5315
that the s of Jonathan was knit to 1Sa 18:1 5315
was knit to the s of David, 1Sa 18:1 5315
LORD lives and as your s lives, 1Sa 20:3 5315
all the desire of your s to do so; 1Sa 23:20 5315
LORD lives, and as your s lives, 1Sa 25:26 5315
over all that your s desires." 2Sa 3:21 5315
blind, who are hated by David's s, 2Sa 5:8 5315
your life and the life of your s, 2Sa 11:11 5315
"As your s lives, my lord the 2Sa 14:19 5315
their heart and with all their s, 1Ki 2:4 5315
all their heart and with all their s 1Ki 8:48 5315
for her s is troubled within her; 2Ki 4:27 5315
with all his heart and all his s, 2Ki 23:3 5315
with all his heart and with all his s 2Ki 23:25 5315
your s to seek the LORD your God; 1Ch 22:19 5315
with all their s in the land of their 2Ch 6:38 5315
with all their heart and s; 2Ch 15:12 5315
all his heart and with all his s, 2Ch 34:31 5315
And life to the bitter of s, Jb 3:20 5315
"My s refuses to touch them; Jb 6:7 5315
in the bitterness of my s. Jb 7:11 5315
my s would choose suffocation, Jb 7:15 5315
speak in the bitterness of my s. Jb 10:1 5315
another dies with a bitter s, Jb 21:25 5315
And what His s desires, that He Jb 23:13 5315
Almighty, who has embittered my s, Jb 27:2 5315
now my s is poured out within me; Jb 30:16 5315
Was not my s grieved for the needy? Jb 30:25 5315
He keeps back his s from the pit, Jb 33:18 5315
bread, And his s favorite food. Jb 33:20 5315
"Then his s draws near to the Jb 33:22 5315
He has redeemed my s from going Jb 33:28 5315
To bring back his s from the pit, Jb 33:30 5315
Many are saying of my s, Ps 3:2 5315
And my s is greatly dismayed; Ps 6:3 5315
Return, O LORD, rescue my s; Ps 6:4 5315
Or he will tear my s like a lion, Ps 7:2 5315
enemy pursue my s and overtake it; Ps 7:5 5315
How can you say to my s, Ps 11:1 5315
one who loves violence His s hates. Ps 11:5 5315
long shall I take counsel in my s, Ps 13:2 5315
will not abandon my s to Sheol; Ps 16:10 5315
Deliver my s from the wicked with Ps 17:13 5315
LORD is perfect, restoring the s; Ps 19:7 5315
Deliver my s from the sword, My Ps 22:20 5315
he who cannot keep his s alive. Ps 22:29 5315
He restores my s; Ps 23:3 5315
not lifted up his s to falsehood And Ps 24:4 5315
To You, O LORD, I lift up my s. Ps 25:1 5315
His s will abide in prosperity, Ps 25:13 5315
Guard my s and deliver me; Ps 25:20 5315
take my s away along with sinners, Ps 26:9 5315
have brought up my s from Sheol; Ps 30:3 5315
That my s may sing praise to You and Ps 30:12 3519b
have known the troubles of my s, Ps 31:7 5315
from grief, my s and my body also. Ps 31:9 5315
To deliver their s from death And Ps 33:19 5315
Our s waits for the LORD; Ps 33:20 5315
My s will make its boast in the Ps 34:2 5315
LORD redeems the s of His servants, Ps 34:22 5315
Say to my s, "I am your salvation." Ps 35:3 5315
cause they dug a pit for my s. Ps 35:7 5315
my s shall rejoice in the LORD; Ps 35:9 5315
good, To the bereavement of my s. Ps 35:12 5315
I humbled my s with fasting, Ps 35:13 5315
Rescue my s from their ravages, My Ps 35:17 5315
Heal my s, for I have sinned Ps 41:4 5315
brooks, So my s pants for You, Ps 42:1 5315
My s thirsts for God, for the Ps 42:2 5315
and I pour out my s within me. Ps 42:4 5315
Why are you in despair, O my s? Ps 42:5 5315
God, my s is in despair within me; Ps 42:6 5315
Why are you in despair, O my s? Ps 42:11 5315
Why are you in despair, O my s? Ps 43:5 5315
our s has sunk down into the dust; Ps 44:25 5315
the redemption of his s is costly, Ps 49:8 5315
But God will redeem my s from the Ps 49:15 5315

Context	Reference	Number
The Lord is the sustainer of my s.	Ps 54:4	5315
He will redeem my s in peace from	Ps 55:18	5315
have delivered my s from death,	Ps 56:13	5315
me, For my s takes refuge in You;	Ps 57:1	5315
My s is among lions;	Ps 57:4	5315
My s is bowed down;	Ps 57:6	5315
My s *waits* in silence for God only;	Ps 62:1	5315
My s, wait in silence for God	Ps 62:5	5315
My s thirsts for You, my flesh	Ps 63:1	5315
My s is satisfied as with marrow	Ps 63:5	5315
My s clings to You;	Ps 63:8	5315
tell of what He has done for my s.	Ps 66:16	5315
When I wept in my s with fasting,	Ps 69:10	5315
draw near to my s *and* redeem it;	Ps 69:18	5315
those who are adversaries of my s	Ps 71:13	5315
And my s, which You have redeemed.	Ps 71:23	5315
Do not deliver the s of Your	Ps 74:19	5315
My s refused to be comforted.	Ps 77:2	5315
He did not spare their s from death,	Ps 78:50	5315
My s longed and even yearned for	Ps 84:2	5315
Preserve my s, for I am a godly	Ps 86:2	5315
Make glad the s of Your servant,	Ps 86:4	5315
to You, O Lord, I lift up my s.	Ps 86:4	5315
And You have delivered my s from	Ps 86:13	5315
For my s has had enough troubles,	Ps 88:3	5315
O LORD, why do You reject my s?	Ps 88:14	5315
Can he deliver his s from the power	Ps 89:48	5315
My s would soon have dwelt in *the*	Ps 94:17	5315
me, Your consolations delight my s.	Ps 94:19	5315
Bless the LORD, O my s,	Ps 103:1	5315
Bless the LORD, O my s,	Ps 103:2	5315
Bless the LORD, O my s!	Ps 103:22	5315
Bless the LORD, O my s!	Ps 104:1	5315
Bless the LORD, O my s.	Ps 104:35	5315
Their s fainted within them.	Ps 107:5	5315
He has satisfied the thirsty s,	Ps 107:9	5315
And the hungry s He has filled	Ps 107:9	5315
Their s abhorred all kinds of food,	Ps 107:18	5315
Their s melted away in *their* misery.	Ps 107:26	5315
will sing praises, even with my s.	Ps 108:1	3519b
those who speak evil against my s.	Ps 109:20	5315
him from those who judge his s.	Ps 109:31	5315
Return to your rest, O my s,	Ps 116:7	5315
You have rescued my s from death,	Ps 116:8	5315
My s is crushed with longing After	Ps 119:20	5315
My s cleaves to the dust;	Ps 119:25	5315
My s weeps because of grief;	Ps 119:28	5315
My s languishes for Your salvation;	Ps 119:81	5315
Therefore my s observes them.	Ps 119:129	5315
My s keeps Your testimonies, And I	Ps 119:167	5315
my s live that it may praise You,	Ps 119:175	5315
Deliver my s, O LORD, from lying	Ps 120:2	5315
Too long has my s had its dwelling	Ps 120:6	5315
He will keep your s.	Ps 121:7	5315
Our s is greatly filled With the	Ps 123:4	5315
would have swept over our s;	Ps 124:4	5315
would have swept over our s."	Ps 124:5	5315
Our s has escaped as a bird out of	Ps 124:7	5315
wait for the LORD, my s does wait,	Ps 130:5	5315
My s *waits* for the Lord More than	Ps 130:6	5315
I have composed and quieted my s;	Ps 131:2	5315
My s is like a weaned child within	Ps 131:2	5315
me bold with strength in my s.	Ps 138:3	5315
And my s knows it very well.	Ps 139:14	5315
No one cares for my s.	Ps 142:4	5315
"Bring my s out of prison, So	Ps 142:7	5315
the enemy has persecuted my s;	Ps 143:3	5315
My s *longs* for You, as a parched	Ps 143:6	5315
For to You I lift up my s.	Ps 143:8	5315
bring my s out of trouble.	Ps 143:11	5315
all those who afflict my s,	Ps 143:12	5315
Praise the LORD, O my s!	Ps 146:1	5315
will be pleasant to your s;	Pr 2:10	5315
So they will be life to your s And	Pr 3:22	5315
The s of the sluggard craves and	Pr 13:4	5315
the s of the diligent is made fat.	Pr 13:4	5315
Desire realized is sweet to the s,	Pr 13:19	5315
Sweet to the s and healing to the	Pr 16:24	5315
his lips are the snare of his s.	Pr 18:7	5315
He who gets wisdom loves his own s;	Pr 19:8	5315
keeps the commandment keeps his s,	Pr 19:16	5315
The s of the wicked desires evil;	Pr 21:10	5315
Guards his s from troubles.	Pr 21:23	5315
rod And rescue his s from Sheol.	Pr 23:14	5315
He not know *it* who keeps your s?	Pr 24:12	5315
that wisdom is thus for your s;	Pr 24:14	5315
he refreshes the s of his masters.	Pr 25:13	5315
Like cold water to a weary s,	Pr 25:25	5315
He will also delight your s.	Pr 29:17	5315
his s lacks nothing of all that he	Ec 6:2	5315
but his s is not satisfied with	Ec 6:3	5315
is better than what the s desires.	Ec 6:9	5315
"Tell me, O you whom my s loves,	SS 1:7	5315
I sought him Whom my s loves;	SS 3:1	5315
I must seek him whom my s loves.'	SS 3:2	5315
you seen him whom my s loves?'	SS 3:3	5315
When I found him whom my s loves;	SS 3:4	5315
my s set me *Over* the chariots of	SS 6:12	5315
fruitful garden, both s and body,	Is 10:18	5315
His s trembles within him.	Is 15:4	5315
laborers will be grieved in s.	Is 19:10	5315
At night my s longs for You,	Is 26:9	5315
'I composed *my* s until morning.	Is 38:13	5315
because of the bitterness of my s.	Is 38:15	5315
It is You who has kept my s from	Is 38:17	5315
chosen one *in whom* My s delights.	Is 42:1	5315
a result of the anguish of His s,	Is 53:11	5315
LORD, My s will exult in my God;	Is 61:10	5315
And their s delights in their	Is 66:3	5315
My s, my soul! I am in anguish!	Jer 4:19	4578
My soul, my s! I am in anguish!	Jer 4:19	4578
Because you have heard, O my s,	Jer 4:19	5315
I have given the beloved of My s	Jer 12:7	5315
My s will sob in secret for *such*	Jer 13:17	5315
He has delivered the s of the needy	Jer 20:13	5315
I will fill the s of the priests with	Jer 31:14	5315
all My heart and with all My s.	Jer 32:41	5315
comforter, One who restores my s.	La 1:16	5315
My s has been rejected from peace;	La 3:17	5315
Surely my s remembers And is bowed	La 3:20	5315
"The LORD is my portion," says my s,	La 3:24	5315
My eyes bring pain to my s Because	La 3:51	5315
the s of the father as well as the	Ezk 18:4	5315
as well as the s of the son is Mine.	Ezk 18:4	5315
The s who sins will die.	Ezk 18:4	5315
eyes and the delight of your s;	Ezk 24:21	5315
rejoiced with all the scorn of your s	Ezk 25:6	5315
have taken vengeance with scorn of s	Ezk 25:15	5315
will weep for you in bitterness of s	Ezk 27:31	5315
joy *and* with scorn of s,	Ezk 36:5	5315
and begged with *all* his s to die,	Jon 4:8	5315
of my body for the sin of my s?	Mi 6:7	5315
man speaks the desire of his s;	Mi 7:3	5315
His s is not right within him;	Hab 2:4	5315
for my s was impatient with them,	Zch 11:8	5315
and their s also was weary of me.	Zch 11:8	5315
but are unable to kill the s;	Mt 10:28	*5590*
destroy both s and body in hell.	Mt 10:28	*5590*
IN WHOM MY S IS WELL-PLEASED;	Mt 12:18	*5590*
whole world and forfeits his s?	Mt 16:26	*5590*
a man give in exchange for his s?	Mt 16:26	*5590*
YOUR HEART, AND WITH ALL YOUR S,	Mt 22:37	*5590*
"My s is deeply grieved, to the	Mt 26:38	*5590*
whole world, and forfeit his s?	Mk 8:36	*5590*
a man give in exchange for his s?	Mk 8:37	*5590*
YOUR HEART, AND WITH ALL YOUR S,	Mk 12:30	*5590*
"My s is deeply grieved to the	Mk 14:34	*5590*
"My s exalts the Lord,	Lk 1:46	*5590*
a sword will pierce even your own s	Lk 2:35	*5590*
YOUR HEART, AND WITH ALL YOUR S,	Lk 10:27	*5590*
'And I will say to my s,	Lk 12:19	*5590*
"S, you have many goods laid up	Lk 12:19	*5590*
night your s is required of you;	Lk 12:20	*5590*
"Now My s has become troubled;	Jn 12:27	*5590*
WILL NOT ABANDON MY S TO HADES,	Ac 2:27	*5590*
that every s that does not heed that	Ac 3:23	*5590*
believed were of one heart and s;	Ac 4:32	*5590*
for every s of man who does evil,	Ro 2:9	*5590*
MAN, Adam, BECAME A LIVING S."	1Co 15:45	*5590*
But I call God as witness to my s,	2Co 1:23	*5590*
and may your spirit and s and body	1Th 5:23	*5590*
as the division of s and spirit,	Heb 4:12	*5590*
we have as an anchor of the s,	Heb 6:19	*5590*
BACK, MY S HAS NO PLEASURE IN HIM.	Heb 10:38	*5590*
faith to the preserving of the s.	Heb 10:39	*5590*
way will save his s from death and	Jas 5:20	*5590*
which wage war against the s.	1Pe 2:11	*5590*
felt *his* righteous s tormented day	2Pe 2:8	*5590*
health, just as your s prospers.	3Jn 1:2	*5590*

SOUL'S

Context	Reference	Number
Lord, You have pleaded my s cause;	La 3:58	5315

SOULS

Context	Reference	Number
month, you shall humble your s and	Lv 16:29	5315
you, that you may humble your s;	Lv 16:31	5315
to make atonement for your s;	Lv 17:11	5315
and you shall humble your s and	Lv 23:27	5315
you, and you shall humble your s;	Lv 23:32	5315
in all your hearts and in all your s	Jos 23:14	5315
And the s of the wounded cry out;	Jb 24:12	5315
preserves the s of His godly ones;	Ps 97:10	5315
life, And he who is wise wins s.	Pr 11:30	5315
memory, is the desire of *our* s.	Is 26:8	5315
you will find rest for your s.	Jer 6:16	5315
"Behold, all s are Mine;	Ezk 18:4	5315
YOU WILL FIND REST FOR YOUR S.	Mt 11:29	*5590*
were added about three thousand s.	Ac 2:41	*5590*
strengthening the s of the disciples,	Ac 14:22	*5590*
their words, unsettling your s,	Ac 15:24	*5590*
spend and be expended for your s.	2Co 12:15	*5590*
for they keep watch over your s as	Heb 13:17	*5590*
which is able to save your s.	Jas 1:21	*5590*
faith the salvation of your s.	1Pe 1:9	*5590*
purified your s for a sincere love of	1Pe 1:22	*5590*
Shepherd and Guardian of your s.	1Pe 2:25	*5590*
entrust their s to a faithful Creator	1Pe 4:19	*5590*
from sin, enticing unstable s,	2Pe 2:14	*5590*
the s of those who had been slain	Rv 6:9	*5590*
s of those who had been beheaded	Rv 20:4	*5590*

SOUND

Context	Reference	Number
They heard the s of the LORD	Gn 3:8	6963
I heard the s of You in the garden,	Gn 3:10	6963
and a very loud trumpet s,	Ex 19:16	6963
When the s of the trumpet grew	Ex 19:19	6963
flashes and the s of the trumpet and	Ex 20:18	6963
Joshua heard the s of the people as	Ex 32:17	6963
"There is a s of war in the camp."	Ex 32:17	6963
It is not the s of the cry of triumph,	Ex 32:18	6963
is it the s of the cry of defeat;	Ex 32:18	6963
But the s of singing I hear."	Ex 32:18	6963
'You shall then s a ram's horn	Lv 25:9	5674a
s a horn all through your land.	Lv 25:9	5674a
And the s of a driven leaf will	Lv 26:36	6963
s an alarm with the trumpets,	Nu 10:9	7321
LORD heard the s of your words,	Dt 1:34	6963
you heard the s of words, but you	Dt 4:12	6963
you hear the s of the trumpet,	Jos 6:5	6963
people heard the s of the trumpet,	Jos 6:20	6963
for he was s asleep and exhausted.	Jg 4:21	7290a
"At the s of those who divide	Jg 5:11	6963
because a s sleep from the LORD	1Sa 26:12	8639
when you hear the s of marching in	2Sa 5:24	6963
shouting and the s of the trumpet.	2Sa 6:15	6963
as you hear the s of the trumpet,	2Sa 15:10	6963
Joab heard the s of the trumpet,	1Ki 1:41	6963
When Ahijah heard the s of her feet	1Ki 14:6	6963
s of the roar of a *heavy* shower."	1Ki 18:41	6963
the fire a s of a gentle blowing.	1Ki 19:12	6963
there was no s or response.	2Ki 4:31	6963
Is not the s of his master's feet	2Ki 6:32	6963
a s of chariots and a sound of horses,	2Ki 7:6	6963
of chariots and a s of horses,	2Ki 7:6	6963
even the s of a great army,	2Ki 7:6	6963
when you hear the s of marching	1Ch 14:15	6963
to s aloud cymbals of bronze;	1Ch 15:19	8085
shouting, and with s of the horn,	1Ch 15:28	6963
for those who should s aloud,	1Ch 16:42	8085
to s the alarm against you.	2Ch 13:12	7321
distinguish the s of the shout of joy	Ezr 3:13	6963
s of the weeping of the people,	Ezr 3:13	6963
and the s was heard far away.	Ezr 3:13	6963
you hear the s of the trumpet,	Ne 4:20	6963
For s wisdom has two sides.	Jb 11:6	8454
With Him are strength and s wisdom,	Jb 12:16	8454
And rejoice at the s of the flute.	Jb 21:12	6963
flute to the s of those who weep.	Jb 30:31	6963
I have heard the s of *your* words:	Jb 33:8	6963
night, When s sleep falls on men,	Jb 33:15	8639
Listen to the s of my words.	Jb 34:16	6963
Heed the s of my cry for help, my	Ps 5:2	6963
deep at the s of Your waterfalls;	Ps 42:7	6963
The LORD, with the s of a trumpet.	Ps 47:5	6963
peoples, And s His praise abroad,	Ps 66:8	8085, 6963
The skies gave forth a s;	Ps 77:17	6963
The s of Your thunder was in the	Ps 77:18	6963
the people who know the joyful s!	Ps 89:15	8643
With the lyre and the s of melody.	Ps 98:5	6963
With trumpets and the s of the horn	Ps 98:6	6963
At the s of Your thunder they	Ps 104:7	6963
cannot make a s with their throat.	Ps 115:7	1897
The s of joyful shouting and	Ps 118:15	6963
Praise Him with trumpet s;	Ps 150:3	8629
He stores up s wisdom for the	Pr 2:7	8454
Keep s wisdom and discretion,	Pr 3:21	8454
For I give you s teaching;	Pr 4:2	2896a
"Counsel is mine and s wisdom;	Pr 8:14	8454
He quarrels against all s wisdom.	Pr 18:1	8454
bird of the heavens will carry the s and	Ec 10:20	6963
the s of the grinding mill is low,	Ec 12:4	6963
will arise at the s of the bird,	Ec 12:4	6963
the head There is nothing s in it,	Is 1:6	4974
A s of tumult on the mountains,	Is 13:4	6963
A s of the uproar of kingdoms, Of	Is 13:4	6963
to you at the s of your cry;	Is 30:19	6963
heart as when one marches to *the* s	Is 30:29	
At the s of the tumult peoples flee;	Is 33:3	6963
with the s of joyful shouting,	Is 48:20	6963
Thanksgiving and s of a melody.	Is 51:3	6963
of weeping and the s of crying.	Is 65:19	6963
O my soul, The s of the trumpet,	Jer 4:19	6963
And hear the s of the trumpet?	Jer 4:21	6963
At the s of the horseman and	Jer 4:29	6963
'Listen to the s of the trumpet!'	Jer 6:17	6963
At the s of the neighing of his	Jer 8:16	6963
The s of a report!	Jer 10:22	6963
the s of the millstones and the	Jer 25:10	6963
the s of the cry of the shepherds,	Jer 25:36	6963
'I have heard a s of terror, Of	Jer 30:5	6963
not see war or hear the s of a trumpet	Jer 42:14	6963
"Its s moves along like a serpent;	Jer 46:22	6963
"The s of an outcry from	Jer 48:3	6963
There is a s of fugitives and refugees	Jer 50:28	6963
The s of an outcry from Babylon,	Jer 51:54	6963
I also heard the s of their wings	Ezk 1:24	6963
like the s of abundant waters	Ezk 1:24	6963
a s of tumult like the sound of an	Ezk 1:24	6963
tumult like the s of an army camp;	Ezk 1:24	6963
a great rumbling s behind me,	Ezk 3:12	6963
s of the wings of the living	Ezk 3:13	6963
the s of the wheels beside them,	Ezk 3:13	6963
them, even a great rumbling s.	Ezk 3:13	6963
the s of the wings of the cherubim	Ezk 10:5	6963
Because of the s of his roaring.	Ezk 19:7	6963
"The s of a carefree multitude	Ezk 23:42	6963
I will silence the s of your songs,	Ezk 26:13	1995
and the s of your harps will be	Ezk 26:13	6963
coastlands shake at the s of your fall	Ezk 26:15	6963
"At the s of the cry of your pilots	Ezk 27:28	6963
the nations quake at the s of its fall	Ezk 31:16	6963
he who hears the s of the trumpet	Ezk 33:4	6963
'He heard the s of the trumpet but	Ezk 33:5	6963
was like the s of many waters;	Ezk 43:2	6963
moment you hear the s of the horn,	Da 3:5	7032a
peoples heard the s of the horn,	Da 3:7	7032a
man who hears the s of the horn,	Da 3:10	7032a
moment you hear the s of the horn,	Da 3:15	7032a
because of the s of the boastful words	Da 7:11	7032a
and the s of his words like the	Da 10:6	6963
his words like the s of a tumult.	Da 10:6	6963
But I heard the s of his words;	Da 10:9	6963
as I heard the s of his words,	Da 10:9	6963
S an alarm at Beth-aven:	Hos 5:8	7321
s an alarm on My holy mountain!	Jl 2:1	7321
war cries and the s of a trumpet.	Am 2:2	6963
listen to the s of your harps.	Am 5:23	2172
improvise to the s of the harp,	Am 6:5	6310

lain down and fallen **s** asleep. **Jon 1:5** 7290a
it is **s** wisdom to fear Your name: **Mi 6:9** 8454
are moaning like the **s** of doves, **Na 2:7** 6963
At the **s** my lips quivered. **Hab 3:16** 6963
the **s** of a cry from the Fish Gate, **Zph 1:10** 6963
is a **s** of the shepherds' wail, **Zch 11:3** 6963
is a **s** of the young lions' roar, **Zch 11:3** 6963
do not **s** a trumpet before you, **Mt 6:2** *4537*
when the **s** of your greeting **Lk 1:44** *5456*
has received him back safe and **s**.' **Lk 15:27** *5198*
wishes and you hear the **s** of it, **Jn 3:8** *5456*
And when this **s** occurred, the **Ac 2:6** *5456*
to think so as to have **s** judgment, **Ro 12:3** *4993*
flute or harp, in producing a **s**, **1Co 14:7** *5456*
bugle produces an indistinct **s**, **1Co 14:8** *5456*
for the trumpet will **s**, **1Co 15:52** *4537*
if we are of **s** mind, it is for you. **2Co 5:13** *4993*
else is contrary to **s** teaching, **1Tm 1:10** *5198*
the **s** doctrine which you have been **1Tm 4:6** *2570*
and does not agree with **s** words, **1Tm 6:3** *5198*
Retain the standard of **s** words **2Tm 1:13** *5198*
they will not endure **s** doctrine; **2Tm 4:3** *5198*
to exhort in **s** doctrine and to refute **Ti 1:9** *5198*
that they may be **s** in the faith, **Ti 1:13** *5198*
which are fitting for **s** doctrine. **Ti 2:1** *5198*
dignified, sensible, **s** in faith, **Ti 2:2** *5198*
s *in* speech which is beyond **Ti 2:8** *5199*
blast of a trumpet and the **s** of words **Heb 12:19** *5456*
and the sound of words which **s** *was* **Heb 12:19**
be of **s** judgment and sober *spirit* **1Pe 4:7** *4993*
behind me a loud voice like *the* **s** **Rv 1:10**
was like the **s** of many waters. **Rv 1:15** *5456*
like *the* **s** of a trumpet speaking **Rv 4:1**
prepared themselves to **s** them. **Rv 8:6** *4537*
three angels who are about to **s**!" **Rv 8:13** *4537*
and the **s** of their wings was like **Rv 9:9** *5456*
wings was like the **s** of chariots, **Rv 9:9** *5456*
angel, when he is about to **s**, **Rv 10:7** *4537*
like the **s** of many waters and like **Rv 14:2** *5456*
and like the **s** of loud thunder, **Rv 14:2** *5456*
which I heard *was* like the **s** **Rv 14:2**
"And the **s** of harpists and **Rv 18:22** *5456*
and the **s** of a mill will not be **Rv 18:22** *5456*
and like the **s** of many waters **Rv 19:6** *5456*
the **s** of mighty peals of thunder, **Rv 19:6** *5456*

SOUNDED

When I have **s** out my father about **1Sa 20:12** 2713
also sang and the trumpets **s**; **2Ch 29:28** 2690
little ones have **s** out a cry *of distress.* **Jer 48:4** 8085
word of the Lord has **s** forth from **1Th 1:8** *1837*
The first **s**, and there came **Rv 8:7** *4537*
The second angel **s**, **Rv 8:8** *4537*
The third angel **s**, **Rv 8:10** *4537*
The fourth angel **s**, **Rv 8:12** *4537*
Then the fifth angel **s**, **Rv 9:1** *4537*
Then the sixth angel **s**, **Rv 9:13** *4537*
Then the seventh angel **s**; **Rv 11:15** *4537*

SOUNDING

you shall blow without **s** an alarm. **Nu 10:7** 7321
The sweet **s** lyre with the harp. **Ps 81:2** 5273b
little farther on they took another **s** **Ac 27:28** *1001*

SOUNDINGS

They took **s** and found *it to* **Ac 27:28** *1001*

SOUNDNESS

There is no **s** in my flesh because **Ps 38:3** 4974
And there is no **s** in my flesh. **Ps 38:7** 4974

SOUNDS

When the ram's horn **s** a long blast, **Ex 19:13** 4900
cymbals, to raise **s** of joy. **1Ch 15:16** 6963
"**S** of terror are in his ears; **Jb 15:21** 6963
"As often as the trumpet **s** he **Jb 39:25**
More than the **s** of many waters, **Ps 93:4** 6963
tumult of their voices **s** forth. **Jer 51:55** 5414
and **s** and peals of thunder. **Rv 4:5** *5456*
there followed peals of thunder and **s** **Rv 8:5** *5456*
lightning and **s** and peals of thunder **Rv 11:19** *5456*
and **s** and peals of thunder; **Rv 16:18** *5456*

SOUR

'The fathers have eaten **s** grapes, **Jer 31:29** 1155
each man who eats the **s** grapes, **Jer 31:30** 1155
'The fathers eat the **s** grapes, **Ezk 18:2** 1155
sponge, he filled it with **s** wine and **Mt 27:48** *3690*
and filled a sponge with **s** wine, **Mk 15:36** *3690*
up to Him, offering Him **s** wine, **Lk 23:36** *3690*
jar full of **s** wine was standing there; **Jn 19:29** *3690*
they put a sponge full of the **s** wine **Jn 19:29** *3690*
Jesus had received the **s** wine, **Jn 19:30** *3690*

SOURCE

"Its rocks are the **s** of sapphires, **Jb 28:6** 4725
"The baptism of John was from what **s**, **Mt 21:25**
Him the **s** of eternal salvation, **Heb 5:9** *159a*
What is the **s** of quarrels and **Jas 4:1** *4159*
Is not the **s** your pleasures that **Jas 4:1** *1782*

SOUTH

and to the north and to the **s**; **Gn 28:14** 5045
twenty boards for the **s** side. **Ex 26:18** 8486
of the tabernacle toward the **s**; **Ex 26:35** 8486
On the **s** side *there shall be* **Ex 27:9** 5045, 8486
twenty boards for the **s** side; **Ex 36:23** 5045, 8486
for the **s** side the hangings of the **Ex 38:9** 5045, 8486
on the **s** side of the tabernacle. **Ex 40:24** 5045
"On the **s** side *shall be* the **Nu 2:10** 8486
on the **s** side shall set out; **Nu 10:6** 8486
the **s** to the ascent of Akrabbim and **Nu 34:4** 5045
shall be to the **s** of Kadesh-barnea; **Nu 34:4** 5045
on the **s** side two thousand cubits, **Nu 35:5** 5045
the west and north and **s** and east, **Dt 3:27** 8486
possession of the sea and the **s**." **Dt 33:23** 1864
s of Chinneroth and in the lowland **Jos 11:2** 5045
Beth-jeshimoth, and on the **s**, **Jos 12:3** 8486
to the **s**, all the land of the **Jos 13:4** 8486
of Zin at the extreme **s**. **Jos 15:1** 8486
Their **s** border was from the **Jos 15:2** 5045
from the bay that turns to the **s**. **Jos 15:2** 5045
went up by the **s** of Kadesh-barnea **Jos 15:3** 5045
This shall be your **s** border. **Jos 15:4** 5045
which is on the **s** of the valley; **Jos 15:7** 5045
slope of the Jebusite on the **s** **Jos 15:8** 5045
in the **s** were Kabzeel and Eder and **Jos 15:21** 5045
The **s** side *belonged* to Ephraim and **Jos 17:10** 5045
stay in its territory on the **s**, **Jos 18:5** 5045
lies on the **s** of lower Beth-horon. **Jos 18:13** 5045
Then the **s** side *was* from the edge **Jos 18:15** 5045
Sea, at the **s** end of the Jordan. **Jos 18:19** 5045
This *was* the **s** border. **Jos 18:19** 5045
it reached to Zebulun on the **s** and **Jos 19:34** 5045
Judah which is in the **s** of Arad; **Jg 1:16** 5045
and on the **s** side of Lebonah." **Jg 21:19** 5045
the other on the **s** opposite Geba. **1Sa 14:5** 5045
David rose from the **s** side and **1Sa 20:41** 5045
which is on the **s** of Jeshimon? **1Sa 23:19** 3225
the Arabah to the **s** of Jeshimon. **1Sa 23:24** 3225
they went out to the **s** of Judah, **2Sa 24:7** 5045
three facing west, three facing **s**, **1Ki 7:25** 5045
the house eastward toward the **s**. **1Ki 7:39** 5045
to the east, west, north and **s**. **1Ch 9:24** 5045
For Obed-edom *it fell* to the **s**, **1Ch 26:15** 5045
four daily, on the **s** four daily, **1Ch 26:17** 5045
three facing west, three facing **s** and **2Ch 4:4** 5045
And the chambers of the **s**; **Jb 9:9** 8486
"Out of the **s** comes the storm, **Jb 37:9** 2315
land is still because of the **s** wind? **Jb 37:17** 1864
Stretching his wings toward the **s**? **Jb 39:26** 8486
His power He directed the **s** wind. **Ps 78:26** 8486
The north and the **s**, **Ps 89:12** 3225
From the north and from the **s**. **Ps 107:3** 3220
O LORD, As the streams in the **S**. **Ps 126:4** 5045
Blowing toward the **s**, **Ec 1:6** 1864
toward the **s** or toward the north, **Ec 11:3** 1864
wind, And come, *wind of* the **s**; **SS 4:16** 8486
to the **s**, 'Do not hold *them* back.' **Is 43:6** 8486
sister, who lives **s** of you, **Ezk 16:46** 3225
and speak out against the **s** and **Ezk 20:46** 1864
whole surface from **s** to north will **Ezk 20:47** 5045
against all flesh from **s** *to* north. **Ezk 21:4** 5045
and on it to the **s** *there was a* **Ezk 40:2** 5045
Then he led me toward the **s**, **Ezk 40:24** 1864
there was a gate toward the **s**; **Ezk 40:24** 1864
court had a gate toward the **s**; **Ezk 40:27** 1864
from gate to gate toward the **s**, **Ezk 40:27** 1864
to the inner court by the **s** gate; **Ezk 40:28** 1864
and he measured the **s** gate **Ezk 40:28** 1864
gate, with its front toward the **s**, **Ezk 40:44** 1864
and one at the side of the **s** gate **Ezk 40:44**
chamber which faces toward the **s**, **Ezk 40:45** 1864
and another doorway toward the **s**; **Ezk 41:11** 1864
chambers which were toward the **s** **Ezk 42:12** 1864
north chambers *and* the **s** chambers, **Ezk 42:13** 1864
On the **s** side he measured five **Ezk 42:18** 1864
shall go out by way of the **s** gate. **Ezk 46:9** 5045
he who enters by way of the **s** gate **Ezk 46:9** 5045
of the house, from **s** of the altar. **Ezk 47:1** 5045
was trickling from the **s** side. **Ezk 47:2** 3233
"The **s** side toward the south **Ezk 47:19** 5045
"The south side toward the **s** **Ezk 47:19** 8486
is the **s** side toward the south. **Ezk 47:19** 8486
is the south side toward the **s**. **Ezk 47:19** 5045
from the **s** border to a point **Ezk 47:20**
and toward the **s** 25,000 in length; **Ezk 48:10** 5045
cubits, the **s** side 4,500 *cubits,* **Ezk 48:16** 5045
250 *cubits,* on the **s** 250 *cubits,* **Ezk 48:17** 5045
at the **s** side toward the south, **Ezk 48:28** 5045
at the south side toward the **s**, **Ezk 48:28** 8486
"On the **s** side, 4,500 *cubits* **Ezk 48:33** 5045
exceedingly great toward the **s**, **Da 8:9** 5045
king of the **S** will grow strong, **Da 11:5** 5045
and the daughter of the king of the **S** **Da 11:6** 5045
the realm of the king of the **S**, **Da 11:9** 5045
"The king of the **S** will be **Da 11:11** 5045
rise up against the king of the **S**; **Da 11:14** 5045
forces of the **S** will not stand *their* **Da 11:15** 5045
king of the **S** with a large army; **Da 11:25** 5045
so the king of the **S** will mobilize **Da 11:25** 5045
will return and come into the **S**, **Da 11:29** 5045
king of the **S** will collide with him, **Da 11:40** 5045
ones go forth to the **s** country. **Zch 6:6** 8486
march in the storm winds of the **s**. **Zch 9:14** 8486
and the other half toward the **s**. **Zch 14:4** 5045
Geba to Rimmon **s** of Jerusalem; **Zch 14:10** 5045
"*The* Queen of *the* **S** will rise up **Mt 12:42** *3558*
"The Queen of the **S** will rise up **Lk 11:31** *3558*
"And when *you see* a **s** wind blowing, **Lk 12:55** *3558*
and west and from north and **s**, **Lk 13:29** *3558*
"Get up and go **s** to the road **Ac 8:26** *3314*
When a moderate **s** wind came up, **Ac 27:13** *3558*
a day later a **s** wind sprang up, **Ac 28:13** *3558*
three gates on the **s** and three gates **Rv 21:13** *3558*

SOUTHEAST

side *of the house* toward the **s**. **2Ch 4:10** 5045, 6924b

SOUTHERN

'Your **s** sector shall extend from **Nu 34:3** 5045
and your **s** border shall extend **Nu 34:3** 5045

SOUTHWARD

and **s** and eastward and westward; **Gn 13:14** 5045
on the **s** side of the tabernacle, **Nu 3:29** 8486
s to the wilderness of Zin at the **Jos 15:1** 5045
Then it proceeded **s** to the ascent **Jos 15:3** 5045
then the border went **s** to the **Jos 17:7** 3225
brook of Kanah, **s** of the brook **Jos 17:9** 5045
side of Luz (that is, Bethel) **s**; **Jos 18:13** 5045
turned round on the west side **s**, **Jos 18:14** 5045
which *lies* before Beth-horon **s**; **Jos 18:14** 5045
to the slope of the Jebusite **s**, **Jos 18:16** 5045
westward, northward, and **s**, **Da 8:4** 5045

SOUTHWEST

of Crete, facing **s** and northwest, **Ac 27:12** *3047*

SOVEREIGN

He who is the blessed and only **S**, **1Tm 6:15** *1413*

SOVEREIGNTY

And His **s** rules over all. **Ps 103:19** 4438
And **s** from Damascus And the **Is 17:3** 4467
s has been removed from you, **Da 4:31** 4437
so I was reestablished in my **s**, **Da 4:36** 4437
king, the Most High God granted **s**, **Da 5:18** 4437
'Then the **s**, the dominion and the **Da 7:27** 4437
for his **s** will be uprooted and **Da 11:4** 4438

SOW

for you, and you may **s** the land. **Gn 47:23** 2232
"You shall **s** your land for **Ex 23:10** 2232
from what you **s** in the field; **Ex 23:16** 2232
you shall not **s** your field with **Lv 19:19** 2232
'Six years you shall **s** your field, **Lv 25:3** 2232
you shall not **s** your field nor **Lv 25:4** 2232
you shall not **s**, nor reap its **Lv 25:11** 2232
if we do not **s** or gather in our crops **Lv 25:20** 2232
you will **s** your seed uselessly, **Lv 26:16** 2232
where you used to **s** your seed and **Dt 11:10** 2232
all the produce from what you **s**, **Dt 14:22** 2233
"You shall not **s** your vineyard **Dt 22:9** 2232
the same, and in the third year **s**, **2Ki 19:29** 2232
those who **s** trouble harvest it. **Jb 4:8** 2232
Let me **s** and another eat, And let **Jb 31:8** 2232
And **s** fields and plant vineyards, **Ps 107:37** 2232
Those who **s** in tears shall reap **Ps 126:5** 2232
He who watches the wind will not **s** **Ec 11:4** 2232
S your seed in the morning and do **Ec 11:6** 2232
And **s** dill and scatter cummin And **Is 28:25** 6327a
which you will **s** in the ground, **Is 30:23** 2232
be, you who **s** beside all waters, **Is 32:20** 2232
the same, and in the third year **s**, **Is 37:30** 2232
ground, And do not **s** among thorns. **Jer 4:3** 2232
"when I will **s** the house of Israel **Jer 31:27** 2232
a house, and you shall not **s** seed and **Jer 35:7** 2232
I will **s** her for Myself in the land. **Hos 2:23** 2232
For they **s** the wind And they reap **Hos 8:7** 2232
S with a view to righteousness, **Hos 10:12** 2232
"You will **s** but you will not reap. **Mi 6:15** 2232
of the air, that they do not **s**, **Mt 6:26** *4687*
"Behold, the sower went out to **s**; **Mt 13:3** *4687*
you not **s** good seed in your field? **Mt 13:27** *4687*
man, reaping where you did not **s** and **Mt 25:24** *4687*
that I reap where I did not **s** and **Mt 25:26** *4687*
Behold, the sower went out to **s**; **Mk 4:3** *4687*
"The sower went out to **s** his seed; **Lk 8:5** *4687*
for they neither **s** nor reap; **Lk 12:24** *4687*
and reap what you did not **s**.' **Lk 19:21** *4687*
and reaping what I did not **s**? **Lk 19:22** *4687*
That which you **s** does not come to **1Co 15:36** *4687*
and that which you **s**, **1Co 15:37** *4687*
do not **s** the body which is to be, **1Co 15:37** *4687*
"A **s**, after washing, *returns* to **2Pe 2:22** *5300*

SOWED

Now Isaac **s** in that land and **Gn 26:12** 2232
razed the city and **s** it with salt. **Jg 9:45** 2232
and as he **s**, some *seeds* fell **Mt 13:4** *4687*
man who **s** good seed in his field. **Mt 13:24** *4687*
and **s** tares among the wheat, **Mt 13:25** *1986b*
a man took and **s** in his field; **Mt 13:31** *4687*
the enemy who **s** them is the devil, **Mt 13:39** *4687*
and as he **s**, some fell beside the **Lk 8:5** *4687*
If we **s** spiritual things in you, **1Co 9:11** *4687*

SOWER

furnishing seed to the **s** and bread **Is 55:10** 2232
"Cut off the **s** from Babylon And **Jer 50:16** 2232
"Behold, the **s** went out to sow; **Mt 13:3** *4687*
"Hear then the parable of the **s**. **Mt 13:18** *4687*
Behold, the **s** went out to sow; **Mk 4:3** *4687*
"The **s** sows the word. **Mk 4:14** *4687*
"The **s** went out to sow his seed; **Lk 8:5** *4687*
He who supplies seed to the **s** and **2Co 9:10** *4687*

SOWING

seed for **s** which is to be sown, **Lv 11:37** 2221
'When you are **s** the eighth year, **Lv 25:22** 2232
gathering will last until **s** time. **Lv 26:5** 2232
morning or evening **s** will succeed, **Ec 11:6**
as he was **s**, some *seed* fell beside **Mk 4:4** *4687*
supply and multiply your seed for **s** **2Co 9:10**

SOWN

seed for sowing which is to be **s**, **Lv 11:37** 2232
which has not been plowed or **s**, **Dt 21:4** 2232
of the seed which you have **s** and **Dt 22:9** 2232
For it was when Israel had **s**, **Jg 6:3** 2232
Light is **s** *like seed* for the righteous And **Ps 97:11** 2232
s fields by the Nile Will become dry, **Is 19:7** 4218
Scarcely have they been **s**, **Is 40:24** 2232
the things **s** in it to spring up, **Is 61:11** 2221
wilderness, Through a land not **s**. **Jer 2:2** 2232
They have **s** wheat and have reaped **Jer 12:13** 2232

and you will be cultivated and **s**. Ezk 36:9 2232
"You have **s** much, but harvest Hg 1:6 2232
away what has been **s** in his heart. Mt 13:19 *4687*
on whom seed was **s** beside the road. Mt 13:19 *4687*
seed was **s** on the rocky places, Mt 13:20 *4687*
whom seed was **s** among the thorns, Mt 13:22 *4687*
whom seed was **s** on the good soil, Mt 13:23 *4687*
the road where the word is **s**; Mk 4:15 *4687*
the word which has been **s** in them. Mk 4:15 *4687*
seed was **s** on the rocky *places,* Mk 4:16 *4687*
whom seed was **s** among the thorns; Mk 4:18 *4687*
whom seed was **s** on the good soil; Mk 4:20 *4687*
seed, which, when **s** upon the soil, Mk 4:31 *4687*
yet when it is **s**, it grows up and Mk 4:32 *4687*
It is **s** a perishable *body,* it is 1Co 15:42 *4687*
it is **s** in dishonor, it is raised 1Co 15:43 *4687*
it is **s** in weakness, it is raised 1Co 15:43 *4687*
it is **s** a natural body, it is 1Co 15:44 *4687*
fruit is righteousness is **s** in peace Jas 3:18 *4687*

SOWS
But he who **s** righteousness *gets* a Pr 11:18 2232
He who **s** iniquity will reap vanity, Pr 22:8 2232
treader of grapes him who **s** seed; Am 9:13 4900
'The one who **s** the good seed is Mt 13:37 *4687*
"The sower **s** the word. Mk 4:14 *4687*
that he who **s** and he who reaps may Jn 4:36 *4687*
'One **s** and another reaps.' Jn 4:37 *4687*
he who **s** sparingly will also reap 2Co 9:6 *4687*
and he who **s** bountifully will 2Co 9:6 *4687*
for whatever a man **s**, Ga 6:7 *4687*
For the one who **s** to his own flesh Ga 6:8 *4687*
but the one who **s** to the Spirit Ga 6:8 *4687*

SPACE
me, and put a **s** between droves." Gn 32:16 7305
to shed light on the **s** in front of it. Ex 25:37 5676
him within the **s** of a full year, Lv 25:30 4390
according to the clear **s** on each, 1Ki 7:36 4626
parts of the **s** behind the wall, Ne 4:13 4725
stretches out the north over empty **s** Jb 26:7 8414
But the free **s** between the side Ezk 41:9 5117
the side chambers toward the free **s** Ezk 41:11 5117
free **s** *was* five cubits all around. Ezk 41:11 5117, 4725
because the galleries took more **s** Ezk 42:5
cubits for its open **s** round about. Ezk 45:2 4054

SPACES
for dwellings and for open **s**; Ezk 48:15 4054
"The city shall have open **s**: Ezk 48:17 4054

SPACIOUS
that land to a good and **s** land, Ex 3:8 7342
to a secure people with a **s** land; Jg 18:10 7342, 3027
Now the city was large and **s**, Ne 7:4 1419
a roomy house With **s** upper rooms, Jer 22:14 7304

SPADE
shall have a **s** among your tools, Dt 23:13 3489

SPAIN
whenever I go to **S** Ro 15:24 *4681*
I will go on by way of you to **S**. Ro 15:28 *4681*

SPAN
a **s** in length and a span in width. Ex 28:16 2239
a span in length and a **s** in width. Ex 28:16 2239
a **s** long and a span wide when Ex 39:9 2239
and a **s** wide when folded double. Ex 39:9 2239
height was six cubits and a **s**. 1Sa 17:4 2239
Remember what my **s** of life is; Ps 89:47 2465
marked off the heavens by the **s**, Is 40:12 2239
on its edge round about one **s**; Ezk 43:13 2239
add a *single* hour to his life's **s**? Lk 12:25 *2244*

SPARE
not **s** the place for the sake of the fifty Gn 18:24 5375
then I will **s** the whole place on Gn 18:26 5375
man intimately, **s** for yourselves. Nu 31:18 2421a
nor shall you **s** or conceal him. Dt 13:8 2550
and **s** my father and my mother and Jos 2:13 2421a
all that he has, and do not **s** him; 1Sa 15:3 2550
If they **s** us, we will live; 2Ki 7:4 2421a
in your power, only **s** his life." Jb 2:6 8104
He did not **s** their soul from death, Ps 78:50 2820
not **s** in the day of vengeance. Pr 6:34 2550
vengeance and will not **s** a man." Is 47:3 6293
curtains of your dwellings, **s** not; Is 54:2 2820
He will not **s** them nor have pity Jer 21:7 2347
So do not **s** her young men; Jer 51:3 2550
have no pity and I will not **s**. Ezk 5:11 2550
no pity on you, nor will I **s** *you,* Ezk 7:4 2550
will show no pity nor will I **s**. Ezk 7:9 2550
will have no pity nor will I **s**; Ezk 8:18 2550
your eye have pity and do not **s**. Ezk 9:5 2550
will have no pity nor will I **s**, Ezk 9:10 2550
s a few of them from the sword, Ezk 12:16 3498
"**S** Your people, O LORD, And do not Jl 2:17 2347
I will **s** them no longer. Am 7:8 5674a
I will **s** them no longer. Am 8:2 5674a
and I will **s** them as a man spares Mal 3:17 2550
He who did not **s** His own Son, but Ro 8:32 *5339*
God did not **s** the natural branches, Ro 11:21 *5339*
branches, He will not **s** you, either. Ro 11:21 *5339*
life, and I am trying to **s** you. 1Co 7:28 *5339*
to **s** you I did not come again 2Co 1:23 *5339*
I come again I will not **s** *anyone,* 2Co 13:2 *5339*
if God did not **s** angels when they 2Pe 2:4 *5339*
and did not **s** the ancient world, 2Pe 2:5 *5339*

SPARED
Egyptians, but **s** our homes.' " Ex 12:27 5337
"Have you **s** all the women? Nu 31:15 2421a
and all she had, Joshua **s**; Jos 6:25 2421a
But Saul and the people **s** Agag and 1Sa 15:9 2550
for the people **s** the best of the 1Sa 15:15 2550
But the king **s** Mephibosheth, the 2Sa 21:7 2550
my master has **s** this Naaman the 2Ki 5:20 2820
So will you be **s**? 2Ki 19:11 5337
So will you be **s**? Is 37:11 5337
He has not **s** All the habitations of La 2:2 2550
You have slain *and* have not **s**. La 3:43 2550
"Yet My eye **s** them rather than Ezk 20:17 2347
and whomever he wished he **s** alive; Da 5:19 2418

SPARES
No man **s** his brother. Is 9:19 2550
man **s** his own son who serves him." Mal 3:17 2550

SPARING
"For it will hurl at him without **s**; Jb 27:22 2550
her, do not be **s** with *your* arrows, Jer 50:14 2550
He has thrown down without **s**, La 2:17 2550
You have slaughtered, not **s**. La 2:21 2550
slay nations without **s**? Hab 1:17 2550
in among you, not **s** the flock; Ac 20:29 *5339*

SPARINGLY
and feed him **s** with bread and 1Ki 22:27 3906
and feed him **s** with bread and 2Ch 18:26 3906
he who sows **s** will also reap 2Co 9:6 *5340*
sows sparingly will also reap **s** 2Co 9:6 *5340*

SPARK
become tinder, His work also a **s**. Is 1:31 5213

SPARKLES
it is red, When it **s** in the cup, Pr 23:31 5414, 5869

SPARKLING
workmanship *was* like **s** beryl, Ezk 1:16 5869
stones of a crown, **S** in His land. Zch 9:16 5264

SPARKS
born for trouble, As **s** fly upward. Jb 5:7 1121, 7565
S of fire leap forth. Jb 41:19 3590

SPARROW
Like a **s** in *its* flitting, like a Pr 26:2 6833

SPARROWS
"Are not two **s** sold for a cent? Mt 10:29 *4765*
you are more valuable than many **s**. Mt 10:31 *4765*
"Are not five **s** sold for two cents? Lk 12:6 *4765*
you are more valuable than many **s**. Lk 12:7 *4765*

SPAT
Then they **s** in His face and beat Mt 26:67 *1716*
They **s** on Him, and took the Mt 27:30 *1716*
had said this, He **s** on the ground, Jn 9:6 *4429*

SPEAK
I have ventured to **s** to the Lord, Gn 18:27 1696
Lord not be angry, and I shall **s**; Gn 18:30 1696
I have ventured to **s** to the Lord; Gn 18:31 1696
and I shall **s** only this once; Gn 18:32 1696
And he said, "**S** on." Gn 24:33 1696
so we cannot **s** to you bad or good. Gn 24:50 1696
I heard your father **s** to your Gn 27:6 1696
careful that you do not **s** to Jacob Gn 31:24 1696
careful not to **s** either good or bad Gn 31:29 1696
shall **s** to Esau when you find him; Gn 32:19 1696
went out to Jacob to **s** with him. Gn 34:6 1696
could not **s** to him on friendly terms. Gn 37:4 1696
Why does my lord **s** such words as Gn 44:7 1696
we say to my lord? What can we **s**? Gn 44:16 1696
please **s** a word in my lord's ears, Gn 44:18 1696
your sight, please **s** to Pharaoh, Gn 50:4 1696
"You are to **s** to him and put Ex 4:15 1696
he shall **s** for you to the people; Ex 4:16 1696
came to Pharaoh to **s** in Your name, Ex 5:23 1696
s to Pharaoh king of Egypt all Ex 6:29 1696
of Egypt all that I **s** to you." Ex 6:29 1696
You shall **s** all that I command you, Ex 7:2 1696
and your brother Aaron shall **s** to Ex 7:2 1696
"Go to Pharaoh and **s** to him, Ex 9:1 1696
"**S** now in the hearing of the people Ex 11:2 1696
"**S** to all the congregation of Israel, Ex 12:3 1696
s to them, saying, Ex 16:12 1696
shall **s** to the sons of Israel." Ex 19:6 1696
people may hear when I **s** with you and Ex 19:9 1696
"**S** to us yourself and we will Ex 20:19 1696
but let not God **s** to us, or we Ex 20:19 1696
I will **s** to you about all that I Ex 25:22 1696
"You shall **s** to all the Ex 28:3 1696
meet with you, to **s** to you there. Ex 29:42 1696
You shall **s** to the sons of Israel, Ex 30:31 1696
for you, **s** to the sons of Israel, Ex 31:13 1696
"Why should the Egyptians **s**, Ex 32:12 559
and the LORD would **s** with Moses. Ex 33:9 1696
used to **s** to Moses face to face, Ex 33:11 1696
in before the LORD to **s** with Him, Ex 34:34 1696
until he went in to **s** with Him. Ex 34:35 1696
"**S** to the sons of Israel and say Lv 1:2 1696
"**S** to the sons of Israel, saying, Lv 4:2 1696
may **s** thoughtlessly with an oath, Lv 5:4 981
"**S** to Aaron and to his sons, Lv 6:25 1696
"**S** to the sons of Israel, saying, Lv 7:23 1696
"**S** to the sons of Israel, saying, Lv 7:29 1696
to the sons of Israel you shall **s**, Lv 9:3 1696
"**S** to the sons of Israel, saying, Lv 11:2 1696
"**S** to the sons of Israel, saying: Lv 12:2 1696
"**S** to the sons of Israel, and say Lv 15:2 1696
"**S** to Aaron and to his sons and Lv 17:2 1696
"**S** to the sons of Israel and say Lv 18:2 1696
"**S** to all the congregation of the Lv 19:2 1696
"**S** to the priests, the sons of Lv 21:1 559
"**S** to Aaron, saying, Lv 21:17 1696
"**S** to Aaron and to his sons and Lv 22:18 1696
"**S** to the sons of Israel and say Lv 23:2 1696
"**S** to the sons of Israel and say Lv 23:10 1696
"**S** to the sons of Israel, saying, Lv 23:24 1696
"**S** to the sons of Israel, saying, Lv 23:34 1696
You shall **s** to the sons of Israel, Lv 24:15 1696
"**S** to the sons of Israel and say Lv 25:2 1696
"**S** to the sons of Israel and say Lv 27:2 1696
"**S** to the sons of Israel, Nu 5:6 1696
"**S** to the sons of Israel and say Nu 5:12 1696
"**S** to the sons of Israel and say Nu 6:2 1696
"**S** to Aaron and to his sons, Nu 6:23 1696
the tent of meeting to **s** with Him, Nu 7:89 1696
"**S** to Aaron and say to him, Nu 8:2 1696
"**S** to the sons of Israel, saying, Nu 9:10 1696
come down and **s** with you there, Nu 11:17 1696
I shall **s** with him in a dream. Nu 12:6 1696
With him I **s** mouth to mouth, Even Nu 12:8 1696
afraid To **s** against My servant, Nu 12:8 1696
"**S** to the sons of Israel and say Nu 15:2 1696
"**S** to the sons of Israel and say Nu 15:18 1696
"**S** to the sons of Israel, and Nu 15:38 1696
"**S** to the congregation, saying, Nu 16:24 1696
"**S** to the sons of Israel, and get Nu 17:2 1696
you shall **s** to the Levites and say Nu 18:26 1696
"**S** to the sons of Israel that they Nu 19:2 1696
s to the rock before their eyes, Nu 20:8 1696
to you as the LORD may **s** to me." Nu 22:8 1696
what else the LORD will **s** to me." Nu 22:19 1696
which I **s** to you shall you do." Nu 22:20 1696
but you shall **s** only the word Nu 22:35 1696
Am I able to **s** anything at all? Nu 22:38 1696
in my mouth, that I shall **s**." Nu 22:38 1696
to Balak, and you shall **s** thus." Nu 23:5 1696
"Must I not be careful to **s** what Nu 23:12 1696
to Balak, and thus you shall **s**." Nu 23:16 1696
the LORD speaks, that I will **s**'? Nu 24:13 1696
you shall **s** to the sons of Israel, Nu 27:8 1696
"**S** to the sons of Israel and say Nu 33:51 1696
"**S** to the sons of Israel and say Nu 35:10 1696
S to Me no more of this matter. Dt 3:26 1696
then **s** to us all that the LORD our Dt 5:27 1696
that I may **s** to you all the Dt 5:31 1696
and he shall **s** to them all that I Dt 18:18 1696
words which he shall **s** in My name, Dt 18:19 1696
I have not commanded him to **s**, Dt 18:20 1696
come near and **s** to the people. Dt 20:2 1696
officers also shall **s** to the people, Dt 20:5 1696
officers shall **s** further to the people and Dt 20:8 1696
shall summon him and **s** to him. Dt 25:8 1696
that I may **s** these words in their Dt 31:28 1696
"Give ear, O heavens, and let me **s**; Dt 32:1 1696
LORD had commanded Joshua to **s** Jos 4:10 1696
"**S** to the sons of Israel, saying, Jos 20:2 1696
and they did not **s** of going up Jos 22:33 559
that it is You who **s** with me. Jg 6:17 1696
against me that I may **s** once more; Jg 6:39 1696
"**S**, now, in the hearing of all Jg 9:2 1696
went after her to **s** tenderly to her Jg 19:3 1696
it, take counsel and **s** up!" Jg 19:30 1696
'**S**, LORD, for Your servant is 1Sa 3:9 1696
"**S**, for Your servant is listening." 1Sa 3:10 1696
then do you **s** to me in this way?" 1Sa 9:21 1696
And he said to him, "**S**!" 1Sa 15:16 1696
"**S** to David secretly, saying, 1Sa 18:22 1696
I will **s** with my father about you; 1Sa 19:3 1696
Saul did not **s** anything that day, 1Sa 20:26 1696
man that no one can **s** to him." 1Sa 25:17 1696
let your maidservant **s** to you, 1Sa 25:24 1696
and in addition Abner went to **s** in 2Sa 3:19 1696
the gate to **s** with him privately, 2Sa 3:27 1696
did I **s** a word with one of the 2Sa 7:7 1696
therefore, please **s** to the king, 2Sa 13:13 1696
Absalom did not **s** to Amnon either 2Sa 13:22 1696
and **s** to him in this manner." 2Sa 14:3 1696
s a word to my lord the king." 2Sa 14:12 1696
And he said, "**S**." 2Sa 14:12 1696
"Now the reason I have come to **s** 2Sa 14:15 1696
'Let me now **s** to the king, perhaps 2Sa 14:15 1696
"Let my lord the king please **s**." 2Sa 14:18 1696
we carry out his plan? If not, you **s**." 2Sa 17:6 1696
out and **s** kindly to your servants, 2Sa 19:7 1696
"**S** to the elders of Judah, 2Sa 19:11 1696
Why do you still **s** of your affairs? 2Sa 19:29 1696
here that I may **s** with you.' " 2Sa 20:16 1696
"Go and **s** to David, 2Sa 24:12 1696
And she said, "**S**." 1Ki 2:14 1696
And she said to him, "**S**." 1Ki 2:16 1696
"Please **s** to Solomon the king, 1Ki 2:17 559
I will **s** to the king for you." 1Ki 2:18 1696
Solomon to **s** to him for Adonijah. 1Ki 2:19 1696
and **s** good words to them, 1Ki 12:7 1696
But you shall **s** to them, 1Ki 12:10 1696
"**S** to Rehoboam the son of 1Ki 12:23 559
"You shall **s** to him, saying, 1Ki 21:19 1696
And you shall **s** to him, saying, 1Ki 21:19 1696
of one of them, and **s** favorably." 1Ki 22:13 1696
LORD says to me, that I shall **s**." 1Ki 22:14 1696
s to me nothing but the truth 1Ki 22:16 1696
LORD pass from me to **s** to you?" 1Ki 22:24 1696
LORD you **s** in your bedroom." 2Ki 6:12 1696
"**S** now to your servants in 2Ki 18:26 1696
and do not **s** with us in Judean in 2Ki 18:26 1696
and to you to **s** these words, 2Ki 18:27 1696
S of all His wonders. 1Ch 16:9 7878
"Go and **s** to David, saying, 1Ch 21:10 1696
them and **s** good words to them, 2Ch 10:7 1696
"**S** to Rehoboam the son of 2Ch 11:3 559
one of them and **s** favorably." 2Ch 18:12 1696
what my God says, that I will **s**." 2Ch 18:13 1696
s to me nothing but the truth in the 2Ch 18:15 1696

LORD pass from me to **s** to you?" **2Ch 18:23** 1696
of Israel, and to **s** against Him, **2Ch 32:17** 559
and female singers **s** about Josiah **2Ch 35:25** 559
able to **s** the language of Judah, **Ne 13:24** 1696
was the custom of the king so *to* **s** **Es 1:13**
will **s** in *the same way* to all the king's **Es 1:18** 559
s to the king about hanging Mordecai **Es 6:4** 559
"You **s** as one of the foolish **Jb 2:10** 1696
s in the anguish of my spirit, **Jb 7:11** 1696
"*Then* I would **s** and not fear Him; **Jb 9:35** 1696
s in the bitterness of my soul. **Jb 10:1** 1696
"But would that God might **s**, **Jb 11:5** 1696
"Or **s** to the earth, and let it **Jb 12:8** 7878
"But I would **s** to the Almighty, **Jb 13:3** 1696
"Will you **s** what is unjust for **Jb 13:7** 1696
And **s** what is deceitful for Him? **Jb 13:7** 1696
silent before me so that I may **s**; **Jb 13:13** 1696
Or let me **s**, then reply to me. **Jb 13:22** 1696
"I too could **s** like you, If I **Jb 16:4** 1696
"If I **s**, my pain is not lessened, **Jb 16:6** 1696
I rise up and they **s** against me. **Jb 19:18** 1696
"Bear with me that I may **s**; **Jb 21:3** 1696
you will **s** with confidence, And the **Jb 22:29** 559
certainly will not **s** unjustly, **Jb 27:4** 1696
my words they did not **s** again, **Jb 29:22** 8138
Now Elihu had waited to **s** to Job **Jb 32:4** 1697
"I thought age should **s**, **Jb 32:7** 1696
I wait, because they do not **s**, **Jb 32:16** 1696
"Let me **s** that I may get relief; **Jb 32:20** 1696
And my lips **s** knowledge sincerely. **Jb 33:3** 4448a
Keep silent, and let me **s**. **Jb 33:31** 1696
S, for I desire to justify you. **Jb 33:32** 1696
it be told Him that I would **s**? **Jb 37:20** 1696
Or will he **s** to you soft words? **Jb 41:3** 1696
'Hear, now, and I will **s**; **Jb 42:4** 1696
Then He will **s** to them in His **Ps 2:5** 1696
destroy those who **s** falsehood; **Ps 5:6** 1696
They **s** falsehood to one another; **Ps 12:2** 1696
and with a double heart they **s**. **Ps 12:2** 1696
With their mouth they **s** proudly. **Ps 17:10** 1696
Who **s** peace with their neighbors, **Ps 28:3** 1696
Which **s** arrogantly against the **Ps 31:18** 1696
For they do not **s** peace, But they **Ps 35:20** 1696
If I would declare and **s** of them, **Ps 40:5** 1696
My enemies **s** evil against me, **Ps 41:5** 559
My mouth will **s** wisdom, **Ps 49:3** 1696
"Hear, O My people, and I will **s**; **Ps 50:7** 1696
sit and **s** against your brother; **Ps 50:20** 1696
are justified when You **s** **Ps 51:4** 1696
Do you indeed **s** righteousness, O **Ps 58:1** 1696
who **s** lies go astray from birth. **Ps 58:3** 1696
those who **s** lies will be stopped. **Ps 63:11** 1696
and wickedly **s** of oppression; **Ps 73:8** 1696
They **s** from on high. **Ps 73:8** 1696
If I had said, "I will **s** thus," **Ps 73:15** 5608
Do not **s** with insolent pride.' " **Ps 75:5** 1696
I am so troubled that I cannot **s**. **Ps 77:4** 1696
For He will **s** peace to His people, **Ps 85:8** 1696
forth *words*, they **s** arrogantly; **Ps 94:4** 1696
S of all His wonders. **Ps 105:2** 7878
Who can **s** of the mighty deeds of **Ps 106:2** 4448a
those who **s** evil against my soul. **Ps 109:20** 1696
have mouths, but they cannot **s**; **Ps 115:5** 1696
I will also **s** of Your testimonies **Ps 119:46** 1696
I am *for* peace, but when I **s**, **Ps 120:7** 1696
When they **s** with their enemies in **Ps 127:5** 1696
have mouths, but they do not **s**; **Ps 135:16** 1696
For they **s** against You wickedly, **Ps 139:20** 559
Whose mouths **s** deceit, And whose **Ps 144:8** 1696
Men shall **s** of the power of **Ps 145:6** 559
s of the glory of Your kingdom And **Ps 145:11** 1696
will **s** the praise of the LORD, **Ps 145:21** 1696
for I will **s** noble things; **Pr 8:6** 1696
man who listens *to the truth* will **s** **Pr 21:28** 1696
Do not **s** in the hearing of a fool, **Pr 23:9** 1696
When your lips **s** what is right. **Pr 23:16** 1696
to be silent and a time to **s**. **Ec 3:7** 1696
do not **s** according to this word, **Is 8:20** 559
He will **s** to this people Through **Is 28:11** 1696
From the earth you will **s**, **Is 29:4** 1696
is right, **S** to us pleasant words, **Is 30:10** 1696
will hasten to **s** clearly. **Is 32:4** 1696
and to **s** error against the LORD, **Is 32:6** 1696
"**S** now to your servants in Aramaic **Is 36:11** 1696
and do not **s** with us in Judean in **Is 36:11** 1696
and to you to **s** these words, **Is 36:12** 1696
"**S** kindly to Jerusalem; **Is 40:2** 1696
come forward, then let them **s**; **Is 41:1** 1696
I, the LORD, **s** righteousness **Is 45:19** 1696
They trust in confusion and **s** lies; **Is 59:4** 1696
"It is I who **s** in righteousness, **Is 63:1** 1696
Behold, I do not know how to **s**, **Jer 1:6** 1696
all that I command you, you shall **s**. **Jer 1:7** 1696
and **s** to them all which I command **Jer 1:17** 1696
to the great And will **s** to them, **Jer 5:5** 1696
To whom shall I **s** and give warning **Jer 6:10** 1696
"For I did not **s** to your fathers, **Jer 7:22** 1696
You shall **s** all these words to them, **Jer 7:27** 1696
And does not **s** the truth, **Jer 9:5** 1696
taught their tongue to **s** lies; **Jer 9:5** 1696
S, "Thus says the LORD, **Jer 9:22** 1696
field are they, And they cannot **s**; **Jer 10:5** 1696
and **s** to the men of Judah and to **Jer 11:2** 1696
you are to **s** this word to them, **Jer 13:12** 559
"At one moment I might **s** **Jer 18:7** 1696
"Or at another moment I might **s** **Jer 18:9** 1696
s to the men of Judah and against **Jer 18:11** 559
You To **s** good on their behalf, **Jer 18:20** 1696
For each time I **s**, I cry aloud; **Jer 20:8** 1696

Him Or **s** anymore in His name," **Jer 20:9** 1696
of Judah, and there **s** this word **Jer 22:1** 1696
They **s** a vision of their own **Jer 23:16** 1696
I did not **s** to them, But they **Jer 23:21** 1696
has My word **s** My word in truth. **Jer 23:28** 1696
and **s** to all the cities of Judah who **Jer 26:2** 1696
I have commanded you to **s** to them. **Jer 26:2** 1696
him to **s** to all the people, **Jer 26:8** 1696
the LORD has sent me to you to **s** **Jer 26:15** 1696
or your sorcerers who **s** to you, **Jer 27:9** 559
words of the prophets who **s** to you, **Jer 27:14** 559
this word which I am about to **s** **Jer 28:7** 1696
"Go and **s** to Hananiah, saying, **Jer 28:13** 559
the Nehelamite you shall **s**, **Jer 29:24** 559
"Once again they will **s** this word **Jer 31:23** 559
he will **s** with him face to face **Jer 32:4** 1696
'Go and **s** to Zedekiah king of **Jer 34:2** 559
he will **s** with you face to face, **Jer 34:3** 1696
of the Rechabites and **s** to them, **Jer 35:2** 1696
and **s** to Ebed-melech the Ethiopian, **Jer 39:16** 559
For each time you **s** about him you **Jer 48:27** 1697
your feet that I may **s** with you!" **Ezk 2:1** 1696
"But you shall **s** My words to them **Ezk 2:7** 1696
go, **s** to the house of Israel." **Ezk 3:1** 1696
and **s** with My words to them. **Ezk 3:4** 1696
My words which I will **s** to you **Ezk 3:10** 1696
and **s** to them and tell them, **Ezk 3:11** 1696
or **s** out to warn the wicked from **Ezk 3:18** 1696
and there I will **s** to you." **Ezk 3:22** 1696
"But when I **s** to you, I will open **Ezk 3:27** 1696
"For I the LORD will **s**, **Ezk 12:25** 1696
word I **s** will be performed. **Ezk 12:25** 1696
will **s** the word and perform it," **Ezk 12:25** 1696
word I **s** will be performed, **Ezk 12:28** 1696
a false vision and **s** a lying divination **Ezk 13:7** 559
"Therefore **s** to them and tell **Ezk 14:4** 1696
is prevailed upon to **s** a word, **Ezk 14:9** 1696
and **s** a parable to the house of **Ezk 17:2** 4911b
of man, **s** to the elders of Israel and **Ezk 20:3** 1696
of man, **s** to the house of Israel and **Ezk 20:27** 1696
and **s** out against the south and **Ezk 20:46** 5197
and **s** against the sanctuaries and **Ezk 21:2** 5197
"**S** a parable to the rebellious house **Ezk 24:3** 4911b
'**S** to the house of Israel, **Ezk 24:21** 559
you will **s** and be mute no longer. **Ezk 24:27** 1696
S and say, 'Thus says the Lord GOD, **Ezk 29:3** 1696
shall **s** of him *and* his helpers from **Ezk 32:21** 1696
man, **s** to the sons of your people and **Ezk 33:2** 1696
you do not **s** to warn the wicked **Ezk 33:8** 1696
of the houses, **s** to one another, **Ezk 33:30** 1696
of your people **s** to you saying, **Ezk 37:18** 559
'**S** to every kind of bird and to **Ezk 39:17** 559
you have agreed together to **s** lying **Da 2:9** 560
He will **s** out against the Most High **Da 7:25** 4449
"May my lord **s**, for you have **Da 10:19** 1696
and they will **s** lies *to each other* **Da 11:27** 1696
and will **s** monstrous things **Da 11:36** 1696
wilderness And **s** kindly to her. **Hos 2:14** 1696
them, but they **s** lies against Me. **Hos 7:13** 1696
They **s** *mere* words, With worthless **Hos 10:4** 1696
you **s** against the house of Isaac.' **Am 7:16** 5197
'Do not **s** out,' *so* they speak out. **Mi 2:6** 5197
'Do not speak out,' *so* they **s** out. **Mi 2:6** 5197
they do not **s** out concerning these **Mi 2:6** 5197
'I will **s** out to you concerning **Mi 2:11** 5197
of violence, Her residents **s** lies, **Mi 6:12** 1696
watch to see what He will **s** to me, **Hab 2:1** 1696
"**S** now to Zerubbabel the son of **Hg 2:2** 559
"**S** to Zerubbabel governor of **Hg 2:21** 559
"Run, **s** to that young man, **Zch 2:4** 1696
s the truth to one another; **Zch 8:16** 1696
He will **s** peace to the nations; **Zch 9:10** 1696
For the teraphim **s** iniquity, **Zch 10:2** 1696
"For it is not you who **s**, **Mt 10:20** *2980*
in the darkness, **s** in the light; **Mt 10:27** *3004*
Jesus began to **s** to the crowds **Mt 11:7** *3004*
you, being evil, **s** what is good? **Mt 12:34** *2980*
every careless word that people **s**, **Mt 12:36** *2980*
outside, seeking to **s** to Him. **Mt 12:46** *2980*
outside seeking to **s** to You." **Mt 12:47** *2980*
do You **s** to them in parables?" **Mt 13:10** *2980*
"Therefore I **s** to them in parables; **Mt 13:13** *2980*
not **s** to them without a parable. **Mt 13:34** *2980*
did not **s** to you concerning bread? **Mt 16:11** *3004*
not permitting the demons to **s**, **Mk 1:34** *2980*
"Why does this man **s** that way? **Mk 2:7** *2980*
not **s** to them without a parable; **Mk 4:34** *2980*
deaf to hear and the mute to **s**." **Mk 7:37** *2980*
soon afterward to **s** evil of Me. **Mk 9:39** *2551*
He began to **s** to them in parables: **Mk 12:1** *2980*
for it is not you who **s**, **Mk 13:11** *2980*
they will **s** with new tongues; **Mk 16:17** *2980*
and I have been sent to **s** to you and **Lk 1:19** *2980*
you shall be silent and unable to **s** **Lk 1:20** *2980*
out, he was unable to **s** to them; **Lk 1:22** *2980*
he *began* to **s** in praise of God. **Lk 1:64** *2980*
and continued to **s** of Him to all **Lk 2:38** *2980*
He would not allow them to **s**, **Lk 4:41** *2980*
to you when all men **s** well of you, **Lk 6:26** *3004*
dead man sat up and began to **s**. **Lk 7:15** *2980*
to **s** to the crowds about John, **Lk 7:24** *3004*
what you are to **s** in your defense, **Lk 12:11** *626*
that You **s** and teach correctly, **Lk 20:21** *3004*
The two disciples heard him **s**, **Jn 1:37** *2980*
One of the two who heard John **s** **Jn 1:40**
to you, we **s** of what we know **Jn 3:11** *2980*
"I who **s** to you am *He*." **Jn 4:26** *2980*
"Why do You **s** with her?" **Jn 4:27** *2980*
God or *whether* I **s** from Myself. **Jn 7:17** *2980*

to **s** and to judge concerning you, **Jn 8:26** *2980*
Him, these I **s** to the world." **Jn 8:26** *2980*
but I **s** these things as the Father **Jn 8:28** *2980*
"I **s** the things which I have seen **Jn 8:38** *2980*
"But because I **s** the truth, you **Jn 8:45** *3004*
If I **s** truth, why do you not **Jn 8:46** *3004*
of age, he will **s** for himself." **Jn 9:21** *2980*
I did not **s** on My own initiative, **Jn 12:49** *2980*
what to say and what to **s**. **Jn 12:49** *2980*
therefore the things I **s**, **Jn 12:50** *2980*
I **s** just as the Father has told Me." **Jn 12:50** *2980*
"I do not **s** of all of you. **Jn 13:18** *3004*
I do not **s** on My own initiative, **Jn 14:10** *2980*
"I will not **s** much more with you, **Jn 14:30** *2980*
He will not **s** on His own initiative, **Jn 16:13** *2980*
but whatever He hears, He will **s**; **Jn 16:13** *2980*
I will no longer **s** to you in figurative **Jn 16:25** *2980*
and these things I **s** in the world so **Jn 17:13** *2980*
"You do not **s** to me? **Jn 19:10** *2980*
and began to **s** with other tongues, **Ac 2:4** *2980*
hearing them **s** in his own language. **Ac 2:6** *2980*
let us warn them to **s** no longer to **Ac 4:17** *2980*
they commanded them not to **s** or **Ac 4:18** *5350*
Your bond-servants may **s** Your word **Ac 4:29** *2980*
s the word of God with boldness. **Ac 4:31** *2980*
stand and **s** to the people in the **Ac 5:20** *2980*
not to **s** in the name of Jesus, **Ac 5:40** *2980*
"We have heard him **s** blasphemous **Ac 6:11** *2980*
and he will **s** words to you by **Ac 11:14** *2980*
"And as I began to **s**, **Ac 11:15** *2980*
Holy Spirit to **s** the word in Asia; **Ac 16:6** *2980*
to **s** out boldly in the synagogue. **Ac 18:26** *3955*
allow me to **s** to the people." **Ac 21:39** *2980*
'YOU SHALL NOT **S** EVIL OF A RULER **Ac 23:5** *3004*
governor had nodded for him to **s**, **Ac 24:10** *3004*
and sent for Paul and heard him **s** **Ac 24:24**
You are permitted to **s** for yourself. **Ac 26:1** *3004*
I **s** to him also with confidence, **Ac 26:26** *2980*
to see you and to **s** with you, **Ac 28:20** *4354*
I will not presume to **s** of anything **Ro 15:18** *2980*
Yet we do **s** wisdom among those who **1Co 2:6** *2980*
but we **s** God's wisdom in a mystery **1Co 2:7** *2980*
which things we also **s**, **1Co 2:13** *2980*
not **s** to you as to spiritual men, **1Co 3:1** *2980*
I **s** as to wise men; **1Co 10:15** *3004*
All do not **s** with tongues, do they? **1Co 12:30** *2980*
If I **s** with the tongues of men and **1Co 13:1** *2980*
a child, I used to **s** like a child, **1Co 13:11** *2980*
in a tongue does not **s** to men but **1Co 14:2** *2980*
unless I **s** to you either by way of **1Co 14:6** *2980*
I **s** in tongues more than you all; **1Co 14:18** *2980*
to **s** five words with my mind so **1Co 14:19** *2980*
STRANGERS I WILL **S** TO THIS PEOPLE, **1Co 14:21** *2980*
together and all **s** in tongues, **1Co 14:23** *2980*
let him **s** to himself and to God. **1Co 14:28** *2980*
Let two or three prophets **s**, **1Co 14:29** *2980*
for they are not permitted to **s**, **1Co 14:34** *2980*
for a woman to **s** in church. **1Co 14:35** *2980*
and do not forbid to **s** in tongues. **1Co 14:39** *2980*
I **s** *this* to your shame. **1Co 15:34** *2980*
we **s** in Christ in the sight of God. **2Co 2:17** *2980*
also believe, therefore we also **s**, **2Co 4:13** *2980*
I **s** as to children **2Co 6:13** *3004*
I do not **s** to condemn you, **2Co 7:3** *3004*
not to **s** of you **2Co 9:4** *3004*
I **s** in foolishness **2Co 11:21** *3004*
I **s** as if insane **2Co 11:23** *2980*
which a man is not permitted to **s**. **2Co 12:4** *2980*
I **s** in terms of human relations: **Ga 3:15** *3004*
laying aside falsehood, **S** TRUTH EACH **Eph 4:25** *2980*
disgraceful even to **s** of the things **Eph 5:12** *3004*
in *proclaiming* it I may **s** boldly, **Eph 6:20** *3955*
may speak boldly, as I ought to **s**. **Eph 6:20** *2980*
to **s** the word of God without fear. **Php 1:14** *2980*
Not that I **s** from want, **Php 4:11** *3004*
we may **s** forth the mystery of Christ, **Col 4:3** *2980*
it clear in the way I ought to **s**. **Col 4:4** *2980*
the boldness in our God to **s** to you **1Th 2:2** *2980*
with the gospel, so we **s**, **1Th 2:4** *2980*
we ourselves **s** proudly of you **2Th 1:4** *1461a*
s the things which are fitting for **Ti 2:1** *2980*
These things **s** and exhort and **Ti 2:15** *2980*
I want you to **s** confidently, **Ti 3:8** *1226*
And, so to **s**, through Abraham even **Heb 7:9** *3004*
things we cannot now **s** in detail. **Heb 9:5** *3004*
hear, slow to **s** *and* slow to anger; **Jas 1:19** *2980*
So **s** and so act as those who are **Jas 2:12** *2980*
Do not **s** against one another, **Jas 4:11** *2635*
they **s** *as* from the world, **1Jn 4:5** *2980*
to come to you and **s** face to face, **2Jn 1:12** *2980*
and we will **s** face to face. **3Jn 1:14** *2980*
they **s** arrogantly, flattering **Jude 1:16** *2980*
the image of the beast would even **s** **Rv 13:15** *2980*

SPEAKER

because he was the chief **s**. **Ac 14:12** *3056*

SPEAKING

as He had finished **s** to Abraham **Gn 18:33** 1696
Before he had finished **s**, **Gn 24:15** 1696
I had finished **s** in my heart, **Gn 24:45** 1696
While he was still **s** with them, **Gn 29:9** 1696
it is my mouth which is **s** to you. **Gn 45:12** 1696
s with him upon Mount Sinai, **Ex 31:18** 1696
shone because of his **s** with Him. **Ex 34:29** 1696
Moses had finished **s** with them, **Ex 34:33** 1696
he heard the voice **s** to him from **Nu 7:89** 1696
As he finished **s** all these words, **Nu 16:31** 1696
God **s** from the midst of the fire, **Dt 4:33** 1696
I am **s** today in your hearing, **Dt 5:1** 1696

God **s** from the midst of the fire, **Dt 5:26** 1696
"Know this day that I *am* not **s** **Dt 11:2**
have finished **s** to the people, **Dt 20:9** 1696
s all these words to all Israel, **Dt 32:45** 1696
When he had finished **s**, **Jg 15:17** 1696
Hannah, she was **s** in her heart, **1Sa 1:13** 1696
when he had finished **s** to Saul, **1Sa 18:1** 1696
finished **s** these words to Saul, **1Sa 24:16** 1696
As soon as he had finished **s**, **2Sa 13:36** 1696
For in **s** this word the king is as **2Sa 14:13** 1696
are still there **s** with the king, **1Ki 1:14** 1696
she was still **s** with the king, **1Ki 1:22** 1696
While he was still **s**, **1Ki 1:42** 1696
they were **s** about his good deeds **Ne 6:19** 559
While he was still **s**, **Jb 1:16** 1696
While he was still **s**, **Jb 1:17** 1696
While he was still **s**, **Jb 1:18** 1696
with no one **s** a word to him, **Jb 2:13** 1696
But who can refrain from **s**? **Jb 4:2** 4405
evil And your lips from **s** deceit. **Ps 34:13** 1696
Falsehood more than **s** what is right **Ps 52:3** 1696
And every mouth is **s** foolishness. **Is 9:17** 1696
Egypt will be **s** the language of Canaan **Is 19:18** 1696
in that day I am the one who is **s**, **Is 52:6** 1696
of the finger and **s** wickedness, **Is 58:9** 1696
own pleasure And **s** *your own* word, **Is 58:13** 1696
our God, **S** oppression and revolt, **Is 59:13** 1696
and while they are still **s**, **Is 65:24** 1696
to you, rising up early and **s**, **Jer 7:13** 1696
people heard Jeremiah **s** these words **Jer 26:7** 1696
When Jeremiah finished **s** all **Jer 26:8** 1696
Jeremiah was **s** to all the people, **Jer 38:1** 1696
people, by **s** such words to them; **Jer 38:4** 1696
and they ceased **s** with him, since **Jer 38:27** 2790b
on my face and heard a voice **s**. **Ezk 1:28** 1696
and I heard *Him* **s** to me. **Ezk 2:2** 1696
man, listen to what I am **s** to you; **Ezk 2:8** 1696
'Is he not *just* **s** parables?'" **Ezk 20:49** 4911b
heard one **s** to me from the house, **Ezk 43:6** 1696
words which the horn was **s**; **Da 7:11** 4449
Then I heard a holy one **s**, **Da 8:13** 1696
to that particular one who was **s**, **Da 8:13** 1696
Now while I was **s** and praying, and **Da 9:20** 1696
while I was still **s** in prayer, **Da 9:21** 1696
angel who was **s** with me said to me, **Zch 1:9** 1696
was **s** with me with gracious words, **Zch 1:13** 1696
who was **s** with me said to me, **Zch 1:14** 1696
to the angel who was **s** with me, **Zch 1:19** 1696
angel who was **s** with me was going **Zch 2:3** 1696
angel who was **s** with me returned and **Zch 4:1** 1696
angel who was **s** with me saying, **Zch 4:4** 1696
So the angel who was **s** with me **Zch 4:5** 1696
angel who was **s** with me went out and **Zch 5:5** 1696
to the angel who was **s** with me, **Zch 5:10** 1696
to the angel who was **s** with me, **Zch 6:4** 1696
s to the priests who belong to the **Zch 7:3** 559
He was still **s** to the crowds, **Mt 12:46** *2980*
marveled as they saw the mute **s**, **Mt 15:31** *2980*
While he was still **s**, **Mt 17:5** *2980*
that He was **s** about them. **Mt 21:45** *3004*
While He was still **s**, **Mt 26:47** *2980*
and He was **s** the word to them. **Mk 2:2** *2980*
and began **s** to them in parables, **Mk 3:23** *3004*
He was **s** the word to them, **Mk 4:33** *2980*
While He was still **s**, **Mk 5:35** *2980*
removed, and he *began* **s** plainly. **Mk 7:35** *2980*
Immediately while He was still **s**, **Mk 14:43** *2980*
And all were **s** well of Him, and **Lk 4:22** *3140*
When He had finished **s**, **Lk 5:4** *2980*
While He was still **s**, **Lk 8:49** *2980*
He *began* **s** to them about the **Lk 9:11** *2980*
were **s** of His departure which He **Lk 9:31** *3004*
And He *began* **s** a parable to the **Lk 14:7** *3004*
While He was still **s**, **Lk 22:47** *2980*
Immediately, while he was still **s**, **Lk 22:60** *2980*
while He was **s** to us on the road, **Lk 24:32** *2980*
He was **s** of the temple of His body. **Jn 2:21** *3004*
that He had been **s** with a woman, **Jn 4:27** *2980*
Yet no one was **s** openly of Him for **Jn 7:13** *2980*
"Look, He is **s** publicly, and **Jn 7:26** *2980*
He had been **s** to them about the **Jn 8:27** *3004*
that He was **s** of literal sleep. **Jn 11:13** *3004*
to know of which one He was **s**. **Jn 13:22** *3004*
"Tell *us* who it is of whom He is **s**." **Jn 13:24** *3004*
"Lo, now You are **s** plainly and **Jn 16:29** *2980*
and **s** of the things concerning the **Ac 1:3** *3004*
not all these who are **s** Galileans? **Ac 2:7** *2980*
s of the mighty deeds of God." **Ac 2:11** *2980*
As they were **s** to the people, **Ac 4:1** *2980*
cannot stop **s** about what we have seen **Ac 4:20** *2980*
the Spirit with which he was **s**. **Ac 6:10** *2980*
who was **s** to him on Mount Sinai, **Ac 7:38** *2980*
s out boldly in the name of the **Ac 9:28** *3955*
the angel who was **s** to him had **Ac 10:7** *2980*
Peter was still **s** these words, **Ac 10:44** *2980*
s with tongues and exalting God. **Ac 10:46** *2980*
But Peter began **s** and *proceeded* **Ac 11:4**
s the word to no one except to **Ac 11:19** *2980*
and *began* **s** to the Greeks also, **Ac 11:20** *2980*
who, **s** to them, were urging them to **Ac 13:43** *4354*
s boldly *with reliance* upon the Lord, **Ac 14:3** *3955*
After they had stopped **s**, **Ac 15:13** *4601*
and we sat down and began **s** to the **Ac 16:13** *2980*
but go on **s** and do not be silent; **Ac 18:9** *2980*
he was **s** and teaching accurately **Ac 18:25** *2980*
s with tongues and prophesying. **Ac 19:6** *2980*
s out boldly for three months, **Ac 19:8** *3955*
s evil of the Way before the **Ac 19:9** *2551*
men will arise, **s** perverse things, **Ac 20:30** *2980*

voice of the One who was **s** to me. **Ac 22:9** *2980*
(I am **s** in human terms.) **Ro 3:5** *3004*
I am **s** in human terms because of **Ro 6:19** *3004*
I am **s** to those who know the law), **Ro 7:1** *2980*
I am **s** to you who are Gentiles. **Ro 11:13** *3004*
I am not **s** these things according **1Co 9:8** *2980*
is He **s** altogether for our sake? **1Co 9:10** *3004*
no one **s** by the Spirit of God says, **1Co 12:3** *2980*
if I come to you **s** in tongues, **1Co 14:6** *2980*
For you will be **s** into the air. **1Co 14:9** *2980*
I am not **s** *this* as a command, but **2Co 8:8** *3004*
for I will be **s** the truth; **2Co 12:6** *3004*
God that we have been **s** in Christ; **2Co 12:19** *2980*
This is allegorically **s**, **Ga 4:24** *238*
but **s** the truth in love, we are to **Eph 4:15** *226*
s to one another in psalms and **Eph 5:19** *2980*
but I am **s** with reference to Christ **Eph 5:32** *3004*
hindering us from **s** to the Gentiles **1Th 2:16** *2980*
come, concerning which we are **s**. **Heb 2:5** *2980*
though we are **s** in this way. **Heb 6:9** *2980*
you do not refuse Him who is **s**. **Heb 12:25** *2980*
EVIL AND HIS LIPS FROM **S** DECEIT. **1Pe 3:10** *2980*
is to do so as one who is **s** **1Pe 4:11** *2980*
donkey, **s** with a voice of a man, **2Pe 2:16** *5350*
For **s** out arrogant *words* of vanity **2Pe 2:18** *5350*
s in them of these things, **2Pe 3:16** *2980*
see the voice that was **s** with me. **Rv 1:12** *2980*
the sound of a trumpet **s** with me, **Rv 4:1** *2980*
heaven, *I heard* again **s** with me, **Rv 10:8** *2980*
to him a mouth **s** arrogant words **Rv 13:5** *2980*

SPEAKS

I know that he **s** fluently. **Ex 4:14** 1696
"When Pharaoh **s** to you, saying, **Ex 7:9** 1696
just as a man **s** to his friend. **Ex 33:11** 1696
'Whatever the LORD **s**, **Nu 23:26** 1696
What the LORD **s**, that I will **Nu 24:13** 1696
seen today that God **s** with man, **Dt 5:24** 1696
to us all that the LORD our God **s** **Dt 5:27** 1696
'But the prophet who **s** a word **Dt 18:20** 1696
or which he **s** in the name of other **Dt 18:20** 1696
prophet **s** in the name of the LORD, **Dt 18:22** 1696
mouth **s** boldly against my enemies, **1Sa 2:1** 7337
"Whoever **s** to you, bring him to **2Sa 14:10** 1696
one who **s** in the language of his own **Es 1:22** 1696
as one of the foolish women **s**. **Jb 2:10** 1696
my mouth, My tongue in my mouth **s**. **Jb 33:2** 1696
"Indeed God **s** once, Or twice, *yet* **Jb 33:14** 1696
'Job **s** without knowledge, And his **Jb 34:35** 1696
The tongue that **s** great things; **Ps 12:3** 1696
And **s** truth in his heart. **Ps 15:2** 1696
Transgression **s** to the ungodly **Ps 36:1** 5002
wisdom, And his tongue **s** justice. **Ps 37:30** 1696
comes to see *me*, he **s** falsehood; **Ps 41:6** 1696
Behold, He **s** forth with His voice, **Ps 68:33** 5414
He who **s** falsehood shall not **Ps 101:7** 1696
of aliens, Whose mouth **s** deceit And **Ps 144:11** 1696
the man who **s** perverse things; **Pr 2:12** 1696
He who **s** truth tells what is right, **Pr 12:17** 6315
There is one who **s** rashly like the **Pr 12:18** 981
And he who **s** right is loved. **Pr 16:13** 1696
When he **s** graciously, do not **Pr 26:25** 6963
For the LORD **s**, "Sons I have reared **Is 1:2** 1696
But now the LORD **s**, **Is 16:14** 1696
For the sea **s**, the stronghold of **Is 23:4** 559
For a fool **s** nonsense, And his **Is 32:6** 1696
the needy one **s** what is right. **Is 32:7** 1696
righteously and **s** with sincerity, **Is 33:15** 1696
tongue is a deadly arrow; It **s** deceit; **Jer 9:8** 1696
mouth one **s** peace to his neighbor, **Jer 9:8** 1696
the word which the LORD **s** to you, **Jer 10:1** 1696
Who is there who **s** and it comes to **La 3:37** 559
voice of God Almighty when He **s**. **Ezk 10:5** 1696
nation or tongue that **s** anything **Da 3:29** 560
abhor him who **s** *with* integrity. **Am 5:10** 1696
a great man **s** the desire of his soul; **Mi 7:3** 1696
Spirit of your Father who **s** in you. **Mt 10:20** *2980*
"Whoever **s** a word against the Son of **Mt 12:32** *3004*
but whoever **s** against the Holy Spirit, **Mt 12:32** *3004*
For the mouth **s** out of that which **Mt 12:34** *2980*
'HE WHO **S** EVIL OF FATHER OR **Mt 15:4** *2551*
'HE WHO **S** EVIL OF FATHER OR **Mk 7:10** *2551*
"Who is this *man* who **s** blasphemies? **Lk 5:21** *2980*
for his mouth **s** from that which **Lk 6:45** *2980*
"And everyone who **s** a word against **Lk 12:10** *3004*
from the earth and **s** of the earth. **Jn 3:31** *2980*
He whom God has sent **s** the words **Jn 3:34** *2980*
"He who **s** from himself seeks his **Jn 7:18** *2980*
a man spoken the way this man **s**." **Jn 7:46** *2980*
Whenever he **s** a lie, he speaks **Jn 8:44** *2980*
a lie, he **s** from his own *nature*, **Jn 8:44** *2980*
This man incessantly **s** against this **Ac 6:13** *2980*
it **s** to those who are under the **Ro 3:19** *2980*
just as David also **s** of the blessing **Ro 4:6** *3004*
righteousness based on faith **s** as **Ro 10:6** *3004*
For one who **s** in a tongue does not **1Co 14:2** *2980*
but in *his* spirit he **s** mysteries. **1Co 14:2** *2980*
But one who prophesies **s** to men **1Co 14:3** *2980*
One who **s** in a tongue edifies himself; **1Co 14:4** *2980*
than one who **s** in tongues, **1Co 14:5** *2980*
be to the one who **s** a barbarian, **1Co 14:11** *2980*
one who **s** will be a barbarian to me. **1Co 14:11** *2980*
let one who **s** in a tongue pray that **1Co 14:13** *2980*
If anyone **s** in a tongue, *it should* **1Co 14:27** *2980*
proof of the Christ who **s** in me, **2Co 13:3** *2980*
though he is dead, he still **s**. **Heb 11:4** *2980*
s better than *the blood* of Abel. **Heb 12:24** *2980*
the Scripture **s** to no purpose: **Jas 4:5** *3004*
He who **s** against a brother or **Jas 4:11** *2635*
his brother, **s** against the law and **Jas 4:11** *2635*

Whoever **s**, *is to do so* as one **1Pe 4:11** *2980*

SPEAR

and took a **s** in his hand, **Nu 25:7** 7420
Not a shield or a **s** was seen Among **Jg 5:8** 7420
neither sword nor **s** was found in the **1Sa 13:22** 2595
The shaft of his **s** was like a weaver's **1Sa 17:7** 2595
and the head of his **s** *weighed* six **1Sa 17:7** 2595
"You come to me with a sword, a **s**, **1Sa 17:45** 2595
does not deliver by sword or by **s**; **1Sa 17:47** 2595
and a **s** *was* in Saul's hand. **1Sa 18:10** 2595
Saul hurled the **s** for he thought, **1Sa 18:11** 2595
his house with his **s** in his hand, **1Sa 19:9** 2595
pin David to the wall with the **s**, **1Sa 19:10** 2595
he stuck the **s** into the wall. **1Sa 19:10** 2595
his **s** at him to strike him down; **1Sa 20:33** 2595
there not a **s** or a sword on hand? **1Sa 21:8** 2595
the height with his **s** in his hand, **1Sa 22:6** 2595
with his **s** stuck in the ground at **1Sa 26:7** 2595
please let me strike him with the **s** **1Sa 26:8** 2595
but now please take the **s** that is **1Sa 26:11** 2595
So David took the **s** and the jug of **1Sa 26:12** 2595
And now, see where the king's **s** is and **1Sa 26:16** 2595
"Behold the **s** of the king! **1Sa 26:22** 2595
behold, Saul was leaning on his **s**. **2Sa 1:6** 2595
belly with the butt end of the **s**, **2Sa 2:23** 2595
that the **s** came out at his back. **2Sa 2:23** 2595
the weight of whose **s** was three **2Sa 21:16** 7013
shaft of whose **s** was like a weaver's **2Sa 21:19** 2595
with iron and the shaft of a **s**, **2Sa 23:7** 2595
And he swung his **s** against three **2Sa 23:18** 2595
the Egyptian *had* a **s** in his hand, **2Sa 23:21** 2595
snatched the **s** from the Egyptian's **2Sa 23:21** 2595
and killed him with his own **s**. **2Sa 23:21** 2595
he lifted up his **s** against three **1Ch 11:11** 2595
and he swung his **s** against three **1Ch 11:20** 2595
hand *was* a **s** like a weaver's beam, **1Ch 11:23** 2595
snatched the **s** from the Egyptian's **1Ch 11:23** 2595
and killed him with his own **s**. **1Ch 11:23** 2595
who could handle shield and **s**, **1Ch 12:8** 7420
who bore shield and **s** *were* 6,800, **1Ch 12:24** 7420
them 37,000 with shield and **s**. **1Ch 12:34** 2595
shaft of whose **s** *was* like a weaver's **1Ch 20:5** 2595
go to war *and* handle **s** and shield. **2Ch 25:5** 7420
him, The flashing **s** and javelin. **Jb 39:23** 2595
Nor the **s**, the dart or the javelin. **Jb 41:26** 2595
Draw also the **s** and the battle-axe **Ps 35:3** 2595
the bow and cuts the **s** in two; **Ps 46:9** 2595
"They seize bow and **s**; **Jer 6:23** 3591
At the radiance of Your gleaming **s**. **Hab 3:11** 2595
soldiers pierced His side with a **s**, **Jn 19:34** *3057*

SPEARMEN

horsemen and two hundred **s**." **Ac 23:23** *1187*

SPEARS

the Hebrews will make swords or **s**." **1Sa 13:19** 2595
So he took three **s** in his hand and **2Sa 18:14** 7626
the **s** and shields that *had been* King **2Ki 11:10** 2595
He put shields and **s** in every **2Ch 11:12** 7420
bearing large shields and **s**, **2Ch 14:8** 7420
to the captains of hundreds the **s** **2Ch 23:9** 2595
for all the army shields, **s**, **2Ch 26:14** 7420
in families with their swords, **s** and **Ne 4:13** 7420
while half of them held the **s**, **Ne 4:16** 7420
half of them holding **s** from dawn **Ne 4:21** 7420
Or his head with fishing **s**? **Jb 41:7** 6767b
men, whose teeth are **s** and arrows And **Ps 57:4** 2595
and their **s** into pruning hooks. **Is 2:4** 2595
Polish the **s**, Put on the **Jer 46:4** 7420
bows and arrows, war clubs and **s** **Ezk 39:9** 7420
And your pruning hooks into **s**; **Jl 3:10** 7420
And their **s** into pruning hooks; **Mi 4:3** 2595
And the cypress **s** are **Na 2:3**
Swords flashing, **s** gleaming, **Na 3:3** 2595
You pierced with his own **s** **Hab 3:14** 4294

SPECIAL

to the LORD to fulfill a **s** vow or **Lv 22:21** 6381
a man or woman makes a **s** vow, **Nu 6:2** 6381
or a sacrifice to fulfill a **s** vow, **Nu 15:3** 6381
a sacrifice, to fulfill a **s** vow, **Nu 15:8** 6381
take **s** note of that person and do not **2Th 3:14** *4593*
and you pay **s** attention to the one **Jas 2:3** *1914*
As each one has received a **s** gift, **1Pe 4:10**

SPECIES

For every **s** of beasts and birds, **Jas 3:7** *5449*

SPECIFIC

to be **s**, that the Gentiles are **Eph 3:6**

SPECIFICALLY

If I **s** say to the lad, **1Sa 20:21** 559

SPECIFICATIONS

house of God according to its **s** and **2Ch 24:13** 4971

SPECIFIED

the days which the king had **s** for **Da 1:18** 559

SPECK

regarded as a **s** of dust on the scales; **Is 40:15** 7834
s that is in your brother's eye, **Mt 7:3** *2595*
'Let me take the **s** out of your eye,' **Mt 7:4** *2595*
take the **s** out of your brother's eye. **Mt 7:5** *2595*
s that is in your brother's eye, **Lk 6:41** *2595*
take out the **s** that is in your eye,' **Lk 6:42** *2595*
will see clearly to take out the **s** **Lk 6:42** *2595*

SPECKLED

there every **s** and spotted sheep and **Gn 30:32** 5348
the spotted and **s** among the goats; **Gn 30:32** 5348
Every one that is not **s** and spotted **Gn 30:33** 5348
the **s** and spotted female goats, **Gn 30:35** 5348
flocks brought forth striped, **s**, **Gn 30:39** 5348
'The **s** shall be your wages,' then **Gn 31:8** 5348
all the flock brought forth **s**; **Gn 31:8** 5348

which were mating *were* striped, **s**, **Gn 31:10** 5348
which are mating are striped, **s**, **Gn 31:12** 5348
like a **s** bird of prey to Me? **Jer 12:9** 6641

SPECTACLE
you vile, And set you up as a **s**. **Na 3:6** 7210
who came together for *this* **s**, **Lk 23:48** *2335*
we have become a **s** to the world, **1Co 4:9** *2302*
made a public **s** through reproaches **Heb 10:33** *2301*

SPECULATION
which give rise to mere **s** rather **1Tm 1:4** *1567b*

SPECULATIONS
but they became futile in their **s**, **Ro 1:21** *1261*
destroying **s** and every lofty thing **2Co 10:5** *3053*
But refuse foolish and ignorant **s**, **2Tm 2:23** *2214*

SPED
He **s** upon the wings of the wind. **Ps 18:10** 1675

SPEECH
of Lamech, Give heed to my **s**, **Gn 4:23** 565a
not understand one another's **s**." **Gn 11:7** 8193
am slow of **s** and slow of tongue." **Ex 4:10** 6310
to me, for I am unskilled in **s**?" **Ex 6:12** 8193
"Behold, I am unskilled in **s**; **Ex 6:30** 8193
the rain, My **s** distill as the dew, **Dt 32:2** 565a
a warrior, one prudent in **s**, **1Sa 16:18** 1697
"He deprives the trusted ones of **s** **Jb 12:20** 8193
"Listen carefully to my **s**, **Jb 13:17** 4405
"Listen carefully to my **s**, **Jb 21:2** 4405
a liar, And make my **s** worthless?" **Jb 24:25** 4405
again, And my **s** dropped on them. **Jb 29:22** 4405
now, Job, please hear my **s**, **Jb 33:1** 4405
Your ear to me, hear my **s**. **Ps 17:6** 565a
Day to day pours forth **s**, **Ps 19:2** 561
There is no **s**, nor are there words; **Ps 19:3** 561
His **s** was smoother than butter, **Ps 55:21** 6310
aimed bitter **s** *as* their arrow, **Ps 64:3** 1697
a deceitful mouth And put devious **s** **Pr 4:24** 8193
And smoother than oil is her **s**; **Pr 5:3** 2441
And sweetness of **s** increases **Pr 16:21** 8193
Excellent **s** is not fitting for a fool, **Pr 17:7** 8193
Than he who is perverse in **s** and is **Pr 19:1** 8193
of heart *And* whose **s** is gracious, **Pr 22:11** 8193
Do not let your **s** cause you to sin **Ec 5:6** 6310
Because their **s** and their actions **Is 3:8** 3956
your **s** will whisper from the dust. **Is 29:4** 565a
people of unintelligible **s** which no **Is 33:19** 8193
sent to a people of unintelligible **s** **Ezk 3:5** 8193
to many peoples of unintelligible **s** **Ezk 3:6** 8193
This figure of **s** Jesus spoke to them, **Jn 10:6** *3942*
and are not using a figure of **s**. **Jn 16:29** *3942*
by their smooth and flattering **s** they **Ro 16:18** *2129*
Him, in all **s** and all knowledge, **1Co 1:5** *3056*
gospel, not in cleverness of **s**, **1Co 1:17** *3056*
superiority of **s** or of wisdom, **1Co 2:1** *3056*
unless you utter by the tongue **s** **1Co 14:9** *3056*
we use great boldness in *our* **s**, **2Co 3:12** *3954*
and his **s** contemptible." **2Co 10:10** *3056*
But even if I am unskilled in **s**, **2Co 11:6** *3056*
and abusive **s** from your mouth. **Col 3:8** *148*
Let your **s** always be with grace, **Col 4:6** *3056*
we never came with flattering **s**, **1Th 2:5** *3056*
rather in **s**, conduct, love, faith *and* **1Tm 4:12** *3056*
sound *in* **s** which is beyond reproach, **Ti 2:8** *3056*

SPEECHLESS
was opened and I was no longer **s**. **Ezk 33:22** 481
toward the ground and became **s**. **Da 10:15** 481
When he fashions **s** idols. **Hab 2:18** 483
wedding clothes?' And the man was **s**. **Mt 22:12** *5392*
men who traveled with him stood **s**, **Ac 9:7** *1753a*

SPEED
"Let Him make **s**, let Him hasten **Is 5:19** 4116
it will come with **s** swiftly. **Is 5:26** 4120

SPEEDILY
carried *them* **s** to all the lay people. **2Ch 35:13** 7323
May evil hunt the violent man **s**." **Ps 140:11** 4073
your recovery will **s** spring forth; **Is 58:8** 4120
s I will return your recompense on **Jl 3:4** 4120

SPEEDY
Swift is the booty, **s** is the prey. **Is 8:1** 2363a

SPELL
or one who casts a **s**, **Dt 18:11** 2267

SPELLS
Or a skillful caster of **s**. **Ps 58:5** 2267
In spite of the great power of your **s**. **Is 47:9** 2267
"Stand *fast* now in your **s** And in **Is 47:12** 2267

SPELT
wheat and the **s** were not ruined, **Ex 9:32** 3698
beans, lentils, millet and **s**, **Ezk 4:9** 3698

SPEND
servant's house, and **s** the night, **Gn 19:2** 3885a
shall **s** the night in the square." **Gn 19:2** 3885a
"**S** the night here, and I will **Nu 22:8** 3885a
"You may **s** the money for **Dt 14:26** 5414
"Please be willing to **s** the night, **Jg 19:6** 3885a
please **s** the night. **Jg 19:9** 3885a
s the night here that your heart **Jg 19:9** 3885a
was not willing to **s** the night, **Jg 19:10** 3885a
Jebusites and **s** the night in it." **Jg 19:11** 3885a
s the night in Gibeah or Ramah." **Jg 19:13** 3885a
into *his* house to **s** the night. **Jg 19:15** 3885a
s the night in the open square." **Jg 19:20** 3885a
to **s** the night at Gibeah which **Jg 20:4** 3885a
not **s** the night with the people. **2Sa 17:8** 3885a
'Do not **s** the night at the fords **2Sa 17:16** 3885a
s the night within Jerusalem so that **Ne 4:22** 3885a
"Why do you **s** the night in front **Ne 13:21** 3885a
"They **s** their days in prosperity, **Jb 21:13** 1086
"They **s** the night naked, without **Jb 24:7** 3885a
will he **s** the night at your manger? **Jb 39:9** 3885a
He will **s** them like a shadow. **Ec 6:12** 6213a
Let us **s** the night in the villages. **SS 7:11** 3885a
the birds of prey will **s** the summer **Is 18:6** 7019b
the beasts of the earth will **s** harvest **Is 18:6** 2778b
of Arabia you must **s** the night, **Is 21:13** 3885a
you **s** money for what is not bread, **Is 55:2** 8254
and **s** the night in secret places; **Is 65:4** 3885a
Thus will I **s** My wrath on them. **Ezk 6:12** 3615
you and **s** My anger against you **Ezk 7:8** 3615
"Thus I will **s** My wrath on the **Ezk 13:15** 3615
Come, **s** the night in sackcloth O **Jl 1:13** 3885a
and it will **s** the night within **Zch 5:4** 3885a
s two hundred denarii on bread and **Mk 6:37** *59*
and whatever more you **s**, **Lk 10:35** *4325*
He would go out and **s** the night on **Lk 21:37** *835*
strangers visiting there used to **s** their **Ac 17:21** *2119*
would not have to **s** time in Asia; **Ac 20:16** *5551*
northwest, and **s** the winter *there*. **Ac 27:12** *3914*
with you, or even **s** the winter, **1Co 16:6** *3914*
I will most gladly **s** and be expended **2Co 12:15** *1159*
decided to **s** the winter there. **Ti 3:12** *3914*
you may **s** *it* on your pleasures. **Jas 4:3** *1159*
and **s** a year there and engage in **Jas 4:13** *4160*

SPENDING
after **s** the full number of days, **Lk 2:43** *5048*
s time with them and baptizing. **Jn 3:22** *1304*
to Caesarea and was **s** time there. **Ac 12:19** *1304*
While they were **s** many days there, **Ac 25:14** *1304*
s our life in malice and envy, **Ti 3:3** *1236*

SPENT
him ate and drank and **s** the night. **Gn 24:54** 3885a
place and **s** the night there, **Gn 28:11** 3885a
and **s** the night on the mountain. **Gn 31:54** 3885a
So he **s** the night there. **Gn 32:13** 3885a
himself **s** that night in the camp. **Gn 32:21** 3885a
When the money was all **s** in **Gn 47:15** 8552
my lord that our money is all **s**, **Gn 47:18** 8552
strength will be **s** uselessly, **Lv 26:20** 8552
The people **s** all day and all **Nu 11:32** 6965
days, the days that you **s** *there*. **Dt 1:46** 3427
camp and **s** the night in the camp. **Jos 6:11** 3885a
but Joshua **s** that night among the **Jos 8:9** 3885a
and Joshua **s** that night in the **Jos 8:13** 1980
that he **s** the night there again. **Jg 19:7** 3885a
They **s** the night around the **1Ch 9:27** 3885a
s the night outside Jerusalem. **Ne 13:20** 3885a
For my life is **s** with sorrow And **Ps 31:10** 3615
For all this His anger is not **s**, **Is 5:25** 7725
indignation *against you* will be **s** and **Is 10:25** 3615
I have **s** My strength for nothing **Is 49:4** 3615
that my days have been **s** in shame? **Jer 20:18** 3615
'Thus My anger will be **s** and **Ezk 5:13** 3615
when I have **s** My wrath upon them. **Ezk 5:13** 3615
Until I have **s** My wrath on you. **Ezk 24:13** 5117
palace and **s** the night fasting, **Da 6:18** 1006b
and **s** the night there. **Mt 21:17** *835*
and had **s** all that she had and was **Mk 5:26** *1159*
and He **s** the whole night in prayer **Lk 6:12** *1273*
"Now when he had **s** everything, a **Lk 15:14** *1159*
Therefore they **s** a long time *there* **Ac 14:3** *1304*
And they **s** a long time with the **Ac 14:28** *1304*
After they had **s** time *there*, **Ac 15:33** *4160*
And having **s** some time *there*, he **Ac 18:23** *4160*
And *there* he **s** three months, and **Ac 20:3** *4160*
After he had **s** not more than **Ac 25:6** *1304*
which from the beginning was **s** **Ac 26:4** *1096*
night and a day I have **s** in the deep **2Co 11:25** *4160*

SPEW
that the land will not **s** you out, **Lv 18:28** 7006a
you to live will not **s** you out. **Lv 20:22** 7006a

SPEWED
land has **s** out its inhabitants. **Lv 18:25** 7006a
as it has **s** out the nation which **Lv 18:28** 7006a

SPHERE
but within the measure of the **s** **2Co 10:13** *2583*
we will be, within our **s**, enlarged **2Co 10:15** *2583*
accomplished in the **s** of another. **2Co 10:16** *2583*

SPICE
and the **s** and the oil for the **Ex 35:28** 1314
there had never been **s** like that **2Ch 9:9** 1314
and cinnamon and **s** and incense and **Rv 18:13** *299a*

SPICED
I would give you **s** wine to drink **SS 8:2** 7544

SPICES
s for the anointing oil and for **Ex 25:6** 1314
also for yourself the finest of **s**: **Ex 30:23** 1314
"Take for yourself **s**, **Ex 30:34** 5561
s with pure frankincense; **Ex 30:34** 5561
and **s** for the anointing oil, **Ex 35:8** 1314
the pure, fragrant incense of **s**, **Ex 37:29** 5561
with camels carrying **s** and very **1Ki 10:2** 1314
amount of **s** and precious stones. **1Ki 10:10** 1314
Never again did such abundance of **s** **1Ki 10:10** 1314
and gold, garments, weapons, **s**, **1Ki 10:25** 1314
the silver and the gold and the **s** **2Ki 20:13** 1314
and the frankincense and the **s**. **1Ch 9:29** 1314
prepared the mixing of the **s**. **1Ch 9:30** 1314
retinue, with camels carrying **s** and **2Ch 9:1** 1314
amount of **s** and precious stones; **2Ch 9:9** 1314
and gold, garments, weapons, **s**, **2Ch 9:24** 1314
place which he had filled with **s** **2Ch 16:14** 1314
silver, gold, precious stones, **s**, **2Ch 32:27** 1314
s and the cosmetics for women **Es 2:12** 1314
of your oils Than all *kinds* of **s**! **SS 4:10** 1314
along with all the finest **s**. **SS 4:14** 1314
Let its **s** be wafted abroad. **SS 4:16** 1314
stag On the mountains of **s**." **SS 8:14** 1314
gold and the **s** and the precious oil **Is 39:2** 1314
'You will die in peace; and as **s** **Jer 34:5**
so they will burn **s** for you; **Jer 34:5**
the flesh well And mix in the **s**, **Ezk 24:10** 7543
with the best of all *kinds* of **s**, **Ezk 27:22** 1314
of James, and Salome, bought **s**, **Mk 16:1** *759*
and prepared **s** and perfumes. **Lk 23:56** *759*
the **s** which they had prepared. **Lk 24:1** *759*
it in linen wrappings with the **s**, **Jn 19:40** *759*

SPIDER'S
fragile, And whose trust a **s** web. **Jb 8:14** 5908
built his house like the **s** web, **Jb 27:18**
adders' eggs and weave the **s** web; **Is 59:5** 5908

SPIED
So they went up and **s** out the land **Nu 13:21** 8446
of the land which they had **s** out, **Nu 13:32** 8446
of those who had **s** out the land, **Nu 14:6** 8446
of days which you **s** out the land, **Nu 14:34** 8446
valley of Eshcol and **s** it out. **Dt 1:24** 7270
two men who had **s** out the land, **Jos 6:22** 7270
So the men went up and **s** out Ai. **Jos 7:2** 7270
The house of Joseph **s** out Bethel **Jg 1:23** 8446

SPIES
"You are **s**; you have come to look **Gn 42:9** 7270
men, your servants are not **s**." **Gn 42:11** 7270
"It is as I said to you, you are **s**; **Gn 42:14** 7270
of Pharaoh, surely you are **s**." **Gn 42:16** 7270
and took us for **s** of the country. **Gn 42:30** 7270
'We are honest men; we are not **s**. **Gn 42:31** 7270
I may know that you are not **s**, **Gn 42:34** 7270
the son of Nun sent two men as **s** **Jos 2:1** 7270
So the young men who were **s** went **Jos 6:23** 7270
The **s** saw a man coming out of **Jg 1:24** 8104
David sent out **s**, and he knew that **1Sa 26:4** 7270
But Absalom sent **s** throughout all **2Sa 15:10** 7270
"From there he **s** out food; **Jb 39:29** 2658
The wicked **s** upon the righteous And **Ps 37:32** 6822
s who pretended to be righteous, **Lk 20:20** *1455*
she had welcomed the **s** in peace. **Heb 11:31** *2685*

SPILLED
and are like water **s** on the ground **2Sa 14:14** 5064
the skins and it will be **s** out, **Lk 5:37** *1632b*

SPIN
they do not toil nor do they **s**, **Mt 6:28** *3514*
they neither toil nor **s**; **Lk 12:27** *3514*

SPINDLE
And her hands grasp the **s**. **Pr 31:19** 6418

SPIRIT
and the **S** of God was moving over **Gn 1:2** 7307
"My **S** shall not strive with man **Gn 6:3** 7307
was the breath of the **s** of life, **Gn 7:22** 7307
morning his **s** was troubled, **Gn 41:8** 7307
man like this, in whom is a divine **s** **Gn 41:38** 7307
s of their father Jacob revived. **Gn 45:27** 7307
have endowed with the **s** of wisdom, **Ex 28:3** 7307
him with the **S** of God in wisdom, **Ex 31:3** 7307
everyone whose **s** moved him came **Ex 35:21** 7307
has filled him with the **S** of God, **Ex 35:31** 7307
if a **s** of jealousy comes over him **Nu 5:14** 7307
or if a **s** of jealousy comes over **Nu 5:14** 7307
or when a **s** of jealousy comes over **Nu 5:30** 7307
take of the **S** who is upon you, **Nu 11:17** 7307
and He took of the **S** who was upon **Nu 11:25** 7307
And when the **S** rested upon them, **Nu 11:25** 7307
And the **S** rested upon them **Nu 11:26** 7307
LORD would put His **S** upon them!" **Nu 11:29** 7307
he has had a different **s** and has **Nu 14:24** 7307
and the **S** of God came upon him. **Nu 24:2** 7307
of Nun, a man in whom is the **S**, **Nu 27:18** 7307
the LORD your God hardened his **s** **Dt 2:30** 7307
was filled with the **s** of wisdom, **Dt 34:9** 7307
there was no **s** in them any longer **Jos 5:1** 7307
The **S** of the LORD came upon him, **Jg 3:10** 7307
S of the LORD came upon Gideon; **Jg 6:34** 7307
Then God sent an evil **s** between **Jg 9:23** 7307
Now the **S** of the LORD came upon **Jg 11:29** 7307
And the **S** of the LORD began to **Jg 13:25** 7307
The **S** of the LORD came upon **Jg 14:6** 7307
Then the **S** of the LORD came upon **Jg 14:19** 7307
And the **S** of the LORD came upon **Jg 15:14** 7307
lord, I am a woman oppressed in **s**; **1Sa 1:15** 7307
"Then the **S** of the LORD will come **1Sa 10:6** 7307
S of God came upon him mightily, **1Sa 10:10** 7307
Then the **S** of God came upon Saul **1Sa 11:6** 7307
and the **S** of the LORD came **1Sa 16:13** 7307
Now the **S** of the LORD departed **1Sa 16:14** 7307
evil **s** from the LORD terrorized him. **1Sa 16:14** 7307
evil **s** from God is terrorizing you. **1Sa 16:15** 7307
the evil **s** from God is on you, **1Sa 16:16** 7307
the *evil* **s** from God came to Saul, **1Sa 16:23** 7307
the evil **s** would depart from him. **1Sa 16:23** 7307
evil **s** from God came mightily upon **1Sa 18:10** 7307
was an evil **s** from the LORD on Saul **1Sa 19:9** 7307
the **S** of God came upon the **1Sa 19:20** 7307
the **S** of God came upon him also, **1Sa 19:23** 7307
then his **s** revived. **1Sa 30:12** 7307
"The **S** of the LORD spoke by me, **2Sa 23:2** 7307
LORD, there was no more **s** in her. **1Ki 10:5** 7307
the **S** of the LORD will carry you **1Ki 18:12** 7307
your **s** is so sullen that you are not **1Ki 21:5** 7307
"Then a **s** came forward and stood **1Ki 22:21** 7307
be a deceiving **s** in the mouth of all **1Ki 22:22** 7307
the LORD has put a deceiving **s** in **1Ki 22:23** 7307
"How did the **S** of the LORD pass **1Ki 22:24** 7307
let a double portion of your **s** be **2Ki 2:9** 7307

"The **s** of Elijah rests on Elisha."	**2Ki 2:15**	7307
perhaps the **S** of the LORD has	**2Ki 2:16**	7307
I will put a **s** in him so that he	**2Ki 19:7**	7307
of Israel stirred up the **s** of Pul,	**1Ch 5:26**	7307
even the **s** of Tilgath-pilneser	**1Ch 5:26**	7307
Then the **S** came upon Amasai, who	**1Ch 12:18**	7307
Now the **S** of God came on Azariah	**2Ch 15:1**	7307
"Then a **s** came forward and stood	**2Ch 18:20**	7307
'I will go and be a deceiving **s** in	**2Ch 18:21**	7307
the LORD has put a deceiving **s** in	**2Ch 18:22**	7307
"How did the **S** of the LORD pass	**2Ch 18:23**	7307
S of the LORD came upon Jahaziel	**2Ch 20:14**	7307
the **s** of the Philistines and the Arabs	**2Ch 21:16**	7307
Then the **S** of God came on	**2Ch 24:20**	7307
the LORD stirred up the **s** of Cyrus	**2Ch 36:22**	7307
the LORD stirred up the **s** of Cyrus	**Ezr 1:1**	7307
everyone whose **s** God had stirred	**Ezr 1:5**	7307
gave Your good **S** to instruct them,	**Ne 9:20**	7307
admonished them by Your **S** through	**Ne 9:30**	7307
"Then a **s** passed by my face;	**Jb 4:15**	7307
Their poison my **s** drinks;	**Jb 6:4**	7307
will speak in the anguish of my **s**,	**Jb 7:11**	7307
And Your care has preserved my **s**.	**Jb 10:12**	7307
should turn your **s** against God And	**Jb 15:13**	7307
"My **s** is broken, my days are	**Jb 17:1**	7307
And the **s** of my understanding	**Jb 20:3**	7307
whose **s** was expressed through you?	**Jb 26:4**	5397
"But it is a **s** in man, And the	**Jb 32:8**	7307
The **s** within me constrains me.	**Jb 32:18**	7307
"The **S** of God has made me, And	**Jb 33:4**	7307
He should gather to Himself His **s**	**Jb 34:14**	7307
Into Your hand I commit my **s**;	**Ps 31:5**	7307
And in whose **s** there is no deceit!	**Ps 32:2**	7307
saves those who are crushed in **s**.	**Ps 34:18**	7307
And renew a steadfast **s** within me.	**Ps 51:10**	7307
do not take Your Holy **S** from me.	**Ps 51:11**	7307
And sustain me with a willing **s**.	**Ps 51:12**	7307
sacrifices of God are a broken **s**;	**Ps 51:17**	7307
He will cut off the **s** of princes;	**Ps 76:12**	7307
I sigh, then my **s** grows faint.	**Ps 77:3**	7307
And my **s** ponders:	**Ps 77:6**	7307
whose **s** was not faithful to God.	**Ps 78:8**	7307
You take away their **s**,	**Ps 104:29**	7307
You send forth Your **S**,	**Ps 104:30**	7307
were rebellious against His **S**,	**Ps 106:33**	7307
Where can I go from Your **S**?	**Ps 139:7**	7307
my **s** was overwhelmed within me,	**Ps 142:3**	7307
my **s** is overwhelmed within me;	**Ps 143:4**	7307
me quickly, O LORD, my **s** fails;	**Ps 143:7**	7307
Let Your good **S** lead me on level	**Ps 143:10**	7307
His **s** departs, he returns to the	**Ps 146:4**	7307
I will pour out my **s** on you;	**Pr 1:23**	7307
perversion in it crushes the **s**.	**Pr 15:4**	7307
the heart is sad, the **s** is broken.	**Pr 15:13**	7307
And a haughty **s** before stumbling.	**Pr 16:18**	7307
It is better to be humble in **s** with	**Pr 16:19**	7307
he who rules his **s**, than he who	**Pr 16:32**	7307
But a broken **s** dries up the bones.	**Pr 17:22**	7307
he who has a cool **s** is a man of	**Pr 17:27**	7307
The **s** of a man can endure his	**Pr 18:14**	7307
a broken **s** who can bear it?	**Pr 18:14**	7307
The **s** of man is the lamp of the	**Pr 20:27**	5397
man who has no control over his **s**.	**Pr 25:28**	7307
But a humble **s** will obtain honor.	**Pr 29:23**	7307
Patience of **s** is better than	**Ec 7:8**	7307
is better than haughtiness of **s**.	**Ec 7:8**	7307
and the **s** will return to God who	**Ec 12:7**	7307
by the **s** of judgment and the	**Is 4:4**	7307
of judgment and the **s** of burning,	**Is 4:4**	7307
S of the LORD will rest on Him,	**Is 11:2**	7307
The **s** of wisdom and understanding,	**Is 11:2**	7307
The **s** of counsel and strength,	**Is 11:2**	7307
The **s** of knowledge and the fear of	**Is 11:2**	7307
"Then the **s** of the Egyptians will	**Is 19:3**	7307
within her a **s** of distortion;	**Is 19:14**	7307
my **s** within me seeks You	**Is 26:9**	7307
A **s** of justice for him who sits in	**Is 28:6**	7307
like that of a **s** from the ground,	**Is 29:4**	178
poured over you a **s** of deep sleep,	**Is 29:10**	7307
make an alliance, but not of My **S**,	**Is 30:1**	7307
their horses are flesh and not **s**;	**Is 31:3**	7307
Until the **S** is poured out upon us	**Is 32:15**	7307
And His **S** has gathered them.	**Is 34:16**	7307
I will put a **s** in him so that he	**Is 37:7**	7307
in all these is the life of my **s**;	**Is 38:16**	7307
has directed the **S** of the LORD,	**Is 40:13**	7307
I have put My **S** upon Him;	**Is 42:1**	7307
it And **s** to those who walk in it,	**Is 42:5**	7307
pour out My **S** on your offspring And	**Is 44:3**	7307
Lord GOD has sent Me, and His **S**."	**Is 48:16**	7307
a wife forsaken and grieved in **s**,	**Is 54:6**	7307
also with the contrite and lowly of **s**	**Is 57:15**	7307
In order to revive the **s** of the lowly	**Is 57:15**	7307
the **s** would grow faint before Me,	**Is 57:16**	7307
"My **S** which is upon you, and My	**Is 59:21**	7307
The **S** of the Lord GOD is upon me,	**Is 61:1**	7307
praise instead of a **s** of fainting.	**Is 61:3**	7307
rebelled And grieved His Holy **S**;	**Is 63:10**	7307
Where is He who put His Holy **S** in	**Is 63:11**	7307
The **S** of the LORD gave them rest.	**Is 63:14**	7307
you will wail with a broken **s**.	**Is 65:14**	7307
who is humble and contrite of **s**,	**Is 66:2**	7307
of Leb-kamai The **s** of a destroyer.	**Jer 51:1**	7307
the **s** of the kings of the Medes,	**Jer 51:11**	7307
My **s** is greatly troubled;	**La 1:20**	4578
tears, My **s** is greatly troubled;	**La 2:11**	4578
wherever the **s** was about to go,	**Ezk 1:12**	7307
Wherever the **s** was about to go,	**Ezk 1:20**	7307
for the **s** of the living beings *was*	**Ezk 1:20**	7307
for the **s** of the living beings *was*	**Ezk 1:21**	7307
S entered me and set me on my feet	**Ezk 2:2**	7307
Then the **S** lifted me up, and I	**Ezk 3:12**	7307
S lifted me up and took me away;	**Ezk 3:14**	7307
embittered in the rage of my **s**,	**Ezk 3:14**	7307
The **S** then entered me and made me	**Ezk 3:24**	7307
and the **S** lifted me up between	**Ezk 8:3**	7307
for the **s** of the living beings *was*	**Ezk 10:17**	7307
the **S** lifted me up and brought me	**Ezk 11:1**	7307
the **S** of the LORD fell upon me,	**Ezk 11:5**	7307
and put a new **s** within them.	**Ezk 11:19**	7307
And the **S** lifted me up and brought	**Ezk 11:24**	7307
by the **S** of God to the exiles in	**Ezk 11:24**	7307
their own **s** and have seen nothing.	**Ezk 13:3**	7307
a new heart and a new **s**!	**Ezk 18:31**	7307
be feeble, every **s** will faint and	**Ezk 21:7**	7307
heart and put a new **s** within you;	**Ezk 36:26**	7307
"I will put My **S** within you	**Ezk 36:27**	7307
me out by the **S** of the LORD and	**Ezk 37:1**	7307
"I will put My **S** within you and	**Ezk 37:14**	7307
I will have poured out My **S** on	**Ezk 39:29**	7307
And the **S** lifted me up and brought	**Ezk 43:5**	7307
and his **s** was troubled and his	**Da 2:1**	7307
and my **s** is anxious to understand	**Da 2:3**	7307
in whom is a **s** of the holy gods;	**Da 4:8**	7308
that a **s** of the holy gods is in you	**Da 4:9**	7308
a **s** of the holy gods is in you.'	**Da 4:18**	7308
in whom is a **s** of the holy gods;	**Da 5:11**	7308
was because an extraordinary **s**,	**Da 5:12**	7308
that a **s** of the gods is in you,	**Da 5:14**	7308
and his **s** became so proud that he	**Da 5:20**	7308
he possessed an extraordinary **s**,	**Da 6:3**	7308
my **s** was distressed within me,	**Da 7:15**	7308
For a **s** of harlotry has led *them*	**Hos 4:12**	7307
a **s** of harlotry is within them,	**Hos 5:4**	7307
will pour out My **S** on all mankind;	**Jl 2:28**	7307
will pour out My **S** in those days.	**Jl 2:29**	7307
'Is the **S** of the LORD impatient?	**Mi 2:7**	7307
With the **S** of the LORD	**Mi 3:8**	7307
the men Who are stagnant in **s**,	**Zph 1:12**	8105
LORD stirred up the **s** of Zerubbabel	**Hg 1:14**	7307
and the **s** of Joshua the son of	**Hg 1:14**	7307
s of all the remnant of the people;	**Hg 1:14**	7307
My **S** is abiding in your midst;	**Hg 2:5**	7307
might nor by power, but by My **S**,'	**Zch 4:6**	7307
the LORD of hosts had sent by His **S**	**Zch 7:12**	7307
and forms the **s** of man within him,	**Zch 12:1**	7307
S of grace and of supplication,	**Zch 12:10**	7307
and the unclean **s** from the land.	**Zch 13:2**	7307
so who has a remnant of the **S**.	**Mal 2:15**	7307
Take heed then to your **s**,	**Mal 2:15**	7307
"So take heed to your **s**,	**Mal 2:16**	7307
to be with child by the Holy **S**.	**Mt 1:18**	4151
conceived in her is of the Holy **S**.	**Mt 1:20**	4151
He will baptize you with the Holy **S**	**Mt 3:11**	4151
the **S** of God descending as a dove	**Mt 3:16**	4151
Then Jesus was led up by the **S**	**Mt 4:1**	4151
"Blessed are the poor in **s**,	**Mt 5:3**	4151
but *it is* the **S** of your Father who	**Mt 10:20**	4151
I WILL PUT MY **S** UPON HIM, AND HE	**Mt 12:18**	4151
I cast out demons by the **S** of God,	**Mt 12:28**	4151
blasphemy against the **S** shall not be	**Mt 12:31**	4151
speaks against the Holy **S**,	**Mt 12:32**	4151
the unclean **s** goes out of a man,	**Mt 12:43**	4151
how does David in the **S** call Him	**Mt 22:43**	4151
the **s** is willing, but the flesh is	**Mt 26:41**	4151
loud voice, and yielded up His **s**.	**Mt 27:50**	4151
Father and the Son and the Holy **S**,	**Mt 28:19**	4151
baptize you with the Holy **S**."	**Mk 1:8**	4151
and the **S** like a dove descending	**Mk 1:10**	4151
Immediately the **S** impelled Him	**Mk 1:12**	4151
their synagogue with an unclean **s**;	**Mk 1:23**	4151
the unclean **s** cried out with a loud	**Mk 1:26**	4151
aware in His **s** that they were	**Mk 2:8**	4151
blasphemes against the Holy **S**	**Mk 3:29**	4151
"He has an unclean **s**."	**Mk 3:30**	4151
tombs with an unclean **s** met Him,	**Mk 5:2**	4151
out of the man, you unclean **s**!"	**Mk 5:8**	4151
little daughter had an unclean **s**	**Mk 7:25**	4151
Sighing deeply in His **s**,	**Mk 8:12**	4151
with a **s** which makes him mute;	**Mk 9:17**	4151
the **s** threw him into a convulsion,	**Mk 9:20**	4151
He rebuked the unclean **s**,	**Mk 9:25**	4151
"You deaf and mute **s**,	**Mk 9:25**	4151
"David himself said in the Holy **S**,	**Mk 12:36**	4151
who speak, but *it is* the Holy **S**.	**Mk 13:11**	4151
the **s** is willing, but the flesh is	**Mk 14:38**	4151
he will be filled with the Holy **S** while	**Lk 1:15**	4151
Him in the **s** and power of Elijah,	**Lk 1:17**	4151
"The Holy **S** will come upon you,	**Lk 1:35**	4151
was filled with the Holy **S**.	**Lk 1:41**	4151
my **s** has rejoiced in God my Savior.	**Lk 1:47**	4151
was filled with the Holy **S**,	**Lk 1:67**	4151
grow and to become strong in **s**,	**Lk 1:80**	4151
and the Holy **S** was upon him.	**Lk 2:25**	4151
been revealed to him by the Holy **S**	**Lk 2:26**	4151
he came in the **S** into the temple;	**Lk 2:27**	4151
He will baptize you with the Holy **S**	**Lk 3:16**	4151
and the Holy **S** descended upon Him	**Lk 3:22**	4151
Jesus, full of the Holy **S**,	**Lk 4:1**	4151
led around by the **S** in the wilderness	**Lk 4:1**	4151
to Galilee in the power of the **S**,	**Lk 4:14**	4151
"THE **S** OF THE LORD IS UPON ME,	**Lk 4:18**	4151
by the **s** of an unclean demon,	**Lk 4:33**	4151
unclean **s** to come out of the man.	**Lk 8:29**	4151
And her **s** returned, and she got	**Lk 8:55**	4151
and a **s** seizes him, and he	**Lk 9:39**	4151
But Jesus rebuked the unclean **s**,	**Lk 9:42**	4151
know what kind of **s** you are of;	**Lk 9:55**	4151
He rejoiced greatly in the Holy **S**,	**Lk 10:21**	4151
heavenly Father give the Holy **S** to	**Lk 11:13**	4151
the unclean **s** goes out of a man,	**Lk 11:24**	4151
who blasphemes against the Holy **S**,	**Lk 12:10**	4151
for the Holy **S** will teach you in	**Lk 12:12**	4151
had had a sickness caused by a **s**;	**Lk 13:11**	4151
INTO YOUR HANDS I COMMIT MY **S**."	**Lk 23:46**	4151
thought that they were seeing a **s**.	**Lk 24:37**	4151
for a **s** does not have flesh and	**Lk 24:39**	4151
"I have seen the **S** descending	**Jn 1:32**	4151
'He upon whom you see the **S**	**Jn 1:33**	4151
One who baptizes in the Holy **S**.'	**Jn 1:33**	4151
one is born of water and the **S** he	**Jn 3:5**	4151
which is born of the **S** is spirit.	**Jn 3:6**	4151
which is born of the Spirit is **s**.	**Jn 3:6**	4151
everyone who is born of the **S**."	**Jn 3:8**	4151
He gives the **S** without measure.	**Jn 3:34**	4151
worship the Father in **s** and truth;	**Jn 4:23**	4151
"God is **s**, and those who worship	**Jn 4:24**	4151
Him must worship in **s** and truth."	**Jn 4:24**	4151
"It is the **S** who gives life;	**Jn 6:63**	4151
spoken to you are **s** and are life.	**Jn 6:63**	4151
But this He spoke of the **S**,	**Jn 7:39**	4151
for the **S** was not yet *given*,	**Jn 7:39**	4151
weeping, He was deeply moved in **s**	**Jn 11:33**	4151
this, He became troubled in **s**,	**Jn 13:21**	4151
that is the **S** of truth, whom the	**Jn 14:17**	4151
"But the Helper, the Holy **S**,	**Jn 14:26**	4151
Father, *that is* the **S** of truth who	**Jn 15:26**	4151
"But when He, the **S** of truth,	**Jn 16:13**	4151
bowed His head and gave up His **s**.	**Jn 19:30**	4151
"Receive the Holy **S**.	**Jn 20:22**	4151
after He had by the Holy **S** given	**Ac 1:2**	4151
will be baptized with the Holy **S**	**Ac 1:5**	4151
when the Holy **S** has come upon you;	**Ac 1:8**	4151
which the Holy **S** foretold by the	**Ac 1:16**	4151
they were all filled with the Holy **S**	**Ac 2:4**	4151
the **S** was giving them utterance.	**Ac 2:4**	4151
THAT I WILL POUR FORTH OF MY **S**	**Ac 2:17**	4151
THOSE DAYS POUR FORTH OF MY **S**	**Ac 2:18**	4151
Father the promise of the Holy **S**,	**Ac 2:33**	4151
receive the gift of the Holy **S**.	**Ac 2:38**	4151
Peter, filled with the Holy **S**,	**Ac 4:8**	4151
who by the Holy **S**, *through* the	**Ac 4:25**	4151
were all filled with the Holy **S** and	**Ac 4:31**	4151
your heart to lie to the Holy **S** and	**Ac 5:3**	4151
put the **S** of the Lord to the test?	**Ac 5:9**	4151
and *so is* the Holy **S**,	**Ac 5:32**	4151
full of the **S** and of wisdom,	**Ac 6:3**	4151
full of faith and of the Holy **S**,	**Ac 6:5**	4151
the **S** with which he was speaking.	**Ac 6:10**	4151
are always resisting the Holy **S**;	**Ac 7:51**	4151
But being full of the Holy **S**,	**Ac 7:55**	4151
"Lord Jesus, receive my **s**!"	**Ac 7:59**	4151
they might receive the Holy **S**.	**Ac 8:15**	4151
they were receiving the Holy **S**.	**Ac 8:17**	4151
S was bestowed through the laying	**Ac 8:18**	4151
my hands may receive the Holy **S**."	**Ac 8:19**	4151
Then the **S** said to Philip,	**Ac 8:29**	4151
the **S** of the Lord snatched Philip	**Ac 8:39**	4151
and be filled with the Holy **S**."	**Ac 9:17**	4151
and in the comfort of the Holy **S**,	**Ac 9:31**	4151
on the vision, the **S** said to him,	**Ac 10:19**	4151
God anointed Him with the Holy **S**	**Ac 10:38**	4151
the Holy **S** fell upon all those who	**Ac 10:44**	4151
because the gift of the Holy **S** had	**Ac 10:45**	4151
who have received the Holy **S** just	**Ac 10:47**	4151
"The **S** told me to go with	**Ac 11:12**	4151
speak, the Holy **S** fell upon them just	**Ac 11:15**	4151
be baptized with the Holy **S**.'	**Ac 11:16**	4151
full of the Holy **S** and of faith.	**Ac 11:24**	4151
began to indicate by the **S** that there	**Ac 11:28**	4151
Lord and fasting, the Holy **S** said,	**Ac 13:2**	4151
So, being sent out by the Holy **S**,	**Ac 13:4**	4151
as Paul, filled with the Holy **S**,	**Ac 13:9**	4151
with joy and with the Holy **S**.	**Ac 13:52**	4151
to them giving them the Holy **S**,	**Ac 15:8**	4151
"For it seemed good to the Holy **S**	**Ac 15:28**	4151
forbidden by the Holy **S** to speak	**Ac 16:6**	4151
S of Jesus did not permit them;	**Ac 16:7**	4151
slave-girl having a **s** of divination	**Ac 16:16**	4151
and turned and said to the **s**,	**Ac 16:18**	4151
his **s** was being provoked within	**Ac 17:16**	4151
and being fervent in **s**,	**Ac 18:25**	4151
Did you receive the Holy **S** when	**Ac 19:2**	4151
heard whether there is a Holy **S**."	**Ac 19:2**	4151
them, the Holy **S** came on them,	**Ac 19:6**	4151
evil **s** answered and said to them,	**Ac 19:15**	4151
the man, in whom was the evil **s**,	**Ac 19:16**	4151
Paul purposed in the **S** to go to	**Ac 19:21**	4151
"And now, behold, bound in **S**,	**Ac 20:22**	4151
the Holy **S** solemnly testifies to me	**Ac 20:23**	4151
the Holy **S** has made you overseers,	**Ac 20:28**	4151
they kept telling Paul through the **S**	**Ac 21:4**	4151
"This is what the Holy **S** says:	**Ac 21:11**	4151
nor an angel, nor a **s**,	**Ac 23:8**	4151
suppose a **s** or an angel has spoken	**Ac 23:9**	4151
"The Holy **S** rightly spoke through	**Ac 28:25**	4151
according to the **S** of holiness,	**Ro 1:4**	4151
whom I serve in my **s** in the	**Ro 1:9**	4151
which is of the heart, by the **S**,	**Ro 2:29**	4151
the Holy **S** who was given to us.	**Ro 5:5**	4151
so that we serve in newness of the **S**	**Ro 7:6**	4151
law of the **S** of life in Christ Jesus	**Ro 8:2**	4151
the flesh but according to the **S**.	**Ro 8:4**	4151
those who are according to the **S**,	**Ro 8:5**	4151
the Spirit, the things of the **S**.	**Ro 8:5**	4151
mind set on the **S** is life and peace,	**Ro 8:6**	4151
are not in the flesh but in the **S**,	**Ro 8:9**	4151

indeed the **S** of God dwells in you. **Ro 8:9** *4151*
does not have the **S** of Christ, **Ro 8:9** *4151*
yet the **s** is alive because of **Ro 8:10** *4151*
S of Him who raised Jesus from the **Ro 8:11** *4151*
through His **S** who dwells in you. **Ro 8:11** *4151*
if by the **S** you are putting to death **Ro 8:13** *4151*
who are being led by the **S** of God, **Ro 8:14** *4151*
you have not received a **s** of slavery **Ro 8:15** *4151*
you have received a **s** of adoption **Ro 8:15** *4151*
The **S** Himself testifies with **Ro 8:16** *4151*
Himself testifies with our **s** **Ro 8:16** *4151*
having the first fruits of the **S**, **Ro 8:23** *4151*
way the **S** also helps our weakness; **Ro 8:26** *4151*
but the **S** Himself intercedes for **Ro 8:26** *4151*
knows what the mind of the **S** is, **Ro 8:27** *4151*
testifies with me in the Holy **S**, **Ro 9:1** *4151*
"GOD GAVE THEM A **S** OF STUPOR, **Ro 11:8** *4151*
behind in diligence, fervent in **s**, **Ro 12:11** *4151*
and peace and joy in the Holy **S**. **Ro 14:17** *4151*
hope by the power of the Holy **S**. **Ro 15:13** *4151*
sanctified by the Holy **S**. **Ro 15:16** *4151*
wonders, in the power of the **S**; **Ro 15:19** *4151*
Christ and by the love of the **S**, **Ro 15:30** *4151*
in demonstration of the **S** and of **1Co 2:4** *4151*
God revealed *them* through the **S**; **1Co 2:10** *4151*
for the **S** searches all things, **1Co 2:10** *4151*
of a man except the **s** of the man which **1Co 2:11** *4151*
no one knows except the **S** of God. **1Co 2:11** *4151*
received, not the **s** of the world, **1Co 2:12** *4151*
world, but the **S** who is from God, **1Co 2:12** *4151*
but in those taught by the **S**, **1Co 2:13** *4151*
accept the things of the **S** of God, **1Co 2:14** *4151*
that the **S** of God dwells in you? **1Co 3:16** *4151*
with love and a **s** of gentleness? **1Co 4:21** *4151*
absent in body but present in **s**, **1Co 5:3** *4151*
assembled, and I with you in **s**, **1Co 5:4** *4151*
that his **s** may be saved in the day **1Co 5:5** *4151*
Christ and in the **S** of our God. **1Co 6:11** *4151*
to the Lord is one **s** *with Him.* **1Co 6:17** *4151*
your body is a temple of the Holy **S** **1Co 6:19** *4151*
may be holy both in body and **s**; **1Co 7:34** *4151*
that I also have the **S** of God. **1Co 7:40** *4151*
one speaking by the **S** of God says, **1Co 12:3** *4151*
is Lord," except by the Holy **S**. **1Co 12:3** *4151*
of gifts, but the same **S**. **1Co 12:4** *4151*
is given the manifestation of the **S** **1Co 12:7** *4151*
the word of wisdom through the **S**, **1Co 12:8** *4151*
knowledge according to the same **S**; **1Co 12:8** *4151*
to another faith by the same **S**, **1Co 12:9** *4151*
gifts of healing by the one **S**, **1Co 12:9** *4151*
the same **S** works all these things, **1Co 12:11** *4151*
For by one **S** we were all baptized **1Co 12:13** *4151*
were all made to drink of one **S**. **1Co 12:13** *4151*
but in *his* **s** he speaks mysteries. **1Co 14:2** *4151*
if I pray in a tongue, my **s** prays, **1Co 14:14** *4151*
I will pray with the **s** and I **1Co 14:15** *4151*
I will sing with the **s** and I **1Co 14:15** *4151*
if you bless in the **s** *only,* **1Co 14:16** *4151*
last Adam *became* a life-giving **s**. **1Co 15:45** *4151*
have refreshed my **s** and yours. **1Co 16:18** *4151*
also sealed us and gave *us* the **S** **2Co 1:22** *4151*
I had no rest for my **s**, **2Co 2:13** *4151*
but with the **S** of the living God, **2Co 3:3** *4151*
not of the letter but of the **S**; **2Co 3:6** *4151*
kills, but the **S** gives life. **2Co 3:6** *4151*
how will the ministry of the **S** **2Co 3:8** *4151*
Now the Lord is the **S**, **2Co 3:17** *4151*
and where the **S** of the Lord is, **2Co 3:17** *4151*
just as from the Lord, the **S**. **2Co 3:18** *4151*
But having the same **s** of faith, **2Co 4:13** *4151*
who gave to us the **S** as a pledge. **2Co 5:5** *4151*
in kindness, in the Holy **S**, **2Co 6:6** *4151*
all defilement of flesh and **s**, **2Co 7:1** *4151*
his **s** has been refreshed by you all. **2Co 7:13** *4151*
you receive a different **s** which you **2Co 11:4** *4151*
not conduct ourselves in the same **s** **2Co 12:18** *4151*
and the fellowship of the Holy **S**, **2Co 13:14** *4151*
did you receive the **S** by the works **Ga 3:2** *4151*
Having begun by the **S**, **Ga 3:3** *4151*
who provides you with the **S** and **Ga 3:5** *4151*
would receive the promise of the **S** **Ga 3:14** *4151*
God has sent forth the **S** **Ga 4:6** *4151*
who was born according to the **S**, **Ga 4:29** *4151*
For we through the **S**, **Ga 5:5** *4151*
But I say, walk by the **S**, **Ga 5:16** *4151*
the flesh sets its desire against the **S**, **Ga 5:17** *4151*
and the **S** against the flesh; **Ga 5:17** *4151*
But if you are led by the **S**, **Ga 5:18** *4151*
But the fruit of the **S** is love, **Ga 5:22** *4151*
If we live by the **S**, **Ga 5:25** *4151*
Spirit, let us also walk by the **S**. **Ga 5:25** *4151*
such a one in a **s** of gentleness; **Ga 6:1** *4151*
but the one who sows to the **S** **Ga 6:8** *4151*
from the **S** reap eternal life. **Ga 6:8** *4151*
Lord Jesus Christ be with your **s**. **Ga 6:18** *4151*
in Him with the Holy **S** of promise, **Eph 1:13** *4151*
may give to you a **s** of wisdom and **Eph 1:17** *4151*
of the **s** that is now working in **Eph 2:2** *4151*
our access in one **S** to the Father. **Eph 2:18** *4151*
into a dwelling of God in the **S**. **Eph 2:22** *4151*
apostles and prophets in the **S**; **Eph 3:5** *4151*
through His **S** in the inner man, **Eph 3:16** *4151*
to preserve the unity of the **S** in the **Eph 4:3** *4151*
There is one body and one **S**, **Eph 4:4** *4151*
be renewed in the **s** of your mind, **Eph 4:23** *4151*
Do not grieve the Holy **S** of God, **Eph 4:30** *4151*
but be filled with the **S**, **Eph 5:18** *4151*
SALVATION, and the sword of the **S**, **Eph 6:17** *4151*
pray at all times in the **S**, **Eph 6:18** *4151*
provision of the **S** of Jesus Christ, **Php 1:19** *4151*
you are standing firm in one **s**, **Php 1:27** *4151*
there is any fellowship of the **S**, **Php 2:1** *4151*
the same love, united in **s**, **Php 2:2** *4861*
For I have no one *else* of kindred **s** **Php 2:20** *2473*
who worship in the **S** of God and **Php 3:3** *4151*
Let your gentle **s** be known to all **Php 4:5** *4151*
Lord Jesus Christ be with your **s**. **Php 4:23** *4151*
informed us of your love in the **S**. **Col 1:8** *4151*
nevertheless I am with you in **s**, **Col 2:5** *4151*
also in power and in the Holy **S** **1Th 1:5** *4151*
with the joy of the Holy **S**, **1Th 1:6** *4151*
in person, not in **s** **1Th 2:17** *2588*
God who gives His Holy **S** to you. **1Th 4:8** *4151*
Do not quench the **S**; **1Th 5:19** *4151*
and may your **s** and soul and body **1Th 5:23** *4151*
or be disturbed either by a **s** or a **2Th 2:2** *4151*
through sanctification by the **S** and **2Th 2:13** *4151*
flesh, Was vindicated in the **S**, **1Tm 3:16** *4151*
But the **S** explicitly says that in **1Tm 4:1** *4151*
doing nothing in a **s** *of* **1Tm 5:21**
God has not given us a **s** of timidity, **2Tm 1:7** *4151*
the Holy **S** who dwells in us, **2Tm 1:14** *4151*
The Lord be with your **s**. **2Tm 4:22** *4151*
and renewing by the Holy **S**, **Ti 3:5** *4151*
Lord Jesus Christ be with your **s**. **Phm 1:25** *4151*
by gifts of the Holy **S** according to **Heb 2:4** *4151*
just as the Holy **S** says, **Heb 3:7** *4151*
as the division of soul and **s**, **Heb 4:12** *4151*
been made partakers of the Holy **S**, **Heb 6:4** *4151*
The Holy **S** *is* signifying this, **Heb 9:8** *4151*
who through the eternal **S** offered **Heb 9:14** *4151*
Holy **S** also testifies to us; **Heb 10:15** *4151*
and has insulted the **S** of grace? **Heb 10:29** *4151*
as the body without *the* **s** is dead, **Jas 2:26** *4151*
"He jealously desires the **S** which **Jas 4:5** *4151*
by the sanctifying work of the **S**, **1Pe 1:2** *4151*
the **S** of Christ within them was **1Pe 1:11** *4151*
by the Holy **S** sent from heaven **1Pe 1:12** *4151*
keep sober *in* **s**, fix your hope **1Pe 1:13**
quality of a gentle and quiet **s**, **1Pe 3:4** *4151*
kindhearted, and humble in **s**; **1Pe 3:8** *5012b*
flesh, but made alive in the **s**; **1Pe 3:18** *4151*
they may live in the **s** according to **1Pe 4:6** *4151*
be of sound judgment and sober **s** **1Pe 4:7**
because the **S** of glory and of God **1Pe 4:14** *4151*
Be of sober **s**, be on the alert. **1Pe 5:8**
men moved by the Holy **S** spoke **2Pe 1:21** *4151*
us, by the **S** whom He has given us. **1Jn 3:24** *4151*
Beloved, do not believe every **s**, **1Jn 4:1** *4151*
By this you know the **S** of God: **1Jn 4:2** *4151*
every **s** that confesses that Jesus **1Jn 4:2**
and every **s** that does not confess **1Jn 4:3** *4151*
this is the **s** of the antichrist, **1Jn 4:3**
By this we know the **s** of truth and **1Jn 4:6** *4151*
of truth and the **s** of error. **1Jn 4:6** *4151*
because He has given us of His **S**. **1Jn 4:13** *4151*
It is the **S** who testifies, because **1Jn 5:6** *4151*
because the **S** is the truth. **1Jn 5:6** *4151*
the **S** and the water and the blood; **1Jn 5:8** *4151*
worldly-minded, devoid of the **S**. **Jude 1:19** *4151*
praying in the Holy **S**, **Jude 1:20** *4151*
I was in the **S** on the Lord's day, **Rv 1:10** *4151*
what the **S** says to the churches. **Rv 2:7** *4151*
what the **S** says to the churches. **Rv 2:11** *4151*
what the **S** says to the churches. **Rv 2:17** *4151*
what the **S** says to the churches.' **Rv 2:29** *4151*
what the **S** says to the churches.' **Rv 3:6** *4151*
what the **S** says to the churches.' **Rv 3:13** *4151*
what the **S** says to the churches. **Rv 3:22** *4151*
Immediately I was in the **S**; **Rv 4:2** *4151*
"Yes," says the **S**, **Rv 14:13** *4151*
he carried me away in the **S** into a **Rv 17:3** *4151*
and a prison of every unclean **s**, **Rv 18:2** *4151*
of Jesus is the **s** of prophecy." **Rv 19:10** *4151*
he carried me away in the **S** to a **Rv 21:10** *4151*
The **S** and the bride say, **Rv 22:17** *4151*

SPIRITIST
a **s** shall surely be put to death. **Lv 20:27** 3049
a spell, or a medium, or a **s**, **Dt 18:11** 3049

SPIRITISTS
'Do not turn to mediums or **s**; **Lv 19:31** 3049
who turns to mediums and to **s**, **Lv 20:6** 3049
land those who were mediums and **s**. **1Sa 28:3** 3049
are mediums and **s** from the land. **1Sa 28:9** 3049
and dealt with mediums and **s**. **2Ki 21:6** 3049
Josiah removed the mediums and the **s** **2Ki 23:24** 3049
and dealt with mediums and **s**. **2Ch 33:6** 3049
Consult the mediums and the **s** **Is 8:19** 3049
of the dead And to mediums and **s**. **Is 19:3** 3049

SPIRITS
God of the **s** of all flesh, **Nu 16:22** 7307
the God of the **s** of all flesh, **Nu 27:16** 7307
happened when they were in high **s**, **Jg 16:25** 3820
"The departed **s** tremble Under the **Jb 26:5** 7496
departed **s** rise *and* praise You? **Ps 88:10** 7496
arouses for you the **s** of the dead, **Is 14:9** 7496
the departed **s** will not rise; **Is 26:14** 7496
will give birth to the departed **s**. **Is 26:19** 7496
"These are the four **s** of heaven, **Zch 6:5** 7307
and He cast out the **s** with a word, **Mt 8:16** *4151*
them authority over unclean **s**, **Mt 10:1** *4151*
with it seven other **s** more wicked **Mt 12:45** *4151*
He commands even the unclean **s**, **Mk 1:27** *4151*
Whenever the unclean **s** saw Him, **Mk 3:11** *4151*
the unclean **s** entered the swine; **Mk 5:13** *4151*
them authority over the unclean **s**; **Mk 6:7** *4151*
power He commands the unclean **s** and **Lk 4:36** *4151*
who were troubled with unclean **s** **Lk 6:18** *4151*
and afflictions and evil **s**; **Lk 7:21** *4151*
healed of evil **s** and sicknesses: **Lk 8:2** *4151*
that the **s** are subject to you, **Lk 10:20** *4151*
seven other **s** more evil than itself, **Lk 11:26** *4151*
sick or afflicted with unclean **s**, **Ac 5:16** *4151*
case of many who had unclean **s**, **Ac 8:7** *4151*
left them and the evil **s** went out. **Ac 19:12** *4151*
name over those who had the evil **s** **Ac 19:13** *4151*
another the distinguishing of **s**, **1Co 12:10** *4151*
s of prophets are subject to prophets **1Co 14:32** *4151*
paying attention to deceitful **s** and **1Tm 4:1** *4151*
Are they not all ministering **s**, **Heb 1:14** *4151*
be subject to the Father of **s**, **Heb 12:9** *4151*
s of *the* righteous made perfect, **Heb 12:23** *4151*
to the **s** *now* in prison, **1Pe 3:19** *4151*
but test the **s** to see whether they **1Jn 4:1** *4151*
seven **S** who are before His throne, **Rv 1:4** *4151*
He who has the seven **S** of God and **Rv 3:1** *4151*
which are the seven **S** of God; **Rv 4:5** *4151*
which are the seven **S** of God, **Rv 5:6** *4151*
three unclean **s** like frogs; **Rv 16:13** *4151*
for they are **s** of demons, **Rv 16:14** *4151*
the God of the **s** of the prophets, **Rv 22:6** *4151*

SPIRITUAL
I may impart some **s** gift to you, **Ro 1:11** *4152*
For we know that the Law is **s**, **Ro 7:14** *4152*
is your **s** service of worship. **Ro 12:1** *3050*
have shared in their **s** things, **Ro 15:27** *4152*
combining **s** *thoughts* with spiritual **1Co 2:13** *4152*
spiritual *thoughts* with **s** *words.* **1Co 2:13** *4152*
he who is **s** appraises all things, **1Co 2:15** *4152*
not speak to you as to **s** men, **1Co 3:1** *4152*
If we sowed **s** things in you, is it **1Co 9:11** *4152*
and all ate the same **s** food; **1Co 10:3** *4152*
and all drank the same **s** drink, **1Co 10:4** *4152*
they were drinking from a **s** rock **1Co 10:4** *4152*
Now concerning **s** *gifts,* brethren, **1Co 12:1** *4152*
yet desire earnestly **s** *gifts,* **1Co 14:1** *4152*
since you are zealous of **s** *gifts,* **1Co 14:12** *4151*
thinks he is a prophet or **s**, **1Co 14:37** *4152*
body, it is raised a **s** body. **1Co 15:44** *4152*
body, there is also a **s** *body.* **1Co 15:44** *4152*
However, the **s** is not first, but **1Co 15:46** *4152*
not first, but the natural; then the **s**. **1Co 15:46** *4152*
you who are **s**, restore such a one **Ga 6:1** *4152*
blessed us with every **s** blessing in **Eph 1:3** *4152*
in psalms and hymns and **s** songs, **Eph 5:19** *4152*
against the **s** *forces* of wickedness **Eph 6:12** *4152*
in all **s** wisdom and understanding, **Col 1:9** *4152*
with psalms *and* hymns *and* **s** songs, **Col 3:16** *4152*
Do not neglect the **s** gift within you, **1Tm 4:14** *5486*
are being built up as a **s** house for a **1Pe 2:5** *4152*
to offer up **s** sacrifices **1Pe 2:5** *4152*

SPIRITUALLY
because they are **s** appraised. **1Co 2:14** *4153*

SPIT
her father had but **s** in her face, **Nu 12:14** 3417
off his foot and **s** in his face; **Dt 25:9** 3417
And I am one at whom men **s**. **Jb 17:6** 8611
"They will mock Him and **s** on Him, **Mk 10:34** *1716*
Some began to **s** at Him, **Mk 14:65** *1716*
mocked and mistreated and **s** upon, **Lk 18:32** *1716*
I will **s** you out of My mouth. **Rv 3:16** *1692*

SPITE
'Yet if in **s** of this you do not **Lv 26:27**
'Yet in **s** of this, when they are **Lv 26:44**
637, 1571
in **s** *of* all the good that I do **1Sa 2:32**
is hope for Israel in **s** of this. **Ezr 10:2** 5921
In **s** *of* this I shall be confident. **Ps 27:3**
In **s** of all this they still sinned And **Ps 78:32**
In **s** *of* all this, His anger does **Is 9:12**
In **s** *of* all this, His anger does **Is 9:17**
In **s** *of* all this, His anger does **Is 9:21**
In **s** *of* all this, His anger does **Is 10:4**
In **s** of your many sorceries, **Is 47:9**
In **s** of the great power of your **Is 47:9**
But in **s** of all these things, **Jer 2:34** 5921
"Yet in **s** of all this her **Jer 3:10**
to other gods in order to **s** Me. **Jer 7:18** 3707
"Do they **s** Me?" declares the LORD. **Jer 7:19** 3707
"Is it not themselves *they* **s**, **Jer 7:19**
who in **s** of the terror resulting **Ezk 32:30**

SPITS
if the man with the discharge **s** on **Lv 15:8** 7556

SPITTING
do not refrain from **s** at my face. **Jb 30:10** 7536
My face from humiliation and **s**. **Is 50:6** 7536
after **s**, He touched his tongue *with* **Mk 7:33** *4429*
and after **s** on his eyes and **Mk 8:23** *4429*
head with a reed, and **s** on Him, **Mk 15:19** *1716*

SPITTLE
let me alone until I swallow my **s**? **Jb 7:19** 7536
ground, and made clay of the **s**, **Jn 9:6** *4427*

SPLASHED
you shall wash what was **s** on. **Lv 6:27** 5137a

SPLASHES
any of its blood **s** on a garment, **Lv 6:27** 5137a

SPLENDID
great and **s** cities which you did **Dt 6:10** 2896a
S and majestic is His work, **Ps 111:3** 1935
And there your **s** chariots will be, **Is 22:18** 3519b
fruit *and* become a **s** vine."' **Ezk 17:8** 155
and you sat on a **s** couch with a **Ezk 23:41** 3519a
things that were luxurious and **s** have **Rv 18:14** *2986*

SPLENDIDLY
horsemen, all of them **s** attired, **Ezk 38:4** 4358
Those who are **s** clothed and live **Lk 7:25** *1741*

SPLENDOR
tell my father of all my **s** in Egypt, **Gn 45:13** 3519b
S and majesty are before Him, **1Ch 16:27** 1935
glory and the **s** of his great majesty **Es 1:4** 3366
it shone Or the moon going in **s**, **Jb 31:26** 3368
"Out of the north comes golden **s**; **Jb 37:22** 2091
displayed Your **s** above the heavens! **Ps 8:1** 1935
S and majesty You place upon **Ps 21:5** 1935
One, *In* Your **s** and Your majesty! **Ps 45:3** 1935
You have made his **s** to cease And **Ps 89:44** 2892b
S and majesty are before Him, **Ps 96:6** 1935
You are clothed with **s** and majesty, **Ps 104:1** 1935
On the glorious **s** of Your majesty And **Ps 145:5** 1926
and from the **s** of His majesty. **Is 2:10** 1926
And the **s** of His majesty, **Is 2:19** 1926
the LORD and the **s** of His majesty, **Is 2:21** 1926
And Jerusalem's **s**, her multitude, **Is 5:14** 1926
all the **s** of Kedar will terminate; **Is 21:16** 3519b
for the master!' or, 'Alas for his **s**!' **Jer 22:18** 1935
been broken, A staff of **s**!' **Jer 48:17** 8597
for it was perfect because of My **s** **Ezk 16:14** 1926
they set forth your **s**. **Ezk 27:10** 1926
of your wisdom And defile your **s**. **Ezk 28:7** 3314
your wisdom by reason of your **s**. **Ezk 28:17** 3314
was large and of extraordinary **s**, **Da 2:31** 2122
And my majesty and **s** were restored **Da 4:36** 2122
children you take My **s** forever. **Mi 2:9** 1926
the LORD will restore the **s** of Jacob **Na 2:2** 1347b
of Jacob Like the **s** of Israel, **Na 2:2** 1347b
His **s** covers the heavens, And the **Hab 3:3** 1935
joyously living in **s** every day. **Lk 16:19** *2988*

SPLINTERS
vine a waste And my fig tree **s**. **Jl 1:7** 7111

SPLIT
he **s** wood for the burnt offering, **Gn 22:3** 1234
a hoof, thus making **s** hoofs, **Lv 11:3** 8156
the hoof, thus making a **s** hoof, **Lv 11:7** 8156
hoof but do not make a **s** *hoof*, **Lv 11:26** 8156
ground that was under them **s** open; **Nu 16:31** 1234
hoof in two *and* chews the cud, **Dt 14:6** 8156
But God **s** the hollow place that is **Jg 15:19** 1234
and they **s** the wood of the cart **1Sa 6:14** 1234
the altar shall be **s** apart and the **1Ki 13:3** 7167
The altar also was **s** apart and the **1Ki 13:5** 7167
land quake, You have **s** it open; **Ps 60:2** 6480
He **s** the rocks in the wilderness And **Ps 78:15** 1234
asunder, The earth is **s** through, **Is 24:19** 6565b
He **s** the rock and the water **Is 48:21** 1234
Him And the valleys will be **s**, **Mi 1:4** 1234
Mount of Olives will be **s** in its middle **Zch 14:4** 1234
and the rocks were **s**. **Mt 27:51** *4977*
The sky was **s** apart like a **Rv 6:14** *673*
great city was **s** into three parts, **Rv 16:19** *1096*

SPLIT-OPEN
and I will make them like **s** figs **Jer 29:17** 8182

SPLITS
mercy He **s** my kidneys open; **Jb 16:13** 6398
and he who **s** logs may be **Ec 10:9** 1234

SPOIL
in the evening he divides the **s**." **Gn 49:27** 7998
overtake, I will divide the **s**; **Ex 15:9** 7998
took all the **s** and all the prey, **Nu 31:11** 7998
and the prey and the **s** to Moses, **Nu 31:12** 7998
the booty that remained from the **s** **Nu 31:32** 957
s of the cities which we had captured. **Dt 2:35** 7998
s of the cities we took as our booty. **Dt 3:7** 7998
that is in the city, all its **s**, **Dt 20:14** 7998
you shall use the **s** of your enemies **Dt 20:14** 7998
when I saw among the **s** a beautiful **Jos 7:21** 7998
you shall take only its **s** and its **Jos 8:2** 7998
only the cattle and the **s** of that city **Jos 8:27** 7998
All the **s** of these cities and **Jos 11:14** 7998
divide the **s** of your enemies with **Jos 22:8** 7998
are they not dividing the **s**? **Jg 5:30** 7998
To Sisera a **s** of dyed work, A **Jg 5:30** 7998
A **s** of dyed work embroidered, **Jg 5:30** 7998
give me an earring from his **s**." **Jg 8:24** 7998
threw an earring there from his **s**. **Jg 8:25** 7998
thirty of them and took their **s** and **Jg 14:19** 2488
freely today of the **s** of their enemies **1Sa 14:30** 7998
people rushed greedily upon the **s**, **1Sa 14:32** 7998
take **s** among them until the morning **1Sa 14:36** 962
but rushed upon the **s** and did what **1Sa 15:19** 7998
"But the people took *some* of the **s**, **1Sa 15:21** 7998
dancing because of all the great **s** **1Sa 30:16** 7998
s or anything that they had taken **1Sa 30:19** 7998
"This is David's **s**." **1Sa 30:20** 7998
we will not give them any of the **s** **1Sa 30:22** 7998
he sent *some* of the **s** to the elders **1Sa 30:26** 7998
the **s** of the enemies of the LORD: **1Sa 30:26** 7998
and take for yourself his **s**." **2Sa 2:21** 2488
raid and brought much **s** with them; **2Sa 3:22** 7998
and from the **s** of Hadadezer, **2Sa 8:12** 7998
he brought out the **s** of the city in **2Sa 12:30** 7998
Now therefore, Moab, to the **s**!" **2Ki 3:23** 7998
and **s** to all their enemies; **2Ki 21:14** 4933
he brought out the **s** of the city, **1Ch 20:2** 7998
They dedicated part of the **s** won **1Ch 26:27** 7998
sheep from the **s** they had brought. **2Ch 15:11** 7998
his people came to take their **s**, **2Ch 20:25** 7998
they were three days taking the **s** **2Ch 20:25** 7998
and sent all their **s** to the king of **2Ch 24:23** 7998
of them and plundered much **s**. **2Ch 25:13** 961
also a great deal of **s** from them, **2Ch 28:8** 7998
and brought the **s** to Samaria. **2Ch 28:8** 7998
armed men left the captives and the **s** **2Ch 28:14** 957
all their naked ones from the **s**; **2Ch 28:15** 7998
and women, and to plunder their **s**, **Es 8:11** 7998
friends for a share *of the* **s**, **Jb 17:5**
those who hate us have taken **s** **Ps 44:10** 8154
at home will divide the **s**!" **Ps 68:12** 7998
word, As one who finds great **s**. **Ps 119:162** 7998
We will fill our houses with **s**; **Pr 1:13** 7998
to divide the **s** with the proud. **Pr 16:19** 7998
s of Samaria will be carried away **Is 8:4** 7998
rejoice when they divide the **s**. **Is 9:3** 7998
So that widows may be their **s** **Is 10:2** 7998
Your **s** is gathered *as* the **Is 33:4** 7998
the prey of an abundant **s** will be **Is 33:23** 7998
And a **s**, with none to say, **Is 42:22** 4933
Who gave Jacob up for **s**, **Is 42:24** 4933
to the wicked of the earth as **s**, **Ezk 7:21** 7998
give you for **s** to the nations. **Ezk 25:7** 957
she will become **s** for the nations. **Ezk 26:5** 957
they will make a **s** of your riches **Ezk 26:12** 7997b
capture her **s** and seize her plunder; **Ezk 29:19** 7998
to capture **s** and to seize plunder, **Ezk 38:12** 7998
'Have you come to capture **s**? **Ezk 38:13** 7998
goods, to capture great **s**? **Ezk 38:13** 7998
the **s** of those who despoiled them and **Ezk 39:10** 7997b
the **s** taken from you will be divided **Zch 14:1** 7998

SPOILED
was **s** in the hand of the potter; **Jer 18:4** 7843

SPOILER
embroidery on the neck of the **s**?' **Jg 5:30** 7998

SPOILS
a tenth part of all *the* **s**, was **Heb 7:2**
gave a tenth of the choicest **s**. **Heb 7:4** *205*

SPOKE
Then God **s** to Noah, saying, **Gn 8:15** 1696
Then God **s** to Noah and to his sons **Gn 9:8** 559
the name of the LORD who **s** to her, **Gn 16:13** 1696
He **s** to Him yet again and said, **Gn 18:29** 1696
went out and **s** to his sons-in-law, **Gn 19:14** 1696
of his army, **s** to Abraham, **Gn 21:22** 559
Isaac **s** to Abraham his father **Gn 22:7** 559
dead, and **s** to the sons of Heth, **Gn 23:3** 1696
And he **s** with them, saying, **Gn 23:8** 1696
He **s** to Ephron in the hearing **Gn 23:13** 1696
land of my birth, and who **s** to me and **Gn 24:7** 1696
while Isaac **s** to his son Esau. **Gn 27:5** 1696
he **s** thus, 'The speckled shall be **Gn 31:8** 559
and if he **s** thus, **Gn 31:8** 559
of your father **s** to me last night, **Gn 31:29** 559
the girl and **s** tenderly to her. **Gn 34:3** 1696
So Shechem **s** to his father Hamor, **Gn 34:4** 559
But Hamor **s** with them, saying, **Gn 34:8** 1696
and **s** to the men of their city, **Gn 34:20** 1696
As she **s** to Joseph day after day, **Gn 39:10** 1696
she **s** to him with these words, **Gn 39:17** 1696
of his wife, which she **s** to him, **Gn 39:19** 1696
the chief cupbearer **s** to Pharaoh, **Gn 41:9** 1696
So Pharaoh **s** to Joseph, **Gn 41:17** 1696
to them and **s** to them harshly. **Gn 42:7** 1696
he returned to them and **s** to them, **Gn 42:24** 1696
of the land, **s** harshly with us, **Gn 42:30** 1696
Then Reuben **s** to his father, **Gn 42:37** 559
Judah **s** to him, however, saying, **Gn 43:3** 559
and **s** to him at the entrance of **Gn 43:19** 1696
old father well, of whom you **s**? **Gn 43:27** 559
brother, of whom you **s** to me?" **Gn 43:29** 559
them and **s** these words to them. **Gn 44:6** 1696
God **s** to Israel in visions of **Gn 46:2** 559
Joseph **s** to the household of Pharaoh **Gn 50:4** 1696
Joseph wept when they **s** to him. **Gn 50:17** 1696
them and **s** kindly to them. **Gn 50:21** 1696
the king of Egypt **s** to the Hebrew **Ex 1:15** 559
and Aaron **s** all the words which **Ex 4:30** 1696
went out and **s** to the people, **Ex 5:10** 559
God **s** further to Moses and said to **Ex 6:2** 1696
Moses **s** thus to the sons of Israel, **Ex 6:9** 1696
Now the LORD **s** to Moses, saying, **Ex 6:10** 1696
But Moses **s** before the LORD, **Ex 6:12** 1696
the LORD **s** to Moses and to Aaron, **Ex 6:13** 1696
They were the ones who **s** to **Ex 6:27** 1696
the day when the LORD **s** to Moses **Ex 6:28** 1696
that the LORD **s** to Moses, saying, **Ex 6:29** 1696
when they **s** to Pharaoh. **Ex 7:7** 1696
Now the LORD **s** to Moses and Aaron, **Ex 7:8** 559
Then the LORD **s** to Moses, saying, **Ex 13:1** 1696
Now the LORD **s** to Moses, saying, **Ex 14:1** 1696
word that we **s** to you in Egypt, **Ex 14:12** 1696
It came about as Aaron **s** to **Ex 16:10** 1696
And the LORD **s** to Moses, saying, **Ex 16:11** 1696
Moses **s** and God answered him with **Ex 19:19** 1696
Then the LORD **s** to Moses, **Ex 19:21** 559
Then God **s** all these words, **Ex 20:1** 1696
Then the LORD **s** to Moses, saying, **Ex 25:1** 1696
The LORD also **s** to Moses, saying, **Ex 30:11** 1696
The LORD **s** to Moses, saying, **Ex 30:17** 1696
Moreover, the LORD **s** to Moses, **Ex 30:22** 1696
Now the LORD **s** to Moses, saying, **Ex 31:1** 1696
The LORD **s** to Moses, saying, **Ex 31:12** 559
Then the LORD **s** to Moses, **Ex 32:7** 1696
Then the LORD **s** to Moses, **Ex 33:1** 1696
and Moses **s** to them. **Ex 34:31** 1696
and whenever he came out and **s** to **Ex 34:34** 1696
Moses **s** to all the **Ex 35:4** 559
Then the LORD **s** to Moses, saying, **Ex 40:1** 1696
LORD called to Moses and **s** to him **Lv 1:1** 1696
Then the LORD **s** to Moses, saying, **Lv 4:1** 1696
Then the LORD **s** to Moses, saying, **Lv 5:14** 1696
Then the LORD **s** to Moses, saying, **Lv 6:1** 1696
Then the LORD **s** to Moses, saying, **Lv 6:8** 1696
Then the LORD **s** to Moses, saying, **Lv 6:19** 1696
Then the LORD **s** to Moses, saying, **Lv 6:24** 1696
Then the LORD **s** to Moses, saying, **Lv 7:22** 1696
Then the LORD **s** to Moses, saying, **Lv 7:28** 1696
Then the LORD **s** to Moses, saying, **Lv 8:1** 1696
"It is what the LORD **s**, **Lv 10:3** 1696
The LORD then **s** to Aaron, saying, **Lv 10:8** 1696
Then Moses **s** to Aaron, and to his **Lv 10:12** 1696
But Aaron **s** to Moses, **Lv 10:19** 1696
The LORD **s** again to Moses and to **Lv 11:1** 1696
Then the LORD **s** to Moses, saying, **Lv 12:1** 1696
the LORD **s** to Moses and to Aaron, **Lv 13:1** 1696
Then the LORD **s** to Moses, saying, **Lv 14:1** 1696
further **s** to Moses and to Aaron, **Lv 14:33** 1696
LORD also **s** to Moses and to Aaron, **Lv 15:1** 1696
Now the LORD **s** to Moses after the **Lv 16:1** 1696
Then the LORD **s** to Moses, saying, **Lv 17:1** 1696
Then the LORD **s** to Moses, saying, **Lv 18:1** 1696
Then the LORD **s** to Moses, saying: **Lv 19:1** 1696
Then the LORD **s** to Moses, saying, **Lv 20:1** 1696
Then the LORD **s** to Moses, saying, **Lv 21:16** 1696
So Moses **s** to Aaron and to his **Lv 21:24** 1696
Then the LORD **s** to Moses, saying, **Lv 22:1** 1696
Then the LORD **s** to Moses, saying, **Lv 22:17** 1696
Then the LORD **s** to Moses, saying, **Lv 22:26** 1696
The LORD **s** again to Moses, saying, **Lv 23:1** 1696
Then the LORD **s** to Moses, saying, **Lv 23:9** 1696
Again the LORD **s** to Moses, saying, **Lv 23:23** 1696
The LORD **s** to Moses, saying, **Lv 23:26** 1696
Again the LORD **s** to Moses, saying, **Lv 23:33** 1696
Then the LORD **s** to Moses, saying, **Lv 24:1** 1696
Then the LORD **s** to Moses, saying, **Lv 24:13** 1696
Moses **s** to the sons of Israel, **Lv 24:23** 1696
then **s** to Moses at Mount Sinai, **Lv 25:1** 1696
Again, the LORD **s** to Moses, **Lv 27:1** 1696
Then the LORD **s** to Moses in the **Nu 1:1** 1696
the LORD **s** to Moses and to Aaron, **Nu 2:1** 1696
LORD **s** with Moses on Mount Sinai. **Nu 3:1** 1696
Then the LORD **s** to Moses, saying, **Nu 3:5** 1696
Again the LORD **s** to Moses, saying, **Nu 3:11** 1696
Then the LORD **s** to Moses in the **Nu 3:14** 1696
Then the LORD **s** to Moses, saying, **Nu 3:44** 1696
the LORD **s** to Moses and to Aaron, **Nu 4:1** 1696
the LORD **s** to Moses and to Aaron, **Nu 4:17** 1696
Then the LORD **s** to Moses, saying, **Nu 4:21** 1696
Then the LORD **s** to Moses, saying, **Nu 5:1** 1696
Then the LORD **s** to Moses, saying, **Nu 5:5** 1696
Then the LORD **s** to Moses, saying, **Nu 5:11** 1696
Again the LORD **s** to Moses, saying, **Nu 6:1** 1696
Then the LORD **s** to Moses, saying, **Nu 6:22** 1696
Then the LORD **s** to Moses, saying, **Nu 7:4** 559
the two cherubim, so He **s** to him. **Nu 7:89** 1696
Then the LORD **s** to Moses, saying, **Nu 8:1** 1696
Again the LORD **s** to Moses, saying, **Nu 8:5** 1696
Now the LORD **s** to Moses, saying, **Nu 8:23** 1696
Thus the LORD **s** to Moses in the **Nu 9:1** 1696
Then the LORD **s** to Moses, saying, **Nu 9:9** 1696
The LORD **s** further to Moses, **Nu 10:1** 1696
down in the cloud and **s** to him; **Nu 11:25** 1696
Then Miriam and Aaron **s** against **Nu 12:1** 1696
Then the LORD **s** to Moses saying, **Nu 13:1** 1696
and they **s** to all the congregation **Nu 14:7** 559
The LORD **s** to Moses and Aaron, **Nu 14:26** 1696
When Moses **s** these words to **Nu 14:39** 1696
Now the LORD **s** to Moses, saying, **Nu 15:1** 1696
Then the LORD **s** to Moses, saying, **Nu 15:17** 1696
The LORD also **s** to Moses, saying, **Nu 15:37** 559
he **s** to Korah and all his company, **Nu 16:5** 1696
the LORD **s** to Moses and Aaron, **Nu 16:20** 1696
Then the LORD **s** to Moses, saying, **Nu 16:23** 1696
and he **s** to the congregation, **Nu 16:26** 1696
Then the LORD **s** to Moses, saying, **Nu 16:36** 1696
and the LORD **s** to Moses, saying, **Nu 16:44** 1696
Then the LORD **s** to Moses, saying, **Nu 17:1** 1696
Moses therefore **s** to the sons of **Nu 17:6** 1696
the sons of Israel **s** to Moses, **Nu 17:12** 559
Then the LORD **s** to Aaron, **Nu 18:8** 1696
Then the LORD **s** to Moses, saying, **Nu 18:25** 1696
the LORD **s** to Moses and Aaron, **Nu 19:1** 1696
thus contended with Moses and **s**, **Nu 20:3** 559
and the LORD **s** to Moses, saying, **Nu 20:7** 1696
Then the LORD **s** to Moses and Aaron **Nu 20:23** 559
people **s** against God and Moses, **Nu 21:5** 1696
Then the LORD **s** to Moses, saying, **Nu 25:10** 1696
Then the LORD **s** to Moses, saying, **Nu 25:16** 1696
that the LORD **s** to Moses and to **Nu 26:1** 559
So Moses and Eleazar the priest **s** **Nu 26:3** 1696
Then the LORD **s** to Moses, saying, **Nu 26:52** 1696
Then the LORD **s** to Moses, saying, **Nu 27:6** 559
Then Moses **s** to the LORD, saying, **Nu 27:15** 1696
Then the LORD **s** to Moses, saying, **Nu 28:1** 1696
Moses **s** to the sons of Israel **Nu 29:40** 559
Then Moses **s** to the heads of the **Nu 30:1** 1696
Then the LORD **s** to Moses, saying, **Nu 31:1** 1696
Moses **s** to the people, saying, **Nu 31:3** 1696
Then the LORD **s** to Moses, saying, **Nu 31:25** 559
sons of Reuben came and **s** to Moses **Nu 32:2** 559
and the sons of Reuben **s** to Moses, **Nu 32:25** 559
Then the LORD **s** to Moses in the **Nu 33:50** 1696
Then the LORD **s** to Moses, saying, **Nu 34:1** 1696
Then the LORD **s** to Moses, saying, **Nu 34:16** 1696
Now the LORD **s** to Moses in the **Nu 35:1** 1696
Then the LORD **s** to Moses, saying, **Nu 35:9** 1696
came near and **s** before Moses and **Nu 36:1** 1696
These are the words which Moses **s** **Dt 1:1** 1696
Moses **s** to the children of Israel, **Dt 1:3** 1696
"The LORD our God **s** to us at Horeb, **Dt 1:6** 1696
"I **s** to you at that time, **Dt 1:9** 559

"So I **s** to you, but you would not	Dt 1:43	1696
the Red Sea, as the LORD **s** to me,	Dt 2:1	1696
"And the LORD **s** to me, saying,	Dt 2:2	559
that the LORD **s** to me, saying,	Dt 2:17	1696
"Then the LORD **s** to you from the	Dt 4:12	1696
the day the LORD **s** to you at Horeb	Dt 4:15	1696
Moses **s** to the sons of Israel,	Dt 4:45	1696
"The LORD **s** to you face to face	Dt 5:4	1696
"These words the LORD **s** to all	Dt 5:22	1696
of your words when you **s** to me,	Dt 5:28	1696
"The LORD **s** further to me,	Dt 9:13	559
as the LORD your God **s** to him.)	Dt 10:9	1696
concerning which he **s** to you,	Dt 13:2	1696
Levitical priests **s** to all Israel,	Dt 27:9	1696
by the way about which I **s** to you,	Dt 28:68	559
just as He **s** to you and as He	Dt 29:13	1696
and **s** these words to all Israel.	Dt 31:1	1696
Then Moses **s** in the hearing of all	Dt 31:30	1696
Then Moses came and **s** all the	Dt 32:44	1696
The LORD **s** to Moses that very	Dt 32:48	1696
LORD **s** to Joshua the son of Nun,	Jos 1:1	559
it to you, just as I **s** to Moses.	Jos 1:3	1696
And Joshua **s** to the priests,	Jos 3:6	559
Jordan, the LORD **s** to Joshua,	Jos 4:1	559
just as the LORD **s** to Joshua,	Jos 4:8	1696
of our country **s** to us,	Jos 9:11	559
called for them and **s** to them,	Jos 9:22	1696
Then Joshua **s** to the LORD in the	Jos 10:12	1696
their inheritance, as He **s** to him.	Jos 13:14	1696
the word which the LORD **s** to Moses	Jos 14:6	1696
has let me live, just as He **s**,	Jos 14:10	1696
the LORD **s** this word to Moses,	Jos 14:10	1696
which the LORD **s** on that day,	Jos 14:12	1696
the sons of Joseph **s** to Joshua,	Jos 17:14	1696
Joshua **s** to the house of Joseph,	Jos 17:17	559
Then the LORD **s** to Joshua, saying,	Jos 20:1	1696
of which I **s** to you through Moses,	Jos 20:2	1696
They **s** to them at Shiloh in	Jos 21:2	1696
to your brothers, as He **s** to them;	Jos 22:4	1696
and they **s** with them saying,	Jos 22:15	1696
and **s** to the heads of the families	Jos 22:21	1696
of Gad and the sons of Manasseh **s**,	Jos 22:30	1696
God **s** concerning you has failed;	Jos 23:14	1696
God **s** to you have come upon you,	Jos 23:15	1696
of the LORD which He **s** to us;	Jos 24:27	1696
the angel of the LORD **s** these words	Jg 2:4	1696
Penuel and **s** similarly to them;	Jg 8:8	1696
So he **s** also to the men of Penuel,	Jg 8:9	559
and **s** to them and to the whole	Jg 9:1	1696
And his mother's relatives **s** all	Jg 9:3	1696
Gaal **s** again and said,	Jg 9:37	1696
and Jephthah **s** all his words	Jg 11:11	1696
you the man who **s** to the woman?"	Jg 13:11	1696
they **s** to the owner of the house,	Jg 19:22	559
and **s** to the sons of Benjamin	Jg 21:13	1696
of whom Boaz **s** was passing by,	Ru 4:1	1696
"What is the word that He **s** to you?	1Sa 3:17	1696
all the words that He **s** to you."	1Sa 3:17	1696
Samuel **s** to all the house of Israel,	1Sa 7:3	559
So Samuel **s** all the words of the	1Sa 8:10	559
the man of whom I **s** to you!	1Sa 9:17	559
Samuel **s** with Saul on the roof.	1Sa 9:25	1696
to Gibeah of Saul and **s** these words	1Sa 11:4	1696
and he **s** these same words;	1Sa 17:23	1696
Then David **s** to the men who were	1Sa 17:26	559
heard when he **s** to the men;	1Sa 17:28	1696
words which David **s** were heard,	1Sa 17:31	1696
servants **s** these words to David.	1Sa 18:23	1696
to these words *which* David **s**.	1Sa 18:24	1696
Then Jonathan **s** well of David to	1Sa 19:4	1696
they **s** to Nabal according to all	1Sa 25:9	1696
Abigail at Carmel, they **s** to her,	1Sa 25:40	1696
and the woman **s** to Saul, saying,	1Sa 28:12	559
accordingly as He **s** through me;	1Sa 28:17	1696
to your words which you **s** to me.	1Sa 28:21	1696
the people **s** of stoning him,	1Sa 30:6	559
also **s** in the hearing of Benjamin;	2Sa 3:19	1696
this vision, so Nathan **s** to David.	2Sa 7:17	1696
we **s** to him and he did not listen	2Sa 12:18	1696
the woman of Tekoa **s** to the king,	2Sa 14:4	559
Then she **s**, saying,	2Sa 20:18	559
the Gibeonites and **s** to them	2Sa 21:2	559
And David **s** the words of this song	2Sa 22:1	1696
"The Spirit of the LORD **s** by me,	2Sa 23:2	1696
said, The Rock of Israel **s** to me,	2Sa 23:3	1696
Then David **s** to the LORD when he	2Sa 24:17	559
Then Nathan **s** to Bathsheba the	1Ki 1:11	559
promise which He **s** concerning me,	1Ki 2:4	1696
"Thus **s** Joab, and thus he	1Ki 2:30	1696
Thus they **s** before the king.	1Ki 3:22	1696
was the living one **s** to the king,	1Ki 3:26	559
He also **s** 3,000 proverbs, and his	1Ki 4:32	1696
He **s** of trees, from the cedar	1Ki 4:33	1696
he **s** also of animals and birds and	1Ki 4:33	1696
as the LORD **s** to David my father,	1Ki 5:5	1696
which I **s** to David your father.	1Ki 6:12	1696
who **s** with His mouth to my father	1Ki 8:15	1696
has fulfilled His word which He **s**;	1Ki 8:20	1696
as You **s** through Moses Your servant,	1Ki 8:53	1696
she **s** with him about all that was	1Ki 10:2	1696
of Israel came and **s** to Rehoboam,	1Ki 12:3	1696
Then they **s** to him, saying,	1Ki 12:7	1696
men who grew up with him **s** to him,	1Ki 12:10	1696
say to this people who **s** to you,	1Ki 12:10	1696
and he **s** to them according to the	1Ki 12:14	1696
which the LORD **s** through Ahijah	1Ki 12:15	1696
s to me by the word of the LORD,	1Ki 13:18	1696
of the LORD which He **s** to him."	1Ki 13:26	1696
Then he **s** to his sons, saying,	1Ki 13:27	1696

buried him, he **s** to his sons,	1Ki 13:31	559
who **s** concerning me *that I would*	1Ki 14:2	1696
He **s** through His servant Ahijah	1Ki 14:18	1696
which He **s** by His servant Ahijah	1Ki 15:29	1696
which He **s** against Baasha through	1Ki 16:12	1696
He **s** by Joshua the son of Nun.	1Ki 16:34	1696
LORD which He **s** through Elijah.	1Ki 17:16	1696
Then a man of God came near and **s**	1Ki 20:28	559
Ahab **s** to Naboth, saying,	1Ki 21:2	1696
I **s** to Naboth the Jezreelite and	1Ki 21:6	1696
to summon Micaiah **s** to him saying,	1Ki 22:13	1696
the word of the LORD which He **s**.	1Ki 22:38	1696
you and **s** these words to you?"	2Ki 1:7	1696
to the word of Elisha which he **s**.	2Ki 2:22	1696
"Thus and thus **s** the girl who is	2Ki 5:4	1696
came near and **s** to him and said,	2Ki 5:13	1696
who **s** when the king came down to	2Ki 7:17	1696
Now Elisha **s** to the woman whose	2Ki 8:1	1696
which He **s** by His servant Elijah	2Ki 9:36	1696
s concerning the house of Ahab,	2Ki 10:10	1696
He **s** through His servant Elijah."	2Ki 10:10	1696
of the LORD which He **s** to Elijah.	2Ki 10:17	1696
which He **s** through His servant	2Ki 14:25	1696
of the LORD which He **s** to Jehu,	2Ki 15:12	1696
as He **s** through all His servants	2Ki 17:23	1696
So they **s** to the king of Assyria,	2Ki 17:26	559
Now the LORD **s** through His	2Ki 21:10	1696
and they **s** to her.	2Ki 22:14	1696
you heard what I **s** against this place	2Ki 22:19	1696
and he **s** kindly to him and set his	2Ki 25:28	1696
Then David **s** to the chiefs of the	1Ch 15:16	559
this vision, so Nathan **s** to David.	1Ch 17:15	1696
The LORD **s** to Gad, David's	1Ch 21:9	1696
he **s** in the name of the LORD.	1Ch 21:19	1696
Solomon **s** to all Israel, to	2Ch 1:2	559
who **s** with His mouth to my father	2Ch 6:4	1696
has fulfilled His word which He **s**;	2Ch 6:10	1696
she **s** with him about all that was	2Ch 9:1	1696
Israel came, they **s** to Rehoboam,	2Ch 10:3	1696
They **s** to him, saying,	2Ch 10:7	1696
men who grew up with him **s** to him,	2Ch 10:10	1696
say to the people who **s** to you,	2Ch 10:10	1696
He **s** to them according to the	2Ch 10:14	1696
which He **s** through Ahijah the	2Ch 10:15	1696
the son of Oded the prophet **s**,	2Ch 15:8	
to summon Micaiah **s** to him saying,	2Ch 18:12	1696
Then Hezekiah **s** encouragingly to	2Ch 30:22	1696
gate, and **s** encouragingly to them,	2Ch 32:6	1696
His servants **s** further against	2Ch 32:16	1696
They **s** of the God of Jerusalem	2Ch 32:19	1696
LORD **s** to him and gave him a sign.	2Ch 32:24	559
LORD **s** to Manasseh and his people,	2Ch 33:10	1696
and the words of the seers who **s**	2Ch 33:18	1696
and they **s** to her regarding this.	2Ch 34:22	1696
the prophet who **s** for the LORD.	2Ch 36:12	6310
came to them and **s** to them thus,	Ezr 5:3	560
He **s** in the presence of his	Ne 4:2	559
fear, I rose and **s** to the nobles,	Ne 4:14	559
And **s** with them from heaven;	Ne 9:13	1696
half **s** in the language of Ashdod,	Ne 13:24	1696
Then Esther **s** to Hathach and	Es 4:10	559
who **s** good on behalf of the king!"	Es 7:9	1696
Then Esther **s** again to the king,	Es 8:3	1696
and one who **s** for the welfare of his	Es 10:3	1696
the Buzite **s** out and said,	Jb 32:6	6030a
For He **s**, and it was done;	Ps 33:9	559
Then I **s** with my tongue:	Ps 39:3	1696
my mouth **s** when I was in distress.	Ps 66:14	1696
Then they **s** against God;	Ps 78:19	1696
Once You **s** in vision to Your godly	Ps 89:19	1696
He **s** to them in the pillar of	Ps 99:7	1696
He **s**, and there came a swarm of	Ps 105:31	559
He **s**, and locusts came, And young	Ps 105:34	559
Spirit, He **s** rashly with his lips.	Ps 106:33	981
He **s** and raised up a stormy wind,	Ps 107:25	559
My heart went out *to him* as he **s**.	SS 5:6	1696
Then the LORD **s** again to Ahaz,	Is 7:10	1696
Again the LORD **s** to me further,	Is 8:5	1696
For thus the LORD **s** to me with	Is 8:11	559
LORD **s** earlier concerning Moab.	Is 16:13	1696
at that time the LORD **s** through	Is 20:2	1696
I **s**, but you did not hear.	Is 65:12	1696
I **s**, but they did not listen.	Is 66:4	1696
"and I **s** to you, rising up early	Jer 7:13	1696
which I never commanded or **s** of,	Jer 19:5	1696
"I **s** to you in your prosperity;	Jer 22:21	1696
which Jeremiah the prophet **s** to	Jer 25:2	1696
prophets **s** to the officials and to all	Jer 26:11	559
Then Jeremiah **s** to all the	Jer 26:12	559
elders of the land rose up and **s** to all	Jer 26:17	559
he **s** to all the people of Judah,	Jer 26:18	559
I **s** words like all these to	Jer 27:12	1696
Then I **s** to the priests and to all	Jer 27:16	1696
s to me in the house of the LORD	Jer 28:1	559
Then the prophet Jeremiah **s** to the	Jer 28:5	559
Hananiah **s** in the presence of	Jer 28:11	559
words which the LORD **s** concerning	Jer 30:4	1696
Then Jeremiah the prophet **s** all	Jer 34:6	1696
because I **s** to them but they did	Jer 35:17	1696
from the day I *first* **s** to you,	Jer 36:2	1696
He **s** through Jeremiah the prophet.	Jer 37:2	1696
king's palace and **s** to the king,	Jer 38:8	1696
Then Johanan the son of Kareah **s**	Jer 40:15	559
which Jeremiah the prophet **s** to	Jer 45:1	1696
message which the LORD **s** to Jeremiah	Jer 46:13	1696
the LORD **s** concerning Babylon,	Jer 50:1	1696
purposed and performed What He **s**	Jer 51:12	1696
Then he **s** kindly to him and set	Jer 52:32	1696
As He **s** to me the Spirit	Ezk 2:2	1696

and He **s** with me and said to me,	Ezk 3:24	1696
And He **s** to the man clothed in	Ezk 10:2	559
I **s** to the people in the morning,	Ezk 24:18	1696
"Are you the one of whom I **s** in	Ezk 38:17	1696
Chaldeans **s** to the king in Aramaic:	Da 2:4	1696
he went and **s** to him as follows:	Da 2:24	560
presence and **s** to him as follows:	Da 2:25	560
'He shouted out and **s** as follows:	Da 4:14	560
The king **s** and said to the wise	Da 5:7	6032
the queen **s** and said,	Da 5:10	6032
The king **s** and said to Daniel,	Da 5:13	6032
the king and **s** to him as follows:	Da 6:6	560
Then they approached and **s** before	Da 6:12	560
answered and **s** before the king,	Da 6:13	560
The king **s** and said to Daniel,	Da 6:16	6032
The king **s** and said to Daniel,	Da 6:20	6032
Then Daniel **s** to the king,	Da 6:21	4449
who **s** in Your name to our kings,	Da 9:6	1696
then I opened my mouth and **s** and	Da 10:16	1696
Now as soon as he **s** to me, I	Da 10:19	1696
the LORD first **s** through Hosea,	Hos 1:2	1696
at Bethel And there He **s** with us,	Hos 12:4	1696
When Ephraim **s**, *there was*	Hos 13:1	1696
s by the commission of the LORD to	Hg 1:13	559
He **s** and said to those who	Zch 3:4	6030a
Then I **s** and said to the angel who	Zch 6:4	6030a
out to me and **s** to me saying,	Zch 6:8	1696
those who **s** in the day that	Zch 8:9	
feared the LORD **s** to one another,	Mal 3:16	1696
was cast out, the mute man **s**;	Mt 9:33	*2980*
so that the mute man **s** and saw.	Mt 12:22	*2980*
And He **s** many things to them in	Mt 13:3	*2980*
He **s** another parable to them,	Mt 13:33	*2980*
Jesus **s** to the crowds in parables,	Mt 13:34	*2980*
But immediately Jesus **s** to them,	Mt 14:27	*2980*
the house, Jesus **s** to him first,	Mt 17:25	*4399*
Jesus **s** to them again in parables,	Mt 22:1	*3004*
Then Jesus **s** to the crowds and	Mt 23:1	*2980*
And Jesus came up and **s** to them,	Mt 28:18	*2980*
they **s** to Jesus about her.	Mk 1:30	*3004*
He **s** with them and said to them,	Mk 6:50	*2980*
was deaf and **s** with difficulty,	Mk 7:32	*3424*
They **s** to them just as Jesus	Mk 11:6	*3004*
He **s** the parable against them.	Mk 12:12	*3004*
burning bush, how God **s** to him,	Mk 12:26	*3004*
As He **s** to our fathers, To Abraham	Lk 1:55	*2980*
As He **s** by the mouth of His holy	Lk 1:70	*2980*
And He also **s** a parable to them:	Lk 6:39	*3004*
to Him, He **s** by way of a parable:	Lk 8:4	*3004*
had gone out, the mute man **s**;	Lk 11:14	*2980*
s to the lawyers and Pharisees,	Lk 14:3	*3004*
and they **s**, saying to Him,	Lk 20:2	*3004*
He **s** this parable against them.	Lk 20:19	*3004*
Remember how He **s** to you while He	Lk 24:6	*2980*
"These are My words which I **s** to	Lk 24:44	*2980*
the word that Jesus **s** to him and	Jn 4:50	*3004*
But this He **s** of the Spirit, whom	Jn 7:39	*3004*
Then Jesus again **s** to them,	Jn 8:12	*2980*
These words He **s** in the treasury,	Jn 8:20	*2980*
As He **s** these things, many came to	Jn 8:30	*2980*
figure of speech Jesus **s** to them,	Jn 10:6	*3004*
These things Jesus **s**,	Jn 12:36	*2980*
Isaiah the prophet which he **s**:	Jn 12:38	*3004*
he saw His glory, and he **s** of Him.	Jn 12:41	*2980*
the word I **s** is what will judge	Jn 12:48	*2980*
Jesus **s** these things;	Jn 17:1	*2980*
to fulfill the word which He **s**,	Jn 18:9	*3004*
went out and **s** to the doorkeeper,	Jn 18:16	*3004*
and I **s** nothing in secret.	Jn 18:20	*2980*
who have heard what I **s** to them;	Jn 18:21	*2980*
word of Jesus which He **s**,	Jn 18:32	*3004*
s of the resurrection of the Christ,	Ac 2:31	*2980*
all things about which God **s** by the	Ac 3:21	*2980*
"But God **s** to this effect, that	Ac 7:6	*2980*
just as He who **s** to Moses directed	Ac 7:44	*2980*
angel of the Lord **s** to Philip saying,	Ac 8:26	*2980*
Barnabas **s** out boldly and said,	Ac 13:46	*3955*
and **s** in such a manner that a	Ac 14:1	*2980*
man was listening to Paul as he **s**,	Ac 14:9	*2980*
And they **s** the word of the Lord to	Ac 16:32	*2980*
s to them in the Hebrew dialect,	Ac 21:40	*4377*
"The Holy Spirit rightly **s**	Ac 28:25	*2980*
I wish that you all **s** in tongues,	1Co 14:5	*2980*
"I BELIEVED, THEREFORE I **S**,"	2Co 4:13	*2980*
we **s** all things to you in truth,	2Co 7:14	*2980*
after He **s** long ago to the fathers	Heb 1:1	*2980*
Moses **s** nothing concerning priests.	Heb 7:14	*2980*
you, who **s** the word of God to you;	Heb 13:7	*2980*
who **s** in the name of the Lord.	Jas 5:10	*2980*
by the Holy Spirit **s** from God.	2Pe 1:21	*2980*
like a lamb and he **s** as a dragon.	Rv 13:11	*2980*
seven bowls came and **s** with me,	Rv 17:1	*2980*
last plagues came and **s** with me,	Rv 21:9	*2980*
The one who **s** with me had a	Rv 21:15	*2980*

SPOKEN

forth as the LORD had **s** to him;	Gn 12:4	1696
Abraham what He has **s** about him."	Gn 18:19	1696
the town of which you have **s**.	Gn 19:21	1696
time of which God had **s** to him.	Gn 21:2	1696
master's son, as the LORD has **s**."	Gn 24:51	1696
the place where He had **s** with him.	Gn 35:13	1696
the place where He had **s** with him,	Gn 35:14	1696
place where God had **s** with him,	Gn 35:15	1696
"It is as I have **s** to Pharaoh:	Gn 41:28	1696
of Joseph that he had **s** to them,	Gn 45:27	1696
since You have **s** to Your servant;	Ex 4:10	1696
which the LORD had **s** to Moses.	Ex 4:30	1696
just as the LORD had **s** to Moses.	Ex 9:12	1696
as the LORD had **s** through Moses.	Ex 9:35	1696

All that the LORD has **s** we will do! Ex 19:8 1696
that I have **s** to you from heaven. Ex 20:22 1696
All the words which the LORD has **s** Ex 24:3 1696
All that the LORD has **s** we will do, Ex 24:7 1696
this land of which I have **s** I will give Ex 32:13 559
do this thing of which you have **s**; Ex 33:17 1696
LORD had **s** to him on Mount Sinai. Ex 34:32 1696
LORD has **s** to them through Moses Lv 10:11 1696
For the LORD had **s** to Moses, Nu 1:48 1696
just as the LORD had **s** to Moses, Nu 5:4 1696
LORD indeed **s** only through Moses? Nu 12:2 1696
Has He not **s** through us as well?" Nu 12:2 1696
'just as you have **s** in My hearing, Nu 14:28 1696
'I, the LORD, have **s**, Nu 14:35 1696
which the LORD has **s** to Moses, Nu 15:22 1696
LORD had **s** to him through Moses. Nu 16:40 1696
Then Aaron took *it* as Moses had **s**, Nu 16:47 1696
have **s** against the LORD and you; Nu 21:7 1696
Balak did just as Balaam had **s**, Nu 23:2 1696
"What has the LORD **s**?" Nu 23:17 1696
Or has He **s**, and will He not make Nu 23:19 1696
as the LORD had **s** through Moses. Nu 27:23 1696
God of your fathers, has **s** to you. Dt 1:21 1696
people which they have **s** to you. Dt 5:28 1696
done well in all that they have **s**. Dt 5:28 1696
before you, as the LORD has **s**. Dt 6:19 1696
just as the LORD has **s** to you. Dt 9:3 1696
words which the LORD had **s** with you Dt 9:10 1696
LORD had **s** to you on the mountain Dt 10:4 1696
you set foot, as He has **s** to you. Dt 11:25 1696
'They have **s** well. Dt 18:17 1696
word which the LORD has not **s**?' Dt 18:21 1696
thing which the LORD has not **s**. Dt 18:22 1696
prophet has **s** it presumptuously; Dt 18:22 1696
the LORD your God, as He has **s**." Dt 26:19 1696
of you, just as the LORD has **s**. Dt 31:3 1696
just as Moses had **s** to them; Jos 4:12 1696
when Joshua had **s** to the people, Jos 6:8 559
just as the leaders had **s** to them. Jos 9:21 1696
all that the LORD had **s** to Moses, Jos 11:23 1696
them out as the LORD has **s**." Jos 14:12 1696
as the LORD had **s** and as the LORD Jg 2:15 1696
and did as the LORD had **s** to him; Jg 6:27 1696
Israel through me, as You have **s**, Jg 6:36 1696
through me, as You have **s**." Jg 6:37 1696
have **s** kindly to your maidservant, Ru 2:13 1696
for I have **s** until now out of my 1Sa 1:16 1696
I have **s** concerning his house, 1Sa 3:12 1696
of which you and I have **s**, 1Sa 20:23 1696
good that He has **s** concerning you, 1Sa 25:30 1696
"As God lives, if you had not **s**, 2Sa 2:27 1696
For the LORD has **s** of David, 2Sa 3:18 559
with the maids of whom you have **s**, 2Sa 6:22 559
for You have **s** also of the house 2Sa 7:19 1696
the word that You have **s** 2Sa 7:25 1696
it forever, and do as You have **s**, 2Sa 7:25 1696
For You, O Lord GOD, have **s**; 2Sa 7:29 1696
that my lord the king has **s**. 2Sa 14:19 1696
"Ahithophel has **s** thus. 2Sa 17:6 1696
if Adonijah has not **s** this word 1Ki 2:23 1696
which He had **s** concerning the 1Ki 2:27 1696
"Do as he has **s** and fall upon him 1Ki 2:31 1696
You have **s** with Your mouth and 1Ki 8:24 1696
which You have **s** to Your servant, 1Ki 8:26 1696
this people who have **s** to me, 1Ki 12:9 1696
is the sign which the LORD has **s**, 1Ki 13:3 1696
words which he had **s** to the king, 1Ki 13:11 1696
for the LORD has **s** *it*." 1Ki 14:11 1696
the Jezreelite had **s** to him; 1Ki 21:4 1696
Of Jezebel also has the LORD **s**, 1Ki 21:23 1696
safely the LORD has not **s** by me." 1Ki 22:28 1696
of the LORD which Elijah had **s**. 2Ki 1:17 1696
Would you be **s** for to the king or 2Ki 4:13 1696
the man of God had **s** to the king, 2Ki 7:18 1696
that the LORD has **s** against him: 2Ki 19:21 1696
will do the thing that He has **s**: 2Ki 20:9 1696
LORD which you have **s** is good." 2Ki 20:19 1696
which He had **s** through His 2Ki 24:2 1696
have I **s** a word with any of the 1Ch 17:6 1696
but You have **s** of Your servant's 1Ch 17:17 1696
let the word that You have **s** 1Ch 17:23 1696
forever, and do as You have **s**. 1Ch 17:23 1696
just as He has **s** concerning you. 1Ch 22:11 1696
oil and wine, of which he has **s**. 2Ch 2:15 559
You have **s** with Your mouth and 2Ch 6:15 1696
You have **s** to Your servant David. 2Ch 6:17 1696
this people, who have **s** to me, 2Ch 10:9 1696
the LORD has not **s** by me." 2Ch 18:27 1696
as the LORD has **s** concerning the 2Ch 23:3 1696
king's words which he had **s** to me. Ne 2:18 559
Now it was when they had **s** daily Es 3:4 559
Even the word **s** gently with you? Jb 15:11
Then after I have **s**, Jb 21:3 1696
"Surely you have **s** in my hearing, Jb 33:8 559
"Once I have **s**, and I will not Jb 40:5 1696
the LORD had **s** these words to Job, Jb 42:7 1696
because you have not **s** of Me what Jb 42:7 1696
have not **s** of Me what is right, Jb 42:8 1696
I have **s** of Your faithfulness and Ps 40:10 559
Mighty One, God, the LORD, has **s**, Ps 50:1 1696
God has **s** in His holiness: Ps 60:6 1696
Once God has **s**; Twice I have heard Ps 62:11 1696
For my enemies have **s** against me; Ps 71:10 559
Glorious things are **s** of you, Ps 87:3 1696
God has **s** in His holiness: Ps 108:7 1696
They have **s** against me with a Ps 109:2 1696
a word **s** in right circumstances. Pr 25:11 1696
seriously all words which are **s**, Ec 7:21 1696
On the day when she is **s** for? SS 8:8 1696

the mouth of the LORD has **s**. Is 1:20 1696
the LORD God of Israel has **s**." Is 21:17 1696
be cut off, for the LORD has **s**." Is 22:25 1696
for the LORD has **s** this word. Is 24:3 1696
For the LORD has **s**. Is 25:8 1696
Or the rogue be **s** of *as* generous. Is 32:5 559
that the LORD has **s** against him: Is 37:22 1696
will do this thing that He has **s**: Is 38:7 1696
For He has **s** to me, and He Himself Is 38:15 559
word of the LORD which you have **s** Is 39:8 1696
For the mouth of the LORD has **s**." Is 40:5 1696
"I have not **s** in secret, In some Is 45:19 1696
Truly I have **s**; truly I will bring it to Is 46:11 1696
"I, even I, have **s**; Is 48:15 1696
the first I have not **s** in secret, Is 48:16 1696
For the mouth of the LORD has **s**." Is 58:14 1696
Your lips have **s** falsehood, Your Is 59:3 1696
be **s** of *as* ministers of our God. Is 61:6 7121
have **s** And have done evil things, Jer 3:5 1696
Because I have **s**, I have purposed Jer 4:28 1696
"Because you have **s** this word, Jer 5:14 1696
They have **s** what is not right; Jer 8:6 1696
whom the mouth of the LORD has **s**, Jer 9:12 1696
be haughty, For the LORD has **s**. Jer 13:15 1696
nor commanded them nor **s** to them; Jer 14:14 1696
if that nation against which I have **s** Jer 18:8 1696
'What has the LORD **s**?' Jer 23:35 1696
'What has the LORD **s**?' Jer 23:37 1696
I have **s** to you again and again, Jer 25:3 1696
For he has **s** to us in the name of Jer 26:16 1696
as the LORD has **s** to that nation Jer 27:13 1696
have **s** words in My name falsely, Jer 29:23 1696
which I have **s** to you in a book. Jer 30:2 1696
as often as I have **s** against him, Jer 31:20 1696
what You have **s** has come to pass; Jer 32:24 1696
fulfill the good word which I have **s** Jer 33:14 1696
observed what this people have **s**, Jer 33:24 1696
For I have **s** the word," Jer 34:5 1696
I have **s** to you again and again; Jer 35:14 1696
I have **s** to you concerning Israel and Jer 36:2 1696
the LORD which He had **s** to him Jer 36:4 1696
The LORD has **s** to you, O remnant Jer 42:19 1696
the message that you have **s** to us Jer 44:16 1696
you have **s** with your mouths and Jer 44:25 1696
have **s** in My zeal when I have Ezk 5:13 1696
I, the LORD, have **s**. Ezk 5:15 1696
I, the LORD, have **s**.' " Ezk 5:17 1696
but it is not I who have **s**? Ezk 13:7 1696
have **s** falsehood and seen a lie, Ezk 13:8 1696
know that I, the LORD, have **s**." Ezk 17:21 1696
I have **s**, and I will perform *it*." Ezk 17:24 1696
I, the LORD, have **s**." Ezk 21:17 1696
for I, the LORD, have **s**.' " Ezk 21:32 1696
I, the LORD, have **s** and will act. Ezk 22:14 1696
Lord GOD,' when the LORD has not **s**. Ezk 22:28 1696
for I have **s**,' declares the Lord Ezk 23:34 1696
"I, the LORD, have **s**; Ezk 24:14 1696
midst of the sea, for I have **s**,' Ezk 26:5 1696
no more, for I the LORD have **s**," Ezk 26:14 1696
hand of strangers, For I have **s**!' Ezk 28:10 1696
I the LORD have **s**." Ezk 30:12 1696
'Thus you have **s**, saying, Ezk 33:10 559
I the LORD have **s**. Ezk 34:24 1696
revilings which you have **s** against Ezk 35:12 559
"And you have **s** arrogantly Ezk 35:13
1431, 6310
the enemy has **s** against you, Ezk 36:2 559
I have **s** against the rest of the nations Ezk 36:5 1696
I have **s** in My jealousy and in My Ezk 36:6 1696
I, the LORD, have **s** and will do it." Ezk 36:36 1696
I, the LORD, have **s** and done it," Ezk 37:14 1696
for it is I who have **s**," Ezk 39:5 1696
"That is the day of which I have **s**. Ezk 39:8 1696
His words which He had **s** against us Da 9:12 1696
And when he had **s** this word to me, Da 10:11 1696
When he had **s** to me according Da 10:15 1696
I have also **s** to the prophets, And Hos 12:10 1696
nation," for the LORD has **s**. Jl 3:8 1696
which the LORD has **s** against you, Am 3:1 1696
The Lord GOD has **s**! Am 3:8 1696
house of Esau," For the LORD has **s**. Ob 1:18 1696
mouth of the LORD of hosts has **s**. Mi 4:4 1696
for you have **s** falsely in the name Zch 13:3 1696
'What have we **s** against You?' Mal 3:13 1696
s by the Lord through the prophet Mt 1:22 *3004*
what had been **s** by the Lord Mt 2:15 *3004*
what had been **s** through Jeremiah Mt 2:17 *3004*
fulfill what was **s** through the Mt 2:23 *3004*
was **s** through Isaiah the prophet: Mt 4:14 *3004*
was **s** through Isaiah the prophet Mt 8:17 *3004*
was **s** through Isaiah the prophet: Mt 12:17 *3004*
fulfill what was **s** through the prophet Mt 13:35 *3004*
He had **s** to them about John the Mt 17:13 *3004*
fulfill what was **s** through the prophet Mt 21:4 *3004*
what was **s** to you by God: Mt 22:31 *3004*
s of through Daniel the prophet, Mt 24:15 *3004*
also be **s** of in memory of her." Mt 26:13 *2980*
that which was **s** through Jeremiah Mt 27:9 *3004*
overhearing what was being **s**, Mk 5:36 *2980*
also be **s** of in memory of her." Mk 14:9 *2980*
when the Lord Jesus had **s** to them, Mk 16:19 *2980*
had been **s** to her by the Lord." Lk 1:45 *2980*
And when the voice had **s**, Lk 9:36 *1096*
Now when He had **s**, a Pharisee Lk 11:37 *2980*
"Teacher, You have **s** well." Lk 20:39 *3004*
in all that the prophets have **s**! Lk 24:25 *2980*
and the word which Jesus had **s**. Jn 2:22 *3004*
the words that I have **s** to you are Jn 6:63 *2980*
"Never has a man **s** the way this man Jn 7:46 *2980*

"We know that God has **s** to Moses, Jn 9:29 *2980*
Now Jesus had **s** of his death, but Jn 11:13 *3004*
"An angel has **s** to Him." Jn 12:29 *2980*
"These things I have **s** to you while Jn 14:25 *2980*
of the word which I have **s** to you. Jn 15:3 *2980*
"These things I have **s** to you so Jn 15:11 *2980*
"If I had not come and **s** to them, Jn 15:22 *2980*
"These things I have **s** to you so Jn 16:1 *2980*
"But these things I have **s** to you, Jn 16:4 *2980*
s to you in figurative language; Jn 16:25 *2980*
"These things I have **s** to you, Jn 16:33 *2980*
When Jesus had **s** these words, He Jn 18:1 *3004*
"I have **s** openly to the world; Jn 18:20 *2980*
"If I have **s** wrongly, testify Jn 18:23 *2980*
And when He had **s** this, He said to Jn 21:19 *3004*
was **s** of through the prophet Joel: Ac 2:16 *3004*
all the prophets who have **s**, Ac 3:24 *2980*
and **s** the word of the Lord, Ac 8:25 *2980*
he had **s** out boldly in the name of Ac 9:27 *3955*
man well **s** of by the entire nation Ac 10:22 *3140*
to decay, He has **s** in this way: Ac 13:34 *3004*
thing **s** of in the Prophets may not Ac 13:40 *3004*
be **s** to them the next Sabbath. Ac 13:42 *2980*
contradicting the things **s** by Paul, Ac 13:45 *2980*
word of God be **s** to you first Ac 13:46 *2980*
When they had **s** the word in Perga, Ac 14:25 *2980*
and he was well **s** of by the brethren Ac 16:2 *3140*
respond to the things **s** by Paul. Ac 16:14 *2980*
over the word which he had **s**, Ac 20:38 *3004*
and well **s** of by all the Jews who Ac 22:12 *3140*
spirit or an angel has **s** to him?" Ac 23:9 *2980*
or **s** anything bad about you. Ac 28:21 *2980*
that it is **s** against everywhere." Ac 28:22 *483*
being persuaded by the things **s**, Ac 28:24 *3004*
after Paul had **s** one *parting* word, Ac 28:25 *3004*
[When he had **s** these words, Ac 28:29 *3004*
to that which had been **s**, Ro 4:18 *3004*
you a good thing be **s** of as evil; Ro 14:16 *987*
how will it be known what is **s**? 1Co 14:9 *2980*
Our mouth has **s** freely to you, O 2Co 6:11 *455*
were **s** to Abraham and to his seed. Ga 3:16 *3004*
our doctrine will not be **s** against. 1Tm 6:1 *987*
last days has **s** to us in His Son, Heb 1:2 *2980*
For if the word **s** through angels Heb 2:2 *2980*
at the first **s** through the Lord, Heb 2:3 *2980*
things which were to be **s** later; Heb 3:5 *2980*
have **s** of another day after that. Heb 4:8 *2980*
are **s** belongs to another tribe, Heb 7:13 *3004*
commandment had been **s** by Moses Heb 9:19 *2980*
further word be **s** to them. Heb 12:19 *4369*
remember the words **s** beforehand 2Pe 3:2 *4275b*
of the Lord and Savior **s** by your 2Pe 3:2
sinners have **s** against Him." Jude 1:15 *2980*
the words that were **s** beforehand by Jude 1:17 *4275b*
the seven peals of thunder had **s**, Rv 10:4 *2980*
the seven peals of thunder have **s** and Rv 10:4 *2980*

SPOKES
Their axles, their rims, their **s**, 1Ki 7:33 2839

SPOKESMAN
worthless, You will become My **s**. Jer 15:19 6310
He would be **s** to this people. Mi 2:11 5197

SPOKESMEN
s have transgressed against Me. Is 43:27 3917b

SPONGE
one of them ran, and taking a **s**, Mt 27:48 *4699*
ran and filled a **s** with sour wine, Mk 15:36 *4699*
so they put a **s** full of the sour Jn 19:29 *4699*

SPOONS
bowls and the **s** and the firepans, 1Ki 7:50 3709
the shovels, the snuffers, the **s**, 2Ki 25:14 3709
the snuffers, the bowls, the **s** and 2Ch 4:22 3709

SPORT
in a Hebrew to us to make **s** of us; Gn 39:14 6711
us, came in to me to make **s** of me; Gn 39:17 6711
me through and make **s** of me." 1Sa 31:4 5953a
which You have formed to **s** in it. Ps 104:26 7832
wickedness is like **s** to a fool, Pr 10:23 7814

SPOT
swelling or a scab or a bright **s**, Lv 13:2 934
"But if the bright **s** is white on Lv 13:4 934
or a reddish-white, bright **s**, Lv 13:19 934
the bright **s** remains in its place and Lv 13:23 934
of the burn becomes a bright **s**, Lv 13:24 934
hair in the bright **s** has turned white Lv 13:25 934
is no white hair in the bright **s** and Lv 13:26 934
the bright **s** remains in its place and Lv 13:28 934
for a scab, and for a bright **s** Lv 14:56 934
he fell there and died on the **s**. 2Sa 2:23 8478
Or if any **s** has stuck to my hands, Jb 31:7 3971
no **s** or wrinkle or any such thing; Eph 5:27 *4696*

SPOTLESS
as of a lamb unblemished and **s**, 1Pe 1:19 *784*
by Him in peace, **s** and blameless, 2Pe 3:14 *784*

SPOTS
bright **s** on the skin of the body, Lv 13:38 934
of the body, *even* white bright **s**, Lv 13:38 934
and if the bright **s** on the skin of Lv 13:39 934
his skin Or the leopard his **s**? Jer 13:23 2272

SPOTTED
there every speckled and **s** sheep and Gn 30:32 2921
s and speckled among the goats; Gn 30:32 2921
not speckled and **s** among the goats Gn 30:33 2921
that day the striped and **s** male goats Gn 30:35 2921
the speckled and **s** female goats, Gn 30:35 2921
forth striped, speckled, and **s**. Gn 30:39 2921

SPOUTS
But the mouth of fools **s** folly. Pr 15:2 5042

and its seven lamps on it with seven s Zch 4:2 4166

SPRANG

and fire s up from the rock and Jg 6:21 5927
and immediately they s up, Mt 13:5 *1816*
and immediately it s up because it Mk 4:5 *1816*
and a day later a south wind s up, Ac 28:13 *1920*

SPRAWL

of ivory And s on their couches, Am 6:4 5628

SPRAWLERS'

And the s banqueting will pass away. Am 6:7 5628

SPREAD

of the Canaanite were s abroad. Gn 10:18 6327a
and you will s out to the west Gn 28:14 6555
When the famine was s over all Gn 41:56
and the more they s out, Ex 1:12 6555
I will s out my hands to the LORD; Ex 9:29 6566
and s out his hands to the LORD; Ex 9:33 6566
shall have *their* wings s upward, Ex 25:20 6566
and unleavened wafers s with oil; Ex 29:2 4886
cherubim had *their* wings s upward, Ex 37:9 6566
He s the tent over the Ex 40:19 6566
or unleavened wafers s with oil. Lv 2:4 4886
and unleavened wafers s with oil, Lv 7:12 4886
infection has not s on the skin, Lv 13:5 6581
the mark has not s on the skin, Lv 13:6 6581
and if the scab has s on the skin, Lv 13:8 6581
in its place and does not s, Lv 13:23 6581
place and has not s in the skin, Lv 13:28 6581
and if the scale has not s and Lv 13:32 6581
the scale has not s in the skin and Lv 13:34 6581
if the scale has s in the skin, Lv 13:36 6581
if the mark has s in the garment, Lv 13:51 6581
the mark has not s in the garment, Lv 13:53 6581
even though the mark has not s, Lv 13:55 6581
the mark has indeed s in the walls Lv 14:39 6581
mark has indeed s in the house, Lv 14:44 6581
and the mark has not indeed s in Lv 14:48 6581
s over *it* a cloth of pure blue, Nu 4:6 6566
they shall also s a cloth of blue and Nu 4:7 6566
"They shall s over them a Nu 4:8 6566
they shall s a blue cloth and cover it Nu 4:11 6566
and s a purple cloth over it. Nu 4:13 6566
they shall s a cover of porpoise skin Nu 4:14 6566
and unleavened wafers s with oil, Nu 6:15 4886
and they s *them* out for themselves Nu 11:32 7849
And they shall s the garment Dt 22:17 6566
He s His wings and caught them, Dt 32:11 6566
So they s out a garment, and every Jg 8:25 6566
in Judah, and s out in Lehi. Jg 15:9 6566
So s your covering over your maid, Ru 3:9 6566
When the battle s, Israel was 1Sa 4:2 5203
and the battle s beyond Beth-aven. 1Sa 14:23 5674a
they were s over all the land, 1Sa 30:16 5203
and s themselves out in the valley 2Sa 5:18 5203
and s themselves out in the valley of 2Sa 5:22 5203
and s it over the well's mouth and 2Sa 17:19 6566
was s over the whole countryside, 2Sa 18:8 6327a
and s it for herself on the rock, 2Sa 21:10 5186
wings of the cherubim were s out, 1Ki 6:27 6566
and he s the gold on the cherubim 1Ki 6:32 7286
For the cherubim s *their* wings 1Ki 8:7 6566
and s out his hands toward heaven. 1Ki 8:22 6566
with his hands s toward heaven. 1Ki 8:54 6566
it in water and s it on his face, 2Ki 8:15 6566
LORD and s it out before the LORD. 2Ki 19:14 6566
cherubim that s out *their wings* 1Ch 28:18 6566
For the cherubim s their wings 2Ch 5:8 6566
of Israel and s out his hands. 2Ch 6:12 6566
and s out his hands toward heaven. 2Ch 6:13 6566
Hence his fame s afar, for he was 2Ch 26:15 3318
As soon as the order s, 2Ch 31:5 6555
fame s throughout all the provinces; Es 9:4 1980
his shoots s out over his garden. Jb 8:16 3318
right And s out your hand to Him Jb 11:13 6566
'My root is s out to the waters, Jb 29:19 6605a
you, with Him, s out the skies, Jb 37:18 7554
Then You s them abroad. Ps 44:2 7971
I have s out my hands to You. Ps 88:9 7849
He s a cloud for a covering, And Ps 105:39 6566
To Him who s out the earth above Ps 136:6 7554
They have s a net by the wayside; Ps 140:5 6566
useless to s the *baited* net In the Pr 1:17 2219
"I have s my couch with coverings Pr 7:16 7234
The lips of the wise s knowledge, Pr 15:7 2219
you s out your hands *in prayer*, Is 1:15 6566
And the s of its wings will fill Is 8:8 4298
Maggots are s out *as your bed* Is 14:11 3331
Its tendrils s themselves out *and* Is 16:8 5203
And those who s nets on the waters Is 19:8 6566
the table, they s out the cloth, Is 21:5 6823
And he will s out his hands in the Is 25:11 6566
mast firmly, Nor s out the sail. Is 33:23 6566
LORD and s it out before the LORD. Is 37:14 6566
Who s out the earth and its Is 42:5 7554
My right hand s out the heavens; Is 48:13 2946
"For you will s abroad to the Is 54:3 6555
"I have s out My hands all day Is 65:2 6566
They will s them out to the sun, Jer 8:2 7849
he will s his canopy over them. Jer 43:10 5186
And s out his wings against Moab. Jer 48:40 6566
s out His wings against Bozrah; Jer 49:22 6566
He has s a net for my feet; La 1:13 6566
Their wings were s out above; Ezk 1:11 6504
s out over their heads. Ezk 1:22 5186
When He s it out before me, it was Ezk 2:10 6566
fire will s to all the house of Israel. Ezk 5:4 3318
"I will also s My net over him, Ezk 12:13 6566
and s them among the countries. Ezk 12:15 2219
so I s My skirt over you and Ezk 16:8 6566
and you s your legs to every Ezk 16:25 6589
"I will s My net over him, Ezk 17:20 6566
And they s their net over him; Ezk 19:8 6566
of many waters as it s them out. Ezk 31:5 7971
"Now I will s My net over you Ezk 32:3 6566
who s terror in the land of the Ezk 32:23 5414
Mizpah And a net s out on Tabor. Hos 5:1 6566
go, I will s My net over them; Hos 7:12 6566
the dawn is s over the mountains, Jl 2:2 6566
and I will s refuse on your faces, Mal 2:3 2219
The news about Him s throughout all Mt 4:24 *565*
This news s throughout all that land. Mt 9:26 *1831*
and s the news about Him throughout all Mt 9:31 *1310*
s their coats in the road, Mt 21:8 *4766*
story was widely s among the Jews, Mt 28:15 *1310*
Immediately the news about Him s Mk 1:28 *1831*
it freely and to s the news around, Mk 1:45 *1310*
many s their coats in the road, Mk 11:8 *4766*
and others s leafy branches which Mk 11:8
and news about Him s through all Lk 4:14 *1831*
not s any further among the people, Ac 4:17 *1268*
the word of the Lord was being s Ac 13:49 *1308*
sin, and so death s to all men, Ro 5:12 *1330*
the things of the gospel *has* s 2Co 8:18
the word of the Lord will s rapidly 2Th 3:1 *5143*
their talk will s like gangrene. 2Tm 2:17 *3542*
will s His tabernacle over them. Rv 7:15 *4637*

SPREADING

and s his hands toward this house; 1Ki 8:38 6566
and s his hands toward this house, 2Ch 6:29 6566
understand the s of the clouds, Jb 36:29 4666
violent man S himself like a Ps 37:35 6168
neighbor Is s a net for his steps. Pr 29:5 6566
and cut away the s branches. Is 18:5 5189
And s out the earth all alone, Is 44:24 7554
And for s out sackcloth and ashes Is 58:5 3331
s vine with its branches turned Ezk 17:6 5628
'She will be a place for the s of nets Ezk 26:5 4894b
will be a place for the s of nets. Ezk 26:14 4894b
will be a place for the s of nets. Ezk 47:10 4894a
the trees and s them in the road. Mt 21:8 *4766*
And the report about Him was s into Lk 4:37 *1607*
news about Him was s even farther, Lk 5:15 *1330*
were s their coats on the road. Lk 19:36 *5291*
The word of God kept on s; Ac 6:7 *837*
that the grace which is s to more 2Co 4:15 *4121*

SPREADS

breaks out and s to thorn bushes, Ex 22:6 4672
if the scab s farther on the skin after Lv 13:7 6581
and if it s farther on the skin, Lv 13:22 6581
If it s farther in the skin, then Lv 13:27 6581
"But if the scale s farther in Lv 13:35 6581
moon And s His cloud over it. Jb 26:9 6576
He s His lightning about Him, Jb 36:30 6566
He s out *like* a threshing sledge Jb 41:30 7502
evil, Who s strife. Pr 6:14 7971
one who s strife among brothers. Pr 6:19 7971
And he who s slander is a fool. Pr 10:18 3318
A perverse man s strife, And a Pr 16:28 7971
mouth of the wicked s iniquity. Pr 19:28 1104
a swimmer s out *his hands* to swim, Is 25:11 6566
And s them out like a tent to dwell in Is 40:22 4969

SPRIG

"I will also take *a* s from Ezk 17:22

SPRIGS

And put forth s like a plant. Jb 14:9 7105b
Then He will cut off the s with Is 18:5 2150

SPRING

by a s of water in the wilderness, Gn 16:7 5871a
by the s on the way to Shur. Gn 16:7 5871a
"Behold, I am standing by the s, Gn 24:13 5871a
she went down to the s and filled Gn 24:16 5871a
ran outside to the man at the s. Gn 24:29 5871a
standing by the camels at the s. Gn 24:30 5871a
"So I came today to the s, Gn 24:42 5871a
behold, I am standing by the s, Gn 24:43 5871a
and went down to the s and drew, Gn 24:45 5871a
bough, A fruitful bough by a s; Gn 49:22 5869
'Nevertheless a s or a cistern Lv 11:36 4599
Israel sang this song: "S up, O well! Nu 21:17 5927
border curved to the s of the waters Jos 15:9 4599
and camped beside the s of Harod; Jg 7:1 5871a
by the s which is in Jezreel. 1Sa 29:1 5871a
then it happened in the s, 2Sa 11:1 8666
He went out to the s of water and 2Ki 2:21 4161
the land in the s of the year. 2Ki 13:20 935
Then it happened in the s, 1Ch 20:1 8666
And out of the dust others will s. Jb 8:19 6779
their mouth as for the s rain. Jb 29:23 4456
valley of Baca they make it a s Ps 84:6 4599
the horn of David to s forth; Ps 132:17 6779
is like a cloud with the s rain. Pr 16:15 4456
Like a trampled s and a polluted Pr 25:26 4599
rock garden locked, a s sealed up. SS 4:12 4599
"*You are* a garden s, SS 4:15 4599
a shoot will s from the stem of Jesse Is 11:1 3318
Before they s forth I proclaim *them* Is 42:9 6779
new, Now it will s forth; Is 43:19 6779
And they will s up among the grass Is 44:4 6779
And righteousness s up with it. Is 45:8 6779
recovery will speedily s forth; Is 58:8 6779
And like a s of water whose waters Is 58:11 4161
the things sown in it to s up, Is 61:11 6779
To s up before all the nations. Is 61:11 6779
And there has been no s rain. Jer 3:3 4456
the autumn rain and the s rain, Jer 5:24 4456
righteous Branch of David to s forth Jer 33:15 6779
the s rain watering the earth." Hos 6:3 4456
dry And his s will be dried up; Hos 13:15 4599
And a s will go out from the house Jl 3:18 4599
Does a trap s up from the earth Am 3:5 5927
when the s crop began to sprout. Am 7:1 3954
the s crop *was* after the king's Am 7:1 3954
the LORD at the time of the s rain Zch 10:1 4456
from the s of the water of life Rv 21:6 *4077*

SPRINGING

a well of water s up to eternal life." Jn 4:14 *242*
no root of bitterness s up causes Heb 12:15 *5453*

SPRINGS

he is the Anah who found the hot s Gn 36:24 3222
where there *were* twelve s of water Ex 15:27 5871a
in Elim there were twelve s of water Nu 33:9 5871a
of water, of fountains and s, Dt 8:7 8415
Negev, give me also s of water." Jos 15:19 1543
the upper s and the lower springs. Jos 15:19 1543
the upper springs and the lower s. Jos 15:19 1543
Negev, give me also s of water." Jg 1:15 1543
the upper s and the lower springs. Jg 1:15 1543
the upper springs and the lower s. Jg 1:15 1543
When the tender grass s out 2Sa 23:4
"Go through the land to all the s 1Ki 18:5 4599
good tree and stop all s of water, 2Ki 3:19 4599
So they stopped all the s of water 2Ki 3:25 4599
second year what s from the same, 2Ki 19:29 5501b
the s which *were* outside the city, 2Ch 32:3 5871a
stopped up all the s and the stream 2Ch 32:4 4599
you entered into the s of the sea Or Jb 38:16 5033
broke open s and torrents; Ps 74:15 4599
Truth s from the earth, Ps 85:11 6779
"All my s *of joy* are in you." Ps 87:7 4599
He sends forth s in the valleys; Ps 104:10 4599
And s of water into a thirsty ground Ps 107:33 4161
And a dry land into s of water; Ps 107:35 4161
For from it *flow* the s of life. Pr 4:23 8444
Should your s be dispersed abroad, Pr 5:16 4599
were no s abounding with water. Pr 8:24 4599
the s of the deep became fixed, Pr 8:28 5871a
water From the s of salvation. Is 12:3 4599
the world and all that s from it. Is 34:1 6631
And the thirsty ground s of water; Is 35:7 4002
second year what s from the same, Is 37:30 5501b
And s in the midst of the valleys; Is 41:18 4599
And will guide them to s of water. Is 49:10 4002
These are s without water and 2Pe 2:17 *4077*
them to s of the water of life; Rv 7:17 *4077*
the rivers and on the s of waters. Rv 8:10 *4077*
earth and sea and s of waters." Rv 14:7 *4077*
the rivers and the s of waters; Rv 16:4 *4077*

SPRINKLE

and s it around on the altar. Ex 29:16 2236b
and s the *rest of the* blood around Ex 29:20 2236b
and s *it* on Aaron and on his Ex 29:21 5137a
s the blood around on the altar that Lv 1:5 2236b
s its blood around on the altar. Lv 1:11 2236b
s the blood around on the altar. Lv 3:2 2236b
s its blood around on the altar. Lv 3:8 2236b
s its blood around on the altar. Lv 3:13 2236b
and s some of the blood seven Lv 4:6 5137a
and s *it* seven times before the Lv 4:17 5137a
'He shall also s some of the blood Lv 5:9 5137a
s its blood around on the altar. Lv 7:2 2236b
"He shall then s seven times the Lv 14:7 5137a
with his finger s some of the oil Lv 14:16 5137a
priest shall s some of the oil that is in Lv 14:27 5137a
and s the house seven times. Lv 14:51 5137a
s *it* with his finger on the mercy seat Lv 16:14 5137a
he shall s some of the blood with his Lv 16:14 5137a
and s it on the mercy seat and in Lv 16:15 5137a
he shall s some of the blood on it Lv 16:19 5137a
"The priest shall s the blood Lv 17:6 2236b
s purifying water on them, Nu 8:7
You shall s their blood on the Nu 18:17 2236b
and s some of its blood toward the Nu 19:4 5137a
and s *it* on the tent and on all Nu 19:18 5137a
'Then the clean *person* shall s on Nu 19:19 5137a
and s on it all the blood of the 2Ki 16:15 2236b
Thus He will s many nations, Kings Is 52:15 5137a
"Then I will s clean water on you, Ezk 36:25 2236b
on it and to s blood on it. Ezk 43:18 2236b

SPRINKLED

half of the blood he s on the altar. Ex 24:6 2236b
the blood and s *it* on the people, Ex 24:8 2236b
He s some of it on the altar Lv 8:11 5137a
s the blood around on the altar. Lv 8:19 2236b
Moses then s *the rest of* the blood Lv 8:24 2236b
on the altar and s it on Aaron, Lv 8:30 5137a
and he s it around on the altar. Lv 9:12 2236b
and he s it around on the altar. Lv 9:18 2236b
water for impurity was not s on him Nu 19:13 2236b
water for impurity has not been s on Nu 19:20 2236b
some of her blood was s on the wall 2Ki 9:33 5137a
s the blood of his peace offerings on 2Ki 16:13 2236b
the blood and s it on the altar. 2Ch 29:22 2236b
rams and s the blood on the altar; 2Ch 29:22 2236b
also and s the blood on the altar. 2Ch 29:22 2236b
the priests s the blood *which they* 2Ch 30:16 2236b
and while the priests s the blood 2Ch 35:11 2236b
"I have s my bed With myrrh, Pr 7:17 5130
lifeblood is s on My garments, Is 63:3 5137a
Gray hairs also are s on him, Hos 7:9 2236b
and s both the book itself and all Heb 9:19 *4472*
he s both the tabernacle and all the Heb 9:21 *4472*
having our hearts s *clean* from an Heb 10:22 *4472*
new covenant, and to the s blood, Heb 12:24 *4473*
Christ and be s with His blood: 1Pe 1:2 *4473*

SPRINKLES
belong to the priest who **s** the blood **Lv 7:14** 2236b
And he who **s** the water for **Nu 19:21** 5137a

SPRINKLING
the ashes of a heifer **s** those who **Heb 9:13** *4472*
Passover and the **s** of the blood, **Heb 11:28** *4378*

SPROUT
"Let the earth **s** vegetation: **Gn 1:11** 1876
rod of the man whom I choose will **s**. **Nu 17:5** 6524a
does trouble **s** from the ground, **Jb 5:6** 6779
is cut down, that it will **s** again, **Jb 14:7** 2498
to make the seeds of grass to **s**? **Jb 38:27** 6779
root, Israel will blossom and **s**, **Is 27:6** 6524a
earth And making it bear and **s**, **Is 55:10** 6779
a horn **s** for the house of Israel, **Ezk 29:21** 6779
His shoots will **s**, And his beauty **Hos 14:6** 1980
when the spring crop began to **s**. **Am 7:1** 5927

SPROUTED
no plant of the field had yet **s**, **Gn 2:5** 6779
by the east wind, **s** up after them. **Gn 41:6** 6779
by the east wind, **s** up after them; **Gn 41:23** 6779
the house of Levi had **s** and put forth **Nu 17:8** 6524a
when the wicked **s** up like grass And **Ps 92:7** 6524a
"Then it **s** and became a low, **Ezk 17:6** 6779
"But when the wheat **s** and bore grain, **Mt 13:26** *985*

SPROUTING
that all its **s** leaves wither? **Ezk 17:9** 6780

SPROUTS
which **s** for you out of the field. **Ex 10:5** 6779
they are like grass which **s** anew. **Ps 90:5** 2498
morning it flourishes and **s** anew; **Ps 90:6** 2498
as the earth brings forth its **s**, **Is 61:11** 6780
And judgment **s** like poisonous **Hos 10:4** 6524a
and the seed **s** and grows—how, **Mk 4:27** *985*

SPUN
skilled women **s** with their hands, **Ex 35:25** 2901
and brought what they had **s**, **Ex 35:25** 4299
with a skill **s** the goats' *hair.* **Ex 35:26** 2901

SPURN
"How long will this people **s** Me? **Nu 14:11** 5006
and **s** Me and break My covenant. **Dt 31:20** 5006
And the enemy **s** Your name forever? **Ps 74:10** 5006

SPURNED
any of those who **s** Me see it. **Nu 14:23** 5006
that these men have **s** the LORD." **Nu 16:30** 5006
"The LORD saw *this,* and **s** *them* **Dt 32:19** 5006
Why has the wicked **s** God? **Ps 10:13** 5006
a foolish people has **s** Your name. **Ps 74:18** 5006
s the covenant of Your servant; **Ps 89:39** 5010
s the counsel of the Most High. **Ps 107:11** 5006
my counsel, They **s** all my reproof. **Pr 1:30** 5006
And my heart **s** reproof! **Pr 5:12** 5006

SPURNS
greedy man curses *and* **s** the LORD. **Ps 10:3** 5006

SPURS
Rezin And **s** their enemies on, **Is 9:11** 5526a

SPY
they may **s** out the land of Canaan, **Nu 13:2** 8446
whom Moses sent to **s** out the land; **Nu 13:16** 8446
them to **s** out the land of Canaan, **Nu 13:17** 8446
which we passed through to **s** out **Nu 14:7** 8446
men whom Moses sent to **s** out the **Nu 14:36** 8446
men who went to **s** out the land. **Nu 14:38** 8446
Moses sent to **s** out Jazer, **Nu 21:32** 7270
whom Joshua sent to **s** out Jericho. **Jos 6:25** 7270
"Go up and **s** out the land." **Jos 7:2** 7270
Kadesh-barnea to **s** out the land, **Jos 14:7** 7270
s out the land and to search it; **Jg 18:2** 7270
men who went to **s** out the country **Jg 18:14** 7270
Now the five men who went to **s** out **Jg 18:17** 7270
to **s** it out and overthrow it?" **2Sa 10:3** 7270
overthrow and to **s** out the land?" **1Ch 19:3** 7270
had sneaked in to **s** out our liberty **Ga 2:4** *2684*

SPYING
they returned from **s** out the land, **Nu 13:25** 8446
which we have gone, in **s** it out, **Nu 13:32** 8446

SQUADS
four **s** of soldiers to guard him, **Ac 12:4** *5069*

SQUANDERED
he **s** his estate with loose living. **Lk 15:13** *1287*

SQUANDERING
to him as **s** his possessions. **Lk 16:1** *1287*

SQUARE
shall spend the night in the **s**." **Gn 19:2** 7339
the altar shall be **s**, **Ex 27:1** 7251
"It shall be **s** *and* folded double, **Ex 28:16** 7251
its width a cubit, it shall be **s**, **Ex 30:2** 7251
a cubit long and a cubit wide, **s**, **Ex 37:25** 7251
long, and five cubits wide, **s**, **Ex 38:1** 7251
It was **s**; they made the breastpiece **Ex 39:9** 7251
its booty into the middle of its open **s** **Dt 13:16** 7339
down in the open **s** of the city, **Jg 19:15** 7339
in the open **s** of the city; **Jg 19:17** 7339
spend the night in the open **s**." **Jg 19:20** 7339
them from the open **s** of Beth-shan, **2Sa 21:12** 7339
and their borders were **s**, **1Ki 7:31** 7251
them into the **s** on the east. **2Ch 29:4** 7339
to him in the **s** at the city gate, **2Ch 32:6** 7339
open **s** *before* the house of God, **Ezr 10:9** 7339
people gathered as one man at the **s** **Ne 8:1** 7339
He read from it before the **s** **Ne 8:3** 7339
and in the **s** at the Water Gate and **Ne 8:16** 7339
in the **s** at the Gate of Ephraim. **Ne 8:16** 7339
city **s** in front of the king's gate. **Es 4:6** 7339
on horseback through the city **s**, **Es 6:9** 7339
on horseback through the city **s**, **Es 6:11** 7339
When I took my seat in the **s**, **Jb 29:7** 7339
She lifts her voice in the **s**; **Pr 1:20** 7339
A lion is in the open **s**!" **Pr 26:13** 7339
yourself a high place in every **s**. **Ezk 16:24** 7339
made your high place in every **s**, **Ezk 16:31** 7339
guardrooms *were* six cubits **s** **Ezk 40:12** 7251
measured the court, a *perfect* **s**, **Ezk 40:47** 7251
The doorposts of the nave were **s**; **Ezk 41:21** 7251
twelve wide, **s** in its four sides. **Ezk 43:16** 7251
there shall be for the holy place a **s** **Ezk 45:2** 7251
set apart the holy allotment, a **s**, **Ezk 48:20** 7243
The city is laid out as a **s**, **Rv 21:16** *5068b*

SQUARED
doorposts *had* **s** *artistic* frames, **1Ki 7:5** 7251

SQUARES
now in the streets, now in the **s**, **Pr 7:12** 7339
In the streets and in the **s** I must **SS 3:2** 7339
in their **s** Everyone is wailing, **Is 15:3** 7339
And seek in her open **s**, **Jer 5:1** 7339
The young men from the town **s**. **Jer 9:21** 7339
They rush wildly in the **s**, **Na 2:4** 7339

SQUEEZED
and **s** them into Pharaoh's cup, **Gn 40:11** 7818
the next morning and **s** the fleece, **Jg 6:38** 2115

SQUIRMING
you and saw you **s** in your blood, **Ezk 16:6** 947
and bare and **s** in your blood. **Ezk 16:22** 947

STABILITY
king gives **s** to the land by justice, **Pr 29:4** 5975
He will be the **s** of your times, **Is 33:6** 530
and the **s** of your faith in Christ. **Col 2:5** *4733*

STACHYS
in Christ, and **S** my beloved. **Ro 16:9** *4720*

STACKED
so that **s** grain or the standing **Ex 22:6** 1430a

STACKING
Like the **s** of grain in its season. **Jb 5:26** 5927

STACTE
spices, **s** and onycha and galbanum, **Ex 30:34** 5198b

STAFF
with my **s** *only* I crossed this Jordan, **Gn 32:10** 4731
and your **s** that is in your hand." **Gn 38:18** 4294
ring and cords and **s** are these?" **Gn 38:25** 4294
ruler's **s** from between his feet, **Gn 49:10** 2710
And he said, "A **s**." **Ex 4:2** 4294
it, and it became a **s** in his hand **Ex 4:4** 4294
shall take in your hand this **s**, **Ex 4:17** 4294
took the **s** of God in his hand. **Ex 4:20** 4294
'Take your **s** and throw *it* down **Ex 7:9** 4294
and Aaron threw his **s** down before **Ex 7:10** 4294
For each one threw down his **s** and **Ex 7:12** 4294
Aaron's **s** swallowed up their staffs. **Ex 7:12** 4294
and you shall take in your hand the **s** **Ex 7:15** 4294
with the **s** that is in my hand, **Ex 7:17** 4294
'Take your **s** and stretch out your **Ex 7:19** 4294
And he lifted up the **s** and struck **Ex 7:20** 4294
hand with your **s** over the rivers, **Ex 8:5** 4294
'Stretch out your **s** and strike the **Ex 8:16** 4294
stretched out his hand with his **s**, **Ex 8:17** 4294
Moses stretched out his **s** toward **Ex 9:23** 4294
Moses stretched out his **s** over the **Ex 10:13** 4294
feet, and your **s** in your hand; **Ex 12:11** 4731
lift up your **s** and stretch out **Ex 14:16** 4294
and take in your hand your **s** with **Ex 17:5** 4294
with the **s** of God in my hand." **Ex 17:9** 4294
and walks around outside on his **s**, **Ex 21:19** 4938b
'When I break your **s** of bread, **Lv 26:26** 4294
those who wield the **s** of office. **Jg 5:14** 7626
the end of the **s** that was in his hand **Jg 6:21** 4938b
he put out the end of the **s** that **1Sa 14:27** 4294
end of the **s** that was in my hand. **1Sa 14:43** 4294
man, he attached him to his **s**. **1Sa 14:52**
loins and take my **s** in your hand, **2Ki 4:29** 4938b
and lay my **s** on the lad's face." **2Ki 4:29** 4938b
and laid the **s** on the lad's face, **2Ki 4:31** 4938b
on the **s** of this crushed reed, **2Ki 18:21** 4938b
Your rod and Your **s**, they comfort me. **Ps 23:4** 4938b
He broke the whole **s** of bread. **Ps 105:16** 4294
and the **s** on their shoulders, **Is 9:4** 4294
the rod of My anger And the **s** in **Is 10:5** 4294
and lifts up his **s** against you, **Is 10:24** 4294
and His **s** will be over the sea and **Is 10:26** 4294
LORD has broken the **s** of the wicked **Is 14:5** 4294
on the **s** of this crushed reed, **Is 36:6** 4938b
been broken, A **s** of splendor!' **Jer 48:17** 4731
break the **s** of bread in Jerusalem, **Ezk 4:16** 4294
you and break the **s** of bread. **Ezk 5:16** 4294
Because they have been *only* a **s** **Ezk 29:6** 4938b
his **s** in his hand because of age. **Zch 8:4** 4938b
I took my **s** Favor and cut it **Zch 11:10** 4731
I cut in pieces my second **s** Union, **Zch 11:14** 4731
two coats, or sandals, or a **s**; **Mt 10:10** *4464*
their journey, except a mere **s** **Mk 6:8** *4464*
for *your* journey, neither a **s**, **Lk 9:3** *4464*
leaning on the top of his **s**. **Heb 11:21** *4464*
given me a measuring rod like a **s**; **Rv 11:1** *4464*

STAFFS
Aaron's staff swallowed up their **s**. **Ex 7:12** 4294
the scepter *and* with their **s**." **Nu 21:18** 4938b
And I took for myself two **s**: **Zch 11:7** 4731

STAG
is like a gazelle or a young **s**. **SS 2:9** 354
young **s** on the mountains of Bether **SS 2:17** 354
young **s** On the mountains of spices **SS 8:14** 354

STAGES
journeyed by **s** from the wilderness **Ex 17:1** 4550
went upward by **s** on all sides of the **Ezk 41:7** 4605

STAGGER
makes them **s** like a drunken man. **Jb 12:25** 8582
us wine to drink that makes us **s**. **Ps 60:3** 8653
with wine and **s** from strong drink: **Is 28:7** 8582
by wine, they **s** from strong drink; **Is 28:7** 8582
They **s**, but not with strong drink. **Is 29:9** 5128
"They will drink and **s** and **Jer 25:16** 1607
"So two or three cities would **s** **Am 4:8** 5128
"People will **s** from sea to sea **Am 8:12** 5128

STAGGERED
reeled and **s** like a drunken man, **Ps 107:27** 5128

STAGGERING
And those who are **s** to slaughter, **Pr 24:11** 4131

STAGGERS
As a drunken man **s** in his vomit. **Is 19:14** 8582

STAGNANT
the men Who are **s** in spirit, **Zph 1:12** 7087a

STAIN
s of your iniquity is before Me," **Jer 2:22** 3799
keep the commandment without **s** **1Tm 6:14** *784*

STAINED
garments, And I **s** all My raiment. **Is 63:3** 1351

STAINS
They are **s** and blemishes, reveling **2Pe 2:13** *4696*

STAIRS
by winding **s** to the middle *story,* **1Ki 6:8** 3883
When he got to the **s**, **Ac 21:35** *304*
Paul, standing on the **s**, **Ac 21:40** *304*

STAIRWAY
and his **s** by which he went up to **1Ki 10:5** 5930b
He brought the shadow on the **s** back **2Ki 20:11** 4609b
it had gone down on the **s** of Ahaz. **2Ki 20:11** 4609b
and his **s** by which he went up to **2Ch 9:4** 5930b
by the **s** of the wall above the house **Ne 12:37** 4608
I will cause the shadow on the **s**, **Is 38:8** 4609b
with the sun on the **s** of Ahaz, **Is 38:8** 4609b
the **s** on which it had gone down. **Is 38:8** 4609b
and its **s** *had* eight steps. **Ezk 40:31** 4608
side, and its **s** *had* eight steps. **Ezk 40:34** 4608
side, and its **s** had eight steps. **Ezk 40:37** 4608
and at the **s** by which it was **Ezk 40:49** 4609b

STAKES
Its **s** will never be pulled up, Nor **Is 33:20** 3489

STALK
of grain came up on a single **s**, **Gn 41:5** 7070
and good, came up on a single **s**; **Gn 41:22** 7070

STALKS
and hidden them in the **s** of flax **Jos 2:6** 6086
the pestilence that **s** in darkness, **Ps 91:6** 1980
I will take hold of its fruit **s**.' **SS 7:8** 5577

STALL
calves from the midst of the **s**, **Am 6:4** 4770
skip about like calves from the **s**. **Mal 4:2** 4770
his ox or his donkey from the **s** and **Lk 13:15** *5336*

STALLIONS
the sound of the neighing of his **s** **Jer 8:16** 47
noise of the galloping hoofs of his **s**, **Jer 47:3** 47
threshing heifer And neigh like **s**, **Jer 50:11** 47

STALLS
Solomon had 40,000 **s** of horses **1Ki 4:26** 723a
Now Solomon had 4,000 **s** for horses **2Ch 9:25** 723a
And there be no cattle in the **s**, **Hab 3:17** 7517

STALWART
s will not strengthen his power, **Am 2:14** 2389

STAMMERERS
tongue of the **s** will hasten to speak **Is 32:4** 5926

STAMMERING
s lips and a foreign tongue, **Is 28:11** 3934
Of a **s** tongue which no one **Is 33:19** 3932

STAMP
'Clap your hand, **s** your foot and **Ezk 6:11** 7554

STAMPED
I crushed *and* **s** them as the mire **2Sa 22:43** 7554
floor At the time it is **s** firm; **Jer 51:33** 1869
clapped your hands and **s** your feet **Ezk 25:6** 7554

STAND
But they said, "**S** aside." **Gn 19:9** 5066
Why do you **s** outside since I have **Gn 24:31** 5975
The magicians could not **s** **Ex 9:11** 5975
s before Pharaoh and say to him, **Ex 9:13** 3320
S by and see the salvation of the **Ex 14:13** 3320
I will **s** before you there on the **Ex 17:6** 5975
sit *as judge* and all the people **s** about **Ex 18:14** 5324
utensils, and the laver and its **s**. **Ex 30:28** 3653b
utensils, and the laver and its **s**, **Ex 31:9** 3653b
all the people would arise and **s**, **Ex 33:8** 5324
and **s** at the entrance of the tent; **Ex 33:9** 5975
and you shall **s** *there* on the rock; **Ex 33:21** 5324
its utensils, the basin and its **s**; **Ex 35:16** 3653b
its utensils, the laver and its **s**; **Ex 39:39** 3653b
shall anoint the laver and its **s**, **Ex 40:11** 3653b
utensils, and the basin and its **s**, **Lv 8:11** 3653b
nor shall any woman **s** before an **Lv 18:23** 5975
to **s** up before your enemies. **Lv 26:37** 8617
priest values it, so it shall **s**. **Lv 27:14** 6965
to your valuation it shall **s**. **Lv 27:17** 6965
of the men who shall **s** with you: **Nu 1:5** 5975
and have her **s** before the LORD, **Nu 5:16** 5975
priest shall then have the woman **s** **Nu 5:18** 5975
make the woman **s** before the LORD, **Nu 5:30** 5975
"You shall have the Levites **s** **Nu 8:13** 5975
them take their **s** there with you. **Nu 11:16** 3320
and to **s** before the congregation **Nu 16:9** 5975
He took his **s** between the dead **Nu 16:48** 5975

the angel of the LORD took his **s** in	**Nu 22:22**	3320
"**S** beside your burnt offering,	**Nu 23:3**	3320
"**S** here beside your burnt offering while	**Nu 23:15**	3320
and have him **s** before Eleazar the	**Nu 27:19**	5975
shall **s** before Eleazar the priest,	**Nu 27:21**	5975
to her, then all her vows shall **s** and	**Nu 30:4**	6965
she has bound herself shall **s**.	**Nu 30:4**	6965
she has bound herself shall **s**;	**Nu 30:5**	6965
then her vows shall **s** and her	**Nu 30:7**	6965
she has bound herself shall **s**.	**Nu 30:7**	6965
herself, shall **s** against her.	**Nu 30:9**	6965
her, then all her vows shall **s** and	**Nu 30:11**	6965
which she bound herself shall **s**.	**Nu 30:11**	6965
the obligation of herself shall not **s**;	**Nu 30:12**	6965
everything that can **s** the fire,	**Nu 31:23**	935
But whatever cannot **s** the fire you	**Nu 31:23**	935
'But as for you, **s** here by Me,	**Dt 5:31**	5975
no man will be able to **s** before	**Dt 7:24**	3320
Who can **s** before the sons of Anak?	**Dt 9:2**	3320
to **s** before the LORD to serve Him	**Dt 10:8**	5975
"No man will be able to **s** before you;	**Dt 11:25**	3320
to **s** and serve in the name of the	**Dt 18:5**	5975
who **s** there before the LORD.	**Dt 18:7**	5975
dispute shall **s** before the LORD,	**Dt 19:17**	5975
these shall **s** on Mount Gerizim to	**Dt 27:12**	5975
these shall **s** on Mount Ebal:	**Dt 27:13**	5975
"You **s** today, all of you, before	**Dt 29:10**	5324
but both with those who **s** here	**Dt 29:15**	5975
"No man will *be able to* **s** before	**Jos 1:5**	3320
shall **s** *still* in the Jordan.' "	**Jos 3:8**	5975
from above will **s** in one heap."	**Jos 3:13**	5975
sons of Israel cannot **s** before their	**Jos 7:12**	6965
You cannot **s** before your enemies	**Jos 7:13**	6965
not one of them shall **s** before you."	**Jos 10:8**	5975
"O sun, **s** still at Gibeon, And O	**Jos 10:12**	1826a
and shall **s** at the entrance of the	**Jos 20:4**	5975
no longer **s** before their enemies.	**Jg 2:14**	5975
"**S** in the doorway of the tent,	**Jg 4:20**	5975
made him **s** between the pillars.	**Jg 16:25**	5975
took their **s** in the assembly of	**Jg 20:2**	3320
"Who is able to **s** before the LORD,	**1Sa 6:20**	5975
"So now, take your **s**,	**1Sa 12:7**	3320
take your **s** and see this great	**1Sa 12:16**	3320
then we will **s** in our place and	**1Sa 14:9**	5975
"Let David now **s** before me,	**1Sa 16:22**	5975
for forty days and took his **s**.	**1Sa 17:16**	3320
I will go out and **s** beside my father	**1Sa 19:3**	5975
'Please **s** beside me and kill me,	**2Sa 1:9**	5975
and **s** beside the way to the gate;	**2Sa 15:2**	5975
"Turn aside and **s** here."	**2Sa 18:30**	3320
he took his **s** in the midst of the plot,	**2Sa 23:12**	3320
the length of each **s** was four	**1Ki 7:27**	4350
Now each **s** had four bronze wheels	**1Ki 7:30**	4350
axles of the wheels *were* on the **s**.	**1Ki 7:32**	4350
at the four corners of each **s**;	**1Ki 7:34**	4350
its supports *were* part of the **s** itself.	**1Ki 7:34**	4350
On the top of the **s** *there was*	**1Ki 7:35**	4350
and on the top of the **s** its stays	**1Ki 7:35**	4350
so that the priests could not **s** to	**1Ki 8:11**	5975
blessed are these your servants who **s**	**1Ki 10:8**	5975
of Israel lives, before whom I **s**,	**1Ki 17:1**	5975
of hosts lives, before whom I **s**,	**1Ki 18:15**	5975
and **s** on the mountain before the	**1Ki 19:11**	5975
of hosts lives, before whom I **s**,	**2Ki 3:14**	5975
and **s** and call on the name of the	**2Ki 5:11**	5975
the LORD lives, before whom I **s**,	**2Ki 5:16**	5975
two kings did not **s** before him;	**2Ki 10:4**	5975
how then can we **s**?"	**2Ki 10:4**	5975
their **s** in the midst of the plot and	**1Ch 11:14**	3320
They are to **s** every morning to	**1Ch 23:30**	5975
so that the priests could not **s** to	**2Ch 5:14**	5975
blessed are these your servants who **s**	**2Ch 9:7**	5975
so that no one can **s** against You.	**2Ch 20:6**	3320
we will **s** before this house and	**2Ch 20:9**	5975
s and see the salvation of the	**2Ch 20:17**	5975
has chosen you to **s** before Him,	**2Ch 29:11**	5975
and Benjamin to **s** *with him.*	**2Ch 34:32**	5975
s in the holy place according to	**2Ch 35:5**	5975
s before You because of this."	**Ezr 9:15**	5975
we are not able to **s** in the open.	**Ezr 10:13**	5975
took their **s** in the house of God.	**Ne 12:40**	5975
whether Mordecai's reason would **s**;	**Es 3:4**	5975
not **s** up or tremble before him,	**Es 5:9**	6965
and no one could **s** before them,	**Es 9:2**	5975
have helped the tottering to **s**,	**Jb 4:4**	6965
in his house, but it does not **s**;	**Jb 8:15**	5975
He will take His **s** on the earth.	**Jb 19:25**	6965
"They abhor me *and* **s** aloof from me,	**Jb 30:10**	7368
I **s** up, and You turn Your	**Jb 30:20**	5975
I **s** up in the assembly *and* cry out	**Jb 30:28**	6965
yourselves before me, take your **s**.	**Jb 33:5**	3320
S and consider the wonders of God.	**Jb 37:14**	5975
And they **s** forth like a garment.	**Jb 38:14**	3320
And he does not **s** still at the	**Jb 39:24**	539
down the wicked where they **s**.	**Jb 40:12**	8478
then is he that can **s** before Me?	**Jb 41:10**	3320
Nor **s** in the path of sinners,	**Ps 1:1**	5975
wicked will not **s** in the judgment,	**Ps 1:5**	6965
kings of the earth take their **s** And	**Ps 2:2**	3320
shall not **s** before Your eyes;	**Ps 5:5**	3320
Why do You **s** afar off, O LORD?	**Ps 10:1**	5975
glorify Him, And **s** in awe of Him,	**Ps 22:23**	1481c
And who may **s** in His holy place?	**Ps 24:3**	6965
have made my mountain to **s** strong;	**Ps 30:7**	5975
of the world **s** in awe of Him.	**Ps 33:8**	1481c
my friends **s** aloof from my plague;	**Ps 38:11**	5975
And my kinsmen **s** afar off.	**Ps 38:11**	5975
the earth **s** in awe of Your signs;	**Ps 65:8**	3372a
And who may **s** in Your presence when	**Ps 76:7**	5975
made the waters **s** up like a heap.	**Ps 78:13**	5324
His **s** in His own congregation;	**Ps 82:1**	5324
I would rather **s** at the threshold	**Ps 84:10**	5605
And have not made him **s** in battle.	**Ps 89:43**	6965
s up for me against evildoers?	**Ps 94:16**	6965
Who will take his **s** for me against	**Ps 94:16**	3320
an accuser **s** at his right hand.	**Ps 109:6**	5975
They **s** this day according to Your	**Ps 119:91**	5975
iniquities, O Lord, who could **s**?	**Ps 130:3**	5975
who **s** in the house of the LORD,	**Ps 135:2**	5975
Who can **s** before His cold?	**Ps 147:17**	5975
the paths meet, she takes her **s**;	**Pr 8:2**	5324
the house of the righteous will **s**.	**Pr 12:7**	5975
counsel of the LORD will **s**.	**Pr 19:21**	6965
He will **s** before kings;	**Pr 22:29**	3320
He will not **s** before obscure men.	**Pr 22:29**	3320
not **s** in the place of great men;	**Pr 25:6**	5975
But who can **s** before jealousy?	**Pr 27:4**	5975
and this will **s** by him in his	**Ec 8:15**	3867a
ones **s** idle because they are few,	**Ec 12:3**	988
not **s** nor shall it come to pass.	**Is 7:7**	6965
a proposal, but it will not **s**,	**Is 8:10**	6965
s as a signal for the peoples;	**Is 11:10**	5975
as I have planned so it will **s**,	**Is 14:24**	6965
I **s** continually by day on the	**Is 21:8**	5975
and incense altars will not **s**.	**Is 27:9**	6965
your pact with Sheol will not **s**;	**Is 28:18**	6965
s in awe of the God of Israel.	**Is 29:23**	6206
themselves, let them **s** up,	**Is 44:11**	5975
"**S** *fast* now in your spells And in	**Is 47:12**	5975
S up and save you from what will	**Is 47:13**	5975
I call to them, they **s** together.	**Is 48:13**	5975
Let us **s** up to each other;	**Is 50:8**	5975
will **s** and pasture your flocks,	**Is 61:5**	5975
Seek refuge, do not **s** *still,*	**Jer 4:6**	5975
"**S** by the ways and see and ask	**Jer 6:16**	5975
"**S** in the gate of the LORD's	**Jer 7:2**	5975
and **s** before Me in this house,	**Jer 7:10**	5975
donkeys **s** on the bare heights,	**Jer 14:6**	5975
and Samuel were to **s** before Me,	**Jer 15:1**	5975
Before Me you will **s**;	**Jer 15:19**	5975
"Go and **s** in the public gate,	**Jer 17:19**	5975
'**S** in the court of the LORD's	**Jer 26:2**	5975
will **s** on its rightful place.	**Jer 30:18**	3427
My covenant *for* day and night **s**	**Jer 33:25**	
man to **s** before Me always.	**Jer 35:19**	5975
to **s** *for you* before the Chaldeans who	**Jer 40:10**	5975
there will know whose word will **s**,	**Jer 44:28**	6965
surely **s** against you for harm.'	**Jer 44:29**	6965
And take your **s** with helmets *on!*	**Jer 46:4**	3320
your **s** and get yourself ready,	**Jer 46:14**	3320
They do not **s** because the LORD has	**Jer 46:15**	5975
They did not **s** *their ground.*	**Jer 46:21**	5975
"**S** by the road and keep watch, O	**Jer 48:19**	5975
The fugitives **s** without strength;	**Jer 48:45**	5975
shepherd who can **s** against Me?"	**Jer 49:19**	5975
shepherd who can **s** before Me?"	**Jer 50:44**	5975
of the LORD against Babylon **s**,	**Jer 51:29**	6965
against whom I am not able to **s**.	**La 1:14**	6965
s on your feet that I may speak	**Ezk 2:1**	5975
me and made me **s** on my feet,	**Ezk 3:24**	5975
still, the wheels would **s** still;	**Ezk 10:17**	5975
Israel to **s** in the battle on the day of	**Ezk 13:5**	5975
s in the gap before Me for the land,	**Ezk 22:30**	5975
They will **s** on the land,	**Ezk 27:29**	5975
ones **s** *erect* in their height.	**Ezk 31:14**	5975
and they shall **s** before them to	**Ezk 44:11**	5975
and they shall **s** before Me to	**Ezk 44:15**	5975
they shall take their **s** to judge;	**Ezk 44:24**	5975
and **s** by the post of the gate.	**Ezk 46:2**	5975
that fishermen will **s** beside it;	**Ezk 47:10**	5975
made to **s** on two feet like a man;	**Da 7:4**	6966
other beasts could **s** before him nor	**Da 8:4**	5975
touched me and made me **s** upright.	**Da 8:18**	5975
about to tell you and **s** upright,	**Da 10:11**	5975
the South will not **s** *their ground,*	**Da 11:15**	5975
will be no strength to make a **s**.	**Da 11:15**	5975
a **s** *for him* or be on his side.	**Da 11:17**	5975
but he will not **s**, for schemes	**Da 11:25**	5975
There they **s**! Will not the battle	**Hos 10:9**	5975
the bow will not **s** *his ground,*	**Am 2:15**	5975
How can Jacob **s**, For he is small?"	**Am 7:2**	6965
How can Jacob **s**, for he is small?"	**Am 7:5**	6965
"Do not **s** at the fork of the	**Ob 1:14**	5975
Who can **s** before His indignation?	**Na 1:6**	5975
I will **s** on my guard post And	**Hab 2:1**	5975
will **s** on the Mount of Olives,	**Zch 14:4**	5975
rot while they **s** on their feet,	**Zch 14:12**	5975
And who can **s** when He appears?	**Mal 3:2**	5975
s on the pinnacle of the temple,	**Mt 4:5**	*2476*
for they love to **s** and pray in the	**Mt 6:5**	*2476*
against itself will not **s**.	**Mt 12:25**	*2476*
how then will his kingdom **s**?	**Mt 12:26**	*2476*
"The men of Nineveh will **s** up	**Mt 12:41**	*450*
that a boat should **s** ready for Him	**Mk 3:9**	*4342*
itself, that kingdom cannot **s**.	**Mk 3:24**	*2476*
that house will not be able to **s**.	**Mk 3:25**	*2476*
and is divided, he cannot **s**,	**Mk 3:26**	*2476*
s up! He is calling for you."	**Mk 10:49**	*1453*
"Whenever you **s** praying,	**Mk 11:25**	*4739*
and you will **s** before governors	**Mk 13:9**	*2476*
s on the pinnacle of the temple,	**Lk 4:9**	*2476*
himself, how will his kingdom **s**?	**Lk 11:18**	*2476*
"The men of Nineveh will **s** up	**Lk 11:32**	*450*
s outside and knock on the door,	**Lk 13:25**	*2476*
And He said to him, "**S** up and go;	**Lk 17:19**	*450*
and to **s** before the Son of Man."	**Lk 21:36**	*2476*
and does not **s** in the truth because	**Jn 8:44**	*4739*
why do you **s** looking into the sky?	**Ac 1:11**	*2476*
taking his **s** with the eleven,	**Ac 2:14**	*2476*
KINGS OF THE EARTH TOOK THEIR **S**,	**Ac 4:26**	*3936*
s and speak to the people in the	**Ac 5:20**	*2476*
"**S** up; I too am *just* a man."	**Ac 10:26**	*450*
I that I could **s** in God's way?"	**Ac 11:17**	*2967*
"**S** upright on your feet."	**Ac 14:10**	*450*
to go up to Jerusalem and **s** trial	**Ac 25:9**	*2919*
there **s** trial on these matters.	**Ac 25:20**	*2919*
'But get up and **s** on your feet;	**Ac 26:16**	*2476*
I **s** to this day testifying both to	**Ac 26:22**	*2476*
you must **s** before Caesar;	**Ac 27:24**	*3936*
into this grace in which we **s**;	**Ro 5:2**	*2476*
according to *His* choice would **s**,	**Ro 9:11**	*3306*
unbelief, but you **s** by your faith.	**Ro 11:20**	*2476*
and he will **s**, for the Lord is	**Ro 14:4**	*2476*
the Lord is able to make him **s**.	**Ro 14:4**	*2476*
For we will all **s** before the	**Ro 14:10**	*3936*
you received, in which also you **s**,	**1Co 15:1**	*2476*
on the alert, **s** firm in the faith,	**1Co 16:13**	*4739*
that you will be able to **s** firm	**Eph 6:11**	*2476*
having done everything, to **s** firm.	**Eph 6:13**	*2476*
S firm therefore, HAVING GIRDED	**Eph 6:14**	*2476*
in this way **s** firm in the Lord,	**Php 4:1**	*4739*
his **s** on *visions* he has seen,	**Col 2:18**	*1687*
that you may **s** perfect and fully	**Col 4:12**	*2476*
live, if you **s** firm in the Lord.	**1Th 3:8**	*4739*
s firm and hold to the traditions	**2Th 2:15**	*4739*
"You **s** over there, or sit down by	**Jas 2:3**	*2476*
is the true grace of God. **S** firm in it!	**1Pe 5:12**	*2476*
you **s** in the presence of His glory	**Jude 1:24**	*2476*
'Behold, I **s** at the door and knock;	**Rv 3:20**	*2476*
and who is able to **s**?"	**Rv 6:17**	*2476*
the seven angels who **s** before God,	**Rv 8:2**	*2476*
s before the Lord of the earth.	**Rv 11:4**	*2476*
will **s** at a distance because of	**Rv 18:15**	*2476*

STANDARD

shekels of silver, commercial **s**.	**Gn 23:16**	5674a
'There shall be one **s** for you;	**Lv 24:22**	4941
camp, and each man by his own **s**,	**Nu 1:52**	1714
shall camp, each by his own **s**,	**Nu 2:2**	1714
be of the **s** of the camp of Judah,	**Nu 2:3**	1714
"On the south side *shall be* the **s**	**Nu 2:10**	1714
"On the west side *shall be* the **s**	**Nu 2:18**	1714
"On the north side *shall be* the **s**	**Nu 2:25**	1714
The **s** of the camp of the sons	**Nu 10:14**	1714
Next the **s** of the camp of Reuben,	**Nu 10:18**	1714
Next the **s** of the camp of the sons	**Nu 10:22**	1714
Then the **s** of the camp of the sons	**Nu 10:25**	1714
fiery *serpent,* and set it on a **s**;	**Nu 21:8**	5251
serpent and set it on the **s**;	**Nu 21:9**	5251
to the **s** of a man of high degree,	**1Ch 17:17**	8447
to the old **s** *was* sixty cubits,	**2Ch 3:3**	4060a
lift up a **s** to the distant nation,	**Is 5:26**	5251
will lift up a **s** for the nations And	**Is 11:12**	5251
Lift up a **s** on the bare hill,	**Is 13:2**	5251
as a **s** is raised on the mountains,	**Is 18:3**	5251
his princes will be terrified at the **s**,"	**Is 31:9**	5251
And set up My **s** to the peoples;	**Is 49:22**	5251
lift up a **s** over the peoples.	**Is 62:10**	5251
"Lift up a **s** toward Zion!	**Jer 4:6**	5251
How long must I see the **s** And	**Jer 4:21**	5251
Proclaim it and lift up a **s**.	**Jer 50:2**	5251
their **s** shall be according to the	**Ezk 45:11**	4971
and by your **s** of measure, it will	**Mt 7:2**	*3358*
By your **s** of measure it will be	**Mk 4:24**	*3358*
For by your **s** of measure it will	**Lk 6:38**	*3358*
was devout by the **s** of the Law,	**Ac 22:12**	*3358*
let us keep living by that same **s**	**Php 3:16**	
Retain the **s** of sound words which	**2Tm 1:13**	*5296*

STANDARDS

man in his place by their **s**.	**Nu 2:17**	1714
shall set out last by their **s**."	**Nu 2:31**	1714
Moses, so they camped by their **s**,	**Nu 2:34**	1714
have set up their own **s** for signs.	**Ps 74:4**	226

STANDING

three men were **s** opposite him;	**Gn 18:2**	5324
and he was **s** by them under the	**Gn 18:8**	5975
Abraham was still **s** before the LORD.	**Gn 18:22**	5975
"Behold, I am **s** by the spring,	**Gn 24:13**	5324
was **s** by the camels at the spring.	**Gn 24:30**	5975
behold, I am **s** by the spring, and	**Gn 24:43**	5324
and behold, he was **s** by the Nile.	**Gn 41:1**	5975
I was **s** on the bank of the Nile;	**Gn 41:17**	5975
which you are **s** is holy ground."	**Ex 3:5**	5975
so that stacked grain or the **s** grain	**Ex 22:6**	7054
of acacia wood, **s** upright.	**Ex 26:15**	5975
s at the entrance of the tent,	**Ex 33:10**	5975
of acacia wood, **s** upright.	**Ex 36:20**	5975
the angel of the LORD **s** in the way	**Nu 22:23**	5324
the angel of the LORD **s** in the way	**Nu 22:31**	5324
you were **s** in the way against me.	**Nu 22:34**	5324
was **s** beside his burnt offering,	**Nu 23:6**	5324
was **s** beside his burnt offering,	**Nu 23:17**	5324
while I was **s** between the LORD and	**Dt 5:5**	5975
to put the sickle to the **s** grain.	**Dt 16:9**	7054
you enter your neighbor's **s** grain,	**Dt 23:25**	7054
sickle in your neighbor's **s** grain.	**Dt 23:25**	7054
where the priests' feet are **s** firm,	**Jos 4:3**	4673
the ark of the covenant were **s**,	**Jos 4:9**	4673
the priests who carried the ark were **s**	**Jos 4:10**	5975
a man was **s** opposite him with his	**Jos 5:13**	5975
place where you are **s** is holy."	**Jos 5:15**	5975
judges were **s** on both sides of the ark	**Jos 8:33**	5975
the **s** grain of the Philistines,	**Jg 15:5**	7054
both the shocks and the **s** grain,	**Jg 15:5**	7054
and pass on, but you remain **s** now,	**1Sa 9:27**	5975
to the men who were **s** by him,	**1Sa 17:26**	5975
Samuel **s** *and* presiding over them,	**1Sa 19:20**	5975

his servants were s around him.	1Sa 22:6	5324
who was s by the servants of Saul,	1Sa 22:9	5324
servants were s by with clothes torn.	2Sa 13:31	5324
all the assembly of Israel was s.	1Ki 8:14	5975
and two lions s beside the arms.	1Ki 10:19	5975
Twelve lions were s there on	1Ki 10:20	5975
s by the altar to burn incense.	1Ki 13:1	5975
road, with the donkey s beside it;	1Ki 13:24	5975
lion also was s beside the body.	1Ki 13:24	5975
and the lion s beside the body;	1Ki 13:25	5975
and the lion s beside the body;	1Ki 13:28	5975
and all the host of heaven s by	1Ki 22:19	5975
Now the watchman was s on the	2Ki 9:17	5975
the king was s by the pillar,	2Ki 11:14	5975
Asherah also remained s in Samaria.	2Ki 13:6	5975
And the angel of the LORD was s by	1Ch 21:15	5975
LORD s between earth and heaven,	1Ch 21:16	5975
and lyres, s east of the altar,	2Ch 5:12	5975
all the assembly of Israel was s.	2Ch 6:3	5975
and all Israel was s.	2Ch 7:6	5975
and two lions s beside the arms.	2Ch 9:18	5975
Twelve lions were s there on	2Ch 9:19	5975
s on His right and on His left.	2Ch 18:18	5975
All Judah was s before the LORD,	2Ch 20:13	5975
s by his pillar at the entrance,	2Ch 23:13	5975
hot, and while they are s *guard*,	Ne 7:3	5975
for he was s above all the people;	Ne 8:5	
Esther the queen s in the court,	Es 5:2	5975
"Behold, Haman is s in the court."	Es 6:5	5975
the gallows s at Haman's house	Es 7:9	5975
waters were s above the mountains.	Ps 104:6	5975
Our feet are s Within your gates,	Ps 122:2	5975
Behold, he is s behind our wall,	SS 2:9	5975
the reaper gathering the s grain,	Is 17:5	7054
were s in the house of the LORD,	Jer 28:5	5975
with all the women who were s by,	Jer 44:15	5975
the glory of the LORD was s there,	Ezk 3:23	5975
S in front of them were seventy	Ezk 8:11	5975
the son of Shaphan s among them,	Ezk 8:11	5975
Now the cherubim were s on the	Ezk 10:3	5975
and he was s in the gateway.	Ezk 40:3	5975
while a man was s beside me.	Ezk 43:6	5975
splendor, was s in front of you,	Da 2:31	6966
myriads upon myriads were s before	Da 7:10	6966
approached one of those who were s	Da 7:16	6966
horns was s in front of the canal.	Da 8:3	5975
had seen s in front of the canal,	Da 8:6	5975
s before me was one who looked	Da 8:15	5975
So he came near to where I was s,	Da 8:17	5977
said to him who was s before me,	Da 10:16	5975
and behold, two others were s,	Da 12:5	5975
The s grain has no heads;	Hos 8:7	7054
the Lord was s by a vertical wall with	Am 7:7	5324
I saw the Lord s beside the altar,	Am 9:1	5324
and he was s among the myrtle	Zch 1:8	5975
And the man who was s among the	Zch 1:10	5975
who was s among the myrtle trees and	Zch 1:11	5975
s before the angel of the LORD,	Zch 3:1	5975
and Satan s at his right hand to	Zch 3:1	5975
garments and s before the angel.	Zch 3:3	5975
who were s before him,	Zch 3:4	5975
the angel of the LORD was s by.	Zch 3:5	5975
access among these who are s *here*.	Zch 3:7	5975
who are s by the Lord of the whole	Zch 4:14	5975
going forth after s before the Lord	Zch 6:5	3320
the broken, or sustain the one s,	Zch 11:16	5324
and brothers were s outside,	Mt 12:46	*2476*
and Your brothers are s outside	Mt 12:47	*2476*
crowd was s on the beach.	Mt 13:2	*2476*
some of those who are s here who	Mt 16:28	*2476*
others s idle in the market place;	Mt 20:3	*2476*
he went out and found others s	Mt 20:6	*2476*
been s here idle all day long?'	Mt 20:6	*2476*
the prophet, s in the holy place	Mt 24:15	*2476*
some of those who were s there,	Mt 27:47	*2476*
s outside they sent *word* to Him and	Mk 3:31	*4739*
some of those who are s here who	Mk 9:1	*2476*
s where it should not be	Mk 13:14	*2476*
who was s right in front of Him,	Mk 15:39	*3936*
s to the right of the altar of incense	Lk 1:11	*2476*
And s over her, He rebuked the	Lk 4:39	*2186*
was s by the lake of Gennesaret;	Lk 5:1	*2476*
and s behind *Him* at His feet,	Lk 7:38	*2476*
and Your brothers are s outside,	Lk 8:20	*2476*
there are some of those s here who	Lk 9:27	*2476*
glory and the two men s with Him.	Lk 9:32	*4921*
tax collector, s some distance away,	Lk 18:13	*2476*
and the scribes were s there,	Lk 23:10	*2476*
Galilee were s at a distance,	Lk 23:49	*2476*
John was s with two of his disciples,	Jn 1:35	*2476*
of the people s around I said it,	Jn 11:42	*4026*
betraying Him, was s with them.	Jn 18:5	*2476*
Peter was s at the door outside.	Jn 18:16	*2476*
and the officers were s *there*,	Jn 18:18	*2476*
with them, s and warming himself.	Jn 18:18	*2476*
officers s nearby struck Jesus,	Jn 18:22	*3936*
Peter was s and warming himself.	Jn 18:25	*2476*
But s by the cross of Jesus	Jn 19:25	*2476*
disciple whom He loved s nearby,	Jn 19:26	*3936*
jar full of sour wine was s there;	Jn 19:29	*2749*
was s outside the tomb weeping;	Jn 20:11	*2476*
around and saw Jesus s *there*,	Jn 20:14	*2476*
who had been healed s with them,	Ac 4:14	*2476*
and the guards s at the doors;	Ac 5:23	*2476*
you put in prison are s in the temple	Ac 5:25	*2476*
PLACE ON WHICH YOU ARE S IS HOLY	Ac 7:33	*2476*
Jesus s at the right hand of God;	Ac 7:55	*2476*
the Son of Man s at the right hand	Ac 7:56	*2476*
had seen the angel s in his house,	Ac 11:13	*2476*
Peter was s in front of the gate.	Ac 12:14	*2476*
was s and appealing to him,	Ac 16:9	*2476*
a disciple of long s with whom we	Ac 21:16	*744*
permission, Paul, s on the stairs,	Ac 21:40	*2476*
came to me, and s near said to me,	Ac 22:13	*2186*
shed, I also was s by approving,	Ac 22:20	*2186*
to the centurion who was s by,	Ac 22:25	*2476*
Ananias commanded those s beside	Ac 23:2	*3936*
I shouted out while s among them,	Ac 24:21	*2476*
"I am s before Caesar's tribunal,	Ac 25:10	*2476*
"And now I am s trial for the	Ac 26:6	*2476*
for in your faith you are s firm.	2Co 1:24	*2476*
therefore keep s firm and do not	Ga 5:1	*4739*
that you are s firm in one spirit,	Php 1:27	*4739*
obtain for themselves a high s and	1Tm 3:13	*898*
the outer tabernacle is still s,	Heb 9:8	*4714b*
the Judge is s right at the door.	Jas 5:9	*2476*
a door s open in heaven,	Rv 4:1	
behold, a throne was s in heaven,	Rv 4:2	*2749*
and the elders a Lamb s,	Rv 5:6	*2476*
After this I saw four angels s at	Rv 7:1	*2476*
s before the throne and before the	Rv 7:9	*2476*
And all the angels were s around	Rv 7:11	*2476*
Then the angel whom I saw s on the	Rv 10:5	*2476*
the Lamb *was* s on Mount Zion,	Rv 14:1	*2476*
his name, s on the sea of glass,	Rv 15:2	*2476*
s at a distance because of the	Rv 18:10	*2476*
Then I saw an angel s in the sun	Rv 19:17	*2476*
the small, s before the throne,	Rv 20:12	*2476*

STANDPOINT

From the s of the gospel they are	Ro 11:28	*2596*
but from the s of *God's* choice	Ro 11:28	*2596*

STANDS

by the hand of a man who s in	Lv 16:21	
eye, while Your cloud s over them;	Nu 14:14	5975
until he s before the congregation	Nu 35:12	5975
the son of Nun, who s before you,	Dt 1:38	5975
priest who s there to serve the LORD	Dt 17:12	5975
heap of stones that s to this day,	Jos 7:26	
it a great heap of stones *that* s	Jos 8:29	
until he s before the congregation	Jos 20:6	5975
he s before the congregation.	Jos 20:9	5975
where the LORD's tabernacle s,	Jos 22:19	7931
Then he made the ten s of bronze;	1Ki 7:27	4350
This was the design of the s:	1Ki 7:28	4350
He made the ten s like this:	1Ki 7:37	4350
each of the ten s *was* one basin.	1Ki 7:38	4350
Then he set the s, five on the	1Ki 7:39	4350
and the ten s with the ten basins	1Ki 7:43	4350
with the ten basins on the s;	1Ki 7:43	4350
Ahaz cut off the borders of the s,	2Ki 16:17	4350
and the s and the bronze sea which	2Ki 25:13	4350
and the s which Solomon had made	2Ki 25:16	4350
He also made the s and he made the	2Ch 4:14	4350
and he made the basins on the s,	2Ch 4:14	4350
My foot s on a level place;	Ps 26:12	5975
The counsel of the LORD s forever,	Ps 33:11	5975
s the queen in gold from Ophir.	Ps 45:9	5324
For He s at the right hand of the	Ps 109:31	5975
established the earth, and it s.	Ps 119:90	5975
my heart s in awe of Your words.	Ps 119:161	6342
And s to judge the people.	Is 3:13	5975
Even the Asherim and incense s.	Is 17:8	2553
And by noble plans he s.	Is 32:8	6965
But the word of our God s forever.	Is 40:8	6965
it in its place and it s *there*.	Is 46:7	5975
And righteousness s far away;	Is 59:14	5975
the sea, concerning the s and	Jer 27:19	4350
LORD and the s and the bronze sea,	Jer 52:17	4350
were under the sea, *and* the s,	Jer 52:20	4350
the king of Babylon s at the parting	Ezk 21:21	5975
Yet there is no one who s firmly	Da 10:21	2388
the great prince who s *guard* over	Da 12:1	5975
who s in the presence of God,	Lk 1:19	*3936*
you s One whom you do not know.	Jn 1:26	*4739*
bridegroom, who s and hears him,	Jn 3:29	*2476*
by this *name* this man s here before	Ac 4:10	*3936*
To his own master he s or falls;	Ro 14:4	*4739*
But he who s firm in his heart,	1Co 7:37	*2476*
let him who thinks he s take heed	1Co 10:12	*2476*
the firm foundation of God s,	2Tm 2:19	*2476*
Every priest s daily ministering	Heb 10:11	*2476*
who s on the sea and on the land."	Rv 10:8	*2476*

STAR

A s shall come forth from Jacob,	Nu 24:17	3556
from heaven, O s of the morning,	Is 14:12	1966
the s of your gods which you made	Am 5:26	3556
For we saw His s in the east and	Mt 2:2	*792*
the exact time the s appeared.	Mt 2:7	*792*
and the s, which they had seen	Mt 2:9	*792*
When they saw the s,	Mt 2:10	*792*
AND THE S OF THE GOD ROMPHA,	Ac 7:43	*798*
for s differs from star in glory.	1Co 15:41	*792*
for star differs from s in glory.	1Co 15:41	*792*
morning s arises in your hearts.	2Pe 1:19	*5459*
and I will give him the morning s.	Rv 2:28	*792*
and a great s fell from heaven,	Rv 8:10	*792*
name of the s is called Wormwood;	Rv 8:11	*792*
and I saw a s from heaven which	Rv 9:1	*792*
of David, the bright morning s."	Rv 22:16	*792*

STARE

They look, they s at me;	Ps 22:17	7200
not s at me because I am swarthy,	SS 1:6	7200

STARING

"Why are you s at one another?"	Gn 42:1	7200

STARS

He made the s also.	Gn 1:16	3556
the heavens, and count the s,	Gn 15:5	3556
your seed as the s of the heavens and	Gn 22:17	3556
descendants as the s of heaven,	Gn 26:4	3556
eleven s were bowing down to me."	Gn 37:9	3556
as the s of the heavens,	Ex 32:13	3556
like the s of heaven in number.	Dt 1:10	3556
the sun and the moon and the s,	Dt 4:19	3556
as numerous as the s of heaven.	Dt 10:22	3556
as numerous as the s of heaven,	Dt 28:62	3556
"The s fought from heaven, From	Jg 5:20	3556
multiply Israel as the s of heaven.	1Ch 27:23	3556
from dawn until the s appeared.	Ne 4:21	3556
sons numerous as the s of heaven,	Ne 9:23	3556
the s of its twilight be darkened;	Jb 3:9	3556
shine, And sets a seal upon the s;	Jb 9:7	3556
Look also at the distant s,	Jb 22:12	3556
the s are not pure in His sight,	Jb 25:5	3556
When the morning s sang together	Jb 38:7	3556
Your fingers, The moon and the s,	Ps 8:3	3556
The moon and s to rule by night,	Ps 136:9	3556
He counts the number of the s;	Ps 147:4	3556
Praise Him, all s of light!	Ps 148:3	3556
the moon and the s are darkened,	Ec 12:2	3556
For the s of heaven and their	Is 13:10	3556
my throne above the s of God,	Is 14:13	3556
And see who has created these s,	Is 40:26	
Those who prophesy by the s,	Is 47:13	3556
fixed order of the moon and the s	Jer 31:35	3556
the heavens and darken their s;	Ezk 32:7	3556
some of the s to fall to the earth,	Da 8:10	3556
like the s forever and ever.	Da 12:3	3556
And the s lose their brightness.	Jl 2:10	3556
And the s lose their brightness.	Jl 3:15	3556
you set your nest among the s,	Ob 1:4	3556
traders more than the s of heaven	Na 3:16	3556
AND THE S WILL FALL from the sky,	Mt 24:29	*792*
THE S WILL BE FALLING from heaven,	Mk 13:25	*792*
be signs in sun and moon and s,	Lk 21:25	*798*
sun nor s appeared for many days,	Ac 27:20	*798*
moon, and another glory of the s;	1Co 15:41	*792*
AS THE S OF HEAVEN IN NUMBER,	Heb 11:12	*798*
wandering s, for whom the black	Jude 1:13	*792*
In His right hand He held seven s	Rv 1:16	*792*
"As for the mystery of the seven s	Rv 1:20	*792*
the seven s are the angels of the	Rv 1:20	*792*
the seven s in His right hand,	Rv 2:1	*792*
Spirits of God and the seven s,	Rv 3:1	*792*
s of the sky fell to the earth,	Rv 6:13	*792*
and a third of the s were struck,	Rv 8:12	*792*
on her head a crown of twelve s;	Rv 12:1	*792*
away a third of the s of heaven and	Rv 12:4	*792*

START

that day the LORD will s *His* threshing	Is 27:12	
you shall s from My sanctuary."	Ezk 9:6	2490c

STARTED

he who s the fire shall surely	Ex 22:6	1197a
the sons of Israel s out boldly in the	Nu 33:3	3318
undertook what they had s to do,	Es 9:23	2490c
So they s with the elders who *were*	Ezk 9:6	2490c
s giving them to the disciples,	Mt 15:36	
and s giving them to His disciples	Mk 8:6	
Now Jesus s on His way with them;	Lk 7:6	
An argument s among them as to	Lk 9:46	*1525*
Jesus spoke to him and s off.	Jn 4:50	*4198*
they s *to* cross the sea to	Jn 6:17	
Lord, they s back to Jerusalem,	Ac 8:25	*5290*
we left and s on our journey,	Ac 21:5	*4198*
and s on our way up to Jerusalem.	Ac 21:15	*305*
and s off for Damascus in order to	Ac 22:5	*4198*

STARTING

Moses recorded their s places	Nu 33:2	4161
according to their s places.	Nu 33:2	4161
but rather that a riot was s,	Mt 27:24	*1096*
all over Judea, s from Galilee even	Lk 23:5	*757*
all Judea, s from Galilee,	Ac 10:37	*757*

STARTLED

the man was s and bent forward;	Ru 3:8	2729
He looked and s the nations.	Hab 3:6	5425a
But they were s and frightened and	Lk 24:37	*4422*

STARVE

He will s all the gods of the earth;	Zph 2:11	7329

STATE

the sea returned to its normal s at	Ex 14:27	386
s his case in the hearing of the elders	Jos 20:4	1696
the people and the s of the war.	2Sa 11:7	7965
and s *the case* in order before	Ps 50:21	6186a
S a proposal, but it will not	Is 8:10	1696
our case together; S your *cause*,	Is 43:26	5608
will return to their former s,	Ezk 16:55	6927
will *also* return to your former s.	Ezk 16:55	6927
and the last s of that man becomes	Mt 12:45	
for the humble s of His bondslave;	Lk 1:48	*5014*
people were in a s of expectation	Lk 3:15	*4328*
last s of that man becomes worse	Lk 11:26	
transform the body of our humble s	Php 3:21	*5014*
the last s has become worse for	2Pe 2:20	

STATED

"This man s, 'I am able to destroy	Mt 26:61	*5346*
You have truly s that HE IS ONE,	Mk 12:32	*3004*

STATELY

things which are s in *their* march,	Pr 30:29	3190
four which are s when they walk:	Pr 30:29	3190
He has no s form or majesty That	Is 53:2	
bear fruit and become a s cedar.	Ezk 17:23	117

STATEMENT

or the rash s of her lips by which she	Nu 30:6	4008
the rash s of her lips by which she	Nu 30:8	4008
"The s is true, according to the	Da 6:12	4406

as soon as the king heard this s, Da 6:14 4406
let your s be, 'Yes, yes' *or* 'No, no' Mt 5:37 *3056*
offended when they heard this s?" Mt 15:12 *3056*
"Not all men *can* accept this s, Mt 19:11 *3056*
when the young man heard this s, Mt 19:22 *3056*
They seized upon that s, Mk 9:10 *3056*
they did not understand *this* s, Mk 9:32 *4487*
Him in order to trap Him in a s. Mk 12:13 *3056*
was very perplexed at *this* s, Lk 1:29 *3056*
they made known the s which had Lk 2:17 *4487*
the s which He had made to them. Lk 2:50 *4487*
they did not understand this s, Lk 9:45 *4487*
afraid to ask Him about this s. Lk 9:45 *4487*
and *the meaning of* this s was Lk 18:34 *4487*
they might catch Him in some s, Lk 20:20 *3056*
"This is a difficult s; Jn 6:60 *3056*
"What is this s that He said, Jn 7:36 *3056*
Pilate heard this s, Jn 19:8 *3056*
The s found approval with the Ac 6:5 *3056*
They listened to him up to this s, Ac 22:22 *3056*
other than for this one s which I Ac 24:21 *5456*
in the s, "YOU SHALL LOVE Ga 5:14
It is a trustworthy s, deserving full 1Tm 1:15 *3056*
It is a trustworthy s: 1Tm 3:1 *3056*
It is a trustworthy s deserving full 1Tm 4:9 *3056*
It is a trustworthy s: 2Tm 2:11 *3056*
This is a trustworthy s; Ti 3:8 *3056*

STATEMENTS

Zelophehad are right in *their* s. Nu 27:7 1696
sons of Joseph are right in *their* s. Nu 36:5 1696

STATING

And He was s the matter plainly. Mk 8:32 *2980*
s that he should be examined by Ac 22:24 *3004*
s nothing but what the Prophets Ac 26:22 *3004*

STATION

and s yourself to meet him on the Ex 7:15 5324
Tomorrow I will s myself on the Ex 17:9 5324
he said to his servants, "S *yourselves.* 1Ki 20:12 7760
s yourselves, stand and see the 2Ch 20:17 3320
"Go, s the lookout, let him Is 21:6 5975
I will pull you down from your s. Is 22:19 4612
Post a strong guard, S sentries, Jer 51:12 6965
post And s myself on the rampart; Hab 2:1 3320

STATIONED

garden of Eden He s the cherubim and Gn 3:24 7931
and s them around the tent. Nu 11:24 5975
So they s the people, all the army Jos 8:13 7760
and he s them in the chariot cities 1Ki 10:26 5148
And he s in Bethel the priests of 1Ki 12:32 5975
s *themselves* against the city. 1Ki 20:12 7760
Now Jehu had s for himself eighty 2Ki 10:24 7760
being s until now at the king's 1Ch 9:18
and he s them in the chariot cities 2Ch 1:14 5117
and he s them in the chariot cities 2Ch 9:25 5117
He s all the people, each man 2Ch 23:10 5975
He s the gatekeepers of the 2Ch 23:19 5975
He then s the Levites in the house 2Ch 29:25 5975
then I s *men* in the lowest parts Ne 4:13 5975
and I s the people in families Ne 4:13 5975
Then I s some of my servants at Ne 13:19 5975
I am s every night at my guard post. Is 21:8 5324

STATIONS

They stood at their s after their 2Ch 30:16 5977
and the priests stood at their s 2Ch 35:10 5977
were also at their s according to 2Ch 35:15 4612

STATUE

there was a single great s; Da 2:31 6755
that s, which was large and of Da 2:31 6755
head of that s *was made* of fine gold, Da 2:32 6755
it struck the s on its feet of iron and Da 2:34 6755
But the stone that struck the s Da 2:35 6755

STATURE

the boy Samuel was growing in s 1Sa 2:26 1432
or at the height of his s, 1Sa 16:7 6967
where there was a man of *great* s 2Sa 21:20 4055
a man of *great* s five cubits tall. 1Ch 11:23 4060a
where there was a man of *great* s 1Ch 20:6 4060a
"Your s is like a palm tree, And SS 7:7 6967
Those also who are tall in s will be Is 10:33 6967
of Cush And the Sabeans, men of s, Is 45:14 4060a
for the heads of *persons* of every s Ezk 13:18 6967
"Because it is high in s and Ezk 31:10 6967
may not be exalted in their s, Ezk 31:14 6967
kept increasing in wisdom and s, Lk 2:52 *2244*
the crowd, for he was small in s. Lk 19:3 *2244*
to the measure of the s which Eph 4:13 *2244*

STATUTE

Joseph made it a s concerning Gn 47:26 2706
made for them a s and regulation, Ex 15:25 2706
it shall be a perpetual s Ex 27:21 2708
It *shall be* a s forever to him and Ex 28:43 2708
the priesthood by a perpetual s. Ex 29:9 2708
shall be a perpetual s for them, Ex 30:21 2706
'It is a perpetual s throughout Lv 3:17 2708
it is a perpetual s throughout your Lv 10:9 2708
shall be a permanent s for you: Lv 16:29 2708
it is a permanent s. Lv 16:31 2708
shall have this as a permanent s, Lv 16:34 2708
This shall be a permanent s to Lv 17:7 2708
It is to be a perpetual s Lv 23:14 2708
It is to be a perpetual s in all Lv 23:21 2708
It is to be a perpetual s Lv 23:31 2708
It *shall be* a perpetual s throughout Lv 23:41 2708
it shall be a perpetual s throughout Lv 24:3 2708
according to all the s of the Passover Nu 9:12 2708
according to the s of the Passover Nu 9:14 2708
you shall have one s, Nu 9:14 2708
this shall be for you a perpetual s Nu 10:8 2708
there shall be one s for you and Nu 15:15 2708
a perpetual s throughout your Nu 15:15 2708
it shall be a perpetual s throughout Nu 18:23 2708
"This is the s of the law which Nu 19:2 2708
and it shall be a perpetual s to Nu 19:10 2708
shall be a perpetual s for them. Nu 19:21 2708
"This is the s of the law which Nu 31:21 2708
a s and an ordinance in Shechem. Jos 24:25 2706
that he made it a s and an 1Sa 30:25 2706
confirmed it to Jacob for a s, 1Ch 16:17 2706
For it is a s for Israel, An Ps 81:4 2706
And the s that He gave them. Ps 99:7 2706
He confirmed it to Jacob for a s, Ps 105:10 2706
that the king should establish a s and Da 6:7 7010
or s which the king establishes may Da 6:15 7010

STATUTES

commandments, My s and My laws." Gn 26:5 2708
commandments, and keep all His s, Ex 15:26 2706
known the s of God and His laws." Ex 18:16 2706
teach them the s and the laws, Ex 18:20 2706
to teach the sons of Israel all the s Lv 10:11 2706
you shall not walk in their s. Lv 18:3 2708
My judgments and keep My s, Lv 18:4 2708
shall keep My s and My judgments, Lv 18:5 2708
are to keep My s and My judgments Lv 18:26 2708
'You are to keep My s. Lv 19:19 2708
'You shall thus observe all My s and Lv 19:37 2708
shall keep My s and practice them; Lv 20:8 2708
'You are therefore to keep all My s Lv 20:22 2708
'You shall thus observe My s and Lv 25:18 2708
'If you walk in My s and keep My Lv 26:3 2708
if, instead, you reject My s, Lv 26:15 2708
and their soul abhorred My s. Lv 26:43 2708
These are the s and ordinances and Lv 26:46 2706
shall observe it according to all its s Nu 9:3 2708
These are the s which the LORD Nu 30:16 2706
listen to the s and the judgments Dt 4:1 2706
I have taught you s and judgments Dt 4:5 2706
who will hear all these s and say, Dt 4:6 2706
what great nation is there that has s Dt 4:8 2706
time to teach you s and judgments, Dt 4:14 2706
"So you shall keep His s and His Dt 4:40 2706
these are the testimonies and the s Dt 4:45 2706
the s and the ordinances which I Dt 5:1 2706
you all the commandments and the s Dt 5:31 2706
the s and the judgments which the Dt 6:1 2706
all His s and His commandments Dt 6:2 2708
His s which He has commanded you. Dt 6:17 2706
'What *do* the testimonies and the s Dt 6:20 2706
us to observe all these s, Dt 6:24 2706
keep the commandment and the s Dt 7:11 2706
His s which I am commanding you Dt 8:11 2708
the LORD's commandments and His s Dt 10:13 2708
and always keep His charge, His s, Dt 11:1 2708
you shall be careful to do all the s Dt 11:32 2706
"These are the s and the judgments Dt 12:1 2706
be careful to observe these s. Dt 16:12 2706
the words of this law and these s, Dt 17:19 2706
you to do these s and ordinances. Dt 26:16 2706
walk in His ways and keep His s, Dt 26:17 2706
His s which I command you today." Dt 27:10 2706
s with which I charge you today, Dt 28:15 2708
and His s which He commanded you. Dt 28:45 2708
keep His commandments and His s Dt 30:10 2708
and His s and His judgments, Dt 30:16 2708
And *as for* His s, I did not depart 2Sa 22:23 2708
walk in His ways, to keep His s, 1Ki 2:3 2708
in the s of his father David, 1Ki 3:3 2708
keeping My s and commandments, 1Ki 3:14 2706
if you will walk in My s and 1Ki 6:12 2708
and His s and His ordinances, 1Ki 8:58 2706
to walk in His s and to keep His 1Ki 8:61 2706
will keep My s and My ordinances, 1Ki 9:4 2706
and My s which I have set before you 1Ki 9:6 2708
not kept My covenant and My s, 1Ki 11:11 2708
observing My s and My ordinances, 1Ki 11:33 2708
My commandments and My s; 1Ki 11:34 2708
My s and My commandments, 1Ki 11:38 2708
My s according to all the law 2Ki 17:13 2708
They rejected His s and His 2Ki 17:15 2706
nor do they follow their s or 2Ki 17:34 2708
"The s and the ordinances and 2Ki 17:37 2706
His s with all *his* heart and all *his* soul 2Ki 23:3 2708
if you are careful to observe the s 1Ch 22:13 2706
Your testimonies and Your s, 1Ch 29:19 2706
will keep My s and My ordinances, 2Ch 7:17 2706
if you turn away and forsake My s 2Ch 7:19 2708
and commandment, s and ordinances, 2Ch 19:10 2706
according to all the law, the s and 2Ch 33:8 2706
and His testimonies and His s with 2Ch 34:31 2706
teach *His* s and ordinances in Israel. Ezr 7:10 2706
of the LORD and His s to Israel: Ezr 7:11 2706
kept the commandments, nor the s, Ne 1:7 2706
laws, Good s and commandments. Ne 9:13 2706
laid down for them commandments, s Ne 9:14 2706
and His ordinances and His s; Ne 10:29 2706
I did not put away His s from me. Ps 18:22 2708
What right have you to tell of My s Ps 50:16 2706
If they violate My s And Ps 89:31 2708
So that they might keep His s And Ps 105:45 2706
may be established To keep Your s! Ps 119:5 2706
I shall keep Your s; Ps 119:8 2706
O LORD; Teach me Your s. Ps 119:12 2706
I shall delight in Your s; Ps 119:16 2708
Your servant meditates on Your s. Ps 119:23 2706
Teach me Your s. Ps 119:26 2706
me, O LORD, the way of Your s, Ps 119:33 2706
And I will meditate on Your s. Ps 119:48 2706
Your s are my songs In the house of Ps 119:54 2706
O LORD; Teach me Your s. Ps 119:64 2706
Teach me Your s. Ps 119:68 2706
afflicted, That I may learn Your s. Ps 119:71 2706
my heart be blameless in Your s, Ps 119:80 2706
the smoke, I do not forget Your s. Ps 119:83 2706
my heart to perform Your s Forever, Ps 119:112 2706
have regard for Your s continually. Ps 119:117 2706
all those who wander from Your s, Ps 119:118 2706
And teach me Your s. Ps 119:124 2706
Your servant, And teach me Your s. Ps 119:135 2706
I will observe Your s. Ps 119:145 2706
For they do not seek Your s. Ps 119:155 2706
For You teach me Your s. Ps 119:171 2706
His s and His ordinances to Israel. Ps 147:19 2706
Woe to those who enact evil s And Is 10:1 2706
transgressed laws, violated s, Is 24:5 2706
nor walked in My law or My s, Jer 44:10 2708
His law, His s or His testimonies, Jer 44:23 2708
and against My s more than the lands Ezk 5:6 2708
and have not walked in My s.' Ezk 5:6 2708
you *and* have not walked in My s, Ezk 5:7 2708
for you have not walked in My s Ezk 11:12 2706
that they may walk in My s and Ezk 11:20 2708
if he walks in My s and My Ezk 18:9 2708
My ordinances, and walks in My s; Ezk 18:17 2708
observed all My s and done them, Ezk 18:19 2708
observes all My s and practices justice Ezk 18:21 2708
"I gave them My s and Ezk 20:11 2708
They did not walk in My s and Ezk 20:13 2708
My ordinances, and as for My s, Ezk 20:16 2708
not walk in the s of your fathers or Ezk 20:18 2706
walk in My s and keep My Ezk 20:19 2708
they did not walk in My s, Ezk 20:21 2708
ordinances, but had rejected My s Ezk 20:24 2708
"I also gave them s that were Ezk 20:25 2706
walks by the s which ensure life Ezk 33:15 2708
you and cause you to walk in My s, Ezk 36:27 2706
in My ordinances and keep My s Ezk 37:24 2708
all its designs, all its s, Ezk 43:11 2708
its whole design and all its s and Ezk 43:11 2708
'These are the s for the altar on Ezk 43:18 2708
all the s of the house of the LORD Ezk 44:5 2708
shall also keep My laws and My s Ezk 44:24 2708
the LORD And have not kept His s; Am 2:4 2706
"The s of Omri And all the works Mi 6:16 2708
"But did not My words and My s, Zch 1:6 2706
you have turned aside from My s and Mal 3:7 2706
even the s and ordinances which I Mal 4:4 2706

STATUTORY

and it shall be a s ordinance to Nu 27:11 2708
shall be for a s ordinance to you Nu 35:29 2708

STAY

do not s anywhere in the valley; Gn 19:17 5975
for he was afraid to s in Zoar; Gn 19:30 3427
"S here with the donkey, and I Gn 22:5 3427
"Let the girl s with us *a few* days Gn 24:55 3427
s in the land of which I shall Gn 26:2 7931
"S with him a few days, until your Gn 27:44 3427
give her to another man; s with me." Gn 29:19 3427
S *with me;* I have divined that Gn 30:27
go, and you shall s no longer." Ex 9:28 5975
but he shall s outside his tent Lv 14:8 3427
please, you also s here tonight, Nu 22:19 3427
but do not s *there* yourselves; Jos 10:19 5975
Judah shall s in its territory on Jos 18:5 5975
and the house of Joseph shall s in Jos 18:5 5975
And why did Dan s in ships? Jg 5:17 1481a
to s wherever he might find *a* Jg 17:8 1481a
s wherever I may find *a place.*" Jg 17:9 1481a
one, but s here with my maids. Ru 2:8 1692
'You should s close to my servants Ru 2:21 1692
the LORD and s there forever." 1Sa 1:22 3427
and s in a secret place and hide 1Sa 19:2 3427
"Hurry, be quick, do not s!" 1Sa 20:38 5975
my father and my mother come *and* s 1Sa 22:3
"Do not s in the stronghold; 1Sa 22:5 3427
"S with me; do not be afraid, for 1Sa 22:23 3427
"S at Jericho until your beards grow 2Sa 10:5 3427
"S here today also, and tomorrow 2Sa 11:12 3427
belongs to Sidon, and s there; 1Ki 17:9 3427
"S here please, for the LORD has 2Ki 2:2 3427
"Elisha, please s here, for the 2Ki 2:4 3427
"Please s here, for the LORD has 2Ki 2:6 3427
Enjoy your glory and s at home; 2Ki 14:10 3427
"S at Jericho until your beards grow 1Ch 19:5 3427
Now s at home; for why should you 2Ch 25:19 3427
calamity, But the LORD was my s. Ps 18:18 4937a
Who s up late in the evening that Is 5:11 309
the outcasts of Moab s with you; Is 16:4 1481a
own life as booty and s alive.' Jer 38:2 2421a
and s with him among the people; Jer 40:5 3427
s in the land and serve the king Jer 40:9 3427
I am going to s at Mizpah to stand Jer 40:10 3427
'If you will indeed s in this land, Jer 42:10 3427
"We will not s in this land," Jer 42:13 3427
for bread, and we will s there"; Jer 42:14 3427
to s in the land of Judah. Jer 43:4 3427
Be at rest and s still. Jer 47:6 1826a
They s in the strongholds; Jer 51:30 3427
Do not s! Remember the LORD from Jer 51:50 5975
or of the immigrants who s in Israel Ezk 14:7 1481a
the aliens who s in your midst, Ezk 47:22 1481a
he will also s *for a time* in the Da 11:16 5975
"You shall s with me for many days. Hos 3:3 3427
So that he does not s at home. Hab 2:5 5115b
and s at his house until you leave Mt 10:11 *3306*
s there until you leave town. Mk 6:10 *3306*

the doorkeeper to **s** on the alert. **Mk 13:34** *1127*
Whatever house you enter, **s** there **Lk 9:4** *3306*
"**S** in that house, eating **Lk 10:7** *3306*
today I must **s** at your house." **Lk 19:5** *3306*
"**S** with us, for it is *getting* **Lk 24:29** *3306*
So He went in to **s** with them. **Lk 24:29** *3306*
but you are to **s** in the city until **Lk 24:49** *2523*
were asking Him to **s** with them; **Jn 4:40** *3306*
s away from these men and let them **Ac 5:38** *868*
asked him to **s** on for a few days. **Ac 10:48** *1961*
their **s** in the land of Egypt, **Ac 13:17** *3940*
Lord, come into my house and **s**." **Ac 16:15** *3306*
asked him to **s** for a longer time, **Ac 18:20** *3306*
to **s** with them for seven days; **Ac 28:14** *1961*
Paul was allowed to **s** by himself, **Ac 28:16** *3306*
and perhaps I will **s** with you, **1Co 16:6** *2650*
the time of your **s** *on earth;* **1Pe 1:17** *3940*

STAYED
from Zoar, and **s** in the mountains, **Gn 19:30** 3427
and he **s** in a cave, he and his two **Gn 19:30** 3427
And he **s** with him a month. **Gn 29:14** 3427
with Laban, and **s** until now; **Gn 32:4** 309
Now Joseph **s** in Egypt, he and his **Gn 50:22** 3427
and the people **s** at Kadesh. **Nu 20:1** 3427
and we **s** in Egypt a long time, **Nu 20:15** 3427
the leaders of Moab **s** with Balaam. **Nu 22:8** 3427
s long enough at this mountain. **Dt 1:6** 3427
s on the mountain forty days and **Dt 10:10** 5975
So she **s** close by the maids of **Ru 2:23** 1692
and Samuel went and **s** in Naioth. **1Sa 19:18** 3427
"When you have **s** for three days, **1Sa 20:19** 8027
and they **s** with him all the time **1Sa 22:4** 3427
David **s** in the wilderness in **1Sa 23:14** 3427
and David **s** at Horesh while **1Sa 23:18** 3427
and **s** in the wilderness of Maon. **1Sa 23:25** 3427
s in the strongholds of Engedi. **1Sa 23:29** 3427
two hundred **s** with the baggage. **1Sa 25:13** 3427
But David **s** at Jerusalem. **2Sa 11:1** 3427
the king while he **s** at Mahanaim, **2Sa 19:32** 7871
and all Israel **s** there six months, **1Ki 11:16** 3427
they went to Damascus and **s** there, **1Ki 11:24** 3427
But David **s** at Jerusalem. **1Ch 20:1** 3427
but Haman **s** to beg for his life **Es 7:7** 5975
And so the plague was **s**. **Ps 106:30** 6113
and Jeremiah **s** there many days. **Jer 37:16** 3427
and Jeremiah **s** in the court of the **Jer 38:13** 3427
So Jeremiah **s** in the court of the **Jer 38:28** 3427
So he **s** among the people. **Jer 39:14** 3427
and **s** with him among the people **Jer 40:6** 3427
they went and **s** in Geruth Chimham, **Jer 41:17** 3427
but **s** out in unpopulated areas; **Mk 1:45** *1510*
and so He **s** by the seashore. **Mk 5:21** *1510*
Mary **s** with her about three months, **Lk 1:56** *3306*
boy Jesus **s** behind in Jerusalem. **Lk 2:43** *5278*
and they **s** with Him that day, for **Jn 1:39** *3306*
and they **s** there a few days. **Jn 2:12** *3306*
and He **s** there two days. **Jn 4:40** *3306*
things to them, He **s** in Galilee. **Jn 7:9** *3306*
He then **s** two days *longer* in the **Jn 11:6** *3306*
but Mary **s** at the house. **Jn 11:20** *2516*
and there He **s** with the disciples. **Jn 11:54** *3306*
Peter **s** many days in Joppa with a **Ac 9:43** *3306*
Paul and Barnabas **s** in Antioch, **Ac 15:35** *1304*
he **s** with them and they were **Ac 18:3** *3306*
he himself **s** in Asia for a while. **Ac 19:22** *1907*
and there we **s** seven days. **Ac 20:6** *1304*
disciples, we **s** there seven days; **Ac 21:4** *1961*
we **s** with them for a day. **Ac 21:7** *3306*
one of the seven, we **s** with him. **Ac 21:8** *3306*
we **s** there for three days. **Ac 28:12** *1961*
And he **s** two full years in his own **Ac 28:30** *1696*
and **s** with him fifteen days. **Ga 1:18** *1961*

STAYING
over the tabernacle, **s** above it, **Nu 9:22** 7931
and he was **s** there. **Jg 17:7** 1481a
there was a certain Levite **s** in the **Jg 19:1** 1481a
Ephraim, and he was **s** in Gibeah, **Jg 19:16** 1481a
were **s** in Geba of Benjamin while the **1Sa 13:16** 3427
Saul was **s** in the outskirts of **1Sa 14:2** 3427
and David was **s** in the wilderness. **1Sa 26:3** 3427
Judah are **s** in temporary shelters, **2Sa 11:11** 3427
"Behold, he is **s** in Jerusalem, **2Sa 16:3** 3427
and Ahimaaz were **s** at En-rogel, **2Sa 17:17** 5975
to the widow with whom I am **s**, **1Ki 17:20** 1481a
to him while he was **s** at Jericho; **2Ki 2:18** 3427
shepherds **s** out in the fields and **Lk 2:8** *63*
where are You **s**?" **Jn 1:38** *3306*
came and saw where He was **s**; **Jn 1:39** *3306*
baptizing, and He was **s** there. **Jn 10:40** *3306*
the upper room where they were **s**; **Ac 1:13** *2650*
he is **s** with a tanner **Ac 10:6** *3579*
also called Peter, was **s** there. **Ac 10:18** *3579*
he is **s** at the house of Simon *the* **Ac 10:32** *3579*
at the house in which we were **s**, **Ac 11:11**
were **s** in this city for some days. **Ac 16:12** *1304*
As we were **s** there for some days, **Ac 21:10** *1961*

STAYS
or your sojourner who **s** with you. **Ex 20:10**
or your sojourner who **s** with you, **Dt 5:14**
his share be who **s** by the baggage; **1Sa 30:24** 3427
on the top of the stand its **s** and its **1Ki 7:35** 3027
He engraved on the plates of its **s** **1Ki 7:36** 3027
'He who **s** in this city will die by **Jer 38:2** 3427
the tribe with which the alien **s**, **Ezk 47:23** 1481a
s awake and keeps his clothes, **Rv 16:15** *1127*

STEAD
one of his sons who is priest in his **s** **Ex 29:30** 8478

STEADFAST
the men of Judah remained **s** to **2Sa 20:2** 1692
And you would be **s** and not fear. **Jb 11:15** 3332
And renew a **s** spirit within me. **Ps 51:10** 3559
My heart is **s**, O God, my heart is **Ps 57:7** 3559
steadfast, O God, my heart is **s**; **Ps 57:7** 3559
their heart was not **s** toward Him, **Ps 78:37** 3559
My heart is **s**, O God; **Ps 108:1** 3559
His heart is **s**, trusting in the **Ps 112:7** 3559
He who is **s** in righteousness *will* **Pr 11:19** 3653a
"The **s** of mind You will keep in **Is 26:3** 5564
my beloved brethren, be **s**, **1Co 15:58** *1476*
faith firmly established and **s**, **Col 1:23** *1476*
a *hope* both sure and **s** and one **Heb 6:19** *949*

STEADFASTNESS
attaining of all **s** and patience; **Col 1:11** *5281*
s of hope in our Lord Jesus Christ in **1Th 1:3** *5281*
of God and into the **s** of Christ. **2Th 3:5** *5281*
men and fall from your own **s**, **2Pe 3:17** *4740*

STEADILY
water receded **s** from the earth, **Gn 8:3** 1980
The water decreased **s** until the tenth **Gn 8:5** 1980
and David grew **s** stronger, but the **2Sa 3:1** 1980
He fixed his gaze **s** *on him* until he **2Ki 8:11** 7760

STEADY
hands were **s** until the sun set. **Ex 17:12** 530
constant dripping on a day of **s** rain **Pr 27:15** 5464

STEAL
but why did you **s** my gods?" **Gn 31:30** 1589
How then could we **s** silver or gold **Gn 44:8** 1589
"You shall not **s**. **Ex 20:15** 1589
'You shall not **s**, nor deal **Lv 19:11** 1589
'You shall not **s**. **Dt 5:19** 1589
people who are humiliated **s** away **2Sa 19:3** 1589
What I did not **s**, I then have to **Ps 69:4** 1497
Or that I not be in want and **s**, **Pr 30:9** 1589
"Will you **s**, murder, and commit **Jer 7:9** 1589
"who **s** My words from each other. **Jer 23:30** 1589
not **s** *only* until they had enough? **Ob 1:5** 1589
and where thieves break in and **s**. **Mt 6:19** *2813*
thieves do not break in or **s**; **Mt 6:20** *2813*
YOU SHALL NOT **S**; **Mt 19:18** *2813*
His disciples may come and **s** Him **Mt 27:64** *2813*
DO NOT COMMIT ADULTERY, DO NOT **S**, **Mk 10:19** *2813*
ADULTERY, DO NOT MURDER, DO NOT **S**, **Lk 18:20** *2813*
"The thief comes only to **s** and **Jn 10:10** *2813*
who preach that one shall not **s**, **Ro 2:21** *2813*
one shall not steal, do you **s**? **Ro 2:21** *2813*
SHALL NOT MURDER, YOU SHALL NOT **S**, **Ro 13:9** *2813*
He who steals must **s** no longer; but **Eph 4:28** *2813*

STEALING
is swearing, deception, murder, **s** **Hos 4:2** 1589

STEALS
"If a man **s** an ox or a sheep and **Ex 22:1** 1589
A tempest **s** him away in the night. **Jb 27:20** 1589
Men do not despise a thief if he **s** **Pr 6:30** 1589
surely everyone who **s** will be **Zch 5:3** 1589
He who **s** must steal no longer; **Eph 4:28** *2813*

STEALTH
went by **s** into the city that day, **2Sa 19:3** 1589
together to seize Jesus by **s** and **Mt 26:4** *1388*
seeking how to seize Him by **s** and **Mk 14:1** *1388*

STEALTHILY
"Now a word was brought to me **s**, **Jb 4:12** 1589
eyes **s** watch for the unfortunate. **Ps 10:8** 6845

STEEDS
the dashing of his valiant **s**. **Jg 5:22** 47
and straw for the horses and swift **s** **1Ki 4:28** 7409
on **s** sired by the royal stud. **Es 8:10** 7409
went out, riding on the royal **s**; **Es 8:14** 7409
the horses, And mount the **s**, **Jer 46:4** 6571a

STEEL
s When he is prepared *to march,* **Na 2:3** 6393

STEEP
the secret place of the **s** pathway, **SS 2:14** 4095
come and settle on the **s** ravines, **Is 7:19** 1327
the **s** pathways will collapse and **Ezk 38:20** 4095
Like water poured down a **s** place. **Mi 1:4** 4174
the whole herd rushed down the **s** **Mt 8:32** *2911*
down the **s** bank into the sea, **Mk 5:13** *2911*
down the **s** bank into the lake and **Lk 8:33** *2911*

STEM
will spring from the **s** of Jesse, **Is 11:1** 1503

STENCH
The canals will emit a **s**, **Is 19:6** 2186b
corpses will give off their **s**, **Is 34:3** 889
And its **s** will arise and its foul **Jl 2:20** 889
And I made the **s** of your camp rise **Am 4:10** 889
by this time there will be a **s**, **Jn 11:39** *3605*

STEP
hardly a **s** between me and death." **1Sa 20:3** 6587
him, And harry him at every **s**. **Jb 18:11** 7272
"If my **s** has turned from the way, **Jb 31:7** 838
in battle, *Then* I would **s** on them, **Is 27:4** 6585

STEPHANAS
baptize also the household of **S**; **1Co 1:16** *4734*
(you know the household of **S**, **1Co 16:15** *4734*
of **S** and Fortunatus and Achaicus, **1Co 16:17** *4734*

STEPHEN
and they chose **S**, a man full of faith **Ac 6:5** *4736*
And **S**, full of grace and power, **Ac 6:8** *4736*
Asia, rose up and argued with **S**. **Ac 6:9** *4736*
They went on stoning **S** as he **Ac 7:59** *4736*
Some devout men buried **S**, **Ac 8:2** *4736*
that occurred in connection with **S** **Ac 11:19** *4736*
blood of Your witness **S** was being **Ac 22:20** *4736*

STEPPED
and he **s** down after making the sin **Lv 9:22** 3381
s in was made well from whatever **Jn 5:4** *1684*

STEPPING
that they were **s** on one another, **Lk 12:1** *2662*
s aside, *began* to inquire of him **Ac 23:19** *402*

STEPS
shall not go up by **s** to My altar, **Ex 20:26** 4609b
hand, And they followed in Your **s**; **Dt 33:3** 7272
"You enlarge my **s** under me, **2Sa 22:37** 6806
There were six **s** to the throne and **1Ki 10:19** 4609b
lions were standing there on the six **s** *1Ki* **10:20** 4609b
placed it under him on the bare **s**, **2Ki 9:13** 4609b
shall the shadow go forward ten **s** **2Ki 20:9** 4609b
ten steps or go back ten **s**?" **2Ki 20:9** 4609b
for the shadow to decline ten **s**; **2Ki 20:10** 4609b
the shadow turn backward ten **s**." **2Ki 20:10** 4609b
the shadow on the stairway back ten **s** **2Ki 20:11** 4609b
From the algum trees the king made **s** **2Ch 9:11** 4546
There were six **s** to the throne **2Ch 9:18** 4609b
lions were standing there on the six **s** **2Ch 9:19** 4609b
at the king's garden as far as the **s** **Ne 3:15** 4609b
they went directly up the **s** of the city **Ne 12:37** 4609b
"For now You number my **s**, **Jb 14:16** 6806
own feet, And he **s** on the webbing. **Jb 18:8** 1980
When my **s** were bathed in butter, **Jb 29:6** 1978
see my ways And number all my **s**? **Jb 31:4** 6806
declare to Him the number of my **s**; **Jb 31:37** 6806
of a man, And He sees all his **s**. **Jb 34:21** 6806
My **s** have held fast to Your paths. **Ps 17:5** 804a
have now surrounded us in our **s**; **Ps 17:11** 838
You enlarge my **s** under me, **Ps 18:36** 6806
The **s** of a man are established by **Ps 37:23** 4703
His **s** do not slip. **Ps 37:31** 804a
And our **s** have not deviated from **Ps 44:18** 804a
they lurk, They watch my **s**, **Ps 56:6** 6119
They have prepared a net for my **s**; **Ps 57:6** 6471
My **s** had almost slipped. **Ps 73:2** 804a
walk, your **s** will not be impeded; **Pr 4:12** 6806
to death, Her **s** take hold of Sheol. **Pr 5:5** 6806
the sensible man considers his **s**. **Pr 14:15** 804a
way, But the LORD directs his **s**. **Pr 16:9** 6806
Man's **s** are *ordained* by the LORD, **Pr 20:24** 4703
Is spreading a net for his **s**. **Pr 29:5** 6471
Guard your **s** as you go to the house **Ec 5:1** 7272
eyes, And go along with mincing **s** And **Is 3:16** 2952
the **s** of the helpless." **Is 26:6** 6471
of Ahaz, to go back ten **s**." **Is 38:8** 4609b
So the sun's *shadow* went back ten **s** **Is 38:8** 4609b
a man who walks to direct his **s**. **Jer 10:23** 6806
They hunted our **s** So that we could **La 4:18** 6806
which faced east, went up its **s** and **Ezk 40:6** 4609b
and it was reached by seven **s**, **Ezk 40:22** 4609b
There were seven **s** going up to it, **Ezk 40:26** 4609b
and its stairway *had* eight **s**. **Ezk 40:31** 4609b
and its stairway *had* eight **s**. **Ezk 40:34** 4609b
and its stairway had eight **s**. **Ezk 40:37** 4609b
and its **s** shall face the east." **Ezk 43:17** 4609b
another **s** down before me." **Jn 5:7** *2597*
s of the faith of our father Abraham **Ro 4:12** *2487*
spirit *and walk* in the same **s**? **2Co 12:18** *2487*
for you to follow in His **s**, **1Pe 2:21** *2487*

STERN
him and causes his **s** face to beam. **Ec 8:1** 5797
Jesus Himself was in the **s**, **Mk 4:38** *4403*
they cast four anchors from the **s** **Ac 27:29** *4403*
but the **s** *began* to be broken up by **Ac 27:41** *4403*

STERNLY
And Jesus **s** warned them: **Mt 9:30** *1690*
crowd **s** told them to be quiet **Mt 20:31** *2008*
And He **s** warned him and **Mk 1:43** *1690*
Many were **s** telling him to be quiet, **Mk 10:48** *2008*
were **s** telling him to be quiet; **Lk 18:39** *2008*

STEW
When Jacob had cooked **s**, **Gn 25:29** 5138
Jacob gave Esau bread and lentil **s**; **Gn 25:34** 5138
boil **s** for the sons of the prophets." **2Ki 4:38** 5138
and sliced them into the pot of **s**, **2Ki 4:39** 5138
as they were eating of the **s**, **2Ki 4:40** 5138

STEWARD
with them, he said to his house **s**, **Gn 43:16** 834, 5921
they came near to Joseph's house **s**, **Gn 43:19** 376, 834, 5921
Then he commanded his house **s**, **Gn 44:1** 834, 5921
when Joseph said to his house **s**, **Gn 44:4** 834, 5921
"Come, go to this **s**, **Is 22:15** 5532a
the wife of Chuza, Herod's **s**, **Lk 8:3** *2012*
is the faithful and sensible **s**, **Lk 12:42** *3623*
must be above reproach as God's **s**, **Ti 1:7** *3623*

STEWARDS
and **s** of the mysteries of God. **1Co 4:1** *3623*
it is required of **s** that one be found **1Co 4:2** *3623*
good **s** of the manifold grace of God **1Pe 4:10** *3623*

STEWARDSHIP
will, I have a **s** entrusted to me. **1Co 9:17** *3622*
have heard of the **s** of God's grace **Eph 3:2** *3622*
minister according to the **s** from God **Col 1:25** *3622*

STICK
and struck the donkey with his **s**. **Nu 22:27** 4731
He took his **s** in his hand and **1Sa 17:40** 4731
him the place, he cut off a **s** and **2Ki 6:6** 6086
bones which were not seen **s** out. **Jb 33:21** 8192
a mass And the clods **s** together? **Jb 38:38** 1692
your mouth And **s** out your tongue? **Is 57:4** 748

tongue **s** to the roof of your mouth Ezk 3:26 1692
take for yourself one **s** and write on Ezk 37:16 6086
take another **s** and write on it, Ezk 37:16 6086
the **s** of Ephraim and all the house Ezk 37:16 6086
one to another into one **s**, Ezk 37:17 6086
I will take the **s** of Joseph, Ezk 37:19 6086
them with it, with the **s** of Judah, Ezk 37:19 6086
of Judah, and make them one **s**, Ezk 37:19 6086
a **s** on the surface of the water. Hos 10:7 7110b

STICKS
dog, that you come to me with **s**?" 1Sa 17:43 4731
a widow was there gathering **s**; 1Ki 17:10 6086
I am gathering a few **s** that I may 1Ki 17:12 6086
friend who **s** closer than a brother. Pr 18:24 1695
"The **s** on which you write Ezk 37:20 6086
Paul had gathered a bundle of **s** Ac 28:3 *5434*

STIFFEN
heart, and **s** your neck no longer. Dt 10:16 7185
not **s** your neck like your fathers, 2Ch 30:8 7185

STIFFENED
s their neck like their fathers, 2Ki 17:14 7185
But he **s** his neck and hardened his 2Ch 36:13 7185
shoulder and **s** their neck, Ne 9:29 7185
their ear, but **s** their neck; Jer 7:26 7185
but **s** their necks in order not to Jer 17:23 7185
because they have **s** their necks so Jer 19:15 7185

STIFFENS
and grinds his teeth and **s** out. Mk 9:18 *3583*

STIFF-NECKED
"You men who are **s** and Ac 7:51 *4644*

STIFLED
sword, While he **s** his compassion; Am 1:11 7843

STILL
Abraham was **s** standing before the Gn 18:22 5750
gave gifts while he was **s** living, Gn 25:6 5750
"Behold, it is **s** high day; Gn 29:7 5750
While he was **s** speaking with them, Gn 29:9 5750
"Do we **s** have any portion or Gn 31:14 5750
and when there was **s** some distance Gn 35:16 5750
with his brothers while he was **s** Gn 37:2
Now he had **s** another dream, and Gn 37:9 5750
"Lo, I have had **s** another dream; Gn 37:9 5750
She bore **s** another son and Gn 38:5 5750
you **s** had *another* brother?" Gn 43:6 5750
'Is your father **s** alive? Gn 43:7 5750
of whom you spoke? Is he **s** alive?" Gn 43:27 5750
our father is well; he is **s** alive." Gn 43:28 5750
to Joseph's house, he was **s** there, Gn 44:14 5750
Is my father **s** alive?" Gn 45:3 5750
and there are **s** five years in Gn 45:6 5750
s five years of famine *to come*, Gn 45:11 5750
"Joseph is **s** alive, and indeed he Gn 45:26 5750
my son Joseph is **s** alive. Gn 45:28 5750
your face, that you are **s** alive." Gn 46:30 5750
when there was **s** some distance to Gn 48:7 5750
and see if they are **s** alive." Ex 4:18 5750
"**S** you exalt yourself against My Ex 9:17 5750
And they **s** *continued* bringing to Ex 36:3 5750
he was unaware, **s** he is guilty and Lv 5:17
and carried them **s** in their tunics to Lv 10:5
s eat old things from the crop, Lv 25:22
'If there are **s** many years, he Lv 25:51 5750
s go out in the year of jubilee, Lv 25:54
meat was **s** between their teeth, Nu 11:33 5750
his uncleanness is **s** on him. Nu 19:13 5750
to add **s** more to the burning anger Nu 32:14 5750
while I am **s** alive with you today, Dt 31:27 5750
you shall stand **s** in the Jordan.'" Jos 3:8
"O sun, stand **s** at Gibeon, And O Jos 10:12 1826a
So the sun stood **s**, Jos 10:13 1826a
"I am **s** as strong today as I was Jos 14:11 5750
is **s** in Ophrah of the Abiezrites. Jg 6:24 5750
"The people are **s** too many; Jg 7:4 5750
afraid, because he was **s** a youth. Jg 8:20 5750
And will you sit **s**? Jg 18:9 2814
"But if you **s** do wickedly, both 1Sa 12:25 7489a
as for Saul, he *was* **s** in Gilgal, 1Sa 13:7 5750
"If I am **s** alive, will you 1Sa 20:14 5750
because my life **s** lingers in me.' 2Sa 1:9 5750
had fallen and died, stood **s**. 2Sa 2:23 5975
to eat bread while it was **s** day; 2Sa 3:35 5750
"There is **s** a son of Jonathan who 2Sa 9:3 5750
while the child was **s** alive, 2Sa 12:18
He said, "While the child was **s** 2Sa 12:22
better for me **s** to be there." 2Sa 14:32 5750
So he turned aside and stood **s**. 2Sa 18:30 5975
do you **s** speak of your affairs? 2Sa 19:29 5750
saw that all the people stood **s**, 2Sa 20:12 5975
everyone who came by him stood **s**. 2Sa 20:12 5975
the eyes of my lord the king **s** 2Sa 24:3
s there speaking with the king, 1Ki 1:14 5750
she was **s** speaking with the king, 1Ki 1:22 5750
While he was **s** speaking, behold, 1Ki 1:42 5750
The people were **s** sacrificing on 1Ki 3:2 7534
Solomon while he was **s** alive, 1Ki 12:6
And he said, "Is he **s** alive? 1Ki 20:32 5750
and we are **s** doing nothing to take 1Ki 22:3 2814
the people **s** sacrificed and burnt 1Ki 22:43 5750
And he said, "Yes, I know; be **s**." 2Ki 2:3 2814
he answered, "Yes, I know; be **s**." 2Ki 2:5 2814
While he was **s** talking with them, 2Ki 6:33 5750
the people **s** sacrificed and burned 2Ki 12:3 5750
the people **s** sacrificed and burned 2Ki 14:4 5750
the people **s** sacrificed and burned 2Ki 15:4 5750
the people **s** sacrificed and burned 2Ki 15:35 5750
But every nation **s** made gods of 2Ki 17:29
while he was **s** restricted because 1Ch 12:1 5750
"What more can David **s** *say* to 1Ch 17:18 5750
is **s** young and inexperienced and 1Ch 29:1
Solomon while he was **s** alive, 2Ch 10:6
The land is **s** ours because we 2Ch 14:7 5750
people **s** sacrificed in the high places, 2Ch 33:17 5750
his reign while he was **s** a youth, 2Ch 34:3 5750
"Be **s**, for the day is holy; Ne 8:11 2013
they were **s** talking with him, Es 6:14 5750
While he was **s** speaking, another Jb 1:16 5750
While he was **s** speaking, another Jb 1:17 5750
While he was **s** speaking, another Jb 1:18 5750
And he **s** holds fast his integrity, Jb 2:3 5750
"Do you **s** hold fast your integrity? Jb 2:9 5750
"It stood **s**, but I could not Jb 4:16 5975
"But it is **s** my consolation, And Jb 6:10 5750
it is **s** green *and* not cut down, Jb 8:12 5750
"Why do the wicked **s** live, Jb 21:7
land is **s** because of the south wind? Jb 37:17 8252
he does not stand **s** at the voice of Jb 39:24 539
your heart upon your bed, and be **s**. Ps 4:4 1826a
I **s** declare Your wondrous deeds. Ps 71:17 5704, 2008
The earth feared and was **s** Ps 76:8 8252
they **s** continued to sin against Him, Ps 78:17 5750
In spite of all this they **s** sinned And Ps 78:32 5750
be silent and, O God, do not be **s**. Ps 83:1 8252
its waves rise, You **s** them. Ps 89:9 7623a
They will **s** yield fruit in old age; Ps 92:14 5750
He caused the storm to be **s**, Ps 107:29 1827
When I awake, I am **s** with You. Ps 139:18 5750
For **s** my prayer is against their Ps 141:5 5750
wise man and he will be **s** wiser, Pr 9:9 5750
rises also while it is **s** night And Pr 31:15 5750
Among those who will come later **s**. Ec 1:11
than the living who are **s** living. Ec 4:2 5728
I am **s** seeking but have not found. Ec 7:28 5750
s I know that it will be well for Ec 8:12 3588, 1571
But His hand is **s** stretched out. Is 5:25 5750
And His hand is **s** stretched out. Is 9:12 5750
And His hand is **s** stretched out. Is 9:17 5750
what is on the right hand but **s** Is 9:20
And His hand is **s** stretched out. Is 9:21 5750
And His hand is **s** stretched out. Is 10:4 5750
The treacherous one **s** deals Is 21:2
and the destroyer **s** destroys. Is 21:2
I have kept **s** and restrained Myself. Is 42:14 2790b
and while they are **s** speaking, Is 65:24 5750
man, Will he **s** return to her? Jer 3:1 5750
do not stand **s**, For I am Jer 4:6
Why are we sitting **s**? Jer 8:14 3427
I certainly **s** remember him; Jer 31:20 5750
while he was **s** confined in the Jer 33:1 5750
Now Jeremiah was **s** coming in Jer 37:4
As Jeremiah was **s** not going back, Jer 40:5 5750
Be at rest and stay **s**. Jer 47:6 1826a
and whenever those stood **s**, Ezk 1:21 5975
those stood still, these stood **s**. Ezk 1:21 5975
whenever they stood **s**, Ezk 1:24 5975
whenever they stood **s**, Ezk 1:25 5975
will see **s** greater abominations." Ezk 8:6 7725
"Yet you will see **s** greater Ezk 8:13 7725
Yet you will see **s** greater Ezk 8:15 7725
When the cherubim stood **s**, Ezk 10:17 5975
still, the wheels would stand **s**; Ezk 10:17 5975
and they stood **s** at the entrance Ezk 10:19 5975
can it **s** be made into anything! Ezk 15:5 5750
them and **s** were not satisfied. Ezk 16:28 1571
"Will you **s** say, "I am a god," Ezk 28:9 559
'They have gone down, they lie **s**, Ezk 32:21 7901
of the furnace of blazing fire **s** Da 3:23
while I was **s** speaking in prayer, Da 9:21 5750
the end is **s** *to come* at the appointed Da 11:27 5750
s *to come* at the appointed time. Da 11:35 5750
were **s** three months until harvest. Am 4:7 5750
while I was **s** in my *own* country? Jon 4:2 5704
'Is the seed **s** in the barn? Hg 2:19 5750
if anyone **s** prophesies, Zch 13:3 5750
Child and His mother while it was **s** Mt 2:14
was **s** speaking to the crowds, Mt 12:46 *2089*
s lacking in understanding also? Mt 15:16 *188*
but **s** others, Jeremiah, or one of Mt 16:14
While he was **s** speaking, a bright cloud Mt 17:5 *2089*
what am I **s** lacking?" Mt 19:20 *2089*
s sleeping and resting? Mt 26:45 *3062*
While He was **s** speaking, Mt 26:47 *2089*
when He was **s** alive that deceiver Mt 27:63 *2089*
morning, while it was **s** dark, Mk 1:35 *3029*
and said to the sea, "Hush, be **s**." Mk 4:39 *5392*
Do you **s** have no faith Mk 4:40 *3768*
While He was **s** speaking, they came Mk 5:35 *2089*
s sleeping and resting? Mk 14:41 *3062*
while He was **s** speaking, Mk 14:43 *2089*
While He was **s** speaking, someone Lk 8:49 *2089*
While he was **s** approaching, Lk 9:42 *2089*
been done, and **s** there is room.' Lk 14:22 *2089*
while the other is **s** far away, Lk 14:32 *2089*
But while he was **s** a long way off, Lk 15:20 *2089*
"One thing you **s** lack; Lk 18:22 *2089*
While He was **s** speaking, behold, a Lk 22:47 *2089*
while he was **s** speaking, Lk 22:60 *2089*
to you while He was **s** in Galilee, Lk 24:6 *2089*
And they stood **s**, looking sad. Lk 24:17 *2476*
While they **s** could not believe Lk 24:41 *2089*
to you while I was **s** with you, Lk 24:44 *2089*
S others were saying, Jn 7:41
S others were saying, "No, but Jn 9:9
but was **s** in the place where Jn 11:30 *2089*
to the tomb, while it was **s** dark, Jn 20:1 *2089*
s breathing threats and murder Ac 9:1 *2089*
Peter was **s** speaking these words, Ac 10:44 *2089*
I also **s** being judged as a sinner? Ro 3:7 *2089*
For while we were **s** helpless, Ro 5:6 *2089*
we who died to sin **s** live in it? Ro 6:2 *2089*
"Why does He **s** find fault? Ro 9:19 *2089*
for you are **s** fleshly. 1Co 3:3 *2089*
I show you a **s** more excellent way. 1Co 12:31 *2089*
you are **s** in your sins. 1Co 15:17 *2089*
If I were **s** trying to please men, Ga 1:10 *2089*
I was **s** unknown by sight to Ga 1:22
if I **s** preach circumcision, Ga 5:11 *2089*
why am I **s** persecuted? Ga 5:11 *2089*
that your love may abound **s** more Php 1:9 *2089*
that you excel **s** more. 1Th 4:1 *3123*
you, brethren, to excel **s** more, 1Th 4:10 *3123*
that while I was **s** with you, 2Th 2:5 *2089*
as long as it is **s** called "Today," Heb 3:13
in **s** ministering to the saints. Heb 6:10
for he was **s** in the loins of his Heb 7:10 *2089*
And this is clearer **s**, Heb 7:15 *2089*
outer tabernacle is **s** standing, Heb 9:8 *2089*
though he is dead, he **s** speaks. Heb 11:4 *2089*
are **s** directed by a very small Jas 3:4
two woes are **s** coming after these Rv 9:12 *2089*
one who does wrong, **s** do wrong; Rv 22:11 *2089*
one who is filthy, **s** be filthy; Rv 22:11 *2089*
s practice righteousness; Rv 22:11 *2089*
is holy, **s** keep himself holy." Rv 22:11 *2089*

STILLS
Who **s** the roaring of the seas, Ps 65:7 7623a

STIMULATE
how to **s** my body with wine while Ec 2:3 4900
how to **s** one another to love and Heb 10:24 *3948*

STING
O Sheol, where is your **s**? Hos 13:14 6986
O DEATH, WHERE IS YOUR **S**?" 1Co 15:55 *2759*
The **s** of death is sin, and the 1Co 15:56 *2759*

STINGS
a serpent And **s** like a viper. Pr 23:32 6567b
of a scorpion when it **s** a man. Rv 9:5 *3817*
have tails like scorpions, and **s**; Rv 9:10 *2759*

STINK
Dead flies make a perfumer's oil **s**, Ec 10:1 887
Their fish **s** for lack of water And Is 50:2 887

STINKWEED
wheat, And **s** instead of barley." Jb 31:40 890

STIR
LORD began to **s** him in Mahaneh-dan, Jg 13:25 6470
And the innocent will **s** up Jb 17:8 5782
S up Yourself, and awake to my Ps 35:23 5782
and Manasseh, **s** up Your power And Ps 80:2 5782
They continually **s** up wars. Ps 140:2 1481b
to **s** up the Medes against them, Is 13:17 5782
"He will **s** up his strength Da 11:25 5782
Who ceases to **s** up *the fire* From Hos 7:4 5782
And I will **s** up your sons, O Zion, Zch 9:13 5782
began to **s** up all the crowd Ac 21:27 *4797*
to **s** you up by way of reminder, 2Pe 1:13 *1326*

STIRRED
he was deeply **s** over his brother, Gn 43:30 3648
Everyone whose heart **s** him and Ex 35:21 5375
All the women whose heart **s** Ex 35:26 5375
skill, everyone whose heart **s** him, Ex 36:2 5375
When it is *well* **s**, you shall bring Lv 6:21 7246
well **s** fine flour mixed with oil. Lv 7:12 7246
the city was **s** because of them, Ru 1:19 1949
that my son has **s** up my servant 1Sa 22:8 6965
the LORD has **s** you up against me, 1Sa 26:19 5496
deeply **s** over her son and said, 1Ki 3:26 3648
God of Israel **s** up the spirit of Pul, 1Ch 5:26 5782
Then the LORD **s** up against Jehoram 2Ch 21:16 5782
the LORD **s** up the spirit of Cyrus king 2Ch 36:22 5782
the LORD **s** up the spirit of Cyrus Ezr 1:1 5782
everyone whose spirit God had **s** to Ezr 1:5 5782
He will be **s** up as in the valley of Is 28:21 7264
And a great storm is being **s** up Jer 25:32 5782
So the LORD **s** up the spirit of Hg 1:14 5782
Jerusalem, all the city was **s**, Mt 21:10 *4579*
But the chief priests **s** up the Mk 15:11 *383*
into the pool and **s** up the water; Jn 5:4 *5015*
the pool when the water is **s** up, Jn 5:7 *5015*
The sea *began* to be **s** up Jn 6:18 *1326*
And they **s** up the people, the Ac 6:12 *4787*
Jews who disbelieved **s** up the minds Ac 14:2 *1892*
They **s** up the crowd and the Ac 17:8 *5015*
the Egyptian who some time ago **s** up Ac 21:38 *387*
your zeal has **s** up most of them. 2Co 9:2 *2042*

STIRRING
are **s** up the city against you. Jg 9:31 6696a
four winds of heaven were **s** up the Da 7:2 1519
after the **s** up of the water, Jn 5:4 *5016*
agitating and **s** up the crowds. Ac 17:13 *5015*
I am **s** up your sincere mind by way 2Pe 3:1 *1326*

STIRRINGS
The **s** of Your heart and Your Is 63:15 1995

STIRS
"Like an eagle that **s** up its nest, Dt 32:11 5782
Hatred **s** up strife, But love Pr 10:12 5782
But a harsh word **s** up anger. Pr 15:1 5927
A hot-tempered man **s** up strife, Pr 15:18 1624
An arrogant man **s** up strife, But Pr 28:25 1624
An angry man **s** up strife, And a Pr 29:22 1624
who **s** up the sea and its waves Is 51:15 7280a
Who **s** up the sea so that its waves Jer 31:35 7280a
"He **s** up the people, teaching all Lk 23:5 *383*
a fellow who **s** up dissension among Ac 24:5 *2795*

STOCK
their **s** taken root in the earth, Is 40:24 1503

STOCKS
"You put my feet in the **s** Jb 13:27 5465
'He puts my feet in the **s**; Jb 33:11 5465
and put him in the **s** that were at Jer 20:2 4115
released Jeremiah from the **s**, Jer 20:3 4115
in the **s** and in the iron collar, Jer 29:26 4115
and fastened their feet in the **s**. Ac 16:24 *3586*

STOIC
and **S** philosophers were conversing Ac 17:18 *4770*

STOLE
then Rachel **s** the household idols Gn 31:19 1589
"If what he **s** is actually found Ex 22:4 1591
so Absalom **s** away the hearts of 2Sa 15:6 1589
and **s** him from among the king's sons 2Ki 11:2 1589
and **s** him from among the king's 2Ch 22:11 1589
s Him away while we were asleep.' Mt 28:13 *2813*

STOLEN
with me, will be considered **s**." Gn 30:33 1589
not know that Rachel had **s** them. Gn 31:32 1589
s by day or stolen by night. Gn 31:39 1589
stolen by day or **s** by night. Gn 31:39 1589
and it is **s** from the man's house, Ex 22:7 1589
"But if it is actually **s** from him, Ex 22:12 1589
ban and have both **s** and deceived. Jos 7:11 1589
the men of Judah **s** you away, 2Sa 19:41 1589
who had **s** them from the open 2Sa 21:12 1589
"**S** water is sweet; Pr 9:17 1589

STOMACH
a curse shall go into your **s**, Nu 5:22 4578
and the two cheeks and the **s**. Dt 18:3 6896
Yet his food in his **s** is changed Jb 20:14 4578
the **s** of the wicked is in need. Pr 13:25 990
mouth his **s** will be satisfied; Pr 18:20 990
but the full **s** of the rich man Ec 5:12 7647
filled his **s** with my delicacies; Jer 51:34 3770
"Son of man, feed your **s** and Ezk 3:3 990
and Jonah was in the **s** of the fish Jon 1:17 4578
his God from the **s** of the fish, Jon 2:1 4578
into the mouth passes into the **s**, Mt 15:17 *2836*
not go into his heart, but into his **s**, Mk 7:19 *2836*
"And he would have gladly filled his **s** Lk 15:16 *2836*
Food is for the **s** and the stomach 1Co 6:13 *2836*
stomach and the **s** is for food 1Co 6:13 *2836*
a little wine for the sake of your **s** 1Tm 5:23 *4751*
it will make your **s** bitter, Rv 10:9 *2836*
eaten it, my **s** was made bitter. Rv 10:10 *2836*

STOMACHS
nor can they fill their **s**, Ezk 7:19 4578

STONE
bdellium and the onyx **s** are there. Gn 2:12 68
And they used brick for **s**, Gn 11:3 68
and took the **s** that he had put Gn 28:18 68
"This **s**, which I have set up Gn 28:22 68
Now the **s** on the mouth of the well Gn 29:2 68
the **s** from the mouth of the well and Gn 29:3 68
and put the **s** back in its place on Gn 29:3 68
the **s** from the mouth of the well; Gn 29:8 68
the **s** from the mouth of the well and Gn 29:10 68
Jacob took a **s** and set it up *as* a Gn 31:45 68
spoken with him, a pillar of **s**, Gn 35:14 68
is the Shepherd, the **S** of Israel), Gn 49:24 68
of wood and in *vessels of* **s**.'" Ex 7:19 68
eyes, will they not then **s** us? Ex 8:26 5619
down into the depths like a **s**. Ex 15:5 68
arm they are motionless as **s**; Ex 15:16 68
little more and they will **s** me." Ex 17:4 5619
took a **s** and put it under him, Ex 17:12 68
If you make an altar of **s** for Me, Ex 20:25 68
other with a **s** or with *his* fist, Ex 21:18 68
and I will give you the **s** tablets Ex 24:12 68
six of their names on the one **s** and Ex 28:10 68
the remaining six on the other **s**, Ex 28:10 68
of the testimony, tablets of **s**, Ex 31:18 68
s tablets like the former ones, Ex 34:1 68
So he cut out two **s** tablets like Ex 34:4 68
he took two **s** tablets in his hand. Ex 34:4 68
the people of the land shall **s** him Lv 20:2 7275
let all the congregation **s** him. Lv 24:14 7275
congregation shall certainly **s** him. Lv 24:16 7275
nor shall you place a figured **s** in Lv 26:1 68
said to **s** them with stones. Nu 14:10 7275
all the congregation shall **s** him Nu 15:35 7275
If he struck him down with a **s** in Nu 35:17 68
or with any deadly object of **s**, Nu 35:23 68
He wrote them on two tablets of **s**. Dt 4:13 68
work of man's hands, wood and **s**, Dt 4:28 68
He wrote them on two tablets of **s** Dt 5:22 68
to receive the tablets of **s**, Dt 9:9 68
LORD gave me the two tablets of **s** Dt 9:10 68
LORD gave me the two tablets of **s** Dt 9:11 68
tablets of **s** like the former ones, Dt 10:1 68
tablets of **s** like the former ones, Dt 10:3 68
"So you shall **s** him to death Dt 13:10 5619
and you shall **s** them to death. Dt 17:5 5619
men of his city shall **s** him to death; Dt 21:21 7275
men of her city shall **s** her to death Dt 22:21 5619
and you shall **s** them to death; Dt 22:24 5619
serve other gods, wood and **s**. Dt 28:36 68
serve other gods, wood and **s**, Dt 28:64 68
and their idols *of* wood, **s**, Dt 29:17 68
you take up a **s** on his shoulder, Jos 4:5 68
the **s** of Bohan the son of Reuben. Jos 15:6 68
the **s** of Bohan the son of Reuben. Jos 18:17 68
and he took a large **s** and set it Jos 24:26 68
this **s** shall be for a witness Jos 24:27 68
Jerubbaal, seventy men, on one **s**. Jg 9:5 68
his sons, seventy men, on one **s**, Jg 9:18 68
sling a **s** at a hair and not miss. Jg 20:16 68
there where there *was* a large **s**; 1Sa 6:14 68
gold, and put them on the large **s**; 1Sa 6:15 68
The large **s** on which they set the 1Sa 6:18 68
Then Samuel took a **s** and set it 1Sa 7:12 68
roll a great **s** to me today." 1Sa 14:33 68
and took from it a **s** and slung *it*, 1Sa 17:49 68
And the **s** sank into his forehead, 1Sa 17:49 68
Philistine with a sling and a **s**, 1Sa 17:50 68
you shall remain by the **s** Ezel. 1Sa 20:19 68
him so that he became *as* a **s**. 1Sa 25:37 68
gold, and *in it was* a precious **s**; 2Sa 12:30 68
not even a small **s** is found there." 2Sa 17:13 6872b
at the large **s** which is in Gibeon, 2Sa 20:8 68
and fatlings by the **s** of Zoheleth, 1Ki 1:9 68
80,000 hewers *of* **s** 1Ki 5:15
built of **s** prepared at the quarry, 1Ki 6:7 68
was cedar, there was no **s** seen. 1Ki 6:18 68
three rows of cut **s** and a row of 1Ki 6:36 1496
of **s** cut according to measure, 1Ki 7:9 1496
s cut according to measure, 1Ki 7:11 1496
all around *had* three rows of cut **s** 1Ki 7:12 1496
tablets of **s** which Moses put there at 1Ki 8:9 68
take him out and **s** him to death." 1Ki 21:10 5619
and each one threw a **s** on every 2Ki 3:25 68
and for buying timber and hewn **s** 2Ki 12:12 68
it and put it on a pavement of **s**. 2Ki 16:17 68
work of men's hands, wood and **s**. 2Ki 19:18 68
and hewn **s** to repair the house. 2Ki 22:6 68
and there was a precious **s** in it; 1Ch 20:2 68
also timber and **s** I have prepared, 1Ch 22:14 68
and masons of **s** and carpenters, 1Ch 22:15 68
80,000 men to quarry **s** in 2Ch 2:2
silver, bronze, iron, **s** and wood, 2Ch 2:14 68
to the builders to buy quarried **s** and 2Ch 34:11 68
would break their **s** wall down!" Ne 4:3 68
Like a **s** into raging waters. Ne 9:11 68
"Water becomes hard like **s**, Jb 38:30 68
"His heart is as hard as a **s**, Jb 41:24 68
not strike your foot against a **s**. Ps 91:12 68
The **s** which the builders rejected Ps 118:22 68
Has become the chief corner **s**. Ps 118:22
And its **s** wall was broken down. Pr 24:31 68
Like one who binds a **s** in a sling, Pr 26:8 68
into it, And he who rolls a **s**, Pr 26:27 68
A **s** is heavy and the sand weighty, Pr 27:3 68
a **s** to strike and a rock to Is 8:14 68
"Behold, I am laying in Zion a **s**, Is 28:16 68
in Zion a stone, a tested **s**, Is 28:16 68
work of men's hands, wood and **s**. Is 37:19 68
And to a **s**, 'You gave me birth.' Jer 2:27 68
They will not take from you *even* a **s** Jer 51:26 68
a corner Nor a **s** for foundations, Jer 51:26 68
you will tie a **s** to it and throw Jer 51:63 68
has blocked my ways with hewn **s**; La 3:9 1496
the pit And have placed a **s** on me. La 3:53 68
something like a sapphire **s**, Ezk 10:1 68
like the gleam of a Tarshish **s**. Ezk 10:9 68
And I will take the heart of **s** Ezk 11:19 68
and they will **s** you and cut you to Ezk 16:40 7275
of the lands, serving wood and **s**.' Ezk 20:32 68
'The company will **s** them with Ezk 23:47 7275
Every precious **s** was your covering: Ezk 28:13 68
and I will remove the heart of **s** Ezk 36:26 68
there were four tables of hewn **s**, Ezk 40:42 68
a **s** was cut out without hands, Da 2:34 69
But the **s** that struck the statue Da 2:35 69
a **s** was cut out of the mountain Da 2:45 69
of bronze, iron, wood and **s**. Da 5:4 69
gold, of bronze, iron, wood and **s**, Da 5:23 69
A **s** was brought and laid over Da 6:17 69
their altars are like the **s** heaps Hos 12:11 1530
have built houses of well-hewn **s**, Am 5:11 1496
grasshoppers Settling in the **s** walls Na 3:17
the **s** will cry out from the wall, Hab 2:11 68
To a mute **s**, 'Arise!' Hab 2:19 68
before one **s** was placed on another Hg 2:15 68
s that I have set before Joshua; Zch 3:9 68
on one **s** are seven eyes. Zch 3:9 68
he will bring forth the top **s** with Zch 4:7 68
I will make Jerusalem a heavy **s** for Zch 12:3 68
STRIKE YOUR FOOT AGAINST A **S**.'" Mt 4:6 *3037*
asks for a loaf, will give him a **s**? Mt 7:9 *3037*
'THE **S** WHICH THE BUILDERS Mt 21:42 *3037*
THIS BECAME THE CHIEF CORNER **S**; Mt 21:42
he who falls on this **s** will be broken Mt 21:44 *3037*
not one **s** here will be left upon Mt 24:2 *3037*
and he rolled a large **s** against Mt 27:60 *3037*
guard they set a seal on the **s**. Mt 27:66 *3037*
rolled away the **s** and sat upon it. Mt 28:2 *3037*
'THE **S** WHICH THE BUILDERS Mk 12:10 *3037*
THIS BECAME THE CHIEF CORNER **S**; Mk 12:10
Not one **s** will be left upon Mk 13:2 *3037*
and he rolled a **s** against the Mk 15:46 *3037*
"Who will roll away the **s** for us Mk 16:3 *3037*
that the **s** had been rolled away, Mk 16:4 *3037*
tell this **s** to become bread." Lk 4:3 *3037*
STRIKE YOUR FOOT AGAINST A **S**.'" Lk 4:11 *3037*
not leave in you one **s** upon another, Lk 19:44 *3037*
all the people will **s** us to death, Lk 20:6 *2642*
'THE **S** WHICH THE BUILDERS Lk 20:17 *3037*
THIS BECAME THE CHIEF CORNER **S**'? Lk 20:17
Everyone who falls on that **s** will be Lk 20:18 *3037*
will not be left one **s** upon another Lk 21:6 *3037*
the **s** rolled away from the tomb, Lk 24:2 *3037*
Now there were six **s** waterpots set Jn 2:6 *3035*
commanded us to **s** such women; Jn 8:5 *3034*
the first to throw a **s** at her." Jn 8:7 *3037*
picked up stones again to **s** Him. Jn 10:31 *3034*
"For a good work we do not **s** You, Jn 10:33 *3034*
were just now seeking to **s** You, Jn 11:8 *3034*
and a **s** was lying against it. Jn 11:38 *3037*
Jesus said, "Remove the **s**." Jn 11:39 *3037*
So they removed the **s**. Jn 11:41 *3037*
and saw the **s** *already* taken away Jn 20:1 *3037*
the **S** WHICH WAS REJECTED by you, Ac 4:11 *3037*
WHICH BECAME THE CHIEF CORNER **S**. Ac 4:11
rulers, to mistreat and to **s** them, Ac 14:5 *3036*
is like gold or silver or **s**, Ac 17:29 *3037*
stumbled over the stumbling **s**, Ro 9:32 *3037*
I LAY IN ZION A **S** OF STUMBLING AND Ro 9:33 *3037*
living God, not on tablets of **s** but 2Co 3:3 *3035*
Jesus Himself being the corner **s**, Eph 2:20
coming to Him as to a living **s** which 1Pe 2:4 *3037*
"BEHOLD, I LAY IN ZION A CHOICE **S**, 1Pe 2:6 *3037*
A CHOICE STONE, A PRECIOUS CORNER **S**, 1Pe 2:6
"THE **S** WHICH THE BUILDERS 1Pe 2:7 *3037*
THIS BECAME THE VERY CORNER **S**," 1Pe 2:7
"A **S** OF STUMBLING AND A ROCK OF 1Pe 2:8 *3037*
and I will give him a white **s**, Rv 2:17 *5586*
and a new name written on the **s** Rv 2:17 *5586*
who was sitting *was* like a jasper **s** Rv 4:3 *3037*
and of brass and of **s** and of wood, Rv 9:20 *3035*
Then a strong angel took up a **s** Rv 18:21 *3037*
was like a very costly **s**, Rv 21:11 *3037*
as a **s** of crystal-clear jasper. Rv 21:11 *3037*
with every kind of precious **s**. Rv 21:19 *3037*
The first foundation **s** was jasper; Rv 21:19 *2310b*

STONECUTTERS
and to the masons and the **s**, 2Ki 12:12 2672, 68
and he set **s** to hew out stones to 1Ch 22:2 2672
s and masons of stone and 1Ch 22:15 2672

STONED
shall surely be **s** or shot through; Ex 19:13 5619
the ox shall surely be **s** and its Ex 21:28 5619
the ox shall be **s** and its owner Ex 21:29 5619
of silver, and the ox shall be **s**. Ex 21:32 5619
They shall be **s** with stones, their Lv 20:27 7275
the camp and **s** him with stones. Lv 24:23 7275
and **s** him to death with stones, Nu 15:36 7275
And all Israel **s** them with stones; Jos 7:25 7275
after they had **s** them with stones. Jos 7:25 5619
and all Israel **s** him to death. 1Ki 12:18 7275
and **s** him to death with stones. 1Ki 21:13 5619
"Naboth has been **s** and is dead." 1Ki 21:14 5619
Naboth had been **s** and was dead, 1Ki 21:15 5619
the sons of Israel **s** him to death. 2Ch 10:18 7275
they **s** him to death in the court of 2Ch 24:21 7275
and killed another, and **s** a third. Mt 21:35 *3036*
people, that they might be **s**). Ac 5:26 *3034*
they **s** Paul and dragged him out of Ac 14:19 *3034*
beaten with rods, once I was **s**, 2Co 11:25 *3034*
They were **s**, they were sawn in Heb 11:37 *3034*
THE MOUNTAIN, IT WILL BE **S**." Heb 12:20 *3036*

STONEMASONS
cedar trees and carpenters and **s**; 2Sa 5:11 2796, 68

STONE'S
from them about a **s** throw, Lk 22:41 *3037*

STONES
he took one of the **s** of the place Gn 28:11 68
Jacob said to his kinsmen, "Gather **s**. Gn 31:46 68
So they took **s** and made a heap, Gn 31:46 68
you shall not build it of cut **s**, Ex 20:25 1496
onyx **s** and setting stones for the Ex 25:7 68
onyx stones and setting **s** for Ex 25:7 68
"You shall take two onyx **s** Ex 28:9 68
you shall engrave the two **s** Ex 28:11 68
"You shall put the two **s** on Ex 28:12 68
as **s** of memorial for the sons of Ex 28:12 68
shall mount on it four rows of **s**; Ex 28:17 68
"The **s** shall be according to Ex 28:21 68
in the cutting of **s** for settings, Ex 31:5 68
and onyx **s** and setting stones for Ex 35:9 68
and onyx stones and setting **s** for Ex 35:9 68
The rulers brought the onyx **s** Ex 35:27 68
and the **s** for setting for the ephod Ex 35:27 68
in the cutting of **s** for settings and Ex 35:33 68
They made the onyx **s**, Ex 39:6 68
memorial **s** for the sons of Israel, Ex 39:7 68
they mounted four rows of **s** on it. Ex 39:10 68
The **s** were corresponding to Ex 39:14 68
shall order them to tear out the **s** Lv 14:40 68
they shall take other **s** and replace Lv 14:42 68
other stones and replace *those* **s**, Lv 14:42 68
he has torn out the **s** and scraped Lv 14:43 68
tear down the house, its **s**, Lv 14:45 68
the land shall stone him with **s**. Lv 20:2 68
They shall be stoned with **s**, Lv 20:27 68
the camp and stoned him with **s**. Lv 24:23 68
said to stone them with **s**. Nu 14:10 68
congregation shall stone him with **s** Nu 15:35 68
and stoned him to death with **s**, Nu 15:36 68
and destroy all their figured **s**, Nu 33:52 4906
a land whose **s** are iron, and out Dt 8:9 68
shall set up for yourself large **s** and Dt 27:2 68
set up on Mount Ebal, these **s**, Dt 27:4 68
the LORD your God, an altar of **s**; Dt 27:5 68
of the LORD your God of uncut **s**, Dt 27:6 68
"You shall write on the **s** all Dt 27:8 68
'Take up for yourselves twelve **s** Jos 4:3 68
'What do these **s** mean to you?' Jos 4:6 68
So these **s** shall become a memorial Jos 4:7 68
took up twelve **s** from the middle of Jos 4:8 68
Then Joshua set up twelve **s** in the Jos 4:9 68

Those twelve s which they had	Jos 4:20	68
'What are these s?'	Jos 4:21	68
And all Israel stoned them with s;	Jos 7:25	68
after they had stoned them with s.	Jos 7:25	68
heap of s that stands to this day,	Jos 7:26	68
heap of s *that stands* to this day.	Jos 8:29	68
law of Moses, an altar of uncut s on	Jos 8:31	68
He wrote there on the s a copy of	Jos 8:32	68
the LORD threw large s from	Jos 10:11	68
Roll large s against the mouth of	Jos 10:18	68
s over the mouth of the cave,	Jos 10:27	68
five smooth s from the brook,	1Sa 17:40	68
He threw s at David and at all	2Sa 16:6	68
and cast s and threw dust at him.	2Sa 16:13	68
over him a very great heap of s.	2Sa 18:17	68
and they quarried great s,	1Ki 5:17	68
quarried great stones, costly s,	1Ki 5:17	68
of the house with cut s.	1Ki 5:17	68
and the s to build the house.	1Ki 5:18	68
All these were of costly s,	1Ki 7:9	68
The foundation was of costly s,	1Ki 7:10	68
of costly stones, *even* large s,	1Ki 7:10	68
s of ten cubits and stones of	1Ki 7:10	68
ten cubits and s of eight cubits.	1Ki 7:10	68
And above were costly s,	1Ki 7:11	68
and very much gold and precious s.	1Ki 10:2	68
amount of spices and precious s.	1Ki 10:10	68
of almug trees and precious s.	1Ki 10:11	68
as common as s in Jerusalem,	1Ki 10:27	68
they carried away the s of Ramah	1Ki 15:22	68
Elijah took twelve s according	1Ki 18:31	68
So with the s he built an altar in	1Ki 18:32	68
the wood and the s and the dust,	1Ki 18:38	68
head a bread cake *baked on* hot s,	1Ki 19:6	7531a
and stoned him to death with s.	1Ki 21:13	68
good piece of land with s.' "	2Ki 3:19	68
Kir-hareseth *only* they left its s;	2Ki 3:25	68
Then he demolished its s,	2Ki 23:15	68
the right hand and the left *to sling* s	1Ch 12:2	68
he set stonecutters to hew out s to	1Ch 22:2	68
of wood, onyx s and inlaid *stones,*	1Ch 29:2	68
onyx stones and inlaid s, stones	1Ch 29:2	68
and inlaid *stones,* s of antimony and	1Ch 29:2	68
antimony and s of various colors,	1Ch 29:2	7553
and all kinds of precious s and	1Ch 29:2	68
Whoever possessed *precious* s	1Ch 29:8	68
as plentiful in Jerusalem as s,	2Ch 1:15	68
80,000 to quarry s in the mountains	2Ch 2:18	
adorned the house with precious s;	2Ch 3:6	68
amount of gold and precious s;	2Ch 9:1	68
amount of spices and precious s;	2Ch 9:9	68
algum trees and precious s.	2Ch 9:10	68
as common as s in Jerusalem,	2Ch 9:27	68
they carried away the s of Ramah	2Ch 16:6	68
body armor, bows and sling s.	2Ch 26:14	68
of shooting arrows and great s.	2Ch 26:15	68
for silver, gold, precious s,	2Ch 32:27	68
which is being built with huge s,	Ezr 5:8	69
with three layers of huge s and	Ezr 6:4	69
Can they revive the s from the	Ne 4:2	68
mother-of-pearl and precious s.	Es 1:6	5508
in league with the s of the field,	Jb 5:23	68
"Is my strength the strength of s,	Jb 6:12	68
rock pile, He grasps a house of s.	Jb 8:17	68
Water wears away s,	Jb 14:19	68
Ophir among the s of the brooks,	Jb 22:24	6697
servants find pleasure in her s And	Ps 102:14	68
A time to throw s and a time to	Ec 3:5	68
stones and a time to gather s;	Ec 3:5	68
He who quarries s may be hurt by	Ec 10:9	68
of David, Built with rows of s	SS 4:4	8530
dug it all around, removed its s,	Is 5:2	5619
But we will rebuild with smooth s;	Is 9:10	1496
Who go down to the s of the pit Like	Is 14:19	68
s like pulverized chalk stones;	Is 27:9	68
stones like pulverized chalk s;	Is 27:9	68
I will set your s in antimony,	Is 54:11	68
your entire wall of precious s.	Is 54:12	68
"Among the smooth s of	Is 57:6	
bronze, And instead of s, iron.	Is 60:17	68
Remove the s, lift up a standard	Is 62:10	68
committed adultery with s and trees.	Jer 3:9	68
"Take *some* large s in your hands	Jer 43:9	68
over these s that I have hidden;	Jer 43:10	68
The sacred s are poured out At the	La 4:1	68
The company will stone them with s	Ezk 23:47	68
and throw your s and your timbers	Ezk 26:12	68
and with all *kinds* of precious s and	Ezk 27:22	68
in the midst of the s of fire.	Ezk 28:14	68
From the midst of the s of fire.	Ezk 28:16	68
him with gold, silver, costly s and	Da 11:38	68
pour her s down into the valley And	Mi 1:6	68
it with its timber and s."	Zch 5:4	68
and trample on the sling s;	Zch 9:15	68
For *they are as* the s of a crown,	Zch 9:16	68
that from these s God is able to	Mt 3:9	*3037*
that these s become bread."	Mt 4:3	*3037*
and s those who are sent to her!	Mt 23:37	*3036*
and gashing himself with s.	Mk 5:5	*3037*
behold what wonderful s and what	Mk 13:1	*3037*
that from these s God is able to	Lk 3:8	*3037*
prophets and s those sent to her!	Lk 13:34	*3036*
silent, the s will cry out!"	Lk 19:40	*3037*
with beautiful s and votive gifts,	Lk 21:5	*3037*
Jews picked up s to throw at Him,	Jn 8:59	*3037*
Jews picked up s again to stone Him.	Jn 10:31	*3037*
with gold, silver, precious s,	1Co 3:12	*3037*
death, in letters engraved on s,	2Co 3:7	*3037*
you also, as living s,	1Pe 2:5	*3037*
gold and precious s and pearls,	Rv 17:4	*3037*
of gold and silver and precious s	Rv 18:12	*3037*
gold and precious s and pearls;	Rv 18:16	*3037*
the city had twelve foundation s,	Rv 21:14	*2310b*
The foundation s of the city wall	Rv 21:19	*2310b*

STONING

because the people spoke of s him,	1Sa 30:6	5619
for which of them are you s Me?"	Jn 10:32	*3034*
out of the city, they *began* s *him*	Ac 7:58	*3036*
They went on s Stephen as he	Ac 7:59	*3036*

STONY

live in s wastes in the wilderness,	Jer 17:6	2788

STOOD

where he had s before the LORD;	Gn 19:27	5975
the LORD s above it and said,	Gn 28:13	5324
my sheaf rose up and also s erect;	Gn 37:7	5324
and they s by the *other* cows on	Gn 41:3	5975
old when he s before Pharaoh,	Gn 41:46	5975
down to Egypt and s before Joseph.	Gn 43:15	5975
before all those who s by him,	Gn 45:1	5324
His sister s at a distance to	Ex 2:4	3320
but Moses s up and helped them and	Ex 2:17	6965
from a kiln, and s before Pharaoh;	Ex 9:10	5975
before them and s behind them.	Ex 14:19	5975
flowing waters s up like a heap;	Ex 15:8	5324
and the people s about Moses from	Ex 18:13	5975
s at the foot of the mountain.	Ex 19:17	3320
they trembled and s at a distance.	Ex 20:18	5975
So the people s at a distance,	Ex 20:21	5975
Moses s in the gate of the camp,	Ex 32:26	5975
descended in the cloud and s there	Ex 34:5	3320
came near and s before the LORD.	Lv 9:5	5975
and s at the doorway of the tent,	Nu 12:5	5975
and they s at the doorway of the	Nu 16:18	5975
s at the doorway of their tents,	Nu 16:27	5324
Then the angel of the LORD s in a	Nu 22:24	5975
and s in a narrow place where	Nu 22:26	5975
They s before Moses and before	Nu 27:2	5975
"*Remember* the day you s before	Dt 4:10	5975
and s at the foot of the mountain,	Dt 4:11	5975
the pillar of cloud s at the doorway	Dt 31:15	5975
above s *and* rose up in one heap,	Jos 3:16	5975
ark of the covenant of the LORD s	Jos 3:17	5975
Half of them s in front of Mount	Jos 8:33	
So the sun s still, and the moon	Jos 10:13	1826a
any cities that s on their mounds,	Jos 11:13	5975
all their enemies s before them;	Jos 21:44	5975
no man has s before you to this day.	Jos 23:9	5975
said to all who s against him,	Jg 6:31	5975
s in his place around the camp;	Jg 7:21	5975
and s on the top of Mount Gerizim,	Jg 9:7	5975
and s in the entrance of the city gate	Jg 9:35	5975
and s in the entrance of the city gate;	Jg 9:44	5975
s by the entrance of the gate.	Jg 18:16	5324
while the priest s by the entrance	Jg 18:17	5324
s before it to *minister* in those	Jg 20:28	5975
the woman who s here beside you,	1Sa 1:26	5324
s and called as at other times,	1Sa 3:10	3320
women who s by her said to her,	1Sa 4:20	5324
s there where there *was* a large stone;	1Sa 6:14	5975
and when he s among the people,	1Sa 10:23	3320
The Philistines s on the	1Sa 17:3	5975
while Israel s on the mountain on the	1Sa 17:3	5975
He s and shouted to the ranks	1Sa 17:8	5975
Then David ran and s over the	1Sa 17:51	5975
to his servants who s around him,	1Sa 22:7	5324
and s on top of the mountain at a	1Sa 26:13	5975
"So I s beside him and killed	2Sa 1:10	5975
had fallen and died, s still.	2Sa 2:23	5975
s on the top of a certain hill.	2Sa 2:25	5975
The elders of his household s	2Sa 12:17	6965
So the king s beside the gate, and	2Sa 18:4	5975
you yourself would have s aloof."	2Sa 18:13	3320
So he turned aside and s still.	2Sa 18:30	5975
Now there s by him one of Joab's	2Sa 20:11	5975
saw that all the people s still,	2Sa 20:12	5975
everyone who came by him s still.	2Sa 20:12	5975
the city, and it s by the rampart;	2Sa 20:15	5975
presence and s before the king.	1Ki 1:28	5975
s before the ark of the covenant of	1Ki 3:15	5975
came to the king and s before him.	1Ki 3:16	5975
It s on twelve oxen, three facing	1Ki 7:25	5975
Then Solomon s before the altar of	1Ki 8:22	5975
And he s and blessed all the	1Ki 8:55	5975
and s in the entrance of the cave.	1Ki 19:13	5975
and s before the LORD and said,	1Ki 22:21	5975
and s opposite *them* at a distance,	2Ki 2:7	5975
the two of them s by the Jordan.	2Ki 2:7	5975
and s by the bank of the Jordan.	2Ki 2:13	5975
summoned and s on the border.	2Ki 3:21	5975
had called her, she s before him.	2Ki 4:12	5975
called her, she s in the doorway.	2Ki 4:15	5975
and s at the doorway of the house	2Ki 5:9	5975
and came and s before him,	2Ki 5:15	5975
went in and s before his master.	2Ki 5:25	5975
he came and s before him and said,	2Ki 8:9	5975
morning he went out and s	2Ki 10:9	5975
The guards s each with his	2Ki 11:11	5975
he revived and s up on his feet.	2Ki 13:21	6965
they came and s by the conduit of	2Ki 18:17	5975
Then Rabshakeh s and cried with a	2Ki 18:28	5975
The king s by the pillar and	2Ki 23:3	5975
brother Asaph s at his right hand,	1Ch 6:39	5975
Then Satan s up against Israel and	1Ch 21:1	5975
and they s on their feet facing	2Ch 3:13	5975
It s on twelve oxen, three facing	2Ch 4:4	5975
Then he s before the altar of the	2Ch 6:12	5975
and he s on it, knelt on his knees	2Ch 6:13	5975
The priests s at their posts	2Ch 7:6	5975
Levites who were in all Israel s with	2Ch 11:13	3320
Then Abijah s on Mount Zemaraim,	2Ch 13:4	6965
and s before the LORD and said,	2Ch 18:20	5975
Then Jehoshaphat s in the assembly	2Ch 20:5	5975
s up to praise the LORD God of	2Ch 20:19	6965
went out, Jehoshaphat s and said,	2Ch 20:20	5975
and he s above the people and said	2Ch 24:20	5975
The Levites s with the *musical*	2Ch 29:26	5975
They s at their stations after	2Ch 30:16	5975
Then the king s in his place and	2Ch 34:31	5975
and the priests s at their	2Ch 35:10	5975
priest s up with Urim and Thummim.	Ezr 2:63	5975
Jeshua *with* his sons and brothers s	Ezr 3:9	5975
the priests s in their apparel	Ezr 3:10	5975
the priest s up and said to them,	Ezr 10:10	6965
while the trumpeter s near me.	Ne 4:18	
Ezra the scribe s at a wooden	Ne 8:4	5975
And beside him s Mattithiah,	Ne 8:4	5975
he opened it, all the people s up.	Ne 8:5	5975
and s and confessed their sins and	Ne 9:2	5975
While they s in their place, they	Ne 9:3	6965
on the Levites' platform s Jeshua,	Ne 9:4	6965
s opposite them in *their* service	Ne 12:9	
s in the inner court of the king's	Es 5:1	5975
Esther arose and s before the king.	Es 8:4	5975
"It s still, but I could not	Jb 4:16	5975
And the old men arose *and* s.	Jb 29:8	5975
But we have risen and s upright.	Ps 20:8	5749a
He commanded, and it s fast.	Ps 33:9	5975
one s in the breach before Him,	Ps 106:23	5975
Then Phinehas s up and interposed,	Ps 106:30	5975
My wisdom also s by me.	Ec 2:9	5975
Seraphim s above Him, each having	Is 6:2	5975
And he s by the conduit of the	Is 36:2	5975
Then Rabshakeh s and cried with a	Is 36:13	5975
Remember how I s before You To	Jer 18:20	5975
and he s in the court of the	Jer 19:14	5975
has s in the council of the LORD,	Jer 23:18	5975
"But if they had s in My council,	Jer 23:22	5975
officials who s beside the king.	Jer 36:21	5975
and whenever those s still,	Ezk 1:21	5975
those stood still, these s still.	Ezk 1:21	5975
whenever they s still, they	Ezk 1:24	5975
whenever they s still, they	Ezk 1:25	5975
in and s beside the bronze altar.	Ezk 9:2	5975
he entered and s beside a wheel.	Ezk 10:6	5975
When the cherubim s still,	Ezk 10:17	5975
temple and s over the cherubim.	Ezk 10:18	5975
and they s still at the entrance	Ezk 10:19	5975
and s over the mountain which is	Ezk 11:23	5975
came to life and s on their feet,	Ezk 37:10	5975
extended to the wall which s on	Ezk 41:6	
came in and s before the king.	Da 2:2	5975
and they s before the image that	Da 3:3	6966
was astounded and s up in haste;	Da 3:24	6966
this word to me, I s up trembling.	Da 10:11	5975
"On the day that you s aloof,	Ob 1:11	5975
He s and surveyed the earth;	Hab 3:6	5975
Sun *and* moon s in their places;	Hab 3:11	5975
Me and s in awe of My name.	Mal 2:5	2865
s over *the place* where the Child was.	Mt 2:9	*2476*
high priest s up and said to Him,	Mt 26:62	*450*
Now Jesus s before the governor,	Mt 27:11	*2476*
of those who s by drew his sword,	Mk 14:47	*3936*
Some s up and *began* to give	Mk 14:57	*450*
The high priest s up *and came*	Mk 14:60	*450*
angel of the Lord suddenly s before	Lk 2:9	*2186*
on the Sabbath, and s up to read.	Lk 4:16	*450*
with them and s on a level place;	Lk 6:17	*2476*
a child and s him by His side,	Lk 9:47	*2476*
lawyer s up and put Him to the test,	Lk 10:25	*450*
men who s at a distance met Him;	Lk 17:12	*2476*
"The Pharisee s and was praying	Lk 18:11	*2476*
who have s by Me in My trials;	Lk 22:28	*1265*
And the people s by, looking on.	Lk 23:35	*2476*
s near them in dazzling clothing;	Lk 24:4	*2186*
And they s still, looking sad.	Lk 24:17	*2476*
He Himself s in their midst	Lk 24:36	*2476*
that s on the other side of the sea	Jn 6:22	*2476*
the feast, Jesus s and cried out,	Jn 7:37	*2476*
another as they s in the temple,	Jn 11:56	*2476*
crowd *of people* who s by and heard	Jn 12:29	*2476*
Jesus came and s in their midst and	Jn 20:19	*2476*
been shut, and s in their midst and	Jn 20:26	*2476*
breaking, Jesus s on the beach;	Jn 21:4	*2476*
men in white clothing s beside them.	Ac 1:10	*3936*
At this time Peter s up in the	Ac 1:15	*450*
he s upright and *began* to walk;	Ac 3:8	*2476*
they s them before the Council.	Ac 5:27	*2476*
s up in the Council and gave	Ac 5:34	*450*
traveled with him s speechless,	Ac 9:7	*2476*
the widows s beside him,	Ac 9:39	*3936*
s before me in shining garments,	Ac 10:30	*2476*
One of them named Agabus s up	Ac 11:28	*450*
Paul s up, and motioning with	Ac 13:16	*450*
while the disciples s around him,	Ac 14:20	*2944*
Pharisees who had believed s up,	Ac 15:5	*1817*
Peter s up and said to them,	Ac 15:7	*450*
So Paul s in the midst of the	Ac 17:22	*2476*
the scribes of the Pharisaic party s up	Ac 23:9	*450*
the Lord s at his side and said,	Ac 23:11	*2186*
found when I s before the Council,	Ac 24:20	*2476*
down from Jerusalem s around him,	Ac 25:7	*4026*
"When the accusers s up,	Ac 25:18	*2476*
The king s up and the governor	Ac 26:30	*450*
Paul s up in their midst and said,	Ac 27:21	*2476*
and whom I serve s before me,	Ac 27:23	*3936*
EAT AND DRINK, AND S UP TO PLAY."	1Co 10:7	*450*

his face, because he s condemned. Ga 2:11
But the Lord s with me and 2Tm 4:17 3936
angel came and s at the altar, Rv 8:3 2476
them, and they s on their feet; Rv 11:11 2476
And the dragon s before the woman Rv 12:4 2476
dragon s on the sand of the seashore. Rv 13:1 2476
by the sea, s at a distance, Rv 18:17 2476

STOOP
house tremble, and mighty men s, Ec 12:3 5791
and I am not fit to s down and Mk 1:7 2955

STOOPED
They s over, they have bowed down Is 46:2 7164
But Jesus s down and with His Jn 8:6 2955
Again He s down and wrote on Jn 8:8 2634a
she s and looked into the tomb; Jn 20:11 3879

STOOPING
s and looking in, he saw the linen Lk 24:12 3879
and s and looking in, he saw the Jn 20:5 3879

STOOPS
Bel has bowed down, Nebo s over; Is 46:1 7164

STOP
make our sons s fearing the LORD.' Jos 22:25 1115
heavy shower does not s you.'" 1Ki 18:44 6113
tree and s all springs of water, 2Ki 3:19 5640
S! Why should you be struck down? 2Ch 25:16 2308
S for your own sake from 2Ch 35:21 2308
a decree to make these men s *work,* Ezr 4:21 989
and they did not s them until a Ezr 5:5 989
them and put a s to the work." Ne 4:11 7673a
Why should the work s while I Ne 6:3 7673a
Because they s *and* no longer answer? Jb 32:16 5975
here shall your proud waves s'? Jb 38:11 7896
S regarding man, whose breath *of* Is 2:22 2308
s you from playing the harlot, Ezk 16:41 7673a
S your expropriations from My Ezk 45:9 7311
he will put a s to sacrifice and grain Da 9:27 7673a
put a s to his scorn against him; Da 11:18 7673a
"Lord GOD, please s! Am 7:5 2308
Now they are fleeing; "S, stop," Na 2:8 5975
Now they are fleeing; "Stop, s," Na 2:8 5975
"S weeping, for she has not died, Lk 8:52 3361
But Jesus answered and said, "S! Lk 22:51 1439
of Jerusalem, s weeping for Me, Lk 23:28 3361
s making My Father's house a place Jn 2:16 3361
"S clinging to Me, for I have not Jn 20:17 3361
for we cannot s speaking about what we Ac 4:20 3361
And he ordered the chariot to s; Ac 8:38 2476
S depriving one another, except by 1Co 7:5 3361
as you ought, and s sinning; 1Co 15:34 3361
of the elders said to me, "S weeping; Rv 5:5 3361

STOPPED
and they s building the city. Gn 11:8 2308
the Philistines s up by filling them Gn 26:15 5640
for the Philistines had s them up Gn 26:18 5640
Then she s bearing. Gn 29:35 5975
Leah saw that she had s bearing, Gn 30:9 5975
the sea, until he s measuring *it,* Gn 41:49 2308
sun stood still, and the moon s, Jos 10:13 5975
sun s in the middle of the sky and Jos 10:13 5975
him, and they s at the last house. 2Sa 15:17 5975
So they s all the springs of water 2Ki 3:25 5640
not one vessel more." And the oil s. 2Ki 4:6 5975
he struck *it* three times and s. 2Ki 13:18 5975
fortifying Ramah and s his work. 2Ch 16:5 7673a
Then the prophet s and said, 2Ch 25:16 2308
s up all the springs and the stream 2Ch 32:4 5640
who s the upper outlet of the waters 2Ch 32:30 5640
Jews and s them by force of arms. Ezr 4:23 989
and it was s until the second year Ezr 4:24 989
they s at the Gate of the Guard. Ne 12:39 5975
"The princes s talking And put Jb 29:9 6113
of those who speak lies will be s. Ps 63:11 5534a
"But since we s burning sacrifices to Jer 44:18 2308
And *its* many waters were s up, Ezk 31:15 3607
have s giving heed to the LORD. Hos 4:10 5800a
the sea, and the sea s its raging. Jon 1:15 5975
and s their ears from hearing. Zch 7:11 3513
got into the boat, the wind s. Mt 14:32 2869
And Jesus s and called them, and Mt 20:32 2476
boat with them, and the wind s; Mk 6:51 2869
And Jesus s and said, Mk 10:49 2476
and the surging waves, and they s, Lk 8:24 3973
and immediately her hemorrhage s. Lk 8:44 2476
And Jesus s and commanded that he Lk 18:40 2476
Zaccheus s and said to the Lord, Lk 19:8 2476
After they had s speaking, Ac 15:13 4601
the soldiers, they s beating Paul. Ac 21:32 3973
this boasting of mine will not be s 2Co 11:10 5420

STOPPING
pour down unceasingly, Without s, La 3:49 2014

STOPS
a deaf cobra that s up its ear, Ps 58:4 331
ceases, The noise of revelers s, Is 24:8 2308
He who s his ears from hearing Is 33:15 331

STORAGE
they built for Pharaoh s cities, Ex 1:11 4543
the s cities which Solomon had, 1Ki 9:19 4543
s cities which he had built in Hamath 2Ch 8:4 4543
all the s cities that Solomon had, 2Ch 8:6 4543
put *them* in your s vessels, Jer 40:10

STORE
and s up the grain for food in the Gn 41:35 6651
'Is it not laid up in s with Me, Dt 32:34 3647
all that your fathers have laid up in s 2Ki 20:17 686
and all the s cities of Naphtali. 2Ch 16:4 4543
fortresses and s cities in Judah. 2Ch 17:12 4543
Wise men s up knowledge, But with Pr 10:14 6845
all that your fathers have laid up in s Is 39:6 686
the LORD has kept the calamity in s Da 9:14 8245
"Do not s up for yourselves Mt 6:19 2343
"But s up for yourselves treasures Mt 6:20 2343
I have no place to s my crops?' Lk 12:17 4863
I will s all my grain and my goods. Lk 12:18 4863

STORED
Thus Joseph s up grain in great Gn 41:49 6651
of the produce of the vineyards s 1Ch 27:27
the treasures were s in Babylon. Ezr 6:1 5182
the years s up for the ruthless. Jb 15:20 6845
times not s up by the Almighty, Jb 24:1 6845
have s up for those who fear You, Ps 31:19 6845
the wealth of the sinner is s up for Pr 13:22 6845
which they have acquired and s up Is 15:7 6486
it will not be s up or hoarded, Is 23:18 686
Ephraim is bound up; His sin is s up. Hos 13:12 6845
that you have s up your treasure! Jas 5:3 2343

STOREHOUSE
LORD will open for you His good s, Dt 28:12 214
south, and to his sons went the s. 1Ch 26:15 624
daily, and at the s two by two. 1Ch 26:17 624
our God, to the chambers of the s. Ne 10:38 214
"Bring the whole tithe into the s, Mal 3:10 214

STOREHOUSES
then Joseph opened all the s, Gn 41:56 834
Adiel had charge of the king's s. 1Ch 27:25 214
charge of the s in the country, 1Ch 27:25 214
the temple, its buildings, its s, 1Ch 28:11 1597
for the s of the house of God and 1Ch 28:12 214
for the s of the dedicated things; 1Ch 28:12 214
in any manner or concerning the s. 2Ch 8:15 214
s also for the produce of grain, 2Ch 32:28 4543
watch at the s of the gates. Ne 12:25 624
grain, wine and oil into the s. Ne 13:12 214
In charge of the s I appointed Ne 13:13 214
you entered the s of the snow, Jb 38:22 214
have you seen the s of the hail, Jb 38:22 214
He lays up the deeps in s. Ps 33:7 214
brings out the wind from His s. Jer 10:13 214
brings forth the wind from His s. Jer 51:16 214
The s are desolate, The barns are Jl 1:17 214

STOREROOM
king's palace to *a place* beneath the s Jer 38:11 214
they have no s nor barn Lk 12:24 5009

STORES
Joash had charge of the s of oil. 1Ch 27:28 214
officers in them and s of food, 2Ch 11:11 214
over the chambers for the s, Ne 12:44 214
'God s away a man's iniquity for Jb 21:19 6845
He s up sound wisdom for the Pr 2:7 6845
for we have s of wheat, barley, Jer 41:8 4301
"So is the man who s up treasure for Lk 12:21 2343

STORIES
he built s encompassing the walls of 1Ki 6:5 3330b
the s against the whole house, 1Ki 6:10 3330b
The side chambers were in three s, Ezk 41:6
round about their three s, Ezk 41:16
to gallery in three s. Ezk 42:3
For they *were* in three s and had Ezk 42:6

STORING
you are s up wrath for yourself in the Ro 2:5 2343
s up for themselves the treasure 1Tm 6:19 597

STORK
and the s, the heron in its kinds, Lv 11:19 2624
the s, and the heron in their Dt 14:18 2624
And the s, whose home is the fir trees Ps 104:17 2624
s in the sky Knows her seasons; Jer 8:7 2624
had wings like the wings of a s, Zch 5:9 2624

STORM
chaff which the s carries away? Jb 21:18 5492a
And You dissolve me in a s. Jb 30:22 8663
"Out of the south comes the s, Jb 37:9 5492a
LORD answered Job out of the s and Jb 40:6 5591b
And terrify them with Your s. Ps 83:15 5492a
He caused the s to be still, So Ps 107:29 5591b
When your dread comes like a s And Pr 1:27 7584
youth will s against the elder And Is 3:5 7292
protection from the s and the rain. Is 4:6 2230
his distress, A refuge from the s, Is 25:4 2230
Is like a *rain* s *against* a wall. Is 25:4 2230
As a s of hail, a tempest of Is 28:2 2230
a s of mighty overflowing waters, Is 28:2 2230
wind And a shelter from the s, Is 32:2 2230
And the s carries them away like Is 40:24 5591b
away, And the s will scatter them; Is 41:16 5591b
the s of the LORD has gone forth Jer 23:19 5591b
And a great s is being stirred up Jer 25:32 5591a
a s wind was coming from the Ezk 1:4 5591b
go up, you will come like a s; Ezk 38:9 7724b
king of the North will s against him Da 11:40 8175a
And a s on the day of tempest. Am 1:14 5591a
there was a great s on the sea so that Jon 1:4 5591a
this great s *has come* upon you." Jon 1:12 5591a
In whirlwind and s is His way, Na 1:3 8183
"but I scattered them with a s wind Zch 7:14 5590
march in the s winds of the south. Zch 9:14 5591b
The LORD who makes the s clouds; Zch 10:1 2385
there arose a great s on the sea, Mt 8:24 4578
'*There will be* a s today, for the Mt 16:3 5494
and no small s was assailing *us,* Ac 27:20 5494
water and mists driven by a s, 2Pe 2:17 2978

STORMED
They s in to scatter us; Hab 3:14 5590

STORMIER
was becoming *even* s against them. Jon 1:13 5590

STORM-TOSSED
"O afflicted one, s, Is 54:11 5590
day as we were being violently s, Ac 27:18 5492

STORMY
From the s wind *and* tempest." Ps 55:8 5584
He spoke and raised up a s wind, Ps 107:25 5591b
S wind, fulfilling His word; Ps 148:8 5591b
sea was becoming increasingly s. Jon 1:11 5590

STORY
The lowest s *was* five cubits wide, 1Ki 6:6 3330b
by winding stairs to the middle s, 1Ki 6:8
another, and thirty in each s; Ezk 41:6 6471
were wider at each successive s, Ezk 41:7 4605
thus one went up from the lowest s Ezk 41:7
the highest by way of the second s. Ezk 41:7
and this s was widely spread among Mt 28:15 3056

STOUT
disease among his s warriors; Is 10:16 4924a

STOUTEST
And killed some of their s ones, Ps 78:31 4924a

STOUTHEARTED
The s were plundered, Ps 76:5 47, 3820

STOVE
an oven or a s shall be smashed; Lv 11:35 3600

STRAGGLER
And there is no s in his ranks. Is 14:31 909

STRAGGLERS
attacked among you all the s at your Dt 25:18 2826

STRAIGHT
will go up every man s ahead." Jos 6:5 5048
into the city, every man s ahead, Jos 6:20 5048
And the cows took the s way in the 1Sa 6:12 3474
Make Your way s before me. Ps 5:8 3474
He led them also by a s way, Ps 107:7 3477
And He will make your paths s. Pr 3:6 3474
gaze be fixed s in front of you. Pr 4:25 3474
by, Who are making their paths s: Pr 9:15 3474
a man of understanding walks s. Pr 15:21 3474
On a s path in which they will Jer 31:9 3477
farther s ahead to the hill Gareb; Jer 31:39 5048
Their legs were s and their Ezk 1:7 3477
they moved, each went s forward. Ezk 1:9
413, 5676, 6440
And each went s forward; Ezk 1:12
413, 5676, 6440
their wings *were stretched out* s, Ezk 1:23 3477
Each one went s ahead. Ezk 10:22
413, 5676, 6440
he entered but shall go s out. Ezk 46:9 3318
the walls, Each one s before her, Am 4:3 5048
And twist everything that is s, Mi 3:9 3477
OF THE LORD, MAKE HIS PATHS S!'" Mt 3:3 2117
OF THE LORD, MAKE HIS PATHS S.'" Mk 1:3 2117
"Let us go s to Bethlehem then, Lk 2:15 1330
WAY OF THE LORD, MAKE HIS PATHS S. Lk 3:4 2117
THE CROOKED WILL BECOME S, Lk 3:5 2117
'MAKE S THE WAY OF THE LORD,' as Jn 1:23 2116
and go to the street called S, Ac 9:11 2117
crooked the s ways of the Lord? Ac 13:10 2117
we ran a s course to Samothrace, Ac 16:11 2113
we ran a s course to Cos and the Ac 21:1 2113
and make s paths for your feet, so Heb 12:13 3717

STRAIGHTEN
who is able to s what He has bent? Ec 7:13 8626
double, and could not s up at all. Lk 13:11 352b
s up and lift up your heads, Lk 21:28 352b

STRAIGHTENED
What is crooked cannot be s and Ec 1:15 8626
persisted in asking Him, He s up, Jn 8:7 352b

STRAIGHTENING
S up, Jesus said to her, "Woman, Jn 8:10 352b

STRAIGHTFORWARD
are all s to him who understands, Pr 8:9 5228
they were not s about the truth of Ga 2:14 3716

STRAIN
who s out a gnat and swallow a Mt 23:24 1368

STRAINED
have s themselves to no profit. Jer 12:13 2470a

STRAINING
Seeing them s at the oars, for Mk 6:48 928

STRAIT
Israel saw that they were in a s 1Sa 13:6 6862b

STRAND
With a single s of your necklace. SS 4:9 6060

STRANDS
A cord of three s is not quickly Ec 4:12

STRANGE
offer any s incense on this altar, Ex 30:9 2114a
offered s fire before the LORD, Lv 10:1 2114a
they offered s fire before the LORD in Nu 3:4 2114a
offered s fire before the LORD. Nu 26:61 2114a
outside *the family* to a s man. Dt 25:5 2114a
with the s gods of the land, Dt 31:16 5236
"They made Him jealous with s *gods;* Dt 32:16 2114a
Or extended our hands to a s god, Ps 44:20 2114a
"Let there be no s god among you; Ps 81:9 2114a
Jacob from a people of s language, Ps 114:1 3937
To deliver you from the s woman, Pr 2:16 2114a
Your eyes will see s things And Pr 23:33 2114a
them with vine slips of a s *god.* Is 17:10 2114a
And there was no s *god* among you; Is 43:12 2114a
They are regarded as a s thing. Hos 8:12 2114a
seems to be a proclaimer of s deities, Ac 17:18 3581
some s things to our ears; Ac 17:20 3579
"BY MEN OF S TONGUES AND BY THE 1Co 14:21 2084

men not to teach **s** doctrines, 1Tm 1:3 *2085*
away by varied and **s** teachings; Heb 13:9 *3581*
s thing were happening to you; 1Pe 4:12 *3581*
immorality and went after **s** flesh, Jude 1:7 *2087*

STRANGER

am a **s** and a sojourner among you; Gn 23:4 1616
"But if a **s** sojourns with you, Ex 12:48 1616
to the **s** who sojourns among you." Ex 12:49 1616
not wrong a **s** or oppress him, Ex 22:21 1616
"You shall not oppress a **s**, Ex 23:9 1616
know the feelings of a **s**, Ex 23:9 1616
female slave, as well as your **s**, Ex 23:12 1616
them for the needy and for the **s**. Lv 19:10 1616
a **s** resides with you in your land, Lv 19:33 1616
'The **s** who resides with you shall Lv 19:34 1616
for the **s** as well as the native, Lv 24:22 1616
him, like a **s** or a sojourner, Lv 25:35 1616
'Now if the means of a **s** or of a Lv 25:47 1616
to a **s** who is sojourning with you, Lv 25:47 1616
and the **s** and the orphan and the Dt 16:11 1616
the **s** and the orphan and the widow Dt 16:14 1616
give it to the Levite, to the **s**, Dt 26:12 1616
LORD, the **s** as well as the native. Jos 8:33 1616
for the **s** who sojourns among them, Jos 20:9 1616
was no **s** with us in the house, 1Ki 3:18 2114a
and my maids consider me a **s**. Jb 19:15 2114a
For I am a **s** with You, A Ps 39:12 1616
They slay the widow and the **s** And Ps 94:6 1616
I am a **s** in the earth; Ps 119:19 1616
Have given a pledge for a **s**, Pr 6:1 2114a
He who is guarantor for a **s** will surely Pr 11:15 2114a
And a **s** does not share its joy. Pr 14:10 2114a
when he becomes surety for a **s**; Pr 20:16 2114a
A **s**, and not your own lips. Pr 27:2 5237
when he becomes surety for a **s**; Pr 27:13 2114a
Why are You like a **s** in the land Jer 14:8 1616
mistreat *or* do violence to the **s**, Jer 22:3 1616
or the orphan, the **s** or the poor; Zch 7:10 1616
I was a **s**, and you invited Me in; Mt 25:35 *3581*
'And when did we see You a **s**, Mt 25:38 *3581*
I was a **s**, and you did not invite Mt 25:43 *3581*
You hungry, or thirsty, or a **s**, Mt 25:44 *3581*
A **s** they simply will not follow, Jn 10:5 *245*

STRANGER'S

to the descendants of a **s** family, Lv 25:47 1616

STRANGERS

your descendants will be **s** in a land Gn 15:13 1616
you were **s** in the land of Egypt. Ex 22:21 1616
also were **s** in the land of Egypt. Ex 23:9 1616
the **s** who were living among them. Jos 8:35 1616
in number, Very few, and **s** in it, 1Ch 16:19 1481a
For **s** have risen against me And Ps 54:3 2114a
in number, Very few, and **s** in it. Ps 105:12 1481a
And let **s** plunder the product of Ps 109:11 2114a
The LORD protects the **s**; Ps 146:9 1616
s will be filled with your strength Pr 5:10 2114a
alone And not for **s** with you. Pr 5:17 2114a
Your fields—**s** are devouring them Is 1:7 2114a
is desolation, as overthrown by **s**. Is 1:7 2114a
And **s** will eat in the waste places Is 5:17 1481a
then **s** will join them and attach Is 14:1 1616
A palace of **s** is a city no more, Is 25:2 2114a
S will stand and pasture your flocks, Is 61:5 2114a
For I have loved **s**, Jer 2:25 2114a
have scattered your favors to the **s** Jer 3:13 2114a
so you will serve **s** in a land that is Jer 5:19 2114a
and **s** will no longer make them Jer 30:8 2114a
has been turned over to **s**, La 5:2 2114a
and deliver you into the hands of **s** Ezk 11:9 2114a
takes **s** instead of her husband! Ezk 16:32 2114a
behold, I will bring **s** upon you, Ezk 28:7 2114a
uncircumcised By the hand of **s**, Ezk 28:10 2114a
that is in it, By the hand of **s**; Ezk 30:12 2114a
S devour his strength, Yet he does Hos 7:9 2114a
it yield, **s** would swallow it up. Hos 8:7 2114a
s will pass through it no more. Jl 3:17 2114a
day that **s** carried off his wealth, Ob 1:11 2114a
from their sons or from **s**?" Mt 17:25 *245*
When Peter said, "From **s**," Mt 17:26 *245*
Potter's Field as a burial place for **s**. Mt 27:7 *3581*
they do not know the voice of **s**." Jn 10:5 *245*
(Now all the Athenians and the **s** Ac 17:21 *3581*
BY THE LIPS OF **S** I WILL SPEAK TO 1Co 14:21 *2087*
and **s** to the covenants of promise, Eph 2:12 *3581*
you are no longer **s** and aliens, Eph 2:19 *3581*
if she has shown hospitality to **s**, 1Tm 5:10 *3580*
were **s** and exiles on the earth. Heb 11:13 *3581*
neglect to show hospitality to **s**, Heb 13:2 *5381*
I urge you as aliens and **s** to abstain 1Pe 2:11 *3927*
and especially *when they are* **s**; 3Jn 1:5 *3581*

STRANGLED

his house in order, and **s** himself; 2Sa 17:23 2614
and from what is **s** and from blood. Ac 15:20 *4156*
from things **s** and from fornication; Ac 15:29 *4156*
from what is **s** and from fornication. Ac 21:25 *4156*

STRAP

undone, Nor its sandal **s** broken. Is 5:27 8288

STRATEGIC

A **s** day came when Herod on his Mk 6:21 *2121*

STRATEGY

And I will confound their **s**, Is 19:3 6098

STRAW

"We have plenty of both **s** and feed, Gn 24:25 8401
he gave **s** and feed to the camels, Gn 24:32 8401
to give the people **s** to make brick Ex 5:7 8401
go and gather **s** for themselves. Ex 5:7 8401
'I am not going to give you *any* **s**. Ex 5:10 8401
'You go *and* get **s** for yourselves Ex 5:11 8401
of Egypt to gather stubble for **s**. Ex 5:12 8401
amount, just as when you had **s**." Ex 5:13 8401
is no **s** given to your servants, Ex 5:16 8401
for you will be given no **s**, Ex 5:18 8401
both **s** and fodder for our donkeys, Jg 19:19 8401
s for the horses and swift steeds to 1Ki 4:28 8401
"Are they as **s** before the wind, Jb 21:18 8401
"He regards iron as **s**, Jb 41:27 8401
the lion will eat **s** like the ox. Is 11:7 8401
As **s** is trodden down in the water of Is 25:10 4963
the lion will eat **s** like the ox; Is 65:25 8401
drifting **s** To the desert wind. Jer 13:24 7179
s have *in common* with grain?" Jer 23:28 8401
precious stones, wood, hay, **s**, 1Co 3:12 *2562*

STRAY

her ways, Do not **s** into her paths. Pr 7:25 8582
s from the words of knowledge. Pr 19:27 7686
You cause us to **s** from Your ways And Is 63:17 8582
house of Israel may no longer **s** from Ezk 14:11 8582

STRAYED

to them, for they have **s** from Me! Hos 7:13 5074

STRAYING

ox or his sheep **s** away, Dt 22:1 5080
and search for the one that is **s**? Mt 18:12 *4105*
For some men, **s** from these things, 1Tm 1:6 *795*
you were continually **s** like sheep, 1Pe 2:25 *4105*

STRAYS

if any among you **s** from the truth and Jas 5:19 *4105*

STREAM

them and sent them across the **s**. Gn 32:23 5158a
stopped up all the springs and the **s** 2Ch 32:4 5158a
The **s** of God is full of water; Ps 65:9 6388
The **s** would have swept over our Ps 124:4 5158a
And all the nations will **s** to it. Is 2:2 5102a
from the flowing **s** of the Euphrates Is 27:12 7642b
For He will come like a rushing **s** Is 59:19 5104
the nations like an overflowing **s**; Is 66:12 5158a
indeed be to me like a deceptive **s** Jer 15:18
That extends its roots by a **s** And Jer 17:8 3105
nations will no longer **s** to him. Jer 51:44 5102a
like an ever-flowing **s**. Am 5:24 5158a
And the peoples will **s** to it. Mi 4:1 5102a

STREAMS

over their rivers, over their **s**, Ex 7:19 2975
over the **s** and over the pools, Ex 8:5 2975
"He does not look at the **s**, Jb 20:17 6390
"He dams up the **s** from flowing, Jb 28:11 5104
rock poured out for me **s** of oil! Jb 29:6 6388
tree *firmly* planted by **s** of water, Ps 1:3 6388
whose **s** make glad the city of God, Ps 46:4 6388
You dried up ever-flowing **s**. Ps 74:15 5104
brought forth **s** also from the rock Ps 78:16 5140
out, And **s** were overflowing; Ps 78:20 5158a
And their **s**, they could not drink. Ps 78:44 5140
My eyes shed **s** of water, Because Ps 119:136 6388
O LORD, As the **s** in the South. Ps 126:4 650
abroad, **S** of water in the streets? Pr 5:16 6388
And **s** *flowing* from Lebanon." SS 4:15 5140
are like doves Beside **s** of water, SS 5:12 650
He will strike it into seven **s** And Is 11:15 5158a
The **s** of Egypt will thin out and Is 19:6 2975
and on every high hill there will be **s** Is 30:25 6388
Like **s** of water in a dry country, Is 32:2 6388
Its **s** will be turned into pitch, Is 34:9 5158a
wilderness And **s** in the Arabah. Is 35:6 5158a
land And **s** on the dry ground; Is 44:3 5140
grass Like poplars by **s** of water.' Is 44:4 2988
make them walk by **s** of waters, Jer 31:9 5158a
My eyes run down with **s** of water La 3:48 6388
the mountains of Israel, by the **s**, Ezk 34:13 650

STREET

doors of your house into the **s**, Jos 2:19 2351
he and Samuel went out into the **s**. 1Sa 9:26 2351
who see me in the **s** flee from me. Ps 31:11 2351
Wisdom shouts in the **s**, Pr 1:20 2351
through the **s** near her corner; Pr 7:8 7784
and the doors on the **s** are shut as Ec 12:4 7784
while mourners go about in the **s**. Ec 12:5 7784
Nor make His voice heard in the **s**. Is 42:2 2351
helpless at the head of every **s**, Is 51:20 2351
s for those who walk over *it*." Is 51:23 2351
For truth has stumbled in the **s**, Is 59:14 7339
Pour *it* out on the children in the **s** Jer 6:11 2351
of bread daily from the bakers' **s**, Jer 37:21 2351
In the **s** the sword slays; La 1:20 2351
hunger At the head of every **s**." La 2:19 2351
out At the corner of every **s**. La 4:1 2351
high place at the top of every **s** and Ezk 16:25 1870
shrine at the beginning of every **s** and Ezk 16:31 1870
to pieces At the head of every **s**; Na 3:10 2351
synagogues and on the **s** corners so Mt 6:5 *4116*
tied at the door, outside in the **s**; Mk 11:4 *296*
and go to the **s** called Straight, Ac 9:11 *4505*
went out and went along one **s**, Ac 12:10 *4505*
And their dead bodies *will lie* in the **s** Rv 11:8 *4116*
the **s** of the city was pure gold, Rv 21:21 *4116*
in the middle of its **s**. Rv 22:2 *4116*

STREETS

Proclaim it not in the **s** of Ashkelon, 2Sa 1:20 2351
stamped them as the mire of the **s**. 2Sa 22:43 2351
make **s** for yourself in Damascus, 1Ki 20:34 2351
them out as the mire of the **s**. Ps 18:42 2351
deceit do not depart from her **s**. Ps 55:11 7339
Let there be no outcry in our **s**! Ps 144:14 7339
At the head of the noisy **s** she Pr 1:21
abroad, Streams of water in the **s**? Pr 5:16 7339
She is now in the **s**, Pr 7:12 2351
I will be killed in the **s**!" Pr 22:13 7339
In the **s** and in the squares I must SS 3:2 7784
refuse in the middle of the **s**. Is 5:25 2351
them down like mud in the **s**. Is 10:6 2351
In their **s** they have girded Is 15:3 2351
There is an outcry in the **s** Is 24:11 2351
their brave men cry in the **s**, Is 33:7 2351
restorer of the **s** in which to dwell. Is 58:12 5410b
fro through the **s** of Jerusalem, Jer 5:1 2351
Judah and in the **s** of Jerusalem? Jer 7:17 2351
from the **s** of Jerusalem the voice of Jer 7:34 2351
cut off the children from the **s**, Jer 9:21 2351
Judah and in the **s** of Jerusalem, Jer 11:6 2351
and as many as the **s** of Jerusalem Jer 11:13 2351
thrown out into the **s** of Jerusalem Jer 14:16 2351
in the **s** of Jerusalem that are desolate Jer 33:10 2351
Judah and in the **s** of Jerusalem, Jer 44:6 2351
Judah and in the **s** of Jerusalem? Jer 44:9 2351
Judah and in the **s** of Jerusalem; Jer 44:17 2351
Judah and in the **s** of Jerusalem, Jer 44:21 2351
and in its **s** there is lamentation Jer 48:38 7339
her young men will fall in her **s**, Jer 49:26 7339
her young men will fall in her **s**, Jer 50:30 7339
And pierced through in their **s**." Jer 51:4 2351
infants faint In the **s** of the city. La 2:11 7339
wounded man In the **s** of the city, La 2:12 7339
On the ground in the **s** Lie young La 2:21 2351
delicacies Are desolate in the **s**; La 4:5 2351
They are not recognized in the **s**; La 4:8 2351
They wandered, blind, in the **s**; La 4:14 2351
that we could not walk in our **s**; La 4:18 7339
fling their silver into the **s** and Ezk 7:19 2351
city, filling its **s** with them." Ezk 11:6 2351
horses he will trample all your **s**. Ezk 26:11 2351
to her And blood to her **s**, Ezk 28:23 2351
plazas, And in all the **s** they say, Am 5:16 2351
trampled down Like mire of the **s**. Mi 7:10 2351
The chariots race madly in the **s**, Na 2:4 2351
I have made their **s** desolate, Zph 3:6 2351
again sit in the **s** of Jerusalem, Zch 8:4 7339
'And the **s** of the city will be Zch 8:5 7339
boys and girls playing in its **s**.' Zch 8:5 7339
And gold like the mire of the **s**. Zch 9:3 2351
in the mire of the **s** in battle; Zch 10:5 2351
do in the synagogues and in the **s**, Mt 6:2 *4505*
ANYONE HEAR HIS VOICE IN THE **S**. Mt 12:19 *4116*
Those slaves went out into the **s** Mt 22:10 *3598*
you, go out into its **s** and say, Lk 10:10 *4116*
and You taught in our **s** Lk 13:26 *4116*
'Go out at once into the **s** and Lk 14:21 *4116*
carried the sick out into the **s** and Ac 5:15 *4116*

STRENGTH

no longer yield its **s** to you; Gn 4:12 3581b
served your father with all my **s**. Gn 31:6 3581b
Israel collected his **s** and sat up in Gn 48:2 2388
might and the beginning of my **s**, Gn 49:3 202
"The LORD is my **s** and song, And Ex 15:2 5797
In Your **s** You have guided *them* to Ex 15:13 5797
'Your **s** will be spent uselessly, Lv 26:20 3581b
and you will have *no* **s** to stand Lv 26:37 8617
for by Your **s** You brought up Nu 14:13 3581b
'My power and the **s** of my hand Dt 8:17 6108
for he is the beginning of his **s**; Dt 21:17 202
When He sees that *their* **s** is gone, Dt 32:36 3027
as my **s** was then, so my strength is Jos 14:11 3581b
strength was then, so my **s** is now, Jos 14:11 3581b
O my soul, march on with **s**. Jg 5:21 5797
"Go in this your **s** and deliver Jg 6:14 3581b
for as the man, so is his **s**." Jg 8:21 1369
his **s** returned and he revived. Jg 15:19 7307
and see where his great **s** *lies* and Jg 16:5 3581b
"Please tell me where your great **s** is Jg 16:6 3581b
So his **s** was not discovered. Jg 16:9 3581b
told me where your great **s** is." Jg 16:15 3581b
then my **s** will leave me and I Jg 16:17 3581b
afflict him, and his **s** left him. Jg 16:19 3581b
But the feeble gird on **s**. 1Sa 2:4 2428
And He will give **s** to His king, 1Sa 2:10 5797
I will break your **s** and the strength 1Sa 2:31 2220
will break your strength and the **s** of 1Sa 2:31 2220
also there was no **s** in him, 1Sa 28:20 3581b
have **s** when you go on *your* way." 1Sa 28:22 3581b
there was no **s** in them to weep. 1Sa 30:4 3581b
have girded me with **s** for battle; 2Sa 22:40 2428
and went in the **s** of that food 1Ki 19:8 3581b
Jehu drew his bow with his full **s** 2Ki 9:24 3027
'I have counsel and **s** for the war.' 2Ki 18:20 1369
and there is no **s** to *deliver*. 2Ki 19:3 3581b
their inhabitants were short of **s**, 2Ki 19:26 3027
Seek the LORD and His **s**; 1Ch 16:11 5797
Him, **S** and joy are in His place. 1Ch 16:27 5797
Ascribe to the LORD glory and **s**. 1Ch 16:28 5797
able men with **s** for the service, 1Ch 26:8 3581b
recover **s** in the days of Abijah; 2Ch 13:20 3581b
powerful and those who have no **s**; 2Ch 14:11 3581b
"The **s** of the burden bearers is Ne 4:10 3581b
the joy of the LORD is your **s**." Ne 8:10 4581
of his authority and **s**, Es 10:2 1369
"What is my **s**, that I should wait? Jb 6:11 3581b
"Is my **s** the strength of stones, Jb 6:12 3581b
"Is my strength the **s** of stones, Jb 6:12 3581b
"Wise in heart and mighty in **s**, Jb 9:4 3581b
"With Him are **s** and sound wisdom, Jb 12:16 5797
"His **s** is famished, And calamity Jb 18:12 202
"One dies in his full **s**, Jb 21:23 6106
And the **s** of the orphans has been Jb 22:9 2220
you have saved the arm without **s**! Jb 26:2 5797
was the **s** of their hands to me? Jb 30:2 3581b

is mighty in **s** of understanding. **Jb 36:5** 3581b
Or all the forces of *your* **s**? **Jb 36:19** 3581b
"Will you trust him because his **s** **Jb 39:11** 3581b
the valley, and rejoices in *his* **s**; **Jb 39:21** 3581b
"Behold now, his **s** in his loins And **Jb 40:16** 3581b
his limbs, Or his mighty **s**, **Jb 41:12** 1369
"In his neck lodges **s**, **Jb 41:22** 5797
babes You have established **s** Because **Ps 8:2** 5797
"I love You, O LORD, my **s**." **Ps 18:1** 2391
The God who girds me with **s** And **Ps 18:32** 2428
have girded me with **s** for battle; **Ps 18:39** 2428
the saving **s** of His right hand. **Ps 20:6** 1369
in Your **s** the king will be glad, **Ps 21:1** 5797
Be exalted, O LORD, in Your **s**; **Ps 21:13** 5797
My **s** is dried up like a potsherd, **Ps 22:15** 3581b
The LORD is my **s** and my shield; **Ps 28:7** 5797
The LORD is their **s**, **Ps 28:8** 5797
Ascribe to the LORD glory and **s**. **Ps 29:1** 5797
LORD will give **s** to His people; **Ps 29:11** 5797
Be to me a rock of **s**, **Ps 31:2** 4581
For You are my **s**. **Ps 31:4** 4581
My **s** has failed because of my **Ps 31:10** 3581b
A warrior is not delivered by great **s**. **Ps 33:16** 3581b
it deliver anyone by its great **s**. **Ps 33:17** 2428
He is their **s** in time of trouble. **Ps 37:39** 4581
My heart throbs, my **s** fails me; **Ps 38:10** 3581b
For You are the God of my **s**; **Ps 43:2** 4581
God is our refuge and **s**, **Ps 46:1** 5797
Because of his **S** I will watch for **Ps 59:9** 5797
as for me, I shall sing of Your **s**; **Ps 59:16** 5797
O my **s**, I will sing praises to **Ps 59:17** 5797
A tower of **s** against the enemy. **Ps 61:3** 5797
The rock of my **s**, my refuge is in **Ps 62:7** 5797
establishes the mountains by His **s**, **Ps 65:6** 3581b
Your God has commanded your **s**; **Ps 68:28** 5797
Ascribe **s** to God; **Ps 68:34** 5797
Israel And His **s** is in the skies. **Ps 68:34** 5797
gives **s** and power to the people. **Ps 68:35** 5797
Do not forsake me when my **s** fails. **Ps 71:9** 3581b
declare Your **s** to *this* generation, **Ps 71:18** 2220
But God is the **s** of my heart and **Ps 73:26** 6697
divided the sea by Your **s**; **Ps 74:13** 5797
You have made known Your **s** **Ps 77:14** 5797
And His **s** and His wondrous works **Ps 78:4** 5807
And gave up His **s** to captivity And **Ps 78:61** 5797
Sing for joy to God our **s**; **Ps 81:1** 5797
is the man whose **s** is in You, **Ps 84:5** 5797
They go from **s** to strength, *Every* **Ps 84:7** 2428
They go from strength to **s**, **Ps 84:7** 2428
Oh grant Your **s** to Your servant, And **Ps 86:16** 5797
have become like a man without **s**, **Ps 88:4** 353
For You are the glory of their **s**, **Ps 89:17** 5797
seventy years, Or if due to **s**, **Ps 90:10** 1369
clothed and girded Himself with **s**; **Ps 93:1** 5797
S and beauty are in His sanctuary. **Ps 96:6** 5797
Ascribe to the LORD glory and **s**. **Ps 96:7** 5797
The **s** of the King loves justice; **Ps 99:4** 5797
He has weakened my **s** in the way; **Ps 102:23** 3581b
LORD, you His angels, Mighty in **s**, **Ps 103:20** 3581b
Seek the LORD and His **s**; **Ps 105:4** 5797
The LORD is my **s** and song, And He **Ps 118:14** 5797
You and the ark of Your **s**. **Ps 132:8** 5797
made me bold with **s** in my soul. **Ps 138:3** 5797
the Lord, the **s** of my salvation, **Ps 140:7** 5797
is our Lord and abundant in **s**; **Ps 147:5** 3581b
not delight in the **s** of the horse; **Ps 147:10** 1369
strangers will be filled with your **s** **Pr 5:10** 3581b
revenue *comes* by the **s** of the ox. **Pr 14:4** 3581b
The glory of young men is their **s**, **Pr 20:29** 3581b
of distress, Your **s** is limited. **Pr 24:10** 3581b
Do not give your **s** to women, **Pr 31:3** 2428
She girds herself with **s** And **Pr 31:17** 5797
S and dignity are her clothing, **Pr 31:25** 5797
"Wisdom is better than **s**." **Ec 9:16** 1369
edge, then he must exert more **s**. **Ec 10:10** 2428
for **s** and not for drunkenness. **Ec 10:17** 1369
The spirit of counsel and **s**, **Is 11:2** 1369
For the LORD GOD is my **s** and song, **Is 12:2** 5797
A **s** to those who repel the **Is 28:6** 1369
In quietness and trust is your **s**." **Is 30:15** 1369
Be their **s** every morning, Our **Is 33:2** 2220
'Your counsel and **s** for the war **Is 36:5** 1369
and there is no **s** to deliver. **Is 37:3** 3581b
their inhabitants were short of **s**, **Is 37:27** 3027
of His might and the **s** of *His* power **Is 40:26** 533
He gives **s** to the weary, And to **Is 40:29** 3581b
wait for the LORD Will gain new **s**; **Is 40:31** 3581b
And let the peoples gain new **s**; **Is 41:1** 3581b
also gets hungry and his **s** fails; **Is 44:12** 3581b
in the LORD are righteousness and **s**. **Is 45:24** 5797
spent My **s** for nothing and vanity; **Is 49:4** 3581b
of the LORD, And My God is My **s**), **Is 49:5** 5797
Awake, awake, put on **s**, **Is 51:9** 5797
awake, Clothe yourself in your **s**, **Is 52:1** 5797
You found renewed **s**, **Is 57:10** 3027
places, And give **s** to your bones; **Is 58:11** 2502b
Marching in the greatness of His **s**? **Is 63:1** 3581b
O LORD, my **s** and my stronghold, **Jer 16:19** 5797
in mankind And makes flesh his **s**, **Jer 17:5** 2220
The fugitives stand without **s**; **Jer 48:45** 3581b
Their **s** is exhausted, They are **Jer 51:30** 1369
fled without **s** Before the pursuer. **La 1:6** 3581b
He has made my **s** fail. **La 1:14** 3581b
to restore their **s** themselves. **La 1:19** 5315
has cut off All the **s** of Israel; **La 2:3** 7161
"My **s** has perished, And *so has* my **La 3:18** 5331
And neither by great **s** nor by many **Ezk 17:9** 2220
and those who were its **s** lived **Ezk 31:17** 2220
the kingdom, the power, the **s** and **Da 2:37** 8632b
the ram had no **s** to withstand him. **Da 8:7** 3581b
yet no **s** was left in me, for my **Da 10:8** 3581b
pallor, and I retained no **s**. **Da 10:8** 3581b
upon me, and I have retained no **s**. **Da 10:16** 3581b
there remains just now no **s** in me, **Da 10:17** 3581b
to me, I received **s** and said, **Da 10:19** 2388
with them and display *great* **s**. **Da 11:7** 2388
will be no **s** to make a stand. **Da 11:15** 3581b
"He will stir up his **s** and **Da 11:25** 3581b
will display **s** and take action. **Da 11:32** 2388
Strangers devour his **s**, **Hos 7:9** 3581b
Will pull down your **s** from you And **Am 3:11** 5797
"Have we not by our *own* **s** taken **Am 6:13** 2392
His flock In the **s** of the LORD, **Mi 5:4** 5797
"Though they are at full **s** **Na 1:12**
your back, summon all *your* **s**. **Na 2:1** 3581b
They whose **s** is their god." **Hab 1:11** 3581b
The Lord GOD is my **s**, **Hab 3:19** 2428
YOUR MIND, AND WITH ALL YOUR **S**.' **Mk 12:30** *2479*
UNDERSTANDING AND WITH ALL THE **S**, **Mk 12:33** *2479*
YOUR SOUL, AND WITH ALL YOUR **S**, **Lk 10:27** *2479*
praying that you may have **s** **Lk 21:36** *2729*
But Saul kept increasing in **s** and **Ac 9:22** *1743*
who had no **s** in his feet, **Ac 14:8** *102*
the weaknesses of those without **s** **Ro 15:1** *102*
burdened excessively, beyond our **s**, **2Co 1:8** *1411*
the working of the **s** of His might **Eph 1:19** *2904*
Lord and in the **s** of His might. **Eph 6:10** *2904*
serving by the **s** which God supplies; **1Pe 4:11** *2479*
was like the sun shining in its **s**. **Rv 1:16** *1411*
which is mixed in full **s** in the cup **Rv 14:10** *194*

STRENGTHEN

and encourage him and **s** him, **Dt 3:28** 553
me and please **s** me just this time, **Jg 16:28** 2388
s yourself and observe and see **1Ki 20:22** 2388
to **s** the kingdom under his rule. **2Ki 15:19** 2388
to make great and to **s** everyone. **1Ch 29:12** 2388
But now, *O God,* **s** my hands. **Ne 6:9** 2388
"I could **s** you with my mouth, And **Jb 16:5** 553
You will **s** their heart, You will **Ps 10:17** 3559
My arm also will **s** him. **Ps 89:21** 553
S me according to Your word. **Ps 119:28** 6965
the exhausted, and **s** the feeble. **Is 35:3** 553
I will **s** you, surely I will help **Is 41:10** 553
your cords And **s** your pegs. **Is 54:2** 2388
And they **s** the hands of evildoers, **Jer 23:14** 2388
'For I will **s** the arms of the king **Ezk 30:24** 2388
'Thus I will **s** the arms of the **Ezk 30:25** 2388
bind up the broken and **s** the sick; **Ezk 34:16** 2388
the stalwart will not **s** his power, **Am 2:14** 553
S your back, summon all *your* **Na 2:1** 2388
S your fortifications! **Na 3:14** 2388
"I will **s** the house of Judah, **Zch 10:6** 1396
"And I will **s** them in the LORD, **Zch 10:12** 1396
turned again, **s** your brothers." **Lk 22:32** *4741*
to **s** and encourage you as to your **1Th 3:2** *4741*
comfort and **s** your hearts in every **2Th 2:17** *4741*
and He will **s** and protect you from **2Th 3:3** *4741*
s the hands that are weak and the **Heb 12:12** *461*
s your hearts, for the coming of **Jas 5:8** *4741*
confirm, **s** *and* establish you. **1Pe 5:10** *4599*
up, and **s** the things that remain, **Rv 3:2** *4741*

STRENGTHENED

So the LORD **s** Eglon the king of **Jg 3:12** 2388
and afterward your hands will be **s** **Jg 7:11** 2388
who **s** his hands to kill his **Jg 9:24** 2388
David **s** himself in the LORD his God **1Sa 30:6** 2388
who are with you will also be **s**." **2Sa 16:21** 2388
He also **s** the fortresses and put **2Ch 11:11** 2388
in every city and **s** them greatly. **2Ch 11:12** 2388
They **s** the kingdom of Judah **2Ch 11:17** 2388
Rehoboam **s** himself in Jerusalem and **2Ch 12:13** 2388
seventh year Jehoiada **s** himself, **2Ch 23:1** 2388
to its specifications and **s** it. **2Ch 24:13** 553
Now Amaziah **s** himself and led his **2Ch 25:11** 2388
and **s** the Millo *in* the city of **2Ch 32:5** 2388
Thus I was **s** according to the hand **Ezr 7:28** 2388
many, And you have **s** weak hands. **Jb 4:3** 2388
And you have **s** feeble knees. **Jb 4:4** 553
son whom You have **s** for Yourself. **Ps 80:15** 553
He has **s** the bars of your gates; **Ps 147:13** 2388
who are sickly you have not **s**, **Ezk 34:4** 2388
touched me again and **s** me. **Da 10:18** 2388
lord speak, for you have **s** me." **Da 10:19** 2388
I trained *and* **s** their arms, **Hos 7:15** 2388
his feet and his ankles were **s**. **Ac 3:7** *4732*
name of Jesus which has **s** this man **Ac 3:16** *4732*
and he took food and was **s**. **Ac 9:19** *1765*
encouraged and **s** the brethren with **Ac 15:32** *1991*
were being **s** in the faith, **Ac 16:5** *4732*
be **s** to eat things sacrificed to **1Co 8:10** *3618*
to be **s** with power through His **Eph 3:16** *2901*
s with all power, according to His **Col 1:11** *1412*
Jesus our Lord, who has **s** me, **1Tm 1:12** *1743*
the Lord stood with me and **s** me, **2Tm 4:17** *1743*
for the heart to be **s** by grace, **Heb 13:9** *950*

STRENGTHENING

afflicted him instead of **s** him. **2Ch 28:20** 2388
heaven appeared to Him, **s** Him. **Lk 22:43** *1765*
s the souls of the disciples, **Ac 14:22** *1991*
Syria and Cilicia, **s** the churches. **Ac 15:41** *1991*
and Phrygia, **s** all the disciples. **Ac 18:23** *4741*

STRENGTHENS

Wisdom **s** a wise man more than ten **Ec 7:19** 5810
all things through Him who **s** me. **Php 4:13** *1743*

STRETCH

and now, he might **s** out his hand, **Gn 3:22** 7971
s out your hand against the lad, **Gn 22:12** 7971
"So I will **s** out My hand and **Ex 3:20** 7971
"**S** out your hand and grasp *it* by **Ex 4:4** 7971
when I **s** out My hand on Egypt and **Ex 7:5** 5186
s out your hand over the waters of **Ex 7:19** 5186
'**S** out your hand with your staff **Ex 8:5** 5186
'**S** out your staff and strike the **Ex 8:16** 5186
"**S** out your hand toward the sky, **Ex 9:22** 5186
"**S** out your hand over the land of **Ex 10:12** 5186
"**S** out your hand toward the sky, **Ex 10:21** 5186
s out your hand over the sea and **Ex 14:16** 5186
"**S** out your hand over the sea so **Ex 14:26** 5186
Yet He did not **s** out His hand **Ex 24:11** 7971
"Like valleys that **s** out, **Nu 24:6** 5186
"**S** out the javelin that is in **Jos 8:18** 5186
to **s** out my hand against him, **1Sa 24:6** 7971
not **s** out my hand against my lord, **1Sa 24:10** 7971
for who can **s** out his hand against **1Sa 26:9** 7971
that I should **s** out my hand against **1Sa 26:11** 7971
but I refused to **s** out my hand **1Sa 26:23** 7971
How is it you were not afraid to **s** out **2Sa 1:14** 7971
'I will **s** over Jerusalem the **2Ki 21:13** 5186
in a heap of ruins **s** out *his* hand, **Jb 30:24** 7971
quickly **s** out her hands to God. **Ps 68:31** 7323
The LORD will **s** forth Your strong **Ps 110:2** 7971
You will **s** forth Your hand against **Ps 138:7** 7971
I **s** out my hands to You; **Ps 143:6** 6566
S forth Your hand from on high; **Ps 144:7** 7971
is too short on which to **s** out, **Is 28:20** 8311
So the LORD will **s** out His hand, **Is 31:3** 5186
And He will **s** over it the line of **Is 34:11** 5186
S out the curtains of your **Is 54:2** 5186
For I will **s** out My hand Against **Jer 6:12** 5186
There is no one to **s** out my tent **Jer 10:20** 5186
So I will **s** out My hand against **Jer 15:6** 5186
I will **s** out My hand against you, **Jer 51:25** 5186
I will **s** out My hand against them **Ezk 6:14** 5186
and I will **s** out My hand against **Ezk 14:9** 5186
and I **s** out My hand against it, **Ezk 14:13** 5186
"I will also **s** out My hand **Ezk 25:13** 5186
I will **s** out My hand against the **Ezk 25:16** 5186
I will **s** out My hand against you And **Ezk 35:3** 5186
"Then he will **s** out his hand **Da 11:42** 7971
they **s** out beside every altar, **Am 2:8** 5186
"So I will **s** out My hand against **Zph 1:4** 5186
And He will **s** out His hand against **Zph 2:13** 5186
"**S** out your hand!" **Mt 12:13** *1614*
"**S** out your hand." **Mk 3:5** *1614*
"**S** out your hand!" **Lk 6:10** *1614*
old, you will **s** out your hands and **Jn 21:18** *1614*

STRETCHED

Abraham **s** out his hand and **Gn 22:10** 7971
But Israel **s** out his right hand **Gn 48:14** 7971
he **s** out his hand and caught it, **Ex 4:4** 7971
So Aaron **s** out his hand over the **Ex 8:6** 5186
Aaron **s** out his hand with his staff, **Ex 8:17** 5186
Moses **s** out his staff toward the sky, **Ex 9:23** 5186
So Moses **s** out his staff over the **Ex 10:13** 5186
Moses **s** out his hand toward the sky **Ex 10:22** 5186
Moses **s** out his hand over the sea; **Ex 14:21** 5186
Moses **s** out his hand over the sea, **Ex 14:27** 5186
"You **s** out Your right hand, **Ex 15:12** 5186
So Joshua **s** out the javelin that **Jos 8:18** 5186
and when he had **s** out his hand, **Jos 8:19** 5186
hand with which he **s** out the javelin **Jos 8:26** 5186
Ehud **s** out his left hand, took **Jg 3:21** 7971
When the angel **s** out his hand **2Sa 24:16** 7971
Jeroboam **s** out his hand from the **1Ki 13:4** 7971
his hand which he **s** out against him **1Ki 13:4** 7971
Then he **s** himself upon the child **1Ki 17:21** 4058
hands, and he **s** himself on him; **2Ki 4:34** 1457
and went up and **s** himself on him; **2Ki 4:35** 1457
in his hand **s** out over Jerusalem. **1Ch 21:16** 5186
s out my hands to the LORD my **Ezr 9:5** 6566
because he had **s** out his hands **Es 8:7** 7971
he has **s** out his hand against God **Jb 15:25** 5186
Or who **s** the line on it? **Jb 38:5** 5186
hand was **s** out without weariness; **Ps 77:2** 5064
I **s** out my hand and no one paid **Pr 1:24** 5186
And He has **s** out His hand against **Is 5:25** 5186
But His hand is still **s** out. **Is 5:25** 5186
away And His hand is still **s** out. **Is 9:12** 5186
away And His hand is still **s** out. **Is 9:17** 5186
away And His hand is still **s** out. **Is 9:21** 5186
away And His hand is still **s** out. **Is 10:4** 5186
is **s** out against all the nations. **Is 14:26** 5186
He has **s** His hand out over the sea, **Is 23:11** 5186
veil which is **s** over all nations. **Is 25:7** 5259
created the heavens and **s** them out, **Is 42:5** 5186
I **s** out the heavens with My hands **Is 45:12** 5186
your Maker, Who **s** out the **Is 51:13** 5186
Then the LORD **s** out His hand and **Jer 1:9** 7971
He has **s** out the heavens. **Jer 10:12** 5186
Your tendrils **s** across the sea, **Jer 48:32** 5674a
He **s** out the heavens. **Jer 51:15** 5186
The adversary has **s** out his hand **La 1:10** 6566
He has **s** out a line, He has not **La 2:8** 5186
the expanse their wings *were* **s** *out* **Ezk 1:23**
He **s** out the form of a hand **Ezk 8:3** 7971
Then the cherub **s** out his hand **Ezk 10:7** 7971
I have **s** out My hand against you **Ezk 16:27** 5186
I have **s** out My hand against you and **Ezk 25:7** 5186
He **s** out his hand with scoffers, **Hos 7:5** 4900
line will be **s** over Jerusalem." **Zch 1:16** 5186
Jesus **s** out His hand and touched him, **Mt 8:3** *1614*
He **s** it out, and it was **Mt 12:13** *1614*
Immediately Jesus **s** out His hand **Mt 14:31** *1614*
compassion, Jesus **s** out His hand **Mk 1:41** *1614*
And he **s** it out, and his hand was **Mk 3:5** *1614*
And He **s** out His hand and touched **Lk 5:13** *1614*

when they **s** him out with thongs, Ac 22:25 *4385*
Then Paul **s** out his hand and Ac 26:1 *1614*
DAY LONG I HAVE **S** OUT MY HANDS Ro 10:21 *1600b*

STRETCHED-OUT
And as for His **s** hand, who can Is 14:27 5186

STRETCHER
down through the tiles with his **s**, Lk 5:19 *2826*
and pick up your **s** and go home." Lk 5:24 *2826*

STRETCHES
to Rimmon which **s** to Neah. Jos 19:13 8388a
Who alone **s** out the heavens And Jb 9:8 5186
"He **s** out the north over empty Jb 26:7 5186
She **s** out her hands to the distaff, Pr 31:19 7971
she **s** out her hands to the needy. Pr 31:20 7971
Who **s** out the heavens like a Is 40:22 5186
Zion **s** out her hands; La 1:17 6566
he **s** it out against the land of Egypt. Ezk 30:25 5186
the LORD who **s** out the heavens, Zch 12:1 5186

STRETCHING
S his wings toward the south? Jb 39:26 6566
S out heaven like a *tent* curtain. Ps 104:2 5186
S out the heavens by Myself And Is 44:24 5186
for breath, **S** out her hands, Jer 4:31 6566
will have no one **s** a measuring line Mi 2:5 7993
And **s** out His hand toward His Mt 12:49 *1614*

STRICKEN
For I have been **s** all day long And Ps 73:14 5060
Where will you be **s** again, Is 1:5 5221
As those who are utterly **s**. Is 16:7 5218a
Yet we ourselves esteemed Him **s**, Is 53:4 5060
Why have You **s** us so that we are Jer 14:19 5221
being **s** For lack of the fruits of La 4:9 1856
Ephraim is **s**, their root is dried Hos 9:16 5221

STRICT
And He gave them **s** orders that no Mk 5:43 *4183*
"We gave you **s** orders not to Ac 5:28 *3852*

STRICTER
such we will incur a **s** judgment. Jas 3:1 *3173*

STRICTEST
to the **s** sect of our religion. Ac 26:5 *198a*

STRICTLY
father **s** put the people under oath, 1Sa 14:28 7650
judgment be executed upon him **s**, Ezr 7:26 629
s according to the law of our fathers Ac 22:3 *195*

STRIDE
"His vigorous **s** is shortened, And Jb 18:7 6806

STRIFE
s between the herdsmen of Abram's Gn 13:7 7379
there be no **s** between you and me, Gn 13:8 4808
during the **s** of the congregation, Nu 27:14 4808
load and burden of you and your **s**? Dt 1:12 7379
at great **s** with the sons of Ammon; Jg 12:2 7379
a shelter from the **s** of tongues. Ps 31:20 7379
seen violence and **s** in the city. Ps 55:9 7379
evil, Who spreads **s**. Pr 6:14 4066
one who spreads **s** among brothers. Pr 6:19 4090
Hatred stirs up **s**, But love covers Pr 10:12 4090
insolence comes nothing but **s**, Pr 13:10 4683
A hot-tempered man stirs up **s**, Pr 15:18 4066
A perverse man spreads **s**, Pr 16:28 4066
a house full of feasting with **s**. Pr 17:1 7379
The beginning of **s** is *like* letting out Pr 17:14 4066
He who loves transgression loves **s**; Pr 17:19 4683
A fool's lips bring **s**, Pr 18:6 7379
The *cast* lot puts an end to **s** Pr 18:18 4066
Keeping away from **s** is an honor Pr 20:3 7379
Even **s** and dishonor will cease. Pr 22:10 1779
who passes by *and* meddles with **s** Pr 26:17 7379
So is a contentious man to kindle **s**. Pr 26:21 7379
An arrogant man stirs up **s**, Pr 28:25 4066
An angry man stirs up **s**, Pr 29:22 4066
the churning of anger produces **s**. Pr 30:33 7379
you fast for contention and **s** and Is 58:4 4683
As a man of **s** and a man of Jer 15:10 7379
S exists and contention arises. Hab 1:3 7379
full of envy, murder, **s**, Ro 1:29 *2054*
sensuality, not in **s** and jealousy. Ro 13:13 *2054*
there is jealousy and **s** among you, 1Co 3:3 *2054*
that perhaps *there will be* **s**, 2Co 12:20 *2054*
idolatry, sorcery, enmities, **s**, Ga 5:20 *2054*
Christ even from envy and **s**, Php 1:15 *2054*
words, out of which arise envy, **s**, 1Tm 6:4 *2054*
and **s** and disputes about the Law, Ti 3:9 *2054*

STRIKE
and **s** Egypt with all My miracles Ex 3:20 5221
I will **s** the water that is in the Ex 7:17 5221
staff and **s** the dust of the earth, Ex 8:16 5221
and will **s** down all the firstborn Ex 12:12 5221
you when I **s** the land of Egypt. Ex 12:13 5221
and you shall **s** the rock, and Ex 17:6 5221
and **s** a woman with child so that she Ex 21:22 5062
s you seven times for your sins. Lv 26:24 5221
to the Midianites and **s** them; Nu 25:17 5221
you shall surely **s** the inhabitants Dt 13:15 5221
you shall **s** all the men in it with Dt 20:13 5221
to **s** down an innocent person.' Dt 27:25 5221
"The LORD will **s** you on the knees Dt 28:35 5221
The sons of Israel did not **s** Jos 9:18 5221
to **s** and kill some of the people as Jg 20:31 5221
and Benjamin began to **s** and kill Jg 20:39 5221
"Go and **s** the inhabitants of Jg 21:10 5221
'Now go and **s** Amalek and utterly 1Sa 15:3 5221
and I will **s** you down and remove 1Sa 17:46 5221
his spear at him to **s** him down; 1Sa 20:33 5221
please let me **s** him with the spear 1Sa 26:8 5221
I will not **s** him the second time." 1Sa 26:8 5221
lives, surely the LORD will **s** him, 1Sa 26:10 5062
Why should I **s** you to the ground? 2Sa 2:22 5221
"Whoever would **s** the Jebusites, 2Sa 5:8 5221
s the army of the Philistines." 2Sa 5:24 5221
'**S** Amnon,' then put him to death. 2Sa 13:28 5221
s the city with the edge of the sword. 2Sa 15:14 5221
Then I will **s** down the king alone, 2Sa 17:2 5221
you not **s** him there to the ground? 2Sa 18:11 5221
and did not **s** him again, and he 2Sa 20:10 5221
"For the LORD will **s** Israel, 1Ki 14:15 5221
"Please **s** me." But the man refused 1Ki 20:35 5221
But the man refused to **s** him. 1Ki 20:35 5221
another man and said, "Please **s** me. 1Ki 20:37 5221
'Then you shall **s** every fortified city 2Ki 3:19 5221
"**S** this people with blindness, I 2Ki 6:18 5221
s the house of Ahab your master, 2Ki 9:7 5221
"**S** the ground," and he struck *it* 2Ki 13:18 5221
shall **s** Aram *only* three times." 2Ki 13:19 5221
s the army of the Philistines." 1Ch 14:15 5221
LORD is going to **s** your people, 2Ch 21:14 5062
And commands it to **s** the mark. Jb 36:32 6293
Raise a song, **s** the timbrel, The Ps 81:2 5414
him, And **s** those who hate him. Ps 89:23 5062
do not **s** your foot against a stone. Ps 91:12 5062
Nor to **s** the noble for *their* Pr 17:26 5221
S a scoffer and the naive may Pr 19:25 5221
Although you **s** him with the rod, he Pr 23:13 5221
You shall **s** him with the rod Pr 23:14 5221
And they **s** *bargains* with the Is 2:6 5606
a stone to **s** and a rock to stumble Is 8:14 5063
And He will **s** the earth with the Is 11:4 5221
He will **s** it into seven streams And Is 11:15 5221
Which used to **s** the peoples in Is 14:6 5221
The LORD will **s** Egypt, Is 19:22 5062
scorching heat or sun **s** them down; Is 49:10 5221
I gave My back to those who **s** *Me,* Is 50:6 5221
and to **s** with a wicked fist. Is 58:4 5221
neighbors who **s** at the inheritance Jer 12:14 5060
let us **s** at him with *our* tongue, Jer 18:18 5221
"I will also **s** down the inhabitants Jer 21:6 5221
and he will **s** them down with the Jer 21:7 5221
also come and **s** the land of Egypt; Jer 43:11 5221
take one third and **s** *it* with the sword Ezk 5:2 5221
through the city after him and **s**; Ezk 9:5 5221
My people, therefore **s** *your* thigh. Ezk 21:12 5606
s your bow from your left hand and Ezk 39:3 5221
And He will **s** the waves in the sea, Zch 10:11 5221
and they will **s** the land, and I Zch 11:6 3807
s every horse with bewilderment and Zch 12:4 5221
while I **s** every horse of the Zch 12:4 5221
"**S** the Shepherd that the sheep Zch 13:7 5221
plague with which the LORD will **s** all Zch 14:12 5062
S YOUR FOOT AGAINST A STONE.'" Mt 4:6 *4350*
'I WILL **S** DOWN THE SHEPHERD, AND Mt 26:31 *3960*
'I WILL **S** DOWN THE SHEPHERD, AND Mk 14:27 *3960*
NOT **S** YOUR FOOT AGAINST A STONE.'" Lk 4:11 *4350*
"Lord, shall we **s** with the sword?" Lk 22:49 *3960*
but if rightly, why do you **s** Me?" Jn 18:23 *1194*
beside him to **s** him on the mouth. Ac 23:2 *5180*
"God is going to **s** you, you Ac 23:3 *5180*
and to **s** the earth with every plague, Rv 11:6 *3960*
so that with it He may **s** down Rv 19:15 *3960*

STRIKES
"He who **s** a man so that he dies Ex 21:12 5221
"He who **s** his father or his Ex 21:15 5221
If men have a quarrel and one **s** the Ex 21:18 5221
"If a man **s** his male or Ex 21:20 5221
"If a man **s** the eye of his Ex 21:26 5221
and **s** his friend so that he dies Dt 19:5 4672
him and **s** him so that he dies, Dt 19:11 5221
he who **s** his neighbor in secret.' Dt 27:24 5221
"Whoever **s** down a Jebusite first 1Ch 11:6 5221
"He **s** them like the wicked In a Jb 34:26 5606
do not fear the Assyrian who **s** you Is 10:24 5221
terrified, *When* He **s** with the rod. Is 30:31 5221
wither as soon as the east wind **s** it Ezk 17:10 5060

STRIKING
And a boy for **s** me; Gn 4:23 2250
"Why are you **s** your companion?" Ex 2:13 5221
the hand of the one who is **s** him, Dt 25:11 5221
angel who was **s** down the people, 2Sa 24:17 5221
will strike Egypt, **s** but healing; Is 19:22 5062
the **s** of Him who has struck them, Is 27:7 5221
As they were **s** *the people* Ezk 9:8 5221
It is made *for* **s** like lightning, Ezk 21:15
I will make *you* sick, **s** you down, Mi 6:13 5221
oppressed by **s** down the Egyptian. Ac 7:24 *3960*
But **s** a reef where two seas met, Ac 27:41 *4045*

STRING
birds and cedar wood and a scarlet **s** Lv 14:4 8439b
and the scarlet **s** and the hyssop, Lv 14:6 8439b
wood and a scarlet **s** and hyssop, Lv 14:49 8439b
and the hyssop and the scarlet **s**, Lv 14:51 8439b
the hyssop and with the scarlet **s**. Lv 14:52 8439b
as a **s** of tow snaps when it touches Jg 16:9 6616
make ready their arrow upon the **s** To Ps 11:2 3499b

STRINGED
Out of ivory palaces **s** instruments Ps 45:8 4482a
Him with **s** instruments and pipe. Ps 150:4 4482a
will play my songs on **s** instruments Is 38:20 5058
director, on my **s** instruments. Hab 3:19 5058

STRINGS
to Him with a harp of ten **s**. Ps 33:2 6218
Upon a harp of ten **s** I will sing Ps 144:9 6218
Your neck with **s** of beads." SS 1:10 2737
Pluck the **s** skillfully, sing many Is 23:16 5059

STRIP
and **s** Aaron of his garments and Nu 20:26 6584
Philistines came to **s** the slain, 1Sa 31:8 6584
after him only to **s** *the slain.* 2Sa 23:10 6584
Philistines came to **s** the slain, 1Ch 10:8 6584
"Who can **s** off his outer armor? Jb 41:13 1540
S, undress and put *sackcloth* on Is 32:11 6584
Remove your veil, **s** off the skirt, Is 47:2 2834
S away her branches, For they are Jer 5:10 5493
places, **s** you of your clothing, Ezk 16:39 6584
'They will also **s** you of your clothes Ezk 23:26 6584
and **s** off their embroidered Ezk 26:16 6584
S off its foliage and scatter its Da 4:14 5426
Or I will **s** her naked And expose her Hos 2:3 6584
You **s** the robe off the garment From Mi 2:8 6584
S off their skin from them, Mi 3:3 6584

STRIPED
So he removed on that day the **s** Gn 30:35 6124
and the flocks brought forth **s**, Gn 30:39 6124
and made the flocks face toward the **s** Gn 30:40 6124
'The **s** shall be your wages,' then Gn 31:8 6124
all the flock brought forth **s**. Gn 31:8 6124
goats which were mating *were* **s**, Gn 31:10 6124
male goats which are mating are **s**, Gn 31:12 6124

STRIPES
trees, and peeled white **s** in them, Gn 30:37 6479
number of **s** according to his guilt. Dt 25:2
him with many more **s** than these and Dt 25:3 4347
rod And their iniquity with **s**. Ps 89:32 5061
S that wound scour away evil, And Pr 20:30 2250

STRIPPED
that they **s** Joseph of his tunic, Gn 37:23 6584
So the sons of Israel **s** themselves Ex 33:6 5337
Moses had **s** Aaron of his garments Nu 20:28 6584
Jonathan **s** himself of the robe 1Sa 18:4 6584
He also **s** off his clothes, and 1Sa 19:24 6584
his head and **s** off his weapons, 1Sa 31:9 6584
So they **s** him and took his head 1Ch 10:9 6584
"He has **s** my honor from me And Jb 19:9 6584
without cause, And **s** men naked. Jb 22:6 6584
siege towers, they **s** its palaces, Is 23:13 6209
I Myself have also **s** your skirts off Jer 13:26 2834
"But I have **s** Esau bare, I have Jer 49:10 2834
their land will be **s** of its fullness Ezk 12:19 3456
s them bare and cast *them* away; Jl 1:7 2834
She is **s**, she is carried away, And Na 2:7 1540
They **s** Him and put a scarlet Mt 27:28 *1562*
and they **s** him and beat him, Lk 10:30 *1562*
garment on (for he was **s** *for work),* Jn 21:7 *1131*

STRIPPING
has left, the **s** locust has eaten. Jl 1:4 2625
The creeping locust, the **s** locust and Jl 2:25 2625

STRIPS
to calve And **s** the forests bare Ps 29:9 2834
creeping locust **s** and flies away. Na 3:16 6584

STRIVE
My Spirit shall not **s** with man Gn 6:3 1777
Did he ever **s** with Israel, or did Jg 11:25 7378
For they are many *who* **s** with me. Ps 55:18
He will not always **s** *with us,* Ps 103:9 7378
those who keep the law **s** with them. Pr 28:4 1624
"**S** to enter through the narrow door; Lk 13:24 *75*
to **s** together with me in your Ro 15:30 *4865*
For it is for this we labor and **s**, 1Tm 4:10 *75*

STRIVEN
you have **s** with God and with men Gn 32:28 8280

STRIVING
"Cease **s** and know that I am God; Ps 46:10
all is vanity and **s** after wind. Ec 1:14 7469
that this also is **s** after wind. Ec 1:17 7475
all was vanity and **s** after wind and Ec 2:11 7469
is futility and **s** after wind. Ec 2:17 7469
man get in all his labor and in his **s** Ec 2:22 7475
too is vanity and **s** after wind. Ec 2:26 7469
too is vanity and **s** after wind. Ec 4:4 7469
full of labor and **s** after wind. Ec 4:6 7469
too is vanity and **s** after wind. Ec 4:16 7475
is futility and a **s** after wind. Ec 6:9 7469
Or am I **s** to please men? Ga 1:10 *2212*
with one mind **s** together for the Php 1:27 *4866*
I labor, **s** according to His power, Col 1:29 *75*
blood in your **s** against sin; Heb 12:4 *464*

STROKE
spear to the ground with one **s**, 1Sa 26:8 6471
my people, to whom the **s** *was due?* Is 53:8 5061
or **s** shall pass from the Law Mt 5:18 *2762*
for one **s** of a letter of the Law to fail. Lk 16:17 *2762*

STROKES
men and the **s** of the sons of men, 2Sa 7:14 5061
And **s** *reach* the innermost parts. Pr 20:30 4347
peoples in fury with unceasing **s**, Is 14:6 4347

STRONG
"Issachar is a **s** donkey, Lying Gn 49:14 1634
shifted *the wind* to a very **s** west wind Ex 10:19 2389
back by a **s** east wind all night and Ex 14:21 5794
"Do not drink wine or **s** drink, Lv 10:9 7941
abstain from wine and **s** drink; Nu 6:3 7941
whether made from wine or **s** drink, Nu 6:3 7941
people who live in it are **s** *or* weak, Nu 13:18 2389
people who live in the land are **s**, Nu 13:28 5794
for they are too **s** for us." Nu 13:31 2389
a heavy force and with a **s** hand. Nu 20:20 2389
shall pour out a drink offering of **s** drink Nu 28:7 7941
Your greatness and Your **s** hand; Dt 3:24 2389
so that you may be **s** and go in and Dt 11:8 2388
or sheep, or wine, or **s** drink, Dt 14:26 7941
have you drunk wine or **s** drink, Dt 29:6 7941
"Be **s** and courageous, do not be Dt 31:6 2388
"Be **s** and courageous, for you Dt 31:7 2388
"Be **s** and courageous, for you Dt 31:23 2388

“Be **s** and courageous, for you **Jos 1:6** 2388
“Only be **s** and very courageous; **Jos 1:7** 2388
Be **s** and courageous! **Jos 1:9** 2388
only be **s** and courageous.” **Jos 1:18** 2388
Be **s** and courageous, for thus the **Jos 10:25** 2388
“I am still as **s** today as I was **Jos 14:11** 2389
when the sons of Israel became **s**, **Jos 17:13** 2388
of iron *and* though they are **s**.” **Jos 17:18** 2389
and **s** nations from before you; **Jos 23:9** 6099
came about when Israel became **s**, **Jg 1:28** 2388
power of the house of Joseph grew **s**, **Jg 1:35** 3513
But there was a **s** tower in the **Jg 9:51** 5797
not to drink wine or **s** drink, **Jg 13:4** 7941
you shall not drink wine or **s** drink **Jg 13:7** 7941
vine nor drink wine or **s** drink, **Jg 13:14** 7941
out of the **s** came something sweet.” **Jg 14:14** 5794
saw that they were too **s** for him, **Jg 18:26** 2389
drunk neither wine nor **s** drink, **1Sa 1:15** 7941
therefore, let your hands be **s** and **2Sa 2:7** 2388
that Abner was making himself **s** in **2Sa 3:6** 2388
“If the Arameans are too **s** for me, **2Sa 10:11** 2388
sons of Ammon are too **s** for you, **2Sa 10:11** 2388
“Be **s**, and let us show ourselves **2Sa 10:12** 2388
And the conspiracy was **s**, **2Sa 15:12** 533
“He delivered me from my **s** enemy, **2Sa 22:18** 5794
me, for they were too **s** for me. **2Sa 22:18** 553
“God is my **s** fortress; **2Sa 22:33** 2428
Be **s**, therefore, and show yourself **1Ki 2:2** 2388
And a great and **s** wind was rending **1Ki 19:11** 2389
with your servants fifty **s** men, **2Ki 2:16** 2428
thousand, all **s** and fit for war, **2Ki 24:16** 1368
gave him **s** support in his kingdom, **1Ch 11:10** 2388
“If the Arameans are too **s** for me, **1Ch 19:12** 2388
sons of Ammon are too **s** for you, **1Ch 19:12** 2388
“Be **s**, and let us show ourselves **1Ch 19:13** 2388
Be **s** and courageous, do not fear **1Ch 22:13** 2388
“Be **s** and courageous, and act; **1Ch 28:20** 2388
of Rehoboam was established and **s** **2Ch 12:1** 2393
who proved too **s** for Rehoboam, **2Ch 13:7** 553
you, be **s** and do not lose courage, **2Ch 15:7** 2388
do go, do *it*, be **s** for the battle; **2Ch 25:8** 2388
of Egypt, for he became very **s**. **2Ch 26:8** 2388
marvelously helped until he *was* **s**. **2Ch 26:15** 2388
But when he became **s**, **2Ch 26:16** 2393
“Be **s** and courageous, do not fear **2Ch 32:7** 2388
that you may be **s** and eat the good **Ezr 9:12** 2388
Your great power and by Your **s** hand. **Ne 1:10** 2389
of power, behold, *He is* the **s** one! **Jb 9:19** 533
And loosens the belt of the **s**. **Jb 12:21** 650
to the downpour and the rain, ‘Be **s**.’ **Jb 37:6** 5797
the skies, **S** as a molten mirror? **Jb 37:18** 2389
“Their offspring become **s**, **Jb 39:4** 2492a
“*His* **s** scales are *his* pride, Shut **Jb 41:15** 4651
He delivered me from my **s** enemy, **Ps 18:17** 5794
rejoices as a **s** man to run his course. **Ps 19:5** 1368
S *bulls* of Bashan have encircled **Ps 22:12** 47
The LORD **s** and mighty, The LORD **Ps 24:8** 5808
Be **s** and let your heart take **Ps 27:14** 2388
have made my mountain to stand **s**; **Ps 30:7** 5797
Be **s** and let your heart take **Ps 31:24** 2388
from him who is too **s** for him, **Ps 35:10** 2389
But my enemies are vigorous *and* **s**, **Ps 38:19** 6105a
And was **s** in his *evil* desire.” **Ps 52:7** 5810
Show Yourself **s**, O God, who have **Ps 68:28** 5810
For You are my **s** refuge. **Ps 71:7** 5797
You made **s** for Yourself. **Ps 80:17** 553
You have a **s** arm; **Ps 89:13** 1369
LORD will stretch forth Your **s** scepter **Ps 110:2** 5797
a **s** hand and an outstretched arm, **Ps 136:12** 2389
For they are too **s** for me. **Ps 142:6** 553
And the hope of **s** men perishes. **Pr 11:7** 202
of the LORD there is **s** confidence, **Pr 14:26** 5797
The name of the LORD is a **s** tower; **Pr 18:10** 5797
A rich man's wealth is his **s** city, **Pr 18:11** 5797
is harder to be won than a **s** city, **Pr 18:19** 5797
Wine is a mocker, **s** drink a brawler, **Pr 20:1** 7941
And a bribe in the bosom, **s** wrath. **Pr 21:14** 5794
For their Redeemer is **s**; **Pr 23:11** 2389
A wise man is **s**, And a man of **Pr 24:5** 5797
The ants are not a **s** people, **Pr 30:25** 5794
Or for rulers to desire **s** drink, **Pr 31:4** 7941
Give **s** drink to him who is perishing, **Pr 31:6** 7941
strength And makes her arms **s**. **Pr 31:17** 553
For love is as **s** as death, **SS 8:6** 5794
The **s** man will become tinder, **Is 1:31** 2634
that they may pursue **s** drink, **Is 5:11** 7941
And valiant men in mixing **s** drink, **Is 5:22** 7941
on them the **s** and abundant waters **Is 8:7** 6099
their **s** cities will be like forsaken **Is 17:9** 4581
S drink is bitter to those who **Is 24:9** 7941
a **s** people will glorify You; **Is 25:3** 5794
“We have a **s** city; **Is 26:1** 5797
the Lord has a **s** and mighty *agent;* **Is 28:2** 2389
wine and stagger from **s** drink: **Is 28:7** 7941
and the prophet reel with **s** drink, **Is 28:7** 7941
wine, they stagger from **s** drink; **Is 28:7** 7941
stagger, but not with **s** drink. **Is 29:9** 7941
horsemen because they are very **s**, **Is 31:1** 6105a
them And young bulls with **s** ones; **Is 34:7** 47
And says to his brother, “Be **s**!” **Is 41:6** 2388
“Bring forward your **s** *arguments,*” **Is 41:21** 6110
and working it with his **s** arm. **Is 44:12** 3581b
will divide the booty with the **s**; **Is 53:12** 6099
let us drink heavily of **s** drink; **Is 56:12** 7941
His right hand and by His **s** arm, **Is 62:8** 5797
a wind too **s** for this—will come at **Jer 4:12** 4392
and with a **s** hand and with an **Jer 32:21** 2389
“Their Redeemer is **s**, **Jer 50:34** 2389
Post a **s** guard, Station sentries, **Jer 51:12** 2388
The Lord has rejected all my **s** men **La 1:15** 47
the hand of the LORD was **s** on me. **Ezk 3:14** 2389
the pride of the **s** ones cease, **Ezk 7:24** 5794
‘And it had **s** branches *fit* for **Ezk 19:11** 5797
Its **s** branch was torn off So that **Ezk 19:12** 5797
there is not in it a **s** branch, **Ezk 19:14** 5797
endure, or can your hands be **s** in **Ezk 22:14** 2388
and your **s** pillars will come down **Ezk 26:11** 5797
it may be **s** to hold the sword. **Ezk 30:21** 2388
arms, both the **s** and the broken; **Ezk 30:22** 2389
“The **s** among the mighty ones **Ezk 32:21** 410
the fat and the **s** I will destroy. **Ezk 34:16** 2389
be a fourth kingdom as **s** as iron; **Da 2:40** 8624
so some of the kingdom will be **s** **Da 2:42** 8624
‘The tree grew large and became **s** And **Da 4:11** 8631
which became large and grew **s**, **Da 4:20** 8631
you have become great and grown **s**, **Da 4:22** 8631
and terrifying and extremely **s**; **Da 7:7** 8624
he becomes **s** through his riches, **Da 11:2** 2393
the king of the South will grow **s**, **Da 11:5** 2388
For **s** is he who carries out His **Jl 2:11** 6099
cedars And he *was* **s** as the oaks; **Am 2:9** 2634
city which goes forth a thousand **s** **Am 5:3**
one which goes forth a hundred **s** **Am 5:3**
forth *with* destruction upon the **s**, **Am 5:9** 5794
And the outcasts a **s** nation, **Mi 4:7** 6099
fourth chariot **s** dappled horses. **Zch 6:3** 554
“When the **s** ones went out, they **Zch 6:7** 554
‘Let your hands be **s**, **Zch 8:9** 2388
let your hands be **s**.’ **Zch 8:13** 2388
‘A **s** support for us are the **Zch 12:5** 556
can anyone enter the **s** man's house **Mt 12:29** 2478
unless he first binds the **s** *man?* **Mt 12:29** 2478
no one can enter the **s** man's house **Mk 3:27** 2478
unless he first binds the **s** man, **Mk 3:27** 2478
no one was **s** enough to subdue him. **Mk 5:4** 2480
grow and to become **s** in spirit, **Lk 1:80** 2901
continued to grow and become **s**, **Lk 2:40** 2901
“When a **s** *man,* fully armed, **Lk 11:21** 2478
consider whether he is **s** enough **Lk 14:31** 1415
I am not **s** enough to dig; **Lk 16:3** 2480
up because a **s** wind was blowing. **Jn 6:18** 3173
in unbelief but grew **s** in faith, **Ro 4:20** 1743
Now we who are **s** ought to bear the **Ro 15:1** 1415
to shame the things which are **s**, **1Co 1:27** 2478
we are weak, but you are **s**; **1Co 4:10** 2478
in the faith, act like men, be **s**. **1Co 16:13** 2901
“His letters are weighty and **s**, **2Co 10:10** 2478
for when I am weak, then I am **s**. **2Co 12:10** 1415
ourselves are weak but you are **s**; **2Co 13:9** 1415
Finally, be **s** in the Lord and in **Eph 6:10** 1743
be **s** in the grace that is in Christ **2Tm 2:1** 1743
would have **s** encouragement **Heb 6:18** 2478
sword, from weakness were made **s**, **Heb 11:34** 1412
great and are driven by **s** winds, **Jas 3:4** 4642
you, young men, because you are **s**, **1Jn 2:14** 2478
And I saw a **s** angel proclaiming **Rv 5:2** 2478
the **s** and every slave and free man hid **Rv 6:15** 2478
I saw another **s** angel coming **Rv 10:1** 2478
and they were not **s** enough, **Rv 12:8** 2480
the Lord God who judges her is **s**. **Rv 18:8** 2478
great city, Babylon, the **s** city! **Rv 18:10** 2478
Then a **s** angel took up a stone like **Rv 18:21** 2478

STRONGER

people shall be **s** than the other; **Gn 25:23** 553
the **s** of the flock were mating, **Gn 30:41** 7194
were Laban's and the **s** Jacob's. **Gn 30:42** 7194
nations greater and **s** than you, **Dt 7:1** 6099
And what is **s** than a lion?” **Jg 14:18** 5794
eagles, They were **s** than lions. **2Sa 1:23** 1396
and David grew steadily **s**, **2Sa 3:1** 2388
make your battle against the city **s** **2Sa 11:25** 2388
since he was **s** than she, he **2Sa 13:14** 2388
therefore they were **s** than we; **1Ki 20:23** 2388
surely we will be **s** than they. **1Ki 20:23** 2388
surely we will be **s** than they.” **1Ki 20:25** 2388
hands will grow **s** and stronger. **Jb 17:9** 555
hands will grow stronger and **s**. **Jb 17:9**
made them **s** than their adversaries. **Ps 105:24** 6105a
with him who is **s** than he is. **Ec 6:10** 8623
Or your fetters will be made **s**; **Is 28:22** 2388
the hand of him who was **s** than he. **Jer 31:11** 2389
“But when someone **s** than he attacks **Lk 11:22** 2478
the weakness of God is **s** than men. **1Co 1:25** 2478
We are not **s** than He, are we? **1Co 10:22** 2478

STRONGEST

take action against the **s** of fortresses **Da 11:39** 4581

STRONGHOLD

on the top of this **s** in an orderly **Jg 6:26** 4581
the time that David was in the **s**. **1Sa 22:4** 4686b
“Do not stay in the **s**; **1Sa 22:5** 4686b
David and his men went up to the **s**. **1Sa 24:22** 4686b
David captured the **s** of Zion, **2Sa 5:7** 4686b
So David lived in the **s** and **2Sa 5:9** 4686b
of it, he went down to the **s**. **2Sa 5:17** 4686b
my salvation, my **s** and my refuge; **2Sa 22:3** 4869
David was then in the **s**, **2Sa 23:14** 4686b
David captured the **s** of Zion **1Ch 11:5** 4686b
Then David dwelt in the **s**; **1Ch 11:7** 4679
David was then in the **s**, **1Ch 11:16** 4686b
David in the **s** in the wilderness, **1Ch 12:8** 4679
and Judah came to the **s** to David. **1Ch 12:16** 4679
will be a **s** for the oppressed, **Ps 9:9** 4869
A **s** in times of trouble; **Ps 9:9** 4869
the horn of my salvation, my **s**. **Ps 18:2** 4869
rock of strength, A **s** to save me. **Ps 31:2** 4686b
The God of Jacob is our **s**. **Ps 46:7** 4869
The God of Jacob is our **s**. **Ps 46:11** 4869
Has made Himself known as a **s**. **Ps 48:3** 4869
watch for You, For God is my **s**. **Ps 59:9** 4869
morning, For You have been my **s** **Ps 59:16** 4869
For God is my **s**, the God who shows **Ps 59:17** 4869
is my rock and my salvation, My **s**; **Ps 62:2** 4869
is my rock and my salvation, My **s**; **Ps 62:6** 4869
But the LORD has been my **s**, **Ps 94:22** 4869
fortress, My **s** and my deliverer, **Ps 144:2** 4869
of the LORD is a **s** to the upright, **Pr 10:29** 4581
down the **s** in which they trust. **Pr 21:22** 5797
the sea speaks, the **s** of the sea, **Is 23:4** 4581
Tarshish, For your **s** is destroyed. **Is 23:14** 4581
wage war against her and her **s**, **Is 29:7** 4685d
O LORD, my strength and my **s**, **Jer 16:19** 4581
The lofty **s** has been put to shame **Jer 48:1** 4869
she should fortify her lofty **s**, **Jer 51:53** 5797
day when I take from them their **s**, **Ezk 24:25** 4581
My wrath on Sin, The **s** of Egypt; **Ezk 30:15** 4581
And a **s** to the sons of Israel. **Jl 3:16** 4581
good, A **s** in the day of trouble, **Na 1:7** 4581
Return to the **s**, O prisoners who **Zch 9:12** 1225

STRONGHOLDS

mountains and the caves and the **s**. **Jg 6:2** 4679
stayed in the wilderness in the **s**, **1Sa 23:14** 4679
hiding with us in the **s** at Horesh, **1Sa 23:19** 4679
and stayed in the **s** of Engedi. **1Sa 23:29** 4679
their **s** you will set on fire, and **2Ki 8:12** 4013
You have brought his **s** to ruin. **Ps 89:40** 4013
Canaan to demolish its **s**. **Is 23:11** 4581
against you, He has ruined your **s**. **Jer 48:18** 4013
And the **s** have been seized, **Jer 48:41** 4679
fighting, They stay in the **s**; **Jer 51:30** 4679
The **s** of the daughter of Judah; **La 2:2** 4013
He has destroyed its **s** And **La 2:5** 4013
and those who are in the **s** and in **Ezk 33:27** 4679
will devise his schemes against **s**, **Da 11:24** 4013

STRONGLY

Yet he urged them **s**, **Gn 19:3** 3966
that He may **s** support those whose **2Ch 16:9** 2388

STRUCK

But the LORD **s** Pharaoh and his **Gn 12:17** 5060
They **s** the men who were at the **Gn 19:11** 5221
he **s** down the Egyptian and hid him **Ex 2:12** 5221
s the water that *was* in the Nile, **Ex 7:20** 5221
after the LORD had **s** the Nile. **Ex 7:25** 5221
and **s** the dust of the earth, **Ex 8:17** 5221
I had put forth My hand and **s** you **Ex 9:15** 5221
The hail **s** all that was in the **Ex 9:25** 5221
the hail also **s** every plant of the **Ex 9:25** 5221
that the LORD **s** all the firstborn in **Ex 12:29** 5221
staff with which you **s** the Nile, **Ex 17:5** 5221
he who **s** him shall go unpunished; **Ex 21:19** 5221
and in and is **s** so that he dies, **Ex 22:2** 5221
be **s** down before your enemies; **Lv 26:17** 5062
day that I **s** down all the firstborn **Nu 3:13** 5221
day that I **s** down all the firstborn **Nu 8:17** 5221
and the LORD **s** the people with a **Nu 11:33** 5221
you will be **s** down before your **Nu 14:42** 5062
and **s** them and beat them down as **Nu 14:45** 5221
and **s** the rock twice with his rod; **Nu 20:11** 5221
Then Israel **s** him with the edge of **Nu 21:24** 5221
but Balaam **s** the donkey to turn **Nu 22:23** 5221
the wall, so he **s** her again. **Nu 22:25** 5221
and **s** the donkey with his stick. **Nu 22:27** 5221
you have **s** me these three times?” **Nu 22:28** 5221
s your donkey these three times? **Nu 22:32** 5221
and he **s** his hands together; **Nu 24:10** 5606
the LORD had **s** down among them. **Nu 33:4** 5221
he **s** him down with an iron object, **Nu 35:16** 5221
‘If he **s** him down with a stone **Nu 35:17** 5221
if he **s** him with a wooden object **Nu 35:18** 5221
or if he **s** him down with his hand **Nu 35:21** 5221
the one who **s** him shall surely be **Nu 35:21** 5221
and it is not known who has **s** him, **Dt 21:1** 5221
The men of Ai **s** down about **Jos 7:5** 5221
and **s** them down on the descent, **Jos 7:5** 5221
s it with the edge of the sword. **Jos 8:24** 5221
and **s** them as far as Azekah and **Jos 10:10** 5221
s them and put them to death, **Jos 10:26** 5221
and **s** it and its king with the **Jos 10:28** 5221
and he **s** it and every person who **Jos 10:30** 5221
and **s** it and every person who *was* **Jos 10:32** 5221
s it with the edge of the sword; **Jos 10:35** 5221
They captured it and **s** it and **Jos 10:37** 5221
and they **s** them with the edge of **Jos 10:39** 5221
Thus Joshua **s** all the land, the **Jos 10:40** 5221
Joshua **s** them from **Jos 10:41** 5221
and they **s** them until no survivor **Jos 11:8** 5221
and **s** its king with the sword; **Jos 11:10** 5221
They **s** every person who was in **Jos 11:11** 5221
and he **s** them with the edge of the **Jos 11:12** 5221
but they **s** every man with the edge **Jos 11:14** 5221
he captured all their kings and **s** them **Jos 11:17** 5221
s them and dispossessed them. **Jos 13:12** 5221
Moses **s** with the chiefs of Midian, **Jos 13:21** 5221
Then they **s** it with the edge of **Jos 19:47** 5221
because he **s** his neighbor without **Jos 20:5** 5221
and **s** it with the edge of the sword **Jg 1:8** 5221
s Sheshai and Ahiman and Talmai. **Jg 1:10** 5221
and they **s** the Canaanites living **Jg 1:17** 5221
and they **s** the city with the edge **Jg 1:25** 5221
They **s** down at that time about **Jg 3:29** 5221
who **s** down six hundred Philistines **Jg 3:31** 5221
Then she **s** Sisera, she smashed his **Jg 5:26** 1986
the tent and **s** it so that it fell, **Jg 7:13** 5221
He **s** them with a very great **Jg 11:33** 5221
He **s** them ruthlessly with a **Jg 15:8** 5221
and **s** them with the edge of the **Jg 18:27** 5221

"They are **s** down before us, as at Jg 20:32 5062
the LORD **s** Benjamin before Israel, Jg 20:35 5062
also deployed and **s** all the city with Jg 20:37 5221
s them with the edge of the sword, Jg 20:48 5221
it was not His hand that **s** us; 1Sa 6:9 5060
He **s** down some of the men of 1Sa 6:19 5221
He **s** down of all the people, 1Sa 6:19 5221
the LORD had **s** the people with a 1Sa 6:19 5221
and **s** them down as far as below 1Sa 7:11 5221
and **s** down the Ammonites until the 1Sa 11:11 5221
They **s** among the Philistines 1Sa 14:31 5221
beard and **s** him and killed him. 1Sa 17:35 5221
and **s** the Philistine on his 1Sa 17:49 5221
s the Philistine and killed him; 1Sa 17:50 5221
and **s** down two hundred men among 1Sa 18:27 5221
in his hand and **s** the Philistine, 1Sa 19:5 5221
And he **s** Nob the city of the 1Sa 22:19 5221
and sheep *he* **s** with the edge of 1Sa 22:19 5221
and **s** them with a great slaughter. 1Sa 23:5 5221
the LORD **s** Nabal 1Sa 25:38 5062
So he **s** him and he died. 2Sa 1:15 5221
therefore Abner **s** him in the belly 2Sa 2:23 5221
But the servants of David had **s** 2Sa 2:31 5221
and there he **s** him in the belly so 2Sa 3:27 5221
and they **s** him in the belly; 2Sa 4:6 5221
they **s** him and killed him and 2Sa 4:7 5221
and **s** down the Philistines from 2Sa 5:25 5221
and God **s** him down there for his 2Sa 6:7 5221
and **s** down Shobach the commander 2Sa 10:18 5221
that he may be **s** down and die." 2Sa 11:15 5221
'Who **s** down Abimelech the son of 2Sa 11:21 5221
You have **s** down Uriah the Hittite 2Sa 12:9 5221
Then the LORD **s** the child that 2Sa 12:15 5062
Absalom has **s** down all the king's 2Sa 13:30 5221
so one **s** the other and killed him. 2Sa 14:6 5221
over the one who **s** his brother, 2Sa 14:7 5221
and **s** Absalom and killed him. 2Sa 18:15 5221
so he **s** him in the belly with it and 2Sa 20:10 5221
Philistines **s** down Saul in Gilboa. 2Sa 21:12 5221
s the Philistine and killed him. 2Sa 21:17 5221
the Hushathite **s** down Saph, 2Sa 21:18 5221
David's brother, **s** him down. 2Sa 21:21 5221
He arose and **s** the Philistines 2Sa 23:10 5221
defended it and **s** the Philistines; 2Sa 23:12 5221
and had **s** down every male in Edom 1Ki 11:15 5221
Baasha **s** him down at Gibbethon, 1Ki 15:27 5221
he **s** down all the household of 1Ki 15:29 5221
of Jeroboam, and because he **s** it. 1Ki 16:7 5221
in and **s** him and put him to death in 1Ki 16:10 5221
and has also **s** down the king." 1Ki 16:16 5221
out and **s** the horses and chariots, 1Ki 20:21 5221
And the man **s** him, wounding him. 1Ki 20:37 5221
s Micaiah on the cheek and said, 1Ki 22:24 5221
and **s** the king of Israel in a joint of 1Ki 22:34 5221
it together and **s** the waters, 2Ki 2:8 5221
him and **s** the waters and said, 2Ki 2:14 5221
And when he also had **s** the waters, 2Ki 2:14 5221
arose and **s** the Moabites, 2Ki 3:24 5221
slingers went about *it* and **s** it. 2Ki 3:25 5221
So He **s** them with blindness 2Ki 6:18 5221
he arose by night and **s** the Edomites 2Ki 8:21 5221
and **s** down Joash at the house of 2Ki 12:20 5221
of Shomer, his servants, **s** *him* 2Ki 12:21 5221
he **s** *it* three times and stopped. 2Ki 13:18 5221
should have **s** five or six times, 2Ki 13:19 5221
then you would have **s** Aram until 2Ki 13:19 5221
The LORD **s** the king, so that 2Ki 15:5 5060
conspired against him and **s** him 2Ki 15:10 5221
and **s** Shallum son of Jabesh in 2Ki 15:14 5221
Then Menahem **s** Tiphsah and all who 2Ki 15:16 5221
open *to him;* therefore he **s** *it* 2Ki 15:16 5221
against him and **s** him in Samaria, 2Ki 15:25 5221
and **s** him and put him to death and 2Ki 15:30 5221
and **s** 185,000 in the camp of the 2Ki 19:35 5221
Then the king of Babylon **s** them 2Ki 25:21 5221
came with ten men and **s** Gedaliah 2Ki 25:25 5221
the Philistines **s** down Jonathan, 1Ch 10:2 5221
it, and **s** down the Philistines; 1Ch 11:14 5221
s down the two *sons of* Ariel of 1Ch 11:22 5221
so He **s** him down because he put 1Ch 13:10 5221
and they **s** down the army of the 1Ch 14:16 5221
Joab **s** Rabbah and overthrew it. 1Ch 20:1 5221
with this thing, so He **s** Israel. 1Ch 21:7 5221
and the LORD **s** him and he died. 2Ch 13:20 5062
They also **s** down those who owned 2Ch 14:15 5221
s Micaiah on the cheek and said, 2Ch 18:23 5221
and **s** the king of Israel in a joint of 2Ch 18:33 5221
and **s** down the Edomites who were 2Ch 21:9 5221
and **s** down 10,000 of the sons of 2Ch 25:11 5221
and **s** down 3,000 of them and 2Ch 25:13 5221
Why should you be **s** down?" 2Ch 25:16 5221
and cursed them and **s** some of them Ne 13:25 5221
Thus the Jews **s** all their enemies Es 9:5 5221
s the four corners of the house, Jb 1:19 5060
For the hand of God has **s** me. Jb 19:21 5060
"Behold, He **s** the rock so that Ps 78:20 5221
He **s** down their vines also and Ps 105:33 5221
He also **s** down all the firstborn Ps 105:36 5221
"They **s** me, *but* I did not become Pr 23:35 5221
me, They **s** me *and* wounded me; SS 5:7 5221
hand against them and **s** them down. Is 5:25 5221
not turn back to Him who **s** them, Is 9:13 5221
again rely on the one who **s** them, Is 10:20 5221
the rod that **s** you is broken; Is 14:29 5221
striking of Him who has **s** them, Is 27:7 5221
has struck them, has He **s** them? Is 27:7 5221
and **s** 185,000 in the camp of the Is 37:36 5221
unjust gain I was angry and **s** him; Is 57:17 5221
For in My wrath I **s** you, Is 60:10 5221

"In vain I have **s** your sons; Jer 2:30 5221
men **s** down by the sword in battle. Jer 18:21 5221
s down Gedaliah the son of Ahikam, Jer 41:2 5221
Ishmael also **s** down all the Jews Jer 41:3 5221
he had **s** down because of Gedaliah, Jer 41:9 5221
after he had **s** down Gedaliah the Jer 41:16 5221
of Nethaniah had **s** down Gedaliah Jer 41:18 5221
Then the king of Babylon **s** them Jer 52:27 5221
and **s** down *the people* in the city. Ezk 9:7 5221
and it **s** the statue on its feet of Da 2:34 4223
But the stone that **s** the statue Da 2:35 4223
and he **s** the ram and shattered his Da 8:7 5221
whose account this calamity *has* **s** Jon 1:7
account *has* this calamity **s** Jon 1:8
You **s** the head of the house of Hab 3:13 4272
s the slave of the high priest and Mt 26:51 *3960*
s the slave of the high priest and Mk 14:47 *3817*
They were all **s** with astonishment Lk 5:26 *2983*
one of them **s** the slave of Lk 22:50 *3960*
it and **s** the high priest's slave, Jn 18:10 *3817*
one of the officers standing nearby **s** Jn 18:22 *1325, 4475*
he **s** Peter's side and woke him Ac 12:7 *3960*
an angel of the Lord **s** him because Ac 12:23 *3960*
When they had **s** them with many Ac 16:23 *2007*
of the Law order me to be **s**?" Ac 23:3 *5180*
s down, but not destroyed; 2Co 4:9 *2598*
moon and a third of the stars were **s**, Rv 8:12 *4141*

STRUCTURE

temple and to finish this **s**?" Ezr 5:3 846
this temple and to finish this **s**?' Ezr 5:9 846
south *there was* a **s** like a city. Ezk 40:2 4011
the **s** surrounding the temple went Ezk 41:7
the design of the house, its **s**, Ezk 43:11 8499

STRUGGLE

"If men **s** with each other and Ex 21:22 5327b
All the days of my **s** I will wait Until Jb 14:14 6635
For our **s** is not against flesh and Eph 6:12 *3823*
my **s** in *the cause of* the gospel, Php 4:3 *4866*
how great a **s** I have on your behalf Col 2:1 *73*

STRUGGLED

children **s** together within her; Gn 25:22 7533
woman's son and a man of Israel **s** Lv 24:10 5327b
two of them **s** together in the field, 2Sa 14:6 5327b

STRUGGLING

a man and his countryman, are **s** Dt 25:11 5327b

STRUT

The wicked **s** about on every side Ps 12:8 1980

STRUTTING

The **s** rooster, the male goat also, Pr 30:31 2223, 4975

STUBBLE

of Egypt to gather **s** for straw. Ex 5:12 7179
Slingstones are turned into **s** for him. Jb 41:28 7179
"Clubs are regarded as **s**; Jb 41:29 7179
as a tongue of fire consumes **s** And Is 5:24 7179
chaff, you will give birth to **s**; Is 33:11 7179
storm carries them away like **s**. Is 40:24 7179
"Behold, they have become like **s**, Is 47:14 7179
a flame of fire consuming the **s**, Jl 2:5 7179
the house of Esau *will be* as **s**. Ob 1:18 7179
consumed As **s** completely withered. Na 1:10 7179

STUBBORN

"Pharaoh's heart is **s**; Ex 7:14 3515
Pharaoh was **s** about letting us go, Ex 13:15 7185
possess, for you are a **s** people. Dt 9:6 7186, 6203
and indeed, it is a **s** people. Dt 9:13 7186, 6203
any man has a **s** and rebellious son Dt 21:18 5637
son of ours is **s** and rebellious, Dt 21:20 5637
their practices or their **s** ways. Jg 2:19 7186
They became **s** and would not listen Ne 9:16 7185, 6203
So they became **s** and appointed a Ne 9:17 7185, 6203
And they turned a **s** shoulder and Ne 9:29 5637
A **s** and rebellious generation, Ps 78:8 5637
has a **s** and rebellious heart; Jer 5:23 5637
who are **s** and obstinate children, Ezk 2:4 7186, 6440
house of Israel is **s** and obstinate. Ezk 3:7 2389, 4696
is **s** Like a stubborn heifer, Hos 4:16 5637
is stubborn Like a **s** heifer, Hos 4:16 5637
and turned a **s** shoulder and Zch 7:11 5637

STUBBORNLY

All of them are **s** rebellious, Jer 6:28 5637

STUBBORN-MINDED

"Listen to Me, you **s**, Is 46:12 47, 3820

STUBBORNNESS

do not look at the **s** of this people Dt 9:27 7190
though I walk in the **s** of my heart Dt 29:19 8307
I know your rebellion and your **s**; Dt 31:27 7186, 6203
them over to the **s** of their heart, Ps 81:12 8307
after the **s** of their evil heart. Jer 3:17 8307
and in the **s** of their evil heart, Jer 7:24 8307
walked after the **s** of their heart and Jer 9:14 8307
one, in the **s** of his evil heart; Jer 11:8 8307
who walk in the **s** of their hearts Jer 13:10 8307
to the **s** of his own evil heart, Jer 16:12 8307
to the **s** of his evil heart.' Jer 18:12 8307
walks in the **s** of his own heart, Jer 23:17 8307
But because of your **s** and Ro 2:5 *4643*

STUBS

two **s** of smoldering firebrands, Is 7:4 2180

STUCK

that he **s** the spear into the wall 1Sa 19:10 5221
spear **s** in the ground at his head; 1Sa 26:7 4600
their tongue **s** to their palate. Jb 29:10 1692
Or if any spot has **s** to my hands, Jb 31:7 1692
and the prow **s** fast and remained Ac 27:41 *2043*

STUD

on steeds sired by the royal **s**. Es 8:10 7424

STUDIED

are **s** by all who delight in them. Ps 111:2 1875

STUDY

heart to **s** the law of the LORD and Ezr 7:10 1875

STUFF

a swallow of that red **s** there, Gn 25:30 123

STUMBLE

'They will therefore **s** over each Lv 26:37 3782
They **s** and perish before You. Ps 9:3 3782
So they will make him **s**; Ps 64:8 3782
And nothing causes them to **s**. Ps 119:165 4383
And your foot will not **s**. Pr 3:23 5062
And if you run, you will not **s**. Pr 4:12 3782
sleep unless they make *someone* **s**. Pr 4:16 3782
They do not know over what they **s**. Pr 4:19 3782
the wicked **s** in *time of* calamity. Pr 24:16 3782
to strike and **s** a rock to **s** over, Is 8:14 4383
"Many will **s** over them, Then Is 8:15 3782
That they may go and **s** backward, Is 28:13 3782
And he who helps will **s** And he who Is 31:3 3782
And vigorous young men **s** badly, Is 40:30 3782
We **s** at midday as in the twilight, Is 59:10 3782
in the wilderness, they did not **s**; Is 63:13 3782
And they will **s** against them, Jer 6:21 3782
feet **s** On the dusky mountains, Jer 13:16 5062
persecutors will **s** and not prevail. Jer 20:11 3782
path in which they will not **s**; Jer 31:9 3782
"The arrogant one will **s** and Jer 50:32 3782
he will not **s** because of it in the Ezk 33:12 3782
cause your nation to **s** any longer," Ezk 36:15 3782
s and fall and be found no more. Da 11:19 3782
So you will **s** by day, And the Hos 4:5 3782
the prophet also will **s** with you Hos 4:5 3782
and Ephraim **s** in their iniquity; Hos 5:5 3782
But transgressors will **s** in them. Hos 14:9 3782
They **s** in their march, They hurry Na 2:5 3782
They **s** over the dead bodies! Na 3:3 3782
caused many to **s** by the instruction; Mal 2:8 3782
"If your right eye makes you **s**, Mt 5:29 *4624*
If your right hand makes you **s**, Mt 5:30 *4624*
ones who believe in Me to **s**, Mt 18:6 *4624*
hand or your foot causes you to **s**, Mt 18:8 *4624*
"If your eye causes you to **s**, Mt 18:9 *4624*
little ones who believe to **s**, Mk 9:42 *4624*
"If your hand causes you to **s**, Mk 9:43 *4624*
"If your foot causes you to **s**, Mk 9:45 *4624*
"If your eye causes you to **s**, Mk 9:47 *4624*
cause one of these little ones to **s**. Lk 17:2 *4624*
"Does this cause you to **s**? Jn 6:61 *4624*
walks in the day, he does not **s**, Jn 11:9 *4350*
they did not **s** so as to fall, Ro 11:11 *4417*
if food causes my brother to **s**, 1Co 8:13 *4624*
I will not cause my brother to **s**. 1Co 8:13 *4624*
For we all **s** in many *ways.* Jas 3:2 *4417*
anyone does not **s** in what he says, Jas 3:2 *4417*
for they **s** because they are 1Pe 2:8 *4350*
these things, you will never **s**; 2Pe 1:10 *4417*

STUMBLED

and my enemies, they **s** and fell. Ps 27:2 3782
tribes there was not one who **s**. Ps 105:37 3782
They **s** and there was none to help. Ps 107:12 3782
For Jerusalem has **s** and Is 3:8 3782
For truth has **s** in the street, And Is 59:14 3782
And they have **s** from their ways, Jer 18:15 3782
Euphrates They have **s** and fallen. Jer 46:6 3782
one warrior has **s** over another, Jer 46:12 3782
"They have repeatedly **s**; Jer 46:16 3782
And youths **s** under *loads* of wood. La 5:13 3782
Judah also has **s** with them. Hos 5:5 3782
you have **s** because of your iniquity. Hos 14:1 3782
They **s** over the stumbling stone, Ro 9:32 *4350*

STUMBLES

not let your heart be glad when he **s** Pr 24:17 3782
No one in it is weary or **s**, Is 5:27 3782
anyone walks in the night, he **s**, Jn 11:10 *4350*
anything by which your brother **s**. Ro 14:21 *4350*
whole law and yet **s** in one *point,* Jas 2:10 *4417*

STUMBLING

nor place a **s** block before the blind, Lv 19:14 4383
But at my **s** they rejoiced and Ps 35:15 6761
from death, Indeed my feet from **s**, Ps 56:13 1762
for me, my feet came close to **s**, Ps 73:2 5186
eyes from tears, My feet from **s**. Ps 116:8 1762
And a haughty spirit before **s**. Pr 16:18 3783
s blocks before this people. Jer 6:21 4383
has become an occasion of **s**. Ezk 7:19 4383
the **s** block of their iniquity. Ezk 14:3 4383
face the **s** block of his iniquity, Ezk 14:4 4383
face the **s** block of his iniquity, Ezk 14:7 4383
may not become a **s** block to you. Ezk 18:30 4383
and became a **s** block of iniquity to Ezk 44:12 4383
out of His kingdom all **s** blocks, Mt 13:41 *4625*

You are a **s** block to Me; Mt 16:23 *4625*
the world because of *its* **s** blocks! Mt 18:7 *4625*
is inevitable that **s** blocks come; Mt 18:7 *4625*
through whom the **s** block comes! Mt 18:7 *4625*
that **s** blocks come, Lk 17:1 *4625*
you so that you may be kept from **s**. Jn 16:1 *4624*
They stumbled over the **s** stone, Ro 9:32 *4348*
STONE OF **S** AND A ROCK OF OFFENSE, Ro 9:33 *4348*
AND A **S** BLOCK AND A RETRIBUTION TO Ro 11:9 *4625*
or a **s** block in a brother's way. Ro 14:13 *4625*
crucified, to Jews a **s** block and 1Co 1:23 *4625*
become a **s** block to the weak. 1Co 8:9 *4348*
Then the **s** block of the cross has Ga 5:11 *4625*
STONE OF **S** AND A ROCK OF OFFENSE 1Pe 2:8 *4348*
there is no cause for **s** in him. 1Jn 2:10 *4625*
Him who is able to keep you from **s**, Jude 1:24 *679*
kept teaching Balak to put a **s** block Rv 2:14 *4625*

STUMP
And its **s** dies in the dry soil, Jb 14:8 1503
Whose **s** remains when it is felled. Is 6:13 4676
The holy seed is its **s**." Is 6:13 4676
Yet leave the **s** with its roots in the Da 4:15 6136a
yet leave the **s** with its roots in the Da 4:23 6136a
leave the **s** with the roots of the tree Da 4:26 6136a

STUNNED
But he was **s**, for he did not Gn 45:26 6313

STUNTED
has an overgrown or **s** *member,* Lv 22:23 7038

STUPID
as beasts, As **s** in your eyes? Jb 18:3 2933
The **s** and the senseless alike Ps 49:10 3684
Nor does a **s** man understand this: Ps 92:6 3684
when will you understand, **s** ones? Ps 94:8 3684
But he who hates reproof is **s**. Pr 12:1 1198
Surely I am more **s** than any man, Pr 30:2 1198
wisest advisers has become **s**. Is 19:11 1197b
They are **s** children And have no Jer 4:22 5530
But they are altogether **s** and Jer 10:8 1197b
Every man is **s**, devoid of Jer 10:14 1197b
For the shepherds have become **s** Jer 10:21 1197b
All mankind is **s**, devoid of Jer 51:17 1197b

STUPOR
"GOD GAVE THEM A SPIRIT OF **S**, Ro 11:8 *2659*

STYLUS
"That with an iron **s** and lead Jb 19:24 5842
is written down with an iron **s**; Jer 17:1 5842

SUAH
The sons of Zophah *were* **S**, 1Ch 7:36 5477

SUBDUE
and fill the earth, and **s** it; Gn 1:28 3533
and He will **s** them before you, Dt 9:3 3665
And I will **s** all your enemies. 1Ch 17:10 3665
"Let us completely **s** them." Ps 74:8 3238
"I would quickly **s** their enemies And Ps 81:14 3665
You **s** the uproar of aliens; Is 25:5 3665
hand, To **s** nations before him And Is 45:1 7286
ones and will **s** three kings. Da 7:24 8214
no one was strong enough to **s** him. Mk 5:4 *1150*

SUBDUED
and the land is **s** before the LORD, Nu 32:22 3533
and the land is **s** before you, Nu 32:29 3533
and the land was **s** before them. Jos 18:1 3533
So Moab was **s** that day under the Jg 3:30 3665
So God **s** on that day Jabin the Jg 4:23 3665
was **s** before the sons of Israel, Jg 8:28 3665
were **s** before the sons of Israel. Jg 11:33 3665
So the Philistines were **s** and they 1Sa 7:13 3665
the Philistines and **s** them; 2Sa 8:1 3665
all the nations which he had **s**: 2Sa 8:11 3533
You have **s** under me those who 2Sa 22:40 3766
defeated the Philistines and **s** them 1Ch 18:1 3665
of the giants, and they were **s**. 1Ch 20:4 3665
and the land is **s** before the LORD 1Ch 22:18 3533
sons of Israel were **s** at that time, 2Ch 13:18 3665
And You **s** before them the inhabitants Ne 9:24 3665
You have **s** under me those who Ps 18:39 3766
And **s** the choice men of Israel. Ps 78:31 3766
And they were **s** under their power. Ps 106:42 3665
Which **s** the nations in anger with Is 14:6 7287a
leaped on them and **s** all of them Ac 19:16 *2634b*

SUBDUES
for me, And **s** peoples under me. Ps 18:47 1696
He **s** peoples under us And nations Ps 47:3 1696
Who **s** my people under me. Ps 144:2 7286
A gift in secret **s** anger, Pr 21:14 3711
nations before him And **s** kings. Is 41:2 7287a

SUBJECT
not **s** him to a slave's service. Lv 25:39 5647
them and became **s** to forced labor. Jg 1:30
over the men **s** to forced labor. 1Ki 4:6
And it will again be **s** to burning, Is 6:13
sons of Ammon will be **s** to them. Is 11:14 4928
demons are **s** to us in Your name." Lk 10:17 *5293*
that the spirits are **s** to you, Lk 10:20 *5293*
does not **s** itself to the law of God, Ro 8:7 *5293*
they did not **s** themselves to the Ro 10:3 *5293*
spirits of prophets are **s** to prophets; 1Co 14:32 *5293*
but are to **s** themselves, just as 1Co 14:34 *5293*
be **s** again to a yoke of slavery. Ga 5:1 *1758*
and be **s** to one another in the Eph 5:21 *5293*
Wives, *be* **s** to your own husbands, Eph 5:22
But as the church is **s** to Christ, Eph 5:24 *5293*
even to **s** all things to Himself. Php 3:21 *5293*
Wives, be **s** to your husbands, as Col 3:18 *5293*
being **s** to their own husbands, Ti 2:5 *5293*
Urge bondslaves to be **s** to their Ti 2:9 *5293*
Remind them to be **s** to rulers, Ti 3:1 *5293*
not **s** to angels the world to come, Heb 2:5 *5293*
He left nothing that is not **s** to him. Heb 2:8 *506*
were **s** to slavery all their lives. Heb 2:15 *1777*
be **s** to the Father of spirits, Heb 12:9 *5293*
likewise, be **s** to *your* elders; 1Pe 5:5 *5293*

SUBJECTED
the creation was **s** to futility, Ro 8:20 *5293*
willingly, but because of Him who **s** it, Ro 8:20 *5293*
When all things are **s** to Him, 1Co 15:28 *5293*
then the Son Himself also will be **s** to 1Co 15:28 *5293*
the One who **s** all things to Him, 1Co 15:28 *5293*
not yet see all things **s** to him. Heb 2:8 *5293*
and powers had been **s** to Him. 1Pe 3:22 *5293*

SUBJECTING
For in **s** all things to him, He Heb 2:8 *5293*

SUBJECTION
and brought them into **s** for male Jer 34:11 3533
and you brought them into **s** to be Jer 34:16 3533
that the kingdom might be in **s**, Ezk 17:14 8217
and He continued in **s** to them; Lk 2:51 *5293*
be in **s** to the governing authorities. Ro 13:1 *5293*
it is necessary to be in **s**, Ro 13:5 *5293*
ALL THINGS IN **S** UNDER HIS FEET. 1Co 15:27 *5293*
"All things are put in **s**," 1Co 15:27 *5293*
who put all things in **s** to Him. 1Co 15:27 *5293*
that you also be in **s** to such men 1Co 16:16 *5293*
But we did not yield in **s** to them Ga 2:5 *5292*
all things in **s** under His feet, Eph 1:22 *5293*
ALL THINGS IN **S** UNDER HIS FEET." Heb 2:8 *5293*

SUBJECTS
to question Him closely on many **s**, Lk 11:53 *4183*

SUBJUGATE
s for yourselves the people of Judah 2Ch 28:10 3533

SUBJUGATION
has a day of panic, **s** and confusion Is 22:5 4001

SUBMISSIVE
be **s** to your masters with all 1Pe 2:18 *5293*
be **s** to your own husbands so that 1Pe 3:1 *5293*
being **s** to their own husbands; 1Pe 3:5 *5293*

SUBMISSIVENESS
receive instruction with entire **s**. 1Tm 2:11 *5292*

SUBMIT
and **s** yourself to her authority." Gn 16:9 6031a
Foreigners **s** to me. Ps 18:44 3584
do you **s** yourself to decrees, Col 2:20 *1379*
Obey your leaders and **s** *to them* Heb 13:17 *5226*
S therefore to God. Jas 4:7 *5293*
S yourselves for the Lord's sake 1Pe 2:13 *5293*

SUBMITTED
We have **s** to Egypt *and* Assyria to La 5:6 5414, 3027
and I **s** to them the gospel which I Ga 2:2 *394*

SUBSEQUENT
the land because of that **s** famine; Gn 41:31 310
s to the one which appeared to me Da 8:1 310

SUBSEQUENTLY
s destroyed those who did not Jude 1:5 *1208*

SUBSIDE
And **s** like the Nile of Egypt. Am 8:8 8257

SUBSIDED
over the earth, and the water **s**. Gn 8:1 7918
Then their anger toward him **s** Jg 8:3 7503
the anger of King Ahasuerus had **s**, Es 2:1 7918
Mordecai, and the king's anger **s**. Es 7:10 7918

SUBSIDES
days, until your brother's fury **s**, Gn 27:44 7725
your brother's anger against you **s** and Gn 27:45 7725
Nile And **s** like the Nile of Egypt; Am 9:5 8257

SUBSTANCE
"O LORD, bless his **s**, Dt 33:11 2428
eyes have seen my unformed **s**; Ps 139:16 1564
He must give all the **s** of his house. Pr 6:31 1952
but the **s** belongs to Christ. Col 2:17 *4983*

SUBSTITUTE
it and its **s** shall become holy. Lv 27:10 8545
it and its **s** shall become holy. Lv 27:33 8545
Who **s** darkness for light and light Is 5:20 7760
Who **s** bitter for sweet and sweet Is 5:20 7760

SUBVERT
ashamed, for they **s** me with a lie; Ps 119:78 5791

SUBVERTS
and **s** the cause of the just. Ex 23:8 5557
But wickedness **s** the sinner. Pr 13:6 5557

SUCATHITES
the Shimeathites *and* the **S**. 1Ch 2:55 7756

SUCCEED
of the LORD, when it will not **s**? Nu 14:41 6743b
that you may **s** in all that you do 1Ki 2:3 7919a
"Go up and **s**, and the LORD will 1Ki 22:15 6743b
fathers, for you will not **s**." 2Ch 13:12 6743b
"Go up to Ramoth-gilead and **s**, 2Ch 18:11 6743b
"Go up and **s**, for they will be 2Ch 18:14 6743b
trust in His prophets and **s**." 2Ch 20:20 6743b
devised a plot, They will not **s**. Ps 21:11 3201
But with many counselors they **s**. Pr 15:22 6965
morning or evening sowing will **s**, Ec 11:6 3787
you will not **s** Jer 32:5 6743b
Will he **s**? Will he who does such Ezk 17:15 6743b
cause deceit to **s** by his influence; Da 8:25 6743b
but it will not **s**, for the end is Da 11:27 6743b
of God I may **s** in coming to you. Ro 1:10 *2137*

SUCCEEDED
and Abiathar **s** Ahithophel; 1Ch 27:34 310
Felix was **s** by Porcius Festus, Ac 24:27 *1240*

SUCCEEDING
care and is **s** in their hands. Ezr 5:8 6744
And without **s** *in the matter* for Is 55:11 6743b

SUCCESS
Abraham, please grant me **s** today, Gn 24:12 7136a
you may have **s** wherever you go. Jos 1:7 7919a
and then you will have **s**. Jos 1:8 7919a
"The God of heaven will give us **s**; Ne 2:20 6743b
that their hands cannot attain **s**. Jb 5:12 8454
has the advantage of giving **s**. Ec 10:10 3787
So this Daniel enjoyed **s** in the Da 6:28 6744

SUCCESSFUL
had made his journey **s** or not. Gn 24:21 6743b
with you to make your journey **s**, Gn 24:40 6743b
make my journey on which I go **s**; Gn 24:42 6743b
with Joseph, so he became a **s** man. Gn 39:2 6743b
be with you that you may be **s**, 1Ch 22:11 6743b
And the elders of the Jews were **s** Ezr 6:14 6744
and make Your servant **s** today and Ne 1:11 6743b
him, and He will make his ways **s**. Is 48:15 6743b

SUCCESSFULLY
and **s** completed all that he had 2Ch 7:11 6743b

SUCCESSIVE
with you, for all **s** generations; Gn 9:12 5769
temple were wider at each **s** story. Ezk 41:7 4605

SUCCESSIVELY
he left and passed **s** through Ac 18:23 *2517*

SUCCESSORS
from Samuel and *his* **s** onward, Ac 3:24 *2517*

SUCCOTH
Jacob journeyed to **S**, Gn 33:17 5523
therefore the place is named **S**. Gn 33:17 5523
journeyed from Rameses to **S**, Ex 12:37 5523
Then they set out from **S** and Ex 13:20 5523
from Rameses and camped in **S**. Nu 33:5 5523
They journeyed from **S** and Nu 33:6 5523
and Beth-nimrah and **S** and Zaphon, Jos 13:27 5523
He said to the men of **S**, Jg 8:5 5523
The leaders of **S** said, Jg 8:6 5523
just as the men of **S** had answered. Jg 8:8 5523
a youth from **S** and questioned him. Jg 8:14 5523
the princes of **S** and its elders, Jg 8:14 5523
He came to the men of **S** and said, Jg 8:15 5523
the men of **S** with them. Jg 8:16 5523
ground between **S** and Zarethan. 1Ki 7:46 5523
clay ground between **S** and Zeredah. 2Ch 4:17 5523
and measure out the valley of **S**. Ps 60:6 5523
And measure out the valley of **S**. Ps 108:7 5523

SUCCOTH-BENOTH
The men of Babylon made **S**, 2Ki 17:30 5524

SUCH
Far be it from You to do **s** a thing, Gn 18:25 2088
a savory dish for me **s** as I love, Gn 27:4 3512c
for your father, **s** as he loves. Gn 27:9 3512c
savory food **s** as his father loved. Gn 27:14 3512c
and **s** shall be my wages. Gn 30:32
s a thing ought not to be done. Gn 34:7 3651
s as I had never seen for ugliness Gn 41:19 2007
my lord speak **s** words as these? Gn 44:7
your servants to do **s** a thing. Gn 44:7 2088
s a man as I can indeed practice Gn 44:15 3644
for **s** is the period required for Gn 50:3 3651
s as has not been *seen* in Egypt Ex 9:18 834
s as had not been in all the land Ex 9:24 834
s as there has not been *before* and Ex 11:6 834, 3644
and **s** as shall never be again. Ex 11:6 3644
that you have brought **s** great sin Ex 32:21
anyone who is clean may eat **s** Lv 7:19
for **s** a one has made naked his Lv 20:19
a person who touches any **s** shall Lv 22:6
nor shall you accept any **s** from Lv 22:25 428
any **s** that one gives to the LORD Lv 27:9 834
who can do **s** works and mighty acts Dt 3:24
that they had **s** a heart in them, Dt 5:29 2088
do **s** a wicked thing among you. Dt 13:11 2088
"But if it has any defect, **s** *as* Dt 15:21
do **s** an evil thing among you. Dt 19:20 2088
But do not commit **s** an act of folly Jg 19:24 2088
"Why do you do **s** things, the evil 1Sa 2:23 428
and he is **s** a worthless man that 1Sa 25:17
s a thing is not done in Israel; 2Sa 13:12 3651
have you planned **s** a thing against 2Sa 14:13 2088
"**S** is not the case. 2Sa 20:21 3651
is the city making **s** an uproar?" 1Ki 1:41
did **s** abundance of spices come in 1Ki 10:10 1931
s almug trees have not come in 1Ki 10:12 3651
"In **s** and such a place shall be 2Ki 6:8 6423
and **s** a place shall be my camp." 2Ki 6:8 492
in heaven, could **s** a thing be?" 2Ki 7:19 2088
I am bringing **s** calamity on 2Ki 21:12
Surely **s** a Passover had not been 2Ki 23:22 2088
s as none of the kings who were 2Ch 1:12 834, 3651
celebrated **s** a Passover as Josiah did 2Ch 35:18
who has put **s** *a thing* as this in Ezr 7:27
"**S** things as you are saying have Ne 6:8 428
And could one **s** as I go into the Ne 6:11 3644
royalty for **s** a time as this?" Es 4:14
"Indeed, you have now become **s**, Jb 6:21 3808
does not know **s** things as these? Jb 12:3 3644
your spirit against God And allow **s** Jb 15:13
"I have heard many **s** things; Jb 16:2 428
"Surely **s** are the dwellings of Jb 18:21 428
And many **s** *decrees* are with Him. Jb 23:14 1992a
me, And **s** as breathe out violence. Ps 27:12
For **s** is God, Our God forever and Ps 48:14 2088

S knowledge is too wonderful for Ps 139:6
The wicked does not understand s Pr 29:7
s days as have never come since the Is 7:17 834
S *will be* the portion of those who Is 17:14 2088
'Behold, s is our hope, where we Is 20:6 3541
He who is too *impoverished* for s Is 40:20
"Who has heard s a thing? Is 66:8 2088
Who has seen s things? Is 66:8 428
there has been s *a thing* as this! Jer 2:10
"And on a nation s as this Shall I Jer 5:9 834
'On a nation s as this Shall I not Jer 5:29 834
"On a nation s as this Shall I Jer 9:9 834
My soul will sob in secret for s Jer 13:17
by speaking s words to them; Jer 38:4 428
the people who were giving him s Jer 44:20
S were their faces. Ezk 1:11
S *was* the appearance of the Ezk 1:28 1931
Will he who does s things escape? Ezk 17:15 428
how can s a servant of my lord talk Da 10:17 2088
of my lord talk with s as my lord? Da 10:17 2088
a time of distress s as never occurred Da 12:1 834
at s a time the prudent person Am 5:13 1931
With s an offering on your part, Mal 1:9 2088
your light shine before men in s a way Mt 5:16 3779
I have not found s great faith Mt 8:10 5118
who had given s authority to men. Mt 9:8 5108
to satisfy s a large crowd?" Mt 15:33 5118
whoever receives one s child in My Mt 18:5 5108
of heaven belongs to s as these." Mt 19:14 5108
s as has not occurred since the Mt 24:21 3634
to s an extent that Jesus could no Mk 1:45 5620
to s an extent that they could not Mk 3:20 5620
And s a very large crowd Mk 4:1
With many s parables He was Mk 4:33 5108
and s miracles as these performed Mk 6:2 5108
s as the washing of cups and Mk 7:4
you do many things s as that." Mk 7:13 3946
of God belongs to s as these. Mk 10:14 5108
tribulation s as has not occurred since Mk 13:19 3634
have I found s great faith." Lk 7:9 5118
man about whom I hear s things?" Lk 9:9 5108
of God belongs to s as these. Lk 18:16 5108
for s people the Father seeks to Jn 4:23 5108
commanded us to stone s women; Jn 8:5 5108
who is a sinner perform s signs?" Jn 9:16 5108
the land for s and such a price?" Ac 5:8 5118
the land for such and s a price?" Ac 5:8 5118
to s an extent that they even Ac 5:15 5620
and spoke in s a manner that a Ac 14:1 3779
keep yourselves free from s things, Ac 15:29 3779
there occurred s a sharp disagreement Ac 15:39
he, having received s a command, Ac 16:24 5108
Away with s a fellow from the earth, Ac 22:22 5108
not of s crimes as I was expecting, Ac 25:18 3739
loss how to investigate s matters, Ac 25:20 3778
this day, might become s as I am, Ac 26:29 5108
that those who practice s things are Ro 1:32 5108
upon those who practice s things. Ro 2:2 5108
on those who practice s things and Ro 2:3 5108
For s men are slaves, not of our Ro 16:18 5108
and immorality of s a kind as does 1Co 5:1 5108
I have decided to deliver s a one 1Co 5:5 5108
not even to eat with s a one. 1Co 5:11 5108
S were some of you; but you were 1Co 6:11 3778
is not under bondage in s *cases,* 1Co 7:15 5108
Yet s will have trouble in this life, 1Co 7:28 5108
no s thing as an idol in the world, 1Co 8:4
Run in s a way that you may win. 1Co 9:24 3779
Therefore I run in s a way, 1Co 9:26 3779
I box in s a way, as not beating 1Co 9:26 3779
you but s as is common to man; 1Co 10:13 442
you also be in subjection to s men 1Co 16:16 5108
Therefore acknowledge s men. 1Co 16:18 5108
Sufficient for s a one is this 2Co 2:6 5108
otherwise s a one might be 2Co 2:7 5108
S confidence we have through Christ 2Co 3:4 5108
Therefore having s a hope, 2Co 3:12 5108
Let s a person consider this, that 2Co 10:11 5108
s persons *we are* also in deed when 2Co 10:11 5108
For s men are false apostles, 2Co 11:13 5108
Apart from s external things, 2Co 11:28
s a man was caught up to the third 2Co 12:2 5108
And I know how s a man 2Co 12:3 5108
On behalf of s a man I will boast; 2Co 12:5 5108
those who practice s things will not Ga 5:21 5108
against s things there is no law. Ga 5:23 5108
restore s a one in a spirit of Ga 6:1 5108
but only s *a word* as is good for Eph 4:29 5100
no spot or wrinkle or any s thing; Eph 5:27 5108
submit yourself to decrees, s as, Col 2:20
Now s persons we command and 2Th 3:12 5108
Avoid s men as these. 2Tm 3:5
s as happened to me at Antioch, 2Tm 3:11 3634
knowing that s a man is perverted Ti 3:11 5108
since I am s a person as Paul, Phm 1:9 5108
who has become s not on the basis Heb 7:16
for us to have s a high priest, Heb 7:26 5108
we have s a high priest, who has Heb 8:1 5108
For those who say s things make it Heb 11:14 5108
who has endured s hostility by sinners Heb 12:3 5108
sound of words which *sound was* s Heb 12:19
with s sacrifices God is pleased. Heb 13:16 5108
knowing that as s we will incur a Jas 3:1
is set aflame by s a small fire! Jas 3:5 2245
we will go to s and such a city, Jas 4:13 3592
we will go to such and s a city, Jas 4:13 3592
all s boasting is evil. Jas 4:16 5108
For s is the will of God that by 1Pe 2:15 3779
s an utterance as this was made to 2Pe 1:17 5107
and s we are. For this reason 1Jn 3:1
we ought to support s men, 3Jn 1:8 5108
s as there had not been since man Rv 16:18 3634
for in one hour s great wealth has Rv 18:17 5118

SUCK

He made him s honey from the rock, Dt 32:13 3243
why the breasts, that I should s? Jb 3:12 3243
"His young ones also s up blood; Jb 39:30 5966
will also s the milk of nations And Is 60:16 3243
And s the breast of kings; Is 60:16 3243
That you may s and be delighted Is 66:11 4711

SUCKLING

Samuel took a s lamb and 1Sa 7:9 2461
ewes with s lambs He brought him To Ps 78:71 5763

SUCKS

"He s the poison of cobras; Jb 20:16 3243

SUDDEN

I will appoint over you a s terror, Lv 26:16 928
you, And s dread terrifies you, Jb 22:10 6597
utterly swept away by s terrors! Ps 73:19 1091
And their years in s terror. Ps 78:33 928
Do not be afraid of s fear Nor Pr 3:25 6597

SUDDENLY

'But if a man dies very s beside Nu 6:9 6597
S the LORD said to Moses Nu 12:4 6597
if he pushed him s without enmity, Nu 35:22 6621
So Joshua came upon them s by Jos 10:9 6597
came upon them s by the waters of Jos 11:7 6597
because the thing came about s. 2Ch 29:36 6597
"If the scourge kills s, Jb 9:23 6597
And s they go down to Sheol. Jb 21:13 7281
back, they will s be ashamed. Ps 6:10 7281
S they shoot at him, and do not Ps 64:4 6597
S they will be wounded. Ps 64:7 6597
his calamity will come s; Pr 6:15 6597
S he follows her As an ox goes to Pr 7:22 6597
For their calamity will rise s, Pr 24:22 6597
Will s be broken beyond remedy. Pr 29:1 6621
evil time when it s falls on them. Ec 9:12 6597
And it will happen instantly, s. Is 29:5 6597
collapse comes s in an instant, Is 30:13 6597
will come on you s in one day: Is 47:9 7281
do not know Will come on you s. Is 47:11 6597
S I acted, and they came to pass. Is 48:3 6597
S my tents are devastated, My Jer 4:20 6597
For s the destroyer Will come upon Jer 6:26 6597
I will s bring down on her Anguish Jer 15:8 6597
You s bring raiders upon them; Jer 18:22 6597
S Babylon has fallen and been Jer 51:8 6597
S the fingers of a man's hand Da 5:5 8160
"Will not your creditors rise up s, Hab 2:7 6621
seek, will s come to His temple; Mal 3:1 6597
he should come s and find you asleep. Mk 13:36 1810
an angel of the Lord s stood before Lk 2:9
And s there appeared with the Lk 2:13 1810
seizes him, and he s screams, Lk 9:39 1810
not come on you s like a trap; Lk 21:34 160
two men s stood near them in Lk 24:4
And s there came from heaven a Ac 2:2 869
and s a light from heaven flashed Ac 9:3 1810
an angel of the Lord s appeared and Ac 12:7
s there came a great earthquake, Ac 16:26 869
a very bright light s flashed from Ac 22:6 1810
to swell up or s fall down dead. Ac 28:6 869
destruction will come upon them s 1Th 5:3 160

SUE

"If anyone wants to s you and Mt 5:40 2919

SUES

No one s righteously and no one Is 59:4 7121

SUET

and the s over the wood which is Lv 1:8 6309
pieces with its head and its s, Lv 1:12 6309
and the pieces and the s in smoke. Lv 8:20 6309

SUFFER

will s *for* your unfaithfulness, Nu 14:33 5375
or if they s the fate of all men, Nu 16:29 6485
and you will s severe sickness, a 2Ch 21:15
young lions do lack and s hunger; Ps 34:10 7456
I s Your terrors; I am overcome. Ps 88:15 5375
a stranger will surely s for it, Pr 11:15 7489a
companion of fools will s harm. Pr 13:20 7489a
And an idle man will s hunger. Pr 19:15 7456
that the king might not s loss. Da 6:2 5142
Even the flocks of sheep s. Jl 1:18 816
and s many things from the elders Mt 16:21 3958
also the Son of Man is going to s at Mt 17:12 3958
the Son of Man must s many things Mk 8:31 3958
that He will s many things and be Mk 9:12 3958
"The Son of Man must s many things Lk 9:22 3958
"But first He must s many things Lk 17:25 3958
this Passover with you before I s; Lk 22:15 3958
necessary for the Christ to s these Lk 24:26 3958
that the Christ would s and rise Lk 24:46 3958
HADES, NOR DID His flesh S DECAY. Ac 2:31 3708
that His Christ would s, Ac 3:18 3958
worthy to s shame for *His* name. Ac 5:41 718
he must s for My name's sake." Ac 9:16 3958
the Christ had to s and rise again Ac 17:3 3958
that the Christ was to s, Ac 26:23 3805
if indeed we s with *Him* so that Ro 8:17 4841
is burned up, he will s loss; 1Co 3:15 2210
all the members s with it; 1Co 12:26 4841
same sufferings which we also s; 2Co 1:6 3958
not s loss in anything through us. 2Co 7:9 2210
Did you s so many things in Ga 3:4 3958
Him, but also to s for His sake, Php 1:29 3958
we were going to s affliction; 1Th 3:4 2346
For this reason I also s these things, 2Tm 1:12 3958
S hardship with *me,* as a good 2Tm 2:3 4777
for which I s hardship even to 2Tm 2:9 2553
He would have needed to s often Heb 9:26 3958
when you do what is right and s *for it* 1Pe 2:20 3958
s for the sake of righteousness, 1Pe 3:14 3958
that you s for doing what is right 1Pe 3:17 3958
those also who s according to 1Pe 4:19 3958
not fear what you are about to s. Rv 2:10 3958

SUFFERED

give birth and she s severe labor. Gn 35:16 7185
for last night I s greatly in a Mt 27:19 3958
because they s this *fate?* Lk 13:2 3958
off into the fire and s no harm. Ac 28:5 3958
not take into account a wrong s, 1Co 13:5
I have s the loss of all things, Php 3:8 2210
but after we had already s and 1Th 2:2 4310a
s shipwreck in regard to their faith. 1Tm 1:19 3489
tempted in that which He has s, Heb 2:18 3958
from the things which He s. Heb 5:8 3958
His own blood, s outside the gate. Heb 13:12 3958
since Christ also s for you, 1Pe 2:21 3958
since Christ has s in the flesh, 1Pe 4:1 3958
because he who has s in the flesh 1Pe 4:1 3958
you have s for a little while, 1Pe 5:10 3958

SUFFERING

those s with various diseases Mt 4:24 4912
a woman who had been s from a Mt 9:20 131
Simon's mother-in-law was s from a Lk 4:38 4912
was a man s from dropsy. Lk 14:2 5203
"And we indeed *are* s justly, Lk 23:41
Himself alive after His s, Ac 1:3 3958
of having abundance and s need. Php 4:12 5302
God, for which indeed you are s. 2Th 1:5 3958
but join with *me* in s for the gospel 2Tm 1:8 4777
because of the s of death crowned Heb 2:9 3804
example, brethren, of s and patience, Jas 5:10 2552
Is anyone among you s? Jas 5:13 2553
up under sorrows when s unjustly. 1Pe 2:19 3958
while s, He uttered no threats, 1Pe 2:23 3958
the same experiences of s are being 1Pe 5:9 3804
s wrong as the wages of doing 2Pe 2:13

SUFFERINGS

for I am aware of their s. Ex 3:7 4341
s of this present time are not worthy Ro 8:18 3804
For just as the s of Christ are 2Co 1:5 3804
the same s which we also suffer; 2Co 1:6 3804
that as you are sharers of our s, 2Co 1:7 3804
and the fellowship of His s, Php 3:10 3804
I rejoice in my s for your sake, Col 1:24 3804
for you also endured the same s at 1Th 2:14 3958
persecutions, *and* s, 2Tm 3:11 3804
author of their salvation through s. Heb 2:10 3804
you endured a great conflict of s, Heb 10:32 3804
as He predicted the s of Christ and 1Pe 1:11 3804
that you share the s of Christ, 1Pe 4:13 3804
and witness of the s of Christ, 1Pe 5:1 3804

SUFFERS

"Why is light given to him who s, Jb 3:20 6001a
hand of everyone who s will come Jb 20:22 6001a
the kingdom of heaven s violence, Mt 11:12 971
s the pains of childbirth together Ro 8:22 4944
And if one member s, 1Co 12:26 3958
Make sure that none of you s as a 1Pe 4:15 3958
but if *anyone* s as a Christian, 1Pe 4:16

SUFFICE

if the dust of Samaria will s for 1Ki 20:10 8230b

SUFFICIENCY

always having all s in everything, 2Co 9:8 841

SUFFICIENT

For the material they had was s Ex 36:7 1767
as to find s for its redemption, Lv 25:26 1767
'But if he has not found s means Lv 25:28 1767
of a sojourner with you becomes s, Lv 25:47 5381
for them, to be s for them? Nu 11:22 4672
for them, to be s for them?" Nu 11:22 4672
generously lend him s for his need Dt 15:8 1767
consecrated themselves in s numbers 2Ch 30:3 1767
but her gain will become s food Is 23:18 7654
worth of bread is not s for them, Jn 6:7 714
S for such a one is this punishment 2Co 2:6 2425
"My grace is s for you, for power 2Co 12:9 714
the time already past is s *for* 1Pe 4:3 713

SUFFOCATION

So that my soul would choose s, Jb 7:15 4267

SUIT

of silver a year, a s of clothes, Jg 17:10 6187
any man had a s to come to the king 2Sa 15:2 7379
every man who has any s or cause 2Sa 15:4 7379

SUITABLE

make him a helper s for him." Gn 2:18 5048
was not found a helper s for him. Gn 2:20 5048
indeed a place s for livestock, Nu 32:1 4725
harbor was not s for wintering, Ac 27:12 428
an administration s to the fullness of Eph 1:10 3588

SUKKIIM

the Lubim, the S and the 2Ch 12:3 5525

SULLEN

went to his house s and vexed, 1Ki 20:43 5620
So Ahab came into his house s and 1Ki 21:4 5620
How is it that your spirit is so s that 1Ki 21:5 5620

SUM

For I do not know the s *of them.* Ps 71:15 5615
The s of Your word is truth, And Ps 119:160 7218
How vast is the s of them! Ps 139:17 7218
large s of money to the soldiers, Mt 28:12 2425

had purchased for a s of money from Ac 7:16 5092
citizenship with a large s of money." Ac 22:28 2774
To s up, all of you be harmonious, 1Pe 3:8 5056

SUMMARY
and related the *following* s of it. Da 7:1 7217

SUMMED
it is s up in this saying, Ro 13:9 346

SUMMER
cold and heat, And s and winter, Gn 8:22 7019c
of raisins, a hundred s fruits, 2Sa 16:1 7019c
and the bread and s fruit for the 2Sa 16:2 7019c
away *as* with the fever heat of s. Ps 32:4 7019c
You have made s and winter. Ps 74:17 7019c
Prepares her food in the s Pr 6:8 7019c
He who gathers in s is a son who Pr 10:5 7019c
Like snow in s and like rain in Pr 26:1 7019c
they prepare their food in the s; Pr 30:25 7019c
For the shouting over your s fruits Is 16:9 7019c
the birds of prey will spend the s Is 18:6 7019b
like the first-ripe fig prior to s, Is 28:4 7019c
"Harvest is past, s is ended, Jer 8:20 7019c
gather in wine and s fruit and oil and Jer 40:10 7019c
and s fruit in great abundance. Jer 40:12 7019c
Upon your s fruits and your grape Jer 48:32 7019c
chaff from the s threshing floors; Da 2:35 7007
house together with the s house; Am 3:15 7019c
there was a basket of s fruit. Am 8:1 7019c
"A basket of s fruit." Am 8:2 7019c
will be in s as well as in winter. Zch 14:8 7019c
leaves, you know that s is near; Mt 24:32 2330
leaves, you know that s is near. Mk 13:28 2330
for yourselves that s is now near. Lk 21:30 2330

SUMMING
the s up of all things in Christ, Eph 1:10 346

SUMMIT
as David was coming to the s, 2Sa 15:32 7218
had passed a little beyond the s, 2Sa 16:1 7218
Journey down from the s of Amana, SS 4:8 7218
From the s of Senir and Hermon, SS 4:8 7218
to Me, *Like* the s of Lebanon; Jer 22:6 7218
And the s of Carmel dries up." Am 1:2 7218
they hide on the s of Carmel, Am 9:3 7218

SUMMON
city shall s him and speak to him. Dt 25:8 7121
someone to s Ahimelech the priest, 1Sa 22:11 7121
messenger who went to s Micaiah 1Ki 22:13 7121
Now, s all the prophets of Baal, 2Ki 10:19 7121
messenger who went to s Micaiah 2Ch 18:12 7121
matter of justice, who can s Him? Jb 9:19 3259
That I will s My servant Eliakim Is 22:20 7121
Me, and who will s Me *into court?* Jer 49:19 3259
"S many against Babylon, All Jer 50:29 8085
Me, and who will s Me *into court?* Jer 50:44 3259
S against her the kingdoms of Jer 51:27 8085
your back, s all *your* strength. Na 2:1 553
when I find time I will s you." Ac 24:25 3333

SUMMONED
Then Jacob s his sons and said, Gn 49:1 7121
Then Moses s all Israel and said Dt 5:1 7121
Moses s all Israel and said to them, Dt 29:2 7121
Then Joshua s the Reubenites and Jos 22:1 7121
and he sent and s Balaam the son Jos 24:9 7121
Now she sent and s Barak the son Jg 4:6 7121
The men of Israel were s from Jg 7:23 6817
So all the men of Ephraim were s and Jg 7:24 6817
Then the sons of Ammon were s and Jg 10:17 6817
Then the men of Ephraim were s, Jg 12:1 6817
people were then s to Saul at Gilgal. 1Sa 13:4 6817
Then Saul s the people and 1Sa 15:4 8085
So Saul s all the people for war, 1Sa 23:8 8085
to put on armor and older were s and 2Ki 3:21 6817
So they sent and s him. 2Ch 10:3 7121
So the king s Jehoiada the chief 2Ch 24:6 7121
in her and she was s by name. Es 2:14 7121
Then the king's scribes were s on Es 3:12 7121
Then Esther s Hathach from the Es 4:5 7121
to the inner court who is not s, Es 4:11 7121
And I have not been s to come to Es 4:11 7121
And s the earth from the rising of Ps 50:1 7121
"After many days you will be s; Ezk 38:8 6485
Let Daniel now be s and Da 5:12 7123
Jesus s His twelve disciples Mt 10:1 4341
s those whom He Himself wanted, Mk 3:13 4341
And He s the twelve and began to Mk 6:7 4341
And He s the crowd with His Mk 8:34 4341
"And he s one of the servants and Lk 15:26 4341
"And he s each one of his Lk 16:5 4341
Pilate s the chief priests and Lk 23:13 4779
into the Praetorium, and s Jesus and Jn 18:33 5455
And when they had s them, Ac 4:18 2564
So the twelve s the congregation Ac 6:2 4341
he s two of his servants and a Ac 10:7 5455
This man s Barnabas and Saul and Ac 13:7 4341
After *Paul* had been s, Ac 24:2 2564

SUMMONING
use them for s the congregation and Nu 10:2 4744
for I am s a sword against all the Jer 25:29 7121
"Then s him, his lord said to Mt 18:32 4341
by this time, and s the centurion, Mk 15:44 4341
S two of his disciples, John sent Lk 7:19 4341

SUMMONS
Then Moses sent a s to Dathan and Nu 16:12 7121
He s the heavens above, And the Ps 50:4 7121

SUMS
people were putting in large s. Mk 12:41 4183

SUN
Now when the s was going down, a Gn 15:12 8121
It came about when the s had set, Gn 15:17 8121
The s had risen over the earth Gn 19:23 8121
there, because the s had set; Gn 28:11 8121
Now the s rose upon him just as he Gn 32:31 8121
the s and the moon and eleven Gn 37:9 8121
but when the s grew hot, it would Ex 16:21 8121
hands were steady until the s set. Ex 17:12 8121
"*But* if the s has risen on him, Ex 22:3 8121
it to him before the s sets, Ex 22:26 8121
'But when the s sets, he will be Lv 22:7 8121
see the s and the moon and the stars, Dt 4:19 8121
or the s or the moon or any of the Dt 17:3 8121
"When the s goes down you shall Dt 24:13 8121
on his day before the s sets, Dt 24:15 8121
with the choice yield of the s, Dt 33:14 8121
Sea toward the setting of the s will Jos 1:4 8121
"O s, stand still at Gibeon, And Jos 10:12 8121
So the s stood still, and the moon Jos 10:13 8121
And the s stopped in the middle of Jos 10:13 8121
Sea toward the setting of the s. Jos 23:4 8121
rising of the s in its might." Jg 5:31 8121
morning, as soon as the s is up, Jg 9:33 8121
day before the s went down, Jg 14:18 2775a
and the s set on them near Gibeah Jg 19:14 8121
by the time the s is hot, 1Sa 11:9 8121
and when the s was going down, 2Sa 2:24 8121
else before the s goes down." 2Sa 3:35 8121
all Israel, and under the s.' " 2Sa 12:12 8121
of the morning *when* the s rises, 2Sa 23:4 8121
and the s shone on the water, 2Ki 3:22 8121
to the s and to the moon and to 2Ki 23:5 8121
kings of Judah had given to the s, 2Ki 23:11 8121
burned the chariots of the s with fire. 2Ki 23:11 8121
be opened until the s is hot, Ne 7:3 8121
"He thrives before the s, Jb 8:16 8121
Who commands the s not to shine, Jb 9:7 2775a
looked at the s when it shone Or Jb 31:26 216
He has placed a tent for the s, Ps 19:4 8121
from the rising of the s to its setting. Ps 50:1 8121
of a woman which never see the s. Ps 58:8 8121
fear You while the s *endures,* Ps 72:5 8121
increase as long as the s *shines;* Ps 72:17 8121
have prepared the light and the s. Ps 74:16 8121
the LORD God is a s and shield; Ps 84:11 8121
And his throne as the s before Me. Ps 89:36 8121
The s knows the place of its Ps 104:19 8121
When the s rises they withdraw And Ps 104:22 8121
From the rising of the s to its Ps 113:3 8121
The s will not smite you by day, Ps 121:6 8121
The s to rule by day, For His Ps 136:8 8121
Praise Him, s and moon; Ps 148:3 8121
work Which he does under the s? Ec 1:3 8121
the s rises and the sun sets; Ec 1:5 8121
the sun rises and the s sets; Ec 1:5 8121
there is nothing new under the s. Ec 1:9 8121
which have been done under the s, Ec 1:14 8121
there was no profit under the s. Ec 2:11 8121
which had been done under the s Ec 2:17 8121
which I had labored under the s, Ec 2:18 8121
by acting wisely under the s. Ec 2:19 8121
which I had labored under the s. Ec 2:20 8121
with which he labors under the s? Ec 2:22 8121
I have seen under the s *that* in Ec 3:16 8121
which were being done under the s. Ec 4:1 8121
activity that is done under the s. Ec 4:3 8121
again at vanity under the s. Ec 4:7 8121
seen all the living under the s throng Ec 4:15 8121
which I have seen under the s: Ec 5:13 8121
labor in which he toils under the s Ec 5:18 8121
an evil which I have seen under the s Ec 6:1 8121
It never sees the s and it never Ec 6:5 8121
will be after him under the s? Ec 6:12 8121
advantage to those who see the s. Ec 7:11 8121
deed that has been done under the s Ec 8:9 8121
is nothing good for a man under the s Ec 8:15 8121
God has given him under the s. Ec 8:15 8121
which has been done under the s. Ec 8:17 8121
in all that is done under the s, Ec 9:3 8121
in all that is done under the s. Ec 9:6 8121
He has given to you under the s; Ec 9:9 8121
you have labored under the s. Ec 9:9 8121
I again saw under the s that the Ec 9:11 8121
came to see as wisdom under the s, Ec 9:13 8121
an evil I have seen under the s, Ec 10:5 8121
is good for the eyes to see the s. Ec 11:7 8121
before the s and the light, the moon Ec 12:2 8121
swarthy, For the s has burned me. SS 1:6 8121
the full moon, As pure as the s, SS 6:10 2535
The s will be dark when it rises And Is 13:10 8121
will be abashed and the s ashamed, Is 24:23 2535
will be as the light of the s, Is 30:26 2535
the light of the s will be seven Is 30:26 2535
which has gone down with the s on Is 38:8 8121
From the rising of the s he will call Is 41:25 8121
from the rising to the setting of the s Is 45:6 8121
heat or s strike them down; Is 49:10 8121
glory from the rising of the s, Is 59:19 8121
you have the s for light by day, Is 60:19 8121
"Your s will no longer set, Nor Is 60:20 8121
will spread them out to the s, Jer 8:2 8121
s has set while it was yet day; Jer 15:9 8121
Who gives the s for light by day And Jer 31:35 8121
themselves eastward toward the s. Ezk 8:16 8121
I will cover the s with a cloud And Ezk 32:7 8121
The s and the moon grow dark And Jl 2:10 8121
s will be turned into darkness And Jl 2:31 8121
The s and moon grow dark And the Jl 3:15 8121
"That I will make the s go down Am 8:9 8121
When the s came up Jon 4:8 8121
the s beat down on Jonah's head Jon 4:8 8121
s will go down on the prophets, Mi 3:6 8121
The s rises and they flee, And the Na 3:17 8121
S *and* moon stood in their places; Hab 3:11 8121
"For from the rising of the s even Mal 1:11 8121
the s of righteousness will rise with Mal 4:2 8121
for He causes His s to rise on *the* Mt 5:45 2246
"But when the s had risen, they Mt 13:6 2246
WILL SHINE FORTH AS THE S Mt 13:43 2246
and His face shone like the s, Mt 17:2 2246
those days THE S WILL BE DARKENED, Mt 24:29 2246
came, after the s had set, Mk 1:32 2246
"And after the s had risen, it Mk 4:6 2246
THE S WILL BE DARKENED AND Mk 13:24 2246
to the tomb when the s had risen. Mk 16:2 2246
While the s was setting, all Lk 4:40 2246
be signs in s and moon and stars, Lk 21:25 2246
the s was obscured; Lk 23:45 2246
S WILL BE TURNED INTO DARKNESS Ac 2:20 2246
and not see the s for a time." Ac 13:11 2246
from heaven, brighter than the s, Ac 26:13 2246
neither s nor stars appeared for Ac 27:20 2246
There is one glory of the s, 1Co 15:41 2246
not let the s go down on your anger, Eph 4:26 2246
the s rises with a scorching wind and Jas 1:11 2246
the s shining in its strength Rv 1:16 2246
and the s became black as sackcloth Rv 6:12 2246
ascending from the rising of the s, Rv 7:2 2246
will the s beat down on them, Rv 7:16 2246
and a third of the s and a third Rv 8:12 2246
and the s and the air were darkened Rv 9:2 2246
head, and his face was like the s, Rv 10:1 2246
a woman clothed with the s, Rv 12:1 2246
poured out his bowl upon the s, Rv 16:8 2246
I saw an angel standing in the s, Rv 19:17 2246
And the city has no need of the s Rv 21:23 2246
of a lamp nor the light of the s, Rv 22:5 2246

SUNDOWN
and at s he may reenter the camp. Dt 23:11 8121, 935

SUNG
His work, Of which men have s. Jb 36:24 7891
song will be s in the land of Judah: Is 26:1 7891

SUNK
"On what were its bases s? Jb 38:6 2883
The nations have s down in the pit Ps 9:15 2883
Your arrows have s deep into me, Ps 38:2 5181
our soul has s down into the dust; Ps 44:25 7743
I have s in deep mire, and there Ps 69:2 2883
your feet were s in the mire, Jer 38:22 2883
Her gates have s into the ground, La 2:9 2883

SUNLIGHT
His radiance is like the s; Hab 3:4 216

SUNRISE
camp on the east side toward the s Nu 2:3 4217
the tent of meeting toward the s, Nu 3:38 4217
beyond the Jordan toward the s." Jos 1:15 4217, 8121
beyond the Jordan toward the s, Jos 12:1 4217, 8121
from Sarid to the east toward the s Jos 19:12 4217, 8121
toward the s to Gath-hepher, Jos 19:13 4217
the S from on high will visit us, Lk 1:78 395

SUNRISING
Jericho, eastward toward the s." Nu 34:15 4217

SUN'S
So the s *shadow* went back ten Is 38:8 8121

SUNSET
west of the way toward the s, Dt 11:30 8121, 3996
the Passover in the evening at s, Dt 16:6 8121, 935
and at s Joshua gave command and Jos 8:29 8121, 935
about at s that Joshua gave Jos 10:27 8121, 935
throughout the army close to s, 1Ki 22:36 8121, 935
and at s he died. 2Ch 18:34 8121, 935
the dawn and the s shout for joy. Ps 65:8 6153
and even until s he kept exerting Da 6:14 4606, 8122

SUNSHINE
the earth, Through s after rain.' 2Sa 23:4 5051
Like dazzling heat in the s, Is 18:4 216

SUPERFICIALLY
the brokenness of My people s, Jer 6:14 7043
of the daughter of My people s, Jer 8:11 7043

SUPERFLUOUS
For it is s for me to write to you 2Co 9:1 4053

SUPERIOR
For who regards you as s? 1Co 4:7 1252

SUPERIORITY
I did not come with s of speech or 1Co 2:1 5247

SUPERVISE
The chief jailer did not s Gn 39:23 7200
mountains and 3,600 to s them. 2Ch 2:2 5329
with foremen over them to s: 2Ch 34:12 5329

SUPERVISED
and s all the workmen from job to 2Ch 34:13 5329

SUPERVISORS
3,600 to make the people work. 2Ch 2:18 5329
hands of the s and the workmen." 2Ch 34:17 6485

SUPH
in the Arabah opposite **S**, Dt 1:1 5489
SUPHAH
"Waheb in **S**, And the wadis of the Nu 21:14 5492b
SUPPER
So they made Him a **s** there, Jn 12:2 *1173*
During **s**, the devil having Jn 13:2 *1173*
up from **s**, and laid aside His Jn 13:4 *1173*
back on His bosom at the **s** Jn 21:20 *1173*
it is not to eat the Lord's **S**, 1Co 11:20 *1173*
each one takes his own **s** first; 1Co 11:21 *1173*
way *He took* the cup also after **s**, 1Co 11:25 *1172*
to the marriage **s** of the Lamb.' " Rv 19:9 *1173*
assemble for the great **s** of God, Rv 19:17 *1173*
SUPPLANTED
for he has **s** me these two times? Gn 27:36 6117
SUPPLANTS
when she **s** her mistress. Pr 30:23 3423
SUPPLICATION
not go very far away. Make **s** for me. Ex 8:28 6279
and I shall make **s** to the LORD Ex 8:29 6279
Pharaoh and made **s** to the LORD. Ex 8:30 6279
"Make **s** to the LORD, for there Ex 9:28 6279
and make **s** to the LORD your God, Ex 10:17 6279
Pharaoh and made **s** to the LORD. Ex 10:18 6279
of Your servant and to his **s**, 1Ki 8:28 8467
"Listen to the **s** of Your servant 1Ki 8:30 8467
and make **s** to You in this house, 1Ki 8:33 2603a
whatever prayer or **s** is made by 1Ki 8:38 8467
heaven their prayer and their **s**, 1Ki 8:45 8467
and repent and make **s** to You in 1Ki 8:47 2603a
then hear their prayer and their **s** in 1Ki 8:49 8467
may be open to the **s** of Your servant 1Ki 8:52 8467
and to the **s** of Your people Israel, 1Ki 8:52 8467
entire prayer and **s** to the LORD, 1Ki 8:54 8467
I have made **s** before the LORD, 1Ki 8:59 2603a
have heard your prayer and your **s**, 1Ki 9:3 8467
of Your servant and to his **s**, 2Ch 6:19 8467
make **s** before You in this house, 2Ch 6:24 2603a
whatever prayer or **s** is made by 2Ch 6:29 8467
heaven their prayer and their **s**, 2Ch 6:35 8467
and repent and make **s** to You in 2Ch 6:37 2603a
by his entreaty and heard his **s**, 2Ch 33:13 8467
The LORD has heard my **s**, Ps 6:9 8467
He has heard the voice of my **s**. Ps 28:6 8469
called, And to the Lord I made **s**: Ps 30:8 2603a
And do not hide Yourself from my **s**. Ps 55:1 8467
Let my **s** come before You; Ps 119:170 8467
I make **s** with my voice to the LORD. Ps 142:1 2603a
They will make **s** to you: Is 45:14 6419
cause the enemy to make **s** to you Jer 15:11 6293
And by **s** I will lead them; Jer 31:9 8469
their **s** will come before the LORD, Jer 36:7 8467
found Daniel making petition and **s** Da 6:11 2604
and presenting my **s** before the Da 9:20 8467
the Spirit of grace and of **s**, Zch 12:10 8469
by prayer and **s** with thanksgiving Php 4:6 *1162*
SUPPLICATIONS
"Listen to the **s** of Your servant 2Ch 6:21 8469
place, their prayer and **s**, 2Ch 6:39 8467
"Will he make many **s** to you, Jb 41:3 8469
Hear the voice of my **s** when I cry Ps 28:2 8469
You heard the voice of my **s** Ps 31:22 8469
give heed to the voice of my **s**! Ps 86:6 8469
He hears My voice *and* my **s**. Ps 116:1 8469
be attentive To the voice of my **s**. Ps 130:2 8469
ear, O LORD, to the voice of my **s**. Ps 140:6 8469
prayer, O LORD, Give ear to my **s**! Ps 143:1 8469
The poor man utters **s**, Pr 18:23 8469
and the **s** of the sons of Israel; Jer 3:21 8469
God to seek *Him by* prayer and **s**, Da 9:3 8469
of Your servant and to his **s**, Da 9:17 8469
for we are not presenting our **s** Da 9:18 8469
"At the beginning of your **s** Da 9:23 8469
He offered up both prayers and **s** Heb 5:7 *2428*
SUPPLIED
(Hiram king of Tyre had **s** Solomon 1Ki 9:11 5375
they **s** *us* with all we needed. Ac 28:10 *2007*
s what was lacking on your part. 1Co 16:17 *378*
Macedonia they fully **s** my need, 2Co 11:9 *4322*
I am amply **s**, having received from Php 4:18 *4137*
being **s** and held together by the Col 2:19 *2023*
will be abundantly **s** to you. 2Pe 1:11 *2023*
SUPPLIES
flock with a keeper and took *the* **s** 1Sa 17:20
large **s** in the cities of Judah, 2Ch 17:13 4399
And **s** belts to the tradesmen. Pr 31:24 5414
Now He who **s** seed to the sower and 2Co 9:10 *2023*
by what every joint **s**, Eph 4:16 *2024*
richly **s** us with all things to enjoy. 1Tm 6:17 *3930*
serving by the strength which God **s**; 1Pe 4:11 *5524*
SUPPLY
and Gomorrah and all their food **s**, Gn 14:11 400
'You will eat the old **s** and Lv 26:10 3462
1,000 out of 10,000 to **s** food for the Jg 20:10 3947
and his warriors to cut off the **s** 2Ch 32:3
we cast lots for the **s** of wood *among* Ne 10:34 7133b
and *I arranged* for the **s** of wood Ne 13:31 7133b
and Judah Both **s** and support, Is 3:1 4937b
and support, the whole **s** of bread And Is 3:1 4937a
bread And the whole **s** of water; Is 3:1 4937a
it, destroy its **s** of bread, Ezk 14:13 4294
time your abundance *being a* **s** 2Co 8:14
their abundance also may become *a* **s** 2Co 8:14
will **s** and multiply your seed for 2Co 9:10 *5524*
And my God will **s** all your needs Php 4:19 *4137*
in your faith **s** moral excellence, 2Pe 1:5 *2023*
SUPPLYING
fully **s** the needs of the saints, 2Co 9:12 *4322*
SUPPORT
calamity, But the LORD was my **s**. 2Sa 22:19 4937a
gave him strong **s** in his kingdom, 1Ch 11:10 2388
He may strongly **s** those whose heart 2Ch 16:9 2388
place **s** him with silver and gold, Ezr 1:4 5375
nobles did not **s** the work of their Ne 3:5 935, 6677
Nor will He **s** the evildoers. Jb 8:20 2388, 3027
Because I saw I had **s** in the gate, Jb 31:21 5833
You **s** my lot. Ps 16:5 8551
sanctuary And **s** you from Zion! Ps 20:2 5582
let no one **s** him. Pr 28:17 8551
then there was nothing to **s** him. Ec 5:14 3027
and Judah Both supply and **s**, Is 3:1 4938a
those who **s** Egypt will fall And Ezk 30:6 5564
"He will take from you its **s**." Mi 1:11 5979
'A strong **s** for us are the Zch 12:5 556
for the worker is worthy of his **s**. Mt 10:10 *5160*
who were contributing to their **s** Lk 8:3 *1247*
in the **s** of the saints, 2Co 8:4 *1248*
the pillar and **s** of the truth. 1Tm 3:15 *1477*
Therefore we ought to **s** such men, 3Jn 1:8 *5274*
SUPPORTED
and Aaron and Hur **s** his hands, Ex 17:12 8551
and **s** Rehoboam the son of Solomon 2Ch 11:17 553
and they **s** the people and the Ezr 8:36 5375
with security, and they are **s**; Jb 24:23 8172
as he who **s** her in *those* times. Da 11:6 2388
At my first defense no one **s** me, 2Tm 4:16 *3854*
SUPPORTING
of God were with them **s** them. Ezr 5:2 5583
and Shabbethai the Levite **s** them. Ezr 10:15 5826
they used **s** cables in undergirding Ac 27:17 *996*
SUPPORTS
axles, and its four feet had **s**; 1Ki 7:30 3802
cast **s** with wreaths at each side. 1Ki 7:30 3802
Now *there were* four **s** at the four 1Ki 7:34 3802
s *were* part of the stand itself. 1Ki 7:34 3802
king made of the almug trees **s** for 1Ki 10:12 4552
He **s** the fatherless and the widow, Ps 146:9 5749a
The LORD **s** the afflicted; Ps 147:6 5749a
that it is not you who **s** the root, Ro 11:18 *941*
but the root **s** you. Ro 11:18
SUPPOSE
"**S** there are fifty righteous Gn 18:24 194
"**S** the fifty righteous are Gn 18:28 194
"**S** forty are found there?" Gn 18:29 194
s thirty are found there?" Gn 18:30 194
s twenty are found there?" Gn 18:31 194
s ten are found there?" Gn 18:32 194
"**S** the woman is not willing Gn 24:5 194
'**S** the woman does not follow me.' Gn 24:39 194
"Do not let my lord **s** they have 2Sa 13:32 559
and do not **s** that you can say to Mt 3:9 *1380*
for they **s** that they will be heard Mt 6:7 *1380*
I **s** the one whom he forgave more." Lk 7:43 *5274*
"**S** one of you has a Lk 11:5 *5101*
"Now **s** one of you fathers is Lk 11:11 *5101*
"Do you **s** that I came to grant Lk 12:51 *1380*
"Do you **s** that these Galileans Lk 13:2 *1380*
"Or do you **s** that those eighteen Lk 13:4 *1380*
I **s** that even the world itself Jn 21:25 *3633*
these men are not drunk, as you **s**, Ac 2:15 *5274*
'What do you **s** that I am? Ac 13:25 *5282*
s a spirit or an angel has spoken Ac 23:9 *1487, 1161*
But do you **s** this, O man, when you Ro 2:3 *3049*
who **s** that godliness is a means of 1Tm 6:5 *3543*
SUPPOSED
sea, they **s** that it was a ghost, Mk 6:49 *1380*
but **s** Him to be in the caravan, Lk 2:44 *3543*
as was **s**, the son of Joseph, Lk 3:23 *3543*
and they **s** that the kingdom of God Lk 19:11 *1380*
"And he **s** that his brethren Ac 7:25 *3543*
and they **s** that Paul had brought Ac 21:29 *3543*
SUPPOSES
anyone **s** that he knows anything, 1Co 8:2 *1380*
SUPPOSING
s that she was going to the tomb Jn 11:31 *1380*
For some were **s**, because Judas had Jn 13:29 *1380*
S Him to be the gardener, Jn 20:15 *1380*
out of the city, **s** him to be dead. Ac 14:19 *3543*
where we were **s** that there would Ac 16:13 *3543*
s that the prisoners had escaped. Ac 16:27 *3543*
s that they had attained their Ac 27:13 *1380*
SUPPRESS
who **s** the truth in unrighteousness, Ro 1:18 *2722*
SUPREME
be guilty before the **s** court; Mt 5:22 *4892*
SUR
third also *shall be* at the gate **S**, 2Ki 11:6 5495
SURE
"Be **s** to observe what I am Ex 34:11
be **s** your sin will find you out. Nu 32:23 3045
"Only be **s** not to eat the blood, Dt 12:23 2388
"Go now, make more **s**, 1Sa 23:22 3559
The testimony of the LORD is **s**, Ps 19:7 539
All His precepts are **s**. Ps 111:7 539
the upright, he makes his way **s**. Pr 21:29 3559
His water will be **s**. Is 33:16 539
of Israel I declare what is **s**. Hos 5:9 539
"But be **s** of this, that if the Mt 24:43 *1097*
yet be **s** of this, that the kingdom Lk 10:11 *1097*
"But be **s** of this, that if the Lk 12:39 *1097*
"Now I know for **s** that the Lord Ac 12:11 *230*
HOLY *and* **S** *blessings* OF DAVID.' Ac 13:34 *4103*
with me saw the light, to be **s**, Ac 22:9 *3303a*
be **s** that it is those who are of Ga 3:7 *1097*
Some, to be **s**, are preaching Php 1:15 *3303a*
are matters which have, to be **s**, Col 2:23 *3303a*
I am **s** that *it is* in you as well. 2Tm 1:5 *3982*
a *hope* both **s** and steadfast and Heb 6:19 *804*
Make **s** *that* your character is Heb 13:5
for we are **s** that we have a good Heb 13:18 *3982*
Make **s** that none of you suffers as a 1Pe 4:15
the prophetic word *made* more **s**, 2Pe 1:19 *949*
Little children, make **s** no one 1Jn 3:7
SURELY
you eat from it you will **s** die." Gn 2:17 4191
"You **s** will not die! Gn 3:4 4191
"**S** I will require your lifeblood; Gn 9:5 389
your money shall **s** be circumcised; Gn 17:13 4135
"I will **s** return to you at this Gn 18:10 7725
since Abraham will **s** become a Gn 18:18 1961
her, know that you shall **s** die, Gn 20:7 4191
s there is no fear of God in this Gn 20:11 7534
wife shall **s** be put to death." Gn 26:11 4191
"**S** the LORD is in this place, and Gn 28:16 403
I will **s** give a tenth to You." Gn 28:22 6237
"**S** you are my bone and my flesh." Gn 29:14 389
s now my husband will love me." Gn 29:32 3588
for I have **s** hired you with my Gn 30:16 7936
"**S** all the wealth which God has Gn 31:16 3588
s now you would have sent me away Gn 31:42 3588
'I will **s** prosper you and make Gn 32:12 3190
Joseph has **s** been torn to pieces!" Gn 37:33 2963
"**S** I will go down to Sheol in Gn 37:35 3588
of Pharaoh, **s** you are spies." Gn 42:16 3588
s by now we could have returned Gn 43:10 3588
"**S** he is torn in pieces," Gn 44:28 389
I will also **s** bring you up again; Gn 46:4 5927
but God will **s** take care of you and Gn 50:24 6485
"God will **s** take care of you, and Gn 50:25 6485
"**S** the matter has become known." Ex 2:14 403
"I have **s** seen the affliction of Ex 3:7 7200
he will **s** drive you out from here Ex 11:1 1644
"God will **s** take care of you Ex 13:19 6485
"You will **s** wear out, both Ex 18:18 5034b
shall **s** be put to death. Ex 19:12 4191
he shall **s** be stoned or shot through; Ex 19:13 5619
he dies shall **s** be put to death. Ex 21:12 4191
shall **s** be put to death. Ex 21:15 4191
shall **s** be put to death. Ex 21:16 4191
shall **s** be put to death. Ex 21:17 4191
he shall **s** be fined as the woman's Ex 21:22 6064
the ox shall **s** be stoned and its Ex 21:28 5619
it, he shall **s** pay ox for ox, Ex 21:36 7999a
He shall **s** make restitution; Ex 22:3 7999a
he who started the fire shall **s** make Ex 22:6 7999a
Whoever lies with an animal shall **s** Ex 22:19 4191
out to Me, I will **s** hear his cry; Ex 22:23 8085
you shall **s** return it to him. Ex 23:4 7725
you shall **s** release *it* with him. Ex 23:5 5800a
it will **s** be a snare to you." Ex 23:33 3588
'You shall **s** observe My sabbaths; Ex 31:13 389
Everyone who profanes it shall **s** be Ex 31:14 4191
shall **s** be put to death. Ex 31:15 4191
priest shall **s** pronounce him unclean Lv 13:44 2930
you may **s** reprove your neighbor, Lv 19:17 3198
Molech, shall **s** be put to death; Lv 20:2 4191
he shall **s** be put to death; Lv 20:9 4191
the adulteress shall **s** be put to death Lv 20:10 4191
both of them shall **s** be put to death, Lv 20:11 4191
both of them shall **s** be put to death; Lv 20:12 4191
they shall **s** be put to death. Lv 20:13 4191
he shall **s** be put to death; Lv 20:15 4191
they shall **s** be put to death. Lv 20:16 4191
spiritist shall **s** be put to death. Lv 20:27 4191
shall **s** be put to death; Lv 24:16 4191
being, he shall **s** be put to death. Lv 24:17 4191
he shall **s** be put to death. Lv 27:29 4191
it, for we will **s** overcome it." Nu 13:30 3201
"**S** all the men who have seen My Nu 14:22 3588
My hearing, so I will **s** do to you; Nu 14:28
'**S** you shall not come into the Nu 14:30 518
s this I will do to all this evil Nu 14:35 518, 3808
"The man shall **s** be put to death; Nu 15:35 4191
firstborn of man you shall **s** redeem, Nu 18:15 6299
I would **s** have killed you just now, Nu 22:33 3588
"They shall **s** die in the wilderness." Nu 26:65 4191
You shall **s** give them a hereditary Nu 27:7 5414
murderer shall **s** be put to death. Nu 35:16 4191
murderer shall **s** be put to death. Nu 35:17 4191
murderer shall **s** be put to death. Nu 35:18 4191
one who struck him shall **s** be put to Nu 35:21 4191
but he shall **s** be put to death. Nu 35:31 4191
'**S** this great nation is a wise and Dt 4:6 7534
that you will **s** perish quickly Dt 4:26 6
you today that you will **s** perish. Dt 8:19 6
"But you shall **s** kill him; Dt 13:9 2026
you shall **s** strike the inhabitants Dt 13:15 5221
"You shall **s** tithe all the Dt 14:22 6237
since the LORD will **s** bless you in Dt 15:4 1288
you shall **s** set a king over you Dt 17:15 7760
shall **s** bury him on the same day Dt 21:23 6912
your God will **s** require it of you. Dt 23:21 1875
shall **s** return the pledge to him, Dt 24:13 7725
you today that you shall **s** perish. Dt 30:18 6
"But I will **s** hide My face in Dt 31:18 5641
"**S** the LORD has given all the Jos 2:24 3588
'**S** the land on which your foot has Jos 14:9 518, 3808
"I will **s** go with you; Jg 4:9 1980

“**S** I will be with you, and you **Jg 6:16** 3588
“We will **s** give *them*.” **Jg 8:25** 5414
s we will do as you have said.” **Jg 11:10**
518, 3808
“We will **s** die, for we have seen **Jg 13:22** 4191
I will **s** take revenge on you, **Jg 15:7**
3588, 518
yet **s** we will not kill you.” **Jg 15:13** 4191
“**S** they are defeated before us, **Jg 20:39**
389, 5062
“He shall **s** be put to death.” **Jg 21:5** 4191
but we will **s** return with you to **Ru 1:10** 3588
“They must **s** burn the fat first, **1Sa 2:16** 6999
but you shall **s** return to Him a **1Sa 6:3** 7725
all that he says **s** comes true. **1Sa 9:6** 935
S there is no one like him among **1Sa 10:24** 3588
Jonathan my son, he shall **s** die.” **1Sa 14:39**
3588, 4191
more also, for you shall **s** die, **1Sa 14:44** 4191
“**S** the bitterness of death is **1Sa 15:32** 403
“**S** the LORD’s anointed is before **1Sa 16:6** 389
S he is coming up to defy Israel. **1Sa 17:25** 3588
is not clean, **s** *he is* not clean.” **1Sa 20:26** 3588
him to me, for he must **s** die.” **1Sa 20:31** 1121
“**S** women have been kept from us **1Sa 21:5**
3588, 518
“You shall **s** die, Ahimelech, you **1Sa 22:16** 4191
there, that he would **s** tell Saul. **1Sa 22:22** 5046
I know that you will **s** be king, **1Sa 24:20** 4427a
“**S** in vain I have guarded all **1Sa 25:21** 389
s there would not have been left **1Sa 25:34**
3588, 518
lives, **s** the LORD will strike him, **1Sa 26:10**
3588, 518
LORD lives, *all* of you must **s** die, **1Sa 26:16** 3588
accomplish much and **s** prevail.” **1Sa 26:25** 3201
“He has **s** made himself odious **1Sa 27:12** 887
for you will **s** overtake them, **1Sa 30:8** 5381
and you will **s** rescue *all*.” **1Sa 30:8** 5337
s then the people would have gone **2Sa 2:27** 3588
for I will **s** show kindness to you **2Sa 9:7** 6213a
s the man who has done this **2Sa 12:5** 3588
that is born to you shall **s** die.” **2Sa 12:14** 4191
“For we will **s** die and are like **2Sa 14:14** 4191
now, I will **s** do this thing; **2Sa 14:21** 3588
s wherever my lord the king may **2Sa 15:21**
3588, 518
all Israel be **s** gathered to you, **2Sa 17:11** 622
I myself will **s** go out with you also **2Sa 18:2** 3318
s not a man will pass the night **2Sa 19:7** 518
‘They will **s** ask *advice* at Abel,’ **2Sa 20:18** 7592
I will **s** buy *it* from you for a price, **2Sa 24:24** 7069
“**S** Solomon your son shall be king **1Ki 1:13** 3588
‘**S** your son Solomon shall be king **1Ki 1:17** 3588
s as I vowed to you by the LORD **1Ki 1:30** 3588
s Adonijah shall be put to death **1Ki 2:24** 3588
for certain that you shall **s** die; **1Ki 2:37** 4191
and go anywhere, you shall **s** die’? **1Ki 2:42** 4191
“I have **s** built You a lofty **1Ki 8:13** 1129
for they will **s** turn your heart **1Ki 11:2** 403
I will **s** tear the kingdom from you, **1Ki 11:11** 7167
you must **s** let me go.” **1Ki 11:22** 7971
“For the thing shall **s** come to **1Ki 13:32** 1961
s there shall be neither dew nor **1Ki 17:1** 518
I will **s** show myself to him today.” **1Ki 18:15** 3588
‘**S**, I sent to you saying, **1Ki 20:5** 3588
and **s** we will be stronger than **1Ki 20:23**
518, 3808
and **s** we will be stronger than **1Ki 20:25**
518, 3808
S there was no one like Ahab who **1Ki 21:25** 7534
“**S** it is the king of Israel,” **1Ki 22:32** 389
gone up, but you shall **s** die. **2Ki 1:4** 4191
gone up, but shall **s** die.’ ” ’ ” **2Ki 1:6** 4191
have gone up, but shall **s** die.’ ” **2Ki 1:16** 4191
the kings have **s** fought together, **2Ki 3:23** 2717c
‘He will **s** come out to me and **2Ki 5:11** 3318
‘You will **s** recover,’ but the **2Ki 8:10** 2421a
me that you would **s** recover.” **2Ki 8:14** 2421a
‘**S** I have seen yesterday the blood **2Ki 9:26**
518, 3808
“The LORD will **s** deliver us, and **2Ki 18:30** 5337
S such a Passover had not been **2Ki 23:22** 3588
S at the command of the LORD it **2Ki 24:3** 389
but I will **s** buy *it* for the full price; **1Ch 21:24** 7069
now on you will **s** have wars.” **2Ch 16:9** 3588
S, *do* you not *have* transgressions **2Ch 28:10** 7534
that **s** God had not sent him, **Ne 6:12** 2009
him, but will **s** fall before him.” **Es 6:13** 5307
he will **s** curse You to Your face.” **Jb 1:11**
518, 3808
S now He would rouse Himself for **Jb 8:6** 3588
“He will **s** reprove you If you **Jb 13:10** 3198
“**S** mockers are with me, And my **Jb 17:2**
518, 3808
“**S** such are the dwellings of the **Jb 18:21** 389
s He would pay attention to me. **Jb 23:6** 389
He will **s** try to flee from its power. **Jb 27:22** 1272
“**S** there is a mine for silver And **Jb 28:1** 3588
S I would carry it on my shoulder, **Jb 31:36**
518, 3808
“**S** you have spoken in my hearing, **Jb 33:8** 389
“**S**, God will not act wickedly, **Jb 34:12**
637, 551
“**S** God will not listen to an **Jb 35:13** 389
“**S** the mountains bring him food, **Jb 40:20** 5608
“I will **s** tell of the decree of **Ps 2:7** 3588
and I will **s** give the nations as **Ps 2:8**
S You lift me above those **Ps 18:48** 637
S goodness and lovingkindness will **Ps 23:6** 389
S in a flood of great waters they **Ps 32:6** 7534
S every man at his best is a mere **Ps 39:5** 389
“**S** every man walks about as a **Ps 39:6** 389
S they make an uproar for nothing; **Ps 39:6** 389
S every man is a mere breath. **Ps 39:11** 389
my complaint and am **s** distracted, **Ps 55:2** 1949
“**S** there is a reward for the **Ps 58:11** 389
S there is a God who judges on **Ps 58:11** 389
S the LORD will dwell *there* **Ps 68:16** 637
S God will shatter the head of His **Ps 68:21** 389
S God is good to Israel, To those **Ps 73:1** 389
S in vain I have kept my heart **Ps 73:13** 389
S You set them in slippery **Ps 73:18** 389
S all the wicked of the earth must **Ps 75:8** 389
S I will remember Your wonders of **Ps 77:11** 3588
S His salvation is near to those **Ps 85:9** 389
S Your servants find pleasure in **Ps 102:14** 3588
O LORD, **s** I am Your servant, I am **Ps 116:16** 3588
of the LORD I will **s** cut them off. **Ps 118:10** 3588
of the LORD I will **s** cut them off. **Ps 118:11** 3588
of the LORD I will **s** cut them off. **Ps 118:12** 3588
S I have composed and quieted my **Ps 131:2**
518, 3808
“**S** I will not enter my house, Nor **Ps 132:3** 518
“**S** the darkness will overwhelm **Ps 139:11** 389
S the righteous will give thanks **Ps 140:13** 389
a stranger will **s** suffer for it, **Pr 11:15** 7451b
the diligent *lead* **s** to advantage, **Pr 21:5** 389
who is hasty *comes* **s** to poverty. **Pr 21:5** 389
S there is a future, And your hope **Pr 23:18**
3588, 518
S she lurks as a robber, And **Pr 23:28** 637
S I am more stupid than any man, **Pr 30:2** 3588
or His son’s name? **S** you know! **Pr 30:4** 3588
“God has **s** tested them in order **Ec 3:18**
s a live dog is better than a dead **Ec 9:4** 3588
S you will be ashamed of the oaks **Is 1:29** 3588
“**S**, many houses shall become **Is 5:9** 518, 3808
you **s** shall not last. **Is 7:9** 3588
“**S**, just as I have intended so it **Is 14:24**
518, 3808
S in a night Ar of Moab is **Is 15:1** 3588
S in a night Kir of Moab is **Is 15:1** 3588
S on the road to Horonaim they **Is 15:5** 3588
S the grass is withered, the **Is 15:6** 3588
S I will bring added *woes* upon **Is 15:9** 3588
“**S** this iniquity shall not be **Is 22:14** 518
He will **s** be gracious to you at **Is 30:19** 2603a
“The LORD will **s** deliver us, this **Is 36:15** 5337
“The LORD will **s** save me; **Is 38:20**
S the people are grass. **Is 40:7** 403
strengthen you, **s** I will help you, **Is 41:10** 637
S I will uphold you with My **Is 41:10** 637
S there was no one who declared, **Is 41:26** 637
S there was no one who proclaimed, **Is 41:26** 637
S there was no one who heard your **Is 41:26** 637
S he cuts cedars for himself, and **Is 44:14**
‘**S**, God is with you, and there is **Is 45:14** 389
s I will do it. **Is 46:11**
“**S** My hand founded the earth, And **Is 48:13** 637
Yet **s** the justice *due* to Me is **Is 49:4** 403
s put on all of them as jewels and **Is 49:18** 3588
S now you will be too cramped **Is 49:19** 3588
S, thus says the LORD, **Is 49:25** 3588
S our griefs He Himself bore, And **Is 53:4** 403
“The LORD will **s** separate me from **Is 56:3** 914
“**S** the coastlands will wait for **Is 60:9** 3588
“**S**, they are My people, Sons who **Is 63:8** 389
S His anger is turned away from me.’ **Jer 2:35** 389
“**S**, as a woman treacherously **Jer 3:20** 403
“**S**, the hills are a deception, A **Jer 3:23** 403
S in the LORD our God Is the **Jer 3:23** 403
S You have utterly deceived this **Jer 4:10** 403
lives,’ **S** they swear falsely.” **Jer 5:2** 3651
“I will **s** snatch them away,” **Jer 8:13** 5486
but they **s** will not save them in **Jer 11:12** 3467
“**S** I will set you free for **Jer 15:11**
518, 3808
S I will cause the enemy to make **Jer 15:11**
518, 3808
S the law is not going to be lost **Jer 18:18** 3588
Then you will **s** be ashamed and **Jer 22:22** 3588
s thus says the LORD, **Jer 23:38** 3651
I will **s** forget you and cast you **Jer 23:39** 5382
“You shall **s** drink! **Jer 25:28** 8354
“I have **s** heard Ephraim grieving, **Jer 31:18** 8085
I will **s** have mercy on him,” **Jer 31:20** 7355
but he will **s** be given into the **Jer 32:4** 5414
for you will **s** be captured and **Jer 34:3** 8610
“We will **s** report all these words **Jer 36:16** 5046
Chaldeans will **s** go away from us,” **Jer 37:9** 1980
s I will not put you to death nor **Jer 38:16** 518
My words will **s** stand against you **Jer 44:29** 6965
I will **s** destroy the city and its **Jer 46:8**
“**S** one shall come *who looms up* **Jer 46:18** 3588
“**S** it will no *more* be found, Even **Jer 46:23** 3588
s they will drag them off, *even* **Jer 49:20**
518, 3808
s He will make their pasture **Jer 49:20**
518, 3808
s they will drag them off, *even* **Jer 50:45**
518, 3808
s He will make their pasture **Jer 50:45**
518, 3808
“**S** I will fill you with a **Jer 51:14**
3588, 518
S this is the day for which we **La 2:16** 389
S against me He has turned His **La 3:3** 389
S my soul remembers And is bowed **La 3:20** 2142
S the whole house of Israel is **Ezk 3:7** 3588
‘You will **s** die,’ **Ezk 3:18** 4191
he shall **s** live because he took **Ezk 3:21** 2421a
‘**s**, because you have defiled My **Ezk 5:11**
518, 3808
‘**S** in the country of the king who **Ezk 17:16**
518, 3808
s My oath which he despised and My **Ezk 17:19**
518, 3808
“you are **s** not going to use this **Ezk 18:3** 518
is righteous *and* will **s** live,” **Ezk 18:9** 2421a
he will **s** be put to death; **Ezk 18:13** 4191
father’s iniquity, he will **s** live. **Ezk 18:17** 2421a
and done them, he shall **s** live. **Ezk 18:19** 2421a
righteousness, he shall **s** live; **Ezk 18:21** 2421a
he had committed, he shall **s** live; **Ezk 18:28** 2421a
“**s** with a mighty hand and with an **Ezk 20:33**
518, 3808
later you will **s** listen to Me, **Ezk 20:39**
518, 369
‘O wicked man, you will **s** die,’ **Ezk 33:8** 4191
“**S** our transgressions and our **Ezk 33:10** 3588
to the righteous he will **s** live, **Ezk 33:13** 2421a
‘You will **s** die,’ and he turns **Ezk 33:14** 4191
iniquity, he shall **s** live; **Ezk 33:15** 2421a
and righteousness; he shall **s** live. **Ezk 33:16** 2421a
s those who are in the waste **Ezk 33:27**
518, 3808
So when it comes to pass—as **s** it will **Ezk 33:33** 2009
“**s** because My flock has become a **Ezk 34:8**
518, 3808
“**S** in the fire of My jealousy I **Ezk 36:5**
518, 3808
s the nations which are around you **Ezk 36:7**
518, 3808
there will **s** be a great earthquake **Ezk 38:19**
518, 3808
“**S** your God is a God of gods and **Da 2:47**
4481, 7187, 1768
S they have committed crime. **Hos 6:9** 3588
S the calf of Samaria will be **Hos 8:6** 3588
S now they will say, **Hos 10:3** 3588
“**S** I have become rich, I have **Hos 12:8** 389
S they are worthless. **Hos 12:11** 389
day of the LORD is coming; **S** it is **Jl 2:1** 3588
S His camp is very great, For **Jl 2:11** 3588
S the Lord GOD does nothing Unless **Am 3:7** 3588
“I will **s** assemble all of you, **Mi 2:12** 622
I will **s** gather the remnant of Israel. **Mi 2:12** 6908
“**S** the stone will cry out from **Hab 2:11** 3588
“**S** Moab will be like Sodom And **Zph 2:9** 3588
‘**S** you will revere Me, Accept **Zph 3:7** 389
s everyone who steals will be **Zch 5:3** 3588
“**S** not I, Lord?” **Mt 26:22** *3385*
“**S** it is not I, Rabbi?” **Mt 26:25** *3385*
“**S** you too are *one* of them; **Mt 26:73** *230*
say to Him one by one, “**S** not I?” **Mk 14:19** *3385*
“**S** you are *one* of them, for you **Mk 14:70** *230*
“**S** the Christ is not going to **Jn 7:41** *3361*
“**S** He will not kill Himself, will **Jn 8:22** *3385*
“**S** You are not greater than our **Jn 8:53** *3361*
“**S** no one can refuse the water **Ac 10:47** *3385*
I say, **s** they have never heard, **Ro 10:18** *3361*
But I say, **s** Israel did not know, **Ro 10:19** *3361*
“I WILL **S** BLESS YOU AND I WILL **Heb 6:14**
3375, 2127
YOU AND I WILL **S** MULTIPLY YOU.” **Heb 6:14** *4129*

SURETY
“I myself will be **s** for him; **Gn 43:9** 6148
your servant became **s** for the lad to **Gn 44:32** 6148
Be **s** for Your servant for good; **Ps 119:122** 6148
have become **s** for your neighbor, **Pr 6:1** 6148
when he becomes **s** for a stranger; **Pr 20:16** 6148
when he becomes **s** for a stranger; **Pr 27:13** 6148

SURF
one who doubts is like the **s** of the sea **Jas 1:6** *2830*

SURFACE
was over the **s** of the deep, **Gn 1:2** 6440
moving over the **s** of the waters. **Gn 1:2** 6440
that is on the **s** of all the earth, **Gn 1:29** 6440
water the whole **s** of the ground. **Gn 2:6** 6440
ark floated on the **s** of the water. **Gn 7:18** 6440
was on the **s** of all the earth. **Gn 8:9** 6440
the **s** of the ground was dried up. **Gn 8:13** 6440
shall cover the **s** of the land, **Ex 10:5** 5869
covered the **s** of the whole land, **Ex 10:15** 5869
on the **s** of the wilderness there **Ex 16:14** 6440
it over the **s** of the water and **Ex 32:20** 6440
and appears deeper than the **s**, **Lv 14:37** 7023
deep on the **s** of the ground. **Nu 11:31** 6440
they cover the **s** of the land, **Nu 22:5** 5869
and they cover the **s** of the land; **Nu 22:11** 5869
on the **s** of the water; **Jb 24:18** 6440
a circle on the **s** of the waters At **Jb 26:10** 6440
the **s** of the deep is imprisoned. **Jb 38:30** 6440
Its **s** was covered with nettles, **Pr 24:31** 6440
your bread on the **s** of the waters, **Ec 11:1** 6440
vessels on the **s** of the waters. **Is 18:2** 6440
devastates it, distorts its **s** and **Is 24:1** 6440
Does he not level its **s** And **Is 28:25** 6440
be as dung on the **s** of the ground **Jer 16:4** 6440
and the whole **s** from south to **Ezk 20:47** 6440
over all the **s** of the earth, **Ezk 34:6** 6440
very many on the **s** of the valley; **Ezk 37:2** 6440
those left on the **s** of the ground, **Ezk 39:14** 6440
west over the **s** of the whole earth **Da 8:5** 6440
a stick on the **s** of the water. **Hos 10:7** 6440

them out on the s of the earth, Am 5:8 6440

SURGE

the rivers whose waters s about? Jer 46:7 1607
the rivers whose waters s about; Jer 46:8 1607
horses, On the s of many waters. Hab 3:15 2563b

SURGING

rebuked the wind and the s waves, Lk 8:24 *2830*

SURMISE

the sailors *began* to s that they were Ac 27:27 *5282*

SURPASS

You s the report that I heard. 2Ch 9:6 3254
'Whom do you s in beauty? Ezk 32:19 5276

SURPASSED

Have s the blessings of my ancestors Gn 49:26 1396
Solomon's wisdom s the wisdom 1Ki 4:30 7235a

SURPASSES

that unless your righteousness s Mt 5:20 *4052*
because of the glory that s *it.* 2Co 3:10 *5235*
love of Christ which s knowledge, Eph 3:19 *5235*
of God, which s all comprehension, Php 4:7 *5242*

SURPASSING

and s greatness was added to me. Da 4:36 3493
that the s greatness of the power 2Co 4:7 *5236*
of the s grace of God in you. 2Co 9:14 *5235*
s greatness of the revelations, 2Co 12:7 *5236*
s greatness of His power toward us Eph 1:19 *5235*
might show the s riches of His grace Eph 2:7 *5235*
the s value of knowing Christ Jesus Php 3:8 *5242*

SURPLUS

they all put in out of their s, Mk 12:44 *4052*
out of their s put into the offering; Lk 21:4 *4052*

SURPRISED

he was s that He had not first Lk 11:38 *2296*
they are s that you do not run 1Pe 4:4 *3579*
do not be s at the fiery ordeal 1Pe 4:12 *3579*
Do not be s, brethren, if the world 1Jn 3:13 *2296*

SURPRISING

Therefore it is not s if his 2Co 11:15 *3173*

SURRENDER

men of Keilah s me into his hand? 1Sa 23:11 5462
"Will the men of Keilah s me and 1Sa 23:12 5462
"They will s you." 1Sa 23:12 5462
be to s him into the king's hand." 1Sa 23:20 5462
How can I s you, O Israel? Hos 11:8 4042
and if I s my body to be burned, 1Co 13:3 *3860*

SURROUND

the gods of the peoples who s you, Dt 6:14 5439
and they will s us and cut off our Jos 7:9 5437
"Then you shall s the king, each 2Ki 11:8
5362b, 5439, 5921
and s *them* with walls and towers, 2Ch 14:7 5437
"The Levites will s the king, 2Ch 23:7
5362b, 5439
"His arrows s me. Without mercy He Jb 16:13 5437
"Therefore snares s you, Jb 22:10 5439
The willows of the brook s him. Jb 40:22 5437
You s him with favor as with Ps 5:12 5849a
me, My deadly enemies who s me. Ps 17:9 5362b
s me with songs of deliverance. Ps 32:7 5437
LORD, lovingkindness shall s him. Ps 32:10 5437
Clouds and thick darkness s Him; Ps 97:2 5439
As the mountains s Jerusalem, Ps 125:2 5439
"As for the head of those who s me, Ps 140:9 5437
The righteous will s me, Ps 142:7 5437
more than the lands which s her; Ezk 5:6 5439
than the nations which s you Ezk 5:7 5439
of the nations which s you,' Ezk 5:7 5439
among the nations which s you, Ezk 5:14 5439
horror to the nations who s you when Ezk 5:15 5439
their graves s them. Ezk 32:26 5439
For the wicked s the righteous; Hab 1:4 3803
up a barricade against you, and s you Lk 19:43 *4033*

SURROUNDED

the men of Sodom, s the house, Gn 19:4 5437
they s *the place* and lay in wait Jg 16:2 5437
worthless fellows, s the house, Jg 19:22 5437
rose up against me and s the house Jg 20:5 5437
They s Benjamin, pursued them Jg 20:43 3803
The cords of Sheol s me; 2Sa 22:6 5437
because of the wars which s him, 1Ki 5:3 5437
they came by night and s the city. 2Ki 6:14 5362b
struck the Edomites who had s him 2Ki 8:21 5437
after the nations which s them, 2Ki 17:15 5439
They have now s us in our steps; Ps 17:11 5437
The cords of Sheol s me; Ps 18:5 5437
Many bulls have s me; Ps 22:12 5437
For dogs have s me; Ps 22:16 5437
For evils beyond number have s me; Ps 40:12 661
have s me like water all day long; Ps 88:17 5437
also s me with words of hatred, Ps 109:3 5437
All nations s me; Ps 118:10 5437
They s me, yes, they surrounded me; Ps 118:11 5437
surrounded me, yes, they s me; Ps 118:11 5437
They s me like bees; Ps 118:12 5437
and a great king came to it, s it and Ec 9:14 5437
you see Jerusalem s by armies, Lk 21:20 *2944*
and s the camp of the saints and the Rv 20:9 *2943a*

SURROUNDING

the food from its own s fields. Gn 41:48 5439
which have no s wall shall be Lv 25:31 5439
the cities of the s land. Nu 32:33 5439
you rest from all your s enemies, Dt 25:19 5439
Judah, with its s pasture lands. Jos 21:11 5439
each had its s pasture lands; Jos 21:42 5439
for Saul and his men were s David 1Sa 23:26 5849a
was *known* in all the s nations. 1Ki 4:31 5439
to a cubit, completely s the sea; 1Ki 7:24 5362b
and in the s area of Jerusalem, 2Ki 23:5 4524
from the Millo even to the s area; 1Ch 11:8 5439
the LORD, and for all the s rooms, 1Ch 28:12 5439
down the Edomites who were s him 2Ch 21:9 5437
far as Naphtali, in their s ruins, 2Ch 34:6 5439
and all the nations s us saw *it,* Ne 6:16 5439
the appearance of the s radiance. Ezk 1:28 5439
those s *you* who despise you. Ezk 16:57 5439
The side chambers s the temple Ezk 41:7 5437
Because the structure s the temple Ezk 41:7 4141
and come, all you s nations, Jl 3:11 5439
sit to judge All the s nations. Jl 3:12 5439
"An enemy, even one s the land, Am 3:11 5439
of the Nile, With water s her, Na 3:8 5439
and on the left all the s peoples, Zch 12:6 5439
the s nations will be gathered, Zch 14:14 5439
they sent *word* into all that s district Mt 14:35 *4066*
all the s district of Galilee. Mk 1:28 *4066*
they may go into the s countryside Mk 6:36 *2945*
spread through all the s district. Lk 4:14 *4066*
every locality in the s district. Lk 4:37 *4066*
Judea and in all the s district. Lk 7:17 *4066*
of the Gerasenes and the s district Lk 8:37 *4066*
that they may go into the s villages Lk 9:12 *2945*
and Derbe, and the s region; Ac 14:6 *4066*
so great a cloud of witnesses s us, Heb 12:1 *4029*

SURROUNDS

When the iniquity of my foes s me, Ps 49:5 5437
Your faithfulness also s You. Ps 89:8 5439
So the LORD s His people From this Ps 125:2 5439
the great one slain, which s them, Ezk 21:14 2314
Ephraim s Me with lies And the Hos 11:12 5437

SURVEY

the land between them to s it; 1Ki 18:6 5674a

SURVEYED

He stood and s the earth; Hab 3:6 4058

SURVIVAL

for our good always and for our s, Dt 6:24 2421a

SURVIVE

even those who s in this city from Jer 21:7 7604
and you and your household will s. Jer 38:17 2421a
how then can we s?" Ezk 33:10 2421a
infants and they would not s. Ac 7:19 *2225*

SURVIVED

those who s fled to the hill country. Gn 14:10 7604
fire, as you have heard *it,* and s? Dt 4:33 2421a
left of those who s or escaped. Jos 8:22 8300
days of the elders who s Joshua, Jos 24:31
748, 3117, 310
days of the elders who s Joshua, Jg 2:7
748, 3117, 310
Those who s were scattered, 1Sa 11:11 7604
escaped *and* had s the captivity, Ne 1:2 7604
remnant there in the province who s Ne 1:3 7604
"The people who s the sword Found Jer 31:2 8300
there was no one who escaped or s La 2:22 8300

SURVIVES

"If, however, he s a day or two, Ex 21:21 5975

SURVIVING

spoke to Aaron, and to his s sons, Lv 10:12 3498
Aaron's s sons Eleazar and Ithamar, Lv 10:16 3498
The s remnant of the house of Judah 2Ki 19:30 7604
The s remnant of the house of Judah Is 37:31 7604

SURVIVOR

children of every city. We left no s. Dt 2:34 8300
we smote them until no s was left. Dt 3:3 8300
person who was in it. He left no s. Jos 10:28 8300
He left no s in it. Jos 10:30 8300
people until he had left him no s. Jos 10:33 8300
He left no s, according to all Jos 10:37 8300
person *who was* in it. He left no s. Jos 10:39 8300
He left no s, but he utterly Jos 10:40 8300
them until no s was left to them. Jos 11:8 8300
until he left him without a s. 2Ki 10:11 8300
'Every s, at whatever place he Ezr 1:4 7604
Nor any s where he sojourned. Jb 18:19 8300
It will consume the s in his tent. Jb 20:26 8300
be no s of the house of Esau," Ob 1:18 8300

SURVIVORS

and the s *who* remained of them had Jos 10:20 8300
"Then s came down to the nobles; Jg 5:13 8300
inheritance for the s of Benjamin, Jg 21:17 6413
remnant, and out of Mount Zion s. 2Ki 19:31 6413
"His s will be buried because of Jb 27:15 8300
LORD of hosts Had left us a few s, Is 1:9 8300
the adornment of the s of Israel. Is 4:2 6413
cut off from Babylon name and s, Is 14:22 7605
And it will kill off your s. Is 14:30 7611
remnant and out of Mount Zion s. Is 37:32 6413
send s from them to the nations: Is 66:19 6412b
So I will give over their s to Jer 15:9 7611
and they will have no s or Jer 42:17 8300
'So there will be no refugees or s Jer 44:14 8300
'Even when their s escape, they Ezk 7:16 6412a
s will be left in it who will be Ezk 14:22 6413
and the s will be scattered to Ezk 17:21 7604
and your s will fall by the sword. Ezk 23:25 319
your s will be consumed by the Ezk 23:25 319
among the s whom the LORD calls. Jl 2:32 8300
do not imprison their s In the day Ob 1:14 8300

SUSA

the Babylonians, the men of S, Ezr 4:9 7801
while I was in S the capitol, Ne 1:1 7800
throne which *was* at the citadel in S, Es 1:2 7800
who were present at the citadel in S, Es 1:5 7800
young virgin to the citadel of S, Es 2:3 7800
there was at the citadel in S a Jew Es 2:5 7800
were gathered to the citadel of S Es 2:8 7800
was issued at the citadel in S; Es 3:15 7800
the city of S was in confusion. Es 3:15 7800
issued in S for their destruction, Es 4:8 7800
all the Jews who are found in S, Es 4:16 7800
was given out at the citadel in S. Es 8:14 7800
city of S shouted and rejoiced. Es 8:15 7800
At the citadel in S the Jews Es 9:6 7800
who were killed at the citadel in S Es 9:11 7800
sons of Haman at the citadel in S. Es 9:12 7800
be granted to the Jews who are in S Es 9:13 7800
and an edict was issued in S, Es 9:14 7800
The Jews who were in S Es 9:15 7800
and killed three hundred men in S, Es 9:15 7800
But the Jews who were in S Es 9:18 7800
looking I was in the citadel of S, Da 8:2 7800

SUSANNA

of Chuza, Herod's steward, and S, Lk 8:3 *4677*

SUSI

of Manasseh, Gaddi the son of S; Nu 13:11 5485

SUSPENSE

"How long will You keep us in s? Jn 10:24
5590, 142

SUSPICION

Saul looked at David with s from 1Sa 18:9 5870b

SUSPICIONS

strife, abusive language, evil s, 1Tm 6:4 *5283*

SUSTAIN

s them while dwelling together, Gn 13:6 5375
not s them because of their livestock. Gn 36:7 5375
you falter, then you are to s him, Lv 25:35 2388
"S yourself with a piece of Jg 19:5 5582
"Please s yourself, and wait Jg 19:8 5582
I will s you in Jerusalem with me." 2Sa 19:33 3557
LORD will s him upon his sickbed; Ps 41:3 5582
And s me with a willing spirit. Ps 51:12 5564
upon the LORD and He will s you; Ps 55:22 3557
S me according to Your word, that I Ps 119:116 5564
"S me with raisin cakes, Refresh SS 2:5 5564
to s the weary one with a word. Is 50:4 5790
the broken, or s the one standing, Zch 11:16 3557

SUSTAINED

grain and new wine I have s him. Gn 27:37 5564
and he had s the king while he 2Sa 19:32 3557
You I have been s from *my* birth; Ps 71:6 5564

SUSTAINER

of life and a s of your old age; Ru 4:15 3557
The Lord is the s of my soul. Ps 54:4 5564

SUSTAINS

body s in its skin a burn by fire, Lv 13:24 1961
I awoke, for the LORD s me. Ps 3:5 5564
But the LORD s the righteous. Ps 37:17 5564
oil, And food which s man's heart. Ps 104:15 5582
The LORD s all who fall And Ps 145:14 5564

SUSTENANCE

s for his father on the journey. Gn 45:23 4202
leave no s in Israel as well as no Jg 6:4 4241
guard and provided them with s, 2Sa 20:3 3557
And let them seek s far from Ps 109:10
household, And s for your maidens. Pr 27:27 2425b

SWADDLING

And thick darkness its s band, Jb 38:9 2854

SWALLOW

have a s of that red stuff there, Gn 25:30 3938
"The earth may s us up!" Nu 16:34 1104
Why would you s up the inheritance 2Sa 20:19 1104
me that I should s up or destroy! 2Sa 20:20 1104
let me alone until I s my spittle? Jb 7:19 1104
he has attained And cannot s *it;* Jb 20:18 1104
LORD will s them up in His wrath, Ps 21:9 1104
me Nor the deep s me up, Ps 69:15 1104
And the s a nest for herself, Ps 84:3 1866
Let us s them alive like Sheol, Pr 1:12 1104
flitting, like a s in *its* flying, Pr 26:2 1866
And on this mountain He will s up Is 25:7 1104
He will s up death for all time, Is 25:8 1104
"Like a s, *like* a crane, so I Is 38:14 5483a
it yield, strangers would s it up. Hos 8:7 1104
They will drink and s And Ob 1:16 3886a
appointed a great fish to s Jonah, Jon 1:17 1104
wicked s up Those more righteous Hab 1:13 1104
strain out a gnat and s a camel! Mt 23:24 *2666*

SWALLOWED

The thin ears s up the seven Gn 41:7 1104
thin ears s the seven good ears. Gn 41:24 1104
Aaron's staff s up their staffs. Ex 7:12 1104
Your right hand, The earth s them. Ex 15:12 1104
opened its mouth and s them up, Nu 16:32 1104
and s them up along with Korah, Nu 26:10 1104
earth opened its mouth and s them, Dt 11:6 1104
a man say that he would be s up? Jb 37:20 1104
"We have s him up!" Ps 35:25 1104
The earth opened and s up Dathan, Ps 106:17 1104
Then they would have s us alive, Ps 124:3 1104
those who s you will be far away. Is 49:19 1104
He has s me like a monster, He has Jer 51:34 1104
I will make what he has s come out Jer 51:44 1105
The Lord has s up; La 2:2 1104
He has s up Israel; La 2:5 1104
He has s up all its palaces, La 2:5 1104
"We have s *her* up! La 2:16 1104
Israel is s up; They are now among Hos 8:8 1104
"DEATH IS S UP in victory. 1Co 15:54 *2666*
is mortal will be s up by life. 2Co 5:4 *2666*

SWALLOWS
ground opens its mouth and **s** them **Nu 16:30** 1104
"He **s** riches, But will vomit them **Jb 20:15** 1104
wise, But a foolish man **s** it up. **Pr 21:20** 1104
as it is in his hand, He **s** it. **Is 28:4** 1104

SWAMPED
began to be **s** and to be in danger. **Lk 8:23** *4845*

SWAMPS
for the hedgehog and **s** of water, **Is 14:23** 98
"But its **s** and marshes will not **Ezk 47:11** 1207

SWARM
"The Nile will **s** with frogs, **Ex 8:3** 8317
things which **s** on the earth: **Lv 11:29** 8317
any of the swarming things that **s**; **Lv 11:43** 8317
things that **s** on the earth. **Lv 11:44** 7430
a **s** of bees and honey were in the **Jg 14:8** 5712
and there came a **s** of flies *And* **Ps 105:31** 6157

SWARMED
the waters **s** after their kind, **Gn 1:21** 8317
Their land **s** with frogs *Even* in **Ps 105:30** 8317

SWARMING
cattle and beasts and every **s** thing **Gn 7:21** 8318
or a carcass of unclean **s** things, **Lv 5:2** 8318
the unclean among the **s** things **Lv 11:29** 8318
unclean among all the **s** things; **Lv 11:31** 8318
'Now every **s** thing that swarms on **Lv 11:41** 8318
in respect to every **s** thing that **Lv 11:42** 8318
any of the **s** things that swarm; **Lv 11:43** 8318
unclean with any of the **s** things **Lv 11:44** 8318
has left, the **s** locust has eaten; **Jl 1:4** 697
And what the **s** locust has left, **Jl 1:4** 697
years That the **s** locust has eaten, **Jl 2:25** 697
yourself like the **s** locust. **Na 3:15** 697
guardsmen are like the **s** locust. **Na 3:17** 697

SWARMS
teem with **s** of living creatures, **Gn 1:20** 8318
thing that **s** upon the earth, **Gn 7:21** 8317
I will send **s** of insects on you **Ex 8:21** 6157
will be full of **s** of insects, **Ex 8:21** 6157
no **s** of insects will be there, **Ex 8:22** 6157
And there came great **s** of insects **Ex 8:24** 6157
laid waste because of the **s** of insects **Ex 8:24** 6157
s of insects may depart from Pharaoh **Ex 8:29** 6157
the **s** of insects from Pharaoh, **Ex 8:31** 6157
swarming thing that **s** on the earth **Lv 11:41** 8317
thing that **s** on the earth, **Lv 11:42** 8317
everything that **s** on the earth, **Lv 11:46** 8317
He sent among them **s** of flies which **Ps 78:45** 6157
In which are **s** without number, **Ps 104:25** 7431
every living creature which **s** in every **Ezk 47:9** 8317

SWARTHY
"Do not stare at me because I am **s**, **SS 1:6** 7840

SWEAR
s to me here by God that you will **Gn 21:23** 7650
Abraham said, "I **s** it." **Gn 21:24** 7650
and I will make you **s** by the LORD, **Gn 24:3** 7650
"My master made me **s**, **Gn 24:37** 7650
And Jacob said, "First **s** to me"; **Gn 25:33** 7650
He said, "**S** to me." So he swore **Gn 47:31** 7650
'My father made me **s**, **Gn 50:5** 7650
your father, as he made you **s**." **Gn 50:6** 7650
Joseph made the sons of Israel **s**, **Gn 50:25** 7650
made the sons of Israel solemnly **s**, **Ex 13:19** 7650
shall not **s** falsely by My name, **Lv 19:12** 7650
s with the oath of the curse, **Nu 5:21** 7650
worship Him and **s** by His name. **Dt 6:13** 7650
Him, and you shall **s** by His name. **Dt 10:20** 7650
please **s** to me by the LORD, **Jos 2:12** 7650
to you which you have made us **s**, **Jos 2:17** 7650
oath which you have made us **s**." **Jos 2:20** 7650
gods, or make *anyone* **s** *by them*, **Jos 23:7** 7650
"**S** to me that you will not kill **Jg 15:12** 7650
"So now **s** to me by the LORD that **1Sa 24:21** 7650
"**S** to me by God that you will not **1Sa 30:15** 7650
servants, for I **s** by the LORD, **2Sa 19:7** 7650
'Let King Solomon **s** to me today **1Ki 1:51** 7650
"Did I not make you **s** by the LORD **1Ki 2:42** 7650
s that they could not find you. **1Ki 18:10** 7650
had made him **s** *allegiance* by God. **2Ch 36:13** 7650
hair, and made them **s** by God, **Ne 13:25** 7650
so is the one who is afraid to **s**. **Ec 9:2** 7621
"I want you to **s**, O daughters of **SS 8:4** 7650
every tongue will **s** *allegiance*. **Is 45:23** 7650
Who **s** by the name of the LORD And **Is 48:1** 7650
earth Will **s** by the God of truth; **Is 65:16** 7650
And you will **s**, 'As the LORD lives,' **Jer 4:2** 7650
lives,' Surely they **s** falsely." **Jer 5:2** 7650
commit adultery and **s** falsely, **Jer 7:9** 7650
of My people, to **s** by My name, **Jer 12:16** 7650
taught My people to **s** by Baal, **Jer 12:16** 7650
obey these words, I **s** by Myself," **Jer 22:5** 7650
who **s** by the guilt of Samaria, **Am 8:14** 7650
who bow down *and* **s** to the LORD **Zph 1:5** 7650
to the LORD and *yet* **s** by Milcom, **Zph 1:5** 7650
and against those who **s** falsely, **Mal 3:5** 7650
Then he began to curse and **s**, **Mt 26:74** *3660*
But he began to curse and **s**, **Mk 14:71** *3660*
And to whom did He **s** that they **Heb 3:18** *3660*
He could **s** by no one greater, **Heb 6:13** *3660*
For men **s** by one greater *than* **Heb 6:16** *3660*
above all, my brethren, do not **s**, **Jas 5:12** *3660*

SWEARER
as the **s** is, so is the one who is **Ec 9:2** 7650

SWEARING
and **s** *allegiance* to the LORD of hosts **Is 19:18** 7650
There is **s**, deception, murder, **Hos 4:2** 422

SWEARS
'Or if a person **s** thoughtlessly **Lv 5:4** 7650
He **s** to his own hurt and does not **Ps 15:4** 7650
Everyone who **s** by Him will glory, **Ps 63:11** 7650
And he who **s** in the earth will **Is 65:16** 7650
and everyone who **s** will be purged **Zch 5:3** 7650
the one who **s** falsely by My name; **Zch 5:4** 7650
'Whoever **s** by the temple, *that* is **Mt 23:16** *3660*
whoever **s** by the gold of the temple is **Mt 23:16** *3660*
'Whoever **s** by the altar, *that* is **Mt 23:18** *3660*
whoever **s** by the offering on it, **Mt 23:18** *3660*
"Therefore, whoever **s** **Mt 23:20** *3660*
s *both* by the altar and by **Mt 23:20** *3660*
"And whoever **s** by the temple, **Mt 23:21** *3660*
s *both* by the temple and by Him **Mt 23:21** *3660*
"And whoever **s** by heaven, swears **Mt 23:22** *3660*
s *both* by the throne of God and by **Mt 23:22** *3660*

SWEAT
By the **s** of your face You will **Gn 3:19** 2188
with *anything which makes them* **s**. **Ezk 44:18** 3154
His **s** became like drops of blood, **Lk 22:44** *2402*

SWEEP
"Will You indeed **s** away the **Gn 18:23** 5595
will You indeed **s** *it* away and not **Gn 18:24** 5595
clean **s** of the house of Jeroboam, **1Ki 14:10** 1197a
you, and will utterly **s** you away, **1Ki 21:21** 1197a
will **s** them away with a whirlwind, **Ps 58:9** 8175a
"Then it will **s** on into Judah, it **Is 8:8** 2498
and I will **s** it with the broom of **Is 14:23** 2894
As windstorms in the Negev **s** on, **Is 21:1** 2498
hail will **s** away the refuge of lies **Is 28:17** 3261
wind will **s** away all your shepherds, **Jer 22:22** 7462a
"Then they will **s** through *like* **Hab 1:11** 2498
not light a lamp and **s** the house **Lk 15:8** *4563*

SWEEPING
Wrath has gone forth, A **s** tempest; **Jer 30:23** 1641

SWEEPS
as one **s** away dung until it is all **1Ki 14:10** 1197a

SWEET
waters, and the waters became **s**. **Ex 15:25** 4985
handfuls of finely ground **s** incense, **Lv 16:12** 5561
out of the strong came something **s**." **Jg 14:14** 4966
And the **s** psalmist of Israel, **2Sa 23:1** 5273b
eat of the fat, drink of the **s**, **Ne 8:10** 4477
"Though evil is **s** in his mouth **Jb 20:12** 4985
We who had **s** fellowship together **Ps 55:14** 4985
The **s** sounding lyre with the harp. **Ps 81:2** 5273b
How **s** are Your words to my taste! **Ps 119:103** 4452
lie down, your sleep will be **s**. **Pr 3:24** 6149
"Stolen water is **s**; **Pr 9:17** 4985
Desire realized is **s** to the soul, **Pr 13:19** 6149
S to the soul and healing to the **Pr 16:24** 4966
Bread obtained by falsehood is **s** to **Pr 20:17** 6156
honey from the comb is **s** to your **Pr 24:13** 4966
man any bitter thing is **s**. **Pr 27:7** 4966
a man's counsel is **s** to his friend. **Pr 27:9** 4986
And his fruit was **s** to my taste. **SS 2:3** 4966
For your voice is **s**, **SS 2:14** 6156
instead of **s** perfume there will be **Is 3:24** 1314
Who substitute bitter for **s** and **Is 5:20** 4966
for sweet and **s** for bitter! **Is 5:20** 4966
bought Me not **s** cane with money, **Is 43:24** 7070
their own blood as with **s** wine; **Is 49:26** 6071
the **s** cane from a distant land? **Jer 6:20** 2896a
and it was **s** as honey in my mouth. **Ezk 3:3** 4966
and **s** cane were among your **Ezk 27:19** 7070
On account of the **s** wine That is **Jl 1:5** 6071
mountains will drip with **s** wine, **Jl 3:18** 6071
the mountains will drip **s** wine And **Am 9:13** 6071
"They are full of **s** wine." **Ac 2:13** *1098*
the **s** aroma of the knowledge of Him **2Co 2:14** *3744*
mouth it will be **s** as honey." **Rv 10:9** *1099*
and in my mouth it was **s** as honey; **Rv 10:10** *1099*

SWEETER
"What is **s** than honey? **Jg 14:18** 4966
S also than honey and the **Ps 19:10** 4966
s than honey to my mouth! **Ps 119:103**

SWEETLY
worm feeds **s** till he is no **Jb 24:20** 4985

SWEETNESS
I leave my **s** and my good fruit, **Jg 9:11** 4987
s of speech increases persuasiveness. **Pr 16:21** 4986
"His mouth is *full of* **s**. **SS 5:16** 4477

SWEET-SCENTED
a bed of balsam, Banks of **s** herbs; **SS 5:13** 4840

SWELL
waste away and your abdomen **s**; **Nu 5:21** 6639
make your abdomen **s** and your **Nu 5:22** 6638
her abdomen will **s** and her thigh **Nu 5:27** 6638
did your foot **s** these forty years. **Dt 8:4** 1216
wear out, nor did their feet **s**. **Ne 9:21** 1216
s up or suddenly fall down dead. **Ac 28:6** *4092b*

SWELLING
a **s** or a scab or a bright spot, **Lv 13:2** 7613
if there is a white **s** in the skin, **Lv 13:10** 7613
there is quick raw flesh in the **s**, **Lv 13:10** 7613
is a white **s** or a reddish-white, **Lv 13:19** 7613
is dim, it is the **s** from the burn; **Lv 13:28** 7613
and if the **s** of the infection is **Lv 13:43** 7613
and for a **s**, and for a scab, and **Lv 14:56** 7613
the mountains quake at its **s** pride. **Ps 46:3** 1346
You rule the **s** of the sea; **Ps 89:9** 1348

SWEPT
or you will be **s** away in the **Gn 19:15** 5595
mountains, or you will be **s** away." **Gn 19:17** 5595
and the LORD **s** the sea *back* by a **Ex 14:21** 1980
you will be **s** away in all their sin." **Nu 16:26** 5595
"The torrent of Kishon **s** them away, **Jg 5:21** 1640
and your king will be **s** away." **1Sa 12:25** 5595
to be **s** away before your foes, **1Ch 21:12** 5595
utterly **s** away by sudden terrors! **Ps 73:19** 5486
have **s** them away like a flood, **Ps 90:5** 2229
stream would have **s** over our soul; **Ps 124:4** 5674a
waters would have **s** over our soul." **Ps 124:5** 5674a
But it is **s** away by injustice. **Pr 13:23** 5595
The downpour of waters **s** by. **Hab 3:10** 5674a
comes, it finds *it* unoccupied, **s**, **Mt 12:44** *4563*
it finds it **s** and put in order. **Lk 11:25** *4563*
his tail **s** away a third of the stars **Rv 12:4** *4951*
her to be **s** away with the flood. **Rv 12:15** *4216*

SWERVE
He caused their chariot wheels to **s**, **Ex 14:25** 5493

SWIFT
and straw for the horses and **s** steeds **1Ki 4:28** 7409
and *they were* as **s** as the gazelles **1Ch 12:8** 4116
loosed the bonds of the **s** donkey, **Jb 39:5** 6171
sun that the race is not to the **s** and **Ec 9:11** 7031
S is the booty, speedy is the prey. **Is 8:1** 4116
Go, **s** messengers, to a nation tall **Is 18:2** 7031
the LORD is riding on a **s** cloud and **Is 19:1** 7031
"And we will ride on **s** *horses*," **Is 30:16** 7031
those who pursue you shall be **s**. **Is 30:16** 7043
You are a **s** young camel entangling **Jer 2:23** 7031
And the turtledove and the **s** and **Jer 8:7** 5483a
Let not the **s** man flee, Nor the **Jer 46:6** 7031
"Flight will perish from the **s**, **Am 2:14** 7031
The **s** of foot will not escape, **Am 2:15** 7031
and I will be a **s** witness against **Mal 3:5** 4116
"THEIR FEET ARE **S** TO SHED BLOOD, **Ro 3:15** *3691*
s destruction upon themselves. **2Pe 2:1** *5031*

SWIFTER
They were **s** than eagles, They were **2Sa 1:23** 7043
days are **s** than a weaver's shuttle, **Jb 7:6** 7043
"Now my days are **s** than a runner; **Jb 9:25** 7043
His horses are **s** than eagles. **Jer 4:13** 7043
Our pursuers were **s** Than the eagles **La 4:19** 7031
"Their horses are **s** than leopards **Hab 1:8** 7043

SWIFT-FOOTED
and Asahel *was as* **s** as one of the **2Sa 2:18** 7031, 7272

SWIFTLY
His word runs very **s**. **Ps 147:15** 4120
behold, it will come with speed **s**. **Is 5:26** 7031
And his calamity has **s** hastened. **Jer 48:16** 3966
one will fly **s** like an eagle And **Jer 48:40** 1675
s and speedily I will return your **Jl 3:4** 7031

SWIM
Every night I make my bed **s**, **Ps 6:6** 7811
swimmer spreads out *his hands* to **s**, **Is 25:11** 7811
had risen, *enough* water to **s** in, **Ezk 47:5** 7813
that none *of them* would **s** away **Ac 27:42** *1579*
that those who could **s** should jump **Ac 27:43** *2860*

SWIMMER
a **s** spreads out *his hands* to swim, **Is 25:11** 7811

SWINDLER
cursed be the **s** who has a male in **Mal 1:14** 5230
or a reviler, or a drunkard, or a **s** **1Co 5:11** *727*

SWINDLERS
s, unjust, adulterers, or even **Lk 18:11** *727*
world, or with the covetous and **s**, **1Co 5:10** *727*
drunkards, nor revilers, nor **s**, **1Co 6:10** *727*

SWINE
do not throw your pearls before **s**, **Mt 7:6** *5519*
a herd of many **s** feeding **Mt 8:30** *5519*
out, send us into the herd of **s**." **Mt 8:31** *5519*
came out and went into the **s**, **Mt 8:32** *5519*
s feeding nearby on the mountain. **Mk 5:11** *5519*
"Send us into the **s** so that we may **Mk 5:12** *5519*
the unclean spirits entered the **s**; **Mk 5:13** *5519*
man, and *all* about the **s**. **Mk 5:16** *5519*
s feeding there on the mountain; **Lk 8:32** *5519*
Him to permit them to enter the **s**. **Lk 8:32**
of the man and entered the **s**; **Lk 8:33** *5519*
him into his fields to feed **s**. **Lk 15:15** *5519*
the pods that the **s** were eating, **Lk 15:16** *5519*

SWINE'S
As a ring of gold in a **s** snout **Pr 11:22** 2386
Who eat **s** flesh, And the broth of **Is 65:4** 2386
is like one who offers **s** blood; **Is 66:3** 2386
in the center, Who eat **s** flesh, **Is 66:17** 2386

SWING
and **s** to and fro far from men. **Jb 28:4** 5128

SWINGING
trees by **s** an axe against them; **Dt 20:19** 5080
had two leaves, two **s** leaves; **Ezk 41:24** 5437

SWINGS
s the axe to cut down the tree, **Dt 19:5** 5080

SWIRL
It will **s** down on the head of the **Jer 23:19** 2342a

SWIRLING
north, The wind continues **s** along; **Ec 1:6** 5437

SWOOP
They will **s** down on the slopes **Is 11:14** 5774a
will mount up and **s** like an eagle and **Jer 49:22** 1675

SWOOPING
like an eagle **s** *down* to devour. **Hab 1:8** 2363a

SWOOPS
of the earth, as the eagle **s** down, **Dt 28:49** 1675
Like an eagle that **s** on its prey. **Jb 9:26** 2907

SWORD
the flaming **s** which turned every **Gn 3:24** 2719
"By your **s** you shall live, **Gn 27:40** 2719

daughters like captives of the **s**? **Gn 31:26** 2719
each took his **s** and came upon the **Gn 34:25** 2719
Shechem with the edge of the **s**, **Gn 34:26** 2719
Amorite with my **s** and my bow." **Gn 48:22** 2719
with pestilence or with the **s**." **Ex 5:3** 2719
a **s** in their hand to kill us." **Ex 5:21** 2719
I will draw out my **s**, **Ex 15:9** 2719
his people with the edge of the **s**. **Ex 17:13** 2719
me from the **s** of Pharaoh." **Ex 18:4** 2719
and I will kill you with the **s**, **Ex 22:24** 2719
of you put his **s** upon his thigh, **Ex 32:27** 2719
no **s** will pass through your land. **Lv 26:6** 2719
will fall before you by the **s**; **Lv 26:7** 2719
will fall before you by the **s**. **Lv 26:8** 2719
'I will also bring upon you a **s** **Lv 26:25** 2719
and will draw out a **s** after you, **Lv 26:33** 2719
will flee as though from the **s**, **Lv 26:36** 2719
other as if *running* from the **s**, **Lv 26:37** 2719
into this land, to fall by the **s**? **Nu 14:3** 2719
you, and you will fall by the **s**, **Nu 14:43** 2719
one who has been slain with a **s** or **Nu 19:16** 2719
come out with the **s** against you." **Nu 20:18** 2719
struck him with the edge of the **s**, **Nu 21:24** 2719
way with his drawn **s** in his hand, **Nu 22:23** 2719
If there had been a **s** in my hand, **Nu 22:29** 2719
way with his drawn **s** in his hand; **Nu 22:31** 2719
Balaam the son of Beor with the **s**. **Nu 31:8** 2719
that city with the edge of the **s**, **Dt 13:15** 2719
its cattle with the edge of the **s**. **Dt 13:15** 2719
men in it with the edge of the **s**. **Dt 20:13** 2719
and with fiery heat and with the **s** **Dt 28:22** 2719
'Outside the **s** will bereave, And **Dt 32:25** 2719
If I sharpen My flashing **s**, **Dt 32:41** 2719
And My **s** will devour flesh, **Dt 32:42** 2719
help And the **s** of your majesty! **Dt 33:29** 2719
him with his **s** drawn in his hand, **Jos 5:13** 2719
donkey, with the edge of the **s**. **Jos 6:21** 2719
were fallen by the edge of the **s** **Jos 8:24** 2719
struck it with the edge of the **s**. **Jos 8:24** 2719
sons of Israel killed with the **s**. **Jos 10:11** 2719
its king with the edge of the **s**; **Jos 10:28** 2719
was in it with the edge of the **s**. **Jos 10:30** 2719
was in it with the edge of the **s**, **Jos 10:32** 2719
struck it with the edge of the **s**; **Jos 10:35** 2719
were in it with the edge of the **s**. **Jos 10:37** 2719
them with the edge of the **s**, **Jos 10:39** 2719
and struck its king with the **s**; **Jos 11:10** 2719
was in it with the edge of the **s**, **Jos 11:11** 2719
them with the edge of the **s**, **Jos 11:12** 2719
every man with the edge of the **s**, **Jos 11:14** 2719
s among *the rest of* their slain. **Jos 13:22** 2719
they struck it with the edge of the **s** **Jos 19:47** 2719
but not by your **s** or your bow. **Jos 24:12** 2719
struck it with the edge of the **s** and **Jg 1:8** 2719
the city with the edge of the **s**, **Jg 1:25** 2719
himself a **s** which had two edges, **Jg 3:16** 2719
took the **s** from his right thigh **Jg 3:21** 2719
not draw the **s** out of his belly; **Jg 3:22** 2719
the edge of the **s** before Barak; **Jg 4:15** 2719
Sisera fell by the edge of the **s**; **Jg 4:16** 2719
the **s** of Gideon the son of Joash, **Jg 7:14** 2719
"A **s** for the LORD and for Gideon!" **Jg 7:20** 2719
the LORD set the **s** of one against **Jg 7:22** 2719
But the youth did not draw his **s**, **Jg 8:20** 2719
"Draw your **s** and kill me, **Jg 9:54** 2719
them with the edge of the **s**; **Jg 18:27** 2719
foot soldiers who drew the **s**. **Jg 20:2** 2719
26,000 men who draw the **s**, **Jg 20:15** 2719
400,000 men who draw the **s**; **Jg 20:17** 2719
all these drew the **s**. **Jg 20:25** 2719
that day, all who draw the **s**. **Jg 20:35** 2719
the city with the edge of the **s**. **Jg 20:37** 2719
were 25,000 men who draw the **s**; **Jg 20:46** 2719
them with the edge of the **s**, **Jg 20:48** 2719
with the edge of the **s**, **Jg 21:10** 2719
that neither **s** nor spear was found **1Sa 13:22** 2719
man's **s** was against his fellow, **1Sa 14:20** 2719
the people with the edge of the **s**. **1Sa 15:8** 2719
your **s** has made women childless, **1Sa 15:33** 2719
David girded his **s** over his **1Sa 17:39** 2719
"You come to me with a **s**, **1Sa 17:45** 2719
does not deliver by **s** or by spear; **1Sa 17:47** 2719
but there was no **s** in David's hand. **1Sa 17:50** 2719
over the Philistine and took his **s** **1Sa 17:51** 2719
his **s** and his bow and his belt. **1Sa 18:4** 2719
there not a spear or a **s** on hand? **1Sa 21:8** 2719
I brought neither my **s** nor my **1Sa 21:8** 2719
"The **s** of Goliath the Philistine, **1Sa 21:9** 2719
the **s** of Goliath the Philistine. **1Sa 22:10** 2719
you have given him bread and a **s** **1Sa 22:13** 2719
priests with the edge of the **s**, **1Sa 22:19** 2719
he struck with the edge of the **s**. **1Sa 22:19** 2719
"Each *of you* gird on his **s**." **1Sa 25:13** 2719
So each man girded on his **s**. **1Sa 25:13** 2719
And David also girded on his **s**, **1Sa 25:13** 2719
Draw your **s** and pierce me through **1Sa 31:4** 2719
So Saul took his **s** and fell on it. **1Sa 31:4** 2719
fell on his **s** and died with him. **1Sa 31:5** 2719
because they had fallen by the **s**. **2Sa 1:12** 2719
s of Saul did not return empty. **2Sa 1:22** 2719
his **s** in his opponent's side; **2Sa 2:16** 2719
"Shall the **s** devour forever? **2Sa 2:26** 2719
a distaff, or who falls by the **s**, **2Sa 3:29** 2719
for the **s** devours one as well as **2Sa 11:25** 2719
down Uriah the Hittite with the **s**, **2Sa 12:9** 2719
with the **s** of the sons of Ammon. **2Sa 12:9** 2719
the **s** shall never depart from your **2Sa 12:10** 2719
the city with the edge of the **s**." **2Sa 15:14** 2719
that day than the **s** devoured. **2Sa 18:8** 2719

and over it was a belt with a **s** in **2Sa 20:8** 2719
Amasa was not on guard against the **s** **2Sa 20:10** 2719
was girded with a new **s**, and he **2Sa 21:16** 2719
hand was weary and clung to the **s**, **2Sa 23:10** 2719
valiant men who drew the **s**, **2Sa 24:9** 2719
put his servant to death with the **s**. **1Ki 1:51** 2719
not put you to death with the **s**.' **1Ki 2:8** 2719
he and killed them with the **s**, **1Ki 2:32** 2719
The king said, "Get me a **s**." **1Ki 3:24** 2719
they brought a **s** before the king. **1Ki 3:24** 2719
all the prophets with the **s**. **1Ki 19:1** 2719
killed Your prophets with the **s**. **1Ki 19:10** 2719
killed Your prophets with the **s**. **1Ki 19:14** 2719
who escapes from the **s** of Hazael, **1Ki 19:17** 2719
who escapes from the **s** of Jehu, **1Ki 19:17** 2719
with your **s** and with your bow? **2Ki 6:22** 2719
men you will kill with the **s**, **2Ki 8:12** 2719
them with the edge of the **s**; **2Ki 10:25** 2719
her put to death with the **s**." **2Ki 11:15** 2719
put Athaliah to death with the **s** **2Ki 11:20** 2719
I will make him fall by the **s** in his **2Ki 19:7** 2719
Sharezer killed him with the **s**; **2Ki 19:37** 2719
shield and **s** and shot with bow and **1Ch 5:18** 2719
Draw your **s** and thrust me through **1Ch 10:4** 2719
Saul took his **s** and fell on it. **1Ch 10:4** 2719
likewise fell on his **s** and died. **1Ch 10:5** 2719
were 1,100,000 men who drew the **s**; **1Ch 21:5** 2719
was 470,000 men who drew the **s**. **1Ch 21:5** 2719
while the **s** of your enemies **1Ch 21:12** 2719
three days of the **s** of the LORD, **1Ch 21:12** 2719
with his drawn **s** in his hand **1Ch 21:16** 2719
he put his **s** back in its sheath. **1Ch 21:27** 2719
by the **s** of the angel of the LORD. **1Ch 21:30** 2719
'Should evil come upon us, the **s**, **2Ch 20:9** 2719
he killed all his brothers with the **s**, **2Ch 21:4** 2719
her, put to death with the **s**." **2Ch 23:14** 2719
put Athaliah to death with the **s**. **2Ch 23:21** 2719
our fathers have fallen by the **s**, **2Ch 29:9** 2719
killed him there with the **s**. **2Ch 32:21** 2719
who slew their young men with the **s** **2Ch 36:17** 2719
Those who had escaped from the **s** **2Ch 36:20** 2719
the kings of the lands, to the **s**, **Ezr 9:7** 2719
each *wore* his **s** girded at his side **Ne 4:18** 2719
struck all their enemies with the **s**, **Es 9:5** 2719
servants with the edge of the **s**, **Jb 1:15** 2719
servants with the edge of the **s**, **Jb 1:17** 2719
saves from the **s** of their mouth, **Jb 5:15** 2719
in war from the power of the **s**. **Jb 5:20** 2719
And he is destined for the **s**. **Jb 15:22** 2719
be afraid of the **s** for yourselves, **Jb 19:29** 2719
brings the punishment of the **s**, **Jb 19:29** 2719
many, they are destined for the **s**; **Jb 27:14** 2719
hear, they shall perish by the **s** And **Jb 36:12** 2719
he does not turn back from the **s**. **Jb 39:22** 2719
Let his maker bring near his **s**. **Jb 40:19** 2719
s that reaches him cannot avail, **Jb 41:26** 2719
not repent, He will sharpen His **s**; **Ps 7:12** 2719
soul from the wicked with Your **s**, **Ps 17:13** 2719
Deliver my soul from the **s**, **Ps 22:20** 2719
The wicked have drawn the **s** and **Ps 37:14** 2719
s will enter their own heart, **Ps 37:15** 2719
by their own **s** they did not possess **Ps 44:3** 2719
in my bow, Nor will my **s** save me. **Ps 44:6** 2719
Gird Your **s** on *Your* thigh, O Mighty **Ps 45:3** 2719
And their tongue a sharp **s**. **Ps 57:4** 2719
over to the power of the **s**; **Ps 63:10** 2719
sharpened their tongue like a **s**. **Ps 64:3** 2719
arrows, The shield and the **s** **Ps 76:3** 2719
delivered His people to the **s**, **Ps 78:62** 2719
His priests fell by the **s**, **Ps 78:64** 2719
also turn back the edge of his **s** And **Ps 89:43** 2719
David His servant from the evil **s**. **Ps 144:10** 2719
And a two-edged **s** in their hand, **Ps 149:6** 2719
wormwood, Sharp as a two-edged **s**. **Pr 5:4** 2719
rashly like the thrusts of a **s**, **Pr 12:18** 2719
Like a club and a **s** and a sharp **Pr 25:18** 2719
"All of them are wielders of the **s**, **SS 3:8** 2719
Each man has his **s** at his side, **SS 3:8** 2719
You will be devoured by the **s**." **Is 1:20** 2719
will not lift up **s** against nation, **Is 2:4** 2719
Your men will fall by the **s** And **Is 3:25** 2719
is captured will fall by the **s**. **Is 13:15** 2719
slain who are pierced with a **s**, **Is 14:19** 2719
from the swords, From the drawn **s**, **Is 21:15** 2719
slain were not slain with the **s**, **Is 22:2** 2719
His fierce and great and mighty **s**, **Is 27:1** 2719
Assyrian will fall by a **s** not of man, **Is 31:8** 2719
a **s** not of man will devour him. **Is 31:8** 2719
So he will not escape the **s**, **Is 31:8** 2719
For My **s** is satiated in heaven, **Is 34:5** 2719
The **s** of the LORD is filled with **Is 34:6** 2719
I will make him fall by the **s** in his **Is 37:7** 2719
his sons killed him with the **s**; **Is 37:38** 2719
He makes them like dust with his **s**, **Is 41:2** 2719
has made My mouth like a sharp **s**, **Is 49:2** 2719
and destruction, famine and **s**; **Is 51:19** 2719
I will destine you for the **s**, **Is 65:12** 2719
by fire And by His **s** on all flesh, **Is 66:16** 2719
Your **s** has devoured your prophets **Jer 2:30** 2719
whereas a **s** touches the throat." **Jer 4:10** 2719
And we will not see **s** or famine. **Jer 5:12** 2719
They will demolish with the **s** your **Jer 5:17** 2719
the road, For the enemy has a **s**, **Jer 6:25** 2719
and I will send the **s** after them **Jer 9:16** 2719
The young men will die by the **s**, **Jer 11:22** 2719
For a **s** of the LORD is devouring **Jer 12:12** 2719
to make an end of them by the **s**, **Jer 14:12** 2719
'You will not see the **s** nor will you **Jer 14:13** 2719
'There will be no **s** or famine in **Jer 14:15** 2719

by **s** and famine those prophets shall **Jer 14:15** 2719
because of the famine and the **s**; **Jer 14:16** 2719
Behold, those slain with the **s**! **Jer 14:18** 2719
And those *destined* for the **s**, **Jer 15:2** 2719
destined for the sword, to the **s**; **Jer 15:2** 2719
"the **s** to slay, the dogs to drag **Jer 15:3** 2719
give over their survivors to the **s** **Jer 15:9** 2719
come to an end by **s** and famine, **Jer 16:4** 2719
them up to the power of the **s**; **Jer 18:21** 2719
struck down by the **s** in battle. **Jer 18:21** 2719
I will cause them to fall by the **s** **Jer 19:7** 2719
fall by the **s** of their enemies. **Jer 20:4** 2719
and will slay them with the **s**. **Jer 20:4** 2719
city from the pestilence, the **s** and **Jer 21:7** 2719
them down with the edge of the **s**. **Jer 21:7** 2719
dwells in this city will die by the **s** **Jer 21:9** 2719
'I will send the **s**, **Jer 24:10** 2719
s that I will send among them." **Jer 25:16** 2719
s which I will send among you." **Jer 25:27** 2719
for I am summoning a **s** against all **Jer 25:29** 2719
He has given them to the **s**,' **Jer 25:31** 2719
the fierceness of the oppressing **s** **Jer 25:38** 2719
Jehoiakim, who slew him with a **s** and **Jer 26:23** 2719
punish that nation with the **s**, **Jer 27:8** 2719
die, you and your people, by the **s**, **Jer 27:13** 2719
I am sending upon them the **s**, **Jer 29:17** 2719
'I will pursue them with the **s**, **Jer 29:18** 2719
"The people who survived the **s** **Jer 31:2** 2719
against it, because of the **s**, **Jer 32:24** 2719
hand of the king of Babylon by **s**, **Jer 32:36** 2719
siege ramps and against the **s**, **Jer 33:4** 2719
'You will not die by the **s**. **Jer 34:4** 2719
'to the **s**, to the pestilence and **Jer 34:17** 2719
stays in this city will die by the **s** **Jer 38:2** 2719
and you will not fall by the **s**; **Jer 39:18** 2719
with the **s** and put to death the **Jer 41:2** 2719
s, which you are afraid of, **Jer 42:16** 2719
to reside there will die by the **s**, **Jer 42:17** 2719
that you will die by the **s**, **Jer 42:22** 2719
and those for the **s** to the sword. **Jer 43:11** 2719
and those for the sword to the **s**. **Jer 43:11** 2719
they will fall by the **s** *and* meet their **Jer 44:12** 2719
will die by the **s** and famine; **Jer 44:12** 2719
punished Jerusalem, with the **s**, **Jer 44:13** 2719
met our end by the **s** and by famine **Jer 44:18** 2719
of Egypt will meet their end by the **s** **Jer 44:27** 2719
'Those who escape the **s** will **Jer 44:28** 2719
And the **s** will devour and be **Jer 46:10** 2719
s has devoured those around you.' **Jer 46:14** 2719
Away from the **s** of the oppressor.' **Jer 46:16** 2719
"Ah, **s** of the LORD, How long will **Jer 47:6** 2719
The **s** will follow after you. **Jer 48:2** 2719
who restrains his **s** from blood. **Jer 48:10** 2719
'And I will send out the **s** after **Jer 49:37** 2719
From before the **s** of the oppressor **Jer 50:16** 2719
Put all her young bulls to the **s**; **Jer 50:27** 2717c
"A **s** against the Chaldeans," **Jer 50:35** 2719
"A **s** against the oracle priests, **Jer 50:36** 2719
A **s** against her mighty men, and **Jer 50:36** 2719
"A **s** against their horses and **Jer 50:37** 2719
A **s** against her treasures, and **Jer 50:37** 2719
You who have escaped the **s**, **Jer 51:50** 2719
In the street the **s** slays; **La 1:20** 2719
my young men Have fallen by the **s**. **La 2:21** 2719
Better are those slain with the **s** **La 4:9** 2719
the **s** in the wilderness. **La 5:9** 2719
you, son of man, take a sharp **s**; **Ezk 5:1** 2719
strike *it* with the **s** all around the **Ezk 5:2** 2719
I will unsheathe a **s** behind them. **Ezk 5:2** 2719
will fall by the **s** around you, **Ezk 5:12** 2719
I will unsheathe a **s** behind them. **Ezk 5:12** 2719
and I will bring the **s** on you. **Ezk 5:17** 2719
am going to bring a **s** on you, **Ezk 6:3** 2719
will have those who escaped the **s** **Ezk 6:8** 2719
of Israel, which will fall by **s**, **Ezk 6:11** 2719
he who is near will fall by the **s**, **Ezk 6:12** 2719
'The **s** is outside and the plague **Ezk 7:15** 2719
is in the field will die by the **s**; **Ezk 7:15** 2719
"You have feared a **s**; **Ezk 11:8** 2719
so I will bring a **s** upon you," **Ezk 11:8** 2719
"You will fall by the **s**. **Ezk 11:10** 2719
I will draw out a **s** after them. **Ezk 12:14** 2719
spare a few of them from the **s**, **Ezk 12:16** 2719
bring a **s** on that country and say, **Ezk 14:17** 2719
'Let the **s** pass through the **Ezk 14:17** 2719
s, famine, wild beasts and plague **Ezk 14:21** 2719
all his troops will fall by the **s**, **Ezk 17:21** 2719
and I will draw My **s** out of its **Ezk 21:3** 2719
therefore My **s** will go forth from **Ezk 21:4** 2719
have drawn My **s** out of its sheath. **Ezk 21:5** 2719
'A **s**, a sword sharpened And also **Ezk 21:9** 2719
a **s** sharpened And also polished! **Ezk 21:9** 2719
the **s** is sharpened and polished, **Ezk 21:11** 2719
They are delivered over to the **s** **Ezk 21:12** 2719
the **s** be doubled the third time, **Ezk 21:14** 2719
third time, the **s** for the slain. **Ezk 21:14** 2719
is the **s** for the great one slain, **Ezk 21:14** 2719
I have given the glittering **s**. **Ezk 21:15** 2719
for the **s** of the king of Babylon **Ezk 21:19** 2719
"You shall mark a way for the **s** **Ezk 21:20** 2719
'A **s**, a sword is drawn, polished **Ezk 21:28** 2719
'A sword, a **s** is drawn, polished **Ezk 21:28** 2719
but they slew her with the **s**. **Ezk 23:10** 2719
your survivors will fall by the **s**. **Ezk 23:25** 2719
left behind will fall by the **s**. **Ezk 24:21** 2719
to Dedan they will fall by the **s**. **Ezk 25:13** 2719
mainland will be slain by the **s**, **Ezk 26:6** 2719
on the mainland with the **s**; **Ezk 26:8** 2719
will slay your people with the **s**; **Ezk 26:11** 2719

By the s upon her on every side; Ezk 28:23 2719
I will bring upon you a s Ezk 29:8 2719
"A s will come upon Egypt, Ezk 30:4 2719
will fall with them by the s. Ezk 30:5 2719
will fall within her by the s," Ezk 30:6 2719
of Pi-beseth Will fall by the s, Ezk 30:17 2719
it may be strong to hold the s. Ezk 30:21 2719
make the s fall from his hand. Ezk 30:22 2719
Babylon and put My s in his hand; Ezk 30:24 2719
when I put My s into the hand of Ezk 30:25 2719
to those who were slain by the s; Ezk 31:17 2719
those who were slain by the s. Ezk 31:18 2719
when I brandish My s before them; Ezk 32:10 2719
"The s of the king of Babylon Ezk 32:11 2719
of those who are slain by the s. Ezk 32:20 2719
She is given over to the s; Ezk 32:20 2719
uncircumcised, slain by the s.' Ezk 32:21 2719
them are slain, fallen by the s, Ezk 32:22 2719
them are slain, fallen by the s, Ezk 32:23 2719
of them slain, fallen by the s, Ezk 32:24 2719
all uncircumcised, slain by the s Ezk 32:25 2719
were slain by the s uncircumcised, Ezk 32:26 2719
and lie with those slain by the s. Ezk 32:28 2719
laid with those slain by the s; Ezk 32:29 2719
with those slain by the s and Ezk 32:30 2719
all his hordes slain by the s, Ezk 32:31 2719
along with those slain by the s, Ezk 32:32 2719
'If I bring a s upon a land, and Ezk 33:2 2719
sees the s coming upon the land and Ezk 33:3 2719
and a s comes and takes him away, Ezk 33:4 2719
'But if the watchman sees the s Ezk 33:6 2719
and a s comes and takes a person Ezk 33:6 2719
"You rely on your s, Ezk 33:26 2719
waste places will fall by the s, Ezk 33:27 2719
to the power of the s at the time of Ezk 35:5 2719
those slain by the s will fall. Ezk 35:8 2719
land that is restored from the s, Ezk 38:8 2719
"I will call for a s against Ezk 38:21 2719
man's s will be against his brother. Ezk 38:21 2719
and all of them fell by the s. Ezk 39:23 2719
they will fall by s and by flame, Da 11:33 2719
will not deliver them by bow, s, Hos 1:7 2719
And I will abolish the bow, the s and Hos 2:18 2719
Their princes will fall by the s Hos 7:16 2719
The s will whirl against their Hos 11:6 2719
They will fall by the s, Hos 13:16 2719
he pursued his brother with the s, Am 1:11 2719
I slew your young men by the s Am 4:10 2719
house of Jeroboam with the s." Am 7:9 2719
'Jeroboam will die by the s and Am 7:11 2719
your daughters will fall by the s, Am 7:17 2719
slay the rest of them with the s; Am 9:1 2719
command the s that it slay them, Am 9:4 2719
of My people will die by the s, Am 9:10 2719
will not lift up s against nation, Mi 4:3 2719
the land of Assyria with the s, Mi 5:6 2719
do preserve I will give to the s. Mi 6:14 2719
a s will devour your young lions; Na 2:13 2719
you, The s will cut you down; Na 3:15 2719
will be slain by My s." Zph 2:12 2719
everyone by the s of another.' Hg 2:22 2719
I will make you like a warrior's s. Zch 9:13 2719
A s will be on his arm And on his Zch 11:17 2719
"Awake, O s, against My Shepherd, Zch 13:7 2719
not come to bring peace, but a s. Mt 10:34 *3162*
Jesus reached and drew out his s, Mt 26:51 *3162*
"Put your s back into its place; Mt 26:52 *3162*
those who take up the s shall perish Mt 26:52 *3162*
the sword shall perish by the s. Mt 26:52 *3162*
of those who stood by drew his s, Mk 14:47 *3162*
and a s will pierce even your own Lk 2:35 *4501b*
will fall by the edge of the s, Lk 21:24 *3162*
whoever has no s is to sell his coat Lk 22:36 *3162*
shall we strike with the s?" Lk 22:49 *3162*
Simon Peter then, having a s, Jn 18:10 *3162*
"Put the s into the sheath; Jn 18:11 *3162*
of John put to death with a s. Ac 12:2 *3162*
he drew his s and was about to kill Ac 16:27 *3162*
or nakedness, or peril, or s? Ro 8:35 *3162*
does not bear the s for nothing; Ro 13:4 *3162*
and the s of the Spirit, Eph 6:17 *3162*
and sharper than any two-edged s, Heb 4:12 *3162*
fire, escaped the edge of the s, Heb 11:34 *3162*
they were put to death with the s; Heb 11:37 *3162*
His mouth came a sharp two-edged s; Rv 1:16 *4501b*
One who has the sharp two-edged s Rv 2:12 *4501b*
them with the s of My mouth. Rv 2:16 *4501b*
and a great s was given to him. Rv 6:4 *3162*
to kill with s and with famine and Rv 6:8 *4501b*
if anyone kills with the s, Rv 13:10 *3162*
with the s he must be killed. Rv 13:10 *3162*
beast who had the wound of the s Rv 13:14 *3162*
From His mouth comes a sharp s, Rv 19:15 *4501b*
And the rest were killed with the s Rv 19:21 *4501b*

SWORDS

s are implements of violence. Gn 49:5 4380
the Hebrews will make s or spears." 1Sa 13:19 2719
according to their custom with s and 1Ki 18:28 2719
took with him 700 men who drew s, 2Ki 3:26 2719
people in families with their s, Ne 4:13 2719
than oil, Yet they were drawn s. Ps 55:21 6609
S are in their lips, For, *they* Ps 59:7 2719
of *man* whose teeth are *like* s And Pr 30:14 2719
hammer their s into plowshares and Is 2:4 2719
For they have fled from the s, Is 21:15 2719
cut you to pieces with their s. Ezk 16:40 2719
and cut them down with their s; Ezk 23:47 2719
And they will draw their s Against Ezk 28:7 2719
And they will draw their s against Ezk 30:11 2719
"By the s of the mighty ones I Ezk 32:12 2719
s were laid under their heads; Ezk 32:27 2719
shield, all of them wielding s; Ezk 38:4 2719
Beat your plowshares into s And Jl 3:10 2719
hammer their s into plowshares Mi 4:3 2719
Horsemen charging, S flashing, Na 3:3 2719
large crowd with s and clubs, Mt 26:47 *3162*
"Have you come out with s and Mt 26:55 *3162*
by a crowd with s and clubs, Mk 14:43 *3162*
Have you come out with s and clubs Mk 14:48 *3162*
"Lord, look, here are two s." Lk 22:38 *3162*
Have you come out with s and clubs Lk 22:52 *3162*

SWORDSMEN

for the fallen were 120,000 s. Jg 8:10 376, 8025, 2719

SWORE

who spoke to me and who s to me, Gn 24:7 7650
s to him concerning this matter. Gn 24:9 7650
so he s to him, and sold his Gn 25:33 7650
which I s to your father Abraham. Gn 26:3 7650
So Jacob s by the fear of his Gn 31:53 7650
So he s to him. Then Israel bowed Gn 47:31 7650
land which I s to give to Abraham, Ex 6:8 5375, 3027
He s to your fathers to give you, Ex 13:5 7650
He s to you and to your fathers, Ex 13:11 7650
Your servants to whom You s by Ex 32:13 7650
the land of which I s to Abraham, Ex 33:1 7650
anything about which he s falsely; Lv 6:5 7650
to the land which You s to their Nu 11:12 7650
land which I s to their fathers, Nu 14:23 7650
land in which I s to settle you, Nu 14:30 5375, 3027
burned in that day, and He s, Nu 32:10 7650
see the land which I s to Abraham, Nu 32:11 7650
LORD s to give to your fathers, Dt 1:8 7650
which I s to give your fathers, Dt 1:35 7650
and s that I would not cross the Dt 4:21 7650
your fathers which He s to them. Dt 4:31 7650
land which He s to your fathers, Dt 6:10 7650
the LORD s to *give* your fathers, Dt 6:18 7650
which He s to your forefathers, Dt 7:8 7650
which He s to your forefathers. Dt 7:12 7650
in the land which He s to your Dt 7:13 7650
s *to give* to your forefathers. Dt 8:1 7650
which He s to your fathers, Dt 8:18 7650
which the LORD s to your fathers, Dt 9:5 7650
s to their fathers to give them.' Dt 10:11 7650
land which the LORD s to your fathers Dt 11:9 7650
s to your fathers to give them, Dt 11:21 7650
LORD s to our fathers to give us.' Dt 26:3 7650
as You s to our fathers.' Dt 26:15 7650
people to Himself, as He s to you, Dt 28:9 7650
s to your fathers to give you. Dt 28:11 7650
you and as He s to your fathers, Dt 29:13 7650
which the LORD s to your fathers, Dt 30:20 7650
honey, which I s to their fathers, Dt 31:20 7650
them into the land which I s." Dt 31:21 7650
into the land which I s to them, Dt 31:23 7650
is the land which I s to Abraham, Dt 34:4 7650
I s to their fathers to give them. Jos 1:6 7650
congregation s *an oath* to them. Jos 9:15 7650
for the oath which we s to them." Jos 9:20 7650
"So Moses s on that day, saying, Jos 14:9 7650
David s to Saul. 1Sa 24:22 7650
Thus the king s to him. 2Sa 19:23 7650
Then the men of David s to him, 2Sa 21:17 7650
you s to your maidservant by the 1Ki 1:17 7650
Jordan, I s to him by the LORD, 1Ki 2:8 7650
Then King Solomon s by the LORD, 1Ki 2:23 7650
Gedaliah s to them and their 2Ki 25:24 7650
order to possess The land which You s Ne 9:15 5375, 3027
Which You s to David in Your Ps 89:49 7650
"Therefore I s in My anger, Truly Ps 95:11 7650
Therefore He s to them That He Ps 106:26 5375, 3027
How he s to the LORD And vowed to Ps 132:2 7650
When I s that the waters of Noah Is 54:9 7650
which I s to your forefathers, Jer 11:5 7650
and gave them this land, which You s Jer 32:22 7650
Zedekiah s to Jeremiah in secret Jer 38:16 7650
s to them and to their men, Jer 40:9 7650
I also s to you and entered into a Ezk 16:8 7650
chose Israel and s to the descendants Ezk 20:5 5375, 3027
land of Egypt, when I s to them, Ezk 20:5 5375, 3027
on that day I s to them, to bring Ezk 20:6 5375, 3027
"Also I s to them in the Ezk 20:15 5375, 3027
"Also I s to them in the Ezk 20:23 5375, 3027
land which I s to give to them, Ezk 20:28 5375, 3027
I s to give to your forefathers. Ezk 20:42 5375, 3027
for I s to give it to your Ezk 47:14 5375, 3027
and s by Him who lives forever Da 12:7 7650
Which You s to our forefathers From Mi 7:20 7650
And he s to her, Mk 6:23 *3660*
which He s to Abraham our father, Lk 1:73 *3660*
As I S IN MY WRATH, Heb 3:11 *3660*
"As I S IN MY WRATH, THEY SHALL Heb 4:3 *3660*
no one greater, He s by Himself, Heb 6:13 *3660*
and s by Him who lives forever and Rv 10:6 *3660*

SWORN

have s to the LORD God Most High, Gn 14:22 7311, 3027
"By Myself I have s, Gn 22:16 7650
and he said, "The LORD has s; Ex 17:16 3027, 5921, 3678
and lied about it and s falsely, Lv 6:3 7650
camp, as the LORD had s to them. Dt 2:14 7650
which He had s to our fathers.' Dt 6:23 7650
just as He has s to your fathers, Dt 13:17 7650
just as He has s to your fathers, Dt 19:8 7650
the LORD has s to their fathers Dt 31:7 7650
to whom the LORD had s that He Jos 5:6 7650
the LORD had s to their fathers Jos 5:6 7650
of there, as you have s to her." Jos 6:22 7650
leaders of the congregation had s to Jos 9:18 7650
"We have s to them by the LORD, Jos 9:19 7650
He had s to give to their fathers, Jos 21:43 7650
that He had s to their fathers, Jos 21:44 7650
which I have s to your fathers; Jg 2:1 7650
and as the LORD had s to them, Jg 2:15 7650
the men of Israel had s in Mizpah, Jg 21:1 7650
since we have s by the LORD not to Jg 21:7 7650
For the sons of Israel had s, Jg 21:18 7650
I have s to the house of Eli that the 1Sa 3:14 7650
inasmuch as we have s to each 1Sa 20:42 7650
if as the LORD has s to David, 2Sa 3:9 7650
O king, s to your maidservant, 1Ki 1:13 7650
for they had s with their whole 2Ch 15:15 7650
And has not s deceitfully. Ps 24:4 7650
I have s to David My servant, Ps 89:3 7650
"Once I have s by My holiness; Ps 89:35 7650
The LORD has s and will not change Ps 110:4 7650
I have s and I will confirm it, Ps 119:106 7650
The LORD has s to David A truth Ps 132:11 7650
my ears the LORD of hosts *has* s, Is 5:9
The LORD of hosts has s saying, Is 14:24 7650
"I have s by Myself, The word has Is 45:23 7650
So I have s that I will not be Is 54:9 7650
The LORD has s by His right hand Is 62:8 7650
And s by those who are not gods. Jer 5:7 7650
'Behold, I have s by My great name Jer 44:26 7650
"For I have s by Myself," Jer 49:13 7650
LORD of hosts has s by Himself: Jer 51:14 7650
they have s solemn oaths. Ezk 21:23
'I have s that surely the nations Ezk 36:7 5375, 3027
therefore I have s against them," Ezk 44:12 5375, 3027
Lord GOD has s by His holiness, Am 4:2 7650
The Lord GOD has s by Himself, Am 6:8 7650
LORD has s by the pride of Jacob, Am 8:7 7650
The rods of chastisement were s. Hab 3:9 7621
and knew that GOD HAD S TO HIM Ac 2:30 *3660*
LORD HAS S AND WILL NOT CHANGE Heb 7:21 *3660*

SWUNG

And he s his spear against three 2Sa 23:18 5782
and he s his spear against three 1Ch 11:20 5782
He who sat on the cloud s His sickle Rv 14:16 *906*
angel s his sickle to the earth and Rv 14:19 *906*

SYCAMORE

s trees that are in the lowland. 1Ki 10:27 8256
and s trees in the Shephelah; 1Ch 27:28 8256
s trees that are in the lowland. 2Ch 9:27 8256
And their s trees with frost. Ps 78:47 8256
a herdsman and a grower of s figs. Am 7:14 8256
climbed up into a s tree in order to Lk 19:4 *4809*

SYCAMORES

as plentiful as s in the lowland. 2Ch 1:15 8256
The s have been cut down, But we Is 9:10 8256

SYCHAR

to a city of Samaria called S, Jn 4:5 *4965*

SYENE

from Migdol *to* S and even to the Ezk 29:10 5482a
From Migdol *to* S They will fall Ezk 30:6 5482a

SYMBOL

they are men who are a s, Zch 3:8 4159
the woman ought to have *a* s *of* 1Co 11:10
which *is* a s for the present time. Heb 9:9 *3850b*

SYMPATHETIC

sum up, all of you be harmonious, s, 1Pe 3:8 *4835*

SYMPATHIZE

to s with him and comfort him. Jb 2:11 5110
who cannot s with our weaknesses, Heb 4:15 *4834*

SYMPATHY

And I looked for s, Ps 69:20 5110
For you showed s to the prisoners and Heb 10:34 *4834*

SYNAGOGUE

a s official came and bowed down Mt 9:18
from there, He went into their s. Mt 12:9 *4864*
and *began* teaching them in their s, Mt 13:54 *4864*
entered the s and *began* to teach. Mk 1:21 *4864*
there was a man in their s with an Mk 1:23 *4864*
after they came out of the s, Mk 1:29 *4864*
He entered again into a s; Mk 3:1 *4864*
One of the s officials named Jairus Mk 5:22 *752*
from the *house of* the s official, Mk 5:35 *752*
spoken, said to the s official, Mk 5:36 *752*
to the house of the s official; Mk 5:38 *752*
came, He began to teach in the s; Mk 6:2 *4864*
He entered the s on the Sabbath, Lk 4:16 *4864*
eyes of all in the s were fixed on Lk 4:20 *4864*
the people in the s were filled with Lk 4:28 *4864*
In the s there was a man Lk 4:33 *4864*
Then He got up and *left* the s, Lk 4:38 *4864*
He entered the s and was teaching; Lk 6:6 *4864*
it was he who built us our s." Lk 7:5 *4864*

and he was an official of the **s**; Lk 8:41 *4864*
from *the house of* the **s** official, Lk 8:49 *752*
But the **s** official, indignant Lk 13:14 *752*
These things He said in the **s** as Jn 6:59 *4864*
he was to be put out of the **s**. Jn 9:22 *656*
they would be put out of the **s**; Jn 12:42 *656*
will make you outcasts from the **s**, Jn 16:2 *656*
was called the **S** of the Freedmen, Ac 6:9 *4864*
they went into the **s** and sat down. Ac 13:14 *4864*
the **s** officials sent to them, Ac 13:15 *752*
meeting of the **s** had broken up, Ac 13:43 *4864*
entered the **s** of the Jews together, Ac 14:1 *4864*
where there was a **s** of the Jews. Ac 17:1 *4864*
they went into the **s** of the Jews. Ac 17:10 *4864*
So he was reasoning in the **s** with Ac 17:17 *4864*
And he was reasoning in the **s** Ac 18:4 *4864*
whose house was next to the **s**. Ac 18:7 *4864*
Crispus, the leader of the **s**, Ac 18:8 *752*
of Sosthenes, the leader of the **s**, Ac 18:17 *752*
Now he himself entered the **s** and Ac 18:19 *4864*
to speak out boldly in the **s**. Ac 18:26 *4864*
And he entered the **s** and continued Ac 19:8 *4864*
that in one **s** after another I used to Ac 22:19 *4864*
and are not, but are a **s** of Satan. Rv 2:9 *4864*
cause *those* of the **s** of Satan, Rv 3:9 *4864*

SYNAGOGUES
all Galilee, teaching in their **s** and Mt 4:23 *4864*
as the hypocrites do in the **s** and in Mt 6:2 *4864*
they love to stand and pray in the **s** Mt 6:5 *4864*
and villages, teaching in their **s** Mt 9:35 *4864*
and scourge you in their **s**; Mt 10:17 *4864*
and the chief seats in the **s**, Mt 23:6 *4864*
them you will scourge in your **s**, Mt 23:34 *4864*
their **s** throughout all Galilee, Mk 1:39 *4864*
and chief seats in the **s** and Mk 12:39 *4864*
and you will be flogged in *the* **s**, Mk 13:9 *4864*
He *began* teaching in their **s** and Lk 4:15 *4864*
on preaching in the **s** of Judea. Lk 4:44 *4864*
you love the chief seats in the **s** Lk 11:43 *4864*
When they bring you before the **s** Lk 12:11 *4864*
He was teaching in one of the **s** on Lk 13:10 *4864*
places, and chief seats in the **s** and Lk 20:46 *4864*
delivering you to the **s** and prisons, Lk 21:12 *4864*
I always taught in **s** and Jn 18:20 *4864*
asked for letters from him to the **s** Ac 9:2 *4864*
began to proclaim Jesus in the **s**, Ac 9:20 *4864*
word of God in the **s** of the Jews; Ac 13:5 *4864*
he is read in the **s** every Sabbath." Ac 15:21 *4864*
in the temple, nor in the **s**, Ac 24:12 *4864*
I punished them often in all the **s**, Ac 26:11 *4864*

SYNTYCHE
I urge Euodia and I urge **S** to live Php 4:2 *4941*

SYRACUSE
After we put in at **S**, Ac 28:12 *4946*

SYRIA
about Him spread throughout all **S**; Mt 4:24 *4947*
while Quirinius was governor of **S**. Lk 2:2 *4947*
to the brethren in Antioch and **S** Ac 15:23 *4947*
traveling through **S** and Cilicia, Ac 15:41 *4947*
brethren and put out to sea for **S**, Ac 18:18 *4947*
as he was about to set sail for **S**, Ac 20:3 *4947*
sailing to **S** and landed at Tyre; Ac 21:3 *4947*
into the regions of **S** and Cilicia. Ga 1:21 *4947*

SYRIAN
cleansed, but only Naaman the **S**." Lk 4:27 *4948*

SYROPHOENICIAN
woman was a Gentile, of the **S** race. Mk 7:26 *4949*

SYRTIS
run aground on *the shallows* of **S**, Ac 27:17 *4950*

T

TAANACH
the king of **T**, one; Jos 12:21 8590
inhabitants of **T** and its towns, Jos 17:11 8590
they allotted **T** with its pasture Jos 21:25 8590
villages, or **T** and its villages, Jg 1:27 8590
At **T** near the waters of Megiddo; Jg 5:19 8590
son of Ahilud, *in* **T** and Megiddo, 1Ki 4:12 8590
with its towns, **T** with its towns, 1Ch 7:29 8590

TAANATH-SHILOH
border turned about eastward to **T** and Jos 16:6 8387

TABBAOTH
sons of Hasupha, the sons of **T**, Ezr 2:43 2884
sons of Hasupha, the sons of **T**, Ne 7:46 2884

TABBATH
as the edge of Abel-meholah, by **T**. Jg 7:22 2888

TABEEL
Bishlam, Mithredath, **T** and Ezr 4:7 2870b
set up the son of **T** as king in the Is 7:6 2870a

TABERAH
name of that place was called **T**, Nu 11:3 8404
"Again at **T** and at Massah and at Dt 9:22 8404

TABERNACLE
as the pattern of the **t** and the Ex 25:9 4908
"Moreover you shall make the **t** Ex 26:1 4908
clasps so that the **t** will be a unit. Ex 26:6 4908
goats' *hair* for a tent over the **t**; Ex 26:7 4908
shall lap over the back of the **t**. Ex 26:12 4908
shall lap over the sides of the **t** Ex 26:13 4908
boards for the **t** of acacia wood, Ex 26:15 4908
do for all the boards of the **t**. Ex 26:17 4908
shall make the boards for the **t**: Ex 26:18 4908
and for the second side of the **t**, Ex 26:20 4908
"For the rear of the **t**, Ex 26:22 4908
the corners of the **t** at the rear. Ex 26:23 4908
the boards of one side of the **t**, Ex 26:26 4908
boards of the other side of the **t**, Ex 26:27 4908
for the boards of the side of the **t** Ex 26:27 4908
"Then you shall erect the **t** Ex 26:30 4908
side of the **t** toward the south; Ex 26:35 4908
You shall make the court of the **t**. Ex 27:9 4908
"All the utensils of the **t** *used* in all Ex 27:19 4908
the **t**, its tent and its covering, Ex 35:11 4908
doorway at the entrance of the **t**; Ex 35:15 4908
the pegs of the **t** and the pegs of Ex 35:18 4908
work made the **t** with ten curtains; Ex 36:8 4908
the clasps, so the **t** was a unit. Ex 36:13 4908
goats' *hair* for a tent over the **t**; Ex 36:14 4908
boards for the **t** of acacia wood, Ex 36:20 4908
did for all the boards of the **t**. Ex 36:22 4908
He made the boards for the **t**: Ex 36:23 4908
Then for the second side of the **t**, Ex 36:25 4908
For the rear of the **t**, Ex 36:27 4908
the corners of the **t** at the rear. Ex 36:28 4908
the boards of one side of the **t**, Ex 36:31 4908
boards of the other side of the **t**, Ex 36:32 4908
and five bars for the boards of the **t** Ex 36:32 4908
All the pegs of the **t** and of Ex 38:20 4908
number of the things for the **t**, Ex 38:21 4908
the **t** of the testimony, Ex 38:21 4908
and all the pegs of the **t** and all Ex 38:31 4908
work of the **t** of the tent of meeting Ex 39:32 4908
They brought the **t** to Moses, Ex 39:33 4908
for the service of the **t**, Ex 39:40 4908
set up the **t** of the tent of meeting. Ex 40:2 4908
the veil for the doorway to the **t**. Ex 40:5 4908
in front of the doorway of the **t** Ex 40:6 4908
the **t** and all that is in it, Ex 40:9 4908
the month, the **t** was erected. Ex 40:17 4908
Moses erected the **t** and laid its Ex 40:18 4908
He spread the tent over the **t** Ex 40:19 4908
He brought the ark into the **t**, Ex 40:21 4908
on the north side of the **t**, Ex 40:22 4908
table, on the south side of the **t**. Ex 40:24 4908
the veil for the doorway of the **t**. Ex 40:28 4908
the doorway of the **t** of the tent Ex 40:29 4908
all around the **t** and the altar, Ex 40:33 4908
glory of the LORD filled the **t**. Ex 40:34 4908
glory of the LORD filled the **t**. Ex 40:35 4908
was taken up from over the **t**, Ex 40:36 4908
the cloud of the LORD was on the **t** Ex 40:38 4908
the **t** and all that was in it, Lv 8:10 4908
My **t** that is among them." Lv 15:31 4908
the LORD before the **t** of the LORD, Lv 17:4 4908
over the **t** of the testimony, Nu 1:50 4908
the **t** and all its furnishings, Nu 1:50 4908
they shall also camp around the **t**. Nu 1:50 4908
"So when the **t** is to set out, the Nu 1:51 4908
and when the **t** encamps, the Nu 1:51 4908
around the **t** of the testimony, Nu 1:53 4908
keep charge of the **t** of the testimony Nu 1:53 4908
to do the service of the **t**. Nu 3:7 4908
to do the service of the **t**. Nu 3:8 4908
to camp behind the **t** westward, Nu 3:23 4908
involved the **t** and the tent, Nu 3:25 4908
is around the **t** and the altar, Nu 3:26 4908
on the southward side of the **t**, Nu 3:29 4908
on the northward side of the **t**. Nu 3:35 4908
involved the frames of the **t**, Nu 3:36 4908
to camp before the **t** eastward, Nu 3:38 4908
the **t** and of all that is in it, Nu 4:16 4908
they shall carry the curtains of the **t** Nu 4:25 4908
is around the **t** and the altar, Nu 4:26 4908
the boards of the **t** and its bars Nu 4:31 4908
the dust that is on the floor of the **t** Nu 5:17 4908
Moses had finished setting up the **t**, Nu 7:1 4908
they presented them before the **t**. Nu 7:3 4908
on the day that the **t** was erected Nu 9:15 4908
erected the cloud covered the **t**, Nu 9:15 4908
the appearance of fire over the **t**, Nu 9:15 4908
as the cloud settled over the **t**, Nu 9:18 4908
lingered over the **t** for many days, Nu 9:19 4908
remained a few days over the **t**, Nu 9:20 4908
the cloud lingered over the **t**, Nu 9:22 4908
from over the **t** of the testimony; Nu 10:11 4908
Then the **t** was taken down; Nu 10:17 4908
Merari, who were carrying the **t**, Nu 10:17 4908
and the **t** was set up before their Nu 10:21 4908
the service of the **t** of the LORD, Nu 16:9 4908
comes near to the **t** of the LORD, Nu 17:13 4908
defiles the **t** of the LORD; Nu 19:13 4908
charge of the **t** of the LORD." Nu 31:30 4908
kept charge of the **t** of the LORD, Nu 31:47 4908
LORD, where the LORD's **t** stands, Jos 22:19 4908
our God which is before His **t**." Jos 22:29 4908
about in a tent, even in a **t**. 2Sa 7:6 4908
the **t** of the tent of meeting, 1Ch 6:32 4908
service of the **t** of the house of God. 1Ch 6:48 4908
the priests before the **t** of the LORD 1Ch 16:39 4908
For the **t** of the LORD, which Moses 1Ch 21:29 4908
will no longer need to carry the **t** and 1Ch 23:26 4908
there before the **t** of the LORD, 2Ch 1:5 4908
He will conceal me in His **t**; Ps 27:5 5520
His **t** is in Salem; Ps 76:2 5520
treated His **t** like a garden *booth;* La 2:6 7900
TOOK ALONG THE **T** OF MOLOCH AND Ac 7:43 *4633*
"Our fathers had the **t** of testimony Ac 7:44 *4633*
I WILL REBUILD THE **T** OF DAVID Ac 15:16 *4633*
the sanctuary and in the true **t**, Heb 8:2 *4633*
when he was about to erect the **t**; Heb 8:5 *4633*
For there was a **t** prepared, the Heb 9:2 *4633*
there was a **t** which is called the Heb 9:3 *4633*
entering the outer **t** performing Heb 9:6 *4633*
the outer **t** is still standing, Heb 9:8 *4633*
the greater and more perfect **t**, Heb 9:11 *4633*
the same way he sprinkled both the **t** Heb 9:21 *4633*
those who serve the **t** have no right Heb 13:10 *4633*
will spread His **t** over them. Rv 7:15 *4637*
to blaspheme His name and His **t**, Rv 13:6 *4633*
and the temple of the **t** of testimony Rv 15:5 *4633*
"Behold, the **t** of God is among men, Rv 21:3 *4633*

TABERNACLES
wish, I will make three **t** here, Mt 17:4 *4633*
let us make three **t**, Mk 9:5 *4633*
let us make three **t**: Lk 9:33 *4633*

TABITHA
was a disciple named **T** Ac 9:36 *5000*
to the body, he said, "**T**, arise." Ac 9:40 *5000*

TABLE
portions to them from his own **t**, Gn 43:34 6440
You shall make a **t** of acacia wood, Ex 25:23 7979
for the poles to carry the **t**. Ex 25:27 7979
with them the **t** may be carried. Ex 25:28 7979
on the **t** before Me at all times. Ex 25:30 7979
shall set the **t** outside the veil, Ex 26:35 7979
and the lampstand opposite the **t** Ex 26:35 7979
shall put the **t** on the north side. Ex 26:35 7979
and the **t** and all its utensils, Ex 30:27 7979
the **t** also and its utensils, and Ex 31:8 7979
the **t** and its poles, and all its Ex 35:13 7979
Then he made the **t** of acacia wood, Ex 37:10 7979
for the poles to carry the **t**. Ex 37:14 7979
them with gold, to carry the **t**. Ex 37:15 7979
the utensils which were on the **t**, Ex 37:16 7979
the **t**, all its utensils, and the Ex 39:36 7979
"You shall bring in the **t** and Ex 40:4 7979
put the **t** in the tent of meeting on Ex 40:22 7979
tent of meeting, opposite the **t**, Ex 40:24 7979
the pure *gold* **t** before the LORD. Lv 24:6 7979
duties *involved* the ark, the **t**, Nu 3:31 7979
the **t** of the bread of the Presence Nu 4:7 7979
to gather up *scraps* under my **t**; Jg 1:7 7979
he has not come to the king's **t**." 1Sa 20:29 7979
Jonathan arose from the **t** in fierce 1Sa 20:34 7979
you shall eat at my **t** regularly." 2Sa 9:7 7979
shall eat at my **t** regularly." 2Sa 9:10 7979
So Mephibosheth ate at David's **t** 2Sa 9:11 7979
he ate at the king's **t** regularly. 2Sa 9:13 7979
among those who ate at your own **t**. 2Sa 19:28 7979
be among those who eat at your **t**; 1Ki 2:7 7979
all who came to King Solomon's **t**, 1Ki 4:27 7979
the golden altar and the golden **t** on 1Ki 7:48 7979
the food of his **t**, the seating of 1Ki 10:5 7979
they were sitting down at the **t**, 1Ki 13:20 7979
Asherah, who eat at Jezebel's **t**." 1Ki 18:19 7979
a **t** and a chair and a lampstand; 2Ki 4:10 7979
tables of showbread, for each **t**; 1Ch 28:16 7979
the food at his **t**, the seating of 2Ch 9:4 7979
showbread is *set* on the clean **t**, 2Ch 13:11 7979
and the **t** of showbread with all of 2Ch 29:18 7979
there were at my **t** one hundred and Ne 5:17 7979
that which was set on your **t** was Jb 36:16 7979
You prepare a **t** before me in Ps 23:5 7979
t before them become a snare; Ps 69:22 7979
God prepare a **t** in the wilderness? Ps 78:19 7979
like olive plants Around your **t**. Ps 128:3 7979
She has also set her **t**; Pr 9:2 7979
"While the king was at his **t**, SS 1:12 4524
They set the **t**, they spread out Is 21:5 7979
mountain, Who set a **t** for Fortune, Is 65:11 7979
couch with a **t** arranged before it on Ezk 23:41 7979
You will be glutted at My **t** with Ezk 39:20 7979
the **t** that is before the LORD." Ezk 41:22 7979
they shall come near to My **t** to Ezk 44:16 7979
lies *to each other* at the same **t**; Da 11:27 7979
t of the LORD is to be despised.' Mal 1:7 7979
'The **t** of the Lord is defiled, and Mal 1:12 7979
and recline *at the* **t** with Abraham, Mt 8:11
as Jesus was reclining *at the* **t** Mt 9:10
fall from their masters' **t**." Mt 15:27 *5132*
on His head as He reclined *at the* **t**. Mt 26:7
Jesus was reclining *at the* **t** with Mt 26:20
that He was reclining *at the* **t** in Mk 2:15
even the dogs under the **t** feed on Mk 7:28 *5132*
and reclining *at the* **t**, there Mk 14:3
As they were reclining *at the* **t** Mk 14:18
as they were reclining *at the* **t**; Mk 16:14
who were reclining *at the* **t** Lk 5:29
house and reclined *at the* **t**. Lk 7:36
that He was reclining *at the* **t** in Lk 7:37
Those who were reclining *at the* **t** Lk 7:49
and reclined *at the* **t**. Lk 11:37
and have them recline *at the* **t**, Lk 12:37
and will recline *at the* **t** in Lk 13:29
out the places of honor *at the* **t**, Lk 14:7
of all who are at the **t** with you. Lk 14:10 *4873*
those who were reclining *at the* **t** Lk 14:15
were falling from the rich man's **t**; Lk 16:21 *5132*
He reclined *at the* **t**, Lk 22:14
betraying Me is with Mine on the **t**. Lk 22:21 *5132*
the one who reclines *at the* **t** or Lk 22:27
not the one who reclines *at the* **t**? Lk 22:27
and drink at My **t** in My kingdom, Lk 22:30 *5132*
When He had reclined *at the* **t** Lk 24:30
one of those reclining *at the* **t** Jn 12:2
His garments and reclined *at the* **t** Jn 13:12
no one of those reclining *at the* **t** Jn 13:28
THEIR **T** BECOME A SNARE AND A TRAP, Ro 11:9 *5132*
cannot partake of the **t** of the Lord 1Co 10:21 *5132*

of the Lord and the **t** of demons. **1Co 10:21** *5132*
and the **t** and the sacred bread; **Heb 9:2** *5132*

TABLES
by weight for the **t** of showbread, **1Ch 28:16** 7979
and silver for the silver **t**; **1Ch 28:16** 7979
He also made ten **t** and placed them **2Ch 4:8** 7979
the **t** with the bread of the Presence **2Ch 4:19** 7979
the **t** are full of filthy vomit, **Is 28:8** 7979
the gate *were* two **t** on each side, **Ezk 40:39** 7979
toward the north, *were* two **t**; **Ezk 40:40** 7979
the porch of the gate *were* two **t**. **Ezk 40:40** 7979
Four **t** *were* on each side next to **Ezk 40:41** 7979
eight **t** on which they slaughter **Ezk 40:41** 7979
there were four **t** of hewn stone, **Ezk 40:42** 7979
on the **t** *was* the flesh of the offering. **Ezk 40:43** 7979
the **t** of the moneychangers and the **Mt 21:12** *5132*
the **t** of the moneychangers and the **Mk 11:15** *5132*
money changers seated *at their* **t**. **Jn 2:14**
and overturned their **t**; **Jn 2:15** *5132*
word of God in order to serve **t**. **Ac 6:2** *5132*
budded, and the **t** of the covenant; **Heb 9:4** *4109*

TABLET
Write them on the **t** of your heart. **Pr 3:3** 3871
Write them on the **t** of your heart. **Pr 7:3** 3871
"Take for yourself a large **t** and **Is 8:1** 1549
write it on a **t** before them And **Is 30:8** 3871
engraved upon the **t** of their heart And **Jer 17:1** 3871
And he asked for a **t** and **Lk 1:63** *4093*

TABLETS
and I will give you the stone **t** **Ex 24:12** 3871
Moses the two **t** of the testimony, **Ex 31:18** 3871
of the testimony, **t** of stone, **Ex 31:18** 3871
t of the testimony in his hand, **Ex 32:15** 3871
t which were written on both sides; **Ex 32:15** 3871
The **t** were God's work, and the **Ex 32:16** 3871
God's writing engraved on the **t**. **Ex 32:16** 3871
and he threw the **t** from his hands **Ex 32:19** 3871
two stone **t** like the former ones, **Ex 34:1** 3871
and I will write on the **t** the **Ex 34:1** 3871
the former **t** which you shattered. **Ex 34:1** 3871
two stone **t** like the former ones, **Ex 34:4** 3871
he took two stone **t** in his hand. **Ex 34:4** 3871
he wrote on the **t** the words of the **Ex 34:28** 3871
t of the testimony *were* in Moses' **Ex 34:29** 3871
He wrote them on two **t** of stone. **Dt 4:13** 3871
He wrote them on two **t** of stone **Dt 5:22** 3871
to receive the **t** of stone, **Dt 9:9** 3871
the **t** of the covenant which the **Dt 9:9** 3871
"The LORD gave me the two **t** **Dt 9:10** 3871
LORD gave me the two **t** of stone, **Dt 9:11** 3871
of stone, the **t** of the covenant. **Dt 9:11** 3871
and the two **t** of the covenant were **Dt 9:15** 3871
I took hold of the two **t** and threw **Dt 9:17** 3871
t of stone like the former ones, **Dt 10:1** 3871
'I will write on the **t** the **Dt 10:2** 3871
the former **t** which you shattered, **Dt 10:2** 3871
t of stone like the former ones, **Dt 10:3** 3871
with the two **t** in my hand. **Dt 10:3** 3871
"He wrote on the **t**, **Dt 10:4** 3871
the **t** in the ark which I had made; **Dt 10:5** 3871
two **t** of stone which Moses put there **1Ki 8:9** 3871
nothing in the ark except the two **t** **2Ch 5:10** 3871
the vision And inscribe *it* on **t**, **Hab 2:2** 3871
the living God, not on **t** of stone but **2Co 3:3** *4109*
stone but on **t** of human hearts. **2Co 3:3** *4109*

TABOR
The border reached to **T** and **Jos 19:22** 8396
'Go and march to Mount **T**, **Jg 4:6** 8396
of Abinoam had gone up to Mount **T**. **Jg 4:12** 8396
So Barak went down from Mount **T** **Jg 4:14** 8396
were they whom you killed at **T**?" **Jg 8:18** 8396
will come as far as the oak of **T**, **1Sa 10:3** 8396
lands, **T** with its pasture lands; **1Ch 6:77** 8396
T and Hermon shout for joy at Your **Ps 89:12** 8396
up like **T** among the mountains, **Jer 46:18** 8396
Mizpah And a net spread out on **T**. **Hos 5:1** 8396

TABRIMMON
them to Ben-hadad the son of **T**, **1Ki 15:18** 2886

TACKLE
Your **t** hangs slack; **Is 33:23** 2256a
day they threw the ship's **t** overboard **Ac 27:19** *4631*

TADMOR
He built **T** in the wilderness **2Ch 8:4** 8412

TAHAN
of **T**, the family of the Tahanites. **Nu 26:35** 8465
Resheph, Telah his son, **T** his son, **1Ch 7:25** 8465

TAHANITES
of Tahan, the family of the **T**. **Nu 26:35** 8470

TAHASH
also bore Tebah and Gaham and **T** **Gn 22:24** 8477

TAHATH
from Makheloth and camped at **T**. **Nu 33:26** 8480
They journeyed from **T** and **Nu 33:27** 8480
T his son, Uriel his son, Uzziah **1Ch 6:24** 8480
the son of **T**, the son of Assir, **1Ch 6:37** 8480
and Bered his son, **T** his son, **1Ch 7:20** 8480
son, Eleadah his son, **T** his son, **1Ch 7:20** 8480

TAHCHEMONITE
Josheb-basshebeth a **T**, **2Sa 23:8** 8461

TAHPANHES
"Also the men of Memphis and **T** **Jer 2:16** 8471
and went in as far as **T**. **Jer 43:7** 8471
of the LORD came to Jeremiah in **T**, **Jer 43:8** 8471
entrance of Pharaoh's palace in **T**, **Jer 43:9** 8471
who were living in Migdol, **T**, **Jer 44:1** 8471
Proclaim also in Memphis and **T**; **Jer 46:14** 8471

TAHPENES
wife, the sister of **T** the queen. **1Ki 11:19** 8472
sister of **T** bore him his son Genubath, **1Ki 11:20** 8472
whom **T** weaned in Pharaoh's house; **1Ki 11:20** 8472

TAHREA
of Micah *were* Pithon, Melech, **T** **1Ch 9:41** 8475

TAHTIM-HODSHI
to Gilead and to the land of **T**, **2Sa 24:6** 8483

TAIL
your hand and grasp *it* by its **t** **Ex 4:4** 2180
fat from the ram and the fat **t**, **Ex 29:22** 451
the entire fat **t** which he shall **Lv 3:9** 451
the fat **t** and the fat that covers **Lv 7:3** 451
He took the fat, and the fat **t**, **Lv 8:25** 451
ox and from the ram, the fat **t**, **Lv 9:19** 451
make you the head and not the **t**, **Dt 28:13** 2180
the head, and you will be the **t**. **Dt 28:44** 2180
and turned *the foxes* **t** to tail and **Jg 15:4** 2180
and turned *the foxes* tail to **t** and **Jg 15:4** 2180
"He bends his **t** like a cedar; **Jb 40:17** 2180
cuts off head and **t** from Israel, **Is 9:14** 2180
who teaches falsehood is the **t**. **Is 9:15** 2180
for Egypt Which *its* head or **t**, **Is 19:15** 2180
his **t** swept away a third of the stars **Rv 12:4** *3769*

TAILS
torch in the middle between two **t**. **Jg 15:4** 2180
They have **t** like scorpions, **Rv 9:10** *3769*
and in their **t** is their power to **Rv 9:10** *3769*
is in their mouths and in their **t**; **Rv 9:19** *3769*
for their **t** are like serpents and **Rv 9:19** *3769*

TAKE
and **t** also from the tree of life, **Gn 3:22** 3947
t for yourself some of all food **Gn 6:21** 3947
"You shall **t** with you of every **Gn 7:2** 3947
here is your wife, **t** her and go." **Gn 12:19** 3947
me and **t** the goods for yourself." **Gn 14:21** 3947
that I will not **t** a thread or a **Gn 14:23** 3947
"I will **t** nothing except what the **Gn 14:24**
let them **t** their share." **Gn 14:24** 3947
t your wife and your two **Gn 19:15** 3947
"You shall **t** these seven ewe **Gn 21:30** 3947
"**T** now your son, your only son, **Gn 22:2** 3947
that you shall not **t** a wife for my **Gn 24:3** 3947
and **t** a wife for my son Isaac." **Gn 24:4** 3947
should I **t** your son back to the **Gn 24:5** 7725
that you do not **t** my son back there! **Gn 24:6** 7725
t a wife for my son from there." **Gn 24:7** 3947
only do not **t** my son back there." **Gn 24:8** 7725
'You shall not **t** a wife for my son **Gn 24:37** 3947
and **t** a wife for my son.' **Gn 24:38** 3947
and you shall **t** a wife for my son **Gn 24:40** 3947
to **t** the daughter of my master's **Gn 24:48** 3947
Rebekah before you, **t** *her* and go, **Gn 24:51** 3947
"Now then, please **t** your gear, **Gn 27:3** 5375
"You shall not **t** a wife from the **Gn 28:1** 3947
and from there **t** to yourself a **Gn 28:2** 3947
to **t** to himself a wife from there, **Gn 28:6** 3947
"You shall not **t** a wife from the **Gn 28:6** 3947
keep me on this journey that I **t**, **Gn 28:20** 1980
matter for you to **t** my husband? **Gn 30:15** 3947
you **t** my son's mandrakes also?" **Gn 30:15** 3947
that you would **t** your daughters **Gn 31:31** 1497
and **t** *it* for yourself." **Gn 31:32** 3947
you **t** wives besides my daughters, **Gn 31:50** 3947
then **t** my present from my hand, **Gn 33:10** 3947
"Please **t** my gift which has been **Gn 33:11** 3947
"Let us **t** our journey and go, and **Gn 33:12** 5265
t our daughters for yourselves. **Gn 34:9** 3947
t your daughters for ourselves, **Gn 34:16** 3947
we will **t** our daughter and go." **Gn 34:17** 3947
Let us **t** their daughters in marriage, **Gn 34:21** 3947
"Let us not **t** his life." **Gn 37:21** 5221
"Let Pharaoh **t** action to appoint **Gn 41:34** 6213a
and **t** *grain for* the famine **Gn 42:33** 3947
no more, and you would **t** Benjamin; **Gn 42:36** 3947
t some of the best products of the **Gn 43:11** 3947
"**T** double *the* money in your hand, **Gn 43:12** 3947
and **t** back in your hand the money **Gn 43:12** 7725
"**T** your brother also, and arise, **Gn 43:13** 3947
and **t** us for slaves with our **Gn 43:18** 3947
If you **t** this one also from me, **Gn 44:29** 3947
and **t** your father and your **Gn 45:18** 3947
t wagons from the land of Egypt **Gn 45:19** 3947
but God will surely **t** care of you and **Gn 50:24** 6485
"God will surely **t** care of you, **Gn 50:25** 6485
"**T** this child away and nurse him **Ex 2:9** 1980
then you shall **t** some water from **Ex 4:9** 3947
and the water which you **t** from the **Ex 4:9** 3947
shall **t** in your hand this staff, **Ex 4:17** 3947
'Then I will **t** you for My people, **Ex 6:7** 3947
'**T** your staff and throw *it* down **Ex 7:9** 3947
and you shall **t** in your hand the **Ex 7:15** 3947
'**T** your staff and stretch out your **Ex 7:19** 3947
"**T** for yourselves handfuls of **Ex 9:8** 3947
T heed, for evil is in your mind. **Ex 10:10** 7200
for we shall **t** some of them to **Ex 10:26** 3947
one to **t** a lamb for themselves, **Ex 12:3** 3947
are to **t** one according to the number **Ex 12:4** 3947
you may **t** it from the sheep or **Ex 12:5** 3947
they shall **t** some of the blood and **Ex 12:7** 3947
"Go and **t** for yourselves lambs **Ex 12:21** 3947
"You shall **t** a bunch of hyssop **Ex 12:22** 3947
"**T** both your flocks and your **Ex 12:32** 3947
"God will surely **t** care of you **Ex 13:19** 6485
He did not **t** away the pillar of **Ex 13:22** 4185
you shall **t** an omer apiece **Ex 16:16** 3947
"**T** a jar and put an omerful of **Ex 16:33** 3947
and **t** with you some of the elders of **Ex 17:5** 3947
and **t** in your hand your staff with **Ex 17:5** 3947
"You shall not **t** the name of the **Ex 20:7** 5375
are to **t** him *even* from My altar, **Ex 21:14** 3947
and shall **t** care of him until he **Ex 21:19** 7495
"If you ever **t** your neighbor's cloak **Ex 22:26** 2254a
"You shall not **t** a bribe, **Ex 23:8** 3947
and **t** possession of the land. **Ex 23:30** 5157
"They shall **t** the gold and **Ex 28:5** 3947
"You shall **t** two onyx stones **Ex 28:9** 3947
and Aaron shall **t** away the **Ex 28:38** 5375
t one young bull and two rams **Ex 29:1** 3947
"You shall **t** the garments, **Ex 29:5** 3947
you shall **t** the anointing oil and **Ex 29:7** 3947
"You shall **t** some of the **Ex 29:12** 3947
"You shall **t** all the fat that **Ex 29:13** 3947
"You shall also **t** the one ram, **Ex 29:15** 3947
slaughter the ram and shall **t** its blood **Ex 29:16** 3947
"Then you shall **t** the other ram, **Ex 29:19** 3947
and **t** some of its blood and put *it* **Ex 29:20** 3947
"Then you shall **t** some of the **Ex 29:21** 3947
"You shall also **t** the fat from **Ex 29:22** 3947
You shall **t** them from their hands, **Ex 29:25** 3947
you shall **t** the breast of Aaron's ram **Ex 29:26** 3947
"You shall **t** the ram of **Ex 29:31** 3947
"When you **t** a census of the sons **Ex 30:12** 5375
You shall **t** the atonement money **Ex 30:16** 3947
"**T** also for yourself the finest **Ex 30:23** 3947
"**T** for yourself spices, stacte **Ex 30:34** 3947
Now Moses used to **t** the tent and **Ex 33:7** 3947
"Then I will **t** My hand away and **Ex 33:23** 5493
t us as Your own possession." **Ex 34:9** 5157
and you might **t** some of his daughters **Ex 34:16** 3947
he would **t** off the veil until he **Ex 34:34** 5493
'**T** from among you a contribution **Ex 35:5** 3947
"Then you shall **t** the anointing oil **Ex 40:9** 3947
'He shall also **t** away its crop **Lv 1:16** 5493
and shall **t** from it his handful of **Lv 2:2** 7061
'The priest then shall **t** up from **Lv 2:9** 7311
'Then the anointed priest is to **t** **Lv 4:5** 3947
'Then the priest is to **t** some of **Lv 4:25** 3947
'The priest shall **t** some of **Lv 4:30** 3947
'The priest is to **t** some of **Lv 4:34** 3947
and the priest shall **t** his handful **Lv 5:12** 7061
and he shall **t** up the ashes *to* **Lv 6:10** 7311
'Then he shall **t** off his garments **Lv 6:11** 6584
"**T** Aaron and his sons with him, **Lv 8:2** 3947
'**T** for yourself a calf, a bull, **Lv 9:2** 3947
'**T** a male goat for a sin offering, **Lv 9:3** 3947
"**T** the grain offering that is **Lv 10:12** 3947
then she shall **t** two turtledoves **Lv 12:8** 3947
give orders to **t** two live clean birds **Lv 14:4** 3947
for the live bird, he shall **t** it **Lv 14:6** 3947
t two male lambs without defect, **Lv 14:10** 3947
"Then the priest shall **t** the one **Lv 14:12** 3947
"The priest shall then **t** some of **Lv 14:14** 3947
also **t** some of the log of oil, **Lv 14:15** 3947
then he is to **t** one male lamb for **Lv 14:21** 3947
"The priest shall **t** the lamb **Lv 14:24** 3947
and the priest is to **t** some of the **Lv 14:25** 3947
"Then they shall **t** other stones **Lv 14:42** 3947
and he shall **t** other plaster and **Lv 14:42** 3947
and he shall **t** *them* outside the **Lv 14:45** 3318
he shall **t** two birds and cedar **Lv 14:49** 3947
"Then he shall **t** the cedar wood **Lv 14:51** 3947
he shall **t** for himself two turtledoves **Lv 15:14** 3947
she shall **t** for herself two turtledoves **Lv 15:29** 3947
"He shall **t** from the **Lv 16:5** 3947
"He shall **t** the two goats and **Lv 16:7** 3947
"He shall **t** a firepan full of **Lv 16:12** 3947
he shall **t** some of the blood of **Lv 16:14** 3947
and shall **t** some of the blood of **Lv 16:18** 3947
and **t** off the linen garments which **Lv 16:23** 6584
nor shall you **t** her son's daughter **Lv 18:17** 3947
'You shall not **t** vengeance, nor **Lv 19:18** 5358
'They shall not **t** a woman who is **Lv 21:7** 3947
nor shall they **t** a woman divorced **Lv 21:7** 3947
shall **t** a wife in her virginity. **Lv 21:13** 3947
by harlotry, these he may not **t**; **Lv 21:14** 3947
you shall **t** for yourselves the foliage **Lv 23:40** 3947
"Then you shall **t** fine flour and **Lv 24:5** 3947
not **t** usurious interest from him, **Lv 25:36** 3947
"**T** a census of all the congregation **Nu 1:2** 5375
nor shall you **t** their census among **Nu 1:49** 5375
and they shall **t** care of it; **Nu 1:50** 8334
out, the Levites shall **t** it down; **Nu 1:51** 3381
You shall **t** the Levites for Me, **Nu 3:41** 3947
"**T** the Levites instead of all the **Nu 3:45** 3947
you shall **t** five shekels apiece, **Nu 3:47** 3947
you shall **t** *them* in terms of the **Nu 3:47** 3947
"**T** a census of the descendants of **Nu 4:2** 5375
they shall **t** down the veil of the screen **Nu 4:5** 3381
"Then they shall **t** a blue cloth **Nu 4:9** 3947
t all the utensils of service, **Nu 4:12** 3947
t away the ashes from the altar, **Nu 4:13** 1878
"**T** a census of the sons of **Nu 4:22** 5375
and the priest shall **t** holy water **Nu 5:17** 3947
and he shall **t** some of the dust **Nu 5:17** 3947
The priest shall have her **t** an oath **Nu 5:19** 7650
'The priest shall **t** the grain **Nu 5:25** 3947
and the priest shall **t** a handful **Nu 5:26** 7061
and **t** the dedicated hair of his **Nu 6:18** 3947
'The priest shall **t** the ram's **Nu 6:19** 3947
"**T** the Levites from among the **Nu 8:6** 3947
"Then let them **t** a bull with its **Nu 8:8** 3947
you shall **t** for a sin offering. **Nu 8:8** 3947
them **t** their stand there with you. **Nu 11:16** 3320
t of the Spirit who is upon you, **Nu 11:17** 680
go up and **t** possession of it, **Nu 13:30** 3423
shall **t** possession of it. **Nu 14:24** 3423

t censers for yourselves, Korah	Nu 16:6	3947
"Each of you **t** his firepan	Nu 16:17	3947
that he shall **t** up the censers out	Nu 16:37	7311
"**T** your censer and put in it fire	Nu 16:46	3947
'When you **t** from the sons of	Nu 18:26	3947
'Next Eleazar the priest shall **t**	Nu 19:4	3947
'The priest shall **t** cedar wood	Nu 19:6	3947
they shall **t** some of the ashes of the	Nu 19:17	3947
'A clean person shall **t** hyssop	Nu 19:18	3947
T the rod; and you and your brother	Nu 20:8	3947
"**T** Aaron and his son Eleazar and	Nu 20:25	3947
I will **t** you to another place;	Nu 23:27	3947
"**T** all the leaders of the people	Nu 25:4	3947
"**T** a census of all the	Nu 26:2	5375
"**T** *a census of the people* from	Nu 26:4	
"**T** Joshua the son of Nun, a man	Nu 27:18	3947
"**T** full vengeance for the sons of	Nu 31:2	5358
t a count of the booty that was	Nu 31:26	5375
t it from their half and give it	Nu 31:29	3947
you shall **t** one drawn out of every	Nu 31:30	3947
do not **t** us across the Jordan."	Nu 32:5	5674a
and you shall **t** possession of the	Nu 33:53	3423
"You shall **t** one leader of	Nu 34:18	3947
you shall **t** more from the larger	Nu 35:8	7235a
you shall **t** less from the smaller;	Nu 35:8	4591
you shall not **t** ransom for the	Nu 35:31	3947
'You shall not **t** ransom for	Nu 35:32	3947
go up, **t** possession, as the LORD,	Dt 1:21	3423
begin to **t** possession and contend	Dt 2:24	3423
city which we did not **t** from them:	Dt 3:4	3947
go in and **t** possession of the land	Dt 4:1	3423
you, nor **t** away from it,	Dt 4:2	1639
t possession of this good land.	Dt 4:22	3423
"Or has a god tried to go to **t**	Dt 4:34	3947
today, and **t** it to your heart,	Dt 4:39	7725
'You shall not **t** the name of the	Dt 5:11	5375
t their daughters for your sons.	Dt 7:3	3947
on them, nor **t** it for yourselves,	Dt 7:25	3947
show partiality nor **t** a bribe.	Dt 10:17	3947
you shall **t** and go to the place	Dt 12:26	5375
not add to nor **t** away from it.	Dt 12:32	1639
then you shall **t** an awl and pierce	Dt 15:17	3947
and you shall not **t** a bribe,	Dt 16:19	3947
the way is long, and **t** his life,	Dt 19:6	5221
elders of his city shall send and **t** him	Dt 19:12	3947
you shall **t** as booty for yourself;	Dt 20:14	962
shall **t** a heifer of the herd,	Dt 21:3	3947
and you **t** them away captive,	Dt 21:10	7617
t her as a wife for yourself,	Dt 21:11	3947
not **t** the mother with the young;	Dt 22:6	3947
the young you may **t** for yourself,	Dt 22:7	3947
and her mother shall **t** and bring out	Dt 22:15	3947
shall **t** the man and chastise him,	Dt 22:18	3947
"A man shall not **t** his father's	Dt 22:30	3947
to **t** her again to be his wife,	Dt 24:4	3947
"No one shall **t** a handmill or an	Dt 24:6	2254a
enter his house to **t** his pledge.	Dt 24:10	5670
nor **t** a widow's garment in pledge.	Dt 24:17	2254a
and **t** her to himself as wife and	Dt 25:5	3947
not desire to **t** his brother's wife,	Dt 25:7	3947
'I do not desire to **t** her,'	Dt 25:8	3947
that you shall **t** some of the first	Dt 26:2	3947
"Then the priest shall **t** the	Dt 26:4	3947
"**T** this book of the law and place	Dt 31:26	3947
"**T** to your heart all the words	Dt 32:46	7760
T possession of the sea and the	Dt 33:23	3423
"**T** up the ark of the covenant and	Jos 3:6	5375
t for yourselves twelve men from	Jos 3:12	3947
"**T** for yourselves twelve men from	Jos 4:2	3947
'**T** up for yourselves twelve stones	Jos 4:3	5375
you **t** up a stone on his shoulder,	Jos 4:5	7311
"**T** up the ark of the covenant,	Jos 6:6	5375
do not covet *them* and **t** some of	Jos 6:18	3947
made them **t** an oath at that time,	Jos 6:26	7650
T all the people of war with you	Jos 8:1	3947
you shall **t** only its spoil and its	Jos 8:2	962
and **t** possession of the city,	Jos 8:7	3423
'**T** provisions in your hand for the	Jos 9:11	3947
not **t** possession of these cities,	Jos 17:12	3423
to **t** possession of the land which the	Jos 18:3	3423
and they shall **t** him into the city	Jos 20:4	622
stands, and **t** possession among us.	Jos 22:19	270
"So **t** diligent heed to yourselves	Jos 23:11	8104
But Manasseh did not **t** possession	Jg 1:27	3423
and **t** with you ten thousand men	Jg 4:6	3947
journey that you are about to **t**,	Jg 4:9	1980
Barak, and **t** away your captives,	Jg 5:12	7617
"**T** the meat and the unleavened	Jg 6:20	3947
"**T** your father's bull and a	Jg 6:25	3947
and **t** a second bull and offer a	Jg 6:26	3947
and **t** the waters before them,	Jg 7:24	3920
come and **t** refuge in my shade;	Jg 9:15	2620
"If you **t** me back to fight	Jg 11:9	7725
did not **t** away the land of Moab nor	Jg 11:15	3947
LORD, and I cannot **t** *it* back."	Jg 11:35	7725
that you go to **t** a wife from the	Jg 14:3	3947
When he returned later to **t** her,	Jg 14:8	3947
I will surely **t** revenge on you,	Jg 15:7	5358
no man will **t** me into his house.	Jg 19:18	622
Only let me **t** *care of* all your	Jg 19:20	
Consider it, **t** counsel and speak up!	Jg 19:30	5779
how did this wickedness **t** place?"	Jg 20:3	1961
"And we will **t** 10 men out of 100	Jg 20:10	3947
come out to **t** part in the dances,	Jg 21:21	2342a
because we did not **t** for each man	Jg 21:22	3947
that you should **t** notice of me,	Ru 2:10	5234
up the priest would **t** for himself.	1Sa 2:14	3947
will not **t** boiled meat from you,	1Sa 2:15	3947
then **t** as much as you desire,"	1Sa 2:16	3947
if not, I will **t** it by force."	1Sa 2:16	3947
Let us **t** to ourselves from Shiloh	1Sa 4:3	3947
"**T** courage and be men, O	1Sa 4:9	2388
"Now therefore, **t** and prepare a	1Sa 6:7	3947
the cart and **t** their calves home,	1Sa 6:7	7725
"**T** the ark of the LORD and place	1Sa 6:8	3947
come down and **t** it up to you."	1Sa 6:21	5927
he will **t** your sons and place *them*	1Sa 8:11	3947
"He will also **t** your daughters	1Sa 8:13	3947
"He will **t** the best of your	1Sa 8:14	3947
"He will **t** a tenth of your	1Sa 8:15	6237
"He will also **t** your male	1Sa 8:16	3947
"He will **t** a tenth of your	1Sa 8:17	6237
"**T** now with you one of the	1Sa 9:3	3947
"So now, **t** your stand, that I may	1Sa 12:7	3320
t your stand and see this great	1Sa 12:16	3320
t spoil among them until the morning	1Sa 14:36	962
"**T** a heifer with you and say,	1Sa 16:2	3947
David would **t** the harp and play *it*	1Sa 16:23	3947
"**T** now for your brothers an ephah	1Sa 17:17	3947
to **t** vengeance on the king's	1Sa 18:25	5358
Saul sent messengers to **t** David,	1Sa 19:14	3947
Saul sent messengers to **t** David,	1Sa 19:20	3947
if you would **t** it for yourself,	1Sa 21:9	3947
would take it for yourself, **t** *it.*	1Sa 21:9	3947
lying in wait for my life to **t** it.	1Sa 24:11	3947
"Shall I then **t** my bread and my	1Sa 25:11	3947
to Abigail, to **t** her as his wife.	1Sa 25:39	3947
us to you to **t** you as his wife."	1Sa 25:40	3947
but now please **t** the spear that is	1Sa 26:11	3947
the young men come over and **t** it.	1Sa 26:22	3947
and **t** hold of one of the young men	2Sa 2:21	270
and **t** for yourself his spoil."	2Sa 2:21	3947
And he was unwilling to **t** from his	2Sa 12:4	3947
t your wives before your eyes and	2Sa 12:11	3947
do not **t** this matter to heart."	2Sa 13:20	7896
the king **t** the report to heart,	2Sa 13:33	7760
Yet God does not **t** away life,	2Sa 14:14	5375
and **t** hold of him and kiss him.	2Sa 15:5	2388
Return and **t** back your brothers;	2Sa 15:20	7725
the king would **t** *it* to heart.	2Sa 19:19	7760
"Let him even **t** it all, since my	2Sa 19:30	3947
t your lord's servants and pursue	2Sa 20:6	3947
God, my rock, in whom I **t** refuge,	2Sa 22:3	2620
shield to all who **t** refuge in Him.	2Sa 22:31	2620
please **t** away the iniquity of Your	2Sa 24:10	5674a
"Let my lord the king **t** and offer	2Sa 24:22	3947
"**T** with you the servants of your	1Ki 1:33	3947
if only your sons **t** heed to their	1Ki 8:25	8104
neighbor and is made to **t** an oath,	1Ki 8:31	422
so that they **t** them away captive	1Ki 8:46	7617
if they **t** thought in the land	1Ki 8:47	7725
"**T** for yourself ten pieces;	1Ki 11:31	3947
I will not **t** the whole kingdom out	1Ki 11:34	3947
but I will **t** the kingdom from his	1Ki 11:35	3947
'I will **t** you, and you shall	1Ki 11:37	3947
"**T** ten loaves with you, *some*	1Ki 14:3	3947
now, O LORD, **t** my life, for I am	1Ki 19:4	3947
they seek my life, to **t** it away."	1Ki 19:10	3947
they seek my life, to **t** it away."	1Ki 19:14	3947
will **t** in their hand and carry away	1Ki 20:6	7760
come out for peace, **t** them alive;	1Ki 20:18	8610
come out for war, **t** them alive."	1Ki 20:18	8610
Then **t** him out and stone him to	1Ki 21:10	3318
t possession of the vineyard of	1Ki 21:15	3423
Jezreelite, to **t** possession of it.	1Ki 21:16	3423
gone down to **t** possession of it.	1Ki 21:18	3423
doing nothing to **t** it out of the hand	1Ki 22:3	3947
"**T** Micaiah and return him to Amon	1Ki 22:26	3947
around and **t** me out of the fight;	1Ki 22:34	3318
about to **t** up Elijah by a whirlwind	2Ki 2:1	5927
the LORD will **t** away your master	2Ki 2:3	3947
the LORD will **t** away your master	2Ki 2:5	3947
and the creditor has come to **t** my	2Ki 4:1	3947
loins and **t** my staff in your hand,	2Ki 4:29	3947
he said, "**T** up your son."	2Ki 4:36	5375
so please **t** a present from your	2Ki 5:15	3947
whom I stand, I will **t** nothing."	2Ki 5:16	3947
And he urged him to **t** *it,*	2Ki 5:16	3947
him and **t** something from him."	2Ki 5:20	3947
"Be pleased to **t** two talents."	2Ki 5:23	3947
each of us **t** from there a beam,	2Ki 6:2	3947
"**T** it up for yourself."	2Ki 6:7	7311
is, that I may send and **t** him."	2Ki 6:13	3947
has sent to **t** away my head?	2Ki 6:32	5493
let some *men* **t** five of the horses	2Ki 7:13	3947
"**T** a gift in your hand and go to	2Ki 8:8	3947
and **t** this flask of oil in your	2Ki 9:1	3947
"Then **t** the flask of oil and pour	2Ki 9:3	3947
"**T** a horseman and send him to	2Ki 9:17	3947
"**T** *him* up and cast him into the	2Ki 9:25	5375
t and cast him into the property,	2Ki 9:26	5375
my voice, **t** the heads of the men,	2Ki 10:6	3947
"**T** them alive." So they took them	2Ki 10:14	8610
the priests **t** it for themselves,	2Ki 12:5	3947
Now therefore **t** no *more* money from	2Ki 12:7	3947
t no *more* money from the people,	2Ki 12:8	3947
"**T** a bow and arrows."	2Ki 13:15	3947
"**T** the arrows," and he took them.	2Ki 13:18	3947
"**T** there one of the priests whom	2Ki 17:27	1980
until I come and **t** you away to a	2Ki 18:32	3947
house of Judah will again **t** root	2Ki 19:30	
"**T** a cake of figs."	2Ki 20:7	3947
came down to **t** their livestock.	1Ch 7:21	3947
So David did not **t** the ark with	1Ch 13:13	5493
and I will not **t** My lovingkindness	1Ch 17:13	5493
please **t** away the iniquity of Your	1Ch 21:8	5674a
Thus says the LORD, '**T** for yourself	1Ch 21:11	6901
"**T** *it* for yourself;	1Ch 21:23	3947
not **t** what is yours for the LORD,	1Ch 21:24	5375
your sons **t** heed to their way,	2Ch 6:16	8104
and is made to **t** an oath,	2Ch 6:22	422
so that they **t** them away captive	2Ch 6:36	7617
if they **t** thought in the land	2Ch 6:37	7725
"**T** Micaiah and return him to Amon	2Ch 18:25	3947
around and **t** me out of the fight	2Ch 18:33	3318
his people came to **t** their spoil,	2Ch 20:25	962
would come, empty the chest, **t** it,	2Ch 24:11	5375
so that they might **t** the city.	2Ch 32:18	3920
"**T** me away, for I am badly	2Ch 35:23	5674a
bronze *chains* to **t** him to Babylon.	2Ch 36:6	1980
"**T** these utensils, go *and* deposit	Ezr 5:15	5376
t their daughters to your sons,	Ezr 9:12	5375
t oath that they would do	Ezr 10:5	7650
now, let us **t** counsel together."	Ne 6:7	3289
or **t** their daughters for our sons.	Ne 10:30	3947
nor **t** of their daughters for your	Ne 13:25	5375
desired was given her to **t** with her	Es 2:13	935
"**T** quickly the robes and the	Es 6:10	3947
And **t** it to a *place of* thorns,	Jb 5:5	3947
And **t** away my iniquity?	Jb 7:21	5674a
I do not **t** notice of myself;	Jb 9:21	3045
then You would **t** note of me,	Jb 10:14	8104
should I **t** my flesh in my teeth And	Jb 13:14	5375
He will **t** His stand on the earth.	Jb 19:25	6965
"But He knows the way I **t**;	Jb 23:10	5973
They **t** the widow's ox for a pledge.	Jb 24:3	2254a
against the poor they **t** a pledge.	Jb 24:9	2254a
And they **t** away the sheaves from	Jb 24:10	5375
"Will he **t** delight in the Almighty	Jb 27:10	6026
And my gnawing *pains* **t** no rest.	Jb 30:17	7901
my Maker would soon **t** me away.	Jb 32:22	5375
before me, **t** your stand.	Jb 33:5	3320
and justice **t** hold *of you.*	Jb 36:17	8551
t hold of the ends of the earth,	Jb 38:13	270
you may **t** it to its territory And	Jb 38:20	3947
you **t** him for a servant forever?	Jb 41:4	3947
t for yourselves seven bulls and	Jb 42:8	3947
kings of the earth **t** their stand And	Ps 2:2	3320
And the rulers **t** counsel together	Ps 2:2	3245
T warning, O judges of the earth.	Ps 2:10	3256
are all who **t** refuge in Him!	Ps 2:12	2620
all who **t** refuge in You be glad,	Ps 5:11	2620
that You **t** thought of him,	Ps 8:4	2142
vexation to **t** it into Your hand.	Ps 10:14	5414
In the LORD I **t** refuge;	Ps 11:1	2620
long shall I **t** counsel in my soul,	Ps 13:2	7896
he **t** a bribe against the innocent.	Ps 15:5	3947
me, O God, for I **t** refuge in You.	Ps 16:1	2620
I **t** their names upon my lips.	Ps 16:4	5375
O Savior of those who **t** refuge at	Ps 17:7	2620
God, my rock, in whom I **t** refuge;	Ps 18:2	2620
shield to all who **t** refuge in Him.	Ps 18:30	2620
ashamed, for I **t** refuge in You.	Ps 25:20	2620
Do not **t** my soul away *along* with	Ps 26:9	622
me, But the LORD will **t** me up.	Ps 27:10	622
and let your heart **t** courage;	Ps 27:14	553
They schemed to **t** away my life.	Ps 31:13	3947
for those who **t** refuge in You,	Ps 31:19	2620
and let your heart **t** courage,	Ps 31:24	553
And none of those who **t** refuge in	Ps 34:22	2620
T hold of buckler and shield And	Ps 35:2	2388
And the children of men **t** refuge	Ps 36:7	2620
Because they **t** refuge in Him.	Ps 37:40	2620
"I shall **t** no young bull out of	Ps 50:9	3947
to **t** My covenant in your mouth?	Ps 50:16	5375
do not **t** Your Holy Spirit from me.	Ps 51:11	3947
As they have waited *to* **t** my life.	Ps 56:6	
of Your wings I will **t** refuge Until	Ps 57:1	2620
Let me **t** refuge in the shelter of	Ps 61:4	2620
LORD and will **t** refuge in Him;	Ps 64:10	2620
and see, and **t** care of this vine,	Ps 80:14	6485
Who will **t** his stand for me	Ps 94:16	3320
do not **t** me away in the midst of	Ps 102:24	5927
You **t** away their spirit,	Ps 104:29	622
That they might **t** possession of	Ps 105:44	3423
Let another **t** his office.	Ps 109:8	3947
It is better to **t** refuge in the LORD	Ps 118:8	2620
It is better to **t** refuge in the LORD	Ps 118:9	2620
T away reproach and contempt from	Ps 119:22	1556
And do not **t** the word of truth	Ps 119:43	5337
If I **t** the wings of the dawn, If I	Ps 139:9	5375
Your enemies **t** *Your name* in vain.	Ps 139:20	5375
In You I **t** refuge;	Ps 141:8	2620
I **t** refuge in You.	Ps 143:9	3680
shield and He in whom I **t** refuge,	Ps 144:2	2620
that You **t** knowledge of him?	Ps 144:3	3045
He does not **t** pleasure in the legs of	Ps 147:10	7521
life to those who **t** hold of her,	Pr 3:18	2388
T hold of instruction;	Pr 4:13	2388
Her steps **t** hold of Sheol.	Pr 5:5	8551
Can a man **t** fire in his bosom And	Pr 6:27	2846
"**T** my instruction and not silver,	Pr 8:10	3947
T his garment when he becomes	Pr 20:16	3947
And **t** the life of those who rob	Pr 22:23	6906
he **t** your bed from under you?	Pr 22:27	3947
T away the dross from the silver,	Pr 25:4	1898
T away the wicked before the	Pr 25:5	1898
T his garment when he becomes	Pr 27:13	3947
to those who **t** refuge in Him.	Pr 30:5	2620
and how to **t** hold of folly,	Ec 2:3	270
and there is nothing to **t** from it,	Ec 3:14	1639
He will **t** nothing from the fruit	Ec 5:15	5375
do not **t** seriously all words which	Ec 7:21	5414
will **t** hold of its fruit stalks.'	SS 7:8	270
those who **t** care of its fruit."	SS 8:12	5201
And I **t** no pleasure in the blood	Is 1:11	2654a
In that day the Lord will **t** away	Is 3:18	5493

Context	Reference	Number
seven women will t hold of one man	Is 4:1	2388
t away our reproach!"	Is 4:1	622
And t away the rights of the ones	Is 5:23	5493
"T care and be calm, have no fear	Is 7:4	8104
"T for yourself a large tablet	Is 8:1	3947
I will t to Myself faithful witnesses	Is 8:2	5749b
the Lord does not t pleasure in their	Is 9:17	8055
and anguish will t hold of *them;*	Is 13:8	270
silver or t pleasure in gold.	Is 13:17	2654a
The peoples will t them along	Is 14:2	3947
they will t their captors captive and	Is 14:2	1961
that you will t up this taunt	Is 14:4	5375
arise and t possession of the earth	Is 14:21	3423
and t your shoes off your feet."	Is 20:2	2502a
Nor did you t into consideration	Is 22:11	7200
T *your* harp, walk about the city,	Is 23:16	3947
days to come Jacob will t root,	Is 27:6	8327
To t refuge in the safety of	Is 30:2	5756
pieces To t fire from a hearth Or	Is 30:14	2846
The lame will t the plunder.	Is 33:23	962
"T courage, fear not.	Is 35:4	2388
until I come and t you away to a	Is 36:17	3947
house of Judah will again t root	Is 37:31	
"Let them t a cake of figs and	Is 38:21	5375
to us what is going to t place;	Is 41:22	7136a
events that are going to t place.	Is 44:7	935
"T the millstones and grind meal.	Is 47:2	3947
I will t vengeance and will not	Is 47:3	3947
Nor is there one to t her by the	Is 51:18	2388
up, *And* a breath will t *them away.*	Is 57:13	3947
you will t delight in the LORD,	Is 58:14	6026
LORD, t no rest for yourselves;	Is 62:6	
like the wind, t us away.	Is 64:6	5375
arouses himself to t hold of You;	Is 64:7	2388
"I will also t some of them for	Is 66:21	3947
And I will t you one from a city	Jer 3:14	3947
And look now and t note.	Jer 5:1	3045
But they refused to t correction.	Jer 5:3	3947
And t up a lamentation on the bare	Jer 7:29	5375
I will t up a weeping and wailing,	Jer 9:10	5375
haste and t up a wailing for us,	Jer 9:18	5375
t away from you your disaster,	Jer 11:15	5674a
"T the waistband that you have	Jer 13:4	3947
t from there the waistband which I	Jer 13:6	3947
"T a lowly seat, For your	Jer 13:18	3427
Will not pangs t hold of you Like	Jer 13:21	270
LORD, Remember me, t notice of me,	Jer 15:15	6485
And t vengeance for me on my	Jer 15:15	5358
view of Your patience, t me away;	Jer 15:15	3947
"You shall not t a wife for	Jer 16:2	3947
"T heed for yourselves, and do	Jer 17:21	8104
not to listen or t correction.	Jer 17:23	3947
and t some of the elders of	Jer 19:1	
will plunder them, t them away and	Jer 20:5	3947
him And t our revenge on him."	Jer 20:10	3947
t all the families of the north,'	Jer 25:9	3947
I will t from them the voice of joy	Jer 25:10	6
"T this cup of the wine of wrath	Jer 25:15	3947
if they refuse to t the cup from	Jer 25:28	3947
king of Babylon did not t when he	Jer 27:20	3947
'T wives and become the fathers of	Jer 29:6	3947
and t wives for your sons and give	Jer 29:6	3947
you will t up your tambourines,	Jer 31:4	5710b
king of Babylon, and he will t it;	Jer 32:3	3920
he will t Zedekiah to Babylon,	Jer 32:5	1980
"T these deeds, this sealed deed	Jer 32:14	3947
have reached the city to t it;	Jer 32:24	3920
of Babylon, and he will t it.	Jer 32:28	3920
it and t it and burn it with fire;	Jer 34:22	3920
"T a scroll and write on it all	Jer 36:2	3947
"T in your hand the scroll from	Jer 36:14	3947
"T again another scroll and write	Jer 36:28	3947
to t possession of *some* property there	Jer 37:12	2505a
"T thirty men from here under	Jer 38:10	3947
"T him and look after him, and do	Jer 39:12	3947
the son of Shaphan, to t him home.	Jer 39:14	3318
t place before you on that day.	Jer 39:16	1961
son of Nethaniah to t your life?"	Jer 40:14	5221
Why should he t your life, so that	Jer 40:15	5221
"T *some* large stones in your	Jer 43:9	3947
will burn them and t them captive.	Jer 43:12	7617
'And I will t away the remnant of	Jer 44:12	3947
And t your stand with helmets *on!*	Jer 46:4	3320
'T your stand and get yourself	Jer 46:14	3320
Then Israel will t possession of his	Jer 49:2	3423
"They will t away their tents and	Jer 49:29	3947
T vengeance on her;	Jer 50:15	5358
"They will not t from you	Jer 51:26	3947
t into your heart all My words	Ezk 3:10	3947
"But as for you, t wheat, barley,	Ezk 4:9	3947
you, son of man, t a sharp sword;	Ezk 5:1	3947
t and use it *as* a barber's razor	Ezk 5:1	3947
Then t scales for weighing and	Ezk 5:1	3947
Then you shall t one third and	Ezk 5:2	3947
"T also a few in number from them	Ezk 5:3	3947
"T again some of them and throw them	Ezk 5:4	3947
"T fire from between the whirling	Ezk 10:6	3947
And I will t the heart of stone	Ezk 11:19	5493
or can *men* t a peg from it on	Ezk 15:3	3947
your clothing, t away your jewels,	Ezk 16:39	3947
"I will also t *a sprig* from the	Ezk 17:22	3947
money on interest or t increase,	Ezk 18:8	3947
does not t interest or increase,	Ezk 18:17	3947
t up a lamentation for the princes	Ezk 19:1	5375
the turban and t off the crown;	Ezk 21:26	7311
t your sons and your daughters;	Ezk 23:25	3947
and t away your beautiful jewels.	Ezk 23:26	3947
in hatred, t all your property,	Ezk 23:29	3947
"T the choicest of the flock, And	Ezk 24:5	3947
T out of it piece after piece,	Ezk 24:6	3318
wrath to come up to t vengeance,	Ezk 24:8	5358
I am about to t from you the	Ezk 24:16	3947
I t from them their stronghold,	Ezk 24:25	3947
"They will t up a lamentation	Ezk 26:17	5375
man, t up a lamentation over Tyre;	Ezk 27:2	5375
they will t up a lamentation for you	Ezk 27:32	5375
t up a lamentation over the king	Ezk 28:12	5375
in Egypt, They t away her wealth,	Ezk 30:4	3947
t up a lamentation over Pharaoh	Ezk 32:2	5375
and the people of the land t one	Ezk 33:2	3947
trumpet and does not t warning,	Ezk 33:4	2094b
trumpet but did not t warning;	Ezk 33:5	2094b
'I t no pleasure in the death of	Ezk 33:11	2654a
"For I will t you from the nations,	Ezk 36:24	3947
t for yourself one stick and write	Ezk 37:16	3947
t another stick and write on it,	Ezk 37:16	3947
I will t the stick of Joseph,	Ezk 37:19	3947
I will t the sons of Israel from	Ezk 37:21	3947
gold, to t away cattle and goods,	Ezk 38:13	3947
t you up from the remotest parts	Ezk 39:2	5927
"They will not t wood from	Ezk 39:10	5375
and they will t the spoil of those	Ezk 39:10	7997b
'You shall t some of its	Ezk 43:20	3947
t the bull for the sin offering,	Ezk 43:21	3947
but shall t virgins from the offspring	Ezk 44:22	3947
they shall t their stand to judge;	Ezk 44:24	5975
you shall t a young bull without	Ezk 45:18	3947
"The priest shall t some of	Ezk 45:19	3947
prince shall not t from the people's	Ezk 46:18	3947
T me into the king's presence, and	Da 2:24	5954
will t place in the latter days.	Da 2:28	1934
what would t place in the future;	Da 2:29	1934
known to you what will t place.	Da 2:29	1934
what will t place in the future;	Da 2:45	1934
O Lord, listen and t action!	Da 9:19	6213a
t courage and be courageous!"	Da 10:19	2388
he will t into captivity to Egypt,	Da 11:8	935
But she will not t a stand *for him*	Da 11:17	5975
and he will t action and *then*	Da 11:28	6213a
at the holy covenant and t action;	Da 11:30	6213a
display strength and t action.	Da 11:32	6213a
"He will t action against the	Da 11:39	6213a
t to yourself a wife of harlotry and	Hos 1:2	3947
I will t back My grain at harvest	Hos 2:9	3947
I will also t away My wool and My	Hos 2:9	5337
new wine t away the understanding.	Hos 4:11	3947
go up to Beth-aven And t the oath:	Hos 4:15	7650
Weeds will t over their treasures	Hos 9:6	3423
T words with you and return to the	Hos 14:2	3947
"T away all iniquity And receive	Hos 14:2	5375
And he will t root like *the cedars*	Hos 14:5	5221
That you might t possession of the	Am 2:10	3423
will t you away with meat hooks,	Am 4:2	5375
which I t up for you as a dirge,	Am 5:1	5375
"T away from Me the noise of your	Am 5:23	5493
From there will My hand t them;	Am 9:2	3947
them out and t them from there;	Am 9:3	3947
O LORD, please t my life from me,	Jon 4:3	3947
"He will t from you its support."	Mi 1:11	3947
them, And houses, and t *them* away.	Mi 2:2	5375
they will t up against you a taunt	Mi 2:4	5375
you t My splendor forever.	Mi 2:9	3947
LORD t delight in thousands of rams,	Mi 6:7	7521
knows those who t refuge in Him.	Na 1:7	2620
T hold of the brick mold!	Na 3:14	2388
t up a taunt-song against him,	Hab 2:6	5375
And they will t refuge in the name	Zph 3:12	2620
'But now t courage, Zerubbabel,'	Hg 2:4	2388
't courage also, Joshua son of	Hg 2:4	2388
you people of the land t courage,'	Hg 2:4	2388
'I will t you, Zerubbabel, son of	Hg 2:23	3947
"T *an offering* from the exiles,	Zch 6:10	3947
"T silver and gold, make an	Zch 6:11	3947
And it will t place if you	Zch 6:15	1961
"T again for yourself the	Zch 11:15	3947
and t of them and boil in them.	Zch 14:21	3947
and if you do not t it to heart to	Mal 2:2	7760
T heed then to your spirit, and	Mal 2:15	8104
"So t heed to your spirit, that	Mal 2:16	8104
do not be afraid to t Mary as your	Mt 1:20	*3880*
T the Child and His mother and flee	Mt 2:13	*3880*
t the Child and His mother,	Mt 2:20	*3880*
to sue you and t your shirt,	Mt 5:40	*2983*
Let me t the speck out of your eye,'	Mt 7:4	*1544b*
first t the log out of your own eye,	Mt 7:5	*1544b*
t the speck out of your brother's eye.	Mt 7:5	*1544b*
"T courage, son; your sins are	Mt 9:2	*2293*
"Daughter, t courage;	Mt 9:22	*2293*
t back your *blessing of* peace.	Mt 10:13	*1994*
"And he who does not t his cross	Mt 10:38	*2983*
"And blessed is he who does not t	Mt 11:6	*4624*
and violent men t it by force.	Mt 11:12	*726*
"T My yoke upon you and learn	Mt 11:29	*142*
Sabbath, will he not t hold of it and	Mt 12:11	*2902*
and t out the wicked from among	Mt 13:49	*873*
"T courage, it is I;	Mt 14:27	*2293*
not good to t the children's bread	Mt 15:26	*2983*
deny himself, and t up his cross and	Mt 16:24	*142*
t the first fish that comes up;	Mt 17:27	*142*
T that and give it to them for you	Mt 17:27	*2983*
you, t one or two more with you,	Mt 18:16	*3880*
'T what is yours and go,	Mt 20:14	*142*
for *those things* must t place,	Mt 24:6	*1096*
until all these things t place.	Mt 24:34	*1096*
t away the talent from him,	Mt 25:28	*142*
and did not t care of You?'	Mt 25:44	*1247*
and said, "T, eat; this is My body."	Mt 26:26	*2983*
for all those who t up the sword	Mt 26:52	*2983*
go and t word to My brethren to	Mt 28:10	*518*
they went out to t custody of Him;	Mk 3:21	*2902*
"T care what you listen to.	Mk 4:24	*991*
t nothing for *their* journey,	Mk 6:8	*142*
"T courage; it is I, do not be afraid."	Mk 6:50	*2293*
not good to t the children's bread	Mk 7:27	*2983*
And they had forgotten to t bread,	Mk 8:14	*2983*
deny himself, and t up his cross and	Mk 8:34	*142*
t pity on us and help us!"	Mk 9:22	*4697*
"T courage, stand up!	Mk 10:49	*2293*
those things must t place;	Mk 13:7	*1096*
"But t heed; behold, I have told you	Mk 13:23	*991*
until all these things t place.	Mk 13:30	*1096*
"T heed, keep on the alert;	Mk 13:33	*991*
and said, "T *it;* this is My body."	Mk 14:22	*2983*
but He did not t it.	Mk 15:23	*2983*
to decide what each man should t.	Mk 15:24	*142*
Elijah will come to t Him down."	Mk 15:36	*2507*
the day when these things t place,	Lk 1:20	*1096*
to t away my disgrace among men."	Lk 1:25	*851*
not t money from anyone by force,	Lk 3:14	*1286*
let me t out the speck that is in	Lk 6:42	*1544b*
first t the log out of your own eye,	Lk 6:42	*1544b*
you will see clearly to t out the speck	Lk 6:42	*1544b*
"Blessed is he who does not t	Lk 7:23	*4624*
"So t care how you listen;	Lk 8:18	*991*
"T nothing for *your* journey,	Lk 9:3	*142*
himself, and t up his cross daily and	Lk 9:23	*142*
innkeeper and said, 'T care of him;	Lk 10:35	*1959*
t your ease, eat, drink *and* be	Lk 12:19	*373*
do not t the place of honor,	Lk 14:8	*2625*
'T your bill, and sit down quickly	Lk 16:6	*1209*
'T your bill, and write eighty.'	Lk 16:7	*1209*
must not go down to t them out;	Lk 17:31	*142*
t up what you did not lay down and	Lk 19:21	*142*
'T the mina away from him and	Lk 19:24	*142*
things are about to t place?"	Lk 21:7	*1096*
these things must t place first,	Lk 21:9	*1096*
these things begin to t place,	Lk 21:28	*1096*
away until all things t place.	Lk 21:32	*1096*
things that are about to t place,	Lk 21:36	*1096*
"T this and share it among	Lk 22:17	*2983*
whoever has a money belt is to t	Lk 22:36	*142*
now and t it to the headwaiter."	Jn 2:8	*5342*
"T these things away;	Jn 2:16	*142*
to come and t Him by force to	Jn 6:15	*726*
My life so that I may t it again.	Jn 10:17	*2983*
I have authority to t it up again.	Jn 10:18	*2983*
Romans will come and t away both	Jn 11:48	*142*
nor do you t into account that it	Jn 11:50	*3049*
for He will t of Mine and will	Jn 16:14	*2983*
and no one *will* t your joy away	Jn 16:22	*142*
have tribulation, but t courage;	Jn 16:33	*2293*
You to t them out of the world,	Jn 17:15	*142*
"T Him yourselves, and judge Him	Jn 18:31	*2983*
"T Him yourselves and crucify	Jn 19:6	*2983*
he might t away the body of Jesus;	Jn 19:38	*142*
laid Him, and I will t Him away."	Jn 20:15	*142*
'LET ANOTHER MAN T HIS OFFICE.'	Ac 1:20	*2983*
Lord, t note of their threats,	Ac 4:29	*1896*
and signs and wonders t place	Ac 4:30	*1096*
t care what you propose to do with	Ac 5:35	*4337*
'T OFF THE SANDALS FROM YOUR FEET,	Ac 7:33	*3089*
"Therefore t heed, so that	Ac 13:40	*991*
Barnabas wanted to t John, called	Ac 15:37	*4838*
not t him along who had deserted	Ac 15:38	*4838*
from there to t Paul on board;	Ac 20:13	*353*
t them and purify yourself along	Ac 21:24	*3880*
and t him away from them by force,	Ac 23:10	*726*
at his side and said, "T courage;	Ac 23:11	*2293*
since you can t note of the fact	Ac 24:11	*1921*
Moses said was going to t place;	Ac 26:22	*1096*
them all to t some food,	Ac 27:33	*3335*
I encourage you to t some food,	Ac 27:34	*3335*
LORD WILL NOT T INTO ACCOUNT."	Ro 4:8	*3049*
WHEN I T AWAY THEIR SINS."	Ro 11:27	*851*
Never t your own revenge, beloved,	Ro 12:19	*1556*
Shall I then t away the members of	1Co 6:15	*142*
But t care that this liberty of	1Co 8:9	*991*
right to t along a believing wife,	1Co 9:5	*4013*
he stands t heed that he does not fall.	1Co 10:12	*991*
t into account a wrong *suffered,*	1Co 13:5	*3049*
those who t pride in appearance and	2Co 5:12	*2744*
did not t any advantage of you,	2Co 12:18	*4122*
t care that you are not consumed by one	Ga 5:15	*991*
t up the full armor of God,	Eph 6:13	*353*
And t THE HELMET OF SALVATION, and	Eph 6:17	*1209*
"T heed to the ministry which you	Col 4:17	*991*
t special note of that person and do	2Th 3:14	*4593*
how will he t care of the church of	1Tm 3:5	*1959*
T pains with these things;	1Tm 4:15	*3191*
we cannot t anything out of it either	1Tm 6:7	*1627*
t hold of the eternal life to	1Tm 6:12	*1949*
so that they may t hold of that	1Tm 6:19	*1949*
T care, brethren, that there	Heb 3:12	*991*
would have strong encouragement to t	Heb 6:18	*2902*
of bulls and goats to t away sins.	Heb 10:4	*851*
which can never t away sins;	Heb 10:11	*4014*
T notice that our brother Timothy	Heb 13:23	*1097*
t the prophets who spoke in the	Jas 5:10	*2983*
appeared in order to t away sins;	1Jn 3:5	*142*
things which must soon t place;	Rv 1:1	*1096*
will t place after these things.	Rv 1:19	*1096*
so that no one will t your crown.	Rv 3:11	*2983*
must t place after these things."	Rv 4:1	*1096*
"Worthy are You to t the book and	Rv 5:9	*2983*
granted to t peace from the earth,	Rv 6:4	*2983*
t the book which is open in the	Rv 10:8	*2983*
"T it and eat it;	Rv 10:9	*2983*

things which must soon t place. Rv 22:6 1096
one who wishes t the water of life Rv 22:17 2983
God will t away his part from the Rv 22:19 851

TAKEN

rib which He had t from the man, Gn 2:22 3947
Because she was t out of Man." Gn 2:23 3947
Because from it you were t; Gn 3:19 3947
the ground from which he was t. Gn 3:23 3947
vengeance will be t on him sevenfold Gn 4:15 5358
woman was t into Pharaoh's house. Gn 12:15 3947
his relative had been t captive, Gn 14:14 7617
of the woman whom you have t, Gn 20:3 3947
and has t away your blessing." Gn 27:35 3947
now he has t away my blessing." Gn 27:36 3947
"God has t away my reproach." Gn 30:23 622
"Jacob has t away all that was Gn 31:1 3947
"Thus God has t away your Gn 31:9 5337
all the wealth which God has t away Gn 31:16 5337
Now Rachel had t the household Gn 31:34 3947
Joseph had been t down to Egypt; Gn 39:1 3381
who had t him down there. Gn 39:1 3381
that you have t us away to die in the Ex 14:11 3947
or two, no vengeance shall be t; Ex 21:21 5358
whenever the cloud was t up from Ex 40:36 5927
but if the cloud was not t up, Ex 40:37 5927
until the day when it was t up. Ex 40:37 5927
t the breast of the wave offering Lv 7:34 3947
shall be t outside the camp, Lv 16:27 3318
I have t the Levites from among Nu 3:12 3947
I have t them for Myself instead Nu 8:16 3947
"But I have t the Levites instead Nu 8:18 3947
Then the tabernacle was t down; Nu 10:17 3381
not t a single donkey from them, Nu 16:15 5375
I Myself have t your fellow Nu 18:6 3947
t all his land out of his hand, Nu 21:26 3947
"Your servants have t a census of Nu 31:49 5375
The men of war had t booty, Nu 31:53 962
"But the LORD has t you and Dt 4:20 3947
to his wife whom he has t. Dt 24:5 3947
the woman had t the two men and Jos 2:4 3947
which they had t from the Jordan, Jos 4:20 3947
ark of the LORD t around the city, Jos 6:11 5437
And they have even t some of the Jos 7:11 3947
the one who is t with the things Jos 7:15 3920
and the tribe of Judah was t. Jos 7:16 3920
near man by man, and Zabdi was t. Jos 7:17 3920
from the tribe of Judah, was t. Jos 7:18 3920
of the sons of Simeon *was* t from Jos 19:9 3947
of silver which were t from you, Jg 17:2 3947
have t away my gods which I made, Jg 18:24 3947
that has t place among you? Jg 20:12 1961
For they had t a great oath Jg 21:5 1961
And the ark of God was t; 1Sa 4:11 3947
and the ark of God has been t." 1Sa 4:17 3947
the news that the ark of God was t 1Sa 4:19 3947
because the ark of God was t and 1Sa 4:21 3947
for the ark of God was t." 1Sa 4:22 3947
The cities which the Philistines had t 1Sa 7:14 3947
tribe of Benjamin was t by lot. 1Sa 10:20 3920
and the Matrite family was t. 1Sa 10:21 3920
And Saul the son of Kish was t; 1Sa 10:21 3920
Whose ox have I t, or whose donkey 1Sa 12:3 3947
I taken, or whose donkey have I t, 1Sa 12:3 3947
or from whose hand have I t a bribe 1Sa 12:3 3947
t anything from any man's hand." 1Sa 12:4 3947
And Jonathan and Saul were t, 1Sa 14:41 3920
And Jonathan was t. 1Sa 14:42 3920
Saul had t the kingdom over Israel, 1Sa 14:47 3920
in its place when it was t away. 1Sa 21:6 3947
had also t Ahinoam of Jezreel, 1Sa 25:43 3947
and I have t my life in my hand and 1Sa 28:21 7760
daughters had been t captive. 1Sa 30:3 7617
two wives had been t captive, 1Sa 30:5 7617
of all the great spoil that they had t 1Sa 30:16 3947
all that the Amalekites had t, 1Sa 30:18 3947
that they had t for themselves; 1Sa 30:19 3947
had t Ish-bosheth the son of Saul and 2Sa 2:8 3947
have t his wife to be your wife, 2Sa 12:9 3947
have t the wife of Uriah the Hittite 2Sa 12:10 3947
"The LORD also has t away your sin; 2Sa 12:13 5674a
you are t in your own evil, for 2Sa 16:8
Now Absalom in his lifetime had t 2Sa 18:18 3947
or has anything been t for us?" 2Sa 19:42 5375
Because they cannot be t in hand; 2Sa 23:6 3947
Solomon has even t his seat on the 1Ki 1:46 3427
he has t hold of the horns of the 1Ki 1:51 270
where they have been t captive, 1Ki 8:47 7617
of those who have t them captive, 1Ki 8:47 7617
enemies who have t them captive, 1Ki 8:48 7617
those who have t them captive, 1Ki 8:50 7617
the high places were not t away; 1Ki 15:14 5493
Zimri saw that the city was t, 1Ki 16:18 3920
and also t possession?" 1Ki 21:19 3423
the high places were not t away; 1Ki 22:43 5493
for you before I am t from you." 2Ki 2:9 3947
you see me when I am t from you, 2Ki 2:10 3947
perhaps the Spirit of the LORD has t 2Ki 2:16 5375
When he had t him and brought him 2Ki 4:20 5375
and had t captive a little girl 2Ki 5:2 7617
you kill those you have t captive 2Ki 6:22 7617
the high places were not t away; 2Ki 12:3 5493
the cities which he had t in war from 2Ki 13:25 3947
the high places were not t away; 2Ki 14:4 5493
the high places were not t away; 2Ki 15:4 5493
the high places were not t away; 2Ki 15:35 5493
whose altars Hezekiah has t away, 2Ki 18:22 5493
you will beget, will be t away; 2Ki 20:18 3947
for the king of Babylon had t all 2Ki 24:7 3947
one father's household t for 1Ch 24:6 270
for Eleazar and one t for Ithamar. 1Ch 24:6 270
which his father David had t; 2Ch 2:17 5608
the land where they are t captive, 2Ch 6:37 7617
where they have been t captive, 2Ch 6:38 7617
For he had t eighteen wives and 2Ch 11:21 5375
Now when Jehoram had t over the 2Ch 21:4 6965
of Judah, and had t Beth-shemesh, 2Ch 28:18 3920
'Has not the same Hezekiah t away 2Ch 32:12 5493
t from the temple in Jerusalem, Ezr 5:14 5312
"For they have t some of their Ezr 9:2 5375
who had been t into exile from Es 2:6 1540
that Esther was t to the king's Es 2:8 3947
who had t her as his daughter, Es 2:15 3947
So Esther was t to King Ahasuerus Es 2:16 3947
which he had t away from Haman, Es 8:2 5674a
LORD gave and the LORD has t away. Jb 1:21 3947
"For you have t pledges of your Jb 22:6 2254a
lives, who has t away my right, Jb 27:2 5493
"Iron is t from the dust, And Jb 28:2 3947
But God has t away my right; Jb 34:5 5493
mighty are t away without a hand. Jb 34:20 5493
my God, in You I have t refuge; Ps 7:1 2620
In You, O LORD, I have t refuge; Ps 31:1 2620
those who hate us have t spoil for Ps 44:10 8154
have t account of my wanderings; Ps 56:8 5608
In You, O LORD, I have t refuge; Ps 71:1 2620
You have t hold of my right hand. Ps 73:23 270
He has t a bag of money with him, Pr 7:20 3947
who are being t away to death, Pr 24:11 3947
For I have t all this to my heart Ec 9:1 5414
not t care of my own vineyard. SS 1:6 5201
"I have t off my dress, How can I SS 5:3 6584
had t from the altar with tongs. Is 6:6 3947
and your iniquity is t away and Is 6:7 5493
Gladness and joy are t away from Is 16:10 622
you who were found were t captive Is 22:3 631
Those *just* t from the breast? Is 28:9 6267
be broken, snared and t captive. Is 28:13 3920
whose altars Hezekiah has t away and Is 36:7 5493
you will beget, will be t away, Is 39:7 3947
has their stock t root in the earth, Is 40:24 8327
I have t from the ends of the earth, Is 41:9 2388
Whom I have t by the right hand, Is 45:1 2388
the prey be t from the mighty man, Is 49:24 3947
of the mighty man will be t away, Is 49:25 3947
I have t out of your hand the cup Is 51:22 3947
that My people have been t away Is 52:5 3947
and judgment He was t away; Is 53:8 3947
And devout men are t away, Is 57:1 622
righteous man is t away from evil, Is 57:1 622
both husband and wife shall be t, Jer 6:11 3920
I mourn, dismay has t hold of me. Jer 8:21 2388
them, they have also t root; Jer 12:2 8327
of the LORD has been t captive. Jer 13:17 7617
Nebuchadnezzar had t into exile Jer 29:1 1540
when he had t him bound in chains Jer 40:1 3947
had t Jeremiah and said to him, Jer 40:2 3947
cities that you have t over." Jer 40:10 8610
people whom Ishmael had t captive Jer 41:14 7617
And have t refuge in flight, Jer 46:5 5127
So gladness and joy are t away Jer 48:33 622
sons have been t away captive And Jer 48:46 3947
Why then has Malcam t possession Jer 49:1 3423
Distress and pangs have t hold of Jer 49:24 270
From there she will be t captive. Jer 50:9 3920
wood be t from it to make anything, Ezk 15:3 3947
they have t bribes to shed blood; Ezk 22:12 3947
you have t interest and profits, Ezk 22:12 3947
t treasure and precious things; Ezk 22:25 3947
have t vengeance with scorn of soul Ezk 25:15 5358
They have t a cedar from Lebanon Ezk 27:5 3947
But had he t warning, he would Ezk 33:5 2094b
he is t away in his iniquity; Ezk 33:6 3947
back what he has t by robbery, Ezk 33:15 1500
"The city has been t." Ezk 33:21 5221
and you have been t up in the talk Ezk 36:3 5927
year after the city was t, Ezk 40:1 5221
his father had t out of the temple Da 5:2 5312
that had been t out of the temple, Da 5:3 5312
and *his* glory was t away from him. Da 5:20 5709
Daniel to be t up out of the den. Da 6:23 5559b
So Daniel was t up out of the den and Da 6:23 5559b
beasts, their dominion was t away, Da 7:12 5709
and his dominion will be t away, Da 7:26 5709
the LORD has t no delight in them. Hos 8:13 7521
you have t My silver and My gold, Jl 3:5 3947
"On garments t as pledges Am 2:8 2254a
t Karnaim for ourselves?" Am 6:13 3947
The LORD has t away *His* judgments Zph 3:15 5493
I have t your iniquity away from Zch 3:4 5674a
when the spoil t from you will be Zch 14:1
you bring what was t by robbery and Mal 1:13 1497
and you will be t away with it. Mal 2:3 5375
that John had been t into custody, Mt 4:12 3860
bridegroom is t away from them, Mt 9:15 522
he has shall be t away from him. Mt 13:12 142
'Be t up and cast into the sea,' Mt 21:21 142
the kingdom of God will be t away Mt 21:43 142
one will be t and one will be left. Mt 24:40 3880
one will be t and one will be left. Mt 24:41 3880
what he does have shall be t away. Mt 25:29 142
He had t a cup and given thanks, Mt 26:27 2983
"But all this has t place to Mt 26:56 1096
John had been t into custody, Mk 1:14 3860
bridegroom is t away from them, Mk 2:20 522
he has shall be t away from him." Mk 4:25 142
'Be t up and cast into the sea,' Mk 11:23 142
And when He had t a cup *and* given Mk 14:23 2983
but *this has* t *place* to Mk 14:49
census be t of all the inhabited earth Lk 2:1 583
This was the first census t while Lk 2:2 1096
catch of fish which they had t; Lk 5:9 4815
bridegroom is t away from them, Lk 5:35 522
he has shall be t away from him." Lk 8:18 142
shall not be t away from her." Lk 10:42 851
have t away the key of knowledge; Lk 11:52 142
one will be t and the other will Lk 17:34 3880
one will be t and the other will Lk 17:35 3880
one will be t and the other will Lk 17:36 3880
what he does have shall be t away. Lk 19:26 142
He had t a cup *and* given thanks, Lk 22:17 1209
had t *some* bread *and* given thanks, Lk 22:19 2983
these things which had t place. Lk 24:14 4819
"No one has t it away from Me, Jn 10:18 142
their feet, and t His garments and Jn 13:12 2983
and *that* they might be t away. Jn 19:31 142
already t away from the tomb. Jn 20:1 142
t away the Lord out of the tomb, Jn 20:2 142
"Because they have t away my Lord, Jn 20:13 142
until the day when He was t up Ac 1:2 353
been t up from you into heaven, Ac 1:11 353
until the day that He was t up Ac 1:22 353
that a noteworthy miracle has t place Ac 4:16 1096
HIS JUDGMENT WAS T AWAY; Ac 8:33 142
the object was t up into the sky. Ac 10:16 353
them and t his leave of them, Ac 20:1 782
the investigation has t place, Ac 25:26 1096
without eating, having t nothing. Ac 27:33 4355
advantage would be t of us by Satan 2Co 2:11 4122
to the Lord, the veil is t away. 2Co 3:16 4014
I have not t advantage of you 2Co 12:17 4122
and He has t it out of the way, Col 2:14 142
But we, brethren, having been t 1Th 2:17 642
so until he is t out of the way. 2Th 2:7 1096
on in the world, T up in glory. 1Tm 3:16 353
resurrection has already t place, 2Tm 2:18 1096
For every high priest t from among Heb 5:1 2983
we who have t refuge would have Heb 6:18 2703
who has t His seat at the right Heb 8:1 2523
death has t place for the redemption Heb 9:15 1096
FOR SIN YOU HAVE T NO PLEASURE Heb 10:6 2106
NOR HAVE YOU T PLEASURE *in them*" Heb 10:8 2106
By faith Enoch was t up so that he Heb 11:5 3346a
that before his being t up he was Heb 11:5 3331
When He had t the book, the Rv 5:8 2983
You have t Your great power and Rv 11:17 2983

TAKES

if Jacob t a wife from the Gn 27:46 3947
unpunished who t His name in vain. Ex 20:7 5375
"If he t to himself another Ex 21:10 3947
there is a man who t his sister, Lv 20:17 3947
is a man who t his brother's wife, Lv 20:21 3947
man t the life of any human being, Lv 24:17 5221
'The one who t the life of an Lv 24:18 5221
according to his vow which he t, Nu 6:21 5087
or t an oath to bind himself with Nu 30:2 7650
unpunished who t His name in vain. Dt 5:11 5375
"If any man t a wife and goes in Dt 22:13 3947
a man t a wife and marries her, Dt 24:1 3947
"When a man t a new wife, he Dt 24:5 3947
And My hand t hold on justice, Dt 32:41 270
that the tribe which the LORD t *by lot* Jos 7:14 3920
family which the LORD t shall come Jos 7:14 3920
the household which the LORD t Jos 7:14 3920
t away the reproach from Israel? 1Sa 17:26 5493
leper, or who t hold of a distaff, 2Sa 3:29 2388
and he comes *and* t an oath before 1Ki 8:31 422
boast like him who t *it* off.' " 1Ki 20:11 6605a
and he comes *and* t an oath before 2Ch 6:22 422
And t away the discernment of the Jb 12:20 3947
And horror t hold of my flesh. Jb 21:6 270
You are not a God who t pleasure Ps 5:4 2655
Nor t up a reproach against his Ps 15:3 5375
is the man who t refuge in Him! Ps 34:8 2620
me, For my soul t refuge in You; Ps 57:1 2620
God t His stand in His own Ps 82:1 5324
the LORD t pleasure in His people; Ps 149:4 7521
It t away the life of its possessors. Pr 1:19 3947
And he t the way to her house, Pr 7:8 6805
the paths meet, she t her stand; Pr 8:2 5324
But the wicked t his place. Pr 11:8 935
who t off a garment on a cold day, Pr 25:20 5710a
Like one who t a dog by the ears Pr 26:17 2388
a man who t bribes overthrows it. Pr 29:4 8641
for *He* t no delight in fools. Ec 5:4
man, And the living t *it* to heart. Ec 7:2 5414
and t a cypress or an oak and Is 44:14 3947
and t one of them and warms himself; Is 44:15 3947
the son of man who t hold of it; Is 56:2 2388
and no man t it to heart; Is 57:1 7760
But he who t refuge in Me will Is 57:13 2620
who t strangers instead of her Ezk 16:32 3947
money on interest and t increase; Ezk 18:13 3947
and a sword comes and t him away, Ezk 33:4 3947
comes and t a person from them, Ezk 33:6 3947
on you The one who t possession, Mi 1:15 3423
LORD t vengeance on His adversaries Na 1:2 5358
Before the decree t effect Zph 2:2 3205
and t along with it seven other Mt 12:45 3880
t away the word which has been sown Mk 4:15 142
and whoever t away your coat, do Lk 6:29 142
and whoever t away what is yours, Lk 6:30 142
t away the word from their heart Lk 8:12 142
he t away from him all his armor Lk 11:22 142
t *along* seven other spirits more evil Lk 11:26 3880
who t away the sin of the world! Jn 1:29 142
does not bear fruit, He t away; Jn 15:2 142
I said that He t of Mine Jn 16:15 2983

each one **t** his own supper first; **1Co 11:21** *4301*
you, anyone **t** advantage of you, **2Co 11:20** *2983*
that no one **t** you captive through **Col 2:8** *4812*
he **t** his seat in the temple of God, **2Th 2:4** *2523*
And no one **t** the honor to himself, **Heb 5:4** *2983*
t place a change of law also. **Heb 7:12** *1096*
He **t** away the first in order to **Heb 10:9** *337*
if anyone **t** away from the words of **Rv 22:19** *851*

TAKING
him on the journey you are **t**, **Gn 42:38** 1980
he would be **t** a life in pledge. **Dt 24:6** 2254a
t with him his servant and a pair **Jg 19:3**
while he was **t** his midday rest. **2Sa 4:5** 7901
even **t** all the shields of gold **1Ki 14:26** 3947
partiality or the **t** of a bribe." **2Ch 19:7** 4727
And they were three days **t** the spoil **2Ch 20:25** 962
and are **t** on themselves a curse **Ne 10:29** 935
"I have seen the foolish **t** root, **Jb 5:3** 8327
not **t** from his descendants rulers **Jer 33:26** 3947
the house of Judah by **t** vengeance, **Ezk 25:12** 5358
"Where are they **t** the ephah?" **Zch 5:10** 1980
because you are not **t** *it* to heart. **Mal 2:2** 7760
one of them ran, and **t** a sponge, **Mt 27:48** *2983*
raised her up, **t** her by the hand, **Mk 1:31** *2902*
T the child by the hand, He said to **Mk 5:41** *2902*
and **t** the seven loaves, He gave **Mk 8:6** *2983*
T the blind man by the hand, He **Mk 8:23** *1949*
T a child, He set him before them, **Mk 9:36** *2983*
them, and **t** him in His arms, **Mk 9:36** *1723*
T them with Him, He withdrew by **Lk 9:10** *3880*
my master is **t** the management away **Lk 16:3** *851*
man, **t** up what I did not lay down and **Lk 19:22** *142*
and **t** a towel, He girded Himself **Jn 13:4** *2983*
t his stand with the eleven, **Ac 2:14** *2476*
wonders and signs were **t** place **Ac 2:43** *1096*
they were **t** their meals together **Ac 2:46** *3335*
and they were **t** note of him as **Ac 3:10** *1921*
signs and wonders were **t** place **Ac 5:12** *1096*
prison, and **t** them out he said, **Ac 5:19** *1806*
signs and great miracles **t** place, **Ac 8:13** *1096*
mission, **t** along with *them* John, **Ac 12:25** *4838*
t from among the Gentiles a people **Ac 15:14** *2983*
and **t** along some wicked men from **Ac 17:5** *4355*
but **t** leave of them and saying, **Ac 18:21** *657*
with us, **t** us to Mnason of Cyprus, **Ac 21:16** *71*
and **t** hold of Paul they dragged **Ac 21:30** *1949*
t opportunity through the **Ro 7:8** *2983*
t an opportunity through the **Ro 7:11** *2983*
but **t** my leave of them, I went on **2Co 2:13** *657*
t precaution so that no one will **2Co 8:20** *4724*
and *we are* **t** every thought captive **2Co 10:5** *163*
t wages *from them* to serve you; **2Co 11:8** *2983*
with Barnabas, **t** Titus along also. **Ga 2:1** *4838*
t up the shield of faith with **Eph 6:16** *353*
t the form of a bond-servant, **Php 2:7** *2983*
t his stand on *visions* he has **Col 2:18** *1687*
not without **t** blood, which he **Heb 9:7**

TALEBEARER
He who goes about as a **t** reveals **Pr 11:13** 7400
rebellious, Going about as a **t**. **Jer 6:28** 7400

TALENT
be made from a **t** of pure gold, **Ex 25:39** 3603
utensils from a **t** of pure gold. **Ex 37:24** 3603
hundred talents, a **t** for a socket. **Ex 38:27** 3603
and its weight *was* a **t** of gold, **2Sa 12:30** 3603
else you shall pay a **t** of silver.' **1Ki 20:39** 3603
Please give them a **t** of silver and **2Ki 5:22** 3603
talents of silver and a **t** of gold. **2Ki 23:33** 3603
he found it to weigh a **t** of gold, **1Ch 20:2** 3603
of silver and one **t** of gold. **2Ch 36:3** 3603
"But he who received the one **t** **Mt 25:18**
one also who had received the one **t** **Mt 25:24** *5007*
away and hid your **t** in the ground. **Mt 25:25** *5007*
take away the **t** from him, **Mt 25:28** *5007*

TALENTS
was 29 **t** and 730 shekels, **Ex 38:24** 3603
was 100 **t** and 1,775 shekels, **Ex 38:25** 3603
The hundred **t** of silver were **Ex 38:27** 3603
hundred sockets for the hundred **t**, **Ex 38:27** 3603
of the wave offering was 70 **t** and **Ex 38:29** 3603
sent to the king 120 **t** of gold. **1Ki 9:14** 3603
and twenty **t** of gold from there, **1Ki 9:28** 3603
a hundred and twenty **t** of gold, **1Ki 10:10** 3603
in one year was 666 **t** of gold, **1Ki 10:14** 3603
from Shemer for two **t** of silver; **1Ki 16:24** 3603
and took with him ten **t** of silver **2Ki 5:5** 3603
"Be pleased to take two **t**." **2Ki 5:23** 3603
and bound two **t** of silver in two **2Ki 5:23** 3603
gave Pul a thousand **t** of silver **2Ki 15:19** 3603
three hundred **t** of silver and thirty **2Ki 18:14** 3603
of silver and thirty **t** of gold. **2Ki 18:14** 3603
a fine of one hundred **t** of silver and **2Ki 23:33** 3603
sons of Ammon sent 1,000 **t** of silver **1Ch 19:6** 3603
house of the LORD 100,000 **t** of gold **1Ch 22:14** 3603
of gold and 1,000,000 **t** of silver, **1Ch 22:14** 3603
namely, 3,000 **t** of gold, of the **1Ch 29:4** 3603
and 7,000 **t** of refined silver, **1Ch 29:4** 3603
5,000 **t** and 10,000 darics of gold, **1Ch 29:7** 3603
of gold, and 10,000 **t** of silver, **1Ch 29:7** 3603
of silver, and 18,000 **t** of brass, **1Ch 29:7** 3603
of brass, and 100,000 **t** of iron. **1Ch 29:7** 3603
fine gold, *amounting* to 600 **t**. **2Ch 3:8** 3603
four hundred and fifty **t** of gold and **2Ch 8:18** 3603
one hundred and twenty **t** of gold and **2Ch 9:9** 3603
in one year was 666 **t** of gold, **2Ch 9:13** 3603
for one hundred **t** of silver. **2Ch 25:6** 3603
what *shall we* do for the hundred **t** **2Ch 25:9** 3603
that year one hundred **t** of silver, **2Ch 27:5** 3603
a fine of one hundred **t** of silver and **2Ch 36:3** 3603
even up to 100 **t** of silver, 100 **Ezr 7:22** 3604
into their hands 650 **t** of silver, **Ezr 8:26** 3603
and silver utensils *worth* 100 **t**, **Ezr 8:26** 3603
worth 100 talents, *and* 100 gold **t**, **Ezr 8:26** 3603
I will pay ten thousand **t** of silver **Es 3:9** 3603
one who owed him ten thousand **t** was **Mt 18:24** *5007*
"To one he gave five **t**, **Mt 25:15** *5007*
the one who had received the five **t** **Mt 25:16** *5007*
with them, and gained five more **t**. **Mt 25:16**
one who *had received* the two **t** **Mt 25:17**
The one who had received the five **t** **Mt 25:20** *5007*
came up and brought five more **t**, **Mt 25:20** *5007*
you entrusted five **t** to me. **Mt 25:20** *5007*
See, I have gained five more **t**.' **Mt 25:20** *5007*
one who *had received* the two **t** **Mt 25:22** *5007*
'Master, you entrusted two **t** to me. **Mt 25:22** *5007*
See, I have gained two more **t**.' **Mt 25:22** *5007*
it to the one who has the ten **t**.' **Mt 25:28** *5007*

TALES
we did not follow cleverly devised **t** **2Pe 1:16** *3454*

TALITHA
the hand, He said to her, "**T** kum!" **Mk 5:41** *5008*

TALK
t of them when you sit in your house **Dt 6:7** 1696
know *very well* the man and his **t**." **2Ki 9:11** 7879
"Should he argue with useless **t**, **Jb 15:3** 1697
understanding and then we can **t**. **Jb 18:2** 1696
They **t** of laying snares secretly; **Ps 64:5** 5608
who sit in the gate **t** about me, **Ps 69:12** 7878
princes sit *and* **t** against me, **Ps 119:23** 1696
Your kingdom And **t** of Your power; **Ps 145:11** 1696
you awake, they will **t** to you. **Pr 6:22** 7878
But mere **t** *leads* only to poverty. **Pr 14:23** 1697
And their lips **t** of trouble. **Pr 24:2** 1696
your fellow citizens who **t** about **Ezk 33:30** 1696
you have been taken up in the **t** and **Ezk 36:3** 8193
how can such a servant of my lord **t** **Da 10:17** 1696
the way you **t** gives you away." **Mt 26:73** *2981*
must be no filthiness and silly **t**, **Eph 5:4** *3473*
their **t** will spread like gangrene. **2Tm 2:17** *3056*

TALKATIVE
And a **t** man be acquitted? **Jb 11:2** 8193

TALKED
on his face, and God **t** with him, **Gn 17:3** 1696
afterward his brothers **t** with him. **Gn 45:15** 1696
he went down and **t** to the woman; **Jg 14:7** 1696
While Saul **t** to the priest, **1Sa 14:19** 1696
officials hear that I have **t** with you **Jer 38:25** 1696
The king **t** with them, and out **Da 1:19** 1696
gave *me* instruction and **t** with me and **Da 9:22** 1696
all these matters were being **t** about **Lk 1:65** *1255*
road, and that He had **t** to him, **Ac 9:27** *2980*
As he **t** with him, he entered and **Ac 10:27** *4926*
he **t** with them a long while until **Ac 20:11** *3656*

TALKERS
men, empty **t** and deceivers, **Ti 1:10** *3151*

TALKING
When He finished **t** with him, **Gn 17:22** 1696
t of them when you sit in your **Dt 11:19** 1696
As he was **t** with them, behold, the **1Sa 17:23** 1696
As they were going along and **t**, **2Ki 2:11** 1696
While he was still **t** with them, **2Ki 6:33** 1696
Now the king was **t** with Gehazi, **2Ki 8:4** 1696
As he was **t** with him, **2Ch 25:16** 1696
While they were still **t** with him, **Es 6:14** 1696
"The princes stopped **t** And **Jb 29:9** 4405
the beginning of his **t** is folly and **Ec 10:13** 1697, 6310
Now while he was **t** with me, **Da 8:18** 1696
appeared to them, **t** with Him. **Mt 17:3** *4814*
not know what you are **t** about." **Mt 26:70** *3004*
and they were **t** with Jesus. **Mk 9:4** *4814*
understand what you are **t** about." **Mk 14:68** *3004*
know this man you are **t** about!" **Mk 14:71** *3004*
and they *began* **t** with one another **Lk 4:36** *4814*
behold, two men were **t** with Him; **Lk 9:30** *4814*
some were **t** about the temple, **Lk 21:5** *3004*
not know what you are **t** about." **Lk 22:60** *3004*
And they were **t** with each other about **Lk 24:14** *3656*
While they were **t** and discussing, **Lk 24:15** *3656*
He is the one who is **t** with you." **Jn 9:37** *2980*
do not know what He is **t** about." **Jn 16:18** *2980*
And he was **t** and arguing with the **Ac 9:29** *2980*
break bread, Paul *began* **t** to them, **Ac 20:7** *1256*
and as Paul kept on **t**, **Ac 20:9** *1256*
they *began* **t** to one another, **Ac 26:31** *2980*
t about things not proper *to mention* **1Tm 5:13** *2980*

TALL
numerous, and **t** as the Anakim. **Dt 2:10** 7311
numerous, and **t** as the Anakim, **Dt 2:21** 7311
a people great and **t**, **Dt 9:2** 7311
And I cut down its **t** cedars *and* **2Ki 19:23** 6967
of *great* stature five cubits **t**. **1Ch 11:23**
Those also who are **t** in stature will **Is 10:33** 7311
to a nation **t** and smooth, **Is 18:2** 4900
hosts From a people **t** and smooth, **Is 18:7** 4900
And I cut down its **t** cedars *and* **Is 37:24** 6967
Then you grew up, became **t** and **Ezk 16:7** 1431

TALLER
people are bigger and **t** than we; **Dt 1:28** 7311
he was **t** than any of the people. **1Sa 9:2** 1364
he was **t** than any of the people **1Sa 10:23** 1361b

TALMAI
where Ahiman, Sheshai and **T**, **Nu 13:22** 8526
Sheshai and Ahiman and **T**, **Jos 15:14** 8526
struck Sheshai and Ahiman and **T**. **Jg 1:10** 8526
son of Maacah, the daughter of **T**, **2Sa 3:3** 8526
and went to **T** the son of Ammihud, **2Sa 13:37** 8526
the daughter of **T** king of Geshur; **1Ch 3:2** 8526

TALMON
were Shallum and Akkub and **T** **1Ch 9:17** 2929
the sons of Ater, the sons of **T**, **Ezr 2:42** 2929
the sons of Ater, the sons of **T**, **Ne 7:45** 2929
Also the gatekeepers, Akkub, **T** and **Ne 11:19** 2929
Bakbukiah, Obadiah, Meshullam, **T** **Ne 12:25** 2929

TAMAR
his firstborn, and her name *was* **T**. **Gn 38:6** 8559
Judah said to his daughter-in-law **T**, **Gn 38:11** 8559
So **T** went and lived in her **Gn 38:11** 8559
It was told to **T**, **Gn 38:13** 8559
T has played the harlot, **Gn 38:24** 8559
of Perez whom **T** bore to Judah, **Ru 4:12** 8559
beautiful sister whose name was **T**, **2Sa 13:1** 8559
so frustrated because of his sister **T** **2Sa 13:2** 8559
"I am in love with **T**, **2Sa 13:4** 8559
'Please let my sister **T** come and **2Sa 13:5** 8559
"Please let my sister **T** come and **2Sa 13:6** 8559
David sent to the house for **T**, **2Sa 13:7** 8559
So **T** went to her brother Amnon's **2Sa 13:8** 8559
Then Amnon said to **T**, **2Sa 13:10** 8559
So **T** took the cakes which she had **2Sa 13:10** 8559
T put ashes on her head and **2Sa 13:19** 8559
So **T** remained and was desolate in **2Sa 13:20** 8559
he had violated his sister **T**. **2Sa 13:22** 8559
day that he violated his sister **T**. **2Sa 13:32** 8559
and one daughter whose name was **T**; **2Sa 14:27** 8559
Baalath and **T** in the wilderness, **1Ki 9:18** 8559
T his daughter-in-law bore him **1Ch 2:4** 8559
and **T** *was* their sister. **1Ch 3:9** 8559
shall extend from **T** as far as the **Ezk 47:19** 8559
the border shall be from **T** to the **Ezk 48:28** 8559
the father of Perez and Zerah by **T**, **Mt 1:3** *2283*

TAMARISK
planted a **t** tree at Beersheba, **Gn 21:33** 815
under the **t** tree on the height **1Sa 22:6** 815
them under the **t** tree at Jabesh, **1Sa 31:13** 815

TAMBOURINE
from the high place with harp, **t**, **1Sa 10:5** 8596
by lyre and harp, by **t** and flute, **Is 5:12** 8596

TAMBOURINES
meet him with **t** and with dancing. **Jg 11:34** 8596
to meet King Saul, with **t**, **1Sa 18:6** 8596
wood, and with lyres, harps, **t**, **2Sa 6:5** 8596
songs and with lyres, harps, **t**, **1Ch 13:8** 8596
midst of the maidens beating **t**. **Ps 68:25** 8608
The gaiety of **t** ceases, The noise **Is 24:8** 8596
be with *the music of* **t** and lyres; **Is 30:32** 8596
Again you will take up your **t**, **Jer 31:4** 8596

TAME
But no one can **t** the tongue; **Jas 3:8** *1150*

TAMED
and creatures of the sea, is **t** and **Jas 3:7** *1150*
and has been **t** by the human race. **Jas 3:7** *1150*

TAMMUZ
were sitting there weeping for **T**. **Ezk 8:14** 8542

TANGLED
Like **t** thorns, And like those who **Na 1:10** 5440

TANHUMETH
the son of **T** the Netophathite, **2Ki 25:23** 8576
Kareah, and Seraiah the son of **T**, **Jer 40:8** 8576

TANNER
days in Joppa with a **t** **Ac 9:43** *1038*
with a **t** *named* Simon, **Ac 10:6** *1038*
house of Simon the **t** by the sea.' **Ac 10:32** *1038*

TAPHATH
T the daughter of Solomon was his **1Ki 4:11** 2955

TAPPUAH
the king of **T**, one; **Jos 12:17** 8599
Zanoah and En-gannim, **T** and Enam, **Jos 15:34** 8599
From **T** the border continued **Jos 16:8** 8599
land of **T** belonged to Manasseh, **Jos 17:8** 8599
but **T** on the border of Manasseh **Jos 17:8** 8599
Korah and **T** and Rekem and Shema. **1Ch 2:43** 8600b

TAR
stone, and they used **t** for mortar. **Gn 11:3** 2564
of Siddim was full of **t** pits; **Gn 14:10** 2564
covered it over with **t** and pitch. **Ex 2:3** 2564

TARALAH
and Rekem and Irpeel and **T**, **Jos 18:27** 8634

TAREA
of Micah *were* Pithon, Melech, **T** and **1Ch 8:35** 8390

TARES
and sowed **t** among the wheat, **Mt 13:25** *2215*
then the **t** became evident also. **Mt 13:26** *2215*
How then does it have **t**?' **Mt 13:27** *2215*
while you are gathering up the **t**, **Mt 13:29** *2215*
"First gather up the **t** and bind **Mt 13:30** *2215*
parable of the **t** of the field." **Mt 13:36** *2215*
t are the sons of the evil *one;* **Mt 13:38** *2215*
"So just as the **t** are gathered **Mt 13:40** *2215*

TARGET
the side, as though I shot at a **t**. **1Sa 20:20** 4307
Why have You set me as Your **t**, **Jb 7:20** 4645
He has also set me up as His **t**. **Jb 16:12** 4307
And set me as a **t** for the arrow. **La 3:12** 4307

TARRIES
Though it **t**, wait for it; **Hab 2:3** 4102

TARRY
the hoofbeats of his chariots **t**?' **Jg 5:28** 309

TARSHISH
sons of Javan *were* Elishah and **T**, **Gn 10:4** 8659

- the king had at sea the ships of **T** — 1Ki 10:22 — 8659
- the ships of **T** came bringing gold — 1Ki 10:22 — 8659
- Jehoshaphat made ships of **T** to go — 1Ki 22:48 — 8659
- The sons of Javan *were* Elishah, **T**, — 1Ch 1:7 — 8659
- Ehud, Chenaanah, Zethan, **T** and — 1Ch 7:10 — 8659
- the king had ships which went to **T** — 2Ch 9:21 — 8659
- the ships of **T** came bringing gold — 2Ch 9:21 — 8659
- with him to make ships to go to **T**, — 2Ch 20:36 — 8659
- were broken and could not go to **T**. — 2Ch 20:37 — 8659
- Carshena, Shethar, Admatha, **T**, — Es 1:14 — 8659
- You break the ships of **T**. — Ps 48:7 — 8659
- Let the kings of **T** and of the — Ps 72:10 — 8659
- Against all the ships of **T** And — Is 2:16 — 8659
- Wail, O ships of **T**, — Is 23:1 — 8659
- Pass over to **T**; Wail, O inhabitants — Is 23:6 — 8659
- like the Nile, O daughter of **T**, — Is 23:10 — 8659
- Wail, O ships of **T**, — Is 23:14 — 8659
- the ships of **T** *will come* first, — Is 60:9 — 8659
- **T**, Put, Lud, Meshech, Tubal and — Is 66:19 — 8659
- Beaten silver is brought from **T**, — Jer 10:9 — 8659
- *was* like the gleam of a **T** stone. — Ezk 10:9 — 8659
- "**T** was your customer because of — Ezk 27:12 — 8659
- "The ships of **T** were the carriers — Ezk 27:25 — 8659
- and Dedan and the merchants of **T** — Ezk 38:13 — 8659
- Jonah rose up to flee to **T** from the — Jon 1:3 — 8659
- found a ship which was going to **T**, — Jon 1:3 — 8659
- down into it to go with them to **T** — Jon 1:3 — 8659
- to forestall this I fled to **T**, — Jon 4:2 — 8659

TARSUS
- Judas for a man from **T** named Saul, — Ac 9:11 — *5018*
- Caesarea and sent him away to **T**. — Ac 9:30 — *5019*
- he left for **T** to look for Saul; — Ac 11:25 — *5019*
- "I am a Jew of **T** in Cilicia, a — Ac 21:39 — *5018*
- "I am a Jew, born in **T** of Cilicia, — Ac 22:3 — *5019*

TARTAK
- and the Avvites made Nibhaz and **T**; — 2Ki 17:31 — 8662

TARTAN
- Then the king of Assyria sent **T** — 2Ki 18:17 — 8661

TASK
- for the **t** is too heavy for you; — Ex 18:18 — 1697
- the **t** *be done* in one or two days, — Ezr 10:13 — 4399
- and it was their **t** to distribute — Ne 13:13 — 5921
- and the Levites, each in his **t**, — Ne 13:30 — 4399
- *It* is a grievous **t** *which* God has — Ec 1:13 — 6045
- his **t** is painful and grievous; — Ec 2:23 — 6045
- He has given the **t** of gathering and — Ec 2:26 — 6045
- I have seen the **t** which God has — Ec 3:10 — 6045
- is vanity and it is a grievous **t**. — Ec 4:8 — 6045
- to know wisdom and to see the **t** — Ec 8:16 — 6045
- To do His **t**, His unusual task, And — Is 28:21 — 4639
- To do His task, His unusual **t**, — Is 28:21 — 4639
- *assigning* to each one his **t**, — Mk 13:34 — *2041*
- we may put in charge of this **t**. — Ac 6:3 — *5532*

TASKMASTER
- do not hear the voice of the **t**. — Jb 3:18 — 5065

TASKMASTERS
- So they appointed **t** over them to — Ex 1:11 — 8269, 4522
- to their cry because of their **t**, — Ex 3:7 — 5065
- Pharaoh commanded the **t** over the — Ex 5:6 — 5065
- So the **t** of the people and their — Ex 5:10 — 5065
- The **t** pressed them, saying, — Ex 5:13 — 5065
- whom Pharaoh's **t** had set over them, — Ex 5:14 — 5065

TASSEL
- that they shall put on the **t** of each — Nu 15:38 — 6734
- "It shall be a **t** for you to — Nu 15:39 — 6734

TASSELS
- they shall make for themselves **t** on — Nu 15:38 — 6734
- "You shall make yourself **t** on the — Dt 22:12 — 1434
- lengthen the **t** *of their garments.* — Mt 23:5 — *2899*

TASTE
- Esau, because he had a **t** for game, — Gn 25:28 — 6310
- its **t** was like wafers with honey. — Ex 16:31 — 2940
- and its **t** was as the taste of — Nu 11:8 — 2940
- as the **t** of cakes baked with oil. — Nu 11:8 — 2940
- if I **t** bread or anything else — 2Sa 3:35 — 2938
- **t** what I eat or what I drink? — 2Sa 19:35 — 2938
- is there any **t** in the white of an egg? — Jb 6:6 — 2940
- O **t** and see that the LORD is good; — Ps 34:8 — 2938
- How sweet are Your words to my **t**! — Ps 119:103 — 2441
- Those who go to **t** mixed wine. — Pr 23:30 — 2713
- from the comb is sweet to your **t**; — Pr 24:13 — 2441
- And his fruit was sweet to my **t**. — SS 2:3 — 2441
- beast, herd, or flock **t** a thing. — Jon 3:7 — 2938
- will not **t** death until they see the — Mt 16:28 — *1089*
- will not **t** death until they see the — Mk 9:1 — *1089*
- will not **t** death until they see the — Lk 9:27 — *1089*
- invited shall **t** of my dinner.'" — Lk 14:24 — *1089*
- word, he will never **t** of death.' — Jn 8:52 — *1089*
- a solemn oath to **t** nothing until we — Ac 23:14 — *1089*
- "Do not handle, do not **t**, — Col 2:21 — *1089*
- God He might **t** death for everyone. — Heb 2:9 — *1089*

TASTED
- So none of the people **t** food. — 1Sa 14:24 — 2938
- I **t** a little of this honey. — 1Sa 14:29 — 2938
- "I indeed **t** a little honey with — 1Sa 14:43 — 2938
- When Belshazzar **t** the wine, he — Da 5:2 — 2942
- When the headwaiter **t** the water — Jn 2:9 — *1089*
- have **t** of the heavenly gift and have — Heb 6:4 — *1089*
- and have **t** the good word of God — Heb 6:5 — *1089*
- have **t** the kindness of the Lord. — 1Pe 2:3 — *1089*

TASTELESS
- something **t** be eaten without salt, — Jb 6:6 — 8602a
- but if the salt has become **t**, — Mt 5:13 — *3471*
- but if even salt has become **t**, — Lk 14:34 — *3471*

TASTES
- words, As the palate **t** its food? — Jb 12:11 — 2938
- tests words As the palate **t** food. — Jb 34:3 — 2938

TASTING
- soul, Never even **t** *anything* good. — Jb 21:25 — 398
- after **t** *it,* He was unwilling to drink — Mt 27:34 — *1089*

TASTY
- I did not eat any **t** food, — Da 10:3 — 2536b

TATTENAI
- At that time **T**, the governor of — Ezr 5:3 — 8674
- *is* the copy of the letter which **T**, — Ezr 5:6 — 8674
- "Now *therefore,* **T**, governor of — Ezr 6:6 — 8674
- Then **T**, the governor of *the* — Ezr 6:13 — 8674

TATTOO
- make any **t** marks on yourselves: — Lv 19:28 — 3793, 7085

TAUGHT
- I have **t** you statutes and — Dt 4:5 — 3925
- and **t** it to the sons of Israel. — Dt 31:22 — 3925
- the sons of Israel might be **t** war, — Jg 3:2 — 3925
- and **t** them how they should fear — 2Ki 17:28 — 3384
- They **t** in Judah, *having* the — 2Ch 17:9 — 3925
- of Judah and **t** among the people. — 2Ch 17:9 — 3925
- Levites who **t** all Israel *and* who — 2Ch 35:3 — 995
- and the Levites who **t** the people — Ne 8:9 — 995
- God, You have **t** me from my youth, — Ps 71:17 — 3925
- For You Yourself have **t** me. — Ps 119:102 — 3384
- Then he **t** me and said to me, — Pr 4:4 — 3384
- in the LORD, I have **t** you today, — Pr 22:19 — 3045
- the oracle which his mother **t** him: — Pr 31:1 — 3256
- Preacher also **t** the people knowledge — Ec 12:9 — 3925
- And *who* **t** Him in the path of — Is 40:14 — 3925
- of justice and **t** Him knowledge And — Is 40:14 — 3925
- your sons will be **t** of the LORD; — Is 54:13 — 3928
- wicked women You have **t** your ways. — Jer 2:33 — 3925
- have **t** their tongue to speak lies; — Jer 9:5 — 3925
- Baals, as their fathers **t** them," — Jer 9:14 — 3925
- they **t** My people to swear by Baal, — Jer 12:16 — 3925
- And you yourself had **t** them — Jer 13:21 — 3925
- though *I* **t** them, teaching again — Jer 32:33 — 3925
- and they have not **t** the difference — Ezk 22:26 — 3045
- Yet it is I who **t** Ephraim to walk, — Hos 11:3 — 7270
- Him all that they had done and **t**. — Mk 6:30 — *1321*
- to say, as He **t** in the temple, — Mk 12:35 — *1321*
- about the things you have been **t**. — Lk 1:4 — *2727*
- as John also **t** his disciples." — Lk 11:1 — *1321*
- and You **t** in our streets'; — Lk 13:26 — *1321*
- 'AND THEY SHALL ALL BE **T** OF GOD.' — Jn 6:45 — *1318*
- synagogue as He **t** in Capernaum. — Jn 6:59 — *1321*
- treasury, as He **t** in the temple; — Jn 8:20 — *1321*
- these things as the Father **t** Me. — Jn 8:28 — *1321*
- I always **t** in synagogues and in — Jn 18:20 — *1321*
- and **t** considerable numbers; — Ac 11:26 — *1321*
- not in words **t** by human wisdom, — 1Co 2:13 — *1318*
- but in those **t** by the Spirit, — 1Co 2:13 — *1318*
- received it from man, nor was I **t** it, — Ga 1:12 — *1321*
- The one who is **t** the word — Ga 6:6 — *2727*
- heard Him and have been **t** in Him, — Eph 4:21 — *1321*
- are **t** by God to love one another; — 1Th 4:9 — *2312*
- the traditions which you were **t**, — 2Th 2:15 — *1321*
- they will be **t** not to blaspheme. — 1Tm 1:20 — *3811*
- a lie, and just as it has **t** you, — 1Jn 2:27 — *1321*

TAUNT
- and a **t** among all the people where — Dt 28:37 — 8148
- **t** the armies of the living God?" — 1Sa 17:26 — 2778a
- "And now I have become their **t**, — Jb 30:9 — 5058
- **t** against the king of Babylon, — Is 14:4 — 4912
- a **t** and a curse in all places — Jer 24:9 — 8148
- day they will take up against you a **t** — Mi 2:4 — 4912

TAUNTED
- concerning whom you **t** me, — Jg 8:15 — 2778a
- **t** the armies of the living God." — 1Sa 17:36 — 2778a
- armies of Israel, whom you have **t**. — 1Sa 17:45 — 2778a
- When he **t** Israel, Jonathan the — 1Ch 20:7 — 2778a
- With which they have **t** My people — Zph 2:8 — 2778a
- because they have **t** and become — Zph 2:10 — 2778a

TAUNTING
- "I have heard the **t** of Moab And — Zph 2:8 — 2781

TAUNTS
- He who oppresses the poor **t** his Maker, — Pr 14:31 — 2778a
- He who mocks the poor **t** his Maker; — Pr 17:5 — 2778a

TAUNT-SONG
- of these take up a **t** against him, — Hab 2:6 — 4912

TAX
- "Levy a **t** for the LORD from — Nu 31:28 — 4371
- it is not allowed to impose **t**, — Ezr 7:24 — 4061
- have borrowed money for the king's **t** — Ne 5:4 — 4060b
- Do not even the **t** collectors do — Mt 5:46 — *5057*
- Matthew, sitting in the **t** collector's — Mt 9:9 — *5058*
- many **t** collectors and sinners came — Mt 9:10 — *5057*
- "Why is your Teacher eating with the **t** — Mt 9:11 — *5057*
- Thomas and Matthew the **t** collector; — Mt 10:3 — *5057*
- a friend of **t** collectors and sinners!' — Mt 11:19 — *5057*
- who collected the two-drachma **t** — Mt 17:24
- teacher not pay the two-drachma **t**?" — Mt 17:24
- him be to you as a Gentile and a **t** — Mt 18:17 — *5057*
- "Truly I say to you that the **t** — Mt 21:31 — *5057*
- but the **t** collectors and prostitutes — Mt 21:32 — *5057*
- Alphaeus sitting in the **t** booth, — Mk 2:14 — *5058*
- and many **t** collectors and sinners — Mk 2:15 — *5057*
- eating with the sinners and **t** collectors, — Mk 2:16 — *5057*
- eating and drinking with **t** collectors — Mk 2:16 — *5057*
- And *some* **t** collectors also came — Lk 3:12 — *5057*
- noticed a **t** collector — Lk 5:27 — *5058*
- Levi sitting in the **t** booth, — Lk 5:27 — *5058*
- a great crowd of **t** collectors — Lk 5:29 — *5057*
- eat and drink with the **t** collectors — Lk 5:30 — *5057*
- people and the **t** collectors — Lk 7:29 — *5057*
- a friend of **t** collectors and sinners!' — Lk 7:34 — *5057*
- Now all the **t** collectors — Lk 15:1 — *5057*
- and the other a **t** collector. — Lk 18:10 — *5057*
- or even like this **t** collector. — Lk 18:11 — *5057*
- "But the **t** collector, standing some — Lk 18:13 — *5057*
- he was a chief **t** collector and he was — Lk 19:2 — *754*
- **t** to whom tax *is due* — Ro 13:7 — *5411*
- tax to whom **t** *is due* — Ro 13:7 — *5411*

TAXED
- but he **t** the land in order to give — 2Ki 23:35 — 6186b

TAXES
- **t** of *the provinces* beyond the River — Ezr 6:8 — 4061
- lawful for us to pay **t** to Caesar, — Lk 20:22 — *5411*
- and forbidding to pay **t** to Caesar, — Lk 23:2 — *5411*
- because of this you also pay **t**, — Ro 13:6 — *5411*

TEACH
- and **t** you what you are to say." — Ex 4:12 — 3384
- I will **t** you what you are to do. — Ex 4:15 — 3384
- then **t** them the statutes and the — Ex 18:20 — 2094b
- "He also has put in his heart to **t**, — Ex 35:34 — 3384
- and so as to **t** the sons of Israel — Lv 10:11 — 3384
- to **t** when they are unclean and — Lv 14:57 — 3384
- that they may **t** their children." — Dt 4:10 — 3925
- to **t** you statutes and judgments, — Dt 4:14 — 3925
- judgments which you shall **t** them, — Dt 5:31 — 3925
- God has commanded *me* to **t** you, — Dt 6:1 — 3925
- You shall **t** them diligently to — Dt 6:7 — 8150
- "You shall **t** them to your — Dt 11:19 — 3925
- according to all that they **t** you. — Dt 17:10 — 3384
- terms of the law which they **t** you, — Dt 17:11 — 3384
- so that they may not **t** you — Dt 20:18 — 3925
- the Levitical priests **t** you; — Dt 24:8 — 3384
- and **t** it to the sons of Israel; — Dt 31:19 — 3925
- shall **T** Your ordinances to Jacob, — Dt 33:10 — 3384
- he may **t** us what to do for the boy — Jg 13:8 — 3384
- and he told *them* to **t** the sons of — 2Sa 1:18 — 3925
- **t** them the good way in which they — 1Ki 8:36 — 3384
- and let him **t** them the custom of — 2Ki 17:27 — 3384
- **t** them the good way in which they — 2Ch 6:27 — 3384
- to **t** in the cities of Judah; — 2Ch 17:7 — 3925
- and to **t** *His* statutes and — Ezr 7:10 — 3925
- and you may **t** anyone who is — Ezr 7:25 — 3046
- "**T** me, and I will be silent; — Jb 6:24 — 3384
- "Will they not **t** you *and* tell — Jb 8:10 — 3384
- the beasts, and let them **t** you; — Jb 12:7 — 3384
- to the earth, and let it **t** you; — Jb 12:8 — 3384
- "Can anyone **t** God knowledge, In — Jb 21:22 — 3925
- increased years should **t** wisdom. — Jb 32:7 — 3045
- silent, and I will **t** you wisdom." — Jb 33:33 — 502
- **T** me what I do not see; — Jb 34:32 — 3384
- "**T** us what we shall say to Him; — Jb 37:19 — 3045
- Your ways, O LORD; **T** me Your paths. — Ps 25:4 — 3925
- Lead me in Your truth and **t** me, — Ps 25:5 — 3925
- **T** me Your way, O LORD, And lead me — Ps 27:11 — 3384
- I will instruct you and **t** you in — Ps 32:8 — 3384
- I will **t** you the fear of the LORD. — Ps 34:11 — 3925
- right hand **t** You awesome things. — Ps 45:4 — 3384
- I will **t** transgressors Your ways, — Ps 51:13 — 3925
- should **t** them to their children, — Ps 78:5 — 3045
- **T** me Your way, O LORD; — Ps 86:11 — 3384
- So **t** us to number our days, That — Ps 90:12 — 3045
- And whom You **t** out of Your law; — Ps 94:12 — 3925
- That he might **t** his elders wisdom. — Ps 105:22 — 2449
- **T** me Your statutes. — Ps 119:12 — 3925
- **T** me Your statutes. — Ps 119:26 — 3925
- **T** me, O LORD, the way of Your — Ps 119:33 — 3384
- **T** me Your statutes. — Ps 119:64 — 3925
- **T** me good discernment and — Ps 119:66 — 3925
- **T** me Your statutes. — Ps 119:68 — 3925
- O LORD, And **t** me Your ordinances. — Ps 119:108 — 3925
- And **t** me Your statutes. — Ps 119:124 — 3925
- servant, And **t** me Your statutes. — Ps 119:135 — 3925
- For You **t** me Your statutes. — Ps 119:171 — 3925
- My testimony which I will **t** them, — Ps 132:12 — 3925
- **T** me the way in which I should — Ps 143:8 — 3045
- **T** me to do Your will, For You are — Ps 143:10 — 3925
- be still wiser, **T** a righteous man and — Pr 9:9 — 3045
- He may **t** us concerning His ways And — Is 2:3 — 3384
- "To whom would He **t** knowledge, — Is 28:9 — 3384
- **T** your daughters wailing, And — Jer 9:20 — 3925
- "They will not **t** again, — Jer 31:34 — 3925
- they shall **t** My people *the* — Ezk 44:23 — 3384
- and *he ordered him* to **t** them the — Da 1:4 — 3925
- That He may **t** us about His ways — Mi 4:2 — 3384
- His mouth and *began* to **t** them, — Mt 5:2 — *1321*
- to **t** and preach in their cities. — Mt 11:1 — *1321*
- and **t** the way of God in truth, — Mt 22:16 — *1321*
- the synagogue and *began* to **t**. — Mk 1:21 — *1321*
- He began to **t** again by the sea. — Mk 4:1 — *1321*
- He began to **t** in the synagogue; — Mk 6:2 — *1321*
- He began to **t** them many things. — Mk 6:34 — *1321*
- And He began to **t** them that the — Mk 8:31 — *1321*
- He once more *began* to **t** them. — Mk 10:1 — *1321*
- And He *began* to **t** and say to them, — Mk 11:17 — *1321*
- but **t** the way of God in truth. — Mk 12:14 — *1321*
- **t** us to pray just as John also — Lk 11:1 — *1321*
- for the Holy Spirit will **t** you in — Lk 12:12 — *1321*
- that You speak and **t** correctly, — Lk 20:21 — *1321*
- but **t** the way of God in truth. — Lk 20:21 — *1321*
- into the temple, and *began to* **t**. — Jn 7:14 — *1321*
- the Greeks, and **t** the Greeks, — Jn 7:35 — *1321*
- He sat down and *began* to **t** them. — Jn 8:2 — *1321*
- My name, He will **t** you all things, — Jn 14:26 — *1321*
- all that Jesus began to do and **t**, — Ac 1:1 — *1321*
- or **t** at all in the name of Jesus. — Ac 4:18 — *1321*
- about daybreak and *began* to **t**. — Ac 5:21 — *1321*
- you, therefore, who **t** another, — Ro 2:21 — *1321*
- another, do you not **t** yourself? — Ro 2:21 — *1321*
- as I **t** everywhere in every church. — 1Co 4:17 — *1321*

Does not even nature itself t you 1Co 11:14 *1321*
men not to t strange doctrines, 1Tm 1:3 *2085*
But I do not allow a woman to t or 1Tm 2:12 *1321*
hospitable, able to t, 1Tm 3:2 *1317*
Prescribe and t these things. 1Tm 4:11 *1321*
T and preach these *principles.* 1Tm 6:2 *1321*
who will be able to t others also. 2Tm 2:2 *1321*
but be kind to all, able to t, 2Tm 2:24 *1317*
teaching things they should not t Ti 1:11 *1321*
have need again for someone to t you Heb 5:12 *1321*
NOT T EVERYONE HIS FELLOW CITIZEN, Heb 8:11 *1321*
have no need for anyone to t you; 1Jn 2:27 *1321*

TEACHER
great, the t *as well* as the pupil. 1Ch 25:8 995
Who is a t like Him? Jb 36:22 4175b
your T will no longer hide Himself, Is 30:20 4175b
but your eyes will behold your T. Is 30:20 4175b
it, *Or* an image, a t of falsehood? Hab 2:18 3384
And that is *your* t? Hab 2:19 3384
"T, I will follow You wherever Mt 8:19 *1320*
"Why is your T eating with the Mt 9:11 *1320*
"A disciple is not above his t, Mt 10:24 *1320*
disciple that he become like his t, Mt 10:25 *1320*
"T, we want to see a sign from Mt 12:38 *1320*
t not pay the two-drachma *tax?"* Mt 17:24 *1320*
"T, what good thing shall I do Mt 19:16 *1320*
"T, we know that You are truthful Mt 22:16 *1320*
"T, Moses said, 'IF A MAN DIES HAVING Mt 22:24 *1320*
T, which is the great commandment Mt 22:36 *1320*
for One is your T, and you are all Mt 23:8 *1320*
'The T says, "My time is near; Mt 26:18 *1320*
"T, do You not care that we are Mk 4:38 *1320*
why trouble the T anymore?" Mk 5:35 *1320*
"T, I brought You my son, Mk 9:17 *1320*
"T, we saw someone casting out Mk 9:38 *1320*
"Good T, what shall I do to Mk 10:17 *1320*
"T, I have kept all these things Mk 10:20 *1320*
"T, we want You to do for us Mk 10:35 *1320*
"T, we know that You are Mk 12:14 *1320*
"T, Moses wrote for us that IF A Mk 12:19 *1320*
"Right, T; You have truly stated Mk 12:32 *1320*
"T, behold what wonderful stones Mk 13:1 *1320*
'The T says, "Where is My guest Mk 14:14 *1320*
"T, what shall we do?" Lk 3:12 *1320*
"A pupil is not above his t; Lk 6:40 *1320*
fully trained, will be like his t. Lk 6:40 *1320*
And he replied, "Say it, T." Lk 7:40 *1320*
do not trouble the T anymore." Lk 8:49 *1320*
"T, I beg You to look at my son, Lk 9:38 *1320*
"T, what shall I do to inherit Lk 10:25 *1320*
"T, when You say this, You insult Lk 11:45 *1320*
"T, tell my brother to divide the Lk 12:13 *1320*
"Good T, what shall I do to Lk 18:18 *1320*
"T, rebuke Your disciples." Lk 19:39 *1320*
"T, we know that You speak and Lk 20:21 *1320*
"T, Moses wrote for us that IF A Lk 20:28 *1320*
"T, You have spoken well." Lk 20:39 *1320*
"T, when therefore will these Lk 21:7 *1320*
'The T says to you, Lk 22:11 *1320*
"Rabbi (which translated means T), Jn 1:38 *1320*
You have come from God *as* a t; Jn 3:2 *1320*
"Are you the t of Israel and do Jn 3:10 *1320*
"T, this woman has been caught in Jn 8:4 *1320*
"The T is here and is calling Jn 11:28 *1320*
"You call Me T and Lord; Jn 13:13 *1320*
"If I then, the Lord and the T, Jn 13:14 *1320*
"Rabboni!" (which means, T). Jn 20:16 *1320*
named Gamaliel, a t of the Law, Ac 5:34 *3547*
the foolish, a t of the immature, Ro 2:20 *1320*
as a t of the Gentiles in faith 1Tm 2:7 *1320*
a preacher and an apostle and a t. 2Tm 1:11 *1320*

TEACHERS
and for Joiarib and Elnathan, t. Ezr 8:16 995
I have more insight than all my t, Ps 119:99 3925
not listened to the voice of my t, Pr 5:13 4175b
sitting in the midst of the t, Lk 2:46 *1320*
Pharisees and t of the law sitting Lk 5:17 *3547*
that was *there,* prophets and t: Ac 13:1 *1320*
second prophets, third t, 1Co 12:28 *1320*
All are not t, are they? 1Co 12:29 *1320*
and some *as* pastors and t, Eph 4:11 *1320*
wanting to be t of the Law, even 1Tm 1:7 *3547*
they will accumulate for themselves t 2Tm 4:3 *1320*
by this time you ought to be t, Heb 5:12 *1320*
Let not many *of you* become t, Jas 3:1 *1320*
will also be false t among you, 2Pe 2:1 *5572*

TEACHES
"For your guilt t your mouth, And Jb 15:5 502
Who t us more than the beasts of Jb 35:11 502
And He t the humble His way. Ps 25:9 3925
Even He who t man knowledge? Ps 94:10 3925
prophet who t falsehood is the tail. Is 9:15 3384
God instructs and t him properly. Is 28:26 3384
your God, who t you to profit, Is 48:17 3925
commandments, and t others Mt 5:19 *1321*
but whoever keeps and t *them,* Mt 5:19 *1321*
or he who t, in his teaching; Ro 12:7 *1321*
all good things with the one who t Ga 6:6 *2727*
His anointing t you about all things, 1Jn 2:27 *1321*
she t and leads My bond-servants Rv 2:20 *1321*

TEACHING
which I am t you to perform, Dt 4:1 3925
"Let my t drop as the rain, My Dt 32:2 3948
without a t priest and without law. 2Ch 15:3 3384
'My t is pure, And I am innocent Jb 11:4 3948
And do not forsake your mother's t; Pr 1:8 8451
My son, do not forget my t, Pr 3:1 8451
For I give you sound t; Pr 4:2 3948
do not forsake the t of your mother; Pr 6:20 8451
is a lamp and the t is light; Pr 6:23 8451
And my t as the apple of your eye. Pr 7:2 8451
The t of the wise is a fountain of Pr 13:14 8451
t of kindness is on her tongue. Pr 31:26 8451
I taught them, t again and again, Jer 32:33 3925
Galilee, t in their synagogues and Mt 4:23 *1321*
crowds were amazed at His t; Mt 7:28 *1322*
t them as *one* having authority, Mt 7:29 *1321*
villages, t in their synagogues and Mt 9:35 *1321*
and *began* t them in their synagogue, Mt 13:54 *1321*
T AS DOCTRINES THE PRECEPTS OF MEN.' Mt 15:9 *1321*
but of the t of the Pharisees and Mt 16:12 *1322*
people came to Him while He was t, Mt 21:23 *1321*
they were astonished at His t. Mt 22:33 *1322*
I used to sit in the temple t and you Mt 26:55 *1321*
t them to observe all that I Mt 28:20 *1321*
They were amazed at His t; Mk 1:22 *1322*
t them as *one* having authority, Mk 1:22 *1321*
A new t with authority! Mk 1:27 *1322*
coming to Him, and He was t them. Mk 2:13 *1321*
t them many things in parables, Mk 4:2 *1321*
and was saying to them in His t, Mk 4:2 *1322*
was going around the villages t. Mk 6:6 *1321*
T AS DOCTRINES THE PRECEPTS OF MEN.' Mk 7:7 *1321*
For He was t His disciples and Mk 9:31 *1321*
crowd was astonished at His t. Mk 11:18 *1322*
In His t He was saying: Mk 12:38 *1322*
I was with you in the temple t, Mk 14:49 *1321*
And He *began* t in their synagogues Lk 4:15 *1321*
and He was t them on the Sabbath; Lk 4:31 *1321*
and they were amazed at His t, Lk 4:32 *1322*
t the people from the boat. Lk 5:3 *1321*
One day He was t; Lk 5:17 *1321*
entered the synagogue and was t; Lk 6:6 *1321*
And He was t in one of the Lk 13:10 *1321*
city and village to another, t, Lk 13:22 *1321*
And He was t daily in the temple; Lk 19:47 *1321*
while He was t the people in the Lk 20:1 *1321*
the day He was t in the temple, Lk 21:37 *1321*
stirs up the people, t all over Judea, Lk 23:5 *1321*
"My t is not Mine, but His who Jn 7:16 *1322*
His will, he will know of the t, Jn 7:17 *1322*
out in the temple, t and saying, Jn 7:28 *1321*
in sins, and are you t us?" Jn 9:34 *1321*
His disciples, and about His t. Jn 18:19 *1322*
the apostles' t and to fellowship, Ac 2:42 *1322*
greatly disturbed because they were t Ac 4:2 *1321*
in the temple and t the people!" Ac 5:25 *1321*
not to continue t in this name, Ac 5:28 *1321*
have filled Jerusalem with your t and Ac 5:28 *1322*
they kept right on t and preaching Ac 5:42 *1321*
being amazed at the t of the Lord. Ac 13:12 *1322*
Judea and *began* t the brethren, Ac 15:1 *1321*
in Antioch, t and preaching with Ac 15:35 *1321*
"May we know what this new t is Ac 17:19 *1322*
t the word of God among them. Ac 18:11 *1321*
he was speaking and t accurately Ac 18:25 *1321*
and t you publicly and from house Ac 20:20 *1321*
that you are t all the Jews who Ac 21:21 *1321*
and t concerning the Lord Jesus Ac 28:31 *1321*
to that form of t to which you were Ro 6:17 *1322*
or he who teaches, in his t; Ro 12:7 *1319*
hindrances contrary to the t which Ro 16:17 *1322*
knowledge or of prophecy or of t? 1Co 14:6 *1322*
each one has a psalm, has a t, 1Co 14:26 *1322*
and t every man with all wisdom, Col 1:28 *1321*
with all wisdom t and admonishing Col 3:16 *1321*
else is contrary to sound t, 1Tm 1:10 *1319*
Scripture, to exhortation and t. 1Tm 4:13 *1319*
to yourself and to your t; 1Tm 4:16 *1319*
who work hard at preaching and t. 1Tm 5:17 *1319*
Now you followed my t, 2Tm 3:10 *1319*
by God and profitable for t, 2Tm 3:16 *1319*
for he vigorously opposed our t. 2Tm 4:15 *3056*
which is in accordance with the t, Ti 1:9 *1322*
t things they should not *teach* for Ti 1:11 *1321*
to much wine, t what is good, Ti 2:3 *2567*
the elementary t about the Christ, Heb 6:1 *3056*
does not abide in the t of Christ, 2Jn 1:9 *1322*
the one who abides in the t, 2Jn 1:9 *1322*
to you and does not bring this t, 2Jn 1:10 *1322*
some who hold the t of Balaam, Rv 2:14 *1322*
who kept t Balak to put a Rv 2:14 *1321*
way hold the t of the Nicolaitans. Rv 2:15 *1322*
Thyatira, who do not hold this t, Rv 2:24 *1322*

TEACHINGS
to walk in His t which He set Da 9:10 8451
the commandments and t of men? Col 2:22 *1319*
away by varied and strange t; Heb 13:9 *1322*

TEAM
I shatter the farmer and his t, Jer 51:23 6776
the chariot to the t of horses, Mi 1:13

TEAR
"T off the gold rings which are Ex 32:2 6561
has any gold, let them t it off.' Ex 32:24 6561
you are to t down their altars and Ex 34:13 5422
'Then he shall t it by its wings, Lv 1:17 8156
your heads nor t your clothes, Lv 10:6 6533
then he shall t it out of the garment Lv 13:56 7167
shall order them to t out the stones Lv 14:40 2502a
shall therefore t down the house, Lv 14:45 5422
his head nor t his clothes; Lv 21:10 6533
And t down all the sons of Sheth. Nu 24:17 7175a
you shall t down their altars, and Dt 7:5 5422
"You shall t down their altars Dt 12:3 5422
you shall t down their altars.' Jg 2:2 5422
I will t down this tower." Jg 8:9 5422
"T your clothes and gird on 2Sa 3:31 7167
surely t the kingdom from you, 1Ki 11:11 7167
but I will t it out of the hand of 1Ki 11:12 7167
I will not t away all the kingdom, 1Ki 11:13 7167
I will t the kingdom out of the 1Ki 11:31 7167
"O you who t yourself in your Jb 18:4 2963
"Let us t their fetters apart And Ps 2:3 5423
Or he will t my soul like a lion, Ps 7:2 2963
is like a lion that is eager to t, Ps 17:12 2963
He will t them down and not build Ps 28:5 2040
God, Or I will t *you* in pieces, Ps 50:22 2963
up and t you away from *your* tent, Ps 52:5 5255
The LORD will t down the house of Pr 15:25 5255
A time to t down and a time to Ec 3:3 6555
A time to t apart and a time to Ec 3:7 7167
neck and will t off their bonds; Jer 30:8 5423
build you up and not t you down, Jer 42:10 2040
I have built I am about to t down, Jer 45:4 2040
"So I will t down the wall which Ezk 13:14 2040
and I will t them from your arms; Ezk 13:20 7167
"I will also t off your veils and Ezk 13:21 7167
and they will t down your shrines, Ezk 16:39 2040
And he learned to t *his* prey; Ezk 19:3 2963
lion, He learned to t *his* prey; Ezk 19:6 2963
its fragments And t your breasts; Ezk 23:34 5423
I, even I, will t to pieces and go Hos 5:14 2963
And I will t open their chests; Hos 13:8 7167
As a wild beast would t them. Hos 13:8 1234
Who t off their skin from them And Mi 3:2 1497
t down all your fortifications. Mi 5:11 2040
And I will t off your shackles." Na 1:13 5423
fat *sheep* and t off their hoofs. Zch 11:16 6561
"They may build, but I will t down; Mal 1:4 2040
eye makes you stumble, t it out and Mt 5:29 *1807*
and turn and t you to pieces. Mt 7:6 *4486*
garment, and a worse t results. Mt 9:16 *4978*
the old, and a worse t results. Mk 2:21 *4978*
otherwise he will both t the new, Lk 5:36 *4977*
I will t down my barns and build Lk 12:18 *2507*
"Let us not t it, but cast lots Jn 19:24 *4977*
Do not t down the work of God for Ro 14:20 *2647*
God will wipe every t from their Rv 7:17 *1144*
He will wipe away every t from Rv 21:4 *1144*

TEARING
like a roaring lion t the prey. Ezk 22:25 2963
her are like wolves t the prey, Ezk 22:27 2963
T his clothes, the high priest said, Mk 14:63 *1284*
for building up and not for t down. 2Co 13:10 *2506*

TEARS
down as a lion, And t the arm, Dt 33:20 2963
he tore him as one t a young goat Jg 14:6 8156
your prayer, I have seen your t; 2Ki 20:5 1832
"Behold, He t down, and it cannot Jb 12:14 2040
I dissolve my couch with my t. Ps 6:6 1832
Do not be silent at my t; Ps 39:12 1832
My t have been my food day and Ps 42:3 1832
Put my t in Your bottle. Ps 56:8 1832
have fed them with the bread of t, Ps 80:5 1832
You have made them to drink t in Ps 80:5 1832
soul from death, My eyes from t, Ps 116:8 1832
Those who sow in t shall reap with Ps 126:5 1832
the foolish t it down with her own Pr 14:1 2040
behold *I saw* the t of the oppressed Ec 4:1 1832
is wailing, dissolved in t. Is 15:3 1065
I will drench you with my t, Is 16:9 1832
GOD will wipe t away from all faces, Is 25:8 1832
your prayer, I have seen your t; Is 38:5 1832
And my eyes a fountain of t, Jer 9:1 1832
for us, That our eyes may shed t And Jer 9:18 1832
weep And flow down with t, Jer 13:17 1832
Let my eyes flow down with t night Jer 14:17 1832
weeping And your eyes from t; Jer 31:16 1832
And her t are on her cheeks; La 1:2 1832
My eyes fail because of t, La 2:11 1832
Let *your* t run down like a river La 2:18 1832
weep, and your t shall not come. Ezk 24:16 1832
through, Tramples down and t, Mi 5:8 2963
the altar of the LORD with t, Mal 2:13 1832
"No one t a piece of cloth from a new Lk 5:36 *4977*
began to wet His feet with her t, Lk 7:38 *1144*
she has wet My feet with her t and Lk 7:44 *1144*
with all humility and with t and with Ac 20:19 *1144*
cease to admonish each one with t. Ac 20:31 *1144*
heart I wrote to you with many t; 2Co 2:4 *1144*
see you, even as I recall your t, 2Tm 1:4 *1144*
supplications with loud crying and t Heb 5:7 *1144*
though he sought for it with t. Heb 12:17 *1144*

TEBAH
also bore T and Gaham and Tahash Gn 22:24 2875

TEBALIAH
Hilkiah the second, T the third, 1Ch 26:11 2882

TEBETH
tenth month which is the month T, Es 2:16 2887

TEEM
"Let the waters t with swarms of Gn 1:20 8317

TEEMING
among all the t life of the water, Lv 11:10 8318
or if a man touches any t things by Lv 22:5 8318
"And all the t life with wings Dt 14:19 8318

TEETH
wine, And his t white from milk. Gn 49:12 8127
meat was still between their t, Nu 11:33 8127
And the t of beasts I will send Dt 32:24 8127
t of the young lions are broken. Jb 4:10 8127
should I take my flesh in my t And Jb 13:14 8127
He has gnashed at me with His t; Jb 16:9 8127
escaped *only* by the skin of my t. Jb 19:20 8127

And snatched the prey from his **t**.	Jb 29:17	8127
Around his **t** there is terror.	Jb 41:14	8127
shattered the **t** of the wicked.	Ps 3:7	8127
They gnashed at me with their **t**.	Ps 35:16	8127
And gnashes at him with his **t**.	Ps 37:12	8127
whose **t** are spears and arrows And	Ps 57:4	8127
shatter their **t** in their mouth;	Ps 58:6	8127
He will gnash his **t** and melt away;	Ps 112:10	8127
given us to be torn by their **t**.	Ps 124:6	8127
Like vinegar to the **t** and smoke	Pr 10:26	8127
kind of *man* whose **t** are *like* swords And	Pr 30:14	8127
swords And his jaw **t** *like* knives,	Pr 30:14	4973
"Your **t** are like a flock of *newly*	SS 4:2	8127
"Your **t** are like a flock of ewes	SS 6:6	8127
And the children's **t** are set on edge.'	Jer 31:29	8127
grapes, his **t** will be set on edge.	Jer 31:30	8127
They hiss and gnash *their* **t**.	La 2:16	8127
He has broken my **t** with gravel;	La 3:16	8127
the children's **t** are set on edge'?	Ezk 18:2	8127
were in its mouth between its **t**;	Da 7:5	8128
and it had large iron **t**.	Da 7:7	8128
with its **t** of iron and its claws	Da 7:19	8128
Its **t** are the teeth of a lion, And	Jl 1:6	8127
Its teeth are the **t** of a lion,	Jl 1:6	8127
"But I gave you also cleanness of **t** in	Am 4:6	8127
something to bite with their **t**,	Mi 3:5	8127
things from between their **t**.	Zch 9:7	8127
be weeping and gnashing of **t**."	Mt 8:12	*3599*
be weeping and gnashing of **t**.	Mt 13:42	*3599*
be weeping and gnashing of **t**.	Mt 13:50	*3599*
be weeping and gnashing of **t**.'	Mt 22:13	*3599*
there will be weeping and gnashing of **t**.	Mt 24:51	*3599*
be weeping and gnashing of **t**.	Mt 25:30	*3599*
foams *at the mouth,* and grinds his **t** and	Mk 9:18	*3599*
will be weeping and gnashing of **t**	Lk 13:28	*3599*
began gnashing their **t** at him.	Ac 7:54	*3599*
their **t** were like *the teeth* of lions.	Rv 9:8	*3599*
and their teeth were like *the* **t**	Rv 9:8	
TEHAPHNEHES		
"In **T** the day will be dark	Ezk 30:18	8471
TEHINNAH		
and **T** the father of Ir-nahash.	1Ch 4:12	8468
TEKEL		
'MENE, MENE, **T**, UPHARSIN.'	Da 5:25	8625b
"'**T**'—you have been weighed on	Da 5:27	8625b
TEKOA		
So Joab sent to **T** and brought a	2Sa 14:2	8620
the woman of **T** spoke to the king,	2Sa 14:4	8621
The woman of **T** said to the king,	2Sa 14:9	8621
bore him Ashhur the father of **T**.	1Ch 2:24	8620
Ashhur, the father of **T**,	1Ch 4:5	8620
Thus he built Bethlehem, Etam, **T**,	2Ch 11:6	8620
went out to the wilderness of **T**;	2Ch 20:20	8620
Now blow a trumpet in **T** And	Jer 6:1	8620
was among the sheepherders from **T**,	Am 1:1	8620
TEKOITE		
Ira the son of Ikkesh the **T**,	2Sa 23:26	8621
Ira the son of Ikkesh the **T**,	1Ch 11:28	8621
was Ira the son of Ikkesh the **T**;	1Ch 27:9	8621
TEKOITES		
next to him the **T** made repairs,	Ne 3:5	8621
After them the **T** repaired another	Ne 3:27	8621
TEL-ABIB		
beside the river Chebar at **T**,	Ezk 3:15	8512
TELAH		
son *along* with Resheph, **T** his son,	1Ch 7:25	8520
TELAIM		
the people and numbered them in **T**,	1Sa 15:4	2923
TELASSAR		
the sons of Eden who *were* in **T**?	2Ki 19:12	8515
the sons of Eden who *were* in **T**?	Is 37:12	8515
TELEM		
Ziph and **T** and Bealoth,	Jos 15:24	2928
Shallum, **T** and Uri.	Ezr 10:24	2928
TEL-HARSHA		
who came up from Tel-melah, **T**,	Ezr 2:59	8521
they who came up from Tel-melah, **T**,	Ne 7:61	8521
TELL		
Why did you not **t** me that she was	Gn 12:18	5046
you did not **t** me, nor did I	Gn 21:26	5046
mountains of which I will **t** you."	Gn 22:2	559
Please **t** me, is there room for us	Gn 24:23	5046
and truly with my master, **t** me;	Gn 24:49	5046
the land of which I shall **t** you.	Gn 26:2	559
T me, what shall your wages be?"	Gn 29:15	5046
and deceive me, and did not **t** me so	Gn 31:27	5046
and I have sent to **t** my lord,	Gn 32:5	5046
"Please **t** me your name."	Gn 32:29	5046
please **t** me where they are	Gn 37:16	5046
T *it* to me, please."	Gn 40:8	5608
"Did I not **t** you,	Gn 42:22	559
"Now you must **t** my father of all	Gn 45:13	5046
"I will go up and **t** Pharaoh,	Gn 46:31	5046
"Assemble yourselves that I may **t**	Gn 49:1	5046
t Pharaoh king of Egypt to let the	Ex 6:11	1696
"The honor is yours to **t** me:	Ex 8:9	
may **t** in the hearing of your son,	Ex 10:2	5608
You shall **t** your son on that day,	Ex 13:8	5046
"**T** the sons of Israel to turn	Ex 14:2	1696
T the sons of Israel to go forward.	Ex 14:15	1696
of Jacob and **t** the sons of Israel:	Ex 19:3	5046
"**T** the sons of Israel to raise a	Ex 25:2	1696
known, if he does not **t** *it,*	Lv 5:1	5046
house shall come and **t** the priest,	Lv 14:35	5046
"**T** your brother Aaron that he	Lv 16:2	1696
"**T** Aaron and his sons to be	Lv 22:2	1696

and they will **t** *it* to the	Nu 14:14	559
and **t** them that they shall make	Nu 15:38	559
the word which I **t** you."	Nu 22:35	1696
He shows me I will **t** you."	Nu 23:3	5046
"Did I not **t** you,	Nu 23:26	1696
"Did I not **t** your messengers whom	Nu 24:12	1696
to the verdict which they **t** you,	Dt 17:11	5046
Your elders, and they will **t** you.	Dt 32:7	5046
if you do not **t** this business of ours;	Jos 2:14	5046
if you **t** this business of ours,	Jos 2:20	5046
your mouth, until the day I **t** you,	Jos 6:10	559
and **t** me now what you have done.	Jos 7:19	5046
from, nor did he **t** me his name.	Jg 13:6	5046
but he did not **t** his father or	Jg 14:6	5046
but he did not **t** them that he had	Jg 14:9	5046
if you will indeed **t** it to me	Jg 14:12	5046
"But if you are unable to **t** me,	Jg 14:13	5046
they could not **t** the riddle in three	Jg 14:14	5046
that he will **t** us the riddle,	Jg 14:15	5046
so should I **t** you?"	Jg 14:16	5046
"Please **t** me where your great	Jg 16:6	5046
now please **t** me how you may be	Jg 16:10	5046
t me how you may be bound."	Jg 16:13	5046
"**T** *us,* how did this wickedness	Jg 20:3	1696
he will **t** you what you shall do."	Ru 3:4	5046
but if not, **t** me that I may know;	Ru 4:4	5046
was afraid to **t** the vision to Eli.	1Sa 3:15	5046
the man came to **t** *it* in the city,	1Sa 4:13	5046
T us how we shall send it to its	1Sa 6:2	3045
t them of the procedure of the king	1Sa 8:9	5046
perhaps he can **t** us about our	1Sa 9:6	5046
of God and he will **t** us our way."	1Sa 9:8	5046
t me where the seer's house is."	1Sa 9:18	5046
t you all that is on your mind.	1Sa 9:19	5046
t me what Samuel said to you."	1Sa 10:15	5046
But he did not **t** him about the	1Sa 10:16	5046
But he did not **t** his father.	1Sa 14:1	5046
us and we will **t** you something."	1Sa 14:12	3045
"**T** me what you have done."	1Sa 14:43	5046
and let me **t** you what the LORD	1Sa 15:16	5046
anything, then I will **t** you."	1Sa 19:3	5046
then would I not **t** you about it?"	1Sa 20:9	5046
"Who will **t** me if your father	1Sa 20:10	5046
that he would surely **t** Saul.	1Sa 22:22	5046
Israel, I pray, **t** Your servant."	1Sa 23:11	5046
young men and they will **t** you.	1Sa 25:8	5046
she did not **t** her husband Nabal.	1Sa 25:19	5046
so she did not **t** him anything at	1Sa 25:36	5046
"Otherwise they will **t** about us,	1Sa 27:11	5046
"How did things go? Please **t** me."	2Sa 1:4	5046
"**T** *it* not in Gath, Proclaim it	2Sa 1:20	5046
all that Joab had sent him *to* **t**.	2Sa 11:22	
to **t** him that the child was dead,	2Sa 12:18	5046
we **t** him that the child is dead,	2Sa 12:18	559
Will you not **t** me?"	2Sa 13:4	5046
send quickly and **t** David,	2Sa 17:16	5046
a maidservant would go and **t** them,	2Sa 17:17	5046
they would go and **t** King David,	2Sa 17:17	5046
t the king what you have seen."	2Sa 18:21	5046
Please **t** Joab, 'Come here that I may	2Sa 20:16	559
to **t** them who shall sit on the	1Ki 1:20	5046
He will **t** you what will happen to	1Ki 14:3	5046
and **t** Ahab and he cannot find you,	1Ki 18:12	5046
"**T** my lord the king,	1Ki 20:9	559
"**T** *him,* 'Let not him who girds on	1Ki 20:11	1696
"Did I not **t** you that he would	1Ki 22:18	559
T me, what do you have in the	2Ki 4:2	5046
the pace for me unless I **t** you."	2Ki 4:24	559
"Will you **t** me which of us is for	2Ki 6:11	5046
us go and **t** the king's household."	2Ki 7:9	5046
"I will now **t** you what the	2Ki 7:12	5046
"It is a lie, **t** us now."	2Ki 9:12	5046
leave the city to go **t** *it* in Jezreel."	2Ki 9:15	5046
'**T** the man who sent you to me,	2Ki 22:15	559
T of His glory among the nations,	1Ch 16:24	5608
"Go and **t** David My servant,	1Ch 17:4	559
I **t** you that the LORD will build a	1Ch 17:10	5046
"Did I not **t** you that he would	2Ch 18:17	559
"**T** the man who sent you to Me,	2Ch 34:23	559
I did not **t** anyone what my God was	Ne 2:12	5046
I alone have escaped to **t** you."	Jb 1:15	5046
I alone have escaped to **t** you."	Jb 1:16	5046
I alone have escaped to **t** you."	Jb 1:17	5046
I alone have escaped to **t** you."	Jb 1:19	5046
"Will they not teach you *and* **t** you,	Jb 8:10	559
the heavens, and let them **t** you.	Jb 12:7	5046
"I will **t** you, listen to me;	Jb 15:17	2331a
and afraid to **t** you what I think.	Jb 32:6	2331a
to me, I too will **t** what I think.	Jb 32:10	2331a
share, I also will **t** my opinion.	Jb 32:17	2331a
"Behold, let me **t** you, you are	Jb 33:12	6030a
T *Me,* if you have understanding,	Jb 38:4	5046
T *Me,* if you know all this.	Jb 38:18	5046
t of the decree of the LORD:	Ps 2:7	5608
I will **t** of all Your wonders.	Ps 9:1	5608
That I may **t** of all Your praises,	Ps 9:14	5608
will **t** of Your name to my brethren;	Ps 22:22	5608
may **t** *it* to the next generation.	Ps 48:13	5608
I were hungry I would not **t** you	Ps 50:12	559
have you to **t** of My statutes And	Ps 50:16	5608
And I will **t** of what He has done	Ps 66:16	5608
And they **t** of the pain of those	Ps 69:26	5608
mouth shall **t** of Your righteousness	Ps 71:15	5608
That I may **t** of all Your works.	Ps 73:28	5608
But **t** to the generation to come	Ps 78:4	5608
and **t** *them* to their children,	Ps 78:6	5608
we will **t** of Your praise.	Ps 79:13	5608
T of His glory among the nations,	Ps 96:3	5608
That *men* may **t** of the name of the	Ps 102:21	5608

And **t** of His works with joyful	Ps 107:22	5608
And **t** of the works of the LORD.	Ps 118:17	5608
And I will **t** of Your greatness.	Ps 145:6	5608
Man is not able to **t** *it.*	Ec 1:8	1696
and **t** himself that his labor is good.	Ec 2:24	7200
For who can **t** a man what will be	Ec 6:12	5046
who can **t** him when it will happen?	Ec 8:7	5046
t him what will come after him?	Ec 10:14	5046
"**T** me, O you whom my soul loves,	SS 1:7	5046
As to what you will **t** him:	SS 5:8	5046
"So now let Me **t** you what I am	Is 5:5	3045
"Go, and **t** this people:	Is 6:9	559
Please let them **t** you, And let	Is 19:12	5046
then you are to **t** them,	Jer 15:2	559
when you **t** this people all these words	Jer 16:10	5046
the words that I **t** you,	Jer 19:2	1696
I will **t** you great and mighty things,	Jer 33:3	5046
"**T** us, please, how did you write	Jer 36:17	5046
"If I **t** you, will you not	Jer 38:15	5046
'**T** us now what you said to the	Jer 38:25	5046
that the LORD your God may **t** us	Jer 42:3	5046
I will **t** you the whole message	Jer 42:4	5046
the LORD our God says, **t** us so,	Jer 42:20	5046
in whatever He has sent me to **t**	Jer 42:21	
To **t** the king of Babylon That his	Jer 51:31	5046
and speak to them and **t** them,	Ezk 3:11	559
that they may **t** all their abominations	Ezk 12:16	5608
But **t** them, "The days draw near as	Ezk 12:23	1696
so **t** those who plaster *it* over	Ezk 13:11	559
speak to them and **t** them,	Ezk 14:4	559
"Will you not **t** us what these	Ezk 24:19	5046
to **t** the king his dreams.	Da 2:2	5046
T the dream to your servants, and	Da 2:4	560
king **t** the dream to his servants,	Da 2:7	560
therefore **t** me the dream, that I	Da 2:9	560
now we will **t** its interpretation	Da 2:36	560
t *me* the visions of my dream which	Da 4:9	560
t *me* its interpretation,	Da 4:18	560
issued, and I have come to **t** *you,*	Da 9:23	5046
the words that I am about to **t** you	Da 10:11	1696
I will **t** you what is inscribed in	Da 10:21	5046
"And now I will **t** you the truth.	Da 11:2	5046
T your sons about it, And *let* your	Jl 1:3	5608
And *let* your sons **t** their	Jl 1:3	
Then they said to him, "**T** us, now!	Jon 1:8	5046
which I am going to **t** you."	Jon 3:2	1696
T it not in Gath, Weep not at all.	Mi 1:10	5046
will do no wrong And **t** no lies,	Zph 3:13	1696
lying visions And **t** false dreams;	Zch 10:2	1696
and remain there until I **t** you;	Mt 2:13	*3004*
"See that you **t** no one;	Mt 8:4	*3004*
"What I **t** you in the darkness,	Mt 10:27	*3004*
I **t** you, and one who is more than a	Mt 11:9	*3004*
and warned them not to **t** who He was.	Mt 12:16	*5318*
"But I **t** you that every careless	Mt 12:36	*3004*
t no one that He was the Christ.	Mt 16:20	*3004*
"**T** the vision to no one until the	Mt 17:9	*3004*
to them, **t** it to the church;	Mt 18:17	*3004*
one thing, which if you **t** Me,	Mt 21:24	*3004*
I will also **t** you by what	Mt 21:24	*3004*
"Neither will I **t** you by what	Mt 21:27	*3004*
'**T** those who have been invited,	Mt 22:4	*3004*
"**T** us then, what do You	Mt 22:17	*3004*
all that they **t** you, do and observe	Mt 23:3	*3004*
"**T** us, when will these things happen,	Mt 24:3	*3004*
t us whether You are the Christ,	Mt 26:63	*3004*
nevertheless I **t** you, hereafter	Mt 26:64	*3004*
"Go quickly and **t** His disciples	Mt 28:7	*3004*
And He earnestly warned them not to **t**	Mk 3:12	*5318*
gave them orders not to **t** anyone;	Mk 7:36	*3004*
warned them to **t** no one about Him.	Mk 8:30	*3004*
took the twelve aside and began to **t**	Mk 10:32	*3004*
and *then* I will **t** you by what	Mk 11:29	*3004*
"Nor will I **t** you by what	Mk 11:33	*3004*
"**T** us, when will these things be,	Mk 13:4	*3004*
"But go, **t** His disciples and	Mk 16:7	*3004*
t this stone to become bread."	Lk 4:3	*3004*
And He ordered him to **t** no one,	Lk 5:14	*3004*
to **t** no one what had happened.	Lk 8:56	*3004*
them not to **t** this to anyone,	Lk 9:21	*3004*
Then **t** her to help me."	Lk 10:40	*3004*
"I **t** you, even though he will not	Lk 11:8	*3004*
yes, I **t** you, it shall be charged	Lk 11:51	*3004*
yes, I **t** you, fear Him!	Lk 12:5	*3004*
t my brother to divide the *family*	Lk 12:13	*3004*
but I **t** you, not even Solomon in all	Lk 12:27	*3004*
I **t** you, no, but rather division;	Lk 12:51	*3004*
"I **t** you, no, but unless you	Lk 13:3	*3004*
"I **t** you, no, but unless you	Lk 13:5	*3004*
for many, I **t** you, will seek to	Lk 13:24	*3004*
'I **t** you, I do not know where you	Lk 13:27	*3004*
"Go and **t** that fox,	Lk 13:32	*3004*
'For I **t** you, none of those men	Lk 14:24	*3004*
"I **t** you that in the same way,	Lk 15:7	*3004*
"In the same way, I **t** you,	Lk 15:10	*3004*
"I **t** you, on that night there	Lk 17:34	*3004*
"I **t** you that He will bring about	Lk 18:8	*3004*
"I **t** you, this man went to	Lk 18:14	*3004*
things, Jesus went on to **t** a parable,	Lk 19:11	*3004*
"I **t** you that to everyone who	Lk 19:26	*3004*
"I **t** you, if these become silent,	Lk 19:40	*3004*
"**T** us by what authority You are	Lk 20:2	*3004*
ask you a question, and you **t** Me:	Lk 20:3	*3004*
"Nor will I **t** you by what	Lk 20:8	*3004*
to **t** the people this parable:	Lk 20:9	*3004*
"For I **t** you that this which is	Lk 22:37	*3004*
"If You are the Christ, **t** us."	Lk 22:67	*3004*
"If I **t** you, you will not believe;	Lk 22:67	*3004*
if I **t** you heavenly things?	Jn 3:12	*3004*

If You are the Christ, **t** us plainly." **Jn 10:24** *3004*
"**T** *us* who it is of whom He is **Jn 13:24** *3004*
"But I **t** you the truth, it is to **Jn 16:7** *3004*
will **t** you plainly of the Father. **Jn 16:25** *518*
or did others **t** you about Me?" **Jn 18:34** *3004*
t me where you have laid Him, **Jn 20:15** *3004*
"**T** me whether you sold the land **Ac 5:8** *3004*
"Please **t** *me,* of whom does **Ac 8:34** *3004*
"Therefore do this that we **t** you. **Ac 21:23** *3004*
"**T** me, are you a Roman?" **Ac 22:27** *3004*
since he has something to **t** you." **Ac 23:18** *2980*
"**T** no one that you have notified **Ac 23:22** *1583*
let these men themselves **t** what **Ac 24:20** *3004*
Behold, I **t** you a mystery; **1Co 15:51** *3004*
T me, you who want to be under **Ga 4:21** *3004*
you, and now I **t** you even weeping, **Php 3:18** *3004*
time will fail me if I **t** of Gideon, **Heb 11:32** *1334*
I will **t** you the mystery of the **Rv 17:7** *3004*

TELLING
by not **t** him that he was fleeing. **Gn 31:20** 5046
you treat me so badly by **t** the man **Gn 43:6** 5046
How long will you refrain from **t** **2Sa 2:26** 559
"When you have finished **t** all the **2Sa 11:19** 1696
heavens are **t** of the glory of God; **Ps 19:1** 5608
"Look, the prophets are **t** them, **Jer 14:13** 559
you are **t** a lie about Ishmael." **Jer 40:16** 1696
had finished **t** all the people all **Jer 43:1** 1696
said to Jeremiah, "You are **t** a lie! **Jer 43:2** 1696
the one who was **t** Him and said, **Mt 12:48** *3004*
teaching His disciples and **t** them, **Mk 9:31** *3004*
were sternly **t** him to be quiet, **Mk 10:48** *2008*
And He was also **t** them a parable: **Lk 5:36** *3004*
And He *began* **t** this parable: **Lk 13:6** *3004*
Now He was **t** them a parable to **Lk 18:1** *3004*
were sternly **t** him to be quiet; **Lk 18:39** *2008*
t these things to the apostles. **Lk 24:10** *3004*
While they were **t** these things, **Lk 24:36** *2980*
am **t** you before *it* comes to pass, **Jn 13:19** *3004*
"What is this thing He is **t** us, **Jn 16:17** *3004*
he knows that he is **t** the truth, **Jn 19:35** *3004*
than **t** or hearing something new.) **Ac 17:21** *3004*
t the people to believe in Him who **Ac 19:4** *3004*
and they kept **t** Paul through the **Ac 21:4** *3004*
t them not to circumcise their **Ac 21:21** *3004*
I am **t** the truth in Christ, I am **Ro 9:1** *3004*
your enemy by **t** you the truth? **Ga 4:16** *226*
we *kept* **t** you in advance that we **1Th 3:4** *4302*
you, I was **t** you these things? **2Th 2:5** *3004*
I am **t** the truth, I am not lying **1Tm 2:7** *3004*
t him to give me the little book. **Rv 10:9** *3004*
t those who dwell on the earth to **Rv 13:14** *3004*

TELLS
whatever Sarah **t** you, listen to **Gn 21:12** 559
t the king of Israel the words **2Ki 6:12** 5046
When he goes outside, he **t** it. **Ps 41:6** 1696
who speaks truth **t** what is right, **Pr 12:17** 5046
And he who **t** lies will not escape. **Pr 19:5** 6315
And he who **t** lies will perish. **Pr 19:9** 6315
He hears the oath but **t** nothing. **Pr 29:24** 5046
A father **t** his sons about Your **Is 38:19** 3045
deal with him just as he **t** you." **Jer 39:12** 1696

TEL-MELAH
are those who came up from **T**, **Ezr 2:59** 8528
were they who came up from **T**, **Ne 7:61** 8528

TEMA
Hadad and **T**, Jetur, Naphish and **Gn 25:15** 8485
Mishma, Dumah, Massa, Hadad, **T**, **1Ch 1:30** 8485
"The caravans of **T** looked, The **Jb 6:19** 8485
O inhabitants of the land of **T**, **Is 21:14** 8485
and Dedan, **T**, Buz and all who cut **Jer 25:23** 8485

TEMAH
the sons of Sisera, the sons of **T**, **Ezr 2:53** 8547
the sons of Sisera, the sons of **T**, **Ne 7:55** 8547

TEMAN
The sons of Eliphaz were **T**, **Gn 36:11** 8487
firstborn of Esau, are chief **T**, **Gn 36:15** 8487
chief Kenaz, chief **T**, **Gn 36:42** 8487
The sons of Eliphaz *were* **T**, **1Ch 1:36** 8487
chief Kenaz, chief **T**, **1Ch 1:53** 8487
there no longer any wisdom in **T**? **Jer 49:7** 8487
against the inhabitants of **T**: **Jer 49:20** 8487
of man, set your face toward **T**, **Ezk 20:46** 8487
from **T** even to Dedan they will **Ezk 25:13** 8487
"So I will send fire upon **T** And **Am 1:12** 8487
mighty men will be dismayed, O **T**, **Ob 1:9** 8487
God comes from **T**, And the Holy **Hab 3:3** 8487

TEMANITE
from his own place, Eliphaz the **T**, **Jb 2:11** 8489
Then Eliphaz the **T** answered, **Jb 4:1** 8489
Then Eliphaz the **T** responded, **Jb 15:1** 8489
Then Eliphaz the **T** responded, **Jb 22:1** 8489
the LORD said to Eliphaz the **T**, **Jb 42:7** 8489
So Eliphaz the **T** and Bildad the **Jb 42:9** 8489

TEMANITES
Husham of the land of the **T** **Gn 36:34** 8489
Husham of the land of the **T** **1Ch 1:45** 8489

TEMENI
bore him Ahuzzam, Hepher, **T** and **1Ch 4:6** 8488

TEMPER
A fool always loses his **t**, **Pr 29:11** 7307
If the ruler's **t** rises against **Ec 10:4** 7307

TEMPERATE
the husband of one wife, **t**, **1Tm 3:2** *3524*
not malicious gossips, but **t**, **1Tm 3:11** *3524*
Older men are to be **t**, **Ti 2:2** *3524*

TEMPERS
will be strife, jealousy, angry **t**, **2Co 12:20** *2372*

TEMPEST
"For He bruises me with a **t** And **Jb 9:17** 8183
A **t** steals him away in the night. **Jb 27:20** 5492a
come, Amid the **t** they roll on. **Jb 30:14** 7724b
From the stormy wind *and* **t**." **Ps 55:8** 5591a
So pursue them with Your **t** And **Ps 83:15** 5591a
storm of hail, a **t** of destruction, **Is 28:2** 8178b
With whirlwind and **t** and the flame **Is 29:6** 5591b
forth in wrath, Even a whirling **t**; **Jer 23:19** 5591a
Behold, the **t** of the LORD! **Jer 30:23** 5591b
has gone forth, A sweeping **t**; **Jer 30:23** 5591a
And a storm on the day of **t**. **Am 1:14** 5492a

TEMPESTUOUS
Him, And it is very **t** around Him. **Ps 50:3** 8175a

TEMPLE
"Where is the **t** prostitute who **Gn 38:21** 6945
has been no **t** prostitute here." **Gn 38:21** 6945
has been no **t** prostitute here.' " **Gn 38:22** 6945
him and drove the peg into his **t**, **Jg 4:21** 7541
dead with the tent peg in his **t**. **Jg 4:22** 7541
she shattered and pierced his **t**. **Jg 5:26** 7541
chamber of the **t** of El-berith. **Jg 9:46** 1004
the doorpost of the **t** of the LORD. **1Sa 1:9** 1964
and Samuel was lying down in the **t** **1Sa 3:3** 1964
his weapons in the **t** of Ashtaroth, **1Sa 31:10** 1004
And from His **t** He heard my voice, **2Sa 22:7** 1964
the doors of the **t** of the LORD, **2Ki 18:16** 1964
to bring out of the **t** of the LORD **2Ki 23:4** 1964
chosen, and the **t** of which I said, **2Ki 23:27** 1004
had made in the **t** of the LORD, **2Ki 24:13** 1964
bronze vessels which were used in **t** **2Ki 25:14**
with the three officers of the **t**. **2Ki 25:18** 5592b
the Levites and the **t** servants. **1Ch 9:2** 5411
lived in the chambers *of the* **t** **1Ch 9:33**
the plan of the porch *of the* **t**, **1Ch 28:11**
for the **t** is not for man, but for **1Ch 29:1** 1002
already provided for the holy **t**, **1Ch 29:3** 1004
do *them* all, and to build the **t**, **1Ch 29:19** 1002
the pillars in front of the **t**, **2Ch 3:17** 1964
them and he set them in the **t**, **2Ch 4:7** 1964
tables and placed them in the **t**, **2Ch 4:8** 1964
for he entered the **t** of the LORD **2Ch 26:16** 1964
did not enter the **t** of the LORD. **2Ch 27:2** 1964
they found in the **t** of the LORD **2Ch 29:16** 1964
he had entered the **t** of his god, **2Ch 32:21** 1004
Josiah had set the **t** in order, **2Ch 35:20** 1004
and put them in his **t** at Babylon. **2Ch 36:7** 1964
The **t** servants: the sons of Ziha, **Ezr 2:43** 5411
All the **t** servants and the sons **Ezr 2:58** 5411
and the **t** servants lived in their **Ezr 2:70** 5411
the foundation of the **t** of the LORD **Ezr 3:6** 1964
the workmen in the **t** of God. **Ezr 3:9** 1004
foundation of the **t** of the LORD, **Ezr 3:10** 1964
old men who had seen the first **t**, **Ezr 3:12** 1004
people of the exile were building a **t** **Ezr 4:1** 1964
issued you a decree to rebuild this **t** **Ezr 5:3** 1005
issued you a decree to rebuild this **t** **Ezr 5:9** 1005
rebuilding the **t** that was built many **Ezr 5:11** 1005
who destroyed this **t** and deported **Ezr 5:12** 1005
had taken from the **t** in Jerusalem, **Ezr 5:14** 1965
brought them to the **t** of Babylon, **Ezr 5:14** 1965
Cyrus took from the **t** of Babylon and **Ezr 5:14** 1965
deposit them in the **t** in Jerusalem and **Ezr 5:15** 1965
the **t**, the place where sacrifices are **Ezr 6:3** 1005
Nebuchadnezzar took from the **t** **Ezr 6:5** 1965
places in the **t** in Jerusalem; **Ezr 6:5** 1965
This **t** was completed on the **Ezr 6:15** 1005
for the dedication of this **t** of God **Ezr 6:17** 1005
and the **t** servants went up to **Ezr 7:7** 5411
the **t** servants at the place **Ezr 8:17** 5411
and 220 of the **t** servants, whom **Ezr 8:20** 5411
of the fortress which is by the **t**, **Ne 2:8** 1004
The **t** servants living in Ophel **Ne 3:26** 5411
as far as the house of the **t** servants **Ne 3:31** 5411
in the house of God, within the **t**, **Ne 6:10** 1964
let us close the doors of the **t**, **Ne 6:10** 1964
I go into the **t** to save his life? **Ne 6:11** 1964
The **t** servants: the sons of Ziha, **Ne 7:46** 5411
All the **t** servants and the sons of **Ne 7:60** 5411
of the people, the **t** servants and **Ne 7:73** 5411
the singers, the **t** servants and **Ne 10:28** 5411
the **t** servants and the descendants **Ne 11:3** 5411
who performed the work of the **t**, **Ne 11:12** 1004
the **t** servants were living in Ophel, **Ne 11:21** 5411
were in charge of the **t** servants. **Ne 11:21** 5411
At Your holy **t** I will bow in **Ps 5:7** 1964
The LORD is in His holy **t**; **Ps 11:4** 1964
He heard my voice out of His **t**, **Ps 18:6** 1964
LORD And to meditate in His **t**. **Ps 27:4** 1964
And in His **t** everything says, **Ps 29:9** 1964
O God, In the midst of Your **t**. **Ps 48:9** 1964
goodness of Your house, Your holy **t**. **Ps 65:4** 1964
Because of Your **t** at Jerusalem **Ps 68:29** 1964
They have defiled Your holy **t**; **Ps 79:1** 1964
I will bow down toward Your holy **t** **Ps 138:2** 1964
train of His robe filling the **t**. **Is 6:1** 1964
the **t** was filling with smoke. **Is 6:4** 1004
gone up to the **t** and *to* Dibon, **Is 15:2** 1004
And of the **t**, 'Your foundation will **Is 44:28** 1964
from the city, a voice from the **t**, **Is 66:6** 1964
'This is the **t** of the LORD, the **Jer 7:4** 1964
of the LORD, the **t** of the LORD, **Jer 7:4** 1964
of the LORD, the **t** of the LORD.' **Jer 7:4** 1964
figs set before the **t** of the LORD! **Jer 24:1** 1964
LORD our God, Vengeance for His **t**. **Jer 50:28** 1964
of the LORD, vengeance for His **t**. **Jer 51:11** 1964
bronze vessels which were used in **t** **Jer 52:18**
with the three officers of the **t**. **Jer 52:24** 5592b
the entrance to the **t** of the LORD, **Ezk 8:16** 1964
with their backs to the **t** of the LORD **Ezk 8:16** 1964
been, to the threshold of the **t**. **Ezk 9:3** 1004
the elders who *were* before the **t**. **Ezk 9:6** 1004
"Defile the **t** and fill the courts **Ezk 9:7** 1004
standing on the right side of the **t** **Ezk 10:3** 1004
cherub to the threshold of the **t**, **Ezk 10:4** 1004
the **t** was filled with the cloud and **Ezk 10:4** 1004
departed from the threshold of the **t** **Ezk 10:18** 1004
the outside of the **t** all around, **Ezk 40:5** 1004
priests who keep charge of the **t**; **Ezk 40:45** 1004
the altar was in front of the **t**. **Ezk 40:47** 1004
he brought me to the porch of the **t** **Ezk 40:48** 1004
he measured the wall of the **t**, **Ezk 41:5** 1004
into the wall of the **t** *itself.* **Ezk 41:6** 1004
The side chambers surrounding the **t** **Ezk 41:7**
the structure surrounding the **t** went **Ezk 41:7** 1004
by stages on all sides of the **t**, **Ezk 41:7** 1004
the width of the **t** *increased* as it **Ezk 41:7** 1004
side chambers belonging to the **t** **Ezk 41:9** 1004
all around the **t** on every side. **Ezk 41:10** 1004
Then he measured the **t**, **Ezk 41:13** 1004
Also the width of the front of the **t** **Ezk 41:14** 1004
the length of those facing the **t** *was* **Ezk 42:8** 1964
describe the **t** to the house of Israel, **Ezk 43:10** 1004
his father had taken out of the **t** **Da 5:2** 1965
that had been taken out of the **t**, **Da 5:3** 1965
sacrifices with **t** prostitutes; **Hos 4:14** 6945
look again toward Your holy **t**.' **Jon 2:4** 1964
came to You, Into Your holy **t**. **Jon 2:7** 1964
you, The Lord from His holy **t**. **Mi 1:2** 1964
And the mountain of the **t** *will* **Mi 3:12** 1004
"But the LORD is in His holy **t**. **Hab 2:20** 1964
on that day all who leap on the **t** **Zph 1:9**
bring wood and rebuild the **t**, **Hg 1:8** 1004
saw this **t** in its former glory? **Hg 2:3** 1004
stone was placed on another in the **t** **Hg 2:15** 1964
the **t** of the LORD was founded, **Hg 2:18** 1964
a **t** for her in the land of Shinar; **Zch 5:11** 1004
He will build the **t** of the LORD. **Zch 6:12** 1964
who will build the **t** of the LORD, **Zch 6:13** 1964
a reminder in the **t** of the LORD to **Zch 6:14** 1964
and build the **t** of the LORD." **Zch 6:15** 1964
the end that the **t** might be built. **Zch 8:9** 1964
seek, will suddenly come to His **t**; **Mal 3:1** 1964
stand on the pinnacle of the **t**, **Mt 4:5** *2413*
priests in the **t** break the Sabbath and **Mt 12:5** *2413*
greater than the **t** is here. **Mt 12:6** *2413*
And Jesus entered the **t** and drove **Mt 21:12** *2413*
were buying and selling in the **t**, **Mt 21:12** *2413*
and *the* lame came to Him in the **t**, **Mt 21:14** *2413*
shouting in the **t**, "Hosanna **Mt 21:15** *2413*
When He entered the **t**, **Mt 21:23** *2413*
'Whoever swears by the **t**, **Mt 23:16** *3485*
swears by the gold of the **t** is **Mt 23:16** *3485*
or the **t** that sanctified the gold? **Mt 23:17** *3485*
"And whoever swears by the **t**, **Mt 23:21** *3485*
swears *both* by the **t** and by Him **Mt 23:21** *846*
between the **t** and the altar. **Mt 23:35** *3485*
Jesus came out from the **t** and **Mt 24:1** *2413*
point out the **t** buildings to Him. **Mt 24:1** *2413*
Every day I used to sit in the **t** **Mt 26:55** *2413*
'I am able to destroy the **t** of God **Mt 26:61** *3485*
threw the pieces of silver into the **t** **Mt 27:5** *3485*
to put them into the **t** treasury, **Mt 27:6** *2878b*
"You who *are going to* destroy the **t** **Mt 27:40** *3485*
the veil of the **t** was torn in two **Mt 27:51** *3485*
Jerusalem *and came* into the **t**; **Mk 11:11** *2413*
And He entered the **t** and began to **Mk 11:15** *2413*
were buying and selling in the **t**, **Mk 11:15** *2413*
to carry merchandise through the **t**. **Mk 11:16** *2413*
And as He was walking in the **t**, **Mk 11:27** *2413*
to say, as He taught in the **t**, **Mk 12:35** *2413*
As He was going out of the **t**, **Mk 13:1** *2413*
Mount of Olives opposite the **t**, **Mk 13:3** *2413*
I was with you in the **t** teaching, **Mk 14:49** *2413*
destroy this **t** made with hands, **Mk 14:58** *3485*
You who *are going to* destroy the **t** **Mk 15:29** *3485*
And the veil of the **t** was torn in **Mk 15:38** *3485*
he was chosen by lot to enter the **t** **Lk 1:9** *3485*
wondering at his delay in the **t**. **Lk 1:21** *3485*
he had seen a vision in the **t**; **Lk 1:22** *3485*
he came in the Spirit into the **t**; **Lk 2:27** *2413*
She never left the **t**, **Lk 2:37** *2413*
days they found Him in the **t**, **Lk 2:46** *2413*
stand on the pinnacle of the **t**, **Lk 4:9** *2413*
Two men went up into the **t** to pray, **Lk 18:10** *2413*
Jesus entered the **t** and began to **Lk 19:45** *2413*
He was teaching daily in the **t**; **Lk 19:47** *2413*
He was teaching the people in the **t** **Lk 20:1** *2413*
some were talking about the **t**, **Lk 21:5** *2413*
the day He was teaching in the **t**, **Lk 21:37** *2413*
to Him in the **t** to listen to Him. **Lk 21:38** *2413*
the chief priests and officers of the **t** **Lk 22:52** *2413*
I was with you daily in the **t**, **Lk 22:53** *2413*
the veil of the **t** was torn in two. **Lk 23:45** *3485*
and were continually in the **t** praising **Lk 24:53** *2413*
And He found in the **t** those who **Jn 2:14** *2413*
and drove *them* all out of the **t**, **Jn 2:15** *2413*
"Destroy this **t**, and in three **Jn 2:19** *3485*
forty-six years to build this **t**, **Jn 2:20** *3485*
was speaking of the **t** of His body. **Jn 2:21** *3485*
Jesus found him in the **t** and **Jn 5:14** *2413*
feast Jesus went up into the **t**, **Jn 7:14** *2413*
Jesus cried out in the **t**, **Jn 7:28** *2413*
morning He came again into the **t**, **Jn 8:2** *2413*
treasury, as He taught in the **t**; **Jn 8:20** *2413*
Himself and went out of the **t**. **Jn 8:59** *2413*
Jesus was walking in the **t** in the **Jn 10:23** *2413*

another as they stood in the **t**, Jn 11:56 2413
in synagogues and in the **t**, Jn 18:20 2413
continuing with one mind in the **t**, Ac 2:46 2413
and John were going up to the **t** at Ac 3:1 2413
at the gate of the **t** which is called Ac 3:2 2413
of those who were entering the **t**. Ac 3:2 2413
and John about to go into the **t**, Ac 3:3 2413
and he entered the **t** with them, Ac 3:8 2413
Beautiful Gate of the **t** to *beg* alms, Ac 3:10 2413
and the captain of the **t** *guard* Ac 4:1 2413
and speak in the **t** to the people Ac 5:20 2413
entered into the **t** about daybreak and Ac 5:21 2413
when the captain of the **t** *guard* and Ac 5:24 2413
are standing in the **t** and teaching Ac 5:25 2413
in the **t** and from house to house, Ac 5:42 2413
The priest of Zeus, whose **t** was Ac 14:13
the **t** of the great goddess Artemis Ac 19:27 2413
of the **t** of the great Artemis and Ac 19:35 3511
along with them, went into the **t** giving Ac 21:26 2413
Asia, upon seeing him in the **t**, Ac 21:27 2413
he has even brought Greeks into the **t** Ac 21:28 2413
Paul had brought him into the **t**. Ac 21:29 2413
they dragged him out of the **t**, Ac 21:30 2413
and was praying in the **t**, Ac 22:17 2413
he even tried to desecrate the **t**; Ac 24:6 2413
"Neither in the **t**, Ac 24:12 2413
they found me *occupied* in the **t**, Ac 24:18 2413
against the **t** or against Caesar." Ac 25:8 2413
some Jews seized me in the **t** and Ac 26:21 2413
and the giving of the Law and the **t** Ro 9:4
not know that you are a **t** of God and 1Co 3:16 3485
If any man destroys the **t** of God, 1Co 3:17 3485
him, for the **t** of God is holy, 1Co 3:17 3485
your body is a **t** of the Holy Spirit 1Co 6:19 3485
knowledge, dining in an idol's **t**, 1Co 8:10 1493
services eat the *food* of the **t**, 1Co 9:13 2413
what agreement has the **t** of God 2Co 6:16 3485
we are the **t** of the living God; 2Co 6:16 3485
growing into a holy **t** in the Lord, Eph 2:21 3485
he takes his seat in the **t** of God, 2Th 2:4 3485
him a pillar in the **t** of My God, Rv 3:12 3485
serve Him day and night in His **t**; Rv 7:15 3485
"Get up and measure the **t** of God Rv 11:1 3485
the court which is outside the **t** and Rv 11:2 3485
And the **t** of God which is in Rv 11:19 3485
of His covenant appeared in His **t**, Rv 11:19 3485
another angel came out of the **t**, Rv 14:15 3485
out of the **t** which is in heaven, Rv 14:17 3485
the **t** of the tabernacle of testimony Rv 15:5 3485
seven plagues came out of the **t**, Rv 15:6 3485
And the **t** was filled with smoke Rv 15:8 3485
no one was able to enter the **t** until Rv 15:8 3485
I heard a loud voice from the **t**, Rv 16:1 3485
a loud voice came out of the **t** from Rv 16:17 3485
I saw no **t** in it, for the Lord Rv 21:22 3485
Almighty and the Lamb are its **t**. Rv 21:22 3485

TEMPLES
Your **t** are like a slice of a SS 4:3 7541
"Your **t** are like a slice of a SS 6:7 7541
who clip the hair on their **t**; Jer 9:26 6285
I shall set fire to the **t** of the gods of Jer 43:12 1004
and the **t** of the gods of Egypt he Jer 43:13 1004
My precious treasures to your **t**, Jl 3:5 1964
not dwell in **t** made with hands; Ac 17:24 5499
neither robbers of **t** nor blasphemers Ac 19:37 2417
You who abhor idols, do you rob **t**? Ro 2:22 2416

TEMPORAL
the things which are seen are **t**, 2Co 4:18 4340

TEMPORARY
Judah are staying in **t** shelters, 2Sa 11:11 5521
with the kings in the **t** shelters, 1Ki 20:12 5521
himself drunk in the **t** shelters 1Ki 20:16 5521
no *firm* root in himself, but is *only* **t**, Mt 13:21 4340
in themselves, but are *only* **t**; Mk 4:17 4340

TEMPT
so that Satan will not **t** you 1Co 7:5 3985
and He Himself does not **t** anyone. Jas 1:13 3985

TEMPTATION
'And do not lead us into **t**, Mt 6:13 3986
that you may not enter into **t**; Mt 26:41 3986
that you may not come into **t**; Mk 14:38 3986
the devil had finished every **t**, Lk 4:13 3986
while, and in time of **t** fall away. Lk 8:13 3986
And lead us not into **t**.' " Lk 11:4 3986
Pray that you may not enter into **t**." Lk 22:40 3986
pray that you may not enter into **t**." Lk 22:46 3986
No **t** has overtaken you but such as 1Co 10:13 3986
but with the **t** will provide the 1Co 10:13 3986
those who want to get rich fall into **t** 1Tm 6:9 3986
how to rescue the godly from **t**, 2Pe 2:9 3986

TEMPTED
Again and again they **t** God, Ps 78:41 5254
Yet they **t** and rebelled against Ps 78:56 5254
And **t** God in the desert. Ps 106:14 5254
wilderness to be **t** by the devil. Mt 4:1 3985
forty days being **t** by Satan; Mk 1:13 3985
forty days, being **t** by the devil. Lk 4:2 3985
will not allow you to be **t** beyond 1Co 10:13 3985
so that you too will not be **t**. Ga 6:1 3985
that the tempter might have **t** you, 1Th 3:5 3985
He Himself was **t** in that which He Heb 2:18 3985
come to the aid of those who are **t**. Heb 2:18 3985
been **t** in all things as *we are,* Heb 4:15 3985
were sawn in two, they were **t**, Heb 11:37 3985
Let no one say when he is **t**, Jas 1:13 3985
"I am being **t** by God"; Jas 1:13 3985
for God cannot be **t** by evil, Jas 1:13 551
But each one is **t** when he is Jas 1:14 3985

TEMPTER
And the **t** came and said to Him, Mt 4:3 3985
that the **t** might have tempted you, 1Th 3:5 3985

TEN
were nine hundred and **t** years, Gn 5:14 6235
t years in the land of Canaan, Gn 16:3 6235
suppose **t** are found there?" Gn 18:32 6235
destroy *it* on account of the **t**." Gn 18:32 6235
Then the servant took **t** camels Gn 24:10 6235
wrists weighing **t** shekels in gold, Gn 24:22 6235
stay with us *a few* days, say **t**; Gn 24:55 6218
Become thousands of **t** thousands, Gn 24:60 7233
me and changed my wages **t** times; Gn 31:7 6235
and you changed my wages **t** times. Gn 31:41 6235
colts, forty cows and **t** bulls, Gn 32:15 6235
female donkeys and **t** male donkeys. Gn 32:15 6235
Then **t** brothers of Joseph went Gn 42:3 6235
t donkeys loaded with the best Gn 45:23 6235
and **t** female donkeys loaded with Gn 45:23 6235
lived one hundred and **t** years. Gn 50:22 6235
age of one hundred and **t** years; Gn 50:26 6235
make the tabernacle with **t** curtains Ex 26:1 6235
"**T** cubits *shall be* the length of Ex 26:16 6235
t pillars and their ten sockets. Ex 27:12 6235
ten pillars and their **t** sockets. Ex 27:12 6235
the covenant, the **T** Commandments. Ex 34:28 6235
the tabernacle with **t** curtains; Ex 36:8 6235
T cubits *was* the length of each Ex 36:21 6235
t pillars and their ten sockets; Ex 38:12 6235
ten pillars and their **t** sockets; Ex 38:12 6235
of you will chase **t** thousand, Lv 26:8 7233
t women will bake your bread in Lv 26:26 6235
and for the female **t** shekels. Lv 27:5 6235
and for the female **t** shekels. Lv 27:7 6235
one gold pan of **t** *shekels,* full of Nu 7:14 6235
one gold pan of **t** *shekels,* full of Nu 7:20 6235
one gold pan of **t** *shekels,* full of Nu 7:26 6235
one gold pan of **t** *shekels,* full of Nu 7:32 6235
one gold pan of **t** *shekels,* full of Nu 7:38 6235
one gold pan of **t** *shekels,* full of Nu 7:44 6235
one gold pan of **t** *shekels,* full of Nu 7:50 6235
one gold pan of **t** *shekels,* full of Nu 7:56 6235
one gold pan of **t** *shekels,* full of Nu 7:62 6235
one gold pan of **t** *shekels,* full of Nu 7:68 6235
one gold pan of **t** *shekels,* full of Nu 7:74 6235
one gold pan of **t** *shekels,* full of Nu 7:80 6235
weighing **t** *shekels* apiece, Nu 7:86 6235
days, nor five days, nor **t** days, Nu 11:19 6235
gathered least gathered **t** homers) Nu 11:32 6235
have put Me to the test these **t** times Nu 14:22 6235
t bulls, two rams, fourteen male Nu 29:23 6235
the **T** Commandments; and He wrote Dt 4:13 6235
the **T** Commandments which the LORD Dt 10:4 6235
And two put **t** thousand to flight, Dt 32:30 7233
the midst of **t** thousand holy ones; Dt 33:2 7233
are the **t** thousands of Ephraim, Dt 33:17 7233
t cities with their villages. Jos 15:57 6235
there fell **t** portions to Manasseh, Jos 17:5 6235
the sons of Kohath received **t** cities Jos 21:5 6235
rest of the sons of Kohath were **t**. Jos 21:26 6235
and with him **t** chiefs, one chief Jos 22:14 6235
being one hundred and **t** years old. Jos 24:29 6235
defeated **t** thousand men at Bezek. Jg 1:4 6235
at the age of one hundred and **t**. Jg 2:8 6235
time about **t** thousand Moabites, Jg 3:29 6235
and take with you **t** thousand men Jg 4:6 6235
t thousand men went up with him; Jg 4:10 6235
with **t** thousand men following him. Jg 4:14 6235
Gideon took **t** men of his servants Jg 6:27 6235
and he judged Israel **t** years. Jg 12:11 6235
and I will give you **t** *pieces* of silver Jg 17:10 6235
When **t** thousand choice men from Jg 20:34 6235
they lived there about **t** years. Ru 1:4 6235
took **t** men of the elders of the city Ru 4:2 6235
Am I not better to you than **t** sons? 1Sa 1:8 6235
roasted grain and these **t** loaves and 1Sa 17:17 6235
"Bring also these **t** cuts of cheese 1Sa 17:18 6235
And David his **t** thousands." 1Sa 18:7 7233
ascribed to David **t** thousands, 1Sa 18:8 7233
And David his **t** thousands'?" 1Sa 21:11 7233
So David sent **t** young men; and 1Sa 25:5 6235
About **t** days later, the 1Sa 25:38 6235
And David his **t** thousands'?" 1Sa 29:5 7233
t concubines to keep the house. 2Sa 15:16 6235
you are worth **t** thousand of us; 2Sa 18:3 6235
t *pieces* of silver and a belt." 2Sa 18:11 6235
And **t** young men who carried Joab's 2Sa 18:15 6235
"We have **t** parts in the king, 2Sa 19:43 6235
and the king took the **t** women, 2Sa 20:3 6235
t fat oxen, twenty pasture-fed 1Ki 4:23 6235
front of the house *was* **t** cubits. 1Ki 6:3 6235
of olive wood, each **t** cubits high. 1Ki 6:23 6235
of the other wing *were* **t** cubits. 1Ki 6:24 6235
The other cherub *was* **t** cubits; 1Ki 6:25 6235
of the one cherub *was* **t** cubits, 1Ki 6:26 6235
stones of **t** cubits and stones of 1Ki 7:10 6235
metal **t** cubits from brim to brim, 1Ki 7:23 6235
around encircling it **t** to a cubit, 1Ki 7:24 6235
he made the **t** stands of bronze; 1Ki 7:27 6235
He made the **t** stands like this: 1Ki 7:37 6235
He made **t** basins of bronze, 1Ki 7:38 6235
each of the **t** stands *was* one basin. 1Ki 7:38 6235
and the **t** stands with the ten 1Ki 7:43 6235
with the **t** basins on the stands; 1Ki 7:43 6235
"Take for yourself **t** pieces; 1Ki 11:31 6235
of Solomon and give you **t** tribes 1Ki 11:31 6235
and give it to you, *even* **t** tribes. 1Ki 11:35 6235
"Take **t** loaves with you, *some* 1Ki 14:3 6235
and took with him **t** talents of silver 2Ki 5:5 6235
of gold and **t** changes of clothes. 2Ki 5:5 6235
and **t** chariots and 10,000 footmen, 2Ki 13:7 6235
and reigned **t** years in Samaria. 2Ki 15:17 6235
shall the shadow go forward **t** steps 2Ki 20:9 6235
ten steps or go back **t** steps?" 2Ki 20:9 6235
for the shadow to decline **t** steps; 2Ki 20:10 6235
shadow turn backward **t** steps." 2Ki 20:10 6235
shadow on the stairway back **t** steps 2Ki 20:11 6235
men of valor, **t** thousand captives, 2Ki 24:14 6235
came with **t** men and struck 2Ki 25:25 6235
the half of Manasseh, **t** cities. 1Ch 6:61 6235
in width and **t** cubits in height. 2Ch 4:1 6235
sea, **t** cubits from brim to brim, 2Ch 4:2 6235
it *and* all around it, **t** cubits, 2Ch 4:3 6235
made **t** basins in which to wash, 2Ch 4:6 6235
he made the **t** golden lampstands 2Ch 4:7 6235
He also made **t** tables and placed 2Ch 4:8 6235
land was undisturbed for **t** years 2Ch 14:1 6235
t thousand kors of wheat and ten 2Ch 27:5 6235
of wheat and **t** thousand of barley. 2Ch 27:5 6235
he reigned three months and **t** days 2Ch 36:9 6235
and with them **t** of their brothers; Ezr 8:24 6235
them came and told us **t** times, Ne 4:12 6235
and once in **t** days all sorts of Ne 5:18 6235
one out of **t** to live in Jerusalem, Ne 11:1 6235
and I will pay **t** thousand talents Es 3:9 6235
the **t** sons of Haman the son of Es 9:10 6235
t sons of Haman at the citadel in Susa. Es 9:12 6235
let Haman's **t** sons be hanged on Es 9:13 6235
and Haman's **t** sons were hanged. Es 9:14 6235
t times you have insulted me; Jb 19:3 6235
I will not be afraid of **t** thousands Ps 3:6 7233
to Him with a harp of **t** strings. Ps 33:2 6218
And **t** thousand at your right hand, Ps 91:7 7233
Upon a harp of **t** strings I will Ps 144:9 6218
and **t** thousands in our fields; Ps 144:13 7232a
a wise man more than **t** rulers who Ec 7:19 6235
Outstanding among **t** thousand. SS 5:10 7233
"For **t** acres of vineyard will Is 5:10 6235
of Ahaz, to go back **t** steps." Is 38:8 6235
the sun's *shadow* went back **t** steps Is 38:8 6235
of the king, along with **t** men, Jer 41:1 6235
the son of Nethaniah and the **t** men Jer 41:2 6235
But **t** men who were found among Jer 41:8 6235
at the end of **t** days Jer 42:7 6235
width of the gateway, **t** cubits, Ezk 40:11 6235
width of the entrance *was* **t** cubits and Ezk 41:2 6235
was an inner walk **t** cubits wide, Ezk 42:4 6235
kor (*which is* **t** baths *or* a homer, Ezk 45:14 6235
a homer, for **t** baths are a homer); Ezk 45:14 6235
test your servants for **t** days, Da 1:12 6235
matter and tested them for **t** days. Da 1:14 6235
At the end of **t** days their Da 1:15 6235
he found them **t** times better than Da 1:20 6235
before it, and it had **t** horns. Da 7:7 6236
the **t** horns that *were* on its head and Da 7:20 6236
'As for the **t** horns, out of this Da 7:24 6236
this kingdom **t** kings will arise; Da 7:24 6236
him **t** thousand *precepts* of My law, Hos 8:12 7239
Will have **t** left to the house of Israel Am 5:3 6235
if **t** men are left in one house, Am 6:9 6235
rams, In **t** thousand rivers of oil? Mi 6:7 7233
measures, there would be only **t**; Hg 2:16 6235
cubits and its width **t** cubits." Zch 5:2 6235
'In those days **t** men from all the Zch 8:23 6235
who owed him **t** thousand talents was Mt 18:24 3463
the **t** became indignant with the Mt 20:24 1176
will be comparable to **t** virgins, Mt 25:1 1176
to the one who has the **t** talents.' Mt 25:28 1176
the **t** began to feel indignant with Mk 10:41 1176
strong enough with **t** thousand *men* Lk 14:31 1176
if she has **t** silver coins and Lk 15:8 1176
t leprous men who stood at a Lk 17:12 1176
"Were there not **t** cleansed? Lk 17:17 1176
"And he called **t** of his slaves, Lk 19:13 1176
his slaves, and gave them **t** minas and Lk 19:13 1176
your mina has made **t** minas more.' Lk 19:16 1176
be in authority over **t** cities.' Lk 19:17 1176
to the one who has the **t** minas.' Lk 19:24 1176
'Master, he has **t** minas *already.*' Lk 19:25 1176
than eight or **t** days among them, Ac 25:6 1176
than **t** thousand words in a tongue. 1Co 14:19 3463
you will have tribulation for **t** days. Rv 2:10 1176
having seven heads and **t** horns, Rv 12:3 1176
having **t** horns and seven heads, Rv 13:1 1176
and on his horns *were* **t** diadems, Rv 13:1 1176
having seven heads and **t** horns. Rv 17:3 1176
the seven heads and the **t** horns. Rv 17:7 1176
"The **t** horns which you saw Rv 17:12 1176
horns which you saw are **t** kings who Rv 17:12 1176
"And the **t** horns which you saw, Rv 17:16 1176

TENANTS
are sojourners before You, and **t**, 1Ch 29:15 8453

TEND
to **t** his father's flock at Bethlehem. 1Sa 17:15 7462a
Like a shepherd He will **t** His flock, Is 40:11 7462a
over them and they will **t** them; Jer 23:4 7462a
He said to him, "**T** My lambs." Jn 21:15 1006
Jesus said to him, "**T** My sheep. Jn 21:17 1006

TENDER
and took a **t** and choice calf and Gn 18:7 7390
When the **t** grass *springs* out of 2Sa 23:4 1877
because your heart was **t** and you 2Ki 22:19 7401
"Because your heart was **t** and you 2Ch 34:27 7401
T and the only son in the sight of Pr 4:3 7390
is withered, the **t** grass died out, Is 15:6 1877
you shall no longer be called **t** and Is 47:1 7390
grew up before Him like a **t** shoot, Is 53:2 3126

of its young twigs a **t** one and **Ezk 17:22** 7390
its branch has already become **t** and **Mt 24:32** *527*
its branch has already become **t** and **Mk 13:28** *527*
Because of the **t** mercy of our God, **Lk 1:78** *4698*

TENDER-HEARTED
Be kind to one another, **t**, **Eph 4:32** *2155*

TENDERLY
loved the girl and spoke **t** to her. **Gn 34:3** 3820
and went after her to speak **t** to her **Jg 19:3** 3820
a nursing *mother* **t** cares for her own **1Th 2:7** *2282*

TENDING
and behold, he is **t** the sheep." **1Sa 16:11** 7462a
servant was **t** his father's sheep. **1Sa 17:34** 7462a
we were with them **t** the sheep. **1Sa 25:16** 7462a
the shepherds who are **t** My people: **Jer 23:2** 7462a
having a slave plowing or **t** sheep, **Lk 17:7** *4165*

TENDRILS
Its **t** spread themselves out *and* **Is 16:8** 7976
Your **t** stretched across the sea, **Jer 48:32** 5189

TENDS
He who **t** the fig tree will eat its **Pr 27:18** 5341
Or who **t** a flock and does not use **1Co 9:7** *4165*

TENONS
shall be two **t** for each board, **Ex 26:17** 3027
sockets under one board for its two **t** **Ex 26:19** 3027
under another board for its two **t**; **Ex 26:19** 3027
There were two **t** for each board, **Ex 36:22** 3027
sockets under one board for its two **t** **Ex 36:24** 3027
under another board for its two **t**. **Ex 36:24** 3027

TENS
of hundreds, of fifties and of **t**. **Ex 18:21** 6235
of hundreds, of fifties and of **t**. **Ex 18:25** 6235
of hundreds, of fifties and of **t**, **Dt 1:15** 6235
will cause **t** of thousands to fall; **Da 11:12** 7239

TEN-STRINGED
With the **t** lute and with the harp **Ps 92:3** 6218

TENT
uncovered himself inside his **t**. **Gn 9:21** 168
east of Bethel, and pitched his **t**, **Gn 12:8** 168
his **t** had been at the beginning, **Gn 13:3** 168
Then Abram moved his **t** and came **Gn 13:18** 167
while he was sitting at the **t** door in **Gn 18:1** 168
ran from the **t** door to meet them and **Gn 18:2** 168
hurried into the **t** to Sarah, **Gn 18:6** 168
"There, in the **t**." **Gn 18:9** 168
Sarah was listening at the **t** door, **Gn 18:10** 168
her into his mother Sarah's **t**, **Gn 24:67** 168
the LORD, and pitched his **t** there; **Gn 26:25** 168
Jacob had pitched his **t** in the hill **Gn 31:25** 168
So Laban went into Jacob's **t** and **Gn 31:33** 168
Jacob's tent and into Leah's **t** **Gn 31:33** 168
and into the **t** of the two maids, **Gn 31:33** 168
he went out of Leah's **t** and entered **Gn 31:33** 168
Leah's tent and entered Rachel's **t**. **Gn 31:33** 168
And Laban felt through all the **t** but **Gn 31:34** 168
land where he had pitched his **t** **Gn 33:19** 168
and pitched his **t** beyond the tower **Gn 35:21** 168
each of you has in his **t**.' " **Ex 16:16** 168
welfare and went into the **t**. **Ex 18:7** 168
hair for a **t** over the tabernacle; **Ex 26:7** 168
curtain at the front of the **t**. **Ex 26:9** 168
the loops and join the **t** together so **Ex 26:11** 168
over in the curtains of the **t**, **Ex 26:12** 168
length of the curtains of the **t**, **Ex 26:13** 168
You shall make a covering for the **t** **Ex 26:14** 168
a screen for the doorway of the **t** **Ex 26:36** 168
"In the **t** of meeting, outside the **Ex 27:21** 168
when they enter the **t** of meeting, **Ex 28:43** 168
the doorway of the **t** of meeting and **Ex 29:4** 168
the bull before the **t** of meeting, **Ex 29:10** 168
the doorway of the **t** of meeting. **Ex 29:11** 168
when he enters the **t** of meeting **Ex 29:30** 168
the doorway of the **t** of meeting. **Ex 29:32** 168
the **t** of meeting before the LORD, **Ex 29:42** 168
the **t** of meeting and the altar; **Ex 29:44** 168
the service of the **t** of meeting, **Ex 30:16** 168
the **t** of meeting and the altar, **Ex 30:18** 168
when they enter the **t** of meeting, **Ex 30:20** 168
you shall anoint the **t** of meeting **Ex 30:26** 168
the testimony in the **t** of meeting where **Ex 30:36** 168
the **t** of meeting, and the ark of **Ex 31:7** 168
and all the furniture of the **t**, **Ex 31:7** 168
Moses used to take the **t** and pitch **Ex 33:7** 168
and he called it the **t** of meeting. **Ex 33:7** 168
would go out to the **t** of meeting **Ex 33:7** 168
whenever Moses went out to the **t**, **Ex 33:8** 168
each at the entrance of his **t**, **Ex 33:8** 168
Moses until he entered the **t**. **Ex 33:8** 168
Whenever Moses entered the **t**, **Ex 33:9** 168
stand at the entrance of the **t**; **Ex 33:9** 168
standing at the entrance of the **t**, **Ex 33:10** 168
each at the entrance of his **t**. **Ex 33:10** 168
man, would not depart from the **t**. **Ex 33:11** 168
its **t** and its covering, **Ex 35:11** 168
for the work of the **t** of meeting **Ex 35:21** 168
hair for a **t** over the tabernacle; **Ex 36:14** 168
of bronze to join the **t** together so **Ex 36:18** 168
for the **t** of rams' skins dyed red, **Ex 36:19** 168
a screen for the doorway of the **t**, **Ex 36:37** 168
the doorway of the **t** of meeting. **Ex 38:8** 168
the doorway of the **t** of meeting, **Ex 38:30** 168
the tabernacle of the **t** of meeting **Ex 39:32** 168
the **t** and all its furnishings: **Ex 39:33** 168
the veil for the doorway of the **t**; **Ex 39:38** 168
tabernacle, for the **t** of meeting; **Ex 39:40** 168
tabernacle of the **t** of meeting. **Ex 40:2** 168
tabernacle of the **t** of meeting. **Ex 40:6** 168
the **t** of meeting and the altar and **Ex 40:7** 168
to the doorway of the **t** of meeting **Ex 40:12** 168
He spread the **t** over the **Ex 40:19** 168
covering of the **t** on top of it, **Ex 40:19** 168
put the table in the **t** of meeting on **Ex 40:22** 168
the lampstand in the **t** of meeting, **Ex 40:24** 168
the gold altar in the **t** of meeting **Ex 40:26** 168
tabernacle of the **t** of meeting, **Ex 40:29** 168
the **t** of meeting and the altar and **Ex 40:30** 168
they entered the **t** of meeting, **Ex 40:32** 168
cloud covered the **t** of meeting, **Ex 40:34** 168
not able to enter the **t** of meeting **Ex 40:35** 168
spoke to him from the **t** of meeting, **Lv 1:1** 168
the doorway of the **t** of meeting, **Lv 1:3** 168
the doorway of the **t** of meeting. **Lv 1:5** 168
the doorway of the **t** of meeting, **Lv 3:2** 168
slay it before the **t** of meeting, **Lv 3:8** 168
slay it before the **t** of meeting, **Lv 3:13** 168
the **t** of meeting before the LORD, **Lv 4:4** 168
and bring it to the **t** of meeting, **Lv 4:5** 168
the LORD in the **t** of meeting; **Lv 4:7** 168
the doorway of the **t** of meeting. **Lv 4:7** 168
bring it before the **t** of meeting. **Lv 4:14** 168
of the bull to the **t** of meeting; **Lv 4:16** 168
the LORD in the **t** of meeting; **Lv 4:18** 168
the doorway of the **t** of meeting. **Lv 4:18** 168
in the court of the **t** of meeting. **Lv 6:16** 168
in the court of the **t** of meeting. **Lv 6:26** 168
blood is brought into the **t** of meeting **Lv 6:30** 168
the doorway of the **t** of meeting." **Lv 8:3** 168
the doorway of the **t** of meeting, **Lv 8:4** 168
the doorway of the **t** of meeting, **Lv 8:31** 168
the doorway of the **t** of meeting **Lv 8:33** 168
the doorway of the **t** of meeting, **Lv 8:35** 168
to the front of the **t** of meeting, **Lv 9:5** 168
Aaron went into the **t** of meeting. **Lv 9:23** 168
the doorway of the **t** of meeting, **Lv 10:7** 168
you come into the **t** of meeting, **Lv 10:9** 168
the doorway of the **t** of meeting a **Lv 12:6** 168
stay outside his **t** for seven days. **Lv 14:8** 168
the doorway of the **t** of meeting. **Lv 14:11** 168
the doorway of the **t** of meeting, **Lv 14:23** 168
the doorway of the **t** of meeting and **Lv 15:14** 168
the doorway of the **t** of meeting. **Lv 15:29** 168
the doorway of the **t** of meeting. **Lv 16:7** 168
thus he shall do for the **t** of meeting **Lv 16:16** 168
no one shall be in the **t** of meeting **Lv 16:17** 168
the **t** of meeting and the altar, **Lv 16:20** 168
shall come into the **t** of meeting and **Lv 16:23** 168
t of meeting and for the altar. **Lv 16:33** 168
it to the doorway of the **t** of meeting **Lv 17:4** 168
at the doorway of the **t** of meeting **Lv 17:5** 168
the doorway of the **t** of meeting, **Lv 17:6** 168
doorway of the **t** of meeting to offer **Lv 17:9** 168
the doorway of the **t** of meeting, **Lv 19:21** 168
of testimony in the **t** of meeting, **Lv 24:3** 168
of Sinai, in the **t** of meeting, **Nu 1:1** 168
shall camp around the **t** of meeting **Nu 2:2** 168
"Then the **t** of meeting shall set **Nu 2:17** 168
before the **t** of meeting, **Nu 3:7** 168
furnishings of the **t** of meeting, **Nu 3:8** 168
sons of Gershon in the **t** of meeting **Nu 3:25** 168
involved the tabernacle and the **t**, **Nu 3:25** 168
the doorway of the **t** of meeting, **Nu 3:25** 168
t of meeting toward the sunrise, **Nu 3:38** 168
do the work in the **t** of meeting. **Nu 4:3** 168
of Kohath in the **t** of meeting, **Nu 4:4** 168
are the things in the **t** of meeting **Nu 4:15** 168
do the work in the **t** of meeting. **Nu 4:23** 168
the **t** of meeting *with* its covering **Nu 4:25** 168
the doorway of the **t** of meeting, **Nu 4:25** 168
Gershonites in the **t** of meeting, **Nu 4:28** 168
do the work of the **t** of meeting. **Nu 4:30** 168
their service in the **t** of meeting: **Nu 4:31** 168
their service in the **t** of meeting, **Nu 4:33** 168
for work in the **t** of meeting. **Nu 4:35** 168
was serving in the **t** of meeting, **Nu 4:37** 168
for work in the **t** of meeting. **Nu 4:39** 168
was serving in the **t** of meeting, **Nu 4:41** 168
for work in the **t** of meeting. **Nu 4:43** 168
of carrying in the **t** of meeting. **Nu 4:47** 168
the doorway of the **t** of meeting. **Nu 6:10** 168
the doorway of the **t** of meeting, **Nu 6:13** 168
the doorway of the **t** of meeting, **Nu 6:18** 168
the service of the **t** of meeting, **Nu 7:5** 168
went into the **t** of meeting **Nu 7:89** 168
Levites before the **t** of meeting. **Nu 8:9** 168
go in to serve the **t** of meeting. **Nu 8:15** 168
of Israel at the **t** of meeting and **Nu 8:19** 168
in the **t** of meeting before Aaron and **Nu 8:22** 168
in the work of the **t** of meeting. **Nu 8:24** 168
brothers in the **t** of meeting, **Nu 8:26** 168
the **t** of the testimony, **Nu 9:15** 168
cloud was lifted from over the **t**, **Nu 9:17** 168
the doorway of the **t** of meeting. **Nu 10:3** 168
each man at the doorway of his **t**; **Nu 11:10** 168
bring them to the **t** of meeting, **Nu 11:16** 168
and stationed them around the **t**. **Nu 11:24** 168
but had not gone out to the **t**), **Nu 11:26** 168
come out to the **t** of meeting." **Nu 12:4** 168
and stood at the doorway of the **t**, **Nu 12:5** 168
had withdrawn from over the **t**, **Nu 12:10** 168
LORD appeared in the **t** of meeting **Nu 14:10** 168
the doorway of the **t** of meeting, **Nu 16:18** 168
the doorway of the **t** of meeting. **Nu 16:19** 168
turned toward the **t** of meeting, **Nu 16:42** 168
to the front of the **t** of meeting, **Nu 16:43** 168
the doorway of the **t** of meeting, **Nu 16:50** 168
then deposit them in the **t** of meeting **Nu 17:4** 168
LORD in the **t** of the testimony. **Nu 17:7** 168
went into the **t** of the testimony; **Nu 17:8** 168
are before the **t** of the testimony. **Nu 18:2** 168
and the obligation of all the **t**, **Nu 18:3** 168
obligations of the **t** of meeting, **Nu 18:4** 168
for all the service of the **t**; **Nu 18:4** 168
the service for the **t** of meeting. **Nu 18:6** 168
the service of the **t** of meeting. **Nu 18:21** 168
come near the **t** of meeting again, **Nu 18:22** 168
the service of the **t** of meeting, **Nu 18:23** 168
your service in the **t** of meeting. **Nu 18:31** 168
toward the front of the **t** of meeting **Nu 19:4** 168
is the law when a man dies in a **t**: **Nu 19:14** 168
everyone who comes into the **t** and **Nu 19:14** 168
who is in the **t** shall be unclean **Nu 19:14** 168
and sprinkle *it* on the **t** and on **Nu 19:18** 168
the doorway of the **t** of meeting and **Nu 20:6** 168
the doorway of the **t** of meeting. **Nu 25:6** 168
the man of Israel into the **t** and **Nu 25:8** 6898
the doorway of the **t** of meeting, **Nu 27:2** 168
and brought it to the **t** of meeting **Nu 31:54** 168
yourselves at the **t** of meeting, **Dt 31:14** 168
themselves at the **t** of meeting. **Dt 31:14** 168
in the **t** in a pillar of cloud, **Dt 31:15** 168
stood at the doorway of the **t**. **Dt 31:15** 168
concealed in the earth inside my **t** **Jos 7:21** 168
messengers, and they ran to the **t**; **Jos 7:22** 168
it was concealed in his **t** with the **Jos 7:22** 168
They took them from inside the **t** **Jos 7:23** 168
t and all that belonged to him; **Jos 7:24** 168
and set up the **t** of meeting there; **Jos 18:1** 168
the doorway of the **t** of meeting. **Jos 19:51** 168
and had pitched his **t** as far away **Jg 4:11** 168
fled away on foot to the **t** of Jael **Jg 4:17** 168
he turned aside to her into the **t**, **Jg 4:18** 168
"Stand in the doorway of the **t**, **Jg 4:20** 168
took a **t** peg and seized a hammer **Jg 4:21** 168
dead with the **t** peg in his temple. **Jg 4:22** 3489
blessed is she of women in the **t**. **Jg 5:24** 168
out her hand for the **t** peg, **Jg 5:26** 3489
men of Israel, each to his **t**, **Jg 7:8** 168
it came to the **t** and struck it so **Jg 7:13** 168
down so that the **t** lay flat." **Jg 7:13** 168
"Not one of us will go to his **t**, **Jg 20:8** 168
the doorway of the **t** of meeting. **1Sa 2:22** 168
and every man fled to his **t**; **1Sa 4:10** 168
rest of the people, each to his **t**. **1Sa 13:2** 168
but he put his weapons in his **t**. **1Sa 17:54** 168
set it in its place inside the **t** which **2Sa 6:17** 168
ark of God dwells within **t** curtains. **2Sa 7:2** 3407
I have been moving about in a **t**, **2Sa 7:6** 168
a **t** for Absalom on the roof, **2Sa 16:22** 168
all Israel fled, each to his **t**. **2Sa 18:17** 168
Israel had fled, each to his **t**. **2Sa 19:8** 168
from the city, each to his **t**. **2Sa 20:22** 168
then took the horn of oil from the **t** **1Ki 1:39** 168
And Joab fled to the **t** of the LORD **1Ki 2:28** 168
Joab had fled to the **t** of the LORD, **1Ki 2:29** 168
Benaiah came to the **t** of the LORD and **1Ki 2:30** 168
ark of the LORD and the **t** of meeting **1Ki 8:4** 168
utensils, which were in the **t**, **1Ki 8:4** 168
entered one **t** and ate and drank, **2Ki 7:8** 168
they returned and entered another **t** **2Ki 7:8** 168
and they fled each to his **t**. **2Ki 14:12** 168
tabernacle of the **t** of meeting, **1Ch 6:32** 168
keepers of the thresholds of the **t**; **1Ch 9:19** 168
the entrance of the **t** of meeting. **1Ch 9:21** 168
the LORD, *even* the house of the **t**, **1Ch 9:23** 168
of God and pitched a **t** for it. **1Ch 15:1** 168
ark of God and placed it inside the **t** **1Ch 16:1** 168
but I have gone from **t** to tent and **1Ch 17:5** 168
but I have gone from tent to **t** and **1Ch 17:5** 168
keep charge of the **t** of meeting, **1Ch 23:32** 168
for God's **t** of meeting was there, **2Ch 1:3** 168
pitched a **t** for it in Jerusalem. **2Ch 1:4** 168
which *was* at the **t** of meeting, **2Ch 1:6** 168
at Gibeon, from the **t** of meeting, **2Ch 1:13** 168
the ark and the **t** of meeting and all **2Ch 5:5** 168
holy utensils which *were* in the **t**; **2Ch 5:5** 168
for the **t** of the testimony?" **2Ch 24:6** 168
and they fled each to his **t**. **2Ch 25:22** 168
will know that your **t** is secure, **Jb 5:24** 168
t of the wicked will be no longer." **Jb 8:22** 168
"The light in his **t** is darkened, **Jb 18:6** 168
torn from the security of his **t**, **Jb 18:14** 168
dwells in his **t** nothing of his; **Jb 18:15** 168
against me And camp around my **t**. **Jb 19:12** 168
consume the survivor in his **t**. **Jb 20:26** 168
the nobleman, And where is the **t**, **Jb 21:28** 168
unrighteousness far from your **t**, **Jb 22:23** 168
friendship of God *was* over my **t**; **Jb 29:4** 168
"Have the men of my **t** not said, **Jb 31:31** 168
O Lord, who may abide in Your **t**? **Ps 15:1** 168
He has placed a **t** for the sun, **Ps 19:4** 168
In the secret place of His **t** He will **Ps 27:5** 168
And I will offer in His **t** sacrifices **Ps 27:6** 168
up and tear you away from *your* **t**, **Ps 52:5** 168
Let me dwell in Your **t** forever; **Ps 61:4** 168
The **t** which He had pitched among **Ps 78:60** 168
He also rejected the **t** of Joseph, **Ps 78:67** 168
will any plague come near your **t**. **Ps 91:10** 168
Stretching out heaven like a **t** **Ps 104:2**
t of the upright will flourish. **Pr 14:11** 168
Nor will the Arab pitch *his* **t** there, **Is 13:20** 167
in faithfulness in the **t** of David; **Is 16:5** 168
A **t** which will not be folded **Is 33:20** 168
"Like a shepherd's **t** my dwelling **Is 38:12** 168
spreads them out like a **t** to dwell in. **Is 40:22** 168
"Enlarge the place of your **t**; **Is 54:2** 168

My **t** is destroyed, And all my **Jer 10:20** 168
There is no one to stretch out my **t** **Jer 10:20** 168
a traveler who has pitched his **t** **Jer 14:8** 168
among them, each man in his **t**, **Jer 37:10** 168
for themselves Their **t** curtains, **Jer 49:29** 3407
In the **t** of the daughter of Zion **La 2:4** 168
The **t** curtains of the land of **Hab 3:7** 3407
cornerstone, From them the **t** peg, **Zch 10:4** 3489
if the earthly **t** which is our house **2Co 5:1** *4636*
For indeed while we are in this **t**, **2Co 5:4** *4636*

TENT-CORD
their **t** plucked up within them? **Jb 4:21** 3499b

TENTH
steadily until the **t** month; **Gn 8:5** 6224
in the **t** month, on the first day **Gn 8:5** 6224
He gave him a **t** of all. **Gn 14:20** 4643
I will surely give a **t** to You." **Gn 28:22** 6237
'On the **t** of this month they are **Ex 12:3** 6218
(Now an omer is a **t** of an ephah.) **Ex 16:36** 6224
he shall bring the **t** of an ephah **Lv 5:11** 6224
the **t** of an ephah of fine flour as **Lv 6:20** 6224
month, on the **t** day of the month, **Lv 16:29** 6218
the **t** day of this seventh month is **Lv 23:27** 6218
on the **t** day of the seventh month; **Lv 25:9** 6218
For every **t** part of herd or flock, **Lv 27:32** 4643
t one shall be holy to the LORD. **Lv 27:32** 6224
On the **t** day *it was* Ahiezer the **Nu 7:66** 6224
also a **t** of an ephah of fine flour **Nu 28:5** 6224
and a **t** *of an ephah* of fine flour **Nu 28:13** 6241
'A **t** *of an ephah* you shall offer **Nu 28:21** 6241
a **t** for each of the seven lambs; **Nu 28:29** 6241
on the **t** day of this seventh month **Nu 29:7** 6218
a **t** for each of the seven lambs; **Nu 29:10** 6241
and a **t** for each of the fourteen **Nu 29:15** 6241
even to the **t** generation, **Dt 23:2** 6224
even to the **t** generation, **Dt 23:3** 6224
Jordan on the **t** of the first month **Jos 4:19** 6218
"He will take a **t** of your seed **1Sa 8:15** 6237
"He will take a **t** of your flocks, **1Sa 8:17** 6237
on the **t** day of the tenth month, **2Ki 25:1** 6218
on the tenth day of the **t** month, **2Ki 25:1** 6224
Jeremiah the **t**, Machbannai the **1Ch 12:13** 6224
for Jeshua, the **t** for Shecaniah, **1Ch 24:11** 6224
the **t** to Shimei, his sons and his **1Ch 25:17** 6224
The **t** for the tenth month *was* **1Ch 27:13** 6224
The tenth for the **t** month *was* **1Ch 27:13** 6224
first day of the **t** month to investigate **Ezr 10:16** 6224
shall bring up the **t** of the tithes to **Ne 10:38** 4643
t month which is the month Tebeth, **Es 2:16** 6224
there will be a **t** portion in it, **Is 6:13** 6224
the **t** year of Zedekiah king of Judah, **Jer 32:1** 6224
king of Judah, in the **t** month, **Jer 39:1** 6224
on the **t** *day* of the tenth month, **Jer 52:4** 6218
on the tenth *day* of the **t** month, **Jer 52:4** 6224
on the **t** *day* of the fifth month, **Jer 52:12** 6218
month, on the **t** of the month, **Ezk 20:1** 6218
in the ninth year, in the **t** month, **Ezk 24:1** 6224
month, on the **t** of the month, **Ezk 24:1** 6218
In the **t** year, in the tenth *month,* **Ezk 29:1** 6224
In the tenth year, in the **t** *month,* **Ezk 29:1** 6224
on the fifth of the **t** month, **Ezk 33:21** 6224
the year, on the **t** of the month, **Ezk 40:1** 6218
bath will contain a **t** of a homer **Ezk 45:11** 4643
and the ephah a **t** of a homer; **Ezk 45:11** 6224
a **t** of a bath from *each* kor **Ezk 45:14** 4643
fast of the **t** *months* will become joy, **Zch 8:19** 6224
day, for it was about the **t** hour. **Jn 1:39** *1182*
a **t** part of all *the spoils,* **Heb 7:2** *1181*
gave a **t** of the choicest spoils. **Heb 7:4** *1181*
to collect a **t** from the people, **Heb 7:5** *586b*
them collected a **t** from Abraham and **Heb 7:6** *1183*
and a **t** of the city fell; **Rv 11:13** *1182*
the **t**, chrysoprase; **Rv 21:20** *1182*

TENT-MAKERS
for by trade they were **t**. **Ac 18:3** *4635*

TENTS
who dwell in **t** and *have* livestock. **Gn 4:20** 168
let him dwell in the **t** of Shem; **Gn 9:27** 168
also had flocks and herds and **t**. **Gn 13:5** 168
and moved his **t** as far as Sodom. **Gn 13:12** 167
was a peaceful man, living in **t**. **Gn 25:27** 168
from the **t** of these wicked men, **Nu 16:26** 168
stood at the doorway of their **t**, **Nu 16:27** 168
How fair are your **t**, O Jacob, **Nu 24:5** 168
you grumbled in your **t** and said, **Dt 1:27** 168
"Return to your **t**." **Dt 5:30** 168
them, their households, their **t**, **Dt 11:6** 168
you are to return to your **t**. **Dt 16:7** 168
forth, And, Issachar, in your **t**. **Dt 33:18** 168
people set out from their **t** to cross **Jos 3:14** 168
turn now and go to your **t**, **Jos 22:4** 168
away, and they went to their **t**. **Jos 22:6** 168
Joshua sent them away to their **t**, **Jos 22:7** 168
"Return to your **t** with great riches **Jos 22:8** 168
with their livestock and their **t**, **Jg 6:5** 168
who lived in **t** on the east of Nobah **Jg 8:11** 168
Every man to his **t**, **2Sa 20:1** 168
Then they went to their **t** joyful **1Ki 8:66** 168
To your **t**, O Israel! **1Ki 12:16** 168
So Israel departed to their **t**. **1Ki 12:16** 168
and left their **t** and their horses **2Ki 7:7** 168
and the **t** just as they were." **2Ki 7:10** 168
but *his* army fled to their **t**. **2Ki 8:21** 168
lived in their **t** as formerly. **2Ki 13:5** 168
of Judah, and attacked their **t** and **1Ch 4:41** 168
so that they occupied their **t** **1Ch 5:10** 168
he sent the people to their **t**, **2Ch 7:10** 168
Every man to your **t**, **2Ch 10:16** 168
So all Israel departed to their **t**. **2Ch 10:16** 168
not let wickedness dwell in your **t**; **Jb 11:14** 168
"The **t** of the destroyers prosper, **Jb 12:6** 168
fire consumes the **t** of the corrupt. **Jb 15:34** 168
May none dwell in their **t**. **Ps 69:25** 168
of their virility in the **t** of Ham. **Ps 78:51** 168
tribes of Israel dwell in their **t**. **Ps 78:55** 168
The **t** of Edom and the Ishmaelites, **Ps 83:6** 168
Than dwell in the **t** of wickedness. **Ps 84:10** 168
But grumbled in their **t**; **Ps 106:25** 168
salvation is in the **t** of the righteous; **Ps 118:15** 168
For I dwell among the **t** of Kedar! **Ps 120:5** 168
of Jerusalem, Like the **t** of Kedar, **SS 1:5** 168
goats By the **t** of the shepherds. **SS 1:8** 4908
Suddenly my **t** are devastated, My **Jer 4:20** 168
will pitch *their* **t** around her, **Jer 6:3** 168
restore the fortunes of the **t** of Jacob **Jer 30:18** 168
in **t** you shall dwell all your days, **Jer 35:7** 168
"We have only dwelt in **t**, **Jer 35:10** 168
take away their **t** and their flocks; **Jer 49:29** 168
will pitch the **t** of his royal pavilion **Da 11:45** 168
Thorns *will be* in their **t**. **Hos 9:6** 168
I will make you live in **t** again, **Hos 12:9** 168
the **t** of Cushan under distress, **Hab 3:7** 168
LORD also will save the **t** of Judah **Zch 12:7** 168
from the LORD cut off from the **t** of Jacob **Mal 2:12** 168
dwelling in **t** with Isaac and Jacob, **Heb 11:9** *4633*

TERAH
years, and became the father of **T**; **Gn 11:24** 8646
after he became the father of **T**, **Gn 11:25** 8646
T lived seventy years, and **Gn 11:26** 8646
records of the generations of **T**. **Gn 11:27** 8646
T became the father of Abram, **Gn 11:27** 8646
died in the presence of his father **T** **Gn 11:28** 8646
T took Abram his son, and Lot **Gn 11:31** 8646
The days of **T** were two hundred **Gn 11:32** 8646
and **T** died in Haran. **Gn 11:32** 8646
from Tahath and camped at **T**. **Nu 33:27** 8646
They journeyed from **T** and **Nu 33:28** 8646
lived beyond the River, *namely,* **T**, **Jos 24:2** 8646
Serug, Nahor, **T**, **1Ch 1:26** 8646
the son of Abraham, the son of **T**, **Lk 3:34** *2291*

TERAPHIM
the spiritists and the **t** and the idols **2Ki 23:24** 8655
For the **t** speak iniquity, And the **Zch 10:2** 8655

TEREBINTH
Like a **t** or an oak Whose stump **Is 6:13** 424
hills, Under oak, poplar and **t**, **Hos 4:13** 424

TERESH
at the king's gate, Bigthan and **T**, **Es 2:21** 8657
concerning Bigthana and **T**, **Es 6:2** 8657

TERMINATE
all the splendor of Kedar will **t**; **Is 21:16** 3615

TERMINATION
and its **t** shall be to the south of **Nu 34:4** 8444
and its **t** shall be at the sea. **Nu 34:5** 8444
and the **t** of the border shall be **Nu 34:8** 8444
and its **t** shall be at Hazar-enan. **Nu 34:9** 8444
its **t** shall be at the Salt Sea. **Nu 34:12** 8444

TERMS
not speak to him on friendly **t**. **Gn 37:4** 7965
in **t** *of* the shekel of **Lv 5:15**
in **t** of the shekel of the sanctuary **Nu 3:47**
in **t** of the shekel of the sanctuary, **Nu 3:50**
do according to the **t** of the verdict **Dt 17:10** 6310
"According to the **t** of the law **Dt 17:11** 6310
it, you shall offer it **t** of peace. **Dt 20:10** 7121
"Shall He recompense on your **t**, **Jb 34:33** 5973
containing the **t** and conditions **Jer 32:11** 4687
a delegation and asks for **t** of peace. **Lk 14:32** *4314*
(I am speaking in human **t**.) **Ro 3:5** *2596*
I am speaking in human **t** because **Ro 6:19** *442*
I speak in **t** of human relations: **Ga 3:15** *2596*

TERRACE
them in the mortar in the brick **t** **Jer 43:9**

TERRAIN
And the rugged **t** a broad valley; **Is 40:4** 7406

TERRIBLE
all that great and **t** wilderness **Dt 1:19** 3372a
the great and **t** wilderness, **Dt 8:15** 3372a
You a name by great and **t** things, **1Ch 17:21** 3372a
His majestic snorting is **t**. **Jb 39:20** 367
lop off the boughs with a **t** crash; **Is 10:33** 4637
the great and **t** day of the LORD. **Mal 4:5** 3372a
throwing him into **t** convulsions, **Mk 9:26** *4183*
And so **t** was the sight, *that* Moses **Heb 12:21** *5398*

TERRIBLY
and they were **t** frightened. **Lk 2:9** *3173*

TERRIFIED
and the men of Benjamin were **t**; **Jg 20:41** 926
to Saul and saw that he was **t**, **1Sa 28:21** 926
all the guests of Adonijah were **t**; **1Ki 1:49** 2729
for he was **t** by the sword of the **1Ch 21:30** 1204
for they were **t** because of the **Ezr 3:3** 367
Haman became **t** before the king **Es 7:6** 1204
When I consider, I am **t** of Him. **Jb 23:15** 6342
And the contempt of families **t** me, **Jb 31:34** 2865
the torrents of ungodliness **t** me. **Ps 18:4** 1204
They were **t**, they fled in alarm. **Ps 48:5** 926
Ramah is **t**, and Gibeah of Saul has **Is 10:29** 2729
They will be **t**, **Is 13:8** 926
I cannot hear, so **t** I cannot see. **Is 21:3** 926
Assyria will be **t**, *When* He strikes **Is 30:31** 2865
he will not be **t** at their voice **Is 31:4** 2865
his princes will be **t** at the standard **Is 31:9** 2865
Sinners in Zion are **t**; **Is 33:14** 6342
And do not be **t** by the signs of **Jer 10:2** 2865
the nations are **t** by them; **Jer 10:2** 2865
be afraid any longer, nor be **t**, **Jer 23:4** 2865
They are **t**, They are drawing back, **Jer 46:5** 2844b
fire, And the men of war are **t**. **Jer 51:32** 926
sea Will be **t** at your passing.' " **Ezk 26:18** 926
You have become **t** And you will **Ezk 27:36** 1091
You have become **t** And you will **Ezk 28:19** 1091
of *its* beasts by which you **t** them, **Hab 2:17** 2865
they were **t**, and said, "It is a **Mt 14:26** *5015*
face down to the ground and were **t**. **Mt 17:6** *5399*
for they all saw Him and were **t**. **Mk 6:50** *5015*
for they became **t**. **Mk 9:6** *1630*
and disturbances, do not be **t**; **Lk 21:9** *4422*
and as *the women* were **t** and bowed **Lk 24:5** *1719*
and the rest were **t** and gave glory **Rv 11:13** *1719*

TERRIFIES
you, And sudden dread **t** you, **Jb 22:10** 926

TERRIFY
and **t** him, so that all the people **2Sa 17:2** 2729
the wall, to frighten and **t** them, **2Ch 32:18** 926
Let the blackness of the day **t** it. **Jb 3:5** 1204
with dreams And **t** me by visions; **Jb 7:14** 1204
me, And let not dread of Him **t** me. **Jb 9:34** 1204
"Will not His majesty **t** you, **Jb 13:11** 1204
let not the dread of You **t** me. **Jb 13:21** 1204
"Distress and anguish **t** him, **Jb 15:24** 1204
no fear of me should **t** you, **Jb 33:7** 1204
His anger And **t** them in His fury, **Ps 2:5** 926
And **t** them with Your storm. **Ps 83:15** 926
craftsmen have come to **t** them, **Zch 1:21** 2729
as if I would **t** you by my letters. **2Co 10:9** *1629*

TERRIFYING
the wilderness, from a **t** land. **Is 21:1** 3372a
dreadful and **t** and extremely strong; **Da 7:7** 368b
a complete end, Indeed a **t** one, **Zph 1:18** 926
The LORD will be **t** to them, **Zph 2:11** 3372a
a **t** expectation of judgment **Heb 10:27** *5398*
It is a **t** thing to fall into the **Heb 10:31** *5398*

TERRITORIES
land with its cities with *their* **t**, **Nu 32:33** 1367
These are *the* **t** which Moses **Jos 13:32**
Now these are *the* **t** which **Jos 14:1**
tumors, both Ashdod and its **t**. **1Sa 5:6** 1366
his sons through all the **t** of Judah **2Ch 11:23** 776

TERRITORY
The **t** of the Canaanite **Gn 10:19** 1366
smite your whole **t** with frogs. **Ex 8:2** 1366
I will bring locusts into your **t**. **Ex 10:4** 1366
and settled in all the **t** of Egypt; **Ex 10:14** 1366
was left in all the **t** of Egypt. **Ex 10:19** 1366
a town on the edge of your **t**. **Nu 20:16** 1366
until we pass through your **t**.' " **Nu 20:17** 1366
Israel to pass through his **t**; **Nu 20:21** 1366
"You will pass through the **t** of **Dt 2:4** 1366
be seen with you in all your **t**, **Dt 16:4** 1366
three parts the **t** of your land which **Dt 19:3** 1366
the LORD your God enlarges your **t**, **Dt 19:8** 1366
have olive trees throughout your **t** **Dt 28:40** 1366
of the sun will be your **t**. **Jos 1:4** 1366
and the **t** of Og king of Bashan, **Jos 12:4** 1366
and the **t** of the Geshurites and **Jos 13:11** 1366
Their **t** was from Aroer, which **Jos 13:16** 1366
Their **t** was Jazer, and all the **Jos 13:25** 1366
Their **t** was from Mahanaim, all **Jos 13:30** 1366
to the **t** of the Japhletites, **Jos 16:3** 1366
as far as the **t** of lower Beth-horon **Jos 16:3** 1366
was the **t** of the sons of Ephraim **Jos 16:5** 1366
Judah shall stay in its **t** on the south **Jos 18:5** 1366
house of Joseph shall stay in their **t** **Jos 18:5** 1366
and the **t** of their lot lay between **Jos 18:11** 1366
And the **t** of their inheritance was **Jos 19:10** 1366
Their **t** was to Jezreel and **Jos 19:18** 1366
Their **t** was Helkath and Hali **Jos 19:25** 1366
The **t** of their inheritance was **Jos 19:41** 1366
with the **t** over against Joppa. **Jos 19:46** 1366
The **t** of the sons of Dan **Jos 19:47** 1366
And they buried him in the **t** of **Jos 24:30** 1366
up with me into the **t** allotted me, **Jg 1:3** 1486
you into the **t** allotted you." **Jg 1:3** 1486
And Judah took Gaza with its **t** and **Jg 1:18** 1366
t and Ekron with its territory. **Jg 1:18** 1366
territory and Ekron with its **t**. **Jg 1:18** 1366
And they buried him in the **t** of **Jg 2:9** 1366
they did not enter the **t** of Moab, **Jg 11:18** 1366
Israel to pass through his **t**; **Jg 11:20** 1366
all the **t** of the Amorites, **Jg 11:22** 1366
her throughout the **t** of Israel. **Jg 19:29** 1366
way of its own **t** to Beth-shemesh, **1Sa 6:9** 1366
and Israel delivered their **t** from **1Sa 7:14** 1366
in the **t** of Benjamin at Zelzah; **1Sa 10:2** 1366
throughout the **t** of Israel. **1Sa 11:3** 1366
sent *them* throughout the **t** of Israel **1Sa 11:7** 1366
me anymore in all the **t** of Israel, **1Sa 27:1** 1366
throughout all the **t** of Israel, **1Ki 1:3** 1366
eat Jezebel in the **t** of Jezreel, **2Ki 9:10** 2506
them throughout the **t** of Israel: **2Ki 10:32** 1366
as far as Gaza and its **t**, **2Ki 18:8** 1366
their **t** from the tribe of Ephraim. **1Ch 6:66** 1366
throughout all the **t** of Israel.' **1Ch 21:12** 1366
That you may take it to its **t** And **Jb 38:20** 1366
of flies *And* gnats in all their **t**. **Ps 105:31** 1366
shattered the trees of their **t**. **Ps 105:33** 1366
has gone around the **t** of Moab, **Is 15:8** 1366
will return to their own **t**. **Jer 31:17** 1366
to remove them far from their **t**, **Jl 3:6** 1366
Or is their **t** greater than yours? **Am 6:2** 1366
possess the **t** of Ephraim **Ob 1:19** 7704
of Ephraim and the **t** of Samaria, **Ob 1:19** 7704

land And when he tramples our **t**. Mi 5:6 1366
become arrogant against their **t**. Zph 2:8 1366
men will call them the wicked **t**, Mal 1:4 1366

TERROR

the **t** of you will be on every beast Gn 9:2 2844a
t *and* great darkness fell upon him. Gn 15:12 367
there was a great **t** upon the Gn 35:5 2847
"**T** and dread fall upon them; Ex 15:16 367
"I will send My **t** ahead of you, Ex 23:27 367
will appoint over you a sudden **t**, Lv 26:16 928
and with great **t** and with signs and Dt 26:8 4172
and you will be *an example of* **t** Dt 28:25 2113
sword will bereave, And inside **t** Dt 32:25 367
the great **t** which Moses performed Dt 34:12 4172
the **t** of you has fallen on us, Jos 2:9 367
He has made them an object of **t**, 2Ch 29:8 2113
such, You see a **t** and are afraid. Jb 6:21 2866
"Sounds of **t** are in his ears; Jb 15:21 6343
calamity from God is a **t** to me, Jb 31:23 6343
Around his teeth there is **t**. Jb 41:14 367
of the earth will no longer cause **t**. Ps 10:18 6206
of many, **T** is on every side; Ps 31:13 4032
And their years in sudden **t**. Ps 78:33 928
not be afraid of the **t** by night, Ps 91:5 6343
The **t** of a king is like the Pr 20:2 367
is **t** to the workers of iniquity. Pr 21:15 4288
From the **t** of the LORD and from Is 2:10 6343
ground Before the **t** of the LORD And Is 2:19 6343
Before the **t** of the LORD and the Is 2:21 6343
evening time, behold, *there is* **t**! Is 17:14 1091
of Judah will become a **t** to Egypt; Is 19:17 2283
T and pit and snare Confront you, Is 24:17 6343
sheer **t** to understand what it means Is 28:19 2113
Your heart will meditate on **t**: Is 33:18 367
And from **t**, for it will not come Is 54:14 4288
has a sword, **T** is on every side. Jer 6:25 4032
a time of healing, but behold, **t**! Jer 8:15 1205
a time of healing, but behold, **t**! Jer 14:19 1205
Do not be a **t** to me; Jer 17:17 4288
I am going to make you a **t** to Jer 20:4 4032
"**T** on every side! Denounce *him;* Jer 20:10 4032
'I will make them a **t** *and an* Jer 24:9 2113
and I will make them a **t** to all Jer 29:18 2113
'I have heard a sound of **t**, Jer 30:5 2731
arm and with great **t**; Jer 32:21 4172
and I will make you a **t** to all the Jer 34:17 2113
T is on every side!" Jer 46:5 4032
object of **t** to all around him." Jer 48:39 4288
"**T**, pit and snare are *coming* Jer 48:43 6343
one who flees from the **t** Will fall Jer 48:44 6343
I am going to bring **t** upon you," Jer 49:5 6343
"As for the **t** of you, The Jer 49:16 8606
'**T** on every side!' Jer 49:29 4032
give them over to **t** and plunder. Ezk 23:46 2113
her **t** On all her inhabitants! Ezk 26:17 2851
t in the land of the living. Ezk 32:23 2851
their **t** in the land of the living and Ezk 32:24 2851
their **t** was instilled in the land of the Ezk 32:25 2851
their **t** in the land of the living. Ezk 32:26 2851
though the **t** of *these* heroes *was* Ezk 32:27 2851
the **t** resulting from their might, Ezk 32:30 2851
"Though I instilled a **t** of him in Ezk 32:32 2851

TERRORIZE

us go up against Judah and **t** it, Is 7:6 6973

TERRORIZED

evil spirit from the LORD **t** him. 1Sa 16:14 1204

TERRORIZING

an evil spirit from God is **t** you. 1Sa 16:15 1204

TERRORS

outstretched arm and by great **t**, Dt 4:34 4172
t of God are arrayed against me. Jb 6:4 1161
"All around **t** frighten him, And Jb 18:11 1091
march him before the king of **t**. Jb 18:14 1091
T come upon him, Jb 20:25 367
with the **t** of thick darkness. Jb 24:17 1091
"**T** overtake him like a flood; Jb 27:20 1091
"**T** are turned against me; They Jb 30:15 1091
t of death have fallen upon me. Ps 55:4 367
utterly swept away by sudden **t**! Ps 73:19 1091
I suffer Your **t**; I am overcome. Ps 88:15 367
Your **t** have destroyed me. Ps 88:16 1161
And the **t** of Sheol came upon me; Ps 116:3 4712
a high place and of **t** on the road; Ec 12:5 2849
against the **t** of the night. SS 3:8 6343
feast My **t** on every side; La 2:22 4032
"I will bring **t** on you and you Ezk 26:21 1091
be **t** and great signs from heaven. Lk 21:11 *5400*

TERTIUS

I, **T**, who write this letter, greet Ro 16:22 *5060*

TERTULLUS

with an attorney *named* **T**, Ac 24:1 *5061*
summoned, **T** began to accuse him, Ac 24:2 *5061*

TEST

every day, that I may **t** them, Ex 16:4 5254
Why do you **t** the LORD?" Ex 17:2 5254
God has come in order to **t** you, Ex 20:20 5254
yet have put Me to the **t** these ten Nu 14:22 5254
not put the LORD your God to the **t**, Dt 6:16 5254
you, and that He might **t** you, Dt 8:16 5254
in order to **t** Israel by them, Jg 2:22 5254
LORD left, to **t** Israel by them Jg 3:1 5254
make a **t** once more with the fleece, Jg 6:39 5254
and I will **t** them for you there. Jg 7:4 6884
to **t** him with difficult questions. 1Ki 10:1 5254
she came to Jerusalem to **t** Solomon 2Ch 9:1 5254
God left him *alone only* to **t** him, 2Ch 32:31 5254
"Does not the ear **t** words, Jb 12:11 974
His eyelids **t** the sons of men. Ps 11:4 974
T my mind and my heart. Ps 26:2 6884
in their heart they put God to the **t** Ps 78:18 5254
now, I will **t** you with pleasure. Ec 2:1 5254
not ask, nor will I **t** the LORD!" Is 7:12 5254
search the heart, I **t** the mind, Jer 17:10 974
You who **t** the righteous, Jer 20:12 974
t your servants for ten days, Da 1:12 5254
And **t** them as gold is tested. Zch 13:9 974
My house, and **t** Me now in this," Mal 3:10 974
they also **t** God and escape.' " Mal 3:15 974
PUT THE LORD YOUR GOD TO THE **T**.' " Mt 4:7 *1598*
Him a sign from heaven, to **t** Him. Mk 8:11 *3985*
PUT THE LORD YOUR GOD TO THE **T**.' " Lk 4:12 *1598*
stood up and put Him to the **t**, Lk 10:25 *1598*
Others, to **t** *Him,* were Lk 11:16 *3985*
This He was saying to **t** him, Jn 6:6 *3985*
the Spirit of the Lord to the **t**? Ac 5:9 *3985*
why do you put God to the **t** by Ac 15:10 *3985*
fire itself will **t** the quality of each 1Co 3:13 *1381a*
that I might put you to the **t**, 2Co 2:9 *1382*
T yourselves *to see* if you are in 2Co 13:5 *3985*
unless indeed you fail the **t**? 2Co 13:5 *96b*
we ourselves do not fail the **t**. 2Co 13:6 *96b*
but **t** the spirits to see whether 1Jn 4:1 *1381a*
and you put to the **t** those who Rv 2:2 *3985*
to **t** those who dwell on the Rv 3:10 *3985*

TESTED

these things, that God **t** Abraham, Gn 22:1 5254
by this you will be **t**: Gn 42:15 974
that your words may be **t**, Gn 42:16 974
regulation, and there He **t** them. Ex 15:25 5254
and because they **t** the LORD, Ex 17:7 5254
the test, as you **t** *Him* at Massah. Dt 6:16 5254
to walk, for he had not **t** *them.* 1Sa 17:39 5254
these, for I have not **t** *them.*" 1Sa 17:39 5254
The word of the LORD is **t**; 2Sa 22:31 6884
have **t** me and You find nothing; Ps 17:3 6884
"When your fathers **t** Me, Ps 95:9 5254
pass, The word of the LORD **t** him. Ps 105:19 6884
And each *is* **t** by the praise Pr 27:21
Every word of God is **t**; Pr 30:5 6884
"God has surely **t** them in order Ec 3:18 1305
I **t** all this with wisdom, *and* I Ec 7:23 5254
laying in Zion a stone, a **t** stone, Is 28:16 976
I have **t** you in the furnace of Is 48:10 977
matter and **t** them for ten days. Da 1:14 5254
And test them as gold is **t**. Zch 13:9 974
whom we have often **t** and found 2Co 8:22 *1381a*
These men must also first be **t**; 1Tm 3:10 *1381a*
By faith Abraham, when he was **t**, Heb 11:17 *3985*
perishable, even though **t** by fire, 1Pe 1:7 *1381a*
into prison, so that you will be **t**, Rv 2:10 *3985*

TESTER

assayer *and* a **t** among My people, Jer 6:27 4013

TESTICLES

or eczema or scabs or crushed **t**. Lv 21:20 810
'Also anything *with its* **t** Lv 22:24

TESTIFIED

for your mouth has **t** against you, 2Sa 1:16 6030a
the worthless men **t** against him, 1Ki 21:13 5749b
though they **t** against them, they 2Ch 24:19 5749b
that today I have **t** against you. Jer 42:19 5749b
John **t** about Him and cried out, Jn 1:15 *3140*
John **t** saying, "I have seen Jn 1:32 *3140*
"I myself have seen, and have **t** Jn 1:34 *3140*
to whom you have **t**, behold, He is Jn 3:26 *3140*
of the word of the woman who **t**, Jn 4:39 *3140*
For Jesus Himself **t** that a prophet Jn 4:44 *3140*
and he has **t** to the truth. Jn 5:33 *3140*
He has **t** of Me. You have neither Jn 5:37 *3140*
became troubled in spirit, and **t** and Jn 13:21 *3140*
And he who has seen has **t**, and his Jn 19:35 *3140*
he solemnly **t** and kept on exhorting Ac 2:40 *1263*
when they had solemnly **t** and Ac 8:25 *1263*
concerning whom He also **t** and said Ac 13:22 *3140*
"And God, who knows the heart, **t** Ac 15:8 *3140*
because we **t** against God that He 1Co 15:15 *3140*
who **t** the good confession before 1Tm 6:13 *3140*
But one has **t** somewhere, saying, Heb 2:6 *1263*
that He has **t** concerning His Son. 1Jn 5:9 *3140*
very glad when brethren came and **t** to 3Jn 1:3 *3140*
and they have **t** to your love before 3Jn 1:6 *3140*
who **t** to the word of God and to Rv 1:2 *3140*

TESTIFIES

up against me, It **t** to my face. Jb 16:8 6030a
the pride of Israel **t** against him, Hos 5:5 6030a
the pride of Israel **t** against him, Hos 7:10 6030a
of that He **t**; and no one receives Jn 3:32 *3140*
"There is another who **t** of Me, Jn 5:32 *3140*
"I am He who **t** about Jn 8:18 *3140*
Father who sent Me **t** about Me." Jn 8:18 *3140*
the Holy Spirit solemnly **t** to me in Ac 20:23 *1263*
The Spirit Himself **t** with our spirit Ro 8:16 *4828*
my conscience **t** with me in the Holy Ro 9:1 *4828*
And the Holy Spirit also **t** to us; Heb 10:15 *3140*
It is the Spirit who **t**, because 1Jn 5:6 *3140*
He who **t** to these things says, Rv 22:20 *3140*

TESTIFY

nor shall you **t** in a dispute so as Ex 23:2 6030a
he hears a public adjuration *to* **t** Lv 5:1
I **t** against you today that you Dt 8:19 5749b
this song will **t** before them as a Dt 31:21 6030a
him, and let them **t** against him, 1Ki 21:10 5749b
And your own lips **t** against you. Jb 15:6 6030a
O Israel, I will **t** against you; Ps 50:7 5749b
You, And our sins **t** against us; Is 59:12 6030a
our iniquities **t** against us, Jer 14:7 6030a
t against the house of Jacob," Am 3:13 5749b
"So you **t** against yourselves, that Mt 23:31 *3140*
many things they **t** against You?" Mt 27:13 *2649*
He came as a witness, to **t** about Jn 1:7 *3140*
but *he came* to **t** about the Light. Jn 1:8 *3140*
because He did not need anyone to **t** Jn 2:25 *3140*
we speak of what we know and **t** of Jn 3:11 *3140*
"If I *alone* **t** about Myself, My Jn 5:31 *3140*
the very works that I do—**t** Jn 5:36 *3140*
it is these that **t** about Me; Jn 5:39 *3140*
but it hates Me because I **t** of it, Jn 7:7 *3140*
"Even if I **t** about Myself, My Jn 8:14 *3140*
these **t** of Me. Jn 10:25 *3140*
continued to **t** *about Him.* Jn 12:17 *3140*
He will **t** about Me, Jn 15:26 *3140*
and you *will* **t** also, because you Jn 15:27 *3140*
t of the wrong; but if rightly, why Jn 18:23 *3140*
to **t** to the truth. Everyone who is Jn 18:37 *3140*
and solemnly to **t** that this is the Ac 10:42 *1263*
to **t** solemnly of the gospel of the Ac 20:24 *1263*
"Therefore, I **t** to you this day Ac 20:26 *3143*
the Council of the elders can **t**. Ac 22:5 *3140*
if they are willing to **t**, Ac 26:5 *3140*
For I **t** about them that they have a Ro 10:2 *3140*
For I **t** that according to their 2Co 8:3 *3140*
And I **t** again to every man who Ga 5:3 *3143*
For I **t** for him that he has a deep Col 4:13 *3140*
and we have seen and **t** and proclaim 1Jn 1:2 *3140*
We have seen and **t** that the Father 1Jn 4:14 *3140*
For there are three that **t**: 1Jn 5:7 *3140*
I, Jesus, have sent My angel to **t** to Rv 22:16 *3140*
I **t** to everyone who hears the Rv 22:18 *3140*

TESTIFYING

these men are **t** against You?" Mt 26:62 *2649*
these men are **t** against You?" Mk 14:60 *2649*
"You are **t** about Yourself; Your Jn 8:13 *3140*
This is the disciple who is **t** to Jn 21:24 *3140*
who was **t** to the word of His grace, Ac 14:3 *3140*
solemnly **t** to the Jews that Jesus Ac 18:5 *1263*
solemnly **t** to both Jews and Greeks Ac 20:21 *1263*
day **t** both to small and great, Ac 26:22 *3143*
by solemnly **t** about the kingdom of Ac 28:23 *1263*
God also **t** with them, both by signs Heb 2:4 *3140*
righteous, God **t** about his gifts, Heb 11:4 *3140*
t that this is the true grace of God. 1Pe 5:12 *1957*

TESTIMONIES

these are the **t** and the statutes Dt 4:45 5713b
and His **t** and His statutes which Dt 6:17 5713b
'What *do* the **t** and the statutes Dt 6:20 5713b
His ordinances, and His **t**, 1Ki 2:3 5715
keep His commandments and His **t** 2Ki 23:3 5715
Your **t** and Your statutes, 1Ch 29:19 5715
keep His commandments and His **t** 2Ch 34:31 5715
who keep His covenant and His **t**. Ps 25:10 5713b
High God And did not keep His **t**, Ps 78:56 5713b
Your **t** are fully confirmed; Ps 93:5 5713b
They kept His **t** And the statute Ps 99:7 5713b
are those who observe His **t**, Ps 119:2 5713b
have rejoiced in the way of Your **t**, Ps 119:14 5715
from me, For I observe Your **t**. Ps 119:22 5713b
Your **t** also are my delight; Ps 119:24 5713b
I cling to Your **t**; Ps 119:31 5715
Incline my heart to Your **t** And Ps 119:36 5715
also speak of Your **t** before kings And Ps 119:46 5713b
ways And turned my feet to Your **t**. Ps 119:59 5713b
to me, Even those who know Your **t**. Ps 119:79 5713b
I shall diligently consider Your **t**. Ps 119:95 5713b
For Your **t** are my meditation. Ps 119:99 5715
I have inherited Your **t** forever, Ps 119:111 5715
Therefore I love Your **t**. Ps 119:119 5713b
That I may know Your **t**. Ps 119:125 5713b
Your **t** are wonderful; Ps 119:129 5715
You have commanded Your **t** in Ps 119:138 5713b
Your **t** are righteous forever; Ps 119:144 5715
save me And I shall keep Your **t**. Ps 119:146 5713b
Of old I have known from Your **t** That Ps 119:152 5713b
I do not turn aside from Your **t**. Ps 119:157 5715
My soul keeps Your **t**, Ps 119:167 5713b
I keep Your precepts and Your **t**, Ps 119:168 5713b
in His law, His statutes or His **t**, Jer 44:23 5715

TESTIMONY

so Aaron placed it before the **T**, Ex 16:34 5715
You shall put into the ark the **t** Ex 25:16 5715
in the ark you shall put the **t** which Ex 25:21 5715
which are upon the ark of the **t**, Ex 25:22 5715
shall bring in the ark of the **t** there Ex 26:33 5715
the mercy seat on the ark of the **t** Ex 26:34 5715
the veil which is before the **t**, Ex 27:21 5715
that is near the ark of the **t**, Ex 30:6 5715
that is over *the ark of* the **t**, Ex 30:6 5715
of meeting and the ark of the **t**, Ex 30:26 5715
put part of it before the **t** in the tent Ex 30:36 5715
tent of meeting, and the ark of **t**, Ex 31:7 5715
Moses the two tablets of the **t**, Ex 31:18 5715
two tablets of the **t** in his hand, Ex 32:15 5715
tablets of the **t** *were* in Moses' hand Ex 34:29 5715
the tabernacle of the **t**, Ex 38:21 5715
the ark of the **t** and its poles and Ex 39:35 5715
place the ark of the **t** there, Ex 40:3 5715
incense before the ark of the **t**, Ex 40:5 5715
he took the **t** and put *it* into the ark, Ex 40:20 5715
and screened off the ark of the **t**, Ex 40:21 5715
seat that is on *the ark of* the **t**, Lv 16:13 5715
Outside the veil of **t** in the tent of Lv 24:3 5715
over the tabernacle of the **t**, Nu 1:50 5715
around the tabernacle of the **t**, Nu 1:53 5715
of the tabernacle of the **t**." Nu 1:53 5715
cover the ark of the **t** with it; Nu 4:5 5715

seat that was on the ark of the **t**, **Nu 7:89** 5715
the tabernacle, the tent of the **t**, **Nu 9:15** 5715
from over the tabernacle of the **t**; **Nu 10:11** 5715
tent of meeting in front of the **t**, **Nu 17:4** 5715
the LORD in the tent of the **t**. **Nu 17:7** 5715
Moses went into the tent of the **t**; **Nu 17:8** 5715
the rod of Aaron before the **t** to be **Nu 17:10** 5715
you are before the tent of the **t**. **Nu 18:2** 5715
to death on the **t** of one witness. **Nu 35:30** 6030a
the priests who carry the ark of the **t** **Jos 4:16** 5715
crown on him and *gave him* the **t**; **2Ki 11:12** 5715
crown on him, and *gave him* the **t** and **2Ch 23:11** 5715
of Israel for the tent of the **t**?" **2Ch 24:6** 5715
The **t** of the LORD is sure, making **Ps 19:7** 5715
For He established a **t** in Jacob And **Ps 78:5** 5715
established it for a **t** in Joseph When **Ps 81:5** 5715
I may keep the **t** of Your mouth. **Ps 119:88** 5715
And My **t** which I will teach them, **Ps 132:12** 5713b
Myself faithful witnesses for **t**, **Is 8:2** 5749b
Bind up the **t**, seal the law among **Is 8:16** 8584
To the law and to the **t**! **Is 8:20** 8584
commanded, as a **t** to them." **Mt 8:4** *3142*
a **t** to them and to the Gentiles. **Mt 10:18** *3142*
be preached in the whole world as a **t** **Mt 24:14** *3142*
to obtain false **t** against Jesus, **Mt 26:59** *5577a*
commanded, as a **t** to them." **Mk 1:44** *3142*
your feet for a **t** against them." **Mk 6:11** *3142*
kings for My sake, as a **t** to them. **Mk 13:9** *3142*
kept trying to obtain **t** against Jesus **Mk 14:55** *3141*
were giving false **t** against Him, **Mk 14:56** *5576*
but their **t** was not consistent. **Mk 14:56** *3141*
began to give false **t** against Him, **Mk 14:57** *5576*
in this respect was their **t** consistent. **Mk 14:59** *3141*
commanded, as a **t** to them." **Lk 5:14** *3142*
your feet as a **t** against them." **Lk 9:5** *3142*
lead to an opportunity for your **t**. **Lk 21:13** *3142*
"What further need do we have of **t**? **Lk 22:71** *3141*
This is the **t** of John, when the Jews **Jn 1:19** *3141*
and you do not accept our **t**. **Jn 3:11** *3140*
and no one receives His **t**. **Jn 3:32** *3140*
"He who has received His **t** has set **Jn 3:33** *3141*
about Myself, My **t** is not true. **Jn 5:31** *3141*
t which He gives about Me is true. **Jn 5:32** *3141*
"But the **t** which I receive is not **Jn 5:34** *3141*
"But the **t** which I have is greater **Jn 5:36** *3141*
which I have is greater than *the* **t** **Jn 5:36**
Your **t** is not true." **Jn 8:13** *3141*
My **t** is true, for I know where I **Jn 8:14** *3140*
that the **t** of two men is true. **Jn 8:17** *3141*
and his **t** is true; and he knows that **Jn 19:35** *3140*
and we know that his **t** is true. **Jn 21:24** *3141*
power the apostles were giving **t** to **Ac 4:33** *3142*
tabernacle of **t** in the wilderness, **Ac 7:44** *3142*
will not accept your **t** about Me.' **Ac 22:18** *3141*
t concerning Christ was confirmed **1Co 1:6** *3142*
proclaiming to you the **t** of God. **1Co 2:1** *3142*
is this: the **t** of our conscience, **2Co 1:12** *3142*
THE **T** OF TWO OR THREE WITNESSES. **2Co 13:1** *4750*
our **t** to you was believed. **2Th 1:10** *3142*
the **t** *given* at the proper time. **1Tm 2:6** *3142*
be ashamed of the **t** of our Lord or **2Tm 1:8** *3142*
This **t** is true. For this reason reprove **Ti 1:13** *3141*
for a **t** of those things which were **Heb 3:5** *3142*
Moses dies without mercy on *the* **t** **Heb 10:28**
the **t** that he was righteous, **Heb 11:4** *3140*
If we receive the **t** of men, **1Jn 5:9** *3141*
the **t** of God is greater; for **1Jn 5:9** *3141*
for the **t** of God is this, that He **1Jn 5:9** *3141*
believes in the Son of God has the **t** **1Jn 5:10** *3141*
because he has not believed in the **t** **1Jn 5:10** *3141*
And the **t** is this, that God has **1Jn 5:11** *3141*
received a *good* **t** from everyone, **3Jn 1:12** *3140*
and we add our **t**, and you know that **3Jn 1:12** *3140*
and you know that our **t** is true. **3Jn 1:12** *3140*
God and to the **t** of Jesus Christ, **Rv 1:2** *3141*
word of God and the **t** of Jesus. **Rv 1:9** *3141*
the **t** which they had maintained; **Rv 6:9** *3141*
When they have finished their **t**, **Rv 11:7** *3141*
because of the word of their **t**, **Rv 12:11** *3141*
of God and hold to the **t** of Jesus. **Rv 12:17** *3141*
the temple of the tabernacle of **t** in **Rv 15:5** *3142*
brethren who hold the **t** of Jesus; **Rv 19:10** *3141*
For the **t** of Jesus is the spirit **Rv 19:10** *3141*
beheaded because of their **t** of Jesus **Rv 20:4** *3141*

TESTING

that He might humble you, **t** you, **Dt 8:2** 5254
for the LORD your God is **t** you to **Dt 13:3** 5254
They were for **t** Israel, **Jg 3:4** 5254
"For *there is* a **t**; **Ezk 21:13** 976
t Jesus, they asked Him to show them a **Mt 16:1** *3985*
Some Pharisees came to Jesus, **t** Him **Mt 19:3** *3985*
"Why are you **t** Me, you hypocrites? **Mt 22:18** *3985*
asked Him *a question*, **t** Him, **Mt 22:35** *3985*
Pharisees came up to Jesus, **t** Him, **Mk 10:2** *3985*
"Why are you **t** Me? **Mk 12:15** *3985*
They were saying this, **t** Him, **Jn 8:6** *3985*
YOUR FATHERS TRIED *Me* BY **T** *Me*, **Heb 3:9** *1381b*
t of your faith produces endurance **Jas 1:3** *1383*
which comes upon you for your **t**, **1Pe 4:12** *3986*
will keep you from the hour of **t**, **Rv 3:10** *3986*

TESTS

"For the ear **t** words As the **Jb 34:3** 974
LORD **t** the righteous and the wicked **Ps 11:5** 974
for gold, But the LORD **t** hearts. **Pr 17:3** 974

TETRARCH

the **t** heard the news about Jesus, **Mt 14:1** *5068a*
Judea, and Herod was **t** of Galilee, **Lk 3:1** *5067b*
Philip was **t** of the region of Ituraea **Lk 3:1** *5067b*
and Lysanias was **t** of Abilene, **Lk 3:1** *5067b*
But when Herod the **t** was reprimanded **Lk 3:19** *5068a*
Now Herod the **t** heard of all that **Lk 9:7** *5068a*
been brought up with Herod the **t**, **Ac 13:1** *5068a*

TEXT

and the **t** of the letter was **Ezr 4:7** 3791
He also gave him a copy of the **t** **Es 4:8** 3791

THADDAEUS

James the son of Alphaeus, and **T**; **Mt 10:3** *2280b*
James the son of Alphaeus, and **T**, **Mk 3:18** *2280b*

THAN

more crafty **t** any beast of the field **Gn 3:1** 4480
Cursed are you more **t** all cattle, **Gn 3:14** 4480
more **t** every beast of the field; **Gn 3:14** 4480
we will treat you worse **t** them." **Gn 19:9** 4480
shall be stronger **t** the other; **Gn 25:23** 4480
is none other **t** the house of God, **Gn 28:17** 3588, 518
better that I give her to you **t** **Gn 29:19** 4480
he loved Rachel more **t** Leah, **Gn 29:30** 4480
Now he was more respected **t** all **Gn 34:19** 4480
loved Joseph more **t** all his sons, **Gn 37:3** 4480
loved him more **t** all his brothers; **Gn 37:4** 4480
"She is more righteous **t** I, **Gn 38:26** 4480
no one greater in this house **t** I, **Gn 39:9** 4480
throne I will be greater **t** you." **Gn 41:40** 4480
brother shall be greater **t** he, **Gn 48:19** 4480
one portion more **t** your brothers, **Gn 48:22** 5921
Israel are more and mightier **t** we. **Ex 1:9** 4480
t to die in the wilderness." **Ex 14:12** 4480
LORD is greater **t** all the gods; **Ex 18:11** 4480
god, other **t** to the LORD alone, **Ex 22:20** 1115
not pay less **t** the half shekel, **Ex 30:15** 4480
more **t** enough for the construction **Ex 36:5** 4480
more **t** enough for all the work, **Ex 36:7** 3498
be deeper **t** the skin of his body, **Lv 13:3** 4480
appear to be deeper **t** the skin, **Lv 13:4** 4480
it appears to be lower **t** the skin, **Lv 13:20** 4480
not lower **t** the skin and is faded, **Lv 13:21** 4480
appears to be deeper **t** the skin, **Lv 13:25** 4480
and it is no deeper **t** the skin, **Lv 13:26** 4480
appears to be deeper **t** the skin and **Lv 13:30** 4480
to be no deeper **t** the skin and **Lv 13:31** 4480
the scale is no deeper **t** the skin, **Lv 13:32** 4480
to be no deeper **t** the skin, **Lv 13:34** 4480
and appears deeper **t** the surface, **Lv 14:37** 4480
if he is poorer **t** your valuation, **Lv 27:8** 4480
a man other **t** your husband has had **Nu 5:20** 1107
was very humble, more **t** any man **Nu 12:3** 4480
nation greater and mightier **t** they **Nu 14:12** 4480
more distinguished **t** the former. **Nu 22:15** 4480
his king shall be higher **t** Agag, **Nu 24:7** 4480
you a thousand-fold more **t** you are and **Dt 1:11**
people are bigger and taller **t** we; **Dt 1:28** 4480
greater and mightier **t** you, **Dt 4:38** 4480
greater and stronger **t** you, **Dt 7:1** 4480
more in number **t** any of the peoples **Dt 7:7** 4480
'These nations are greater **t** I; **Dt 7:17** 4480
greater and mightier **t** you, **Dt 9:1** 4480
mightier and greater **t** they.' **Dt 9:14** 4480
greater and mightier **t** you. **Dt 11:23** 4480
and people more numerous **t** you, **Dt 20:1** 4480
with many more stripes **t** these and **Dt 25:3** 5921
multiply you more **t** your fathers. **Dt 30:5** 4480
"More blessed **t** sons is Asher; **Dt 33:24** 4480
and because it was greater **t** Ai, **Jos 10:2** 4480
more who died from the hailstones **t** **Jos 10:11** 4480
more corruptly **t** their fathers, **Jg 2:19** 4480
"This is nothing less **t** the sword **Jg 7:14** 1115, 518
better **t** the vintage of Abiezer? **Jg 8:2** 4480
better **t** Balak the son of Zippor, **Jg 11:25** 4480
"What is sweeter **t** honey? **Jg 14:18** 4480
And what is stronger **t** a lion?" **Jg 14:18** 4480
sister more beautiful **t** she? **Jg 15:2** 4480
more **t** those whom he killed in his life **Jg 16:30** 4480
for it is harder for me **t** for you, **Ru 1:13** 4480
last kindness to be better **t** the first **Ru 3:10** 4480
there is a relative closer **t** I. **Ru 3:12** 4480
and is better to you **t** seven sons, **Ru 4:15** 4480
I not better to you **t** ten sons?" **1Sa 1:8** 4480
not a more handsome person **t** he **1Sa 9:2** 4480
he was taller **t** any of the people. **1Sa 9:2** 4480
he was taller **t** any of the people **1Sa 10:23** 4480
to obey is better **t** sacrifice, **1Sa 15:22** 4480
And to heed **t** the fat of rams. **1Sa 15:22** 4480
your neighbor, who is better **t** you. **1Sa 15:28** 4480
more wisely **t** all the servants of Saul **1Sa 18:30** 4480
"You are more righteous **t** I; **1Sa 24:17** 4480
There is nothing better for me **t** **1Sa 27:1** 3588
They were swifter **t** eagles, **2Sa 1:23** 4480
They were stronger **t** lions. **2Sa 1:23** 4480
wonderful **T** the love of women. **2Sa 1:26** 4480
I will be more lightly esteemed **t** this **2Sa 6:22** 4480
since he was stronger **t** she, **2Sa 13:14** 4480
greater **t** the love with which he had **2Sa 13:15** 4480
is greater **t** the other that you have **2Sa 13:16** 4480
better **t** the counsel of Ahithophel. **2Sa 17:14** 4480
that day **t** the sword devoured. **2Sa 18:8** 4480, 834
will be worse for you **t** all the evil **2Sa 19:7** 4480
have more *claim* on David **t** you. **2Sa 19:43** 4480
harsher **t** the words of the men of **2Sa 19:43** 4480
but he delayed longer **t** the set **2Sa 20:5** 4480
will do us more harm **t** Absalom; **2Sa 20:6** 4480
and make his throne greater **t** the **1Ki 1:37** 4480
name of Solomon better **t** your name **1Ki 1:47** 4480
his throne greater **t** your throne!' **1Ki 1:47** 4480
men more righteous and better **t** he **1Ki 2:32** 4480
For he was wiser **t** all men, **1Ki 4:31** 4480
all men, **t** Ethan the Ezrahite, **1Ki 4:31** 4480
So King Solomon became greater **t** **1Ki 10:23** 4480
is thicker **t** my father's loins! **1Ki 12:10** 4480
more evil **t** all who were before you, **1Ki 14:9** 4480
provoked Him to jealousy more **t** all **1Ki 14:22** 4480
acted more wickedly **t** all who *were* **1Ki 16:25** 4480
more **t** all who were before him. **1Ki 16:30** 4480
t all the kings of Israel who were **1Ki 16:33** 4480
I am not better **t** my fathers." **1Ki 19:4** 4480
therefore they were stronger **t** we; **1Ki 20:23** 4480
we will be stronger **t** they. **1Ki 20:23** 4480
we will be stronger **t** they." **1Ki 20:25** 4480
I will give you a better vineyard **t** it **1Ki 21:2** 4480
better **t** all the waters of Israel? **2Ki 5:12** 4480
there, more **t** once or twice. **2Ki 6:10**
more **t** those who are with them." **2Ki 6:16** 4480
but they found nothing more of her **t** **2Ki 9:35** 3588, 518
of the army not more **t** fifty horsemen **2Ki 13:7** 3588, 518
seduced them to do evil more **t** the **2Ki 21:9** 4480
having done wickedly more **t** all **2Ki 21:11** 4480
was more honorable **t** his brothers, **1Ch 4:9** 4480
more bronze **t** could be weighed; **1Ch 22:3**
t the descendants of Ithamar, **1Ch 24:4** 4480
greater is our God **t** all the gods. **2Ch 2:5** 4480
So King Solomon became greater **t** **2Ch 9:22** 4480
is thicker **t** my father's loins! **2Ch 10:10** 4480
daughter of Absalom more **t** all his **2Ch 11:21** 4480
more **t** they could carry. **2Ch 20:25** 4480
own family, who were better **t** you, **2Ch 21:13** 4480
much more to give you **t** this." **2Ch 25:9** 4480
themselves **t** the priests. **2Ch 29:34** 4480
Passover otherwise **t** prescribed. **2Ch 30:18**
us is greater **t** the one with him. **2Ch 32:7** 4480
to do more evil **t** the nations whom **2Ch 33:9** 4480
us less **t** our iniquities *deserve*, **Ezr 9:13** 4480
man and feared God more **t** many. **Ne 7:2** 4480
another who is more worthy **t** she. **Es 1:19** 4480
loved Esther more **t** all the women, **Es 2:17** 4480
with him more **t** all the virgins, **Es 2:17** 4480
escape any more **t** all the Jews. **Es 4:13** 4480
king desire to honor more **t** me?" **Es 6:6** 4480
it more **t** for hidden treasures, **Jb 3:21** 4480
be heavier **t** the sand of the seas; **Jb 6:3** 4480
are swifter **t** a weaver's shuttle, **Jb 7:6** 4480
Death rather **t** my pains. **Jb 7:15** 4480
my days are swifter **t** a runner; **Jb 9:25** 4480
Deeper **t** Sheol, what can you know? **Jb 11:8** 4480
"Its measure is longer **t** the earth And **Jb 11:9** 4480
the earth And broader **t** the sea. **Jb 11:9** 4480
life would be brighter **t** noonday; **Jb 11:17** 4480
are among us, Older **t** your father. **Jb 15:10** 4480
mouth more **t** my necessary food. **Jb 23:12** 4480
"But now those younger **t** I mock me, **Jb 30:1** 4480
they were years older **t** he. **Jb 32:4** 4480
in this, For God is greater **t** man. **Jb 33:12** 4480
flesh become fresher **t** in youth, **Jb 33:25** 4480
'My righteousness is more **t** God's'? **Jb 35:2** 4480
I have, more **t** if I had sinned?' **Jb 35:3** 4480
the clouds—they are higher **t** you. **Jb 35:5** 4480
us more **t** the beasts of the earth And **Jb 35:11** 4480
wiser **t** the birds of the heavens?' **Jb 35:11** 4480
days of Job more **t** his beginning; **Jb 42:12** 4480
More **t** when their grain and new **Ps 4:7** 4480
made him a little lower **t** God, **Ps 8:5** 4480
They are more desirable **t** gold, **Ps 19:10** 4480
than gold, yes, **t** much fine gold; **Ps 19:10** 4480
Sweeter also **t** honey and the **Ps 19:10** 4480
T the abundance of many wicked. **Ps 37:16** 4480
more numerous **t** the hairs of my **Ps 40:12** 4480
You are fairer **t** the sons of men; **Ps 45:2** 4480
me, and I shall be whiter **t** snow. **Ps 51:7** 4480
You love evil more **t** good, **Ps 52:3** 4480
Falsehood more **t** speaking what is **Ps 52:3** 4480
His speech was smoother **t** butter, **Ps 55:21** 4480
His words were softer **t** oil, **Ps 55:21** 4480
me to the rock that is higher **t** I. **Ps 61:2** 4480
are together lighter **t** breath. **Ps 62:9** 4480
lovingkindness is better **t** life, **Ps 63:3** 4480
are more **t** the hairs of my head; **Ps 69:4** 4480
it will please the LORD better **t** an ox **Ps 69:31** 4480
majestic **t** the mountains of prey. **Ps 76:4** 4480
is better **t** a thousand *outside*. **Ps 84:10** 4480
T dwell in the tents of wickedness. **Ps 84:10** 4480
LORD loves the gates of Zion More **t** **Ps 87:2** 4480
More **t** the sounds of many waters, **Ps 93:4** 4480
T the mighty breakers of the sea, **Ps 93:4**
them stronger **t** their adversaries. **Ps 105:24** 4480
better to take refuge in the LORD **T** **Ps 118:8** 4480
better to take refuge in the LORD **T** **Ps 118:9** 4480
law of Your mouth is better to me **T** **Ps 119:72** 4480
make me wiser **t** my enemies, **Ps 119:98** 4480
more insight **t** all my teachers, **Ps 119:99** 4480
I understand more **t** the aged, **Ps 119:100** 4480
Yes, sweeter **t** honey to my mouth! **Ps 119:103** 4480
for the Lord More **t** the watchmen **Ps 130:6** 4480
more **t** the watchmen for the morning. **Ps 130:6**
is better **t** the profit of silver And **Pr 3:14** 4480
silver And her gain better **t** fine gold. **Pr 3:14** 4480
She is more precious **t** jewels; **Pr 3:15** 4480
And smoother **t** oil is her speech; **Pr 5:3** 4480
knowledge rather **t** choicest gold. **Pr 8:10** 4480
"For wisdom is better **t** jewels; **Pr 8:11** 4480
"My fruit is better **t** gold, **Pr 8:19** 4480
And my yield *better* **t** choicest silver. **Pr 8:19** 4480
T he who honors himself and lacks **Pr 12:9** 4480

T great treasure and turmoil with **Pr 15:16** 4480
T a fattened ox *served* with hatred. **Pr 15:17** 4480
T great income with injustice. **Pr 16:8** 4480
better it is to get wisdom **t** gold! **Pr 16:16** 4480
T to divide the spoil with the **Pr 16:19** 4480
slow to anger is better **t** the mighty, **Pr 16:32** 4480
spirit, **t** he who captures a city. **Pr 16:32** 4480
T a house full of feasting with strife. **Pr 17:1** 4480
T a hundred blows into a fool. **Pr 17:10** 4480
Rather **t** a fool in his folly. **Pr 17:12** 4480
harder to be won **t** a strong city, **Pr 18:19** 4480
friend who sticks closer **t** a brother. **Pr 18:24** 4480
T he who is perverse in speech **Pr 19:1** 4480
better to be a poor man **t** a liar. **Pr 19:22** 4480
by the LORD more **t** sacrifice. **Pr 21:3** 4480
T in a house shared with a **Pr 21:9** 4480
T with a contentious and vexing **Pr 21:19** 4480
to be more desired **t** great wealth, **Pr 22:1** 4480
Favor is better **t** silver and gold. **Pr 22:1** 4480
T for you to be placed lower in **Pr 25:7** 4480
corner of the roof **T** in a house shared **Pr 25:24** 4480
is more hope for a fool **t** for him. **Pr 26:12** 4480
wiser in his own eyes **T** seven men **Pr 26:16** 4480
a fool is heavier **t** both of them. **Pr 27:3** 4480
rebuke **T** love that is concealed. **Pr 27:5** 4480
who is near **t** a brother far away. **Pr 27:10** 4480
T he who is crooked though he be **Pr 28:6** 4480
find *more* favor **T** he who flatters **Pr 28:23** 4480
is more hope for a fool **t** for him. **Pr 29:20** 4480
Surely I am more stupid **t** any man, **Pr 30:2** 4480
and increased wisdom more **t** all who **Ec 1:16** 5921
I possessed flocks and herds larger **t** **Ec 2:7** 4480
increased more **t** all who preceded me **Ec 2:9** 4480
There is nothing better for a man **t** **Ec 2:24**
nothing better for them **t** to rejoice **Ec 3:12**
3588, 518
nothing is better **t** that man should **Ec 3:22** 4480
more **t** the living who are still living. **Ec 4:2** 4480
But better *off* **t** both of them is **Ec 4:3** 4480
One hand full of rest is better **t** **Ec 4:6** 4480
Two are better **t** one because they **Ec 4:9** 4480
yet wise lad is better **t** an old **Ec 4:13** 4480
and draw near to listen rather **t** **Ec 5:1** 4480
better that you should not vow **t** that **Ec 5:5** 4480
"Better the miscarriage **t** he, **Ec 6:3** 4480
it is better off **t** he. **Ec 6:5** 4480
is better **t** what the soul desires. **Ec 6:9** 4480
with him who is stronger **t** he is. **Ec 6:10** 4480
name is better **t** a good ointment, **Ec 7:1** 4480
is better **t** the day of one's birth. **Ec 7:1** 4480
T to go to a house of feasting, **Ec 7:2** 4480
Sorrow is better **t** laughter, **Ec 7:3** 4480
T for one to listen to the song of fools **Ec 7:5** 4480
matter is better **t** its beginning; **Ec 7:8** 4480
is better **t** haughtiness of spirit. **Ec 7:8** 4480
former days were better **t** these?" **Ec 7:10** 4480
t ten rulers who are in a city. **Ec 7:19** 4480
more bitter **t** death the woman **Ec 7:26** 4480
live dog is better **t** a dead lion. **Ec 9:4** 4480
"Wisdom is better **t** strength." **Ec 9:16** 4480
better **t** the shouting of a ruler among **Ec 9:17** 4480
Wisdom is better **t** weapons of war, **Ec 9:18** 4480
is weightier **t** wisdom *and* honor. **Ec 10:1** 4480
For your love is better **t** wine. **SS 1:2** 4480
will extol your love more **t** wine. **SS 1:4** 4480
much better is your love **t** wine, **SS 4:10** 4480
your oils **T** all *kinds* of spices! **SS 4:10** 4480
were greater **t** those of Jerusalem and **Is 10:10** 4480
mortal man scarcer **t** pure gold And **Is 13:12** 4480
And mankind **t** the gold of Ophir. **Is 13:12** 4480
regarded by Him as less **t** nothing **Is 40:17** 4480
was marred more **t** any man And **Is 52:14** 4480
His form more **t** the sons of men. **Is 52:14** 4480
T the sons of the married woman," **Is 54:1** 4480
heavens are higher **t** the earth, **Is 55:9** 4480
So are My ways higher **t** your ways **Is 55:9** 4480
And My thoughts **t** your thoughts. **Is 55:9** 4480
a name better **t** that of sons and **Is 56:5** 4480
near me, For I am holier **t** you!' **Is 65:5** 4480
more righteous **t** treacherous Judah. **Jer 3:11** 4480
His horses are swifter **t** eagles. **Jer 4:13** 4480
made their faces harder **t** rock; **Jer 5:3** 4480
did more evil **t** their fathers. **Jer 7:26** 4480
death will be chosen rather **t** life **Jer 8:3** 4480
before Me **T** the sand of the seas; **Jer 15:8** 4480
even more **t** your forefathers; **Jer 16:12** 4480
The heart is more deceitful **t** all else **Jer 17:9** 4480
hand of him who was stronger **t** he. **Jer 31:11** 4480
they are *now* more numerous **t** locusts **Jer 46:23** 4480
"More **t** the weeping for Jazer I **Jer 48:32** 4480
Is greater **t** the sin of Sodom, **La 4:6** 4480
ones were purer **t** snow, **La 4:7** 4480
snow, They were whiter **t** milk; **La 4:7** 4480
were more ruddy *in* body **t** corals, **La 4:7** 4480
appearance is blacker **t** soot, **La 4:8** 4480
sword **T** those slain with hunger; **La 4:9** 4480
swifter **T** the eagles of the sky; **La 4:19** 4480
"Like emery harder **t** flint I have **Ezk 3:9** 4480
more wickedly **t** the nations and **Ezk 5:6** 4480
t the lands which surround her; **Ezk 5:6** 4480
'Because you have more turmoil **t** **Ezk 5:7** 4480
t the wilderness toward Diblah; **Ezk 6:14** 4480
tumult rather **t** joyful shouting **Ezk 7:7** 3808
greater abominations **t** these." **Ezk 8:15** 4480
wood of the vine *better* **t** any wood **Ezk 15:2** 4480
more corruptly in all your conduct **t** **Ezk 16:47** 4480
your abominations more **t** they. **Ezk 16:51** 4480
you acted more abominably **t** they, **Ezk 16:52** 4480
they are more in the right **t** you. **Ezk 16:52** 4480

"rather **t** that he should turn **Ezk 18:23** 3808
them rather **t** destroying them, **Ezk 20:17** 4480
more corrupt in her lust **t** she, **Ezk 23:11** 4480
more **t** the harlotries of her sister. **Ezk 23:11** 4480
Behold, you are wiser **t** Daniel; **Ezk 28:3** 4480
loftier **t** all the trees of the field **Ezk 31:5** 4480
treat you better **t** at the first. **Ezk 36:11** 4480
took more *space* away from them **t** **Ezk 42:5** 4480
more **t** the lower and middle ones. **Ezk 42:6** 4480
looking more haggard **t** the youths **Da 1:10** 4480
they were fatter **t** all the youths who **Da 1:15** 4480
ten times better **t** all the magicians **Da 1:20** 5921
me more **t** in any *other* living man, **Da 2:30** 4481
more **t** it was usually heated. **Da 3:19**
5922, 1768
larger in appearance **t** its associates. **Da 7:20** 4481
but one *was* longer **t** the other, **Da 8:3** 4480
far more riches **t** all *of them;* **Da 11:2** 4480
a greater multitude **t** the former, **Da 11:13** 4480
it was better for me then **t** now!' **Hos 2:7** 4480
in loyalty rather **t** sacrifice, **Hos 6:6** 3808
of God rather **t** burnt offerings. **Hos 6:6** 4480
Are they better **t** these kingdoms, **Am 6:2** 4480
their territory greater **t** yours? **Am 6:2** 4480
death is better to me **t** life." **Jon 4:3** 4480
"Death is better to me **t** life." **Jon 4:8** 4480
there are more **t** 120,000 persons who **Jon 4:11** 4480
Are you better **t** No-amon, Which **Na 3:8** 4480
increased your traders more **t** the stars **Na 3:16** 4480
"Their horses are swifter **t** leopards **Hab 1:8** 4480
keener **t** wolves in the evening. **Hab 1:8** 4480
up Those more righteous **t** they? **Hab 1:13** 4480
with disgrace rather **t** honor. **Hab 2:16** 4480
will be greater **t** the former,' **Hg 2:9** 4480
coming after me is mightier **t** I, **Mt 3:11**
t for your whole body to be thrown **Mt 5:29**
2532, 3361
t for your whole body to go into **Mt 5:30**
2532, 3361
what more are you doing **t** *others?* **Mt 5:47**
Is not life more **t** food, **Mt 6:25**
food, and the body more **t** clothing? **Mt 6:25**
you not worth much more **t** they? **Mt 6:26**
day of judgment **t** for that city. **Mt 10:15** *2228*
are more valuable **t** many sparrows. **Mt 10:31**
loves father or mother more **t** Me **Mt 10:37** *5228*
loves son or daughter more **t** Me **Mt 10:37** *5228*
and one who is more **t** a prophet. **Mt 11:9**
anyone greater **t** John the Baptist! **Mt 11:11**
kingdom of heaven is greater **t** he. **Mt 11:11**
in *the* day of judgment **t** for you. **Mt 11:22** *2228*
the day of judgment, **t** for you." **Mt 11:24** *2228*
greater **t** the temple is here. **Mt 12:6**
valuable then is a man **t** a sheep! **Mt 12:12**
something greater **t** Jonah is here. **Mt 12:41**
greater **t** Solomon is here. **Mt 12:42**
spirits more wicked **t** itself, **Mt 12:45**
man becomes worse **t** the first. **Mt 12:45**
this is smaller **t** all *other* seeds, **Mt 13:32**
it is larger **t** the garden plants and **Mt 13:32**
t to have two hands or two feet **Mt 18:8** *2228*
with one eye, **t** to have two eyes **Mt 18:9** *2228*
he rejoices over it more **t** over **Mt 18:13** *2228*
t for a rich man to enter the **Mt 19:24** *2228*
group of slaves larger **t** the first; **Mt 21:36**
more **t** twelve legions of angels? **Mt 26:53**
deception will be worse **t** the first." **Mt 27:64**
One is coming who is mightier **t** I, **Mk 1:7**
smaller **t** all the seeds that are upon **Mk 4:31**
larger **t** all the garden plants and **Mk 4:32**
and did not have more **t** one loaf **Mk 8:14** *1508*
crippled, **t**, having your two hands, **Mk 9:43** *2228*
life lame, **t**, having your two feet, **Mk 9:45** *2228*
with one eye, **t**, having two eyes, **Mk 9:47** *2228*
t for a rich man to enter the kingdom **Mk 10:25** *2228*
commandment greater **t** these." **Mk 12:31**
is much more **t** all burnt offerings **Mk 12:33**
this poor widow put in more **t** all **Mk 12:43**
t what you have been ordered to." **Lk 3:13** *3844*
One is coming who is mightier **t** I, **Lk 3:16**
and one who is more **t** a prophet. **Lk 7:26**
there is no one greater **t** John; **Lk 7:28**
kingdom of God is greater **t** he." **Lk 7:28**
no more **t** five loaves and two fish, **Lk 9:13** *2228*
day for Sodom **t** for that city. **Lk 10:12** *2228*
Sidon in the judgment **t** for you. **Lk 10:14** *2228*
"But when someone stronger **t** he **Lk 11:22**
other spirits more evil **t** itself, **Lk 11:26**
man becomes worse **t** the first." **Lk 11:26**
greater **t** Solomon is here. **Lk 11:31**
something greater **t** Jonah is here. **Lk 11:32**
are more valuable **t** many sparrows. **Lk 12:7**
"For life is more **t** food, **Lk 12:23**
food, and the body more **t** clothing. **Lk 12:23**
more valuable you are **t** the birds! **Lk 12:24**
greater sinners **t** all *other* Galileans **Lk 13:2** *3844*
were *worse* culprits **t** all the men **Lk 13:4** *3844*
someone more distinguished **t** you **Lk 14:8**
t over ninety-nine righteous **Lk 15:7** *2228*
men have more **t** enough bread, **Lk 15:17** *4052*
own kind **t** the sons of light. **Lk 16:8** *5228*
t for one stroke of a letter of the Law **Lk 16:17** *2228*
t that he would cause one of **Lk 17:2** *2228*
justified rather **t** the other; **Lk 18:14** *3844*
t for a rich man to enter the **Lk 18:25** *2228*
widow put in more **t** all *of them;* **Lk 21:3**
after me has a higher rank **t** I, **Jn 1:15**
a Man who has a higher rank **t** I, **Jn 1:30**
see greater things **t** these." **Jn 1:50**

the darkness rather **t** the Light **Jn 3:19** *2228*
baptizing more disciples **t** John **Jn 4:1** *2228*
not greater **t** our father Jacob, **Jn 4:12**
will show Him greater works **t** these, **Jn 5:20**
greater **t** *the testimony of* John; **Jn 5:36**
signs **t** those which this man has, **Jn 7:31**
not greater **t** our father Abraham, **Jn 8:53**
them to Me, is greater **t** all; **Jn 10:29**
men rather **t** the approval of God. **Jn 12:43** *2228*
slave is not greater **t** his master, **Jn 13:16**
greater **t** the one who sent him. **Jn 13:16**
greater *works* **t** these he will do; **Jn 14:12**
for the Father is greater **t** I. **Jn 14:28**
"Greater love has no one **t** this, **Jn 15:13**
'A slave is not greater **t** his master.' **Jn 15:20**
disciple ran ahead faster **t** Peter and **Jn 20:4**
do you love Me more **t** these?" **Jn 21:15**
give heed to you rather **t** to God, **Ac 4:19** *2228*
the man was more **t** forty years old **Ac 4:22**
"We must obey God rather **t** men. **Ac 5:29** *2228*
no greater burden **t** these essentials: **Ac 15:28** *4133*
were more noble-minded **t** those in **Ac 17:11**
their time in nothing other **t** telling **Ac 17:21** *2228*
It is more blessed to give **t** to receive **Ac 20:35** *2228*
more **t** forty who formed this plot. **Ac 23:13**
for more **t** forty of them are lying **Ac 23:21**
no more **t** twelve days ago I went up **Ac 24:11**
other **t** for this one statement **Ac 24:21** *2228*
spent not more **t** eight or ten days **Ac 25:6**
light from heaven, brighter **t** the sun **Ac 26:13** *5228*
t by what was being said by Paul. **Ac 27:11** *2228*
the creature rather **t** the Creator, **Ro 1:25** *3844*
Are we better **t** they? **Ro 3:9**
of himself **t** he ought to think; **Ro 12:3** *3844*
nearer to us **t** when we believed. **Ro 13:11** *2228*
foolishness of God is wiser **t** men, **1Co 1:25**
weakness of God is stronger **t** men. **1Co 1:25**
other **t** the one which is laid, **1Co 3:11** *3844*
it is better to marry **t** to burn **1Co 7:9** *2228*
better for me to die **t** have any man **1Co 9:15** *2228*
We are not stronger **t** He, **1Co 10:22**
t one who speaks in tongues, **1Co 14:5** *2228*
I speak in tongues more **t** you all; **1Co 14:18**
rather **t** ten thousand words in a **1Co 14:19** *2228*
He appeared to more **t** five hundred **1Co 15:6** *1883*
I labored even more **t** all of them, **1Co 15:10**
t what you read and understand, **2Co 1:13** *2228*
no one will credit me with more **t** he **2Co 12:6** *5228*
T OF THE ONE WHO HAS A HUSBAND." **Ga 4:27** *2228*
rather **t** from pure motives, **Php 1:17** *3756*
as more important **t** yourselves; **Php 2:3**
More **t** that, I count all things to **Php 3:8** *3304*
a gift more **t** once for my needs. **Php 4:16** *2532*
rather **t** according to Christ. **Col 2:8**
2532, 3756
as for the Lord rather **t** for men, **Col 3:23**
2532, 3756
I, Paul, more **t** once **1Th 2:18** *2532*
mere speculation rather **t** *furthering* **1Tm 1:4** *2228*
of our Lord was more **t** abundant, **1Tm 1:14** *5250*
and is worse **t** an unbeliever. **1Tm 5:8**
she is not less **t** sixty years old, **1Tm 5:9**
pleasure rather **t** lovers of God, **2Tm 3:4** *2228*
as a slave, but more **t** a slave, **Phm 1:16** *5228*
will do even more **t** what I say. **Phm 1:21** *5228*
as much better **t** the angels, **Heb 1:4**
a more excellent name **t** they. **Heb 1:4** *3844*
A LITTLE WHILE LOWER **T** THE ANGELS; **Heb 2:7** *3844*
a little while lower **t** the angels, **Heb 2:9** *3844*
worthy of more glory **t** Moses, **Heb 3:3** *3844*
house has more honor **t** the house. **Heb 3:3**
and sharper **t** any two-edged sword, **Heb 4:12** *5228*
For men swear by one greater **t** **Heb 6:16**
with better sacrifices **t** these. **Heb 9:23** *3844*
to God a better sacrifice **t** Cain, **Heb 11:4** *3844*
t to enjoy the passing pleasures **Heb 11:25** *2228*
reproach of Christ greater riches **t** **Heb 11:26**
speaks better **t** *the blood* of Abel. **Heb 12:24** *3844*
being more precious **t** gold which is **1Pe 1:7**
rather **t** for doing what is wrong. **1Pe 3:17** *2228*
become worse for them **t** the first. **2Pe 2:20**
righteousness, **t** having known it, **2Pe 2:21** *2228*
for God is greater **t** our heart and **1Jn 3:20**
greater is He who is in you **t** he **1Jn 4:4** *2228*
I have no greater joy **t** this, **3Jn 1:4**
of late are greater **t** at first. **Rv 2:19**

THANK

t and praise the LORD God of Israel **1Ch 16:4** 3034
to **t** and to praise the LORD, **1Ch 23:30** 3034
"Now therefore, our God, we **t** You, **1Ch 29:13** 3034
and bring sacrifices and **t** offerings **2Ch 29:31** 8426
sacrifices and **t** offerings, **2Ch 29:31** 8426
offerings and **t** offerings on it; **2Ch 33:16** 8426
And with my song I shall **t** Him. **Ps 28:7** 3034
I will render **t** offerings to You. **Ps 56:12** 8426
"For Sheol cannot **t** You, **Is 38:18** 3034
who bring a **t** offering into the house **Jer 33:11** 8426
"Offer a **t** offering also from **Am 4:5** 8426
"He does not **t** the slave because **Lk 17:9** *5485*
I **t** You that I am not like other **Lk 18:11** *2168*
I **t** You that You have heard Me. **Jn 11:41** *2168*
I **t** my God through Jesus Christ **Ro 1:8** *2168*
I **t** my God always concerning you for **1Co 1:4** *2168*
I **t** God that I baptized none of **1Co 1:14** *2168*
I **t** God, I speak in tongues more **1Co 14:18** *2168*
I **t** my God in all my remembrance **Php 1:3** *2168*
this reason we also constantly **t** God **1Th 2:13** *2168*
I **t** Christ Jesus our Lord, who has **1Tm 1:12** *5485*
I **t** God, whom I serve with a clear **2Tm 1:3** *5485*

I t my God always, making mention Phm 1:4 2168

THANKED

If his loins have not t me, Jb 31:20 1288
them, he t God and took courage. Ac 28:15 2168

THANKFUL

were called in one body; and be t. Col 3:15 2170

THANKFULNESS

most excellent Felix, with all t. Ac 24:3 2169
If I partake with t, 1Co 10:30 5485
singing with t in your hearts to God. Col 3:16 5485

THANKS

"Therefore I will give t to You, 2Sa 22:50 3034
relatives to give t to the LORD. 1Ch 16:7 3034
Oh give t to the LORD, call upon 1Ch 16:8 3034
O give t to the LORD, for *He is* 1Ch 16:34 3034
To give t to Your holy name, 1Ch 16:35 3034
by name, to give t to the LORD, 1Ch 16:41 3034
in giving t and praising the LORD. 1Ch 25:3 3034
"Give t to the LORD, for His 2Ch 20:21 3034
offerings and giving t to the LORD 2Ch 30:22 3034
to minister and to give t and to 2Ch 31:2 3034
praising and giving t to the LORD, Ezr 3:11 3034
them, to praise *and* give t, Ne 12:24 3034
In Sheol who will give You t? Ps 6:5 3034
I will give t to the LORD Ps 7:17 3034
t to the LORD with all my heart; Ps 9:1 3034
give t to You among the nations, Ps 18:49 3034
ones, And give t to His holy name. Ps 30:4 3034
I will give t to You forever. Ps 30:12 3034
Give t to the LORD with the lyre; Ps 33:2 3034
I will give You t in the great Ps 35:18 3034
will give t to Your name forever. Ps 44:8 3034
will give You t forever and ever. Ps 45:17 3034
I will give You t forever, Ps 52:9 3034
I will give t to Your name, O LORD, Ps 54:6 3034
I will give t to You, O Lord, Ps 57:9 3034
We give t to You, O God, we give Ps 75:1 3034
thanks to You, O God, we give t, Ps 75:1 3034
Will give t to You forever; Ps 79:13 3034
I will give t to You, O Lord my Ps 86:12 3034
It is good to give t to the LORD And Ps 92:1 3034
And give t to His holy name. Ps 97:12 3034
Give t to Him, bless His name. Ps 100:4 3034
Oh give t to the LORD, call upon Ps 105:1 3034
Oh give t to the LORD, for He is Ps 106:1 3034
To give t to Your holy name And Ps 106:47 3034
Oh give t to the LORD, for He is Ps 107:1 3034
Let them give t to the LORD for Ps 107:8 3034
Let them give t to the LORD for Ps 107:15 3034
Let them give t to the LORD for Ps 107:21 3034
Let them give t to the LORD for Ps 107:31 3034
I will give t to You, O LORD, Ps 108:3 3034
give t abundantly to the LORD; Ps 109:30 3034
I will give t to the LORD with all *my* Ps 111:1 3034
Give t to the LORD, for He is good; Ps 118:1 3034
them, I shall give t to the LORD. Ps 118:19 3034
I shall give t to You, for You Ps 118:21 3034
are my God, and I give t to You; Ps 118:28 3034
Give t to the LORD, for He is good; Ps 118:29 3034
I shall give t to You with Ps 119:7 3034
midnight I shall rise to give t to You Ps 119:62 3034
To give t to the name of the LORD. Ps 122:4 3034
Give t to the LORD, for He is good, Ps 136:1 3034
Give t to the God of gods, For His Ps 136:2 3034
Give t to the Lord of lords, For Ps 136:3 3034
Give t to the God of heaven, For Ps 136:26 3034
give You t with all my heart; Ps 138:1 3034
And give t to Your name for Your Ps 138:2 3034
kings of the earth will give t to You Ps 138:4 3034
I will give t to You, for I am Ps 139:14 3034
righteous will give t to Your name; Ps 140:13 3034
So that I may give t to Your name; Ps 142:7 3034
Your works shall give t to You, Ps 145:10 3034
"I will give t to You, O LORD; Is 12:1 3034
"Give t to the LORD, call on His Is 12:4 3034
You, I will give t to Your name; Is 25:1 3034
is the living who give t to You, Is 38:19 3034
"Give t to the LORD of hosts, For Jer 33:11 3034
my fathers, I give t and praise, Da 2:23 3029
and giving t before his God, Da 6:10 3029
and giving t, He broke them and Mt 15:36 2168
He had taken a cup and given t, Mt 26:27 2168
loaves, He gave t and broke them, Mk 8:6 2168
He had taken a cup *and* given t, Mk 14:23 2168
came up and *began* giving t to God, Lk 2:38 437
face at His feet, giving t to Him. Lk 17:16 2168
He had taken a cup *and* given t, Lk 22:17 2168
had taken *some* bread *and* given t, Lk 22:19 2168
and having given t, Jn 6:11 2168
bread after the Lord had given t. Jn 6:23 2168
gave t to God in the presence of all Ac 27:35 2168
not honor Him as God or give t Ro 1:21 2168
But t be to God that though you Ro 6:17 5485
T be to God through Jesus Christ Ro 7:25 5485
the Lord, for he gives t to God; Ro 14:6 2168
does not eat, and gives t to God. Ro 14:6 2168
to whom not only do I give t, Ro 16:4 2168
that for which I give t? 1Co 10:30 2168
and when He had given t, 1Co 11:24 2168
"Amen" at your giving of t, 1Co 14:16 2169
For you are giving t well enough, 1Co 14:17 2168
but t be to God, who gives us the 1Co 15:57 5485
that t may be given by many 2Co 1:11 2168
But t be to God, who always leads 2Co 2:14 5485
may cause the giving of t to abound 2Co 4:15 2169
But t be to God who puts the same 2Co 8:16 5485
T be to God for His indescribable 2Co 9:15 5485
do not cease giving t for you, Eph 1:16 2168
fitting, but rather giving of t. Eph 5:4 2169
always giving t for all things in Eph 5:20 2168
We give t to God, the Father of Col 1:3 2168
giving t to the Father, who has Col 1:12 2168
giving t through Him to God the Col 3:17 2168
We give t to God always for all of 1Th 1:2 2168
For what t can we render to God 1Th 3:9 2169
in everything give t; 1Th 5:18 2168
always to give t to God for you, 2Th 1:3 2168
always give t to God for you, 2Th 2:13 2168
of lips that give t to His name. Heb 13:15 3670
t to Him who sits on the throne, Rv 4:9 2169
"We give You t, O Lord God, the Rv 11:17 2168

THANKSGIVING

'If he offers it by way of t, Lv 7:12 8426
with the sacrifice of t he shall offer Lv 7:12 8426
sacrifice of his peace offerings for t, Lv 7:13 8426
for the flesh of the sacrifice of his t Lv 7:15 8426
a sacrifice of t to the LORD, Lv 22:29 8426
in beginning the t at prayer, Ne 11:17 3034
was in charge of the songs of t, Ne 12:8 1960
with hymns of t and with songs *to* Ne 12:27 8426
of praise and hymns of t to God. Ne 12:46 3034
may proclaim with the voice of t And Ps 26:7 8426
God, With the voice of joy and t, Ps 42:4 8426
"Offer to God a sacrifice of t And Ps 50:14 8426
He who offers a sacrifice of t honors Ps 50:23 8426
And magnify Him with t. Ps 69:30 8426
come before His presence with t, Ps 95:2 8426
Enter His gates with t Ps 100:4 8426
them also offer sacrifices of t, Ps 107:22 8426
I shall offer a sacrifice of t, Ps 116:17 8426
Sing to the LORD with t; Ps 147:7 8426
in her, T and sound of a melody. Is 51:3 8426
bringing sacrifices of t to the house Jer 17:26 8426
'From them will proceed t And Jer 30:19 8426
to You With the voice of t. Jon 2:9 8426
through us is producing t to God. 2Co 9:11 2169
with t let your requests be made Php 4:6 2169
alert in it with *an attitude of* t; Col 4:2 2169
t and honor and power and might, Rv 7:12 2169

THANKSGIVINGS

overflowing through many t to God. 2Co 9:12 2169
and prayers, petitions *and* t, 1Tm 2:1 2169

THAT'S

"T right! As you have said, so it Ezr 10:12

THEATER

rushed with one accord into the t, Ac 19:29 2302
urged him not to venture into the t. Ac 19:31 2302

THEBES

I am going to punish Amon of T, Jer 46:25 4996
Zoan And execute judgments on T. Ezk 30:14 4996
also cut off the hordes of T. Ezk 30:15 4996
in anguish, T will be breached And Ezk 30:16 4996

THEBEZ

Then Abimelech went to T, Jg 9:50 8405
camped against T and captured it. Jg 9:50 8405
the wall so that he died at T? 2Sa 11:21 8405

THEFT

then he shall be sold for his t. Ex 22:3 1591

THEFTS

adulteries, fornications, t, Mt 15:19 2829
evil thoughts, fornications, t, Mk 7:21 2829
their immorality nor of their t. Rv 9:21 2809

THEIRS

strangers in a land that is not t, Gn 15:13 1992a
five times as much as any of t. Gn 43:34
t *was* the service of the holy *objects,* Nu 7:9 5921, 1992a
them up with all that is t, Nu 16:30 1992a
every offering of t, Nu 18:9
the sons of Reuben have received t Nu 34:14
The cities shall be t to live in; Nu 35:3 1992a
This shall become t as pasture Nu 35:5 1992a
of Levi, for the lot was t first. Jos 21:10 1992a
But nothing of t was missing, 1Sa 30:19 1992a
(for t was the *first* lot), 1Ch 6:54 1992a
according to these works of t, Ne 6:14
land, Everlasting joy will be t. Is 61:7 1992a
whose word will stand, Mine or t. Jer 44:28 4480, 1992a
thing in Israel shall be t. Ezk 44:29 4480, 1992a
Destruction is t, for they have Hos 7:13
dwelling places which are not t. Hab 1:6
comeliness and beauty *will be* t! Zch 9:17
for t is the kingdom of heaven. Mt 5:3 846
for t is the kingdom of heaven. Mt 5:10 846
put my seal on this fruit of t, Ro 15:28 846

THEME

My heart overflows with a good t; Ps 45:1 1697

THEMSELVES

and made t loin coverings. Gn 3:7 1992a
and the man and his wife hid t Gn 3:8
and they took wives for t, Gn 6:2
Abram and Nahor took wives for t. Gn 11:29
so that they wearied t *trying* to Gn 19:11
seven ewe lambs of the flock by t. Gn 21:28 905
mean, which you have set by t?" Gn 21:29 905
him by himself, and them by t, Gn 43:32 905
Egyptians who ate with him by t, Gn 43:32 905
also join t to those who hate us, Ex 1:10
them go and gather straw for t. Ex 5:7 1992a
down to me and bow t before me, Ex 11:8
are each one to take a lamb for t, Ex 12:3
prepared any provisions for t. Ex 12:39
minor dispute they t will judge. Ex 18:22
minor dispute they t would judge. Ex 18:26
near to the LORD consecrate t, Ex 19:22
as your stranger, may refresh t. Ex 23:12
You shall join five curtains by t Ex 26:9 905
and the *other* six curtains by t, Ex 26:9 905
land of Egypt, have corrupted t. Ex 32:7
have made for t a molten calf, Ex 32:8
have made a god of gold for t. Ex 32:31
Israel stripped t of their ornaments Ex 33:6
He joined five curtains by t Ex 36:16 905
and *the other* six curtains by t. Ex 36:16 905
purified t from sin and washed Nu 8:21
but they t shall do no work. Nu 8:26
congregation shall gather t to you Nu 10:3
they spread *them* out for t Nu 11:32
they shall make for t tassels on the Nu 15:38
they assembled t against Moses and Nu 20:2
Israel joined t to Baal of Peor, Nu 25:3
have joined t to Baal of Peor." Nu 25:5
gathered t together against the LORD Nu 27:3
those who are left and hide t from Dt 7:20
have made a molten image for t.' Dt 9:12
presented t at the tent of meeting. Dt 31:14
Even our enemies t judge this. Dt 32:31
of that city as plunder for t, Jos 8:27
that they gathered t together with Jos 9:2
feet, and worn-out clothes on t; Jos 9:5
nation avenged t of their enemies. Jos 10:13
hidden t in the cave at Makkedah. Jos 10:16
the cave where they had hidden t, Jos 10:27
sons of Israel assembled t at Shiloh, Jos 18:1
sons of Israel gathered t at Shiloh to Jos 22:12
and they presented t before God. Jos 24:1
them, and bowed t down to them; Jg 2:12
gods and bowed t down to them. Jg 2:17
took their daughters for t as wives, Jg 3:6
the sons of Israel made for t the dens Jg 6:2
the sons of the east assembled t; Jg 6:33
the city fled there and shut t in; Jg 9:51
fellows gathered t about Jephthah, Jg 11:3
an inheritance for t to live in, Jg 18:1
Dan set up for t the graven image; Jg 18:30
So they set up for t Micah's Jg 18:31
encouraged t and arrayed for Jg 20:22
they had arrayed t the first day. Jg 20:22
day and arrayed t against Gibeah as Jg 20:30
place and arrayed t at Baal-tamar; Jg 20:33
took for t Moabite women *as* wives; Ru 1:4 1992a
were full hire t out for bread, 1Sa 2:5
his sons brought a curse on t and 1Sa 3:13 1992a
then the people hid t in caves, 1Sa 13:6
When both of them revealed t 1Sa 14:11
holes where they have hidden t." 1Sa 14:11
the men of Israel who had hidden t 1Sa 14:22
men have kept t from women." 1Sa 21:4
that they had taken for t; 1Sa 30:19 1992a
and spread t out in the valley of 2Sa 5:18
and spread t out in the valley of 2Sa 5:22
and Maacah *were* by t in the field. 2Sa 10:8 905
Israel, they gathered t together. 2Sa 10:15
And the Arameans arrayed t to meet 2Sa 10:17
daughters of the king dressed t in 2Sa 13:18
All the men of Israel assembled t to 1Ki 8:2
For they also built for t high places 1Ki 14:23
choose one ox for t and cut it up, 1Ki 18:23
and cut t according to their custom 1Ki 18:28
So they stationed t against 1Ki 20:12
(now the harlots bathed t *there*), 1Ki 22:38
bowed t to the ground before him. 2Ki 2:15
the camp to hide t in the field, 2Ki 7:12
of Judah, and made a king over t. 2Ki 8:20
let the priests take it for t, 2Ki 12:5
they built for t high places in 2Ki 17:9
They set for t *sacred* pillars 2Ki 17:10
God and made for t molten images, 2Ki 17:16
and sold t to do evil in the sight 2Ki 17:17
and appointed from among t priests 2Ki 17:32
Levites consecrated t to bring up the 1Ch 15:14
they had made t odious to David, 1Ch 19:6
to hire for t chariots and horsemen 1Ch 19:6
they hired for t 32,000 chariots, 1Ch 19:7
had come were by t in the field. 1Ch 19:9 905
arrayed t against the Arameans. 1Ch 19:10
they arrayed t against the sons of 1Ch 19:11
four sons *who were* with him hid t. 1Ch 21:20
All the men of Israel assembled t to 2Ch 5:3
who were present had sanctified t, 2Ch 5:11
and the singers were to make t heard 2Ch 5:13
by My name humble t and pray and 2Ch 7:14
and the king humbled t and said, 2Ch 12:6
the LORD saw that they humbled t, 2Ch 12:7
"They have humbled t *so* I will not 2Ch 12:7
things which they took for t, 2Ch 20:25
Judah and set up a king over t. 2Ch 21:8
their brothers, consecrated t, 2Ch 29:15
other priests had consecrated t. 2Ch 29:34
to consecrate t than the priests. 2Ch 29:34
the priests had not consecrated t in 2Ch 30:3
humbled t and came to Jerusalem. 2Ch 30:11
and Levites were ashamed of t, 2Ch 30:15
of themselves, and consecrated t 2Ch 30:15
who had not consecrated t; 2Ch 30:17
and Zebulun, had not purified t, 2Ch 30:18
number of priests consecrated t. 2Ch 30:24
devote t to the law of the LORD. 2Ch 31:4
consecrated t faithfully in holiness. 2Ch 31:18
for t and for the priests, 2Ch 35:14
for t and for the priests, 2Ch 35:14
Levites had purified t together; Ezr 6:20

brothers the priests and for **t**. Ezr 6:20
those who had separated **t** from the Ezr 6:21
Levites have not separated **t** from Ezr 9:1
as wives for **t** and for their sons, Ezr 9:2
they going to restore *it* for **t**? Ne 4:2
them and made booths for **t**, Ne 8:16
separated **t** from all foreigners, Ne 9:2
"Even when they made for **t** A calf Ne 9:18
who had separated **t** from the peoples Ne 10:28
and are taking on **t** a curse and an Ne 10:29
singers had built **t** villages around Ne 12:29
and the Levites purified **t**; Ne 12:30
the Levites that they should purify **t** Ne 13:22
day to avenge **t** on their enemies. Es 8:13
Jews **t** gained the mastery over those Es 9:1 1992a
lives and rid **t** of their enemies, Es 9:16 5117
the Jews rid **t** of their enemies, Es 9:22 5117
and made a custom for **t** and Es 9:27
all those who allied **t** with them, Es 9:27
just as they had established for **t** and Es 9:31 5315
came to present **t** before the LORD, Jb 1:6
came to present **t** before the LORD, Jb 2:1
earth, Who rebuilt ruins for **t**; Jb 3:14
They have massed **t** against me. Jb 16:10
are made to hide **t** altogether. Jb 24:4
houses, They shut **t** up by day; Jb 24:16
The young men saw me and hid **t**, Jb 29:8
workers of iniquity may hide **t**. Jb 34:22
that they have magnified **t**. Jb 36:9
have set **t** against me round about. Ps 3:6
rejoiced and gathered **t** together; Ps 35:15
dishonor who magnify **t** over me. Ps 35:26
delight **t** in abundant prosperity. Ps 37:11
would magnify **t** against me." Ps 38:16
hate us have taken spoil for **t**. Ps 44:10
have assembled **t** *as* the people of the Ps 47:9
For, lo, the kings assembled **t**, Ps 48:4
They **t** have fallen into the midst Ps 57:6
they run and set **t** against me. Ps 59:4
hold fast to **t** an evil purpose; Ps 64:5
the hills gird **t** with rejoicing. Ps 65:12
Let not the rebellious exalt **t**. Ps 66:7
And let *men* bless **t** by him; Ps 72:17
And our enemies laugh among **t**. Ps 80:6
those who hate You have exalted **t**. Ps 83:2 7218
All who do wickedness vaunt **t**. Ps 94:4
They band **t** together against the Ps 94:21
images, Who boast **t** of idols; Ps 97:7
They joined **t** also to Baal-peor, Ps 106:28
And let them cover **t** with their Ps 109:29
scoffers delight **t** in scoffing And Pr 1:22
when the wicked rise, men hide **t**. Pr 28:12
When the wicked rise, men hide **t**; Pr 28:28
of men with which to occupy **t**. Ec 3:10
Which they made for **t** to worship, Is 2:20
For they have brought evil on **t**. Is 3:9
attach **t** to the house of Jacob. Is 14:1
they have girded **t** with sackcloth; Is 15:3
Its tendrils spread **t** out *and* passed Is 16:8
for the craftsmen **t** are mere men. Is 44:11 1992a
Let them all assemble **t**, Is 44:11
But have **t** gone into captivity. Is 46:2 5315
They cannot deliver **t** from the Is 47:14 5315
they call **t** after the holy city And Is 48:2
foreigners who join **t** to the LORD, Is 56:6
they cover **t** with their works; Is 59:6
bow **t** at the soles of your feet; Is 60:14
and purify **t** *to go* to the gardens, Is 66:17
waters, To hew for **t** cisterns, Jer 2:13
the nations will bless **t** in Him, Jer 4:2
"Is it not **t** *they spite*, to their Jer 7:19
They weary **t** committing iniquity. Jer 9:5
They have strained **t** to no profit. Jer 12:13
They will carry off for **t** Their tent Jer 49:29
that they may join **t** to the LORD Jer 50:5
for food To restore their lives **t**. La 1:11
food to restore their strength **t**. La 1:19
They have girded **t** with sackcloth. La 2:10
"Depart! Unclean!" they cried of **t**. La 4:15
and they will loathe **t** in their Ezk 6:9
They will gird **t** with sackcloth Ezk 7:18
they were prostrating **t** eastward Ezk 8:16
and no longer defile **t** with all their Ezk 14:11
they could *only* deliver **t**," Ezk 14:14 5315
They would deliver only **t** by their Ezk 14:20 5315
They will set **t** against you on Ezk 23:24
guilt, and avenged **t** upon them," Ezk 25:12
They will clothe **t** with trembling; Ezk 26:16
"Also they will make **t** bald for Ezk 27:31
for you And gird **t** with sackcloth; Ezk 27:31
of Israel who have been feeding **t**! Ezk 34:2
fed **t** and did not feed My flock; Ezk 34:8
shepherds will not feed **t** anymore, Ezk 34:10
who appropriated My land for **t** as Ezk 36:5
you will **t** endure their insults. Ezk 36:7 1992a
longer defile **t** with their idols, Ezk 37:23
they shall not gird **t** with Ezk 44:18
not go to a dead person to defile **t**; Ezk 44:25
had a husband, they may defile **t**. Ezk 44:25
living creatures fed **t** from it. Da 4:12
them, and they ran away to hide **t**. Da 10:7
lift **t** up in order to fulfill the vision, Da 11:14
will appoint for **t** one leader, Hos 1:11
For *the men* **t** go apart with Hos 4:14 1992a
and new wine they assemble **t**, Hos 7:14
gold they have made idols for **t**, Hos 8:4
their bread will be for **t** *alone;* Hos 9:4 5315
Baal-peor and devoted **t** to shame, Hos 9:10
And make for **t** molten images, Hos 13:2
David have composed songs for **t**, Am 6:5
anoint **t** with the finest of oils, Am 6:6
And though they conceal **t** from My Am 9:3
and authority originate with **t**. Hab 1:7
clothe **t** with foreign garments. Zph 1:8
"Many nations will join **t** to Zch 2:11
empty the golden *oil* from **t**?" Zch 4:12
by itself and their wives by **t**; Zch 12:12 905
by itself and their wives by **t**; Zch 12:12 905
by itself and their wives by **t**; Zch 12:13 905
by itself and their wives by **t**; Zch 12:13 905
by itself and their wives by **t**. Zch 12:14 905
some of the scribes said to **t**, Mt 9:3 1438
the villages and buy food for **t**." Mt 14:15 1438
They began to discuss *this* among **t**, Mt 16:7 1438
them up on a high mountain by **t**. Mt 17:1 2398
also eunuchs who made **t** eunuchs Mt 19:12 1438
the twelve *disciples* aside by **t**, Mt 20:17 2398
And they *began* reasoning among **t**, Mt 21:25 1438
saw the son, they said among **t**, Mt 21:38 1438
Sadducees, they gathered **t** together. Mt 22:34
seated **t** in the chair of Moses; Mt 23:2 2523
but they **t** are unwilling to move Mt 23:4 846
"Then they **t** also will answer, Mt 25:44 846
divided up His garments among **t** by Mt 27:35
so that they debated among **t**, Mk 1:27 846
were reasoning that way within **t**, Mk 2:8 1438
and they have no *firm* root in **t**, Mk 4:17 1438
the boat to a secluded place by **t**. Mk 6:32 2398
and buy **t** something to eat." Mk 6:36 1438
do not eat unless they cleanse **t**; Mk 7:4
them up on a high mountain by **t**. Mk 9:2
2398, 3441
They *began* reasoning among **t**, Mk 11:31 1438
divided up His garments among **t**, Mk 15:24
mocking *Him* among **t** and saying, Mk 15:31 240
He appeared to the eleven **t** as they Mk 16:14 846
But they **t** were filled with rage, Lk 6:11 846
rejected God's purpose for **t**, Lk 7:30 1438
table with Him began to say to **t**, Lk 7:49 1438
some people who trusted in **t** that Lk 18:9 1438
They reasoned among **t**, Lk 20:5 1438
And they began to discuss among **t** Lk 22:23 1438
dividing up His garments among **t**. Lk 23:34
for they **t** also went to the feast. Jn 4:45 846
they **t** got into the small boats, Jn 6:24 846
before the Passover to purify **t**. Jn 11:55 1438
believe because of the works **t**. Jn 14:11 846
and *yet* they **t** are in the world, Jn 17:11 846
may have My joy made full in **t**. Jn 17:13 1438
that they **t** also may be sanctified Jn 17:19 846
was cold and they were warming **t**; Jn 18:18
and they **t** did not enter into the Jn 18:28 846
continually devoting **t** to prayer, Ac 1:14 4342
tongues as of fire distributing **t**, Ac 2:3
devoting **t** to the apostles' teaching Ac 2:42 4342
who **t** will also report the same Ac 15:27 846
and Silas, also being prophets **t**, Ac 15:32 846
let them come **t** and bring us out." Ac 16:37 846
they **t** understand that in one Ac 22:19 846
and bound **t** under an oath, Ac 23:12 1438
bound **t** under a curse not to eat or Ac 23:21 1438
in God, which these men cherish **t**, Ac 24:15 846
"Or else let these men **t** tell Ac 24:20 846
in this way let **t** be driven along. Ac 27:17
and they **t** also took food. Ac 27:36 846
having a great dispute among **t**. Ac 28:29 1438
having the Law, are a law to **t**, Ro 2:14 1438
did not subject **t** to the righteousness Ro 10:3
will receive condemnation upon **t**. Ro 13:2 1438
devoting **t** to this very thing. Ro 13:6 4342
to speak, but are to subject **t**, 1Co 14:34
devoted **t** for ministry to the saints 1Co 16:15 1438
live might no longer live for **t**, 2Co 5:15 1438
but they first gave **t** to the Lord 2Co 8:5 1438
with some of those who commend **t**; 2Co 10:12 1438
when they measure **t** by themselves and 2Co 10:12 1438
when they measure themselves by **t** and 2Co 10:12 1438
and compare **t** with themselves, 2Co 10:12 1438
and compare themselves with **t**, 2Co 10:12 1438
disguising **t** as apostles of Christ. 2Co 11:13
servants also disguise **t** as servants 2Co 11:15
you would even mutilate **t**. Ga 5:12
do not even keep the Law **t**, Ga 6:13 846
have given **t** over to sensuality for Eph 4:19 1438
For they **t** report about us what 1Th 1:9 846
to adorn **t** with proper clothing, 1Tm 2:9 1438
obtain for **t** a high standing and great 1Tm 3:13 1438
and pierced **t** with many griefs. 1Tm 6:10 1438
storing up for **t** the treasure of a 1Tm 6:19 1438
they will accumulate for **t** teachers 2Tm 4:3 1438
One of **t**, a prophet of their own, Ti 1:12 846
again crucify to **t** the Son of God and Heb 6:6 1438
men swear by one greater *than* **t**, Heb 6:16
but the heavenly things **t** with Heb 9:23 846
not merely hearers who delude **t**. Jas 1:22 1438
them that they were not serving **t**, 1Pe 1:12 1438
who hoped in God, used to adorn **t**, 1Pe 3:5 1438
bringing swift destruction upon **t**. 2Pe 2:1 1438
they **t** are slaves of corruption; 2Pe 2:19 846
you without fear, caring for **t**; Jude 1:12 1438
test those who call **t** apostles, Rv 2:2 1438
hid **t** in the caves and among the Rv 6:15 1438
trumpets prepared **t** to sound them. Rv 8:6 848
for they have kept **t** chaste. Rv 14:4 1510

THEN

T God said, "Let there be light" Gn 1:3
T God said, "Let there be an Gn 1:6
T God said, "Let the waters below Gn 1:9
T God said, "Let the earth sprout Gn 1:11
T God said, "Let there be lights in Gn 1:14
T God said, "Let the waters teem Gn 1:20
T God said, "Let the earth bring Gn 1:24
T God said, "Let Us make man in Gn 1:26
T God said, "Behold, I have given Gn 1:29
T God blessed the seventh day and Gn 2:3
T the LORD God formed man of dust Gn 2:7
T the LORD God took the man and Gn 2:15
T the LORD God said, Gn 2:18
t He took one of his ribs and Gn 2:21
T the eyes of both of them were Gn 3:7
T the LORD God called to the man, Gn 3:9
T the LORD God said to the woman, Gn 3:13
T to Adam He said, Gn 3:17
T the LORD God said, Gn 3:22
T the LORD said to Cain, Gn 4:6
T the LORD said to Cain, Gn 4:9
T Cain went out from the presence Gn 4:16
T Lamech seventy-sevenfold." Gn 4:24
T *men* began to call upon the name Gn 4:26 227
T the days of Adam after he became Gn 5:4
T Seth lived eight hundred and Gn 5:7
T Enosh lived eight hundred and Gn 5:10
T Kenan lived eight hundred and Gn 5:13
T Mahalalel lived eight hundred Gn 5:16
T Jared lived eight hundred years Gn 5:19
T Enoch walked with God three Gn 5:22
T Methuselah lived seven hundred Gn 5:26
T Lamech lived five hundred and Gn 5:30
T the LORD said, Gn 6:3
T the LORD saw that the wickedness Gn 6:5
T God said to Noah, Gn 6:13
T the LORD said to Noah, Gn 7:1
T Noah and his sons and his wife Gn 7:7
T the flood came upon the earth Gn 7:17
T it came about at the end of Gn 8:6
T he sent out a dove from him, to Gn 8:8
T he put out his hand and took Gn 8:9
T he waited yet another seven Gn 8:12
T Noah removed the covering of the Gn 8:13
T God spoke to Noah, saying, Gn 8:15
T Noah built an altar to the LORD, Gn 8:20
T God spoke to Noah and to his Gn 9:8
the cloud, **t** I will look upon it, Gn 9:16
T Noah began farming and planted a Gn 9:20
the Canaanite *was* **t** in the land. Gn 12:6 227
T he proceeded from there to the Gn 12:8
T Pharaoh called Abram and said, Gn 12:18
Now **t**, here is your wife, take her Gn 12:19
were dwelling **t** in the land. Gn 13:7 227
left, **t** I will go to the right; Gn 13:9
right, **t** I will go to the left." Gn 13:9
t your descendants can also be Gn 13:16
T Abram moved his tent and came Gn 13:18
T they turned back and came to Gn 14:7
T they took all the goods of Sodom Gn 14:11
T a fugitive came and told Abram Gn 14:13
T after his return from the defeat Gn 14:17
T behold, the word of the LORD Gn 15:4
T he believed in the LORD; Gn 15:6
T he brought all these to Him and Gn 15:10
"**T** in the fourth generation they Gn 15:16
T the angel of the LORD said to Gn 16:9
T she called the name of the LORD Gn 16:13
T God said to Abraham, Gn 17:15
T I will bless her, and she shall Gn 17:16
T Abraham fell on his face and Gn 17:17
T Abraham took Ishmael his son, Gn 17:23
T they said to him, Gn 18:9
T the men rose up from there, and Gn 18:16
T the men turned away from there Gn 18:22
t I will spare the whole place on Gn 18:26
T he said, "Oh may the Lord not be Gn 18:30
T he said, "Oh may the Lord not be Gn 18:32
t you may rise early and go on Gn 19:2
T the *two* men said to Lot, Gn 19:12
T the LORD rained on Sodom and Gn 19:24
T the firstborn said to the Gn 19:31
t you go in and lie with him, that Gn 19:34
t he sojourned in Gerar. Gn 20:1
T God said to him in the dream, Gn 20:6
T Abimelech called Abraham and Gn 20:9
Abimelech **t** took sheep and oxen Gn 20:14
T the LORD took note of Sarah as Gn 21:1
T Abraham circumcised his son Gn 21:4
T she went and sat down opposite Gn 21:16
T God opened her eyes and she saw Gn 21:19
T Abraham set seven ewe lambs of Gn 21:28
T they came to the place of which Gn 22:9
T Abraham raised his eyes and Gn 22:13
T the angel of the LORD called to Gn 22:15
T Abraham rose from before his Gn 23:3
T Ephron answered Abraham, saying Gn 23:14
T Abraham said to him, Gn 24:6
t you will be free from this my Gn 24:8
T the servant took ten camels from Gn 24:10
T the servant ran to meet her, and Gn 24:17
T the man bowed low and worshiped Gn 24:26
T the girl ran and told her Gn 24:28
T Laban unloaded the camels, and Gn 24:32
t you will be free from my oath, Gn 24:41 227
"**T** I asked her, and said, Gn 24:47
T Laban and Bethuel replied, Gn 24:50
T he and the men who were with him Gn 24:54
T they called Rebekah and said to Gn 24:58
T Rebekah arose with her maids, Gn 24:61
T she took her veil and covered Gn 24:65
T Isaac brought her into his Gn 24:67

T his sons Isaac and Ishmael **Gn 25:9**
it is so, why **t** am I *this way?*" **Gn 25:22**
of what *use* **t** is the birthright to me? **Gn 25:32**
T Jacob gave Esau bread and lentil **Gn 25:34**
T Abimelech called Isaac and said, **Gn 26:9**
How **t** did you say, **Gn 26:9**
T Abimelech said to Isaac, **Gn 26:16**
T Isaac dug again the wells of **Gn 26:18**
T they dug another well, and they **Gn 26:21**
T he went up from there to **Gn 26:23**
T Abimelech came to him from Gerar **Gn 26:26**
T he made them a feast, and they **Gn 26:30**
t Isaac sent them away and they **Gn 26:31**
"Now **t**, please take your gear, **Gn 27:3**
"**T** you shall bring *it* to your **Gn 27:10**
t I will be as a deceiver in his **Gn 27:12**
T Rebekah took the best garments **Gn 27:15**
T he came to his father and said, **Gn 27:18**
T Isaac said to Jacob, **Gn 27:21**
T his father Isaac said to him, **Gn 27:26**
T he also made savory food, and **Gn 27:31**
T Isaac trembled violently, and **Gn 27:33**
"Who was he **t** that hunted game **Gn 27:33** 645
T he said, "Is he not rightly named **Gn 27:36**
Now as for you **t**, what can I do, **Gn 27:37** 645
T Isaac his father answered and **Gn 27:39**
t I will kill my brother Jacob." **Gn 27:41**
T I will send and get you from **Gn 27:45**
T Isaac sent Jacob away, and he **Gn 28:5**
T Jacob departed from Beersheba **Gn 28:10**
T Jacob awoke from his sleep and **Gn 28:16**
T Jacob made a vow, saying, **Gn 28:20**
safety, **t** the LORD will be my God. **Gn 28:21**
T Jacob went on his journey, and **Gn 29:1**
they would **t** roll the stone from **Gn 29:3**
t we water the sheep." **Gn 29:8**
T Jacob kissed Rachel, and lifted **Gn 29:11**
T he related to Laban all these **Gn 29:13**
T Laban said to Jacob, **Gn 29:15**
T Jacob said to Laban, **Gn 29:21**
Why **t** have you deceived me?" **Gn 29:25**
T she conceived again and bore a **Gn 29:33**
T she stopped bearing. **Gn 29:35**
T Jacob's anger burned against **Gn 30:2**
T Rachel said, "God has vindicated **Gn 30:6**
T Leah said, "How fortunate!" **Gn 30:11**
T Leah said, "Happy am I! **Gn 30:13**
T Rachel said to Leah, **Gn 30:14**
t Leah went out to meet him and **Gn 30:16**
T Leah said, "God has given me my **Gn 30:18**
T Leah said, "God has endowed me **Gn 30:20**
T God remembered Rachel, and God **Gn 30:22**
T Jacob took fresh rods of poplar **Gn 30:37**
T the LORD said to Jacob, **Gn 31:3**
t all the flock brought forth **Gn 31:8**
t all the flock brought forth **Gn 31:8**
"**T** the angel of God said to me in **Gn 31:11**
now **t**, do whatever God has said to **Gn 31:16**
T Jacob arose and put his children **Gn 31:17**
t Rachel stole the household idols **Gn 31:19**
t he took his kinsmen with him and **Gn 31:23**
T Laban said to Jacob, **Gn 31:26**
T Jacob replied to Laban, **Gn 31:31**
T he went out of Leah's tent and **Gn 31:33**
T Jacob became angry and contended **Gn 31:36**
T Laban replied to Jacob, **Gn 31:43**
T Jacob took a stone and set it up **Gn 31:45**
T Jacob offered a sacrifice on the **Gn 31:54**
T Laban departed and returned to **Gn 31:55**
T Jacob sent messengers before him **Gn 32:3**
T Jacob was greatly afraid and **Gn 32:7**
t the company which is left will **Gn 32:8**
T he selected from what he had **Gn 32:13**
t you shall say, **Gn 32:18**
T he commanded also the second and **Gn 32:19**
T afterward I will see his face; **Gn 32:20**
T Jacob was left alone, and a man **Gn 32:24**
T he said, "Let me go, for the dawn **Gn 32:26**
T Jacob asked him and said, **Gn 32:29**
T Jacob lifted his eyes and **Gn 33:1**
T Esau ran to meet him and **Gn 33:4**
T the maids came near with their **Gn 33:6**
t take my present from my hand, **Gn 33:10**
T Esau said, "Let us take our **Gn 33:12**
T he erected there an altar and **Gn 33:20**
T Hamor the father of Shechem went **Gn 34:6**
t I will give whatever you say to **Gn 34:11**
t we will give our daughters to **Gn 34:16**
t we will take our daughter and go." **Gn 34:17**
T Jacob said to Simeon and Levi, **Gn 34:30**
T God said to Jacob, **Gn 35:1**
T God appeared to Jacob again when **Gn 35:9**
T God went up from him in the **Gn 35:13**
T they journeyed from Bethel; **Gn 35:16**
T Israel journeyed on and pitched **Gn 35:21**
t Simeon and Levi and Judah and **Gn 35:23**
T Esau took his wives and his sons **Gn 36:6**
These **t** are *the records of* the **Gn 36:9**
T Bela died, and Jobab the son of **Gn 36:33**
T Jobab died, and Husham of the **Gn 36:34**
T Husham died, and Hadad the son **Gn 36:35**
T Hadad died, and Samlah of **Gn 36:36**
T Samlah died, and Shaul of **Gn 36:37**
T Shaul died, and Baal-hanan the **Gn 36:38**
T Baal-hanan the son of Achbor **Gn 36:39**
T Joseph had a dream, and when he **Gn 37:5**
T his brothers said to him, **Gn 37:8**
T his brothers went to pasture **Gn 37:12**
T he said to him, **Gn 37:14**

T the man said, "They have moved **Gn 37:17**
"Now **t**, come and let us kill him **Gn 37:20**
T let us see what will become of **Gn 37:20**
T they sat down to eat a meal. **Gn 37:25**
T some Midianite traders passed **Gn 37:28**
T he examined it and said, **Gn 37:33**
T all his sons and all his **Gn 37:35**
T she conceived again and bore a **Gn 38:4**
T Judah said to Onan, **Gn 38:8**
T Judah said to his **Gn 38:11**
T she arose and departed, and **Gn 38:19**
T Judah said, "Let her keep them, **Gn 38:23**
T Judah said, "Bring her out and let **Gn 38:24**
his brother came out. **T** she said, **Gn 38:29**
How **t** could I do this great evil and **Gn 39:9**
T she spoke to him with these **Gn 39:17**
T it came about after these things **Gn 40:1**
T the cupbearer and the baker for **Gn 40:5**
T they said to him, **Gn 40:8**
T Joseph said to them, **Gn 40:8**
T Joseph said to him, **Gn 40:12**
T Joseph answered and said, **Gn 40:18**
T behold, seven other cows came up **Gn 41:3**
and fat cows. **T** Pharaoh awoke. **Gn 41:4**
T behold, seven ears, thin and **Gn 41:6**
T Pharaoh awoke, and behold, *it* **Gn 41:7**
T the chief cupbearer spoke to **Gn 41:9**
T Pharaoh sent and called for **Gn 41:14**
Joseph **t** answered Pharaoh, saying, **Gn 41:16**
just as ugly as before. **T** I awoke. **Gn 41:21**
T I told it to the magicians, but **Gn 41:24**
"**T** let them gather all the food **Gn 41:35**
T Pharaoh said to his servants, **Gn 41:38**
T Pharaoh took off his signet ring **Gn 41:42**
T Pharaoh named Joseph **Gn 41:45**
t there was famine in all the **Gn 41:54**
t Joseph opened all the **Gn 41:56**
T ten brothers of Joseph went down **Gn 42:3**
T they said to him, **Gn 42:10**
T they said to one another, **Gn 42:21**
T Joseph gave orders to fill their **Gn 42:25**
T he said to his brothers, **Gn 42:28**
T Reuben spoke to his father, **Gn 42:37**
t you will bring my gray hair down **Gn 42:38**
T Israel said, "Why did you treat me **Gn 43:6**
t let me bear the blame before you **Gn 43:9**
T their father Israel said to **Gn 43:11**
"If *it must be* so, **t** do this: **Gn 43:11** 645
t they arose and went down to **Gn 43:15**
T he brought Simeon out to them. **Gn 43:23**
T the man brought the men into **Gn 43:24**
T he asked them about their **Gn 43:27**
T he washed his face and came out; **Gn 43:31**
T he commanded his house steward, **Gn 44:1**
How **t** could we steal silver or **Gn 44:8**
T they hurried, each man lowered **Gn 44:11**
T they tore their clothes, and **Gn 44:13**
T Judah approached him, and said, **Gn 44:18**
"**T** you said to your servants, **Gn 44:21**
is with us, **t** we will go down; **Gn 44:26**
t let me bear the blame before my **Gn 44:32**
T Joseph could not control himself **Gn 45:1**
T Joseph said to his brothers, **Gn 45:3**
T Joseph said to his brothers, **Gn 45:4**
T he fell on his brother **Gn 45:14**
T Pharaoh said to Joseph, **Gn 45:17**
T the sons of Israel did so; **Gn 45:21**
T they went up from Egypt, and **Gn 45:25**
T Israel said, "It is enough; my son **Gn 45:28**
T Jacob arose from Beersheba; **Gn 46:5**
T Israel said to Joseph, **Gn 46:30**
T Joseph went in and told Pharaoh, **Gn 47:1**
T Pharaoh said to his brothers, **Gn 47:3**
T Pharaoh said to Joseph, **Gn 47:5**
t put them in charge of my **Gn 47:6**
T Joseph brought his father Jacob **Gn 47:7**
T Joseph said, "Give up your **Gn 47:16**
T Joseph said to the people, **Gn 47:23**
T Israel bowed *in worship* at the **Gn 47:31**
T Jacob said to Joseph, **Gn 48:3**
T Joseph brought them close to **Gn 48:10**
T Joseph took them from his knees, **Gn 48:12**
T Israel said to Joseph, **Gn 48:21**
T Jacob summoned his sons and **Gn 49:1**
to your father's bed; **T** you defiled *it* **Gn 49:4** 227
T he charged them and said to **Gn 49:29**
T Joseph fell on his father's **Gn 50:1**
t I will return.' " **Gn 50:5**
T his brothers also came and fell **Gn 50:18**
T Joseph made the sons of Israel **Gn 50:25**
T the king of Egypt spoke to the **Ex 1:15**
son, **t** you shall put him to death; **Ex 1:16**
is a daughter, **t** she shall live." **Ex 1:16**
T Pharaoh commanded all his **Ex 1:22**
T she put the child into it and **Ex 2:3**
T his sister said to Pharaoh's **Ex 2:7**
T Pharaoh's daughter said to her, **Ex 2:9**
T Moses was afraid and **Ex 2:14**
T the shepherds came and drove **Ex 2:17**
said to his daughters, "Where is he **t**? **Ex 2:20**
T she gave birth to a son, and he **Ex 2:22**
T He said, "Do not come near here; **Ex 3:5**
T Moses hid his face, **Ex 3:6**
T Moses said to God, **Ex 3:13**
T Moses said, **Ex 4:1**
T He said, "Throw it on the ground **Ex 4:3**
T He said, "Put your hand into your **Ex 4:7**
t you shall take some water from **Ex 4:9**
T Moses said to the LORD, **Ex 4:10**

"Now **t** go, and I, even I, will be **Ex 4:12**
T the anger of the LORD burned **Ex 4:14**
T Moses departed and returned to **Ex 4:18**
"**T** you shall say to Pharaoh, **Ex 4:22**
T Zipporah took a flint and cut **Ex 4:25**
T Moses and Aaron went and **Ex 4:29**
He **t** performed the signs in the **Ex 4:30**
t they bowed low and worshiped. **Ex 4:31**
T they said, "The God of the **Ex 5:3**
T the foremen of the sons of **Ex 5:15**
T Moses returned to the LORD and **Ex 5:22**
T the LORD said to Moses, **Ex 6:1**
'**T** I will take you for My people, **Ex 6:7**
how **t** will Pharaoh listen to me, **Ex 6:12**
T the LORD spoke to Moses and to **Ex 6:13**
how **t** will Pharaoh listen to me?" **Ex 6:30**
T the LORD said to Moses, **Ex 7:1**
t I will lay My hand on Egypt and **Ex 7:4**
miracle,' **t** you shall say to Aaron, **Ex 7:9**
T Pharaoh also called for *the* wise **Ex 7:11**
T the LORD said to Moses, **Ex 7:14**
T the LORD said to Moses, **Ex 7:19**
T Pharaoh turned and went into his **Ex 7:23**
T the LORD said to Moses, **Ex 8:1**
T the LORD said to Moses, **Ex 8:5**
T Pharaoh called for Moses and **Ex 8:8**
T he said, "Tomorrow." So he said, **Ex 8:10**
T Moses and Aaron went out from **Ex 8:12**
T the LORD said to Moses, **Ex 8:16**
T the magicians said to Pharaoh, **Ex 8:19**
T the LORD did so. **Ex 8:24**
eyes, will they not **t** stone us? **Ex 8:26**
T Moses said, "Behold, I am going **Ex 8:29**
T the LORD said to Moses, **Ex 9:1**
T the LORD said to Moses and **Ex 9:8**
T the LORD said to Moses, **Ex 9:13**
you would **t** have been cut off from **Ex 9:15**
T Pharaoh sent for Moses and **Ex 9:27**
T the LORD said to Moses, **Ex 10:1**
'**T** your houses shall be filled and **Ex 10:6**
T he said to them, **Ex 10:10**
T the LORD said to Moses, **Ex 10:12**
T Pharaoh hurriedly called for **Ex 10:16**
T the LORD said to Moses, **Ex 10:21**
T Pharaoh called to Moses, and **Ex 10:24**
T Pharaoh said to him, **Ex 10:28**
T the LORD said to Moses, **Ex 11:9**
t he and his neighbor nearest to **Ex 12:4**
t the whole assembly of the **Ex 12:6**
T Moses called for all the elders **Ex 12:21**
T the sons of Israel went and did **Ex 12:28**
T he called for Moses and Aaron at **Ex 12:31**
him, **t** he may eat of it. **Ex 12:44** 227
and **t** let him come near to **Ex 12:48** 227
T all the sons of Israel did *so;* **Ex 12:50**
T the LORD spoke to Moses, saying, **Ex 13:1**
it, **t** you shall break its neck; **Ex 13:13**
t you shall say to him, **Ex 13:14**
T they set out from Succoth and **Ex 13:20**
T the Egyptians chased after them **Ex 14:9**
T they said to Moses, **Ex 14:11**
T the LORD said to Moses, **Ex 14:15**
"**T** the Egyptians will know that I **Ex 14:18**
T Moses stretched out his hand **Ex 14:21**
T the Egyptians took up the **Ex 14:23**
T the LORD said to Moses, **Ex 14:26**
t the LORD overthrew the Egyptians **Ex 14:27**
T Moses and the sons of Israel **Ex 15:1** 227
"**T** the chiefs of Edom were **Ex 15:15** 227
T Moses led Israel from the Red **Ex 15:22**
T he cried out to the LORD, and **Ex 15:25**
T they came to Elim where there **Ex 15:27**
T they set out from Elim, and all **Ex 16:1**
T the LORD said to Moses, **Ex 16:4**
T Moses said to Aaron, **Ex 16:9**
t he said to them, **Ex 16:23**
T the LORD said to Moses, **Ex 16:28**
T Moses said, "This is what the **Ex 16:32**
T all the congregation of the sons **Ex 17:1**
T the LORD said to Moses, **Ex 17:5**
T Amalek came and fought against **Ex 17:8**
T they took a stone and put it **Ex 17:12**
T the LORD said to Moses, **Ex 17:14**
T Jethro, Moses' father-in-law, **Ex 18:5**
T Moses went out to meet his **Ex 18:7**
T Jethro, Moses' father-in-law, **Ex 18:12**
t teach them the statutes and the **Ex 18:20**
you, **t** you will be able to endure, **Ex 18:23**
T Moses bade his father-in-law **Ex 18:27**
'Now **t**, if you will indeed obey My **Ex 19:5**
t you shall be My own possession **Ex 19:5**
T Moses told the words of the **Ex 19:9**
T the LORD spoke to Moses, **Ex 19:21**
T the LORD said to him, **Ex 19:24**
T God spoke all these words, **Ex 20:1**
T they said to Moses, **Ex 20:19**
T the LORD said to Moses, **Ex 20:22**
t his wife shall go out with him. **Ex 21:3**
t his master shall bring him to **Ex 21:6**
t he shall bring him to the door **Ex 21:6**
t he shall let her be redeemed. **Ex 21:8**
t she shall go out for nothing, **Ex 21:11**
t I will appoint you a place to **Ex 21:13**
t he who struck him shall go **Ex 21:19**
t you shall appoint *as a penalty* **Ex 21:23**
t he shall give for the redemption **Ex 21:30**
t they shall sell the live ox and **Ex 21:35**
t he shall be sold for his theft. **Ex 22:3**
t the owner of the house shall **Ex 22:8**

t I will be an enemy to your Ex 23:22
T He said to Moses, Ex 24:1
T Moses came and recounted to the Ex 24:3
T he arose early in the morning, Ex 24:4
T he took the book of the covenant Ex 24:7
T Moses went up with Aaron, Nadab Ex 24:9
T Moses went up to the mountain, Ex 24:15
T the LORD spoke to Moses, saying, Ex 25:1
“**T** you shall make a lampstand of Ex 25:31
“**T** you shall make its lamps seven Ex 25:37
“**T** you shall make curtains of Ex 26:7
“**T** you shall make the boards for Ex 26:15
“**T** you shall make bars of acacia Ex 26:26
“**T** you shall erect the tabernacle Ex 26:30
“**T** bring near to yourself Aaron Ex 28:1
“**T** you shall bring Aaron and his Ex 29:4
“**T** you shall take the anointing Ex 29:7
“**T** you shall bring the bull Ex 29:10
“**T** you shall cut the ram into its Ex 29:17
“**T** you shall take the other ram, Ex 29:19
“**T** you shall take some of the Ex 29:21
“**T** you shall take the breast of Ex 29:26
t you shall burn the remainder Ex 29:34
t the altar shall be most holy, Ex 29:37
t each one of them shall give a Ex 30:12
T the LORD said to Moses, Ex 30:34
T all the people tore off the gold Ex 32:3
T the LORD spoke to Moses, Ex 32:7
“Now **t** let Me alone, that My Ex 32:10
T Moses entreated the LORD his Ex 32:11
T Moses turned and went down from Ex 32:15
T Moses said to Aaron, Ex 32:21
t Moses stood in the gate of the Ex 32:26
T Moses said, “Dedicate yourselves Ex 32:29
T Moses returned to the LORD, and Ex 32:31
T the LORD smote the people, Ex 32:35
T the LORD spoke to Moses, Ex 33:1
T Moses said to the LORD, Ex 33:12
T he said to Him, Ex 33:15
“For how **t** can it be known that I Ex 33:16 645
T Moses said, “I pray You, show me Ex 33:18
T the LORD said, Ex 33:21
“**T** I will take My hand away and Ex 33:23
T the LORD passed by in front of Ex 34:6
T God said, “Behold, I am going to Ex 34:10
it, **t** you shall break its neck. Ex 34:20
T the LORD said to Moses, Ex 34:27
T Moses called to them, and Aaron Ex 34:31
T Moses assembled all the Ex 35:1
T all the congregation of the sons Ex 35:20
T all whose hearts moved them, Ex 35:22
T Moses said to the sons of Ex 35:30
T Moses called Bezalel and Oholiab Ex 36:2
T he made curtains of goats’ *hair* Ex 36:14
T he made the boards for the Ex 36:20
T for the second side of the Ex 36:25
T he made bars of acacia wood, Ex 36:31
T he made the table of acacia Ex 37:10
T he made the lampstand of pure Ex 37:17
T he made the altar of incense of Ex 37:25
T he made the altar of burnt Ex 38:1
T he made the court: Ex 38:9
T they hammered out gold sheets Ex 39:3
T they put the two gold cords in Ex 39:17
T he made the robe of the ephod of Ex 39:22
T the LORD spoke to Moses, saying, Ex 40:1
“**T** you shall take the anointing Ex 40:9
“**T** you shall bring Aaron and his Ex 40:12
T he took the testimony and put *it* Ex 40:20
T he put the table in the tent of Ex 40:22
T he placed the lampstand in the Ex 40:24
T he placed the gold altar in the Ex 40:26
T he set up the veil for the Ex 40:28
T the cloud covered the tent of Ex 40:34
t they did not set out until the Ex 40:37
T the LORD called to Moses and Lv 1:1
‘He shall **t** skin the burnt Lv 1:6
‘**T** Aaron’s sons the priests Lv 1:8
‘He shall **t** cut it into its pieces Lv 1:12
t he shall bring his offering from Lv 1:14
‘**T** he shall tear it by its wings, Lv 1:17
shall **t** bring it to Aaron’s sons the Lv 2:2
‘The priest **t** shall take up from Lv 2:9
‘You shall **t** put oil on it and lay Lv 2:15
‘**T** Aaron’s sons shall offer *it* up Lv 3:5
t he shall offer it before the Lv 3:7
‘**T** the priest shall offer *it* up in Lv 3:11
t he shall offer it before the Lv 3:12
T the LORD spoke to Moses, saying, Lv 4:1
t let him offer to the LORD a bull Lv 4:3
‘**T** the anointed priest is to take Lv 4:5
t the assembly shall offer a bull Lv 4:14
‘**T** the elders of the congregation Lv 4:15
‘**T** the anointed priest is to bring Lv 4:16
‘**T** he is to bring out the bull to Lv 4:21
‘**T** the priest is to take some of Lv 4:25
t he shall bring for his offering Lv 4:28
‘**T** he shall remove all its fat, Lv 4:31
‘**T** he shall remove all its fat, Lv 4:35
tell *it,* **t** he will bear his guilt. Lv 5:1
is unclean, **t** he will be guilty. Lv 5:2
him, and **t** he comes to know *it,* Lv 5:3
him, and **t** he comes to know *it,* Lv 5:4
t he shall bring to the LORD his Lv 5:7
‘The second he shall **t** prepare as Lv 5:10
t for his offering for that which Lv 5:11
t *the rest* shall become the Lv 5:13
T the LORD spoke to Moses, saying, Lv 5:14
t he shall bring his guilt Lv 5:15

The priest shall **t** make atonement Lv 5:16
“He is **t** to bring to the priest a Lv 5:18
T the LORD spoke to Moses, saying, Lv 6:1
t it shall be, when he sins and Lv 6:4
“**T** he shall bring to the priest Lv 6:6
T the LORD spoke to Moses, saying, Lv 6:8
‘**T** he shall take off his garments Lv 6:11
‘**T** one *of them* shall lift up from Lv 6:15
T the LORD spoke to Moses, saying, Lv 6:19
T the LORD spoke to Moses, saying, Lv 6:24
t it shall be scoured and rinsed Lv 6:28
‘**T** he shall offer from it all its Lv 7:3
t along with the sacrifice of Lv 7:12
T the LORD spoke to Moses, saying, Lv 7:22
T the LORD spoke to Moses, saying, Lv 7:28
T the LORD spoke to Moses, saying, Lv 8:1
T Moses had Aaron and his sons Lv 8:6
t placed the breastpiece on him, Lv 8:8
Moses **t** took the anointing oil and Lv 8:10
T he poured some of the anointing Lv 8:12
T he brought the bull of the sin Lv 8:14
T he poured out *the rest of* the Lv 8:15
T he presented the ram of the Lv 8:18
T he presented the second ram, the Lv 8:22
Moses **t** sprinkled *the rest of* the Lv 8:24
He **t** put all *these* on the hands of Lv 8:27
T Moses took them from their hands Lv 8:28
T Moses said to Aaron and to his Lv 8:31
“**T** to the sons of Israel you Lv 9:3
Moses **t** said to Aaron, Lv 9:7
t make the offering for the Lv 9:7
he **t** offered up in smoke on the Lv 9:10
T he slaughtered the burnt Lv 9:12
T he presented the people’s Lv 9:15
T he slaughtered the ox and the Lv 9:18
T Aaron lifted up his hands toward Lv 9:22
T fire came out from before the Lv 9:24
T Moses said to Aaron, Lv 10:3
T Moses said to Aaron and to his Lv 10:6
The LORD **t** spoke to Aaron, saying, Lv 10:8
T Moses spoke to Aaron, and to his Lv 10:12
until evening, **t** it becomes clean. Lv 11:32
T the LORD spoke to Moses, saying, Lv 12:1
t she shall be unclean for seven Lv 12:2
‘**T** she shall remain in the blood Lv 12:4
t she shall be unclean for two Lv 12:5
‘**T** he shall offer it before the Lv 12:7
t she shall take two turtledoves Lv 12:8
T the LORD spoke to Moses and to Lv 13:1
t he shall be brought to Aaron the Lv 13:2
t the priest shall isolate *him who* Lv 13:4
t the priest shall isolate him for Lv 13:5
t the priest shall pronounce him Lv 13:6
t the priest shall pronounce him Lv 13:8
t he shall be brought to the Lv 13:9
‘The priest shall **t** look, Lv 13:10
t the priest shall look, and Lv 13:13
t he shall come to the priest, Lv 13:16
t the priest shall pronounce clean Lv 13:17
t it shall be shown to the priest; Lv 13:19
t the priest shall pronounce him Lv 13:20
t the priest shall isolate him for Lv 13:21
t the priest shall pronounce him Lv 13:22
t the priest shall look at it. Lv 13:25
t the priest shall isolate him for Lv 13:26
t the priest shall pronounce him Lv 13:27
t the priest shall look at the Lv 13:30
t the priest shall pronounce him Lv 13:30
t the priest shall isolate *the* Lv 13:31
t he shall shave himself, but he Lv 13:33
“**T** on the seventh day the priest Lv 13:34
t the priest shall look at him, Lv 13:36
t the priest shall look, and if Lv 13:39
“**T** the priest shall look at him; Lv 13:43
“**T** the priest shall look at the Lv 13:50
“He shall **t** look at the mark on Lv 13:51
t the priest shall order them to Lv 13:54
“**T** if the priest looks, and Lv 13:56
t he shall tear it out of the Lv 13:56
it shall **t** be washed a second time Lv 13:58
T the LORD spoke to Moses, saying, Lv 14:1
t the priest shall give orders to Lv 14:4
“He shall **t** sprinkle seven times Lv 14:7
The one to be cleansed shall **t** wash Lv 14:8
He shall **t** wash his clothes and Lv 14:9
“**T** the priest shall take the one Lv 14:12
“The priest shall **t** take some of Lv 14:14
the priest shall **t** dip his Lv 14:16
T afterward, he shall slaughter Lv 14:19
t he is to take one male lamb for Lv 14:21
“**T** the eighth day he shall bring Lv 14:23
“The priest shall **t** put some of Lv 14:28
“He shall **t** offer one of the Lv 14:30
t the one who owns the house shall Lv 14:35
“The priest shall **t** command that Lv 14:36
t the priest shall come out of the Lv 14:38
t the priest shall order them to Lv 14:40
“**T** they shall take other stones Lv 14:42
t the priest shall come in and Lv 14:44
t the priest shall pronounce the Lv 14:48
“To cleanse the house **t**, Lv 14:49
“**T** he shall take the cedar wood Lv 14:51
‘Whoever **t** touches any of the Lv 15:10
t he shall count off for himself Lv 15:13
he shall **t** wash his clothes and Lv 15:13
‘**T** on the eighth day he shall take Lv 15:14
‘**T** on the eighth day she shall Lv 15:29
T he shall bathe his body in water Lv 16:4
“**T** Aaron shall offer the bull for Lv 16:6

“**T** Aaron shall offer the goat on Lv 16:9
“**T** Aaron shall offer the bull of Lv 16:11
“**T** he shall slaughter the goat of Lv 16:15
“**T** he shall go out to the altar Lv 16:18
“**T** Aaron shall lay both of his Lv 16:21
“**T** Aaron shall come into the tent Lv 16:23
“**T** he shall offer up in smoke the Lv 16:25
t afterward he shall come into the Lv 16:26
“**T** the one who burns them shall Lv 16:28
t afterward he shall come into the Lv 16:28
T the LORD spoke to Moses, saying, Lv 17:1
“**T** you shall say to them, Lv 17:8
t he will become clean. Lv 17:15
body, **t** he shall bear his guilt.” Lv 17:16
T the LORD spoke to Moses, saying, Lv 18:1
T the LORD spoke to Moses, saying: Lv 19:1
t you shall count their fruit as Lv 19:23
T the LORD spoke to Moses, saying, Lv 20:1
t I Myself will set My face Lv 20:5
T the LORD said to Moses, Lv 21:1
T the LORD spoke to Moses, saying, Lv 21:16
T the LORD spoke to Moses, saying, Lv 22:1
t he shall add to it a fifth of it Lv 22:14
T the LORD spoke to Moses, saying, Lv 22:17
T the LORD spoke to Moses, saying, Lv 22:26
‘**T** on the fifteenth day of the Lv 23:6
T the LORD spoke to Moses, saying, Lv 23:9
t you shall bring in the sheaf of Lv 23:10
‘Its grain offering shall **t** be Lv 23:13
t you shall present a new grain Lv 23:16
‘The priest shall **t** wave them with Lv 23:20
T the LORD spoke to Moses, saying, Lv 24:1
“**T** you shall take fine flour and Lv 24:5
T the LORD spoke to Moses, saying, Lv 24:13
t let all the congregation stone Lv 24:14
his God, **t** he will bear his sin. Lv 24:15
T Moses spoke to the sons of Lv 24:23
The LORD **t** spoke to Moses at Lv 25:1
t the land shall have a sabbath to Lv 25:2
‘You shall **t** sound a ram’s horn Lv 25:9
‘**T** the land will yield its Lv 25:19
t I will so order My blessing for Lv 25:21
t his nearest kinsman is to come Lv 25:25
t he shall calculate the years Lv 25:27
t what he has sold shall remain in Lv 25:28
t his redemption right remains Lv 25:29
t the house that is in the walled Lv 25:30
falter, **t** you are to sustain him, Lv 25:35
‘He shall **t** go out from you, he Lv 25:41
‘**T**, too, *it is* out of the sons of Lv 25:45
t he shall have redemption right Lv 25:48
‘He **t** with his purchaser shall Lv 25:50
t I shall give you rains in their Lv 26:4
t I will punish you seven times Lv 26:18
‘If **t**, you act with hostility Lv 26:21
t I will act with hostility Lv 26:24
t I will act with wrathful Lv 26:28
‘I **t** will destroy your high Lv 26:30
‘**T** the land will enjoy its Lv 26:34 227
t the land will rest and enjoy its Lv 26:34 227
they **t** make amends for their iniquity Lv 26:41 227
t I will remember My covenant with Lv 26:42
t your valuation shall be fifty Lv 27:3
t your valuation shall be thirty Lv 27:4
t your valuation for the male shall be Lv 27:5
t your valuation shall be five Lv 27:6
t your valuation shall be fifteen Lv 27:7
t he shall be placed before the Lv 27:8
t both it and its substitute shall Lv 27:10
t he shall place the animal before Lv 27:11
t he shall add one-fifth of it to Lv 27:13
t the priest shall value it as Lv 27:14
t he shall add one-fifth of your Lv 27:15
t your valuation shall be Lv 27:16
t the priest shall calculate the Lv 27:18
t he shall add one-fifth of your Lv 27:19
t the priest shall calculate for Lv 27:23
t he shall redeem it according to Lv 27:27
t it shall be sold according to Lv 27:27
t both it and its substitute shall Lv 27:33
T the LORD spoke to Moses in the Nu 1:1
“These **t** are the names of the men Nu 1:5
T they registered by ancestry in Nu 1:18
“**T** *comes* the tribe of Zebulun, Nu 2:7
“**T** *comes* the tribe of Gad, and Nu 2:14
“**T** the tent of meeting shall set Nu 2:17
“**T** *comes* the tribe of Benjamin, Nu 2:22
“**T** *comes* the tribe of Naphtali, Nu 2:29
These **t** are the names of the sons Nu 3:2
T the LORD spoke to Moses, saying, Nu 3:5
T the LORD spoke to Moses in the Nu 3:14
These **t** are the sons of Levi by Nu 3:17
T the LORD said to Moses, Nu 3:40
T the LORD spoke to Moses, saying, Nu 3:44
T Moses gave the ransom money to Nu 3:51
T the LORD spoke to Moses and to Nu 4:1
“**T** they shall take a blue cloth Nu 4:9
“**T** they shall take away the ashes Nu 4:13
T the LORD spoke to Moses and to Nu 4:17
T the LORD spoke to Moses, saying, Nu 4:21
T the LORD spoke to Moses, saying, Nu 5:1
T the LORD spoke to Moses, saying, Nu 5:5
t he shall confess his sins which Nu 5:7
T the LORD spoke to Moses, saying, Nu 5:11
the man shall **t** bring his wife to the Nu 5:15
‘**T** the priest shall bring her near Nu 5:16
‘The priest shall **t** have the woman Nu 5:18
(**t** the priest shall have the woman Nu 5:21
‘The priest shall **t** write these Nu 5:23

'**T** he shall make the woman drink **Nu 5:24**
the water, **t** it shall come about, **Nu 5:27**
she will **t** be free and conceive **Nu 5:28**
he shall **t** make the woman stand **Nu 5:30**
t he shall shave his head on the **Nu 6:9**
'**T** on the eighth day he shall **Nu 6:10**
'**T** the priest shall present *them* **Nu 6:16**
'The Nazirite shall **t** shave his **Nu 6:18**
'**T** the priest shall wave them for **Nu 6:20**
T the LORD spoke to Moses, saying, **Nu 6:22**
Israel, and I **t** will bless them." **Nu 6:27**
T the leaders of Israel, the heads **Nu 7:2**
t they presented them before the **Nu 7:3**
T the LORD spoke to Moses, saying, **Nu 7:4**
T the LORD said to Moses, **Nu 7:11**
T the LORD spoke to Moses, saying, **Nu 8:1**
"**T** let them take a bull with its **Nu 8:8**
"Aaron **t** shall present the **Nu 8:11**
t offer the one for a sin offering **Nu 8:12**
"**T** after that the Levites may go **Nu 8:15**
T after that the Levites went in **Nu 8:22**
T the LORD spoke to Moses, saying, **Nu 9:9**
that person shall **t** be cut off from **Nu 9:13**
sons of Israel would **t** set out; **Nu 9:17**
T according to the command of the **Nu 9:20**
only one is blown, **t** the leaders, **Nu 10:4**
t you shall sound an alarm with **Nu 10:9**
T the cloud settled down in the **Nu 10:12**
T the tabernacle was taken down; **Nu 10:17**
T the Kohathites set out, carrying **Nu 10:21**
T the standard of the camp of the **Nu 10:25**
T Moses said to Hobab the son of **Nu 10:29**
T he said, "Please do not leave us, **Nu 10:31**
T it came about when the ark set **Nu 10:35**
"**T** I will come down and speak **Nu 11:17**
T the LORD came down in the cloud **Nu 11:25**
T Joshua the son of Nun, the **Nu 11:28**
T Moses returned to the camp, *both* **Nu 11:30**
T Miriam and Aaron spoke against **Nu 12:1**
T the LORD came down in a pillar **Nu 12:5**
Why **t** were you not afraid To speak **Nu 12:8**
T Aaron said to Moses, **Nu 12:11**
T the LORD spoke to Moses saying, **Nu 13:1**
These **t** *were* their names: **Nu 13:4**
t go up into the hill country. **Nu 13:17**
Make an effort **t** to get some of **Nu 13:20**
T they came to the valley of **Nu 13:23**
T Caleb quieted the people before **Nu 13:30**
T all the congregation lifted up **Nu 14:1**
T Moses and Aaron fell on their **Nu 14:5**
t He will bring us into this land and **Nu 14:8**
T the glory of the LORD appeared **Nu 14:10**
"**T** the Egyptians will hear of it, **Nu 14:13**
t the nations who have heard of **Nu 14:15**
"Why **t** are you transgressing the **Nu 14:41** 2088
T the Amalekites and the **Nu 14:45**
t make an offering by fire to the **Nu 15:3**
t you shall offer with the bull a **Nu 15:9**
T the LORD spoke to Moses, saying, **Nu 15:17**
t it shall be, that when you eat **Nu 15:19**
t it shall be, if it is done **Nu 15:24**
'**T** the priest shall make atonement **Nu 15:25**
t he shall offer a one year old **Nu 15:27**
T the LORD said to Moses, **Nu 15:35**
T Moses said to Korah, **Nu 16:8**
T Moses sent a summons to Dathan **Nu 16:12**
T Moses became very angry and said **Nu 16:15**
T the LORD spoke to Moses and **Nu 16:20**
T the LORD spoke to Moses, saying, **Nu 16:23**
T Moses arose and went to Dathan **Nu 16:25**
t the LORD has not sent me. **Nu 16:29**
t you will understand that these **Nu 16:30**
T the LORD spoke to Moses, saying, **Nu 16:36**
T Moses and Aaron came to the **Nu 16:43**
T they fell on their faces. **Nu 16:45**
t bring it quickly to the **Nu 16:46**
T Aaron took *it* as Moses had **Nu 16:47**
T Aaron returned to Moses at the **Nu 16:50**
T the LORD spoke to Moses, saying, **Nu 17:1**
"You shall **t** deposit them in the **Nu 17:4**
Moses **t** brought out all the rods **Nu 17:9**
T the sons of Israel spoke to **Nu 17:12**
T the LORD spoke to Aaron, **Nu 18:8**
T the LORD said to Aaron, **Nu 18:20**
T the LORD spoke to Moses, saying, **Nu 18:25**
t you shall present an offering **Nu 18:26**
t *the rest* shall be reckoned to **Nu 18:30**
T the LORD spoke to Moses and **Nu 19:1**
T the heifer shall be burned in **Nu 19:5**
'The priest shall **t** wash his **Nu 19:7**
and **t** he will be clean; but if **Nu 19:12**
'**T** for the unclean *person* they **Nu 19:17**
'**T** the clean *person* shall sprinkle **Nu 19:19**
T the sons of Israel, the whole **Nu 20:1**
"Why **t** have you brought the **Nu 20:4**
T Moses and Aaron came in from the **Nu 20:6**
T the glory of the LORD appeared **Nu 20:6**
T Moses lifted up his hand and **Nu 20:11**
From Kadesh Moses **t** sent **Nu 20:14**
water, **t** I will pay its price. **Nu 20:19**
T the LORD spoke to Moses and **Nu 20:23**
T Moses and Eleazar came down from **Nu 20:28**
t he fought against Israel and **Nu 21:1**
t I will utterly destroy their **Nu 21:2**
t they utterly destroyed them and **Nu 21:3**
T they set out from Mount Hor by **Nu 21:4**
T the LORD said to Moses, **Nu 21:8**
T Israel sang this song: **Nu 21:17** 227
T Israel sent messengers to Sihon, **Nu 21:21**

T Israel struck him with the edge **Nu 21:24**
T we have laid waste even to **Nu 21:30**
T they turned and went up by the **Nu 21:33**
T the sons of Israel journeyed, **Nu 22:1**
T God came to Balaam and said, **Nu 22:9**
T Balak again sent leaders, more **Nu 22:15**
Please come **t**, curse this people **Nu 22:17**
T the angel of the LORD stood in a **Nu 22:24**
T Balaam said to the donkey, **Nu 22:29**
T the LORD opened the eyes of **Nu 22:31**
Now **t**, if it is displeasing to **Nu 22:34**
T Balak said to Balaam, **Nu 22:37**
T it came about in the morning **Nu 22:41**
T Balaam said to Balak, **Nu 23:1**
T Balaam said to Balak, **Nu 23:3**
T the LORD put a word in Balaam's **Nu 23:5**
T Balak said to Balaam, **Nu 23:11**
T Balak said to him, **Nu 23:13**
T the LORD met Balaam and put a **Nu 23:16**
T he took up his discourse and **Nu 23:18**
has blessed, **t** I cannot revoke it. **Nu 23:20**
T Balak said to Balaam, **Nu 23:25**
T Balak said to Balaam, **Nu 23:27**
T Balak's anger burned against **Nu 24:10**
T he took up his discourse and said, **Nu 24:23**
T Balaam arose and departed and **Nu 24:25**
T behold, one of the sons of **Nu 25:6**
T the LORD spoke to Moses, saying, **Nu 25:10**
T the LORD spoke to Moses, saying, **Nu 25:16**
T it came about after the plague, **Nu 26:1**
T the LORD spoke to Moses, saying, **Nu 26:52**
T the daughters of Zelophehad, the **Nu 27:1**
T the LORD spoke to Moses, saying, **Nu 27:6**
t you shall transfer his **Nu 27:8**
t you shall give his inheritance **Nu 27:9**
t you shall give his inheritance **Nu 27:10**
t you shall give his inheritance **Nu 27:11**
T the LORD said to Moses, **Nu 27:12**
T Moses spoke to the LORD, saying, **Nu 27:15**
T he laid his hands on him and **Nu 27:23**
T the LORD spoke to Moses, saying, **Nu 28:1**
'**T** the drink offering with it *shall be* a **Nu 28:7**
'**T** on the sabbath day two male **Nu 28:9**
'**T** at the beginning of each of **Nu 28:11**
'**T** on the fourteenth day of the **Nu 28:16**
'**T** on the tenth day of this **Nu 29:7**
'**T** on the fifteenth day of the **Nu 29:12**
'**T** on the second day: **Nu 29:17**
'**T** on the third day: **Nu 29:20**
'**T** on the fourth day: **Nu 29:23**
'**T** on the fifth day: **Nu 29:26**
'**T** on the sixth day: **Nu 29:29**
'**T** on the seventh day: **Nu 29:32**
T Moses spoke to the heads of the **Nu 30:1**
her, **t** all her vows shall stand and **Nu 30:4**
t her vows shall stand and her **Nu 30:7**
t he shall annul her vow which she **Nu 30:8**
her, **t** all her vows shall stand and **Nu 30:11**
t whatever proceeds out of her **Nu 30:12**
t he confirms all her vows or all **Nu 30:14**
them, **t** he shall bear her guilt." **Nu 30:15**
T the LORD spoke to Moses, saying, **Nu 31:1**
T they burned all their cities **Nu 31:10**
T Eleazar the priest said to the **Nu 31:21**
T the LORD spoke to Moses, saying, **Nu 31:25**
T the officers who were over the **Nu 31:48**
T they came near to him and said, **Nu 32:16**
t afterward you shall return and **Nu 32:22**
t you shall give them the land of **Nu 32:29**
T the sons of Israel journeyed **Nu 33:5**
T Aaron the priest went up to **Nu 33:38**
T they journeyed from Mount Hor and **Nu 33:41**
T the LORD spoke to Moses in the **Nu 33:50**
t you shall drive out all the **Nu 33:52**
t it shall come about that those **Nu 33:55**
T the LORD spoke to Moses, saying, **Nu 34:1**
'**T** your border shall turn **Nu 34:4**
T the LORD spoke to Moses, saying, **Nu 34:16**
T the LORD spoke to Moses, saying, **Nu 35:9**
t you shall select for yourselves **Nu 35:11**
t the congregation shall judge **Nu 35:24**
t their inheritance will be added **Nu 36:4**
T Moses commanded the sons of **Nu 36:5**
"**T** I charged your judges at that **Dt 1:16**
"**T** we set out from Horeb, and **Dt 1:19**
"**T** all of you approached me and **Dt 1:22**
"**T** they took *some* of the fruit of **Dt 1:25**
"**T** I said to you, **Dt 1:29**
"**T** the LORD heard the sound of **Dt 1:34**
"**T** you said to me, **Dt 1:41**
"**T** you returned and wept before **Dt 1:45**
"**T** we turned and set out for the **Dt 2:1**
"**T** the LORD said to me, **Dt 2:9**
"**T** Sihon with all his people came **Dt 2:32**
"**T** we turned and went up the road **Dt 3:1**
"**T** I commanded you at that time, **Dt 3:18**
T you may return every man to his **Dt 3:20**
"**T** the LORD spoke to you from the **Dt 4:12**
T Moses set apart three cities **Dt 4:41** 227
T Moses summoned all Israel and **Dt 5:1**
'Now **t** why should we die? **Dt 5:25**
God any longer, **t** we will die. **Dt 5:25**
t speak to us all that the LORD **Dt 5:27**
"**T** it shall come about when the **Dt 6:10**
t watch yourself, that you do not forget **Dt 6:12**
t you shall say to your son, **Dt 6:21**
t you shall utterly destroy them. **Dt 7:2**
t the anger of the LORD will be **Dt 7:4**
"**T** it shall come about, because **Dt 7:12**

t your heart will become proud and **Dt 8:14**
"Know, **t**, *it is* not because of **Dt 9:6**
t I remained on the mountain forty **Dt 9:9**
"**T** the LORD said to me, **Dt 9:12**
t you rebelled against the command **Dt 9:23**
"**T** I turned and came down from **Dt 10:5**
"**T** the LORD said to me, **Dt 10:11**
t the LORD will drive out all **Dt 11:23**
t it shall come about that the **Dt 12:11**
t you may eat meat, whatever you **Dt 12:20**
t you may slaughter of your herd **Dt 12:21**
"**T** all Israel will hear and be **Dt 13:11**
t you shall investigate and search **Dt 13:14**
"**T** you shall gather all its booty **Dt 13:16**
t you shall exchange *it* for money, **Dt 14:25**
t he may cry to the LORD against **Dt 15:9**
t he shall serve you six years, **Dt 15:12**
t you shall take an awl and pierce **Dt 15:17**
"**T** you shall celebrate the Feast **Dt 16:10**
t you shall inquire thoroughly. **Dt 17:4**
t you shall bring out that man or **Dt 17:5**
t you shall arise and go up to the **Dt 17:8**
"**T** all the people will hear and **Dt 17:13**
t he shall serve in the name of **Dt 18:7**
t you shall add three more cities for **Dt 19:9**
t the elders of his city shall **Dt 19:12**
t both the men who have the **Dt 19:17**
t you shall do to him just as he **Dt 19:19**
"**T** the officers shall speak **Dt 20:8**
t all the people who are **Dt 20:11**
you, **t** you shall besiege it. **Dt 20:12**
t your elders and your judges **Dt 21:2**
"**T** the priests, the sons of Levi, **Dt 21:5**
t you shall bring her home to your **Dt 21:12**
t you shall let her go wherever **Dt 21:14**
t it shall be in the day he wills **Dt 21:16**
t his father and mother shall **Dt 21:19**
"**T** all the men of his city shall **Dt 21:21**
t you shall bring it home to your **Dt 22:2**
t you shall restore it to him. **Dt 22:2**
a wife and goes in to her and **t** **Dt 22:13**
t the girl's father and her mother **Dt 22:15**
t they shall bring out the girl to **Dt 22:21**
woman, **t** both of them shall die, **Dt 22:22**
t you shall bring them both out to **Dt 22:24**
t only the man who lies with her **Dt 22:25**
t the man who lay with her shall **Dt 22:29**
t he must go outside the camp; **Dt 23:10**
t you may eat grapes until you are **Dt 23:24**
t you may pluck the heads with **Dt 23:25**
t her former husband who sent her **Dt 24:4**
sells him, **t** that thief shall die; **Dt 24:7**
t it shall be if the wicked man **Dt 25:2**
the judge shall **t** make him lie down **Dt 25:2**
t his brother's wife shall go up **Dt 25:7**
"**T** the elders of his city shall **Dt 25:8**
t his brother's wife shall come to **Dt 25:9**
t you shall cut off her hand; **Dt 25:12**
"**T** it shall be, when you enter **Dt 26:1**
"**T** the priest shall take the **Dt 26:4**
"**T** we cried to the LORD, the God **Dt 26:7**
t you shall give it to the Levite, **Dt 26:12**
T Moses and the elders of Israel **Dt 27:1**
T Moses and the Levitical priests **Dt 27:9**
"The Levites shall **t** answer and **Dt 27:14**
"**T** you shall eat the offspring of **Dt 28:53**
t the LORD will bring **Dt 28:59**
"**T** you shall be left few in **Dt 28:62**
"**T** the LORD will single him out **Dt 29:21**
"**T** *men* will say, **Dt 29:25**
t the LORD your God will restore **Dt 30:3**
"**T** the LORD your God will prosper **Dt 30:9**
T Moses called to Joshua and said **Dt 31:7**
T Moses commanded them, saying, **Dt 31:10**
T the LORD said to Moses, **Dt 31:14**
"**T** My anger will be kindled **Dt 31:17**
t they will turn to other gods and **Dt 31:20**
"**T** it shall come about, when many **Dt 31:21**
T He commissioned Joshua the son **Dt 31:23**
how much more, **t**, after my death? **Dt 31:27**
T Moses spoke in the hearing of **Dt 31:30**
T he forsook God who made him, **Dt 32:15**
T He said, 'I will hide My face from **Dt 32:20**
T Moses came and spoke all the **Dt 32:44**
"**T** die on the mountain where you **Dt 32:50**
"**T** he provided the first *part* for **Dt 33:21**
T the LORD said to him, **Dt 34:4**
t the days of weeping *and* mourning **Dt 34:8**
for **t** you will make your way **Jos 1:8** 227
and **t** you will have success. **Jos 1:8** 227
T Joshua commanded the officers of **Jos 1:10**
T you shall return to your own **Jos 1:15**
T Joshua the son of Nun sent two **Jos 2:1**
T she let them down by a rope **Jos 2:15**
T afterward you may go on your way." **Jos 2:16**
t we shall be free from the oath **Jos 2:20**
T the two men returned and came **Jos 2:23**
T Joshua rose early in the morning; **Jos 3:1**
t you shall set out from your **Jos 3:3**
T Joshua said to the people, **Jos 3:5**
T Joshua said to the sons of **Jos 3:9**
"Now **t**, take for yourselves **Jos 3:12**
t you shall say to them, **Jos 4:7**
T Joshua set up twelve stones in **Jos 4:9**
t you shall inform your children, **Jos 4:22**
T the LORD said to Joshua, **Jos 5:9**
t on the seventh day you shall **Jos 6:4**
T he said to the people, **Jos 6:7**
T you shall shout!" **Jos 6:10**

t they came into the camp and Jos 6:11
T on the seventh day Jos 6:15
T Joshua made them take an oath at Jos 6:26
T Joshua tore his clothes and fell Jos 7:6
'In the morning **t** you shall come Jos 7:14
T Joshua said to Achan, Jos 7:19
t I coveted them and took them; Jos 7:21
T Joshua and all Israel with him, Jos 7:24
"**T** I and all the people who are Jos 8:5
"**T** it will be when you have Jos 8:8
T all the people of war who *were* Jos 8:11
T the LORD said to Joshua, Jos 8:18
t all Israel returned to Ai and Jos 8:24
T Joshua built an altar to the Jos 8:30 227
T afterward he read all the words Jos 8:34
how **t** shall we make a covenant Jos 9:7
T Joshua said to them, Jos 9:8
now **t**, make a covenant with us." Jos 9:11
T the sons of Israel set out and Jos 9:17
T Joshua called for them and spoke Jos 9:22
T the men of Gibeon sent *word* to Jos 10:6
T Joshua spoke to the LORD in the Jos 10:12 227
T Joshua and all Israel with him Jos 10:15
T Joshua said, "Open the mouth of Jos 10:22
Joshua **t** said to them, Jos 10:25
T Joshua and all Israel with him Jos 10:29
T Horam king of Gezer came up to Jos 10:33 227
T Joshua and all Israel with him Jos 10:36
T Joshua and all Israel with him Jos 10:38
T it came about, when Jabin king Jos 11:1
T the LORD said to Joshua, Jos 11:6
T Joshua turned back at that time, Jos 11:10
T Joshua came at that time and cut Jos 11:21
T the sons of Judah drew near to Jos 14:6
as my strength was **t**, Jos 14:11 227
"Now **t**, give me this hill country Jos 14:12
T the land had rest from war. Jos 14:15
T it proceeded southward to the Jos 15:3
t went up by the south of Jos 15:3
T the border went up to Jos 15:6
T the border went up the valley of Jos 15:8
t the border curved to Baalah Jos 15:9
T the border curved to Shikkeron Jos 15:11
T he went up from there against Jos 15:15
T she said, "Give me a blessing; Jos 15:19
T the lot for the sons of Joseph Jos 16:1
T the border went westward at Jos 16:6
t reached Jericho and came out at Jos 16:7
t the border went southward to the Jos 17:7
T the sons of Joseph spoke to Jos 17:14
T the whole congregation of the Jos 18:1
t they shall return to me. Jos 18:4
T the men arose and went, and Jos 18:8
t I will cast lots for you here Jos 18:8
t the border went up to the side Jos 18:12
T the south side *was* from the edge Jos 18:15
T the second lot fell to Simeon, Jos 19:1
T their border went up to the west Jos 19:11
Maralah, it **t** touched Dabbesheth and Jos 19:11
T it turned from Sarid to the east Jos 19:12
t it proceeded on north to Cabul, Jos 19:27
t the border turned to Hosah, and Jos 19:29
T the border turned westward to Jos 19:34
T they struck it with the edge of Jos 19:47
T the LORD spoke to Joshua, Jos 20:1
t they shall not deliver the Jos 20:5
T the manslayer shall return to Jos 20:6 227
T the heads of households of the Jos 21:1
T the lot came out for the Jos 21:4
T the cities from the tribe of Jos 21:20
T Joshua summoned the Reubenites Jos 22:1 227
T the sons of Israel sent to the Jos 22:13
t cross into the land of the Jos 22:19
T the sons of Reuben and the sons Jos 22:21
in time to come, **t** we shall say, Jos 22:28
T Phinehas the son of Eleazar the Jos 22:32
"Be very firm, **t**, to keep and do Jos 23:6
t the anger of the LORD will burn Jos 23:16
T Joshua gathered all the tribes Jos 24:1
'**T** I took your father Abraham from Jos 24:3
'**T** I sent Moses and Aaron, and I Jos 24:5
'**T** I brought you into the land of Jos 24:8
'**T** Balak the son of Zippor, king Jos 24:9
'**T** I sent the hornet before you Jos 24:12
T Joshua said to the people, Jos 24:19
t He will turn and do you harm and Jos 24:20
T Joshua dismissed the people, Jos 24:28
T Judah said to Simeon his Jg 1:3
T the sons of Judah fought against Jg 1:8
T from there he went against the Jg 1:11
T it came about when she came *to* Jg 1:14
T she alighted from her donkey, Jg 1:14
T Judah went with Simeon his Jg 1:17
T they gave Hebron to Caleb, as Jg 1:20
T the Amorites forced the sons of Jg 1:34
T Joshua the son of Nun, the Jg 2:8
T the sons of Israel did evil in Jg 2:11
T the LORD raised up judges who Jg 2:16
T the anger of the LORD was Jg 3:8
T the land had rest forty years. Jg 3:11
T Ehud went out into the vestibule Jg 3:23
T the sons of Israel again did Jg 4:1
T Barak said to her, Jg 4:8
you will go with me, **t** I will go; Jg 4:8
T Deborah arose and went with Jg 4:9
T they told Sisera that Barak the Jg 4:12
t she covered him. Jg 4:19
T Deborah and Barak the son of Jg 5:1
T war *was* in the gates. Jg 5:8 227
T the people of the LORD went down Jg 5:11 227
"**T** survivors came down to the Jg 5:13 227
T fought the kings of Canaan At Jg 5:19 227
"**T** the horses' hoofs beat From Jg 5:22 227
T she struck Sisera, she smashed Jg 5:26
T the sons of Israel did what was Jg 6:1
T the angel of the LORD came and Jg 6:11
T Gideon said to him, Jg 6:13
why **t** has all this happened to us? Jg 6:13
t show me a sign that it is You Jg 6:17
T Gideon went in and prepared a Jg 6:19
T the angel of the LORD put out Jg 6:21
T the angel of the LORD vanished Jg 6:21
T Gideon built an altar there to Jg 6:24
T Gideon took ten men of his Jg 6:27
T the men of the city said to Jg 6:30
T all the Midianites and the Jg 6:33
T Gideon said to God, Jg 6:36
t I will know that You will Jg 6:37
T Gideon said to God, Jg 6:39
T Jerubbaal (that is, Gideon) and all Jg 7:1
T the LORD said to Gideon, Jg 7:4
t you also blow the trumpets all Jg 7:18
T the men of Ephraim said to him, Jg 8:1
T their anger toward him subsided Jg 8:3 227
T Gideon and the 300 men who were Jg 8:4
t I will thrash your bodies with Jg 8:7
T Gideon the son of Joash returned Jg 8:13
T *the youth* wrote down for him the Jg 8:14
T he said to Zebah and Zalmunna, Jg 8:18
T Zebah and Zalmunna said, Jg 8:21
T the men of Israel said to Jg 8:22
T Jerubbaal the son of Joash went Jg 8:29
T it came about, as soon as Gideon Jg 8:33
T he went to his father's house at Jg 9:5
"**T** the trees said to the fig Jg 9:10
"**T** the trees said to the vine, Jg 9:12
if **t** you have dealt in truth and Jg 9:19
T Jotham escaped and fled, and Jg 9:21
T God sent an evil spirit between Jg 9:23
T Gaal the son of Ebed said, Jg 9:28
T I would remove Abimelech." Jg 9:29
T Zebul said to him, Jg 9:38
T Abimelech remained at Arumah, Jg 9:41
T Abimelech and the company who Jg 9:44
the other two companies **t** dashed Jg 9:44
t he razed the city and sowed it Jg 9:45
T he said to the people who *were* Jg 9:48
T Abimelech went to Thebez, and he Jg 9:50
T he called quickly to the young Jg 9:54
T he died and was buried in Shamir. Jg 10:2
T the sons of Israel again did Jg 10:6
T the sons of Israel cried out to Jg 10:10
T the sons of Ammon were summoned Jg 10:17
T Jephthah said to the elders of Jg 11:7
T Jephthah went with the elders of Jg 11:11
T Israel sent messengers to the Jg 11:17
'**T** they went through the Jg 11:18
Israel, are you **t** to possess it? Jg 11:23
t he passed through Mizpah of Jg 11:29
t it shall be that whatever comes Jg 11:31
T he said, "Go." So he sent her away Jg 11:38
T the men of Ephraim were Jg 12:1
Why **t** have you come up to me this Jg 12:3
T Jephthah gathered all the men of Jg 12:4
t they would say to him, Jg 12:6
T they seized him and slew him at Jg 12:6
T Jephthah the Gileadite died and Jg 12:7
T Ibzan died and was buried in Jg 12:10
T Elon the Zebulunite died and was Jg 12:12
T Abdon the son of Hillel the Jg 12:15
T the angel of the LORD appeared Jg 13:3
T the woman came and told her Jg 13:6
T Manoah entreated the LORD and Jg 13:8
T Manoah arose and followed his Jg 13:11
T Manoah said to the angel of the Jg 13:15
t offer it to the LORD." Jg 13:16
T Manoah knew that he was the Jg 13:21 227
T the woman gave birth to a son Jg 13:24
T Samson went down to Timnah and Jg 14:1
T his father and his mother said Jg 14:3
T Samson went down to Timnah with Jg 14:5
T his father went down to the Jg 14:10
T Samson said to them, Jg 14:12
t I will give you thirty linen Jg 14:12
t you shall give me thirty linen Jg 14:13
T it came about on the fourth day Jg 14:15
She **t** told the riddle to the sons Jg 14:17
T the Spirit of the LORD came upon Jg 14:19
Samson **t** said to them, Jg 15:3
T the Philistines said, Jg 15:6
T the Philistines went up and Jg 15:9
T 3,000 men of Judah went down to Jg 15:11
What **t** is this that you have done Jg 15:11
T they bound him with two new Jg 15:13
T Samson said, "With the jawbone Jg 15:16
T he became very thirsty, and he Jg 15:18
light, **t** we will kill him." Jg 16:2
t he put them on his shoulders and Jg 16:3
T we will each give you eleven Jg 16:5
t I will become weak and be like Jg 16:7
T the lords of the Philistines Jg 16:8
T Delilah said to Samson, Jg 16:10
t I will become weak and be like Jg 16:11
T Delilah said to Samson, Jg 16:13
t I will become weak and be like Jg 16:13
T she said to him, Jg 16:15
t my strength will leave me and I Jg 16:17
T the lords of the Philistines Jg 16:18
T she began to afflict him, and Jg 16:19
T the Philistines seized him and Jg 16:21
T Samson said to the boy who was Jg 16:26
T Samson called to the LORD and Jg 16:28
T his brothers and all his Jg 16:31
He **t** returned the eleven hundred Jg 17:3
T the man departed from the city, Jg 17:8
Micah **t** said to him, Jg 17:10
T Micah said, "Now I know that Jg 17:13
T the five men departed and came Jg 18:7
T from the family of the Danites, Jg 18:11
T the five men who went to spy out Jg 18:14
T they turned and departed, and Jg 18:21
T they took what Micah had made Jg 18:27
T her husband arose and went after Jg 19:3
T the man arose to go, but his Jg 19:7
T tomorrow you may arise early for Jg 19:9
T behold, an old man was coming Jg 19:16
T the man, the owner of the house, Jg 19:23
t let her go at the approach of Jg 19:25
t behold, his concubine was lying at Jg 19:27
T he placed her on the donkey; Jg 19:28
T all the sons of Israel from Dan Jg 20:1
T all the people arose as one man, Jg 20:8
T the tribes of Israel sent men Jg 20:12
"Now **t**, deliver up the men, the Jg 20:13
T the men of Israel besides Jg 20:17
T the LORD said, "Judah *shall go up* Jg 20:18
T the sons of Benjamin came out of Jg 20:21
T the sons of Israel came against Jg 20:24
T all the sons of Israel and all Jg 20:26
T all the men of Israel arose from Jg 20:33
T the men of Israel turned in the Jg 20:39
T the men of Israel turned, and Jg 20:41
The men of Israel **t** turned back Jg 20:48
T the sons of Israel said, Jg 21:5
T the whole congregation sent *word* Jg 21:13
T the elders of the congregation Jg 21:16
t you shall come out of the Jg 21:21
T Elimelech, Naomi's husband, died; Ru 1:3
T both Mahlon and Chilion also Ru 1:5
T she arose with her Ru 1:6
T she kissed them, and they lifted up Ru 1:9
T she said, "Behold, your Ru 1:15
T Boaz said to his servant who was Ru 2:5
T Boaz said to Ruth, Ru 2:8
T she fell on her face, bowing to Ru 2:10
T she said, "I have found favor in Ru 2:13
T she beat out what she had Ru 2:17
Her mother-in-law **t** said to her, Ru 2:19
T Ruth the Moabitess said, Ru 2:21
T Naomi her mother-in-law said to Ru 3:1
t he will tell you what you shall Ru 3:4
T he said, "May you be blessed of Ru 3:10
redeem you, **t** I will redeem you, Ru 3:13
T she went into the city. Ru 3:15
T she said, "Wait, my daughter, Ru 3:18
T he said to the closest relative, Ru 4:3
T Boaz said, "On the day you buy Ru 4:5
T Boaz said to the elders and all Ru 4:9
T the women said to Naomi, Ru 4:14
T Naomi took the child and laid Ru 4:16
T Elkanah her husband said to her, 1Sa 1:8
T Hannah rose after eating and 1Sa 1:9
t I will give him to the LORD all 1Sa 1:11
T Eli said to her, 1Sa 1:14
T Eli answered and said, 1Sa 1:17
T they arose early in the morning 1Sa 1:19
T the man Elkanah went up with all 1Sa 1:21
t I will bring him, that he may 1Sa 1:22
T they slaughtered the bull, and 1Sa 1:25
T Hannah prayed and said, 1Sa 2:1
T Elkanah went to his home at 1Sa 2:11
T he would thrust it into the pan, 1Sa 2:14
t take as much as you desire," 1Sa 2:16
as you desire," **t** he would say, 1Sa 2:16
T Eli would bless Elkanah and his 1Sa 2:20
T a man of God came to Eli and 1Sa 2:27
T he ran to Eli and said, 1Sa 3:5
T Eli discerned that the LORD was 1Sa 3:8
T the LORD came and stood and 1Sa 3:10
T he opened the doors of the house 1Sa 3:15
T Eli called Samuel and said, 1Sa 3:16
T they understood that the ark of 1Sa 4:6
T the man came hurriedly and told 1Sa 4:14
T the one who brought the news 1Sa 4:17
T the Philistines took the ark of 1Sa 5:2
T you will be healed and it will 1Sa 6:3 227
T they said, "What shall be the guilt 1Sa 6:4
"Why **t** do you harden your hearts 1Sa 6:6
T send it away that it may go. 1Sa 6:8
t He has done us this great evil. 1Sa 6:9
t we will know that it was not 1Sa 6:9
T the men did so, and took two 1Sa 6:10
T Samuel spoke to all the house of 1Sa 7:3
T Samuel said, "Gather all Israel to 1Sa 7:5
T the sons of Israel said to 1Sa 7:8
T Samuel took a stone and set it 1Sa 7:12
T his return *was* to Ramah, for his 1Sa 7:17
T all the elders of Israel 1Sa 8:4
"Now **t**, listen to their voice; 1Sa 8:9
"**T** you will cry out in that day 1Sa 8:18
T they passed through the land of 1Sa 9:4
T he passed through the land of 1Sa 9:4
T Saul said to his servant, 1Sa 9:7
T Saul said to his servant, 1Sa 9:10
T Saul approached Samuel in the 1Sa 9:18
Why **t** do you speak to me in this 1Sa 9:21
T Samuel took Saul and his servant 1Sa 9:22

T the cook took up the leg with 1Sa 9:24
T Samuel took the flask of oil, 1Sa 10:1
t you will find two men close to 1Sa 10:2
"**T** you will go on further from 1Sa 10:3
"**T** the Spirit of the LORD will 1Sa 10:6
T it happened when he turned his 1Sa 10:9
T he brought the tribe of Benjamin 1Sa 10:21
T Samuel told the people the 1Sa 10:25
T, if there is no one to deliver 1Sa 11:3
T the messengers came to Gibeah of 1Sa 11:4
T the Spirit of God came upon Saul 1Sa 11:6
T the dread of the LORD fell on 1Sa 11:7
T the men of Jabesh said, 1Sa 11:10
T the people said to Samuel, 1Sa 11:12
T Samuel said to the people, 1Sa 11:14
T Samuel said to all Israel, 1Sa 12:1
T Samuel said to the people, 1Sa 12:6
t the LORD sent Moses and Aaron 1Sa 12:8
"**T** the LORD sent Jerubbaal and 1Sa 12:11
t both you and also the king who 1Sa 12:14
t the hand of the LORD will be 1Sa 12:15
T you will know and see that your 1Sa 12:17
T all the people said to Samuel, 1Sa 12:19
"You must not turn aside, for **t** 1Sa 12:21
T Saul blew the trumpet throughout 1Sa 13:3
people were **t** summoned to Saul at 1Sa 13:4
t the people hid themselves in 1Sa 13:6
T Samuel arose and went up from 1Sa 13:15
T Jonathan said to the young man 1Sa 14:6
T Jonathan said, 1Sa 14:8
t we will stand in our place and 1Sa 14:9
'Come up to us,' **t** we will go up, 1Sa 14:10
T Jonathan climbed up on his hands 1Sa 14:13
T Saul said to Ahijah, 1Sa 14:18
T Saul and all the people who *were* 1Sa 14:20
T one of the people said, 1Sa 14:28
T Jonathan said, 1Sa 14:29
T they told Saul, saying, 1Sa 14:33
T Saul said, "Let us go down after 1Sa 14:36
T he said to all Israel, 1Sa 14:40
T Saul said to Jonathan, 1Sa 14:43
T Saul went up from pursuing the 1Sa 14:46
T Samuel said to Saul, 1Sa 15:1
T Saul summoned the people and 1Sa 15:4
T the word of the LORD came to 1Sa 15:10
t turned and proceeded on down to 1Sa 15:12
"What **t** is this bleating of the 1Sa 15:14
T Samuel said to Saul, 1Sa 15:16
"Why **t** did you not obey the voice 1Sa 15:19
T Saul said to Samuel, 1Sa 15:20
T Saul said to Samuel, 1Sa 15:24
T he said, "I have sinned; 1Sa 15:30
T Samuel said, "Bring me Agag, 1Sa 15:32
T Samuel went to Ramah, but Saul 1Sa 15:34
T Jesse called Abinadab and made 1Sa 16:8
T Samuel said to Jesse, 1Sa 16:11
T Samuel took the horn of oil and 1Sa 16:13
Saul's servants **t** said to him, 1Sa 16:15
T one of the young men said 1Sa 16:18
T David came to Saul and attended 1Sa 16:21
T a champion came out from the 1Sa 17:4
t we will become your servants; 1Sa 17:9
t you shall become our servants 1Sa 17:9
T Jesse said to David his son, 1Sa 17:17
T David left his baggage in the 1Sa 17:22
T David spoke to the men who were 1Sa 17:26
T he turned away from him to 1Sa 17:30
T Saul said to David, 1Sa 17:33
T Saul clothed David with his 1Sa 17:38
T the Philistine came on and 1Sa 17:41
T David said to the Philistine, 1Sa 17:45
T it happened when the Philistine 1Sa 17:48
T David ran and stood over the 1Sa 17:51
T David took the Philistine's head 1Sa 17:54
T Jonathan made a covenant with 1Sa 18:3
T Saul became very angry, for this 1Sa 18:8
T Saul said to David, 1Sa 18:17
T Saul commanded his servants, 1Sa 18:22
Saul **t** said, "Thus you shall say to 1Sa 18:25
T David brought their foreskins, 1Sa 18:27
t Saul was even more afraid of 1Sa 18:29
T the commanders of the 1Sa 18:30
anything, **t** I will tell you." 1Sa 19:3
T Jonathan spoke well of David to 1Sa 19:4
Why **t** will you sin against 1Sa 19:5
T Jonathan called David, and 1Sa 19:7
T Saul sent messengers to David's 1Sa 19:11
T Saul sent messengers to see 1Sa 19:15
T Saul sent messengers to take 1Sa 19:20
T he himself went to Ramah and 1Sa 19:22
T David fled from Naioth in Ramah, 1Sa 20:1
T Jonathan said to David, 1Sa 20:4
If your father misses me at all, **t** say 1Sa 20:6
for why **t** should you bring me to 1Sa 20:8 2088
t would I not tell you about it?" 1Sa 20:9
T David said to Jonathan, 1Sa 20:10
T Jonathan said to David, 1Sa 20:12
shall I not **t** send to you and make 1Sa 20:12 227
T Jonathan said to him, 1Sa 20:18
side of you, get them,' **t** come; 1Sa 20:21
t Jonathan rose up and Abner sat 1Sa 20:25
Jonathan **t** answered Saul, 1Sa 20:28
T Saul's anger burned against 1Sa 20:30
T Saul hurled his spear at him to 1Sa 20:33
T Jonathan arose from the table in 1Sa 20:34
T Jonathan gave his weapons to his 1Sa 20:40
T he rose and departed, 1Sa 20:42
T David came to Nob to Ahimelech 1Sa 21:1
how much more **t** today will their 1Sa 21:5
T the priest said, 1Sa 21:9
T David arose and fled that day 1Sa 21:10
T Achish said to his servants, 1Sa 21:14
T he left them with the king of 1Sa 22:4
T Saul heard that David and the 1Sa 22:6
T Doeg the Edomite, who was 1Sa 22:9
T the king sent someone to summon 1Sa 22:11
Saul **t** said to him, 1Sa 22:13
T Ahimelech answered the king and 1Sa 22:14
T the king said to Doeg, 1Sa 22:18
T David said to Abiathar, 1Sa 22:22
T they told David, saying, 1Sa 23:1
How much more **t** if we go to Keilah 1Sa 23:3
T David inquired of the LORD once 1Sa 23:4
T David said, "O LORD God of 1Sa 23:10
T David said, "Will the men of 1Sa 23:12
T David and his men, about six 1Sa 23:13
T Ziphites came up to Saul at 1Sa 23:19
"Now **t**, O king, come down 1Sa 23:20
T they arose and went to Ziph 1Sa 23:24
T Saul took three thousand chosen 1Sa 24:2
T David arose and cut off the edge 1Sa 24:4
T Saul lifted up his voice and 1Sa 24:16
T Samuel died; and all Israel 1Sa 25:1
in David's name; **t** they waited. 1Sa 25:9
"Shall I **t** take my bread and my 1Sa 25:11
T Abigail hurried and took two 1Sa 25:18
own hand, now **t** let your enemies and 1Sa 25:26
t the life of my lord shall be 1Sa 25:29
t remember your maidservant." 1Sa 25:31
T David said to Abigail, 1Sa 25:32
T Abigail came to Nabal, and 1Sa 25:36
T David sent a proposal to 1Sa 25:39
T Abigail quickly arose, and rode 1Sa 25:42
T the Ziphites came to Saul at 1Sa 26:1
David **t** arose and came to the 1Sa 26:5
T David said to Ahimelech 1Sa 26:6
T Abishai said to David, 1Sa 26:8
T David crossed over to the other 1Sa 26:13
T Abner replied, 1Sa 26:14
Why **t** have you not guarded your 1Sa 26:15
T Saul recognized David's voice 1Sa 26:17
"Why **t** is my lord pursuing his 1Sa 26:18 2088
"Now **t**, do not let my blood fall 1Sa 26:20
T Saul said, "I have sinned. Return, 1Sa 26:21
T Saul said to David, 1Sa 26:25
T David said to himself, 1Sa 27:1
Saul **t** will despair of searching 1Sa 27:1
T David said to Achish, 1Sa 27:5
T he returned and came to Achish. 1Sa 27:9
T Saul said to his servants, 1Sa 28:7
T Saul disguised himself by 1Sa 28:8
Why are you **t** laying a snare for 1Sa 28:9
T the woman said, 1Sa 28:11
T Samuel said to Saul, 1Sa 28:15
"Why **t** do you ask me, since the 1Sa 28:16
T Saul immediately fell full 1Sa 28:20
T they arose and went away that 1Sa 28:25
T the commanders of the 1Sa 29:3
T Achish called David and said to 1Sa 29:6
"Now **t** arise early in the morning 1Sa 29:10
T it happened when David and his 1Sa 30:1
T David and the people who were 1Sa 30:4
T David said to Abiathar the 1Sa 30:7
t his spirit revived. 1Sa 30:12
T David said to him, 1Sa 30:15
t David approached the people and 1Sa 30:21
T all the wicked and worthless men 1Sa 30:22
T David said, "You must not do so, 1Sa 30:23
T Saul said to his armor bearer, 1Sa 31:4
t the Philistines came and lived 1Sa 31:7
T David said to him, 2Sa 1:3
"**T** he said to me, 2Sa 1:9
T David took hold of his clothes 2Sa 1:11
T David said to him, 2Sa 1:14
T David chanted with this lament 2Sa 1:17
T it came about afterwards that 2Sa 2:1
T the men of Judah came and there 2Sa 2:4
T Abner said to Joab, 2Sa 2:14
T Abner looked behind him and 2Sa 2:20
How **t** could I lift up my face to 2Sa 2:22
T Abner called to Joab and said, 2Sa 2:26
surely **t** the people would have 2Sa 2:27 227
Abner and his men **t** went through 2Sa 2:29
T Joab returned from following 2Sa 2:30
T Joab and his men went all night 2Sa 2:32
T Abner was very angry over the 2Sa 3:8
T Abner sent messengers to David 2Sa 3:12
T Abner said to him, 2Sa 3:16
"Now **t**, do *it!* For the LORD has 2Sa 3:18
T Abner and twenty men with him 2Sa 3:20
T Joab came to the king and said, 2Sa 3:24
why **t** have you sent him away and 2Sa 3:24 2088
T David said to Joab and to all 2Sa 3:31
T all the people came to persuade 2Sa 3:35
T the king said to his servants, 2Sa 3:38
T they brought the head of 2Sa 4:8
T David commanded the young men, 2Sa 4:12
T all the tribes of Israel came to 2Sa 5:1
t they anointed David king over 2Sa 5:3
T Hiram king of Tyre sent 2Sa 5:11
T David inquired of the LORD, 2Sa 5:19
trees, **t** you shall act promptly, 2Sa 5:24 227
for **t** the LORD will have gone out 2Sa 5:24 227
T David did so, just as the LORD 2Sa 5:25
T it happened *as* the ark of the 2Sa 6:16
T all the people departed each to 2Sa 6:19
T David the king went in and sat 2Sa 7:18
T David defeated Hadadezer, the 2Sa 8:3
T David put garrisons among the 2Sa 8:6
T David said, "Is there yet anyone 2Sa 9:1
T King David sent and brought him 2Sa 9:5
T the king called Saul's servant 2Sa 9:9
T Ziba said to the king, 2Sa 9:11
T David said, "I will show kindness 2Sa 10:2
your beards grow, and **t** return." 2Sa 10:5
for me, **t** you shall help me, 2Sa 10:11
you, **t** I will come to help you. 2Sa 10:11
T Joab returned from *fighting* 2Sa 10:14
T it happened in the spring, at 2Sa 11:1
T David sent to Joab, *saying,* 2Sa 11:6
T David said to Uriah, 2Sa 11:8
Shall I **t** go to my house to eat 2Sa 11:11
T David said to Uriah, 2Sa 11:12
T Joab sent and reported to David 2Sa 11:18
t you shall say, 'Your servant Uriah 2Sa 11:21
T David said to the messenger, 2Sa 11:25
t she bore him a son. 2Sa 11:27
T the LORD sent Nathan to David. 2Sa 12:1
T David's anger burned greatly 2Sa 12:5
Nathan **t** said to David, 2Sa 12:7
T David said to Nathan, 2Sa 12:13
T the LORD struck the child that 2Sa 12:15
T it happened on the seventh day 2Sa 12:18
How **t** can we tell him that the 2Sa 12:18
T he came to his own house, and 2Sa 12:20
T his servants said to him, 2Sa 12:21
T David comforted his wife 2Sa 12:24
T he took the crown of their king 2Sa 12:30
T David and all the people 2Sa 12:31
T Amnon said to him, 2Sa 13:4
Jonadab **t** said to him, 2Sa 13:5
T David sent to the house for 2Sa 13:7
T Amnon said to Tamar, 2Sa 13:10
T Amnon hated her with a very 2Sa 13:15
T he called his young man who 2Sa 13:17
T his attendant took her out and 2Sa 13:18
T Absalom her brother said to her, 2Sa 13:20
T Absalom said, "If not, please let 2Sa 13:26
'Strike Amnon,' **t** put him to death. 2Sa 13:28
T all the king's sons arose and 2Sa 13:29
T the king arose, tore his clothes 2Sa 13:31
t go to the king and speak to him 2Sa 14:3
T the king said to the woman, 2Sa 14:8
T she said, "Please let the king 2Sa 14:11
T the woman said, 2Sa 14:12
"Why **t** have you planned such a 2Sa 14:13
"**T** your maidservant said, 2Sa 14:17
T the king answered and said to 2Sa 14:18
T the king said to Joab, 2Sa 14:21
t Joab said, "Today your servant 2Sa 14:22
T Absalom sent for Joab, to send 2Sa 14:29
T Joab arose, came to Absalom at 2Sa 14:31
T Absalom would say to him, 2Sa 15:3
t every man who has any suit or 2Sa 15:4
t I will serve the LORD.'" 2Sa 15:8
of the trumpet, **t** you shall say, 2Sa 15:10
T two hundred men went with 2Sa 15:11
T a messenger came to David, 2Sa 15:13
T the king's servants said to the 2Sa 15:15
T the king said to Ittai the 2Sa 15:19
t He will bring me back again and 2Sa 15:25
T all the people who were with him 2Sa 15:30
me, **t** you will be a burden to me. 2Sa 15:33
t you can thwart the counsel of 2Sa 15:34
T the king said, 2Sa 16:3
T Abishai the son of Zeruiah said 2Sa 16:9
'Curse David,' **t** who shall say, 2Sa 16:10
T David said to Abishai and to all 2Sa 16:11
T Absalom and all the people, the 2Sa 16:15
T Hushai said to Absalom, 2Sa 16:18
T Absalom said to Ahithophel, 2Sa 16:20
t all Israel will hear that you 2Sa 16:21
T I will strike down the king 2Sa 17:2
t all the people will be at peace." 2Sa 17:3
T Absalom said, "Now call Hushai 2Sa 17:5
t all Israel shall bring ropes to 2Sa 17:13
T Absalom and all the men of 2Sa 17:14
T Hushai said to Zadok and to 2Sa 17:15
T Absalom's servants came to the 2Sa 17:20
T David and all the people who 2Sa 17:22
T David came to Mahanaim. 2Sa 17:24
T David numbered the people who 2Sa 18:1
T the king said to them, 2Sa 18:4
T the people went out into the 2Sa 18:6
T Joab said to the man who had 2Sa 18:11
Why **t** did you not strike him there 2Sa 18:11
t you yourself would have stood 2Sa 18:13
T Joab said, "I will not waste time 2Sa 18:14
T Joab blew the trumpet, and the 2Sa 18:16
T Ahimaaz the son of Zadok said, 2Sa 18:19
T Joab said to the Cushite, 2Sa 18:21
T Ahimaaz ran by way of the plain 2Sa 18:23
T the watchman saw another man 2Sa 18:26
T the king said, 2Sa 18:30
T the king said to the Cushite, 2Sa 18:32
T it was told Joab, 2Sa 19:1
T Joab came into the house to the 2Sa 19:5
today, **t** you would be pleased. 2Sa 19:6 227
t all the people came before the 2Sa 19:8
Now **t**, why are you silent about 2Sa 19:10
T King David sent to Zadok and 2Sa 19:11
Why **t** should you be the last to 2Sa 19:12
The king **t** returned and came as 2Sa 19:15
T Shimei the son of Gera, the 2Sa 19:16
T they kept crossing the ford to 2Sa 19:18
David **t** said, "What have I to do 2Sa 19:22
T Mephibosheth the son of Saul 2Sa 19:24

Why **t** should your servant be an	2Sa 19:35	
The king **t** kissed Barzillai and	2Sa 19:39	
T all the men of Judah answered	2Sa 19:42	
Why **t** are you angry about this	2Sa 19:42	
Why **t** did you treat us with	2Sa 19:43	
T David came to his house at	2Sa 20:3	
T the king said to Amasa,	2Sa 20:4	
T Joab and Abishai his brother	2Sa 20:10	
T a wise woman called from the	2Sa 20:16	
T she said to him, "Listen to the	2Sa 20:17	
T she spoke, saying,	2Sa 20:18	
T the woman wisely came to all the	2Sa 20:22	
T the Gibeonites said to him,	2Sa 21:4	
T he gave them into the hands of	2Sa 21:9	
t David went and took the bones of	2Sa 21:12	
T Ishbi-benob, who was among the	2Sa 21:16	
T the men of David swore to him,	2Sa 21:17	227
t Sibbecai the Hushathite struck	2Sa 21:18	227
"**T** the earth shook and quaked,	2Sa 22:8	
"**T** the channels of the sea	2Sa 22:16	
"**T** I pulverized them as the dust	2Sa 22:43	
T three of the thirty chief men	2Sa 23:13	
David was **t** in the stronghold,	2Sa 23:14	227
Philistines was **t** in Bethlehem.	2Sa 23:14	227
T Benaiah the son of Jehoiada, the	2Sa 23:20	
T they came to Gilead and to the	2Sa 24:6	
T David said to Gad,	2Sa 24:14	
T David spoke to the LORD when he	2Sa 24:17	
T Araunah said, "Why has my lord	2Sa 24:21	
T Nathan spoke to Bathsheba the	1Ki 1:11	
Why **t** has Adonijah become king?'	1Ki 1:13	
T Bathsheba bowed and prostrated	1Ki 1:16	
T Nathan said, "My lord the king,	1Ki 1:24	
T King David said,	1Ki 1:28	
T Bathsheba bowed with her face to	1Ki 1:31	
T King David said,	1Ki 1:32	
"**T** you shall come up after him,	1Ki 1:35	
Zadok the priest **t** took the horn	1Ki 1:39	
T they blew the trumpet, and all	1Ki 1:39	
T Adonijah said,	1Ki 1:42	
T all the guests of Adonijah were	1Ki 1:49	
T David slept with his fathers and	1Ki 2:10	
T he said, "I have something *to say*	1Ki 2:14	
T he said, "Please speak to Solomon	1Ki 2:17	
t he had a throne set for the	1Ki 2:19	
T she said, "I am making one small	1Ki 2:20	
T King Solomon swore by the LORD,	1Ki 2:23	
T to Abiathar the priest the king	1Ki 2:26	
T Solomon sent Benaiah the son of	1Ki 2:29	
T Benaiah the son of Jehoiada went	1Ki 2:34	
Shimei **t** said to the king,	1Ki 2:38	
T Shimei arose and saddled his	1Ki 2:40	
"Why **t** have you not kept the oath	1Ki 2:43	
T Solomon formed a marriage	1Ki 3:1	
T Solomon said, "You have shown	1Ki 3:6	
t I will prolong your days."	1Ki 3:14	
T Solomon awoke, and behold, it	1Ki 3:15	
T two women who were harlots came	1Ki 3:16	227
T the other woman said,	1Ki 3:22	
T the king said,	1Ki 3:23	
T the woman whose child *was* the	1Ki 3:26	
T the king said,	1Ki 3:27	
T Solomon sent *word* to Hiram,	1Ki 5:2	
T you shall accomplish my desire	1Ki 5:9	
Solomon **t** gave Hiram 20,000 kors	1Ki 5:11	
T the king commanded, and they	1Ki 5:17	
t I will carry out My word with	1Ki 6:12	
T he built the walls of the house	1Ki 6:15	
T he prepared an inner sanctuary	1Ki 6:19	
T he carved all the walls of the	1Ki 6:29	
T he made the hall of pillars;	1Ki 7:6	
T he made the ten stands of bronze;	1Ki 7:27	
T he set the stands, five on the	1Ki 7:39	
T Solomon assembled the elders of	1Ki 8:1	227
T all the elders of Israel came,	1Ki 8:3	
T the priests brought the ark of	1Ki 8:6	
T Solomon said, "The LORD has said	1Ki 8:12	227
T the king faced about and blessed	1Ki 8:14	
T Solomon stood before the altar	1Ki 8:22	
t hear in heaven and act and	1Ki 8:32	
t hear in heaven, and forgive	1Ki 8:34	
t hear in heaven and forgive	1Ki 8:36	
t hear in heaven Your dwelling	1Ki 8:39	
t hear in heaven their prayer and	1Ki 8:45	
t hear their prayer and their	1Ki 8:49	
T they went to their tents joyful	1Ki 8:66	
t I will establish the throne of	1Ki 9:5	
t I will cut off Israel from the	1Ki 9:7	
t King Solomon gave Hiram twenty	1Ki 9:11	227
for her, **t** he built the Millo.	1Ki 9:24	227
T she said to the king,	1Ki 10:6	
T she turned and went to her own	1Ki 10:13	
T Solomon built a high place for	1Ki 11:7	227
T the LORD raised up an adversary	1Ki 11:14	
T Pharaoh said to him,	1Ki 11:22	
T Jeroboam the son of Nebat, an	1Ki 11:26	
T Ahijah took hold of the new	1Ki 11:30	
'**T** it will be, that if you listen	1Ki 11:38	
t I will be with you and build you	1Ki 11:38	
T Rehoboam went to Shechem, for	1Ki 12:1	
T they sent and called him, and	1Ki 12:3	
T he said to them,	1Ki 12:5	
for three days, **t** return to me."	1Ki 12:5	
T they spoke to him, saying,	1Ki 12:7	
t they will be your servants	1Ki 12:7	
T Jeroboam and all the people came	1Ki 12:12	
T King Rehoboam sent Adoram, who	1Ki 12:18	
T Jeroboam built Shechem in the	1Ki 12:25	
t the heart of this people will	1Ki 12:27	
T he went up to the altar which he	1Ki 12:33	
T he gave a sign the same day,	1Ki 13:3	
T the king said to the man of God,	1Ki 13:7	
T he said to his sons,	1Ki 13:13	
T he said to him,	1Ki 13:15	
T he spoke to his sons, saying,	1Ki 13:27	
T Jeroboam's wife arose and	1Ki 14:17	
T it happened as often as the king	1Ki 14:28	
T Asa took all the silver and the	1Ki 15:18	
T King Asa made a proclamation to	1Ki 15:22	
T Baasha the son of Ahijah of the	1Ki 15:27	
T Zimri went in and struck him and	1Ki 16:10	
T Omri and all Israel with him	1Ki 16:17	
T the people of Israel were	1Ki 16:21	227
T the word of the LORD came to	1Ki 17:8	
T Elijah said to her,	1Ki 17:13	
T he took him from her bosom and	1Ki 17:19	
T he stretched himself upon the	1Ki 17:21	
T the woman said to Elijah,	1Ki 17:24	
T Ahab said to Obadiah,	1Ki 18:5	
he will **t** kill me."	1Ki 18:14	
"Now **t** send *and* gather to me all	1Ki 18:19	
T Elijah said to the people,	1Ki 18:22	
"**T** you call on the name of your	1Ki 18:24	
T they took the ox which was given	1Ki 18:26	
T Elijah said to all the people,	1Ki 18:30	
T he arranged the wood and cut the	1Ki 18:33	
T the fire of the LORD fell and	1Ki 18:38	
T Elijah said to them,	1Ki 18:40	
T the hand of the LORD was on	1Ki 18:46	
T Jezebel sent a messenger to	1Ki 19:2	
T he looked and behold, there was	1Ki 19:6	
T he came there to a cave and	1Ki 19:9	
T he said, "I have been very zealous	1Ki 19:14	
my mother, **t** I will follow you."	1Ki 19:20	
T he arose and followed Elijah and	1Ki 19:21	
T he sent messengers to the city	1Ki 20:2	
T the messengers returned and	1Ki 20:5	
T the king of Israel called all	1Ki 20:7	
T the king of Israel replied,	1Ki 20:11	
T he said, "Who shall begin the	1Ki 20:14	
T he mustered the young men of the	1Ki 20:15	
T he said, "If they have come out for	1Ki 20:18	
T the prophet came near to the	1Ki 20:22	
T we will fight against them in	1Ki 20:25	
T a man of God came near and spoke	1Ki 20:28	
T he said, "Go, bring him."	1Ki 20:33	
T Ben-hadad came out to him,	1Ki 20:33	
T he said to him,	1Ki 20:36	
T he found another man and said,	1Ki 20:37	
t your life shall be for his life,	1Ki 20:39	
T he hastily took the bandage away	1Ki 20:41	
T take him out and stone him to	1Ki 21:10	
T the two worthless men came in	1Ki 21:13	
T they sent *word* to Jezebel,	1Ki 21:14	
T the word of the LORD came to	1Ki 21:17	
T the word of the LORD came to	1Ki 21:28	
T the king of Israel gathered the	1Ki 22:6	
T the king of Israel called an	1Ki 22:9	
T Zedekiah the son of Chenaanah	1Ki 22:11	
T the messenger who went to summon	1Ki 22:13	
T the king said to him,	1Ki 22:16	
T the king of Israel said to	1Ki 22:18	
"**T** a spirit came forward and	1Ki 22:21	
T He said, 'You are to entice *him*	1Ki 22:22	
T Zedekiah the son of Chenaanah	1Ki 22:24	
T the king of Israel said,	1Ki 22:26	
T a cry passed throughout the army	1Ki 22:36	
T Ahaziah the son of Ahab said to	1Ki 22:49	227
shall surely die.' " **T** Elijah departed.	2Ki 1:4	
T *the king* sent to him a captain	2Ki 1:9	
T fire came down from heaven and	2Ki 1:10	
T the fire of God came down from	2Ki 1:12	
T he said to him,	2Ki 1:16	
T the sons of the prophets who	2Ki 2:3	
T Elijah said to him,	2Ki 2:6	
T he took hold of his own clothes	2Ki 2:12	
T the men of the city said to	2Ki 2:19	
T he went up from there to Bethel;	2Ki 2:23	
T two female bears came out of the	2Ki 2:24	
T he went and sent *word* to	2Ki 3:7	
T the king of Israel said,	2Ki 3:10	
'**T** you shall strike every	2Ki 3:19	
T they said, "This is blood;	2Ki 3:23	
T he took his oldest son who was	2Ki 3:27	
T he said, "Go, borrow vessels at	2Ki 4:3	
T she came and told the man of God.	2Ki 4:7	
T he said to Gehazi his servant,	2Ki 4:12	
"What **t** is to be done for her?"	2Ki 4:14	
T he said, "At this season next year	2Ki 4:16	
lap until noon, and **t** died.	2Ki 4:20	
T she called to her husband and	2Ki 4:22	
T she saddled a donkey and said to	2Ki 4:24	
T she said, "Did I ask for a son from	2Ki 4:28	
T he said to Gehazi,	2Ki 4:29	
T Gehazi passed on before them and	2Ki 4:31	
T he returned and walked in the	2Ki 4:35	
T she went in and fell at his feet	2Ki 4:37	
T one went out into the field to	2Ki 4:39	
T there was no harm in the pot.	2Ki 4:41	
T he would cure him of his leprosy."	2Ki 5:3	227
T the king of Aram said,	2Ki 5:5	
T his servants came near and spoke	2Ki 5:13	
How much more **t**, when he says	2Ki 5:13	
T he said to him,	2Ki 5:26	
T one said, "Please be willing to go	2Ki 6:3	
T the man of God said,	2Ki 6:6	
T Elisha prayed and said,	2Ki 6:17	
T Elisha said to them,	2Ki 6:19	
T the king of Israel when he saw	2Ki 6:21	
T he said, "May God do so to me	2Ki 6:31	
T Elisha said, "Listen to the word of	2Ki 7:1	
T he said, "Behold, you will see it	2Ki 7:2	
t the famine is in the city and we	2Ki 7:4	
T they said to one another,	2Ki 7:9	
T the king arose in the night and	2Ki 7:12	
T the messengers returned and told	2Ki 7:15	
T a measure of fine flour *was sold*	2Ki 7:16	
T the royal officer answered the	2Ki 7:19	
T Elisha came to Damascus.	2Ki 8:7	
T Elisha said to him,	2Ki 8:10	
T he answered, "Because I know the	2Ki 8:12	
T Hazael said, "But what is your	2Ki 8:13	
being **t** the king of Judah,	2Ki 8:16	
T Joram crossed over to Zair, and	2Ki 8:21	
T Libnah revolted at the same time.	2Ki 8:22	227
T he went with Joram the son of	2Ki 8:28	
T Ahaziah the son of Jehoram king	2Ki 8:29	
"**T** take the flask of oil and pour	2Ki 9:3	
T open the door and flee and do	2Ki 9:3	
T he opened the door and fled.	2Ki 9:10	
T they hurried and each man took	2Ki 9:13	
t let no one escape *or* leave	2Ki 9:15	
T Jehu rode in a chariot and went	2Ki 9:16	
T he sent out a second horseman,	2Ki 9:19	
T Joram said, "Get ready."	2Ki 9:21	
T *Jehu* said to Bidkar his officer,	2Ki 9:25	
Now **t**, take and cast him into the	2Ki 9:26	
T his servants carried him in a	2Ki 9:28	
T he lifted up his face to the	2Ki 9:32	
how **t** can we stand?"	2Ki 10:4	
T he wrote a letter to them a	2Ki 10:6	
"Know **t** that there shall fall to	2Ki 10:10	645
T he arose and departed and went	2Ki 10:12	
T Jehu gathered all the people and	2Ki 10:18	
T Jehu sent throughout Israel and	2Ki 10:21	
T they went in to offer sacrifices	2Ki 10:24	
T it came about, as soon as he had	2Ki 10:25	
T he made a covenant with them and	2Ki 11:4	
"**T** you shall surround the king,	2Ki 11:8	
T he brought the king's son out	2Ki 11:12	
T Athaliah tore her clothes and	2Ki 11:14	
T Jehoiada made a covenant between	2Ki 11:17	
T Jehoash said to the priests,	2Ki 12:4	
T King Jehoash called for Jehoiada	2Ki 12:7	
T Hazael king of Aram went up and	2Ki 12:17	227
T he went away from Jerusalem.	2Ki 12:18	
T Jehoahaz entreated the favor of	2Ki 13:4	
T he said to the king of Israel,	2Ki 13:16	
t Elisha laid his hands on the	2Ki 13:16	
T Elisha said, "Shoot!" And he shot.	2Ki 13:17	
T he said, "Take the arrows,"	2Ki 13:18	
t you would have struck Aram until	2Ki 13:19	227
T Jehoash the son of Jehoahaz took	2Ki 13:25	
T Amaziah sent messengers to	2Ki 14:8	227
T Jehoash king of Israel captured	2Ki 14:13	
T they brought him on horses and	2Ki 14:20	
T Shallum the son of Jabesh	2Ki 15:10	
T Menahem son of Gadi went up from	2Ki 15:14	
T Menahem struck Tiphsah and all	2Ki 15:16	227
T Menahem exacted the money from	2Ki 15:20	
T Pekah son of Remaliah, his	2Ki 15:25	
T Rezin king of Aram and Pekah son	2Ki 16:5	227
t the king approached the altar	2Ki 16:12	
T King Ahaz commanded Urijah the	2Ki 16:15	
T King Ahaz cut off the borders of	2Ki 16:17	
T the king of Assyria invaded the	2Ki 17:5	
T they made their sons and their	2Ki 17:17	
T Jeroboam drove Israel away from	2Ki 17:21	
T the king of Assyria commanded,	2Ki 17:27	
T the king of Assyria carried	2Ki 18:11	
T Hezekiah king of Judah sent to	2Ki 18:14	
T the king of Assyria sent Tartan	2Ki 18:17	
T Rabshakeh said to them,	2Ki 18:19	
"How **t** can you repulse one	2Ki 18:24	
T Eliakim the son of Hilkiah, and	2Ki 18:26	
T Rabshakeh stood and cried with a	2Ki 18:28	
T Eliakim the son of Hilkiah, who	2Ki 18:37	
T he sent Eliakim who was over the	2Ki 19:2	
T Rabshakeh returned and found the	2Ki 19:8	
T Hezekiah took the letter from	2Ki 19:14	
T Isaiah the son of Amoz sent to	2Ki 19:20	
'**T** this shall be the sign for you:	2Ki 19:29	
T it happened that night that the	2Ki 19:35	
T he turned his face to the wall and	2Ki 20:2	
T Isaiah said, "Take a cake of figs."	2Ki 20:7	
T Isaiah the prophet came to King	2Ki 20:14	
T Isaiah said to Hezekiah,	2Ki 20:16	
T Hezekiah said to Isaiah,	2Ki 20:19	
T he set the carved image of	2Ki 21:7	
T the people of the land killed	2Ki 21:24	
T Hilkiah the high priest said to	2Ki 22:8	
T the king commanded Hilkiah the	2Ki 22:12	
T the king sent, and they gathered	2Ki 23:1	
T the king commanded Hilkiah the	2Ki 23:4	
T he brought all the priests from	2Ki 23:8	
T he demolished its stones, ground	2Ki 23:15	
T he said, "What is this monument	2Ki 23:17	
t he returned to Jerusalem.	2Ki 23:20	
T the king commanded all the	2Ki 23:21	
T the people of the land took	2Ki 23:30	
t he turned and rebelled against	2Ki 24:1	
T he led away into exile all	2Ki 24:14	
T the king of Babylon made his	2Ki 24:17	
T the city was broken into, and	2Ki 25:4	
T they captured the king and	2Ki 25:6	
t put out the eyes of Zedekiah and	2Ki 25:7	
T the rest of the people who were	2Ki 25:11	

T the captain of the guard took 2Ki 25:18
T the king of Babylon struck them 2Ki 25:21
T all the people, both small and 2Ki 25:26
of Ishmael *was* Nebaioth, **t** Kedar, 1Ch 1:29
T Hadad died. Now the chiefs of 1Ch 1:51
firstborn, **t** Abinadab the second, 1Ch 2:13
were Ram the firstborn, **t** Bunah, 1Ch 2:25
were Jeiel the chief, **t** Zechariah 1Ch 5:7
t Janai and Shaphat in Bashan. 1Ch 5:12
T to the rest of the sons of 1Ch 6:61
T he went in to his wife, and she 1Ch 7:23
firstborn son *was* Abdon, **t** Zur, 1Ch 8:30
firstborn son *was* Abdon, **t** Zur, 1Ch 9:36
T Saul said to his armor bearer, 1Ch 10:4
T all Israel gathered to David at 1Ch 11:1
T David and all Israel went to 1Ch 11:4
T David dwelt in the stronghold; 1Ch 11:7
David was **t** in the stronghold, 1Ch 11:16 227
Philistines *was* **t** in Bethlehem. 1Ch 11:16 227
The chief was Ahiezer, **t** Joash, 1Ch 12:3
T Jeremiah, Jahaziel, Johanan, 1Ch 12:4
T some of the sons of Benjamin and 1Ch 12:16
T the Spirit came upon Amasai, who 1Ch 12:18
T David received them and made 1Ch 12:18
T David consulted with the 1Ch 13:1
T all the assembly said that they 1Ch 13:4
T David became angry because of 1Ch 13:11
T David took more wives at 1Ch 14:3
T the LORD said to him, 1Ch 14:10
t you shall go out to battle, 1Ch 14:15 227
T the fame of David went out into 1Ch 14:17
T David said, "No one is to carry 1Ch 15:2 227
T David called for Zadok and 1Ch 15:11
T David spoke to the chiefs of the 1Ch 15:16
t Jeiel, Shemiramoth, Jehiel, 1Ch 16:5
T on that day David first assigned 1Ch 16:7 227
T the trees of the forest will 1Ch 16:33 227
T say, "Save us, O God of our 1Ch 16:35
T all the people said, 1Ch 16:36
T all the people departed each to 1Ch 16:43
T Nathan said to David, 1Ch 17:2
T David the king went in and sat 1Ch 17:16
T David put *garrisons* among the 1Ch 18:6
T he put garrisons in Edom, and 1Ch 18:13
T David said, "I will show kindness 1Ch 19:2
T *certain persons* went and told 1Ch 19:5
your beards grow, and **t** return." 1Ch 19:5
for me, **t** you shall help me; 1Ch 19:12
strong for you, **t** I will help you. 1Ch 19:12
T Joab came to Jerusalem. 1Ch 19:15
T it happened in the spring, at 1Ch 20:1
T David and all the people 1Ch 20:3
t Sibbecai the Hushathite killed 1Ch 20:4 227
T Satan stood up against Israel 1Ch 21:1
T David lifted up his eyes and saw 1Ch 21:16
T David and the elders, covered 1Ch 21:16
T the angel of the LORD commanded 1Ch 21:18
T David said to Ornan, 1Ch 21:22
T David built an altar to the LORD 1Ch 21:26
T David said, "This is the house of 1Ch 22:1
T he called for his son Solomon, 1Ch 22:6
"**T** you will prosper, if you are 1Ch 22:13 227
T they cast lots *for* his son 1Ch 26:14
T King David rose to his feet and 1Ch 28:2
T David gave to his son Solomon 1Ch 28:11
T David said to his son Solomon, 1Ch 28:20
T King David said to the entire 1Ch 29:1
Who **t** is willing to consecrate 1Ch 29:5
T the rulers of the fathers' 1Ch 29:6
T the people rejoiced because they 1Ch 29:9
T David said to all the assembly, 1Ch 29:20
T Solomon sat on the throne of the 1Ch 29:23
T he died in a ripe old age, full 1Ch 29:28
T Solomon and all the assembly 2Ch 1:3
T Solomon sent *word* to Huram the 2Ch 2:3
T Huram, king of Tyre, answered in 2Ch 2:11
T Huram continued, 2Ch 2:12
"Now **t**, let my lord send to his 2Ch 2:15
T Solomon began to build the house 2Ch 3:1
T he made two sculptured cherubim 2Ch 3:10
T he made a bronze altar, twenty 2Ch 4:1
T he made the ten golden 2Ch 4:7
T he made the court of the priests 2Ch 4:9
T Solomon assembled to Jerusalem 2Ch 5:2 227
T all the elders of Israel came, 2Ch 5:4
T the priests brought the ark of 2Ch 5:7
t the house, the house of the LORD, 2Ch 5:13
T Solomon said, "The LORD has said 2Ch 6:1 227
T the king faced about and blessed 2Ch 6:3
T he stood before the altar of the 2Ch 6:12
t hear from heaven and act 2Ch 6:23
t hear from heaven and 2Ch 6:25
t hear in heaven and forgive 2Ch 6:27
t hear from heaven Your 2Ch 6:30
t hear from heaven, from Your 2Ch 6:33
t hear from heaven their 2Ch 6:35
t hear from heaven, from Your 2Ch 6:39
T the king and all the people 2Ch 7:4
T Solomon consecrated the middle 2Ch 7:7
T on the twenty-third day of the 2Ch 7:10
T the LORD appeared to Solomon at 2Ch 7:12
ways, **t** I will hear from heaven, 2Ch 7:14
t I will establish your royal 2Ch 7:18
t I will uproot you from My land 2Ch 7:20
T Solomon went to Hamath-zobah and 2Ch 8:3
T Solomon brought Pharaoh's 2Ch 8:11
T Solomon offered burnt offerings 2Ch 8:12 227
T Solomon went to Ezion-geber and 2Ch 8:17 227
T she said to the king, 2Ch 9:5
T she gave the king one hundred 2Ch 9:9
T she turned and went to her own 2Ch 9:12
T Rehoboam went to Shechem, for 2Ch 10:1
T King Rehoboam consulted with the 2Ch 10:6
t they will be your servants 2Ch 10:7
T King Rehoboam sent Hadoram, who 2Ch 10:18
T Rehoboam took as a wife Mahalath 2Ch 11:18
T Shemaiah the prophet came to 2Ch 12:5
T King Rehoboam made shields of 2Ch 12:10
guards came and carried them and **t** 2Ch 12:11
T Abijah stood on Mount Zemaraim, 2Ch 13:4
T the men of Judah raised a war 2Ch 13:15
t it was that God routed Jeroboam 2Ch 13:15
T Asa called to the LORD his God and 2Ch 14:11
T they returned to Jerusalem. 2Ch 14:15
He **t** restored the altar of the 2Ch 15:8
T Asa brought out silver and gold 2Ch 16:2
T King Asa brought all Judah, and 2Ch 16:6
T Asa was angry with the seer and 2Ch 16:10
son **t** became king in his place, 2Ch 17:1
T in the third year of his reign 2Ch 17:7
T the king of Israel assembled the 2Ch 18:5
T the king of Israel called an 2Ch 18:8
T the messenger who went to summon 2Ch 18:12
T the king said to him, 2Ch 18:15
T the king of Israel said to 2Ch 18:17
"**T** a spirit came forward and 2Ch 18:20
T He said, 'You are to entice *him* 2Ch 18:21
T Zedekiah the son of Chenaanah 2Ch 18:23
T the king of Israel said, 2Ch 18:25
T Jehoshaphat the king of Judah 2Ch 19:1
"Now **t** let the fear of the LORD 2Ch 19:7
T he charged them saying, 2Ch 19:9
T some came and reported to 2Ch 20:2
T Jehoshaphat stood in the 2Ch 20:5
T in the midst of the assembly the 2Ch 20:14
T on the fourth day they assembled 2Ch 20:26
T Eliezer the son of Dodavahu of 2Ch 20:37
T Jehoshaphat slept with his 2Ch 21:1
T Jehoram crossed over with his 2Ch 21:9
T Libnah revolted at the same time 2Ch 21:10 227
T a letter came to him from Elijah 2Ch 21:12
T the LORD stirred up against 2Ch 21:16
T the inhabitants of Jerusalem 2Ch 22:1
T all the assembly made a covenant 2Ch 23:3
T Jehoiada the priest gave to the 2Ch 23:9
T they brought out the king's son 2Ch 23:11
T Athaliah tore her clothes and 2Ch 23:13
T Jehoiada made a covenant between 2Ch 23:16
t the king's scribe and the chief 2Ch 24:11
T the Spirit of God came on 2Ch 24:20
T Amaziah his son became king in 2Ch 24:27
T Amaziah dismissed them, the 2Ch 25:10
T the anger of the LORD burned 2Ch 25:15
T the prophet stopped and said, 2Ch 25:16
T Amaziah king of Judah took 2Ch 25:17
T Joash king of Israel captured 2Ch 25:23
T they brought him on horses and 2Ch 25:28
T Azariah the priest entered after 2Ch 26:17
T some of the heads of the sons of 2Ch 28:12
T the men who were designated by 2Ch 28:15
t they returned to Samaria. 2Ch 28:15
T he said to them, 2Ch 29:5
T the Levites arose: 2Ch 29:12
T the Levites received *it* to carry 2Ch 29:16
T they consecrated the house of 2Ch 29:17
T they went in to King Hezekiah 2Ch 29:18
T King Hezekiah arose early and 2Ch 29:20
T they brought the male goats of 2Ch 29:23
He **t** stationed the Levites in the 2Ch 29:25
T Hezekiah gave the order to offer 2Ch 29:27
T Hezekiah said, 2Ch 29:31
T Hezekiah and all the people 2Ch 29:36
T they slaughtered the Passover 2Ch 30:15
T Hezekiah spoke encouragingly to 2Ch 30:22
T the whole assembly decided to 2Ch 30:23
T the Levitical priests arose and 2Ch 30:27
T all the sons of Israel returned 2Ch 31:1
T Hezekiah questioned the priests 2Ch 31:9
T Hezekiah commanded *them* to 2Ch 31:11
T he put the carved image of the 2Ch 33:7
T Manasseh knew that the LORD *was* 2Ch 33:13
T he put army commanders in all 2Ch 33:14
T he burned the bones of the 2Ch 34:5
T he returned to Jerusalem. 2Ch 34:7
T they gave *it* into the hands of 2Ch 34:10
T Shaphan brought the book to the 2Ch 34:16
T the king commanded Hilkiah, 2Ch 34:20
T the king sent and gathered all 2Ch 34:29
T the king stood in his place and 2Ch 34:31
T Josiah celebrated the Passover 2Ch 35:1
T they removed the burnt offerings 2Ch 35:12
T Jeremiah chanted a lament for 2Ch 35:25
T the people of the land took 2Ch 36:1
T the king of Egypt deposed him at 2Ch 36:3
T they burned the house of God and 2Ch 36:19
T the heads of fathers' *households* Ezr 1:5
T Jeshua the son of Jozadak and Ezr 3:2
T they gave money to the masons Ezr 3:7
T Jeshua *with* his sons and Ezr 3:9
T the people of the land Ezr 4:4
t *wrote* Rehum the commander and Ezr 4:9 116
T the king sent an answer to Ezr 4:17
T as soon as the copy of King Ezr 4:23 116
T work on the house of God in Ezr 4:24 116
t Zerubbabel the son of Shealtiel Ezr 5:2 116
T we told them accordingly what Ezr 5:4 116
and **t** a written reply be returned Ezr 5:5 116
"**T** we asked those elders and said Ezr 5:9 116
'**T** that Sheshbazzar came *and* laid Ezr 5:16 116
and from **t** until now it has been Ezr 5:16 116
T King Darius issued a decree, and Ezr 6:1 116
T Tattenai, the governor of *the* Ezr 6:13 116
T they appointed the priests to Ezr 6:18
T they slaughtered the Passover Ezr 6:20
T I proclaimed a fast there at the Ezr 8:21
T I set apart twelve of the Ezr 8:24
T I said to them, Ezr 8:28
T we journeyed from the river Ezr 8:31
T they delivered the king's edicts Ezr 8:36
T everyone who trembled at the Ezr 9:4
T Ezra rose and made the leading Ezr 10:5
T Ezra rose from before the house Ezr 10:6
T Ezra the priest stood up and Ezr 10:10
T all the assembly replied Ezr 10:12
T I was very much afraid. Ne 2:2
T the king said to me, Ne 2:4
T the king said to me, the queen Ne 2:6
T I came to the governors *of the* Ne 2:9
T I passed on to the Fountain Gate Ne 2:14
T I entered the Valley Gate again Ne 2:15
T I said to them, Ne 2:17
T they said, "Let us arise and build." Ne 2:18
T Eliashib the high priest arose Ne 3:1
t I stationed *men* in the lowest Ne 4:13
t all of us returned to the wall, Ne 4:15
T I was very angry when I had Ne 5:6
T they were silent and could not Ne 5:8
T they said, "We will give *it* back Ne 5:12
T the people did according to this Ne 5:13
t Sanballat and Geshem sent *a* Ne 6:2
T Sanballat sent his servant to me Ne 6:5
T I sent *a message* to him saying, Ne 6:8
T I perceived that surely God had Ne 6:12
T Tobiah sent letters to frighten Ne 6:19
t I put Hanani my brother, Ne 7:2
T I said to them, Ne 7:3
T my God put it into my heart to Ne 7:5
T I found the book of the Ne 7:5
T Ezra the priest brought the law Ne 8:2
T Ezra blessed the LORD the great Ne 8:6
t they bowed low and worshiped the Ne 8:6
T Nehemiah, who was the governor, Ne 8:9
T he said to them, Ne 8:10
T on the second day the heads of Ne 8:13
T the Levites, Jeshua, Kadmiel, Ne 9:5
"**T** You performed signs and Ne 9:10
"**T** You came down on Mount Ne 9:13
T I had the leaders of Judah come Ne 12:31
T the two choirs took their stand Ne 12:40
T I gave an order and they Ne 13:9
T I gathered them together and Ne 13:11
All Judah **t** brought the tithe of Ne 13:12
T I reprimanded the nobles of Ne 13:17
T I stationed some of my servants Ne 13:19
T I warned them and said to them, Ne 13:21
"Do we **t** hear about you that you Ne 13:27
T the king became very angry and Es 1:12
T the king said to the wise men Es 1:13
t all women will give honor to Es 1:20
T the king's attendants, who Es 2:2
"**T** let the young lady who pleases Es 2:4
T the king gave a great banquet, Es 2:18
t Mordecai was sitting at the Es 2:19
T the king's servants who were at Es 3:3
T Haman said to King Ahasuerus, Es 3:8
T the king took his signet ring Es 3:10
T the king's scribes were summoned Es 3:12
T Esther's maidens and her eunuchs Es 4:4
T Esther summoned Hathach from the Es 4:5
T Esther spoke to Hathach and Es 4:10
T Mordecai told *them* to reply to Es 4:13
T Esther told *them* to reply to Es 4:15
T the king said to her, Es 5:3
T the king said, Es 5:5
T Haman went out that day glad and Es 5:9
T Haman recounted to them the Es 5:11
T Zeresh his wife and all his Es 5:14
t go joyfully with the king to the Es 5:14
T the king's servants who attended Es 6:3
T Haman said to the king, Es 6:7
T the king said to Haman, Es 6:10
T Mordecai returned to the king's Es 6:12
T his wise men and Zeresh his wife Es 6:13
T Queen Esther replied, Es 7:3
T King Ahasuerus asked Queen Es 7:5
T Haman became terrified before Es 7:6
T the king said, Es 7:8
T Harbonah, one of the eunuchs who Es 7:9
T Esther spoke again to the king, Es 8:3
T she said, "If it pleases the king Es 8:5
T Mordecai went out from the Es 8:15
What **t** have they done in the rest Es 9:12
T said Esther, "If it pleases the king, Es 9:13
T Mordecai recorded these events, Es 9:20
T Queen Esther, daughter of Es 9:29
T Satan answered the LORD and Jb 1:7
T Satan answered the LORD, Jb 1:9
T the LORD said to Satan, Jb 1:12
T Job arose and tore his robe and Jb 1:20
T Satan answered the LORD and Jb 2:2
T Satan went out from the presence Jb 2:7
T his wife said to him, Jb 2:9
T they sat down on the ground with Jb 2:13
I would have slept **t**, Jb 3:13 227
T Eliphaz the Temanite answered, Jb 4:1
"**T** a spirit passed by my face; Jb 4:15
was silence, **t** I heard a voice: Jb 4:16

T Job answered, Jb 6:1
"For **t** it would be heavier than Jb 6:3 6258
T You frighten me with Jb 7:14
"Why **t** do You not pardon my Jb 7:21
T Bildad the Shuhite answered, Jb 8:1
T He delivered them into the power Jb 8:4
his place, **T** it will deny him, Jb 8:18
T Job answered, Jb 9:1
"How **t** can I answer Him, *And* Jb 9:14 637, 3588
If *it is* not *He,* **t** who is it? Jb 9:24 645
Why **t** should I toil in vain? Jb 9:29 2088
"**T** I would speak and not fear Jb 9:35
t You would take note of me, Jb 10:14
'Why **t** have You brought me out of Jb 10:18
'**T** Zophar the Naamathite answered, Jb 11:1
Know **t** that God forgets a part of Jb 11:6
"**T**, indeed, you could lift up Jb 11:15 227
"**T** you would trust, because there Jb 11:18
T Job responded, Jb 12:1
"Truly **t** you are the people, And Jb 12:2 3588
nations great, **t** destroys them; Jb 12:23
the nations, **t** leads them away. Jb 12:23
T let come on me what may. Jb 13:13
For **t** I would be silent and die. Jb 13:19 6258
T I will not hide from Your face: Jb 13:20 227
"**T** call, and I will answer; Jb 13:22
Or let me speak, **t** reply to me. Jb 13:22
T Eliphaz the Temanite responded, Jb 15:1
T Job answered, Jb 16:1
T Bildad the Shuhite responded, Jb 18:1
understanding and **t** we can talk. Jb 18:2 310
T Job responded, Jb 19:1
Know **t** that God has wronged me And Jb 19:6 645
"**T** be afraid of the sword for Jb 19:29
T Zophar the Naamathite answered, Jb 20:1
T Job answered, Jb 21:1
T after I have spoken, you may Jb 21:3
"How **t** will you vainly comfort Jb 21:34
T Eliphaz the Temanite responded, Jb 22:1
T the Almighty will be your gold Jb 22:25
"For **t** you will delight in the Jb 22:26 227
T Job replied, Jb 23:1
a little while, **t** they are gone; Jb 24:24
T Bildad the Shuhite answered, Jb 25:1
"How **t** can a man be just with God? Jb 25:4
T Job responded, Jb 26:1
T Job continued his discourse and Jb 27:1
Why **t** do you act foolishly? Jb 27:12 2088
"Where **t** does wisdom come from? Jb 28:20
T He saw it and declared it; Jb 28:27 227
"**T** I thought, 'I shall die in my nest, Jb 29:18
"When I expected good, **t** evil came; Jb 30:26
waited for light, **t** darkness came. Jb 30:26
How **t** could I gaze at a virgin? Jb 31:1
What **t** could I do when God arises? Jb 31:14
T these three men ceased answering Jb 32:1
T He opens the ears of men, And Jb 33:16 227
"**T** his soul draws near to the Jb 33:22
T let him be gracious to him, and Jb 33:24
T he will pray to God, and He will Jb 33:26
"**T** if you have anything to say, Jb 33:32
T Elihu continued and said, Jb 34:1
He keeps quiet, who **t** can condemn? Jb 34:29
His face, who **t** can behold Him, Jb 34:29
T Elihu continued and said, Jb 35:1
T Elihu continued and said, Jb 36:1
T He declares to them their work Jb 36:9
"**T** indeed, He enticed you from Jb 36:16
"**T** the beast goes into its lair And Jb 37:8
T the LORD answered Job out of the Jb 38:1
"You know, for you were born **t**, Jb 38:21 227
T the LORD said to Job, Jb 40:1
T Job answered the LORD and said, Jb 40:3
T the LORD answered Job out of the Jb 40:6
"**T** I will also confess to you, Jb 40:14
Who **t** is he that can stand before Jb 41:10
T Job answered the LORD and said, Jb 42:1
T all his brothers and all his Jb 42:11
T He will speak to them in His Ps 2:5 227
T the earth shook and quaked; Ps 18:7
T the channels of water appeared, Ps 18:15
T I beat them fine as the dust Ps 18:42
T I will be blameless, And I Ps 19:13 227
T he passed away, and lo, he was Ps 37:36
T I spoke with my tongue: Ps 39:3
T I said, "Behold, I come; Ps 40:7 227
T I will go to the altar of God, Ps 43:4
T You planted them; Ps 44:2
T You spread them abroad. Ps 44:2
T the King will desire your beauty. Ps 45:11
They saw *it,* **t** they were amazed; Ps 48:5 3651
T I will teach transgressors Your Ps 51:13
T my tongue will joyfully sing of Ps 51:14
T You will delight in righteous Ps 51:19 227
T young bulls will be offered on Ps 51:19 227
reproaches me, **T** I could bear *it;* Ps 55:12
T I could hide myself from him. Ps 55:12
T my enemies will turn back in the Ps 56:9 227
T all men will fear, And they Ps 64:9
not steal, I **t** have to restore. Ps 69:4 227
T I perceived their end. Ps 73:17
T I was senseless and ignorant; Ps 73:22
I remember God, **t** I am disturbed; Ps 77:3
I sigh, **t** my spirit grows faint. Ps 77:3
T I said, "It is my grief, Ps 77:10
T He led them with the cloud by Ps 78:14
T they spoke against God; Ps 78:19
T He let *them* fall in the midst of Ps 78:28
He killed them, **t** they sought Him, Ps 78:34
T the Lord awoke as *if from* sleep, Ps 78:65
T we shall not turn back from You; Ps 80:18
T those who sing as well as those Ps 87:7
T I will punish their transgression Ps 89:32
T all the trees of the forest will Ps 96:12 227
T He confirmed it to Jacob for a Ps 105:10
T He brought them out with silver Ps 105:37
T they believed His words; Ps 106:12
T they despised the pleasant land; Ps 106:24
T Phinehas stood up and interposed, Ps 106:30
T He gave them into the hand of Ps 106:41
T they cried out to the LORD in Ps 107:6
T they cried out to the LORD in Ps 107:13
T they cried out to the LORD in Ps 107:19
T they cried to the LORD in their Ps 107:28
T they were glad because they were Ps 107:30
T I called upon the name of the Ps 116:4
T I shall not be ashamed When I Ps 119:6 227
T I would have perished in my Ps 119:92 227
T they would have swallowed us Ps 124:3 233
T the waters would have engulfed Ps 124:4 233
T the raging waters would have Ps 124:5 233
T our mouth was filled with Ps 126:2 227
T they said among the nations, Ps 126:2 227
"**T** they will call on me, but I Pr 1:28 227
T you will discern the fear of the Pr 2:5 227
T you will discern righteousness Pr 2:9 227
T you will walk in your way Pr 3:23 227
T he taught me and said to me, Pr 4:4
Now **t**, *my* sons, listen to me And Pr 5:7
Do this **t**, my son, and deliver Pr 6:3 645
T I was beside Him, *as* a master Pr 8:30
pride comes, **t** comes dishonor, Pr 11:2
when he goes his way, **t** he boasts. Pr 20:14 227
How **t** can man understand his way? Pr 20:24
find *it,* **t** there will be a future, Pr 24:14
Afterwards, **t**, build your house. Pr 24:27
T your poverty will come *as* a Pr 24:34
south, **T** turning toward the north, Ec 1:6
T I became great and increased Ec 2:9
T I said to myself, Ec 2:15
Why **t** have I been extremely wise?" Ec 2:15 227
t he gives his legacy to one who Ec 2:21
T I looked again at all the acts Ec 4:1
T I looked again at vanity under Ec 4:7
t there was nothing to support him. Ec 5:14
t I say, "Better Ec 6:3
What **t** is the advantage to a man? Ec 6:11
So **t**, I have seen the wicked Ec 8:10
Go **t**, eat your bread in Ec 9:7
t he must exert more strength. Ec 10:10
t the dust will return to the Ec 12:7
T I became in his eyes as one who SS 8:10 227
"**T** I will restore your judges as Is 1:26
t the LORD will create over the Is 4:5
T He expected *it* to produce *good* Is 5:2
T the lambs will graze as in their Is 5:17
T I said, "Woe is me, for I am ruined Is 6:5
T one of the seraphim flew to me with Is 6:6
T I heard the voice of the Lord, Is 6:8
T I said, "Here am I. Send me!" Is 6:8
T I said, "Lord, how long?" Is 6:11
T the LORD said to Isaiah, Is 7:3
T the LORD spoke again to Ahaz, Is 7:10
T he said, "Listen now, O house of Is 7:13
T the LORD said to me, Is 8:1
T the LORD said to me, Is 8:3
"**T** it will sweep on into Judah, Is 8:8
"**T** He shall become a sanctuary; Is 8:14
T they will fall and be broken; Is 8:15
T they will look to the earth, and Is 8:22
From **t** on and forevermore. Is 9:7 6258
T a shoot will spring from the Is 11:1
T in that day Is 11:10
T it will happen on that day that Is 11:11
T the jealousy of Ephraim will Is 11:13
T you will say on that day, Is 12:1
t strangers will join them and Is 14:1
T his yoke will be removed from Is 14:25
"How **t** will one answer the Is 14:32
T, like fleeing birds *or* scattered Is 16:2
T He will cut off the sprigs with Is 18:5
"**T** the spirit of the Egyptians Is 19:3
Well **t**, where are your wise men? Is 19:12 645
"**T** they will be dismayed and Is 20:5
T the lookout called, Is 21:8
T your choicest valleys were full Is 22:7
T you counted the houses of Is 22:10
"**T** it will come about in that Is 22:20
"**T** I will set the key of the Is 22:22
T she will go back to her harlot's Is 23:17
T it will be that he who flees the Is 24:18
T the moon will be abashed and the Is 24:23
T I would step on them, I would Is 27:4
T hail will sweep away the refuge Is 28:17
T you become its trampling *place.* Is 28:18
T you will be brought low; Is 29:4
T the book will be given to the Is 29:12
T the Lord said, Is 29:13
T He will give *you* rain for the Is 30:23
T the eyes of those who see will Is 32:3
T justice will dwell in the Is 32:16
T my people will live in a Is 32:18
T the prey of an abundant spoil Is 33:23 227
T the eyes of the blind will be Is 35:5 227
T the lame will leap like a deer, Is 35:6 227
T Eliakim the son of Hilkiah, who Is 36:3
T Rabshakeh said to them, Is 36:4
"How **t** can you repulse one Is 36:9
T Eliakim and Shebna and Joah said Is 36:11
T Rabshakeh stood and cried with a Is 36:13
T Eliakim the son of Hilkiah, who Is 36:22
T he sent Eliakim who was over the Is 37:2
T Rabshakeh returned and found the Is 37:8
T Hezekiah took the letter from Is 37:14
T Isaiah the son of Amoz sent *word* Is 37:21
"**T** this shall be the sign for you: Is 37:30
T the angel of the LORD went out and Is 37:36
T Hezekiah turned his face to the Is 38:2
T the word of the LORD came to Is 38:4
T Hezekiah had said, Is 38:22
T Isaiah the prophet came to King Is 39:3
T Isaiah said to Hezekiah, Is 39:5
T Hezekiah said to Isaiah, Is 39:8
T the glory of the LORD will be Is 40:5
T he answered, "What shall I call Is 40:6
To whom **t** will you liken God? Is 40:18
"To whom **t** will you liken Me That Is 40:25
come forward, **t** let them speak; Is 41:1 227
T it becomes *something* for a man Is 44:15
T I make the rest of it into an Is 44:19
"Now, **t**, hear this, you sensual Is 47:8
T your well-being would have been Is 48:18
"**T** you will say in your heart, Is 49:21
T I blessed him and multiplied him." Is 51:2
sky, **T** look to the earth beneath; Is 51:6
t the Assyrian oppressed them Is 52:4
"**T** your light will break out like Is 58:8 227
"**T** you will call, and the LORD Is 58:9 227
T your light will rise in Is 58:10
T you will take delight in the Is 58:14 227
T His own arm brought salvation to Is 59:16
"**T** you will see and be radiant, Is 60:5 227
T you will know that I, the LORD, Is 60:16
"**T** all your people *will be* Is 60:21
T they will rebuild the ancient Is 61:4
T their offspring will be known Is 61:9
T His people remembered the days Is 63:11
Where **t** is a house you could build Is 66:1 2088
T you will see *this,* and your Is 66:14
"**T** they shall bring all your Is 66:20
"**T** they will go forth and look Is 66:24
T I said, "Alas, Lord GOD! Behold, Jer 1:6
T the LORD stretched out His hand Jer 1:9
T the LORD said to me, Jer 1:12
T the LORD said to me, Jer 1:14
How **t** have you turned yourself Jer 2:21
T the LORD said to me in the days Jer 3:6
"**T** I will give you shepherds Jer 3:15
"**T** I said, 'How I would set you Jer 3:19
"**T** you should return to Me. Jer 4:1
T the nations will bless Jer 4:2
T I said, "Ah, Lord GOD! Surely Jer 4:10
seeks truth, **T** I will pardon her. Jer 5:1
T I said, "They are only the poor, Jer 5:4
t you shall say to them, Jer 5:19
t I will let you dwell in this Jer 7:7
t come and stand before Me in this Jer 7:10
"**T** I will make to cease from the Jer 7:34
"Why **t** has this people, Jer 8:5
Why **t** has not the health of the Jer 8:22 3588
T I said, "Amen, Jer 11:5
T the LORD said to me, Jer 11:9
"**T** the cities of Judah and the Jer 11:12
T You showed me their deeds. Jer 11:18 227
T how can you compete with horses? Jer 12:5
"**T** if they will really learn Jer 12:16
t I will uproot that nation, Jer 12:17
T the word of the LORD came to me Jer 13:3
T I went to the Euphrates and dug, Jer 13:7
T the word of the LORD came to me, Jer 13:8
t say to them, 'Thus says the LORD, Jer 13:13
T you also can do good Who are Jer 13:23
T the LORD said to me, Jer 14:14
T the LORD said to me, Jer 15:1
t you are to tell them, Jer 15:2
"**T** I will cause your enemies to Jer 15:14
"If you return, **t** I will restore you Jer 15:19
"**T** I will make you to this people Jer 15:20
"**T** you are to say to them, Jer 16:11
t there will come in through the Jer 17:25
t I will kindle a fire in its Jer 17:27
T I went down to the potter's Jer 18:3
T the word of the LORD came to me Jer 18:5
t I will think better of the good Jer 18:10
"So now **t**, speak to the men of Jer 18:11
T they said, "Come and let us devise Jer 18:18
"**T** go out to the valley of Jer 19:2
"**T** you are to break the jar in Jer 19:10
T Jeremiah came from Topheth, Jer 19:14
T in my heart it becomes like a Jer 20:9
T Jeremiah said to them, Jer 21:3
"**T** afterwards," declares the LORD, Jer 21:7
"**T** *say* to the household of the Jer 21:11
t kings will enter the gates of Jer 22:4
"**T** they will answer, Jer 22:9
T it was well with him. Jer 22:15 227
afflicted and needy; **T** it was well. Jer 22:16 227
T you will surely be ashamed and Jer 22:22 227
"**T** I Myself will gather the Jer 23:3
T they will live on their own soil." Jer 23:8
T they would have announced My Jer 23:22
t you shall say to them, Jer 23:33
"**T** as for the prophet or the Jer 23:34
T the LORD said to me, Jer 24:3
T the word of the LORD came to me, Jer 24:4
'**T** it will be when seventy years Jer 25:12

T I took the cup from the LORD's Jer 25:17
to drink, **t** you will say to them, Jer 25:28
t I will make this house like Jer 26:6
T the priests and the prophets Jer 26:11
T Jeremiah spoke to all the Jer 26:12
T the officials and all the people Jer 26:16
T some of the elders of the land Jer 26:17
t the king sought to put him to Jer 26:21
T King Jehoiakim sent men to Egypt: Jer 26:22
t many nations and great kings Jer 27:7
T I spoke to the priests and to Jer 27:16
'**T** I will bring them back and Jer 27:22
T the prophet Jeremiah spoke to Jer 28:5
t that prophet will be known *as* Jer 28:9
T Hananiah the prophet took the Jer 28:10
T the prophet Jeremiah went his Jer 28:11
T Jeremiah the prophet said to Jer 28:15
'**T** you will call upon Me and come Jer 29:12
now **t**, why have you not rebuked Jer 29:27
T came the word of the LORD to Jer 29:30
"**T** the virgin will rejoice in Jer 31:13 227
"**T** the offspring of Israel also Jer 31:36
T I will also cast off all the Jer 31:37
t it will turn to Goah. Jer 31:39
"**T** Hanamel my uncle's son came to Jer 32:8
T I knew that this was the word of Jer 32:8
"**T** I took the deeds of purchase, Jer 32:11
of Neriah, **t** I prayed to the LORD, Jer 32:16
T the word of the LORD came to Jer 32:26
T the word of the LORD came to Jer 33:1
t My covenant may also be broken Jer 33:21
t I would reject the descendants Jer 33:26 1571
T Jeremiah the prophet spoke all Jer 34:6
T the word of the LORD came to Jer 34:12
T I took Jaazaniah the son of Jer 35:3
T I set before the men of the Jer 35:5
T the word of the LORD came to Jer 35:12
T you will dwell in the land which I Jer 35:15
T Jeremiah said to the house of Jer 35:18
t I will forgive their iniquity Jer 36:3
T Jeremiah called Baruch the son Jer 36:4
T Baruch read from the book the Jer 36:10
T all the officials sent Jehudi Jer 36:14
T Baruch said to them, Jer 36:18
T the officials said to Baruch, Jer 36:19
T the king sent Jehudi to get the Jer 36:21
T the word of the LORD came to Jer 36:27
T Jeremiah took another scroll and Jer 36:32
T the word of the LORD came to Jer 37:6
T the officials were angry at Jer 37:15
T he said, "You will be given into Jer 37:17
"Where **t** are your prophets who Jer 37:19
T King Zedekiah gave commandment, Jer 37:21
T the officials said to the king, Jer 38:4
T they took Jeremiah and cast him Jer 38:6
T the king commanded Ebed-melech Jer 38:10
T Ebed-melech the Ethiopian said Jer 38:12
T King Zedekiah sent and had Jer 38:14
T Jeremiah said to Zedekiah, Jer 38:15
T Jeremiah said to Zedekiah, Jer 38:17
king of Babylon, **t** you will live, Jer 38:17
t this city will be given over to Jer 38:18
T King Zedekiah said to Jeremiah, Jer 38:19
'**T** behold, all of the women who Jer 38:22
T Zedekiah said to Jeremiah, Jer 38:24
t you are to say to them, Jer 38:26
T all the officials came to Jer 38:27
T all the officials of the king of Jer 39:3
T the king of Babylon slew the Jer 39:6
He **t** blinded Zedekiah's eyes and Jer 39:7
Go on back **t** to Gedaliah the son Jer 40:5
T Jeremiah went to Mizpah to Jer 40:6
T Gedaliah the son of Ahikam, the Jer 40:9
T all the Jews returned from all Jer 40:12
T Johanan the son of Kareah spoke Jer 40:15
T Ishmael the son of Nethaniah Jer 41:6
T Ishmael took captive all the Jer 41:10
T Johanan the son of Kareah and Jer 41:16
T all the commanders of the Jer 42:1
T Jeremiah the prophet said to Jer 42:4
T they said to Jeremiah, Jer 42:5
T he called for Johanan the son of Jer 42:8
t I will build you up and not tear Jer 42:10
t in that case listen to the word Jer 42:15
t the sword, Jer 42:16
T the word of the LORD came to Jer 43:8
'Now **t** thus says the LORD God of Jer 44:7
and **t** to return to the land of Judah, Jer 44:14
T all the men who were aware that Jer 44:15
for **t** we had plenty of food Jer 44:17
T Jeremiah said to all the people, Jer 44:20
T Jeremiah said to all the people, Jer 44:24
T all the remnant of Judah who Jer 44:28
T they said, 'Get up! And let us go Jer 46:16
Why **t** has Malcam taken possession Jer 49:1
T Israel will take possession of Jer 49:2
And who **t** is the shepherd who can Jer 49:19 2088
'**T** I will set My throne in Elam Jer 49:38
And who **t** is the shepherd who can Jer 50:44 2088
"**T** heaven and earth and all that Jer 51:48
T Jeremiah said to Seraiah, Jer 51:61
t see that you read all these Jer 51:61
T the city was broken into, and Jer 52:7
T they captured the king and Jer 52:9
T he blinded the eyes of Zedekiah; Jer 52:11
T Nebuzaradan the captain of the Jer 52:15
T the captain of the guard took Jer 52:24
T the king of Babylon struck them Jer 52:27
T he spoke kindly to him and set Jer 52:32

T He will have compassion La 3:32
T I noticed from the appearance of Ezk 1:27
T He said to me, Ezk 2:1
T He said to me, Ezk 2:3
T I looked, and behold, a hand was Ezk 2:9
T He said to me, Ezk 3:1
T I ate it, and it was sweet as honey Ezk 3:3
T He said to me, Ezk 3:4
T the Spirit lifted me up, and I Ezk 3:12
T I came to the exiles who lived Ezk 3:15
The Spirit **t** entered me and made Ezk 3:24
"**T** lay siege against it, build a Ezk 4:2
"**T** get yourself an iron plate and Ezk 4:3
"**T** you shall set your face toward Ezk 4:7
T the LORD said, Ezk 4:13
T He said to me, Ezk 4:15
T take scales for weighing and Ezk 5:1
T you shall take one third and Ezk 5:2
t they will know that I, the LORD, Ezk 5:13
t I will also intensify the Ezk 5:16
"**T** those of you who escape will Ezk 6:9
"**T** they will know that I am the Ezk 6:10
"**T** you will know that I am the Ezk 6:13
t you will know that I am the LORD!' Ezk 7:4
t you will know that I, the LORD, Ezk 7:9
t robbers will enter and profane Ezk 7:22
t they will seek a vision from a Ezk 7:26
T I looked, and behold, a likeness Ezk 8:2
T He said to me, Ezk 8:5
T He brought me to the entrance of Ezk 8:7
T He said to me, Ezk 8:12
T He brought me to the entrance of Ezk 8:14
T He brought me into the inner Ezk 8:16
T He cried out in my hearing with Ezk 9:1
T the glory of the God of Israel Ezk 9:3
T He said to me, Ezk 9:9
T behold, the man clothed in linen Ezk 9:11
T I looked, and behold, in the Ezk 10:1
T the glory of the LORD went up Ezk 10:4
T the cherub stretched out his Ezk 10:7
T I looked, and behold, four Ezk 10:9
T the cherubim rose up. Ezk 10:15
T the glory of the LORD departed Ezk 10:18
T the Spirit of the LORD fell upon Ezk 11:5
T I fell on my face and cried out Ezk 11:13
T the word of the LORD came to me, Ezk 11:14
T they will be My people, and I Ezk 11:20
T the cherubim lifted up their Ezk 11:22
T I told the exiles all the things Ezk 11:25
T the word of the LORD came to me Ezk 12:1
T you will go out at evening in Ezk 12:4
T in the evening I dug through the Ezk 12:7
"**T** say to the people of the land, Ezk 12:19
T the word of the LORD came to me Ezk 12:21
T the word of the LORD came to me Ezk 13:1
T some elders of Israel came to me Ezk 14:1
and **t** comes to the prophet, Ezk 14:4
and **t** comes to the prophet to Ezk 14:7
T the word of the LORD came to me Ezk 14:12
t you will be comforted for the Ezk 14:22
"**T** they will comfort you when you Ezk 14:23
T the word of the LORD came to me Ezk 15:1
is it **t** useful for anything? Ezk 15:4
T you will know that I am the Ezk 15:7
T the word of the LORD came to me Ezk 16:1
T you grew up, became tall and Ezk 16:7
"**T** I passed by you and saw you, Ezk 16:8
"**T** I bathed you with water, Ezk 16:9
"**T** your fame went forth among the Ezk 16:14
"**T** you took your embroidered Ezk 16:18
"**T** it came about after all your Ezk 16:23
T I will stop you from playing Ezk 16:41
"**T** you will remember your ways Ezk 16:61
T it sprouted and became a low, Ezk 17:6
T I will bring him to Babylon and Ezk 17:20
T the word of the LORD came to me Ezk 18:1
"**T** he may have a violent son who Ezk 18:10
'**T** nations heard about him; Ezk 19:4
'**T** nations set against him On Ezk 19:8
T I resolved to pour out My wrath Ezk 20:8
T I resolved to pour out My wrath Ezk 20:13
t they saw every high hill and Ezk 20:28
"**T** I said to them, Ezk 20:29
"**T** you will know that I am the Ezk 20:44
T I said, "Ah Lord GOD! They are Ezk 20:49
T the word of the LORD came to me Ezk 22:1
T cause her to know all her Ezk 22:2
"Behold, **t**, I smite My hand at Ezk 22:13
t I became disgusted with her, as Ezk 23:18
T you will gnaw its fragments And Ezk 23:34
T declare to them their Ezk 23:36
"**T** I said concerning her who was Ezk 23:43
"**T** set it empty on its coals So Ezk 24:11
T I said to them, Ezk 24:20
t you will know that I am the Lord Ezk 24:24
"**T** all the princes of the sea Ezk 26:16
t I will bring you down with Ezk 26:20
T they will know that I am the Ezk 28:22
T they will know that I am the Ezk 28:23
t they will know that I am the Ezk 28:24
t they will live in their land Ezk 28:25
T they will know that I am the Ezk 28:26
"**T** all the inhabitants of Egypt Ezk 29:6
T they will know that I am the Ezk 29:9
T they will know that I am the Ezk 29:16
T they will know that I am the Ezk 29:21
T the pride of her power will Ezk 30:18
T they will know that I am the Ezk 30:25
t they will know that I am the Ezk 30:26

"**T** I will make their waters Ezk 32:14 227
T they shall know that I am the Ezk 32:15
t he who hears the sound of the Ezk 33:4
how **t** can we survive?" Ezk 33:10
Why **t** will you die, O house of Ezk 33:11
iniquity, **t** he shall die in it. Ezk 33:18
T the word of the LORD came to me Ezk 33:23
Should you **t** possess the land? Ezk 33:25
Should you **t** possess the land?" ' Ezk 33:26
"**T** they will know that I am the Ezk 33:29
t they will know that a prophet has Ezk 33:33
T the word of the LORD came to me Ezk 34:1
"**T** I will set over them one Ezk 34:23
T they will know that I am the Ezk 34:27
"**T** they will know that I, the Ezk 34:30
T you will know that I am the LORD. Ezk 35:4
T you will know that I am the LORD. Ezk 35:9
"**T** you will know that I, the Ezk 35:12
T they will know that I am the Ezk 35:15
T the word of the LORD came to me Ezk 36:16
T the nations will know that I am Ezk 36:23
"**T** I will sprinkle clean water on Ezk 36:25
"**T** you will remember your evil Ezk 36:31
"**T** the nations that are left Ezk 36:36
T they will know that I am the Ezk 36:38
T He said to me, Ezk 37:9
T He said to me, Ezk 37:11
"**T** you will know that I am the Ezk 37:13
T you will know that I, the LORD, Ezk 37:14
t take another stick and write on Ezk 37:16
"**T** join them for yourself one to Ezk 37:17
"**T** those who inhabit the cities Ezk 39:9
t he will set up a marker by it Ezk 39:15
t I shall be sanctified through Ezk 39:27
"**T** they will know that I am the Ezk 39:28
and **t** gathered them *again* to their Ezk 39:28
T he went to the gate which faced Ezk 40:6
T he measured the porch of the Ezk 40:8
T he brought me into the outer Ezk 40:17
T he measured the width from the Ezk 40:19
T he led me toward the south, and Ezk 40:24
T he brought me to the inner court Ezk 40:28
T he brought me to the north gate; Ezk 40:35
T he brought me to the porch of Ezk 40:48
T he brought me to the nave and Ezk 41:1
T he went inside and measured each Ezk 41:3
T he measured the wall of the Ezk 41:5
T he measured the temple, a Ezk 41:13
T he brought me out into the outer Ezk 42:1
T he said to me, Ezk 42:13
t they shall not go out into the Ezk 42:14
t they shall approach that which Ezk 42:14
T he led me to the gate, the gate Ezk 43:1
T I heard one speaking to me from Ezk 43:6
T He brought me back by the way of Ezk 44:1
T He brought me by way of the Ezk 44:4
t they shall put on other garments Ezk 44:19
T the priests shall provide his Ezk 46:2
of the gate and **t** go out; Ezk 46:2
T he shall go out, and the gate Ezk 46:12
t it shall return to the prince. Ezk 46:17
T he brought me through the Ezk 46:19
T he brought me out into the outer Ezk 46:21
T he said to me, Ezk 46:24
T he brought me back to the door Ezk 47:1
T he brought me back to the bank Ezk 47:6
T he said to me, Ezk 47:8
t they go toward the sea, being Ezk 47:8
T the king ordered Ashpenaz, the Da 1:3
T the commander of the officials Da 1:7
T you would make me forfeit my Da 1:10
"**T** let our appearance be observed Da 1:13
T at the end of the days which the Da 1:18
T the king gave orders to call in Da 2:2
T the Chaldeans spoke to the king Da 2:4
T Daniel replied with discretion Da 2:14 116
T Arioch informed Daniel about the Da 2:15 116
T Daniel went to his house and Da 2:17 116
T the mystery was revealed to Da 2:19 116
T Daniel blessed the God of heaven; Da 2:19 116
T Arioch hurriedly brought Daniel Da 2:25 116
"**T** the iron, the clay, the Da 2:35 116
t another third kingdom of bronze, Da 2:39
"**T** there will be a fourth kingdom Da 2:40
T King Nebuchadnezzar fell on his Da 2:46 116
T the king promoted Daniel and Da 2:48 116
T Nebuchadnezzar the king sent Da 3:2
T the satraps, the prefects and Da 3:3 116
T the herald loudly proclaimed: Da 3:4
T Nebuchadnezzar in rage and anger Da 3:13 116
t these men were brought before Da 3:13 116
T Nebuchadnezzar was filled with Da 3:19 116
T these men were tied up in their Da 3:21 116
T Nebuchadnezzar the king was Da 3:24 116
T Nebuchadnezzar came near to the Da 3:26 116
T Shadrach, Meshach and Abed-nego Da 3:26 116
T the king caused Shadrach, Da 3:30 116
"**T** the magicians, the conjurers, Da 4:7 116
"**T** Daniel, whose name is Da 4:19 116
T they brought the gold vessels Da 5:3 116
T the king's face grew pale and Da 5:6 116
T all the king's wise men came in, Da 5:8 116
T King Belshazzar was greatly Da 5:9 116
T Daniel was brought in before the Da 5:13 116
T Daniel answered and said before Da 5:17 116
"**T** the hand was sent from Him and Da 5:24 116
T Belshazzar gave orders, and they Da 5:29 116
T this Daniel began distinguishing Da 6:3 116
T the commissioners and satraps Da 6:4 116

T these men said,	Da 6:5	116
T these commissioners and satraps	Da 6:6	116
T these men came by agreement and	Da 6:11	116
T they approached and spoke before	Da 6:12	116
T they answered and spoke before	Da 6:13	116
T, as soon as the king heard this	Da 6:14	116
T these men came by agreement to	Da 6:15	116
T the king gave orders, and Daniel	Da 6:16	116
T the king went off to his palace	Da 6:18	116
T the king arose at dawn, at	Da 6:19	116
T Daniel spoke to the king,	Da 6:21	116
T the king was very pleased and	Da 6:23	116
The king **t** gave orders, and they	Da 6:24	
T Darius the king wrote to all the	Da 6:25	116
t he wrote the dream down *and*	Da 7:1	116
"**T** I kept looking because of the	Da 7:11	116
"**T** I desired to know the exact	Da 7:19	116
'**T** the sovereignty, the dominion and	Da 7:27	
T I lifted my eyes and looked, and	Da 8:3	
T the male goat magnified *himself*	Da 8:8	
T I heard a holy one speaking, and	Da 8:13	
t the holy place will be properly	Da 8:14	
T I, Daniel, was exhausted and	Da 8:27	
T I got up *again* and carried on	Da 8:27	
in prayer, **t** the man Gabriel,	Da 9:21	
"**T** after the sixty-two weeks the	Da 9:26	
T behold, a hand touched me and	Da 10:10	
T he said to me,	Da 10:12	
t behold, Michael, one of the	Da 10:13	
t I opened my mouth and spoke and	Da 10:16	
T *this* one with human appearance	Da 10:18	
T he said, "Do you understand why	Da 10:20	
T a fourth will gain far more	Da 11:2	
"**T** the king of the South will	Da 11:5	
"**T** the latter will enter the	Da 11:9	
T the latter will raise a great	Da 11:11	
"**T** the king of the North will	Da 11:15	
"**T** he will turn his face to the	Da 11:18	
"**T** in his place one will arise	Da 11:20	
"**T** he will return to his land	Da 11:28	
and he will take action and **t**	Da 11:28	
"**T** the king will do as he	Da 11:36	
"**T** he will stretch out his hand	Da 11:42	
T I, Daniel, looked and behold,	Da 12:5	
t you will enter into rest and	Da 12:13	
T she conceived again and gave	Hos 1:6	
T she will say, 'I will go back to my	Hos 2:7	
it was better for me **t** than now!'	Hos 2:7	227
"And **t** I will uncover her	Hos 2:10	6258
"**T** I will give her her vineyards	Hos 2:15	
T you will know the LORD.	Hos 2:20	
T the LORD said to me,	Hos 3:1	
T I said to her,	Hos 3:3	
T Ephraim went to Assyria And sent	Hos 5:13	
T they will say to the mountains,	Hos 10:8	
T the LORD will be zealous for His	Jl 2:18	
"**T** I will make up to you for the	Jl 2:25	
T My people will never be put to	Jl 2:26	
T I will enter into judgment with	Jl 3:2	
T you will know that I am the LORD	Jl 3:17	
"**T** I raised up some of your sons	Am 2:11	
T I would send rain on one city	Am 4:7	
T go down to Gath of the	Am 6:2	
T one's uncle, or his undertaker,	Am 6:10	
T he will answer, "Keep quiet.	Am 6:10	
T I said, "Lord GOD, please stop!	Am 7:5	
T the Lord said, "Behold I am about	Am 7:8	
T I will rise up against the	Am 7:9	
T Amaziah, the priest of Bethel,	Am 7:10	
T Amaziah said to Amos,	Am 7:12	
T Amos replied to Amaziah,	Am 7:14	
T the LORD said to me,	Am 8:2	
"**T** I will turn your festivals	Am 8:10	
T I will slay the rest of them	Am 9:1	
"**T** your mighty men will be	Ob 1:9	
"**T** the house of Jacob will be	Ob 1:18	
T *those of* the Negev will possess	Ob 1:19	
T the sailors became afraid and	Jon 1:5	
T they said to him,	Jon 1:8	
T the men became extremely	Jon 1:10	
T the sea will become calm for	Jon 1:12	
T they called on the LORD and	Jon 1:14	
T the men feared the LORD greatly,	Jon 1:16	
T Jonah prayed to the LORD his God	Jon 2:1	
T the LORD commanded the fish, and	Jon 2:10	
T Jonah began to go through the	Jon 3:4	
T the people of Nineveh believed	Jon 3:5	
t God relented concerning the	Jon 3:10	
T Jonah went out from the city and	Jon 4:5	
T God said to Jonah,	Jon 4:9	
T the LORD said,	Jon 4:10	
covet fields and **t** seize *them*,	Mi 2:2	
T they will cry out to the LORD,	Mi 3:4	227
T they will hammer their swords	Mi 4:3	
T the remainder of His brethren	Mi 5:3	
T we will raise against him Seven	Mi 5:5	
T the remnant of Jacob Will be	Mi 5:7	
T their confusion will occur.	Mi 7:4	6258
T my enemy will see, And shame	Mi 7:10	
"**T** they will sweep through *like*	Hab 1:11	227
T the LORD answered me and said,	Hab 2:2	
"**T** it will come about on the day	Zph 1:8	
"For **t** I will give to the peoples	Zph 3:9	227
For **t** I will remove from your	Zph 3:11	227
T the word of the LORD came by	Hg 1:3	
T Zerubbabel the son of Shealtiel,	Hg 1:12	
T Haggai, the messenger of the	Hg 1:13	
T Haggai said, "If one who is	Hg 2:13	
T Haggai said,	Hg 2:14	

T the word of the LORD came a	Hg 2:20	
T they repented and said,	Zch 1:6	
T I said, "My lord, what are these?"	Zch 1:9	
T the angel of the LORD said	Zch 1:12	
T I lifted up my eyes and looked,	Zch 1:18	
T the LORD showed me four	Zch 1:20	
T I lifted up my eyes and looked,	Zch 2:1	
T you will know that the LORD of	Zch 2:9	
T I will dwell in your midst, and	Zch 2:11	
T he showed me Joshua the high	Zch 3:1	
T I said, "Let them put a clean	Zch 3:5	
t you will also govern My house	Zch 3:7	
T the angel who was speaking with	Zch 4:1	
T I said to the angel	Zch 4:4	
T he said to me,	Zch 4:6	
T you will know that the LORD of	Zch 4:9	
T I said to him,	Zch 4:11	
T he said, "These are the two	Zch 4:14	
T I lifted up my eyes again and	Zch 5:1	
T he said to me,	Zch 5:3	
T the angel who was speaking with	Zch 5:5	
T he said, "This is Wickedness!"	Zch 5:8	
T I lifted up my eyes and looked,	Zch 5:9	
T he said to me,	Zch 5:11	
T I spoke and said to the angel	Zch 6:4	
T He cried out to me and spoke to	Zch 6:8	
"**T** say to him, 'Thus says the LORD	Zch 6:12	
T you will know that the LORD of	Zch 6:15	
T the word of the LORD of hosts	Zch 7:4	
T the word of the LORD came to	Zch 7:8	
T the word of the LORD of hosts	Zch 8:1	
T Jerusalem will be called the	Zch 8:3	
T the word of the LORD of hosts	Zch 8:18	
T they also will be a remnant for	Zch 9:7	
T the LORD will appear over them,	Zch 9:14	
T I annihilated the three	Zch 11:8	
T I said, "I will not pasture you.	Zch 11:9	
T the LORD said to me,	Zch 11:13	
T I cut in pieces my second staff Union,	Zch 11:14	
"**T** the clans of Judah will say in	Zch 12:5	
t his father and mother who gave	Zch 13:3	
T he will say, '*Those* with which I	Zch 13:6	
T the LORD will go forth and fight	Zch 14:3	
T the LORD, my God, will come, *and*	Zch 14:5	
T it will come about that any who	Zch 14:16	
t no *rain will fall* on them;	Zch 14:18	
T if I am a father, where is My	Mal 1:6	
"**t** I will send the curse upon	Mal 2:2	
"**T** you will know that I have sent	Mal 2:4	
Take heed **t** to your spirit, and	Mal 2:15	
"**T** the offering of Judah and	Mal 3:4	
"**T** I will draw near to you for	Mal 3:5	
"**T** I will rebuke the devourer for	Mal 3:11	
T those who feared the LORD spoke	Mal 3:16	227
T Herod secretly called the magi and	Mt 2:7	5119
T, opening their treasures, they	Mt 2:11	2532
T when Herod saw that he had been	Mt 2:16	5119
T what had been spoken through	Mt 2:17	5119
T after being warned *by God* in a	Mt 2:22	1161
T Jerusalem was going out to him,	Mt 3:5	5119
T Jesus arrived from Galilee at	Mt 3:13	5119
T he permitted Him.	Mt 3:15	5119
T Jesus was led up by the Spirit	Mt 4:1	5119
forty nights, He **t** became hungry.	Mt 4:2	5306
T the devil took Him into the holy	Mt 4:5	5119
T Jesus said to him,	Mt 4:10	5119
T the devil left Him;	Mt 4:11	5119
"Whoever **t** annuls one of the	Mt 5:19	3767
and **t** come and present your	Mt 5:24	5119
"Pray, **t**, in this way:	Mt 6:9	3767
t your Father will not forgive	Mt 6:15	3761
so **t** if your eye is clear, your	Mt 6:22	3767
If **t** the light that is in you is	Mt 6:23	3767
"Do not worry **t**,	Mt 6:31	3767
and **t** you will see clearly to take	Mt 7:5	5119
"If you **t**, being evil, know how	Mt 7:11	3767
"So **t**, you will know them by	Mt 7:20	686
"And **t** I will declare to them,	Mt 7:23	5119
T a scribe came and said to Him,	Mt 8:19	2532
T He got up and rebuked the winds	Mt 8:26	5119
t He said to the paralytic	Mt 9:6	5119
T it happened that as Jesus was	Mt 9:10	2532
T the disciples of John came to	Mt 9:14	5119
from them, and **t** they will fast.	Mt 9:15	5119
T He touched their eyes, saying,	Mt 9:29	5119
T He said to His disciples,	Mt 9:37	5119
T He began to denounce the cities	Mt 11:20	5119
"How much more valuable **t** is a man	Mt 12:12	3767
So **t**, it is lawful to do good on	Mt 12:12	5620
T He said to the man,	Mt 12:13	5119
T a demon-possessed man	Mt 12:22	5119
how **t** will his kingdom stand?	Mt 12:26	3767
t the kingdom of God has come upon	Mt 12:28	686
And **t** he will plunder his house.	Mt 12:29	5119
T some of the scribes and	Mt 12:38	5119
"**T** it says, 'I will return to my house	Mt 12:44	5119
"**T** it goes and takes along with	Mt 12:45	5119
"Hear **t** the parable of the sower.	Mt 13:18	3767
t the tares became evident also.	Mt 13:26	5119
How **t** does it have tares?'	Mt 13:27	3767
'Do you want us, **t**, to go and	Mt 13:28	3767
T He left the crowds and went	Mt 13:36	5119
"**T** THE RIGHTEOUS WILL SHINE FORTH	Mt 13:43	5119
Where **t** *did* this man *get* all these	Mt 13:56	3767
T some Pharisees and scribes came	Mt 15:1	5119
T the disciples came and said to	Mt 15:12	5119
T Jesus said to her,	Mt 15:28	5119
T they understood that He did not	Mt 16:12	5119
T He warned the disciples that	Mt 16:20	5119

T Jesus said to His disciples,	Mt 16:24	5119
and WILL **T** REPAY EVERY MAN	Mt 16:27	5119
"Why **t** do the scribes say that	Mt 17:10	3767
T the disciples understood that He	Mt 17:13	5119
T the disciples came to Jesus	Mt 17:19	5119
"**T** the sons are exempt.	Mt 17:26	686
"Who **t** is greatest in the kingdom	Mt 18:1	686
Whoever **t** humbles himself as this	Mt 18:4	3767
T Peter came and said to Him,	Mt 18:21	5119
"**T** summoning him, his lord said	Mt 18:32	5119
"Why **t** did Moses command to GIVE	Mt 19:7	3767
T *some* children were brought to	Mt 19:13	5119
T he said to Him, "Which ones?"	Mt 19:18	
"**T** who can be saved?"	Mt 19:25	686
T Peter said to Him,	Mt 19:27	5119
what **t** will there be for us?"	Mt 19:27	686
T the mother of the sons of	Mt 20:20	5119
t Jesus sent two disciples,	Mt 21:1	5119
'**T** why did you not believe him?'	Mt 21:25	3767
T he said to his slaves,	Mt 22:8	5119
"**T** the king said to the servants,	Mt 22:13	5119
T the Pharisees went and plotted	Mt 22:15	5119
"Tell us **t**, what do You think? Is	Mt 22:17	3767
T He said to them, "Then render to	Mt 22:21	5119
"**T** render to Caesar the things	Mt 22:21	3767
"**T** how does David in the Spirit	Mt 22:43	3767
"If David **t** calls Him	Mt 22:45	3767
T Jesus spoke to the crowds	Mt 23:1	5119
"Fill up, **t**, the measure *of the*	Mt 23:32	2532
"**T** they will deliver you to	Mt 24:9	5119
nations, and **t** the end will come.	Mt 24:14	5119
t those who are in Judea must flee	Mt 24:16	5119
"For **t** there will be a great	Mt 24:21	5119
"**T** if anyone says to you,	Mt 24:23	5119
"And **t** the sign of the Son of Man	Mt 24:30	5119
and **t** all the tribes of the earth	Mt 24:30	5119
"**T** there will be two men in the	Mt 24:40	5119
"Who **t** is the faithful and	Mt 24:45	686
"**T** the kingdom of heaven will be	Mt 25:1	5119
"**T** all those virgins rose and	Mt 25:7	5119
"Be on the alert **t**, for you do	Mt 25:13	3767
'**T** you ought to have put my money	Mt 25:27	3767
t He will sit on His glorious	Mt 25:31	5119
"**T** the King will say to those on	Mt 25:34	5119
"**T** the righteous will answer Him,	Mt 25:37	5119
"**T** He will also say to those on	Mt 25:41	5119
"**T** they themselves also will	Mt 25:44	5119
"**T** He will answer them, '	Mt 25:45	5119
T the chief priests and the elders	Mt 26:3	5119
T one of the twelve, named Judas	Mt 26:14	5119
From **t** on he *began* looking for	Mt 26:16	5119
T Jesus said to them,	Mt 26:31	5119
T Jesus came with them to a place	Mt 26:36	5119
T He said to them,	Mt 26:38	5119
T He came to the disciples and	Mt 26:45	5119
T they came and laid hands on	Mt 26:50	5119
T Jesus said to him,	Mt 26:52	5119
"How **t** will the Scriptures be	Mt 26:54	3767
T all the disciples left Him and	Mt 26:56	5119
T the high priest tore his robes and	Mt 26:65	5119
T they spat in His face and beat	Mt 26:67	5119
T he began to curse and swear,	Mt 26:74	5119
T when Judas, who had betrayed	Mt 27:3	5119
T that which was spoken through	Mt 27:9	5119
T Pilate said to Him,	Mt 27:13	5119
"**T** what shall I do with Jesus who	Mt 27:22	3767
T he released Barabbas for them;	Mt 27:26	5119
T the soldiers of the governor	Mt 27:27	5119
T Pilate ordered it to be given	Mt 27:58	5119
T Jesus said to them,	Mt 28:10	5119
Just **t** there was a man in their	Mk 1:23	2117
and **t** they will fast in that day.	Mk 2:20	5119
and **t** he will plunder his house.	Mk 3:27	5119
T His mother and His brothers arrived,	Mk 3:31	2532
t, when affliction or persecution	Mk 4:17	1534
first the blade, **t** the head,	Mk 4:28	1535b
t the mature grain in the head.	Mk 4:28	1535b
"Who **t** is this, that even the	Mk 4:41	686
T He got into the boat with them,	Mk 6:51	2532
T again He laid His hands on his	Mk 8:25	1534
T a cloud formed, overshadowing	Mk 9:7	2532
"**T** who can be saved?"	Mk 10:26	2532
T they came to Jericho. And as He	Mk 10:46	2532
T they came to Jerusalem. And He	Mk 11:15	2532
and **t** I will tell you by what	Mk 11:29	
'**T** why did you not believe him?'	Mk 11:31	3767
T they sent some of the Pharisees	Mk 12:13	2532
t those who are in Judea must flee	Mk 13:14	5119
"And **t** if anyone says to you,	Mk 13:21	5119
"**T** they will see THE SON OF MAN	Mk 13:26	5119
t He will send forth the angels,	Mk 13:27	5119
T Judas Iscariot, who was one of	Mk 14:10	2532
T Pilate questioned Him again,	Mk 15:4	2532
"**T** what shall I do with Him whom	Mk 15:12	3767
T they brought Him to the place	Mk 15:22	2532
So **t**, when the Lord Jesus had	Mk 16:19	3767
and **t** returned to her home.	Lk 1:56	
"What **t** will this child *turn out*	Lk 1:66	686
"Let us go straight to Bethlehem **t**,	Lk 2:15	1211
His name was **t** called Jesus,	Lk 2:21	
t he took Him into his arms, and	Lk 2:28	2532
and **t** as a widow to the age of	Lk 2:37	
T, after three days they found Him	Lk 2:46	2532
"**T** what shall we do?"	Lk 3:10	3767
T He got up and *left*	Lk 4:38	2532
t they will fast in those days."	Lk 5:35	5119
and **t** you will see clearly to take	Lk 6:42	5119
"To what **t** shall I compare the	Lk 7:31	3767
T He said to her, "Your sins have	Lk 7:48	2532

t the devil comes and takes away **Lk 8:12** *1534*
"Who **t** is this, that He commands **Lk 8:25** *686*
T they sailed to the country of **Lk 8:26** *2532*
T He took the five loaves and the two **Lk 9:16** *2532*
T a voice came out of the cloud, **Lk 9:35** *2532*
T Jesus said to him, "Go and do **Lk 10:37** *1161*
T tell her to help me." **Lk 10:40** *3767*
T He said to them, "Suppose one of **Lk 11:5** *2532*
"If you **t**, being evil, know how **Lk 11:13** *3767*
t the kingdom of God has come upon **Lk 11:20** *686*
"**T** it goes and takes *along* seven **Lk 11:26** *5119*
"**T** watch out that the light in **Lk 11:35** *3767*
t all things are clean for you. **Lk 11:41** *2400*
T He said to them, "Beware, and be **Lk 12:15** *2532*
"**T** he said, 'This is what I will **Lk 12:18** *2532*
"If **t** you cannot do even a very **Lk 12:26** *3767*
"Who **t** is the faithful and **Lk 12:42** *686*
t He will answer and say to you, **Lk 13:25** *2532*
"**T** you will begin to say, **Lk 13:26** *5119*
and **t** in disgrace you proceed to **Lk 14:9** *5119*
t you will have honor in the sight **Lk 14:10** *5119*
T the head of the household became **Lk 14:21** *5119*
"So **t**, none of you can be My **Lk 14:33** *3767*
"**T** he said to another, **Lk 16:7** *1899*
"**T** I beg you, father, that you **Lk 16:27** *3767*
T Jesus answered and said, "Were **Lk 17:17** *2532*
"**T** who can be saved?" **Lk 18:26** *2532*
T He took the twelve aside and said **Lk 18:31** *2532*
kingdom for himself, and **t** return. **Lk 19:12**
'**T** why did you not put my money **Lk 19:23** *2532*
"**T** he said to the bystanders, **Lk 19:24** *2532*
t, will the owner of the vineyard do **Lk 20:15** *3767*
"What **t** is this that is written: **Lk 20:17** *3767*
"**T** render to Caesar the things **Lk 20:25** *5106*
T He said to them, "How *is it* **Lk 20:41** *2532*
T He continued by saying to them, **Lk 21:10** *5119*
t recognize that her desolation is **Lk 21:20** *5119*
"**T** those who are in Judea **Lk 21:21** *5119*
"**T** they will see THE SON OF MAN **Lk 21:27** *5119*
T He told them a parable: "Behold **Lk 21:29** *2532*
T came the *first* day of Unleavened **Lk 22:7** *1161*
T Jesus said to the chief priests **Lk 22:52** *2532*
"Are You the Son of God, **t**?" **Lk 22:70** *3767*
T they said, "What further need do **Lk 22:71** *2532*
T the whole body of them got up **Lk 23:1** *2532*
T Pilate said to the chief priests **Lk 23:4** *2532*
"**T** they will begin TO SAY TO THE **Lk 23:30** *5119*
T they returned and prepared spices **Lk 23:56** *22532*
T beginning with Moses and with all **Lk 24:27** *2532*
T their eyes were opened and they **Lk 24:31** *2532*
T He opened their minds to **Lk 24:45** *5119*
"What **t**? Are you Elijah?" **Jn 1:21** *3767*
T they said to him, "Who are you, **Jn 1:22** *3767*
"Why **t** are you baptizing, if you **Jn 1:25** *3767*
t *he serves* the poorer *wine;* **Jn 2:10**
The Jews **t** said to Him, "What sign **Jn 2:18** *3767*
The Jews **t** said, "It took forty-six **Jn 2:20** *3767*
where **t** do You get that living water **Jn 4:11** *3767*
and **t** comes the harvest'? **Jn 4:35**
T they said to him, "Yesterday at **Jn 4:52** *3767*
whoever **t** first, after the **Jn 5:4** *3767*
T Jesus went up on the mountain, **Jn 6:3** *2532*
Jesus **t** took the loaves, and having **Jn 6:11** *3767*
T, when they had rowed about three **Jn 6:19** *3767*
"What **t** do You do for a sign, **Jn 6:30** *3767*
Jesus **t** said to them, "Truly, **Jn 6:32** *3767*
T they said to Him, "Lord, always **Jn 6:34** *3767*
T the Jews *began* to argue with **Jn 6:52** *3767*
"*What* **t** if you see the **Jn 6:62** *3767*
feast, **t** He Himself also went up, **Jn 7:10** *5119*
The Jews **t** were astonished, saying, **Jn 7:15** *3767*
T Jesus cried out in the temple, **Jn 7:28** *3767*
you, **t** I go to Him who sent Me. **Jn 7:33** *2532*
The Jews **t** said to one another, **Jn 7:35** *3767*
The officers **t** came to the chief **Jn 7:45** *3767*
The Pharisees **t** answered them, "You **Jn 7:47** *3767*
what **t** do You say?" **Jn 8:5** *3767*
T Jesus again spoke to them, saying, **Jn 8:12** *3767*
T He said again to them, "I go away, **Jn 8:21** *3767*
Man, **t** you will know that I am *He,* **Jn 8:28** *5119*
t you are truly disciples of Mine; **Jn 8:31**
"How **t** were your eyes opened?" **Jn 9:10** *3767*
T the Pharisees also were asking him **Jn 9:15** *3767*
The Jews **t** did not believe *it* of **Jn 9:18** *3767*
T how does he now see?" **Jn 9:19** *3767*
He **t** answered, "Whether He is a **Jn 9:25** *3767*
The Jews **t** gathered around Him, **Jn 10:24** *3767*
He **t** stayed two days *longer* in the **Jn 11:6** *5119*
T after this He said to the **Jn 11:7** *1899*
The disciples **t** said to Him, "Lord, **Jn 11:12** *3767*
So Jesus **t** said to them plainly, **Jn 11:14** *3767*
Martha **t** said to Jesus, "Lord, if **Jn 11:21** *3767*
T the Jews who were with her in **Jn 11:31** *3767*
So they removed the stone. **T** Jesus **Jn 11:41** *1161*
Mary **t** took a pound of very costly **Jn 12:3** *3767*
The large crowd of the Jews **t** learned **Jn 12:9** *3767*
t they remembered that these **Jn 12:16** *5119*
these **t** came to Philip, who was from **Jn 12:21** *3767*
"Father, glorify Your name." **T** a **Jn 12:28** *3767*
The crowd **t** answered Him, "We have **Jn 12:34** *3767*
T He poured water into the basin, **Jn 13:5** *1534*
t *wash* not only my feet, but **Jn 13:9**
"If I **t**, the Lord and the **Jn 13:14** *3767*
Jesus **t** answered, "That is the one **Jn 13:26** *3767*
morsel, Satan **t** entered into him. **Jn 13:27** *5119*
what **t** has happened that You are **Jn 14:22** *2532*
Some of His disciples **t** said to **Jn 16:17** *3767*
Judas **t**, having received the *Roman* **Jn 18:3** *3767*
Simon Peter **t**, having a sword, drew **Jn 18:10** *3767*

T the slave-girl who kept the door **Jn 18:17** *3767*
The high priest **t** questioned Jesus **Jn 18:19** *3767*
Peter **t** denied *it* again, **Jn 18:27** *3767*
T they led Jesus from Caiaphas into **Jn 18:28** *3767*
t My servants would be fighting so **Jn 18:36** *3767*
do you wish **t** that I release for **Jn 18:39** *3767*
Pilate **t** took Jesus and scourged Him. **Jn 19:1** *3767*
Jesus **t** came out, wearing the crown **Jn 19:5** *3767*
So he **t** handed Him over to them **Jn 19:16** *5119*
T the soldiers, when they had **Jn 19:23** *3767*
When Jesus **t** saw His mother, **Jn 19:26** *3767*
T He said to the disciple, **Jn 19:27** *1534*
T the Jews, because it was the day **Jn 19:31** *3767*
come to the tomb **t** also **Jn 20:8** *5119*
The disciples **t** rejoiced when they **Jn 20:20** *3767*
T He said to Thomas, **Jn 20:27** *1534*
and **t** they were not able to haul **Jn 21:6** *3765*
T they returned to Jerusalem from **Ac 1:12** *5119*
So **t**, those who had received his **Ac 2:41** *3767*
T Peter, filled with the Holy **Ac 4:8** *5119*
T Peter *said* to her, **Ac 5:9** *1161*
T the captain went along with the **Ac 5:26** *5119*
of Jesus, and **t** released them. **Ac 5:40**
T they secretly induced men to **Ac 6:11** *5119*
"**T** he left the land of **Ac 7:4** *5119*
"**T** Joseph sent *word* and invited **Ac 7:14** *2532*
T falling on his knees, he cried out **Ac 7:60** *2532*
T they *began* laying their hands on **Ac 8:17** *5119*
T the Spirit said to Philip, "Go up **Ac 8:29** *2532*
T Philip opened his mouth, **Ac 8:35** *2532*
Now **t**, we are all here present **Ac 10:33** *3767*
T Peter answered, **Ac 10:46** *5119*
T they asked him to stay on for a **Ac 10:48** *5119*
"Well **t**, God has granted to the **Ac 11:18** *686*
So **t** those who were scattered **Ac 11:19** *3767*
T when he arrived and witnessed **Ac 11:23**
T he left and went to another place. **Ac 12:17** *2532*
T he went down from Judea to **Ac 12:19** *1161*
T, when they had fasted and prayed **Ac 13:3** *5119*
T the proconsul believed when he **Ac 13:12** *5119*
"**T** they asked for a king, and God **Ac 13:21** *2532*
T it seemed good to the apostles **Ac 15:22** *5119*
T immediately the brethren sent Paul **Ac 17:14** *5119*
"Being **t** the children of God, we **Ac 17:29** *3767*
T he left there and went to the house **Ac 18:7** *2532*
"Into what **t** were you baptized?" **Ac 19:3** *3767*
So **t**, some were shouting one thing **Ac 19:32** *3767*
"So **t**, if Demetrius and the **Ac 19:38** *3767*
daybreak, and **t** left. **Ac 20:11** *3779*
T we went on board the ship, and **Ac 21:6** *2532*
T Paul answered, **Ac 21:13** *5119*
"What, **t**, is *to be done?* **Ac 21:22** *3767*
T Paul took the men, and the next **Ac 21:26** *5119*
T all the city was provoked, **Ac 21:30** *2532*
T the commander came up and took **Ac 21:33** *5119*
"**T** you are not the Egyptian who **Ac 21:38** *686*
and **t** they raised their voices **Ac 22:22**
T Paul said to him, **Ac 23:3** *5119*
and **t** we arrested him. **Ac 24:6** *2532*
T he gave orders to the centurion for **Ac 24:23** *2532*
Festus **t**, having arrived in **Ac 25:1** *3767*
Festus **t** answered that Paul was **Ac 25:4** *3767*
"If, **t**, I am a wrongdoer and have **Ac 25:11** *3767*
T when Festus had conferred with **Ac 25:12** *5119*
T Agrippa *said* to Festus, **Ac 25:22** *2532*
T Paul stretched out his hand and **Ac 26:1** *5119*
"So **t**, all Jews know my manner of **Ac 26:4** *3767*
"So **t**, I thought to myself that I **Ac 26:9** *3767*
and *also* at Jerusalem and **t** **Ac 26:20**
from **t** on all hope of our being **Ac 27:20** *3062*
T Paul stood up in their midst and **Ac 27:21** *5119*
T the soldiers cut away the ropes **Ac 27:32** *5119*
t we found out that the island was **Ac 28:1** *5119*
T what advantage has the Jew? **Ro 3:1** *3767*
What **t**? If some did not believe, **Ro 3:3** *1063*
What **t**? Are we better than they? **Ro 3:9** *3767*
Where **t** is boasting? **Ro 3:27** *3767*
Do we **t** nullify the Law through **Ro 3:31** *3767*
What **t** shall we say that Abraham, **Ro 4:1** *3767*
blessing **t** on the circumcised, **Ro 4:9** *3767*
How **t** was it credited? **Ro 4:10** *3767*
Much more **t**, having now been **Ro 5:9** *3767*
So **t** as through one transgression **Ro 5:18** *686*
What shall we say **t**? **Ro 6:1** *3767*
What **t**? Shall we sin because we are **Ro 6:15** *3767*
what benefit were you **t** deriving **Ro 6:21** *5119*
So **t**, if while her husband is **Ro 7:3** *686*
What shall we say **t**? **Ro 7:7** *3767*
So **t**, the Law is holy, and the **Ro 7:12** *5620*
I find **t** the principle that evil **Ro 7:21** *686*
So **t**, on the one hand I myself **Ro 7:25** *686*
So **t**, brethren, we are under **Ro 8:12** *686*
What **t** shall we say to these things? **Ro 8:31** *3767*
What shall we say **t**? **Ro 9:14** *3767*
So **t** it *does* not *depend* on the man **Ro 9:16** *686*
So **t** He has mercy on whom He **Ro 9:18** *686*
You will say to me **t**, **Ro 9:19** *3767*
What shall we say **t**? **Ro 9:30** *3767*
How **t** will they call on Him in **Ro 10:14** *3767*
I say **t**, God has not rejected His **Ro 11:1** *3767*
In the same way **t**, there has also **Ro 11:5** *3767*
What **t**? What Israel is seeking, **Ro 11:7** *3767*
I say **t**, they did not stumble so **Ro 11:11** *3767*
Inasmuch **t** as I am an apostle of **Ro 11:13** *3767*
You will say **t**, "Branches were **Ro 11:19** *3767*
Behold **t** the kindness and severity **Ro 11:22** *3767*
So **t** each one of us will give **Ro 14:12** *686*
So **t** we pursue the things **Ro 14:19** *686*
What **t** is Apollos? **1Co 3:5** *3767*

So **t** neither the one who plants **1Co 3:7** *5620*
So **t** let no one boast in men. **1Co 3:21** *5620*
and **t** each man's praise will come **1Co 4:5** *5119*
for **t** you would have to go out of **1Co 5:10** *686*
Actually, **t**, it is already a **1Co 6:7** *3767*
Shall I **t** take away the members of **1Co 6:15** *3767*
I think **t** that this is good in **1Co 7:26** *3767*
So **t** both he who gives his own **1Co 7:38** *5620*
What **t** is my reward? **1Co 9:18** *3767*
They **t** *do it* to receive a **1Co 9:25** *3767*
What do I mean **t**? **1Co 10:19** *3767*
Whether, **t**, you eat or drink or **1Co 10:31** *3767*
So **t**, my brethren, when you come **1Co 11:33** *5620*
third teachers, **t** miracles, **1Co 12:28** *1899*
miracles, **t** gifts of healings, **1Co 12:28** *1899*
mirror dimly, but **t** face to face; **1Co 13:12** *5119*
but **t** I will know fully just as I **1Co 13:12** *5119*
If **t** I do not know the meaning of **1Co 14:11** *3767*
What is *the outcome* **t**? **1Co 14:15** *3767*
So **t** tongues are for a sign, not **1Co 14:22** *5620*
What is *the outcome* **t**, **1Co 14:26** *3767*
to Cephas, **t** to the twelve. **1Co 15:5** *1534*
t He appeared to James, then to **1Co 15:7** *1899*
to James, **t** to all the apostles; **1Co 15:7** *1534*
Whether **t** *it was* I or they, so we **1Co 15:11** *3767*
raised, **t** our preaching is vain, **1Co 15:14** *686*
T those also who have fallen **1Co 15:18** *686*
t *comes* the end, when He hands **1Co 15:24** *1534*
t the Son Himself also will be **1Co 15:28** *5119*
why **t** are they baptized for them? **1Co 15:29** *2532*
but the natural; **t** the spiritual. **1Co 15:46** *1899*
t will come about the saying that **1Co 15:54** *5119*
who **t** makes me glad but the one **2Co 2:2** *2532*
for when I am weak, **t** I am strong. **2Co 12:10** *5119*
T three years later I went up to **Ga 1:18** *1899*
T I went into the regions of Syria **Ga 1:21** *1899*
T after an interval of fourteen **Ga 2:1** *1899*
is Christ **t** a minister of sin? **Ga 2:17** *686*
Law, **t** Christ died needlessly." **Ga 2:21** *686*
So **t**, does He who provides you with **Ga 3:5** *3767*
So **t** those who are of faith are **Ga 3:9** *5620*
Why the Law **t**? It was added **Ga 3:19** *3767*
Is the Law **t** contrary to the **Ga 3:21** *3767*
t righteousness would indeed have **Ga 3:21**
t you are Abraham's descendants, **Ga 3:29** *686*
if a son, **t** an heir through God. **Ga 4:7** *2532*
Where **t** is that sense of blessing **Ga 4:15** *3767*
So **t**, brethren, we are not **Ga 4:31** *1352*
T the stumbling block of the cross **Ga 5:11** *686*
and **t** he will have *reason for* **Ga 6:4** *5119*
So **t**, while we have opportunity, **Ga 6:10** *686*
So **t** you are no longer strangers **Eph 2:19** *686*
So **t** do not be foolish, but **Eph 5:17**
1223, 3778
What **t**? Only that in every way, **Php 1:18** *1063*
So **t**, my beloved, just as you have **Php 2:12** *5620*
Receive him **t** in the Lord with all **Php 2:29** *3767*
t you also will be revealed with **Col 3:4** *5119*
Finally **t**, brethren, we request **1Th 4:1** *3767*
T we who are alive and remain **1Th 4:17** *1899*
t destruction will come upon them **1Th 5:3** *5119*
t let us not sleep as others do, **1Th 5:6** *686*
T that lawless one will be revealed **2Th 2:8** *5119*
So **t**, brethren, stand firm and **2Th 2:15** *686*
t he is not to eat, either. **2Th 3:10** *3754*
First of all, **t**, I urge that **1Tm 2:1** *3767*
who was first created, *and* **t** Eve. **1Tm 2:13** *1534*
An overseer, **t**, must be above **1Tm 3:2** *3767*
t let them serve as deacons if **1Tm 3:10** *1534*
If **t** you regard me a partner, **Phm 1:17** *3767*
and **t** have fallen away, it is **Heb 6:6**
and **t** also king of Salem, **Heb 7:2** *1899*
and **t** for the *sins* of the people, **Heb 7:27** *1899*
"**T** I SAID, 'BEHOLD, I HAVE COME **Heb 10:7** *5119*
t He said, "BEHOLD, I HAVE COME **Heb 10:9** *5119*
WRITE THEM," *He* **t** *says,* **Heb 10:16**
t you are illegitimate children **Heb 12:8** *686*
And His voice shook the earth **t**, **Heb 12:26** *5119*
Through Him **t**, let us continually **Heb 13:15** *3767*
T when lust has conceived, it **Jas 1:15** *1534*
above is first pure, **t** peaceable, **Jas 3:17** *1899*
little while and **t** vanishes away. **Jas 4:14** *1899*
Is anyone among you suffering? **T** **Jas 5:13**
Is anyone among you sick? **T** he **Jas 5:14**
T he prayed again, and the sky **Jas 5:18** *2532*
This precious value, **t**, is for you **1Pe 2:7** *3767*
t the Lord knows how to rescue **2Pe 2:9**
T I turned to see the voice that was **Rv 1:12** *2532*
T I *began* to weep greatly because **Rv 5:4** *2532*
T I looked, and I heard the voice of **Rv 5:11** *2532*
T I saw when the Lamb broke one of **Rv 6:1** *2532*
T the kings of the earth **Rv 6:15** *2532*
T one of the elders answered, saying **Rv 7:13** *2532*
T the angel took the censer **Rv 8:5** *2532*
T I looked, and I heard an eagle **Rv 8:13** *2532*
T the fifth angel sounded, and I saw **Rv 9:1** *2532*
T out of the smoke came locusts upon **Rv 9:3** *2532*
T the sixth angel sounded, and I **Rv 9:13** *2532*
T the angel whom I saw standing on **Rv 10:5** *2532*
t the mystery of God is finished, **Rv 10:7** *2532*
T the voice which I heard from heaven, **Rv 10:8** *2532*
T there was given me a measuring rod **Rv 11:1** *2532*
T they went up into heaven in **Rv 11:12** *2532*
T the seventh angel sounded; **Rv 11:15** *2532*
T another sign appeared in heaven: **Rv 12:3** *2532*
T the woman fled into the wilderness **Rv 12:6** *2532*
T I heard a loud voice in heaven, **Rv 12:10** *2532*
T I saw a beast coming up out of **Rv 13:1** *2532*
T I saw another beast coming up out **Rv 13:11** *2532*

T I looked, and behold, the Lamb	Rv 14:1	2532
T another angel, a third one,	Rv 14:9	2532
T I looked, and behold, a white	Rv 14:14	2532
T He who sat on the cloud swung His	Rv 14:16	2532
T another angel, the one who has	Rv 14:18	2532
T I saw another sign in heaven,	Rv 15:1	2532
T one of the four living creatures	Rv 15:7	2532
T I heard a loud voice from	Rv 16:1	2532
T the third *angel* poured out his	Rv 16:4	2532
T the fifth *angel* poured out his	Rv 16:10	2532
T the seventh *angel* poured out	Rv 16:17	2532
T one of the seven angels who had	Rv 17:1	2532
T a strong angel took up a stone like	Rv 18:21	2532
T I heard *something* like	Rv 19:6	2532
T he said to me, "Write, 'Blessed	Rv 19:9	2532
T I fell at his feet to worship him.	Rv 19:10	2532
T I saw an angel standing in the sun,	Rv 19:17	2532
T I saw an angel coming down from	Rv 20:1	2532
T I saw thrones, and they sat on	Rv 20:4	2532
T I saw a great white throne and Him	Rv 20:11	2532
T death and Hades were thrown into	Rv 20:14	2532
T I saw a new heaven and a new earth;	Rv 21:1	2532
T He said to me, "It is done. I am	Rv 21:6	2532
T one of the seven angels who had	Rv 21:9	2532
T he showed me a river of the water	Rv 22:1	2532

THEOPHILUS

order, most excellent **T**,	Lk 1:3	2321
The first account I composed, **T**,	Ac 1:1	2321

THERE

"Let **t** be light";	Gn 1:3	
"Let there be light"; and **t** was light.	Gn 1:3	
And **t** was evening and there was	Gn 1:5	
was evening and **t** was morning,	Gn 1:5	
"Let **t** be an expanse in the midst	Gn 1:6	
And **t** was evening and there was	Gn 1:8	
was evening and **t** was morning,	Gn 1:8	
T was evening and there was morning,	Gn 1:13	
was evening and **t** was morning,	Gn 1:13	
"Let **t** be lights in the expanse	Gn 1:14	
T was evening and there was morning,	Gn 1:19	
was evening and **t** was morning,	Gn 1:19	
T was evening and there was morning,	Gn 1:23	
was evening and **t** was morning,	Gn 1:23	
And **t** was evening and there was	Gn 1:31	
was evening and **t** was morning,	Gn 1:31	
and **t** was no man to cultivate the	Gn 2:5	
and **t** He placed the man whom He	Gn 2:8	8033
and from **t** it divided and became	Gn 2:10	8033
land of Havilah, where **t** is gold.	Gn 2:11	8033
bdellium and the onyx stone are **t**.	Gn 2:12	8033
but for Adam **t** was not found a	Gn 2:20	
t went into the ark to Noah by	Gn 7:9	
and it flew here and **t** until the	Gn 8:7	7725
neither shall **t** again be a flood	Gn 9:11	
the land of Shinar and settled **t**.	Gn 11:2	8033
down and **t** confuse their language,	Gn 11:7	8033
LORD scattered them abroad from **t**	Gn 11:8	8033
because **t** the LORD confused the	Gn 11:9	8033
and from **t** the LORD scattered them	Gn 11:9	8033
as far as Haran, and settled **t**.	Gn 11:31	8033
So he built an altar **t** to the LORD	Gn 12:7	8033
Then he proceeded from **t** to the	Gn 12:8	8033
and **t** he built an altar to the	Gn 12:8	8033
Now **t** was a famine in the land;	Gn 12:10	
went down to Egypt to sojourn **t**,	Gn 12:10	8033
which he had made **t** formerly;	Gn 13:4	8033
and **t** Abram called on the name of	Gn 13:4	8033
And **t** was strife between the	Gn 13:7	
"Please let **t** be no strife	Gn 13:8	
t he built an altar to the LORD.	Gn 13:18	8033
t *appeared* a smoking oven and a	Gn 15:17	
"**T**, in the tent."	Gn 18:9	2009
Then the men rose up from **t**,	Gn 18:16	8033
Then the men turned away from **t**	Gn 18:22	8033
"Suppose **t** are fifty righteous	Gn 18:24	3426
it if I find forty-five **t**."	Gn 18:28	8033
"Suppose forty are found **t**?"	Gn 18:29	8033
suppose thirty are found **t**?"	Gn 18:30	8033
not do *it* if I find thirty **t**."	Gn 18:30	8033
suppose twenty are found **t**?"	Gn 18:31	8033
suppose ten are found **t**?"	Gn 18:32	8033
Please, let me escape **t**	Gn 19:20	8033
"Hurry, escape **t**, for I cannot do	Gn 19:22	8033
do anything until you arrive **t**."	Gn 19:22	8033
and **t** is not a man on earth to	Gn 19:31	369
Now Abraham journeyed from **t**	Gn 20:1	8033
surely **t** is no fear of God in this	Gn 20:11	369
t the two of them took an oath.	Gn 21:31	8033
and **t** he called on the name of the	Gn 21:33	8033
and offer him **t** as a burnt	Gn 22:2	8033
and I and the lad will go over **t**;	Gn 22:5	5704, 3541
and Abraham built the altar **t** and	Gn 22:9	8033
me that I may bury my dead **t**."	Gn 23:13	8033
do not take my son back **t**!	Gn 24:6	8033
take a wife for my son from **t**.	Gn 24:7	8033
only do not take my son back **t**."	Gn 24:8	8033
is **t** room for us to lodge in your	Gn 24:23	3426
t Abraham was buried with Sarah	Gn 25:10	8033
behold, **t** were twins in her womb.	Gn 25:24	
a swallow of that red stuff **t**,	Gn 25:30	
Now **t** was a famine in the land,	Gn 26:1	
when he had been **t** a long time,	Gn 26:8	8033
And Isaac departed from **t** and	Gn 26:17	8033
valley of Gerar, and settled **t**.	Gn 26:17	8033
found **t** a well of flowing water,	Gn 26:19	8033
He moved away from **t** and dug	Gn 26:22	8033
he went up from **t** to Beersheba.	Gn 26:23	8033
So he built an altar **t** and	Gn 26:25	8033
the LORD, and pitched his tent **t**;	Gn 26:25	8033
and **t** Isaac's servants dug a well.	Gn 26:25	8033
'Let **t** now be an oath between us,	Gn 26:28	
me two choice young goats from **t**,	Gn 27:9	8033
I will send and get you from **t**.	Gn 27:45	8033
and from **t** take to yourself a wife	Gn 28:2	8033
to take to himself a wife from **t**,	Gn 28:6	8033
place and spent the night **t**,	Gn 28:11	8033
of sheep were lying **t** beside it,	Gn 29:2	8033
all the flocks were gathered **t**,	Gn 29:3	8033
removing from **t** every speckled and	Gn 30:32	8033
heap, and they ate **t** by the heap.	Gn 31:46	8033
So he spent the night **t**.	Gn 32:13	8033
And he blessed him **t**.	Gn 32:29	8033
But he said, "What need is **t**?	Gn 33:15	
Then he erected **t** an altar and	Gn 33:20	8033
go up to Bethel and live **t**	Gn 35:1	8033
and make an altar **t** to God,	Gn 35:1	8033
and I will make an altar **t** to God,	Gn 35:3	8033
t was a great terror upon the	Gn 35:5	
He built an altar **t**,	Gn 35:7	8033
because **t** God had revealed Himself	Gn 35:7	8033
and when **t** was still some distance	Gn 35:16	
Now **t** were twelve sons of Jacob	Gn 35:22	
"The boy is not **t**; as for me,	Gn 37:30	
Judah saw **t** a daughter of a	Gn 38:2	8033
'**T** has been no temple prostitute	Gn 38:21	
'**T** has been no temple prostitute	Gn 38:22	
behold, **t** were twins in her womb.	Gn 38:27	
who had taken him down **t**.	Gn 39:1	8033
and with him **t** he did not concern	Gn 39:6	
"**T** is no one greater in this	Gn 39:9	369
men of the household was **t** inside.	Gn 39:11	8033
and he was **t** in the jail.	Gn 39:20	8033
so that whatever was done **t**,	Gn 39:22	8033
and **t** is no one to interpret it."	Gn 40:8	369
t *was* a vine in front of me;	Gn 40:9	
t *were* three baskets of white	Gn 40:16	
and in the top basket **t** *were* some	Gn 40:17	
the Nile **t** came up seven cows,	Gn 41:2	
but **t** was no one who could	Gn 41:8	369
"Now a Hebrew youth *was* with us **t**,	Gn 41:12	8033
but **t** was no one who could explain	Gn 41:24	369
t is no one so discerning and wise	Gn 41:39	369
t was famine in all the lands,	Gn 41:54	
all the land of Egypt **t** was bread.	Gn 41:54	
saw that **t** was grain in Egypt,	Gn 42:1	3426
heard that **t** is grain in Egypt;	Gn 42:2	3426
go down **t** and buy *some* for us from	Gn 42:2	8033
tested, whether **t** is truth in you.	Gn 42:16	
for **t** was an interpreter between	Gn 42:23	
their grain and departed from **t**.	Gn 42:26	8033
that they were to eat a meal **t**.	Gn 43:25	8033
he entered his chamber and wept **t**.	Gn 43:30	8033
to Joseph's house, he was still **t**,	Gn 44:14	8033
So **t** was no man with him when	Gn 45:1	
and **t** are still five years in	Gn 45:6	
five years in which **t** will be neither	Gn 45:6	369
"**T** I will also provide for you,	Gn 45:11	8033
for **t** are still five years of	Gn 45:11	
I will make you a great nation **t**.	Gn 46:3	8033
t *were* fourteen persons in all.	Gn 46:22	
t *were* seven persons in all.	Gn 46:25	
for **t** is no pasture for your	Gn 47:4	369
Now **t** was no food in all the land,	Gn 47:13	369
T is nothing left for my lord	Gn 47:18	
when **t** was still some distance to	Gn 48:7	
I buried her **t** on the way to Ephrath	Gn 48:7	8033
From **t** is the Shepherd, the Stone	Gn 49:24	8033
"**T** they buried Abraham and his	Gn 49:31	8033
t they buried Isaac and his wife	Gn 49:31	8033
wife Rebekah, and **t** I buried Leah	Gn 49:31	8033
of Canaan, **t** you shall bury me."	Gn 50:5	8033
T also went up with him both	Gn 50:9	
they lamented **t** with a very great	Gn 50:10	8033
when he saw **t** was no one *around*,	Ex 2:12	369
"Is **t** not your brother Aaron the	Ex 4:14	
"**T** is no straw given to your	Ex 5:16	369
and **t** will be blood throughout	Ex 7:19	
t is no one like the LORD our God.	Ex 8:10	369
Pharaoh saw that **t** was relief,	Ex 8:15	
and **t** were gnats on man and beast.	Ex 8:17	
so **t** were gnats on man and beast.	Ex 8:18	
no swarms of insects will be **t**,	Ex 8:22	8033
And **t** came great swarms of insects	Ex 8:24	
t was not even one of the	Ex 9:7	
t is no one like Me in all the earth	Ex 9:14	369
So **t** was hail, and fire flashing	Ex 9:24	
of Israel *were*, **t** was no hail.	Ex 9:26	
for **t** has been enough of God's	Ex 9:28	
and **t** will be hail no longer,	Ex 9:29	
T had never been so *many* locusts,	Ex 10:14	
nor would **t** be so *many* again.	Ex 10:14	
that **t** may be darkness over the	Ex 10:21	
and **t** was thick darkness in all	Ex 10:22	
And until we arrive **t**,	Ex 10:26	8033
t shall be a great cry in all the	Ex 11:6	
such as **t** has not been *before* and	Ex 11:6	
'Seven days **t** shall be no leaven	Ex 12:19	
and **t** was a great cry in Egypt,	Ex 12:30	
for **t** was no home where there was	Ex 12:30	369
home where **t** was not someone dead.	Ex 12:30	369
t shall be a feast to the LORD.	Ex 13:6	
"Is it because **t** were no graves	Ex 14:11	369
and **t** was the cloud along with the	Ex 14:20	
T He made for them a statute and	Ex 15:25	8033
regulation, and **t** He tested them.	Ex 15:25	8033
where **t** *were* twelve springs of water	Ex 15:27	
they camped **t** beside the waters.	Ex 15:27	8033
and in the morning **t** was a layer	Ex 16:13	
t was a fine flake-like thing,	Ex 16:14	
foul nor was **t** any worm in it.	Ex 16:24	
the sabbath, **t** will be none."	Ex 16:26	
and **t** was no water for the people	Ex 17:1	369
the people thirsted **t** for water;	Ex 17:3	8033
before you **t** on the rock at Horeb;	Ex 17:6	8033
and **t** Israel camped in front of	Ex 19:2	8033
that **t** were thunder and lightning	Ex 19:16	
yet **t** is no injury,	Ex 21:22	
"But if **t** is *any further* injury,	Ex 21:23	
t will be no bloodguiltiness on	Ex 22:2	369
t will be bloodguiltiness on his	Ex 22:3	
"**T** shall be no one miscarrying or	Ex 23:26	
and under His feet **t** appeared to	Ex 24:10	
Me on the mountain and remain **t**,	Ex 24:12	8033
"**T** I will meet with you; and from	Ex 25:22	8033
"**T** *shall be* two tenons for each	Ex 26:17	
"**T** shall be eight boards with their	Ex 26:25	
the testimony **t** within the veil;	Ex 26:33	8033
On the south side **t** *shall be*	Ex 27:9	
for the north side in length **t**	Ex 27:11	
t *shall be* a screen of twenty cubits	Ex 27:16	
"**T** shall be an opening at its	Ex 28:32	
around its opening **t** shall be a	Ex 28:32	
and **t** *shall be* one-tenth *of an*	Ex 29:40	
meet with you, to speak to you **t**.	Ex 29:42	8033
meet **t** with the sons of Israel,	Ex 29:43	8033
T *shall be* perpetual incense	Ex 30:8	
that **t** will be no plague among them	Ex 30:12	
t shall be an equal part of each.	Ex 30:34	
t is a sabbath of complete rest,	Ex 31:15	
"**T** is a sound of war in the camp."	Ex 32:17	
"Behold, **t** is a place by Me, and	Ex 33:21	
and you shall stand **t** on the rock;	Ex 33:21	
and present yourself **t** to Me on	Ex 34:2	8033
stood **t** with him as he called upon	Ex 34:5	8033
So he was **t** with the LORD forty	Ex 34:28	8033
T *were* two tenons for each board,	Ex 36:22	
T were eight boards with their	Ex 36:30	
T were six branches going out of its	Ex 37:18	
In the lampstand **t** *were* four cups	Ex 37:20	
For the north side **t** *were* one	Ex 38:11	
For the west side **t** *were* hangings	Ex 38:12	
place the ark of the testimony **t**,	Ex 40:3	8033
and **t** was fire in it by night,	Ex 40:38	
offering, **t** is one law for them;	Lv 7:7	
and eat it **t** together with the	Lv 8:31	8033
and if **t** is a white swelling in	Lv 13:10	
and **t** is quick raw flesh in the	Lv 13:10	
and in the place of the boil **t** is	Lv 13:19	
t are no white hairs in it and it	Lv 13:21	369
t is no white hair in the bright	Lv 13:26	369
t is thin yellowish hair in it,	Lv 13:30	
and **t** is no black hair in it,	Lv 13:31	369
t occurs a reddish-white	Lv 13:42	
whom **t** is an infection of leprosy,	Lv 14:32	
on which **t** is seminal emission,	Lv 15:17	
so that **t** is a seminal emission,	Lv 15:18	
place, and shall leave them **t**.	Lv 16:23	8033
freedom, **t** shall be punishment;	Lv 19:20	
'If **t** *is* anyone who curses his	Lv 20:9	
'If **t** *is* a man who commits	Lv 20:10	
'If **t** *is* a man who lies with his	Lv 20:11	
'If **t** *is* a man who lies with his	Lv 20:12	
'If **t** *is* a man who lies with a	Lv 20:13	
'If **t** *is* a man who marries	Lv 20:14	
that **t** will be no immorality in	Lv 20:14	
'If **t** *is* a man who lies with an	Lv 20:15	
'If **t** *is* a woman who approaches	Lv 20:16	
'If **t** *is* a man who takes his	Lv 20:17	
'If **t** *is* a man who lies with a	Lv 20:18	
'If **t** *is* a man who lies with his	Lv 20:20	
'If **t** *is* a man who takes his	Lv 20:21	
t shall be no defect in it.	Lv 22:21	
t is a sabbath of complete rest,	Lv 23:3	
t is the Feast of Unleavened Bread	Lv 23:6	
t shall be seven complete sabbaths.	Lv 23:15	
"If **t** is any person who will not	Lv 23:29	
'**T** shall be one standard for you;	Lv 24:22	
'If **t** are still many years, he	Lv 25:51	
t shall be a man of each tribe,	Nu 1:4	
that **t** will be no wrath on the	Nu 1:53	
t *were* 8,600, performing	Nu 3:28	
and **t** is no witness against her	Nu 5:13	369
that **t** will be no plague among the	Nu 8:19	
But **t** were *some* men who were	Nu 9:6	
t the sons of Israel would camp.	Nu 9:17	8033
T is nothing at all to look at	Nu 11:6	369
them take their stand **t** with you.	Nu 11:16	8033
come down and speak with you **t**,	Nu 11:17	8033
Now **t** went forth a wind from the	Nu 11:31	
because **t** they buried the people	Nu 11:34	8033
If **t** is a prophet among you, I,	Nu 12:6	
"Go up **t** into the Negev;	Nu 13:17	2088
Are **t** trees in it or not?	Nu 13:20	3426
and from **t** cut down a branch with a	Nu 13:23	8033
sons of Israel cut down from **t**.	Nu 13:24	8033
we saw the descendants of Anak **t**.	Nu 13:28	8033
"**T** also we saw the Nephilim	Nu 13:33	8033
and **t** they will die.' "	Nu 14:35	8033
will be **t** in front of you,	Nu 14:43	8033
t shall be one statute for you and	Nu 15:15	
'**T** is to be one law and one	Nu 15:16	
for **t** is one rod for the head *of*	Nu 17:3	
that **t** will no longer be wrath on	Nu 18:5	
and on the persons who were **t**,	Nu 19:18	8033
Miriam died **t** and was buried there.	Nu 20:1	8033

died there and was buried **t**.	**Nu 20:1**	8033
T was no water for the congregation,	**Nu 20:2**	
nor is **t** water to drink."	**Nu 20:5**	369
to his people, and will die **t**."	**Nu 20:26**	8033
Aaron died **t** on the mountain top.	**Nu 20:28**	8033
For **t** is no food and no water, and	**Nu 21:5**	369
From **t** they set out and camped in	**Nu 21:12**	8033
From **t** they journeyed and camped	**Nu 21:13**	8033
From **t** *they continued* to Beer,	**Nu 21:16**	8033
the Amorites who *were* **t**.	**Nu 21:32**	8033
until **t** was no remnant left him;	**Nu 21:35**	
t is a people who came out of	**Nu 22:11**	
where **t** was no way to turn to the	**Nu 22:26**	369
If **t** had been a sword in my hand,	**Nu 22:29**	3426
and he saw from **t** a portion of the	**Nu 22:41**	8033
and curse them for me from **t**."	**Nu 23:13**	8033
I myself meet *the* LORD over **t**."	**Nu 23:15**	3541
"For **t** is no omen against Jacob,	**Nu 23:23**	
Nor is **t** any divination against Israel	**Nu 23:23**	
you curse them for me from **t**."	**Nu 23:27**	8033
But among these **t** was not a man of	**Nu 26:64**	
So **t** were furnished from the	**Nu 31:5**	
remain **t** in the cities of Gilead;	**Nu 32:26**	8033
and in Elim **t** were twelve springs	**Nu 33:9**	
and they camped **t**.	**Nu 33:9**	8033
now it was **t** that the people had	**Nu 33:14**	8033
command of the LORD, and died **t** in	**Nu 33:38**	8033
person unintentionally may flee **t**.	**Nu 35:11**	8033
person unintentionally may flee **t**.	**Nu 35:15**	8033
saw the sons of the Anakim **t**."	**Dt 1:28**	8033
'Not even you shall enter **t**.	**Dt 1:37**	8033
before you, he shall enter **t**;	**Dt 1:38**	8033
of good or evil, shall enter **t**,	**Dt 1:39**	8033
the days that you spent **t**.	**Dt 1:46**	
(The Emim lived **t** formerly, a	**Dt 2:10**	
t was no city that was too high	**Dt 2:36**	
t was not a city which we did not	**Dt 3:4**	
for what god is **t** in heaven or on	**Dt 3:24**	
"For what great nation is **t** that	**Dt 4:7**	
"Or what great nation is **t** that	**Dt 4:8**	
"**T** you will serve gods, the work of	**Dt 4:28**	8033
"But from **t** you will seek the	**Dt 4:29**	8033
t is no other besides Him.	**Dt 4:35**	369
on the earth below; **t** is no other.	**Dt 4:39**	369
that a manslayer might flee **t**,	**Dt 4:42**	8033
LORD your God brought you out of **t**	**Dt 5:15**	8033
'For who is **t** of all flesh who	**Dt 5:26**	
from **t** in order to bring us in,	**Dt 6:23**	8033
t will be no male or female	**Dt 7:14**	
ground where **t** was no water;	**Dt 8:15**	369
and **t** they are, as the LORD	**Dt 10:5**	8033
T Aaron died and there he was	**Dt 10:6**	8033
Aaron died and **t** he was buried	**Dt 10:6**	8033
From **t** they set out to Gudgodah,	**Dt 10:7**	8033
that **t** will be no rain and the ground	**Dt 11:17**	
to establish His name **t** for His	**Dt 12:5**	8033
dwelling, and **t** you shall come.	**Dt 12:5**	8033
"**T** you shall bring your burnt	**Dt 12:6**	8033
"**T** also you and your households	**Dt 12:7**	8033
t you shall bring all that I	**Dt 12:11**	8033
t you shall offer your burnt	**Dt 12:14**	8033
and **t** you shall do all that I	**Dt 12:14**	8033
and **t** you shall eat in the	**Dt 14:26**	8033
t will be no poor among you,	**Dt 15:4**	
"If **t** is a poor man with you, one	**Dt 15:7**	
that **t** is no base thought in your	**Dt 15:9**	
t shall be a solemn assembly to the	**Dt 16:8**	
"If **t** is found in your midst, in	**Dt 17:2**	
who stands **t** to serve the LORD	**Dt 17:12**	8033
who stand **t** before the LORD.	**Dt 18:7**	8033
"**T** shall not be found among you	**Dt 18:10**	
so that any manslayer may flee **t**.	**Dt 19:3**	8033
manslayer who may flee **t** and live:	**Dt 19:4**	8033
"But if **t** is a man who hates his	**Dt 19:11**	
city shall send and take him from **t**	**Dt 19:12**	8033
break the heifer's neck **t** in the valley	**Dt 21:4**	8033
"If **t** is a girl who is a virgin	**Dt 22:23**	
t is no sin in the girl worthy of	**Dt 22:26**	369
out, but **t** was no one to save her.	**Dt 22:27**	369
"If **t** is among you any man who is	**Dt 23:10**	
outside the camp and go out **t**,	**Dt 23:12**	8033
LORD your God redeemed you from **t**;	**Dt 24:18**	8033
"If **t** is a dispute between men	**Dt 25:1**	
down to Egypt and sojourned **t**,	**Dt 26:5**	8033
but **t** he became a great, mighty	**Dt 26:5**	8033
shall build **t** an altar to the LORD	**Dt 27:5**	8033
peace offerings and eat **t**,	**Dt 27:7**	8033
and **t** will be no one to frighten	**Dt 28:26**	369
but **t** will be nothing you can do.	**Dt 28:32**	369
and **t** you shall serve other gods,	**Dt 28:36**	8033
and **t** you shall serve other gods,	**Dt 28:64**	8033
and **t** will be no resting place	**Dt 28:65**	
but **t** the LORD will give you a	**Dt 28:65**	8033
And **t** you will offer yourselves	**Dt 28:68**	8033
slaves, but **t** will be no buyer."	**Dt 28:68**	
t will not be among you a man or	**Dt 29:18**	3426
t will not be among you a root	**Dt 29:18**	3426
from **t** the LORD your God will	**Dt 30:4**	8033
and from **t** He will bring you back.	**Dt 30:4**	8033
remain **t** as a witness against you.	**Dt 31:26**	8033
And **t** was no foreign god with him.	**Dt 32:12**	369
And **t** is no understanding in them.	**Dt 32:28**	369
is gone, And **t** is none *remaining,*	**Dt 32:36**	657
am He, And **t** is no god besides Me;	**Dt 32:39**	369
And **t** is no one who can deliver	**Dt 32:39**	369
distance, but you shall not go **t**,	**Dt 32:52**	8033
At His right hand **t** was flashing	**Dt 33:2**	
T they will offer righteous	**Dt 33:19**	8033
For **t** the ruler's portion was	**Dt 33:21**	8033
"**T** is none like the God of	**Dt 33:26**	369
but you shall not go over **t**."	**Dt 34:4**	8033
the servant of the LORD died **t** in	**Dt 34:5**	8033
name was Rahab, and lodged **t**.	**Jos 2:1**	8033
hide yourselves **t** for three days until	**Jos 2:16**	8033
and remained **t** for three days	**Jos 2:22**	8033
they lodged **t** before they crossed.	**Jos 3:1**	8033
t shall be between you and it a	**Jos 3:4**	
place and put them down **t**.	**Jos 4:8**	8033
and they are **t** to this day.	**Jos 4:9**	8033
and **t** was no spirit in them any	**Jos 5:1**	
woman and all she has out of **t**,	**Jos 6:22**	8033
not make all the people toil up **t**,	**Jos 7:3**	8033
men from the people went up **t**,	**Jos 7:4**	8033
"**T** are things under the ban in	**Jos 7:13**	
Now **t** *was* a valley between him	**Jos 8:11**	
But he did not know that **t** *was* an	**Jos 8:14**	
He wrote **t** on the stones a	**Jos 8:32**	8033
T was not a word of all that Moses	**Jos 8:35**	
t *were* more who died from	**Jos 10:11**	
T was no day like that before it or	**Jos 10:14**	
but do not stay **t** yourselves;	**Jos 10:19**	
t was no one left who breathed.	**Jos 11:11**	
T was not a city which made peace	**Jos 11:19**	
T were no Anakim left in the land	**Jos 11:22**	
on that day that Anakim *were* **t**,	**Jos 14:12**	8033
Caleb drove out from **t** the three	**Jos 15:14**	8033
Then he went up from **t** against the	**Jos 15:15**	8033
t fell ten portions to Manasseh,	**Jos 17:5**	
clear a place for yourself **t** in the land	**Jos 17:15**	8033
and set up the tent of meeting **t**;	**Jos 18:1**	8033
T remained among the sons of Israel	**Jos 18:2**	
and **t** Joshua divided the land to	**Jos 18:10**	8033
t the border continued to Luz,	**Jos 18:13**	8033
The border extended *from* **t**	**Jos 18:14**	
From **t** it continued eastward	**Jos 19:13**	8033
and proceeded from **t** to Hukkok;	**Jos 19:34**	8033
without premeditation, may flee **t**,	**Jos 20:3**	8033
person unintentionally may flee **t**,	**Jos 20:9**	8033
built an altar **t** by the Jordan,	**Jos 22:10**	8033
he took a large stone and set it up **t**	**Jos 24:26**	8033
him to Jerusalem and he died **t**.	**Jg 1:7**	8033
Then from **t** he went against the	**Jg 1:11**	8033
he drove out from **t** the three sons	**Jg 1:20**	8033
and **t** they sacrificed to the LORD.	**Jg 2:5**	8033
and **t** arose another generation	**Jg 2:10**	
for **t** *was* peace between Jabin	**Jg 4:17**	
'Is **t** anyone here?'	**Jg 4:20**	3426
T they shall recount the righteous	**Jg 5:11**	8033
Among the divisions of Reuben **T**	**Jg 5:15**	
Among the divisions of Reuben **T**	**Jg 5:16**	
Where he bowed, **t** he fell dead.	**Jg 5:27**	8033
Then Gideon built an altar **t** to	**Jg 6:24**	8033
If **t** is dew on the fleece only,	**Jg 6:37**	
let **t** be dew on all the ground."	**Jg 6:39**	
and I will test them for you **t**.	**Jg 7:4**	8033
He went up from **t** to Penuel and	**Jg 8:8**	8033
threw an earring **t** from his spoil.	**Jg 8:25**	8033
all Israel played the harlot with it **t**,	**Jg 8:27**	8033
and went to Beer and remained **t**	**Jg 9:21**	8033
But **t** was a strong tower in the	**Jg 9:51**	
fled **t** and shut themselves in;	**Jg 9:51**	8033
Thus **t** fell at that time 42,000 of	**Jg 12:6**	
T was a certain man of Zorah, of	**Jg 13:2**	
"Is **t** no woman among the	**Jg 14:3**	369
and Samson made a feast **t**,	**Jg 14:10**	8033
went to Gaza and saw a harlot **t**,	**Jg 16:1**	8033
lords of the Philistines were **t**.	**Jg 16:27**	8033
Now **t** was a man of the hill	**Jg 17:1**	
days **t** was no king in Israel;	**Jg 17:6**	369
Now **t** was a young man from	**Jg 17:7**	
and he was staying **t**.	**Jg 17:7**	8033
days **t** was no king of Israel;	**Jg 18:1**	369
the house of Micah, and lodged **t**.	**Jg 18:2**	8033
and they turned aside **t** and	**Jg 18:3**	8033
for **t** was no ruler humiliating	**Jg 18:7**	369
a place where **t** is no lack of	**Jg 18:10**	369
They passed from **t** to the hill	**Jg 18:13**	8033
"Do you know that **t** are in these	**Jg 18:14**	3426
They turned aside **t** and came	**Jg 18:15**	8033
the land went up *and* entered **t**,	**Jg 18:17**	8033
And **t** was no one to deliver *them,*	**Jg 18:28**	369
when **t** was no king in Israel,	**Jg 19:1**	369
that **t** was a certain Levite	**Jg 19:1**	
was **t** for a period of four months.	**Jg 19:2**	8033
they ate and drank and lodged **t**.	**Jg 19:4**	8033
that he spent the night **t** again.	**Jg 19:7**	8033
And **t** were with him a pair of	**Jg 19:10**	
They turned aside **t** in order	**Jg 19:15**	8033
of Ephraim, *for* I am from **t**,	**Jg 19:18**	8033
"Yet **t** is both straw and fodder	**Jg 19:19**	3426
t is no lack of anything."	**Jg 19:19**	369
let us go," but **t** was no answer.	**Jg 19:28**	369
thus they remained **t** before the	**Jg 20:26**	8033
of God *was* **t** in those days,	**Jg 20:27**	8033
sat **t** before God until evening,	**Jg 21:2**	8033
arose early and built an altar **t** and	**Jg 21:4**	8033
"Who is **t** among all the tribes of	**Jg 21:5**	
"What one is **t** of the tribes of	**Jg 21:8**	
inhabitants of Jabesh-gilead was **t**.	**Jg 21:9**	8033
12,000 of the valiant warriors **t**,	**Jg 21:10**	8033
They said, "**T** *must be* an	**Jg 21:17**	
t is a feast of the LORD from year	**Jg 21:19**	
departed from **t** at that time,	**Jg 21:24**	8033
each one of them went out from **t**	**Jg 21:24**	8033
days **t** was no king in Israel;	**Jg 21:25**	369
that **t** was a famine in the land.	**Ru 1:1**	
the land of Moab and remained **t**.	**Ru 1:2**	8033
And they lived **t** about ten years.	**Ru 1:4**	8033
will die, and **t** I will be buried.	**Ru 1:17**	8033
t is a relative closer than I.	**Ru 3:12**	3426
up to the gate and sat down **t**,	**Ru 4:1**	8033
for **t** is no one but you to redeem	**Ru 4:4**	369
Now **t** was a certain man from	**1Sa 1:1**	8033
Phinehas, were priests to the LORD **t**.	**1Sa 1:3**	8033
the LORD and stay **t** forever."	**1Sa 1:22**	8033
And he worshiped the LORD **t**.	**1Sa 1:28**	8033
"**T** is no one holy like the LORD,	**1Sa 2:2**	369
Indeed, **t** is no one besides You,	**1Sa 2:2**	369
Nor is **t** any rock like our God.	**1Sa 2:2**	369
to all the Israelites who came **t**.	**1Sa 2:14**	8033
so that **t** will not be an old man in	**1Sa 2:31**	
and from **t** they carried the ark of	**1Sa 4:4**	8033
were **t** with the ark of the	**1Sa 4:4**	8033
for **t** fell of Israel thirty	**1Sa 4:10**	
and **t** has also been a great slaughter	**1Sa 4:17**	
For **t** was a deadly confusion	**1Sa 5:11**	
the hand of God was very heavy **t**.	**1Sa 5:11**	8033
on which **t** has never been a yoke;	**1Sa 6:7**	
t where there *was* a large stone;	**1Sa 6:14**	8033
there where **t** was a large stone;	**1Sa 6:14**	8033
fasted on that day and said **t**,	**1Sa 7:6**	8033
So **t** was peace between Israel and	**1Sa 7:14**	
was to Ramah, for his house *was* **t**,	**1Sa 7:17**	8033
was there, and **t** he judged Israel;	**1Sa 7:17**	8033
he built **t** an altar to the LORD.	**1Sa 7:17**	8033
"No, but **t** shall be a king over	**1Sa 8:19**	
Now **t** was a man of Benjamin whose	**1Sa 9:1**	
and **t** was not a more handsome	**1Sa 9:2**	369
but *they were* not **t**.	**1Sa 9:4**	
t is a man of God in this city,	**1Sa 9:6**	
Now let us go **t**, perhaps he can	**1Sa 9:6**	8033
t is no present to bring to the man	**1Sa 9:7**	369
you will go on further from **t**,	**1Sa 10:3**	8033
and **t** three men going up to God at	**1Sa 10:3**	8033
as you have come **t** to the city,	**1Sa 10:5**	8033
When they came to the hill **t**,	**1Sa 10:10**	8033
A man **t** said,	**1Sa 10:12**	
		4480, 8033
So they ran and took him from **t**,	**1Sa 10:23**	8033
Surely **t** is no one like him among	**1Sa 10:24**	369
if **t** is no one to deliver us,	**1Sa 11:3**	369
Gilgal and renew the kingdom **t**."	**1Sa 11:14**	8033
and **t** they made Saul king before	**1Sa 11:15**	8033
T they also offered sacrifices of	**1Sa 11:15**	8033
and **t** Saul and all the men of	**1Sa 11:15**	8033
t was a sharp crag on the one	**1Sa 14:4**	
And **t** was a trembling in the camp,	**1Sa 14:15**	
and they went here and **t**.	**1Sa 14:16**	
and his armor bearer were not **t**.	**1Sa 14:17**	
and **t** *was* very great confusion.	**1Sa 14:20**	
and **t** was honey on the ground.	**1Sa 14:25**	
t *was* a flow of honey; but no	**1Sa 14:26**	
ox with him and slaughtered *it* **t**.	**1Sa 14:34**	8033
"**T** remains yet the youngest, and	**1Sa 16:11**	
know that **t** is a God in Israel,	**1Sa 17:46**	3426
but **t** was no sword in David's hand.	**1Sa 17:50**	369
When **t** was war again, David went	**1Sa 19:8**	
Now **t** was an evil spirit from the	**1Sa 19:9**	
He proceeded **t** to Naioth in Ramah;	**1Sa 19:23**	8033
t is hardly a step between me and	**1Sa 20:3**	
sacrifice **t** for the whole family.'	**1Sa 20:6**	8033
But if **t** is iniquity in me, put me	**1Sa 20:8**	3426
if **t** is good *feeling* toward David,	**1Sa 20:12**	
t is safety for you and no harm,	**1Sa 20:21**	
"**T** is no ordinary bread on hand,	**1Sa 21:4**	369
hand, but **t** is consecrated bread;	**1Sa 21:4**	3426
for **t** was no bread there but the	**1Sa 21:6**	
for there was no bread **t** but the	**1Sa 21:6**	8033
servants of Saul was **t** that day,	**1Sa 21:7**	8033
"Now is **t** not a spear or a sword	**1Sa 21:8**	3426
t is no other except it here."	**1Sa 21:9**	369
"**T** is none like it;	**1Sa 21:9**	369
So David departed from **t** and	**1Sa 22:1**	8033
of it, they went down **t** to him.	**1Sa 22:1**	8033
Now **t** were about four hundred men	**1Sa 22:2**	
David went from **t** to Mizpah of	**1Sa 22:3**	8033
that **t** is no one who discloses to me	**1Sa 22:8**	369
and **t** is none of you who is sorry	**1Sa 22:8**	369
day, when Doeg the Edomite was **t**,	**1Sa 22:22**	8033
haunt is, *and* who has seen him **t**;	**1Sa 23:22**	8033
David went up from **t** and	**1Sa 23:29**	8033
on the way, where **t** *was* a cave;	**1Sa 24:3**	8033
t is no evil or rebellion in my hands,	**1Sa 24:11**	369
Now **t** *was* a man in Maon whose	**1Sa 25:2**	
T are many servants today who are	**1Sa 25:10**	
surely **t** would not have been left	**1Sa 25:34**	
T is nothing better for me than to	**1Sa 27:1**	369
in the country, that I may live **t**;	**1Sa 27:5**	8033
t is a woman who is a medium at	**1Sa 28:7**	
also **t** was no strength in him, for	**1Sa 28:20**	
wept until **t** was no strength in them	**1Sa 30:4**	369
came to Jabesh and burned them **t**.	**1Sa 31:12**	8033
For **t** the shield of the mighty was	**2Sa 1:21**	8033
So David went up **t**,	**2Sa 2:2**	8033
and **t** anointed David king over the	**2Sa 2:4**	8033
the three sons of Zeruiah were **t**,	**2Sa 2:18**	8033
he fell **t** and died on the spot.	**2Sa 2:23**	8033
Now **t** was a long war between the	**2Sa 3:1**	
It came about while **t** was war	**2Sa 3:6**	
and **t** he struck him in the belly	**2Sa 3:27**	8033
and may **t** not fail from the house	**2Sa 3:29**	
been aliens **t** until this day).	**2Sa 4:3**	8033
Baal-perazim and defeated them **t**;	**2Sa 5:20**	8033
They abandoned their idols **t**,	**2Sa 5:21**	8033
to bring up from **t** the ark of God	**2Sa 6:2**	8033
and God struck him down **t** for his	**2Sa 6:7**	8033
and he died **t** by the ark of God.	**2Sa 6:7**	8033

Context	Reference	Number
for **t** is none like You, and there	**2Sa 7:22**	369
and **t** is no God besides You,	**2Sa 7:22**	369
"Is **t** yet anyone left of the	**2Sa 9:1**	3426
Now **t** was a servant of the house	**2Sa 9:2**	
"Is **t** not yet anyone of the house	**2Sa 9:3**	657
"**T** is still a son of Jonathan who	**2Sa 9:3**	
of their army, and he died **t**.	**2Sa 10:18**	8033
where he knew **t** *were* valiant men.	**2Sa 11:16**	
"**T** were two men in one city, the	**2Sa 12:1**	
to Geshur, and was **t** three years.	**2Sa 13:38**	8033
brought a wise woman from **t** and	**2Sa 14:2**	8033
and **t** was no one to separate them,	**2Sa 14:6**	369
his head **t** was no defect in him.	**2Sa 14:25**	
To Absalom **t** were born three sons,	**2Sa 14:27**	
next to mine, and he has barley **t**;	**2Sa 14:30**	8033
better for me still to be **t**."	**2Sa 14:32**	8033
and if **t** is iniquity in me, let	**2Sa 14:32**	3426
t also your servant will be."	**2Sa 15:21**	8033
God to Jerusalem and remained **t**.	**2Sa 15:29**	8033
Abiathar the priests with you **t**?	**2Sa 15:35**	8033
their two sons are with them **t**,	**2Sa 15:36**	8033
t came out from there a man of the	**2Sa 16:5**	
there came out from **t** a man of the	**2Sa 16:5**	8033
weary and he refreshed himself **t**.	**2Sa 16:14**	8033
'**T** has been a slaughter among the	**2Sa 17:9**	
even a small stone is found **t**."	**2Sa 17:13**	8033
The people of Israel were defeated **t**	**2Sa 18:7**	8033
slaughter **t** that day was great,	**2Sa 18:7**	8033
For the battle **t** was spread over	**2Sa 18:8**	8033
not strike him **t** to the ground?	**2Sa 18:11**	8033
and **t** is nothing hidden from the king	**2Sa 18:13**	
t is good news in his mouth."	**2Sa 18:25**	
T were a thousand men of Benjamin	**2Sa 19:17**	
a worthless fellow happened to be **t**	**2Sa 20:1**	8033
Now **t** stood by him one of Joab's	**2Sa 20:11**	
Now **t** was a famine in the days of	**2Sa 21:1**	
bones of Jonathan his son from **t**,	**2Sa 21:13**	8033
t was war again with the Philistines	**2Sa 21:18**	
T was war with the Philistines again	**2Sa 21:19**	
T was war at Gath again, where there	**2Sa 21:20**	
where **t** was a man of *great* stature	**2Sa 21:20**	
looked, but **t** was none to save;	**2Sa 22:42**	369
Philistines who were gathered **t** to	**2Sa 23:9**	8033
where **t** was a plot of ground full	**2Sa 23:11**	8033
and **t** were in Israel eight hundred	**2Sa 24:9**	
Or shall **t** be three days'	**2Sa 24:13**	
David built **t** an altar to the LORD and	**2Sa 24:25**	8033
you are still **t** speaking with the king	**1Ki 1:14**	8033
anoint him **t** as king over Israel,	**1Ki 1:34**	8033
have come up from **t** rejoicing,	**1Ki 1:45**	8033
t is with you Shimei the son of	**1Ki 2:8**	
may **t** be peace from the LORD	**1Ki 2:33**	
a house in Jerusalem and live **t**,	**1Ki 2:36**	8033
do not go out from **t** to any place.	**1Ki 2:36**	8033
because **t** was no house built for	**1Ki 3:2**	
went to Gibeon to sacrifice **t**,	**1Ki 3:4**	8033
so that **t** has been no one like you	**1Ki 3:12**	
so that **t** will not be any among	**1Ki 3:13**	
T was no stranger with us in the	**1Ki 3:18**	369
t is neither adversary nor	**1Ki 5:4**	369
for you know that **t** is no one	**1Ki 5:6**	369
and I will have them broken up **t**,	**1Ki 5:9**	8033
and **t** was peace between Hiram and	**1Ki 5:12**	
and **t** was neither hammer nor axe	**1Ki 6:7**	
T was cedar on the house within,	**1Ki 6:18**	
was cedar, **t** was no stone seen.	**1Ki 6:18**	369
to place **t** the ark of the covenant of	**1Ki 6:19**	8033
T *were artistic window* frames in	**1Ki 7:4**	
T were nets of network	**1Ki 7:17**	
T *were* capitals on the two	**1Ki 7:20**	
the frames **t** *was* a pedestal above,	**1Ki 7:29**	
and also on its opening **t** *were*	**1Ki 7:31**	
Now **t** *were* four supports at	**1Ki 7:34**	
On the top of the stand **t** *was* a	**1Ki 7:35**	
they are **t** to this day.	**1Ki 8:8**	8033
T was nothing in the ark except	**1Ki 8:9**	369
stone which Moses put **t** at Horeb,	**1Ki 8:9**	8033
a house that My name might be **t**,	**1Ki 8:16**	8033
"**T** I have set a place for the ark,	**1Ki 8:21**	8033
t is no God like You in heaven	**1Ki 8:23**	369
'My name shall be **t**,'	**1Ki 8:29**	8033
are shut up and **t** is no rain,	**1Ki 8:35**	
"If **t** is famine in the land, if	**1Ki 8:37**	
in the land, if **t** is pestilence,	**1Ki 8:37**	
if **t** is blight *or* mildew,	**1Ki 8:37**	
plague, whatever sickness **t** *is,*	**1Ki 8:37**	
(for **t** is no man who does not sin)	**1Ki 8:46**	369
t is no one else.	**1Ki 8:60**	369
because **t** he offered the burnt	**1Ki 8:64**	8033
by putting My name **t** forever,	**1Ki 9:3**	8033
My heart will be **t** perpetually.	**1Ki 9:3**	8033
and twenty talents of gold from **t**,	**1Ki 9:28**	8033
LORD, **t** was no more spirit in her.	**1Ki 10:5**	
T *were* six steps to the throne and	**1Ki 10:19**	
Twelve lions were standing **t**	**1Ki 10:20**	8033
all Israel stayed **t** six months,	**1Ki 11:16**	8033
went to Damascus and stayed **t**,	**1Ki 11:24**	
country of Ephraim, and lived **t**.	**1Ki 12:25**	
went out from **t** and built Penuel.	**1Ki 12:25**	8033
t came a man of God from Judah to	**1Ki 13:1**	
eat no bread, nor drink water **t**;	**1Ki 13:17**	8033
behold, Ahijah the prophet is **t**,	**1Ki 14:2**	8033
of Israel to put His name **t**.	**1Ki 14:21**	8033
T were also male cult prostitutes in	**1Ki 14:24**	
T was war between Rehoboam	**1Ki 14:30**	
T was war between Rehoboam	**1Ki 15:6**	
And **t** was war between Abijam and	**1Ki 15:7**	
Now **t** was war between Asa and	**1Ki 15:16**	
"*Let* **t** *be* a treaty between you	**1Ki 15:19**	
T was war between Asa and Baasha	**1Ki 15:32**	
surely **t** shall be neither dew nor	**1Ki 17:1**	
the ravens to provide for you **t**."	**1Ki 17:4**	8033
because **t** was no rain in the land.	**1Ki 17:7**	
belongs to Sidon, and stay **t**;	**1Ki 17:9**	8033
a widow **t** to provide for you."	**1Ki 17:9**	8033
a widow was **t** gathering sticks;	**1Ki 17:10**	8033
that **t** was no breath left in him.	**1Ki 17:17**	
t is no nation or kingdom where my	**1Ki 18:10**	3426
But **t** was no voice and no one	**1Ki 18:26**	369
but **t** was no voice, no one	**1Ki 18:29**	369
the brook Kishon, and slew them **t**.	**1Ki 18:40**	8033
for **t** is the sound of the roar of	**1Ki 18:41**	
and looked and said, "**T** is nothing."	**1Ki 18:43**	369
wind, and **t** was a heavy shower.	**1Ki 18:45**	
to Judah, and left his servant **t**.	**1Ki 19:3**	8033
t was an angel touching him,	**1Ki 19:5**	2088
t was at his head a bread cake	**1Ki 19:6**	
Then he came **t** to a cave and	**1Ki 19:9**	8033
there to a cave and lodged **t**;	**1Ki 19:9**	8033
So he departed from **t** and found	**1Ki 19:19**	8033
and **t** *were* thirty-two kings with	**1Ki 20:1**	
of the provinces, and **t** were 232;	**1Ki 20:15**	
your servant was busy here and **t**,	**1Ki 20:40**	2008
Surely **t** was no one like Ahab who	**1Ki 21:25**	
"Is **t** not yet a prophet of the	**1Ki 22:7**	369
"**T** is yet one man by whom we may	**1Ki 22:8**	
(now the harlots bathed themselves **t**	**1Ki 22:38**	
Now **t** was no king in Edom;	**1Ki 22:47**	369
'Is it because **t** is no God in	**2Ki 1:3**	369
'Is it because **t** is no God in	**2Ki 1:6**	369
is it because **t** is no God in Israel to	**2Ki 1:16**	369
and they were divided here and **t**,	**2Ki 2:8**	2008
t *appeared* a chariot of fire	**2Ki 2:11**	
they were divided here and **t**;	**2Ki 2:14**	2008
t are with your servants fifty	**2Ki 2:16**	3426
t shall not be from there death or	**2Ki 2:21**	
there shall not be from **t** death or	**2Ki 2:21**	8033
Then he went up from **t** to Bethel;	**2Ki 2:23**	8033
He went from **t** to Mount Carmel,	**2Ki 2:25**	8033
and from **t** he returned to Samaria.	**2Ki 2:25**	8033
and **t** was no water for the army or	**2Ki 3:9**	
"Is **t** not a prophet of the LORD	**2Ki 3:11**	369
And **t** came great wrath against	**2Ki 3:27**	
"**T** is not one vessel more."	**2Ki 4:6**	369
Now **t** came a day when Elisha	**2Ki 4:8**	
where **t** was a prominent woman,	**2Ki 4:8**	
by, he turned in **t** to eat food.	**2Ki 4:8**	8033
and let us set a bed for him **t**,	**2Ki 4:10**	8033
to us, *that* he can turn in **t**."	**2Ki 4:10**	8033
One day he came **t** and turned in to	**2Ki 4:11**	8033
t is the Shunammite.	**2Ki 4:25**	1975
but **t** was no sound or	**2Ki 4:31**	369
When Elisha returned to Gilgal, **t**	**2Ki 4:38**	
of God, **t** is death in the pot."	**2Ki 4:40**	
Then **t** was no harm in the pot.	**2Ki 4:41**	
that **t** is a prophet in Israel."	**2Ki 5:8**	3426
that **t** is no God in all the earth,	**2Ki 5:15**	369
the house of Rimmon to worship **t**,	**2Ki 5:18**	8033
and each of us take from **t** a beam,	**2Ki 6:2**	8033
and let us make a place **t** for	**2Ki 6:2**	8033
off a stick and threw *it* in **t**,	**2Ki 6:6**	8033
the Arameans are coming down **t**."	**2Ki 6:9**	8033
him, so that he guarded himself **t**,	**2Ki 6:10**	8033
and chariots and a great army **t**,	**2Ki 6:14**	8033
T was a great famine in Samaria;	**2Ki 6:25**	
Now **t** were four leprous men at the	**2Ki 7:3**	
is in the city and we will die **t**;	**2Ki 7:4**	8033
behold, **t** was no one there.	**2Ki 7:5**	369
behold, there was no one **t**.	**2Ki 7:5**	8033
carried from **t** silver and gold and	**2Ki 7:8**	8033
tent and carried from **t** *also,*	**2Ki 7:8**	8033
and behold, **t** was no one there,	**2Ki 7:10**	369
and behold, there was no one **t**,	**2Ki 7:10**	8033
"When you arrive **t**, search out	**2Ki 9:2**	8033
to Jezreel, for Joram was lying **t**.	**2Ki 9:16**	8033
"**T** *is* treachery, O Ahaziah!"	**2Ki 9:23**	
But he fled to Megiddo and died **t**.	**2Ki 9:27**	8033
t shall fall to the earth nothing of	**2Ki 10:10**	
Now when he had departed from **t**,	**2Ki 10:15**	8033
so that **t** was not a man left who	**2Ki 10:21**	
"Search and see that **t** is	**2Ki 10:23**	3426
house, she was put to death **t**.	**2Ki 11:16**	8033
t was much money in the chest,	**2Ki 12:10**	
But **t** were not made for the house	**2Ki 12:13**	
But **t** passed by a wild beast that	**2Ki 14:9**	
him to Lachish and killed him **t**.	**2Ki 14:19**	8033
for **t** was neither bond nor free,	**2Ki 14:26**	
nor was **t** any helper for Israel.	**2Ki 14:26**	369
and did not remain **t** in the land.	**2Ki 15:20**	8033
and have lived **t** to this day.	**2Ki 16:6**	8033
and **t** they burned incense on all	**2Ki 17:11**	8033
the beginning of their living **t**,	**2Ki 17:25**	8033
"Take **t** one of the priests whom	**2Ki 17:27**	8033
exile and let him go and live **t**;	**2Ki 17:27**	8033
so that after him **t** was none like	**2Ki 18:5**	
and **t** is no strength to *deliver.*	**2Ki 19:3**	369
to this city or shoot an arrow **t**;	**2Ki 19:32**	8033
T was nothing in his house nor in	**2Ki 20:13**	
t is nothing among my treasuries	**2Ki 20:15**	
if **t** will be peace and truth in	**2Ki 20:19**	
and he smashed them **t** and	**2Ki 23:12**	8033
that *were* **t** on the mountain,	**2Ki 23:16**	8033
priests of the high places who *were* **t**	**2Ki 23:20**	8033
Before him **t** was no king like	**2Ki 23:25**	
'My name shall be **t**.' "	**2Ki 23:27**	8033
him to Egypt, and he died **t**.	**2Ki 23:34**	8033
He carried out from **t** all the	**2Ki 24:13**	8033
that **t** was no food for the people of	**2Ki 25:3**	
and **t** he reigned seven years and	**1Ch 3:4**	8033
they lived **t** with the king for his	**1Ch 4:23**	8033
those who lived **t** formerly *were*	**1Ch 4:40**	8033
and the Meunites who were found **t**,	**1Ch 4:41**	8033
t was pasture there for their flocks.	**1Ch 4:41**	
there was pasture **t** for their flocks.	**1Ch 4:41**	8033
and have lived **t** to this day.	**1Ch 4:43**	8033
after the ark rested **t**.	**1Ch 6:31**	
inhabitants of the land, *were* **t**.	**1Ch 11:4**	8033
gathered together **t** to battle,	**1Ch 11:13**	8033
and **t** was a plot of ground full of	**1Ch 11:13**	
From the Gadites **t** came over	**1Ch 12:8**	
since **t** is no wrong in my hands,	**1Ch 12:17**	
t defected to him from Manasseh:	**1Ch 12:20**	
until **t** was a great army like the	**1Ch 12:22**	
t were 50,000 who went out in the	**1Ch 12:33**	
Of Naphtali **t** *were* 1,000	**1Ch 12:34**	
in battle formation, **t** *were* 28,600.	**1Ch 12:35**	
Of Asher **t** *were* 40,000 who went	**1Ch 12:36**	
t *were* 120,000 with all *kinds*	**1Ch 12:37**	
They were **t** with David three days,	**1Ch 12:39**	8033
T was joy indeed in Israel.	**1Ch 12:40**	
to bring up from **t** the ark of God,	**1Ch 13:6**	8033
and he died **t** before God.	**1Ch 13:10**	8033
and David defeated them **t**;	**1Ch 14:11**	8033
They abandoned their gods **t**;	**1Ch 14:12**	8033
So he left Asaph and his relatives **t**	**1Ch 16:37**	8033
"O LORD, **t** is none like You,	**1Ch 17:20**	369
nor is **t** any God besides You,	**1Ch 17:20**	369
and **t** was a precious stone in it;	**1Ch 20:2**	
And **t** was war with the Philistines	**1Ch 20:5**	
Again **t** was war at Gath, where	**1Ch 20:6**	
where **t** was a man of *great* stature	**1Ch 20:6**	
David built an altar to the LORD **t** and	**1Ch 21:26**	8033
Jebusite, he offered sacrifice **t**.	**1Ch 21:28**	8033
t are many workmen with you,	**1Ch 22:15**	
and the iron **t** is no limit.	**1Ch 22:16**	369
t *were* sixteen heads of fathers'	**1Ch 24:4**	
the divisions of the gatekeepers **t**	**1Ch 26:1**	
On the east **t** were six Levites, on	**1Ch 26:17**	
At the Parbar on the west **t** *were*	**1Ch 26:18**	
"Now behold, **t** *are*	**1Ch 28:21**	
like a shadow, and **t** is no hope.	**1Ch 29:15**	369
for God's tent of meeting was **t**,	**2Ch 1:3**	8033
was **t** before the tabernacle of the	**2Ch 1:5**	8033
Solomon went up **t** before the	**2Ch 1:6**	8033
and they are **t** to this day.	**2Ch 5:9**	8033
T was nothing in the ark except	**2Ch 5:10**	369
the two tablets which Moses put **t**	**2Ch 5:10**	
a house that My name might be **t**,	**2Ch 6:5**	8033
Jerusalem that My name might be **t**,	**2Ch 6:6**	8033
"**T** I have set the ark in which is	**2Ch 6:11**	8033
t is no god like You in heaven or	**2Ch 6:14**	369
that *You would* put Your name **t**,	**2Ch 6:20**	8033
heavens are shut up and **t** is no rain	**2Ch 6:26**	
"If **t** is famine in the land, if	**2Ch 6:28**	
in the land, if **t** is pestilence,	**2Ch 6:28**	
if **t** is blight or mildew,	**2Ch 6:28**	
if **t** is locust or grasshopper,	**2Ch 6:28**	
plague or whatever sickness **t** *is,*	**2Ch 6:28**	
(for **t** is no man who does not sin)	**2Ch 6:36**	369
for **t** he offered the burnt	**2Ch 7:7**	8033
the heavens so that **t** is no rain,	**2Ch 7:13**	
that My name may be **t** forever,	**2Ch 7:16**	8033
My heart will be **t** perpetually.	**2Ch 7:16**	8033
and settled the sons of Israel **t**.	**2Ch 8:2**	8033
and took from **t** four hundred and	**2Ch 8:18**	8033
t had never been spice like that	**2Ch 9:9**	
T *were* six steps to the throne	**2Ch 9:18**	
Twelve lions were standing **t**	**2Ch 9:19**	8033
of Israel, to put His name **t**.	**2Ch 12:13**	8033
And **t** *were* wars between Rehoboam	**2Ch 12:15**	
Now **t** was war between Abijah and	**2Ch 13:2**	
and **t** was no one at war with him	**2Ch 14:6**	369
t is no one besides You to help	**2Ch 14:11**	369
for **t** was much plunder in them.	**2Ch 14:14**	
"In those times **t** was no	**2Ch 15:5**	369
for **t** is reward for your work."	**2Ch 15:7**	3426
And **t** was no more war until the	**2Ch 15:19**	
"*Let* **t** *be* a treaty between you	**2Ch 16:3**	
"Is **t** not yet a prophet of the	**2Ch 18:6**	369
"**T** is yet one man by whom we may	**2Ch 18:7**	
"But **t** is *some* good in you, for	**2Ch 19:3**	4672
You a sanctuary **t** for Your name,	**2Ch 20:8**	
the spoil because **t** was so much.	**2Ch 20:25**	
for **t** they blessed the LORD.	**2Ch 20:26**	8033
So **t** was no one of the house of	**2Ch 22:9**	369
house, they put her to death **t**.	**2Ch 23:15**	8033
they saw that **t** was much money,	**2Ch 24:11**	
But **t** passed by a wild beast that	**2Ch 25:18**	
him to Lachish and killed him **t**.	**2Ch 25:27**	8033
and they hurried him out of **t**,	**2Ch 26:20**	8033
But a prophet of the LORD was **t**,	**2Ch 28:9**	8033
its villages, and they settled **t**.	**2Ch 28:18**	8033
T *were* also many burnt offerings	**2Ch 29:35**	
For **t** *were* many in the assembly	**2Ch 30:17**	
So **t** was great joy in Jerusalem,	**2Ch 30:26**	
because **t** was nothing like this in	**2Ch 30:26**	
t *were* men who were designated by	**2Ch 31:19**	
'Who *was* **t** among all the gods of	**2Ch 32:14**	
killed him **t** with the sword.	**2Ch 32:21**	8033
T had not been celebrated a Passover	**2Ch 35:18**	
His people, until **t** was no remedy.	**2Ch 36:16**	369
Whoever **t** is among you of all His	**2Ch 36:23**	
'Whoever **t** is among you of all His	**Ezr 1:3**	
and afterward **t** *was* a continual	**Ezr 3:5**	
house, which is **t** in Babylon,	**Ezr 5:17**	8536
t was written in it as follows:	**Ezr 6:2**	
the River, keep away from **t**.	**Ezr 6:6**	8536

who has caused His name to dwell **t** **Ezr 6:12** 8536
t *went up* Ezra son of Seraiah, **Ezr 7:1**
t will not be wrath against **Ezr 7:23**
I did not find any Levites **t**. **Ezr 8:15** 8033
I proclaimed a fast **t** at the river of **Ezr 8:21** 8033
princes and all Israel present **t** **Ezr 8:25**
and remained **t** three days. **Ezr 8:32** 8033
until **t** is no remnant nor any who **Ezr 9:14** 369
yet now **t** is hope for Israel in **Ezr 10:2** 3426
Although he went **t**, **Ezr 10:6** 8033
"But **t** are many people; it is the **Ezr 10:13**
Of the sons of Immer **t** *were* **Ezr 10:20**
Of Levites **t** *were* Jozabad, **Ezr 10:23**
Of the singers **t** *was* Eliashib; **Ezr 10:24**
Of Israel, of the sons of Parosh **t** **Ezr 10:25**
Of the sons of Nebo **t** *were* Jeiel, **Ezr 10:43**
"The remnant **t** in the province **Ne 1:3** 8033
I will gather them from **t** and will **Ne 1:9** 8033
to Jerusalem and was **t** three days. **Ne 2:11** 8033
and **t** was no animal with me except **Ne 2:12** 369
but **t** was no place for my mount to **Ne 2:14** 369
is failing, Yet **t** is much rubbish; **Ne 4:10**
of the trumpet, rally to us **t**. **Ne 4:20** 8033
Now **t** was a great outcry of the **Ne 5:1**
For **t** were those who said, **Ne 5:2** 3426
T were others who said, "We are **Ne 5:3** 3426
Also **t** were those who said, **Ne 5:4** 3426
were gathered **t** for the work. **Ne 5:16** 8033
Moreover, **t** *were* at my table one **Ne 5:17**
of whom **t** *were* 7,337; and they **Ne 7:67**
And **t** was great rejoicing. **Ne 8:17**
and on the eighth day **t** *was* a **Ne 8:18**
t are the utensils of the **Ne 10:39** 8033
For **t** *was* a commandment from **Ne 11:23**
t *were* leaders of the singers, **Ne 12:46**
and **t** was found written in it that **Ne 13:1**
and I returned **t** the utensils of **Ne 13:9** 8033
Also men of Tyre were living **t** *who* **Ne 13:16**
nations **t** was no king like him, **Ne 13:26**
T *were hangings of* fine white **Es 1:6**
to the law, **t** was no compulsion, **Es 1:8** 369
and **t** will be plenty of contempt **Es 1:18**
Now **t** was at the citadel in Susa **Es 2:5**
"**T** is a certain people scattered **Es 3:8** 3426
t was great mourning among the **Es 4:3**
For the Jews **t** was light and **Es 8:16**
t was gladness and joy for the **Es 8:17**
T was a man in the land of Uz whose **Jb 1:1**
Now **t** was a day when the sons of **Jb 1:6**
For **t** is no one like him on the **Jb 1:8** 369
womb, And naked I shall return **t**. **Jb 1:21** 8033
Again **t** was a day when the sons of **Jb 2:1** •
For **t** is no one like him on the **Jb 2:3** 369
"**T** the wicked cease from raging, **Jb 3:17** 8033
And **t** the weary are at rest. **Jb 3:17** 8033
"The small and the great are **t**, **Jb 3:19** 8033
Who long for death, but **t** is none, **Jb 3:21** 369
T *was* silence, then I heard a **Jb 4:16**
is **t** anyone who will answer you? **Jb 5:1** 3426
gate, And **t** is no deliverer. **Jb 5:4** 369
Or is **t** any taste in the white of **Jb 6:6** 3426
"For the despairing man **t** *should* **Jb 6:14**
They came **t** and were confounded. **Jb 6:20** 5704
"Desist now, let **t** be no injustice; **Jb 6:29**
"Is **t** injustice on my tongue? **Jb 6:30** 3426
"**T** is no umpire between us, Who **Jb 9:33** 3426
Yet **t** is no deliverance from Your **Jb 10:7** 369
would trust, because **t** is hope; **Jb 11:18** 3426
And **t** will be no escape for them; **Jb 11:20**
a man, and **t** can be no release. **Jb 12:14**
"For **t** is hope for a tree, When **Jb 14:7** 3426
"Is **t** *no* limit to windy words? **Jb 16:3**
t is no violence in my hands, **Jb 16:17**
And let **t** be no *resting* place for **Jb 16:18**
Who is **t** that will be my guarantor? **Jb 17:3**
"**T** dwells in his tent nothing of **Jb 18:15**
for help, but **t** is no justice. **Jb 19:7** 369
that you may know **t** is judgment." **Jb 19:29**
"Is **t** any pleasure to the **Jb 22:3**
"**T** the upright would reason with **Jb 23:7** 8033
I go forward but He is not **t**, **Jb 23:8**
"Is **t** any number to His troops? **Jb 25:3** 3426
"Surely **t** is a mine for silver And **Jb 28:1** 3426
And when Elihu saw that **t** was no **Jb 32:5** 369
t was no one who refuted Job, **Jb 32:12** 369
innocent and **t** is no guilt in me. **Jb 33:9**
"If **t** is an angel *as* mediator for **Jb 33:23** 3426
"**T** is no darkness or deep shadow **Jb 34:22** 369
"**T** they cry out, but He does not **Jb 35:12** 8033
t is yet more to be said in God's **Jb 36:2**
"From **t** he spies out food; **Jb 39:29** 8033
where the slain are, **t** is he." **Jb 39:30** 8033
the beasts of the field play **t**. **Jb 40:20** 8033
Around his teeth **t** is terror. **Jb 41:14**
"**T** is no deliverance for him in **Ps 3:2** 369
T is nothing reliable in what they **Ps 5:9** 369
For **t** is no mention of You in **Ps 6:5** 369
away, while **t** is none to deliver. **Ps 7:2** 369
If **t** is injustice in my hands, **Ps 7:3** 3426
All his thoughts are, "**T** is no God." **Ps 10:4** 369
has said in his heart, "**T** is no God." **Ps 14:1** 369
T is no one who does good. **Ps 14:1** 369
see if **t** are any who understand, **Ps 14:2** 3426
T is no one who does good, not **Ps 14:3** 369
T they are in great dread, For God **Ps 14:5** 8033
hand **t** are pleasures forever. **Ps 16:11**
for help, but **t** was none to save, **Ps 18:41** 369
T is no speech, nor are there **Ps 19:3** 369
is no speech, nor are **t** words; **Ps 19:3** 369
And **t** is nothing hidden from its **Ps 19:6** 369
In keeping them **t** is great reward. **Ps 19:11**
For **t** is none to help. **Ps 22:11** 369
"What profit is **t** in my blood, if **Ps 30:9**
in whose spirit **t** is no deceit! **Ps 32:2** 369
those who fear Him **t** is no want. **Ps 34:9** 369
T is no fear of God before his **Ps 36:1** 369
T the doers of iniquity have **Ps 36:12** 8033
for his place and he will not be **t**. **Ps 37:10**
T is no soundness in my flesh **Ps 38:3** 369
T is no health in my bones because **Ps 38:3** 369
And **t** is no soundness in my flesh. **Ps 38:7** 369
T is none to compare with You. **Ps 40:5** 369
T is a river whose streams make **Ps 46:4**
Panic seized them **t**, **Ps 48:6** 8033
pieces, and **t** will be none to deliver. **Ps 50:22** 369
has said in his heart, "**T** is no God," **Ps 53:1** 369
T is no one who does good. **Ps 53:1** 369
if **t** is anyone who understands, **Ps 53:2** 3426
T is no one who does good, not **Ps 53:3** 369
T they were in great fear *where* no **Ps 53:5** 8033
With whom **t** is no change, And who **Ps 55:19** 369
t is a reward for the righteous; **Ps 58:11**
t is a God who judges on earth!" **Ps 58:11** 3426
weary land where **t** is no water. **Ps 63:1**
T will be silence before You, *and* **Ps 65:1**
T let us rejoice in Him! **Ps 66:6** 8033
Almighty scattered the kings **t**, **Ps 68:14**
Surely the LORD will dwell **t** **Ps 68:16**
that the LORD God may dwell **t**. **Ps 68:18**
T is Benjamin, the youngest, **Ps 68:27** 8033
deep mire, and **t** is no foothold; **Ps 69:2** 369
for sympathy, but **t** was none, **Ps 69:20** 369
they may dwell **t** and possess it. **Ps 69:35** 8033
him, for **t** is no one to deliver." **Ps 71:11** 369
May **t** be abundance of grain in the **Ps 72:16**
For **t** are no pains in their death, **Ps 73:4** 369
is **t** knowledge with the Most High? **Ps 73:11** 3426
T is no longer any prophet, Nor is **Ps 74:9** 369
Nor is **t** any among us who knows **Ps 74:9**
T He broke the flaming arrows, The **Ps 76:3** 8033
Your arrows flashed here and **t**. **Ps 77:17**
And **t** was no one to bury them. **Ps 79:3** 369
Let **t** be known among the nations **Ps 79:10**
"Let **t** be no strange god among you; **Ps 81:9**
T is no one like You among the **Ps 86:8** 369
Nor are **t** any works like Yours. **Ps 86:8** 369
'This one was born **t**.' " **Ps 87:4** 8033
"This one was born **t**." **Ps 87:6** 8033
t is no unrighteousness in Him. **Ps 92:15**
T is the sea, great and broad, In **Ps 104:25** 2088
T the ships move along, *And* **Ps 104:26** 8033
and **t** came a swarm of flies *And* **Ps 105:31**
tribes **t** was not one who stumbled. **Ps 105:37** 369
T were those who dwelt in darkness **Ps 107:10**
stumbled and **t** was none to help. **Ps 107:12** 369
t He makes the hungry to dwell, **Ps 107:36** 8033
Let **t** be none to extend **Ps 109:12**
t thrones were set for judgment, **Ps 122:5** 8033
But **t** is forgiveness with You, **Ps 130:4**
with the LORD **t** is lovingkindness, **Ps 130:7**
"**T** I will cause the horn of David **Ps 132:17** 8033
For **t** the LORD commanded the **Ps 133:3** 8033
Nor is **t** any breath at all in **Ps 135:17** 3426
Babylon, **T** we sat down and wept, **Ps 137:1** 8033
For **t** our captors demanded of us **Ps 137:3** 8033
before **t** is a word on my tongue, **Ps 139:4** 369
If I ascend to heaven, You are **t**; **Ps 139:8** 8033
bed in Sheol, behold, You are **t**. **Ps 139:8**
Even **t** Your hand will lead me, And **Ps 139:10** 8033
When as yet **t** was not one of them. **Ps 139:16**
see if **t** be any hurtful way in me, **Ps 139:24**
For **t** is no one who regards me; **Ps 142:4** 369
T is no escape for me; **Ps 142:4**
Let **t** *be* no outcry in our streets! **Ps 144:14**
man, in whom **t** is no salvation. **Ps 146:3** 369
broken and **t** will be no healing. **Pr 6:15** 369
T are six things which the LORD **Pr 6:16** 1992a
T is nothing crooked or perverted **Pr 8:8** 369
"When **t** were no depths I was **Pr 8:24** 369
When **t** were no springs abounding **Pr 8:24** 369
established the heavens, I was **t**, **Pr 8:27** 8033
does not know that the dead are **t**, **Pr 9:18** 8033
When **t** are many words, **Pr 10:19**
wicked perish, **t** is joyful shouting. **Pr 11:10**
Where **t** is no guidance the people **Pr 11:14** 369
of counselors **t** is victory. **Pr 11:14**
T is one who scatters, and **Pr 11:24** 3426
And **t** is one who withholds what is **Pr 11:24**
T is one who speaks rashly like **Pr 12:18** 3426
And in *its* pathway **t** is no death. **Pr 12:28**
T is one who pretends to be rich, **Pr 13:7** 3426
among the upright **t** is good will. **Pr 14:9**
T is a way *which seems* right to a **Pr 14:12** 3426
In all labor **t** is profit, But mere **Pr 14:23**
the LORD **t** is strong confidence, **Pr 14:26**
T is a way *which seems* right to a **Pr 16:25** 3426
Why is **t** a price in the hand of a **Pr 17:16**
But **t** is a friend who sticks **Pr 18:24** 3426
your son while **t** is hope, **Pr 19:18** 3426
T is gold, and an abundance of **Pr 20:15** 3426
T is precious treasure and oil in **Pr 21:20**
T is no wisdom and no **Pr 21:30** 369
"**T** is a lion outside; **Pr 22:13**
Surely **t** is a future, And your **Pr 23:18** 3426
of counselors **t** is victory. **Pr 24:6**
find *it,* then **t** will be a future, **Pr 24:14** 3426
For **t** will be no future for the **Pr 24:20**
And **t** comes out a vessel for the **Pr 25:4**
T is more hope for a fool than for **Pr 26:12**
"**T** is a lion in the road! **Pr 26:13**
out, And where **t** is no whisperer, **Pr 26:20** 369
For **t** are seven abominations in **Pr 26:25**
And **t** *will be* goats' milk enough **Pr 27:27**
triumph, **t** is great glory, **Pr 28:12**
rages or laughs, and **t** is no rest. **Pr 29:9** 369
Where **t** is no vision, the people **Pr 29:18** 369
t will be no response. **Pr 29:19** 369
T is more hope for a fool than for **Pr 29:20**
T is a kind of *man* who curses his **Pr 30:11**
T is a kind who is pure in his own **Pr 30:12**
T is a kind—oh how lofty are his **Pr 30:13**
T is a kind of *man* whose teeth are **Pr 30:14**
T are three things that will not **Pr 30:15** 1992a
T are three things which are too **Pr 30:18** 1992a
T are three things which are **Pr 30:29** 1992a
to its place it rises **t** *again.* **Ec 1:5** 8033
rivers flow, **T** they flow again. **Ec 1:7** 8033
t is nothing new under the sun. **Ec 1:9** 369
Is **t** anything of which one might **Ec 1:10** 3426
T is no remembrance of earlier **Ec 1:11** 369
T will be for them no remembrance **Ec 1:11**
in much wisdom **t** is much grief, **Ec 1:18**
until I could see what good **t** is **Ec 2:3**
and **t** was no profit under the sun. **Ec 2:11** 369
For **t** is no lasting remembrance of **Ec 2:16** 369
When **t** is a man who has labored **Ec 2:21** 3426
T is nothing better for a man *than* **Ec 2:24** 369
T is an appointed time for **Ec 3:1**
And **t** is a time for every event **Ec 3:1**
What profit is **t** to the worker **Ec 3:9**
I know that **t** is nothing better **Ec 3:12** 369
t is nothing to add to it and **Ec 3:14** 369
and **t** is nothing to take from it, **Ec 3:14** 369
place of justice **t** is wickedness and **Ec 3:16** 8033
of righteousness **t** is wickedness. **Ec 3:16** 8033
matter and for every deed is **t**. **Ec 3:17** 8033
and **t** is no advantage for man over **Ec 3:19** 369
T was a certain man without a **Ec 4:8** 3426
yet **t** was no end to all his labor. **Ec 4:8** 369
t is not another to lift him up. **Ec 4:10** 369
T is no end to all the people, to **Ec 4:16** 369
and in many words **t** is emptiness. **Ec 5:7**
and **t** are higher officials over **Ec 5:8**
T is a grievous evil *which* I have **Ec 5:13** 3426
then **t** was nothing to support him. **Ec 5:14** 369
T is an evil which I have seen **Ec 6:1** 3426
For **t** are many words which **Ec 6:11** 3426
t is a righteous man who perishes **Ec 7:15** 3426
and **t** is a wicked man who prolongs **Ec 7:15** 3426
t is not a righteous man on earth **Ec 7:20** 369
For **t** is a proper time and **Ec 8:6** 3426
and **t** is no discharge in the time **Ec 8:8** 369
T is futility which is done on the **Ec 8:14** 3426
t are righteous men to whom it **Ec 8:14** 3426
t are evil men to whom it happens **Ec 8:14** 3426
for **t** is nothing good for a man **Ec 8:15** 369
T is one fate for the righteous **Ec 9:2**
that **t** is one fate for all men. **Ec 9:3**
joined with all the living, **t** is hope; **Ec 9:4** 3426
for **t** is no activity or planning **Ec 9:10** 369
T was a small city with few men in **Ec 9:14**
But **t** was found in it a poor wise **Ec 9:15**
T is an evil I have seen under the **Ec 10:5** 3426
t is no profit for the charmer. **Ec 10:11** 369
the tree falls, **t** it lies. **Ec 11:3** 8033
And **t** is no blemish in you. **SS 4:7** 369
"**T** are sixty queens and eighty **SS 6:8** 1992a
T I will give you my love. **SS 7:12** 8033
T your mother was in labor with **SS 8:5** 8033
T she was in labor *and* gave you **SS 8:5** 8033
the head **T** is nothing sound in it, **Is 1:6** 369
And **t** will be none to quench *them.* **Is 1:31** 369
t is no end to their treasures; **Is 2:7** 369
And **t** is no end to their chariots. **Is 2:7** 369
t is neither bread nor cloak; **Is 3:7** 369
perfume **t** will be putrefaction; **Is 3:24**
T will be a shelter to *give* shade **Is 4:6**
"What more was **t** to do for My **Is 5:4**
to field, Until **t** is no more room, **Is 5:8**
t is darkness *and* distress; **Is 5:30**
t will be a tenth portion in it, **Is 6:13**
t used to be a thousand vines, **Is 7:23**
People will come **t** with bows and **Is 7:24** 8033
you will not go **t** for fear of briars **Is 7:25** 8033
But **t** will be no *more* gloom for **Is 9:1**
T will be no end to the increase **Is 9:7** 369
And **t** was not one that flapped its **Is 10:14**
And **t** will be a highway from **Is 11:16**
Just as **t** was for Israel In the **Is 11:16**
will the Arab pitch *his* tent **t**, **Is 13:20** 8033
make *their flocks* lie down **t**. **Is 13:20** 8033
desert creatures will lie down **t**, **Is 13:21** 8033
owls; Ostriches also will live **t**, **Is 13:21** 8033
and shaggy goats will frolic **t**. **Is 13:21** 8033
t is no straggler in his ranks. **Is 14:31** 369
died out, **T** is no green thing. **Is 15:6**
In the vineyards also **t** will be no **Is 16:10**
And **t** will be no one to frighten **Is 17:2** 369
At evening time, behold, **t** *is* **Is 17:14**
T will be no work for Egypt Which **Is 19:15**
In that day **t** will be an altar to **Is 19:19**
In that day **t** will be a highway **Is 19:23**
Instead, **t** is gaiety and gladness, **Is 22:13**
T you will die And there your **Is 22:18** 8033
And **t** your splendid chariots will **Is 22:18** 8033
Tarshish, **T** is no more restraint. **Is 23:10** 369
even **t** you will find no rest." **Is 23:12** 8033

T is an outcry in the streets	**Is 24:11**	
T the calf will graze, And there	**Is 27:10**	8033
And **t** it will lie down and feed on	**Is 27:10**	8033
A little here, a little **t**.' "	**Is 28:10**	8033
line, A little here, a little **t**,"	**Is 28:13**	8033
on every high hill **t** will be streams	**Is 30:25**	
But **t** the majestic *One*, the LORD,	**Is 33:21**	8033
The people who dwell **t** will be	**Is 33:24**	
t is no one there *Whom* they may	**Is 34:12**	369
there is no one **t** *Whom* they may	**Is 34:12**	8033
the night monster will settle **t**	**Is 34:14**	8033
make its nest and lay *eggs* **t**,	**Is 34:15**	8033
the hawks will be gathered **t**,	**Is 34:15**	8033
A highway will be **t**,	**Is 35:8**	8033
No lion will be **t**, Nor will any	**Is 35:9**	8033
These will not be found **t**.	**Is 35:9**	8033
But the redeemed will walk **t**,	**Is 35:9**	
and **t** is no strength to deliver.	**Is 37:3**	369
to this city or shoot an arrow **t**;	**Is 37:33**	8033
T was nothing in his house nor in	**Is 39:2**	
t is nothing among my treasuries	**Is 39:4**	
"For **t** will be peace and truth in	**Is 39:8**	
are seeking water, but **t** is none,	**Is 41:17**	369
Surely **t** was no one who declared,	**Is 41:26**	369
t was no one who proclaimed,	**Is 41:26**	369
Surely **t** was no one who heard your	**Is 41:26**	369
"But when I look, **t** is no one,	**Is 41:28**	369
And **t** is no counselor among them	**Is 41:28**	369
Before Me **t** was no God formed, And	**Is 43:10**	
And **t** will be none after Me.	**Is 43:10**	
And **t** is no savior besides Me.	**Is 43:11**	369
t was no strange *god* among you;	**Is 43:12**	369
And **t** is none who can deliver out	**Is 43:13**	369
last, And **t** is no God besides Me.	**Is 44:6**	369
Is **t** any God besides Me, Or is	**Is 44:8**	3426
Me, Or is **t** any *other* Rock?	**Is 44:8**	369
nor is **t** knowledge or	**Is 44:19**	
"Is **t** not a lie in my right hand?"	**Is 44:20**	
"I am the LORD, and **t** is no other;	**Is 45:5**	369
Besides Me **t** is no God.	**Is 45:5**	369
sun That **t** is no one besides Me.	**Is 45:6**	369
I am the LORD, and **t** is no other,	**Is 45:6**	369
is with you, and **t** is none else,	**Is 45:14**	369
"I am the LORD, and **t** is none else.	**Is 45:18**	369
And **t** is no other God besides Me,	**Is 45:21**	369
T is none except Me.	**Is 45:21**	369
For I am God, and **t** is no other.	**Is 45:22**	369
set it in its place and it stands **t**.	**Is 46:7**	
For I am God, and **t** is no other;	**Is 46:9**	369
I am God, and **t** is no one like Me,	**Is 46:9**	
'I am, and **t** is no one besides me.	**Is 47:8**	657
'I am, and **t** is no one besides me.'	**Is 47:10**	657
T will be no coal to warm by *Nor*	**Is 47:14**	369
T is none to save you.	**Is 47:15**	369
the time it took place, I was **t**.	**Is 48:16**	8033
"**T** is no peace for the wicked,"	**Is 48:22**	369
"Why was **t** no man when I came?	**Is 50:2**	369
called, *why* was **t** none to answer?	**Is 50:2**	369
T is none to guide her among all	**Is 51:18**	369
Nor is **t** one to take her by the	**Is 51:18**	369
the first into Egypt to reside **t**;	**Is 52:4**	8033
Depart, depart, go out from **t**,	**Is 52:11**	8033
Nor was **t** any deceit in His mouth.	**Is 53:9**	
do not return **t** without watering the	**Is 55:10**	8033
also went up **t** to offer sacrifice.	**Is 57:7**	8033
"**T** is no peace," says my God,	**Is 57:21**	369
t is no justice in their tracks;	**Is 59:8**	369
hope for justice, but **t** is none,	**Is 59:11**	369
His sight that **t** was no justice.	**Is 59:15**	369
And He saw that **t** was no man, And	**Is 59:16**	369
that **t** was no one to intercede;	**Is 59:16**	369
the peoples **t** was no man with Me.	**Is 63:3**	369
looked, and **t** was no one to help,	**Is 63:5**	369
and **t** was no one to uphold;	**Is 63:5**	369
T is no one who calls on Your name,	**Is 64:7**	369
it, for **t** is benefit in it,'	**Is 65:8**	
it, And My servants will dwell **t**.	**Is 65:9**	8033
And **t** will no longer be heard in	**Is 65:19**	
"No longer will **t** be in it an	**Is 65:20**	
t has been such *a thing* as this!	**Jer 2:10**	
And **t** has been no spring rain.	**Jer 3:3**	
tree, and she was a harlot **t**.	**Jer 3:6**	8033
looked, and behold, **t** was no man,	**Jer 4:25**	369
man, If **t** is one who does justice,	**Jer 5:1**	3426
whose midst **t** is only oppression.	**Jer 6:6**	
'Peace, peace,' But **t** is no peace.	**Jer 6:14**	369
house and proclaim **t** this word and	**Jer 7:2**	8033
because **t** is no *other* place.	**Jer 7:32**	369
'Peace, peace,' But **t** is no peace.	**Jer 8:11**	369
"**T** will be no grapes on the vine And	**Jer 8:13**	369
cities And let us perish **t**,	**Jer 8:14**	8033
Adders, for which **t** is no charm,	**Jer 8:17**	369
Is **t** no balm in Gilead?	**Jer 8:22**	369
Is there no physician there?	**Jer 8:22**	369
Is there no physician **t**?	**Jer 8:22**	8033
T is none like You, O LORD;	**Jer 10:6**	369
kingdoms, **T** is none like You.	**Jer 10:7**	369
When He utters His voice, **t** *is* a	**Jer 10:13**	
And **t** is no breath in them.	**Jer 10:14**	
T is no one to stretch out my tent	**Jer 10:20**	369
T is no peace for anyone.	**Jer 12:12**	369
hide it **t** in a crevice of the rock	**Jer 13:4**	8033
and take from **t** the waistband which	**Jer 13:6**	8033
which I commanded you to hide **t**."	**Jer 13:6**	8033
up, And **t** is no one to open *them*;	**Jer 13:19**	369
t has been no rain on the land;	**Jer 14:4**	
her young, Because **t** is no grass.	**Jer 14:5**	
eyes fail For **t** is no vegetation.	**Jer 14:6**	369
'**T** will be no sword or famine in	**Jer 14:15**	
and **t** will be no one to bury	**Jer 14:16**	369
Are **t** any among the idols of the	**Jer 14:22**	3426
and **t** you will serve other gods	**Jer 16:13**	8033
then **t** will come in through the	**Jer 17:25**	
and **t** I will announce My words to	**Jer 18:2**	8033
the potter's house, and **t** he was,	**Jer 18:3**	2009
and proclaim **t** the words that I	**Jer 19:2**	8033
t is no *other* place for burial.	**Jer 19:11**	369
enter Babylon, and **t** you will die and	**Jer 20:6**	8033
die and **t** you will be buried,	**Jer 20:6**	8033
of Judah, and **t** speak this word	**Jer 22:1**	8033
"He will never return **t**;	**Jer 22:11**	8033
t he will die and not see this	**Jer 22:12**	8033
were not born, and **t** you will die.	**Jer 22:26**	8033
Is **t** *anything* in the hearts of the	**Jer 23:26**	3426
t was also a man who prophesied in	**Jer 26:20**	
be **t** until the day I visit them,'	**Jer 27:22**	8033
multiply **t** and do not decrease.	**Jer 29:6**	8033
Of dread, and **t** is no peace.	**Jer 30:5**	369
day is great, **T** is none like it;	**Jer 30:7**	369
'**T** is no one to plead your cause;	**Jer 30:13**	369
"For **t** will be a day when	**Jer 31:6**	3426
"**T** is hope for your future,"	**Jer 31:17**	3426
"How long will you go here and **t**,	**Jer 31:22**	2559
he will be **t** until I visit him,"	**Jer 32:5**	8033
t will be heard in this place,	**Jer 33:10**	
'**T** will again be in this place	**Jer 33:12**	
behold, all the officials were sitting **t**	**Jer 36:12**	8033
and **t** were *only* wounded men left	**Jer 37:10**	
some property **t** among the people.	**Jer 37:12**	
		4480, 8033
the son of Hananiah was **t**;	**Jer 37:13**	8033
and Jeremiah stayed **t** many days.	**Jer 37:16**	8033
"Is **t** a word from the LORD?"	**Jer 37:17**	3426
And Jeremiah said, "**T** is!"	**Jer 37:17**	3426
scribe, that I may not die **t**."	**Jer 37:20**	8033
t was no water but only mud,	**Jer 38:6**	369
t is no more bread in the city."	**Jer 38:9**	369
and took from **t** worn-out clothes	**Jer 38:11**	8033
house of Jonathan to die **t**.' "	**Jer 38:26**	8033
eating bread together **t** in Mizpah,	**Jer 41:1**	8033
the Chaldeans who were found **t**,	**Jer 41:3**	8033
for bread, and we will stay **t**";	**Jer 42:14**	8033
Egypt and go in to reside **t**,	**Jer 42:15**	8033
overtake you **t** in the land of Egypt;	**Jer 42:16**	8033
follow closely after you **t** *in* Egypt,	**Jer 42:16**	8033
and you will die **t**.	**Jer 42:16**	8033
to reside **t** will die by the sword,	**Jer 42:17**	8033
are not to enter Egypt to reside **t**	**Jer 43:2**	8033
and he will depart from **t** safely.	**Jer 43:12**	8033
the land of Egypt to reside **t**,	**Jer 44:12**	8033
'So **t** will be no refugees or	**Jer 44:14**	
entered the land of Egypt to reside **t**	**Jer 44:14**	8033
gone to the land of Egypt to reside **t**	**Jer 44:28**	8033
For **t** will be a slaughter for the	**Jer 46:10**	
T is no healing for you.	**Jer 46:11**	369
They cried **t**, 'Pharaoh king of Egypt	**Jer 46:17**	8033
T He has assigned it."	**Jer 47:7**	8033
"**T** is praise for Moab no longer;	**Jer 48:2**	369
t are gashes on all the hands and	**Jer 48:37**	
t is lamentation everywhere;	**Jer 48:38**	3605
t no longer any wisdom in Teman?	**Jer 49:7**	369
I will bring you down from **t**,"	**Jer 49:16**	8033
"no one will live **t**,	**Jer 49:18**	8033
T is an outcry! The noise of it has	**Jer 49:21**	
T is anxiety by the sea, It cannot	**Jer 49:23**	
No one will live **t**,	**Jer 49:33**	8033
And **t** will be no nation To which	**Jer 49:36**	8033
and **t** will be no inhabitant in it.	**Jer 50:3**	
From **t** she will be taken captive.	**Jer 50:9**	8033
of Israel, but **t** will be none;	**Jer 50:20**	369
T is a sound of fugitives and	**Jer 50:28**	
on every side, Let **t** be no escape.	**Jer 50:29**	
the desert creatures will live **t**	**Jer 50:39**	
"No man will live **t**,	**Jer 50:40**	8033
When He utters His voice, **t** *is* a	**Jer 51:16**	
And **t** is no breath in them.	**Jer 51:17**	
so that **t** will be nothing dwelling	**Jer 51:62**	
t was no food for the people	**Jer 52:6**	
T were ninety-six exposed	**Jer 52:23**	
t were 4,600 persons in all.	**Jer 52:30**	
Look and see if **t** is any pain like	**La 1:12**	3426
T is no one to comfort her;	**La 1:17**	369
T is no one to comfort me;	**La 1:21**	369
And **t** was no one who escaped or	**La 2:22**	
in the dust, Perhaps **t** is hope.	**La 3:29**	3426
Who is **t** who speaks and it comes	**La 3:37**	2088
are worn out, **t** is no rest for us.	**La 5:5**	
T is no one to deliver us from	**La 5:8**	369
and **t** the hand of the LORD came	**Ezk 1:3**	8033
Within it **t** were figures	**Ezk 1:5**	
t was something that looked like	**Ezk 1:13**	
t was one wheel on the earth	**Ezk 1:15**	
the heads of the living beings **t**	**Ezk 1:22**	
And **t** came a voice from above the	**Ezk 1:25**	
t was something resembling a throne,	**Ezk 1:26**	
and **t** *was* a radiance around Him.	**Ezk 1:27**	
and I sat **t** seven days where they	**Ezk 3:15**	8033
The hand of the LORD was on me **t**,	**Ezk 3:22**	8033
and **t** I will speak to you."	**Ezk 3:22**	8033
glory of the LORD was standing **t**,	**Ezk 3:23**	8033
seek peace, but **t** will be none.	**Ezk 7:25**	369
hand of the Lord GOD fell on me **t**.	**Ezk 8:1**	8033
from His loins and downward **t** *was*	**Ezk 8:2**	
glory of the God of Israel *was* **t**,	**Ezk 8:4**	8033
were sitting **t** weeping for Tammuz.	**Ezk 8:14**	8033
t *were* twenty-five men at	**Ezk 11:1**	
"When they come **t**, they will	**Ezk 11:18**	8033
not see it, though he will die **t**.	**Ezk 12:13**	8033
"For **t** will no longer be any	**Ezk 12:24**	
when **t** is no peace.	**Ezk 13:10**	369
T will also be in My anger a	**Ezk 13:13**	
peace for her when **t** is no peace,'	**Ezk 13:16**	369
which you hunt lives **t** as birds and	**Ezk 13:20**	8033
"But **t** was another great eagle	**Ezk 17:7**	
and enter into judgment with him **t**	**Ezk 17:20**	8033
t is not in it a strong branch,	**Ezk 19:14**	
they offered **t** their sacrifices and	**Ezk 20:28**	8033
and **t** they presented the	**Ezk 20:28**	8033
T also they made their soothing	**Ezk 20:28**	8033
and **t** they poured out their	**Ezk 20:28**	8033
and **t** I will enter into judgment	**Ezk 20:35**	8033
"**t** the whole house of Israel, all	**Ezk 20:40**	8033
t I will accept them and there I will	**Ezk 20:40**	8033
and **t** I will seek your	**Ezk 20:40**	8033
"**T** you will remember your ways	**Ezk 20:43**	8033
"For **t** *is* a testing; and what	**Ezk 21:13**	
in My wrath and I will lay you **t**	**Ezk 22:20**	
"**T** is a conspiracy of her	**Ezk 22:25**	
"Son of man, **t** were two women,	**Ezk 23:2**	
t their breasts were pressed and	**Ezk 23:3**	8033
and **t** their virgin bosom was	**Ezk 23:3**	8033
To the pot in which **t** is rust And	**Ezk 24:6**	
T is no secret that is a match for	**Ezk 28:3**	
And I placed you **t**. You were on	**Ezk 28:14**	
"And **t** will be no more for the	**Ezk 28:24**	
t they will be a lowly kingdom.	**Ezk 29:14**	8033
And **t** will no longer be a prince	**Ezk 30:13**	
I break **t** the yoke bars of Egypt.	**Ezk 30:18**	8033
"Assyria is **t** and all her company;	**Ezk 32:22**	8033
"Elam is **t** and all her hordes	**Ezk 32:24**	8033
and all their hordes are **t**;	**Ezk 32:26**	8033
"**T** also is Edom, its kings and	**Ezk 32:29**	8033
"**T** also are the chiefs of the	**Ezk 32:30**	8033
and **t** was no one to search or seek	**Ezk 34:6**	369
T they will lie down on good	**Ezk 34:14**	8033
them,' although the LORD was **t**,	**Ezk 35:10**	8033
t *were* very many on the surface	**Ezk 37:2**	
as I prophesied, **t** was a noise,	**Ezk 37:7**	
but **t** was no breath in them.	**Ezk 37:8**	369
t will surely be a great earthquake	**Ezk 38:19**	
give Gog a burial ground **t** in Israel,	**Ezk 39:11**	8033
bury Gog **t** with all his horde,	**Ezk 39:11**	8033
leave none of them **t** any longer.	**Ezk 39:28**	8033
was upon me and He brought me **t**.	**Ezk 40:1**	8033
and on it to the south **t** *was* a	**Ezk 40:2**	
So He brought me **t**;	**Ezk 40:3**	8033
t was a man whose appearance was	**Ezk 40:3**	
t was a wall on the outside of the	**Ezk 40:5**	
and **t** *were* five cubits between	**Ezk 40:7**	
T *was* a barrier *wall* one	**Ezk 40:12**	
T *were* shuttered windows	**Ezk 40:16**	
And **t** *were* windows all around	**Ezk 40:16**	
t *were* chambers and a pavement	**Ezk 40:17**	
t was a gate toward the south;	**Ezk 40:24**	
T *were* seven steps going up to it,	**Ezk 40:26**	
T *were* porches all around,	**Ezk 40:30**	
t they rinse the burnt offering.	**Ezk 40:38**	8033
For the burnt offering **t** *were*	**Ezk 40:42**	
Also **t** were carved on them, on the	**Ezk 41:25**	
and **t** *was* a threshold of wood on	**Ezk 41:25**	
T *were* latticed windows and palm	**Ezk 41:26**	
facing the building, **t** *were* chambers.	**Ezk 42:10**	
T they shall lay the most holy	**Ezk 42:13**	8033
without laying **t** their garments	**Ezk 42:14**	8033
"Out of this **t** shall be for the	**Ezk 45:2**	
t *was* a place at the extreme rear	**Ezk 46:19**	8033
in every corner of the court **t** *was*	**Ezk 46:21**	
In the four corners of the court **t**	**Ezk 46:22**	
T *was* a row *of masonry* round	**Ezk 46:23**	
on the bank of the river **t** *were*	**Ezk 47:7**	
And **t** will be very many fish, for	**Ezk 47:9**	
many fish, for these waters go **t** and	**Ezk 47:9**	8033
from Engedi to Eneglaim **t** will be	**Ezk 47:10**	
t you shall give *him* his	**Ezk 47:23**	8033
'The LORD is **t**.' "	**Ezk 48:35**	8033
me, **t** is only one decree for you.	**Da 2:9**	
"**T** is not a man on earth who	**Da 2:10**	383
and **t** is no one else who could	**Da 2:11**	383
t is a God in heaven who reveals	**Da 2:28**	383
t was a single great statue;	**Da 2:31**	
"After you **t** will arise	**Da 2:39**	
"Then **t** will be a fourth kingdom	**Da 2:40**	
"**T** are certain Jews whom you have	**Da 3:12**	383
and what god is **t** who can deliver	**Da 3:15**	
inasmuch as **t** is no other god who	**Da 3:29**	383
t *was* a tree in the midst of	**Da 4:10**	
in case **t** may be a prolonging of	**Da 4:27**	
"**T** is a man in your kingdom in	**Da 5:11**	383
nor was **t** anyone to rescue from	**Da 8:4**	369
and **t** was none to rescue the ram	**Da 8:7**	
and in its place **t** came up four	**Da 8:8**	
and **t** was none to explain *it*.	**Da 8:27**	369
for under the whole heaven **t** has	**Da 9:12**	
until Messiah the Prince **t** *will be*	**Da 9:25**	
even to the end **t** will be war;	**Da 9:26**	
t was a certain man dressed in	**Da 10:5**	
left **t** with the kings of Persia.	**Da 10:13**	8033
t remains just now no strength in	**Da 10:17**	
Yet **t** is no one who stands firmly	**Da 10:21**	369
for **t** will be no strength to make	**Da 11:15**	369
And **t** will be a time of distress	**Da 12:1**	
t was a nation until that time;	**Da 12:1**	
t *will be* 1,290 days.	**Da 12:11**	
give her her vineyards from **t**,	**Hos 2:15**	8033
sing **t** as in the days of her youth,	**Hos 2:15**	8033
Because **t** is no faithfulness or	**Hos 4:1**	369
T *is* swearing, deception,	**Hos 4:2**	

and **t** will be none to deliver.	**Hos 5:14**	369
T they have dealt treacherously	**Hos 6:7**	8033
Ephraim's harlotry is **t**,	**Hos 6:10**	8033
t is a harvest appointed for you,	**Hos 6:11**	
And **t** is *only* hostility in the	**Hos 9:8**	
Indeed, I came to hate them **t**!	**Hos 9:15**	8033
have sinned, O Israel; **T** they stand!	**Hos 10:9**	8033
at Bethel And **t** He spoke with us,	**Hos 12:4**	8033
Is **t** iniquity *in* Gilead?	**Hos 12:11**	
When Ephraim spoke, **t** *was*	**Hos 13:1**	
Me, For **t** is no savior besides Me.	**Hos 13:4**	369
T I will also devour them like a	**Hos 13:8**	8033
Because **t** is no pasture for them;	**Jl 1:18**	369
So **t** is a great and mighty people;	**Jl 2:2**	
T has never been *anything* like it,	**Jl 2:2**	
Nor will **t** be again after it To	**Jl 2:2**	
LORD your God, And **t** is no other;	**Jl 2:27**	369
T will be those who escape,	**Jl 2:32**	
will enter into judgment with them **t**	**Jl 3:2**	8033
nations, And gather yourselves **t**.	**Jl 3:11**	8033
For **t** I will sit to judge All the	**Jl 3:12**	8033
ground when **t** is no bait in it?	**Am 3:5**	369
withheld the rain from you While **t**	**Am 4:7**	
T is none to raise her up.	**Am 5:2**	369
"**T** is wailing in all the plazas,	**Am 5:16**	
"And in all the vineyards **t** *is*	**Am 5:17**	
And go from **t** to Hamath the great,	**Am 6:2**	8033
and **t** eat bread and there do your	**Am 7:12**	8033
bread and **t** do your prophesying!	**Am 7:12**	8033
t *was* a basket of summer fruit.	**Am 8:1**	
From **t** will My hand take them;	**Am 9:2**	8033
From **t** will I bring them down.	**Am 9:2**	8033
them out and take them from **t**;	**Am 9:3**	8033
From **t** I will command the serpent	**Am 9:3**	8033
From **t** I will command the sword	**Am 9:4**	8033
From **t** I will bring you down,"	**Ob 1:4**	8033
(**T** is no understanding in him.)	**Ob 1:7**	369
Zion **t** will be those who escape,	**Ob 1:17**	
So that **t** will be no survivor of	**Ob 1:18**	
and **t** was a great storm on the sea	**Jon 1:4**	
T he made a shelter for himself	**Jon 4:5**	8033
the great city in which **t** are more	**Jon 4:11**	3426
Because **t** is no answer from God.	**Mi 3:7**	369
Is **t** no king among you, Or has	**Mi 4:9**	369
T you will be rescued;	**Mi 4:10**	8033
T the LORD will redeem you From	**Mi 4:10**	8033
tears, And **t** is none to rescue.	**Mi 5:8**	369
t yet a man in the wicked house,	**Mi 6:10**	
T is not a cluster of grapes to	**Mi 7:1**	369
And **t** is no upright *person* among	**Mi 7:2**	369
For **t** is no limit to the treasure	**Na 2:9**	369
T fire will consume you, The sword	**Na 3:15**	8033
And **t** is no one to regather *them.*	**Na 3:18**	369
T is no relief for your breakdown,	**Na 3:19**	369
t is no breath at all inside it.	**Hab 2:19**	369
And **t** is the hiding of His power.	**Hab 3:4**	8033
And **t** be no fruit on the vines,	**Hab 3:17**	369
And **t** be no cattle in the stalls,	**Hab 3:17**	369
"**T** will be the sound of a cry	**Zph 1:10**	
So that **t** will be no inhabitant.	**Zph 2:5**	369
am, and **t** is no one besides me."	**Zph 2:15**	657
but **t** *is* not *enough* to be	**Hg 1:6**	
but **t** *is* not *enough* to become	**Hg 1:6**	
and what they offer **t** is unclean.	**Hg 2:14**	8033
measures, **t** would be only ten;	**Hg 2:16**	
measures, **t** would be *only* twenty.	**Hg 2:16**	
t *were* four horns.	**Zch 1:18**	
t *was* a man with a measuring line	**Zch 2:1**	
Ho **t**! Flee from the land of the north	**Zch 2:6**	1945
t *was* a flying scroll.	**Zch 5:1**	
and **t** two women were coming out	**Zch 5:9**	
be set **t** on her own pedestal."	**Zch 5:11**	8033
'For before those days **t** was no	**Zch 8:10**	
t was no peace because of his	**Zch 8:10**	369
'For **t** *will be* peace for	**Zch 8:12**	
because **t** is no shepherd.	**Zch 10:2**	369
T is a sound of the shepherds'	**Zch 11:3**	
T is a sound of the young lions'	**Zch 11:3**	
"In that day **t** will be great	**Zch 12:11**	
that day **t** will be no light;	**Zch 14:6**	
at evening time **t** will be light.	**Zch 14:7**	
it, and **t** will no longer be a curse,	**Zch 14:11**	
hosts, **t** will be no rain on them.	**Zch 14:17**	
In that day **t** will *be inscribed* on	**Zch 14:20**	
And **t** will no longer be a	**Zch 14:21**	
"Oh that **t** were one among you who	**Mal 1:10**	
so that **t** may be food in My house,	**Mal 3:10**	
and remain **t** until I tell you;	**Mt 2:13**	*1563*
remained **t** until the death of Herod	**Mt 2:15**	*1563*
Herod, he was afraid to go **t**.	**Mt 2:22**	*1563*
from **t** He saw two other brothers,	**Mt 4:21**	*1564*
and **t** remember that your brother	**Mt 5:23**	*2546*
leave your offering **t** before the altar	**Mt 5:24**	*1563*
you, you will not come out of **t**	**Mt 5:26**	*1564*
is, **t** your heart will be also.	**Mt 6:21**	*1563*
what man is **t** among you who,	**Mt 7:9**	
and **t** are many who enter through it.	**Mt 7:13**	*1510*
and **t** are few who find it.	**Mt 7:14**	*1510*
in that place **t** will be weeping	**Mt 8:12**	*1563*
t arose a great storm on the sea,	**Mt 8:24**	
Now **t** was a herd of many swine	**Mt 8:30**	
As Jesus went on from **t**,	**Mt 9:9**	*1564*
As Jesus went on from **t**,	**Mt 9:27**	*1564*
for **t** is nothing concealed that will	**Mt 10:26**	
He departed from **t** to teach and	**Mt 11:1**	*1564*
among those born of women **t** has	**Mt 11:11**	
Departing from **t**,	**Mt 12:9**	*1564*
And a man *was* **t** whose hand was	**Mt 12:10**	
"What man is **t** among you	**Mt 12:11**	
aware of *this,* withdrew from **t**.	**Mt 12:15**	*1564*
itself, and they go in and live **t**;	**Mt 12:45**	*1563*
in that place **t** will be weeping	**Mt 13:42**	
t will be weeping and gnashing of	**Mt 13:50**	*1563*
parables, He departed from **t**.	**Mt 13:53**	*1564*
He did not do many miracles **t**	**Mt 13:58**	*1563*
He withdrew from **t** in a boat	**Mt 14:13**	*1564*
T were about five thousand men who	**Mt 14:21**	
it was evening, He was **t** alone.	**Mt 14:23**	*1563*
Jesus went away from **t**,	**Mt 15:21**	*1564*
Departing from **t**,	**Mt 15:29**	*1564*
on the mountain, He was sitting **t**.	**Mt 15:29**	*1563*
"And in the morning, '**T** *will be*	**Mt 16:3**	
t are some of those who are	**Mt 16:28**	
'Move from here to **t**,'	**Mt 17:20**	*1563*
My name, I am **t** in their midst."	**Mt 18:20**	*1563*
Him, and He healed them **t**.	**Mt 19:2**	*1563*
"For **t** are eunuchs who were born	**Mt 19:12**	
and **t** are eunuchs who were made	**Mt 19:12**	
and **t** are *also* eunuchs who made	**Mt 19:12**	
hands on them, He departed from **t**.	**Mt 19:15**	*1564*
T is *only* One who is good;	**Mt 19:17**	
what then will **t** be for us?"	**Mt 19:27**	
you will find a donkey tied **t**	**Mt 21:2**	
to Bethany, and spent the night **t**.	**Mt 21:17**	*1563*
"No longer shall **t** ever be *any*	**Mt 21:19**	
T was a landowner who PLANTED A	**Mt 21:33**	
and as many as you find **t**,	**Mt 22:9**	
he saw a man **t** who was not dressed in	**Mt 22:11**	*1563*
in that place **t** will be weeping	**Mt 22:13**	*1563*
(who say **t** is no resurrection)	**Mt 22:23**	
"Now **t** were seven brothers with us;	**Mt 22:25**	
and in various places **t** will be	**Mt 24:7**	
t will be a great tribulation,	**Mt 24:21**	
'**T** *He is,*' do not believe *him.*	**Mt 24:23**	*5602*
is, **t** the vultures will gather.	**Mt 24:28**	*1563*
t will be two men in the field;	**Mt 24:40**	
t will be weeping and gnashing	**Mt 24:51**	*1563*
"But at midnight **t** was a shout,	**Mt 25:6**	
t will not be enough for us and	**Mt 25:9**	
in that place **t** will be weeping	**Mt 25:30**	*1563*
here while I go over **t** and pray."	**Mt 26:36**	*1563*
him and said to those who were **t**,	**Mt 26:71**	*1563*
began to keep watch over Him **t**.	**Mt 27:36**	*1563*
some of those who were standing **t**,	**Mt 27:47**	*1563*
Many women were **t** looking on	**Mt 27:55**	*1563*
t came a rich man from Arimathea,	**Mt 27:57**	
And Mary Magdalene was **t**,	**Mt 27:61**	*1563*
into Galilee, **t** you will see Him;	**Mt 28:7**	*1563*
and **t** they will see Me."	**Mt 28:10**	*1563*
Just then **t** was a man in their	**Mk 1:23**	
a secluded place, and was praying **t**.	**Mk 1:35**	*2546*
so that I may preach **t** also;	**Mk 1:38**	*1563*
so that **t** was no longer room,	**Mk 2:2**	
some of the scribes were sitting **t**	**Mk 2:6**	*1563*
for **t** were many of them, and they	**Mk 2:15**	
and a man was **t** whose hand was	**Mk 3:1**	*1563*
And **t** arose a fierce gale of wind,	**Mk 4:37**	
Now **t** was a large herd of swine	**Mk 5:11**	
Jesus went out from **t**	**Mk 6:1**	*1564*
And He could do no miracle **t**	**Mk 6:5**	*1563*
stay **t** until you leave town.	**Mk 6:10**	*1563*
to you, as you go out from **t**,	**Mk 6:11**	*1564*
(For **t** were many *people* coming and	**Mk 6:31**	
and ran **t** together on foot	**Mk 6:33**	*1563*
cities, and got **t** ahead of them.	**Mk 6:33**	*4281*
T were five thousand men who ate	**Mk 6:44**	
country and began to carry here and **t**	**Mk 6:55**	*4064*
and **t** are many other things which	**Mk 7:4**	
t is nothing outside the man which	**Mk 7:15**	
Jesus got up and went away from **t**	**Mk 7:24**	*1564*
when **t** was again a large crowd	**Mk 8:1**	
About four thousand were **t**;	**Mk 8:9**	
t are some of those who are	**Mk 9:1**	
From **t** they went out and *began*	**Mk 9:30**	*2547*
for **t** is no one who will perform	**Mk 9:39**	
from **t** to the region of Judea and	**Mk 10:1**	*1564*
t is no one who has left house or	**Mk 10:29**	
you will find a colt tied **t**, on	**Mk 11:2**	
(who say that **t** is no resurrection)	**Mk 12:18**	
"**T** were seven brothers;	**Mk 12:20**	
T is no other commandment greater	**Mk 12:31**	
AND **T** IS NO ONE ELSE BESIDES HIM;	**Mk 12:32**	
t will be earthquakes in various	**Mk 13:8**	
t will *also* be famines.	**Mk 13:8**	
'Behold, *He is* **t**'; do not believe *him;*	**Mk 13:21**	*1563*
t might be a riot of the people."	**Mk 14:2**	
t came a woman with an alabaster	**Mk 14:3**	
prepare for us **t**."	**Mk 14:15**	*1563*
T were also *some* women looking on	**Mk 15:40**	
and **t** *were* many other women who	**Mk 15:41**	
t you will see Him, just as He	**Mk 16:7**	*1563*
t was a priest named	**Lk 1:5**	
that **t** would be a fulfillment of what	**Lk 1:45**	
"**T** is no one among your relatives	**Lk 1:61**	
While they were **t**,	**Lk 2:6**	*1563*
because **t** was no room for them in	**Lk 2:7**	
In the same region **t** were *some*	**Lk 2:8**	
t has been born for you a Savior	**Lk 2:11**	
And suddenly **t** appeared with the	**Lk 2:13**	
t was a man in Jerusalem whose	**Lk 2:25**	
And **t** was a prophetess, Anna the	**Lk 2:36**	
they went up **t** according to	**Lk 2:42**	
t were many widows in Israel in	**Lk 4:25**	
"And **t** were many lepers in Israel	**Lk 4:27**	
In the synagogue **t** was a man	**Lk 4:33**	
t *was* a man covered with leprosy;	**Lk 5:12**	
and **t** were *some* Pharisees and	**Lk 5:17**	
and teachers of the law sitting **t**,	**Lk 5:17**	
and **t** was a great crowd of	**Lk 5:29**	
and **t** was a man there whose right	**Lk 6:6**	
there was a man **t** whose right hand	**Lk 6:6**	*1563*
and **t** *was* a large crowd of His	**Lk 6:17**	
"For **t** is no good tree which	**Lk 6:43**	
t is no one greater than John;	**Lk 7:28**	
t was a woman in the city who was	**Lk 7:37**	
Now **t** was a herd of many swine	**Lk 8:32**	
swine feeding **t** on the mountain;	**Lk 8:32**	*1563*
t came a man named Jairus,	**Lk 8:41**	
Whatever house you enter, stay **t**	**Lk 9:4**	*1563*
t were about five thousand men.)	**Lk 9:14**	
t are some of those standing here	**Lk 9:27**	
"If a man of peace is **t**,	**Lk 10:6**	*1563*
itself, and they go in and live **t**;	**Lk 11:26**	*1563*
When He left **t**,	**Lk 11:53**	*2547*
"But **t** is nothing covered up that	**Lk 12:2**	
and **t** I will store all my grain	**Lk 12:18**	*1563*
is, **t** your heart will be also.	**Lk 12:34**	*1563*
on *your* way **t** make an effort	**Lk 12:58**	
you will not get out of **t** until	**Lk 12:59**	*1564*
Now on the same occasion **t** were	**Lk 13:1**	
t was a woman who for eighteen	**Lk 13:11**	
"**T** are six days in which work	**Lk 13:14**	
are **t** *just* a few who are being	**Lk 13:23**	
"In that place **t** will be weeping	**Lk 13:28**	*1510*
And **t** in front of Him was a	**Lk 14:2**	*2400*
been done, and still **t** is room.'	**Lk 14:22**	
t will be *more* joy in heaven over	**Lk 15:7**	
t is joy in the presence of the	**Lk 15:10**	
and **t** he squandered his estate	**Lk 15:13**	*1563*
"**T** was a rich man who had	**Lk 16:1**	
"Now **t** was a rich man,	**Lk 16:19**	
and you **t** is a great chasm fixed,	**Lk 16:26**	
none may cross over from **t** to us.'	**Lk 16:26**	*1564*
"Were **t** not ten cleansed?	**Lk 17:17**	
'Look, here *it is!*' or, '**T** *it is!*'	**Lk 17:21**	*1563*
"They will say to you, 'Look **t**!	**Lk 17:23**	*1563*
t will be two in one bed;	**Lk 17:34**	
"**T** will be two women grinding at	**Lk 17:35**	
t also the vultures will be	**Lk 17:37**	*1563*
saying, "In a certain city **t** was a	**Lk 18:2**	*1510*
"**T** was a widow in that city,	**Lk 18:3**	
t is no one who has left house or	**Lk 18:29**	
t was a man called by the name of	**Lk 19:2**	
t, as you enter, you will find a	**Lk 19:30**	*3739*
Now **t** came to Him some of the	**Lk 20:27**	
say that **t** is no resurrection),	**Lk 20:27**	
"Now **t** were seven brothers;	**Lk 20:29**	
in which **t** will not be left one stone	**Lk 21:6**	
and **t** will be great earthquakes,	**Lk 21:11**	
and **t** will be terrors and great	**Lk 21:11**	
for **t** will be great distress upon	**Lk 21:23**	
"**T** will be signs in sun and moon	**Lk 21:25**	
furnished upper room; prepare it **t**."	**Lk 22:12**	*1563*
And **t** arose also a dispute among	**Lk 22:24**	
and the scribes were standing **t**,	**Lk 23:10**	
t they crucified Him and the	**Lk 23:33**	*1563*
Now **t** was also an inscription	**Lk 23:38**	
of the criminals who were hanged **t**	**Lk 23:39**	
T came a man sent from God, whose	**Jn 1:6**	
T was the true Light which, coming	**Jn 1:9**	
in whom **t** is no deceit!"	**Jn 1:47**	*1510*
On the third day **t** was a	**Jn 2:1**	
and the mother of Jesus was **t**;	**Jn 2:1**	*1563*
Now **t** were six stone waterpots set	**Jn 2:6**	
there were six stone waterpots set **t**	**Jn 2:6**	*1563*
and they stayed **t** a few days.	**Jn 2:12**	*1563*
Now **t** was a man of the Pharisees,	**Jn 3:1**	
and **t** He was spending time with	**Jn 3:22**	*1563*
because **t** was much water there;	**Jn 3:23**	
because there was much water **t**;	**Jn 3:23**	*1563*
Therefore **t** arose a discussion on	**Jn 3:25**	*1096*
and Jacob's well was **t**.	**Jn 4:6**	*1563*
T came a woman of Samaria to draw	**Jn 4:7**	
'**T** are yet four months, and *then*	**Jn 4:35**	
and He stayed **t** two days.	**Jn 4:40**	*1563*
He went forth from **t** into Galilee.	**Jn 4:43**	*1564*
t was a royal official	**Jn 4:46**	
things **t** was a feast of the Jews,	**Jn 5:1**	
Now **t** is in Jerusalem by the sheep	**Jn 5:2**	
A man was **t**	**Jn 5:5**	*1563*
When Jesus saw him lying **t**,	**Jn 5:6**	
while **t** was a crowd in *that* place.	**Jn 5:13**	
"**T** is another who testifies	**Jn 5:32**	
and **t** He sat down with His disciples.	**Jn 6:3**	*1563*
"**T** is a lad here who has five	**Jn 6:9**	
Now **t** was much grass in the place.	**Jn 6:10**	
t was no other small boat there,	**Jn 6:22**	
there was no other small boat **t**,	**Jn 6:22**	*1563*
T came other small boats from	**Jn 6:23**	
saw that Jesus was not **t**,	**Jn 6:24**	*1563*
"But **t** are some of you who do not	**Jn 6:64**	
T was much grumbling among	**Jn 7:12**	
t is no unrighteousness in Him.	**Jn 7:18**	
because **t** is no truth in him.	**Jn 8:44**	
t is One who seeks and judges.	**Jn 8:50**	
And **t** was a division among them.	**Jn 9:16**	
baptizing, and He was staying **t**.	**Jn 10:40**	*1563*
Many believed in Him **t**.	**Jn 10:42**	*1563*
You, and are You going **t** again?"	**Jn 11:8**	*1563*
"Are **t** not twelve hours in the day?	**Jn 11:9**	*1563*
for your sakes that I was not **t**,	**Jn 11:15**	*1563*
was going to the tomb to weep **t**.	**Jn 11:31**	*1563*
by this time **t** will be a stench,	**Jn 11:39**	
but went away from **t** to the	**Jn 11:54**	*1564*
t He stayed with the disciples.	**Jn 11:54**	*2546*
So they made Him a supper **t**,	**Jn 12:2**	*1563*
of the Jews then learned that He was **t**;	**Jn 12:9**	*1563*

Context	Reference	Number
Now **t** were some Greeks among	**Jn 12:20**	*1563*
I am, **t** My servant will be also;	**Jn 12:26**	*1563*
T was reclining on Jesus' bosom	**Jn 13:23**	
t you may be also.	**Jn 14:3**	
the Kidron, where **t** was a garden,	**Jn 18:1**	
often met **t** with His disciples.	**Jn 18:2**	*1563*
came **t** with lanterns and torches	**Jn 18:3**	*1563*
and the officers were standing **t**,	**Jn 18:18**	
T they crucified Him, and with Him	**Jn 19:18**	*3699*
full of sour wine was standing **t**;	**Jn 19:29**	
He was crucified **t** was a garden,	**Jn 19:41**	
was nearby, they laid Jesus **t**.	**Jn 19:42**	*1563*
he saw the linen wrappings lying **t**;	**Jn 20:5**	
he saw the linen wrappings lying **t**,	**Jn 20:6**	
around and saw Jesus standing **t**,	**Jn 20:14**	
and although **t** were so many, the	**Jn 21:11**	
And **t** are also many other things	**Jn 21:25**	
twenty persons was **t** together),	**Ac 1:15**	
And suddenly **t** came from heaven a	**Ac 2:2**	
And **t** appeared to them tongues as	**Ac 2:3**	
t were Jews living in Jerusalem,	**Ac 2:5**	
and that day **t** were added about	**Ac 2:41**	
and Annas the high priest *was* **t**,	**Ac 4:6**	
"And **t** is salvation in no one else;	**Ac 4:12**	
for **t** is no other name under	**Ac 4:12**	
"For truly in this city **t** were	**Ac 4:27**	
For **t** was not a needy person among	**Ac 4:34**	
Now **t** elapsed an interval of about	**Ac 5:7**	
From **t**, after his father died,	**Ac 7:4**	*2547*
heard that **t** was grain in Egypt,	**Ac 7:12**	
he sent our fathers **t** the first	**Ac 7:12**	
"And Jacob went down to Egypt and **t**	**Ac 7:15**	
"*From* **t** they were removed to	**Ac 7:16**	
until **T** AROSE ANOTHER KING OVER	**Ac 7:18**	
t came the voice of the Lord:	**Ac 7:31**	
'OR WHAT PLACE IS **T** FOR MY REPOSE?	**Ac 7:49**	
So **t** was much rejoicing in that	**Ac 8:8**	
t was a man named Simon,	**Ac 8:9**	
t was an Ethiopian eunuch,	**Ac 8:27**	
Now **t** was a disciple at	**Ac 9:10**	
And immediately **t** fell from his	**Ac 9:18**	
T he found a man named Aeneas, who	**Ac 9:33**	*1563*
Now in Joppa **t** was a disciple	**Ac 9:36**	
having heard that Peter was **t**,	**Ac 9:38**	*1722, 846*
Now **t** *was* a man at Caesarea named	**Ac 10:1**	
and **t** were in it all *kinds of*	**Ac 10:12**	
also called Peter, was staying **t**.	**Ac 10:18**	*1759a*
But **t** were some of them, men of	**Ac 11:20**	
t would certainly be a great famine	**Ac 11:28**	
t was no small disturbance among	**Ac 12:18**	
Caesarea and was spending time **t**.	**Ac 12:19**	
Now **t** were at Antioch, in the	**Ac 13:1**	
in the church that was **t**,	**Ac 13:1**	
and from **t** they sailed to Cyprus.	**Ac 13:4**	*1564*
Therefore they spent a long time **t**	**Ac 14:3**	
and **t** they continued to preach the	**Ac 14:7**	*2546*
From **t** they sailed to Antioch,	**Ac 14:26**	*2547*
After **t** had been much debate,	**Ac 15:7**	
After they had spent time **t**,	**Ac 15:33**	
seemed good to Silas to remain **t**.	**Ac 15:34**	*847*
And **t** occurred such a sharp	**Ac 15:39**	
a disciple was **t**, named Timothy,	**Ac 16:1**	*1563*
and from **t** to Philippi, which is a	**Ac 16:12**	*2547*
that **t** would be a place of prayer;	**Ac 16:13**	
t came a great earthquake,	**Ac 16:26**	
t was a synagogue of the Jews.	**Ac 17:1**	
saying that **t** is another king,	**Ac 17:7**	
Berea also, they came **t** as	**Ac 17:13**	*2546*
and Silas and Timothy remained **t**.	**Ac 17:14**	*1563*
Athenians and the strangers visiting **t**	**Ac 17:21**	
Then he left **t** and went to	**Ac 18:7**	*1564*
And he settled **t** a year and six	**Ac 18:11**	
but if **t** are questions about words	**Ac 18:15**	
to Ephesus, and he left them **t**.	**Ac 18:19**	*847*
And having spent some time **t**, he	**Ac 18:23**	
whether **t** is a Holy Spirit."	**Ac 19:2**	
T were in all about twelve men.	**Ac 19:7**	
"After I have been **t**,	**Ac 19:21**	*1563*
About that time **t** occurred no	**Ac 19:23**	
"Not only is **t** danger that	**Ac 19:27**	
what man is **t** after all who does	**Ac 19:35**	
since **t** is no *real* cause *for it,*	**Ac 19:40**	
And **t** he spent three months,	**Ac 20:3**	
and **t** we stayed seven days.	**Ac 20:6**	*3699*
T were many lamps in the upper room	**Ac 20:8**	
And **t** was a young man	**Ac 20:9**	
from **t** to take Paul on board;	**Ac 20:13**	*1564*
Sailing from **t**,	**Ac 20:15**	*2547*
knowing what will happen to me **t**,	**Ac 20:22**	*1722, 846*
to Rhodes and from **t** to Patara;	**Ac 21:1**	*2547*
for **t** the ship was to unload its	**Ac 21:3**	*1566*
disciples, we stayed **t** seven days;	**Ac 21:4**	*847*
When our days **t** were ended,	**Ac 21:5**	
we were staying **t** for some days,	**Ac 21:10**	
how many thousands **t** are among the	**Ac 21:20**	
t is nothing to the things which they	**Ac 21:24**	
and when **t** was a great hush, he	**Ac 21:40**	
even those who were **t** to Jerusalem	**Ac 22:5**	*1566*
and **t** you will be told of all that	**Ac 22:10**	*2546*
of by all the Jews who lived **t**,	**Ac 22:12**	
t occurred a dissension between the	**Ac 23:7**	
say that **t** is no resurrection,	**Ac 23:8**	
And **t** occurred a great uproar;	**Ac 23:9**	
T were more than forty who formed	**Ac 23:13**	
"When I was informed that **t**	**Ac 23:30**	
that **t** shall certainly be a	**Ac 24:15**	
t *were* some Jews from Asia	**Ac 24:18**	

Context	Reference	Number
men among you go **t** with me,	**Ac 25:5**	
and if **t** is anything wrong about	**Ac 25:5**	
they were spending many days **t**,	**Ac 25:14**	*1563*
"**T** is a man who was left as a	**Ac 25:14**	
t stand trial on these matters.	**Ac 25:20**	*2546*
From **t** we put out to sea and	**Ac 27:4**	*2547*
T the centurion found an Alexandrian	**Ac 27:6**	*2546*
decision to put out to sea from **t**,	**Ac 27:12**	*1564*
and spend the winter **t**.	**Ac 27:12**	
But before very long **t** rushed down	**Ac 27:14**	
for **t** will be no loss of life	**Ac 27:22**	
we stayed **t** for three days.	**Ac 28:12**	
From **t** we sailed around and	**Ac 28:13**	*3606*
T we found *some* brethren, and were	**Ac 28:14**	*3757*
came from **t** as far as the Market	**Ac 28:15**	*2547*
t was no ground for putting me to	**Ac 28:18**	
T *will be* tribulation	**Ro 2:9**	
For **t** is no partiality with God.	**Ro 2:11**	
"**T** IS NONE RIGHTEOUS, NOT EVEN	**Ro 3:10**	
T IS NONE WHO UNDERSTANDS, THERE	**Ro 3:11**	
T IS NONE WHO SEEKS FOR GOD;	**Ro 3:11**	
T IS NONE WHO DOES GOOD, THERE IS	**Ro 3:12**	
DOES GOOD, **T** IS NOT EVEN ONE."	**Ro 3:12**	
"**T** IS NO FEAR OF GOD BEFORE THEIR	**Ro 3:18**	
for **t** is no distinction;	**Ro 3:22**	
wrath, but where **t** is no law,	**Ro 4:15**	
is no law, **t** also is no violation.	**Ro 4:15**	
is not imputed when **t** is no law.	**Ro 5:13**	
t resulted condemnation to all men,	**Ro 5:18**	
t resulted justification of life to all	**Ro 5:18**	
Therefore **t** is now no condemnation	**Ro 8:1**	
only this, but **t** was Rebekah also,	**Ro 9:10**	
T is no injustice with God, is	**Ro 9:14**	
is no injustice with God, is **t**?	**Ro 9:14**	
T THEY SHALL BE CALLED SONS OF THE	**Ro 9:26**	*1563*
For **t** is no distinction between	**Ro 10:12**	
t has also come to be at the	**Ro 11:5**	
For **t** is no authority except from	**Ro 13:1**	
and if **t** is any other commandment,	**Ro 13:9**	
"**T** SHALL COME THE ROOT OF JESSE,	**Ro 15:12**	
to be helped on my way **t** by you,	**Ro 15:24**	*1563*
and that **t** be no divisions among you,	**1Co 1:10**	
that **t** are quarrels among you.	**1Co 1:11**	
that **t** were not many wise	**1Co 1:26**	
For since **t** is jealousy and strife	**1Co 3:3**	
that **t** is immorality among you,	**1Co 5:1**	
that **t** is not among you one wise	**1Co 6:5**	*1762*
we know that **t** is no such thing as	**1Co 8:4**	
and that **t** is no God but one.	**1Co 8:4**	
For even if **t** are so-called gods	**1Co 8:5**	
t are many gods and many lords,	**1Co 8:5**	
yet for us **t** is *but* one God, the	**1Co 8:6**	
Since **t** is one bread, we who are	**1Co 10:17**	
For **t** must also be factions among	**1Co 11:19**	
Now **t** are varieties of gifts, but	**1Co 12:4**	
And **t** are varieties of ministries,	**1Co 12:5**	
T are varieties of effects, but	**1Co 12:6**	
But now **t** are many members, but	**1Co 12:20**	
that **t** may be no division in	**1Co 12:25**	
Love never fails; but if **t** *are*	**1Co 13:8**	
if **t** *are* tongues, they will	**1Co 13:8**	
if **t** *is* knowledge, it will be	**1Co 13:8**	
T are, perhaps, a great many kinds	**1Co 14:10**	
but if **t** is no interpreter, he	**1Co 14:28**	
that **t** is no resurrection of the dead	**1Co 15:12**	
But if **t** is no resurrection of the	**1Co 15:13**	
flesh, but **t** is one *flesh* of men,	**1Co 15:39**	
T are also heavenly bodies and	**1Co 15:40**	
T is one glory of the sun, and	**1Co 15:41**	
If **t** is a natural body, there is	**1Co 15:44**	
body, **t** is also a spiritual *body*.	**1Co 15:44**	
to me, and **t** are many adversaries.	**1Co 16:9**	
that with me **t** will be yes,	**2Co 1:17**	
the Lord is, **t** is liberty.	**2Co 3:17**	
so that just as **t** *was*	**2Co 8:11**	
so **t** *may be* also	**2Co 8:11**	
your need, that **t** may be equality;	**2Co 8:14**	
t is the daily pressure on me *of*	**2Co 11:28**	
t was given me a thorn in the	**2Co 12:7**	
that perhaps **t** *will be* strife,	**2Co 12:20**	
only **t** are some who are disturbing	**Ga 1:7**	
T is neither Jew nor Greek, there	**Ga 3:28**	*1762*
t is neither slave nor free man,	**Ga 3:28**	*1762*
man, **t** is neither male nor female;	**Ga 3:28**	*1762*
against such things **t** is no law.	**Ga 5:23**	
that by revelation **t** was made	**Eph 3:3**	
T *is* one body and one Spirit,	**Eph 4:4**	
tossed here and **t** by waves and	**Eph 4:14**	*2831*
and **t** *must be no* filthiness	**Eph 5:4**	
and **t** is no partiality with Him.	**Eph 6:9**	
Therefore if **t** is any encouragement	**Php 2:1**	
if **t** is any consolation of love,	**Php 2:1**	
if **t** is any fellowship of the	**Php 2:1**	
if **t** is any excellence and if	**Php 4:8**	
t is no *distinction between* Greek and	**Col 3:11**	*1762*
For **t** is one God, *and* one mediator	**1Tm 2:5**	
Now in a large house **t** are not	**2Tm 2:20**	
in the future **t** is laid up for me	**2Tm 4:8**	
For **t** are many rebellious men,	**Ti 1:10**	
decided to spend the winter **t**.	**Ti 3:12**	*1563*
that **t** not be in any one of you	**Heb 3:12**	
So **t** remains a Sabbath rest for	**Heb 4:9**	
And **t** is no creature hidden from	**Heb 4:13**	
what further need *was* **t** for	**Heb 7:11**	
of necessity **t** takes place a	**Heb 7:12**	
t is a setting aside of a former	**Heb 7:18**	
and on the other hand **t** is a	**Heb 7:19**	
since **t** are those who offer the	**Heb 8:4**	
t would have been no occasion	**Heb 8:7**	

Context	Reference	Number
For **t** was a tabernacle prepared,	**Heb 9:2**	
t was a tabernacle which is called	**Heb 9:3**	
t must of necessity be the death	**Heb 9:16**	
of blood **t** is no forgiveness.	**Heb 9:22**	
But in those *sacrifices* **t** is a	**Heb 10:3**	
Now where **t** is forgiveness of	**Heb 10:18**	
t is no longer *any* offering for	**Heb 10:18**	
t no longer remains a sacrifice	**Heb 10:26**	
t was born even of one man,	**Heb 11:12**	
for what son is **t** whom *his* father	**Heb 12:7**	
that **t** *be* no immoral or godless	**Heb 12:16**	
with whom **t** is no variation or	**Jas 1:17**	*1762*
and **t** also comes in a poor man in	**Jas 2:2**	
"You stand over **t**, or sit down by	**Jas 2:3**	*1563*
t is disorder and every evil thing.	**Jas 3:16**	*1563*
T is *only* one Lawgiver and Judge,	**Jas 4:12**	
and spend a year **t** and engage in	**Jas 4:13**	*1563*
For what credit is **t** if,	**1Pe 2:20**	
Who is **t** to harm you if you	**1Pe 3:13**	
just as **t** will also be false	**2Pe 2:1**	
in Him **t** is no darkness at all.	**1Jn 1:5**	
t is no cause for stumbling in him.	**1Jn 2:10**	
and in Him **t** is no sin.	**1Jn 3:5**	
T is no fear in love;	**1Jn 4:18**	
For **t** are three that testify:	**1Jn 5:7**	*1510*
T is a sin *leading* to death;	**1Jn 5:16**	
t is a sin not *leading* to death.	**1Jn 5:17**	
the last time **t** will be mockers,	**Jude 1:18**	
because you have **t** some who hold	**Rv 2:14**	*1563*
and **t** *was* a rainbow around	**Rv 4:3**	
And **t** *were* seven lamps of fire	**Rv 4:5**	
and before the throne **t** *was*	**Rv 4:6**	
And **t** was given to each of them a	**Rv 6:11**	
and **t** was a great earthquake;	**Rv 6:12**	
t was silence in heaven for about	**Rv 8:1**	
and **t** followed peals of thunder	**Rv 8:5**	
sounded, and **t** came hail and fire,	**Rv 8:7**	
that **t** will be delay no longer,	**Rv 10:6**	
Then **t** was given me a measuring rod	**Rv 11:1**	
hour **t** was a great earthquake,	**Rv 11:13**	
and **t** were loud voices in heaven,	**Rv 11:15**	
and **t** were flashes of lightning	**Rv 11:19**	
so that **t** she would be nourished	**Rv 12:6**	*1563*
And **t** was war in heaven, Michael	**Rv 12:7**	
and **t** was no longer a place found	**Rv 12:8**	
T was given to him a mouth speaking	**Rv 13:5**	
And **t** were flashes of lightning	**Rv 16:18**	
and **t** was a great earthquake, such	**Rv 16:18**	
such as **t** had not been since man	**Rv 16:18**	
away, and **t** is no longer *any* sea.	**Rv 21:1**	
t will no longer be *any* death;	**Rv 21:4**	
t will no longer be *any* mourning,	**Rv 21:4**	
T *were* three gates on the east	**Rv 21:13**	
(for **t** will be no night there)	**Rv 21:25**	
(for there will be no night **t**)	**Rv 21:25**	*1563*
T will no longer be any curse;	**Rv 22:3**	
t will no longer be *any* night;	**Rv 22:5**	

THEREAFTER

Context	Reference	Number
T Samuel called the people	**1Sa 10:17**	
in the sight of all nations **t**.	**2Ch 32:23**	4480, 310, 3651
who would live ungodly *lives* **t**;	**2Pe 2:6**	*3195*

THEREBY

Context	Reference	Number
and die **t** because they profane it;	**Lv 22:9**	
T good will come to you.	**Jb 22:21**	
Bear one another's burdens, and **t**	**Ga 6:2**	*3779*
upon anyone *too* hastily and **t**	**1Tm 5:22**	*3366*

THEREFORE

Context	Reference	Number
t the LORD God sent him out from	**Gn 3:23**	
"**T** whoever kills Cain, vengeance	**Gn 4:15**	3651
t it is said, "Like Nimrod a mighty	**Gn 10:9**	5921, 3651
T its name was called Babel,	**Gn 11:9**	5921, 3651
T he treated Abram well for her	**Gn 12:16**	
T the well was called	**Gn 16:14**	5921, 3651
T the name of the town was called	**Gn 19:22**	5921, 3651
t I did not let you touch her.	**Gn 20:6**	5921, 3651
"Now **t**, restore the man's wife,	**Gn 20:7**	
T she said to Abraham,	**Gn 21:10**	
now **t**, swear to me here by God	**Gn 21:23**	
T he called that place Beersheba,	**Gn 21:31**	5921, 3651
T his name was called Edom.	**Gn 25:30**	5921, 3651
t the name of the city is	**Gn 26:33**	5921, 3651
"Now **t**, my son, listen to me as I	**Gn 27:8**	
"Now **t**, my son, obey my voice,	**Gn 27:43**	
should you **t** serve me for nothing?	**Gn 29:15**	
He has **t** given me this *son* also."	**Gn 29:33**	
T he was named Levi.	**Gn 29:34**	5921, 3651
T she named him Judah.	**Gn 29:35**	5921, 3651
T she named him Dan.	**Gn 30:6**	5921, 3651
"**T** he may lie with you tonight in	**Gn 30:15**	3651
T it was named Galeed,	**Gn 31:48**	5921, 3651
T, to this day the sons of Israel	**Gn 32:32**	5921, 3651
t the place is named Succoth.	**Gn 33:17**	5921, 3651
t let them live in the land and	**Gn 34:21**	

He said, **t**, "I will send you a young goat Gn 38:17
t this distress has come upon us." Gn 42:21
5921, 3651
"Now, **t**, when I come to your Gn 44:30
"Now, **t**, please let your servant Gn 44:33
"Now, **t**, it was not you who sent Gn 45:8
Now, **t**, please let your servants Gn 47:4
T, they did not sell their land. Gn 47:22
5921, 3651
Now **t**, please let me go up and Gn 50:5
T it was named Abel-mizraim, Gn 50:11
5921, 3651
"So **t**, do not be afraid; Gn 50:21
"**T**, come now, and I will send you Ex 3:10
they are lazy, **t** they cry out, Ex 5:8
5921, 3651
t you say, 'Let us go *and* sacrifice Ex 5:17
5921, 3651
"Say, **t**, to the sons of Israel, Ex 6:6 3651
"Now **t** send, bring your livestock Ex 9:19
"Now **t**, please forgive my sin Ex 10:17
"**T**, our livestock too shall go Ex 10:26
t you shall observe this day Ex 12:17
"**T**, you shall keep this ordinance Ex 13:10
T, I sacrifice to the LORD the Ex 13:15
5921, 3651
t it was named Marah. Ex 15:23
5921, 3651
t He gives you bread for two days Ex 16:29
5921, 3651
T the people quarreled with Moses Ex 17:2
t the LORD blessed the sabbath day Ex 20:11
5921, 3651
t you shall not eat *any* flesh torn Ex 22:31
"**T** you are to observe the sabbath, Ex 31:14
Now **t**, put off your ornaments from Ex 33:5
"Now **t**, I pray You, if I have Ex 33:13
So Aaron, **t**, kept silent. Lv 10:3
Consecrate yourselves **t**, Lv 11:44
T, the priest shall pronounce him Lv 13:25
"He shall **t** tear down the house, Lv 14:45
"**T** I said to the sons of Israel, Lv 17:12
5921, 3651
T I said to the sons of Israel, Lv 17:14
t I have brought its punishment Lv 18:25
You shall consecrate yourselves **t** Lv 20:7
'You are **t** to keep all My statutes Lv 20:22
and **t** I have abhorred them. Lv 20:23
'You are **t** to make a distinction Lv 20:25
'You shall consecrate him, **t**, Lv 21:8
'They shall **t** keep My charge, so Lv 22:9
'What, **t**, belongs to the Levites Lv 25:33
'They will **t** stumble over each Lv 26:37
'If, **t**, a man wishes to redeem Lv 27:31
Aaron **t** did so; he mounted its lamps Nu 8:3
Moses **t** said to them, Nu 9:8
The people **t** cried out to Moses, Nu 11:2
The LORD **t** said to Moses, Nu 11:16
T the LORD will give you meat and Nu 11:18
t He slaughtered them in the Nu 14:16
"**T** you and all your company are Nu 16:11 3651
Moses **t** spoke to the sons of Israel, Nu 17:6
t I have said concerning them, Nu 18:24
5921, 3651
t you shall not bring this Nu 20:12 3651
T it is said in the Book of the Nu 21:14
5921, 3651
T those who use proverbs say, Nu 21:27
5921, 3651
"Now, **t**, please come, curse this Nu 22:6
"**T**, flee to your place now. Nu 24:11
"**T** say, 'Behold, I give him My Nu 25:12 3651
"Now **t**, kill every male among the Nu 31:17
t He chose their descendants after Dt 4:37
"Know **t** today, and take it to Dt 4:39
t the LORD your God commanded you Dt 5:15
5921, 3651
"Know **t** that the LORD your God, Dt 7:9
"**T**, you shall keep the Dt 7:11
"**T**, you shall keep the Dt 8:6
"Know **t** today that it is the LORD Dt 9:3
T, Levi does not have a portion or Dt 10:9
5921, 3651
shall **t** love the LORD your God, Dt 11:1
"You shall **t** keep every Dt 11:8
"You shall **t** impress these words Dt 11:18
t I command you, saying, Dt 15:11
5921, 3651
t I command you this today. Dt 15:15
5921, 3651
"**T**, I command you, saying, Dt 19:7
5921, 3651
you, **t** your camp must be holy; Dt 23:14
t I am commanding you to do this Dt 24:18
5921, 3651
t I am commanding you to do this Dt 24:22
5921, 3651
"**T** it shall come about when the Dt 25:19
You shall **t** be careful to do them Dt 26:16
shall **t** obey the LORD your God, Dt 27:10
t you shall serve your enemies Dt 28:48
"**T**, the anger of the LORD burned Dt 29:27
"Now **t**, write this song for Dt 31:19
now **t** arise, cross this Jordan, Jos 1:2
"Now, **t**, please swear to me by the Jos 2:12
t the anger of the LORD burned Jos 7:1
"**T** the sons of Israel cannot Jos 7:12
T the name of that place has been Jos 7:26
5921, 3651

now **t**, make a covenant with us." Jos 9:6
"Now **t**, you are cursed, and you Jos 9:23
t we feared greatly for our lives Jos 9:24
T Adoni-zedek king of Jerusalem Jos 10:3
"Now **t**, apportion this land for Jos 13:7
T, Hebron became the inheritance Jos 14:14
5921, 3651
t turn now and go to your tents, Jos 22:4
"**T** we said, 'Let us build an altar, Jos 22:26
"**T** we said, 'It shall also come about Jos 22:28
"Now, **t**, fear the LORD and serve Jos 24:14
"Now **t**, put away the foreign gods Jos 24:23
"**T** I also said, Jg 2:3
T they took the key and opened Jg 3:25
T on that day he named him Jg 6:32
"Now **t** come, proclaim in the Jg 7:3
T it shall be that he of whom I Jg 7:4
"Now **t**, if you have dealt in Jg 9:16
"Would, **t**, that this people were Jg 9:29
"Now **t**, arise by night, you and Jg 9:32
t I will no longer deliver you. Jg 10:13 3651
t, return them peaceably now." Jg 11:13
'I **t** have not sinned against you, Jg 11:27
"Now **t**, be careful not to drink Jg 13:4
now **t**, get her for me as a wife." Jg 14:2
T he named it En-hakkore, which Jg 15:19
5921, 3651
now **t**, I will return them to you." Jg 17:3
T they called that place Jg 18:12
5921, 3651
Now **t**, consider what you should do." Jg 18:14
T, they turned their backs before Jg 20:42
you **t** wait until they were grown? Ru 1:13 3860
Would you **t** refrain from marrying? Ru 1:13 3860
"Wash yourself **t**, and anoint Ru 3:3
"**T** the LORD God of Israel 1Sa 2:30 3651
"**T** I have sworn to the house of Eli 1Sa 3:14 3651
t, be men and fight." 1Sa 4:9
T neither the priests of Dagon nor 1Sa 5:5
5921, 3651
They sent **t** and gathered all the 1Sa 5:11
"Now **t**, take and prepare a new 1Sa 6:7
Now **t**, go up for you will find him 1Sa 9:13
T it became a proverb: 1Sa 10:12
5921, 3651
Now **t**, present yourselves before 1Sa 10:19
T they inquired further of the 1Sa 10:22
"Now **t**, here is the king whom you 1Sa 12:13
T I said, 'Now the Philistines will 1Sa 13:12
t, he put out the end of the staff 1Sa 14:27
T, Saul said to the LORD, the God 1Sa 14:41
now **t**, listen to the words of the 1Sa 15:1
"Now **t**, please pardon my sin and 1Sa 15:25
T Saul removed him from his 1Sa 18:13
T Saul said to David, 1Sa 18:21
now **t**, become the king's 1Sa 18:22
Now **t**, please be on guard in the 1Sa 19:2
T they say, "Is Saul also among the 1Sa 19:24
5921, 3651
"**T** deal kindly with your servant, 1Sa 20:8
T now, send and bring him to me, 1Sa 20:31
"Now **t**, what do you have on hand? 1Sa 21:3
t they called that place the Rock 1Sa 23:28
5921, 3651
"The LORD **t** be judge and decide 1Sa 24:15
May the LORD **t** reward you with 1Sa 24:19
T let *my* young men find favor in 1Sa 25:8
"Now **t**, know and consider what 1Sa 25:17
"Now **t**, my lord, as the LORD 1Sa 25:26
now **t**, please let me strike him 1Sa 26:8
"Now **t**, please let my lord the 1Sa 26:19
t Ziklag has belonged to the kings 1Sa 27:6 3651
t he will become my servant 1Sa 27:12
t I have called you, that you may 1Sa 28:15
t tomorrow you and your sons will 1Sa 28:19
"Now **t** return and go in peace, 1Sa 29:7
"Now **t**, let your hands be strong and 2Sa 2:7
T that place was called 2Sa 2:16
t Abner struck him in the belly 2Sa 2:23
T they say, "The blind or the lame 2Sa 5:8
5921, 3651
T he named that place Baal-perazim. 2Sa 5:20
5921, 3651
t I will celebrate before the LORD. 2Sa 6:21
"Now **t**, thus you shall say to My 2Sa 7:8
"Now **t**, O LORD God, the word that 2Sa 7:25
t Your servant has found courage to 2Sa 7:27
5921, 3651
"Now **t**, may it please You to 2Sa 7:29
'Now **t**, the sword shall never 2Sa 12:10
David **t** inquired of God for the 2Sa 12:16
"Now **t**, gather the rest of the 2Sa 12:28
Now **t**, please speak to the king, 2Sa 13:13
"Now **t**, do not let my lord the 2Sa 13:33
go **t**, bring back the young man 2Sa 14:21
T he said to his servants, 2Sa 14:30
Now **t**, let me see the king's face, 2Sa 14:32
T David said to Ittai, 2Sa 15:22
T Zadok and Abiathar returned the 2Sa 15:29
"Now **t**, send quickly and tell 2Sa 17:16
t now it is better that you *be* 2Sa 18:3
"Now **t** arise, go out and speak 2Sa 19:7
t behold, I have come today, the 2Sa 19:20
t do what is good in your sight. 2Sa 19:27
t we also have more *claim* on David 2Sa 19:43
"**T** the LORD has recompensed me 2Sa 22:25
"**T** I will give thanks to You, O 2Sa 22:50
5921, 3651
T he would not drink it. 2Sa 23:17

t he became their commander; 2Sa 23:19
Be strong, **t**, and show yourself a 1Ki 2:2
"Now **t**, do not let him go 1Ki 2:9
"Now **t**, as the LORD lives, who 1Ki 2:24
t the LORD shall return your evil 1Ki 2:44
"Now **t**, command that they cut for 1Ki 5:6
"Now **t**, O LORD, the God of 1Ki 8:25
"Now **t**, O God of Israel, let Your 1Ki 8:26
"Let your heart **t** be wholly 1Ki 8:61
t the LORD has brought all this 1Ki 9:9
5921, 3651
forever, **t** He made you king, 1Ki 10:9
sought **t** to put Jeroboam to death; 1Ki 11:40
t lighten the hard service of your 1Ki 12:4
t the LORD has given him to the 1Ki 13:26
t behold, I am bringing calamity 1Ki 14:10 3651
T all Israel made Omri, 1Ki 16:16
t they were stronger than we; 1Ki 20:23
5921, 3651
t I will give all this great 1Ki 20:28
t your life shall go for his life, 1Ki 20:42
"**T**, hear the word of the LORD. 1Ki 22:19 3651
"Now **t**, behold, the LORD has put 1Ki 22:23
"Now **t** thus says the LORD, 2Ki 1:4 3651
T you shall not come down from the 2Ki 1:6 3651
t you shall not come down from the 2Ki 1:16 3651
They sent **t** fifty men; 2Ki 2:17
Now **t**, Moab, to the spoil!" 2Ki 3:23
"**T**, the leprosy of Naaman shall 2Ki 5:27
Now **t** come, and let us go over to 2Ki 7:4
T they arose and fled in the 2Ki 7:7
Now **t** come, let us go and tell the 2Ki 7:9
t they have gone from the camp to 2Ki 7:12
took **t** two chariots with horses, 2Ki 7:14
T they returned and told him. 2Ki 9:36
Now **t** take no *more* money from your 2Ki 12:7
not open *to him*; **t** he struck *it* 2Ki 15:16
t the LORD sent lions among them 2Ki 17:25
"Now **t**, come, make a bargain with 2Ki 18:23
T, offer a prayer for the remnant 2Ki 19:4
"**T** their inhabitants were short of 2Ki 19:26
T I will put My hook in your nose, 2Ki 19:28
"**T** thus says the LORD concerning 2Ki 19:32 3651
t thus says the LORD, the God of 2Ki 21:12 3651
t My wrath burns against this 2Ki 22:17
"**T**, behold, I will gather you to 2Ki 22:20 3651
T Saul took his sword and fell on 1Ch 10:4
T He killed him and turned the 1Ch 10:14
t it was called the city of David. 1Ch 11:7
5921, 3651
T he would not drink it. 1Ch 11:19
T they named that place 1Ch 14:11
5921, 3651
"Now, **t**, thus shall you say to My 1Ch 17:7
t Your servant has found *courage* 1Ch 17:25
5921, 3651
T, Joab departed and went 1Ch 21:4
Now, **t**, consider what answer I 1Ch 21:12
T now I will make preparation for 1Ch 22:5
arise, **t**, and build the sanctuary 1Ch 22:19
"Now **t**, our God, we thank You, 1Ch 29:13
"Now **t**, O LORD, the God of 2Ch 6:16
"Now **t**, O LORD, the God of 2Ch 6:17
"Now **t** arise, O LORD God, to Your 2Ch 6:41
t He has brought all this 2Ch 7:22
5921, 3651
t He made you king over them, 2Ch 9:8
now **t** lighten the hard service of 2Ch 10:4
t the army of the king of Aram has 2Ch 16:7
5921, 3651
"**T**, hear the word of the LORD. 2Ch 18:18 3651
"Now **t**, behold, the LORD has put a 2Ch 18:22
T they have named that place 2Ch 20:26
5921, 3651
"Now **t**, listen to me and return 2Ch 28:11
"**T** the wrath of the LORD was 2Ch 29:8
t their brothers the Levites 2Ch 29:34
t, the Levites *were* over the 2Ch 30:17
"Now **t**, do not let Hezekiah 2Ch 32:15
t wrath came on him and on Judah 2Ch 32:25
T the LORD brought the commanders 2Ch 33:11
t My wrath will be poured out on 2Ch 34:25
t the Levites prepared for 2Ch 35:14
T He brought up against them the 2Ch 36:17
t they were considered unclean *and* Ezr 2:62
t we have sent and informed the Ezr 4:14
5922, 1836
t that city was laid waste. Ezr 4:15
5922, 1836
"Now **t**, Tattenai, governor of Ezr 6:6
with this money, **t**, you shall Ezr 7:17
3606, 6903, 1836
"Now **t**, make confession to the Ezr 10:11
t we His servants will arise and Ne 2:20
t let us get grain that we may eat Ne 5:2
T, I held a great assembly against Ne 5:7
t you are rebuilding the wall. Ne 6:6
5921, 3651
t they were considered unclean *and* Ne 7:64
"**T** You delivered them into Ne 9:27
T You abandoned them to the Ne 9:28
T You gave them into the Ne 9:30
"Now **t**, our God, the great, the Ne 9:32
t Haman sought to destroy all the Es 3:6
T the Jews of the rural areas, who Es 9:19
5921, 3651
T they called these days Purim Es 9:26
5921, 3651

seas; **T** my words have been rash. Jb 6:3
5921, 3651
"**T** I will not restrain my mouth; Jb 7:11 1571
t I say, 'He destroys the guiltless and Jb 9:22
5921, 3651
T You will not exalt *them.* Jb 17:4
5921, 3651
"**T** my disquieting thoughts make Jb 20:2 3651
T his prosperity does not endure. Jb 20:21
5921, 3651
"**T** snares surround you, And Jb 22:10
5921, 3651
"**T**, I would be dismayed at His Jb 23:15
5921, 3651
Or in his disaster **t** cry out for help? Jb 30:24 3651
"**T** my harp is turned to mourning, Jb 30:31
T I was shy and afraid to tell you Jb 32:6
5921, 3651
"**T**, listen to me, you men of Jb 34:10 3651
"**T** He knows their works, And He Jb 34:25 3651
T declare what you know. Jb 34:33
T men fear Him; He does not regard Jb 37:24 3651
"**T** I have declared that which I Jb 42:3 3651
T I retract, And I repent in dust Jb 42:6
5921, 3651
"Now **t**, take for yourselves seven Jb 42:8
T the wicked will not stand in the Ps 1:5
5921, 3651
Now **t**, O kings, show discernment; Ps 2:10
T my heart is glad and my glory Ps 16:9 3651
T the LORD has recompensed me Ps 18:24
T I will give thanks to You among Ps 18:49
5921, 3651
T He instructs sinners in the way. Ps 25:8
5921, 3651
T my heart exults, And with my Ps 28:7
T, let everyone who is godly pray Ps 32:6
5921, 2088
T I remember You from the land of Ps 42:6
5921, 3651
T God has blessed You forever. Ps 45:2
5921, 3651
T God, Your God, has anointed You Ps 45:7
5921, 3651
T the peoples will give You Ps 45:17
5921, 3651
T we will not fear, though the Ps 46:2
5921, 3651
T pride is their necklace; Ps 73:6 3651
T his people return to this place, Ps 73:10 3651
T the LORD heard and was full of Ps 78:21 3651
loved Me, **t** I will deliver him; Ps 91:14
"**T** I swore in My anger, Truly Ps 95:11 834
T He said that He would destroy Ps 106:23
T He swore to them That He would Ps 106:26
T the anger of the LORD was Ps 106:40
T He humbled their heart with Ps 107:12
T He will lift up *His* head. Ps 110:7
5921, 3651
T I shall call *upon Him* as long as Ps 116:2
T I will look *with satisfaction* Ps 118:7
T I hate every false way. Ps 119:104
5921, 3651
T I love Your testimonies. Ps 119:119 3651
T I love Your commandments Above Ps 119:127
5921, 3651
T I esteem right all *Your* precepts Ps 119:128
5921, 3651
T my soul observes them. Ps 119:129
5921, 3651
very pure, **T** Your servant loves it. Ps 119:140
Depart from me, **t**, men of Ps 139:19
T my spirit is overwhelmed within Ps 143:4
T his calamity will come suddenly; Pr 6:15
5921, 3651
"**T** I have come out to meet you, Pr 7:15
5921, 3651
Now **t**, *my* sons, listen to me, And Pr 7:24
"Now **t**, *O* sons, listen to me, For Pr 8:32
T do not associate with a gossip. Pr 20:19
T I completely despaired of all Ec 2:20
t let your words be few. Ec 5:2
5921, 3651
t the hearts of the sons of men Ec 8:11
5921, 3651
T the maidens love you. SS 1:3
5921, 3651
T the Lord GOD of hosts, The Is 1:24
T the Lord will afflict the scalp Is 3:17
T My people go into exile for Is 5:13 3651
T Sheol has enlarged its throat Is 5:14 3651
T, as a tongue of fire consumes Is 5:24 3651
"**T** the Lord Himself will give you Is 7:14 3651
"Now **t**, behold, the Lord is about Is 8:7 3651
T the LORD raises against them Is 9:11
T the Lord does not take pleasure Is 9:17
5921, 3651
T the Lord, the GOD of hosts, will Is 10:16 3651
T thus says the Lord GOD of hosts, Is 10:24 3651
T you will joyously draw water Is 12:3
T all hands will fall limp, And Is 13:7
5921, 3651
T I will make the heavens Is 13:13
5921, 3651
T the armed men of Moab cry aloud; Is 15:4
5921, 3651
T the abundance *which* they have Is 15:7
5921, 3651
T Moab will wail; Is 16:7 3651
T I will weep bitterly for Jazer, Is 16:9
5921, 3651
T my heart intones like a harp for Is 16:11
5921, 3651
T you plant delightful plants And Is 17:10
5921, 3651
T I say, "Turn your eyes away from Is 22:4
5921, 3651
T in that day the Lord GOD of Is 22:12
T, a curse devours the earth, and Is 24:6
5921, 3651
T, the inhabitants of the earth Is 24:6
5921, 3651
T glorify the LORD in the east, Is 24:15
5921, 3651
T a strong people will glorify Is 25:3
5921, 3651
T You have punished and destroyed Is 26:14 3651
T through this Jacob's iniquity Is 27:9 3651
T their Maker will not have Is 27:11 3651
5921, 3651
T, hear the word of the LORD, O Is 28:14 3651
T thus says the Lord GOD, Is 28:16 3651
T behold, I will once again deal Is 29:14 3651
T thus says the LORD, who redeemed Is 29:22 3651
"**T** the safety of Pharaoh will be Is 30:3
T, I have called her Is 30:7 3651
T thus says the Holy One of Is 30:12 3651
T this iniquity will be to you Is 30:13 3651
flee on horses," **T** you shall flee! Is 30:16 3651
5921, 3651
T those who pursue you shall be Is 30:16
5921, 3651
T the LORD longs to be gracious to Is 30:18 3651
And **t** He waits on high to have Is 30:18 3651
"Now **t**, come make a bargain with Is 36:8
T, offer a prayer for the remnant Is 37:4
"**T** their inhabitants were short Is 37:27
T I will put My hook in your nose And Is 37:29
"**T**, thus says the LORD concerning Is 37:33 3651
T I declared *them* to you long ago, Is 48:5
T, I am not disgraced; Is 50:7
5921, 3651
T, I have set My face like flint, Is 50:7
5921, 3651
T, please hear this, you Is 51:21 3651
"Now **t**, what do I have here," Is 52:5
"**T** My people shall know My name; Is 52:6 3651
t in that day I am the one who is Is 52:6 3651
T, I will allot Him a portion with Is 53:12 3651
strength, **T** you did not faint. Is 57:10 3651
5921, 3651
T justice is far from us, And Is 59:9
5921, 3651
T they will possess a double Is 61:7 3651
T He turned Himself to become Is 63:10
T I will measure their former work Is 65:7
T, thus says the Lord GOD, Is 65:13 3651
"**T** I will yet contend with you," Jer 2:9 3651
Know **t** and see that it is evil and Jer 2:19
T even the wicked women You have Jer 2:33 3651
"**T** the showers have been Jer 3:3
T a lion from the forest will Jer 5:6
5921, 3651
T, thus says the LORD, the God of Jer 5:14 3651
T they have become great and rich. Jer 5:27
5921, 3651
T they shall fall among those who Jer 6:15 3651
"**T** hear, O nations, And know, O Jer 6:18 3651
T, thus says the LORD, Jer 6:21 3651
t, I will do to the house which is Jer 7:14
T thus says the Lord GOD, Jer 7:20 3651
"**T**, behold, days are coming," Jer 7:32 3651
"**T** I will give their wives to Jer 8:10 3651
T they shall fall among those who Jer 8:12 3651
T thus says the LORD of hosts, Jer 9:7 3651
t thus says the LORD of hosts, the Jer 9:15 3651
T they have not prospered, And all Jer 10:21
5921, 3651
t I brought on them all the words Jer 11:8
T thus says the LORD, Jer 11:11 3651
"**T** do not pray for this people, Jer 11:14
T thus says the LORD concerning Jer 11:21 3651
t, thus says the LORD of hosts, Jer 11:22 3651
T I have come to hate her. Jer 12:8
5921, 3651
"**T** you are to speak this word to Jer 13:12
"**T** I will scatter them like Jer 13:24
T the LORD does not accept them; Jer 14:10
"**T** thus says the LORD concerning Jer 14:15 3651
T we hope in You, For You are Jer 14:22
T, thus says the LORD, Jer 15:19 3651
"**T** behold, days are coming," Jer 16:14 3651
"**T** behold, I am going to make Jer 16:21 3651
"**T** thus says the LORD, Jer 18:13 3651
T, give their children over to Jer 18:21 3651
t, behold, days are coming," Jer 19:6 3651
T my persecutors will stumble and Jer 20:11
5921, 3651
T thus says the LORD in regard to Jer 22:18 3651
T thus says the LORD God of Israel Jer 23:2 3651
"**T** behold, *the* days are coming," Jer 23:7 3651
"**T** their way will be like Jer 23:12 3651
"**T** thus says the LORD of hosts Jer 23:15 3651
"**T** behold, I am against the Jer 23:30 3651
"**T** behold, I will surely forget Jer 23:39 3651
"**T** thus says the LORD of hosts, Jer 25:8 3651
"**T** you shall prophesy against Jer 25:30 3651
"Now **t** amend your ways and your Jer 26:13 3651
"**T** thus says the LORD, Jer 28:16 3651
"You, **t**, hear the word of the Jer 29:20
t thus says the LORD, Jer 29:32 3651
'**T** all who devour you will be Jer 30:16 3651
T I have drawn you with Jer 31:3
5921, 3651
T My heart yearns for him; Jer 31:20
5921, 3651
t You have made all this calamity Jer 32:23
T thus says the LORD, Jer 32:28 3651
"Now **t** thus says the LORD God of Jer 32:36 3651
"**T** thus says the LORD, Jer 34:17 3651
"**T** thus says the LORD, the God of Jer 35:17 3651
t thus says the LORD of hosts, the Jer 35:19 3651
'**T** thus says the LORD concerning Jer 36:30 3651
t this thing has happened to you. Jer 40:3
T you should now clearly Jer 42:22
"**T** My wrath and My anger were Jer 44:6
"**T** thus says the LORD of hosts, Jer 44:11 3651
t this calamity has befallen you, Jer 44:23
5921, 3651
T he retains his flavor, And his Jer 48:11
5921, 3651
"**T** behold, the days are coming," Jer 48:12 3651
"**T** I will wail for Moab, Even Jer 48:31
5921, 3651
"**T** My heart wails for Moab like Jer 48:36
5921, 3651
T they have lost the abundance it Jer 48:36
5921, 3651
"**T** behold, the days are coming," Jer 49:2 3651
T hear the plan of the LORD which Jer 49:20 3651
"**T**, her young men will fall in Jer 49:26 3651
"**T** thus says the LORD of hosts, Jer 50:18 3651
"**T** her young men will fall in her Jer 50:30 3651
"**T** the desert creatures will live Jer 50:39 3651
T hear the plan of the LORD which Jer 50:45 3651
T the nations are going mad. Jer 51:7
5921, 3651
T thus says the LORD, Jer 51:36 3651
T behold, days are coming When I Jer 51:47 3651
"**T** behold, the days are coming," Jer 51:52 3651
T she has become an unclean thing. La 1:8
5921, 3651
T she has fallen astonishingly; La 1:9
recall to my mind, **T** I have hope. La 3:21
5921, 3651
"**T** I have hope in Him." La 3:24
5921, 3651
"**T**, thus says the Lord GOD, Ezk 5:7 3651
t, thus says the Lord GOD, Ezk 5:8 3651
'**T**, fathers will eat *their* sons Ezk 5:10 3651
t I will also withdraw, Ezk 5:11
t I will make it an abhorrent Ezk 7:20
5921, 3651
"**T**, I will bring the worst of the Ezk 7:24
"**T**, I indeed will deal in wrath. Ezk 8:18
"**T**, prophesy against them, son of Ezk 11:4 3651
"**T**, thus says the Lord GOD, Ezk 11:7 3651
"**T** say, 'Thus says the Lord GOD, Ezk 11:16 3651
T say, 'Thus says the Lord GOD, "I Ezk 11:17 3651
"**T**, son of man, prepare for Ezk 12:3
"**T** say to them, Ezk 12:23 3651
"**T** say to them, Ezk 12:28 3651
T, thus says the Lord GOD, Ezk 13:8 3651
t behold, I am against you, Ezk 13:8 3651
T, thus says the Lord GOD, Ezk 13:13 3651
T, thus says the Lord GOD, Ezk 13:20 3651
t, you women will no longer see Ezk 13:23 3651
"**T** speak to them and tell them, Ezk 14:4 3651
"**T** say to the house of Israel, Ezk 14:6 3651
"**T**, thus says the Lord GOD, Ezk 15:6 3651
T, O harlot, hear the word of the Ezk 16:35 3651
t, behold, I will gather all your Ezk 16:37 3651
T I removed them when I saw *it.* Ezk 16:50
T, thus says the Lord GOD, Ezk 17:19 3651
"**T** I will judge you, O house of Ezk 18:30 3651
"**T**, repent and live." Ezk 18:32
"**T**, son of man, speak to the Ezk 20:27 3651
"**T**, say to the house of Israel, Ezk 20:30 3651
t My sword will go forth from its Ezk 21:4 3651
My people, **t** strike *your* thigh. Ezk 21:12 3651
"You **t**, son of man, prophesy and Ezk 21:14
"**T**, thus says the Lord GOD, Ezk 21:24 3651
t I have made you a reproach to Ezk 22:4
5921, 3651
"**T**, thus says the Lord GOD, Ezk 22:19 3651
all of you have become dross, **t**, Ezk 22:19 3651
"**T**, I gave her into the hand of Ezk 23:9 3651
"**T**, O Oholibah, thus says the Ezk 23:22 3651
t I will give her cup into your Ezk 23:31
"**T**, thus says the Lord GOD, Ezk 23:35 3651
'**T**, thus says the Lord GOD, Ezk 24:6 3651
'**T**, thus says the Lord GOD, Ezk 24:9 3651
t, behold, I am going to give you Ezk 25:4 3651
t, behold, I have stretched out My Ezk 25:7 3651
t, behold, I am going to deprive Ezk 25:9 3651
t thus says the Lord GOD, Ezk 25:13 3651
T, they will act in Edom according Ezk 25:14
t thus says the Lord GOD, Ezk 25:16 3651
t thus says the Lord GOD, Ezk 26:3 3651
T thus says the Lord GOD, Ezk 28:6 3651
T, behold, I will bring strangers Ezk 28:7 3651
T I have cast you as profane From Ezk 28:16
T I have brought fire from the Ezk 28:18
'**T** thus says the Lord GOD, Ezk 29:8 3651
t, behold, I am against you and Ezk 29:10 3651
T thus says the Lord GOD, Ezk 29:19 3651
"**T** thus says the Lord GOD, Ezk 30:22 3651

Context	Reference	Number
'**T** its height was loftier than all	Ezk 31:5	5921, 3651
'**T** thus says the Lord GOD,	Ezk 31:10	3651
t I will give it into the hand of	Ezk 31:11	
"**T** say to them,	Ezk 33:25	3651
T, you shepherds, hear the word of	Ezk 34:7	3651
t, you shepherds, hear the word of	Ezk 34:9	3651
T, thus says the Lord GOD to them,	Ezk 34:20	3651
t, I will deliver My flock, and	Ezk 34:22	
t as I live," declares the Lord GOD,	Ezk 35:6	3651
t bloodshed will pursue you.	Ezk 35:6	
t as I live," declares the Lord GOD,	Ezk 35:11	3651
t prophesy and say,	Ezk 36:3	3651
'**T**, O mountains of Israel, hear	Ezk 36:4	3651
t thus says the Lord GOD,	Ezk 36:5	3651
"**T** prophesy concerning the land	Ezk 36:6	3651
"**T** thus says the Lord GOD,	Ezk 36:7	3651
t you will no longer devour men	Ezk 36:14	3651
"**T** I poured out My wrath on them	Ezk 36:18	
"**T** say to the house of Israel,	Ezk 36:22	3651
"**T** prophesy and say to them,	Ezk 37:12	3651
"**T** prophesy, son of man, and say	Ezk 38:14	3651
T thus says the Lord GOD,	Ezk 39:25	3651
t the width of the temple	Ezk 41:7	5921, 3651
t *the upper chambers* were set back	Ezk 42:6	5921, 3651
t it shall be shut.	Ezk 44:2	
t I have sworn against them,"	Ezk 44:12	5921, 3651
t declare to me the dream and its	Da 2:6	3861a
t tell me the dream, that I may	Da 2:9	3861a
T, Daniel went in to Arioch, whom	Da 2:24	3606, 6903, 1836
T at that time, when all the	Da 3:7	3606, 6903, 1836
"**T** I make a decree that any	Da 3:29	
'**T**, O king, may my advice be	Da 4:27	3861a
T King Darius signed the document,	Da 6:9	3606, 6903, 1836
"**T** the LORD has kept the	Da 9:14	
t he will be disheartened and	Da 11:30	
"**T**, behold, I will hedge up her	Hos 2:6	3651
"**T**, I will take back My grain at	Hos 2:9	3651
"**T**, behold, I will allure her,	Hos 2:14	3651
T the land mourns, And everyone	Hos 4:3	5921, 3651
T your daughters play the harlot And	Hos 4:13	5921, 3651
T I am like a moth to Ephraim And	Hos 5:12	
T I have hewn *them* in pieces by	Hos 6:5	5921, 3651
T a tumult will arise among your	Hos 10:14	
T, return to your God, Observe	Hos 12:6	
T they will be like the morning	Hos 13:3	3651
T they forgot Me.	Hos 13:6	5921, 3651
T I will punish you for all your	Am 3:2	5921, 3651
T, thus says the Lord GOD,	Am 3:11	3651
"**T** thus I will do to you, O	Am 4:12	3651
T because you impose heavy rent	Am 5:11	3651
T at such a time the prudent	Am 5:13	3651
T thus says the LORD God of	Am 5:16	3651
"**T**, I will make you go into exile	Am 5:27	
T, they will now go into exile at	Am 6:7	3651
T I will deliver up *the* city and	Am 6:8	
"**T**, thus says the LORD,	Am 7:17	3651
T in order to forestall this I	Jon 4:2	5921, 3651
"**T** now, O LORD, please take my	Jon 4:3	
T you will give parting gifts On	Mi 1:14	3651
T thus says the LORD,	Mi 2:3	3651
"**T** you will have no one	Mi 2:5	3651
T *it will be* night for you	Mi 3:6	3651
T, on account of you Zion will be	Mi 3:12	3651
T He will give them *up* until the	Mi 5:3	3651
T I will give you up for	Mi 6:16	4616
T the law is ignored And justice	Hab 1:4	5921, 3651
T justice comes out perverted.	Hab 1:4	5921, 3651
T they rejoice and are glad.	Hab 1:15	5921, 3651
T they offer a sacrifice to their	Hab 1:16	5921, 3651
Will they **t** empty their net And	Hab 1:17	5921, 3651
"**T**, as I live," declares the LORD	Zph 2:9	3651
"**T** wait for Me,"	Zph 3:8	3651
Now **t**, thus says the LORD of	Hg 1:5	
"**T**, because of you the sky has	Hg 1:10	5921, 3651
"**T** say to them, 'Thus says the LORD	Zch 1:3	
'**T** thus says the LORD,	Zch 1:16	3651
t great wrath came from the LORD	Zch 7:12	
T *the people* wander like sheep,	Zch 10:2	5921, 3651
t you, O sons of Jacob, are not	Mal 3:6	
"**T** bear fruit in keeping	Mt 3:8	3767
t every tree that does not bear good	Mt 3:10	3767
"**T** if you are presenting your	Mt 5:23	3767
"**T** you are to be perfect, as your	Mt 5:48	3767
"In everything, **t**, treat people	Mt 7:12	3767
"**T** everyone who hears these words	Mt 7:24	3767
"**T** beseech the Lord of the	Mt 9:38	3767
"**T** do not fear them, for there is	Mt 10:26	3767
"**T** everyone who confesses Me before	Mt 10:32	3767
"**T** I say to you, any sin and	Mt 12:31	1223, 3778
"**T** I speak to them in parables;	Mt 13:13	1223, 3778
"**T** every scribe who has become a	Mt 13:52	1223, 3778
What **t** God has joined together,	Mt 19:6	3767
"**T** when the owner of the vineyard	Mt 21:40	3767
"**T** I say to you, the kingdom of	Mt 21:43	1223, 3778
'Go **t** to the main highways, and as	Mt 22:9	3767
"In the resurrection, **t**, whose wife	Mt 22:28	3767
t all that they tell you, do and	Mt 23:3	3767
t you will receive greater	Mt 23:14	1223, 3778
"**T**, whoever swears by the altar, swears	Mt 23:20	3767
"**T**, behold, I am sending you	Mt 23:34	1223, 3778
"**T** when you see the ABOMINATION	Mt 24:15	3767
"**T** be on the alert, for you do	Mt 24:42	3767
'**T** take away the talent from him,	Mt 25:28	3767
"**T**, give orders for the grave to	Mt 27:64	3767
"Go **t** and make disciples of all	Mt 28:19	3767
"What **t** God has joined together,	Mk 10:9	3767
"**T** I say to you, all things for	Mk 11:24	1223, 3778
"**T**, be on the alert	Mk 13:35	3767
"**T** bear fruits in keeping	Lk 3:8	3767
"**T** if You worship before me, it	Lk 4:7	3767
t beseech the Lord of the harvest	Lk 10:2	3767
"If **t** your whole body is full of	Lk 11:36	3767
"**T**, salt is good;	Lk 14:34	3767
"**T** if you have not been faithful in	Lk 16:11	3767
"In the resurrection **t**,	Lk 20:33	3767
"**T** David calls Him 'Lord,'	Lk 20:44	3767
when **t** will these things happen?	Lk 21:7	3767
"**T** I will punish Him and release Him."	Lk 23:16	3767
t I will punish Him and release Him."	Lk 23:22	3767
T there arose a discussion on	Jn 3:25	3767
T when the Lord knew that	Jn 4:1	3767
T the Samaritan woman said to Him,	Jn 4:9	3767
T He came again to Cana of Galilee	Jn 4:46	3767
For this reason **t** the Jews were	Jn 5:18	3767
T Jesus answered and was saying to	Jn 5:19	3767
T Jesus, lifting up His eyes	Jn 6:5	3767
T when the people saw the sign which	Jn 6:14	3767
T they said to Him, "What shall we	Jn 6:28	3767
T the Jews were grumbling about Him,	Jn 6:41	3767
T many of His disciples, when they	Jn 6:60	3767
T His brothers said to Him, "Leave	Jn 7:3	3767
T Jesus said, "For a little while	Jn 7:33	3767
Some of the people **t**,	Jn 7:40	3767
"**T** I said to you that you will die	Jn 8:24	3767
t you also do the things which you	Jn 8:38	3767
T they picked up stones to throw	Jn 8:59	3767
T the neighbors, and those who	Jn 9:8	3767
T some of the Pharisees were	Jn 9:16	3767
T they were seeking again to seize	Jn 10:39	3767
T Thomas, who is called Didymus,	Jn 11:16	3767
Martha **t**, when she heard that	Jn 11:20	3767
T, when Mary came where Jesus was,	Jn 11:32	3767
When Jesus **t** saw her weeping, and	Jn 11:33	3767
T many of the Jews who came to Mary,	Jn 11:45	3767
T the chief priests and the	Jn 11:47	3767
T Jesus no longer continued to walk	Jn 11:54	3767
Jesus, **t**, six days before the	Jn 12:1	3767
T Jesus said, "Let her alone, so	Jn 12:7	3767
t the things I speak, I speak just	Jn 12:50	3767
T Jesus said to him, "What you do,	Jn 13:27	3767
T when he had gone out, Jesus said,	Jn 13:31	3767
t I said that He takes of Mine	Jn 16:15	1223, 3778
"**T** you too have grief now;	Jn 16:22	3767
T He again asked them, "Whom do you	Jn 18:7	3767
T Pilate went out to them and said,	Jn 18:29	3767
T Pilate entered again into	Jn 18:33	3767
T Pilate said to Him, "So You are a	Jn 18:37	3767
T when Pilate heard this statement,	Jn 19:8	3767
T when Pilate heard these words, he	Jn 19:13	3767
They took Jesus, **t**, and He went	Jn 19:17	3767
T many of the Jews read this inscription,	Jn 19:20	3767
T the soldiers did these things.	Jn 19:25	3767
T when Jesus had received the sour	Jn 19:30	3767
T because of the Jewish day of	Jn 19:42	3767
T many other signs Jesus also	Jn 20:30	3767
T that disciple whom Jesus loved said	Jn 21:7	3767
T this saying went out among	Jn 21:23	3767
"**T** it is necessary that of the men	Ac 1:21	3767
T MY HEART WAS GLAD AND MY TONGUE	Ac 2:26	1223, 3778
"**T** having been exalted to the	Ac 2:33	3767
"**T** let all the house of Israel	Ac 2:36	3767
"**T** repent and return, so that your	Ac 3:19	3767
"**T**, brethren, select from among	Ac 6:3	1161
T, those who had been scattered	Ac 8:4	3767
"**T** repent of this wickedness of	Ac 8:22	3767
T send to Joppa and invite Simon,	Ac 10:32	3767
"**T** if God gave to them the same gift	Ac 11:17	3767
"**T** He also says in another *Psalm*,	Ac 13:35	1360
"**T** let it be known to you,	Ac 13:38	3767
"**T** take heed, so that the thing	Ac 13:40	3767
T they spent a long time *there*	Ac 14:3	3767
T, being sent on their way by the	Ac 15:3	3767
"Now **t** why do you put God to the	Ac 15:10	3767
"**T** it is my judgment that we do	Ac 15:19	1352
"**T** we have sent Judas and Silas,	Ac 15:27	3767
T come out now and go in peace."	Ac 16:36	3767
T many of them believed, along with	Ac 17:12	3767
T what you worship in ignorance,	Ac 17:23	3767
"**T** having overlooked the times of	Ac 17:30	3767
"**T**, I testify to you this day	Ac 20:26	1360
"**T** be on the alert, remembering	Ac 20:31	1352
"**T** do this that we tell you.	Ac 21:23	3767
T those who were about to examine	Ac 22:29	3767
"Now **t**, you and the Council	Ac 23:15	3767
t he also used to send for him	Ac 24:26	1352
"**T**," he said, "let the influential men	Ac 25:5	3767
T I have brought him before you	Ac 25:26	1352
t I beg you to listen to me	Ac 26:3	1352
"**T**, keep up your courage, men,	Ac 27:25	1352
"**T** I encourage you to take some	Ac 27:34	1352
"For this reason, **t**, I requested	Ac 28:20	3767
"**T** let it be known to you that this	Ac 28:28	3767
T God gave them over in the lusts	Ro 1:24	1352
T you have no excuse, everyone	Ro 2:1	1352
you, **t**, who teach another, do you	Ro 2:21	3767
T IT WAS ALSO CREDITED TO HIM AS	Ro 4:22	1352
T, having been justified by faith,	Ro 5:1	3767
T, just as through one man sin	Ro 5:12	1223, 3778
T we have been buried with Him	Ro 6:4	3767
T do not let sin reign in your	Ro 6:12	3767
T what benefit were you then	Ro 6:21	3767
T, my brethren, you also were made	Ro 7:4	5620
T did that which is good become *a*	Ro 7:13	3767
T there is now no condemnation for	Ro 8:1	686
T I urge you, brethren, by	Ro 12:1	3767
T whoever resists authority has	Ro 13:2	5620
T it is necessary to be in subjection,	Ro 13:5	1352
Love does no wrong to a neighbor; **t**	Ro 13:10	3767
T let us lay aside the deeds of	Ro 13:12	3767
t whether we live or die, we are	Ro 14:8	3767
T let us not judge one another	Ro 14:13	3767
T do not let what is for you a	Ro 14:16	3767
T, accept one another, just as	Ro 15:7	1352
"**T** I WILL GIVE PRAISE TO YOU	Ro 15:9	1223, 3778
T in Christ Jesus I have found	Ro 15:17	3767
T, when I have finished this, and	Ro 15:28	3767
t I am rejoicing over you, but I	Ro 16:19	3767
T do not go on passing judgment	1Co 4:5	5620
T I exhort you, be imitators of me.	1Co 4:16	3767
T let us celebrate the feast, not	1Co 5:8	5620
t glorify God in your body.	1Co 6:20	1211
T concerning the eating of things	1Co 8:4	3767
T, if food causes my brother to	1Co 8:13	1355
T I run in such a way, as not	1Co 9:26	5106
T let him who thinks he stands	1Co 10:12	5620
T, my beloved, flee from idolatry.	1Co 10:14	1355
T the woman ought to have *a symbol*	1Co 11:10	1223, 3778
T when you meet together, it is	1Co 11:20	3767
T whoever eats the bread or drinks	1Co 11:27	5620
T I make known to you that no one	1Co 12:3	1352
T let one who speaks in a tongue	1Co 14:13	1352
T if the whole church assembles	1Co 14:23	3767
T, my brethren, desire earnestly	1Co 14:39	5620
T, my beloved brethren, be	1Co 15:58	5620
T acknowledge such men.	1Co 16:18	3767
T, I was not vacillating when I	2Co 1:17	3767
t also through Him is our Amen to	2Co 1:20	1352
T having such a hope, we use great	2Co 3:12	3767
T, since we have this ministry, as	2Co 4:1	1223, 3778
"I BELIEVED, **T** I SPOKE,"	2Co 4:13	1352
we also believe, **t** we also speak,	2Co 4:13	1352
T we do not lose heart, but though	2Co 4:16	1352
T, being always of good courage,	2Co 5:6	3767
T we also have as our ambition,	2Co 5:9	1352
T, knowing the fear of the Lord, we	2Co 5:11	3767
that one died for all, **t** all died;	2Co 5:14	686
T from now on we recognize no one	2Co 5:16	5620
T if anyone is in Christ, *he is* a	2Co 5:17	5620
T, we are ambassadors for Christ,	2Co 5:20	3767
"**T**, COME OUT FROM THEIR MIDST AND	2Co 6:17	1352
T, having these promises, beloved,	2Co 7:1	3767
T openly before the churches,	2Co 8:24	3767
T it is not surprising if his	2Co 11:15	3767
Most gladly, **t**, I will rather	2Co 12:9	3767
T I am well content with	2Co 12:10	1352
T, be sure that it is those who	Ga 3:7	686
T the Law has become our tutor *to*	Ga 3:24	5620
T you are no longer a slave, but a	Ga 4:7	5620
t keep standing firm and do not be	Ga 5:1	3767
T remember that formerly you, the	Eph 2:11	1352
T I ask you not to lose heart at	Eph 3:13	1352
T I, the prisoner of the Lord,	Eph 4:1	3767
T it says, "WHEN HE ASCENDED ON	Eph 4:8	1352
T, laying aside falsehood, SPEAK	Eph 4:25	1352
T be imitators of God, as beloved	Eph 5:1	3767
T do not be partakers with them;	Eph 5:7	3767
T be careful how you walk, not as	Eph 5:15	3767
T, take up the full armor of God,	Eph 6:13	1223, 3778
Stand firm **t**, HAVING GIRDED YOUR	Eph 6:14	3767
T if there is any encouragement in	Php 2:1	3767
T I hope to send him immediately,	Php 2:23	3767
T I have sent him all the more	Php 2:28	3767
Let us **t**, as many as are perfect,	Php 3:15	3767
T, my beloved brethren whom I long	Php 4:1	5620
T as you have received Christ Jesus	Col 2:6	3767
T no one is to act as your judge	Col 2:16	3767
T if you have been raised up with	Col 3:1	3767
T consider the members of your	Col 3:5	3767
T when we could endure *it* no	1Th 3:1	1352
T comfort one another with these	1Th 4:18	5620
T encourage one another and build	1Th 5:11	1352
t, we ourselves speak proudly of	2Th 1:4	5620

T I want the men in every place to 1Tm 2:8 3767
T, I want younger widows to get 1Tm 5:14 3767
T do not be ashamed of the 2Tm 1:8 3767
You t, my son, be strong in the 2Tm 2:1 3767
T, if anyone cleanses himself from 2Tm 2:21 3767
T, though I have enough confidence Phm 1:8 1352
T GOD, YOUR GOD, HAS ANOINTED Heb 1:9 1223, 3778
T, since the children share in flesh Heb 2:14 3767
T, He had to be made like His Heb 2:17 3606
T, holy brethren, partakers of a Heb 3:1 3606
T, just as the Holy Spirit says, Heb 3:7 1352
"T I WAS ANGRY WITH THIS Heb 3:10 1352
T, let us fear if, while a Heb 4:1 3767
T, since it remains for some to Heb 4:6 3767
T let us be diligent to enter that Heb 4:11 3767
T, since we have a great high priest Heb 4:14 3767
T let us draw near with confidence to Heb 4:16 3767
T leaving the elementary teaching Heb 6:1 1352
T He is able also to save forever Heb 7:25 3606
T even the first covenant was not Heb 9:18 3606
T it was necessary for the copies Heb 9:23 3767
T, when He comes into the world, Heb 10:5 1352
T, brethren, since we have Heb 10:19 3767
T, do not throw away your Heb 10:35 3767
T there was born even of one man, Heb 11:12 1352
T God is not ashamed to be called Heb 11:16 1352
T, since we have so great a cloud Heb 12:1 5105
T, strengthen the hands that are Heb 12:12 1352
T, since we receive a kingdom Heb 12:28 1352
T Jesus also, that He might Heb 13:12 1352
T, putting aside all filthiness and Jas 1:21 1352
T whoever wishes to be a friend of Jas 4:4 3767
T it says, "GOD IS OPPOSED TO THE Jas 4:6 1352
Submit t to God. Resist the devil Jas 4:7 3767
T, to one who knows the right Jas 4:17 3767
T be patient, brethren, until Jas 5:7 3767
T, confess your sins to one Jas 5:16 3767
T, prepare your minds for action, 1Pe 1:13 1352
T, putting aside all malice and 1Pe 2:1 3767
T, since Christ has suffered in 1Pe 4:1 3767
t, be of sound judgment and sober 1Pe 4:7 3767
T, those also who suffer 1Pe 4:19 5620
T, I exhort the elders among you, 1Pe 5:1 3767
T humble yourselves under the mighty 1Pe 5:6 3767
T, brethren, be all the more 2Pe 1:10 1352
T, I will always be ready to 2Pe 1:12 1352
T, beloved, since you look for 2Pe 3:14 1352
You t, beloved, knowing this 2Pe 3:17 3767
t they speak as from the world, 1Jn 4:5 1223, 3778
T we ought to support such men, 3Jn 1:8 3767
"T write the things which you have Rv 1:19 3767
'T remember from where you have Rv 2:5 3767
'T repent; or else I am coming to Rv 2:16 3767
T if you do not wake up, I will come Rv 3:3 3767
t be zealous and repent. Rv 3:19 3767

THEREON

with the poles t, as Moses had 1Ch 15:15 5921

THESE

T are the records of the Gn 6:9 428
T three were the sons of Noah, Gn 9:19 428
t the whole earth was populated. Gn 9:19 428
Now t are the records of the Gn 10:1 428
From t the coastlands of the Gn 10:5 428
T are the sons of Ham, according Gn 10:20 428
all t were the sons of Joktan. Gn 10:29 428
T are the sons of Shem, according Gn 10:31 428
T are the families of the sons of Gn 10:32 428
and out of t the nations were Gn 10:32 428
T are the records of the Gn 11:10 428
Now t are the records of the Gn 11:27 428
All t came as allies to the valley Gn 14:3 428
and t were allies with Abram. Gn 14:13 1992a
After t things the word of the Gn 15:1 428
Then he brought all t to Him and Gn 15:10 428
which passed between t pieces. Gn 15:17 428
only do nothing to t men, Gn 19:8 411
all t things in their hearing; Gn 20:8 428
"What do t seven ewe lambs mean, Gn 21:29 428
"You shall take t seven ewe lambs Gn 21:30
Now it came about after t things, Gn 22:1 428
Now it came about after t things, Gn 22:20 428
t eight Milcah bore to Nahor, Gn 22:23 428
t were the years of the life of Gn 23:1
mother's household about t things. Gn 24:28 428
All t were the sons of Keturah. Gn 25:4 428
T are all the years of Abraham's life Gn 25:7 428
Now t are the records of the Gn 25:12 428
and t are the names of the sons of Gn 25:13 428
T are the sons of Ishmael and Gn 25:16 428
of Ishmael and t are their names, Gn 25:16 428
T are the years of the life of Gn 25:17 428
Now t are the records of the Gn 25:19 428
I will give all t lands, Gn 26:3 411
give your descendants all t lands; Gn 26:4 411
he has supplanted me t two times? Gn 27:36 2088
the daughters of Heth, like t, Gn 27:46 428
he related to Laban all t things. Gn 29:13 428
"T twenty years I have been with Gn 31:38 2088
"T twenty years I have been in Gn 31:41 2088
can I do this day to t my daughters Gn 31:43 428
and to whom do t animals in front Gn 32:17 428
then you shall say, 'T belong Gn 32:18
"Who are t with you?" Gn 33:5 428
"T men are friendly with us; Gn 34:21 428
T are the sons of Jacob who were Gn 35:26 428
Now t are the records of the Gn 36:1 428
T are the sons of Esau who were Gn 36:5 428
T then are the records of the Gn 36:9 428
T are the names of Esau's sons: Gn 36:10 428
T are the sons of Esau's wife Adah. Gn 36:12 428
T are the sons of Reuel: Nahath Gn 36:13 428
T were the sons of Esau's wife Gn 36:13 428
T were the sons of Esau's wife Gn 36:14 428
T are the chiefs of the sons of Gn 36:15 428
T are the chiefs descended from Gn 36:16 428
t are the sons of Adah. Gn 36:16 428
T are the sons of Reuel, Esau's son: Gn 36:17 428
T are the chiefs descended from Gn 36:17 428
t are the sons of Esau's wife Gn 36:17 428
T are the sons of Esau's wife Gn 36:18 428
T are the chiefs descended from Gn 36:18 428
T are the sons of Esau Gn 36:19 428
and t are their chiefs. Gn 36:19 428
T are the sons of Seir the Horite, Gn 36:20 428
T are the chiefs descended from Gn 36:21 428
T are the sons of Shobal: Alvan Gn 36:23 428
T are the sons of Zibeon: Aiah Gn 36:24 428
T are the children of Anah: Dishon, Gn 36:25 428
T are the sons of Dishon: Hemdan Gn 36:26 428
T are the sons of Ezer: Gn 36:27 428
T are the sons of Dishan: Gn 36:28 428
T are the chiefs descended from Gn 36:29 428
T are the chiefs descended from Gn 36:30 428
Now t are the kings who reigned in Gn 36:31 428
Now t are the names of the chiefs Gn 36:40 428
T are the chiefs of Edom Gn 36:43 428
T are the records of the Gn 37:2 428
the man to whom t things belong." Gn 38:25 428
ring and cords and staff are t?" Gn 38:25 428
It came about after t events Gn 39:7 428
she spoke to him with t words, Gn 39:17 428
Then it came about after t things Gn 40:1 428
of t good years that are coming, Gn 41:35 428
So he gathered all the food of t Gn 41:48
all t things are against me." Gn 42:36
them and spoke t words to them. Gn 44:6 428
my lord speak such words as t? Gn 44:7 428
has been in the land t two years, Gn 45:6 2088
Now t are the names of the sons of Gn 46:8 428
T are the sons of Leah, whom she Gn 46:15 428
T are the sons of Zilpah, whom Gn 46:18 428
bore to Jacob t sixteen persons. Gn 46:18 428
T are the sons of Rachel, who were Gn 46:22 428
T are the sons of Bilhah, whom Gn 46:25 428
Rachel, and she bore t to Jacob; Gn 46:25 428
t things that Joseph was told, Gn 48:1 428
Joseph's sons, he said, "Who are t?" Gn 48:8 428
All t are the twelve tribes of Gn 49:28 428
Now t are the names of the sons of Ex 1:1 428
they will not believe even t two signs Ex 4:9 428
T are the heads of their fathers' Ex 6:14 428
t are the families of Reuben. Ex 6:14 428
t are the families of Simeon. Ex 6:15 428
T are the names of the sons of Levi Ex 6:16 428
T are the families of the Levites Ex 6:19 428
t are the families of the Ex 6:24 428
T are the heads of the fathers' Ex 6:25 428
that I may perform t signs of Mine Ex 10:1 428
"All t your servants will Ex 11:8 428
all t wonders before Pharaoh; Ex 11:10 428
and t people who are with you, Ex 18:18 2088
and you shall place t over them Ex 18:21
and all t people also will go to Ex 18:23 2088
T are the words that you shall Ex 19:6 428
and set before them all t words Ex 19:7 428
Then God spoke all t words, Ex 20:1 428
"Now t are the ordinances which Ex 21:1 428
not do t three things for her, Ex 21:11 428
in accordance with all t words." Ex 24:8 428
of pure gold, with all t utensils. Ex 25:39 428
"T are the garments which they shall Ex 28:4 428
and you shall put all t in the Ex 29:24 3605
make of t a holy anointing oil, Ex 30:25
"Write down t words, for in Ex 34:27 428
for in accordance with t words I Ex 34:27 428
"T are the things that the LORD Ex 35:1 428
is made of t things to the LORD, Lv 2:8 428
it, he will be guilty in one of t. Lv 5:4 428
he becomes guilty in one of t, Lv 5:5 428
he has committed from one of t, Lv 5:13 428
'T the LORD had commanded to be Lv 7:36 834
He then put all t on the hands of Lv 8:27
When things like t happened to me, Lv 10:19 428
'T are the creatures which you may Lv 11:2 2088
you are not to eat of t, Lv 11:4 2088
'T you may eat, whatever is in the Lv 11:9 2088
'T, moreover, you shall detest Lv 11:13 428
'Yet t you may eat among all the Lv 11:21 2088
'T of them you may eat: Lv 11:22 428
'By t, moreover, you will be made Lv 11:24 428
'Now t are to you the unclean Lv 11:29 2088
'T are to you the unclean among Lv 11:31 428
(t are holy garments). Lv 16:4 1992a
yourselves by any of t things; Lv 18:24 428
for by all t the nations which I Lv 18:24 428
not do any of t abominations, Lv 18:26 428
you have done all t abominations, Lv 18:27 411
does any of t abominations, Lv 18:29 428
you, for they did all t things, Lv 20:23 428
by harlotry, t he may not take; Lv 21:14 428
appointed times are t: Lv 23:2 428
'T are the appointed times of the Lv 23:4 428
'T are the appointed times of the Lv 23:37 428
if he is not redeemed by t means, Lv 25:54 428
not carry out all t commandments, Lv 26:14 428
'If also after t things you do Lv 26:18 428
'And if by t things you are not Lv 26:23 428
T are the statutes and ordinances Lv 26:46 428
T are the commandments which the Lv 27:34 428
"T then are the names of the men Nu 1:5 428
"T are they who were called of Nu 1:16 428
So Moses and Aaron took t men who Nu 1:17 428
T are the ones who were numbered, Nu 1:44 428
T are the numbered men of the sons Nu 2:32 428
Now t are the records of the Nu 3:1 428
T then are the names of the sons Nu 3:2 428
T are the names of the sons of Nu 3:3 428
T then are the sons of Levi by Nu 3:17 428
T are the names of the sons of Nu 3:18 428
T are the families of the Levites Nu 3:20 428
t were the families of the Nu 3:21 428
t were the families of the Nu 3:27 428
t were the families of Merari. Nu 3:33 428
T are the things in the tent of Nu 4:15 428
T are the numbered men of the Nu 4:37 428
T are the numbered men of the Nu 4:41 428
T are the numbered men of the Nu 4:45 428
thus t were his numbered men, just Nu 4:49
then write t curses on a scroll, Nu 5:23 428
"Accept t things from them, Nu 7:5
T then were their names: Nu 13:4 428
T are the names of the men whom Nu 13:16 428
have put Me to the test t ten times Nu 14:22 2088
When Moses spoke t words to Nu 14:39 428
shall do t things in this manner, Nu 15:13 428
do not observe all t commandments, Nu 15:22 428
you put out the eyes of t men? Nu 16:14 1992a
from the tents of t wicked men, Nu 16:26 428
has sent me to do all t deeds; Nu 16:28 428
"If t men die the death of all Nu 16:29 428
t men have spurned the LORD." Nu 16:30 428
he finished speaking all t words, Nu 16:31 428
"As for the censers of t men who Nu 16:38 428
Israel took all t cities and Nu 21:25 428
"Who are t men with you?" Nu 22:9 428
have struck me t three times?" Nu 22:28 2088
struck your donkey t three times? Nu 22:32 2088
aside from me t three times. Nu 22:33 2088
in blessing them t three times! Nu 24:10 2088
T are the families of the Nu 26:7 428
T are the Dathan and Abiram who Nu 26:9 1931
T are the families of the Nu 26:14 428
T are the families of the sons of Nu 26:18 428
T are the families of Judah Nu 26:22 428
T are the families of Issachar Nu 26:25 428
T are the families of the Nu 26:27 428
T are the sons of Gilead: Nu 26:30 428
T are the families of Manasseh; Nu 26:34 428
T are the sons of Ephraim Nu 26:35 428
T are the sons of Shuthelah: of Eran, Nu 26:36 428
T are the families of the sons of Nu 26:37 428
T are the sons of Joseph according Nu 26:37 428
T are the sons of Benjamin Nu 26:41 428
T are the sons of Dan according to Nu 26:42 428
T are the families of Dan Nu 26:42 428
T are the families of the sons of Nu 26:47 428
T are the families of Naphtali Nu 26:50 428
T are those who were numbered of Nu 26:51 428
"Among t the land shall be Nu 26:53 428
T are those who were numbered of Nu 26:57 428
T are the families of Levi: Nu 26:58 428
T are those who were numbered by Nu 26:63 428
But among t there was not a man of Nu 26:64 428
and t are the names of his Nu 27:1 428
(T are the waters of Meribah of Nu 27:14 1992a
'You shall present t besides the Nu 28:23 428
'You shall present t to the LORD Nu 29:39 428
T are the statutes which the LORD Nu 30:16 428
t caused the sons of Israel, Nu 31:16 2007
you will destroy all t people." Nu 32:15 2088
T are the journeys of the sons of Nu 33:1 428
and t are their journeys according Nu 33:2 428
"T are the names of the men who Nu 34:17 428
"T are the names of the men: of Nu 34:19 428
T are those whom the LORD Nu 34:29 428
'T six cities shall be for refuge Nu 35:15 428
avenger according to t ordinances. Nu 35:24 428
'T things shall be for a statutory Nu 35:29 428
T are the commandments and the Nu 36:13 428
T are the words which Moses spoke Dt 1:1 428
'Not one of t men, this evil Dt 1:35 428
T forty years the LORD your God Dt 2:7 2088
"All t were cities fortified with Dt 3:5 428
your God has done to t two kings; Dt 3:21 428
will hear all t statutes and say, Dt 4:6 428
all t things have come upon you, Dt 4:30 428
to one of t cities he might live: Dt 4:42 411
t are the testimonies and the Dt 4:45 428
"T words the LORD spoke to all Dt 5:22 428
"T words, which I am commanding you Dt 6:6 428
us to observe all t statutes, Dt 6:24 428
because you listen to t judgments Dt 7:12 428
'T nations are greater than I; Dt 7:17 428
your God will clear away t nations Dt 7:22 411
in the wilderness t forty years, Dt 8:2 2088
did your foot swell t forty years. Dt 8:4 2088
because of the wickedness of t nations Dt 9:4 428
because of the wickedness of t nations Dt 9:5 428
done t great and awesome things Dt 10:21 428
therefore impress t words of mine Dt 11:18 428
the LORD will drive out all t nations Dt 11:23 428
"T are the statutes and the Dt 12:1 428
all t words which I command you, Dt 12:28 428
'How do t nations serve their Dt 12:30 428

"**T** are the animals which you may	**Dt 14:4**	2088
you are not to eat of **t** among	**Dt 14:7**	2088
"**T** you may eat of all that are in	**Dt 14:9**	2088
"But **t** are the ones which you	**Dt 14:12**	2088
be careful to observe **t** statutes.	**Dt 16:12**	428
words of this law and **t** statutes,	**Dt 17:19**	428
"For whoever does **t** things is	**Dt 18:12**	428
and because of **t** detestable things	**Dt 18:12**	428
flee to one of **t** cities and live;	**Dt 19:5**	428
for yourself, besides **t** three.	**Dt 19:9**	428
and he flees to one of **t** cities,	**Dt 19:11**	411
of the cities of **t** nations nearby.	**Dt 20:15**	428
"Only in the cities of **t** peoples	**Dt 20:16**	428
for whoever does **t** things is an	**Dt 22:5**	428
for both of **t** are an abomination	**Dt 23:18**	
him with many more stripes than **t** and	**Dt 25:3**	428
"For everyone who does **t** things,	**Dt 25:16**	428
to do **t** statutes and ordinances.	**Dt 26:16**	428
set up on Mount Ebal, **t** stones,	**Dt 27:4**	428
t shall stand on Mount Gerizim to	**Dt 27:12**	428
t shall stand on Mount Ebal:	**Dt 27:13**	428
"All **t** blessings will come	**Dt 28:2**	428
that all **t** curses will come upon	**Dt 28:15**	428
"So all **t** curses shall come on	**Dt 28:45**	428
T are the words of the covenant	**Dt 29:1**	428
all of **t** things have come upon you,	**Dt 30:1**	428
inflict all **t** curses on your enemies	**Dt 30:7**	428
and spoke **t** words to all Israel.	**Dt 31:1**	428
will destroy **t** nations before you,	**Dt 31:3**	428
that **t** evils have come upon us?'	**Dt 31:17**	428
that I may speak **t** words in their	**Dt 31:28**	428
all **t** words to all Israel,	**Dt 32:45**	428
'What do **t** stones mean to you?'	**Jos 4:6**	428
So **t** stones shall become a	**Jos 4:7**	428
'What are **t** stones?'	**Jos 4:21**	428
"**T** wineskins which we filled were	**Jos 9:13**	428
and **t** our clothes and our sandals	**Jos 9:13**	428
Now **t** five kings had fled and	**Jos 10:16**	428
and bring **t** five kings out to me	**Jos 10:22**	428
and brought **t** five kings out to	**Jos 10:23**	428
brought **t** kings out to Joshua,	**Jos 10:24**	428
feet on the necks of **t** kings."	**Jos 10:24**	428
Joshua captured all **t** kings	**Jos 10:42**	428
of **t** kings having agreed to meet,	**Jos 11:5**	428
was the head of all **t** kingdoms.	**Jos 11:10**	428
all the cities of **t** kings,	**Jos 11:12**	428
spoil of **t** cities and the cattle,	**Jos 11:14**	428
war a long time with all **t** kings.	**Jos 11:18**	428
Now **t** are the kings of the land	**Jos 12:1**	428
Now **t** are the kings of the land	**Jos 12:7**	428
T are *the territories* which Moses	**Jos 13:32**	428
Now **t** are *the territories* which	**Jos 14:1**	428
as He spoke, **t** forty-five years,	**Jos 14:10**	2088
t *were* the male descendants of	**Jos 17:2**	428
and **t** are the names of his	**Jos 17:3**	428
t cities *belonged* to Ephraim	**Jos 17:9**	428
not take possession of **t** cities,	**Jos 17:12**	428
t cities as far as Baalath-beer,	**Jos 19:8**	428
t cities with their villages.	**Jos 19:16**	428
t cities with their villages.	**Jos 19:31**	428
t cities with their villages.	**Jos 19:48**	428
T are the inheritances which	**Jos 19:51**	428
He shall flee to one of **t** cities,	**Jos 20:4**	428
T were the appointed cities for	**Jos 20:9**	428
Levites from their inheritance **t** cities	**Jos 21:3**	428
gave by lot to the Levites **t** cities	**Jos 21:8**	428
They gave **t** cities which are	**Jos 21:9**	428
nine cities from **t** two tribes.	**Jos 21:16**	428
All **t** *were* the cities of the sons	**Jos 21:40**	
T cities each had its surrounding	**Jos 21:42**	428
thus *it was* with all **t** cities.	**Jos 21:42**	428
brothers **t** many days to this day,	**Jos 22:3**	2088
your God has done to all **t** nations	**Jos 23:3**	428
I have apportioned to you **t** nations	**Jos 23:4**	428
will not associate with **t** nations,	**Jos 23:7**	428
nations, **t** which remain among you,	**Jos 23:7**	428
cling to the rest of **t** nations,	**Jos 23:12**	428
nations, **t** which remain among you,	**Jos 23:12**	428
not continue to drive **t** nations out	**Jos 23:13**	428
and who did **t** great signs in our	**Jos 24:17**	428
And Joshua wrote **t** words in the	**Jos 24:26**	428
It came about after **t** things	**Jos 24:29**	428
the angel of the LORD spoke **t** words	**Jg 2:4**	428
Now **t** are the nations which the	**Jg 3:1**	428
T *nations are:* the five lords of	**Jg 3:3**	
mother's relatives spoke all **t** words	**Jg 9:3**	428
He have shown us all **t** things,	**Jg 13:23**	428
You have deceived me **t** three times	**Jg 16:15**	2088
"Do you know that there are in **t**	**Jg 18:14**	428
When **t** went into Micah's house	**Jg 18:18**	428
let us approach one of **t** places;	**Jg 19:13**	
Out of all **t** people 700 choice men	**Jg 20:16**	2088
all **t** were men of war.	**Jg 20:17**	2088
all **t** drew the sword.	**Jg 20:25**	428
all **t** were valiant warriors.	**Jg 20:44**	428
all **t** were valiant warriors.	**Jg 20:46**	428
"**T** six *measures* of barley he gave	**Ru 3:17**	428
t are the generations of Perez:	**Ru 4:18**	428
that I hear from all **t** people?	**1Sa 2:23**	428
us from the hand of **t** mighty gods?	**1Sa 4:8**	428
T are the gods who smote the	**1Sa 4:8**	428
T are the golden tumors which	**1Sa 6:17**	428
he judged Israel in all **t** places.	**1Sa 7:16**	428
shall be when **t** signs come to you,	**1Sa 10:7**	428
spoke **t** words in the hearing of the	**1Sa 11:4**	
mightily when he heard **t** words,	**1Sa 11:6**	428
the garrison of **t** uncircumcised;	**1Sa 14:6**	428
names of his two daughters *were* **t**:	**1Sa 14:49**	
"The LORD has not chosen **t**."	**1Sa 16:10**	428

"Are **t** all the children?"	**1Sa 16:11**	
heard **t** words of the Philistine,	**1Sa 17:11**	428
roasted grain and **t** ten loaves and	**1Sa 17:17**	2088
"Bring also **t** ten cuts of cheese	**1Sa 17:18**	428
and he spoke **t** same words;	**1Sa 17:23**	428
"I cannot go with **t**,	**1Sa 17:39**	428
servants spoke **t** words to David.	**1Sa 18:23**	428
to **t** words *which* David spoke.	**1Sa 18:24**	428
his servants told David **t** words,	**1Sa 18:26**	428
and Jonathan told him all **t** words.	**1Sa 19:7**	428
David took **t** words to heart and	**1Sa 21:12**	428
I go and attack **t** Philistines?"	**1Sa 23:2**	428
David persuaded his men with **t**	**1Sa 24:7**	
finished speaking **t** words to Saul,	**1Sa 24:16**	428
to all **t** words in David's name;	**1Sa 25:9**	428
told him according to all **t** words.	**1Sa 25:12**	428
his wife told him **t** things,	**1Sa 25:37**	428
"What *are* **t** Hebrews *doing here?*"	**1Sa 29:3**	428
who has been with me **t** days,	**1Sa 29:3**	2088
me these days, or *rather* **t** years,	**1Sa 29:3**	2088
it not *be* with the heads of **t** men?	**1Sa 29:4**	1992a
otherwise **t** uncircumcised will come	**1Sa 31:4**	428
T were born to David at Hebron.	**2Sa 3:5**	428
and **t** men the sons of Zeruiah are	**2Sa 3:39**	428
Now **t** are the names of those who	**2Sa 5:14**	428
all **t** words and all this vision,	**2Sa 7:17**	428
also dedicated **t** to the LORD,	**2Sa 8:11**	
to you many more things like **t**!	**2Sa 12:8**	2007
King David heard of all **t** matters,	**2Sa 13:21**	428
and it was he who put all **t** words	**2Sa 14:19**	428
"Why do you have **t**?"	**2Sa 16:2**	428
T four were born to the giant in	**2Sa 21:22**	428
Now **t** are the last words of David.	**2Sa 23:1**	428
T are the names of the mighty men	**2Sa 23:8**	428
T things the three mighty men did.	**2Sa 23:17**	428
T *things* Benaiah the son of	**2Sa 23:22**	428
but **t** sheep, what have they done?	**2Sa 24:17**	428
T were his officials: Azariah	**1Ki 4:2**	428
T are their names: Ben-hur, in	**1Ki 4:8**	428
All **t** were of costly stones, of	**1Ki 7:9**	428
even all **t** utensils which Hiram	**1Ki 7:45**	428
"And may **t** words of mine, with	**1Ki 8:59**	428
"What are **t** cities which you have	**1Ki 9:13**	428
T *were* the chief officers who	**1Ki 9:23**	428
how blessed are **t** your servants	**1Ki 10:8**	428
Solomon held fast to **t** in love.	**1Ki 11:2**	1992a
t also they related to their	**1Ki 13:11**	
be neither dew nor rain **t** years,	**1Ki 17:1**	428
Now it came about after **t** things that	**1Ki 17:17**	428
done all **t** things at Your word.	**1Ki 18:36**	428
So **t** went out from the city, the	**1Ki 20:19**	428
Now it came about after **t** things that	**1Ki 21:1**	428
about when Ahab heard **t** words,	**1Ki 21:27**	428
'With **t** you will gore the	**1Ki 22:11**	428
'**T** have no master.	**1Ki 22:17**	428
the mouth of all **t** your prophets;	**1Ki 22:23**	428
you and spoke **t** words to you?"	**2Ki 1:7**	428
the lives of **t** fifty servants of yours	**2Ki 1:13**	428
'I have purified **t** waters;	**2Ki 2:21**	428
For the LORD has called **t** three	**2Ki 3:10**	428
the LORD has called **t** three kings	**2Ki 3:13**	428
and pour out into all **t** vessels,	**2Ki 4:4**	428
"O LORD, open the eyes of **t** *men*,	**2Ki 6:20**	428
When **t** lepers came to the	**2Ki 7:8**	428
killed him, but who killed all **t**?	**2Ki 10:9**	428
sin, from **t** Jehu did not depart,	**2Ki 10:29**	
while **t** nations feared the LORD,	**2Ki 17:41**	428
and to you to speak **t** words,	**2Ki 18:27**	428
"What did **t** men say, and from	**2Ki 20:14**	428
of Judah has done **t** abominations,	**2Ki 21:11**	428
who proclaimed **t** things.	**2Ki 23:16**	428
proclaimed **t** things which you have	**2Ki 23:17**	428
and **t** the king of Babylon brought	**2Ki 24:16**	
all **t** vessels was beyond weight.	**2Ki 25:16**	428
pillar was like **t** with network.	**2Ki 25:17**	428
all **t** *were* the sons of Joktan.	**1Ch 1:23**	428
T are their genealogies:	**1Ch 1:29**	428
t *were* the sons of Ishmael.	**1Ch 1:31**	428
All **t** were the sons of Keturah.	**1Ch 1:33**	428
Now **t** are the kings who reigned in	**1Ch 1:43**	428
T *were* the chiefs of Edom.	**1Ch 1:54**	428
T are the sons of Israel:	**1Ch 2:1**	428
t three were born to him by	**1Ch 2:3**	
and **t** were her sons:	**1Ch 2:18**	428
All **t** were the sons of Machir, the	**1Ch 2:23**	428
T were the sons of Jerahmeel.	**1Ch 2:33**	428
T were the sons of Caleb.	**1Ch 2:50**	428
from **t** came the Zorathites and the	**1Ch 2:53**	428
Now **t** were the sons of David who	**1Ch 3:1**	428
T were born to him in Jerusalem:	**1Ch 3:5**	428
All **t** *were* the sons of David,	**1Ch 3:9**	
T *were* the families of the	**1Ch 4:2**	428
T *were* the sons of Etam: Jezreel,	**1Ch 4:3**	428
T *were* the sons of Hur, the	**1Ch 4:4**	428
T were the sons of Naarah.	**1Ch 4:6**	428
T are the men of Recah.	**1Ch 4:12**	428
(And **t** are the sons of Bithia the	**1Ch 4:17**	428
T were the potters and the	**1Ch 4:23**	1992a
T *were* their cities until the	**1Ch 4:31**	428
T *were* their settlements, and they	**1Ch 4:33**	2088
t mentioned by name *were* leaders	**1Ch 4:38**	428
T, recorded by name, came in	**1Ch 4:41**	428
T *were* the sons of Abihail, the	**1Ch 5:14**	428
All of **t** were enrolled in the	**1Ch 5:17**	
T were the heads of their fathers'	**1Ch 5:24**	428
T are the names of the sons of	**1Ch 6:17**	428
And **t** are the families of the	**1Ch 6:19**	428
Now **t** are those whom David	**1Ch 6:31**	428
T are those who served with their	**1Ch 6:33**	428

T are the sons of Aaron: Eleazar his	**1Ch 6:50**	428
Now **t** are their settlements	**1Ch 6:54**	428
t cities which are mentioned by	**1Ch 6:65**	428
All **t** *were* the sons of Becher.	**1Ch 7:8**	428
All **t** *were* sons of Jediael,	**1Ch 7:11**	428
T *were* the sons of Gilead the son	**1Ch 7:17**	428
In **t** lived the sons of Joseph the	**1Ch 7:29**	428
T were the sons of Japhlet.	**1Ch 7:33**	428
All **t** *were* the sons of Asher,	**1Ch 7:40**	428
T are the sons of Ehud: these are	**1Ch 8:6**	428
t are the heads of fathers'	**1Ch 8:6**	428
T were his sons, heads of fathers'	**1Ch 8:10**	428
T were heads of the fathers'	**1Ch 8:28**	428
six sons, and **t** *were* their names:	**1Ch 8:38**	428
All **t** *were* the sons of Azel.	**1Ch 8:38**	428
t *were* of the sons of Benjamin.	**1Ch 8:40**	428
All **t** *were* heads of fathers'	**1Ch 9:9**	428
T *were* the gatekeepers for the	**1Ch 9:18**	1992a
All **t** who were chosen to be	**1Ch 9:22**	
T were enrolled by genealogy in	**1Ch 9:22**	1992a
Now **t** are the singers, heads of	**1Ch 9:33**	428
T were heads of fathers'	**1Ch 9:34**	428
had six sons whose names are **t**:	**1Ch 9:44**	428
T were the sons of Azel.	**1Ch 9:44**	428
otherwise **t** uncircumcised will	**1Ch 10:4**	428
Now **t** are the heads of the mighty	**1Ch 11:10**	428
T *constitute* the list of	**1Ch 11:11**	428
Shall I drink the blood of **t** men	**1Ch 11:19**	428
T things the three mighty men did.	**1Ch 11:19**	428
T *things* Benaiah the son of	**1Ch 11:24**	428
Now **t** are the ones who came to	**1Ch 12:1**	428
T of the sons of Gad were captains	**1Ch 12:14**	428
T are the ones who crossed the	**1Ch 12:15**	428
Now **t** are the numbers of the	**1Ch 12:23**	428
All **t**, being men of war who could	**1Ch 12:38**	428
T are the names of the children born	**1Ch 14:4**	428
According to all **t** words and	**1Ch 17:15**	428
to make known all **t** great things.	**1Ch 17:19**	
King David also dedicated **t** to the	**1Ch 18:11**	
T were descended from the giants	**1Ch 20:8**	411
but **t** sheep, what have they done?	**1Ch 21:17**	428
Of **t**, 24,000 were to oversee the	**1Ch 23:4**	428
T were the heads of the fathers'	**1Ch 23:9**	428
T four *were* the sons of Shimei.	**1Ch 23:10**	428
T were the sons of Levi according	**1Ch 23:24**	428
of the descendants of Aaron *were* **t**:	**1Ch 24:1**	
T were their offices for their	**1Ch 24:19**	428
T *were* the sons of the Levites	**1Ch 24:30**	428
T also cast lots just as their	**1Ch 24:31**	1992a
All **t** *were* the sons of Heman the	**1Ch 25:5**	428
All **t** were under the direction of	**1Ch 25:6**	428
t *were* of the sons of Obed-edom;	**1Ch 26:8**	428
To **t** divisions of the gatekeepers,	**1Ch 26:12**	428
T were the divisions of the	**1Ch 26:19**	428
t Hebronites were investigated	**1Ch 26:31**	
T *were* the princes of the tribes	**1Ch 27:22**	428
All **t** were overseers of the	**1Ch 27:31**	428
willingly offered all **t** *things;*	**1Ch 29:17**	428
Now **t** are the foundations which	**2Ch 3:3**	428
The wings of **t** cherubim extended	**2Ch 3:13**	428
t utensils in great quantities,	**2Ch 4:18**	428
T were the chief officers of King	**2Ch 8:10**	428
how blessed are **t** your servants	**2Ch 9:7**	428
"Let us build **t** cities and	**2Ch 14:7**	428
Now when Asa heard **t** words and the	**2Ch 15:8**	428
T are they who served the king,	**2Ch 17:19**	428
With **t** you shall gore the Arameans until	**2Ch 18:10**	428
'**T** have no master.	**2Ch 18:16**	428
in the mouth of **t** your prophets,	**2Ch 18:22**	428
All **t** *were* the sons of Jehoshaphat	**2Ch 21:2**	428
Now **t** are those who conspired	**2Ch 24:26**	428
all **t** were for a burnt offering to	**2Ch 29:32**	428
After **t** acts of faithfulness	**2Ch 32:1**	428
t were from the king's possessions.	**2Ch 35:7**	428
Now **t** are the people of the	**Ezr 2:1**	428
T came with Zerubbabel, Jeshua,	**Ezr 2:2**	834
Now **t** are those who came up from	**Ezr 2:59**	428
T searched *among* their ancestral	**Ezr 2:62**	428
a decree to make **t** men stop *work*,	**Ezr 4:21**	479
t King Cyrus took from the temple	**Ezr 5:14**	1994
"Take **t** utensils, go *and* deposit	**Ezr 5:15**	429
you are to do for **t** elders of Judah	**Ezr 6:8**	479
the full cost is to be paid to **t** people	**Ezr 6:8**	479
Now after **t** things, in the reign	**Ezr 7:1**	428
Now **t** are the heads of their	**Ezr 8:1**	428
last ones, **t** being their names,	**Ezr 8:13**	428
when **t** things had been completed,	**Ezr 9:1**	428
peoples who commit **t** abominations?	**Ezr 9:14**	428
All **t** had married foreign wives,	**Ezr 10:44**	428
When I heard **t** words,	**Ne 1:4**	428
"What are **t** feeble Jews doing?	**Ne 4:2**	
heard their outcry and **t** words.	**Ne 5:6**	428
king, according to **t** reports.	**Ne 6:6**	428
the king according to **t** reports.	**Ne 6:7**	428
according to **t** works of theirs,	**Ne 6:14**	428
T are the people of the province	**Ne 7:6**	428
T *were* they who came up from	**Ne 7:61**	428
T searched *among* their ancestral	**Ne 7:64**	428
T *were* the priests.	**Ne 10:8**	428
Now **t** are the heads of the	**Ne 11:3**	428
Now **t** are the sons of Benjamin:	**Ne 11:7**	428
Now **t** are the priests and the	**Ne 12:1**	428
T were the heads of the priests	**Ne 12:7**	428
T *served* in the days of Joiakim	**Ne 12:26**	428
king of Israel sin regarding **t** things?	**Ne 13:26**	428
When **t** days were completed,	**Es 1:5**	428
After **t** things when the anger of	**Es 2:1**	428
After **t** events King Ahasuerus	**Es 3:1**	428
to the king for **t** thirty days."	**Es 4:11**	2088

Then Mordecai recorded **t** events, Es 9:20 428
Therefore they called **t** days Purim Es 9:26 428
would not fail to celebrate **t** two days Es 9:27 428
So **t** days were to be remembered Es 9:28 428
and **t** days of Purim were not to Es 9:28 428
to establish **t** days of Purim at Es 9:31 428
established **t** customs for Purim, Es 9:32 428
"How long will you say **t** things, Jb 8:2 428
'Yet **t** things You have concealed Jb 10:13 428
does not know such things as **t**? Jb 12:3 428
"Who among all **t** does not know Jb 12:9 428
"**T** ten times you have insulted Jb 19:3 2088
t are the fringes of His ways; Jb 26:14 428
Then **t** three men ceased answering Jb 32:1 428
does all **t** oftentimes with men, Jb 33:29 428
"For by **t** He judges peoples; Jb 36:31
LORD had spoken **t** words to Job, Jb 42:7 428
t things will never be shaken. Ps 15:5 428
T things I remember and I pour Ps 42:4 428
"**T** things you have done and I Ps 50:21 428
T who speak lies go astray from Ps 58:3
Behold, **t** are the wicked; Ps 73:12 428
Let him give heed to **t** things, Ps 107:43 428
T also are sayings of the wise. Pr 24:23 428
T also are proverbs of Solomon Pr 25:1 428
former days were better than **t**?" Ec 7:10 428
not found a woman among all **t**. Ec 7:28 428
you to judgment for all **t** things. Ec 11:9 428
and masters of **t** collections are Ec 12:11
And **t** ruins will be under your Is 3:6 2088
fainthearted because of **t** two stubs Is 7:4 428
"Inasmuch as **t** people have Is 8:6 2088
And **t** also reel with wine and Is 28:7 428
Not one of **t** will be missing; Is 34:16 2007
T will not be found there. Is 35:9
and to you to speak **t** words, Is 36:12 428
'Who among all the gods of **t** lands Is 36:20 428
behold, all of **t** were dead. Is 37:36
"O Lord, by **t** things *men* Is 38:16
in all **t** is the life of my spirit; Is 38:16
"What did **t** men say, and from Is 39:3 428
And see who has created **t** *stars,* Is 40:26 428
T are the things I will do, And I Is 42:16 428
"Remember **t** things, O Jacob, And Is 44:21 428
I am the LORD who does all **t**. Is 45:7 428
T things you did not consider Nor Is 47:7 428
"But **t** two things will come on Is 47:9 428
among them has declared **t** things? Is 48:14 428
"Behold, **t** will come from afar; Is 49:12 428
And lo, **t** *will come* from the Is 49:12 428
And **t** from the land of Sinim." Is 49:12 428
Even **t** may forget, but I will not Is 49:15 428
'Who has begotten **t** for me, Is 49:21 428
And who has reared **t**? Is 49:21 428
From where did **t** come?' " Is 49:21 428
T two things have befallen you; Is 51:19 2007
I relent concerning **t** things? Is 57:6 428
"Who are **t** who fly like a cloud And Is 60:8 428
You restrain Yourself at **t** things, Is 64:12 428
T are smoke in My nostrils, Is 65:5 428
"For My hand made all **t** things, Is 66:2 428
all **t** things came into being," Is 66:2 428
But in spite of all **t** things, Jer 2:34 428
'After she has done all **t** things she Jer 3:7 428
and proclaim **t** words toward the Jer 3:12 428
Have brought **t** things to you. Jer 4:18 428
"Shall I not punish **t** *people,*" Jer 5:9 428
our God done all **t** things to us?' Jer 5:19 428
iniquities have turned **t** away, Jer 5:25 428
'Shall I not punish **t** *people?*' Jer 5:29 428
who enter by **t** gates to worship the Jer 7:2 428
you may do all **t** abominations?' Jer 7:10 428
you have done all **t** things," Jer 7:13 428
shall speak all **t** words to them, Jer 7:27 428
I not punish them for **t** things?" Jer 9:9 428
for I delight in **t** things," Jer 9:24 428
portion of Jacob is not like **t**; Jer 10:16 428
"Proclaim all **t** words in the Jer 11:6 428
'Why have **t** things happened to me?' Jer 13:22 428
one who has done all **t** things. Jer 14:22 428
when you tell this people all **t** words Jer 16:10 428
who come in through **t** gates: Jer 17:20 428
Jeremiah prophesying **t** things, Jer 20:1 428
and your people who enter **t** gates. Jer 22:2 428
"But if you will not obey **t** words, Jer 22:5 428
"I did not send **t** prophets, Jer 23:21 428
even **t** prophets of the deception Jer 23:26 428
'Like **t** good figs, so I will Jer 24:5 428
t twenty-three years the word of Jer 25:3 2088
against all **t** nations round about; Jer 25:9 428
and **t** nations will serve the king Jer 25:11 428
prophesy against them all **t** words, Jer 25:30 428
heard Jeremiah speaking **t** words Jer 26:7 428
officials of Judah heard **t** things, Jer 26:10 428
sent me to you to speak all **t** words Jer 26:15 428
"Now I have given all **t** lands Jer 27:6 428
all **t** to Zedekiah king of Judah, Jer 27:12 428
iron on the neck of all **t** nations, Jer 28:14 428
Now **t** are the words of the letter Jer 29:1 428
Now **t** are the words which the LORD Jer 30:4 428
I have done **t** things to you. Jer 30:15 428
Israel, Return to **t** your cities. Jer 31:21 428
"Take **t** deeds, this sealed deed Jer 32:14 428
prophet spoke all **t** words to Zedekiah Jer 34:6 428
report all **t** words to the king." Jer 36:16 428
how did you write all **t** words? Jer 36:17 428
"He dictated all **t** words to me, Jer 36:18 428
heard all **t** words were not afraid, Jer 36:24 428
t men have acted wickedly in all Jer 38:9 428
"Now put **t** worn-out clothes and Jer 38:12 428
t men who are seeking your life." Jer 38:16 428
t words and you will not die. Jer 38:24 428
with all **t** words which the king had Jer 38:27 428
that is, all **t** words Jer 43:1 428
over **t** stones that I have hidden; Jer 43:10 428
when he had written down **t** words Jer 45:1 428
will scatter them to all **t** winds; Jer 49:36 428
portion of Jacob is not like **t**; Jer 51:19 428
all **t** words which have been Jer 51:60 428
that you read all **t** words aloud, Jer 51:61 428
bronze of all **t** vessels was beyond Jer 52:20 428
And the second pillar was like **t**, Jer 52:22 428
T are the people whom Jer 52:28 2088
"For **t** things I weep; La 1:16 428
Of **t** things the Lord does not approve. La 3:36
of **t** things our eyes are dim; La 5:17 428
Whenever those went, **t** went; Ezk 1:21 428
those stood still, **t** stood still. Ezk 1:21
"When you have completed **t**, Ezk 4:6 428
greater abominations than **t**." Ezk 8:15 428
T are the living beings that I saw Ezk 10:20 1931
t are the men who devise iniquity Ezk 11:2 428
t men have set up their idols in Ezk 14:3 428
even *though* **t** three men, Noah, Ezk 14:14 428
t three men were in its midst, Ezk 14:16 428
t three men were in its midst, Ezk 14:18 428
you to do any of **t** things for you, Ezk 16:5 428
"while you do all **t** things, Ezk 16:30 428
have enraged Me by all **t** things, Ezk 16:43 428
you not know what **t** things *mean?'* Ezk 17:12 428
allegiance, yet did all **t** things; Ezk 17:18 428
does any of **t** things to a brother Ezk 18:10 428
did not do any of **t** things), Ezk 18:11 428
has committed all **t** abominations, Ezk 18:13 428
'**T** things will be done to you Ezk 23:30 428
what **t** things that you are doing Ezk 24:19 428
for **t** they were your customers. Ezk 27:21
though the terror of **t** heroes Ezk 32:27
"**T** Pharaoh will see, and he will Ezk 32:31
they who live in **t** waste places in Ezk 33:24 428
'**T** two nations and these two lands Ezk 35:10
and **t** two lands will be mine, Ezk 35:10
'**T** are the people of the LORD; Ezk 36:20 428
"Son of man, can **t** bones live?" Ezk 37:3 428
"Prophesy over **t** bones and say Ezk 37:4 428
"Thus says the Lord GOD to **t** bones, Ezk 37:5 428
O breath, and breathe on **t** slain, Ezk 37:9 428
t bones are the whole house of Ezk 37:11 428
declare to us what you mean by **t**? Ezk 37:18 428
T are the sons of Zadok, who from Ezk 40:46 1992a
Below **t** chambers *was* the Ezk 42:9 428
"And **t** are the measurements of Ezk 43:13 428
'**T** are the statutes for the altar Ezk 43:18 428
t four in the corners *were* the Ezk 46:22 428
"**T** are the boiling places where Ezk 46:24 428
"**T** waters go out toward the Ezk 47:8 428
many fish, for **t** waters go there and Ezk 47:9 428
"Now **t** are the names of the tribes: Ezk 48:1 428
The holy allotment shall be for **t**, Ezk 48:10 428
"**T** *shall be* its measurements: Ezk 48:16 428
t are their *several* portions," Ezk 48:29 428
"**T** are the exits of the city: Ezk 48:30 428
As for **t** four youths, God gave Da 1:17 428
crush and break all **t** in pieces. Da 2:40 459
and put an end to all **t** kingdoms, Da 2:44 459
T men, O king, have disregarded Da 3:12 479
then **t** men were brought before the Da 3:13 479
Then **t** men were tied up in their Da 3:21 479
But **t** three men, Shadrach, Meshach Da 3:23 479
saw in regard to **t** men that the fire Da 3:27 479
had no effect on the bodies of **t** men Da 3:27
and **t** fantasies *as I lay* on Da 4:5
'Now **t** *were* the visions in my Da 4:10
that **t** satraps might be Da 6:2 459
Then **t** men said, Da 6:5 479
Then **t** commissioners and satraps Da 6:6 459
Then **t** men came by agreement and Da 6:11 479
Then **t** men came by agreement to Da 6:15 479
me the interpretation of **t** things: Da 7:16
'**T** great beasts, which are four *in* Da 7:17 459
spoken to me according to **t** words, Da 10:15 428
stands firmly with me against **t** *forces* Da 10:21 428
but **t** will be rescued out of his Da 11:41 428
will awake, **t** to everlasting life, Da 12:2 428
conceal **t** words and seal up the Da 12:4
will it be until the end of **t** Da 12:6
all **t** *events* will be completed. Da 12:7 428
will be the outcome of **t** *events?*" Da 12:8 428
for **t** words are concealed Da 12:9
'**T** are my wages Which my lovers Hos 2:12 1992a
wise, let him understand **t** things; Hos 14:9 428
"**T** who pant after the *very* dust Am 2:7
"**t** who hoard up violence and Am 3:10
Are they better than **t** kingdoms, Am 6:2 428
not speak out concerning **t** things, Mi 2:6 428
Are **t** His doings? Mi 2:7 428
through **t** things their catch is large, Hab 1:16 1992a
"Will not all of **t** take up a Hab 2:6 428
from a corpse touches any of **t**, Hg 2:13 428
"My lord, what are **t**?" Zch 1:9 428
"I will show you what **t** are." Zch 1:9 428
"**T** are those whom the LORD has Zch 1:10 428
been indignant **t** seventy years?" Zch 1:12 2088
speaking with me, "What are **t**?" Zch 1:19 428
"**T** are the horns which have Zch 1:19 428
"What are **t** coming to do?" Zch 1:21 428
"**T** are the horns which have Zch 1:21 428
but **t** *craftsmen* have come to Zch 1:21 428
among **t** who are standing *here.* Zch 3:7 428
"What are **t**, my lord?" Zch 4:4 428
"Do you not know what **t** are?" Zch 4:5 428
But **t** seven will be glad when they Zch 4:10 428
in the hand of Zerubbabel—**t** Zch 4:10
"What are **t** two olive trees on Zch 4:11 428
"Do you not know what **t** are?" Zch 4:13 428
"**T** are the two anointed ones who Zch 4:14 428
"What are **t**, my lord?" Zch 6:4 428
"**T** are the four spirits of Zch 6:5 428
as I have done **t** many years?" Zch 7:3 2088
seventh months **t** seventy years, Zch 7:5 2088
'Are not **t** the words which the Zch 7:7
you who are listening in **t** days to Zch 8:9 428
listening in these days to **t** words Zch 8:9 428
people to inherit all **t** *things.* Zch 8:12 428
so I have again purposed in **t** days Zch 8:15 428
'**T** are the things which you should Zch 8:16 428
for all **t** are what I hate,' Zch 8:17 428
are **t** wounds between your arms?' Zch 13:6 428
that from **t** stones God is able to Mt 3:9 *3778*
that **t** stones become bread." Mt 4:3 *3778*
"All **t** things I will give You, if Mt 4:9 *3778*
of the least of **t** commandments, Mt 5:19 *3778*
anything beyond **t** is of evil. Mt 5:37 *3778*
clothed himself like one of **t**. Mt 6:29 *3778*
Gentiles eagerly seek all **t** things; Mt 6:32 *3778*
knows that you need all **t** things. Mt 6:32 *3778*
t things will be added to you. Mt 6:33 *3778*
who hears **t** words of Mine and Mt 7:24 *3778*
who hears **t** words of Mine and Mt 7:26 *3778*
When Jesus had finished **t** words, Mt 7:28 *3778*
He was saying **t** things to them, Mt 9:18 *3778*
names of the twelve apostles are **t**: Mt 10:2 *3778*
T twelve Jesus sent out after Mt 10:5 *3778*
gives to one of **t** little ones even a cup Mt 10:42 *3778*
As **t** men were going *away,* Jesus Mt 11:7 *3778*
that You have hidden **t** things from Mt 11:25 *3778*
All **t** things Jesus spoke to the Mt 13:34 *3778*
t are the sons of the kingdom; Mt 13:38 *3778*
you understood all **t** things?" Mt 13:51 *3778*
Jesus had finished **t** parables, Mt 13:53 *3778*
this man *get* this wisdom and **t** Mt 13:54
did this man *get* all **t** things?" Mt 13:56 *3778*
"**T** are the things which defile Mt 15:20 *3778*
whoever causes one of **t** little ones Mt 18:6 *3778*
not despise one of **t** little ones, Mt 18:10 *3778*
that one of **t** little ones perish. Mt 18:14 *3778*
When Jesus had finished **t** words, Mt 19:1 *3778*
of heaven belongs to such as **t**." Mt 19:14 *5108*
"All **t** things I have kept; Mt 19:20 *3778*
'**T** last men have worked *only* one Mt 20:12 *3778*
t two sons of mine may sit one Mt 20:21 *3778*
You hear what **t** *children* are saying?" Mt 21:16 *3778*
authority are You doing **t** things, Mt 21:23 *3778*
by what authority I do **t** things. Mt 21:24 *3778*
by what authority I do **t** things. Mt 21:27 *3778*
"On **t** two commandments depend the Mt 22:40 *3778*
but **t** are the things you should Mt 23:23 *3778*
all **t** things will come upon this Mt 23:36 *3778*
"Do you not see all **t** things? Mt 24:2 *3778*
"Tell us, when will **t** things happen, Mt 24:3 *3778*
"But all **t** things are *merely* the Mt 24:8 *3778*
too, when you see all **t** things, Mt 24:33 *3778*
until all **t** things take place. Mt 24:34 *3778*
it to one of **t** brothers of Mine, Mt 25:40 *3778*
do it to one of the least of **t**, Mt 25:45 *3778*
"**T** will go away into eternal Mt 25:46 *3778*
Jesus had finished all **t** words, Mt 26:1 *3778*
What is it that **t** men are Mt 26:62 *3778*
are you reasoning about **t** things in Mk 2:8 *3778*
"**T** are the ones who are beside Mk 4:15 *3778*
t are the ones on whom seed was Mk 4:16 *3778*
t are the ones who have heard the Mk 4:18 *3778*
"Where did this man *get* **t** things, Mk 6:2 *3778*
as **t** performed by His hands? Mk 6:2 *5108*
that is why **t** miraculous powers Mk 6:14 *3588*
"All **t** evil things proceed from Mk 7:23 *3778*
desolate place to satisfy **t** people?" Mk 8:4 *3778*
He ordered **t** to be served as well. Mk 8:7 *3778*
Whoever causes one of **t** little ones Mk 9:42 *3778*
of God belongs to such as **t**. Mk 10:14 *5108*
I have kept all **t** things from my Mk 10:20 *3778*
But at **t** words he was saddened, and Mk 10:22 *3588*
authority are You doing **t** things, Mk 11:28 *3778*
this authority to do **t** things?" Mk 11:28 *3778*
by what authority I do **t** things. Mk 11:29 *3778*
by what authority I do **t** things." Mk 11:33 *3778*
commandment greater than **t**." Mk 12:31 *3778*
t will receive greater Mk 12:40 *3778*
"Do you see **t** great buildings? Mk 13:2 *3778*
"Tell us, when will **t** things be, Mk 13:4 *3778*
sign when all **t** things are going to be Mk 13:4 *3778*
T things are *merely* the beginning Mk 13:8 *3778*
when you see **t** things happening, Mk 13:29 *3778*
until all **t** things take place. Mk 13:30 *3778*
that **t** men are testifying against You Mk 14:60 *3778*
"**T** signs will accompany those who Mk 16:17 *3778*
[*And they promptly reported all* **t** Mk 16:20
the day when **t** things take place, Lk 1:20 *3778*
After **t** days Elizabeth his Lk 1:24 *3778*
and all **t** matters were being Lk 1:65 *3778*
Mary treasured all **t** things, Lk 2:19 *3778*
and His mother treasured all **t** Lk 2:51
from **t** stones God is able to raise up Lk 3:8 *3778*
with rage as they heard **t** things; Lk 4:28 *3778*
to him about all **t** things. Lk 7:18 *3778*
As He said **t** things, He would call Lk 8:8 *3778*
and **t** have no *firm* root; Lk 8:13 *3778*

t are the ones who have heard, Lk 8:14 *3778*
t are the ones who have heard the Lk 8:15 *3778*
"My mother and My brothers are **t** Lk 8:21 *3778*
and buy food for all **t** people." Lk 9:13 *3778*
Some eight days after **t** sayings, Lk 9:28 *3778*
as **t** were leaving *Him,* Peter said Lk 9:33 *846*
"Let **t** words sink into your ears; Lk 9:44 *3778*
that You have hidden **t** things from Lk 10:21 *3778*
"Which of **t** three do you think Lk 10:36 *3778*
While Jesus was saying **t** things, Lk 11:27 *3778*
but **t** are the things you should Lk 11:42 *3778*
Under **t** circumstances, after so Lk 12:1 *3739*
clothed himself like one of **t**. Lk 12:27 *3778*
"For all **t** things the nations of Lk 12:30 *3778*
knows that you need **t** things. Lk 12:30 *3778*
t things will be added to you. Lk 12:31 *3778*
"Do you suppose that **t** Galileans Lk 13:2 *3778*
inquiring what **t** things could be. Lk 15:26 *3778*
were listening to all **t** things and Lk 16:14 *3778*
one of **t** little ones to stumble. Lk 17:2 *3778*
of God belongs to such as **t**. Lk 18:16 *5108*
"All **t** things I have kept from *my* Lk 18:21 *3778*
But when he had heard **t** things, Lk 18:23 *3778*
disciples understood none of **t** things, Lk 18:34 *3778*
they were listening to **t** things, Lk 19:11 *3778*
kingdom, he ordered that **t** slaves, Lk 19:15 *3778*
"But **t** enemies of mine, who did Lk 19:27 *3778*
After He had said **t** things, Lk 19:28 *3778*
"I tell you, if **t** become silent, Lk 19:40 *3778*
authority You are doing **t** things, Lk 20:2 *3778*
by what authority I do **t** things." Lk 20:8 *3778*
will come and destroy **t** vine-growers Lk 20:16 *3778*
T will receive greater condemnation." Lk 20:47 *3778*
"*As for* **t** things which you are Lk 21:6 *3778*
when therefore will **t** things happen? Lk 21:7 *3778*
sign when **t** things are about to take Lk 21:7 *3778*
t things must take place first, Lk 21:9 *3778*
"But before all **t** things, they Lk 21:12 *3778*
because **t** are days of vengeance, Lk 21:22 *3778*
when **t** things begin to take place, Lk 21:28 *3778*
when you see **t** things happening, Lk 21:31 *3778*
have strength to escape all **t** things Lk 21:36 *3778*
do **t** things when the tree is green, Lk 23:31 *3778*
at a distance, seeing **t** things. Lk 23:49 *3778*
reported all **t** things to the eleven Lk 24:9 *3778*
telling **t** things to the apostles. Lk 24:10 *3778*
But **t** words appeared to them as Lk 24:11 *3778*
t things which had taken place. Lk 24:14 *3778*
"What are **t** words that you are Lk 24:17 *3778*
have happened here in **t** days?" Lk 24:18 *3778*
third day since **t** things happened. Lk 24:21 *3778*
Christ to suffer **t** things and to enter Lk 24:26 *3778*
While they were telling **t** things, Lk 24:36 *3778*
"**T** are My words which I spoke to Lk 24:44 *3778*
"You are witnesses of **t** things. Lk 24:48 *3778*
T things took place in Bethany Jn 1:28 *3778*
will see greater things than **t**." Jn 1:50 *3778*
"Take **t** things away; Jn 2:16 *3778*
us as your authority for doing **t** Jn 2:18 *3778*
for no one can do **t** signs that You Jn 3:2 *3778*
"How can **t** things be?" Jn 3:9 *3778*
and do not understand **t** things? Jn 3:10 *3778*
After **t** things Jesus and His Jn 3:22 *3778*
After **t** things there was a feast Jn 5:1 *3778*
In **t** lay a multitude of those who Jn 5:3 *3778*
was doing **t** things on the Sabbath. Jn 5:16 *3778*
t things the Son also does in like Jn 5:19 *3778*
will show Him greater works than **t**, Jn 5:20 *3778*
t things so that you may be saved. Jn 5:34 *3778*
it is **t** that testify about Me; Jn 5:39 *1565*
After **t** things Jesus went away to Jn 6:1 *3778*
we to buy bread, so that **t** may eat?" Jn 6:5 *3778*
what are **t** for so many people?" Jn 6:9 *3778*
T things He said in the synagogue as Jn 6:59 *3778*
After **t** things Jesus was Jn 7:1 *3778*
If You do **t** things, show Yourself Jn 7:4 *3778*
Having said **t** things to them, Jn 7:9 *3778*
muttering **t** things about Him, Jn 7:32 *3778*
when they heard **t** words, Jn 7:40 *3778*
T words He spoke in the treasury, Jn 8:20 *3778*
Him, **t** I speak to the world." Jn 8:26 *3778*
but I speak **t** things as the Father Jn 8:28 *3778*
As He spoke **t** things, many came to Jn 8:30 *3778*
who were with Him heard **t** things and Jn 9:40 *3778*
among the Jews because of **t** words. Jn 10:19 *3778*
"**T** are not the sayings of one Jn 10:21 *3778*
name, **t** testify of Me. Jn 10:25 *3778*
When He had said **t** things, Jn 11:43 *3778*
T things His disciples did not Jn 12:16 *3778*
that **t** things were written of Him, Jn 12:16 *3778*
they had done **t** things to Him. Jn 12:16 *3778*
t then came to Philip, who Jn 12:21 *3778*
T things Jesus spoke, Jn 12:36 *3778*
T things Isaiah said because he Jn 12:41 *3778*
"If you know **t** things, you are Jn 13:17 *3778*
greater *works* than **t** he will do; Jn 14:12 *3778*
"**T** things I have spoken to you while Jn 14:25 *3778*
"**T** things I have spoken to you so Jn 15:11 *3778*
"But all **t** things they will do to Jn 15:21 *3778*
"**T** things I have spoken to you so Jn 16:1 *3778*
"**T** things they will do because they Jn 16:3 *3778*
"But **t** things I have spoken to Jn 16:4 *3778*
T things I did not say to you Jn 16:4 *3778*
I have said **t** things to you, Jn 16:6 *3778*
"**T** things I have spoken to you in Jn 16:25 *3778*
"**T** things I have spoken to you, Jn 16:33 *3778*
Jesus spoke **t** things; and lifting up Jn 17:1 *3778*
and **t** things I speak in the world so Jn 17:13 *3778*
"I do not ask on behalf of **t** alone, Jn 17:20 *3778*

and **t** have known that You sent Jn 17:25 *3778*
When Jesus had spoken **t** words, Jn 18:1 *3778*
you seek Me, let **t** go their way," Jn 18:8 *3778*
Pilate heard **t** words, Jn 19:13 *3778*
the soldiers did **t** things. Jn 19:25 *3778*
For **t** things came to pass Jn 19:36 *3778*
After **t** things Joseph of Arimathea, Jn 19:38 *3778*
that He had said **t** things to her. Jn 20:18 *3778*
but **t** have been written so that you Jn 20:31 *3778*
After **t** things Jesus manifested Jn 21:1 *3778*
do you love Me more than **t**?" Jn 21:15 *3778*
who is testifying to **t** things Jn 21:24 *3778*
these things and wrote **t** things Jn 21:24 *3778*
To **t** He also presented Himself Ac 1:3 *3739*
And after He had said **t** things, Ac 1:9 *3778*
T all with one mind were Ac 1:14 *3778*
one of **t** *must* become a witness Ac 1:22 *3778*
one of **t** two You have chosen Ac 1:24 *3778*
are not all **t** who are speaking Ac 2:7 *3778*
"For **t** men are not drunk, as you Ac 2:15 *3778*
"Men of Israel, listen to **t** words: Ac 2:22 *3778*
onward, also announced **t** days. Ac 3:24 *3778*
"What shall we do with **t** men? Ac 4:16 *3778*
And as he heard **t** words, Ananias Ac 5:5 *3778*
over all who heard of **t** things. Ac 5:11 *3778*
the chief priests heard **t** words, Ac 5:24 *3778*
"And we are witnesses of **t** things; Ac 5:32 *3778*
what you propose to do with **t** men. Ac 5:35 *3778*
stay away from **t** men and let them Ac 5:38 *3778*
And **t** they brought before the Ac 6:6 *3739*
"Are **t** things so?" Ac 7:1 *3778*
MY HAND WHICH MADE ALL **T** THINGS?' Ac 7:50 *3778*
Peter was still speaking **t** words, Ac 10:44 *3778*
the water for **t** to be baptized Ac 10:47 *3778*
T six brethren also went with me Ac 11:12 *3778*
"Report **t** things to James and the Ac 12:17 *3778*
"After **t** things He gave *them* Ac 13:20 *3778*
fulfilled **t** by condemning *Him.* Ac 13:27
t things might be spoken to them Ac 13:42 *3778*
"Men, why are you doing **t** things? Ac 14:15 *3778*
you should turn from **t** vain things Ac 14:15 *3778*
Even saying **t** things, Ac 14:18 *3778*
'AFTER **T** THINGS I will return, AND Ac 15:16 *3778*
MAKES **T** THINGS KNOWN FROM LONG AGO. Ac 15:18 *3778*
greater burden than **t** essentials: Ac 15:28 *3778*
"**T** men are bond-servants of the Ac 16:17 *3778*
"**T** men are throwing our city into Ac 16:20 *3778*
jailer reported **t** words to Paul, Ac 16:36 *3778*
The policemen reported **t** words Ac 16:38 *3778*
"**T** men who have upset the world Ac 17:6 *3778*
authorities who heard **t** things. Ac 17:8 *3778*
Now **t** were more noble-minded than Ac 17:11 *3778*
to see whether **t** things were so. Ac 17:11 *3778*
know what **t** things mean." Ac 17:20 *3778*
After **t** things he left Athens and Ac 18:1 *3778*
to be a judge of **t** matters." Ac 18:15 *3778*
concerned about any of **t** things. Ac 18:17 *3778*
Now after **t** things were finished, Ac 19:21 *3778*
t he gathered together with the Ac 19:25 *3739*
"So, since **t** are undeniable Ac 19:36 *3778*
"For you have brought **t** men *here* Ac 19:37 *3778*
But **t** had gone on ahead and were Ac 20:5 *3778*
"You yourselves know that **t** hands Ac 20:34 *3778*
When he had said **t** things, Ac 20:36 *3778*
After **t** days we got ready and Ac 21:15 *3778*
have notified me of **t** things." Ac 23:22 *3778*
When **t** had come to Caesarea Ac 23:33 *3748*
yourself concerning all **t** matters you Ac 24:8 *3778*
asserting that **t** things were so. Ac 24:9 *3778*
which **t** men cherish themselves, Ac 24:15 *3778*
"Or else let **t** men themselves Ac 24:20 *3778*
trial before me on **t** *charges?*" Ac 25:9 *3778*
is *true* of which **t** men accuse me, Ac 25:11 *3778*
there stand trial on **t** matters. Ac 25:20 *3778*
the king knows about **t** matters, Ac 26:26 *3778*
none of **t** things escape his notice; Ac 26:26 *3778*
as I am, except for **t** chains." Ac 26:29 *3778*
"Unless **t** men remain in the ship, Ac 27:31 *3778*
[When he had spoken **t** words, Ac 28:29 *3778*
t, not having the Law, are a law to Ro 2:14 *3778*
Spirit of God, **t** are sons of God. Ro 8:14 *3778*
and **t** whom He predestined, He also Ro 8:30 *3778*
and **t** whom He called, He also Ro 8:30 *3778*
and **t** whom He justified, He also Ro 8:30 *3778*
then shall we say to **t** things? Ro 8:31 *3778*
But in all **t** things we Ro 8:37 *3778*
how much more will **t** who are the Ro 11:24 *3778*
so **t** also now have been Ro 11:31 *3778*
further place for me in **t** regions, Ro 15:23 *3778*
Now **t** things, brethren, I have 1Co 4:6 *3778*
not write **t** things to shame you, 1Co 4:14 *3778*
I am not speaking **t** things 1Co 9:8 *3778*
does not the Law also say **t** things? 1Co 9:8 *3778*
But I have used none of **t** things. 1Co 9:15 *3778*
And I am not writing **t** things so 1Co 9:15 *3778*
Now **t** things happened as examples 1Co 10:6 *3778*
Now **t** things happened to them as 1Co 10:11 *3778*
same Spirit works all **t** things, 1Co 12:11 *3778*
t we bestow more abundant honor, 1Co 12:23 *3778*
faith, hope, love, abide **t** three; 1Co 13:13 *3778*
but the greatest of **t** is love. 1Co 13:13 *3778*
And who is adequate for **t** things? 2Co 2:16 *3778*
Now all **t** things are from God, 2Co 5:18
Therefore, having **t** promises, 2Co 7:1 *3778*
am writing **t** things while absent, 2Co 13:10 *3778*
for **t** *women* are two covenants: one Ga 4:24 *3778*
for **t** are in opposition to one Ga 5:17 *3778*
carousing, and things like **t**, Ga 5:21 *3778*
T *are* in accordance with Eph 1:19

for because of **t** things the wrath Eph 5:6 *3778*
I ask you also to help **t** women who Php 4:3 *3778*
dwell on **t** things. Php 4:8 *3778*
and seen in me, practice **t** things, Php 4:9 *3778*
T are matters which have, to be Col 2:23 *3748*
For it is because of **t** things Col 3:6 *3739*
Beyond all **t** things *put on* love, Col 3:14 *3778*
t are the only fellow workers for Col 4:11 *3778*
would be disturbed by **t** afflictions; 1Th 3:3 *3778*
is *the* avenger in all **t** things, 1Th 4:6 *3778*
comfort one another with **t** words. 1Th 4:18 *3778*
T will pay the penalty of eternal 2Th 1:9 *3748*
you, I was telling you **t** things? 2Th 2:5 *3778*
some men, straying from **t** things, 1Tm 1:6 *3739*
t are Hymenaeus and Alexander, 1Tm 1:20 *3739*
T men must also first be tested; 1Tm 3:10 *3778*
I am writing **t** things to you, 1Tm 3:14 *3778*
pointing out **t** things to the brethren, 1Tm 4:6 *3778*
Prescribe and teach **t** things. 1Tm 4:11 *3778*
Take pains with **t** things; 1Tm 4:15 *3778*
persevere in **t** things, 1Tm 4:16 *846*
Prescribe **t** things as well, so 1Tm 5:7 *3778*
to maintain **t** *principles* without bias, 1Tm 5:21 *3778*
Teach and preach **t** *principles.* 1Tm 6:2 *3778*
with **t** we shall be content. 1Tm 6:8 *3778*
But flee from **t** things, you man of 1Tm 6:11 *3778*
reason I also suffer **t** things, 2Tm 1:12 *3778*
t to faithful men 2Tm 2:2 *3778*
Remind *them* of **t** things, and 2Tm 2:14 *3778*
cleanses himself from **t** *things,* 2Tm 2:21 *3778*
Avoid such men as **t**. 2Tm 3:5 *3778*
so **t** *men* also oppose the truth, 2Tm 3:8 *3778*
T things speak and exhort and Ti 2:15 *3778*
and concerning **t** things I want you Ti 3:8 *3778*
T things are good and profitable Ti 3:8 *3778*
in **t** last days has spoken to us in Heb 1:2 *3778*
t are descended from Abraham. Heb 7:5
one concerning whom **t** things are Heb 7:13 *3778*
but of **t** things we cannot now Heb 9:5 *3739*
Now when **t** things have been so Heb 9:6 *3778*
the heavens to be cleansed with **t**, Heb 9:23 *3778*
with better sacrifices than **t**. Heb 9:23 *3778*
there is forgiveness of **t** things, Heb 10:18 *3778*
All **t** died in faith, without Heb 11:13 *3778*
And all **t**, having gained approval Heb 11:39 *3778*
t things ought not to be this way. Jas 3:10 *3778*
in **t** things which now have been 1Pe 1:12 *846*
but has appeared in **t** last times 1Pe 1:20 *3588*
For by **t** He has granted to us His 2Pe 1:4 *3739*
For if **t** *qualities* are yours and 2Pe 1:8 *3778*
For he who lacks **t** *qualities* is 2Pe 1:9 *3778*
as long as you practice **t** things, 2Pe 1:10 *3778*
ready to remind you of **t** things, 2Pe 1:12 *3778*
be able to call **t** things to mind. 2Pe 1:15 *3778*
But **t**, like unreasoning animals, 2Pe 2:12 *3778*
T are springs without water and 2Pe 2:17 *3778*
Since all **t** things are to be 2Pe 3:11 *3778*
since you look for **t** things, 2Pe 3:14 *3778*
speaking in them of **t** things, 2Pe 3:16 *3778*
T things we write, so that our joy 1Jn 1:4 *3778*
I am writing **t** things to you so 1Jn 2:1 *3778*
T things I have written to you 1Jn 2:26 *3778*
T things I have written to you who 1Jn 5:13 *3778*
since they in the same way as **t** Jude 1:7 *3778*
Yet in the same way **t** men, Jude 1:8 *3778*
But **t** men revile the things which Jude 1:10 *3778*
by **t** things they are destroyed. Jude 1:10 *3778*
T are the men who are hidden Jude 1:12 *3778*
It was also about **t** men *that* Enoch, Jude 1:14 *3778*
T are grumblers, finding fault, Jude 1:16 *3778*
T are the ones who cause Jude 1:19 *3778*
will take place after **t** things. Rv 1:19 *3778*
After **t** things I looked, and Rv 4:1 *3778*
must take place after **t** things." Rv 4:1 *3778*
After **t** things I looked, and Rv 7:9 *3778*
"**T** who are clothed in the white Rv 7:13 *3778*
"**T** are the ones who come out of Rv 7:14 *3778*
are still coming after **t** things. Rv 9:12 *3778*
was killed by **t** three plagues, Rv 9:18 *3778*
who were not killed by **t** plagues, Rv 9:20 *3778*
T are the two olive trees and the Rv 11:4 *3778*
T have the power to shut up the Rv 11:6 *3778*
because **t** two prophets tormented Rv 11:10 *3778*
T are the ones who have not been Rv 14:4 *3778*
T *are* the ones who follow the Lamb Rv 14:4 *3778*
T have been purchased from among Rv 14:4 *3778*
After **t** things I looked, and the Rv 15:5 *3778*
because You judged **t** things; Rv 16:5 *3778*
who has the power over **t** plagues, Rv 16:9 *3778*
"**T** have one purpose, and they give Rv 17:13 *3778*
"**T** will wage war against the Rv 17:14 *3778*
t will hate the harlot and will Rv 17:16 *3778*
After **t** things I saw another angel Rv 18:1 *3778*
"The merchants of **t** things, Rv 18:15 *3778*
After **t** things I heard something like Rv 19:1 *3778*
"**T** are true words of God." Rv 19:9 *3778*
t two were thrown alive into the Rv 19:20 *3588*
after **t** things he must be released Rv 20:3 *3778*
over **t** the second death has no Rv 20:6 *3778*
t words are faithful and true." Rv 21:5 *3778*
overcomes will inherit **t** things, Rv 21:7 *3778*
"**T** words are faithful and true"; Rv 22:6 *3778*
one who heard and saw **t** things. Rv 22:8 *3778*
the angel who showed me **t** things. Rv 22:8 *3778*
My angel to testify to you **t** things Rv 22:16 *3778*
He who testifies to **t** things says, Rv 22:20 *3778*

THESSALONIANS

Aristarchus and Secundus of the **T**, Ac 20:4 *2331*
Timothy, To the church of the **T** 1Th 1:1 *2331*

and Timothy, To the church of the **T** **2Th 1:1** *2331*

THESSALONICA

and Apollonia, they came to **T**, **Ac 17:1** *2332*
more noble-minded than those in **T**, **Ac 17:11** *2332*
But when the Jews of **T** found out **Ac 17:13** *2332*
by Aristarchus, a Macedonian of **T**. **Ac 27:2** *2331*
for even in **T** you sent *a gift* more **Php 4:16** *2332*
has deserted me and gone to **T**; **2Tm 4:10** *2332*

THEUDAS

"For some time ago **T** rose up, **Ac 5:36** *2333*

THICK

and there was **t** darkness in all **Ex 10:22** 653
I will come to you in a **t** cloud, **Ex 19:9** 5672
and a **t** cloud upon the mountain **Ex 19:16** 3515
while Moses approached the **t** cloud **Ex 20:21** 6205
darkness, cloud and **t** gloom. **Dt 4:11** 6205
of the cloud and *of* the **t** gloom, **Dt 5:22** 6205
You are grown fat, **t**, and sleek **Dt 32:15** 5666
the **t** branches of a great oak. **2Sa 18:9** 7730
With **t** darkness under His feet. **2Sa 22:10** 6205
of waters, **t** clouds of the sky. **2Sa 22:12** 5645
It was a handbreadth **t**, **1Ki 7:26** 5672
He would dwell in the **t** cloud. **1Ki 8:12** 6205
It was a handbreadth **t**, **2Ch 4:5** 5672
He would dwell in the **t** cloud. **2Ch 6:1** 6205
He judge through the **t** darkness? **Jb 22:13** 6205
is the same to him as **t** darkness, **Jb 24:17** 6757
with the terrors of **t** darkness. **Jb 24:17** 6757
moisture He loads the **t** cloud; **Jb 37:11** 5645
about the layers of the **t** clouds, **Jb 37:16** 5645
And **t** darkness its swaddling band, **Jb 38:9** 6205
With **t** darkness under His feet. **Ps 18:9** 6205
of waters, **t** clouds of the skies. **Ps 18:11** 5645
before Him passed His **t** clouds, **Ps 18:12** 5645
and **t** darkness surround Him; **Ps 97:2** 6205
transgressions like a **t** cloud And **Is 44:22** 5645
Israel, Or a land of **t** darkness? **Jer 2:31** 3991
was five cubits **t** all around, **Ezk 41:12** 7341
A day of clouds and **t** darkness. **Jl 2:2** 6205
A day of clouds and **t** darkness, **Zph 1:15** 6205

THICKER

finger is **t** than my father's loins! **1Ki 12:10** 5666
finger is **t** than my father's loins! **2Ch 10:10** 5666

THICKEST

lodging place, its **t** forest. **2Ki 19:23** 3759
to its highest peak, its **t** forest. **Is 37:24** 3759

THICKET

ram caught in the **t** by his horns; **Gn 22:13** 5442
"A lion has gone up from his **t**, **Jer 4:7** 5441
you do in the **t** of the Jordan? **Jer 12:5** 1347b
like a lion from the **t** of the Jordan **Jer 50:44** 1347b

THICKETS

hid themselves in caves, in **t**, **1Sa 13:6** 2336
sets the **t** of the forest aflame And **Is 9:18** 5442
He will cut down the **t** of the forest **Is 10:34** 5442
In the **t** of Arabia you must spend **Is 21:13** 3293a
They go into the **t** and climb among **Jer 4:29** 5645
like a lion from the **t** of the Jordan **Jer 49:19** 1347b

THICKNESS

and four fingers in **t**, **Jer 52:21** 5672
So he measured the **t** of the wall, **Ezk 40:5** 7341
The **t** of the outer wall of the **Ezk 41:9** 7341
In the **t** of the wall of the court **Ezk 42:10** 7341

THIEF

the **t** is caught while breaking in and **Ex 22:2** 1590
man's house, if the **t** is caught, **Ex 22:7** 1590
"If the **t** is not caught, then the **Ex 22:8** 1590
sells him, then that **t** shall die; **Dt 24:7** 1590
needy, And at night he is as a **t**. **Jb 24:14** 1590
shout against them as *against* a **t**, **Jb 30:5** 1590
"When you see a **t**, you are **Ps 50:18** 1590
Men do not despise a **t** if he **Pr 6:30** 1590
He who is a partner with a **t** hates **Pr 29:24** 1590
"As the **t** is shamed when he is **Jer 2:26** 1590
The **t** enters in, Bandits raid **Hos 7:1** 1590
through the windows like a **t**. **Jl 2:9** 1590
"and it will enter the house of the **t** **Zch 5:4** 1590
of the night the **t** was coming, **Mt 24:43** *2812*
in heaven, where no **t** comes near nor **Lk 12:33** *2812*
at what hour the **t** was coming, **Lk 12:39** *2812*
other way, he is a **t** and a robber. **Jn 10:1** *2812*
"The **t** comes only to steal and **Jn 10:10** *2812*
the poor, but because he was a **t**, **Jn 12:6** *2812*
come just like a **t** in the night. **1Th 5:2** *2812*
day would overtake you like a **t**; **1Th 5:4** *2812*
of you suffers as a murderer, or **t**, **1Pe 4:15** *2812*
of the Lord will come like a **t**, **2Pe 3:10** *2812*
not wake up, I will come like a **t**, **Rv 3:3** *2812*
("Behold, I am coming like a **t**. **Rv 16:15** *2812*

THIEVES

are rebels And companions of **t**; **Is 1:23** 1590
Or was he caught among **t**? **Jer 48:27** 1590
If **t** *came* by night, They would **Jer 49:9** 1590
"If **t** came to you, If robbers by **Ob 1:5** 1590
and where **t** break in and steal. **Mt 6:19** *2812*
where **t** do not break in or steal; **Mt 6:20** *2812*
came before Me are **t** and robbers, **Jn 10:8** *2812*
nor **t**, nor *the* covetous, nor **1Co 6:10** *2812*

THIGH

"Please place your hand under my **t**, **Gn 24:2** 3409
under the **t** of Abraham his master, **Gn 24:9** 3409
he touched the socket of his **t**; **Gn 32:25** 3409
so the socket of Jacob's **t** was **Gn 32:25** 3409
and he was limping on his **t**. **Gn 32:31** 3409
which is on the socket of the **t**, **Gn 32:32** 3409
he touched the socket of Jacob's **t** **Gn 32:32** 3409
place now your hand under my **t** and **Gn 47:29** 3409
that is on them and the right **t** **Ex 29:22** 7785
and the **t** of the heave offering which **Ex 29:27** 7785
of you put his sword upon his **t**, **Ex 32:27** 3409
'You shall give the right **t** to **Lv 7:32** 7785
t shall be his as *his* portion. **Lv 7:33** 7785
and the **t** of the contribution from **Lv 7:34** 7785
and their fat and the right **t**. **Lv 8:25** 7785
of fat and on the right **t**. **Lv 8:26** 7785
But the breasts and the right **t** **Lv 9:21** 7785
and the **t** of the offering you may **Lv 10:14** 7785
"The **t** offered by lifting up and **Lv 10:15** 7785
LORD's making your **t** waste away **Nu 5:21** 3409
swell and your **t** waste away." **Nu 5:22** 3409
swell and her **t** will waste away, **Nu 5:27** 3409
and the **t** offered by lifting up; **Nu 6:20** 7785
offering and like the right **t**. **Nu 18:18** 7785
he bound it on his right **t** under his **Jg 3:16** 3409
took the sword from his right **t** and **Jg 3:21** 3409
Gird Your sword on *Your* **t**, **Ps 45:3** 3409
I was instructed, I smote on *my* **t**; **Jer 31:19** 3409
people, therefore strike *your* **t**. **Ezk 21:12** 3409
pieces, Every good piece, the **t** and **Ezk 24:4** 3409
To lay him open from **t** to neck **Hab 3:13** 3247
on His **T** He has a name written, **Rv 19:16** *3382*

THIGHS

from the loins even to the **t**. **Ex 28:42** 3409
And made his **t** heavy with flesh. **Jb 15:27** 3689
sinews of his **t** are knit together. **Jb 40:17** 6344
its belly and its **t** of bronze, **Da 2:32** 3410

THIN

t and scorched by the east wind, **Gn 41:6** 1851
The **t** ears swallowed up the **Gn 41:7** 1851
and lo, seven ears, withered, **t**, **Gn 41:23** 1851
and the **t** ears swallowed the seven **Gn 41:24** 1851
and the seven **t** ears scorched by **Gn 41:27** 7534
there is **t** yellowish hair in it, **Lv 13:30** 1851
The streams of Egypt will **t** out and **Is 19:6** 1809

THING

over every creeping **t** that creeps on **Gn 1:26** 7431
over every living **t** that moves on **Gn 1:28** 2416a
to every **t** that moves on the earth **Gn 1:30** 3605
of every living **t** of all flesh, **Gn 6:19** 2416a
of every creeping **t** of the ground **Gn 6:20** 7431
every living **t** that I have made." **Gn 7:4** 3351
and every creeping **t** that creeps **Gn 7:14** 7431
every swarming **t** that swarms upon **Gn 7:21** 8318
He blotted out every living **t** that **Gn 7:23** 3351
every living **t** of all flesh that is with **Gn 8:17** 2421b
every creeping **t** that creeps on the **Gn 8:17** 7431
Every beast, every creeping **t**, **Gn 8:19** 7431
again destroy every living **t**, **Gn 8:21** 2416a
"Every moving **t** that is alive **Gn 9:3** 7431
be it from You to do such a **t**, **Gn 18:25** 1697
that you have done this **t**?" **Gn 20:10** 1697
"I do not know who has done this **t**; **Gn 21:26** 1697
because you have done this **t** and **Gn 22:16** 1697
If you will do this *one* **t** for me, **Gn 30:31** 1697
he had done a disgraceful **t** in Israel **Gn 34:7** 5039
for such a **t** ought not to be done. **Gn 34:7** 3651
"We cannot do this **t**, **Gn 34:14** 1697
man did not delay to do the **t**, **Gn 34:19** 1697
from your servants to do such a **t**. **Gn 44:7** 1697
"Why have you done this **t**, **Ex 1:18** 1697
LORD will do this **t** in the land." **Ex 9:5** 1697
the LORD did this **t** on the next **Ex 9:6** 1697
there was a fine flake-like **t**, **Ex 16:14** 2636
"What is this **t** that you are **Ex 18:14** 1697
"The **t** that you are doing is not **Ex 18:17** 1697
do this **t** and God *so* commands you, **Ex 18:23** 1697
any lost **t** about which one says, **Ex 22:9** 9
this **t** of which you have spoken; **Ex 33:17** 1697
for it is a fearful **t** that I am **Ex 34:10** 3372a
t which the LORD has commanded, **Ex 35:4** 1697
a **t** most holy, of the offerings to **Lv 2:3** 6944
a **t** most holy of the offerings to **Lv 2:10** 6944
if a person touches any unclean **t**, **Lv 5:2** 1697
he has sinned against the holy **t**, **Lv 5:16** 6944
him or the lost **t** which he found, **Lv 6:4** 9
It shall be an offensive **t**, **Lv 7:18** 6292
or any unclean detestable **t**, **Lv 7:21** 8263
"This is the **t** which the LORD has **Lv 8:5** 1697
"This is the **t** which the LORD has **Lv 9:6** 1697
so it shall be a **t** perpetually due **Lv 10:15** 2706
'Now every swarming **t** that swarms **Lv 11:41** 8318
every swarming **t** that swarms on **Lv 11:42** 8318
living **t** that moves in the waters and **Lv 11:46** 2416a
shall not touch any consecrated **t**, **Lv 12:4** 6944
the **t** in which the mark occurs and **Lv 13:54**
and whoever sits on the **t** on which **Lv 15:6** 3627
'Whoever touches any **t** on **Lv 15:22** 3627
on the **t** on which she is sitting, **Lv 15:23** 3627
and every **t** on which she sits **Lv 15:26** 3627
profaned the holy **t** of the LORD; **Lv 19:8** 6944
LORD brings about an entirely new **t** **Nu 16:30** 1278
Every devoted **t** in Israel shall be **Nu 18:14** 2764a
'The **t** which you have said to do **Dt 1:14** 1697
'The **t** pleased me and I took **Dt 1:23** 1697
you have not lacked a **t**." **Dt 2:7** 1697
been done like this great **t**, **Dt 4:32** 1697
"I took your sinful **t**, the calf **Dt 9:21**
every living **t** that followed them, **Dt 11:6** 3351
do such a wicked **t** among you. **Dt 13:11** 1697
shall not eat any detestable **t**. **Dt 14:3** 8441
because for this **t** the LORD your **Dt 15:10** 1697
detestable **t** to the LORD your God. **Dt 17:1** 8441
if it is true and the **t** certain **Dt 17:4** 1697
detestable **t** has been done in Israel, **Dt 17:4** 8441
if the **t** does not come about or **Dt 18:22** 1697
t which the LORD has not spoken. **Dt 18:22** 1697
again do such an evil **t** among you. **Dt 19:20** 1697
keep yourself from every evil **t**. **Dt 23:9** 1697
I am commanding you to do this **t**. **Dt 24:18** 1697
I am commanding you to do this **t**. **Dt 24:22** 1697
a disgraceful **t** in Israel.' " **Jos 7:15** 5039
of you, and have done this **t**. **Jos 9:24** 1697
"Who did this **t**?" **Jg 6:29** 1697
the son of Joash did this **t**." **Jg 6:29** 1697
is this **t** you have done to us, **Jg 8:1** 1697
"Let this **t** be done for me; **Jg 11:37** 1697
drink, nor eat any unclean **t**. **Jg 13:4** 2931
drink nor eat any unclean **t**, **Jg 13:7** 2932a
drink, nor eat any unclean **t**; **Jg 13:14** 2932a
the **t** which we will do to Gibeah; **Jg 20:9** 1697
This is the **t** that you shall do: **Jg 21:11** 1697
I am about to do a **t** in Israel at **1Sa 3:11** 1697
But the **t** was displeasing in the **1Sa 8:6** 1697
see this great **t** which the LORD will **1Sa 12:16** 1697
to another and said the same **t**; **1Sa 17:30** 1697
answered the same **t** as before. **1Sa 17:30** 1697
Saul, the **t** was agreeable to him. **1Sa 18:20** 1697
my father hide this **t** from me? **1Sa 20:2** 1697
I should do this **t** to my lord, **1Sa 24:6** 1697
"This **t** that you have done is not **1Sa 26:16** 1697
come upon you for this **t**." **1Sa 28:10** 1697
has done this **t** to you this day. **1Sa 28:18** 1697
you, because you have done this **t**. **2Sa 2:6** 1697
you, but I demand one **t** of you, **2Sa 3:13** 1697
and to do a great **t** for You and **2Sa 7:23** 1420
this good **t** to Your servant. **2Sa 7:28** 2899b
your soul, I will not do this **t**." **2Sa 11:11** 1697
'Do not let this **t** displease you, **2Sa 11:25** 1697
But the **t** that David had done was **2Sa 11:27** 1697
he did this **t** and had no compassion **2Sa 12:6** 1697
will do this **t** before all Israel, **2Sa 12:12** 1697
"What is this **t** that you have done? **2Sa 12:21** 1697
such a **t** is not done in Israel; **2Sa 13:12** 3651
do not do this disgraceful **t**! **2Sa 13:12** 5039
have you planned such a **t** against **2Sa 14:13** 2088
your servant Joab has done this **t**. **2Sa 14:20** 1697
now, I will surely do this **t**; **2Sa 14:21** 1697
lord the king delight in this **t**?" **2Sa 24:3** 1697
t been done by my lord the king, **1Ki 1:27** 1697
that Solomon had asked this **t**. **1Ki 3:10** 1697
"Because you have asked this **t** **1Ki 3:11** 1697
commanded him concerning this **t**, **1Ki 11:10** 1697
this **t** has come from Me. **1Ki 12:24** 1697
Now this **t** became a sin, for the **1Ki 12:30** 1697
"For the **t** shall surely come to **1Ki 13:32** 1697
a trivial **t** for him to walk in the sins **1Ki 16:31** 7043
do, but this **t** I cannot do.' " **1Ki 20:9** 1697
"Do this **t**: remove the kings, **1Ki 20:24** 1697
"You have asked a hard **t**. **2Ki 2:10** 7185
slight **t** in the sight of the LORD; **2Ki 3:18** 7043
told you *to do some* great **t**, **2Ki 5:13** 1697
of Aram was enraged over this **t**; **2Ki 6:11** 1697
in heaven, could this **t** be?" **2Ki 7:2** 1697
in heaven, could such a **t** be?" **2Ki 7:19** 1697
every kind of good **t** of Damascus, **2Ki 8:9** 2898
that he should do this great **t**?" **2Ki 8:13** 1697
"This is the **t** that you shall do: **2Ki 11:5** 1697
"You shall not do this **t**." **2Ki 17:12** 1697
will do the **t** that He has spoken: **2Ki 20:9** 1697
for the **t** was right in the eyes of **1Ch 13:4** 1697
"This was a small **t** in Your eyes, **1Ch 17:17** 6994
this good **t** to Your servant. **1Ch 17:26** 2899b
Why does my lord seek this **t**? **1Ch 21:3** 2088
God was displeased with this **t**, **1Ch 21:7** 1697
in that I have done this **t**. **1Ch 21:8** 1697
to his house, for this **t** is from Me. **2Ch 11:4** 1697
"This is the **t** which you shall do: **2Ch 23:4** 1697
and every unclean **t** which they **2Ch 29:16** 2932a
because the **t** came about suddenly. **2Ch 29:36** 1697
Thus the **t** was right in the sight **2Ch 30:4** 1697
who has put *such a* **t** as this in **Ezr 7:27**
"What is this **t** you are doing? **Ne 2:19** 1697
"The **t** which you are doing is not **Ne 5:9** 1697
of houses full of every good **t**, **Ne 9:25** 2898
"What is this evil **t** you are doing, **Ne 13:17** 1697
is the life of every living **t**, **Jb 12:10** 2416a
I am decaying like a rotten **t**, **Jb 13:28** 7538
"You will also decree a **t**, **Jb 22:28** 561
And searches after every green **t**. **Jb 39:8** 3387
And the peoples devising a vain **t**? **Ps 2:1** 7385b
One **t** I have asked from the LORD, **Ps 27:4** 259
not be in want of any good **t**. **Ps 34:10** 2896b
"A wicked **t** is poured out upon **Ps 41:8** 1697
No good **t** does He withhold from **Ps 84:11** 2896b
set no worthless **t** before my eyes; **Ps 101:3** 1697
incline my heart to any evil **t**, **Ps 141:4** 1697
the desire of every living **t**. **Ps 145:16** 2416a
He who finds a wife finds a good **t** **Pr 18:22** 2896b
knowledge are a more precious **t**. **Pr 20:15** 3627
man any bitter **t** is sweet. **Pr 27:7** 4751
It is good that you grasp one **t** and **Ec 7:18** 2088
"*adding* one **t** to another to find **Ec 7:27** 259
Is it too slight a **t** for you to **Is 7:13** 4592
died out, There is no green **t**. **Is 15:6** 3418
will scatter them as an impure **t**, **Is 30:22** 1739
will do this **t** that He has spoken: **Is 38:7** 1697
Or the **t** you are making *say*, **Is 45:9** 6467
"It is too small a **t** that You **Is 49:6** 7043
"Who has heard such a **t**? **Is 66:8** 2088
And see if there has been such *a* **t** **Jer 2:10**
"But the shameful **t** has consumed **Jer 3:24** 1322
An appalling and horrible **t** Has **Jer 5:30** 8186a
you have set up to the shameful **t**, **Jer 11:13** 1322
Has done a most appalling **t**. **Jer 18:13** 8186b

a **t** which I never commanded or **Jer 19:5**
men will indeed perform this **t**, **Jer 22:4** 1697
of Samaria I saw an offensive **t**: **Jer 23:13** 8604
I have seen a horrible **t**: **Jer 23:14** 8186a
For the LORD has created a new **t** **Jer 31:22** 2319
this **t** has happened to you. **Jer 40:3** 1697
"Do not do this **t**, for you are **Jer 40:16** 1697
and the **t** that we should do." **Jer 42:3** 1697
this abominable **t** which I hate." **Jer 44:4** 1697
she has become an unclean **t**. **La 1:8** 5206
become an unclean **t** among them. **La 1:17** 5079
gold will become an abhorrent **t**; **Ezk 7:19** 5079
make it an abhorrent **t** to them. **Ezk 7:20** 5079
Is it too light a **t** for the house **Ezk 8:17** 7043
'Is it too slight a **t** for you that **Ezk 34:18** 4592
every devoted **t** in Israel shall be **Ezk 44:29** 2764a
the **t** which the king demands is **Da 2:11** 4406
Israel I have seen a horrible **t**; **Hos 6:10** 8186b
They are regarded as a strange **t**. **Hos 8:12** 2114a
The **t** itself will be carried to **Hos 10:6**
beast, herd, or flock taste a **t**. **Jon 3:7** 3972
"You have devised a shameful **t** **Hab 2:10** 1322
"This is another **t** you do: **Mal 2:13** 8145
what good **t** shall I do that I may **Mt 19:16** *18*
ninth hour, and did the same **t**. **Mt 20:5** *5615*
"I will also ask you one **t**, **Mt 21:24** *3056*
to the second and said the same **t**; **Mt 21:30** *5615*
and they did the same **t** to them. **Mt 21:36** *5615*
the disciples said the same **t** too. **Mt 26:35** *3668*
time, saying the same **t** once more. **Mt 26:44** *3056*
"One **t** you lack: go and sell all you **Mk 10:21** *1520*
they all were saying the same **t** also **Mk 14:31** *5615*
and see this **t** that has happened **Lk 2:15** *4487*
but *only* one **t** is necessary, for **Lk 10:42** *1520*
cannot do even a very little **t**, **Lk 12:26** *1646*
He who is faithful in a very little **t** **Lk 16:10** *1646*
who is unrighteous in a very little **t** **Lk 16:10** *1646*
"One **t** you still lack; **Lk 18:22** *1520*
been faithful in a very little **t**, **Lk 19:17** *1646*
be who was going to do this **t**. **Lk 22:23** *3778*
any good **t** come out of Nazareth?" **Jn 1:46** *18*
one **t** I do know, that though I **Jn 9:25** *1520*
"Well, here is an amazing **t**, **Jn 9:30** *2298*
"What is this **t** He is telling us, **Jn 16:17** *3778*
you yourselves know the **t** which **Ac 10:37** *4487*
so that the **t** spoken of in the **Ac 13:40** *3004*
some were shouting one **t** and some **Ac 19:32**
shouting one **t** *and* some another, **Ac 21:34**
but I am doing the very **t** I hate. **Ro 7:15** *3739*
I do the very **t** I do not want *to do*, **Ro 7:16** *3778*
I am doing the very **t** I do not want, **Ro 7:20** *3778*
depth, nor any other created **t**, **Ro 8:39** *2937*
The **t** molded will not say to the **Ro 9:20** *4110*
devoting themselves to this very **t**. **Ro 13:6** *3778*
do not let what is for you a good **t** **Ro 14:16** *18*
But to me it is a very small **t** **1Co 4:3** *1646*
no such **t** as an idol in the world, **1Co 8:4** *3762*
That a **t** sacrificed to idols is **1Co 10:19** *1494*
This is the very **t** I wrote you, **2Co 2:3** *846*
what earnestness this very **t**, **2Co 7:11** *846*
every lofty **t** raised up against the **2Co 10:5** *5313*
very **t** I also was eager to do. **Ga 2:10** *846*
only **t** I want to find out from you: **Ga 3:2** *3441*
no spot or wrinkle or any such **t**; **Eph 5:27** *5108*
whatever good **t** each one does, **Eph 6:8** *18*
For I am confident of this very **t**, **Php 1:6** *846*
with God a **t** to be grasped, **Php 2:6** *725*
one **t** *I do:* forgetting what *lies* behind **Php 3:13** *1520*
knowledge of every good **t** which is in **Phm 1:6** *18*
It is a terrifying **t** to fall into **Heb 10:31** *5398*
equip you in every good **t** to do His **Heb 13:21** *18*
Every good **t** given and every **Jas 1:17** *1394*
is disorder and every evil **t**. **Jas 3:16** *4229*
one who knows *the* right **t** to do and **Jas 4:17** *2570*
so that in the **t** in which they **1Pe 2:12**
the **t** in which you are slandered, **1Pe 3:16**
as though some strange **t** were **1Pe 4:12** *3581*
And every created **t** which is in **Rv 5:13** *2938*
of the earth, nor any green **t**, **Rv 9:4** *5515*
every living **t** in the sea died. **Rv 16:3** *5590*

THINGS

cattle and creeping **t** and beasts **Gn 1:24** 7431
from man to animals to creeping **t** **Gn 6:7** 7431
t and to birds of the sky, **Gn 7:23** 7431
After these **t** the word of the LORD **Gn 15:1** 1697
told all these **t** in their hearing; **Gn 20:8** 1697
me **t** that ought not to be done." **Gn 20:9** 4639
Now it came about after these **t**, **Gn 22:1** 1697
Now it came about after these **t**, **Gn 22:20** 1697
a variety of good **t** of his master's **Gn 24:10** 2898
mother's household about these **t**. **Gn 24:28** 1697
he also gave precious **t** to her **Gn 24:53** 4030
Isaac all the **t** that he had done. **Gn 24:66** 1697
he related to Laban all these **t**. **Gn 29:13** 1697
the man to whom these **t** belong." **Gn 38:25** 428
Then it came about after these **t** **Gn 40:1** 1697
all these **t** are against me." **Gn 42:36**
loaded with the best **t** of Egypt, **Gn 45:23** 2898
Now it came about after these **t**, **Gn 48:1** 1697
"If he will not do these three **t** **Ex 21:11**
take away the iniquity of the holy **t** **Ex 28:38** 6944
"Thus they shall eat those **t** by **Ex 29:33**
"These are the **t** that the LORD **Ex 35:1** 1697
This is the number of the **t** for **Ex 38:21** 6491a
is made of these **t** to the LORD, **Lv 2:8** 428
a grain offering of early ripened **t** **Lv 2:14** 1061
offering of your early ripened **t**. **Lv 2:14** 1061
sins unintentionally in any of the **t** **Lv 4:2** 4687
and they commit any of the **t** which **Lv 4:13** 4687
any one of all the **t** which the LORD **Lv 4:22** 4687
in doing any of the **t** which the LORD **Lv 4:27** 4687
a carcass of unclean swarming **t**, **Lv 5:2** 8318
against the LORD's holy **t**, **Lv 5:15** 6944
if a person sins and does any of the **t** **Lv 5:17**
to any one of the **t** a man may do; **Lv 6:3**
will be forgiven for any one of the **t** **Lv 6:7**
Aaron and his sons did all the **t** **Lv 8:36** 1697
When **t** like these happened to me, **Lv 10:19**
they are detestable **t** to you, **Lv 11:10** 8263
the swarming **t** which swarm on the **Lv 11:29** 8318
unclean among all the swarming **t**; **Lv 11:31** 8318
any of the swarming **t** that swarm; **Lv 11:43** 8318
swarming **t** that swarm on the earth. **Lv 11:44** 8318
'Whoever then touches any of the **t** **Lv 15:10**
yourselves by any of these **t**; **Lv 18:24** 428
you, for they did all these **t**, **Lv 20:23** 428
or if a man touches any teeming **t** by **Lv 22:5** 8318
can still eat old **t** from the crop, **Lv 25:22** 3465
'If also after these **t** you **Lv 26:18** 428
by these **t** you are not turned to Me, **Lv 26:23** 428
concerning the most holy **t**. **Nu 4:4** 6944
These are the **t** in the tent of **Nu 4:15** 4853a
"Accept *these* **t** from them, that **Nu 7:5**
shall do these **t** in this manner, **Nu 15:13** 428
'These **t** shall be for a **Nu 35:29** 428
time all the **t** that you should do. **Dt 1:18** 1697
the **t** which your eyes have seen and **Dt 4:9** 1697
all these **t** have come upon you, **Dt 4:30** 1697
all good **t** which you did not fill, **Dt 6:11** 2898
has done these great and awesome **t** **Dt 10:21** 3372a
"Only your holy **t** which you may **Dt 12:26** 6944
the detestable **t** of those nations. **Dt 18:9** 8441
whoever does these **t** is detestable to **Dt 18:12** 428
because of these detestable **t** the LORD **Dt 18:12** 8441
do according to all their detestable **t** **Dt 20:18** 8441
for whoever does these **t** is an **Dt 22:5** 428
"For everyone who does these **t**, **Dt 25:16** 428
heart, for the abundance of all **t**; **Dt 28:47** 3605
and in the lack of all **t**; **Dt 28:48** 3605
The secret **t** belong to the LORD our **Dt 29:29** 5641
but the **t** revealed belong to us **Dt 29:29** 1540
all of these **t** have come upon you, **Dt 30:1** 1697
venom of crawling **t** of the dust. **Dt 32:24** 2119a
the impending **t** are hastening upon **Dt 32:35** 6264
land, With the choice **t** of heaven, **Dt 33:13** 4022
best **t** of the ancient mountains, **Dt 33:15** 7218
choice **t** of the everlasting hills, **Dt 33:15** 4022
choice **t** of the earth and its fullness, **Dt 33:16** 4022
"Just as we obeyed Moses in all **t**, **Jos 1:17** 3605
from the **t** under the ban, **Jos 6:18** 2764a
take some of the **t** under the ban, **Jos 6:18** 2764a
in regard to the **t** under the ban, **Jos 7:1** 2764a
took some of the **t** under the ban, **Jos 7:1** 2764a
taken some of the **t** under the ban **Jos 7:11** 2764a
also put *them* among their own **t**. **Jos 7:11** 3627
you destroy the **t** under the ban **Jos 7:12** 2764a
are **t** under the ban in your midst, **Jos 7:13** 2764a
have removed the **t** under the ban **Jos 7:13** 2764a
who is taken with the **t** under the ban **Jos 7:15** 2764a
in the **t** under the ban, **Jos 22:20** 2764a
It came about after these **t** **Jos 24:29** 1697
He have shown us all these **t**, **Jg 13:23** 428
nor would He have let us hear **t** **Jg 13:23**
"Why do you do such **t**, **1Sa 2:23** 1697
the evil **t** that I hear from all **1Sa 2:23** 1697
"How did **t** go, my son?" **1Sa 4:16** 1697
you would go after futile **t** which can **1Sa 12:21** 8414
what great **t** He has done for you. **1Sa 12:24** 1431
the choicest of the **t** devoted to **1Sa 15:21** 2764a
his wife told him these **t**, **1Sa 25:37** 1697
David said to him, "How did **t** go? **2Sa 1:4** 1697
You and awesome **t** for Your land, **2Sa 7:23** 3372a
to you many more **t** like these! **2Sa 12:8**
order to change the appearance of **t** **2Sa 14:20** 1697
with me, Ordered in all **t**, **2Sa 23:5** 3605
These **t** the three mighty men did. **2Sa 23:17** 428
These **t** Benaiah the son of **2Sa 23:22**
"I am offering you three **t**; **2Sa 24:12** 7969
and birds and creeping **t** and fish. **1Ki 4:33** 7431
t dedicated by his father David, **1Ki 7:51** 6944
dedicated **t** of his father and his own **1Ki 15:15** 6944
father and his own dedicated **t**: **1Ki 15:15** 6944
Now it came about after these **t** that **1Ki 17:17** 1697
have done all these **t** at Your word. **1Ki 18:36** 1697
Now it came about after these **t** that **1Ki 21:1** 1697
great **t** that Elisha has done." **2Ki 8:4** 1419
"All the money of the sacred **t** **2Ki 12:4** 6944
king of Judah took all the sacred **t** **2Ki 12:18** 6944
and his own sacred **t** and all the **2Ki 12:18** 6944
The sons of Israel did **t** secretly **2Ki 17:9** 1697
did evil **t** provoking the LORD. **2Ki 17:11** 1697
who proclaimed these **t**. **2Ki 23:16** 1697
from Judah and proclaimed these **t** **2Ki 23:17** 1697
the **t** which were baked in pans. **1Ch 9:31** 4639
These **t** the three mighty men did. **1Ch 11:19** 428
These **t** Benaiah the son of **1Ch 11:24**
to make known all these great **t**. **1Ch 17:19** 1420
a name by great and terrible **t**, **1Ch 17:21** 3372a
"I offer you three **t**; **1Ch 21:10** 7969
in the purifying of all holy **t**, **1Ch 23:28** 6944
storehouses of the dedicated **t**; **1Ch 28:12** 6944
house of my God the gold for the **t** **1Ch 29:2**
and the silver for the **t** *of* **1Ch 29:2**
and the bronze for the **t** *of* **1Ch 29:2**
the iron for the **t** *of* iron, **1Ch 29:2**
and wood for the **t** *of* wood, onyx **1Ch 29:2**
of gold for the **t** *of* gold and of **1Ch 29:5**
of gold and of silver for the **t** **1Ch 29:5**
For all **t** come from You, and from **1Ch 29:14** 3605
have willingly offered all these **t**; **1Ch 29:17**
to rinse **t** for the burnt offering; **2Ch 4:6** 4639
t that *were* in the house of God: **2Ch 4:19** 3627
And Solomon brought in the **t** that **2Ch 5:1**
the dedicated **t** of his father and his **2Ch 15:18** 6944
father and his own dedicated **t**: **2Ch 15:18** 6944
and valuable **t** which they took for **2Ch 20:25** 3627
of silver, gold and precious **t**, **2Ch 21:3** 4030
even used the holy **t** of the house of **2Ch 24:7** 6944
The consecrated **t** were 600 **2Ch 29:33** 6944
who showed good insight *in the* **t** **2Ch 30:22**
the tithes and the consecrated **t**; **2Ch 31:12** 6944
for the LORD and the most holy **t**. **2Ch 31:14** 6944
they boiled the holy **t** in pots, **2Ch 35:13** 6944
should not eat from the most holy **t** **Ezr 2:63** 6944
Now after these **t**, in the reign of **Ezr 7:1** 1697
when these **t** had been completed, **Ezr 9:1** 428
may be strong and eat the good **t** **Ezr 9:12**
"Such **t** as you are saying have **Ne 6:8** 1697
should not eat from the most holy **t** **Ne 7:65** 6944
for the holy **t** and for the sin **Ne 10:33** 6944
of Israel sin regarding these **t**? **Ne 13:26** 428
After these **t** when the anger of **Es 2:1** 1697
Who does great and unsearchable **t**, **Jb 5:9** 2714
"How long will you say these **t**, **Jb 8:2** 428
t searched out by their fathers. **Jb 8:8** 2714
Who does great **t**, unfathomable, **Jb 9:10** 1419
'Yet these **t** You have concealed **Jb 10:13** 428
who does not know such **t** as these? **Jb 12:3**
"Only two **t** do not do to me, Then **Jb 13:20** 8147
You write bitter **t** against me **Jb 13:26** 4846
"I have heard many such **t**; **Jb 16:2** 7227a
He filled their houses with good **t**; **Jb 22:18**
t which we cannot comprehend. **Jb 37:5** 1419
"I know that You can do all **t**, **Jb 42:2** 3605
T too wonderful for me, **Jb 42:3** 6381
You have put all **t** under his feet, **Ps 8:6** 3605
The tongue that speaks great **t**; **Ps 12:3** 1419
He who does these **t** will never be **Ps 15:5** 428
him with the blessings of good **t**; **Ps 21:3** 2896b
ask me of **t** that I do not know. **Ps 35:11**
These **t** I remember and I pour out **Ps 42:4** 428
right hand teach You awesome **t**. **Ps 45:4** 3372a
"These **t** you have done and I **Ps 50:21** 428
To God who accomplishes *all* **t** for **Ps 57:2**
You who have done great **t**; **Ps 71:19** 1419
Glorious **t** are spoken of you, O **Ps 87:3** 3513
song, For He has done wonderful **t**, **Ps 98:1** 6381
satisfies your years with good **t**, **Ps 103:5** 2896b
Who had done great **t** in Egypt, **Ps 106:21** 1419
Ham *And* awesome **t** by the Red Sea. **Ps 106:22**
Let him give heed to these **t**, **Ps 107:43** 428
Who humbles Himself to behold *The* **t** **Ps 113:6**
behold Wonderful **t** from Your law. **Ps 119:18** 6381
For all **t** are Your servants. **Ps 119:91** 3605
LORD has done great **t** for them." **Ps 126:2** 1431
The LORD has done great **t** for us; **Ps 126:3** 1431
Or in **t** too difficult for me. **Ps 131:1** 6381
Who devise evil **t** in *their* hearts; **Ps 140:2** 7451a
Creeping **t** and winged fowl; **Ps 148:10** 7431
the man who speaks perverse **t**; **Pr 2:12** 8419
are six **t** which the LORD hates, **Pr 6:16** 2007
"Listen, for I will speak noble **t**; **Pr 8:6** 5057
of my lips *will reveal* right **t**. **Pr 8:6** 4339
all desirable **t** cannot compare with **Pr 8:11** 2656
But he who pursues worthless **t** **Pr 12:11**
of the wicked pours out evil **t**. **Pr 15:28** 7451a
eyes *does so* to devise perverse **t**; **Pr 16:30** 8419
Have I not written to you excellent **t** **Pr 22:20** 7991c
Your eyes will see strange **t** And **Pr 23:33** 2114a
your mind will utter perverse **t**. **Pr 23:33** 8419
seek the LORD understand all **t**. **Pr 28:5** 3605
Two **t** I asked of You, Do not **Pr 30:7** 8147
are three **t** that will not be satisfied, **Pr 30:15** 7969
There are three **t** which are too **Pr 30:18** 7969
Under three **t** the earth quakes, **Pr 30:21** 7969
Four **t** are small on the earth, But **Pr 30:24** 702
There are three **t** which are **Pr 30:29** 7969
All **t** are wearisome; **Ec 1:8** 1697
is no remembrance of earlier **t**; **Ec 1:11** 7223
of the later **t** which will occur, **Ec 1:11** 314
When good **t** increase, those who **Ec 5:11** 2899b
soul is not satisfied with good **t** and **Ec 6:3** 2899b
years twice and does not enjoy good **t** **Ec 6:6** 2899b
activity of God who makes all **t**. **Ec 11:5** 3605
you to judgment for all these **t**. **Ec 11:9** 428
song, for He has done excellent **t**; **Is 12:5** 1348
You turn **t** around! Shall **Is 29:16**
"O Lord, by *these* **t** *men* live, **Is 38:16**
Declare the **t** that are going to **Is 41:23** 857
the former **t** have come to pass, **Is 42:9** 7223
come to pass, Now I declare new **t**; **Is 42:9** 2319
These are the **t** I will do, And I **Is 42:16** 1697
You have seen many **t**, **Is 42:20** 7227a
And proclaim to us the former **t**? **Is 43:9** 7223
"Do not call to mind the former **t**, **Is 43:18** 7223
things, Or ponder **t** of the past. **Is 43:18** 6931
declare to them the **t** that are coming **Is 44:7** 857
their precious **t** are of no profit; **Is 44:9** 2530
"Remember these **t**, O Jacob, And **Is 44:21** 428
"I, the LORD, am the maker of all **t**, **Is 44:24** 3605
"Ask Me about the **t** to come **Is 45:11** 857
Declaring **t** that are upright. **Is 45:19** 4339
t that you carry are burdensome, **Is 46:1** 5385
"Remember the former **t** long past, **Is 46:9** 7223
times **t** which have not been done, **Is 46:10**
These **t** you did not consider Nor **Is 47:7** 428
"But these two **t** will come on **Is 47:9** 8147

“I declared the former **t** long ago Is 48:3 7223
to you new **t** from this time, Is 48:6 2319
hidden **t** which you have not known. Is 48:6 5341
among them has declared these **t**? Is 48:14 428
These two **t** have befallen you; Is 51:19 8147
Shall I relent concerning these **t**? Is 57:6 428
the **t** sown in it to spring up, Is 61:11 2221
awesome **t** which we did not expect, Is 64:3 3372a
our precious **t** have become a ruin. Is 64:11 4261
You restrain Yourself at these **t**, Is 64:12 428
And the former **t** will not be Is 65:17 7223
“For My hand made all these **t**, Is 66:2 428
all these **t** came into being,” Is 66:2 428
Who has seen such **t**? Is 66:8 428
Who eat swine’s flesh, detestable **t** and Is 66:17 8263
To eat its fruit and its good **t**. Jer 2:7 2898
walked after **t** that did not profit. Jer 2:8
But in spite of all these **t**, Jer 2:34 428
have spoken And have done evil **t**, Jer 3:5 7451a
‘After she has done all these **t** she Jer 3:7 428
your detested **t** from My presence, Jer 4:1 8251
deeds Have brought these **t** to you. Jer 4:18 428
our God done all these **t** to us?” Jer 5:19 428
you have done all these **t**,” Jer 7:13 4639
“they have set their detestable **t** Jer 7:30 8251
I not punish them for these **t**?” Jer 9:9 428
for I delight in these **t**,” Jer 9:24 428
they may say nice **t** to you.” Jer 12:6 2899b
‘Why have these **t** happened to me?’ Jer 13:22 428
the one who has done all these **t**. Jer 14:22 428
Futility and **t** of no profit.” Jer 16:19 3276
Jeremiah prophesying these **t**, Jer 20:1 1697
its produce and all its costly **t**; Jer 20:5 3366
officials of Judah heard these **t**, Jer 26:10 1697
I have done these **t** to you. Jer 30:15 428
“But they put their detestable **t** Jer 32:34 8251
I will tell you great and mighty **t**, Jer 33:3 1219
you seeking great **t** for yourself? Jer 45:5 1419
remembers all her precious **t** La 1:7 4262
his hand Over all her precious **t**, La 1:10 4261
They have given their precious **t** La 1:11 4262
“For these **t** I weep; La 1:16 428
these the Lord does not approve. La 3:36
Because of these **t** our eyes are dim; La 5:17 428
and their detestable **t** with it; Ezk 7:20 8251
every form of creeping **t** and Ezk 8:10 7431
and beasts *and* detestable **t**, Ezk 8:10 8263
they will remove all its detestable **t** Ezk 11:18 8251
detestable **t** and abominations, Ezk 11:21 8251
the **t** that the LORD had shown me. Ezk 11:25 1697
you to do any of these **t** for you, Ezk 16:5 428
“while you do all these **t**, Ezk 16:30 4639
have enraged Me by all these **t**, Ezk 16:43 428
you not know what these **t** *mean?*’ Ezk 17:12 428
Will he who does such **t** escape? Ezk 17:15 428
allegiance, yet did all these **t**, Ezk 17:18 428
does any of these **t** to a brother Ezk 18:10 428
did not do any of these **t**), Ezk 18:11 428
you, the detestable **t** of his eyes, Ezk 20:7 8251
the detestable **t** of their eyes, Ezk 20:8 8251
harlot after their detestable **t**? Ezk 20:30 8251
your gifts, with all your holy **t**. Ezk 20:40 6944
all the evil **t** that you have done. Ezk 20:43 7451a
You have despised My holy **t** and Ezk 22:8 6944
taken treasure and precious **t**; Ezk 22:25 3366
law and have profaned My holy **t**; Ezk 22:26 6944
‘These **t** will be done to you Ezk 23:30 428
t that you are doing mean for us?” Ezk 24:19 428
idols, or with their detestable **t**, Ezk 37:23 8251
t that creep on the earth, Ezk 38:20 7431
LORD shall eat the most holy **t**. Ezk 42:13 6944
they shall lay the most holy **t**, Ezk 42:13 6944
charge of My holy **t** yourselves, Ezk 44:8 6944
nor come near to any of My holy **t**, Ezk 44:13 6944
to the **t** that are most holy; Ezk 44:13 6944
reveals the profound and hidden **t**; Da 2:22 5642a
iron crushes and shatters all **t**, Da 2:40 3606
me the interpretation of these **t**: Da 7:16 4406
monstrous **t** against the God of gods; Da 11:36 6381
over all the precious **t** of Egypt; Da 11:43 2536b
And the creeping **t** of the ground. Hos 2:18 7431
wise, let him understand these **t**; Hos 14:9 428
up, For it has done great **t**.” Jl 2:20 1431
For the LORD has done great **t**. Jl 2:21 1431
not speak out concerning these **t**, Mi 2:6 428
creeping **t** without a ruler over them Hab 1:14 7431
through these **t** their catch is large, Hab 1:16 1992a
“I will completely remove all **t** Zph 1:2
has despised the day of small **t**? Zch 4:10 6996a
this people to inherit all these **t**. Zch 8:12
are the **t** which you should do: Zch 8:16 1697
detestable **t** from between their teeth Zch 9:7 8251
“All these **t** I will give You, if Mt 4:9 3778
the Gentiles eagerly seek all these **t**; Mt 6:32 3778
knows that you need all these **t**. Mt 6:32 3778
all these **t** will be added to you. Mt 6:33 3778
He was saying these **t** to them, Mt 9:18 3778
that You have hidden these **t** from Mt 11:25 3778
“All **t** have been handed over to Mt 11:27 3956
spoke many **t** to them in parables, Mt 13:3 4183
All these **t** Jesus spoke to the Mt 13:34 3778
I WILL UTTER T HIDDEN SINCE THE Mt 13:35 2928
“Have you understood all these **t**?” Mt 13:51 3778
of his treasure **t** new and old.” Mt 13:52 2537
did this man *get* all these **t**?” Mt 13:56 3778
“But the **t** that proceed out of Mt 15:18
are the **t** which defile the man; Mt 15:20
and suffer many **t** from the elders Mt 16:21 4183
is coming and will restore all **t**; Mt 17:11 3956

“All these **t** I have kept; Mt 19:20 3778
but with God all **t** are possible.” Mt 19:26 3956
the wonderful **t** that He had done, Mt 21:15 2297
“And all **t** you ask in prayer, Mt 21:22 3956
authority are You doing these **t**, Mt 21:23 3778
by what authority I do these **t**. Mt 21:24 3778
by what authority I do these **t**. Mt 21:27 3778
to Caesar the **t** that are Caesar’s; Mt 22:21
and to God the **t** that are God’s.” Mt 22:21
for they say **t** and do not do Mt 23:3
but these are the **t** you should Mt 23:23
all these **t** will come upon this Mt 23:36 3778
“Do you not see all these **t**? Mt 24:2 3778
“Tell us, when will these **t** happen, Mt 24:3 3778
for *those* **t** must take place, but Mt 24:6
“But all these **t** are *merely* the Mt 24:8 3778
the **t** out that are in his house. Mt 24:17
you too, when you see all these **t**, Mt 24:33 3778
away until all these **t** take place. Mt 24:34 3778
You were faithful with a few **t**, Mt 25:21 3641
will put you in charge of many **t**; Mt 25:21 4183
You were faithful with a few **t**, Mt 25:23 3641
will put you in charge of many **t**; Mt 25:23 4183
many **t** they testify against You?” Mt 27:13 4214
and the **t** that were happening, Mt 27:54
about these **t** in your hearts? Mk 2:8 3778
teaching them many **t** in parables, Mk 4:2 4183
the desires for other **t** enter in and Mk 4:19 3062
great **t** the Lord has done for you, Mk 5:19 3745
great **t** Jesus had done for him; Mk 5:20 3745
“Where did this man *get* these **t**, Mk 6:2 3778
and He began to teach them many **t**. Mk 6:34 4183
and there are many other **t** which Mk 7:4 4183
and you do many **t** such as that.” Mk 7:13 4183
but the **t** which proceed out of the Mk 7:15
“All these evil **t** proceed from Mk 7:23 4190
“He has done all **t** well; Mk 7:37 3956
the Son of Man must suffer many **t** Mk 8:31 4183
does first come and restore all **t**. Mk 9:12 3956
that He will suffer many **t** and Mk 9:12 4183
All **t** are possible to him who Mk 9:23 3956
all these **t** from my youth up.” Mk 10:20 3778
for all **t** are possible with God.” Mk 10:27 3956
all **t** for which you pray and ask, Mk 11:24 3956
authority are You doing these **t**, Mk 11:28 3778
this authority to do these **t**?” Mk 11:28 3778
by what authority I do these **t**. Mk 11:29 3778
by what authority I do these **t**. Mk 11:33 3778
to Caesar the **t** that are Caesar’s, Mk 12:17
and to God the **t** that are God’s.” Mk 12:17
“Tell us, when will these **t** be, Mk 13:4 3778
sign when all these **t** are going to be Mk 13:4 3778
those **t** must take place; Mk 13:7
These **t** are *merely* the beginning Mk 13:8 3778
when you see these **t** happening, Mk 13:29 3778
away until all these **t** take place. Mk 13:30 3778
All **t** are possible for You; Mk 14:36 3956
an account of the **t** accomplished Lk 1:1 4229
about the **t** you have been taught. Lk 1:4 3056
the day when these **t** take place, Lk 1:20 3778
Mighty One has done great **t** for me; Lk 1:49 3173
FILLED THE HUNGRY WITH GOOD T; Lk 1:53 18
wondered at the **t** which were told Lk 2:18
But Mary treasured all these **t**, Lk 2:19 4487
amazed at the **t** which were being said Lk 2:33
all *these* **t** in her heart. Lk 2:51 4487
the wicked **t** which Herod had done, Lk 3:19 4190
with rage as they heard these **t**; Lk 4:28 3778
“We have seen remarkable **t** today.” Lk 5:26 3861
reported to him about all these **t**. Lk 7:18 3778
As He said these **t**, He would call Lk 8:8 3778
great **t** God has done for you.” Lk 8:39 3745
great **t** Jesus had done for him. Lk 8:39 3745
man about whom I hear such **t**?” Lk 9:9 5108
“The Son of Man must suffer many **t** Lk 9:22 4183
any of the **t** which they had seen. Lk 9:36
that You have hidden these **t** from Lk 10:21 3778
“All **t** have been handed over to Lk 10:22 3956
the eyes which see the **t** you see, Lk 10:23
wished to see the **t** which you see, Lk 10:24
and to hear the **t** which you hear, Lk 10:24
and bothered about so many **t**; Lk 10:41 4183
While Jesus was saying these **t**, Lk 11:27 3778
and then all **t** are clean for you. Lk 11:41 3956
but these are the **t** you should Lk 11:42 3778
“For all these **t** the nations of Lk 12:30 3778
knows that you need these **t**. Lk 12:30 3778
and these **t** will be added to you. Lk 12:31 3778
the glorious **t** being done by Him. Lk 13:17 1741
inquiring what these **t** could be. Lk 15:26 3778
were listening to all these **t** and Lk 16:14 3778
life you received your good **t**, Lk 16:25 18
and likewise Lazarus bad **t**; Lk 16:25 2556
he did the **t** which were commanded, Lk 17:9
all the **t** which are commanded you, Lk 17:10 3956
“But first He must suffer many **t** Lk 17:25 4183
All these **t** I have kept from *my* Lk 18:21 3778
But when He had heard these **t**, Lk 18:23 3778
“The **t** that are impossible with people Lk 18:27 102
and all **t** which are written Lk 18:31 3956
disciples understood none of these **t**, Lk 18:34 3778
comprehend the **t** that were said. Lk 18:34
they were listening to these **t**, Lk 19:11 3778
After He had said these **t**, Lk 19:28 3778
you, the **t** which make for peace! Lk 19:42
authority You are doing these **t**, Lk 20:2 3778
by what authority I do these **t**.” Lk 20:8 3778
to Caesar the **t** that are Caesar’s, Lk 20:25
and to God the **t** that are God’s.” Lk 20:25

these **t** which you are looking at, Lk 21:6 3778
when therefore will these **t** happen? Lk 21:7 3778
these **t** are about to take place?” Lk 21:7 3778
for these **t** must take place first, Lk 21:9 3778
“But before all these **t**, Lk 21:12 3778
so that all **t** which are Lk 21:22 3956
expectation of the **t** which are coming Lk 21:26
when these **t** begin to take place, Lk 21:28 3778
when you see these **t** happening, Lk 21:31 3778
pass away until all **t** take place. Lk 21:32 3956
t that are about to take place, Lk 21:36 3778
saying many other **t** against Him, Lk 22:65 4183
do these **t** when the tree is green, Lk 23:31 3778
at a distance, seeing these **t**. Lk 23:49 3778
reported all these **t** to the eleven Lk 24:9 3778
telling these **t** to the apostles. Lk 24:10 3778
all these **t** which had taken place. Lk 24:14 3778
unaware of the **t** which have happened Lk 24:18
And He said to them, “What **t**?” Lk 24:19 4169
“The **t** about Jesus the Nazarene, Lk 24:19
third day since these **t** happened. Lk 24:21 3778
for the Christ to suffer these **t** and Lk 24:26 3778
He explained to them the **t** Lk 24:27
While they were telling these **t**, Lk 24:36 3778
that all **t** which are written about Lk 24:44 3956
“You are witnesses of these **t**. Lk 24:48 3778
All **t** came into being through Him, and Jn 1:3 3956
These **t** took place in Bethany Jn 1:28 3778
will see greater **t** than these.” Jn 1:50 3173
“Take these **t** away; Jn 2:16 3778
us as your authority for doing these **t**?” Jn 2:18 3778
“How can these **t** be?” Jn 3:9 3778
and do not understand these **t**? Jn 3:10 3778
If I told you earthly **t** and you Jn 3:12 1919
believe if I tell you heavenly **t**? Jn 3:12 2032
After these **t** Jesus and His Jn 3:22 3778
and has given all **t** into His hand. Jn 3:35 3956
He will declare all **t** to us.” Jn 4:25 537a
me all the **t** that I *have* done; Jn 4:29 3956
me all the **t** that I *have* done.” Jn 4:39 3956
having seen all the **t** that He did Jn 4:45 3956
After these **t** there was a feast of Jn 5:1 3778
was doing these **t** on the Sabbath. Jn 5:16 3778
these **t** the Son also does in like Jn 5:19 3778
all **t** that He Himself is doing; Jn 5:20 3956
say these **t** so that you may be saved. Jn 5:34 3778
After these **t** Jesus went away to Jn 6:1 3778
These **t** He said in the synagogue as Jn 6:59 3778
After these **t** Jesus was walking in Jn 7:1 3778
If You do these **t**, show Yourself Jn 7:4 3778
Having said these **t** to them, Jn 7:9 3778
muttering these **t** about Him, Jn 7:32 3778
“I have many **t** to speak and to Jn 8:26 4183
and the **t** which I heard from Him, Jn 8:26
I speak these **t** as the Father taught Jn 8:28 3778
the **t** that are pleasing to Him.” Jn 8:29 701
As He spoke these **t**, Jn 8:30 3778
“I speak the **t** which I have seen Jn 8:38
therefore you also do the **t** which Jn 8:38
who were with Him heard these **t** and Jn 9:40 3778
did not understand what those **t** were Jn 10:6
When He had said these **t**, Jn 11:43 3778
them the **t** which Jesus had done. Jn 11:46
These **t** His disciples did not Jn 12:16 3778
that these **t** were written of Him, Jn 12:16 3778
that they had done these **t** to Him. Jn 12:16 3778
These **t** Jesus spoke, and He Jn 12:36 3778
These **t** Isaiah said because he Jn 12:41 3778
therefore the **t** I speak, I speak Jn 12:50
had given all **t** into His hands, Jn 13:3 3956
“If you know these **t**, Jn 13:17 3778
t we have need of for the feast”; Jn 13:29
“These **t** I have spoken to you while Jn 14:25 3778
My name, He will teach you all **t**, Jn 14:26 3956
“These **t** I have spoken to you so Jn 15:11 3778
for all **t** that I have heard from Jn 15:15 3956
“But all these **t** they will do to Jn 15:21 3778
“These **t** I have spoken to you so Jn 16:1 3778
“These **t** they will do because Jn 16:3 3778
“But these **t** I have spoken to Jn 16:4 3778
These **t** I did not say to you Jn 16:4 3778
I have said these **t** to you, Jn 16:6 3778
“I have many more **t** to say to you, Jn 16:12 4183
All **t** that the Father has are Mine; Jn 16:15 3956
“These **t** I have spoken to you in Jn 16:25 3778
“Now we know that You know all **t**, Jn 16:30 3956
“These **t** I have spoken to you, Jn 16:33 3778
Jesus spoke these **t**; Jn 17:1 3778
and all **t** that are Mine are Yours, Jn 17:10 3956
and these **t** I speak in the world so Jn 17:13 3778
the **t** that were coming upon Him, Jn 18:4 3956
the soldiers did these **t**. Jn 19:25 3778
all **t** had already been accomplished, Jn 19:28 3956
For these **t** came to pass Jn 19:36 3778
After these **t** Joseph of Arimathea, Jn 19:38 3778
that He had said these **t** to her. Jn 20:18 3778
After these **t** Jesus manifested Jn 21:1 3778
“Lord, You know all **t**; Jn 21:17 3956
who is testifying to these **t** Jn 21:24 3778
these things and wrote these **t** Jn 21:24 3778
also many other **t** which Jesus did, Jn 21:25 4183
t concerning the kingdom of God. Ac 1:3
And after He had said these **t**, Ac 1:9 3778
together and had all **t** in common; Ac 2:44 537a
“But the **t** which God announced Ac 3:18
until *the* period of restoration of all **t** Ac 3:21 3956
AND THE PEOPLES DEVISE FUTILE T? Ac 4:25 2756
all **t** were common property to them Ac 4:32 3956
and over all who heard of these **t**. Ac 5:11 3778

Context	Reference	Number
"And we are witnesses of these **t**;	Ac 5:32	*4487*
"Are these **t** so?"	Ac 7:1	*3778*
MY HAND WHICH MADE ALL THESE **T**?'	Ac 7:50	*3778*
witnesses of all the **t** He did	Ac 10:39	*3956*
Report these **t** to James and the	Ac 12:17	*3778*
"After these **t** He gave *them*	Ac 13:20	*3778*
who believes is freed from all **t**,	Ac 13:39	*3956*
begging that these **t** might be spoken	Ac 13:42	*4487*
contradicting the **t** spoken by Paul,	Ac 13:45	*2980*
"Men, why are you doing these **t**?	Ac 14:15	*3778*
from these vain **t** to a living God,	Ac 14:15	*3152*
Even saying these **t**,	Ac 14:18	*3778*
they *began* to report all **t** that	Ac 14:27	*3745*
'AFTER THESE **T** I will return, AND	Ac 15:16	*3778*
MAKES THESE **T** KNOWN FROM LONG AGO.	Ac 15:18	*3778*
abstain from **t** contaminated by idols	Ac 15:20	*234*
the same **t** by word *of mouth.*	Ac 15:27	*846*
that you abstain from **t** sacrificed	Ac 15:29	*1494*
and from blood and from **t** strangled	Ac 15:29	*4156*
keep yourselves free from such **t**,	Ac 15:29	*3739*
respond to the **t** spoken by Paul.	Ac 16:14	*2980*
authorities who heard these **t**.	Ac 17:8	*3778*
to see whether these **t** were so.	Ac 17:11	*3778*
some strange **t** to our ears;	Ac 17:20	*3579*
know what these **t** mean."	Ac 17:20	*3778*
made the world and all **t** in it,	Ac 17:24	*3956*
to all *people* life and breath and all **t**;	Ac 17:25	*3956*
After these **t** he left Athens and	Ac 18:1	*3778*
concerned about any of these **t**.	Ac 18:17	*3778*
accurately the **t** concerning Jesus,	Ac 18:25	
Now after these **t** were finished,	Ac 19:21	*3778*
will arise, speaking perverse **t**,	Ac 20:30	*1294*
When he had said these **t**,	Ac 20:36	*3778*
to relate one by one the **t** which God	Ac 21:19	
there is nothing to the **t** which they	Ac 21:24	
you have notified me of these **t**."	Ac 23:22	*3778*
the **t** of which we accuse him."	Ac 24:8	
asserting that these **t** were so.	Ac 24:9	*3778*
but if none of those **t** is *true* of	Ac 25:11	
"In regard to all the **t** of which	Ac 26:2	*3956*
I had to do many **t** hostile to the	Ac 26:9	*4183*
only to the **t** which you have seen,	Ac 26:16	
t in which I will appear to you;	Ac 26:16	
none of these **t** escape his notice;	Ac 26:26	*3778*
others on various **t** from the ship.	Ac 27:44	*5100*
being persuaded by the **t** spoken,	Ac 28:24	*3004*
do those **t** which are not proper,	Ro 1:28	
such **t** are worthy of death,	Ro 1:32	*5108*
you who judge practice the same **t**.	Ro 2:1	*846*
upon those who practice such **t**.	Ro 2:2	*5108*
on those who practice such **t** and	Ro 2:3	*5108*
do instinctively the **t** of the Law,	Ro 2:14	
approve the **t** that are essential,	Ro 2:18	
t of which you are now ashamed?	Ro 6:21	
the outcome of those **t** is death.	Ro 6:21	*1565*
their minds on the **t** of the flesh,	Ro 8:5	
the Spirit, the **t** of the Spirit.	Ro 8:5	
God causes all **t** to work together	Ro 8:28	*3956*
What then shall we say to these **t**?	Ro 8:31	*3778*
with Him freely give us all **t**?	Ro 8:32	*3956*
But in all these **t** we	Ro 8:37	*3778*
nor principalities, nor **t** present,	Ro 8:38	*1764*
nor things present, nor **t** to come,	Ro 8:38	*3195*
BRING GOOD NEWS OF GOOD **T**!"	Ro 10:15	*18*
through Him and to Him are all **t**.	Ro 11:36	*3956*
has faith that he may eat all **t**,	Ro 14:2	*3956*
So then we pursue the **t** which	Ro 14:19	
All **t** indeed are clean, but they	Ro 14:20	*3956*
boasting in **t** pertaining to God.	Ro 15:17	
have shared in their spiritual **t**,	Ro 15:27	*4152*
to them also in material **t**.	Ro 15:27	*4559*
but God has chosen the foolish **t**	1Co 1:27	*3474*
has chosen the weak **t** of the world	1Co 1:27	*772*
to shame the **t** which are strong,	1Co 1:27	
base **t** of the world and the despised	1Co 1:28	*36*
has chosen, the **t** that are not,	1Co 1:28	
He may nullify the **t** that are,	1Co 1:28	
"**T** WHICH EYE HAS NOT SEEN AND EAR	1Co 2:9	
for the Spirit searches all **t**,	1Co 2:10	*3956*
the **t** freely given to us by God,	1Co 2:12	*5483*
which **t** we also speak, not in	1Co 2:13	
accept the **t** of the Spirit of God,	1Co 2:14	
he who is spiritual appraises all **t**,	1Co 2:15	*3956*
For all **t** belong to you,	1Co 3:21	*3956*
or **t** present or things to come;	1Co 3:22	*1764*
or things present or **t** to come;	1Co 3:22	*3195*
all **t** belong to you,	1Co 3:22	*3956*
bring to light the **t** hidden in the	1Co 4:5	*2927*
Now these **t**, brethren, I have	1Co 4:6	*3778*
of the world, the dregs of all **t**,	1Co 4:13	*3956*
I do not write these **t** to shame you,	1Co 4:14	*3778*
All **t** are lawful for me, but not	1Co 6:12	*3956*
me, but not all **t** are profitable.	1Co 6:12	*3956*
All **t** are lawful for me, but I	1Co 6:12	*3956*
concerning the **t** about which you	1Co 7:1	
concerned about the **t** of the Lord,	1Co 7:32	
about the **t** of the world,	1Co 7:33	
concerned about the **t** of the Lord,	1Co 7:34	
about the **t** of the world,	1Co 7:34	
concerning **t** sacrificed to idols,	1Co 8:1	*1494*
eating of **t** sacrificed to idols,	1Co 8:4	*1494*
the Father, from whom are all **t** and	1Co 8:6	*3956*
Jesus Christ, by whom are all **t**,	1Co 8:6	*3956*
to eat **t** sacrificed to idols?	1Co 8:10	*1494*
I am not speaking these **t** according	1Co 9:8	*3778*
does not the Law also say these **t**?	1Co 9:8	*3778*
If we sowed spiritual **t** in you,	1Co 9:11	*4152*
we reap material **t** from you?	1Co 9:11	*4559*
this right, but we endure all **t** so	1Co 9:12	*3956*
But I have used none of these **t**.	1Co 9:15	*3778*
And I am not writing these **t** so	1Co 9:15	*3778*
I have become all **t** to all men,	1Co 9:22	*3956*
all **t** for the sake of the gospel,	1Co 9:23	*3956*
exercises self-control in all **t**.	1Co 9:25	*3956*
these **t** happened as examples for us,	1Co 10:6	*3778*
that we would not crave evil **t**	1Co 10:6	*2556*
Now these **t** happened to them as an	1Co 10:11	*3778*
t which the Gentiles sacrifice,	1Co 10:20	
All **t** are lawful, but not all	1Co 10:23	*3956*
but not all **t** are profitable.	1Co 10:23	*3956*
All **t** are lawful, but not all	1Co 10:23	*3956*
are lawful, but not all **t** edify.	1Co 10:23	*3956*
as I also please all men in all **t**,	1Co 10:33	*3956*
and all **t** originate from God.	1Co 11:12	*3956*
who works all **t** in all *persons.*	1Co 12:6	*3956*
the same Spirit works all these **t**,	1Co 12:11	*3778*
bears all **t**, believes all things,	1Co 13:7	*3956*
bears all things, believes all **t**,	1Co 13:7	*3956*
believes all things, hopes all **t**,	1Co 13:7	*3956*
hopes all things, endures all **t**.	1Co 13:7	*3956*
a man, I did away with childish **t**.	1Co 13:11	
Yet *even* lifeless **t**,	1Co 14:7	*895*
Let all **t** be done for edification.	1Co 14:26	*3956*
let him recognize that the **t** which	1Co 14:37	
But all **t** must be done properly and	1Co 14:40	*3956*
FOR HE HAS PUT ALL **T** IN	1Co 15:27	*3956*
"All **t** are put in subjection,"	1Co 15:27	*3956*
put all **t** in subjection to Him.	1Co 15:27	*3956*
When all **t** are subjected to Him,	1Co 15:28	*3956*
One who subjected all **t** to Him,	1Co 15:28	*3956*
whether you are obedient in all **t**.	2Co 2:9	*3956*
And who is adequate for these **t**?	2Co 2:16	*3778*
the **t** hidden because of shame,	2Co 4:2	*2927*
For all **t** *are* for your sakes, so	2Co 4:15	*3956*
look not at the **t** which are seen,	2Co 4:18	
but at the **t** which are not seen;	2Co 4:18	
the **t** which are seen are temporal,	2Co 4:18	
but the **t** which are not seen are	2Co 4:18	
the old **t** passed away;	2Co 5:17	*744*
behold, new **t** have come.	2Co 5:17	*2537*
Now all *these* **t** are from God, who	2Co 5:18	*3956*
nothing yet possessing all **t**.	2Co 6:10	*3956*
as we spoke all **t** to you in truth,	2Co 7:14	*3956*
him the brother whose fame in *the* **t**	2Co 8:18	
and found diligent in many **t**,	2Co 8:22	*4183*
looking at **t** as they are outwardly.	2Co 10:7	
made *this* evident to you in all **t**.	2Co 11:6	*3956*
Apart from *such* external **t**,	2Co 11:28	
I am writing these **t** while absent,	2Co 13:10	*3778*
Did you suffer so many **t** in	Ga 3:4	*5118*
DOES NOT ABIDE BY ALL **T** WRITTEN	Ga 3:10	*3956*
the elemental **t** of the world.	Ga 4:3	*4747*
weak and worthless elemental **t**,	Ga 4:9	*4747*
may not do the **t** that you please.	Ga 5:17	
carousing, and **t** like these,	Ga 5:21	
who practice such **t** will not inherit	Ga 5:21	*5108*
against such **t** there is no law.	Ga 5:23	*5108*
all good **t** with the one who teaches	Ga 6:6	*18*
the summing up of all **t** in Christ,	Eph 1:10	*3956*
t in the heavens and things on	Eph 1:10	
the heavens and **t** on the earth.	Eph 1:10	
who works all **t** after the counsel of	Eph 1:11	*3956*
He put all **t** in subjection under His	Eph 1:22	*3956*
as head over all **t** to the church,	Eph 1:22	*3956*
hidden in God who created all **t**;	Eph 3:9	*3956*
that He might fill all **t**.)	Eph 4:10	*3956*
for because of these **t** the wrath	Eph 5:6	*3778*
t which are done by them in secret.	Eph 5:12	
But all **t** become visible when they	Eph 5:13	*3956*
always giving thanks for all **t** in	Eph 5:20	*3956*
masters, do the same **t** to them,	Eph 6:9	*846*
approve the **t** that are excellent,	Php 1:10	
Do all **t** without grumbling or	Php 2:14	*3956*
as soon as I see how **t** *go* with me;	Php 2:23	*3588*
To write the same **t** *again* is no	Php 3:1	*846*
But whatever **t** were gain to me,	Php 3:7	*3748*
those **t** I have counted as loss for	Php 3:7	*3778*
I count all **t** to be loss in view	Php 3:8	*3956*
I have suffered the loss of all **t**,	Php 3:8	*3956*
who set their minds on earthly **t**.	Php 3:19	*1919*
even to subject all **t** to Himself.	Php 3:21	*3956*
dwell on these **t**.	Php 4:8	*3778*
The **t** you have learned and	Php 4:9	*3739*
and seen in me, practice these **t**,	Php 4:9	*3778*
I can do all **t** through Him who	Php 4:13	*3956*
For by Him all **t** were created,	Col 1:16	*3956*
all **t** have been created through Him	Col 1:16	*3956*
He is before all **t**,	Col 1:17	*3956*
and in Him all **t** hold together.	Col 1:17	*3956*
Him to reconcile all **t** to Himself,	Col 1:20	*3956*
t on earth or things in heaven.	Col 1:20	
things on earth or **t** in heaven.	Col 1:20	
t which are a *mere* shadow of what	Col 2:17	
t destined to perish with use)	Col 2:22	
Christ, keep seeking the **t** above,	Col 3:1	
Set your mind on the **t** above,	Col 3:2	
not on the **t** that are on earth.	Col 3:2	
For it is because of these **t**	Col 3:6	*3739*
Beyond all these **t** *put on* love,	Col 3:14	*3778*
obedient to your parents in all **t**,	Col 3:20	*3956*
in all **t** obey those who are your	Col 3:22	*3956*
is *the* avenger in all these **t**,	1Th 4:6	*3778*
you, I was telling you these **t**?	2Th 2:5	*3778*
some men, straying from these **t**,	1Tm 1:6	*3739*
but temperate, faithful in all **t**.	1Tm 3:11	*3956*
I am writing these **t** to you,	1Tm 3:14	*3778*
out these **t** to the brethren,	1Tm 4:6	*3778*
godliness is profitable for all **t**,	1Tm 4:8	*3956*
Prescribe and teach these **t**.	1Tm 4:11	*3778*
Take pains with these **t**;	1Tm 4:15	*3778*
persevere in these **t**,	1Tm 4:16	*846*
Prescribe these **t** as well, so that	1Tm 5:7	*3778*
talking about **t** not proper *to mention*	1Tm 5:13	*1189b*
But flee from these **t**,	1Tm 6:11	*3778*
of God, who gives life to all **t**,	1Tm 6:13	*3956*
supplies us with all **t** to enjoy.	1Tm 6:17	*3956*
this reason I also suffer these **t**,	2Tm 1:12	*3778*
The **t** which you have heard	2Tm 2:2	
For this reason I endure all **t** for	2Tm 2:10	*3956*
Remind *them* of these **t**,	2Tm 2:14	*3778*
cleanses himself from these **t**,	2Tm 2:21	
continue in the **t** you have learned	2Tm 3:14	*3739*
But you, be sober in all **t**,	2Tm 4:5	*3956*
teaching **t** they should not *teach* for	Ti 1:11	*3739*
To the pure, all **t** are pure;	Ti 1:15	*3956*
speak the **t** which are fitting for	Ti 2:1	
in all **t** show yourself to be an	Ti 2:7	*3956*
These **t** speak and exhort and	Ti 2:15	*3778*
and concerning these **t** I want you	Ti 3:8	*3778*
These **t** are good and profitable	Ti 3:8	*3778*
whom He appointed heir of all **t**,	Heb 1:2	*3956*
upholds all **t** by the word of His	Heb 1:3	*3956*
YOU HAVE PUT ALL **T** IN SUBJECTION	Heb 2:8	*3956*
For in subjecting all **t** to him,	Heb 2:8	*3956*
do not yet see all **t** subjected to him.	Heb 2:8	*3956*
for Him, for whom are all **t**,	Heb 2:10	*3956*
and through whom are all **t**,	Heb 2:10	*3956*
made like His brethren in all **t**,	Heb 2:17	*3956*
priest in **t** pertaining to God,	Heb 2:17	
but the builder of all **t** is God.	Heb 3:4	*3956*
t which were to be spoken later;	Heb 3:5	
but all **t** are open and laid bare	Heb 4:13	*3956*
been tempted in all **t** as *we are,*	Heb 4:15	*3956*
of men in **t** pertaining to God,	Heb 5:1	
from the **t** which He suffered.	Heb 5:8	
we are convinced of better **t**	Heb 6:9	*2909*
and **t** that accompany salvation,	Heb 6:9	
so that by two unchangeable **t**	Heb 6:18	*4229*
concerning whom these **t** are spoken	Heb 7:13	*3778*
copy and shadow of the heavenly **t**,	Heb 8:5	*2032*
"THAT YOU MAKE all **T** ACCORDING TO	Heb 8:5	*3956*
t we cannot now speak in detail.	Heb 9:5	*3739*
these **t** have been so prepared,	Heb 9:6	*3778*
high priest of the good **t** to come,	Heb 9:11	*18*
all **t** are cleansed with blood,	Heb 9:22	*3956*
copies of the **t** in the heavens to be	Heb 9:23	
but the heavenly **t** themselves with	Heb 9:23	*2032*
only a shadow of the good **t** to come	Heb 10:1	*18*
come *and* not the very form of **t**,	Heb 10:1	*4229*
there is forgiveness of these **t**,	Heb 10:18	*3778*
Now faith is the assurance of **t**	Heb 11:1	
for, the conviction of **t** not seen.	Heb 11:1	*4229*
made out of **t** which are visible.	Heb 11:3	
by God about **t** not yet seen,	Heb 11:7	
For those who say such **t** make it	Heb 11:14	*5108*
Esau, even regarding **t** to come.	Heb 11:20	*3195*
of those **t** which can be shaken,	Heb 12:27	
can be shaken, as of created **t**,	Heb 12:27	*4160*
so that those **t** which cannot	Heb 12:27	
ourselves honorably in all **t**.	Heb 13:18	*3956*
and *yet* it boasts of great **t**.	Jas 3:5	*3173*
these **t** ought not to be this way.	Jas 3:10	*3778*
in these **t** which now have been	1Pe 1:12	*846*
t into which angels long to look.	1Pe 1:12	
were not redeemed with perishable **t**	1Pe 1:18	*5349*
The end of all **t** is near;	1Pe 4:7	*3956*
so that in all **t** God may be	1Pe 4:11	*3956*
as long as you practice these **t**,	2Pe 1:10	*3778*
be ready to remind you of these **t**,	2Pe 1:12	*3778*
be able to call these **t** to mind.	2Pe 1:15	*3778*
Since all these **t** are to be	2Pe 3:11	*3778*
since you look for these **t**,	2Pe 3:14	*3778*
speaking in them of these **t**,	2Pe 3:16	*3778*
are some **t** hard to understand,	2Pe 3:16	*5100*
These **t** we write, so that our	1Jn 1:4	*3778*
I am writing these **t** to you	1Jn 2:1	*3778*
the world nor the **t** in the world.	1Jn 2:15	
These **t** I have written to you	1Jn 2:26	*3778*
anointing teaches you about all **t**,	1Jn 2:27	*3956*
than our heart and knows all **t**.	1Jn 3:20	*3956*
do the **t** that are pleasing in His sight	1Jn 3:22	
These **t** I have written to you who	1Jn 5:13	*3778*
have many **t** to write to you, I	2Jn 1:12	*4183*
I had many **t** to write to you, but	3Jn 1:13	*4183*
you know all **t** once for all,	Jude 1:5	*3956*
t which they do not understand;	Jude 1:10	
the **t** which they know by instinct,	Jude 1:10	
by these **t** they are destroyed.	Jude 1:10	*3778*
and of all the harsh **t** which	Jude 1:15	*4642*
t which must soon take place;	Rv 1:1	
the **t** which are written in it;	Rv 1:3	
the **t** which you have seen,	Rv 1:19	
have seen, and the **t** which are,	Rv 1:19	
and the **t** which will take place	Rv 1:19	
will take place after these **t**.	Rv 1:19	*3778*
'But I have a few **t** against you,	Rv 2:14	*3641*
to eat **t** sacrificed to idols and	Rv 2:14	*1494*
and eat **t** sacrificed to idols.	Rv 2:20	*1494*
not known the deep **t** of Satan,	Rv 2:24	*901*
and strengthen the **t** that remain,	Rv 3:2	*3062*
After these **t** I looked, and	Rv 4:1	*3778*
must take place after these **t**."	Rv 4:1	*3778*
for You created all **t**,	Rv 4:11	*3956*
and on the sea, and all **t** in them,	Rv 5:13	*3956*
After these **t** I looked, and	Rv 7:9	*3778*
are still coming after these **t**.	Rv 9:12	*3778*
"Seal up the **t** which the seven	Rv 10:4	

CREATED HEAVEN AND THE **T** IN IT,	Rv 10:6	
IT, AND THE EARTH AND THE **T** IN IT,	Rv 10:6	
IT, AND THE SEA AND THE **T** IN IT,	Rv 10:6	
After these **t** I looked, and the	Rv 15:5	*3778*
because You judged these **t**;	Rv 16:5	*3778*
the unclean **t** of her immorality,	Rv 17:4	*169*
After these **t** I saw another angel	Rv 18:1	*3778*
and all **t** that were luxurious and	Rv 18:14	
"The merchants of these **t**,	Rv 18:15	*3778*
After these **t** I heard something like	Rv 19:1	*3778*
after these **t** he must be released	Rv 20:3	*3778*
judged from the **t** which were written	Rv 20:12	
the first **t** have passed away."	Rv 21:4	*4413*
"Behold, I am making all **t** new."	Rv 21:5	*3956*
overcomes will inherit these **t**,	Rv 21:7	*3778*
t which must soon take place.	Rv 22:6	
the one who heard and saw these **t**.	Rv 22:8	*3778*
the angel who showed me these **t**.	Rv 22:8	*3778*
to you these **t** for the churches.	Rv 22:16	*3778*
He who testifies to these **t** says,	Rv 22:20	*3778*

THINK

"Do you **t** that David is honoring	2Sa 10:3	5869
"I **t** the running of the first one	2Sa 18:27	7200
"Do you **t** that David is honoring	1Ch 19:3	5869
and afraid to tell you what I **t**.	Jb 32:6	1843
to me, I too will tell what I **t**.'	Jb 32:10	1843
t this is according to justice?	Jb 35:2	2803
would **t** the deep to be gray-haired.	Jb 41:32	2803
of man, that You **t** of him?	Ps 144:3	2803
then I will **t** better of the good	Jer 18:10	5162
"So you **t**, house of Israel, for I	Ezk 11:5	559
"Do not **t** that I came to abolish	Mt 5:17	*3543*
"Do not **t** that I came to bring	Mt 10:34	*3543*
"What do you **t**, Simon?	Mt 17:25	*1380*
"What do you **t**? If any man has a	Mt 18:12	*1380*
"But what do you **t**?	Mt 21:28	*1380*
"Tell us then, what do You **t**?	Mt 22:17	*1380*
"What do you **t** about the Christ,	Mt 22:42	*1380*
an hour when you do not **t** *He will.*	Mt 24:44	*1380*
"Or do you **t** that I cannot appeal	Mt 26:53	*1380*
what do you **t**?" They answered,	Mt 26:66	*1380*
"Which of these three do you **t**	Lk 10:36	*1380*
because you **t** that in them you	Jn 5:39	*1380*
"Do not **t** that I will accuse you	Jn 5:45	*1380*
What do you **t**; that He will not come	Jn 11:56	*1380*
who kills you to **t** that he is offering	Jn 16:2	*1380*
we ought not to **t** that the Divine	Ac 17:29	*3543*
Or do you **t** lightly of the riches	Ro 2:4	*2706*
not to **t** more highly of himself than	Ro 12:3	*5252*
of himself than he ought to **t**;	Ro 12:3	*5426*
to **t** so as to have sound judgment,	Ro 12:3	*5426*
For, I **t**, God has exhibited us	1Co 4:9	*1380*
I **t** then that this is good in view	1Co 7:26	*3543*
and I **t** that I also have the	1Co 7:40	*1380*
to speak like a child, **t** like a child,	1Co 13:11	*5426*
I say, let no one **t** me foolish;	2Co 11:16	*1380*
beyond all that we ask or **t**,	Eph 3:20	*3539*
that you always **t** kindly of us,	1Th 3:6	*2192, 3417*
punishment do you **t** he will deserve	Heb 10:29	*1380*
Or do you **t** that the Scripture	Jas 4:5	*1380*

THINKING

t, "the men of the place might	Gn 26:7	
t, "David cannot enter here."	2Sa 5:6	559
were *trying* to frighten us, **t**,	Ne 6:9	559
"Why are you **t** evil in your hearts?	Mt 9:4	*1760*
But He knew what they were **t**,	Lk 6:8	*1261*
what they were **t** in their heart,	Lk 9:47	*1261*
do not be children in your **t**;	1Co 14:20	*5424*
be infants, but in your **t** be mature.	1Co 14:20	*5424*
All this time you have been **t** that	2Co 12:19	*1380*
t to cause me distress in my	Php 1:17	*3633*
And indeed if they had been **t** of	Heb 11:15	*3421*

THINKS

For as he **t** within himself, so he	Pr 23:7	8176
even what he **t** he has shall be	Lk 8:18	*1380*
him who **t** anything to be unclean,	Ro 14:14	*3049*
If any man among you **t** that he is	1Co 3:18	*1380*
But if any man **t** that he is acting	1Co 7:36	*3543*
Therefore let him who **t** he stands	1Co 10:12	*1380*
anyone **t** he is a prophet or spiritual,	1Co 14:37	*1380*
For if anyone **t** he is something	Ga 6:3	*1380*
anyone **t** himself to be religious,	Jas 1:26	*1380*

THIRD

and there was morning, a **t** day.	Gn 1:13	7992
The name of the **t** river is Tigris;	Gn 2:14	7992
with lower, second, and **t** decks.	Gn 6:16	7992
On the **t** day Abraham raised his	Gn 22:4	7992
on the **t** day that Jacob had fled,	Gn 31:22	7992
also the second and the **t**,	Gn 32:19	7992
Now it came about on the **t** day,	Gn 34:25	7992
Thus it came about on the **t** day,	Gn 40:20	7992
Joseph said to them on the **t** day,	Gn 42:18	7992
the **t** generation of Ephraim's sons;	Gn 50:23	8029
In the **t** month after the sons of	Ex 19:1	7992
let them be ready for the **t** day,	Ex 19:11	7992
for on the **t** day the LORD will	Ex 19:11	7992
"Be ready for the **t** day;	Ex 19:15	7969
So it came about on the **t** day,	Ex 19:16	7992
on the **t** and the fourth generations	Ex 20:5	8029
and a bulb under the **t** pair of	Ex 25:35	
and the **t** row a jacinth, an agate	Ex 28:19	7992
to the **t** and fourth generations."	Ex 34:7	8029
and a bulb under the **t** pair of	Ex 37:21	
and the **t** row, a jacinth, an	Ex 39:12	7992
t day shall be burned with fire.	Lv 7:17	7992
should *ever* be eaten on the **t** day,	Lv 7:18	7992
t day shall be burned with fire.	Lv 19:6	7992
it is eaten at all on the **t** day,	Lv 19:7	7992
And they shall set out **t**.	Nu 2:24	7992
On the **t** day *it was* Eliab the son	Nu 7:24	7992
the **t** and the fourth *generations*.'	Nu 14:18	8029
the **t** day and on the seventh day,	Nu 19:12	7992
the **t** day and on the seventh day,	Nu 19:12	7992
the **t** day and on the seventh day;	Nu 19:19	7992
a bull and a **t** of a hin for the ram	Nu 28:14	7992
'Then on the **t** day:	Nu 29:20	7992
the **t** day and on the seventh day.	Nu 31:19	7992
on the **t** and the fourth *generations*	Dt 5:9	8029
"At the end of every **t** year you	Dt 14:28	7969
"The sons of the **t** generation who	Dt 23:8	7992
of your increase in the **t** year,	Dt 26:12	7992
came to their cities on the **t** day.	Jos 9:17	7992
and its towns, the **t** is Napheth.	Jos 17:11	7969
Now the **t** lot came up for the sons	Jos 19:10	7992
the sons of Benjamin on the **t** day	Jg 20:30	7992
Samuel again for the **t** time.	1Sa 3:8	7992
him Abinadab, and the **t** Shammah.	1Sa 17:13	7992
sent messengers again the **t** time,	1Sa 19:21	7992
in the field until the **t** evening.	1Sa 20:5	7992
this time tomorrow, *or* the **t** day,	1Sa 20:12	7992
men came to Ziklag on the **t** day,	1Sa 30:1	7992
On the **t** day,	2Sa 1:2	7992
and the **t**, Absalom the son of	2Sa 3:3	7992
one **t** under the command of Joab,	2Sa 18:2	7992
one **t** under the command of Abishai	2Sa 18:2	7992
and one **t** under the command of	2Sa 18:2	7992
on the **t** day after I gave birth,	1Ki 3:18	7992
and the **t** *was* seven cubits wide;	1Ki 6:6	7992
and from the middle to the **t**.	1Ki 6:8	7992
people came to Rehoboam on the **t** day	1Ki 12:12	7992
"Return to me on the **t** day."	1Ki 12:12	7992
the **t** year of Asa king of Judah and	1Ki 15:28	7969
the **t** year of Asa king of Judah,	1Ki 15:33	7969
LORD came to Elijah in the **t** year,	1Ki 18:1	7992
"Do it a **t** time,"	1Ki 18:34	8027
time," and they did it a **t** time.	1Ki 18:34	8027
In the **t** year	1Ki 22:2	7992
he again sent the captain of a **t** fifty	2Ki 1:13	7992
the **t** captain of fifty went up,	2Ki 1:13	7992
one **t** of you, who come in on the	2Ki 11:5	7992
t also *shall be* at the gate Sur,	2Ki 11:6	7992
t at the gate behind the guards),	2Ki 11:6	7992
about in the **t** year of Hoshea,	2Ki 18:1	7969
the same, and in the **t** year sow,	2Ki 19:29	7992
On the **t** day you shall go up to	2Ki 20:5	7992
the house of the LORD the **t** day?"	2Ki 20:8	7992
Abinadab the second, Shimea the **t**,	1Ch 2:13	7992
t *was* Absalom the son of Maacah,	1Ch 3:2	7992
was Jehoiakim, the **t** Zedekiah,	1Ch 3:15	7992
Ashbel the second, Aharah the **t**,	1Ch 8:1	7992
the second and Eliphelet the **t**.	1Ch 8:39	7992
Obadiah the second, Eliab the **t**,	1Ch 12:9	7992
Jahaziel the **t** and Jekameam the	1Ch 23:19	7992
the **t** for Harim, the fourth for	1Ch 24:8	7992
the second, Jahaziel the **t**,	1Ch 24:23	7992
the **t** to Zaccur, his sons and his	1Ch 25:10	7992
the second, Zebadiah the **t**,	1Ch 26:2	7992
Jehozabad the second, Joah the **t**,	1Ch 26:4	7992
the second, Tebaliah the **t**,	1Ch 26:11	7992
The **t** commander of the army for	1Ch 27:5	7992
army for the **t** month *was* Benaiah,	1Ch 27:5	7992
came to Rehoboam on the **t** day	2Ch 10:12	7992
"Return to me on the **t** day."	2Ch 10:12	7992
t month of the fifteenth year of Asa's	2Ch 15:10	7992
Then in the **t** year of his reign he	2Ch 17:7	7969
one **t** of you, of the priests and	2Ch 23:4	7992
one **t** *shall be* at the king's house,	2Ch 23:5	7992
a **t** at the Gate of the Foundation;	2Ch 23:5	7992
in the second and in the **t** year.	2Ch 27:5	7992
In the **t** month they began to make	2Ch 31:7	7992
on the **t** day of the month Adar;	Ezr 6:15	8532
to contribute yearly one **t** of a shekel	Ne 10:32	7992
in the **t** year of his reign he	Es 1:3	7969
Now it came about on the **t** day	Es 5:1	7992
at that time in the **t** month	Es 8:9	7992
Keziah, and the **t** Keren-happuch.	Jb 42:14	7992
t *party* with Egypt and Assyria,	Is 19:24	7992
the same, and in the **t** year sow,	Is 37:30	7992
brought to him at the **t** entrance that	Jer 38:14	7992
"One **t** you shall burn in the fire	Ezk 5:2	7992
Then you shall take one **t** and	Ezk 5:2	7992
one **t** you shall scatter to the wind;	Ezk 5:2	7992
'One **t** of you will die by plague	Ezk 5:12	7992
one **t** will fall by the sword	Ezk 5:12	7992
one **t** I will scatter to every wind,	Ezk 5:12	7992
a man, the **t** the face of a lion,	Ezk 10:14	7992
the sword be doubled the **t** time,	Ezk 21:14	7992
the eleventh year, in the **t** *month*,	Ezk 31:1	7992
and a **t** of a hin of oil to moisten	Ezk 46:14	7992
In the **t** year of the reign of	Da 1:1	7969
then another **t** kingdom of bronze,	Da 2:39	8523
as **t** *ruler* in the kingdom."	Da 5:7	8533a
as the **t** *ruler* in the kingdom."	Da 5:16	8531
as the **t** *ruler* in the kingdom.	Da 5:29	8531
the **t** year of the reign of Belshazzar	Da 8:1	7969
In the **t** year of Cyrus king of	Da 10:1	7969
He will raise us up on the **t** day	Hos 6:2	7992
with the **t** chariot white horses,	Zch 6:3	7992
But the **t** will be left in it.	Zch 13:8	7992
bring the **t** part through the fire,	Zch 13:9	7992
and be raised up on the **t** day.	Mt 16:21	*5154*
He will be raised on the **t** day."	Mt 17:23	*5154*
"And he went out about the **t** hour	Mt 20:3	*5154*
the **t** day He will be raised up."	Mt 20:19	*5154*
killed another, and stoned a **t**.	Mt 21:35	*3739*
so also the second, and the **t**,	Mt 22:26	*5154*
and went away and prayed a **t** time,	Mt 26:44	*5154*
to be made secure until the **t** day,	Mt 27:64	*5154*
and the **t** likewise;	Mk 12:21	*5154*
And He came the **t** time, and said	Mk 14:41	*5154*
t hour when they crucified Him.	Mk 15:25	*5154*
and be raised up on the **t** day."	Lk 9:22	*5154*
second watch, or even in the **t**,	Lk 12:38	*5154*
and the **t** *day* I reach My goal.'	Lk 13:32	*5154*
the **t** day He will rise again."	Lk 18:33	*5154*
"And he proceeded to send a **t**;	Lk 20:12	*5154*
and the **t** married her;	Lk 20:31	*5154*
And he said to them the **t** time,	Lk 23:22	*5154*
and the **t** day rise again."	Lk 24:7	*5154*
it is the **t** day since these things	Lk 24:21	*5154*
again from the dead the **t** day,	Lk 24:46	*5154*
On the **t** day there was a	Jn 2:1	*5154*
This is now the **t** time that Jesus	Jn 21:14	*5154*
He said to him the **t** time,	Jn 21:17	*5154*
because He said to him the **t** time,	Jn 21:17	*5154*
it is *only* the **t** hour of the day;	Ac 2:15	*5154*
"God raised Him up on the **t** day and	Ac 10:40	*5154*
and fell down from the **t** floor and	Ac 20:9	*5152*
ready by the **t** hour of the night	Ac 23:23	*5154*
and on the **t** day they threw the	Ac 27:19	*5154*
second prophets, **t** teachers,	1Co 12:28	*5154*
and that He was raised on the **t** day	1Co 15:4	*5154*
man was caught up to the **t** heaven.	2Co 12:2	*5154*
Here for this **t** time I am ready to	2Co 12:14	*5154*
is the **t** time I am coming to you.	2Co 13:1	*5154*
and the **t** creature had a face like	Rv 4:7	*5154*
When He broke the **t** seal,	Rv 6:5	*5154*
the **t** living creature saying,	Rv 6:5	*5154*
a **t** of the earth was burned up,	Rv 8:7	*5154*
a **t** of the trees were burned up,	Rv 8:7	*5154*
and a **t** of the sea became blood,	Rv 8:8	*5154*
and a **t** of the creatures which	Rv 8:9	*5154*
a **t** of the ships were destroyed.	Rv 8:9	*5154*
The **t** angel sounded, and a	Rv 8:10	*5154*
and it fell on a **t** of the rivers	Rv 8:10	*5154*
a **t** of the waters became wormwood,	Rv 8:11	*5154*
and a **t** of the sun and a third of	Rv 8:12	*5154*
third of the sun and a **t** of the moon	Rv 8:12	*5154*
and a **t** of the stars were struck,	Rv 8:12	*5154*
so that a **t** of them would be	Rv 8:12	*5154*
day would not shine for a **t** of it,	Rv 8:12	*5154*
they would kill a **t** of mankind.	Rv 9:15	*5154*
A **t** of mankind was killed by these	Rv 9:18	*5154*
the **t** woe is coming quickly.	Rv 11:14	*5154*
away a **t** of the stars of heaven and	Rv 12:4	*5154*
Then another angel, a **t** one,	Rv 14:9	*5154*
Then the **t** *angel* poured out his	Rv 16:4	*5154*
the **t**, chalcedony;	Rv 21:19	*5154*

THIRST

and our livestock with **t**?"	Ex 17:3	6772
send against you, in hunger, in **t**,	Dt 28:48	6772
and now shall I die of **t** and fall	Jg 15:18	6772
over to die by hunger and by **t**,	2Ch 32:11	6772
from a rock for them for their **t**,	Ne 9:15	6772
gave them water for their **t**.	Ne 9:20	6772
They tread wine presses but **t**.	Jb 24:11	6770
And for my **t** they gave me vinegar	Ps 69:21	6772
The wild donkeys quench their **t**.	Ps 104:11	6772
their multitude is parched with **t**.	Is 5:13	6772
faint And his **t** is not quenched.	Is 29:8	5315
their tongue is parched with **t**;	Is 41:17	6772
They did not **t** when He led	Is 48:21	6770
"They will not hunger or **t**,	Is 49:10	6770
for lack of water And die of **t**.	Is 50:2	6772
unshod And your throat from **t**;	Jer 2:25	6773
roof of its mouth because of **t**;	La 4:4	6772
desert land And slay her with **t**.	Hos 2:3	6772
famine for bread or a **t** for water,	Am 8:11	6772
the young men will faint from **t**.	Am 8:13	6772
hunger and **t** for righteousness,	Mt 5:6	*1372*
of this water will **t** again;	Jn 4:13	*1372*
I will give him shall never **t**;	Jn 4:14	*1372*
who believes in Me will never **t**.	Jn 6:35	*1372*
sleepless nights, in hunger and **t**,	2Co 11:27	*1373*
hunger no longer, nor **t** anymore;	Rv 7:16	*1372*

THIRSTED

But the people **t** there for water;	Ex 17:3	6770

THIRSTS

My soul **t** for God, for the living	Ps 42:2	6770
My soul **t** for You, my flesh	Ps 63:1	6770
Every one who **t**, come to the	Is 55:1	6771
I will give to the one who **t** from	Rv 21:6	*1372*

THIRSTY

t ground where there was no water;	Dt 8:15	6774
water to drink, for I am **t**."	Jg 4:19	6770
Then he became very **t**,	Jg 15:18	6770
When you are **t**, go to the water	Ru 2:9	6770
weary and **t** in the wilderness."	2Sa 17:29	6771
They were hungry and **t**;	Ps 107:5	6771
For He has satisfied the **t** soul,	Ps 107:9	8264
springs of water into a **t** ground;	Ps 107:33	6774
And if he is **t**, give him water to	Pr 25:21	6771
Bring water for the **t**,	Is 21:14	6771
Or as when a **t** man dreams	Is 29:8	6771
And to withhold drink from the **t**.	Is 32:6	6771
And the **t** ground springs of water;	Is 35:7	6774
I will pour out water on the **t** *land*	Is 44:3	6771
will drink, but you will be **t**.	Is 65:13	6770
wilderness, In a dry and **t** land.	Ezk 19:13	6772
I was **t**, and you gave Me	Mt 25:35	*1372*
or **t**, and give You *something* to drink?	Mt 25:37	*1372*
I was **t**, and you gave Me nothing	Mt 25:42	*1372*
when did we see You hungry, or **t**,	Mt 25:44	*1372*
me this water, so I will not be **t** nor	Jn 4:15	*1372*

and **t** is the gate of heaven." Gn 28:17 2088
keep me on **t** journey that I take, Gn 28:20 2088
"**T** stone, which I have set up as a Gn 28:22 2088
"What is **t** you have done to me? Gn 29:25 2088
"Complete the week of **t** one, Gn 29:27 2088
therefore given me **t** *son* also." Gn 29:33 2088
"Now **t** time my husband will Gn 29:34 6471
"**T** time I will praise the LORD." Gn 29:35 6471
If you will do **t** *one* thing for me, Gn 30:31 2088
father he has made all **t** wealth." Gn 31:1 2088
now arise, leave **t** land, Gn 31:13 2088
But what can I do **t** day to these Gn 31:43
"**T** heap is a witness between you Gn 31:48 2088
between you and me **t** day." Gn 31:48
"Behold **t** heap and behold the Gn 31:51 2088
"**T** heap is a witness, and the Gn 31:52 2088
pass by **t** heap to you for harm, Gn 31:52 2088
pass by **t** heap and this pillar to me, Gn 31:52 2088
by this heap and **t** pillar to me, Gn 31:52 2088
"**T** is God's camp." Gn 32:2 2088
my staff *only* I crossed **t** Jordan, Gn 32:10 2088
"After **t** manner you shall speak Gn 32:19 2088
to **t** day the sons of Israel do not Gn 32:32 2088
all **t** company which I have met?" Gn 33:8 2088
"Get me **t** young girl for a wife." Gn 34:4 2088
"We cannot do **t** thing, to give Gn 34:14 2088
"Only on **t** *condition* will we Gn 34:15 2088
"Only on **t** *condition* will the men Gn 34:22 2088
pillar of Rachel's grave to **t** day. Gn 35:20
to **t** dream which I have had; Gn 37:6
"What is **t** dream that you have had? Gn 37:10 2088
"Here comes **t** dreamer! Gn 37:19 1976
But Reuben heard **t** and rescued Gn 37:21
t pit that is in the wilderness, Gn 37:22 2088
to their father and said, "We found **t**; Gn 37:32 2088
After all, I sent **t** young goat, Gn 38:23 2088
"**T** one came out first." Gn 38:28 2088
no one greater in **t** house than I, Gn 39:9 2088
How then could I do **t** great evil and Gn 39:9 2088
"**T** is what your slave did to me," Gn 39:19
1697, 428
"**T** is the interpretation of it: Gn 40:12 2088
and get me out of **t** house. Gn 40:14 2088
"**T** is its interpretation: Gn 40:18 2088
"Can we find a man like **t**, Gn 41:38 2088
God has informed you of all **t**, Gn 41:39 2088
by **t** you will be tested: Gn 42:15 2088
you shall not go from **t** place Gn 42:15 2088
"Do **t** and live, for I fear God: Gn 42:18 2088
t distress has come upon us." Gn 42:21 2088
is **t** that God has done to us?" Gn 42:28 2088
'By **t** I will know that you are Gn 42:33 2088
"If *it must be* so, then do **t**: Gn 43:11 2088
So the men took **t** present, and Gn 43:15 2088
"Is **t** your youngest brother, of Gn 43:29 2088
'Is not **t** the one from which my Gn 44:5 2088
have done wrong in doing **t**.' " Gn 44:5 834
"What is **t** deed that you have done? Gn 44:15 2088
"Far be it from me to do **t**. Gn 44:17 2088
If you take **t** one also from me, Gn 44:29 2088
Do **t**: load your beasts and go to the Gn 45:17 2088
'Do **t**: take wagons from the land of Gn 45:19 2088
the land of Egypt *valid* to **t** day, Gn 47:26 2088
and will give **t** land to your Gn 48:4 2088
my shepherd all my life to **t** day, Gn 48:15 2088
for **t** one is the firstborn. Gn 48:18 2088
and **t** is what their father said to Gn 49:28 2088
"**T** is a grievous mourning for the Gn 50:11 2088
to bring about **t** present result, Gn 50:20 2088
and bring you up from **t** land to Gn 50:24 2088
"Why have you done **t** thing, Ex 1:18 2088
"**T** is one of the Hebrews' Ex 2:6 2088
"Take **t** child away and nurse him Ex 2:9 2088
So he looked **t** way and that, and Ex 2:12 3541
When Pharaoh heard of **t** matter, Ex 2:15 2088
now and see **t** marvelous sight, Ex 3:3 2088
and **t** shall be the sign to you Ex 3:12 2088
shall worship God at **t** mountain." Ex 3:12 2088
T is My name forever, Ex 3:15 2088
and **t** is My memorial-name to all Ex 3:15 2088
"I will grant **t** people favor Ex 3:21 2088
shall take in your hand **t** staff, Ex 4:17 2088
you deal **t** way with your servants? Ex 5:15 3541
You brought harm to **t** people? Ex 5:22 2088
he has done harm to **t** people, Ex 5:23 2088
"By **t** you shall know that I am Ex 7:17 2088
house with no concern even for **t**. Ex 7:23 2088
"**T** is the finger of God." Ex 8:19 1931
Tomorrow **t** sign will occur. Ex 8:23 2088
hardened his heart **t** time also, Ex 8:32 2088
will do **t** thing in the land." Ex 9:5 2088
LORD did **t** thing on the next Ex 9:6 2088
"For **t** time I will send all My Ex 9:14 2088
for **t** reason I have allowed you to Ex 9:16 2088
"Behold, about **t** time tomorrow, I Ex 9:18 2088
"I have sinned **t** time; Ex 9:27 6471
upon the earth until **t** day.' " Ex 10:6 2088
long will **t** man be a snare to us? Ex 10:7 2088
please forgive my sin only **t** once, Ex 10:17 6471
only remove **t** death from me." Ex 10:17 2088
"**T** month shall be the beginning Ex 12:2 2088
'On the tenth of **t** month they are Ex 12:3 2088
'Now you shall eat it in **t** manner: Ex 12:11 3602
t day will be a memorial to you, Ex 12:14 2088
for on **t** very day I brought your Ex 12:17 2088
therefore you shall observe **t** day Ex 12:17 2088
"And you shall observe **t** event as Ex 12:24 2088
you shall observe **t** rite. Ex 12:25 2088
'What does **t** rite mean to you?' Ex 12:26 2088

t night is for the LORD, to be Ex 12:42 2088
"**T** is the ordinance of the Ex 12:43 2088
of Israel are to celebrate **t**. Ex 12:47 2088
"Remember **t** day in which you went Ex 13:3 2088
LORD brought you out from **t** place. Ex 13:3 2088
"On **t** day in the month of Abib, Ex 13:4
observe **t** rite in this month. Ex 13:5 2088
observe this rite in **t** month. Ex 13:5 2088
you shall keep **t** ordinance at its Ex 13:10 2088
in time to come, saying, 'What is **t**?' Ex 13:14 2088
"What is **t** we have done, that we Ex 14:5 2088
have you dealt with us in **t** way, Ex 14:11 2088
"Is **t** not the word that we spoke Ex 14:12 2088
of Israel sang **t** song to the LORD, Ex 15:1 2088
T is my God, and I will praise Him; Ex 15:2 2088
have brought us out into **t** wilderness Ex 16:3 2088
kill **t** whole assembly with hunger." Ex 16:3 2088
Moses said, "**T** *will happen* when Ex 16:8
"**T** is what the LORD has Ex 16:16 2088
"**T** is what the LORD meant: Ex 16:23 1931
"**T** is what the LORD has Ex 16:32 2088
"What shall I do to **t** people? Ex 17:4 2088
"Write **t** in a book as a memorial and Ex 17:14 2088
"What is **t** thing that you are Ex 18:14 2088
"If you do **t** thing and God *so* Ex 18:23 2088
'**T** is it,' the case of both Ex 22:9 2088
"**T** is the contribution which you are Ex 25:3 2088
"Now **t** is what you shall do to Ex 29:1 2088
"Now **t** is what you shall offer on Ex 29:38 2088
"You shall put **t** altar in Ex 30:6
any strange incense on **t** altar, Ex 30:9
"**T** is what everyone who is Ex 30:13 2088
'**T** shall be a holy anointing oil Ex 30:31 2088
for **t** is a sign between Me Ex 31:13 2088
as for **t** Moses, the man who Ex 32:1 2088
He took **t** from their hand, Ex 32:4
"**T** is your god, O Israel, who Ex 32:4 428
Now when Aaron saw **t**, he built Ex 32:5
'**T** is your god, O Israel, who Ex 32:8 428
"I have seen **t** people, and Ex 32:9 2088
and all **t** land of which I have Ex 32:13 2088
"What did **t** people do to you, Ex 32:21 2088
for **t** Moses, the man who brought Ex 32:23 2088
the fire, and out came **t** calf." Ex 32:24 2088
t people has committed a great Ex 32:31 2088
When the people heard **t** sad word, Ex 33:4 2088
'Bring up **t** people!' Ex 33:12 2088
that **t** nation is Your people." Ex 33:13 2088
"I will also do **t** thing of which Ex 33:17 2088
what I am commanding you **t** day: Ex 34:11
"**T** is the thing which the LORD Ex 35:4 2088
T is the number of the things for Ex 38:21 428
had commanded, **t** they had done. Ex 39:43 3651
'**T** is the law for the burnt Lv 6:9 2088
'Now **t** is the law of the grain Lv 6:14 2088
"**T** is the offering which Aaron Lv 6:20 2088
'**T** is the law of the sin offering: Lv 6:25 2088
'Now **t** is the law of the guilt Lv 7:1 2088
'Now **t** is the law of the sacrifice Lv 7:11 2088
'Of **t** he shall present one of Lv 7:14
"**T** is that which is consecrated to Lv 7:35 2088
T is the law of the burnt Lv 7:37 2088
"**T** is the thing which the LORD Lv 8:5 2088
to do as has been done **t** day, Lv 8:34 2088
"**T** is the thing which the LORD Lv 9:6 2088
t very day they presented their Lv 10:19
T is the law regarding the animal and Lv 11:46 2088
T is the law for her who bears *a* Lv 12:7 2088
T is the law for the mark of Lv 13:59 2088
"**T** shall be the law of the leper Lv 14:2 2088
"**T** is the law *for him* in whom Lv 14:32 2088
T is the law for any mark of Lv 14:54 2088
T is the law of leprosy. Lv 14:57 2088
'**T**, moreover, shall be his Lv 15:3 2088
T is the law for the one with a Lv 15:32 2088
shall enter the holy place with **t**: Lv 16:3 2088
"**T** shall be a permanent statute Lv 16:29 2088
for it is on **t** day that atonement Lv 16:30 2088
have **t** as a permanent statute, Lv 16:34 2088
'**T** is what the LORD has commanded, Lv 17:2 2088
T shall be a permanent statute to Lv 17:7 2088
'Until **t** same day, until you have Lv 23:14 2088
'On **t** same day you shall make a Lv 23:21 2088
the tenth day of **t** seventh month Lv 23:27 2088
not do any work on **t** same day, Lv 23:28 2088
not humble himself on **t** same day, Lv 23:29 2088
who does any work on **t** same day, Lv 23:30 2088
'On the fifteenth of **t** seventh month Lv 23:34 2088
'On **t** year of jubilee each of you Lv 25:13 2088
house sale in the city of **t** possession Lv 25:33 2088
I, in turn, will do **t** to you: Lv 26:16 2088
'Yet if in spite of **t** you Lv 26:27 2088
'Yet in spite of **t**, when they are Lv 26:44 2088
"**T** is the work of the descendants Nu 4:4 2088
"But do **t** to them that they may Nu 4:19 2088
"**T** is the service of the families Nu 4:24 2088
"**T** is the service of the families Nu 4:28 2088
"Now **t** is the duty of their Nu 4:31 2088
"**T** is the service of the families Nu 4:33 2088
be immune to **t** water of bitterness Nu 5:19 428
and **t** water that brings a curse Nu 5:22 428
'**T** is the law of jealousy: Nu 5:29 2088
shall apply all **t** law to her. Nu 5:30 2088
'Now **t** is the law of the Nazirite Nu 6:13 2088
"**T** is the law of the Nazirite who Nu 6:21 2088
T *was* the offering of Nahshon the Nu 7:17 2088
T *was* the offering of Nethanel the Nu 7:23 2088
T *was* the offering of Eliab the Nu 7:29 2088
T *was* the offering of Elizur the Nu 7:35 2088

T *was* the offering of Shelumiel Nu 7:41 2088
T *was* the offering of Eliasaph the Nu 7:47 2088
T *was* the offering of Elishama the Nu 7:53 2088
T *was* the offering of Gamaliel the Nu 7:59 2088
T *was* the offering of Abidan the Nu 7:65 2088
T *was* the offering of Ahiezer the Nu 7:71 2088
T *was* the offering of Pagiel the Nu 7:77 2088
T *was* the offering of Ahira the Nu 7:83 2088
T *was* the dedication *offering* for Nu 7:84 2088
T *was* the dedication *offering* for Nu 7:88 2088
Now **t** was the workmanship of the Nu 8:4 2088
"**T** is what *applies* to the Levites: Nu 8:24 2088
"On the fourteenth day of **t** month, Nu 9:3 2088
and **t** shall be for you a perpetual Nu 10:8
T was the order of march of the Nu 10:28 428
all to look at except **t** manna." Nu 11:6
the burden of all **t** people on me? Nu 11:11 2088
it I who conceived all **t** people? Nu 11:12 2088
get meat to give to all **t** people? Nu 11:13 2088
am not able to carry all **t** people, Nu 11:14 2088
about a day's journey on **t** side Nu 11:31 3541
do not account **t** sin to us, in Nu 12:11
and honey, and **t** is its fruit. Nu 13:27 2088
that we had died in **t** wilderness! Nu 14:2 2088
the LORD bringing us into **t** land, Nu 14:3 2088
then He will bring us into **t** land and Nu 14:8 2088
"How long will **t** people spurn Me? Nu 14:11 2088
You brought up **t** people from Nu 14:13 2088
it to the inhabitants of **t** land. Nu 14:14 2088
are in the midst of **t** people, Nu 14:14 2088
You slay **t** people as one man, Nu 14:15 2088
LORD could not bring **t** people into Nu 14:16 2088
the iniquity of **t** people according Nu 14:19 2088
You also have forgiven **t** people, Nu 14:19 2088
shall I bear with **t** evil congregation Nu 14:27 2088
will fall in **t** wilderness, Nu 14:29 2088
will fall in **t** wilderness. Nu 14:32 2088
surely **t** I will do to all this Nu 14:35 2088
I will do to all **t** evil congregation Nu 14:35 2088
In **t** wilderness they shall be Nu 14:35 2088
shall do these things in **t** manner, Nu 15:13 3602
When Moses heard **t**, he fell on Nu 16:4
"Do **t**: take censers for yourselves, Nu 16:6 2088
from among **t** congregation, Nu 16:21 2088
"By **t** you shall know that the Nu 16:28 2088
for **t** is not my doing. Nu 16:28
away from among **t** congregation, Nu 16:45 2088
"**T** shall be yours from the most Nu 18:9 2088
"**T** also is yours, the offering of Nu 18:11 2088
"**T** is the statute of the law Nu 19:2 2088
'**T** is the law when a man dies in a Nu 19:14 2088
LORD's assembly into **t** wilderness, Nu 20:4 2088
bring us in to **t** wretched place? Nu 20:5 2088
water for you out of **t** rock?" Nu 20:10 2088
you shall not bring **t** assembly into Nu 20:12 2088
deliver **t** people into my hand, Nu 21:2 2088
and we loathe **t** miserable food." Nu 21:5
Then Israel sang **t** song: Nu 21:17 2088
"Now **t** horde will lick up all Nu 22:4
curse **t** people for me since they Nu 22:6 2088
then, curse **t** people for me.' " Nu 22:17 2088
with a wall on **t** side and a wall on Nu 22:24 2088
ridden all your life to **t** day? Nu 22:30 2088
what **t** people will do to your people Nu 24:14 2088
"Go up to **t** mountain of Abarim, Nu 27:12 2088
'**T** is the offering by fire which Nu 28:3 2088
'**T** *is* the burnt offering of Nu 28:10
t is the burnt offering of each Nu 28:14 2088
On the fifteenth day of **t** month *shall* Nu 28:17 2088
'After **t** manner you shall present Nu 28:24 428
on the tenth day of **t** seventh month Nu 29:7 2088
"**T** is the word which the LORD has Nu 30:1 2088
"**T** is the statute of the law Nu 31:21 2088
let **t** land be given to your Nu 32:5 2088
"**T** is what your fathers did when Nu 32:8 3541
fallen to us on **t** side of the Jordan Nu 32:19
"If you will do **t**, if you will Nu 32:20 2088
and **t** land shall be yours for a Nu 32:22 2088
t is the land that shall fall to Nu 34:2 2088
t shall be your west border. Nu 34:6 2088
'And **t** shall be your north border: Nu 34:7 2088
T shall be your north border. Nu 34:9 2088
T shall be your land according to Nu 34:12 2088
"**T** is the land that you are to Nu 34:13 2088
T shall become theirs as pasture Nu 35:5 2088
"**T** is what the LORD has commanded Nu 36:6 2088
Moses undertook to expound **t** law, Dt 1:5 2088
stayed long enough at **t** mountain. Dt 1:6 2088
you are **t** day like the stars of Dt 1:10
until you came to **t** place.' Dt 1:31 2088
"But for all **t**, you did not trust Dt 1:32 2088
of these men, **t** evil generation, Dt 1:35 2088
who **t** day have no knowledge of Dt 1:39
circled **t** mountain long enough. Dt 2:3 2088
through **t** great wilderness. Dt 2:7 2088
in their place even to **t** day. Dt 2:22 2088
'**T** day I will begin to put the Dt 2:25 2088
possession of **t** land at that time. Dt 3:12 2088
Havvoth-jair, *as it is* to **t** day.) Dt 3:14
given you **t** land to possess it; Dt 3:18 2088
Speak to Me no more of **t** matter. Dt 3:26 2088
you shall not cross over **t** Jordan. Dt 3:27 2088
go across at the head of **t** people, Dt 3:28 2088
'Surely **t** great nation is a wise Dt 4:6 2088
judgments as righteous as **t** whole law Dt 4:8 2088
"For I will die in **t** land, Dt 4:22 2088
take possession of **t** good land. Dt 4:22 2088
been done like **t** great thing, Dt 4:32 2088
Now **t** is the law which Moses set Dt 4:44 2088

make **t** covenant with our fathers,	**Dt 5:3**	2088
For **t** great fire will consume us;	**Dt 5:25**	2088
the voice of the words of **t** people	**Dt 5:28**	2088
"Now **t** is the commandment, the	**Dt 6:1**	2088
careful to observe all **t** commandment	**Dt 6:25**	2088
of my hand made me **t** wealth.'	**Dt 8:17**	2088
to your fathers, as *it is* **t** day.	**Dt 8:18**	2088
brought me in to possess **t** land,'	**Dt 9:4**	2088
giving you **t** good land to possess,	**Dt 9:6**	2088
until you arrived at **t** place,	**Dt 9:7**	2088
'I have seen **t** people, and indeed,	**Dt 9:13**	2088
look at the stubbornness of **t** people	**Dt 9:27**	2088
to bless in His name until **t** day.	**Dt 10:8**	2088
above all peoples, as *it is* **t** day.	**Dt 10:15**	2088
"Know **t** day that I *am* not	**Dt 11:2**	
until you came to **t** place;	**Dt 11:5**	2088
careful to keep all **t** commandment	**Dt 11:22**	2088
"You shall not act like **t** toward the	**Dt 12:4**	3651
t abomination has been done among	**Dt 13:14**	2088
"**T** is the manner of remission:	**Dt 15:2**	2088
all **t** commandment which I am	**Dt 15:5**	2088
because for **t** thing the LORD your	**Dt 15:10**	2088
therefore I command you **t** today.	**Dt 15:15**	2088
t detestable thing has been done	**Dt 17:4**	2088
woman who has done **t** evil deed to	**Dt 17:5**	2088
shall write for himself a copy of **t** law	**Dt 17:18**	2088
words of **t** law and these statutes,	**Dt 17:19**	2088
"Now **t** shall be the priests' due	**Dt 18:3**	2088
"**T** is according to all that you	**Dt 18:16**	
me not see **t** great fire anymore,	**Dt 18:16**	2088
"Now **t** is the case of the	**Dt 19:4**	2088
observe all **t** commandment which	**Dt 19:9**	2088
'Our hands did not shed **t** blood,	**Dt 21:7**	2088
'**T** son of ours is stubborn and	**Dt 21:20**	2088
'I took **t** woman, *but* when I came	**Dt 22:14**	2088
my daughter to **t** man for a wife,	**Dt 22:16**	2088
But **t** is the evidence of my	**Dt 22:17**	428
"But if **t** charge is true, that	**Dt 22:20**	2088
and murders him, so is **t** case.	**Dt 22:26**	2088
I am commanding you to do **t** thing.	**Dt 24:18**	2088
I am commanding you to do **t** thing.	**Dt 24:22**	2088
'I declare **t** day to the LORD my	**Dt 26:3**	
and He has brought us to **t** place and	**Dt 26:9**	2088
place and has given us **t** land,	**Dt 26:9**	2088
"**T** day the LORD your God commands	**Dt 26:16**	2088
on them all the words of **t** law,	**Dt 27:3**	2088
words of **t** law very distinctly."	**Dt 27:8**	2088
T day you have become a people for	**Dt 27:9**	2088
the words of **t** law by doing them.'	**Dt 27:26**	2088
to observe all the words of **t** law	**Dt 28:58**	2088
law which are written in **t** book,	**Dt 28:58**	2088
fear **t** honored and awesome name,	**Dt 28:58**	2088
not written in the book of **t** law,	**Dt 28:61**	2088
"Yet to **t** day the LORD has not	**Dt 29:4**	2088
"When you reached **t** place,	**Dt 29:7**	2088
words of **t** covenant to do them,	**Dt 29:9**	2088
I making **t** covenant and this oath,	**Dt 29:14**	2088
I making this covenant and **t** oath,	**Dt 29:14**	2088
he hears the words of **t** curse,	**Dt 29:19**	2088
curse which is written in **t** book	**Dt 29:20**	2088
are written in **t** book of the law.	**Dt 29:21**	2088
has the LORD done thus to **t** land?	**Dt 29:24**	2088
Why **t** great outburst of anger?'	**Dt 29:24**	2088
curse which is written in **t** book;	**Dt 29:27**	2088
another land, as *it is* **t** day.'	**Dt 29:28**	2088
observe all the words of **t** law.	**Dt 29:29**	2088
are written in **t** book of the law,	**Dt 30:10**	2088
"For **t** commandment which I	**Dt 30:11**	2088
for **t** is your life and the length	**Dt 30:20**	1931
'You shall not cross **t** Jordan.'	**Dt 31:2**	2088
for you shall go with **t** people	**Dt 31:7**	2088
So Moses wrote **t** law and gave it	**Dt 31:9**	2088
you shall read **t** law in front of	**Dt 31:11**	2088
to observe all the words of **t** law.	**Dt 31:12**	2088
and **t** people will arise and play	**Dt 31:16**	2088
write **t** song for yourselves,	**Dt 31:19**	2088
so that **t** song may be a	**Dt 31:19**	2088
that **t** song will testify before	**Dt 31:21**	2088
Moses wrote **t** song the same day,	**Dt 31:22**	2088
finished writing the words of **t** law	**Dt 31:24**	2088
"Take **t** book of the law and place	**Dt 31:26**	2088
of Israel the words of **t** song,	**Dt 31:30**	2088
"The LORD saw **t**,	**Dt 32:19**	
the LORD has not done all **t**."	**Dt 32:27**	2088
were wise, that they understood **t**,	**Dt 32:29**	2088
our enemies themselves judge **t**.	**Dt 32:31**	
and spoke all the words of **t** song	**Dt 32:44**	2088
even all the words of **t** law.	**Dt 32:46**	2088
And by **t** word you will prolong	**Dt 32:47**	2088
"Go up to **t** mountain of the	**Dt 32:49**	2088
Now **t** is the blessing with which	**Dt 33:1**	2088
And **t** regarding Judah;	**Dt 33:7**	2088
"**T** is the land which I swore to	**Dt 34:4**	2088
knows his burial place to **t** day.	**Dt 34:6**	2088
therefore arise, cross **t** Jordan,	**Jos 1:2**	2088
this Jordan, you and all **t** people,	**Jos 1:2**	2088
"From the wilderness and **t** Lebanon,	**Jos 1:4**	2088
for you shall give **t** people	**Jos 1:6**	2088
"**T** book of the law shall not	**Jos 1:8**	2088
days you are to cross **t** Jordan,	**Jos 1:11**	2088
rest and will give you **t** land.'	**Jos 1:13**	2088
do not tell **t** business of ours;	**Jos 2:14**	2088
"We *shall be* free from **t** oath to	**Jos 2:17**	2088
you tie **t** cord of scarlet thread	**Jos 2:18**	2088
if you tell **t** business of ours,	**Jos 2:20**	2088
have not passed **t** way before."	**Jos 3:4**	2088
"**T** day I will begin to exalt you	**Jos 3:7**	2088
"By **t** you shall know that the	**Jos 3:10**	2088
"Let **t** be a sign among you, so	**Jos 4:6**	2088

and they are there to **t** day.	**Jos 4:9**	2088
crossed **t** Jordan on dry ground.'	**Jos 4:22**	2088
T is the reason why Joshua	**Jos 5:4**	2088
place is called Gilgal to **t** day.	**Jos 5:9**	2088
in the midst of Israel to **t** day,	**Jos 6:25**	2088
up and builds **t** city Jericho;	**Jos 6:26**	2088
bring **t** people over the Jordan,	**Jos 7:7**	2088
of Israel, and **t** is what I did:	**Jos 7:20**	2088
The LORD will trouble you **t** day."	**Jos 7:25**	2088
of stones that stands to **t** day,	**Jos 7:26**	2088
the valley of Achor to **t** day.	**Jos 7:26**	2088
no place to flee **t** way or that,	**Jos 8:20**	2008
some on **t** side and some on that	**Jos 8:22**	2088
forever, a desolation until **t** day.	**Jos 8:28**	2088
of stones *that stands* to **t** day.	**Jos 8:29**	2088
"**T** our bread *was* warm *when* we	**Jos 9:12**	2088
"**T** we will do to them, even let	**Jos 9:20**	2088
of you, and have done **t** thing.	**Jos 9:24**	2088
the altar of the LORD, to **t** day,	**Jos 9:27**	2088
mouth of the cave, to **t** very day.	**Jos 10:27**	2088
for tomorrow at **t** time I will	**Jos 11:6**	2088
"**T** is the land that remains:	**Jos 13:2**	2088
apportion **t** land for an	**Jos 13:7**	2088
live among Israel until **t** day.	**Jos 13:13**	2088
T was the inheritance of the sons	**Jos 13:23**	2088
T is the inheritance of the sons	**Jos 13:28**	2088
the LORD spoke **t** word to Moses,	**Jos 14:10**	2088
give me **t** hill country about which	**Jos 14:12**	2088
the Kenizzite until **t** day,	**Jos 14:14**	2088
T shall be your south border.	**Jos 15:4**	2088
T is the border around the sons of	**Jos 15:12**	2088
T is the inheritance of the tribe	**Jos 15:20**	2088
of Judah at Jerusalem until **t** day.	**Jos 15:63**	2088
Now **t** was the territory of	**Jos 16:5**	
T is the inheritance of the tribe	**Jos 16:8**	2088
in the midst of Ephraim to **t** day,	**Jos 16:10**	2088
Now **t** was the lot for the tribe	**Jos 17:1**	
T *was* the west side.	**Jos 18:14**	2088
T *was* the south border.	**Jos 18:19**	2088
T *was* the inheritance of the sons	**Jos 18:20**	2088
T is the inheritance of the sons	**Jos 18:28**	2088
T *was* the inheritance of the tribe	**Jos 19:8**	2088
T *was* the inheritance of the sons	**Jos 19:16**	2088
T *was* the inheritance of the tribe	**Jos 19:23**	2088
T *was* the inheritance of the tribe	**Jos 19:31**	2088
T *was* the inheritance of the tribe	**Jos 19:39**	2088
T *was* the inheritance of the tribe	**Jos 19:48**	2088
brothers these many days to **t** day,	**Jos 22:3**	2088
'What is **t** unfaithful act which	**Jos 22:16**	2088
from following the LORD **t** day,	**Jos 22:16**	
to rebel against the LORD **t** day?	**Jos 22:16**	
not cleansed ourselves to **t** day,	**Jos 22:17**	2088
t day from following the LORD?	**Jos 22:18**	
LORD do not save us **t** day!	**Jos 22:22**	2088
we have done **t** out of concern,	**Jos 22:24**	2088
shall also come about if they say **t**	**Jos 22:28**	
from following the LORD **t** day,	**Jos 22:29**	
have not committed **t** unfaithful act	**Jos 22:31**	2088
God, as you have done to **t** day.	**Jos 23:8**	2088
man has stood before you to **t** day.	**Jos 23:9**	2088
until you perish from off **t** good land	**Jos 23:13**	2088
destroyed you from off **t** good land	**Jos 23:15**	2088
t stone shall be for a witness	**Jos 24:27**	2088
of Benjamin in Jerusalem to **t** day.	**Jg 1:21**	2088
it Luz which is its name to **t** day.	**Jg 1:26**	2088
with the inhabitants of **t** land;	**Jg 2:2**	2088
what is **t** you have done?	**Jg 2:2**	2088
"Because **t** nation has	**Jg 2:20**	2088
For **t** is the day in which the LORD	**Jg 4:14**	2088
the presence of the LORD, **T** Sinai,	**Jg 5:5**	2088
why then has all **t** happened to us?	**Jg 6:13**	2088
"Go in **t** your strength and	**Jg 6:14**	2088
bread and lay them on **t** rock,	**Jg 6:20**	1975
To **t** day it is still in Ophrah of	**Jg 6:24**	2088
your God on the top of **t** stronghold	**Jg 6:26**	2088
"Who did **t** thing?"	**Jg 6:29**	2088
the son of Joash did **t** thing."	**Jg 6:29**	2088
'**T** one shall go with you,' he	**Jg 7:4**	2088
'**T** one shall not go with you,' he	**Jg 7:4**	2088
"**T** is nothing less than the sword	**Jg 7:14**	2088
is **t** thing you have done to us,	**Jg 8:1**	2088
I will tear down **t** tower."	**Jg 8:9**	2088
Jerubbaal and his house **t** day,	**Jg 9:19**	2088
that **t** people were under my	**Jg 9:29**	2088
Is **t** not the people whom you	**Jg 9:38**	2088
are called Havvoth-jair to **t** day.	**Jg 10:4**	2088
only please deliver us **t** day."	**Jg 10:15**	2088
"For **t** reason we have now	**Jg 11:8**	3651
"Let **t** thing be done for me;	**Jg 11:37**	2088
then have you come up to me **t** day to	**Jg 12:3**	2088
When Manoah and his wife saw **t**,	**Jg 13:20**	
hear *things* like **t** at this time."	**Jg 13:23**	2088
hear *things* like this at **t** time."	**Jg 13:23**	
the young men customarily did **t**.	**Jg 14:10**	3651
to impoverish us? Is **t** not *so?*"	**Jg 14:15**	
"**T** time I shall be blameless in	**Jg 15:3**	6471
the Philistines said, "Who did **t**?"	**Jg 15:6**	2088
"Since you act like **t**,	**Jg 15:7**	2088
is **t** that you have done to us?"	**Jg 15:11**	2088
"You have given **t** great deliverance	**Jg 15:18**	2088
which is in Lehi to **t** day.	**Jg 15:19**	2088
After **t** it came about that he	**Jg 16:4**	3651
please strengthen me just **t** time,	**Jg 16:28**	2088
And what are you doing in **t** *place?*	**Jg 18:3**	2088
that place Mahaneh-dan to **t** day;	**Jg 18:12**	2088
and let us turn aside into **t** city	**Jg 19:11**	2088
t man has come into my house,	**Jg 19:23**	2088
do not commit **t** act of folly.	**Jg 19:23**	2088
an act of folly against **t** man."	**Jg 19:24**	2088

"Nothing like **t** has *ever* happened	**Jg 19:30**	2088
from the land of Egypt to **t** day.	**Jg 19:30**	2088
how did **t** wickedness take place?"	**Jg 20:3**	2088
"But now **t** is the thing which we	**Jg 20:9**	2088
"What is **t** wickedness that has	**Jg 20:12**	2088
may put them to death and remove **t**	**Jg 20:13**	
has **t** come about in Israel,	**Jg 21:3**	2088
"**T** is the thing that you shall do:	**Jg 21:11**	2088
and the women said, "Is **t** Naomi?"	**Ru 1:19**	2088
"Whose young woman is **t**?"	**Ru 2:5**	2088
do not go on from **t** one,	**Ru 2:8**	2088
"Remain **t** night, and when morning	**Ru 3:13**	
Now **t** was *the custom* in former	**Ru 4:7**	2088
and **t** was the *manner of*	**Ru 4:7**	2088
will give you by **t** young woman."	**Ru 4:12**	2088
Now **t** man would go up from his	**1Sa 1:3**	1931
"For **t** boy I prayed, and the LORD	**1Sa 1:27**	2088
LORD give you children from **t** woman	**1Sa 2:20**	2088
'**T** will be the sign to you which	**1Sa 2:34**	2088
"What *does* the noise of **t** great shout	**1Sa 4:6**	2088
nothing like **t** has happened before.	**1Sa 4:7**	2088
the noise of **t** commotion *mean?*"	**1Sa 4:14**	2088
of Dagon in Ashdod to **t** day.	**1Sa 5:5**	2088
then He has done us **t** great evil.	**1Sa 6:9**	2088
witness to **t** day in the field of Joshua	**1Sa 6:18**	2088
stand before the LORD, **t** holy God?	**1Sa 6:20**	2088
them up from Egypt even to **t** day	**1Sa 8:8**	2088
"**T** will be the procedure of the	**1Sa 8:11**	2088
there is a man of God in **t** city,	**1Sa 9:6**	2088
the LORD had revealed **t** to	**1Sa 9:15**	
"About **t** time tomorrow I will	**1Sa 9:16**	
T one shall rule over My people."	**1Sa 9:17**	2088
do you speak to me in **t** way?"	**1Sa 9:21**	2088
"How can **t** one deliver us?"	**1Sa 10:27**	2088
make *it* with you on **t** condition,	**1Sa 11:2**	2088
a man shall be put to death **t** day,	**1Sa 11:13**	2088
you from my youth even to **t** day.	**1Sa 12:2**	2088
and His anointed is witness **t** day	**1Sa 12:5**	2088
Egypt and settled them in **t** place.	**1Sa 12:8**	2088
see **t** great thing which the LORD	**1Sa 12:16**	2088
for we have added to all our sins **t**	**1Sa 12:19**	
You have committed all **t** evil,	**1Sa 12:20**	2088
and **t** shall be the sign to us."	**1Sa 14:10**	2088
I tasted a little of **t** honey.	**1Sa 14:29**	2088
see how **t** sin has happened today.	**1Sa 14:38**	2088
"May God do **t** *to me* and more	**1Sa 14:44**	3541
t great deliverance in Israel?	**1Sa 14:45**	2088
he has worked with God **t** day."	**1Sa 14:45**	2088
"What then is **t** bleating of the	**1Sa 15:14**	2088
"The LORD has not chosen **t** one	**1Sa 16:8**	2088
"The LORD has not chosen **t** one	**1Sa 16:9**	2088
"Arise, anoint him; for **t** is he."	**1Sa 16:12**	2088
"I defy the ranks of Israel **t** day;	**1Sa 17:10**	2088
an ephah of **t** roasted grain and these	**1Sa 17:17**	2088
you seen **t** man who is coming up?	**1Sa 17:25**	2088
the man who kills **t** Philistine and	**1Sa 17:26**	1975
who is **t** uncircumcised Philistine,	**1Sa 17:26**	2088
him in accord with **t** word,	**1Sa 17:27**	2088
go and fight with **t** Philistine."	**1Sa 17:32**	2088
not able to go against **t** Philistine	**1Sa 17:33**	2088
and **t** uncircumcised Philistine	**1Sa 17:36**	2088
from the hand of **t** Philistine."	**1Sa 17:37**	2088
"**T** day the LORD will deliver you	**1Sa 17:46**	2088
the army of the Philistines **t** day to	**1Sa 17:46**	2088
and that all **t** assembly may know	**1Sa 17:47**	2088
"Abner, whose son is **t** young man?"	**1Sa 17:55**	2088
for **t** saying displeased him;	**1Sa 18:8**	2088
"Why have you deceived me like **t**	**1Sa 19:17**	3602
my father hide **t** thing from me?	**1Sa 20:2**	2088
'Do not let Jonathan know **t**,	**1Sa 20:3**	2088
my father about **t** time tomorrow,	**1Sa 20:12**	
the arrows are on **t** side of you,	**1Sa 20:21**	2008
For **t** reason he has not come to	**1Sa 20:29**	3651
"Is **t** not David the king of the	**1Sa 21:11**	2088
not sing of **t** one as they danced,	**1Sa 21:11**	2088
that you have brought **t** one to act	**1Sa 21:15**	2088
Shall **t** one come into my house?"	**1Sa 21:15**	2088
lie in ambush, as *it is* **t** day."	**1Sa 22:8**	2088
lying in ambush as *it is* **t** day?"	**1Sa 22:13**	2088
at all of **t** whole affair."	**1Sa 22:15**	2088
t *is* the day of which the LORD	**1Sa 24:4**	
I should do **t** thing to my lord,	**1Sa 24:6**	2088
t day your eyes have seen that the	**1Sa 24:10**	2088
"Is **t** your voice, my son David?"	**1Sa 24:16**	2088
what you have done to me **t** day.	**1Sa 24:19**	2088
that **t** *man* has in the wilderness,	**1Sa 25:21**	2088
pay attention to **t** worthless man,	**1Sa 25:25**	2088
"Now let **t** gift which your	**1Sa 25:27**	2088
t will not cause grief or a	**1Sa 25:31**	2088
who sent you **t** day to meet me,	**1Sa 25:32**	2088
have kept me **t** day from bloodshed	**1Sa 25:33**	2088
"**T** thing that you have done is	**1Sa 26:16**	2088
"Is **t** your voice, my son David?"	**1Sa 26:17**	2088
was precious in your sight **t** day.	**1Sa 26:21**	2088
highly valued in my sight **t** day,	**1Sa 26:24**	2088
to the kings of Judah to **t** day.	**1Sa 27:6**	2088
come upon you for **t** thing."	**1Sa 28:10**	2088
has done **t** thing to you this day.	**1Sa 28:18**	2088
has done this thing to you **t** day.	**1Sa 28:18**	2088
"Is **t** not David, the servant of	**1Sa 29:3**	2088
day he deserted *to me* to **t** day?"	**1Sa 29:3**	2088
For with what could **t** *man* make	**1Sa 29:4**	2088
"Is **t** not David, of whom they	**1Sa 29:5**	2088
day of your coming to me to **t** day.	**1Sa 29:6**	2088
when I came before you to **t** day,	**1Sa 29:8**	2088
"Shall I pursue **t** band?	**1Sa 30:8**	2088
you bring me down to **t** band?"	**1Sa 30:15**	2088
I will bring you down to **t** band."	**1Sa 30:15**	2088
"**T** is David's spoil."	**1Sa 30:20**	2088

will listen to you in **t** matter? 1Sa 30:24 2088
an ordinance for Israel to **t** day. 1Sa 30:25 2088
Then David chanted with **t** lament 2Sa 1:17 2088
t kindness to Saul your lord, 2Sa 2:5 2088
also will show **t** goodness to you, 2Sa 2:6 2088
because you have done **t** thing. 2Sa 2:6 2088
I do not accomplish **t** for him, 2Sa 3:9 3651
man has fallen **t** day in Israel? 2Sa 3:38 2088
been aliens there until **t** day). 2Sa 4:3 2088
the king vengeance **t** day on Saul 2Sa 4:8 2088
is called Perez-uzzah to **t** day. 2Sa 6:8 2088
will be more lightly esteemed than **t** 2Sa 6:22 2088
Israel from Egypt, even to **t** day; 2Sa 7:6 2088
all these words and all **t** vision, 2Sa 7:17 2088
that You have brought me **t** far? 2Sa 7:18 1988
"And yet **t** was insignificant in 2Sa 7:19 2088
And **t** is the custom of man, O Lord 2Sa 7:19 2088
You have done all **t** greatness to 2Sa 7:21 2088
"For **t** reason You are great, O 2Sa 7:22 3651
courage to pray **t** prayer to You. 2Sa 7:27 2088
t good thing to Your servant. 2Sa 7:28 2088
Now after **t** it came about that 2Sa 8:1 3651
"Is **t** not Bathsheba, the daughter 2Sa 11:3 2088
soul, I will not do **t** thing." 2Sa 11:11 2088
'Do not let **t** thing displease you, 2Sa 11:25 2088
who has done **t** deserves to die, 2Sa 12:5 2088
because he did **t** thing and had no 2Sa 12:6 2088
will do **t** thing before all Israel, 2Sa 12:12 2088
because by **t** deed you have given 2Sa 12:14 2088
is **t** thing that you have done? 2Sa 12:21 2088
Now it was after **t** that Absalom 2Sa 13:1 3651
do not do **t** disgraceful thing! 2Sa 13:12 2088
because **t** wrong in sending me away 2Sa 13:16 2088
throw **t** woman out of my *presence,* 2Sa 13:17 2088
for in **t** manner the virgin 2Sa 13:18 3651
do not take **t** matter to heart." 2Sa 13:20 2088
by the intent of Absalom **t** has been 2Sa 13:32 2088
and speak to him in **t** manner." 2Sa 14:3 2088
For in speaking **t** word the king is 2Sa 14:13 2088
reason I have come to speak **t** word 2Sa 14:15 2088
hand of Joab with you in all **t**?" 2Sa 14:19 2088
servant Joab has done **t** thing. 2Sa 14:20 2088
now, I will surely do **t** thing; 2Sa 14:21 2088
Now it came about after **t** that 2Sa 15:1 3651
In **t** manner Absalom dealt with 2Sa 15:6 2088
"Why should **t** dead dog curse my 2Sa 16:9 2088
how much more now **t** Benjamite? 2Sa 16:11 2088
me instead of his cursing **t** day." 2Sa 16:12 2088
"Is **t** your loyalty to your friend? 2Sa 16:17 2088
For whom the LORD, **t** people, 2Sa 16:18 2088
"**T** time the advice that 2Sa 17:7 2088
"**T** is what Ahithophel counseled 2Sa 17:15 2088
and **t** is what I have counseled. 2Sa 17:15 2088
called Absalom's Monument to **t** day. 2Sa 18:18 2088
not the man to carry news **t** day, 2Sa 18:20 2088
"**T** one also is bringing good news." 2Sa 18:26 2088
"**T** is a good man and comes with 2Sa 18:27 2088
for the LORD has freed you **t** day 2Sa 18:31
for I know **t** day that if Absalom 2Sa 19:6
and **t** will be worse for you than 2Sa 19:7 2088
not Shimei be put to death for **t**, 2Sa 19:21 2088
you should **t** day be an adversary to 2Sa 19:22
king compensate me *with* **t** reward? 2Sa 19:36 2088
then are you angry about **t** matter? 2Sa 19:42 2088
Now it came about after **t** that 2Sa 21:18 3651
David spoke the words of **t** song to 2Sa 22:1 2088
me, O LORD, that I should do **t**. 2Sa 23:17 2088
the king delight in **t** thing?" 2Sa 24:3 2088
"Has **t** thing been done by my lord 1Ki 1:27 2088
I will indeed do so **t** day." 1Ki 1:30 2088
T is the noise which you have 1Ki 1:45 1931
t word against his own life. 1Ki 2:23 2088
not put you to death at **t** time, 1Ki 2:26 2088
for him **t** great lovingkindness, 1Ki 3:6 2088
sit on his throne, as *it is* **t** day. 1Ki 3:6 2088
judge **t** great people of Yours?" 1Ki 3:9 2088
that Solomon had asked **t** thing. 1Ki 3:10 2088
"Because you have asked **t** thing 1Ki 3:11 2088
t woman and I live in the same 1Ki 3:17 2088
that **t** woman also gave birth to a 1Ki 3:18 2088
"**T** woman's son died in the night, 1Ki 3:19 2088
'**T** is my son who is living, and 1Ki 3:23 2088
a wise son over **t** great people." 1Ki 5:7 2088
t house which you are building, 1Ki 6:12 2088
like **t** hall for Pharaoh's daughter, 1Ki 7:8 2088
T was the design of the stands: 1Ki 7:28 2088
He made the ten stands like **t**: 1Ki 7:37 2088
they are there to **t** day. 1Ki 8:8 2088
it with Your hand as it is **t** day. 1Ki 8:24 2088
how much less **t** house which I have 1Ki 8:27 2088
open toward **t** house night and day, 1Ki 8:29 2088
servant shall pray toward **t** place. 1Ki 8:29 2088
when they pray toward **t** place; 1Ki 8:30 2088
before Your altar in **t** house, 1Ki 8:31 2088
supplication to You in **t** house, 1Ki 8:33 2088
and they pray toward **t** place and 1Ki 8:35 2088
his hands toward **t** house; 1Ki 8:38 2088
he comes and prays toward **t** house, 1Ki 8:42 2088
t house which I have built is called 1Ki 8:43 2088
had finished praying **t** entire prayer 1Ki 8:54 2088
His commandments, as at **t** day." 1Ki 8:61 2088
I have consecrated **t** house which 1Ki 9:3 2088
"And **t** house will become a heap 1Ki 9:8 2088
thus to **t** land and to **t** house?' 1Ki 9:8 2088
thus to this land and to **t** house?' 1Ki 9:8 2088
all **t** adversity on them.' " 1Ki 9:9 2088
called the land of Cabul to **t** day. 1Ki 9:13 2088
Now **t** is the account of the forced 1Ki 9:15 2088
forced laborers, even to **t** day. 1Ki 9:21 2088
nor have they been seen to **t** day. 1Ki 10:12 2088
commanded him concerning **t** thing, 1Ki 11:10 2088
"Because you have done **t**, 1Ki 11:11 2088
Now **t** was the reason why he 1Ki 11:27 2088
the descendants of David for **t**, 1Ki 11:39 2088
counsel *me* to answer **t** people?" 1Ki 12:6 2088
be a servant to **t** people today, 1Ki 12:7 2088
t people who have spoken to me, 1Ki 12:9 2088
say to **t** people who spoke to you, 1Ki 12:10 2088
the house of David to **t** day. 1Ki 12:19 2088
t thing has come from Me. 1Ki 12:24 2088
"If **t** people go up to offer 1Ki 12:27 2088
then the heart of **t** people will 1Ki 12:27 2088
Now **t** thing became a sin, for the 1Ki 12:30 2088
"**T** is the sign which the LORD has 1Ki 13:3 2088
bread or drink water in **t** place. 1Ki 13:8 2088
drink water with you in **t** place. 1Ki 13:16 2088
After **t** event Jeroboam did not 1Ki 13:33 2088
T event became sin to the house of 1Ki 13:34 2088
I would be king over **t** people. 1Ki 14:2 2088
cut off the house of Jeroboam **t** day 1Ki 14:14 2088
will uproot Israel from **t** good land 1Ki 14:15 2088
let **t** child's life return to him." 1Ki 17:21 2088
"Is **t** you, Elijah my master?" 1Ki 18:7 2088
"Is **t** you, you troubler of Israel?" 1Ki 18:17 2088
that **t** people may know that You, 1Ki 18:37 2088
them by tomorrow about **t** time." 1Ki 19:2
but about **t** time tomorrow I will 1Ki 20:6
how **t** man is looking for trouble; 1Ki 20:7 2088
do, but **t** thing I cannot do.' " 1Ki 20:9 2088
When *Ben-hadad* heard **t** message, 1Ki 20:12 2088
you seen all **t** great multitude? 1Ki 20:13 2088
"Do **t** thing: remove the kings, 1Ki 20:24 2088
I will give all **t** great multitude into 1Ki 20:28 2088
Now the men took **t** as an omen, 1Ki 20:33
will let you go with **t** covenant." 1Ki 20:34
a man to me and said, 'Guard **t** man; 1Ki 20:39 2088
said **t** while another said that. 1Ki 22:20 3541
"Put **t** man in prison and feed 1Ki 22:27 2088
I will recover from **t** sickness." 2Ki 1:2 2088
situation of **t** city is pleasant, 2Ki 2:19
have been purified to **t** day, 2Ki 2:22 2088
'Make **t** valley full of trenches.' 2Ki 3:16 2088
'**T** is but a slight thing in 2Ki 3:18 2088
they said, "**T** is blood; the kings have 2Ki 3:23 2088
I perceive that **t** is a holy man of 2Ki 4:9 1931
"Call **t** Shunammite." 2Ki 4:12 2088
careful for us with all **t** care; 2Ki 4:13 2088
"At **t** season next year you will 2Ki 4:16 2088
"Call **t** Shunammite." 2Ki 4:36 2088
I set **t** before a hundred men?" 2Ki 4:43 2088
"And now as **t** letter comes to 2Ki 5:6 2088
that **t** man is sending *word* to me 2Ki 5:7 2088
"In **t** matter may the LORD pardon 2Ki 5:18 2088
pardon your servant in **t** matter." 2Ki 5:18 2088
has spared **t** Naaman the Aramean, 2Ki 5:20 2088
that you do not pass **t** place, 2Ki 6:9 2088
of Aram was enraged over **t** thing; 2Ki 6:11 2088
"Strike **t** people with blindness, 2Ki 6:18 2088
"**T** is not the way, nor is this 2Ki 6:19 2088
is not the way, nor is **t** the city; 2Ki 6:19 2090
Now it came about after **t**, 2Ki 6:24 3651
"**T** woman said to me, 2Ki 6:28 2088
Do you see how **t** son of a murderer 2Ki 6:32 2088
"Behold, **t** evil is from the LORD; 2Ki 6:33 2088
'Tomorrow about **t** time a measure 2Ki 7:1
in heaven, could **t** thing be?" 2Ki 7:2 2088
T day is a day of good news, but 2Ki 7:9 2088
will be *sold* tomorrow about **t** time 2Ki 7:18
t is the woman and this is her 2Ki 8:5 2088
is the woman and **t** is her son, 2Ki 8:5 2088
I recover from **t** sickness?' " 2Ki 8:8 2088
I recover from **t** sickness?' " 2Ki 8:9 2088
that he should do **t** great thing?" 2Ki 8:13 2088
revolted against Judah to **t** day. 2Ki 8:22 2088
take **t** flask of oil in your hand and 2Ki 9:1 2088
did **t** mad fellow come to you?" 2Ki 9:11 2088
"If **t** is your mind, *then* let no 2Ki 9:15
LORD laid **t** oracle against him: 2Ki 9:25 2088
I will repay you in **t** property,' 2Ki 9:26 2088
Ahaziah the king of Judah saw **t**, 2Ki 9:27
to **t** cursed woman and bury her, 2Ki 9:34 2088
"**T** is the word of the LORD, which 2Ki 9:36 1931
"**T** is Jezebel." 2Ki 9:37 2088
Now, when **t** letter comes to you, 2Ki 10:2 2088
Jezreel tomorrow about **t** time." 2Ki 10:6
and made it a latrine to **t** day. 2Ki 10:27
"**T** is the thing that you shall do: 2Ki 11:5 2088
and named it Joktheel to **t** day. 2Ki 14:7 2088
T is the word of the LORD which He 2Ki 15:12 1931
and have lived there to **t** day. 2Ki 16:6 2088
Now **t** came about because the sons 2Ki 17:7
"You shall not do **t** thing." 2Ki 17:12 2088
own land to Assyria until **t** day. 2Ki 17:23 2088
To **t** day they do according to the 2Ki 17:34 2088
fathers did, so they do to **t** day. 2Ki 17:41 2088
is **t** confidence that you have? 2Ki 18:19 2088
on the staff of **t** crushed reed, 2Ki 18:21 2088
before **t** altar in Jerusalem'? 2Ki 18:22 2088
against **t** place to destroy it? 2Ki 18:25 2088
'Go up against **t** land and destroy it.' 2Ki 18:25 2088
and **t** city will not be given into 2Ki 18:30 2088
'**T** day is a day of distress, 2Ki 19:3 2088
"**T** is the word that the LORD has 2Ki 19:21 2088
'Then **t** shall be the sign for you: 2Ki 19:29 2088
eat **t** year what grows of itself, 2Ki 19:29 2088
zeal of the LORD will perform **t**. 2Ki 19:31 2088
He will not come to **t** city or shoot 2Ki 19:32 2088
he shall not come to **t** city," 2Ki 19:33 2088
'For I will defend **t** city to save 2Ki 19:34 2088
and I will deliver you and **t** city 2Ki 20:6 2088
and I will defend **t** city for My 2Ki 20:6 2088
"**T** shall be the sign to you from 2Ki 20:9 2088
fathers have laid up in store to **t** day 2Ki 20:17 2088
"In **t** house and in Jerusalem, 2Ki 21:7 2088
from Egypt, even to **t** day.' " 2Ki 21:15 2088
words of **t** book that has been found 2Ki 22:13 2088
listened to the words of **t** book, 2Ki 22:13 2088
I bring evil on **t** place and on its 2Ki 22:16 2088
My wrath burns against **t** place, 2Ki 22:17 2088
heard what I spoke against **t** place 2Ki 22:19 2088
evil which I will bring on **t** place 2Ki 22:20 2088
to carry out the words of **t** covenant 2Ki 23:3 2088
that were written in **t** book. 2Ki 23:3 2088
"What is **t** monument that I see?" 2Ki 23:17 1975
in **t** book of the covenant." 2Ki 23:21 2088
t Passover was observed to the 2Ki 23:23 2088
t city which I have chosen, 2Ki 23:27 2088
through the anger of the LORD **t** 2Ki 24:20
destroyed them utterly to **t** day, 1Ch 4:41 2088
and have lived there to **t** day. 1Ch 4:43 2088
to the river of Gozan, to **t** day. 1Ch 5:26 2088
before my God that I should do **t**. 1Ch 11:19 2088
that place Perez-uzza to **t** day. 1Ch 13:11 2088
that I brought up Israel to **t** day, 1Ch 17:5 2088
and according to all **t** vision, 1Ch 17:15 2088
that You have brought me **t** far? 1Ch 17:16 1988
"**T** was a small thing in Your eyes, 1Ch 17:17 2088
You have wrought all **t** greatness, 1Ch 17:19 2088
t good thing to Your servant. 1Ch 17:26 2088
Now after **t** it came about that 1Ch 18:1 3651
Now it came about after **t**, 1Ch 19:1 3651
Now it came about after **t**, 1Ch 20:4 3651
Why does my lord seek **t** thing? 1Ch 21:3 2088
God was displeased with **t** thing, 1Ch 21:7 2088
in that I have done **t** thing. 1Ch 21:8 2088
"Give me the site of **t** threshing 1Ch 21:22
"**T** is the house of the LORD God, 1Ch 22:1 2088
and **t** is the altar of burnt 1Ch 22:1 2088
T Shelomoth and his relatives had 1Ch 26:26 1931
all of **t** was in the care of 1Ch 26:28
Now **t** *is* the enumeration of 1Ch 27:1
T Benaiah *was* the mighty man of 1Ch 27:6 1931
and because of **t**, wrath came upon 1Ch 27:24 2088
"All **t**," *said David,* 1Ch 28:19
all the details of **t** pattern." 1Ch 28:19
himself **t** day to the LORD?" 1Ch 29:5
able to offer as generously as **t**? 1Ch 29:14 2088
all **t** abundance that we have 1Ch 29:16 2088
preserve **t** forever in the 1Ch 29:18 2088
out and come in before **t** people, 2Ch 1:10 2088
rule **t** great people of Yours?" 2Ch 1:10 2088
"Because you had **t** in mind, and 2Ch 1:11 2088
t *being required* forever in Israel. 2Ch 2:4 2088
and they are there to **t** day. 2Ch 5:9 2088
it with Your hand, as it is **t** day. 2Ch 6:15 2088
how much less **t** house which I have 2Ch 6:18 2088
open toward **t** house day and night, 2Ch 6:20 2088
servant shall pray toward **t** place. 2Ch 6:20 2088
when they pray toward **t** place; 2Ch 6:21 2088
before Your altar in **t** house, 2Ch 6:22 2088
before You in **t** house, 2Ch 6:24 2088
they pray toward **t** place and confess 2Ch 6:26 2088
his hands toward **t** house, 2Ch 6:29 2088
they come and pray toward **t** house, 2Ch 6:32 2088
that they may know that **t** house 2Ch 6:33 2088
t city which You have chosen and 2Ch 6:34 2088
to the prayer *offered* in **t** place. 2Ch 6:40 2088
and have chosen **t** place for Myself 2Ch 7:12 2088
to the prayer *offered* in **t** place. 2Ch 7:15 2088
have chosen and consecrated **t** house 2Ch 7:16 2088
and **t** house which I have 2Ch 7:20 2088
"As for **t** house, which was 2Ch 7:21 2088
thus to **t** land and to this house?' 2Ch 7:21 2088
thus to this land and to **t** house?' 2Ch 7:21 2088
all **t** adversity on them.' " 2Ch 7:22 2088
as forced laborers to **t** day. 2Ch 8:8 2088
counsel *me* to answer **t** people?" 2Ch 10:6 2088
"If you will be kind to **t** people 2Ch 10:7 2088
give that we may answer **t** people, 2Ch 10:9 2088
the house of David to **t** day. 2Ch 10:19 2088
for **t** thing is from Me. 2Ch 11:4 2088
have come against **t** multitude. 2Ch 14:11 2088
You have acted foolishly in **t**. 2Ch 16:9 2088
for he was enraged at him for **t**. 2Ch 16:10 2088
T was their muster according to their 2Ch 17:14 428
one said **t** while another said that. 2Ch 18:19 3602
"Put **t** *man* in prison and feed 2Ch 18:26 2088
Now it came about after **t** that the 2Ch 20:1 3651
drive out the inhabitants of **t** land 2Ch 20:7 2088
before **t** house and before You 2Ch 20:9 2088
(for Your name is in **t** house) 2Ch 20:9 2088
powerless before **t** great multitude 2Ch 20:12 2088
because of **t** great multitude, 2Ch 20:15 2088
'You *need* not fight in **t** *battle;* 2Ch 20:17 2088
After **t** Jehoshaphat king of 2Ch 20:35 3651
revolted against Judah to **t** day. 2Ch 21:10 2088
So after all **t** the LORD smote him 2Ch 21:18 2088
"**T** is the thing which you shall 2Ch 23:4 2088
Now it came about after **t** that 2Ch 24:4 3651
and Jerusalem for **t** their guilt. 2Ch 24:18 2088
much more to give you than **t**." 2Ch 25:9 2088
you, because you have done **t** and 2Ch 25:16 2088
The Ammonites also paid him **t** 2Ch 27:5 2088
t same King Ahaz became yet more 2Ch 28:22 1931
our wives are in captivity for **t**. 2Ch 29:9 2088
all **t** *continued* until the burnt 2Ch 29:28 2088
and will return to **t** land. 2Ch 30:9 2088

Context	Reference	No.
because there was nothing like **t**	2Ch 30:26	2088
Now when all **t** was finished, all	2Ch 31:1	2088
t great quantity is left over."	2Ch 31:10	2088
After **t** Sennacherib king of	2Ch 32:9	2088
deceive you or mislead you like **t**,	2Ch 32:15	2088
They called **t** out *with a* loud	2Ch 32:18	
prayed about **t** and cried out to	2Ch 32:20	2088
"In **t** house and in Jerusalem,	2Ch 33:7	2088
Now after **t** he built the outer	2Ch 33:14	3651
all that is written in **t** book."	2Ch 34:21	2088
and they spoke to her regarding **t**.	2Ch 34:22	2088
on **t** place and on its inhabitants,	2Ch 34:24	2088
will be poured out on **t** place and	2Ch 34:25	2088
you heard His words against **t** place	2Ch 34:27	2088
I will bring on **t** place and on its	2Ch 34:28	2088
of the covenant written in **t** book.	2Ch 34:31	2088
They did **t** also with the bulls.	2Ch 35:12	3651
reign **t** Passover was celebrated.	2Ch 35:19	2088
After all **t**, when Josiah had set	2Ch 35:20	2088
in their lamentations to **t** day.	2Ch 35:25	
Now **t** *was* their number:	Ezr 1:9	428
the foundation of **t** house was laid	Ezr 3:12	2088
t is the copy of the letter which	Ezr 4:11	1836
that **t** city may not be rebuilt	Ezr 4:21	1791
in carrying out **t** *matter;*	Ezr 4:22	1836
a decree to rebuild **t** temple and to	Ezr 5:3	1836
and to finish **t** structure?"	Ezr 5:3	1836
were reconstructing **t** building.	Ezr 5:4	1836
T *is* the copy of the letter which	Ezr 5:6	
and **t** work is going on with great	Ezr 5:8	1791
to rebuild **t** temple and to finish this	Ezr 5:9	1836
temple and to finish **t** structure?'	Ezr 5:9	1836
who destroyed **t** temple and	Ezr 5:12	1836
decree to rebuild **t** house of God.	Ezr 5:13	1836
t house of God at Jerusalem;	Ezr 5:17	1791
decision concerning **t** *matter."*	Ezr 5:17	1836
"Leave **t** work on the house of God	Ezr 6:7	1791
t house of God on its site.	Ezr 6:7	1791
the rebuilding of **t** house of God:	Ezr 6:8	1791
that any man who violates **t** edict,	Ezr 6:11	1836
a refuse heap on account of **t**.	Ezr 6:11	1836
t house of God in Jerusalem.	Ezr 6:12	1791
have issued **t** decree, let *it*	Ezr 6:12	
T temple was completed on the third	Ezr 6:15	1836
the dedication of **t** house of God	Ezr 6:16	1836
the dedication of **t** temple of God	Ezr 6:17	1836
T Ezra went up from Babylon, and	Ezr 7:6	1931
Now **t** is the copy of the decree	Ezr 7:11	2088
with **t** money, therefore, you shall	Ezr 7:17	1836
or servants of **t** house of God.	Ezr 7:24	1836
a thing as **t** in the king's heart,	Ezr 7:27	2088
our God concerning **t** *matter,*	Ezr 8:23	2088
foremost in **t** unfaithfulness."	Ezr 9:2	2088
When I heard about **t** matter,	Ezr 9:3	2088
Since the days of our fathers to **t** day	Ezr 9:7	2088
and to open shame, as *it is* **t** day.	Ezr 9:7	2088
God, what shall we say after **t**?	Ezr 9:10	2088
given us an escaped remnant as **t**,	Ezr 9:13	2088
escaped remnant, as *it is* **t** day;	Ezr 9:15	2088
stand before You because of **t**."	Ezr 9:15	2088
is hope for Israel in spite of **t**.	Ezr 10:2	2088
"Arise! For **t** matter is your	Ezr 10:4	
would do according to **t** proposal;	Ezr 10:5	2088
trembling because of **t** matter and	Ezr 10:9	
transgressed greatly in **t** matter.	Ezr 10:13	2088
t matter is turned away from us."	Ezr 10:14	2088
the son of Tikvah opposed **t**,	Ezr 10:15	2088
him compassion before **t** man."	Ne 1:11	2088
T is nothing but sadness of heart."	Ne 2:2	2088
"What is **t** thing you are doing?	Ne 2:19	2088
Please, let us leave off **t** usury.	Ne 5:10	2088
to them **t** very day their fields,	Ne 5:11	
would do according to **t** promise.	Ne 5:12	2088
who does not fulfill **t** promise;	Ne 5:13	2088
people did according to **t** promise.	Ne 5:13	2088
myself to the work on **t** wall;	Ne 5:16	2088
Yet for all **t** I did not demand the	Ne 5:18	2088
servitude was heavy on **t** people.	Ne 5:18	2088
all that I have done for **t** people.	Ne 5:19	2088
to me four times in **t** manner,	Ne 6:4	2088
He was hired for **t** reason,	Ne 6:13	4616
for they recognized that **t** work	Ne 6:16	2088
"**T** day is holy to the LORD your	Ne 8:9	1931
for **t** day is holy to our Lord.	Ne 8:10	
on the twenty-fourth day of **t** month	Ne 9:1	2088
a name for Yourself as *it is* **t** day.	Ne 9:10	2088
'**T** is your God Who brought you up	Ne 9:18	2088
of the kings of Assyria to **t** day.	Ne 9:32	2088
"Now because of all **t** We are	Ne 9:38	2088
Now prior to **t**, Eliashib the	Ne 13:4	2088
all **t** *time* I was not in Jerusalem,	Ne 13:6	2088
Remember me for **t**, O my God, and	Ne 13:14	2088
is **t** evil thing you are doing,	Ne 13:17	2088
God brought on us and on **t** city	Ne 13:18	2088
and on this city all **t** trouble?	Ne 13:18	2088
For **t** also remember me, O my God,	Ne 13:22	2088
you have committed all **t** great evil	Ne 13:27	2088
"**T** day the ladies of Persia	Es 1:18	2088
T word pleased the king	Es 1:21	
would go in to the king in **t** way:	Es 2:13	2088
they should be ready for **t** day.	Es 3:14	2088
learn what **t** *was* and why it *was.*	Es 4:5	2088
if you remain silent at **t** time,	Es 4:14	2088
royalty for such a time as **t**?"	Es 4:14	2088
may the king and Haman come **t** day	Es 5:4	
"Yet all of **t** does not satisfy me	Es 5:13	2088
been bestowed on Mordecai for **t**?"	Es 6:3	2088
and an enemy is **t** wicked Haman!"	Es 7:6	2088
the Jews would be ready for **t** day	Es 8:13	2088
T *was done* on the thirteenth day	Es 9:17	
of the instructions in **t** letter,	Es 9:26	2088
both what they had seen in **t**	Es 9:26	3602
t second letter about Purim.	Es 9:29	2088
Through all **t** Job did not sin nor	Jb 1:22	2088
In all **t** Job did not sin with his lips.	Jb 2:10	2088
three friends heard of all **t** adversity	Jb 2:11	2088
"Behold **t**; we have investigated	Jb 5:27	2088
"Behold, **t** is the joy of His way;	Jb 8:19	1931
"In truth I know that **t** is so;	Jb 9:2	
I know that **t** is within You:	Jb 10:13	2088
the hand of the LORD has done **t**,	Jb 12:9	2088
"Behold, my eye has seen all **t**,	Jb 13:1	
"**T** also will be my salvation, For	Jb 13:16	1931
upright will be appalled at **t**,	Jb 17:8	2088
And **t** is the place of him who does	Jb 18:21	2088
"Do you know **t** from of old, From	Jb 20:4	2088
"**T** is the wicked man's portion	Jb 20:29	2088
let **t** be your *way of* consolation.	Jb 21:2	2088
"**T** is the portion of a wicked man	Jb 27:13	2088
tell you, you are not right in **t**,	Jb 33:12	2088
if *you have* understanding, hear **t**;	Jb 34:16	2088
think **t** is according to justice?	Jb 35:2	2088
have preferred **t** to affliction.	Jb 36:21	2088
"At **t** also my heart trembles, And	Jb 37:1	2088
"Listen to **t**, O Job, Stand and	Jb 37:14	2088
"Who is **t** that darkens counsel By	Jb 38:2	2088
Tell *Me,* if you know all **t**.	Jb 38:18	
'Who is **t** that hides counsel	Jb 42:3	2088
After **t**, Job lived 140 years,	Jb 42:16	2088
O LORD my God, if I have done **t**,	Ps 7:3	2088
him from **t** generation forever.	Ps 12:7	2098
whose portion is in **t** life,	Ps 17:14	
T is the generation of those who	Ps 24:6	2088
Who is **t** King of glory?	Ps 24:10	2088
In *spite of* **t** I shall be confident.	Ps 27:3	2088
T poor man cried, and the LORD	Ps 34:6	2088
By **t** I know that You are pleased	Ps 41:11	2088
All **t** has come upon us, but we	Ps 44:17	2088
Would not God find **t** out?	Ps 44:21	2088
Hear **t**, all peoples;	Ps 49:1	2088
T is the way of those who are	Ps 49:13	2088
"Now consider **t**, you who forget	Ps 50:22	2088
T I know, that God is for me.	Ps 56:9	2088
Twice I have heard **t**:	Ps 62:11	2098
Until I declare Your strength to **t**	Ps 71:18	
his people return to **t** place,	Ps 73:10	1988
When I pondered to understand **t**,	Ps 73:16	2088
And **t** Mount Zion, where You have	Ps 74:2	2088
Remember **t**, O LORD, that the enemy	Ps 74:18	2088
well mixed, and He pours out of **t**;	Ps 75:8	2088
In spite of all **t** they still sinned And	Ps 78:32	2088
To **t** hill country which His right	Ps 78:54	2088
and see, and take care of **t** vine,	Ps 80:14	2088
'**T** one was born there.' "	Ps 87:4	2088
"**T** one and that one were born in	Ps 87:5	376
"**T** one was born there."	Ps 87:6	2088
does a stupid man understand **t**:	Ps 92:6	2088
Zion heard **t** and was glad,	Ps 97:8	
T will be written for the	Ps 102:18	2088
Let **t** be the reward of my accusers	Ps 109:20	2088
let them know that **t** is Your hand;	Ps 109:27	2088
From **t** time forth and forever.	Ps 113:2	6258
From **t** time forth and forever.	Ps 115:18	6258
T is the gate of the LORD;	Ps 118:20	2088
T is the LORD's doing;	Ps 118:23	2088
T is the day which the LORD has	Ps 118:24	2088
T is my comfort in my affliction,	Ps 119:50	2088
T has become mine, That I observe	Ps 119:56	2088
They stand **t** day according to	Ps 119:91	
in From **t** time forth and forever.	Ps 121:8	6258
From **t** time forth and forever.	Ps 125:2	6258
From **t** time forth and forever.	Ps 131:3	6258
"**T** is My resting place forever;	Ps 132:14	2088
T is an honor for all His godly	Ps 149:9	1931
Do **t** then, my son, and deliver	Pr 6:3	2088
"See, we did not know **t**,"	Pr 24:12	2088
the oppressor have **t** in common:	Pr 29:13	6298
T is the way of an adulterous	Pr 30:20	3651
"See **t**, it is new"?	Ec 1:10	2088
t also is striving after wind.	Ec 1:17	2088
t was my reward for all my labor.	Ec 2:10	2088
"**T** too is vanity."	Ec 2:15	2088
wisely under the sun. **T** too is vanity.	Ec 2:19	2088
T too is vanity and a great evil.	Ec 2:21	2088
mind does not rest. **T** too is vanity.	Ec 2:23	2088
T also I have seen that it is	Ec 2:24	2090
T too is vanity and striving after	Ec 2:26	2088
T too is vanity and striving after	Ec 4:4	2088
T too is vanity and it is a	Ec 4:8	2088
for **t** too is vanity and striving	Ec 4:16	2088
with its income. **T** too is vanity.	Ec 5:10	2088
T also is a grievous evil	Ec 5:16	2090
for **t** is his reward.	Ec 5:18	1931
t is the gift of God.	Ec 5:19	2090
T is vanity and a severe	Ec 6:2	2088
T too is futility and a striving	Ec 6:9	2088
the fool; And **t** too is futility.	Ec 7:6	2088
from wisdom that you ask about **t**.	Ec 7:10	2088
I tested all **t** with wisdom, *and* I	Ec 7:23	2090
"Behold, I have discovered **t**,"	Ec 7:27	2088
"Behold, I have found only **t**,	Ec 7:29	2088
All **t** I have seen and applied my	Ec 8:9	2088
T too is futility.	Ec 8:10	2088
I say that **t** too is futility.	Ec 8:14	2088
and **t** will stand by him in his	Ec 8:15	1931
For I have taken all **t** to my heart	Ec 9:1	2088
T is an evil in all that is done	Ec 9:3	2088
for **t** is your reward in life and	Ec 9:9	1931
Also **t** I came to see as wisdom	Ec 9:13	2090
But beyond **t**, my son, be warned:	Ec 12:12	1992a
because **t** *applies to* every person.	Ec 12:13	2088
"What is **t** coming up from the	SS 3:6	2088
T is my beloved and this is my	SS 5:16	2088
is my beloved and **t** is my friend,	SS 5:16	2088
'Who is **t** that grows like the	SS 6:10	2088
t coming up from the wilderness	SS 8:5	2088
of you **t** trampling of My courts?	Is 1:12	2088
On **t** account the anger of the LORD	Is 5:25	3651
For all **t** His anger is not spent,	Is 5:25	2088
"Behold, **t** has touched your lips;	Is 6:7	2088
"Go, and tell **t** people:	Is 6:9	2088
hearts of **t** people insensitive,	Is 6:10	2088
to walk in the way of **t** people,	Is 8:11	2088
that **t** people call a conspiracy,	Is 8:12	2088
do not speak according to **t** word,	Is 8:20	2088
LORD of hosts will accomplish **t**.	Is 9:7	2088
t, His anger does not turn away	Is 9:12	2088
For those who guide **t** people are	Is 9:16	2088
t, His anger does not turn away	Is 9:17	2088
t, His anger does not turn away	Is 9:21	2088
t, His anger does not turn away	Is 10:4	2088
hand and by my wisdom I did **t**,	Is 10:13	
t be known throughout the earth.	Is 12:5	2088
that you will take up **t** taunt	Is 14:4	2088
'Is **t** the man who made the earth	Is 14:16	2088
"**T** is the plan devised against	Is 14:26	2088
and **t** is the hand that is	Is 14:26	2088
that King Ahaz died **t** oracle came:	Is 14:28	2088
T is the word which the LORD spoke	Is 16:13	2088
"So the inhabitants of **t** coastland	Is 20:6	2008
For **t** reason my loins are full of	Is 21:3	3651
"Surely **t** iniquity shall not be	Is 22:14	2088
"Come, go to **t** steward, To	Is 22:15	2088
Is **t** your jubilant *city,* Whose	Is 23:7	2088
Who has planned **t** against Tyre,	Is 23:8	2088
t is the people *which* was not;	Is 23:13	2088
for the LORD has spoken **t** word.	Is 24:3	2088
for all peoples on **t** mountain;	Is 25:6	2088
And on **t** mountain He will swallow	Is 25:7	2088
t is our God for whom we have	Is 25:9	2088
T is the LORD for whom we have	Is 25:9	2088
the LORD will rest on **t** mountain,	Is 25:10	2088
In that day **t** song will be sung in	Is 26:1	2088
Therefore through **t** Jacob's	Is 27:9	2088
And **t** will be the full price of	Is 27:9	2088
He will speak to **t** people Through	Is 28:11	2088
t people who are in Jerusalem,	Is 28:14	2088
T also comes from the LORD of	Is 28:29	2088
is literate, saying, "Please read **t**,"	Is 29:11	2088
is illiterate, saying, "Please read **t**."	Is 29:12	2088
"Because **t** people draw near with	Is 29:13	2088
deal marvelously with **t** people,	Is 29:14	2088
For **t** is a rebellious people,	Is 30:9	1931
"Since you have rejected **t** word And	Is 30:12	2088
Therefore **t** iniquity will be to	Is 30:13	2088
"**T** is the way, walk in it,"	Is 30:21	2088
is **t** confidence that you have?	Is 36:4	2088
on the staff of **t** crushed reed,	Is 36:6	2088
'You shall worship before **t** altar'?	Is 36:7	2088
against **t** land to destroy it?	Is 36:10	2088
'Go up against **t** land and destroy	Is 36:10	2088
t city will not be given into the	Is 36:15	2088
'**T** day is a day of distress,	Is 37:3	2088
t is the word that the LORD has	Is 37:22	2088
"Then **t** shall be the sign for you:	Is 37:30	2088
eat **t** year what grows of itself,	Is 37:30	
LORD of hosts will perform **t**." '	Is 37:32	2088
'He will not come to **t** city	Is 37:33	2088
and he will not come to **t** city,'	Is 37:34	2088
'For I will defend **t** city to save	Is 37:35	2088
"I will deliver you and **t** city	Is 38:6	2088
and I will defend **t** city."	Is 38:6	2088
"**T** shall be the sign to you from	Is 38:7	2088
do **t** thing that He has spoken:	Is 38:7	2088
fathers have laid up in store to **t** day	Is 39:6	2088
the hand of the LORD has done **t**,	Is 41:20	2088
Who has declared **t** from	Is 41:26	
But **t** is a people plundered and	Is 42:22	1931
Who among you will give ear to **t**?	Is 42:23	2088
Who among them can declare **t** And	Is 43:9	2088
"**T** one will say,	Is 44:5	2088
over **t** half he eats meat as he	Is 44:16	
Who has announced **t** from of old?	Is 45:21	2088
"Remember **t**, and be assured;	Is 46:8	2088
"Now, then, hear **t**, you sensual	Is 47:8	2088
"Hear **t**, O house of Jacob, who	Is 48:1	2088
"You have heard; look at all **t**.	Is 48:6	
to you new things from **t** time,	Is 48:6	6258
"Come near to Me, listen to **t**:	Is 48:16	2088
of joyful shouting, proclaim **t**,	Is 48:20	2088
T you will have from My hand:	Is 50:11	2088
Therefore, please hear **t**,	Is 51:21	2088
"For **t** is like the days of Noah	Is 54:9	2088
T is the heritage of the servants	Is 54:17	2088
"How blessed is the man who does **t**,	Is 56:2	2088
it a fast like **t** which I choose,	Is 58:5	2088
Will you call **t** a fast, even an	Is 58:5	2088
"Is **t** not the fast which I	Is 58:6	2088
Me, **t** is My covenant with them,"	Is 59:21	2088
Who is **t** who comes from Edom,	Is 63:1	2088
T One who is majestic in His	Is 63:1	2088
"But to **t** one I will look, To him	Is 66:2	2088
Then you will see **t**, and your	Is 66:14	
I have appointed you **t** day over	Jer 1:10	2088
there has been such *a thing* as **t**!	Jer 2:10	2088
"Be appalled, O heavens, at **t**,	Jer 2:12	2088
"Have you not done **t** to yourself By	Jer 2:17	2088

"From **t** *place* also you will go Jer 2:37 2088
"Yet in spite of all **t** her Jer 3:10 2088
from our youth even to **t** day. Jer 3:25 2088
"For **t**, put on sackcloth, Lament Jer 4:8 2088
deceived **t** people and Jerusalem, Jer 4:10 2088
said to **t** people and to Jerusalem, Jer 4:11 2088
a wind too strong for **t** Jer 4:12 428
T is your evil. How bitter! Jer 4:18 2088
"For **t** the earth shall mourn And Jer 4:28 2088
on a nation such as **t** Shall I not Jer 5:9 2088
"Because you have spoken **t** word, Jer 5:14 2088
your mouth fire And **t** people wood, Jer 5:14 2088
"Declare **t** in the house of Jacob Jer 5:20 2088
hear **t**, O foolish and senseless Jer 5:21 2088
'But **t** people has a stubborn and Jer 5:23 2088
as **t** Shall I not avenge Myself?' Jer 5:29 2088
T is the city to be punished, In Jer 6:6 1931
am bringing disaster on **t** people, Jer 6:19 2088
stumbling blocks before **t** people. Jer 6:21 2088
house and proclaim there **t** word and Jer 7:2 2088
I will let you dwell in **t** place. Jer 7:3 2088
'**T** is the temple of the LORD, the Jer 7:4 1992a
shed innocent blood in **t** place, Jer 7:6 2088
I will let you dwell in **t** place, Jer 7:7 2088
and stand before Me in **t** house, Jer 7:10 2088
'Has **t** house, which is called by Jer 7:11 2088
for you, do not pray for **t** people, Jer 7:16 2088
will be poured out on **t** place, Jer 7:20 2088
"But **t** is what I commanded them, Jer 7:23 2088
of the land of Egypt until **t** day, Jer 7:25 2088
'**T** is the nation that did not obey Jer 7:28 2088
'The dead bodies of **t** people Jer 7:33 2088
that remains of **t** evil family, Jer 8:3 2088
"Why then has **t** people, Jer 8:5 2088
"On a nation such as **t** Shall I not Jer 9:9 2088
wise man that may understand **t**? Jer 9:12 2088
I will feed them, **t** people, Jer 9:15 2088
but let him who boasts boast of **t**, Jer 9:24 2088
inhabitants of the land At **t** time, Jer 10:18 2088
"Truly **t** is a sickness, And I Jer 10:19 2088
"Hear the words of **t** covenant, Jer 11:2 2088
not heed the words of **t** covenant Jer 11:3 2088
and honey, as *it is* **t** day. Jer 11:5 2088
words of **t** covenant and do them. Jer 11:6 2088
the land of Egypt, even to **t** day, Jer 11:7 2088
them all the words of **t** covenant, Jer 11:8 2088
do not pray for **t** people, Jer 11:14 2088
'**T** wicked people, who refuse to Jer 13:10 2088
let them be just like **t** waistband which Jer 13:10 2088
you are to speak **t** word to them, Jer 13:12 2088
to fill all the inhabitants of **t** land Jer 13:13 2088
"**T** is your lot, the portion Jer 13:25 2088
Thus says the LORD to **t** people, Jer 14:10 2088
pray for the welfare of **t** people. Jer 14:11 2088
you lasting peace in **t** place.' " Jer 14:13 2088
will be no sword or famine in **t** land Jer 14:15 2088
"You will say **t** word to them, Jer 14:17 2088
heart would not be with **t** people; Jer 15:1 2088
"Then I will make you to **t** people Jer 15:20 2088
sons or daughters in **t** place." Jer 16:2 2088
and daughters born in **t** place, Jer 16:3 2088
fathers who beget them in **t** land: Jer 16:3 2088
My peace from **t** people," Jer 16:5 2088
men and small will die in **t** land; Jer 16:6 2088
going to eliminate from **t** place, Jer 16:9 2088
when you tell **t** people all these words Jer 16:10 2088
all **t** great calamity against us? Jer 16:10 2088
'So I will hurl you out of **t** land Jer 16:13 2088
T time I will make them know My Jer 16:21 2088
in through the gates of **t** city Jer 17:24 2088
through the gates of **t** city kings and Jer 17:25 2088
and **t** city will be inhabited Jer 17:25 2088
deal with you as **t** potter *does?*" Jer 18:6 2088
Who ever heard the like of **t**? Jer 18:13 428
to bring a calamity upon **t** place, Jer 19:3 2088
and have made **t** an alien place Jer 19:4 2088
and *because* they have filled **t** place Jer 19:4 2088
"when **t** place will no longer be Jer 19:6 2088
of Judah and Jerusalem in **t** place, Jer 19:7 2088
"I will also make **t** city a Jer 19:8 2088
I break **t** people and this city, Jer 19:11 2088
I break this people and **t** city, Jer 19:11 2088
"**T** is how I will treat this Jer 19:12 3651
t place and its inhabitants," Jer 19:12 2088
"so as to make **t** city like Topheth. Jer 19:12 2088
I am about to bring on **t** city and Jer 19:15 2088
over all the wealth of **t** city, Jer 20:5 2088
them into the center of **t** city. Jer 21:4 2088
down the inhabitants of **t** city, Jer 21:6 2088
in **t** city from the pestilence, Jer 21:7 2088
"You shall also say to **t** people, Jer 21:8 2088
"He who dwells in **t** city will die Jer 21:9 2088
For I have set My face against **t** city Jer 21:10 2088
of Judah, and there speak **t** word Jer 22:1 2088
shed innocent blood in **t** place. Jer 22:3 2088
men will indeed perform **t** thing, Jer 22:4 2088
will enter the gates of **t** house, Jer 22:4 2088
"that **t** house will become a Jer 22:5 2088
Many nations will pass by **t** city; Jer 22:8 2088
LORD done thus to **t** great city?' Jer 22:8 2088
who went forth from **t** place, Jer 22:11 2088
will die and not see **t** land again. Jer 22:12 2088
T has been your practice from your Jer 22:21 2088
"Is **t** man Coniah a despised, Jer 22:28 2088
'Write **t** man down childless, A man Jer 22:30 2088
And **t** is His name by which He will Jer 23:6 2088
t people the slightest benefit," Jer 23:32 2088
"Now when **t** people or the prophet Jer 23:33 2088
'Because you said **t** word, Jer 23:38 2088
whom I have sent out of **t** place Jer 24:5 2088
I will bring them again to **t** land; Jer 24:6 2088
of Jerusalem who remain in **t** land and Jer 24:8 2088
king of Judah, even to **t** day, Jer 25:3 2088
will bring them against **t** land and Jer 25:9 2088
'**T** whole land will be a desolation Jer 25:11 2088
it, all that is written in **t** book which Jer 25:13 2088
"Take **t** cup of the wine of wrath Jer 25:15 2088
and a curse, as it is **t** day; Jer 25:18 2088
am beginning to work calamity in **t** Jer 25:29
Judah, **t** word came from the LORD, Jer 26:1 2088
I will make **t** house like Shiloh, Jer 26:6 2088
and **t** city I will make a curse to Jer 26:6 2088
'**T** house will be like Shiloh and Jer 26:9 2088
and **t** city will be desolate, Jer 26:9 2088
"A death sentence for **t** man! Jer 26:11 2088
For he has prophesied against **t** city Jer 26:11 2088
sent me to prophesy against **t** house Jer 26:12 2088
and against **t** city all the words that Jer 26:12 2088
on yourselves, and on **t** city and Jer 26:15 2088
"No death sentence for **t** man! Jer 26:16 2088
and he prophesied against **t** city Jer 26:20 2088
against this city and against **t** land Jer 26:20 2088
t word came to Jeremiah from the Jer 27:1 2088
the priests and to all **t** people, Jer 27:16 2088
Why should **t** city become a ruin? Jer 27:17 2088
vessels that are left in **t** city, Jer 27:19 2088
and restore them to **t** place.' " Jer 27:22 2088
I am going to bring back to **t** place Jer 28:3 2088
took away from **t** place and carried Jer 28:3 2088
to bring back to **t** place Jeconiah Jer 28:4 2088
exiles, from Babylon to **t** place. Jer 28:6 2088
"Yet hear now **t** word which I am Jer 28:7 2088
have made **t** people trust in a lie. Jer 28:15 2088
T year you are going to die, Jer 28:16
(**T** was after King Jeconiah and the Jer 29:2
you, to bring you back to **t** place. Jer 29:10 2088
the people who dwell in **t** city, Jer 29:16 2088
Zephaniah the priest read **t** Jer 29:29 2088
have anyone living among **t** people, Jer 29:32 2088
latter days you will understand **t**. Jer 30:24
"Once again they will speak **t** Jer 31:23 2088
At **t** I awoke and looked, and my Jer 31:26 2088
But **t** is the covenant which I Jer 31:33 2088
"If **t** fixed order departs From Jer 31:36 428
I am about to give **t** city into the Jer 32:3 2088
that **t** was the word of the LORD. Jer 32:8 1931
deeds, **t** sealed deed of purchase and Jer 32:14 2088
deed of purchase and **t** open deed, Jer 32:14 2088
again be bought in **t** land." Jer 32:15 2088
and even to **t** day both in Israel Jer 32:20 2088
a name for Yourself, as at **t** day. Jer 32:20 2088
and gave them **t** land, which You Jer 32:22 2088
all **t** calamity come upon them. Jer 32:23 2088
I am about to give **t** city into the Jer 32:28 2088
who are fighting against **t** city will Jer 32:29 2088
set **t** city on fire and burn it, Jer 32:29 2088
"Indeed **t** city has been to Me *a* Jer 32:31 2088
that they built it, even to **t** day, Jer 32:31 2088
that they should do **t** abomination, Jer 32:35 2088
t city of which you say, Jer 32:36 2088
and I will bring them back to **t** Jer 32:37 2088
and will faithfully plant them in **t** land Jer 32:41 2088
t great disaster on this people, Jer 32:42 2088
this great disaster on **t** people, Jer 32:42 2088
bought in **t** land of which you say, Jer 32:43 2088
concerning the houses of **t** city, Jer 33:4 2088
I have hidden My face from **t** city Jer 33:5 2088
there will be heard in **t** place, Jer 33:10 2088
be in **t** place which is waste, Jer 33:12 2088
and **t** is *the name* by which she Jer 33:16 2088
what **t** people have spoken, Jer 33:24 2088
I am giving **t** city into the hand Jer 34:2 2088
I will bring them back to **t** city; Jer 34:22 2088
they do not drink *wine* to **t** day, Jer 35:14 2088
t people has not listened to Me. Jer 35:16 2088
t word came to Jeremiah from Jer 36:1 2088
the days of Josiah, even to **t** day. Jer 36:2 2088
has pronounced against **t** people." Jer 36:7 2088
"You have burned **t** scroll, Jer 36:29 2088
certainly come and destroy **t** land, Jer 36:29 2088
return and fight against **t** city, Jer 37:8 2088
up and burn **t** city with fire.' " Jer 37:10 2088
servants, or against **t** people, Jer 37:18 2088
against you or against **t** land'? Jer 37:19 2088
'He who stays in **t** city will die Jer 38:2 2088
'**T** city will certainly be given Jer 38:3 2088
"Now let **t** man be put to death, Jer 38:4 2088
the men of war who are left in **t** city Jer 38:4 2088
for **t** man is not seeking the Jer 38:4 2088
seeking the well-being of **t** people but Jer 38:4 2088
lives, who made **t** life for us, Jer 38:16 2088
t city will not be burned with Jer 38:17 2088
then **t** city will be given over to Jer 38:18 2088
t is the word which the LORD has Jer 38:21 2088
t city will be burned with fire.' " Jer 38:23 2088
bring My words on **t** city for disaster Jer 39:16 2088
t calamity against this place; Jer 40:2 2088
this calamity against **t** place; Jer 40:2 2088
t thing has happened to you. Jer 40:3 2088
"Do not do **t** thing, for you are Jer 40:16 2088
God, *that is* for all **t** remnant; Jer 42:2 2088
'If you will indeed stay in **t** land, Jer 42:10 2088
"We will not stay in **t** land," Jer 42:13 2088
you will see **t** place no more." Jer 42:18 2088
t day they are in ruins and no one Jer 44:2 2088
t abominable thing which I hate." Jer 44:4 2088
and a desolation as it is **t** day. Jer 44:6 2088
not become contrite even to **t** day, Jer 44:10 2088
remember them and did not *all* **t** Jer 44:21
an inhabitant, as *it is* **t** day. Jer 44:22 2088
t calamity has befallen you, Jer 44:23 2088
befallen you, as *it has* **t** day." Jer 44:23 2088
'**T** will be the sign to you,' Jer 44:29 2088
am going to punish you in **t** place, Jer 44:29 2088
T *is* the message which Jeremiah Jer 45:1
Who is **t** that rises like the Nile, Jer 46:7 2088
T *is* the message which the LORD Jer 46:13
t is the vengeance of the LORD: Jer 50:15 1931
and **t** last one *who* has broken his Jer 50:17 2088
For **t** is the LORD's time of Jer 51:6 1931
concerning **t** place to cut it off, Jer 51:62 2088
as you finish reading **t** scroll, Jer 51:63 2088
through the anger of the LORD **t** Jer 52:3
nothing to all you who pass **t** way? La 1:12
"Is **t** the city of which they La 2:15 2088
Surely **t** is the day for which we La 2:16 2088
T I recall to my mind, Therefore I La 3:21 2088
Because of **t** our heart is faint, La 5:17 2088
And **t** was their appearance: Ezk 1:5 2088
against Me to **t** very day. Ezk 2:3 2088
eat **t** scroll, and go, speak to the Ezk 3:1 2088
my mouth, and He fed me **t** scroll. Ezk 3:2 2088
t scroll which I am giving you." Ezk 3:3 2088
T is a sign to the house of Israel. Ezk 4:3 1931
says the Lord GOD, '**T** is Jerusalem; Ezk 5:5 2088
inflict **t** disaster on them." Ezk 6:10 2088
north of the altar gate *was* **t** idol Ezk 8:5 2088
He said to me, "Do you see **t**, Ezk 8:15
He said to me, "Do you see **t**, Ezk 8:17
and give evil advice in **t** city, Ezk 11:2 2088
T *city* is the pot and we are the Ezk 11:3 1931
multiplied your slain in **t** city, Ezk 11:6 2088
the flesh and **t** *city* is the pot; Ezk 11:7 1931
"**T** *city* will not be a pot for Ezk 11:11 1931
t land has been given us as a Ezk 11:15 1931
"**T** burden *concerns* the prince in Ezk 12:10 2088
what is **t** proverb you *people* have Ezk 12:22 2088
"I will make **t** proverb cease so Ezk 12:23 2088
even with **t** you were not satisfied Ezk 16:29 2088
"so that you will not commit **t** Ezk 16:43
who quotes proverbs will quote **t** Ezk 16:44
t was the guilt of your sister Ezk 16:49 2088
t vine bent its roots toward him Ezk 17:7 2088
"What do you mean by using **t** Ezk 18:2 2088
use **t** proverb in Israel anymore. Ezk 18:3 2088
T is a lamentation, and has become Ezk 19:14 1931
"Yet in **t** your fathers have Ezk 20:27 2088
name is called Bamah to **t** day." Ezk 20:29 2088
with all your idols to **t** day. Ezk 20:31
t *will* no longer *be* the same. Ezk 21:26 2088
T also will be no more until He Ezk 21:27 2088
"Now her sister Oholibah saw **t**, Ezk 23:11
"Again, they have done **t** to Me: Ezk 23:38 2088
the name of the day, **t** very day. Ezk 24:2 2088
siege to Jerusalem **t** very day. Ezk 24:2 2088
"**T** is a lamentation and they Ezk 32:16 1931
"I am not doing **t** for your sake," Ezk 36:32
'**T** desolate land has become like Ezk 36:35 1976
"**T** also I will let the house of Ezk 36:37 2088
"**T** is the chamber which faces Ezk 40:45 2090
"**T** is the most holy *place*." Ezk 41:4 2088
"**T** is the table that is before Ezk 41:22 2088
He said to me, "Son of man, **t** *is* Ezk 43:7
"**T** is the law of the house: Ezk 43:12 2088
Behold, **t** is the law of the house. Ezk 43:12 2088
and **t** *shall be* the *height* of the Ezk 43:13 2088
"**T** gate shall be shut; Ezk 44:2 2088
they made My covenant void—**t** Ezk 44:7
"Out of **t** there shall be for the Ezk 45:2 2088
"From **t** area you shall Ezk 45:3 2088
"**T** shall be his land for a Ezk 45:8
"**T** is the offering that you shall Ezk 45:13 2088
shall give to **t** offering for the prince Ezk 45:16 2088
feast, he shall provide like **t**, Ezk 45:25 428
"**T** is the place where the priests Ezk 46:20 2088
have you seen **t**?" Then he Ezk 47:6
"**T** *shall be* the boundary by which Ezk 47:13 2088
and **t** land shall fall to you as an Ezk 47:14 2088
"**T** *shall be* the boundary of Ezk 47:15 2088
T is the north side. Ezk 47:17
T is the east side. Ezk 47:18
T is the south side toward the Ezk 47:19
T is the west side. Ezk 47:20 2088
"So you shall divide **t** land among Ezk 47:21 2088
alienate **t** choice *portion* of land; Ezk 48:14
"**T** is the land which you shall Ezk 48:29 2088
So he listened to them in **t** matter Da 1:14 2088
anything like **t** of any magician, Da 2:10 1836
Because of **t** the king became Da 2:12 1836
of heaven concerning **t** mystery, Da 2:18 1836
T was your dream and the visions Da 2:28 1836
t mystery has not been revealed to Da 2:30 1836
T *was* the dream; now we will tell its Da 2:36 1836
been able to reveal **t** mystery." Da 2:47 1836
For **t** reason at that time certain Da 3:8 1836
you an answer concerning **t** matter. Da 3:16 1836
For **t** reason, because the king's Da 3:22 1836
who is able to deliver in **t** way." Da 3:29 1836
"**T** sentence is by the decree of Da 4:17
'**T** is the dream *which* I, King Da 4:18 1836
t is the interpretation, O king, Da 4:24 1836
and **t** is the decree of the Most Da 4:24 1932
"All **t** happened to Nebuchadnezzar Da 4:28
'Is **t** not Babylon the great, which Da 4:30 1668
"Any man who can read **t** Da 5:7 1836
"**T** *was* because an extraordinary Da 5:12
problems were found in **t** Daniel, Da 5:12

that they might read t inscription	Da 5:15	1836
heart, even though you knew all t,	Da 5:22	1836
and t inscription was written out.	Da 5:24	1836
"Now t is the inscription that	Da 5:25	1836
"T is the interpretation of the	Da 5:26	1836
Then t Daniel began distinguishing	Da 6:3	1836
ground of accusation against t Daniel	Da 6:5	1836
as the king heard t statement,	Da 6:14	1836
So t Daniel enjoyed success in the	Da 6:28	1836
"After t I kept looking, and	Da 7:6	1836
"After t I kept looking in the	Da 7:7	1836
t horn possessed eyes like the	Da 7:8	1668
him the exact meaning of all t.	Da 7:16	1836
of t kingdom ten kings will arise;	Da 7:24	
"At t point the revelation ended.	Da 7:28	3542
give t *man* an understanding of the	Da 8:16	1975
but to us open shame, as it is t day	Da 9:7	2088
all t calamity has come on us;	Da 9:13	2088
a name for Yourself, as it is t day	Da 9:15	2088
left alone and saw t great vision;	Da 10:8	2088
when he had spoken t word to me,	Da 10:11	2088
set your heart on understanding t	Da 10:12	
Then t one with human appearance	Da 10:18	
but t last time it will not turn	Da 11:29	
one on t bank of the river and	Da 12:5	2008
Hear t, O priests!	Hos 5:1	2088
have they sought Him, for all t.	Hos 7:10	2088
T *will be* their derision in the	Hos 7:16	2097
For from Israel is even t!	Hos 8:6	1931
Let Israel know t! The prophet	Hos 9:7	
Hear t, O elders, And listen, all	Jl 1:2	2088
Has *anything like* t happened in	Jl 1:2	2088
"It will come about after t	Jl 2:28	3651
Proclaim t among the nations:	Jl 3:9	2088
Is t not so, O sons of Israel?"	Am 2:11	2088
Hear t word which the LORD has	Am 3:1	2088
Hear t word, you cows of Bashan	Am 4:1	2088
Because I will do t to you,	Am 4:12	2088
Hear t word which I take up for	Am 5:1	2088
The LORD changed His mind about t.	Am 7:3	2088
The LORD changed His mind about t.	Am 7:6	2088
"T too shall not be,"	Am 7:6	1931
Hear t, you who trample the needy,	Am 8:4	2088
"Because of t will not the land	Am 8:8	2088
Declares the LORD who does t.	Am 9:12	2088
exiles of t host of the sons of Israel,	Ob 1:20	2088
t calamity *has struck* us."	Jon 1:7	2088
account *has* t calamity *struck* us?	Jon 1:8	2088
"How could you do t?"	Jon 1:10	2088
t great storm *has come* upon you."	Jon 1:12	2088
us perish on account of t man's life	Jon 1:14	2088
was not t what I said while I was	Jon 4:2	2088
to forestall t I fled to Tarshish,	Jon 4:2	
All t is for the rebellion of	Mi 1:5	2088
of t I must lament and wail,	Mi 1:8	2088
I am planning against t family a	Mi 2:3	2088
For t is no place of rest Because	Mi 2:10	2088
He would be spokesman to t people.	Mi 2:11	2088
Now hear t, heads of the house of	Mi 3:9	2088
T One will be *our* peace. When	Mi 5:5	2088
the remnant of Baal from t place,	Zph 1:4	2088
T they will have in return for	Zph 2:10	2088
T is the exultant city Which	Zph 2:15	2088
T people says, "The time has not	Hg 1:2	2088
while t house *lies* desolate?"	Hg 1:4	2088
saw t temple in its former glory?	Hg 2:3	2088
I will fill t house with glory,'	Hg 2:7	2088
'The latter glory of t house will	Hg 2:9	2088
'and in t place I will give	Hg 2:9	2088
and touches bread with t fold,	Hg 2:12	
said, "'So is t people.	Hg 2:14	2088
And so is t nation before Me,'	Hg 2:14	2088
do consider from t day onward:	Hg 2:15	2088
'Do consider from t day onward,	Hg 2:18	2088
t day on I will bless *you*.'"	Hg 2:19	2088
Is t not a brand plucked from the	Zch 3:2	2088
"T is the word of the LORD to	Zch 4:6	2088
laid the foundation of t house,	Zch 4:9	2088
"T is the curse that is going	Zch 5:3	2088
now your eyes and see what t is	Zch 5:5	2088
"T is the ephah going forth."	Zch 5:6	2088
"T is their appearance in all the	Zch 5:6	2088
and t is a woman sitting inside	Zch 5:7	2088
"T is Wickedness!"	Zch 5:8	2088
remnant of t people in those days,	Zch 8:6	2088
of t people as in the former days,'	Zch 8:11	2088
the remnant of t people to inherit all	Zch 8:12	2088
T very day I am declaring that I	Zch 9:12	2088
Now t will be the plague with	Zch 14:12	2088
So also like t plague will be the	Zch 14:15	2088
T will be the punishment of Egypt,	Zch 14:19	2088
eyes will see t and you will say,	Mal 1:5	
"And now t commandment is for	Mal 2:1	2088
I have sent t commandment to you,	Mal 2:4	2088
"*As* for the man who does t,	Mal 2:12	
"T is another thing you do: you	Mal 2:13	2088
My house, and test Me now in t,"	Mal 3:10	2088
But when he had considered t,	Mt 1:20	*3778*
Now all t took place to fulfill	Mt 1:22	*3778*
When Herod the king heard t, he	Mt 2:3	
for t is what has been written by	Mt 2:5	*3779*
T *was* to fulfill what had been	Mt 2:15	
T *was* to fulfill what was spoken	Mt 2:23	
For t is the one referred to by	Mt 3:3	*3778*
"Permit *it* at t time;	Mt 3:15	*737*
for in t way it is fitting for us	Mt 3:15	*3779*
"T is My beloved Son, in whom I	Mt 3:17	*3778*
T *was* to fulfill what was spoken	Mt 4:14	
"Pray, then, in t way:	Mt 6:9	*3779*
'Give us t day our daily bread.	Mt 6:11	*4594*
"For t reason I say to you, do	Mt 6:25	*3778*
for t is the Law and the Prophets.	Mt 7:12	*3778*
and I say to t one,	Mt 8:9	*3778*
to my slave, 'Do t!' and he does *it*	Mt 8:9	*3778*
Now when Jesus heard t, He	Mt 8:10	
T *was* to fulfill what was spoken	Mt 8:17	
"What kind of a man is t,	Mt 8:27	*3778*
"T *fellow* blasphemes."	Mt 9:3	*3778*
But when the crowds saw t, they	Mt 9:8	
When the Pharisees saw t, they	Mt 9:11	
But when Jesus heard t,	Mt 9:12	
"But go and learn what t means: 'I	Mt 9:13	
T news spread throughout all that	Mt 9:26	*3778*
believe that I am able to do t?"	Mt 9:28	*3778*
"See that no one knows *about* t!"	Mt 9:30	
"Nothing like t has ever been seen	Mt 9:33	*3779*
"T is the one about whom it is	Mt 11:10	*3778*
what shall I compare t generation?	Mt 11:16	*3778*
it would have remained to t day.	Mt 11:23	*4594*
"Yes, Father, for t way was	Mt 11:26	*3779*
But when the Pharisees saw t,	Mt 12:2	
"But if you had known what t means,	Mt 12:7	
But Jesus, aware of t, withdrew	Mt 12:15	
T *was* to fulfill what was spoken	Mt 12:17	
"T man cannot be the Son of	Mt 12:23	*3778*
But when the Pharisees heard t,	Mt 12:24	
"T man casts out demons only by	Mt 12:24	*3778*
For t reason they will be your judges.	Mt 12:27	
		1223, 3778
be forgiven him, either in t age or	Mt 12:32	*3778*
with t generation at the judgment,	Mt 12:41	*3778*
South will rise up with t generation	Mt 12:42	*3778*
also be with t evil generation."	Mt 12:45	*3778*
HEART OF T PEOPLE HAS BECOME DULL,	Mt 13:15	*3778*
T is the one on whom seed was sown	Mt 13:19	*3778*
t is the man who hears the word and	Mt 13:20	*3778*
t is the man who hears the word,	Mt 13:22	*3778*
t is the man who hears the word	Mt 13:23	*3778*
'An enemy has done t!'	Mt 13:28	*3778*
and t is smaller than all *other*	Mt 13:32	*3739*
T *was* to fulfill what was spoken	Mt 13:35	
"Where *did* t man *get* this wisdom and	Mt 13:54	*3778*
"Where *did* this man *get* t wisdom and	Mt 13:54	*3778*
"Is not t the carpenter's son?	Mt 13:55	*3778*
did t man *get* all these things?"	Mt 13:56	*3778*
"T is John the Baptist;	Mt 14:2	*3778*
and when the people heard *of* t,	Mt 14:13	
"T place is desolate and the hour is	Mt 14:15	*3588*
by t you invalidated	Mt 15:6	
'T PEOPLE HONORS ME WITH THEIR	Mt 15:8	*3778*
of the mouth, t defiles the man."	Mt 15:11	*3778*
when they heard t statement?"	Mt 15:12	*3588*
would we get so many loaves in t	Mt 15:33	
They began to discuss t among	Mt 16:7	
But Jesus, aware of t,	Mt 16:8	
flesh and blood did not reveal t	Mt 16:17	
upon t rock I will build My church;	Mt 16:18	*3778*
T shall never happen to You."	Mt 16:22	*3778*
"T is My beloved Son, with whom I	Mt 17:5	*3778*
When the disciples heard t, they	Mt 17:6	
seed, you will say to t mountain,	Mt 17:20	*3778*
"But t kind does not go out	Mt 17:21	*3778*
then humbles himself as t child,	Mt 18:4	*3778*
"For t reason the kingdom of	Mt 18:23	*3778*
'FOR T REASON A MAN SHALL LEAVE HIS	Mt 19:5	*3778*
beginning it has not been t way.	Mt 19:8	*3779*
the man with his wife is like t,	Mt 19:10	*3779*
all men *can* accept t statement,	Mt 19:11	*3778*
He who is able to accept t, let	Mt 19:12	
the young man heard t statement,	Mt 19:22	*3778*
When the disciples heard t, they	Mt 19:25	
"With people t is impossible, but	Mt 19:26	*3778*
I wish to give to t last man the same	Mt 20:14	*3778*
on *My* left, t is not Mine to give,	Mt 20:23	*3778*
And hearing t, the ten became	Mt 20:24	
"It is not t way among you, but	Mt 20:26	*3779*
T took place to fulfill what was	Mt 21:4	*3778*
city was stirred, saying, "Who is t?"	Mt 21:10	*3778*
"T is the prophet Jesus, from	Mt 21:11	*3778*
Seeing t, the disciples were	Mt 21:20	
but even if you say to t mountain,	Mt 21:21	*3778*
and who gave You t authority?"	Mt 21:23	*3778*
and you, seeing t, did not even	Mt 21:32	
'T is the heir; come, let us kill him and	Mt 21:38	*3778*
T BECAME THE CHIEF CORNER *stone*;	Mt 21:42	*3778*
T CAME ABOUT FROM THE LORD, AND IT	Mt 21:42	*3778*
"And he who falls on t stone will	Mt 21:44	*3778*
Whose likeness and inscription is t?	Mt 22:20	*3778*
And hearing t, they were amazed,	Mt 22:22	
When the crowds heard t, they	Mt 22:33	
"T is the great and foremost	Mt 22:38	*3778*
will come upon t generation.	Mt 23:36	*3778*
"T gospel of the kingdom shall be	Mt 24:14	*3778*
t generation will not pass away	Mt 24:34	*3778*
"But be sure of t, that if the	Mt 24:43	*1565*
"For t reason you also must be ready;	Mt 24:44	*3778*
were indignant when they saw t,	Mt 26:8	
saw *this*, and said, "Why t waste?	Mt 26:8	*3778*
"For t *perfume* might have been	Mt 26:9	*3778*
But Jesus, aware of t,	Mt 26:10	
she poured t perfume on My body,	Mt 26:12	*3778*
wherever t gospel is preached in	Mt 26:13	*3778*
what t woman has done will also	Mt 26:13	*3778*
and said, "Take, eat; t is My body."	Mt 26:26	*3778*
for t is My blood of the covenant,	Mt 26:28	*3778*
I will not drink of t fruit of the	Mt 26:29	*3778*
fall away because of Me t night,	Mt 26:31	*3778*
I say to you that t *very* night,	Mt 26:34	*3778*
possible, let t cup pass from Me;	Mt 26:39	*3778*
if t cannot pass away unless I	Mt 26:42	*3778*
that it must happen t way?"	Mt 26:54	*3779*
"But all t has taken place to	Mt 26:56	*3778*
"T man stated, 'I am able to destroy	Mt 26:61	*3778*
"T man was with Jesus of Nazareth."	Mt 26:71	*3778*
For t reason that field has been	Mt 27:8	*1352*
the Field of Blood to t day.	Mt 27:8	*4594*
"I am innocent of t Man's blood;	Mt 27:24	*3778*
"T IS JESUS THE KING OF	Mt 27:37	*3778*
"T man is calling for Elijah."	Mt 27:47	*3778*
"Truly t was the Son of God!"	Mt 27:54	*3778*
T man went to Pilate and asked for	Mt 27:58	*3778*
"And if t should come to the	Mt 28:14	*3778*
and t story was widely spread	Mt 28:15	*3778*
among the Jews, *and is* to t day.	Mt 28:15	*4594*
saying, "What is t? A new teaching	Mk 1:27	*3778*
"Why does t man speak that way?	Mk 2:7	*3778*
have never seen anything like t."	Mk 2:12	*3779*
And hearing t, Jesus said to them,	Mk 2:17	
When His own people heard *of* t,	Mk 3:21	
"Listen *to* t! Behold,	Mk 4:3	
"Do you not understand t parable?	Mk 4:13	*3778*
"Who then is t, that even the	Mk 4:41	*3778*
to see the woman who had done t.	Mk 5:32	*3778*
that no one should know about t,	Mk 5:43	*3778*
"Where did t man *get* these	Mk 6:2	*3778*
and what is t wisdom given to Him,	Mk 6:2	
"Is not t the carpenter, the son	Mk 6:3	*3778*
When his disciples heard *about* t,	Mk 6:29	
"T place is desolate and it is	Mk 6:35	*3588*
'T PEOPLE HONORS ME WITH THEIR	Mk 7:6	*3778*
"Because of t answer go;	Mk 7:29	*3778*
to find enough bread here in t	Mk 8:4	
does t generation seek for a sign?	Mk 8:12	*3778*
will be given to t generation."	Mk 8:12	*3778*
And Jesus, aware of t,	Mk 8:17	
in t adulterous and sinful generation,	Mk 8:38	*3778*
"T is My beloved Son, listen to	Mk 9:7	*3778*
has t been happening to him?"	Mk 9:21	*3778*
"T kind cannot come out by	Mk 9:29	*3778*
But they did not understand t	Mk 9:32	
"Whoever receives one child like t	Mk 9:37	*5108*
heart he wrote you t commandment.	Mk 10:5	*3778*
"FOR T REASON A MAN SHALL LEAVE	Mk 10:7	*3778*
questioning Him about t again.	Mk 10:10	*3778*
But when Jesus saw t,	Mk 10:14	
on *My* left, t is not Mine to give;	Mk 10:40	
Hearing t, the ten began to	Mk 10:41	
"But it is not t way among you, but	Mk 10:43	*3779*
'Why are you doing t?'	Mk 11:3	*3778*
priests and the scribes heard t,	Mk 11:18	
you, whoever says to t mountain,	Mk 11:23	*3778*
t authority to do these things?"	Mk 11:28	*3778*
'T is the heir; come, let us kill him,	Mk 12:7	*3778*
"Have you not even read t Scripture:	Mk 12:10	*3778*
T BECAME THE CHIEF CORNER *stone*	Mk 12:10	*3778*
T CAME ABOUT FROM THE LORD, AND IT	Mk 12:11	*3778*
Whose likeness and inscription is t?"	Mk 12:16	*3778*
"Is t not the reason you are	Mk 12:24	*3778*
"The second is t,	Mk 12:31	*3778*
t poor widow put in more than all	Mk 12:43	*3778*
t generation will not pass away	Mk 13:30	*3778*
"Why has t perfume been wasted?	Mk 14:4	*3778*
"For t perfume might have been	Mk 14:5	*3778*
what t woman has done will also	Mk 14:9	*3778*
They were glad when they heard t,	Mk 14:11	
and said, "Take *it*; t is My body."	Mk 14:22	*3778*
"T is My blood of the covenant,	Mk 14:24	*3778*
that t very night, before a rooster crows	Mk 14:30	*3778*
remove t cup from Me;	Mk 14:36	*3778*
but t *has taken place* to	Mk 14:49	
destroy t temple made with hands,	Mk 14:58	*3778*
Not even in t respect was	Mk 14:59	*3779*
"T is *one* of them!"	Mk 14:69	*3778*
"I do not know t man you are	Mk 14:71	*3778*
"Let t Christ, the King of	Mk 15:32	
"Truly t man was the Son of God!"	Mk 15:39	*3778*
wondered if He was dead by t time,	Mk 15:44	*2235*
ascertaining t from the centurion,	Mk 15:45	
"How will I know t *for certain?*	Lk 1:18	*3778*
you and to bring you t good news.	Lk 1:19	*3778*
"T is the way the Lord has dealt	Lk 1:25	*3779*
But she was very perplexed at t	Lk 1:29	
kind of salutation t was.	Lk 1:29	*3778*
"How can t be, since I am a virgin?"	Lk 1:34	*3778*
Now at t time Mary arose and went	Lk 1:39	*3778*
from t time on all generations	Lk 1:48	*3568*
will t child *turn out to be*?"	Lk 1:66	*3778*
T was the first census taken while	Lk 2:2	*3778*
"T *will be* a sign for you: you	Lk 2:12	*3778*
and see t thing that has happened	Lk 2:15	*3778*
When they had seen t,	Lk 2:17	
had been told them about t Child.	Lk 2:17	*3778*
t man was righteous and devout,	Lk 2:25	*3778*
t *Child* is appointed for the fall	Lk 2:34	*3778*
why have You treated us t way?	Lk 2:48	*3779*
Herod also added t to them all:	Lk 3:20	*3778*
tell t stone to become bread."	Lk 4:3	*3778*
You all t domain and its glory;	Lk 4:6	*3778*
"Today t Scripture has been	Lk 4:21	*3778*
"Is t not Joseph's son?"	Lk 4:22	*3778*
you will quote t proverb to Me,	Lk 4:23	*3778*
"What is t message?	Lk 4:36	*3778*
for I was sent for t purpose."	Lk 4:43	*3778*
When they had done t,	Lk 5:6	*3778*
is t *man* who speaks blasphemies?	Lk 5:21	*3778*
It was at t time that He went	Lk 6:12	*3778*
worthy for You to grant t to him;	Lk 7:4	*3778*

for t reason I did not even	Lk 7:7	1352
and I say to t one,	Lk 7:8	3778
to my slave, 'Do t!' and he does it.	Lk 7:8	3778
Now when Jesus heard t,	Lk 7:9	3778
T report concerning Him went out all	Lk 7:17	3778
"T is the one about whom it is	Lk 7:27	3778
and the tax collectors heard t,	Lk 7:29	3778
I compare the men of t generation,	Lk 7:31	3778
who had invited Him saw t,	Lk 7:39	3778
"If t man were a prophet He would	Lk 7:39	3778
t woman is who is touching Him,	Lk 7:39	3588
"Do you see t woman?	Lk 7:44	3778
"For t reason I say to you, her	Lk 7:47	3739
is t *man* who even forgives sins?"	Lk 7:49	3778
Him as to what t parable meant.	Lk 8:9	3778
"Now the parable is t:	Lk 8:11	3778
and riches and pleasures of t	Lk 8:14	3778
"Who then is t, that He commands	Lk 8:25	3778
But when Jesus heard t, He	Lk 8:50	3778
but who is t man about whom I hear	Lk 9:9	3778
were aware of t and followed Him;	Lk 9:11	3778
them not to tell t to anyone,	Lk 9:21	3778
While he was saying t,	Lk 9:34	3778
"T is My Son, *My* Chosen One;	Lk 9:35	3778
did not understand t statement,	Lk 9:45	3778
to ask Him about t statement.	Lk 9:45	3778
t child in My name receives Me,	Lk 9:48	3778
you, t is the one who is great."	Lk 9:48	3778
His disciples James and John saw t,	Lk 9:54	3778
Now after t the Lord appointed	Lk 10:1	3778
'Peace *be* to t house.'	Lk 10:5	3778
yet be sure of t, that the kingdom	Lk 10:11	3778
"Nevertheless do not rejoice in t,	Lk 10:20	3778
for t way was well-pleasing in Your	Lk 10:21	3779
DO T AND YOU WILL LIVE."	Lk 10:28	3778
"T generation is a wicked	Lk 11:29	3778
the Son of Man be to t generation.	Lk 11:30	3778
rise up with the men of t generation	Lk 11:31	3778
with t generation at the judgment	Lk 11:32	3778
"Teacher, when You say t,	Lk 11:45	3778
"For t reason also the wisdom of	Lk 11:49	3778
be charged against t generation,	Lk 11:50	3778
be charged against t generation.'	Lk 11:51	3778
'T is what I will do:	Lk 12:18	3778
T *very* night your soul is required	Lk 12:20	3778
"For t reason I say to you, do	Lk 12:22	3778
"But be sure of t, that if the	Lk 12:39	3778
You addressing t parable to us,	Lk 12:41	3778
do you not analyze t present time?	Lk 12:56	3778
because they suffered t *fate?*	Lk 13:2	3778
And He *began* telling t parable:	Lk 13:6	3778
on t fig tree without finding any.	Lk 13:7	3778
'Let it alone, sir, for t year too,	Lk 13:8	3778
"And t woman, a daughter of	Lk 13:16	3778
from t bond on the Sabbath day?"	Lk 13:16	3778
As He said t, all His	Lk 13:17	3778
And they could make no reply to t.	Lk 14:6	3778
'Give *your* place to t man,' and then	Lk 14:9	3778
at the table with Him heard t,	Lk 14:15	3778
back and reported t to his master.	Lk 14:21	3778
'T man began to build and was not	Lk 14:30	3778
"T man receives sinners and eats	Lk 15:2	3778
So He told them t parable,	Lk 15:3	3778
for t son of mine was dead and	Lk 15:24	3778
but when t son of yours came, who	Lk 15:30	3778
for t brother of yours was dead	Lk 15:32	3778
and t *manager* was reported to him	Lk 16:1	3778
'What is t I hear about you?	Lk 16:2	3778
for the sons of t age are more	Lk 16:8	3778
for I am in agony in t flame.'	Lk 16:24	3778
'And besides all t, between us and	Lk 16:26	3778
also come to t place of torment.'	Lk 16:28	3778
you would say to t mulberry tree,	Lk 17:6	3778
to God, except t foreigner?"	Lk 17:18	3778
and be rejected by t generation.	Lk 17:25	3778
yet because t widow bothers me, I	Lk 18:5	3778
And He also told t parable to	Lk 18:9	3778
"The Pharisee stood and was praying t	Lk 18:11	3778
or even like t tax collector.	Lk 18:11	3778
t man went to his house	Lk 18:14	3778
When Jesus heard t, He said to	Lk 18:22	3778
at t time and in the age to come,	Lk 18:30	3778
the meaning of t statement was hidden	Lk 18:34	3778
began to inquire what t was.	Lk 18:36	3778
salvation has come to t house,	Lk 19:9	3778
'Do business *with* t until I come	Lk 19:13	3778
not want t man to reign over us.'	Lk 19:14	3778
"If you had known in t day,	Lk 19:42	3778
one who gave You t authority?"	Lk 20:2	3778
to tell the people t parable:	Lk 20:9	3778
and t one also they wounded and	Lk 20:12	3778
saying, 'T is the heir; let us kill him	Lk 20:14	3778
"What then is t that is written:	Lk 20:17	3778
T BECAME THE CHIEF CORNER *stone*'?	Lk 20:17	3778
He spoke t parable against them.	Lk 20:19	3778
"The sons of t age marry and are	Lk 20:34	3778
t poor widow put in more than all	Lk 21:3	3778
the land and wrath to t people	Lk 21:23	3778
t generation will not pass away	Lk 21:32	3778
earnestly desired to eat t Passover	Lk 22:15	3778
t and share it among yourselves;	Lk 22:17	3778
"T is My body which is given for	Lk 22:19	3778
do t in remembrance of Me."	Lk 22:19	3778
"T cup which is poured out for	Lk 22:20	3778
be who was going to do t thing.	Lk 22:23	3778
"But *it is* not t way with you,	Lk 22:26	3779
that t which is written must be	Lk 22:37	3778
are willing, remove t cup from Me;	Lk 22:42	3778
and said, "Stop! No more of t."	Lk 22:51	3778

but t hour and the power of	Lk 22:53	3778
"T man was with Him too."	Lk 22:56	3778
"Certainly t man also was with	Lk 22:59	3778
"We found t man misleading our	Lk 23:2	3778
"I find no guilt in t man."	Lk 23:4	3778
Galilee even as far as t place."	Lk 23:5	5602
"You brought t man to me as one	Lk 23:14	3778
I have found no guilt in t man	Lk 23:14	3778
"Away with t man, and release for	Lk 23:18	3778
"Why, what evil has t man done?	Lk 23:22	3778
Himself if t is the Christ of God,	Lk 23:35	3778
"T IS THE KING OF THE JEWS."	Lk 23:38	3778
t man has done nothing wrong."	Lk 23:41	3778
Having said t, He breathed His	Lk 23:46	3778
"Certainly t man was innocent."	Lk 23:47	3778
who came together for t spectacle,	Lk 23:48	3778
t man went to Pilate and asked for	Lk 23:52	3778
While they were perplexed about t,	Lk 24:4	3778
Indeed, besides all t,	Lk 24:21	3778
And when He had said t,	Lk 24:40	3778
"T was He of whom I said,	Jn 1:15	3778
T is the testimony of John, when	Jn 1:19	3778
"T is He on behalf of whom I	Jn 1:30	3778
t is the One who baptizes in the	Jn 1:33	3778
that t is the Son of God."	Jn 1:34	3778
T beginning of *His* signs Jesus did	Jn 2:11	3778
After t He went down to Capernaum,	Jn 2:12	3778
"Destroy t temple, and in three	Jn 2:19	3778
forty-six years to build t temple,	Jn 2:20	3778
remembered that He said t;	Jn 2:22	3778
t man came to Jesus by night and	Jn 3:2	3778
"T is the judgment, that the Light	Jn 3:19	3778
So t joy of mine has been made	Jn 3:29	3778
His testimony has set his seal to t,	Jn 3:33	3778
Everyone who drinks of t water will	Jn 4:13	3778
"Sir, give me t water, so I will	Jn 4:15	3778
t you have said truly."	Jn 4:18	3778
fathers worshiped in t mountain,	Jn 4:20	3778
coming when neither in t mountain nor	Jn 4:21	3778
At t point His disciples came,	Jn 4:27	3778
t is not the Christ, is it?"	Jn 4:29	3778
"For in t *case* the saying is	Jn 4:37	3778
know that t One is indeed the Savior	Jn 4:42	3778
T is again a second sign that	Jn 4:54	3778
For t reason the Jews were	Jn 5:16	3778
For t reason therefore the Jews	Jn 5:18	3778
"Do not marvel at t;	Jn 5:28	3778
T He was saying to test him, for He	Jn 6:6	3778
"T is truly the Prophet who	Jn 6:14	3778
"T is the work of God, that you	Jn 6:29	3778
"Lord, always give us t bread."	Jn 6:34	3778
"T is the will of Him who sent Me,	Jn 6:39	3778
"For t is the will of My Father,	Jn 6:40	3778
"Is not t Jesus, the son of	Jn 6:42	3778
"T is the bread which comes down	Jn 6:50	3778
if anyone eats of t bread,	Jn 6:51	3778
t man give us *His* flesh to eat?"	Jn 6:52	3778
"T is the bread which came down	Jn 6:58	3778
eats t bread will live forever."	Jn 6:58	3778
when they heard t said, "This	Jn 6:60	3778
"T is a difficult statement;	Jn 6:60	3778
that His disciples grumbled at t,	Jn 6:61	3778
"Does t cause you to stumble?	Jn 6:61	3778
"For t reason I have said to you,	Jn 6:65	3778
As a result of t many of His	Jn 6:66	3778
I do not go up to t feast because	Jn 7:8	3778
"How has t man become learned,	Jn 7:15	3778
"For t reason Moses has given you	Jn 7:22	3778
"Is t not the man whom they are	Jn 7:25	3778
really know that t is the Christ,	Jn 7:26	3778
we know where t man is from;	Jn 7:27	3778
signs than those which t man has,	Jn 7:31	3778
"Where does t man intend to go	Jn 7:35	3778
"What is t statement that He	Jn 7:36	3778
But t He spoke of the Spirit, whom	Jn 7:39	3778
"T certainly is the Prophet."	Jn 7:40	3778
"T is the Christ."	Jn 7:41	3778
man spoken the way t man speaks."	Jn 7:46	3779
"But t crowd which does not	Jn 7:49	3778
t woman has been caught in	Jn 8:4	3778
They were saying t,	Jn 8:6	3778
you are of t world, I am not of	Jn 8:23	3778
this world, I am not of t world.	Jn 8:23	3778
t Abraham did not do.	Jn 8:40	3778
for t reason you do not hear *them,*	Jn 8:47	3778
who sinned, t man or his parents,	Jn 9:2	3778
"*It was* neither *that* t man sinned,	Jn 9:3	3778
When He had said t,	Jn 9:6	3778
"Is not t the one who used to sit	Jn 9:8	3778
Others were saying, "T is he,"	Jn 9:9	3778
"T man is not from God, because	Jn 9:16	3778
"Is t your son, who you say was	Jn 9:19	3778
"We know that t is our son, and	Jn 9:20	3778
His parents said t because they	Jn 9:22	3778
For t reason his parents said,	Jn 9:23	3778
we know that t man is a sinner."	Jn 9:24	3778
but as for t man, we do not know	Jn 9:29	3778
"If t man were not from God, He	Jn 9:33	3778
"For judgment I came into t world,	Jn 9:39	3778
T figure of speech Jesus spoke to	Jn 10:6	3778
sheep, which are not of t fold;	Jn 10:16	3778
"For t reason the Father loves	Jn 10:17	3778
T commandment I received from My	Jn 10:18	3778
John said about t man was true."	Jn 10:41	3778
But when Jesus heard t, He said,	Jn 11:4	3778
"T sickness is not to end	Jn 11:4	3778
after t He said to the disciples,	Jn 11:7	3778
he sees the light of t world.	Jn 11:9	3778
T He said, and after that He said	Jn 11:11	3778

Do you believe t?"	Jn 11:26	3778
When she had said t,	Jn 11:28	3778
"Could not t man, who opened the	Jn 11:37	3778
have kept t man also from dying?"	Jn 11:37	3778
by t time there will be a stench,	Jn 11:39	2235
t man is performing many signs.	Jn 11:47	3778
"If we let Him *go on* like t,	Jn 11:48	3779
Now he did not say t on his own	Jn 11:51	3778
"Why was t perfume not sold for	Jn 12:5	3778
Now he said t, not because he was	Jn 12:6	3778
For t reason also the people	Jn 12:18	3778
that He had performed t sign.	Jn 12:18	3778
and he who hates his life in t world	Jn 12:25	3778
'Father, save Me from t hour'?	Jn 12:27	3778
for t purpose I came to this hour.	Jn 12:27	3778
for this purpose I came to t hour.	Jn 12:27	3778
"T voice has not come for My	Jn 12:30	3778
"Now judgment is upon t world;	Jn 12:31	3778
the ruler of t world will be cast out.	Jn 12:31	3778
But He was saying t to indicate	Jn 12:33	3778
Who is t Son of Man?"	Jn 12:34	3778
T *was* to fulfill the word of	Jn 12:38	3778
For t reason they could not believe,	Jn 12:39	3778
out of t world to the Father,	Jn 13:1	3778
for t reason He said,	Jn 13:11	3778
When Jesus had said t,	Jn 13:21	3778
what purpose He had said t to him.	Jn 13:28	3778
"By t all men will know that you	Jn 13:35	3778
"My Father is glorified by t,	Jn 15:8	3778
"T is My commandment, that you	Jn 15:12	3778
"Greater love has no one than t,	Jn 15:13	3778
"T I command you, that you love	Jn 15:17	3778
because of t the world hates you.	Jn 15:19	
		1223, 3778
"But *they have done* t to fulfill	Jn 15:25	3778
ruler of t world has been judged.	Jn 16:11	3778
"What is t thing He is telling	Jn 16:17	3778
"What is t that He says,	Jn 16:18	3778
you deliberating together about t,	Jn 16:19	3778
by t we believe that You came from	Jn 16:30	3778
"T is eternal life, that they may	Jn 17:3	3778
not also *one* of t man's disciples,	Jn 18:17	3778
When He had said t,	Jn 18:22	3778
do you bring against t Man?"	Jn 18:29	3778
"If t Man were not an evildoer,	Jn 18:30	3778
saying t on your own initiative,	Jn 18:34	3778
"My kingdom is not of t world.	Jn 18:36	3778
If My kingdom were of t world,	Jn 18:36	3778
My kingdom is not of t realm."	Jn 18:36	1782
For t I have been born, and for	Jn 18:37	3778
for t I have come into the world,	Jn 18:37	3778
And when he had said t,	Jn 18:38	3778
"Not t Man, but Barabbas."	Jn 18:40	3778
Pilate heard t statement,	Jn 19:8	3778
for t reason he who delivered Me	Jn 19:11	3778
As a result of t Pilate made	Jn 19:12	3778
"If you release t Man, you are no	Jn 19:12	3778
many of the Jews read t inscription,	Jn 19:20	3778
t *was* to fulfill the Scripture:	Jn 19:24	3778
After t, Jesus, knowing that all	Jn 19:28	3778
When she had said t,	Jn 20:14	3778
And when He had said t,	Jn 20:20	3778
And when He had said t,	Jn 20:22	3778
which are not written in t book;	Jn 20:30	3778
He manifested *Himself* in t way.	Jn 21:1	3779
T is now the third time that Jesus	Jn 21:14	3778
Now t He said, signifying by what	Jn 21:19	3778
And when He had spoken t,	Jn 21:19	3778
"Lord, and what about t man?"	Jn 21:21	3778
Therefore t saying went out among	Jn 21:23	3778
T is the disciple who is	Jn 21:24	3778
is it at t time You are restoring	Ac 1:6	3778
T Jesus, who has been taken up	Ac 1:11	3778
At t time Peter stood up in	Ac 1:15	3778
his share in t ministry."	Ac 1:17	3778
(Now t man acquired a field with	Ac 1:18	3778
to occupy t ministry and	Ac 1:25	3778
And when t sound occurred, the	Ac 2:6	3778
"What does t mean?"	Ac 2:12	3778
Jerusalem, let t be known to you and	Ac 2:14	3778
but t is what was spoken of	Ac 2:16	3778
t *Man,* delivered over by the	Ac 2:23	3778
and his tomb is with us to t day.	Ac 2:29	3778
"T Jesus God raised up again, to	Ac 2:32	3778
t which you both see and hear.	Ac 2:33	3778
t Jesus whom you crucified."	Ac 2:36	3778
Now when they heard t, they were	Ac 2:37	3778
Be saved from t perverse generation!	Ac 2:40	3778
But when Peter saw t, he replied	Ac 3:12	3778
of Israel, why are you amazed at t,	Ac 3:12	3778
t man whom you see and know;	Ac 3:16	3778
has given him t perfect health	Ac 3:16	3778
in what name, have you done t?"	Ac 4:7	3778
to how t man has been made well,	Ac 4:9	3778
by t *name* this man stands here	Ac 4:10	3778
by this *name* t man stands here before	Ac 4:10	3778
no longer to any man in t name."	Ac 4:17	3778
on whom t miracle of healing had	Ac 4:22	3778
And when they heard t, they	Ac 4:24	3778
"For truly in t city there were	Ac 4:27	3778
conceived t deed in your heart?	Ac 5:4	3778
the whole message of t Life."	Ac 5:20	3778
Upon hearing t, they entered	Ac 5:21	3778
them as to what would come of t.	Ac 5:24	3778
to continue teaching in t name,"	Ac 5:28	3778
to bring t man's blood upon us."	Ac 5:28	3778
But when they heard t,	Ac 5:33	3778
"After t man, Judas of Galilee	Ac 5:37	3778
for if t plan or action is	Ac 5:38	3778

Now at **t** time while the disciples	**Ac 6:1**	3778
we may put in charge of **t** task.	**Ac 6:3**	3778
"**T** man incessantly speaks against	**Ac 6:13**	3778
speaks against **t** holy place and	**Ac 6:13**	3778
heard him say that **t** Nazarene,	**Ac 6:14**	3778
will destroy **t** place and alter the	**Ac 6:14**	3778
God had him move to **t** country in	**Ac 7:4**	3778
"But God spoke to **t** effect,	**Ac 7:6**	3779
COME OUT AND SERVE ME IN **T** PLACE.'	**Ac 7:7**	3778
was at **t** time that Moses was born;	**Ac 7:20**	3739
"At **t** remark, MOSES FLED AND	**Ac 7:29**	3778
"**T** Moses whom they disowned,	**Ac 7:35**	3778
"**T** man led them out, performing	**Ac 7:36**	3778
"**T** is the Moses who said to the	**Ac 7:37**	3778
"**T** is the one who was in the	**Ac 7:38**	3778
FOR **T** MOSES WHO LED US OUT OF THE	**Ac 7:40**	3778
Now when they heard **t**,	**Ac 7:54**	3778
do not hold **t** sin against them!"	**Ac 7:60**	3778
Having said **t**, he fell asleep.	**Ac 7:60**	3778
"**T** man is what is called the	**Ac 8:10**	3778
"Give **t** authority to me as well,	**Ac 8:19**	3778
no part or portion in **t** matter,	**Ac 8:21**	3778
repent of **t** wickedness of yours,	**Ac 8:22**	3778
(**T** is a desert *road.*)	**Ac 8:26**	3778
"Go up and join **t** chariot."	**Ac 8:29**	3778
which he was reading was **t**:	**Ac 8:32**	3778
of whom does the prophet say **t**?	**Ac 8:34**	3778
and beginning from **t** Scripture he	**Ac 8:35**	3778
have heard from many about **t** man,	**Ac 9:13**	3778
"Is **t** not he who in Jerusalem	**Ac 9:21**	3778
those who called on **t** name,	**Ac 9:21**	3778
that **t** *Jesus* is the Christ.	**Ac 9:22**	3778
t woman was abounding with deeds	**Ac 9:36**	3778
T happened three times,	**Ac 10:16**	3778
"Four days ago to **t** hour,	**Ac 10:30**	3778
t is the One who has been appointed	**Ac 10:42**	3778
"**T** happened three times,	**Ac 11:10**	3778
When they heard **t**,	**Ac 11:18**	3778
Now at **t** time some prophets came	**Ac 11:27**	3778
And **t** took place in the *reign* of	**Ac 11:28**	3748
And **t** they did, sending it in	**Ac 11:30**	3739
And when he realized **t**, he went	**Ac 12:12**	
T man summoned Barnabas and Saul	**Ac 13:7**	3778
"The God of **t** people Israel chose	**Ac 13:17**	3778
"From the descendants of **t** man,	**Ac 13:23**	3778
message of **t** salvation has been sent.	**Ac 13:26**	3778
that God has fulfilled **t** *promise*	**Ac 13:33**	3778
to decay, He has spoken in **t** way:	**Ac 13:34**	3779
When the Gentiles heard **t**,	**Ac 13:48**	
T man was listening to Paul as he	**Ac 14:9**	3778
and elders concerning **t** issue.	**Ac 15:2**	3778
together to look into **t** matter.	**Ac 15:6**	3778
"With **t** the words of the	**Ac 15:15**	3778
and they sent **t** letter by them,	**Ac 15:23**	
Paul wanted **t** man to go with him;	**Ac 16:3**	3778
staying in **t** city for some days.	**Ac 16:12**	3778
continued doing **t** for many days.	**Ac 16:18**	3778
"**T** Jesus whom I am proclaiming to	**Ac 17:3**	3778
t idle babbler wish to say?"	**Ac 17:18**	3778
"May we know what **t** new teaching	**Ac 17:19**	3778
found an altar with **t** inscription,	**Ac 17:23**	3739
in ignorance, **t** I proclaim to you.	**Ac 17:23**	3778
hear you again concerning **t**."	**Ac 17:32**	3778
I have many people in **t** city."	**Ac 18:10**	3778
"**T** man persuades men to worship	**Ac 18:13**	3778
T man had been instructed in the	**Ac 18:25**	3778
When they heard **t**,	**Ac 19:5**	
T took place for two years, so that	**Ac 19:10**	3778
Jewish chief priest, were doing **t**.	**Ac 19:14**	3778
T became known to all, both Jews	**Ac 19:17**	3778
depends upon **t** business.	**Ac 19:25**	3778
t Paul has persuaded and turned	**Ac 19:26**	3778
danger that **t** trade of ours fall into	**Ac 19:27**	3778
When they heard **t** and were filled	**Ac 19:28**	
"But if you want anything beyond **t**,	**Ac 19:39**	
and in **t** connection we will be	**Ac 19:40**	3739
for **t** disorderly gathering."	**Ac 19:40**	3778
After saying **t** he dismissed the	**Ac 19:41**	3778
"Therefore, I testify to you **t** day	**Ac 20:26**	4594
in **t** manner you must help the weak	**Ac 20:35**	3779
Now **t** man had four virgin	**Ac 21:9**	3778
"**T** is what the Holy Spirit says:	**Ac 21:11**	3592
'In **t** way the Jews at Jerusalem	**Ac 21:11**	3779
will bind the man who owns **t** belt	**Ac 21:11**	3778
When we had heard **t**,	**Ac 21:12**	3778
"Therefore do **t** that we tell you.	**Ac 21:23**	3778
T is the man who preaches to all	**Ac 21:28**	3778
people and the Law and **t** place;	**Ac 21:28**	3778
and has defiled **t** holy place."	**Ac 21:28**	3778
Cilicia, but brought up in **t** city,	**Ac 22:3**	3778
I persecuted **t** Way to the death,	**Ac 22:4**	3778
listened to him up to **t** statement,	**Ac 22:22**	3778
When the centurion heard **t**, he	**Ac 22:26**	
For **t** man is a Roman."	**Ac 22:26**	3778
"I acquired **t** citizenship with a	**Ac 22:28**	3778
before God up to **t** day."	**Ac 23:1**	3778
As he said **t**, there occurred a	**Ac 23:7**	3778
"We find nothing wrong with **t** man;	**Ac 23:9**	3778
more than forty who formed **t** plot.	**Ac 23:13**	3778
"Lead **t** young man to the	**Ac 23:17**	3778
asked me to lead **t** young man to you	**Ac 23:18**	3778
he wrote a letter having **t** form:	**Ac 23:25**	3778
"When **t** man was arrested by the	**Ac 23:27**	3778
being carried out for **t** nation,	**Ac 24:2**	3778
we acknowledge **t** in every way	**Ac 24:3**	
"For we have found **t** man a real	**Ac 24:5**	3778
you have been a judge to **t** nation,	**Ac 24:10**	3778
"But **t** I admit to you, that	**Ac 24:14**	3778
"In view of **t**, I also do my best	**Ac 24:16**	3778
other than for **t** one statement	**Ac 24:21**	3778
you see **t** man about whom all	**Ac 25:24**	3778
And for **t** hope, O King, I am being	**Ac 26:7**	3739
"And **t** is just what I did in	**Ac 26:10**	3739
for **t** purpose I have appeared to	**Ac 26:16**	3778
"For **t** reason *some* Jews seized me	**Ac 26:21**	3778
I stand to **t** day testifying both	**Ac 26:22**	3778
Paul was saying **t** in his defense,	**Ac 26:24**	3778
t has not been done in a corner.	**Ac 26:26**	3778
but also all who hear me **t** day,	**Ac 26:29**	4594
"**T** man is not doing anything	**Ac 26:31**	3778
"**T** man might have been set free	**Ac 26:32**	3778
they let down the sea anchor and in **t**	**Ac 27:17**	3779
and incurred **t** damage and loss.	**Ac 27:21**	3778
"For **t** very night an angel of the	**Ac 27:23**	3778
for **t** is for your preservation,	**Ac 27:34**	3778
Having said **t**, he took bread	**Ac 27:35**	3778
"Undoubtedly **t** man is a murderer,	**Ac 28:4**	3778
After **t** had happened, the rest	**Ac 28:9**	3778
"For **t** reason, therefore, I	**Ac 28:20**	3778
for I am wearing **t** chain for the	**Ac 28:20**	3778
for concerning **t** sect, it is known	**Ac 28:22**	3778
'GO TO **T** PEOPLE AND SAY	**Ac 28:26**	3778
HEART OF **T** PEOPLE HAS BECOME DULL,	**Ac 28:27**	3778
that **t** salvation of God has been	**Ac 28:28**	3778
For **t** reason God gave them over to	**Ro 1:26**	3778
But do you suppose **t**,	**Ro 2:3**	3778
T *was* to demonstrate His	**Ro 3:25**	
Is **t** blessing then on the	**Ro 4:9**	3778
For **t** reason *it is* by faith, in	**Ro 4:16**	3778
into **t** grace in which we stand;	**Ro 5:2**	3778
And not only **t**, but we also exult	**Ro 5:3**	
And not only **t**, but we also exult	**Ro 5:11**	
knowing **t**, that our old self was	**Ro 6:6**	3778
and **t** commandment, which was to	**Ro 7:10**	3778
me free from the body of **t** death?	**Ro 7:24**	3778
sufferings of **t** present time are not	**Ro 8:18**	3588
And not only **t**, but also we	**Ro 8:23**	
For **t** is the word of promise:	**Ro 9:9**	3778
"AT **T** TIME I WILL COME, AND SARAH	**Ro 9:9**	3778
And not only **t**, but there was	**Ro 9:10**	
"FOR **T** VERY PURPOSE I RAISED YOU	**Ro 9:17**	3778
"Why did you make me like **t**,"	**Ro 9:20**	3779
TO HEAR NOT, DOWN TO **T** VERY DAY."	**Ro 11:8**	4594
to be uninformed of **t** mystery	**Ro 11:25**	3778
"**T** IS MY COVENANT WITH THEM, WHEN	**Ro 11:27**	3778
do not be conformed to **t** world,	**Ro 12:2**	3778
because of **t** you also pay taxes,	**Ro 13:6**	3778
themselves to **t** very thing.	**Ro 13:6**	3778
For **t**, "YOU SHALL NOT COMMIT	**Ro 13:9**	3588
it is summed up in **t** saying,	**Ro 13:9**	3778
Do **t**, knowing the time, that	**Ro 13:11**	3778
For to **t** end Christ died and lived	**Ro 14:9**	3778
but rather determine **t**	**Ro 14:13**	3778
For he who in **t** *way* serves Christ	**Ro 14:18**	3778
For **t** reason I have often been	**Ro 15:22**	1352
Therefore, when I have finished **t**,	**Ro 15:28**	3778
put my seal on **t** fruit of theirs,	**Ro 15:28**	3778
I, Tertius, who write **t** letter,	**Ro 16:22**	3588
Now I mean **t**, that each one of you	**1Co 1:12**	3778
Where is the debater of **t** age?	**1Co 1:20**	3778
a wisdom, however, not of **t** age nor	**1Co 2:6**	3778
age nor of the rulers of **t** age,	**1Co 2:6**	3778
none of the rulers of **t** age has	**1Co 2:8**	3778
thinks that he is wise in **t** age,	**1Co 3:18**	3778
For the wisdom of **t** world is	**1Co 3:19**	3778
Let a man regard us in **t** manner,	**1Co 4:1**	3779
In **t** case, moreover, it is	**1Co 4:2**	5602
yet I am not by **t** acquitted;	**1Co 4:4**	3778
To **t** present hour we are both	**1Co 4:11**	3588
For **t** reason I have sent to you	**1Co 4:17**	3778
the one who had done **t** deed would	**1Co 5:2**	3778
judged him who has so committed **t**,	**1Co 5:3**	3778
the immoral people of **t** world,	**1Co 5:10**	3778
How much more matters of **t** life?	**1Co 6:3**	
dealing with matters of **t** life,	**1Co 6:4**	
I say **t** to your shame. *Is it*	**1Co 6:5**	
You do **t** even to *your*	**1Co 6:8**	3778
But **t** I say by way of concession,	**1Co 7:6**	3778
gift from God, one in **t** manner,	**1Co 7:7**	3779
each, in **t** manner let him walk.	**1Co 7:17**	3779
I think then that **t** is good in	**1Co 7:26**	3778
such will have trouble in **t** life,	**1Co 7:28**	3588
But **t** I say, brethren, the time	**1Co 7:29**	3778
form of **t** world is passing away.	**1Co 7:31**	3778
T I say for your own benefit; not to	**1Co 7:35**	3778
has decided **t** in his own heart,	**1Co 7:37**	3778
not all men have **t** knowledge;	**1Co 8:7**	3588
But take care that **t** liberty of	**1Co 8:9**	3778
to those who examine me is **t**:	**1Co 9:3**	3778
we did not use **t** right,	**1Co 9:12**	3778
For if I do **t** voluntarily, I have	**1Co 9:17**	3778
"**T** is meat sacrificed to idols,"	**1Co 10:28**	3778
But in giving **t** instruction, I do	**1Co 11:17**	3778
In **t** I will not praise you.	**1Co 11:22**	3778
"**T** is My body, which is for you;	**1Co 11:24**	3778
do **t** in remembrance of Me."	**1Co 11:24**	3778
"**T** cup is the new covenant in My	**1Co 11:25**	3778
do **t**, as often as you drink *it,* in	**1Co 11:25**	3778
you eat **t** bread and drink the cup,	**1Co 11:26**	3778
For **t** reason many among you are	**1Co 11:30**	3778
it is not for **t** reason any the	**1Co 12:15**	3778
it is not for **t** reason any the	**1Co 12:16**	3778
I WILL SPEAK TO **T** PEOPLE,	**1Co 14:21**	3778
But if anyone does not recognize **t**	**1Co 14:38**	
hoped in Christ in **t** life only,	**1Co 15:19**	3778
I speak **t** to your shame.	**1Co 15:34**	
Now I say **t**, brethren, that flesh	**1Co 15:50**	3778
For **t** perishable must put on the	**1Co 15:53**	3778
and **t** mortal must put on	**1Co 15:53**	3778
But when **t** perishable will have	**1Co 15:54**	3778
and **t** mortal will have put on	**1Co 15:54**	3778
For our proud confidence is **t**:	**2Co 1:12**	3778
In **t** confidence I intended at	**2Co 1:15**	3778
when I intended to do **t**,	**2Co 1:17**	3778
I determined **t** for my own sake,	**2Co 2:1**	3778
T is the very thing I wrote you, so	**2Co 2:3**	3778
t punishment which *was inflicted* by	**2Co 2:6**	3778
For to **t** end also I wrote, so that	**2Co 2:9**	3778
in **t** case has no glory because	**2Co 3:10**	3778
for until **t** very day at the	**2Co 3:14**	4594
to **t** day whenever Moses is read,	**2Co 3:15**	4594
since we have **t** ministry,	**2Co 4:1**	3778
in whose case the god of **t** world	**2Co 4:4**	3778
t treasure in earthen vessels,	**2Co 4:7**	3778
For indeed in **t** *house* we groan,	**2Co 5:2**	3778
For indeed while we are in **t** tent,	**2Co 5:4**	3588
us for **t** very purpose is God,	**2Co 5:5**	3778
controls us, having concluded **t**,	**2Co 5:14**	3778
yet now we know *Him in* **t** *way*	**2Co 5:16**	
what earnestness **t** very thing,	**2Co 7:11**	3778
this very thing, **t** godly sorrow,	**2Co 7:11**	3588
t reason we have been comforted.	**2Co 7:13**	3778
and **t**, not as we had expected,	**2Co 8:5**	
in you **t** gracious work as well.	**2Co 8:6**	3778
abound in **t** gracious work also.	**2Co 8:7**	3778
I am not speaking **t** as a command,	**2Co 8:8**	
I give *my* opinion in **t** matter,	**2Co 8:10**	3778
for **t** is to your advantage,	**2Co 8:10**	3778
begin a year ago not only to do **t**,	**2Co 8:10**	
For **t** is not for the ease of	**2Co 8:13**	
at **t** present time your abundance	**2Co 8:14**	3588
and not only **t**, but he has also	**2Co 8:19**	
travel with us in **t** gracious work,	**2Co 8:19**	3778
administration of **t** generous gift;	**2Co 8:20**	3778
about **t** ministry to the saints;	**2Co 9:1**	3588
may not be made empty in **t** case,	**2Co 9:3**	3778
be put to shame by **t** confidence.	**2Co 9:4**	3778
Now **t** *I say,* he who sows sparingly	**2Co 9:6**	3778
For the ministry of **t** service is	**2Co 9:12**	3778
Because of the proof given by **t**	**2Co 9:13**	3778
consider **t** again within himself,	**2Co 10:7**	3778
Let such a person consider **t**,	**2Co 10:11**	3778
you bear **t** beautifully.	**2Co 11:4**	
in every way we have made **t**	**2Co 11:6**	
t boasting of mine will not be	**2Co 11:10**	3778
in **t** confidence of boasting.	**2Co 11:17**	3778
but I refrain *from* **t**, so	**2Co 12:6**	
of the revelations, for **t** reason,	**2Co 12:7**	1352
Concerning **t** I implored the Lord	**2Co 12:8**	3778
Forgive me **t** wrong!	**2Co 12:13**	3778
Here for **t** third time I am ready	**2Co 12:14**	3778
All **t** time you have been thinking	**2Co 12:19**	3819
T is the third time I am coming to	**2Co 13:1**	3778
not recognize **t** about yourselves,	**2Co 13:5**	
t we also pray for, that you be	**2Co 13:9**	3778
For **t** reason I am writing these	**2Co 13:10**	3778
us from **t** present evil age,	**Ga 1:4**	3588
T is the only thing I want to find	**Ga 3:2**	3778
What I am saying is **t**:	**Ga 3:17**	3778
T is allegorically speaking,	**Ga 4:24**	3748
Now **t** Hagar is Mount Sinai in	**Ga 4:25**	3588
T persuasion *did* not *come* from Him	**Ga 5:8**	3588
a man sows, **t** he will also reap.	**Ga 6:7**	3778
And those who will walk by **t** rule,	**Ga 6:16**	3778
For **t** reason I too, having heard	**Eph 1:15**	3778
that is named, not only in **t** age but	**Eph 1:21**	3778
to the course of **t** world,	**Eph 2:2**	3778
For **t** reason I, Paul, the prisoner	**Eph 3:1**	3778
By referring to **t**,	**Eph 3:4**	3739
of all saints, **t** grace was given,	**Eph 3:8**	3778
T *was* in accordance with	**Eph 3:11**	
For **t** reason I bow my knees	**Eph 3:14**	3778
(Now **t** *expression,* "He ascended,"	**Eph 4:9**	3588
So **t** I say, and affirm together with	**Eph 4:17**	3778
you did not learn Christ in **t** way,	**Eph 4:20**	3779
For **t** you know with certainty,	**Eph 5:5**	3778
For **t** reason it says,	**Eph 5:14**	1352
FOR **T** REASON A MAN SHALL LEAVE HIS	**Eph 5:31**	3778
T mystery is great;	**Eph 5:32**	3778
in the Lord, for **t** is right.	**Eph 6:1**	3778
t he will receive back from the	**Eph 6:8**	3778
the world forces of **t** darkness,	**Eph 6:12**	3778
in the Spirit, and with **t** in view,	**Eph 6:18**	846
him to you for **t** very purpose,	**Eph 6:22**	3778
I am confident of **t** very thing,	**Php 1:6**	3778
me to feel **t** way about you all,	**Php 1:7**	3778
And **t** I pray, that your love may	**Php 1:9**	3778
and in **t** I rejoice. Yes, and I	**Php 1:18**	3778
for I know that **t** will turn out	**Php 1:19**	3778
t *will mean* fruitful labor for me;*	**Php 1:22**	3778
Convinced of **t**,	**Php 1:25**	3778
Have **t** attitude in yourselves	**Php 2:5**	3778
For **t** reason also, God highly	**Php 2:9**	1352
as are perfect, have **t** attitude;	**Php 3:15**	3778
in **t** way stand firm in the Lord, my	**Php 4:1**	3779
For **t** reason also, since the day	**Col 1:9**	3778
Of **t** *church* I was made a minister	**Col 1:25**	
of **t** mystery among the Gentiles,	**Col 1:27**	3778
For **t** purpose also I labor,	**Col 1:29**	3739
I say **t** so that no one will	**Col 2:4**	3778
for **t** is well-pleasing to the Lord.	**Col 3:20**	3778
him to you for **t** very purpose,	**Col 4:8**	3778

When **t** letter is read among you, Col 4:16 3588
write **t** greeting with my own hand. Col 4:18 3588
For **t** reason we also 1Th 2:13 3778
that we have been destined for **t**. 1Th 3:3 3778
For **t** reason, when I could endure 1Th 3:5 3778
for **t** reason, brethren, in all our 1Th 3:7 3778
For **t** is the will of God, your 1Th 4:3 3778
So, he who rejects **t** is not 1Th 4:8
For **t** we say to you by the word of 1Th 4:15 3778
for **t** is God's will for you in 1Th 5:18 3778
have **t** letter read to all the brethren. 1Th 5:27 3588
T *is* a plain indication of God's 2Th 1:5
To **t** end also we pray for you 2Th 1:11 3739
For **t** reason God will send 2Th 2:11 3778
It was for **t** He called you 2Th 2:14 3739
we do not have the right *to* **t**, 2Th 3:9
you, we used to give you **t** order: 2Th 3:10 3778
obey our instruction in **t** letter, 2Th 3:14 3588
write **t** greeting with my own hand, 2Th 3:17 3588
and **t** is a distinguishing mark in 2Th 3:17 3739
t is the way I write. 2Th 3:17 3779
Yet for **t** reason I found mercy, 1Tm 1:16 3778
T command I entrust to you, 1Tm 1:18 3778
T is good and acceptable in the 1Tm 2:3 3778
For **t** I was appointed a 1Tm 2:7 3739
it is for **t** we labor and strive, 1Tm 4:10 3778
for as you do **t** you will ensure 1Tm 4:16 3778
for **t** is acceptable in the sight 1Tm 5:4 3778
who are rich in **t** present world 1Tm 6:17 3588
For **t** reason I remind you to 2Tm 1:6 3739
For **t** reason I also suffer these 2Tm 1:12 3739
For **t** reason I endure all things 2Tm 2:10 3778
of God stands, having **t** seal, 2Tm 2:19 3778
But realize **t**, that in the last 2Tm 3:1 3778
having loved **t** present world, 2Tm 4:10 3588
For **t** reason I left you in Crete, Ti 1:5 3778
T testimony is true. Ti 1:13 3778
For **t** reason reprove them severely Ti 1:13 3739
T is a trustworthy statement; Ti 3:8 3588
For perhaps he was for **t** reason Phm 1:15 3778
am writing **t** with my own hand, Phm 1:19
For **t** reason we must pay much Heb 2:1 3778
I WAS ANGRY WITH **T** GENERATION, Heb 3:10 3778
and again in **t** *passage*, Heb 4:5 3778
by **t** time you ought to be teachers, Heb 5:12 3588
And **t** we will do, if God permits. Heb 6:3 3778
though we are speaking in **t** way. Heb 6:9 3779
T hope we have as an anchor of the Heb 6:19 3739
For **t** Melchizedek, king of Salem, Heb 7:1 3778
Now observe how great **t** man was Heb 7:4 3778
In **t** case mortal men receive Heb 7:8 5602
And **t** is clearer still, if another Heb 7:15
because **t** He did once for all when Heb 7:27 3778
point in what has been said *is* **t**: Heb 8:1
is necessary that **t** *high priest* also Heb 8:3 3778
"FOR **T** IS THE COVENANT THAT I Heb 8:10 3778
t is called the holy place. Heb 9:2 3748
The Holy Spirit *is* signifying **t**, Heb 9:8 3778
that is to say, not of **t** creation; Heb 9:11 3778
For **t** reason He is the Heb 9:15 3778
"**T** IS THE BLOOD OF THE COVENANT Heb 9:20 3778
once and after **t** *comes* judgment, Heb 9:27 3778
By **t** will we have been sanctified Heb 10:10 3739
"**T** IS THE COVENANT THAT I WILL Heb 10:16 3778
T *expression*, "Yet once more," Heb 12:27 3588
for by **t** some have entertained Heb 13:2 3778
do **t** with joy and not with grief, Heb 13:17 3778
t would be unprofitable for you. Heb 13:17 3778
I urge *you* all the more to do **t**, Heb 13:19 3778
bear with **t** word of exhortation, Heb 13:22 3588
T you know, my beloved brethren. Jas 1:19
t man will be blessed in what he Jas 1:25 3778
t man's religion is worthless. Jas 1:26 3778
sight of *our* God and Father is **t**: Jas 1:27 3778
not God choose the poor of **t** world Jas 2:5 3588
things ought not to be **t** way. Jas 3:10 3779
T wisdom is not that which comes Jas 3:15 3778
live and also do **t** or that." Jas 4:15 3778
In **t** you greatly rejoice, even 1Pe 1:6 3739
As to **t** salvation, the prophets 1Pe 1:10 3739
And **t** is the word which was 1Pe 1:25 3778
For **t** is contained in Scripture: 1Pe 2:6
T precious value, then, is for you 1Pe 2:7 3588
T BECAME THE VERY CORNER *stone*," 1Pe 2:7 3778
t *doom* they were also appointed. 1Pe 2:8 3739
For **t** *finds* favor, if for the sake 1Pe 2:19 3778
endure it, **t** *finds* favor with God. 1Pe 2:20 3778
have been called for **t** purpose, 1Pe 2:21 3778
For in **t** way in former times the 1Pe 3:5 3779
In *all* **t**, they are surprised 1Pe 4:4 3739
For the gospel has for **t** purpose 1Pe 4:6 3778
but is to glorify God in **t** name. 1Pe 4:16 3778
that **t** is the true grace of God. 1Pe 5:12 3778
Now for **t** very reason also, 2Pe 1:5 3778
for in **t** way the entrance into the 2Pe 1:11 3779
as I am in **t** *earthly* dwelling, 2Pe 1:13 3778
such an utterance as **t** was made to 2Pe 1:17
"**T** is My beloved Son with whom I 2Pe 1:17 3778
and we ourselves heard **t** utterance 2Pe 1:18 3778
But know **t** first of all, that no 2Pe 1:20 3778
is overcome, by **t** he is enslaved. 2Pe 2:19 3778
T is now, beloved, the second 2Pe 3:1 3778
Know **t** first of all, that in the 2Pe 3:3 3778
For when they maintain **t**, 2Pe 3:5 3778
let **t** one *fact* escape your notice, 2Pe 3:8 3778
are to be destroyed in **t** way, 2Pe 3:11 3779
beloved, knowing **t** beforehand, 2Pe 3:17
T is the message we have heard from 1Jn 1:5 3778
By **t** we know that we have come 1Jn 2:3 3778
By **t** we know that we are in Him: 1Jn 2:5 3778
from **t** we know that it is the last 1Jn 2:18 3606
T is the antichrist, the one who 1Jn 2:22 3778
T is the promise which He Himself 1Jn 2:25 3778
For **t** reason the world does not 1Jn 3:1 3778
And everyone who has **t** hope *fixed* 1Jn 3:3 3778
Son of God appeared for **t** purpose, 1Jn 3:8 3778
By **t** the children of God and the 1Jn 3:10 3778
For **t** is the message which you 1Jn 3:11 3778
We know love by **t**, that He laid 1Jn 3:16 3778
We will know by **t** that we are of 1Jn 3:19 3778
T is His commandment, that we 1Jn 3:23 3778
We know by **t** that He abides in us, 1Jn 3:24 3778
By **t** you know the Spirit of God: 1Jn 4:2 3778
t is the *spirit* of the 1Jn 4:3 3778
By **t** we know the spirit of truth 1Jn 4:6 3778
By **t** the love of God was 1Jn 4:9 3778
In **t** is love, not that we loved 1Jn 4:10 3778
By **t** we know that we abide in Him 1Jn 4:13 3778
By **t**, love is perfected with us, 1Jn 4:17 3778
He is, so also are we in **t** world. 1Jn 4:17 3778
t commandment we have from Him, 1Jn 4:21 3778
By **t** we know that we love the 1Jn 5:2 3778
For **t** is the love of God, that we 1Jn 5:3 3778
and **t** is the victory that has 1Jn 5:4 3778
T is the One who came by water and 1Jn 5:6 3778
for the testimony of God is **t**, 1Jn 5:9 3778
And the testimony is **t**, 1Jn 5:11 3778
life, and **t** life is in His Son. 1Jn 5:11 3778
T is the confidence which we have 1Jn 5:14 3778
that he should make request for **t**. 1Jn 5:16 1565
T is the true God and eternal 1Jn 5:20 3778
And **t** is love, that we walk 2Jn 1:6 3778
T is the commandment, just as you 2Jn 1:6 3778
T is the deceiver and the 2Jn 1:7 3778
you and does not bring **t** teaching, 2Jn 1:10 3778
I have no greater joy than **t**, 3Jn 1:4 3778
For **t** reason, if I come, I will 3Jn 1:10 3778
and not satisfied with **t**, 3Jn 1:10 3778
marked out for **t** condemnation, Jude 1:4 3778
seven golden lampstands, says **t**: Rv 2:1 3592
'But I have **t** against you, that Rv 2:4
'Yet **t** you do have, that you hate Rv 2:6 3778
and has come to life, says **t**: Rv 2:8 3592
the sharp two-edged sword says **t**: Rv 2:12 3592
are like burnished bronze, says **t**: Rv 2:18 3592
'But I have **t** against you, that Rv 2:20
who do not hold **t** teaching, Rv 2:24 3778
God and the seven stars, says **t**: Rv 3:1 3592
shuts and no one opens, says **t**: Rv 3:7 3592
of the creation of God, says **t**: Rv 3:14 3592
After **t** I saw four angels standing Rv 7:1 3778
"For **t** reason, they are before Rv 7:15 3778
And **t** is how I saw in the vision Rv 9:17 3779
he must be killed in **t** way. Rv 11:5 3779
"For **t** reason, rejoice, O heavens Rv 12:12 3778
"For **t** reason in one day her Rv 18:8 3778
T is the first resurrection. Rv 20:5 3778
T is the second death, the lake of Rv 20:14 3778
words of the prophecy of **t** book." Rv 22:7 3778
who heed the words of **t** book. Rv 22:9 3778
words of the prophecy of **t** book, Rv 22:10 3778
words of the prophecy of **t** book: Rv 22:18 3778
which are written in **t** book; Rv 22:18 3778
words of the book of **t** prophecy, Rv 22:19 3778
city, which are written in **t** book. Rv 22:19 3778

THISTLE

Thorn and **t** will grow on their altars; Hos 10:8 1863

THISTLES

thorns and **t** it shall grow for you; Gn 3:18 1863
was completely overgrown with **t**; Pr 24:31 7057
and **t** in its fortified cities; Is 34:13 2336
though **t** and thorns are with you Ezk 2:6 5621
thorn *bushes* nor figs from **t**, Mt 7:16 5146
but if it yields thorns and **t**, Heb 6:8 5146

THOMAS

T and Matthew the tax collector; Mt 10:3 2381
Bartholomew, and Matthew, and **T**, Mk 3:18 2381
and Matthew and **T**; Lk 6:15 2381
T, who is called Jn 11:16 2381
T said to Him, "Lord, we do not Jn 14:5 2381
But **T**, one of the twelve, called Jn 20:24 2381
were again inside, and **T** with them. Jn 20:26 2381
Then He said to **T**, Jn 20:27 2381
T answered and said to Him, Jn 20:28 2381
Simon Peter, and **T** called Didymus, Jn 21:2 2381
James and Andrew, Philip and **T**, Ac 1:13 2381

THONG

will not take a thread or a sandal **t** Gn 14:23 8288
and untie the **t** of His sandals. Mk 1:7 2438
fit to untie the **t** of His sandals; Lk 3:16 2438
the **t** of whose sandal I am not Jn 1:27 2438

THONGS

they stretched him out with **t**, Ac 22:25 2438

THORN

out and spreads to **t** bushes, Ex 22:6 6975
"The **t** bush which was in Lebanon 2Ki 14:9 2336
Lebanon, and trampled the **t** bush. 2Ki 14:9 2336
"The **t** bush which was in Lebanon 2Ch 25:18 2336
Lebanon and trampled the **t** bush. 2Ch 25:18 2336
Like a **t** *which* falls into the hand Pr 26:9 2336
crackling of **t** bushes under a pot, Ec 7:6 5518b
the cliffs, on all the **t** bushes and Is 7:19 5285
Instead of the **t** bush the cypress will Is 55:13 5285
a prickling brier or a painful **t** from Ezk 28:24 6975
T and thistle will grow on their Hos 10:8 6975
The most upright like a **t** hedge. Mi 7:4 4534
are not gathered from **t** *bushes* Mt 7:16 173
IN THE FLAME OF A BURNING **T** BUSH Ac 7:30 942
who appeared to him in the **t** bush. Ac 7:35 942
was given me a **t** in the flesh, 2Co 12:7 4647

THORNS

"Both **t** and thistles it shall Gn 3:18 6975
your eyes and as **t** in your sides, Nu 33:55 6796
on your sides and **t** in your eyes, Jos 23:13 6796
but they will become *as* **t** in your Jg 2:3
I will thrash your bodies with the **t** Jg 8:7 6975
t of the wilderness and briers, Jg 8:16 6975
them will be thrust away like **t**, 2Sa 23:6 6975
And take it to a *place of* **t**, Jb 5:5 6791
your pots can feel *the fire of* **t** He Ps 58:9 329
were extinguished as a fire of **t**; Ps 118:12 6975
the lazy is as a hedge of **t**, Pr 15:19 2312
T *and* snares are in the way of the Pr 22:5 6791
"Like a lily among the **t**, SS 2:2 2336
But briars and **t** will come up. Is 5:6 7898
silver, will become briars and **t**. Is 7:23 7898
all the land will be briars and **t**. Is 7:24 7898
go there for fear of briars and **t**; Is 7:25 7898
It consumes briars and **t**; Is 9:18 7898
burn and devour his **t** and his briars Is 10:17 7898
give Me briars *and* **t** in battle, Is 27:4 7898
which **t** *and* briars shall come up; Is 32:13 6975
t which are burned in the fire. Is 33:12 6975
T will come up in its fortified Is 34:13 5518b
ground, And do not sow among **t**. Jer 4:3 6975
have sown wheat and have reaped **t**, Jer 12:13 6975
though thistles and **t** are with you Ezk 2:6 5544
I will hedge up her way with **t**, Hos 2:6 5518b
T *will be* in their tents. Hos 9:6 2336
O Death, where are your **t**? Hos 13:14 1698
Like tangled **t**, And like those who Na 1:10 5518b
"Others fell among the **t**, Mt 13:7 173
the **t** came up and choked them out. Mt 13:7 173
on whom seed was sown among the **t**, Mt 13:22 173
And after twisting together a crown of **t**, Mt 27:29 173
"Other *seed* fell among the **t**, Mk 4:7 173
and the **t** came up and choked it, Mk 4:7 173
on whom seed was sown among the **t**, Mk 4:18 173
and after twisting a crown of **t**, Mk 15:17 174
For men do not gather figs from **t**, Lk 6:44 173
"Other *seed* fell among the **t**; Lk 8:7 173
and the **t** grew up with it and Lk 8:7 173
The *seed* which fell among the **t**, Lk 8:14 173
soldiers twisted together a crown of **t** Jn 19:2 173
crown of **t** and the purple robe. Jn 19:5 174
but if it yields **t** and thistles, Heb 6:8 173

THOROUGH

case by a more **t** investigation; Ac 23:15 199

THOROUGHLY

us make bricks and burn *them* **t**." Gn 11:3 8316
and search out and inquire **t**. Dt 13:14 3190
of it, then you shall inquire **t**. Dt 17:4 3190
The judges shall investigate **t** Dt 19:18 3190
his images they broke in pieces **t**, 2Ki 11:18 3190
Wash me **t** from my iniquity And Ps 51:2 7235a
"They will **t** glean as the vine Jer 6:9 5953b
he will **t** deal with it. Ezk 31:11 6213a
will **t** clear His threshing floor; Mt 3:12 1245b
to **t** clear His threshing floor, Lk 3:17 1245a
inquire somewhat more **t** about him. Ac 23:20 199
ON THE EARTH, **T** AND QUICKLY." Ro 9:28 4931

THOSE

he was the father of **t** who dwell Gn 4:20
all **t** who play the lyre and pipe. Gn 4:21
were on the earth in **t** days, Gn 6:4 1992a
T were the mighty men who *were* of Gn 6:4 1992a
T that entered, male and female of Gn 7:16
t that were with him in the ark. Gn 7:23
And I will bless **t** who bless you, Gn 12:3
But **t** who survived fled to the Gn 14:10
and He overthrew **t** cities, Gn 19:25 411
The gate of **t** who hate them." Gn 24:60
Cursed be **t** who curse you, And Gn 27:29
And blessed be **t** who bless you." Gn 27:29
and all **t** who followed the droves, Gn 32:19
buy grain among **t** who were coming, Gn 42:5
before all **t** who stood by him, Gn 45:1
for **t** of your households and as food Gn 47:24
join themselves to **t** who hate us, Ex 1:10
Now it came about in **t** days, Ex 2:11 1992a
about in *the course of* **t** many days Ex 2:23 1992a
t who rise up against You; Ex 15:7
truth, **t** who hate dishonest gain; Ex 18:21
generations of **t** who hate Me, Ex 20:5
to **t** who love Me and keep My Ex 20:6
"Thus they shall eat **t** things by Ex 29:33
All the skillful men among **t** Ex 36:8
The silver of **t** of the congregation Ex 38:25
over to **t** who were numbered, Ex 38:26
'By **t** who come near Me I will be Lv 10:3
these, among **t** which chew the cud, Lv 11:4
or among **t** which divide the hoof: Lv 11:4
fins and scales, **t** in the water, Lv 11:9
t which have above their feet Lv 11:21
take other stones and replace **t** Lv 14:42
t persons who do *so* shall be cut Lv 18:29
t who play the harlot after him, Lv 20:5
a male as **t** who lie with a woman, Lv 20:13
and **t** who are born in his house Lv 22:11 1992a
'**T** *that are* blind or fractured or Lv 22:22
besides **t** *of* the sabbaths of Lv 23:38
t who live as aliens with you. Lv 25:6
and **t** who hate you will rule over Lv 26:17
'As for **t** of you who may be left, Lv 26:36
'So **t** of you who may be left will Lv 26:39

"Now **t** who camp on the east side	**Nu 2:3**	
"**T** who camp next to him *shall be*	**Nu 2:5**	
"**T** who camp next to him *shall be*	**Nu 2:12**	
"**T** who camp next to him *shall be*	**Nu 2:27**	
and had the oversight of **t** who	**Nu 3:32**	
Now **t** who were to camp before the	**Nu 3:38**	
the ransom of **t** who are in excess	**Nu 3:48**	
money from **t** who were in excess,	**Nu 3:49**	
beyond **t** ransomed by the Levites;	**Nu 3:49**	
T men said to him, "*Though* we	**Nu 9:7**	1992a
And let **t** who hate You flee	**Nu 10:35**	
Now the people became like **t** who	**Nu 11:1**	
among **t** who had been registered,	**Nu 11:26**	
of **t** who had spied out the land,	**Nu 14:6**	
any of **t** who spurned Me see it.	**Nu 14:23**	
even **t** men who brought out the	**Nu 14:37**	
alive out of **t** men who went to spy	**Nu 14:38**	1992a
T who found him gathering wood	**Nu 15:33**	
But **t** who died by the plague were	**Nu 16:49**	
t who died on account of Korah.	**Nu 16:49**	
of **t** which they give to the LORD,	**Nu 18:12**	
T *were* the waters of Meribah,	**Nu 20:13**	1992a
Therefore **t** who use proverbs say,	**Nu 21:27**	
T who died by the plague were 24,000.	**Nu 25:9**	
and **t** who were numbered of them	**Nu 26:7**	
to **t** who were numbered of them,	**Nu 26:18**	
to **t** who were numbered of them,	**Nu 26:22**	
to **t** who were numbered of them,	**Nu 26:25**	
to **t** who were numbered of them,	**Nu 26:27**	
and **t** who were numbered of them	**Nu 26:34**	
to **t** who were numbered of them,	**Nu 26:37**	
and **t** who were numbered of them	**Nu 26:41**	
to **t** who were numbered of them,	**Nu 26:43**	
to **t** who were numbered of them,	**Nu 26:47**	
and **t** who were numbered of them	**Nu 26:50**	
These are **t** who were numbered of	**Nu 26:51**	
to **t** who were numbered of them.	**Nu 26:54**	
These are **t** who were numbered	**Nu 26:57**	
T who were numbered of them	**Nu 26:62**	
These are **t** who were numbered by	**Nu 26:63**	
not a man of **t** who were numbered	**Nu 26:64**	
he was not among the company of **t**	**Nu 27:3**	
portion of **t** who went out to war,	**Nu 31:36**	
until the entire generation of **t**	**Nu 32:13**	
t whom you let remain of them *will*	**Nu 33:55**	
These are **t** whom the LORD	**Nu 34:29**	
They married **t** from the families	**Nu 36:12**	
t which the LORD your God has	**Dt 4:19**	
with all **t** of us alive here today.	**Dt 5:3**	428
generations of **t** who hate Me,	**Dt 5:9**	
to **t** who love Me and keep My	**Dt 5:10**	
with **t** who love Him and keep His	**Dt 7:9**	
but repays **t** who hate Him to their	**Dt 7:10**	
until **t** who are left and hide	**Dt 7:20**	
these among **t** which chew the cud,	**Dt 14:7**	
t that divide the hoof in two:	**Dt 14:7**	
judge who is *in office* in **t** days,	**Dt 17:9**	1992a
from **t** who offer a sacrifice,	**Dt 18:3**	
detestable things of **t** nations.	**Dt 18:9**	1992a
"For **t** nations, which you shall	**Dt 18:14**	428
listen to **t** who practice	**Dt 18:14**	
who will be *in office* in **t** days.	**Dt 19:17**	1992a
"Among **t** nations you shall	**Dt 28:65**	1992a
seen, **t** great signs and wonders.	**Dt 29:3**	1992a
but both with **t** who stand here	**Dt 29:15**	
and with **t** who are not with	**Dt 29:15**	
and serve the gods of **t** nations;	**Dt 29:18**	1992a
enemies and on **t** who hate you,	**Dt 30:7**	
So I will make them jealous with **t**	**Dt 32:21**	
And I will repay **t** who hate Me.	**Dt 32:41**	
Shatter the loins of **t** who rise up	**Dt 33:11**	
against him, And **t** who hate him,	**Dt 33:11**	
And **t** are the ten thousands of	**Dt 33:17**	1992a
And **t** are the thousands of Manasseh."	**Dt 33:17**	1992a
and as soon as **t** who were pursuing	**Jos 2:7**	
and when **t** who carried the ark	**Jos 3:15**	
and **t** which were flowing down	**Jos 3:16**	
T twelve stones which they had taken	**Jos 4:20**	428
left of **t** who survived or escaped.	**Jos 8:22**	
than **t** whom the sons of Israel killed	**Jos 10:11**	
of the Philistines and all **t** *of*	**Jos 13:2**	
both **t** who are in Beth-shean and	**Jos 17:16**	
and **t** who are in the valley of	**Jos 17:16**	
t who went to describe the land,	**Jos 18:8**	
one who is high priest in **t** days.	**Jos 20:6**	1992a
the hands of **t** who plundered them.	**Jg 2:16**	
because of **t** who oppressed and	**Jg 2:18**	
LORD allowed **t** nations to remain,	**Jg 2:23**	428
t who had not experienced it	**Jg 3:2**	7534
"At the sound of **t** who divide	**Jg 5:11**	
"From Ephraim **t** whose root is in	**Jg 5:14**	
t who wield the staff of office.	**Jg 5:14**	
But let **t** who love Him be like the	**Jg 5:31**	
Now the number of **t** who lapped,	**Jg 7:6**	
Gideon went up by the way of **t** who	**Jg 8:11**	
chamber on fire over **t** *inside,*	**Jg 9:49**	
you are among **t** who trouble me;	**Jg 11:35**	
clothes to **t** who told the riddle.	**Jg 14:19**	
than **t** whom he killed in his life.	**Jg 16:30**	
In **t** days there was no king in	**Jg 17:6**	1992a
In **t** days there was no king of	**Jg 18:1**	1992a
and in **t** days the tribe of the	**Jg 18:1**	1992a
Now it came about in **t** days,	**Jg 19:1**	1992a
of God *was* there in **t** days,	**Jg 20:27**	1992a
before it to *minister* in **t** days),	**Jg 20:28**	1992a
while **t** who came out of the cities	**Jg 20:42**	
do for wives for **t** who are left,	**Jg 21:7**	1992a
do for wives for **t** who are left,	**Jg 21:16**	
to their number from **t** who danced,	**Jg 21:23**	
In **t** days there was no king in	**Jg 21:25**	1992a
it before **t** who are sitting *here,*	**Ru 4:4**	
"**T** who were full hire themselves	**1Sa 2:5**	
But **t** who were hungry cease *to*	**1Sa 2:5**	
"**T** who contend with the LORD will	**1Sa 2:10**	
for **t** who honor Me I will honor,	**1Sa 2:30**	
and **t** who despise Me will be	**1Sa 2:30**	
from the LORD was rare in **t** days,	**1Sa 3:1**	1992a
t who are invited will eat.	**1Sa 9:13**	
at the head of **t** who were invited,	**1Sa 9:22**	
t signs came about on that day.	**1Sa 10:9**	428
T who survived were scattered, so	**1Sa 11:11**	
the hands of **t** who plundered them.	**1Sa 14:48**	
t few sheep in the wilderness?	**1Sa 17:28**	2007
t who seek evil against my lord,	**1Sa 25:26**	
Now it came about in **t** days that	**1Sa 28:1**	1992a
Saul had removed from the land **t**	**1Sa 28:3**	
how he has cut off **t** who are	**1Sa 28:9**	
where **t** left behind remained.	**1Sa 30:9**	
wicked and worthless men among **t**	**1Sa 30:22**	
to **t** who were in Bethel, and to	**1Sa 30:27**	
and to **t** who were in Ramoth of the	**1Sa 30:27**	
and to **t** who were in Jattir,	**1Sa 30:27**	
and to **t** who were in Aroer, and to	**1Sa 30:28**	
and to **t** who were in Siphmoth,	**1Sa 30:28**	
and to **t** who were in Eshtemoa,	**1Sa 30:28**	
and to **t** who were in Racal, and to	**1Sa 30:29**	
and to **t** who were in the cities of	**1Sa 30:29**	
and to **t** who were in the cities of	**1Sa 30:29**	
and to **t** who were in Hormah, and	**1Sa 30:30**	
and to **t** who were in Bor-ashan,	**1Sa 30:30**	
and to **t** who were in Athach,	**1Sa 30:30**	
and to **t** who were in Hebron, and	**1Sa 30:31**	
with **t** who were beyond the Jordan,	**1Sa 31:7**	
Now these are the names of **t** who	**2Sa 5:14**	
which he gave in **t** days,	**2Sa 16:23**	1992a
t who are with him are valiant men.	**2Sa 17:10**	
all **t** who rose up against you."	**2Sa 18:31**	
by loving **t** who hate you, and by	**2Sa 19:6**	
you, and by hating **t** who love you.	**2Sa 19:6**	
among **t** who ate at your own table.	**2Sa 19:28**	
"I am of **t** who are peaceable *and*	**2Sa 20:19**	
bones of **t** who had been hanged.	**2Sa 21:13**	
strong enemy, From **t** who hated me,	**2Sa 22:18**	
under me **t** who rose up against me.	**2Sa 22:40**	
And I destroyed **t** who hated me.	**2Sa 22:41**	
me above **t** who rise up against me;	**2Sa 22:49**	
be among **t** who eat at your table;	**1Ki 2:7**	
the name of the LORD until **t** days.	**1Ki 3:2**	1992a
T deputies provided for King Solomon	**1Ki 4:27**	428
of **t** who have taken them captive,	**1Ki 8:47**	
t who have taken them captive,	**1Ki 8:50**	
for **t** who are with us are more	**2Ki 6:16**	
more than **t** who are with them."	**2Ki 6:16**	
Would you kill **t** you have taken	**2Ki 6:22**	
In **t** days the LORD began to cut	**2Ki 10:32**	1992a
with **t** who were to go out on the	**2Ki 11:9**	
the hands of **t** who did the work,	**2Ki 12:11**	
gave that to **t** who did the work,	**2Ki 12:14**	
to pay to **t** who did the work,	**2Ki 12:15**	
In **t** days the LORD began to send	**2Ki 15:37**	1992a
for until **t** days the sons of	**2Ki 18:4**	1992a
nor *among* **t** who were before him.	**2Ki 18:5**	
'Did the gods of **t** nations which	**2Ki 19:12**	
In **t** days Hezekiah became mortally	**2Ki 20:1**	1992a
people of the land killed all **t** who	**2Ki 21:24**	
also **t** who burned incense to Baal,	**2Ki 23:5**	
T are the Kenites who came from	**1Ch 2:55**	1992a
for **t** who lived there formerly	**1Ch 4:40**	
Now these are **t** whom David	**1Ch 6:31**	
are **t** who served with their sons:	**1Ch 6:33**	
and all **t** of his house died	**1Ch 10:6**	
they put to flight all **t** in the valleys,	**1Ch 12:15**	
Moreover **t** who were near to them,	**1Ch 12:40**	
Let the heart of **t** who seek the LORD	**1Ch 16:10**	
for **t** who should sound aloud,	**1Ch 16:42**	
households of **t** of them who were	**1Ch 23:24**	
well as **t** of his younger brother.	**1Ch 24:31**	
and the number of **t** who performed	**1Ch 25:1**	376
t twenty years of age and under,	**1Ch 27:23**	
or the life of **t** who hate you,	**2Ch 1:11**	
nor **t** who will come after you."	**2Ch 1:12**	
t of my lord David your father.	**2Ch 2:14**	2450
T from all the tribes of Israel who	**2Ch 11:16**	
at war with him during **t** years,	**2Ch 14:6**	428
and **t** who have no strength;	**2Ch 14:11**	
struck down **t** who owned livestock,	**2Ch 14:15**	
"In **t** times there was no	**2Ch 15:5**	1992a
and Benjamin and **t** from Ephraim,	**2Ch 15:9**	
t whose heart is completely His.	**2Ch 16:9**	
apart from **t** whom the king put in	**2Ch 17:19**	
t who hate the LORD and so *bring*	**2Ch 19:2**	
he appointed **t** who sang to the	**2Ch 20:21**	
and **t** who praised *Him* in holy attire,	**2Ch 20:21**	
with **t** who were to go out on the	**2Ch 23:8**	
king and Jehoiada gave it to **t** who	**2Ch 24:12**	
are **t** who conspired against him:	**2Ch 24:26**	
and he took a census of **t** from	**2Ch 25:5**	
arose against **t** who were coming	**2Ch 28:12**	
and all **t** who were willing *brought*	**2Ch 29:31**	
that He may return to **t** of you who	**2Ch 30:6**	
before **t** who led them captive and	**2Ch 30:9**	
of Israel and **t** living in Judah.	**2Ch 30:25**	
there among all the gods of **t** nations	**2Ch 32:14**	428
In **t** days Hezekiah became mortally	**2Ch 32:24**	1992a
of **t** who had sacrificed to them.	**2Ch 34:4**	
t who are left in Israel and in Judah,	**2Ch 34:21**	
So Hilkiah and **t** whom the king	**2Ch 34:22**	
T who had escaped from the sword he	**2Ch 36:20**	7611
All **t** about them encouraged	**Ezr 1:6**	
are **t** who came up from Tel-melah,	**Ezr 2:59**	
t elders and said to them thus,	**Ezr 5:9**	479
all **t** who had separated themselves	**Ezr 6:21**	
t who know the laws of your God;	**Ezr 7:25**	
genealogical enrollment of **t** who	**Ezr 8:1**	
disposed to all **t** who seek Him,	**Ezr 8:22**	
against all **t** who forsake Him."	**Ezr 8:22**	
t of the Canaanites,	**Ezr 9:1**	
t who tremble at the commandment	**Ezr 10:3**	
all **t** in our cities who have married	**Ezr 10:14**	
lovingkindness for **t** who love Him	**Ne 1:5**	
though **t** of you who have been	**Ne 1:9**	
T who were rebuilding the wall and	**Ne 4:17**	
t who carried burdens took *their* load	**Ne 4:17**	
For there were **t** who said,	**Ne 5:2**	
Also there were **t** who said,	**Ne 5:4**	
besides **t** who came to us from the	**Ne 5:17**	
Also in **t** days many letters went	**Ne 6:17**	1992a
found the book of the genealogy of **t**	**Ne 7:5**	
and women, **t** who could understand;	**Ne 8:3**	
The entire assembly of **t** who	**Ne 8:17**	
and all **t** who had separated	**Ne 10:28**	
all **t** who had knowledge and	**Ne 10:28**	
In **t** days I saw in Judah some who	**Ne 13:15**	1992a
In **t** days I also saw that the Jews	**Ne 13:23**	1992a
in **t** days as King Ahasuerus sat on	**Es 1:2**	1992a
In **t** days, while Mordecai was	**Es 2:21**	1992a
from **t** who guarded the door,	**Es 2:21**	
their laws are different from **t**	**Es 3:8**	
of **t** who carry on the *king's* business,	**Es 3:9**	
the mastery over **t** who hated them.	**Es 9:1**	
hands on **t** who sought their harm;	**Es 9:2**	
and **t** who were doing the king's	**Es 9:3**	
they pleased to **t** who hated them.	**Es 9:5**	
On that day the number of **t** who	**Es 9:11**	
kill 75,000 of **t** who hated them;	**Es 9:16**	
because on **t** days the Jews rid	**Es 9:22**	
and for all **t** who allied	**Es 9:27**	
"Let **t** curse it who curse the	**Jb 3:8**	
t who plow iniquity And those who	**Jb 4:8**	
And **t** who sow trouble harvest it.	**Jb 4:8**	
t who dwell in houses of clay,	**Jb 4:19**	
He sets on high **t** who are lowly,	**Jb 5:11**	
And **t** who mourn are lifted to	**Jb 5:11**	
"**T** who hate you will be clothed	**Jb 8:22**	
As prepared for **t** whose feet slip.	**Jb 12:5**	
And **t** who provoke God are secure,	**Jb 12:6**	
"**T** in the west are appalled at	**Jb 18:20**	
And **t** in the east are seized with	**Jb 18:20**	
"**T** who live in my house and my	**Jb 19:15**	
t I love have turned against me.	**Jb 19:19**	2088
T who have seen him will say,	**Jb 20:7**	
In that He judges **t** on high?	**Jb 21:22**	
t who know Him not see His days?	**Jb 24:1**	
t who rebel against the light;	**Jb 24:13**	
So does Sheol **t** *who* have	**Jb 24:19**	
"But now **t** younger than I mock	**Jb 30:1**	6810
"Fools, even **t** without a name,	**Jb 30:8**	1121
flute to the sound of **t** who weep.	**Jb 30:31**	
disaster to **t** who work iniquity?	**Jb 31:3**	
And his life to **t** who bring death.	**Jb 33:22**	
destroy **t** who speak falsehood;	**Ps 5:6**	
That **t** who love Your name may exult	**Ps 5:11**	
Save me from all **t** who pursue me,	**Ps 7:1**	
And **t** who know Your name will put	**Ps 9:10**	
have not forsaken **t** who seek You.	**Ps 9:10**	
my affliction from **t** who hate me,	**Ps 9:13**	
who honors **t** who fear the LORD;	**Ps 15:4**	
The sorrows of **t** who have bartered	**Ps 16:4**	
O Savior of **t** who take refuge at	**Ps 17:7**	
From **t** who rise up *against them.*	**Ps 17:7**	
enemy, And from **t** who hated me,	**Ps 18:17**	
under me **t** who rose up against me.	**Ps 18:39**	
And I destroyed **t** who hated me.	**Ps 18:40**	
me above **t** who rise up against me;	**Ps 18:48**	
hand will find out **t** who hate you.	**Ps 21:8**	
pay my vows before **t** who fear Him.	**Ps 22:25**	
T who seek Him will praise the	**Ps 22:26**	
All **t** who go down to the dust will	**Ps 22:29**	
The world, and **t** who dwell in it.	**Ps 24:1**	
the generation of **t** who seek Him,	**Ps 24:6**	
none of **t** who wait for You will	**Ps 25:3**	
T who deal treacherously without	**Ps 25:3**	
To **t** who keep His covenant and His	**Ps 25:10**	
of the LORD is for **t** who fear Him,	**Ps 25:14**	
like **t** who go down to the pit.	**Ps 28:1**	
And with **t** who work iniquity,	**Ps 28:3**	
I hate **t** who regard vain idols,	**Ps 31:6**	
T who see me in the street flee	**Ps 31:11**	
and from **t** who persecute me.	**Ps 31:15**	
stored up for **t** who fear You,	**Ps 31:19**	
for **t** who take refuge in You,	**Ps 31:19**	
of the LORD is on **t** who fear Him,	**Ps 33:18**	
On **t** who hope for His	**Ps 33:18**	
encamps around **t** who fear Him,	**Ps 34:7**	
For to **t** who fear Him there is no	**Ps 34:9**	
saves **t** who are crushed in spirit.	**Ps 34:18**	
And **t** who hate the righteous will	**Ps 34:21**	
And none of **t** who take refuge in	**Ps 34:22**	
LORD, with **t** who contend with me;	**Ps 35:1**	
against **t** who fight against me.	**Ps 35:1**	
battle-axe to meet **t** who pursue me;	**Ps 35:3**	
Let **t** be ashamed and dishonored	**Ps 35:4**	
Let **t** be turned back and	**Ps 35:4**	
Do not let **t** who are wrongfully my	**Ps 35:19**	
Nor let **t** who hate me without	**Ps 35:19**	
t who are quiet in the land.	**Ps 35:20**	
Let **t** be ashamed and humiliated	**Ps 35:26**	

Let **t** be clothed with shame and	Ps 35:26	
lovingkindness to **t** who know You,	Ps 36:10	
off, But **t** who wait for the LORD,	Ps 37:9	
slay **t** who are upright in conduct.	Ps 37:14	
For **t** blessed by Him will inherit	Ps 37:22	
t cursed by Him will be cut off.	Ps 37:22	
T who seek my life lay snares *for*	Ps 38:12	
And **t** who seek to injure me have	Ps 38:12	
many are **t** who hate me wrongfully.	Ps 38:19	
And **t** who repay evil for good,	Ps 38:20	
nor to **t** who lapse into falsehood.	Ps 40:4	
Let **t** be ashamed and humiliated	Ps 40:14	
Let **t** be turned back and	Ps 40:14	
Let **t** be appalled because of their	Ps 40:15	
Let **t** who love Your salvation say	Ps 40:16	
down **t** who rise up against us.	Ps 44:5	
have put to shame **t** who hate us.	Ps 44:7	
And **t** who hate us have taken spoil	Ps 44:10	
and a derision to **t** around us.	Ps 44:13	
Even **t** who trust in their wealth And	Ps 49:6	
is the way of **t** who are foolish,	Ps 49:13	
And of **t** after them who approve	Ps 49:13	
T who have made a covenant with Me	Ps 50:5	
t who were at peace with him;	Ps 55:20	
among **t** who breathe forth fire,	Ps 57:4	
from **t** who rise up against me.	Ps 59:1	
Deliver me from **t** who do iniquity And	Ps 59:2	
given a banner to **t** who fear You,	Ps 60:4	
of **t** who fear Your name.	Ps 61:5	
But **t** who seek my life to destroy	Ps 63:9	1992a
For the mouths of **t** who speak lies	Ps 63:11	
the tumult of **t** who do iniquity,	Ps 64:2	
t who hate Him flee before Him.	Ps 68:1	
T who hate me without a cause are	Ps 69:4	
T who would destroy me are	Ps 69:4	
May **t** who wait for You not be	Ps 69:6	
May **t** who seek You not be	Ps 69:6	
reproaches of **t** who reproach You	Ps 69:9	
T who sit in the gate talk about	Ps 69:12	
pain of **t** whom You have wounded.	Ps 69:26	
And **t** who love His name will dwell	Ps 69:36	
Let **t** be ashamed and humiliated	Ps 70:2	
Let **t** be turned back and	Ps 70:2	
Let **t** be turned back because of	Ps 70:3	
And let **t** who love Your salvation	Ps 70:4	
And **t** who watch for my life have	Ps 71:10	
Let **t** who are adversaries of my	Ps 71:13	
And may **t** from the city flourish	Ps 72:16	
To **t** who are pure in heart!	Ps 73:1	
t who are far from You will	Ps 73:27	
all **t** who are unfaithful to You.	Ps 73:27	
The uproar of **t** who rise against	Ps 74:23	
and derision to **t** around us.	Ps 79:4	
preserve **t** who are doomed to die.	Ps 79:11	1121
"**T** who hate the LORD would	Ps 81:15	
And **t** who hate You have exalted	Ps 83:2	
are **t** who dwell in Your house!	Ps 84:4	
from **t** who walk uprightly.	Ps 84:11	
is near to **t** who fear Him,	Ps 85:9	
That **t** who hate me may see *it* and	Ps 86:17	
and Babylon among **t** who know Me;	Ps 87:4	
Then **t** who sing as well as those	Ps 87:7	
t who play the flutes *shall say,*	Ps 87:7	
among **t** who go down to the pit;	Ps 88:4	
above all **t** who are around Him?	Ps 89:7	
him, And strike **t** who hate him.	Ps 89:23	
me against **t** who do wickedness?	Ps 94:16	
Let all **t** be ashamed who serve	Ps 97:7	
The world and **t** who dwell in it.	Ps 98:7	
among **t** who called on His name;	Ps 99:6	
hate the work of **t** who fall away;	Ps 101:3	7846
of the LORD all **t** who do iniquity.	Ps 101:8	
T who deride me have used my *name*	Ps 102:8	
free **t** who were doomed to death,	Ps 102:20	1121
toward **t** who fear Him.	Ps 103:11	
has compassion on **t** who fear Him.	Ps 103:13	
to everlasting on **t** who fear Him,	Ps 103:17	
To **t** who keep His covenant And	Ps 103:18	
of **t** who seek the LORD be glad.	Ps 105:3	
blessed are **t** who keep justice,	Ps 106:3	
And **t** who hated them ruled over	Ps 106:41	1992a
There were **t** who dwelt in darkness	Ps 107:10	
T who go down to the sea in ships,	Ps 107:23	
wickedness of **t** who dwell in it.	Ps 107:34	
And of **t** who speak evil against my	Ps 109:20	
him from **t** who judge his soul.	Ps 109:31	
has given food to **t** who fear Him;	Ps 111:5	
all **t** who do *His commandments;*	Ps 111:10	
T who make them will become like	Ps 115:8	
He will bless **t** who fear the LORD,	Ps 115:13	
Oh let **t** who fear the LORD say,	Ps 118:4	
is for me among **t** who help me;	Ps 118:7	
satisfaction on **t** who hate me.	Ps 118:7	
are **t** whose way is blameless,	Ps 119:1	
are **t** who observe His testimonies,	Ps 119:2	
companion of all **t** who fear You,	Ps 119:63	
And of **t** who keep Your precepts.	Ps 119:63	
May **t** who fear You see me and be	Ps 119:74	
May **t** who fear You turn to me,	Ps 119:79	
Even **t** who know Your testimonies.	Ps 119:79	
judgment on **t** who persecute me?	Ps 119:84	
I hate **t** who are double-minded,	Ps 119:113	
t who wander from Your statutes,	Ps 119:118	
manner with **t** who love Your name.	Ps 119:132	
T who follow after wickedness draw	Ps 119:150	
T who love Your law have great	Ps 119:165	
dwelling With **t** who hate peace.	Ps 120:6	
the scoffing of **t** who are at ease,	Ps 123:4	
T who trust in the LORD Are as	Ps 125:1	
good, O LORD, to **t** who are good And	Ps 125:4	
And to **t** who are upright in their	Ps 125:4	
But as for **t** who turn aside to	Ps 125:5	
of Zion, We were like **t** who dream.	Ps 126:1	
T who sow in tears shall reap with	Ps 126:5	
Nor do **t** who pass by say,	Ps 129:8	
T who make them will be like them,	Ps 135:18	
Do I not hate **t** who hate You, O	Ps 139:21	
loathe **t** who rise up against You?	Ps 139:21	
for the head of **t** who surround me,	Ps 140:9	
the snares of **t** who do iniquity.	Ps 141:9	
like **t** who have long been dead.	Ps 143:3	
like **t** who go down to the pit.	Ps 143:7	
destroy all **t** who afflict my soul,	Ps 143:12	
the desire of **t** who fear Him;	Ps 145:19	
raises up **t** who are bowed down;	Ps 146:8	
The LORD favors **t** who fear Him,	Ps 147:11	
T who wait for His lovingkindness.	Ps 147:11	
as **t** who go down to the pit;	Pr 1:12	
shield to **t** who walk in integrity,	Pr 2:7	
From **t** who leave the paths of	Pr 2:13	
of life to **t** who take hold of her,	Pr 3:18	
good from **t** to whom it is due,	Pr 3:27	
they are life to **t** who find them And	Pr 4:22	
And right to **t** who find knowledge.	Pr 8:9	
"I love **t** who love me;	Pr 8:17	
And **t** who diligently seek me will	Pr 8:17	
endow **t** who love me with wealth,	Pr 8:21	
All **t** who hate me love death."	Pr 8:36	
Calling to **t** who pass by, Who are	Pr 9:15	
is the lazy one to **t** who send him.	Pr 10:26	
in the heart of **t** who devise evil,	Pr 12:20	
But **t** who deal faithfully are His	Pr 12:22	
wisdom is with **t** who receive counsel.	Pr 13:10	
But **t** who love the rich are many.	Pr 14:20	
will be to **t** who devise good.	Pr 14:22	
And **t** who love it will eat its	Pr 18:21	
take the life of **t** who rob them.	Pr 22:23	
not be among **t** who give pledges,	Pr 22:26	
t who become guarantors for debts.	Pr 22:26	
T who linger long over wine, Those	Pr 23:30	
T who go to taste mixed wine.	Pr 23:30	
Deliver **t** who are being taken away	Pr 24:11	
And **t** who are staggering to	Pr 24:11	
with **t** who are given to change,	Pr 24:21	
But to **t** who rebuke the *wicked*	Pr 24:25	
messenger to **t** who send him,	Pr 25:13	
a fool or who hires **t** who pass by.	Pr 26:10	
A lying tongue hates **t** it crushes,	Pr 26:28	
T who forsake the law praise the	Pr 28:4	
But **t** who keep the law strive with	Pr 28:4	
But **t** who seek the LORD understand	Pr 28:5	
to **t** who take refuge in Him.	Pr 30:5	
Among **t** who will come later *still.*	Ec 1:11	
t who consume them increase.	Ec 5:11	
When **t** riches were lost through a	Ec 5:14	1931
an advantage to **t** who see the sun.	Ec 7:11	
not deliver **t** who practice it.	Ec 8:8	
t who used to go in and out from	Ec 8:10	
will be well for **t** who fear God,	Ec 8:12	
and **t** who look through windows	Ec 12:3	
the lips of **t** who fall asleep.	SS 7:9	
t who take care of its fruit."	SS 8:12	
And **t** who forsake the LORD will	Is 1:28	
T who guide you lead *you* astray And	Is 3:12	
Woe to **t** who add house to house	Is 5:8	
Woe to **t** who rise early in the	Is 5:11	
Woe to **t** who drag iniquity with	Is 5:18	
Woe to **t** who call evil good, and	Is 5:20	
Woe to **t** who are wise in their own	Is 5:21	
Woe to **t** who are heroes in	Is 5:22	
T who live in a dark land, The	Is 9:2	
For **t** who guide this people are	Is 9:16	
And **t** who are guided by them are	Is 9:16	
Woe to **t** who enact evil statutes And	Is 10:1	
And to **t** who constantly record	Is 10:1	
than **t** of Jerusalem and Samaria,	Is 10:10	
a club wielding **t** who lift it,	Is 10:15	
and **t** of the house of Jacob who	Is 10:20	
T also who are tall in stature	Is 10:33	
t who are lofty will be abased.	Is 10:33	
And **t** who harass Judah will be cut	Is 11:13	
"**T** who see you will gaze at you,	Is 14:16	
"**T** who are most helpless will eat,	Is 14:30	
As **t** who are utterly stricken.	Is 16:7	
the portion of **t** who plunder us And	Is 17:14	
And the lot of **t** who pillage us.	Is 17:14	
And all **t** who cast a line into the	Is 19:8	
And **t** who spread nets on the	Is 19:8	
T *who are* the cornerstone of her	Is 19:13	
for **t** who dwell in the presence of	Is 23:18	
and **t** who live in it are held	Is 24:6	
drink is bitter to **t** who drink it.	Is 24:9	
brought low **t** who dwell on high,	Is 26:5	
and **t** who were perishing in the	Is 27:13	
Of **t** who are overcome with wine!	Is 28:1	
A strength to **t** who repel the	Is 28:6	
T *just* weaned from milk?	Is 28:9	
T *just* taken from the breast?	Is 28:9	
Woe to **t** who deeply hide their	Is 29:15	
"**T** who err in mind will know	Is 29:24	
And **t** who criticize will accept	Is 29:24	
t who pursue you shall be swift.	Is 30:16	
are all **t** who long for Him.	Is 30:18	
t who go down to Egypt for help	Is 31:1	
eyes of **t** who see will not be blinded	Is 32:3	
ears of **t** who hear will listen.	Is 32:3	
Say to **t** with anxious heart,	Is 35:4	
'Did the gods of **t** nations which	Is 37:12	
In **t** days Hezekiah became mortally	Is 38:1	1992a
T who go down to the pit cannot	Is 38:18	
Yet **t** who wait for the LORD Will	Is 40:31	
all **t** who are angered at you will	Is 41:11	
T who contend with you will be as	Is 41:11	376
will seek **t** who quarrel with you,	Is 41:12	376
T who war with you will be as	Is 41:12	376
And spirit to **t** who walk in it,	Is 42:5	
And **t** who dwell in darkness from	Is 42:7	
islands, and **t** who dwell on them.	Is 42:10	
T who fashion a graven image are	Is 44:9	
"**T** who lavish gold from the purse	Is 46:6	
T who prophesy by the stars,	Is 47:13	
T who predict by the new moons,	Is 47:13	
"So have **t** become to you with	Is 47:15	
Saying to **t** who are bound,	Is 49:9	
forth,' To **t** who are in darkness,	Is 49:9	
And **t** who swallowed you will be	Is 49:19	
T who hopefully wait for Me will	Is 49:23	
I gave My back to **t** who strike *Me,*	Is 50:6	
to **t** who pluck out the beard;	Is 50:6	
street for **t** who walk over *it.*"	Is 51:23	
"**T** who rule over them howl, and	Is 52:5	
Even **t** I will bring to My holy	Is 56:7	
to them, to **t** *already* gathered."	Is 56:8	
And the breath *of* **t** *whom* I have	Is 57:16	
"**T** from among you will rebuild	Is 58:12	
We grope like **t** who have no eyes;	Is 59:10	
Among **t** who are vigorous *we are*	Is 59:10	
And to **t** who turn from	Is 59:20	
All **t** from Sheba will come;	Is 60:6	
"The sons of **t** who afflicted	Is 60:14	
And all **t** who despised you will	Is 60:14	
To grant **t** who mourn *in* Zion,	Is 61:3	
But **t** who garner it will eat it and	Is 62:9	
And **t** who gather it will drink it	Is 62:9	
We have become *like* **t** over whom	Is 63:19	
Like **t** who were not called by Your	Is 63:19	
by **t** who did not ask *for Me;*	Is 65:1	
be found by **t** who did not seek Me.	Is 65:1	
offspring of **t** blessed by the LORD,	Is 65:23	
And **t** slain by the LORD will be	Is 66:16	
"**T** who sanctify and purify	Is 66:17	
And **t** who handle the law did not	Jer 2:8	
has rejected **t** in whom you trust,	Jer 2:37	
"It shall be in **t** days when	Jer 3:16	1992a
"In **t** days the house of Judah	Jer 3:18	1992a
And sworn by **t** who are not gods.	Jer 5:7	
"Yet even in **t** days,"	Jer 5:18	1992a
they shall fall among **t** who fall;	Jer 6:15	
they shall fall among **t** who fall;	Jer 8:12	
and all **t** inhabiting the desert	Jer 9:26	
t who deal in treachery at ease?	Jer 12:1	
wickedness of **t** who dwell in it,	Jer 12:4	
and see **T** coming from the north.	Jer 13:20	
t prophets shall meet their end!	Jer 14:15	1992a
Behold, **t** slain with the sword!	Jer 14:18	
T *destined* for death, to death;	Jer 15:2	
And **t** *destined* for the sword, to	Jer 15:2	
And **t** *destined* for famine, to	Jer 15:2	
And **t** *destined* for captivity, to	Jer 15:2	
T who turn away on earth will be	Jer 17:13	
Let **t** who persecute me be put to	Jer 17:18	
the hand of **t** who seek their life;	Jer 19:7	
t who seek their life will distress	Jer 19:9	
even **t** who survive in this city	Jer 21:7	
hand of **t** who seek their lives;	Jer 21:7	
hand of **t** who are seeking your life,	Jer 22:25	
into the hand of **t** whom you dread,	Jer 22:25	
keep saying to **t** who despise Me,	Jer 23:17	
I am against **t** who have prophesied	Jer 23:32	
shout like **t** who tread *the grapes,*	Jer 25:30	
"**T** slain by the LORD on that day	Jer 25:33	
similar to all **t** of Jeremiah.	Jer 26:20	
And **t** who plunder you will be for	Jer 30:16	
And the voice of **t** who celebrate;	Jer 30:19	
"In **t** days they will not say	Jer 31:29	1992a
house of Israel after **t** days,"	Jer 31:33	1992a
the bride, the voice of **t** who say,	Jer 33:11	
and of **t** who bring a thank	Jer 33:11	
'In **t** days and at that time I will	Jer 33:15	1992a
'In **t** days Judah will be saved	Jer 33:16	1992a
the hand of **t** who seek their life.	Jer 34:20	
the hand of **t** who seek their life,	Jer 34:21	
and **t** women will say,	Jer 38:22	1992a
t of the poorest of the land who	Jer 40:7	
t who are *meant* for death *will be*	Jer 43:11	
and **t** for captivity to captivity,	Jer 43:11	
and **t** for the sword to the sword.	Jer 43:11	
t who were living in Migdol,	Jer 44:1	
t who live in the land of Egypt,	Jer 44:13	
'**T** who escape the sword will return	Jer 44:28	
the hand of **t** who seek his life,	Jer 44:30	
sword has devoured **t** around you.'	Jer 46:14	
Pharaoh and **t** who trust in him.	Jer 46:25	
of **t** who are seeking their lives,	Jer 46:26	
The city and **t** who live in it;	Jer 47:2	
send to him **t** who tip *vessels,*	Jer 48:12	
t who were not sentenced to drink	Jer 49:12	
I will scatter to all the winds **t** who	Jer 49:32	
And before **t** who seek their lives;	Jer 49:37	
"In **t** days and at that time,"	Jer 50:4	1992a
'In **t** days and at that time,'	Jer 50:20	1992a
t whom I leave as a remnant.'	Jer 50:20	
Babylon, All **t** who bend the bow:	Jer 50:29	
has given me into the hands Of **t**	La 1:14	
T whom I bore and reared,	La 2:22	
Like **t** who have long been dead.	La 3:6	
is good to **t** who wait for Him,	La 3:25	

T who ate delicacies Are desolate	**La 4:5**	
T reared in purple Embrace ash	**La 4:5**	
Better are **t** slain with the sword	**La 4:9**	
sword Than **t** slain with hunger;	**La 4:9**	
Whenever **t** went, these went;	**Ezk 1:21**	
and *whenever* **t** stood still, these	**Ezk 1:21**	
whenever **t** rose from the earth,	**Ezk 1:21**	
destruction of **t** whom I will send to	**Ezk 5:16**	
for you will have **t** who escaped	**Ezk 6:8**	
"Then **t** of you who escape will	**Ezk 6:9**	
will also consume **t** in the city.	**Ezk 7:15**	
are **t** to whom the inhabitants of	**Ezk 11:15**	
"But as for **t** whose hearts go	**Ezk 11:21**	
sight, as **t** going into exile.	**Ezk 12:4**	
and say to **t** who prophesy from	**Ezk 13:2**	
so tell **t** who plaster *it* over with	**Ezk 13:11**	
on **t** who have plastered it over with	**Ezk 13:15**	
t lives whom you hunt as birds.	**Ezk 13:20**	
to the desire of **t** who hate you,	**Ezk 16:27**	
from **t** women in your harlotries,	**Ezk 16:34**	
even all **t** whom you loved *and* all	**Ezk 16:37**	
loved *and* all **t** whom you hated.	**Ezk 16:37**	
t surrounding *you* who despise you.	**Ezk 16:57**	
and **t** who transgress against Me;	**Ezk 20:38**	
"**T** who are near and those who are	**Ezk 22:5**	
t who are far from you will mock	**Ezk 22:5**	
into the hand of **t** whom you hate,	**Ezk 23:28**	
of **t** from whom you were alienated.	**Ezk 23:28**	
with **t** who go down to the pit,	**Ezk 26:20**	
with **t** who go down to the pit,	**Ezk 26:20**	
"**T** from Beth-togarmah gave horses	**Ezk 27:14**	
And you will die the death of **t**	**Ezk 28:8**	
In the hands of **t** who wound you?	**Ezk 28:9**	
t who support Egypt will fall And	**Ezk 30:6**	
with **t** who go down to the pit."	**Ezk 31:14**	
with **t** who go down to the pit;	**Ezk 31:16**	
to **t** who were slain by the sword;	**Ezk 31:17**	
and **t** who were its strength lived	**Ezk 31:17**	
t who were slain by the sword.	**Ezk 31:18**	
When I smite all **t** who live in it,	**Ezk 32:15**	
with **t** who go down to the pit;	**Ezk 32:18**	
of **t** who are slain by the sword.	**Ezk 32:20**	
with **t** who went down to the pit.	**Ezk 32:24**	
with **t** who go down to the pit;	**Ezk 32:25**	
and lie with **t** slain by the sword.	**Ezk 32:28**	
laid with **t** slain by the sword;	**Ezk 32:29**	
and with **t** who go down to the pit.	**Ezk 32:29**	
with **t** slain by the sword and	**Ezk 32:30**	
with **t** who go down to the pit.	**Ezk 32:30**	
along with **t** slain by the sword,	**Ezk 32:32**	
surely **t** who are in the waste	**Ezk 33:27**	
and **t** who are in the strongholds	**Ezk 33:27**	
Prophesy and say to **t** shepherds,	**Ezk 34:2**	
"**T** who are sickly you have not	**Ezk 34:4**	
the hand of **t** who enslaved them.	**Ezk 34:27**	
t slain by the sword will fall.	**Ezk 35:8**	
will go against **t** who are at rest,	**Ezk 38:11**	
who prophesied in **t** days for *many*	**Ezk 38:17**	1992a
fire upon Magog and **t** who inhabit	**Ezk 39:6**	
"Then **t** who inhabit the cities of	**Ezk 39:9**	
the spoil of **t** who despoiled them and	**Ezk 39:10**	
plunder of **t** who plundered them,"	**Ezk 39:10**	
of **t** who pass by east of the sea,	**Ezk 39:11**	
and it will block off **t** who would	**Ezk 39:11**	
t who were passing through,	**Ezk 39:14**	
even **t** left on the surface of the	**Ezk 39:14**	
"As **t** who pass through the	**Ezk 39:15**	
according to **t** same measurements.	**Ezk 40:24**	428
all around like **t** other windows;	**Ezk 40:25**	428
according to **t** same measurements.	**Ezk 40:28**	428
according to **t** same measurements.	**Ezk 40:29**	428
according to **t** same measurements.	**Ezk 40:32**	428
according to **t** same measurements.	**Ezk 40:33**	428
according to **t** same measurements,	**Ezk 40:35**	428
trees like **t** carved on the walls;	**Ezk 41:25**	
the length of **t** facing the temple	**Ezk 42:8**	
"In the days of **t** kings the	**Da 2:44**	581
t men who carried up Shadrach,	**Da 3:22**	479
dream applied to **t** who hate you and	**Da 4:19**	
to humble **t** who walk in pride."	**Da 4:37**	
and they brought **t** men who had	**Da 6:24**	479
"I approached one of **t** who were	**Da 7:16**	
for **t** who love Him and keep His	**Da 9:4**	
t who are nearby and those who are	**Da 9:7**	
those who are nearby and **t** who are	**Da 9:7**	
a reproach to all **t** around us.	**Da 9:16**	
In **t** days, I, Daniel, had been	**Da 10:2**	1992a
along with **t** who brought her in and	**Da 11:6**	
well as he who supported her in **t**	**Da 11:6**	
"Now in **t** times many will rise up	**Da 11:14**	1992a
"**T** who eat his choice food will	**Da 11:26**	
t who forsake the holy covenant.	**Da 11:30**	
t who act wickedly toward the	**Da 11:32**	
"**T** who have insight among the people	**Da 11:33**	
Some of **t** who have insight will fall,	**Da 11:35**	
honor to **t** who acknowledge *him*	**Da 11:39**	
"Many of **t** who sleep in the	**Da 12:2**	
"**T** who have insight will shine	**Da 12:3**	
and **t** who lead the many to	**Da 12:3**	
but **t** who have insight will	**Da 12:10**	
say to **t** who were not My people,	**Hos 2:23**	
t who contend with the priest.	**Hos 4:4**	
become like **t** who move a boundary;	**Hos 5:10**	
T who live in his shadow Will	**Hos 14:7**	
will pour out My Spirit in **t** days.	**Jl 2:29**	1992a
There will be **t** who escape,	**Jl 2:32**	
in **t** days and at that time,	**Jl 3:1**	1992a
T after which their fathers walked.	**Am 2:4**	
the wine of **t** who have been fined.	**Am 2:8**	

For **t** who turn justice into	**Am 5:7**	
Woe to **t** who are at ease in Zion And	**Am 6:1**	7600
And to **t** who *feel* secure in the	**Am 6:1**	
T who recline on beds of ivory And	**Am 6:4**	
"*As for* **t** who swear by the guilt	**Am 8:14**	
And all **t** who dwell in it mourn,	**Am 9:5**	
T who say, 'The calamity will not	**Am 9:10**	
Zion there will be **t** who escape,	**Ob 1:17**	
Then **t** *of* the Negev will possess	**Ob 1:19**	
And **t** *of* the Shephelah	**Ob 1:19**	
"**T** who regard vain idols Forsake	**Jon 2:8**	
Woe to **t** who scheme iniquity, Who	**Mi 2:1**	
From **t** returned from war.	**Mi 2:8**	
Even **t** whom I have afflicted.	**Mi 4:6**	
He knows **t** who take refuge in Him.	**Na 1:7**	
And like **t** who are drunken with	**Na 1:10**	
favor On **t** who deal treacherously?	**Hab 1:13**	
up **T** more righteous than they?	**Hab 1:13**	
And **t** who collect from you awaken?	**Hab 2:7**	
Their exultation *was* like **t** Who	**Hab 3:14**	
"And **t** who bow down on the	**Zph 1:5**	
And **t** who bow down *and* swear to	**Zph 1:5**	
And **t** who have turned back from	**Zph 1:6**	
And **t** who have not sought the LORD	**Zph 1:6**	
"I will gather **t** who grieve about	**Zph 3:18**	
"These are **t** whom the LORD has	**Zch 1:10**	
He spoke and said to **t** who	**Zch 3:4**	
t who are going to the land of the	**Zch 6:8**	
"**T** who are far off will come	**Zch 6:15**	
remnant of this people in **t** days,	**Zch 8:6**	1992a
t who *spoke* in the day that	**Zch 8:9**	
'For before **t** days there was no	**Zch 8:10**	1992a
'In **t** days ten men from all the	**Zch 8:23**	1992a
"**T** who buy them slay them and go	**Zch 11:5**	
and *each of* **t** who sell them says,	**Zch 11:5**	
and let **t** who are left eat one	**Zch 11:9**	
'**T** with which I was wounded in	**Zch 13:6**	
forth and fight against **t** nations,	**Zch 14:3**	1992a
cattle that will be in **t** camps.	**Zch 14:15**	1992a
and against **t** who swear falsely,	**Mal 3:5**	
and against **t** who oppress the wage	**Mal 3:5**	
and **t** who turn aside the alien and	**Mal 3:5**	
Then **t** who feared the LORD spoke	**Mal 3:16**	
t who fear the LORD and who esteem	**Mal 3:16**	
for **t** who sought the Child's life	**Mt 2:20**	*3588*
in **t** days John the Baptist came,	**Mt 3:1**	*1565*
AND **T** WHO WERE SITTING IN THE	**Mt 4:16**	*3588*
t suffering with various diseases	**Mt 4:24**	
"Blessed are **t** who mourn, for	**Mt 5:4**	*3588*
"Blessed are **t** who hunger and	**Mt 5:6**	*3588*
"Blessed are **t** who have been	**Mt 5:10**	*3588*
and pray for **t** who persecute you	**Mt 5:44**	*3588*
"For if you love **t** who love you,	**Mt 5:46**	*3588*
what is good to **t** who ask Him!	**Mt 7:11**	*3588*
and said to **t** who were following,	**Mt 8:10**	*3588*
"*It is* not **t** who are healthy who	**Mt 9:12**	*3588*
a physician, but **t** who are sick.	**Mt 9:12**	*3588*
Do not fear **t** who kill the body	**Mt 10:28**	*3588*
T who wear soft *clothing are* in	**Mt 11:8**	*3588*
among **t** born of women there has	**Mt 11:11**	
him to eat nor for **t** with him,	**Mt 12:4**	*3588*
and **t** who commit lawlessness,	**Mt 13:41**	*3588*
And **t** who were in the boat	**Mt 14:33**	*3588*
the heart, and **t** defile the man.	**Mt 15:18**	*2548*
bringing with them **t** *who were*	**Mt 15:30**	
And **t** who ate were four thousand	**Mt 15:38**	*3588*
there are some of **t** who are	**Mt 16:28**	*3588*
t who collected the two-drachma	**Mt 17:24**	*3588*
only **t** to whom it has been given.	**Mt 19:11**	
and to **t** he said,	**Mt 20:4**	*1565*
"When **t** *hired* about the	**Mt 20:9**	*3588*
"When **t** *hired* first came,	**Mt 20:10**	*3588*
but it is for **t** for whom it has	**Mt 20:23**	
and **t** who followed, were	**Mt 21:9**	*3588*
drove out all **t** who were buying and	**Mt 21:12**	*3588*
seats of **t** who were selling doves.	**Mt 21:12**	*3588*
will he do to **t** vine-growers?"	**Mt 21:40**	*1565*
"He will bring **t** wretches to a	**Mt 21:41**	*846*
to call **t** who had been invited to the	**Mt 22:3**	*3588*
'Tell **t** who have been invited,	**Mt 22:4**	*3588*
armies and destroyed **t** murderers	**Mt 22:7**	*1565*
but **t** who were invited were not	**Mt 22:8**	*3588*
"**T** slaves went out into the streets	**Mt 22:10**	*1565*
allow **t** who are entering to go in.	**Mt 23:13**	*3588*
of **t** who murdered the prophets.	**Mt 23:31**	*3588*
and stones **t** who are sent to her!	**Mt 23:37**	*3588*
for **t** *things* must take place,	**Mt 24:6**	
then **t** who are in Judea must flee	**Mt 24:16**	*3588*
"But woe to **t** who are pregnant	**Mt 24:19**	*3588*
to those who are pregnant and to **t**	**Mt 24:19**	*3588*
to those who are nursing babies in **t**	**Mt 24:19**	*3588*
Unless **t** days had been cut short,	**Mt 24:22**	*1565*
elect **t** days will be cut short.	**Mt 24:22**	*1565*
after the tribulation of **t** days	**Mt 24:29**	*1565*
"For as in **t** days	**Mt 24:38**	*1565*
"Then all **t** virgins rose and	**Mt 25:7**	*1565*
and **t** who were ready went in with	**Mt 25:10**	*3588*
master of **t** slaves came and settled	**Mt 25:19**	*1565*
King will say to **t** on His right,	**Mt 25:34**	*3588*
He will also say to **t** on His left,	**Mt 25:41**	*3588*
one of **t** who were with Jesus	**Mt 26:51**	*3588*
for all **t** who take up the sword	**Mt 26:52**	*3588*
T who had seized Jesus led Him away	**Mt 26:57**	*3588*
him and said to **t** who were there,	**Mt 26:71**	*3588*
And **t** passing by were hurling	**Mt 27:39**	*3588*
some of **t** who were standing there,	**Mt 27:47**	*3588*
and **t** who were with him keeping	**Mt 27:54**	*3588*
In **t** days Jesus came	**Mk 1:9**	*1565*
ill and **t** who were demon-possessed.	**Mk 1:32**	*3588*

"*It is* not **t** who are healthy who	**Mk 2:17**	*3588*
a physician, but **t** who are sick;	**Mk 2:17**	*3588*
it to **t** who were with him?"	**Mk 2:26**	*3588*
with the result that all **t** who had	**Mk 3:10**	
summoned **t** whom He Himself wanted,	**Mk 3:13**	
at **t** who were sitting around Him,	**Mk 3:34**	*3588*
but **t** who are outside get	**Mk 4:11**	*1565*
"And **t** are the ones on whom seed	**Mk 4:20**	*1565*
T who had seen it described to them	**Mk 5:16**	*3588*
on their pallets **t** who were sick,	**Mk 6:55**	*3588*
In **t** days, when there was again a	**Mk 8:1**	*1565*
there are some of **t** who are	**Mk 9:1**	*3588*
"How hard it will be for **t** who	**Mk 10:23**	*3588*
and **t** who followed were fearful.	**Mk 10:32**	*3588*
t for whom it has been prepared."	**Mk 10:40**	
t who are recognized as rulers of the	**Mk 10:42**	*3588*
T who went in front and those who	**Mk 11:9**	*3588*
in front and **t** who followed	**Mk 11:9**	*3588*
began to drive out **t** who were buying	**Mk 11:15**	*3588*
seats of **t** who were selling doves;	**Mk 11:15**	*3588*
"But **t** vine-growers said to one	**Mk 12:7**	*1565*
t *things* must take place;	**Mk 13:7**	
then **t** who are in Judea must flee	**Mk 13:14**	*3588*
"But woe to **t** who are pregnant	**Mk 13:17**	*3588*
to those who are pregnant and to **t**	**Mk 13:17**	*3588*
to those who are nursing babies in **t**	**Mk 13:17**	*3588*
"For **t** days will be a *time of*	**Mk 13:19**	*1565*
Lord had shortened **t** days,	**Mk 13:20**	
"But in **t** days, after that	**Mk 13:24**	*1565*
one of **t** who stood by	**Mk 14:47**	*3588*
T passing by were hurling abuse at	**Mk 15:29**	*3588*
T who were crucified with Him were	**Mk 15:32**	*3588*
to **t** who had been with Him,	**Mk 16:10**	*3588*
because they had not believed **t**	**Mk 16:14**	*3588*
accompany **t** who have believed:	**Mk 16:17**	*3588*
t who from the beginning	**Lk 1:2**	*3588*
GENERATION TOWARD **T** WHO FEAR HIM.	**Lk 1:50**	*3588*
He has scattered **t** *who were* proud	**Lk 1:51**	
And has exalted **t** who were humble.	**Lk 1:52**	
came on all **t** living around them;	**Lk 1:65**	*3588*
TO SHINE UPON **T** WHO SIT IN	**Lk 1:79**	*3588*
Now in **t** days a decree went out	**Lk 2:1**	*1565*
continued to speak of Him to all **t**	**Lk 2:38**	*3588*
And He ate nothing during **t** days,	**Lk 4:2**	*1565*
TO SET FREE **T** WHO ARE OPPRESSED,	**Lk 4:18**	
While the sun was setting, all **t** who	**Lk 4:40**	*3745*
"*It is* not **t** who are well who	**Lk 5:31**	*3588*
a physician, but **t** who are sick.	**Lk 5:31**	*3588*
then they will fast in **t** days."	**Lk 5:35**	*1565*
he and **t** who were with him,	**Lk 6:3**	*3588*
and **t** who were troubled with	**Lk 6:18**	*3588*
do good to **t** who hate you,	**Lk 6:27**	*3588*
bless **t** who curse you, pray for	**Lk 6:28**	*3588*
you, pray for **t** who mistreat you.	**Lk 6:28**	*3588*
"If you love **t** who love you,	**Lk 6:32**	*3588*
even sinners love **t** who love them.	**Lk 6:32**	*3588*
do good to **t** who do good to you,	**Lk 6:33**	*3588*
"If you lend to **t** from whom	**Lk 6:34**	
When **t** who had been sent	**Lk 7:10**	*3588*
T who are splendidly clothed and live	**Lk 7:25**	*3588*
among **t** born of women there is no	**Lk 7:28**	
T who were reclining *at the table*	**Lk 7:49**	*3588*
and **t** from the various cities were	**Lk 8:4**	*3588*
"**T** beside the road are those who	**Lk 8:12**	*3588*
the road are **t** who have heard;	**Lk 8:12**	*3588*
T on the rocky *soil are* those who,	**Lk 8:13**	
Those on the rocky *soil are* **t** who,	**Lk 8:13**	
t who come in may see the light.	**Lk 8:16**	*3588*
Now on one of **t** days Jesus	**Lk 8:22**	
T who had seen it reported to them	**Lk 8:36**	*3588*
as for **t** who do not receive you,	**Lk 9:5**	
curing **t** who had need of healing.	**Lk 9:11**	*3588*
there are some of **t** standing here	**Lk 9:27**	*3588*
and reported to no one in **t** days	**Lk 9:36**	*1565*
me to say good-bye to **t** at home."	**Lk 9:61**	*3588*
and heal **t** in it who are sick, and	**Lk 10:9**	*3588*
Holy Spirit to **t** who ask Him?"	**Lk 11:13**	*3588*
are **t** who hear the word of God and	**Lk 11:28**	*3588*
t who enter may see the light.	**Lk 11:33**	*3588*
and you hindered **t** who were entering."	**Lk 11:52**	*3588*
be afraid of **t** who kill the body and	**Lk 12:4**	*3588*
"Blessed are **t** slaves whom the	**Lk 12:37**	*1565*
them so, blessed are **t** *slaves.*	**Lk 12:38**	*1565*
t eighteen on whom the tower in	**Lk 13:4**	*1565*
prophets and stones **t** sent to her!	**Lk 13:34**	*3588*
When one of **t** who were reclining	**Lk 14:15**	*3588*
to say to **t** who had been invited,	**Lk 14:17**	*3588*
none of **t** men who were invited	**Lk 14:24**	*1565*
"You are **t** who justify yourselves	**Lk 16:15**	*3588*
so that **t** who wish to come	**Lk 16:26**	*3588*
"How hard it is for **t** who are	**Lk 18:24**	*3588*
T who led the way were sternly	**Lk 18:39**	*3588*
So **t** who were sent went away and	**Lk 19:32**	*3588*
to drive out **t** who were selling,	**Lk 19:45**	*3588*
but **t** who are considered worthy to	**Lk 20:35**	*3588*
"Then **t** who are in Judea must flee	**Lk 21:21**	*3588*
and **t** who are in the midst of	**Lk 21:21**	*3588*
and **t** who are in the country	**Lk 21:21**	*3588*
"Woe to **t** who are pregnant and	**Lk 21:23**	*3588*
to those who are pregnant and to **t**	**Lk 21:23**	*3588*
to those who are nursing babies in **t**	**Lk 21:23**	*3588*
for it will come upon all **t** who	**Lk 21:35**	*3588*
and **t** who have authority over them	**Lk 22:25**	*3588*
"You are **t** who have stood by	**Lk 22:28**	*3588*
When **t** who were around Him saw	**Lk 22:49**	*3588*
"Some of **t** who were with us	**Lk 24:24**	*3588*
eleven and **t** who were with them,	**Lk 24:33**	*3588*
and **t** who were His own did not	**Jn 1:11**	*3588*
even to **t** who believe in His name,	**Jn 1:12**	*3588*

Context	Reference	No.
give an answer to **t** who sent us?	**Jn 1:22**	*3588*
And He found in the temple **t** who	**Jn 2:14**	*3588*
and to **t** who were selling the	**Jn 2:16**	*3588*
and **t** who worship Him must worship	**Jn 4:24**	*3588*
a multitude of **t** who were sick,	**Jn 5:3**	*3588*
and **t** who hear will live.	**Jn 5:25**	*3588*
t who did the good *deeds* to a	**Jn 5:29**	*3588*
t who committed the evil *deeds* to	**Jn 5:29**	*3588*
was performing on **t** who were sick.	**Jn 6:2**	*3588*
distributed to **t** who were seated;	**Jn 6:11**	*3588*
were left over by **t** who had eaten.	**Jn 6:13**	*3588*
signs than **t** which this man has,	**Jn 7:31**	*3588*
whom **t** who believed in Him were to	**Jn 7:39**	*3588*
to **t** Jews who had believed Him,	**Jn 8:31**	*3588*
and **t** who previously saw him as a	**Jn 9:8**	*3588*
that **t** who do not see may see,	**Jn 9:39**	*3588*
that **t** who see may become blind."	**Jn 9:39**	*3588*
T of the Pharisees who were with	**Jn 9:40**	*3588*
not understand what **t** things were	**Jn 10:6**	
but Lazarus was one of **t** reclining	**Jn 12:2**	*3588*
some Greeks among **t** who were	**Jn 12:20**	*3588*
Now no one of **t** reclining *at the*	**Jn 13:28**	*3588*
but of **t** whom You have given Me;	**Jn 17:9**	
but for **t** also who believe in Me	**Jn 17:20**	*3588*
"Of **t** whom You have given Me I	**Jn 18:9**	
Question **t** who have heard what I	**Jn 18:21**	*3588*
a guide to **t** who arrested Jesus.	**Ac 1:16**	*3588*
I WILL IN **T** DAYS POUR FORTH OF MY	**Ac 2:18**	*1565*
t who had received his word were	**Ac 2:41**	*3588*
And all **t** who had believed were	**Ac 2:44**	*3588*
day by day **t** who were being saved.	**Ac 2:47**	*3588*
of **t** who were entering the temple.	**Ac 3:2**	*3588*
But many of **t** who had heard the	**Ac 4:4**	*3588*
the congregation of **t** who believed	**Ac 4:32**	*3588*
the feet of **t** who have buried your	**Ac 5:9**	*3588*
God has given to **t** who obey Him."	**Ac 5:32**	*3588*
and all **t** who followed him were	**Ac 5:37**	
They killed **t** who had	**Ac 7:52**	*3588*
t who had been scattered went	**Ac 8:4**	*3588*
All **t** hearing him continued to	**Ac 9:21**	*3588*
t who called on this name,	**Ac 9:21**	*3588*
Peter was traveling through all **t**	**Ac 9:32**	
t who were his personal attendants,	**Ac 10:7**	
the Holy Spirit fell upon all **t**	**Ac 10:44**	*3588*
t who were circumcised took issue	**Ac 11:2**	*3588*
So then **t** who were scattered	**Ac 11:19**	*3588*
and he went about seeking **t** who	**Ac 13:11**	
and **t** among you who fear God,	**Ac 13:26**	*3588*
"For **t** who live in Jerusalem, and	**Ac 13:27**	*3588*
appeared to **t** who came up with Him	**Ac 13:31**	*3588*
not trouble **t** who are turning to God	**Ac 15:19**	*3588*
in every city **t** who preach him,	**Ac 15:21**	*3588*
peace to **t** who had sent them out.	**Ac 15:33**	*3588*
of the Jews who were in **t** parts,	**Ac 16:3**	*1565*
policemen, saying, "Release **t** men."	**Ac 16:35**	*1565*
than **t** in Thessalonica,	**Ac 17:11**	*3588*
Now **t** who escorted Paul brought	**Ac 17:15**	*3588*
with **t** who happened to be present.	**Ac 17:17**	*3588*
he greatly helped **t** who had	**Ac 18:27**	*3588*
attempted to name over **t** who had	**Ac 19:13**	*3588*
Many also of **t** who had believed	**Ac 19:18**	*3588*
And many of **t** who practiced magic	**Ac 19:19**	*3588*
two of **t** who ministered to him,	**Ac 19:22**	*3588*
he had gone through **t** districts and	**Ac 20:2**	*1565*
among all **t** who are sanctified.	**Ac 20:32**	*3588*
the Jews of **t** who have believed,	**Ac 21:20**	*3588*
to bring even **t** who were there to	**Ac 22:5**	*3588*
"And **t** who were with me saw	**Ac 22:9**	*3588*
by the hand by **t** who were with me and	**Ac 22:11**	*3588*
and beat **t** who believed in You.	**Ac 22:19**	*3588*
coats of **t** who were slaying him.'	**Ac 22:20**	*3588*
Therefore **t** who were about to	**Ac 22:29**	*3588*
commanded **t** standing beside him to	**Ac 23:2**	*3588*
but if none of **t** things is *true* of	**Ac 25:11**	
and **t** who were journeying with me.	**Ac 26:13**	*3588*
inheritance among **t** who have been	**Ac 26:18**	*3588*
both to **t** of Damascus first,	**Ac 26:20**	*3588*
and **t** who were sitting with them,	**Ac 26:30**	*3588*
all **t** who are sailing with you.'	**Ac 27:24**	*3588*
and commanded that **t** who could	**Ac 27:43**	*3588*
Paul called together **t** who were the	**Ac 28:17**	*3588*
do **t** things which are not proper,	**Ro 1:28**	*3588*
that **t** who practice such things	**Ro 1:32**	*3588*
approval to **t** who practice them.	**Ro 1:32**	*3588*
upon **t** who practice such things.	**Ro 2:2**	*3588*
when you pass judgment on **t** who	**Ro 2:3**	*3588*
to **t** who by perseverance in doing	**Ro 2:7**	*3588*
but to **t** who are selfishly	**Ro 2:8**	*3588*
a light to **t** who are in darkness,	**Ro 2:19**	*3588*
speaks to **t** who are under the Law,	**Ro 3:19**	*3588*
Christ for all **t** who believe;	**Ro 3:22**	*3588*
"BLESSED ARE **T** WHOSE LAWLESS	**Ro 4:7**	
father of circumcision to **t** who not	**Ro 4:12**	*3588*
if **t** who are of the Law are heirs,	**Ro 4:14**	*3588*
not only to **t** who are of the Law,	**Ro 4:16**	*3588*
but also to **t** who are of the faith	**Ro 4:16**	*3588*
as **t** who believe in Him who raised	**Ro 4:24**	*3588*
even over **t** who had not sinned in	**Ro 5:14**	*3588*
much more **t** who receive the	**Ro 5:17**	*3588*
to God as **t** alive from the dead,	**Ro 6:13**	
the outcome of **t** things is death.	**Ro 6:21**	*1565*
speaking to **t** who know the law),	**Ro 7:1**	
for **t** who are in Christ Jesus.	**Ro 8:1**	*3588*
For **t** who are according to the	**Ro 8:5**	*3588*
but **t** who are according to the	**Ro 8:5**	*3588*
and **t** who are in the flesh cannot	**Ro 8:8**	*3588*
for good to **t** who love God,	**Ro 8:28**	*3588*
to **t** who are called according to	**Ro 8:28**	*3588*
For **t** whom He foreknew, He also	**Ro 8:29**	*3739*
CALL **T** WHO WERE NOT MY PEOPLE,	**Ro 9:25**	*3588*
"HOW BEAUTIFUL ARE THE FEET OF **T**	**Ro 10:15**	*3588*
FOUND BY **T** WHO DID NOT SEEK ME,	**Ro 10:20**	*3588*
TO **T** WHO DID NOT ASK FOR ME."	**Ro 10:20**	*3588*
but **t** who were chosen obtained it,	**Ro 11:7**	*1589*
to **t** who fell, severity, but to	**Ro 11:22**	*3588*
Bless **t** who persecute you;	**Ro 12:14**	*3588*
Rejoice with **t** who rejoice, and	**Ro 12:15**	*3588*
rejoice, and weep with **t** who weep.	**Ro 12:15**	
and **t** which exist are established	**Ro 13:1**	*3588*
bear the weaknesses of **t** without	**Ro 15:1**	*3588*
"THE REPROACHES OF **T** WHO	**Ro 15:3**	*3588*
t who are disobedient in Judea,	**Ro 15:31**	*3588*
Greet **t** who are of the *household*	**Ro 16:10**	*3588*
t of the *household* of Narcissus,	**Ro 16:11**	*3588*
keep your eye on **t** who cause	**Ro 16:17**	*3588*
to **t** who have been sanctified in	**1Co 1:2**	
is foolishness to **t** who are perishing,	**1Co 1:18**	*3588*
preached to save **t** who believe.	**1Co 1:21**	*3588*
but to **t** who are the called, both	**1Co 1:24**	*3588*
wisdom among **t** who are mature;	**1Co 2:6**	*3588*
ALL THAT GOD HAS PREPARED FOR **T** WHO	**1Co 2:9**	*3588*
but in **t** taught by the Spirit,	**1Co 2:13**	
the words of **t** who are arrogant but	**1Co 4:19**	*3588*
judge **t** who are within *the church?*	**1Co 5:12**	*3588*
But **t** who are outside, God judges.	**1Co 5:13**	*3588*
t who have wives should be as	**1Co 7:29**	*3588*
and **t** who weep, as though they did	**1Co 7:30**	*3588*
and **t** who rejoice, as though they	**1Co 7:30**	*3588*
and **t** who buy, as though they did	**1Co 7:30**	*3588*
and **t** who use the world, as though	**1Co 7:31**	*3588*
to **t** who examine me is this:	**1Co 9:3**	*3588*
Do you not know that **t** who perform	**1Co 9:13**	*3588*
and **t** who attend regularly to the	**1Co 9:13**	*3588*
So also the Lord directed **t** who	**1Co 9:14**	*3588*
to **t** who are under the Law, as	**1Co 9:20**	*3588*
might win **t** who are under the Law;	**1Co 9:20**	*3588*
to **t** who are without law, as	**1Co 9:21**	*3588*
I might win **t** who are without law.	**1Co 9:21**	*3588*
that **t** who run in a race all run,	**1Co 9:24**	*3588*
are not **t** who eat the sacrifices	**1Co 10:18**	*3588*
so that **t** who are approved	**1Co 11:19**	*3588*
God and shame **t** who have nothing?	**1Co 11:22**	*3588*
and **t** *members* of the body which	**1Co 12:23**	*3588*
for a sign, not to **t** who believe but	**1Co 14:22**	*3588*
unbelievers but to **t** who believe.	**1Co 14:22**	*3588*
Then **t** also who have fallen asleep	**1Co 15:18**	*3588*
first fruits of **t** who are asleep.	**1Co 15:20**	*3588*
after that **t** who are Christ's at	**1Co 15:23**	*3588*
what will **t** do who are baptized	**1Co 15:29**	*3588*
so also are **t** who are earthy;	**1Co 15:48**	*3588*
so also are **t** who are heavenly.	**1Co 15:48**	*3588*
comfort **t** who are in any affliction	**2Co 1:4**	*3588*
t who ought to make me rejoice;	**2Co 2:3**	*3588*
among **t** who are being saved and	**2Co 2:15**	*3588*
and among **t** who are perishing;	**2Co 2:15**	*3588*
is veiled to **t** who are perishing,	**2Co 4:3**	*3588*
t who take pride in appearance and	**2Co 5:12**	*3588*
some of **t** who commend themselves;	**2Co 10:12**	*3588*
cut off opportunity from **t** who desire	**2Co 11:12**	*3588*
any of **t** whom I have sent to you,	**2Co 12:17**	*3588*
and I may mourn over many of **t** who	**2Co 12:21**	*3588*
say in advance to **t** who have sinned	**2Co 13:2**	*3588*
to **t** who were apostles before me;	**Ga 1:17**	*3588*
to **t** who were of reputation,	**Ga 2:2**	*3588*
t who were of high reputation	**Ga 2:6**	*3588*
t who were of reputation	**Ga 2:6**	*3588*
it is **t** who are of faith who are sons	**Ga 3:7**	*3588*
So then **t** who are of faith are	**Ga 3:9**	*3588*
might be given to **t** who believe.	**Ga 3:22**	*3588*
redeem **t** who were under the Law,	**Ga 4:5**	*3588*
to **t** which by nature are no gods.	**Ga 4:8**	*3588*
wish that **t** who are troubling you	**Ga 5:12**	*3588*
that **t** who practice such things will	**Ga 5:21**	*3588*
Now **t** who belong to Christ Jesus	**Ga 5:24**	*3588*
t who are of the household of	**Ga 6:10**	*3588*
T who desire to make a good	**Ga 6:12**	*3745*
For **t** who are circumcised do not	**Ga 6:13**	*3588*
And **t** who will walk by this rule,	**Ga 6:16**	*3745*
AND PEACE TO **T** WHO WERE NEAR;	**Eph 2:17**	*3588*
it will give grace to **t** who hear.	**Eph 4:29**	*3588*
be obedient to **t** who are your	**Eph 6:5**	*3588*
Grace be with all **t** who love our	**Eph 6:24**	*3588*
t who are in heaven and on earth	**Php 2:10**	*3588*
interests, not **t** of Christ Jesus.	**Php 2:21**	*3588*
t things I have counted as loss	**Php 3:7**	*3778*
and observe **t** who walk according	**Php 3:17**	*3588*
especially **t** of Caesar's household.	**Php 4:22**	*3588*
and for **t** who are at Laodicea,	**Col 2:1**	*3588*
and for all **t** who have not	**Col 2:1**	
as **t** who have been chosen of God,	**Col 3:12**	
t who are your masters on earth,	**Col 3:22**	*3588*
as **t** who *merely* please men,	**Col 3:22**	
deep concern for you and for **t** who	**Col 4:13**	*3588*
brethren, about **t** who are asleep,	**1Th 4:13**	*3588*
God will bring with Him **t** who have	**1Th 4:14**	*3588*
precede **t** who have fallen asleep.	**1Th 4:15**	*3588*
For **t** who sleep do their sleeping	**1Th 5:7**	*3588*
and **t** who get drunk get drunk at	**1Th 5:7**	*3588*
that you appreciate **t** who	**1Th 5:12**	*3588*
with affliction **t** who afflict you,	**2Th 1:6**	*3588*
dealing out retribution to **t** who	**2Th 1:8**	*3588*
to **t** who do not obey the gospel of	**2Th 1:8**	*3588*
of wickedness for **t** who perish,	**2Th 2:10**	*3588*
but for **t** who are lawless and	**1Tm 1:9**	
for **t** who kill their fathers or	**1Tm 1:9**	
as an example for **t** who would	**1Tm 1:16**	*3588*
with **t** outside *the church,*	**1Tm 3:7**	*3588*
For **t** who have served well as	**1Tm 3:13**	*3588*
shared in by **t** who believe and know	**1Tm 4:3**	*3588*
an example of **t** who believe.	**1Tm 4:12**	*3588*
yourself and for **t** who hear you.	**1Tm 4:16**	*3588*
especially for **t** of his household,	**1Tm 5:8**	
if she has assisted **t** in distress,	**1Tm 5:10**	
assist **t** who are widows indeed.	**1Tm 5:16**	*3588*
especially **t** who work hard at	**1Tm 5:17**	*3588*
T who continue in sin, rebuke in	**1Tm 5:20**	*3588*
and **t** which are otherwise cannot	**1Tm 5:25**	*3588*
T who have believers as	**1Tm 6:2**	*3588*
because **t** who partake of the	**1Tm 6:2**	*3588*
words, **t** of our Lord Jesus Christ,	**1Tm 6:3**	*3588*
But **t** who want to get rich fall	**1Tm 6:9**	*3588*
Instruct **t** who are rich in this	**1Tm 6:17**	*3588*
for the sake of **t** who are chosen,	**2Tm 2:10**	*3588*
"The Lord knows **t** who are His,"	**2Tm 2:19**	*3588*
with **t** who call on the Lord from a	**2Tm 2:22**	*3588*
t who are in opposition,	**2Tm 2:25**	*3588*
For among them are **t** who enter	**2Tm 3:6**	*3588*
for the faith of **t** chosen of God	**Ti 1:1**	
and to refute **t** who contradict.	**Ti 1:9**	*3588*
especially **t** of the circumcision,	**Ti 1:10**	*3588*
but to **t** who are defiled and	**Ti 1:15**	*3588*
so that **t** who have believed God	**Ti 3:8**	*3588*
Greet **t** who love us in *the* faith.	**Ti 3:15**	*3588*
of **t** who will inherit salvation?	**Heb 1:14**	*3588*
confirmed to us by **t** who heard,	**Heb 2:3**	*3588*
t who are sanctified are all from one	**Heb 2:11**	*3588*
and might free **t** who through	**Heb 2:15**	
to the aid of **t** who are tempted.	**Heb 2:18**	*3588*
for a testimony of **t** things which	**Heb 3:5**	*3588*
did not all **t** who came out of	**Heb 3:16**	*3588*
Was it not with **t** who sinned,	**Heb 3:17**	*3588*
but to **t** who were disobedient?	**Heb 3:18**	*3588*
united by faith in **t** who heard.	**Heb 4:2**	*3588*
and **t** who formerly had good news	**Heb 4:6**	*3588*
He became to all **t** who obey Him	**Heb 5:9**	*3588*
For in the case of **t** who have once	**Heb 6:4**	*3588*
brings forth vegetation useful to **t** for	**Heb 6:7**	*1565*
but imitators of **t** who through	**Heb 6:12**	*3588*
And **t** indeed of the sons of Levi	**Heb 7:5**	*3588*
He is able also to save forever **t** who	**Heb 7:25**	*3588*
need daily, like **t** high priests,	**Heb 7:27**	*3588*
since there are **t** who offer the	**Heb 8:4**	*3588*
THE HOUSE OF ISRAEL AFTER **T** DAYS,	**Heb 8:10**	*1565*
t who have been defiled sanctify	**Heb 9:13**	*3588*
t who have been called may receive	**Heb 9:15**	*3588*
sin, to **t** who eagerly await Him.	**Heb 9:28**	*3588*
make perfect **t** who draw near.	**Heb 10:1**	*3588*
But in **t** *sacrifices* there is a	**Heb 10:3**	*846*
for all time **t** who are sanctified.	**Heb 10:14**	*3588*
WILL MAKE WITH THEM AFTER **T** DAYS,	**Heb 10:16**	*1565*
with **t** who were so treated.	**Heb 10:33**	*3588*
But we are not of **t** who shrink	**Heb 10:39**	
but of **t** who have faith to the	**Heb 10:39**	
is a rewarder of **t** who seek Him.	**Heb 11:6**	*3588*
For **t** who say such things make it	**Heb 11:14**	*3588*
along with **t** who were disobedient,	**Heb 11:31**	*3588*
FOR **T** WHOM THE LORD LOVES HE	**Heb 12:6**	
to **t** who have been trained by it,	**Heb 12:11**	*3588*
sound was such that **t** who heard	**Heb 12:19**	*3588*
For if **t** did not escape when they	**Heb 12:25**	*1565*
of **t** things which can be shaken,	**Heb 12:27**	*3588*
t things which cannot be shaken	**Heb 12:27**	*3588*
them, *and* **t** who are ill-treated,	**Heb 13:3**	*3588*
Remember **t** who led you, who spoke	**Heb 13:7**	*3588*
t who were so occupied were not	**Heb 13:9**	*3588*
from which **t** who serve the	**Heb 13:10**	*3588*
For the bodies of **t** animals whose	**Heb 13:11**	*3778*
as **t** who will give an account.	**Heb 13:17**	
T from Italy greet you.	**Heb 13:24**	*3588*
has promised to **t** who love Him.	**Jas 1:12**	*3588*
He promised to **t** who love Him?	**Jas 2:5**	*3588*
as **t** who are to be judged by *the*	**Jas 2:12**	*3588*
sown in peace by **t** who make peace.	**Jas 3:18**	*3588*
and the outcry of **t** who did the	**Jas 5:4**	*3588*
We count **t** blessed who endured.	**Jas 5:11**	*3588*
Christ, To **t** who reside as aliens,	**1Pe 1:1**	
through **t** who preached the gospel	**1Pe 1:12**	*3588*
but for **t** who disbelieve,	**1Pe 2:7**	*3588*
and the praise of **t** who do right.	**1Pe 2:14**	
only to **t** who are good and gentle,	**1Pe 2:18**	*3588*
also to **t** who are unreasonable.	**1Pe 2:18**	*3588*
LORD IS AGAINST **T** WHO DO EVIL."	**1Pe 3:12**	
t who revile your good behavior in	**1Pe 3:16**	*3588*
preached even to **t** who are dead,	**1Pe 4:6**	
what *will be* the outcome for **t** who	**1Pe 4:17**	*3588*
t also who suffer according to	**1Pe 4:19**	*3588*
it over **t** allotted to your charge,	**1Pe 5:3**	*3588*
To **t** who have received a faith of	**2Pe 1:1**	*3588*
having made them an example to **t**	**2Pe 2:6**	
and especially **t** who indulge the	**2Pe 2:10**	*3588*
will in the destruction of **t** creatures	**2Pe 2:12**	*3778*
t who barely escape from the ones	**2Pe 2:18**	*3588*
but also for **t** *of* the whole world.	**1Jn 2:2**	
t who are trying to deceive you.	**1Jn 2:26**	*3588*
God will for him give life to **t** who	**1Jn 5:16**	*3588*
t who do not acknowledge Jesus	**2Jn 1:7**	*3588*
he forbids **t** who desire *to do so*	**3Jn 1:10**	*3588*
of James, To **t** who are the called,	**Jude 1:1**	*3588*
t who were long beforehand marked	**Jude 1:4**	*3588*
destroyed **t** who did not believe.	**Jude 1:5**	*3588*
who reads and **t** who hear the words	**Rv 1:3**	*3588*
see Him, even **t** who pierced Him;	**Rv 1:7**	
t who call themselves apostles,	**Rv 2:2**	*3588*
and the blasphemy by **t** who say	**Rv 2:9**	*3588*
and **t** who commit adultery with her	**Rv 2:22**	*3588*
'Behold, I will cause **t** of	**Rv 3:9**	
test **t** who dwell on the earth.	**Rv 3:10**	*3588*

'**T** whom I love, I reprove and Rv 3:19 *3745*
the souls of **t** who had been slain Rv 6:9 *3588*
on **t** who dwell on the earth?" Rv 6:10 *3588*
the number of **t** who were sealed, Rv 7:4 *3588*
woe to **t** who dwell on the earth, Rv 8:13 *3588*
And in **t** days men will seek death Rv 9:6 *1565*
the horses and **t** who sat on them: Rv 9:17 *3588*
altar, and **t** who worship in it. Rv 11:1 *3588*
T from the peoples and tribes Rv 11:9
And **t** who dwell on the earth *will* Rv 11:10 *3588*
t who dwell on the earth. Rv 11:10 *3588*
upon **t** who were watching them. Rv 11:11 *3588*
saints and **t** who fear Your name, Rv 11:18 *3588*
destroy **t** who destroy the earth." Rv 11:18 *3588*
and his feet were like **t** of a Rv 13:2
that is, **t** who dwell in heaven. Rv 13:6 *3588*
the earth and **t** who dwell in it Rv 13:12 *3588*
And he deceives **t** who dwell on the Rv 13:14 *3588*
telling **t** who dwell on the earth Rv 13:14 *3588*
preach to **t** who live on the earth, Rv 14:6 *3588*
t who worship the beast and his Rv 14:11 *3588*
and **t** who had been victorious Rv 15:2 *3588*
and **t** who dwell on the earth were Rv 17:2 *3588*
And **t** who dwell on the earth, Rv 17:8 *3588*
and **t** who are with Him *are the* Rv 17:14 *3588*
'Blessed are **t** who are invited to Rv 19:9 *3588*
flesh of horses and of **t** who sit on Rv 19:18 *3588*
by which he deceived **t** who had Rv 19:20 *3588*
and **t** who worshiped his image; Rv 19:20 *3588*
And I *saw* the souls of **t** who had Rv 20:4 *3588*
and **t** who had not worshiped the Rv 20:4
but only **t** whose names are written Rv 21:27 *3588*
t who heed the words of this book. Rv 22:9 *3588*
Blessed are **t** who wash their robes, Rv 22:14 *3588*

THOUGH

even **t** blameless? Gn 20:4
"**T** you have felt through all my Gn 31:37 3588
"**T** I am Pharaoh, yet without Gn 41:44
Philistines, even **t** it was near; Ex 13:17 3588
t the people are so obstinate, Ex 34:9 3588
things, **t** it is hidden from him and Lv 5:2
not to be done, **t** he was unaware, Lv 5:17
the camel, for **t** it chews cud, it Lv 11:4
shaphan, for **t** it chews cud, Lv 11:5
rabbit also, for **t** it chews cud, Lv 11:6
pig, for **t** it divides the hoof, Lv 11:7
t the one who touches their Lv 11:36
'**T** if water is put on the seed and Lv 11:38
even **t** the mark has not spread, Lv 13:55
as **t** in her menstrual impurity; Lv 15:25
will flee as **t** from the sword, Lv 26:36 4499
Those men said to him, "**T** we Nu 9:7
"**T** Balak were to give me his Nu 22:18 518
'**T** Balak were to give me his house Nu 24:13 518
for **t** they chew the cud, Dt 14:7
t he was not deserving of death, Dt 19:6
'I have peace **t** I walk in the Dt 29:19 3588
For **t** it is a forest, you shall Jos 17:18
even **t** they have chariots of iron Jos 17:18 3588
of iron *and* **t** they are strong." Jos 17:18 3588
"**T** you detain me, I will not eat Jg 13:16 518
young goat **t** he had nothing in his hand; Jg 14:6
t I am not like one of your Ru 2:13
t it is in Jonathan my son, 1Sa 14:39 3588, 518
t you were little in your own 1Sa 15:17 518
the side, as **t** I shot at a target. 1Sa 20:20
t it was an ordinary journey; 1Sa 21:5
t you are lying in wait for my 1Sa 24:11
I am weak today, **t** anointed king; 2Sa 3:39
as **t** it had been a trivial thing 1Ki 16:31
t not like his father and his 2Ki 3:2 7534
t the Chaldeans were all around 2Ki 25:4
T Judah prevailed over his 1Ch 5:2 3588
t they testified against them, 2Ch 24:19
t not according to the purification 2Ch 30:19
t those of you who have been Ne 1:9 518
your face sad **t** you are not sick? Ne 2:2
"**T** your beginning was insignificant Jb 8:7
"For **t** I were right, I could not Jb 9:15 518
"**T** I am righteous, my mouth will Jb 9:20 518
T I am guiltless, He will declare Jb 9:20
"**T** I say, 'I will forget my complaint, Jb 9:27 518
have been as **t** I had not been, Jb 10:19 3512c
"**T** He slay me, I will hope in Him. Jb 13:15 2005
"**T** its roots grow old in the Jb 14:8 518
"**T** his loftiness reaches the Jb 20:6 518
"**T** evil is sweet in his mouth Jb 20:12 518
T he desires it and will not let Jb 20:13
"**T** his sons are many, they are Jb 27:14 518
"**T** he piles up silver like dust And Jb 27:16 518
t *I am* without transgression.' Jb 34:6
T her labor be in vain, *she* is Jb 39:16
t the Jordan rushes to his mouth. Jb 40:23 3588
T they intended evil against You Ps 21:11 3588
Even **t** I walk through the valley Ps 23:4 3588
T a host encamp against me, My Ps 27:3 518
T war arise against me, In *spite* Ps 27:3 518
as **t** it were my friend or brother; Ps 35:14
fear, **t** the earth should change And Ps 46:2
And **t** the mountains slip into the Ps 46:2
T its waters roar *and* foam, Though Ps 46:3
T the mountains quake at its Ps 46:3
T while he lives he congratulates Ps 49:18 3588
t *men* praise you when you do well Ps 49:18
Who eat up My people *as* **t** they Ps 53:4
tried Me, **t** they had seen My work. Ps 95:9 1571
Even **t** princes sit *and* talk Ps 119:23
T I have become like a wineskin in Ps 119:83 3588
For **t** the LORD is exalted, Yet He Ps 138:6 3588
T I walk in the midst of trouble, Ps 138:7 518
T He scoffs at the scoffers, Yet Pr 3:34 518
be satisfied **t** you give many gifts. Pr 6:35 3588
T *his* hatred covers itself with Pr 26:26
T you pound a fool in a mortar Pr 27:22 518
he who is crooked **t** he be rich. Pr 28:6
For **t** he understands, there will Pr 29:19
even **t** he was born poor in his Ec 4:14 3588
t a man's trouble is heavy upon him. Ec 8:6 3588
t one should never sleep day or night Ec 8:16 3588
t man should seek laboriously, Ec 8:17 7945, 834
and **t** the wise man should say, Ec 8:17 518
Yes, even **t** you multiply prayers, Is 1:15 3588
"**T** your sins are as scarlet, They Is 1:18 518
T they are red like crimson, They Is 1:18 518
For **t** your people, O Israel, may Is 10:22 518
T they had fled far away. Is 22:3
T the wicked is shown favor, He Is 26:10
Even **t** *the* needy one speaks what Is 32:7
T youths grow weary and tired, And Is 40:30
are blind, even **t** they have eyes, Is 43:8
the deaf, even **t** they have ears. Is 43:8
of honor **T** you have not known Me. Is 45:4
gird you, **t** you have not known Me; Is 45:5
T one may cry to it, it cannot Is 46:7 637
t Abraham does not know us And Is 63:16 3588
T the waves toss, yet they cannot Jer 5:22
T they roar, yet they cannot cross Jer 5:22
t they will cry to Me, yet I will Jer 11:11
"Even **t** Moses and Samuel were to Jer 15:1 518
And **t** they fight against you, They Jer 15:20
"even **t** Coniah the son of Jer 22:24 518
t *I* taught them, teaching again Jer 32:33
Even **t** Elnathan and Delaiah and Jer 36:25 1571
Even **t** they are *now* more numerous Jer 46:23 3588
T you make your nest as high as an Jer 49:16 3588
"**T** Babylon should ascend to the Jer 51:53 3588
And **t** she should fortify her lofty Jer 51:53 3588
t the Chaldeans were all around Jer 52:7
t thistles and thorns are with you Ezk 2:6 3588
t they are a rebellious house." Ezk 3:9 3588
and **t** they cry in My ears with a Ezk 8:18
"**T** I had removed them far away Ezk 11:16 3588
and **t** I had scattered them among Ezk 11:16 3588
t they are a rebellious house. Ezk 12:3 3588
not see it, **t** he will die there. Ezk 12:13
even **t** these three men, Ezk 14:14
t these three men were in its Ezk 14:16
even **t** these three men were in Ezk 14:18
even **t** Noah, Daniel and Job were Ezk 14:20
and I set My face against them. **T** Ezk 15:7
"Behold, **t** it is planted, will it Ezk 17:10
(**t** he himself did not do any of Ezk 18:11
t you will be sought, you will Ezk 26:21
T you are a man and not God, In Ezk 28:9
t they instilled their terror in Ezk 32:26 3588
t the terror of *these* heroes *was* Ezk 32:27 3588
"**T** I instilled a terror of him in Ezk 32:32 3588
as **t** *they were* rams, lambs, Ezk 39:18
heart, even **t** you knew all this, Da 5:22 6903
t not to his *own* descendants, Da 11:4
t not in anger nor in battle. Da 11:20
t they turn to other gods and love Hos 3:1
T you, Israel, play the harlot, Do Hos 4:15 518
T the pride of Israel testifies Hos 7:10
Even **t** they hire *allies* among the Hos 8:10 3588
T I wrote for him ten thousand Hos 8:12
T they bring up their children, Hos 9:12 3588, 518
Even **t** they bear children, I will Hos 9:16 3588
T they call them to *the One* on Hos 11:7
T he flourishes among the reeds, Hos 13:15 3558
T his height *was* like the height Am 2:9
T you have built houses of Am 5:11
"Even **t** you offer up to Me burnt Am 5:22 518
"**T** they dig into Sheol, From Am 9:2 518
And **t** they ascend to heaven, From Am 9:2 518
"**T** they hide on the summit of Carmel, Am 9:3 518
And **t** they conceal themselves from Am 9:3 518
"And **t** they go into captivity Am 9:4 518
"**T** you build high like the eagle, Ob 1:4 518
T you set your nest among the Ob 1:4 518
T all the peoples walk Each in the Mi 4:5 3588
T I fall I will rise; Mi 7:8 3588
T I dwell in darkness, the LORD is Mi 7:8 3588
"**T** they are at full *strength* and Na 1:12 518
T I have afflicted you, I will Na 1:12
Even **t** devastators have devastated Na 2:2 3588
T Nineveh *was* like a pool of water Na 2:8
T it tarries, wait for it; Hab 2:3 518
T the fig tree should not blossom And Hab 3:17 3588
T the yield of the olive should Hab 3:17
T the flock should be cut off from Hab 3:17
and Sidon, **t** they are very wise. Zch 9:2 3588
be as **t** I had not rejected them, Zch 10:6 3512c
T Edom says, "We have been beaten Mal 1:4 3588
t she is your companion and your Mal 2:14
"*Even* **t** all may fall away because Mt 26:33 *1487*
even **t** many false witnesses came Mt 26:60
t it is smaller than all the seeds Mk 4:31
"*Even* **t** all may fall away, yet I Mk 14:29 *1487*
even **t** he will not get up and give Lk 11:8 *1487*
'Even **t** I do not fear God nor Lk 18:4 *1487*
He acted as **t** He were going farther. Lk 24:28 *4364*
that **t** I was blind, now I see." Jn 9:25
do them, **t** you do not believe Me, Jn 10:38 *2579*
But **t** He had performed so many Jn 12:37
ground, and **t** his eyes were open, Ac 9:8
"And **t** they found no ground for Ac 13:28
T SOMEONE SHOULD DESCRIBE IT TO Ac 13:41 *1437*
hands, as **t** He needed anything, Ac 17:25
t He is not far from each one of Ac 17:27 *2532, 1065*
as **t** you were going to determine Ac 23:15 *5613*
as **t** they were going to inquire Ac 23:20 *5613*
and **t** he has been saved from the Ac 28:4
t I had done nothing against our Ac 28:17
For even **t** they knew God, they did Ro 1:21
t having the letter *of the Law* and Ro 2:27 *1223*
true, **t** every man *be found* a liar, Ro 3:4 *1161*
t perhaps for the good man someone Ro 5:7 *1063*
God that **t** you were slaves of sin, Ro 6:17
t she is joined to another man. Ro 7:3
t the body is dead because of sin, Ro 8:10 *3303a*
as **t** the word of God has failed. Ro 9:6 *3754*
for **t** *the twins* were not yet born and Ro 9:11
"**T** THE NUMBER OF THE SONS OF Ro 9:27 *1437*
faith, but as **t** *it were* by works. Ro 9:32 *5613*
as **t** I were not coming to you. 1Co 4:18 *5613*
t absent in body but present in 1Co 5:3 *3303a*
this, as **t** I were present. 1Co 5:3 *5613*
should be as **t** they had none; 1Co 7:29 *5613*
who weep, as **t** they did not weep; 1Co 7:30 *5613*
as **t** they did not rejoice; 1Co 7:30 *5613*
buy, as **t** they did not possess; 1Co 7:30 *5613*
as **t** they did not make full use of 1Co 7:31 *5613*
For **t** I am free from all *men,* I 1Co 9:19
t not being myself under the Law, 1Co 9:20
t not being without the law of God 1Co 9:21
of the body, **t** they are many, 1Co 12:12
but **t** our outer man is decaying, 2Co 4:16 *1487, 2532*
even **t** we have known Christ 2Co 5:16 *1487*
as **t** God were making an appeal 2Co 5:20 *5613*
For **t** I caused you sorrow by my 2Co 7:8 *1487, 2532*
t I did regret it—*for* I see that 2Co 7:8 *1487, 2532*
you sorrow, **t** only for a while 2Co 7:8 *1487, 2532*
t He was rich, yet for your sake He 2Co 8:9
For **t** we walk in the flesh, we do 2Co 10:3
necessary, **t** it is not profitable; 2Co 12:1 *3303a*
apostles, even **t** I am a nobody. 2Co 12:11 *1487*
and **t** now absent I say in advance 2Co 13:2
t we may appear unapproved. 2Co 13:7 *5613*
who was with me, **t** he was a Greek, Ga 2:3
even **t** it is *only* a man's covenant, Ga 3:15 *3676*
For even **t** I am absent in body, Col 2:5 *1487*
as **t** seasoned with salt, so that Col 4:6
even **t** as apostles of Christ we 1Th 2:6
even **t** they do not understand 1Tm 1:7
even **t** I was formerly a blasphemer 1Tm 1:13
t I have enough confidence in Phm 1:8
For **t** by this time you ought to be Heb 5:12 *2532*
t we are speaking in this way. Heb 6:9 *1487, 2532*
t he is dead, he still speaks. Heb 11:4
as **t** *they were passing* through dry Heb 11:29 *5613*
t he sought for it with tears. Heb 12:17 *2539*
as **t** in prison with them, Heb 13:3 *5613*
t they are so great and are driven Jas 3:4
even **t** now for a little while, 1Pe 1:6
perishable, even **t** tested by fire, 1Pe 1:7 *1161*
and **t** you have not seen Him, you 1Pe 1:8
Him, and **t** you do not see Him now, 1Pe 1:8
that **t** they are judged in the 1Pe 4:6 *3303a*
as **t** some strange thing were 1Pe 4:12 *5613*
even **t** you *already* know *them,* 2Pe 1:12 *2539*
Now I ask you, lady, not as **t** *I* 2Jn 1:5
T I have many things to write to you, 2Jn 1:12
t you know all things once for Jude 1:5

THOUGHT

"Because I **t**, surely there is no Gn 20:11 559
for I **t** that you would take your Gn 31:31 559
for he **t**, "*I am afraid* that he too Gn 38:11 559
saw her, he **t** she *was* a harlot, Gn 38:15 2803
there is no base **t** in your heart, Dt 15:9 1697
t that you hated her intensely; Jg 15:2 559
"So I **t** to inform you, saying, Ru 4:4 559
So Eli **t** she was drunk. 1Sa 1:13 2803
he looked at Eliab and **t**, 1Sa 16:6 559
Saul hurled the spear for he **t**, 1Sa 18:11 559
For Saul **t**, "My hand shall not be 1Sa 18:17 559
Saul **t**, "I will give her to him 1Sa 18:21 559
for he **t**, "It is an accident, he is not 1Sa 20:26 559
and **t** he was bringing good news, 2Sa 4:10 5869
if they take **t** in the land where 1Ki 8:47 3820
"Behold, I **t**, 'He will surely come 2Ki 5:11 559
servant of Elisha the man of God, **t**, 2Ki 5:20 559
For he **t**, "Is it not so, if there will 2Ki 20:19 559
if they take **t** in the land where 2Ch 6:37 3824
and **t** to break into them for 2Ch 32:1 559
"Then I **t**, 'I shall die in my nest, Jb 29:18 559
"I **t** age should speak, And Jb 32:7 559
man that You take **t** of him, Ps 8:4 2142
We have **t** on Your lovingkindness, O Ps 48:9 1819
Their inner **t** is *that* their Ps 49:11 7130
You **t** that I was just like you; Ps 50:21 1819
For the inward **t** and the heart of Ps 64:6 7130
You understand my **t** from afar. Ps 139:2 7454
hasty in word or impulsive in **t** Ec 5:2 3820
For he **t**, "For there will be peace Is 39:8 559
not remember Me Nor give *Me* a **t**? Is 57:11 3820
the age of one hundred Will be **t** Is 65:20
"I **t**, 'After she has done all Jer 3:7 559

t that they would receive more; **Mt 20:10** *3543*
she **t**, "If I just touch His garments, **Mk 5:28** *3004*
and **t** that they were seeing a spirit. **Lk 24:37** *1380*
but they **t** that He was speaking of **Jn 11:13** *1380*
because you **t** you could obtain the **Ac 8:20** *3543*
but **t** he was seeing a vision. **Ac 12:9** *1380*
formed by the art and **t** of man. **Ac 17:29** *1761*
I **t** to myself that I had to do **Ac 26:9** *1380*
So I **t** it necessary to urge the **2Co 9:5** *2233*
and *we are* taking every **t** captive **2Co 10:5** *3540*
But I **t** it necessary to send to **Php 2:25** *2233*
we **t** it best to be left behind at **1Th 3:1** *2106*

THOUGHTLESSLY
'Or if a person swears **t** with his **Lv 5:4** 981
a man may speak **t** with an oath, **Lv 5:4** 981

THOUGHTS
every intent of the **t** of his heart **Gn 6:5** 4284
understands every intent of the **t**. **1Ch 28:9** 4284
Amid disquieting **t** from the visions **Jb 4:13** 8174b
my disquieting **t** make me respond, **Jb 20:2** 8174b
"Behold, I know your **t**, **Jb 21:27** 4284
All his **t** are, "There is no God." **Ps 10:4** 4209
have done, And Your **t** toward us; **Ps 40:5** 4284
their **t** are against me for evil. **Ps 56:5** 4284
Your **t** are very deep. **Ps 92:5** 4284
The LORD knows the **t** of man, **Ps 94:11** 4284
my anxious **t** multiply within me, **Ps 94:19** 8312
How precious also are Your **t** to me, **Ps 139:17** 7454
Try me and know my anxious **t**; **Ps 139:23** 8312
In that very day his **t** perish. **Ps 146:4** 6250
The **t** of the righteous are just, **Pr 12:5** 4284
And the unrighteous man his **t**; **Is 55:7** 4284
"For My **t** are not your thoughts, **Is 55:8** 4284
"For My thoughts are not your **t**, **Is 55:8** 4284
ways And My **t** than your thoughts. **Is 55:9** 4284
ways And My thoughts than your **t**. **Is 55:9** 4284
Their **t** are thoughts of iniquity, **Is 59:7** 4284
Their thoughts are **t** of iniquity, **Is 59:7** 4284
not good, following their own **t**, **Is 65:2** 4284
I know their works and their **t**; **Is 66:18** 4284
your wicked **t** Lodge within you? **Jer 4:14** 4284
of Israel, for I know your **t**. **Ezk 11:5** 4609a, 7307
that **t** will come into your mind and **Ezk 38:10** 1697
your **t** turned to what would take **Da 2:29** 7476
may understand the **t** of your mind. **Da 2:30** 7476
for a while as his **t** alarmed him. **Da 4:19** 7476
grew pale and his **t** alarmed him **Da 5:6** 7476
Do not let your **t** alarm you or **Da 5:10** 7476
my **t** were greatly alarming me and **Da 7:28** 7476
declares to man what are His **t**, **Am 4:13** 7808
do not know the **t** of the LORD, **Mi 4:12** 4284
And Jesus knowing their **t** said, **Mt 9:4** *1761*
knowing their **t** Jesus said to them, **Mt 12:25** *1761*
"For out of the heart come evil **t**, **Mt 15:19** *1261*
heart of men, proceed the evil **t**, **Mk 7:21** *1261*
proud in the **t** of their heart. **Lk 1:51** *1271*
to the end that **t** from many hearts **Lk 2:35** *1261*
But He knew their **t** and **Lk 11:17** *1270*
and their **t** alternately accusing **Ro 2:15** *3053*
For who among men knows the **t** of **1Co 2:11**
Even so the **t** of God no one knows **1Co 2:11**
combining spiritual **t** with **1Co 2:13**
able to judge the **t** and intentions **Heb 4:12** *1761*

THOUSAND
your brother a **t** pieces of silver; **Gn 20:16** 505
about six hundred **t** men on foot, **Ex 12:37** 505
and about three **t** men of the people **Ex 32:28** 505
a hundred of you will chase ten **t**, **Lv 26:8** 7233
"A **t** from each tribe of all the **Nu 31:4** 505
of Israel, a **t** from each tribe, **Nu 31:5** 505
tribe, twelve **t** armed for war. **Nu 31:5** 505
sent them, a **t** from each tribe, **Nu 31:6** 505
city outward a **t** cubits around. **Nu 35:4** 505
on the east side two **t** cubits, **Nu 35:5** 505
on the south side two **t** cubits, **Nu 35:5** 505
and on the west side two **t** cubits, **Nu 35:5** 505
on the north side two **t** cubits, **Nu 35:5** 505
"How could one chase a **t**, **Dt 32:30** 505
And two put ten **t** to flight, **Dt 32:30** 7233
from the midst of ten **t** holy ones; **Dt 33:2** 7233
or three **t** men need go up to Ai; **Jos 7:3** 505
So about three **t** men from the **Jos 7:4** 505
of your men puts to flight a **t**, **Jos 23:10** 505
they defeated ten **t** men at Bezek. **Jg 1:4** 505
at that time about ten **t** Moabites, **Jg 3:29** 505
and take with you ten **t** men from **Jg 4:6** 505
and ten **t** men went up with him; **Jg 4:10** 505
with ten **t** men following him. **Jg 4:14** 505
was seen Among forty **t** in Israel. **Jg 5:8** 505
died, about a **t** men and women. **Jg 9:49** 505
it and killed a **t** men with it. **Jg 15:15** 505
a donkey I have killed a **t** men." **Jg 15:16** 505
When ten **t** choice men from all **Jg 20:34** 505
four **t** men on the battlefield. **1Sa 4:2** 505
of Israel thirty **t** foot soldiers. **1Sa 4:10** 505
weighed five **t** shekels of bronze. **1Sa 17:5** 505
to the commander of *their* **t**, **1Sa 17:18** 505
him as his commander of a **t**; **1Sa 18:13** 505
Saul took three **t** chosen men from **1Sa 24:2** 505
t sheep and a thousand goats. **1Sa 25:2** 505
thousand sheep and a **t** goats. **1Sa 25:2** 505
him three **t** chosen men of Israel, **1Sa 26:2** 505
chosen men of Israel, thirty **t**. **2Sa 6:1** 505
But you are worth ten **t** of us; **2Sa 18:3** 505
a **t** *pieces of* silver in my hand, **2Sa 18:12** 505
were a **t** men of Benjamin with him, **2Sa 19:17** 505
in Israel eight hundred **t** valiant men **2Sa 24:9** 505
of Judah were five hundred **t** men. **2Sa 24:9** 505
and seventy **t** men of the people **2Sa 24:15** 505
a **t** burnt offerings on that altar. **1Ki 3:4** 505
it could hold two **t** baths. **1Ki 7:26** 505
six **t** *shekels* of gold and ten changes **2Ki 5:5** 505
and Menahem gave Pul a **t** talents **2Ki 15:19** 505
and I will give you two **t** horses, **2Ki 18:23** 505
men of valor, ten **t** captives, **2Ki 24:14** 505
All the men of valor, seven **t**, **2Ki 24:16** 505
craftsmen and the smiths, one **t**, **2Ki 24:16** 505
a hundred and the greatest to a **t**. **1Ch 12:14** 505
He commanded to a **t** generations, **1Ch 16:15** 505
offered a **t** burnt offerings on it. **2Ch 1:6** 505
ten **t** kors of wheat and ten **2Ch 27:5** 505
kors of wheat and ten **t** of barley. **2Ch 27:5** 505
and a **t** cubits of the wall to the **Ne 3:13** 505
and I will pay ten **t** talents of silver **Es 3:9** 505
not answer Him once in a **t** *times.* **Jb 9:3** 505
mediator for him, One out of a **t**, **Jb 33:23** 505
is Mine, The cattle on a **t** hills. **Ps 50:10** 505
courts is better than a **t** *outside.* **Ps 84:10** 505
For a **t** years in Your sight Are **Ps 90:4** 505
A **t** may fall at your side And ten **Ps 91:7** 505
And ten **t** at your right hand, **Ps 91:7** 7233
He commanded to a **t** generations, **Ps 105:8** 505
If the *other* man lives a **t** years twice **Ec 6:6** 505
I have found one man among a **t**, **Ec 7:28** 505
On which are hung a **t** shields, **SS 4:4** 505
ruddy, Outstanding among ten **t**. **SS 5:10** 7233
Each one was to bring a **t** *shekels* **SS 8:11** 505
The **t** *shekels* are for you, **SS 8:12** 505
where there used to be a **t** vines, **Is 7:23** 505
valued at a **t** *shekels* of silver, **Is 7:23** 505
One **t** *will flee* at the threat of **Is 30:17** 505
and I will give you two **t** horses, **Is 36:8** 505
his hand, he measured a **t** cubits, **Ezk 47:3** 505
he measured a **t** and led me through **Ezk 47:4** 505
he measured a **t** and led me through **Ezk 47:4** 505
Again he measured a **t**; **Ezk 47:5** 505
great feast for a **t** of his nobles, **Da 5:1** 506
wine in the presence of the **t**. **Da 5:1** 506
for him ten **t** *precepts* of My law, **Hos 8:12** 7239
The city which goes forth a **t** *strong* **Am 5:3** 505
of rams, In ten **t** rivers of oil? **Mi 6:7** 7233
were about five **t** men who ate, **Mt 14:21** *4000*
And those who ate were four **t** men, **Mt 15:38** *5070*
the five loaves of the five **t**, **Mt 16:9** *4000*
"Or the seven loaves of the four **t**, **Mt 16:10** *5070*
one who owed him ten **t** talents was **Mt 18:24** *3463*
into the sea, about two **t** *of them* **Mk 5:13** *1367*
five **t** men who ate the loaves. **Mk 6:44** *4000*
About four **t** were *there* **Mk 8:9** *5070*
the five loaves for the five **t**, **Mk 8:19** *4000*
I broke the seven for the four **t**, **Mk 8:20** *5070*
(For there were about five **t** men.) **Lk 9:14** *4000*
he is strong enough with ten **t** *men* **Lk 14:31** *5505*
coming against him with twenty **t**? **Lk 14:31** *5505*
sat down, in number about five **t**. **Jn 6:10** *4000*
there were added about three **t** souls. **Ac 2:41** *5153*
the men came to be about five **t**. **Ac 4:4** *5505*
found it fifty **t** pieces of silver. **Ac 19:19** *3461*
led the four **t** men of the Assassins **Ac 21:38** *5070*
I HAVE KEPT for Myself SEVEN **T** MEN **Ro 11:4** *2035*
and twenty-three **t** fell in one day. **1Co 10:8** *5505*
than ten **t** words in a tongue. **1Co 14:19** *3463*
the Lord one day is like a **t** years, **2Pe 3:8** *5507*
years, and a **t** years like one day. **2Pe 3:8** *5507*
one hundred and forty-four **t** **Rv 7:4** *5505*
of Judah, twelve **t** *were* sealed, **Rv 7:5** *5505*
from the tribe of Reuben twelve **t**, **Rv 7:5** *5505*
from the tribe of Gad twelve **t**, **Rv 7:5** *5505*
the tribe of Asher twelve **t**, from **Rv 7:6** *5505*
the tribe of Naphtali twelve **t**, **Rv 7:6** *5505*
the tribe of Manasseh twelve **t**, **Rv 7:6** *5505*
the tribe of Simeon twelve **t**, from **Rv 7:7** *5505*
from the tribe of Levi twelve **t**, **Rv 7:7** *5505*
the tribe of Issachar twelve **t**, **Rv 7:7** *5505*
the tribe of Zebulun twelve **t**, **Rv 7:8** *5505*
from the tribe of Joseph twelve **t**, **Rv 7:8** *5505*
of Benjamin, twelve **t** *were* sealed. **Rv 7:8** *5505*
seven **t** people were killed in **Rv 11:13** *5505*
one **t** two hundred and sixty days. **Rv 12:6** *5507*
Him one hundred and forty-four **t**, **Rv 14:1** *5505*
one hundred and forty-four **t** who **Rv 14:3** *5505*
and bound him for a **t** years; **Rv 20:2** *5507*
until the **t** years were completed; **Rv 20:3** *5507*
reigned with Christ for a **t** years. **Rv 20:4** *5507*
until the **t** years were completed. **Rv 20:5** *5507*
will reign with Him for a **t** years. **Rv 20:6** *5507*
When the **t** years are completed, **Rv 20:7** *5507*

THOUSAND-FOLD
increase you a **t** more than you are and **Dt 1:11** 505, 6471

THOUSANDS
sister, Become **t** of ten thousands, **Gn 24:60** 505
sister, Become thousands of ten **t**, **Gn 24:60** 7233
these over them *as* leaders of **t**, **Ex 18:21** 505
over the people, leaders of **t**, **Ex 18:25** 505
but showing lovingkindness to **t**, **Ex 20:6** 505
who keeps lovingkindness for **t**, **Ex 34:7** 505
LORD, *To* the myriad **t** of Israel." **Nu 10:36** 505
furnished from the **t** of Israel, **Nu 31:5** 505
the captains of **t** and the captains of **Nu 31:14** 505
who were over the **t** of the army, **Nu 31:48** 505
the captains of **t** and the captains of **Nu 31:48** 505
the captains of **t** and the captains of **Nu 31:52** 505
the captains of **t** and of hundreds, **Nu 31:54** 505
them heads over you, leaders of **t** and **Dt 1:15** 505
but showing lovingkindness to **t**, **Dt 5:10** 505
those are the ten **t** of Ephraim, **Dt 33:17** 7233
And those are the **t** of Manasseh." **Dt 33:17** 505
household among the **t** of Israel. **Jos 22:14** 505
commanders of **t** and of fifties, **1Sa 8:12** 505
"Saul has slain his **t**, **1Sa 18:7** 505
thousands, And David his ten **t**." **1Sa 18:7** 7233
"They have ascribed to David ten **t**, **1Sa 18:8** 7233
but to me they have ascribed **t**. **1Sa 18:8** 505
'Saul has slain his **t**, **1Sa 21:11** 505
thousands, And David his ten **t**'?" **1Sa 21:11** 7233
make you all commanders of **t** and **1Sa 22:7** 505
out among all the **t** of Judah." **1Sa 23:23** 505
on by hundreds and by **t**, **1Sa 29:2** 505
'Saul has slain his **t**, **1Sa 29:5** 505
thousands, And David his ten **t**'?" **1Sa 29:5** 7233
set over them commanders of **t** and **2Sa 18:1** 505
people went out by hundreds and **t**. **2Sa 18:4** 505
Elihu and Zillethai, captains of **t** **1Ch 12:20** 505
consulted with the captains of the **t** **1Ch 13:1** 505
of Israel and the captains over **t**, **1Ch 15:25** 505
the commanders of **t** and hundreds, **1Ch 26:26** 505
commanders of **t** and of hundreds, **1Ch 27:1** 505
the king, and the commanders of **t**, **1Ch 28:1** 505
commanders of **t** and of hundreds, **1Ch 29:6** 505
to the commanders of **t** and of **2Ch 1:2** 505
of Judah, commanders of **t**, **2Ch 17:14** 505
commanders of **t** and commanders of **2Ch 25:5** 505
will not be afraid of ten **t** of people **Ps 3:6** 7233
God are myriads, **t** upon thousands; **Ps 68:17** 8136
God are myriads, thousands upon **t**; **Ps 68:17** 505
Than **t** of gold and silver *pieces.* **Ps 119:72** 505
And our flocks bring forth **t** and **Ps 144:13** 505
thousands and ten **t** in our fields; **Ps 144:13** 7232a
who shows lovingkindness to **t**, **Jer 32:18** 505
T upon thousands were attending **Da 7:10** 506
upon **t** were attending Him, **Da 7:10** 506
he will cause tens of **t** to fall; **Da 11:12** 7239
LORD take delight in **t** of rams, **Mi 6:7** 505
after so many **t** of people **Lk 12:1** *3461*
how many **t** there are among the **Ac 21:20** *3461*
came with many **t** of His holy ones, **Jude 1:14** *3461*
of myriads, and **t** of thousands, **Rv 5:11** *5505*
of myriads, and thousands of **t**, **Rv 5:11** *5505*

THOUSANDTH
His lovingkindness to a **t** generation **Dt 7:9** 505

THRASH
then I will **t** your bodies with the **Jg 8:7** 1758

THREAD
that I will not take a **t** or a **Gn 14:23** 2339
midwife took and tied a scarlet **t** **Gn 38:28**
came out who had the scarlet **t** on **Gn 38:30**
you tie this cord of scarlet **t** in **Jos 2:18** 2339
the ropes from his arms like a **t**. **Jg 16:12** 2339
"Your lips are like a scarlet **t**, **SS 4:3** 2339

THREADS
cut *them* into **t** to be woven in *with* **Ex 39:3** 6616
twisted **t** of chainwork for the capitals **1Ki 7:17** 1434
of your head are like purple **t**; **SS 7:5** 713

THREAT
will flee at the **t** of one *man* **Is 30:17** 1606
You will flee at the **t** of five **Is 30:17** 1606

THREATENED
to injure me have **t** destruction, **Ps 38:12** 1696
For the waters have **t** my life. **Ps 69:1** 935, 5704
When they had **t** them further, **Ac 4:21** *4324*

THREATENING
today, for the sky is red and **t**.' **Mt 16:3** *4768*
give up **t**, knowing that both their **Eph 6:9** *547*

THREATS
will bring upon you all the **t**, **Jos 23:15** 7451a, 1697
now, Lord, take note of their **t**, **Ac 4:29** *547*
still breathing **t** and murder **Ac 9:1** *547*
while suffering, He uttered no **t**, **1Pe 2:23** *546*

THREE
walked with God **t** hundred years **Gn 5:22** 7969
t hundred and sixty-five years. **Gn 5:23** 7969
Noah became the father of **t** sons: **Gn 6:10** 7969
of the ark **t** hundred cubits, **Gn 6:15** 7969
the **t** wives of his sons with them, **Gn 7:13** 7969
These **t** *were* the sons of Noah, **Gn 9:19** 7969
Noah lived **t** hundred and fifty **Gn 9:28** 7969
lived four hundred and **t** years after **Gn 11:13** 7969
Shelah lived four hundred and **t** years **Gn 11:15** 7969
his house, **t** hundred and eighteen, **Gn 14:14** 7969
"Bring Me a **t** year old heifer, **Gn 15:9** 8027
and a **t** year old female goat, **Gn 15:9** 8027
female goat, and a **t** year old ram, **Gn 15:9** 8027
t men were standing opposite him; **Gn 18:2** 7969
prepare **t** measures of fine flour, **Gn 18:6** 7969
t flocks of sheep were lying there **Gn 29:2** 7969
because I have borne him **t** sons." **Gn 29:34** 7969
And he put *a distance of* **t** days' **Gn 30:36** 7969
Now it was about **t** months later **Gn 38:24** 7969
and on the vine *were* **t** branches. **Gn 40:10** 7969
the **t** branches are three days; **Gn 40:12** 7969
the three branches are **t** days; **Gn 40:12** 7969
within **t** more days Pharaoh will **Gn 40:13** 7969
there were **t** baskets of white **Gn 40:16** 7969
the **t** baskets are three days; **Gn 40:18** 7969
the three baskets are **t** days; **Gn 40:18** 7969
within **t** more days Pharaoh will **Gn 40:19** 7969
all together in prison for **t** days. **Gn 42:17** 7969
but to Benjamin he gave **t** hundred **Gn 45:22** 7969
she hid him for **t** months. **Ex 2:2** 7969

let us go a **t** days' journey into Ex 3:18 7969
let us go a **t** days' journey into Ex 5:3 7969
"We must go a **t** days' journey Ex 8:27 7969
all the land of Egypt for **t** days. Ex 10:22 7969
rise from his place for **t** days, Ex 10:23 7969
and they went **t** days in the Ex 15:22 7969
not do these **t** *things* for her, Ex 21:11 7969
"**T** times a year you shall Ex 23:14 7969
"**T** times a year all your males Ex 23:17 7969
t branches of the lampstand from Ex 25:32 7969
and **t** branches of the lampstand Ex 25:32 7969
"**T** cups *shall be* shaped like Ex 25:33 7969
and **t** cups shaped like almond Ex 25:33 7969
and its height shall be **t** cubits. Ex 27:1 7969
their **t** pillars and their three sockets. Ex 27:14 7969
three pillars and their **t** sockets. Ex 27:14 7969
their **t** pillars and their three sockets. Ex 27:15 7969
three pillars and their **t** sockets. Ex 27:15 7969
and about **t** thousand men of the Ex 32:28 7969
"**T** times a year all your males Ex 34:23 7969
when you go up **t** times a year to Ex 34:24 7969
t branches of the lampstand from Ex 37:18 7969
and **t** branches of the lampstand Ex 37:18 7969
t cups shaped like almond Ex 37:19 7969
and **t** cups shaped like almond Ex 37:19 7969
wide, square, and **t** cubits high. Ex 38:1 7969
with their **t** pillars and their Ex 38:14 7969
three pillars and their **t** sockets, Ex 38:14 7969
with their **t** pillars and their Ex 38:15 7969
three pillars and their **t** sockets. Ex 38:15 7969
T years it shall be forbidden to Lv 19:23 7969
bring forth the crop for **t** years. Lv 25:21 7969
shall be **t** shekels of silver. Lv 27:6 7969
mount of the LORD **t** days' journey, Nu 10:33 7969
in front of them for the **t** days, Nu 10:33 7969
"You **t** come out to the tent of Nu 12:4 7969
So the **t** of them came out. Nu 12:4 7969
have struck me these **t** times?" Nu 22:28 7969
struck your donkey these **t** times? Nu 22:32 7969
aside from me these **t** times. Nu 22:33 7969
in blessing them these **t** times! Nu 24:10 7969
and they went **t** days' journey in Nu 33:8 7969
'You shall give **t** cities across Nu 35:14 7969
t cities in the land of Canaan; Nu 35:14 7969
Then Moses set apart **t** cities Dt 4:41 7969
"**T** times in a year all your males Dt 16:16 7969
of two witnesses or **t** witnesses, Dt 17:6 7969
you shall set aside **t** cities for Dt 19:2 7969
and divide into **t** parts the Dt 19:3 8027
set aside **t** cities for yourself.' Dt 19:7 7969
add **t** more cities for yourself, Dt 19:9 7969
for yourself, besides these **t**. Dt 19:9 7969
the evidence of two or **t** witnesses Dt 19:15 7969
for within **t** days you are to cross Jos 1:11 7969
hide yourselves there for **t** days until Jos 2:16 7969
and remained there for **t** days Jos 2:22 7969
At the end of **t** days Jos 3:2 7969
t thousand men need go up to Ai; Jos 7:3 7969
So about **t** thousand men from the Jos 7:4 7969
It came about at the end of **t** days Jos 9:16 7969
out from there the **t** sons of Anak: Jos 15:14 7969
"Provide for yourselves **t** men Jos 18:4 7969
Kartan with its pasture lands; **t** cities. Jos 21:32 7969
out from there the **t** sons of Anak. Jg 1:20 7969
the 300 men into **t** companies, Jg 7:16 7969
When the **t** companies blew the Jg 7:20 7969
Abimelech ruled over Israel **t** years. Jg 9:22 7969
and divided them into **t** companies, Jg 9:43 7969
of the Arnon, **t** hundred years, Jg 11:26 7969
not tell the riddle in **t** days. Jg 14:14 7969
went and caught **t** hundred foxes, Jg 15:4 7969
You have deceived me these **t** times Jg 16:15 7969
and he remained with him **t** days. Jg 19:4 7969
birth to **t** sons and two daughters. 1Sa 2:21 7969
which were lost **t** days ago, 1Sa 9:20 7969
and there **t** men going up to God at 1Sa 10:3 7969
meet you, one carrying **t** young goats, 1Sa 10:3 7969
carrying **t** loaves of bread, 1Sa 10:3 7969
put the people in **t** companies; 1Sa 11:11 7969
of the Philistines in **t** companies: 1Sa 13:17 7969
The **t** older sons of Jesse had 1Sa 17:13 7969
And the names of his **t** sons who 1Sa 17:13 7969
Now the **t** oldest followed Saul, 1Sa 17:14 7969
"When you have stayed for **t** days, 1Sa 20:19 8027
I will shoot **t** arrows to the side, 1Sa 20:20 7969
to the ground, and bowed **t** times. 1Sa 20:41 7969
Then Saul took **t** thousand chosen 1Sa 24:2 7969
and he had **t** thousand sheep and a 1Sa 25:2 7969
t thousand chosen men of Israel, 1Sa 26:2 7969
water for **t** days and three nights. 1Sa 30:12 7969
water for three days and **t** nights. 1Sa 30:12 7969
when I fell sick **t** days ago. 1Sa 30:13 7969
Thus Saul died with his **t** sons, 1Sa 31:6 7969
his **t** sons fallen on Mount Gilboa. 1Sa 31:8 7969
the **t** sons of Zeruiah were there, 2Sa 2:18 7969
that **t** hundred and sixty men died. 2Sa 2:31 7969
of Obed-edom the Gittite **t** months, 2Sa 6:11 7969
to Geshur, and was there **t** years. 2Sa 13:38 7969
To Absalom there were born **t** sons, 2Sa 14:27 7969
So he took **t** spears in his hand 2Sa 18:14 7969
men of Judah for me within **t** days, 2Sa 20:4 7969
in the days of David for **t** years, 2Sa 21:1 7969
was **t** hundred *shekels* of bronze 2Sa 21:16 7969
one of the **t** mighty men with David 2Sa 23:9 7969
Then **t** of the thirty chief men 2Sa 23:13 7969
So the **t** mighty men broke through 2Sa 23:16 7969
These things the **t** mighty men did. 2Sa 23:17 7969
swung his spear against **t** hundred 2Sa 23:18 7969
and had a name as well as the **t**. 2Sa 23:18 7969

he did not attain to the **t**. 2Sa 23:19 7969
name as well as the **t** mighty men. 2Sa 23:22 7969
but he did not attain to the **t**. 2Sa 23:23 7969
"I am offering you **t** things; 2Sa 24:12 7969
Or will you flee **t** months before 2Sa 24:13 7969
be **t** days' pestilence in your land? 2Sa 24:13 7969
came about at the end of **t** years, 1Ki 2:39 7969
He built the inner court with **t** rows 1Ki 6:36 7969
artistic window frames in **t** rows, 1Ki 7:4 7969
was opposite window in **t** ranks. 1Ki 7:4 7969
was opposite window in **t** ranks. 1Ki 7:5 7969
great court all around *had* **t** rows of 1Ki 7:12 7969
on twelve oxen, **t** facing north, 1Ki 7:25 7969
three facing north, **t** facing west, 1Ki 7:25 7969
three facing west, **t** facing south, 1Ki 7:25 7969
facing south, and **t** facing east; 1Ki 7:25 7969
cubits and its height **t** cubits. 1Ki 7:27 7969
Now **t** times in a year Solomon 1Ki 9:25 7969
t minas of gold on each shield, 1Ki 10:17 7969
once every **t** years the ships of 1Ki 10:22 7969
and **t** hundred concubines, 1Ki 11:3 7969
"Depart for **t** days, then return 1Ki 12:5 7969
He reigned **t** years in Jerusalem; 1Ki 15:2 7969
himself upon the child **t** times, 1Ki 17:21 7969
T years passed without war between 1Ki 22:1 7969
and they searched **t** days but 2Ki 2:17 7969
the LORD has called these **t** kings 2Ki 3:10 7969
the LORD has called these **t** kings 2Ki 3:13 7969
or **t** officials looked down at him. 2Ki 9:32 7969
he struck it **t** times and stopped. 2Ki 13:18 7969
shall strike Aram *only* **t** times." 2Ki 13:19 7969
T times Joash defeated him and 2Ki 13:25 7969
Samaria and besieged it **t** years. 2Ki 17:5 7969
end of **t** years they captured it; 2Ki 18:10 7969
required of Hezekiah king of Judah **t** 2Ki 18:14 7969
he reigned **t** months in Jerusalem; 2Ki 23:31 7969
became his servant *for* **t** years; 2Ki 24:1 7969
he reigned **t** months in Jerusalem; 2Ki 24:8 7969
of the capital was **t** cubits, 2Ki 25:17 7969
with the **t** officers of the temple. 2Ki 25:18 7969
these **t** were born to him by 1Ch 2:3 7969
the **t** sons of Zeruiah *were* Abshai, 1Ch 2:16 7969
Elioenai, Hizkiah and Azrikam, **t**. 1Ch 3:23 7969
The sons of Benjamin *were* **t**: 1Ch 7:6 7969
Thus Saul died with his **t** sons, 1Ch 10:6 7969
he lifted up his spear against **t** 1Ch 11:11 7969
who *was* one of the **t** mighty men. 1Ch 11:12 7969
Now **t** of the thirty chief men went 1Ch 11:15 7969
So the **t** broke through the camp of 1Ch 11:18 7969
These things the **t** mighty men did. 1Ch 11:19 7969
swung his spear against **t** hundred 1Ch 11:20 7969
Of the **t** in the second *rank* he was 1Ch 11:21 7969
he did not attain to the *first* **t**. 1Ch 11:21 7969
name as well as the **t** mighty men. 1Ch 11:24 7969
but he did not attain to the **t**. 1Ch 11:25 7969
They were there with David **t** days, 1Ch 12:39 7969
of Obed-edom in his house **t** months; 1Ch 13:14 7969
"I offer you **t** things; 1Ch 21:10 7969
either **t** years of famine, or three 1Ch 21:12 7969
or **t** months to be swept away 1Ch 21:12 7969
t days of the sword of the LORD, 1Ch 21:12 7969
the first and Zetham and Joel, **t**. 1Ch 23:8 7969
Shelomoth and Haziel and Haran, **t**. 1Ch 23:9 7969
The sons of Mushi *were* **t**: 1Ch 23:23 7969
sons and **t** daughters to Heman. 1Ch 25:5 7969
twelve oxen, **t** facing the north, 2Ch 4:4 7969
facing the north, **t** facing west, 2Ch 4:4 7969
three facing west, **t** facing south and 2Ch 4:4 7969
facing south and **t** facing east; 2Ch 4:4 7969
cubits wide and **t** cubits high, 2Ch 6:13 7969
new moons and the **t** annual feasts 2Ch 8:13 7969
using **t** hundred shekels of gold on 2Ch 9:16 7969
once every **t** years the ships of 2Ch 9:21 7969
"Return to me again in **t** days." 2Ch 10:5 7969
the son of Solomon for **t** years, 2Ch 11:17 7969
of David and Solomon for **t** years. 2Ch 11:17 7969
He reigned **t** years in Jerusalem; 2Ch 13:2 7969
And they were **t** days taking the 2Ch 20:25 7969
he reigned **t** months in Jerusalem. 2Ch 36:2 7969
and he reigned **t** months and ten 2Ch 36:9 7969
with **t** layers of huge stones and Ezr 6:4 8532
Ahava, where we camped for **t** days; Ezr 8:15 7969
and remained there **t** days. Ezr 8:32 7969
would not come within **t** days, Ezr 10:8 7969
at Jerusalem within the **t** days. Ezr 10:9 7969
to Jerusalem and was there **t** days. Ne 2:11 7969
do not eat or drink for **t** days, Es 4:16 7969
and killed **t** hundred men in Susa, Es 9:15 7969
and **t** daughters were born to him. Jb 1:2 7969
invite their **t** sisters to eat and drink Jb 1:4 7969
"The Chaldeans formed **t** bands and Jb 1:17 7969
Now when Job's **t** friends heard of Jb 2:11 7969
these **t** men ceased answering Job, Jb 32:1 7969
his anger burned against his **t** friends Jb 32:3 7969
no answer in the mouth of the **t** men Jb 32:5 7969
He had seven sons and **t** daughters. Jb 42:13 7969
There are **t** things that will not Pr 30:15 7969
There are **t** things which are too Pr 30:18 7969
Under **t** things the earth quakes, Pr 30:21 7969
There are **t** things which are Pr 30:29 7969
A cord of **t** *strands* is not quickly Ec 4:12 8027
"Within **t** years, as a hired man Is 16:14 7969
or **t** olives on the topmost bough, Is 17:6 7969
naked and barefoot **t** years as a sign Is 20:3 7969
Jehudi had read **t** or four columns, Jer 36:23 7969
with the **t** officers of the temple. Jer 52:24 7969
t hundred and ninety days; Ezk 4:5 7969
side, **t** hundred and ninety days. Ezk 4:9 7969
even *though* these **t** men, Ezk 14:14 7969

these **t** men were in its midst, Ezk 14:16 7969
these **t** men were in its midst, Ezk 14:18 7969
the east *numbered* **t** on each side; Ezk 40:10 7969
the **t** of them had the same Ezk 40:10 7969
It had **t** guardrooms on each side; Ezk 40:21 7969
gate was **t** cubits on each side. Ezk 40:48 7969
side chambers were in **t** stories, Ezk 41:6 7969
round about their **t** stories, Ezk 41:16 7969
altar *was* of wood, **t** cubits high and Ezk 41:22 7969
to gallery in **t** stories. Ezk 42:3 7992
For they *were* in **t** stories and had Ezk 42:6 8027
Israel, **t** gates toward the north: Ezk 48:31 7969
4,500 *cubits,* shall be **t** gates: Ezk 48:32 7969
by measurement, shall be **t** gates: Ezk 48:33 7969
4,500 *cubits, shall be* **t** gates: Ezk 48:34 7969
they should be educated **t** years, Da 1:5 7969
But these **t** men, Shadrach, Meshach Da 3:23 8532
"Was it not **t** men we cast bound Da 3:24 8532
and over them **t** commissioners Da 6:2 8532
on his knees **t** times a day, Da 6:10 8532
his petition **t** times a day." Da 6:13 8532
and **t** ribs *were* in its mouth Da 7:5 8532
and **t** of the first horns were Da 7:8 8532
and before which **t** *of them* fell, Da 7:20 8532
ones and will subdue **t** kings. Da 7:24 8532
been mourning for **t** entire weeks. Da 10:2 7969
the entire **t** weeks were completed. Da 10:3 7969
t more kings are going to arise in Da 11:2 7969
"For **t** transgressions of Damascus Am 1:3 7969
"For **t** transgressions of Gaza and Am 1:6 7969
"For **t** transgressions of Tyre and Am 1:9 7969
"For **t** transgressions of Edom and Am 1:11 7969
"For **t** transgressions of the sons Am 1:13 7969
"For **t** transgressions of Moab and Am 2:1 7969
"For **t** transgressions of Judah Am 2:4 7969
"For **t** transgressions of Israel Am 2:6 7969
morning, Your tithes every **t** days. Am 4:4 7969
were still **t** months until harvest. Am 4:7 7969
"So two or **t** cities would stagger Am 4:8 7969
the fish **t** days and three nights. Jon 1:17 7969
the fish three days and **t** nights. Jon 1:17 7969
great city, a **t** days' walk. Jon 3:3 7969
the **t** shepherds in one month, Zch 11:8 7969
for just as JONAH WAS **T** DAYS AND Mt 12:40 *5140*
WAS THREE DAYS AND **T** NIGHTS IN Mt 12:40 *5140*
so will the Son of Man be **t** days Mt 12:40 *5140*
three days and **t** nights in the Mt 12:40 *5140*
took and hid in **t** pecks of flour Mt 13:33 *5140*
have remained with Me now **t** days Mt 15:32 *5140*
I will make **t** tabernacles here, Mt 17:4 *5140*
THE MOUTH OF TWO OR **T** WITNESSES Mt 18:16 *5140*
"For where two or **t** have gathered Mt 18:20 *5140*
you will deny Me **t** times." Mt 26:34 *5151*
and to rebuild it in **t** days.' " Mt 26:61 *5140*
crows, you will deny Me **t** times." Mt 26:75 *5151*
temple and rebuild it in **t** days, Mt 27:40 *5140*
'After **t** days I *am to* rise again.' Mt 27:63 *5140*
have remained with Me now **t** days Mk 8:2 *5140*
and after **t** days rise again. Mk 8:31 *5140*
let us make **t** tabernacles, one Mk 9:5 *5140*
He will rise **t** days later." Mk 9:31 *5140*
t days later He will rise again." Mk 10:34 *5140*
sold for over **t** hundred denarii, Mk 14:5 *5145*
you yourself will deny Me **t** times." Mk 14:30 *5151*
and in **t** days I will build another Mk 14:58 *5140*
twice, you will deny Me **t** times." Mk 14:72 *5151*
temple and rebuild it in **t** days, Mk 15:29 *5140*
stayed with her about **t** months, Lk 1:56 *5140*
after **t** days they found Him in the Lk 2:46 *5140*
up for **t** years and six months, Lk 4:25 *5140*
let us make **t** tabernacles: Lk 9:33 *5140*
"Which of these **t** do you think Lk 10:36 *5140*
'Friend, lend me **t** loaves; Lk 11:5 *5140*
will be divided, **t** against two and Lk 12:52 *5140*
against two and two against **t**. Lk 12:52 *5140*
for **t** years I have come looking Lk 13:7 *5140*
took and hid in **t** pecks of flour Lk 13:21 *5140*
denied **t** times that you know Me." Lk 22:34 *5151*
today, you will deny Me **t** times." Lk 22:61 *5151*
in **t** days I will raise it up." Jn 2:19 *5140*
will You raise it up in **t** days?" Jn 2:20 *5140*
had rowed about **t** or four miles, Jn 6:19
1501, 4002
not sold for **t** hundred denarii and Jn 12:5 *5145*
crow until you deny Me **t** times. Jn 13:38 *5151*
were added about **t** thousand souls. Ac 2:41 *5153*
an interval of about **t** hours, Ac 5:7 *5140*
t months in his father's home. Ac 7:20 *5140*
And he was **t** days without sight, Ac 9:9 *5140*
This happened **t** times, Ac 10:16 *5151*
"Behold, **t** men are looking for you. Ac 10:19 *5140*
"This happened **t** times, Ac 11:10 *5151*
at that moment **t** men appeared Ac 11:11 *5140*
and for **t** Sabbaths reasoned with Ac 17:2 *5140*
speaking out boldly for **t** months, Ac 19:8 *5140*
And *there* he spent **t** months, Ac 20:3 *5140*
night and day for a period of **t** years Ac 20:31 *5148*
t days later went up to Jerusalem Ac 25:1 *5140*
entertained us courteously **t** days. Ac 28:7 *5140*
At the end of **t** months we set Ac 28:11 *5140*
we stayed there for **t** days. Ac 28:12 *5140*
of Appius and **T** Inns to meet us; Ac 28:15 *5140*
After **t** days Paul called together Ac 28:17 *5140*
faith, hope, love, abide these **t**; 1Co 13:13 *5140*
should be by two or at the most **t**, 1Co 14:27 *5140*
Let two or **t** prophets speak, 1Co 14:29 *5140*
T times I was beaten with rods, 2Co 11:25 *5151*
stoned, **t** times I was shipwrecked, 2Co 11:25 *5151*
I implored the Lord **t** times that it 2Co 12:8 *5151*

TESTIMONY OF TWO OR **T** WITNESSES. **2Co 13:1** *5140*
Then **t** years later I went up to **Ga 1:18** *5140*
the basis of two or **t** witnesses. **1Tm 5:19** *5140*
testimony of two or **t** witnesses. **Heb 10:28** *5140*
for **t** months by his parents, **Heb 11:23** *5150*
earth for **t** years and six months. **Jas 5:17** *5140*
For there are **t** that testify: **1Jn 5:7** *5140*
and the **t** are in agreement. **1Jn 5:8** *5140*
and **t** quarts of barley for a **Rv 6:6** *5140*
t angels who are about to sound!" **Rv 8:13** *5140*
was killed by these **t** plagues, **Rv 9:18** *5140*
dead bodies for **t** and a half days, **Rv 11:9** *5140*
But after the **t** and a half days **Rv 11:11** *5140*
t unclean spirits like frogs; **Rv 16:13** *5140*
great city was split into **t** parts, **Rv 16:19** *5140*
There were **t** gates on the east and **Rv 21:13** *5140*
and **t** gates on the north and three **Rv 21:13** *5140*
and **t** gates on the south and three **Rv 21:13** *5140*
the south and **t** gates on the west. **Rv 21:13** *5140*

THREE-PRONGED
with a **t** fork in his hand. **1Sa 2:13** 7969, 8127

THREE-TENTHS
and **t** *of an ephah* of fine flour **Lv 14:10** 7969, 6241
grain offering of **t** *of an ephah* of fine **Nu 15:9** 7969, 6241
and **t** *of an ephah* of fine flour **Nu 28:12** 7969, 6241
t *of an ephah* for a bull and **Nu 28:20** 7969, 6241
oil: **t** *of an ephah* for each bull, **Nu 28:28** 7969, 6241
oil: **t** *of an ephah* for the bull, **Nu 29:3** 7969, 6241
oil: **t** *of an ephah* for the bull, **Nu 29:9** 7969, 6241
t *of an ephah* for each of the **Nu 29:14** 7969, 6241

THREE-YEAR-OLD
with a **t** bull and one ephah of **1Sa 1:24** 7969

THRESH
does not continue to **t** it forever. **Is 28:28** 1758
it, He does not **t** it longer. **Is 28:28** 1854
You will **t** the mountains and **Is 41:15** 1758
a trained heifer that loves to **t**, **Hos 10:11** 1758
"Arise and **t**, daughter of Zion, **Mi 4:13** 1758
and the thresher *to* **t** in hope of **1Co 9:10** *248*

THRESHED
O my **t** *people,* and my afflicted of **Is 21:10** 4098
is not **t** with a threshing sledge, **Is 28:27** 1758
Because they **t** Gilead with **Am 1:3** 1758

THRESHER
and the **t** *to thresh* in hope of **1Co 9:10** *248*

THRESHING
they came to the **t** floor of Atad, **Gn 50:10** 1637
mourning at the **t** floor of Atad, **Gn 50:11** 1637
your **t** will last for you until **Lv 26:5** 1786
as the offering of the **t** floor, **Nu 15:20** 1637
the grain from the **t** floor or the full **Nu 18:27** 1637
as the product of the **t** floor, **Nu 18:30** 1637
your flock and from your **t** floor **Dt 15:14** 1637
your **t** floor and your wine vat; **Dt 16:13** 1637
not muzzle the ox while he is **t**. **Dt 25:4** 1758
a fleece of wool on the **t** floor. **Jg 6:37** 1637
barley at the **t** floor tonight. **Ru 3:2** 1637
and go down to the **t** floor; **Ru 3:3** 1637
So she went down to the **t** floor **Ru 3:6** 1637
the woman came to the **t** floor." **Ru 3:14** 1637
and are plundering the **t** floors." **1Sa 23:1** 1637
they came to the **t** floor of Nacon, **2Sa 6:6** 1637
t floor of Araunah the Jebusite. **2Sa 24:16** 1637
t floor of Araunah the Jebusite." **2Sa 24:18** 1637
"To buy the **t** floor from you, in **2Sa 24:21** 1637
the **t** sledges and the yokes of the **2Sa 24:22** 4173
So David bought the **t** floor and **2Sa 24:24** 1637
at the **t** floor at the entrance of **1Ki 22:10** 1637
From the **t** floor, or from the wine **2Ki 6:27** 1637
and made them like the dust at **t**. **2Ki 13:7** 1758
came to the **t** floor of Chidon, **1Ch 13:9** 1637
the **t** floor of Ornan the Jebusite. **1Ch 21:15** 1637
the **t** floor of Ornan the Jebusite. **1Ch 21:18** 1637
And Ornan was **t** wheat. **1Ch 21:20** 1758
and went out from the **t** floor and **1Ch 21:21** 1637
"Give me the site of *this* **t** floor, **1Ch 21:22** 1637
the **t** sledges for wood and the wheat **1Ch 21:23** 4173
the **t** floor of Ornan the Jebusite, **1Ch 21:28** 1637
the **t** floor of Ornan the Jebusite. **2Ch 3:1** 1637
and *they* were sitting at the **t** floor **2Ch 18:9** 1637
And gather *it from* your **t** floor? **Jb 39:12** 1637
out *like* a **t** sledge on the mire. **Jb 41:30** 2742a
And drives the **t** wheel over them. **Pr 20:26** 212
and my afflicted of the **t** floor! **Is 21:10** 1637
that day the LORD will start *His* **t** **Is 27:12** 2251
is not threshed with a **t** sledge, **Is 28:27** 2742a
sharp **t** sledge with double edges; **Is 41:15** 4173
you skip about like a **t** heifer **Jer 50:11** 1758
daughter of Babylon is like a **t** floor **Jer 51:33** 1637
chaff from the summer **t** floors; **Da 2:35** 147
harlots' earnings on every **t** floor. **Hos 9:1** 1637
T floor and wine press will not **Hos 9:2** 1637
is blown away from the **t** floor And **Hos 13:3** 1637
t floors will be full of grain, **Jl 2:24** 1637
them like sheaves to the **t** floor. **Mi 4:12** 1637
will thoroughly clear His **t** floor; **Mt 3:12** *257*
to thoroughly clear His **t** floor, **Lk 3:17** *257*
NOT MUZZLE THE OX WHILE HE IS **T**." **1Co 9:9** *248*
NOT MUZZLE THE OX WHILE HE IS **T**," **1Tm 5:18** *248*

THRESHOLD
house with her hands on the **t**. **Jg 19:27** 5592b
his hands *were* cut off on the **t**; **1Sa 5:4** 4670
tread on the **t** of Dagon in Ashdod **1Sa 5:5** 4670
pillars and a **t** in front of them. **1Ki 7:6** 5646
was entering the **t** of the house, **1Ki 14:17** 5592b
priests who guarded the **t** put in it **2Ki 12:9** 5592b
at the **t** of the house of my God Than **Ps 84:10** 5605
had been, to the **t** of the temple. **Ezk 9:3** 4670
the cherub to the **t** of the temple, **Ezk 10:4** 4670
departed from the **t** of the temple **Ezk 10:18** 4670
and measured the **t** of the gate, **Ezk 40:6** 5592b
the other **t** *was* one rod in width. **Ezk 40:6** 5592b
And the **t** of the gate by the porch **Ezk 40:7** 5592b
three stories, opposite the **t**, **Ezk 41:16** 5592b
and *there was* a **t** of wood on the **Ezk 41:25** 5646
setting their **t** by My threshold and **Ezk 43:8** 5592b
setting their threshold by My **t** and **Ezk 43:8** 5592b
he shall worship at the **t** of the gate **Ezk 46:2** 4670
from under the **t** of the house **Ezk 47:1** 4670
day all who leap on the *temple* **t**, **Zph 1:9** 4670
Desolation *will be* on the **t**; **Zph 2:14** 5592b

THRESHOLDS
keepers of the **t** of the tent; **1Ch 9:19** 5592b
be gatekeepers at the **t** were 212. **1Ch 9:22** 5592b
the beams, the **t** and its walls and **2Ch 3:7** 5592b
And the foundations of the **t** **Is 6:4** 5592b
The **t**, the latticed windows and **Ezk 41:16** 5592b
chambers of the house and the **t**. **Ezk 41:26** 5646
capitals so that the **t** will shake, **Am 9:1** 5592b

THREW
took him and **t** him into the pit. **Gn 37:24** 7993
So he **t** it on the ground, and it **Ex 4:3** 7993
foreskin and **t** it at Moses' feet, **Ex 4:25** 5060
and Aaron **t** his staff down before **Ex 7:10** 7993
For each one **t** down his staff and **Ex 7:12** 7993
and Moses **t** it toward the sky, and **Ex 9:10** 2236b
and he **t** *it* into the waters, and **Ex 15:25** 7993
and he **t** the tablets from his **Ex 32:19** 7993
to me, and I **t** it into the fire, **Ex 32:24** 7993
or **t** something at him lying in **Nu 35:20** 7993
or **t** something at him without **Nu 35:22** 7993
tablets and **t** them from my hands and **Dt 9:17** 7993
and I **t** its dust into the brook **Dt 9:21** 7993
and **t** it at the entrance of the **Jos 8:29** 7993
the LORD **t** large stones from **Jos 10:11** 7993
t them into the cave where they had **Jos 10:27** 7993
and every one of them **t** an earring **Jg 8:25** 7993
certain woman **t** an upper millstone **Jg 9:53** 7993
he **t** the jawbone from his hand; **Jg 15:17** 7993
He **t** stones at David and at **2Sa 16:6** 5619
and cast stones and **t** dust at him. **2Sa 16:13** 6080
t a garment over him when he saw **2Sa 20:12** 7993
son of Bichri and **t** it to Joab. **2Sa 20:22** 7993
to him and **t** his mantle on him. **1Ki 19:19** 7993
water and **t** salt in it and said, **2Ki 2:21** 7993
and each one **t** a stone on every **2Ki 3:25** 7993
He **t** it into the pot **2Ki 4:41** 7993
off a stick and **t** *it* in there, **2Ki 6:6** 7993
So they **t** her down, and some of **2Ki 9:33** 8058
and the royal officers **t** *them* out, **2Ki 10:25** 7993
and **t** its dust on the graves of **2Ki 23:6** 7993
and **t** their dust into the brook **2Ki 23:12** 7993
and **t** them down from the top of **2Ch 25:12** 7993
and he **t** *them* outside the city. **2Ch 33:15** 7993
I **t** all of Tobiah's household goods **Ne 13:8** 7993
and they **t** dust over their heads **Jb 2:12** 2236b
my hand **t** a kiss from my mouth, **Jb 31:27** 5401a
cut it with a scribe's knife and **t** *it* **Jer 36:23** 7993
and they **t** the cargo which was in **Jon 1:5** 2904
up Jonah, **t** him into the sea, **Jon 1:15** 2904
And he **t** her down into the middle **Zch 5:8** 7993
t them to the potter in the house of **Zch 11:13** 7993
but the bad they **t** away. **Mt 13:48** *906*
and went and **t** him in prison until **Mt 18:30** *906*
and **t** him out of the vineyard and **Mt 21:39** *1544b*
And he **t** the pieces of silver into **Mt 27:5** *4496*
spirit **t** him into a convulsion, **Mk 9:20** *4952*
and **t** him out of the vineyard. **Mk 12:8** *1544b*
and **t** him into a convulsion. **Lk 9:42** *4952*
took and **t** into his own garden; **Lk 13:19** *906*
they **t** their coats on the colt **Lk 19:35** *1977*
"So they **t** him out of the vineyard **Lk 20:15** *1544b*
and **t** himself into the sea. **Jn 21:7** *906*
blows, they **t** them into prison, **Ac 16:23** *906*
t them into the inner prison and **Ac 16:24** *906*
they **t** the ship's tackle overboard **Ac 27:19** *4496*
the altar, and **t** it to the earth; **Rv 8:5** *906*
heaven and **t** them to the earth. **Rv 12:4** *906*
and **t** them into the great wine press **Rv 14:19** *906*
"And they **t** dust on their heads **Rv 18:19** *906*
millstone and **t** it into the sea, **Rv 18:21** *906*
and he **t** him into the abyss, and shut **Rv 20:3** *906*

THRILL
And your heart will **t** and rejoice; **Is 60:5** 6342

THRIVE
'Thus says the Lord GOD, "Will it **t**? **Ezk 17:9** 6743b
though it is planted, will it **t**? **Ezk 17:10** 6743b

THRIVES
"He **t** before the sun, And his **Jb 8:16** 7373a

THROAT
Their **t** is an open grave; **Ps 5:9** 1627
my **t** is parched; My eyes fail while **Ps 69:3** 1627
cannot make a sound with their **t**. **Ps 115:7** 1627
And put a knife to your **t** If **Pr 23:2** 3930
Sheol has enlarged its **t** and opened **Is 5:14** 5315
unshod And your **t** from thirst; **Jer 2:25** 1627
whereas a sword touches the **t**." **Jer 4:10** 5315
"THEIR **T** IS AN OPEN GRAVE, WITH **Ro 3:13** *2995*

THROBS
My heart **t**, my strength fails me; **Ps 38:10** 5503

THRONE
in the **t** I will be greater than you." **Gn 41:40** 3678
of the Pharaoh who sits on his **t**, **Ex 11:5** 3678
firstborn of Pharaoh who sat on his **t** **Ex 12:29** 3678
he sits on the **t** of his kingdom, **Dt 17:18** 3678
and to establish the **t** of David **2Sa 3:10** 3678
I will establish the **t** of his kingdom **2Sa 7:13** 3678
your **t** shall be established forever. **2Sa 7:16** 3678
king and his **t** are guiltless." **2Sa 14:9** 3678
me, and he shall sit on my **t**"? **1Ki 1:13** 3678
me and he shall sit on my **t**.' **1Ki 1:17** 3678
shall sit on the **t** of my lord the king **1Ki 1:20** 3678
me, and he shall sit on my **t**'? **1Ki 1:24** 3678
sit on the **t** of my lord the king **1Ki 1:27** 3678
he shall sit on my **t** in my place'; **1Ki 1:30** 3678
sit on my **t** and be king in my place; **1Ki 1:35** 3678
and make his **t** greater than the **1Ki 1:37** 3678
the **t** of my lord King David!" **1Ki 1:37** 3678
his seat on the **t** of the kingdom. **1Ki 1:46** 3678
his **t** greater than your throne!' **1Ki 1:47** 3678
his throne greater than your **t**!' **1Ki 1:47** 3678
who has granted one to sit on my **t** **1Ki 1:48** 3678
lack a man on the **t** of Israel.' **1Ki 2:4** 3678
And Solomon sat on the **t** of David **1Ki 2:12** 3678
before her, and sat on his **t**; **1Ki 2:19** 3678
had a **t** set for the king's mother, **1Ki 2:19** 3678
set me on the **t** of David my father and **1Ki 2:24** 3678
and his house and his **t**, **1Ki 2:33** 3678
and the **t** of David shall be **1Ki 2:45** 3678
given him a son to sit on his **t**, **1Ki 3:6** 3678
will set on your **t** in your place, **1Ki 5:5** 3678
He made the hall of the **t** where he **1Ki 7:7** 3678
David and sit on the **t** of Israel, **1Ki 8:20** 3678
a man to sit on the **t** of Israel, **1Ki 8:25** 3678
then I will establish the **t** of **1Ki 9:5** 3678
not lack a man on the **t** of Israel.' **1Ki 9:5** 3678
you to set you on the **t** of Israel; **1Ki 10:9** 3678
the king made a great **t** of ivory **1Ki 10:18** 3678
There were six steps to the **t** and **1Ki 10:19** 3678
a round top to the **t** at its rear, **1Ki 10:19** 3678
king, as soon as he sat on his **t**, **1Ki 16:11** 3678
Judah were sitting each on his **t**, **1Ki 22:10** 3678
I saw the LORD sitting on His **t**, **1Ki 22:19** 3678
and set *him* on his father's **t**, **2Ki 10:3** 3678
shall sit on the **t** of Israel." **2Ki 10:30** 3678
And he sat on the **t** of the kings. **2Ki 11:19** 3678
and Jeroboam sat on his **t**; **2Ki 13:13** 3678
shall sit on the **t** of Israel." **2Ki 15:12** 3678
set his **t** above the throne of the kings **2Ki 25:28** 3678
set his throne above the **t** of the kings **2Ki 25:28** 3678
I will establish his **t** forever. **1Ch 17:12** 3678
his **t** shall be established forever. **1Ch 17:14** 3678
I will establish the **t** of his kingdom **1Ch 22:10** 3678
on the **t** of the kingdom of the LORD **1Ch 28:5** 3678
Solomon sat on the **t** of the LORD **1Ch 29:23** 3678
David and sit on the **t** of Israel, **2Ch 6:10** 3678
a man to sit on the **t** of Israel, **2Ch 6:16** 3678
then I will establish your royal **t** as I **2Ch 7:18** 3678
setting you on His **t** as king for the **2Ch 9:8** 3678
the king made a great **t** of ivory **2Ch 9:17** 3678
There were six steps to the **t** **2Ch 9:18** 3678
in gold attached to the **t**, **2Ch 9:18** 3678
Judah were sitting each on his **t**, **2Ch 18:9** 3678
I saw the LORD sitting on His **t**, **2Ch 18:18** 3678
placed the king upon the royal **t**. **2Ch 23:20** 3678
t which *was* at the citadel in Susa, **Es 1:2** 3678
on his royal **t** in the throne room, **Es 5:1** 3678
on his royal throne in the **t** room, **Es 5:1** 4438
on the **t** He has seated them forever, **Jb 36:7** 3678
sat on the **t** judging righteously. **Ps 9:4** 3678
established His **t** for judgment, **Ps 9:7** 3678
the LORD's **t** is in heaven; **Ps 11:4** 3678
Your **t**, O God, is forever and ever; **Ps 45:6** 3678
nations, God sits on His holy **t**. **Ps 47:8** 3678
up your **t** to all generations." **Ps 89:4** 3678
are the foundation of Your **t**; **Ps 89:14** 3678
And his **t** as the days of heaven. **Ps 89:29** 3678
And his **t** as the sun before Me. **Ps 89:36** 3678
And cast his **t** to the ground. **Ps 89:44** 3678
Your **t** is established from of old; **Ps 93:2** 3678
Can a **t** of destruction be allied **Ps 94:20** 3678
are the foundation of His **t**. **Ps 97:2** 3678
established His **t** in the heavens, **Ps 103:19** 3678
your body I will set upon your **t**. **Ps 132:11** 3678
shall sit upon your **t** forever." **Ps 132:12** 3678
a **t** is established on righteousness. **Pr 16:12** 3678
A king who sits on the **t** of justice **Pr 20:8** 3678
he upholds his **t** by righteousness. **Pr 20:28** 3678
And his **t** will be established in **Pr 25:5** 3678
His **t** will be established forever. **Pr 29:14** 3678
I saw the Lord sitting on a **t**, **Is 6:1** 3678
t of David and over his kingdom, **Is 9:7** 3678
raise my **t** above the stars of God, **Is 14:13** 3678
A **t** will even be established in **Is 16:5** 3678
And he will become a **t** of glory to **Is 22:23** 3678
Sit on the ground without a **t**, **Is 47:1** 3678
"Heaven is My **t** and the earth is **Is 66:1** 3678
and they will set each one his **t** **Jer 1:15** 3678
'The **T** of the LORD,' and all the **Jer 3:17** 3678
kings that sit for David on his **t**, **Jer 13:13** 3678
not disgrace the **t** of Your glory; **Jer 14:21** 3678
A glorious **t** on high from the **Jer 17:12** 3678
princes sitting on the **t** of David, **Jer 17:25** 3678

of Judah, who sits on David's **t**, **Jer 22:2** 3678
sitting in David's place on his **t**, **Jer 22:4** 3678
will prosper Sitting on the **t** of David **Jer 22:30** 3678
king who sits on the **t** of David, **Jer 29:16** 3678
on the **t** of the house of Israel; **Jer 33:17** 3678
not have a son to reign on his **t**, **Jer 33:21** 3678
no one to sit on the **t** of David, **Jer 36:30** 3678
and I am going to set his **t** *right* **Jer 43:10** 3678
'Then I will set My **t** in Elam **Jer 49:38** 3678
he spoke kindly to him and set his **t** **Jer 52:32** 3678
Your **t** is from generation to **La 5:19** 3678
was something resembling a **t**, **Ezk 1:26** 3678
and on that which resembled a **t**, **Ezk 1:26** 3678
in appearance resembling a **t**, **Ezk 10:1** 3678
of the king who put him on the **t**, **Ezk 17:16** 4427a
this is the place of My **t** and the **Ezk 43:7** 3678
he was deposed from his royal **t** and **Da 5:20** 3764
His **t** *was* ablaze with flames, Its **Da 7:9** 3764
of Nineveh, he arose from his **t**, **Jon 3:6** 3678
honor and sit and rule on His **t**. **Zch 6:13** 3678
He will be a priest on His **t**, **Zch 6:13** 3678
by heaven, for it is the **t** of God, **Mt 5:34** *2362*
of Man will sit on His glorious **t**, **Mt 19:28** *2362*
swears *both* by the **t** of God and by **Mt 23:22** *2362*
He will sit on His glorious **t**. **Mt 25:31** *2362*
Him the **t** of His father David; **Lk 1:32** *2362*
one OF HIS DESCENDANTS ON HIS **T**, **Ac 2:30** *2362*
'HEAVEN IS MY **T**, AND EARTH IS THE **Ac 7:49** *2362*
"YOUR **T**, O GOD, IS FOREVER AND **Heb 1:8** *2362*
with confidence to the **t** of grace, **Heb 4:16** *2362*
t of the Majesty in the heavens, **Heb 8:1** *2362*
at the right hand of the **t** of God. **Heb 12:2** *2362*
seven Spirits who are before His **t**, **Rv 1:4** *2362*
you dwell, where Satan's **t** is; **Rv 2:13** *2362*
him to sit down with Me on My **t**, **Rv 3:21** *2362*
sat down with My Father on His **t**. **Rv 3:21** *2362*
a **t** was standing in heaven, **Rv 4:2** *2362*
heaven, and One sitting on the **t**. **Rv 4:2** *2362*
there was a rainbow around the **t**, **Rv 4:3** *2362*
Around the **t** *were* twenty-four **Rv 4:4** *2362*
Out from the **t** come flashes of **Rv 4:5** *2362*
of fire burning before the **t**, **Rv 4:5** *2362*
before the **t** *there was something* like **Rv 4:6** *2362*
in the center and around the **t**, **Rv 4:6** *2362*
thanks to Him who sits on the **t**, **Rv 4:9** *2362*
down before Him who sits on the **t**, **Rv 4:10** *2362*
cast their crowns before the **t**, **Rv 4:10** *2362*
right hand of Him who sat on the **t** **Rv 5:1** *2362*
And I saw between the **t** **Rv 5:6** *2362*
hand of Him who sat on the **t**. **Rv 5:7** *2362*
the voice of many angels around the **t** **Rv 5:11** *2362*
"To Him who sits on the **t**, **Rv 5:13** *2362*
presence of Him who sits on the **t**, **Rv 6:16** *2362*
before the **t** and before the Lamb, **Rv 7:9** *2362*
to our God who sits on the **t**, **Rv 7:10** *2362*
the angels were standing around the **t** **Rv 7:11** *2362*
they fell on their faces before the **t** **Rv 7:11** *2362*
they are before the **t** of God; **Rv 7:15** *2362*
and He who sits on the **t** will **Rv 7:15** *2362*
for the Lamb in the center of the **t** **Rv 7:17** *2362*
altar which was before the **t**. **Rv 8:3** *2362*
was caught up to God and to His **t**. **Rv 12:5** *2362*
and his **t** and great authority. **Rv 13:2** *2362*
they sang a new song before the **t** **Rv 14:3** *2362*
his bowl on the **t** of the beast **Rv 16:10** *2362*
came out of the temple from the **t**, **Rv 16:17** *2362*
God who sits on the **t** saying, **Rv 19:4** *2362*
And a voice came from the **t**, **Rv 19:5** *2362*
I saw a great white **t** and Him who **Rv 20:11** *2362*
the small, standing before the **t**, **Rv 20:12** *2362*
I heard a loud voice from the **t**, **Rv 21:3** *2362*
And He who sits on the **t** said, **Rv 21:5** *2362*
from the **t** of God and of the Lamb, **Rv 22:1** *2362*
and the **t** of God and of the Lamb **Rv 22:3** *2362*

THRONES

For there **t** were set for judgment, **Ps 122:5** 3678
The **t** of the house of David. **Ps 122:5** 3678
kings of the nations from their **t**. **Is 14:9** 3678
set his throne above the **t** of the kings **Jer 52:32** 3678
the sea will go down from their **t**, **Ezk 26:16** 3678
kept looking Until **t** were set up, **Da 7:9** 3764
I will overthrow the **t** of kingdoms **Hg 2:22** 3678
you also shall sit upon twelve **t**, **Mt 19:28** *2362*
brought down rulers from *their* **t**, **Lk 1:52** *2362*
and you will sit on **t** judging the **Lk 22:30** *2362*
whether **t** or dominions or rulers **Col 1:16** *2362*
the throne *were* twenty-four **t**; **Rv 4:4** *2362*
and upon the **t** *I saw* twenty-four **Rv 4:4** *2362*
who sit on their **t** before God, **Rv 11:16** *2362*
Then I saw **t**, and they sat on **Rv 20:4** *2362*

THRONG

will praise You among a mighty **t**. **Ps 35:18** 5971a
I used to go along with the **t** *and* lead **Ps 42:4** 5519
in the house of God in the **t**. **Ps 55:14** 7285a
The princes of Judah *in* their **t**, **Ps 68:27** 7277
seen all the living under the sun **t** to **Ec 4:15** 1980
and a great **t** of people from all **Lk 6:17** *4128*

THRONGS

his own spears The head of his **t**. **Hab 3:14** 6518

THROUGH

Abram passed **t** the land as far **Gn 12:6** 5674a
the land **t** its length and breadth; **Gn 13:17**
I will obtain children **t** her." **Gn 16:2** 4480
preserve our family **t** our father." **Gn 19:32** 4480
preserve our family **t** our father." **Gn 19:34** 4480
for **t** Isaac your descendants shall **Gn 21:12** 4480
Philistines looked out **t** a window, **Gn 26:8** 1157
t her I too may have children." **Gn 30:3** 4480
me pass **t** your entire flock today, **Gn 30:32**
And Laban felt **t** all the tent but **Gn 31:34** 4959
you have felt **t** all my goods, **Gn 31:37** 4959
and went **t** all the land of Egypt. **Gn 41:46** 5674a
scattered **t** all the land of Egypt **Ex 5:12**
blood was **t** all the land of Egypt. **Ex 7:21**
gnats **t** all the land of Egypt.' " **Ex 8:16**
gnats **t** all the land of Egypt. **Ex 8:17**
beast **t** all the land of Egypt." **Ex 9:9**
proclaim My name **t** all the earth. **Ex 9:16**
the field **t** all the land of Egypt, **Ex 9:25**
as the LORD had spoken **t** Moses. **Ex 9:35** 3027
the field **t** all the land of Egypt. **Ex 10:15**
'For I will go **t** the land of Egypt **Ex 12:12** 5674a
pass **t** to smite the Egyptians; **Ex 12:23** 5674a
t Pharaoh and all his army, **Ex 14:4**
the sons of Israel shall go **t** the midst **Ex 14:16** 935
t Pharaoh and all his army, **Ex 14:17**
t his chariots and his horsemen. **Ex 14:17**
LORD, when I am honored **t** Pharaoh, **Ex 14:18**
t his chariots and his horsemen." **Ex 14:18**
Israel went **t** the midst of the sea on **Ex 14:22** 935
t the pillar of fire and cloud and **Ex 14:24**
dry land **t** the midst of the sea, **Ex 14:29**
dry land **t** the midst of the sea. **Ex 15:19**
shall surely be stoned or shot **t**; **Ex 19:13** 3384
not break **t** to the LORD to gaze, **Ex 19:21** 2040
break **t** to come up to the LORD, **Ex 19:24** 2040
shall pass **t** from end to end. **Ex 26:28** 1272
shall ordain them **t** seven days. **Ex 29:35**
had commanded **t** Moses to be done, **Ex 35:29** 3027
He made the middle bar to pass **t** in **Ex 36:33** 1272
entrusted *to him*, or **t** robbery, **Lv 6:2**
he will ordain you **t** seven days. **Lv 8:33**
the LORD had commanded **t** Moses. **Lv 8:36** 3027
LORD has spoken to them **t** Moses." **Lv 10:11** 3027
t any of the swarming things that **Lv 11:43**
sound a horn all **t** your land. **Lv 25:9**
proclaim a release **t** the land to all its **Lv 25:10**
no sword will pass **t** your land. **Lv 26:6** 5674a
of Israel **t** Moses at Mount Sinai. **Lv 26:46** 3027
commandment of the LORD **t** Moses. **Nu 4:37** 3027
commandment of the LORD **t** Moses. **Nu 4:45** 3027
commandment of the LORD **t** Moses, **Nu 4:49** 3027
the command of the LORD **t** Moses. **Nu 9:23** 3027
commandment of the LORD **t** Moses. **Nu 10:13** 3027
LORD indeed spoken only **t** Moses? **Nu 12:2**
Has He not spoken **t** us as well?" **Nu 12:2**
"The land **t** which we have gone, **Nu 13:32** 5674a
"The land which we passed **t** to **Nu 14:7** 5674a
LORD has commanded you **t** Moses, **Nu 15:23** 3027
to all the people **t** error. **Nu 15:26**
LORD had spoken to him **t** Moses. **Nu 16:40** 3027
'Please let us pass **t** your land. **Nu 20:17**
pass **t** field or through vineyard; **Nu 20:17** 5674a
pass through field or **t** vineyard; **Nu 20:17**
we pass **t** your territory.' " **Nu 20:17** 5674a
"You shall not pass **t** us, **Nu 20:18** 5674a
Let me only pass **t** on my feet, **Nu 20:19** 5674a
"You shall not pass **t**." **Nu 20:20** 5674a
Israel to pass **t** his territory; **Nu 20:21** 5674a
"Let me pass **t** your land. **Nu 21:22** 5674a
we have passed **t** your border." **Nu 21:22** 5674a
Israel to pass **t** his border. **Nu 21:23** 5674a
crush **t** the forehead of Moab, **Nu 24:17** 4272
tent and pierced both of them **t**, **Nu 25:8** 1856
Israel and the woman, **t** the body. **Nu 25:8** 413
as the LORD had spoken **t** Moses. **Nu 27:23** 3027
Israel, **t** the counsel of Balaam, **Nu 31:16**
fire, you shall pass **t** the fire, **Nu 31:23** 5674a
fire you shall pass **t** the water. **Nu 31:23** 5674a
and passed **t** the midst of the sea **Nu 33:8**
to the sons of Israel **t** Moses in the **Nu 36:13** 3027
and went **t** all that great and **Dt 1:19**
"You will pass **t** the territory of **Dt 2:4**
t this great wilderness. **Dt 2:7**
And we turned and passed **t** by the **Dt 2:8** 5674a
and pass **t** the valley of Arnon. **Dt 2:24** 5674a
'Let me pass **t** your land, I will **Dt 2:27**
drink, only let me pass **t** on foot, **Dt 2:28** 5674a
willing for us to pass **t** his land; **Dt 2:30**
t the great and terrible wilderness, **Dt 8:15**
have redeemed **t** Your greatness, **Dt 9:26**
pierce it **t** his ear into the door, **Dt 15:17**
or his daughter pass **t** the fire, **Dt 18:10**
we came **t** the midst of the nations **Dt 29:16**
of the nations **t** which you passed; **Dt 29:16** 5674a
And **t** the skies in His majesty. **Dt 33:26**
"Pass **t** the midst of the camp and **Jos 1:11**
them down by a rope **t** the window, **Jos 2:15** 1157
window **t** which you let us down, **Jos 2:18**
went **t** the midst of the camp; **Jos 3:2** 5674a
as the LORD commanded **t** Moses, **Jos 14:2** 3027
and continued **t** Timnah. **Jos 15:10** 5674a
t the hill country to Bethel. **Jos 16:1**
they may arise and walk **t** the land **Jos 18:4**
walk **t** the land and describe it, **Jos 18:8**
men went and passed **t** the land, **Jos 18:9**
up **t** the hill country westward, **Jos 18:12**
of which I spoke to you **t** Moses, **Jos 20:2** 3027
"The LORD commanded **t** Moses to **Jos 21:2** 3027
as the LORD had commanded **t** Moses. **Jos 21:8** 3027
the command of the LORD **t** Moses. **Jos 22:9** 3027
led him **t** all the land of Canaan, **Jos 24:3**
preserved us **t** all the way in which **Jos 24:17**
peoples **t** whose midst we passed. **Jos 24:17**
commanded their fathers **t** Moses. **Jg 3:4** 3027
and it went **t** into the ground; **Jg 4:21** 6795
mother of Sisera **t** the lattice, **Jg 5:28** 1157
"If You will deliver Israel **t** me, **Jg 6:36** 3027
You will deliver Israel **t** me, **Jg 6:37** 3027
So the young man pierced him **t**, **Jg 9:54** 1856
and Israel went **t** the wilderness **Jg 11:16**
"Please let us pass **t** your land," **Jg 11:17**
'Then they went **t** the wilderness **Jg 11:18**
pass **t** your land to our place." **Jg 11:19**
Israel to pass **t** his territory; **Jg 11:20**
he passed **t** Gilead and Manasseh; **Jg 11:29** 5674a
then he passed **t** Mizpah of Gilead, **Jg 11:29** 5674a
t the entire tribe of Benjamin, **Jg 20:12**
t the offspring which the LORD **Ru 4:12** 4480
He passed **t** the hill country **1Sa 9:4**
passed **t** the land of Shalishah, **1Sa 9:4**
they passed **t** the land of Shaalim, **1Sa 9:4**
t the land of the Benjamites, **1Sa 9:4**
Michal let David down **t** a window, **1Sa 19:12** 1157
either **t** prophets or by dreams; **1Sa 28:15** 3027
done accordingly as He spoke **t** me; **1Sa 28:17** 3027
sword and pierce me **t** with it, **1Sa 31:4** 1856
pierce me **t** and make sport of me. **1Sa 31:4** 1856
went **t** the Arabah all that night; **2Sa 2:29**
David's soul, **t** the water tunnel." **2Sa 5:8**
"The LORD has broken **t** my enemies **2Sa 5:20** 6555
sent *word* **t** Nathan the prophet, **2Sa 12:25** 3027
made them pass **t** the brickkiln. **2Sa 12:31**
thrust them **t** the heart of Absalom **2Sa 18:14**
went **t** all the tribes of Israel to Abel **2Sa 20:14** 5674a
the earth, **T** sunshine after rain.' **2Sa 23:4** 4480
t the camp of the Philistines, **2Sa 23:16** 1234
now **t** all the tribes of Israel, **2Sa 24:2**
had gone about **t** the whole land, **2Sa 24:8**
spoke **t** Moses Your servant, **1Ki 8:53** 3027
He promised **t** Moses His servant. **1Ki 8:56** 3027
which the LORD spoke **t** Ahijah the **1Ki 12:15** 3027
which He spoke **t** His servant Ahijah **1Ki 14:18** 3027
the word of the LORD **t** the prophet **1Ki 16:7** 3027
against Baasha **t** Jehu the prophet, **1Ki 16:12** 3027
the LORD which He spoke **t** Elijah. **1Ki 17:16** 3027
"Go **t** the land to all the springs **1Ki 18:5**
And Ahaziah fell **t** the lattice in **2Ki 1:2** 1157
to break **t** to the king of Edom; **2Ki 3:26** 1234
a lamp to him **t** his sons always. **2Ki 8:19**
and the arrow went **t** his heart and **2Ki 9:24** 3318
He spoke **t** His servant Elijah." **2Ki 10:10** 3027
which He spoke **t** His servant Jonah **2Ki 14:25** 3027
even made his son pass **t** the fire, **2Ki 16:3**
t all His prophets *and* every seer, **2Ki 17:13** 3027
you **t** My servants the prophets." **2Ki 17:13** 3027
their daughters pass **t** the fire, **2Ki 17:17**
t all His servants the prophets. **2Ki 17:23** 3027
"**T** your messengers you have **2Ki 19:23** 3027
He made his son pass **t** the fire, **2Ki 21:6**
spoke **t** His servants the prophets, **2Ki 21:10** 3027
pass **t** the fire for Molech. **2Ki 23:10**
t His servants the prophets. **2Ki 24:2** 3027
For **t** the anger of the LORD *this* **2Ki 24:20** 5921
sword and thrust me **t** with it, **1Ch 10:4** 1856
to the word of the LORD **t** Samuel. **1Ch 11:3** 3027
t the camp of the Philistines and **1Ch 11:18** 1234
broken **t** my enemies by my hand, **1Ch 14:11** 6555
to them **t** Aaron their father, **1Ch 24:19** 3027
which He spoke **t** Ahijah the **2Ch 10:15** 3027
t all the territories of Judah and **2Ch 11:23** 6555
of the LORD **t** the sons of David, **2Ch 13:8** 3027
the fortified cities **t** all Judah. **2Ch 17:19**
and came **t** the upper gate to the **2Ch 23:20** 8432
understanding **t** the vision of God; **2Ch 26:5**
was from the LORD **t** His prophets. **2Ch 29:25** 3027
t the country of Ephraim and **2Ch 30:10**
stream which flowed **t** the region, **2Ch 32:4** 8432
He made his sons pass **t** the fire in **2Ch 33:6**
the ordinances *given* **t** Moses." **2Ch 33:8** 3027
building **t** the prophesying of Haggai **Ezr 6:14**
to pass **t** until I come to Judah, **Ne 2:7** 5674a
the LORD had commanded **t** Moses **Ne 8:14** 3027
So they passed **t** the midst of the **Ne 9:11**
and law, **T** Your servant Moses. **Ne 9:14** 3027
them by Your Spirit **t** Your prophets, **Ne 9:30** 3027
God's law, which was given **t** Moses, **Ne 10:29** 3027
on horseback **t** the city square, **Es 6:9**
on horseback **t** the city square, **Es 6:11**
T all this Job did not sin nor did **Jb 1:22**
breaks **t** me with breach after breach **Jb 16:14** 6555
Can He judge **t** the thick darkness? **Jb 22:13** 1157
t the cleanness of your hands." **Jb 22:30**
whose spirit was expressed **t** you? **Jb 26:4** 4480
"He hews out channels **t** the rocks, **Jb 28:10**
by His light I walked **t** darkness; **Jb 29:3**
"As **t** a wide breach they come, **Jb 30:14**
passes **t** the paths of the seas. **Ps 8:8** 5674a
line has gone out **t** all the earth, **Ps 19:4**
glory is great **t** Your salvation, **Ps 21:5**
And **t** the lovingkindness of the **Ps 21:7**
Even though I walk **t** the valley of **Ps 23:4**
body wasted away **T** my groaning **Ps 32:3**
T You we will push back our **Ps 44:5**
T Your name we will trample down **Ps 44:5**
Go **t** her palaces, **Ps 48:13** 6448
T God we shall do valiantly, And **Ps 60:12**
They passed **t** the river on foot; **Ps 66:6**
We went **t** fire and through water, **Ps 66:12**
We went through fire and **t** water, **Ps 66:12**
for Him who rides **t** the deserts, **Ps 68:4**
You marched **t** the wilderness, **Ps 68:7**
wait for You not be ashamed **t** me, **Ps 69:6**
seek You not be dishonored **t** me, **Ps 69:6**
their tongue parades **t** the earth. **Ps 73:9**
sea and caused them to pass **t** **Ps 78:13** 5674a

Context	Reference	Number
Passing **t** the valley of Baca they	**Ps 84:6**	
And He led them **t** the deeps, as	**Ps 106:9**	
the deeps, as **t** the wilderness.	**Ps 106:9**	
and bowed down **T** oppression,	**Ps 107:39**	4480
T God we will do valiantly	**Ps 108:13**	
I shall enter **t** them, I shall give	**Ps 118:19**	
The righteous will enter **t** it.	**Ps 118:20**	
Revive me **t** Your righteousness.	**Ps 119:40**	
Israel pass **t** the midst of it,	**Ps 136:14**	
led His people **t** the wilderness,	**Ps 136:16**	
house I looked out **t** my lattice,	**Pr 7:6**	1157
t the street near her corner;	**Pr 7:8**	
an arrow pierces **t** his liver;	**Pr 7:23**	6398
But **t** knowledge the righteous will	**Pr 11:9**	
T insolence comes nothing but	**Pr 13:10**	
who has understanding sees **t** him.	**Pr 28:11**	2713
For the dream comes **t** much effort and	**Ec 5:3**	
the voice of a fool **t** many words.	**Ec 5:3**	
riches were lost **t** a bad investment	**Ec 5:14**	
may bite him who breaks **t** a wall.	**Ec 10:8**	6555
T indolence the rafters sag, and	**Ec 10:18**	
and **t** slackness the house leaks.	**Ec 10:18**	
those who look **t** windows grow dim;	**Ec 12:3**	
wall, He is looking **t** the windows,	**SS 2:9**	4480
He is peering **t** the lattice.	**SS 2:9**	4480
extended his hand **t** the opening,	**SS 5:4**	4480
Flowing gently **t** the lips of	**SS 7:9**	
it will overflow and pass **t**,	**Is 8:8**	5674a
They will pass **t** the land	**Is 8:21**	
Aiath, He has passed **t** Migron;	**Is 10:28**	
They have gone **t** the pass, *saying,*	**Is 10:29**	5674a
who is found will be thrust **t**,	**Is 13:15**	1856
spoke **t** Isaiah the son of Amoz,	**Is 20:2**	3027
asunder, The earth is split **t**,	**Is 24:19**	6565b
But **t** You alone we confess Your	**Is 26:13**	
Therefore **t** this Jacob's iniquity	**Is 27:9**	
T stammering lips and a foreign	**Is 28:11**	
the overwhelming scourge passes **t**,	**Is 28:18**	5674a
"As often as it passes **t**,	**Is 28:19**	5674a
after morning it will pass **t**,	**Is 28:19**	5674a
T a land of distress and anguish,	**Is 30:6**	
will pass **t** it forever and ever.	**Is 34:10**	
"**T** your servants you have	**Is 37:24**	3027
"When you pass **t** the waters, I	**Is 43:2**	
And **t** the rivers, they will not	**Is 43:2**	
When you walk **t** the fire, you will	**Is 43:2**	1119
Who makes a way **t** the sea And a	**Is 43:16**	
And a path **t** the mighty waters,	**Is 43:16**	
bronze and cut **t** their iron bars.	**Is 45:2**	1438
when He led them **t** the deserts.	**Is 48:21**	
pierced **t** for our transgressions,	**Is 53:5**	2490a
and hated With no one passing **t**,	**Is 60:15**	5674a
Go **t**, go through the gates,	**Is 62:10**	5674a
Go through, go **t** the gates,	**Is 62:10**	5674a
Who led them **t** the depths?	**Is 63:13**	
the wilderness, **T** a land not sown.	**Jer 2:2**	
Who led us **t** the wilderness,	**Jer 2:6**	
T a land of deserts and of pits,	**Jer 2:6**	
T a land of drought and of deep	**Jer 2:6**	
T a land that no one crossed And	**Jer 2:6**	
fro **t** the streets of Jerusalem,	**Jer 5:1**	
"Go up **t** her vine rows and	**Jer 5:10**	
T deceit they refuse to know Me,"	**Jer 9:6**	
waste so that no one passes **t**,	**Jer 9:10**	5674a
a desert, so that no one passes **t**?	**Jer 9:12**	5674a
death has come up **t** our windows;	**Jer 9:21**	
t which the kings of Judah come in	**Jer 17:19**	
who come in **t** these gates:	**Jer 17:20**	
in **t** the gates of Jerusalem.	**Jer 17:21**	
"to bring no load in **t** the gates	**Jer 17:24**	
will come in **t** the gates of this city	**Jer 17:25**	
coming in **t** the gates of Jerusalem on	**Jer 17:27**	
to pass **t** *the fire* to Molech,	**Jer 32:35**	5674a
He spoke **t** Jeremiah the prophet.	**Jer 37:2**	3027
by way of the king's garden **t** the gate	**Jer 39:4**	
orders about Jeremiah **t** Nebuzaradan	**Jer 39:11**	3027
Chaldeans, **t** Jeremiah the prophet:	**Jer 50:1**	3027
And pierced **t** in their streets."	**Jer 51:4**	1856
And **t** which no son of man passes.	**Jer 51:43**	5674a
For **t** the anger of the LORD *this*	**Jer 52:3**	5921
So that no prayer can pass **t**.	**La 3:44**	5674a
bloodshed also will pass **t** you,	**Ezk 5:17**	
"Son of man, now dig **t** the wall."	**Ezk 8:8**	
So I dug **t** the wall, and behold,	**Ezk 8:8**	
"Go **t** the midst of the city, *even*	**Ezk 9:4**	
even **t** the midst of Jerusalem,	**Ezk 9:4**	
Go **t** the city after him and strike;	**Ezk 9:5**	
"Dig a hole **t** the wall in their	**Ezk 12:5**	
in their sight and go out **t** it.	**Ezk 12:5**	
I dug **t** the wall with my hands;	**Ezk 12:7**	
dig a hole **t** the wall to bring *it* out.	**Ezk 12:12**	
from Me **t** all their idols."	**Ezk 14:5**	
wild beasts to pass **t** the land and	**Ezk 14:15**	
pass **t** it because of the beasts,	**Ezk 14:15**	5674a
'Let the sword pass **t** the country	**Ezk 14:17**	
causing them to pass **t** *the fire.*	**Ezk 16:21**	5674a
nakedness uncovered **t** your harlotries	**Ezk 16:36**	
all their firstborn to pass **t** *the fire*	**Ezk 20:26**	5674a
your sons to pass **t** the fire,	**Ezk 20:31**	
I will disperse you **t** the lands,	**Ezk 22:15**	
pass **t** *the fire* to them as food.	**Ezk 23:37**	5674a
"A man's foot will not pass **t** it,	**Ezk 29:11**	
of a beast will not pass **t** it,	**Ezk 29:11**	
so that no one will pass **t**.	**Ezk 33:28**	5674a
flock wandered **t** all the mountains	**Ezk 34:6**	
the one who passes **t** and returns.	**Ezk 35:7**	5674a
when I am sanctified **t** you	**Ezk 38:16**	
I spoke in former days **t** My servants	**Ezk 38:17**	3027
will constantly pass **t** the land,	**Ezk 39:14**	

Context	Reference	Number
burying those who were passing **t**,	**Ezk 39:14**	5674a
"As those who pass **t** the land	**Ezk 39:15**	
who pass through the land pass **t**	**Ezk 39:15**	5674a
then I shall be sanctified **t** them	**Ezk 39:27**	
Then he brought me **t** the entrance,	**Ezk 46:19**	
cubits, and he led me **t** the water,	**Ezk 47:3**	5674a
a thousand and led me **t** the water,	**Ezk 47:4**	5674a
a thousand and led me **t** *the water,*	**Ezk 47:4**	5674a
"And **t** his shrewdness He will	**Da 8:25**	5921
us **t** His servants the prophets.	**Da 9:10**	3027
as he becomes strong **t** his riches,	**Da 11:2**	
on coming and overflow and pass **t**,	**Da 11:10**	5674a
t the Jewel of *his* kingdom;	**Da 11:20**	5674a
overflow *them* and pass **t**.	**Da 11:40**	5674a
When the LORD first spoke **t** Hosea,	**Hos 1:2**	
t the prophets I gave parables.	**Hos 12:10**	3027
But **t** Baal he did wrong and died.	**Hos 13:1**	
When they burst **t** the defenses,	**Jl 2:8**	1157
enter **t** the windows like a thief.	**Jl 2:9**	1157
strangers will pass **t** it no more.	**Jl 3:17**	
"You will go out **t** breaches *in*	**Am 4:3**	
I will pass **t** the midst of you,"	**Am 5:17**	
to go **t** the city one day's walk;	**Jon 3:4**	
They break out, pass **t** the gate and	**Mi 2:13**	5674a
of sheep, Which, if he passes **t**,	**Mi 5:8**	5674a
will the wicked one pass **t** you;	**Na 1:15**	
sweep **t** *like* the wind and pass on.	**Hab 1:11**	2498
Because **t** these things their catch	**Hab 1:16**	
You marched **t** the earth;	**Hab 3:12**	
His Spirit **t** the former prophets;	**Zch 7:12**	3027
will pass **t** the sea *of* distress	**Zch 10:11**	
of Jerusalem **t** the LORD of hosts,	**Zch 12:5**	
pierce him **t** when he prophesies.	**Zch 13:3**	1856
bring the third part **t** the fire,	**Zch 13:9**	
of the LORD to Israel **t** Malachi.	**Mal 1:1**	3027
fulfill what was spoken by the Lord **t**	**Mt 1:22**	*1223*
what had been spoken by the Lord **t**	**Mt 2:15**	*1223*
what had been spoken **t** Jeremiah	**Mt 2:17**	*1223*
fulfill what was spoken **t** the prophets	**Mt 2:23**	*1223*
was spoken **t** Isaiah the prophet:	**Mt 4:14**	*1223*
"Enter **t** the narrow gate; for	**Mt 7:13**	*1223*
and there are many who enter **t** it.	**Mt 7:13**	*1223*
was spoken **t** Isaiah the prophet	**Mt 8:17**	*1223*
Jesus was going **t** all the cities	**Mt 9:35**	*4013*
you will not finish *going* **t**	**Mt 10:23**	
t the grainfields on the Sabbath,	**Mt 12:1**	*1223*
was spoken **t** Isaiah the prophet:	**Mt 12:17**	*1223*
man, it passes **t** waterless places	**Mt 12:43**	*1223*
what was spoken **t** the prophet	**Mt 13:35**	*1223*
but woe to that man **t** whom the	**Mt 18:7**	*1223*
camel to go **t** the eye of a needle,	**Mt 19:24**	*1223*
fulfill what was spoken **t** the prophet	**Mt 21:4**	*1223*
spoken of **t** Daniel the prophet,	**Mt 24:15**	*1223*
that which was spoken **t** Jeremiah	**Mt 27:9**	*1223*
that He was passing **t** the grainfields	**Mk 2:23**	*1223*
t Sidon to the Sea of Galilee,	**Mk 7:31**	*1223*
out and *began* to go **t** Galilee,	**Mk 9:30**	*1223*
a camel to go **t** the eye of a needle	**Mk 10:25**	*1223*
to carry merchandise **t** the temple.	**Mk 11:16**	*1223*
Jesus Himself sent out **t** *them from*	**Mk 16:20**	
t all the surrounding district.	**Lk 4:14**	*2596*
But passing **t** their midst, He went	**Lk 4:30**	*1223*
let him down **t** the tiles with his	**Lk 5:19**	*1223*
He was passing **t** *some* grainfields on	**Lk 6:1**	*1223*
passes **t** waterless places seeking rest,	**Lk 11:24**	*1223*
And He was passing **t** from one city	**Lk 13:22**	*1279*
"Strive to enter **t** the narrow door;	**Lk 13:24**	*1223*
but woe to him **t** whom they come!	**Lk 17:1**	*1223*
camel to go **t** the eye of a needle than	**Lk 18:25**	*1223*
written **t** the prophets about the Son	**Lk 18:31**	*1223*
entered Jericho and was passing **t**.	**Lk 19:1**	*1330*
He was about to pass **t** that way.	**Lk 19:4**	*1330*
All things came into being **t** Him,	**Jn 1:3**	*1223*
that all might believe **t** him.	**Jn 1:7**	*1223*
and the world was made **t** Him,	**Jn 1:10**	*1223*
For the Law was given **t** Moses;	**Jn 1:17**	*1223*
were realized **t** Jesus Christ.	**Jn 1:17**	*1223*
the world might be saved **t** Him.	**Jn 3:17**	*1223*
And He had to pass **t** Samaria.	**Jn 4:4**	
		1330, 1223
if anyone enters **t** Me,	**Jn 10:9**	*1223*
one comes to the Father but **t** Me.	**Jn 14:6**	*1223*
who believe in Me **t** their word;	**Jn 17:20**	*1223*
was spoken of **t** the prophet Joel:	**Ac 2:16**	*1223*
God performed **t** Him in your midst,	**Ac 2:22**	*1223*
were taking place **t** the apostles.	**Ac 2:43**	*1223*
and the faith which *comes* **t** Him	**Ac 3:16**	*1223*
miracle has taken place **t** them is	**Ac 4:16**	*1223*
who by the Holy Spirit, **t**	**Ac 4:25**	
t the name of Your holy servant Jesus."	**Ac 4:30**	*1223*
granting them deliverance **t** him,	**Ac 7:25**	*1223*
t the laying on of the apostles' hands,	**Ac 8:18**	*1223*
and as he passed **t** he kept	**Ac 8:40**	*1330*
him down **t** *an opening in* the wall,	**Ac 9:25**	*1223*
was traveling **t** all *those regions,*	**Ac 9:32**	*1330*
preaching peace **t** Jesus Christ	**Ac 10:36**	*1223*
prophets bear witness that **t** His name	**Ac 10:43**	*1223*
they had gone **t** the whole island	**Ac 13:6**	*1330*
that **t** Him forgiveness of sins is	**Ac 13:38**	*1223*
and **t** Him everyone who believes is	**Ac 13:39**	*1722*
not be freed **t** the Law of Moses.	**Ac 13:39**	*1722*
being spread **t** the whole region.	**Ac 13:49**	*1223*
"**T** many tribulations we must	**Ac 14:22**	*1223*
They passed **t** Pisidia and came	**Ac 14:24**	*1330*
t both Phoenicia and Samaria,	**Ac 15:3**	*1330*
t the grace of the Lord Jesus,	**Ac 15:11**	*1223*
done **t** them among the Gentiles.	**Ac 15:12**	*1223*
was traveling **t** Syria and Cilicia,	**Ac 15:41**	*1330*
they were passing **t** the cities,	**Ac 16:4**	*1279*

Context	Reference	Number
They passed **t** the Phrygian and	**Ac 16:6**	*1330*
t Amphipolis and Apollonia,	**Ac 17:1**	*1353*
"For while I was passing **t** and	**Ac 17:23**	*1330*
t a Man whom He has appointed,	**Ac 17:31**	*1722*
he left and passed successively **t**	**Ac 18:23**	*1330*
those who had believed **t** grace,	**Ac 18:27**	*1223*
Paul passed **t** the upper	**Ac 19:1**	*1330*
had passed **t** Macedonia and Achaia,	**Ac 19:21**	*1330*
When he had gone **t** those districts	**Ac 20:2**	*1330*
decided to return **t** Macedonia.	**Ac 20:3**	*1223*
upon me **t** the plots of the Jews;	**Ac 20:19**	*1722*
they kept telling Paul **t** the Spirit	**Ac 21:4**	*1223*
among the Gentiles **t** his ministry.	**Ac 21:19**	*1223*
we have **t** you attained much peace,	**Ac 24:2**	*1223*
When we had sailed **t** the sea	**Ac 27:5**	*1277*
wanting to bring Paul safely **t**,	**Ac 27:43**	*1295*
they had been brought safely **t**,	**Ac 28:1**	*1295*
rightly spoke **t** Isaiah the prophet	**Ac 28:25**	*1223*
promised beforehand **t** His prophets	**Ro 1:2**	*1223*
t whom we have received grace and	**Ro 1:5**	*1223*
my God **t** Jesus Christ for you all,	**Ro 1:8**	*1223*
understood **t** what has been made,	**Ro 1:20**	
the secrets of men **t** Christ Jesus.	**Ro 2:16**	*1223*
the Law, **t** your breaking the Law,	**Ro 2:23**	*1223*
But if **t** my lie the truth of God	**Ro 3:7**	*1722*
for **t** the Law *comes* the knowledge	**Ro 3:20**	*1223*
even *the* righteousness of God **t** faith	**Ro 3:22**	*1223*
a gift by His grace **t** the redemption	**Ro 3:24**	*1223*
propitiation in His blood **t** faith.	**Ro 3:25**	*1223*
the uncircumcised **t** faith is one.	**Ro 3:30**	*1223*
we then nullify the Law **t** faith?	**Ro 3:31**	*1223*
of the world was not **t** the Law,	**Ro 4:13**	*1223*
but **t** the righteousness of faith.	**Ro 4:13**	*1223*
with God **t** our Lord Jesus Christ,	**Ro 5:1**	*1223*
t whom also we have obtained our	**Ro 5:2**	*1223*
within our hearts **t** the Holy Spirit	**Ro 5:5**	*1223*
saved from the wrath *of God* **t** Him.	**Ro 5:9**	*1223*
to God **t** the death of His Son,	**Ro 5:10**	*1223*
in God **t** our Lord Jesus Christ,	**Ro 5:11**	*1223*
t whom we have now received the	**Ro 5:11**	*1223*
just as **t** one man sin entered into	**Ro 5:12**	*1223*
into the world, and death **t** sin,	**Ro 5:12**	*1223*
which came **t** the one who sinned;	**Ro 5:16**	*1223*
the one, death reigned **t** the one,	**Ro 5:17**	*1223*
will reign in life **t** the One,	**Ro 5:17**	*1223*
So then as **t** one transgression	**Ro 5:18**	*1223*
even so **t** one act of righteousness	**Ro 5:18**	*1223*
For as **t** the one man's disobedience	**Ro 5:19**	*1223*
even so **t** the obedience of the One	**Ro 5:19**	*1223*
so grace would reign **t** righteousness	**Ro 5:21**	*1223*
life **t** Jesus Christ our Lord.	**Ro 5:21**	*1223*
with Him **t** baptism into death,	**Ro 6:4**	*1223*
dead **t** the glory of the Father,	**Ro 6:4**	*1223*
to the Law **t** the body of Christ,	**Ro 7:4**	*1223*
come to know sin except **t** the Law;	**Ro 7:7**	*1223*
opportunity **t** the commandment,	**Ro 7:8**	*1223*
opportunity **t** the commandment,	**Ro 7:11**	*1223*
deceived me and **t** it killed me.	**Ro 7:11**	*1223*
my death **t** that which is good,	**Ro 7:13**	*1223*
that **t** the commandment sin would	**Ro 7:13**	*1223*
be to God **t** Jesus Christ our Lord!	**Ro 7:25**	*1223*
do, weak as it was **t** the flesh,	**Ro 8:3**	*1223*
t His Spirit who dwells in you.	**Ro 8:11**	*1223*
conquer **t** Him who loved us.	**Ro 8:37**	*1223*
"**T** ISAAC YOUR DESCENDANTS WILL BE	**Ro 9:7**	*1722*
t Him and to Him are all things.	**Ro 11:36**	*1223*
For **t** the grace given to me I say	**Ro 12:3**	*1223*
that **t** perseverance and the	**Ro 15:4**	*1223*
what Christ has accomplished **t** me,	**Ro 15:18**	*1223*
the only wise God, **t** Jesus Christ,	**Ro 16:27**	*1223*
t whom you were called into	**1Co 1:9**	*1223*
the world **t** its wisdom did not *come to*	**1Co 1:21**	*1223*
t the foolishness of the message	**1Co 1:21**	*1223*
us God revealed *them* **t** the Spirit;	**1Co 2:10**	*1223*
Servants **t** whom you believed, even	**1Co 3:5**	*1223*
will be saved, yet so as **t** fire.	**1Co 3:15**	*1223*
I became your father **t** the gospel.	**1Co 4:15**	*1223*
will also raise us up **t** His power.	**1Co 6:14**	*1223*
husband is sanctified **t** his wife,	**1Co 7:14**	*1722*
wife is sanctified **t** her	**1Co 7:14**	*1722*
all things, and we *exist* **t** Him.	**1Co 8:6**	*1223*
For **t** your knowledge he who is	**1Co 8:11**	*1722*
cloud and all passed **t** the sea;	**1Co 10:1**	*1330*
the man *has his birth* **t** the woman;	**1Co 11:12**	*1223*
the word of wisdom **t** the Spirit,	**1Co 12:8**	*1223*
victory **t** our Lord Jesus Christ.	**1Co 15:57**	*1223*
to you after I go **t** Macedonia,	**1Co 16:5**	*1330*
for I am going **t** Macedonia;	**1Co 16:5**	*1330*
our comfort is abundant **t** Christ.	**2Co 1:5**	*1223*
in helping us **t** your prayers,	**2Co 1:11**	
on us **t** *the prayers of* many.	**2Co 1:11**	*1223*
therefore also **t** Him is our Amen to	**2Co 1:20**	*1223*
our Amen to the glory of God **t** us.	**2Co 1:20**	*1223*
and manifests **t** us the sweet aroma	**2Co 2:14**	*1223*
we have **t** Christ toward God.	**2Co 3:4**	*1223*
reconciled us to Himself **t** Christ and	**2Co 5:18**	*1223*
though God were making an appeal **t**	**2Co 5:20**	*1223*
not suffer loss in anything **t** us.	**2Co 7:9**	*1537*
but as proving **t** the earnestness	**2Co 8:8**	*1223*
t His poverty might become rich.	**2Co 8:9**	
has spread **t** all the churches;	**2Co 8:18**	*1223*
which **t** us is producing	**2Co 9:11**	*1223*
t many thanksgivings to God.	**2Co 9:12**	*1223*
hardship, **t** many sleepless nights,	**2Co 11:27**	*1722*
a basket **t** a window in the wall,	**2Co 11:33**	*1223*
I have not taken advantage of you **t**	**2Co 12:17**	*1223*
from men nor **t** the agency of man,	**Ga 1:1**	*1223*
agency of man, but **t** Jesus Christ and	**Ga 1:1**	*1223*
it **t** a revelation of Jesus Christ.	**Ga 1:12**	*1223*

womb and called me **t** His grace, **Ga 1:15** *1223*
Law but **t** faith in Christ Jesus, **Ga 2:16** *1223*
"For **t** the Law I died to the Law, **Ga 2:19** *1223*
if righteousness *comes* **t** the Law, **Ga 2:21** *1223*
the promise of the Spirit **t** faith. **Ga 3:14** *1223*
having been ordained **t** angels by **Ga 3:19** *1223*
of God **t** faith in Christ Jesus. **Ga 3:26** *1223*
and if a son, then an heir **t** God. **Ga 4:7** *1223*
by the free woman **t** the promise. **Ga 4:23** *1223*
For we **t** the Spirit, by faith, are **Ga 5:5**
but faith working **t** love. **Ga 5:6** *1223*
but **t** love serve one another. **Ga 5:13** *1223*
t which the world has been **Ga 6:14** *1223*
as sons **t** Jesus Christ to Himself, **Eph 1:5** *1223*
we have redemption **t** His blood, **Eph 1:7** *1223*
grace you have been saved **t** faith; **Eph 2:8** *1223*
in one body to God **t** the cross, **Eph 2:16** *1223*
for **t** Him we both have our access **Eph 2:18** *1223*
in Christ Jesus **t** the gospel, **Eph 3:6** *1223*
made known **t** the church to the rulers **Eph 3:10** *1223*
confident access **t** faith in Him. **Eph 3:12** *1223*
t His Spirit in the inner man, **Eph 3:16** *1223*
may dwell in your hearts **t** faith; **Eph 3:17** *1223*
is over all and **t** all and in all. **Eph 4:6** *1223*
which *comes* **t** Jesus Christ, **Php 1:11** *1223*
for my deliverance **t** your prayers **Php 1:19** *1223*
Jesus **t** my coming to you again. **Php 1:26** *1223*
that which is **t** faith in Christ, **Php 3:9** *1223*
things **t** Him who strengthens me. **Php 4:13** *1722*
all things have been created **t** **Col 1:16** *1223*
and **t** Him to reconcile all things **Col 1:20** *1223*
peace **t** the blood of His cross; **Col 1:20** *1223*
t Him, *I say,* whether things on **Col 1:20** *1223*
you in His fleshly body **t** death, **Col 1:22** *1223*
no one takes you captive **t** philosophy **Col 2:8** *1223*
Him **t** faith in the working of God, **Col 2:12** *1223*
having triumphed over them **t** Him. **Col 2:15** *1722*
thanks **t** Him to God the Father. **Col 3:17** *1223*
comforted about you **t** your faith; **1Th 3:7** *1223*
salvation **t** our Lord Jesus Christ, **1Th 5:9** *1223*
t sanctification by the Spirit and faith **2Th 2:13** *1722*
this He called you **t** our gospel, **2Th 2:14** *1223*
preserved **t** the bearing of children **1Tm 2:15** *1223*
on you **t** prophetic utterance **1Tm 4:14** *1223*
you **t** the laying on of my hands. **2Tm 1:6** *1223*
immortality to light **t** the gospel, **2Tm 1:10** *1223*
t the Holy Spirit who dwells in **2Tm 1:14** *1223*
wisdom that leads to salvation **t** faith **2Tm 3:15** *1223*
t me the proclamation might be **2Tm 4:17** *1223*
richly **t** Jesus Christ our Savior, **Ti 3:6** *1223*
may become effective **t** the knowledge **Phm 1:6** *1722*
saints have been refreshed **t** you, **Phm 1:7** *1223*
for I hope that **t** your prayers I **Phm 1:22** *1223*
t whom also He made the world. **Heb 1:2** *1223*
if the word spoken **t** angels proved **Heb 2:2** *1223*
at the first spoken **t** the Lord, **Heb 2:3** *1223*
things, and **t** whom are all things, **Heb 2:10** *1223*
of their salvation **t** sufferings. **Heb 2:10** *1223*
that **t** death He might render **Heb 2:14** *1223*
who **t** fear of death were subject to **Heb 2:15** *1223*
saying **t** David after so long a **Heb 4:7** *1722*
fall, **t** *following* the same example **Heb 4:11** *1722*
who has passed **t** the heavens, **Heb 4:14** *1330*
who **t** faith and patience inherit the **Heb 6:12** *1223*
so to speak, **t** Abraham even Levi, **Heb 7:9** *1223*
was **t** the Levitical priesthood **Heb 7:11** *1223*
hope, **t** which we draw near to God. **Heb 7:19** *1223*
an oath **t** the One who said to Him, **Heb 7:21** *1223*
those who draw near to God **t** Him, **Heb 7:25** *1223*
He entered **t** the greater and more **Heb 9:11** *1223*
t the blood of goats and calves, **Heb 9:12** *1223*
and calves, but **t** His own blood, **Heb 9:12** *1223*
who **t** the eternal Spirit offered **Heb 9:14** *1223*
sanctified **t** the offering of the body of **Heb 10:10** *1223*
He inaugurated for us **t** the veil, **Heb 10:20** *1223*
t reproaches and tribulations, **Heb 10:33**
t which he obtained the testimony **Heb 11:4** *1223*
about his gifts, and **t** faith, **Heb 11:4** *1223*
By faith they passed **t** the Red Sea **Heb 11:29** *1224*
they were passing **t** dry land; **Heb 11:29** *1223*
gained approval **t** their faith, **Heb 11:39** *1223*
t which those who were so **Heb 13:9** *1722*
sanctify the people **t** His own blood, **Heb 13:12** *1223*
T Him then, let us continually **Heb 13:15** *1223*
t the blood of the eternal covenant, **Heb 13:20** *1722*
in His sight, **t** Jesus Christ, **Heb 13:21** *1223*
hope **t** the resurrection of Jesus Christ **1Pe 1:3** *1223*
protected by the power of God **t** faith **1Pe 1:5** *1223*
t those who preached the gospel to **1Pe 1:12** *1223*
who **t** Him are believers in God, **1Pe 1:21** *1223*
t the living and enduring word of **1Pe 1:23** *1223*
acceptable to God **t** Jesus Christ. **1Pe 2:5** *1223*
were brought safely **t** *the* water. **1Pe 3:20** *1223*
t the resurrection of Jesus Christ, **1Pe 3:21** *1223*
may be glorified **t** Jesus Christ, **1Pe 4:11** *1223*
T Silvanus, our faithful brother **1Pe 5:12** *1223*
t the true knowledge of Him who **2Pe 1:3** *1223*
t which the world at that time was **2Pe 3:6** *1223*
world so that we might live **t** Him. **1Jn 4:9** *1223*
Savior, **t** Jesus Christ our Lord, **Jude 1:25** *1223*

THROUGHOUT

after you **t** their generations for an **Gn 17:7**
after you **t** their generations. **Gn 17:9**
be circumcised **t** your generations, **Gn 17:12**
be blood **t** all the land of Egypt, **Ex 7:19**
the field, **t** the land of Egypt." **Ex 9:22**
t your generations you are to **Ex 12:14**
observe this day **t** your generations as **Ex 12:17**
of Israel **t** their generations. **Ex 12:42**
shall be eaten **t** the seven days; **Ex 13:7**
of it be kept **t** your generations, **Ex 16:32**
to be kept **t** your generations." **Ex 16:33**
cubits, and the width fifty **t**, **Ex 27:18**
a perpetual statute **t** their generations **Ex 27:21**
burnt offering **t** your generations **Ex 29:42**
the LORD **t** your generations. **Ex 30:8**
once a year **t** your generations. **Ex 30:10**
descendants **t** their generations." **Ex 30:21**
oil to Me **t** your generations. **Ex 30:31**
Me and you **t** your generations, **Ex 31:13**
the sabbath **t** their generations **Ex 31:16**
was circulated **t** the camp, **Ex 36:6**
priesthood **t** their generations." **Ex 40:15**
T all their journeys whenever **Ex 40:36**
For **t** all their journeys, the **Ex 40:38**
perpetual statute **t** your generations **Lv 3:17**
ordinance **t** your generations, **Lv 6:18**
forever **t** their generations.' " **Lv 7:36**
statute **t** your generations **Lv 10:9**
to them **t** their generations." **Lv 17:7**
of your offspring **t** their generations **Lv 21:17**
your descendants **t** your generations **Lv 22:3**
a perpetual statute **t** your generations **Lv 23:14**
places **t** your generations. **Lv 23:21**
a perpetual statute **t** your generations **Lv 23:31**
statute **t** your generations; **Lv 23:41**
statute **t** your generations. **Lv 24:3**
its purchaser **t** his generations; **Lv 25:30**
statute **t** your generations. **Nu 10:8**
people weeping **t** their families, **Nu 11:10**
be among you **t** your generations, **Nu 15:14**
statute **t** your generations; **Nu 15:15**
an offering **t** your generations. **Nu 15:21**
and onward **t** your generations, **Nu 15:23**
garments **t** their generations, **Nu 15:38**
statute **t** your generations, **Nu 18:23**
month **t** the months of the year. **Nu 28:14**
ordinance to you **t** your generations **Nu 35:29**
towns **t** Israel where he resides, **Dt 18:6** 4480, 3605
have olive trees **t** your territory **Dt 28:40** 3605
you trusted come down **t** your land, **Dt 28:52** 3605
shall besiege you in all your towns **t** **Dt 28:52** 3605
He sent messengers **t** Manasseh, **Jg 6:35** 3605
another even **t** the whole army; **Jg 7:22** 3605
sent messengers **t** all the hill country **Jg 7:24** 3605
her **t** the territory of Israel. **Jg 19:29** 3605
cut her in pieces and sent her **t** the **Jg 20:6** 3605
out of 100 **t** the tribes of Israel, **Jg 20:10** 3605
was a deadly confusion **t** the city; **1Sa 5:11** 3605
t the territory of Israel. **1Sa 11:3** 3605
sent *them* **t** the territory of Israel **1Sa 11:7** 3605
Saul blew the trumpet **t** the land, **1Sa 13:3** 3605
t the land of the Philistines, **1Sa 31:9** 5439
spies **t** all the tribes of Israel, **2Sa 15:10**
t all the tribes of Israel, **2Sa 19:9**
t all the territory of Israel, **1Ki 1:3**
the house was finished **t** all its parts **1Ki 6:38**
passed **t** the army close to sunset, **1Ki 22:36** 5674a
Then Jehu sent **t** Israel and all **2Ki 10:21** 3605
them **t** the territory of Israel: **2Ki 10:32** 3605
t all the land east of Gilead. **1Ch 5:10** 5921
All their cities **t** their families **1Ch 6:60**
departed and went **t** all Israel, **1Ch 21:4**
t all the territory of Israel.' **1Ch 21:12**
famous and glorious **t** all lands. **1Ch 22:5**
t all the months of the year, **1Ch 27:1**
eyes of the LORD move to and fro **t** **2Ch 16:9** 3605
and they went **t** all the cities of **2Ch 17:9** 5437
and proclaimed a fast **t** all Judah. **2Ch 20:3** 5921
They went **t** Judah and gathered **2Ch 23:2** 5437
of hundreds **t** Judah and Benjamin; **2Ch 25:5** 3605
to circulate a proclamation **t** all Israel **2Ch 30:5**
The couriers went **t** all Israel **2Ch 30:6**
altars **t** all Judah and Benjamin, **2Ch 31:1** 4480
Thus Hezekiah did **t** all Judah; **2Ch 31:20**
altars **t** the land of Israel. **2Ch 34:7** 3605
T his lifetime they did not turn **2Ch 34:33** 3605
sent a proclamation **t** his kingdom, **2Ch 36:22** 3605
a proclamation **t** all his kingdom, **Ezr 1:1**
proclamation **t** Judah and Jerusalem **Ezr 10:7**
make is heard **t** all his kingdom, **Es 1:20**
who *were* **t** the whole kingdom of **Es 3:6**
Jews assembled in their cities **t** all the **Es 9:2**
fame spread **t** all the provinces; **Es 9:4**
and celebrated **t** every generation, **Es 9:28**
T all generations I will not be **Ps 10:6**
as the moon, **t** all generations. **Ps 72:5**
When he went **t** the land of Egypt. **Ps 81:5** 5921
Your years are **t** all generations. **Ps 102:24**
continues **t** all generations; **Ps 119:90**
O LORD, **t** all generations. **Ps 135:13**
endures **t** all generations. **Ps 145:13**
T his life *he* also eats in **Ec 5:17** 3605
will stand by him in his toils **t** **Ec 8:15**
is in their hearts **t** their lives. **Ec 9:3**
Let this be known **t** the earth. **Is 12:5** 3605
places for sin **t** your borders. **Jer 17:3** 3605
wounded will groan **t** her land. **Jer 51:52** 3605
"So **t** all their habitations I **Ezk 6:14**
they were dispersed **t** the lands. **Ezk 36:19**
like a pool of water **t** her days, **Na 2:8** 4480
people Who march **t** the earth **Hab 1:6** 4800
range to and fro **t** the earth." **Zch 4:10** 3605
Jesus was going **t** all Galilee, **Mt 4:23** *4013*
The news about Him spread **t** all Syria; **Mt 4:24** *1519*
This news spread **t** all that land. **Mt 9:26** *1519*
out and spread the news about Him **t** **Mt 9:31** *1722*
their synagogues **t** all Galilee, **Mk 1:39** *1519*
proclaiming **t** the whole city what **Lk 8:39** *2596*
Departing, they *began* going **t** **Lk 9:6** *1330*
t the regions of Judea and Samaria **Ac 8:1** *2596*
So the church **t** all Judea and **Ac 9:31** *2596*
which took place **t** all Judea, **Ac 10:37** *2596*
the brethren who were **t** Judea heard **Ac 11:1** *2596*
among all the Jews **t** the world, **Ac 24:5** *2596*
then **t** all the region of Judea, **Ac 26:20**
proclaimed **t** the whole world. **Ro 1:8** *1722*
BE PROCLAIMED **T** THE WHOLE EARTH." **Ro 9:17** *1722*
all the saints who are **t** Achaia: **2Co 1:1** *3650*
known **t** the whole praetorian guard **Php 1:13** *1722*
as aliens, scattered **t** Pontus, **1Pe 1:1** *1290*

THROW

and **t** him into one of the pits; **Gn 37:20** 7993
T him into this pit that is in the **Gn 37:22** 7993
"**T** it on the ground." **Ex 4:3** 7993
and **t** *it* down before Pharaoh, **Ex 7:9** 7993
and let Moses **t** it toward the sky **Ex 9:8** 2236b
you shall **t** it to the dogs. **Ex 22:31** 7993
and **t** into confusion all the **Ex 23:27** 2000
and **t** them away at an unclean place **Lv 14:40** 7993
and will **t** them into great confusion **Dt 7:23** 1949
Did not a woman **t** an upper **2Sa 11:21** 7993
t this woman out of my *presence,* **2Sa 13:17** 7971
He said, "**T** her down." **2Ki 9:33** 8058
or **t** up a siege ramp against it. **2Ki 19:32** 8210
Over Edom I shall **t** My shoe; **Ps 60:8** 7993
Over Edom I shall **t** My shoe; **Ps 108:9** 7993
T in your lot with us, We shall **Pr 1:14** 5307
A time to **t** stones and a time to **Ec 3:5** 7993
to keep and a time to **t** away. **Ec 3:6** 7993
or **t** up a siege ramp against it. **Is 37:33** 8210
cedars And **t** *them* on the fire. **Jer 22:7** 5307
t it into the middle of the Euphrates **Jer 51:63** 7993
of them and **t** them into the fire and **Ezk 5:4** 7993
and **t** your stones and your timbers **Ezk 26:12** 7760
the priests shall **t** salt on them, **Ezk 43:24** 7993
"Pick me up and **t** me into the sea. **Jon 1:12** 2904
"I will **t** filth on you And make **Na 3:6** 7993
to **t** down the horns of the nations **Zch 1:21** 3034
"**T** it to the potter, *that* **Zch 11:13** 7993
the Son of God, **t** Yourself down; **Mt 4:6** *906*
tear it out and **t** it from you; **Mt 5:29** *906*
cut it off and **t** it from you; **Mt 5:30** *906*
do not **t** your pearls before swine, **Mt 7:6** *906*
and will **t** them into the furnace of **Mt 13:42** *906*
and will **t** them into the furnace of **Mt 13:50** *906*
bread and **t** it to the dogs." **Mt 15:26** *906*
go to the sea and **t** in a hook, **Mt 17:27** *906*
cut it off and **t** it from you; **Mt 18:8** *906*
pluck it out and **t** it from you. **Mt 18:9** *906*
and **t** him into the outer darkness; **Mt 22:13** *1544b*
"**T** out the worthless slave into **Mt 25:30** *1544b*
bread and **t** it to the dogs." **Mk 7:27** *906*
t it out; it is better for you to **Mk 9:47** *1544b*
of God, **t** Yourself down from here; **Lk 4:9** *906*
in order to **t** Him down the cliff. **Lk 4:29** *2630*
the officer **t** you into prison. **Lk 12:58** *906*
will **t** up a barricade against you, **Lk 19:43** *3925a*
from them about a stone's **t**, **Lk 22:41** *1000*
the first to **t** a stone at her." **Jn 8:7** *906*
they picked up stones to **t** at Him, **Jn 8:59** *906*
do not **t** away your confidence, **Heb 10:35** *577*
'Behold, I will **t** her on a bed *of* **Rv 2:22** *906*

THROWING

T him into convulsions, the unclean **Mk 1:26** *4682*
t him into terrible convulsions, **Mk 9:26** *4682*
T aside his cloak, he jumped up **Mk 10:50** *577*
men are **t** our city into confusion, **Ac 16:20** *1613*
t off their cloaks and tossing dust **Ac 22:23** *4496*
by **t** out the wheat into the sea. **Ac 27:38** *1544b*

THROWN

will be **t** to you over the wall." **2Sa 20:21** 7993
and his body was **t** on the road, **1Ki 13:24** 7993
by and saw the body **t** on the road, **1Ki 13:25** 7993
and found his body **t** on the road **1Ki 13:28** 7993
had **t** away in their haste. **2Ki 7:15** 7993
is **t** into the net by his own feet, **Jb 18:8** 7971
t down by the sides of the rock, **Ps 141:6** 8058
So their slain will be **t** out, **Is 34:3** 7993
be **t** out into the streets of Jerusalem **Jer 14:16** 7993
Dragged off and **t** out beyond the **Jer 22:19** 7993
In His wrath He has **t** down The **La 2:2** 2040
They have **t** dust on their heads; **La 2:10** 5927
He has **t** down without sparing, And **La 2:17** 2040
were **t** out into the open field, **Ezk 16:5** 7993
the mountains also will be **t** down, **Ezk 38:20** 2040
place of His sanctuary was **t** down. **Da 8:11** 7993
is cut down and **t** into the fire. **Mt 3:10** *906*
except to be **t** out and trampled **Mt 5:13** *906*
officer, and you be **t** into prison. **Mt 5:25** *906*
your whole body to be **t** into hell. **Mt 5:29** *906*
tomorrow is **t** into the furnace, **Mt 6:30** *906*
is cut down and **t** into the fire. **Mt 7:19** *906*
"It has often **t** him both into **Mk 9:22** *906*
is cut down and **t** into the fire." **Lk 3:9** *906*
when the demon had **t** him down in **Lk 4:35** *4496*
tomorrow is **t** into the furnace, **Lk 12:28** *906*
but yourselves being **t** out. **Lk 13:28** *1544b*
or for the manure pile; it is **t** out. **Lk 14:35** *906*
neck and he were **t** into the sea, **Lk 17:2** *4496*
was one who had been **t** into prison **Lk 23:19** *906*
had been **t** into prison for insurrection **Lk 23:25** *906*
had not yet been **t** into prison. **Jn 3:24** *906*
in Me, he is **t** away as a branch and **Jn 15:6** *906*
Romans, and have **t** us into prison; **Ac 16:37** *906*

and they were t to the earth; Rv 8:7 906
mountain burning with fire was t Rv 8:8 906
And the great dragon was t down, Rv 12:9 906
he was t down to the earth, and Rv 12:9 906
his angels were t down with him. Rv 12:9 906
of our brethren has been t down, Rv 12:10 906
that he was t down to the earth, Rv 12:13 906
city, be t down with violence, Rv 18:21 906
these two were t alive into the lake Rv 19:20 906
devil who deceived them was t into Rv 20:10 906
death and Hades were t into the Rv 20:14 906
he was t into the lake of fire. Rv 20:15 906

THROWS
Like a madman who t Firebrands, Pr 26:18 3384
and it t him into a convulsion Lk 9:39 *4682*

THRUSH
the swift and the t Observe the time Jer 8:7 5693

THRUST
He will t them out from before Jos 23:5 1920
thigh and t it into his belly. Jg 3:21 8628
Then he would t it into the pan, 1Sa 2:14 5221
his opponent by the head and t 2Sa 2:16
t them through the heart of Absalom 2Sa 18:14 8628
every one of them will be t away 2Sa 23:6 5074
sword and t me through with it, 1Ch 10:4 1856
skin And t my horn in the dust. Jb 16:15 5953d
They t aside my feet and build up Jb 30:12 7971
their transgressions t them out, Ps 5:10 5080
have been t down and cannot rise. Ps 36:12 1760
They have counseled only to t him Ps 62:4 5080
wicked is t down by his wrongdoing, Pr 14:32 1760
Nor to t aside the righteous in Pr 18:5 5186
who is found will be t through, Is 13:15 1856
you will be t down to Sheol, Is 14:15 3381
because the LORD has t them down. Jer 46:15 1920
and t at all the weak with your Ezk 34:21 1920

THRUSTING
t them out of their possession; Ezk 46:18 3238

THRUSTS
rashly like the t of a sword, Pr 12:18 4094a

THUMB
and on the t of his right hand and Lv 8:23 931
and on the t of their right hand and Lv 8:24 931
and on the t of his right hand and Lv 14:14 931
and on the t of his right hand, Lv 14:17 931
and on the t of his right hand and Lv 14:25 931
and on the t of his right hand and Lv 14:28 931

THUMBS
and on the t of their right hands Ex 29:20 931
and cut off his t and big toes. Jg 1:6 931
"Seventy kings with their t and Jg 1:7 931

THUMMIM
of judgment the Urim and the T, Ex 28:30 8550
he put the Urim and the T. Lv 8:8 8550
"*Let* Your T and Your Urim *belong* to Dt 33:8 8550
a priest stood up with Urim and T. Ezr 2:63 8550
a priest arose with Urim and T. Ne 7:65 8550

THUNDER
sky, and the LORD sent t and hail, Ex 9:23 6963
been enough of God's t and hail; Ex 9:28 6963
the t will cease and there will Ex 9:29 6963
and the t and the hail ceased, and Ex 9:33 6963
and the hail and the t had ceased, Ex 9:34 6963
that there were t and lightning Ex 19:16 6963
spoke and God answered him with t. Ex 19:19 6963
All the people perceived the t Ex 20:18 6963
them He will t in the heavens, 1Sa 2:10 7481
the LORD thundered with a great t on 1Sa 7:10 6963
LORD, that He may send t and rain. 1Sa 12:17 6963
the LORD sent t and rain that day; 1Sa 12:18 6963
But His mighty t, who can Jb 26:14 7482
closely to the t of His voice, Jb 37:2 7267
from afar, And the t of the captains Jb 39:25 7482
can you t with a voice like His? Jb 40:9 7481
sound of Your t was in the whirlwind Ps 77:18 7482
you in the hiding place of t; Ps 81:7 7482
sound of Your t they hurried away. Ps 104:7 7482
t and earthquake and loud noise, Is 29:6 7482
Boanerges, which means, "Sons of T" Mk 3:17 *1027*
and sounds and peals of t. Rv 4:5 *1027*
saying as with a voice of t, Rv 6:1 *1027*
and there followed peals of t and Rv 8:5 *1027*
peals of t uttered their voices. Rv 10:3 *1027*
the seven peals of t had spoken, Rv 10:4 *1027*
the seven peals of t have spoken and Rv 10:4 *1027*
of lightning and sounds and peals of t Rv 11:19 *1027*
and like the sound of loud t, Rv 14:2 *1027*
and sounds and peals of t; Rv 16:18 *1027*
like the sound of mighty peals of t, Rv 19:6 *1027*

THUNDERBOLT
the rain And a course for the t, Jb 28:26
6963, 2385
for the flood, Or a way for the t, Jb 38:25
6963, 2385

THUNDERED
But the LORD t with a great 1Sa 7:10 7481
"The LORD t from heaven, And the 2Sa 22:14 7481
The LORD also t in the heavens, Ps 18:13 7481
it were saying that it had t; Jn 12:29
1027, 1096

THUNDERING
the clouds, The t of His pavilion? Jb 36:29 8663

THUNDERS
He t with His majestic voice, Jb 37:4 7481
"God t with His voice wondrously, Jb 37:5 7481
The God of glory t, Ps 29:3 7481

THUS
T the heavens and the earth were Gn 2:1
T Noah did; according to all that Gn 6:22
T He blotted out every living Gn 7:23
t they came to the land of Canaan. Gn 12:5
T they separated from each other. Gn 13:11
t shall My covenant be in your Gn 17:13
T it came about, when God Gn 19:29
T both the daughters of Lot were Gn 19:36
T they sent away their sister Gn 24:59
t Isaac was comforted after his Gn 24:67
T Esau despised his birthright. Gn 25:34
"If he spoke t, Gn 31:8 3541
and if he spoke t, Gn 31:8 3541
T God has taken away your Gn 31:9
"T I was: by day the heat Gn 31:40
"T you shall say to my lord Esau: Gn 32:4 3541
'T says your servant Jacob, Gn 32:4 3541
T he urged him and he took *it*. Gn 33:11
"T you shall live with us, and Gn 34:10
T He called him Israel. Gn 35:10
T they brought Joseph into Egypt. Gn 37:28
t the LORD's blessing was upon all Gn 39:5
T it came about on the third day, Gn 40:20
T Joseph stored up grain in great Gn 41:49
And t it was done for them. Gn 42:25 3651
"T it came about when we went up Gn 44:24
T your servants will bring the Gn 44:31
'T says your son Joseph, Gn 45:9 3541
T the land became Pharaoh's. Gn 47:20
T he put Ephraim before Manasseh. Gn 48:20
T his sons did for him as he had Gn 50:12 3651
'T you shall say to Joseph, Gn 50:17 3541
"T you shall say to the sons of Ex 3:14 3541
"T you shall say to the sons of Ex 3:15 3541
T you will plunder the Egyptians." Ex 3:22
'T says the LORD, Ex 4:22 3541
"T says the LORD, the God of Ex 5:1 3541
"T says Pharaoh, Ex 5:10 3541
Moses spoke t to the sons of Israel, Ex 6:9 3651
LORD commanded them, t they did. Ex 7:6 3651
and t they did just as the LORD Ex 7:10 3651
'T says the LORD, Ex 7:17 3541
'T says the LORD, Ex 8:1 3541
'T says the LORD, Ex 8:20 3541
'T says the LORD, the God of the Ex 9:1 3541
'T says the LORD, the God of the Ex 9:13 3541
'T says the LORD, the God of the Ex 10:3 3541
"T may the LORD be with you, if Ex 10:10 3651
T nothing green was left on tree Ex 10:15
'T says the LORD, Ex 11:4 3541
T they plundered the Egyptians. Ex 12:36
"T I will harden Pharaoh's heart, Ex 14:4
T the one did not come near the Ex 14:20
T the LORD saved Israel that day Ex 14:30
T his hands were steady until the Ex 17:12
"T you shall say to the house of Ex 19:3 3541
"T you shall say to the sons of Ex 20:22 3541
t you shall do for all the boards Ex 26:17 3651
t it shall be with both of them: Ex 26:24 3651
"T they shall eat those things by Ex 29:33
"T you shall do to Aaron and to his Ex 29:35 3602
"T says the LORD, the God of Ex 32:27 3541
T the LORD used to speak to Moses Ex 33:11
T the people were restrained from Ex 36:6
t he did for all the boards of the Ex 36:22 3651
t he did with both of them for the Ex 36:29 3651
T all the work of the tabernacle Ex 39:32
T Moses did; according to all that Ex 40:16
T Moses finished the work. Ex 40:33
t he shall do with it. Lv 4:20 3651
T the priest shall make atonement Lv 4:26
T the priest shall make atonement Lv 4:31
T the priest shall make atonement Lv 4:35
T Aaron and his sons did all the Lv 8:36
for t I have been commanded. Lv 10:13 3651
a hoof, t making split hoofs, Lv 11:3
the hoof, t making a split hoof, Lv 11:7
t you shall be holy, for I am holy.' " Lv 11:45
T the priest shall look, and if Lv 14:3
T the priest shall make atonement Lv 14:20
"He shall t cleanse the house Lv 14:52
"T you shall keep the sons of Lv 15:31
and t he shall do for the tent of Lv 16:16 3651
shall t put on the linen garments, Lv 16:32
'T you are to keep My charge, that Lv 18:30
shall t observe all My statutes and Lv 19:37
t both of them shall be cut off Lv 20:18
'T you are to be holy to Me, for I Lv 20:26
'You shall t celebrate it *as a* Lv 23:41
T the one who kills an animal Lv 24:21
T the sons of Israel did, just as Lv 24:23
'You shall t consecrate the Lv 25:10
'You shall t observe My statutes and Lv 25:18
'T for every piece of your Lv 25:24
You will t eat your food to the Lv 26:5
'T all the tithe of the land, of Lv 27:30
T the sons of Israel did; Nu 1:54
T the sons of Israel did; Nu 2:34
"You shall t give the Levites to Nu 3:9
t *these were* his numbered men, Nu 4:49
Moses, t the sons of Israel did. Nu 5:4 3651
'T you shall bless the sons of Nu 6:23 3541
"T you shall do to them, for their Nu 8:7 3541
"T you shall separate the Levites Nu 8:14
T did Moses and Aaron and all the Nu 8:20
T you shall deal with the Levites Nu 8:26 3602
T the LORD spoke to Moses in the Nu 9:1
T they set out from the mount of Nu 10:33
You are going to deal t with me, Nu 11:15 3602
T they told him, and said, Nu 13:27
'T it shall be done for each ox, Nu 15:11 3602
T Korah assembled all the Nu 16:19
T I will lessen from upon Myself Nu 17:5
T Moses did; just as the LORD had Nu 17:11
"And they shall t attend to your Nu 18:3
The people t contended with Moses Nu 20:3
You shall t bring forth water for Nu 20:8
"T your brother Israel has said, Nu 20:14 3541
T Edom refused to allow Israel to Nu 20:21
T the name of the place was called Nu 21:3
T Israel lived in the land of the Nu 21:31
"T says Balak the son of Zippor, Nu 22:16 3541
to Balak, and you shall speak t." Nu 23:5 3541
to Balak, and t you shall speak." Nu 23:16 3541
t it will be withdrawn from our Nu 36:3
"T no inheritance of the sons of Nu 36:7
"T no inheritance shall be Nu 36:9
"T we took the land at that time Dt 3:8
that you should do t in the land Dt 4:5 3651
"But t you shall do to them: Dt 7:5 3541
"T you are to know in your heart Dt 8:5
shall not behave t toward the LORD Dt 12:31 3651
t you shall purge the evil from Dt 17:12
T you shall purge the evil from Dt 19:19
"T you shall not show pity: Dt 19:21
"T you shall do to all the cities Dt 20:15 3651
"T you shall do with his donkey, Dt 22:3 3651
t you shall purge the evil from Dt 22:21
t you shall purge the evil from Dt 22:22
T you shall purge the evil from Dt 22:24
"T it is done to the man who does Dt 25:9 3602
has the LORD done t to this land? Dt 29:24 3662
"Do you t repay the LORD, O Dt 32:6 2088
T the sons of Israel did as Joshua Jos 4:8 3651
T the second day they marched Jos 6:14
t the LORD, the God of Israel, has Jos 7:13 3541
T he did to them, and delivered Jos 9:26 3651
for t the LORD will do to all your Jos 10:25 3602
T he did to the king of Makkedah Jos 10:28
T he did to its king just as he Jos 10:30
T Joshua struck all the land, the Jos 10:40
T Joshua took all that land: Jos 11:16
T the land had rest from war. Jos 11:23
T the sons of Israel did just as Jos 14:5 3651
T there fell ten portions to Jos 17:5
whom the LORD has t far blessed?" Jos 17:14 3541
T they gave them Kiriath-arba, Jos 21:11
t *it was* with all these cities. Jos 21:42 3651
"T says the whole congregation of Jos 22:16 3541
"T says the LORD, the God of Jos 24:2 3541
T I gave them into your hand. Jos 24:11
t it shall be for a witness Jos 24:27
t they provoked the LORD to anger. Jg 2:12
"T let all Your enemies perish, Jg 5:31 3651
"T says the LORD, the God of Jg 6:8 3541
T the sons of Israel did not Jg 8:34
T he said to them, Jg 9:7
T God repaid the wickedness of Jg 9:56
t they forsook the LORD and did Jg 10:6
"T says Jephthah, Jg 11:15 3541
T it became a custom in Israel, Jg 11:39
T there fell at that time 42,000 Jg 12:6
t burning up both the shocks and Jg 15:5
T he had judged Israel twenty Jg 16:31
"T and so has Micah done to me, Jg 18:4 2090
T all the men of Israel were Jg 20:11
t they remained there before the Jg 20:26
T 18,000 men of Benjamin fell; Jg 20:44
T may the LORD do to me, and Ru 1:17 3541
T she came and has remained from Ru 2:7
T they did in Shiloh to all the 1Sa 2:14 3602
T the sin of the young men was 1Sa 2:17
"T says the LORD, 1Sa 2:27 3541
T Samuel grew and the LORD was 1Sa 3:19
T the word of Samuel came to all 1Sa 4:1
T he judged Israel forty years. 1Sa 4:18
"T far the LORD has helped us." 1Sa 7:12 2008
"T says the LORD, the God of 1Sa 10:18 3541
T Samuel brought all the tribes of 1Sa 10:20
t I will make it a reproach on all 1Sa 11:2
t you shall say to the men of 1Sa 11:9 3541
"T says the LORD of hosts, 1Sa 15:2 3541
T Jesse made seven of his sons 1Sa 16:10
"T it will be done for the man 1Sa 17:27 3541
T David prevailed over the 1Sa 17:50
"T you shall say to David, 1Sa 18:25 3541
T Saul was David's enemy 1Sa 18:29
T David delivered the inhabitants 1Sa 23:5
T he said to him, 1Sa 23:17
and t you shall say, 1Sa 25:6 3541
T Saul died with his three sons, 1Sa 31:6
T they buried Abner in Hebron; 2Sa 3:32
t the LORD has given my lord the 2Sa 4:8
T the ark of the LORD remained in 2Sa 6:11
'T says the LORD, 2Sa 7:5 3541
t you shall say to My servant 2Sa 7:8 3541
'T says the LORD of hosts, 2Sa 7:8 3541
"T you shall say to Joab, 2Sa 11:25 3541
T says the LORD God of Israel, 2Sa 12:7 3541
"T says the LORD, 2Sa 12:11 3541
And t he did to all the cities of 2Sa 12:31 3651
T they will extinguish my coal 2Sa 14:7
T he came to the king and 2Sa 14:33
"But if He should say t, 2Sa 15:26 3541
T Shimei said when he cursed, 2Sa 16:7 3541
"Ahithophel has spoken t. 2Sa 17:6
1697, 2088

t Ahithophel has counseled against **2Sa 17:21** 3602
t he died and was buried in the **2Sa 17:23**
And **t** he said as he walked, **2Sa 18:33** 3541
T he turned the hearts of all the **2Sa 19:14**
T the king swore to him. **2Sa 19:23**
and **t** they ended *the dispute.* **2Sa 20:18** 3651
T David said to the Gibeonites, **2Sa 21:3**
t they did all that the king **2Sa 21:14**
'**T** the LORD says, **2Sa 24:12** 3541
T the LORD was moved by prayer **2Sa 24:25**
T may the LORD, the God of my lord **1Ki 1:36** 3651
"The king has also said **t**, **1Ki 1:48** 3602
"**T** the king has said, **1Ki 2:30** 3541
"**T** spoke Joab, and thus he **1Ki 2:30** 3541
Joab, and **t** he answered me." **1Ki 2:30** 3541
T the kingdom was established in **1Ki 2:46**
T they spoke before the king. **1Ki 3:22**
t Solomon would give Hiram year by **1Ki 5:11** 3541
t he made side chambers all around. **1Ki 6:5**
T he set up the pillars at the **1Ki 7:21**
T all the work that King Solomon **1Ki 7:51**
'Why has the LORD done **t** to this **1Ki 9:8** 3602
T also he did for all his foreign **1Ki 11:8** 3651
for **t** says the LORD, the God of **1Ki 11:31** 3541
'**T** I will afflict the descendants **1Ki 11:39**
T the time that Solomon reigned in **1Ki 11:42**
"**T** you shall say to this people **1Ki 12:10** 3541
'**T** says the LORD, **1Ki 12:24** 3541
t he did in Bethel, sacrificing to **1Ki 12:32** 3651
"O altar, altar, **t** says the LORD, **1Ki 13:2** 3541
"**T** says the LORD, **1Ki 13:21** 3541
You shall say **t** and thus to her, **1Ki 14:5** 2090
You shall say thus and **t** to her, **1Ki 14:5** 2088
'**T** says the LORD God of Israel, **1Ki 14:7** 3541
T Zimri destroyed all the **1Ki 16:12**
T Ahab did more to provoke the **1Ki 16:33**
"For **t** says the LORD God of **1Ki 17:14** 3541
"**T** says Ben-hadad, **1Ki 20:2** 3541
"**T** says Ben-hadad, **1Ki 20:5** 3541
"**T** says the LORD, **1Ki 20:13** 3541
"**T** says the LORD, **1Ki 20:14** 3541
"**T** says the LORD, **1Ki 20:28** 3541
"**T** says the LORD, **1Ki 20:42** 3541
"**T** says the LORD, **1Ki 21:19** 3541
'**T** says the LORD, **1Ki 21:19** 3541
"**T** says the LORD, **1Ki 22:11** 3541
the prophets were prophesying **t**, **1Ki 22:12** 3651
'**T** says the king, **1Ki 22:27** 3541
"Now therefore **t** says the LORD, **2Ki 1:4** 3541
"**T** says the LORD, **2Ki 1:6** 3541
"O man of God, **t** says the king, **2Ki 1:11** 3541
"**T** says the LORD, **2Ki 1:16** 3541
"**T** says the LORD, **2Ki 2:21** 3541
"**T** says the LORD, **2Ki 3:16** 3541
"For **t** says the LORD, **2Ki 3:17** 3541
T they destroyed the cities; **2Ki 3:25**
they may eat, for **t** says the LORD, **2Ki 4:43** 3541
"**T** and thus spoke the girl who is **2Ki 5:4** 2088
"Thus and **t** spoke the girl who is **2Ki 5:4** 2088
t he warned him, so that he **2Ki 6:10**
t says the LORD, **2Ki 7:1** 3541
'**T** says the LORD, **2Ki 9:3** 3541
"**T** says the LORD, the God of **2Ki 9:6** 3541
"**T** and thus he said to me, **2Ki 9:12** 2088
"Thus and **t** he said to me, **2Ki 9:12** 2088
'**T** says the LORD, **2Ki 9:12** 3541
"**T** says the king, **2Ki 9:18** 3541
"**T** says the king, **2Ki 9:19** 3541
T Jehu eradicated Baal out of **2Ki 10:28**
t Urijah the priest made *it,* **2Ki 16:11** 3651
'**T** says the great king, the king **2Ki 18:19** 3541
"**T** says the king, **2Ki 18:29** 3541
for **t** says the king of Assyria, **2Ki 18:31** 3541
"**T** says Hezekiah, **2Ki 19:3** 3541
"**T** you shall say to your master, **2Ki 19:6** 3541
'**T** says the LORD, **2Ki 19:6** 3541
"**T** you shall say to Hezekiah king **2Ki 19:10** 3541
"**T** says the LORD, the God of **2Ki 19:20** 3541
'Therefore **t** says the LORD **2Ki 19:32** 3541
"**T** says the LORD, **2Ki 20:1** 3541
'**T** says the LORD, the God of your **2Ki 20:5** 3541
therefore **t** says the LORD, the God **2Ki 21:12** 3541
"**T** says the LORD God of Israel, **2Ki 22:15** 3541
t says the LORD, **2Ki 22:16** 3541
the LORD **t** shall you say to him, **2Ki 22:18** 3541
'**T** says the LORD God of Israel, **2Ki 22:18** 3541
T Saul died with his three sons, **1Ch 10:6**
T the ark of God remained with the **1Ch 13:14**
T all Israel brought up the ark of **1Ch 15:28**
'**T** says the LORD, **1Ch 17:4** 3541
t shall you say to My servant **1Ch 17:7** 3541
'**T** says the LORD of hosts, **1Ch 17:7** 3541
T the Arameans were not willing to **1Ch 19:19**
And **t** David did to all the cities **1Ch 20:3** 3651
'**T** says the LORD, **1Ch 21:10** 3541
"**T** says the LORD, **1Ch 21:11** 3541
T they are to keep charge of the **1Ch 23:32**
of Ithamar, they divided them **t**: **1Ch 24:4**
T they were divided by lot, the **1Ch 24:5**
T Solomon made all these utensils **2Ch 4:18**
T all the work that Solomon **2Ch 5:1**
T the king and all the people **2Ch 7:5**
T Solomon finished the house of **2Ch 7:11**
'Why has the LORD done **t** to this **2Ch 7:21** 3602
T all the work of Solomon was **2Ch 8:16**
"**T** you shall say to the people **2Ch 10:10** 3541
T you shall say to them, **2Ch 10:10** 3541
'**T** says the LORD, **2Ch 11:4** 3541
T he built Bethlehem, Etam, Tekoa, **2Ch 11:6**

"**T** says the LORD, **2Ch 12:5** 3541
T the sons of Israel were subdued **2Ch 13:18**
"**T** says the LORD, **2Ch 18:10** 3541
the prophets were prophesying **t**, **2Ch 18:11** 3651
'**T** says the king, **2Ch 18:26** 3541
"**T** you shall do in the fear of **2Ch 19:9** 3541
T you shall do and you will not be **2Ch 19:10** 3541
t says the LORD to you, **2Ch 20:15** 3541
"**T** says the LORD God of your **2Ch 21:12** 3541
T be with the king when he comes **2Ch 23:7**
T they did daily and collected **2Ch 24:11** 3541
'**T** God has said, **2Ch 24:20** 3541
T Joash the king did not remember **2Ch 24:22**
T they executed judgment on Joash. **2Ch 24:24**
T the service of the house of the **2Ch 29:35**
T the thing was right in the sight **2Ch 30:4**
T Hezekiah did throughout all Judah; **2Ch 31:20** 2088
"**T** says Sennacherib king of **2Ch 32:10** 3541
T Manasseh misled Judah and the **2Ch 33:9**
"**T** says the LORD, the God of **2Ch 34:23** 3541
t says the LORD, **2Ch 34:24** 3541
the LORD, **t** you will say to him, **2Ch 34:26** 3541
'**T** says the LORD God of Israel **2Ch 34:26** 3541
T the sons of Israel who were **2Ch 35:17**
"**T** says Cyrus king of Persia, **2Ch 36:23** 3541
"**T** says Cyrus king of Persia, **Ezr 1:2** 3541
came to them and spoke to them **t**, **Ezr 5:3** 3652
to him in which it was written **t**: **Ezr 5:7** 1836
those elders and said to them **t**, **Ezr 5:9** 3660
"**T** they answered us, saying, **Ezr 5:11** 3660
T I was strengthened according to **Ezr 7:28**
T I weighed into their hands 650 **Ezr 8:26**
T we came to Jerusalem and **Ezr 8:32**
T in Judah it was said, **Ne 4:10**
"**T** may God shake out every man **Ne 5:13** 3602
even **t** may he be shaken out and **Ne 5:13** 3602
T we will not neglect the house of **Ne 10:39**
T I purified them from everything **Ne 13:30**
And **t** I will go in to the king, **Es 4:16** 3651
'**T** it shall be done to the man **Es 6:9** 3602
"**T** it shall be done to the man **Es 6:11** 3602
he, who would presume to do **t**?" **Es 7:5** 3651
T the Jews struck all their **Es 9:5**
T the Jews undertook what they had **Es 9:23**
T Job did continually. **Jb 1:5** 3602
"**T** it is hidden from the eyes of **Jb 28:21**
'**T** far you shall come, but no **Jb 38:11** 6311
T I have seen You in the **Ps 63:2**
for **t** You prepare the earth. **Ps 65:9** 3651
"I will speak **t**," **Ps 73:15** 3644
T He remembered that they were but **Ps 78:39**
T Jacob sojourned in the land of **Ps 105:23**
T He rebuked the Red Sea and it **Ps 106:9**
T they exchanged their glory For **Ps 106:20**
T they provoked *Him* to anger with **Ps 106:29**
T they became unclean in their **Ps 106:39**
T they have repaid me evil for **Ps 109:5**
for **t** shall the man be blessed Who **Ps 128:4** 3651
has not dealt **t** with any nation; **Ps 147:20** 3651
that wisdom is **t** for your soul; **Pr 24:14** 3651
"**T** I shall do to him as he has **Pr 24:29** 3651
T I considered all my activities **Ec 2:11**
T I hated all the fruit of my **Ec 2:18**
as a man is born, **t** will he die. **Ec 5:16** 3651
in the city where they did **t**. **Ec 8:10** 3651
beloved, That **t** you adjure us?" **SS 5:9** 3602
T they shall both burn together And **Is 1:31**
T He looked for justice, but **Is 5:7**
t says the Lord GOD: **Is 7:7** 3541
For **t** the LORD spoke to me with **Is 8:11** 3541
t says the Lord GOD of hosts, **Is 10:24** 3541
T I will punish the world for its **Is 13:11**
For **t** the LORD has told me, **Is 18:4** 3541
T the LORD will make Himself known **Is 19:21**
For **t** the Lord says to me, **Is 21:6** 3541
For **t** the Lord said to me, **Is 21:16** 3541
T says the Lord GOD of hosts, **Is 22:15** 3541
For **t** it will be in the midst of **Is 24:13** 3541
pains, **T** were we before You, **Is 26:17** 3651
Therefore **t** says the Lord GOD, **Is 28:16** 3541
T the multitude of all the nations **Is 29:8** 3651
Therefore **t** says the LORD, who **Is 29:22** 3541
t says the Holy One of Israel, **Is 30:12** 3541
For **t** the Lord GOD, the Holy One **Is 30:15** 3541
For **t** says the LORD to me, **Is 31:4** 3541
T their land will be soaked with **Is 34:7**
'**T** says the great king, the king **Is 36:4** 3541
"**T** says the king, **Is 36:14** 3541
for **t** says the king of Assyria, **Is 36:16** 3541
"**T** says Hezekiah, **Is 37:3** 3541
"**T** you shall say to your master, **Is 37:6** 3541
'**T** says the LORD, **Is 37:6** 3541
"**T** you shall say to Hezekiah king **Is 37:10** 3541
"**T** says the LORD, the God of **Is 37:21** 3541
t says the LORD concerning the **Is 37:33** 3541
"**T** says the LORD, **Is 38:1** 3541
'**T** says the LORD, the God of your **Is 38:5** 3541
T says God the LORD, Who created **Is 42:5** 3541
But now, **t** says the LORD, your **Is 43:1** 3541
T says the LORD your Redeemer, the **Is 43:14** 3541
T says the LORD, Who makes a way **Is 43:16** 3541
T says the LORD who made you And **Is 44:2** 3541
"**T** says the LORD, the King of **Is 44:6** 3541
T says the LORD, your Redeemer, **Is 44:24** 3541
T says the LORD to Cyrus His **Is 45:1** 3541
T says the LORD, the Holy One of **Is 45:11** 3541
T says the LORD, **Is 45:14** 3541
For **t** says the LORD, who created **Is 45:18** 3541
T says the LORD, your Redeemer, **Is 48:17** 3541

T says the LORD, the Redeemer of **Is 49:7** 3541
T says the LORD, **Is 49:8** 3541
T says the Lord GOD, **Is 49:22** 3541
Surely, **t** says the LORD, **Is 49:25** 3541
T says the LORD, **Is 50:1** 3541
T says your Lord, the LORD, even **Is 51:22** 3541
For **t** says the LORD, **Is 52:3** 3541
For **t** says the Lord GOD, **Is 52:4** 3541
T He will sprinkle many nations, **Is 52:15** 3651
T says the LORD, **Is 56:1** 3541
For **t** says the LORD, **Is 56:4** 3541
For **t** says the high and exalted **Is 57:15** 3541
T says the LORD, **Is 65:8** 3541
Therefore, **t** says the Lord GOD, **Is 65:13** 3541
T says the LORD, **Is 66:1** 3541
T all these things came into **Is 66:2**
For **t** says the LORD, **Is 66:12** 3541
'**T** says the LORD, **Jer 2:2** 3541
T says the LORD, **Jer 2:5** 3541
For **t** says the LORD to the men of **Jer 4:3** 3541
For **t** says the LORD, **Jer 4:27** 3541
T it will be done to them!" **Jer 5:13** 3541
Therefore, **t** says the LORD, the **Jer 5:14** 3541
For **t** says the LORD of hosts, **Jer 6:6** 3541
T says the LORD of hosts, **Jer 6:9** 3541
T says the LORD, **Jer 6:16** 3541
Therefore, **t** says the LORD, **Jer 6:21** 3541
T says the LORD, **Jer 6:22** 3541
T says the LORD of hosts, the God **Jer 7:3** 3541
Therefore **t** says the Lord GOD, **Jer 7:20** 3541
T says the LORD of hosts, the God **Jer 7:21** 3541
'**T** says the LORD, **Jer 8:4** 3541
t says the LORD of hosts, **Jer 9:7** 3541
t says the LORD of hosts, **Jer 9:15** 3541
T says the LORD of hosts, **Jer 9:17** 3541
"**T** says the LORD, **Jer 9:22** 3541
T says the LORD, **Jer 9:23** 3541
T says the LORD, **Jer 10:2** 3541
T you shall say to them, **Jer 10:11** 1836
For **t** says the LORD, **Jer 10:18** 3541
'**T** says the LORD, the God of **Jer 11:3** 3541
Therefore **t** says the LORD, **Jer 11:11** 3541
Therefore **t** says the LORD **Jer 11:21** 3541
t says the LORD of hosts, **Jer 11:22** 3541
T says the LORD concerning all My **Jer 12:14** 3541
T the LORD said to me, **Jer 13:1** 3541
"**T** says the LORD, **Jer 13:9** 3541
'**T** says the LORD, the God of **Jer 13:12** 3541
'**T** says the LORD, **Jer 13:13** 3541
T says the LORD to this people, **Jer 14:10** 3541
"Therefore **t** says the LORD **Jer 14:15** 3541
are to tell them, '**T** says the LORD: **Jer 15:2** 3541
Therefore, **t** says the LORD, **Jer 15:19** 3541
For **t** says the LORD concerning the **Jer 16:3** 3541
For **t** says the LORD, **Jer 16:5** 3541
For **t** says the LORD of hosts, the **Jer 16:9** 3541
T says the LORD, **Jer 17:5** 3541
T the LORD said to me, **Jer 17:19** 3541
'**T** says the LORD, **Jer 17:21** 3541
'**T** says the LORD, **Jer 18:11** 3541
"Therefore **t** says the LORD, **Jer 18:13** 3541
T says the LORD, **Jer 19:1** 3541
t says the LORD of hosts, the God **Jer 19:3** 3541
'**T** says the LORD of hosts, **Jer 19:11** 3541
"**T** says the LORD of hosts, the **Jer 19:15** 3541
"For **t** says the LORD, **Jer 20:4** 3541
'**T** says the LORD God of Israel, **Jer 21:4** 3541
'**T** says the LORD, **Jer 21:8** 3541
O house of David, **t** says the LORD: **Jer 21:12** 3541
T says the LORD, **Jer 22:1** 3541
'**T** says the LORD, **Jer 22:3** 3541
For **t** says the LORD concerning the **Jer 22:6** 3541
'Why has the LORD done **t** to this **Jer 22:8** 3602
For **t** says the LORD in regard to **Jer 22:11** 3541
Therefore **t** says the LORD in **Jer 22:18** 3541
"**T** says the LORD, **Jer 22:30** 3541
Therefore **t** says the LORD God of **Jer 23:2** 3541
"Therefore **t** says the LORD of **Jer 23:15** 3541
T says the LORD of hosts, **Jer 23:16** 3541
"**T** will each of you say to his **Jer 23:35** 3541
"**T** you will say to *that* prophet, **Jer 23:37** 3541
surely **t** says the LORD, **Jer 23:38** 3541
"**T** says the LORD God of Israel, **Jer 24:5** 3541
indeed, **t** says the LORD **Jer 24:8** 3541
t says the LORD of hosts, **Jer 25:8** 3541
For **t** the LORD, the God of Israel, **Jer 25:15** 3541
'**T** says the LORD of hosts, the God **Jer 25:27** 3541
'**T** says the LORD of hosts: **Jer 25:28** 3541
T says the LORD of hosts, **Jer 25:32** 3541
"**T** says the LORD, **Jer 26:2** 3541
'**T** says the LORD, **Jer 26:4** 3541
'**T** the LORD of hosts has said, **Jer 26:18** 3541
t says the LORD to **Jer 27:2** 3541
'**T** says the LORD of hosts, the God **Jer 27:4** 3541
t you shall say to your masters, **Jer 27:4** 3541
'**T** says the LORD: Do not listen to **Jer 27:16** 3541
"For **t** says the LORD of hosts **Jer 27:19** 3541
"Yes, **t** says the LORD of hosts, **Jer 27:21** 3541
"**T** says the LORD of hosts, the **Jer 28:2** 3541
'**T** says the LORD, **Jer 28:11** 3541
'**T** says the LORD, **Jer 28:13** 3541
'For **t** says the LORD of hosts, the **Jer 28:14** 3541
"Therefore **t** says the LORD, **Jer 28:16** 3541
"**T** says the LORD of hosts, the **Jer 29:4** 3541
"For **t** says the LORD of hosts, **Jer 29:8** 3541
"For **t** says the LORD, **Jer 29:10** 3541
for **t** says the LORD concerning the **Jer 29:16** 3541
t says the LORD of hosts, **Jer 29:17** 3541
"**T** says the LORD of hosts, the **Jer 29:21** 3541

“**T** says the LORD of hosts, the Jer 29:25 3541
‘**T** says the LORD concerning Jer 29:31 3541
therefore **t** says the LORD, Jer 29:32 3541
“**T** says the LORD, the God of Jer 30:2 3541
“For **t** says the LORD, Jer 30:5 3541
“For **t** says the LORD, Jer 30:12 3541
“**T** says the LORD, Jer 30:18 3541
“**T** says the LORD, Jer 31:2 3541
For **t** says the LORD, Jer 31:7 3541
T says the LORD, Jer 31:15 3541
T says the LORD, Jer 31:16 3541
T says the LORD of hosts, the God Jer 31:23 3541
T says the LORD, Who gives the sun Jer 31:35 3541
T says the LORD, Jer 31:37 3541
“**T** says the LORD, Jer 32:3 3541
‘**T** says the LORD of hosts, the God Jer 32:14 3541
‘For **t** says the LORD of hosts, the Jer 32:15 3541
Therefore **t** says the LORD, Jer 32:28 3541
“Now therefore **t** says the LORD Jer 32:36 3541
“For **t** says the LORD, Jer 32:42 3541
“**T** says the LORD who made *the* Jer 33:2 3541
“For **t** says the LORD God of Jer 33:4 3541
“**T** says the LORD, Jer 33:10 3541
“**T** says the LORD of hosts, Jer 33:12 3541
“For **t** says the LORD, Jer 33:17 3541
“**T** says the LORD, Jer 33:20 3541
T they despise My people, no Jer 33:24
“**T** says the LORD, Jer 33:25 3541
“**T** says the LORD God of Israel, Jer 34:2 3541
‘**T** says the LORD, ‘Behold, I Jer 34:2 3541
T says the LORD concerning you, Jer 34:4 3541
“**T** says the LORD God of Israel, Jer 34:13 3541
“Therefore **t** says the LORD, Jer 34:17 3541
“**T** says the LORD of hosts, the Jer 35:13 3541
“Therefore **t** says the LORD, the Jer 35:17 3541
“**T** says the LORD of hosts, the Jer 35:18 3541
t says the LORD of hosts, Jer 35:19 3541
‘**T** says the LORD, Jer 36:29 3541
‘Therefore **t** says the LORD Jer 36:30 3541
“**T** says the LORD God of Israel, Jer 37:7 3541
‘**T** you are to say to the king of Jer 37:7 3541
“**T** says the LORD, Jer 37:9 3541
“**T** says the LORD, Jer 38:2 3541
“**T** says the LORD, Jer 38:3 3541
“**T** says the LORD God of hosts, Jer 38:17 3541
‘**T** says the LORD of hosts, the God Jer 39:16 3541
t Ishmael the son of Nethaniah Jer 41:10
“**T** says the LORD the God of Jer 42:9 3541
T says the LORD of hosts, the God Jer 42:15 3541
For **t** says the LORD of hosts, the Jer 42:18 3541
‘**T** says the LORD of hosts, the God Jer 43:10 3541
“**T** says the LORD of hosts, the Jer 44:2 3541
then **t** says the LORD God of hosts, Jer 44:7 3541
t says the LORD of hosts, Jer 44:11 3541
t your land has become a ruin, an Jer 44:22
t says the LORD of hosts, the God Jer 44:25 3541
“**T** says the LORD, Jer 44:30 3541
“**T** says the LORD the God of Jer 45:2 3541
“**T** you are to say to him, Jer 45:4 3541
‘**T** says the LORD, Jer 45:4 3541
T says the LORD: “Behold, waters Jer 47:2 3541
T says the LORD of hosts, the God Jer 48:1 3541
For **t** says the LORD: Jer 48:40 3541
T far the judgment on Moab. Jer 48:47 2008
T says the LORD: “Does Israel have Jer 49:1 3541
T says the LORD of hosts, Jer 49:7 3541
For **t** says the LORD, Jer 49:12 3541
T says the LORD, Jer 49:28 3541
“**T** says the LORD of hosts, Jer 49:35 3541
t says the LORD of hosts, Jer 50:18 3541
T says the LORD of hosts, Jer 50:33 3541
T says the LORD: “Behold, I am Jer 51:1 3541
For **t** says the LORD of hosts, the Jer 51:33 3541
Therefore **t** says the LORD, Jer 51:36 3541
T says the LORD of hosts, Jer 51:58 3541
T far are the words of Jeremiah. Jer 51:64 2008
With whom have You dealt **t**? La 2:20 3541
‘**T** says the Lord GOD.’ Ezk 2:4 3541
‘**T** says the Lord GOD.’ ” Ezk 3:11 3541
‘**T** says the Lord GOD.’ Ezk 3:27 3541
t you shall bear the iniquity of Ezk 4:5
“**T** will the sons of Israel eat Ezk 4:13 3602
“**T** says the Lord GOD, Ezk 5:5 3541
“Therefore, **t** says the Lord GOD, Ezk 5:7 3541
therefore, **t** says the Lord GOD, Ezk 5:8 3541
‘**T** My anger will be spent and I Ezk 5:13
T says the Lord GOD to the Ezk 6:3 3541
“**T** says the Lord GOD, Ezk 6:11 3541
T will I spend My wrath on them. Ezk 6:12
t they will know that I am the Ezk 6:14
t says the Lord GOD to the land of Ezk 7:2 3541
“**T** says the Lord GOD, Ezk 7:5 3541
T they went out and struck down Ezk 9:7
“**T** says the LORD, Ezk 11:5 3541
‘Therefore, **t** says the Lord GOD, Ezk 11:7 3541
“**T** you will know that I am the Ezk 11:12
‘**T** says the Lord GOD, Ezk 11:16 3541
‘**T** says the Lord GOD, Ezk 11:17 3541
‘**T** says the Lord GOD, Ezk 12:10 3541
‘**T** says the Lord GOD concerning Ezk 12:19 3541
‘**T** says the Lord GOD, Ezk 12:23 3541
‘**T** says the Lord GOD, Ezk 12:28 3541
‘**T** says the Lord GOD, Ezk 13:3 3541
Therefore, **t** says the Lord GOD, Ezk 13:8 3541
Therefore, **t** says the Lord GOD, Ezk 13:13 3541
“**T** I will spend My wrath on the Ezk 13:15
‘**T** says the Lord GOD, Ezk 13:18 3541
Therefore, **t** says the Lord GOD, Ezk 13:20 3541
T you will know that I am the LORD.” Ezk 13:23

‘**T** says the Lord GOD, Ezk 14:4 3541
‘**T** says the Lord GOD, Ezk 14:6 3541
T they will be My people, and I Ezk 14:11
For **t** says the Lord GOD, Ezk 14:21 3541
“Therefore, **t** says the Lord GOD, Ezk 15:6 3541
“**T** I will make the land desolate, Ezk 15:8
‘**T** says the Lord GOD to Jerusalem, Ezk 16:3 3541
“**T** you were adorned with gold and Ezk 16:13
“**T** you are different from those Ezk 16:34
t you are different.” Ezk 16:34
T says the Lord GOD, Ezk 16:36 3541
“**T** I will judge you like women Ezk 16:38
“**T** they were haughty and Ezk 16:50
T you have made your sisters Ezk 16:51
For **t** says the Lord GOD, Ezk 16:59 3541
“**T** I will establish My covenant Ezk 16:62
‘**T** says the Lord GOD, Ezk 17:3 3541
‘**T** says the Lord GOD, Ezk 17:9 3541
Therefore, **t** says the Lord GOD, Ezk 17:19 3541
T says the Lord GOD, Ezk 17:22 3541
‘**T** says the Lord GOD, Ezk 20:3 3541
‘**T** says the Lord GOD, Ezk 20:5 3541
‘**T** says the Lord GOD, Ezk 20:27 3541
‘**T** says the Lord GOD, Ezk 20:30 3541
T you will know that I am the LORD. Ezk 20:38
of Israel,” **t** says the Lord GOD, Ezk 20:39 3541
t says the Lord GOD, Ezk 20:47 3541
‘**T** says the LORD, Ezk 21:3 3541
“**T** all flesh will know that I, Ezk 21:5
‘**T** says the LORD.’ Ezk 21:9 3541
“Therefore, **t** says the Lord GOD, Ezk 21:24 3541
t says the Lord GOD, Ezk 21:26 3541
‘**T** says the Lord GOD concerning Ezk 21:28 3541
‘**T** says the Lord GOD, Ezk 22:3 3541
T you have brought your day near Ezk 22:4
“Therefore, **t** says the Lord GOD, Ezk 22:19 3541
‘**T** says the Lord GOD,’ when the Ezk 22:28 3541
“**T** I have poured out My Ezk 22:31
T she became a byword Ezk 23:10
“**T** you longed for the lewdness of Ezk 23:21
O Oholibah, **t** says the Lord GOD, Ezk 23:22 3541
“**T** I will make your lewdness and Ezk 23:27
“For **t** says the Lord GOD, Ezk 23:28 3541
“**T** says the Lord GOD, Ezk 23:32 3541
“Therefore, **t** says the Lord GOD, Ezk 23:35 3541
T they have committed adultery Ezk 23:37
lo, **t** they did within My house. Ezk 23:39 3541
adultery with her when she is **t**?’ Ezk 23:43
T they went in to Oholah and to Ezk 23:44 3651
“For **t** says the Lord GOD, Ezk 23:46 3541
‘**T** I will make lewdness cease Ezk 23:48
t you will know that I am the Lord Ezk 23:49
“**T** says the Lord GOD, Ezk 24:3 3541
‘Therefore, **t** says the Lord GOD, Ezk 24:6 3541
‘Therefore, **t** says the Lord GOD, Ezk 24:9 3541
“**T** says the Lord GOD, Ezk 24:21 3541
‘**T** Ezekiel will be a sign to you; Ezk 24:24
T you will be a sign to them, and Ezk 24:27
T says the Lord GOD, Ezk 25:3 3541
T you will know that I am the LORD.” Ezk 25:5
‘For **t** says the Lord GOD, Ezk 25:6 3541
T you will know that I am the LORD.” Ezk 25:7
‘**T** says the Lord GOD, Ezk 25:8 3541
“**T** I will execute judgments on Ezk 25:11
‘**T** says the Lord GOD, Ezk 25:12 3541
therefore **t** says the Lord GOD, Ezk 25:13 3541
t they will know My vengeance,” Ezk 25:14
‘**T** says the Lord GOD, Ezk 25:15 3541
therefore **t** says the Lord GOD, Ezk 25:16 3541
therefore **t** says the Lord GOD, Ezk 26:3 3541
For **t** says the Lord GOD, Ezk 26:7 3541
T says the Lord GOD to Tyre, Ezk 26:15 3541
For **t** says the Lord GOD, Ezk 26:19 3541
‘**T** says the Lord GOD, Ezk 27:3 3541
‘**T** says the Lord GOD, Ezk 28:2 3541
Therefore **t** says the Lord GOD, Ezk 28:6 3541
‘**T** says the Lord GOD, Ezk 28:12 3541
‘**T** says the Lord GOD, Ezk 28:22 3541
‘**T** says the Lord GOD, Ezk 28:25 3541
‘**T** says the Lord GOD, Ezk 29:3 3541
‘Therefore **t** says the Lord GOD, Ezk 29:8 3541
‘For **t** says the Lord GOD, Ezk 29:13 3541
Therefore **t** says the Lord GOD, Ezk 29:19 3541
‘**T** says the Lord GOD, Ezk 30:2 3541
‘**T** says the LORD, Ezk 30:6 3541
‘**T** says the Lord GOD, Ezk 30:10 3541
‘**T** says the Lord GOD, Ezk 30:13 3541
“**T** I will execute judgments on Ezk 30:19
“Therefore **t** says the Lord GOD, Ezk 30:22 3541
‘**T** I will strengthen the arms of Ezk 30:25
‘Therefore **t** says the Lord GOD, Ezk 31:10 3541
“**T** says the Lord GOD, Ezk 31:15 3541
t equal in glory and greatness? Ezk 31:18 3602
T says the Lord GOD, Ezk 32:3 3541
For **t** says the Lord GOD, Ezk 32:11 3541
‘**T** you have spoken, saying, Ezk 33:10 3651
‘**T** says the Lord GOD, Ezk 33:25 3541
“**T** you shall say to them, Ezk 33:27 3541
‘**T** says the Lord GOD, Ezk 33:27 3541
‘**T** says the Lord GOD, Ezk 34:2 3541
‘**T** says the Lord GOD, Ezk 34:10 3541
For **t** says the Lord GOD, Ezk 34:11 3541
My flock, **t** says the Lord GOD, Ezk 34:17 3541
t says the Lord GOD to them, Ezk 34:20 3541
‘**T** says the Lord GOD, Ezk 35:3 3541
‘**T** says the Lord GOD, Ezk 35:14 3541
‘**T** says the Lord GOD, Ezk 36:2 3541
‘**T** says the Lord GOD, Ezk 36:3 3541
T says the Lord GOD to the Ezk 36:4 3541

therefore **t** says the Lord GOD, Ezk 36:5 3541
“**T** says the Lord GOD, Ezk 36:6 3541
“Therefore **t** says the Lord GOD, Ezk 36:7 3541
T you will know that I am the LORD. Ezk 36:11
“**T** says the Lord GOD, Ezk 36:13 3541
‘**T** says the Lord GOD, Ezk 36:22 3541
‘**T** says the Lord GOD, Ezk 36:33 3541
‘**T** says the Lord GOD, Ezk 36:37 3541
“**T** says the Lord GOD to these Ezk 37:5 3541
‘**T** says the Lord GOD, Ezk 37:9 3541
‘**T** says the Lord GOD, Ezk 37:12 3541
‘**T** says the Lord GOD, Ezk 37:19 3541
‘**T** says the Lord GOD, Ezk 37:21 3541
‘**T** says the Lord GOD, Ezk 38:3 3541
‘**T** says the Lord GOD, Ezk 38:10 3541
‘**T** says the Lord GOD, Ezk 38:14 3541
‘**T** says the Lord GOD, Ezk 38:17 3541
‘**T** says the Lord GOD, Ezk 39:1 3541
son of man, **t** says the Lord GOD, Ezk 39:17 3541
Therefore **t** says the Lord GOD, Ezk 39:25 3541
and **t** one went up from the lowest Ezk 41:7 3651
t *were* the side chambers of the Ezk 41:26
“Son of man, **t** says the Lord GOD, Ezk 43:18 3541
t you shall cleanse it and make Ezk 43:20
‘**T** says the Lord GOD, Ezk 44:6 3541
‘**T** says the Lord GOD, Ezk 44:9 3541
‘**T** says the Lord GOD, Ezk 45:9 3541
‘**T** says the Lord GOD, Ezk 45:18 3541
“**T** you shall do on the seventh *day* Ezk 45:20 3651
‘**T** says the Lord GOD, Ezk 46:1 3541
“**T** they shall provide the lamb, Ezk 46:15
‘**T** says the Lord GOD, Ezk 46:16 3541
T says the Lord GOD, Ezk 47:13 3541
and **t** they said to it, Da 7:5 3652
“**T** he said: ‘The fourth beast will be Da 7:23 3652
“**T** He has confirmed His words Da 9:12
T it will be done to you at Bethel Hos 10:15 3602
“**T** you will know that I am in the Jl 2:27
T says the LORD, Am 1:3 3541
T says the LORD, Am 1:6 3541
T says the LORD, Am 1:9 3541
T says the LORD, Am 1:11 3541
T says the LORD, Am 1:13 3541
T says the LORD, Am 2:1 3541
T says the LORD, Am 2:4 3541
T says the LORD, Am 2:6 3541
Therefore, **t** says the Lord GOD, Am 3:11 3541
T says the LORD, Am 3:12 3541
“Therefore **t** I will do to you, O Am 4:12 3541
For **t** says the Lord GOD, Am 5:3 3541
For **t** says the LORD to the house Am 5:4 3541
And **t** may the LORD God of hosts be Am 5:14 3651
t says the LORD God of hosts, Am 5:16 3541
T the Lord GOD showed me, and Am 7:1 3541
T the Lord GOD showed me, and Am 7:4 3541
T He showed me, and behold, the Am 7:7 3541
“For **t** Amos says, Am 7:11 3541
“Therefore, **t** says the LORD, Am 7:17 3541
T the Lord GOD showed me, and Am 8:1 3541
T says the Lord GOD concerning Ob 1:1 3541
Therefore **t** says the LORD, Mi 2:3 3541
T says the LORD concerning the Mi 3:5 3541
T says the LORD, Na 1:12 3541
“**T** says the LORD of hosts, Hg 1:2 3541
t says the LORD of hosts, Hg 1:5 3541
T says the LORD of hosts, Hg 1:7 3541
“For **t** says the LORD of hosts, Hg 2:6 3541
“**T** says the LORD of hosts, Hg 2:11 3541
“**T** says the LORD of hosts, Zch 1:3 3541
“**T** says the LORD of hosts, Zch 1:4 3541
“**T** says the LORD of hosts, Zch 1:14 3541
‘Therefore **t** says the LORD, Zch 1:16 3541
‘**T** says the LORD of hosts, Zch 1:17 3541
For **t** says the LORD of hosts, Zch 2:8 3541
“**T** says the LORD of hosts, Zch 3:7 3541
“**T** says the LORD of hosts, Zch 6:12 3541
T, He will be a priest on His Zch 6:13
“**T** has the LORD of hosts said, Zch 7:9 3541
T the land is desolated behind Zch 7:14
“**T** says the LORD of hosts, Zch 8:2 3541
“**T** says the LORD, Zch 8:3 3541
“**T** says the LORD of hosts, Zch 8:4 3541
“**T** says the LORD of hosts, Zch 8:6 3541
“**T** says the LORD of hosts, Zch 8:7 3541
“**T** says the LORD of hosts, Zch 8:9 3541
“For **t** says the LORD of hosts, Zch 8:14 3541
“**T** says the LORD of hosts, Zch 8:19 3541
“**T** says the LORD of hosts, Zch 8:20 3541
“**T** says the LORD of hosts, Zch 8:23 3541
T says the LORD my God, Zch 11:4 3541
and **t** the afflicted of the flock Zch 11:11 3651
T declares the LORD who Zch 12:1
t says the LORD of hosts, Mal 1:4 3541
t observing the traditions of Mk 7:3
t invalidating the word of God by Mk 7:13
(**T** *He* declared all foods clean.) Mk 7:19
“**T** it is written, that the Christ Lk 24:46 3779
was sitting **t** by the well. Jn 4:6 3779
leaning back **t** on Jesus' bosom, Jn 13:25 3779
would suffer, He has **t** fulfilled. Ac 3:18 3779
and **t** we came to Rome. Ac 28:14 3779
And **t** I aspired to preach the Ro 15:20 3779
t establishing peace, Eph 2:15
t incurring condemnation, 1Tm 5:12
and **t** gone astray from the faith. 1Tm 6:21
‘He who overcomes will **t** be clothed Rv 3:5 3779

THWART

then you can **t** the counsel of 2Sa 15:34 6565a
to **t** the good counsel of Ahithophel, 2Sa 17:14 6565a

THWARTED
advice of the cunning is quickly t. Jb 5:13 4116
that no purpose of Yours can be t. Jb 42:2 1219
"Devise a plan, but it will be t; Is 8:10 6565a
THWARTS
But He t the way of the wicked. Ps 146:9 5791
THYATIRA
from the city of T, a seller of Ac 16:14 2363
to Smyrna and to Pergamum and to T Rv 1:11 2363
"And to the angel of the church in T Rv 2:18 2363
the rest who are in T, who do not Rv 2:24 2363
TIBERIAS
side of the Sea of Galilee (or T). Jn 6:1 5085
There came other small boats from T Jn 6:23 5085
to the disciples at the Sea of T, Jn 21:1 5085
TIBERIUS
year of the reign of T Caesar, Lk 3:1 5086
TIBHATH
Also from T and from Cun, cities 1Ch 18:8 2880
TIBNI
followed T the son of Ginath, 1Ki 16:21 8402
who followed T the son of Ginath. 1Ki 16:22 8402
And T died and Omri became king. 1Ki 16:22 8402
TICKLED
but wanting to have their ears t, 2Tm 4:3 2833
TIDAL
king of Elam, and T king of Goiim, Gn 14:1 8413
king of Elam and T king of Goiim Gn 14:9 8413
TIDINGS
Proclaim good t of His salvation 1Ch 16:23 1319
proclaimed glad t of righteousness Ps 40:9 1319
women who proclaim the good t are Ps 68:11 1319
Proclaim good t of His salvation Ps 96:2 1319
He will not fear evil t; Ps 112:7 8052
TIE
you t this cord of scarlet thread Jos 2:18 7194
T them around your neck. Pr 6:21 6029
t your sash securely about him. Is 22:21 2388
you will t a stone to it and throw Jer 51:63 7194
were in his army to t up Shadrach, Da 3:20 3729
"They t up heavy burdens and Mt 23:4 1195
TIED
t a scarlet thread on his hand, Gn 38:28 7194
ephod, with which he t it to him. Lv 8:7 640
has no covering t down on it, Nu 19:15 6616
and she t the scarlet cord in the Jos 2:21 7194
the horses t and the donkeys tied, 2Ki 7:10 631
the horses tied and the donkeys t, 2Ki 7:10 631
high priest came up and t it in bags 2Ki 12:10 6696a
men were t up in their trousers, Da 3:21 3729
of blazing fire still t up. Da 3:23 3729
you will find a donkey t there and Mt 21:2 1210
it, you will find a colt t there, Mk 11:2 1210
They went away and found a colt t at Mk 11:4 1210
you enter, you will find a colt t Lk 19:30 1210
TIES
"He t his foal to the vine, And Gn 49:11 631
TIGHT
pride, Shut up as with a t seal. Jb 41:15 6862a
TIGHTLY
Now Jericho was t shut because of Jos 6:1 5462
"If they bind me t with new ropes Jg 16:11 631
And roll you t like a ball, To be Is 22:18 6801
of many colors and t wound cords, Ezk 27:24 723b
TIGLATH-PILESER
T king of Assyria came and 2Ki 15:29 8407
messengers to T king of Assyria, 2Ki 16:7 8407
to meet T king of Assyria, 2Ki 16:10 8407
TIGRIS
The name of the third river is T; Gn 2:14 2313
the great river, that is, the T, Da 10:4 2313
TIKVAH
the wife of Shallum the son of T, 2Ki 22:14 8616
the son of T opposed this, Ezr 10:15 8616
TILES
through the t with his stretcher, Lk 5:19 2766
TILGATH-PILNESER
whom T king of Assyria carried 1Ch 5:6 8407
the spirit of T king of Assyria, 1Ch 5:26 8407
So T king of Assyria came against 2Ch 28:20 8407
TILL
bread, T you return to the ground, Gn 3:19 5704
t he is no longer remembered. Jb 24:20 5704
T I die I will not put away my Jb 27:5 5704
of peace t the moon is no more. Ps 72:7 5704
"and they will t it and dwell in it." Jer 27:11 5647
TILLED
workers who t the soil. 1Ch 27:26 5656
those for whose sake it is also t, Heb 6:7 1090
TILLER
but Cain was a t of the ground. Gn 4:2 5647
I am a t of the ground, for a man Zch 13:5
376, 5647
TILLS
He who t his land will have plenty Pr 12:11 5647
He who t his land will have plenty Pr 28:19 5647
TILON
Amnon and Rinnah, Benhanan and T. 1Ch 4:20 8436
TIMAEUS
named Bartimaeus, the son of T, Mk 10:46 5090
TIMBER
who knows how to cut t like the 1Ki 5:6 6086
the cedar and cypress t. 1Ki 5:8 6086
of the cedar and cypress t. 1Ki 5:10 6086
Solomon with cedar and cypress t 1Ki 9:11 6086
its t with which Baasha had built. 1Ki 15:22 6086
and for buying t and hewn stone to 2Ki 12:12 6086
buying t and hewn stone to repair 2Ki 22:6 6086
quantities of cedar t to David. 1Ch 22:4 6086
also t and stone I have prepared, 1Ch 22:14 6086
cypress and algum t from Lebanon, 2Ch 2:8 6086
know how to cut t of Lebanon; 2Ch 2:8 6086
to prepare t in abundance for me, 2Ch 2:9 6086
the woodsmen who cut the t, 2Ch 2:10 6086
whatever t you need from Lebanon and 2Ch 2:16 6086
away the stones of Ramah and its t 2Ch 16:6 6086
buy quarried stone and t for couplings 2Ch 34:11 6086
a t shall be drawn from his house Ezr 6:11 636
that he may give me t to make Ne 2:8 6086
sedan chair From the t of Lebanon. SS 3:9 6086
consume it with its t and stones." Zch 5:4 6086
TIMBERS
the house, its stones, and its t, Lv 14:45 6086
and prepared the t and the stones 1Ki 5:18 6086
to the house with t of cedar. 1Ki 6:10 6086
and t of cedar logs beyond number, 1Ch 22:4 6086
huge stones and one layer of t. Ezr 6:4 636
and throw your stones and your t Ezk 26:12 6086
TIMBREL
with songs, with t and with lyre; Gn 31:27 8596
sister, took the t in her hand, Ex 15:20 8596
"They sing to the t and harp And Jb 21:12 8596
Raise a song, strike the t, Ps 81:2 8596
praises to Him with t and lyre. Ps 149:3 8596
Praise Him with t and dancing; Ps 150:4 8596
TIMBRELS
after her with t and with dancing. Ex 15:20 8596
TIME
in the course of t that Cain brought Gn 4:3 3117
righteous man, blameless in his t; Gn 6:9 1755
be righteous before Me in this t. Gn 7:1 1755
return to you at this t next year; Gn 18:10 6256
At the appointed t I will return to Gn 18:14 4150
to you, at this t next year, Gn 18:14 6256
at the appointed t of which God Gn 21:2 4150
Now it came about at that t that Gn 21:22 6256
to Abraham a second t from heaven, Gn 22:15 8145
by the well of water at evening t, Gn 24:11 6256
the t when women go out to draw Gn 24:11 6256
when he had been there a long t, Gn 26:8 3117
it is not t for the livestock to Gn 29:7 6256
me my wife, for my t is completed, Gn 29:21 3117
"Now this t my husband will Gn 29:34 6471
"This t I will praise the LORD." Gn 29:35 6471
"And it came about at the t when Gn 31:10 6256
And it came about at that t, Gn 38:1 6256
Now after a considerable t Shua's Gn 38:12 3117
when the t of mourning was ended, Gn 38:12 5162
at the t she was giving birth, Gn 38:27 6256
from the t he made him overseer in Gn 39:5 227
were in confinement for some t. Gn 40:4 3117
asleep and dreamed a second t; Gn 41:5 8145
was returned in our sacks the first t Gn 43:18 8462
came down the first t to buy food, Gn 43:20 8462
and wept on his neck a long t. Gn 46:29 5750
the t for Israel to die drew near, Gn 47:29 3117
neither recently nor in t past, Ex 4:10 8032a
At that t she said, Ex 4:26 227
hardened his heart this t also, Ex 8:32 6471
The LORD set a definite t, Ex 9:5 4150
"For this t I will send all My Ex 9:14 6471
"Behold, about this t tomorrow, Ex 9:18 6256
"I have sinned this t; Ex 9:27 6471
Now the t that the sons of Israel Ex 12:40 4186
its appointed t from year to year. Ex 13:10 4150
your son asks you in t to come, Ex 13:14 4279
shall only pay for his loss of t, Ex 21:19 7674
the appointed t in the month Abib, Ex 23:15 4150
appointed t in the month of Abib, Ex 34:18 4150
even during plowing t and harvest Ex 34:21 2758
it shall then be washed a second t Lv 13:58 8145
during the t that he has quarantined Lv 14:46 3117
like her uncleanness at that t. Lv 15:26 5079
not enter at any t into the holy place Lv 16:2 6256
you have the t of the seven sabbaths Lv 25:8 3117
will last until sowing t. Lv 26:5 2233
at the t when the LORD spoke with Nu 3:1 3117
the Passover at its appointed t. Nu 9:2 4150
observe it at its appointed t; Nu 9:3 4150
at its appointed t among the sons of Nu 9:7 4150
of the LORD at its appointed t. Nu 9:13 4150
you blow an alarm the second t, Nu 10:6 8145
So they moved out for the first t Nu 10:13 7223
Now the t was the time of the Nu 13:20 3117
the t of the first ripe grapes. Nu 13:20 3117
and we stayed in Egypt a long t, Nu 20:15 3117
Zippor was king of Moab at that t. Nu 22:4 6256
At the proper t it shall be said Nu 23:23 6256
to Me, at their appointed t.' Nu 28:2 4150
if the manslayer at any t goes Nu 35:26 3318
"I spoke to you at that t, Dt 1:9 6256
I charged your judges at that t, Dt 1:16 6256
"I commanded you at that t Dt 1:18 6256
"Now the t that it took for us to Dt 2:14 3117
captured all his cities at that t and Dt 2:34 6256
captured all his cities at that t; Dt 3:4 6256
"Thus we took the land at that t Dt 3:8 6256
possession of this land at that t. Dt 3:12 6256
"Then I commanded you at that t, Dt 3:18 6256
"I commanded Joshua at that t, Dt 3:21 6256
pleaded with the LORD at that t, Dt 3:23 6256
The LORD commanded me at that t to Dt 4:14 6256
God is giving you for all t." Dt 4:40 3117
enmity toward him in t past; Dt 4:42 8032a
the LORD and you at that t, Dt 5:5 6256
your son asks you in t to come, Dt 6:20 4279
LORD listened to me that t also. Dt 9:19 6471
prayed for Aaron at the same t. Dt 9:20 6256
"At that t the LORD said to me, Dt 10:1 6256
At that t the LORD set apart the Dt 10:8 6256
and forty nights like the first t, Dt 10:10 3117
LORD listened to me that t also; Dt 10:10 6471
the t that you came out of Egypt. Dt 16:6 4150
from the t you begin to put the sickle Dt 16:9
"When you besiege a city a long t, Dt 20:19 3117
priest who is in office at that t and Dt 26:3 3117
at the t of the year of remission Dt 31:10 4150
the t for you to die is near; Dt 31:14 3117
In due t their foot will slip; Dt 32:35 6256
Since that t no prophet has risen in Dt 34:10 5750
"It came about when it was t to Jos 2:5
ask their fathers in t to come, Jos 4:21 4279
At that t the LORD said to Joshua, Jos 5:2 6256
the sons of Israel the second t." Jos 5:2 8145
At the seventh t, Jos 6:16 6471
made them take an oath at that t, Jos 6:26 6256
kings and their lands at one t, Jos 10:42 6471
for tomorrow at this t I will Jos 11:6 6256
Then Joshua turned back at that t, Jos 11:10 6256
Joshua waged war a long t with all Jos 11:18 3117
Then Joshua came at that t and cut Jos 11:21 6256
from the t that the LORD spoke Jos 14:10 227
'In t to come your sons may say to Jos 22:24 4279
not say to our sons in t to come, Jos 22:27 4279
to our generations in t to come, Jos 22:28 4279
in the wilderness for a long t. Jos 24:7 3117
They struck down at that t about ten Jg 3:29 6256
was judging Israel at that t. Jg 4:4 6256
you in the t of your distress." Jg 10:14 6256
not recover them within that t? Jg 11:26 6256
fell at that t 42,000 of Ephraim. Jg 12:6 6256
hear things like this at this t." Jg 13:23 6256
Now at that t the Philistines were Jg 14:4 6256
while, in the t of wheat harvest, Jg 15:1 3117
"This t I shall be blameless in Jg 15:3 6471
please strengthen me just this t, Jg 16:28 6471
all the t that the house of God Jg 18:31 3117
Benjamin returned at that t, Jg 21:14 6256
departed from there at that t, Jg 21:24 6256
It came about in due t, 1Sa 1:20 3117
It happened at that t as Eli 1Sa 3:2 3117
called Samuel again for the third t. 1Sa 3:8 7992
And about the t of her death the 1Sa 4:20 6256
Kiriath-jearim, the t was long, 1Sa 7:2 3117
"About this t tomorrow I will 1Sa 9:16 6256
for you until the appointed t, 1Sa 9:24 4150
'Tomorrow, by the t the sun is hot, 1Sa 11:9
to the appointed t set by Samuel, 1Sa 13:8 4150
at that t with the sons of Israel. 1Sa 14:18 3117
it came about at the t when Merab, 1Sa 18:19 6256
"For a second t you may be my 1Sa 18:21 8147
sent messengers again the third t, 1Sa 19:21 7992
my father about this t tomorrow, 1Sa 20:12 6256
stayed with him all the t that David 1Sa 22:4 3117
all the t we were with them 1Sa 25:16 3117
not strike him the second t." 1Sa 26:8 8138
all the t he has lived in the country of 1Sa 27:11 3117
The t that David was king in 2Sa 2:11
4557, 3117
the t when kings go out to battle, 2Sa 11:1 6256
When the t of mourning was over, 2Sa 11:27
So he sent again a second t, 2Sa 14:29 8145
your father's servant in t past, 2Sa 15:34 227
"This t the advice that 2Sa 17:7 6471
will not waste t here with you." 2Sa 18:14 3176
he delayed longer than the set t 2Sa 20:5 4150
hundred slain by him at one t; 2Sa 23:8 6471
and came to David in the harvest t 2Sa 23:13 7105a
the morning until the appointed t, 2Sa 24:15 6256
never crossed him at any t by asking 1Ki 1:6 3117
As David's t to die drew near, he 1Ki 2:1 3117
not put you to death at this t, 1Ki 2:26 3117
observed the feast at that t, 1Ki 8:65 6256
appeared to Solomon a second t, 1Ki 9:2 8145
It came about at that t, 1Ki 11:29 6256
Thus the t that Solomon reigned in 1Ki 11:42 3117
At that t Abijah the son of 1Ki 14:1 6256
The t that Jeroboam reigned 1Ki 14:20 3117
But in the t of his old age he was 1Ki 15:23 6256
the t of the offering of the evening 1Ki 18:29
"Do it a second t," 1Ki 18:34 8138
time," and they did it a second t. 1Ki 18:34 8138
"Do it a third t," 1Ki 18:34 8027
time," and they did it a third t. 1Ki 18:34 8027
At the t of the offering of the evening 1Ki 18:36 3117
It came about at the seventh t, 1Ki 18:44
them by tomorrow about this t." 1Ki 19:2 6256
the LORD came again a second t 1Ki 19:7 8145
but about this t tomorrow I will 1Ki 20:6 6256
went out of Samaria at that t and 2Ki 3:6 3117
the t of offering the sacrifice, 2Ki 3:20
Is it a t to receive money and to 2Ki 5:26 6256
'Tomorrow about this t a measure 2Ki 7:1 6256
will be sold tomorrow about this t 2Ki 7:18 6256
Libnah revolted at the same t. 2Ki 8:22 6256
letter to them a second t saying, 2Ki 10:6 8145
Jezreel tomorrow about this t." 2Ki 10:6 6256
Now the t which Jehu reigned over 2Ki 10:36 3117
At that t Rezin king of Aram 2Ki 16:6 6256
At that t Hezekiah cut off the 2Ki 18:16 6256
At that t Berodach-baladan a son 2Ki 20:12 6256

At that **t** the servants of	2Ki 24:10	6256
from **t** to time *to be* with them;	1Ch 9:25	6256
from time to **t** *to be* with them;	1Ch 9:25	6256
hundred whom he killed at one **t**.	1Ch 11:11	6471
the **t** when kings go out *to battle,*	1Ch 20:1	6256
At that **t**, when David saw that the	1Ch 21:28	6256
high place at Gibeon at that **t**.	1Ch 21:29	6256
the son of David king a second **t**,	1Ch 29:22	8145
feast at that **t** for seven days,	2Ch 7:8	6256
of Israel were subdued at that **t**,	2Ch 13:18	6256
At that **t** Hanani the seer came to	2Ch 16:7	6256
some of the people at the same **t**.	2Ch 16:10	6256
at the same **t** against his rule,	2Ch 21:10	6256
it came about in the course of **t**,	2Ch 21:19	3117
From the **t** that Amaziah turned	2Ch 25:27	6256
At that **t** King Ahaz sent to the	2Ch 28:16	6256
Now in the **t** of his distress this	2Ch 28:22	6256
could not celebrate it at that **t**,	2Ch 30:3	6256
celebrated the Passover at that **t**,	2Ch 35:17	6256
At that **t** Tattenai, the governor	Ezr 5:3	2166
the weight was recorded at that **t**.	Ezr 8:34	6256
me, and I gave him a definite **t**.	Ne 2:6	2165
At that **t** I also said to the people,	Ne 4:22	6256
although at that **t** I had not set	Ne 6:1	6256
to me in the same manner a fifth **t**	Ne 6:5	6471
You in the **t** of their distress,	Ne 9:27	6256
But during all this **t** I was not	Ne 13:6	
After some **t**, however, I asked	Ne 13:6	3117
From that **t** on they did not come	Ne 13:21	6256
gathered together the second **t**,	Es 2:19	8145
if you remain silent at this **t**,	Es 4:14	6256
royalty for such a **t** as this?"	Es 4:14	6256
every **t** I see Mordecai the Jew sitting	Es 5:13	6256
at that **t** in the third month	Es 8:9	6256
to their appointed **t** annually.	Es 9:27	2165
will be accomplished before his **t**,	Jb 15:32	3117
were snatched away before their **t**,	Jb 22:16	6256
And opens their ear in **t** *of*	Jb 36:15	
reserved for the **t** of distress,	Jb 38:23	6256
the **t** the mountain goats give birth?	Jb 39:1	6256
do you know the **t** they give birth?	Jb 39:2	6256
fiery oven in the **t** of your anger;	Ps 21:9	6256
in a **t** when You may be found;	Ps 32:6	6256
not be ashamed in the **t** of evil,	Ps 37:19	6256
is their strength in **t** of trouble.	Ps 37:39	6256
You, O LORD, at an acceptable **t**;	Ps 69:13	6256
not cast me off in the **t** of old age;	Ps 71:9	6256
"When I select an appointed **t**,	Ps 75:2	4150
And their **t** *of punishment* would be	Ps 81:15	6256
For it is **t** to be gracious to her,	Ps 102:13	6256
her, For the appointed **t** has come.	Ps 102:13	4150
the **t** that his word came to pass,	Ps 105:19	6256
From this **t** forth and forever.	Ps 113:2	6258
From this **t** forth and forever.	Ps 115:18	6258
It is **t** for the LORD to act, *For*	Ps 119:126	6256
in From this **t** forth and forever.	Ps 121:8	6258
From this **t** forth and forever.	Ps 125:2	6258
From this **t** forth and forever.	Ps 131:3	6258
give them their food in due **t**.	Ps 145:15	6256
lamp will go out in **t** of darkness.	Pr 20:20	380
But the wicked stumble in **t** *of*	Pr 24:16	
the cold of snow in the **t** of harvest	Pr 25:13	3117
a faithless man in **t** of trouble.	Pr 25:19	3117
is an appointed **t** for everything.	Ec 3:1	2165
And there is a **t** for every event	Ec 3:1	6256
A **t** to give birth and a time to	Ec 3:2	6256
to give birth and a **t** to die;	Ec 3:2	6256
A **t** to plant and a time to uproot	Ec 3:2	6256
and a **t** to uproot what is planted.	Ec 3:2	6256
A **t** to kill and a time to heal;	Ec 3:3	6256
A time to kill and a **t** to heal;	Ec 3:3	6256
A **t** to tear down and a time to	Ec 3:3	6256
to tear down and a **t** to build up.	Ec 3:3	6256
A **t** to weep and a time to laugh;	Ec 3:4	6256
A time to weep and a **t** to laugh;	Ec 3:4	6256
A **t** to mourn and a time to dance.	Ec 3:4	6256
A time to mourn and a **t** to dance.	Ec 3:4	6256
A **t** to throw stones and a time to	Ec 3:5	6256
stones and a **t** to gather stones;	Ec 3:5	6256
A **t** to embrace and a time to shun	Ec 3:5	6256
and a **t** to shun embracing.	Ec 3:5	6256
A **t** to search and a time to give	Ec 3:6	6256
and a **t** to give up as lost;	Ec 3:6	6256
A **t** to keep and a time to throw	Ec 3:6	6256
to keep and a **t** to throw away.	Ec 3:6	6256
A **t** to tear apart and a time to	Ec 3:7	6256
apart and a **t** to sew together;	Ec 3:7	6256
A **t** to be silent and a time to	Ec 3:7	6256
to be silent and a **t** to speak.	Ec 3:7	6256
A **t** to love and a time to hate;	Ec 3:8	6256
A time to love and a **t** to hate;	Ec 3:8	6256
A **t** for war and a time for peace.	Ec 3:8	6256
A time for war and a **t** for peace.	Ec 3:8	6256
everything appropriate in its **t**.	Ec 3:11	6256
for a **t** for every matter and for	Ec 3:17	6256
Why should you die before your **t**?	Ec 7:17	6256
knows the proper **t** and procedure.	Ec 8:5	6256
For there is a proper **t** and	Ec 8:6	6256
is no discharge in the **t** of war,	Ec 8:8	4421
your clothes be white all the **t**,	Ec 9:8	6256
t and chance overtake them all.	Ec 9:11	6256
Moreover, man does not know his **t**:	Ec 9:12	6256
sons of men are ensnared at an evil **t**	Ec 9:12	6256
princes eat at the appropriate **t**	Ec 10:17	6256
The **t** has arrived for pruning *the*	SS 2:12	6256
"He will eat curds and honey at the **t**	Is 7:15	
Will again recover the second **t** with	Is 11:11	8145
Her *fateful* **t** also will soon come	Is 13:22	6256
At evening **t**, behold, *there is*	Is 17:14	6256

will spend harvest **t** on them.	Is 18:6	2778b
At that **t** a gift of homage will be	Is 18:7	6256
at that **t** the LORD spoke through	Is 20:2	6256
will swallow up death for all **t**,	Is 25:8	5331
the pregnant woman approaches *the* **t**	Is 26:17	
That it may serve in the **t** to come	Is 30:8	3117
also in the **t** of distress.	Is 33:2	6256
At that **t** Merodach-baladan son of	Is 39:1	6256
"I have kept silent for a long **t**,	Is 42:14	5769
From the **t** that I established the	Is 44:7	
to you new things from this **t**,	Is 48:6	6258
secret, From the **t** it took place,	Is 48:16	6256
"In a favorable **t** I have answered	Is 49:8	6256
Was I not silent even for a long **t**	Is 57:11	5769
LORD, will hasten it in its **t**."	Is 60:22	6256
We continued in them a long **t**;	Is 64:5	5769
the **t** is coming to gather all	Is 66:18	
LORD came to me a second **t** saying,	Jer 1:13	8145
In *the* **t** *of* her heat who can turn	Jer 2:24	
But in the **t** of their trouble they	Jer 2:27	6256
save you In the **t** of your trouble;	Jer 2:28	6256
"At that **t** they will call Jerusalem	Jer 3:17	6256
In that **t** it will be said to this	Jer 4:11	6256
At the **t** that I punish them, They	Jer 6:15	6256
"At that **t**," declares the LORD,	Jer 8:1	6256
Observe the **t** of their migration;	Jer 8:7	6256
At the **t** of their punishment they	Jer 8:12	6256
For a **t** of healing, but behold,	Jer 8:15	6256
In the **t** of their punishment they	Jer 10:15	6256
inhabitants of the land At this **t**,	Jer 10:18	6471
them in the **t** of their disaster.	Jer 11:12	6256
of the LORD came to me a second **t**,	Jer 13:3	8145
Its Savior in **t** of distress,	Jer 14:8	6256
And for a **t** of healing, but	Jer 14:19	6256
supplication to you In a **t** of disaster	Jer 15:11	6256
of disaster and a **t** of distress.	Jer 15:11	6256
before your eyes and in your **t**,	Jer 16:9	3117
This **t** I will make them know My	Jer 16:21	6471
with them in the **t** of Your anger!	Jer 18:23	6256
For each **t** I speak, I cry aloud;	Jer 20:8	1767
until the **t** of his own land comes;	Jer 27:7	6256
it is the **t** of Jacob's distress,	Jer 30:7	6256
"At that **t**," declares the LORD,	Jer 31:1	6256
Now at that **t** the army of the king	Jer 32:2	227
that they may last a long **t**."	Jer 32:14	3117
came to Jeremiah the second **t**,	Jer 33:1	8145
'In those days and at that **t** I	Jer 33:15	6256
will not be at their appointed **t**,	Jer 33:20	6256
vineyards and fields at that **t**.	Jer 39:10	3117
has let the appointed **t** pass by!'	Jer 46:17	4150
them, The **t** of their punishment.	Jer 46:21	6256
For each **t** you speak about him you	Jer 48:27	1767
upon him At the **t** I punish him.	Jer 49:8	6256
"In those days and at that **t**,"	Jer 50:4	6256
the sickle at the **t** of harvest;	Jer 50:16	6256
'In those days and at that **t**,'	Jer 50:20	6256
come, The **t** of their punishment.	Jer 50:27	6256
The **t** when I will punish you.	Jer 50:31	6256
this is the LORD's **t** of vengeance;	Jer 51:6	6256
In the **t** of their punishment they	Jer 51:18	6256
floor At the **t** it is stamped firm;	Jer 51:33	6256
the **t** of harvest will come for her."	Jer 51:33	6256
He has called an appointed **t**	La 1:15	4150
you shall lie down a second **t**,	Ezk 4:6	8145
you shall eat it from **t** to time.	Ezk 4:10	6256
you shall eat it from time to **t**.	Ezk 4:10	6256
you shall drink it from **t** to time.	Ezk 4:11	6256
you shall drink it from time to **t**.	Ezk 4:11	6256
The **t** has come, the day is near	Ezk 7:7	6256
'The **t** has come, the day has	Ezk 7:12	6256
who say, '*The* **t** is not near to	Ezk 11:3	
you were at the **t** for love;	Ezk 16:8	6256
the sword be doubled the third **t**,	Ezk 21:14	7992
t of the punishment of the end,'	Ezk 21:25	6256
t of the punishment of the end.	Ezk 21:29	6256
midst, so that her **t** will come,	Ezk 22:3	6256
forsake her harlotries from *the* **t**	Ezk 23:8	
A **t** *of doom* for the nations.	Ezk 30:3	6256
And He opened my mouth at the **t**	Ezk 33:22	5704
sword at the **t** of their calamity,	Ezk 35:5	6256
at the **t** of the punishment	Ezk 35:5	6256
They answered a second **t** and said,	Da 2:7	8579
that you are bargaining for **t**,	Da 2:8	5732
the king that he would give him **t**,	Da 2:16	2166
were crushed all at the same **t** and	Da 2:35	2298
Therefore at that **t**,	Da 3:7	2166
at that **t** certain Chaldeans came	Da 3:8	2166
seven periods of **t** pass over him.	Da 4:16	5732
seven periods of **t** pass over him,"	Da 4:23	5732
periods of **t** will pass over you,	Da 4:25	5732
periods of **t** will pass over you until	Da 4:32	5732
At that **t** my reason returned to me.	Da 4:36	2166
them for an appointed period of **t**.	Da 7:12	5732
and the **t** arrived when the saints	Da 7:22	2166
be given into his hand for a **t**,	Da 7:25	5732
for a time, times, and half a **t**.	Da 7:25	5732
pertains to the **t** of the end."	Da 8:17	6256
to the appointed **t** of the end.	Da 8:19	4150
the **t** of the evening offering.	Da 9:21	6256
he will also stay *for a* **t** in	Da 11:16	
he will come in a **t** of tranquility	Da 11:21	7962
"In a **t** of tranquility he will	Da 11:24	7962
strongholds, but *only* for a **t**.	Da 11:24	6256
still *to come* at the appointed **t**.	Da 11:27	4150
"At the appointed **t** he will	Da 11:29	4150
but this last **t** it will not turn	Da 11:29	314
make them pure until the end **t**;	Da 11:35	6256
still *to come* at the appointed **t**.	Da 11:35	4150
"At the end **t** the king of the	Da 11:40	6256

"Now at that **t** Michael, the great	Da 12:1	6256
And there will be a **t** of distress	Da 12:1	6256
there was a nation until that **t**;	Da 12:1	6256
and at that **t** your people,	Da 12:1	6256
up the book until the end of **t**;	Da 12:4	6256
be for a **t**, times, and half *a time;*	Da 12:7	4150
and half *a* **t**; and as soon as	Da 12:7	
and sealed up until the end **t**.	Da 12:9	6256
From the **t** that the regular sacrifice	Da 12:11	6256
will take back My grain at harvest **t**	Hos 2:9	6256
For it is **t** to seek the LORD Until	Hos 10:12	6256
For it is not the **t** that he should	Hos 13:13	6256
in those days and at that **t**,	Jl 3:1	6256
at such a **t** the prudent person	Am 5:13	6256
keeps silent, for it is an evil **t**.	Am 5:13	6256
make it like a **t** *of* mourning	Am 8:10	
LORD came to Jonah the second **t**,	Jon 3:1	8145
For it will be an evil **t**.	Mi 2:3	6256
hide His face from them at that **t**	Mi 3:4	6256
He will give them *up* until the **t**	Mi 5:3	6256
Because at that **t** He will be great	Mi 5:4	6258
Who has appointed its **t**?	Mi 6:9	
At that **t** she will be trampled down	Mi 7:10	6258
vision is yet for the appointed **t**;	Hab 2:3	4150
"It will come about at that **t**	Zph 1:12	6256
I am going to deal at that **t** With all	Zph 3:19	6256
"At that **t** I will bring you in,	Zph 3:20	6256
the **t** when I gather you together;	Zph 3:20	6256
"The **t** has not come, *even* the	Hg 1:2	6256
even the **t** for the house of the LORD	Hg 1:2	6256
"Is it **t** for you yourselves to	Hg 1:4	6256
from that **t** *when* one came to a	Hg 2:16	1961
word of the LORD came a second **t** to	Hg 2:20	8145
I answered the second **t** and said to	Zch 4:12	8145
the LORD at the **t** of the spring rain	Zch 10:1	6256
at evening **t** there will be light.	Zch 14:7	6256
t of the deportation to Babylon.	Mt 1:11	1909
from them the exact **t** the star appeared.	Mt 2:7	5550
according to the **t** which he had	Mt 2:16	5550
"Permit *it* at this **t**;	Mt 3:15	737
From that **t** Jesus began to preach	Mt 4:17	5119
here to torment us before the **t**?"	Mt 8:29	2540
At that **t** Jesus said,	Mt 11:25	2540
At that **t** Jesus went through the	Mt 12:1	2540
and in the **t** of the harvest I will	Mt 13:30	2540
At that **t** Herod the tetrarch heard	Mt 14:1	2540
From that **t** Jesus began to	Mt 16:21	5119
At that **t** the disciples came to Jesus	Mt 18:1	5610
"When the harvest **t** approached,	Mt 21:34	2540
"At that **t** many will fall	Mt 24:10	5119
at what **t** of the night the thief was	Mt 24:43	5438
them their food at the proper **t**?	Mt 24:45	2540
master is not coming for a long **t**,'	Mt 24:48	5549
"Now after a long **t** the master of	Mt 25:19	5550
'The Teacher says, "My **t** is near;	Mt 26:18	2540
away again a second **t** and prayed,	Mt 26:42	1208
went away and prayed a third **t**,	Mt 26:44	5154
At that **t** Jesus said to the crowds	Mt 26:55	5610
At that **t** they were holding a notorious	Mt 27:16	5119
At that **t** two robbers were	Mt 27:38	5119
"The **t** is fulfilled, and the	Mk 1:15	2540
the **t** of Abiathar *the* high priest,	Mk 2:26	1909
they did not even have **t** to eat.)	Mk 6:31	2119
"At the *harvest* **t** he sent a	Mk 12:2	2540
will be a **t** *of* tribulation	Mk 13:19	
know when the *appointed* **t** will come.	Mk 13:33	2540
to betray Him at an opportune **t**.	Mk 14:11	2122
And He came the third **t**,	Mk 14:41	5154
a rooster crowed a second **t**.	Mk 14:72	1208
wondered if He was dead by this **t**,	Mk 15:44	2235
be fulfilled in their proper **t**."	Lk 1:20	2540
Now at this **t** Mary arose and went	Lk 1:39	2250
from this **t** on all generations	Lk 1:48	3568
Now the **t** had come for Elizabeth	Lk 1:57	5550
of the world in a moment of **t**.	Lk 4:5	5550
left Him until an opportune **t**.	Lk 4:13	2540
in the **t** of Elisha the prophet;	Lk 4:27	1909
It was at this **t** that He went	Lk 6:12	2250
At that very **t** He cured many	Lk 7:21	5610
but she, since the **t** I came in,	Lk 7:45	
and in **t** of temptation fall away.	Lk 8:13	2540
put on any clothing for a long **t**,	Lk 8:27	5550
At that very **t** He rejoiced greatly	Lk 10:21	5610
their rations at the proper **t**?	Lk 12:42	2540
master will be a long **t** in coming,'	Lk 12:45	5549
do you not analyze this present **t**?	Lk 12:56	2540
at that **t** some Pharisees approached,	Lk 13:31	5610
you will not see Me until *the* **t**	Lk 13:35	
since that **t** the gospel of	Lk 16:16	5119
at this **t** and in the age to come,	Lk 18:30	2540
the **t** of your visitation."	Lk 19:44	2540
went on a journey for a long **t**.	Lk 20:9	5550
"At the *harvest* **t** he sent a	Lk 20:10	2540
'The **t** is near.'	Lk 21:8	2540
also was in Jerusalem at that **t**.	Lk 23:7	2250
wanted to see Him for a long **t**,	Lk 23:8	5550
And he said to them the third **t**,	Lk 23:22	5154
No one has seen God at any **t**;	Jn 1:18	4455
He cannot enter a second **t** into	Jn 3:4	1208
there He was spending **t** with them	Jn 3:22	1304
been a long **t** *in that condition,*	Jn 5:6	5550
neither heard His voice at any **t** nor	Jn 5:37	4455
"My **t** is not yet here, but	Jn 7:6	2540
but your **t** is always opportune.	Jn 7:6	2540
My **t** has not yet fully come."	Jn 7:8	2540
So a second **t** they called the man	Jn 9:24	1208
"Since the beginning of **t** it has	Jn 9:32	165
At that **t** the Feast of the	Jn 10:22	5119
by this **t** there will be a stench,	Jn 11:39	2235

This is now the third t that Jesus Jn 21:14 5154
He said to him again a second t, Jn 21:16 1208
He said to him the third t, Jn 21:17 5154
He said to him the third t, Jn 21:17 5154
is it at this t You are restoring Ac 1:6 5550
At this t Peter stood up in Ac 1:15 2250
who have accompanied us all the t Ac 1:21 5550
His holy prophets from ancient t. Ac 3:21 165
put the men outside for a short t. Ac 5:34 1024
"For some t ago Theudas rose up, Ac 5:36 2250
Now at this t while the disciples Ac 6:1 2250
our fathers *there* the first t. Ac 7:12 4413
"But as the t of the promise was Ac 7:17 5550
was at this t that Moses was born; Ac 7:20 2540
"At that t they made a calf Ac 7:41 2250
our fathers, until the t of David. Ac 7:45 2250
he had for a long t astonished them Ac 8:11 5550
it happened at that t that she fell Ac 9:37 2250
a voice *came* to him a second t, Ac 10:15 1208
from heaven answered a second t, Ac 11:9 1208
Now at this t some prophets came Ac 11:27 2250
Now about that t Herod the king Ac 12:1 2540
Caesarea and was spending t there. Ac 12:19 1304
and not see the sun for a t." Ac 13:11 2540
Therefore they spent a long t Ac 14:3 5550
spent a long t with the disciples. Ac 14:28 5550
After they had spent t *there,* Ac 15:33 5550
spend their t in nothing other than Ac 17:21 2119
asked him to stay for a longer t, Ac 18:20 5550
And having spent some t *there,* Ac 18:23 5550
About that t there occurred no Ac 19:23 2540
would not have to spend t in Asia; Ac 20:16 5551
how I was with you the whole t, Ac 20:18 5550
Egyptian who some t ago stirred up a Ac 21:38 2250
at that very t I looked up at him. Ac 22:13 5610
the present, and when I find t I Ac 24:25 2540
At the same t too, he was hoping Ac 24:26 260
to Jerusalem (*at the same* t, Ac 25:3
about me for a long t, Ac 26:5 509
"In a short t you will persuade Ac 26:28 3641
that whether in a short or long t, Ac 26:29 3173
When considerable t had passed Ac 27:9 5550
had gone a long t without food, Ac 27:21 776
at the same t they were loosening the Ac 27:40 260
But after they had waited a long t Ac 28:6
righteousness at the present t, Ro 3:26 2540
at the right t Christ died for the Ro 5:6 2540
the sufferings of this present t are not Ro 8:18 2540
"AT THIS T I WILL COME, AND SARAH Ro 9:9 2540
come to be at the present t a remnant Ro 11:5 2540
Do this, knowing the t, Ro 13:11 2540
on passing judgment before the t, 1Co 4:5 2540
except by agreement for a t, 1Co 7:5 2540
the t has been shortened, 1Co 7:29 2540
Who at any t serves as a soldier 1Co 9:7 4218
five hundred brethren at one t, 1Co 15:6 2178
to remain with you for some t, 1Co 16:7 5550
no *at the same* t? 2Co 1:17
ACCEPTABLE T I LISTENED TO YOU, 2Co 6:2 2540
Behold, now is "THE ACCEPTABLE T," 2Co 6:2 2540
at this present t your abundance 2Co 8:14 2540
third t I am ready to come to you, 2Co 12:14 5154
All this t you have been thinking 2Co 12:19 3819
is the third t I am coming to you. 2Co 13:1 5154
said when present the second t, 2Co 13:2 1208
when the fullness of the t came, Ga 4:4 5550
However at that t, when you did Ga 4:8 5119
the gospel to you the first t; Ga 4:13 4387
But as at that t he who was born Ga 4:29 5119
for in due t we will reap if we Ga 6:9 2540
at that t separate from Christ, Eph 2:12 2540
making the most of your t, Eph 5:16 2540
praying at the same t for us as well, Col 4:3 260
that in his t he will be revealed. 2Th 2:6 2540
testimony *given* at the proper t. 1Tm 2:6 2540
same t they also learn *to be* idle, 1Tm 5:13 260
He will bring about at the proper t 1Tm 6:15 2540
For the t will come when they will 2Tm 4:3 2540
the t of my departure has come. 2Tm 4:6 2540
but at the proper t manifested, Ti 1:3 2540
same t also prepare me a lodging, Phm 1:22 260
through David after so long a t just Heb 4:7 5550
find grace to help in t of need. Heb 4:16 2121
by this t you ought to be teachers, Heb 5:12 5550
is a symbol for the present t. Heb 9:9 2540
imposed until a t of reformation. Heb 9:10 2540
will appear a second t for salvation Heb 9:28 1208
ministering and offering t after time Heb 10:11 4178
time after t the same sacrifices, Heb 10:11 4178
one sacrifice for sins for all t, Heb 10:12 1336
waiting from that t onward UNTIL Heb 10:13 3062
He has perfected for all t those who Heb 10:14 1336
even beyond the proper t of life, Heb 11:11 2540
For t will fail me if I tell of Heb 11:32 5550
For they disciplined us for a short t Heb 12:10 2250
to be revealed in the last t. 1Pe 1:5 2540
seeking to know what person or t 1Pe 1:11 2540
the t of your stay *on earth;* 1Pe 1:17 5550
so as to live the rest of the t in 1Pe 4:2 5550
For the t already past is 1Pe 4:3 5550
For *it is* t for judgment to begin 1Pe 4:17 2540
He may exalt you at the proper t, 1Pe 5:6 2540
at any t after my departure you will 2Pe 1:15 1539
the world at that t was destroyed, 2Pe 3:6 5119
No one has seen God at any t; 1Jn 4:12 4455
In the last t there will be mockers, Jude 1:18 5550
before all t and now and forever. Jude 1:25 165
for the t is near. Rv 1:3 2540
'I gave her t to repent, Rv 2:21 5550
and the t *came* for the dead to be Rv 11:18 2540
and *the* t to reward Your Rv 11:18
that he has *only* a short t." Rv 12:12 2540
for a t and times and half a time, Rv 12:14 2540
for a time and times and half a t, Rv 12:14 2540
And a second t they said, Rv 19:3 1208
he must be released for a short t. Rv 20:3 5550
of this book, for the t is near. Rv 22:10 2540

TIMELY
And how delightful is a t word! Pr 15:23 6256

TIMES
he has supplanted me these two t? Gn 27:36 6471
me and changed my wages ten t; Gn 31:7 4489
and you changed my wages ten t. Gn 31:41 4489
bowed down to the ground seven t, Gn 33:3 6471
five t as much as any of theirs. Gn 43:34 3027
them judge the people at all t; Ex 18:22 6256
They judged the people at all t; Ex 18:26 6256
"Three t a year you shall Ex 23:14 7272
"Three t a year all your males Ex 23:17 6471
on the table before Me at all t. Ex 25:30 8548
"Three t a year all your males Ex 34:23 6471
go up three t a year to appear before Ex 34:24 6471
the blood seven t before the LORD, Lv 4:6 6471
it seven t before the LORD, Lv 4:17 6471
some of it on the altar seven t and Lv 8:11 6471
"He shall then sprinkle seven t Lv 14:7 6471
the oil seven t before the LORD. Lv 14:16 6471
left palm seven t before the LORD. Lv 14:27 6471
and sprinkle the house seven t. Lv 14:51 6471
the blood with his finger seven t. Lv 16:14 6471
some of the blood on it seven t and Lv 16:19 6471
'The LORD's appointed t which you Lv 23:2 4150
My appointed t are these: Lv 23:2 4150
are the appointed t of the LORD, Lv 23:4 4150
at the t appointed for them. Lv 23:4 4150
are the appointed t of the LORD Lv 23:37 4150
the appointed t of the LORD. Lv 23:44 4150
for yourself, seven t seven years, Lv 25:8 6471
you seven t more for your sins. Lv 26:18 7651
seven t according to your sins. Lv 26:21 7651
strike you seven t for your sins. Lv 26:24 7651
punish you seven t for your sins. Lv 26:28 7651
have put Me to the test these ten t Nu 14:22 6471
offering or in your appointed t, Nu 15:3 4150
of the tent of meeting seven t. Nu 19:4 6471
have struck me these three t?" Nu 22:28 7272
struck your donkey these three t? Nu 22:32 7272
aside from me these three t. Nu 22:33 7272
he did not go as at other t to Nu 24:1 6471
in blessing them these three t! Nu 24:10 6471
to the LORD at your appointed t, Nu 29:39 4150
"Three t in a year all your males Dt 16:16 6471
may beat him forty t *but* no more, Dt 25:3 705
march around the city seven t, Jos 6:4 6471
city in the same manner seven t; Jos 6:15 6471
marched around the city seven t. Jos 6:15 6471
'From ancient t your fathers lived Jos 24:2 5769
You have deceived me these three t Jg 16:15 6471
I will go out as at other t and shake Jg 16:20 6471
against Gibeah as at other t. Jg 20:30 6471
some of the people as at other t, Jg 20:31 6471
Now this was *the custom* in former t Ru 4:7 6440
stood and called as at other t, 1Sa 3:10 6471
to the ground, and bowed three t. 1Sa 20:41 6471
of the land from ancient t, 1Sa 27:8 5769
"In t past you were seeking for 2Sa 3:17
1571, 8032a, 8543
a hundred t as many as they are, 2Sa 24:3 6471
Now three t in a year Solomon 1Ki 9:25 6471
himself upon the child three t, 1Ki 17:21 6471
And he said, "Go back" seven t. 1Ki 18:43 6471
"How many t must I adjure you to 1Ki 22:16 6471
the lad sneezed seven t and the lad 2Ki 4:35 6471
"Go and wash in the Jordan seven t, 2Ki 5:10 6471
dipped *himself* seven t in the Jordan, 2Ki 5:14 6471
he struck *it* three t and stopped. 2Ki 13:18 6471
should have struck five or six t, 2Ki 13:19 6471
shall strike Aram *only* three t." 2Ki 13:19 6471
Three t Joash defeated him and 2Ki 13:25 6471
From ancient t I planned it. 2Ki 19:25
3117, 6924a
"In t past, even when Saul was 1Ch 11:2
1571, 8032a, 8543
men who understood the t, 1Ch 12:32 6256
a hundred t as many as they are! 1Ch 21:3 6471
"In those t there was no 2Ch 15:5 6256
"How many t must I adjure you to 2Ch 18:15 6471
foreign wives come at appointed t, Ezr 10:14 6256
near them came and told us ten t, Ne 4:12 6471
to me four t in this manner, Ne 6:4 6471
And many t You rescued them Ne 9:28 6256
the new moon, for the appointed t, Ne 10:33 4150
households, at fixed t annually, Ne 10:34 6256
of David and Asaph, in ancient t, Ne 12:46 6924a
the supply of wood at appointed t Ne 13:31 6256
to the wise men who understood the t Es 1:13 6256
of Purim at their appointed t, Es 9:31 2165
with instructions for their t of fasting Es 9:31 6685
not answer Him once in a thousand t. Jb 9:3
"These ten t you have insulted Jb 19:3 6471
t not stored up by the Almighty, Jb 24:1 6256
Will he call on God at all t? Jb 27:10 6256
A stronghold in t of trouble; Ps 9:9 6256
You hide *Yourself* in t of trouble? Ps 10:1 6256
His ways prosper at all t; Ps 10:5 6256
on the earth, refined seven t. Ps 12:6 7659
My t are in Your hand; Ps 31:15 6256
I will bless the LORD at all t; Ps 34:1 6256
Trust in Him at all t, Ps 62:8 6256
heavens, which are from ancient t; Ps 68:33 6924a
practice righteousness at all t! Ps 106:3 6256
Many t He would deliver them; Ps 106:43 6471
After Your ordinances at all t. Ps 119:20 6256
Seven t a day I praise You, Ps 119:164 7651
"Many t they have persecuted me Ps 129:1 7227a
"Many t they have persecuted me Ps 129:2 7227a
her breasts satisfy you at all t; Pr 5:19 6256
from the earliest t of the earth. Pr 8:23 6924a
A friend loves at all t, Pr 17:17 6256
For a righteous man falls seven t, Pr 24:16 7651
have many t cursed others. Ec 7:22 6471
a sinner does evil a hundred t Ec 8:12
in earlier t He treated the land Is 9:1 6256
the sun will be seven t *brighter,* Is 30:26 7659
will be the stability of your t, Is 33:6 6256
it, From ancient t I planned it. Is 37:26
3117, 6924a
Or from former t, that we may say, Is 41:26 6440
from ancient t things which have not Is 46:10 6924a
from ancient t prophesied against Jer 28:8 5769
and he prophesies of t far off.' Ezk 12:27 6256
he found them ten t better than Da 1:20 3027
who changes the t and the epochs; Da 2:21 5732
to heat the furnace seven t more than Da 3:19 2298
kneeling on his knees three t a day, Da 6:10 2166
his petition three t a day." Da 6:13 2166
make alterations in t and in law; Da 7:25 2166
hand for a time, t, and half a time. Da 7:25 5732
and moat, even in t of distress. Da 9:25 6256
he who supported her in *those* t. Da 11:6 6256
"Now in those t many will rise up Da 11:14 6256
be for a time, t, and half *a time;* Da 12:7 4150
cannot *discern* the signs of the t? Mt 16:3 2540
and I forgive him? Up to seven t? Mt 18:21 2034
do not say to you, up to seven t, Mt 18:22 2034
times, but up to seventy t seven. Mt 18:22 1441
will receive many t as much, Mt 19:29 4179
you will deny Me three t." Mt 26:34 5151
crows, you will deny Me three t." Mt 26:75 5151
he will receive a hundred t as much Mk 10:30 1542
you yourself will deny Me three t." Mk 14:30 5151
twice, you will deny Me three t." Mk 14:72 5151
a crop a hundred t as great." Lk 8:8 1542
For it had seized him many t; Lk 8:29 5550
he sins against you seven t a day, Lk 17:4 2034
a day, and returns to you seven t, Lk 17:4 2034
that at all t they ought to pray and Lk 18:1 3842
receive many t as much at this time Lk 18:30 4179
I will give back four t as much." Lk 19:8 5073
t of the Gentiles are fulfilled. Lk 21:24 2540
"But keep on the alert at all t, Lk 21:36 2540
denied three t that you know Me." Lk 22:34 5151
today, you will deny Me three t." Lk 22:61 5151
crow until you deny Me three t. Jn 13:38 5151
It is not for you to know t or epochs Ac 1:7 5550
in order that t of refreshing may Ac 3:19 2540
This happened three t, Ac 10:16 5151
"This happened three t, Ac 11:10 5151
determined *their* appointed t and Ac 17:26 2540
overlooked the t of ignorance, Ac 17:30 5550
For whatever was written in earlier t Ro 15:4 4270
beaten t without number, 2Co 11:23 5234
Five t I received from the Jews 2Co 11:24 3999
Three t I was beaten with rods, 2Co 11:25 5151
stoned, three t I was shipwrecked, 2Co 11:25 5151
I implored the Lord three t that it 2Co 12:8 5151
suitable to the fullness of the t, Eph 1:10 2540
pray at all t in the Spirit, Eph 6:18 2540
Now as to the t and the epochs, 1Th 5:1 5550
Spirit explicitly says that in later t 1Tm 4:1 2540
last days difficult t will come. 2Tm 3:1 2540
these last t for the sake of you 1Pe 1:20 5550
in former t the holy women also, 1Pe 3:5 4218
for a time and t and half a time, Rv 12:14 2540

TIMID
when he was young and t and could 2Ch 13:7
7390, 3824

TIMIDITY
God has not given us a spirit of t, 2Tm 1:7 1167

TIMNA
T was a concubine of Esau's Gn 36:12 8555
and Lotan's sister was T. Gn 36:22 8555
chief T, chief Alvah, chief Gn 36:40 8555
Omar, Zephi, Gatam, Kenaz, T and 1Ch 1:36 8555
and Lotan's sister *was* T. 1Ch 1:39 8555
chief T, chief Aliah, chief 1Ch 1:51 8555

TIMNAH
went up to his sheepshearers at T, Gn 38:12 8553
your father-in-law is going up to T Gn 38:13 8553
Enaim, which is on the road to T; Gn 38:14 8553
and continued through T. Jos 15:10 8553
Kain, Gibeah and T; Jos 15:57 8553
and Elon and T and Ekron, Jos 19:43 8553
Then Samson went down to T and Jg 14:1 8553
to Timnah and saw a woman in T, Jg 14:1 8553
"I saw a woman in T, Jg 14:2 8553
Then Samson went down to T with Jg 14:5 8553
came as far as the vineyards of T; Jg 14:5 8553
its villages, T with its villages, 2Ch 28:18 8553

TIMNATH-HERES
territory of his inheritance in T, Jg 2:9 8556a

TIMNATH-SERAH
T in the hill country of Ephraim. Jos 19:50 8556b
territory of his inheritance in T, Jos 24:30 8556b

Context	Reference	Number
TIMNITE		
"Samson, the son-in-law of the **T**,	**Jg 15:6**	8554
TIMON		
and Philip, Prochorus, Nicanor, **T**,	**Ac 6:5**	*5096*
TIMOTHY		
disciple was there, named **T**,	**Ac 16:1**	*5095*
and Silas and **T** remained there.	**Ac 17:14**	*5095*
receiving a command for Silas and **T**	**Ac 17:15**	*5095*
and **T** came down from Macedonia,	**Ac 18:5**	*5095*
ministered to him, **T** and Erastus,	**Ac 19:22**	*5095*
and Gaius of Derbe, and **T**,	**Ac 20:4**	*5095*
T my fellow worker greets you, and	**Ro 16:21**	*5095*
this reason I have sent to you **T**,	**1Co 4:17**	*5095*
Now if **T** comes, see that he is	**1Co 16:10**	*5095*
will of God, and **T** *our* brother,	**2Co 1:1**	*5095*
by me and Silvanus and **T**	**2Co 1:19**	*5095*
Paul and **T**, bond-servants of	**Php 1:1**	*5095*
Jesus to send **T** to you shortly,	**Php 2:19**	*5095*
will of God, and **T** our brother,	**Col 1:1**	*5095*
Paul and Silvanus and **T**, To the	**1Th 1:1**	*5095*
and we sent **T**, our brother and	**1Th 3:2**	*5095*
that **T** has come to us from you,	**1Th 3:6**	*5095*
Paul and Silvanus and **T**, To the	**2Th 1:1**	*5095*
To **T**, *my* true child in *the* faith:	**1Tm 1:2**	*5095*
This command I entrust to you, **T**,	**1Tm 1:18**	*5095*
O **T**, guard what has been entrusted	**1Tm 6:20**	*5095*
To **T**, my beloved son:	**2Tm 1:2**	*5095*
Christ Jesus, and **T** our brother,	**Phm 1:1**	*5095*
our brother **T** has been released,	**Heb 13:23**	*5095*
TIN		
the iron, the **t** and the lead,	**Nu 31:22**	913
all of them are bronze and **t** and	**Ezk 22:18**	913
iron and lead and **t** into the furnace	**Ezk 22:20**	913
with silver, iron, **t** and	**Ezk 27:12**	913
TINDER		
The strong man will become **t**,	**Is 1:31**	5296
TINGLE		
of everyone who hears it will **t**.	**1Sa 3:11**	6750
of it, both his ears will **t**.	**2Ki 21:12**	6750
everyone that hears of it will **t**.	**Jer 19:3**	6750
TINKLE		
And **t** the bangles on their feet,	**Is 3:16**	5913
TINKLING		
and its **t** shall be heard when he	**Ex 28:35**	6963
TIP		
t the water jars of the heavens,	**Jb 38:37**	7901
send to him those who **t** *vessels*,	**Jer 48:12**	6808
vessels, and they will **t** him over,	**Jer 48:12**	6808
that he may dip the **t** of his finger	**Lk 16:24**	*206*
TIPHSAH		
of the River, from **T** even to Gaza,	**1Ki 4:24**	8607
Then Menahem struck **T** and all who	**2Ki 15:16**	8607
TIRAS		
Javan and Tubal and Meshech and **T**.	**Gn 10:2**	8494
Javan, Tubal, Meshech and **T**.	**1Ch 1:5**	8494
TIRATHITES		
who lived at Jabez *were* the **T**,	**1Ch 2:55**	8654
TIRED		
"I am **t** of living because of the	**Gn 27:46**	6973
earth Does not become weary or **t**.	**Is 40:28**	3021
Though youths grow weary and **t**,	**Is 40:30**	3021
They will run and not get **t**,	**Is 40:31**	3021
"You were **t** out by the length of	**Is 57:10**	3021
footmen and they have **t** you out,	**Jer 12:5**	3811
I am **t** of relenting!	**Jer 15:6**	3811
TIRESOME		
'My, how **t** it is!'	**Mal 1:13**	8513
TIRHAKAH		
say concerning **T** king of Cush,	**2Ki 19:9**	8640
say concerning **T** king of Cush,	**Is 37:9**	8640
TIRHANAH		
concubine, bore Sheber and **T**.	**1Ch 2:48**	8647
TIRIA		
Ziph and Ziphah, **T** and Asarel.	**1Ch 4:16**	8493
TIRZAH		
Noah, Hoglah, Milcah and **T**.	**Nu 26:33**	8656
Noah and Hoglah and Milcah and **T**.	**Nu 27:1**	8656
Mahlah, **T**, Hoglah, Milcah and	**Nu 36:11**	8656
the king of **T**, one:	**Jos 12:24**	8656
and Noah, Hoglah, Milcah and **T**.	**Jos 17:3**	8656
arose and departed and came to **T**.	**1Ki 14:17**	8656
Ramah and remained in **T**.	**1Ki 15:21**	8656
became king over all Israel at **T**,	**1Ki 15:33**	8656
his fathers and was buried in **T**,	**1Ki 16:6**	8656
became king over Israel at **T**,	**1Ki 16:8**	8656
Now he *was* at **T** drinking himself	**1Ki 16:9**	8656
who *was* over the household at **T**.	**1Ki 16:9**	8656
Zimri reigned seven days at **T**.	**1Ki 16:15**	8656
Gibbethon and besieged **T**.	**1Ki 16:17**	8656
he reigned six years at **T**.	**1Ki 16:23**	8656
son of Gadi went up from **T** and	**2Ki 15:14**	8656
were in it and its borders from **T**,	**2Ki 15:16**	8656
"You are as beautiful as **T**,	**SS 6:4**	8656
TISHBITE		
Now Elijah the **T**, who was of the	**1Ki 17:1**	8664b
of the LORD came to Elijah the **T**,	**1Ki 21:17**	8664b
of the LORD came to Elijah the **T**,	**1Ki 21:28**	8664b
of the LORD said to Elijah the **T**,	**2Ki 1:3**	8664b
"It is Elijah the **T**."	**2Ki 1:8**	8664b
spoke by His servant Elijah the **T**,	**2Ki 9:36**	8664b
TITHE		
'Thus all the **t** of the land, of	**Lv 27:30**	4643
wishes to redeem part of his **t**,	**Lv 27:31**	4643
I have given all the **t** in Israel for	**Nu 18:21**	4643
"For the **t** of the sons of Israel,	**Nu 18:24**	4643
you take from the sons of Israel the **t**	**Nu 18:26**	4643
it to the LORD, a **t** of the tithe.	**Nu 18:26**	4643
it to the LORD, a tithe of the **t**.	**Nu 18:26**	4643
your gates the **t** of your grain or	**Dt 12:17**	4643
"You shall surely **t** all the	**Dt 14:22**	6237
His name, the **t** of your grain,	**Dt 14:23**	4643
you are not able to bring *the* **t**,	**Dt 14:24**	4643
t of your produce in that year,	**Dt 14:28**	4643
paying all the **t** of your increase in	**Dt 26:12**	4643
in abundantly the **t** of all.	**2Ch 31:5**	4643
in the **t** of oxen and sheep,	**2Ch 31:6**	4643
and the **t** of sacred gifts which	**2Ch 31:6**	4643
t of our ground to the Levites,	**Ne 10:37**	4643
then brought the **t** of the grain,	**Ne 13:12**	4643
the whole **t** into the storehouse,	**Mal 3:10**	4643
you **t** mint and dill and cummin,	**Mt 23:23**	*586b*
For you pay **t** of mint and rue and	**Lk 11:42**	*586b*
TITHES		
offering to the LORD from your **t**,	**Nu 18:28**	4643
your sacrifices, your **t**,	**Dt 12:6**	4643
your **t** and the contribution of	**Dt 12:11**	4643
the **t** and the consecrated things;	**2Ch 31:12**	4643
the **t** in all the rural towns.	**Ne 10:37**	6237
when the Levites receive **t**,	**Ne 10:38**	6237
shall bring up the tenth of the **t** to	**Ne 10:38**	4643
the first fruits and the **t**,	**Ne 12:44**	4643
the utensils and the **t** of grain,	**Ne 13:5**	4643
morning, Your **t** every three days.	**Am 4:4**	4643
In **t** and offerings.	**Mal 3:8**	4643
I pay **t** of all that I get.'	**Lk 18:12**	*586a*
In this case mortal men receive **t**,	**Heb 7:8**	*1181*
Abraham even Levi, who received **t**,	**Heb 7:9**	*1181*
Levi, who received tithes, paid **t**,	**Heb 7:9**	*1183*
TITHING		
in the third year, the year of **t**,	**Dt 26:12**	4643
TITIUS		
of a man named **T** Justus,	**Ac 18:7**	*5102a*
TITLE		
I have given you a **t** of honor	**Is 45:4**	3655
TITUS		
spirit, not finding **T** my brother;	**2Co 2:13**	*5103*
comforted us by the coming of **T**;	**2Co 7:6**	*5103*
even much more for the joy of **T**,	**2Co 7:13**	*5103*
our boasting before **T** proved to be	**2Co 7:14**	*5103*
So we urged **T** that as he	**2Co 8:6**	*5103*
on your behalf in the heart of **T**.	**2Co 8:16**	*5103*
As for **T**, *he is* my partner and	**2Co 8:23**	*5103*
I urged **T** *to go*, and I sent the	**2Co 12:18**	*5103*
T did not take any advantage of	**2Co 12:18**	*5103*
Barnabas, taking **T** along also.	**Ga 2:1**	*5103*
But not even **T**, who was with me,	**Ga 2:3**	*5103*
gone to Galatia, **T** to Dalmatia.	**2Tm 4:10**	*5103*
To **T**, my true child in a common	**Ti 1:4**	*5103*
TIZITE		
and Joha his brother, the **T**,	**1Ch 11:45**	8491
TOAH		
the son of Eliel, the son of **T**,	**1Ch 6:34**	8430
TOB		
and lived in the land of **T**;	**Jg 11:3**	2897
get Jephthah from the land of **T**;	**Jg 11:5**	2897
and the men of **T** with 12,000 men.	**2Sa 10:6**	382a
Rehob and the men of **T** and Maacah	**2Sa 10:8**	382a
TOBADONIJAH		
Adonijah, Tobijah and **T**,	**2Ch 17:8**	2899a
TOBIAH		
sons of Delaiah, the sons of **T**,	**Ezr 2:60**	2900
and **T** the Ammonite official heard	**Ne 2:10**	2900
and **T** the Ammonite official,	**Ne 2:19**	2900
Now **T** the Ammonite *was* near him	**Ne 4:3**	2900
when Sanballat, **T**,	**Ne 4:7**	2900
it was reported to Sanballat, **T**,	**Ne 6:1**	2900
T and Sanballat had hired him.	**Ne 6:12**	2900
T and Sanballat according to these	**Ne 6:14**	2900
from the nobles of Judah to **T**,	**Ne 6:17**	2900
T sent letters to frighten me.	**Ne 6:19**	2900
sons of Delaiah, the sons of **T**,	**Ne 7:62**	2900
of our God, being related to **T**,	**Ne 13:4**	2900
evil that Eliashib had done for **T**,	**Ne 13:7**	2900
TOBIAH'S		
and **T** *letters* came to them.	**Ne 6:17**	2900
I threw all of **T** household goods out	**Ne 13:8**	2900
TOBIJAH		
Jehonathan, Adonijah, **T** and	**2Ch 17:8**	2900
from the exiles, from Heldai, **T** and	**Zch 6:10**	2900
temple of the LORD to Helem, **T**,	**Zch 6:14**	2900
TOCHEN		
were Etam, Ain, Rimmon, **T** and	**1Ch 4:32**	8507
TODAY		
nor did I hear of it until **t**."	**Gn 21:26**	3117
please grant me success **t**,	**Gn 24:12**	3117
"So I came **t** to the spring, and	**Gn 24:42**	3117
pass through your entire flock **t**,	**Gn 30:32**	3117
"Why are your faces so sad **t**?"	**Gn 40:7**	3117
make mention **t** of my *own* offenses.	**Gn 41:9**	3117
the youngest is with our father **t**,	**Gn 42:13**	3117
the youngest is with our father **t** in	**Gn 42:32**	3117
I have **t** bought you and your land	**Gn 47:23**	3117
have you come *back* so soon **t**?"	**Ex 2:18**	3117
either yesterday or **t** in making brick	**Ex 5:14**	3117
He will accomplish for you **t**;	**Ex 14:13**	3117
Egyptians whom you have seen **t**,	**Ex 14:13**	3117
"Eat it **t**, for today is a sabbath	**Ex 16:25**	3117
for **t** is a sabbath to the LORD;	**Ex 16:25**	3117
t you will not find it in the	**Ex 16:25**	3117
consecrate them **t** and tomorrow,	**Ex 19:10**	3117
"Dedicate yourselves **t** to the LORD	**Ex 32:29**	3117
bestow a blessing upon you **t**."	**Ex 32:29**	3117
for **t** the LORD will appear to you.' "	**Lv 9:4**	3117
if I had eaten a sin offering **t**,	**Lv 10:19**	3117
'**T** you shall cross over Ar,	**Dt 2:18**	3117
him into your hand, as *he is* **t**.	**Dt 2:30**	3117
to the LORD your God are alive **t**.	**Dt 4:4**	3117
which I am setting before you **t**?	**Dt 4:8**	3117
for His own possession, as **t**.	**Dt 4:20**	3117
earth to witness against you **t**,	**Dt 4:26**	3117
for an inheritance, as it is **t**.	**Dt 4:38**	3117
"Know therefore **t**, and take it to	**Dt 4:39**	3117
which I am giving you **t**,	**Dt 4:40**	3117
I am speaking **t** in your hearing,	**Dt 5:1**	3117
with all those of us alive here **t**.	**Dt 5:3**	3117
we have seen **t** that God speaks with	**Dt 5:24**	3117
which I am commanding you **t**,	**Dt 6:6**	3117
and for our survival, as *it is* **t**.	**Dt 6:24**	3117
which I am commanding you **t**,	**Dt 7:11**	3117
that I am commanding you **t**	**Dt 8:1**	3117
which I am commanding you **t**;	**Dt 8:11**	3117
I testify against you **t** that you will	**Dt 8:19**	3117
You are crossing over the Jordan **t** to	**Dt 9:1**	3117
"Know therefore **t** that it is the	**Dt 9:3**	3117
am commanding you **t** for your good?	**Dt 10:13**	3117
which I am commanding you **t**,	**Dt 11:8**	3117
which I am commanding you **t**,	**Dt 11:13**	3117
you **t** a blessing and a curse:	**Dt 11:26**	3117
God, which I am commanding you **t**;	**Dt 11:27**	3117
way which I am commanding you **t**,	**Dt 11:28**	3117
which I am setting before you **t**.	**Dt 11:32**	3117
at all what we are doing here **t**,	**Dt 12:8**	3117
which I am commanding you **t**,	**Dt 13:18**	3117
which I am commanding you **t**.	**Dt 15:5**	3117
therefore I command you this **t**.	**Dt 15:15**	3117
which I command you **t**,	**Dt 19:9**	3117
the battle against your enemies **t**.	**Dt 20:3**	3117
"You have **t** declared the LORD to	**Dt 26:17**	3117
LORD has **t** declared you to be His	**Dt 26:18**	3117
which I command you **t**.	**Dt 27:1**	3117
stones, as I am commanding you **t**,	**Dt 27:4**	3117
statutes which I command you **t**."	**Dt 27:10**	3117
which I command you **t**,	**Dt 28:1**	3117
your God, which I charge you **t**,	**Dt 28:13**	3117
the words which I command you **t**,	**Dt 28:14**	3117
with which I charge you **t**,	**Dt 28:15**	3117
"You stand **t**, all of you, before	**Dt 29:10**	3117
your God is making with you **t**,	**Dt 29:12**	3117
that He may establish you **t** as His	**Dt 29:13**	3117
with those who stand here with us **t** in	**Dt 29:15**	3117
those who are not with us here **t**	**Dt 29:15**	3117
heart turns away **t** from the LORD	**Dt 29:18**	3117
to all that I command you **t**,	**Dt 30:2**	3117
which I command you **t**.	**Dt 30:8**	3117
which I command you **t**	**Dt 30:11**	3117
before you **t** life and prosperity,	**Dt 30:15**	3117
I command you **t** to love the LORD	**Dt 30:16**	3117
I declare to you **t** that you shall	**Dt 30:18**	3117
earth to witness against you **t**,	**Dt 30:19**	3117
a hundred and twenty years old **t**;	**Dt 31:2**	3117
which they are developing **t**,	**Dt 31:21**	3117
while I am still alive with you **t**,	**Dt 31:27**	3117
with which I am warning you **t**,	**Dt 32:46**	3117
"**T** I have rolled away the	**Jos 5:9**	3117
I am eighty-five years old **t**.	**Jos 14:10**	3117
"I am still as strong **t** as I was	**Jos 14:11**	3117
If you rebel against the LORD **t**,	**Jos 22:18**	3117
"**T** we know that the LORD is in	**Jos 22:31**	3117
t I am going the way of all the	**Jos 23:14**	3117
choose for yourselves **t** whom you	**Jos 24:15**	3117
risen against my father's house **t**	**Jg 9:18**	3117
judge **t** between the sons of Israel	**Jg 11:27**	3117
should be *missing* **t** in Israel?"	**Jg 21:3**	3117
tribe is cut off from Israel **t**.	**Jg 21:6**	3117
"Where did you glean **t** and where	**Ru 2:19**	3117
with whom I worked **t** is Boaz."	**Ru 2:19**	3117
rest until he has settled it **t**."	**Ru 3:18**	3117
"You are witnesses **t** that I have	**Ru 4:9**	3117
you are witnesses **t**."	**Ru 4:10**	3117
not left you without a redeemer **t**,	**Ru 4:14**	3117
"Why has the LORD defeated us **t**	**1Sa 4:3**	3117
escaped from the battle line **t**."	**1Sa 4:16**	3117
for he has come into the city **t**,	**1Sa 9:12**	3117
a sacrifice on the high place **t**.	**1Sa 9:12**	3117
for you shall eat with me **t**;	**1Sa 9:19**	3117
"When you go from me **t**,	**1Sa 10:2**	3117
"But you have **t** rejected your God,	**1Sa 10:19**	3117
for **t** the LORD has accomplished	**1Sa 11:13**	3117
"Is it not the wheat harvest **t**?	**1Sa 12:17**	3117
be the man who eats food **t**.' "	**1Sa 14:28**	3117
if only the people had eaten freely **t**	**1Sa 14:30**	3117
roll a great stone to me **t**."	**1Sa 14:33**	3117
see how this sin has happened **t**.	**1Sa 14:38**	3117
the kingdom of Israel from you **t** and	**1Sa 15:28**	3117
time you may be my son-in-law **t**."	**1Sa 18:21**	3117
the meal, either yesterday or **t**?"	**1Sa 20:27**	3117
t will their vessels *be holy*?"	**1Sa 21:5**	3117
begin to inquire of God for him **t**?	**1Sa 22:15**	3117
LORD had given you **t** into my hand	**1Sa 24:10**	3117
You have declared **t** that you have	**1Sa 24:18**	3117
There are many servants **t** who are	**1Sa 25:10**	3117
"**T** God has delivered your enemy	**1Sa 26:8**	3117
for they have driven me out **t** so	**1Sa 26:19**	3117
LORD delivered you into *my* hand **t**,	**1Sa 26:23**	3117
"Where have you made a raid **t**?"	**1Sa 27:10**	3117
T I show kindness to the house of	**2Sa 3:8**	3117
and yet **t** you charge me with a	**2Sa 3:8**	3117
"I am weak **t**, though anointed	**2Sa 3:39**	3117
of Israel distinguished himself **t**!	**2Sa 6:20**	3117
He uncovered himself **t** in the eyes	**2Sa 6:20**	3117

“Stay here **t** also, and tomorrow I **2Sa 11:12** 3117
“**T** your servant knows that I have **2Sa 14:22** 3117
shall I **t** make you wander with us, **2Sa 15:20** 3117
‘**T** the house of Israel will **2Sa 16:3** 3117
you shall carry no news **t** because **2Sa 18:20** 3117
“**T** you have covered with shame **2Sa 19:5** 3117
who **t** have saved your life and the **2Sa 19:5** 3117
For you have shown **t** that princes **2Sa 19:6** 3117
alive and all of us were dead **t**, **2Sa 19:6** 3117
therefore behold, I have come **t**, **2Sa 19:20** 3117
man be put to death in Israel **t**? **2Sa 19:22** 3117
that I am king over Israel **t**?” **2Sa 19:22** 3117
“For he has gone down **t** and has **1Ki 1:25** 3117
granted one to sit on my throne **t** **1Ki 1:48** 3117
‘Let King Solomon swear to me **t** **1Ki 1:51** 3117
Adonijah shall be put to death **t**.” **1Ki 2:24** 3117
“Blessed be the LORD **t**, **1Ki 5:7** 3117
Your servant prays before You **t**; **1Ki 8:28** 3117
be a servant to this people **t**, **1Ki 12:7** 3117
surely show myself to him **t**.” **1Ki 18:15** 3117
t let it be known that You are **1Ki 18:36** 3117
deliver them into your hand **t**, **1Ki 20:13** 3117
your master from over you **t**?” **2Ki 2:3** 3117
your master from over you **t**?” **2Ki 2:5** 3117
“Why will you go to him **t**? **2Ki 4:23** 3117
your son that we may eat him **t**, **2Ki 6:28** 3117
son of Shaphat remains on him **t**.” **2Ki 6:31** 3117
“The Valley of Beracah” until **t**. **2Ch 20:26** 3117
I am not *coming* against you **t** but **2Ch 35:21** 3117
and make Your servant successful **t** **Ne 1:11** 3117
“Behold, we are slaves **t**, **Ne 9:36** 3117
to do according to the edict of **t**; **Es 9:13** 3117
“Even **t** my complaint is rebellion; **Jb 23:2** 3117
My Son, **T** I have begotten You. **Ps 2:7** 3117
T, if you would hear His voice, **Ps 95:7** 3117
T I have paid my vows. **Pr 7:14** 3117
in the LORD, I have taught you **t**, **Pr 22:19** 3117
Yet **t** he will halt at Nob; **Is 10:32** 3117
give thanks to You, as I do **t**; **Is 38:19** 3117
before **t** you have not heard them, **Is 48:7** 3117
And tomorrow will be like **t**, **Is 56:12**
2088, 3117
You do not fast like *you do* **t** to **Is 58:4** 3117
I have made you **t** as a fortified city **Jer 1:18** 3117
I am freeing you **t** from the chains **Jer 40:4** 3117
t I have testified against you. **Jer 42:19** 3117
So I have told you **t**, **Jer 42:21** 3117
which is *alive* **t** and tomorrow is **Mt 6:30** *4594*
‘*There will be* a storm **t**, **Mt 16:3** *4594*
‘Son, go work **t** in the vineyard.’ **Mt 21:28** *4594*
for **t** in the city of David there **Lk 2:11** *4594*
“**T** this Scripture has been **Lk 4:21** *4594*
We have seen remarkable things **t**.” **Lk 5:26** *4594*
which is *alive* **t** and tomorrow is **Lk 12:28** *4594*
and perform cures **t** and tomorrow, **Lk 13:32** *4594*
t and tomorrow and the next *day* **Lk 13:33** *4594*
for **t** I must stay at your house.” **Lk 19:5** *4594*
“**T** salvation has come to this **Lk 19:9** *4594*
the rooster will not crow **t** until you **Lk 22:34** *4594*
“Before a rooster crows **t**, **Lk 22:61** *4594*
t you shall be with Me in Paradise.” **Lk 23:43** *4594*
if we are on trial **t** for a benefit **Ac 4:9** *4594*
MY SON; **T** I HAVE BEGOTTEN YOU.’ **Ac 13:33** *4594*
for God just as you all are **t**. **Ac 22:3** *4594*
I am on trial before you **t**.’ ” **Ac 24:21** *4594*
to make my defense before you **t**; **Ac 26:2** *4594*
“**T** is the fourteenth day that you **Ac 27:33** *4594*
MY SON, **T** I HAVE BEGOTTEN YOU”? **Heb 1:5** *4594*
“**T** IF YOU HEAR HIS VOICE **Heb 3:7** *4594*
long as it is *still* called “**T**,” **Heb 3:13** *4594*
“**T** IF YOU HEAR HIS VOICE, DO NOT **Heb 3:15** *4594*
again fixes a certain day, “**T**,” **Heb 4:7** *4594*
“**T** IF YOU HEAR HIS VOICE, DO NOT **Heb 4:7** *4594*
MY SON, **T** I HAVE BEGOTTEN YOU”; **Heb 5:5** *4594*
yesterday and **t** and forever. **Heb 13:8** *4594*
“**T** or tomorrow we will go to **Jas 4:13** *4594*

TODAY'S
riot in connection with **t** events, **Ac 19:40** *4594*

TOE
on the big **t** of his right foot. **Lv 8:23** 931
on the big **t** of their right foot. **Lv 8:24** 931
on the big **t** of his right foot, **Lv 14:14** 931
on the big **t** of his right foot, **Lv 14:17** 931
on the big **t** of his right foot. **Lv 14:25** 931
on the big **t** of his right foot, **Lv 14:28** 931

TOES
on the big **t** of their right feet, **Ex 29:20** 931
and cut off his thumbs and big **t**. **Jg 1:6** 931, 7272
their thumbs and their big **t** cut off **Jg 1:7** 931, 7272
each hand and six **t** on each foot, **2Sa 21:20** 676
who had twenty-four fingers and **t**, **1Ch 20:6** 676
fingers on each hand and six **t** **1Ch 20:6**
In that you saw the feet and **t**, **Da 2:41** 677
“*As* the **t** of the feet *were* **Da 2:42** 677

TOGARMAH
were Ashkenaz and Riphath and **T**. **Gn 10:3** 8425
were Ashkenaz, Diphath, and **T**. **1Ch 1:6** 8425

TOGETHER
and they sewed fig leaves **t** and **Gn 3:7** 8609
t with those that were with him in **Gn 7:23**
and they went out **t** from Ur of the **Gn 11:31** 854
not sustain them while dwelling **t**, **Gn 13:6** 3164a
they were not able to remain **t**. **Gn 13:6** 3164a
So the two of them walked on **t**. **Gn 22:6** 3164a
So the two of them walked on **t**. **Gn 22:8** 3164a
arose and went **t** to Beersheba; **Gn 22:19** 3164a
children struggled **t** within her; **Gn 25:22**
they will gather **t** against me and **Gn 34:30**
too great for them to live **t**, **Gn 36:7** 3164a
he put them all **t** in prison for three **Gn 42:17** 622
“Gather **t** and hear, O sons of **Gn 49:2**
and gather the elders of Israel **t** and **Ex 3:16**
the people answered **t** and said, **Ex 19:8** 3164a
the loops and join the tent **t** so **Ex 26:11** 2266
and **t** they shall be complete to **Ex 26:24** 3164a
sons of Levi gathered **t** to him. **Ex 32:26**
of bronze to join the tent **t** so **Ex 36:18** 2266
and **t** they were complete to its **Ex 36:29** 3164a
and eat it there **t** with the bread **Lv 8:31**
t with the cedar wood and the **Lv 14:6**
t with the grain offering. **Lv 14:31** 5921
breed **t** two kinds of your cattle; **Lv 19:19** 7250
of two kinds of material mixed **t**. **Lv 19:19** 8162
you gather **t** into your cities, **Lv 26:25**
they assembled all the congregation **t** **Nu 1:18**
t with the basket of unleavened **Nu 6:17** 5921
t with the breast offered by **Nu 6:20** 5921
of the sea be gathered **t** for them, **Nu 11:22**
who are gathered **t** against Me. **Nu 14:35**
t with some of the sons of Israel, **Nu 16:2**
They assembled **t** against Moses and **Nu 16:3**
are gathered **t** against the LORD; **Nu 16:11**
Balaam, and he struck his hands **t**; **Nu 24:10** 5606
who gathered themselves **t** against **Nu 27:3**
t with their pasture lands. **Nu 35:7**
plow with an ox and a donkey **t**. **Dt 22:10** 3164a
mixed of wool and linen **t**. **Dt 22:11** 3164a
“When brothers live **t** and one of **Dt 25:5** 3164a
his countryman, are struggling **t**, **Dt 25:11** 3164a
gathered, The tribes of Israel **t**. **Dt 33:5** 3162
city were called **t** to pursue them, **Jos 8:16** 2199
that they gathered themselves **t** **Jos 9:2** 3164a
of Eglon, gathered **t** and went up, **Jos 10:5**
encamped **t** at the waters of Merom, **Jos 11:5** 3164a
t with the cities which were set **Jos 16:9**
Zebulun and Naphtali **t** to Kedesh, **Jg 4:10** 2199
Sisera called **t** all his chariots, **Jg 4:13** 2199
were called **t** to follow him. **Jg 6:34** 2199
also were called **t** to follow him; **Jg 6:35** 2199
and all Beth-millo assembled **t**, **Jg 9:6**
tower of Shechem were gathered **t**. **Jg 9:47**
And the sons of Israel gathered **t** and **Jg 10:17**
you, that you have assembled **t**?” **Jg 18:23** 2199
them sat down and ate and drank **t**; **Jg 19:6** 3164a
all the elders of Israel gathered **t** **1Sa 8:4**
Samuel called the people **t** to the **1Sa 10:17** 6817
that no two of them were left **t**. **1Sa 11:11** 3162
me a man that we may fight **t**.” **1Sa 17:10** 3162
they kissed each other and wept **t**, **1Sa 20:41**
376, 7453
gathered **t** and mourned for him, **1Sa 25:1**
the Philistines gathered **t** and came **1Sa 28:4**
Saul gathered all Israel **t** and they **1Sa 28:4**
his servants **t** with the woman urged **1Sa 28:23** 1571
Philistines gathered **t** all their armies **1Sa 29:1**
and all his men on that day **t**. **1Sa 31:6** 3164a
so they fell down **t**. **2Sa 2:16** 3164a
of Benjamin gathered **t** behind Abner **2Sa 2:25**
he had gathered all the people **t**, **2Sa 2:30**
they gathered themselves **t**. **2Sa 10:15** 3162
he gathered all Israel **t** and crossed **2Sa 10:17**
And it grew up **t** with him and his **2Sa 12:3** 3164a
his servants were whispering **t**, **2Sa 12:19**
gather the rest of the people **t** **2Sa 12:28**
of them struggled **t** in the field, **2Sa 14:6** 5327b
they were gathered **t** and also went **2Sa 20:14**
so that the seven of them fell **t**; **2Sa 21:9** 3162
birth to a child, and we were **t**. **1Ki 3:18** 3164a
her own land **t** with her servants. **1Ki 10:13**
t with 450 prophets of Baal **1Ki 18:19**
the prophets **t** at Mount Carmel. **1Ki 18:20** 6908
of Israel gathered the prophets **t**, **1Ki 22:6**
folded it **t** and struck the waters, **2Ki 2:8** 1563
has called these three kings **t** **2Ki 3:13**
the kings have surely fought **t**, **2Ki 3:23** 2717c
riding **t** after Ahab his father, **2Ki 9:25** 6776
and all *those* of his house died **t**. **1Ch 10:6** 3164a
in his kingdom, **t** with all Israel, **1Ch 11:10** 5973
were gathered **t** there to battle, **1Ch 11:13**
So David assembled all Israel **t**, **1Ch 13:5**
gathered **t** the sons of Aaron and **1Ch 15:4**
And the sons of Ammon gathered **t** **1Ch 19:7**
he gathered all Israel **t** and crossed **1Ch 19:17**
And he gathered **t** all the leaders **1Ch 23:2**
t with some of the Meunites, **2Ch 20:1** 5973
Judah gathered **t** to seek help from **2Ch 20:4**
t with his sons and his wives, **2Ch 21:17** 1571
when Ahaz gathered **t** the utensils **2Ch 28:24**
t with a freewill offering for the **Ezr 1:4** 5973
the people gathered **t** as one man to **Ezr 3:1**
but we ourselves will **t** build to **Ezr 4:3** 3162
Levites had purified themselves **t**; **Ezr 6:20** 259
t with the elders and judges of **Ezr 10:14** 5973
was joined **t** to half its *height*, **Ne 4:6** 7194
All of them conspired **t** to **Ne 4:8** 3164a
let us meet **t** at Chephirim in the **Ne 6:2** 3164a
come now, let us take counsel **t**.” **Ne 6:7** 3164a
“Let us meet **t** in the house of **Ne 6:10** 3259
The whole assembly **t** *was* 42,360, **Ne 7:66** 259
t with the singers and the **Ne 12:45**
Then I gathered them **t** and **Ne 13:11**
were gathered **t** the second time, **Es 2:19**
and they made an appointment **t** to **Jb 2:11** 3164a
“The prisoners are at ease **t**; **Jb 3:18** 3162
the balances **t** with my calamity! **Jb 6:2** 3162
Him, That we may go to court **t**. **Jb 9:32** 3164a
knit me **t** with bones and sinews? **Jb 10:11** 5526b
Shall we **t** go down into the dust?” **Jb 17:16** 3162
“His troops come **t**, And build up **Jb 19:12** 3162
“**T** they lie down in the dust, And **Jb 21:26** 3162
the nettles they are gathered **t**. **Jb 30:7** 5596
me, And its furrows weep **t**; **Jb 31:38** 3162
All flesh would perish **t**, **Jb 34:15** 3162
When the morning stars sang **t** And **Jb 38:7** 3162
a mass And the clods stick **t**? **Jb 38:38** 1692
“Hide them in the dust **t**; **Jb 40:13** 3162
sinews of his thighs are knit **t**. **Jb 40:17** 8276
folds of his flesh are joined **t**, **Jb 41:23** 1692
And the rulers take counsel **t** **Ps 2:2** 3162
t they have become corrupt; **Ps 14:3** 3164a
they took counsel **t** against me, **Ps 31:13** 3162
the waters of the sea **t** as a heap; **Ps 33:7**
me, And let us exalt His name **t**. **Ps 34:3** 3164a
and gathered themselves **t**; **Ps 35:15**
not know gathered **t** against me, **Ps 35:15**
those be ashamed and humiliated **t** **Ps 40:14** 3162
who hate me whisper **t** against me; **Ps 41:7** 3162
themselves, They passed by **t**. **Ps 48:4** 3164a
low and high, Rich and poor **t**. **Ps 49:2** 3162
t they have become corrupt; **Ps 53:3** 3164a
We who had sweet fellowship **t** **Ps 55:14** 3164a
They are **t** lighter than breath. **Ps 62:9** 3162
for my life have consulted **t**, **Ps 71:10** 3164a
t against Your treasured ones. **Ps 83:3**
have conspired **t** with one mind; **Ps 83:5** 3164a
and truth have met **t**; **Ps 85:10**
They band themselves **t** against the **Ps 94:21** 1413
Let the mountains sing **t** for joy **Ps 98:8** 3162
When the peoples are gathered **t**, **Ps 102:22** 3164a
LORD, The small **t** with the great. **Ps 115:13** 5973
built As a city that is compact **t**; **Ps 122:3** 3164a
For brothers to dwell **t** in unity! **Ps 133:1** 3162
tear apart and a time to sew **t**; **Ec 3:7** 8609
if two lie down **t** they keep warm, **Ec 4:11**
me after you *and* let us run **t**! **SS 1:4**
“Come now, and let us reason **t**,” **Is 1:18**
and sinners will be crushed **t**, **Is 1:28** 3164a
Thus they shall both burn **t** And **Is 1:31** 3164a
And **t** they are against Judah. **Is 9:21** 3164a
the young lion and the fatling **t**; **Is 11:6** 3164a
Their young will lie down **t**, **Is 11:7** 3164a
T they will plunder the sons of **Is 11:14** 3164a
kingdoms, Of nations gathered **t**! **Is 13:4**
left **t** for mountain birds of prey, **Is 18:6** 3164a
All your rulers have fled **t**, **Is 22:3** 3162
were found were taken captive **t**, **Is 22:3** 3164a
They will be gathered **t** *Like* **Is 24:22** 626
But *the Lord* will lay low his pride **t** **Is 25:11** 5973
all of them will come to an end **t**. **Is 31:3** 3164a
And all flesh will see *it* **t**; **Is 40:5** 3164a
Let us come **t** for judgment. **Is 41:1** 3164a
T with the box tree and the **Is 41:19** 3164a
look about us and fear **t**. **Is 41:23** 3164a
All the nations have gathered **t** So **Is 43:9** 3164a
lie down **t** *and not* rise again; **Is 43:17** 3164a
let us argue our case **t**; **Is 43:26** 3162
let them **t** be put to shame. **Is 44:11** 3162
will go away **t** in humiliation. **Is 45:16** 3164a
Draw near **t**, you fugitives of the **Is 45:20** 3164a
Indeed, let them consult **t**. **Is 45:21** 3164a
over, they have bowed down **t**; **Is 46:2** 3164a
When I call to them, they stand **t**. **Is 48:13** 3164a
All of them gather **t**, **Is 49:18**
voices, They shout joyfully **t**; **Is 52:8** 3164a
Break forth, shout joyfully **t**, **Is 52:9** 3164a
They all gather **t**, they come to **Is 60:4**
Kedar will be gathered **t** to you, **Is 60:7**
the box tree and the cypress **t**, **Is 60:13** 3164a
iniquities of their fathers **t**,” **Is 65:7** 3164a
wolf and the lamb will graze **t**, **Is 65:25** 259
and they will come **t** from the land **Jer 3:18** 3164a
on the gathering of young men **t**; **Jer 6:11** 3164a
Their fields and their wives **t**; **Jer 6:12** 3164a
against them, Fathers and sons **t**; **Jer 6:21** 3164a
both the fathers and the sons **t**,” **Jer 13:14** 3164a
she who is in labor with child, **t**; **Jer 31:8** 3164a
And the young men and the old, **t**, **Jer 31:13** 3164a
all its cities will dwell **t** in it, **Jer 31:24** 3164a
eating bread **t** there in Mizpah, **Jer 41:1** 3164a
t with Jeremiah the prophet and **Jer 43:6**
both of them have fallen down **t**. **Jer 46:12** 3164a
turned back *and* have fled away **t**; **Jer 46:21** 3164a
And Chemosh will go off into exile **T** **Jer 48:7** 3164a
For Malcam will go into exile **T** **Jer 49:3** 3164a
no one to gather the fugitives **t**. **Jer 49:5**
“Gather yourselves **t** and come **Jer 49:14**
“They will roar **t** like young lions, **Jer 51:38** 3164a
Like rams **t** with male goats. **Jer 51:40** 5973
By His hand they are knit **t**. **La 1:14** 8276
They have languished **t**. **La 2:8** 3164a
prophesy and clap *your* hands **t**; **Ezk 21:14**
413, 3709
“I will also clap My hands **t**, **Ezk 21:17**
413, 3709
will not be brought **t** or gathered. **Ezk 29:5** 622
and the bones came **t**, **Ezk 37:7** 7126
For you have agreed **t** to speak **Da 2:9** 2164
and his knees began knocking **t**. **Da 5:6** 1668
and the governors have consulted **t** **Da 6:7** 3272b
sons of Israel will be gathered **t**, **Hos 1:11** 3164a
exile, He and his princes **t**,” **Am 1:15** 3164a
Do two men walk **t** unless they have **Am 3:3** 3164a
house **t** with the summer house; **Am 3:15** 5971a
put them **t** like sheep in the fold; **Mi 2:12** 3162
So they weave it **t**. **Mi 7:3** 5686
gather them **t** in their fishing net. **Hab 1:15**

Gather yourselves **t**, **Zph 2:1**
at the time when I gather you **t**; **Zph 3:20**
them every ruler, *all* of them **t**. **Zch 10:4** 3164a
whistle for them to gather them **t**, **Zch 10:8**
before they came **t** she was found **Mt 1:18** *4905*
Gathering **t** all the chief **Mt 2:4** *4863*
both to grow **t** until the harvest; **Mt 13:30** *4885*
they were gathering **t** in Galilee, **Mt 17:22** *4962*
three have gathered **t** in My name, **Mt 18:20** *4863*
What therefore God has joined **t**, **Mt 19:6** *4801*
and gathered **t** all they found, **Mt 22:10** *4863*
plotted **t** how they might trap Him **Mt 22:15** *4824*
they gathered themselves **t**. **Mt 22:34**
1909, 3588, 846
the Pharisees were gathered **t**, **Mt 22:41** *4863*
wanted to gather your children **t**, **Mt 23:37** *1996*
THEY WILL GATHER **T** His elect from **Mt 24:31** *1996*
elders of the people were gathered **t** **Mt 26:3** *4863*
t to seize Jesus by stealth and **Mt 26:4** *4823*
and the elders were gathered **t**. **Mt 26:57** *4863*
the elders of the people conferred **t** **Mt 27:1**
And they conferred **t** and with the **Mt 27:7** *4824*
So when the people gathered **t**, **Mt 27:17** *4863*
And after twisting **t** a crown of **Mt 27:29**
Pharisees gathered **t** with Pilate, **Mt 27:62** *4863*
with the elders and consulted **t**, **Mt 28:12** *4824*
And many were gathered **t**, **Mk 2:2** *4863*
apostles gathered **t** with Jesus; **Mk 6:30** *4863*
and ran there **t** on foot from all the **Mk 6:33** *4936*
"What therefore God has joined **t**, **Mk 10:9** *4801*
will gather **t** His elect from the four **Mk 13:27** *1996*
elders and the scribes gathered **t**. **Mk 14:53** *4905*
called **t** the whole *Roman* cohort. **Mk 15:16** *4779*
and discussed **t** what they might do **Lk 6:11**
4314, 240
measure—pressed down, shaken **t**, **Lk 6:38** *4531*
a large crowd was coming **t**, **Lk 8:4** *4896*
And He called the twelve **t**, **Lk 9:1** *4779*
of people had gathered **t** that **Lk 12:1** *1996*
wanted to gather your children **t**, **Lk 13:34** *1996*
he calls **t** his friends and his **Lk 15:6** *4779*
calls **t** her friends and neighbors, **Lk 15:9** *4779*
the younger son gathered everything **t** **Lk 15:13** *4863*
the courtyard and had sat down **t**, **Lk 22:55** *4776*
But they cried out all **t**, **Lk 23:18** *3826*
who came **t** for this spectacle, **Lk 23:48** *4836*
and found gathered **t** the eleven **Lk 24:33** *120a*
and he who reaps may rejoice **t**. **Jn 4:36** *3674*
order that He might also gather **t** **Jn 11:52** *4863*
day on they planned **t** to kill Him. **Jn 11:53** *1011*
"Are you deliberating **t** about this, **Jn 16:19**
3326, 240
glorify Me **t** with Yourself, **Jn 17:5** *3844*
temple, where all the Jews come **t**; **Jn 18:20** *4905*
And the soldiers twisted **t** a crown of **Jn 19:2**
The two were running **t**; **Jn 20:4** *3674*
two others of His disciples were **t**. **Jn 21:2** *3674*
Gathering them **t**, **Ac 1:4** *4871a*
So when they had come **t**, **Ac 1:6** *4905*
and twenty persons was there **t**), **Ac 1:15**
1909, 3588, 846
they were all **t** in one place. **Ac 2:1** *3674*
occurred, the crowd came **t**, **Ac 2:6** *4905*
all those who had believed were **t** and **Ac 2:44**
1909, 3588, 846
they were taking their meals **t** **Ac 2:46** *3335*
all the people ran **t** to them at **Ac 3:11** *4936*
were gathered **t** in Jerusalem; **Ac 4:5** *4863*
WERE GATHERED **T** AGAINST THE LORD **Ac 4:26**
1909, 3588, 846
gathered **t** against Your holy servant **Ac 4:27** *4863*
the place where they had gathered **t** **Ac 4:31** *4863*
"Why is it that you have agreed **t** **Ac 5:9** *4856*
of Jerusalem were coming **t**, **Ac 5:16** *4905*
came, they called the Council **t**, **Ac 5:21** *4779*
to them as they were fighting **t**, **Ac 7:26** *3164*
congregation in the wilderness **t** with **Ac 7:38** *3326*
Jews plotted **t** to do away with him, **Ac 9:23** *4823*
and had called **t** his relatives and **Ac 10:24** *4779*
were gathered **t** and were praying. **Ac 12:12** *4867*
entered the synagogue of the Jews **t**, **Ac 14:1**
2596, 3588, 846
arrived and gathered the church **t**, **Ac 14:27** *4863*
the elders came **t** to look into this **Ac 15:6** *4863*
gathered the congregation **t**, **Ac 15:30** *4863*
The crowd rose up **t** against them, **Ac 16:22** *4911*
spoke the word of the Lord to him **t** **Ac 16:32** *4862*
brought their books **t** and *began* **Ac 19:19** *4851a*
these he gathered **t** with the **Ac 19:25** *4867*
for what reason they had come **t**. **Ac 19:32** *4905*
we were gathered **t** to break bread, **Ac 20:7** *4863*
room where we were gathered **t**. **Ac 20:8** *4863*
provoked, and the people rushed **t** **Ac 21:30** *4890*
Agrippa came **t** with Bernice **Ac 25:23** *2532*
After three days Paul called **t** those **Ac 28:17** *4779*
Jews, and when they came **t**, **Ac 28:17** *4905*
that I may be encouraged **t** with you **Ro 1:12** *4837*
ASIDE, **T** THEY HAVE BECOME USELESS; **Ro 3:12** *260*
pains of childbirth **t** until now. **Ro 8:22**
4959, 4944
God causes all things to work **t** for **Ro 8:28** *4903*
to strive **t** with me in your **Ro 15:30** *4865*
come **t** again so that Satan will **1Co 7:5**
1909, 3588, 846
because you come **t** not for the **1Co 11:17** *4905*
when you come **t** as a church, **1Co 11:18** *4905*
Therefore when you meet **t**, **1Co 11:20**
1909, 3588, 846
brethren, when you come **t** to eat, **1Co 11:33** *4905*
you will not come **t** for judgment. **1Co 11:34** *4905*
the whole church assembles **t** **1Co 14:23**
1909, 3588, 846
And working **t** *with Him,* we also **2Co 6:1** *4903*
Do not be bound **t** with unbelievers; **2Co 6:14** *2086*
to die **t** and to live together. **2Co 7:3** *4880*
to die together and to live **t**. **2Co 7:3** *4800*
made us alive **t** with Christ **Eph 2:5** *4806*
being fitted **t**, is growing into a **Eph 2:21** *4883*
in whom you also are being built **t** **Eph 2:22** *4925*
being fitted and held **t** by what **Eph 4:16**
4822, 4883
and affirm **t** with the Lord, **Eph 4:17** *1722*
with one mind striving **t** for the faith **Php 1:27** *4866*
the gospel, **t** with Clement also and **Php 4:3** *3326*
and in Him all things hold **t**. **Col 1:17** *4921*
having been knit **t** in love, **Col 2:2** *4822*
He made you alive **t** with Him, **Col 2:13** *4806*
held **t** by the joints and ligaments, **Col 2:19** *4822*
alive and remain will be caught up **t** **1Th 4:17** *260*
or asleep, we will live **t** with Him. **1Th 5:10** *260*
and our gathering **t** to Him, **2Th 2:1** *1997*
forsaking our own assembling **t**, **Heb 10:25** *1997*
is in Babylon, chosen **t** with you, **1Pe 5:13** *4899*
to gather them **t** for the war of **Rv 16:14** *4863*
And they gathered them **t** to the **Rv 16:16** *4863*
to gather them **t** for the war; **Rv 20:8** *4863*

TOHU
the son of Elihu, the son of **T**, **1Sa 1:1** 8459

TOI
Now when **T** king of Hamath heard **2Sa 8:9** 8583
T sent Joram his son to King David **2Sa 8:10** 8583
Hadadezer had been at war with **T**. **2Sa 8:10** 8583

TOIL
In **t** you will eat of it All the **Gn 3:17** 6093
our work and from the **t** of our hands **Gn 5:29** 6093
affliction and the **t** of my hands, **Gn 31:42** 3018
and our **t** and our oppression; **Dt 26:7** 5999
make all the people **t** up there, **Jos 7:3** 3021
Why then should I **t** in vain? **Jb 9:29** 3021
and in your **t** in which you have **Ec 9:9** 5999
The **t** of a fool *so* wearies him **Ec 10:15** 5999
So the peoples will **t** for nothing, **Jer 51:58** 3021
"She has wearied *Me* with **t**, **Ezk 24:12** 8383
of hosts That peoples **t** for fire, **Hab 2:13** 3021
they do not **t** nor do they spin, **Mt 6:28** *2872*
they neither **t** nor spin; **Lk 12:27** *2872*
and we **t**, working with our own **1Co 4:12** *2872*
your **t** is not *in* vain in the Lord. **1Co 15:58** *2873*
I did not run in vain nor **t** in vain. **Php 2:16** *2872*
deeds and your **t** and perseverance, **Rv 2:2** *2873*

TOILED
"I have **t** in vain, I have spent **Is 49:4** 3021

TOILS
worker from that in which he **t**? **Ec 3:9** 6001b
to him who **t** for the wind? **Ec 5:16** 5998
labor in which he **t** under the sun **Ec 5:18** 5998
and this will stand by him in his **t** **Ec 8:15** 5999

TOKEN
sign and **t** against Egypt and Cush, **Is 20:3** 4159

TOKHATH
the wife of Shallum the son of **T**, **2Ch 34:22** 8445

TOLA
T and Puvvah and Iob and Shimron. **Gn 46:13** 8439a
of **T**, the family of the Tolaites; **Nu 26:23** 8439a
Abimelech died, **T** the son of Puah, **Jg 10:1** 8439a
T, Puah, Jashub and Shimron. **1Ch 7:1** 8439a
The sons of **T** *were* Uzzi, **1Ch 7:2** 8439a
The sons of **T** *were* mighty men of **1Ch 7:2** 8439a

TOLAD
at Bilhah, Ezem, **T**, **1Ch 4:29** 8434

TOLAITES
of Tola, the family of the **T**; **Nu 26:23** 8440

TOLD
"Who **t** you that you were naked? **Gn 3:11** 5046
Cain **t** Abel his brother. **Gn 4:8** 559
and **t** his two brothers outside. **Gn 9:22** 5046
came and **t** Abram the Hebrew. **Gn 14:13** 5046
and **t** all these things in their hearing; **Gn 20:8** 1696
the place of which God had **t** him. **Gn 22:3** 559
the place of which God had **t** him; **Gn 22:9** 559
things, that it was **t** Abraham, **Gn 22:20** 5046
Then the girl ran and **t** her **Gn 24:28** 5046
eat until I have **t** my business." **Gn 24:33** 1696
The servant **t** Isaac all the **Gn 24:66** 5608
Isaac's servants came in and **t** him **Gn 26:32** 5046
I have done as you **t** me. **Gn 27:19** 1696
Jacob **t** Rachel that he was a **Gn 29:12** 5046
son, and she ran and **t** her father. **Gn 29:12** 5046
When it was **t** Laban on the third **Gn 31:22** 5046
and when he **t** it to his brothers, **Gn 37:5** 5046
It was **t** to Tamar, **Gn 38:13** 5046
cupbearer **t** his dream to Joseph, **Gn 40:9** 5608
And Pharaoh **t** them his dreams, but **Gn 41:8** 5608
Then I **t** it to the magicians, but **Gn 41:24** 559
God has **t** to Pharaoh what He is **Gn 41:25** 5046
they **t** him all that had happened **Gn 42:29** 5046
And he did as Joseph had **t** *him.* **Gn 44:2** 1696
we **t** him the words of my lord. **Gn 44:24** 5046
They **t** him, saying, **Gn 45:26** 5046
When they **t** him all the words of **Gn 45:27** 1696
Then Joseph went in and **t** Pharaoh, **Gn 47:1** 5046
these things that Joseph was **t**, **Gn 48:1** 559
When it was **t** to Jacob, **Gn 48:2** 5046
Moses **t** Aaron all the words of **Ex 4:28** 5046
in trouble because they were **t**, **Ex 5:19** 559
was **t** that the people had fled, **Ex 14:5** 5046
the congregation came and **t** Moses, **Ex 16:22** 5046
Joshua did as Moses **t** him, **Ex 17:10** 559
Moses **t** his father-in-law all **Ex 18:8** 5608
Then Moses **t** the words of the **Ex 19:9** 5046
down to the people and **t** them. **Ex 19:25** 559
lead the people where I **t** you. **Ex 32:34** 1696
So Moses **t** the sons of Israel to **Nu 9:4** 1696
So Moses went out and **t** the people **Nu 11:24** 1696
man ran and **t** Moses and said, **Nu 11:27** 5046
Thus they **t** him, and said, **Nu 13:27** 5608
is **t** you and you have heard of it, **Dt 17:4** 5046
It was **t** the king of Jericho, **Jos 2:2** 559
it was certainly **t** your servants that **Jos 9:24** 5046
It was **t** Joshua, saying, **Jos 10:17** 5046
did to them as the LORD had **t** him; **Jos 11:9** 559
Then they **t** Sisera that Barak the **Jg 4:12** 5046
which our fathers **t** us about, **Jg 6:13** 5608
Now when they **t** Jotham, he went **Jg 9:7** 5046
and it was **t** to Abimelech. **Jg 9:25** 5046
field, and it was **t** to Abimelech. **Jg 9:42** 5046
It was **t** Abimelech that all **Jg 9:47** 5046
the woman came and **t** her husband, **Jg 13:6** 559
ran quickly and **t** her husband, **Jg 13:10** 5046
back and **t** his father and mother, **Jg 14:2** 5046
people, and have not **t** *it* to me." **Jg 14:16** 5046
not **t** *it* to my father or mother; **Jg 14:16** 5046
he **t** her because she pressed him **Jg 14:17** 5046
She then **t** the riddle to the sons **Jg 14:17** 5046
clothes to those who **t** the riddle. **Jg 14:19** 5046
When it was **t** to the Gazites, **Jg 16:2**
have deceived me and **t** me lies; **Jg 16:10** 1696
have deceived me and **t** me lies; **Jg 16:13** 1696
not **t** me where your great strength is. **Jg 16:15** 5046
So he **t** her all *that was* in his **Jg 16:17** 5046
t her all *that was* in his heart, **Jg 16:18** 5046
t me all *that is* in his heart." **Jg 16:18** 5046
So she **t** her mother-in-law with **Ru 2:19** 5046
And she **t** her all that the man had **Ru 3:16** 5046
"For I have **t** him that I am about **1Sa 3:13** 5046
So Samuel **t** him everything and hid **1Sa 3:18** 5046
the man came hurriedly and **t** Eli. **1Sa 4:14** 5046
"He **t** us plainly that the donkeys **1Sa 10:16** 5046
Then Samuel **t** the people the **1Sa 10:25** 1696
went and **t** the men of Jabesh; **1Sa 11:9** 5046
Then they **t** Saul, saying, **1Sa 14:33** 5046
So Jonathan **t** him and said, **1Sa 14:43** 5046
and it was **t** Samuel, saying, **1Sa 15:12** 5046
were heard, they **t** *them* to Saul, **1Sa 17:31** 5046
When they **t** Saul, the thing was **1Sa 18:20** 5046
his servants **t** David these words, **1Sa 18:26** 5046
Now Saul **t** Jonathan his son and **1Sa 19:1** 1696
So Jonathan **t** David saying, **1Sa 19:2** 5046
Jonathan **t** him all these words. **1Sa 19:7** 5046
But Michal, David's wife, **t** him, **1Sa 19:11** 5046
and **t** him all that Saul had done **1Sa 19:18** 5046
It was **t** Saul, saying, **1Sa 19:19** 5046
When it was **t** Saul, he sent **1Sa 19:21** 5046
Abiathar **t** David that Saul had **1Sa 22:21** 5046
Then they **t** David, saying, **1Sa 23:1** 5046
When it was **t** Saul that David had **1Sa 23:7** 5046
When it was **t** Saul that David had **1Sa 23:13** 5046
I am **t** that he is very cunning. **1Sa 23:22** 559
went to seek *him,* they **t** David, **1Sa 23:25** 5046
the Philistines, he was **t**, **1Sa 24:1** 5046
and they came and **t** him according **1Sa 25:12** 5046
one of the young men **t** Abigail, **1Sa 25:14** 5046
his wife **t** him these things, **1Sa 25:37** 5046
Now it was **t** Saul that David had **1Sa 27:4** 5046
said to the young man who **t** him, **2Sa 1:5** 5046
The young man who **t** him said, **2Sa 1:6** 5046
said to the young man who **t** him, **2Sa 1:13** 5046
and he **t** *them* to teach the sons of **2Sa 1:18** 559
And they **t** David, saying, **2Sa 2:4** 5046
was with him arrived, they **t** Joab, **2Sa 3:23** 5046
when one **t** me, saying, **2Sa 4:10** 5046
Now it was **t** King David, saying, **2Sa 6:12** 5046
When they **t** *it* to David, he sent **2Sa 10:5** 5046
Now when it was **t** David, he **2Sa 10:17** 5046
and she sent and **t** David, **2Sa 11:5** 5046
Now when they **t** David, saying, **2Sa 11:10** 5046
Joab came to the king and **t** him, **2Sa 14:33** 5046
Now someone **t** David, saying, **2Sa 15:31** 5046
curses, and if the LORD has **t** him, **2Sa 16:10** 559
him curse, for the LORD has **t** him. **2Sa 16:11** 559
a lad did see them and **t** Absalom; **2Sa 17:18** 5046
well and went and **t** King David; **2Sa 17:21** 5046
man saw *it,* he **t** Joab and said, **2Sa 18:10** 5046
said to the man who had **t** him, **2Sa 18:11** 5046
watchman called and **t** the king. **2Sa 18:25** 5046
Then it was **t** Joab, **2Sa 19:1** 5046
When they **t** all the people, **2Sa 19:8** 5046
When it was **t** David what Rizpah **2Sa 21:11** 5046
So Gad came to David and **t** him, **2Sa 24:13** 5046
They **t** the king, saying, **1Ki 1:23** 5046
Now it was **t** Solomon, saying, **1Ki 1:51** 5046
It was **t** King Solomon that **1Ki 2:29** 5046
And they **t** Shimei, saying, **1Ki 2:39** 5046
It was **t** Solomon that Shimei **1Ki 2:41** 5046
And behold, the half was not **t** me. **1Ki 10:7** 5046
and his sons came and **t** him all **1Ki 13:11** 5608
so they came and **t** *it* in the city **1Ki 13:25** 1696
"Has it not been **t** to my master **1Ki 18:13** 5046
went to meet Ahab and **t** him; **1Ki 18:16** 5046
Now Ahab **t** Jezebel all that Elijah **1Ki 19:1** 5046
Ben-hadad sent out and they **t** him, **1Ki 20:17** 5046
she came and **t** the man of God. **2Ki 4:7** 5046
it from me and has not **t** me." **2Ki 4:27** 5046
he returned to meet him and **t** him, **2Ki 4:31** 5046
Naaman went in and **t** his master, **2Ki 5:4** 5046

t you *to do some* great thing, 2Ki 5:13 1696
which the man of God had **t** him; 2Ki 6:10 559
And it was **t** him, saying, 2Ki 6:13 5046
of the city, and they **t** them, 2Ki 7:10 5046
and **t** *it* within the king's 2Ki 7:11 5046
returned and **t** the king. 2Ki 7:15 5046
Aram was sick, and it was **t** him, 2Ki 8:7 5046
"He **t** me that you would surely 2Ki 8:14 559
Therefore they returned and **t** him. 2Ki 9:36 5046
When the messenger came and **t** him, 2Ki 10:8 5046
and **t** him the words of Rabshakeh. 2Ki 18:37 5046
the scribe **t** the king saying, 2Ki 22:10 5046
And the men of the city **t** him, 2Ki 23:17 559
went and **t** David about the men. 1Ch 19:5 5046
When it was **t** David, he gathered 1Ch 19:17 5046
of your wisdom was not **t** me. 2Ch 9:6 5046
the scribe **t** the king saying, 2Ch 34:18 5046
those whom the king had **t** went to 2Ch 34:22
Then we **t** them accordingly what Ezr 5:4 560
and I **t** them what to say to Iddo Ezr 8:17
7760, 1697, 6310
nor had I as yet **t** the Jews, Ne 2:16 5046
I **t** them how the hand of my Ne 2:18 5046
near them came and **t** us ten times, Ne 4:12 559
And You **t** them to enter in order to Ne 9:15 559
You had **t** their fathers to enter Ne 9:23 559
for Esther did what Mordecai **t** her Es 2:20 5046
Mordecai and he **t** Queen Esther, Es 2:22 5046
that they **t** Haman to see whether Es 3:4 5046
he had **t** them that he was a Jew. Es 3:4 5046
for they had **t** him *who* the people Es 3:6 5046
and her eunuchs came and **t** her, Es 4:4 5046
Mordecai **t** him all that had Es 4:7 5046
Mordecai **t** *them* to reply to Esther, Es 4:13 559
Esther **t** *them* to reply to Mordecai, Es 4:15 559
What wise men have **t**, Jb 15:18 5046
Shall it be **t** Him that I would speak Jb 37:20 5608
went and did as the LORD **t** them; Jb 42:9 1696
It will be **t** of the Lord to the Ps 22:30 5608
our ears, Our fathers have **t** us The Ps 44:1 5608
known, And our fathers have **t** us. Ps 78:3 5608
With my lips I have **t** of All the Ps 119:13 5608
I have **t** of my ways, and You have Ps 119:26 5608
For thus the LORD has **t** me, Is 18:4 559
and **t** him the words of Rabshakeh. Is 36:22 5046
what had not been **t** them they will Is 52:15 5608
So I have **t** you today, but you Jer 42:21 5046
Then I **t** the exiles all the things Ezk 11:25 1696
So he **t** me and made known to me Da 7:16 560
mornings Which has been **t** is true; Da 8:26 559
the LORD, because he had **t** them. Jon 1:10 5046
and falsehood Had **t** lies *and said,* Mi 2:11 3576
He has **t** you, O man, what is good; Mi 6:8 5046
would not believe if you were **t**. Hab 1:5 5608
heard that the ancients were **t**, Mt 5:21 3004
heard that the ancients were **t**, Mt 5:33 3004
crowd sternly **t** them to be quiet Mt 20:31 2008
"Behold, I have **t** you in advance. Mt 24:25 4275b
behold, I have **t** you." Mt 28:7 3004
And He **t** His disciples that a boat Mk 3:9 3004
Him and **t** Him the whole truth. Mk 5:33 3004
They **t** Him, saying, Mk 8:28 3004
I **t** Your disciples to cast it out, Mk 9:18 3004
to them just as Jesus had **t** *them,* Mk 11:6 3004
I have **t** you everything in advance. Mk 13:23 4275b
found *it* just as He had **t** them; Mk 14:16 3004
just as He **t** you.' " Mk 16:7 3004
had been **t** them about this Child. Lk 2:17 2980
were **t** them by the shepherds. Lk 2:18 2980
and seen, just as had been **t** them. Lk 2:20 2980
And He **t** them a parable, saying, Lk 12:16 3004
So He **t** them this parable, Lk 15:3 3004
And He also **t** this parable to Lk 18:9 3004
They **t** him that Jesus of Lk 18:37 518
found it just as He had **t** them. Lk 19:32 3004
Then He **t** them a parable: Lk 21:29 3004
everything just as He had **t** them; Lk 22:13 3004
of the Lord, how He had **t** him, Lk 22:61 3004
"If I **t** you earthly things and Jn 3:12 3004
see a man who **t** me all the things Jn 4:29 3004
"He **t** me all the things that I Jn 4:39 3004
and **t** the Jews that it was Jesus Jn 5:15 3004
Me, a man who has **t** you the truth, Jn 8:40 2980
"I **t** you already and you did not Jn 9:27 3004
"I **t** you, and you do not believe; Jn 10:25 3004
and **t** them the things which Jesus Jn 11:46 3004
Philip came and **t** Andrew; Jn 12:22 3004
and Philip came and **t** Jesus. Jn 12:22 3004
just as the Father has **t** Me." Jn 12:50 3004
were not so, I would have **t** you; Jn 14:2 3004
I have **t** you before it happens, Jn 14:29 3004
may remember that I **t** you of them. Jn 16:4 3004
"I **t** you that I am *He;* Jn 18:8 3004
it will be **t** you what you must do." Ac 9:6 2980
"The Spirit **t** me to go with Ac 11:12 3004
and they have been **t** about you, Ac 21:21 2727
which they have been **t** about you, Ac 21:24 2727
and there you will be **t** of all Ac 22:10 2980
went to the commander and **t** him, Ac 22:26 518
entered the barracks and **t** Paul. Ac 23:16 518
turn out exactly as I have been **t**. Ac 27:25 2980
many walk, of whom I often **t** you, Php 3:18 3004
just as we also **t** you before and 1Th 4:6 4275b
and they were **t** that they should Rv 6:11 3004
They were **t** not to hurt Rv 9:4 3004

TOLERABLE
it will be more **t** for *the* land of Mt 10:15 414
it will be more **t** for Tyre and Mt 11:22 414
will be more **t** for the land of Sodom Mt 11:24 414
be more **t** in that day for Sodom than Lk 10:12 414
"But it will be more **t** for Tyre Lk 10:14 414

TOLERANCE
of the riches of His kindness and **t** Ro 2:4 463
showing **t** for one another in love, Eph 4:2 430

TOLERATE
For you, being *so* wise, **t** 2Co 11:19 430
For you **t** it if anyone enslaves you, 2Co 11:20 430
and that you cannot **t** evil men, Rv 2:2 941
you, that you **t** the woman Jezebel, Rv 2:20 863

TOLL
not pay tribute, custom or **t**, Ezr 4:13 1983
custom and **t** were paid to them. Ezr 4:20 1983
allowed to impose tax, tribute or **t** Ezr 7:24 1983

TOMB
in the **t** of his father Joash, Jg 8:32 6913
in the **t** of Manoah his father. Jg 16:31 6913
will find two men close to Rachel's **t** 1Sa 10:2 6900
father's **t** which was in Bethlehem. 2Sa 2:32 6913
and buried him in his own **t**. 2Ki 23:30 6900
They buried him in his own **t** 2Ch 16:14 6913
not been, Carried from womb to **t**.' Jb 10:19 6913
Men will keep watch over *his* **t**. Jb 21:32 1430b
lie in glory, Each in his own **t**. Is 14:18 1004
you have been cast out of your **t** Is 14:19 6913
have hewn a **t** for yourself here, Is 22:16 6913
You who hew a **t** on the height, Is 22:16 6913
and laid it in his own new **t**, Mt 27:60 3419
stone against the entrance of the **t** Mt 27:60 3419
And they left the **t** quickly Mt 28:8 3419
away his body and laid it in a **t**. Mk 6:29 3419
and laid Him in a **t** which had been Mk 15:46 3418
against the entrance of the **t**. Mk 15:46 3419
they came to the **t** when the sun had Mk 16:2 3418
us from the entrance of the **t**?" Mk 16:3 3419
Entering the **t**, Mk 16:5 3419
They went out and fled from the **t**, Mk 16:8 3419
laid Him in a **t** cut into the rock, Lk 23:53 3418
saw the **t** and how His body was Lk 23:55 3419
dawn, they came to the **t** bringing Lk 24:1 3418
the stone rolled away from the **t**, Lk 24:2 3419
and returned from the **t** and Lk 24:9 3419
But Peter got up and ran to the **t**; Lk 24:12 3419
at the **t** early in the morning, Lk 24:22 3419
those who were with us went to the **t** Lk 24:24 3419
already been in the **t** four days. Jn 11:17 3419
was going to the **t** to weep there. Jn 11:31 3419
moved within, came to the **t**. Jn 11:38 3419
He called Lazarus out of the **t** and Jn 12:17 3419
and in the garden a new **t** in Jn 19:41 3419
since the **t** was nearby, Jn 19:42 3419
Magdalene came early to the **t**, Jn 20:1 3419
already taken away from the **t**. Jn 20:1 3419
taken away the Lord out of the **t**, Jn 20:2 3419
and they were going to the **t**. Jn 20:3 3419
Peter and came to the **t** first; Jn 20:4 3419
following him, and entered the **t**; Jn 20:6 3419
disciple who had first come to the **t** Jn 20:8 3419
standing outside the **t** weeping; Jn 20:11 3419
she stooped and looked into the **t**; Jn 20:11 3419
and his **t** is with us to this day. Ac 2:29 3418
and laid in the **t** which Abraham Ac 7:16 3418
the cross and laid Him in a **t**. Ac 13:29 3419
dead bodies to be laid in a **t**. Rv 11:9 3418

TOMBS
but not in the **t** of the kings. 2Ch 21:20 6913
bury him in the **t** of the kings. 2Ch 24:25 6913
into the **t** of the kings of Israel; 2Ch 28:27 6913
section of the **t** of the sons of David; 2Ch 32:33 6913
buried in the **t** of his fathers. 2Ch 35:24 6913
city, the place of my fathers' **t**, Ne 2:3 6913
to the city of my fathers' **t**, Ne 2:5 6913
a point opposite the **t** of David, Ne 3:16 6913
as they were coming out of the **t**. Mt 8:28 3419
For you are like whitewashed **t** Mt 23:27 5028
For you build the **t** of the prophets Mt 23:29 5028
The **t** were opened, Mt 27:52 3419
and coming out of the **t** after His Mt 27:53 3419
immediately a man from the **t** with Mk 5:2 3419
he had his dwelling among the **t**. Mk 5:3 3418
among the **t** and in the mountains, Mk 5:5 3418
living in a house, but in the **t**. Lk 8:27 3418
For you are like concealed **t**, Lk 11:44 3419
you build the **t** of the prophets, Lk 11:47 3419
and you build *their* **t**. Lk 11:48
all who are in the **t** will hear His Jn 5:28 3419

TOMORROW
Then he said, "**T**." Ex 8:10 4279
T this sign will occur. Ex 8:23 4279
servants, and from his people **t**; Ex 8:29 4279
"**T** the LORD will do this thing in Ex 9:5 4279
"Behold, about this time **t**, Ex 9:18 4279
t I will bring locusts into your Ex 10:4 4279
T is a sabbath observance, a holy Ex 16:23 4279
T I will station myself on the top Ex 17:9 4279
and consecrate them today and **t**, Ex 19:10 4279
"**T** *shall be* a feast to the LORD." Ex 32:5 4279
'Consecrate yourselves for **t**, Nu 11:18 4279
turn **t** and set out to the Nu 14:25 4279
"**T** morning the LORD will show who Nu 16:5 1242
in the presence of the LORD **t**; Nu 16:7 4279
be present before the LORD **t**, Nu 16:16 4279
for **t** the LORD will do wonders Jos 3:5 4279
'Consecrate yourselves for **t**, Jos 7:13 4279
for **t** at this time I will deliver Jos 11:6 4279
whole congregation of Israel **t**. Jos 22:18 4279
Then **t** you may arise early for Jg 19:9 4279
for **t** I will deliver them into Jg 20:28 4279
"About this time **t** I will send 1Sa 9:16 4279
'**T**, by the time the sun is hot, 1Sa 11:9 4279
"**T** we will come out to you, and 1Sa 11:10 4279
t you will be put to death." 1Sa 19:11 4279
"Behold, **t** is the new moon, and I 1Sa 20:5 4279
out my father about this time **t**, 1Sa 20:12 4279
"**T** is the new moon, and you will 1Sa 20:18 4279
therefore **t** you and your sons will 1Sa 28:19 4279
also, and **t** I will let you go." 2Sa 11:12 4279
of them by **t** about this time." 1Ki 19:2 4279
but about this time **t** I will send 1Ki 20:6 4279
today, and we will eat my son **t**.' 2Ki 6:28 4279
'**T** about this time a measure of 2Ki 7:1 4279
will be *sold* **t** about this time at 2Ki 7:18 4279
me at Jezreel **t** about this time." 2Ki 10:6 4279
'**T** go down against them. 2Ch 20:16 4279
t go out to face them, for the 2Ch 20:17 4279
t I will do as the king says." Es 5:8 4279
and **t** also I am invited by her Es 5:12 4279
let **t** also be granted to the Jews Es 9:13 4279
come back, And **t** I will give *it,*" Pr 3:28 4279
Do not boast about **t**, Pr 27:1 4279
eat and drink, for **t** we may die." Is 22:13 4279
And **t** will be like today, only Is 56:12 4279
and **t** is thrown into the furnace, Mt 6:30 839
"So do not worry about **t**; Mt 6:34 839
for **t** will care for itself. Mt 6:34 839
and **t** is thrown into the furnace, Lk 12:28 839
and perform cures today and **t**, Lk 13:32 839
on today and **t** and the next *day* Lk 13:33 839
bring Paul down **t** to the Council, Ac 23:20 839
"**T**," he said, "you shall hear him." Ac 25:22 839
US EAT AND DRINK, FOR **T** WE DIE. 1Co 15:32 839
"Today or **t** we will go to such Jas 4:13 839
what your life will be like **t**. Jas 4:14 839

TONE
with you now and to change my **t**, Ga 4:20 5456

TONES
produce a distinction in the **t**, 1Co 14:7 5353

TONGS
flowers and the lamps and the **t**, 1Ki 7:49 4457
the lamps, and the **t** of gold, 2Ch 4:21 4457
had taken from the altar with **t**. Is 6:6 4457

TONGUE
am slow of speech and slow of **t**." Ex 4:10 3956
who laps the water with his **t** as Jg 7:5 3956
by me, And His word was on my **t**. 2Sa 23:2 3956
hidden from the scourge of the **t**, Jb 5:21 3956
"Is there injustice on my **t**? Jb 6:30 3956
And he hides it under his **t**, Jb 20:12 3956
The viper's **t** slays him. Jb 20:16 3956
Nor will my **t** mutter deceit. Jb 27:4 3956
And their **t** stuck to their palate. Jb 29:10 3956
my mouth, My **t** in my mouth speaks. Jb 33:2 3956
Or press down his **t** with a cord? Jb 41:1 3956
They flatter with their **t**. Ps 5:9 3956
his **t** is mischief and wickedness. Ps 10:7 3956
The **t** that speaks great things; Ps 12:3 3956
"With our **t** we will prevail; Ps 12:4 3956
He does not slander with his **t**, Ps 15:3 3956
And my **t** cleaves to my jaws; Ps 22:15 3956
Keep your **t** from evil And your Ps 34:13 3956
And my **t** shall declare Your Ps 35:28 3956
wisdom, And his **t** speaks justice. Ps 37:30 3956
That I may not sin with my **t**; Ps 39:1 3956
Then I spoke with my **t**: Ps 39:3 3956
My **t** is the pen of a ready writer. Ps 45:1 3956
in evil And your **t** frames deceit. Ps 50:19 3956
Then my **t** will joyfully sing of Ps 51:14 3956
Your **t** devises destruction, Like a Ps 52:2 3956
words that devour, O deceitful **t**. Ps 52:4 3956
arrows And their **t** a sharp sword. Ps 57:4 3956
sharpened their **t** like a sword. Ps 64:3 3956
Their own **t** is against them; Ps 64:8 3956
And He was extolled with my **t**. Ps 66:17 3956
The **t** of your dogs *may have* its Ps 68:23 3956
My **t** also will utter Your Ps 71:24 3956
their **t** parades through the earth. Ps 73:9 3956
And lied to Him with their **t**. Ps 78:36 3956
spoken against me with a lying **t**. Ps 109:2 3956
Let my **t** sing of Your word, For all Ps 119:172 3956
lying lips, From a deceitful **t**. Ps 120:2 3956
be done to you, You deceitful **t**? Ps 120:3 3956
And our **t** with joyful shouting; Ps 126:2 3956
May my **t** cling to the roof of my Ps 137:6 3956
before there is a word on my **t**, Ps 139:4 3956
Haughty eyes, a lying **t**, Pr 6:17 3956
the smooth **t** of the adulteress. Pr 6:24 3956
The **t** of the righteous is *as* Pr 10:20 3956
the perverted **t** will be cut out. Pr 10:31 3956
the **t** of the wise brings healing. Pr 12:18 3956
a lying **t** is only for a moment. Pr 12:19 3956
The **t** of the wise makes knowledge Pr 15:2 3956
A soothing **t** is a tree of life, Pr 15:4 3956
answer of the **t** is from the LORD. Pr 16:1 3956
pays attention to a destructive **t**. Pr 17:4 3956
life are in the power of the **t**, Pr 18:21 3956
acquisition of treasures by a lying **t** Pr 21:6 3956
He who guards his mouth and his **t**, Pr 21:23 3956
And a soft **t** breaks the bone. Pr 25:15 3956
forth rain, And a backbiting **t**, Pr 25:23 3956
A lying **t** hates those it crushes, Pr 26:28 3956
Than he who flatters with the **t**. Pr 28:23 3956
teaching of kindness is on her **t**. Pr 31:26 3956
Honey and milk are under your **t**, SS 4:11 3956
as a **t** of fire consumes stubble And Is 5:24 3956
destroy The **t** of the Sea of Egypt; Is 11:15 3956
stammering lips and a foreign **t**, Is 28:11 3956

His t is like a consuming fire; Is 30:27 3956
And the t of the stammerers will Is 32:4 3956
t which no one understands. Is 33:19 3956
And the t of the mute will shout Is 35:6 3956
their t is parched with thirst; Is 41:17 3956
every t will swear *allegiance.* Is 45:23 3956
GOD has given Me the t of disciples, Is 50:4 3956
And every t that accuses you in Is 54:17 3956
your mouth And stick out your t? Is 57:4 3956
Your t mutters wickedness. Is 59:3 3956
They bend their t *like* their bow; Jer 9:3 3956
have taught their t to speak lies; Jer 9:5 3956
"Their t is a deadly arrow; Jer 9:8 3956
let us strike at him with *our* t, Jer 18:18 3956
The t of the infant cleaves To the La 4:4 3956
I will make your t stick to the Ezk 3:26 3956
nation or t that speaks anything Da 3:29 3961
of the insolence of their t. Hos 7:16 3956
t is deceitful in their mouth. Mi 6:12 3956
Nor will a deceitful t Be found in Zph 3:13 3956
their t will rot in their mouth. Zch 14:12 3956
He touched his t *with the saliva;* Mk 7:33 *1100*
impediment of his t was removed, Mk 7:35 *1100*
mouth was opened and his t *loosed,* Lk 1:64 *1100*
finger in water and cool off my t, Lk 16:24 *1100*
HEART WAS GLAD AND MY T EXULTED; Ac 2:26 *1100*
EVERY T SHALL GIVE PRAISE TO GOD. Ro 14:11 *1100*
one who speaks in a t does not 1Co 14:2 *1100*
One who speaks in a t edifies himself 1Co 14:4 *1100*
unless you utter by the t speech that 1Co 14:9 *1100*
let one who speaks in a t pray that 1Co 14:13 *1100*
For if I pray in a t, 1Co 14:14 *1100*
than ten thousand words in a t. 1Co 14:19 *1100*
has a revelation, has a t, 1Co 14:26 *1100*
If anyone speaks in a t, 1Co 14:27 *1100*
and that every t will confess Php 2:11 *1100*
and yet does not bridle his t but Jas 1:26 *1100*
the t is a small part of the body, Jas 3:5 *1100*
And the t is a fire, the *very* Jas 3:6 *1100*
the t is set among our members as Jas 3:6 *1100*
But no one can tame the t; Jas 3:8 *1100*
MUST KEEP HIS T FROM EVIL AND HIS LIPS 1Pe 3:10 *1100*
us not love with word or with t, 1Jn 3:18 *1100*
tribe and t and people and nation. Rv 5:9 *1100*
tribe and people and t and nation Rv 13:7 *1100*
nation and tribe and t and people; Rv 14:6 *1100*

TONGUES

in a shelter from the strife of t. Ps 31:20 3956
Confuse, O Lord, divide their t, Ps 55:9 3956
They sharpen their t as a serpent; Ps 140:3 3956
to gather all nations and t. Is 66:18 3956
"who use their t and declare, Jer 23:31 3956
they will speak with new t; Mk 16:17 *1100*
And there appeared to them t as of Ac 2:3 *1100*
and began to speak with other t, Ac 2:4 *1100*
we hear them in our *own* t speaking Ac 2:11 *1100*
speaking with t and exalting God. Ac 10:46 *1100*
speaking with t and prophesying. Ac 19:6 *1100*
WITH THEIR T THEY KEEP DECEIVING, Ro 3:13 *1100*
to another *various* kinds of t, 1Co 12:10 *1100*
another the interpretation of t. 1Co 12:10 *1100*
various kinds of t. 1Co 12:28 *1100*
All do not speak with t, 1Co 12:30 *1100*
with the t of men and of angels, 1Co 13:1 *1100*
if *there are* t, they will cease; 1Co 13:8 *1100*
I wish that you all spoke in t, 1Co 14:5 *1100*
than one who speaks in t, 1Co 14:5 *1100*
if I come to you speaking in t, 1Co 14:6 *1100*
I speak in t more than you all; 1Co 14:18 *1100*
"BY MEN OF STRANGE T AND BY THE 1Co 14:21 *2084*
So then t are for a sign, not to 1Co 14:22 *1100*
together and all speak in t, 1Co 14:23 *1100*
and do not forbid to speak in t. 1Co 14:39 *1100*
and *all* tribes and peoples and t, Rv 7:9 *1100*
and nations and t and kings." Rv 10:11 *1100*
from the peoples and tribes and t Rv 11:9 *1100*
gnawed their t because of pain, Rv 16:10 *1100*
and multitudes and nations and t. Rv 17:15 *1100*

TONIGHT

are the men who came to you t? Gn 19:5 3915
let us make him drink wine t also; Gn 19:34 3915
"Therefore he may lie with you t Gn 30:15 3915
Now please, you also stay here t, Nu 22:19 3915
the sons of Israel have come here t Jos 2:2 3915
place where you will lodge t.' " Jos 4:3 3915
if I should even have a husband t Ru 1:12 3915
barley at the threshing floor t. Ru 3:2 3915
"If you do not save your life t, 1Sa 19:11 3915
I may arise and pursue David t. 2Sa 17:1 3915

TOO

"My punishment is t great to bear! Gn 4:13 4480
they will be t many to count." Gn 16:10 3808
Is anything t difficult for the LORD? Gn 18:14 4480
for you are t powerful for us." Gn 26:16 3966
and they quarreled over it t, Gn 26:21 1571
and his eyes were t dim to see, Gn 27:1 4480
her I t may have children." Gn 30:3 1571
which is t great to be numbered.' " Gn 32:12 4480
their property had become t great Gn 36:7 4480
he t may die like his brothers." Gn 38:11 1571
"Therefore, our livestock t Ex 10:26 1571
household is t small for a lamb, Ex 12:4 4480
for the task is t heavy for you; Ex 18:18 4480
field become t numerous for you. Ex 23:29 5921
Consider t, that this nation is Ex 33:13
'He t, who eats some of its Lv 11:40
he t shall wash his clothes and Lv 15:8
'Then, t, *it is* out of the sons of Lv 25:45 1571
The Levites, t, purified Nu 8:21
because it is t burdensome for me. Nu 11:14 4480
for they are t strong for us." Nu 13:31 4480
me since they are t mighty for me; Nu 22:6 4480
you t will be gathered to your Nu 27:13 1571
The case that is t hard for you, Dt 1:17 4480
no city that was t high for us; Dt 2:36 4480
beasts would grow t numerous for you. Dt 7:22 5921
to put His name is t far from you, Dt 12:21
chooses to set His name is t far away Dt 14:24
is t difficult for you to decide, Dt 17:8 4480
today is not t difficult for you, Dt 30:11 4480
of Ephraim is t narrow for you." Jos 17:15
of Judah was t large for them; Jos 19:9 4480
because he was t afraid of his Jg 6:27
people who are with you are t many Jg 7:2 4480
"The people are still t many; Jg 7:4
that they were t strong for him, Jg 18:26 4480
for I am t old to have a husband. Ru 1:12 4480
and he t prophesied before Samuel 1Sa 19:24 1571
two hundred who were t exhausted 1Sa 30:10 4480
were t exhausted to follow David, 1Sa 30:21 4480
of Zeruiah are t difficult for me. 2Sa 3:39 4480
the Arameans are t strong for me, 2Sa 10:11 4480
of Ammon are t strong for you, 2Sa 10:11 4480
and if *that had been* t little, 2Sa 12:8
the Jordan and the king crossed t 2Sa 19:39
me, for they were t strong for me. 2Sa 22:18 4480
a great people who are t many to be 1Ki 3:8 4480
because *they were* t many; 1Ki 7:47 3966
was t small to hold the burnt offering 1Ki 8:64 4480
"It is t much for you to go up to 1Ki 12:28 4480
the journey is t great for you." 1Ki 19:7 4480
the battle was t fierce for him, 2Ki 3:26 4480
we are living is t limited for us. 2Ki 6:1 4480
"Shoot him t, in the chariot." 2Ki 9:27 1571
the Arameans are t strong for me, 1Ch 19:12 4480
of Ammon are t strong for you, 1Ch 19:12 4480
who proved t strong for Rehoboam, 2Ch 13:7 5921
But the priests were t few, 2Ch 29:34
Are the consolations of God t small Jb 15:11 4480
"I t could speak like you, If I Jb 16:4 1571
That t would have been an iniquity Jb 31:28 1571
me, I t will tell what I think.' Jb 32:10 637
"I t will answer my share, I also Jb 32:17 637
I t have been formed out of the Jb 33:6 1571
Things t wonderful for me, Jb 42:3 4480
me, for they were t mighty for me. Ps 18:17 4480
from him who is t strong for him, Ps 35:10 4480
burden they weigh t much for me. Ps 38:4 4480
They would be t numerous to count. Ps 40:5 4480
T long has my soul had its Ps 120:6
Or in things t difficult for me. Ps 131:1 4480
knowledge is t wonderful for me; Ps 139:6 4480
It is t high, I cannot attain to Ps 139:6
For they are t strong for me. Ps 142:6 4480
A man of t *many* friends *comes* Pr 18:24
Wisdom is t exalted for a fool, He Pr 24:7
which are t wonderful for me, Pr 30:18 4480
And behold, it t was futility. Ec 2:1 1571
"This t is vanity." Ec 2:15 1571
This t is vanity. Ec 2:19 1571
This t is vanity and a great evil. Ec 2:21 1571
This t is vanity. Ec 2:23 1571
This t is vanity and striving Ec 2:26 1571
This t is vanity and striving Ec 4:4 1571
This t is vanity and it is a Ec 4:8 1571
for this t is vanity and striving Ec 4:16 1571
This t is vanity. Ec 5:10 1571
This t is futility and a striving Ec 6:9 1571
the fool; And this t is futility. Ec 7:6 1571
This t is futility. Ec 8:10 1571
I say that this t is futility. Ec 8:14 1571
Is it t slight a thing for you to Is 7:13 4480
bed is t short on which to stretch Is 28:20 4480
blanket is t small to wrap oneself in. Is 28:20
He who is t impoverished for *such* Is 40:20
"It is t small a thing that You Is 49:6 4480
be t cramped for the inhabitants, Is 49:19 4480
'The place is t cramped for me; Is 49:20
a wind t strong for this Jer 4:12 4480
But they t, with one accord, have Jer 5:5
'You t have done evil, *even* more Jer 16:12
Nothing is t difficult for You, Jer 32:17 4480
is anything t difficult for Me?" Jer 32:27 4480
For even they t have turned back Jer 46:21 1571
You t, Madmen, will be silenced; Jer 48:2 1571
Is it t light a thing for the Ezk 8:17
but, as if that were t little, Ezk 16:47 6985
'Is it t slight a thing for you Ezk 34:18 4480
"This t shall not be," Am 7:6 1571
You t were as one of them. Ob 1:11 1571
T little to be among the clans of Mi 5:2
And Egypt t, without limits. Na 3:9
You t will become drunk, You will Na 3:11 1571
You t will search for a refuge Na 3:11 1571
eyes are t pure to approve evil, Hab 1:13 4480
'If it is t difficult in the sight Zch 8:6 6381
also be t difficult in My sight?' Zch 8:6 6381
Gaza t will writhe in great pain; Zch 9:5
I t may come and worship Him." Mt 2:8 *2532*
'You go into the vineyard t.' Mt 20:7 *2532*
"So, you t, outwardly appear Mt 23:28 *2532*
So, you t, when you see all Mt 24:33 *2532*
not be enough for us and you t; Mt 25:9
disciples said the same thing t. Mt 26:35 *2532*
You t were with Jesus the Galilean. Mt 26:69 *2532*
"Surely you t are *one* of them; Mt 26:73 *2532*
"Even so, you t, when you see Mk 13:29 *2532*
them, for you are a Galilean t." Mk 14:70 *2532*
You say this, You insult us t." Lk 11:45 *2532*
"You t, be ready; Lk 12:40 *2532*
it alone, sir, for this year t, Lk 13:8 *2532*
"So you t, when you do all the Lk 17:10 *2532*
come to this house, because he, t, Lk 19:9 *2532*
"This man was with Him t." Lk 22:56 *2532*
"You are *one* of them t!" Lk 22:58 *2532*
Him, for he is a Galilean t." Lk 22:59 *2532*
The prophets died t; Jn 8:53 *2532*
want to become His disciples t, Jn 9:27 *2532*
"We are not blind t, Jn 9:40 *2532*
"Therefore you t have grief now; Jn 16:22 *2532*
people after him; he t perished, Ac 5:37 *2548*
I t am *just* a man." Ac 10:26 *2532*
At the same time t, Ac 24:26 *2532*
we t might walk in newness of life. Ro 6:4 *2532*
with groanings t deep for words; Ro 8:26 *215*
For I t am an Israelite, a Ro 11:1 *2532*
root is holy, the branches are t. Ro 11:16 *2532*
is it t much if we reap 1Co 9:11 *3173*
in order not to say t much 2Co 2:5 *1912*
gathered MUCH DID NOT HAVE T MUCH, 2Co 8:15 *4121*
so that you t will not be tempted. Ga 6:1 *2532*
For this reason I t, Eph 1:15 *2532*
Among them we t all formerly lived Eph 2:3 *2532*
and that t, from God. Php 1:28
You t, *I urge you,* rejoice in Php 2:18 *2532*
you t have a Master in heaven. Col 4:1 *2532*
Do not lay hands upon anyone t 1Tm 5:22
so t the rich man in the midst of Jas 1:11 *2532*
You t be patient; Jas 5:8 *2532*
so that you t may have fellowship 1Jn 1:3 *2532*
Anyone who goes t far and does not 2Jn 1:9 *4254*

TOOK

Then the LORD God t the man and Gn 2:15 3947
then He t one of his ribs and Gn 2:21 3947
she t from its fruit and ate; Gn 3:6 3947
Lamech t to himself two wives: Gn 4:19 3947
and he was not, for God t him. Gn 5:24 3947
and they t wives for themselves, Gn 6:2 3947
he put out his hand and t her, Gn 8:9 3947
and t of every clean animal and of Gn 8:20 3947
But Shem and Japheth t a garment Gn 9:23 3947
and Nahor t wives for themselves. Gn 11:29 3947
Terah t Abram his son, and Lot Gn 11:31 3947
Abram t Sarai his wife and Lot Gn 12:5 3947
so that I t her for my wife? Gn 12:19 3947
Then they t all the goods of Sodom Gn 14:11 3947
They also t Lot, Abram's Gn 14:12 3947
And He t him outside and said, Gn 15:5 3318
wife Sarai t Hagar the Egyptian, Gn 16:3 3947
Then Abraham t Ishmael his son, Gn 17:23 3947
and t a tender and choice calf and Gn 18:7 3947
He t curds and milk and the Gn 18:8 3947
king of Gerar sent and t Sarah. Gn 20:2 3947
Abimelech then t sheep and oxen Gn 20:14 3947
t note of Sarah as He had said, Gn 21:1 6485
and t bread and a skin of water and Gn 21:14 3947
and his mother t a wife for him Gn 21:21 3947
Abraham t sheep and oxen and Gn 21:27 3947
there the two of them t an oath. Gn 21:31 7650
and t two of his young men with Gn 22:3 3947
Abraham t the wood of the Gn 22:6 3947
and he t in his hand the fire and Gn 22:6 3947
and t the knife to slay his son. Gn 22:10 3947
and Abraham went and t the ram and Gn 22:13 3947
who t me from my father's house Gn 24:7 3947
Then the servant t ten camels from Gn 24:10 3947
the man t a gold ring Gn 24:22 3947
servant t Rebekah and departed. Gn 24:61 3947
t her veil and covered herself. Gn 24:65 3947
Sarah's tent, and he t Rebekah, Gn 24:67 3947
Now Abraham t another wife, whose Gn 25:1 3947
forty years old when he t Rebekah, Gn 25:20 3947
Then Rebekah t the best garments Gn 27:15 3947
He t away my birthright, and Gn 27:36 3947
and he t one of the stones of the Gn 28:11 3947
and t the stone that he had put Gn 28:18 3947
evening he t his daughter Leah, Gn 29:23 3947
she t her maid Zilpah and gave her Gn 30:9 3947
Then Jacob t fresh rods of poplar Gn 30:37 3947
then he t his kinsmen with him and Gn 31:23 3947
Then Jacob t a stone and set it up Gn 31:45 3947
So they t stones and made a heap, Gn 31:46 3947
and t his two wives and his two maids Gn 32:22 3947
He t them and sent them across Gn 32:23 3947
Thus he urged him and he t *it.* Gn 33:11 3947
t her and lay with her by force. Gn 34:2 3947
each t his sword and came upon the Gn 34:25 3947
and t Dinah from Shechem's house, Gn 34:26 3947
They t their flocks and their Gn 34:28 3947
Esau t his wives from the Gn 36:2 3947
Then Esau t his wives and his sons Gn 36:6 3947
and they t him and threw him into Gn 37:24 3947
So they t Joseph's tunic, and Gn 37:31 3947
and he t her and went in to her. Gn 38:2 3947
t a wife for Er his firstborn, Gn 38:6 3947
the LORD, so the LORD t his life. Gn 38:7 4191
so He t his life also. Gn 38:10 4191
it t place while she was giving Gn 38:28 1961
and the midwife t and tied a Gn 38:28 3947
t him and put him into the jail, Gn 39:20 3947
of them, and he t care of them; Gn 40:4 8334
so I t the grapes and squeezed Gn 40:11 3947
Then Pharaoh t off his signet ring Gn 41:42 5493
he t Simeon from them and bound Gn 42:24 3947
and t us for spies of the country. Gn 42:30 5414
So the men t this present, and Gn 43:15 3947

Context	Reference	Number
and they **t** double *the* money in	**Gn 43:15**	3947
He **t** portions to them from his	**Gn 43:34**	5375
They **t** their livestock and	**Gn 46:6**	3947
He **t** five men from among his	**Gn 47:2**	3947
So he **t** his two sons Manasseh and	**Gn 48:1**	3947
Then Joseph **t** them from his knees,	**Gn 48:12**	3318
Joseph **t** them both, Ephraim	**Gn 48:13**	3947
which I **t** from the hand of the	**Gn 48:22**	3947
woman **t** the child and nursed him.	**Ex 2:9**	3947
Israel, and God **t** notice *of them.*	**Ex 2:25**	3045
his bosom, and when he **t** it out,	**Ex 4:6**	3318
and when he **t** it out of his bosom,	**Ex 4:7**	3318
So Moses **t** his wife and his sons	**Ex 4:20**	3947
t the staff of God in his hand.	**Ex 4:20**	3947
Then Zipporah **t** a flint and cut	**Ex 4:25**	3947
So they **t** soot from a kiln, and	**Ex 9:10**	3947
west wind which **t** up the locusts and	**Ex 10:19**	5375
So the people **t** their dough before	**Ex 12:34**	5375
t the bones of Joseph with him,	**Ex 13:19**	3947
ready and **t** his people with him;	**Ex 14:6**	3947
he **t** six hundred select chariots,	**Ex 14:7**	3947
the Egyptians **t** up the pursuit,	**Ex 14:23**	7291
sister, **t** the timbrel in her hand,	**Ex 15:20**	3947
t a stone and put it under him,	**Ex 17:12**	3947
t Moses' wife Zipporah,	**Ex 18:2**	3947
t a burnt offering and sacrifices	**Ex 18:12**	3947
Moses **t** half of the blood and	**Ex 24:6**	3947
Then he **t** the book of the covenant	**Ex 24:7**	3947
So Moses **t** the blood and sprinkled	**Ex 24:8**	3947
He **t** *this* from their hand, and	**Ex 32:4**	3947
He **t** the calf which they had	**Ex 32:20**	3947
t two stone tablets in his hand.	**Ex 34:4**	3947
Then he **t** the testimony and put *it*	**Ex 40:20**	3947
restore what he **t** by robbery or	**Lv 6:4**	1497
Moses then **t** the anointing oil and	**Lv 8:10**	3947
Moses slaughtered *it* and **t** the blood	**Lv 8:15**	3947
He also **t** all the fat that was on	**Lv 8:16**	3947
t some of its blood and put it on the	**Lv 8:23**	3947
He **t** the fat, and the fat	**Lv 8:25**	3947
he **t** one unleavened cake and one	**Lv 8:26**	3947
Then Moses **t** them from their hands	**Lv 8:28**	3947
Moses also **t** the breast and	**Lv 8:29**	3947
So Moses **t** some of the anointing	**Lv 8:30**	3947
So they **t** what Moses had commanded	**Lv 9:5**	3947
and **t** the goat of the sin offering	**Lv 9:15**	3947
t their respective firepans,	**Lv 10:1**	3947
So Moses and Aaron **t** these men who	**Nu 1:17**	3947
So Moses **t** the ransom money from	**Nu 3:49**	3947
he **t** the money in terms of the shekel	**Nu 3:50**	3947
So Moses **t** the carts and the oxen and	**Nu 7:6**	3947
and He **t** of the Spirit who was	**Nu 11:25**	680
Peleth, sons of Reuben, **t** *action,*	**Nu 16:1**	3947
So they each **t** his *own* censer and	**Nu 16:18**	3947
So Eleazar the priest **t** the bronze	**Nu 16:39**	3947
Aaron **t** *it* as Moses had spoken,	**Nu 16:47**	3947
He **t** his stand between the	**Nu 16:48**	5975
looked, and each man **t** his rod.	**Nu 17:9**	3947
t the rod from before the LORD,	**Nu 20:9**	3947
and **t** some of them captive.	**Nu 21:1**	7617
and **t** possession of his land from	**Nu 21:24**	3423
Israel **t** all these cities and	**Nu 21:25**	3947
and the angel of the LORD **t** his	**Nu 22:22**	3320
the morning that Balak **t** Balaam and	**Nu 22:41**	3947
He **t** up his discourse and said,	**Nu 23:7**	5375
I **t** you to curse my enemies, but	**Nu 23:11**	3947
he **t** him to the field of Zophim,	**Nu 23:14**	3947
he **t** up his discourse and said,	**Nu 23:18**	5375
So Balak **t** Balaam to the top of	**Nu 23:28**	3947
He **t** up his discourse and said,	**Nu 24:3**	5375
He **t** up his discourse and said,	**Nu 24:15**	5375
and **t** up his discourse and said,	**Nu 24:20**	5375
and **t** up his discourse and said,	**Nu 24:21**	5375
he **t** up his discourse and said,	**Nu 24:23**	5375
and **t** a spear in his hand,	**Nu 25:7**	3947
and he **t** Joshua and set him before	**Nu 27:22**	3947
They **t** all the spoil and all	**Nu 31:11**	3947
t one drawn out of every fifty,	**Nu 31:47**	3947
the priest **t** the gold from them,	**Nu 31:51**	3947
So Moses and Eleazar the priest **t**	**Nu 31:54**	3947
Manasseh went to Gilead and **t** it,	**Nu 32:39**	3920
of Manasseh went and **t** its towns,	**Nu 32:41**	3920
and **t** Kenath and its villages,	**Nu 32:42**	3920
"So I **t** the heads of your tribes,	**Dt 1:15**	3947
me and I **t** twelve of your men,	**Dt 1:23**	3947
"Then they **t** *some* of the fruit of	**Dt 1:25**	3947
and He was angry and **t** an oath,	**Dt 1:34**	7650
"Now the time that it **t** for us to	**Dt 2:14**	1980
"We **t** only the animals as our	**Dt 2:35**	962
of the cities we **t** as our booty.	**Dt 3:7**	962
"Thus we **t** the land at that time	**Dt 3:8**	3947
"So we **t** possession of this land	**Dt 3:12**	3423
Jair the son of Manasseh **t** all the	**Dt 3:14**	3947
They **t** possession of his land	**Dt 4:47**	3423
"I **t** hold of the two tablets	**Dt 9:17**	8610
"I **t** your sinful *thing,* the	**Dt 9:21**	3947
'I **t** this woman, *but* when I came	**Dt 22:14**	3947
dies who **t** her to be his wife,	**Dt 24:3**	3947
and we **t** their land and gave it as	**Dt 29:8**	3947
So they **t** up the ark of the	**Jos 3:6**	5375
and **t** up twelve stones from the	**Jos 4:8**	5375
priests **t** up the ark of the LORD.	**Jos 6:12**	5375
ahead, and they **t** the city.	**Jos 6:20**	3920
t some of the things under the	**Jos 7:1**	3947
he **t** the family of the Zerahites;	**Jos 7:17**	3920
then I coveted them and **t** them;	**Jos 7:21**	3947
They **t** them from inside the	**Jos 7:23**	3947
him, **t** Achan the son of Zerah,	**Jos 7:24**	3947
And he **t** about 5,000 men and set	**Jos 8:12**	3947
But they **t** alive the king of Ai	**Jos 8:23**	8610
Israel **t** only the cattle and the	**Jos 8:27**	962
t his body down from the tree and	**Jos 8:29**	3381
and **t** worn-out sacks on their	**Jos 9:4**	3947
our bread *was* warm *when* we **t** it for	**Jos 9:12**	6719b
Israel **t** some of their provisions,	**Jos 9:14**	3947
and they **t** them down from the	**Jos 10:27**	3381
sons of Israel **t** as their plunder;	**Jos 11:14**	962
Thus Joshua **t** all that land:	**Jos 11:16**	3947
they **t** them all in battle.	**Jos 11:19**	3947
So Joshua **t** the whole land,	**Jos 11:23**	3947
'Then I **t** your father Abraham from	**Jos 24:3**	3947
and you **t** possession of their land	**Jos 24:8**	3423
and he **t** a large stone and set it	**Jos 24:26**	3947
And Judah **t** Gaza with its	**Jg 1:18**	3920
and they **t** possession of the hill	**Jg 1:19**	3423
and they **t** their daughters for	**Jg 3:6**	3947
t the sword from his right thigh	**Jg 3:21**	3947
they **t** the key and opened them,	**Jg 3:25**	3947
t a tent peg and seized a hammer	**Jg 4:21**	3947
They **t** no plunder in silver.	**Jg 5:19**	3947
Then Gideon **t** ten men of his	**Jg 6:27**	3947
So the 300 men **t** the people's	**Jg 7:8**	3947
and they **t** the waters as far as	**Jg 7:24**	3920
He **t** the elders of the city,	**Jg 8:16**	3947
and **t** the crescent ornaments which	**Jg 8:21**	3947
So he **t** his people and divided	**Jg 9:43**	3947
and Abimelech **t** an axe in his hand	**Jg 9:48**	3947
"Because Israel **t** away my land	**Jg 11:13**	3947
I **t** my life in my hands and	**Jg 12:3**	7760
Manoah **t** the young goat with the grain	**Jg 13:19**	3947
thirty of them and **t** their spoil and	**Jg 14:19**	3947
hundred foxes, and **t** torches,	**Jg 15:4**	3947
because he **t** his wife and gave her	**Jg 15:6**	3947
so he reached out and **t** it and	**Jg 15:15**	3947
t hold of the doors of the city gate	**Jg 16:3**	270
So Delilah **t** new ropes and bound	**Jg 16:12**	3947
Delilah **t** the seven locks of his	**Jg 16:14**	3947
household came down, **t** him,	**Jg 16:31**	5375
the silver is with me; I **t** it."	**Jg 17:2**	3947
his mother **t** two hundred *pieces of*	**Jg 17:4**	3947
and **t** the graven image and the	**Jg 18:17**	3947
house and **t** the graven image,	**Jg 18:18**	3947
and he **t** the ephod and household	**Jg 18:20**	3947
Then they **t** what Micah had made	**Jg 18:27**	3947
who **t** a concubine for himself from	**Jg 19:1**	3947
for no one **t** them into *his* house	**Jg 19:15**	622
So he **t** him into his house and	**Jg 19:21**	935
he **t** a knife and laid hold of his	**Jg 19:29**	3947
t their stand in the assembly of	**Jg 20:2**	3320
"And I **t** hold of my concubine and	**Jg 20:6**	270
and **t** wives according to their	**Jg 21:23**	5375
They **t** for themselves Moabite	**Ru 1:4**	5375
t *it* up and went into the city,	**Ru 2:18**	5375
She also **t** *it* out and gave Naomi	**Ru 2:18**	3318
who **t** notice of you be blessed."	**Ru 2:19**	5234
He **t** ten men of the elders of	**Ru 4:2**	3947
So Boaz **t** Ruth, and she became his	**Ru 4:13**	3947
Then Naomi **t** the child and laid	**Ru 4:16**	3947
weaned him, she **t** him up with her,	**1Sa 1:24**	5927
Now the Philistines **t** the ark of	**1Sa 5:1**	3947
Then the Philistines **t** the ark of	**1Sa 5:2**	3947
So they **t** Dagon and set him in his	**1Sa 5:3**	3947
and **t** two milch cows and hitched	**1Sa 6:10**	3947
And the cows **t** the straight way in	**1Sa 6:12**	3474
The Levites **t** down the ark of	**1Sa 6:15**	3381
came and **t** the ark of the LORD and	**1Sa 7:1**	5927
Samuel **t** a suckling lamb and	**1Sa 7:9**	3947
Then Samuel **t** a stone and set it	**1Sa 7:12**	3947
t bribes and perverted justice.	**1Sa 8:3**	3947
Then Samuel **t** Saul and his servant	**1Sa 9:22**	3947
Then the cook **t** up the leg with	**1Sa 9:24**	7311
Then Samuel **t** the flask of oil,	**1Sa 10:1**	3947
So they ran and **t** him from there,	**1Sa 10:23**	3947
He **t** a yoke of oxen and cut	**1Sa 11:7**	3947
and **t** sheep and oxen and calves,	**1Sa 14:32**	3947
the people **t** *some* of the spoil,	**1Sa 15:21**	3947
Then Samuel **t** the horn of oil and	**1Sa 16:13**	3947
Jesse **t** a donkey *loaded with*	**1Sa 16:20**	3947
for forty days and **t** his stand.	**1Sa 17:16**	3320
t *the supplies* and went as Jesse had	**1Sa 17:20**	5375
came and **t** a lamb from the flock,	**1Sa 17:34**	5375
And David **t** them off.	**1Sa 17:39**	5493
He **t** his stick in his hand and	**1Sa 17:40**	3947
t from it a stone and slung *it,*	**1Sa 17:49**	3947
and **t** his sword and drew it out of its	**1Sa 17:51**	3947
Then David **t** the Philistine's head	**1Sa 17:54**	3947
Abner **t** him and brought him before	**1Sa 17:57**	3947
Saul **t** him that day and did	**1Sa 18:2**	3947
"For he **t** his life in his hand	**1Sa 19:5**	7760
Michal **t** the household idol	**1Sa 19:13**	3947
David **t** these words to heart and	**1Sa 21:12**	7760
Then Saul **t** three thousand chosen	**1Sa 24:2**	3947
and **t** two hundred *loaves* of bread	**1Sa 25:18**	3947
So David **t** the spear and the jug	**1Sa 26:12**	3947
alive, and he **t** away the sheep,	**1Sa 27:9**	3947
and she **t** flour, kneaded it and	**1Sa 28:24**	3947
and they **t** captive the women *and*	**1Sa 30:2**	7617
Saul **t** his sword and fell on it.	**1Sa 31:4**	3947
and **t** the body of Saul and the	**1Sa 31:12**	3947
They **t** their bones and buried	**1Sa 31:13**	3947
And I **t** the crown which *was* on his	**2Sa 1:10**	3947
Then David **t** hold of his clothes	**2Sa 1:11**	2388
And they **t** up Asahel and buried	**2Sa 2:32**	5375
sent and **t** her from *her* husband,	**2Sa 3:15**	3947
Joab **t** him aside into the middle	**2Sa 3:27**	5186
Now all the people **t** note *of it,*	**2Sa 3:36**	5234
and his nurse **t** him up and fled.	**2Sa 4:4**	5375
And they **t** his head and traveled	**2Sa 4:7**	3947
But they **t** the head of Ish-bosheth	**2Sa 4:12**	3947
Meanwhile David **t** more concubines	**2Sa 5:13**	3947
the ark of God and **t** hold of it,	**2Sa 6:6**	270
but David **t** it aside to the house	**2Sa 6:10**	5186
"I **t** you from the pasture, from	**2Sa 7:8**	3947
him, as I **t** *it* away from Saul,	**2Sa 7:15**	5493
and David **t** control of the chief	**2Sa 8:1**	3947
David **t** the shields of gold	**2Sa 8:7**	3947
t a very large amount of bronze.	**2Sa 8:8**	3947
So Hanun **t** David's servants and	**2Sa 10:4**	3947
David sent messengers and **t** her,	**2Sa 11:4**	3947
he **t** the poor man's ewe lamb and	**2Sa 12:4**	3947
Then he **t** the crown of their king	**2Sa 12:30**	3947
And she **t** dough, kneaded *it,* made	**2Sa 13:8**	3947
She **t** the pan and dished *them*	**2Sa 13:9**	3947
So Tamar **t** the cakes which she had	**2Sa 13:10**	3947
he **t** hold of her and said to her,	**2Sa 13:11**	2388
Then his attendant **t** her out and	**2Sa 13:18**	3318
And the woman **t** a covering and	**2Sa 17:19**	3947
and the battle **t** place in the	**2Sa 18:6**	1961
So he **t** three spears in his hand	**2Sa 18:14**	3947
They **t** Absalom and cast him	**2Sa 18:17**	3947
and the king **t** the ten women,	**2Sa 20:3**	3947
And Joab **t** Amasa by the beard with	**2Sa 20:9**	270
So the king **t** the two sons of	**2Sa 21:8**	3947
And Rizpah the daughter of Aiah **t**	**2Sa 21:10**	3947
then David went and **t** the bones of	**2Sa 21:12**	3947
"He sent from on high, He **t** me;	**2Sa 22:17**	3947
But he **t** his stand in the midst of	**2Sa 23:12**	3320
and **t** *it* and brought *it* to David.	**2Sa 23:16**	5375
Zadok the priest then **t** the horn	**1Ki 1:39**	3947
went and **t** hold of the horns of	**1Ki 1:50**	2388
and **t** hold of the horns of the altar.	**1Ki 2:28**	2388
and **t** Pharaoh's daughter and	**1Ki 3:1**	3947
and **t** my son from beside me while	**1Ki 3:20**	3947
and the priests **t** up the ark.	**1Ki 8:3**	5375
and **t** four hundred and twenty	**1Ki 9:28**	3947
and they **t** men with them from	**1Ki 11:18**	3947
Then Ahijah **t** hold of the new	**1Ki 11:30**	8610
So the prophet **t** up the body of	**1Ki 13:29**	5375
He **t** away the treasures of the	**1Ki 14:26**	3947
king's house, and he **t** everything,	**1Ki 14:26**	3947
Then Asa **t** all the silver and the	**1Ki 15:18**	3947
Then he **t** him from her bosom and	**1Ki 17:19**	3947
Elijah **t** the child and	**1Ki 17:23**	3947
Obadiah **t** a hundred prophets	**1Ki 18:4**	3947
Then they **t** the ox which was given	**1Ki 18:26**	3947
Elijah **t** twelve stones	**1Ki 18:31**	3947
and **t** the pair of oxen and	**1Ki 19:21**	3947
Now the men **t** this as an omen, and	**1Ki 20:33**	5172
and he **t** him up into the chariot.	**1Ki 20:33**	5927
"The cities which my father **t**	**1Ki 20:34**	3947
Then he hastily **t** the bandage away	**1Ki 20:41**	5493
So they **t** him outside the city and	**1Ki 21:13**	3318
Elijah **t** his mantle and folded	**2Ki 2:8**	3947
Then he **t** hold of his own clothes	**2Ki 2:12**	2388
He also **t** up the mantle of Elijah	**2Ki 2:13**	7311
He **t** the mantle of Elijah that	**2Ki 2:14**	3947
he **t** with him 700 men who drew	**2Ki 3:26**	3947
Then he **t** his oldest son who was	**2Ki 3:27**	3947
and she **t** up her son and went out.	**2Ki 4:37**	5375
He departed and **t** with him ten	**2Ki 5:5**	3947
he **t** them from their hand and	**2Ki 5:24**	3947
So he put out his hand and **t** it.	**2Ki 6:7**	3947
They **t** therefore two chariots with	**2Ki 7:14**	3947
meet him and **t** a gift in his hand,	**2Ki 8:9**	3947
he **t** the cover and dipped it	**2Ki 8:15**	3947
Then they hurried and each man **t**	**2Ki 9:13**	3947
them, they **t** the king's sons	**2Ki 10:7**	3947
So they **t** them alive and killed	**2Ki 10:14**	8610
and he **t** him up to him into the	**2Ki 10:15**	5927
t Joash the son of Ahaziah and	**2Ki 11:2**	3947
And each one of them **t** his men who	**2Ki 11:9**	3947
He **t** the captains of hundreds	**2Ki 11:19**	3947
But Jehoiada the priest **t** a chest	**2Ki 12:9**	3947
Jehoash king of Judah **t** all	**2Ki 12:18**	3947
So he **t** a bow and arrows.	**2Ki 13:15**	3947
"Take the arrows," and he **t** them.	**2Ki 13:18**	3947
Jehoash the son of Jehoahaz **t** again	**2Ki 13:25**	3947
of Salt 10,000 and **t** Sela by war,	**2Ki 14:7**	8610
He **t** all the gold and silver	**2Ki 14:14**	3947
All the people of Judah **t** Azariah,	**2Ki 14:21**	3947
Ahaz **t** the silver and gold	**2Ki 16:8**	3947
he also **t** down the sea from the	**2Ki 16:17**	3381
Then Hezekiah **t** the letter from	**2Ki 19:14**	3947
they **t** and laid *it* on the boil,	**2Ki 20:7**	3947
and he sent and **t** the bones from	**2Ki 23:16**	3947
Then the people of the land **t**	**2Ki 23:30**	3947
But he **t** Jehoahaz away and brought	**2Ki 23:34**	3947
So the king of Babylon **t** him	**2Ki 24:12**	3947
They **t** away the pots, the	**2Ki 25:14**	3947
The captain of the guard also **t**	**2Ki 25:15**	3947
Then the captain of the guard **t**	**2Ki 25:18**	3947
From the city he **t** one	**2Ki 25:19**	3947
the captain of the guard **t** them and	**2Ki 25:20**	3947
t the towns of Jair from them,	**1Ch 2:23**	3947
daughter of Pharaoh, whom Mered **t**	**1Ch 4:17**	3947
They **t** away their cattle:	**1Ch 5:21**	7617
t a wife for Huppim and Shuppim,	**1Ch 7:15**	3947
them in and when they **t** them out.	**1Ch 9:28**	3318
Saul **t** his sword and fell on it.	**1Ch 10:4**	3947
So they stripped him and **t** his head	**1Ch 10:9**	5375
arose and **t** away the body of Saul	**1Ch 10:12**	5375
They **t** their stand in the	**1Ch 11:14**	3320
and **t** *it* and brought *it* to David;	**1Ch 11:18**	5375
but **t** it aside to the house of	**1Ch 13:13**	5186
David **t** more wives at Jerusalem,	**1Ch 14:3**	3947
"I **t** you from the pasture, from	**1Ch 17:7**	3947
as I **t** it from him who was before	**1Ch 17:13**	5493
t Gath and its towns from the hand	**1Ch 18:1**	3947

David t from him 1,000 1Ch 18:4 3920
David t the shields of gold 1Ch 18:7 3947
t a very large amount of bronze, 1Ch 18:8 3947
So Hanun t David's servants and 1Ch 19:4 3947
David t the crown of their 1Ch 20:2 3947
the sons of Kish, t them *as wives.* 1Ch 23:22 5375
He t pleasure in me to make *me* king 1Ch 28:4 7521
and the Levites t up the ark. 2Ch 5:4 5375
and t from there four hundred and 2Ch 8:18 3947
Then Rehoboam t as a wife Mahalath 2Ch 11:18 3947
After her he t Maacah the 2Ch 11:20 3947
and t the treasures of the house 2Ch 12:9 3947
He t everything; he even took the 2Ch 12:9 3947
he even t the golden shields which 2Ch 12:9 3947
and t fourteen wives to himself, 2Ch 13:21 5375
he t courage and removed the 2Ch 15:8 2388
He t great pride in the ways 2Ch 17:6 1361b
which they t for themselves, 2Ch 20:25 5337
t Joash the son of Ahaziah, 2Ch 22:11 3947
and t captains of hundreds: 2Ch 23:1 3947
And each one of them t his men who 2Ch 23:8 3947
He t the captains of hundreds, 2Ch 23:20 3947
Jehoiada t two wives for him, 2Ch 24:3 5375
and he t a census of those from 2Ch 25:5 6485
Amaziah king of Judah t counsel 2Ch 25:17 3289
He t all the gold and silver 2Ch 25:24
all the people of Judah t Uzziah, 2Ch 26:1 3947
and they t also a great deal of spoil 2Ch 28:8 962
by name arose, t the captives, 2Ch 28:15 2388
Although Ahaz t a portion out of the 2Ch 28:21 2505a
and the priests t the blood and 2Ch 29:22 6901
And he t courage and rebuilt all 2Ch 32:5 2388
chains and t him to Babylon. 2Ch 33:11 1980
So his servants t him out of the 2Ch 35:24 5674a
land t Joahaz the son of Josiah, 2Ch 36:1 3947
But Neco t Joahaz his brother and 2Ch 36:4 3947
who t a wife from the daughters of Ezr 2:61 3947
t from the temple of Babylon and Ezr 5:14 5312
which Nebuchadnezzar t from the Ezr 6:5 5312
so they t the oath. Ezr 10:5 7650
and I t up the wine and gave it to Ne 2:1 5375
t *their* load with one hand doing the Ne 4:17 6006
each t his weapon *even to* Ne 4:23
So I called the priests and t an Ne 5:12 7650
and t from them bread and wine Ne 5:15 3947
who t a wife of the daughters of Ne 7:63 3947
They t possession of the land Ne 9:22 3423
They t possession of houses full Ne 9:25 3423
Then the two choirs t their stand Ne 12:40 5975
Now it t place in the days of Es 1:1 1961
t her as his own daughter. Es 2:7 3947
Then the king t his signet ring Es 3:10 5493
So Haman t the robe and the horse, Es 6:11 3947
The king t off his signet ring Es 8:2 5493
the Sabeans attacked and t them. Jb 1:15 3947
made a raid on the camels and t them Jb 1:17 3947
And he t a potsherd to scrape Jb 2:8 3947
again t up his discourse and said, Jb 29:1 5375
When I t my seat in the square, Jb 29:7 3559
He sent from on high, He t me; Ps 18:16 3947
t counsel together against me, Ps 31:13 3245
He who t me from my mother's womb; Ps 71:6 1491
And t him from the sheepfolds; Ps 78:70 3947
t deep root and filled the land. Ps 80:9 8327
I t great delight and sat down, SS 2:3 2530
the walls t away my shawl from me. SS 5:7 5375
Elam t up the quiver With the Is 22:6 5375
And the horsemen t up fixed Is 22:7 7896
Then Hezekiah t the letter from Is 37:14 3947
Before they t place I proclaimed Is 48:5 935
secret, From the time it t place, Is 48:16 1961
and I t the waistband from the Jer 13:7 3947
I t the cup from the LORD's hand and Jer 25:17 3947
t away from this place and carried to Jer 28:3 3947
Then Hananiah the prophet t the Jer 28:10 3947
in the day I t them by the hand to Jer 31:32 2388
"Then I t the deeds of purchase, Jer 32:11 3947
came in and t possession of it, Jer 32:23 3423
and t back the male servants and the Jer 34:11 7725
and each man t back his male Jer 34:16 7725
I t Jaazaniah the son of Jeremiah, Jer 35:3 3947
So Baruch the son of Neriah t the Jer 36:14 3947
and he t it out of the chamber of Jer 36:21 3947
Then Jeremiah t another scroll and Jer 36:32 3947
King Zedekiah sent and t him *out;* Jer 37:17 3947
Then they t Jeremiah and cast him Jer 38:6 3947
So Ebed-melech t the men under his Jer 38:11 3947
and t from there worn-out clothes and Jer 38:11 3947
they even sent and t Jeremiah out Jer 39:14 3947
Then Ishmael t captive all the Jer 41:10 7617
the son of Nethaniah t them captive Jer 41:10 7617
So they t all the men and went to Jer 41:12 3947
t from Mizpah all the remnant of the Jer 41:16 3947
forces t the entire remnant of Judah Jer 43:5 3947
And all who t them captive have Jer 50:33 7617
They also t away the pots, the Jer 52:18 3947
the guard also t away the bowls, Jer 52:19 3947
Then the captain of the guard t Jer 52:24 3947
He also t from the city one Jer 52:25 3947
t them and brought them to the king Jer 52:26 3947
Spirit lifted me up and t me away; Ezk 3:14 3947
surely live because he t warning; Ezk 3:21 2094b
t *some* and put *it* into the hands Ezk 10:7 5375
in linen, who t *it* and went out. Ezk 10:7 3947
"You t some of your clothes, Ezk 16:16 3947
"You also t your beautiful jewels Ezk 16:17 3947
"Then you t your embroidered Ezk 16:18 3947
you t your sons and daughters whom Ezk 16:20 3947
lovers with whom you t pleasure, Ezk 16:37 6149

and t away the top of the cedar. Ezk 17:3 3947
"He also t some of the seed of Ezk 17:5 3947
Jerusalem, t its king and princes and Ezk 17:12 3947
'He t one of the royal family Ezk 17:13 3947
t away the mighty of the land, Ezk 17:13 3947
She t another of her cubs And made Ezk 19:5 3947
"So I t them out of the land of Ezk 20:10 3318
they t her sons and her daughters, Ezk 23:10 3947
they both t the same way. Ezk 23:13 3947
they t hold of you with the hand, Ezk 29:7 8610
galleries t more *space* away from them Ezk 42:5 398
the Ancient of Days t *His* seat; Da 7:9 3488
t possession of the kingdom. Da 7:22 2631
t Gomer the daughter of Diblaim, Hos 1:3 3947
to walk, I t them in My arms; Hos 11:3 3947
womb he t his brother by the heel, Hos 12:3 6117
anger And I t him away in My wrath. Hos 13:11 3947
"But the LORD t me from following Am 7:15 3947
And I t for myself two staffs: Zch 11:7 3947
I t my staff Favor and cut Zch 11:10 3947
So I t the thirty *shekels* of Zch 11:13 3947
Now all this t place to fulfill Mt 1:22 *1096*
him, and t *Mary* as his wife, Mt 1:24 *3880*
Joseph got up and t the Child and Mt 2:14 *3880*
t the Child and His mother, Mt 2:21 *3880*
devil t Him into the holy city and Mt 4:5 *3880*
t Him to a very high mountain and Mt 4:8 *3880*
"HE HIMSELF T OUR INFIRMITIES AND Mt 8:17 *2983*
He entered and t her by the hand, Mt 9:25 *2902*
a man t and sowed in his field; Mt 13:31 *2983*
is like leaven, which a woman t and Mt 13:33 *2983*
And they t offense at Him. Mt 13:57 *4624*
and t away the body and buried it; Mt 14:12 *142*
He t the five loaves and the two Mt 14:19 *2983*
out His hand and t hold of him, Mt 14:31 *1949*
t the seven loaves and the fish; Mt 15:36 *2983*
Peter t Him aside and began to Mt 16:22 *4355*
Six days later Jesus t with Mt 17:1 *3880*
He t the twelve *disciples* aside by Mt 20:17 *3880*
This t place to fulfill what was Mt 21:4 *1096*
t his slaves and beat one, Mt 21:35 *2983*
"They t him, and threw him Mt 21:39 *2983*
flood came and t them all away; Mt 24:39 *142*
to ten virgins, who t their lamps and Mt 25:1 *2983*
when the foolish t their lamps, Mt 25:3 *2983*
lamps, they t no oil with them, Mt 25:3 *2983*
but the prudent t oil in flasks Mt 25:4 *2983*
were eating, Jesus t *some* bread, Mt 26:26 *2983*
And He t with Him Peter and the Mt 26:37 *3880*
t the pieces of silver and said, Mt 27:6 *2983*
T THE THIRTY PIECES OF SILVER, Mt 27:9 *2983*
he t water and washed his hands in Mt 27:24 *2983*
soldiers of the governor t Jesus into Mt 27:27 *3880*
and t the reed and *began* to beat Mt 27:30 *2983*
they t the *scarlet* robe off Him Mt 27:31 *1562*
And Joseph t the body and wrapped Mt 27:59 *2983*
And they came up and t hold of His Mt 28:9 *2902*
And they t the money and did as Mt 28:15 *2983*
they t Him along with them in Mk 4:36 *3880*
He t along the child's father and Mk 5:40 *3880*
And they t offense at Him. Mk 6:3 *4624*
they came and t away his body and Mk 6:29 *142*
And He t the five loaves and the Mk 6:41 *2983*
Jesus t him aside from the Mk 7:33 *618*
And Peter t Him aside and began to Mk 8:32 *4355*
Jesus t with Him Peter and James Mk 9:2 *3880*
But Jesus t him by the hand and Mk 9:27 *2902*
And He t them in His arms and Mk 10:16 *1723*
And again He t the twelve aside Mk 10:32 *3880*
"They t him, and beat him and Mk 12:3 *2983*
"They t him, and killed him and Mk 12:8 *2983*
and the first t a wife, and died leaving Mk 12:20 *2983*
they were eating, He t *some* bread, Mk 14:22 *2983*
And He t with Him Peter and James Mk 14:33 *3880*
t Him away into the palace Mk 15:16 *520*
Him, they t the purple robe off Him Mk 15:20 *1562*
bought a linen cloth, t Him down, Mk 15:46 *2507*
then he t Him into his arms, and Lk 2:28 *1209*
and t and ate the consecrated Lk 6:4 *2983*
t her by the hand and called, Lk 8:54 *2902*
Then He t the five loaves and the Lk 9:16 *2983*
He t along Peter and John and Lk 9:28 *3880*
t a child and stood him by His Lk 9:47 *1949*
him to an inn and t care of him. Lk 10:34 *1959*
"On the next day he t out two Lk 10:35 *1544b*
t and threw into his own garden; Lk 13:19 *2983*
which a woman t and hid in three Lk 13:21 *2983*
And He t hold of him and healed Lk 14:4 *1949*
Then He t the twelve aside and said Lk 18:31 *3880*
and the first t a wife and died Lk 20:29 *2983*
And in the same way *He* t the cup Lk 22:20
And he t it down and wrapped it in Lk 23:53 *2507*
He t the bread and blessed *it,* Lk 24:30 *2983*
He t it and ate *it* before them. Lk 24:43 *2983*
These things t place in Bethany Jn 1:28 *1096*
So they t it *to him.* Jn 2:8 *5342*
"It t forty-six years to build Jn 2:20
Jesus then t the loaves Jn 6:11 *2983*
Dedication t place at Jerusalem; Jn 10:22 *1096*
Mary then t a pound of very Jn 12:3 *2983*
t the branches of the palm trees and Jn 12:13 *2983*
morsel, He t and gave it to Judas, Jn 13:26 *2983*
Pilate then t Jesus Jn 19:1 *2983*
They t Jesus, therefore, and He Jn 19:17 *3880*
t His outer garments and made four Jn 19:23 *2983*
t her into his own *household.* Jn 19:27 *2983*
t away His body. Jn 19:38 *142*
So they t the body of Jesus and Jn 19:40 *2983*
Jesus came and t the bread and Jn 21:13 *2983*

KINGS OF THE EARTH T THEIR STAND, Ac 4:26 *3936*
They t his advice; Ac 5:40 *3982*
t shrewd advantage of our race and Ac 7:19 *2686*
Pharaoh's daughter t him away and Ac 7:21 *337*
he defended him and t vengeance Ac 7:24 *4160*
'YOU ALSO T ALONG THE TABERNACLE Ac 7:43 *353*
t food and was strengthened. Ac 9:19 *2983*
but his disciples t him by night and Ac 9:25 *2983*
But Barnabas t hold of him and Ac 9:27 *1949*
t place throughout all Judea, Ac 10:37 *1096*
were circumcised t issue with him, Ac 11:2 *1252*
And this t place in the *reign* of Ac 11:28 *1096*
t his seat on the rostrum and Ac 12:21 *2523*
an inheritance—*all of which* t Ac 13:19
they t Him down from the cross and Ac 13:29 *2507*
and Barnabas t Mark with him and Ac 15:39 *3880*
and he t him and circumcised him Ac 16:3 *2983*
And he t them that *very* hour of Ac 16:33 *3880*
And they t him and brought him to Ac 17:19 *1949*
And they all t hold of Sosthenes, Ac 18:17 *1949*
t leave of the brethren and put Ac 18:18 *657*
they t him aside and explained to Ac 18:26 *4355*
them and t away the disciples, Ac 19:9 *873*
This t place for two years, so Ac 19:10 *1096*
They t away the boy alive, and Ac 20:12 *71*
we t him on board and came to Ac 20:14 *353*
he t Paul's belt and bound his own Ac 21:11 *142*
Then Paul t the men, and the next Ac 21:26 3880
At once he t along *some* Ac 21:32 *3880*
came up and t hold of him, Ac 21:33 *1949*
So he t him and led him to the Ac 23:18 *3880*
The commander t him by the Ac 23:19 *1949*
t Paul and brought him by night to Ac 23:31 *353*
violence t him out of our hands, Ac 24:7 *520*
and on the next day he t his seat Ac 25:6 *2523*
day t my seat on the tribunal and Ac 25:17 *2523*
They t soundings and found *it* Ac 27:28 *1001*
they t another sounding and found Ac 27:28 *1001*
he t bread and gave thanks to God Ac 27:35 *2983*
and they themselves also t food. Ac 27:36 *4355*
he thanked God and t courage. Ac 28:15 *2983*
in which He was betrayed t bread; 1Co 11:23 *2983*
In the same way *He* t the cup also 1Co 11:25
no one, we t advantage of no one. 2Co 7:2 *4122*
that I am, I t you in by deceit. 2Co 12:16 *2983*
but t pleasure in wickedness. 2Th 2:12 *2106*
THE DAY WHEN I T THEM BY THE HAND Heb 8:9 *1949*
he t the blood of the calves and Heb 9:19 *2983*
NOT FOUND BECAUSE GOD T HIM UP; Heb 11:5 *3346a*
and t the book out of the right hand Rv 5:7 *2983*
Then the angel t the censer Rv 8:5 *2983*
I t the little book out of the Rv 10:10 *2983*
Then a strong angel t up a stone Rv 18:21 *142*

TOOL

for if you wield your t on it, Ex 20:25 2719
and fashioned it with a graving t and Ex 32:4 2747
you shall not wield an iron t on Dt 27:5
which no man had wielded an iron t; Jos 8:31
nor any iron t heard in the house 1Ki 6:7 3627
man shapes iron into a cutting t and Is 44:12 4621
of a craftsman with a cutting t. Jer 10:3 4621

TOOLS

shall have a spade among your t, Dt 23:13 240

TOOTH

eye for eye, t for tooth, hand for Ex 21:24 8127
eye for eye, tooth for t, Ex 21:24 8127
a t of his male or female slave, Ex 21:27 8127
him go free on account of his t. Ex 21:27 8127
eye for eye, t for tooth; Lv 24:20 8127
eye for eye, tooth for t; Lv 24:20 8127
life, eye for eye, t for tooth, Dt 19:21 8127
life, eye for eye, tooth for t, Dt 19:21 8127
Like a bad t and an unsteady foot Pr 25:19 8127
FOR AN EYE, AND A T FOR A TOOTH.' Mt 5:38 *3599*
FOR AN EYE, AND A TOOTH FOR A T.' Mt 5:38 *3599*

TOP

finish it to a cubit from the t; Gn 6:16 4605
whose t *will reach* into heaven, Gn 11:4 7218
him on the altar, on t of the wood. Gn 22:9 4605
with its t reaching to heaven; Gn 28:12 7218
a pillar and poured oil on its t. Gn 28:18 7218
and in the t basket *there were* Gn 40:17 5945a
will station myself on the t of the hill Ex 17:9 7218
Hur went up to the t of the hill. Ex 17:10 7218
Sinai, to the t of the mountain; Ex 19:20 7218
Moses to the t of the mountain, Ex 19:20 7218
consuming fire on the mountain t. Ex 24:17 7218
the mercy seat on t of the ark, Ex 25:21 4605
to its t to the first ring; Ex 26:24 7218
at its t in the middle of it; Ex 28:32 7218
its t and its sides all around, Ex 30:3 1406
to Me on the t of the mountain. Ex 34:2 7218
to its t to the first ring; Ex 36:29 7218
its t and its sides all around, Ex 37:26 1406
opening of the robe was *at the* t Ex 39:23
covering of the tent on t of it, Ex 40:19 4605
the mercy seat on t of the ark. Ex 40:20 4605
on the t or on the front of it. Lv 13:55 7146
porpoise skin that is on t of it, Nu 4:25 4605
died there on the mountain t. Nu 20:28 7218
at the t of Pisgah which overlooks Nu 21:20 7218
I see him from the t of the rocks, Nu 23:9 7218
of Zophim, to the t of Pisgah, Nu 23:14 7218
Balak took Balaam to the t of Peor Nu 23:28 7218
'Go up to the t of Pisgah and lift Dt 3:27 7218
to Mount Nebo, to the t of Pisgah, Dt 34:1 7218
went up to the t of the mountain Jos 15:8 7218
From the t of the mountain the Jos 15:9 7218

altar to the LORD your God on the **t** Jg 6:26 7218
stood on the **t** of Mount Gerizim, Jg 9:7 7218
up to the **t** of the mountain which is Jg 16:3 7218
and stood on **t** of the mountain at 1Sa 26:13 7218
stood on the **t** of a certain hill. 2Sa 2:25 7218
were on the **t** of the pillars; 1Ki 7:17 7218
were on the **t** of the pomegranates; 1Ki 7:18 7218
which *were* on the **t** of the pillars in 1Ki 7:19 7218
On the **t** of the pillars was 1Ki 7:22 7218
and the sea *was set* on **t** of them, 1Ki 7:25 4605
the crown at the **t** *was* a cubit, 1Ki 7:31 4605
On the **t** of the stand *there* 1Ki 7:35 7218
and on the **t** of the stand its 1Ki 7:35 7218
were on the **t** of the two pillars, 1Ki 7:41 7218
were on the **t** of the pillars; 1Ki 7:41 7218
round **t** to the throne at its rear, 1Ki 10:19 7218
Elijah went up to the **t** of Carmel; 1Ki 18:42 7218
was sitting on the **t** of the hill. 2Ki 1:9 7218
on the **t** of each *was* five cubits. 2Ch 3:15 7218
and the sea *was set* on **t** of them and 2Ch 4:4 4605
two capitals on **t** of the pillars, 2Ch 4:12 7218
which were on **t** of the pillars, 2Ch 4:12 7218
them to the **t** of the cliff and 2Ch 25:12 7218
them down from the **t** of the cliff 2Ch 25:12 7218
of Judah come up on **t** of the wall, Ne 12:31
4480, 5921
to the right on **t** of the wall toward Ne 12:31
4480, 5921
and touched the **t** of the scepter. Es 5:2 7218
the earth on **t** of the mountains; Ps 72:16 7218
t of the heights beside the way, Pr 8:2 7218
who lies down on the **t** of a mast. Pr 23:34 7218
left as a flag on a mountain **t** And Is 30:17 7218
place at the **t** of every street and Ezk 16:25 7218
on **t** of all your *other* abominations. Ezk 16:43 5921
and took away the **t** of the cedar. Ezk 17:3 6788
a sprig from the lofty **t** of the cedar Ezk 17:22 6788
And its **t** was among the clouds. Ezk 31:3 6788
and has set its **t** among the clouds, Ezk 31:10 6788
nor set their **t** among the clouds, Ezk 31:14 6788
entire area on the **t** of the mountain Ezk 43:12 7218
gold with its bowl on the **t** of it, Zch 4:2 7218
lamps which are on the **t** of it; Zch 4:2 7218
he will bring forth the **t** stone with Zch 4:7 7222
was torn in two from **t** to bottom; Mt 27:51 *509*
was torn in two from **t** to bottom. Mk 15:38 *509*
leaning on the **t** of his staff. Heb 11:21 *206*

TOPAZ

be a row of ruby, **t** and emerald; Ex 28:17 6357
first row *was* a row of ruby, **t**, Ex 39:10 6357
"The **t** of Ethiopia cannot equal Jb 28:19 6357
The ruby, the **t** and the diamond; Ezk 28:13 6357
the ninth, **t**; the tenth, chrysoprase; Rv 21:20 *5116*

TOPHEL

between Paran and **T** and Laban and Dt 1:1 8603

TOPHETH

He also defiled **T**, which is in the 2Ki 23:10 8612
For **T** has long been ready, Indeed, Is 30:33 8613
have built the high places of **T**, Jer 7:31 8612
"when it will no longer be called **T**, Jer 7:32 8612
for they will bury in **T** because Jer 7:32 8612
T or the valley of Ben-hinnom, Jer 19:6 8612
and they will bury in **T** because Jer 19:11 8612
"so as to make this city like **T**. Jer 19:12 8612
will be defiled like the place **T**, Jer 19:13 8612
Then Jeremiah came from **T**, Jer 19:14 8612

TOPMOST

or three olives on the **t** bough, Is 17:6
7218, 534
plucked off the **t** of its young twigs Ezk 17:4 7218
pluck from the **t** of its young twigs Ezk 17:22 7218

TOPPLE

in order to **t** the wall. 2Sa 20:15 5307

TOPS

the **t** of the mountains became Gn 8:5 7218
their **t** and their bands with gold; Ex 36:38 7218
and the overlaying of their **t**, Ex 38:17 7218
and the overlaying of their **t** and Ex 38:19 7218
their **t** and made bands for them. Ex 38:28 7218
him on the **t** of the mountains, Jg 9:25 7218
from the **t** of the mountains." Jg 9:36 7218
in the **t** of the balsam trees, 2Sa 5:24 7218
to set on the **t** of the pillars; 1Ki 7:16 7218
were on the **t** of the pillars; 1Ki 7:42 6440
in the **t** of the balsam trees, 1Ch 14:15 7218
them on the **t** of the pillars; 2Ch 3:16 7218
the **t** of the heights of the city: Pr 9:3 1610
joy from the **t** of the mountains. Is 42:11 7218
on all the **t** of the mountains, Ezk 6:13 7218
sacrifices on the **t** of the mountains Hos 4:13 7218
leap on the **t** of the mountains, Jl 2:5 7218
lodge in the **t** of her pillars; Zph 2:14 3730

TORCH

and a flaming **t** which passed between Gn 15:17 3940
and put one **t** in the middle Jg 15:4 3940
like a **t** that is burning. Is 62:1 3940
and a flaming **t** among sheaves, Zch 12:6 3940
from heaven, burning like a **t**, Rv 8:10 *2985*

TORCHES

them, with **t** inside the pitchers. Jg 7:16 3940
they held the **t** in their left Jg 7:20 3940
three hundred foxes, and took **t**, Jg 15:4 3940
When he had set fire to the **t**, Jg 15:5 3940
"Out of his mouth go burning **t**; Jb 41:19 3940
like **t** darting back and forth Ezk 1:13 3940
his eyes were like flaming **t**, Da 10:6 3940
Their appearance is like **t**, Na 2:4 3940
with lanterns and **t** and weapons. Jn 18:3 *2985*

TORE

so he **t** his garments. Gn 37:29 7167
So Jacob **t** his clothes, and put Gn 37:34 7167
Then they **t** their clothes, and Gn 44:13 7167
Then all the people **t** off the gold Ex 32:3 6561
out the land, **t** their clothes; Nu 14:6 7167
Then Joshua **t** his clothes and fell Jos 7:6 7167
He **t** down the tower of Penuel Jg 8:17 5422
he **t** his clothes and said, Jg 11:35 7167
so that he **t** him as one tears a Jg 14:6 8156
the edge of his robe, and it **t**. 1Sa 15:27 7167
hold of his clothes and **t** them, 2Sa 1:11 7167
and **t** her long-sleeved garment 2Sa 13:19 7167
t his clothes and lay on the 2Sa 13:31 7167
him and **t** it into twelve pieces. 1Ki 11:30 7167
and **t** the kingdom away from the 1Ki 14:8 7167
that he **t** his clothes and put on 1Ki 21:27 7167
clothes and **t** them in two pieces. 2Ki 2:12 7167
t up forty-two lads of their number. 2Ki 2:24 1234
he **t** his clothes and said, 2Ki 5:7 7167
he **t** his clothes 2Ki 6:30 7167
Athaliah **t** her clothes and cried, 2Ki 11:14 7167
the house of Baal, and **t** it down; 2Ki 11:18 5422
t down the wall of Jerusalem from 2Ki 14:13 6555
heard *it*, he **t** his clothes, 2Ki 19:1 7167
of the law, he **t** his clothes. 2Ki 22:11 7167
places, **t** down the *sacred* pillars, 2Ch 14:3 7665
Athaliah **t** her clothes and said, 2Ch 23:13 7167
the house of Baal and **t** it down, 2Ch 23:17 5422
and **t** down the wall of Jerusalem 2Ch 25:23 6555
They **t** down the altars of the 2Ch 34:4 5422
he also **t** down the altars and beat 2Ch 34:7 5422
of the law, he **t** his clothes. 2Ch 34:19 7167
before Me, **t** your clothes and 2Ch 34:27 7167
I **t** my garment and my robe, Ezr 9:3 7167
had been done, he **t** his clothes, Es 4:1 7167
t his robe and shaved his head, Jb 1:20 7167
And each of them **t** his robe and Jb 2:12 7167
And **t** down houses to fortify Is 22:10 5422
heard *it*, he **t** his clothes, Is 37:1 7167
your yoke *And* **t** off your bonds; Jer 2:20 5423
You broke and **t** all their hands; Ezk 29:7 1234
His anger also **t** continually, And Am 1:11 2963
The lion **t** enough for his cubs, Na 2:12 2963
Then the high priest **t** his robes and Mt 26:65 *1284*
they **t** their robes and rushed out Ac 14:14 *1284*
magistrates **t** their robes off them and Ac 16:22 *4048*

TORMENT

"How long will you **t** me And Jb 19:2 3013
You will lie down in **t**. Is 50:11 4620
here to **t** us before the time?" Mt 8:29 *928*
implore You by God, do not **t** me!" Mk 5:7 *928*
I beg You, do not **t** me." Lk 8:28 *928*
he lifted up his eyes, being in **t**, Lk 16:23 *931*
also come to this place of **t**.' Lk 16:28 *931*
a messenger of Satan to **t** me—to 2Co 12:7 *2852*
anyone, but to **t** for five months; Rv 9:5 *928*
and their **t** was like the torment Rv 9:5 *929*
torment was like the **t** of a scorpion Rv 9:5 *929*
the smoke of their **t** goes up forever Rv 14:11 *929*
degree give her **t** and mourning; Rv 18:7 *929*
because of the fear of her **t**, Rv 18:10 *929*
because of the fear of her **t**, Rv 18:15 *929*

TORMENTED

fearfully **t**." Mt 8:6 *928*
felt *his* righteous soul **t** day 2Pe 2:8 *928*
t those who dwell on the earth. Rv 11:10 *928*
and he will be **t** with fire and Rv 14:10 *928*
and they will be **t** day and night Rv 20:10 *928*

TORMENTORS

of us songs, And our **t** mirth, Ps 137:3 8437
put it into the hand of your **t**, Is 51:23 3013

TORN

"That which was **t** *of beasts* I did Gn 31:39 2966
has surely been **t** to pieces!" Gn 37:33 2963
"Surely he is **t** in pieces," Gn 44:28 2963
"If it is all **t** to pieces, let Ex 22:13 2963
for what has been **t** to pieces. Ex 22:13 2966
flesh **t** to pieces in the field; Ex 22:31 2966
of mail, so that it will not be **t**. Ex 28:32 7167
opening, so that it would not be **t**. Ex 39:23 7167
the fat of an animal **t** *by beasts* may Lv 7:24 2966
infection, his clothes shall be **t**, Lv 13:45 6533
after he has **t** out the stones and Lv 14:43 2502a
which dies or is **t** *by beasts*, Lv 17:15 2966
which dies or is **t** *by beasts*, Lv 22:8 2966
bruised or crushed or **t** or cut, Lv 22:24 5423
donkey shall be **t** away from you, Dt 28:31 1497
and you will be **t** from the land Dt 28:63 5255
worn-out and **t** and mended, Jos 9:4 1234
were new, and behold, they are **t**; Jos 9:13 1234
the altar of Baal was **t** down, Jg 6:28 5422
he has **t** down the altar of Baal, Jg 6:30 5422
someone has **t** down his altar." Jg 6:31 5422
because he had **t** down his altar. Jg 6:32 5422
clothes **t** and dust on his head. 1Sa 4:12 7167
"The LORD has **t** the kingdom of 1Sa 15:28 7167
for the LORD has **t** the kingdom out 1Sa 28:17 7167
clothes **t** and dust on his head. 2Sa 1:2 7167
were standing by with clothes **t**. 2Sa 13:31 7167
Archite met him with his coat **t** and 2Sa 15:32 7167
which has **t** him and killed him, 1Ki 13:26 7665
eaten the body nor **t** the donkey. 1Ki 13:28 7665
of the LORD which had been **t** down. 1Ki 18:30 2040
t down Your altars and killed Your 1Ki 19:10 2040
t down Your altars and killed Your 1Ki 19:14 2040
king of Israel had **t** his clothes, 2Ki 5:8 7167
"Why have you **t** your clothes? 2Ki 5:8 7167
When He had **t** Israel from the 2Ki 17:21 7167
came to Hezekiah with their clothes **t** 2Ki 18:37 7167
and you have **t** your clothes and 2Ki 22:19 7167
with my garment and my robe **t**, Ezr 9:5 7167
anger has **t** me and hunted me down, Jb 16:9 2963
are past, my plans are **t** apart, Jb 17:11 5423
t from the security of his tent, Jb 18:14 5423
given us to be **t** by their teeth. Ps 124:6 2964
mouth of the wicked it is **t** down. Pr 11:11 2040
strands is not quickly **t** apart. Ec 4:12 5423
Nor any of its cords be **t** apart. Is 33:20 5423
came to Hezekiah with their clothes **t** Is 36:22 7167
out of them will be **t** in pieces, Jer 5:6 2963
clothes **t** and their bodies gashed, Jer 41:5 7167
Her walls have been **t** down. Jer 50:15 2040
aside my ways and **t** me to pieces; La 3:11 6582
died of itself or was **t** by beasts, Ezk 4:14 2966
Its strong branch was **t** off So that Ezk 19:12 6561
And her foundations are **t** down. Ezk 30:4 2040
death or has been **t** to pieces. Ezk 44:31 2966
you will be **t** limb from limb and Da 2:5 5648
Meshach and Abed-nego shall be **t** Da 3:29 5648
For He has **t** *us*, but He will heal Hos 6:1 2963
desolate, The barns are **t** down, Jl 1:17 2040
prey And his dens with **t** flesh. Na 2:12 2966
which will not be **t** down." Mt 24:2 *2647*
the veil of the temple was **t** in two Mt 27:51 *4977*
chains had been **t** apart by him and Mk 5:4 *1288*
which will not be **t** down." Mk 13:2 *2647*
was **t** in two from top to bottom. Mk 15:38 *4977*
which will not be **t** down." Lk 21:6 *2647*
veil of the temple was **t** in two. Lk 23:45 *4977*
were so many, the net was not **t**. Jn 21:11 *4977*
was afraid Paul would be **t** to pieces Ac 23:10 *1288*
THEY HAVE **T** DOWN YOUR ALTARS, Ro 11:3 *2679*
tent which is our house is **t** down, 2Co 5:1 *2647*

TORRENT

"The **t** of Kishon swept them away, Jg 5:21 5158a
swept them away, The ancient **t**, Jg 5:21 5158a
The ancient torrent, the **t** Kishon. Jg 5:21 5158a
and Jabin at the **t** of Kishon, Ps 83:9 5158a
breath is like an overflowing **t**, Is 30:28 5158a
the LORD, like a **t** of brimstone, Is 30:33 5158a
north And become an overflowing **t**, Jer 47:2 5158a
the **t** burst against that house and Lk 6:48 *4215*
and the **t** burst against it and Lk 6:49 *4215*

TORRENTIAL

who are with him, a **t** rain, Ezk 38:22 7857

TORRENTS

t of destruction overwhelmed me; 2Sa 22:5 5158a
Like the **t** of wadis which vanish, Jb 6:15 650
Its **t** wash away the dust of the Jb 14:19 5599a
the **t** of ungodliness terrified me. Ps 18:4 5158a
broke open springs and **t**; Ps 74:15 5158a

TORTURED

and others were **t**, not accepting Heb 11:35 *5178*

TORTURERS

handed him over to the **t** until he Mt 18:34 *930*

TOSS

its waters **t** up refuse and mud. Is 57:20 1644
Though the waves **t**, Jer 5:22 1607

TOSSED

the Nile, And it will be **t** about And Am 8:8 1644
t here and there by waves and Eph 4:14 *2831*
the sea, driven and **t** by the wind. Jas 1:6 *4494*

TOSSES

And **t** me into the hands of the Jb 16:11 3399

TOSSING

And I am continually **t** until dawn. Jb 7:4 5076
But the wicked are like the **t** sea, Is 57:20 1644
cloaks and **t** dust into the air, Ac 22:23 *906*

TOTAL

"The **t** of the numbered men of the Nu 2:9 3605
"The **t** of the numbered men of the Nu 2:16 3605
"The **t** of the numbered men of the Nu 2:24 3605
"The **t** of the numbered men of the Nu 2:31 3605
the **t** of the numbered men of the Nu 2:32 3605
The **t** number of the heads of the 2Ch 26:12 3605

TOTALED

areas along the east *side* **t** a Ezk 41:14

TOTALLY

was ruined, it was **t** worthless. Jer 13:7 3605
waistband which is **t** worthless. Jer 13:10 3605
t destroy the house of Jacob," Am 9:8 8045
His arm will be **t** withered And Zch 11:17 3001

TOTTER

it will not **t** forever and ever. Ps 104:5 4131
They **t** *when rendering* judgment. Is 28:7 6328
prepare an idol that will not **t**. Is 40:20 4131
with nails, *So that* it will not **t**. Is 41:7 4131
hammers So that it will not **t**. Jer 10:4 6328

TOTTERED

made an uproar, the kingdoms **t**; Ps 46:6 4131

TOTTERING

words have helped the **t** to stand, Jb 4:4 3782
a leaning wall, like a **t** fence? Ps 62:3 1760

TOTTERS

Heal its breaches, for it **t**. Ps 60:2 4131
a drunkard And it **t** like a shack, Is 24:20 5110

TOU

Now when **T** king of Hamath heard 1Ch 18:9 8583
Hadadezer had been at war with **T**. 1Ch 18:10 8583

TOUCH

'You shall not eat from it or **t** it, Gn 3:3 5060

therefore I did not let you t her. Gn 20:6 5060
mountain or t the border of it; Ex 19:12 5060
'No hand shall t him, but he shall Ex 19:13 5060
their flesh nor t their carcasses; Lv 11:8 5060
shall not t any consecrated thing, Lv 12:4 5060
not t the holy objects and die. Nu 4:15 5060
t nothing that belongs to them, Nu 16:26 5060
their flesh nor t their carcasses. Dt 14:8 5060
Israel, and now we cannot t them. Jos 9:19 5060
the servants not to t you. Ru 2:9 5060
and he will not t you anymore." 2Sa 14:10 5060
"Do not t My anointed ones, And 1Ch 16:22 5060
hand now and t all that he has; Jb 1:11 5060
now, and t his bone and his flesh; Jb 2:5 5060
Even in seven evil will not t you. Jb 5:19 5060
"My soul refuses to t them; Jb 6:7 5060
"Do not t My anointed ones, And Ps 105:15 5060
T the mountains, that they may Ps 144:5 5060
out from there, T nothing unclean; Is 52:11 5060
no one could t their garments. La 4:14 5060
"Depart, depart, do not t!" La 4:15 5060
not t any man on whom is the mark; Ezk 9:6 5066
"If I only t His garment, I will Mt 9:21 681
just t the fringe of His cloak; Mt 14:36 681
around Him in order to t Him. Mk 3:10 681
"If I just t His garments, I Mk 5:28 681
just t the fringe of His cloak; Mk 6:56 681
Jesus and implored Him to t him. Mk 8:22 681
to Him so that He might t them; Mk 10:13 681
people were trying to t Him, Lk 6:19 681
"Someone did t Me, for I was Lk 8:46 681
will not even t the burdens with one Lk 11:46 4379
to Him so that He would t them, Lk 18:15 681
t Me and see, for a spirit does Lk 24:39 5584
good for a man not to t a woman. 1Co 7:1 681
"AND DO NOT T WHAT IS UNCLEAN 2Co 6:17 681
handle, do not taste, do not t!" Col 2:21 2345
the firstborn would not t them. Heb 11:28 2345
and the evil one does not t him. 1Jn 5:18 681

TOUCHED

just as we have not t you and have Gn 26:29 5060
him, he t the socket of his thigh; Gn 32:25 5060
because he t the socket of Jacob's Gn 32:32 5060
and on the one who t the bone or Nu 19:18 5060
and whoever has t any slain, Nu 31:19 5060
to Maralah, it then t Dabbesheth and Jos 19:11 6293
the south and t Asher on the west, Jos 19:34 6293
t the meat and the unleavened bread; Jg 6:21 5060
hearts God had t went with him. 1Sa 10:26 5060
a second time and t him and said, 1Ki 19:7 5060
And when the man t the bones of 2Ki 13:21 5060
cubits, t the wall of the house, 2Ch 3:11 5060
t the wing of the other cherub. 2Ch 3:11 5060
cubits, t the wall of the house; 2Ch 3:12 5060
near and t the top of the scepter. Es 5:2 5060
He t my mouth with it and said, Is 6:7 5060
"Behold, this has t your lips; Is 6:7 5060
out His hand and t my mouth, Jer 1:9 5060
How it has t your heart!" Jer 4:18 5060
their wings t one another; Ezk 1:9 2266
he t me and made me stand upright. Da 8:18 5060
a hand t me and set me trembling Da 10:10 5060
t me again and strengthened me. Da 10:18 5060
stretched out His hand and t him, Mt 8:3 681
He t her hand, and the fever Mt 8:15 681
Him and t the fringe of His cloak; Mt 9:20 681
Then He t their eyes, saying, Mt 9:29 681
and as many as t it were cured. Mt 14:36 681
came to them and t them and said, Mt 17:7 681
compassion, Jesus t their eyes; Mt 20:34 681
stretched out His hand and t him, Mk 1:41 681
crowd behind Him and t His cloak. Mk 5:27 681
"Who t My garments?" Mk 5:30 681
and You say, 'Who t Me?' " Mk 5:31 681
as many as t it were being cured. Mk 6:56 681
He t his tongue with the saliva; Mk 7:33 681
stretched out His hand and t him, Lk 5:13 681
And He came up and t the coffin; Lk 7:14 681
and t the fringe of His cloak, Lk 8:44 681
"Who is the one who t Me?" Lk 8:45 681
the reason why she had t Him, Lk 8:47 681
And He t his ear and healed him. Lk 22:51 681
come to a mountain that can be t Heb 12:18 5584
what we have looked at and t with our 1Jn 1:1 5584

TOUCHES

"He who t this man or his wife Gn 26:11 5060
whoever t the mountain shall Ex 19:12 5060
whatever t the altar shall be holy. Ex 29:37 5060
whatever t them shall be holy. Ex 30:29 5060
if a person t any unclean thing, Lv 5:2 5060
'Or if he t human uncleanness, of Lv 5:3 5060
Whoever t them will become Lv 6:18 5060
'Anyone who t its flesh will Lv 6:27 5060
'Also the flesh that t anything Lv 7:19 5060
When anyone t anything unclean, Lv 7:21 5060
whoever t their carcasses becomes Lv 11:24 5060
whoever t them becomes unclean. Lv 11:26 5060
whoever t their carcasses becomes Lv 11:27 5060
whoever t them when they are dead Lv 11:31 5060
though the one who t their carcass Lv 11:36 5060
the one who t its carcass becomes Lv 11:39 5060
who t his bed shall wash his Lv 15:5 5060
'Also whoever t the person with Lv 15:7 5060
'Whoever then t any of the things Lv 15:10 5060
the one with the discharge t without Lv 15:11 5060
the person with the discharge t Lv 15:12 5060
and whoever t her shall be unclean Lv 15:19 5060
'Anyone who t her bed shall Lv 15:21 5060
'Whoever t any thing on which Lv 15:22 5060
she is sitting, when he t it, Lv 15:23 5060
whoever t them shall be unclean Lv 15:27 5060
And if one t anything made unclean Lv 22:4 5060
or if a man t any teeming things by Lv 22:5 5060
a person who t any such shall be Lv 22:6 5060
'The one who t the corpse of any Nu 19:11 5060
'Anyone who t a corpse, the body Nu 19:13 5060
anyone who in the open field t one Nu 19:16 5060
and he who t the water for Nu 19:21 5060
unclean person t shall be unclean; Nu 19:22 5060
and the person who t it shall be Nu 19:22 5060
a string of tow snaps when it t fire. Jg 16:9 7381a
But the man who t them Must be 2Sa 23:7 5060
It t you, and you are dismayed. Jb 4:5 5060
And his head t the clouds, Jb 20:6 5060
He t the mountains, and they smoke. Ps 104:32 5060
Whoever t her will not go Pr 6:29 5060
whereas a sword t the throat." Jer 4:10 5060
who t the land so that it melts, Am 9:5 5060
and t bread with this fold, Hg 2:12 5060
one who is unclean from a corpse t Hg 2:13 5060
plunder you, for he who t you, Zch 2:8 5060
you, t the apple of His eye. Zch 2:8 5060
"IF EVEN A BEAST T THE MOUNTAIN, Heb 12:20 2345

TOUCHING

of the one was t the one wall, 1Ki 6:27 5060
other cherub was t the other wall. 1Ki 6:27 5060
So their wings were t each other 1Ki 6:27 5060
behold, there was an angel t him, 1Ki 19:5 5060
each had two t another being, and Ezk 1:11 2266
the living beings t one another and Ezk 3:13 5401a
whole earth without t the ground; Da 8:5 5060
a human being was t my lips; Da 10:16 5060
person this woman is who is t Him, Lk 7:39 681

TOUGHNESS

it will have in it the t of iron, Da 2:41 5326

TOW

snapped the cords as a string of t Jg 16:9 5296

TOWARD

God planted a garden t the east, Gn 2:8 4480
The dove came to him t evening Gn 8:11
from Sidon as you go t Gerar, Gn 10:19
as you go t Sodom and Gomorrah and Gn 10:19
from Mesha as you go t Sephar, Gn 10:30
on, continuing t the Negev. Gn 12:9
"Now look t the heavens, and Gn 15:5
there, and looked down t Sodom; Gn 18:16 5921, 6440
away from there and went t Sodom, Gn 18:22
looked down t Sodom and Gomorrah, Gn 19:28 5921, 6440
and t all the land of the valley, Gn 19:28 5921, 6440
there t the land of the Negev, Gn 20:1
and His truth t my master; Gn 24:27 4480, 5973
meditate in the field t evening; Gn 24:63 6437
of Egypt as one goes t Assyria; Gn 25:18
from Beersheba and went t Haran. Gn 28:10
made the flocks face t the striped Gn 30:40 413
not friendly t him as formerly. Gn 31:2 5973
is not friendly t me as formerly, Gn 31:5 413
face t the hill country of Gilead. Gn 31:21
his right hand t Israel's left, Gn 48:13 4480
his left hand t Israel's right, Gn 48:13 4480
And his flank shall be t Sidon. Gn 49:13 5921
and let Moses throw it t the sky Ex 9:8
and Moses threw it t the sky, Ex 9:10
"Stretch out your hand t the sky, Ex 9:22 5921
stretched out his staff t the sky, Ex 9:23 5921
"Stretch out your hand t the sky, Ex 10:21 5921
stretched out his hand t the sky, Ex 10:22 5921
a change of heart t the people, Ex 14:5 413
that they looked t the wilderness, Ex 16:10 413
presumptuously t his neighbor, Ex 21:14 5921
do not be rebellious t him, Ex 23:21
are to be turned t the mercy seat. Ex 25:20 413
of the tabernacle t the south; Ex 26:35
is t the inner side of the ephod. Ex 28:26 413
bow low t the earth and worship. Ex 34:8 413
with their faces t each other; Ex 37:9 413
cherubim were t the mercy seat. Ex 37:9 413
lifted up his hands t the people Lv 9:22 413
'So I will turn t you and make you Lv 26:9 413
camp on the east side t the sunrise Nu 2:3
the tent of meeting t the sunrise, Nu 3:38
As Aaron turned t Miriam, behold, Nu 12:10 413
they turned t the tent of meeting, Nu 16:42 413
t the front of the tent of meeting Nu 19:4 413
he set his face t the wilderness. Nu 24:1 413
side of the Jordan t the east." Nu 32:19
t the LORD and toward Israel, Nu 32:22 4480
toward the LORD and t Israel, Nu 32:22 4480
eastward t the sunrising." Nu 34:15
having enmity t him in time past; Dt 4:42
west of the way t the sunset, Dt 11:30
act like this t the LORD your God. Dt 12:4
behave thus t the LORD your God, Dt 12:31
is hostile t your poor brother, Dt 15:9
shall be hostile t his brother and Dt 28:54
his brother and t the wife he cherishes Dt 28:54
t the rest of his children who remain, Dt 28:54
shall be hostile t the husband she Dt 28:56
and t her son and daughter, Dt 28:56
and t her afterbirth which issues Dt 28:57
and t her children whom she bears; Dt 28:57
"They have acted corruptly t Him, Dt 32:5
Sea t the setting of the sun will Jos 1:4
beyond the Jordan t the sunrise." Jos 1:15
down t the sea of the Arabah, Jos 3:16 5921
javelin that is in your hand t Ai, Jos 8:18 413
that was in his hand t the city. Jos 8:18 413
coast of the Great Sea t Lebanon, Jos 9:1 413, 4136
Mount Halak, that rises t Seir, Jos 11:17
beyond the Jordan t the sunrise, Jos 12:1
the Sea of Chinneroth t the east, Jos 12:3
Sea, eastward t Beth-jeshimoth, Jos 12:3 1870
beyond the Jordan t the west, Jos 12:7
Mount Halak, which rises t Seir; Jos 12:7
and all of Lebanon, t the east, Jos 13:5
and turned northward t Gilgal Jos 15:7 413
the valley of Rephaim t the north. Jos 15:8
sons of Judah t the border of Edom Jos 15:21 413
from Sarid to the east t the sunrise Jos 19:12
t the sunrise to Gath-hepher, Jos 19:13
It turned t the east to Beth-dagon Jos 19:27
to Judah at the Jordan t the east. Jos 19:34
Sea t the setting of the sun. Jos 23:4
as far as Beth-shittah t Zererah, Jg 7:22
Then their anger t him subsided Jg 8:3 4480, 5921
went up from the altar t heaven, Jg 13:20
a young lion came roaring t him. Jg 14:5 7122
t the direction of the wilderness, Jg 20:42 413
down opposite Gibeah t the east. Jg 20:43 4480
rest turned and fled t the wilderness Jg 20:45
men turned and fled t the wilderness Jg 20:47
Samuel was coming out t them to go 1Sa 9:14 7122
one company turned t Ophrah, 1Sa 13:17 413, 1870
company turned t Beth-horon, 1Sa 13:18 1870
company turned t the border which 1Sa 13:18 1870
valley of Zeboim t the wilderness. 1Sa 13:18
David ran quickly t the battle line 1Sa 17:48
if there is good feeling t David, 1Sa 20:12 413
his men were coming down t her; 1Sa 25:20 7122
Uzzah reached out t the ark of God 2Sa 6:6 413
heart was inclined t Absalom. 2Sa 14:1 5921
over t the way of the wilderness. 2Sa 15:23 5921, 6440
"I was also blameless t Him, 2Sa 22:24
of the valley of Gad and t Jazer. 2Sa 24:5 413
stretched out his hand t Jerusalem 2Sa 24:16
his servants crossing over t him; 2Sa 24:20 5921
and uprightness of heart t You; 1Ki 3:6 5973
of the house eastward t the south. 1Ki 7:39 4480, 4136
and spread out his hands t heaven. 1Ki 8:22
open t this house night and day, 1Ki 8:29 413
t the place of which You have 1Ki 8:29 413
servant shall pray t this place. 1Ki 8:29 413
when they pray t this place; 1Ki 8:30 413
and they pray t this place and 1Ki 8:35 413
spreading his hands t this house; 1Ki 8:38 413
he comes and prays t this house, 1Ki 8:42 413
and they pray to the LORD t the city 1Ki 8:44 1870
and pray to You t their land 1Ki 8:48 1870
with his hands spread t heaven. 1Ki 8:54
good was found t the LORD God 1Ki 14:13 413
"Go up now, look t the sea." 1Ki 18:43 1870
"Open the window t the east," 2Ki 13:17
side of the house t the southeast. 2Ch 4:10
and spread out his hands t heaven. 2Ch 6:13
open t this house day and night, 2Ch 6:20 413
t the place of which You have 2Ch 6:20 413
servant shall pray t this place. 2Ch 6:20 413
when they pray t this place; 2Ch 6:21 413
and they pray t this place and 2Ch 6:26 413
spreading his hands t this house, 2Ch 6:29 413
they come and pray t this house, 2Ch 6:32 413
and they pray to You t this city 2Ch 6:34 1870
and pray t their land which You 2Ch 6:38 1870
and t the house which I have built 2Ch 6:38
they looked t the multitude, 2Ch 20:24 413
heart of the king of Assyria t them Ezr 6:22 5921
front of the Water Gate t the east Ne 3:26
that they acted arrogantly t them, Ne 9:10 5921
top of the wall t the Refuse Gate. Ne 12:31
dust over their heads t the sky. Jb 2:12
me And increase Your anger t me; Jb 10:17 5973
They do not turn t the vineyards. Jb 24:18 1870
Stretching his wings t the south? Jb 39:26
eyes are continually t the LORD, Ps 25:15 413
up my hands t Your holy sanctuary. Ps 28:2 413
eyes of the LORD are t the righteous Ps 34:15 413
Be not envious t wrongdoers. Ps 37:1
have done, And Your thoughts t us; Ps 40:5 413
in His deeds t the sons of men. Ps 66:5 5921
footsteps t the perpetual ruins; Ps 74:3
heart was not steadfast t Him, Ps 78:37 5973
Your indignation t us to cease. Ps 85:4 5973
Your lovingkindness t me is great, Ps 86:13 5921
T evening it fades and withers Ps 90:6
t those who fear Him. Ps 103:11 5921
O LORD, in Your favor t Your people; Ps 106:4
LORD For all His benefits t me? Ps 116:12 5921
His lovingkindness is great t us, Ps 117:2 5921
I will bow down t Your holy temple Ps 138:2 413
For my eyes are t You, O GOD, the Ps 141:8 413
is t a servant who acts wisely, Pr 14:35
is t him who acts shamefully. Pr 14:35
wings Like an eagle that flies t Pr 23:5
Blowing t the south, Then turning Ec 1:6 413
south, Then turning t the north, Ec 1:6 413
heart directs him t the right, Ec 10:2
man's heart directs him t the left. Ec 10:2

t the south or toward the north,	Ec 11:3	
toward the south or t the north,	Ec 11:3	
Lebanon, Which faces t Damascus.	SS 7:4	6440
his heart inclines t wickedness:	Is 32:6	
goodness t the house of Israel,	Is 63:7	
compassion are restrained t me.	Is 63:15	413
will be indignant t His enemies.	Is 66:14	854
these words t the north and say,	Jer 3:12	
"Lift up a standard t Zion!	Jer 4:6	
examine my heart's *attitude* t You.	Jer 12:3	854
of the Horse Gate t the east,	Jer 31:40	
and he went out t the Arabah.	Jer 39:4	1870
he has become arrogant t the LORD;	Jer 48:26	5921
he has become arrogant t the LORD.	Jer 48:42	5921
heart and hands T God in heaven;	La 3:41	413
And no hands were turned t her.	La 4:6	
out straight, one t the other;	Ezk 1:23	413
set your face t it so that it is under	Ezk 4:3	413
your face t the siege of Jerusalem	Ezk 4:7	413
face t the mountains of Israel,	Ezk 6:2	413
than the wilderness t Diblah;	Ezk 6:14	
your eyes now t the north."	Ezk 8:5	1870
So I raised my eyes t the north,	Ezk 8:5	1870
LORD's house which *was* t the north;	Ezk 8:14	413
LORD and their faces t the east;	Ezk 8:16	
themselves eastward t the sun.	Ezk 8:16	
with its branches turned t him,	Ezk 17:6	413
this vine bent its roots t him and	Ezk 17:7	5921
and sent out its branches t him from	Ezk 17:7	
"Son of man, set your face t Teman,	Ezk 20:46	1870
of man, set your face t Jerusalem,	Ezk 21:2	413
set your face t the sons of Ammon and	Ezk 25:2	413
"Son of man, set your face t Sidon,	Ezk 28:21	413
face t Gog of the land of Magog,	Ezk 38:2	413
The guardrooms of the gate t	Ezk 40:10	1870
windows *looking* t the guardrooms,	Ezk 40:16	413
and t their side pillars within	Ezk 40:16	413
the gate which faced t the east;	Ezk 40:22	1870
Then he led me t the south, and	Ezk 40:24	1870
there was a gate t the south;	Ezk 40:24	1870
court had a gate t the south;	Ezk 40:27	1870
from gate to gate t the south,	Ezk 40:27	1870
porches *were* t the outer court;	Ezk 40:31	413
into the inner court t the east.	Ezk 40:32	1870
porches *were* t the outer court;	Ezk 40:34	
pillars *were* t the outer court;	Ezk 40:37	
up to the gateway t the north,	Ezk 40:40	
gate, with its front t the south,	Ezk 40:44	1870
the south gate facing t the north.	Ezk 40:44	1870
chamber which faces t the south,	Ezk 40:45	1870
the chamber which faces t the north	Ezk 40:46	1870
the side chambers t the free space	Ezk 41:11	
consisted of one doorway t the north	Ezk 41:11	1870
and another doorway t the south;	Ezk 41:11	
separate area at the side t the west	Ezk 41:12	1870
face t the palm tree on one side and	Ezk 41:19	413
a young lion's face t the palm tree	Ezk 41:19	413
outer court, the way t the north;	Ezk 42:1	1870
opposite the building t the north.	Ezk 42:1	413
t the outer court facing the	Ezk 42:7	1870
the wall of the court t the east,	Ezk 42:10	1870
the chambers which were t the south	Ezk 42:12	1870
in front of the wall t the east,	Ezk 42:12	1870
the gate which faced t the east and	Ezk 42:15	1870
gate, the gate facing t the east;	Ezk 43:1	1870
way of the gate facing t the east.	Ezk 43:4	1870
on the west side t the west and on	Ezk 45:7	
and on the east side t the east,	Ezk 45:7	
at the extreme rear t the west.	Ezk 46:19	
threshold of the house t the east,	Ezk 47:1	
When the man went out t the east	Ezk 47:3	
waters go out t the eastern region	Ezk 47:8	413
then they go t the sea, being made	Ezk 47:8	
and on the north t the north is	Ezk 47:17	
"The south side t the south	Ezk 47:19	
is the south side t the south.	Ezk 47:19	
t the north beside Hamath,	Ezk 48:1	
t the north 25,000 *cubits in*	Ezk 48:10	
t the west 10,000 in width,	Ezk 48:10	
width, t the east 10,000 in width,	Ezk 48:10	
and t the south 25,000 in length;	Ezk 48:10	
shall be 10,000 *cubits* t the east and	Ezk 48:18	
the east and 10,000 t the west;	Ezk 48:18	
the allotment t the east border	Ezk 48:21	5704
of the 25,000 t the west border,	Ezk 48:21	5921
at the south side t the south,	Ezk 48:28	
Israel, three gates t the north:	Ezk 48:31	
expression was altered t Shadrach,	Da 3:19	5922
raised my eyes t heaven and	Da 4:34	
he had windows open t Jerusalem);	Da 6:10	5049
and also t you, O king, I have	Da 6:22	6925
horns t the four winds of heaven.	Da 8:8	
exceedingly great t the south,	Da 8:9	413
toward the south, t the east,	Da 8:9	413
east, and t the Beautiful *Land.*	Da 8:9	413
I turned my face t the ground and	Da 10:15	
parceled out t the four points of the	Da 11:4	
face t the fortresses of his own land,	Da 11:19	
who act wickedly t the covenant,	Da 11:32	
right hand and his left t heaven,	Da 12:7	413
so I will also be t you."	Hos 3:3	413
direct their desire t their iniquity.	Hos 4:8	413
look again t Your holy temple.'	Jon 2:4	413
It hastens t the goal and it will	Hab 2:3	
tribes of Israel, are t the LORD),	Zch 9:1	
the mountain will move t the north	Zch 14:4	
and the other half t the south.	Zch 14:4	
half of them t the eastern sea and	Zch 14:8	413
the other half t the western sea;	Zch 14:8	413
and the people t whom the LORD is	Mal 1:4	
out His hand t His disciples,	Mt 12:49	*1909*
two fish, and looking up t heaven,	Mt 14:19	*1519*
on the water and came t Jesus.	Mt 14:29	*4314*
dawn t the first *day* of the week,	Mt 28:1	*1519*
two fish, and looking up t heaven,	Mk 6:41	*1519*
GENERATION T THOSE WHO FEAR HIM.	Lk 1:50	
displayed His great mercy t her;	Lk 1:58	*3326*
To show mercy t our fathers, And	Lk 1:72	*3326*
And turning His gaze t His disciples,	Lk 6:20	*1519*
Turning t the woman, He said	Lk 7:44	*4314*
He was traveling t Jerusalem.	Lk 9:53	*1519*
"The one who showed mercy t him."	Lk 10:37	*3326*
himself, and is not rich t God."	Lk 12:21	*1519*
us, for it is *getting* t evening,	Lk 24:29	*4314*
Jews and Greeks of repentance t God	Ac 20:21	*1519*
in their desire t one another,	Ro 1:27	*1519*
demonstrates His own love t us,	Ro 5:8	*1519*
set on the flesh is hostile t God;	Ro 8:7	*1519*
do not be arrogant t the branches;	Ro 11:18	*2620*
Be of the same mind t one another;	Ro 12:16	*1519*
unbecomingly t his virgin *daughter,*	1Co 7:36	*1909*
His grace t me did not prove vain;	1Co 15:10	*1519*
the world, and especially t you.	2Co 1:12	*4314*
we have through Christ t God.	2Co 3:4	*4314*
abounds all the more t you,	2Co 7:15	*1519*
you, but bold t you when absent!	2Co 10:1	*1519*
in me, and who is not weak t you,	2Co 13:3	*1519*
the power of God *directed* t you.	2Co 13:4	*1519*
of His power t us who believe.	Eph 1:19	*1519*
in kindness t us in Christ Jesus.	Eph 2:7	*1909*
I press on t the goal for the	Php 3:14	*1519*
with wisdom t outsiders,	Col 4:5	*4314*
your faith t God has gone forth,	1Th 1:8	*4314*
we behaved t you believers;	1Th 2:10	
you do practice it t all the brethren	1Th 4:10	*1519*
you will behave properly t outsiders	1Th 4:12	*4314*
love of each one of you t one another	2Th 1:3	*1519*
which you have t the Lord Jesus and	Phm 1:5	*4314*
Lord Jesus and t all the saints;	Phm 1:5	*1519*
dead works and of faith t God,	Heb 6:1	*1909*
which you have shown t His name,	Heb 6:10	*1519*
with the world is hostility t God?	Jas 4:4	
if for the sake of conscience t God	1Pe 2:19	
"FOR THE EYES OF THE LORD ARE T	1Pe 3:12	*1909*
with humility t one another,	1Pe 5:5	
slowness, but is patient t you,	2Pe 3:9	*1519*

TOWEL

and taking a t, He girded Himself	Jn 13:4	*3012*
the t with which He was girded.	Jn 13:5	*3012*

TOWER

a t whose top *will reach* into heaven	Gn 11:4	4026
the t which the sons of men had built	Gn 11:5	4026
his tent beyond the t of Eder.	Gn 35:21	4029
safely, I will tear down this t."	Jg 8:9	4026
He tore down the t of Penuel	Jg 8:17	4026
all the leaders of the t of Shechem	Jg 9:46	4026
all the leaders of the t of Shechem	Jg 9:47	4026
men of the t of Shechem also died,	Jg 9:49	4026
a strong t in the center of the city,	Jg 9:51	4026
they went up on the roof of the t.	Jg 9:51	4026
to the t and fought against it,	Jg 9:52	4026
approached the entrance of the t	Jg 9:52	4026
is a t of deliverance to His king,	2Sa 22:51	4023a
the watchman was standing on the t	2Ki 9:17	4026
the wall to the T of the Hundred	Ne 3:1	4026
the Hundred *and* the T of Hananel.	Ne 3:1	4026
section and the T of Furnaces.	Ne 3:11	4026
the t projecting from the upper house	Ne 3:25	4026
the east and the projecting t.	Ne 3:26	4026
in front of the great projecting t	Ne 3:27	4026
the wall, above the T of Furnaces,	Ne 12:38	4026
the Fish Gate, the T of Hananel and	Ne 12:39	4026
Hananel and the T of the Hundred,	Ne 12:39	4026
A t of strength against the enemy.	Ps 61:3	4026
name of the LORD is a strong t;	Pr 18:10	4026
"Your neck is like the t of David	SS 4:4	4026
"Your neck is like a t of ivory,	SS 7:4	4026
nose is like the t of Lebanon,	SS 7:4	4026
Against every high t,	Is 2:15	4026
He built a t in the middle of it And	Is 5:2	4026
T of Hananel to the Corner Gate.	Jer 31:38	4026
"As for you, t of the flock,	Mi 4:8	4026
and from the T of Hananel to the	Zch 14:10	4026
A WINE PRESS IN IT, AND BUILT A T,	Mt 21:33	*4444*
THE WINE PRESS AND BUILT A T,	Mk 12:1	*4444*
eighteen on whom the t in Siloam fell	Lk 13:4	*4444*
you, when he wants to build a t,	Lk 14:28	*4444*

TOWERS

in the villages and in the t.	1Ch 27:25	4026
surround *them* with walls and t,	2Ch 14:7	4026
Uzziah built t in Jerusalem at the	2Ch 26:9	4026
He built t in the wilderness	2Ch 26:10	4026
to be on the t and on the corners for	2Ch 26:15	4026
and t on the wooded *hills.*	2Ch 27:4	4026
broken down and erected t on it,	2Ch 32:5	4026
and go around her; Count her t;	Ps 48:12	4026
wall, and my breasts were like t;	SS 8:10	4026
Hyenas will howl in their fortified t	Is 13:22	
erected their siege t,	Is 23:13	969a
raise up battle t against you.	Is 29:3	4694
great slaughter, when the t fall.	Is 30:25	4026
Where is he who counts the t?"	Is 33:18	4026
will come up in its fortified t,	Is 34:13	759
the fortified t of Ben-hadad."	Jer 49:27	759
heaven And t up to the very skies.	Jer 51:9	5375
'He destroyed their fortified t	Ezk 19:7	759
of Tyre and break down her t;	Ezk 26:4	4026
axes he will break down your t.	Ezk 26:9	4026
and the Gammadim were in your t.	Ezk 27:11	4026
cities And the high corner t.	Zph 1:16	6438
Their corner t are in ruins.	Zph 3:6	6438

TOWN

this t is near *enough* to flee to,	Gn 19:20	5892b
the t of which you have spoken.	Gn 19:21	5892b
the name of the t was called Zoar.	Gn 19:22	5892b
a t on the edge of your territory.	Nu 20:16	5892b
A flame from the t of Sihon;	Nu 21:28	7151
it to the alien who is in your t,	Dt 14:21	8179
the Levite who is in your t,	Dt 14:27	8179
and shall deposit *it* in your t.	Dt 14:28	8179
and the widow who are in your t,	Dt 14:29	8179
and the Levite who is in your t,	Dt 16:11	8179
and the alien who is in your t,	Dt 31:12	8179
full of noise, You boisterous t,	Is 22:2	5892b
The young men from the t squares.	Jer 9:21	7339
been deserted, The t of My joy!	Jer 49:25	7151
To the t and all its inhabitants.	Hab 2:8	7151
And founds a t with violence!	Hab 2:12	7151
To the t and all its inhabitants.	Hab 2:17	7151
Now *the* t *of* Bethel had sent	Zch 7:2	
stay there until you leave t.	Mk 6:10	*1564*
the crowd, the t clerk said,	Ac 19:35	*1122*

TOWNS

of Manasseh went and took its t,	Nu 32:41	2333
besides a great many unwalled t.	Dt 3:5	5892b
in any of your t in your land	Dt 15:7	8179
sacrifice the Passover in any of your t	Dt 16:5	8179
and the widow who are in your t.	Dt 16:14	8179
judges and officers in all your t	Dt 16:18	8179
in your midst, in any of your t,	Dt 17:2	8179
if a Levite comes from any of your t	Dt 18:6	8179
he shall choose in one of your t	Dt 23:16	8179
who is in your land in your t	Dt 24:14	8179
that they may eat in your t and	Dt 26:12	8179
"It shall besiege you in all your t	Dt 28:52	8179
and it shall besiege you in all your t	Dt 28:52	8179
will oppress you in all your t.	Dt 28:55	8179
enemy will oppress you in your t.	Dt 28:57	8179
of Bashan, and all the t of Jair,	Jos 13:30	2333
with its t and its villages;	Jos 15:45	1323
Ashdod, its t and its villages;	Jos 15:47	1323
Gaza, its t and its villages;	Jos 15:47	1323
Manasseh had Beth-shean and its t	Jos 17:11	1323
its towns and Ibleam and its t,	Jos 17:11	1323
the inhabitants of Dor and its t,	Jos 17:11	1323
inhabitants of En-dor and its t,	Jos 17:11	1323
inhabitants of Taanach and its t,	Jos 17:11	1323
inhabitants of Megiddo and its t,	Jos 17:11	1323
who are in Beth-shean and its t and	Jos 17:16	1323
the t of Jair, the son of Manasseh,	1Ki 4:13	2333
high places in all their t,	2Ki 17:9	5892b
Aram took the t of Jair from them,	1Ch 2:23	2333
in Gilead, in Bashan and in its t,	1Ch 5:16	1323
were Bethel with its t,	1Ch 7:28	1323
and to the west Gezer with its t,	1Ch 7:28	1323
and Shechem with its t as far as	1Ch 7:28	1323
towns as far as Ayyah with its t,	1Ch 7:28	1323
of Manasseh, Beth-shean with its t,	1Ch 7:29	1323
its towns, Taanach with its t,	1Ch 7:29	1323
its towns, Megiddo with its t,	1Ch 7:29	1323
with its towns, Dor with its t.	1Ch 7:29	1323
who built Ono and Lod, with its t;	1Ch 8:12	1323
took Gath and its t from the hand of	1Ch 18:1	1323
the tithes in all the rural t.	Ne 10:37	5892b
lived in Kiriath-arba and its t,	Ne 11:25	1323
and its towns, in Dibon and its t,	Ne 11:25	1323
in Beersheba and its t,	Ne 11:27	1323
Ziklag, in Meconah and in its t,	Ne 11:28	1323
and its fields, Azekah and its t.	Ne 11:30	1323
and Aija, at Bethel and its t,	Ne 11:31	1323
areas, who live in the rural t,	Es 9:19	5892b
to bring on this city and all its t the	Jer 19:15	5892b
And her t will be set on fire.	Jer 49:2	1323
go somewhere else to the t nearby,	Mk 1:38	*2969*

TRACE

so that not a t of them was found.	Da 2:35	870

TRACED

the one whose genealogy is not t	Heb 7:6	*1075*

TRACHONITIS

of the region of Ituraea and T,	Lk 3:1	*5139*

TRACKED

T with bloody *footprints.*	Hos 6:8	6121a

TRACKS

death And her t *lead* to the dead;	Pr 2:18	4570
there is no justice in their t;	Is 59:8	4570

TRACT

and who owned a t of land, sold it	Ac 4:37	*68*

TRADE

live and t in it and acquire	Gn 34:10	5503
them live in the land and t in it,	Gn 34:21	5503
and you may t in the land.'"	Gn 42:34	5503
by your t You have increased your	Ezk 28:5	7404
"By the abundance of your t You	Ezk 28:16	7404
In the unrighteousness of your t You	Ezk 28:18	7404
and because he was of the same t,	Ac 18:3	*3673*
for by t they were tent-makers.	Ac 18:3	*5078*
t of ours fall into disrepute,	Ac 19:27	*3313*

TRADED

"Dedan t with you in saddlecloths	Ezk 27:20	7402
Sheba and Raamah, they t with you;	Ezk 27:22	7402
Asshur *and* Chilmad t with you.	Ezk 27:23	7402
t with you in choice garments,	Ezk 27:24	7402
My people, T a boy for a harlot And	Jl 3:3	5414

went and t with them, and gained Mt 25:16 2038b
TRADERS
Then some Midianite t passed by, Gn 37:28 5503
besides *that* from the t and the 1Ki 10:15 376, 8446
the king's t procured them from 2Ch 1:16 5503
which the t and merchants brought; 2Ch 9:14 376, 8446
Once or twice the t and merchants Ne 13:20 7402
"Will the t bargain over him? Jb 41:6 2271
t were the honored of the earth? Is 23:8 3667b
he set it in a city of t. Ezk 17:4 7402
and Meshech, they were your t; Ezk 27:13 7402
"The sons of Dedan were your t. Ezk 27:15 7402
land of Israel, they were your t; Ezk 27:17 7402
"The t of Sheba and Raamah, they Ezk 27:22 7402
Canneh, Eden, the t of Sheba, Ezk 27:23 7402
You have increased your t more Na 3:16 7402
TRADES
with the workmen of similar t, Ac 19:25
TRADESMEN
them, And supplies belts to the t. Pr 31:24 3667b
TRADING
As to the riches of his t, Jb 20:18 8545
TRADITION
Me consists of t learned *by rote,* Is 29:13 4687, 376
break the t of the elders? Mt 15:2 *3862*
of God for the sake of your t? Mt 15:3 *3862*
of God for the sake of your t. Mt 15:6 *3862*
according to the t of the elders, Mk 7:5 *3862*
God, you hold to the t of men." Mk 7:8 *3862*
of God in order to keep your t. Mk 7:9 *3862*
your t which you have handed down; Mk 7:13 *3862*
according to the t of men, Col 2:8 *3862*
the t which you received from us. 2Th 3:6 *3862*
TRADITIONS
observing the t of the elders; Mk 7:3 *3862*
and hold firmly to the t, 1Co 11:2 *3862*
zealous for my ancestral t. Ga 1:14 *3862*
hold to the t which you were taught, 2Th 2:15 *3862*
TRAFFICKED
have t with you from your youth; Is 47:15 5503
TRAIL
Go forth on the t of the flock And SS 1:8 6119
TRAIN
T up a child in the way he should Pr 22:6 2596
with the t of His robe filling the Is 6:1 7757
horsemen in pairs, A t of donkeys, Is 21:7 7393
A train of donkeys, a t of camels, Is 21:7 7393
never again will they t for war. Mi 4:3 3925
TRAINED
captive, he led out his t men, Gn 14:14 2593
men of valor, men t for war, 1Ch 12:8 6635
who were t in singing to the LORD, 1Ch 25:7 3925
I t *and* strengthened their arms, Hos 7:15 3256
a t heifer that loves to thresh, Hos 10:11 3925
after he has been fully t, Lk 6:40 *2675*
senses t to discern good and evil. Heb 5:14 *1128*
to those who have been t by it, Heb 12:11 *1128*
souls, having a heart t in greed, 2Pe 2:14 *1128*
TRAINING
for t in righteousness; 2Tm 3:16 *3809*
TRAINS
"He t my hands for battle, So 2Sa 22:35 3925
He t my hands for battle, So that Ps 18:34 3925
my rock, Who t my hands for war, Ps 144:1 3925
TRAITOR
Judas Iscariot, who became a t. Lk 6:16 *4273*
TRAMPLE
Or that a wild beast may t them. Jb 39:15 1758
him t my life down to the ground And Ps 7:5 7429
Through Your name we will t down Ps 44:5 947
and the serpent you will t down. Ps 91:13 7429
pasturing oxen and for sheep to t. Is 7:25 4823
And to t them down like mud in the Is 10:6 4823
and I will t him on My mountains. Is 14:25 947
"The foot will t it, The feet of Is 26:6 7429
horses he will t all your streets. Ezk 26:11 7429
Hear this, you who t the needy, Am 8:4 7602b
devour and t on the sling stones; Zch 9:15 3533
or they will t them under their feet, Mt 7:6 *2662*
TRAMPLED
the people t on him at the gate, 2Ki 7:17 7429
the people t on him at the gate and 2Ki 7:20 7429
horses, and he t her under foot. 2Ki 9:33 7429
in Lebanon, and t the thorn bush. 2Ki 14:9 7429
in Lebanon and t the thorn bush. 2Ch 25:18 7429
O God, for man has t upon me; Ps 56:1 7602b
foes have t upon me all day long, Ps 56:2 7602b
Like a t spring and a polluted Pr 25:26 7511
wall and it will become t ground. Is 5:5 4823
of the pit Like a t corpse. Is 14:19 947
The lords of the nations have t Is 16:8 1986
My anger And t them in My wrath; Is 63:3 7429
They have t down My field; Jer 12:10 947
and t down the remainder with its Da 7:7 7512
and t down the remainder with its Da 7:19 7512
him to the ground and t on him, Da 8:7 7429
to the earth, and it t them down. Da 8:10 7429
holy place and the host to be t?" Da 8:13 4823
At that time she will be t down Like Mi 7:10 4823
In anger You t the nations. Hab 3:12 1758
You t on the sea with Your horses, Hab 3:15 1869
out and t under foot by men. Mt 5:13 *2662*
and it was t under foot and the Lk 8:5 *2662*
and Jerusalem will be t under foot Lk 21:24 *3961*
has t under foot the Son of God, Heb 10:29 *2662*
TRAMPLES
And t down the waves of the sea; Jb 9:8 1869
He reproaches him who t upon me. Ps 57:3 7602b
land, When he t on our citadels, Mi 5:5 1869
land And when he t our territory. Mi 5:6 1869
passes through, T down and tears, Mi 5:8 7429
TRAMPLING
T under foot the pieces of silver; Ps 68:30 7511
of you this t of My courts? Is 1:12 7429
Then you become its t *place.* Is 28:18 4823
TRANCE
preparations, he fell into a t; Ac 10:10 *1611*
and in a t I saw a vision, a Ac 11:5 *1611*
the temple, that I fell into a t, Ac 22:17 *1611*
TRANQUIL
A t heart is life to the body, But Pr 14:30 4832
so that we may lead a t and 1Tm 2:2 *2263*
TRANQUILITY
but he will come in a time of t Da 11:21 7962
"In a time of t he will enter the Da 11:24 7962
TRANSCRIBED
men of Hezekiah, king of Judah, t. Pr 25:1 6275
TRANSFER
and you shall t the inheritance of Nu 27:7 5674a
then you shall t his inheritance Nu 27:8 5674a
to t the kingdom from the house of 2Sa 3:10 5674a
TRANSFERRED
shall be t from tribe to tribe, Nu 36:7 5437
"Thus no inheritance shall be t Nu 36:9 5437
and t her and her maids to the Es 2:9 8132
and t us to the kingdom of His Col 1:13 *3179*
TRANSFIGURED
And He was t before them; Mt 17:2 *3339*
And He was t before them; Mk 9:2 *3339*
TRANSFORM
who will t the body of our humble Php 3:21 *3345*
TRANSFORMED
'They t the beauty of His Ezk 7:20 7760
be t by the renewing of your mind, Ro 12:2 *3339*
are being t into the same image 2Co 3:18 *3339*
TRANSGRESS
"When you t the covenant of the Jos 23:16 5674a
'Why do you t the commandments of 2Ch 24:20 5674a
purposed that my mouth will not t. Ps 17:3 5674a
water would not t His command, Pr 8:29 5674a
for a piece of bread a man will t. Pr 28:21 6586
rebels and those who t against Me; Ezk 20:38 6586
"Enter Bethel and t; Am 4:4 6586
"Why do you yourselves t the Mt 15:3 *3845*
and that no man t and defraud his 1Th 4:6 *5233*
TRANSGRESSED
I have not t or forgotten any of Dt 26:13 5674a
and they have also t My covenant Jos 7:11 5674a
he has t the covenant of the LORD, Jos 7:15 5674a
"Because this nation has t My Jg 2:20 5674a
I have indeed t the command of the 1Sa 15:24 5674a
which they have t against You, 1Ki 8:50 6586
their God, but t His covenant, 2Ki 18:12 5674a
we have t greatly in this matter. Ezr 10:13 6586
its inhabitants, for they t laws, Is 24:5 5674a
your spokesmen have t against Me. Is 43:27 6586
of the men Who have t against Me. Is 66:24 6586
The rulers also t against Me, And Jer 2:8 6586
You have all t against Me," Jer 2:29 6586
That you have t against the LORD Jer 3:13 6586
by which they have t against Me. Jer 33:8 6586
the men who have t My covenant, Jer 34:18 5674a
We have t and rebelled, You have La 3:42 6586
t against Me to this very day. Ezk 2:3 6586
all Israel has t Your law and turned Da 9:11 5674a
Adam they have t the covenant; Hos 6:7 5674a
Because they have t My covenant And Hos 8:1 5674a
TRANSGRESSING
you t the commandment of the LORD, Nu 14:41 5674a
LORD your God, by t His covenant, Dt 17:2 5674a
"Why are you t the king's command?" Es 3:3 5674a
T and denying the LORD, And Is 59:13 6586
TRANSGRESSION
Jacob said to Laban, "What is my t? Gn 31:36 6588
the t of your brothers and their Gn 50:17 6588
the t of the servants of the God Gn 50:17 6588
for he will not pardon your t, Ex 23:21 6588
who forgives iniquity, t and sin; Ex 34:7 6588
forgiving iniquity and t; Nu 14:18 6588
not forgive your t or your sins. Jos 24:19 6588
forgive the t of your maidservant; 1Sa 25:28 6588
then do You not pardon my t Jb 7:21 6588
them into the power of their t. Jb 8:4 6588
"My t is sealed up in a bag, And Jb 14:17 6588
'I am pure, without t; Jb 33:9 6588
incurable, *though I am* without t.' Jb 34:6 6588
Nor has He acknowledged t well, Jb 35:15 6588
I shall be acquitted of great t. Ps 19:13 6588
blessed is he whose t is forgiven, Ps 32:1 6588
T speaks to the ungodly within his Ps 36:1 6588
me, Not for my t nor for my sin, Ps 59:3 6588
I will punish their t with the rod Ps 89:32 6588
are many words, t is unavoidable, Pr 10:19 6588
is ensnared by the t of his lips, Pr 12:13 6588
He who conceals a t seeks love, But Pr 17:9 6588
He who loves t loves strife; Pr 17:19 6588
it is his glory to overlook a t. Pr 19:11 6588
By the t of a land many are its Pr 28:2 6588
his mother And says, "It is not a t," Pr 28:24 6588
By t an evil man is ensnared, But Pr 29:6 6588
the wicked increase, t increases; Pr 29:16 6588
a hot-tempered man abounds in t. Pr 29:22 6588
shack, For its t is heavy upon it, Is 24:20 6588
For the t of my people, to whom the Is 53:8 6588
And declare to My people their t And Is 58:1 6588
those who turn from t in Jacob," Is 59:20 6588
deliver him in the day of his t, Ezk 33:12 6588
And on account of t the host will Da 8:12 6588
apply, while the t causes horror, Da 8:13 6588
your holy city, to finish the t, Da 9:24 6588
In Gilgal multiply t! Am 4:4 6586
the free gift is not like the t. Ro 5:15 *3900*
by the t of the one the many died, Ro 5:15 *3900*
the judgment *arose* from one t Ro 5:16
For if by the t of the one, death Ro 5:17 *3900*
So then as through one t there Ro 5:18 *3900*
came in so that the t would increase; Ro 5:20 *3900*
But by their t salvation *has come* Ro 11:11 *3900*
if their t is riches for the world Ro 11:12 *3900*
being deceived, fell into t. 1Tm 2:14 *3847*
and every t and disobedience Heb 2:2 *3847*
received a rebuke for his own t, 2Pe 2:16 *3892*
TRANSGRESSIONS
of Israel and because of their t Lv 16:16 6588
t in regard to all their sins; Lv 16:21 6588
and all their t which they have 1Ki 8:50 6588
do you not *have* t of your own 2Ch 28:10 819
"Have I covered my t like Adam, Jb 31:33 6588
And if your t are many, what do Jb 35:6 6588
to them their work And their t, Jb 36:9 6588
In the multitude of their t thrust Ps 5:10 6588
the sins of my youth or my t; Ps 25:7 6588
"I will confess my t to the LORD"; Ps 32:5 6588
"Deliver me from all my t; Ps 39:8 6588
of Your compassion blot out my t. Ps 51:1 6588
For I know my t, And my sin is Ps 51:3 6588
As for our t, You forgive Ps 65:3 6588
far has He removed our t from us. Ps 103:12 6588
up strife, But love covers all t. Pr 10:12 6588
He who conceals his t will not Pr 28:13 6588
wipes out your t for My own sake, Is 43:25 6588
wiped out your t like a thick cloud Is 44:22 6588
for your t your mother was sent Is 50:1 6588
He was pierced through for our t, Is 53:5 6588
our t are multiplied before You, Is 59:12 6588
For our t are with us, And we know Is 59:12 6588
pieces, Because their t are many, Jer 5:6 6588
Because of the multitude of her t; La 1:5 6588
"The yoke of my t is bound; La 1:14 6588
have dealt with me For all my t; La 1:22 6588
defile themselves with all their t. Ezk 14:11 6588
"All his t which he has committed Ezk 18:22 6588
all his t which he had committed, Ezk 18:28 6588
and turn away from all your t, Ezk 18:30 6588
your t which you have committed and Ezk 18:31 6588
in that your t are uncovered, Ezk 21:24 6588
our t and our sins are upon us, Ezk 33:10 6588
things, or with any of their t; Ezk 37:23 6588
according to their t I dealt with Ezk 39:24 6588
"For three t of Damascus and for Am 1:3 6588
"For three t of Gaza and for four Am 1:6 6588
"For three t of Tyre and for four Am 1:9 6588
"For three t of Edom and for four Am 1:11 6588
"For three t of the sons of Ammon Am 1:13 6588
"For three t of Moab and for four Am 2:1 6588
"For three t of Judah and for Am 2:4 6588
"For three t of Israel and for Am 2:6 6588
the day that I punish Israel's t, Am 3:14 6588
For I know your t are many and Am 5:12 6588
if you forgive others for their t, Mt 6:14 *3900*
Father will not forgive your t. Mt 6:15 *3900*
in heaven will also forgive you your t. Mk 11:25 *3900*
is in heaven forgive your t." Mk 11:26 *3900*
was delivered over because of our t, Ro 4:25 *3900*
the free gift *arose* from many t Ro 5:16 *3900*
It was added because of t, Ga 3:19 *3847*
even when we were dead in our t, Eph 2:5 *3900*
When you were dead in your t Col 2:13 *3900*
Him, having forgiven us all our t, Col 2:13 *3900*
for the redemption of the t that were Heb 9:15 *3847*
TRANSGRESSOR
but if you are a t of the Law, Ro 2:25 *3848*
circumcision are a t of the Law? Ro 2:27 *3848*
I prove myself to be a t. Ga 2:18 *3848*
you have become a t of the law. Jas 2:11 *3848*
TRANSGRESSORS
t will be altogether destroyed; Ps 37:38 6586
Then I will teach t Your ways, Ps 51:13 6586
But t and sinners will be crushed Is 1:28 6586
Recall it to mind, you t. Is 46:8 6586
And was numbered with the t; Is 53:12 6586
of many, And interceded for the t. Is 53:12 6586
When the t have run *their course,* Da 8:23 6586
them, But t will stumble in them. Hos 14:9 6586
"And He was numbered with t." Mk 15:28 *459*
'AND HE WAS NUMBERED WITH T'; Lk 22:37 *459*
and are convicted by the law as t. Jas 2:9 *3848*
TRANSIENT
my days; Let me know how t I am. Ps 39:4 2310
TRANSLATED
in Aramaic and t *from* Aramaic. Ezr 4:7 8638
us has been t and read before me. Ezr 4:18 6568
which t means, "GOD WITH US." Mt 1:23 *3177*
t means, "Little girl, I say to you, Mk 5:41 *3177*
Golgotha, which is t, Place of a Skull Mk 15:22 *3177*
which is t, "MY GOD, MY GOD, WHY Mk 15:34 *3177*
"Rabbi (which t means Teacher), Jn 1:38 *3177*

the Messiah" (which **t** means Christ). Jn 1:41 *3177*
Cephas" (which is **t** Peter). Jn 1:42 *2059*
pool of Siloam" (which is **t**, Sent). Jn 9:7 *2059*
t means Son of Encouragement), Ac 4:36 *3177*
t *in Greek* is called Dorcas), Ac 9:36 *1329*
magician (for so his name is **t**) Ac 13:8 *3177*

TRANSLATING
t to give the sense so that they Ne 8:8 6567a

TRANSLATION
of all, by the **t** *of his name,* Heb 7:2 *2059*

TRANSMIT
that they will not **t** holiness to the Ezk 44:19 6942
to **t** holiness to the people." Ezk 46:20 6942

TRANSPARENT
city was pure gold, like **t** glass. Rv 21:21 *1306b*

TRANSPORTERS
Now Solomon had 70,000 **t**, 1Ki 5:15 5449, 5375

TRAP
will be a snare and a **t** to you, Jos 23:13 4170
heel, *And* a **t** snaps shut on him. Jb 18:9 6782
And a **t** for him on the path. Jb 18:10 4434
are in peace, *may it become* a **t**. Ps 69:22 4170
The proud have hidden a **t** for me, Ps 140:5 6341a
the **t** which they have set for me, Ps 141:9 6341a
walk They have hidden a **t** for me. Ps 142:3 6341a
It is a **t** for a man to say rashly, Pr 20:25 4170
And a snare and a **t** for the Is 8:14 4170
They set a **t**, They catch men. Jer 5:26 4889
Does a bird fall into a **t** on the Am 3:5 6341a
Does a **t** spring up from the earth Am 3:5 6341a
they might **t** Him in what He said. Mt 22:15 *3802*
in order to **t** Him in a statement. Mk 12:13 *64*
not come on you suddenly like a **t**; Lk 21:34 *3803*
TABLE BECOME A SNARE AND A **T**, Ro 11:9 *2339*

TRAPPED
so that they were **t** in the midst Jos 8:22
net and birds **t** in a snare, Ec 9:12 270
All of them are **t** in caves, Or are Is 42:22 6351

TRAPPER
you from the snare of the **t** And Ps 91:3 3353
a bird out of the snare of the **t**; Ps 124:7 3369

TRAPPINGS
Whose **t** include bit and bridle to Ps 32:9 5716

TRAVAILED
"I have neither **t** nor given Is 23:4 2342a
and cry aloud, you who have not **t**; Is 54:1 2342a
"Before she **t**, she brought forth; Is 66:7 2342a
As soon as Zion **t**, she also Is 66:8 2342a

TRAVAILS
Behold, he **t** with wickedness, And Ps 7:14 2254a

TRAVEL
they might **t** by day and by night. Ex 13:21 1980
I will **t** only on the highway; Dt 2:27 1980
And you who **t** on the road—sing! Jg 5:10 1980
The unclean will not **t** on it, Is 35:8 5674a
because you **t** around on sea and Mt 23:15 *4013*
t with us in this gracious work, 2Co 8:19 *4898*

TRAVELED
t by way of the Arabah all night. 2Sa 4:7 1980
The men who **t** with him stood Ac 9:7 *4922*
Now when they had **t** through Ac 17:1 *1353*

TRAVELER
and saw the **t** in the open square Jg 19:17 376, 732
"Now a **t** came to the rich man, 2Sa 12:4 1982
I have opened my doors to the **t**. Jb 31:32 734
are desolate, the **t** has ceased, Is 33:8 5674a
Or like a **t** who has pitched his *tent* Jer 14:8 732

TRAVELERS
And **t** went by roundabout ways. Jg 5:6 1980, 5410b
The **t** of Sheba hoped for them. Jb 6:19 1979

TRAVELING
"Behold, it is the **t** couch of SS 3:7
because He was **t** toward Jerusalem. Lk 9:53 *4198*
Now as they were **t** along, Lk 10:38 *4198*
approached and *began* **t** with them. Lk 24:15 *4848*
As he was **t**, it happened that he was Ac 9:3 *4198*
was **t** through all *those regions,* Ac 9:32 *1330*
was **t** through Syria and Cilicia, Ac 15:41 *1330*
Paul's **t** companions from Macedonia. Ac 19:29 *4898*

TRAVERSING
he had not been **t** with his feet. Is 41:3 935

TRAYS
and their **t** *shall be* of pure gold. Ex 25:38 4289
snuffers and its **t** of pure gold. Ex 37:23 4289
and its **t** and all its oil vessels, Nu 4:9 4289

TREACHEROUS
to any *who are* **t** in iniquity. Ps 59:5 898
They turned aside like a **t** bow. Ps 78:57 7423a
I behold the **t** and loathe *them,* Ps 119:158 898
the **t** will be uprooted from it. Pr 2:22 898
crookedness of the **t** will destroy them. Pr 11:3 898
But the **t** will be caught by *their* Pr 11:6 898
the desire of the **t** is violence. Pr 13:2 898
But the way of the **t** is hard. Pr 13:15 898
But he who utters lies is **t**. Pr 14:25 4820
And the **t** is in the place of the Pr 21:18 898
overthrows the words of the **t** man. Pr 22:12 898
like fish caught in a **t** net and Ec 9:12 7451a
The **t** one *still* deals Is 21:2 898
The **t** deal treacherously, And the Is 24:16 898
the **t** deal very treacherously." Is 24:16 898
And he who is **t**, while *others* did Is 33:1 898
and her **t** sister Judah saw it. Jer 3:7 901
her **t** sister Judah did not fear; Jer 3:8 898
t sister Judah did not return to Me Jer 3:10 901
more righteous than **t** Judah. Jer 3:11 898
adulterers, An assembly of **t** men. Jer 9:2 898
Her prophets are reckless, **t** men; Zph 3:4 900
t, reckless, conceited, lovers of 2Tm 3:4 *4273*

TREACHEROUSLY
the men of Shechem dealt **t** with Jg 9:23 898
"You have acted **t**; 1Sa 14:33 898
if I had dealt **t** against his life 2Sa 18:13 8267
But they acted **t** against the God 1Ch 5:25 4603
Those who deal **t** without cause Ps 25:3 898
and acted **t** like their fathers; Ps 78:57 898
The treacherous one *still* deals **t**, Is 21:2 898
The treacherous deal **t**, Is 24:16 898
And the treacherous deal very **t**." Is 24:16 898
others did not deal **t** with him. Is 33:1 898
soon as you cease to deal **t**, Is 33:1 898
others will deal **t** with you. Is 33:1 898
I knew that you would deal very **t**; Is 48:8 898
a woman **t** departs from her lover, Jer 3:20 898
So you have dealt **t** with Me, Jer 3:20 898
Judah Have dealt very **t** with Me," Jer 5:11 898
Even they have dealt **t** with you, Jer 12:6 898
her friends have dealt **t** with her; La 1:2 898
Me by acting **t** against Me. Ezk 20:27 4603
because they acted **t** against Me, Ezk 39:23 4603
have dealt **t** against the LORD, Hos 5:7 898
they have dealt **t** against Me. Hos 6:7 898
with favor On those who deal **t**? Hab 1:13 898
Why do we deal **t** each against his Mal 2:10 898
"Judah has dealt **t**, and an Mal 2:11 898
against whom you have dealt **t**, Mal 2:14 898
and let no one deal **t** against the Mal 2:15 898
spirit, that you do not deal **t**." Mal 2:16 898

TREACHERY
"*There is* **t**, O Ahaziah!" 2Ki 9:23 4820
And they devise **t** all day long. Ps 38:12 4820
all those who deal in **t** at ease? Jer 12:1 899a
will not be remembered for his **t** Ezk 18:24 4604
forget their disgrace and all their **t** Ezk 39:26 4604

TREAD
will **t** upon their high places." Dt 33:29 1869
t on the threshold of Dagon in 1Sa 5:5 1869
They **t** wine presses but thirst. Jb 24:11 1869
And **t** down the wicked where they Jb 40:12 1915
who will **t** down our adversaries. Ps 60:12 947
will **t** upon the lion and cobra, Ps 91:13 1869
who shall **t** down our adversaries. Ps 108:13 947
shout like those who **t** *the grapes,* Jer 25:30 1869
No one will **t** *them* with shouting, Jer 48:33 1869
that you must **t** down with your Ezk 34:18 7429
what you **t** down with your feet and Ezk 34:19 4823
earth and **t** it down and crush it. Da 7:23 1759
Come, **t**, for the wine press is Jl 3:13 3381
He will come down and **t** on the Mi 1:3 1869
You will **t** the olive but will not Mi 6:15 1869
will **t** our iniquities under foot. Mi 7:19 3533
Go into the clay and **t** the mortar! Na 3:14 7429
"You will **t** down the wicked, Mal 4:3 6072
to **t** on serpents and scorpions, Lk 10:19 *3961*
they will **t** under foot the holy city Rv 11:2 *3961*

TREADER
No **t** treads out wine in the Is 16:10 1869
the **t** of grapes him who sows seed; Am 9:13 1869

TREADING
t wine presses on the sabbath, Ne 13:15 1869
T down *the enemy* in the mire of Zch 10:5 947

TREADS
on which the sole of your foot **t** Dt 11:24 1869
on which the sole of your foot **t**, Jos 1:3 1869
treader **t** out wine in the presses, Is 16:10 1869
Even as the potter **t** clay." Is 41:25 7429
Whoever **t** on them does not know Is 59:8 1869
the one who **t** in the wine press? Is 63:2 1869
And **t** on the high places of the earth Am 4:13 1869
and He **t** the wine press of the Rv 19:15 *3961*

TREASON
tore her clothes and cried, "**T**! 2Ki 11:14 7195
her clothes and cried, "Treason! **T**!" 2Ki 11:14 7195
tore her clothes and said, "**T**! 2Ch 23:13 7195
her clothes and said, "Treason! **T**!" 2Ch 23:13 7195

TREASURE
has given you **t** in your sacks; Gn 43:23 4301
and showed them all his **t** house, 2Ki 20:13 5238
the **t** I have of gold and silver, 1Ch 29:3 5459
be conducted in the king's **t** house, Ezr 5:17 1596
belly You fill with Your **t**; Ps 17:14 6840
And **t** my commandments within you, Pr 2:1 6845
And **t** my commandments within you. Pr 7:1 6845
Than great **t** and turmoil with it. Pr 15:16 214
There is precious **t** and oil in the Pr 21:20 214
and the **t** of kings and provinces. Ec 2:8 5459
The fear of the LORD is his **t**. Is 33:6 214
and showed them *all* his **t** house, Is 39:2 5238
have taken **t** and precious things; Ezk 22:25 2633
For there is no limit to the **t** Na 2:9 8499
for where your **t** is, there your Mt 6:21 *2344*
good man brings out of *his* good **t** Mt 12:35 *2344*
the evil man brings out of *his* evil **t** Mt 12:35 *2344*
is like a **t** hidden in the field, Mt 13:44 *2344*
who brings out of his **t** Mt 13:52 *2344*
and you will have **t** in heaven; Mt 19:21 *2344*
and you will have **t** in heaven; Mk 10:21 *2344*
out of the good **t** of his heart Lk 6:45 *2344*
the evil *man* out of the evil **t** Lk 6:45
the man who stores up **t** for himself, Lk 12:21 *2343*
out, an unfailing **t** in heaven, Lk 12:33 *2344*
"For where your **t** is, there your Lk 12:34 *2344*
and you shall have **t** in heaven; Lk 18:22 *2344*
who was in charge of all her **t**; Ac 8:27 *1047*
we have this **t** in earthen vessels, 2Co 4:7 *2344*
the **t** of a good foundation for the 1Tm 6:19 *597*
the **t** which has been entrusted to 2Tm 1:14 *2570, 3866*
that you have stored up your **t**! Jas 5:3 *2343*

TREASURED
to be His people, a **t** possession, Dt 26:18 5459
I have **t** the words of His mouth Jb 23:12 6845
together against Your **t** ones. Ps 83:3 6845
Your word I have **t** in my heart, Ps 119:11 6845
But Mary **t** all these things, Lk 2:19 *4933*
His mother **t** all *these* things in her Lk 2:51 *1301*

TREASURER
by the hand of Mithredath the **t**, Ezr 1:8 1489
Erastus, the city **t** greets you, Ro 16:23 *3623*

TREASURERS
issue a decree to all the **t** who Ezr 7:21 1490
governors, the counselors, the **t**, Da 3:2 1411
governors, the counselors, the **t**, Da 3:3 1411

TREASURES
And the hidden **t** of the sand." Dt 33:19 5603
He took away the **t** of the house 1Ki 14:26 214
LORD and the **t** of the king's house, 1Ki 14:26 214
the **t** of the house of the LORD, 2Ki 24:13 214
and the **t** of the king's house, 2Ki 24:13 214
of the **t** of the house of God and 1Ch 26:20 214
of the **t** of the dedicated gifts. 1Ch 26:20 214
of the **t** of the house of the LORD. 1Ch 26:22 214
of Moses, was officer over the **t**. 1Ch 26:24 214
all the **t** of the dedicated gifts which 1Ch 26:26 214
took the **t** of the house of the LORD 2Ch 12:9 214
and the **t** of the king's palace. 2Ch 12:9 214
and the **t** of the king's house, 2Ch 25:24 214
the **t** of the house of the LORD, 2Ch 36:18 214
and the **t** of the king and of his 2Ch 36:18 214
the **t** were stored in Babylon. Ezr 6:1 1596
dig for it more than for hidden **t**, Jb 3:21 4301
is held in reserve for his **t**, Jb 20:26 6845
search for her as for hidden **t**; Pr 2:4 4301
The acquisition of **t** by a lying tongue Pr 21:6 214
And there is no end to their **t**; Is 2:7 214
peoples And plundered their **t**, Is 10:13 6264
And their **t** on camels' humps, Is 30:6 214
I will give you the **t** of darkness And Is 45:3 214
"Your wealth and your **t** I will Jer 15:13 214
wealth and all your **t** for booty, Jer 17:3 214
even all the **t** of the kings of Judah Jer 20:5 214
in your own achievements and **t**, Jer 48:7 214
daughter Who trusts in her **t**, Jer 49:4 214
A sword against her **t**, Jer 50:37 214
by many waters, Abundant in **t**, Jer 51:13 214
silver, costly stones and **t**. Da 11:38 2536b
the hidden **t** of gold and silver and Da 11:43 4362
will take over their **t** of silver; Hos 9:6 4261
My precious **t** to your temples, Jl 3:5 4261
And his hidden **t** searched out! Ob 1:6 4710
house, *Along with* **t** of wickedness And Mi 6:10 214
Then, opening their **t**, they presented Mt 2:11 *2344*
up for yourselves **t** on earth, Mt 6:19 *2344*
store up for yourselves **t** in heaven, Mt 6:20 *2344*
all the **t** of wisdom and knowledge. Col 2:3 *2344*
riches than the **t** of Egypt; Heb 11:26 *2344*

TREASURIES
store with Me, Sealed up in My **t**? Dt 32:34 214
in the **t** of the house of the LORD. 1Ki 7:51 214
left in the **t** of the house of the LORD 1Ki 15:18 214
LORD and the **t** of the king's house, 1Ki 15:18 214
the **t** of the house of the LORD and 2Ki 12:18 214
and in the **t** of the king's house, 2Ki 14:14 214
and in the **t** of the king's house, 2Ki 16:8 214
and in the **t** of the king's house. 2Ki 18:15 214
and all that was found in his **t**. 2Ki 20:13 214
my **t** that I have not shown them." 2Ki 20:15 214
over the **t** in the house of God. 1Ch 9:26 214
them in the **t** of the house of God. 2Ch 5:1 214
from the **t** of the house of the LORD 2Ch 16:2 214
he made for himself **t** for silver, 2Ch 32:27 214
to put into the king's **t**." Es 3:9 1595
promised to pay to the king's **t** for Es 4:7 1595
brings forth the wind from His **t**. Ps 135:7 214
wealth, That I may fill their **t**. Pr 8:21 214
and all that was found in his **t**. Is 39:2 214
my **t** that I have not shown them." Is 39:4 214
gold and silver for your **t**. Ezk 28:4 214

TREASURY
shall go into the **t** of the LORD." Jos 6:19 214
the **t** of the house of the LORD. Jos 6:24 214
to the **t** of the house of the LORD, 1Ch 29:8 214
they gave to the **t** for the work Ezr 2:69 214
the cost be paid from the royal **t**. Ezr 6:4 1005
paid to these people from the royal **t** Ezr 6:8 5232
provide *for it* from the royal **t**. Ezr 7:20 1596
gave to the **t** 1,000 gold drachmas, Ne 7:70 214
gave into the **t** of the work 20,000 Ne 7:71 214
the vessels into the **t** of his god. Da 1:2 1004, 214
It will plunder *his* **t** of every Hos 13:15 214
to put them into the temple **t**, Mt 27:6 *2878b*
And He sat down opposite the **t**, Mk 12:41 *1049*
were putting money into the **t**; Mk 12:41 *1049*
all the contributors to the **t**; Mk 12:43 *1049*
putting their gifts into the **t**. Lk 21:1 *1049*
These words He spoke in the **t**, Jn 8:20 *1049*

TREAT
we will t you worse than them." Gn 19:9 7489a
"Should he t our sister as a harlot?" Gn 34:31 6213a
"Why did you t me so badly by Gn 43:6 7489a
to t Me as holy in the sight of Nu 20:12 6942
against My command to t Me as holy Nu 27:14 6942
because you did not t Me as holy Dt 32:51 6942
city and we will t you kindly." Jg 1:24 6213a
then did you t us with contempt? 2Sa 19:43 7043
"This is how I will t this place Jer 19:12 6213a
t you better than at the first. Ezk 36:11 3190
How can I t you like Zeboiim? Hos 11:8 7760
'But now I will not t the remnant Zch 8:11
t people the same way you want them Mt 7:12 4160
same way you want them to t you, Mt 7:12 4160
fathers used to t the prophets. Lk 6:23 4160
used to t the false prophets in Lk 6:26 4160
"T others the same way Lk 6:31 4160
you want them to t you. Lk 6:31 4160

TREATED
he t Abram well for her sake; Gn 12:16 3190
So Sarai t her harshly, and she Gn 16:6 6031a
the righteous and the wicked are t Gn 18:25
come near Me I will be t as holy, Lv 10:3 6942
Egyptians t us and our fathers badly Nu 20:15 7489a
t us harshly and afflicted us, Dt 26:6 7489a
in earlier times He t the land of Is 9:1 7043
And He has violently t His La 2:6 2554
"They have t father and mother Ezk 22:7 7043
things and be t with contempt? Mk 9:12 1847
in the head, and t him shamefully. Mk 12:4 718
"Son, why have You t us this way? Lk 2:48 4160
beat him also and t him shamefully and Lk 20:11 818
saw one *of them* being t unjustly, Ac 7:24 91
and Julius t Paul with consideration Ac 27:3 5530
poorly clothed, and are roughly t, 1Co 4:11 2852
For in what respect were you t as 2Co 12:13 2274
sharers with those who were so t. Heb 10:33 390
when you sin and are harshly t, 1Pe 2:20 2852

TREATING
after t Him with contempt and Lk 23:11 1848

TREATISE
in the t of the prophet Iddo. 2Ch 13:22 4097
in the t of the Book of the Kings. 2Ch 24:27 4097

TREATMENT
and severe t of the body, Col 2:23 857

TREATS
"She t her young cruelly, as if Jb 39:16 7188
For son t father contemptuously, Mi 7:6 5034a

TREATY
there be a t between you and me, 1Ki 15:19 1285
break your t with Baasha king of 1Ki 15:19 1285
there be a t between you and me, 2Ch 16:3 1285
break your t with Baasha king of 2Ch 16:3 1285

TREE
t which has fruit yielding seed; Gn 1:29 6086
LORD God caused to grow every t Gn 2:9 6086
the t of life also in the midst of Gn 2:9 6086
and the t of the knowledge of good Gn 2:9 6086
"From any t of the garden you may Gn 2:16 6086
but from the t of the knowledge of Gn 2:17 6086
eat from any t of the garden'?" Gn 3:1 6086
but from the fruit of the t which Gn 3:3 6086
saw that the t was good for food, Gn 3:6 6086
and that the t was desirable to Gn 3:6 6086
Have you eaten from the t of which Gn 3:11 6086
with me, she gave me from the t, Gn 3:12 6086
the t about which I commanded you, Gn 3:17 6086
and take also from the t of life, Gn 3:22 6086
to guard the way to the t of life. Gn 3:24 6086
and rest yourselves under the t; Gn 18:4 6086
by them under the t as they ate. Gn 18:8 6086
planted a tamarisk t at Beersheba, Gn 21:33 815
from you and will hang you on a t, Gn 40:19 6086
shattered every t of the field. Ex 9:25 6086
they will eat every t which sprouts Ex 10:5 6086
Thus nothing green was left on t Ex 10:15 6086
LORD, and the LORD showed him a t; Ex 15:25 6086
the land or of the fruit of the t, Lv 27:30 6086
the hills and under every green t. Dt 12:2 6086
yourself an Asherah of any kind of t Dt 16:21 6086
swings the axe to cut down the t, Dt 19:5 6086
For is the t of the field a man, Dt 20:19 6086
to death, and you hang him on a t, Dt 21:22 6086
shall not hang all night on the t, Dt 21:23 6086
way, in any t or on the ground, Dt 22:6 6086
"When you beat your olive t, Dt 24:20 2132
He hanged the king of Ai on a t Jos 8:29 6086
took his body down from the t and Jos 8:29 6086
to sit under the palm t of Deborah Jg 4:5 8560
and they said to the olive t, Jg 9:8 2132
"But the olive t said to them, Jg 9:9 2132
"Then the trees said to the fig t, Jg 9:10 8384
"But the fig t said to them, Jg 9:11 8384
pomegranate t which is in Migron. 1Sa 14:2 7416
under the tamarisk t on the height 1Sa 22:6 815
under the tamarisk t at Jabesh, 1Sa 31:13 815
man under his vine and his fig t, 1Ki 4:25 8384
and beneath every luxuriant t. 1Ki 14:23 6086
and sat down under a juniper t; 1Ki 19:4 7574
down and slept under a juniper t; 1Ki 19:5 7574
fell every good t and stop all springs 2Ki 3:19 6086
the hills and under every green t. 2Ki 16:4 6086
high hill and under every green t, 2Ki 17:10 6086
each of his vine and each of his fig t 2Ki 18:31 8384
hills and under every green t. 2Ch 28:4 6086
first fruits of all the fruit of every t Ne 10:35 6086
the fruit of every t, Ne 10:37 6086
"For there is hope for a t, Jb 14:7 6086
off his flower like the olive t. Jb 15:33 2132
He has uprooted my hope like a t. Jb 19:10 6086
will be broken like a t. Jb 24:20 6086
t *firmly* planted by streams of water Ps 1:3 6086
a luxuriant t in its native soil. Ps 37:35 249
green olive t in the house of God; Ps 52:8 2132
man will flourish like the palm t, Ps 92:12 8558
the *burning* coals of the broom t. Ps 120:4 7574
She is a t of life to those who Pr 3:18 6086
fruit of the righteous is a t of life, Pr 11:30 6086
desire fulfilled is a t of life. Pr 13:12 6086
A soothing tongue is a t of life, Pr 15:4 6086
He who tends the fig t will eat its Pr 27:18 8384
and whether a t falls toward the Ec 11:3 6086
the north, wherever the t falls, Ec 11:3 6086
the almond t blossoms, the Ec 12:5 8247
t among the trees of the forest, SS 2:3 8598
'The fig t has ripened its figs, SS 2:13 8384
"Your stature is like a palm t, SS 7:7 8558
'I will climb the palm t, SS 7:8 8558
Beneath the apple t I awakened you SS 8:5 8598
no t cutter comes up against us.' Is 14:8
it like the shaking of an olive t, Is 17:6 2132
on the branches of a fruitful t, Is 17:6 6509
As the shaking of an olive t, Is 24:13 2132
Or as *one* withers from the fig t. Is 34:4 8384
The t snake will make its nest Is 34:15 7091
each of his vine and each of his fig t Is 36:16 8384
Selects a t that does not rot; Is 40:20 6086
and the myrtle and the olive t; Is 41:19 8410
with the box t and the cypress, Is 41:19 8391
O forest, and every t in it; Is 44:23 6086
"Behold, I am a dry t." Is 56:3 6086
the oaks, Under every luxuriant t, Is 57:5 6086
to you, The juniper, the box t and Is 60:13 8410
For as the lifetime of a t, Is 65:22 6086
"I see a rod of an almond t." Jer 1:11 8247
under every green t You have lain Jer 2:20 6086
Who say to a t, 'You are my father,' Jer 2:27 6086
high hill and under every green t, Jer 3:6 6086
the strangers under every green t, Jer 3:13 6086
vine And no figs on the fig t, Jer 8:13 8384
"A green olive t, beautiful in Jer 11:16 2132
us destroy the t with its fruit, Jer 11:19 6086
be like a t planted by the water, Jer 17:8 6086
mountains, under every green t and Ezk 6:13 6086
I bring down the high t, Ezk 17:24 6086
the high tree, exalt the low t, Ezk 17:24 6086
the low tree, dry up the green t and Ezk 17:24 6086
tree and make the dry t flourish. Ezk 17:24 6086
every high hill and every leafy t, Ezk 20:28 6086
consume every green t in you, Ezk 20:47 6086
in you, as well as every dry t; Ezk 20:47 6086
rod of My son despising every t? Ezk 21:10 6086
No t in God's garden could compare Ezk 31:8 6086
"Also the t of the field will yield its Ezk 34:27 6086
I will multiply the fruit of the t and Ezk 36:30 6086
side pillar *were* palm t ornaments. Ezk 40:16 8561
and its palm t ornaments *had* the Ezk 40:22 8561
t ornaments on its side pillars, Ezk 40:26 8561
and palm t ornaments *were* on its Ezk 40:31 8561
and palm t ornaments *were* on its Ezk 40:34 8561
and palm t ornaments *were* on its Ezk 40:37 8561
t was between cherub and cherub, Ezk 41:18 8561
toward the palm t on one side and Ezk 41:19 8561
the palm t on the other side; Ezk 41:19 8561
was a t in the midst of the earth Da 4:10 363
t grew large and became strong And Da 4:11 363
"Chop down the t and cut off its Da 4:14 363
'The t that you saw, which became Da 4:20 363
"Chop down the t and destroy it; Da 4:23 363
the stump with the roots of the t, Da 4:26 363
on the fig t in its first *season*. Hos 9:10 8384
beauty will be like the olive t And Hos 14:6 2132
a waste And my fig t splinters. Jl 1:7 8384
dries up And the fig t fails; Jl 1:12 8384
the palm also, and the apple t, Jl 1:12 8598
For the t has borne its fruit, Jl 2:22 6086
The fig t and the vine have Jl 2:22 8384
his vine And under his fig t, Mi 4:4 8384
the fig t should not blossom And Hab 3:17 8384
including the vine, the fig t, Hg 2:19 8384
the pomegranate and the olive t, Hg 2:19 6086
his vine and under *his* fig t.'" Zch 3:10 8384
every t that does not Mt 3:10 1186
"So every good t bears good fruit, Mt 7:17 1186
but the bad t bears bad fruit. Mt 7:17 1186
"A good t cannot produce bad Mt 7:18 1186
can a bad t produce good fruit. Mt 7:18 1186
"Every t that does not bear good Mt 7:19 1186
"Either make the t good and its Mt 12:33 1186
or make the t bad and its fruit Mt 12:33 1186
for the t is known by its fruit. Mt 12:33 1186
garden plants and becomes a t, Mt 13:32 1186
Seeing a lone fig t by the road, Mt 21:19 4808
And at once the fig t withered. Mt 21:19 4808
did the fig t wither *all* at once?" Mt 21:20 4808
do what was done to the fig t, Mt 21:21 4808
learn the parable from the fig t: Mt 24:32 4808
at a distance a fig t in leaf, Mk 11:13 4808
fig t withered from the roots *up*. Mk 11:20 4808
fig t which You cursed has withered Mk 11:21 4808
learn the parable from the fig t: Mk 13:28 4808
every t that does not Lk 3:9 1186
no good t which produces bad fruit, Lk 6:43 1186
a bad t which produces good fruit. Lk 6:43 1186
each t is known by its own fruit. Lk 6:44 1186
"A man had a fig t which Lk 13:6 4808
come looking for fruit on this fig t Lk 13:7 4808
and it grew and became a t, Lk 13:19 1186
you would say to this mulberry t, Lk 17:6 4807
a sycamore t in order to see Him, Lk 19:4 4809
the fig t and all the trees; Lk 21:29 4808
do these things when the t is green, Lk 23:31 3586
when you were under the fig t, Jn 1:48 4808
that I saw you under the fig t, Jn 1:50 4808
of the rich root of the olive t, Ro 11:17 1636
what is by nature a wild olive t, Ro 11:24 65
nature into a cultivated olive t, Ro 11:24 2565
be grafted into their own olive t? Ro 11:24 1636
IS EVERYONE WHO HANGS ON A T" Ga 3:13 3586
Can a fig t, my brethren, produce Jas 3:12 4808
grant to eat of the t of life which Rv 2:7 3586
as a fig t casts its unripe figs Rv 6:13 4808
earth or on the sea or on any t. Rv 7:1 1186
nor any green thing, nor any t, Rv 9:4 1186
of the river was the t of life, Rv 22:2 3586
and the leaves of the t were for Rv 22:2 3586
have the right to the t of life, Rv 22:14 3586
take away his part from the t of life Rv 22:19 3586

TREES
and fruit t on the earth bearing Gn 1:11 6086
their kind, and t bearing fruit with Gn 1:12 6086
From the fruit of the t of the garden Gn 3:2 6086
God among the t of the garden. Gn 3:8 6086
all the t which were in the field, Gn 23:17 6086
of poplar and almond and plane t, Gn 30:37 6196
fruit of the t that the hail had left. Ex 10:15 6086
and plant all kinds of t for food, Lv 19:23 6086
the foliage of beautiful t, Lv 23:40 6086
leafy t and willows of the brook, Lv 23:40 6086
the t of the field will bear their fruit. Lv 26:4 6086
and the t of the land will not yield Lv 26:20 6086
Are there t in it or not? Nu 13:20 6086
of water and seventy palm t, Nu 33:9 8558
olive t which you did not plant, Dt 6:11 2132
vines and fig t and pomegranates, Dt 8:8 8384
you shall not destroy its t by Dt 20:19 6086
"Only the t which you know are Dt 20:20 6086
know are not fruit t you shall destroy Dt 20:20 6086
"You shall have olive t Dt 28:40 2132
"The cricket shall possess all your t Dt 28:42 6086
of Jericho, the city of palm t, Dt 34:3 8558
and he hanged them on five t; Jos 10:26 6086
they hung on the t until evening. Jos 10:26 6086
and they took them down from the t Jos 10:27 6086
possessed the city of the palm t. Jg 3:13 8558
'Once the t went forth to anoint Jg 9:8 6086
and go to wave over the t?' Jg 9:9 6086
"Then the t said to the fig tree, Jg 9:10 6086
fruit, and go to wave over the t?' Jg 9:11 6086
"Then the t said to the vine, Jg 9:12 6086
men, and go to wave over the t?' Jg 9:13 6086
all the t said to the bramble, Jg 9:14 6086
"The bramble said to the t, Jg 9:15 6086
and cut down a branch from the t, Jg 9:48 6086
to David with cedar t and carpenters 2Sa 5:11 6086
at them in front of the balsam t. 2Sa 5:23 1057
in the tops of the balsam t, 2Sa 5:24 1057
He spoke of t, from the cedar 1Ki 4:33 6086
engravings of cherubim, palm t, 1Ki 6:29 8561
them carvings of cherubim, palm t, 1Ki 6:32 8561
on the cherubim and on the palm t. 1Ki 6:32 8561
He carved *on it* cherubim, palm t, 1Ki 6:35 8561
cherubim, lions and palm t, 1Ki 7:36 8561
a very great *number of* almug t and 1Ki 10:11 6086
king made of the almug t supports 1Ki 10:12 6086
almug t have not come in *again* 1Ki 10:12 6086
cedars as plentiful as sycamore t 1Ki 10:27 8256
water and felled all the good t, 2Ki 3:25 6086
to the Jordan, they cut down t. 2Ki 6:4 6086
a land of olive t and honey, 2Ki 18:32 2132
messengers to David with cedar t, 1Ch 14:1 6086
at them in front of the balsam t. 1Ch 14:14 1057
in the tops of the balsam t, 1Ch 14:15 1057
Then the t of the forest will sing 1Ch 16:33 6086
and sycamore t in the Shephelah; 1Ch 27:28 8256
it with palm t and chains. 2Ch 3:5 8561
algum t and precious stones. 2Ch 9:10 6086
From the algum t the king made steps 2Ch 9:11 418
cedars as plentiful as sycamore t 2Ch 9:27 8256
to Jericho, the city of palm t, 2Ch 28:15 8558
and branches of *other* leafy t, Ne 8:15 6086
groves, Fruit t in abundance. Ne 9:25 6086
up *His* axe in a forest of t. Ps 74:5 6086
And their sycamore t with frost. Ps 78:47 8256
Then all the t of the forest will Ps 96:12 6086
t of the LORD drink their fill, Ps 104:16 6086
stork, whose home is the fir t. Ps 104:17 1265
their vines also and their fig t, Ps 105:33 8384
shattered the t of their territory. Ps 105:33 6086
Fruit t and all cedars; Ps 148:9 6086
in them all kinds of fruit t; Ec 2:5 6086
to irrigate a forest of growing t. Ec 2:6 6086
tree among the t of the forest, SS 2:3 6086
With all the t of frankincense, SS 4:14 6086
"I went down to the orchard of nut t SS 6:11 93
shook as the t of the forest shake Is 7:2 6086
And the rest of the t of his forest Is 10:19 6086
the cypress t rejoice over you, Is 14:8 1265
himself among the t of the forest. Is 44:14 6086
And all the t of the field will Is 55:12 6086
adultery with stones and t. Jer 3:9 6086
devour your vines and your fig t; Jer 5:17 8384
"Cut down her t And cast up a Jer 6:6 6097
on man and on beast and on the t Jer 7:20 6086

By green **t** on the high hills.	**Jer 17:2**	6086
is among the **t** of the forest?	**Ezk 15:2**	6086
vine among the **t** of the forest,	**Ezk 15:6**	6086
"All the **t** of the field will	**Ezk 17:24**	6086
your planks of fir **t** from Senir;	**Ezk 27:5**	1265
to all the **t** of the field.	**Ezk 31:4**	6086
was loftier than all the **t** of the field	**Ezk 31:5**	6086
plane **t** could not match its branches	**Ezk 31:8**	6196
branches, And all the **t** of Eden,	**Ezk 31:9**	6086
all the **t** by the waters may not be	**Ezk 31:14**	6086
and all the **t** of the field wilted	**Ezk 31:15**	6086
and all the well-watered **t** of Eden,	**Ezk 31:16**	6086
"To which among the **t** of Eden are	**Ezk 31:18**	6086
brought down with the **t** of Eden	**Ezk 31:18**	6086
carved with cherubim and palm **t**;	**Ezk 41:18**	8561
cherubim and palm **t** were carved,	**Ezk 41:20**	8561
cherubim and palm **t** like those	**Ezk 41:25**	8561
palm **t** on one side and on the other,	**Ezk 41:26**	8561
there *were* very many **t** on the one	**Ezk 47:7**	6086
will grow all *kinds of* **t** for food.	**Ezk 47:12**	6086
will destroy her vines and fig **t**,	**Hos 2:12**	8384
All the **t** of the field dry up.	**Jl 1:12**	6086
burned up all the **t** of the field.	**Jl 1:19**	6086
vineyards, fig **t** and olive trees;	**Am 4:9**	8384
vineyards, fig trees and olive **t**;	**Am 4:9**	2132
fortifications are fig **t** with ripe fruit	**Na 3:12**	8384
myrtle **t** which were in the ravine,	**Zch 1:8**	1918
the myrtle **t** answered and said,	**Zch 1:10**	1918
was standing among the myrtle **t** and	**Zch 1:11**	1918
also two olive **t** by it, one on the	**Zch 4:3**	2132
"What are these two olive **t** on	**Zch 4:11**	2132
Because the glorious **t** have been	**Zch 11:2**	
already laid at the root of the **t**;	**Mt 3:10**	*1186*
were cutting branches from the **t** and	**Mt 21:8**	*1186*
men, for I see *them* like **t**,	**Mk 8:24**	*1186*
already laid at the root of the **t**;	**Lk 3:9**	*1186*
"Behold the fig tree and all the **t**;	**Lk 21:29**	*1186*
took the branches of the palm **t** and	**Jn 12:13**	*5404*
autumn **t** without fruit, doubly	**Jude 1:12**	*1186*
the earth or the sea or the **t** until	**Rv 7:3**	*1186*
a third of the **t** were burned up,	**Rv 8:7**	*1186*
These are the two olive **t** and the	**Rv 11:4**	*1636*

TREMBLE

"The peoples have heard, they **t**;	**Ex 15:14**	7264
lie down with no one making *you* **t**.	**Lv 26:6**	2729
will **t** and be in anguish because	**Dt 2:25**	7264
or panic, or **t** before them,	**Dt 20:3**	6206
do not be afraid or **t** at them,	**Dt 31:6**	6206
Do not **t** or be dismayed, for the	**Jos 1:9**	6206
T before Him, all the earth;	**1Ch 16:30**	2342a
t at the commandment of our God;	**Ezr 10:3**	2730a
did not stand up or **t** before him,	**Es 5:9**	2111
of its place, And its pillars **t**;	**Jb 9:6**	6426
You cause a driven leaf to **t**?	**Jb 13:25**	6206
"The departed spirits **t** Under the	**Jb 26:5**	2342a
"The pillars of heaven **t** And	**Jb 26:11**	7514a
T, and do not sin;	**Ps 4:4**	7264
T before Him, all the earth.	**Ps 96:9**	2342a
LORD reigns, let the peoples **t**;	**Ps 99:1**	7264
T, O earth, before the Lord,	**Ps 114:7**	2342a
that the watchmen of the house **t**,	**Ec 12:3**	2111
He arises to make the earth **t**.	**Is 2:19**	6206
He arises to make the earth **t**.	**Is 2:21**	6206
I will make the heavens **t**,	**Is 13:13**	7264
this the man who made the earth **t**,	**Is 14:16**	7264
idols of Egypt will **t** at His presence,	**Is 19:1**	5128
and they will **t** and be in dread	**Is 19:16**	2729
sea, He has made the kingdoms **t**;	**Is 23:11**	7264
T, you *women* who are at ease;	**Is 32:11**	2729
The ends of the earth **t**;	**Is 41:5**	2729
'Do not **t** and do not be afraid;	**Is 44:8**	6342
let them stand up, let them **t**,	**Is 44:11**	6342
the nations may **t** at Your presence!	**Is 64:2**	7264
the LORD, you who **t** at His word:	**Is 66:5**	2730a
'Do you not **t** in My presence?	**Jer 5:22**	2342a
broken within me, All my bones **t**;	**Jer 23:9**	7363a
and they will fear and **t** because	**Jer 33:9**	7264
secure, with no one making *him* **t**.	**Jer 46:27**	2729
of the people of the land will **t**.	**Ezk 7:27**	926
sit on the ground, **t** every moment and	**Ezk 26:16**	2729
the coastlands will **t** On the day of	**Ezk 26:18**	2729
and they will **t** every moment,	**Ezk 32:10**	2729
and **t** before the God of Daniel;	**Da 6:26**	2112
all the inhabitants of the land **t**,	**Jl 2:1**	7264
the earth quakes, The heavens **t**,	**Jl 2:10**	7493
And the heavens and the earth **t**.	**Jl 3:16**	7493
in a city will not the people **t**?	**Am 3:6**	2729
my bones, And in my place I **t**.	**Hab 3:16**	7264
down With no one to make them **t**."	**Zph 3:13**	2729
they do not **t** when they revile	**2Pe 2:10**	*5141*

TREMBLED

Then Isaac **t** violently, and said,	**Gn 27:33**	2729
the people who *were* in the camp **t**.	**Ex 19:16**	2729
they **t** and stood at a distance.	**Ex 20:18**	5128
the garrison and the raiders **t**,	**1Sa 14:15**	2729
afraid and his heart **t** greatly.	**1Sa 28:5**	2729
Then everyone who **t** at the words	**Ezr 9:4**	2730a
The deeps also **t**.	**Ps 77:16**	7264
The earth **t** and shook.	**Ps 77:18**	7264
The earth saw and **t**.	**Ps 97:4**	2342a
the foundations of the thresholds **t**	**Is 6:4**	5128
language feared and **t** before him;	**Da 5:19**	2112
I heard and my inward parts **t**,	**Hab 3:16**	7264

TREMBLES

"At this also my heart **t**,	**Jb 37:1**	2729
He looks at the earth, and it **t**;	**Ps 104:32**	7460
My flesh **t** for fear of You, And I	**Ps 119:120**	5568
His soul **t** within him.	**Is 15:4**	3415
of spirit, and who **t** at My word.	**Is 66:2**	2730a

TREMBLING

and they *turned* **t** to one another,	**Gn 42:28**	2729
The leaders of Moab, **t** grips them;	**Ex 15:15**	7461a
the LORD will give you a **t** heart,	**Dt 28:65**	7268
'Whoever is afraid and **t**,	**Jg 7:3**	2730a
heart was **t** for the ark of God.	**1Sa 4:13**	2730a
and all the people followed him **t**.	**1Sa 13:7**	2729
And there was a **t** in the camp, in	**1Sa 14:15**	2731
so that it became a great **t**.	**1Sa 14:15**	2731
city came **t** to meet him and said,	**1Sa 16:4**	2729
Ahimelech came **t** to meet David and	**1Sa 21:1**	2729
The foundations of heaven were **t**	**2Sa 22:8**	7264
come **t** out of their fortresses.	**2Sa 22:46**	2296
t because of this matter and the	**Ezr 10:9**	7460
Dread came upon me, and **t**,	**Jb 4:14**	7461b
reverence And rejoice with **t**.	**Ps 2:11**	7461b
mountains were **t** And were shaken,	**Ps 18:7**	7264
come **t** out of their fortresses.	**Ps 18:45**	2727
Fear and **t** come upon me,	**Ps 55:5**	7461a
for has been turned for me into **t**.	**Is 21:4**	2731
T has seized the godless.	**Is 33:14**	7461b
profit, Perhaps you may cause **t**.	**Is 47:12**	6206
"Son of man, eat your bread with **t** and	**Ezk 12:18**	7494
will clothe themselves with **t**;	**Ezk 26:16**	2731
set me **t** on my hands and knees.	**Da 10:10**	5128
this word to me, I stood up **t**.	**Da 10:11**	7460
and they will come **t** to the LORD	**Hos 3:5**	6342
sons will come **t** from the west.	**Hos 11:10**	2729
will come **t** like birds from Egypt And	**Hos 11:11**	2729
When Ephraim spoke, *there was* **t**.	**Hos 13:1**	7578
come **t** out of their fortresses;	**Mi 7:17**	7264
of the land of Midian were **t**.	**Hab 3:7**	7264
But the woman fearing and **t**,	**Mk 5:33**	*5141*
for **t** and astonishment had gripped	**Mk 16:8**	*5156*
came **t** and fell down before Him,	**Lk 8:47**	*5141*
t with fear he fell down before Paul	**Ac 16:29**	*1790*
and in fear and in much **t**,	**1Co 2:3**	*5156*
you received him with fear and **t**.	**2Co 7:15**	*5156*
to the flesh, with fear and **t**,	**Eph 6:5**	*5156*
your salvation with fear and **t**;	**Php 2:12**	*5156*
"I AM FULL OF FEAR and **t**."	**Heb 12:21**	*1790*

TRENCH

and he made a **t** around the altar,	**1Ki 18:32**	8585a
he also filled the **t** with water.	**1Ki 18:35**	8585a
up the water that was in the **t**.	**1Ki 18:38**	8585a

TRENCHES

'Make this valley full of **t**.'	**2Ki 3:16**	1356a

TRESPASS

to **t** against the LORD in the	**Nu 31:16**	4560, 4604
So Saul died for his **t** which he	**1Ch 10:13**	4604
even if anyone is caught in any **t**,	**Ga 6:1**	*3900*

TRESPASSES

not counting their **t** against them,	**2Co 5:19**	*3900*
blood, the forgiveness of our **t**,	**Eph 1:7**	*3900*
you were dead in your **t** and sins,	**Eph 2:1**	*3900*

TRESSES

The king is captivated by *your* **t**.	**SS 7:5**	7298b

TRIAL

before the congregation for **t**.	**Nu 35:12**	4941
if we are on **t** today for a benefit	**Ac 4:9**	*350*
beaten us in public without **t**,	**Ac 16:37**	*178*
I am on **t** for the hope and	**Ac 23:6**	*2919*
I am on **t** before you today.' "	**Ac 24:21**	*2919*
stand **t** before me on these *charges*?"	**Ac 25:9**	*2919*
there stand **t** on these matters.	**Ac 25:20**	*2919*
"And now I am standing **t** for the	**Ac 26:6**	*2919*
and that which was a **t** to you in	**Ga 4:14**	*3986*
IN THE DAY OF **T** IN THE WILDERNESS,	**Heb 3:8**	*3986*
is a man who perseveres under **t**;	**Jas 1:12**	*3986*

TRIALS

from within *another* nation by **t**,	**Dt 4:34**	4531b
the great **t** which your eyes saw	**Dt 7:19**	4531b
great **t** which your eyes have seen,	**Dt 29:3**	4531b
who have stood by Me in My **t**;	**Lk 22:28**	*3986*
and with **t** which came upon me	**Ac 20:19**	*3986*
when you encounter various **t**,	**Jas 1:2**	*3986*
have been distressed by various **t**,	**1Pe 1:6**	*3986*

TRIBAL

t army of the sons of Issachar;	**Nu 10:15**	4294
the **t** army of the sons of Zebulun.	**Nu 10:16**	4294
the **t** army of the sons of Simeon,	**Nu 10:19**	4294
the **t** army of the sons of Gad.	**Nu 10:20**	4294
t army of the sons of Manasseh;	**Nu 10:23**	4294
t army of the sons of Benjamin.	**Nu 10:24**	4294
the **t** army of the sons of Asher;	**Nu 10:26**	4294
t army of the sons of Naphtali.	**Nu 10:27**	4294

TRIBE

the son of Hur, of the **t** of Judah.	**Ex 31:2**	4294
son of Ahisamach, of the **t** of Dan;	**Ex 31:6**	4294
the son of Hur, of the **t** of Judah.	**Ex 35:30**	4294
son of Ahisamach, of the **t** of Dan.	**Ex 35:34**	4294
the son of Hur, of the **t** of Judah,	**Ex 38:22**	4294
son of Ahisamach, of the **t** of Dan,	**Ex 38:23**	4294
of Dibri, of the **t** of Dan.)	**Lv 24:11**	4294
there shall be a man of each **t**,	**Nu 1:4**	4294
numbered men of the **t** of Reuben	**Nu 1:21**	4294
numbered men of the **t** of Simeon	**Nu 1:23**	4294
numbered men of the **t** of Gad	**Nu 1:25**	4294
numbered men of the **t** of Judah	**Nu 1:27**	4294
numbered men of the **t** of Issachar	**Nu 1:29**	4294
numbered men of the **t** of Zebulun	**Nu 1:31**	4294
numbered men of the **t** of Ephraim	**Nu 1:33**	4294
men of the **t** of Manasseh	**Nu 1:35**	4294
men of the **t** of Benjamin	**Nu 1:37**	4294
numbered men of the **t** of Dan	**Nu 1:39**	4294
numbered men of the **t** of Asher	**Nu 1:41**	4294
men of the **t** of Naphtali	**Nu 1:43**	4294
among them by their fathers' **t**.	**Nu 1:47**	4294
t of Levi you shall not number,	**Nu 1:49**	4294
to him *shall be* the **t** of Issachar,	**Nu 2:5**	4294
"*Then comes* the **t** of Zebulun, and	**Nu 2:7**	4294
to him *shall be* the **t** of Simeon,	**Nu 2:12**	4294
"Then *comes* the **t** of Gad, and the	**Nu 2:14**	4294
to him *shall be* the **t** of Manasseh,	**Nu 2:20**	4294
"Then *comes* the **t** of Benjamin,	**Nu 2:22**	4294
to him *shall be* the **t** of Asher,	**Nu 2:27**	4294
"Then *comes* the **t** of Naphtali,	**Nu 2:29**	4294
"Bring the **t** of Levi near and set	**Nu 3:6**	4294
t of the families of the Kohathites	**Nu 4:18**	7626
of Amminadab, of the **t** of Judah;	**Nu 7:12**	4294
from the **t** of Reuben, Shammua the	**Nu 13:4**	4294
from the **t** of Simeon, Shaphat the	**Nu 13:5**	4294
from the **t** of Judah, Caleb the son	**Nu 13:6**	4294
from the **t** of Issachar, Igal the	**Nu 13:7**	4294
from the **t** of Ephraim, Hoshea the	**Nu 13:8**	4294
from the **t** of Benjamin, Palti the	**Nu 13:9**	4294
from the **t** of Zebulun, Gaddiel the	**Nu 13:10**	4294
from the **t** of Joseph, from the	**Nu 13:11**	4294
of Joseph, from the **t** of Manasseh,	**Nu 13:11**	4294
from the **t** of Dan, Ammiel the son	**Nu 13:12**	4294
from the **t** of Asher, Sethur the	**Nu 13:13**	4294
from the **t** of Naphtali, Nahbi the	**Nu 13:14**	4294
from the **t** of Gad, Geuel the son	**Nu 13:15**	4294
also your brothers, the **t** of Levi,	**Nu 18:2**	4294
of Levi, the **t** of your father,	**Nu 18:2**	7626
and saw Israel camping **t** by tribe;	**Nu 24:2**	7626
and saw Israel camping tribe by **t**;	**Nu 24:2**	7626
"A thousand from each **t** of all	**Nu 31:4**	4294
of Israel, a thousand from each **t**,	**Nu 31:5**	4294
sent them, a thousand from each **t**,	**Nu 31:6**	4294
"For the **t** of the sons of Reuben	**Nu 34:14**	4294
and the **t** of the sons of Gad	**Nu 34:14**	4294
leader of every **t** to apportion the land	**Nu 34:18**	4294
of the **t** of Judah, Caleb the son	**Nu 34:19**	4294
Of the **t** of the sons of Simeon,	**Nu 34:20**	4294
"Of the **t** of Benjamin, Elidad the	**Nu 34:21**	4294
the **t** of the sons of Dan a leader,	**Nu 34:22**	4294
of the **t** of the sons of Manasseh a	**Nu 34:23**	4294
t of the sons of Ephraim a leader,	**Nu 34:24**	4294
t of the sons of Zebulun a leader,	**Nu 34:25**	4294
t of the sons of Issachar a leader,	**Nu 34:26**	4294
t of the sons of Asher a leader,	**Nu 34:27**	4294
t of the sons of Naphtali a leader,	**Nu 34:28**	4294
be added to the inheritance of the **t**	**Nu 36:3**	4294
be added to the inheritance of the **t**	**Nu 36:4**	4294
inheritance of the **t** of our fathers."	**Nu 36:4**	4294
"The **t** of the sons of Joseph are	**Nu 36:5**	4294
family of the **t** of their father.'	**Nu 36:6**	4294
be transferred from **t** to tribe,	**Nu 36:7**	4294
be transferred from tribe to **t**,	**Nu 36:7**	4294
inheritance of the **t** of his fathers.	**Nu 36:7**	4294
inheritance of any **t** of the sons of	**Nu 36:8**	4294
the family of the **t** of her father,	**Nu 36:8**	4294
from one **t** to another tribe,	**Nu 36:9**	4294
from one tribe to another **t**,	**Nu 36:9**	4294
t of the family of their father.	**Nu 36:12**	4294
of your men, one man for each **t**.	**Dt 1:23**	7626
the LORD set apart the **t** of Levi	**Dt 10:8**	7626
priests, the whole **t** of Levi,	**Dt 18:1**	7626
a man or woman, or family or **t**,	**Dt 29:18**	7626
of Israel, one man for each **t**.	**Jos 3:12**	7626
the people, one man from each **t**,	**Jos 4:2**	7626
of Israel, one man from each **t**;	**Jos 4:4**	7626
son of Zerah, from the **t** of Judah,	**Jos 7:1**	4294
the **t** which the LORD takes *by lot*	**Jos 7:14**	7626
and the **t** of Judah was taken.	**Jos 7:16**	7626
son of Zerah, from the **t** of Judah,	**Jos 7:18**	4294
Only to the **t** of Levi he did not	**Jos 13:14**	7626
to the **t** of the sons of Reuben	**Jos 13:15**	4294
an inheritance to the **t** of Gad,	**Jos 13:24**	4294
But to the **t** of Levi, Moses did	**Jos 13:33**	7626
the lot for the **t** of the sons of Judah	**Jos 15:1**	4294
This is the inheritance of the **t**	**Jos 15:20**	4294
of the **t** of the sons of Judah toward	**Jos 15:21**	4294
This is the inheritance of the **t**	**Jos 16:8**	4294
was the lot for the **t** of Manasseh,	**Jos 17:1**	4294
from each **t** that I may send them,	**Jos 18:4**	7626
Now the lot of the **t** of the sons	**Jos 18:11**	4294
Now the cities of the **t** of the sons	**Jos 18:21**	4294
to the **t** of the sons of Simeon	**Jos 19:1**	4294
of the **t** of the sons of Simeon	**Jos 19:8**	4294
This *was* the inheritance of the **t**	**Jos 19:23**	4294
lot fell to the **t** of the sons of Asher	**Jos 19:24**	4294
This *was* the inheritance of the **t**	**Jos 19:31**	4294
This *was* the inheritance of the **t**	**Jos 19:39**	4294
lot fell to the **t** of the sons of Dan	**Jos 19:40**	4294
This *was* the inheritance of the **t**	**Jos 19:48**	4294
on the plain from the **t** of Reuben,	**Jos 20:8**	4294
in Gilead from the **t** of Gad,	**Jos 20:8**	4294
in Bashan from the **t** of Manasseh.	**Jos 20:8**	4294
cities by lot from the **t** of Judah and	**Jos 21:4**	4294
and from the **t** of the Simeonites	**Jos 21:4**	4294
and from the **t** of Benjamin.	**Jos 21:4**	4294
from the families of the **t** of Ephraim	**Jos 21:5**	4294
and from the **t** of Dan and from the	**Jos 21:5**	4294
from the families of the **t** of Issachar	**Jos 21:6**	4294
and from the **t** of Asher and from	**Jos 21:6**	4294
Asher and from the **t** of Naphtali	**Jos 21:6**	4294
twelve cities from the **t** of Reuben	**Jos 21:7**	4294
and from the **t** of Gad and from the	**Jos 21:7**	4294
of Gad and from the **t** of Zebulun.	**Jos 21:7**	4294
from the **t** of the sons of Judah	**Jos 21:9**	4294
from the **t** of the sons of Simeon;	**Jos 21:9**	4294
From the **t** of Benjamin, Gibeon	**Jos 21:17**	4294

cities from the **t** of Ephraim were	**Jos 21:20**	4294
From the **t** of Dan, Elteke with	**Jos 21:23**	4294
From the **t** of Issachar, *they*	**Jos 21:28**	4294
From the **t** of Asher, *they gave*	**Jos 21:30**	4294
From the **t** of Naphtali, *they*	**Jos 21:32**	4294
they gave from the **t** of Zebulun,	**Jos 21:34**	4294
From the **t** of Reuben, *they*	**Jos 21:36**	4294
From the **t** of Gad, *they gave*	**Jos 21:38**	4294
the **t** of the Danites was seeking	**Jg 18:1**	7626
to a **t** and a family in Israel?"	**Jg 18:19**	7626
were priests to the **t** of the Danites	**Jg 18:30**	7626
through the entire **t** of Benjamin,	**Jg 20:12**	7626
so that one **t** should be *missing*	**Jg 21:3**	7626
One **t** is cut off from Israel today.	**Jg 21:6**	7626
that a **t** will not be blotted out	**Jg 21:17**	7626
every man to his **t** and family,	**Jg 21:24**	7626
the families of the **t** of Benjamin?	**1Sa 9:21**	7626
t of Benjamin was taken by lot.	**1Sa 10:20**	7626
Then he brought the **t** of Benjamin	**1Sa 10:21**	7626
widow's son from the **t** of Naphtali,	**1Ki 7:14**	4294
but I will give one **t** to your son	**1Ki 11:13**	7626
(but he will have one **t**,	**1Ki 11:32**	7626
'But to his son I will give one **t**,	**1Ki 11:36**	7626
None but the **t** of Judah followed	**1Ki 12:20**	7626
of Judah and the **t** of Benjamin,	**1Ki 12:21**	7626
was left except the **t** of Judah.	**2Ki 17:18**	7626
and from the **t** of Benjamin:	**1Ch 6:60**	4294
by lot, from the family of the **t**,	**1Ch 6:61**	4294
were given from the **t** of Issachar	**1Ch 6:62**	4294
Issachar and from the **t** of Asher,	**1Ch 6:62**	4294
tribe of Asher, the **t** of Naphtali,	**1Ch 6:62**	4294
Naphtali, and the **t** of Manasseh,	**1Ch 6:62**	4294
families, from the **t** of Reuben,	**1Ch 6:63**	4294
the tribe of Reuben, the **t** of Gad and	**1Ch 6:63**	4294
of Gad and the **t** of Zebulun,	**1Ch 6:63**	4294
from the **t** of the sons of Judah,	**1Ch 6:65**	4294
the **t** of the sons of Simeon	**1Ch 6:65**	4294
and the **t** of the sons of Benjamin,	**1Ch 6:65**	4294
territory from the **t** of Ephraim.	**1Ch 6:66**	4294
and from the **t** of Issachar:	**1Ch 6:72**	4294
and from the **t** of Asher:	**1Ch 6:74**	4294
and from the **t** of Naphtali:	**1Ch 6:76**	4294
were given, from the **t** of Zebulun:	**1Ch 6:77**	4294
given them, from the **t** of Reuben:	**1Ch 6:78**	4294
and from the **t** of Gad:	**1Ch 6:80**	4294
were named among the **t** of Levi.	**1Ch 23:14**	7626
to be the **t** of Your inheritance;	**Ps 74:2**	7626
did not choose the **t** of Ephraim,	**Ps 78:67**	7626
But chose the **t** of Judah, Mount	**Ps 78:68**	7626
Israel is the **t** of His inheritance;	**Jer 10:16**	7626
And of the **t** of His inheritance;	**Jer 51:19**	7626
the **t** with which the alien stays,	**Ezk 47:23**	7626
to fear Your name: "Hear, O **t**.	**Mi 6:9**	4294
of Phanuel, of the **t** of Asher.	**Lk 2:36**	*5443*
Kish, a man of the **t** of Benjamin,	**Ac 13:21**	*5443*
of Abraham, of the **t** of Benjamin.	**Ro 11:1**	*5443*
of Israel, of the **t** of Benjamin,	**Php 3:5**	*5443*
are spoken belongs to another **t**,	**Heb 7:13**	*5443*
a **t** with reference to which Moses	**Heb 7:14**	*5443*
Lion that is from the **t** of Judah,	**Rv 5:5**	*5443*
men from every **t** and tongue and	**Rv 5:9**	*5443*
every **t** of the sons of Israel:	**Rv 7:4**	*5443*
the **t** of Judah, twelve thousand	**Rv 7:5**	*5443*
the **t** of Reuben twelve thousand,	**Rv 7:5**	*5443*
from the **t** of Gad twelve thousand,	**Rv 7:5**	*5443*
the **t** of Asher twelve thousand,	**Rv 7:6**	*5443*
the **t** of Naphtali twelve thousand,	**Rv 7:6**	*5443*
the **t** of Manasseh twelve thousand,	**Rv 7:6**	*5443*
the **t** of Simeon twelve thousand,	**Rv 7:7**	*5443*
the **t** of Levi twelve thousand,	**Rv 7:7**	*5443*
the **t** of Issachar twelve thousand,	**Rv 7:7**	*5443*
the **t** of Zebulun twelve thousand,	**Rv 7:8**	*5443*
the **t** of Joseph twelve thousand,	**Rv 7:8**	*5443*
the **t** of Benjamin, twelve thousand	**Rv 7:8**	*5443*
and authority over every **t** and	**Rv 13:7**	*5443*
and **t** and tongue and people;	**Rv 14:6**	*5443*

TRIBES

princes according to their **t**.	**Gn 25:16**	523
people, As one of the **t** of Israel.	**Gn 49:16**	7626
these are the twelve **t** of Israel,	**Gn 49:28**	7626
for the twelve **t** of Israel.	**Ex 24:4**	7626
to his name for the twelve **t**.	**Ex 28:21**	7626
with its name for the twelve **t**.	**Ex 39:14**	7626
the leaders of their fathers' **t**;	**Nu 1:16**	4294
(they were the leaders of the **t**;	**Nu 7:2**	4294
man from each of their fathers' **t**,	**Nu 13:2**	4294
names of the **t** of their fathers.	**Nu 26:55**	4294
heads of the **t** of the sons of Israel,	**Nu 30:1**	4294
from each tribe of all the **t** of Israel	**Nu 31:4**	4294
of the **t** of the sons of Israel.	**Nu 32:28**	4294
to the **t** of your fathers.	**Nu 33:54**	4294
to give to the nine and a half **t**.	**Nu 34:13**	4294
"The two and a half **t** have	**Nu 34:15**	4294
the *other* **t** of the sons of Israel,	**Nu 36:3**	7626
for the **t** of the sons of Israel	**Nu 36:9**	4294
and experienced men from your **t**,	**Dt 1:13**	7626
"So I took the heads of your **t**,	**Dt 1:15**	7626
of tens, and officers for your **t**.	**Dt 1:15**	7626
heads of your **t** and your elders.	**Dt 5:23**	7626
God will choose from all your **t**,	**Dt 12:5**	7626
the LORD chooses in one of your **t**,	**Dt 12:14**	7626
giving you, according to your **t**,	**Dt 16:18**	7626
him and his sons from all your **t**,	**Dt 18:5**	7626
your chiefs, your **t**,	**Dt 29:10**	7626
from all the **t** of Israel,	**Dt 29:21**	7626
of your **t** and your officers,	**Dt 31:28**	7626
The **t** of Israel together.	**Dt 33:5**	7626
twelve men from the **t** of Israel,	**Jos 3:12**	7626
number of the **t** of the sons of Israel.	**Jos 4:5**	7626
number of the **t** of the sons of Israel;	**Jos 4:8**	7626
you shall come near by your **t**.	**Jos 7:14**	7626
and brought Israel near by **t**,	**Jos 7:16**	7626
to their divisions by their **t**.	**Jos 11:23**	7626
and Joshua gave it to the **t** of Israel	**Jos 12:7**	7626
for an inheritance to the nine **t** and	**Jos 13:7**	7626
of the **t** of the sons of Israel	**Jos 14:1**	4294
for the nine **t** and the half-tribe.	**Jos 14:2**	4294
given the inheritance of the two **t**	**Jos 14:3**	4294
For the sons of Joseph were two **t**,	**Jos 14:4**	4294
among the sons of Israel seven **t** who	**Jos 18:2**	7626
the **t** of the sons of Israel distributed	**Jos 19:51**	4294
of the **t** of the sons of Israel.	**Jos 21:1**	4294
nine cities from these two **t**.	**Jos 21:16**	7626
from each of the **t** of Israel;	**Jos 22:14**	4294
as an inheritance for your **t**,	**Jos 23:4**	7626
all the **t** of Israel to Shechem,	**Jos 24:1**	7626
possession among the **t** of Israel.	**Jg 18:1**	7626
even of all the **t** of Israel,	**Jg 20:2**	7626
of 100 throughout the **t** of Israel,	**Jg 20:10**	7626
Then the **t** of Israel sent men	**Jg 20:12**	7626
Who is there among all the **t** of Israel	**Jg 21:5**	7626
"What one is there of the **t** of Israel	**Jg 21:8**	7626
made a breach in the **t** of Israel.	**Jg 21:15**	7626
the **t** of Israel to be My priests,	**1Sa 2:28**	7626
the smallest of the **t** of Israel,	**1Sa 9:21**	7626
by your **t** and by your clans."	**1Sa 10:19**	7626
brought all the **t** of Israel near,	**1Sa 10:20**	7626
made the head of the **t** of Israel?	**1Sa 15:17**	7626
Then all the **t** of Israel came to	**2Sa 5:1**	7626
word with one of the **t** of Israel,	**2Sa 7:7**	7626
is from one of the **t** of Israel."	**2Sa 15:2**	7626
throughout all the **t** of Israel,	**2Sa 15:10**	7626
throughout all the **t** of Israel,	**2Sa 19:9**	7626
he went through all the **t** of Israel	**2Sa 20:14**	7626
now through all the **t** of Israel,	**2Sa 24:2**	7626
Israel and all the heads of the **t**,	**1Ki 8:1**	4294
choose a city out of all the **t** of Israel	**1Ki 8:16**	7626
of Solomon and give you ten **t**	**1Ki 11:31**	7626
chosen from all the **t** of Israel),	**1Ki 11:32**	7626
and give it to you, *even* ten **t**.	**1Ki 11:35**	7626
had chosen from all the **t** of Israel	**1Ki 14:21**	7626
of the **t** of the sons of Jacob,	**1Ki 18:31**	7626
chosen from all the **t** of Israel,	**2Ki 21:7**	7626
Now in charge of the **t** of Israel:	**1Ch 27:16**	7626
the princes of the **t** of Israel.	**1Ch 27:22**	7626
of Israel, the princes of the **t**,	**1Ch 28:1**	7626
the princes of the **t** of Israel,	**1Ch 29:6**	7626
Israel and all the heads of the **t**,	**2Ch 5:2**	4294
choose a city out of all the **t** of Israel	**2Ch 6:5**	7626
Those from all the **t** of Israel	**2Ch 11:16**	7626
chosen from all the **t** of Israel,	**2Ch 12:13**	7626
chosen from all the **t** of Israel,	**2Ch 33:7**	7626
to the number of the **t** of Israel.	**Ezr 6:17**	7625
And made the **t** of Israel dwell in	**Ps 78:55**	7626
And among His **t** there was not one	**Ps 105:37**	7626
To which the **t** go up, even the	**Ps 122:4**	7626
even the **t** of the LORD—An	**Ps 122:4**	7626
who are the cornerstone of her **t**	**Is 19:13**	7626
To raise up the **t** of Jacob and	**Is 49:6**	7626
servants, the **t** of Your heritage.	**Is 63:17**	7626
nations, like the **t** of the lands,	**Ezk 20:32**	4940
of Ephraim, and the **t** of Israel,	**Ezk 37:19**	7626
of Israel according to their **t**."	**Ezk 45:8**	7626
among the twelve **t** of Israel;	**Ezk 47:13**	7626
according to the **t** of Israel.	**Ezk 47:21**	7626
with you among the **t** of Israel.	**Ezk 47:22**	7626
"Now these are the names of the **t**:	**Ezk 48:1**	7626
city, out of all the **t** of Israel,	**Ezk 48:19**	7626
"As for the rest of the **t**:	**Ezk 48:23**	7626
t of Israel for an inheritance,	**Ezk 48:29**	7626
city, named for the **t** of Israel,	**Ezk 48:31**	7626
Among the **t** of Israel I declare	**Hos 5:9**	7626
especially of all the **t** of Israel,	**Zch 9:1**	7626
judging the twelve **t** of Israel.	**Mt 19:28**	*5443*
all the **t** of the earth will mourn,	**Mt 24:30**	*5443*
judging the twelve **t** of Israel.	**Lk 22:30**	*5443*
which our twelve **t** hope to attain,	**Ac 26:7**	*1429*
twelve **t** who are dispersed abroad:	**Jas 1:1**	*5443*
and all the **t** of the earth will	**Rv 1:7**	*5443*
and *all* **t** and peoples and tongues,	**Rv 7:9**	*5443*
Those from the peoples and **t**	**Rv 11:9**	*5443*
twelve **t** of the sons of Israel.	**Rv 21:12**	*5443*

TRIBULATION

"Then they will deliver you to **t**,	**Mt 24:9**	*2347*
"For then there will be a great **t**,	**Mt 24:21**	*2347*
immediately after the **t** of those days	**Mt 24:29**	*2347*
those days will be a *time of* **t** such as	**Mk 13:19**	*2347*
"But in those days, after that **t**,	**Mk 13:24**	*2347*
In the world you have **t**,	**Jn 16:33**	*2347*
There will be **t** and distress for	**Ro 2:9**	*2347*
that **t** brings about perseverance;	**Ro 5:3**	*2347*
Will **t**, or distress, or	**Ro 8:35**	*2347*
in hope, persevering in **t**,	**Ro 12:12**	*2347*
having received the word in much **t**	**1Th 1:6**	*2347*
fellow partaker in the **t** and kingdom	**Rv 1:9**	*2347*
'I know your **t** and your poverty	**Rv 2:9**	*2347*
and you will have **t** for ten days.	**Rv 2:10**	*2347*
adultery with her into great **t**,	**Rv 2:22**	*2347*
ones who come out of the great **t**,	**Rv 7:14**	*2347*

TRIBULATIONS

"Through many **t** we must enter the	**Ac 14:22**	*2347*
this, but we also exult in our **t**,	**Ro 5:3**	*2347*
lose heart at my **t** on your behalf,	**Eph 3:13**	*2347*
through reproaches and **t**,	**Heb 10:33**	*2347*

TRIBUNAL

the next day he took his seat on the **t**	**Ac 25:6**	*968*
"I am standing before Caesar's **t**,	**Ac 25:10**	*968*
next day took my seat on the **t** and	**Ac 25:17**	*968*

TRIBUTE

God with a **t** of a freewill offering	**Dt 16:10**	4530
And the sons of Israel sent **t** by	**Jg 3:15**	4503
He presented the **t** to Eglon king of	**Jg 3:17**	4503
he had finished presenting the **t**,	**Jg 3:18**	4503
the people who had carried the **t**.	**Jg 3:18**	4503
servants to David, bringing **t**.	**2Sa 8:2**	4503
servants to David, bringing **t**.	**2Sa 8:6**	4503
they brought **t** and served Solomon	**1Ki 4:21**	4503
became his servant and paid him **t**.	**2Ki 17:3**	4503
no **t** to the king of Assyria,	**2Ki 17:4**	4503
servants to David, bringing **t**.	**1Ch 18:2**	4503
servants to David, bringing **t**.	**1Ch 18:6**	4503
Judah brought **t** to Jehoshaphat,	**2Ch 17:5**	4503
and silver as **t** to Jehoshaphat;	**2Ch 17:11**	4853a
Ammonites also gave **t** to Uzziah,	**2Ch 26:8**	4503
are finished, they will not pay **t**,	**Ezr 4:13**	4061
beyond the River, and that **t**,	**Ezr 4:20**	4061
t or toll *on* any of the priests,	**Ezr 7:24**	4061
Now King Ahasuerus laid a **t** on the	**Es 10:1**	4522
Send the **t** lamb to the ruler of	**Is 16:1**	
to Assyria As **t** to King Jareb;	**Hos 10:6**	4503
And exact a **t** of grain from them,	**Am 5:11**	4864

TRICKED

that he had been **t** by the magi,	**Mt 2:16**	*1702*

TRICKERY

together with the **t** of his hands.	**Is 25:11**	698
detected their **t** and said to them,	**Lk 20:23**	*3834*
wind of doctrine, by the **t** of men,	**Eph 4:14**	*2940*

TRICKLING

water was **t** from the south side.	**Ezk 47:2**	6379

TRICKS

been hostile to you with their **t**,	**Nu 25:18**	5231

TRIED

this matter, he **t** to kill Moses.	**Ex 2:15**	1245
The magicians **t** with their	**Ex 8:18**	6213a
"Or has a god **t** to go to take for	**Dt 4:34**	5254
over his armor and **t** to walk,	**1Sa 17:39**	2974
Saul **t** to pin David to the	**1Sa 19:10**	1245
When He has **t** me, I shall come	**Jb 23:10**	974
'Job ought to be **t** to the limit,	**Jb 34:36**	974
As silver **t** in a furnace on the earth,	**Ps 12:6**	6884
You have **t** my heart;	**Ps 17:3**	974
The word of the LORD is **t**;	**Ps 18:30**	6884
For You have **t** us, O God;	**Ps 66:10**	974
your fathers tested Me, They **t** Me,	**Ps 95:9**	974
But John **t** to prevent Him, saying,	**Mt 3:14**	
and we **t** to prevent him because he	**Mk 9:38**	
They **t** to give Him wine mixed	**Mk 15:23**	
and **t** to keep Him from going away	**Lk 4:42**	
and we **t** to prevent him because he	**Lk 9:49**	
chief priests **t** to lay hands on Him	**Lk 20:19**	*2212*
he **t** to reconcile them in peace,	**Ac 7:26**	
he even **t** to desecrate the temple;	**Ac 24:6**	*3985*
tribunal, where I ought to be **t**.	**Ac 25:10**	*2919*
I **t** to force them to blaspheme;	**Ac 26:11**	
temple and **t** to put me to death.	**Ac 26:21**	*3987*
measure and **t** to destroy it;	**Ga 1:13**	
which he once **t** to destroy."	**Ga 1:23**	
YOUR FATHERS **T** *ME* BY TESTING *ME*,	**Heb 3:9**	*3985*

TRIES

God **t** the hearts and minds.	**Ps 7:9**	974
Who **t** the feelings and the heart,	**Jer 11:20**	974

TRIGON

sound of the horn, flute, lyre, **t**,	**Da 3:5**	5443
sound of the horn, flute, lyre, **t**,	**Da 3:7**	5443
sound of the horn, flute, lyre, **t**,	**Da 3:10**	5443
sound of the horn, flute, lyre, **t**,	**Da 3:15**	5443

TRIM

shave her head and **t** her nails.	**Dt 21:12**	6213a
only **t** *the hair of* their heads.	**Ezk 44:20**	3697

TRIMMED

for his feet, nor **t** his mustache,	**2Sa 19:24**	6213a
virgins rose and **t** their lamps.	**Mt 25:7**	*2885*

TRIMS

every morning when he **t** the lamps.	**Ex 30:7**	3190
Aaron **t** the lamps at twilight,	**Ex 30:8**	5927

TRIP

Who have purposed to **t** up my feet.	**Ps 140:4**	1760

TRIUMPH

is not the sound of the cry of **t**,	**Ex 32:18**	1369
enemy does not shout in **t** over me.	**Ps 41:11**	7321
When the righteous **t**,	**Pr 28:12**	5970
Shout *in* **t**, O Israel! Rejoice	**Zph 3:14**	
Shout *in* **t**, O daughter of	**Zch 9:9**	
leads us in **t** in Christ,	**2Co 2:14**	*2358*

TRIUMPHANT

"Our hand is **t**, And the LORD has	**Dt 32:27**	7311

TRIUMPHANTLY

God will let me look **t** upon my	**Ps 59:10**	

TRIUMPHED

having **t** over them through Him.	**Col 2:15**	*2358*

TRIUMPHING

That the **t** of the wicked is short,	**Jb 20:5**	7445

TRIUMPHS

mercy **t** over judgment.	**Jas 2:13**	*2620*

TRIVIAL

"Is it **t** in your sight to become	**1Sa 18:23**	7043
as though it had been a **t** thing	**1Ki 16:31**	7043

TROAS

by Mysia, they came down to **T**.	**Ac 16:8**	*5174*
putting out to sea from **T**,	**Ac 16:11**	*5174*
and were waiting for us at **T**.	**Ac 20:5**	*5174*
came to them at **T** within five days;	**Ac 20:6**	*5174*

Now when I came to T for the 2Co 2:12 5174
cloak which I left at T with Carpus, 2Tm 4:13 5174

TROD

of their vineyards and t them, Jg 9:27 1869
and t them down opposite Gibeah Jg 20:43 1869
path Which wicked men have t, Jb 22:15 1869
I also t them in My anger And Is 63:3 1869
I t down the peoples in My anger And Is 63:6 947

TRODDEN

land on which your foot has t will Jos 14:9 1869
"The proud beasts have not t it, Jb 28:8 1869
And Moab will be t down in his Is 25:10 1758
As straw is t down in the water Is 25:10 1758
of Ephraim is t under foot. Is 28:3 7429
"I have t the wine trough alone, Is 63:3 1869
Our adversaries have t it down. Is 63:18 947
The Lord has t as in a wine press La 1:15 1869
wine press was t outside the city, Rv 14:20 3961

TROOP

"For by You I can run upon a t; 2Sa 22:30 1416
Philistines were gathered into a t where 2Sa 23:11 2422a
while the t of the Philistines was 2Sa 23:13 2422a
For by You I can run upon a t; Ps 18:29 1416
behold, here comes a t of riders, Is 21:9 376

TROOPED

And t to the harlot's house. Jer 5:7 1413

TROOPS

with his chariots and his many t Jg 4:7
were 36,000 t of the army for war, 1Ch 7:4 1416
He placed t in all the fortified 2Ch 17:2 2428
I have given to the t of Israel?" 2Ch 25:9 1416
the t which came to him from 2Ch 25:10 1416
But the t whom Amaziah sent back 2Ch 25:13 1121, 1416
ashamed to request from the king t Ezr 8:22 2428
"His t come together, And build Jb 19:12 1416
"Is there any number to His t? Jb 25:3 1416
And dwelt as a king among the t, Jb 29:25 1416
him, his helpers and all his t; Ezk 12:14 102
might give him horses and many t. Ezk 17:15 5971a
all his t will fall by the sword, Ezk 17:21 102
Gomer with all its t; Ezk 38:6 102
parts of the north with all its t Ezk 38:6 102
the land, you and all your t, Ezk 38:9 102
I will rain on him and on his t, Ezk 38:22 102
of Israel, you and all your t and Ezk 39:4 102
ground, not even their choicest t, Da 11:15 5971a
"Now muster yourselves in t, Mi 5:1 1413
in troops, daughter of t; Mi 5:1 1416
ordered the t to go down and take Ac 23:10 4753
them with the t and rescued him, Ac 23:27 4753

TROPHIMUS

and Tychicus and T of Asia. Ac 20:4 5161
had previously seen T the Ephesian Ac 21:29 5161
but T I left sick at Miletus. 2Tm 4:20 5161

TROUBLE

"You have brought t on me by Gn 34:30 5916
"God has made me forget all my t Gn 41:51 5999
were in t because they were told, Ex 5:19 7451b
Nor has He seen t in Israel; Nu 23:21 5999
and they will t you in the land Nu 33:55 6887c
Israel accursed and bring t on it. Jos 6:18 5916
The LORD will t you this day." Jos 7:25 5916
to me now when you are in t?" Jg 11:7 6887a
and you are among those who t me; Jg 11:35 5916
"What is your t?" 2Sa 14:5
see how this man is looking for t; 1Ki 20:7 7463a
should you provoke t so that you 2Ki 14:10 7463a
why should you provoke t so that you, 2Ch 25:19 7463a
us and on this city all this t? Ne 13:18 7463a
the t would not be commensurate Es 7:4 6862b
womb, Or hide t from my eyes. Jb 3:10 5999
And those who sow t harvest it. Jb 4:8 5999
does t sprout from the ground, Jb 5:6 5999
For man is born for t, Jb 5:7 5999
And nights of t are appointed me. Jb 7:3 5999
"For you would forget your t, Jb 11:16 5999
A stronghold in times of t; Ps 9:9 6869a
You hide Yourself in times of t? Ps 10:1 6869a
LORD answer you in the day of t! Ps 20:1 6869a
Be not far from me, for t is near; Ps 22:11 6869a
Look upon my affliction and my t, Ps 25:18 5999
For in the day of t He will Ps 27:5 7463a
You preserve me from t; Ps 32:7 6862b
He is their strength in time of t. Ps 37:39 6869a
LORD will deliver him in a day of t. Ps 41:1 7463a
A very present help in t. Ps 46:1 6869a
Call upon Me in the day of t; Ps 50:15 6869a
He has delivered me from all t, Ps 54:7 6869a
For they bring down t upon me And Ps 55:3 205
They are not in t as other men, Ps 73:5 5999
the day of my t I sought the Lord; Ps 77:2 6869a
Fury and indignation and t, Ps 78:49 6869a
"You called in t and I rescued Ps 81:7 6869a
In the day of my t I shall call upon Ps 86:7 6869a
I will be with him in t; Ps 91:15 6869a
cried out to the LORD in their t; Ps 107:6 6862b
cried out to the LORD in their t; Ps 107:13 6862b
cried out to the LORD in their t; Ps 107:19 6862b
they cried to the LORD in their t, Ps 107:28 6862b
T and anguish have come upon me, Ps 119:143 6862b
In my t I cried to the LORD, And Ps 120:1 6869a
Though I walk in the midst of t, Ps 138:7 6869a
I declare my t before Him. Ps 142:2 6869a
bring my soul out of t. Ps 143:11 6869a
He who winks the eye causes t, Pr 10:10 6094
The righteous is delivered from t, Pr 11:8 6869a
the righteous will escape from t. Pr 12:13 6869a
But the wicked are filled with t. Pr 12:21 7451b
But t is in the income of the Pr 15:6 5916
And their lips talk of t. Pr 24:2 5999
in a faithless man in time of t. Pr 25:19 6869a
And remember his t no more. Pr 31:7 5999
a royal command experiences no t, Ec 8:5 1697, 7451a
though a man's t is heavy upon him. Ec 8:6 7463a
in the time of their t they will say, Jer 2:27 7463a
save you In the time of your t; Jer 2:28 7463a
the womb To look on t and sorrow, Jer 20:18 5999
also t the hearts of many peoples when Ezk 32:9 3707
And Bethel will come to t. Am 5:5 205
A stronghold in the day of t, Na 1:7 6869a
that day, A day of t and distress, Zph 1:15 6869a
Each day has enough t of its own. Mt 6:34 2549
him over and keep you out of t." Mt 28:14 275
why t the Teacher anymore?" Mk 5:35 4660
"Lord, do not t Yourself further, Lk 7:6 4660
do not t the Teacher anymore." Lk 8:49 4660
do not t those who are turning to God Ac 15:19 3926
Yet such will have t in this life, 1Co 7:28 2347
now on let no one cause t for me, Ga 6:17 2873
same things again is no t to me, Php 3:1 3636
bitterness springing up causes t, Heb 12:15 1776

TROUBLED

the morning his spirit was t, Gn 41:8 6470
"Why have you t us? Jos 7:25 5916
"My father has t the land. 1Sa 14:29 5916
grief or a t heart to my lord, 1Sa 25:31 4383
Now David's heart t him after he 2Sa 24:10 5221
"I have not t Israel, but you and 1Ki 18:18 5916
for her soul is t within her; 2Ki 4:27 4843
for God t them with every kind of 2Ch 15:6 2000
I am so t that I cannot speak. Ps 77:4 6470
he who sings songs to a t heart. Pr 25:20 7451a
and a few days You will be t, Is 32:10 7264
Be t, you complacent daughters; Is 32:11 7264
My spirit is greatly t; La 1:20 2560a
of tears, My spirit is greatly t; La 2:11 2560a
They are t in countenance. Ezk 27:35 7481
his spirit was t and his sleep left him Da 2:1 6470
he cried out with a t voice. Da 6:20 6088
Herod the king heard this, he was t, Mt 2:3 5015
began to be very distressed and t. Mk 14:33 85
Zacharias was t when he saw the Lk 1:12 5015
and those who were t with unclean Lk 6:18 1776
"Why are you t, and why do doubts Lk 24:38 5015
deeply moved in spirit and was t, Jn 11:33 5015
"Now My soul has become t; Jn 12:27 5015
said this, He became t in spirit, Jn 13:21 5015
"Do not let your heart be t; Jn 14:1 5015
Do not let your heart be t, Jn 14:27 5015
"Do not be t, for his life is in Ac 20:10 2350b
INTIMIDATION, AND DO NOT BE T, 1Pe 3:14 5015

TROUBLER

"Is this you, you t of Israel?" 1Ki 18:17 5916
Carmi was Achar, the t of Israel, 1Ch 2:7 5916

TROUBLES

evils and t will come upon them; Dt 31:17 6869a
evils and t have come upon them, Dt 31:21 6869a
"From six t He will deliver you, Jb 5:19 6869a
The t of my heart are enlarged; Ps 25:17 6869a
Israel, O God, Out of all his t. Ps 25:22 6869a
You have known the t of my soul, Ps 31:7 6869a
And saved him out of all his t. Ps 34:6 6869a
delivers them out of all their t. Ps 34:17 6869a
shown me many t and distresses Will Ps 71:20 6869a
For my soul has had enough t, Ps 88:3 7463a
He who t his own house will Pr 11:29 5916
He who profits illicitly t his own Pr 15:27 5916
tongue, Guards his soul from t. Pr 21:23 6869a
the former t are forgotten, Is 65:16 6869a

TROUBLESOME

this, It was t in my sight Ps 73:16 5999
or evildoer, or a t meddler; 1Pe 4:15 244

TROUBLING

"What is t you, Queen Esther? Es 5:3
wish that those who are t you Ga 5:12 387

TROUGH

emptied her jar into the t, Gn 24:20 8268
"I have trodden the wine t alone, Is 63:3 6333b

TROUGHS

gutters, even in the watering t, Gn 30:38 8268
t to water their father's flock. Ex 2:16 7298a

TROUSERS

these men were tied up in their t, Da 3:21 5622
singed, nor were their t damaged, Da 3:27 5622

TRUE

word will come t for you or not." Nu 11:23 7136a
the sign or the wonder comes t, Dt 13:2
If it is t and the matter Dt 13:14 571
if it is t and the thing certain Dt 17:4 571
does not come about or come t, Dt 18:22
"But if this charge is t, Dt 22:20 571
Now it is t I am a close relative; Ru 3:12 551
all that he says surely comes t. 1Sa 9:6
"Is it not t, though you were 1Sa 15:17
"It was a t report which I heard 1Ki 10:6 571
"It was a t report which I heard 2Ch 9:5 571
days Israel was without the t God 2Ch 15:3 571
and t before the LORD his God. 2Ch 31:20 571
them just ordinances and t laws, Ne 9:13 571
The judgments of the LORD are t; Ps 19:9 571
righteousness gets a t reward. Pr 11:18 571
Or let them hear and say, "It is t." Is 43:9 571
But the LORD is the t God; Jer 10:10 571
the LORD be a t and faithful witness Jer 42:5 571
t justice between man and man, Ezk 18:8 571
so the dream is t and its Da 2:45 3330a
"Is it t, Shadrach, Meshach and Da 3:14 6656
His works are t and His ways just, Da 4:37 7187
"The statement is t, Da 6:12 3330a
mornings Which has been told is t; Da 8:26 571
the message was t and one of great Da 10:1 571
'Dispense t justice and practice Zch 7:9 571
"T instruction was in his mouth and Mal 2:6 571
will entrust the t riches to you? Lk 16:11 228
There was the t Light which, Jn 1:9 228
his seal to this, that God is t. Jn 3:33 227
when the t worshipers will Jn 4:23 228
"For in this case the saying is t, Jn 4:37 228
about Myself, My testimony is not t. Jn 5:31 227
which He gives about Me is t. Jn 5:32 227
gives you the t bread out of heaven. Jn 6:32 228
"For My flesh is t food, and My Jn 6:55 227
food, and My blood is t drink. Jn 6:55 227
of the One who sent Him, He is t, Jn 7:18 227
Myself, but He who sent Me is t, Jn 7:28 228
Your testimony is not t." Jn 8:13 227
about Myself, My testimony is t, Jn 8:14 227
if I do judge, My judgment is t; Jn 8:16 228
the testimony of two men is t. Jn 8:17 227
you, but He who sent Me is t; Jn 8:26 227
John said about this man was t." Jn 10:41 227
"I am the t vine, and My Father Jn 15:1 228
may know You, the only t God, Jn 17:3 228
testified, and his testimony is t; Jn 19:35 228
and we know that his testimony is t. Jn 21:24 227
all with resolute heart to remain t Ac 11:23
but if none of those things is t Ac 25:11
Rather, let God be found t, Ro 3:4 227
regarded as deceivers and yet t; 2Co 6:8 227
The signs of a t apostle were 2Co 12:12
for we are the t circumcision, Php 3:3
Indeed, t companion, I ask you also Php 4:3 1103
Finally, brethren, whatever is t, Php 4:8 227
in a t knowledge of God's mystery, Col 2:2 1922
is being renewed to a t knowledge Col 3:10 1922
idols to serve a living and t God, 1Th 1:9 228
Timothy, my t child in the faith: 1Tm 1:2 1103
my t child in a common faith: Ti 1:4 1103
This testimony is t. Ti 1:13 227
and in the t tabernacle, Heb 8:2 228
hands, a mere copy of the t one, Heb 9:24 228
that this is the t grace of God. 1Pe 5:12 227
through the t knowledge of Him who 2Pe 1:3 1922
in the t knowledge of our Lord Jesus 2Pe 1:8 1922
them according to the t proverb, 2Pe 2:22 227
you, which is t in Him and in you, 1Jn 2:8 227
the t Light is already shining. 1Jn 2:8 228
things, and is t and is not a lie, 1Jn 2:27 227
that we may know Him who is t 1Jn 5:20 228
true; and we are in Him who is t, 1Jn 5:20 228
This is the t God and eternal life. 1Jn 5:20 228
you know that our testimony is t. 3Jn 1:12 227
He who is holy, who is t, Rv 3:7 228
Amen, the faithful and t Witness, Rv 3:14 228
"How long, O Lord, holy and t, Rv 6:10 228
Righteous and t are Your ways, King Rv 15:3 228
t and righteous are Your judgments." Rv 16:7 228
HIS JUDGMENTS ARE T AND RIGHTEOUS; Rv 19:2 228
"These are t words of God." Rv 19:9 228
on it is called Faithful and T Rv 19:11 228
these words are faithful and t." Rv 21:5 228
"These words are faithful and t"; Rv 22:6 228

TRUER

it is much t that the members of 1Co 12:22 3123

TRULY

deal kindly and t with my master, Gn 24:49 571
"T we are guilty concerning our Gn 42:21 61
"But if you t obey his voice Ex 23:22 8085
"T, I have sinned against the Jos 7:20 546
"But t we have done this out of Jos 22:24 518, 3808
But t as the LORD lives and as 1Sa 20:3 199
"T I am a widow, for my husband 2Sa 14:5 61
"T is not my house so with God? 2Sa 23:5 3588
"T she has no son and her husband 2Ki 4:14 61
"T, O LORD, the kings of Assyria 2Ki 19:17 551
before Me, I t have heard you," 2Ki 22:19 1571
"T He is good, truly His 2Ch 7:3 3588
t His lovingkindness is everlasting. 2Ch 7:3 3588
before Me, I t have heard you," 2Ch 34:27 1571
"T then you are the people, And Jb 12:2 551
"Even if I have t erred, My error Jb 19:4 551
'T our adversaries are cut off, Jb 22:20 518, 3808
"For t my words are not false; Jb 36:4 551
T they shall not enter into My Ps 95:11 518
T, the mouth of the LORD has spoken Is 1:20 3588
them, but will t rely on the LORD, Is 10:20 571
"T, O LORD, the kings of Assyria Is 37:18 551
T, You are a God who hides Is 45:15 403
T I have spoken; truly I will bring it Is 46:11 637
t I will bring it to pass. Is 46:11 637
"For if you t amend your ways and Jer 7:5 3190
if you t practice justice between Jer 7:5 6213a
"T this is a sickness, And I must Jer 10:19 389
T our apostasies have been many, Jer 14:7 3588
for t the LORD has sent me to you Jer 26:15 571
as one whom the LORD has t sent." Jer 28:9 571
"For t I say to you, until heaven Mt 5:18 281
"T I say to you, you will not Mt 5:26 281

T I say to you, they have their Mt 6:2 281
T I say to you, they have their Mt 6:5 281
T I say to you, they have their Mt 6:16 281
"T I say to you, I have not found Mt 8:10 281
"T I say to you, it will be more Mt 10:15 281
for t I say to you, you will not Mt 10:23 281
t I say to you, he shall not lose Mt 10:42 281
"T I say to you, among those Mt 11:11 281
"For t I say to you that many Mt 13:17 281
"T I say to you, there are some Mt 16:28 281
for t I say to you, if you have Mt 17:20 281
"T I say to you, unless you are Mt 18:3 281
that he finds it, t I say to you, Mt 18:13 281
"T I say to you, whatever you Mt 18:18 281
"T I say to you, it is hard for a Mt 19:23 281
"T I say to you, that you who Mt 19:28 281
"T I say to you, if you have Mt 21:21 281
"T I say to you that the Mt 21:31 281
"T I say to you, all these things Mt 23:36 281
T I say to you, not one stone here Mt 24:2 281
"T I say to you, this generation Mt 24:34 281
"T I say to you that he will put Mt 24:47 281
'T I say to you, I do not know you.' Mt 25:12 281
'T I say to you, to the extent Mt 25:40 281
'T I say to you, to the extent Mt 25:45 281
"T I say to you, wherever this Mt 26:13 281
"T I say to you that one of you Mt 26:21 281
"T I say to you that this *very* Mt 26:34 281
"T this was the Son of God!" Mt 27:54 230
"T I say to you, all sins shall Mk 3:28 281
T I say to you, no sign will be Mk 8:12 281
"T I say to you, there are some Mk 9:1 281
of Christ, t I say to you, Mk 9:41 281
"T I say to you, whoever does not Mk 10:15 281
"T I say to you, there is no one Mk 10:29 281
"T I say to you, whoever says to Mk 11:23 281
You have t stated that HE IS ONE, Mk 12:32 1909, 225
"T I say to you, this poor widow Mk 12:43 281
"T I say to you, this generation Mk 13:30 281
"T I say to you, wherever Mk 14:9 281
"T I say to you that one of you Mk 14:18 281
"T I say to you, I will never Mk 14:25 281
"T I say to you, that this Mk 14:30 281
"T this man was the Son of God!" Mk 15:39 230
"T I say to you, no prophet is Lk 4:24 281
t I say to you, that he will gird Lk 12:37 281
"T I say to you that he will put Lk 12:44 230
"T I say to you, whoever does not Lk 18:17 281
"T I say to you, there is no one Lk 18:29 281
"T I say to you, this poor widow Lk 21:3 230
"T I say to you, this generation Lk 21:32 281
"T I say to you, today you shall Lk 23:43 281
"T, truly, I say to you, you Jn 1:51 281
"Truly, t, I say to you, you Jn 1:51 281
"T, truly, I say to you, unless Jn 3:3 281
"Truly, t, I say to you, unless Jn 3:3 281
"T, truly, I say to you, unless Jn 3:5 281
"Truly, t, I say to you, unless Jn 3:5 281
"T, truly, I say to you, we speak Jn 3:11 281
"Truly, t, I say to you, we speak Jn 3:11 281
this you have said t." Jn 4:18 227
"T, truly, I say to you, the Son Jn 5:19 281
"Truly, t, I say to you, the Son Jn 5:19 281
"T, truly, I say to you, he who Jn 5:24 281
"Truly, t, I say to you, he who Jn 5:24 281
"T, truly, I say to you, an hour Jn 5:25 281
"Truly, t, I say to you, an hour Jn 5:25 281
"This is t the Prophet who is to Jn 6:14 230
"T, truly, I say to you, you seek Jn 6:26 281
"Truly, t, I say to you, you seek Jn 6:26 281
"T, truly, I say to you, it is Jn 6:32 281
"Truly, t, I say to you, it is Jn 6:32 281
"T, truly, I say to you, he who Jn 6:47 281
"Truly, t, I say to you, he who Jn 6:47 281
"T, truly, I say to you, unless Jn 6:53 281
"Truly, t, I say to you, unless Jn 6:53 281
then you are t disciples of Mine; Jn 8:31 230
"T, truly, I say to you, everyone Jn 8:34 281
"Truly, t, I say to you, everyone Jn 8:34 281
"T, truly, I say to you, if Jn 8:51 281
"Truly, t, I say to you, if Jn 8:51 281
"T, truly, I say to you, before Jn 8:58 281
"Truly, t, I say to you, before Jn 8:58 281
"T, truly, I say to you, he who Jn 10:1 281
"Truly, t, I say to you, he who Jn 10:1 281
"T, truly, I say to you, I am the Jn 10:7 281
"Truly, t, I say to you, I am the Jn 10:7 281
"T, truly, I say to you, unless a Jn 12:24 281
"Truly, t, I say to you, unless a Jn 12:24 281
"T, truly, I say to you, a slave Jn 13:16 281
"Truly, t, I say to you, a slave Jn 13:16 281
"T, truly, I say to you, he who Jn 13:20 281
"Truly, t, I say to you, he who Jn 13:20 281
"T, truly, I say to you, that one Jn 13:21 281
"Truly, t, I say to you, that one Jn 13:21 281
T, truly, I say to you, a rooster Jn 13:38 281
Truly, t, I say to you, a rooster Jn 13:38 281
"T, truly, I say to you, he who Jn 14:12 281
"Truly, t, I say to you, he who Jn 14:12 281
"T, truly, I say to you, that you Jn 16:20 281
"Truly, t, I say to you, that you Jn 16:20 281
T, truly, I say to you, if you Jn 16:23 281
Truly, t, I say to you, if you Jn 16:23 281
and t understood that I came forth Jn 17:8 230
"T, truly, I say to you, when you Jn 21:18 281
"Truly, t, I say to you, when you Jn 21:18 281
"For t in this city there were Ac 4:27 1909, 225
love of God has t been perfected. 1Jn 2:5 230

TRUMPET
mountain and a very loud t sound, Ex 19:16 7782
the sound of the t grew louder and Ex 19:19 7782
the sound of the t and the mountain Ex 20:18 7782
when you hear the sound of the t, Jos 6:5 7782
people heard the sound of the t, Jos 6:20 7782
that he blew the t in the hill Jg 3:27 7782
and he blew a t, and the Jg 6:34 7782
all who are with me blow the t, Jg 7:18 7782
Saul blew the t throughout the land, 1Sa 13:3 7782
So Joab blew the t; 2Sa 2:28 7782
shouting and the sound of the t. 2Sa 6:15 7782
as you hear the sound of the t, 2Sa 15:10 7782
Then Joab blew the t, 2Sa 18:16 7782
and he blew the t and said, 2Sa 20:1 7782
So he blew the t, and they were 2Sa 20:22 7782
Israel, and blow the t and say, 1Ki 1:34 7782
Then they blew the t, 1Ki 1:39 7782
Joab heard the sound of the t, 1Ki 1:41 7782
on the bare steps, and blew the t, 2Ki 9:13 7782
place you hear the sound of the t, Ne 4:20 7782
stand still at the voice of the t. Jb 39:24 7782
"As often as the t *sounds* he Jb 39:25 7782
The LORD, with the sound of a t. Ps 47:5 7782
Blow the t at the new moon, At the Ps 81:3 7782
Praise Him with t sound; Ps 150:3 7782
it, And as soon as the t is blown, Is 18:3 7782
day that a great t will be blown, Is 27:13 7782
Raise your voice like a t, Is 58:1 7782
"Blow the t in the land; Jer 4:5 7782
O my soul, The sound of the t, Jer 4:19 7782
And hear the sound of the t? Jer 4:21 7782
Now blow a t in Tekoa And raise a Jer 6:1 7782
'Listen to the sound of the t!' Jer 6:17 7782
not see war or hear the sound of a t Jer 42:14 7782
cause a t blast of war to be heard Jer 49:2 8643
land, Blow a t among the nations! Jer 51:27 7782
'They have blown the t and made Ezk 7:14 8619
and blows on the t and warns the Ezk 33:3 7782
he who hears the sound of the t and Ezk 33:4 7782
'He heard the sound of the t but Ezk 33:5 7782
coming and does not blow the t and Ezk 33:6 7782
horn in Gibeah, The t in Ramah. Hos 5:8 2689
Put the t to your lips! Hos 8:1 7782
Blow a t in Zion, And sound an Jl 2:1 7782
Blow a t in Zion, Consecrate a Jl 2:15 7782
war cries and the sound of a t. Am 2:2 7782
If a t is blown in a city will not Am 3:6 7782
A day of t and battle cry Against Zph 1:16 7782
And the Lord GOD will blow the t, Zch 9:14 7782
poor, do not sound a t before you, Mt 6:2 4537
send forth His angels with A GREAT T Mt 24:31 4536
twinkling of an eye, at the last t; 1Co 15:52 4536
for the t will sound, and the dead 1Co 15:52 4537
archangel and with the t of God 1Th 4:16 4536
and to the blast of a t and the Heb 12:19 4536
loud voice like *the sound* of a t, Rv 1:10 4536
the sound of a t speaking with me, Rv 4:1 4536
blasts of the t of the three angels Rv 8:13 4536
to the sixth angel who had the t, Rv 9:14 4536

TRUMPETER
built, while the t *stood* near me. Ne 4:18 8628, 7782

TRUMPETERS
and the t beside the king; 2Ki 11:14 2689
in unison when the t and the 2Ch 5:13 2689
and the t *were* beside the king. 2Ch 23:13 2689
flute-players and t will not be heard Rv 18:22 4538

TRUMPETS
a reminder by blowing *of* t, Lv 23:24
"Make yourself two t of silver, Nu 10:2 2689
Aaron, moreover, shall blow the t; Nu 10:8 2689
shall sound an alarm with the t, Nu 10:9 2689
blow the t over your burnt offerings, Nu 10:10 2689
be to you a day for blowing t. Nu 29:1 8643
the t for the alarm in his hand. Nu 31:6 2689
shall carry seven t of rams' horns Jos 6:4 7782
and the priests shall blow the t. Jos 6:4 7782
priests carry seven t of rams' horns Jos 6:6 7782
carrying the seven t of rams' horns Jos 6:8 7782
LORD went forward and blew the t; Jos 6:8 7782
before the priests who blew the t, Jos 6:9 7782
they continued to blow the t. Jos 6:9 7782
seven t of rams' horns before the ark Jos 6:13 7782
on continually, and blew the t; Jos 6:13 7782
they continued to blow the t. Jos 6:13 7782
time, when the priests blew the t, Jos 6:16 7782
shouted, and *priests* blew the t; Jos 6:20 7782
and their t into their hands. Jg 7:8 7782
and he put t and empty pitchers Jg 7:16 7782
blow the t all around the camp and Jg 7:18 7782
and they blew the t and smashed Jg 7:19 7782
blew the t and broke the pitchers, Jg 7:20 7782
the t in their right hands for blowing, Jg 7:20 7782
When they blew 300 t, Jg 7:22 7782
of the land rejoiced and blew t. 2Ki 11:14 2689
silver cups, snuffers, bowls, t, 2Ki 12:13 2689
tambourines, cymbals and with t. 1Ch 13:8 2689
blew the t before the ark of God. 1Ch 15:24 2689
with sound of the horn, with t, 1Ch 15:28 2689
Jahaziel the priests *blew* t continually 1Ch 16:6 2689
were Heman and Jeduthun *with* t 1Ch 16:42 2689
and twenty priests blowing t 2Ch 5:12 2689
voice accompanied by t and cymbals 2Ch 5:13 2689
priests on the other side blew t; 2Ch 7:6 2690
His priests with the signal t to sound 2Ch 13:12 2689
LORD, and the priests blew the t. 2Ch 13:14 2689
loud voice, with shouting, with t and 2Ch 15:14 2689
and t to the house of the LORD. 2Ch 20:28 2689
of the land rejoiced and blew t, 2Ch 23:13 2689
David, and the priests with the t. 2Ch 29:26 2689
to the LORD also began with the t, 2Ch 29:27 2689
also sang and the t sounded; 2Ch 29:28 2689
stood in their apparel with t, Ezr 3:10 2689
of the sons of the priests with t; Ne 12:35 2689
and Hananiah, with the t; Ne 12:41 2689
With t and the sound of the horn Ps 98:6 2689
and seven t were given to them. Rv 8:2 4536
angels who had the seven t prepared Rv 8:6 4536

TRUNK
the t of Dagon was left to him. 1Sa 5:4

TRUST
"For every breach of t, Ex 22:9 6588
you did not t the LORD your God, Dt 1:32 539
men of Shechem put their t in him. Jg 9:26 982
'But Sihon did not t Israel to Jg 11:20 539
'We t in the LORD our God,' is it 2Ki 18:22 982
Hezekiah make you t in the LORD, 2Ki 18:30 982
Do not let your God in whom you t 2Ki 19:10 982
appointed in their office of t. 1Ch 9:22 530
Levites, were in an office of t, 1Ch 9:26 530
O LORD our God, for we t in You, 2Ch 14:11 8172
put your t in the LORD your God and 2Ch 20:20 539
Put your t in His prophets and 2Ch 20:20 539
'He puts no t even in His servants; Jb 4:18 539
And whose t a spider's web. Jb 8:14 4009
"Then you would t, because there Jb 11:18 982
He puts no t in His holy ones, Jb 15:15 539
"Let him not t in emptiness, Jb 15:31 539
gold, And called fine gold my t, Jb 31:24 4009
"Will you t him because his Jb 39:11 539
righteousness, And t in the LORD. Ps 4:5 982
Your name will put their t in You, Ps 9:10 982
You made me t *when* upon Ps 22:9 982
O my God, in You I t, Ps 25:2 982
But I t in the LORD. Ps 31:6 982
But as for me, I t in You, Ps 31:14 982
Because we t in His holy name. Ps 33:21 982
T in the LORD and do good; Ps 37:3 982
way to the LORD, T also in Him, Ps 37:5 982
and fear And will t in the LORD. Ps 40:3 982
man who has made the LORD his t, Ps 40:4 4009
For I will not t in my bow, Nor Ps 44:6 982
Even those who t in their wealth And Ps 49:6 982
I t in the lovingkindness of God Ps 52:8 982
But I will t in You. Ps 55:23 982
afraid, I will put my t in You. Ps 56:3 982
I praise, In God I have put my t; Ps 56:4 982
In God I have put my t, Ps 56:11 982
T in Him at all times, O people; Ps 62:8 982
Do not t in oppression And do not Ps 62:10 982
You who are the t of all the ends Ps 65:5 4009
And did not t in His salvation. Ps 78:22 982
fortress, My God, in whom I t!" Ps 91:2 982
O Israel, t in the LORD; Ps 115:9 982
O house of Aaron, t in the LORD; Ps 115:10 982
who fear the LORD, t in the LORD; Ps 115:11 982
in the LORD Than to t in man. Ps 118:8 982
in the LORD Than to t in princes. Ps 118:9 982
me, For I t in Your word. Ps 119:42 982
Those who t in the LORD Are as Ps 125:1 982
For I t in You; Teach me the way Ps 143:8 982
Do not t in princes, In mortal Ps 146:3 982
T in the LORD with all your heart And Pr 3:5 982
the stronghold in which they t. Pr 21:22 4009
So that your t may be in the LORD, Pr 22:19 4009
I will t and not be afraid; Is 12:2 982
"T in the LORD forever, For in Is 26:4 982
put your t in oppression and guile, Is 30:12 982
In quietness and t is your strength." Is 30:15 985
And t in chariots because they are Is 31:1 982
'We t in the LORD our God,' is it Is 36:7 982
Hezekiah make you t in the LORD, Is 36:15 982
Do not let your God in whom you t Is 37:10 982
put to shame, Who t in idols, Is 42:17 982
Let him t in the name of the LORD Is 50:10 982
They t in confusion and speak Is 59:4 982
has rejected those in whom you t, Jer 2:37 4009
fortified cities in which you t. Jer 5:17 982
"Do not t in deceptive words, Jer 7:4 982
called by My name, in which you t, Jer 7:14 982
And do not t any brother; Jer 9:4 982
the LORD And whose t is the LORD. Jer 17:7 4009
have made this people t in a lie. Jer 28:15 982
and he has made you t in a lie," Jer 29:31 982
Pharaoh and those who t in him. Jer 46:25 982
your t in your own achievements Jer 48:7 982
And let your widows t in Me." Jer 49:11 982
servants who put their t in Him, Da 3:28 7365
Do not t in a neighbor; Mi 7:5 982
She did not t in the LORD, Zph 3:2 982
that we would not t in ourselves, 2Co 1:9 3982
But I t that you will realize that 2Co 13:6 1679
and I t in the Lord that I myself Php 2:24 3982
"I WILL PUT MY T IN HIM." Heb 2:13 3982

TRUSTED
walls in which you t come down Dt 28:52 982
He t in the LORD, the God of 2Ki 18:5 982
their prayers because they t in Him. 1Ch 5:20 982
because they t in the LORD, 2Ch 13:18 8172
were disappointed for they had t, Jb 6:20 982
"He deprives the t ones of speech And Jb 12:20 539
I have t in Your lovingkindness; Ps 13:5 982
In You our fathers t; Ps 22:4 982
They t and You delivered Ps 22:4 982

In You they t and were not Ps 22:5 982
t in the LORD without wavering. Ps 26:1 982
Even my close friend in whom I t, Ps 41:9 982
But t in the abundance of his Ps 52:7 982
forgotten Me And t in falsehood. Jer 13:25 982
All my t friends, Watching for my Jer 20:10 7965
booty, because you have t in Me," Jer 39:18 982
"But you t in your beauty and Ezk 16:15 982
him, because he had t in his God. Da 6:23 540
Because you have t in your way, Hos 10:13 982
some people who t in themselves that Lk 18:9 3982

TRUSTING
'On what are you t that you are 2Ch 32:10 982
heart is steadfast, t in the LORD. Ps 112:7 982
you are t in deceptive words to no Jer 7:8 982
t in the Lord because of my Php 1:14 3982

TRUSTS
"He t in his house, but it does Jb 8:15 8172
For the king t in the LORD, And Ps 21:7 982
My heart t in Him, and I am helped; Ps 28:7 982
But he who t in the LORD, Ps 32:10 982
blessed is the man who t in You! Ps 84:12 982
save Your servant who t in You. Ps 86:2 982
like them, Everyone who t in them. Ps 115:8 982
them, Yes, everyone who t in them. Ps 135:18 982
He who t in his riches will fall, Pr 11:28 982
blessed is he who t in the LORD. Pr 16:20 982
he who t in the LORD will prosper. Pr 28:25 982
who t in his own heart is a fool, Pr 28:26 982
who t in the LORD will be exalted. Pr 29:25 982
The heart of her husband t in her, Pr 31:11 982
peace, Because he t in You. Is 26:3 982
Cursed is the man who t in mankind Jer 17:5 982
Blessed is the man who t in the LORD Jer 17:7 982
daughter Who t in her treasures, Jer 49:4 982
and he so t in his righteousness Ezk 33:13 982
its maker t in his own handiwork Hab 2:18 982
"HE T IN GOD; LET GOD RESCUE Him Mt 27:43 3982

TRUSTWORTHY
But he who is t conceals a matter. Pr 11:13 539, 7307
A t witness will not lie, Pr 14:5 529
loyalty, But who can find a t man? Pr 20:6 529
and its interpretation is t." Da 2:45 540
of stewards that one be found t. 1Co 4:2 4103
who by the mercy of the Lord is t. 1Co 7:25 4103
It is a t statement, deserving 1Tm 1:15 4103
It is a t statement: 1Tm 3:1 4103
It is a t statement deserving full 1Tm 4:9 4103
It is a t statement: 2Tm 2:11 4103
This is a t statement; Ti 3:8 4103

TRUTH
and His t toward my master; Gn 24:27 571
tested, whether there is t in you. Gn 42:16 571
able men who fear God, men of t, Ex 18:21 571
abounding in lovingkindness and t; Ex 34:6 571
and give me a pledge of t, Jos 2:12 571
and serve Him in sincerity and t; Jos 24:14 571
'If in t you are anointing me as Jg 9:15 571
if you have dealt in t and Jg 9:16 571
if then you have dealt in t and Jg 9:19 571
serve Him in t with all your heart; 1Sa 12:24 571
show lovingkindness and t to you; 2Sa 2:6 571
You are God, and Your words are t, 2Sa 7:28 571
mercy and t be with you." 2Sa 15:20 571
to walk before Me in t with all 1Ki 2:4 571
as he walked before You in t and 1Ki 3:6 571
of the LORD in your mouth is t." 1Ki 17:24 571
to speak to me nothing but the t 1Ki 22:16 571
how I have walked before You in t 2Ki 20:3 571
will be peace and t in my days?" 2Ki 20:19 571
to speak to me nothing but the t 2Ch 18:15 571
namely, words of peace and t, Es 9:30 571
"In t I know that this is so; But Jb 9:2 551
And speaks t in his heart. Ps 15:2 571
Lead me in Your t and teach me, For Ps 25:5 571
t To those who keep His covenant Ps 25:10 571
eyes, And I have walked in Your t. Ps 26:3 571
ransomed me, O LORD, God of t. Ps 31:5 571
Your t from the great congregation. Ps 40:10 571
Your lovingkindness and Your t will Ps 40:11 571
O send out Your light and Your t, Ps 43:3 571
For the cause of t and meekness Ps 45:4 571
desire t in the innermost being, Ps 51:6 571
His lovingkindness and His t. Ps 57:3 571
heavens And Your t to the clouds. Ps 57:10 571
may be displayed because of the t. Ps 60:4 7189b
Appoint lovingkindness and t that Ps 61:7 571
Answer me with Your saving t. Ps 69:13 571
You with a harp, Even Your t, Ps 71:22 571
Lovingkindness and t have met Ps 85:10 571
T springs from the earth, Ps 85:11 571
I will walk in Your t; Ps 86:11 571
abundant in lovingkindness and t. Ps 86:15 571
Lovingkindness and t go before You Ps 89:14 571
And Your t reaches to the skies. Ps 108:4 571
works of His hands are t and justice Ps 111:7 571
performed in t and uprightness. Ps 111:8 571
lovingkindness, because of Your t. Ps 115:1 571
the t of the LORD is everlasting. Ps 117:2 571
do not take the word of t utterly out Ps 119:43 571
righteousness, And Your law is t. Ps 119:142 571
And all Your commandments are t. Ps 119:151 571
The sum of Your word is t, Ps 119:160 571
A t from which He will not turn Ps 132:11 571
for Your lovingkindness and Your t; Ps 138:2 571
To all who call upon Him in t. Ps 145:18 571
Do not let kindness and t leave you; Pr 3:3 571
"For my mouth will utter t; Pr 8:7 571
He who speaks t tells what is right, Pr 12:17 530
But kindness and t will be to Pr 14:22 571
By lovingkindness and t iniquity is Pr 16:6 571
Loyalty and t preserve the king, Pr 20:28 571
But the man who listens to the t Pr 21:28
know the certainty of the words of t Pr 22:21 571
Buy t, and do not sell it, Get Pr 23:23 571
If a king judges the poor with t, Pr 29:14 571
and to write words of t correctly. Ec 12:10 571
who err in mind will know the t, Is 29:24 998
of the hasty will discern the t, Is 32:4 1847
how I have walked before You in t Is 38:3 571
will be peace and t in my days." Is 39:8 571
But not in t nor in righteousness. Is 48:1 571
For t has stumbled in the street, Is 59:14 571
Yes, t is lacking; Is 59:15 571
Will be blessed by the God of t; Is 65:16 543
earth Will swear by the God of t; Is 65:16 543
'As the LORD lives,' In t, Jer 4:2 571
one who does justice, who seeks t, Jer 5:1 530
do not Your eyes look for t? Jer 5:3 530
t has perished and has been cut Jer 7:28 530
Lies and not t prevail in the land; Jer 9:3 530
And does not speak the t, Jer 9:5 571
has My word speak My word in t. Jer 23:28 571
them an abundance of peace and t. Jer 33:6 571
and it will fling t to the ground Da 8:12 571
and giving attention to Your t. Da 9:13 571
is inscribed in the writing of t. Da 10:21 571
"And now I will tell you the t. Da 11:2 571
You will give t to Jacob And Mi 7:20 571
will be called the City of T, Zch 8:3 571
their God in t and righteousness.' Zch 8:8 571
speak the t to one another; Zch 8:16 571
judge with t and judgment for Zch 8:16 571
so love t and peace.' Zch 8:19 571
and teach the way of God in t, Mt 22:16 225
Him and told Him the whole t. Mk 5:33 225
but teach the way of God in t. Mk 12:14 225
so that you may know the exact t Lk 1:4 803
"But I say to you in t, Lk 4:25 225
but teach the way of God in t. Lk 20:21 225
the Father, full of grace and t. Jn 1:14 225
grace and t were realized through Jn 1:17 225
he who practices the t comes to the Jn 3:21 225
worship the Father in spirit and t; Jn 4:23 225
must worship in spirit and t." Jn 4:24 225
and he has testified to the t. Jn 5:33 225
and you will know the t, Jn 8:32 225
and the t will make you free." Jn 8:32 225
Me, a man who has told you the t, Jn 8:40 225
and does not stand in the t because Jn 8:44 225
because there is no t in him. Jn 8:44 225
"But because I speak the t, Jn 8:45 225
If I speak t, why do you not believe Jn 8:46 225
"I am the way, and the t, Jn 14:6 225
that is the Spirit of t, Jn 14:17 225
Father, that is the Spirit of t who Jn 15:26 225
"But I tell you the t, Jn 16:7 225
"But when He, the Spirit of t, Jn 16:13 225
He will guide you into all the t; Jn 16:13 225
"Sanctify them in the t; Jn 17:17 225
Your word is t. Jn 17:17 225
also may be sanctified in t. Jn 17:19 225
world, to testify to the t. Jn 18:37 225
Everyone who is of the t hears My Jn 18:37 225
Pilate said to Him, "What is t?" Jn 18:38 225
he knows that he is telling the t, Jn 19:35 227
but I utter words of sober t. Ac 26:25 225
suppress the t in unrighteousness, Ro 1:18 225
exchanged the t of God for a lie, Ro 1:25 225
ambitious and do not obey the t, Ro 2:8 225
of knowledge and of the t, Ro 2:20 225
t of God abounded to His glory, Ro 3:7 225
I am telling the t in Christ, Ro 9:1 225
on behalf of the t of God to confirm Ro 15:8 225
unleavened bread of sincerity and t. 1Co 5:8 225
but rejoices with the t; 1Co 13:6 225
but by the manifestation of t 2Co 4:2 225
in the word of t, in the power of 2Co 6:7 225
we spoke all things to you in t, 2Co 7:14 225
before Titus proved to be the t. 2Co 7:14 225
As the t of Christ is in me, this 2Co 11:10 225
for I will be speaking the t; 2Co 12:6 225
we can do nothing against the t, 2Co 13:8 225
the truth, but only for the t. 2Co 13:8 225
so that the t of the gospel would Ga 2:5 225
about the t of the gospel, Ga 2:14 225
your enemy by telling you the t? Ga 4:16 226
hindered you from obeying the t? Ga 5:7 225
listening to the message of t, Eph 1:13 225
but speaking the t in love, Eph 4:15 226
in Him, just as t is in Jesus, Eph 4:21 225
and holiness of the t. Eph 4:24 225
laying aside falsehood, SPEAK T EACH Eph 4:25 225
goodness and righteousness and t), Eph 5:9 225
HAVING GIRDED YOUR LOINS WITH T, Eph 6:14 225
way, whether in pretense or in t, Php 1:18 225
previously heard in the word of t, Col 1:5 225
understood the grace of God in t; Col 1:6 225
they did not receive the love of the t 2Th 2:10 225
judged who did not believe the t, 2Th 2:12 225
by the Spirit and faith in the t. 2Th 2:13 225
to come to the knowledge of the t. 1Tm 2:4 225
(I am telling the t, I am not lying) 1Tm 2:7 225
of the Gentiles in faith and t. 1Tm 2:7 225
the pillar and support of the t. 1Tm 3:15 225
those who believe and know the t. 1Tm 4:3 225
mind and deprived of the t, 1Tm 6:5 225
handling the word of t. 2Tm 2:15 225
men who have gone astray from the t 2Tm 2:18 225
leading to the knowledge of the t, 2Tm 2:25 225
to come to the knowledge of the t. 2Tm 3:7 225
so these men also oppose the t, 2Tm 3:8 225
turn away their ears from the t and 2Tm 4:4 225
knowledge of the t which is according Ti 1:1 225
of men who turn away from the t. Ti 1:14 225
receiving the knowledge of the t, Heb 10:26 225
brought us forth by the word of t, Jas 1:18 225
arrogant and so lie against the t. Jas 3:14 225
any among you strays from the t and Jas 5:19 225
Since you have in obedience to the t 1Pe 1:22 225
the t which is present with you. 2Pe 1:12 225
the way of the t will be maligned; 2Pe 2:2 225
we lie and do not practice the t; 1Jn 1:6 225
ourselves and the t is not in us. 1Jn 1:8 225
a liar, and the t is not in him; 1Jn 2:4 225
you because you do not know the t, 1Jn 2:21 225
and because no lie is of the t. 1Jn 2:21 225
or with tongue, but in deed and t. 1Jn 3:18 225
know by this that we are of the t, 1Jn 3:19 225
By this we know the spirit of t and 1Jn 4:6 225
because the Spirit is the t. 1Jn 5:6 225
her children, whom I love in t; 2Jn 1:1 225
but also all who know the t, 2Jn 1:1 225
for the sake of the t which abides 2Jn 1:2 225
Son of the Father, in t and love. 2Jn 1:3 225
of your children walking in t, 2Jn 1:4 225
beloved Gaius, whom I love in t. 3Jn 1:1 225
came and testified to your t, 3Jn 1:3 225
that is, how you are walking in t. 3Jn 1:3 225
of my children walking in the t. 3Jn 1:4 225
may be fellow workers with the t. 3Jn 1:8 225
everyone, and from the t itself; 3Jn 1:12 225

TRUTHFUL
T lips will be established Pr 12:19 571
A t witness saves lives, But he Pr 14:25 571
we know that You are t and teach Mt 22:16 227
"Teacher, we know that You are t and Mk 12:14 227

TRUTHFULLY
"But I say to you t, Lk 9:27 230

TRY
that You t the heart and 1Ch 29:17 974
morning And t him every moment? Jb 7:18 974
surely t to flee from its power. Jb 27:22
Examine me, O LORD, and t me; Ps 26:2 5254
T me and know my anxious thoughts; Ps 139:23 974
for you to t the patience of men, Is 7:13 3811
you will t the patience of my God Is 7:13 3811
Do not t to comfort me concerning Is 22:4 213
You will t to remove for Mi 6:14
and I am going to t them out; Lk 14:19 1381a
sit to t me according to the Law, Ac 23:3 2919
are slandered, we t to conciliate; 1Co 4:13
Nor let us t the Lord, as some of 1Co 10:9 1598
t to compel you to be circumcised, Ga 6:12

TRYING
so that they wearied themselves t Gn 19:11
For all of them were t to Ne 6:9
the rest of the prophets who were t Ne 6:14
And he should cease t forever Ps 49:8
began t to find a ground of accusation Da 6:4 1156
kept t to obtain false testimony Mt 26:59 2212
to obtain testimony against Jesus to Mk 14:55 2212
and they were t to bring him in and Lk 5:18 2212
the people were t to touch Him, Lk 6:19 2212
And he kept t to see Him. Lk 9:9 2212
Zaccheus was t to see who Jesus was, Lk 19:3 2212
the people were t to destroy Him, Lk 19:47 2212
he was t to associate with the Ac 9:26 3985
they were t to go into Bithynia, Ac 16:7 3985
and t to persuade Jews and Greeks. Ac 18:4
were t to escape from the ship and Ac 27:30 2212
and t to persuade them concerning Ac 28:23
life, and I am t to spare you. 1Co 7:28
If I were still t to please men, I Ga 1:10
t to learn what is pleasing to the Eph 5:10 1381a
those who are t to deceive you. 1Jn 2:26

TRYPHAENA
Greet T and Tryphosa, workers in Ro 16:12 5170

TRYPHOSA
Greet Tryphaena and T, Ro 16:12 5173

TUBAL
Javan and T and Meshech and Tiras. Gn 10:2 8422
Gomer, Magog, Madai, Javan, T, 1Ch 1:5 8422
Put, Lud, Meshech, T and Is 66:19 8422
"Javan, T and Meshech, they were Ezk 27:13 8422
T and all their hordes are Ezk 32:26 8422
prince of Rosh, Meshech and T, Ezk 38:2 8422
prince of Rosh, Meshech and T. Ezk 38:3 8422
prince of Rosh, Meshech and T; Ezk 39:1 8422

TUBAL-CAIN
Zillah, she also gave birth to T, Gn 4:22 8423
and the sister of T was Naamah. Gn 4:22 8423

TUBES
"His bones are t of bronze; Jb 40:18 650

TUMBLING
a loaf of barley bread was t into Jg 7:13 2015

TUMORS
with the boils of Egypt and with t Dt 28:27 6076b
them and smote them with t, 1Sa 5:6 6076b
old, so that t broke out on them. 1Sa 5:9 6076b
who did not die were smitten with t 1Sa 5:12 6076b
"Five golden t and five golden 1Sa 6:4 6076b
you shall make likenesses of your t 1Sa 6:5 6076b

and the likenesses of their **t**.	1Sa 6:11	2914
These are the golden **t** which	1Sa 6:17	2914

TUMULT

and your servant, I saw a great **t**,	2Sa 18:29	1995
"He scorns the **t** of the city, The	Jb 39:7	1995
the **t** of those who do iniquity,	Ps 64:2	7285b
waves, And the **t** of the peoples.	Ps 65:7	1995
booted warrior in the *battle* **t**,	Is 9:5	7494
A sound of **t** on the mountains,	Is 13:4	1995
the sound of the **t** peoples flee;	Is 33:3	1995
a deception, A **t** *on* the mountains.	Jer 3:23	1995
is a **t** of waters in the heavens,	Jer 10:13	1995
With the noise of a great **t** He has	Jer 11:16	1999
stallions, The **t** of his chariots,	Jer 47:3	7494
is a **t** of waters in the heavens,	Jer 51:16	1995
t of their voices sounds forth.	Jer 51:55	7588
a sound of **t** like the sound of an	Ezk 1:24	1999
t rather than joyful shouting on the	Ezk 7:7	4103
his words like the sound of a **t**.	Da 10:6	1995
a **t** will arise among your people,	Hos 10:14	7588
And Moab will die amid **t**,	Am 2:2	7588

TUMULTS

and see *the* great **t** within her and *the*	Am 3:9	4103
beatings, in imprisonments, in **t**,	2Co 6:5	*181*

TUMULTUOUS

been engulfed with its **t** waves.	Jer 51:42	1995

TUNED

with harps **t** to alamoth;	1Ch 15:20	
with lyres **t** to the sheminith.	1Ch 15:21	

TUNIC

and he made him a varicolored **t**.	Gn 37:3	3801
they stripped Joseph of his **t**,	Gn 37:23	3801
the varicolored **t** that was on him;	Gn 37:23	3801
So they took Joseph's **t**,	Gn 37:31	3801
and dipped the **t** in the blood;	Gn 37:31	3801
and they sent the varicolored **t**	Gn 37:32	3801
it is your son's **t** or not."	Gn 37:32	3801
"It is my son's **t**,	Gn 37:33	3801
a robe and a **t** of checkered work,	Ex 28:4	3801
the **t** of checkered work of fine linen	Ex 28:39	3801
and put on Aaron the **t** and the	Ex 29:5	3801
He put the **t** on him and girded	Lv 8:7	3801
"He shall put on the holy linen **t**,	Lv 16:4	3801
And I will clothe him with your **t** And	Is 22:21	3801
to every soldier and *also* the **t**;	Jn 19:23	*5509*
now the **t** was seamless, woven in	Jn 19:23	*5509*

TUNICS

For Aaron's sons you shall make **t**;	Ex 28:40	3801
bring his sons and put **t** on them.	Ex 29:8	3801
They made the **t** of finely woven linen	Ex 39:27	3801
bring his sons and put **t** on them;	Ex 40:14	3801
come near and clothed them with **t**,	Lv 8:13	3801
carried them still in their **t** to the	Lv 10:5	3801
festal robes, outer **t**,	Is 3:22	4595
"Do not put on two **t**."	Mk 6:9	*5509*
"The man who has two **t** is to share	Lk 3:11	*5509*
and do not *even* have two **t** apiece.	Lk 9:3	*5509*
and showing all the **t** and garments	Ac 9:39	*5509*

TUNNEL

soul, through the water **t**."	2Sa 5:8	6794b

TURBAN

of checkered work, a **t** and a sash,	Ex 28:4	4701
cord, and it shall be on the **t**;	Ex 28:37	4701
it shall be at the front of the **t**.	Ex 28:37	4701
and shall make a **t** of fine linen,	Ex 28:39	4701
you shall set the **t** on his head and	Ex 29:6	4701
and put the holy crown on the **t**.	Ex 29:6	4701
and the **t** of fine linen, and the	Ex 39:28	4701
it, to fasten it on the **t** above,	Ex 39:31	4701
He also placed the **t** on his head,	Lv 8:9	4701
turban on his head, and on the **t**,	Lv 8:9	4701
and attired with the linen **t**	Lv 16:4	4701
justice was like a robe and a **t**.	Jb 29:14	6797
'Remove the **t** and take off the	Ezk 21:26	4701
Bind on your **t** and put your shoes	Ezk 24:17	6287b
"Let them put a clean **t** on his head."	Zch 3:5	6797
So they put a clean **t** on his head	Zch 3:5	6797

TURBANS

hand mirrors, undergarments, **t** and	Is 3:23	6797
with flowing **t** on their heads,	Ezk 23:15	2871
'Your **t** will be on your heads	Ezk 24:23	6287b
"Linen **t** shall be on their heads and	Ezk 44:18	6287b

TURBID

Which are **t** because of ice *And*	Jb 6:16	6937

TURMOIL

I am not at rest, but **t** comes."	Jb 3:26	7267
Is short-lived and full of **t**.	Jb 14:1	7267
Than great treasure and **t** with it.	Pr 15:16	4103
gives you rest from your pain and **t**	Is 14:3	7267
t to the inhabitants of Babylon.	Jer 50:34	7264
'Because you have more **t** than the	Ezk 5:7	2001a
you, you of ill repute, full of **t**.	Ezk 22:5	4103

TURN

please **t** aside into your servant's	Gn 19:2	5493
t to the right hand or the left."	Gn 24:49	6437
"I must **t** aside now and see this	Ex 3:3	5493
"Tell the sons of Israel to **t** back	Ex 14:2	7725
to **t** aside after a multitude in order to	Ex 23:2	5186
your enemies **t** *their* backs to you.	Ex 23:27	5414
T from Your burning anger and	Ex 32:12	7725
Ingathering at the **t** of the year.	Ex 34:22	8622
'Do not **t** to idols or make for	Lv 19:4	6437
'Do not **t** to mediums or spiritists;	Lv 19:31	6437
'So I will **t** toward you and make	Lv 26:9	6437
I, in **t**, will do this to you:	Lv 26:16	637
t tomorrow and set out to the	Nu 14:25	6437
not **t** off into field or vineyard;	Nu 21:22	5186
donkey to **t** her back into the way.	Nu 22:23	5186
t to the right hand or the left.	Nu 22:26	5186
to you, I will **t** back."	Nu 22:34	7725
the LORD may **t** away from Israel."	Nu 25:4	7725
if you **t** away from following Him,	Nu 32:15	7725
'Then your border shall **t** *direction*	Nu 34:4	5437
'The border shall **t** *direction*	Nu 34:5	5437
'**T** and set your journey, and go to	Dt 1:7	6437
t around and set out for the	Dt 1:40	6437
mountain long enough. *Now* **t** north,	Dt 2:3	6437
I will not **t** aside to the right or	Dt 2:27	5493
you shall not **t** aside to the right	Dt 5:32	5493
"For they will **t** your sons away	Dt 7:4	5493
do not **t** away and serve other gods	Dt 11:16	5493
but **t** aside from the way which I	Dt 11:28	5493
in order that the LORD may **t** from	Dt 13:17	7725
you shall not **t** aside from the	Dt 17:11	5493
himself, or else his heart will **t** away;	Dt 17:17	5493
not **t** aside from the commandment,	Dt 17:20	5493
t to cover up your excrement.	Dt 23:13	7725
among you or He will **t** away from you.	Dt 23:14	7725
and do not **t** aside from any of the	Dt 28:14	5493
if you **t** to the LORD your God with	Dt 30:10	7725
do, for they will **t** to other gods.	Dt 31:18	6437
t to other gods and serve them,	Dt 31:20	6437
will act corruptly and **t** from the way	Dt 31:29	5493
do not **t** from it to the right or	Jos 1:7	5493
they **t** *their* backs before their	Jos 7:12	6437
t now and go to your tents,	Jos 22:4	6437
that you must **t** away this day from	Jos 22:18	7725
to **t** away from following the LORD,	Jos 22:23	7725
rebel against the LORD and **t** away	Jos 22:29	7725
so that you may not **t** aside from	Jos 23:6	5493
then He will **t** and do you harm and	Jos 24:20	7725
and I in **t** will go with you into	Jg 1:3	1571
that they would **t** back and act	Jg 2:19	7725
"**T** aside, my master, turn aside	Jg 4:18	5493
aside, my master, **t** aside to me!	Jg 4:18	5493
and let us **t** aside into this city	Jg 19:11	5493
"We will not **t** aside into the	Jg 19:12	5493
you *or* **t** back from following you;	Ru 1:16	7725
"**T** aside, friend, sit down here."	Ru 4:1	5493
and did not **t** aside to the right	1Sa 6:12	5493
t aside from following the LORD,	1Sa 12:20	5493
"You must not **t** aside,	1Sa 12:21	5493
t yourself, *and* here I am with you	1Sa 14:7	5186
"**T** around and put the priests of	1Sa 22:17	5437
t around and attack the priests."	1Sa 22:18	5437
bow of Jonathan did not **t** back,	2Sa 1:22	5472
and did not **t** to the right or to the left	2Sa 2:19	5186
"**T** to your right or to your left,	2Sa 2:21	5186
to **t** aside from following him.	2Sa 2:21	5493
"**T** aside from following me.	2Sa 2:22	5493
However, he refused to **t** aside;	2Sa 2:23	5493
from telling the people to **t** back	2Sa 2:26	7725
blind and lame will **t** you away";	2Sa 5:6	5493
no one can **t** to the right or to	2Sa 14:19	3231
"Let him **t** to his own house, and	2Sa 14:24	5437
"**T** aside and stand here."	2Sa 18:30	5437
t back until they were consumed.	2Sa 22:38	7725
my enemies **t** *their* backs to me,	2Sa 22:41	5414
that you do and wherever you **t**,	1Ki 2:3	6437
if they **t** to You again and	1Ki 8:33	7725
confess Your name and **t** from their sin	1Ki 8:35	7725
indeed **t** away from following Me,	1Ki 9:6	7725
for they will surely **t** your heart	1Ki 11:2	5186
was a **t** *of events* from the LORD,	1Ki 12:15	5438
"Go away from here and **t** eastward,	1Ki 17:3	6437
for at the **t** of the year the king	1Ki 20:22	8666
At the **t** of the year,	1Ki 20:26	8666
"**T** around and take me out of the	1Ki 22:34	2015
he did not **t** aside from it, doing	1Ki 22:43	5493
to us, *that* he can **t** in there."	2Ki 4:10	5493
to do with peace? **T** behind me."	2Ki 9:18	5437
to do with peace? **T** behind me."	2Ki 9:19	5437
he did not **t** from them.	2Ki 13:2	5493
Nevertheless they did not **t** away	2Ki 13:6	5493
he did not **t** away from all the	2Ki 13:11	5493
"**T** from your evil ways and keep	2Ki 17:13	7725
t fortified cities into ruinous heaps.	2Ki 19:25	
		1961, 7582
And I will **t** you back by the way	2Ki 19:28	7725
the shadow **t** backward ten steps."	2Ki 20:10	7725
nor did he **t** aside to the right or	2Ki 22:2	5493
the LORD did not **t** from the	2Ki 23:26	7725
to **t** the kingdom of Saul to him,	1Ch 12:23	5437
and **t** from their sin when You	2Ch 6:26	7725
do not **t** away the face of Your	2Ch 6:42	7725
face and **t** from their wicked ways,	2Ch 7:14	7725
"But if you **t** away and forsake My	2Ch 7:19	7725
for it was a **t** *of events* from God	2Ch 10:15	5252
"**T** around and take me out of the	2Ch 18:33	2015
it happened at the **t** of the year	2Ch 24:23	8622
burning anger may **t** away from us.	2Ch 29:10	7725
burning anger may **t** away from you.	2Ch 30:8	7725
and will not **t** *His* face away from	2Ch 30:9	5493
and did not **t** aside to the right or to	2Ch 34:2	5493
They in **t** gave *it* to the	2Ch 34:11	
did not **t** from following the LORD	2Ch 34:33	5493
Josiah would not **t** away from him,	2Ch 35:22	5437
At the **t** of the year King	2Ch 36:10	8666
every place where you may **t**,"	Ne 4:12	7725
order to **t** them back to Your law.	Ne 9:29	7725
You or **t** from their evil deeds.	Ne 9:35	7725
when the **t** of each young lady came	Es 2:12	8447
Now when the **t** of Esther, the	Es 2:15	8447
which of the holy ones will you **t**?	Jb 5:1	6437
never **t** Your gaze away from me,	Jb 7:19	8159
"God will not **t** back His anger;	Jb 9:13	7725
would You **t** me into dust again?	Jb 10:9	7725
"**T** Your gaze from him that he may	Jb 14:6	8159
should **t** your spirit against God And	Jb 15:13	7725
He is unique and who can **t** Him?	Jb 23:13	7725
do not **t** toward the vineyards.	Jb 24:18	6437
You **t** Your attention against me.	Jb 30:20	995
may **t** man aside *from his* conduct,	Jb 33:17	5493
greatness of the ransom **t** you aside.	Jb 36:18	5186
'Be careful, do not **t** to evil,	Jb 36:21	6437
he does not **t** back from the sword.	Jb 39:22	7725
They shall **t** back, they will	Ps 6:10	7725
When my enemies **t** back, They	Ps 9:3	7725
not **t** back until they were consumed.	Ps 18:37	7725
my enemies **t** their backs to me,	Ps 18:40	5414
You will make them **t** their back;	Ps 21:12	7896
will remember and **t** to the LORD,	Ps 22:27	7725
T to me and be gracious to me, For	Ps 25:16	6437
not **t** Your servant away in anger;	Ps 27:9	5186
"**T** Your gaze away from me, that I	Ps 39:13	8159
us to **t** back from the adversary;	Ps 44:10	7725
t back in the day when I call;	Ps 56:9	7725
of Your compassion, **t** to me,	Ps 69:16	6437
my greatness And **t** *to* comfort me.	Ps 71:21	5437
T Your footsteps toward the	Ps 74:3	7311
O God *of* hosts, **t** again now, we	Ps 80:14	7725
we shall not **t** back from You;	Ps 80:18	5472
And **t** My hand against their	Ps 81:14	7725
But let them not **t** back to folly.	Ps 85:8	7725
T to me, and be gracious to me;	Ps 86:16	6437
also **t** back the edge of his sword And	Ps 89:43	7725
You **t** man back into dust	Ps 90:3	7725
To **t** away His wrath from	Ps 106:23	7725
O Jordan, that you **t** back?	Ps 114:5	5437
T away my eyes from looking at	Ps 119:37	5674a
T away my reproach which I dread,	Ps 119:39	5674a
Yet I do not **t** aside from Your law.	Ps 119:51	5186
May those who fear You **t** to me,	Ps 119:79	7725
T to me and be gracious to me,	Ps 119:132	6437
not **t** aside from Your testimonies.	Ps 119:157	5186
who **t** aside to their crooked ways,	Ps 125:5	5186
Do not **t** away the face of Your	Ps 132:10	7725
truth from which He will not **t** back	Ps 132:11	7725
"**T** to my reproof, Behold, I will	Pr 1:23	7725
the LORD and **t** away from evil.	Pr 3:7	5493
nor **t** away from the words of my	Pr 4:5	5186
T away from it and pass on.	Pr 4:15	7847
t to the right nor to the left;	Pr 4:27	5186
T your foot from evil.	Pr 4:27	5493
your heart **t** aside to her ways,	Pr 7:25	7847
is naive, let him **t** in here!"	Pr 9:4	5493
is naive, let him **t** in here,"	Pr 9:16	5493
To **t** aside from the snares of	Pr 13:14	5493
it is an abomination to fools to **t**	Pr 13:19	5493
And **t** His anger away from him.	Pr 24:18	7725
aflame, But wise men **t** away anger.	Pr 29:8	7725
T, my beloved, and be like a gazelle	SS 2:17	5437
T your eyes away from me, For	SS 6:5	5437
"I will also **t** My hand against	Is 1:25	7725
t out that when they are hungry,	Is 8:21	6437
this, His anger does not **t** away	Is 9:12	7725
not **t** back to Him who struck them,	Is 9:13	7725
this, His anger does not **t** away	Is 9:17	7725
this, His anger does not **t** away	Is 9:21	7725
this, His anger does not **t** away	Is 10:4	7725
will each **t** to his own people,	Is 13:14	6437
hand, who can **t** it back?"	Is 14:27	7725
"**T** your eyes away from me, Let me	Is 22:4	8159
t and harrow the ground?	Is 28:24	6605a
You **t** *things* around!	Is 29:16	2016
nor shall his face now **t** pale;	Is 29:22	2357
of the way, **t** aside from the path,	Is 30:11	5186
you **t** to the right or to the left.	Is 30:21	3231
That you should **t** fortified cities	Is 37:26	7582
And I will **t** you back by the way	Is 37:29	7725
"**T** to Me and be saved, all the	Is 45:22	6437
righteousness And will not **t** back,	Is 45:23	7725
not disobedient Nor did I **t** back.	Is 50:5	5472
you **t** your foot From doing your	Is 58:13	7725
t from transgression in Jacob,"	Is 59:20	7725
of her heat who can **t** her away?	Jer 2:24	7725
Yet you **t** to Me,"	Jer 3:1	7725
And not **t** away from following Me.'	Jer 3:19	7725
My mind, nor will I **t** from it."	Jer 4:28	7725
Does one **t** away and not repent?	Jer 8:4	7725
Or who will **t** aside to ask about	Jer 15:5	5493
They for their part may **t** to you,	Jer 15:19	7725
for you, you must not **t** to them.	Jer 15:19	7725
Those who **t** away on earth will be	Jer 17:13	5493
Oh **t** back, each of you from his	Jer 18:11	7725
as to **t** away Your wrath from them.	Jer 18:20	7725
I am about to **t** back the weapons	Jer 21:4	5437
anger of the LORD will not **t** back	Jer 23:20	7725
'**T** now everyone from his evil way	Jer 25:5	7725
everyone will **t** from his evil way,	Jer 26:3	7725
anger of the LORD will not **t** back Until	Jer 30:24	7725
I will **t** their mourning into joy And	Jer 31:13	2015
then it will **t** to Goah.	Jer 31:39	5437
that I will not **t** away from them,	Jer 32:40	7725
that they will not **t** away from Me.	Jer 32:40	5493
'**T** now every man from his evil	Jer 35:15	7725
man will **t** from his evil way;	Jer 36:3	7725
everyone will **t** from his evil way,	Jer 36:7	7725
ears to **t** from their wickedness,	Jer 44:5	7725
"Flee away, **t** back, dwell in the	Jer 49:8	6437
them **t** aside *on* the mountains;	Jer 50:6	7725
each **t** back to his own people And	Jer 50:16	6437
faces did not **t** when they moved,	Ezk 1:9	5437
and he does not **t** from his	Ezk 3:19	7725
t from one side to the other until	Ezk 4:8	2015

‘I will also **t** My face from them, **Ezk 7:22** 5437
would not **t** from beside them. **Ezk 10:16** 5437
wicked not to **t** from his wicked way **Ezk 13:22** 7725
“Repent and **t** away from your **Ezk 14:6** 7725
and **t** your faces away from all **Ezk 14:6** 7725
I in **t** will bring your conduct **Ezk 16:43** 1571
should **t** from his ways and live? **Ezk 18:23** 7725
“Repent and **t** away from all your **Ezk 18:30** 7725
“I will **t** the fortunes of **Ezk 29:14** 7725
a wicked man to **t** from his way and **Ezk 33:9** 7725
and he does not **t** from his way, **Ezk 33:9** 7725
wicked **t** from his way and live. **Ezk 33:11** 7725
T back, turn back from your evil **Ezk 33:11** 7725
back, **t** back from your evil ways! **Ezk 33:11** 7725
I am for you, and I will **t** to you, **Ezk 36:9** 6437
“I will **t** you about and put **Ezk 38:4** 7725
to **t** your hand against the waste **Ezk 38:12** 7725
and I will **t** you around, drive **Ezk 39:2** 7725
Your anger and Your wrath **t** away **Da 9:16** 7725
“Then he will **t** his face to the **Da 11:18** 7725
“So he will **t** his face toward the **Da 11:19** 7725
not **t** out the way it did before. **Da 11:29** 1961
“By smooth *words* he will **t** to **Da 11:32** 2610
though they **t** to other gods and **Hos 3:1** 6437
themselves, They **t** away from Me. **Hos 7:14** 5493
They **t**, *but* not upward, They are **Hos 7:16** 7725
All faces **t** pale. **Jl 2:6** 6908
whether He will *not* **t** and relent And **Jl 2:14** 7725
t aside the way of the humble; **Am 2:7** 5186
For those who **t** justice into **Am 5:7** 2015
And **t** aside the poor in the gate. **Am 5:12** 5186
songs of the palace will **t** to wailing **Am 8:3** 3213
t your festivals into mourning **Am 8:10** 2015
that each may **t** from his wicked way **Jon 3:8** 7725
“Who knows, God may **t** and relent and **Jon 3:9** 7725
And I will **t** their shame into **Zph 3:19** 7760
And I will **t** My hand against the **Zch 13:7** 7725
and those who **t** aside the alien and **Mal 3:5** 5186
cheek, **t** the other to him also. **Mt 5:39** *4762*
and do not **t** away from him who **Mt 5:42** *654*
and **t** and tear you to pieces. **Mt 7:6** *4762*
field must not **t** back to get his cloak. **Mt 24:18** *1994*
must not **t** back to get his coat. **Mk 13:16** *1994*
“And he will **t** many of the **Lk 1:16** *1994*
TO **T** THE HEARTS OF THE FATHERS **Lk 1:17** *1994*
“What then will this child **t** *out* **Lk 1:66**
judge **t** you over to the officer, **Lk 12:58** *3860*
who is in the field must not **t** back. **Lk 17:31** *1994*
“And having received it in their **t**, **Ac 7:45** *1237*
seeking to **t** the proconsul away **Ac 13:8** *1294*
you should **t** from these vain things **Ac 14:15** *1994*
that they may **t** from darkness to light **Ac 26:18** *1994*
they should repent and **t** to God, **Ac 26:20** *1994*
that it will **t** out exactly as I **Ac 27:25** *1510*
you learned, and **t** away from them. **Ro 16:17** *1578*
at the most three, and *each* in **t**, **1Co 14:27** *3313*
how is it that you **t** back again to **Ga 4:9** *1994*
only *do* not **t** your freedom **Ga 5:13**
this will **t** out for my deliverance **Php 1:19** *576*
and will **t** away their ears from **2Tm 4:4** *654*
truth and will **t** aside to myths. **2Tm 4:4** *1624*
of men who **t** away from the truth. **Ti 1:14** *654*
who **t** away from Him who *warns* **Heb 12:25** *654*
“HE MUST **T** AWAY FROM EVIL AND DO **1Pe 3:11** *1578*
to **t** away from the holy **2Pe 2:21** *5290*
ungodly persons who **t** the grace of **Jude 1:4** *3346a*
the waters to **t** them into blood, **Rv 11:6** *4762*

TURNED

sword which **t** every direction to **Gn 3:24** 2015
and their faces were **t** away, **Gn 9:23** 322
they **t** back and came to En-mishpat **Gn 14:7** 7725
Then the men **t** away from there and **Gn 18:22** 6437
so they **t** aside to him and entered **Gn 19:3** 5493
LORD has blessed you wherever I **t**. **Gn 30:30** 7272
So he **t** aside to her by the road, **Gn 38:16** 5186
He **t** away from them and wept. **Gn 42:24** 5437
and they **t** trembling to one **Gn 42:28**
LORD saw that he **t** aside to look, **Ex 3:4** 5493
staff and they **t** into serpents. **Ex 7:12** 1961
staff that was **t** into a serpent. **Ex 7:15** 2015
hand, and it will be **t** to blood. **Ex 7:17** 2015
was in the Nile was **t** to blood. **Ex 7:20** 2015
Then Pharaoh **t** and went into his **Ex 7:23** 6437
he **t** and went out from Pharaoh. **Ex 10:6** 6437
and **t** the sea into dry land, **Ex 14:21** 7760
faces of the cherubim are to be **t** **Ex 25:20**
“They have quickly **t** aside from **Ex 32:8** 5493
Then Moses **t** and went down from **Ex 32:15** 6437
if the hair in the infection has **t** white **Lv 13:3** 2015
the hair on it has not **t** white, **Lv 13:4** 2015
skin, and it has **t** the hair white, **Lv 13:10** 2015
has all **t** white *and* he is clean. **Lv 13:13** 2015
if the infection has **t** to white, **Lv 13:17** 2015
and the hair on it has **t** white, **Lv 13:20** 2015
in the bright spot has **t** white and **Lv 13:25** 2015
these things you are not **t** to Me, **Lv 26:23** 3256
As Aaron **t** toward Miriam, behold, **Nu 12:10** 6437
t back from following the LORD. **Nu 14:43** 7725
they **t** toward the tent of meeting, **Nu 16:42** 6437
so Israel **t** away from him. **Nu 20:21** 5186
Then they **t** and went up by the way **Nu 21:33** 6437
the donkey **t** off from the way and **Nu 22:23** 5186
“But the donkey saw me and **t** aside **Nu 22:33** 5186
If she had not **t** aside from me, I **Nu 22:33** 5186
has **t** away My wrath from the sons **Nu 25:11** 7725
Etham and **t** back to Pi-hahiroth, **Nu 33:7** 7725
“They **t** and went up into the **Dt 1:24** 6437
“Then we **t** and set out for the **Dt 2:1** 6437
And we **t** and passed through by the **Dt 2:8** 6437

“Then we **t** and went up the road **Dt 3:1** 6437
They have quickly **t** aside from the **Dt 9:12** 5493
“So I **t** and came down from the **Dt 9:15** 6437
you had **t** aside quickly from the **Dt 9:16** 5493
“Then I **t** and came down from the **Dt 10:5** 6437
for a wife, but he **t** against her; **Dt 22:16** 8130
your God **t** the curse into a blessing **Dt 23:5** 2015
Israel has **t** *their* back before their **Jos 7:8** 2015
and the LORD **t** from the fierceness **Jos 7:26** 7725
the men of Ai **t** back and looked, **Jos 8:20** 6437
wilderness **t** against the pursuers. **Jos 8:20** 2015
t back and slew the men of Ai. **Jos 8:21** 7725
Then Joshua **t** back at that time, **Jos 11:10** 7725
up to Addar and **t** about to Karka. **Jos 15:3** 5437
and **t** northward toward Gilgal **Jos 15:7** 6437
The border **t** about from Baalah **Jos 15:10** 5437
and the border **t** about eastward to **Jos 16:6** 5437
and **t** round on the west side **Jos 18:14** 5437
Then it **t** from Sarid to the east **Jos 19:12** 7725
It **t** toward the east to Beth-dagon **Jos 19:27** 7725
The border **t** to Ramah and to **Jos 19:29** 7725
then the border **t** to Hosah, and it **Jos 19:29** 7725
border **t** westward to Aznoth-tabor and **Jos 19:34** 7725
They **t** aside quickly from the way **Jg 2:17** 5493
But he himself **t** back from the **Jg 3:19** 7725
he **t** aside to her into the tent, **Jg 4:18** 5493
and **t** it upside down so that the **Jg 7:13** 2015
he **t** aside to look at the carcass **Jg 14:8** 5493
and **t** *the foxes* tail to tail and **Jg 15:4** 6437
and they **t** aside there and said **Jg 18:3** 5493
They **t** aside there and came to **Jg 18:15** 5493
Then they **t** and departed, and put **Jg 18:21** 6437
who **t** around and said to Micah, **Jg 18:23** 5437
he **t** and went back to his house. **Jg 18:26** 6437
They **t** aside there in order to **Jg 19:15** 5493
the men of Israel **t** in the battle, **Jg 20:39** 2015
Then the men of Israel **t**, **Jg 20:41** 2015
they **t** their backs before the men **Jg 20:42** 6437
The rest **t** and fled toward the **Jg 20:45** 6437
But 600 men **t** and fled toward the **Jg 20:47** 6437
The men of Israel then **t** back **Jg 20:48** 7725
And he **t** aside and sat down. **Ru 4:1** 5493
but **t** aside after dishonest gain **1Sa 8:3** 5186
he **t** his back to leave Samuel, **1Sa 10:9** 6437
one company **t** toward Ophrah, to **1Sa 13:17** 6437
company **t** toward Beth-horon, **1Sa 13:18** 6437
and another company **t** toward the **1Sa 13:18** 6437
even they also **t** to be with **1Sa 14:21**
and wherever he **t**, he inflicted **1Sa 14:47** 6437
he has **t** back from following Me and **1Sa 15:11** 7725
then **t** and proceeded on down to **1Sa 15:12** 5437
As Samuel **t** to go, *Saul* seized **1Sa 15:27** 5437
Then he **t** away from him to another **1Sa 17:30** 5437
And Doeg the Edomite **t** around and **1Sa 22:18** 5437
So Absalom **t** to his own house and **2Sa 14:24** 5437
So he **t** aside and stood still. **2Sa 18:30** 5437
The victory that day was **t** to **2Sa 19:2** 1961
Thus he **t** the hearts of all the **2Sa 19:14** 5186
kingdom has **t** about and become **1Ki 2:15** 5437
leaves of the one door **t** on pivots, **1Ki 6:34** 1550
leaves of the other door **t** on pivots. **1Ki 6:34** 1550
and all their rear parts **t** inward. **1Ki 7:25**
Then she **t** and went to her own **1Ki 10:13** 6437
and his wives **t** his heart away. **1Ki 11:3** 5186
his wives **t** his heart away after **1Ki 11:4** 5186
heart was **t** away from the LORD, **1Ki 11:9** 5186
and had not **t** aside from anything **1Ki 15:5** 5493
have **t** their heart back again.” **1Ki 18:37** 5437
a man **t** aside and brought a man to **1Ki 20:39** 5493
t away his face and ate no food. **1Ki 21:4** 5437
they **t** aside to fight against him, **1Ki 22:32** 5493
they **t** back from pursuing him. **1Ki 22:33** 7725
by, he **t** in there to eat food. **2Ki 4:8** 5493
and **t** in to the upper chamber and **2Ki 4:11** 5493
So he **t** and went away in a rage. **2Ki 5:12** 6437
man **t** from his chariot to meet you? **2Ki 5:26** 2015
t to them because of His covenant **2Ki 13:23** 6437
Then he **t** his face to the wall and **2Ki 20:2** 5437
Now when Josiah **t**, he saw the **2Ki 23:16** 6437
no king like him who **t** to the LORD **2Ki 23:25** 7725
he **t** and rebelled against him. **2Ki 24:1** 7725
and **t** the kingdom to David the son **1Ch 10:14** 5437
Ornan **t** back and saw the angel, **1Ch 21:20** 7725
all their hindquarters **t** inwards. **2Ch 4:4** 1004
Then she **t** and went to her own **2Ch 9:12** 2015
anger of the LORD **t** away from him, **2Ch 12:12** 7725
When Judah **t** around, behold, they **2Ch 13:14** 6437
they **t** to the LORD God of Israel, **2Ch 15:4** 7725
they **t** aside to fight against him. **2Ch 18:31** 5437
they **t** back from pursuing him. **2Ch 18:32** 7725
and **t** his attention to seek the **2Ch 20:3** 5414
t aside from them and did not destroy **2Ch 20:10** 5493
Amaziah **t** away from following the **2Ch 25:27** 5493
t their faces away from the dwelling **2Ch 29:6** 5437
the LORD, and have **t** *their* backs. **2Ch 29:6** 5414
and had **t** the heart of the king of **Ezr 6:22** 5437
this matter is **t** away from us.” **Ezr 10:14** 7725
And they **t** a stubborn shoulder and **Ne 9:29** 5414
God **t** the curse into a blessing. **Ne 13:2** 2015
it was **t** to the contrary so that **Es 9:1** 2015
t for them from sorrow into gladness **Es 9:22** 2015
those I love have **t** against me. **Jb 19:19** 2015
have kept His way and not **t** aside. **Jb 23:11** 5186
And underneath it is **t** up as fire. **Jb 28:5** 2015
“Terrors are **t** against me; They **Jb 30:15** 2015
my harp is **t** to mourning, **Jb 30:31** 1961
“If my step has **t** from the way, **Jb 31:7** 5186
they **t** aside from following Him, **Jb 34:27** 5493
are **t** into stubble for him. **Jb 41:28** 2015

They have all **t** aside, **Ps 14:3** 5493
t for me my mourning into dancing **Ps 30:11** 2015
Let those be **t** back and humiliated **Ps 35:4** 5472
trust, And has not **t** to the proud, **Ps 40:4** 6437
Let those be **t** back and dishonored **Ps 40:14** 5472
Our heart has not **t** back, **Ps 44:18** 5472
Every one of them has **t** aside; **Ps 53:3** 5472
He **t** the sea into dry land; **Ps 66:6** 2015
Who has not **t** away my prayer Nor **Ps 66:20** 5493
Let those be **t** back and dishonored **Ps 70:2** 5472
Let those be **t** back because of **Ps 70:3** 7725
they **t** back in the day of battle. **Ps 78:9** 2015
And **t** their rivers to blood, And **Ps 78:44** 2015
But **t** back and acted treacherously **Ps 78:57** 5472
t aside like a treacherous bow. **Ps 78:57** 2015
You withdrew all Your fury; You **t** **Ps 85:3** 7725
He **t** their heart to hate His **Ps 105:25** 2015
He **t** their waters into blood And **Ps 105:29** 2015
The Jordan **t** back. **Ps 114:3** 5437
t the rock into a pool of water, **Ps 114:8** 2015
And **t** my feet to Your testimonies. **Ps 119:59** 7725
not **t** aside from Your ordinances, **Ps 119:102** 5493
Be put to shame and **t** backward; **Ps 129:5** 5472
So I **t** to consider wisdom, madness **Ec 2:12** 6437
beloved had **t** away *and* had gone! **SS 5:6** 2559
Where has your beloved **t**, **SS 6:1** 6437
Israel, They have **t** away from Him. **Is 1:4** 2114a
with me, Your anger is **t** away, **Is 12:1** 7725
has been **t** for me into trembling. **Is 21:4** 7760
will be **t** into a fertile field, **Is 29:17** 7725
Its streams will be **t** into pitch, **Is 34:9** 2015
Hezekiah **t** his face to the wall and **Is 38:2** 5437
They will be **t** back *and* be **Is 42:17** 5472
a deceived heart has **t** him aside. **Is 44:20** 5186
Each of us has **t** to his own way; **Is 53:6** 6437
They have all **t** to their own way, **Is 56:11** 6437
Justice is **t** back, And **Is 59:14** 5472
of the sea will be **t** to you, **Is 60:5** 2015
He **t** Himself to become their enemy, **Is 63:10** 2015
How then have you **t** yourself **Jer 2:21** 2015
For they have **t** *their* back to Me, **Jer 2:27** 6437
His anger is **t** away from me.’ **Jer 2:35** 7725
the LORD Has not **t** back from us.” **Jer 4:8** 7725
They have **t** aside and departed. **Jer 5:23** 5493
‘Your iniquities have **t** these away, **Jer 5:25** 5186
houses shall be **t** over to others, **Jer 6:12** 5437
T away in continual apostasy? **Jer 8:5** 7725
Everyone **t** to his course, Like a **Jer 8:6** 7725
“They have **t** back to the iniquities **Jer 11:10** 7725
has **t** back from his wickedness. **Jer 23:14** 7725
And would have **t** them back from **Jer 23:22** 7725
And *why* have all faces **t** pale? **Jer 30:6** 2015
‘For after I **t** back, I repented; **Jer 31:19** 7725
“They have **t** *their* back to **Jer 32:33** 6437
But afterward they **t** around and **Jer 34:11** 7725
t and done what is right in My sight **Jer 34:15** 7725
“Yet you **t** and profaned My name, **Jer 34:16** 7725
they **t** in fear one to another and **Jer 36:16** 6342
sunk in the mire, They **t** back.” **Jer 38:22** 5472
Yet it **t** out that as soon as they **Jer 41:7** 1961
Mizpah **t** around and came back, **Jer 41:14** 5437
For even they too have **t** back *and* **Jer 46:21** 6437
not **t** back for *their* children, **Jer 47:3** 6437
How Moab has **t** his back **Jer 48:39** 6437
She has **t** away to flee, And panic **Jer 49:24** 6437
He has **t** me back; **La 1:13** 7725
Surely against me He has **t** His hand **La 3:3** 2015
He has **t** aside my ways and torn me **La 3:11** 5493
And no hands were **t** toward her. **La 4:6** 2342a
Our inheritance has been **t** **La 5:2** 2015
dancing has been **t** into mourning. **La 5:15** 2015
hearts which **t** away from Me, **Ezk 6:9** 5493
with its branches **t** toward him, **Ezk 17:6** 6437
“Because he considered and **t** away **Ezk 18:28** 7725
And I have **t** you to ashes on the **Ezk 28:18** 5414
iniquity of their having **t** to Egypt. **Ezk 29:16** 6437
He **t** to the west side *and* **Ezk 42:19** 5437
thoughts **t** to what would take place **Da 2:29** 5559b
transgressed Your law and **t** aside, **Da 9:11** 5493
natural color **t** to a deathly pallor, **Da 10:8** 2015
I **t** my face toward the ground and **Da 10:15** 5414
Ephraim has become a cake not **t**. **Hos 7:8** 2015
My heart is **t** over within Me, All **Hos 11:8** 2015
For My anger has **t** away from them. **Hos 14:4** 7725
pastures of the wilderness have **t** **Jl 2:22** 1876
“The sun will be **t** into darkness And **Jl 2:31** 2015
you have **t** justice into poison And **Am 6:12** 2015
that they **t** from their wicked way, **Jon 3:10** 7725
Reproaches will not be **t** back. **Mi 2:6** 5472
t back from following the LORD, **Zph 1:6** 5472
and **t** a stubborn shoulder and **Zch 7:11** 5414
and he **t** many back from iniquity. **Mal 2:6** 7725
you have **t** aside from the way; **Mal 2:8** 5493
you have **t** aside from My statutes and **Mal 3:7** 5493
But He **t** and said to Peter, **Mt 16:23** *4762*
t around in the crowd and said, **Mk 5:30** *1994*
and **t** and said to the crowd **Lk 7:9** *4762*
But He **t** and rebuked them, **Lk 9:55** *4762*
and He **t** and said to them, **Lk 14:25** *4762*
t back, glorifying God with a loud **Lk 17:15** *5290*
you, when once you have **t** again, **Lk 22:32** *1994*
The Lord **t** and looked at Peter. **Lk 22:61** *4762*
And Jesus **t** and saw them **Jn 1:38** *4762*
but your grief will be **t** into joy. **Jn 16:20** *1096*
she had said this, she **t** around and **Jn 20:14** *4762*
She **t** and said to Him in Hebrew, **Jn 20:16** *4762*
Judas **t** aside to go to his own place **Ac 1:25** *3845*
‘THE SUN WILL BE **T** INTO DARKNESS **Ac 2:20** *3344*
in their hearts **t** back to Egypt, **Ac 7:39** *4762*

"But God **t** away and delivered Ac 7:42 *4762*
saw him, and they **t** to the Lord. Ac 9:35 *1994*
number who believed **t** to the Lord. Ac 11:21 *1994*
and **t** and said to the spirit, Ac 16:18 *1994*
this Paul has persuaded and **t** away Ac 19:26 *3179*
ALL HAVE **T** ASIDE, TOGETHER THEY Ro 3:12 *1578*
that my circumstances have **t** out Php 1:12 *2064*
and how you **t** to God from idols to 1Th 1:9 *1994*
t aside to fruitless discussion, 1Tm 1:6 *1624*
already **t** aside to follow Satan. 1Tm 5:15 *1624*
who are in Asia **t** away from me, 2Tm 1:15 *654*
your laughter be **t** into mourning and Jas 4:9 *3346b*
Then I **t** to see the voice that was Rv 1:12 *1994*
And having **t** I saw seven golden Rv 1:12 *1994*

TURNING
not **t** to the right or left, Nu 20:17 5186
t away from following the LORD Jos 22:16 7725
wiping it and **t** it upside down. 2Ki 21:13 2015
t to the LORD God of Israel. 2Ch 36:13 7725
fearing God and **t** away from evil. Jb 1:1 5493
God and **t** away from evil." Jb 1:8 5493
fearing God and **t** away from evil. Jb 2:3 5493
t around by His guidance, Jb 37:12 2015
the wicked, **T** the wicked to ruin. Pr 21:12 5557
south, Then **t** toward the north, Ec 1:6 5437
t their knowledge into foolishness Is 44:25 7725
was angry, And he went on **t** away, Is 57:17 7726
the LORD, And **t** away from our God, Is 59:13 5472
t their faces in its direction; Jer 50:5
would go, without **t** as they went. Ezk 1:12 5437
without **t** as they moved. Ezk 1:17 5437
directions without **t** as they went; Ezk 10:11 5437
faced, without **t** as they went. Ezk 10:11 5437
even **t** aside from Your commandments Da 9:5 5493
LORD our God by **t** from our iniquity Da 9:13 7725
My people are bent on **t** from Me. Hos 11:7 4878
But Jesus **t** and seeing her said, Mt 9:22 *4762*
But **t** around and seeing His Mk 8:33 *1994*
And **t** His gaze toward His disciples, Lk 6:20 *1869*
T toward the woman, He said to Simon, Lk 7:44 *4762*
T to the disciples, He said Lk 10:23 *4762*
But Jesus **t** to them said, Lk 23:28 *4762*
Peter, **t** around, saw the disciple Jn 21:20 *1994*
t every one *of you* from your wicked Ac 3:26 *654*
and prayed, and **t** to the body, Ac 9:40 *1994*
behold, we are **t** to the Gentiles. Ac 13:46 *4762*
not trouble those who are **t** to God Ac 15:19 *1994*

TURNS
the raw flesh **t** again and is changed Lv 13:16 7725
t to mediums and to spiritists, Lv 20:6 6437
in to her and *then* **t** against her, Dt 22:13 8130
if the latter husband **t** against her Dt 24:3 8130
whose heart **t** away today from the Dt 29:18 6437
if your heart **t** away and you will Dt 30:17 6437
from the bay that **t** to the south. Jos 15:2 6437
you know how the matter **t** out; Ru 3:18 5307
He **t** on the right, I cannot see Jb 23:9 5848a
"My skin **t** black on me, And my Jb 30:30 7835
is cautious and **t** away from evil, Pr 14:16 5493
A gentle answer **t** away wrath, But Pr 15:1 7725
Wherever he **t**, he prospers. Pr 17:8 6437
He **t** it wherever He wishes. Pr 21:1 5186
As the door **t** on its hinges, So Pr 26:14 5437
He who **t** away his ear from Pr 28:9 5493
All joy **t** to gloom. Is 24:11 6150
And he who **t** aside from evil makes Is 59:15 5493
darkness, *And* **t** *it* into gloom. Jer 13:16 7896
whose heart **t** away from the LORD. Jer 17:5 5493
I have spoken **t** from its evil, Jer 18:8 7725
she herself groans and **t** away. La 1:8 7725
when a righteous man **t** away from Ezk 3:20 7725
if the wicked man **t** from all his sins Ezk 18:21 7725
man **t** away from his righteousness, Ezk 18:24 7725
man **t** away from his righteousness, Ezk 18:26 7725
when a wicked man **t** away from his Ezk 18:27 7725
day when he **t** from his wickedness; Ezk 33:12 7725
and he **t** from his sin and Ezk 33:14 7725
"When the righteous **t** from his Ezk 33:18 7725
"But when the wicked **t** from his Ezk 33:19 7725
"Stop, stop," But no one **t** back. Na 2:8 6437
"If it **t** out that he finds Mt 18:13 *1096*
shower is coming,' and so it **t** out. Lk 12:54 *1096*
a hot day,' and it **t** out *that way.* Lk 12:55 *1096*
but whenever a person **t** to the Lord, 2Co 3:16 *1994*
the truth and one **t** him back, Jas 5:19 *1994*
t a sinner from the error of his way Jas 5:20 *1994*

TURQUOISE
and the second row a **t**, Ex 28:18 5306
and the second row, a **t**, Ex 39:11 5306
The lapis lazuli, the **t** and Ezk 28:13 5306

TURTLEDOVE
and a three year old ram, and a **t**, Gn 15:9 8449
pigeon or a **t** for a sin offering. Lv 12:6 8449
soul of Your **t** to the wild beast; Ps 74:19 8449
the **t** has been heard in our land. SS 2:12 8449
And the **t** and the swift and the Jer 8:7 8449

TURTLEDOVES
from the **t** or from young pigeons. Lv 1:14 8449
two **t** or two young pigeons, Lv 5:7 8449
for two **t** or two young pigeons, Lv 5:11 8449
take two **t** or two young pigeons, Lv 12:8 8449
and two **t** or two young pigeons Lv 14:22 8449
one of the **t** or young pigeons, Lv 14:30 8449
two **t** or two young pigeons, Lv 15:14 8449
two **t** or two young pigeons and Lv 15:29 8449
on the eighth day he shall bring two **t** Nu 6:10 8449
"A PAIR OF **T** OR TWO YOUNG Lk 2:24 *5167*

TUSKS
ivory **t** and ebony they brought as Ezk 27:15 7161

TUTOR
Law has become our **t** *to lead us* to Ga 3:24 *3807*
come, we are no longer under a **t**. Ga 3:25 *3807*

TUTORED
son of Hachmoni **t** the king's sons. 1Ch 27:32 5973

TUTORS
to have countless **t** in Christ, 1Co 4:15 *3807*

TWELFTH
On the **t** day *it was* Ahira the son Nu 7:78 8147, 6240
before him, and he with the **t**. 1Ki 19:19 8147, 6240
In the **t** year of Joram the son of 2Ki 8:25 8147, 6240
the **t** year of Ahaz king of Judah, 2Ki 17:1 8147, 6240
king of Judah, in the **t** month, 2Ki 25:27 8147, 6240
for Eliashib, the **t** for Jakim, 1Ch 24:12 8147, 6240
the **t** to Hashabiah, his sons and 1Ch 25:19 8147, 6240
The **t** for the twelfth month *was* 1Ch 27:15 8147, 6240
The twelfth for the **t** month *was* 1Ch 27:15 8147, 6240
and in the **t** year he began to 2Ch 34:3 8147, 6240
on the **t** of the first month to go to Ezr 8:31 8147, 6240
in the **t** year of King Ahasuerus, Es 3:7 8147, 6240
month *to month,* until the **t** month, Es 3:7 8147, 6240
the thirteenth *day* of the **t** month, Es 3:13 8147, 6240
the thirteenth *day* of the **t** month Es 8:12 8147, 6240
Now in the **t** month Es 9:1 8147, 6240
king of Judah, in the **t** month, Jer 52:31 8147, 6240
month, on the **t** of the month, Ezk 29:1 8147, 6240
In the **t** year, Ezk 32:1 8147, 6240
the twelfth year, in the **t** *month,* Ezk 32:1 8147, 6240
In the **t** year, Ezk 32:17 8147, 6240
Now in the **t** year of our exile, Ezk 33:21 8147, 6240
the eleventh, jacinth; the **t**, amethyst. Rv 21:20 *1428*

TWELVE
were nine hundred and **t** years, Gn 5:8 8147, 6240
T years they had served Gn 14:4 8147, 6240
become the father of **t** princes, Gn 17:20 8147, 6240
t princes according to their Gn 25:16 8147, 6240
Now there were **t** sons of Jacob Gn 35:22 8147, 6240
servants are **t** brothers *in all,* Gn 42:13 8147, 6240
'We are **t** brothers, sons of our Gn 42:32 8147, 6240
these are the **t** tribes of Israel, Gn 49:28 8147, 6240
where there *were* **t** springs of water Ex 15:27 8147, 6240
t pillars for the twelve tribes of Israel. Ex 24:4 8147, 6240
for the **t** tribes of Israel. Ex 24:4 8147, 6240
t, according to their names; Ex 28:21 8147, 6240
to his name for the **t** tribes. Ex 28:21 8147, 6240
they were **t**, corresponding to Ex 39:14 8147, 6240
with its name for the **t** tribes. Ex 39:14 8147, 6240
flour and bake **t** cakes with it; Lv 24:5 8147, 6240
with the leaders of Israel, **t** men, Nu 1:44 8147, 6240
six covered carts and **t** oxen, Nu 7:3 8147, 6240
t silver dishes, twelve silver Nu 7:84 8147, 6240
silver dishes, **t** silver bowls, Nu 7:84 8147, 6240
twelve silver bowls, **t** gold pans, Nu 7:84 8147, 6240
the **t** gold pans, full of incense, Nu 7:86 8147, 6240
for the burnt offering **t** bulls, Nu 7:87 8147, 6240
twelve bulls, *all* the rams **t**, Nu 7:87 8147, 6240
old with their grain offering **t**, Nu 7:87 8147, 6240
male goats for a sin offering **t**; Nu 7:87 8147, 6240
t rods, from all their leaders Nu 17:2 8147, 6240
their fathers' households, **t** rods, Nu 17:6 8147, 6240
t bulls, two rams, fourteen male Nu 29:17 8147, 6240
tribe, **t** thousand armed for war. Nu 31:5 8147, 6240
and in Elim there were **t** springs Nu 33:9 8147, 6240
me and I took **t** of your men, Dt 1:23 8147, 6240
t men from the tribes of Israel, Jos 3:12 8147, 6240
yourselves **t** men from the people, Jos 4:2 8147, 6240
'Take up for yourselves **t** stones Jos 4:3 8147, 6240
So Joshua called the **t** men whom he Jos 4:4 8147, 6240
and took up **t** stones from the Jos 4:8 8147, 6240
Then Joshua set up **t** stones in the Jos 4:9 8147, 6240
Those **t** stones which they had Jos 4:20 8147, 6240
t cities with their villages. Jos 18:24 8147, 6240
t cities with their villages. Jos 19:15 8147, 6240
their families received **t** cities from Jos 21:7 8147, 6240
and their lot was **t** cities. Jos 21:40 8147, 6240
concubine and cut her in **t** pieces, Jg 19:29 8147, 6240
t for Benjamin and Ish-bosheth the 2Sa 2:15 8147, 6240
and **t** of the servants of David. 2Sa 2:15 8147, 6240
had **t** deputies over all Israel, 1Ki 4:7 8147, 6240
and a line of **t** cubits measured 1Ki 7:15 8147, 6240
It stood on **t** oxen, three facing 1Ki 7:25 8147, 6240
sea and the **t** oxen under the sea; 1Ki 7:44 8147, 6240
T lions were standing there on 1Ki 10:20 8147, 6240
on him and tore it into **t** pieces. 1Ki 11:30 8147, 6240
over Israel *and reigned* **t** years; 1Ki 16:23 8147, 6240
Elijah took **t** stones according 1Ki 18:31 8147, 6240
with **t** pairs *of oxen* before him, 1Ki 19:19 8147, 6240
of Judah, and reigned **t** years. 2Ki 3:1 8147, 6240
t years old when he became king, 2Ki 21:1 8147, 6240
the tribe of Zebulun, **t** cities. 1Ch 6:63 8147, 6240
his relatives and sons *were* **t**; 1Ch 25:9 8147, 6240
his sons and his relatives, **t**; 1Ch 25:10 8147, 6240
his sons and his relatives, **t**; 1Ch 25:11 8147, 6240
his sons and his relatives, **t**; 1Ch 25:12 8147, 6240
his sons and his relatives, **t**; 1Ch 25:13 8147, 6240
his sons and his relatives, **t**; 1Ch 25:14 8147, 6240
his sons and his relatives, **t**; 1Ch 25:15 8147, 6240
his sons and his relatives, **t**; 1Ch 25:16 8147, 6240
his sons and his relatives, **t**; 1Ch 25:17 8147, 6240
his sons and his relatives, **t**; 1Ch 25:18 8147, 6240
his sons and his relatives, **t**; 1Ch 25:19 8147, 6240
his sons and his relatives, **t**; 1Ch 25:20 8147, 6240
his sons and his relatives, **t**; 1Ch 25:21 8147, 6240
his sons and his relatives, **t**; 1Ch 25:22 8147, 6240
his sons and his relatives, **t**; 1Ch 25:23 8147, 6240
his sons and his relatives, **t**; 1Ch 25:24 8147, 6240
his sons and his relatives, **t**; 1Ch 25:25 8147, 6240
his sons and his relatives, **t**; 1Ch 25:26 8147, 6240
his sons and his relatives, **t**; 1Ch 25:27 8147, 6240
his sons and his relatives, **t**; 1Ch 25:28 8147, 6240
his sons and his relatives, **t**; 1Ch 25:29 8147, 6240
his sons and his relatives, **t**; 1Ch 25:30 8147, 6240

his sons and his relatives, **t**. **1Ch 25:31** 8147, 6240
It stood on **t** oxen, three facing **2Ch 4:4** 8147, 6240
one sea with the **t** oxen under it. **2Ch 4:15** 8147, 6240
T lions were standing there on **2Ch 9:19** 8147, 6240
t years old when he became king, **2Ch 33:1** 8147, 6240
apart **t** of the leading priests, **Ezr 8:24** 8147, 6240
of King Artaxerxes, *for* **t** years, **Ne 5:14** 8147, 6240
after the end of her **t** months **Es 2:12** 8147, 6240
and the **t** bronze bulls that were **Jer 52:20** 8147, 6240
and it *was* **t** cubits in **Jer 52:21** 8147, 6240
be **t** *cubits* long by twelve wide, **Ezk 43:16** 8147, 6240
be twelve *cubits* long by **t** wide, **Ezk 43:16** 8147, 6240
among the **t** tribes of Israel; **Ezk 47:13** 8147, 6240
"**T** months later he was walking on **Da 4:29** 8648, 6236
from a hemorrhage for **t** years, **Mt 9:20** *1427*
Jesus summoned His **t** disciples **Mt 10:1** *1427*
names of the **t** apostles are these: **Mt 10:2** *1427*
These **t** Jesus sent out after **Mt 10:5** *1427*
instructions to His **t** disciples, **Mt 11:1** *1427*
the broken pieces, **t** full baskets. **Mt 14:20** *1427*
you also shall sit upon **t** thrones, **Mt 19:28** *1427*
judging the **t** tribes of Israel. **Mt 19:28** *1427*
He took the **t** *disciples* aside by **Mt 20:17** *1427*
Then one of the **t**, named Judas **Mt 26:14** *1427*
at the table with the **t** disciples. **Mt 26:20** *1427*
behold, Judas, one of the **t**, **Mt 26:47** *1427*
more than **t** legions of angels? **Mt 26:53** *1427*
And He appointed **t**, **Mk 3:14** *1427*
And He appointed the **t**: **Mk 3:16** *1427*
His followers, along with the **t**, **Mk 4:10** *1427*
had had a hemorrhage for **t** years, **Mk 5:25** *1427*
for she was **t** years old. **Mk 5:42** *1427*
And He summoned the **t** and began to **Mk 6:7** *1427*
and they picked up **t** full baskets **Mk 6:43** *1427*
They said to Him, "**T**." **Mk 8:19** *1427*
He called the **t** and said to them, **Mk 9:35** *1427*
And again He took the **t** aside and **Mk 10:32** *1427*
left for Bethany with the **t**, **Mk 11:11** *1427*
Iscariot, who was one of the **t**, **Mk 14:10** *1427*
it was evening He came with the **t**. **Mk 14:17** *1427*
"*It is* one of the **t**, **Mk 14:20** *1427*
speaking, Judas, one of the **t**, **Mk 14:43** *1427*
And when He became **t**, **Lk 2:42** *1427*
and chose **t** of them, whom He also **Lk 6:13** *1427*
The **t** were with Him, **Lk 8:1** *1427*
only daughter, about **t** years old, **Lk 8:42** *1427*
who had a hemorrhage for **t** years, **Lk 8:43** *1427*
And He called the **t** together, **Lk 9:1** *1427*
and the **t** came and said to Him, **Lk 9:12** *1427*
were picked up, **t** baskets *full*. **Lk 9:17** *1427*
took the **t** aside and said to them, **Lk 18:31** *1427*
belonging to the number of the **t**. **Lk 22:3** *1427*
judging the **t** tribes of Israel. **Lk 22:30** *1427*
one called Judas, one of the **t**, **Lk 22:47** *1427*
and filled **t** baskets with **Jn 6:13** *1427*
Jesus said to the **t**, **Jn 6:67** *1427*
I Myself not choose you, the **t**, **Jn 6:70** *1427*
Iscariot, for he, one of the **t**, **Jn 6:71** *1427*
"Are there not **t** hours in the day? **Jn 11:9** *1427*
But Thomas, one of the **t**, **Jn 20:24** *1427*
So the **t** summoned the **Ac 6:2** *1427*
and Jacob *of* the **t** patriarchs. **Ac 7:8** *1427*
There were in all about **t** men. **Ac 19:7** *1427*
t days ago I went up to Jerusalem to **Ac 24:11** *1427*
which our **t** tribes hope to attain, **Ac 26:7** *1429*
appeared to Cephas, then to the **t**. **1Co 15:5** *1427*
To the **t** tribes who are dispersed **Jas 1:1** *1427*
of Judah, **t** thousand *were* sealed, **Rv 7:5** *1427*
the tribe of Reuben **t** thousand, **Rv 7:5** *1427*
from the tribe of Gad **t** thousand, **Rv 7:5** *1427*
the tribe of Asher **t** thousand, **Rv 7:6** *1427*
the tribe of Naphtali **t** thousand, **Rv 7:6** *1427*
the tribe of Manasseh **t** thousand, **Rv 7:6** *1427*
the tribe of Simeon **t** thousand, **Rv 7:7** *1427*
from the tribe of Levi **t** thousand, **Rv 7:7** *1427*
the tribe of Issachar **t** thousand, **Rv 7:7** *1427*
the tribe of Zebulun **t** thousand, **Rv 7:8** *1427*
the tribe of Joseph **t** thousand, **Rv 7:8** *1427*
Benjamin, **t** thousand *were* sealed. **Rv 7:8** *1427*
for **t** hundred and sixty days, **Rv 11:3** *5507, 1250*
on her head a crown of **t** stars; **Rv 12:1** *1427*
great and high wall, with **t** gates, **Rv 21:12** *1427*
gates, and at the gates **t** angels; **Rv 21:12** *1427*
t tribes of the sons of Israel. **Rv 21:12** *1427*
the city had **t** foundation stones, **Rv 21:14** *1427*
the **t** names of the twelve apostles **Rv 21:14** *1427*
names of the **t** apostles of the Lamb. **Rv 21:14** *1427*
the **t** gates were twelve pearls; **Rv 21:21** *1427*
the twelve gates were **t** pearls; **Rv 21:21** *1427*
of life, bearing **t** *kinds of* fruit, **Rv 22:2** *1427*

TWENTIETH

month, on the **t** of the month, **Nu 10:11** 6242
So in the **t** year of Jeroboam the **1Ki 15:9** 6242
in the **t** year of Jotham the son of **2Ki 15:30** 6242
for Pethahiah, the **t** for Jehezkel, **1Ch 24:16** 6242
for the **t** to Eliathah, his sons **1Ch 25:27** 6242
ninth month on the **t** of the month, **Ezr 10:9** 6242
the month Chislev, *in* the **t** year, **Ne 1:1** 6242
in the **t** year of King Artaxerxes, **Ne 2:1** 6242
from the **t** year to the **Ne 5:14** 6242

TWENTY

be one hundred and **t** years." **Gn 6:3** 6242
suppose **t** are found there?" **Gn 18:31** 6242
destroy *it* on account of the **t**." **Gn 18:31** 6242
t years I *have been* with you; **Gn 31:38** 6242
"These **t** years I have been in **Gn 31:41** 6242
female goats and **t** male goats, **Gn 32:14** 6242
two hundred ewes and **t** rams, **Gn 32:14** 6242
t female donkeys and ten male **Gn 32:15** 6242
for **t** *shekels* of silver. **Gn 37:28** 6242
t boards for the south side. **Ex 26:18** 6242
of silver under the **t** boards, **Ex 26:19** 6242
on the north side, **t** boards, **Ex 26:20** 6242
and its pillars *shall be* **t**, **Ex 27:10** 6242
with their **t** sockets of bronze; **Ex 27:10** 6242
and its **t** pillars with their **Ex 27:11** 6242
with their **t** sockets of bronze; **Ex 27:11** 6242
shall be a screen of **t** cubits, **Ex 27:16** 6242
(the shekel is **t** gerahs), **Ex 30:13** 6242
from **t** years old and over, **Ex 30:14** 6242
t boards for the south side; **Ex 36:23** 6242
of silver under the **t** boards; **Ex 36:24** 6242
the north side, he made **t** boards, **Ex 36:25** 6242
their **t** pillars, and their twenty **Ex 38:10** 6242
pillars, and their **t** sockets, **Ex 38:10** 6242
their **t** pillars and their twenty **Ex 38:11** 6242
their **t** sockets *were* of bronze, **Ex 38:11** 6242
And the length *was* **t** cubits and **Ex 38:18** 6242
from **t** years old and upward, **Ex 38:26** 6242
t years even to sixty years old, **Lv 27:3** 6242
If it be from five years even to **t** years **Lv 27:5** 6242
for the male shall be **t** shekels and **Lv 27:5** 6242
The shekel shall be **t** gerahs. **Lv 27:25** 6242
from **t** years old and upward, **Nu 1:3** 6242
from **t** years old and upward, **Nu 1:18** 6242
male from **t** years old and upward, **Nu 1:20** 6242
male from **t** years old and upward, **Nu 1:22** 6242
from **t** years old and upward, **Nu 1:24** 6242
from **t** years old and upward, **Nu 1:26** 6242
from **t** years old and upward, **Nu 1:28** 6242
from **t** years old and upward, **Nu 1:30** 6242
from **t** years old and upward, **Nu 1:32** 6242
from **t** years old and upward, **Nu 1:34** 6242
from **t** years old and upward, **Nu 1:36** 6242
from **t** years old and upward, **Nu 1:38** 6242
from **t** years old and upward, **Nu 1:40** 6242
from **t** years old and upward, **Nu 1:42** 6242
from **t** years old and upward, **Nu 1:45** 6242
(the shekel is **t** gerahs), **Nu 3:47** 6242
days, nor ten days, nor **t** days, **Nu 11:19** 6242
from **t** years old and upward, **Nu 14:29** 6242
the sanctuary, which is **t** gerahs. **Nu 18:16** 6242
from **t** years old and upward, **Nu 26:2** 6242
from **t** years old and upward, **Nu 26:4** 6242
from **t** years old and upward, **Nu 32:11** 6242
a hundred and **t** years old today; **Dt 31:2** 6242
and **t** years old when he died, **Dt 34:7** 6242
of Israel severely for **t** years. **Jg 4:3** 6242
the entrance of Minnith, **t** cities, **Jg 11:33** 6242
So he judged Israel **t** years in the **Jg 15:20** 6242
Thus he had judged Israel **t** years. **Jg 16:31** 6242
time was long, for it was **t** years; **1Sa 7:2** 6242
armor bearer made was about **t** men **1Sa 14:14** 6242
Then Abner and **t** men with him came **2Sa 3:20** 6242
had fifteen sons and **t** servants. **2Sa 9:10** 6242
sons and his **t** servants with him; **2Sa 19:17** 6242
the end of nine months and **t** days. **2Sa 24:8** 6242
ten fat oxen, **t** pasture-fed oxen, **1Ki 4:23** 6242
and **t** kors of beaten oil; **1Ki 5:11** 6242
was sixty cubits and its width **t** *cubits* **1Ki 6:2** 6242
the house *was* **t** cubits in length, **1Ki 6:3** 6242
He built **t** cubits on the rear **1Ki 6:16** 6242
sanctuary *was* **t** cubits in length, **1Ki 6:20** 6242
in length, **t** cubits in width, **1Ki 6:20** 6242
in width, and **t** cubits in height, **1Ki 6:20** 6242
end of **t** years in which Solomon **1Ki 9:10** 6242
t cities in the land of Galilee. **1Ki 9:11** 6242
and **t** talents of gold from there, **1Ki 9:28** 6242
a hundred and **t** talents of gold, **1Ki 10:10** 6242
t loaves of barley and fresh ears **2Ki 4:42** 6242
in Samaria, *and reigned* **t** years. **2Ki 15:27** 6242
t years old when he became king, **2Ki 16:2** 6242
LORD, from **t** years old and upward. **1Ch 23:24** 6242
from **t** years old and upward. **1Ch 23:27** 6242
those **t** years of age and under, **1Ch 27:23** 6242
cubits, and the width **t** cubits. **2Ch 3:3** 6242
the width of the house, **t** cubits, **2Ch 3:4** 6242
width of the house *was* **t** cubits, **2Ch 3:8** 6242
and its width *was* **t** cubits; **2Ch 3:8** 6242
of the cherubim *was* **t** cubits; **2Ch 3:11** 6242
these cherubim extended **t** cubits, **2Ch 3:13** 6242
t cubits in length and twenty **2Ch 4:1** 6242
t cubits in width and ten cubits in **2Ch 4:1** 6242
and **t** priests blowing trumpets **2Ch 5:12** 6242
t years in which Solomon had built **2Ch 8:1** 6242
one hundred and **t** talents of gold and **2Ch 9:9** 6242
those from **t** years old and upward and **2Ch 25:5** 6242
t years old when he became king, **2Ch 28:1** 6242
from **t** years old and upwards, **2Ch 31:17** 6242
the Levites from **t** years and older to **Ezr 3:8** 6242
be **t** shekels a day by weight; **Ezk 4:10** 6242
length of the porch *was* **t** cubits **Ezk 40:49** 6242
cubits, and the width, **t** cubits. **Ezk 41:2** 6242
He measured its length, **t** cubits, **Ezk 41:4** 6242
cubits, and the width, **t** cubits, **Ezk 41:4** 6242
and the *outer* chambers *was* **t** cubits **Ezk 41:10** 6242
Opposite the **t** *cubits* which **Ezk 42:3** 6242
"The shekel shall be **t** gerahs; **Ezk 45:12** 6242
t shekels, twenty-five shekels, **Ezk 45:12** 6242
to a *grain* heap of **t** *measures*, **Hg 2:16** 6242
measures, there would be *only* **t**. **Hg 2:16** 6242
its length is **t** cubits and its **Zch 5:2** 6242
against him with **t** thousand? **Lk 14:31** *1501*
t or thirty gallons each. **Jn 2:6** *1417*
and **t** persons was there together), **Ac 1:15** *1501*
and found *it to be* **t** fathoms; **Ac 27:28** *1501*

TWENTY-EIGHT

of each curtain shall be **t** cubits, **Ex 26:2** 6242, 8083
of each curtain was **t** cubits and **Ex 36:9** 6242, 8083
Israel in Samaria *was* **t** years. **2Ki 10:36** 6242, 8083
t sons and sixty daughters. **2Ch 11:21** 6242, 8083

TWENTY-FIFTH

on the **t** of *the month* Elul, **Ne 6:15** 6242, 2568
month, on the **t** of the month, **Jer 52:31** 6242, 2568
In the **t** year of our exile, at the **Ezk 40:1** 6242, 2568

TWENTY-FIRST

the **t** day of the month at evening. **Ex 12:18** 6242, 259
the **t** for Jachin, the **1Ch 24:17** 6242, 259
for the **t** to Hothir, his sons and **1Ch 25:28** 6242, 259
On the **t** of the seventh month, the **Hg 2:1** 6242, 259

TWENTY-FIVE

from **t** years old and upward they **Nu 8:24** 6242, 2568
he reigned **t** years in Jerusalem. **1Ki 22:42** 6242, 2568
t years old when he became king, **2Ki 14:2** 6242, 2568
t years old when he became king, **2Ki 15:33** 6242, 2568
t years old when he became king, **2Ki 18:2** 6242, 2568
t years old when he became king, **2Ki 23:36** 6242, 2568
he reigned in Jerusalem **t** years. **2Ch 20:31** 6242, 2568
t years old when he became king, **2Ch 25:1** 6242, 2568
t years old when he became king, **2Ch 27:1** 6242, 2568
t years old when he became king, **2Ch 27:8** 6242, 2568
king *when he was* **t** years old; **2Ch 29:1** 6242, 2568
t years old when he became king, **2Ch 36:5** 6242, 2568
were about **t** men with their backs **Ezk 8:16** 6242, 2568
there were **t** men at the entrance **Ezk 11:1** 6242, 2568
a width of **t** cubits from *one* door **Ezk 40:13** 6242, 2568
cubits and the width **t** cubits. **Ezk 40:21** 6242, 2568
cubits and the width **t** cubits. **Ezk 40:25** 6242, 2568
cubits long and **t** cubits wide. **Ezk 40:29** 6242, 2568
t cubits long and five cubits wide. **Ezk 40:30** 6242, 2568
cubits long and **t** cubits wide. **Ezk 40:33** 6242, 2568
cubits and the width **t** cubits. **Ezk 40:36** 6242, 2568
twenty shekels, **t** shekels, *and* **Ezk 45:12** 6242, 2568

TWENTY-FOUR

toes on each foot, **t** in number; **2Sa 21:20** 6242, 702
at Tirzah, *and reigned* **t** years. **1Ki 15:33** 6242, 702
who had **t** fingers and toes, **1Ch 20:6** 6242, 702
Around the throne *were* **t** thrones; **Rv 4:4** *1501, 5064*
thrones *I saw* **t** elders sitting, **Rv 4:4** *1501, 5064*
the **t** elders will fall down before **Rv 4:10** *1501, 5064*
t elders fell down before the Lamb, **Rv 5:8** *1501, 5064*
And the **t** elders, who sit on their **Rv 11:16** *1501, 5064*
And the **t** elders and the four **Rv 19:4** *1501, 5064*

TWENTY-FOURTH

for Delaiah, the **t** for Maaziah. **1Ch 24:18** 6242, 702
for the **t** to Romamti-ezer, his **1Ch 25:31** 6242, 702
Now on the **t** day of this month the **Ne 9:1** 6242, 702

On the **t** day of the first month, **Da 10:4** 6242, 702
on the **t** day of the sixth month in **Hg 1:15** 6242, 702
On the **t** of the ninth *month,* in **Hg 2:10** 6242, 702
from the **t** day of the ninth *month;* **Hg 2:18** 6242, 702
on the **t** *day* of the month, **Hg 2:20** 6242, 702
the **t** day of the eleventh month, **Zch 1:7** 6242, 702

TWENTY-NINE
Nahor lived **t** years, and **Gn 11:24** 6242, 8672
all, **t** cities with their villages. **Jos 15:32** 6242, 8672
he reigned **t** years in Jerusalem. **2Ki 14:2** 6242, 8672
he reigned **t** years in Jerusalem; **2Ki 18:2** 6242, 8672
he reigned **t** years in Jerusalem. **2Ch 25:1** 6242, 8672
he reigned **t** years in Jerusalem. **2Ch 29:1** 6242, 8672

TWENTY-ONE
t years old when he became king, **2Ki 24:18** 6242, 259
t years old when he became king, **2Ch 36:11** 6242, 259
t years old when he became king, **Jer 52:1** 6242, 259
was withstanding me for **t** days; **Da 10:13** 6242, 259

TWENTY-SECOND
for Jachin, the **t** for Gamul, **1Ch 24:17** 6242, 8147
for the **t** to Giddalti, his sons **1Ch 25:29** 6242, 8147

TWENTY-SEVEN
Sarah lived one hundred and **t** years **Gn 23:1** 6242, 7651

TWENTY-SEVENTH
month, on the **t** day of the month, **Gn 8:14** 6242, 7651
the **t** year of Asa king of Judah, **1Ki 16:10** 6242, 7651
the **t** year of Asa king of Judah, **1Ki 16:15** 6242, 7651
t year of Jeroboam king of Israel, **2Ki 15:1** 6242, 7651
month, on the **t** *day* of the month, **2Ki 25:27** 6242, 7651
Now in the **t** year, in the first **Ezk 29:17** 6242, 7651

TWENTY-SIXTH
the **t** year of Asa king of Judah, **1Ki 16:8** 6242, 8337a

TWENTY-THIRD
in the **t** year of King Jehoash **2Ki 12:6** 6242, 7969
In the **t** year of Joash the son of **2Ki 13:1** 6242, 7969
the **t** for Delaiah, the **1Ch 24:18** 6242, 7969
for the **t** to Mahazioth, his sons **1Ch 25:30** 6242, 7969
Then on the **t** day of the seventh **2Ch 7:10** 6242, 7969
on the **t** day; and it was written **Es 8:9** 6242, 7969
in the **t** year of Nebuchadnezzar, **Jer 52:30** 6242, 7969

TWENTY-THREE
Aaron was one hundred **t** years old **Nu 33:39** 6242, 7969
He judged Israel **t** years. **Jg 10:2** 6242, 7969
t years old when he became king, **2Ki 23:31** 6242, 7969
t cities in the land of Gilead. **1Ch 2:22** 6242, 7969
t years old when he became king, **2Ch 36:2** 6242, 7969
these **t** years the word of the LORD **Jer 25:3** 6242, 7969
and **t** thousand fell in one day. **1Co 10:8** *1501, 5140*

TWENTY-TWO
t cities with their villages. **Jos 19:30** 6242, 8147
arose and judged Israel **t** years. **Jg 10:3** 6242, 8147
that Jeroboam reigned *was* **t** years; **1Ki 14:20** 6242, 8147
over Israel in Samaria **t** years. **1Ki 16:29** 6242, 8147
t years old when he became king, **2Ki 8:26** 6242, 8147
t years old when he became king, **2Ki 21:19** 6242, 8147
of his father's house **t** captains. **1Ch 12:28** 6242, 8147
became the father of **t** sons and **2Ch 13:21** 6242, 8147
t years old when he became king, **2Ch 22:2** 705, 8147
t years old when he became king, **2Ch 33:21** 6242, 8147

TWICE
repeating of the dream to Pharaoh **t**, **Gn 41:32** 6471
by now we could have returned **t**." **Gn 43:10** 6471
t as much as they gather daily." **Ex 16:5** 4932
day they gathered **t** as much bread, **Ex 16:22** 4932
struck the rock **t** with his rod; **Nu 20:11** 6471
David escaped from his presence **t**. **1Sa 18:11** 6471
Israel, who had appeared to him **t**, **1Ki 11:9** 6471
there, more than once or **t**. **2Ki 6:10** 8147
Once or **t** the traders and **Ne 13:20** 8147
"Indeed God speaks once, Or **t**, **Jb 33:14** 8147
Even **t**, and I will add nothing more." **Jb 40:5** 8147
T I have heard this: **Ps 62:11** 8147
the *other* man lives a thousand years **t** **Ec 6:6** 6471
Distress will not rise up **t**. **Na 1:9** 6471
you make him **t** as much a son of **Mt 23:15** *1362*
very night, before a rooster crows **t**, **Mk 14:30** *1364*
"Before a rooster crows **t**, **Mk 14:72** *1364*
'I fast **t** a week; I pay tithes of all **Lk 18:12** *1364*
you might **t** receive a blessing; **2Co 1:15** *1208*
has mixed, mix **t** as much for her. **Rv 18:6** *1362*

TWIG
are putting the **t** to their nose. **Ezk 8:17** 2156

TWIGS
plucked off the topmost of its young **t** **Ezk 17:4** 3242
from the topmost of its young **t** **Ezk 17:22** 3127

TWILIGHT
of Israel is to kill it at **t**. **Ex 12:6** 6153
'At **t** you shall eat meat, and in **Ex 16:12** 6153
other lamb you shall offer at **t**; **Ex 29:39** 6153
other lamb you shall offer at **t**, **Ex 29:41** 6153
When Aaron trims the lamps at **t**, **Ex 30:8** 6153
month at **t** is the LORD's Passover. **Lv 23:5** 6153
day of this month, at **t**, **Nu 9:3** 6153
fourteenth day of the month, at **t**, **Nu 9:5** 6153
month on the fourteenth day at **t**, **Nu 9:11** 6153
other lamb you shall offer at **t**; **Nu 28:4** 6153
other lamb you shall offer at **t**; **Nu 28:8** 6153
David slaughtered them from the **t** **1Sa 30:17** 5399
They arose at **t** to go to the **2Ki 7:5** 5399
they arose and fled in the **t**, **2Ki 7:7** 5399
the stars of its **t** be darkened; **Jb 3:9** 5399
of the adulterer waits for the **t**, **Jb 24:15** 5399
In the **t**, in the evening, In the **Pr 7:9** 5399
The **t** I longed for has been turned **Is 21:4** 5399
We stumble at midday as in the **t**, **Is 59:10** 5399

TWIN
the **T** Brothers for its figurehead. **Ac 28:11** *1359*

TWINKLING
in a moment, in the **t** of an eye, **1Co 15:52** *4493*

TWINS
behold, there were **t** in her womb. **Gn 25:24** 8420b
behold, there were **t** in her womb. **Gn 38:27** 8420b
washing, All of which bear **t**, **SS 4:2** 8382
like two fawns, **T** of a gazelle Which **SS 4:5** 8420b
washing, All of which bear **t**, **SS 6:6** 8382
like two fawns, **T** of a gazelle. **SS 7:3** 8420b
when she had conceived **t** by one **Ro 9:10**
for though *the* **t** were not yet **Ro 9:11**

TWIST
And **t** everything that is straight, **Mi 3:9** 6140

TWISTED
with ten curtains of fine **t** linen and **Ex 26:1** 7806
scarlet *material* and fine **t** linen; **Ex 26:31** 7806
scarlet *material* and fine **t** linen, **Ex 26:36** 7806
hangings for the court of fine **t** linen **Ex 27:9** 7806
scarlet *material* and fine **t** linen, **Ex 27:16** 7806
five cubits of fine **t** linen, **Ex 27:18** 7806
scarlet *material* and fine **t** linen, **Ex 28:6** 7806
scarlet *material* and fine **t** linen. **Ex 28:8** 7806
shall make them of **t** cordage work, **Ex 28:14** 4020
fine **t** linen you shall make it. **Ex 28:15** 7806
chains of **t** cordage work in pure **Ex 28:22** 1383
of fine **t** linen and blue and **Ex 36:8** 7806
material, and fine **t** linen; **Ex 36:35** 7806
material, and fine **t** linen, **Ex 36:37** 7806
of the court were of fine **t** linen, **Ex 38:9** 7806
all around *were* of fine **t** linen. **Ex 38:16** 7806
material and fine **t** linen. **Ex 38:18** 7806
material, and fine **t** linen, **Ex 39:2** 7806
material, and fine **t** linen, **Ex 39:5** 7806
scarlet *material* and fine **t** linen. **Ex 39:8** 7806
of **t** cordage work in pure gold. **Ex 39:15** 1383
t *linen* on the hem of the robe. **Ex 39:24** 7806
linen breeches of fine **t** linen, **Ex 39:28** 7806
and the sash of fine **t** linen, **Ex 39:29** 7806
and **t** threads of chainwork for the **1Ki 7:17** 1434
Even Leviathan the **t** serpent; **Is 27:1** 6129
And the soldiers **t** together a crown **Jn 19:2** *4120*

TWISTING
And after **t** together a crown of **Mt 27:29** *4120*
and after **t** a crown of thorns, they **Mk 15:17** *4120*

TWITTER
a swallow, *like* a crane, so I **t**; **Is 38:14** 6850

TWO
God made the **t** great lights, **Gn 1:16** 8147
Lamech took to himself **t** wives: **Gn 4:19** 8147
t of every *kind* into the ark, **Gn 6:19** 8147
t of every *kind* will come to you **Gn 6:20** 8147
the animals that are not clean **t**, **Gn 7:2** 8147
and told his **t** brothers outside. **Gn 9:22** 8147
T sons were born to Eber; the name **Gn 10:25** 8147
t years after the flood; **Gn 11:10**
Peleg lived **t** hundred and nine years **Gn 11:19**
Reu lived **t** hundred and seven years **Gn 11:21**
and Serug lived **t** hundred years **Gn 11:23**
were **t** hundred and five years; **Gn 11:32**
these to Him and cut them in **t**, **Gn 15:10** 8432
Now the **t** angels came to Sodom in **Gn 19:1** 8147
I have **t** daughters who have not **Gn 19:8** 8147
Then the **t** men said to Lot, **Gn 19:12**
your wife and your **t** daughters who **Gn 19:15** 8147
the hands of his **t** daughters **Gn 19:16** 8147
and his **t** daughters with him; **Gn 19:30** 8147
in a cave, he and his **t** daughters. **Gn 19:30** 8147
and the **t** of them made a covenant. **Gn 21:27** 8147
there the **t** of them took an oath. **Gn 21:31** 8147
and took **t** of his young men with **Gn 22:3** 8147
the **t** of them walked on together. **Gn 22:6** 8147
the **t** of them walked on together. **Gn 22:8** 8147
t bracelets for her wrists weighing ten **Gn 24:22** 8147
"**T** nations are in your womb; **Gn 25:23** 8147
And **t** peoples will be separated **Gn 25:23** 8147
bring me **t** choice young goats from **Gn 27:9** 8147
has supplanted me these **t** times? **Gn 27:36** 6471
Now Laban had **t** daughters; **Gn 29:16** 8147
and into the tent of the **t** maids, **Gn 31:33** 8147
that they may decide between us **t**. **Gn 31:37** 8147
years for your **t** daughters and **Gn 31:41** 8147
and the camels, into **t** companies; **Gn 32:7** 8147
and now I have become **t** companies. **Gn 32:10** 8147
t hundred female goats and twenty **Gn 32:14**
t hundred ewes and twenty rams, **Gn 32:14**
that same night and took his **t** wives **Gn 32:22** 8147
his **t** maids and his eleven children, **Gn 32:22** 8147
Leah and Rachel and the **t** maids. **Gn 33:1** 8147
t of Jacob's sons, Simeon and Levi, **Gn 34:25** 8147
was furious with his **t** officials, **Gn 40:2** 8147
happened at the end of **t** full years **Gn 41:1**
came, **t** sons were born to Joseph, **Gn 41:50** 8147
"You may put my **t** sons to death **Gn 42:37** 8147
know that my wife bore me **t** sons; **Gn 44:27** 8147
been in the land these **t** years, **Gn 45:6**
were born to him in Egypt were **t**; **Gn 46:27** 8147
So he took his **t** sons Manasseh and **Gn 48:1** 8147
"Now your **t** sons, who were **Gn 48:5** 8147
t Hebrews were fighting with each **Ex 2:13** 8147
will not believe even these **t** signs **Ex 4:9** 8147
blood and put it on the **t** doorposts **Ex 12:7** 8147
to the lintel and the **t** doorposts; **Ex 12:22** 8147
the lintel and on the **t** doorposts, **Ex 12:23** 8147
much bread, **t** omers for each one. **Ex 16:22** 8147
bread for **t** days on the sixth day. **Ex 16:29**
and her **t** sons, of whom one was **Ex 18:3** 8147
wife and her **t** sons with her." **Ex 18:6** 8147
however, he survives a day or **t**, **Ex 21:21**
shall be made by the **t** of them that **Ex 22:11** 8147
wood **t** and a half cubits long, **Ex 25:10**
and **t** rings shall be on one side **Ex 25:12** 8147
and **t** rings on the other side of **Ex 25:12** 8147
t and a half cubits long and one **Ex 25:17**
"You shall make **t** cherubim of gold, **Ex 25:18** 8147
at the **t** ends of the mercy seat. **Ex 25:18** 8147
with the mercy seat at its **t** ends. **Ex 25:19** 8147
from between the **t** cherubim which **Ex 25:22** 8147
t cubits long and one cubit wide **Ex 25:23** 8147
shall be **t** tenons for each board, **Ex 26:17** 8147
t sockets under one board for its **Ex 26:19** 8147
under one board for its **t** tenons **Ex 26:19** 8147
and **t** sockets under another board for **Ex 26:19** 8147
another board for its **t** tenons; **Ex 26:19** 8147
t sockets under one board and two **Ex 26:21** 8147
and **t** sockets under another board. **Ex 26:21** 8147
"You shall make **t** boards for **Ex 26:23** 8147
they shall form the **t** corners. **Ex 26:24** 8147
t sockets under one board and two **Ex 26:25** 8147
and **t** sockets under another board. **Ex 26:25** 8147
shall be on the **t** sides of the altar **Ex 27:7** 8147
"It shall have **t** shoulder pieces **Ex 28:7** 8147
pieces joined to its **t** ends, **Ex 28:7** 8147
"You shall take **t** onyx stones **Ex 28:9** 8147
you shall engrave the **t** stones **Ex 28:11** 8147
"You shall put the **t** stones **Ex 28:12** 8147
on his **t** shoulders for a memorial. **Ex 28:12** 8147
and **t** chains of pure gold; **Ex 28:14** 8147
the breastpiece **t** rings of gold, **Ex 28:23** 8147
and shall put the **t** rings on the **Ex 28:23** 8147
on the **t** ends of the breastpiece. **Ex 28:23** 8147
You shall put the **t** cords of gold **Ex 28:24** 8147
on the **t** rings at the ends **Ex 28:24** 8147
put the *other* **t** ends of the two cords **Ex 28:25** 8147
put the *other* two ends of the **t** cords **Ex 28:25** 8147
cords on the **t** filigree *settings,* **Ex 28:25** 8147
"You shall make **t** rings of gold **Ex 28:26** 8147
on the **t** ends of the breastpiece, **Ex 28:26** 8147
"You shall make **t** rings of gold **Ex 28:27** 8147
t shoulder pieces of the ephod, **Ex 28:27** 8147
bull and **t** rams without blemish, **Ex 29:1** 8147
with the bull and the **t** rams. **Ex 29:3** 8147
and the **t** kidneys and the fat that **Ex 29:13** 8147
and the **t** kidneys and the fat that **Ex 29:22** 8147
t one year old lambs each day, **Ex 29:38** 8147
and its height *shall be* **t** cubits; **Ex 30:2**
"You shall make **t** gold rings **Ex 30:4** 8147
shall make *them* on its **t** side walls **Ex 30:4** 8147
half as much, **t** hundred and fifty, **Ex 30:23**
fragrant cane **t** hundred and fifty, **Ex 30:23**
the **t** tablets of the testimony, **Ex 31:18** 8147
from the mountain with the **t** tablets **Ex 32:15** 8147
"Cut out for yourself **t** stone **Ex 34:1** 8147
So he cut out **t** stone tablets like **Ex 34:4** 8147
took **t** stone tablets in his hand. **Ex 34:4** 8147
the **t** tablets of the testimony *were* in **Ex 34:29** 8147
were **t** tenons for each board, **Ex 36:22** 8147

t sockets under one board for its	**Ex 36:24**	8147
under one board for its **t** tenons	**Ex 36:24**	8147
t sockets under another board for its	**Ex 36:24**	8147
another board for its **t** tenons.	**Ex 36:24**	8147
t sockets under one board and two	**Ex 36:26**	8147
and **t** sockets under another board.	**Ex 36:26**	8147
He made **t** boards for the	**Ex 36:28**	8147
both of them for the **t** corners.	**Ex 36:29**	8147
sockets, **t** under every board.	**Ex 36:30**	8147
length was **t** and a half cubits,	**Ex 37:1**	
even **t** rings on one side of it,	**Ex 37:3**	8147
t rings on the other side of it.	**Ex 37:3**	8147
gold, **t** and a half cubits long and	**Ex 37:6**	
He made **t** cherubim of gold;	**Ex 37:7**	8147
at the **t** ends of the mercy seat;	**Ex 37:7**	8147
with the mercy seat at the **t** ends.	**Ex 37:8**	8147
t cubits long and a cubit wide and	**Ex 37:10**	
wide, square, and **t** cubits high;	**Ex 37:25**	
He made **t** golden rings for it	**Ex 37:27**	8147
for it under its molding, on its **t** sides	**Ex 37:27**	8147
was attached at its **t** *upper* ends.	**Ex 39:4**	8147
They made **t** gold filigree *settings*	**Ex 39:16**	8147
settings and **t** gold rings,	**Ex 39:16**	8147
and put the **t** rings on the two	**Ex 39:16**	8147
on the **t** ends of the breastpiece.	**Ex 39:16**	8147
Then they put the **t** gold cords in	**Ex 39:17**	8147
put the two gold cords in the **t** rings	**Ex 39:17**	8147
put the *other* **t** ends of the two cords	**Ex 39:18**	8147
ends of the **t** cords on the two filigree	**Ex 39:18**	8147
cords on the **t** filigree *settings,*	**Ex 39:18**	8147
They made **t** gold rings and	**Ex 39:19**	8147
on the **t** ends of the breastpiece,	**Ex 39:19**	8147
they made **t** gold rings and placed	**Ex 39:20**	8147
t shoulder pieces of the ephod,	**Ex 39:20**	8147
and the **t** kidneys with the fat	**Lv 3:4**	8147
and the **t** kidneys with the fat	**Lv 3:10**	8147
and the **t** kidneys with the fat	**Lv 3:15**	8147
and the **t** kidneys with the fat	**Lv 4:9**	8147
t turtledoves or two young	**Lv 5:7**	8147
turtledoves or **t** young pigeons,	**Lv 5:7**	8147
are insufficient for **t** turtledoves or	**Lv 5:11**	8147
turtledoves or **t** young pigeons,	**Lv 5:11**	8147
and the **t** kidneys with the fat	**Lv 7:4**	8147
and the **t** rams and the basket of	**Lv 8:2**	8147
and the **t** kidneys and their fat;	**Lv 8:16**	8147
the lobe of the liver and the **t** kidneys	**Lv 8:25**	8147
she shall be unclean for **t** weeks,	**Lv 12:5**	
then she shall take **t** turtledoves	**Lv 12:8**	8147
turtledoves or **t** young pigeons,	**Lv 12:8**	8147
give orders to take **t** live clean birds	**Lv 14:4**	8147
take **t** male lambs without defect,	**Lv 14:10**	8147
and **t** turtledoves or two young	**Lv 14:22**	8147
two turtledoves or **t** young pigeons	**Lv 14:22**	8147
he shall take **t** birds and cedar	**Lv 14:49**	8147
he shall take for himself **t** turtledoves	**Lv 15:14**	8147
turtledoves or **t** young pigeons,	**Lv 15:14**	8147
she shall take for herself **t** turtledoves	**Lv 15:29**	8147
turtledoves or **t** young pigeons and	**Lv 15:29**	8147
the death of the **t** sons of Aaron,	**Lv 16:1**	8147
t male goats for a sin offering and	**Lv 16:5**	8147
"He shall take the **t** goats	**Lv 16:7**	8147
shall cast lots for the **t** goats,	**Lv 16:8**	8147
and **t** handfuls of finely ground	**Lv 16:12**	
together **t** kinds of your cattle;	**Lv 19:19**	3610
your field with **t** kinds of seed,	**Lv 19:19**	3610
t kinds of material mixed together.	**Lv 19:19**	3610
t *loaves* of bread for a wave offering,	**Lv 23:17**	8147
a bull of the herd and **t** rams;	**Lv 23:18**	8147
and **t** male lambs one year old for a	**Lv 23:19**	8147
with **t** lambs before the LORD;	**Lv 23:20**	8147
"You shall set them *in* **t** rows,	**Lv 24:6**	8147
eighth day he shall bring **t** turtledoves	**Nu 6:10**	8147
or **t** young pigeons to the priest,	**Nu 6:10**	8147
a cart for *every* **t** of the leaders	**Nu 7:3**	8147
T carts and four oxen he gave to	**Nu 7:7**	8147
of peace offerings, **t** oxen,	**Nu 7:17**	8147
of peace offerings, **t** oxen,	**Nu 7:23**	8147
of peace offerings, **t** oxen,	**Nu 7:29**	8147
of peace offerings, **t** oxen,	**Nu 7:35**	8147
of peace offerings, **t** oxen,	**Nu 7:41**	8147
of peace offerings, **t** oxen,	**Nu 7:47**	8147
of peace offerings, **t** oxen,	**Nu 7:53**	8147
of peace offerings, **t** oxen,	**Nu 7:59**	8147
of peace offerings, **t** oxen,	**Nu 7:65**	8147
of peace offerings, **t** oxen,	**Nu 7:71**	8147
of peace offerings, **t** oxen,	**Nu 7:77**	8147
of peace offerings, **t** oxen,	**Nu 7:83**	8147
from between the **t** cherubim,	**Nu 7:89**	8147
Whether it was **t** days or a month	**Nu 9:22**	
yourself **t** trumpets of silver,	**Nu 10:2**	8147
and grind *it* between **t** millstones	**Nu 11:8**	
eat, not one day, nor **t** days,	**Nu 11:19**	
t men had remained in the camp;	**Nu 11:26**	8147
and about **t** cubits *deep* on the	**Nu 11:31**	
it on a pole between **t** *men,*	**Nu 13:23**	8147
t hundred and fifty leaders of the	**Nu 16:2**	
t hundred and fifty firepans;	**Nu 16:17**	
consumed the **t** hundred and fifty men	**Nu 16:35**	
and his **t** servants were with him.	**Nu 22:22**	8147
t male lambs one year old without	**Nu 28:3**	8147
t male lambs one year old without	**Nu 28:9**	8147
t bulls and one ram, seven male	**Nu 28:11**	8147
t bulls and one ram and seven male	**Nu 28:19**	8147
aroma to the LORD: **t** young bulls,	**Nu 28:27**	8147
thirteen bulls, **t** rams, fourteen	**Nu 29:13**	8147
two-tenths for each of the **t** rams,	**Nu 29:14**	8147
twelve bulls, **t** rams, fourteen	**Nu 29:17**	8147
eleven bulls, **t** rams, fourteen	**Nu 29:20**	8147
ten bulls, **t** rams, fourteen male	**Nu 29:23**	8147
nine bulls, **t** rams, fourteen male	**Nu 29:26**	8147
eight bulls, **t** rams, fourteen male	**Nu 29:29**	8147
seven bulls, **t** rams, fourteen male	**Nu 29:32**	8147
"The **t** and a half tribes have	**Nu 34:15**	8147
the east side **t** thousand cubits,	**Nu 35:5**	
the south side **t** thousand cubits,	**Nu 35:5**	
the west side **t** thousand cubits,	**Nu 35:5**	
the north side **t** thousand cubits,	**Nu 35:5**	
hand of the **t** kings of the Amorites	**Dt 3:8**	8147
God has done to these **t** kings;	**Dt 3:21**	8147
wrote them on **t** tablets of stone.	**Dt 4:13**	8147
the **t** kings of the Amorites,	**Dt 4:47**	8147
He wrote them on **t** tablets of stone	**Dt 5:22**	8147
"The LORD gave me the **t**	**Dt 9:10**	8147
gave me the **t** tablets of stone,	**Dt 9:11**	8147
and the **t** tablets of the covenant	**Dt 9:15**	8147
the covenant were in my **t** hands.	**Dt 9:15**	8147
"I took hold of the **t** tablets	**Dt 9:17**	8147
Cut out for yourself **t** tablets of stone	**Dt 10:1**	8147
and cut out **t** tablets of stone like the	**Dt 10:3**	8147
with the **t** tablets in my hand.	**Dt 10:3**	8147
has the hoof split in **t** *and* chews the	**Dt 14:6**	8147
those that divide the hoof in **t**:	**Dt 14:7**	8156
the evidence of **t** witnesses or three	**Dt 17:6**	8147
and the **t** cheeks and the stomach.	**Dt 18:3**	3895
on the evidence of **t** or three	**Dt 19:15**	8147
"If a man has **t** wives, the one	**Dt 21:15**	8147
vineyard with **t** kinds of seed,	**Dt 22:9**	3610
"If **t** men, a man and his	**Dt 25:11**	
And **t** put ten thousand to flight,	**Dt 32:30**	8147
Joshua the son of Nun sent **t** men	**Jos 2:1**	8147
taken the **t** men and hidden them,	**Jos 2:4**	8147
did to the **t** kings of the Amorites	**Jos 2:10**	8147
Then the **t** men returned and came	**Jos 2:23**	8147
Joshua said to the **t** men who	**Jos 6:22**	8147
only about **t** or three thousand men	**Jos 7:3**	
t hundred shekels of silver and a bar	**Jos 7:21**	
and all that He did to the **t** kings	**Jos 9:10**	8147
given the inheritance of the **t** tribes	**Jos 14:3**	8147
the sons of Joseph were **t** tribes,	**Jos 14:4**	8147
t cities with their villages.	**Jos 15:60**	8147
nine cities from these **t** tribes.	**Jos 21:16**	8147
with its pasture lands; **t** cities.	**Jos 21:25**	8147
with its pasture lands; **t** cities.	**Jos 21:27**	8147
drove out the **t** kings of the Amorites	**Jos 24:12**	8147
himself a sword which had **t** edges,	**Jg 3:16**	8147
t maidens for every warrior;	**Jg 5:30**	
captured the **t** leaders of Midian,	**Jg 7:25**	8147
captured the **t** kings of Midian,	**Jg 8:12**	8147
the other **t** companies then dashed	**Jg 9:44**	8147
let me alone **t** months, that I may	**Jg 11:37**	8147
So he sent her away for **t** months;	**Jg 11:38**	8147
At the end of **t** months	**Jg 11:39**	8147
in the middle between **t** tails.	**Jg 15:4**	8147
they bound him with **t** new ropes	**Jg 15:13**	8147
doors of the city gate and the **t** posts	**Jg 16:3**	8147
the Philistines for my **t** eyes."	**Jg 16:28**	8147
Samson grasped the **t** middle pillars	**Jg 16:29**	8147
his mother took **t** hundred *pieces*	**Jg 17:4**	
Moab with his wife and his **t** sons.	**Ru 1:1**	8147
t sons *were* Mahlon and Chilion,	**Ru 1:2**	8147
and she was left with her **t** sons.	**Ru 1:3**	8147
of her **t** children and her husband.	**Ru 1:5**	8147
and her **t** daughters-in-law with her;	**Ru 1:7**	8147
said to her **t** daughters-in-law,	**Ru 1:8**	8147
He had **t** wives:	**1Sa 1:2**	8147
And the **t** sons of Eli, Hophni and	**1Sa 1:3**	8147
to three sons and **t** daughters.	**1Sa 2:21**	8147
will come concerning your **t** sons,	**1Sa 2:34**	8147
and the **t** sons of Eli, Hophni and	**1Sa 4:4**	8147
and the **t** sons of Eli, Hophni and	**1Sa 4:11**	8147
the people, and your **t** sons also,	**1Sa 4:17**	8147
prepare a new cart and **t** milch cows	**1Sa 6:7**	8147
and took **t** milch cows and hitched	**1Sa 6:10**	8147
then you will find **t** men close to	**1Sa 10:2**	8147
and give you **t** *loaves* of bread,	**1Sa 10:4**	8147
no **t** of them were left together.	**1Sa 11:11**	8147
and he reigned *forty*-**t** years	**1Sa 13:1**	8147
of his **t** daughters *were these:*	**1Sa 14:49**	8147
and struck down **t** hundred men	**1Sa 18:27**	
So the **t** of them made a covenant	**1Sa 23:18**	8147
t hundred stayed with the baggage.	**1Sa 25:13**	
and took **t** hundred *loaves* of bread	**1Sa 25:18**	
and **t** jugs of wine and five sheep	**1Sa 25:18**	8147
and **t** hundred cakes of figs,	**1Sa 25:18**	
even David with his **t** wives,	**1Sa 27:3**	8147
and went, he and **t** men with him,	**1Sa 28:8**	8147
t wives had been taken captive,	**1Sa 30:5**	8147
for **t** hundred who were too	**1Sa 30:10**	
cake and **t** clusters of raisins,	**1Sa 30:12**	8147
taken, and rescued his **t** wives.	**1Sa 30:18**	8147
David came to the **t** hundred men	**1Sa 30:21**	
David remained **t** days in Ziklag.	**2Sa 1:1**	8147
up there, and his **t** wives also,	**2Sa 2:2**	8147
and he was king for **t** years.	**2Sa 2:10**	8147
Saul's son *had* **t** men who were	**2Sa 4:2**	8147
and he measured **t** lines to put to	**2Sa 8:2**	8147
"There were **t** men in one city,	**2Sa 12:1**	8147
Now it came about after **t** full years	**2Sa 13:23**	
"Your maidservant had **t** sons,	**2Sa 14:6**	8147
but the **t** of them struggled	**2Sa 14:6**	8147
lived **t** full years in Jerusalem,	**2Sa 14:28**	
Then **t** hundred men went with	**2Sa 15:11**	
in peace and your **t** sons with you,	**2Sa 15:27**	8147
their **t** sons are with them there,	**2Sa 15:36**	8147
were **t** hundred loaves of bread,	**2Sa 16:1**	3967
so the **t** of them departed quickly	**2Sa 17:18**	8147
was sitting between the **t** gates;	**2Sa 18:24**	8147
the king took the **t** sons of Rizpah	**2Sa 21:8**	8147
the **t** *sons of* Ariel of Moab.	**2Sa 23:20**	8147
t commanders of the armies of Israel	**1Ki 2:5**	8147
because he fell upon **t** men more	**1Ki 2:32**	8147
that **t** of the servants of Shimei	**1Ki 2:39**	8147
Then **t** women who were harlots came	**1Ki 3:16**	8147
only the **t** of us in the house.	**1Ki 3:18**	8147
"Divide the living child in **t**,	**1Ki 3:25**	8147
and the **t** of them made a covenant.	**1Ki 5:12**	8147
a month *and* **t** months at home.	**1Ki 5:14**	8147
he made **t** cherubim of olive wood,	**1Ki 6:23**	8147
So *he made* **t** doors of olive wood,	**1Ki 6:32**	8147
and **t** doors of cypress wood;	**1Ki 6:34**	8147
the **t** leaves of the one door	**1Ki 6:34**	8147
and the **t** leaves of the other door	**1Ki 6:34**	8147
fashioned the **t** pillars of bronze;	**1Ki 7:15**	8147
made **t** capitals of molten bronze	**1Ki 7:16**	8147
and **t** rows around on the one	**1Ki 7:18**	8147
were capitals on the **t** pillars,	**1Ki 7:20**	8147
pomegranates *numbered* **t** hundred	**1Ki 7:20**	
the gourds were in **t** rows,	**1Ki 7:24**	8147
it could hold **t** thousand baths.	**1Ki 7:26**	
the **t** pillars and the *two* bowls of	**1Ki 7:41**	8147
the two pillars and the **t** bowls	**1Ki 7:41**	
were on the top of the **t** pillars,	**1Ki 7:41**	8147
and the **t** networks to cover the	**1Ki 7:41**	8147
to cover the **t** bowls of the capitals	**1Ki 7:41**	8147
pomegranates for the **t** networks,	**1Ki 7:42**	8147
t rows of pomegranates for each	**1Ki 7:42**	8147
to cover the **t** bowls of the capitals	**1Ki 7:42**	8147
t tablets of stone which Moses put	**1Ki 8:9**	8147
Solomon had built the **t** houses,	**1Ki 9:10**	8147
and **t** lions standing beside the	**1Ki 10:19**	8147
and made **t** golden calves,	**1Ki 12:28**	8147
he reigned over Israel **t** years.	**1Ki 15:25**	8147
at Tirzah, *and reigned* **t** years.	**1Ki 16:8**	
Israel were divided into **t** parts:	**1Ki 16:21**	2677
Shemer for **t** talents of silver;	**1Ki 16:24**	
you hesitate between **t** opinions?	**1Ki 18:21**	8147
"Now let them give us **t** oxen;	**1Ki 18:23**	8147
enough to hold **t** measures of seed.	**1Ki 18:32**	
like **t** little flocks of goats,	**1Ki 20:27**	8147
seat **t** worthless men before him,	**1Ki 21:10**	8147
Then the **t** worthless men came in	**1Ki 21:13**	8147
he reigned **t** years over Israel.	**1Ki 22:51**	
and consumed the first **t** captains	**2Ki 1:14**	8147
So the **t** of them went on.	**2Ki 2:6**	8147
the **t** of them stood by the Jordan.	**2Ki 2:7**	8147
so that the **t** of them crossed over	**2Ki 2:8**	8147
which separated the **t** of them.	**2Ki 2:11**	8147
clothes and tore them in **t** pieces.	**2Ki 2:12**	8147
Then **t** female bears came out of	**2Ki 2:24**	8147
my **t** children to be his slaves."	**2Ki 4:1**	8147
be given **t** mules' load of earth;	**2Ki 5:17**	6776
just now **t** young men of the sons	**2Ki 5:22**	8147
and **t** changes of clothes.' "	**2Ki 5:22**	8147
"Be pleased to take **t** talents."	**2Ki 5:23**	
and bound **t** talents of silver in	**2Ki 5:23**	
bound two talents of silver in **t** bags	**2Ki 5:23**	8147
bags with **t** changes of clothes and	**2Ki 5:23**	8147
gave them to **t** of his servants;	**2Ki 5:23**	8147
and **t** measures of barley for a	**2Ki 7:1**	
therefore **t** chariots with horses,	**2Ki 7:14**	8147
and **t** measures of barley for a shekel,	**2Ki 7:16**	
"**T** measures of barley for a	**2Ki 7:18**	
And **t** or three officials looked	**2Ki 9:32**	8147
the **t** kings did not stand before	**2Ki 10:4**	8147
"Put them in **t** heaps at the	**2Ki 10:8**	8147
"**T** parts of you, *even* all who	**2Ki 11:7**	8147
in Samaria, *and reigned* **t** years.	**2Ki 15:23**	8147
molten images, *even* **t** calves,	**2Ki 17:16**	8147
I will give you **t** thousand horses,	**2Ki 18:23**	
the **t** courts of the house of the LORD.	**2Ki 21:5**	8147
he reigned **t** years in Jerusalem;	**2Ki 21:19**	8147
the **t** courts of the house of the LORD,	**2Ki 23:12**	8147
between the **t** walls beside the king's	**2Ki 25:4**	
The **t** pillars, the one sea, and	**2Ki 25:16**	8147
T sons were born to Eber, the name	**1Ch 1:19**	8147
the father of Tekoa, had **t** wives,	**1Ch 4:5**	8147
down the **t** *sons of* Ariel of Moab.	**1Ch 11:22**	8147
do, their chiefs *were* **t** hundred;	**1Ch 12:32**	
and at the storehouse **t** by two.	**1Ch 26:17**	8147
and at the storehouse two by **t**.	**1Ch 26:17**	8147
the highway and **t** at the Parbar.	**1Ch 26:18**	8147
Then he made **t** sculptured cherubim	**2Ch 3:10**	8147
He also made **t** pillars for the	**2Ch 3:15**	8147
The oxen *were* in **t** rows,	**2Ch 4:3**	8147
the **t** pillars, the bowls and the	**2Ch 4:12**	8147
the bowls and the **t** capitals on	**2Ch 4:12**	
and the **t** networks to cover the	**2Ch 4:12**	8147
to cover the **t** bowls of the capitals	**2Ch 4:12**	8147
pomegranates for the **t** networks,	**2Ch 4:13**	8147
t rows of pomegranates for each	**2Ch 4:13**	8147
to cover the **t** bowls of the capitals	**2Ch 4:13**	8147
nothing in the ark except the **t** tablets	**2Ch 5:10**	8147
t hundred and fifty who ruled over	**2Ch 8:10**	
and **t** lions standing beside the	**2Ch 9:18**	8147
of time, at the end of **t** years,	**2Ch 21:19**	8147
Jehoiada took **t** wives for him,	**2Ch 24:3**	8147
the **t** courts of the house of the LORD.	**2Ch 33:5**	8147
he reigned **t** years in Jerusalem.	**2Ch 33:21**	8147
t utensils of fine shiny bronze,	**Ezr 8:27**	8147
the task *be done* in one or **t** days,	**Ezr 10:13**	8147
and I appointed **t** great choirs,	**Ne 12:31**	8147
Then the **t** choirs took their stand	**Ne 12:40**	8147
t of the king's officials from	**Es 2:21**	8147
t of the king's eunuchs who were	**Es 6:2**	8147
not fail to celebrate these **t** days	**Es 9:27**	8147
For sound wisdom has **t** sides.	**Jb 11:6**	3718
"Only **t** things do not do to me,	**Jb 13:20**	8147

you and against your **t** friends, Jb 42:7 8147
the bow and cuts the spear in **t**; Ps 46:9 7112
cut in **t** the cords of the wicked. Ps 129:4 7112
T things I asked of You, Do not Pr 30:7 8147
The leech has **t** daughters, Pr 30:15 8147
hand full of rest is better than **t** fists Ec 4:6
T are better than one because they Ec 4:9 8147
if **t** lie down together they keep Ec 4:11 8147
who is alone, **t** can resist him. Ec 4:12 8147
"Your **t** breasts are like two fawns, SS 4:5 8147
"Your two breasts are like **t** fawns, SS 4:5 8147
at the dance of the **t** companies? SS 6:13
"Your **t** breasts are like two fawns, SS 7:3 8147
"Your two breasts are like **t** fawns, SS 7:3 8147
And **t** hundred are for those who SS 8:12
with **t** he covered his face, and Is 6:2 8147
and with **t** he covered his feet, Is 6:2 8147
his feet, and with **t** he flew. Is 6:2 8147
these **t** stubs of smoldering firebrands, Is 7:4 8147
the land whose **t** kings you dread Is 7:16 8147
T *or* three olives on the topmost Is 17:6 8147
made a reservoir between the **t** walls Is 22:11 2346
I will give you **t** thousand horses, Is 36:8
"But these **t** things will come on Is 47:9 8147
These **t** things have befallen you; Is 51:19 8147
My people have committed **t** evils: Jer 2:13 8147
from a city and **t** from a family, Jer 3:14 8147
t baskets of figs set before the Jer 24:1 8147
'Within **t** years I am going to Jer 28:3 8145
will I break within **t** full years the Jer 28:11 8145
t families which the LORD chose, Jer 33:24 8147
when they cut the calf in **t** and Jer 34:18
the gate between the **t** walls; Jer 39:4
way of the gate between the **t** walls Jer 52:7
The **t** pillars, the one sea, and Jer 52:20 8147
each had **t** touching another *being,* Ezk 1:11 8147
and **t** covering their bodies. Ezk 1:11 8147
each one also had **t** wings covering Ezk 1:23 8147
make **t** ways for the sword of the Ezk 21:19 8147
way, at the head of the **t** ways, Ezk 21:21 8147
"Son of man, there were **t** women, Ezk 23:2 8147
'These **t** nations and these two Ezk 35:10 8147
and these **t** lands will be mine, Ezk 35:10 8147
they will no longer be **t** nations and Ezk 37:22 8147
longer be divided into **t** kingdoms. Ezk 37:22 8147
and its side pillars, **t** cubits. Ezk 40:9 8147
gate *were* **t** tables on each side, Ezk 40:39 8147
toward the north, *were* **t** tables; Ezk 40:40 8147
porch of the gate *were* **t** tables. Ezk 40:40 8147
pillar of the doorway, **t** cubits, Ezk 41:3 8147
and every cherub had **t** faces, Ezk 41:18 8147
high and its length **t** cubits; Ezk 41:22 8147
Each of the doors had **t** leaves, Ezk 41:24 8147
had two leaves, **t** swinging leaves; Ezk 41:24 8147
t *leaves* for one door and two Ezk 41:24 8147
door and **t** leaves for the other. Ezk 41:24 8147
the lower ledge *shall be* **t** cubits and Ezk 43:14 8147
sheep from *each* flock of **t** hundred Ezk 45:15
Joseph *shall have* **t** portions. Ezk 47:13 8147
to stand on **t** feet like a man; Da 7:4
a ram which had **t** horns was Da 8:3
Now the **t** horns *were* long, but one Da 8:3
to the ram that had the **t** horns, Da 8:6
the ram and shattered his **t** horns, Da 8:7 8147
ram which you saw with the **t** horns Da 8:20
behold, **t** others were standing, Da 12:5 8147
"He will revive us after **t** days; Hos 6:2
t years before the earthquake. Am 1:1
Do **t** men walk together unless they Am 3:3 8147
"So **t** or three cities would Am 4:8 8147
also **t** olive trees by it, one on Zch 4:3 8147
"What are these **t** olive trees on Zch 4:11 8147
"What are the **t** olive branches Zch 4:12 8147
are beside the **t** golden pipes, Zch 4:12 8147
"These are the **t** anointed ones who Zch 4:14 8147
and there **t** women were coming out Zch 5:9 8147
from between the **t** mountains; Zch 6:1 8147
will be between the **t** offices." Zch 6:13 8147
And I took for myself **t** staffs: Zch 11:7 8147
"That **t** parts in it will be cut Zch 13:8 8147
from **t** years old and under, Mt 2:16 *1332*
Sea of Galilee, He saw **t** brothers, Mt 4:18 *1417*
there He saw **t** other brothers, Mt 4:21 *1417*
you to go one mile, go with him **t**. Mt 5:41 *1417*
"No one can serve **t** masters; Mt 6:24 *1417*
t men who were demon-possessed met Mt 8:28 *1417*
there, **t** blind men followed Him, Mt 9:27 *1417*
your journey, or even **t** coats, Mt 10:10 *1417*
not **t** sparrows sold for a cent? Mt 10:29 *1417*
only five loaves and **t** fish." Mt 14:17 *1417*
the five loaves and the **t** fish, Mt 14:19 *1417*
than to have **t** hands or two feet Mt 18:8 *1417*
than to have two hands or **t** feet Mt 18:8 *1417*
with one eye, than to have **t** eyes Mt 18:9 *1417*
you, take one or **t** more with you, Mt 18:16 *1417*
MOUTH OF **T** OR THREE WITNESSES Mt 18:16 *1417*
that if **t** of you agree on earth Mt 18:19 *1417*
where **t** or three have gathered Mt 18:20 *1417*
AND THE **T** SHALL BECOME ONE FLESH'? Mt 19:5 *1417*
"So they are no longer **t**, Mt 19:6 *1417*
these **t** sons of mine may sit one Mt 20:21 *1417*
indignant with the **t** brothers. Mt 20:24 *1417*
t blind men sitting by the road, Mt 20:30 *1417*
then Jesus sent **t** disciples, Mt 21:1 *1417*
A man had **t** sons, and he came to Mt 21:28 *1417*
"Which of the **t** did the will of his Mt 21:31 *1417*
"On these **t** commandments depend Mt 22:40 *1417*
there will be **t** men in the field; Mt 24:40 *1417*
"**T** women *will be* grinding at the Mt 24:41 *1417*
gave five talents, to another, **t**, Mt 25:15 *1417*
the **t** *talents* gained two more. Mt 25:17 *1417*
the two *talents* gained **t** more. Mt 25:17 *1417*
who *had received* the **t** talents Mt 25:22 *1417*
you entrusted **t** talents to me. Mt 25:22 *1417*
I have gained **t** more talents.' Mt 25:22 *1417*
after **t** days the Passover is coming, Mt 26:2 *1417*
Peter and the **t** sons of Zebedee, Mt 26:37 *1417*
But later on **t** came forward, Mt 26:60 *1417*
"Which of the **t** do you want me to Mt 27:21 *1417*
t robbers were crucified with Him, Mt 27:38 *1417*
was torn in **t** from top to bottom; Mt 27:51 *1417*
the sea, about **t** thousand *of them* Mk 5:13 *1367*
"Do not put on **t** tunics." Mk 6:9 *1417*
spend **t** hundred denarii on bread Mk 6:37 *1250*
"Five, and **t** fish." Mk 6:38 *1417*
the five loaves and the **t** fish, Mk 6:41 *1417*
He divided up the **t** fish among them Mk 6:41 *1417*
than, having your **t** hands, Mk 9:43 *1417*
lame, than, having your **t** feet, Mk 9:45 *1417*
with one eye, than, having **t** eyes, Mk 9:47 *1417*
AND THE **T** SHALL BECOME ONE FLESH Mk 10:8 *1417*
so they are no longer **t**, Mk 10:8 *1417*
and John, the **t** sons of Zebedee, Mk 10:35 *1417*
He sent **t** of His disciples, Mk 11:1 *1417*
and put in **t** small copper coins, Mk 12:42 *1417*
Unleavened Bread were **t** days away; Mk 14:1 *1417*
And He sent **t** of His disciples and Mk 14:13 *1417*
They crucified **t** robbers with Him, Mk 15:27 *1417*
the veil of the temple was torn in **t** Mk 15:38 *1417*
in a different form to **t** of them while Mk 16:12 *1417*
TURTLEDOVES OR **T** YOUNG PIGEONS." Lk 2:24 *1417*
"The man who has **t** tunics Lk 3:11 *1417*
and He saw **t** boats lying at the Lk 5:2 *1417*
Summoning **t** of His disciples, Lk 7:19 *1417*
A moneylender had **t** debtors: Lk 7:41 *1417*
do not *even* have **t** tunics apiece. Lk 9:3 *1417*
more than five loaves and **t** fish, Lk 9:13 *1417*
the five loaves and the **t** fish, Lk 9:16 *1417*
t men were talking with Him; Lk 9:30 *1417*
and the **t** men standing with Him. Lk 9:32 *1417*
he took out **t** denarii and gave them Lk 10:35 *1417*
five sparrows sold for **t** cents? Lk 12:6 *1417*
will be divided, three against **t** and Lk 12:52 *1417*
against two and **t** against three. Lk 12:52 *1417*
"A man had **t** sons Lk 15:11 *1417*
"No servant can serve **t** masters; Lk 16:13 *1417*
there will be **t** in one bed; Lk 17:34 *1417*
"There will be **t** women grinding Lk 17:35 *1417*
"**T** men will be in the field; Lk 17:36 *1417*
"**T** men went up into the temple to Lk 18:10 *1417*
He sent **t** of the disciples, Lk 19:29 *1417*
putting in **t** small copper coins. Lk 21:2 *1417*
"Lord, look, here are **t** swords." Lk 22:38 *1417*
T others also, who were criminals, Lk 23:32 *1417*
veil of the temple was torn in **t**. Lk 23:45 *3319*
t men suddenly stood near them in Lk 24:4 *1417*
t of them were going that very day Lk 24:13 *1417*
standing with **t** of his disciples, Jn 1:35 *1417*
The **t** disciples heard him speak, Jn 1:37 *1417*
One of the **t** who heard John *speak* Jn 1:40 *1417*
and He stayed there **t** days. Jn 4:40 *1417*
After the **t** days He went forth Jn 4:43 *1417*
"**T** hundred denarii worth of bread Jn 6:7 *1250*
has five barley loaves and **t** fish, Jn 6:9 *1417*
the testimony of **t** men is true. Jn 8:17 *1417*
He then stayed **t** days *longer* in Jn 11:6 *1417*
near Jerusalem, about **t** miles off; Jn 11:18 *1178b*
Him, and with Him **t** other men, Jn 19:18 *1417*
The **t** were running together; Jn 20:4 *1417*
saw **t** angels in white sitting, Jn 20:12 *1417*
and **t** others of His disciples were Jn 21:2 *1417*
t men in white clothing stood Ac 1:10 *1417*
So they put forward **t** men, Ac 1:23 *1417*
one of these **t** You have chosen Ac 1:24 *1417*
he became the father of **t** sons. Ac 7:29 *1417*
was there, sent **t** men to him, Ac 9:38 *1417*
he summoned **t** of his servants and Ac 10:7 *1417*
was sleeping between **t** soldiers, Ac 12:6 *1417*
two soldiers, bound with **t** chains, Ac 12:6 *1417*
This took place for **t** years, Ac 19:10 *1417*
t of those who ministered to him, Ac 19:22 *1417*
as they shouted for about **t** hours, Ac 19:34 *1417*
him to be bound with **t** chains; Ac 21:33 *1417*
called to him **t** of the centurions and Ac 23:23 *1417*
"Get **t** hundred soldiers ready by Ac 23:23 *1250*
horsemen and **t** hundred spearmen." Ac 23:23 *1250*
But after **t** years had passed, Ac 24:27 *1333*
t hundred and seventy-six persons. Ac 27:37 *1250*
striking a reef where **t** seas met, Ac 27:41 *1337*
And he stayed **t** full years in his Ac 28:30 *1333*
"THE **T** SHALL BECOME ONE FLESH." 1Co 6:16 *1417*
be by **t** or at the most three, 1Co 14:27 *1417*
Let **t** or three prophets speak, 1Co 14:29 *1417*
TESTIMONY OF **T** OR THREE WITNESSES. 2Co 13:1 *1417*
written that Abraham had **t** sons, Ga 4:22 *1417*
for these *women* are **t** covenants: Ga 4:24 *1417*
might make the **t** into one new man, Eph 2:15 *1417*
AND THE **T** SHALL BECOME ONE FLESH. Eph 5:31 *1417*
the basis of **t** or three witnesses. 1Tm 5:19 *1417*
that by **t** unchangeable things in Heb 6:18 *1417*
testimony of **t** or three witnesses. Heb 10:28 *1417*
were stoned, they were sawn in **t**, Heb 11:37 *4249*
t woes are still coming after Rv 9:12 *1417*
horsemen was **t** hundred million; Rv 9:16 *1365a, 3461*
grant *authority* to my **t** witnesses, Rv 11:3 *1417*
These are the **t** olive trees and Rv 11:4 *1417*
the **t** lampstands that stand before the Rv 11:4 *1417*
because these **t** prophets tormented Rv 11:10 *1417*
thousand **t** hundred and sixty days. Rv 12:6 *1250*
But the **t** wings of the great eagle Rv 12:14 *1417*
and he had **t** horns like a lamb and Rv 13:11 *1417*
for a distance of **t** hundred miles. Rv 14:20 *1812*
these **t** were thrown alive into the Rv 19:20 *1417*

TWO-DRACHMA
collected the **t** *tax* came to Peter and Mt 17:24 *1323*
your teacher not pay the **t** *tax?*" Mt 17:24 *1323*

TWO-EDGED
And a **t** sword in their hand, Ps 149:6 6310
as wormwood, Sharp as a **t** sword. Pr 5:4 6310
and sharper than any **t** sword, Heb 4:12 *1366*
of His mouth came a sharp **t** sword; Rv 1:16 *1366*
has the sharp **t** sword says this: Rv 2:12 *1366*

TWOFOLD
LORD increased all that Job had **t**. Jb 42:10 4932
And crush them with **t** destruction! Jer 17:18 4932

TWOS
went into the ark to Noah by **t**, Gn 7:9 8147
by **t** of all flesh in which was the Gn 7:15 8147

TWO-TENTHS
then be **t** *of an ephah* of fine flour Lv 23:13 8147, 6241
offering, made of **t** *of an ephah;* Lv 23:17 8147, 6241
t *of an ephah* shall be *in* each Lv 24:5 8147, 6241
offering **t** *of an ephah* of fine flour Nu 15:6 8147, 6241
and **t** *of an ephah* of fine flour Nu 28:9 8147, 6241
and **t** of fine flour Nu 28:12 8147, 6241
for a bull and **t** for the ram. Nu 28:20 8147, 6241
for each bull, **t** for the one ram, Nu 28:28 8147, 6241
ephah for the bull, **t** for the ram, Nu 29:3 8147, 6241
for the bull, **t** for the one ram, Nu 29:9 8147, 6241
bulls, **t** for each of the two rams, Nu 29:14 8147, 6241

TWO-THIRDS
The charge was **t** of a shekel 1Sa 13:21 6371a

TYCHICUS
and **T** and Trophimus of Asia. Ac 20:4 *5190*
circumstances, how I am doing, **T**, Eph 6:21 *5190*
As to all my affairs, **T**, Col 4:7 *5190*
But **T** I have sent to Ephesus. 2Tm 4:12 *5190*
When I send Artemas or **T** to you, Ti 3:12 *5190*

TYPE
who is a **t** of Him who was to come. Ro 5:14 *5179b*
he also received him back as a **t**. Heb 11:19 *3850b*

TYRANNICAL
and defiled, The **t** city! Zph 3:1 3238

TYRANNUS
daily in the school of **T**. Ac 19:9 *5181*

TYRANT
the captives of a **t** be rescued?" Is 49:24
the prey of the **t** will be rescued; Is 49:25 6184

TYRANTS
'Redeem me from the hand of the **t**'? Jb 6:23 6184
which **t** receive from the Almighty. Jb 27:13 6184
"Alien **t** of the nations have Ezk 31:12 6184
all of them are **t** of the nations, Ezk 32:12 6184

TYRE
and to the fortified city of **T**; Jos 19:29 6865
Then Hiram king of **T** sent 2Sa 5:11 6865
and came to the fortress of **T** and 2Sa 24:7 6865
Hiram king of **T** sent his servants 1Ki 5:1 6865
sent and brought Hiram from **T**. 1Ki 7:13 6865
and his father was a man of **T**, 1Ki 7:14 6876
(Hiram king of **T** had supplied 1Ki 9:11 6865
So Hiram came out from **T** to see 1Ki 9:12 6865
Hiram king of **T** sent messengers 1Ch 14:1 6865
sent *word* to Huram the king of **T**, 2Ch 2:3 6865
Then Huram, king of **T**, 2Ch 2:11 6865
Also men of **T** were living there Ne 13:16 6876
daughter of **T** *will come* with a gift; Ps 45:12 6865
with the inhabitants of **T**; Ps 83:7 6865
Philistia and **T** with Ethiopia: Ps 87:4 6865
The oracle concerning **T**. Is 23:1 6865
For **T** is destroyed, without Is 23:1
be in anguish at the report of **T**. Is 23:5 6865
Who has planned this against **T**, Is 23:8 6865
in that day **T** will be forgotten Is 23:15 6865
it will happen to **T** as *in* the song of Is 23:15 6865
years that the LORD will visit **T**. Is 23:17 6865
and all the kings of **T**, Jer 25:22 6865
sons of Ammon, to the king of **T** and Jer 27:3 6865
To cut off from **T** and Sidon Every Jer 47:4 6865
T has said concerning Jerusalem, Ezk 26:2 6865
'Behold, I am against you, O **T**, Ezk 26:3 6865
They will destroy the walls of **T** and Ezk 26:4 6865
I will bring upon **T** from the north Ezk 26:7 6865
Thus says the Lord GOD to **T**, Ezk 26:15 6865
man, take up a lamentation over **T**; Ezk 27:2 6865
and say to **T**, who dwells at the Ezk 27:3 6865
"O **T**, you have said, Ezk 27:3 6865
Your wise men, O **T**, Ezk 27:8 6865
'Who is like **T**, Like her who is Ezk 27:32 6865
of man, say to the leader of **T**, Ezk 28:2 6865
a lamentation over the king of **T** and Ezk 28:12 6865
his army labor hard against **T**; Ezk 29:18 6865

his army had no wages from **T** for **Ezk 29:18** 6865
in a pleasant meadow like **T**; **Hos 9:13** 6865
"Moreover, what are you to Me, O **T**, **Jl 3:4** 6865
"For three transgressions of **T** **Am 1:9** 6865
will send fire upon the wall of **T** And **Am 1:10** 6865
T and Sidon, though they are very **Zch 9:2** 6865
For **T** built herself a fortress And **Zch 9:3** 6865
if the miracles had occurred in **T** and **Mt 11:21** *5184*
it will be more tolerable for **T** **Mt 11:22** *5184*
into the district of **T** and Sidon. **Mt 15:21** *5184*
and the vicinity of **T** and Sidon, **Mk 3:8** *5184*
away from there to the region of **T**. **Mk 7:24** *5184*
He went out from the region of **T**, **Mk 7:31** *5184*
the coastal region of **T** and Sidon, **Lk 6:17** *5184*
miracles had been performed in **T** **Lk 10:13** *5184*
be more tolerable for **T** and Sidon **Lk 10:14** *5184*
with the people of **T** and Sidon; **Ac 12:20** *5183*
sailing to Syria and landed at **T**; **Ac 21:3** *5184*
we had finished the voyage from **T**, **Ac 21:7** *5184*

TYRIAN
of a Danite woman and a **T** father, **2Ch 2:14** 6876

TYRIANS
for the Sidonians and **T** brought **1Ch 22:4** 6876
oil to the Sidonians and to the **T**, **Ezr 3:7** 6876

U

UCAL
to Ithiel, to Ithiel and **U**: **Pr 30:1** 401

UEL
Maadai, Amram, **U**, **Ezr 10:34** 177b

UGLINESS
such as I had never seen for **u** in all **Gn 41:19** 7455

UGLY
them from the Nile, **u** and gaunt, **Gn 41:3** 7451a
The **u** and gaunt cows ate up **Gn 41:4** 7451a
them, poor and very **u** and gaunt, **Gn 41:19** 7451a
and the lean and **u** cows ate up the **Gn 41:20** 7451a
for they were just as **u** as before. **Gn 41:21** 7451a
"The seven lean and **u** cows **Gn 41:27** 7451a

ULAI
I myself was beside the **U** Canal. **Da 8:2** 195
of a man between *the banks of* **U**, **Da 8:16** 195

ULAM
and his sons *were* **U** and Rakem. **1Ch 7:16** 198
The son of **U** *was* Bedan. **1Ch 7:17** 198
his brother *were* **U** his firstborn, **1Ch 8:39** 198
sons of **U** were mighty men of valor, **1Ch 8:40** 198

ULLA
The sons of **U** *were* Arah, **1Ch 7:39** 5925

UMMAH
Included also *were* **U**, **Jos 19:30** 5981

UMPIRE
"There is no **u** between us, Who **Jb 9:33** 3198

UNABLE
Am I really **u** to honor you?" **Nu 22:37** 3808, 3201
"But if you are **u** to tell me, **Jg 14:13** 3808, 3201
was **u** to build a house for the name **1Ki 5:3** 3808, 3201
Israel were **u** to destroy utterly, **1Ki 9:21** 3808, 3201
And they were **u** to eat. **2Ki 4:40** 3808, 3201
u to skin all the burnt offerings; **2Ch 29:34** 3808, 3201
are **u** To rebuild the wall." **Ne 4:10** 3808, 3201
of them are mute dogs **u** to bark, **Is 56:10** 3808, 3201
But he is **u** to heal you, Or to **Hos 5:13** 3808, 3201
land is **u** to endure all his words. **Am 7:10** 3808, 3201
body but are **u** to kill the soul; **Mt 10:28** *3361, 1410*
Being **u** to get to Him because **Mk 2:4** *3361, 1410*
you shall be silent and **u** to speak **Lk 1:20** *3361, 1410*
out, he was **u** to speak to them; **Lk 1:22** *3756, 1410*
"When they were **u** to repay, he **Lk 7:42** *3361, 2192*
and they were **u** to get to Him **Lk 8:19** *3756, 1410*
and was **u** because of the crowd, **Lk 19:3** *3756, 1410*
they were **u** to catch Him in a saying **Lk 20:26** *3756, 2480*
u to cope with the wisdom and the **Ac 6:10** *3756, 2480*
we will be **u** to account for this **Ac 19:40** *3756, 1410*

UNALTERABLE
spoken through angels proved **u**, **Heb 2:2** *949*

UNANSWERED
"Shall a multitude of words go **u**, **Jb 11:2** 3808, 6030a

UNAPPROACHABLE
immortality and dwells in **u** light, **1Tm 6:16** *676*

UNAPPROVED
even though we may appear **u**. **2Co 13:7** *96b*

UNASSAILABLE
The **u** fortifications of your walls **Is 25:12** 4869
who dwell on high, the **u** city; **Is 26:5** 7682

UNAVOIDABLE
many words, transgression is **u**, **Pr 10:19** 2308, 3808

UNAWARE
though he was **u**, still he is guilty **Lv 5:17** 3045, 3808
But His parents were **u** of it, **Lk 2:43** *3756, 1097*
who walk over *them* are **u** *of it*." **Lk 11:44** *3756, 3609a*
u of the things which have happened **Lk 24:18** *3756, 1097*
I do not want you to be **u**, brethren, **Ro 1:13** *50*
I do not want you to be **u**, brethren, **1Co 10:1** *50*
brethren, I do not want you to be **u**. **1Co 12:1** *50*
we do not want you to be **u**, brethren, **2Co 1:8** *50*

UNAWARES
sword and came upon the city **u**, **Gn 34:25** 983
Let destruction come upon him **u**, **Ps 35:8** 3808, 3045

UNBECOMINGLY
acting **u** toward his virgin *daughter*, **1Co 7:36** *807*
does not act **u**; it does not seek its **1Co 13:5** *807*

UNBELIEF
miracles there because of their **u**. **Mt 13:58** *570*
And He wondered at their **u**. **Mk 6:6** *570*
"I do believe; help my **u**." **Mk 9:24** *570*
for their **u** and hardness of heart, **Mk 16:14** *570*
their **u** will not nullify the **Ro 3:3** *570*
of God, he did not waver in **u** but **Ro 4:20** *570*
they were broken off for their **u**, **Ro 11:20** *570*
they do not continue in their **u**, **Ro 11:23** *570*
because I acted ignorantly in **u**; **1Tm 1:13** *570*
not able to enter because of **u**. **Heb 3:19** *570*

UNBELIEVER
brother has a wife who is an **u**, **1Co 7:12** *571*
an **u** or an ungifted man enters, **1Co 14:24** *571*
a believer in common with an **u**? **2Co 6:15** *571*
the faith and is worse than an **u**. **1Tm 5:8** *571*

UNBELIEVERS
and assign him a place with the **u**. **Lk 12:46** *571*
with brother, and that before **u**? **1Co 6:6** *571*
If one of the **u** invites you and **1Co 10:27** *571*
not to those who believe but to **u**; **1Co 14:22** *571*
not to **u** but to those who believe. **1Co 14:22** *571*
and ungifted men or **u** enter, **1Co 14:23** *571*
Do not be bound together with **u**; **2Co 6:14** *571*

UNBELIEVING
"You **u** and perverted generation, **Mt 17:17** *571*
"O **u** generation, how long shall I **Mk 9:19** *571*
"You **u** and perverted generation, **Lk 9:41** *571*
and do not be **u**, but believing." **Jn 20:27** *571*
And a woman who has an **u** husband, **1Co 7:13** *571*
For the **u** husband is sanctified **1Co 7:14** *571*
and the **u** wife is sanctified **1Co 7:14** *571*
Yet if the **u** one leaves, let him **1Co 7:15** *571*
has blinded the minds of the **u** so **2Co 4:4** *571*
to those who are defiled and **u**, **Ti 1:15** *571*
in any one of you an evil, **u** heart that **Heb 3:12** *570*
cowardly and **u** and abominable **Rv 21:8** *571*

UNBIND
"**U** him, and let him go." **Jn 11:44** *3089*

UNBLEMISHED
shall be an **u** male a year old; **Ex 12:5** 8549
an **u** red heifer in which is no defect **Nu 19:2** 8549
as of a lamb **u** and spotless, **1Pe 1:19** *299b*

UNCEASING
And with **u** complaint in his bones; **Jb 33:19** 386
peoples in fury with **u** strokes, **Is 14:6** 1115, 5627
great sorrow and **u** grief in my heart **Ro 9:2** *88*

UNCEASINGLY
My eyes pour down **u**, **La 3:49** 3808, 1820
as to how **u** I make mention of you, **Ro 1:9** *89*

UNCERTAINTY
fix their hope on the **u** of riches, **1Tm 6:17** *83*

UNCHANGEABLE
so that by two **u** things **Heb 6:18** *276*

UNCHANGEABLENESS
the promise the **u** of His purpose, **Heb 6:17** *276*

UNCHANGING
Because He delights in **u** love. **Mi 7:18** 2617a
to Jacob *And* **u** love to Abraham, **Mi 7:20** 2617a

UNCHASTITY
wife, except for *the* reason of **u**, **Mt 5:32** *4202*

UNCIRCUMCISED
"But an **u** male who is not **Gn 17:14** 6189
give our sister to one who is **u**, **Gn 34:14** 6190
But no **u** person may eat of it. **Ex 12:48** 6189
or if their **u** heart becomes humbled **Lv 26:41** 6189
for they were **u**, because they had **Jos 5:7** 6189
a wife from the **u** Philistines?" **Jg 14:3** 6189
fall into the hands of the **u**?" **Jg 15:18** 6189
over to the garrison of these **u**; **1Sa 14:6** 6189
For who is this **u** Philistine, that **1Sa 17:26** 6189
and this **u** Philistine will be like **1Sa 17:36** 6189
these **u** will come and pierce me **1Sa 31:4** 6189
The daughters of the **u** will exult. **2Sa 1:20** 6189
these **u** will come and abuse me." **1Ch 10:4** 6189
For the **u** and the unclean Will no **Is 52:1** 6189
all who are circumcised and yet **u** **Jer 9:25** 6190
for all the nations are **u**, **Jer 9:26** 6189
house of Israel are **u** of heart." **Jer 9:26** 6189
'You will die the death of the **u** By **Ezk 28:10** 6189
will lie in the midst of the **u**, **Ezk 31:18** 6189
and make your bed with the **u**.' **Ezk 32:19** 6189
gone down, they lie still, the **u**, **Ezk 32:21** 6189
who went down **u** to the lower parts **Ezk 32:24** 6189
they are all **u**, slain by the sword **Ezk 32:25** 6189
of them were slain by the sword **u**, **Ezk 32:26** 6189
beside the fallen heroes of the **u**, **Ezk 32:27** 6189
"But in the midst of the **u** you **Ezk 32:28** 6189
they will lie with the **u** and **Ezk 32:29** 6189
they lay down **u** with those slain by **Ezk 32:30** 6189
will be made to lie down among *the* **u** **Ezk 32:32** 6189
u in heart and uncircumcised in **Ezk 44:7** 6189
in heart and **u** in flesh, **Ezk 44:7** 6189
u in heart and uncircumcised in **Ezk 44:9** 6189
in heart and **u** in flesh, **Ezk 44:9** 6189
stiff-necked and **u** in heart and ears **Ac 7:51** *564*
went to **u** men and ate with them." **Ac 11:3** *203*
So if the **u** man keeps the **Ro 2:26** *203*
he who is physically **u**, **Ro 2:27** *203*
and the **u** through faith is one. **Ro 3:30** *203*
circumcised, or on the **u** also? **Ro 4:9** *203*
While he was circumcised, or **u**? **Ro 4:10** *203*
while circumcised, but while **u**; **Ro 4:10** *203*
of the faith which he had while **u**, **Ro 4:11** *203*
Abraham which he had while **u**. **Ro 4:12** *203*
He is not to become **u**. **1Co 7:18** *1986a*
entrusted with the gospel to the **u**, **Ga 2:7** *203*
Greek and Jew, circumcised and **u**, **Col 3:11** *203*

UNCIRCUMCISION
your circumcision has become **u**. **Ro 2:25** *203*
his **u** be regarded as circumcision? **Ro 2:26** *203*
Has anyone been called in **u**? **1Co 7:18** *203*
is nothing, and **u** is nothing, **1Co 7:19** *203*
circumcision nor **u** means anything, **Ga 5:6** *203*
is circumcision anything, nor **u**, **Ga 6:15** *203*
in the flesh, who are called "**U**" **Eph 2:11** *203*
and the **u** of your flesh, **Col 2:13** *203*

UNCLE
the sons of Aaron's **u** Uzziel, **Lv 10:4** 1730
or his **u**, or his uncle's son, may **Lv 25:49** 1730
Saul's **u** said to him and his servant, **1Sa 10:14** 1730
Saul's **u** said, **1Sa 10:15** 1730
So Saul said to his **u**, **1Sa 10:16** 1730
was Abner the son of Ner, Saul's **u**. **1Sa 14:50** 1730
of Babylon made his **u** Mattaniah king **2Ki 24:17** 1730
Also Jonathan, David's **u**, **1Ch 27:32** 1730
Abihail the **u** of Mordecai who had **Es 2:15** 1730
Hanamel the son of Shallum your **u** **Jer 32:7** 1730
Then one's **u**, or his undertaker, **Am 6:10** 1730

UNCLEAN
if a person touches any **u** thing, **Lv 5:2** 2931
whether a carcass of an **u** beast or **Lv 5:2** 2931
beast or the carcass of **u** cattle **Lv 5:2** 2931
or a carcass of **u** swarming things, **Lv 5:2** 2931
is hidden from him and he is **u**, **Lv 5:2** 2931
may be with which he becomes **u**, **Lv 5:3** 2930
anything **u** shall not be eaten; **Lv 7:19** 2931
When anyone touches anything **u**, **Lv 7:21** 2931
human uncleanness, or an **u** animal, **Lv 7:21** 2931
animal, or any **u** detestable thing, **Lv 7:21** 2931
and between the **u** and the clean, **Lv 10:10** 2931
divide the hoof, it is **u** to you. **Lv 11:4** 2931
divide the hoof, it is **u** to you; **Lv 11:5** 2931
divide the hoof, it is **u** to you; **Lv 11:6** 2931
does not chew cud, it is **u** to you. **Lv 11:7** 2931
they are **u** to you. **Lv 11:8** 2931
moreover, you will be made **u**: **Lv 11:24** 2930
carcasses becomes **u** until evening, **Lv 11:24** 2930
clothes and be **u** until evening. **Lv 11:25** 2930
not chew cud, they are **u** to you: **Lv 11:26** 2931
whoever touches them becomes **u**. **Lv 11:26** 2930
walk on *all* fours, are **u** to you; **Lv 11:27** 2931
carcasses becomes **u** until evening, **Lv 11:27** 2930
clothes and be **u** until evening; **Lv 11:28** 2930
they are **u** to you. **Lv 11:28** 2931
the **u** among the swarming things **Lv 11:29** 2931
u among all the swarming things; **Lv 11:31** 2931
are dead becomes **u** until evening. **Lv 11:31** 2930
when they are dead becomes **u**, **Lv 11:32** 2930
the water and be **u** until evening, **Lv 11:32** 2930
whatever is in it becomes **u** and **Lv 11:33** 2930
which water comes, shall become **u**, **Lv 11:34** 2930
in every vessel shall become **u**. **Lv 11:34** 2930
their carcass may fall becomes **u**; **Lv 11:35** 2930
they are **u** and shall continue as **Lv 11:35** 2931
and shall continue as **u** to you. **Lv 11:35** 2931
touches their carcass shall be **u**. **Lv 11:36** 2930
falls on it, it is **u** to you. **Lv 11:38** 2931
who touches its carcass becomes **u** **Lv 11:39** 2930
clothes and be **u** until evening, **Lv 11:40** 2930
clothes and be **u** until evening. **Lv 11:40** 2930
and you shall not make yourselves **u** **Lv 11:43** 2930
with them so that you become **u**. **Lv 11:43** 2930
you shall not make yourselves **u** with **Lv 11:44** 2930
between the **u** and the clean, **Lv 11:47** 2931
she shall be **u** for seven days, **Lv 12:2** 2930
her menstruation she shall be **u**. **Lv 12:2** 2930
then she shall be **u** for two weeks, **Lv 12:5** 2930
at him, he shall pronounce him **u**. **Lv 13:3** 2930
the priest shall pronounce him **u**; **Lv 13:8** 2930
the priest shall pronounce him **u**; **Lv 13:11** 2930
not isolate him, for he is **u**. **Lv 13:11** 2931
appears on him, he shall be **u**. **Lv 13:14** 2930

and he shall pronounce him **u**; **Lv 13:15** 2930
the raw flesh is **u**, it is leprosy **Lv 13:15** 2930
the priest shall pronounce him **u**; **Lv 13:20** 2930
the priest shall pronounce him **u**; **Lv 13:22** 2930
the priest shall pronounce him **u**; **Lv 13:25** 2930
the priest shall pronounce him **u**; **Lv 13:27** 2930
the priest shall pronounce him **u**; **Lv 13:30** 2930
seek for the yellowish hair; he is **u**. **Lv 13:36** 2931
he is a leprous man, he is **u**. **Lv 13:44** 2931
priest shall surely pronounce him **u**; **Lv 13:44** 2930
cover his mustache and cry, '**U**! **Lv 13:45** 2931
his mustache and cry, 'Unclean! **U**!' **Lv 13:45** 2931
"He shall remain **u** all the days **Lv 13:46** 2930
he has the infection; he is **u**. **Lv 13:46** 2931
is a leprous malignancy, it is **u**. **Lv 13:51** 2931
the mark has not spread, it is **u**; **Lv 13:55** 2931
for pronouncing it clean or **u**. **Lv 13:59** 2930
in the house need not become **u**; **Lv 14:36** 2930
throw them away at an **u** place **Lv 14:40** 2931
at an **u** place outside the city. **Lv 14:41** 2931
malignant mark in the house; it is **u**. **Lv 14:44** 2931
outside the city to an **u** place. **Lv 14:45** 2931
it, becomes **u** until evening. **Lv 14:46** 2930
to teach when they are **u** and **Lv 14:57** 2931
from his body, his discharge is **u**. **Lv 15:2** 2931
with the discharge lies becomes **u**, **Lv 15:4** 2930
on which he sits becomes **u**. **Lv 15:4** 2930
in water and be **u** until evening; **Lv 15:5** 2930
in water and be **u** until evening; **Lv 15:6** 2930
in water and be **u** until evening. **Lv 15:7** 2930
in water and be **u** until evening. **Lv 15:8** 2930
the discharge rides becomes **u**. **Lv 15:9** 2930
him shall be **u** until evening, **Lv 15:10** 2930
in water and be **u** until evening. **Lv 15:10** 2930
in water and be **u** until evening. **Lv 15:11** 2930
in water and be **u** until evening. **Lv 15:16** 2930
with water and be **u** until evening. **Lv 15:17** 2930
in water and be **u** until evening. **Lv 15:18** 2930
and whoever touches her shall be **u** **Lv 15:19** 2930
her menstrual impurity shall be **u**, **Lv 15:20** 2930
on which she sits shall be **u**. **Lv 15:20** 2930
in water and be **u** until evening. **Lv 15:21** 2930
in water and be **u** until evening. **Lv 15:22** 2930
it, he shall be **u** until evening. **Lv 15:23** 2930
on him, he shall be **u** seven days, **Lv 15:24** 2930
bed on which he lies shall be **u**. **Lv 15:24** 2930
in her menstrual impurity; she is **u**. **Lv 15:25** 2931
on which she sits shall be **u**, **Lv 15:26** 2931
whoever touches them shall be **u** **Lv 15:27** 2930
in water and be **u** until evening. **Lv 15:27** 2930
emission so that he is **u** by it, **Lv 15:32** 2930
or a man who lies with an **u** woman. **Lv 15:33** 2931
water, and remain **u** until evening; **Lv 17:15** 2930
the clean animal and the **u**, **Lv 20:25** 2931
between the **u** bird and the clean; **Lv 20:25** 2931
I have separated for you as **u**. **Lv 20:25** 2930
touches anything made **u** by a corpse **Lv 22:4** 2931
things by which he is made **u**, **Lv 22:5** 2930
or any man by whom he is made **u**, **Lv 22:5** 2930
any such shall be **u** until evening, **Lv 22:6** 2930
torn *by beasts*, becoming **u** by it; **Lv 22:8** 2930
it is any **u** animal of the kind **Lv 27:11** 2931
'But if *it is* among the **u** animals, **Lv 27:27** 2931
who is **u** because of a *dead* person. **Nu 5:2** 2931
'He shall not make himself **u** for **Nu 6:7** 2930
were **u** because of *the* dead person, **Nu 9:6** 2931
are **u** because of *the* dead person, **Nu 9:7** 2931
u because of a *dead* person, **Nu 9:10** 2931
the firstborn of **u** animals you shall **Nu 18:15** 2931
priest shall be **u** until evening. **Nu 19:7** 2930
and shall be **u** until evening. **Nu 19:8** 2930
clothes and be **u** until evening; **Nu 19:10** 2930
person shall be **u** for seven days. **Nu 19:11** 2930
sprinkled on him, he shall be **u**; **Nu 19:13** 2931
tent shall be **u** for seven days. **Nu 19:14** 2930
tied down on it, shall be **u**. **Nu 19:15** 2931
grave, shall be **u** for seven days. **Nu 19:16** 2930
'Then for the **u** *person* they shall **Nu 19:17** 2931
clean *person* shall sprinkle on the **u** **Nu 19:19** 2931
'But the man who is **u** and does not **Nu 19:20** 2930
been sprinkled on him, he is **u**. **Nu 19:20** 2931
impurity shall be **u** until evening. **Nu 19:21** 2930
anything that the **u** *person* touches **Nu 19:22** 2931
unclean *person* touches shall be **u**; **Nu 19:22** 2930
it shall be **u** until evening.' " **Nu 19:22** 2930
the **u** and the clean may eat of it, **Dt 12:15** 2931
the **u** and the clean alike may eat **Dt 12:22** 2931
they are **u** for you. **Dt 14:7** 2931
not *chew* the cud, it is **u** for you. **Dt 14:8** 2931
you shall not eat; it is **u** for you. **Dt 14:10** 2931
life with wings are **u** to you; **Dt 14:19** 2931
the **u** and the clean alike *may eat* **Dt 15:22** 2931
among you any man who is **u** because **Dt 23:10** 3808, 2889
I removed any of it while I was **u**, **Dt 26:14** 2931
the land of your possession is **u**, **Jos 22:19** 2931
strong drink, nor eat any **u** thing. **Jg 13:4** 2931
strong drink nor eat any **u** thing, **Jg 13:7** 2932a
strong drink, nor eat any **u** thing; **Jg 13:14** 2932a
would enter *who was* in any way **u**. **2Ch 23:19** 2931
and every **u** thing which they found **2Ch 29:16** 2932a
lambs for everyone who *was* **u**, **2Ch 30:17** 3808, 2889
therefore they were considered **u** **Ezr 2:62** 1351
are entering to possess is an **u** land **Ezr 9:11** 5079
therefore they were considered **u** **Ne 7:64** 1351
can make the clean out of the **u**? **Jb 14:4** 2931
they became **u** in their practices, **Ps 106:39** 2930
for the clean and for the **u**; **Ec 9:2** 2931
Because I am a man of **u** lips, **Is 6:5** 2931
I live among a people of **u** lips; **Is 6:5** 2931
The **u** will not travel on it, But **Is 35:8** 2931
the **u** Will no longer come into you. **Is 52:1** 2931
out from there, Touch nothing **u**; **Is 52:11** 2931
us have become like one who is **u**, **Is 64:6** 2931
broth of **u** meat is *in* their pots. **Is 65:4** 6292
How long will you remain **u**?" **Jer 13:27** 3808, 2891
she has become an **u** thing. **La 1:8** 5206
Jerusalem has become an **u** thing **La 1:17** 5079
Depart! **U**!" they cried of themselves **La 4:15** 2931
eat their bread **u** among the nations **Ezk 4:13** 2931
nor has any **u** meat ever entered my **Ezk 4:14** 6292
I pronounced them **u** because of **Ezk 20:26** 2930
was **u** in her menstrual impurity. **Ezk 22:10** 2931
between the **u** and the clean; **Ezk 22:26** 2931
discern between the **u** and the clean. **Ezk 44:23** 2931
in Assyria they will eat **u** *food*. **Hos 9:3** 2931
you yourself will die upon **u** soil. **Am 7:17** 2931
"If one who is **u** from a corpse **Hg 2:13** 2931
these, will *the latter* become **u**?" **Hg 2:13** 2930
"It will become **u**." **Hg 2:13** 2930
and what they offer there is **u**. **Hg 2:14** 2931
also remove the prophets and the **u** **Zch 13:2** 2932a
them authority over **u** spirits, **Mt 10:1** *169*
the **u** spirit goes out of a man, **Mt 12:43** *169*
synagogue with an **u** spirit; **Mk 1:23** *169*
the **u** spirit cried out with a loud **Mk 1:26** *169*
He commands even the **u** spirits, **Mk 1:27** *169*
Whenever the **u** spirits saw Him, **Mk 3:11** *169*
"He has an **u** spirit." **Mk 3:30** *169*
man from the tombs with an **u** spirit **Mk 5:2** *169*
Come out of the man, you **u** spirit!" **Mk 5:8** *169*
the **u** spirits entered the swine; **Mk 5:13** *169*
them authority over the **u** spirits; **Mk 6:7** *169*
little daughter had an **u** spirit **Mk 7:25** *169*
He rebuked the **u** spirit, **Mk 9:25** *169*
by the spirit of an **u** demon, **Lk 4:33** *169*
power He commands the **u** spirits and **Lk 4:36** *169*
who were troubled with **u** spirits **Lk 6:18** *169*
commanded the **u** spirit to come out **Lk 8:29** *169*
But Jesus rebuked the **u** spirit, **Lk 9:42** *169*
the **u** spirit goes out of a man, **Lk 11:24** *169*
sick or afflicted with **u** spirits, **Ac 5:16** *169*
case of many who had **u** spirits, **Ac 8:7** *169*
eaten anything unholy and **u**." **Ac 10:14** *169*
not call any man unholy or **u**. **Ac 10:28** *169*
nothing unholy or **u** has ever entered **Ac 11:8** *169*
Jesus that nothing is **u** in itself; **Ro 14:14** *2839*
him who thinks anything to be **u**, **Ro 14:14** *2839*
to be unclean, to him it is **u**. **Ro 14:14** *2839*
for otherwise your children are **u**, **1Co 7:14** *169*
"And do not touch what is **u** **2Co 6:17** *169*
and has regarded as **u** the blood of **Heb 10:29** *2839*
three **u** spirits like frogs; **Rv 16:13** *169*
of the **u** things of her immorality, **Rv 17:4** *169*
and a prison of every **u** spirit, **Rv 18:2** *169*
a prison of every **u** and hateful bird. **Rv 18:2** *169*
and nothing **u**, and no one who **Rv 21:27** *2839*

UNCLEANNESS

'Or if he touches human **u**, **Lv 5:3** 2932a
of whatever *sort* his **u** *may* be with **Lv 5:3** 2932a
in his **u**, that person shall be cut off **Lv 7:20** 2932a
anything unclean, whether human **u**, **Lv 7:21** 2932a
the one to be cleansed from his **u**. **Lv 14:19** 2932a
shall be his **u** in his discharge: **Lv 15:3** 2932a
it is his **u** whether his body **Lv 15:3** 2932a
unclean, like her **u** at that time. **Lv 15:26** 2932a
of Israel separated from their **u**, **Lv 15:31** 2932a
so that they will not die in their **u** **Lv 15:31** 2932a
to the LORD, while he has an **u**, **Lv 22:3** 2932a
is made unclean, whatever his **u**; **Lv 22:5** 2932a
you have not gone astray into **u**, **Nu 5:19** 2932a
purify himself from **u** with the water **Nu 19:12** 2398
his **u** is still on him. **Nu 19:13** 2932a
day he shall purify him from **u**, **Nu 19:19** 2398
does not purify himself from **u**, **Nu 19:20** 2398
had purified herself from her **u**, **2Sa 11:4** 2932a
carry the **u** out from the holy place. **2Ch 29:5** 5079
the **u** of the peoples of the lands, **Ezr 9:11** 5079
Her **u** was in her skirts; **La 1:9** 2932a
I will consume your **u** from you. **Ezk 22:15** 2932a
the **u** of a woman in her impurity. **Ezk 36:17** 2932a
I will save you from all your **u**; **Ezk 36:29** 2932a
"According to their **u** and **Ezk 39:24** 2932a
the **u** that brings on destruction, **Mi 2:10** 2932b
full of dead men's bones and all **u**. **Mt 23:27** *167*

UNCLE'S

a man who lies with his **u** wife he has **Lv 20:20** 1733
he has uncovered his **u** nakedness; **Lv 20:20** 1730
or his uncle, or his **u** son, **Lv 25:49** 1730
that is Esther, his **u** daughter, **Es 2:7** 1730
"Then Hanamel my **u** son came to me **Jer 32:8** 1730
at Anathoth from Hanamel my **u** son, **Jer 32:9** 1730
in the sight of Hanamel my **u** *son* **Jer 32:12** 1730

UNCLES'

of Zelophehad married their **u** sons. **Nu 36:11** 1730

UNCLOTHED

because we do not want to be **u** but **2Co 5:4** *1562*

UNCONCERNED

her labor be in vain, *she* is **u**; **Jb 39:16** 1097, 6343

UNCONDEMNED

a man who is a Roman and **u**? **Ac 22:25** *178*

UNCONTROLLED

"**U** as water, you shall not have **Gn 49:4** 6349

UNCOVER

"Do not **u** your heads nor tear **Lv 10:6** 6544a
relative of his to **u** nakedness; **Lv 18:6** 1540
not **u** the nakedness of your father, **Lv 18:7** 1540
you are not to **u** her nakedness. **Lv 18:7** 1540
'You shall not **u** the nakedness of **Lv 18:8** 1540
their nakedness you shall not **u**. **Lv 18:9** 1540
their nakedness you shall not **u**; **Lv 18:10** 1540
you shall not **u** her nakedness. **Lv 18:11** 1540
'You shall not **u** the nakedness of **Lv 18:12** 1540
'You shall not **u** the nakedness of **Lv 18:13** 1540
'You shall not **u** the nakedness of **Lv 18:14** 1540
'You shall not **u** the nakedness of **Lv 18:15** 1540
you shall not **u** her nakedness. **Lv 18:15** 1540
'You shall not **u** the nakedness of **Lv 18:16** 1540
'You shall not **u** the nakedness of **Lv 18:17** 1540
daughter, to **u** her nakedness; **Lv 18:17** 1540
she is alive, to **u** her nakedness. **Lv 18:18** 1540
approach a woman to **u** her nakedness **Lv 18:19** 1540
not **u** the nakedness of your mother's **Lv 20:19** 1540
garments, shall not **u** his head nor **Lv 21:10** 6544a
he will not **u** his father's skirt. **Dt 22:30** 1540
go and **u** his feet and lie down; **Ru 3:4** 1540
strip off the skirt, **U** the leg, **Is 47:2** 1540
"And then I will **u** her lewdness **Hos 2:10** 1540

UNCOVERED

and **u** himself inside his tent. **Gn 9:21** 1540
the hair of his head shall be **u**, **Lv 13:45** 6544a
he has **u** his father's nakedness; **Lv 20:11** 1540
He has **u** his sister's nakedness; **Lv 20:17** 1540
he has **u** his uncle's nakedness; **Lv 20:20** 1540
he has **u** his brother's nakedness. **Lv 20:21** 1540
down, yet having his eyes **u**. **Nu 24:4** 1540
down, yet having his eyes **u**. **Nu 24:16** 1540
he has **u** his father's skirt.' **Dt 27:20** 1540
and **u** his feet and lay down. **Ru 3:7** 1540
He **u** himself today in the eyes of **2Sa 6:20** 1540
and barefoot with buttocks **u**, **Is 20:4** 2834
And Kir **u** the shield. **Is 22:6** 6168
"Your nakedness will be **u**, **Is 47:3** 1540
from Me, you have **u** yourself, **Is 57:8** 1540
I have **u** his hiding places So that **Jer 49:10** 1540
nakedness **u** through your harlotries **Ezk 16:36** 1540
before your wickedness was **u**, **Ezk 16:57** 1540
in that your transgressions are **u**, **Ezk 21:24** 1540
have **u** *their* fathers' nakedness; **Ezk 22:10** 1540
"They **u** her nakedness; **Ezk 23:10** 1540
"She **u** her harlotries and **Ezk 23:18** 1540
harlotries and **u** her nakedness. **Ezk 23:18** 1540
of your harlotries will be **u**, **Ezk 23:29** 1540
The iniquity of Ephraim is **u**, **Hos 7:1** 1540
who has her head **u** while praying or **1Co 11:5** *177*
to pray to God *with her head* **u**? **1Co 11:13** *177*

UNCOVERS

woman and **u** her nakedness, **Lv 20:18** 1540
ones shamelessly **u** himself!" **2Sa 6:20** 1540

UNCUT

of the LORD your God of **u** stones, **Dt 27:6** 8003
of Moses, an altar of **u** stones on **Jos 8:31** 8003

UNDEFENDED

look at the **u** parts of our land." **Gn 42:9** 6172
look at the **u** parts of our land!" **Gn 42:12** 6172

UNDEFILED

a high priest, holy, innocent, **u**, **Heb 7:26** *283*
and the *marriage* bed *is to be* **u**; **Heb 13:4** *283*
Pure and **u** religion in the **Jas 1:27** *283*
and **u** and will not fade away, **1Pe 1:4** *283*

UNDENIABLE

"So, since these are **u** facts, **Ac 19:36** *368*

UNDER

the breath of life, from **u** heaven; **Gn 6:17** 8478
mountains everywhere **u** the heavens **Gn 7:19** 8478
and rest yourselves **u** the tree; **Gn 18:4** 8478
he was standing by them **u** the tree **Gn 18:8** 8478
come **u** the shelter of my roof." **Gn 19:8**
left the boy **u** one of the bushes. **Gn 21:15** 8478
"Please place your hand **u** my thigh, **Gn 24:2** 8478
his hand **u** the thigh of Abraham **Gn 24:9** 8478
the place and put it **u** his head, **Gn 28:11**
the stone that he had put **u** his head **Gn 28:18**
and Jacob hid them **u** the oak which **Gn 35:4** 8478
was buried below Bethel **u** the oak; **Gn 35:8** 8478
supervise anything **u** Joseph's charge **Gn 39:23**
the cities **u** Pharaoh's authority, **Gn 41:35** 8478
place now your hand **u** my thigh and **Gn 47:29** 8478
you to go, except **u** compulsion. **Ex 3:19**
for **u** compulsion he will let them **Ex 6:1**
and **u** compulsion he will drive **Ex 6:1**
u the burdens of the Egyptians, **Ex 6:6** 8478
u the burdens of the Egyptians. **Ex 6:7** 8478
took a stone and put it **u** him, **Ex 17:12** 8478
memory of Amalek from **u** heaven." **Ex 17:14** 8478
from **u** the hand of the Egyptians. **Ex 18:10** 8478
or in the water **u** the earth. **Ex 20:4** 8478
you lying *helpless* **u** its load, **Ex 23:5** 8478
and **u** His feet there appeared to **Ex 24:10** 8478
shall be **u** the *first* pair of branches **Ex 25:35** 8478
a bulb **u** the *second* pair of branches **Ex 25:35** 8478
a bulb **u** the *third* pair of branches **Ex 25:35** 8478
of silver **u** the twenty boards, **Ex 26:19** 8478
two sockets **u** one board for its **Ex 26:19** 8478
and two sockets **u** another board for **Ex 26:19** 8478
two sockets **u** one board and two **Ex 26:21** 8478
and two sockets **u** another board. **Ex 26:21** 8478
two sockets **u** one board and two **Ex 26:25** 8478
and two sockets **u** another board. **Ex 26:25** 8478
hang up the veil **u** the clasps, **Ex 26:33** 8478

Context	Reference	Number
beneath, **u** the ledge of the altar,	Ex 27:5	8478
gold rings for it **u** its molding;	Ex 30:4	8478
of silver **u** the twenty boards;	Ex 36:24	8478
two sockets **u** one board for its	Ex 36:24	8478
and two sockets **u** another board for	Ex 36:24	8478
two sockets **u** one board and two	Ex 36:26	8478
and two sockets **u** another board.	Ex 36:26	8478
sockets, two **u** every board.	Ex 36:30	8478
bulb was **u** the *first* pair of branches	Ex 37:21	8478
a bulb **u** the *second* pair of branches	Ex 37:21	8478
a bulb **u** the *third* pair of branches	Ex 37:21	8478
golden rings for it **u** its molding,	Ex 37:27	8478
network beneath, **u** its ledge,	Ex 38:4	8478
any of the things which were **u** him	Lv 15:10	8478
flock, whatever passes **u** the rod,	Lv 27:32	8478
shall be **u** the direction of Ithamar	Nu 4:28	
u the direction of Ithamar the son	Nu 4:33	
u *the authority of* your husband,	Nu 5:19	8478
u *the authority of* your husband,	Nu 5:20	8478
u *the authority of* her husband,	Nu 5:29	8478
is **u** the sacrifice of peace offerings.	Nu 6:18	8478
u the direction of Ithamar the son	Nu 7:8	
ground that was **u** them split open;	Nu 16:31	8478
the LORD, she lay down **u** Balaam;	Nu 22:27	8478
u her vows or the rash statement	Nu 30:6	5921
he shall annul her vow which she is **u**	Nu 30:8	5921
u the leadership of Moses and	Nu 33:1	
peoples everywhere **u** the heavens,	Dt 2:25	8478
the peoples **u** the whole heaven.	Dt 4:19	8478
or in the water **u** the earth.	Dt 5:8	8478
their name perish from **u** heaven;	Dt 7:24	8478
house, and like it come **u** the ban;	Dt 7:26	2764a
blot out their name from **u** heaven;	Dt 9:14	8478
the hills and **u** every green tree.	Dt 12:2	8478
from that which is put **u** the ban	Dt 13:17	2764a
memory of Amalek from **u** heaven;	Dt 25:19	8478
and the earth which is **u** you,	Dt 28:23	8478
blot out his name from **u** heaven.	Dt 29:20	8478
"The city shall be **u** the ban,	Jos 6:17	2764a
from the things **u** the ban,	Jos 6:18	2764a
take some of the things **u** the ban,	Jos 6:18	2764a
in regard to the things **u** the ban,	Jos 7:1	2764a
took some of the things **u** the ban,	Jos 7:1	2764a
taken some of the things **u** the ban	Jos 7:11	2764a
you destroy the things **u** the ban	Jos 7:12	2764a
things **u** the ban in your midst,	Jos 7:13	2764a
have removed the things **u** the ban	Jos 7:13	2764a
who is taken with the things **u** the ban	Jos 7:15	2764a
in the things **u** the ban,	Jos 22:20	2764a
stone and set it up there **u** the oak	Jos 24:26	8478
to gather up *scraps* **u** my table;	Jg 1:7	8478
it on his right thigh **u** his cloak.	Jg 3:16	8478
that day **u** the hand of Israel.	Jg 3:30	8478
to sit **u** the palm tree of Deborah	Jg 4:5	8478
sat **u** the oak that was in Ophrah,	Jg 6:11	8478
brought *them* out to him **u** the oak and	Jg 6:19	8478
this people were **u** my authority!	Jg 9:29	
u whose wings you have come to	Ru 2:12	8478
u the pomegranate tree which is in	1Sa 14:2	8478
Saul had put the people **u** oath,	1Sa 14:24	422
his father put the people **u** oath;	1Sa 14:27	7650
strictly put the people **u** oath,	1Sa 14:28	7650
u the tamarisk tree on the height	1Sa 22:6	8478
u the tamarisk tree at Jabesh,	1Sa 31:13	8478
all Israel, and **u** the sun.'"	2Sa 12:12	5048
were in it, and set *them* **u** saws,	2Sa 12:31	
one third **u** the command of Joab,	2Sa 18:2	
one third **u** the command of Abishai	2Sa 18:2	
and one third **u** the command of	2Sa 18:2	
u the thick branches of a great oak.	2Sa 18:9	8478
mule that was **u** him kept going.	2Sa 18:9	8478
and placed them **u** guard and	2Sa 20:3	
With thick darkness **u** His feet.	2Sa 22:10	8478
"You enlarge my steps **u** me,	2Sa 22:37	8478
And they fell **u** my feet.	2Sa 22:39	8478
You have subdued **u** me those who	2Sa 22:40	8478
me, And brings down peoples **u** me,	2Sa 22:48	8478
man **u** his vine and his fig tree,	1Ki 4:25	8478
put them **u** the soles of his feet.	1Ki 5:3	8478
U its brim gourds went around	1Ki 7:24	8478
sea and the twelve oxen **u** the sea;	1Ki 7:44	8478
u the wings of the cherubim.	1Ki 8:6	8478
and in all the land **u** his rule.	1Ki 9:19	
and found him sitting **u** an oak;	1Ki 13:14	8478
but put no fire **u** *it;* and I will	1Ki 18:23	
and I will not put a fire **u** *it.*	1Ki 18:23	
but put no fire **u** *it.*"	1Ki 18:25	
and sat down **u** a juniper tree;	1Ki 19:4	8478
down and slept **u** a juniper tree;	1Ki 19:5	8478
revolted from **u** the hand of Judah,	2Ki 8:20	8478
placed it **u** him on the bare steps,	2Ki 9:13	8478
and he trampled her **u** foot.	2Ki 9:33	
u oath in the house of the LORD,	2Ki 11:4	7650
from **u** the hand of the Arameans;	2Ki 13:5	8478
the name of Israel from **u** heaven,	2Ki 14:27	8478
strengthen the kingdom **u** his rule.	2Ki 15:19	
the hills and **u** every green tree.	2Ki 16:4	8478
the bronze oxen which were **u** it and	2Ki 16:17	8478
Egypt from **u** the hand of Pharaoh,	2Ki 17:7	8478
high hill and **u** every green tree,	2Ki 17:10	8478
and the city came **u** siege.	2Ki 24:10	
So the city was **u** siege until the	2Ki 25:2	
their bones **u** the oak in Jabesh,	1Ch 10:12	8478
of the LORD is **u** curtains."	1Ch 17:1	8478
were **u** the direction of Asaph,	1Ch 25:2	5921
u the direction of the king.	1Ch 25:2	5921
u the direction of their father	1Ch 25:3	5921
were **u** the direction of their father	1Ch 25:6	5921
were **u** the direction of the king.	1Ch 25:6	5921
those twenty years of age and **u**,	1Ch 27:23	4295
oxen *were* **u** it *and* all around it,	2Ch 4:3	8478
one sea with the twelve oxen **u** it.	2Ch 4:15	8478
u the wings of the cherubim.	2Ch 5:7	8478
and in all the land **u** his rule.	2Ch 8:6	
the kingdom was undisturbed **u** him.	2Ch 14:5	6440
u the authority of the Levitical priests,	2Ch 23:18	
u commanders of thousands and	2Ch 25:5	
u the direction of Hananiah,	2Ch 26:11	5921
U their direction was an elite army	2Ch 26:13	5921
the hills and **u** every green tree.	2Ch 28:4	8478
u the authority of Conaniah and	2Ch 31:13	4480
U his authority *were* Eden,	2Ch 31:15	5921
remaining in Jerusalem **u** siege?	2Ch 32:10	
now it has been **u** construction and	Ezr 5:16	1124
the Levites carried out repairs **u**	Ne 3:17	
brothers carried out repairs **u**	Ne 3:18	
also placed ourselves **u** obligation	Ne 10:32	5921
u the regulations for the women	Es 2:12	
as she had done when **u** his care.	Es 2:20	
And he hides it **u** his tongue,	Jb 20:12	8478
U the waters and their inhabitants.	Jb 26:5	8478
the cloud does not burst **u** them.	Jb 26:8	8478
And sees everything **u** the heavens.	Jb 28:24	8478
U the nettles they are gathered	Jb 30:7	8478
"**U** the whole heaven He lets it	Jb 37:3	8478
"It is changed like clay **u**	Jb 38:14	
"**U** the lotus plants he lies down,	Jb 40:21	8478
Whatever is **u** the whole heaven is	Jb 41:11	8478
You have put all things **u** his feet,	Ps 8:6	8478
U his tongue is mischief and	Ps 10:7	8478
With thick darkness **u** His feet.	Ps 18:9	8478
You enlarge my steps **u** me,	Ps 18:36	8478
They fell **u** my feet.	Ps 18:38	8478
You have subdued **u** me those who	Ps 18:39	8478
for me, And subdues peoples **u** me.	Ps 18:47	8478
The peoples fall **u** You;	Ps 45:5	8478
He subdues peoples **u** us And	Ps 47:3	8478
under us And nations **u** our feet.	Ps 47:3	8478
Trampling **u** foot the pieces of silver;	Ps 68:30	
u His wings you may seek refuge;	Ps 91:4	8478
they were subdued **u** their power.	Ps 106:42	8478
Poison of a viper is **u** their lips.	Ps 140:3	8478
Who subdues my people **u** me.	Ps 144:2	8478
he take your bed from **u** you?	Pr 22:27	8478
U three things the earth quakes,	Pr 30:21	8478
And **u** four, it cannot bear up	Pr 30:21	8478
U a slave when he becomes king,	Pr 30:22	8478
U an unloved woman when she gets a	Pr 30:23	8478
his work Which he does **u** the sun?	Ec 1:3	8478
there is nothing new **u** the sun.	Ec 1:9	8478
all that has been done **u** heaven.	Ec 1:13	8478
which have been done **u** the sun,	Ec 1:14	8478
for the sons of men to do **u** heaven	Ec 2:3	8478
and there was no profit **u** the sun.	Ec 2:11	8478
which had been done **u** the sun	Ec 2:17	8478
for which I had labored **u** the sun,	Ec 2:18	8478
by acting wisely **u** the sun.	Ec 2:19	8478
for which I had labored **u** the sun.	Ec 2:20	8478
with which he labors **u** the sun?	Ec 2:22	8478
a time for every event **u** heaven	Ec 3:1	8478
I have seen **u** the sun *that* in the	Ec 3:16	8478
which were being done **u** the sun.	Ec 4:1	8478
activity that is done **u** the sun.	Ec 4:3	8478
looked again at vanity **u** the sun.	Ec 4:7	8478
I have seen all the living **u** the sun	Ec 4:15	8478
evil *which* I have seen **u** the sun:	Ec 5:13	8478
one's labor in which he toils **u** the sun	Ec 5:18	8478
an evil which I have seen **u** the sun	Ec 6:1	8478
what will be after him **u** the sun?	Ec 6:12	8478
crackling of thorn bushes **u** a pot,	Ec 7:6	8478
deed that has been done **u** the sun	Ec 8:9	8478
is nothing good for a man **u** the sun	Ec 8:15	8478
which God has given him **u** the sun.	Ec 8:15	8478
which has been done **u** the sun.	Ec 8:17	8478
in all that is done **u** the sun,	Ec 9:3	8478
in all that is done **u** the sun.	Ec 9:6	8478
He has given to you **u** the sun;	Ec 9:9	8478
which you have labored **u** the sun.	Ec 9:9	8478
I again saw **u** the sun that the	Ec 9:11	8478
I came to see as wisdom **u** the sun,	Ec 9:13	8478
is an evil I have seen **u** the sun,	Ec 10:5	8478
"Let his left hand be **u** my head	SS 2:6	8478
Honey and milk are **u** your tongue,	SS 4:11	8478
"Let his left hand be **u** my head And	SS 8:3	8478
ruins will be **u** your charge,"	Is 3:6	8478
And **u** his glory a fire will be	Is 10:16	8478
of Ephraim is trodden **u** foot.	Is 28:3	
and gather *them* **u** its protection.	Is 34:15	
the oaks, **U** every luxuriant tree,	Is 57:5	8478
U the clefts of the crags?	Is 57:5	8478
u every green tree You have lain	Jer 2:20	8478
high hill and **u** every green tree,	Jer 3:6	8478
the strangers **u** every green tree,	Jer 3:13	8478
earth and from **u** the heavens."	Jer 10:11	8460
the ground, You who dwell **u** siege!	Jer 10:17	
not put its neck **u** the yoke of the king	Jer 27:8	
u the yoke of the king of Babylon	Jer 27:11	
u the yoke of the king of Babylon and	Jer 27:12	
u the hands of the one who numbers	Jer 33:13	5921
that were **u** his dominion and all the	Jer 34:1	
men from here **u** your authority and	Jer 38:10	
took the men **u** his authority and	Jer 38:11	
rags **u** your armpits under the ropes	Jer 38:12	8478
rags under your armpits **u** the ropes	Jer 38:12	8478
had put **u** the charge of Gedaliah	Jer 41:10	6485
So the city was **u** siege until the	Jer 52:5	
bronze bulls that were **u** the sea,	Jer 52:20	8478
has gone into exile **u** affliction And	La 1:3	4480
affliction And **u** harsh servitude;	La 1:3	4480
To crush **u** His feet All the	La 3:34	8478
From **u** the heavens of the LORD!	La 3:66	8478
"**U** his shadow We shall live among	La 4:20	
youths stumbled **u** *loads* of wood.	La 5:13	
U their wings on their four sides	Ezk 1:8	8478
U the expanse their wings *were*	Ezk 1:23	8478
toward it so that it is **u** siege,	Ezk 4:3	
the mountains, **u** every green tree and	Ezk 6:13	8478
green tree and **u** every leafy oak	Ezk 6:13	8478
whirling wheels **u** the cherubim and	Ezk 10:2	8478
form of a man's hand **u** their wings.	Ezk 10:8	8478
him, but its roots remained **u** it.	Ezk 17:6	8478
with him, putting him **u** oath.	Ezk 17:13	
of every kind will nest **u** it;	Ezk 17:23	8478
I will make you pass **u** the rod,	Ezk 20:37	8478
And also pile wood **u** the pot.	Ezk 24:5	8478
And **u** its branches all the beasts	Ezk 31:6	8478
great nations lived **u** its shade.	Ezk 31:6	
lived **u** its shade among the nations.	Ezk 31:17	
swords were laid **u** their heads;	Ezk 32:27	8478
were made **u** the rows round about.	Ezk 46:23	8478
from **u** the threshold of the house	Ezk 47:1	8478
the water was flowing down from **u**,	Ezk 47:1	8478
of the field found shade **u** it,	Da 4:12	8460
Let the beasts flee from **u** it And	Da 4:14	8460
u which the beasts of the field	Da 4:21	8460
all the kingdoms **u** the whole heaven	Da 7:27	8460
for **u** the whole heaven there has	Da 9:12	8478
burn incense on the hills, **U** oak,	Hos 4:13	8478
The seeds shrivel **u** their clods;	Jl 1:17	8478
made a shelter for himself and sat **u** it	Jon 4:5	8478
The mountains will melt **u** Him And	Mi 1:4	8478
Each of them will sit **u** his vine	Mi 4:4	8478
under his vine And **u** his fig tree,	Mi 4:4	8478
will tread our iniquities **u** foot.	Mi 7:19	3533
the tents of Cushan **u** distress,	Hab 3:7	8478
invite his neighbor to *sit* **u** *his* vine	Zch 3:10	8478
his vine and **u** *his* fig tree.'"	Zch 3:10	8478
be ashes **u** the soles of your feet	Mal 4:3	8478
from two years old and **u**,	Mt 2:16	*2736*
out and trampled **u** foot by men.	Mt 5:13	*2662*
and put it **u** a basket,	Mt 5:15	*5259*
they will trample them **u** their feet,	Mt 7:6	*2662*
worthy for You to come **u** my roof,	Mt 8:8	*5259*
"For I also am a man **u** authority,	Mt 8:9	*5259*
authority, with soldiers **u** me;	Mt 8:9	*5259*
hen gathers her chicks **u** her wings,	Mt 23:37	*5259*
brought to be put **u** a basket,	Mk 4:21	*5259*
a basket, is it, or **u** a bed?	Mk 4:21	*5259*
OF THE AIR CAN NEST **U** ITS SHADE."	Mk 4:32	*5259*
but even the dogs **u** the table feed	Mk 7:28	*5270*
AND DUG A VAT **U** THE WINE PRESS	Mk 12:1	*5276*
Him and lead Him away **u** guard."	Mk 14:44	*806*
worthy for You to come **u** my roof;	Lk 7:6	*5259*
I also am a man placed **u** authority,	Lk 7:8	*5259*
authority, with soldiers **u** me;	Lk 7:8	*5259*
and it was trampled **u** foot and	Lk 8:5	*2662*
a container, or puts it **u** a bed;	Lk 8:16	*5270*
and shackles and kept **u** guard,	Lk 8:29	*5442*
in a cellar nor **u** a basket,	Lk 11:33	*5259*
U these circumstances, after so	Lk 12:1	*1722*
hen *gathers* her brood **u** her wings,	Lk 13:34	*5259*
Jerusalem will be trampled **u** foot	Lk 21:24	*3961*
since you are **u** the same sentence	Lk 23:40	*1722*
you, when you were **u** the fig tree,	Jn 1:48	*5259*
you that I saw you **u** the fig tree,	Jn 1:50	*5270*
men from every nation **u** heaven.	Ac 2:5	*5259*
for there is no other name **u** heaven	Ac 4:12	*5259*
sold, was it not **u** your control?	Ac 5:4	*1722*
We have four men who are **u** a vow;	Ac 21:23	*2192, 1909*
in this city, educated **u** Gamaliel,	Ac 22:3	*3844, 3588, 4228*
and bound themselves **u** an oath,	Ac 23:12	*332*
bound ourselves **u** a solemn oath	Ac 23:14	*332*
bound themselves **u** a curse not to eat	Ac 23:21	*332*
but **u** no accusation deserving death	Ac 23:29	*2192*
and sailed **u** the shelter of Cyprus	Ac 27:4	*5284*
we sailed **u** the shelter of Crete,	Ac 27:7	*5284*
u the shelter of a small island	Ac 27:16	*5295*
to get the *ship's* boat **u** control.	Ac 27:16	*4031*
I am **u** obligation both to Greeks	Ro 1:14	*3781*
and all who have sinned **u** the Law	Ro 2:12	*1722*
Jews and Greeks are all **u** sin;	Ro 3:9	*5259*
POISON OF ASPS IS **U** THEIR LIPS";	Ro 3:13	*5259*
speaks to those who are **u** the Law,	Ro 3:19	*1722*
over you, for you are not **u** law but	Ro 6:14	*5259*
are not under law but **u** grace.	Ro 6:14	*5259*
we are not **u** law but under grace?	Ro 6:15	*5259*
we are not under law but **u** grace?	Ro 6:15	*5259*
brethren, we are **u** obligation,	Ro 8:12	*3781*
will soon crush Satan **u** your feet.	Ro 16:20	*5259*
is not **u** bondage in such *cases,*	1Co 7:15	*1402*
his heart, being **u** no constraint,	1Co 7:37	*2192*
boast of, for I am **u** compulsion;	1Co 9:16	*1945*
to those who are **u** the Law,	1Co 9:20	*5259*
are under the Law, as **u** the Law though	1Co 9:20	*5259*
though not being myself **u** the Law,	1Co 9:20	*5259*
might win those who are **u** the Law;	1Co 9:20	*5259*
of God but **u** the law of Christ,	1Co 9:21	*1772*
our fathers were all **u** the cloud and	1Co 10:1	*5259*
put all His enemies **u** His feet.	1Co 15:25	*5259*
THINGS IN SUBJECTION **U** HIS FEET.	1Co 15:27	*5259*
not grudgingly or **u** compulsion,	2Co 9:7	*1537*
In Damascus the ethnarch **u** Aretas	2Co 11:32	
works of the Law are **u** a curse;	Ga 3:10	*5259*
has shut up everyone **u** sin,	Ga 3:22	*5259*
we were kept in custody **u** the law,	Ga 3:23	*5259*

come, we are no longer **u** a tutor. **Ga 3:25** *5259*
but he is **u** guardians and managers **Ga 4:2** *5259*
in bondage **u** the elemental things **Ga 4:3** *5259*
born of a woman, born **u** the Law, **Ga 4:4** *5259*
redeem those who were **u** the Law, **Ga 4:5** *5259*
Tell me, you who want to be **u** law, **Ga 4:21** *5259*
that he is **u** obligation to keep **Ga 5:3** *3781*
the Spirit, you are not **u** the Law. **Ga 5:18** *5259*
things in subjection **u** His feet, **Eph 1:22** *5259*
and on earth and **u** the earth, **Php 2:10** *2709*
proclaimed in all creation **u** heaven, **Col 1:23** *5259*
keeping his children **u** control with **1Tm 3:4** *1722*
All who are **u** the yoke as slaves **1Tm 6:1** *5259*
THINGS IN SUBJECTION U HIS FEET." **Heb 2:8** *5270*
committed **u** the first covenant, **Heb 9:15** *1909*
trampled **u** foot the Son of God, **Heb 10:29** *2662*
is a man who perseveres **u** trial; **Jas 1:12**
that you may not fall **u** judgment. **Jas 5:12** *5259*
a person bears up **u** sorrows when **1Pe 2:19** *5297*
oversight not **u** compulsion, **1Pe 5:2** *317*
u the mighty hand of God, **1Pe 5:6** *5259*
keep the unrighteous **u** punishment **2Pe 2:9**
has kept in eternal bonds **u** darkness **Jude 1:6** *5259*
or on the earth or **u** the earth **Rv 5:3** *5270*
and **u** the earth and on the sea, **Rv 5:13** *5270*
they will tread **u** foot the holy city **Rv 11:2** *3961*
the sun, and the moon **u** her feet, **Rv 12:1** *5270*

UNDERGARMENTS
shall put on **u** next to his flesh; **Lv 6:10** 4370
linen **u** shall be next to his body, **Lv 16:4** 4370
hand mirrors, **u**, turbans and **Is 3:23** 5466
linen **u** shall be on their loins; **Ezk 44:18** 4370

UNDERGIRDING
supporting cables in **u** the ship; **Ac 27:17** *5269*

UNDERGO
allow Your Holy One to **u** decay. **Ps 16:10** 7845
That he should not **u** decay. **Ps 49:9** 7845
"But I have a baptism to **u**, **Lk 12:50** *907*
ALLOW YOUR HOLY ONE TO U DECAY. **Ac 2:27** *3708*
ALLOW YOUR HOLY ONE TO U DECAY.' **Ac 13:35** *3708*
whom God raised did not **u** decay. **Ac 13:37** *3708*

UNDERGOING
in **u** the punishment of eternal fire. **Jude 1:7** *5254*

UNDERNEATH
be above, and you will not be **u**, **Dt 28:13** 4295
And **u** are the everlasting arms; **Dt 33:27** 8478
my tent with the silver **u** it." **Jos 7:21** 8478
in his tent with the silver **u** it. **Jos 7:22** 8478
four wheels *were* **u** the borders, **1Ki 7:32** 8478
And **u** it is turned up as fire. **Jb 28:5** 8478
I saw **u** the altar the souls of **Rv 6:9** *5270*

UNDERPARTS
"His **u** are *like* sharp potsherds; **Jb 41:30** 8478

UNDERSTAND
will not **u** one another's speech." **Gn 11:7** 8085
that you may **u** how the LORD makes **Ex 11:7** 3045
then you will **u** that these men **Nu 16:30** 3045
that He might make you **u** that man **Dt 8:3** 3045
whose language you shall not **u**, **Dt 28:49** 8085
yourself discernment to **u** justice, **1Ki 3:11** 8085
servants in Aramaic, for we **u** *it;* **2Ki 18:26** 8085
"the LORD made me **u** in writing by **1Ch 28:19** 7919a
men and women, those who could **u**; **Ne 8:3** 995
What do you **u** that we do not? **Jb 15:9** 995
His mighty thunder, who can **u**?" **Jb 26:14** 995
be wise, Nor may elders **u** justice. **Jb 32:9** 995
u the spreading of the clouds, **Jb 36:29** 995
declared that which I did not **u**, **Jb 42:3** 995
To see if there are any who **u**, **Ps 14:2** 7919a
When I pondered to **u** this, **Ps 73:16** 3045
They do not know nor do they **u**; **Ps 82:5** 995
Nor does a stupid man **u** this: **Ps 92:6** 995
And when will you **u**, stupid ones? **Ps 94:8** 7919a
in Egypt did not **u** Your wonders; **Ps 106:7** 7919a
Make me **u** the way of Your precepts, **Ps 119:27** 995
I **u** more than the aged, Because I **Ps 119:100** 995
You **u** my thought from afar. **Ps 139:2** 995
To **u** a proverb and a figure, The **Pr 1:6** 995
"O naive ones, **u** prudence; And, O **Pr 8:5** 995
O fools, **u** wisdom. **Pr 8:5** 995
of the sensible is to **u** his way, **Pr 14:8** 995
LORD, How then can man **u** his way? **Pr 20:24** 995
Evil men do not **u** justice, But **Pr 28:5** 995
those who seek the LORD **u** all things **Pr 28:5** 995
wicked does not **u** *such* concern. **Pr 29:7** 995
for me, Four which I do not **u**: **Pr 30:18** 3045
not know, My people do not **u**." **Is 1:3** 995
Keep on looking, but do not **u**.' **Is 6:9** 3045
their ears, **U** with their hearts, **Is 6:10** 995
And let them **u** what the LORD of **Is 19:12** 3045
sheer terror to **u** what it means." **Is 28:19** 995
servants in Aramaic, for we **u** *it;* **Is 36:11** 8085
believe Me And **u** that I am He. **Is 43:10** 995
They do not know, nor do they **u**, **Is 44:18** 995
they had not heard they will **u**. **Is 52:15** 995
know, Nor can you **u** what they say. **Jer 5:15** 8085
is the wise man that may **u** this? **Jer 9:12** 995
is desperately sick; Who can **u** it? **Jer 17:9** 3045
In the last days you will clearly **u** it. **Jer 23:20** 995
In the latter days you will **u** this. **Jer 30:24** 995
You should clearly **u** that today I **Jer 42:19** 3045
u that you will die by the sword, **Jer 42:22** 3045
whose words you cannot **u**. **Ezk 3:6** 8085
Perhaps they will **u** though they **Ezk 12:3** 7200
is anxious to **u** the dream." **Da 2:3** 3045
may **u** the thoughts of your mind. **Da 2:30** 3046
which do not see, hear or **u**. **Da 5:23** 3046

the vision, I sought to **u** it; **Da 8:15** 998
u that the vision pertains to the **Da 8:17** 995
u the words that I am about to **Da 10:11** 995
"Do you **u** why I came to you? **Da 10:20** 3045
for me, I heard but could not **u**; **Da 12:8** 995
and none of the wicked will **u**, **Da 12:10** 995
but those who have insight will **u**. **Da 12:10** 995
is wise, let him **u** these things; **Hos 14:9** 995
And they do not **u** His purpose; **Mi 4:12** 995
they do not hear, nor do they **u**. **Mt 13:13** *4920*
KEEP ON HEARING, BUT WILL NOT U; **Mt 13:14** *4920*
AND U WITH THEIR HEART AND RETURN, **Mt 13:15** *4920*
of the kingdom and does not **u** it, **Mt 13:19** *4920*
He said to them, "Hear and **u**. **Mt 15:10** *4920*
"Do you not **u** that everything **Mt 15:17** *3539*
"Do you not yet **u** or remember the **Mt 16:9** *3539*
"How is it that you do not **u** that **Mt 16:11** *3539*
the holy place (let the reader **u**), **Mt 24:15** *3539*
and they did not **u** until the flood **Mt 24:39** *1097*
MAY HEAR AND NOT U, OTHERWISE THEY **Mk 4:12** *4920*
"Do you not **u** this parable? **Mk 4:13** *3609a*
How will you **u** all the parables? **Mk 4:13** *1097*
"Listen to Me, all of you, and **u**: **Mk 7:14** *4920*
Do you not **u** that whatever goes **Mk 7:18** *3539*
Do you not yet see or **u**? **Mk 8:17** *4920*
"Do you not yet **u**?" **Mk 8:21** *4920*
But they did not **u** *this* statement, **Mk 9:32** *50*
that you do not **u** the Scriptures or **Mk 12:24** *3609a*
should not be (let the reader **u**), **Mk 13:14** *3539*
u what you are talking about." **Mk 14:68** *1987*
But they did not **u** the statement **Lk 2:50** *4920*
SEE, AND HEARING THEY MAY NOT U. **Lk 8:10** *4920*
But they did not **u** this statement, **Lk 9:45** *50*
their minds to **u** the Scriptures, **Lk 24:45** *4920*
Israel and do not **u** these things? **Jn 3:10** *1097*
"Why do you not **u** what I am saying? **Jn 8:43** *1097*
but they did not **u** what those **Jn 10:6** *1097*
and **u** that the Father is in Me, **Jn 10:38** *1097*
disciples did not **u** at the first; **Jn 12:16** *1097*
now, but you will **u** hereafter." **Jn 13:7** *1097*
yet they did not **u** the Scripture, **Jn 20:9** *3609a*
but they did not **u**. **Ac 7:25** *4920*
"Do you **u** what you are reading?" **Ac 8:30** *1097*
"I most certainly **u** *now* that God **Ac 10:34** *2638*
but did not **u** the voice of the One **Ac 22:9** *191*
they themselves **u** that in one **Ac 22:19** *1987*
KEEP ON HEARING, BUT WILL NOT U; **Ac 28:26** *4920*
AND U WITH THEIR HEART AND RETURN, **Ac 28:27** *4920*
what I am doing, I do not **u**; **Ro 7:15** *1097*
THEY WHO HAVE NOT HEARD SHALL U." **Ro 15:21** *4920*
to him; and he cannot **u** them, **1Co 2:14** *1097*
But I want you to **u** that Christ is **1Co 11:3** *3609a*
to you than what you read and **u**, **2Co 1:13** *1921*
I hope you will **u** until the end; **2Co 1:13** *1921*
as you also partially did **u** us, **2Co 1:14** *1921*
when you read you can **u** my insight **Eph 3:4** *3539*
u what the will of the Lord is. **Eph 5:17** *4920*
even though they do not **u** either **1Tm 1:7** *3539*
By faith we **u** that the worlds were **Heb 11:3** *3539*
which are some things hard to **u**, **2Pe 3:16** *1425*
the things which they do not **u**; **Jude 1:10** *3609a*

UNDERSTANDING
the Spirit of God in wisdom, in **u**, **Ex 31:3** 8394
in **u** and in knowledge and in all **Ex 35:31** 8394
in whom the LORD has put skill and **u** **Ex 36:1** 8394
for that is your wisdom and your **u** **Dt 4:6** 998
nation is a wise and **u** people.' **Dt 4:6** 995
And there is no **u** in them. **Dt 32:28** 8394
"So give Your servant an **u** heart **1Ki 3:9** 8085
and he was filled with wisdom and **u** **1Ki 7:14** 8394
LORD give you discretion and **u**, **1Ch 22:12** 998
was a counselor, a man of **u**, **1Ch 27:32** 995
endowed with discretion and **u**, **2Ch 2:12** 998
a skilled man, endowed with **u**, **2Ch 2:13** 998
had **u** through the vision of God; **2Ch 26:5** 995
and all who *could* listen with **u**, **Ne 8:2** 995
all those who had knowledge and **u**, **Ne 10:28** 995
aged men, *With* long life is **u**. **Jb 12:12** 8394
To Him belong counsel and **u**. **Jb 12:13** 8394
You have kept their heart from **u**, **Jb 17:4** 7922
Show **u** and then we can talk. **Jb 18:2** 995
spirit of my **u** makes me answer. **Jb 20:3** 998
And by His **u** He shattered Rahab. **Jb 26:12** 8394
And where is the place of **u**? **Jb 28:12** 998
And where is the place of **u**? **Jb 28:20** 998
And to depart from evil is **u**.' " **Jb 28:28** 998
of the Almighty gives them **u**. **Jb 32:8** 995
listen to me, you men of **u**. **Jb 34:10** 3824
"But if *you have* **u**, hear this; **Jb 34:16** 998
"Men of **u** will say to me, And a **Jb 34:34** 3824
He is mighty in strength of **u**. **Jb 36:5** 3820
Tell *Me,* if you have **u**, **Jb 38:4** 998
being Or given **u** to the mind? **Jb 38:36** 998
has not given her a share of **u**. **Jb 39:17** 998
Is it by your **u** that the hawk soars, **Jb 39:26** 998
or as the mule which have no **u**, **Ps 32:9** 995
meditation of my heart *will be* **u**. **Ps 49:3** 8394
Man in *his* pomp, yet without **u**, **Ps 49:20** 995
A good **u** have all those who do *His* **Ps 111:10** 7922
Give me **u**, that I may observe Your **Ps 119:34** 995
Give me **u**, that I may learn Your **Ps 119:73** 995
From Your precepts I get **u**; **Ps 119:104** 995
give me **u**, That I may know Your **Ps 119:125** 995
It gives **u** to the simple. **Ps 119:130** 995
Give me **u** that I may live. **Ps 119:144** 995
Give me **u** according to Your word. **Ps 119:169** 995
His **u** is infinite. **Ps 147:5** 8394
To discern the sayings of **u**, **Pr 1:2** 998
a man of **u** will acquire wise counsel **Pr 1:5** 995

wisdom, Incline your heart to **u**; **Pr 2:2** 8394
Lift your voice for **u**; **Pr 2:3** 8394
His mouth *come* knowledge and **u**. **Pr 2:6** 8394
guard you, **U** will watch over you, **Pr 2:11** 8394
And do not lean on your own **u**. **Pr 3:5** 998
wisdom And the man who gains **u**. **Pr 3:13** 8394
By **u** He established the heavens. **Pr 3:19** 8394
attention that you may gain **u**, **Pr 4:1** 998
Acquire wisdom! Acquire **u**! **Pr 4:5** 998
with all your acquiring, get **u**. **Pr 4:7** 998
wisdom, Incline your ear to my **u**; **Pr 5:1** 8394
And call **u** *your* intimate friend; **Pr 7:4** 998
call, And **u** lift up her voice? **Pr 8:1** 8394
I am **u**, power is mine. **Pr 8:14** 998
To him who lacks **u** she says, **Pr 9:4** 3820
And proceed in the way of **u**." **Pr 9:6** 998
knowledge of the Holy One is **u**. **Pr 9:10** 998
And to him who lacks **u** she says, **Pr 9:16** 3820
for the back of him who lacks **u**. **Pr 10:13** 3820
many, But fools die for lack of **u**. **Pr 10:21** 3820
And *so is* wisdom to a man of **u**. **Pr 10:23** 8394
But a man of **u** keeps silent. **Pr 11:12** 8394
Good **u** produces favor, But the way **Pr 13:15** 7922
is easy to one who has **u**. **Pr 14:6** 995
He who is slow to anger has great **u**, **Pr 14:29** 8394
in the heart of one who has **u**, **Pr 14:33** 995
But a man of **u** walks straight. **Pr 15:21** 8394
who listens to reproof acquires **u**. **Pr 15:32** 3820
to get **u** is to be chosen above silver. **Pr 16:16** 998
The wise in heart will be called **u**, **Pr 16:21** 995
U is a fountain of life to one who **Pr 16:22** 7922
goes deeper into one who has **u** **Pr 17:10** 995
the presence of the one who has **u**, **Pr 17:24** 995
has a cool spirit is a man of **u**. **Pr 17:27** 8394
A fool does not delight in **u**, **Pr 18:2** 8394
He who keeps **u** will find good. **Pr 19:8** 8394
reprove one who has **u** and he will **Pr 19:25** 995
But a man of **u** draws it out. **Pr 20:5** 8394
man who wanders from the way of **u** **Pr 21:16** 7919a
There is no wisdom and no **u** And no **Pr 21:30** 8394
Get wisdom and instruction and **u**. **Pr 23:23** 998
built, And by **u** it is established; **Pr 24:3** 8394
But by a man of **u** *and* knowledge, **Pr 28:2** 995
poor who has **u** sees through him. **Pr 28:11** 995
who is a great oppressor lacks **u**, **Pr 28:16** 8394
And I do not have the **u** of a man. **Pr 30:2** 998
wisdom I did *this,* For I have **u**; **Is 10:13** 995
Him, The spirit of wisdom and **u**, **Is 11:2** 998
to him who formed it, "He has no **u**" **Is 29:16** 995
did He consult and *who* gave Him **u**? **Is 40:14** 995
And informed Him of the way of **u**? **Is 40:14** 8394
His **u** is inscrutable. **Is 40:28** 8394
is there knowledge or **u** to say, **Is 44:19** 8394
they are shepherds who have no **u**; **Is 56:11** 995
will feed you on knowledge and **u**. **Jer 3:15** 7919a
children And have no **u**. **Jer 4:22** 995
And by His **u** He has stretched out **Jer 10:12** 8394
And by His **u** He stretched out the **Jer 51:15** 8394
"By your wisdom and **u** You have **Ezk 28:4** 8394
branch of wisdom, endowed with **u** **Da 1:4** 995
As for every matter of wisdom and **u** **Da 1:20** 998
men And knowledge to men of **u**. **Da 2:21** 999
give this *man* an **u** of the vision." **Da 8:16** 995
forth to give you insight with **u**. **Da 9:22** 998
message and gain **u** of the vision. **Da 9:23** 995
and had an **u** of the vision. **Da 10:1** 998
that you set your heart on **u** *this* and **Da 10:12** 995
"Now I have come to give you an **u** **Da 10:14** 995
people will give **u** to the many; **Da 11:33** 995
and new wine take away the **u**. **Hos 4:11** 3820
the people without **u** are ruined. **Hos 4:14** 995
(There is no **u** in him.) **Ob 1:7** 8394
And **u** from the mountain of Esau? **Ob 1:8** 8394
"Are you still lacking in **u** also? **Mt 15:16** *801*
mistaken, not **u** the Scriptures nor **Mt 22:29** *3609a*
"Are you so lacking in **u** also? **Mk 7:18** *801*
ALL THE HEART AND WITH ALL THE U **Mk 12:33** *4907*
amazed at His **u** and His answers. **Lk 2:47** *4907*
without **u**, untrustworthy, **Ro 1:31** *801*
BY A NATION WITHOUT U WILL I **Ro 10:19** *801*
themselves, they are without **u**. **2Co 10:12** *4920*
being darkened in their **u**, **Eph 4:18** *1271*
in all spiritual wisdom and **u**, **Col 1:9** *4907*
from the full assurance of **u**, **Col 2:2** *4907*
Lord will give you **u** in everything. **2Tm 2:7** *4907*
Who among you is wise and **u**? **Jas 3:13** *1990*
live with *your wives* in an **u** way, **1Pe 3:7** *1108*
God has come, and has given us **u** so **1Jn 5:20** *1271*
Let him who has **u** calculate the **Rv 13:18** *3563*

UNDERSTANDS
u every intent of the thoughts. **1Ch 28:9** 995
"God **u** its way, And He knows its **Jb 28:23** 995
all, He who **u** all their works. **Ps 33:15** 995
To see if there is anyone who **u**, **Ps 53:2** 7919a
Who **u** the power of Your anger **Ps 90:11** 3045
all straightforward to him who **u**, **Pr 8:9** 995
For though he **u**, there will be no **Pr 29:19** 995
stammering tongue which no one **u**. **Is 33:19** 998
are taken away, while no one **u**. **Is 57:1** 995
of this, that he **u** and knows Me, **Jer 9:24** 7919a
man who hears the word and **u** it; **Mt 13:23** *4920*
THERE IS NONE WHO U, **Ro 3:11** *4920*
for no one **u**, but in *his* spirit he **1Co 14:2** *191*
he is conceited *and* **u** nothing; **1Tm 6:4** *1987*

UNDERSTOOD
not know, however, that Joseph **u**, **Gn 42:23** 8085
they were wise, that they **u** this, **Dt 32:29** 7919a
Then they **u** that the ark of the **1Sa 4:6** 3045

the people and all Israel **u** that day **2Sa 3:37** 3045
of Issachar, men who **u** the times, **1Ch 12:32** 998
sense so that they **u** the reading. **Ne 8:8** 995
because they **u** the words which had **Ne 8:12** 995
said to the wise men who **u** the times **Es 1:13** 3045
this, My ear has heard and **u** it. **Jb 13:1** 995
you **u** the expanse of the earth? **Jb 38:18** 995
Have you not **u** from the **Is 40:21** 995
Daniel even **u** all *kinds of* visions **Da 1:17** 995
but he **u** the message and had an **Da 10:1** 995
"Have you **u** all these things?" **Mt 13:51** *4920*
Then they **u** that He did not say to **Mt 16:12** *4920*
Then the disciples **u** that He had **Mt 17:13** *4920*
they **u** that He was speaking about **Mt 21:45** *1097*
for they **u** that He spoke the **Mk 12:12** *1097*
But the disciples **u** none of these things, **Lk 18:34** *4920*
for they **u** that He spoke this **Lk 20:19** *1097*
u that I came forth from You, **Jn 17:8** *1097*
and **u** that they were uneducated **Ac 4:13** *2638*
he supposed that his brethren **u** that **Ac 7:25** *4920*
u through what has been made, **Ro 1:20** *3539*
none of the rulers of this age has **u**; **1Co 2:8** *1097*
for if they had **u** it they would **1Co 2:8** *1097*
and **u** the grace of God in truth; **Col 1:6** *1921*

UNDERTAKE
God may bless you in all that you **u** **Dt 23:20** 3027, 4916a
and rebuke, in all you **u** to do, **Dt 28:20** 3027, 4916a

UNDERTAKEN
inasmuch as many have **u** to compile **Lk 1:1** *2021*

UNDERTAKER
Then one's uncle, or his **u**, **Am 6:10** 8313

UNDERTAKINGS
and rejoice in all your **u** in which **Dt 12:7** 3027, 4916a
the LORD your God in all your **u**. **Dt 12:18** 3027, 4916a
all your work and in all your **u**. **Dt 15:10** 3027, 4916a

UNDERTOOK
Moab, Moses **u** to expound this law, **Dt 1:5** 2974
Jews **u** what they had started to do, **Es 9:23** 6901

UNDERWENT
among his fathers and **u** decay; **Ac 13:36** *3708*

UNDESIRABLE
Or is he an **u** vessel? **Jer 22:28** 369, 2656
broken Moab like an **u** vessel," **Jer 48:38** 369, 2656

UNDETECTED
eyes of her husband and she is **u**, **Nu 5:13** 5641

UNDISCIPLINED
not act in an **u** manner among you, **2Th 3:7** *812*
among you are leading an **u** life, **2Th 3:11** *814*

UNDISTRACTED
to secure **u** devotion to the Lord. **1Co 7:35** *563*

UNDISTURBED
the land was **u** for eighty years. **Jg 3:30** 8252
the land was **u** for forty years. **Jg 5:31** 8252
And the land was **u** for forty years **Jg 8:28** 8252
So they left his bones **u** with the **2Ki 23:18** 4422
The land was **u** for ten years during **2Ch 14:1** 8252
And the kingdom was **u** under him. **2Ch 14:5** 8252
in Judah, since the land was **u**, **2Ch 14:6** 8252
dwellings and in **u** resting places; **Is 32:18** 7600
see Jerusalem, an **u** habitation, **Is 33:20** 7600
And Jacob will return and be **u** **Jer 46:27** 8252
He has also been **u**, *like wine* **Jer 48:11** 8252
house, his possessions are **u** **Lk 11:21** *1722, 1515*

UNDIVIDED
and helped *David* with an **u** heart. **1Ch 12:33** 3808, 3820

UNDO
To **u** the bands of the yoke, **Is 58:6** 5425b

UNDONE
he left nothing **u** of all that the **Jos 11:15** 5493, 3808
Nor is the belt at its waist **u**, **Is 5:27** 6605a
do, And I will not leave them **u**." **Is 42:16** 5800a

UNDOUBTEDLY
"**U** this man is a murderer, and **Ac 28:4** *3843*

UNDRESS
Strip, **u** and put *sackcloth* on **Is 32:11** 6209

UNEDUCATED
they were **u** and untrained men, **Ac 4:13** *62*

UNFADING
will receive the **u** crown of glory. **1Pe 5:4** *262*

UNFAILING
wear out, an **u** treasure in heaven, **Lk 12:33** *413*

UNFAIRNESS
people because of his **u** to her. **Ex 21:8** 898

UNFAITHFUL
wife goes astray and is **u** to him, **Nu 5:12** 4604
and has been **u** to her husband, **Nu 5:27** 4604
'What is this **u** act which you have **Jos 22:16** 4604
or if in an **u** act against the LORD **Jos 22:22** 4604
you have not committed this **u** act **Jos 22:31** 4604
they had been **u** to the LORD, **2Ch 12:2** 4603
and he was **u** to the LORD his God, **2Ch 26:16** 4603
sanctuary, for you have been **u** and **2Ch 26:18** 4603
Judah and was very **u** to the LORD. **2Ch 28:19** 4604
became yet more **u** to the LORD. **2Ch 28:22** 4603
"For our fathers have been **u** and **2Ch 29:6** 4603
who were **u** to the LORD God of **2Ch 30:7** 4603
the priests and the people were very **u** **2Ch 36:14** 4604
"We have been **u** to our God and **Ezr 10:2** 4603
"You have been **u** and have married **Ezr 10:10** 4603
'If you are **u** I will scatter you **Ne 1:8** 4603
all those who are **u** to You. **Ps 73:27** 2181
u act which he has committed against **Ezk 17:20** 4604
because of their **u** deeds which **Da 9:7** 4604

UNFAITHFULLY
"If a person acts **u** and sins **Lv 5:15** 4604
sins and acts **u** against the LORD, **Lv 6:2** 4604
acting **u** against the LORD, **Nu 5:6** 4604
But the sons of Israel acted **u** in **Jos 7:1** 4604
not Achan the son of Zerah act **u** in **Jos 22:20** 4604
evil by acting **u** against our God **Ne 13:27** 4603
because they have acted **u**,' " **Ezk 15:8** 4604

UNFAITHFULNESS
in their **u** which they committed **Lv 26:40** 4603
and they will suffer *for* your **u**, **Nu 14:33** 2184
into exile to Babylon for their **u**. **1Ch 9:1** 4604
during his reign in his **u**, **2Ch 29:19** 4604
by him, and all his sin, his **u**, **2Ch 33:19** 4604
have been foremost in this **u**." **Ezr 9:2** 4604
on account of the **u** of the exiles **Ezr 9:4** 4604
mourning over the **u** of the exiles. **Ezr 10:6** 4604
sins against Me by committing **u**, **Ezk 14:13** 4603

UNFANNED
And **u** fire will devour him; **Jb 20:26** 5301

UNFASTENED
and everyone's chains were **u**. **Ac 16:26** *447*

UNFATHOMABLE
Who does great things, **u**, **Jb 9:10** 2714, 369, 5704
are His judgments and **u** His ways! **Ro 11:33** *421*
Gentiles the **u** riches of Christ, **Eph 3:8** *421*

UNFEELING
They have closed their **u** *heart,* **Ps 17:10** 2459

UNFOLDING
The **u** of Your words gives light; **Ps 119:130** 6608

UNFORMED
eyes have seen my **u** substance; **Ps 139:16** 1564

UNFORTUNATE
eyes stealthily watch for the **u**. **Ps 10:8** 2489
And the **u** fall by his mighty ones. **Ps 10:10** 2489
The **u** commits *himself* to You; **Ps 10:14** 2489
mute, For the rights of all the **u**. **Pr 31:8** 2475, 1121

UNFRUITFUL
water is bad and the land is **u**." **2Ki 2:19** 7921
choke the word, and it becomes **u**. **Mt 13:22** *175*
choke the word, and it becomes **u**. **Mk 4:19** *175*
my spirit prays, but my mind is **u**. **1Co 14:14** *175*
in the **u** deeds of darkness, **Eph 5:11** *175*
needs, so that they will not be **u**. **Ti 3:14** *175*
u in the true knowledge of our Lord **2Pe 1:8** *175*

UNFRUITFULNESS
there death or **u** any longer.' " **2Ki 2:21** 7921

UNGIFTED
the one who fills the place of the **u** **1Co 14:16** *2399*
and **u** men or unbelievers enter, **1Co 14:23** *2399*
an unbeliever or an **u** man enters, **1Co 14:24** *2399*

UNGODLINESS
the torrents of **u** terrified me. **Ps 18:4** 1100
To practice **u** and to speak error **Is 32:6** 2612
all **u** and unrighteousness of men who **Ro 1:18** *763*
HE WILL REMOVE **U** FROM JACOB." **Ro 11:26** *763*
for it will lead to further **u**, **2Tm 2:16** *763*
instructing us to deny **u** and **Ti 2:12** *763*

UNGODLY
speaks to the **u** within his heart; **Ps 36:1** 7563
plead my case against an **u** nation; **Ps 43:1** 2623, 3808
in Him who justifies the **u**, **Ro 4:5** *765*
right time Christ died for the **u**. **Ro 5:6** *765*
rebellious, for the **u** and sinners, **1Tm 1:9** *765*
a flood upon the world of the **u**; **2Pe 2:5** *765*
those who would live **u** **2Pe 2:6** *764*
judgment and destruction of **u** men. **2Pe 3:7** *765*
u persons who turn the grace of **Jude 1:4** *765*
and to convict all the **u** of all **Jude 1:15** *765*
all the ungodly of all their **u** deeds **Jude 1:15** *763*
which they have done in an **u** way, **Jude 1:15** *764*
things which **u** sinners have spoken **Jude 1:15** *763*
following after their own **u** lusts." **Jude 1:18** *763*

UNGRATEFUL
He Himself is kind to **u** and evil *men* **Lk 6:35** *884*
disobedient to parents, **u**, unholy, **2Tm 3:2** *884*

UNGUARDED
they left the city **u** and pursued **Jos 8:17** 6605a

UNHINDERED
Jesus Christ with all openness, **u**. **Ac 28:31** *209*

UNHOLY
eaten anything **u** and unclean." **Ac 10:14** *2839*
cleansed, no *longer* consider **u**." **Ac 10:15** *2839*
not call any man **u** or unclean. **Ac 10:28** *2839*
for nothing **u** or unclean has ever **Ac 11:8** *2839*
cleansed, no longer consider **u**.' **Ac 11:9** *2839*
sinners, for the **u** and profane, **1Tm 1:9** *462*
disobedient to parents, ungrateful, **u**, **2Tm 3:2** *462*

UNIFORMLY
are **u** favorable to the king. **1Ki 22:13** 259, 6310
are **u** favorable to the king. **2Ch 18:12** 259, 6310

UNIMPRESSIVE
but his personal presence is **u** and **2Co 10:10** *772*

UNINFORMED
brethren, to be **u** of this mystery **Ro 11:25** *50*
But we do not want you to be **u**, **1Th 4:13** *50*

UNINTELLIGIBLE
A people of **u** speech which no one **Is 33:19** 6012
being sent to a people of **u** speech **Ezk 3:5** 6012
nor to many peoples of **u** speech or **Ezk 3:6** 6012

UNINTENTIONALLY
'If a person sins **u** in any of the **Lv 4:2** 7684
and **u** does any one of all the things **Lv 4:22** 7684
anyone of the common people sins **u** **Lv 4:27** 7684
sins **u** against the LORD's holy things, **Lv 5:15** 7684
he sinned **u** and did not know *it,* **Lv 5:18** 7684
'But if a man eats a holy *gift* **u**, **Lv 22:14** 7684
then it shall be, if it is done **u**, **Nu 15:24** 7684
'Also if one person sins **u**, **Nu 15:27** 7684
who goes astray when he sins **u**, **Nu 15:28** 7684
who does *anything* **u**, **Nu 15:29** 7684
any person **u** may flee there. **Nu 35:11** 7684
that anyone who kills a person **u** **Nu 35:15** 7684
who **u** slew his neighbor without **Dt 4:42** 1847, 1097
when he kills his friend **u**, **Dt 19:4** 1847, 1097
manslayer who kills any person **u**, **Jos 20:3** 7684
that whoever kills any person **u** **Jos 20:9** 7684

UNION
Favor and the other I called **U**; **Zch 11:7** 2260c
Then I cut in pieces my second staff **U**, **Zch 11:14** 2260c

UNIQUE
"But He is **u** and who can turn Him? **Jb 23:13** 259
But my dove, my perfect one, is **u**: **SS 6:9** 259
'A disaster, **u** disaster, behold it **Ezk 7:5** 259
For it will be a **u** day which is **Zch 14:7** 259

UNISON
in **u** when the trumpeters and the **2Ch 5:13** 259

UNIT
that the tabernacle will be a **u**. **Ex 26:6** 259
tent together so that it will be a **u**. **Ex 26:11** 259
clasps, so the tabernacle was a **u**. **Ex 36:13** 259
together so that it would be a **u**. **Ex 36:18** 259

UNITE
U my heart to fear Your name. **Ps 86:11** 3161

UNITED
Let not my glory be **u** with their **Gn 49:6** 3161
against the city, **u** as one man. **Jg 20:11** 2270
me, my heart shall be **u** with you; **1Ch 12:17** 3162
stood **u** *with* Kadmiel and his sons, **Ezr 3:9** 259
will not be **u** with them in burial, **Is 14:20** 3161
For if we have become **u** with *Him* **Ro 6:5** *4854*
the same love, **u** in spirit, **Php 2:2** *4861*
not **u** by faith in those who heard. **Heb 4:2** *4786*

UNITY
For brothers to dwell together in **u**! **Ps 133:1** 3162
that they may be perfected in **u**, **Jn 17:23** *1520*
to preserve the **u** of the Spirit in the **Eph 4:3** *1775b*
we all attain to the **u** of the faith, **Eph 4:13** *1775b*
which is the perfect bond of **u**. **Col 3:14** *4886*

UNJUST
"Will you speak what is **u** for God, **Jb 13:7** 5767b
wicked And my opponent as the **u**. **Jb 27:7** 5767a
"Is it not calamity to the **u** And **Jb 31:3** 5767a
me from the deceitful and **u** man! **Ps 43:1** 5767b
he who hates **u** gain will prolong *his* **Pr 28:16** 1215
An **u** man is abominable to the **Pr 29:27** 5766
who constantly record **u** decisions, **Is 10:1** 5999
sincerity, He who rejects **u** gain And **Is 33:15** 1215, 4642
own way, Each one to his **u** gain, **Is 56:11** 1215
Because of the iniquity of his **u** gain **Is 57:17** 1215
may devote to the LORD their **u** gain **Mi 4:13** 1215
But the **u** knows no shame. **Zph 3:5** 5767a
swindlers, **u**, adulterers, or even **Lk 18:11** *94*
For God is not **u** so as to forget **Heb 6:10** *94*
once for all, *the* just for the **u**, **1Pe 3:18** *94*

UNJUSTLY
everyone who acts **u** is an **Dt 25:16** 5766
My lips certainly will not speak **u**, **Jb 27:4** 5767b
How long will you judge **u** And **Ps 82:2** 5766
He deals **u** in the land of uprightness **Is 26:10** 5765
is he who makes a fortune, but **u**; **Jer 17:11** 4941, 3808
saw one *of them* being treated **u**, **Ac 7:24** *91*
up under sorrows when suffering **u**. **1Pe 2:19** *95*
u accusing us with wicked words; **3Jn 1:10** *5396*

UNKNOWN
"So the abundance will be **u** in **Gn 41:31** 3045, 3808
inscription, 'TO AN **U** GOD.' **Ac 17:23** *57*
as **u** yet well-known, as dying yet **2Co 6:9** *50*
I was *still* **u** by sight to the **Ga 1:22** *50*

UNLAWFUL
"You yourselves know how **u** it is **Ac 10:28** *111*

UNLEASH
I will even **u** My power upon Ekron, **Am 1:8** 7725

UNLEAVENED
feast for them, and baked **u** bread, **Gn 19:3** 4682
it with **u** bread and bitter herbs. **Ex 12:8** 4682
'Seven days you shall eat **u** bread, **Ex 12:15** 4682
also observe the *Feast of* **U** Bread, **Ex 12:17** 4682
at evening, you shall eat **u** bread, **Ex 12:18** 4682
you shall eat **u** bread.' " **Ex 12:20** 4682
of Egypt into cakes of **u** bread. **Ex 12:39** 4682
seven days you shall eat **u** bread, **Ex 13:6** 4682

"**U** bread shall be eaten Ex 13:7 4682
observe the Feast of **U** Bread; Ex 23:15 4682
seven days you are to eat **u** bread, Ex 23:15 4682
and **u** bread and unleavened cakes Ex 29:2 4682
bread and **u** cakes mixed with oil, Ex 29:2 4682
oil, and **u** wafers spread with oil; Ex 29:2 4682
one wafer from the basket of **u** bread Ex 29:23 4682
observe the Feast of **U** Bread. Ex 34:18 4682
seven days you are to eat **u** bread, Ex 34:18 4682
it shall be **u** cakes of fine flour Lv 2:4 4682
oil, or **u** wafers spread with oil. Lv 2:4 4682
it shall be of fine flour, **u**, Lv 2:5 4682
eaten as **u** cakes in a holy place; Lv 6:16 4682
offer **u** cakes mixed with oil, Lv 7:12 4682
oil, and **u** wafers spread with oil, Lv 7:12 4682
rams and the basket of **u** bread, Lv 8:2 4682
From the basket of **u** bread Lv 8:26 4682
he took one **u** cake and one cake of Lv 8:26 4682
and eat it **u** beside the altar, Lv 10:12 4682
the Feast of **U** Bread to the LORD; Lv 23:6 4682
seven days you shall eat **u** bread. Lv 23:6 4682
and a basket of **u** cakes of fine flour Nu 6:15 4682
oil and **u** wafers spread with oil, Nu 6:15 4682
with the basket of **u** cakes; Nu 6:17 4682
and one **u** cake out of the basket and Nu 6:19 4682
of the basket and one **u** wafer, Nu 6:19 4682
eat it with **u** bread and bitter herbs. Nu 9:11 4682
u bread *shall be* eaten for seven Nu 28:17 4682
you shall eat with it **u** bread, Dt 16:3 4682
"Six days you shall eat **u** bread, Dt 16:8 4682
at the Feast of **U** Bread and at the Dt 16:16 4682
land, **u** cakes and parched *grain*. Jos 5:11 4682
u bread from an ephah of flour; Jg 6:19 4682
"Take the meat and the **u** bread Jg 6:20 4682
touched the meat and the **u** bread; Jg 6:21 4682
consumed the meat and the **u** bread. Jg 6:21 4682
it and baked **u** bread from it. 1Sa 28:24 4682
ate **u** bread among their brothers. 2Ki 23:9 4682
a grain offering, and **u** wafers, 1Ch 23:29 4682
the Feast of **U** Bread, 2Ch 8:13 4682
to celebrate the Feast of **U** Bread 2Ch 30:13 4682
celebrated the Feast of **U** Bread *for* 2Ch 30:21 4682
the Feast of **U** Bread seven days. 2Ch 35:17 4682
they observed the Feast of **U** Bread Ezr 6:22 4682
u bread shall be eaten. Ezk 45:21 4682
Now on the first *day* of **U** Bread Mt 26:17 *106*
Now the Passover and **U** Bread were Mk 14:1 *106*
On the first day of **U** Bread, Mk 14:12 *106*
Now the Feast of **U** Bread, Lk 22:1 *106*
Then came the *first* day of **U** Bread Lk 22:7 *106*
it was during the days of **U** Bread. Ac 12:3 *106*
after the days of **U** Bread, Ac 20:6 *106*
lump, just as you are *in fact* **u**. 1Co 5:7 *106*
u bread of sincerity and truth. 1Co 5:8 *106*

UNLESS
not let you go **u** you bless me." Gn 32:26 3588, 518
u your youngest brother comes here! Gn 42:15 3588, 518
face **u** your brother is with you.' Gn 43:3 1115
u your brother is with you.'" Gn 43:5 1115
'**U** your youngest brother comes Gn 44:23 518, 3808
u our youngest brother is with us.' Gn 44:26 369
u he has bathed his body in water. Lv 22:6 3588, 518
U their Rock had sold them, Dt 32:30 518, 3808, 3588
u, when we come into the land, you Jos 2:18 2009
u you destroy the things under the Jos 7:12 518, 3808
u you had come quickly to meet me, 1Sa 25:34 3588, 3884a
my face **u** you first bring Michal, 2Sa 3:13 3588, 518
the pace for me **u** I tell you." 2Ki 4:24 3588, 518
to the king **u** the king delighted in her Es 2:14 3588, 518
u the king holds out to him the Es 4:11 905, 4480, 834
u I had believed that I would see Ps 27:13 3884a
U the LORD builds the house, They Ps 127:1 518, 3808
U the LORD guards the city, The Ps 127:1 518, 3808
they cannot sleep **u** they do evil; Pr 4:16 518, 3808
sleep **u** they make *someone* stumble. Pr 4:16 518, 3808
U the LORD of hosts Had left us a Is 1:9 3884a
pass, **U** the Lord has commanded *it*? La 3:37 3808
U You have utterly rejected us La 5:22 3588, 518
Daniel **u** we find *it* against him with Da 6:5 3861b
u they have made an appointment? Am 3:3 1115
den **u** he has captured *something*? Am 3:4 1115, 518
U He reveals His secret counsel To Am 3:7 3588, 518
u your righteousness surpasses *that* Mt 5:20 *1437, 3361*
u he first binds the strong *man*? Mt 12:29 *1437, 3361*
u you are converted and become Mt 18:3 *1437, 3361*
"**U** those days had been cut short, Mt 24:22 *1487*
cannot pass away **u** I drink it, Mt 26:42 *1437, 3361*
u he first binds the strong man, Mk 3:27 *1437, 3361*
u they carefully wash their hands, Mk 7:3 *1437, 3361*
not eat **u** they cleanse themselves; Mk 7:4 *1437, 3361*
"**U** the Lord had shortened *those* Mk 13:20 *1487*
u perhaps we go and buy food for Lk 9:13 *1487, 3385*
"I tell you, no, but **u** you repent, Lk 13:3 *1437, 3361*
"I tell you, no, but **u** you repent, Lk 13:5 *1437, 3361*
that You do **u** God is with him." Jn 3:2 *1437, 3361*
I say to you, **u** one is born again he Jn 3:3 *1437, 3361*
u one is born of water and the Jn 3:5 *1437, 3361*
u it has been given him from Jn 3:27 *1437, 3361*
"**U** you *people* see signs and Jn 4:48 *1437, 3361*
u *it is* something He sees the Jn 5:19 *302, 3361*
u the Father who sent Me draws him; Jn 6:44 *1437, 3361*
u you eat the flesh of the Son of Jn 6:53 *1437, 3361*
u it has been granted him from the Jn 6:65 *1437, 3361*
u it first hears from him and Jn 7:51 *1437, 3361*
for **u** you believe that I am *He* Jn 8:24 *1437, 3361*
u a grain of wheat falls into the Jn 12:24 *1437, 3361*
itself **u** it abides in the vine, Jn 15:4 *1437, 3361*
can you **u** you abide in Me. Jn 15:4 *1437, 3361*
u it had been given you from above; Jn 19:11 *1487, 3361*
"**U** I see in His hands the Jn 20:25 *1437, 3361*
could I, **u** someone guides me?" Ac 8:31 *1437, 3361*
"**U** you are circumcised according Ac 15:1 *1437, 3361*
"**U** these men remain in the ship, Ac 27:31 *1437, 3361*
And just as Isaiah foretold, "**U** Ro 9:29 *1508*
will they preach **u** they are sent? Ro 10:15 *1437, 3361*
in tongues, **u** he interprets, 1Co 14:5 *1487, 3361*
u I speak to you either by way of 1Co 14:6 *1437, 3361*
u you utter by the tongue speech 1Co 14:9 *1437, 3361*
to you, **u** you believed in vain. 1Co 15:2 *1487, 3361*
does not come to life **u** it dies; 1Co 15:36 *1437, 3361*
u indeed you fail the test? 2Co 13:5 *1487, 3385*
come **u** the apostasy comes first, 2Th 2:3 *1437, 3361*
u he competes according to the rules 2Tm 2:5 *1437, 3361*
u you repent. Rv 2:5 *1437, 3361*
u they repent of her deeds. Rv 2:22 *1437, 3361*

UNLIFTED
covenant the same veil remains **u**, 2Co 3:14 *343*

UNLOAD
there the ship was to **u** its cargo. Ac 21:3 *670*

UNLOADED
Then Laban **u** the camels, and he Gn 24:32 6605a

UNLOVED
Now the LORD saw that Leah was **u**, Gn 29:31 8130
the LORD has heard that I am **u**, Gn 29:33 8130
the one loved and the other **u**, Dt 21:15 8130
and the **u** have borne him sons, Dt 21:15 8130
firstborn son belongs to the **u**, Dt 21:15 8146
firstborn before the son of the **u**, Dt 21:16 8130
the firstborn, the son of the **u**, Dt 21:17 8130
u woman when she gets a husband, Pr 30:23 8130

UNLOVING
understanding, untrustworthy, **u**, Ro 1:31 *794*
u, irreconcilable, malicious gossips, 2Tm 3:3 *794*

UNMARRIED
But I say to the **u** and to widows 1Co 7:8 *22*
she does leave, she must remain **u**, 1Co 7:11 *22*
One who is **u** is concerned about 1Co 7:32 *22*
The woman who is **u**, 1Co 7:34 *22*

UNMERCIFUL
untrustworthy, unloving, **u**; Ro 1:31 *415a*

UNNATURAL
natural function for that which is **u**, Ro 1:26 *3844, 5449*

UNNI
Jaaziel, Shemiramoth, Jehiel, **U**, 1Ch 15:18 6042
Aziel, Shemiramoth, Jehiel, **U**, 1Ch 15:20 6042
Also Bakbukiah and **U**, Ne 12:9 6042

UNNOTICED
certain persons have crept in **u**, Jude 1:4 *3921*

UNOBSERVED
U, they perish forever. Jb 4:20 1097, 7760

UNOCCUPIED
and when it comes, it finds *it* **u**, Mt 12:44 *4980*

UNPLEASANT
few and **u** have been the years of Gn 47:9 7451a
"Whether *it is* pleasant or **u**, Jer 42:6 7451b

UNPOPULATED
a city, but stayed out in **u** areas; Mk 1:45 *2048*

UNPREPARED
come with me and find you **u**, 2Co 9:4 *532*

UNPRINCIPLED
by the sensual conduct of **u** men 2Pe 2:7 *113*
away by the error of **u** men and 2Pe 3:17 *113*

UNPRODUCTIVE
a burning waste, unsown and **u**, Dt 29:23 6779, 3808

UNPROFITABLE
for they are **u** and worthless. Ti 3:9 *512*
for this would be **u** for you. Heb 13:17 *255*

UNPUNISHED
for the LORD will not leave him **u** Ex 20:7 5352
then he who struck him shall go **u**; Ex 21:19 5352
the owner of the ox shall go **u**. Ex 21:28 5355a
by no means leave *the guilty* **u**, Ex 34:7 5352
for the LORD will not leave him **u** Dt 5:11 5352
therefore, do not let him go **u**, 1Ki 2:9 5352
Whoever touches her will not go **u**. Pr 6:29 5352
the evil man will not go **u**, Pr 11:21 5352
Assuredly, he will not be **u**. Pr 16:5 5352
at calamity will not go **u**. Pr 17:5 5352
A false witness will not go **u**, Pr 19:5 5352
A false witness will not go **u**, Pr 19:9 5352
haste to be rich will not go **u**. Pr 28:20 5352
And will by no means leave you **u**.' Jer 30:11 5352
And by no means leave you **u**." Jer 46:28 5352
by no means leave *the guilty* **u**. Na 1:3 5352
who buy them slay them and go **u**, Zch 11:5 3808, 816

UNQUENCHABLE
burn up the chaff with **u** fire." Mt 3:12 *762*
to go into hell, into the **u** fire, Mk 9:43 *762*
burn up the chaff with **u** fire." Lk 3:17 *762*

UNREASONABLE
but also to those who are **u**. 1Pe 2:18 *4646*

UNREASONING
But these, like **u** animals, born as 2Pe 2:12 *249*
know by instinct, like **u** animals, Jude 1:10 *249*

UNRELIABLE
stream With water that is **u**? Jer 15:18 539, 3808

UNREPENTANT
of your stubbornness and **u** heart Ro 2:5 *279*

UNRESTRAINED
is no vision, the people are **u**, Pr 29:18 6544a
in anger with **u** persecution. Is 14:6 2820, 1097

UNRIGHTEOUS
way And the **u** man his thoughts; Is 55:7 205
rain on *the* righteous and *the* **u**. Mt 5:45 *94*
his master praised the **u** manager Lk 16:8 *93*
and he who is **u** in a very little Lk 16:10 *94*
little thing is **u** also in much. Lk 16:10 *94*
faithful in the *use of* **u** wealth, Lk 16:11 *94*
"Hear what the **u** judge said; Lk 18:6 *93*
God who inflicts wrath is not **u**, Ro 3:5 *94*
dare to go to law before the **u** and 1Co 6:1 *94*
the **u** will not inherit the kingdom 1Co 6:9 *94*
and to keep the **u** under punishment 2Pe 2:9 *94*

UNRIGHTEOUSNESS
our God will have no part in **u** or 2Ch 19:7 5767b
hope, And **u** must shut its mouth. Jb 5:16 5767b
you remove **u** far from your tent, Jb 22:23 5767b
No, in heart you work **u**; Ps 58:2 5767b
my rock, and there is no **u** in Him. Ps 92:15 5767b
But all **u** shuts its mouth. Ps 107:42 5767b
They also do no **u**; Ps 119:3 5767b
created Until **u** was found in you. Ezk 28:15 5767b
In the **u** of your trade You Ezk 28:18 5766
and **u** was not found on his lips; Mal 2:6 5767b
by means of the wealth of **u** Lk 16:9 *93*
is true, and there is no **u** in Him. Jn 7:18 *93*
all ungodliness and **u** of men who Ro 1:18 *93*
men who suppress the truth in **u**, Ro 1:18 *93*
being filled with all **u**, Ro 1:29 *93*
do not obey the truth, but obey **u**, Ro 2:8 *93*
But if our **u** demonstrates the Ro 3:5 *93*
body to sin *as* instruments of **u**; Ro 6:13 *93*
does not rejoice in **u**, 1Co 13:6 *93*
of Beor, who loved the wages of **u**; 2Pe 2:15 *93*
sins and to cleanse us from all **u**. 1Jn 1:9 *93*
All **u** is sin, and there is a sin 1Jn 5:17 *93*

UNRIPE
drop off his **u** grape like the vine, Jb 15:33 1155
as a fig tree casts its **u** figs Rv 6:13 *3653*

UNRULY
Judah is also **u** against God, Even Hos 11:12 7300
you, brethren, admonish the **u**, 1Th 5:14 *813*
every brother who leads an **u** life 2Th 3:6 *814*

UNSALTY
but if the salt becomes **u**, Mk 9:50 *358*

UNSATISFIED
To keep the hungry person **u** And to Is 32:6 7385a

UNSEARCHABLE
Who does great and **u** things, **Jb 5:9** 369, 2714
The number of His years is **u**. **Jb 36:26** 3808, 2714
And His greatness is **u**. **Ps 145:3** 369, 2714
depth, So the heart of kings is **u**. **Pr 25:3** 369, 2714
How **u** are His judgments and **Ro 11:33** *419*
UNSEEN
endured, as seeing Him who is **u**. **Heb 11:27** *517*
UNSETTLING
with *their* words, **u** your souls, **Ac 15:24** *384*
UNSHEATHE
and I will **u** a sword behind them. **Ezk 5:2** 7385a
and I will **u** a sword behind them. **Ezk 5:12** 7385a
UNSHOD
"Keep your feet from being **u** **Jer 2:25** 3182
UNSHRUNK
no one puts a patch of **u** cloth on **Mt 9:16** *46*
No one sews a patch of **u** cloth on **Mk 2:21** *46*
UNSKILLED
to me, for I am **u** in speech?" **Ex 6:12** 6189
"Behold, I am **u** in speech; **Ex 6:30** 6189
But even if I am **u** in speech, **2Co 11:6** *2399*
UNSOLD
"While it remained **u**, did it **Ac 5:4**
UNSOWN
burning waste, **u** and unproductive, **Dt 29:23** 3808, 2232
UNSPARING
And I rejoice in **u** pain, **Jb 6:10** 3808, 2550
UNSTABLE
Her ways are **u**, she does not know **Pr 5:6** 5128
man, **u** in all his ways. **Jas 1:8** *182*
cease from sin, enticing **u** souls, **2Pe 2:14** *793*
which the untaught and **u** distort, **2Pe 3:16** *793*
UNSTAINED
to keep oneself **u** by the world. **Jas 1:27** *784*
UNSTEADY
Like a bad tooth and an **u** foot Is **Pr 25:19** 4571
UNSTOPPED
the ears of the deaf will be **u**. **Is 35:5** 6605a
UNSUSPECTING
the camp when the camp was **u**. **Jg 8:11** 983
off the garment From **u** passers-by, **Mi 2:8** 983
they deceive the hearts of the **u**. **Ro 16:18** *172*
UNTAUGHT
which the **u** and unstable distort, **2Pe 3:16** *261*
UNTIE
u them and bring them to Me. **Mt 21:2** *3089*
and **u** the thong of His sandals. **Mk 1:7** *3089*
u it and bring it *here*. **Mk 11:2** *3089*
not fit to **u** the thong of His sandals; **Lk 3:16** *3089*
each of you on the Sabbath **u** his ox **Lk 13:15** *3089*
u it and bring it *here*. **Lk 19:30** *3089*
sandal I am not worthy to **u**." **Jn 1:27** *3089*
whose feet I am not worthy to **u**.' **Ac 13:25** *3089*
UNTIED
outside in the street; and they **u** it. **Mk 11:4** *3089*
UNTIL
steadily **u** the tenth month; **Gn 8:5** 5704
u the water was dried up from the **Gn 8:7** 5704
do anything **u** you arrive there." **Gn 19:22** 5704
nor did I hear of it **u** today." **Gn 21:26** 1115
u they have finished drinking." **Gn 24:19** 5704, 518
eat **u** I have told my business." **Gn 24:33** 5704, 518
richer **u** he became very wealthy; **Gn 26:13** 5704
u your brother's fury subsides, **Gn 27:44** 5704, 834
u your brother's anger against you **Gn 27:45** 5704
u I have done what I have promised **Gn 28:15** 5704, 834
u all the flocks are gathered, **Gn 29:8** 5704, 834
with Laban, and stayed **u** now; **Gn 32:4** 5704
man wrestled with him **u** daybreak. **Gn 32:24** 5704
u he came near to his brother. **Gn 33:3** 5704
u I come to my lord at Seir." **Gn 33:14** 5704, 834
Jacob kept silent **u** they came in. **Gn 34:5** 5704
house **u** my son Shelah grows up"; **Gn 38:11** 5704
give a pledge **u** you send *it?*" **Gn 38:17** 5704
beside her **u** his master came home. **Gn 39:16** 5704
sea, **u** he stopped measuring *it*, **Gn 41:49** 5704, 3588
from our youth even **u** now, **Gn 46:34** 5704
between his feet, **U** Shiloh comes, **Gn 49:10** 5704, 3588
you have not listened **u** now." **Ex 7:16** 5704
from the day it was founded **u** now. **Ex 9:18** 5704
upon the earth **u** this day.'" **Ex 10:6** 5704
And **u** we arrive there, we **Ex 10:26** 5704
u the fourteenth day of the same **Ex 12:6** 5704
leave any of it over **u** morning, **Ex 12:10** 5704
whatever is left of it **u** morning, **Ex 12:10** 5704
the first day **u** the seventh day, **Ex 12:15** 5704
u the twenty-first day of the month **Ex 12:18** 5704
the door of his house **u** morning. **Ex 12:22** 5704
U Your people pass over, O LORD, **Ex 15:16** 5704
U the people pass over whom You **Ex 15:16** 5704
man leave any of it **u** morning." **Ex 16:19** 5704
some left part of it **u** morning, **Ex 16:20** 5704
put aside to be kept **u** morning." **Ex 16:23** 5704
So they put it aside **u** morning, **Ex 16:24** 5704
u they came to an inhabited land; **Ex 16:35** 5704
they ate the manna **u** they came to **Ex 16:35** 5704
hands were steady **u** the sun set. **Ex 17:12** 5704
from the morning **u** the evening. **Ex 18:13** 5704
you from morning **u** evening?" **Ex 18:14** 5704
of him **u** he is completely healed. **Ex 21:19**
to remain overnight **u** morning. **Ex 23:18** 5704
u you become fruitful and take **Ex 23:30** 5704, 834
here for us **u** we return to you. **Ex 24:14** 5704, 834
of the bread remains **u** morning, **Ex 29:34** 5704
after Moses **u** he entered the tent. **Ex 33:8** 5704
with My hand **u** I have passed by. **Ex 33:22** 5704
to be left over **u** morning. **Ex 34:25**
take off the veil **u** he came out; **Ex 34:34** 5704
u he went in to speak with Him. **Ex 34:35** 5704
u the day when it was taken up. **Ex 40:37** 5704
the altar all night **u** the morning, **Lv 6:9** 5704
leave any of it over **u** morning. **Lv 7:15** 5704
u the day that the period of your **Lv 8:33** 5704
becomes unclean **u** evening, **Lv 11:24** 5704
clothes and be unclean **u** evening. **Lv 11:25** 5704
becomes unclean **u** evening, **Lv 11:27** 5704
clothes and be unclean **u** evening; **Lv 11:28** 5704
dead becomes unclean **u** evening. **Lv 11:31** 5704
water and be unclean **u** evening, **Lv 11:32** 5704
carcass becomes unclean **u** evening. **Lv 11:39** 5704
clothes and be unclean **u** evening, **Lv 11:40** 5704
clothes and be unclean **u** evening. **Lv 11:40** 5704
u the days of her purification are **Lv 12:4** 5704
it, becomes unclean **u** evening. **Lv 14:46** 5704
in water and be unclean **u** evening; **Lv 15:5** 5704
in water and be unclean **u** evening. **Lv 15:6** 5704
in water and be unclean **u** evening. **Lv 15:7** 5704
in water and be unclean **u** evening. **Lv 15:8** 5704
him shall be unclean **u** evening, **Lv 15:10** 5704
in water and be unclean **u** evening. **Lv 15:10** 5704
in water and be unclean **u** evening. **Lv 15:11** 5704
in water and be unclean **u** evening. **Lv 15:16** 5704
water and be unclean **u** evening. **Lv 15:17** 5704
in water and be unclean **u** evening. **Lv 15:18** 5704
her shall be unclean **u** evening. **Lv 15:19** 5704
in water and be unclean **u** evening. **Lv 15:21** 5704
in water and be unclean **u** evening. **Lv 15:22** 5704
it, he shall be unclean **u** evening. **Lv 15:23** 5704
in water and be unclean **u** evening. **Lv 15:27** 5704
tent of meeting **u** he comes out, **Lv 16:17** 5704
and remain unclean **u** evening; **Lv 17:15** 5704
but what remains **u** the third day **Lv 19:6** 5704
with you all night **u** morning. **Lv 19:13** 5704
of the holy *gifts* **u** he is clean. **Lv 22:4** 5704, 834
such shall be unclean **u** evening, **Lv 22:6** 5704
shall leave none of it **u** morning; **Lv 22:30** 5704
'**U** this same day, until you have **Lv 23:14** 5704
u you have brought in the offering **Lv 23:14** 5704
from evening **u** evening you shall **Lv 23:32** 5704
eating *the old* **u** the ninth year **Lv 25:22** 5704
purchaser **u** the year of jubilee; **Lv 25:28** 5704
valid **u** a full year from its sale; **Lv 25:29** 5704
with you **u** the year of jubilee. **Lv 25:40** 5704
remain **u** the year of jubilee, **Lv 25:52** 5704
last for you **u** grape gathering, **Lv 26:5** 5381
gathering will last **u** sowing time. **Lv 26:5** 5381
are left **u** the year of jubilee; **Lv 27:18** 5704
He shall be holy **u** the days are **Nu 6:5** 5704
shall leave none of it **u** morning, **Nu 9:12** 5704
over the tabernacle, **u** morning. **Nu 9:15** 5704
remained from evening **u** morning, **Nu 9:21** 5704
u it comes out of your nostrils **Nu 11:20** 5704, 834
on **u** Miriam was received again. **Nu 12:15** 5704
people, from Egypt even **u** now." **Nu 14:19** 5704
u your corpses lie in the wilderness. **Nu 14:33** 5704
priest shall be unclean **u** evening. **Nu 19:7** 5704
and shall be unclean **u** evening. **Nu 19:8** 5704
clothes and be unclean **u** evening; **Nu 19:10** 5704
shall be unclean **u** evening.'" **Nu 19:21** 5704
it shall be unclean **u** evening.'" **Nu 19:22** 5704
u we pass through your territory.'" **Nu 20:17** 5704, 834
u we have passed through your **Nu 21:22** 5704, 834
u there was no remnant left him; **Nu 21:35** 5704
lie down **u** it devours the prey, **Nu 23:24** 5704
u the entire generation of those **Nu 32:13** 5704
u we have brought them to their **Nu 32:17** 5704, 834, 518
u every one of the sons of Israel has **Nu 32:18** 5704
u He has driven His enemies out **Nu 32:21** 5704
u he stands before the congregation **Nu 35:12** 5704
u the death of the high priest who **Nu 35:25** 5704
u the death of the high priest. **Nu 35:28** 5704
walked **u** you came to this place.' **Dt 1:31** 5704
u we crossed over the brook Zered was **Dt 2:14** 5704, 834
u all the generation of the men of **Dt 2:14** 5704
the camp **u** they all perished. **Dt 2:15** 5704
u I cross over the Jordan into the **Dt 2:29** 5704, 834
smote them **u** no survivor was left. **Dt 3:3** 5704
u the LORD gives rest to your **Dt 3:20** 5704
u those who are left and hide **Dt 7:20** 5704
confusion **u** they are destroyed. **Dt 7:23** 5704
you **u** you have destroyed them. **Dt 7:24** 5704
Egypt **u** you arrived at this place, **Dt 9:7** 5704
small **u** it was as fine as dust; **Dt 9:21** 5704, 834
to bless in His name **u** this day. **Dt 10:8** 5704
u you came to this place; **Dt 11:5** 5704
shall remain overnight **u** morning. **Dt 16:4**
is making war with you **u** it falls. **Dt 20:20** 5704
u your countryman looks for it; **Dt 22:2** 5704
grapes **u** you are fully satisfied, **Dt 23:24**
u you are destroyed and until you **Dt 28:20** 5704
and **u** you perish quickly, **Dt 28:20** 5704
u He has consumed you from the land **Dt 28:21** 5704
will pursue you **u** you perish. **Dt 28:22** 5704
down on you **u** you are destroyed. **Dt 28:24** 5704
overtake you **u** you are destroyed, **Dt 28:45** 5704
your neck **u** He has destroyed you. **Dt 28:48** 5704
your ground **u** you are destroyed, **Dt 28:51** 5704
u they have caused you to perish. **Dt 28:51** 5704
u your high and fortified walls **Dt 28:52** 5704
bring on you **u** you are destroyed. **Dt 28:61** 5704
in a book **u** they were complete, **Dt 31:24** 5704
this song, **u** they were complete: **Dt 31:30** 5704
u the LORD gives your brothers **Jos 1:15** 5704
three days **u** the pursuers return. **Jos 2:16** 5704
days **u** the pursuers returned. **Jos 2:22** 5704
u all the nation had finished **Jos 3:17** 5704, 834
u everything was completed that the **Jos 4:10** 5704
before you **u** you had crossed, **Jos 4:23** 5704
up before us **u** we had crossed; **Jos 4:23** 5704
sons of Israel **u** they had crossed, **Jos 5:1** 5704
the wilderness, **u** all the nation, **Jos 5:6** 5704
in the camp **u** they were healed. **Jos 5:8** 5704
your mouth, **u** the day I tell you, **Jos 6:10** 5704
the ark of the LORD **u** the evening, **Jos 7:6** 5704
u you have removed the things under **Jos 7:13** 5704
after us **u** we have drawn them away **Jos 8:6** 5704
and they slew them **u** no one was **Jos 8:22** 5704
the sword **u** they were destroyed, **Jos 8:24** 5704
u he had utterly destroyed all the **Jos 8:26** 5704
forever, a desolation **u** this day. **Jos 8:28** 5704
king of Ai on a tree **u** evening; **Jos 8:29** 5704
U the nation avenged themselves of **Jos 10:13** 5704
slaughter, **u** they were destroyed, **Jos 10:20** 5704
they hung on the trees **u** evening. **Jos 10:26** 5704
u he had left him no survivor. **Jos 10:33** 5704
u no survivor was left to them. **Jos 11:8** 5704
sword, **u** they had destroyed them. **Jos 11:14** 5704
live among Israel **u** this day. **Jos 13:13** 5704
the Kenizzite **u** this day, **Jos 14:14** 5704
of Judah at Jerusalem **u** this day. **Jos 15:63** 5704
u he stands before the congregation **Jos 20:6** 5704
u the death of the one who is high **Jos 20:6** 5704
u he stands before the congregation. **Jos 20:9** 5704
u you perish from off this good **Jos 23:13** 5704
u He has destroyed you from off **Jos 23:15** 5704
They waited **u** they became anxious; **Jg 3:25** 5704
u they had destroyed Jabin the **Jg 4:24** 5704, 834
in Israel, **U** I, Deborah, arose, **Jg 5:7** 5704
I, Deborah, arose, **U** I arose, **Jg 5:7**
from here, **u** I come *back* to You, **Jg 6:18** 5704
"I will remain **u** you return." **Jg 6:18** 5704
"*Let us wait* **u** the morning light, **Jg 16:2** 5704
Now Samson lay **u** midnight, and at **Jg 16:3** 5704
for **u** that day an inheritance had **Jg 18:1** 5704
u the day of the captivity of the land. **Jg 18:30** 5704
yourself, and wait **u** afternoon"; **Jg 19:8** 5704
abused her all night **u** morning, **Jg 19:25** 5704
her master was, **u** *full* daylight. **Jg 19:26** 5704
wept before the LORD **u** evening, **Jg 20:23** 5704
and fasted that day **u** evening. **Jg 20:26** 5704
sat there before God **u** evening, **Jg 21:2** 5704
therefore wait **u** they were grown? **Ru 1:13** 5704, 834
went **u** they came to Bethlehem. **Ru 1:19** 5704
remained from the morning **u** now; **Ru 2:7** 5704
gleaned in the field **u** evening. **Ru 2:17** 5704
u they have finished all my harvest. **Ru 2:21** 5704, 518
glean **u** the end of the barley harvest **Ru 2:23** 5704
to the man **u** he has finished eating **Ru 3:3** 5704
Lie down **u** morning." **Ru 3:13** 5704
So she lay at his feet **u** morning **Ru 3:14** 5704
u you know how the matter turns **Ru 3:18** 5704, 834
rest **u** he has settled it today." **Ru 3:18** 3588, 518
for I have spoken **u** now out of my **1Sa 1:16** 5704
not go up **u** the child is weaned; **1Sa 1:22** 5704
Remain **u** you have weaned him; **1Sa 1:23** 5704
nursed her son **u** she weaned him. **1Sa 1:23** 5704
So Samuel lay down **u** morning. **1Sa 3:15** 5704
people will not eat **u** he comes, **1Sa 9:13** 5704
kept for you **u** the appointed time, **1Sa 9:24**
You shall wait seven days **u** I come **1Sa 10:8** 5704
Ammonites **u** the heat of the day. **1Sa 11:11** 5704
'Wait **u** we come to you'; **1Sa 14:9** 5704
and **u** I have avenged myself on my **1Sa 14:24** 5704
among them **u** the morning light, **1Sa 14:36** 5704
them **u** they are exterminated.' **1Sa 15:18** 5704
Saul again **u** the day of his death; **1Sa 15:35** 5704
not sit down **u** he comes here." **1Sa 16:11** 5704
u he came to Naioth in Ramah. **1Sa 19:23** 5704
in the field **u** the third evening. **1Sa 20:5** 5704
u I know what God will do for me." **1Sa 22:3** 5704, 834
been left to Nabal **u** the morning light **1Sa 25:34** 5704
at all **u** the morning light. **1Sa 25:36** 5704

wept **u** there was no strength in them **1Sa 30:4** 5704, 834
u the evening of the next day; **1Sa 30:17** 5704
wept and fasted **u** evening for Saul **2Sa 1:12** 5704
night **u** the day dawned at Hebron. **2Sa 2:32**
been aliens there **u** this day). **2Sa 4:3** 5704
at Jericho **u** your beards grow, **2Sa 10:5** 5704
u all the people had finished passing **2Sa 15:24** 5704
u word comes from you to inform me. **2Sa 15:28** 5704
u not even a small stone is found **2Sa 17:13** 5704, 834
upon you from your youth **u** now." **2Sa 19:7** 5704
u the day he came *home* in peace. **2Sa 19:24** 5704
shut up **u** the day of their death, **2Sa 20:3** 5704
u it rained on them from the sky; **2Sa 21:10** 5704
turn back **u** they were consumed. **2Sa 22:38** 5704
struck the Philistines **u** his hand was **2Sa 23:10** 5704, 3588
the morning **u** the appointed time, **2Sa 24:15** 5704
u he had finished building his own **1Ki 3:1** 5704
the name of the LORD **u** those days. **1Ki 3:2** 5704
u the LORD put them under the **1Ki 5:3** 5704
u all the house was finished. **1Ki 6:22** 5704
u I came and my eyes had seen it. **1Ki 10:7** 5704, 834
u he had cut off every male in **1Ki 11:16** 5704
in Egypt **u** the death of Solomon. **1Ki 11:40** 5704
sweeps away dung **u** it is all gone. **1Ki 14:10** 5704
alive, **u** he had destroyed them, **1Ki 15:29** 5704
u the day that the LORD sends rain **1Ki 17:14** 5704
Baal from morning **u** noon saying, **1Ki 18:26** 5704
u the blood gushed out on them. **1Ki 18:28** 5704
they raved **u** the time of the **1Ki 18:29** 5704
Arameans **u** they are consumed.' " **1Ki 22:11** 5704
bread and water **u** I return safely. **1Ki 22:27** 5704
they urged him **u** he was ashamed, **2Ki 2:17** 5704
u in Kir-hareseth *only* they left **2Ki 3:25** 5704
mother, he sat on her lap **u** noon, **2Ki 4:20** 5704
u a donkey's head was sold for **2Ki 6:25** 5704
"Why do we sit here **u** we die? **2Ki 7:3** 5704
if we wait **u** morning light, **2Ki 7:9** 5704
she left the land even **u** now." **2Ki 8:6** 5704
steadily *on him* **u** he was ashamed, **2Ki 8:11** 5704
entrance of the gate **u** morning." **2Ki 10:8** 5704
u he left him without a survivor. **2Ki 10:11** 5704
Samaria, **u** he had destroyed him, **2Ki 10:17** 5704
Aphek **u** you have destroyed *them*." **2Ki 13:17** 5704
u you would have destroyed *it*. **2Ki 13:19** 5704
cast them from His presence **u** now. **2Ki 13:23** 5704
u He had cast them out of His **2Ki 17:20** 5704, 834
u the LORD removed Israel from His **2Ki 17:23** 5704, 834
own land to Assyria **u** this day. **2Ki 17:23** 5704
for **u** those days the sons of Israel **2Ki 18:4** 5704
u I come and take you away to a **2Ki 18:32** 5704
u he had filled Jerusalem from one **2Ki 21:16** 5704, 834
u He cast them out from His presence **2Ki 24:20** 5704
So the city was under siege **u** the **2Ki 25:2** 5704
their cities **u** the reign of David. **1Ch 4:31** 5704
in their place **u** the exile. **1Ch 5:22** 5704
u Solomon had built the house of **1Ch 6:32** 5704
being stationed **u** now at the **1Ch 9:18** 5704
u there was a great army like the **1Ch 12:22** 5704
for **u** now the greatest part of **1Ch 12:29** 5704
at Jericho **u** your beards grow, **1Ch 19:5** 5704, 834
nor forsake you **u** all the work for **1Ch 28:20** 5704
the LORD, and **u** it was finished. **2Ch 8:16** 5704
did not believe their reports **u** I came **2Ch 9:6** 5704, 834
And there was no more war **u** the **2Ch 15:19** 5704
Arameans **u** they are consumed.' " **2Ch 18:10** 5704
water **u** I return safely. **2Ch 18:26** 5704
of the Arameans **u** the evening; **2Ch 18:34** 5704
"The Valley of Beracah" **u** today. **2Ch 20:26** 5704
u your bowels come out because of **2Ch 21:15** 5704
the chest **u** they had finished. **2Ch 24:10** 5704
helped **u** he *was* strong. **2Ch 26:15** 5704, 3588
all this *continued* **u** the burnt offering **2Ch 29:28** 5704
them **u** the work was completed and **2Ch 29:34** 5704
and **u** the *other* priests had **2Ch 29:34** 5704
u they had destroyed them all. **2Ch 31:1** 5704
offerings and the fat **u** night; **2Ch 35:14** 5704
u the wrath of the LORD **2Ch 36:16** 5704
His people, **u** there was no remedy. **2Ch 36:16** 5704
u the rule of the kingdom of Persia, **2Ch 36:20** 5704
u the land had enjoyed its **2Ch 36:21** 5704
u seventy years were complete. **2Ch 36:21**
u a priest stood up with Urim and **Ezr 2:63** 5704
even **u** the reign of Darius king of **Ezr 4:5** 5704
u a decree is issued by me. **Ezr 4:21** 5704
and it was stopped **u** the second **Ezr 4:24** 5704
u a report could come to Darius, **Ezr 5:5** 5705
and from then **u** now it has been **Ezr 5:16** 5705
"Watch and keep *them* **u** you weigh **Ezr 8:29** 5704
appalled **u** the evening offering. **Ezr 9:4** 5704
u there is no remnant nor any who **Ezr 9:14** 5704
u the fierce anger of our God on **Ezr 10:14** 5704
to pass through **u** I come to Judah, **Ne 2:7** 5704, 834
know or see **u** we come among them, **Ne 4:11** 5704, 834
from dawn **u** the stars appeared. **Ne 4:21** 5704
be opened **u** the sun is hot, **Ne 7:3** 5704
u a priest arose with Urim and **Ne 7:65** 5704
Gate from early morning **u** midday, **Ne 8:3** 5704
not open them **u** after the sabbath. **Ne 13:19** 5704
to month, **u** the twelfth month, **Es 3:7**

I am continually tossing **u** dawn. **Jb 7:4** 5704
me alone **u** I swallow my spittle? **Jb 7:19** 5704
U he fulfills his day like a hired **Jb 14:6** 5704
U the heavens are no longer, He will **Jb 14:12** 5704
me **u** Your wrath returns *to You,* **Jb 14:13** 5704
I will wait **U** my change comes. **Jb 14:14** 5704
wickedness **u** You find none. **Ps 10:15**
turn back **u** they were consumed. **Ps 18:37** 5704
He will guide us **u** death. **Ps 48:14** 5921
refuge **U** destruction passes by. **Ps 57:1** 5704
U I declare Your strength to *this* **Ps 71:18** 5704
U I came into the sanctuary of God; **Ps 73:17** 5704
U a pit is dug for the wicked. **Ps 94:13** 5704
work And to his labor **u** evening. **Ps 104:23** 5704
U the time that his word came to **Ps 105:19** 5704
U I make Your enemies a footstool **Ps 110:1** 5704
U he looks *with satisfaction* on **Ps 112:8** 5704
God, **U** He is gracious to us. **Ps 123:2** 5704
U I find a place for the LORD, A **Ps 132:5** 5704
and brighter **u** the full day. **Pr 4:18** 5704
drink our fill of love **u** morning; **Pr 7:18** 5704
U an arrow pierces through his **Pr 7:23** 5704
U another comes and examines him. **Pr 18:17**
blood Will be a fugitive **u** death; **Pr 28:17** 5704
u I could see what good there is **Ec 2:3** 5704, 834
awaken *my* love **U** she pleases." **SS 2:7** 5704
"**U** the cool of the day when the **SS 2:17** 5704
U I had brought him to my mother's **SS 3:4** 5704
awaken *my* love **U** she pleases." **SS 3:5** 5704
"**U** the cool of the day When the **SS 4:6** 5704
awaken *my* love **U** she pleases." **SS 8:4** 5704
to field, **U** there is no more room, **Is 5:8** 5704
"**U** cities are devastated *and* **Is 6:11** 5704, 834, 518
not be forgiven you **U** you die," **Is 22:14** 5704
U indignation runs *its* course. **Is 26:20** 5704
U you are left as a flag on a **Is 30:17** 5704, 518
U the Spirit is poured out upon us **Is 32:15** 5704
u I come and take you away to a **Is 36:17** 5704
From day **u** night You make an **Is 38:12** 5704
"I composed *my soul* **u** morning. **Is 38:13** 5704
From day **u** night You make an **Is 38:13** 5704
U He has established justice in **Is 42:4** 5704
U her righteousness goes forth **Is 62:1** 5704
give Him no rest **u** He establishes **Is 62:7** 5704
u the end of the eleventh year of **Jer 1:3** 5704
u the exile of Jerusalem in the **Jer 1:3** 5704
of the land of Egypt **u** this day, **Jer 7:25** 5704
them **u** I have annihilated them." **Jer 9:16** 5704
U He has performed and carried out **Jer 23:20** 5704
u they are destroyed from the land **Jer 24:10** 5704
u the time of his own land comes; **Jer 27:7** 5704
"**u** I have destroyed it by his **Jer 27:8** 5704
be there **u** the day I visit them,' **Jer 27:22** 5704
not turn back **U** He has performed **Jer 30:24** 5704
and **u** He has accomplished The **Jer 30:24** 5704
he will be there **u** I visit him," **Jer 32:5** 5704
u all the scroll was consumed in **Jer 36:23** 5704
u all the bread in the city was **Jer 37:21** 5704
u the day that Jerusalem was captured. **Jer 38:28** 5704
famine **u** they are completely gone. **Jer 44:27** 5704
destroy *only* **u** they had enough. **Jer 49:9**
after them **U** I have consumed them. **Jer 49:37** 5704
u He cast them out from His presence **Jer 52:3** 5704
So the city was under siege **u** the **Jer 52:5** 5704
in prison **u** the day of his death. **Jer 52:11** 5704
his life **u** the day of his death. **Jer 52:34** 5704
U the LORD looks down And sees **La 3:50** 5704
u you have completed the days of **Ezk 4:8** 5704
for from my youth **u** now I have **Ezk 4:14** 5704
u He comes whose right it is, **Ezk 21:27** 5704
U I have spent My wrath on you. **Ezk 24:13** 5704
U unrighteousness was found in you. **Ezk 28:15** 5704
u you have scattered them abroad, **Ezk 34:21** 5704, 834
marker by it **u** the buriers have buried **Ezk 39:15** 5704
will eat fat **u** you are glutted, **Ezk 39:19**
and drink blood **u** you are drunk, **Ezk 39:19**
shall not be shut **u** the evening. **Ezk 46:2** 5704
be his **u** the year of liberty; **Ezk 46:17** 5704
And Daniel continued **u** the first **Da 1:21** 5704
me **u** the situation is changed; **Da 2:9** 5705, 1768
u a stone was cut out without hands **Da 2:34** 5705, 1768
u seven periods of time pass over **Da 4:23** 5705, 1768
u you recognize that the Most High **Da 4:25** 5705, 1768
u you recognize that the Most High **Da 4:32** 5705, 1768
u his hair had grown like eagles' **Da 4:33** 5705, 1768
u he recognized that the Most High **Da 5:21** 5705, 1768
and even **u** sunset he kept exerting **Da 6:14** 5705
looking **u** its wings were plucked, **Da 7:4** 5705, 1768
looking **U** thrones were set up, **Da 7:9** 5705, 1768
looking **u** the beast was slain, **Da 7:11** 5705, 1768
u the Ancient of Days came and **Da 7:22** 5705, 1768
u Messiah the Prince *there will be* **Da 9:25** 5704
even **u** a complete destruction, **Da 9:27** 5704
u the entire three weeks were **Da 10:3** 5704
make them pure **u** the end time; **Da 11:35** 5704

u the indignation is finished, **Da 11:36** 5704
there was a nation **u** that time; **Da 12:1** 5704
up the book **u** the end of time; **Da 12:4** 5704
be **u** the end of *these* wonders?" **Da 12:6** 5704
and sealed up **u** the end time. **Da 12:9** 5704
place **U** they acknowledge their guilt **Hos 5:15** 5704, 834
of the dough **u** it is leavened. **Hos 7:4** 5704
bereave them **u** not a man is left. **Hos 9:12**
U He comes to rain righteousness on **Hos 10:12** 5704
were still three months **u** harvest. **Am 4:7**
not steal *only* **u** they had enough? **Ob 1:5**
under it in the shade **u** he could see **Jon 4:5** 5704, 834
He will give them *up* **u** the time **Mi 5:3** 5704
U He pleads my case and executes **Mi 7:9** 5704, 834
U no *room* can be found for them. **Zch 10:10**
for you a blessing **u** it overflows. **Mal 3:10** 5704
virgin **u** she gave birth to a Son; **Mt 1:25** *2193*
u it came and stood over *the* **Mt 2:9** *2193*
and remain there **u** I tell you; **Mt 2:13** *2193*
remained there **u** the death of Herod **Mt 2:15** *2193*
you, **u** heaven and earth pass away, **Mt 5:18** *2193*
the Law **u** all is accomplished. **Mt 5:18** *2193*
u you have paid up the last cent. **Mt 5:26** *2193*
stay at his house **u** you leave *that city.* **Mt 10:11** *2193*
of Israel **u** the Son of Man comes. **Mt 10:23** *2193*
From the days of John the Baptist **u** **Mt 11:12** *2193*
and the Law prophesied **u** John. **Mt 11:13** *2193*
U HE LEADS JUSTICE TO VICTORY. **Mt 12:20** *2193*
to grow together **u** the harvest; **Mt 13:30** *2193*
of flour **u** it was all leavened." **Mt 13:33** *2193*
who will not taste death **u** they see **Mt 16:28** *2193*
u the Son of Man has risen from the **Mt 17:9** *2193*
u he should pay back what was owed. **Mt 18:30** *2193*
u he should repay all that was owed **Mt 18:34** *2193*
U I PUT YOUR ENEMIES BENEATH YOUR **Mt 22:44** *2193*
on you will not see Me **u** you say, **Mt 23:39** *2193*
the beginning of the world **u** now, **Mt 24:21** *2193*
u all these things take place. **Mt 24:34** *2193*
u the day that Noah entered the **Mt 24:38** *891*
u the flood came and took them all **Mt 24:39** *2193*
u that day when I drink it new with **Mt 26:29** *2193*
all the land **u** the ninth hour. **Mt 27:45** *2193*
to be made secure **u** the third day, **Mt 27:64** *2193*
stay there **u** you leave town. **Mk 6:10** *2193*
who will not taste death **u** they see **Mk 9:1** *2193*
u the Son of Man rose from **Mk 9:9** *1487, 3361, 3752*
U I PUT YOUR ENEMIES BENEATH YOUR **Mk 12:36** *2193*
creation which God created **u** now, **Mk 13:19** *2193*
u all these things take place. **Mk 13:30** *3360*
u that day when I drink it new in the **Mk 14:25** *2193*
"Sit here **u** I have prayed." **Mk 14:32** *2193*
the whole land **u** the ninth hour. **Mk 15:33** *2193*
unable to speak **u** the day when these **Lk 1:20** *891*
and he lived in the deserts **u** the **Lk 1:80** *2193*
left Him **u** an opportune time. **Lk 4:13** *891*
stay there **u** you leave that city. **Lk 9:4** *2532*
u they see the kingdom of God." **Lk 9:27** *2193*
I am **u** it is accomplished! **Lk 12:50** *2193*
u you have paid the very last cent. **Lk 12:59** *2193*
u I dig around it and put in **Lk 13:8** *2193*
of flour **u** it was all leavened." **Lk 13:21** *2193*
Me **u** *the time* comes when you say, **Lk 13:35** *2193*
one which is lost **u** he finds it? **Lk 15:4** *2193*
search carefully **u** she finds it? **Lk 15:8** *2193*
Prophets *were proclaimed* **u** John; **Lk 16:16** *3360*
u the day that Noah entered the **Lk 17:27** *891*
business *with this* **u** I come *back.*' **Lk 19:13** *1722, 3739*
U I MAKE YOUR ENEMIES **Lk 20:43** *2193*
u the times of the Gentiles are fulfilled. **Lk 21:24** *891*
pass away **u** all things take place. **Lk 21:32** *2193*
I shall never again eat it **u** it is **Lk 22:16** *2193*
on **u** the kingdom of God comes." **Lk 22:18** *2193*
u you have denied three times that **Lk 22:34** *2193*
the whole land **u** the ninth hour, **Lk 23:44** *2193*
to stay in the city **u** you are clothed **Lk 24:49** *2193*
have kept the good wine **u** now." **Jn 2:10** *2193*
"My Father is working **u** now, **Jn 5:17** *2193*
u they called the parents of the **Jn 9:18** *2193*
crow **u** you deny Me three times. **Jn 13:38** *2193*
"**U** now you have asked for nothing **Jn 16:24** *2193*
"If I want him to remain **u** I come, **Jn 21:22** *2193*
"If I want him to remain **u** I come, **Jn 21:23** *2193*
u the day when He was taken up **Ac 1:2** *891*
u the day that He was taken up **Ac 1:22** *2193*
U I MAKE YOUR ENEMIES **Ac 2:35** *2193*
whom heaven must receive **u** *the* **Ac 3:21** *891*
put them in jail **u** the next day, **Ac 4:3** *1519*
U THERE AROSE ANOTHER KING OVER **Ac 7:18** *891*
our fathers, **u** the time of David. **Ac 7:45** *2193*
the cities **u** he came to Caesarea. **Ac 8:40** *2193*
them judges **u** Samuel the prophet. **Ac 13:20** *2193*
prolonged his message **u** midnight. **Ac 20:7** *3360*
them a long while **u** daybreak, **Ac 20:11** *891*
us **u** *we were* out of the city. **Ac 21:5** *2193*
u the sacrifice was offered for **Ac 21:26** *2193*
nor drink **u** they had killed Paul. **Ac 23:12** *2193*
nothing **u** we have killed Paul. **Ac 23:14** *2193*
to eat or drink **u** they slay him; **Ac 23:21** *2193*
custody **u** I send him to Caesar." **Ac 25:21** *2193*
U the day was about to dawn, Paul **Ac 27:33** *891*
Prophets, from morning **u** evening. **Ac 28:23** *2193*
u the Law sin was in the world, **Ro 5:13** *891*
death reigned from Adam **u** Moses, **Ro 5:14** *3360*
of childbirth together **u** now. **Ro 8:22** *891*
u the fullness of the Gentiles has come **Ro 11:25** *891*
but wait **u** the Lord comes who will **1Co 4:5** *2193*

dregs of all things, *even* **u** now. 1Co 4:13 *2193*
accustomed to the idol **u** now, 1Co 8:7 *2193*
the Lord's death **u** He comes. 1Co 11:26 *891*
time, most of whom remain **u** now, 1Co 15:6 *2193*
For He must reign **u** He has put all 1Co 15:25 *891*
remain in Ephesus **u** Pentecost; 1Co 16:8 *2193*
you will understand **u** the end; 2Co 1:13 *2193*
for **u** this very day at the reading 2Co 3:14 *891*
u the seed would come to whom the Ga 3:19 *891*
u the date set by the father. Ga 4:2 *891*
labor **u** Christ is formed in you Ga 4:19 *3360*
u we all attain to the unity of Eph 4:13 *3360*
gospel from the first day **u** now. Php 1:5 *891*
it **u** the day of Christ Jesus. Php 1:6 *891*
and blameless **u** the day of Christ; Php 1:10 *1519*
remain **u** the coming of the Lord, 1Th 4:15 *1519*
so **u** he is taken out of the way. 2Th 2:7 *2193*
U I come, give attention to the 1Tm 4:13 *2193*
u the appearing of our Lord Jesus 1Tm 6:14 *3360*
have entrusted to Him **u** that day. 2Tm 1:12 *1519*
U I make Your enemies A footstool Heb 1:13 *2193*
boast of our hope firm **u** the end. Heb 3:6 *3360*
of our assurance firm **u** the end, Heb 3:14 *3360*
full assurance of hope **u** the end, Heb 6:11 *891*
imposed **u** a time of reformation. Heb 9:10 *3360*
U His enemies be made a footstool Heb 10:13 *2193*
u the coming of the Lord. Jas 5:7 *2193*
u it gets the early and late rains. Jas 5:7 *2193*
u the day dawns and the morning 2Pe 1:19 *2193*
brother is in the darkness **u** now. 1Jn 2:9 *2193*
Be faithful **u** death, and I will Rv 2:10 *891*
what you have, hold fast **u** I come. Rv 2:25 *891*
he who keeps My deeds **u** the end, Rv 2:26 *891*
u *the number of* their fellow Rv 6:11 *2193*
u we have sealed the bond-servants Rv 7:3 *891*
u the seven plagues of the seven Rv 15:8 *891*
u the words of God will be Rv 17:17 *891*
u the thousand years were completed Rv 20:3 *891*
u the thousand years were completed. Rv 20:5 *891*

UNTIMELY
of all, as to one **u** born, 1Co 15:8 *1626*

UNTOUCHED
may sleep satisfied, **u** by evil. Pr 19:23 1077, 6485

UNTRAINED
I was chastised, Like an **u** calf; Jer 31:18 3808, 3925
they were uneducated and **u** men, Ac 4:13 *2399*

UNTRIMMED
your grapes of **u** vines you shall not Lv 25:5 5139
nor gather in *from* its **u** vines. Lv 25:11 5139

UNTRUSTWORTHY
without understanding, **u**, Ro 1:31 *802*

UNTYING
"What are you doing, **u** the colt?" Mk 11:5 *3089*
'Why are you **u** it?' Lk 19:31 *3089*
As they were **u** the colt, Lk 19:33 *3089*
"Why are you **u** the colt?" Lk 19:33 *3089*

UNUSUAL
To do His task, His **u** task, Is 28:21 2114a
had seen nothing **u** happen to him, Ac 28:6 *824*

UNVEILED
with **u** face, beholding as in a mirror 2Co 3:18 *343*

UNVENTED
"Behold, my belly is like **u** wine, Jb 32:19 3808, 6605a

UNWALLED
besides a great many **u** towns. Dt 3:5 6521
up against the land of **u** villages. Ezk 38:11 6519

UNWASHED
to eat with **u** hands does not defile Mt 15:20 *449*
with impure hands, that is, **u**. Mk 7:2 *449*

UNWAVERING
full of mercy and good fruits, **u**, Jas 3:17 *87*

UNWEIGHED
Solomon left all the utensils **u**, 1Ki 7:47

UNWHOLESOME
no **u** word proceed from your mouth, Eph 4:29 *4550*

UNWILLING
against Me and are **u** to obey Me, Lv 26:21 3808, 14
And David was **u** to move the ark of 2Sa 6:10 3808, 14
And he was **u** to take from his own 2Sa 12:4 2550
but he was **u** and would not eat 2Sa 12:17 3808, 14
"But he was **u** and went and Mt 18:30 *3756, 2309*
feast, and they were **u** to come. Mt 22:3 *3756, 2309*
but they themselves are **u** to move Mt 23:4 *3756, 2309*
under her wings, and you were **u**. Mt 23:37 *3756, 2309*
tasting *it,* He was **u** to drink. Mt 27:34 *3756, 2309*
guests, he was **u** to refuse her. Mk 6:26 *3756, 2309*
"For a while he was **u**; Lk 18:4 *3756, 2309*
u to lift up his eyes to heaven, Lk 18:13 *3756, 2309*
and you are **u** to come to Me so that Jn 5:40 *3756, 2309*
for He was **u** to walk in Judea because Jn 7:1 *3756, 2309*
were **u** to be obedient to him, Ac 7:39 *3756, 2309*
I am **u** to be a judge of these Ac 18:15 *3756, 1014*

UNWISE
the Lord, O foolish and **u** people? Dt 32:6 3808, 2450
how you walk, not as **u** men but Eph 5:15 *781*

UNWITTINGLY
'But when you **u** fail and do not Nu 15:22 7686

UNWORTHY
I am **u** of all the lovingkindness Gn 32:10 6994
'We are **u** slaves; we have done *only* Lk 17:10 *888*
judge yourselves **u** of eternal life, Ac 13:46 *3756, 514*
cup of the Lord in an **u** manner, 1Co 11:27 *371*

UPBUILDING
and all for your **u**, beloved. 2Co 12:19 *3619*

UPHARSIN
'MENĒ, MENĒ, TEKĒL, **U**.' Da 5:25 6537b

UPHAZ
from Tarshish, And gold from **U**, Jer 10:9 210
with *a belt of* pure gold of **U**. Da 10:5 210

UPHEAVED
the earth is **u** by His presence, Na 1:5 5375

UPHELD
They are **u** forever and ever; Ps 111:8 5564
His heart is **u**, he will not fear, Ps 112:8 5564
And His righteousness **u** Him. Is 59:16 5564
And My wrath **u** Me. Is 63:5 5564
is ignored And justice is never **u**. Hab 1:4 3318

UPHOLD
You **u** me in my integrity, Ps 41:12 8551
U me that I may be safe, That I Ps 119:117 5582
To establish it and to **u** it with Is 9:7 5582
Surely I will **u** you with My Is 41:10 8551
"Behold, My Servant, whom I **u**; Is 42:1 8551
and there was no one to **u**; Is 63:5 5564

UPHOLDS
And Your right hand **u** me; Ps 18:35 5582
Your right hand **u** me. Ps 63:8 8551
he **u** his throne by righteousness. Pr 20:28 5582
your God, who **u** your right hand, Is 41:13 2388
and **u** all things by the word of Heb 1:3 *5342*

UPLIFTED
withheld, And the **u** arm is broken. Jb 38:15 7311
with an **u** arm He led them out from Ac 13:17 *5308*

UPPER
it was attached at its two **u** ends. Ex 39:4
or an **u** millstone in pledge, Dt 24:6 7393
u springs and the lower springs. Jos 15:19 5942
as far as **u** Beth-horon. Jos 16:5 5945a
u springs and the lower springs. Jg 1:15 5942
an **u** millstone on Abimelech's head, Jg 9:53 7393
woman throw an **u** millstone on him 2Sa 11:21 7393
carried him up to the **u** room where 1Ki 17:19 5944
brought him down from the **u** room 1Ki 17:23 5944
u chamber which *was* in Samaria, 2Ki 1:2 5944
make a little walled **u** chamber and 2Ki 4:10 5944
and turned in to the **u** chamber and 2Ki 4:11 5944
u gate of the house of the Lord. 2Ki 15:35 5945a
by the conduit of the **u** pool, 2Ki 18:17 5945a
the roof, the **u** chamber of Ahaz, 2Ki 23:12 5944
who built lower and **u** Beth-horon, 1Ch 7:24 5945a
its storehouses, its **u** rooms, 1Ch 28:11 5944
overlaid the **u** rooms with gold. 2Ch 3:9 5944
He also built **u** Beth-horon and 2Ch 8:5 5945a
and came through the **u** gate to the 2Ch 23:20 5945a
u gate of the house of the Lord, 2Ch 27:3 5945a
the **u** outlet of the waters of Gihon 2Ch 32:30 5945a
u section of the tombs of the sons 2Ch 32:33 4608
from the **u** house of the king, Ne 3:25 5945a
as far as the **u** room of the corner. Ne 3:31 5944
Between the **u** room of the corner Ne 3:32 5944
lays the beams of His **u** chambers Ps 104:3 5944
the mountains from His **u** chambers; Ps 104:13 5944
end of the conduit of the **u** pool, Is 7:3 5945a
he stood by the conduit of the **u** pool Is 36:2 5945a
that were at the **u** Benjamin Gate, Jer 20:2 5945a
And his **u** rooms without justice, Jer 22:13 5944
roomy house With spacious **u** rooms, Jer 22:14 5944
the scribe, in the **u** court, Jer 36:10 5945a
from the direction of the **u** gate Ezk 9:2 5945a
Now the **u** chambers *were* smaller Ezk 42:5 5945a
therefore *the* **u** *chambers* were set Ezk 42:6
His **u** chambers in the heavens And Am 9:6 4609b
large **u** room furnished *and* ready; Mk 14:15 *311b*
you a large, furnished **u** room; Lk 22:12 *311b*
they went up to the **u** room where Ac 1:13 *5253*
body, they laid it in an **u** room. Ac 9:37 *5253*
they brought him into the **u** room; Ac 9:39 *5253*
Paul passed through the **u** country Ac 19:1 *510*
There were many lamps in the **u** room Ac 20:8 *5253*

UPRIGHT
of acacia wood, standing **u**. Ex 26:15 5975
of acacia wood, standing **u**. Ex 36:20 5975
Let me die the death of the **u**, Nu 23:10 3477
injustice, Righteous and **u** is He. Dt 32:4 3477
the Lord lives, you *have been* **u**, 1Sa 29:6 3477
and the Lord be with the **u**." 2Ch 19:11 2896a
and that man was blameless, **u**, Jb 1:1 3477
the earth, a blameless and **u** man, Jb 1:8 3477
a blameless and **u** man fearing God Jb 2:3 3477
Or where were the **u** destroyed? Jb 4:7 3477
If you are pure and **u**, Jb 8:6 3477
"The **u** will be appalled at this, Jb 17:8 3477
"There the **u** would reason with Him; Jb 23:7 3477
God, Who saves the **u** in heart. Ps 7:10 3477
in darkness at the **u** in heart. Ps 11:2 3477
The **u** will behold His face. Ps 11:7 3477
But we have risen and stood **u**. Ps 20:8 5749a
Good and **u** is the Lord; Ps 25:8 3477
joy, all you who are **u** in heart. Ps 32:11 3477
Praise is becoming to the **u**. Ps 33:1 3477
For the word of the Lord is **u**, Ps 33:4 3477
righteousness to the **u** in heart. Ps 36:10 3477
slay those who are **u** in conduct. Ps 37:14 3477
blameless man, and behold the **u**; Ps 37:37 3477
And the **u** shall rule over them in Ps 49:14 3477
And all the **u** in heart will glory. Ps 64:10 3477
To declare that the Lord is **u**; Ps 92:15 3477
all the **u** in heart will follow it. Ps 94:15 3477
And gladness for the **u** in heart. Ps 97:11 3477
The **u** see it and are glad; Ps 107:42 3477
In the company of the **u** and in the Ps 111:1 3477
generation of the **u** will be blessed. Ps 112:2 3477
arises in the darkness for the **u**; Ps 112:4 3477
O Lord, And **u** are Your judgments. Ps 119:137 3477
those who are **u** in their hearts. Ps 125:4 3477
The **u** will dwell in Your presence. Ps 140:13 3477
stores up sound wisdom for the **u**; Pr 2:7 3477
For the **u** will live in the land And Pr 2:21 3477
But He is intimate with the **u**. Pr 3:32 3477
I have led you in **u** paths. Pr 4:11 3476
the Lord is a stronghold to the **u**, Pr 10:29 8537
integrity of the **u** will guide them, Pr 11:3 3477
righteousness of the **u** will deliver Pr 11:6 3477
By the blessing of the **u** a city is Pr 11:11 3477
mouth of the **u** will deliver them. Pr 12:6 3477
among the **u** there is good will. Pr 14:9 3477
the tent of the **u** will flourish. Pr 14:11 3477
prayer of the **u** is His delight. Pr 15:8 3477
the path of the **u** is a highway. Pr 15:19 3477
highway of the **u** is to depart from Pr 16:17 3477
as for the pure, his conduct is **u**. Pr 21:8 3477
is in the place of the **u**. Pr 21:18 3477
as for the **u**, he makes his way sure. Pr 21:29 3477
He who leads the **u** astray in an Pr 28:10 3477
the **u** are concerned for his life. Pr 29:10 3477
And he who is **u** in the way is Pr 29:27 3477
only this, that God made men **u**, Ec 7:29 3477
O **U** One, make the path of the Is 26:7 3477
Declaring things that are **u**. Is 45:19 4339
Each one who walked in his **u** way. Is 57:2 5228
he touched me and made me stand **u**. Da 8:18 5921, 5977
am about to tell you and stand **u**, Da 10:11 5921, 5977
there is no **u** *person* among men. Mi 7:2 3477
The most **u** like a thorn hedge. Mi 7:4 3477
he stood **u** and *began* to walk; Ac 3:8 *2476*
"Stand **u** on your feet." Ac 14:10 *3717*

UPRIGHTLY
Do you judge **u**, O sons of men? Ps 58:1 4339
He withhold from those who walk **u**. Ps 84:11 8549
do good To the one walking **u**? Mi 2:7 3477
how devoutly and **u** and blamelessly 1Th 2:10 *1346*

UPRIGHTNESS
or for the **u** of your heart that you Dt 9:5 3476
and **u** of heart toward You; 1Ki 3:6 3483
in integrity of heart and **u**, 1Ki 9:4 3476
the heart and delight in **u**, 1Ch 29:17 4339
words are *from* the **u** of my heart, Jb 33:3 3476
Let integrity and **u** preserve me, Ps 25:21 3476
A scepter of **u** is the scepter of Your Ps 45:6 4334
will judge the peoples with **u** And Ps 67:4 4334
They are performed in truth and **u**. Ps 111:8 3477
thanks to You with **u** of heart, Ps 119:7 3476
those who leave the paths of **u** To Pr 2:13 3476
who walks in his **u** fears the Lord, Pr 14:2 3476
to strike the noble for *their* **u**. Pr 17:26 3476
He deals unjustly in the land of **u**, Is 26:10 5228
in the street, And **u** cannot enter. Is 59:14 5228
he walked with Me in peace and **u**, Mal 2:6 4334

UPROAR
is the city making such an **u**?" 1Ki 1:41 1993
so that the city is in an **u**. 1Ki 1:45 1949
Why are the nations in an **u** And Ps 2:1 7283
Surely they make an **u** for nothing; Ps 39:6 1993
The nations made an **u**, Ps 46:6 1993
The **u** of those who rise against Ps 74:23 7588
behold, Your enemies make an **u** Ps 83:2 1993
A sound of the **u** of kingdoms, Of Is 13:4 7588
the **u** of many peoples Who roar Is 17:12 1995
You subdue the **u** of aliens; Is 25:5 7588
"A voice of **u** from the city, a Is 66:6 7588
a mob and set the city in an **u**; Ac 17:5 *2350b*
After the **u** had ceased, Paul Ac 20:1 *2351*
out the facts because of the **u**, Ac 21:34 *2351*
And there occurred a great **u**; Ac 23:9 *2906*
purified, without *any* crowd or **u**. Ac 24:18 *2351*

UPROOT
and He will **u** Israel from this 1Ki 14:15 5428
then I will **u** you from My land 2Ch 7:20 5428
And would **u** all my increase. Jb 31:12 8327
And **u** you from the land of the Ps 52:5 8327
and a time to **u** what is planted. Ec 3:2 6131
"Behold I am about to **u** them from Jer 12:14 5428
will **u** the house of Judah from among Jer 12:14 5428
listen, then I will **u** that nation, Jer 12:17 5428
that nation, **u** and destroy it," Jer 12:17 5428
or concerning a kingdom to **u**, Jer 18:7 5428
I will plant you and not **u** you; Jer 42:10 5428
I have planted I am about to **u**, Jer 45:4 5428

you may **u** the wheat with them. **Mt 13:29** *1610*

UPROOTED
and the LORD **u** them from their **Dt 29:28** 5428
And He has **u** my hope like a tree. **Jb 19:10** 5265
eat, And let my crops be **u**. **Jb 31:8** 8327
ruins, And You have **u** the cities; **Ps 9:6** 5428
the treacherous will be **u** from it. **Pr 2:22** 5255
about that after I have **u** them, **Jer 12:15** 5428
for his sovereignty will be **u** and **Da 11:4** 5428
out at noon And Ekron will be **u**. **Zph 2:4** 6131
Father did not plant shall be **u**. **Mt 15:13** *1610*
'Be **u** and be planted in the sea'; **Lk 17:6** *1610*
without fruit, doubly dead, **u**; **Jude 1:12** *1610*

UPSET
of it, for the oxen nearly **u** *it*. **2Sa 6:6** 8058
ark, because the oxen nearly **u** *it*. **1Ch 13:9** 8058
These men who have **u** the world **Ac 17:6** *387*
and they **u** the faith of some. **2Tm 2:18** *396*

UPSETTING
because they are **u** whole families, **Ti 1:11** *396*

UPSIDE
and turned it **u** down so that the **Jg 7:13** 4605
wiping it and turning it **u** down. **2Ki 21:13** 5921, 6440

UPWARD
shall have *their* wings spread **u**, **Ex 25:20** 4605
cherubim had *their* wings spread **u**, **Ex 37:9** 4605
from twenty years old and **u**, **Ex 38:26** 4605
are from sixty years old and **u**, **Lv 27:7** 4605
from twenty years old and **u**, **Nu 1:3** 4605
from twenty years old and **u**, **Nu 1:18** 4605
male from twenty years old and **u**, **Nu 1:20** 4605
male from twenty years old and **u**, **Nu 1:22** 4605
from twenty years old and **u**, **Nu 1:24** 4605
from twenty years old and **u**, **Nu 1:26** 4605
from twenty years old and **u**, **Nu 1:28** 4605
from twenty years old and **u**, **Nu 1:30** 4605
from twenty years old and **u**, **Nu 1:32** 4605
from twenty years old and **u**, **Nu 1:34** 4605
from twenty years old and **u**, **Nu 1:36** 4605
from twenty years old and **u**, **Nu 1:38** 4605
from twenty years old and **u**, **Nu 1:40** 4605
from twenty years old and **u**, **Nu 1:42** 4605
from twenty years old and **u**, **Nu 1:45** 4605
every male from a month old and **u** **Nu 3:15** 4605
every male from a month old and **u**, **Nu 3:22** 4605
every male from a month old and **u**, **Nu 3:28** 4605
every male from a month old and **u**, **Nu 3:34** 4605
every male from a month old and **u**, **Nu 3:39** 4605
of Israel from a month old and **u**, **Nu 3:40** 4605
of names from a month old and **u**, **Nu 3:43** 4605
from thirty years and **u**, **Nu 4:3** 4605
from thirty years and **u** to fifty years **Nu 4:23** 4605
from thirty years and **u** even to fifty **Nu 4:30** 4605
from thirty years and **u** even to fifty **Nu 4:35** 4605
from thirty years and **u** even to fifty **Nu 4:39** 4605
from thirty years and **u** even to fifty **Nu 4:43** 4605
from thirty years and **u** even to fifty **Nu 4:47** 4605
from twenty-five years old and **u** **Nu 8:24** 4605
from twenty years old and **u**, **Nu 14:29** 4605
from twenty years old and **u**, **Nu 26:2** 4605
from twenty years old and **u**, **Nu 26:4** 4605
every male from a month old and **u**, **Nu 26:62** 4605
from twenty years old and **u**, **Nu 32:11** 4605
of Akrabbim, from Sela and **u**. **Jg 1:36** 4605
the people from his shoulders **u**. **1Sa 10:23** 4605
root downward and bear fruit **u**. **2Ki 19:30** 4605
from thirty years old and **u**, **1Ch 23:3** 4605
LORD, from twenty years old and **u**. **1Ch 23:24** 4605
from twenty years old and **u**. **1Ch 23:27** 4605
those from twenty years old and **u** and **2Ch 25:5** 4605
the males from thirty years old and **u** **2Ch 31:16** 4605
born for trouble, As sparks fly **u**. **Jb 5:7** 1361b
path of life *leads* **u** for the wise That **Pr 15:24** 4605
that the breath of man ascends **u** and **Ec 3:21** 4605
king and their God as they face **u**. **Is 8:21** 4605
they roll **u** in a column of smoke. **Is 9:18** 55
root downward and bear fruit **u**. **Is 37:31** 4605
the appearance of His loins and **u** **Ezk 1:27** 4605
and from His loins and **u** **Ezk 8:2** 4605
went **u** by stages on all sides of the **Ezk 41:7** 4605
were set back from the ground **u**. **Ezk 42:6** 4605
They turn, *but* not **u**, **Hos 7:16** 5920
for the prize of the **u** call of God in **Php 3:14** *507*

UPWARDS
from twenty years old and **u**, **2Ch 31:17** 4605
hearth shall extend **u** four horns. **Ezk 43:15** 4605

UR
his birth, in **U** of the Chaldeans. **Gn 11:28** 218a
together from **U** of the Chaldeans **Gn 11:31** 218a
you out of **U** of the Chaldeans, **Gn 15:7** 218a
Hararite, Eliphal the son of **U**, **1Ch 11:35** 218b
him out from **U** of the Chaldees, **Ne 9:7** 218a

URBANUS
Greet **U**, our fellow worker in Christ **Ro 16:9** *3773*

URGE
"Do not **u** me to leave you *or* turn **Ru 1:16** 6293
I **u** you to keep up your courage, **Ac 27:22** *3867*
I **u** you, brethren, by **Ro 12:1** *3870*
Now I **u** you, brethren, by our Lord **Ro 15:30** *3870*
Now I **u** you, brethren, keep your **Ro 16:17** *3870*
Now I **u** you, brethren **1Co 16:15** *3870*
Wherefore I **u** you to reaffirm *your* **2Co 2:8** *3870*
we also **u** you not to receive the **2Co 6:1** *3870*
So I thought it necessary to **u** the **2Co 9:5** *3870*
Now I, Paul, myself **u** you by the **2Co 10:1** *3870*
You too, *I* **u** *you,* rejoice in **Php 2:18**
I **u** Euodia and I urge Syntyche to **Php 4:2** *3870*
I urge Euodia and I **u** Syntyche to **Php 4:2** *3870*
But we **u** you, brethren, to excel **1Th 4:10** *3870*
We **u** you, brethren, admonish **1Th 5:14** *3870*
I **u** that entreaties *and* prayers, **1Tm 2:1** *3870*
u the young men to be sensible; **Ti 2:6** *3870*
U bondslaves to be subject to **Ti 2:9**
I **u** *you* all the more to do this, **Heb 13:19** *3870*
But I **u** you, brethren, bear with **Heb 13:22** *3870*
I **u** you as aliens and strangers to **1Pe 2:11** *3870*

URGED
Yet he **u** them strongly, so they **Gn 19:3** 6484
morning dawned, the angels **u** Lot, **Gn 19:15** 213
Thus he **u** him and he took *it.* **Gn 33:11** 6484
The Egyptians **u** the people, **Ex 12:33** 2388, 5921
daily with her words and **u** him, **Jg 16:16** 509
but his father-in-law **u** him so **Jg 19:7** 6484
together with the woman **u** him, **1Sa 28:23** 6555
Although he **u** him, he would not **2Sa 13:25** 6555
But when Absalom **u** him, **2Sa 13:27** 6555
they **u** him until he was ashamed, **2Ki 2:17** 6484
And he **u** him to take *it,* but he **2Ki 5:16** 6484
And he **u** him, and bound two **2Ki 5:23** 6555
But they **u** Him, saying, **Lk 24:29** *3849*
had been baptized, she **u** us, **Ac 16:15** *3870*
u him not to venture into the theater. **Ac 19:31** *3870*
So we **u** Titus that as he **2Co 8:6** *3870*
I **u** Titus *to go,* and I sent the **2Co 12:18** *3870*
As I **u** you upon my departure for **1Tm 1:3** *3870*

URGENT
because the king's matter was **u**." **1Sa 21:8** 5169
is the decree from the king *so* **u**?" **Da 2:15** 2685
because the king's command *was* **u** **Da 3:22** 2685

URGENTLY
Did I not **u** send to you to call you? **Nu 22:37** 7971

URGES
for him, For his hunger **u** him *on.* **Pr 16:26** 404

URGING
Meanwhile the disciples were **u** Him, **Jn 4:31** *2065*
were **u** them to continue in the **Ac 13:43** *3982*
and they were **u** him, **Ac 25:2** *3870*
begging us with much **u** for the favor **2Co 8:4** *3874*

URI
by name Bezalel, the son of **U**, **Ex 31:2** 221
by name Bezalel the son of **U**, **Ex 35:30** 221
the son of **U**, the son of Hur, **Ex 38:22** 221
Geber the son of **U**, **1Ki 4:19** 221
Hur became the father of **U**, **1Ch 2:20** 221
U became the father of Bezalel. **1Ch 2:20** 221
altar, which Bezalel the son of **U**, **2Ch 1:5** 221
Shallum, Telem and **U**. **Ezr 10:24** 221

URIAH
the wife of **U** the Hittite?" **2Sa 11:3** 223a
"Send me **U** the Hittite." **2Sa 11:6** 223a
So Joab sent **U** to David. **2Sa 11:6** 223a
When **U** came to him, David asked **2Sa 11:7** 223a
Then David said to **U**, **2Sa 11:8** 223a
And **U** went out of the king's house, **2Sa 11:8** 223a
But **U** slept at the door of the **2Sa 11:9** 223a
"**U** did not go down to his house," **2Sa 11:10** 223a
to his house," David said to **U**, **2Sa 11:10** 223a
U said to David, **2Sa 11:11** 223a
Then David said to **U**, **2Sa 11:12** 223a
So **U** remained in Jerusalem that **2Sa 11:12** 223a
and sent *it* by the hand of **U**. **2Sa 11:14** 223a
"Place **U** in the front line of the **2Sa 11:15** 223a
that he put **U** at the place where **2Sa 11:16** 223a
and **U** the Hittite also died. **2Sa 11:17** 223a
U the Hittite is dead also.' " **2Sa 11:21** 223a
U the Hittite is also dead." **2Sa 11:24** 223a
Now when the wife of **U** heard that **2Sa 11:26** 223a
heard that **U** her husband was dead, **2Sa 11:26** 223a
You have struck down **U** the Hittite **2Sa 12:9** 223a
have taken the wife of **U** the Hittite **2Sa 12:10** 223a
U the Hittite; thirty-seven in all. **2Sa 23:39** 223a
in the case of **U** the Hittite. **1Ki 15:5** 223a
U the Hittite, Zabad the son of **1Ch 11:41** 223a
Meremoth the son of **U** the priest, **Ezr 8:33** 223a
the son of **U** the son of Hakkoz **Ne 3:4** 223a
After him Meremoth the son of **U** **Ne 3:21** 223a
Mattithiah, Shema, Anaiah, **U**, **Ne 8:4** 223a
U the priest and Zechariah the son **Is 8:2** 223a
U the son of Shemaiah from **Jer 26:20** 223b
but **U** heard *it,* and he was afraid **Jer 26:21** 223b
And they brought **U** from Egypt and **Jer 26:23** 223b
Bathsheba who had been the wife of **U**. **Mt 1:6** *3774*

URIAH'S
child that **U** widow bore to David, **2Sa 12:15** 223a

URIEL
Tahath his son, **U** his son, Uzziah **1Ch 6:24** 222
the sons of Kohath, **U** the chief, **1Ch 15:5** 222
and for the Levites, for **U**, **1Ch 15:11** 222
the daughter of **U** of Gibeah. **2Ch 13:2** 222

URIJAH
and King Ahaz sent to **U** the priest **2Ki 16:10** 223a
So **U** the priest built an altar; **2Ki 16:11** 223a
thus **U** the priest made *it,* **2Ki 16:11** 223a
King Ahaz commanded **U** the priest, **2Ki 16:15** 223a
So **U** the priest did according to **2Ki 16:16** 223a

URIM
of judgment the **U** and the Thummim, **Ex 28:30** 224
he put the **U** and the Thummim. **Lv 8:8** 224
judgment of the **U** before the LORD. **Nu 27:21** 224
Your Thummim and Your **U** *belong* to **Dt 33:8** 224
by dreams or by **U** or by prophets. **1Sa 28:6** 224
stood up with **U** and Thummim. **Ezr 2:63** 224
a priest arose with **U** and Thummim. **Ne 7:65** 224

URINE
and drink their own **u** with you?" **2Ki 18:27** 7890
and drink their own **u** with you?" **Is 36:12** 7890

USE
so of what **u** then is **Gn 25:32**
make *any* like it, to **u** as perfume, **Ex 30:38** 7381a
beasts may be put to any other **u**, **Lv 7:24** 4399
any article of which **u** is made **Lv 11:32** 4399
can **u** them as permanent slaves. **Lv 25:46** 5647
u a razor over their whole body and **Nu 8:7** 5674a
and you shall **u** them for summoning **Nu 10:2** 1961
those who **u** proverbs say, **Nu 21:27** 4911b
and has not begun to **u** its fruit? **Dt 20:6** 2490c
another man would begin to **u** its fruit. **Dt 20:6** 2490c
and you shall **u** the spoil of your **Dt 20:14** 398
but you will not **u** its fruit. **Dt 28:30** 2490c
I will **u** My arrows on them. **Dt 32:23** 3615
donkeys and **u** *them* for his work. **1Sa 8:16** 6213a
to the **u** of each lampstand; **1Ch 28:15** 5656
I will **u** force against you." **Ne 13:21** 7971
"Can a vigorous man be of **u** to God, **Jb 22:2** 5532a
of the warriors could **u** his hands. **Ps 76:5** 4672
yourself with lye And **u** much soap, **Jer 2:22** 7235a
"who **u** their tongues and declare, **Jer 23:31** 3947
take and **u** it *as* a barber's razor **Ezk 5:1** 5674a
no longer **u** it as a proverb in Israel. **Ezk 12:23** 4911b
not going to **u** this proverb in Israel **Ezk 18:3** 4911b
of the two ways, to **u** divination; **Ezk 21:21** 7080
be for common **u** for the city, **Ezk 48:15** 2455
nor did I **u** any ointment at all until **Da 10:3** 5480a
do not **u** meaningless repetition as **Mt 6:7** *945*
Why does it even **u** up the ground?' **Lk 13:7** *2673*
you have not been faithful in the **u** **Lk 16:11**
you have not been faithful in *the* **u** **Lk 16:12**
lump one vessel for honorable **u** and **Ro 9:21** *5092*
use and another for common **u**? **Ro 9:21** *819*
and those who **u** the world, as **1Co 7:31** *5530*
they did not make full **u** of it; **1Co 7:31** *2710*
does not **u** the milk of the flock? **1Co 9:7** *2068*
we did not **u** this right, **1Co 9:12** *5530*
so as not to make full **u** of my right **1Co 9:18** *2710*
we **u** great boldness in *our* speech, **2Co 3:12** *5530*
when present I *need* not **u** severity, **2Co 13:10** *5530*
destined to perish with **u**) **Col 2:22** *671*
but **u** a little wine for the sake **1Tm 5:23** *5530*
What **u** is it, my brethren, if someone **Jas 2:14** *3786*
for *their* body, what **u** is that? **Jas 2:16** *3786*
and do not **u** your freedom as a **1Pe 2:16** *2192*
but **u** *it* as bondslaves of God. **1Pe 2:16**

USED
But a mist **u** to rise from the **Gn 2:6**
whole earth **u** the same language **Gn 11:1** 1961
And they **u** brick for stone, and **Gn 11:3** 1961
stone, and they **u** tar for mortar. **Gn 11:3** 1961
the water in the skin was **u** up, **Gn 21:15** 3615
LORD had **u** against the Egyptians, **Ex 14:31** 6213a
the utensils of the tabernacle **u** **Ex 27:19**
Now Moses **u** to take the tent and **Ex 33:7**
Thus the LORD **u** to speak to Moses **Ex 33:11**
the gold that was **u** for the work, **Ex 38:24** 6213a
for which the leather is **u**, **Lv 13:51** 4399
that they may be **u** in the service **Nu 7:5** 5647
which we **u** to eat free in Egypt, **Nu 11:5**
where you **u** to sow your seed and **Dt 11:10**
u to gather up *scraps* under my table; **Jg 1:7**
She **u** to sit under the palm **Jg 4:5**
new ropes which have not been **u**, **Jg 16:11** 4399
He **u** to go annually on circuit **1Sa 7:16**
to inquire of God, he **u** to say, **1Sa 9:9**
Absalom **u** to rise early and **2Sa 15:2**
"Formerly they **u** to say, **2Sa 20:18**
and **u** to pay the king of Israel **2Ki 3:4**
who **u** to pour water on the hands **2Ki 3:11**
witchcraft and **u** divination, **2Ki 21:6** 5172
which were **u** in *temple* service. **2Ki 25:14** 8334
even **u** the holy things of the house **2Ch 24:7** 6213a
practiced witchcraft, **u** divination, **2Ch 33:6** 5172
u it to restore and repair the house. **2Ch 34:10** 5414
His sons **u** to go and hold a **Jb 1:4**
For I **u** to go along with the **Ps 42:4**
me have **u** my *name* as a curse. **Ps 102:8** 7650
those who **u** to go in and out from **Ec 8:10**
my mother, who **u** to instruct me; **SS 8:2**
there **u** to be a thousand vines, **Is 7:23**
u to be cultivated with the hoe, **Is 7:25**
Which **u** to strike the peoples in **Is 14:6**
Whose feet **u** to carry her to **Is 23:7**
a curse will be **u** by all the exiles **Jer 29:22** 3947
which were **u** in *temple* service. **Jer 52:18** 8334
and gold, *Which* they **u** for Baal. **Hos 2:8** 6213a
When she **u** to offer sacrifices to them **Hos 2:13**
"Show Me the coin **u** for **Mt 22:19**
Every day I **u** to sit in the temple **Mt 26:55**
he **u** to enjoy listening to him. **Mk 6:20**
Now at *the* feast he **u** to release **Mk 15:6**
they **u** to follow Him and minister **Mk 15:41**
fathers **u** to treat the prophets. **Lk 6:23**
u to treat the false prophets in **Lk 6:26**
the one who **u** to sit and beg?" **Jn 9:8**
he **u** to pilfer what was put into **Jn 12:6**
younger, you **u** to gird yourself and **Jn 21:18**
whom they **u** to set down every day **Ac 3:2**
who **u** to sit at the Beautiful Gate of **Ac 3:10**
and garments that Dorcas **u** to make **Ac 9:39**
word of the Lord, how He **u** to say, **Ac 11:16**
visiting there **u** to spend their time in **Ac 17:21**
I **u** to imprison and beat those who **Ac 22:19**

he also **u** to send for him quite often Ac 24:26
they **u** supporting cables in Ac 27:17 *5530*
But I have **u** none of these things. 1Co 9:15 *5530*
a child, I **u** to speak like a child, 1Co 13:11
who **u** to put a veil over his face 2Co 3:13
how I **u** to persecute the church of Ga 1:13
he **u** to eat with the Gentiles; Ga 2:12
you, we **u** to give you this order: 2Th 3:10
in God, **u** to adorn themselves, 1Pe 3:5

USEFUL
Or a wise man be **u** to himself? Jb 22:2 5532a
is it *then* **u** for anything? Ezk 15:4 6743b
sanctified, **u** to the Master, 2Tm 2:21 *2173*
for he is **u** to me for service. 2Tm 4:11 *2173*
now is **u** both to you and to me. Phm 1:11 *2173*
vegetation **u** to those for whose sake Heb 6:7 *2111*

USELESS
"Should he argue with **u** talk, Jb 15:3 3808, 5532a
For their deceitfulness is **u**. Ps 119:118 8267
it is **u** to spread the *baited* net In the Pr 1:17 2600
Like the legs *which* are **u** to Pr 26:7 1802a
Looking for help was **u**; La 4:17 1892
"It is **u** either for the soil or Lk 14:35 *3777, 2111*
TOGETHER THEY HAVE BECOME U; Ro 3:12 *889*
of the wise, THAT THEY ARE U." 1Co 3:20 *3152*
wrangle about words, which is **u** 2Tm 2:14 *3762, 5539*
who formerly was **u** to you, Phm 1:11 *890*
that faith without works is **u**? Jas 2:20 *692*
they render you neither **u** nor 2Pe 1:8 *692*

USELESSLY
also, you will sow your seed **u**, Lv 26:16 7385b
'Your strength will be spent **u**, Lv 26:20 7385b
not **u** kindle *fire on* My altar! Mal 1:10 2600

USELESSNESS
because of its weakness and **u** Heb 7:18 *512*

USES
which he indeed **u** for divination? Gn 44:5 5172
the fire, one who **u** divination, Dt 18:10 7080
Who **u** his neighbor's services Jer 22:13 5647
Law is good, if one **u** it lawfully, 1Tm 1:8 *5530*

USING
u 600 *shekels of* gold on each 1Ki 10:16 5927
u three minas of gold on each 1Ki 10:17 5927
u both the right hand and the left 1Ch 12:2
u 600 *shekels of* beaten gold on 2Ch 9:15 5927
u three hundred shekels of gold on 2Ch 9:16 5927
What do you mean by **u** this proverb Ezk 18:2 4911b
and are not **u** a figure of speech. Jn 16:29 *3004*

USUAL
the harp with his hand, as **u**; 1Sa 18:10 3117
The king sat on his seat as **u**, 1Sa 20:25 6471

USUALLY
times more than it was **u** heated. Da 3:19 2370

USURIOUS
'Do not take **u** interest from him, Lv 25:36 8636

USURY
"You are exacting **u**, Ne 5:7 4855
Please, let us leave off this **u**. Ne 5:10 4855
his wealth by interest and **u** Gathers Pr 28:8 8636

UTENSILS
of pure gold, with all these **u**. Ex 25:39 3627
shall make all its **u** of bronze. Ex 27:3 3627
"All the **u** of the tabernacle *used* Ex 27:19 3627
and the table and all its **u**, Ex 30:27 3627
and the lampstand and its **u**, Ex 30:27 3627
of burnt offering and all its **u**, Ex 30:28 3627
the table also and its **u**, Ex 31:8 3627
gold lampstand with all its **u**, Ex 31:8 3627
offering also with all its **u**, Ex 31:9 3627
and its poles, and all its **u**, Ex 35:13 3627
lampstand also for the light and its **u** Ex 35:14 3627
grating, its poles, and all its **u**, Ex 35:16 3627
the **u** which were on the table, Ex 37:16 3627
its **u** from a talent of pure gold. Ex 37:24 3627
He made all the **u** of the altar, Ex 38:3 3627
he made all its **u** of bronze. Ex 38:3 3627
and all the **u** of the altar, Ex 38:30 3627
the table, all its **u**, Ex 39:36 3627
of lamps and all its **u**, Ex 39:37 3627
grating, its poles and all its **u**, Ex 39:39 3627
of burnt offering and all its **u**, Ex 40:10 3627
anointed the altar and all its **u**, Lv 8:11 3627
and the **u** of the sanctuary with Nu 3:31 3627
and they shall put it and all its **u** in a Nu 4:10 3627
shall take all the **u** of service, Nu 4:12 3627
"They shall also put on it all its **u** by Nu 4:14 3627
basins, all the **u** of the altar; Nu 4:14 3627
and the altar and all its **u**; Nu 7:1 3627
silver of the **u** *was* 2,400 *shekels*, Nu 7:85 3627
even all these **u** which Hiram made 1Ki 7:45 3627
Solomon left all the **u** *unweighed*, 1Ki 7:47 3627
the silver and the gold and the **u**, 1Ki 7:51 3627
of meeting and all the holy **u**, 1Ki 8:4 3627
silver and gold and **u**. 1Ki 15:15 3627
all the gold and silver and all the **u** 2Ki 14:14 3627
had charge of the **u** of service, 1Ch 9:28 3627
over the furniture and over all the **u** 1Ch 9:29 3627
and the pillars and the bronze **u**. 1Ch 18:8 3627
and all its **u** for its service." 1Ch 23:26 3627
for all the **u** of service in the house of 1Ch 28:13 3627
for the golden **u**, the weight of 1Ch 28:14
all **u** for every kind of service; 1Ch 28:14 3627
for the silver **u**, the weight *of* 1Ch 28:14
all **u** for every kind of service; 1Ch 28:14 3627
shovels, the forks and all its **u**, 2Ch 4:16 3627
all these **u** in great quantities, 2Ch 4:18 3627
silver and the gold and all the **u**, 2Ch 5:1 3627
the holy **u** which *were* in the tent; 2Ch 5:5 3627
silver and gold and **u**. 2Ch 15:18 3627
into **u** for the house of the LORD, 2Ch 24:14 3627
u for the service and the burnt 2Ch 24:14 3627
and pans and **u** of gold and silver. 2Ch 24:14 3627
and all the **u** which were found in 2Ch 25:24 3627
the **u** of the house of God, 2Ch 28:24 3627
he cut the **u** of the house of God in 2Ch 28:24 3627
burnt offering with all of its **u**, 2Ch 29:18 3627
of showbread with all of its **u**. 2Ch 29:18 3627
all the **u** which King Ahaz had 2Ch 29:19 3627
and silver **u** of the house of God Ezr 5:14 3984
'Take these **u**, go *and* deposit Ezr 5:15 3984
and silver **u** of the house of God, Ezr 6:5 3984
"Also the **u** which are given to Ezr 7:19 3984
the silver, the gold and the **u**, Ezr 8:25 3627
and silver **u** *worth* 100 talents, Ezr 8:26 3627
and two **u** of fine shiny bronze, Ezr 8:27 3627
to the LORD, and the **u** are holy; Ezr 8:28 3627
out silver and gold and the **u**, Ezr 8:30 3627
and the gold and the **u** were weighed Ezr 8:33 3627
there are the **u** of the sanctuary, Ne 10:39 3627
the frankincense, the **u** and Ne 13:5 3627
there the **u** of the house of God Ne 13:9 3627

UTHAI
U the son of Ammihud, the son of 1Ch 9:4 5793
U and Zabbud, and 70 males with Ezr 8:14 5793

UTMOST
Up to the **u** bound of the everlasting Gn 49:26 8379
I hate them with the **u** hatred; Ps 139:22 8503
wrath has come upon them to the **u**. 1Th 2:16 *5056*

UTTER
land of **u** gloom as darkness *itself*, Jb 10:22 5890
of curses and lies which they **u**. Ps 59:12 5608
My tongue also will **u** Your Ps 71:24 1897
I will **u** dark sayings of old, Ps 78:2 5042
Let my lips **u** praise, For You Ps 119:171 5042
They shall eagerly **u** the memory of Ps 145:7 5042
"I was almost in **u** ruin In the Pr 5:14 3605
"For my mouth will **u** truth; Pr 8:7 1897
your mind will **u** perverse things. Pr 23:33 1696
He will **u** a shout, yes, He will Is 42:13 7321
And **u** His voice from His holy Jer 25:30 5414
visions and **u** lying divinations. Ezk 13:9 7080
Egypt an **u** waste and desolation, Ezk 29:10 2721b
u a bitter lamentation *and* say, Mi 2:4 5091
And **u** disgrace *will come* upon your Hab 2:16 7022
I WILL U THINGS HIDDEN SINCE THE Mt 13:35 *2044*
and whatever blasphemies they **u**; Mk 3:28 *987*
but I **u** words of sober truth. Ac 26:25 *669*
unless you **u** by the tongue speech 1Co 14:9 *1325*

UTTERANCE
Nor will I alter the **u** of My lips. Ps 89:34 4161
u of my lips Was in Your presence. Jer 17:16 4161
for I will give you **u** and wisdom Lk 21:15 *4750*
as the Spirit was giving them **u**. Ac 2:4 *669*
and to hear an **u** from His mouth. Ac 22:14 *5456*
in faith and **u** and knowledge and 2Co 8:7 *3056*
and that **u** may be given to me in the Eph 6:19 *3056*
through prophetic **u** with the laying 1Tm 4:14 *4394*
such an **u** as this was made to Him 2Pe 1:17 *5456*
heard this **u** made from heaven 2Pe 1:18 *5456*

UTTERANCES
their **u** to the end of the world. Ps 19:4 4405
"All the **u** of my mouth are in Pr 8:8 561
neither Him nor the **u** of the prophets Ac 13:27 *5456*
do not despise prophetic **u**. 1Th 5:20 *4394*
as one who is speaking the **u** of God; 1Pe 4:11 *3051*

UTTERED
No one **u** a word against any of the Jos 10:21 2782
which you **u** a curse in my hearing, Jg 17:2 422
And the Most High **u** His voice. 2Sa 22:14 5414
but he **u** *his* prophecy against me Ne 6:12 1696
"To whom have you **u** words? Jb 26:4 5046
And the Most High **u** His voice, Ps 18:13 5414
Which my lips **u** And my mouth spoke Ps 66:14 6475
and the judgments **u** by His mouth, Ps 105:5
The deep **u** forth its voice, It Hab 3:10 5414
And Jesus **u** a loud cry, and Mk 15:37 *863*
while suffering, He **u** no threats, 1Pe 2:23 *546*
seven peals of thunder **u** their voices Rv 10:3 *2980*

UTTERING
and **u** from the heart lying words. Is 59:13 1897
a man and a mouth **u** great *boasts*. Da 7:8 4449
eyes and a mouth **u** great *boasts* Da 7:20 4449

UTTERLY
that I will **u** blot out the memory Ex 17:14 4229a
LORD alone, shall be **u** destroyed. Ex 22:20 2763a
but you shall **u** overthrow them and Ex 23:24 2040
I will **u** destroy their cities." Nu 21:2 2763a
then they **u** destroyed them and Nu 21:3 2763a
time and **u** destroyed the men, Dt 2:34 2763a
"We **u** destroyed them, as we Dt 3:6 2763a
of Heshbon, **u** destroying the men, Dt 3:6 2763a
on it, but will be **u** destroyed. Dt 4:26 8045
then you shall **u** destroy them. Dt 7:2 2763a
you shall **u** detest it and you Dt 7:26 8262
it and you shall **u** abhor it, Dt 7:26 8581
"You shall **u** destroy all the Dt 12:2 6
u destroying it and all that is in Dt 13:15 2763a
"But you shall **u** destroy them, Dt 20:17 2763a
and Og, whom you **u** destroyed. Jos 2:10 2763a
They **u** destroyed everything in Jos 6:21 2763a
u destroyed all the inhabitants of Ai. Jos 8:26 2763a
Ai, and had **u** destroyed it Jos 10:1 2763a
he **u** destroyed it and every person Jos 10:28 2763a
and he **u** destroyed that day every Jos 10:35 2763a
And he **u** destroyed it and every Jos 10:37 2763a
and **u** destroyed every person *who* Jos 10:39 2763a
he **u** destroyed all who breathed, Jos 10:40 2763a
of the sword, **u** destroying *them;* Jos 11:11 2763a
the sword, *and* **u** destroyed them; Jos 11:12 2763a
that he might **u** destroy them, Jos 11:20 2763a
Joshua **u** destroyed them with their Jos 11:21 2763a
in Zephath, and **u** destroyed it. Jg 1:17 2763a
'**U** curse its inhabitants; Jg 5:23 779
you shall **u** destroy every man and Jg 21:11 2763a
and **u** destroy all that he has, 1Sa 15:3 2763a
and **u** destroyed all the people 1Sa 15:8 2763a
not willing to destroy them **u**; 1Sa 15:9 2763a
worthless, that they **u** destroyed. 1Sa 15:9 2763a
the rest we have **u** destroyed." 1Sa 15:15 2763a
'Go and **u** destroy the sinners, the 1Sa 15:18 2763a
have **u** destroyed the Amalekites. 1Sa 15:20 2763a
Israel were unable to destroy **u**, 1Ki 9:21 2763a
you, and will **u** sweep you away, 1Ki 21:21 1197a
and destroyed them **u** to this day, 1Ch 4:41 2763a
nations which my fathers **u** destroyed 2Ch 32:14 2763a
u swept away by sudden terrors! Ps 73:19 8552
Do not forsake me **u**! Ps 119:8 5704, 3966
do not take the word of truth **u** out Ps 119:43 5704, 3966
The arrogant **u** deride me, *Yet* I do Ps 119:51 5704, 3966
love, It would be **u** despised." SS 8:7 936
And the land is **u** desolate, Is 6:11 8077
And the LORD will **u** destroy The Is 11:15 2763a
As those who are **u** stricken. Is 16:7 389
of white cloth will be **u** dejected. Is 19:9 954
And the city will be **u** laid low. Is 32:19 8218
He has **u** destroyed them, He has Is 34:2 2763a
turned back *and* be **u** put to shame, Is 42:17 954
And the nations will be **u** ruined. Is 60:12 2717b
Surely You have **u** deceived this Jer 4:10 5378
They will be **u** ashamed, because Jer 20:11 3966
and I will **u** destroy them and Jer 25:9 2763a
Slay and **u** destroy them," Jer 50:21 2763a
up like heaps And **u** destroy her, Jer 50:26 2763a
Unless You have **u** rejected us La 5:22 3988a
"**U** slay old men, young men, Ezk 9:6 4889
and they were **u** astonished, Mk 6:51 *3029, 1537, 4053*
They were **u** astonished, Mk 7:37 *5249*
be **u** destroyed from among the people Ac 3:23 *1842*
sin would become **u** sinful. Ro 7:13 *5236*

UTTERS
mouth of the righteous **u** wisdom, Ps 37:30 1897
in the city she **u** her sayings: Pr 1:21 559
A false witness *who* **u** lies, Pr 6:19 6315
But a false witness **u** lies. Pr 14:5 6315
But he who **u** lies is treacherous. Pr 14:25 6315
The poor man **u** supplications, But Pr 18:23 1696
When He **u** His voice, *there is* a Jer 10:13 5414
When He **u** His voice, *there is* a Jer 51:16 5414
LORD **u** His voice before His army; Jl 2:11 5414
And **u** His voice from Jerusalem, Jl 3:16 5414
And from Jerusalem He **u** His voice; Am 1:2 5414

UZ
U and Hul and Gether and Mash. Gn 10:23 5780
U his firstborn and Buz his Gn 22:21 5780
the sons of Dishan: **U** and Aran. Gn 36:28 5780
Asshur, Arpachshad, Lud, Aram, **U**, 1Ch 1:17 5780
sons of Dishan *were* **U** and Aran. 1Ch 1:42 5780
There was a man in the land of **U** whose Jb 1:1 5780
all the kings of the land of **U**, Jer 25:20 5780
Edom, Who dwells in the land of **U**; La 4:21 5780

UZAI
Palal the son of **U** *made repairs* in Ne 3:25 186

UZAL
and Hadoram and **U** and Diklah Gn 10:27 187
Hadoram, **U**, Diklah, 1Ch 1:21 187
Javan paid for your wares from **U**; Ezk 27:19 187

UZZA
his own house, in the garden of **U**, 2Ki 21:18 5798
in his grave in the garden of **U**, 2Ki 21:26 5798
became the father of **U** and Ahihud. 1Ch 8:7 5798
and **U** and Ahio drove the cart. 1Ch 13:7 5798
U put out his hand to hold the 1Ch 13:9 5798
of the LORD burned against **U**, 1Ch 13:10 5798
of the LORD's outburst against **U**; 1Ch 13:11 5798
the sons of **U**, the sons of Paseah, Ezr 2:49 5798
the sons of Gazzam, the sons of **U**, Ne 7:51 5798

UZZAH
and **U** and Ahio, the sons of 2Sa 6:3 5798
U reached out toward the ark of 2Sa 6:6 5798
of the LORD burned against **U**, 2Sa 6:7 5798
of the LORD's outburst against **U**, 2Sa 6:8 5798
son, Shimei his son, **U** his son, 1Ch 6:29 5804b

UZZEN-SHEERAH
lower and upper Beth-horon, also **U**. 1Ch 7:24 242

UZZI
and Bukki became the father of **U**, 1Ch 6:5 5813
U became the father of Zerahiah, 1Ch 6:6 5813
Bukki his son, **U** his son, Zerahiah 1Ch 6:51 5813
The sons of Tola *were* **U** 1Ch 7:2 5813
The son of **U** *was* Izrahiah. 1Ch 7:3 5813
Ezbon, **U**, Uzziel, Jerimoth and 1Ch 7:7 5813
of Jeroham, and Elah the son of **U**, 1Ch 9:8 5813
son of Zerahiah, son of **U**, Ezr 7:4 5813
Jerusalem was **U** the son of Bani, Ne 11:22 5813

of Joiarib, Mattenai; of Jedaiah, U; Ne 12:19 5813
Maaseiah, Shemaiah, Eleazar, U, Ne 12:42 5813

UZZIA
U the Ashterathite, Shama and 1Ch 11:44 5814

UZZIAH
year of U king of Judah, 2Ki 15:13 5818
year of Jotham the son of U. 2Ki 15:30 5818
Jotham the son of U king of Judah 2Ki 15:32 5818
to all that his father U had done. 2Ki 15:34 5818
his son, Uriel his son, U his son and 1Ch 6:24 5818
And Jonathan the son of U had 1Ch 27:25 5818
all the people of Judah took U, 2Ch 26:1 5818
U was sixteen years old when he 2Ch 26:3 5818
Ammonites also gave tribute to U, 2Ch 26:8 5818
U built towers in Jerusalem at the 2Ch 26:9 5818
U had an army ready for battle, 2Ch 26:11 5818
U prepared for all the army 2Ch 26:14 5818
They opposed U the king and said 2Ch 26:18 5818
"It is not for you, U, 2Ch 26:18 5818
But U, with a censer in his hand 2Ch 26:19 5818
King U was a leper to the day 2Ch 26:21 5818
Now the rest of the acts of U, 2Ch 26:22 5818
So U slept with his fathers, and 2Ch 26:23 5818
to all that his father U had done; 2Ch 27:2 5818
Elijah, Shemaiah, Jehiel and U; Ezr 10:21 5818
Athaiah the son of U, Ne 11:4 5818
he saw during the reigns of U, Is 1:1 5818
the son of Jotham, the son of U, Is 7:1 5818
of Beeri, during the days of U, Hos 1:1 5818
in the days of U king of Judah, Am 1:1 5818
in the days of U king of Judah. Zch 14:5 5818
Joram, and Joram the father of U. Mt 1:8 *3604*
U was the father of Jotham, Mt 1:9 *3604*

UZZIAH'S
In the year of King U death I Is 6:1 5818

UZZIEL
Amram and Izhar and Hebron and U; Ex 6:18 5816
The sons of U: Ex 6:22 5816
the sons of Aaron's uncle U, Lv 10:4 5816
Amram and Izhar, Hebron and U; Nu 3:19 5816
was Elizaphan the son of U. Nu 3:30 5816
Neariah, Rephaiah and U, 1Ch 4:42 5816
were Amram, Izhar, Hebron and U. 1Ch 6:2 5816
were Amram, Izhar, Hebron and U. 1Ch 6:18 5816
Ezbon, Uzzi, U, Jerimoth and Iri. 1Ch 7:7 5816
of the sons of U, Amminadab the 1Ch 15:10 5816
Amram, Izhar, Hebron and U. 1Ch 23:12 5816
The sons of U *were* Micah the first 1Ch 23:20 5816
Of the sons of U, Micah; 1Ch 24:24 5816
Bukkiah, Mattaniah, U, 1Ch 25:4 5816
sons of Jeduthun, Shemaiah and U. 2Ch 29:14 5816
Next to him U the son of Harhaiah Ne 3:8 5816

UZZIELITES
and the family of the U; Nu 3:27 5817
the Hebronites and the U, 1Ch 26:23 5817

V

VACILLATING
not v when I intended to do this, 2Co 1:17
5530, 1644

VAGABOND
poverty will come in like a v And Pr 6:11 1980

VAGRANT
a v and a wanderer on the earth." Gn 4:12 5128
a v and a wanderer on the earth, Gn 4:14 5128

VAIN
name of the LORD your God in v, Ex 20:7 7723
who takes His name in v. Ex 20:7 7723
name of the LORD your God in v, Dt 5:11 7723
who takes His name in v. Dt 5:11 7723
"Surely in v I have guarded all 1Sa 25:21 8267
they followed vanity and became v, 2Ki 17:15 1891
Why then should I toil in v? Jb 9:29 1892
Though her labor be in v, Jb 39:16 7385b
the peoples devising a v thing? Ps 2:1 7385b
I hate those who regard v idols, Ps 31:6 7723
For deliverance by man is in v. Ps 60:11 7723
in v I have kept my heart pure And Ps 73:13 7385b
For deliverance by man is in v. Ps 108:12 7723
They labor in v who build it; Ps 127:1 7723
The watchman keeps awake in v. Ps 127:1 7723
It is v for you to rise up early, Ps 127:2 7723
Your enemies take *Your name* in v. Ps 139:20 7723
Charm is deceitful and beauty is v, Pr 31:30 1892
Egypt, whose help is v and empty. Is 30:7 1892
"I have toiled in v, Is 49:4 7385b
"They will not labor in v, Is 65:23 7385b
"In v I have struck your sons; Jer 2:30 7723
In v you make yourself beautiful. Jer 4:30 7723
In v the refining goes on, But the Jer 6:29 7723
In v have you multiplied remedies; Jer 46:11 7723
I have not said in v that I would Ezk 6:10 2600
not done in v whatever I did to it," Ezk 14:23 2600
"Those who regard v idols Forsake Jon 2:8 7723
They comfort in v. Zch 10:2 7723
'It is v to serve God; Mal 3:14 7723
'BUT IN V DO THEY WORSHIP ME, Mt 15:9 *3155*
'BUT IN V DO THEY WORSHIP ME, Mk 7:7 *3155*
you should turn from these v things Ac 14:15 *3152*
to you, unless you believed in v. 1Co 15:2 *1500*
grace toward me did not prove v; 1Co 15:10 *2756*
raised, then our preaching is v, 1Co 15:14 *2756*
is vain, your faith also is v. 1Co 15:14 *2756*
your toil is not *in* v in the Lord. 1Co 15:58 *2756*
to receive the grace of God in v 2Co 6:1 *2756*
be running, or had run, in v. Ga 2:2 *2756*
Did you suffer so many things in v Ga 3:4 *1500*
in vain—if indeed it was in v? Ga 3:4 *1500*
I have labored over you in v. Ga 4:11 *1500*
I did not run in v nor toil in vain. Php 2:16 *2756*
did not run in vain nor toil in v. Php 2:16 *2756*
our coming to you was not in v, 1Th 2:1 *2756*
you, and our labor would be in v. 1Th 3:5 *2756*

VAINLY
"How then will you v comfort me, Jb 21:34 1892
And do not v hope in robbery; Ps 62:10 1891

VAIZATHA
Parmashta, Arisai, Aridai and V, Es 9:9 2055

VALIANT
all you v men shall cross over Dt 3:18 2428
battle array, all your v warriors, Jos 1:14 2428
with its king *and* the v warriors. Jos 6:2 2428
chose 30,000 men, v warriors, Jos 8:3 2428
with him and all the v warriors. Jos 10:7 2428
Moabites, all robust and v men; Jg 3:29 2428
the dashing of his v steeds. Jg 5:22 47
LORD is with you, O v warrior." Jg 6:12 2428
the Gileadite was a v warrior, Jg 11:1 2428
v men from Zorah and Eshtaol, Jg 18:2 2428
all these were v warriors. Jg 20:44 2428
all these were v warriors. Jg 20:46 2428
12,000 of the v warriors there Jg 21:10 2428
and the v *men* whose hearts God had 1Sa 10:26 2428
saw any mighty man or any v man, 1Sa 14:52 2428
only be a v man for me and fight 1Sa 18:17 2428
v men rose and walked all night, 1Sa 31:12 2428
your hands be strong and be v; 2Sa 2:7
1121, 2428
where he knew there *were* v men. 2Sa 11:16 2428
Be courageous and be v." 2Sa 13:28
1121, 2428
"And even the one who is v, 2Sa 17:10
1121, 2428
those who are with him are v men. 2Sa 17:10 2428
the son of a v man of Kabzeel, 2Sa 23:20 2428
eight hundred thousand v men who 2Sa 24:9 2428
are a v man and bring good news." 1Ki 1:42 2428
the man Jeroboam was a v warrior, 1Ki 11:28 2428
The man was also a v warrior, 2Ki 5:1 2428
of Manasseh, *consisting* of v men, 1Ch 5:18 2428
all the v men arose and took away 1Ch 10:12 2428
the son of a v man of Kabzeel, 1Ch 11:22 2428
Elihu and Semachiah, were v men. 1Ch 26:7 2428
had sons and relatives, 18 v men. 1Ch 26:9 2428
mighty men, even all the v men. 1Ch 28:1 2428
battle with an army of v warriors, 2Ch 13:3 1368
chosen men *who were* v warriors. 2Ch 13:3 2428
all of them were v warriors. 2Ch 14:8 2428
of Judah, and warriors, v men, 2Ch 17:13
2428, 1368
and with him 300,000 v warriors; 2Ch 17:14 2428
and with him 200,000 v warriors; 2Ch 17:16 2428
of Benjamin, Eliada a v warrior, 2Ch 17:17 2428
He hired also 100,000 v warriors 2Ch 25:6 2428
of the households, of v warriors, 2Ch 26:12 2428
eighty priests of the LORD, v men. 2Ch 26:17 2428
120,000 in one day, all v men, 2Ch 28:6 2428
and their brothers, v warriors, Ne 11:14 2428
He drags off the v by His power; Jb 24:22 47
And v men in mixing strong drink, Is 5:22 2428
warriors, And men v for battle'? Jer 48:14 2428
He commanded certain v warriors Da 3:20 2429

VALIANTLY
While Israel performs v. Nu 24:18 2428
acted v and defeated the Amalekites 1Sa 14:48 2428
Through God we shall do v, Ps 60:12 2428
Through God we will do v Ps 108:13 2428
The right hand of the LORD does v. Ps 118:15 2428
The right hand of the LORD does v. Ps 118:16 2428

VALID
concerning the land of Egypt v to Gn 47:26
his redemption right remains v until Lv 25:29
a covenant is v *only* when men are Heb 9:17 *949*

VALLEY
and saw all the v of the Jordan, Gn 13:10 3603
himself all the v of the Jordan, Gn 13:11 3603
settled in the cities of the v, Gn 13:12 3603
came as allies to the v of Siddim Gn 14:3 6010
against them in the v of Siddim, Gn 14:8 6010
Now the v of Siddim was full of Gn 14:10 6010
to meet him at the v of Shaveh Gn 14:17 6010
of Shaveh (that is, the King's V). Gn 14:17 6010
and do not stay anywhere in the v; Gn 19:17 3603
those cities, and all the v, Gn 19:25 3603
and toward all the land of the v, Gn 19:28 3603
God destroyed the cities of the v, Gn 19:29 3603
and camped in the v of Gerar, Gn 26:17 5158a
when Isaac's servants dug in the v Gn 26:19 5158a
he sent him from the v of Hebron, Gn 37:14 6010
Then they came to the v of Eshcol Nu 13:23 5158a
place was called the v of Eshcol, Nu 13:24 5158a
the v that is in the land of Moab, Nu 21:20 1516
they went up to the v of Eshcol and Nu 32:9 5158a
and came to the v of Eshcol and Dt 1:24 5158a
and pass through the v of Arnon. Dt 2:24 5158a
is on the edge of the v of Arnon Dt 2:36 5158a
from the city which is in the v, Dt 2:36 5158a
the v of Arnon to Mount Hermon Dt 3:8 5158a
Aroer, which is by the v of Arnon, Dt 3:12 5158a
even as far as the v of Arnon, Dt 3:16 5158a
the middle of the v as a border Dt 3:16 5158a
in the v opposite Beth-peor. Dt 3:29 1516
in the v opposite Beth-peor, Dt 4:46 1516
is on the edge of the v of Arnon, Dt 4:48 5158a
down to a v with running water, Dt 21:4 5158a
the heifer's neck there in the v. Dt 21:4 5158a
whose neck was broken in the v; Dt 21:6 5158a
and the plain in the v of Jericho, Dt 34:3 1237
him in the v in the land of Moab, Dt 34:6 1516
brought them up to the v of Achor. Jos 7:24 6010
called the v of Achor to this day. Jos 7:26 6010
there was a v between him and Ai. Jos 8:11 1516
that night in the midst of the v. Jos 8:13 6010
And O moon in the v of Aijalon." Jos 10:12 6010
and the v of Mizpeh to the east; Jos 11:8 1237
Baal-gad in the v of Lebanon at the Jos 11:17 1237
from the v of the Arnon as far as Jos 12:1 5158a
on the edge of the v of the Arnon, Jos 12:2 5158a
middle of the v and half of Gilead, Jos 12:2 5158a
from Baal-gad in the v of Lebanon Jos 12:7 1237
on the edge of the v of the Arnon, Jos 13:9 5158a
which is in the middle of the v, Jos 13:9 5158a
on the edge of the v of the Arnon, Jos 13:16 5158a
city which is in the middle of the v Jos 13:16 5158a
Zereth-shahar on the hill of the v, Jos 13:19 6010
and in the v, Beth-haram and Jos 13:27 6010
up to Debir from the v of Achor, Jos 15:7 6010
which is on the south of the v; Jos 15:7 5158a
border went up the v of Ben-hinnom Jos 15:8 1516
the v of Hinnom to the west, Jos 15:8 1516
the v of Rephaim toward the north. Jos 15:8 6010
Canaanites who live in the v land Jos 17:16 6010
who are in the v of Jezreel." Jos 17:16 6010
which is in the v of Ben-hinnom, Jos 18:16 1516
is in the v of Rephaim northward; Jos 18:16 6010
it went down to the v of Hinnom, Jos 18:16 1516
and it ended at the v of Iphtahel. Jos 19:14 1516
and to the v of Iphtahel northward Jos 19:27 1516
not drive out the inhabitants of the v Jg 1:19 6010
allow them to come down to the v; Jg 1:34 6010
Into the v they rushed at his heels; Jg 5:15 6010
and camped in the v of Jezreel. Jg 6:33 6010
by the hill of Moreh in the v. Jg 7:1 6010
of Midian was below him in the v. Jg 7:8 6010
sons of the east were lying in the v Jg 7:12 6010
loved a woman in the v of Sorek, Jg 16:4 5158a
in the v which is near Beth-rehob. Jg 18:28 6010
their wheat harvest in the v, 1Sa 6:13 6010
which overlooks the v of Zeboim 1Sa 13:18 1516
and set an ambush in the v. 1Sa 15:5 5158a
and camped in the v of Elah, 1Sa 17:2 6010
side, with the v between them. 1Sa 17:3 1516
of Israel are in the v of Elah, 1Sa 17:19 6010
the Philistines as far as the v, 1Sa 17:52 1516
whom you killed in the v of Elah, 1Sa 21:9 6010
were on the other side of the v, 1Sa 31:7 6010
out in the v of Rephaim. 2Sa 5:18 6010
out in the v of Rephaim. 2Sa 5:22 6010
18,000 Arameans in the V of Salt. 2Sa 8:13 1516
and we will drag it into the v 2Sa 17:13 5158a
a pillar which is in the King's V, 2Sa 18:18 6010
was camping in the v of Rephaim. 2Sa 23:13 6010
is in the middle of the v of Gad and 2Sa 24:5 5158a
on some mountain or into some v." 2Ki 2:16 1516
'Make this v full of trenches.' 2Ki 3:16 5158a
that v shall be filled with water, 2Ki 3:17 5158a
which is by the v of the Arnon, 2Ki 10:33 5158a
He killed *of* Edom in the V of Salt 2Ki 14:7 1516
is in the v of the son of Hinnom, 2Ki 23:10 1516
even to the east side of the v, 1Ch 4:39 1516
the men of Israel who were in the v 1Ch 10:7 6010
was camping in the v of Rephaim. 1Ch 11:15 6010
made a raid in the v of Rephaim. 1Ch 14:9 6010
made yet another raid in the v. 1Ch 14:13 6010
18,000 Edomites in the V of Salt. 1Ch 18:12 1516
in the v of Zephathah at Mareshah. 2Ch 14:10 1516
you will find them at the end of the v 2Ch 20:16 5158a
assembled in the v of Beracah, 2Ch 20:26 6010
"The V of Beracah" 2Ch 20:26 6010
forth, and went to the V of Salt and 2Ch 25:11 1516
at the Corner Gate and at the V Gate 2Ch 26:9 1516
incense in the v of Ben-hinnom and 2Ch 28:3 1516
it to carry out to the Kidron v. 2Ch 29:16 5158a
the fire in the v of Ben-hinnom; 2Ch 33:6 1516
the west side of Gihon, in the v, 2Ch 33:14 5158a
I went out at night by the V Gate Ne 2:13 1516
Then I entered the V Gate again Ne 2:15 1516
of Zanoah repaired the V Gate. Ne 3:13 1516
him the priests, the men of the v, Ne 3:22 3603
as far as the v of Hinnom. Ne 11:30 1516
Lod and Ono, the v of craftsmen. Ne 11:35 1516
clods of the v will gently cover him; Jb 21:33 5158a
"He paws in the v, and rejoices Jb 39:21 6010
the v of the shadow of death, Ps 23:4 1516
and measure out the v of Succoth. Ps 60:6 6010
Passing through the v of Baca they Ps 84:6 6010
And measure out the v of Succoth. Ps 108:7 6010
ravens of the v will pick it out, Pr 30:17 5158a
To see the blossoms of the v, SS 6:11 5158a
ears of grain In the v of Rephaim. Is 17:5 6010
oracle concerning the v of vision. Is 22:1 1516
and confusion In the v of vision, Is 22:5 1516
Which is at the head of the fertile v Is 28:1 1516
is at the head of the fertile v, Is 28:4 1516
stirred up as in the v of Gibeon, Is 28:21 6010
"Let every v be lifted up, And Is 40:4 1516
And the rugged terrain a broad v; Is 40:4 1237
cattle which go down into the v, Is 63:14 1237
And the v of Achor a resting place Is 65:10 6010
Look at your way in the v! Jer 2:23 1516

is in the v of the son of Hinnom, Jer 7:31 1516
or the v of the son of Hinnom, Jer 7:32 1516
but the v of the Slaughter; Jer 7:32 1516
"Then go out to the v of Ben-hinnom, Jer 19:2 1516
Topheth or the v of Ben-hinnom, Jer 19:6 1516
but rather the v of Slaughter. Jer 19:6 1516
I am against you, O v dweller, Jer 21:13 6010
And the whole v of the dead bodies Jer 31:40 6010
that are in the v of Ben-hinnom Jer 32:35 1516
O remnant of their v, Jer 47:5 6010
The v also will be ruined And the Jer 48:8 6010
Your v is flowing *away,* O Jer 49:4 6010
me down in the middle of the v; Ezk 37:1 1237
very many on the surface of the v; Ezk 37:2 1237
the v of those who pass by east of Ezk 39:11 1516
will call *it* the v of Hamon-gog. Ezk 39:11 1516
buried it in the v of Hamon-gog. Ezk 39:15 1516
of Israel in the v of Jezreel." Hos 1:5 6010
the v of Achor as a door of hope. Hos 2:15 6010
them down to the v of Jehoshaphat. Jl 3:2 6010
come up to the v of Jehoshaphat, Jl 3:12 6010
multitudes in the v of decision! Jl 3:14 6010
LORD is near in the v of decision. Jl 3:14 6010
LORD To water the v of Shittim. Jl 3:18 5158a
the inhabitant from the v of Aven, Am 1:5 1237
pour her stones down into the v And Mi 1:6 1516
east to west by a very large v, Zch 14:4 1516
flee by the v of My mountains, Zch 14:5 1516
for the v of the mountains will Zch 14:5 1516

VALLEYS

and the Canaanites live in the v; Nu 14:25 6010
"Like v that stretch out, Like Nu 24:6 5158a
flowing forth in v and hills; Dt 8:7 1237
possess it, a land of hills and v, Dt 11:11 1237
springs of water and to all the v; 1Ki 18:5 5158a
but He is not a god of *the* v," 1Ki 20:28 6010
put to flight all those in the v, 1Ch 12:15 6010
had charge of the cattle in the v. 1Ch 27:29 6010
So that they dwell in dreadful v, Jb 30:6 5158a
Or will he harrow the v after you? Jb 39:10 6010
And the v are covered with grain; Ps 65:13 6010
the v sank down To the place which Ps 104:8 1237
He sends forth springs in the v; Ps 104:10 5158a
rose of Sharon, The lily of the v." SS 2:1 6010
choicest v were full of chariots, Is 22:7 6010
And springs in the midst of the v; Is 41:18 1237
"How boastful you are about the v! Jer 49:4 6010
the hills, the ravines and the v: Ezk 6:3 1516
the mountains like doves of the v, Ezk 7:16 1516
in all the v its branches have fallen and Ezk 31:12 1516
And fill the v with your refuse. Ezk 32:5 1516
on your hills and in your v and in Ezk 35:8 1516
to the ravines and to the v, Ezk 36:4 1516
to the ravines and to the v, Ezk 36:6 1516
Him And the v will be split, Mi 1:4 6010

VALOR

of a Benjamite, a mighty man of v. 1Sa 9:1 2428
musician, a mighty man of v, 1Sa 16:18 2428
and all the mighty men of v, 2Ki 24:14 2428
All the men of v, 2Ki 24:16 2428
and Jahdiel, mighty men of v, 1Ch 5:24 2428
mighty men of v in their generations 1Ch 7:2 2428
of Issachar *were* mighty men of v, 1Ch 7:5 2428
households, mighty men of v, 1Ch 7:7 2428
20,200 mighty men of v. 1Ch 7:9 2428
17,200 mighty men of v, 1Ch 7:11 2428
choice and mighty men of v, 1Ch 7:40 2428
sons of Ulam were mighty men of v, 1Ch 8:40 2428
the wilderness, mighty men of v, 1Ch 12:8 2428
for they were all mighty men of v, 1Ch 12:21 2428
Simeon, mighty men of v for war, 1Ch 12:25 2428
Zadok, a young man mighty of v, 1Ch 12:28 2428
Ephraim 20,800, mighty men of v, 1Ch 12:30 2428
for they were mighty men of v. 1Ch 26:6 2428

VALUABLE

it was not considered v in the days 1Ki 10:21 3972
silver was not considered v in the 2Ch 9:20 3972
and v things which they took for 2Ch 20:25 2536b
and all kinds of v articles, 2Ch 32:27 2532
v articles of the house of the LORD, 2Ch 36:10 2532
and destroyed all its v articles. 2Ch 36:19 4261
"So do not fear; you are more v Mt 10:31 *1308*
"How much more v then is a man than Mt 12:12 *1308*
you are more v than many sparrows. Lk 12:7 *1308*
more v you are than the birds! Lk 12:24 *1308*

VALUABLES

and the v in front of them. Jg 18:21 3520
goods, with cattle and with v, Ezr 1:6 4030

VALUATION

to your v in silver by shekels, Lv 5:15 6187
the flock, according to your v, Lv 5:18 6187
the flock, according to your v, Lv 6:6 6187
valued according to your v of persons Lv 27:2 6187
'If your v is of the male from Lv 27:3 6187
then your v shall be fifty shekels Lv 27:3 6187
your v shall be thirty shekels. Lv 27:4 6187
v for the male shall be twenty shekels Lv 27:5 6187
then your v shall be five shekels Lv 27:6 6187
and for the female your v shall be Lv 27:6 6187
your v shall be fifteen shekels, Lv 27:7 6187
'But if he is poorer than your v, Lv 27:8 6187
add one-fifth of it to your v. Lv 27:13 6187
one-fifth of your v price to it, Lv 27:15 6187
then your v shall be proportionate Lv 27:16 6187
to your v it shall stand. Lv 27:17 6187
it shall be deducted from your v. Lv 27:18 6187
one-fifth of your v price to it, Lv 27:19 6187
the amount of your v up to the year Lv 27:23 6187
give your v as holy to the LORD. Lv 27:23 6187
'Every v of yours, moreover, shall Lv 27:25 6187
redeem it according to your v and Lv 27:27 6187
shall be sold according to your v. Lv 27:27 6187
you shall redeem them, by your v, Nu 18:16 6187
the land, each according to his v, 2Ki 23:35 6187

VALUE

and the priest shall v him; Lv 27:8 6186b
who vowed, the priest shall v him. Lv 27:8 6186b
shall v it as either good or bad; Lv 27:12 6186b
as you, the priest, v it, Lv 27:12 6187
shall v it as either good or bad; Lv 27:14 6186b
"Man does not know its v, Jb 28:13 6187
Who will not v silver or take Is 13:17 2803
upon finding one pearl of great v, Mt 13:46 *4186*
For indeed circumcision is of v if Ro 2:25 *5623*
of the surpassing v of knowing Christ Php 3:8 *5242*
no v against fleshly indulgence. Col 2:23 *5092*
This precious v, then, is for you 1Pe 2:7 *5092*

VALUED

he *shall be* v according to your Lv 27:2
was highly v in my sight this day, 1Sa 26:24 1431
highly v in the sight of the LORD, 1Sa 26:24 1431
cannot be v in the gold of Ophir, Jb 28:16 5541b
it, Nor can it be v in pure gold. Jb 28:19 5541b
v at a thousand *shekels* of Is 7:23
price at which I was v by them." Zch 11:13 3365

VALUES

as the priest v it, so it shall stand. Lv 27:14 6186b

VANGUARD

And its v into the eastern sea, Jl 2:20 6440

VANIAH

V, Meremoth, Eliashib, Ezr 10:36 2057

VANISH

the torrents of wadis which v, Jb 6:15 5674a
is hot, they v from their place. Jb 6:17 1846
When people v in their place. Jb 36:20 5927
They v—like smoke they vanish away. Ps 37:20 3615
They vanish—like smoke they v away. Ps 37:20 3615
My son, let them not v from your Pr 3:21 3868
But the idols will completely v. Is 2:18 2498
For the sky will v like smoke, Is 51:6 4414a
make *her* loud noise v from her. Jer 51:55 6

VANISHED

angel of the LORD v from his sight. Jg 6:21 1980
and He v from their sight. Lk 24:31 *855*

VANISHES

"When a cloud v, it is gone, So Jb 7:9 3615
a little while and then v away. Jas 4:14 *853*

VANITIES

"Vanity of v," says the Preacher, Ec 1:2 1892
"Vanity of v! All is vanity. Ec 1:2 1892
"Vanity of v," says the Preacher, Ec 12:8 1892

VANITY

they followed v and became vain, 2Ki 17:15 1892
So am I allotted months of v, Jb 7:3 7723
Men of low degree are only v and Ps 62:9 1892
For what v You have created all Ps 89:47 7723
away my eyes from looking at v, Ps 119:37 7723
He who sows iniquity will reap v, Pr 22:8 205
"V of vanities," says the Preacher, Ec 1:2 1892
"V of vanities! All is vanity. Ec 1:2 1892
"Vanity of vanities! All is v." Ec 1:2 1892
all is v and striving after wind. Ec 1:14 1892
and behold all was v and striving Ec 2:11 1892
So I said to myself, "This too is v." Ec 2:15 1892
wisely under the sun. This too is v. Ec 2:19 1892
This too is v and a great evil. Ec 2:21 1892
his mind does not rest. This too is v. Ec 2:23 1892
This too is v and striving after wind. Ec 2:26 1892
for man over beast, for all is v. Ec 3:19 1892
This too is v and striving after wind. Ec 4:4 1892
I looked again at v under the sun. Ec 4:7 1892
This too is v and it is a grievous task Ec 4:8 1892
this too is v and striving after wind. Ec 4:16 1892
with its income. This too is v. Ec 5:10 1892
This is v and a severe affliction. Ec 6:2 1892
"V of vanities," says the Preacher, Ec 12:8 1892
vanities," says the Preacher, "all is v!" Ec 12:8 1892
My strength for nothing and v; Is 49:4 1892
For speaking out arrogant *words* of v 2Pe 2:18 *3153*

VAPOR

by a lying tongue Is a fleeting v, Pr 21:6 1892
BLOOD, AND FIRE, AND V OF SMOKE. Ac 2:19 *822*
You are *just* a v that appears for Jas 4:14 *822*

VAPORS

He causes the v to ascend from the Ps 135:7 5387b

VARIATION

lights, with whom there is no v or Jas 1:17 *3883*

VARICOLORED

and he made him a v tunic. Gn 37:3 6446
the v tunic that was on him; Gn 37:23 6446
and they sent the v tunic and Gn 37:32 6446

VARIED

away by v and strange teachings; Heb 13:9 *4164*

VARIETIES

Now there are v of gifts, but the 1Co 12:4 *1243*
And there are v of ministries, and 1Co 12:5 *1243*
There are v of effects, but 1Co 12:6 *1243*

VARIETY

a v of good things of his master's Gn 24:10 3605

VARIOUS

according to their v chiefs in Gn 36:30
antimony and stones of v colors, 1Ch 29:2 7553
he had filled with spices of v kinds 2Ch 16:14
in golden vessels of v kinds, Es 1:7 8132
yourself high places of v colors and Ezk 16:16 2921
suffering with v diseases and pains, Mt 4:24 *4164*
and in v places there will be Mt 24:7 *2596*
many who were ill with v diseases, Mk 1:34 *4164*
will be earthquakes in v places; Mk 13:8 *2596*
who were sick with v diseases Lk 4:40 *4164*
and those from the v cities were Lk 8:4 *2596*
in v places plagues and famines; Lk 21:11 *2596*
others on v things from the ship. Ac 27:44 *5100*
to another v kinds of tongues, 1Co 12:10
v kinds of tongues. 1Co 12:28
with sins, led on by v impulses, 2Tm 3:6 *4164*
enslaved to v lusts and pleasures, Ti 3:3 *4164*
signs and wonders and by v miracles Heb 2:4 *4164*
to food and drink and v washings, Heb 9:10 *1313*
when you encounter v trials, Jas 1:2 *4164*
have been distressed by v trials, 1Pe 1:6 *4164*

VASHTI

Queen V also gave a banquet for Es 1:9 2060
to bring Queen V before the king Es 1:11 2060
But Queen V refused to come at the Es 1:12 2060
what is to be done with Queen V, Es 1:15 2060
"Queen V has wronged not only the Es 1:16 2060
'King Ahasuerus commanded Queen V Es 1:17 2060
that V may no longer come into Es 1:19 2060
he remembered V and what she had Es 2:1 2060
the king be queen in place of V." Es 2:4 2060
and made her queen instead of V. Es 2:17 2060

VAST

How v is the sum of them! Ps 139:17 6105a
ball, *To be cast* into a v country; Is 22:18 7342
For your ruin is as v as the sea; La 2:13 1419

VAT

the full produce from the wine v. Nu 18:27 3342
and as the product of the wine v. Nu 18:30 3342
floor and from your wine v; Dt 15:14 3342
threshing floor and your wine v; Dt 16:13 3342
it And also hewed out a wine v in it; Is 5:2 3342
and *when* one came to the wine v Hg 2:16 3342
AND DUG A V UNDER THE WINE PRESS Mk 12:1 *5276*

VATS

v will overflow with new wine. Pr 3:10 3342
And the v will overflow with the Jl 2:24 3342
The v overflow, for their Jl 3:13 3342

VAULT

And He walks on the v of heaven.' Jb 22:14 2329

VAULTED

the dungeon, that is, the v cell; Jer 37:16 2588
founded His v dome over the earth, Am 9:6 92

VAUNT

you v yourselves against me And Jb 19:5 1431
who do wickedness v themselves. Ps 94:4 559

VEDAN

"V and Javan paid for your wares Ezk 27:19 2051

VEGETABLE

it with your foot like a v garden. Dt 11:10 3419
that I may have it for a v garden 1Ki 21:2 3419

VEGETABLES

Better is a dish of v where love is Than Pr 15:17 3419
some v to eat and water to drink. Da 1:12 2235a
to drink, and kept giving them v. Da 1:16 2235a
but he who is weak eats v *only.* Ro 14:2 *3001*

VEGETATION

"Let the earth sprout v: Gn 1:11 1877
The earth brought forth v, Gn 1:12 1877
They were as the v of the field 2Ki 19:26 6212a
city flourish like v of the earth. Ps 72:16 6212a
And v for the labor of man, Ps 104:14 6212a
And ate up all v in their land, Ps 105:35 6212a
They were *as* the v of the field Is 37:27 6212a
and hills And wither all their v; Is 42:15 6212a
v of the countryside to wither? Jer 12:4 6212a
Their eyes fail For there is no v. Jer 14:6 6212a
finished eating the v of the land, Am 7:2 6212a
Like showers on v Which do not Mi 5:7 6212a
rain, v in the field to *each* man. Zch 10:1 6212a
brings forth v useful to those for Heb 6:7 *1008*

VEHEMENTLY

standing there, accusing Him v. Lk 23:10 *2159*

VEIL

took her v and covered herself. Gn 24:65 6809
and covered *herself* with a v, Gn 38:14 6809
and removed her v and put on her Gn 38:19 6809
"You shall make a v of blue Ex 26:31 6532
hang up the v under the clasps, Ex 26:33 6532
the testimony there within the v; Ex 26:33 6532
and the v shall serve for you as a Ex 26:33 6532
shall set the table outside the v, Ex 26:35 6532
v which is before the testimony, Ex 27:21 6532
shall put this altar in front of the v Ex 30:6 6532
them, he put a v over his face. Ex 34:33 4533
take off the v until he came out; Ex 34:34 4533
So Moses would replace the v over Ex 34:35 4533
he made the v of blue and purple Ex 36:35 6532
and the sockets of the v; Ex 38:27 6532
skins, and the screening v; Ex 39:34 6532
the v for the doorway of the tent; Ex 39:38 4539
shall screen the ark with the v. Ex 40:3 6532
and set up the v for the doorway Ex 40:5 4539
v for the gateway of the court. Ex 40:8 4539
and set up a v for the screen, Ex 40:21 6532
of the tabernacle, outside the v. Ex 40:22 6532
tent of meeting in front of the v; Ex 40:26 6532
he set up the v for the doorway Ex 40:28 4539
v for the gateway of the court. Ex 40:33 4539

front of the v of the sanctuary. Lv 4:6 6532
the LORD, in front of the v. Lv 4:17 6532
into the holy place inside the v, Lv 16:2 6532
and bring *it* inside the v. Lv 16:12 6532
and bring its blood inside the v and Lv 16:15 6532
only he shall not go in to the v Lv 21:23 6532
"Outside the v of testimony in Lv 24:3 6532
shall take down the v of the screen Nu 4:5 6532
the altar and inside the v, Nu 18:7 6532
He made the v of violet, 2Ch 3:14 6532
eyes are *like* doves behind your v; SS 4:1 6777
of a pomegranate Behind your v. SS 4:3 6777
of a pomegranate Behind your v. SS 6:7 6777
Even the v which is stretched over Is 25:7 4541b
Remove your v, strip off the skirt, Is 47:2 6777
the v of the temple was torn in Mt 27:51 *2665*
And the v of the temple was torn Mk 15:38 *2665*
v of the temple was torn in two. Lk 23:45 *2665*
who used to put a v over his face 2Co 3:13 *2571*
the same v remains unlifted, 2Co 3:14 *2571*
read, a v lies over their heart; 2Co 3:15 *2571*
to the Lord, the v is taken away. 2Co 3:16 *2571*
and one which enters within the v, Heb 6:19 *2665*
Behind the second v there Heb 9:3 *2665*
inaugurated for us through the v, Heb 10:20 *2665*

VEILED
And even if our gospel is v, 2Co 4:3 *2572*
is v to those who are perishing, 2Co 4:3 *2572*

VEILS
one who v herself Beside the flocks SS 1:7 5844a
dangling earrings, bracelets, v, Is 3:19 7479
undergarments, turbans and v. Is 3:23 7289
and make v for the heads of Ezk 13:18 4555
"I will also tear off your v and Ezk 13:21 4555

VENGEANCE
v will be taken on him sevenfold." Gn 4:15 5358
a day or two, no v shall be taken; Ex 21:21 5358
'You shall not take v, Lv 19:18 5358
will execute v for the covenant; Lv 26:25 5359
"Take full v for the sons of Israel Nu 31:2 5360
to execute the LORD's v on Midian. Nu 31:3 5360
'V is Mine, and retribution, In Dt 32:35 5359
I will render v on My adversaries, Dt 32:41 5359
will render v on His adversaries, Dt 32:43 5359
take v on the king's enemies.'" 1Sa 18:25 5358
LORD has given my lord the king v 2Sa 4:8 5360
The God who executes v for me, 2Sa 22:48 5360
The God who executes v for me, Ps 18:47 5360
will rejoice when he sees the v; Ps 58:10 5359
V for the blood of Your servants which Ps 79:10 5360
O Lord, God of v, Ps 94:1 5360
God of v, shine forth! Ps 94:1 5360
To execute v on the nations And Ps 149:7 5360
he will not spare in the day of v. Pr 6:34 5359
For the LORD has a day of v, Is 34:8 5359
Behold, your God will come *with* v; Is 35:4 5359
take v and will not spare a man." Is 47:3 5359
He put on garments of v for clothing Is 59:17 5359
LORD And the day of v of our God; Is 61:2 5359
"For the day of v was in My heart, Is 63:4 5359
heart, Let me see Your v on them, Jer 11:20 5360
take v for me on my persecutors. Jer 15:15 5358
Let me see Your v on them; Jer 20:12 5360
A day of v, so as to avenge Himself Jer 46:10 5360
For this is the v of the LORD: Jer 50:15 5360
Take v on her; As she has done *to* Jer 50:15 5358
in Zion the v of the LORD our God, Jer 50:28 5360
LORD our God, V for His temple. Jer 50:28 5360
For this is the LORD's time of v; Jer 51:6 5360
For it is the v of the LORD, Jer 51:11 5360
of the LORD, v for His temple. Jer 51:11 5360
case And exact full v for you; Jer 51:36 5360
You have seen all their v, La 3:60 5360
cause wrath to come up to take v, Ezk 24:8 5359
the house of Judah by taking v, Ezk 25:12 5359
"I will lay My v on Edom by Ezk 25:14 5360
thus they will know My v," Ezk 25:14 5360
and have taken v with scorn of soul Ezk 25:15 5359
"I will execute great v on them Ezk 25:17 5360
when I lay My v on them. Ezk 25:17 5360
"And I will execute v in anger Mi 5:15 5359
LORD takes v on His adversaries, Na 1:2 5358
because these are days of v, Lk 21:22 *1557*
he defended him and took v for the Ac 7:24 *1557*
"V IS MINE, I WILL REPAY," Ro 12:19 *1557*
"V IS MINE, I WILL REPAY." Heb 10:30 *1557*

VENOM
the v of crawling things of the dust. Dt 32:24 2534
"Their wine is the v of serpents, Dt 32:33 2534
To the v of cobras within him. Jb 20:14 4846
v like the venom of a serpent; Ps 58:4 2534
venom like the v of a serpent; Ps 58:4 2534
Who mix in your v even to make Hab 2:15 2534

VENT
I will give full v to my complaint; Jb 10:1 5800a

VENTURE
who would not v to set the sole of Dt 28:56 5254
v to ask Him any more questions. Mk 12:34 *5111*
with fear and would not v to look. Ac 7:32 *5111*
him not to v into the theater. Ac 19:31
1325, 1438

VENTURED
I have v to speak to the Lord, Gn 18:27 2974
I have v to speak to the Lord; Gn 18:31 2974
the disciples v to question Him, Jn 21:12 *5111*

VENTURES
"If one v a word with you, will Jb 4:2 5254

VERDICT
declare to you the v in the case. Dt 17:9 1697
do according to the terms of the v Dt 17:10 1697
to the v which they tell you, Dt 17:11 4941

VERIFIED
to me, so your words may be v, Gn 42:20 539

VERMILION
of the Chaldeans portrayed with v, Ezk 23:14 8350

VERSES
I address my v to the King; Ps 45:1 4639

VERTICAL
the Lord was standing by a v wall with Am 7:7 594

VERY
made, and behold, it was v good. Gn 1:31 3966
So Cain became v angry and his Gn 4:5 3966
On the v same day Noah and Shem Gn 7:13 6106
that the woman was v beautiful. Gn 12:14 3966
Now Abram was v rich in livestock, Gn 13:2 3966
Your reward shall be v great." Gn 15:1 3966
sun had set, that it was v dark, Gn 15:17 5939
their foreskin in the v same day, Gn 17:23 6106
In the v same day Abraham was Gn 17:26 6106
The girl was v beautiful, Gn 24:16 3966
richer until he became v wealthy; Gn 26:13 3966
and they were v angry because he Gn 34:7 3966
them, poor and v ugly and gaunt, Gn 41:19 3966
for it *will be* v severe. Gn 41:31 3966
because the famine was v severe, Gn 47:13 3966
fruitful and became v numerous. Gn 47:27 3966
and it was a v great company. Gn 50:9 3966
a v great and sorrowful lamentation Gn 50:10 3966
multiplied, and became v mighty. Ex 1:20 3966
But he said, "You are lazy, v Ex 5:17
only you shall not go v far away. Ex 8:28
a v severe pestilence on your livestock Ex 9:3 3966
I will send a v heavy hail, Ex 9:18 3966
the midst of the hail, v severe, Ex 9:24 3966
they were v numerous. Ex 10:14 3966
a v strong west wind which took up Ex 10:19 3966
for on this v day I brought your Ex 12:17 6106
a v large number of livestock. Ex 12:38 3966
and thirty years, to the v day, Ex 12:41 6106
and they became v frightened; Ex 14:10 3966
on that v day they came into the Ex 19:1
and a v loud trumpet sound, Ex 19:16 3966
You shall beat some of it v fine, Ex 30:36 1854
v first of the first fruits of your soil Ex 34:26
this v day they presented their Lv 10:19
to the v corners of your field, Lv 19:9
to the v corners of your field nor Lv 23:22
'But if a man dies v suddenly Nu 6:9 6621
the people with a v severe plague. Nu 11:33 3966
(Now the man Moses was v humble, Nu 12:3 3966
cities are fortified *and* v large; Nu 13:28 3966
out the v bad report of the land Nu 14:37
Moses became v angry and said to Nu 16:15 3966
will be afraid of you. So be v careful; Dt 2:4 3966
mountain burned with fire to the v Dt 4:11
grinding it v small until it was Dt 9:21 3190
cities that are v far from you, Dt 20:15 3966
words of this law v distinctly." Dt 27:8 3190
man who is refined and v delicate Dt 28:54 3966
"But the word is v near you, in Dt 30:14 3966
spoke to Moses that v same day, Dt 32:48 6106
"Only be strong and v courageous; Jos 1:7 3966
after the Passover, on that v day, Jos 5:11 6106
Do not go v far from the city, but Jos 8:4 3966
have come from a v far country Jos 9:9 3966
because of the v long journey." Jos 9:13 3966
'We are v far from you,' when you Jos 9:22 3966
them with a v great slaughter, Jos 10:20 3966
mouth of the cave, to this v day. Jos 10:27 6106
with v many horses and chariots. Jos 11:4 3966
and v much of the land remains to Jos 13:1 3966
"Only be v careful to observe the Jos 22:5 3966
riches and with v much livestock, Jos 22:8 3966
iron, and with v many clothes; Jos 22:8 3966
"Be v firm, then, to keep and do Jos 23:6 3966
Now Eglon was a v fat man. Jg 3:17 3966
So Israel was brought v low because Jg 6:6 3966
struck them with a v great slaughter Jg 11:33 3966
You have brought me v low, Jg 11:35 3766
of the angel of God, v awesome. Jg 13:6 3966
Then he became v thirsty, and he Jg 15:18 3966
land, and behold, it is v good. Jg 18:9 3966
has dealt v bitterly with me. Ru 1:20 3966
"Boast no more so v proudly, 1Sa 2:3 1364
sin of the young men was v great 1Sa 2:17 3966
Now Eli was v old; 1Sa 2:22 3966
and the slaughter was v great, 1Sa 4:10 3966
the city with v great confusion; 1Sa 5:9 3966
the hand of God was v heavy there. 1Sa 5:11 3966
words, and he became v angry. 1Sa 11:6 3966
and there was v great confusion. 1Sa 14:20 3966
And the people were v weary. 1Sa 14:31 3966
Then Saul became v angry, 1Sa 18:8 3966
have been v beneficial to you. 1Sa 19:4 3966
but if he is v angry, know that he 1Sa 20:7 2734
I am told that he is v cunning. 1Sa 23:22 6191
and the man was v rich, and he had 1Sa 25:2 3966
"Yet the men were v good to us, 1Sa 25:15 3966
within him, for he was v drunk; 1Sa 25:36
5704, 3966
"V well, you shall know what your 1Sa 28:2 3651
"V well, I will make you my 1Sa 28:2 3651
was v afraid because of the words of 1Sa 28:20 3966
You have been v pleasant to me. 2Sa 1:26 3966
That day the battle was v severe, 2Sa 2:17 3966

Then Abner was v angry over the 2Sa 3:8 3966
the v name of the LORD of hosts 2Sa 6:2
took a v large amount of bronze. 2Sa 8:8 3966
was v beautiful in appearance. 2Sa 11:2 3966
so that he was v sick. 2Sa 12:15
and Jonadab was a v shrewd man. 2Sa 13:3 3966
hated her with a v great hatred; 2Sa 13:15 3966
all these matters, he was v angry. 2Sa 13:21 3966
all his servants wept v bitterly. 2Sa 13:36 3966
over him a v great heap of stones. 2Sa 18:17 3966
Now Barzillai was v old, 2Sa 19:32 3966
for he was a v great man. 2Sa 19:32 3966
for I have acted v foolishly." 2Sa 24:10 3966
The girl was v beautiful; 1Ki 1:4 3966
And he was also a v handsome man, 1Ki 1:6 3966
Now the king was v old, 1Ki 1:15 3966
"V well; I will speak to the king for 1Ki 2:18 2896a
wisdom and v great discernment 1Ki 4:29 3966
Jerusalem with a v large retinue, 1Ki 10:2 3966
v much gold and precious stones. 1Ki 10:2 3966
and a v great *amount* of spices and 1Ki 10:10 3966
a v great *number of* almug trees 1Ki 10:11 3966
"I have been v zealous for the LORD, 1Ki 19:10 7065
I have been v zealous for the LORD, 1Ki 19:14 7065
v abominably in following idols, 1Ki 21:26 3966
"You know v *well* the man and his 2Ki 9:11
of Israel, *which was* v bitter; 2Ki 14:26 3966
the LORD was v angry with Israel and 2Ki 17:18 3966
Manasseh shed v much innocent blood 2Ki 21:16 3966
1,760 v able men for the work of 1Ch 9:13
were only a few in number, V few, 1Ch 16:19
took a v large amount of bronze, 1Ch 18:8 3966
of the city, a v great amount. 1Ch 20:2 3966
for I have done v foolishly." 1Ch 21:8 3966
LORD, for His mercies are v great. 1Ch 21:13 3966
has sinned and done v wickedly, 1Ch 21:17 7489a
the sons of Rehabiah were v many. 1Ch 23:17 4605
with him, a v great assembly 2Ch 7:8 3966
She had a v large retinue, with 2Ch 9:1 3966
and a v great *amount of* spices and 2Ch 9:9 3966
they carried away v much plunder. 2Ch 14:13 3966
with v many chariots and horsemen? 2Ch 16:8 3966
they made a v great fire for him. 2Ch 16:14
5704, 3966
be v careful what you do, for the 2Ch 19:7
of Israel, with a v loud voice. 2Ch 20:19 4605
a v great army into their hands, 2Ch 24:24 3966
him (for they left him v sick), 2Ch 24:25 7227a
of Egypt, for he became v strong. 2Ch 26:8 4605
and was v unfaithful to the LORD. 2Ch 28:19 4604
second month, a v large assembly. 2Ch 30:13 3966
God had given him v great wealth. 2Ch 32:29 3966
Ophel *with it* and made it v high. 2Ch 33:14 3966
people were v unfaithful *following* all 2Ch 36:14 7235a
house of God, a v large assembly, Ezr 10:1 3966
"We have acted v corruptly Ne 1:7 2254b
Then I was v much afraid. Ne 2:2 3966
it was v displeasing to them that Ne 2:10
7463a, 1419
he became furious and v angry and Ne 4:1 7235a
to be closed, they were v angry. Ne 4:7 3966
Then I was v angry when I had Ne 5:6 3966
to them this v day their fields, Ne 5:11
It was v displeasing to me, so Ne 13:8 3966
Then the king became v angry and Es 1:12 3966
donkeys, and v many servants; Jb 1:3 3966
saw that *his* pain was v great. Jb 2:13 3966
on, also become v powerful? Jb 21:7 2428
And the v ends of the earth as Ps 2:8
The v memory of them has perished. Ps 9:6 1992a
that v destruction let him fall. Ps 35:8
A v present help in trouble. Ps 46:1 3966
it is v tempestuous around Him. Ps 50:3 3966
For we are brought v low. Ps 79:8 3966
Your thoughts are v deep. Ps 92:5 3966
shall be full of sap and v green, Ps 92:14 7488
O LORD my God, You are v great; Ps 104:1 3966
only a few men in number, V few, Ps 105:12
His people to be v fruitful, Ps 105:24 3966
Your word is v pure, Therefore Your Ps 119:140 3966
raze it To its v foundation." Ps 137:7
And my soul knows it v well. Ps 139:14 3966
to my cry, For I am brought v low; Ps 142:6 3966
In that v day his thoughts perish. Ps 146:4
His word runs v swiftly. Ps 147:15 5704
The v flame of the LORD. SS 8:6
"My v own vineyard is at my SS 8:12 7945
"For in a v little while My Is 10:25 4213
will be v small *and* impotent." Is 16:14 4213
attention, v close attention." Is 21:7 7227a
treacherous deal v treacherously." Is 24:16 899a
because they are v strong, Is 31:1 3966
aged you made your yoke v heavy. Is 47:6 3966
you would deal v treacherously; Is 48:8 898
And shudder, be v desolate," Jer 2:12 3966
dealt v treacherously with Me," Jer 5:11 898
be taken, The aged and the v old. Jer 6:11
4392, 3117
'Do we not v well know that every Jer 13:12 3045
And made him v happy. Jer 20:15 8055
One basket had v good figs, like Jer 24:2 3966
the other basket had v bad figs which Jer 24:2 3966
"Figs, the good figs, v good; Jer 24:3 3966
and the bad *figs*, v bad, Jer 24:3 3966
the pride of Moab—he *is* v proud Jer 48:29 3966
And towers up to the v skies. Jer 51:9
me, For I have been v rebellious. La 1:20 4784
against Me to this v day. Ezk 2:3 6106
Judah is v, very great, and the land Ezk 9:9 3966

Israel and Judah is very, **v** great, **Ezk 9:9** 3966
the name of the day, this **v** day. **Ezk 24:2** 6106
siege to Jerusalem this **v** day. **Ezk 24:2** 6106
you were filled and were **v** glorious **Ezk 27:25** 3966
and forest shade, And **v** high, **Ezk 31:3** 6967
there were **v** many on the surface **Ezk 37:2** 3966
and lo, *they were* **v** dry. **Ezk 37:2** 3966
and set me on a **v** high mountain, **Ezk 40:2** 3966
were **v** many trees on the one side **Ezk 47:7** 3966
And there will be **v** many fish, **Ezk 47:9** 3966
the fish of the Great Sea, **v** many. **Ezk 47:10** 3966
became indignant and **v** furious and **Da 2:12** 7690
v *well.* But if you do not **Da 3:15**
Then the king was **v** pleased and **Da 6:23** 7690
again wage war up to his **v** fortress. **Da 11:10**
Surely His camp is **v** great, **Jl 2:11** 3966
is indeed great and **v** awesome, **Jl 2:11** 3966
"These who pant after the **v** dust **Am 2:7**
LORD, Near and coming **v** quickly; **Zph 1:14** 3966
LORD was **v** angry with your fathers. **Zch 1:2** 7110a
"But I am **v** angry with the nations **Zch 1:15** 1419, 7110a
and Sidon, though they are **v** wise. **Zch 9:2** 3966
This **v** day I am declaring that I **Zch 9:12** 1571
east to west by a **v** large valley, **Zch 14:4** 3966
by the magi, he became **v** enraged, **Mt 2:16** *3029*
took Him to a **v** high mountain and **Mt 4:8** *3029*
servant was healed that **v** moment. **Mt 8:13**
"But the **v** hairs of your head are **Mt 10:30** *2532*
for he is a lunatic and is **v** ill; **Mt 17:15** *2560*
they were **v** astonished and said, **Mt 19:25** *4970*
alabaster vial of **v** costly perfume, **Mt 26:7** *927*
say to you that this **v** night, **Mt 26:34**
became **v** frightened and said, **Mt 27:54** *4970*
And such a **v** large crowd **Mk 4:1** *4183*
They became **v** much afraid and **Mk 4:41** *3173*
mind, the **v** man who had had the **Mk 5:15**
he heard him, he was **v** perplexed; **Mk 6:20** *4183*
And although the king was **v** sorry, **Mk 6:26** *4036*
of **v** costly perfume of pure nard; **Mk 14:3** *4185*
that this **v** night, **Mk 14:30** *4594*
to be **v** distressed and troubled. **Mk 14:33** *1568*
for their eyes were **v** heavy; **Mk 14:40**
V early on the first day of the week, **Mk 16:2** *3029*
But she was **v** perplexed at *this* **Lk 1:29** *1298*
At that **v** moment she came up **Lk 2:38** *846*
At that **v** time He cured many **Lk 7:21**
At that **v** time He rejoiced greatly **Lk 10:21** *846*
the Pharisees began to be **v** hostile **Lk 11:53** *1171*
the **v** hairs of your head are all **Lk 12:7** *2532*
Spirit will teach you in that **v** hour **Lk 12:12** *846*
a rich man was **v** productive. **Lk 12:16** *2164*
This **v** night your soul is **Lk 12:20**
cannot do even a **v** little thing, **Lk 12:26** *1646*
you have paid the **v** last cent." **Lk 12:59** *2532*
"He who is faithful in a **v** little thing **Lk 16:10** *1646*
who is unrighteous in a **v** little thing **Lk 16:10** *1646*
these things, he became **v** sad, **Lk 18:23** *4036*
been faithful in a **v** little thing, **Lk 19:17** *1646*
to lay hands on Him that **v** hour, **Lk 20:19** *846*
agony He was praying **v** fervently; **Lk 22:44** *1617*
Herod was **v** glad when he saw Jesus **Lk 23:8** *3029*
with one another that **v** day; **Lk 23:12** *846*
two of them were going that **v** day **Lk 24:13** *846*
And they got up that **v** hour and **Lk 24:33** *846*
accomplish—the **v** works that I do **Jn 5:36** *846*
caught in adultery, in the **v** act. **Jn 8:4** *849a*
the **v** one who had received his sight, **Jn 9:18** *846*
took a pound of **v** costly perfume **Jn 12:3** *4186*
On the **v** night when Herod was **Ac 12:6** *1565*
Now he was **v** angry with the people **Ac 12:20** *2371*
the **v** ones who are now His **Ac 13:31**
And it came out at that **v** moment. **Ac 16:18** *846*
And he took them that **v** hour of **Ac 16:33**
are **v** religious in all respects. **Ac 17:22** *1174*
a **v** bright light suddenly flashed **Ac 22:6** *2425*
at that **v** time I looked up at him. **Ac 22:13** *846*
the Jews, as you also **v** well know. **Ac 25:10** *2573*
But before **v** long there rushed **Ac 27:14** *4183*
"For this **v** night an angel of the **Ac 27:23**
but I am doing the **v** thing I hate. **Ro 7:15** *3778*
the **v** thing I do not want *to do,* **Ro 7:16** *3778*
the **v** evil that I do not want. **Ro 7:19** *3778*
doing the **v** thing I do not want, **Ro 7:20** *3778*
THIS **V** PURPOSE I RAISED YOU UP, **Ro 9:17** *846*
And Isaiah is **v** bold and says, **Ro 10:20** *662*
TO HEAR NOT, DOWN TO THIS **V** DAY." **Ro 11:8** *4594*
devoting themselves to this **v** thing. **Ro 13:6** *846*
But I have written **v** boldly to you **Ro 15:15** *5112*
But to me it is a **v** small thing **1Co 4:3** *1646*
This is the **v** thing I wrote you, **2Co 2:3** *846*
for until this **v** day at the **2Co 3:14** *4594*
us for this **v** purpose is God, **2Co 5:5** *846*
what earnestness this **v** thing, **2Co 7:11** *846*
but being himself **v** earnest, **2Co 8:17**
v thing I also was eager to do. **Ga 2:10** *846*
To me, the **v** least of all saints, **Eph 3:8** *1646*
him to you for this **v** purpose, **Eph 6:22** *846*
I am confident of this **v** thing, **Php 1:6** *846*
Christ, for *that* is **v** much better; **Php 1:23** *4183*
him to you for this **v** purpose, **Col 4:8** *846*
you had become **v** dear to us. **1Th 2:8** *27*
you esteem them **v** highly in love **1Th 5:13** *5239a*
know **v** well what services he rendered **2Tm 1:18** *957*
that is, *sending* my **v** heart, **Phm 1:12**
come *and* not the **v** form of things, **Heb 10:1** *846*
FOR YET IN A **V** LITTLE WHILE, HE **Heb 10:37** *3745*
directed by a **v** small rudder wherever **Jas 3:4** *1646*
And the tongue is a fire, the **v** **Jas 3:6**
THIS BECAME THE **V** CORNER *stone,"* **1Pe 2:7** *2776*
you were called for the **v** purpose **1Pe 3:9** *3778*
Now for this **v** reason also, **2Pe 1:5** *846*
I was **v** glad to find *some* of your **2Jn 1:4** *3029*
For I was **v** glad when brethren **3Jn 1:3** *3029*
every article *made* from **v** costly wood **Rv 18:12** *5093*
brilliance was like a **v** costly stone, **Rv 21:11** *5093*

VESSEL

'Also the earthenware **v** in which **Lv 6:28** 3627
if it was boiled in a bronze **v**, **Lv 6:28** 3627
'As for any earthenware **v** into **Lv 11:33** 3627
unclean and you shall break the **v**. **Lv 11:33**
liquid which may be drunk in every **v** **Lv 11:34** 3627
the one bird in an earthenware **v** **Lv 14:5** 3627
the one bird in an earthenware **v** **Lv 14:50** 3627
an earthenware **v** which the person **Lv 15:12** 3627
wooden **v** shall be rinsed in water. **Lv 15:12** 3627
holy water in an earthenware **v**; **Nu 5:17** 3627
'Every open **v**, which has no **Nu 19:15** 3627
shall be added to them in a **v**. **Nu 19:17** 3627
"Bring me another **v**." **2Ki 4:6** 3627
"There is not one **v** more." **2Ki 4:6** 3627
out of mind; I am like a broken **v**. **Ps 31:12** 3627
there comes out a **v** for the smith; **Pr 25:4** 3627
Like an earthen **v** overlaid with **Pr 26:23** 2789
An earthenware **v** among the vessels **Is 45:9** 2789
their grain offering in a clean **v** to **Is 66:20** 3627
But the **v** that he was making of **Jer 18:4** 3627
so he remade it into another **v**, **Jer 18:4** 3627
even as one breaks a potter's **v**, **Jer 19:11** 3627
Or is he an undesirable **v**? **Jer 22:28** 3627
you will fall like a choice **v**. **Jer 25:34** 3627
not been emptied from **v** to vessel, **Jer 48:11** 3627
not been emptied from vessel to **v**, **Jer 48:11** 3627
Moab like an undesirable **v**," **Jer 48:38** 3627
has set me down *like* an empty **v**; **Jer 51:34** 3627
put them in one **v** and make them **Ezk 4:9** 3627
from it on which to hang any **v**? **Ezk 15:3** 3627
Like a **v** in which no one delights. **Hos 8:8** 3627
seas met, they ran the **v** aground; **Ac 27:41** *3491*
same lump one **v** for honorable use and **Ro 9:21** *4632*
you know how to possess his own **v** **1Th 4:4** *4632*
things, he will be a **v** for honor, **2Tm 2:21** *4632*

VESSELS

both in **v** *of* wood and in **Ex 7:19**
in *vessels of* wood and in **v** *of* **Ex 7:19**
and its trays and all its oil **v**, **Nu 4:9** 3627
and the holy **v** and the trumpets **Nu 31:6** 3627
the **v** of the young men were holy, **1Sa 21:5** 3627
then today will their **v** *be holy?"* **1Sa 21:5** 3627
Solomon's drinking **v** *were* of gold, **1Ki 10:21** 3627
and all the **v** of the house of the **1Ki 10:21** 3627
borrow **v** at large for yourself **2Ki 4:3** 3627
all your neighbors, *even* empty **v**; **2Ki 4:3** 3627
and pour out into all these **v**, **2Ki 4:4** 3627
they were bringing *the* **v** to her **2Ki 4:5**
When the **v** were full, **2Ki 4:6** 3627
bowls, trumpets, any **v** of gold, **2Ki 12:13** 3627
or **v** of silver from the money **2Ki 12:13** 3627
all the **v** that were made for Baal, **2Ki 23:4** 3627
and cut in pieces all the **v** of gold **2Ki 24:13** 3627
and all the bronze **v** which were **2Ki 25:14** 3627
the bronze of all these **v** was beyond **2Ki 25:16** 3627
and the holy **v** of God into the **1Ch 22:19** 3627
Solomon's drinking **v** *were* of gold, **2Ch 9:20** 3627
and all the **v** of the house of the **2Ch 9:20** 3627
in golden **v** of various kinds, **Es 1:7** 3627
Even in papyrus **v** on the surface **Is 18:2** 3627
and issue, all the least of **v**, **Is 22:24** 3627
vessel among the **v** of earth! **Is 45:9** 2789
You who carry the **v** of the LORD. **Is 52:11** 3627
have returned with their **v** empty; **Jer 14:3** 3627
the **v** of the LORD's house will now **Jer 27:16** 3627
that the **v** which are left in the **Jer 27:18** 3627
the **v** that are left in this city, **Jer 27:19** 3627
concerning the **v** that are left in **Jer 27:21** 3627
all the **v** of the LORD's house, **Jer 28:3** 3627
bring back the **v** of the LORD's house **Jer 28:6** 3627
and put *them* in your *storage* **v**, **Jer 40:10** 3627
I will send to him those who tip **v**, **Jer 48:12**
empty his **v** and shatter his jars. **Jer 48:12** 3627
and all the bronze **v** which were **Jer 52:18** 3627
the bronze of all these **v** was beyond **Jer 52:20** 3627
the lives of men and **v** of bronze **Ezk 27:13** 3627
some of the **v** of the house of God; **Da 1:2** 3627
he brought the **v** into the treasury **Da 1:2** 3627
orders to bring the gold and silver **v** **Da 5:2** 3984
Then they brought the gold **v** that **Da 5:3** 3984
have brought the **v** of His house **Da 5:23** 3984
their precious **v** of silver and gold he **Da 11:8** 3627
v of wrath prepared for destruction **Ro 9:22** *4632*
of His glory upon **v** of mercy, **Ro 9:23** *4632*
have this treasure in earthen **v**, **2Co 4:7** *4632*
are not only gold and silver **v**, **2Tm 2:20** *4632*
also **v** of wood and of earthenware, **2Tm 2:20**
and all the **v** of the ministry with the **Heb 9:21** *4632*
AS THE **V** OF THE POTTER ARE BROKEN **Rv 2:27** *4632*

VESTIBULE

Then Ehud went out into the **v** and **Jg 3:23** 4528

VESTURE

His **v** *was* like white snow And the **Da 7:9** 3831

VEXATION

for You have beheld mischief and **v** **Ps 10:14** 3708a
eats in darkness with great **v**, **Ec 5:17** 3707

VEXED

went to his house sullen and **v**, **1Ki 20:43** 2198
came into his house sullen and **v** **1Ki 21:4** 2198
The wicked will see it and be **v**, **Ps 112:10** 3707

VEXING

with a contentious and **v** woman. **Pr 21:19** 3708a

VIAL

alabaster **v** of very costly perfume, **Mt 26:7** *211*
an alabaster **v** of very costly perfume **Mk 14:3** *211*
she broke the **v** and poured it over **Mk 14:3** *211*
brought an alabaster **v** of perfume, **Lk 7:37** *211*

VICINITY

who were in Bethlehem and all its **v**, **Mt 2:16** *3725*
and the **v** of Tyre and Sidon, **Mk 3:8** *4012*
from the cities in the **v** of Jerusalem **Ac 5:16** *4038*

VICIOUS

Nor will any **v** beast go up on it; **Is 35:9** 6530
a matter of wrong or of **v** crime, **Ac 18:14** *4190*

VICTIMS

many are the **v** she has cast down, **Pr 7:26** 2491a
again be **v** of famine in the land, **Ezk 34:29** 622
WAS NOT TO ME THAT YOU OFFERED **V** **Ac 7:42** *4968*

VICTORIES

Command **v** for Jacob. **Ps 44:4** 3444

VICTORIOUS

God is in your midst, A **v** warrior. **Zph 3:17** 3467
and those who had been **v** over **Rv 15:2** *3528*

VICTORIOUSLY

And in Your majesty ride on **v**, **Ps 45:4** 6743b

VICTORY

The **v** that day was turned to **2Sa 19:2** 8668
brought about a great **v** that day; **2Sa 23:10** 8668
the LORD brought about a great **v**. **2Sa 23:12** 8668
him the LORD had given **v** to Aram. **2Ki 5:1** 8668
"The LORD's arrow of **v**, **2Ki 13:17** 8668
even the arrow of **v** over Aram; **2Ki 13:17** 8668
the LORD saved them by a great **v**. **1Ch 11:14** 8668
glory and the **v** and the majesty, **1Ch 29:11** 5331
We will sing for joy over your **v**, **Ps 20:5** 3444
A horse is a false hope for **v**; **Ps 33:17** 8668
arm have gained the **v** for Him. **Ps 98:1** 3467
in abundance of counselors there is **v** **Pr 11:14** 8668
battle, But **v** belongs to the LORD. **Pr 21:31** 8668
in abundance of counselors there is **v** **Pr 24:6** 8668
cry out with shouts of **v** over you." **Jer 51:14**
OUT, UNTIL HE LEADS JUSTICE TO **V**. **Mt 12:20** *3534*
"DEATH IS SWALLOWED UP in **V**. **1Co 15:54** *3534*
"O DEATH, WHERE IS YOUR **V**? **1Co 15:55** *3534*
who gives us the **v** through our Lord **1Co 15:57** *3534*
is the **v** that has overcome the world **1Jn 5:4** *3529*

VIEW

"Go, **v** the land, especially Jericho." **Jos 2:1** 7200
Do not, in **v** of Your patience, take **Jer 15:15**
Offer complaint in **v** of his sins? **La 3:39** 5921
in **v** of the multitude of his idols, **Ezk 14:4**
Sow with a **v** to righteousness, **Hos 10:12**
"In **v** of this, I also do my best **Ac 24:16**
good in **v** of the present distress, **1Co 7:26** *1223*
that you will adopt no other **v**; **Ga 5:10** *5426*
with a **v** to an administration **Eph 1:10** *1519*
with a **v** to the redemption of **Eph 1:14** *1519*
and with this in **v**, be on the alert **Eph 6:18** *1519*
in **v** of your participation in the **Php 1:5** *1909*
be loss in **v** of the surpassing value **Php 3:8** *1223*

VIEWED

and **v** others with contempt: **Lk 18:9** *1848*

VIEWS

to hear from you what your **v** are; **Ac 28:22** *5426*

VIGOR

eye was not dim, nor his **v** abated. **Dt 34:7** 3893
will come to the grave in full **v**, **Jb 5:26** 3624
His bones are full of his youthful **v**, **Jb 20:11** 5934
V had perished from them. **Jb 30:2** 3624
to the days of his youthful **v**; **Jb 33:25** 5934
The first fruits of all their **v**. **Ps 105:36** 202
Or you will give your **v** to others **Pr 5:9** 1935

VIGOROUS

for they are **v** and give birth **Ex 1:19** 2422b
"His **v** stride is shortened, And **Jb 18:7** 202
"Can a **v** man be of use to God, Or **Jb 22:2**
But my enemies are **v** *and* strong, **Ps 38:19** 2416a
And **v** young men stumble badly, **Is 40:30** 970
Among those who are **v** *we are* like **Is 59:10** 820

VIGOROUSLY

And they contended with him **v**. **Jg 8:1** 2394
He will **v** plead their case So **Jer 50:34** 7378
Make it boil **v**. Also seethe its bones **Ezk 24:5** 7571
for he **v** opposed our teaching. **2Tm 4:15** *3029*

VILE

When she has done many **v** deeds? **Jer 11:15** 4209
throw filth on you And make you **v**, **Na 3:6** 5034a

VILENESS

When **v** is exalted among the sons **Ps 12:8** 2149
And your **v** will be in your midst. **Mi 6:14** 3445

VILLAGE

And whatever city or **v** you enter, **Mt 10:11** *2968*
"Go into the **v** opposite you, and **Mt 21:2** *2968*
hand, He brought him out of the **v**; **Mk 8:23** *2968*
"Do not even enter the **v**." **Mk 8:26** *2968*
"Go into the **v** opposite you, and **Mk 11:2** *2968*
from every **v** of Galilee and Judea **Lk 5:17** *2968*
from one city and **v** to another, **Lk 8:1** *2968*
and entered a **v** of the Samaritans to **Lk 9:52** *2968*
And they went on to another **v**. **Lk 9:56** *2968*
along, He entered a **v**; **Lk 10:38** *2968*
from one city and **v** to another, **Lk 13:22** *2968*
As He entered a **v**, **Lk 17:12** *2968*
"Go into the **v** ahead of *you;* there, **Lk 19:30** *2968*
that very day to a **v** named Emmaus, **Lk 24:13** *2968*
the **v** where they were going, **Lk 24:28** *2968*

the v where David was?" Jn 7:42 2968
v of Mary and her sister Martha. Jn 11:1 2968
Jesus had not yet come into the v, Jn 11:30 2968

VILLAGES

these are their names, by their v, Gn 25:16 2691b
'The houses of the v, Lv 25:31 2691b
in Heshbon, and in all her v. Nu 21:25 1323
and they captured its v and Nu 21:32 1323
went and took Kenath and its v, Nu 32:42 1323
who lived in v as far as Gaza, Dt 2:23 2691b
families, the cities and their v. Jos 13:23 2691b
families, the cities and their v. Jos 13:28 2691b
twenty-nine cities with their v. Jos 15:32 2691b
fourteen cities with their v. Jos 15:36 2691b
sixteen cities with their v. Jos 15:41 2691b
nine cities with their v. Jos 15:44 2691b
Ekron, with its towns and its v; Jos 15:45 2691b
the side of Ashdod, with their v. Jos 15:46 2691b
Ashdod, its towns and its v; Jos 15:47 2691b
Gaza, its towns and its v; Jos 15:47 2691b
eleven cities with their v. Jos 15:51 2691b
nine cities with their v. Jos 15:54 2691b
ten cities with their v. Jos 15:57 2691b
six cities with their v. Jos 15:59 2691b
two cities with their v. Jos 15:60 2691b
six cities with their v. Jos 15:62 2691b
all the cities with their v. Jos 16:9 2691b
twelve cities with their v. Jos 18:24 2691b
fourteen cities with their v. Jos 18:28 2691b
thirteen cities with their v; Jos 19:6 2691b
Ashan; four cities with their v; Jos 19:7 2691b
and all the v which were around Jos 19:8 2691b
twelve cities with their v. Jos 19:15 2691b
these cities with their v. Jos 19:16 2691b
sixteen cities with their v. Jos 19:22 2691b
families, the cities with their v. Jos 19:23 2691b
twenty-two cities with their v. Jos 19:30 2691b
these cities with their v. Jos 19:31 2691b
nineteen cities with their v. Jos 19:38 2691b
families, the cities with their v. Jos 19:39 2691b
these cities with their v. Jos 19:48 2691b
the fields of the city and its v they Jos 21:12 2691b
possession of Beth-shean and its v, Jg 1:27 1323
villages, or Taanach and its v, Jg 1:27 1323
the inhabitants of Dor and its v, Jg 1:27 1323
inhabitants of Ibleam and its v, Jg 1:27 1323
inhabitants of Megiddo and its v; Jg 1:27 1323
Israel lived in Heshbon and its v, Jg 11:26 1323
villages, and in Aroer and its v, Jg 11:26 1323
fortified cities and of country v. 1Sa 6:18 3724d
from them, with Kenath and its v, 1Ch 2:23 1323
Their v were Etam, Ain, 1Ch 4:32 2691b
and all their v that were around 1Ch 4:33 2691b
the fields of the city and its v, 1Ch 6:56 2691b
in the v of the Netophathites. 1Ch 9:16 2691b
enrolled by genealogy in their v, 1Ch 9:22 2691b
Their relatives in their v 1Ch 9:25 2691b
country, in the cities, in the v and 1Ch 27:25 3723
several cities, Bethel with its v, 2Ch 13:19 1323
its villages, Jeshanah with its v and 2Ch 13:19 1323
villages and Ephron with its v. 2Ch 13:19 1323
Gederoth, and Soco with its v, 2Ch 28:18 1323
its villages, Timnah with its v, 2Ch 28:18 1323
villages, and Gimzo with its v, 2Ch 28:18 1323
as for the v with their fields, Ne 11:25 2691b
towns, and in Jekabzeel and its v, Ne 11:25 2691b
Zanoah, Adullam, and their v, Ne 11:30 2691b
from the v of the Netophathites, Ne 12:28 2691b
built themselves v around Jerusalem. Ne 12:29 2691b
in the lurking places of the v; Ps 10:8 2691b
Let us spend the night in the v. SS 7:11 3723
up against the land of unwalled v. Ezk 38:11 6519
of Tarshish with all its v Ezk 38:13 3724d
through all the cities and v, Mt 9:35 2968
that they may go into the v and buy Mt 14:15 2968
He was going around the v teaching. Mk 6:6 2968
the surrounding countryside and v Mk 6:36 2968
Wherever He entered v, Mk 6:56 2968
to the v of Caesarea Philippi; Mk 8:27 2968
began going throughout the v, Lk 9:6 2968
they may go into the surrounding v Lk 9:12 2968
to many v of the Samaritans. Ac 8:25 2968

VINDICATE

"For the LORD will v His people, Dt 32:36 1777
V me, O LORD, according to my Ps 7:8 8199
To v the orphan and the oppressed, Ps 10:18 8199
V me, O LORD, for I have walked in Ps 26:1 8199
V me, O God, and plead my case Ps 43:1 8199
Your name, And v me by Your power. Ps 54:1 1777
he v the afflicted of the people, Ps 72:4 8199
V the weak and fatherless; Ps 82:3 8199
"I will v the holiness of My Ezk 36:23 6942

VINDICATED

"God has v me, and has indeed Gn 30:6 1777
I know that I will be v. Jb 13:18 6663
Yet wisdom is v by her deeds." Mt 11:19 1344
wisdom is v by all her children." Lk 7:35 1344
in the flesh, Was v in the Spirit, 1Tm 3:16 1344

VINDICATES

He who v Me is near; Is 50:8 6663

VINDICATION

v before all who are with you, Gn 20:16 3682
joy and rejoice, who favor my v; Ps 35:27 6664
And their v is from Me," Is 54:17 6666
The LORD has brought about our v; Jer 51:10 6666
you the early rain for your v. Jl 2:23 6666
what v of yourselves, what 2Co 7:11 627

VINE

there was a v in front of me; Gn 40:9 1612
and on the v were three branches. Gn 40:10 1612
"He ties his foal to the v, Gn 49:11 1612
his donkey's colt to the choice v; Gn 49:11 8321b
that is produced by the grape v, Nu 6:4 1612
their v is from the vine of Sodom, Dt 32:32 1612
their vine is from the v of Sodom, Dt 32:32 1612
"Then the trees said to the v, Jg 9:12 1612
"But the v said to them, Jg 9:13 1612
not eat anything that comes from the v Jg 13:14 1612
man under his v and his fig tree, 1Ki 4:25 1612
and found a wild v and gathered 2Ki 4:39 1612
and eat each of his v and each of 2Ki 18:31 1612
off his unripe grape like the v, Jb 15:33 1612
You removed a v from Egypt; Ps 80:8 1612
and see, and take care of this v, Ps 80:14 1612
wife shall be like a fruitful v Within Ps 128:3 1612
To see whether the v had budded Or SS 6:11 1612
breasts be like clusters of the v, SS 7:8 1612
Let us see whether the v has budded SS 7:12 1612
planted it with the choicest v. Is 5:2 8321a
for Jazer, for the v of Sibmah; Is 16:9 1612
with v slips of a strange god. Is 17:10 2156
The new wine mourns, The v decays, Is 24:7 1612
fields, for the fruitful v, Is 32:12 1612
away As a leaf withers from the v, Is 34:4 1612
and eat each of his v and each of Is 36:16 1612
"Yet I planted you a choice v, Jer 2:21 8321a
degenerate shoots of a foreign v? Jer 2:21 1612
"Go up through her v rows and Jer 5:10 7795b
They will thoroughly glean as the v Jer 6:9 1612
"There will be no grapes on the v And Jer 8:13 1612
will weep for you, O v of Sibmah! Jer 48:32 1612
how is the wood of the v better Ezk 15:2 1612
the wood of the v among the trees Ezk 15:6 1612
spreading v with its branches Ezk 17:6 1612
So it became a v and yielded Ezk 17:6 1612
this v bent its roots toward him Ezk 17:7 1612
and become a splendid v." Ezk 17:8 1612
was like a v in your vineyard, Ezk 19:10 1612
Israel is a luxuriant v; Hos 10:1 1612
And they will blossom like the v. Hos 14:7 1612
It has made my v a waste And my Jl 1:7 1612
The v dries up And the fig tree Jl 1:12 1612
and the v have yielded in full. Jl 2:22 1612
Each of them will sit under his v Mi 4:4 1612
And destroyed their v branches. Na 2:2 2156
Even including the v, Hg 2:19 1612
invite his neighbor to sit under his v Zch 3:10 1612
the v will yield its fruit, the Zch 8:12 1612
nor will your v in the field cast its Mal 3:11 1612
will not drink of this fruit of the v Mt 26:29 288
never again drink of the fruit of the v Mk 14:25 288
will not drink of the fruit of the v Lk 22:18 288
"I am the true v, and My Father Jn 15:1 288
itself unless it abides in the v, Jn 15:4 288
"I am the v, you are the branches; Jn 15:5 288
olives, or a v produce figs? Jas 3:12 288
clusters from the v of the earth, Rv 14:18 288
clusters from the v of the earth, Rv 14:19 288

VINEDRESSER

true vine, and My Father is the v. Jn 15:1 1092

VINEDRESSERS

of the land to be v and plowmen. 2Ki 25:12 3755
He also had plowmen and v in the 2Ch 26:10 3755
will be your farmers and your v. Is 61:5 3755
of the land to be v and plowmen. Jer 52:16 3755
Be ashamed, O farmers, Wail, O v, Jl 1:11 3755

VINEGAR

he shall drink no v, Nu 6:3 2558
dip your piece of bread in the v." Ru 2:14 2558
my thirst they gave me v to drink. Ps 69:21 2558
Like v to the teeth and smoke to Pr 10:26 2558
on a cold day, or like v on soda, Pr 25:20 2558

VINE-GROWERS

A TOWER, and rented it out to v Mt 21:33 1092
he sent his slaves to the v to receive Mt 21:34 1092
v took his slaves and beat one, Mt 21:35 1092
"But when the v saw the son, they Mt 21:38 1092
what will he do to those v?" Mt 21:40 1092
rent out the vineyard to other v who Mt 21:41 1092
and rented it out to v and went on Mk 12:1 1092
time he sent a slave to the v, Mk 12:2 1092
produce of the vineyard from the v. Mk 12:2 1092
"But those v said to one another, Mk 12:7 1092
He will come and destroy the v, Mk 12:9 1092
a vineyard and rented it out to v, Lk 20:9 1092
time he sent a slave to the v, Lk 20:10 1092
but the v beat him and sent him Lk 20:10 1092
"But when the v saw him, they Lk 20:14 1092
"He will come and destroy these v Lk 20:16 1092

VINES

and your grapes of untrimmed v Lv 25:5 5139
gather in from its untrimmed v. Lv 25:11 5139
or figs or v or pomegranates, Nu 20:5 1612
of v and fig trees and Dt 8:8 1612
destroyed their v with hailstones And Ps 78:47 1612
He struck down their v also and Ps 105:33 1612
time has arrived for pruning the v, SS 2:12
And the v in blossom have given SS 2:13 1612
there used to be a thousand v, Is 7:23 1612
withered, the v of Sibmah as well; Is 16:8 1612
devour your v and your fig trees; Jer 5:17 1612
I will destroy her v and fig trees, Hos 2:12 1612
And there be no fruit on the v, Hab 3:17 1612

VINEYARD

began farming and planted a v. Gn 9:20 3754
man lets a field or v be grazed bare Ex 22:5 3754
field and the best of his own v. Ex 22:5 3754
with your v and your olive grove. Ex 23:11 3754
'Nor shall you glean your v, Lv 19:10 3754
gather the fallen fruit of your v; Lv 19:10 3754
six years you shall prune your v Lv 25:3 3754
sow your field nor prune your v. Lv 25:4 3754
pass through field or through v; Nu 20:17 3754
will not turn off into field or v; Nu 21:22 3754
Who is the man that has planted a v Dt 20:6 3754
sow your v with two kinds of seed, Dt 22:9 3754
increase of the v will become defiled. Dt 22:9 3754
"When you enter your neighbor's v, Dt 23:24 3754
you gather the grapes of your v, Dt 24:21 3754
you shall plant a v, Dt 28:30 3754
Naboth the Jezreelite had a v which 1Ki 21:1 3754
"Give me your v, that I may have 1Ki 21:2 3754
I will give you a better v than it in 1Ki 21:2 3754
'Give me your v for money; 1Ki 21:6 3754
I will give you a v in its place.' 1Ki 21:6 3754
'I will not give you my v.' " 1Ki 21:6 3754
the v of Naboth the Jezreelite." 1Ki 21:7 3754
possession of the v of Naboth, 1Ki 21:15 3754
to the v of Naboth the Jezreelite, 1Ki 21:16 3754
he is in the v of Naboth where he 1Ki 21:18 3754
And glean the v of the wicked. Jb 24:6 3754
by the v of the man lacking sense, Pr 24:30 3754
From her earnings she plants a v. Pr 31:16 3754
I have not taken care of my own v. SS 1:6 3754
"Solomon had a v at Baal-hamon; SS 8:11 3754
He entrusted the v to caretakers. SS 8:11 3754
"My very own v is at my disposal; SS 8:12 3754
is left like a shelter in a v, Is 1:8 3754
"It is you who have devoured the v; Is 3:14 3754
of my beloved concerning His v. Is 5:1 3754
well-beloved had a v on a fertile hill. Is 5:1 3754
Judah, Judge between Me and My v. Is 5:3 3754
more was there to do for My v that Is 5:4 3754
you what I am going to do to My v: Is 5:5 3754
For the v of the LORD of hosts is Is 5:7 3754
"For ten acres of v will yield Is 5:10 3754
"A v of wine, sing of it! Is 27:2 3754
"Many shepherds have ruined My v, Jer 12:10 3754
shall not plant a v or own one; Jer 35:7 3754
we do not have v or field or seed. Jer 35:9 3754
mother was like a vine in your v, Ezk 19:10
country, Planting places for a v. Mi 1:6 3754
to hire laborers for his v. Mt 20:1 290
the day, he sent them into his v. Mt 20:2 290
'You also go into the v, Mt 20:4 290
'You go into the v too.' Mt 20:7 290
owner of the v said to his foreman, Mt 20:8 290
'Son, go work today in the v.' Mt 21:28 290
was a landowner who PLANTED A V Mt 21:33 290
him, and threw him out of the v and Mt 21:39 290
when the owner of the v comes, Mt 21:40 290
rent out the v to other vine-growers who Mt 21:41 290
"A man PLANTED A V AND PUT A Mk 12:1 290
receive some of the produce of the v Mk 12:2 290
him and threw him out of the v. Mk 12:8 290
"What will the owner of the v do? Mk 12:9 290
and will give the v to others. Mk 12:9 290
which had been planted in his v; Lk 13:6 290
"A man planted a v and rented it Lk 20:9 290
him some of the produce of the v; Lk 20:10 290
"The owner of the v said, Lk 20:13 290
they threw him out of the v and Lk 20:15 290
the owner of the v do to them? Lk 20:15 290
and will give the v to others." Lk 20:16 290
Who plants a v and does not eat 1Co 9:7 290

VINEYARD-KEEPER

"And he said to the v, Lk 13:7 289

VINEYARDS

us an inheritance of fields and v. Nu 16:14 3754
stood in a narrow path of the v, Nu 22:24 3754
v and olive trees which you did Dt 6:11 3754
"You shall plant and cultivate v, Dt 28:39 3754
you are eating of v and olive Jos 24:13 3754
gathered the grapes of their v and Jg 9:27 3754
came as far as the v of Timnah; Jg 14:5 3754
along with the v and groves. Jg 15:5 3754
"Go and lie in wait in the v, Jg 21:20 3754
then you shall come out of the v Jg 21:21 3754
and your v and your olive groves and 1Sa 8:14 3754
tenth of your seed and of your v and 1Sa 8:15 3754
give to all of you fields and v? 1Sa 22:7 3754
receive clothes and olive groves and v 2Ki 5:26 3754
new wine, a land of bread and v, 2Ki 18:32 3754
the third year sow, reap, plant v, 2Ki 19:29 3754
the Ramathite had charge of the v; 1Ch 27:27 3754
had charge of the produce of the v 1Ch 27:27 3754
are mortgaging our fields, our v and Ne 5:3 3754
king's tax on our fields and our v. Ne 5:4 3754
fields and v belong to others." Ne 5:5 3754
very day their fields, their v, Ne 5:11 3754
good thing, Hewn cisterns, v, Ne 9:25 3754
They do not turn toward the v. Jb 24:18 3754
And sow fields and plant v, Ps 107:37 3754
myself, I planted v for myself; Ec 2:4 3754
They made me caretaker of the v, SS 1:6 3754
blossoms In the v of Engedi." SS 1:14 3754
foxes that are ruining the v, SS 2:15 3754
While our v are in blossom." SS 2:15 3754
"Let us rise early and go to the v; SS 7:12 3754
In the v also there will be no Is 16:10 3754
new wine, a land of bread and v. Is 36:17 3754
the third year sow, reap, plant v and Is 37:30 3754
also plant v and eat their fruit. Is 65:21 3754

plant v On the hills of Samaria; **Jer 31:5** 3754
"Houses and fields and v will **Jer 32:15** 3754
gave them v and fields at that time. **Jer 39:10** 3754
they will build houses, plant v and **Ezk 28:26** 3754
I will give her her v from there, **Hos 2:15** 3754
devouring Your many gardens and v, **Am 4:9** 3754
You have planted pleasant v, **Am 5:11** 3754
"And in all the v *there is* **Am 5:17** 3754
also plant v and drink their wine, **Am 9:14** 3754
plant v but not drink their wine." **Zph 1:13** 3754

VINTAGE
from your harvest and your v. **Ex 22:29** 1831
better than the v of Abiezer? **Jg 8:2** 1210
For the v is ended, *And the fruit* **Is 32:10** 1210

VIOLATE
he shall not v his word; **Nu 30:2** 2490c
wife, but another man will v her; **Dt 28:30** 7693
"No, my brother, do not v me, **2Sa 13:12** 6031a
If they v My statutes And do not **Ps 89:31** 2490c
"My covenant I will not v, **Ps 89:34** 2490c

VIOLATED
he has v his neighbor's wife. **Dt 22:24** 6031a
his wife because he has v her; **Dt 22:29** 6031a
she, he v her and lay with her. **2Sa 13:14** 6031a
because he had v his sister Tamar. **2Sa 13:22** 6031a
day that he v his sister Tamar. **2Sa 13:32** 6031a
troubler of Israel, who v the ban. **1Ch 2:7** 4603
He has v his covenant. **Ps 55:20** 2490c
transgressed laws, v statutes, **Is 24:5** 2498
Where have you not been v? **Jer 3:2** 7693

VIOLATES
that any man who v this edict, **Ezr 6:11** 8133

VIOLATING
trust in Him, v the king's command, **Da 3:28** 8133

VIOLATION
and in v of the Law order me to be **Ac 23:3** *3891*
is no law, there also is no v. **Ro 4:15** *3847*

VIOLENCE
and the earth was filled with v. **Gn 6:11** 2555
is filled with v because of them; **Gn 6:13** 2555
Their swords are implements of v. **Gn 49:5** 2555
that the v done to the seventy sons **Jg 9:24** 2555
savior, You save me from v. **2Sa 22:3** 2555
And you will not be afraid of v when **Jb 5:21** 7701
"You will laugh at v and famine, **Jb 5:22** 7701
there is no v in my hands, **Jb 16:17** 2555
"Behold, I cry, 'V!' **Jb 19:7** 2555
And He will not do v to justice **Jb 37:23** 6031a
And his v will descend upon his **Ps 7:16** 2555
one who loves v His soul hates. **Ps 11:5** 2555
me, And such as breathe out v. **Ps 27:12** 2555
I have seen v and strife in the city. **Ps 55:9** 2555
you weigh out the v of your hands. **Ps 58:2** 2555
their life from oppression and v, **Ps 72:14** 2555
The garment of v covers them. **Ps 73:6** 2555
are full of the habitations of v. **Ps 74:20** 2555
ways of everyone who gains by v; **Pr 1:19** 1214
Do not envy a man of v And **Pr 3:31** 2555
And drink the wine of v. **Pr 4:17** 2555
mouth of the wicked conceals v. **Pr 10:6** 2555
mouth of the wicked conceals v. **Pr 10:11** 2555
desire of the treacherous is v. **Pr 13:2** 2555
A man of v entices his neighbor And **Pr 16:29** 2555
The v of the wicked will drag them **Pr 21:7** 7701
For their minds devise v, **Pr 24:2** 7701
and drinks v Who sends a message **Pr 26:6** 2555
He had done no v, **Is 53:9** 2555
And an act of v is in their hands. **Is 59:6** 2555
"V will not be heard again in **Is 60:18** 2555
V and destruction are heard in her; **Jer 6:7** 2555
I proclaim v and destruction, **Jer 20:8** 2555
mistreat *or* do v to the stranger, **Jer 22:3** 2554
"May the v *done* to me and to my **Jer 51:35** 2555
And v *will be* in the land With **Jer 51:46** 2555
'V has grown into a rod of **Ezk 7:11** 2555
crimes and the city is full of v. **Ezk 7:23** 2555
that they have filled the land with v **Ezk 8:17** 2555
on account of the v of all who live **Ezk 12:19** 2555
"Her priests have done v to My **Ezk 22:26** 2554
You were internally filled with v, **Ezk 28:16** 2555
put away v and destruction, and **Ezk 45:9** 2555
They employ v, so that bloodshed **Hos 4:2** 6555
He multiplies lies and v. **Hos 12:1** 7701
the v done to the sons of Judah, **Jl 3:19** 2555
"these who hoard up v and **Am 3:10** 2555
you bring near the seat of v? **Am 6:3** 2555
Because of v to your brother Jacob, **Ob 1:10** 2555
from the v which is in his hands. **Jon 3:8** 2555
men of *the* city are full of v, **Mi 6:12** 2555
I cry out to You, "V!" **Hab 1:2** 2555
destruction and v are before me; **Hab 1:3** 2555
"All of them come for v. **Hab 1:9** 2555
bloodshed and v done to the land, **Hab 2:8** 2555
And founds a town with v! **Hab 2:12** 5767b
"For the v done to Lebanon will **Hab 2:17** 2555
bloodshed and v done to the land, **Hab 2:17** 2555
fill the house of their lord with v **Zph 1:9** 2555
They have done v to the law. **Zph 3:4** 2554
the kingdom of heaven suffers v, **Mt 11:12** *971*
to bring them *back* without v **Ac 5:26** *970*
because of the v of the mob; **Ac 21:35** *970*
much v took him out of our hands, **Ac 24:7** *970*
great city, be thrown down with v, **Rv 18:21** *3731*

VIOLENT
You rescue me from the v man. **2Sa 22:49** 2555
was he who cursed me with a v curse **1Ki 2:8** 4834
have kept from the paths of the v. **Ps 17:4** 6530
You rescue me from the v man. **Ps 18:48** 2555
And they hate me with v hatred. **Ps 25:19** 2555
I have seen a wicked, v man **Ps 37:35** 6184
me And v men have sought my life; **Ps 54:3** 6184
band of v men have sought my life, **Ps 86:14** 6184
Preserve me from v men **Ps 140:1** 2555
Preserve me from v men Who **Ps 140:4** 2555
evil hunt the v man speedily." **Ps 140:11** 2555
you from the grasp of the v." **Jer 15:21** 6184
and a v wind will break out. **Ezk 13:11** 5591b
"I will make a v wind break out in **Ezk 13:13** 5591b
may have a v son who sheds blood and **Ezk 18:10** 6530
the v ones among your people will **Da 11:14** 6530
And Jerusalem with v injustice. **Mi 3:10** 5767b
They were so extremely v that no **Mt 8:28** *5467*
and v men take it by force. **Mt 11:12** *973*
from heaven a noise like a v rushing **Ac 2:2** *972*
down from the land a v wind, **Ac 27:14** *5189*
a persecutor and a v aggressor. **1Tm 1:13** *5197*

VIOLENTLY
Then Isaac trembled v, **Gn 27:33** 2731, 1419, 5704, 3966
and the whole mountain quaked v. **Ex 19:18** 3966
Israel, and he deals with him v or **Dt 24:7** 6014b
pushed me v so that I was falling, **Ps 118:13** 1760
through, The earth is shaken v. **Is 24:19** 4131
And He has v treated His **La 2:6** 2554
as we were being v storm-tossed, **Ac 27:18** *4971*

VIOLET
in purple, crimson and v *fabrics,* **2Ch 2:7** 8504
stone and wood, *and* in purple, v, **2Ch 2:14** 8504
He made the veil of v, **2Ch 3:14** 8504
hangings of fine white and v linen **Es 1:6** 8504
V and purple are their clothing; **Jer 10:9** 8504

VIPER
Poison of a v is under their lips. **Ps 140:3** 5919
a serpent And stings like a v. **Pr 23:32** 6848b
serpent's root a v will come out, **Is 14:29** 6848a
and lion, v and flying serpent, **Is 30:6** 660
a v came out because of the heat and **Ac 28:3** *2191*

VIPER'S
The v tongue slays him. **Jb 20:16** 660
child will put his hand on the v den. **Is 11:8** 6848b

VIPERS
"You brood of v, who warned you **Mt 3:7** *2191*
"You brood of v, how can you, **Mt 12:34** *2191*
"You serpents, you brood of v, **Mt 23:33** *2191*
"You brood of v, who warned you **Lk 3:7** *2191*

VIRGIN
The girl was very beautiful, a v, **Gn 24:16** 1330
seduces a v who is not engaged, **Ex 22:16** 1330
also for his v sister, who is near **Lv 21:3** 1330
is to marry a v of his own people, **Lv 21:14** 1330
near her, I did not find her a v,' **Dt 22:14** 1331
"I did not find your daughter a v." **Dt 22:17** 1331
he publicly defamed a v of Israel. **Dt 22:19** 1330
that the girl was not found a v, **Dt 22:20** 1331
girl who is a v engaged to a man, **Dt 22:23** 1330
"If a man finds a girl who is a v, **Dt 22:28** 1330
Both young man and v, **Dt 32:25** 1330
my v daughter and his concubine. **Jg 19:24** 1330
made himself ill, for she was a v, **2Sa 13:2** 1330
the v daughters of the king dressed **2Sa 13:18** 1330
a young v for my lord the king, **1Ki 1:2** 1330
you, The v daughter of Zion; **2Ki 19:21** 1330
no compassion on young man or v, **2Ch 36:17** 1330
may gather every beautiful young v **Es 2:3** 1330
How then could I gaze at a v? **Jb 31:1** 1330
a v will be with child and bear a **Is 7:14** 5959
O crushed v daughter of Sidon. **Is 23:12** 1330
you, The v daughter of Zion; **Is 37:22** 1330
the dust, O v daughter of Babylon; **Is 47:1** 1330
For *as* a young man marries a v, **Is 62:5** 1330
"Can a v forget her ornaments, Or **Jer 2:32** 1330
For the v daughter of my people **Jer 14:17** 1330
The v of Israel Has done a most **Jer 18:13** 1330
will be rebuilt, O v of Israel! **Jer 31:4** 1330
the v will rejoice in the dance, **Jer 31:13** 1330
Return, O v of Israel, Return to **Jer 31:21** 1330
balm, O v daughter of Egypt! **Jer 46:11** 1330
you I shatter young man and v, **Jer 51:22** 1330
press The v daughter of Judah. **La 1:15** 1330
comfort you, O v daughter of Zion? **La 2:13** 1330
there their v bosom was handled. **Ezk 23:3** 1331
and they handled her v bosom and **Ezk 23:8** 1331
Wail like a v girded with sackcloth **Jl 1:8** 1330
The v Israel. She *lies* neglected on **Am 5:2** 1330
BEHOLD, THE V SHALL BE WITH CHILD **Mt 1:23** *3933*
kept her a v until she gave birth to **Mt 1:25** *3756, 1097*
to a v engaged to a man whose name **Lk 1:27** *3933*
"How can this be, since I am a v?" **Lk 1:34** *435, 3756, 1097*
Now this man had four v daughters **Ac 21:9** *3933*
and if a v marries, she has **1Co 7:28** *3933*
woman who is unmarried, and the v, **1Co 7:34** *3933*
unbecomingly toward his v *daughter,* **1Co 7:36** *3933*
heart, to keep his own v *daughter,* **1Co 7:37** *3933*
gives his own v *daughter* in marriage **1Co 7:38** *3933*
I might present you *as* a pure v. **2Co 11:2** *3933*

VIRGINITY
'He shall take a wife in her v. **Lv 21:13** 1331
bring out the *evidence* of the girl's v to **Dt 22:15** 1331
the evidence of my daughter's v.' **Dt 22:17** 1331
and weep because of my v, **Jg 11:37** 1331
on the mountains because of her v. **Jg 11:38** 1331

VIRGIN'S
and the v name was Mary. **Lk 1:27** *3933*

VIRGINS
money equal to the dowry for v. **Ex 22:17** 1330
of Jabesh-gilead 400 young v who had **Jg 21:12** 1330
young v be sought for the king. **Es 2:2** 1330
with him more than all the v, **Es 2:17** 1330
When the v were gathered **Es 2:19** 1330
The v, her companions who follow **Ps 45:14** 1330
And His v had no wedding songs. **Ps 78:63** 1330
Both young men and v; **Ps 148:12** 1330
up young men *nor* reared v." **Is 23:4** 1330
are groaning, Her v are afflicted, **La 1:4** 1330
My v and my young men Have gone **La 1:18** 1330
The v of Jerusalem Have bowed **La 2:10** 1330
My v and my young men Have fallen **La 2:21** 1330
The v in the cities of Judah. **La 5:11** 1330
but shall take v from the offspring of **Ezk 44:22** 1330
the beautiful v And the young men **Am 8:13** 1330
men flourish, and new wine the v. **Zch 9:17** 1330
will be comparable to ten v, **Mt 25:1** *3933*
"Then all those v rose and **Mt 25:7** *3933*
"Later the other v also came, **Mt 25:11** *3933*
concerning v I have no command of **1Co 7:25** *3933*

VIRILITY
The first *issue* of their v in the tents **Ps 78:51** 202

VISIBLE
tops of the mountains became v. **Gn 8:5** 7200
has become v to me in the house.' **Lv 14:35** 7200
v to the end of the whole earth. **Da 4:11** 2379
sky and was v to all the earth **Da 4:20** 2379
granted that He become v, **Ac 10:40** *1717*
But all things become v when they **Eph 5:13** *5319*
everything that becomes v is light. **Eph 5:13** *5319*
and on earth, v and invisible, **Col 1:16** *3707*
not made out of things which are v. **Heb 11:3** *5316*

VISION
of the LORD came to Abram in a v, **Gn 15:1** 4236
make Myself known to him in a v. **Nu 12:6** 4759a
Who sees the v of the Almighty, **Nu 24:4** 4236
Who sees the v of the Almighty, **Nu 24:16** 4236
was afraid to tell the v to Eli. **1Sa 3:15** 4759a
all these words and all this v, **2Sa 7:17** 2384
words and according to all this v, **1Ch 17:15** 2377
understanding through the v of God; **2Ch 26:5** 7200
in the v of Isaiah the prophet, **2Ch 32:32** 2377
Even like a v of the night he is **Jb 20:8** 2384
"In a dream, a v of the night, **Jb 33:15** 2384
You spoke in v to Your godly **Ps 89:19** 2377
Where there is no v, **Pr 29:18** 2377
The v of Isaiah the son of Amoz **Is 1:1** 2377
A harsh v has been shown to me; **Is 21:2** 2380
oracle concerning the valley of v. **Is 22:1** 2384
and confusion In the valley of v, **Is 22:5** 2384
be like a dream, a v of the night. **Is 29:7** 2377
The entire v will be to you **Is 29:11** 2380
are prophesying to you a false v, **Jer 14:14** 2377
speak a v of their own imagination, **Jer 23:16** 2377
prophets find No v from the LORD. **La 2:9** 2377
for the v regarding all their **Ezk 7:13** 2377
they will seek a v from a prophet, **Ezk 7:26** 2377
and brought me in a v by the Spirit **Ezk 11:24** 4758
So the v that I had seen left me. **Ezk 11:24** 4758
days are long and every v fails'? **Ezk 12:22** 2377
as the fulfillment of every v. **Ezk 12:23** 2377
there will no longer be any false v or **Ezk 12:24** 2377
'The v that he sees is for many **Ezk 12:27** 2377
"Did you not see a false v and **Ezk 13:7** 4236
appearance of the v which I saw, **Ezk 43:3** 4758
like the v which I saw when He **Ezk 43:3** 4758
And the visions *were* like the v **Ezk 43:3** 4758
revealed to Daniel in a night v. **Da 2:19** 2376
"I was looking in my v by night, **Da 7:2** 2376
the king a v appeared to me, **Da 8:1** 2377
I looked in the v, **Da 8:2** 2377
and I looked in the v and **Da 8:2** 2377
"How long will the v *about* the **Da 8:13** 2377
When I, Daniel, had seen the v, **Da 8:15** 2377
man an understanding of the v." **Da 8:16** 4758
the v pertains to the time of the end **Da 8:17** 2377
The v of the evenings and mornings **Da 8:26** 4758
But keep the v secret, For *it* **Da 8:26** 2377
but I was astounded at the v, **Da 8:27** 4758
I had seen in the v previously, **Da 9:21** 2377
and gain understanding of the v. **Da 9:23** 4758
to seal up v and prophecy and **Da 9:24** 2377
and had an understanding of the v. **Da 10:1** 4758
Now I, Daniel, alone saw the v, **Da 10:7** 4759a
were with me did not see the v; **Da 10:7** 4759a
left alone and saw this great v; **Da 10:8** 4759a
for the v pertains to the days yet **Da 10:14** 2377
as a result of the v anguish has come **Da 10:16** 4759a
up in order to fulfill the v, **Da 11:14** 2377
The v of Obadiah. **Ob 1:1** 2377
without v, And darkness for you **Mi 3:6** 2377
The book of the v of Nahum **Na 1:1** 2377
"Record the v And inscribe *it* on **Hab 2:2** 2377
v is yet for the appointed time; **Hab 2:3** 2377
will each be ashamed of his v when **Zch 13:4** 2384
"Tell the v to no one until the **Mt 17:9** *3705*
he had seen a v in the temple; **Lk 1:22** *3701*
they had also seen a v of angels who **Lk 24:23** *3701*
and the Lord said to him in a v, **Ac 9:10** *3705*
and he has seen in a v a man named **Ac 9:12** *3705*
he clearly saw in a v an angel of God **Ac 10:3** *3705*
the v which he had seen might be, **Ac 10:17** *3705*
Peter was reflecting on the v, **Ac 10:19** *3705*
and in a trance I saw a v, **Ac 11:5** *3705*

but thought he was seeing a **v**. **Ac 12:9** *3705*
A **v** appeared to Paul in the night: **Ac 16:9** *3705*
When he had seen the **v**, **Ac 16:10** *3705*
said to Paul in the night by a **v**, **Ac 18:9** *3705*
disobedient to the heavenly **v**, **Ac 26:19** *3701*
this is how I saw in the **v** the horses **Rv 9:17** *3706*

VISIONS

God spoke to Israel in **v** of the night **Gn 46:2** 4759a
in those days, **v** were infrequent. **1Sa 3:1** 2377
and in the **v** of Iddo the seer **2Ch 9:29** 2378
thoughts from the **v** of the night, **Jb 4:13** 2384
with dreams And terrify me by **v**; **Jb 7:14** 2384
They reel while having **v**, **Is 28:7** 7203b
"You must not see **v**"; **Is 30:10**
seen for you False and foolish **v**; **La 2:14**
were opened and I saw **v** of God. **Ezk 1:1** 4759a
and brought me in the **v** of God to **Ezk 8:3** 4759a
prophets who see false **v** and utter **Ezk 13:9** 7723
and who see **v** of peace for her **Ezk 13:16** 2377
women will no longer see false **v** or **Ezk 13:23** 7723
while they see for you false **v**, **Ezk 21:29** 7723
seeing false **v** and divining lies for **Ezk 22:28** 7723
In the **v** of God He brought me into **Ezk 40:2** 4759a
And the **v** *were* like the vision **Ezk 43:3** 4759a
all *kinds of* **v** and dreams. **Da 1:17** 2377
This was your dream and the **v** in **Da 2:28** 2376
the **v** in my mind kept alarming me. **Da 4:5** 2376
v of my dream which I have seen, **Da 4:9** 2376
v in my mind *as I lay* on my bed: **Da 4:10** 2376
v in my mind *as I lay* on my bed, **Da 4:13** 2376
Daniel saw a dream and **v** in his mind **Da 7:1** 2376
I kept looking in the night **v**, **Da 7:7** 2376
"I kept looking in the night **v**, **Da 7:13** 2376
the **v** in my mind kept alarming me. **Da 7:15** 2376
prophets, And I gave numerous **v**, **Hos 12:10** 2377
dreams, Your young men will see **v**. **Jl 2:28** 2384
which he envisioned in **v** **Am 1:1** 2372
And the diviners see lying **v** And **Zch 10:2** 8267
AND YOUR YOUNG MEN SHALL SEE **V**, **Ac 2:17** *3706*
I will go on to **v** and revelations of **2Co 12:1** *3701*
taking his stand on **v** he has seen, **Col 2:18**

VISIT

to **v** the daughters of the land. **Gn 34:1** 7200
v Nabal and greet him in my name; **1Sa 25:5** 935, 413
Some years later he went down to **v** **2Ch 18:2**
v your abode and fear no loss. **Jb 5:24** 6485
You **v** the earth and cause **Ps 65:9** 6485
V me with Your salvation, **Ps 106:4** 6485
years that the LORD will **v** Tyre. **Is 23:17** 6485
be there until the day I **v** them,' **Jer 27:22** 6485
I will **v** you and fulfill My good **Jer 29:10** 6485
he will be there until I **v** him," **Jer 32:5** 6485
in prison, and you did not **v** Me.' **Mt 25:43** *1980a*
Sunrise from on high will **v** us, **Lk 1:78** *1980a*
"On the second **v** Joseph made **Ac 7:13**
his mind to **v** his brethren, **Ac 7:23** *1980a*
with a foreigner or to **v** him; **Ac 10:28** *4334*
"Let us return and **v** the brethren **Ac 15:36** *1980a*
to **v** orphans and widows in their **Jas 1:27** *1980a*

VISITATION

recognize the time of your **v**." **Lk 19:44** *1984*
them, glorify God in the day of **v**. **1Pe 2:12** *1984*

VISITED

since you have **v** your servant." **Gn 18:5** 5674a
and **v** a certain Adullamite, **Gn 38:1** 5186
Samson **v** his wife with a young goat **Jg 15:1** 6485
the LORD had **v** His people in giving **Ru 1:6** 6485
The LORD **v** Hannah; **1Sa 2:21** 6485
because He has not **v** *in* His anger, **Jb 35:15** 6485
You have **v** *me* by night; **Ps 17:3** 6485
the LORD of hosts has **v** His flock, **Zch 10:3** 6485
I was sick, and you **v** Me; **Mt 25:36** *1980a*
For He has **v** us and accomplished **Lk 1:68** *1980a*
"God has **v** His people!" **Lk 7:16** *1980a*

VISITING

v the iniquity of the fathers on **Ex 20:5** 6485
v the iniquity of fathers on the **Ex 34:7** 6485
v the iniquity of the fathers on **Nu 14:18** 6485
v the iniquity of the fathers on **Dt 5:9** 6485
"Are You the only one **v** Jerusalem **Lk 24:18** *3939*
Athenians and the strangers **v** there **Ac 17:21** *1927*

VISITORS

around Cyrene, and **v** from Rome, **Ac 2:10** *1927*

VITALITY

My **v** was drained away *as* with the **Ps 32:4** 3955

VOCATION

the boy's mode of life and his **v**?" **Jg 13:12** 4639

VOICE

listened to the **v** of your wife, **Gn 3:17** 6963
The **v** of your brother's blood is **Gn 4:10** 6963
"Adah and Zillah, Listen to my **v**, **Gn 4:23** 6963
Abram listened to the **v** of Sarai. **Gn 16:2** 6963
him, and lifted up her **v** and wept. **Gn 21:16** 6963
for God has heard the **v** of the lad **Gn 21:17** 6963
because you have obeyed My **v**." **Gn 22:18** 6963
only obey my **v**, and go, get *them* **Gn 27:13** 6963
"The **v** is the voice of Jacob, but **Gn 27:22** 6963
"The voice is the **v** of Jacob, **Gn 27:22** 6963
So Esau lifted his **v** and wept. **Gn 27:38** 6963
"Now therefore, my son, obey my **v**, **Gn 27:43** 6963
Rachel, and lifted his **v** and wept. **Gn 29:11** 6963
and has indeed heard my **v** and has **Gn 30:6** 6963
that I raised my **v** and screamed, **Gn 39:15** 6963
as I raised my **v** and screamed, **Gn 39:18** 6963
obey His **v** to let Israel go? **Ex 5:2** 6963
earnest heed to the **v** of the LORD **Ex 15:26** 6963
obey My **v** and keep My covenant, **Ex 19:5** 6963

guard before him and obey his **v**; **Ex 23:21** 6963
obey his **v** and do all that I say, **Ex 23:22** 6963
the people answered with one **v** and **Ex 24:3** 6963
he heard the **v** speaking to him **Nu 7:89** 6963
and have not listened to My **v**, **Nu 14:22** 6963
He heard our **v** and sent an angel **Nu 20:16** 6963
The LORD heard the **v** of Israel **Nu 21:3** 6963
the LORD did not listen to your **v** nor **Dt 1:45** 6963
but you saw no form—only a **v**. **Dt 4:12** 6963
LORD your God and listen to His **v**. **Dt 4:30** 6963
"Has *any* people heard the **v** of God **Dt 4:33** 6963
you hear His **v** to discipline you; **Dt 4:36** 6963
the thick gloom, with a great **v**, **Dt 5:22** 6963
when you heard the **v** from the **Dt 5:23** 6963
we have heard His **v** from the midst **Dt 5:24** 6963
if we hear the **v** of the LORD our **Dt 5:25** 6963
has heard the **v** of the living God **Dt 5:26** 6963
The LORD heard the **v** of your words **Dt 5:28** 6963
'I have heard the **v** of the words **Dt 5:28** 6963
to the **v** of the LORD your God. **Dt 8:20** 6963
Him nor listened to His **v**. **Dt 9:23** 6963
His commandments, listen to His **v**, **Dt 13:4** 6963
to the **v** of the LORD your God, **Dt 13:18** 6963
to the **v** of the LORD your God, **Dt 15:5** 6963
again the **v** of the LORD my God, **Dt 18:16** 6963
and the LORD heard our **v** and saw **Dt 26:7** 6963
to the **v** of the LORD my God; **Dt 26:14** 6963
ordinances, and listen to His **v**. **Dt 26:17** 6963
the men of Israel with a loud **v**, **Dt 27:14** 6963
LORD your God, by obeying His **v**, **Dt 30:20** 6963
"Hear, O LORD, the **v** of Judah, **Dt 33:7** 6963
not listen to the **v** of the LORD, **Jos 5:6** 6963
not shout nor let your **v** be heard nor **Jos 6:10** 6963
LORD listened to the **v** of a man; **Jos 10:14** 6963
have listened to my **v** in all that I **Jos 22:2** 6963
our God and we will obey His **v**." **Jos 24:24** 6963
and has not listened to My **v**, **Jg 2:20** 6963
and lifted his **v** and called out. **Jg 9:7** 6963
God listened to the **v** of Manoah; **Jg 13:9** 6963
recognized the **v** of the young man, **Jg 18:3** 6963
not let your **v** be heard among us, **Jg 18:25** 6963
listen to the **v** of their brothers, **Jg 20:13** 6963
moving, but her **v** was not heard. **1Sa 1:13** 6963
listen to the **v** of their father, **1Sa 2:25** 6963
"Listen to the **v** of the people in **1Sa 8:7** 6963
"Now then, listen to their **v**; **1Sa 8:9** 6963
to listen to the **v** of Samuel, **1Sa 8:19** 6963
"Listen to their **v** and appoint **1Sa 8:22** 6963
I have listened to your **v** in all that **1Sa 12:1** 6963
and listen to His **v** and not rebel **1Sa 12:14** 6963
not listen to the **v** of the LORD, **1Sa 12:15** 6963
did you not obey the **v** of the LORD, **1Sa 15:19** 6963
"I did obey the **v** of the LORD, **1Sa 15:20** 6963
As in obeying the **v** of the LORD? **1Sa 15:22** 6963
people and listened to their **v**. **1Sa 15:24** 6963
listened to the **v** of Jonathan, **1Sa 19:6** 6963
"Is this your **v**, my son David?" **1Sa 24:16** 6963
Saul lifted up his **v** and wept. **1Sa 24:16** 6963
Saul recognized David's **v** and said, **1Sa 26:17** 6963
"Is this your **v**, my son David?" **1Sa 26:17** 6963
"It is my **v**, my lord the king." **1Sa 26:17** 6963
she cried out with a loud **v**; **1Sa 28:12** 6963
listen to the **v** of your maidservant, **1Sa 28:22** 6963
and the king lifted up his **v** and **2Sa 3:32** 6963
and he did not listen to our **v**. **2Sa 12:18** 6963
country was weeping with a loud **v**, **2Sa 15:23** 6963
face and cried out with a loud **v**, **2Sa 19:4** 6963
the **v** of singing men and women? **2Sa 19:35** 6963
And from His temple He heard my **v**, **2Sa 22:7** 6963
And the Most High uttered His **v**. **2Sa 22:14** 6963
assembly of Israel with a loud **v**, **1Ki 8:55** 6963
The LORD heard the **v** of Elijah, **1Ki 17:22** 6963
was no **v** and no one answered. **1Ki 18:26** 6963
"Call out with a loud **v**, **1Ki 18:27** 6963
So they cried with a loud **v** and **1Ki 18:28** 6963
but there was no **v**, **1Ki 18:29** 6963
behold, a **v** *came* to him and said, **1Ki 19:13** 6963
he listened to their **v** and did so. **1Ki 20:25** 6963
not listened to the **v** of the LORD, **1Ki 20:36** 6963
no one there, nor the **v** of man, **2Ki 7:10** 6963
side, and you will listen to my **v**, **2Ki 10:6** 6963
obey the **v** of the LORD their God, **2Ki 18:12** 6963
and cried with a loud **v** in Judean, **2Ki 18:28** 6963
whom have you raised *your* **v**, **2Ki 19:22** 6963
to make themselves heard with one **v** **2Ch 5:13** 6963
and when they lifted up their **v** **2Ch 5:13** 6963
an oath to the LORD with a loud **v**, **2Ch 15:14** 6963
God of Israel, with a very loud **v**. **2Ch 20:19** 6963
and their **v** was heard and their **2Ch 30:27** 6963
They called this out with a loud **v** in **2Ch 32:18** 6963
wept with a loud **v** when the **Ezr 3:12** 6963
replied with a loud **v**, **Ezr 10:12** 6963
they cried with a loud **v** to the LORD **Ne 9:4** 6963
not hear the **v** of the taskmaster. **Jb 3:18** 6963
lion and the **v** of the *fierce* lion, **Jb 4:10** 6963
was silence, then I heard a **v**: **Jb 4:16** 6963
that He was listening to my **v**. **Jb 9:16** 6963
The **v** of the nobles was hushed, **Jb 29:10** 6963
closely to the thunder of His **v**, **Jb 37:2** 6963
"After it, a **v** roars; **Jb 37:4** 6963
He thunders with His majestic **v**, **Jb 37:4** 6963
lightnings when His **v** is heard. **Jb 37:4** 6963
thunders with His **v** wondrously, **Jb 37:5** 6963
you lift up your **v** to the clouds, **Jb 38:34** 6963
still at the **v** of the trumpet. **Jb 39:24** 6963
can you thunder with a **v** like His? **Jb 40:9** 6963
was crying to the LORD with my **v**, **Ps 3:4** 6963
O LORD, You will hear my **v**; **Ps 5:3** 6963
has heard the **v** of my weeping. **Ps 6:8** 6963

He heard my **v** out of His temple, **Ps 18:6** 6963
And the Most High uttered His **v**, **Ps 18:13** 6963
Their **v** is not heard. **Ps 19:3** 6963
proclaim with the **v** of thanksgiving **Ps 26:7** 6963
O LORD, when I cry with my **v**, **Ps 27:7** 6963
Hear the **v** of my supplications **Ps 28:2** 6963
heard the **v** of my supplication. **Ps 28:6** 6963
The **v** of the LORD is upon the **Ps 29:3** 6963
The **v** of the LORD is powerful, The **Ps 29:4** 6963
The **v** of the LORD is majestic. **Ps 29:4** 6963
v of the LORD breaks the cedars; **Ps 29:5** 6963
The **v** of the LORD hews out flames **Ps 29:7** 6963
The **v** of the LORD shakes the **Ps 29:8** 6963
The **v** of the LORD makes the deer **Ps 29:9** 6963
heard the **v** of my supplications **Ps 31:22** 6963
the **v** of joy and thanksgiving, **Ps 42:4** 6963
v of him who reproaches and reviles **Ps 44:16** 6963
He raised His **v**, the earth melted. **Ps 46:6** 6963
Shout to God with the **v** of joy. **Ps 47:1** 6963
Because of the **v** of the enemy, **Ps 55:3** 6963
and murmur, And He will hear my **v**. **Ps 55:17** 6963
does not hear the **v** of charmers, **Ps 58:5** 6963
Hear my **v**, O God, in my complaint; **Ps 64:1** 6963
given heed to the **v** of my prayer. **Ps 66:19** 6963
He speaks forth with His **v**, **Ps 68:33** 6963
forth with His voice, a mighty **v**. **Ps 68:33** 6963
forget the **v** of Your adversaries, **Ps 74:23** 6963
My **v** *rises* to God, and I will cry **Ps 77:1** 6963
My **v** *rises* to God, and He will **Ps 77:1** 6963
My people did not listen to My **v**, **Ps 81:11** 6963
heed to the **v** of my supplications! **Ps 86:6** 6963
The floods have lifted up their **v**, **Ps 93:3** 6963
Today, if you would hear His **v**, **Ps 95:7** 6963
word, Obeying the **v** of His word! **Ps 103:20** 6963
not listen to the **v** of the LORD. **Ps 106:25** 6963
He hears My **v** *and* my supplications. **Ps 116:1** 6963
Hear my **v** according to Your **Ps 119:149** 6963
Lord, hear my **v**! Let Your ears be **Ps 130:2** 6963
To the **v** of my supplications. **Ps 130:2** 6963
to the **v** of my supplications. **Ps 140:6** 6963
Give ear to my **v** when I call to You **Ps 141:1** 6963
I cry aloud with my **v** to the LORD; **Ps 142:1** 6963
I make supplication with my **v** to **Ps 142:1** 6963
She lifts her **v** in the square; **Pr 1:20** 6963
Lift your **v** for understanding; **Pr 2:3** 6963
not listened to the **v** of my teachers, **Pr 5:13** 6963
And understanding lift up her **v**? **Pr 8:1** 6963
And my **v** is to the sons of men. **Pr 8:4** 6963
who blesses his friend with a loud **v** **Pr 27:14** 6963
v of a fool through many words. **Ec 5:3** 6963
God be angry on account of your **v** **Ec 5:6** 6963
And the **v** of the turtledove has **SS 2:12** 6963
see your form, Let me hear your **v**; **SS 2:14** 6963
For your **v** is sweet, And your form **SS 2:14** 6963
A **v**! My beloved was knocking: **SS 5:2** 6963
companions are listening for your **v** **SS 8:13** 6963
trembled at the **v** of him who called **Is 6:4** 6963
Then I heard the **v** of the Lord, **Is 6:8** 6963
Cry aloud with your **v**, **Is 10:30** 6963
bare hill, Raise your **v** to them, **Is 13:2** 6963
v is heard all the way to Jahaz; **Is 15:4** 6963
Give ear and hear my **v**, **Is 28:23** 6963
Your **v** will also be like that of **Is 29:4** 6963
His **v** of authority to be heard, **Is 30:30** 6963
For at the **v** of the LORD Assyria **Is 30:31** 6963
will not be terrified at their **v** **Is 31:4** 6963
who are at ease, *And* hear my **v**; **Is 32:9** 6963
and cried with a loud **v** in Judean and **Is 36:13** 6963
whom have you raised *your* **v** And **Is 37:23** 6963
A **v** is calling, "Clear the way for the **Is 40:3** 6963
A **v** says, "Call out." **Is 40:6** 6963
news, Lift up your **v** mightily, **Is 40:9** 6963
"He will not cry out or raise *His* **v**, **Is 42:2**
make His **v** heard in the street. **Is 42:2** 6963
That obeys the **v** of His servant, **Is 50:10** 6963
Raise your **v** like a trumpet, And **Is 58:1** 6963
to make your **v** heard on high. **Is 58:4** 6963
v of weeping and the sound of crying **Is 65:19** 6963
"A **v** of uproar from the city, a **Is 66:6** 6963
the city, a **v** from the temple, **Is 66:6** 6963
The **v** of the LORD who is rendering **Is 66:6** 6963
And you have not obeyed My **v**,' **Jer 3:13** 6963
A **v** is heard on the bare heights, **Jer 3:21** 6963
the **v** of the LORD our God." **Jer 3:25** 6963
For a **v** declares from Dan, And **Jer 4:15** 6963
Their **v** roars like the sea, And **Jer 6:23** 6963
'Obey My **v**, and I will be your God **Jer 7:23** 6963
that did not obey the **v** of the LORD **Jer 7:28** 6963
the **v** of joy and the voice of gladness **Jer 7:34** 6963
of joy and the **v** of gladness, **Jer 7:34** 6963
the **v** of the bridegroom and the **Jer 7:34** 6963
bridegroom and the **v** of the bride; **Jer 7:34** 6963
have not obeyed My **v** nor walked **Jer 9:13** 6963
a **v** of wailing is heard from Zion, **Jer 9:19** 6963
When He utters His **v**, **Jer 10:13** 6963
'Listen to My **v**, and do according **Jer 11:4** 6963
"Listen to My **v**." **Jer 11:7** 6963
the **v** of rejoicing and the voice **Jer 16:9** 6963
rejoicing and the **v** of gladness, **Jer 16:9** 6963
the **v** of the groom and the voice **Jer 16:9** 6963
the groom and the **v** of the bride. **Jer 16:9** 6963
in My sight by not obeying My **v**, **Jer 18:10** 6963
out, And lift up your **v** in Bashan; **Jer 22:20** 6963
That you have not obeyed My **v**. **Jer 22:21** 6963
I will take from them the **v** of joy **Jer 25:10** 6963
of joy and the **v** of gladness, **Jer 25:10** 6963
the **v** of the bridegroom and the **Jer 25:10** 6963
bridegroom and the **v** of the bride, **Jer 25:10** 6963
His **v** from His holy habitation; **Jer 25:30** 6963

obey the **v** of the LORD your God; Jer 26:13 6963
And the **v** of those who celebrate; Jer 30:19 6963
"A **v** is heard in Ramah, Jer 31:15 6963
"Restrain your **v** from weeping And Jer 31:16 6963
not obey Your **v** or walk in Your law; Jer 32:23 6963
the **v** of joy and the voice of Jer 33:11 6963
of joy and the **v** of gladness, Jer 33:11 6963
the **v** of the bridegroom and the Jer 33:11 6963
bridegroom and the **v** of the bride, Jer 33:11 6963
the bride, the **v** of those who say, Jer 33:11 6963
v of Jonadab the son of Rechab, Jer 35:8 6963
LORD and did not listen to His **v**, Jer 40:3 6963
listen to the **v** of the LORD our God Jer 42:6 6963
to the **v** of the LORD our God." Jer 42:6 6963
to the **v** of the LORD your God, Jer 42:13 6963
did not obey the **v** of the LORD to Jer 43:4 6963
did not obey the **v** of the LORD) Jer 43:7 6963
and not obeyed the **v** of the LORD or Jer 44:23 6963
to Jahaz they have raised their **v**, Jer 48:34 6963
Their **v** roars like the sea; And Jer 50:42 6963
When He utters His **v**, Jer 51:16 6963
You have heard my **v**, La 3:56 6963
went, like the **v** of the Almighty, Ezk 1:24 6963
And there came a **v** from above the Ezk 1:25 6963
on my face and heard a **v** speaking. Ezk 1:28 6963
they cry in My ears with a loud **v**, Ezk 8:18 6963
my hearing with a loud **v** saying, Ezk 9:1 6963
like the **v** of God Almighty when He Ezk 10:5 6963
cried out with a loud **v** and said, Ezk 11:13 6963
So that his **v** would be heard no more Ezk 19:9 6963
lift up the **v** with a battle cry, Ezk 21:22 6963
And they will make their **v** heard Ezk 27:30 6963
song by one who has a beautiful **v** Ezk 33:32 6963
And His **v** was like the sound of Ezk 43:2 6963
king's mouth, a **v** came from heaven, Da 4:31 7032a
he cried out with a troubled **v**. Da 6:20 7032a
And I heard the **v** of a man between Da 8:16 6963
obeyed the **v** of the LORD our God, Da 9:10 6963
turned aside, not obeying Your **v**; Da 9:11 6963
but we have not obeyed His **v**. Da 9:14 6963
LORD utters His **v** before His army; Jl 2:11 6963
And utters His **v** from Jerusalem, Jl 3:16 6963
from Jerusalem He utters His **v**; Am 1:2 6963
You heard my **v**. Jon 2:2 6963
You With the **v** of thanksgiving. Jon 2:9 6963
And let the hills hear your **v**. Mi 6:1 6963
The **v** of the LORD will call to the Mi 6:9 6963
v of your messengers be heard." Na 2:13 6963
The deep uttered forth its **v**, Hab 3:10 6963
She heeded no **v**, She accepted no Zph 3:2 6963
obeyed the **v** of the LORD their God Hg 1:12 6963
"A V WAS HEARD IN RAMAH, WEEPING Mt 2:18 5456
"THE V OF ONE CRYING IN THE Mt 3:3 5456
behold, a **v** out of the heavens said Mt 3:17 5456
ANYONE HEAR HIS V IN THE STREETS. Mt 12:19 5456
and behold, a **v** out of the cloud said Mt 17:5 5456
Jesus cried out with a loud **v**, Mt 27:46 5456
cried out again with a loud **v**, Mt 27:50 5456
THE V OF ONE CRYING IN THE Mk 1:3 5456
and a **v** came out of the heavens: Mk 1:11 5456
spirit cried out with a loud **v** and Mk 1:26 5456
and shouting with a loud **v**, Mk 5:7 5456
and a **v** came out of the cloud, Mk 9:7 5456
Jesus cried out with a loud **v**, Mk 15:34 5456
And she cried out with a loud **v** and Lk 1:42 2906
"THE V OF ONE CRYING IN THE Lk 3:4 5456
dove, and a **v** came out of heaven, Lk 3:22 5456
and he cried out with a loud **v**, Lk 4:33 5456
before Him, and said in a loud **v**, Lk 8:28 5456
Then a **v** came out of the cloud, Lk 9:35 5456
And when the **v** had spoken, Jesus Lk 9:36 5456
women in the crowd raised her **v** and Lk 11:27 5456
glorifying God with a loud **v**, Lk 17:15 5456
to praise God joyfully with a loud **v** Lk 19:37 5456
Jesus, crying out with a loud **v**, Lk 23:46 5456
"I am A V OF ONE CRYING IN THE Jn 1:23 5456
because of the bridegroom's **v**. Jn 3:29 5456
hear the **v** of the Son of God, Jn 5:25 5456
are in the tombs will hear His **v**, Jn 5:28 5456
neither heard His **v** at any time nor Jn 5:37 5456
opens, and the sheep hear his **v**, Jn 10:3 5456
him because they know his **v**. Jn 10:4 5456
do not know the **v** of strangers." Jn 10:5 5456
also, and they will hear My **v**; Jn 10:16 5456
"My sheep hear My **v**, Jn 10:27 5456
He cried out with a loud **v**, Jn 11:43 5456
Then a **v** came out of heaven: Jn 12:28 5456
"This **v** has not come for My sake, Jn 12:30 5456
who is of the truth hears My **v**." Jn 18:37 5456
raised his **v** and declared to them: Ac 2:14 5456
there came the **v** of the Lord: Ac 7:31 5456
But they cried out with a loud **v**, Ac 7:57 5456
knees, he cried out with a loud **v**, Ac 7:60 5456
of them shouting with a loud **v**; Ac 8:7 5456
and heard a **v** saying to him, Ac 9:4 5456
stood speechless, hearing the **v** but Ac 9:7 5456
A **v** came to him, Ac 10:13 5456
a **v** *came* to him a second time, Ac 10:15 5456
"I also heard a **v** saying to me, Ac 11:7 5456
"But a **v** from heaven answered a Ac 11:9 5456
When she recognized Peter's **v**, Ac 12:14 5456
"The **v** of a god and not of a man!" Ac 12:22 5456
said with a loud **v**, Ac 14:10 5456
had done, they raised their **v**, Ac 14:11 5456
But Paul cried out with a loud **v**, Ac 16:28 5456
ground and heard a **v** saying to me, Ac 22:7 5456
did not understand the **v** of the One Ac 22:9 5456
I heard a **v** saying to me in the Ac 26:14 5456
defense, Festus said in a loud **v**, Ac 26:24 5456
"THEIR V HAS GONE OUT INTO ALL Ro 10:18 5353
you may with one **v** glorify the God Ro 15:6 4750
with the **v** of *the* archangel and 1Th 4:16 5456
"TODAY IF YOU HEAR HIS V Heb 3:7 5456
"TODAY IF YOU HEAR HIS V, Heb 3:15 5456
"TODAY IF YOU HEAR HIS V, Heb 4:7 5456
And His **v** shook the earth then, Heb 12:26 5456
speaking with a **v** of a man, 2Pe 2:16 5456
a loud **v** like *the sound* of a trumpet, Rv 1:10 5456
the **v** that was speaking with me. Rv 1:12 5456
and His **v** *was* like the sound of Rv 1:15 5456
hears My **v** and opens the door, Rv 3:20 5456
and the first **v** which I had heard, Rv 4:1 5456
angel proclaiming with a loud **v**, Rv 5:2 5456
and I heard the **v** of many angels Rv 5:11 5456
saying with a loud **v**, Rv 5:12 5456
saying as with a **v** of thunder, Rv 6:1 5456
And I heard *something* like a **v** in the Rv 6:6 5456
the **v** of the fourth living creature Rv 6:7 5456
and they cried out with a loud **v**, Rv 6:10 5456
and he cried out with a loud **v** to Rv 7:2 5456
and they cry out with a loud **v**, Rv 7:10 5456
midheaven, saying with a loud **v**, Rv 8:13 5456
and I heard a **v** from the four Rv 9:13 5456
and he cried out with a loud **v**, Rv 10:3 5456
I heard a **v** from heaven saying, Rv 10:4 5456
days of the **v** of the seventh angel, Rv 10:7 5456
the **v** which I heard from heaven, Rv 10:8 5456
loud **v** from heaven saying to them, Rv 11:12 5456
Then I heard a loud **v** in heaven, Rv 12:10 5456
And I heard a **v** from heaven, like Rv 14:2 5456
and the **v** which I heard *was* like Rv 14:2 5456
and he said with a loud **v**, Rv 14:7 5456
them, saying with a loud **v**, Rv 14:9 5456
And I heard a **v** from heaven, Rv 14:13 5456
crying out with a loud **v** to Him Rv 14:15 5456
and he called with a loud **v** to him Rv 14:18 5456
I heard a loud **v** from the temple, Rv 16:1 5456
and a loud **v** came out of the Rv 16:17 5456
And he cried out with a mighty **v**, Rv 18:2 5456
I heard another **v** from heaven, Rv 18:4 5456
and the **v** of the bridegroom and Rv 18:23 5456
a loud **v** of a great multitude in Rv 19:1 5456
And a **v** came from the throne, Rv 19:5 5456
the **v** of a great multitude and like Rv 19:6 5456
and he cried out with a loud **v**, Rv 19:17 5456
I heard a loud **v** from the throne, Rv 21:3 5456

VOICES

lifted up their **v** and cried, Nu 14:1 6963
people lifted up their **v** and wept. Jg 2:4 6963
lifted up their **v** and wept bitterly. Jg 21:2 6963
they lifted up their **v** and wept. Ru 1:9 6963
lifted up their **v** and wept again; Ru 1:14 6963
people lifted up their **v** and wept. 1Sa 11:4 6963
lifted their **v** and wept until there was 1Sa 30:4 6963
came and lifted their **v** and wept; 2Sa 13:36 6963
him, they raised their **v** and wept. Jb 2:12 6963
lift up *their* **v** among the branches. Ps 104:12 6963
They raise their **v**, Is 24:14 6963
and its cities lift up *their* **v**, Is 42:11
Your watchmen lift up *their* **v**, Is 52:8 6963
lift their **v** against the cities of Judah Jer 4:16 6963
tumult of their **v** sounds forth. Jer 51:55 6963
and they raised their **v**, Lk 17:13 5456
loud **v** asking that He be crucified. Lk 23:23 5456
And their **v** *began* to prevail. Lk 23:23 5456
they lifted their **v** to God with Ac 4:24 5456
then they raised their **v** and said, Ac 22:22 5456
peals of thunder uttered their **v**. Rv 10:3 5456
and there were loud **v** in heaven, Rv 11:15 5456

VOID

The earth was formless and **v**, Gn 1:2 922
but the former days will be **v** Nu 6:12 5307
and behold, *it was* formless and **v**; Jer 4:23 922
"I will make **v** the counsel Jer 19:7 1238b
for they made My covenant **v** Ezk 44:7 6565a
faith is made **v** and the promise is Ro 4:14 2758
cross of Christ would not be made **v** 1Co 1:17 2758

VOLUME

and all measures of **v** and size. 1Ch 23:29 4884

VOLUNTARILY

have **v** vowed to the LORD your God, Dt 23:23 5071
'Give them to us **v**, because we did Jg 21:22 2603a
For if I do this **v**, 1Co 9:17 1635
not under compulsion, but **v**, 1Pe 5:2 1596

VOLUNTEER

Your people will **v** freely in the Ps 110:3 5071

VOLUNTEERED

led in Israel, That the people **v**, Jg 5:2 5068
son of Zichri, who **v** for the LORD, 2Ch 17:16 5068
men who **v** to live in Jerusalem. Ne 11:2 5068

VOLUNTEERS

of Israel, The **v** among the people; Jg 5:9 5068

VOMIT

riches, But will **v** them up; Jb 20:15 7006a
v up the morsel you have eaten, Pr 23:8 7006a
you not have it in excess and **v** it. Pr 25:16 7006a
Like a dog that returns to its **v** Pr 26:11 6892
a drunken man staggers in his **v**. Is 19:14 7006b
the tables are full of filthy **v**, Is 28:8 7006b
"Drink, be drunk, **v**, Jer 25:27 7006c
so Moab will wallow in his **v**, Jer 48:26 7006b
"A DOG RETURNS TO ITS OWN V," 2Pe 2:22 1829

VOMITED

it **v** Jonah up onto the dry land. Jon 2:10 7006a

VOPHSI

of Naphtali, Nahbi the son of **V**; Nu 13:14 2058

VOTE

to death I cast my **v** against them. Ac 26:10 5586

VOTIVE

is a **v** or a freewill offering, Lv 7:16 5088
v or any of their freewill offerings Lv 22:18 5088
all your **v** and freewill offerings, Lv 23:38 5088
besides your **v** offerings and your Nu 29:39 5088
of your hand, your **v** offerings, Dt 12:6 5088
and all your choice **v** offerings Dt 12:11 5088
any of your **v** offerings which you Dt 12:17 5088
you may have and your **v** offerings, Dt 12:26 5088
LORD your God for any **v** offering, Dt 23:18 5088
with beautiful stones and **v** gifts, Lk 21:5 334

VOW

Then Jacob made a **v**, Gn 28:20 5088
pillar, where you made a **v** to Me; Gn 31:13 5088
the LORD to fulfill a special **v** or Lv 22:21 5088
for a **v** it will not be accepted. Lv 22:23 5088
'When a man makes a difficult **v**, Lv 27:2 5088
a man or woman makes a special **v**, Nu 6:2 5087
special vow, the **v** of a Nazirite, Nu 6:2 5088
'All the days of his **v** of separation Nu 6:5 5088
according to his **v** which he takes, Nu 6:21 5087
sacrifice to fulfill a special **v**, Nu 15:3 5088
sacrifice, to fulfill a special **v**, Nu 15:8 5088
So Israel made a **v** to the LORD and Nu 21:2 5088
"If a man makes a **v** to the LORD, Nu 30:2 5088
if a woman makes a **v** to the LORD, Nu 30:3 5088
and her father hears her **v** and her Nu 30:4 5088
then he shall annul her **v** which Nu 30:8 5088
"But the **v** of a widow or of a Nu 30:9 5088
"Every **v** and every binding oath Nu 30:13 5088
which you will **v** to the LORD. Dt 12:11 5087
your votive offerings which you **v**, Dt 12:17 5087
you make a **v** to the LORD your God, Dt 23:21 5088
made a **v** to the LORD and said, Jg 11:30 5088
to the **v** which he had made; Jg 11:39 5088
She made a **v** and said, 1Sa 1:11 5088
yearly sacrifice and *pay* his **v**. 1Sa 1:21 5088
Jonathan made David **v** again 1Sa 20:17 7650
"Please let me go and pay my **v** 2Sa 15:7 5088
"For your servant vowed a **v** while 2Sa 15:8 5088
to You the **v** will be performed. Ps 65:1 5088
When you make a **v** to God, do not Ec 5:4 5088
Pay what you **v**! Ec 5:4 5087
It is better that you should not **v** than Ec 5:5 5087
that you should **v** and not pay. Ec 5:5 5087
make a **v** to the LORD and perform Is 19:21 5088
hair cut, for he was keeping a **v**. Ac 18:18 2171
have four men who are under a **v**; Ac 21:23 2171

VOWED

to the means of the one who **v**, Lv 27:8 5087
if she **v** in her husband's house, Nu 30:10 5087
v to the LORD your God, Dt 23:23 5087
the voice of Jonathan, and Saul **v**, 1Sa 19:6 7650
Yet David **v** again, saying, 1Sa 20:3 7650
Saul **v** to her by the LORD, 1Sa 28:10 7650
but David **v**, saying, 2Sa 3:35 7650
my vow which I have **v** to the LORD, 2Sa 15:7 5087
"For your servant **v** a vow while I 2Sa 15:8 5087
The king **v** and said, 1Ki 1:29 7650
surely as I **v** to you by the LORD 1Ki 1:30 7650
And **v** to the Mighty One of Jacob, Ps 132:2 5087
perform our vows that we have **v**, Jer 44:25 5087
That which I have **v** I will pay. Jon 2:9 5087

VOWING

"However, if you refrain from **v**, Dt 23:22 5087

VOWS

law of the Nazirite who **v** his offering Nu 6:21 5087
her, then all her **v** shall stand and Nu 30:4 5088
none of her **v** or her obligations Nu 30:5 5088
if she should marry while under her **v** Nu 30:6 5088
then her **v** shall stand and her Nu 30:7 5088
her, then all her **v** shall stand and Nu 30:11 5088
out of her lips concerning her **v** or Nu 30:12 5088
then he confirms all her **v** or all Nu 30:14 5088
And you will pay your **v**. Jb 22:27 5088
pay my **v** before those who fear Him Ps 22:25 5088
And pay your **v** to the Most High; Ps 50:14 5088
Your **v** are *binding* upon me, O God; Ps 56:12 5088
For You have heard my **v**, Ps 61:5 5088
That I may pay my **v** day by day. Ps 61:8 5088
I shall pay You my **v**, Ps 66:13 5088
Make **v** to the LORD your God and Ps 76:11 5087
I shall pay my **v** to the LORD, Oh Ps 116:14 5088
I shall pay my **v** to the LORD, Oh Ps 116:18 5088
Today I have paid my **v**. Pr 7:14 5088
And after the **v** to make inquiry. Pr 20:25 5088
And what, O son of my **v**? Pr 31:2 5088
perform our **v** that we have vowed, Jer 44:25 5088
Go ahead and confirm your **v**, Jer 44:25 5088
and certainly perform your **v**!' Jer 44:25 5088
sacrifice to the LORD and made **v**. Jon 1:16 5088
your feasts, O Judah; Pay your **v**. Na 1:15 5088
has a male in his flock and **v** it, Mal 1:14 5087
'YOU SHALL NOT MAKE FALSE V, Mt 5:33 1964
SHALL FULFILL YOUR V TO THE LORD.' Mt 5:33 3727

VOYAGE

we had finished the **v** from Tyre, Ac 21:7 4144
and the **v** was now dangerous, Ac 27:9 4144
I perceive that the **v** will Ac 27:10 4144

VULTURE

eagle and the **v** and the buzzard, Lv 11:13 6538
and the pelican and the carrion **v**, Lv 11:18 7360
eagle and the **v** and the buzzard, Dt 14:12 6538
the pelican, the carrion **v**, Dt 14:17 7360

VULTURES
is, there the v will gather. **Mt 24:28** *105*
there also the v will be gathered." **Lk 17:37** *105*

W

WADI
set out and camped in W Zered. **Nu 21:12** 5158a
have acted deceitfully like a w, **Jb 6:15** 5158a
WADIS
And the w of the Arnon, **Nu 21:14** 5158a
And the slope of the w That extends **Nu 21:15** 5158a
Like the torrents of w which vanish, **Jb 6:15** 5158a
WAFER
of bread *mixed with* oil and one w **Ex 29:23** 7550
of bread *mixed with* oil and one w, **Lv 8:26** 7550
of the basket and one unleavened w, **Nu 6:19** 7550
WAFERS
and its taste was like w with honey. **Ex 16:31** 6838
and unleavened w spread with oil; **Ex 29:2** 7550
or unleavened w spread with oil. **Lv 2:4** 7550
and unleavened w spread with oil, **Lv 7:12** 7550
flour mixed with oil and unleavened w **Nu 6:15** 7550
and unleavened w, or *what is baked* **1Ch 23:29** 7550
WAFTED
Let its spices be w abroad. May my **SS 4:16** 5140
WAG
they w the head, *saying,* **Ps 22:7** 5128
they w their head. **Ps 109:25** 5128
WAGE
came up to Jerusalem to w war; **2Ki 16:5**
the son of Ahab king of Israel to w **2Ch 22:5** 4421
who could w war with great power, to **2Ch 26:13** 6213a
For by wise guidance you will w war, **Pr 24:6** 6213a
went up to Jerusalem to w war **Is 7:1**
multitude of all the nations who w **Is 29:7** 6633
Even all who w war against her **Is 29:7** 6633
of all the nations will be Who w war **Is 29:8** 6633
the LORD of hosts come down to w **Is 31:4** 6633
that he may again w war up to his **Da 11:10** 1624
'For before those days there was no w **Zch 8:10** 7939
there was no wage for man or any w **Zch 8:10** 7939
those who oppress the w earner **Mal 3:5** 7916
Now to the one who works, his w is **Ro 4:4** *3408*
not the source your pleasures that w **Jas 4:1** *4754*
to abstain from fleshly lusts which w **1Pe 2:11** *4754*
and who is able to w war with him?" **Rv 13:4** *4170*
"These will w war against the Lamb, **Rv 17:14** *4170*
WAGED
Joshua w war a long time with all **Jos 11:18** 6213a
'You have shed much blood and have w **1Ch 22:8** 6213a
The dragon and his angels w war, **Rv 12:7** *4170*
WAGES
what shall your w be?" **Gn 29:15** 4909
"God has given me my w because I **Gn 30:18** 7939
He continued, "Name me your w, **Gn 30:28** 7939
and *such* shall be my w. **Gn 30:32** 7939
when you come concerning my w. **Gn 30:33** 7939
has cheated me and changed my w ten **Gn 31:7** 4909
'The speckled shall be your w,' **Gn 31:8** 7939
'The striped shall be your w,' **Gn 31:8** 7939
and you changed my w ten times. **Gn 31:41** 4909
for me and I will give *you* your w." **Ex 2:9** 7939
The w of a hired man are not to **Lv 19:13** 6468
bring the hire of a harlot or the w **Dt 23:18** 4242
"You shall give him his w on his day **Dt 24:15** 7939
and your w be full from the LORD, **Ru 2:12** 4909
and I will give you w for your **1Ki 5:6** 7939
hired man who eagerly waits for his w, **Jb 7:2** 6467
The w of the righteous is life, **Pr 10:16** 6468
The wicked earns deceptive w, But he **Pr 11:18** 7938
she will go back to her harlot's w **Is 23:17** 868
Her gain and her harlot's w will be **Is 23:18** 868
And your w for what does not satisfy? **Is 55:2** 3018
pay And does not give him his w, **Jer 22:13** 6467
But he and his army had no w from **Ezk 29:18** 7939
and it will be w for his army. **Ezk 29:19** 7939
'These are my w Which my lovers have **Hos 2:12** 866
earns w *to put* into a purse with **Hg 1:6** 7939
give *me* my w; but if not, never **Zch 11:12** 7939
thirty *shekels* of silver as my w. **Zch 11:12** 7939
who oppress the wage earner in his w, **Mal 3:5** 7939
the laborers and pay them their w, **Mt 20:8** *3408*
and be content with your w." **Lk 3:14** *3800*
for the laborer is worthy of his w. **Lk 10:7** *3408*
"Already he who reaps is receiving w **Jn 4:36** *3408*
For the w of sin is death, but **Ro 6:23** *3800*
I robbed other churches by taking w **2Co 11:8** *3800*
and "The laborer is worthy of his w." **1Tm 5:18** *3408*
suffering wrong as the w of doing **2Pe 2:13** *3408*
who loved the w of unrighteousness; **2Pe 2:15** *3408*
and in righteousness He judges and w **Rv 19:11** *4170*
WAGGING
abuse at Him, w their heads **Mt 27:39** *2795*
w their heads, and saying, "Ha! **Mk 15:29** *2795*
WAGING
for the Philistines are w war against **1Sa 28:15** 3898a
and that horn was w war with **Da 7:21** 5648
w war against the law of my mind **Ro 7:23** *497*
Michael and his angels w war with **Rv 12:7** *4170*
WAGON
I am weighted down beneath you As a w **Am 2:13** 5699
WAGONS
take w from the land of Egypt for **Gn 45:19** 5699
and Joseph gave them w according to **Gn 45:21** 5699
and when he saw the w that Joseph had **Gn 45:27** 5699
little ones and their wives in the w **Gn 46:5** 5699
chariots and w, and with a company **Ezk 23:24** 1534
shake at the noise of cavalry and w **Ezk 26:10** 1534
WAHEB
"W in Suphah, And the wadis of **Nu 21:14** 2052
WAIL
W, for the day of the LORD is **Is 13:6** 3213
"W, O gate; cry, O city; Melt **Is 14:31** 3213
Its w *goes* as far as Eglaim **Is 15:8** 3215
Therefore Moab will w; everyone of **Is 16:7** 3213
everyone of Moab will w. You will **Is 16:7** 3213
The oracle concerning Tyre. W, **Is 23:1** 3213
Pass over to Tarshish; W, **Is 23:6** 3213
W, O ships of Tarshish, For your **Is 23:14** 3213
And you will w with a broken spirit. **Is 65:14** 3213
Lament and w; For the fierce anger **Jer 4:8** 3213
"W, you shepherds, and cry; **Jer 25:34** 3213
every inhabitant of the land will w. **Jer 47:2** 3213
W and cry out; Declare by the Arnon **Jer 48:20** 3213
"Therefore I will w for Moab, Even **Jer 48:31** 3213
"W, O Heshbon, for Ai has been **Jer 49:3** 3213
W over her! Bring balm for her pain; **Jer 51:8** 3213
"Cry out and w, son of man; for it **Ezk 21:12** 3213
"W, 'Alas for the day!' **Ezk 30:2** 3213
"Son of man, w for the hordes of **Ezk 32:18** 5091
to Me from their heart When they w on **Hos 7:14** 3213
Awake, drunkards, and weep; And w, **Jl 1:5** 3213
W like a virgin girded with sackcloth **Jl 1:8** 421
Be ashamed, O farmers, W, O **Jl 1:11** 3213
W, O ministers of the altar! Come, **Jl 1:13** 3213
Because of this I must lament and w, **Mi 1:8** 3213
A w from the Second Quarter, **Zph 1:10** 3215
"W, O inhabitants of the Mortar, **Zph 1:11** 3213
W, O cypress, for the cedar has **Zch 11:2** 3213
W, O oaks of Bashan, For **Zch 11:2** 3213
There is a sound of the shepherds' w, **Zch 11:3** 3215
WAILED
out into the midst of the city and w **Es 4:1** 2199
How they have w! How Moab has **Jer 48:39** 3213
WAILING
weeping and w; and many lay on **Es 4:3** 4553
and in their squares Everyone is w, **Is 15:3** 3213
goes as far as Eglaim and its w **Is 15:8** 3213
to w, To shaving the head and to **Is 22:12** 4553
I will take up a weeping and w, **Jer 9:10** 5092
And send for the w women, that they **Jer 9:17** 2450
"Let them make haste and take up a w **Jer 9:18** 5092
"For a voice of w is heard from Zion, **Jer 9:19** 5092
Teach your daughters w, And everyone **Jer 9:20** 5092
And the w of the masters of the flock! **Jer 25:36** 3215
"Moreover, in their w they will **Ezk 27:32** 5092
"There is w in all the plazas, **Am 5:16** 4553
in all the vineyards *there is* w, **Am 5:17** 4553
songs of the palace will turn to w in **Am 8:3** 3213
and *people* loudly weeping and w. **Mk 5:38** *214*
WAILS
Moab w over Nebo and Medeba; **Is 15:2** 3213
"Therefore My heart w for Moab like **Jer 48:36** 1993
My heart also w like flutes for **Jer 48:36** 1993
WAIST
sword in its sheath fastened at his w; **2Sa 20:8** 4975
blood of war on his belt about his w, **1Ki 2:5** 4975
Nor is the belt at its w undone, Nor **Is 5:27** 2504
And faithfulness the belt about His w. **Is 11:5** 2504
and put *sackcloth* on *your* w, **Is 32:11** 2504
waistband and put it around your w, **Jer 13:1** 4975
the LORD and put it around my w. **Jer 13:2** 4975
which is around your w, and arise, **Jer 13:4** 4975
'For as the waistband clings to the w **Jer 13:11** 4975
whose w was girded with *a belt of* **Da 10:5** 4975
hair and a leather belt around his w; **Mt 3:4** *3751*
wore a leather belt around his w, **Mk 1:6** *3751*
WAISTBAND
"Go and buy yourself a linen w **Jer 13:1** 232
So I bought the w in accordance with **Jer 13:2** 232
"Take the w that you have bought, **Jer 13:4** 232
Euphrates and take from there the w **Jer 13:6** 232
and I took the w from the place where **Jer 13:7** 232
the w was ruined, it was totally **Jer 13:7** 232
let them be just like this w which is **Jer 13:10** 232
'For as the w clings to the waist of **Jer 13:11** 232
WAIT
"For Your salvation I w, O LORD. **Gn 49:18** 6960a
"But if he did not lie in w *for* **Ex 21:13** 6658a
But to the elders he said, "W here **Ex 24:14** 3427
Moses therefore said to them, "W, **Nu 9:8** 5975
or threw something at him lying in w **Nu 35:20** 6660
something at him without lying in w, **Nu 35:22** 6660
who hates his neighbor and lies in w **Dt 19:11** 693
and lie in w in the field. **Jg 9:32** 693
with him arose by night and lay in w **Jg 9:34** 693
and lay in w in the field; when he **Jg 9:43** 693
surrounded *the place* and lay in w **Jg 16:2** 693
"*Let us* w until the morning **Jg 16:2**
Now she had *men* lying in w in an **Jg 16:9** 693
For the *men* were lying in w in **Jg 16:12** 693
and w until afternoon"; **Jg 19:8** 4102
"Go and lie in w in the vineyards, **Jg 21:20** 693
would you therefore w until they were **Ru 1:13** 7663b
Then she said, "W, my daughter, **Ru 3:18** 3427
You shall w seven days until I come **1Sa 10:8** 3176
"If they say to us, 'W until we **1Sa 14:9** 1826a
Then Samuel said to Saul, "W, **1Sa 15:16** 7503
though you are lying in w for my life **1Sa 24:11** 6658a
"See, I am going to w at the fords **2Sa 15:28** 4102
why should I w for the LORD any **2Ki 6:33** 3176
if we w until morning light, **2Ki 7:9** 2442
open the door and flee and do not w." **2Ki 9:3** 2442
Let it w for light but have none, **Jb 3:9** 6960a
that I should w? And what is my end, **Jb 6:11** 3176
All the days of my struggle I will w **Jb 14:14** 3176
"Shall I w, because they do not **Jb 32:16** 3176
and you must w for Him! **Jb 35:14** 2342a
"W for me a little, and I will show **Jb 36:2** 3803
in *their* dens *And* lie in w in **Jb 38:40** 695
Indeed, none of those who w for You **Ps 25:3** 6960a
For You I w all the day. **Ps 25:5** 6960a
preserve me, For I w for You. **Ps 25:21** 6960a
W for the LORD; Be strong **Ps 27:14** 6960a
Yes, w for the LORD. **Ps 27:14** 6960a
Rest in the LORD and w patiently **Ps 37:7** 2342a
But those who w for the LORD, **Ps 37:9** 6960a
W for the LORD and keep His way, **Ps 37:34** 6960a
"And now, Lord, for what do I w? **Ps 39:7** 6960a
And I will w on Your name, for **Ps 52:9** 6960a
My soul, w in silence for God only, **Ps 62:5** 1826a
My eyes fail while I w for my God. **Ps 69:3** 3176
May those who w for You not be **Ps 69:6** 6960a
They all w for You To give them their **Ps 104:27** 7663b
They did not w for His counsel, **Ps 106:13** 2442
For I w for Your ordinances. **Ps 119:43** 3176
Because I w for Your word. **Ps 119:74** 3176
I w for Your word. **Ps 119:81** 3176
The wicked w for me to destroy me; **Ps 119:95** 6960a
I w for Your word. **Ps 119:114** 3176
I w for Your words. **Ps 119:147** 3176
I w for the LORD, my soul does **Ps 130:5** 6960a
my soul does w, And in His word do **Ps 130:5** 6960a
Those who w for His lovingkindness. **Ps 147:11** 3176
Let us lie in w for blood, **Pr 1:11** 693
But they lie in w for their own blood; **Pr 1:18** 693
The words of the wicked lie in w for **Pr 12:6** 693
W for the LORD, and He will save **Pr 20:22** 6960a
Do not lie in w, O wicked man, **Pr 24:15** 693
And I will w for the LORD who is **Is 8:17** 2442
Be delayed and w, Blind yourselves **Is 29:9** 8539
Yet those who w for the LORD Will **Is 40:31** 6960a
And the coastlands will w expectantly **Is 42:4** 3176
Those who hopefully w for Me will **Is 49:23** 6960a
The coastlands will w for Me, **Is 51:5** 6960a
And for My arm they will w **Is 51:5** 3176
"Surely the coastlands will w for Me; **Is 60:9** 6960a
They watch like fowlers lying in w; **Jer 5:26** 7918
He is to me like a bear lying in w, **La 3:10** 693
The LORD is good to those who w **La 3:25** 6960a
And as raiders w for a man, *So* a **Hos 6:9** 2442
And w for your God continually. **Hos 12:6** 6960a
Like a leopard I will lie in w by **Hos 13:7** 7789
showers on vegetation Which do not w **Mi 5:7** 6960a
All of them lie in w for bloodshed; **Mi 7:2** 693
I will w for the God of my **Mi 7:7** 3176
w for it; For it will certainly come, **Hab 2:3** 2442
Because I must w quietly for the day **Hab 3:16** 5117
"Therefore w for Me," declares **Zph 3:8** 2442
and will come up and w on them. **Lk 12:37** *1247*
but to w for what the Father had **Ac 1:4** *4037*
than forty of them are lying in w for **Ac 23:21** *1748*
with perseverance we w eagerly for it. **Ro 8:25** *553*
but w until the Lord comes who **1Co 4:5**
w for one another. **1Co 11:33** *1551*
from which also we eagerly w for a **Php 3:20** *553*
and to w for His Son from heaven, **1Th 1:10** *362*
WAITED
So he w yet another seven days; **Gn 8:10** 2342a
Then he w yet another seven days, **Gn 8:12** 3176
They w until they became anxious; **Jg 3:25** 2342a
Now he w seven days, according to **1Sa 13:8** 3176
in David's name; then they w. **1Sa 25:9** 5117
So the prophet departed and w for **1Ki 20:38** 5975
and she w on Naaman's wife. **2Ki 5:2** 1961
"To me they listened and w, **Jb 29:21** 3176
"They w for me as for the rain, **Jb 29:23** 3176
When I w for light, then darkness **Jb 30:26** 3176
Now Elihu had w to speak to Job **Jb 32:4** 2442
"Behold, I w for your words, I **Jb 32:11** 3176
I w patiently for the LORD; **Ps 40:1** 6960a
As they have w *to take* my life. **Ps 56:6** 6960a
this is our God for whom we have w **Is 25:9** 6960a
is the LORD for whom we have w; **Is 25:9** 6960a
We have w for You eagerly; Your **Is 26:8** 6960a
we have w for You. Be their strength **Is 33:2** 6960a
We w for peace, but no good **Jer 8:15** 6960a
We w for peace, but nothing good **Jer 14:19** 6960a
Surely this is the day for which we w; **La 2:16** 6960a
They w in ambush for us in **La 4:19** 693
'When she saw, as she w, *That* **Ezk 19:5** 3176
and she got up and w on Him. **Mt 8:15** *1247*
and she w on them. **Mk 1:31** *1247*
and she immediately got up and w on **Lk 4:39** *1247*
But after they had w a long time **Ac 28:6** *4328*
And so, having patiently w, he **Heb 6:15** *3114*
WAITERS
the attendance of his w and their **1Ki 10:5** 8334
WAITING
met Moses and Aaron as they were w **Ex 5:20** 5324
my gates, W at my doorposts. **Pr 8:34** 8104
"How blessed is he who keeps w **Da 12:12** 2442
inhabitant of Maroth Becomes weak w **Mi 1:12** 2342a
who himself was w for the kingdom of **Mk 15:43** *4327*
The people were w for Zacharias, **Lk 1:21** *4328*
for they had all been w for Him. **Lk 8:40** *4328*
"Be like men who are w for their **Lk 12:36** *4327*
who was w for the kingdom of God; **Lk 23:51** *4327*

Context	Reference	Number
[w for the moving of the waters;	Jn 5:3	1551
Now Cornelius was w for them and had	Ac 10:24	4328
Now while Paul was w for them at	Ac 17:16	1551
these had gone on ahead and were w	Ac 20:5	3306
and now they are ready and w for	Ac 23:21	4327
w eagerly for our adoption as	Ro 8:23	553
are w for the hope of righteousness.	Ga 5:5	553
w from that time onward UNTIL HIS	Heb 10:13	1551
when the patience of God kept w in	1Pe 3:20	553
w anxiously for the mercy of our Lord	Jude 1:21	4327
WAITS		
And as a hired man who eagerly w for	Jb 7:2	6960a
"The eye of the adulterer w for	Jb 24:15	8104
Our soul w for the LORD; He is	Ps 33:20	2442
My soul w in silence for God only;	Ps 62:1	
My soul w for the Lord More than	Ps 130:6	
And therefore He w on high to have	Is 30:18	2442
Who acts in behalf of the one who w	Is 64:4	2442
It is good that he w silently For	La 3:26	3175
the anxious longing of the creation w	Ro 8:19	553
The farmer w for the precious produce	Jas 5:7	1551
WAKE		
"Behind him he makes a w to shine;	Jb 41:32	5410a
may sleep a perpetual sleep And not w	Jer 51:39	3364
sleep a perpetual sleep and not w up,"	Jer 51:57	3364
'W up, and strengthen the things	Rv 3:2	1127
Therefore if you do not w up, I will	Rv 3:3	1127
WALK		
"Arise, w about the land through	Gn 13:17	1980
W before Me, and be blameless.	Gn 17:1	1980
whether or not they will w in My	Ex 16:4	1980
them the way in which they are to w	Ex 18:20	1980
'All the winged insects that w on	Lv 11:20	1980
among all the winged insects which w	Lv 11:21	1980
among all the creatures that w on	Lv 11:27	1980
you shall not w in their statutes.	Lv 18:3	1980
'If you w in My statutes and keep My	Lv 26:3	1980
'I will also w among you and be your	Lv 26:12	1980
the bars of your yoke and made you w	Lv 26:13	1980
"You shall w in all the way which	Dt 5:33	1980
you sit in your house and when you w	Dt 6:7	1980
to w in His ways and to fear Him.	Dt 8:6	1980
to w in all His ways and love Him,	Dt 10:12	1980
you sit in your house and when you w	Dt 11:19	1980
to w in all His ways and hold fast to	Dt 11:22	1980
LORD your God commanded you to w.	Dt 13:5	1980
and to w in His ways always—then	Dt 19:9	1980
and that you would w in His ways	Dt 26:17	1980
of the LORD your God and w in His	Dt 28:9	1980
'I have peace though I w in	Dt 29:19	1980
to w in His ways and to keep His	Dt 30:16	1980
so will your leisurely w be.	Dt 33:25	1679
and that they may arise and w through	Jos 18:4	1980
"Go and w through the land	Jos 18:8	1980
to love the LORD your God and w	Jos 22:5	1980
keep the way of the LORD to w in	Jg 2:22	1980
and the house of your father should w	1Sa 2:30	1980
and he will w before My anointed	1Sa 2:35	1980
His sons, however, did not w in his	1Sa 8:3	1980
and your sons do not w in your ways.	1Sa 8:5	1980
sword over his armor and tried to w,	1Sa 17:39	1980
to w in His ways, to keep His	1Ki 2:3	1980
to w before Me in truth with all	1Ki 2:4	1980
"If you w in My ways, keeping My	1Ki 3:14	1980
if you will w in My statutes	1Ki 6:12	1980
lovingkindness to Your servants who w	1Ki 8:23	1980
your sons take heed to their way to w	1Ki 8:25	1980
the good way in which they should w.	1Ki 8:36	1980
to w in all His ways and to keep His	1Ki 8:58	1980
to w in His statutes and to keep His	1Ki 8:61	1980
"As for you, if you will w before	1Ki 9:4	1980
to all that I command you and w in My	1Ki 11:38	1980
had been a trivial thing for him to w	1Ki 16:31	1980
But Jehu was not careful to w in	2Ki 10:31	1980
and did not w in the way of the	2Ki 21:22	1980
to w after the LORD, and to	2Ki 23:3	1980
lovingkindness to Your servants who w	2Ch 6:14	1980
to w in My law as you have walked	2Ch 6:16	1980
the good way in which they should w.	2Ch 6:27	1980
that they may fear You, to w in Your	2Ch 6:31	1980
"As for you, if you w before Me as	2Ch 7:17	1980
a covenant before the LORD to w	2Ch 34:31	1980
should you not w in the fear of our	Ne 5:9	1980
themselves a curse and an oath to w	Ne 10:29	1980
"He makes counselors w barefoot	Jb 12:17	1980
"He makes priests w barefoot	Jb 12:19	1980
How blessed is the man who does not w	Ps 1:1	1980
Even though I w through the valley of	Ps 23:4	1980
But as for me, I shall w in my	Ps 26:11	1980
W about Zion and go around her;	Ps 48:12	5437
So that I may w before God In	Ps 56:13	1980
the covenant of God And refused to w	Ps 78:10	1980
To w in their own devices.	Ps 81:12	1980
That Israel would w in My ways!	Ps 81:13	1980
They w about in darkness; All	Ps 82:5	1980
does He withhold from those who w	Ps 84:11	1980
I will w in Your truth; Unite my	Ps 86:11	1980
they w in the light of Your	Ps 89:15	1980
his sons forsake My law And do not w	Ps 89:30	1980
I will w within my house in	Ps 101:2	1980
but they cannot w; They cannot make	Ps 115:7	1980
I shall w before the LORD In	Ps 116:9	1980
Who w in the law of the LORD.	Ps 119:1	1980
They w in His ways.	Ps 119:3	1980
Make me w in the path of Your	Ps 119:35	1869
And I will w at liberty, For I seek	Ps 119:45	1980
Though I w in the midst of trouble,	Ps 138:7	1980
In the way where I w They have hidden	Ps 142:3	1980
Teach me the way in which I should w;	Ps 143:8	1980
My son, do not w in the way with	Pr 1:15	1980
He is a shield to those who w in	Pr 2:7	1980
leave the paths of uprightness To w	Pr 2:13	1980
So you will w in the way of good men	Pr 2:20	1980
Then you will w in your way securely	Pr 3:23	1980
When you w, your steps will not be	Pr 4:12	1980
When you w about, they will guide	Pr 6:22	1980
Or can a man w on hot coals And his	Pr 6:28	1980
"I w in the way of righteousness,	Pr 8:20	1980
But the blameless in their w	Pr 11:20	1870
four which are stately when they w:	Pr 30:29	1980
knowing how to w before	Ec 6:8	1980
And that we may w in His paths."	Is 2:3	1980
Come, house of Jacob, and let us w	Is 2:5	1980
the daughters of Zion are proud And w	Is 3:16	1980
power and instructed me not to w in	Is 8:11	1980
The people who w in darkness Will see	Is 9:2	1980
into seven streams And make men w	Is 11:15	1869
Take your harp, w about the city,	Is 23:16	5437
w in it," whenever you turn to	Is 30:21	1980
But the redeemed will w there,	Is 35:9	1980
They will w and not become weary.	Is 40:31	1980
on it And spirit to those who w in it,	Is 42:5	1980
whose ways they were not willing to w,	Is 42:24	1980
When you w through the fire,	Is 43:2	1980
They will w behind you, they will	Is 45:14	1980
W in the light of your fire And among	Is 50:11	1980
'Lie down that we may w over you.	Is 51:23	5674a
And like the street for those who w	Is 51:23	5674a
but we w in gloom.	Is 59:9	1980
Who w in the way which is not	Is 65:2	1980
And after them I will w.'	Jer 2:25	1980
nor will they w anymore after	Jer 3:17	1980
those days the house of Judah will w	Jer 3:18	1980
and w in it; And you will find rest	Jer 6:16	1980
'We will not w in it.'	Jer 6:16	1980
go out into the field And do not w on	Jer 6:25	1980
nor w after other gods to your own	Jer 7:6	1980
and offer sacrifices to Baal and w	Jer 7:9	1980
and you will w in all the way which I	Jer 7:23	1980
Because they cannot w! Do not fear	Jer 10:5	6805
who w in the stubbornness of their	Jer 13:10	1980
To w in bypaths, Not on a highway,	Jer 18:15	1980
to w in My law which I have set	Jer 26:4	1980
I will make them w by streams of	Jer 31:9	1980
but they did not obey Your voice or w	Jer 32:23	1980
tell us the way in which we should w	Jer 42:3	1980
He has driven me and made me w In	La 3:2	1980
our steps So that we could not w in	La 4:18	1980
that they may w in My statutes	Ezk 11:20	1980
They did not w in My statutes	Ezk 20:13	1980
they did not w in them; they even	Ezk 20:16	1980
'Do not w in the statutes of your	Ezk 20:18	1980
'I am the LORD your God; w in	Ezk 20:19	1980
they did not w in My statutes, nor	Ezk 20:21	1980
men—My people Israel—to w	Ezk 36:12	1980
Spirit within you and cause you to w	Ezk 36:27	1980
and they will w in My ordinances	Ezk 37:24	1980
the chambers was an inner w ten	Ezk 42:4	4109
and He is able to humble those who w	Da 4:37	1981
to w in His teachings which He set	Da 9:10	1980
Yet it is I who taught Ephraim to w,	Hos 11:3	7270
They will w after the LORD, He	Hos 11:10	1980
And the righteous will w in them,	Hos 14:9	1980
Do two men w together unless they	Am 3:3	1980
great city, a three days' w.	Jon 3:3	4109
to go through the city one day's w;	Jon 3:4	4109
And you will not w haughtily, For it	Mi 2:3	1980
us about His ways And that we may w	Mi 4:2	1980
Though all the peoples w Each in	Mi 4:5	1980
we will w In the name of the LORD	Mi 4:5	1980
And to w humbly with your God?	Mi 6:8	1980
And in their devices you w.	Mi 6:16	1980
And makes me w on my high places.	Hab 3:19	1869
distress on men So that they will w	Zph 1:17	1980
'If you will w in My ways and if you	Zch 3:7	1980
And in His name they will w,"	Zch 10:12	1980
and w'?	Mt 9:5	4043
RECEIVE SIGHT and the lame w,	Mt 11:5	4043
and pick up your pallet and w'?	Mk 2:9	4043
the girl got up and began to w;	Mk 5:42	4043
"Why do Your disciples not w	Mk 7:5	4043
"Beware of the scribes who like to w	Mk 12:38	4043
'Get up and w'?	Lk 5:23	4043
the lame w, the lepers are	Lk 7:22	4043
and the people who w over them	Lk 11:44	4043
who like to w around in long robes,	Lk 20:46	4043
pick up your pallet and w."	Jn 5:8	4043
up his pallet and began to w.	Jn 5:9	4043
'Pick up your pallet and w.' "	Jn 5:11	4043
'Pick up your pallet and w'?"	Jn 5:12	4043
for He was unwilling to w in Judea	Jn 7:1	4043
he who follows Me will not w in	Jn 8:12	4043
Jesus no longer continued to w	Jn 11:54	4043
W while you have the Light, so that	Jn 12:35	4043
you used to gird yourself and w	Jn 21:18	4043
of Jesus Christ the Nazarene—w!"	Ac 3:6	4043
he stood upright and began to w;	Ac 3:8	4043
power or piety we had made him w?	Ac 3:12	4043
And he leaped up and began to w.	Ac 14:10	4043
to circumcise their children nor to w	Ac 21:21	4043
but that you yourself also w orderly,	Ac 21:24	4748
so we too might w in newness of life.	Ro 6:4	4043
who do not w according to the flesh	Ro 8:4	4043
in this manner let him w. And so I	1Co 7:17	4043
for we w by faith, not by sight	2Co 5:7	4043
"I WILL DWELL IN THEM AND W AMONG	2Co 6:16	1704
For though we w in the flesh, we do	2Co 10:3	4043
ourselves in the same spirit and w	2Co 12:18	
But I say, w by the Spirit, and you	Ga 5:16	4043
let us also w by the Spirit.	Ga 5:25	4748
And those who will w by this rule,	Ga 6:16	4748
beforehand so that we would w in them.	Eph 2:10	4043
implore you to w in a manner worthy	Eph 4:1	4043
that you w no longer just as	Eph 4:17	4043
no longer just as the Gentiles also w,	Eph 4:17	4043
and w in love, just as Christ also	Eph 5:2	4043
w as children of Light	Eph 5:8	4043
Therefore be careful how you w, not	Eph 5:15	4043
and observe those who w according to	Php 3:17	4043
For many w, of whom I often told you,	Php 3:18	4043
so that you will w in a manner worthy	Col 1:10	4043
so w in Him,	Col 2:6	4043
so that you would w in a manner	1Th 2:12	4043
as to how you ought to w and please	1Th 4:1	4043
God (just as you actually do w),	1Th 4:1	4043
fellowship with Him and yet w in	1Jn 1:6	4043
but if we w in the Light as He	1Jn 1:7	4043
he abides in Him ought himself to w	1Jn 2:6	4043
And this is love, that we w	2Jn 1:6	4043
that you should w in it.	2Jn 1:6	4043
and they will w with Me in white,	Rv 3:4	4043
which can neither see nor hear nor w;	Rv 9:20	4043
so that he will not w about naked	Rv 16:15	4043
The nations will w by its light,	Rv 21:24	4043
WALKED		
Then Enoch w with God three hundred	Gn 5:22	1980
Enoch w with God; and he was not,	Gn 5:24	1980
Noah w with God.	Gn 6:9	1980
it upon both their shoulders and w	Gn 9:23	1980
So the two of them w on together.	Gn 22:6	1980
So the two of them w on together.	Gn 22:8	1980
before whom I have w, will send	Gn 24:40	1980
whom my fathers Abraham and Isaac w,	Gn 48:15	1980
But the sons of Israel w on dry land	Ex 14:29	1980
but the sons of Israel w on dry land	Ex 15:19	1980
in all the way which you have w until	Dt 1:31	1980
For the sons of Israel w forty years	Jos 5:6	1980
when Israel w in the wilderness;	Jos 14:10	1980
the way in which their fathers had w	Jg 2:17	1980
And I have w before you from my youth	1Sa 12:2	1980
his shield-carrier also w before him.	1Sa 17:7	1980
all the valiant men rose and w all	1Sa 31:12	1980
w all morning, and came to Mahanaim.	2Sa 2:29	1980
And King David w behind the bier.	2Sa 3:31	1980
came David arose from his bed and w	2Sa 11:2	1980
and his head was covered and he w	2Sa 15:30	1980
And thus he said as he w, "O my son	2Sa 18:33	1980
according as he w before You in truth	1Ki 3:6	1980
as your father David w, then I will	1Ki 3:14	1980
way to walk before Me as you have w.'	1Ki 8:25	1980
walk before Me as your father David w,	1Ki 9:4	1980
and they have not w in My ways,	1Ki 11:33	1980
He w in all the sins of his father	1Ki 15:3	1980
and w in the way of his father	1Ki 15:26	1980
and w in the way of Jeroboam	1Ki 15:34	1980
and you have w in the way of Jeroboam	1Ki 16:2	1980
For he w in all the way of Jeroboam	1Ki 16:26	1980
He w in all the way of Asa his father;	1Ki 22:43	1980
in the sight of the LORD and w in	1Ki 22:52	1980
Then he returned and w in the house	2Ki 4:35	1980
He w in the way of the kings of	2Ki 8:18	1980
He w in the way of the house of Ahab	2Ki 8:27	1980
but w in them; and the Asherah also	2Ki 13:6	1980
Israel sin, but he w in them.	2Ki 13:11	1980
But he w in the way of the kings of	2Ki 16:3	1980
and w in the customs of the nations	2Ki 17:8	1980
but w in the customs which Israel had	2Ki 17:19	1980
The sons of Israel w in all the sins	2Ki 17:22	1980
how I have w before You in truth	2Ki 20:3	1980
For he w in all the way that his	2Ki 21:21	1980
in all the way that his father had w,	2Ki 21:21	1980
in the sight of the LORD and w in	2Ki 22:2	1980
"In all places where I have w with	1Ch 17:6	1980
to walk in My law as you have w	2Ch 6:16	1980
walk before Me as your father David w,	2Ch 7:17	1980
for they w in the way of David	2Ch 11:17	1980
He w in the way of his father Asa	2Ch 20:32	1980
He w in the way of the kings of	2Ch 21:6	1980
'Because you have not w in the ways	2Ch 21:12	1980
but have w in the way of the kings of	2Ch 21:13	1980
He also w in the ways of the house of	2Ch 22:3	1980
He also w according to their counsel,	2Ch 22:5	1980
But he w in the ways of the kings of	2Ch 28:2	1980
and w in the ways of his father	2Ch 34:2	1980
Every day Mordecai w back and forth	Es 2:11	1980
And by His light I w through	Jb 29:3	1980
"If I have w with falsehood,	Jb 31:5	1980
into the springs of the sea Or w in	Jb 38:16	1980
for I have w in my integrity,	Ps 26:1	1980
And I have w in Your truth.	Ps 26:3	1980
sweet fellowship together W in	Ps 55:14	1980
how I have w before You in truth	Is 38:3	1980
Each one who w in his upright way.	Is 57:2	1980
That they went far from Me And w	Jer 2:5	1980
the prophets prophesied by Baal And w	Jer 2:8	1980
but w in their own counsels	Jer 7:24	1980
and have not obeyed My voice nor w	Jer 9:13	1980
but have w after the stubbornness of	Jer 9:14	1980
but w, each one, in	Jer 11:8	1980
nor have they feared nor w in My law	Jer 44:10	1980
obeyed the voice of the LORD or w	Jer 44:23	1980
rejected My ordinances and have not w	Ezk 5:6	1980
which surround you and have not w	Ezk 5:7	1980
for you have not w in My statutes	Ezk 11:12	1980
"Yet you have not merely w in their	Ezk 16:47	1980
'And he w about among the lions;	Ezk 19:6	1980

'You have **w** in the way of your	**Ezk 23:31**	1980
You **w** in the midst of the stones of	**Ezk 28:14**	1980
Those after which their fathers **w**.	**Am 2:4**	1980
he **w** with Me in peace and uprightness,	**Mal 2:6**	1980
and that we have **w** in mourning before	**Mal 3:14**	1980
and **w** on the water and came toward	**Mt 14:29**	*4043*
and he looked at Jesus as He **w**,	**Jn 1:36**	*4043*
who had never **w**.	**Ac 14:8**	*4043*
who regard us as if we **w** according to	**2Co 10:2**	*4043*
in which you formerly **w** according to	**Eph 2:2**	*4043*
and in them you also once **w**, when	**Col 3:7**	*4043*
to walk in the same manner as He **w**.	**1Jn 2:6**	*4043*

WALKING

heard the sound of the LORD God **w**	**Gn 3:8**	1980
and Abraham was **w** with them to send	**Gn 18:16**	1980
"Who is that man **w** in the field to	**Gn 24:65**	1980
with her maidens **w** alongside the Nile;	**Ex 2:5**	1980
"Now, here is the king **w** before you,	**1Sa 12:2**	1980
and Ahio was **w** ahead of the ark.	**2Sa 6:4**	1980
Now Solomon loved the LORD, **w** in	**1Ki 3:3**	1980
and keep all My commandments by **w** in	**1Ki 6:12**	1980
w in the way of Jeroboam, and in	**1Ki 16:19**	1980
"From roaming about on the earth and **w**	**Jb 1:7**	1980
"From roaming about on the earth and **w**	**Jb 2:2**	1980
riding on horses and princes **w**	**Ec 10:7**	1980
you are each one **w** according to	**Jer 16:12**	1980
The committing of adultery and **w** in	**Jer 23:14**	1980
I see four men loosed *and* **w**	**Da 3:25**	1981
"Twelve months later he was **w** on	**Da 4:29**	1981
Do not My words do good To the one **w**	**Mi 2:7**	1980
"If a man **w** after wind and falsehood	**Mi 2:11**	1980
Now as Jesus was **w** by the Sea of	**Mt 4:18**	*4043*
w on the sea.	**Mt 14:25**	*4043*
When the disciples saw Him **w** on	**Mt 14:26**	*4043*
and the lame **w**, and the blind seeing;	**Mt 15:31**	*4043*
w on the sea; and He intended to	**Mk 6:48**	*4043*
But when they saw Him **w** on the sea,	**Mk 6:49**	*4043*
like trees, **w** around."	**Mk 8:24**	*4043*
and Jesus was **w** on ahead of them;	**Mk 10:32**	*4254*
And as He was **w** in the temple,	**Mk 11:27**	*4043*
form to two of them while they were **w**	**Mk 16:12**	*4043*
w blamelessly in all the commandments	**Lk 1:6**	*4198*
with one another as you are **w**?" And	**Lk 24:17**	*4043*
they saw Jesus **w** on the sea	**Jn 6:19**	*4043*
His disciples withdrew and were not **w**	**Jn 6:66**	*4043*
After these things Jesus was **w** in	**Jn 7:1**	*4043*
it was winter, and Jesus was **w** in	**Jn 10:23**	*4043*
w and leaping and praising God.	**Ac 3:8**	*4043*
And all the people saw him **w**	**Ac 3:9**	*4043*
you are no longer **w** according to love.	**Ro 14:15**	*4043*
and are you not **w** like mere men?	**1Co 3:3**	*4043*
not **w** in craftiness or adulterating	**2Co 4:2**	*4043*
to find *some* of your children **w**	**2Jn 1:4**	*4043*
how you are **w** in truth.	**3Jn 1:3**	*4043*
to hear of my children **w** in the truth.	**3Jn 1:4**	*4043*

WALKS

if he gets up and **w** around outside on	**Ex 21:19**	1980
'Also whatever **w** on its paws, among	**Lv 11:27**	1980
and whatever **w** on *all* fours,	**Lv 11:42**	1980
"Since the LORD your God **w** in	**Dt 23:14**	1980
And He **w** on the vault of heaven.'	**Jb 22:14**	1980
And **w** with wicked men?	**Jb 34:8**	1980
He who **w** with integrity, and works	**Ps 15:2**	1980
"Surely every man **w** about as a	**Ps 39:6**	1980
He who **w** in a blameless way is	**Ps 101:6**	1980
He **w** upon the wings of the wind;	**Ps 104:3**	1980
Who **w** in His ways.	**Ps 128:1**	1980
Is the one who **w** with a perverse	**Pr 6:12**	1980
He who **w** in integrity walks securely,	**Pr 10:9**	1980
He who walks in integrity **w** securely,	**Pr 10:9**	1980
He who **w** with wise men will be wise,	**Pr 13:20**	1980
He who **w** in his uprightness fears	**Pr 14:2**	1980
But a man of understanding **w** straight.	**Pr 15:21**	1980
Better is a poor man who **w** in his	**Pr 19:1**	1980
A righteous man who **w** in his	**Pr 20:7**	1980
Better is the poor who **w** in his	**Pr 28:6**	1980
He who **w** blamelessly will be	**Pr 28:18**	1980
But he who **w** wisely will be delivered.	**Pr 28:26**	1980
but the fool **w** in darkness.	**Ec 2:14**	1980
Even when the fool **w** along the road,	**Ec 10:3**	1980
He who **w** righteously and speaks with	**Is 33:15**	1980
But it *will* be for him who **w**	**Is 35:8**	1980
That **w** in darkness and has no light?	**Is 50:10**	1980
Nor is it in a man who **w** to direct	**Jer 10:23**	1980
And as for everyone who **w** in	**Jer 23:17**	1980
if he **w** in My statutes and My	**Ezk 18:9**	1980
and **w** in My statutes; he will not	**Ezk 18:17**	1980
w by the statutes which ensure life	**Ezk 33:15**	1980
If anyone **w** in the day, he does not	**Jn 11:9**	*4043*
"But if anyone **w** in the night, he	**Jn 11:10**	*4043*
he who **w** in the darkness does not	**Jn 12:35**	*4043*
his brother is in the darkness and **w**	**1Jn 2:11**	*4043*
the One who **w** among the seven golden	**Rv 2:1**	*4043*

WALL

Its branches run over a **w**.	**Gn 49:22**	7791
and the waters *were like* a **w** to	**Ex 14:22**	2346
and the waters *were like* a **w** to	**Ex 14:29**	2346
which have no surrounding **w** shall be	**Lv 25:31**	2346
with a **w** on this side and a wall	**Nu 22:24**	1447
with a wall on this side and a **w**	**Nu 22:24**	1447
she pressed herself to the **w**	**Nu 22:25**	7023
pressed Balaam's foot against the **w**,	**Nu 22:25**	7023
Levites *shall extend* from the **w**	**Nu 35:4**	7023
for her house was on the city **w**,	**Jos 2:15**	2346
so that she was living on the **w**.	**Jos 2:15**	2346
and the **w** of the city will fall down	**Jos 6:5**	2346
shouted with a great shout and the **w**	**Jos 6:20**	2346
"I will pin David to the **w**."	**1Sa 18:11**	7023
Saul tried to pin David to the **w** with	**1Sa 19:10**	7023
so that he stuck the spear into the **w**.	**1Sa 19:10**	7023
the seat by the **w**; then Jonathan	**1Sa 20:25**	7023
"They were a **w** to us both by night	**1Sa 25:16**	2346
and they fastened his body to the **w**	**1Sa 31:10**	2346
and the bodies of his sons from the **w**	**1Sa 31:12**	2346
know that they would shoot from the **w**?	**2Sa 11:20**	2346
an upper millstone on him from the **w**	**2Sa 11:21**	2346
Why did you go so near the **w**?'	**2Sa 11:21**	2346
shot at your servants from the **w**; so	**2Sa 11:24**	2346
up to the roof of the gate by the **w**,	**2Sa 18:24**	2346
destruction in order to topple the **w**.	**2Sa 20:15**	2346
head will be thrown to you over the **w**."	**2Sa 20:21**	2346
By my God I can leap over a **w**.	**2Sa 22:30**	7791
the house of the LORD and the **w**	**1Ki 3:1**	2346
to the hyssop that grows on the **w**;	**1Ki 4:33**	7023
Against the **w** of the house he built	**1Ki 6:5**	7023
outside he made offsets *in the* **w**	**1Ki 6:6**	
of the one was touching the *one* **w**,	**1Ki 6:27**	7023
other cherub was touching the other **w**.	**1Ki 6:27**	7023
the **w** of Jerusalem, Hazor, Megiddo,	**1Ki 9:15**	2346
and the **w** fell on 27,000 men who were	**1Ki 20:30**	2346
him as a burnt offering on the **w**.	**2Ki 3:27**	2346
of Israel was passing by on the **w** a	**2Ki 6:26**	2346
he was passing by on the **w**	**2Ki 6:30**	2346
of her blood was sprinkled on the **w**	**2Ki 9:33**	7023
came to Jerusalem and tore down the **w**	**2Ki 14:13**	2346
of the people who are on the **w**."	**2Ki 18:26**	2346
and not to the men who sit on the **w**,	**2Ki 18:27**	2346
Then he turned his face to the **w**	**2Ki 20:2**	7023
camped against it and built a siege **w**	**2Ki 25:1**	1785
touched the **w** of the house, and	**2Ch 3:11**	7023
touched the **w** of the house; and	**2Ch 3:12**	7023
him to Jerusalem and tore down the **w**	**2Ch 25:23**	2346
and broke down the **w** of Gath	**2Ch 26:6**	2346
broke down the wall of Gath and the **w**	**2Ch 26:6**	2346
Gath and the wall of Jabneh and the **w**	**2Ch 26:6**	2346
and he built extensively the **w** of	**2Ch 27:3**	2346
he took courage and rebuilt all the **w**	**2Ch 32:5**	2346
and *built* another outside **w**	**2Ch 32:5**	2346
people of Jerusalem who were on the **w**,	**2Ch 32:18**	2346
Now after this he built the outer **w**	**2Ch 33:14**	2346
the house of God and broke down the **w**	**2Ch 36:19**	2346
restore its ruins and to give us a **w**	**Ezr 9:9**	1447
and the **w** of Jerusalem is broken down	**Ne 1:3**	2346
for the **w** of the city and for	**Ne 2:8**	2346
by the ravine and inspected the **w**.	**Ne 2:15**	2346
let us rebuild the **w** of Jerusalem so	**Ne 2:17**	2346
They consecrated the **w** to the Tower	**Ne 3:1**	
Jerusalem as far as the Broad **W**.	**Ne 3:8**	2346
and a thousand cubits of the **w** to	**Ne 3:13**	2346
and the **w** of the Pool of Shelah at	**Ne 3:15**	2346
projecting tower and as far as the **w**	**Ne 3:27**	2346
heard that we were rebuilding the **w**,	**Ne 4:1**	2346
he would break their stone **w** down!"	**Ne 4:3**	2346
So we built the **w** and the whole wall	**Ne 4:6**	2346
So we built the wall and the whole **w**	**Ne 4:6**	2346
ourselves are unable To rebuild the **w**."	**Ne 4:10**	2346
parts of the space behind the **w**,	**Ne 4:13**	2346
then all of us returned to the **w**,	**Ne 4:15**	2346
Those who were rebuilding the **w**	**Ne 4:17**	2346
and we are separated on the **w** far	**Ne 4:19**	2346
applied myself to the work on this **w**;	**Ne 5:16**	2346
our enemies that I had rebuilt the **w**,	**Ne 6:1**	2346
therefore you are rebuilding the **w**.	**Ne 6:6**	2346
So the **w** was completed on	**Ne 6:15**	2346
Now when the **w** was rebuilt and I had	**Ne 7:1**	2346
Now at the dedication of the **w** of	**Ne 12:27**	2346
the gates and the **w**.	**Ne 12:30**	2346
of Judah come up on top of the **w**,	**Ne 12:31**	2346
to the right on top of the **w** toward	**Ne 12:31**	2346
of David by the stairway of the **w**	**Ne 12:37**	2346
them with half of the people on the **w**,	**Ne 12:38**	2346
of Furnaces, to the Broad **W**,	**Ne 12:38**	2346
you spend the night in front of the **w**?	**Ne 13:21**	2346
And by my God I can leap over a **w**.	**Ps 18:29**	7791
Like a leaning **w**, like a tottering	**Ps 62:3**	1447
And like a high **w** in his own	**Pr 18:11**	2346
And its stone **w** was broken down.	**Pr 24:31**	1447
may bite him who breaks through a **w**.	**Ec 10:8**	1447
he is standing behind our **w**, He is	**SS 2:9**	3796
"If she is a **w**, We will build on	**SS 8:9**	2346
"I was a **w**, and my breasts were	**SS 8:10**	2346
Against every fortified **w**,	**Is 2:15**	2346
I will break down its **w** and it will	**Is 5:5**	1447
you saw that the breaches In the **w**	**Is 22:9**	
And tore down houses to fortify the **w**.	**Is 22:10**	2346
like a *rain* storm *against* a **w**.	**Is 25:4**	7023
A bulge in a high **w**, Whose collapse	**Is 30:13**	2346
of the people who are on the **w**."	**Is 36:11**	2346
and not to the men who sit on the **w**,	**Is 36:12**	2346
Hezekiah turned his face to the **w**	**Is 38:2**	7023
And your entire **w** of precious stones.	**Is 54:12**	1366
We grope along the **w** like blind men,	**Is 59:10**	7023
make you to this people A fortified **w**	**Jer 15:20**	2346
who are besieging you outside the **w**;	**Jer 21:4**	2346
the city **w** was breached.	**Jer 39:2**	
"I will set fire to the **w** of	**Jer 49:27**	2346
Even the **w** of Babylon has fallen down!	**Jer 51:44**	2346
"The broad **w** of Babylon will be	**Jer 51:58**	2346
camped against it and built a siege **w**	**Jer 52:4**	1785
LORD determined to destroy The **w**	**La 2:8**	2346
And He has caused rampart and **w** to	**La 2:8**	2346
"O **w** of the daughter of Zion, Let	**La 2:18**	2346
build a siege **w**, raise up a ramp,	**Ezk 4:2**	1785
iron plate and set it up as an iron **w**	**Ezk 4:3**	7023
a hole in the **w**.	**Ezk 8:7**	7023
now dig through the **w**." So I dug	**Ezk 8:8**	7023
So I dug through the **w**, and behold,	**Ezk 8:8**	7023
were carved on the **w** all around.	**Ezk 8:10**	7023
"Dig a hole through the **w** in their	**Ezk 12:5**	7023
in the evening I dug through the **w**	**Ezk 12:7**	7023
They will dig a hole through the **w** to	**Ezk 12:12**	7023
nor did you build the **w** around	**Ezk 13:5**	1443
And when anyone builds a **w**, behold,	**Ezk 13:10**	2434
"Behold, when the **w** has fallen,	**Ezk 13:12**	7023
"So I will tear down the **w** which you	**Ezk 13:14**	7023
"Thus I will spend My wrath on the **w**	**Ezk 13:15**	7023
'The **w** is gone and its plasterers	**Ezk 13:15**	7023
to build a siege **w**.	**Ezk 21:22**	1785
among them who would build up the **w**	**Ezk 22:30**	1447
And she saw men portrayed on the **w**,	**Ezk 23:14**	7023
pathways will collapse and every **w**	**Ezk 38:20**	2346
And behold, there was a **w** on	**Ezk 40:5**	2346
So he measured the thickness of the **w**,	**Ezk 40:5**	2346
There was a barrier **w** one	**Ezk 40:12**	
Then he measured the **w** of the temple,	**Ezk 41:5**	7023
the side chambers extended to the **w**	**Ezk 41:6**	7023
and not be fastened into the **w** of	**Ezk 41:6**	7023
The thickness of the outer **w** of	**Ezk 41:9**	7023
and the **w** of the building *was*	**Ezk 41:12**	7023
and on all the **w** all around inside	**Ezk 41:17**	7023
as well as *on* the **w** of the nave.	**Ezk 41:20**	7023
As for the outer **w** by the side of	**Ezk 42:7**	1447
In the thickness of the **w** of	**Ezk 42:10**	1447
the way in front of the **w** toward	**Ezk 42:12**	1448
it had a **w** all around, the length	**Ezk 42:20**	2346
with *only* the **w** between Me	**Ezk 43:8**	7023
the lampstand on the plaster of the **w**	**Da 5:5**	3797
And I will build a **w** against her so	**Hos 2:6**	1447
They climb the **w** like soldiers; And	**Jl 2:7**	2346
They run on the **w**; They climb into	**Jl 2:9**	2346
"So I will send fire upon the **w** of	**Am 1:7**	2346
"So I will send fire upon the **w** of	**Am 1:10**	2346
"So I will kindle a fire on the **w** of	**Am 1:14**	2346
leans his hand against the **w**	**Am 5:19**	7023
the Lord was standing by a vertical **w**	**Am 7:7**	2346
And **w** up its breaches; I will also	**Am 9:11**	1443
They hurry to her **w**,	**Na 2:5**	2346
Whose **w** *consisted* of the sea?	**Na 3:8**	2346
the stone will cry out from the **w**,	**Hab 2:11**	7023
'will be a **w** of fire around her,	**Zch 2:5**	2346
WHO PLANTED A VINEYARD AND PUT A **W**	**Mt 21:33**	*5418*
MAN PLANTED A VINEYARD AND PUT A **W**	**Mk 12:1**	*5418*
down through *an opening in* the **w**,	**Ac 9:25**	*5038*
you whitewashed **w**! Do you sit to try	**Ac 23:3**	*5109*
in a basket through a window in the **w**,	**2Co 11:33**	*5038*
down the barrier of the dividing **w**,	**Eph 2:14**	*3320*
It had a great and high **w**, with	**Rv 21:12**	*5038*
And the **w** of the city had twelve	**Rv 21:14**	*5038*
and its gates and its **w**.	**Rv 21:15**	*5038*
measured its **w**, seventy-two yards,	**Rv 21:17**	*5038*
The material of the **w** was jasper;	**Rv 21:18**	*5038*
The foundation stones of the city **w**	**Rv 21:19**	*5038*

WALLED

a man sells a dwelling house in a **w**	**Lv 25:29**	2346
then the house that is in the **w** city	**Lv 25:30**	2346
make a little **w** upper chamber	**2Ki 4:10**	7023
"He has **w** up my way so that I cannot	**Jb 19:8**	1443
He has **w** me in so that I cannot go	**La 3:7**	1443

WALLOW

And **w** *in ashes,* you masters of	**Jer 25:34**	6428
so Moab will **w** in his vomit,	**Jer 48:26**	5606
They will **w** in ashes.	**Ezk 27:30**	6428

WALLOWING

But Amasa lay **w** in *his* blood in	**2Sa 20:12**	1556
returns to **w** in the mire."	**2Pe 2:22**	*2946*

WALLS

make *them* on its two side **w**	**Ex 30:4**	6763
and if the mark on the **w** of the house	**Lv 14:37**	7023
the mark has indeed spread in the **w**	**Lv 14:39**	7023
were cities fortified with high **w**,	**Dt 3:5**	2346
towns until your high and fortified **w**	**Dt 28:52**	2346
sixty great cities with **w** and bronze	**1Ki 4:13**	2346
he built stories encompassing the **w**	**1Ki 6:5**	7023
would not be inserted in the **w** of	**1Ki 6:6**	7023
Then he built the **w** of the house on	**1Ki 6:15**	7023
to the ceiling he overlaid *the* **w**	**1Ki 6:15**	
Then he carved all the **w** of the house	**1Ki 6:29**	7023
by way of the gate between the two **w**	**2Ki 25:4**	2346
captain of the guard broke down the **w**	**2Ki 25:10**	2346
to overlay the **w** of the buildings;	**1Ch 29:4**	7023
the thresholds and its **w** and its	**2Ch 3:7**	7023
and he carved cherubim on the **w**.	**2Ch 3:7**	7023
fortified cities *with* **w**, gates	**2Ch 8:5**	2346
cities and surround *them* with **w**	**2Ch 14:7**	2346
and evil city and are finishing the **w**	**Ezr 4:12**	7792
if that city is rebuilt and the **w** are	**Ezr 4:13**	7792
if that city is rebuilt and the **w**	**Ezr 4:16**	7792
and beams are being laid in the **w**;	**Ezr 5:8**	3797
inspecting the **w** of Jerusalem which	**Ne 2:13**	2346
heard that the repair of the **w** of	**Ne 4:7**	2346
"Within the **w** they produce oil;	**Jb 24:11**	7791
Build the **w** of Jerusalem.	**Ps 51:18**	2346
night they go around her upon her **w**,	**Ps 55:10**	2346
You have broken down all his **w**; You	**Ps 89:40**	1448
"May peace be within your **w**,	**Ps 122:7**	2426
that is broken into *and* without **w**	**Pr 25:28**	2346
The guardsmen of the **w** took away my	**SS 5:7**	2346
make for ourselves a breach in its **w**	**Is 7:6**	
A breaking down of **w** And a crying to	**Is 22:5**	7023
made a reservoir between the two **w**	**Is 22:11**	2346
unassailable fortifications of your **w**	**Is 25:12**	2346
He sets up **w** and ramparts for	**Is 26:1**	2346
Your **w** are continually before Me.	**Is 49:16**	2346
will give in My house and within My **w**	**Is 56:5**	2346
"Foreigners will build up your **w**,	**Is 60:10**	2346

But you will call your **w** salvation, **Is 60:18** 2346
On your **w**, O Jerusalem, I have **Is 62:6** 2346
and against all its **w** round about **Jer 1:15** 2346
city and as a pillar of iron and as **w** **Jer 1:18** 2346
through the gate between the two **w**; **Jer 39:4** 2346
and they broke down the **w** of **Jer 39:8** 2346
And rush back and forth inside the **w**; **Jer 49:3** 1448
Her **w** have been torn down. For this **Jer 50:15** 2346
Lift up a signal against the **w** of **Jer 51:12** 2346
by way of the gate between the two **w** **Jer 52:7** 2346
of the guard broke down all the **w** **Jer 52:14** 2346
into the hand of the enemy The **w** of **La 2:7** 2346
they cast up ramps and build siege **w** **Ezk 17:17** 1785
'They will destroy the **w** of Tyre **Ezk 26:4** 2346
and he will make siege **w** against you, **Ezk 26:8** 1785
rams he will direct against your **w**, **Ezk 26:9** 2346
your **w** will shake at the noise of **Ezk 26:10** 2346
break down your **w** and destroy your **Ezk 26:12** 2346
and your army were on your **w**, **Ezk 27:11** 2346
They hung their shields on your **w** **Ezk 27:11** 2346
citizens who talk about you by the **w** **Ezk 33:30** 7023
all of them living without **w** **Ezk 38:11** 2346
area with the building and its **w** **Ezk 41:13** 7023
palm trees like those carved on the **w**; **Ezk 41:25** 7023
out *through* breaches *in the* **w**, **Am 4:3**
will be a day for building your **w**. **Mi 7:11** 1447
grasshoppers Settling in the stone **w** **Na 3:17** 1448
'Jerusalem will be inhabited without **w** **Zch 2:4** 6519
By faith the **w** of Jericho fell down **Heb 11:30** *5038*

WAND
and their *diviner's* **w** informs **Hos 4:12** 4731

WANDER
when God caused me to **w** from my **Gn 20:13** 8582
and He made them **w** in the wilderness **Nu 32:13** 5128
and shall I today make you **w** with us, **2Sa 15:20** 5128
I will not make the feet of Israel **w** **2Ki 21:8** 5110
And makes them **w** in a pathless **Jb 12:24** 8582
When its young cry to God And **w** **Jb 38:41** 8582
"Behold, I would **w** far away, I **Ps 55:7** 5074
They **w** about for food And growl if **Ps 59:15** 5128
And makes them **w** in a pathless **Ps 107:40** 8582
Let his children **w** about and beg; **Ps 109:10** 5128
Do not let me **w** from Your **Ps 119:10** 7686
Who **w** from Your commandments. **Ps 119:21** 7686
You have rejected all those who **w** **Ps 119:118** 7686
And fools will not **w** *on it.* **Is 35:8** 8582
I will **w** about all my years because **Is 38:15** 1718
"Even so they have loved to **w**; they **Jer 14:10** 5128
"**W** away from the midst of Babylon **Jer 50:8** 5110
The herds of cattle **w** aimlessly **Jl 1:18** 943
Therefore *the people* **w** like sheep, **Zch 10:2** 5265

WANDERED
And she departed and **w** about in **Gn 21:14** 8582
And they **w** about from nation to **1Ch 16:20** 1980
And they **w** about from nation to **Ps 105:13** 1980
They **w** in the wilderness in a desert **Ps 107:4** 8582
reached as far as Jazer *and* **w** to **Is 16:8** 8582
Each has **w** in his own way; There is **Is 47:15** 8582
Both man and beast have **w** off, they **Jer 50:3** 5110
They **w**, blind, in the streets; **La 4:14** 5128
So they fled and **w**; *Men* among **La 4:15** 5128
"My flock **w** through all **Ezk 34:6** 7686
and some by longing for it have **w** **1Tm 6:10** *635*

WANDERER
you will be a vagrant and a **w** on **Gn 4:12** 5110
and I will be a vagrant and a **w** on **Gn 4:14** 5110
an exile and a **w**? And who has reared **Is 49:21** 5493

WANDERERS
And they will be **w** among the nations. **Hos 9:17** 5074

WANDERING
he was **w** in the field; and the man **Gn 37:15** 8582
'They are **w** aimlessly in the land; **Ex 14:3** 943
meet your enemy's ox or his donkey **w** **Ex 23:4** 8582
'My father was a **w** Aramean, and he **Dt 26:5** 6
Remember my affliction and my **w**, **La 3:19** 4788
w in deserts and mountains and caves **Heb 11:38** *4105*
w stars, for whom the black darkness **Jude 1:13** *4107*

WANDERINGS
He has known your **w** through this **Dt 2:7** 1980
You have taken account of my **w**; Put **Ps 56:8** 5112

WANDERS
"He **w** about for food, saying, **Jb 15:23** 5074
A man who **w** from the way of **Pr 21:16** 8582
Like a bird that **w** from her nest, So **Pr 27:8** 5074
So is a man who **w** from his home. **Pr 27:8** 5074

WANE
And My righteousness will not **w**. **Is 51:6** 2865
Nor will your moon **w**; For you will **Is 60:20** 622

WANT
said to her, "What do you **w**?" **Jos 15:18**
said to her, "What do you **w**?" **Jg 1:14**
wilderness *and* they were not in **w**; **Ne 9:21** 2637
mountain rains And hug the rock for **w** **Jb 24:8** 1097
They do not **w** to know its ways Nor **Jb 24:13**
"From **w** and famine they are **Jb 30:3** 2639
my shepherd, I shall not **w**. **Ps 23:1** 2637
to those who fear Him there is no **w**. **Ps 34:9** 4270
seek the LORD shall not be in **w** **Ps 34:10** 2637
all my counsel And did not **w** my **Pr 1:25** 14
and yet it results only in **w**. **Pr 11:24** 4270
will come *as* a robber And your **w** **Pr 24:34** 4270
after wealth And does not know that **w** **Pr 28:22** 2639
He who gives to the poor will never **w**, **Pr 28:27** 4270
Or that I not be in **w** and steal, **Pr 30:9** 3423
"I **w** you to swear, O daughters of **SS 8:4**
treat people the same way you **w** them **Mt 7:12** *2309*
we **w** to see a sign from You." **Mt 12:38** *2309*
'Do you **w** us, then, to go **Mt 13:28** *2309*
and I do not **w** to send them away **Mt 15:32** *2309*
"What do you **w** Me to do for you?" **Mt 20:32** *2309*
They said to Him, "Lord, *we* **w** **Mt 20:33**
"Where do You **w** us to prepare for **Mt 26:17** *2309*
"Whom do you **w** me to release for **Mt 27:17** *2309*
"Which of the two do you **w** me to **Mt 27:21** *2309*
"Ask me for whatever you **w** and I **Mk 6:22** *2309*
"I **w** you to give me at once the head **Mk 6:25** *2309*
and He did not **w** anyone to know **Mk 9:30** *2309*
we **w** You to do for us whatever we ask **Mk 10:35** *2309*
And He said to them, "What do you **w** **Mk 10:36** *2309*
"What do you **w** Me to do for you?" **Mk 10:51** *2309*
I **w** to regain my sight!" **Mk 10:51**
"Where do You **w** us to go and prepare **Mk 14:12** *2309*
"Do you **w** me to release for you **Mk 15:9** *2309*
"Treat others the same way you **w** **Lk 6:31** *2309*
do You **w** us to command fire to come **Lk 9:54** *2309*
"What do you **w** Me to do for you?" **Lk 18:41** *2309*
I **w** to regain my sight!" **Lk 18:41**
'We do not **w** this man to reign over **Lk 19:14** *2309*
who did not **w** me to reign over them, **Lk 19:27** *2309*
They said to Him, "Where do You **w** **Lk 22:9** *2309*
"You do not **w** to go away also, do **Jn 6:67** *2309*
and you **w** to do the desires of your **Jn 8:44** *2309*
why do you **w** to hear *it* again? **Jn 9:27** *2309*
You do not **w** to become His disciples **Jn 9:27** *2309*
Jesus said to him, "If I **w** him to **Jn 21:22** *2309*
"If I **w** him to remain until I come, **Jn 21:23** *2309*
so we **w** to know what these things **Ac 17:20** *1014*
"But if you **w** anything beyond this, **Ac 19:39** *1934*
I do not **w** you to be unaware, **Ro 1:13** *2309*
But if I do the very thing I do not **w** **Ro 7:16** *2309*
For the good that I **w**, I do not do, **Ro 7:19** *2309*
the very evil that I do not **w**. **Ro 7:19** *2309*
I am doing the very thing I do not **w**, **Ro 7:20** *2309*
For I do not **w** you, brethren, to be **Ro 11:25** *2309*
Do you **w** to have no fear of authority? **Ro 13:3** *2309*
but I **w** you to be wise in what is **Ro 16:19** *2309*
But I **w** you to be free from concern. **1Co 7:32** *2309*
For I do not **w** you to be unaware, **1Co 10:1** *2309*
and I do not **w** you to become sharers **1Co 10:20** *2309*
the unbelievers invites you and you **w** **1Co 10:27** *2309*
But I **w** you to understand that Christ **1Co 11:3** *2309*
I do not **w** you to be unaware. **1Co 12:1** *2309*
For we do not **w** you to be unaware, **2Co 1:8** *2309*
because we do not **w** to be unclothed **2Co 5:4** *2309*
are some who are disturbing you and **w** **Ga 1:7** *2309*
This is the only thing I **w** to find **Ga 3:2** *2309*
Tell me, you who **w** to be under law, **Ga 4:21** *2309*
Now I **w** you to know, brethren, that **Php 1:12** *1014*
Not that I speak from **w**, for I have **Php 4:11** *5304*
For I **w** you to know how great a **Col 2:1** *2309*
But we do not **w** you to be uninformed, **1Th 4:13** *2309*
Therefore I **w** the men in every place **1Tm 2:8** *1014*
Likewise, *I* **w** women to adorn **1Tm 2:9**
they **w** to get married, **1Tm 5:11** *2309*
Therefore, I **w** younger *widows* to **1Tm 5:14** *1014*
But those who **w** to get rich fall into **1Tm 6:9** *1014*
and concerning these things I **w** you **Ti 3:8** *1014*
but without your consent I did not **w** **Phm 1:14** *2309*
I do not **w** to *do so* with paper **2Jn 1:12** *1014*
and she does not **w** to repent of her **Rv 2:21** *2309*

WANTED
Although Herod **w** to put him to death, **Mt 14:5** *2309*
How often I **w** to gather your children **Mt 23:37** *2309*
any one prisoner whom they **w**. **Mt 27:15** *2309*
summoned those whom He Himself **w**, **Mk 3:13** *2309*
had a grudge against him and **w** to put **Mk 6:19** *2309*
He **w** no one to know *of it;* **Mk 7:24** *2309*
as to what he **w** him called. **Lk 1:62** *2309*
How often I **w** to gather your children **Lk 13:34** *2309*
for he had **w** to see Him for a long **Lk 23:8** *2309*
also of the fish as much as they **w**. **Jn 6:11** *2309*
Some of them **w** to seize Him, but no **Jn 7:44** *2309*
and **w** to offer sacrifice with **Ac 14:13** *2309*
Barnabas **w** to take John, called Mark, **Ac 15:37** *1014*
Paul **w** this man to go with him; **Ac 16:3** *2309*
And when he **w** to go across to Achaia, **Ac 18:27** *1014*
And when Paul **w** to go into **Ac 19:30** *1014*
[We **w** to judge him according to our **Ac 24:6** *2309*
For we **w** to come to you—I, Paul, **1Th 2:18** *2309*

WANTING
being a righteous man and not **w** to **Mt 1:19** *2309*
Pilate, **w** to release Jesus, **Lk 23:20** *2309*
"And **w** to ascertain the charge for **Ac 23:28** *1014*
but the centurion, **w** to bring Paul **Ac 27:43** *1014*
w to be teachers of the Law, even **1Tm 1:7** *2309*
but **w** to have their ears tickled, **2Tm 4:3**

WANTON
But she who gives herself to **w** **1Tm 5:6** *4684*
on the earth and led a life of **w** **Jas 5:5** *4684*

WANTS
"If anyone **w** to sue you and take **Mt 5:40** *2309*
and do not turn away from him who **w** **Mt 5:42** *2309*
"If anyone **w** to be first, he shall **Mk 9:35** *2309*
for Herod **w** to kill You." **Lk 13:31** *2309*
"For which one of you, when he **w** to **Lk 14:28** *2309*
the one who **w** to do good. **Ro 7:21** *2309*
And if anyone **w** to harm them, fire **Rv 11:5** *2309*
so if anyone **w** to harm them, he must **Rv 11:5** *2309*

WAR
that they made **w** with Bera king **Gn 14:2** 4421
will multiply and in the event of **w**, **Ex 1:10** 4421
change their minds when they see **w**, **Ex 13:17** 4421
the LORD will have **w** against **Ex 17:16** 4421
"There is a sound of **w** in the camp." **Ex 32:17** 4421
whoever *is able to* go out to **w** in **Nu 1:3** 6635
whoever *was able to* go out to **w**, **Nu 1:20** 6635
whoever *was able to* go out to **w**, **Nu 1:22** 6635
whoever *was able to* go out to **w**, **Nu 1:24** 6635
whoever *was able to* go out to **w**, **Nu 1:26** 6635
whoever *was able to* go out to **w**, **Nu 1:28** 6635
whoever *was able to* go out to **w**, **Nu 1:30** 6635
whoever *was able to* go out to **w**, **Nu 1:32** 6635
whoever *was able to* go out to **w**, **Nu 1:34** 6635
whoever *was able to* go out to **w**, **Nu 1:36** 6635
whoever *was able to* go out to **w**, **Nu 1:38** 6635
whoever *was able to* go out to **w**, **Nu 1:40** 6635
whoever *was able to* go out to **w**, **Nu 1:42** 6635
whoever *was able to* go out to **w** **Nu 1:45** 6635
"When you go to **w** in your land **Nu 10:9** 4421
whoever is able to go out to **w** in **Nu 26:2** 6635
"Arm men from among you for the **w**, **Nu 31:3** 6635
of Israel you shall send to the **w**." **Nu 31:4** 6635
twelve thousand armed for **w**. **Nu 31:5** 6635
to the **w**, and Phinehas the son of **Nu 31:6** 6635
to the **w** with them, and the holy **Nu 31:6** 6635
So they made **w** against Midian, just **Nu 31:7** 6633
who had come from service in the **w**. **Nu 31:14** 4421
the priest said to the men of **w** who **Nu 31:21** 6635
for the LORD from the men of **w** **Nu 31:28** 4421
from the spoil which the men of **w** had **Nu 31:32** 6635
portion of those who went out to **w**, **Nu 31:36** 6635
from the men who had gone to **w** **Nu 31:42** 6633
have taken a census of men of **w** who **Nu 31:49** 4421
The men of **w** had taken booty, every **Nu 31:53** 6635
"Shall your brothers go to **w** while **Nu 32:6** 4421
before the LORD for the **w**, **Nu 32:20** 4421
everyone who is armed for **w**, will **Nu 32:27** 6635
man of you girded on his weapons of **w**, **Dt 1:41** 4421
nor provoke them to **w**, for I will **Dt 2:9** 4421
all the generation of the men of **w** **Dt 2:14** 4421
it came about when all the men of **w** **Dt 2:16** 4421
by signs and wonders and by **w** and by **Dt 4:34** 4421
but makes **w** against you, then you **Dt 20:12** 4421
to make **w** against it in order to **Dt 20:19** 3898a
against the city that is making **w** **Dt 20:20** 4421
about 40,000 equipped for **w**, crossed **Jos 4:13** 6635
all the men of **w**, died in **Jos 5:4** 4421
the men of **w** who came out of Egypt, **Jos 5:6** 4421
all the men of **w** circling the city **Jos 6:3** 4421
Take all the people of **w** with you **Jos 8:1** 4421
Joshua rose with all the people of **w** **Jos 8:3** 4421
Then all the people of **w** who *were* **Jos 8:11** 4421
he and all the people of **w** with him **Jos 10:7** 4421
said to the chiefs of the men of **w** **Jos 10:24** 4421
So Joshua and all the people of **w** **Jos 11:7** 4421
Joshua waged **w** a long time with all **Jos 11:18** 4421
Thus the land had rest from **w**. **Jos 11:23** 4421
for **w** and for going out and coming in. **Jos 14:11** 4421
Then the land had rest from **w**. **Jos 14:15** 4421
because he was a man of **w**. **Jos 17:1** 4421
at Shiloh to go up against them in **w**. **Jos 22:12** 6635
speak of going up against them in **w** **Jos 22:33** 6635
the sons of Israel might be taught **w**, **Jg 3:2** 4421
When he went out to **w**, the LORD **Jg 3:10** 4421
"New gods were chosen; Then **w** *was* **Jg 5:8** 3901
you are doing me wrong by making **w** **Jg 11:27** 3898a
hundred men armed with weapons of **w** **Jg 18:11** 4421
men armed with their weapons of **w**, **Jg 18:16** 4421
hundred men armed with weapons of **w**. **Jg 18:17** 4421
all these were men of **w**. **Jg 20:17** 4421
harvest and to make his weapons of **w** **1Sa 8:12** 4421
Now the **w** against the Philistines was **1Sa 14:52** 4421
in battle array shouting the **w** cry. **1Sa 17:20** 4421
and Saul set him over the men of **w**. **1Sa 18:5** 4421
When there was **w** again, David went **1Sa 19:8** 4421
So Saul summoned all the people for **w**, **1Sa 23:8** 4421
gathered their armed camps for **w**, to **1Sa 28:1** 6633
for the Philistines are waging **w** **1Sa 28:15** 3898a
And the weapons of **w** perished!" **2Sa 1:27** 4421
Now there was a long **w** between **2Sa 3:1** 4421
It came about while there was **w** **2Sa 3:6** 4421
for Hadadezer had been at **w** with Toi. **2Sa 8:10** 4421
and the people and the state of the **w**. **2Sa 11:7** 4421
to David all the events of the **w**. **2Sa 11:18** 4421
telling all the events of the **w** to **2Sa 11:19** 4421
Now when the Philistines were at **w** **2Sa 21:15** 4421
about after this that there was **w** **2Sa 21:18** 4421
There was **w** with the Philistines **2Sa 21:19** 4421
There was **w** at Gath again, where **2Sa 21:20** 4421
he also shed the blood of **w** in peace. **1Ki 2:5** 4421
And he put the blood of **w** on his belt **1Ki 2:5** 4421
for they were men of **w**, his servants, **1Ki 9:22** 4421
how he made **w** and how he reigned, **1Ki 14:19** 3898a
There was **w** between Rehoboam **1Ki 14:30** 4421
There was **w** between Rehoboam **1Ki 15:6** 4421
And there was **w** between Abijam **1Ki 15:7** 4421
Now there was **w** between Asa **1Ki 15:16** 4421
There was **w** between Asa and Baasha **1Ki 15:32** 4421
or if they have come out for **w**, take **1Ki 20:18** 4421
Three years passed without **w** between **1Ki 22:1** 4421
went with Joram the son of Ahab to **w** **2Ki 8:28** 4421
the cities which he had taken in **w** **2Ki 13:25** 4421
and took Sela by **w**, and named it **2Ki 14:7** 4421
came up to Jerusalem to *wage* **w**; **2Ki 16:5** 4421
have counsel and strength for the **w**.' **2Ki 18:20** 4421
all strong and fit for **w**, and these **2Ki 24:16** 4421
and all the men of **w** *fled* by **2Ki 25:4** 4421
who was overseer of the men of **w**, **2Ki 25:19** 4421
In the days of Saul they made **w** with **1Ch 5:10** 4421
44,760, who went to **w**. **1Ch 5:18** 6635
They made **w** against the Hagrites, **1Ch 5:19** 4421
For many fell slain, because the **w** **1Ch 5:22** 4421
troops of the army for **w**, for they **1Ch 7:4** 4421
ready to go out with the army to **w**. **1Ch 7:11** 4421

for service in **w** was 26,000 1Ch 7:40 4421
mighty men who helped *him* in **w**. 1Ch 12:1 4421
men trained for **w**, who could handle 1Ch 12:8 4421
of the divisions equipped for **w**, who 1Ch 12:23 6635
6,800, equipped for **w**. 1Ch 12:24 6635
mighty men of valor for **w**, 7,100. 1Ch 12:25 6635
with all kinds of weapons of **w** 1Ch 12:33 4421
with all *kinds* of weapons of **w** 1Ch 12:37 6635
All these, being men of **w** who could 1Ch 12:38 4421
for Hadadezer had been at **w** with Tou. 1Ch 18:10 4421
Now it came about after this, that **w** 1Ch 20:4 4421
And there was **w** with the Philistines 1Ch 20:5 4421
Again there was **w** at Gath, where 1Ch 20:6 4421
My name because you are a man of **w** 1Ch 28:3 4421
they were men of **w**, his chief 2Ch 8:9 4421
Now there was **w** between Abijah 2Ch 13:2 4421
Then the men of Judah raised a **w** cry, 2Ch 13:15
when the men of Judah raised the **w** 2Ch 13:15
and there was no one at **w** with him 2Ch 14:6 4421
And there was no more **w** until 2Ch 15:19 4421
so that they did not make **w** against 2Ch 17:10 3898a
with him 180,000 equipped for **w**. 2Ch 17:18 6635
came to make **w** against Jehoshaphat. 2Ch 20:1 4421
son of Ahab king of Israel to wage **w** 2Ch 22:5 4421
able to go to **w** *and* handle 2Ch 25:5 6635
who could wage **w** with great power, 2Ch 26:13 4421
In Jerusalem he made engines *of* **w** 2Ch 26:15
come and that he intended to make **w** 2Ch 32:2 4421
Neco king of Egypt came up to make **w** 2Ch 35:20 3898a
the house with which I am at **w**, 2Ch 35:21 4421
disguised himself in order to make **w** 2Ch 35:22 3898a
but came to make **w** on the plain of 2Ch 35:22 3898a
And in **w** from the power of the sword. Jb 5:20 4421
For the day of **w** and battle? Jb 38:23 7128
the thunder of the captains and the **w** Jb 39:25 8643
Though **w** arise against me, In Ps 27:3 4421
But his heart was **w**; His words were Ps 55:21 7128
the peoples who delight in **w**. Ps 68:30 7128
and the sword and the weapons of **w**. Ps 76:3 4421
They are for **w**. Ps 120:7 4421
Who trains my hands for **w**, Ps 144:1 7128
And make **w** by wise guidance. Pr 20:18 4421
For by wise guidance you will wage **w**, Pr 24:6 4421
A time for **w** and a time for peace. Ec 3:8 4421
is no discharge in the time of **w**, Ec 8:8 4421
Wisdom is better than weapons of **w**, Ec 9:18 7128
Expert in **w**; Each man has his sword SS 3:8 4421
And never again will they learn **w**. Is 2:4 4421
went up to Jerusalem to *wage* **w** Is 7:1 4421
of all the nations who wage **w** against Is 29:7 6633
Even all who wage **w** against her Is 29:7 6633
of all the nations will be Who wage **w** Is 29:8 6633
LORD of hosts come down to wage **w** Is 31:4 6633
'Your counsel and strength for the **w** Is 36:5 4421
Those who **w** with you will be as Is 41:12 4421
arouse *His* zeal like a man of **w**. Is 42:13 4421
He will raise a **w** cry. He will Is 42:13 6873
the trumpet, The alarm of **w**. Jer 4:19 4421
"Prepare **w** against her; Jer 6:4 4421
about to turn back the weapons of **w** Jer 21:4 4421
"I Myself will **w** against you with an Jer 21:5 3898a
of **w** and of calamity and of Jer 28:8 4421
as he is discouraging the men of **w** Jer 38:4 4421
king of Judah and all the men of **w** Jer 39:4 4421
were found there, the men of **w**. Jer 41:3 4421
where we will not see **w** or hear Jer 42:14 4421
I will cause a trumpet blast of **w** to Jer 49:2 4421
And all the men of **w** will be silenced Jer 49:26 4421
And all her men of **w** will be silenced Jer 50:30 4421
My weapon of **w**; And with you I Jer 51:20 4421
And the men of **w** are terrified. Jer 51:32 4421
and all the men of **w** fled and went Jer 52:7 4421
who was overseer of the men of **w**, Jer 52:25 4421
company will not help him in the **w**, Ezk 17:17 4421
your men of **w**. They hung shield Ezk 27:10 4421
gave horses and **w** horses and mules Ezk 27:14 6571a
in merchandise And all your men of **w** Ezk 27:27 4421
down to Sheol with their weapons of **w** Ezk 32:27 4421
w clubs and spears, and for seven Ezk 39:9 4731
with mighty men and all the men of **w**," Ezk 39:20 4421
and that horn was waging **w** with Da 7:21 7129
even to the end there will be **w**; Da 9:26 4421
that he may again wage **w** up to his Da 11:10 1624
extremely large and mighty army for **w**; Da 11:25 4421
the sword and **w** from the land, And Hos 2:18 4421
And like **w** horses, so they run. Jl 2:4
Prepare a **w**; rouse the mighty men! Jl 3:9 4421
consume her citadels Amid **w** cries Am 1:14 8643
With **w** cries and the sound of a Am 2:2 8643
From those returned from **w**. Mi 2:8 4421
in their mouths They declare holy **w**. Mi 3:5 4421
And never again will they train for **w**. Mi 4:3 4421
And the bow of **w** will be cut off. Zch 9:10 4421
all the peoples who have gone to **w** Zch 14:12 6633
waging **w** against the law of my mind Ro 7:23 *497*
we do not **w** according to the flesh, 2Co 10:3 *4754*
became mighty in **w**, put foreign Heb 11:34 *4171*
the source your pleasures that wage **w** Jas 4:1 *4754*
from fleshly lusts which wage **w** 1Pe 2:11 *4754*
and I will make **w** against them with Rv 2:16 *4170*
comes up out of the abyss will make **w** Rv 11:7 *4171*
And there was **w** in heaven, Michael Rv 12:7 *4171*
Michael and his angels waging **w** with Rv 12:7 *4171*
The dragon and his angels waged **w**, Rv 12:7 *4171*
and went off to make **w** with the rest Rv 12:17 *4171*
and who is able to wage **w** with him?" Rv 13:4 *4170*
It was also given to him to make **w** Rv 13:7 *4171*
to gather them together for the **w** of Rv 16:14 *4171*
"These will wage **w** against the Lamb, Rv 17:14 *4170*
righteousness He judges and wages **w**. Rv 19:11 *4170*
and their armies assembled to make **w** Rv 19:19 *4171*
to gather them together for the **w**; Rv 20:8 *4171*

WAR-CLUB
He says, "You are My **w**, *My* Jer 51:20 4661

WARD
And no one can **w** off His hand Or say Da 4:35 4223

WARDROBE
one who *was* in charge of the **w**, 2Ki 10:22 4458
keeper of the **w** (now she lived in 2Ki 22:14 899b
the keeper of the **w** (now she lived 2Ch 34:22 899b

WARES
that from the traders and the **w** 1Ki 10:15 4536
the peoples of the land who bring **w** Ne 10:31 4728
tin and lead they paid for your **w**. Ezk 27:12 5801
and war horses and mules for your **w**. Ezk 27:14 5801
they paid for your **w** with emeralds, Ezk 27:16 5801
"Vedan and Javan paid for your **w** Ezk 27:19 5801
they paid for your **w** with the best of Ezk 27:22 5801
"Your wealth, your **w**, your Ezk 27:27 5801
'When your **w** went out from the seas, Ezk 27:33 5801

WARFARE
And your father is an expert in **w**, 2Sa 17:8 4421
that her **w** has ended, That her Is 40:2 6635
for the weapons of our **w** are not of 2Co 10:4 *4752*

WARM
"This our bread *was* **w** *when* Jos 9:12 2525
but he could not keep **w**. 1Ki 1:1 2552
that my lord the king may keep **w**." 1Ki 1:2 2552
and the flesh of the child became **w**. 2Ki 4:34 2552
if two lie down together they keep **w**, Ec 4:11 2552
but how can one be **w** *alone?* Ec 4:11 2552
I am **w**, I have seen the fire." Is 44:16 2552
There will be no coal to **w** by *Nor* Is 47:14 2552
but no one is **w** *enough;* and he Hg 1:6 2552

WARMED
And if he has not been **w** with Jb 31:20 2552
be **w** and be filled," and yet you do Jas 2:16 *2328*

WARMING
was sitting with the officers and **w** Mk 14:54 *2328*
and seeing Peter **w** himself, she Mk 14:67 *2328*
for it was cold and they were **w** Jn 18:18 *2328*
standing and **w** himself. Jn 18:18 *2328*
Now Simon Peter was standing and **w** Jn 18:25 *2328*

WARMS
abandons her eggs to the earth And **w** Jb 39:14 2552
so he takes one of them and **w** himself; Is 44:15 2552
He also **w** himself and says, "Aha! Is 44:16 2552

WARN
w the people, so that they do not Ex 19:21 5749b
you shall solemnly **w** them and tell 1Sa 8:9 5749b
swear by the LORD and solemnly **w** 1Ki 2:42 5749b
you shall **w** them so that they may not 2Ch 19:10 2094b
from My mouth, **w** them from Me. Ezk 3:17 2094b
and you do not **w** him or speak out to Ezk 3:18 2094b
you do not warn him or speak out to **w** Ezk 3:18 2094b
and you do not speak to **w** Ezk 33:8 2094b
"But if you on your part **w** a wicked Ezk 33:9 2094b
"But I will **w** you whom to fear: Lk 12:5 *5263*
brothers—in order that he may **w** Lk 16:28 *1263*
let us **w** them to speak no longer to Ac 4:17 *546*

WARNED
"The man solemnly **w** us, 'You shall Gn 43:3 5749b
for You **w** us, saying, 'Set bounds Ex 19:23 5749b
of goring and its owner has been **w**, Ex 21:29 5749b
thus he **w** him, so that he guarded 2Ki 6:10 2094b
Yet the LORD **w** Israel 2Ki 17:13 5749b
and His warnings with which He **w** them. 2Ki 17:15 5749b
Then I **w** them and said to them, Ne 13:21 5749b
Moreover, by them Your servant is **w**; Ps 19:11 2094b
But beyond this, my son, be **w**: Ec 12:12 2094b
"Be **w**, O Jerusalem, Or I shall be Jer 6:8 3256
'For I solemnly **w** your fathers in Jer 11:7 5749b
"Yet if you have **w** the wicked and he Ezk 3:19 2094b
since you have not **w** him, he shall Ezk 3:20 2094b
"However, if you have **w** Ezk 3:21 2094b
the trumpet and the people are not **w**, Ezk 33:6 2094b
And having been **w** *by God* in a Mt 2:12 *5537*
Then after being **w** *by God* in a Mt 2:22 *5537*
who **w** you to flee from the wrath to Mt 3:7 *5263*
And Jesus sternly **w** them: "See that Mt 9:30 *1690*
and **w** them not to tell who He was. Mt 12:16 *2008*
Then He **w** the disciples that they Mt 16:20 *2008*
And He sternly **w** him and immediately Mk 1:43 *1690*
And He earnestly **w** them not to tell Mk 3:12 *2008*
And He **w** them to tell no one about Mk 8:30 *2008*
who **w** you to flee from the wrath to Lk 3:7 *5263*
But He **w** them and instructed *them* Lk 9:21 *2008*
also told you before and solemnly **w** 1Th 4:6 *1263*
just as Moses was **w** *by God* when Heb 8:5 *5537*
By faith Noah, being **w** *by God* Heb 11:7 *5537*
escape when they refused him who **w** Heb 12:25 *5537*

WARNING
so that they became a **w**. Nu 26:10 5251
heart all the words with which I am **w** Dt 32:46 5749b
Take **w**, O judges of the earth. Ps 2:10 3256
To whom shall I speak and give **w** That Jer 6:10 5749b
w persistently, saying, "Listen to Jer 11:7 5749b
shall surely live because he took **w**; Ezk 3:21 2094b
a **w** and an object of horror to Ezk 5:15 4148
of the trumpet and does not take **w**, Ezk 33:4 2094b
of the trumpet but did not take **w**; Ezk 33:5 2094b
But had he taken **w**, he would have Ezk 33:5 2094b
from My mouth and give them **w** Ezk 33:7 2094b
man after a first and second **w**, Ti 3:10 *3559*

WARNINGS
He made with their fathers and His **w** 2Ki 17:15 5715

WARNS
land and blows on the trumpet and **w** Ezk 33:3 2094b
who turn away from Him who **w** Heb 12:25

WARP
whether in **w** or woof, of linen or of Lv 13:48 8359
or in the **w** or in the woof, or in Lv 13:49 8359
whether in the **w** or in the woof, Lv 13:51 8359
whether the **w** or the woof, in wool Lv 13:52 8359
either in the **w** or in the woof, Lv 13:53 8359
whether from the **w** or from the woof; Lv 13:56 8359
whether in the **w** or in the woof, or Lv 13:57 8359
"The garment, whether the **w** or Lv 13:58 8359
whether in the **w** or in the woof, Lv 13:59 8359

WARRED
might which he showed and how he **w**, 1Ki 22:45 3898a
Now he went out and **w** against 2Ch 26:6 3898a

WARRING
Now the king of Aram was **w** against 2Ki 6:8 3898a
Nebuchadnezzar king of Babylon is **w** Jer 21:2 3898a
with which you are **w** against the king Jer 21:4 3898a

WARRIOR
"The LORD is a **w**; The LORD Ex 15:3 4421
two maidens for every **w**; Jg 5:30 1397
is with you, O valiant **w**." Jg 6:12 1368
the Gileadite was a valiant **w**, Jg 11:1 1368
a **w**, one prudent in speech, and a 1Sa 16:18 4421
but a youth while he has been a **w** 1Sa 17:33 4421
Now the man Jeroboam was a valiant **w**, 1Ki 11:28 1368
The man was also a valiant **w**, *but* 2Ki 5:1 1368
and of Benjamin, Eliada a valiant **w**, 2Ch 17:17 1368
an angel who destroyed every mighty **w**, 2Ch 32:21 1368
He runs at me like a **w**. Jb 16:14 1368
A **w** is not delivered by great Ps 33:16 1368
Like a **w** overcome by wine. Ps 78:65 1368
Sharp arrows of the **w**, With the Ps 120:4 1368
Like arrows in the hand of a **w**, So Ps 127:4 1368
The mighty man and the **w**, The judge Is 3:2 4421
For every boot of the booted **w** in Is 9:5 5431
The LORD will go forth like a **w**, Is 42:13 1368
For one **w** has stumbled over another, Jer 46:12 1368
Their arrows will be like an expert **w** Jer 50:9 1368
In it the **w** cries out bitterly. Zph 1:14 1368
A victorious **w**. He will exult over Zph 3:17 1368

WARRIOR'S
And I will make you like a **w** sword. Zch 9:13 1368

WARRIORS
and divide the booty between the **w** Nu 31:27 4421
all your valiant **w**, and shall help Jos 1:14 1368
with its king *and* the valiant **w**. Jos 6:2 1368
valiant **w**, and sent them out at Jos 8:3 1368
of war with him and all the valiant **w**. Jos 10:7 1368
of the LORD came down to me as **w**. Jg 5:13 1368
help of the LORD against the **w**.' Jg 5:23 1368
all these were valiant **w**. Jg 20:44 376
all these were valiant **w**. Jg 20:46 376
of the valiant **w** there, Jg 21:10 1121
chosen men who were **w**, to fight 1Ki 12:21 4421
chosen men who were **w**, to fight 2Ch 11:1 4421
the battle with an army of valiant **w**, 2Ch 13:3 1368
chosen men *who were* valiant **w**. 2Ch 13:3 1368
all of them were valiant **w**. 2Ch 14:8 1368
and **w**, valiant men, in Jerusalem. 2Ch 17:13 4421
him 300,000 valiant **w**; 2Ch 17:14 1368
with him 200,000 valiant **w**; 2Ch 17:16 1368
He hired also 100,000 valiant **w** out of 2Ch 25:6 1368
of valiant **w**, was 2,600. 2Ch 26:12 1368
decided with his officers and his **w** 2Ch 32:3 1368
and their brothers, valiant **w**, 128. Ne 11:14 1368
And none of the **w** could use his hands. Ps 76:5 2428
swift and the battle is not to the **w**, Ec 9:11 1368
a wasting disease among his stout **w**; Is 10:16 4924a
I have even called My mighty **w**, My Is 13:3 1368
"How can you say, 'We are mighty **w**, Jer 48:14 1368
He commanded certain valiant **w** who Da 3:20 1401
in your numerous **w**, Hos 10:13 1368
"Even the bravest among the **w** will Am 2:16 1368
The **w** are dressed in scarlet, Na 2:3 376

WARS
it is said in the Book of the **W** of Nu 21:14 4421
who had not experienced any of the **w** Jg 3:1 4421
the LORD his God because of the **w** 1Ki 5:3 4421
much blood and have waged great **w**; 1Ch 22:8 4421
And *there were* **w** between Rehoboam 2Ch 12:15 4421
from now on you will surely have **w**." 2Ch 16:9 4421
even all his **w** and his acts, behold, 2Ch 27:7 4421
He makes **w** to cease to the end of Ps 46:9 4421
They continually stir up **w**. Ps 140:2 4421
"You will be hearing of **w** and rumors Mt 24:6 *4171*
be hearing of wars and rumors of **w**. Mt 24:6 *4171*
"When you hear of **w** and rumors Mk 13:7 *4171*
hear of wars and rumors of **w**, Mk 13:7 *4171*
"When you hear of **w** and disturbances, Lk 21:9 *4171*

WASH
let a little water be brought and **w** Gn 18:4 7364
and **w** your feet; then you may rise Gn 19:2 7364
and water to **w** his feet and the feet Gn 24:32 7364
and let them **w** their garments; Ex 19:10 3526
doorway of the tent of meeting and **w** Ex 29:4 7364
and **w** its entrails and its legs, Ex 29:17 7364
"Aaron and his sons shall **w** their Ex 30:19 7364
they shall **w** with water, so that Ex 30:20 7364
"So they shall **w** their hands Ex 30:21 7364
doorway of the tent of meeting and **w** Ex 40:12 7364
and its legs he shall **w** with water. Lv 1:9 7364
and the legs he shall **w** with water. Lv 1:13 7364

in a holy place you shall **w** what was **Lv 6:27** 3526
up any of their carcasses shall **w** his **Lv 11:25** 3526
who picks up their carcasses shall **w** **Lv 11:28** 3526
who eats some of its carcass shall **w** **Lv 11:40** 3526
one who picks up its carcass shall **w** **Lv 11:40** 3526
And he shall **w** his clothes and be **Lv 13:6** 3526
and he shall **w** his clothes and be **Lv 13:34** 3526
then the priest shall order them to **w** **Lv 13:54** 3526
"The one to be cleansed shall then **w** **Lv 14:8** 3526
He shall then **w** his clothes and bathe **Lv 14:9** 3526
lies down in the house shall **w** his **Lv 14:47** 3526
and whoever eats in the house shall **w** **Lv 14:47** 3526
who touches his bed shall **w** his **Lv 15:5** 3526
shall **w** his clothes and bathe in **Lv 15:6** 3526
the person with the discharge shall **w** **Lv 15:7** 3526
he too shall **w** his clothes and bathe **Lv 15:8** 3526
and he who carries them shall **w** his **Lv 15:10** 3526
rinsed his hands in water shall **w** his **Lv 15:11** 3526
he shall then **w** his clothes and bathe **Lv 15:13** 3526
'Anyone who touches her bed shall **w** **Lv 15:21** 3526
any thing on which she sits shall **w** **Lv 15:22** 3526
them shall be unclean and shall **w** his **Lv 15:27** 3526
the goat as the scapegoat shall **w** his **Lv 16:26** 3526
"Then the one who burns them shall **w** **Lv 16:28** 3526
he shall **w** his clothes and bathe in **Lv 17:15** 3526
"But if he does not **w** *them* **Lv 17:16** 3526
and he shall **w** them off into **Nu 5:23** 4229a
a razor over their whole body and **w** **Nu 8:7** 3526
'The priest shall then **w** his clothes **Nu 19:7** 3526
'The one who burns it shall also **w** **Nu 19:8** 3526
the ashes of the heifer shall **w** his **Nu 19:10** 3526
and he shall **w** his clothes and bathe **Nu 19:19** 3526
the water for impurity shall **w** his **Nu 19:21** 3526
"And you shall **w** your clothes on **Nu 31:24** 3526
is nearest to the slain man shall **w** **Dt 21:6** 7364
"**W** yourself therefore, and anoint **Ru 3:3** 7364
your maidservant is a maid to **w** **1Sa 25:41** 7364
and **w** your feet." And Uriah went **2Sa 11:8** 7364
"Go and **w** in the Jordan seven times, **2Ki 5:10** 7364
Could I not **w** in them and be clean?" **2Ki 5:12** 7364
'**W**, and be clean'?" **2Ki 5:13** 7364
He also made ten basins in which to **w**, **2Ch 4:6** 7364
the sea *was* for the priests to **w** **2Ch 4:6** 7364
"If I should **w** myself with snow And **Jb 9:30** 7364
Its torrents **w** away the dust of **Jb 14:19** 7857
I shall **w** my hands in innocence, **Ps 26:6** 7364
W me thoroughly from my iniquity **Ps 51:2** 3526
W me, and I shall be whiter than **Ps 51:7** 3526
He will **w** his feet in the blood of **Ps 58:10** 7364
"**W** yourselves, make yourselves **Is 1:16** 7364
"Although you **w** yourself with lye **Jer 2:22** 3526
W your heart from evil, O Jerusalem, **Jer 4:14** 3526
anoint your head and **w** your face **Mt 6:17** *3538*
For they do not **w** their hands when **Mt 15:2** *3538*
do not eat unless they carefully **w** **Mk 7:3** *3538*
and said to him, "Go, **w** in **Jn 9:7** *3538*
'Go to Siloam and **w**'; so I went **Jn 9:11** *3538*
and began to **w** the disciples' feet **Jn 13:5** *3538*
do You **w** my feet?" **Jn 13:6** *3538*
"Never shall You **w** my feet!" Jesus **Jn 13:8** *3538*
"If I do not **w** you, you have no **Jn 13:8** *3538*
then **w** not only my feet, but **Jn 13:9**
"He who has bathed needs only to **w** **Jn 13:10** *3538*
ought to **w** one another's feet. **Jn 13:14** *3538*
and **w** away your sins, calling on His **Ac 22:16** *628*
Blessed are those who **w** their robes, **Rv 22:14** *4150*

WASHBOWL
"Moab is My **w**; Over Edom I shall **Ps 60:8** 7366
"Moab is My **w**; Over Edom I shall **Ps 108:9** 7366

WASHED
and they **w** their feet; and he gave **Gn 43:24** 7364
Then he **w** his face and came out; **Gn 43:31** 7364
and they **w** their garments. **Ex 19:14** 3526
it Moses and Aaron and his sons **w** **Ex 40:31** 7364
they **w**, just as the LORD had **Ex 40:32** 7364
Aaron and his sons come near and **w** **Lv 8:6** 7364
After he had **w** the entrails **Lv 8:21** 7364
He also **w** the entrails and the legs, **Lv 9:14** 7364
the article with the mark has been **w**, **Lv 13:55** 3526
mark has faded after it has been **w**, **Lv 13:56** 3526
the mark has departed when you **w** it, **Lv 13:58** 3526
it shall then be **w** a second time **Lv 13:58** 3526
it shall be **w** with water and be **Lv 15:17** 3526
purified themselves from sin and **w** **Nu 8:21** 3526
and they **w** their feet and ate **Jg 19:21** 7364
So David arose from the ground, **w**, **2Sa 12:20** 7364
nor **w** his clothes, from the day **2Sa 19:24** 3526
They **w** the chariot by the pool of **1Ki 22:38** 7857
Whose foundations were **w** away by a **Jb 22:16** 3332
vain I have kept my heart pure And **w** **Ps 73:13** 7364
Yet is not **w** from his filthiness. **Pr 30:12** 7364
I have **w** my feet, How can I dirty **SS 5:3** 7364
When the Lord has **w** away the filth of **Is 4:4** 7364
He has **w** me away. **Jer 51:34** 1740
nor were you **w** with water for **Ezk 16:4** 7364
"Then I bathed you with water, **w** **Ezk 16:9** 7857
he took water and **w** his hands in **Mt 27:24** *633*
that He had not first ceremonially **w** **Lk 11:38** *907*
So he went away and **w**, and came **Jn 9:7** *3538*
so I went away and **w**, and I received **Jn 9:11** *3538*
and I **w**, and I see." **Jn 9:15** *3538*
So when He had **w** their feet, **Jn 13:12** *3538*
w your feet, you also ought to wash **Jn 13:14** *3538*
and when they had **w** her body, they **Ac 9:37** *3068*
that *very* hour of the night and **w** **Ac 16:33** *3068*
but you were **w**, but you were **1Co 6:11** *628*
if she has **w** the saints' feet, if **1Tm 5:10** *3538*
an evil conscience and our bodies **w** **Heb 10:22** *3068*
and they have **w** their robes and made **Rv 7:14** *4150*

WASHES
He **w** his garments in wine, And his **Gn 49:11** 3526

WASHING
for **w**; and you shall put it between **Ex 30:18** 7364
the altar and put water in it for **w**. **Ex 40:30** 7364
Which have come up from *their* **w**, **SS 4:2** 7367
Which have come up from *their* **w**, **SS 6:6** 7367
such as the **w** of cups and pitchers **Mk 7:4** *909*
were **w** their nets. **Lk 5:2** *4150*
having cleansed her by the **w** of water **Eph 5:26** *3067*
by the **w** of regeneration and renewing **Ti 3:5** *3067*
after **w**, *returns* to wallowing in **2Pe 2:22** *3068*

WASHINGS
of instruction about **w** and laying on **Heb 6:2** *909*
only to food and drink and various **w**, **Heb 9:10** *909*

WASTE
his servants and the land was laid **w** **Ex 8:24** 7843
consumption and fever that will **w** **Lv 26:16** 3615
'I will lay **w** your cities as well **Lv 26:31** 2723
desolate and your cities become **w**. **Lv 26:33** 2723
by the LORD's making your thigh **w** **Nu 5:21** 5307
your abdomen swell and your thigh **w** **Nu 5:22** 5307
will swell and her thigh will **w** away, **Nu 5:27** 5307
Then we have laid **w** even to Nophah, **Nu 21:30** 8074
a burning **w**, unsown and unproductive, **Dt 29:23**
And in the howling **w** of a wilderness; **Dt 32:10** 8414
Then Joab said, "I will not **w** time **2Sa 18:14** 3176
and the wicked will not **w** them **1Ch 17:9** 1086
therefore that city was laid **w**. **Ezr 4:15** 2718
"I **w** away; I will not live forever. **Jb 7:16** 3988a
makes them wander in a pathless **w**. **Jb 12:24** 8414
You have laid **w** all my company. **Jb 16:7** 8074
gnaw the dry ground by night in **w** **Jb 30:3** 7724b
To satisfy the **w** and desolate land **Jb 38:27** 7724b
they have devoured Jacob And laid **w** **Ps 79:7** 8074
Or of the destruction that lays **w** at **Ps 91:6** 7703
I have become like an owl of the **w** **Ps 102:6** 2723
A fruitful land into a salt **w**, **Ps 107:34** 4420
makes them wander in a pathless **w**. **Ps 107:40** 8414
And **w** your compliments. **Pr 23:8** 7843
"I will lay it **w**; It will not be **Is 5:6** 1326
And strangers will eat in the **w** **Is 5:17** 2723
the LORD lays the earth **w**, **Is 24:1** 1238b
The earth will be completely laid **w** **Is 24:3** 1238b
"I will lay **w** the mountains **Is 42:15** 2717b
it *and* did not create it a **w** **Is 45:18** 8414
'Seek Me in a **w** place'; I, the **Is 45:19** 8414
"For your **w** and desolate places **Is 49:19** 2723
He will comfort all her **w** places. **Is 51:3** 2723
You **w** places of Jerusalem; For the **Is 52:9** 2723
And they have made his land a **w**; **Jer 2:15** 8047
from his place To make your land a **w**. **Jer 4:7** 8047
Because they are laid **w** so that no **Jer 9:10** 5327c
laid **w** like a desert, so that no one **Jer 9:12** 5327c
And have laid **w** his habitation. **Jer 10:25** 8074
"It is a **w**, without man and without **Jer 33:10** 2720b
again be in this place which is **w**, **Jer 33:12** 2720b
has caused my flesh and my skin to **w** **La 3:4** 1086
be appalled with one another and **w** **Ezk 4:17** 4743
cities will become **w** and the high **Ezk 6:6** 2717b
that your altars may become **w** **Ezk 6:6** 2717b
and make the land more desolate and **w** **Ezk 6:14** 4923
"The inhabited cities will be laid **w** **Ezk 12:20** 2717b
their fortified towers And laid **w** **Ezk 19:7** 2717b
And I will lay it **w**; from Teman even **Ezk 25:13** 2723
now that she is laid **w**,' **Ezk 26:2** 2717b
like the ancient **w** places, with **Ezk 26:20** 2723
Egypt will become a desolation and **w**. **Ezk 29:9** 2723
make the land of Egypt an utter **w** **Ezk 29:10** 2721b
the midst of cities that are laid **w**, **Ezk 29:12** 2717b
they who live in these **w** places in **Ezk 33:24** 2723
surely those who are in the **w** places **Ezk 33:27** 2723
make the land a desolation and a **w**, **Ezk 33:28** 4923
I make the land a desolation and a **w** **Ezk 33:29** 4923
make you a desolation and a **w**. **Ezk 35:3** 4923
"I will lay **w** your cities And you **Ezk 35:4** 2723
"I will make Mount Seir a **w** and a **Ezk 35:7** 8077
cities will be inhabited and the **w** **Ezk 36:10** 2723
and the **w** places will be rebuilt. **Ezk 36:33** 2723
and the **w**, desolate and ruined **Ezk 36:35** 2720b
so will the **w** cities be filled with **Ezk 36:38** 2720b
Israel which had been a continual **w**; **Ezk 38:8** 2723
to turn your hand against the **w** **Ezk 38:12** 2723
It has made my vine a **w** And my fig **Jl 1:7** 8047
Egypt will become a **w**, And Edom will **Jl 3:19** 8077
And the sanctuaries of Israel laid **w**. **Am 7:9** 2717b
she is desolate and **w**! Hearts are **Na 2:10** 1110
Their cities are laid **w**, Without a **Zph 3:6** 6658b
divided against itself is laid **w**; **Mt 12:25** *2049*
"Why this **w**? **Mt 26:8** *684*
divided against itself is laid **w**; **Lk 11:17** *2049*
such great wealth has been laid **w**!' **Rv 18:17** *2049*
for in one hour she has been laid **w**!' **Rv 18:19** *2049*

WASTED
he **w** his seed on the ground in order **Gn 38:9** 7843
'*They will be* **w** by famine, **Dt 32:24** 4198
My eye has **w** away with grief; It has **Ps 6:7** 6244
My eye is **w** away from grief, my soul **Ps 31:9** 6244
And my body has **w** away. **Ps 31:10** 6244
my body **w** away Through my groaning **Ps 32:3** 1086
My eye has **w** away because of **Ps 88:9** 1669
"Why has this perfume been **w**? **Mk 14:4** *684*

WASTELAND
top of Pisgah which overlooks the **w**. **Nu 21:20** 3452
the top of Peor which overlooks the **w**. **Nu 23:28** 3452

WASTES
"His flesh **w** away from sight, **Jb 33:21** 3615
he who keeps company with harlots **w** **Pr 29:3** 6
And it will be as when a sick man **w** **Is 10:18** 4549
But will live in stony **w** in **Jer 17:6** 2788
to the desolate **w** and to the forsaken **Ezk 36:4** 2723

WASTING
But sent a **w** disease among them. **Ps 106:15** 7332
will send a **w** disease among his stout **Is 10:16** 7332

WATCH
"May the LORD **w** between you **Gn 31:49** 6822
At the morning **w**, the LORD **Ex 14:24** 821
"**W** yourself that you make no **Ex 34:12** 8104
"So **w** yourselves carefully, since **Dt 4:15** 8104
"So **w** yourselves, that you do not **Dt 4:23** 8104
then **w** yourself, that you do not **Dt 6:12** 8104
camp at the beginning of the middle **w**, **Jg 7:19** 821
when they had just posted the **w**; **Jg 7:19** 8104
and **w**; and behold, if the daughters **Jg 21:21** 7200
"**W**, if it goes up by the way of its **1Sa 6:9** 7200
midst of the camp at the morning **w** **1Sa 11:11** 821
sent messengers to David's house to **w** **1Sa 19:11** 8104
So it was as Joab kept **w** on the city, **2Sa 11:16** 8104
on the sabbath and keep **w** over **2Ki 11:5** 4931
shall keep **w** over the house for **2Ki 11:6** 4931
shall also keep **w** over the house of **2Ki 11:7** 4931
because the **w** was committed to them; **1Ch 9:27** 4931
"**W** and keep *them* until you weigh **Ezr 8:29** 8245
Talmon and their brethren who kept **w** **Ne 11:19** 8104
Akkub *were* gatekeepers keeping **w** **Ne 12:25** 4929
"You put my feet in the stocks And **w** **Jb 13:27** 8104
Men will keep **w** over *his* tomb. **Jb 21:32** 8245
anyone capture him when he is on **w**, **Jb 40:24** 5869
prayer to You and *eagerly* **w**. **Ps 5:3** 6822
His eyes stealthily **w** for **Ps 10:8** 6845
They attack, they lurk, They **w** my **Ps 56:6** 8104
Because of his strength I will **w** **Ps 59:9** 8104
His eyes keep **w** on the nations; Let **Ps 66:7** 6822
And those who **w** for my life have **Ps 71:10** 8104
Or *as* a **w** in the night. **Ps 90:4** 821
Keep **w** over the door of my lips. **Ps 141:3** 5341
Understanding will **w** over you, **Pr 2:11** 5341
and she will **w** over you. **Pr 4:6** 5341
W over your heart with all diligence, **Pr 4:23** 5341
W the path of your feet And all your **Pr 4:26** 6424
they will **w** over you; And when you **Pr 6:22** 8104
will also hold you by the hand and **w** **Is 42:6** 5341
They **w** like fowlers lying in wait; **Jer 5:26** 7789
so I will **w** over them to build and to **Jer 31:28** 8245
"Stand by the road and keep **w**, **Jer 48:19** 6822
But as for me, I will **w** expectantly **Mi 7:7** 6822
w the road; Strengthen your back, **Na 2:1** 6822
And I will keep **w** to see what He will **Hab 2:1** 6822
But I will **w** over the house of Judah, **Zch 12:4** 6491b, 5869
And in the fourth **w** of the night He **Mt 14:25** *5438*
And Jesus said to them, "**W** out **Mt 16:6** *3708*
remain here and keep **w** with Me." **Mt 26:38** *1127*
you *men* could not keep **w** with Me **Mt 26:40** *1127*
they *began* to keep **w** over Him **Mt 27:36** *5083*
at about the fourth **w** of the night He **Mk 6:48** *5438*
"**W** out! Beware of the leaven of **Mk 8:15** *3708*
remain here and keep **w**." **Mk 14:34** *1127*
Could you not keep **w** for one hour? **Mk 14:37** *1127*
out in the fields and keeping **w** over **Lk 2:8** *5438*
"Then **w** out that the light in you is **Lk 11:35** *4648*
"Whether he comes in the second **w**, **Lk 12:38** *5438*
for they keep **w** over your souls as **Heb 13:17** *69*
W yourselves, that you do not lose **2Jn 1:8** *991*

WATCHED
As in the days when God **w** over me; **Jb 29:2** 8104
"As I have **w** over them to pluck up, **Jer 31:28** 8245
In our watching we have **w** For a **La 4:17** 6822
So they **w** Him, and sent spies who **Lk 20:20** *3906*
in just the same way as you have **w** **Ac 1:11** *2300*
and their enemies **w** them. **Rv 11:12** *2334*

WATCHER
O **w** of men? Why have You set me as **Jb 7:20** 5341
an *angelic* **w**, a holy one, **Da 4:13** 5894
'In that the king saw an *angelic* **w**, **Da 4:23** 5894

WATCHERS
is by the decree of the *angelic* **w** **Da 4:17** 5894

WATCHES
He **w** all my paths.' **Jb 33:11** 8104
I meditate on You in the night **w**, **Ps 63:6** 821
My eyes anticipate the night **w**, **Ps 119:148** 821
And He **w** all his paths. **Pr 5:21** 6424
He who **w** his way preserves his life. **Pr 16:17** 5341
for one official **w** over another **Ec 5:8** 8104
He who **w** the wind will not sow and he **Ec 11:4** 8104
night At the beginning of the night **w**; **La 2:19** 821

WATCHING
that Eli was **w** her mouth. **1Sa 1:12** 8104
on *his* seat by the road eagerly **w**, **1Sa 4:13** 6822
W daily at my gates, Waiting at my **Pr 8:34** 8245
W the evil and the good. **Pr 15:3** 6822
for I am **w** over My word to perform it." **Jer 1:12** 8245
A leopard is **w** their cities. **Jer 5:6** 8245
W for my fall, say: "Perhaps he **Jer 20:10** 8104
'Behold, I am **w** over them for harm **Jer 44:27** 8245
In our **w** we have watched For a nation **La 4:17** 6836
the afflicted of the flock who were **w** **Zch 11:11** 8104

"Keep **w** and praying that you may not	**Mt 26:41**	*1127*
They were **w** Him *to see* if He	**Mk 3:2**	*3906*
"Keep **w** and praying that you may not	**Mk 14:38**	*1127*
The scribes and the Pharisees were **w**	**Lk 6:7**	*3906*
And He said to them, "I was **w** Satan	**Lk 10:18**	*2334*
they were **w** Him closely.	**Lk 14:1**	*3906*
They were also **w** the gates day	**Ac 9:24**	*3906*
guards in front of the door were **w**	**Ac 12:6**	*5083*
and **w** out for the coats of those who	**Ac 22:20**	*5442*
day that you have been constantly **w**	**Ac 27:33**	*4328*
great fear fell upon those who were **w**	**Rv 11:11**	*2334*

WATCHMAN

And the young man who was the **w**	**2Sa 13:34**	6822
and the **w** went up to the roof of	**2Sa 18:24**	6822
The **w** called and told the king.	**2Sa 18:25**	6822
Then the **w** saw another man running;	**2Sa 18:26**	6822
and the **w** called to the gatekeeper	**2Sa 18:26**	6822
The **w** said, "I think the running of	**2Sa 18:27**	6822
Now the **w** was standing on the tower	**2Ki 9:17**	6822
And the **w** reported, "The messenger	**2Ki 9:18**	6822
The **w** reported, "He came even to	**2Ki 9:20**	6822
Or as a hut *which* the **w** has made.	**Jb 27:18**	5341
The **w** keeps awake in vain.	**Ps 127:1**	8104
"**W**, how far gone is the night?	**Is 21:11**	8104
W, how far gone is the night?"	**Is 21:11**	8104
The **w** says, "Morning comes but also	**Is 21:12**	8104
I have appointed you a **w** to the house	**Ezk 3:17**	6822
among them and make him their **w**,	**Ezk 33:2**	6822
'But if the **w** sees the sword coming	**Ezk 33:6**	6822
I have appointed you a **w** for	**Ezk 33:7**	6822
Ephraim *was* a **w** with my God, a	**Hos 9:8**	6822

WATCHMAN'S

Like a **w** hut in a cucumber field,	**Is 1:8**	4412
I will require from the **w** hand.'	**Ezk 33:6**	6822

WATCHMEN

Now Saul's **w** in Gibeah of Benjamin	**1Sa 14:16**	6822
waits for the Lord More than the **w**	**Ps 130:6**	8104
more than the **w** for the morning.	**Ps 130:6**	8104
in the day that the **w** of the house	**Ec 12:3**	8104
"The **w** who make the rounds in	**SS 3:3**	8104
"The **w** who make the rounds in	**SS 5:7**	8104
Listen! Your **w** lift up *their*	**Is 52:8**	6822
His **w** are blind, All of them know	**Is 56:10**	6822
I have appointed **w**; All day and all	**Is 62:6**	8104
'Like **w** of a field they are against	**Jer 4:17**	8104
"And I set **w** over you, *saying*,	**Jer 6:17**	6822
"For there will be a day when **w** On	**Jer 31:6**	5341
The day when you post your **w**, Your	**Mi 7:4**	6822

WATCH-TOWER

from **w** to fortified city.	**2Ki 17:9**	4026
from **w** to fortified city.	**2Ki 18:8**	4026
I stand continually by day on the **w**,	**Is 21:8**	4707
Hill and **w** have become caves forever,	**Is 32:14**	975

WATER

used to rise from the earth and **w**	**Gn 2:6**	8248
Now a river flowed out of Eden to **w**	**Gn 2:10**	8248
even I am bringing the flood of **w**	**Gn 6:17**	4325
hundred years old when the flood of **w**	**Gn 7:6**	4325
him entered the ark because of the **w**	**Gn 7:7**	4325
that the **w** of the flood came upon	**Gn 7:10**	4325
and the **w** increased and lifted up	**Gn 7:17**	4325
The **w** prevailed and increased greatly	**Gn 7:18**	4325
ark floated on the surface of the **w**.	**Gn 7:18**	4325
The **w** prevailed more and more upon	**Gn 7:19**	4325
The **w** prevailed fifteen cubits higher,	**Gn 7:20**	4325
The **w** prevailed upon the earth one	**Gn 7:24**	4325
and the **w** subsided.	**Gn 8:1**	4325
and the **w** receded steadily from	**Gn 8:3**	4325
of one hundred and fifty days the **w**	**Gn 8:3**	4325
The **w** decreased steadily until	**Gn 8:5**	4325
it flew here and there until the **w**	**Gn 8:7**	4325
to see if the **w** was abated from	**Gn 8:8**	4325
for the **w** was on the surface of all	**Gn 8:9**	4325
So Noah knew that the **w** was abated	**Gn 8:11**	4325
the **w** was dried up from the earth.	**Gn 8:13**	4325
shall never again be cut off by the **w**	**Gn 9:11**	4325
and never again shall the **w** become a	**Gn 9:15**	4325
LORD found her by a spring of **w**	**Gn 16:7**	4325
"Please let a little **w** be brought	**Gn 18:4**	4325
and took bread and a skin of **w**	**Gn 21:14**	4325
When the **w** in the skin was used up,	**Gn 21:15**	4325
her eyes and she saw a well of **w**;	**Gn 21:19**	4325
she went and filled the skin with **w**	**Gn 21:19**	4325
to Abimelech because of the well of **w**	**Gn 21:25**	4325
outside the city by the well of **w** at	**Gn 24:11**	4325
the time when women go out to draw **w**.	**Gn 24:11**	7579
of the city are coming out to draw **w**;	**Gn 24:13**	4325
and I will **w** your camels also'	**Gn 24:14**	8248
"Please let me drink a little **w** from	**Gn 24:17**	4325
and **w** to wash his feet and the feet	**Gn 24:32**	4325
"Please let me drink a little **w** from	**Gn 24:43**	4325
and I will **w** your camels also'; so	**Gn 24:46**	8248
Then Isaac dug again the wells of **w**	**Gn 26:18**	4325
and found there a well of flowing **w**,	**Gn 26:19**	4325
"The **w** is ours!" So he named	**Gn 26:20**	4325
"We have found **w**."	**Gn 26:32**	4325
from the mouth of the well and **w**	**Gn 29:3**	8248
W the sheep, and go, pasture them."	**Gn 29:7**	8248
then we **w** the sheep."	**Gn 29:8**	8248
without any **w** in it.	**Gn 37:24**	4325
into Joseph's house and gave them **w**,	**Gn 43:24**	4325
"Uncontrolled as **w**, you shall not	**Gn 49:4**	4325
"Because I drew him out of the **w**."	**Ex 2:10**	4325
and they came to draw **w** and filled	**Ex 2:16**	1802a
water and filled the troughs to **w**	**Ex 2:16**	8248
he even drew the **w** for us and watered	**Ex 2:19**	1802a
then you shall take some **w** from	**Ex 4:9**	4325
and the **w** which you take from	**Ex 4:9**	4325
morning as he is going out to the **w**,	**Ex 7:15**	4325
I will strike the **w** that is in	**Ex 7:17**	4325
will find difficulty in drinking **w**	**Ex 7:18**	4325
and over all their reservoirs of **w**,	**Ex 7:19**	4325
lifted up the staff and struck the **w**	**Ex 7:20**	4325
and all the **w** that *was* in	**Ex 7:20**	4325
that the Egyptians could not drink **w**	**Ex 7:21**	4325
Egyptians dug around the Nile for **w**	**Ex 7:24**	4325
for they could not drink of the **w** of	**Ex 7:24**	4325
as he comes out to the **w**, and say to	**Ex 8:20**	4325
any of it raw or boiled at all with **w**,	**Ex 12:9**	4325
days in the wilderness and found no **w**.	**Ex 15:22**	4325
there *were* twelve springs of **w**	**Ex 15:27**	4325
and there was no **w** for the people to	**Ex 17:1**	4325
"Give us **w** that we may drink."	**Ex 17:2**	4325
But the people thirsted there for **w**;	**Ex 17:3**	4325
and **w** will come out of it, that	**Ex 17:6**	4325
or on the earth beneath or in the **w**	**Ex 20:4**	4325
He will bless your bread and your **w**;	**Ex 23:25**	4325
tent of meeting and wash them with **w**.	**Ex 29:4**	4325
and you shall put **w** in it.	**Ex 30:18**	4325
they shall wash with **w**, so that they	**Ex 30:20**	4325
it over the surface of the **w** and made	**Ex 32:20**	4325
he did not eat bread or drink **w**.	**Ex 34:28**	4325
of meeting and the altar and put **w** in	**Ex 40:7**	4325
tent of meeting and wash them with **w**.	**Ex 40:12**	4325
of meeting and the altar and put **w** in	**Ex 40:30**	4325
and its legs he shall wash with **w**.	**Lv 1:9**	4325
and the legs he shall wash with **w**.	**Lv 1:13**	4325
it shall be scoured and rinsed in **w**.	**Lv 6:28**	4325
come near and washed them with **w**.	**Lv 8:6**	4325
the entrails and the legs with **w**,	**Lv 8:21**	4325
whatever is in the **w**: all that have	**Lv 11:9**	4325
those in the **w**, in the seas or in	**Lv 11:9**	4325
among all the teeming life of the **w**,	**Lv 11:10**	4325
living creatures that are in the **w**,	**Lv 11:10**	4325
'Whatever in the **w** does not have	**Lv 11:12**	4325
is made—it shall be put in the **w**	**Lv 11:32**	4325
on which **w** comes, shall become	**Lv 11:34**	4325
a spring or a cistern collecting **w**	**Lv 11:36**	4325
'Though if **w** is put on the seed	**Lv 11:38**	4325
an earthenware vessel over running **w**.	**Lv 14:5**	4325
that was slain over the running **w**.	**Lv 14:6**	4325
shave off all his hair and bathe in **w**	**Lv 14:8**	4325
his clothes and bathe his body in **w**	**Lv 14:9**	4325
an earthenware vessel over running **w**.	**Lv 14:50**	4325
bird as well as in the running **w**,	**Lv 14:51**	4325
of the bird and with the running **w**,	**Lv 14:52**	4325
shall wash his clothes and bathe in **w**	**Lv 15:5**	4325
shall wash his clothes and bathe in **w**	**Lv 15:6**	4325
shall wash his clothes and bathe in **w**	**Lv 15:7**	4325
shall wash his clothes and bathe in **w**	**Lv 15:8**	4325
shall wash his clothes and bathe in **w**	**Lv 15:10**	4325
without having rinsed his hands in **w**	**Lv 15:11**	4325
shall wash his clothes and bathe in **w**	**Lv 15:11**	4325
wooden vessel shall be rinsed in **w**.	**Lv 15:12**	4325
and bathe his body in running **w**	**Lv 15:13**	4325
he shall bathe all his body in **w**	**Lv 15:16**	4325
it shall be washed with **w** and be	**Lv 15:17**	4325
they shall both bathe in **w** and be	**Lv 15:18**	4325
shall wash his clothes and bathe in **w**	**Lv 15:21**	4325
shall wash his clothes and bathe in **w**	**Lv 15:22**	4325
shall wash his clothes and bathe in **w**	**Lv 15:27**	4325
Then he shall bathe his body in **w**	**Lv 16:4**	4325
"He shall bathe his body with **w** in a	**Lv 16:24**	4325
his clothes and bathe his body with **w**;	**Lv 16:26**	4325
his clothes and bathe his body with **w**,	**Lv 16:28**	4325
shall wash his clothes and bathe in **w**,	**Lv 17:15**	4325
unless he has bathed his body in **w**.	**Lv 22:6**	4325
and the priest shall take holy **w** in	**Nu 5:17**	4325
tabernacle and put *it* into the **w**.	**Nu 5:17**	4325
the hand of the priest is to be the **w**	**Nu 5:18**	4325
be immune to this **w** of bitterness	**Nu 5:19**	4325
and this **w** that brings a curse shall	**Nu 5:22**	4325
and he shall wash them off into the **w**	**Nu 5:23**	4325
he shall make the woman drink the **w**	**Nu 5:24**	4325
so that the **w** which brings a curse	**Nu 5:24**	4325
he shall make the woman drink the **w**.	**Nu 5:26**	4325
'When he has made her drink the **w**,	**Nu 5:27**	4325
that the **w** which brings a curse will	**Nu 5:27**	4325
sprinkle purifying **w** on them,	**Nu 8:7**	4325
his clothes and bathe his body in **w**,	**Nu 19:7**	4325
it shall also wash his clothes in **w**	**Nu 19:8**	4325
in water and bathe his body in **w**,	**Nu 19:8**	4325
the sons of Israel shall keep it as **w**	**Nu 19:9**	4325
himself from uncleanness with the **w**	**Nu 19:12**	4325
Because the **w** for impurity was not	**Nu 19:13**	4325
purification from sin and flowing **w**	**Nu 19:17**	4325
take hyssop and dip *it* in the **w**,	**Nu 19:18**	4325
clothes and bathe *himself* in **w**	**Nu 19:19**	4325
the **w** for impurity has not been	**Nu 19:20**	4325
And he who sprinkles the **w** for	**Nu 19:21**	4325
and he who touches the **w** for impurity	**Nu 19:21**	4325
There was no **w** for the congregation,	**Nu 20:2**	4325
nor is there **w** to drink."	**Nu 20:5**	4325
that it may yield its **w**. You shall	**Nu 20:8**	4325
You shall thus bring forth **w** for them	**Nu 20:8**	4325
shall we bring forth **w** for you out of	**Nu 20:10**	4325
and **w** came forth abundantly,	**Nu 20:11**	4325
we will not even drink **w** from a well.	**Nu 20:17**	4325
my livestock do drink any of your **w**,	**Nu 20:19**	4325
For there is no food and no **w**,	**Nu 21:5**	4325
that I may give them **w**."	**Nu 21:16**	4325
we will not drink **w** from wells.	**Nu 21:22**	4325
"**W** will flow from his buckets,	**Nu 24:7**	4325
Me as holy before their eyes at the **w**."	**Nu 27:14**	4325
but it shall be purified with **w** for	**Nu 31:23**	4325
the fire you shall pass through the **w**.	**Nu 31:23**	4325
Elim there were twelve springs of **w**	**Nu 33:9**	4325
it was there that the people had no **w**	**Nu 33:14**	4325
and you shall also purchase **w** from	**Dt 2:6**	4325
and give me **w** for money so that I may	**Dt 2:28**	4325
likeness of any fish that is in the **w**	**Dt 4:18**	4325
or on the earth beneath or in the **w**	**Dt 5:8**	4325
a land of brooks of **w**, of fountains	**Dt 8:7**	4325
thirsty ground where there was no **w**;	**Dt 8:15**	4325
He brought **w** for you out of the rock	**Dt 8:15**	4325
I neither ate bread nor drank **w**.	**Dt 9:9**	4325
I neither ate bread nor drank **w**,	**Dt 9:18**	4325
a land of brooks of **w**.	**Dt 10:7**	4325
when He made the **w** of the Red Sea to	**Dt 11:4**	4325
where you used to sow your seed and **w**	**Dt 11:10**	8248
drinks **w** from the rain of heaven,	**Dt 11:11**	4325
to pour it out on the ground like **w**.	**Dt 12:16**	4325
pour it out on the ground like **w**.	**Dt 12:24**	4325
you may eat of all that are in **w**:	**Dt 14:9**	4325
to pour it out on the ground like **w**.	**Dt 15:23**	4325
down to a valley with running **w**,	**Dt 21:4**	386
they did not meet you with food and **w**	**Dt 23:4**	4325
he shall bathe himself with **w**,	**Dt 23:11**	4325
wood to the one who draws your **w**,	**Dt 29:11**	4325
heard how the LORD dried up the **w**	**Jos 2:10**	4325
ark were dipped in the edge of the **w**	**Jos 3:15**	4325
of the people melted and became as **w**.	**Jos 7:5**	4325
hewers of wood and drawers of **w** for	**Jos 9:21**	4325
both hewers of wood and drawers of **w**	**Jos 9:23**	4325
day hewers of wood and drawers of **w**	**Jos 9:27**	4325
give me also springs of **w**."	**Jos 15:19**	4325
give me also springs of **w**."	**Jg 1:15**	4325
"Please give me a little **w** to drink,	**Jg 4:19**	4325
Even the clouds dripped **w**.	**Jg 5:4**	4325
"He asked for **w** *and* she gave him	**Jg 5:25**	4325
a bowl full of **w**.	**Jg 6:38**	4325
bring them down to the **w** and I will	**Jg 7:4**	4325
he brought the people down to the **w**.	**Jg 7:5**	4325
separate everyone who laps the **w** with	**Jg 7:5**	4325
rest of the people kneeled to drink **w**.	**Jg 7:6**	4325
place that is in Lehi so that **w** came	**Jg 15:19**	4325
go to the **w** jars and drink from what	**Ru 2:9**	3627
They gathered to Mizpah, and drew **w**	**1Sa 7:6**	4325
young women going out to draw **w**	**1Sa 9:11**	4325
"Shall I then take my bread and my **w**	**1Sa 25:11**	4325
that is at his head and the jug of **w**,	**1Sa 26:11**	4325
David took the spear and the jug of **w**	**1Sa 26:12**	4325
the king's spear is and the jug of **w**	**1Sa 26:16**	4325
and they provided him **w** to drink.	**1Sa 30:11**	4325
For he had not eaten bread or drunk **w**	**1Sa 30:12**	4325
through the **w** tunnel."	**2Sa 5:8**	6794b
"For we will surely die and are like **w**	**2Sa 14:14**	4325
"They have crossed the brook of **w**."	**2Sa 17:20**	4325
"Arise and cross over the **w** quickly	**2Sa 17:21**	4325
"Oh that someone would give me **w** to	**2Sa 23:15**	4325
and drew **w** from the well of Bethlehem	**2Sa 23:16**	4325
nor would I eat bread or drink **w** in	**1Ki 13:8**	4325
nor drink **w**, nor return by the way	**1Ki 13:9**	4325
nor will I eat bread or drink **w** with	**1Ki 13:16**	4325
nor drink **w** there; do not return by	**1Ki 13:17**	4325
that he may eat bread and drink **w**.' "	**1Ki 13:18**	4325
ate bread in his house and drank **w**.	**1Ki 13:19**	4325
returned and eaten bread and drunk **w**	**1Ki 13:22**	4325
"Eat no bread and drink no **w**";	**1Ki 13:22**	4325
as a reed is shaken in the **w**;	**1Ki 14:15**	4325
"Please get me a little **w** in a jar,	**1Ki 17:10**	4325
and provided them with bread and **w**.	**1Ki 18:4**	4325
the land to all the springs of **w**	**1Ki 18:5**	4325
and provided them with bread and **w**?	**1Ki 18:13**	4325
"Fill four pitchers with **w** and pour	**1Ki 18:34**	4325
The **w** flowed around the altar and he	**1Ki 18:35**	4325
and he also filled the trench with **w**.	**1Ki 18:35**	4325
and licked up the **w** that was in	**1Ki 18:38**	4325
and a jar of **w**. So he ate and drank	**1Ki 19:6**	4325
feed him sparingly with bread and **w**	**1Ki 22:27**	4325
but the **w** is bad and the land is	**2Ki 2:19**	4325
He went out to the spring of **w**	**2Ki 2:21**	4325
and there was no **w** for the army or	**2Ki 3:9**	4325
who used to pour **w** on the hands of	**2Ki 3:11**	4325
that valley shall be filled with **w**,	**2Ki 3:17**	4325
good tree and stop all springs of **w**,	**2Ki 3:19**	4325
w came by the way of Edom,	**2Ki 3:20**	4325
and the country was filled with **w**.	**2Ki 3:20**	4325
and the sun shone on the **w**,	**2Ki 3:22**	4325
and the Moabites saw the **w** opposite	**2Ki 3:22**	4325
So they stopped all the springs of **w**	**2Ki 3:25**	4325
the axe head fell into the **w**;	**2Ki 6:5**	4325
Set bread and **w** before them, that	**2Ki 6:22**	4325
he took the cover and dipped it in **w**	**2Ki 8:15**	4325
pool and the conduit and brought **w**	**2Ki 20:20**	4325
"Oh that someone would give me **w** to	**1Ch 11:17**	4325
camp of the Philistines and drew **w**	**1Ch 11:18**	4325
feed him sparingly with bread and **w**	**2Ch 18:26**	4325
to cut off the *supply of* **w** from	**2Ch 32:3**	4325
of Assyria come and find abundant **w**?"	**2Ch 32:4**	4325
he did not eat bread nor drink **w**,	**Ezr 10:6**	4325
as far as the front of the **W** Gate	**Ne 3:26**	4325
took his weapon *even to* the **w**.	**Ne 4:23**	4325
which was in front of the **W** Gate,	**Ne 8:1**	4325
which was in front of the **W** Gate	**Ne 8:3**	4325
and in the square at the **W** Gate	**Ne 8:16**	4325
You brought forth **w** from a rock for	**Ne 9:15**	4325
And You gave them **w** for their thirst.	**Ne 9:20**	4325
the house of David to the **W** Gate	**Ne 12:37**	4325
the sons of Israel with bread and **w**,	**Ne 13:2**	4325
And my cries pour out like **w**.	**Jb 3:24**	4325
gives rain on the earth And sends **w**	**Jb 5:10**	4325
Can the rushes grow without **w**?	**Jb 8:11**	4325
At the scent of **w** it will flourish	**Jb 14:9**	4325
"*As* **w** evaporates from the sea,	**Jb 14:11**	4325
W wears away stones, Its torrents	**Jb 14:19**	4325

Context	Reference	Number
who drinks iniquity like **w**!	Jb 15:16	4325
"To the weary you have given no **w** to	Jb 22:7	4325
And an abundance of **w** covers you.	Jb 22:11	4325
insignificant on the surface of the **w**;	Jb 24:18	4325
Who drinks up derision like **w**,	Jb 34:7	4325
"For He draws up the drops of **w**,	Jb 36:27	4325
"**W** becomes hard like stone,	Jb 38:30	4325
So that an abundance of **w** will cover	Jb 38:34	4325
Or tip the **w** jars of the heavens,	Jb 38:37	5035a
firmly planted by streams of **w**,	Ps 1:3	4325
Then the channels of **w** appeared,	Ps 18:15	4325
I am poured out like **w**, And all my	Ps 22:14	4325
As the deer pants for the **w** brooks,	Ps 42:1	4325
Let them flow away like **w** that runs	Ps 58:7	4325
and weary land where there is no **w**.	Ps 63:1	4325
The stream of God is full of **w**; You	Ps 65:9	4325
You **w** its furrows abundantly, You	Ps 65:10	7301
We went through fire and through **w**,	Ps 66:12	4325
May the flood of **w** not overflow me	Ps 69:15	4325
Like showers that **w** the earth.	Ps 72:6	2222
The clouds poured out **w**; The skies	Ps 77:17	4325
have poured out their blood like **w**	Ps 79:3	4325
They have surrounded me like **w** all	Ps 88:17	4325
He opened the rock and **w** flowed out;	Ps 105:41	4325
into a wilderness And springs of **w**	Ps 107:33	4325
changes a wilderness into a pool of **w**	Ps 107:35	4325
And a dry land into springs of **w**;	Ps 107:35	4325
And it entered into his body like **w**	Ps 109:18	4325
Who turned the rock into a pool of **w**,	Ps 114:8	4325
The flint into a fountain of **w**.	Ps 114:8	4325
My eyes shed streams of **w**, Because	Ps 119:136	4325
Drink **w** from your own cistern	Pr 5:15	4325
from your own cistern And fresh **w**	Pr 5:15	5140
Streams of **w** in the streets?	Pr 5:16	4325
were no springs abounding with **w**.	Pr 8:24	4325
the sea its boundary So that the **w**	Pr 8:29	4325
"Stolen **w** is sweet; And bread	Pr 9:17	4325
of strife is *like* letting out **w**,	Pr 17:14	4325
the heart of a man is *like* deep **w**,	Pr 20:5	4325
heart is *like* channels of **w** in	Pr 21:1	4325
thirsty, give him **w** to drink;	Pr 25:21	4325
Like cold **w** to a weary soul, So	Pr 25:25	4325
As in **w** face *reflects* face, So	Pr 27:19	4325
Earth that is never satisfied with **w**,	Pr 30:16	4325
I made ponds of **w** for myself from	Ec 2:6	4325
A well of fresh **w**, And streams	SS 4:15	4325
are like doves Beside streams of **w**,	SS 5:12	4325
Your drink diluted with **w**.	Is 1:22	4325
away Or as a garden that has no **w**.	Is 1:30	4325
of bread And the whole supply of **w**;	Is 3:1	4325
Therefore you will joyously draw **w**	Is 12:3	4325
for the hedgehog and swamps of **w**,	Is 14:23	4325
Bring **w** for the thirsty,	Is 21:14	4325
As straw is trodden down in the **w** of	Is 25:10	4325
I **w** it every moment. So that no one	Is 27:3	8248
take fire from a hearth Or to scoop **w**	Is 30:14	4325
given you bread of privation and **w** of	Is 30:20	4325
there will be streams running with **w**	Is 30:25	4325
Like streams of **w** in a dry country,	Is 32:2	4325
His **w** will be sure.	Is 33:16	4325
And the thirsty ground springs of **w**;	Is 35:7	4325
"The afflicted and needy are seeking **w**,	Is 41:17	4325
will make the wilderness a pool of **w**	Is 41:18	4325
water And the dry land fountains of **w**.	Is 41:18	4325
'For I will pour out **w** on	Is 44:3	4325
grass Like poplars by streams of **w**.'	Is 44:4	4325
he drinks no **w** and becomes weary.	Is 44:12	4325
He made the **w** flow out of the rock	Is 48:21	4325
He split the rock and the **w** gushed	Is 48:21	4325
And will guide them to springs of **w**.	Is 49:10	4325
Their fish stink for lack of **w**	Is 50:2	4325
And like a spring of **w** whose waters	Is 58:11	4325
as fire causes **w** to boil	Is 64:2	4325
Broken cisterns That can hold no **w**.	Jer 2:13	4325
doomed us And given us poisoned **w**	Jer 8:14	4325
wormwood and give them poisoned **w** to	Jer 9:15	4325
tears And our eyelids flow with **w**.	Jer 9:18	4325
but do not put it in **w**."	Jer 13:1	4325
nobles have sent their servants for **w**;	Jer 14:3	4325
come to the cisterns and found no **w**.	Jer 14:3	4325
me like a deceptive *stream* With **w**	Jer 15:18	4325
will be like a tree planted by the **w**,	Jer 17:8	4325
forsaken the fountain of living **w**,	Jer 17:13	4325
Or is the cold flowing **w** *from a*	Jer 18:14	4325
And make them drink poisonous **w**, For	Jer 23:15	4325
Now in the cistern there was no **w** but	Jer 38:6	4325
My eyes run down with **w**; Because far	La 1:16	4325
Pour out your heart like **w** Before	La 2:19	4325
My eyes run down with streams of **w**	La 3:48	4325
We have to pay for our drinking **w**,	La 5:4	4325
"The **w** you drink shall be the sixth	Ezk 4:11	4325
and drink **w** by measure and in horror,	Ezk 4:16	4325
because bread and **w** will be scarce;	Ezk 4:17	4325
and all knees will become *like* **w**.	Ezk 7:17	4325
bread with trembling and drink your **w**	Ezk 12:18	4325
bread with anxiety and drink their **w**	Ezk 12:19	4325
nor were you washed with **w** for	Ezk 16:4	4325
"Then I bathed you with **w**, washed	Ezk 16:9	4325
that he might **w** it.	Ezk 17:7	8248
faint and all knees will be weak as **w**.	Ezk 21:7	4325
put *it* on and also pour **w** in it;	Ezk 24:3	4325
timbers and your debris into the **w**.	Ezk 26:12	4325
"Then I will sprinkle clean **w** on you,	Ezk 36:25	4325
w was flowing from under	Ezk 47:1	4325
And the **w** was flowing down	Ezk 47:1	4325
w was trickling from the south side.	Ezk 47:2	4325
and he led me through the **w**,	Ezk 47:3	4325
w *reaching* the ankles.	Ezk 47:3	4325
a thousand and led me through the **w**,	Ezk 47:4	4325
w *reaching* the knees. Again he	Ezk 47:4	4325
a thousand and led me through *the* **w**,	Ezk 47:4	
w *reaching* the loins.	Ezk 47:4	4325
for the **w** had risen, *enough*	Ezk 47:5	4325
enough **w** to swim in, a river	Ezk 47:5	4325
will bear every month because their **w**	Ezk 47:12	4325
be given some vegetables to eat and **w**	Da 1:12	4325
Who give *me* my bread and my **w**,	Hos 2:5	4325
them I will pour out My wrath like **w**.	Hos 5:10	4325
Like a stick on the surface of the **w**.	Hos 10:7	4325
For the **w** brooks are dried up	Jl 1:20	4325
the brooks of Judah will flow with **w**;	Jl 3:18	4325
from the house of the LORD To **w**	Jl 3:18	8248
stagger to another city to drink **w**,	Am 4:8	4325
a famine for bread or a thirst for **w**,	Am 8:11	4325
"**W** encompassed me to the point of	Jon 2:5	4325
Do not let them eat or drink **w**.	Jon 3:7	4325
Like **w** poured down a steep place.	Mi 1:4	4325
Nineveh *was* like a pool of **w**	Na 2:8	4325
With **w** surrounding her, Whose	Na 3:8	4325
Draw for yourself **w** for the siege!	Na 3:14	4325
"As for me, I baptize you with **w**	Mt 3:11	*5204*
Jesus came up immediately from the **w**;	Mt 3:16	*5204*
little ones even a cup of cold **w** to	Mt 10:42	
me to come to You on the **w**."	Mt 14:28	*5204*
and walked on the **w** and came toward	Mt 14:29	*5204*
into the fire and often into the **w**.	Mt 17:15	*5204*
he took **w** and washed his hands in	Mt 27:24	*5204*
"I baptized you with **w**; but He will	Mk 1:8	*5204*
Immediately coming up out of the **w**,	Mk 1:10	*5204*
him both into the fire and into the **w**	Mk 9:22	*5204*
"For whoever gives you a cup of **w** to	Mk 9:41	*5204*
will meet you carrying a pitcher of **w**;	Mk 14:13	*5204*
I baptize you with **w**; but One is	Lk 3:16	*5204*
"Put out into the deep **w** and let	Lk 5:4	*899*
you gave Me no **w** for My feet, but	Lk 7:44	*5204*
commands even the winds and the **w**,	Lk 8:25	*5204*
from the stall and lead him away to **w**	Lk 13:15	*4222*
he may dip the tip of his finger in **w**	Lk 16:24	*5204*
will meet you carrying a pitcher of **w**;	Lk 22:10	*5204*
"I baptize in **w**, *but* among you	Jn 1:26	*5204*
I came baptizing in **w**."	Jn 1:31	*5204*
but He who sent me to baptize in **w**	Jn 1:33	*5204*
"Fill the waterpots with **w**." So	Jn 2:7	*5204*
When the headwaiter tasted the **w**	Jn 2:9	*5204*
the servants who had drawn the **w**	Jn 2:9	*5204*
unless one is born of **w**	Jn 3:5	*5204*
because there was much **w** there;	Jn 3:23	*5204*
came a woman of Samaria to draw **w**.	Jn 4:7	*5204*
He would have given you living **w**."	Jn 4:10	*5204*
where then do You get that living **w**?	Jn 4:11	
"Everyone who drinks of this **w** will	Jn 4:13	*5204*
but whoever drinks of the **w** that I	Jn 4:14	*5204*
but the **w** that I will give him will	Jn 4:14	*5204*
him will become in him a well of **w**	Jn 4:14	*5204*
give me this **w**, so I will not be	Jn 4:15	*5204*
of Galilee where He had made the **w**	Jn 4:46	*5204*
into the pool and stirred up the **w**;	Jn 5:4	*5204*
after the stirring up of the **w**,	Jn 5:4	*5204*
to put me into the pool when the **w** is	Jn 5:7	*5204*
being will flow rivers of living **w**.' "	Jn 7:38	*5204*
Then He poured **w** into the basin,	Jn 13:5	*5204*
and immediately blood and **w** came out.	Jn 19:34	*5204*
for John baptized with **w**, but you	Ac 1:5	*5204*
along the road they came to some **w**;	Ac 8:36	*5204*
W! What prevents me from being	Ac 8:36	*5204*
and they both went down into the **w**,	Ac 8:38	*5204*
When they came up out of the **w**,	Ac 8:39	*5204*
"Surely no one can refuse the **w** for	Ac 10:47	*5204*
'John baptized with **w**, but you will	Ac 11:16	*5204*
cleansed her by the washing of **w** with	Eph 5:26	*5204*
No longer drink **w** *exclusively*,	1Tm 5:23	*5202*
with **w** and scarlet wool and hyssop,	Heb 9:19	*5204*
and our bodies washed with pure **w**.	Heb 10:22	*5204*
both fresh and bitter **w**?	Jas 3:11	
Nor *can* salt **w** produce fresh.	Jas 3:12	*5204*
were brought safely through *the* **w**.	1Pe 3:20	*5204*
These are springs without **w** and mists	2Pe 2:17	*504*
and *the* earth was formed out of **w**	2Pe 3:5	*5204*
was formed out of water and by **w**,	2Pe 3:5	*5204*
being flooded with **w**.	2Pe 3:6	*5204*
This is the One who came by **w**	1Jn 5:6	*5204*
not with the **w** only, but with	1Jn 5:6	*5204*
but with the **w** and with the blood.	1Jn 5:6	*5204*
the Spirit and the **w** and the blood;	1Jn 5:8	*5204*
clouds without **w**, carried along by	Jude 1:12	*504*
will guide them to springs of the **w**	Rv 7:17	*5204*
And the serpent poured **w** like a river	Rv 12:15	*5204*
and its **w** was dried up, so that	Rv 16:12	*5204*
who thirsts from the spring of the **w**	Rv 21:6	*5204*
Then he showed me a river of the **w** of	Rv 22:1	*5204*
let the one who wishes take the **w** of	Rv 22:17	*5204*

WATERED

Context	Reference	Number
that it was well **w** everywhere	Gn 13:10	4945b
and she **w** the camels also.	Gn 24:46	8248
for from that well they **w** the flocks.	Gn 29:2	8248
from the mouth of the well and **w**	Gn 29:10	8248
Moses stood up and helped them and **w**	Ex 2:17	8248
he even drew the water for us and **w**	Ex 2:19	8248
of my heart in order to destroy the **w**	Dt 29:19	7302
And he who waters will himself be **w**.	Pr 11:25	3372b
And you will be like a **w** garden,	Is 58:11	7302
And their life will be like a **w**	Jer 31:12	7302
of the Jordan against a perennially **w**	Jer 49:19	
of the Jordan to a perennially **w**	Jer 50:44	
I planted, Apollos **w**, but God was	1Co 3:6	*4222*

WATERFALLS

Context	Reference	Number
calls to deep at the sound of Your **w**;	Ps 42:7	6794b

WATERING

Context	Reference	Number
even in the **w** troughs, where	Gn 30:38	4325
flocks among the **w** places,	Jg 5:11	4857
all the thorn bushes and on all the **w**	Is 7:19	5097
And do not return there without **w**	Is 55:10	7301
flock of two hundred from the **w**	Ezk 45:15	4945b
Like the spring rain **w** the earth."	Hos 6:3	3384

WATERLESS

Context	Reference	Number
"When they become **w**, they are	Jb 6:17	2215
set your prisoners free from the **w**	Zch 9:11	369, 4325
it passes through **w** places seeking	Mt 12:43	*504*
it passes through **w** places seeking	Lk 11:24	*504*

WATERPOT

Context	Reference	Number
So the woman left her **w**, and went	Jn 4:28	*5201*

WATERPOTS

Context	Reference	Number
Now there were six stone **w** set there	Jn 2:6	*5201*
Jesus said to them, "Fill the **w**	Jn 2:7	*5201*

WATERS

Context	Reference	Number
was moving over the surface of the **w**.	Gn 1:2	4325
be an expanse in the midst of the **w**,	Gn 1:6	4325
and let it separate the **w** from	Gn 1:6	4325
let it separate the waters from the **w**."	Gn 1:6	4325
and separated the **w** which were below	Gn 1:7	4325
were below the expanse from the **w**	Gn 1:7	4325
Then God said, "Let the **w** below	Gn 1:9	4325
and the gathering of the **w** He called	Gn 1:10	4325
Then God said, "Let the **w** teem with	Gn 1:20	4325
with which the **w** swarmed after their	Gn 1:21	4325
and fill the **w** in the seas, and let	Gn 1:22	4325
and stretch out your hand over the **w**	Ex 7:19	4325
stretched out his hand over the **w** of	Ex 8:6	4325
so the **w** were divided.	Ex 14:21	4325
and the **w** *were like* a wall to	Ex 14:22	4325
your hand over the sea so that the **w**	Ex 14:26	4325
The **w** returned and covered	Ex 14:28	4325
and the **w** *were like* a wall to	Ex 14:29	4325
"At the blast of Your nostrils the **w**	Ex 15:8	4325
The flowing **w** stood up like a heap;	Ex 15:8	4325
They sank like lead in the mighty **w**.	Ex 15:10	4325
and the LORD brought back the **w**	Ex 15:19	4325
they could not drink the **w** of Marah,	Ex 15:23	4325
and he threw *it* into the **w**,	Ex 15:25	4325
and the **w** became sweet. There He	Ex 15:25	4325
and they camped there beside the **w**.	Ex 15:27	4325
living thing that moves in the **w**	Lv 11:46	4325
Those *were* the **w** of Meribah,	Nu 20:13	4325
rebelled against My command at the **w**	Nu 20:24	4325
Like cedars beside the **w**.	Nu 24:6	4325
And his seed *will be* by many **w**,	Nu 24:7	4325
(These are the **w** of Meribah of	Nu 27:14	4325
midst of the sons of Israel at the **w**	Dt 32:51	4325
With whom You contended at the **w** of	Dt 33:8	4325
'When you come to the edge of the **w**	Jos 3:8	4325
rest in the **w** of the Jordan,	Jos 3:13	4325
the **w** of the Jordan will be cut off,	Jos 3:13	4325
and the **w** which are flowing down	Jos 3:13	4325
the **w** which were flowing down from	Jos 3:16	4325
'Because the **w** of the Jordan were	Jos 4:7	4325
the **w** of the Jordan were cut off.'	Jos 4:7	4325
that the **w** of the Jordan returned to	Jos 4:18	4325
the LORD your God dried up the **w**	Jos 4:23	4325
how the LORD had dried up the **w**	Jos 5:1	4325
came and encamped together at the **w**	Jos 11:5	4325
came upon them suddenly by the **w**	Jos 11:7	4325
and the border continued to the **w** of	Jos 15:7	4325
border curved to the spring of the **w**	Jos 15:9	4325
from the Jordan at Jericho to the **w**	Jos 16:1	4325
and went to the fountain of the **w** of	Jos 18:15	4325
of Canaan At Taanach near the **w**	Jg 5:19	4325
down against Midian and take the **w**	Jg 7:24	4325
were summoned and they took the **w** as	Jg 7:24	4325
before me like the breakthrough of **w**."	2Sa 5:20	4325
I have even captured the city of **w**.	2Sa 12:27	4325
A mass of **w**, thick clouds of the sky.	2Sa 22:12	4325
He drew me out of many **w**.	2Sa 22:17	4325
folded it together and struck the **w**,	2Ki 2:8	4325
that fell from him and struck the **w**	2Ki 2:14	4325
And when he also had struck the **w**,	2Ki 2:14	4325
'I have purified these **w**; there	2Ki 2:21	4325
So the **w** have been purified to this	2Ki 2:22	4325
better than all the **w** of Israel?	2Ki 5:12	4325
his fig tree and drink each of the **w**	2Ki 18:31	4325
"I dug *wells* and drank foreign **w**,	2Ki 19:24	4325
like the breakthrough of **w**."	1Ch 14:11	4325
who stopped the upper outlet of the **w**	2Ch 32:30	4325
Like a stone into raging **w**.	Ne 9:11	4325
As **w** that have passed by, you would	Jb 11:16	4325
"Behold, He restrains the **w**,	Jb 12:15	4325
and heat consume the snow **w**,	Jb 24:19	4325
departed spirits tremble Under the **w**	Jb 26:5	4325
"He wraps up the **w** in His clouds,	Jb 26:8	4325
a circle on the surface of the **w**	Jb 26:10	4325
to the wind And meted out the **w** by	Jb 28:25	4325
'My root is spread out to the **w**,	Jb 29:19	4325
And the expanse of the **w** is frozen.	Jb 37:10	4325
Darkness of **w**, thick clouds of	Ps 18:11	4325
He drew me out of many **w**.	Ps 18:16	4325
He leads me beside quiet **w**.	Ps 23:2	4325
voice of the LORD is upon the **w**;	Ps 29:3	4325
The LORD is over many **w**.	Ps 29:3	4325
Surely in a flood of great **w** they	Ps 32:6	4325
He gathers the **w** of the sea together	Ps 33:7	4325
Though its **w** roar *and* foam,	Ps 46:3	4325
Save me, O God, For the **w** have	Ps 69:1	4325
I have come into deep **w**, and a flood	Ps 69:2	4325
from my foes and from the deep **w**.	Ps 69:14	4325
And **w** of abundance are drunk by them.	Ps 73:10	4325

heads of the sea monsters in the **w**.	**Ps 74:13**	4325
The **w** saw You, O God; The waters	**Ps 77:16**	4325
The waters saw You, O God; The **w**	**Ps 77:16**	4325
sea And Your paths in the mighty **w**,	**Ps 77:19**	4325
And He made the **w** stand up like a	**Ps 78:13**	4325
also from the rock And caused **w** to	**Ps 78:16**	4325
He struck the rock so that **w** gushed	**Ps 78:20**	4325
I proved you at the **w** of Meribah.	**Ps 81:7**	4325
More than the sounds of many **w**,	**Ps 93:4**	4325
beams of His upper chambers in the **w**;	**Ps 104:3**	4325
The **w** were standing above	**Ps 104:6**	4325
He **w** the mountains from His upper	**Ps 104:13**	8248
He turned their **w** into blood	**Ps 105:29**	4325
The **w** covered their adversaries;	**Ps 106:11**	4325
provoked *Him* to wrath at the **w** of	**Ps 106:32**	4325
Who do business on great **w**;	**Ps 107:23**	4325
Then the **w** would have engulfed us,	**Ps 124:4**	4325
Then the raging **w** would have swept	**Ps 124:5**	4325
who spread out the earth above the **w**,	**Ps 136:6**	4325
me and deliver me out of great **w**,	**Ps 144:7**	4325
He causes His wind to blow and the **w**	**Ps 147:18**	4325
And the **w** that are above the heavens!	**Ps 148:4**	4325
And he who **w** will himself be watered.	**Pr 11:25**	7301
words of a man's mouth are deep **w**;	**Pr 18:4**	4325
Who has wrapped the **w** in His garment?	**Pr 30:4**	4325
your bread on the surface of the **w**,	**Ec 11:1**	4325
"Many **w** cannot quench love, Nor	**SS 8:7**	4325
have rejected the gently flowing **w** of	**Is 8:6**	4325
on them the strong and abundant **w** of	**Is 8:7**	4325
knowledge of the LORD As the **w**	**Is 11:9**	4325
For the **w** of Nimrim are desolate.	**Is 15:6**	4325
For the **w** of Dimon are full of blood;	**Is 15:9**	4325
rush on like the rumbling of mighty **w**!	**Is 17:12**	4325
rumble on like the rumbling of many **w**,	**Is 17:13**	4325
vessels on the surface of the **w**. Go,	**Is 18:2**	4325
The **w** from the sea will dry up,	**Is 19:5**	4325
And those who spread nets on the **w**	**Is 19:8**	4325
And you collected the **w** of the lower	**Is 22:9**	4325
between the two walls For the **w** of	**Is 22:11**	4325
And *were* on many **w**. The grain of	**Is 23:3**	4325
Like a storm of mighty overflowing **w**,	**Is 28:2**	4325
away the refuge of lies And the **w**	**Is 28:17**	4325
you who sow beside all **w**, Who let	**Is 32:20**	4325
For **w** will break forth in	**Is 35:6**	4325
his fig tree and drink each of the **w**	**Is 36:16**	4325
'I dug *wells* and drank **w**,	**Is 37:25**	4325
Who has measured the **w** in the hollow	**Is 40:12**	4325
"When you pass through the **w**,	**Is 43:2**	4325
sea And a path through the mighty **w**,	**Is 43:16**	4325
Because I have given **w** in	**Is 43:20**	4325
The **w** of the great deep; Who made	**Is 51:10**	4325
When I swore that the **w** of Noah Would	**Is 54:9**	4325
come to the **w**; And you who have no	**Is 55:1**	4325
And its **w** toss up refuse and mud.	**Is 57:20**	4325
And like a spring of water whose **w** do	**Is 58:11**	4325
Who divided the **w** before them to make	**Is 63:12**	4325
The fountain of living **w**, To hew for	**Jer 2:13**	4325
To drink the **w** of the Nile? Or what	**Jer 2:18**	4325
To drink the **w** of the Euphrates?	**Jer 2:18**	4325
"As a well keeps its **w** fresh, So	**Jer 6:7**	4325
Oh that my head were **w** And my eyes a	**Jer 9:1**	4325
there is a tumult of **w** in	**Jer 10:13**	4325
I will make them walk by streams of **w**,	**Jer 31:9**	4325
Like the rivers whose **w** surge about?	**Jer 46:7**	4325
Even like the rivers whose **w** surge	**Jer 46:8**	4325
Thus says the LORD: "Behold, **w**	**Jer 47:2**	4325
for even the **w** of Nimrim will become	**Jer 48:34**	4325
"A drought on her **w**, and they will	**Jer 50:38**	4325
O you who dwell by many **w**, Abundant	**Jer 51:13**	4325
there is a tumult of **w** in	**Jer 51:16**	4325
And their waves will roar like many **w**;	**Jer 51:55**	4325
W flowed over my head; I said,	**La 3:54**	4325
wings like the sound of abundant **w** as	**Ezk 1:24**	4325
He placed *it* beside abundant **w**;	**Ezk 17:5**	4325
in good soil beside abundant **w**, that	**Ezk 17:8**	4325
Planted by the **w**; It was fruitful	**Ezk 19:10**	4325
of branches Because of abundant **w**.	**Ezk 19:10**	4325
up the deep over you and the great **w**	**Ezk 26:19**	4325
rowers have brought you Into great **w**;	**Ezk 27:26**	4325
by the seas In the depths of the **w**,	**Ezk 27:34**	4325
'The **w** made it grow, the deep made	**Ezk 31:4**	4325
its branches long Because of many **w**	**Ezk 31:5**	4325
For its roots extended to many **w**.	**Ezk 31:7**	4325
so that all the trees by the **w** may	**Ezk 31:14**	4325
And *its* many **w** were stopped up,	**Ezk 31:15**	4325
in your rivers And muddied the **w** with	**Ezk 32:2**	4325
all its cattle from beside many **w**;	**Ezk 32:13**	4325
"Then I will make their **w** settle And	**Ezk 32:14**	4325
that you should drink of the clear **w**,	**Ezk 34:18**	4325
voice was like the sound of many **w**;	**Ezk 43:2**	4325
Then he said to me, "These **w** go out	**Ezk 47:8**	4325
and the **w** *of the sea* become fresh.	**Ezk 47:8**	4325
for these **w** go there and *the others*	**Ezk 47:9**	4325
extend from Tamar as far as the **w**	**Ezk 47:19**	4325
border shall be from Tamar to the **w**	**Ezk 48:28**	4325
who was above the **w** of the river,	**Da 12:6**	4325
who was above the **w** of the river, as	**Da 12:7**	4325
Who calls for the **w** of the sea	**Am 5:8**	4325
"But let justice roll down like **w**	**Am 5:24**	4325
He who calls for the **w** of the sea	**Am 9:6**	4325
Which was situated by the **w** of	**Na 3:8**	4325
As the **w** cover the sea.	**Hab 2:14**	4325
The downpour of **w** swept by. The deep	**Hab 3:10**	4325
On the surge of many **w**.	**Hab 3:15**	4325
And in that day living **w** will flow	**Zch 14:8**	4325
into the sea and perished in the **w**.	**Mt 8:32**	*5204*
[waiting for the moving of the **w**;	**Jn 5:3**	*5204*
the one who plants nor the one who **w**	**1Co 3:7**	*4222*
Now he who plants and he who **w** are	**1Co 3:8**	*4222*
was like the sound of many **w**.	**Rv 1:15**	*5204*
of the rivers and on the springs of **w**.	**Rv 8:10**	*5204*
and a third of the **w** became wormwood,	**Rv 8:11**	*5204*
and many men died from the **w**,	**Rv 8:11**	*5204*
and they have power over the **w** to	**Rv 11:6**	*5204*
like the sound of many **w** and like	**Rv 14:2**	*5204*
the earth and sea and springs of **w**."	**Rv 14:7**	*5204*
into the rivers and the springs of **w**;	**Rv 16:4**	*5204*
And I heard the angel of the **w** saying,	**Rv 16:5**	*5204*
the great harlot who sits on many **w**,	**Rv 17:1**	*5204*
And he said to me, "The **w** which you	**Rv 17:15**	*5204*
and like the sound of many **w** and like	**Rv 19:6**	*5204*

WAVE

and shall **w** them as a wave offering	**Ex 29:24**	5130
and shall wave them as a **w** offering	**Ex 29:24**	8573
and **w** it as a wave offering before	**Ex 29:26**	5130
and wave it as a **w** offering before	**Ex 29:26**	8573
the breast of the **w** offering	**Ex 29:27**	8573
even the gold of the **w** offering, was	**Ex 38:24**	8573
of the **w** offering was 70 talents	**Ex 38:29**	8573
may be presented as a **w** offering	**Lv 7:30**	8573
taken the breast of the **w** offering	**Lv 7:34**	8573
and presented them as a **w** offering	**Lv 8:27**	8573
and presented it for a **w** offering	**Lv 8:29**	8573
Aaron presented as a **w** offering	**Lv 9:21**	8573
"The breast of the **w** offering,	**Lv 10:14**	8573
to present as a **w** offering before	**Lv 10:15**	8573
and present them as a **w** offering	**Lv 14:12**	8573
for a guilt offering as a **w** offering	**Lv 14:21**	8573
shall offer them for a **w** offering	**Lv 14:24**	8573
'He shall **w** the sheaf before the	**Lv 23:11**	5130
after the sabbath the priest shall **w**	**Lv 23:11**	5130
'Now on the day when you **w** the sheaf,	**Lv 23:12**	5130
in the sheaf of the **w** offering;	**Lv 23:15**	8573
of bread for a **w** offering,	**Lv 23:17**	8573
'The priest shall then **w** them with	**Lv 23:20**	5130
the first fruits for a **w** offering	**Lv 23:20**	8573
and he shall **w** the grain offering	**Nu 5:25**	5130
'Then the priest shall **w** them for a	**Nu 6:20**	5130
wave them for a **w** offering	**Nu 6:20**	8573
before the LORD as a **w** offering	**Nu 8:11**	8573
to present them as a **w** offering	**Nu 8:13**	8573
present them as a **w** offering;	**Nu 8:15**	8573
presented them as a **w** offering	**Nu 8:21**	8573
even all the **w** offerings of the sons	**Nu 18:11**	8573
like the breast of a **w** offering	**Nu 18:18**	8573
and go to **w** over the trees?'	**Jg 9:9**	5128
and go to **w** over the trees?'	**Jg 9:11**	5128
and go to **w** over the trees?'	**Jg 9:13**	5128
and **w** his hand over the place	**2Ki 5:11**	5130
Its fruit will **w** like *the cedars of*	**Ps 72:16**	7493
And He will **w** His hand over the River	**Is 11:15**	5130
W the hand that they may enter	**Is 13:2**	5130
which He is going to **w** over them.	**Is 19:16**	5130
who passes by her will hiss *And* **w**	**Zph 2:15**	5128
"For behold, I will **w** My hand over	**Zch 2:9**	5130

WAVED

of the heave offering which was **w**	**Ex 29:27**	5130

WAVER

My presence , And will not **w**,	**Jer 4:1**	5110
he did not **w** in unbelief but grew	**Ro 4:20**	*1252*

WAVERING

trusted in the LORD without **w**.	**Ps 26:1**	4571
the confession of our hope without **w**,	**Heb 10:23**	*186*

WAVES

"For the **w** of death encompassed me;	**2Sa 22:5**	4867
the heavens And tramples down the **w**	**Jb 9:8**	1116
And here shall your proud **w** stop'?	**Jb 38:11**	1530
All Your breakers and Your **w** have	**Ps 42:7**	1530
The roaring of their **w**,	**Ps 65:7**	1530
You have afflicted me with all Your **w**.	**Ps 88:7**	4867
When its **w** rise, You still them.	**Ps 89:9**	1530
The floods lift up their pounding **w**.	**Ps 93:3**	1796
Which lifted up the **w** of the sea.	**Ps 107:25**	1530
So that the **w** of the sea were hushed.	**Ps 107:29**	1530
And your righteousness like the **w** of	**Is 48:18**	1530
who stirs up the sea and its **w** roar	**Is 51:15**	1530
Though the **w** toss, yet they cannot	**Jer 5:22**	1530
Who stirs up the sea so that its **w**	**Jer 31:35**	1530
been engulfed with its tumultuous **w**.	**Jer 51:42**	1530
And their **w** will roar like many	**Jer 51:55**	1530
as the sea brings up its **w**.	**Ezk 26:3**	1530
distress And He will strike the **w**	**Zch 10:11**	1530
the boat was being covered with the **w**;	**Mt 8:24**	*2949*
battered by the **w**; for the wind was	**Mt 14:24**	*2949*
and the **w** were breaking over the boat	**Mk 4:37**	*2949*
rebuked the wind and the surging **w**,	**Lk 8:24**	*2830*
at the roaring of the sea and the **w**,	**Lk 21:25**	*4535*
be broken up by the force *of the* **w**.	**Ac 27:41**	
tossed here and there by **w**	**Eph 4:14**	*2831*
wild **w** of the sea, casting up their	**Jude 1:13**	*2949*

WAVING

up and the breast offered by **w** they	**Lv 10:15**	8573
together with the breast offered by **w**	**Nu 6:20**	8573
and be in dread because of the **w** of	**Is 19:16**	5130

WAX

My heart is like **w**; It is melted	**Ps 22:14**	1749
As **w** melts before the fire, *So*	**Ps 68:2**	1749
The mountains melted like **w** at	**Ps 97:5**	1749
Like **w** before the fire, Like water	**Mi 1:4**	1749

WAY

turned every direction to guard the **w**	**Gn 3:24**	1870
for all flesh had corrupted their **w**	**Gn 6:12**	1870
by the spring on the **w** to Shur.	**Gn 16:7**	1870
his household after him to keep the **w**	**Gn 18:19**	1870
you may rise early and go on your **w**."	**Gn 19:2**	1870
LORD had blessed Abraham in every **w**.	**Gn 24:1**	3605
the LORD has guided me in the **w**	**Gn 24:27**	1870
who had guided me in the right **w** to	**Gn 24:48**	1870
since the LORD has prospered my **w**.	**Gn 24:56**	1870
why then am I *this* **w**?" So she	**Gn 25:22**	
and rose and went on his **w**. Thus	**Gn 25:34**	1980
Now as Jacob went on his **w**,	**Gn 32:1**	1870
So Esau returned that day on his **w** to	**Gn 33:16**	1870
Rachel died and was buried on the **w**	**Gn 35:19**	1870
on their **w** to bring *them* down to	**Gn 37:25**	1980
to point out *the* **w** before him to	**Gn 46:28**	
and I buried her there on the **w** to	**Gn 48:7**	1870
"Dan shall be a serpent in the **w**,	**Gn 49:17**	1870
So he looked this **w** and that,	**Ex 2:12**	3541
about at the lodging place on the **w**	**Ex 4:24**	1870
"Why do you deal this **w** with your	**Ex 5:15**	3541
God did not lead them by the **w** of	**Ex 13:17**	1870
God led the people around by the **w** of	**Ex 13:18**	1870
of cloud by day to lead them on the **w**,	**Ex 13:21**	1870
Why have you dealt with us in this **w**,	**Ex 14:11**	2088
and make known to them the **w** in which	**Ex 18:20**	1870
and he went his **w** into his own land.	**Ex 18:27**	
before you to guard you along the **w**	**Ex 23:20**	1870
have quickly turned aside from the **w**	**Ex 32:8**	1870
and I might destroy you on the **w**."	**Ex 33:3**	1870
'If he offers it by **w** of	**Lv 7:12**	5921
but who has in no **w** been redeemed nor	**Lv 19:20**	6299
set out to the wilderness by the **w** of	**Nu 14:25**	1870
heard that Israel was coming by the **w**	**Nu 21:1**	1870
they set out from Mount Hor by the **w**	**Nu 21:4**	1870
Then they turned and went up by the **w**	**Nu 21:33**	1870
the LORD took his stand in the **w**	**Nu 22:22**	1870
of the LORD standing in the **w**	**Nu 22:23**	1870
the donkey turned off from the **w**	**Nu 22:23**	1870
donkey to turn her back into the **w**.	**Nu 22:23**	1870
a narrow place where there was no **w**	**Nu 22:26**	1870
of the LORD standing in the **w**	**Nu 22:31**	1870
and he bowed all the **w** to the ground.	**Nu 22:31**	1870
because your **w** was contrary to me.	**Nu 22:32**	1870
know that you were standing in the **w**	**Nu 22:34**	1870
and Balak also went his **w**.	**Nu 24:25**	1870
journey from Horeb by the **w** of	**Dt 1:2**	1870
wilderness which you saw on the **w** to	**Dt 1:19**	1870
and bring back to us word of the **w** by	**Dt 1:22**	1870
in all the **w** which you have walked	**Dt 1:31**	1870
who goes before you on *your* **w**,	**Dt 1:33**	1870
to show you the **w** in which you should	**Dt 1:33**	1870
set out for the wilderness by the **w**	**Dt 1:40**	1870
set out for the wilderness by the **w**	**Dt 2:1**	1870
we turned and passed through by the **w**	**Dt 2:8**	1870
"You shall walk in all the **w** which	**Dt 5:33**	1870
your house and when you walk by the **w**	**Dt 6:7**	1870
"You shall remember all the **w** which	**Dt 8:2**	1870
have quickly turned aside from the **w**	**Dt 9:12**	1870
had turned aside quickly from the **w**	**Dt 9:16**	1870
but turn aside from the **w** which I am	**Dt 11:28**	1870
west of the **w** toward the sunset, in	**Dt 11:30**	1870
to seduce you from the **w** in which	**Dt 13:5**	1870
'You shall never again return that **w**.'	**Dt 17:16**	1870
because the **w** is long, and take his	**Dt 19:6**	1870
donkey or his ox fallen down on the **w**,	**Dt 22:4**	1870
come upon a bird's nest along the **w**,	**Dt 22:6**	1870
meet you with food and water on the **w**	**Dt 23:4**	1870
your God did to Miriam on the **w** as	**Dt 24:9**	1870
what Amalek did to you along the **w**	**Dt 25:17**	1870
how he met you along the **w**	**Dt 25:18**	1870
they will come out against you one **w**	**Dt 28:7**	1870
you will go out one **w** against them,	**Dt 28:25**	1870
by the **w** about which I spoke to you,	**Dt 28:68**	1870
act corruptly and turn from the **w**	**Dt 31:29**	1870
for then you will make your **w**	**Jos 1:8**	1870
Then afterward you may go on your **w**."	**Jos 2:16**	1870
that you may know the **w** by which you	**Jos 3:4**	1870
for you have not passed this **w** before."	**Jos 3:4**	1870
died in the wilderness along the **w**	**Jos 5:4**	1870
born in the wilderness along the **w** as	**Jos 5:5**	1870
had not circumcised them along the **w**.	**Jos 5:7**	1870
and fled by the **w** of the wilderness.	**Jos 8:15**	1870
and they had no place to flee this **w**	**Jos 8:20**	2008
and pursued them by the **w** of	**Jos 10:10**	1870
"Now behold, today I am going the **w**	**Jos 23:14**	1870
and preserved us through all the **w** in	**Jos 24:17**	1870
They turned aside quickly from the **w**	**Jg 2:17**	1870
whether they will keep the **w** of the	**Jg 2:22**	1870
Gideon went up by the **w** of those who	**Jg 8:11**	1870
and one company comes by the **w** of	**Jg 9:37**	1870
that we may know whether our **w** on	**Jg 18:5**	1870
that your **w** in which you are going has	**Jg 18:6**	1870
So the sons of Dan went on their **w**;	**Jg 18:26**	1870
So they passed along and went their **w**,	**Jg 19:14**	
the house and went out to go on his **w**,	**Jg 19:27**	1870
and they went on the **w** to return to	**Ru 1:7**	1870
So the woman went her **w** and ate,	**1Sa 1:18**	1870
"Watch, if it goes up by the **w** of	**1Sa 6:9**	1870
And the cows took the straight **w** in	**1Sa 6:12**	1870
man of God and he will tell us our **w**."	**1Sa 9:8**	1870
then do you speak to me in this **w**?"	**1Sa 9:21**	1697
you in the good and right **w**.	**1Sa 12:23**	1870
he set himself against him on the **w**	**1Sa 15:2**	1870
the slain Philistines lay along the **w**	**1Sa 17:52**	1870
He came to the sheepfolds on the **w**,	**1Sa 24:3**	1870
and went on *his* **w**.	**1Sa 24:7**	1870
So David's young men retraced their **w**	**1Sa 25:12**	1870
So David went on his **w**, and Saul	**1Sa 26:25**	1870
strength when you go on *your* **w**."	**1Sa 28:22**	1870
carried *them* off and went their **w**.	**1Sa 30:2**	1870
which is in front of Giah by the **w** of	**2Sa 2:24**	1870
they took his head and traveled by **w**	**2Sa 4:7**	1870
Now it was while they were on the **w**	**2Sa 13:30**	1870
to rise early and stand beside the **w**	**2Sa 15:2**	1870

Context	Reference	No.
the people passed over toward the w	2Sa 15:23	1870
So David and his men went on the w;	2Sa 16:13	1870
Then Ahimaaz ran by w of the plain	2Sa 18:23	1870
"As for God, His w is blameless;	2Sa 22:31	1870
And He sets the blameless in His w.	2Sa 22:33	1870
and they arose and each went on his w.	1Ki 1:49	1870
"I am going the w of all the earth.	1Ki 2:2	1870
'If your sons are careful of their w,	1Ki 2:4	1870
only your sons take heed to their w	1Ki 8:25	1870
the wicked by bringing his w on his	1Ki 8:32	1870
teach them the good w in which they	1Ki 8:36	1870
by whatever w You shall send them,	1Ki 8:44	1870
and returned and went *their* w	1Ki 12:24	1870
nor return by the w which you came.' "	1Ki 13:9	1870
So he went another w and did not	1Ki 13:10	1870
way and did not return by the w which	1Ki 13:10	1870
Their father said to them, "Which w	1Ki 13:12	1870
Now his sons had seen the w which	1Ki 13:12	1870
do not return by going the w which	1Ki 13:17	1870
a lion met him on the w and killed	1Ki 13:24	1870
who brought him back from the w heard	1Ki 13:26	1870
did not return from his evil w, but	1Ki 13:33	1870
and walked in the w of his father	1Ki 15:26	1870
and walked in the w of Jeroboam	1Ki 15:34	1870
and you have walked in the w of	1Ki 16:2	1870
walking in the w of Jeroboam,	1Ki 16:19	1870
For he walked in all the w of	1Ki 16:26	1870
Ahab went one w by himself	1Ki 18:6	1870
by himself and Obadiah went another w	1Ki 18:6	1870
Now as Obadiah was on the w, behold,	1Ki 18:7	1870
return on your w to the wilderness of	1Ki 19:15	1870
and waited for the king by the w,	1Ki 20:38	1870
He walked in all the w of Asa his	1Ki 22:43	1870
of the LORD and walked in the w	1Ki 22:52	1870
in the way of his father and in the w	1Ki 22:52	1870
in the way of his mother and in the w	1Ki 22:52	1870
and as he was going up by the w,	2Ki 2:23	1870
He said, "Which w shall we go up?"	2Ki 3:8	1870
"The w of the wilderness of Edom."	2Ki 3:8	1870
water came by the w of Edom,	2Ki 3:20	1870
and go your w; if you meet any man,	2Ki 4:29	
"This is not the w, nor is this	2Ki 6:19	1870
all the w was full of clothes	2Ki 7:15	1870
He walked in the w of the kings of	2Ki 8:18	1870
He walked in the w of the house of	2Ki 8:27	1870
he fled by the w of the garden	2Ki 9:27	1870
On the w while he was at Beth-eked of	2Ki 10:12	1870
and came by the w of the gate of	2Ki 11:19	1870
But he walked in the w of the kings	2Ki 16:3	1870
The covered w for the sabbath which	2Ki 16:18	4146b
And I will turn you back by the w	2Ki 19:28	1870
"By the w that he came, by the same	2Ki 19:33	1870
For he walked in all the w that his	2Ki 21:21	1870
and did not walk in the w of the	2Ki 21:22	1870
the LORD and walked in all the w	2Ki 22:2	1870
the men of war *fled* by night by w	2Ki 25:4	1870
And they went by w of the Arabah.	2Ki 25:4	1870
the ten golden lampstands in the w	2Ch 4:7	4941
front of the inner sanctuary in the w	2Ch 4:20	4941
only your sons take heed to their w,	2Ch 6:16	1870
the wicked by bringing his w on his	2Ch 6:23	1870
teach them the good w in which they	2Ch 6:27	1870
by whatever w You shall send them,	2Ch 6:34	1870
for they walked in the w of David	2Ch 11:17	1870
He walked in the w of his father Asa	2Ch 20:32	1870
He walked in the w of the kings of	2Ch 21:6	1870
but have walked in the w of the kings	2Ch 21:13	1870
one would enter *who was* in any w	2Ch 23:19	1697
to protect us from the enemy on the w,	Ezr 8:22	1870
the enemy and the ambushes by the w.	Ezr 8:31	1870
and I answered them in the same w.	Ne 6:4	1697
fire by night To light for them the w	Ne 9:12	1870
To guide them on their w,	Ne 9:19	1870
to light for them the w in which they	Ne 9:19	1870
conduct will speak in *the same* w	Es 1:18	
would go in to the king in this w:	Es 2:13	2088
maidens also will fast in the same w.	Es 4:16	3651
"*Why is light given* to a man whose w	Jb 3:23	1870
"Behold, this is the joy of His w;	Jb 8:19	1870
I shall go the w of no return.	Jb 16:22	734
the righteous will hold to his w,	Jb 17:9	1870
"He has walled up my w so that I	Jb 19:8	734
And build up their w against me	Jb 19:12	1870
And let this be your w *of*	Jb 21:2	
"But He knows the w I take; *When*	Jb 23:10	1870
I have kept His w and not turned	Jb 23:11	1870
"God understands its w,	Jb 28:23	1870
"I chose a w for them and sat as	Jb 29:25	1870
"If my step has turned from the w,	Jb 31:7	1870
makes him find it according to his w.	Jb 34:11	734
"Who has appointed Him His w,	Jb 36:23	1870
"Where is the w to the dwelling of	Jb 38:19	1870
"Where is the w that the light is	Jb 38:24	1870
Or a w for the thunderbolt,	Jb 38:25	1870
For the LORD knows the w of	Ps 1:6	1870
But the w of the wicked will perish.	Ps 1:6	1870
and you perish *in* the w, For His	Ps 2:12	1870
Make Your w straight before me.	Ps 5:8	1870
As for God, His w is blameless;	Ps 18:30	1870
me with strength And makes my w	Ps 18:32	1870
He instructs sinners in the w.	Ps 25:8	1870
And He teaches the humble His w.	Ps 25:9	1870
He will instruct him in the w he	Ps 25:12	1870
Teach me Your w, O LORD,	Ps 27:11	1870
instruct you and teach you in the w	Ps 32:8	1870
Let their w be dark and slippery,	Ps 35:6	1870
Commit your w to the LORD, Trust	Ps 37:5	1870
because of him who prospers in his w,	Ps 37:7	1870
And He delights in his w.	Ps 37:23	1870
Wait for the LORD and keep His w,	Ps 37:34	1870
steps have not deviated from Your w,	Ps 44:18	734
This is the w of those who are	Ps 49:13	1870
And to him who orders *his* w	Ps 50:23	1870
That Your w may be known on the	Ps 67:2	1870
Your w, O God, is holy; What god	Ps 77:13	1870
Your w was in the sea And Your paths	Ps 77:19	1870
So that all who pass *that* w pick	Ps 80:12	1870
And will make His footsteps into a w.	Ps 85:13	1870
Teach me Your w, O LORD; I will	Ps 86:11	1870
All who pass along the w plunder him;	Ps 89:41	1870
I will give heed to the blameless w.	Ps 101:2	1870
He who walks in a blameless w is	Ps 101:6	1870
He has weakened my strength in the w;	Ps 102:23	1870
They did not find a w to an inhabited	Ps 107:4	1870
He led them also by a straight w,	Ps 107:7	1870
Fools, because of their rebellious w,	Ps 107:17	1870
How blessed are those whose w is	Ps 119:1	1870
How can a young man keep his w pure?	Ps 119:9	734
I have rejoiced in the w of Your	Ps 119:14	1870
Make me understand the w of Your	Ps 119:27	1870
Remove the false w from me,	Ps 119:29	1870
I have chosen the faithful w; I have	Ps 119:30	1870
I shall run the w of Your	Ps 119:32	1870
Teach me, O LORD, the w of Your	Ps 119:33	1870
restrained my feet from every evil w,	Ps 119:101	734
Therefore I hate every false w.	Ps 119:104	734
I hate every false w.	Ps 119:128	734
And see if there be any hurtful w in	Ps 139:24	1870
And lead me in the everlasting w.	Ps 139:24	1870
In the w where I walk They have	Ps 142:3	734
Teach me the w in which I should walk;	Ps 143:8	1870
But He thwarts the w of the wicked.	Ps 146:9	1870
My son, do not walk in the w with	Pr 1:15	1870
shall eat of the fruit of their own w	Pr 1:31	1870
And He preserves the w of His godly	Pr 2:8	1870
To deliver you from the w of evil,	Pr 2:12	1870
So you will walk in the w of good men	Pr 2:20	1870
Then you will walk in your w securely	Pr 3:23	1870
I have directed you in the w of	Pr 4:11	1870
wicked And do not proceed in the w of	Pr 4:14	1870
The w of the wicked is like darkness;	Pr 4:19	1870
Keep your w far from her And do not	Pr 5:8	1870
And reproofs for discipline are the w	Pr 6:23	1870
And he takes the w to her house,	Pr 7:8	1870
Her house is the w to Sheol,	Pr 7:27	1870
On top of the heights beside the w,	Pr 8:2	1870
Pride and arrogance and the evil w	Pr 8:13	1870
"I walk in the w of righteousness,	Pr 8:20	734
me at the beginning of His w, Before	Pr 8:22	1870
proceed in the w of understanding."	Pr 9:6	1870
The w of the LORD is a stronghold	Pr 10:29	1870
of the blameless will smooth his w,	Pr 11:5	1870
The w of a fool is right in his own	Pr 12:15	1870
But the w of the wicked leads them	Pr 12:26	1870
In the w of righteousness is life,	Pr 12:28	734
Righteousness guards the one whose w	Pr 13:6	1870
But the w of the treacherous is hard.	Pr 13:15	1870
the sensible is to understand his w,	Pr 14:8	1870
There is a w *which seems* right to	Pr 14:12	1870
But its end is the w of death.	Pr 14:12	1870
The w of the wicked is an abomination	Pr 15:9	1870
is for him who forsakes the w;	Pr 15:10	734
The w of the lazy is as a hedge of	Pr 15:19	1870
The mind of man plans his w,	Pr 16:9	1870
He who watches his w preserves his	Pr 16:17	1870
There is a w *which seems* right to	Pr 16:25	1870
But its end is the w of death.	Pr 16:25	1870
his neighbor And leads him in a w	Pr 16:29	1870
It is found in the w of righteousness.	Pr 16:31	1870
The foolishness of man ruins his w,	Pr 19:3	1870
But when he goes his w, then he	Pr 20:14	235
How then can man understand his w?	Pr 20:24	1870
Every man's w is right in his own	Pr 21:2	1870
The w of a guilty man is crooked,	Pr 21:8	1870
A man who wanders from the w of	Pr 21:16	1870
he makes his w sure.	Pr 21:29	1870
Thorns *and* snares are in the w of	Pr 22:5	1870
Train up a child in the w he should	Pr 22:6	1870
And direct your heart in the w.	Pr 23:19	1870
well Is a righteous man who gives w	Pr 25:26	4131
leads the upright astray in an evil w	Pr 28:10	1870
But a child who gets his own w brings	Pr 29:15	7971
And he who is upright in the w is	Pr 29:27	1870
The w of an eagle in the sky,	Pr 30:19	1870
The w of a serpent on a rock,	Pr 30:19	1870
The w of a ship in the middle of	Pr 30:19	1870
And the w of a man with a maid.	Pr 30:19	1870
This is the w of an adulterous woman:	Pr 30:20	1870
I will go my w to the mountain of	SS 4:6	1980
instructed me not to walk in the w of	Is 8:11	1870
by the w of the sea, on the other	Is 9:1	1870
against you, the w Egypt *did*.	Is 10:24	1870
the sea and He will lift it up the w	Is 10:26	1870
Their voice is heard all the w to	Is 15:4	5704
From Sela by w of the wilderness to	Is 16:1	
driven in a firm place will give w;	Is 22:25	4185
The w of the righteous is smooth;	Is 26:7	734
Indeed, *while following* the w of	Is 26:8	734
"Get out of the w, turn aside from	Is 30:11	1870
"This is the w, walk in it,"	Is 30:21	1870
be for him who walks *that* w,	Is 35:8	1870
And I will turn you back by the w	Is 37:29	1870
'By the w that he came, by the same	Is 37:34	1870
A voice is calling, "Clear the w	Is 40:3	1870
knowledge And informed Him of the w	Is 40:14	1870
"My w is hidden from the LORD,	Is 40:27	1870
By a w he had not been traversing	Is 41:3	734
"I will lead the blind by a w they	Is 42:16	1870
Who makes a w through the sea And a	Is 43:16	1870
Each has wandered in his own w;	Is 47:15	5676
Who leads you in the w you should go.	Is 48:17	1870
Each of us has turned to his own w;	Is 53:6	1870
Let the wicked forsake his w	Is 55:7	1870
They have all turned to their own w,	Is 56:11	1870
one who walked in his upright w.	Is 57:2	5228
prepare the w, Remove *every*	Is 57:14	1870
every obstacle out of the w of My	Is 57:14	1870
in the w of his heart.	Is 57:17	1870
They do not know the w of peace,	Is 59:8	1870
Clear the w for the people; Build up,	Is 62:10	1870
Who walk *in* the w which is not	Is 65:2	1870
your God When He led you in the w?	Jer 2:17	1870
Look at your w in the valley! Know	Jer 2:23	1870
"How well you prepare your w To seek	Jer 2:33	1870
go around so much Changing your w?	Jer 2:36	1870
And you have had your w."	Jer 3:5	3201
Because they have perverted their w,	Jer 3:21	1870
For they do not know the w of the	Jer 5:4	1870
For they know the w of the LORD	Jer 5:5	1870
Where the good w is, and walk in it;	Jer 6:16	1870
That you may know and assay their w."	Jer 6:27	1870
and you will walk in all the w which	Jer 7:23	1870
"Do not learn the w of the nations,	Jer 10:2	1870
I know, O LORD, that a man's w	Jer 10:23	1870
Why has the w of the wicked prospered?	Jer 12:1	1870
each of you from his evil w,	Jer 18:11	1870
I set before you the w of life	Jer 21:8	1870
before you the way of life and the w	Jer 21:8	1870
"Therefore their w will be like	Jer 23:12	1870
turned them back from their evil w	Jer 23:22	1870
'Turn now everyone from his evil w	Jer 25:5	1870
everyone will turn from his evil w,	Jer 26:3	1870
Then the prophet Jeremiah went his w.	Jer 28:11	1870
The w by which you went. Return, O	Jer 31:21	1870
I will give them one heart and one w,	Jer 32:39	1870
'Turn now every man from his evil w	Jer 35:15	1870
every man will turn from his evil w;	Jer 36:3	1870
everyone will turn from his evil w,	Jer 36:7	1870
"*In* what w have I sinned	Jer 37:18	
went out of the city at night by w of	Jer 39:4	1870
LORD your God may tell us the w	Jer 42:3	1870
"They will ask for the w to Zion,	Jer 50:5	1870
forth from the city at night by w of	Jer 52:7	1870
And they went by w of the Arabah.	Jer 52:7	1870
it nothing to all you who pass this w?	La 1:12	1870
All who pass along the w Clap their	La 2:15	1870
to warn the wicked from his wicked w	Ezk 3:18	1870
his wickedness or from his wicked w,	Ezk 3:19	1870
wicked not to turn from his wicked w	Ezk 13:22	1870
"Yet you say, 'The w of the Lord	Ezk 18:25	1870
Is My w not right? Is it not your	Ezk 18:25	1870
'The w of the Lord is not right.'	Ezk 18:29	1870
make it at the head of the w to	Ezk 21:19	1870
"You shall mark a w for the sword to	Ezk 21:20	1870
stands at the parting of the w, at	Ezk 21:21	1870
their w I have brought upon their	Ezk 22:31	1870
they both took the same w.	Ezk 23:13	1870
'You have walked in the w of your	Ezk 23:31	1870
speak to warn the wicked from his w,	Ezk 33:8	1870
warn a wicked man to turn from his w	Ezk 33:9	1870
way and he does not turn from his w,	Ezk 33:9	1870
that the wicked turn from his w	Ezk 33:11	1870
'The w of the Lord is not right,'	Ezk 33:17	1870
when it is their own w that is not	Ezk 33:17	1870
"Yet you say, 'The w of the Lord	Ezk 33:20	1870
their w before Me was like	Ezk 36:17	1870
lowest *story* to the highest by w	Ezk 41:7	
the w toward the north; and he	Ezk 42:1	1870
a w of one *hundred* cubits;	Ezk 42:4	1870
The w in front of them *was* like	Ezk 42:11	1870
was an opening at the head of the w,	Ezk 42:12	1870
the w in front of the wall toward	Ezk 42:12	1870
he brought me out by the w of	Ezk 42:15	1870
God of Israel was coming from the w	Ezk 43:2	1870
LORD came into the house by the w	Ezk 43:4	1870
Then He brought me back by the w of	Ezk 44:1	1870
he shall enter by w of the porch of	Ezk 44:3	1870
gate and shall go out by the same w."	Ezk 44:3	1870
Then He brought me by w of the north	Ezk 44:4	1870
"The prince shall enter by w of	Ezk 46:2	1870
he shall go in by w of the porch of	Ezk 46:8	1870
of the gate and go out by the same w.	Ezk 46:8	1870
he who enters by w of the north gate	Ezk 46:9	1870
gate to worship shall go out by w of	Ezk 46:9	1870
And he who enters by w of the south	Ezk 46:9	1870
of the south gate shall go out by w	Ezk 46:9	1870
No one shall return by w of the gate	Ezk 46:9	1870
He brought me out by w of the north	Ezk 47:2	1870
on the outside to the outer gate by w	Ezk 47:2	1870
from the Great Sea *by* the w of	Ezk 47:15	1870
beside the w of Hethlon to	Ezk 48:1	1870
god who is able to deliver in this w."	Da 3:29	
last time it will not turn out the w	Da 11:29	
He said, "Go *your* w, Daniel,	Da 12:9	
"But as for you, go *your* w to	Da 12:13	
I will hedge up her w with thorns,	Hos 2:6	1870
a band of priests murder on the w	Hos 6:9	1870
Because you have trusted in your w,	Hos 10:13	1870
of the helpless Also turn aside the w	Am 2:7	1870
'As the w of Beersheba lives,'	Am 8:14	1870
that each may turn from his wicked w	Jon 3:8	1870
that they turned from their wicked w	Jon 3:10	1870
Go on your w, inhabitant of Shaphir,	Mi 1:11	5674a
In whirlwind and storm is His w,	Na 1:3	1870
you have turned aside from the w;	Mal 2:8	1870
and he will clear the w before Me.	Mal 3:1	1870
they went their w; and the star,	Mt 2:9	*4198*

for their own country by another w.	Mt 2:12	3598
'MAKE READY THE W OF THE LORD, MAKE	Mt 3:3	3598
for in this w it is fitting for us to	Mt 3:15	3779
BY THE W OF THE SEA, BEYOND	Mt 4:15	3598
for in the same w they persecuted	Mt 5:12	3779
light shine before men in such a w	Mt 5:16	3779
law while you are with him on the w,	Mt 5:25	3598
"Pray, then, in this w: 'Our	Mt 6:9	3779
"For in the w you judge, you will	Mt 7:2	2917
treat people the same w you want them	Mt 7:12	3779
for the gate is wide and the w is	Mt 7:13	3598
"For the gate is small and the w is	Mt 7:14	3598
that no one could pass by that w.	Mt 8:28	3598
"Do not go in the w of the	Mt 10:5	3598
WHO WILL PREPARE YOUR W BEFORE YOU.'	Mt 11:10	3598
"Yes, Father, for this w was	Mt 11:26	3779
That is the w it will also be with	Mt 12:45	3779
for they might faint on the w."	Mt 15:32	3598
in the same w that I had mercy on you?'	Mt 18:33	5613
the beginning it has not been this w.	Mt 19:8	3779
are eunuchs who were born that w from	Mt 19:12	3779
and on the w He said to them,	Mt 20:17	3598
"It is not this w among you, but	Mt 20:26	3779
"For John came to you in the w of	Mt 21:32	3598
paid no attention and went their w,	Mt 22:5	565
that You are truthful and teach the w	Mt 22:16	3598
the w a hen gathers her chicks under	Mt 23:37	5158
say that it must happen this w?"	Mt 26:54	3779
for even the w you talk gives you	Mt 26:73	2981
In the same w the chief priests also,	Mt 27:41	3668
Now while they were on their w, some	Mt 28:11	4198
WHO WILL PREPARE YOUR W;	Mk 1:2	3598
'MAKE READY THE W OF THE LORD,	Mk 1:3	3598
"Why does this man speak that w?	Mk 2:7	3779
that they were reasoning that w	Mk 2:8	3779
His disciples began to make their w	Mk 2:23	3598
"In a similar w these are the ones	Mk 4:16	3668
they will faint on the w; and some	Mk 8:3	3598
and on the w He questioned His	Mk 8:27	3598
"What were you discussing on the w?"	Mk 9:33	3598
But they kept silent, for on the w	Mk 9:34	3598
"But it is not this w among you,	Mk 10:43	3779
but teach the w of God in truth.	Mk 12:14	3598
In the same w the chief priests also,	Mk 15:31	3668
saw the w He breathed His last, he	Mk 15:39	3779
they were walking along on their w to	Mk 16:12	4198
"This is the w the Lord has dealt	Lk 1:25	3779
To guide our feet into the w of peace."	Lk 1:79	3598
And everyone was on his w to register	Lk 2:3	4198
came in a hurry and found their w to	Lk 2:16	429
why have You treated us this w?	Lk 2:48	3779
'MAKE READY THE W OF THE LORD,	Lk 3:4	3598
He went His w.	Lk 4:30	4198
and asked him to put out a little w	Lk 5:3	3641
But not finding any w to bring	Lk 5:19	
For in the same w their fathers used	Lk 6:23	2596
the false prophets in the same w.	Lk 6:26	2596
"Treat others the same w you want	Lk 6:31	3668
Now Jesus started on His w with	Lk 7:6	4198
WHO WILL PREPARE YOUR W BEFORE YOU.'	Lk 7:27	3598
He spoke by w of a parable:	Lk 8:4	1223
and as they go on their w they are	Lk 8:14	4198
and greet no one on the w.	Lk 10:4	3598
for this w was well-pleasing in Your	Lk 10:21	3779
it turns out that w.	Lk 12:55	
on your w there make an	Lk 12:58	3598
and proceeding on His w to Jerusalem.	Lk 13:22	4197
"I tell you that in the same w,	Lk 15:7	3779
"In the same w, I tell you, there	Lk 15:10	3779
But while he was still a long w off,	Lk 15:20	3112
and everyone is forcing his w into it.	Lk 16:16	971
While He was on the w to Jerusalem,	Lk 17:11	4198
Those who led the w were sternly	Lk 18:39	4254
He was about to pass through that w.	Lk 19:4	
but teach the w of God in truth.	Lk 20:21	3598
and in the same w all seven died,	Lk 20:31	5615
And in the same w He took the cup	Lk 22:20	5615
"But it is not this w with you,	Lk 22:26	3779
'MAKE STRAIGHT THE W OF THE LORD,'	Jn 1:23	3598
not be thirsty nor come all the w	Jn 4:15	
"Never has a man spoken the w this	Jn 7:46	3779
but climbs up some other w, he is a	Jn 10:1	237a
know the w where I am going."	Jn 14:4	3598
how do we know the w?"	Jn 14:5	3598
Jesus said to him, "I am the w,	Jn 14:6	3598
let these go their w,"	Jn 18:8	5217
"Is that the w You answer the high	Jn 18:22	3779
He manifested Himself in this w.	Jn 21:1	3779
will come in just the same w as you	Ac 1:11	5158
So they went on their w from	Ac 5:41	4198
but went on his w rejoicing.	Ac 8:39	3598
if he found any belonging to the W,	Ac 9:2	3598
as they were on their w	Ac 10:9	3596
was I that I could stand in God's w?"	Ac 11:17	2967
connection with Stephen made their w	Ac 11:19	1330
He has spoken in this w: 'I WILL	Ac 13:34	3779
Therefore, being sent on their w by	Ac 15:3	4311
in the same w as they also are."	Ac 15:11	5158
who are proclaiming to you the w of	Ac 16:17	3598
This man had been instructed in the w	Ac 18:25	3598
him aside and explained to him the w	Ac 18:26	3598
speaking evil of the W before	Ac 19:9	3598
no small disturbance concerning the W.	Ac 19:23	3598
I am on my w to Jerusalem, not	Ac 20:22	4198
'In this w the Jews at Jerusalem	Ac 21:11	3779
we got ready and started on our w up	Ac 21:15	305
"I persecuted this W to the death,	Ac 22:4	3598
"But it happened that as I was on my w,	Ac 22:6	4198
they were shouting against him that w.	Ac 22:24	3779
we acknowledge this in every w	Ac 24:3	3839
that according to the W which they	Ac 24:14	3598
a more exact knowledge about the W,	Ac 24:22	3598
an ambush to kill him on the w).	Ac 25:3	3598
at midday, O King, I saw on the w a	Ac 26:13	3598
we gave w to it and let ourselves	Ac 27:15	1929
let down the sea anchor and in this w	Ac 27:17	3779
and in the same w also the men	Ro 1:27	3668
In the same w the Spirit also helps	Ro 8:26	5615
In the same w then, there has also	Ro 11:5	3779
or a stumbling block in a brother's w.	Ro 14:13	
For he who in this w serves	Ro 14:18	
and to be helped on my w there by you,	Ro 15:24	4311
I will go on by w of you to Spain.	Ro 15:28	1223
But this I say by w of concession,	1Co 7:6	2596
Run in such a w that you may win.	1Co 9:24	3779
Therefore I run in such a w, as not	1Co 9:26	3779
I box in such a w, as not beating	1Co 9:26	3779
the temptation will provide the w of	1Co 10:13	1545
In the same w He took the cup	1Co 11:25	5615
I show you a still more excellent w.	1Co 12:31	3598
you unless I speak to you either by w	1Co 14:6	1722
so that you may send me on my w	1Co 16:6	4311
But send him on his w in peace, so	1Co 16:11	4311
that is, to pass your w into	2Co 1:16	1223
we are afflicted in every w, but	2Co 4:8	3956
yet now we know Him in this w	2Co 5:16	
but by w of equality	2Co 8:13	1537
in every w we have made this	2Co 11:6	3956
you did not learn Christ in this w,	Eph 4:20	3779
not by w of eyeservice, as	Eph 6:6	2596
is only right for me to feel this w	Php 1:7	3778
What then? Only that in every w,	Php 1:18	5158
no w alarmed by your opponents	Php 1:28	3367
rejoice in the same w and share	Php 2:18	846
in this w stand firm in the Lord, my	Php 4:1	3779
and He has taken it out of the w,	Col 2:14	3319
that I may make it clear in the w I	Col 4:4	5613
come from error or impurity or by w	1Th 2:3	1722
and Jesus our Lord direct our w to	1Th 3:11	3598
Let no one in any w deceive you, for	2Th 2:3	5158
so until he is taken out of the w.	2Th 2:7	3319
this is the w I write.	2Th 3:17	3779
I serve with a clear conscience the w	2Tm 1:3	575
the lawyer and Apollos on their w so	Ti 3:13	4311
But if he has wronged you in any w or	Phm 1:18	5100
though we are speaking in this w.	Heb 6:9	3779
In the same w God, desiring even	Heb 6:17	
that the w into the holy place has	Heb 9:8	3598
And in the same w he sprinkled both	Heb 9:21	3668
by a new and living w which He	Heb 10:20	3598
In the same w, was not Rahab	Jas 2:25	3668
and sent them out by another w?	Jas 2:25	3668
these things ought not to be this w.	Jas 3:10	3779
a sinner from the error of his w will	Jas 5:20	3598
silver or gold from your futile w of	1Pe 1:18	391
In the same w, you wives, be	1Pe 3:1	3668
For in this w in former times	1Pe 3:5	3779
You husbands in the same w, live	1Pe 3:7	3668
your wives in an understanding w,	1Pe 3:7	1108
for in this w the entrance into	2Pe 1:11	3779
to stir you up by w of reminder,	2Pe 1:13	1722
and because of them the w of	2Pe 2:2	3598
forsaking the right w, they have	2Pe 2:15	3598
having followed the w of Balaam,	2Pe 2:15	3598
for them not to have known the w of	2Pe 2:21	3598
am stirring up your sincere mind by w	2Pe 3:1	1722
things are to be destroyed in this w,	2Pe 3:11	3779
will do well to send them on their w	3Jn 1:6	4311
since they in the same w as these	Jude 1:7	5158
Yet in the same w these men, also by	Jude 1:8	3668
For they have gone the w of Cain,	Jude 1:11	3598
which they have done in an ungodly w,	Jude 1:15	764
you also have some who in the same w	Rv 2:15	3668
and the night in the same w.	Rv 8:12	3668
he must be killed in this w.	Rv 11:5	3779
so that the w would be prepared for	Rv 16:12	3598

WAYFARER

To prepare for the w who had come to	2Sa 12:4	732

WAYFARERS'

Oh that I had in the desert A w	Jer 9:2	732

WAYFARING

"Have you not asked w men,	Jb 21:29	5674a

WAYS

let me know Your w that I may know	Ex 33:13	1870
to walk in His w and to fear Him.	Dt 8:6	1870
to walk in all His w and love Him,	Dt 10:12	1870
to walk in all His w and hold fast to	Dt 11:22	1870
and to walk in His w always—then	Dt 19:9	1870
and that you would walk in His w	Dt 26:17	1870
way and will flee before you seven w.	Dt 28:7	1870
LORD your God and walk in His w.	Dt 28:9	1870
but you will flee seven w before them,	Dt 28:25	1870
and you will not prosper in your w;	Dt 28:29	1870
to walk in His w and to keep His	Dt 30:16	1870
For all His w are just; A God of	Dt 32:4	1870
LORD your God and walk in all His w	Jos 22:5	1870
their practices or their stubborn w.	Jg 2:19	1870
And travelers went by roundabout w.	Jg 5:6	734
did not walk in his w, but turned	1Sa 8:3	1870
and your sons do not walk in your w.	1Sa 8:5	1870
David was prospering in all his w for	1Sa 18:14	1870
but plans w so that the banished one	2Sa 14:14	4284
"For I have kept the w of the LORD,	2Sa 22:22	1870
to walk in His w, to keep His	1Ki 2:3	1870
"If you walk in My w, keeping My	1Ki 3:14	1870
render to each according to all his w,	1Ki 8:39	1870
to walk in all His w and to keep His	1Ki 8:58	1870
and they have not walked in My w,	1Ki 11:33	1870
that I command you and walk in My w,	1Ki 11:38	1870
"Turn from your evil w and keep My	2Ki 17:13	1870
render to each according to all his w	2Ch 6:30	1870
to walk in Your w as long as they	2Ch 6:31	1870
My face and turn from their wicked w,	2Ch 7:14	1870
and his w and his words are written	2Ch 13:22	1870
He took great pride in the w of the	2Ch 17:6	1870
'Because you have not walked in the w	2Ch 21:12	1870
of Jehoshaphat your father and the w	2Ch 21:12	1870
He also walked in the w of the house	2Ch 22:3	1870
mighty because he ordered his w	2Ch 27:6	1870
But he walked in the w of the kings	2Ch 28:2	1870
the rest of his acts and all his w,	2Ch 28:26	1870
and walked in the w of his father	2Ch 34:2	1870
And the integrity of your w your hope?	Jb 4:6	1870
Nevertheless I will argue my w before	Jb 13:15	1870
even desire the knowledge of Your w.	Jb 21:14	1870
Or profit if you make your w perfect?	Jb 22:3	1870
And light will shine on your w.	Jb 22:28	1870
They do not want to know its w Nor	Jb 24:13	1870
And His eyes are on their w.	Jb 24:23	1870
these are the fringes of His w;	Jb 26:14	1870
feet and build up against me their w	Jb 30:12	734
"Does He not see my w And number all	Jb 31:4	1870
"For His eyes are upon the w of a	Jb 34:21	1870
And had no regard for any of His w;	Jb 34:27	1870
"He is the first of the w of God;	Jb 40:19	1870
His w prosper at all times; Your	Ps 10:5	1870
For I have kept the w of the LORD,	Ps 18:21	1870
Make me know Your w, O LORD;	Ps 25:4	1870
I said, "I will guard my w That I	Ps 39:1	1870
I will teach transgressors Your w,	Ps 51:13	1870
That Israel would walk in My w!	Ps 81:13	1870
To guard you in all your w.	Ps 91:11	1870
And they do not know My w.	Ps 95:10	1870
He made known His w to Moses, His	Ps 103:7	1870
They walk in His w.	Ps 119:3	1870
Oh that my w may be established To	Ps 119:5	1870
on Your precepts And regard Your w.	Ps 119:15	734
I have told of my w, and You have	Ps 119:26	1870
And revive me in Your w.	Ps 119:37	1870
I considered my w And turned my feet	Ps 119:59	1870
For all my w are before You.	Ps 119:168	1870
who turn aside to their crooked w,	Ps 125:5	6128
Who walks in His w.	Ps 128:1	1870
And they will sing of the w of the	Ps 138:5	1870
intimately acquainted with all my w.	Ps 139:3	1870
LORD is righteous in all His w	Ps 145:17	1870
So are the w of everyone who gains by	Pr 1:19	734
paths of uprightness To walk in the w	Pr 2:13	1870
And who are devious in their w;	Pr 2:15	4570
In all your w acknowledge Him,	Pr 3:6	1870
Her w are pleasant ways And all her	Pr 3:17	1870
Her ways are pleasant w And all her	Pr 3:17	1870
And do not choose any of his w.	Pr 3:31	1870
the path of your feet And all your w	Pr 4:26	1870
Her w are unstable, she does not	Pr 5:6	4570
For the w of a man are before	Pr 5:21	1870
Observe her w and be wise,	Pr 6:6	1870
let your heart turn aside to her w,	Pr 7:25	1870
For blessed are they who keep my w.	Pr 8:32	1870
But he who perverts his w will be	Pr 10:9	1870
But he who is devious in his w	Pr 14:2	1870
heart will have his fill of his own w,	Pr 14:14	1870
All the w of a man are clean in his	Pr 16:2	1870
When a man's w are pleasing to the	Pr 16:7	1870
bribe from the bosom To pervert the w	Pr 17:23	734
Or you will learn his w And find a	Pr 22:25	734
And let your eyes delight in my w.	Pr 23:26	1870
Or your w to that which destroys	Pr 31:3	1870
She looks well to the w of her	Pr 31:27	1979
That He may teach us concerning His w	Is 2:3	1870
And in whose w they were not willing	Is 42:24	1870
And I will make all his w smooth;	Is 45:13	1870
and He will make his w successful.	Is 48:15	1870
Nor are your w My ways," declares	Is 55:8	1870
Nor are your ways My w," declares	Is 55:8	1870
So are My w higher than your ways	Is 55:9	1870
So are My ways higher than your w	Is 55:9	1870
"I have seen his w, but I will heal	Is 57:18	1870
day by day and delight to know My w,	Is 58:2	1870
desisting from your own w, From	Is 58:13	1870
do You cause us to stray from Your w	Is 63:17	1870
Who remembers You in Your w.	Is 64:5	1870
As they have chosen their own w,	Is 66:3	1870
a swift young camel entangling her w,	Jer 2:23	1870
wicked women You have taught your w.	Jer 2:33	1870
"Your w and your deeds Have brought	Jer 4:18	1870
"Stand by the w and see and ask	Jer 6:16	1870
"Amend your w and your deeds, and I	Jer 7:3	1870
"For if you truly amend your w	Jer 7:5	1870
"Then if they will really learn the w	Jer 12:16	1870
They did not repent of their w.	Jer 15:7	1870
"For My eyes are on all their w;	Jer 16:17	1870
give to each man according to his w,	Jer 17:10	1870
and reform your w and your deeds." '	Jer 18:11	1870
And they have stumbled from their w,	Jer 18:15	1870
"Now therefore amend your w and your	Jer 26:13	1870
whose eyes are open to all the w of	Jer 32:19	1870
giving to everyone according to his w	Jer 32:19	1870
He has blocked my w with hewn stone;	La 3:9	1870
He has turned aside my w and torn me	La 3:11	1870
Let us examine and probe our w, And	La 3:40	1870
I will judge you according to your w	Ezk 7:3	1870
but I will bring your w upon you,	Ezk 7:4	1870
judge you according to your w	Ezk 7:8	1870
I will repay you according to your w,	Ezk 7:9	1870
you have not merely walked in their w	Ezk 16:47	1870

"Then you will remember your **w** **Ezk 16:61** 1870
than that he should turn from his **w** **Ezk 18:23** 1870
Is it not your **w** that are not right? **Ezk 18:25** 1870
Are My **w** not right, O house of **Ezk 18:29** 1870
Is it not your **w** that are not right? **Ezk 18:29** 1870
"There you will remember your **w** **Ezk 20:43** 1870
not according to your evil **w** or **Ezk 20:44** 1870
make two **w** for the sword of the king **Ezk 21:19** 1870
at the head of the two **w**, to use **Ezk 21:21** 1870
according to your **w** and according to **Ezk 24:14** 1870
"You were blameless in your **w** From **Ezk 28:15** 1870
turn back from your evil **w**! Why then **Ezk 33:11** 1870
judge each of you according to his **w**." **Ezk 33:20** 1870
they defiled it by their **w** and their **Ezk 36:17** 1870
According to their **w** and their deeds **Ezk 36:19** 1870
"Then you will remember your evil **w** **Ezk 36:31** 1870
Be ashamed and confounded for your **w**, **Ezk 36:32** 1870
for all His works are true and His **w** **Da 4:37** 735
hand are your life-breath and your **w**, **Da 5:23** 735
So I will punish them for their **w** And **Hos 4:9** 1870
of a bird catcher is in all his **w**, **Hos 9:8** 1870
will punish Jacob according to his **w**; **Hos 12:2** 1870
For the **w** of the LORD are right, **Hos 14:9** 1870
That He may teach us about His **w** And **Mi 4:2** 1870
His **w** are everlasting. **Hab 3:6** 1979
"Consider your **w**! **Hg 1:5** 1870
"Consider your **w**! **Hg 1:7** 1870
"Return now from your evil **w** **Zch 1:4** 1870
to do to us in accordance with our **w** **Zch 1:6** 1870
'If you will walk in My **w** and if you **Zch 3:7** 1870
just as you are not keeping My **w** but **Mal 2:9** 1870
on BEFORE THE LORD TO PREPARE HIS **W**; **Lk 1:76** *3598*
'YOU HAVE MADE KNOWN TO ME THE **W** **Ac 2:28** *3598*
one *of you* from your wicked **w**." **Ac 3:26** *4189*
cease to make crooked the straight **w** **Ac 13:10** *3598*
all the nations to go their own **w**; **Ac 14:16** *3598*
His judgments and unfathomable His **w**! **Ro 11:33** *3598*
and he will remind you of my **w** which **1Co 4:17** *3598*
in many portions and in many **w**, **Heb 1:1** *4187*
AND THEY DID NOT KNOW MY **W**'; **Heb 3:10** *3598*
unstable in all his **w**. **Jas 1:8** *3598*
For we all stumble in many **w**. If **Jas 3:2**
Righteous and true are Your **w**, King **Rv 15:3** *3598*

WAYSIDE
He will drink from the brook by the **w**; **Ps 110:7** 1870
They have spread a net by the **w**; **Ps 140:5** 4570
a leopard I will lie in wait by the **w**. **Hos 13:7** 1870

WAYWARDNESS
"For the **w** of the naive will kill **Pr 1:32** 4878

WE
So then **I** us pursue the things **Ro 14:19**

WEAK
And Leah's eyes were **w**, but Rachel **Gn 29:17** 7390
who live in it are strong *or* **w**, **Nu 13:18** 7504b
then I will become **w** and be like any **Jg 16:7** 2470a
then I will become **w** and be like any **Jg 16:11** 2470a
then I will become **w** and be like any **Jg 16:13** 2470a
will leave me and I will become **w** **Jg 16:17** 2470a
"I am **w** today, though anointed king; **2Sa 3:39** 7390
And you have strengthened **w** hands. **Jb 4:3** 7504b
"What a help you are to the **w**! **Jb 26:2** 3808
Vindicate the **w** and fatherless; **Ps 82:3** 1800b
Rescue the **w** and needy; Deliver **Ps 82:4** 1800b
My knees are **w** from fasting, **Ps 109:24** 3782
'Even you have been made **w** as we, **Is 14:10** 2470a
will faint and all knees will be **w** as **Ezk 21:7** 1980
and thrust at all the **w** with your **Ezk 34:21** 2470a
Let the **w** say, "I am a mighty man." **Jl 3:10** 2523
the inhabitant of Maroth Becomes **w** **Mi 1:12** 2470a
but the flesh is **w**." **Mt 26:41** *772*
but the flesh is **w**." **Mk 14:38** *772*
in this manner you must help the **w** **Ac 20:35** *770*
Without becoming **w** in faith he **Ro 4:19** *770*
For what the Law could not do, **w** as **Ro 8:3** *770*
Now accept the one who is **w** in faith, **Ro 14:1** *770*
but he who is **w** eats vegetables **Ro 14:2** *770*
and God has chosen the **w** things of **1Co 1:27** *772*
we are **w**, but you are strong; you **1Co 4:10** *772*
and their conscience being **w** is **1Co 8:7** *772*
become a stumbling block to the **w**. **1Co 8:9** *772*
if he is **w**, be strengthened to eat **1Co 8:10** *772*
through your knowledge he who is **w** is **1Co 8:11** *770*
their conscience when it is **w**, you **1Co 8:12** *770*
To the **w** I became weak, that I might **1Co 9:22** *772*
To the weak I became **w**, that I might **1Co 9:22** *772*
that I might win the **w**; I have **1Co 9:22** *772*
For this reason many among you are **w** **1Co 11:30** *772*
I *must* say that we have been **w** **2Co 11:21** *770*
Who is **w** without my being weak? Who **2Co 11:29** *770*
Who is weak without my being **w**? Who **2Co 11:29** *770*
for when I am **w**, then I am strong. **2Co 12:10** *770*
and who is not **w** toward you, but **2Co 13:3** *770*
For we also are **w** in Him, yet we **2Co 13:4** *770*
we rejoice when we ourselves are **w** **2Co 13:9** *770*
it that you turn back again to the **w** **Ga 4:9** *772*
help the **w**, be patient with everyone. **1Th 5:14** *772*
enter into households and captivate **w** **2Tm 3:6** *1133*
men as high priests who are **w**, but **Heb 7:28** *769*
strengthen the hands that are **w** **Heb 12:12** *3935*

WEAKEN
But they did not **w**; You have **Jer 5:3** 2470a

WEAKENED
He has **w** my strength in the way; **Ps 102:23** 6031a
You who have **w** the nations! **Is 14:12** 2522

WEAKER
but the house of Saul grew **w** **2Sa 3:1** 1800b
of the body which seem to be **w** are **1Co 12:22** *772*
as with someone **w**, since she is a **1Pe 3:7** *4160*

WEAKNESS
I will also bring **w** into their hearts **Lv 26:36** 4816
in human terms because of the **w** of **Ro 6:19** *769*
same way the Spirit also helps our **w**; **Ro 8:26** *769*
and the **w** of God is stronger than men. **1Co 1:25** *772*
I was with you in **w** and in fear **1Co 2:3** *769*
it is sown in **w**, it is raised in **1Co 15:43** *769*
I will boast of what pertains to my **w**. **2Co 11:30** *769*
for power is perfected in **w**." Most **2Co 12:9** *769*
indeed He was crucified because of **w**, **2Co 13:4** *769*
since he himself also is beset with **w**; **Heb 5:2** *769*
a former commandment because of its **w** **Heb 7:18** *772*
from **w** were made strong, became **Heb 11:34** *769*

WEAKNESSES
we who are strong ought to bear the **w** **Ro 15:1** *771*
except in regard to *my* **w**. **2Co 12:5** *769*
I will rather boast about my **w**, so **2Co 12:9** *769*
Therefore I am well content with **w**, **2Co 12:10** *769*
who cannot sympathize with our **w**, **Heb 4:15** *769*

WEALTH
to our father he has made all this **w**." **Gn 31:1** 3519b
"Surely all the **w** which God has **Gn 31:16** 6239
they captured and looted all their **w** **Gn 34:29** 2428
strength of my hand made me this **w**.' **Dt 8:17** 2428
He who is giving you power to make **w**, **Dt 8:18** 2428
a man of great **w**, of the family of **Ru 2:1** 2428
and may you achieve **w** in Ephrathah **Ru 4:11** 2428
even from all the mighty men of **w**, **2Ki 15:20** 2428
w or honor, or the life of those who **2Ch 1:11** 5233
And I will give you riches and **w** **2Ch 1:12** 5233
for God had given him very great **w**. **2Ch 32:29** 7399
And the schemer is eager for their **w**. **Jb 5:5** 2428
'Offer a bribe for me from your **w**,' **Jb 6:22** 3581b
nor will his **w** endure; And his grain **Jb 15:29** 2428
And his hands give back his **w**. **Jb 20:10** 202
If I have gloated because my **w** was **Jb 31:25** 2428
Even those who trust in their **w** **Ps 49:6** 2428
alike perish And leave their **w** to **Ps 49:10** 2428
they have increased *in* **w**. **Ps 73:12** 2428
W and riches are in his house, **Ps 112:3** 1952
will find all *kinds* of precious **w**, **Pr 1:13** 1952
Honor the LORD from your **w** **Pr 3:9** 1952
Enduring **w** and righteousness. **Pr 8:18** 1952
To endow those who love me with **w**, **Pr 8:21** 3426
The rich man's **w** is his fortress, **Pr 10:15** 1952
but has great **w**. **Pr 13:7** 1952
The ransom of a man's life is his **w**, **Pr 13:8** 6239
W *obtained* by fraud dwindles, **Pr 13:11** 1952
And the **w** of the sinner is stored up **Pr 13:22** 2428
Great **w** is *in* the house of **Pr 15:6** 2633
A rich man's **w** is his strong city, **Pr 18:11** 1952
W adds many friends, But a poor man **Pr 19:4** 1952
House and **w** are an inheritance from **Pr 19:14** 1952
is to be more desired than great **w**, **Pr 22:1** 6239
Do not weary yourself to gain **w**, **Pr 23:4** 6238
For **w** certainly makes itself **Pr 23:5**
He who increases his **w** by interest **Pr 28:8** 1952
man with an evil eye hastens after **w** **Pr 28:22** 1952
company with harlots wastes *his* **w**. **Pr 29:3** 1952
and my mind has observed a **w** of **Ec 1:16** 7235a
to whom God has given riches and **w**, **Ec 5:19** 5233
to whom God has given riches and **w** **Ec 6:2** 5233
neither is bread to the wise nor **w** to **Ec 9:11** 6239
the **w** of Damascus and the spoil of **Is 8:4** 2428
And where will you leave your **w**? **Is 10:3** 3519b
A **w** of salvation, wisdom **Is 33:6** 2633
treasures of darkness And hidden **w** of **Is 45:3** 4301
The **w** of the nations will come to you. **Is 60:5** 2428
that *men* may bring to you the **w** **Is 60:11** 2428
You will eat the **w** of nations, **Is 61:6** 2428
"Your **w** and your treasures I will **Jer 15:13** 2428
I will give over your **w** and all your **Jer 17:3** 2428
'I will also give over all the **w** of **Jer 20:5** 2633
none of their **w**, nor anything **Ezk 7:11** 1991
the abundance of all *kinds* of **w**; **Ezk 27:12** 1952
the abundance of all *kinds* of **w**, **Ezk 27:18** 1952
"Your **w**, your wares, your **Ezk 27:27** 1952
With the abundance of your **w** and your **Ezk 27:33** 1952
And he will carry off her **w** **Ezk 29:19** 1995
They take away her **w**, And her **Ezk 30:4** 1995
I have found **w** for myself; In all my **Hos 12:8** 202
day that strangers carried off his **w**, **Ob 1:11** 2428
And do not loot their **w** In the day of **Ob 1:13** 2428
LORD their unjust gain And their **w** **Mi 4:13** 2428
is no limit to the treasure—**W** **Na 2:9** 3519b
"Moreover, their **w** will become **Zph 1:13** 2428
and they will come with the **w** of all **Hg 2:7** 2532
will dispossess her And cast her **w** **Zch 9:4** 2428
and the **w** of all the surrounding **Zch 14:14** 2428
You cannot serve God and **w**. **Mt 6:24** *3126*
the world and the deceitfulness of **w** **Mt 13:22** *4149*
So he divided his **w** between them. **Lk 15:12** *979*
who has devoured your **w** with **Lk 15:30** *979*
for yourselves by means of the **w** of **Lk 16:9** *3126*
in the *use of* unrighteous **w**, who **Lk 16:11** *3126*
You cannot serve God and **w**." **Lk 16:13** *3126*
deep poverty overflowed in the **w** of **2Co 8:2** *4149*
and *attaining* to all the **w** that **Col 2:2** *4149*
the earth have become rich by the **w** of **Rv 18:3** *1411*
for in one hour such great **w** has been **Rv 18:17** *4149*
had ships at sea became rich by her **w**, **Rv 18:19** *5094*

WEALTHY
to grow richer until he became very **w**; **Gn 26:13** 1431
presence of his brothers and the **w** **Ne 4:2** 2428
will eat in the waste places of the **w**. **Is 5:17** 4220
hard it will be for those who are **w** **Mk 10:23** *5536*
"How hard it is for those who are **w** **Lk 18:24** *5536*
and have become **w**, and have need of **Rv 3:17** *4147*

WEANED
The child grew and was **w**, **Gn 21:8** 1580
feast on the day that Isaac was **w**. **Gn 21:8** 1580
will not go up until the child is **w**; **1Sa 1:22** 1580
Remain until you have **w** him; only **1Sa 1:23** 1580
and nursed her son until she **w** him. **1Sa 1:23** 1580
Now when she had **w** him, she took him **1Sa 1:24** 1580
whom Tahpenes **w** in Pharaoh's house; **1Ki 11:20** 1580
Like a **w** child *rests* against his **Ps 131:2** 1580
My soul is like a **w** child within me. **Ps 131:2** 1580
And the **w** child will put his hand on **Is 11:8** 1580
Those *just* **w** from milk? Those **Is 28:9** 1580
When she had **w** Lo-ruhamah, she **Hos 1:8** 1580

WEAPON
each man with his **w** in his hand, **2Ch 23:10** 7973
the work and the other holding a **w**. **Ne 4:17** 7973
each *took* his **w** *even to* **Ne 4:23** 7973
"He may flee from the iron **w**, **Jb 20:24** 5402
the fire of coals And brings out a **w** **Is 54:16** 3627
"No **w** that is formed against you **Is 54:17** 3627
My **w** of war; And with you I **Jer 51:20** 3627
each with his destroying **w** in his **Ezk 9:1** 3627
each with his shattering **w** in his **Ezk 9:2** 3627

WEAPONS
And every man of you girded on his **w** **Dt 1:41** 3627
six hundred men armed with **w** of war **Jg 18:11** 3627
six hundred men armed with their **w** of **Jg 18:16** 3627
with the six hundred men armed with **w** **Jg 18:17** 3627
to reap his harvest and to make his **w** **1Sa 8:12** 3627
but he put his **w** in his tent. **1Sa 17:54** 3627
Then Jonathan gave his **w** to his lad **1Sa 20:40** 3627
I brought neither my sword nor my **w** **1Sa 21:8** 3627
off his head and stripped off his **w**, **1Sa 31:9** 3627
They put his **w** in the temple of **1Sa 31:10** 3627
And the **w** of war perished!" **2Sa 1:27** 3627
w, spices, horses, and mules, so **1Ki 10:25** 5402
horses and a fortified city and the **w**, **2Ki 10:2** 5402
each with his **w** in his hand; **2Ki 11:8** 3627
The guards stood each with his **w** in **2Ki 11:11** 3627
battle formation with all kinds of **w** **1Ch 12:33** 3627
with all *kinds* of **w** of war for **1Ch 12:37** 3627
w, spices, horses and mules, so **2Ch 9:24** 5402
each man with his **w** in his hand; **2Ch 23:7** 3627
and made **w** and shields in great **2Ch 32:5** 7973
He goes out to meet the **w**. **Jb 39:21** 5402
also prepared for Himself deadly **w**; **Ps 7:13** 3627
The shield and the sword and the **w** of **Ps 76:3** 4421
Wisdom is better than **w** of war, but **Ec 9:18** 3627
In that day you depended on the **w** of **Is 22:8** 5402
brandishing **w**, He will fight them. **Is 30:32** 8573
As for a rogue, his **w** are evil; **Is 32:7** 3627
I am about to turn back the **w** of war **Jer 21:4** 3627
Each with his **w**; And they will cut **Jer 22:7** 3627
armory And has brought forth the **w** of **Jer 50:25** 3627
'They will come against you with **w**, **Ezk 23:24** 2021
who went down to Sheol with their **w** **Ezk 32:27** 3627
will go out and make fires with the **w** **Ezk 39:9** 5402
for they will make fires with the **w**; **Ezk 39:10** 5402
there with lanterns and torches and **w**. **Jn 18:3** *3696*
by the **w** of righteousness for **2Co 6:7** *3696*
for the **w** of our warfare are not of **2Co 10:4** *3696*

WEAR
give me food to eat and garments to **w**, **Gn 28:20** 3847
"You will surely **w** out, both **Ex 18:18** 5034b
nor **w** a garment upon you of two kinds **Lv 19:19** 5927
and who has been consecrated to **w** **Lv 21:10** 3847
"Your clothing did not **w** out on you, **Dt 8:4** 1086
"A woman shall not **w** man's clothing, **Dt 22:5** 1961
"You shall not **w** a material mixed of **Dt 22:11** 3847
Their clothes did not **w** out, nor did **Ne 9:21** 1086
but the just will **w** *it* **Jb 27:17** 3847
And all of them will **w** out like a **Ps 102:26** 1086
"We will eat our own bread and **w** our **Is 4:1** 3847
And all the host of heaven will **w** **Is 34:4** 4743
they will all **w** out like a garment; **Is 50:9** 1086
And the earth will **w** out like a **Is 51:6** 1086
And My chosen ones will **w** out **Is 65:22** 1086
will be clothed with purple and **w** **Da 5:16**
speak out against the Most High and **w** **Da 7:25** 1080
or 'What will we **w** for clothing?' **Mt 6:31** *4016*
Those who **w** soft *clothing* are in **Mt 11:8** *5409*
but *to* **w** sandals; and *He added* **Mk 6:9** *5265*
yourselves money belts which do not **w** **Lk 12:33** *3822*
by continually coming she will **w** me **Lk 18:5** *5299*

WEARIED
so that they **w** *themselves trying* **Gn 19:11** 3811
Nor **w** you with incense. **Is 43:23** 3021
You have **w** Me with your iniquities. **Is 43:24** 3021
"You are **w** with your many counsels; **Is 47:13** 3811
"She has **w** *Me* with toil, Yet **Ezk 24:12** 3811
And how have I **w** you? Answer Me. **Mi 6:3** 3811
You have **w** the LORD with your **Mal 2:17** 3021
"How have we **w** *Him?*" In that **Mal 2:17** 3021
being **w** from His journey, was **Jn 4:6** *2872*

WEARIES
The toil of a fool *so* **w** him that **Ec 10:15** 3021
When he **w** himself upon *his* high **Is 16:12** 3811

WEARINESS
my hand was stretched out without **w**; **Ps 77:2** 6313
came to me in *my* extreme **w** about **Da 9:21** 3288

WEARING
as a boy **w** a linen ephod. **1Sa 2:18** 2296
was **w** an ephod. And the people did **1Sa 14:3** 5375
and David was **w** a linen ephod. **2Sa 6:14** 2296
To shaving the head and to **w** **Is 22:12** 2296
A young man was following Him, **w** **Mk 14:51** *4016*

w a white robe; and they were amazed. **Mk 16:5** 4016
Jesus then came out, **w** the crown of **Jn 19:5** 5409
for I am **w** this chain for the sake of **Ac 28:20** 4029
special attention to the one who is **w** **Jas 2:3** 5409
and **w** gold jewelry, or putting on **1Pe 3:3** 4025

WEARISOME
All things are **w**; Man is not able to **Ec 1:8** 3023

WEARS
Water **w** away stones, Its torrents **Jb 14:19** 7833

WEARY
your rear when you were faint and **w**; **Dt 25:18** 3023
crossed over, **w** yet pursuing. **Jg 8:4** 5889
for they are **w**, and I am pursuing **Jg 8:5** 5889
give bread to your men who are **w**?' " **Jg 8:15** 3287
And the people were **w**. **1Sa 14:28** 5888
And the people were very **w**. **1Sa 14:31** 5888
people who were with him arrived **w** **2Sa 16:14** 5889
"I will come upon him while he is **w** **2Sa 17:2** 3023
"The people are hungry and **w** **2Sa 17:29** 5889
against the Philistines, David became **w**. **2Sa 21:15** 5888
the Philistines until his hand was **w** **2Sa 23:10** 3021
And there the **w** are at rest. **Jb 3:17** 3019
"To the **w** you have given no water to **Jb 22:7** 5889
I am **w** with my sighing; Every night **Ps 6:6** 3021
In a dry and **w** land where there is no **Ps 63:1** 5889
I am **w** with my crying; my throat is **Ps 69:3** 3021
Do not **w** yourself to gain wealth, **Pr 23:4** 3021
Or he will become **w** of you and hate **Pr 25:17** 7646
Like cold water to a **w** soul, So **Pr 25:25** 5889
He is **w** of bringing it to his mouth **Pr 26:15** 3811
I am **w** of bearing *them.* **Is 1:14** 3811
No one in it is **w** or stumbles, None **Is 5:27** 5889
give rest to the **w**," And, "Here **Is 28:12** 5889
ends of the earth Does not become **w** **Is 40:28** 3286
He gives strength to the **w**, **Is 40:29** 3287
Though youths grow **w** and tired, **Is 40:30** 3286
They will walk and not become **w**. **Is 40:31** 3286
But you have become **w** of Me, O **Is 43:22** 3021
he drinks no water and becomes **w**. **Is 44:12** 3286
A load for the **w** *beast.* **Is 46:1** 5889
That I may know how to sustain the **w** **Is 50:4** 3287
All who seek her will not become **w**; **Jer 2:24** 3286
I am **w** with holding *it* in. **Jer 6:11** 3811
They **w** themselves committing iniquity. **Jer 9:5** 3811
And I am **w** of holding *it* in, And **Jer 20:9** 3811
"For I satisfy the **w** ones **Jer 31:25** 5889
I am **w** with my groaning and have **Jer 45:3** 3021
And nations grow **w** for nothing? **Hab 2:13** 3286
and their soul also was **w** of me. **Zch 11:8** 973a
"Come to Me, all who are **w** **Mt 11:28** 2872
"But, that I may not **w** you any **Ac 24:4** 1465
time we will reap if we do not grow **w**. **Ga 6:9** 1590
do not grow **w** of doing good. **2Th 3:13** 1457b
so that you will not grow **w** and lose **Heb 12:3** 2577
and have not grown **w**. **Rv 2:3** 2872

WEARYING
excessive devotion *to books* is **w** **Ec 12:12** 3024

WEATHER
'*It will be* fair **w**, for the sky **Mt 16:2** 2105

WEAVE
"You shall **w** the tunic of checkered **Ex 28:39** 7660
"If you **w** the seven locks of my hair **Jg 16:13** 707
They hatch adders' eggs and **w** **Is 59:5** 707
So they **w** it together. **Mi 7:3** 5686

WEAVER
the work of a **w**. **Ex 26:36** 7551
the work of a **w**, *with* their four **Ex 27:16** 7551
the work of a **w**. **Ex 28:39** 7551
and of a **w**, as performers of every **Ex 35:35** 707
the work of a **w**; **Ex 36:37** 7551
of the court was the work of the **w**, **Ex 38:18** 7551
and a skillful workman and a **w** in **Ex 38:23** 7551
the work of the **w**, just as the **Ex 39:29** 7551
As a **w** I rolled up my life. He cuts **Is 38:12** 707

WEAVER'S
of his spear was like a **w** beam, **1Sa 17:7** 707
of whose spear was like a **w** beam. **2Sa 21:19** 707
hand *was* a spear like a **w** beam, **1Ch 11:23** 707
whose spear *was* like a **w** beam. **1Ch 20:5** 707
swifter than a **w** shuttle, **Jb 7:6** 708

WEAVERS
linen made from combed flax And the **w** **Is 19:9** 707

WEAVING
where the women were **w** hangings for **2Ki 23:7** 707

WEB
the seven locks of my hair with the **w** **Jg 16:13** 4545
of his hair and wove them into the **w**]. **Jg 16:14** 4545
out the pin of the loom and the **w**. **Jg 16:14** 4545
And whose trust a spider's **w**. **Jb 8:14** 1004
built his house like the spider's **w**, **Jb 27:18**
eggs and weave the spider's **w**; **Is 59:5** 6980

WEBBING
And he steps on the **w**. **Jb 18:8** 7639

WEBS
Their **w** will not become clothing, **Is 59:6** 6980

WEDDING
And His virgins had no **w** songs. **Ps 78:63** 1984b
has crowned him On the day of his **w**, **SS 3:11** 2861
be compared to a king who gave a **w** **Mt 22:2** 1062
those who had been invited to the **w** **Mt 22:3** 1062
come to the **w** feast." ' **Mt 22:4** 1062
'The **w** is ready, but those who were **Mt 22:8** 1062
invite to the **w** feast.' **Mt 22:9** 1062
and the **w** hall was filled with dinner **Mt 22:10** 3567
a man there who was not dressed in **w** **Mt 22:11** 1062
how did you come in here without **w** **Mt 22:12** 1062
were ready went in with him to the **w** **Mt 25:10** 1062
when he returns from the **w** feast, **Lk 12:36** 1062
invited by someone to a **w** feast, **Lk 14:8** 1062
On the third day there was a **w** in **Jn 2:1** 1062
His disciples were invited to the **w**. **Jn 2:2** 1062

WEEDS
W will take over their treasures of **Hos 9:6** 7057
And judgment sprouts like poisonous **w** **Hos 10:4** 7219
W were wrapped around my head. **Jon 2:5** 5488

WEEK
"Complete the **w** of this one, and we **Gn 29:27** 7620
Jacob did so and completed her **w**, **Gn 29:28** 7620
firm covenant with the many for one **w**, **Da 9:27** 7620
but in the middle of the **w** he will **Da 9:27** 7620
toward the first *day* of the **w**, **Mt 28:1** 4521
Very early on the first day of the **w**, **Mk 16:2** 4521
risen early on the first day of the **w**, **Mk 16:9** 4521
'I fast twice a **w**; I pay tithes of **Lk 18:12** 4521
But on the first day of the **w**, at **Lk 24:1** 4521
Now on the first *day* of the **w** **Jn 20:1** 4521
the first *day* of the **w**, and when **Jn 20:19** 4521
On the first day of the **w**, when we **Ac 20:7** 4521
On the first day of every **w** each one **1Co 16:2** 4521

WEEKS
"You shall celebrate the Feast of **W**, **Ex 34:22** 7620
then she shall be unclean for two **w**, **Lv 12:5** 7620
the LORD in your *Feast of* **W**, **Nu 28:26** 7620
"You shall count seven **w** for **Dt 16:9** 7620
you shall begin to count seven **w** from **Dt 16:9** 7620
you shall celebrate the Feast of **W** to **Dt 16:10** 7620
Bread and at the Feast of **W** and at **Dt 16:16** 7620
the Feast of **W** and the Feast of **2Ch 8:13** 7620
Who keeps for us The appointed **w** of **Jer 5:24** 7620
"Seventy **w** have been decreed for **Da 9:24** 7620
the Prince *there will be* seven **w** **Da 9:25** 7620
will be seven weeks and sixty-two **w**; **Da 9:25** 7620
"Then after the sixty-two **w** **Da 9:26** 7620
had been mourning for three entire **w**. **Da 10:2** 7620
at all until the entire three **w** were **Da 10:3** 7620

WEEP
went in to mourn for Sarah and to **w** **Gn 23:2** 1058
and he sought *a place* to **w**; **Gn 43:30** 1058
For they **w** before me, saying, **Nu 11:13** 1058
that I may go to the mountains and **w** **Jg 11:37** 1058
why do you **w** and why do you not eat **1Sa 1:8** 1058
matter with the people that they **w**?" **1Sa 11:5** 1058
there was no strength in them to **w**. **1Sa 30:4** 1058
"O daughters of Israel, **w** over Saul, **2Sa 1:24** 1058
Hazael said, "Why does my lord **w**?" **2Ki 8:12** 1058
do not mourn or **w**." For all **Ne 8:9** 1058
their widows will not be able to **w**. **Jb 27:15** 1058
my flute to the sound of those who **w**. **Jb 30:31** 1058
And its furrows **w** together; **Jb 31:38** 1058
And His widows could not **w**. **Ps 78:64** 1058
A time to **w** and a time to laugh; **Ec 3:4** 1058
even to the high places to **w**. **Is 15:2** 1065
Therefore I will **w** bitterly for Jazer, **Is 16:9** 1058
Let me **w** bitterly, Do not try to **Is 22:4** 1065
you will **w** no longer. He will surely **Is 30:19** 1058
The ambassadors of peace **w** bitterly. **Is 33:7** 1058
That I might **w** day and night For **Jer 9:1** 1058
And my eyes will bitterly **w** And flow **Jer 13:17** 1830
Do not **w** for the dead or mourn for **Jer 22:10** 1058
But **w** continually for the one who **Jer 22:10** 1058
than the weeping for Jazer I will **w** **Jer 48:32** 1058
"For these things I **w**; My eyes run **La 1:16** 1058
shall not mourn and you shall not **w**, **Ezk 24:16** 1058
You will not mourn and you will not **w**, **Ezk 24:23** 1058
And they will **w** for you in bitterness **Ezk 27:31** 1058
Awake, drunkards, and **w**; And wail, **Jl 1:5** 1058
W between the porch and the altar, **Jl 2:17** 1058
Tell it not in Gath, **W** not at all. **Mi 1:10** 1058
"Shall I **w** in the fifth month **Zch 7:3** 1058
and they will **w** bitterly over Him **Zch 12:10** 4843
"Why make a commotion and **w**? **Mk 5:39** 2799
And he began to **w**. **Mk 14:72** 2799
Blessed *are* you who **w** now, for **Lk 6:21** 2799
for you shall mourn and **w**. **Lk 6:25** 2799
"Do not **w**." **Lk 7:13** 2799
and you did not **w**.' **Lk 7:32** 2799
but **w** for yourselves and for your **Lk 23:28** 2799
that she was going to the tomb to **w** **Jn 11:31** 2799
that you will **w** and lament, but **Jn 16:20** 2799
And they *began* to **w** aloud **Ac 20:37** 2805
and **w** with those who weep. **Ro 12:15** 2799
and weep with those who **w**. **Ro 12:15** 2799
and those who **w**, as though they did **1Co 7:30** 2799
as though they did not **w**; and those **1Co 7:30** 2799
Be miserable and mourn and **w**; let **Jas 4:9** 2799
Come now, you rich, **w** and howl for **Jas 5:1** 2799
Then I *began* to **w** greatly because **Rv 5:4** 2799
will **w** and lament over her when they **Rv 18:9** 2799
"And the merchants of the earth **w** **Rv 18:11** 2799

WEEPING
Now Moses heard the people **w** **Nu 11:10** 1058
while they were **w** at the doorway of **Nu 25:6** 1058
then the days of **w** *and* mourning **Dt 34:8** 1065
so that your eyes will fail *from* **w** **1Sa 2:33**
But her husband went with her, **w** as **2Sa 3:16** 1058
While all the country was **w** with a **2Sa 15:23** 1058
each covered his head and went up **w** **2Sa 15:30** 1058
the king is **w** and mourns for Absalom." **2Sa 19:1** 1058
shout of joy from the sound of the **w** **Ezr 3:13** 1065
w and prostrating himself before **Ezr 10:1** 1058
For all the people were **w** when they **Ne 8:9** 1058
w and wailing; and many lay on **Es 4:3** 1065
"My face is flushed from **w**, **Jb 16:16** 1065
LORD has heard the voice of my **w**. **Ps 6:8** 1065
W may last for the night, **Ps 30:5** 1065
bread And mingled my drink with **w** **Ps 102:9** 1065
He who goes to and fro **w**, carrying **Ps 126:6** 1058
For they go up the ascent of Luhith **w**; **Is 15:5** 1065
GOD of hosts called *you* to **w**, **Is 22:12** 1065
longer be heard in her The voice of **w** **Is 65:19** 1065
The **w** *and* the supplications of **Jer 3:21** 1065
"For the mountains I will take up a **w** **Jer 9:10** 1065
"With **w** they will come, And by **Jer 31:9** 1065
Lamentation *and* bitter **w**. Rachel **Jer 31:15** 1065
Rachel is **w** for her children; She **Jer 31:15** 1065
"Restrain your voice from **w** And **Jer 31:16** 1065
w as he went; and as he met them, **Jer 41:6** 1058
They will ascend with continual **w**; **Jer 48:5** 1065
"More than the **w** for Jazer I will **Jer 48:32** 1065
they will go along **w** as they go, **Jer 50:4** 1058
were sitting there **w** for Tammuz. **Ezk 8:14** 1058
And with fasting, **w** and mourning; **Jl 2:12** 1065
bitterly over Him like the bitter **w** **Zch 12:10** 4843
with **w** and with groaning, because He **Mal 2:13** 1065
"A VOICE WAS HEARD IN RAMAH, **W** **Mt 2:18** 2805
RACHEL **W** FOR HER CHILDREN; **Mt 2:18** 2805
in that place there will be **w** **Mt 8:12** 2805
in that place there will be **w** **Mt 13:42** 2805
in that place there will be **w** **Mt 13:50** 2805
in that place there will be **w** **Mt 22:13** 2805
in that place there will be **w** **Mt 24:51** 2805
in that place there will be **w** **Mt 25:30** 2805
and *people* loudly **w** and wailing. **Mk 5:38** 2799
while they were mourning and **w**. **Mk 16:10** 2799
w, she began to wet His feet with **Lk 7:38** 2799
Now they were all **w** and lamenting for **Lk 8:52** 2799
"Stop **w**, for she has not died, but **Lk 8:52** 2799
"In that place there will be **w** **Lk 13:28** 2805
stop **w** for Me, but weep for **Lk 23:28** 2799
When Jesus therefore saw her **w**, **Jn 11:33** 2799
the Jews who came with her *also* **w**, **Jn 11:33** 2799
Mary was standing outside the tomb **w**; **Jn 20:11** 2799
why are you **w**?" She said to them, **Jn 20:13** 2799
why are you **w**? Whom are you seeking?" **Jn 20:15** 2799
w and showing all the tunics **Ac 9:39** 2799
w and breaking my heart? For I am **Ac 21:13** 2799
and now tell you even **w**, *that they* **Php 3:18** 2799
"Stop **w**; behold, the Lion that is **Rv 5:5** 2799
her torment, **w** and mourning, **Rv 18:15** 2799
w and mourning, saying, 'Woe, woe, **Rv 18:19** 2799

WEEPS
my scoffers; My eye **w** to God. **Jb 16:20** 1811
My soul **w** because of grief; **Ps 119:28** 1811
She **w** bitterly in the night And her **La 1:2** 1058

WEIGH
and he found it to **w** a talent of gold, **1Ch 20:2** 4948
"Watch and keep *them* until you **w** **Ezr 8:29** 8254
Let Him **w** me with accurate scales, **Jb 31:6** 8254
Nor should my pressure **w** heavily on **Jb 33:7** 3513
As a heavy burden they **w** too much for **Ps 38:4** 3513
On earth you **w** out the violence of **Ps 58:2** 6424
who lavish gold from the purse And **w** **Is 46:6** 8254
All who **w** out silver will be cut off. **Zph 1:11** 5187
For you **w** men down with burdens hard **Lk 11:46** 5412

WEIGHED
and Abraham **w** out for Ephron **Gn 23:16** 8254
And with Him actions are **w**. **1Sa 2:3** 8505
was clothed with scale-armor which **w** **1Sa 17:5** 4948
and the head of his spear **w** six **1Sa 17:7**
he **w** the hair of his head at 200 shekels **2Sa 14:26** 8254
They gave the money which was **w** out **2Ki 12:11** 8505
and more bronze than could be **w**; **1Ch 22:3** 4948
and I **w** out to them the silver, **Ezr 8:25** 8254
Thus I **w** into their hands 650 talents of **Ezr 8:26** 8254
and the Levites accepted the **w** out **Ezr 8:30** 4948
and the gold and the utensils were **w** **Ezr 8:33** 8254
Everything *was* numbered and **w**, **Ezr 8:34** 4948
"Oh that my grief were actually **w** **Jb 6:2** 8254
Nor can silver be **w** as its price. **Jb 28:15** 8254
Alas, sinful nation, People **w** down **Is 1:4** 3515
And **w** the mountains in a balance **Is 40:12** 8254
and I **w** out the silver for him, **Jer 32:9** 8254
and **w** out the silver on the scales. **Jer 32:10** 8254
The precious sons of Zion, **W** against **La 4:2** 5537
"'TEKEL'—you have been **w** on **Da 5:27** 8625a
So they **w** out thirty *shekels* of **Zch 11:12** 8254
And they **w** out thirty pieces of **Mt 26:15** 2476
they **w** anchor and *began* sailing **Ac 27:13** 142
and captivate weak women **w** **2Tm 3:6** 4987

WEIGHING
the man took a gold ring **w** a **Gn 24:22** 4948
and two bracelets for her wrists **w** **Gn 24:22** 4948
each silver dish **w** one hundred **Nu 7:85**
w ten *shekels* apiece, **Nu 7:86**
Then take scales for **w** and divide **Ezk 5:1** 4948

WEIGHS
Anxiety in a man's heart **w** it down, **Pr 12:25** 7812
But the LORD **w** the motives. **Pr 16:2** 8505
But the LORD **w** the hearts. **Pr 21:2** 8505
Does He not consider *it* who **w** **Pr 24:12** 8505
Where is he who **w**? Where is he who **Is 33:18** 8254

WEIGHT
in measurement of **w**, or capacity. **Lv 19:35** 4948
was one silver dish whose **w** *was* **Nu 7:13** 4948
his offering one silver dish whose **w** **Nu 7:19** 4948
was one silver dish whose **w** *was* **Nu 7:25** 4948
was one silver dish whose **w** *was* **Nu 7:31** 4948
was one silver dish whose **w** *was* **Nu 7:37** 4948
was one silver dish whose **w** *was* **Nu 7:43** 4948
was one silver dish whose **w** *was* **Nu 7:49** 4948
was one silver dish whose **w** *was* **Nu 7:55** 4948
was one silver dish whose **w** *was* **Nu 7:61** 4948

was one silver dish whose w *was* Nu 7:67 4948
was one silver dish whose w *was* Nu 7:73 4948
was one silver dish whose w *was* Nu 7:79 4948
"You shall have a full and just w; Dt 25:15 68
and a bar of gold fifty shekels in w, Jos 7:21 4948
The w of the gold earrings that he Jg 8:26 4948
and its w *was* a talent of gold, 2Sa 12:30 4948
his head at 200 shekels by the king's w. 2Sa 14:26 68
the w of whose spear was three 2Sa 21:16 4948
hundred *shekels* of bronze in w, 2Sa 21:16 4948
the w of the bronze could not be 1Ki 7:47 4948
Now the w of gold which came in to 1Ki 10:14 4948
of all these vessels was beyond w. 2Ki 25:16 4948
gave Ornan 600 shekels of gold by w for 1Ch 21:25 4948
and bronze and iron beyond w, for 1Ch 22:14 4948
for the golden *utensils,* the w 1Ch 28:14 4948
the w *of silver* for all utensils 1Ch 28:14 4948
and the w *of gold* for the golden 1Ch 28:15 4948
with the w of each lampstand and its 1Ch 28:15 4948
and *the* w *of silver* for 1Ch 28:15 4948
with the w of each lampstand and its 1Ch 28:15 4948
and the gold by w for the tables of 1Ch 28:16 4948
and for the golden bowls with the w 1Ch 28:17 4948
and for the silver bowls with the w 1Ch 28:17 4948
altar of incense refined gold by w; 1Ch 28:18 4948
The w of the nails was fifty shekels 2Ch 3:9 4948
for the w of the bronze could not be 2Ch 4:18 4948
Now the w of gold which came to 2Ch 9:13 4948
and all the w was recorded at that Ezr 8:34 4948
"When He imparted w to the wind Jb 28:25 4948
But a just w is His delight. Pr 11:1 68
of all these vessels was beyond w. Jer 52:20 4948
shall be twenty shekels a day by w; Ezk 4:10 4946
and they will eat bread by w and with Ezk 4:16 4948
of the ephah and cast the lead w on Zch 5:8 68
about a hundred pounds w. Jn 19:39
is producing for us an eternal w of 2Co 4:17 *922*

WEIGHTED
"Behold, I am w down beneath you Am 2:13 5781
As a wagon is w down when filled Am 2:13 5781
so that your hearts will not be w Lk 21:34 *916*

WEIGHTIER
so a little foolishness is w than Ec 10:1 3368
and have neglected the w provisions Mt 23:23 *926*

WEIGHTS
just w, a just ephah, and a just Lv 19:36 68
not have in your bag differing w, Dt 25:13 68
All the w of the bag are His Pr 16:11 68
Differing w and differing measures, Pr 20:10 68
Differing w are an abomination to Pr 20:23 68
scales And a bag of deceptive w? Mi 6:11 68

WEIGHTY
A stone is heavy and the sand w, Pr 27:3 5192
For they say, "His letters are w 2Co 10:10 *926*

WELCOME
no prophet is w in his hometown. Lk 4:24 *1184*
from the management people will w me Lk 16:4 *1209*
fears Him and does what is right is w Ac 10:35 *1184*
him and wrote to the disciples to w Ac 18:27 *588*
And I will w you. 2Co 6:17 *1523*
w him); Col 4:10 *1209*

WELCOMED
And as Jesus returned, the people w Lk 8:40 *588*
and a woman named Martha w Him into Lk 10:38 *5264*
and Jason has w them, and they all Ac 17:7 *5264*
who w us and entertained us Ac 28:7 *324*
but having seen them and having w Heb 11:13 *782*
after she had w the spies in peace. Heb 11:31 *1209*

WELCOMING
and w them, He *began* speaking to Lk 9:11 *588*
in his own rented quarters and was w Ac 28:30 *588*

WELFARE
"Go now and see about the w of your Gn 37:14 7965
welfare of your brothers and the w of Gn 37:14 7965
Then he asked them about their w, Gn 43:27 7965
and they asked each other of their w Ex 18:7 7965
and asked him of his w. Jg 18:15 7965
and look into the w of your brothers, 1Sa 17:18 7965
David asked concerning the w of Joab 2Sa 11:7 7965
that someone had come to seek the w Ne 2:10 2899b
people and one who spoke for the w of Es 10:3 7965
"Lo, for *my own* w I had great Is 38:17 7965
"Do not pray for the w of this Jer 14:11 2899b
will turn aside to ask about your w? Jer 15:5 7965
'Seek the w of the city where I have Jer 29:7 7965
for in its w you will have welfare.' Jer 29:7 7965
for in its welfare you will have w.' Jer 29:7 7965
'plans for w and not for calamity Jer 29:11 7965
genuinely be concerned for your w. Php 2:20 *3588*

WELL
"If you do w, will not *your* Gn 4:7 3190
And if you do not do w, sin is Gn 4:7 3190
you are my sister so that it may go w Gn 12:13 3190
Therefore he treated Abram w for her Gn 12:16 3190
that it was w watered everywhere Gn 13:10 4945b
Therefore the w was called Gn 16:14 875
God opened her eyes and she saw a w Gn 21:19 875
to Abimelech because of the w of Gn 21:25 875
that I dug this w." Gn 21:30 875
kneel down outside the city by the w Gn 24:11 875
and ran back to the w to draw, Gn 24:20 875
dug in the valley and found there a w Gn 26:19 875
So he named the w Esek, because they Gn 26:20 875
Then they dug another w, and they Gn 26:21 875
away from there and dug another w, Gn 26:22 875
and there Isaac's servants dug a w. Gn 26:25 875
came in and told him about the w Gn 26:32 875
He looked, and saw a w in the field, Gn 29:2 875
for from that w they watered Gn 29:2 875
Now the stone on the mouth of the w Gn 29:2 875
the stone from the mouth of the w Gn 29:3 875
in its place on the mouth of the w. Gn 29:3 875
And he said to them, "Is it w with Gn 29:6 7965
"It is w, and here is Rachel his Gn 29:6 7965
the stone from the mouth of the w; Gn 29:8 875
the stone from the mouth of the w Gn 29:10 875
"Only keep me in mind when it goes w Gn 40:14 3190
we as w as you and our little ones. Gn 43:8 1571
"Is your old father w, of whom you Gn 43:27 7965
"Your servant our father is w; he Gn 43:28 7965
God has let me see your children as w." Gn 48:11 1571
and he sat down by a w. Ex 2:15 875
the boils were on the magicians as w Ex 9:11
all the firstborn of the cattle as w. Ex 11:5
as w as your stranger, may refresh Ex 23:12
as w as his sons and his sons' Ex 29:21
the woven garments as w, Ex 31:10
ministering in the holy place as w as Ex 39:1
When it is w stirred, you shall Lv 6:21
and cakes *of* w stirred fine flour Lv 7:12
in the blood of the slain bird as w Lv 14:51
you shall make a proclamation as w; Lv 23:21
The alien as w as the native, when Lv 24:16
it shall be for the stranger as w as Lv 24:22
'I will lay waste your cities as w Lv 26:31
and My covenant with Abraham as w, Lv 26:42 637
Has He not spoken through us as w?" Nu 12:2 1571
we will not even drink water from a w. Nu 20:17 875
that is the w where the LORD said Nu 21:16 875
O w! Sing to it! Nu 21:17 875
"The w, which the leaders sank, Nu 21:18 875
that it may go w with you and with Dt 4:40 3190
and your female servant may rest as w Dt 5:14
may be prolonged and that it may go w Dt 5:16 3190
They have done w in all that they Dt 5:28 3190
that it may be w with them and with Dt 5:29 3190
you may live and that it may be w Dt 5:33 2895
that it may be w with you and that Dt 6:3 3190
that it may be w with you and that Dt 6:18 3190
you shall w remember what the LORD Dt 7:18 2142
so that it may be w with you and your Dt 12:25 3190
so that it may be w with you and your Dt 12:28 3190
since he fares w with you; Dt 15:16 2895
'They have spoken w. Dt 18:17 3190
that it may go w with you. Dt 19:13 2895
in order that it may be w with you Dt 22:7 3190
the stranger as w as the native. Jos 8:33
leave no sustenance in Israel as w as Jg 6:4
as w as everyone who kneels to drink." Jg 7:5
and if you have dealt w with Jg 9:16 2899b
that it may be w with you? Ru 3:1 3190
grow dim *and* he could not see w), 1Sa 3:2
Then Saul said to his servant, "W 1Sa 9:10 2896a
and you will be w." 1Sa 16:16 2895
for me now a man who can play w 1Sa 16:17 3190
and Saul would be refreshed and be w, 1Sa 16:23 2895
Then Jonathan spoke w of David to 1Sa 19:4 2896a
Ramah and came as far as the large w 1Sa 19:22 953a
"Your father knows w that I have 1Sa 20:3 3045
for you have dealt w with me, while 1Sa 24:17 2899b
When the LORD deals w with my 1Sa 25:31 3190
David said to Achish, "Very w, you 1Sa 28:2 3651
"Very w, I will make you my 1Sa 28:2 3651
and they brought him back from the w 2Sa 3:26 953a
for the sword devours one as w as 2Sa 11:25
who had a w in his courtyard, 2Sa 17:18 875
that they came up out of the w 2Sa 17:21 875
"All is w." And he prostrated 2Sa 18:28 7965
The king said, "Is it w with 2Sa 18:29 7965
"Is it w with the young man Absalom?" 2Sa 18:32 7965
Joab said to Amasa, "Is it w with 2Sa 20:9 7965
give me water to drink from the w of 2Sa 23:15 877
and drew water from the w of 2Sa 23:16 877
and had a name as w as the three. 2Sa 23:18
and had a name as w as the three 2Sa 23:22
Bathsheba said, "Very w; I will 1Ki 2:18 2896a
you did w that it was in your heart. 1Ki 8:18 2895
"*It will be* w." 2Ki 4:23 7965
'Is it w with you? Is it well with 2Ki 4:26 7965
Is it w with your husband? 2Ki 4:26 7965
Is it w with the child?' " 2Ki 4:26 7965
she answered, "It is w." 2Ki 4:26 7965
and said, "Is all w?" 2Ki 5:21 7965
He said, "All is w. My master has 2Ki 5:22 7965
"Is all w? Why did this mad fellow 2Ki 9:11 7965
"You know *very* w the man and his 2Ki 9:11
"Is it w, Zimri, your master's 2Ki 9:31 7965
as w as the chariots and horses and a 2Ki 10:2
"Because you have done w in 2Ki 10:30 2895
and it will be w with you." 2Ki 25:24 3190
give me water to drink from the w of 1Ch 11:17 953a
Philistines and drew water from the w 1Ch 11:18 953a
and he had a name as w as the thirty. 1Ch 11:20
and had a name as w as the three 1Ch 11:24
head of fathers' *households* as w 1Ch 24:31 5980
the small as w as the great, 1Ch 25:8
the teacher *as* w as the pupil. 1Ch 25:8
you did w that it was in your heart. 2Ch 6:8 2895
because he had done w in Israel 2Ch 24:16 2899b
as w as in Ephraim and Manasseh, 2Ch 31:1
as w as the priests who were enrolled 2Ch 31:17
as w as all the altars which he had 2Ch 33:15
in the direction of the Dragon's W Ne 2:13 5886
as w as wine, grapes, figs and all Ne 13:15 637
according to their language as w as Es 8:9
"But I have intelligence as w as you; Jb 12:3 1571
"Will it be w when He examines you? Jb 13:9 2896a
has He acknowledged transgression w, Jb 35:15 3966
which I made as w as you; He eats Jb 40:15 5973
men praise you when you do w for Ps 49:18 3190
It is w mixed, and He pours out of Ps 75:8 4392
So they ate and were w filled, Ps 78:29 3966
Then those who sing as w as those who Ps 87:7
It is w with the man who is gracious Ps 112:5 2896a
You have dealt w with Your servant, Ps 119:65 2896b
You will be happy and it will be w Ps 128:2 2895
And my soul knows it very w. Ps 139:14 3966
And fresh water from your own w. Pr 5:15 875
When it goes w with the righteous, Pr 11:10 2898
And an adulterous woman is a narrow w. Pr 23:27 875
a trampled spring and a polluted w Pr 25:26 4726
Know w the condition of your flocks, Pr 27:23 3045
She looks w to the ways of her Pr 31:27 6822
God has made the one as w as Ec 7:14 5980
still I know that it will be w for Ec 8:12 2896a
But it will not be w for the evil man Ec 8:13 2896a
the pitcher by the w is shattered Ec 12:6 4002
"*You are* a garden spring, A w SS 4:15 875
the righteous that *it will go* w Is 3:10 2895
will try the patience of my God as w? Is 7:13 1571
the vines of Sibmah *as* w; Is 16:8
W then, where are your wise men? Is 19:12 645
And consider and gain insight as w, Is 41:20 3164a
"You have seen w, for I am watching Jer 1:12 3190
"How w you prepare your way To seek Jer 2:33 3190
"As a w keeps its waters fresh, So Jer 6:7 953a
that it may be w with you.' Jer 7:23 3190
'Do we not very w know that every Jer 13:12 3045
as w as in all the gates of Jerusalem; Jer 17:19
Then it was w with him. Jer 22:15 2895
Then it was w. Is not that what it Jer 22:16 2895
And Jehudi read it to the king as w Jer 36:21
that it may go w with you and you may Jer 38:20 3190
that it may go w with you. Jer 40:9 3190
and said to him, "Are you w aware Jer 40:14 3045
so that it may go w with us when we Jer 42:6 3190
we had plenty of food and were w Jer 44:17 2896a
they and the sons of Judah as w; Jer 50:4 3164a
And the sons of Judah as w; And all Jer 50:33 3164a
the cup will come around to you as w, La 4:21 1571
the prince in Jerusalem as w as all Ezk 12:10
"The days draw near as w as Ezk 12:23
the soul of the father as w as Ezk 18:4
as w as every dry tree; the blazing Ezk 20:47
Boil the flesh w And mix in Ezk 24:10 8552
who has a beautiful voice and plays w Ezk 33:32 3190
opposite the gate on the north as w Ezk 40:23
as w as *on* the wall of the nave. Ezk 41:20
mark w, see with your eyes and hear Ezk 44:5 3820
and mark w the entrance of the house, Ezk 44:5 3820
very w. But if you do not Da 3:15
her in and the one who sired her as w Da 11:6
as w as many animals?" Jon 4:11
Concerning evil, both hands do it w. Mi 7:3 3190
it will be in summer as w as in Zch 14:8
I will get w." Mt 9:21 *4982*
your faith has made you w." At once Mt 9:22 *4982*
At once the woman was made w. Mt 9:22 *4982*
"His master said to him, 'W done, Mt 25:21 *2095*
"His master said to him, 'W done, Mt 25:23 *2095*
wine is lost and the skins *as* w; Mk 2:22
so that she will get w and live." Mk 5:23 *4982*
touch His garments, I will get w." Mk 5:28
your faith has made you w; go in Mk 5:34 *4982*
for His name had become w known; Mk 6:14 *5318*
as w *as* deceit, sensuality, Mk 7:22
"He has done all things w; He makes Mk 7:37 *2573*
He ordered these to be served as w. Mk 8:7 *2532*
your faith has made you w." Mk 10:52 *4982*
that He had answered them w, asked Mk 12:28 *2573*
it seemed fitting for me as w, Lk 1:3 *2532*
And all were speaking w of Him, Lk 4:22 *3140*
do here in your hometown as w.' " Lk 4:23 *2532*
"*It is* not those who are w who Lk 5:31 *5198*
"Woe *to you* when all men speak w Lk 6:26 *2573*
because it had been w built. Lk 6:48 *2573*
was demon-possessed had been made w. Lk 8:36 *4982*
your faith has made you w; go in Lk 8:48 *4982*
and she will be made w." Lk 8:50 *4982*
"Woe to you lawyers as w! For you Lk 11:46 *2532*
or to everyone *else* as w?" Lk 12:41 *2532*
have a son or an ox fall into a w, Lk 14:5 *5421*
your faith has made you w." Lk 17:19 *4982*
your faith has made you w." Lk 18:42 *4982*
"And he said to him, 'W done, Lk 19:17 *1065*
You have spoken w." Lk 20:39 *2573*
and Jacob's w was there. So Jesus, Jn 4:6 *4077*
was sitting thus by the w. It was Jn 4:6 *4077*
have nothing to draw with and the w Jn 4:11 *5421*
who gave us the w, and drank of it Jn 4:12 *5421*
will give him will become in him a w Jn 4:14 *4077*
stepped in was made w from whatever Jn 5:4 *5199*
"Do you wish to get w?" Jn 5:6 *5199*
Immediately the man became w, Jn 5:9 *5199*
"He who made me w was the one who Jn 5:11 *5199*
you have become w; do not sin Jn 5:14 *5199*
that it was Jesus who had made him w. Jn 5:15 *5199*
Me because I made an entire man w on Jn 7:23 *5199*
"W, here is an amazing thing, that Jn 9:30 *1063*
seen and hated Me and My Father as w. Jn 15:24 *2532*
as to how this man has been made w, Ac 4:9 *4982*
and they will carry you out *as* w." Ac 5:9
"Give this authority to me as w, so Ac 8:19 *2532*
And he said, "W, how could I, Ac 8:31 *1063*
Philip as w as the eunuch, and he Ac 8:38 *5037*

a righteous and God-fearing man w Ac 10:22 3140
"W then, God has granted to Ac 11:18 686
seen that he had faith to be made w, Ac 14:9 4982
you will do w. Farewell." Ac 15:29 2095
and he was w spoken of by Ac 16:2 3140
they came there as w, agitating Ac 17:13 2546
When we had heard this, we as w as Ac 21:12 5037
and w spoken of by all the Jews Ac 22:12 3140
as you also very w know. Ac 25:10 2573
and of myself as w. Ro 16:2 846
he will do w. 1Co 7:37 2573
daughter in marriage does w, 1Co 7:38 2573
For you are giving thanks w enough, 1Co 14:17 2573
in you this gracious work as w. 2Co 8:6 2532
Therefore I am w content with 2Co 12:10 2106
the past and to all the rest *as* w, 2Co 13:2
God shows no partiality)—w, Ga 2:6 1063
You were running w; who hindered you Ga 5:7 2573
SO THAT IT MAY BE W WITH YOU, Eph 6:3 2095
the cause of Christ has become w Php 1:13 5318
Nevertheless, you have done w to Php 4:14 2573
praying at the same time for us as w, Col 4:3 2532
For you yourselves know full w that 1Th 5:2 199
you who are afflicted and to us as w 2Th 1:7
one who manages his own household w, 1Tm 3:4 2573
For those who have served w as 1Tm 3:13 2573
Prescribe these things as w, so that 1Tm 5:7 2532
The elders who rule w are to be 1Tm 5:17 2573
I am sure that *it is* in you as w. 2Tm 1:5 2532
on that day—and you know very w 2Tm 1:18 957
owe to me even your own self as w). Phm 1:19 4359
you are doing w. Jas 2:8 2573
But someone may w say, "You Jas 2:18
You do w; the demons also believe, Jas 2:19 2573
able to bridle the whole body as w. Jas 3:2 2532
we direct their entire body as w. Jas 3:3 2532
to which you do w to pay attention as 2Pe 1:19 2573
You will do w to send them on their 3Jn 1:6 2573

WELL-BEING
Causing w and creating calamity; Is 45:7 7965
Then your w would have been like a Is 48:18 7965
The chastening for our w *fell* Is 53:5 7965
And the w of your sons will be Is 54:13 7965
for this man is not seeking the w of Jer 38:4 7965

WELL-BELOVED
Let me sing now for my w Is 5:1 3039
My w had a vineyard on a fertile hill. Is 5:1 3039

WELL-CONCEIVED
"We are ready with a w plot"; Ps 64:6 2664

WELL-DRIVEN
collections are like w nails; Ec 12:11 5193

WELL-FED
"They were w lusty horses, Each Jer 5:8 2109
"Woe to you who are w now, Lk 6:25 1705a

WELL-FORTIFIED
siege ramp and capture a w city; Da 11:15 4013

WELL-HEWN
you have built houses of w stone, Am 5:11 1496

WELL-KNOWN
as unknown yet w, as dying yet 2Co 6:9 1921

WELL-MIXED
is baked in the pan or what is w, 1Ch 23:29 7246

WELL-OFF
For we were w in Egypt." Nu 11:18 2895

WELL-PLEASED
My beloved Son, in whom I am w." Mt 3:17 2106
MY BELOVED IN WHOM MY SOUL is W; Mt 12:18 2106
My beloved Son, with whom I am w; Mt 17:5 2106
My beloved Son, in You I am w." Mk 1:11 2106
My beloved Son, in You I am w." Lk 3:22 2106
God was w through the foolishness 1Co 1:21 2106
with most of them God was not w; 1Co 10:5 2106
we were w to impart to you not 1Th 2:8 2106
My beloved Son with whom I am w" 2Pe 1:17 2106

WELL-PLEASING
for this way was w in Your sight. Mt 11:26 2107
for this way was w in Your sight. Lk 10:21 2107
an acceptable sacrifice, w to God. Php 4:18 2101
things, for this is w to the Lord. Col 3:20 2101
to be w, not argumentative, Ti 2:9 2101

WELL'S
and spread it over the w mouth and 2Sa 17:19 875

WELLS
Now all the w which his father's Gn 26:15 875
Isaac dug again the w of water Gn 26:18 875
we will not drink water from w. Nu 21:22 875
"I dug w and drank foreign 2Ki 19:24
'I dug w and drank waters, Is 37:25

WELL-SET
Instead of w hair, a plucked-out Is 3:24 4748

WELL-WATERED
nor their w mighty ones stand Ezk 31:14 8354
and all the w trees of Eden, the Ezk 31:16 8354

WELTS
sound in it, *Only* bruises, w and Is 1:6 2250

WENT
Then Cain w out from the presence Gn 4:16 3318
w into the ark to Noah by twos, Gn 7:9 935
So they w into the ark to Noah, by Gn 7:15 935
So Noah w out, and his sons and Gn 8:18 3318
w out by their families from the ark Gn 8:19 3318
that land he w forth into Assyria, Gn 10:11 3318
and they w out together from Ur of Gn 11:31 3318
and they w as far as Haran, and Gn 11:31 935
So Abram w forth as the LORD had Gn 12:4 1980
and Lot w with him. Gn 12:4 1980
so Abram w down to Egypt to Gn 12:10 3381
So Abram w up from Egypt to the Gn 13:1 5927
He w on his journeys from the Gn 13:3 1980
Now Lot, who w with Abram, also Gn 13:5 1980
and w in pursuit as far as Dan. Gn 14:14 7291
the king of Sodom w out to meet Gn 14:17 3318
share of the men who w with me, Gn 14:24 1980
He w in to Hagar, and she Gn 16:4 935
with him, God w up from Abraham. Gn 17:22 5927
from there and w toward Sodom, Gn 18:22 1980
Lot w out to them at the doorway, Gn 19:6 3318
Lot w out and spoke to his Gn 19:14 3318
arose early in the morning *and* w Gn 19:27
Lot w up from Zoar, and stayed Gn 19:30 5927
the firstborn w in and lay with her Gn 19:33 935
she w and sat down opposite him, Gn 21:16 1980
and she w and filled the skin with Gn 21:19 1980
and arose and w to the place of Gn 22:3 1980
and Abraham w and took the ram and Gn 22:13 1980
arose and w together to Beersheba; Gn 22:19 1980
and Abraham w in to mourn for Gn 23:2 935
who w in at the gate of his city, Gn 23:10 935
who w in at the gate of his city. Gn 23:18 935
he arose and w to Mesopotamia, Gn 24:10 1980
and she w down to the spring and Gn 24:16 3381
man said to me," he w to the man; Gn 24:30 935
and w down to the spring and drew, Gn 24:45 3381
Isaac w out to meditate in the Gn 24:63 3318
So she w to inquire of the LORD. Gn 25:22 1980
drank, and rose and w on his way. Gn 25:34 1980
So Isaac w to Gerar, to Abimelech Gn 26:1 1980
he w up from there to Beersheba. Gn 26:23 5927
So when Esau w to the field to Gn 27:5 1980
So he w and got *them*, and brought Gn 27:14 1980
and he w to Paddan-aram to Laban, Gn 28:5 1980
and Esau w to Ishmael, and Gn 28:9 1980
from Beersheba and w toward Haran. Gn 28:10 1980
Then Jacob w on his journey, and Gn 29:1 5375
mother's brother, Jacob w up Gn 29:10 5066
and *Jacob* w in to her. Gn 29:23 935
So *Jacob* w in to Rachel also, and Gn 29:30 935
as a wife, and Jacob w in to her. Gn 30:4 935
Reuben w and found mandrakes Gn 30:14 1980
Leah w out to meet him and said, Gn 30:16 3318
So Laban w into Jacob's tent and Gn 31:33 935
Then he w out of Leah's tent and Gn 31:33 3318
Now as Jacob w on his way, the Gn 32:1 1980
w out to visit the daughters of Gn 34:1 3318
Hamor the father of Shechem w out Gn 34:6 3318
All who w out of the gate of Gn 34:24 3318
who w out of the gate of his city. Gn 34:24 3318
from Shechem's house, and w forth. Gn 34:26 3318
Then God w up from him in the Gn 35:13 5927
that Reuben w and lay with Bilhah Gn 35:22 1980
and w to *another* land away from Gn 36:6 1980
brothers w to pasture their father's Gn 37:12 1980
So Joseph w after his brothers and Gn 37:17 1980
and he took her and w in to her. Gn 38:2 935
when he w in to his brother's wife, Gn 38:9 935
So Tamar w and lived in her Gn 38:11 1980
Judah w up to his sheepshearers at Gn 38:12 5927
gave *them* to her and w in to her, Gn 38:18 935
w into the house to do his work, Gn 39:11 935
her hand and fled, and w outside. Gn 39:12 3318
me and fled and w outside." Gn 39:15 3318
And Joseph w forth over the land Gn 41:45 3318
And Joseph w out from the presence Gn 41:46 3318
w through all the land of Egypt. Gn 41:46 5674a
ten brothers of Joseph w down to Gn 42:3 3381
then they arose and w down to Gn 43:15 3381
we w up to your servant my father, Gn 44:24 5927
and the one w out from me, and I Gn 44:28 3318
Then they w up from Egypt, and Gn 45:25 5927
and his sons, who w to Egypt: Gn 46:8 935
Joseph prepared his chariot and w Gn 46:29 5927
Then Joseph w in and told Pharaoh, Gn 47:1 935
and w out from his presence. Gn 47:10 3318
you w up to your father's bed; Gn 49:4 5927
he w up to my couch. Gn 49:4 5927
So Joseph w up to bury his father, Gn 50:7 5927
and with him w up all the servants Gn 50:7 5927
There also w up with him both Gn 50:9 5927
a man from the house of Levi w and Ex 2:1 1980
w and called the child's mother. Ex 2:8 1980
that he w out to his brethren and Ex 2:11 3318
He w out the next day, and Ex 2:13 3318
So he w and met him at the Ex 4:27 1980
Then Moses and Aaron w and Ex 4:29 1980
foremen w out and spoke to Ex 5:10 3318
Then Pharaoh turned and w into his Ex 7:23 935
and Aaron w out from Pharaoh, Ex 8:12 3318
So Moses w out from Pharaoh and Ex 8:30 3318
So Moses w out of the city from Ex 9:33 3318
Moses and Aaron w to Pharaoh Ex 10:3 935
he turned and w out from Pharaoh. Ex 10:6 3318
He w out from Pharaoh and made Ex 10:18 3318
w out from Pharaoh in hot anger. Ex 11:8 3318
the sons of Israel w and did *so;* Ex 12:28 1980
multitude also w up with them, Ex 12:38 5927
LORD w out from the land of Egypt. Ex 12:41 3318
day in which you w out from Egypt, Ex 13:3 3318
and the sons of Israel w up in Ex 13:18 5927
Israel, moved and w behind them; Ex 14:19 1980
The sons of Israel w through Ex 14:22 935
his chariots and his horsemen w in Ex 14:23 935
They w down into the depths like a Ex 15:5 3381
and his horsemen w into the sea, Ex 15:19 935
and all the women w out after her Ex 15:20 3318
and they w out into the wilderness Ex 15:22 3318
and they w three days in the Ex 15:22 1980
some of the people w out to gather, Ex 16:27 3318
Hur w up to the top of the hill. Ex 17:10 5927
w out to meet his father-in-law, Ex 18:7 3318
welfare and w into the tent. Ex 18:7 935
he w his way into his own land. Ex 18:27 1980
Moses w up to God, and the Ex 19:3 5927
So Moses w down from the mountain Ex 19:14 3381
of the mountain, and Moses w up. Ex 19:20 5927
So Moses w down to the people and Ex 19:25 3381
Then Moses w up with Aaron, Nadab Ex 24:9 5927
Moses w up to the mountain of God. Ex 24:13 5927
Then Moses w up to the mountain, Ex 24:15 5927
cloud as he w up to the mountain; Ex 24:18 5927
Then Moses turned and w down from Ex 32:15 3381
sad word, they w into mourning, Ex 33:4 56
whenever Moses w out to the tent, Ex 33:8 3318
morning and w up to Mount Sinai, Ex 34:4 5927
But whenever Moses w in before the Ex 34:34 935
until he w in to speak with Him. Ex 34:35 935
Aaron w into the tent of meeting. Lv 9:23 935
on when he w into the holy place, Lv 16:23 935
w out among the sons of Israel; Lv 24:10 3318
Now when Moses w into the tent of Nu 7:89 935
Then after that the Levites w in Nu 8:22 935
So Moses w out and told the people Nu 11:24 3318
w forth a wind from the LORD and Nu 11:31 5265
So they w up and spied out the Nu 13:21 5927
"We w in to the land where you Nu 13:27 935
men who w to spy out the land. Nu 14:38 1980
they rose up early and w up to the Nu 14:40 5927
But they w up heedlessly to the Nu 14:44 5927
arose and w to Dathan and Abiram, Nu 16:25 1980
to them w down alive to Sheol; Nu 16:33 3381
Moses w into the tent of the testimony Nu 17:8 935
that our fathers w down to Egypt, Nu 20:15 3381
and they w up to Mount Hor in the Nu 20:27 5927
Sihon gathered all his people and w Nu 21:23 3318
"For a fire w forth from Heshbon, Nu 21:28 3318
and w up by the way of Bashan, Nu 21:33 5927
Og the king of Bashan w out with Nu 21:33 3318
of Moab arose and w to Balak and Nu 22:14 1980
and w with the leaders of Moab. Nu 22:21 1980
from the way and w into the field; Nu 22:23 1980
The angel of the LORD w further, Nu 22:26 5674a
So Balaam w along with the leaders Nu 22:35 1980
he w out to meet him at the city Nu 22:36 3318
And Balaam w with Balak, and they Nu 22:39 1980
So he w to a bare hill. Nu 23:3 1980
place, and Balak also w his way. Nu 24:25 1980
and he w after the man of Israel Nu 25:8 935
the congregation w out to meet them Nu 31:13 3318
booty between the warriors who w out Nu 31:27 3318
men of war who w out to battle, Nu 31:28 3318
portion of those who w out to war, Nu 31:36 3318
"For when they w up to the valley Nu 32:9 5927
Manasseh w to Gilead and took it, Nu 32:39 1980
of Manasseh w and took its towns, Nu 32:41 1980
Nobah w and took Kenath and Nu 32:42 1980
and they w three days' journey in Nu 33:8 1980
Then Aaron the priest w up to Nu 33:38 5927
and w through all that great and Dt 1:19 1980
and w up into the hill country, Dt 1:24 5927
and w up into the hill country. Dt 1:43 5927
and w up the road to Bashan, Dt 3:1 5927
"When I w up to the mountain to Dt 9:9 5927
and w up on the mountain with the Dt 10:3 5927
"Your fathers w down to Egypt Dt 10:22 3381
and he w down to Egypt and Dt 26:5 3381
'They w and served other gods Dt 29:26 1980
So Moses w and spoke these words Dt 31:1 1980
So Moses and Joshua w and Dt 31:14 1980
Now Moses w up from the plains of Dt 34:1 5927
So they w and came into the house Jos 2:1 1980
gate at dark, that the men w out; Jos 2:5 3318
I do not know where the men w. Jos 2:5 1980
the officers w through the midst of Jos 3:2 5674a
and w ahead of the people. Jos 3:6 1980
w over all its banks as before. Jos 4:18 1980
Joshua w to him and said to him, Jos 5:13 1980
no one w out and no one came in. Jos 6:1 3318
w forward and blew the trumpets; Jos 6:8 5674a
The armed men w before the Jos 6:9 1980
ark of the LORD w on continually, Jos 6:13 1980
and the armed men w before them and Jos 6:13 1980
the people w up into the city, Jos 6:20 5927
So the young men who were spies w Jos 6:23 935
So the men w up and spied out Ai. Jos 7:2 5927
men from the people w up there, Jos 7:4 5927
and they w to the place of ambush Jos 8:9 1980
and he w up with the elders of Jos 8:10 5927
people of war who *were* with him w up Jos 8:11 5927
w out to meet Israel in battle, Jos 8:14 3318
They w to Joshua to the camp Jos 9:6 1980
Eglon, gathered together and w up, Jos 10:5 5927
So Joshua w up from Gilgal, he and Jos 10:7 5927
him w up from Eglon to Hebron, Jos 10:36 5927
"Nevertheless my brethren who w Jos 14:8 5927
then w up by the south of Jos 15:3 5927
and w up to Addar and turned about Jos 15:3 5927
the border w up to Beth-hoglah, Jos 15:6 5927
and the border w up to the stone Jos 15:6 5927
The border w up to Debir from Jos 15:7 5927
Then the border w up the valley of Jos 15:8 5927
and the border w up to the top of Jos 15:8 5927
and w down to Beth-shemesh and Jos 15:10 3381
Then he w up from there against Jos 15:15 5927
lot for the sons of Joseph w from the Jos 16:1 3318

It **w** from Bethel to Luz, and	**Jos 16:2**	3318
It **w** down westward to the	**Jos 16:3**	3381
Then the border **w** westward at	**Jos 16:6**	3318
It **w** down from Janoah to	**Jos 16:7**	3381
then the border **w** southward to the	**Jos 17:7**	1980
w down to the brook of Kanah,	**Jos 17:9**	3381
Then the men arose and **w**,	**Jos 18:8**	1980
those who **w** to describe the land,	**Jos 18:8**	1980
men **w** and passed through the land,	**Jos 18:9**	1980
then the border **w** up to the side	**Jos 18:12**	5927
and **w** up through the hill country	**Jos 18:12**	5927
the border **w** down to Ataroth-addar,	**Jos 18:13**	3381
and the border **w** westward and went	**Jos 18:15**	3318
and **w** to the fountain of the waters	**Jos 18:15**	3318
The border **w** down to the edge	**Jos 18:16**	3381
it **w** down to the valley of Hinnom,	**Jos 18:16**	3381
southward, and **w** down to En-rogel.	**Jos 18:16**	3381
It extended northward and **w** to	**Jos 18:17**	3318
to En-shemesh and **w** to Geliloth,	**Jos 18:17**	3318
and it **w** down to the stone of	**Jos 18:17**	3381
and **w** down to the Arabah.	**Jos 18:18**	3381
w up to the west and to Maralah,	**Jos 19:11**	5927
for the sons of Dan **w** up and	**Jos 19:47**	5927
away, and they **w** to their tents.	**Jos 22:6**	1980
and his sons **w** down to Egypt.	**Jos 24:4**	3381
through all the way in which we **w**	**Jos 24:17**	1980
So Simeon **w** with him.	**Jg 1:3**	1980
Judah **w** up, and the LORD gave	**Jg 1:4**	5927
Afterward the sons of Judah **w**	**Jg 1:9**	3381
So Judah **w** against the Canaanites	**Jg 1:10**	1980
Then from there he **w** against the	**Jg 1:11**	1980
w up from the city of palms with	**Jg 1:16**	5927
they **w** and lived with the people.	**Jg 1:16**	1980
Judah **w** with Simeon his brother,	**Jg 1:17**	1980
of Joseph **w** up against Bethel,	**Jg 1:22**	5927
The man **w** into the land of the	**Jg 1:26**	1980
the sons of Israel **w** each to his	**Jg 2:6**	1980
Wherever they **w**, the hand of the	**Jg 2:15**	3318
When he **w** out to war, the LORD	**Jg 3:10**	3318
and he **w** and defeated Israel, and	**Jg 3:13**	1980
handle also **w** in after the blade,	**Jg 3:22**	935
Then Ehud **w** out into the vestibule	**Jg 3:23**	3318
and the sons of Israel **w** down with	**Jg 3:27**	3381
So they **w** down after him and	**Jg 3:28**	3381
arose and **w** with Barak to Kedesh.	**Jg 4:9**	1980
ten thousand men **w** up with him;	**Jg 4:10**	5927
Deborah also **w** up with him.	**Jg 4:10**	5927
So Barak **w** down from Mount Tabor	**Jg 4:14**	3381
Jael **w** out to meet Sisera, and	**Jg 4:18**	3318
and **w** secretly to him and drove	**Jg 4:21**	935
and it **w** through into the ground;	**Jg 4:21**	6795
"LORD, when You **w** out from Seir,	**Jg 5:4**	3318
travelers **w** by roundabout ways.	**Jg 5:6**	1980
the people of the LORD **w** down to	**Jg 5:11**	3381
Then Gideon **w** in and prepared a	**Jg 6:19**	935
So he **w** with Purah his servant	**Jg 7:11**	3381
you **w** to fight against Midian?"	**Jg 8:1**	1980
He **w** up from there to Penuel and	**Jg 8:8**	5927
Gideon **w** up by the way of	**Jg 8:11**	5927
Jerubbaal the son of Joash **w** and	**Jg 8:29**	1980
Abimelech the son of Jerubbaal **w** to	**Jg 9:1**	1980
Then he **w** to his father's house at	**Jg 9:5**	935
they **w** and made Abimelech king,	**Jg 9:6**	1980
he **w** and stood on the top of Mount	**Jg 9:7**	1980
"Once the trees **w** forth to anoint	**Jg 9:8**	1980
and **w** to Beer and remained there	**Jg 9:21**	1980
They **w** out into the field and	**Jg 9:27**	3318
w into the house of their god,	**Jg 9:27**	935
Now Gaal the son of Ebed **w** out and	**Jg 9:35**	3318
So Gaal **w** out before the leaders	**Jg 9:39**	3318
the people **w** out to the field,	**Jg 9:42**	3318
So Abimelech **w** up to Mount Zalmon,	**Jg 9:48**	5927
Then Abimelech **w** to Thebez, and he	**Jg 9:50**	1980
w up on the roof of the tower.	**Jg 9:51**	5927
Jephthah, and they **w** out with him.	**Jg 11:3**	3318
elders of Gilead **w** to get Jephthah	**Jg 11:5**	1980
w with the elders of Gilead,	**Jg 11:11**	1980
and Israel **w** through the	**Jg 11:16**	1980
'Then they **w** through the	**Jg 11:18**	1980
he **w** on to the sons of Ammon.	**Jg 11:29**	5674a
that the daughters of Israel **w**	**Jg 11:40**	1980
when the flame **w** up from the altar	**Jg 13:20**	5927
Then Samson **w** down to Timnah and	**Jg 14:1**	3381
Then Samson **w** down to Timnah with	**Jg 14:5**	3381
he **w** down and talked to the woman;	**Jg 14:7**	3381
the honey into his hands and **w** on,	**Jg 14:9**	1980
hands and went on, eating as he **w**.	**Jg 14:9**	1980
his father **w** down to the woman;	**Jg 14:10**	3381
seventh day before the sun **w** down,	**Jg 14:18**	935
and he **w** down to Ashkelon and	**Jg 14:19**	3381
and he **w** up to his father's house.	**Jg 14:19**	5927
Samson **w** and caught three	**Jg 15:4**	1980
and he **w** down and lived in the	**Jg 15:8**	3381
w up and camped in Judah,	**Jg 15:9**	5927
Then 3,000 men of Judah **w** down to	**Jg 15:11**	3381
Now Samson **w** to Gaza and saw a	**Jg 16:1**	1980
a harlot there, and **w** in to her.	**Jg 16:1**	935
So the Levite **w** *in.*	**Jg 17:10**	1980
They **w** up and camped at	**Jg 18:12**	5927
Then the five men who **w** to spy out	**Jg 18:14**	1980
Now the five men who **w** to spy out	**Jg 18:17**	1980
men who went to spy out the land **w**	**Jg 18:17**	5927
When these **w** into Micah's	**Jg 18:18**	935
image and **w** among the people.	**Jg 18:20**	935
So the sons of Dan **w** on their way;	**Jg 18:26**	1980
he turned and **w** back to his house.	**Jg 18:26**	7725
and she **w** away from him to her	**Jg 19:2**	1980
Then her husband arose and **w** after	**Jg 19:3**	1980
they passed along and **w** their way,	**Jg 19:14**	1980
and I **w** to Bethlehem in Judah.	**Jg 19:18**	1980
w out to them and said to them,	**Jg 19:23**	3318
house and **w** out to go on his way,	**Jg 19:27**	3318
the man arose and **w** to his home.	**Jg 19:28**	1980
of Israel arose, **w** up to Bethel,	**Jg 20:18**	5927
The men of Israel **w** out to	**Jg 20:20**	3318
The sons of Israel **w** up and	**Jg 20:23**	5927
Benjamin **w** out against them	**Jg 20:25**	3318
sons of Israel and all the people **w** up	**Jg 20:26**	5927
The sons of Israel **w** up	**Jg 20:30**	5927
The sons of Benjamin **w** out	**Jg 20:31**	3318
And they **w** and returned to their	**Jg 21:23**	1980
and each one of them **w** out from	**Jg 21:24**	3318
man of Bethlehem in Judah **w**	**Ru 1:1**	1980
and they **w** on the way to return to	**Ru 1:7**	1980
w until they came to Bethlehem.	**Ru 1:19**	1980
"I **w** out full, but the LORD has	**Ru 1:21**	1980
So she departed and **w** and gleaned	**Ru 2:3**	935
took *it* up and **w** into the city,	**Ru 2:18**	935
So she **w** down to the threshing	**Ru 3:6**	3381
he **w** to lie down at the end of the	**Ru 3:7**	935
Then she **w** into the city.	**Ru 3:15**	935
Now Boaz **w** up to the gate and sat	**Ru 4:1**	5927
his wife, and he **w** in to her.	**Ru 4:13**	935
she **w** up to the house of the LORD,	**1Sa 1:7**	5927
So the woman **w** her way and ate,	**1Sa 1:18**	1980
Then the man Elkanah **w** up with all	**1Sa 1:21**	5927
Elkanah **w** to his home at Ramah.	**1Sa 2:11**	1980
And they **w** to their own home.	**1Sa 2:20**	1980
So he **w** and lay down.	**1Sa 3:5**	1980
So Samuel arose and **w** to Eli and	**1Sa 3:6**	1980
And he arose and **w** to Eli and	**1Sa 3:8**	1980
Samuel **w** and lay down in his place.	**1Sa 3:9**	1980
Now Israel **w** out to meet the	**1Sa 4:1**	3318
cry of the city **w** up to heaven.	**1Sa 5:12**	5927
they **w** along the highway, lowing	**1Sa 6:12**	1980
the highway, lowing as they **w**,	**1Sa 6:12**	1980
Philistines **w** up against Israel.	**1Sa 7:7**	5927
The men of Israel **w** out of	**1Sa 7:11**	3318
when a man **w** to inquire of God,	**1Sa 9:9**	1980
So they **w** to the city where the	**1Sa 9:10**	1980
they **w** up the slope to the city,	**1Sa 9:11**	5927
So they **w** up to the city.	**1Sa 9:14**	5927
and Samuel **w** out into the street.	**1Sa 9:26**	3318
donkeys which you **w** to look for	**1Sa 10:2**	1980
not be found, we **w** to Samuel."	**1Sa 10:14**	935
Saul also **w** to his house at Gibeah;	**1Sa 10:26**	1980
hearts God had touched **w** with him.	**1Sa 10:26**	1980
w and told the men of Jabesh;	**1Sa 11:9**	935
So all the people **w** to Gilgal,	**1Sa 11:15**	1980
"When Jacob **w** into Egypt and your	**1Sa 12:8**	935
and Saul **w** out to meet him *and* to	**1Sa 13:10**	3318
Then Samuel arose and **w** up from	**1Sa 13:15**	5927
Israel **w** down to the Philistines,	**1Sa 13:20**	3381
the garrison of the Philistines **w** out	**1Sa 13:23**	3318
and they **w** here and *there.*	**1Sa 14:16**	1980
who **w** up with them all around in	**1Sa 14:21**	5927
Then Saul **w** up from pursuing the	**1Sa 14:46**	5927
Philistines **w** to their own place.	**1Sa 14:46**	1980
and **w** on the mission on which the	**1Sa 15:20**	1980
So Samuel **w** back following Saul,	**1Sa 15:31**	7725
Then Samuel **w** to Ramah, but Saul	**1Sa 15:34**	1980
but Saul **w** up to his house at	**1Sa 15:34**	5927
And Samuel arose and **w** to Ramah.	**1Sa 16:13**	1980
sons who **w** to the battle were Eliab	**1Sa 17:13**	1980
but David **w** back and forth from	**1Sa 17:15**	1980, 7725
and **w** as Jesse had commanded him.	**1Sa 17:20**	1980
I **w** out after him and attacked	**1Sa 17:35**	3318
w out wherever Saul sent him,	**1Sa 18:5**	3318
and he **w** out and came in before	**1Sa 18:13**	3318
he **w** out and came in before them.	**1Sa 18:16**	3318
David rose up and **w**,	**1Sa 18:27**	1980
the Philistines **w** out *to battle,*	**1Sa 18:30**	3318
happened as often as they **w** out,	**1Sa 18:30**	3318
David **w** out and fought with the	**1Sa 19:8**	3318
and he **w** out and fled and escaped.	**1Sa 19:12**	1980
and Samuel **w** and stayed in Naioth.	**1Sa 19:18**	1980
Then he himself **w** to Ramah and	**1Sa 19:22**	1980
so that he **w** along prophesying	**1Sa 19:23**	1980
both of them **w** out to the field.	**1Sa 20:11**	3318
Jonathan **w** out into the field	**1Sa 20:35**	3318
while Jonathan **w** into the city.	**1Sa 20:42**	935
and **w** to Achish king of Gath.	**1Sa 21:10**	935
of it, they **w** down there to him.	**1Sa 22:1**	3381
w from there to Mizpah of Moab;	**1Sa 22:3**	1980
w into the forest of Hereth.	**1Sa 22:5**	935
So David and his men **w** to Keilah	**1Sa 23:5**	1980
and they **w** wherever they could go.	**1Sa 23:13**	1980
arose and **w** to David at Horesh,	**1Sa 23:16**	1980
while Jonathan **w** to his house.	**1Sa 23:18**	1980
arose and **w** to Ziph before Saul.	**1Sa 23:24**	1980
Saul and his men **w** to seek *him,*	**1Sa 23:25**	1980
Saul **w** on one side of the mountain,	**1Sa 23:26**	1980
and **w** to meet the Philistines;	**1Sa 23:28**	1980
David **w** up from there and	**1Sa 23:29**	5927
and **w** to seek David and his men in	**1Sa 24:2**	1980
and Saul **w** in to relieve himself.	**1Sa 24:3**	935
left the cave, and **w** on *his* way.	**1Sa 24:7**	1980
Now afterward David arose and **w**	**1Sa 24:8**	3318
And Saul **w** to his home, but David	**1Sa 24:22**	1980
his men **w** up to the stronghold.	**1Sa 24:22**	5927
And David arose and **w** down to the	**1Sa 25:1**	3381
men retraced their way and **w** back;	**1Sa 25:12**	7725
and about four hundred men **w** up	**1Sa 25:13**	5927
as long as we **w** about with them,	**1Sa 25:15**	1980
So Saul arose and **w** down to the	**1Sa 26:2**	3381
Saul's head, and they **w** away,	**1Sa 26:12**	1980
So David **w** on his way, and Saul	**1Sa 26:25**	1980
Now David and his men **w** up and	**1Sa 27:8**	5927
putting on other clothes, and **w**,	**1Sa 28:8**	1980
they arose and **w** away that night.	**1Sa 28:25**	1980
the Philistines **w** up to Jezreel.	**1Sa 29:11**	5927
carried *them* off and **w** their way.	**1Sa 30:2**	1980
So David **w**, he and the six hundred	**1Sa 30:9**	1980
and they **w** out to meet David and	**1Sa 30:21**	3318
w with David said,	**1Sa 30:22**	1980
The battle **w** heavily against Saul,	**1Sa 31:3**	3513
So David **w** up there, and his two	**2Sa 2:2**	5927
w out from Mahanaim to Gibeon with	**2Sa 2:12**	3318
servants of David **w** out and met them	**2Sa 2:13**	3318
So they arose and **w** over by count,	**2Sa 2:15**	5674a
Abner and his men then **w** through	**2Sa 2:29**	1980
Then Joab and his men **w** all night	**2Sa 2:32**	1980
But her husband **w** with her,	**2Sa 3:16**	1980
went with her, weeping as he **w**,	**2Sa 3:16**	1980
and in addition Abner **w** to speak	**2Sa 3:19**	1980
Abner away, and he **w** in peace.	**2Sa 3:21**	1980
Now the king and his men **w** to	**2Sa 5:6**	1980
w up to seek out David;	**2Sa 5:17**	5927
it, he **w** down to the stronghold.	**2Sa 5:17**	3381
And David arose and **w** with all the	**2Sa 6:2**	1980
David **w** and brought up the ark	**2Sa 6:12**	1980
king **w** in and sat before the LORD,	**2Sa 7:18**	935
whom God **w** to redeem for Himself	**2Sa 7:23**	1980
as he **w** to restore his rule at the	**2Sa 8:3**	1980
LORD helped David wherever he **w**.	**2Sa 8:6**	1980
LORD helped David wherever he **w**.	**2Sa 8:14**	1980
Uriah **w** out of the king's house,	**2Sa 11:8**	3318
and in the evening he **w** out to lie	**2Sa 11:13**	3318
w out and fought against Joab,	**2Sa 11:17**	3318
So Nathan **w** to his house.	**2Sa 12:15**	1980
and David fasted and **w** and lay all	**2Sa 12:16**	935
and **w** in to her and lay with her;	**2Sa 12:24**	935
all the people and **w** to Rabbah,	**2Sa 12:29**	1980
w to her brother Amnon's house,	**2Sa 13:8**	1980
So everyone **w** out from him.	**2Sa 13:9**	3318
her hand on her head and **w** away,	**2Sa 13:19**	1980
went away, crying aloud as she **w**.	**2Sa 13:19**	1980
w to Talmai the son of Ammihud,	**2Sa 13:37**	1980
So Joab arose and **w** to Geshur and	**2Sa 14:23**	1980
So he arose and **w** to Hebron.	**2Sa 15:9**	1980
men **w** with Absalom from Jerusalem,	**2Sa 15:11**	1980
who were invited and **w** innocently,	**2Sa 15:11**	1980
So the king **w** out and all his	**2Sa 15:16**	3318
The king **w** out and all the	**2Sa 15:17**	3318
And David **w** up the ascent of the	**2Sa 15:30**	5927
Mount of Olives, and wept as he **w**,	**2Sa 15:30**	5927
and **w** up weeping as they went.	**2Sa 15:30**	5927
and went up weeping as they **w**.	**2Sa 15:30**	5927
So David and his men **w** on the way;	**2Sa 16:13**	1980
and Shimei **w** along on the hillside	**2Sa 16:13**	1980
with him and as he **w** he cursed and	**2Sa 16:13**	1980
and Absalom **w** in to his father's	**2Sa 16:22**	935
and they **w** down into it.	**2Sa 17:18**	3381
well and **w** and told King David;	**2Sa 17:21**	1980
and arose and **w** to his home,	**2Sa 17:23**	1980
who **w** in to Abigail the daughter	**2Sa 17:25**	935
w out by hundreds and thousands.	**2Sa 18:4**	3318
Then the people **w** out into the	**2Sa 18:6**	3318
and the mule **w** under the thick	**2Sa 18:9**	935
and the watchman **w** up to the roof	**2Sa 18:24**	1980
king was deeply moved and **w** up to	**2Sa 18:33**	5927
So the people **w** by stealth into	**2Sa 19:3**	935
and he **w** on to the Jordan with the	**2Sa 19:31**	5674a
Now the king **w** on to Gilgal, and	**2Sa 19:40**	5674a
Gilgal, and Chimham **w** on with him;	**2Sa 19:40**	5674a
w to call out *the men of* Judah,	**2Sa 20:5**	1980
So Joab's men **w** out after him,	**2Sa 20:7**	3318
and they **w** out from Jerusalem to	**2Sa 20:7**	3318
and as he **w** forward, it fell out.	**2Sa 20:8**	3318
Now he **w** through all the tribes of	**2Sa 20:14**	5674a
together and also **w** after him.	**2Sa 20:14**	935
then David **w** and took the bones of	**2Sa 21:12**	1980
David **w** down and his servants with	**2Sa 21:15**	3381
"Smoke **w** up out of His nostrils,	**2Sa 22:9**	5927
chief men **w** down and came to David	**2Sa 23:13**	3381
w in *jeopardy* of their lives?"	**2Sa 23:17**	1980
He also **w** down and killed a lion	**2Sa 23:20**	3381
but he **w** down to him with a club	**2Sa 23:21**	3381
the commanders of the army **w** out	**2Sa 24:4**	3318
they **w** out to the south of Judah,	**2Sa 24:7**	3318
David **w** up according to the	**2Sa 24:19**	5927
and Araunah **w** out and bowed his	**2Sa 24:20**	3318
w in to the king in the bedroom.	**1Ki 1:15**	935
and the Pelethites **w** down and had	**1Ki 1:38**	3381
All the people **w** up after him,	**1Ki 1:40**	5927
they arose and each **w** on his way.	**1Ki 1:49**	1980
w and took hold of the horns of	**1Ki 1:50**	1980
curse on the day I **w** to Mahanaim.	**1Ki 2:8**	1980
So Bathsheba **w** to King Solomon to	**1Ki 2:19**	935
Benaiah the son of Jehoiada **w** up	**1Ki 2:34**	5927
and **w** to Gath to Achish to look	**1Ki 2:40**	1980
And Shimei **w** and brought his	**1Ki 2:40**	1980
and he **w** out and fell upon him so	**1Ki 2:46**	3318
w to Gibeon to sacrifice there,	**1Ki 3:4**	1980
Under its brim gourds **w** around	**1Ki 7:24**	
Then they **w** to their tents joyful	**1Ki 8:66**	1980
They **w** to Ophir and took four	**1Ki 9:28**	935
he **w** up to the house of the LORD,	**1Ki 10:5**	5927
Then she turned and **w** to her own	**1Ki 10:13**	1980
For Solomon **w** after Ashtoreth the	**1Ki 11:5**	1980
w to Damascus and stayed there,	**1Ki 11:24**	1980
when Jeroboam **w** out of Jerusalem,	**1Ki 11:29**	3318
Then Rehoboam **w** to Shechem, for	**1Ki 12:1**	1980
and returned and **w** *their way*	**1Ki 12:24**	1980
And he **w** out from there and built	**1Ki 12:25**	3318
for the people **w** *to worship* before	**1Ki 12:30**	1980

Judah, and he **w** up to the altar; **1Ki 12:32** 5927
Then he **w** up to the altar which he **1Ki 12:33** 5927
and **w** up to the altar to burn **1Ki 12:33** 5927
So he **w** another way and did not **1Ki 13:10** 1980
So he **w** after the man of God and **1Ki 13:14** 1980
So he **w** back with him, and ate **1Ki 13:19** 7725
He **w** and found his body thrown **1Ki 13:28** 1980
did so, and arose and **w** to Shiloh, **1Ki 14:4** 1980
Baasha king of Israel **w** up **1Ki 15:17** 5927
Then Zimri **w** in and struck him **1Ki 16:10** 935
with him **w** up from Gibbethon and **1Ki 16:17** 5927
he **w** into the citadel of the **1Ki 16:18** 935
and **w** to serve Baal and worshiped **1Ki 16:31** 1980
So he **w** and did according to the **1Ki 17:5** 1980
for he **w** and lived by the brook **1Ki 17:5** 1980
So he arose and **w** to Zarephath, **1Ki 17:10** 1980
So she **w** and did according to the **1Ki 17:15** 1980
Elijah **w** to show himself to Ahab. **1Ki 18:2** 1980
Ahab **w** one way by himself and **1Ki 18:6** 1980
Obadiah **w** another way by himself. **1Ki 18:6** 1980
So Obadiah **w** to meet Ahab and **1Ki 18:16** 1980
and Ahab **w** to meet Elijah. **1Ki 18:16** 1980
So Ahab **w** up to eat and drink. **1Ki 18:42** 5927
Elijah **w** up to the top of Carmel; **1Ki 18:42** 5927
So he **w** up and looked and said, **1Ki 18:43** 5927
And Ahab rode and **w** to Jezreel. **1Ki 18:45** 1980
But he himself **w** a day's journey **1Ki 19:4** 1980
and **w** in the strength of that food **1Ki 19:8** 1980
and **w** out and stood in the **1Ki 19:13** 3318
And he **w** up and besieged Samaria and **1Ki 20:1** 5927
They **w** out at noon, while **1Ki 20:16** 3318
men of the rulers of the provinces **w** **1Ki 20:17** 3318
So these **w** out from the city, the **1Ki 20:19** 3318
The king of Israel **w** out and **1Ki 20:21** 3318
w up to Aphek to fight against Israel. **1Ki 20:26** 5927
provisioned and **w** to meet them; **1Ki 20:27** 1980
"Your servant **w** out into the **1Ki 20:39** 3318
king of Israel **w** to his house sullen **1Ki 20:43** 1980
and **w** about despondently. **1Ki 21:27** 1980
Then the messenger who **w** to summon **1Ki 22:13** 1980
Judah **w** up against Ramoth-gilead. **1Ki 22:29** 5927
himself and **w** into the battle. **1Ki 22:30** 935
And he **w** up to him, and behold, he **2Ki 1:9** 5927
the third captain of fifty **w** up, **2Ki 1:13** 5927
and **w** down with him to the king. **2Ki 1:15** 3381
Elijah **w** with Elisha from Gilgal. **2Ki 2:1** 1980
So they **w** down to Bethel. **2Ki 2:2** 3381
So the two of them **w** on. **2Ki 2:6** 1980
the sons of the prophets **w** and stood **2Ki 2:7** 1980
w up by a whirlwind to heaven. **2Ki 2:11** 5927
He **w** out to the spring of water **2Ki 2:21** 3318
Then he **w** up from there to Bethel; **2Ki 2:23** 5927
He **w** from there to Mount Carmel, **2Ki 2:25** 1980
And King Jehoram **w** out of Samaria **2Ki 3:6** 3318
Then he **w** and sent *word* to **2Ki 3:7** 1980
So the king of Israel **w** with the **2Ki 3:9** 1980
the king of Edom **w** down to him. **2Ki 3:12** 3381
and they **w** forward into the land, **2Ki 3:24** 935
slingers **w** about *it* and struck it. **2Ki 3:25** 5437
So she **w** from him and shut the **2Ki 4:5** 1980
the day came that he **w** out to his **2Ki 4:18** 3318
She **w** up and laid him on the **2Ki 4:21** 5927
the door behind him and **w** out. **2Ki 4:21** 3318
So she **w** and came to the man of **2Ki 4:25** 1980
And he **w** up and lay on the child, **2Ki 4:34** 5927
and **w** up and stretched himself on **2Ki 4:35** 5927
Then she **w** in and fell at his feet **2Ki 4:37** 935
and she took up her son and **w** out. **2Ki 4:37** 3318
Then one **w** out into the field to **2Ki 4:39** 3318
Naaman **w** in and told his master, **2Ki 5:4** 935
was furious and **w** away and said, **2Ki 5:11** 1980
So he turned and **w** away in a rage. **2Ki 5:12** 1980
So he **w** down and dipped *himself* **2Ki 5:14** 3381
But he **w** in and stood before his **2Ki 5:25** 935
"Your servant **w** nowhere." **2Ki 5:25** 1980
So he **w** out from his presence a **2Ki 5:27** 3318
So he **w** with them; **2Ki 6:4** 1980
away, and they **w** to their master. **2Ki 6:23** 1980
and **w** up and besieged Samaria. **2Ki 6:24** 5927
and clothes, and **w** and hid *them;* **2Ki 7:8** 1980
there *also,* and **w** and hid *them.* **2Ki 7:8** 1980
They **w** after them to the Jordan, **2Ki 7:15** 1980
So the people **w** out and plundered **2Ki 7:16** 3318
and she **w** with her household and **2Ki 8:2** 1980
and she **w** out to appeal to the **2Ki 8:3** 3318
So Hazael **w** to meet him and took a **2Ki 8:9** 1980
Then he **w** with Joram the son of **2Ki 8:28** 1980
son of Jehoram king of Judah **w** down **2Ki 8:29** 3381
of the prophet, **w** to Ramoth-gilead. **2Ki 9:4** 1980
He arose and **w** into the house, **2Ki 9:6** 935
in a chariot and **w** to Jezreel, **2Ki 9:16** 1980
a horseman **w** to meet him and said, **2Ki 9:18** 1980
and Ahaziah king of Judah **w** out, **2Ki 9:21** 3318
and they **w** out to meet Jehu and **2Ki 9:21** 3318
and the arrow **w** through his heart and **2Ki 9:24** 3318
They **w** to bury her, but they **2Ki 9:35** 1980
morning he **w** out and stood **2Ki 10:9** 3318
and departed and **w** to Samaria. **2Ki 10:12** 1980
they **w** into the house of Baal, **2Ki 10:21** 935
Jehu **w** into the house of Baal **2Ki 10:23** 935
Then they **w** in to offer sacrifices **2Ki 10:24** 935
and **w** to the inner room of the **2Ki 10:25** 1980
All the people of the land **w** to the **2Ki 11:18** 935
Then Hazael king of Aram **w** up and **2Ki 12:17** 5927
Then he **w** away from Jerusalem. **2Ki 12:18** 5927
So Jehoash king of Israel **w** up; **2Ki 14:11** 5927
Then Menahem son of Gadi **w** up from **2Ki 15:14** 5927
and the king of Assyria **w** up **2Ki 16:9** 5927
Now King Ahaz **w** to Damascus to **2Ki 16:10** 1980
the altar and **w** up to it, **2Ki 16:12** 5927
Assyria invaded the whole land and **w** **2Ki 17:5** 5927
and **w** after the nations which **2Ki 17:15**
wherever he **w** he prospered. **2Ki 18:7** 3318
they **w** up and came to Jerusalem. **2Ki 18:17** 5927
And when they **w** up, they came and **2Ki 18:17** 5927
and he **w** up to the house of the **2Ki 19:14** 5927
that the angel of the LORD **w** out and **2Ki 19:35** 3318
Asaiah **w** to Huldah the prophetess, **2Ki 22:14** 1980
The king **w** up to the house of **2Ki 23:2** 5927
Pharaoh Neco king of Egypt **w** up to **2Ki 23:29** 5927
And King Josiah **w** to meet him, and **2Ki 23:29** 1980
king of Babylon **w** up to Jerusalem, **2Ki 24:10** 5927
Jehoiachin the king of Judah **w** out **2Ki 24:12** 3318
And they **w** by way of the Arabah. **2Ki 25:4** 1980
the forces arose and **w** to Egypt; **2Ki 25:26** 935
Afterward Hezron **w** in to the **1Ch 2:21** 935
They **w** to the entrance of Gedor, **1Ch 4:39** 1980
five hundred men **w** to Mount Seir, **1Ch 4:42** 1980
battle, *were* 44,760, who **w** to war. **1Ch 5:18** 3318
and Jehozadak **w** *along* when the **1Ch 6:15** 1980
Then he **w** in to his wife, and she **1Ch 7:23** 935
and all Israel **w** to Jerusalem **1Ch 11:4** 1980
the son of Zeruiah **w** up first, **1Ch 11:6** 5927
men **w** down to the rock to David, **1Ch 11:15** 3381
drink the blood of these men *who* **w** **1Ch 11:19**
He also **w** down and killed a lion **1Ch 11:22** 3381
but he **w** down to him with a club **1Ch 11:23** 3381
David **w** out to meet them, and **1Ch 12:17** 3318
As he **w** to Ziklag there defected **1Ch 12:20** 1980
were 50,000 who **w** out in the army, **1Ch 12:33** 3318
were 40,000 who **w** out in the army **1Ch 12:36** 3318
and all Israel **w** up to Baalah, **1Ch 13:6** 5927
w up in search of David; **1Ch 14:8** 5927
of it and **w** out against them. **1Ch 14:8** 3318
the fame of David **w** out into all the **1Ch 14:17** 3318
who **w** to bring up the ark of the **1Ch 15:25** 1980
Then David the king **w** in and sat **1Ch 17:16** 935
whom God **w** to redeem for Himself **1Ch 17:21** 1980
as he **w** to establish his rule to **1Ch 18:3** 1980
LORD helped David wherever he **w**. **1Ch 18:6** 1980
LORD helped David wherever he **w**. **1Ch 18:13** 1980
w and told David about the men. **1Ch 19:5** 1980
and **w** throughout all Israel, **1Ch 21:4** 1980
So David **w** up at the word of Gad, **1Ch 21:19** 5927
w out from the threshing floor and **1Ch 21:21** 3318
and to his sons **w** the storehouse. **1Ch 26:15**
divisions which came in and **w** out **1Ch 27:1** 3318
w to the high place which was at **2Ch 1:3** 1980
Solomon **w** up there before the **2Ch 1:6** 5927
So Solomon **w** from the high place **2Ch 1:13** 935
Then Solomon **w** to Hamath-zobah and **2Ch 8:3** 1980
Then Solomon **w** to Ezion-geber and **2Ch 8:17** 1980
and they **w** with Solomon's servants **2Ch 8:18** 935
he **w** up to the house of the LORD, **2Ch 9:4** 5927
Then she turned and **w** to her own **2Ch 9:12** 1980
For the king had ships which **w** to **2Ch 9:21** 1980
Then Rehoboam **w** to Shechem, for **2Ch 10:1** 1980
So Asa **w** out to meet him, and they **2Ch 14:10** 3318
and he **w** out to meet Asa and said **2Ch 15:2** 3318
who **w** out or to him who came in, **2Ch 15:5** 3318
and they **w** throughout all the **2Ch 17:9** 5437
w down to *visit* Ahab at Samaria. **2Ch 18:2** 3381
Then the messenger who **w** to summon **2Ch 18:12** 1980
Judah **w** up against Ramoth-gilead. **2Ch 18:28** 5927
himself, and they **w** into battle. **2Ch 18:29** 935
Jehu the son of Hanani the seer **w** out **2Ch 19:2** 3318
Jehoshaphat lived in Jerusalem and **w** **2Ch 19:4** 3318
and **w** out to the wilderness of Tekoa **2Ch 20:20** 3318
and when they **w** out, Jehoshaphat **2Ch 20:20** 3318
w out before the army and said, **2Ch 20:21** 3318
and **w** with Jehoram the son of Ahab **2Ch 22:5** 1980
w down to see Jehoram the son of **2Ch 22:6** 3381
from God, in that he **w** to Joram. **2Ch 22:7** 935
he **w** out with Jehoram against Jehu **2Ch 22:7** 3318
They **w** throughout Judah and **2Ch 23:2** 5437
the people **w** to the house of Baal and **2Ch 23:17** 935
and **w** to the Valley of Salt and **2Ch 25:11** 1980
So Joash king of Israel **w** up, **2Ch 25:21** 5927
Now he **w** out and warred against **2Ch 26:6** 3318
and he **w** out to meet the army **2Ch 28:9** 3318
and **w** in to cleanse the house of **2Ch 29:15** 935
So the priests **w** in to the inner **2Ch 29:16** 935
w in to King Hezekiah and said, **2Ch 29:18** 935
and **w** up to the house of the LORD. **2Ch 29:20** 5927
The couriers **w** throughout all **2Ch 30:6** 1980
w out to the cities of Judah, **2Ch 31:1** 3318
those whom the king had told **w** to **2Ch 34:22** 1980
The king **w** up to the house of **2Ch 34:30** 5927
and Josiah **w** out to engage him. **2Ch 35:20** 3318
w up from Babylon to Jerusalem. **Ezr 1:11** 5927
they **w** in haste to Jerusalem to **Ezr 4:23** 236
there **w** *up* Ezra son of Seraiah, **Ezr 7:1**
This Ezra **w** up from Babylon, and **Ezr 7:6** 5927
and the temple servants **w** up to **Ezr 7:7** 5927
those who **w** up with me from Babylon **Ezr 8:1** 5927
w into the chamber of Jehohanan **Ezr 10:6** 1980
Although he **w** there, he did not **Ezr 10:6** 1980
So I **w** out at night by the Valley **Ne 2:13** 3318
So I **w** up at night by the ravine **Ne 2:15** 5927
repair of the walls of Jerusalem **w** on **Ne 4:7** 5927
Also in those days many letters **w** **Ne 6:17** 1980
All the people **w** away to eat, **Ne 8:12** 1980
So the people **w** out and brought **Ne 8:16** 3318
And Ezra the scribe **w** before them. **Ne 12:36**
At the Fountain Gate they **w** **Ne 12:37** 5927
The couriers **w** out impelled by the **Es 3:15** 3318
and **w** out into the midst of the **Es 4:1** 3318
He **w** as far as the king's **Es 4:2** 935
So Hathach **w** out to Mordecai to **Es 4:6** 3318
So Mordecai **w** away and did just as **Es 4:17** 5674a
Then Haman **w** out that day glad and **Es 5:9** 3318
himself, however, **w** to his house and **Es 5:10** 935
his anger from drinking wine *and* **w** **Es 7:7**
the word **w** out of the king's mouth, **Es 7:8** 3318
by the king's command, **w** out, **Es 8:14** 3318
Then Mordecai **w** out from the **Es 8:15** 3318
Then Satan **w** out from the presence **Jb 2:7** 3318
I **w** out to the gate of the city, **Jb 29:7** 3318
forth, it **w** out from the womb; **Jb 38:8** 3318
Zophar the Naamathite **w** and did **Jb 42:9** 1980
Smoke **w** up out of His nostrils, **Ps 18:8** 5927
I **w** about as though it were my **Ps 35:14** 1980
We **w** through fire and through **Ps 66:12** 935
O God, when You **w** forth before Your **Ps 68:7** 3318
The singers **w** on, the musicians **Ps 68:25** 6923
he **w** throughout the land of Egypt. **Ps 81:5** 3318
So that it **w** hard with Moses on **Ps 106:32** 7489a
they **w** down to the depths; **Ps 107:26** 3381
When Israel **w** forth from Egypt, **Ps 114:1** 3318
Before I was afflicted I **w** astray, **Ps 119:67** 7683
My heart **w** out *to him* as he spoke. **SS 5:6** 3318
"I **w** down to the orchard of nut **SS 6:11** 3381
w up to Jerusalem to *wage* war **Is 7:1** 5927
and he **w** up to the house of the **Is 37:14** 5927
Then the angel of the LORD **w** out and **Is 37:36** 3318
So the sun's *shadow* **w** back ten **Is 38:8** 7725
And they **w** forth from My mouth, **Is 48:3** 3318
"My people **w** down at the first **Is 52:4** 3381
You also **w** up there to offer sacrifice. **Is 57:7** 5927
angry, And he **w** on turning away, **Is 57:17** 1980
That they **w** far from Me And walked **Jer 2:5** 7368
She **w** up on every high hill and **Jer 3:6** 1980
but she **w** and was a harlot also. **Jer 3:8** 1980
and **w** backward and not forward. **Jer 7:24** 1961
I **w** and hid it by the Euphrates, **Jer 13:5** 1980
Then I **w** to the Euphrates and dug, **Jer 13:7** 1980
I **w** down to the potter's house, **Jer 18:3** 3381
who **w** forth from this place, **Jer 22:11** 3318
afraid and fled and **w** to Egypt. **Jer 26:21** 935
and *certain* men with him **w** **Jer 26:22**
exiles of Judah who **w** to Babylon,' **Jer 28:4** 935
the prophet Jeremiah **w** his way. **Jer 28:11** 1980
when it **w** to find its rest." **Jer 31:2** 1980
highway, The way by which you **w**. **Jer 31:21** 1980
he **w** down to the king's house, **Jer 36:12** 3381
scroll in his hand and **w** to them. **Jer 36:14** 935
they **w** to the king in the court, **Jer 36:20** 935
that Jeremiah **w** out from Jerusalem **Jer 37:12** 3318
and Ebed-melech **w** out from the **Jer 38:8** 3318
w into the king's palace to *a place* **Jer 38:11** 935
they fled and **w** out of the **Jer 39:4** 3318
and he **w** out toward the Arabah. **Jer 39:4** 3318
Then Jeremiah **w** to Mizpah to **Jer 40:6** 935
Ishmael the son of Nethaniah **w** out **Jer 41:6** 3318
to meet them, weeping as he **w**; **Jer 41:6** 1980
w to fight with Ishmael the son of **Jer 41:12** 1980
w to Johanan the son of Kareah. **Jer 41:14** 1980
men and **w** to the sons of Ammon. **Jer 41:15** 1980
w and stayed in Geruth Chimham, **Jer 41:17** 1980
and **w** in as far as Tahpanhes. **Jer 43:7** 935
when he **w** with Zedekiah the king **Jer 51:59** 1980
all the men of war fled and **w** forth **Jer 52:7** 3318
And they **w** by way of the Arabah. **Jer 52:7** 1980
moved, each **w** straight forward. **Ezk 1:9** 1980
And each **w** straight forward; **Ezk 1:12** 1980
go, without turning as they **w**. **Ezk 1:12** 1980
Whenever those **w**, these went; **Ezk 1:21** 1980
Whenever those went, these **w**; **Ezk 1:21** 1980
of abundant waters as they **w**, **Ezk 1:24** 1980
and I **w** embittered in the rage of **Ezk 3:14** 1980
I got up and **w** out to the plain; **Ezk 3:23** 3318
And they **w** in and stood beside the **Ezk 9:2** 935
the glory of the God of Israel **w** up **Ezk 9:3** 5927
Thus they **w** out and struck down **Ezk 9:7** 3318
Then the glory of the LORD **w** up **Ezk 10:4** 7311
in linen, who took *it* and **w** out. **Ezk 10:7** 3318
they **w** in *any of* their four **Ezk 10:11** 1980
without turning as they **w**; **Ezk 10:11** 1980
faced, without turning as they **w**. **Ezk 10:11** 1980
Each one **w** straight ahead. **Ezk 10:22** 1980
w up from the midst of the city and **Ezk 11:23** 5927
I **w** out in the dark *and* carried **Ezk 12:7** 3318
"Then your fame **w** forth among the **Ezk 16:14** 3318
continually **w** after their idols. **Ezk 20:16** 1980
"But they **w** in to her as they **Ezk 23:44** 935
Thus they **w** in to Oholah and to **Ezk 23:44** 935
of Judah when they **w** into exile, **Ezk 25:3** 1980
your wares **w** out from the seas, **Ezk 27:33** 3318
"On the day when it **w** down to **Ezk 31:15** 3381
"They also **w** down with it to **Ezk 31:17** 3381
who **w** down uncircumcised to the **Ezk 32:24** 3381
with those who **w** down to the pit. **Ezk 32:24** 3381
who **w** down to Sheol with their **Ezk 32:27** 3381
in shame **w** down with the slain. **Ezk 32:30** 3381
came to the nations where they **w**, **Ezk 36:20** 935
among the nations where they **w**. **Ezk 36:21** 935
among the nations where you **w**. **Ezk 36:22** 935
Israel **w** into exile for their iniquity **Ezk 39:23** 1540
he **w** to the gate which faced east, **Ezk 40:6** 935
which faced east, **w** up its steps and **Ezk 40:6** 5927
as one **w** up to the gateway toward **Ezk 40:40** 5927
Then he **w** inside and measured each **Ezk 41:3** 935
structure surrounding the temple **w** **Ezk 41:7**
temple *increased* as it **w** higher; **Ezk 41:7**
and thus one **w** up from the lowest **Ezk 41:7** 5927
the Levites who **w** far from Me when **Ezk 44:10** 7368
far from Me when Israel **w** astray, **Ezk 44:10** 8582

who **w** astray from Me after their	Ezk 44:10	8582
sons of Israel **w** astray from Me,	Ezk 44:15	8582
When the man **w** out toward the east	Ezk 47:3	3318
when the sons of Israel **w** astray as	Ezk 48:11	8582
astray as the Levites **w** astray.	Ezk 48:11	8582
So the decree **w** forth that the	Da 2:13	5312
So Daniel **w** in and requested of	Da 2:16	5954
Then Daniel **w** to his house and	Da 2:17	236
Therefore, Daniel **w** in to Arioch,	Da 2:24	5954
he **w** and spoke to him as follows:	Da 2:24	236
and his hip joints **w** slack and	Da 5:6	8271
Then the king **w** off to his palace	Da 6:18	236
and **w** in haste to the lions' den.	Da 6:19	236
So he **w** and took Gomer the	Hos 1:3	1980
Then Ephraim **w** to Assyria And sent	Hos 5:13	1980
them, The more they **w** from them;	Hos 11:2	1980
So he **w** down to Joppa, found a	Jon 1:3	3381
and **w** down into it to go with them	Jon 1:3	3381
So Jonah arose and **w** to Nineveh	Jon 3:3	1980
Then Jonah **w** out from the city and	Jon 4:5	3318
an exile, She **w** into captivity;	Na 3:10	1980
They **w** away at the light of Your	Hab 3:11	1980
You **w** forth for the salvation of Your	Hab 3:13	3318
who was speaking with me **w** out and	Zch 5:5	3318
"When the strong ones **w** out,	Zch 6:7	3318
so that no one **w** back and forth,	Zch 7:14	5674a
and for him who **w** out or came in	Zch 8:10	3318
nations that **w** against Jerusalem will	Zch 14:16	935
hearing the king, they **w** their way;	Mt 2:9	4198
in the east, **w** on before them until	Mt 2:9	4254
He **w** up on the mountain;	Mt 5:1	305
came out and **w** into the swine,	Mt 8:32	565
ran away, and **w** to the city and	Mt 8:33	565
And he got up and **w** home.	Mt 9:7	565
As Jesus **w** on from there, He saw a	Mt 9:9	3855
As Jesus **w** on from there, two blind	Mt 9:27	3855
But they **w** out and spread the	Mt 9:31	1831
At that time Jesus **w** through	Mt 12:1	4198
there, He **w** into their synagogue.	Mt 12:9	2064
But the Pharisees **w** out and	Mt 12:14	1831
That day Jesus **w** out of the house	Mt 13:1	1831
"Behold, the sower **w** out to sow;	Mt 13:3	1831
tares among the wheat, and **w** away.	Mt 13:25	565
crowds and **w** into the house.	Mt 13:36	2064
he **w** and sold all that he had and	Mt 13:46	565
and they **w** and reported to Jesus.	Mt 14:12	2064
When He **w** ashore, He saw a	Mt 14:14	1831
He **w** up on the mountain by Himself	Mt 14:23	305
Jesus **w** away from there, and	Mt 15:21	1831
w along by the Sea of Galilee,	Mt 15:29	2064
And He left them and **w** away.	Mt 16:4	565
"But that slave **w** out and found	Mt 18:28	1831
and **w** and threw him in prison	Mt 18:30	565
this statement, he **w** away grieving;	Mt 19:22	565
like a landowner who **w** out early	Mt 20:1	1831
"And he **w** out about the third	Mt 20:3	1831
right I will give you.' And *so* they **w**.	Mt 20:4	565
"Again he **w** out about the sixth	Mt 20:5	1831
about the eleventh *hour* he **w** out and	Mt 20:6	1831
The disciples **w** and did just	Mt 21:6	4198
and **w** out of the city to Bethany,	Mt 21:17	1831
but afterward he regretted it and **w**.	Mt 21:29	565
vine-growers and **w** on a journey.	Mt 21:33	589
paid no attention and **w** their way,	Mt 22:5	565
slaves **w** out into the streets and	Mt 22:10	1831
Then the Pharisees **w** and plotted	Mt 22:15	4198
and leaving Him, they **w** away.	Mt 22:22	565
and **w** out to meet the bridegroom.	Mt 25:1	1831
and those who were ready **w** in with	Mt 25:10	1525
and he **w** on his journey.	Mt 25:15	589
who had received the five talents **w**	Mt 25:16	4198
he who received the one *talent* **w**	Mt 25:18	565
and **w** away and hid your talent in	Mt 25:25	565
Iscariot, **w** to the chief priests	Mt 26:14	4198
they **w** out to the Mount of Olives.	Mt 26:30	1831
And He **w** a little beyond *them,* and	Mt 26:39	4281
He **w** away again a second time and	Mt 26:42	565
w away and prayed a third time,	Mt 26:44	565
Judas **w** to Jesus and said,	Mt 26:49	4334
And he **w** out and wept bitterly.	Mt 26:75	1831
and he **w** away and hanged himself.	Mt 27:5	565
This man **w** to Pilate and asked for	Mt 27:58	4334
entrance of the tomb and **w** away.	Mt 27:60	565
they **w** and made the grave secure,	Mt 27:66	4198
and **w** away to follow Him.	Mk 1:20	565
They **w** into Capernaum;	Mk 1:21	1531
and **w** away to a secluded place,	Mk 1:35	565
And He **w** into their synagogues	Mk 1:39	2064
But he **w** out and began to proclaim	Mk 1:45	1831
and **w** out in the sight of everyone	Mk 2:12	1831
He **w** out again by the seashore;	Mk 2:13	1831
The Pharisees **w** out and	Mk 3:6	1831
And He **w** up on the mountain and	Mk 3:13	305
they **w** out to take custody of Him;	Mk 3:21	1831
Behold, the sower **w** out to sow;	Mk 4:3	1831
And he **w** away and began to	Mk 5:20	565
And He **w** off with him;	Mk 5:24	565
Jesus **w** out from there	Mk 6:1	1831
They **w** out and preached that	Mk 6:12	1831
she **w** out and said to her mother,	Mk 6:24	1831
And he **w** and had him beheaded in	Mk 6:27	565
They **w** away in the boat to a	Mk 6:32	565
When Jesus **w** ashore, He saw a	Mk 6:34	1831
w away from there to the region of Tyre.	Mk 7:24	565
He **w** out from the region of Tyre,	Mk 7:31	1831
and **w** away to the other side.	Mk 8:13	565
Jesus **w** out, along with His	Mk 8:27	1831
From there they **w** out and	Mk 9:30	1831
He **w** from there to the region of	Mk 10:1	2064

was saddened, and he **w** away grieving,	Mk 10:22	565
They **w** away and found a colt	Mk 11:4	565
Those who **w** in front and those	Mk 11:9	4254
He **w** *to see* if perhaps He would	Mk 11:13	2064
to vine-growers and **w** on a journey.	Mk 12:1	589
And *so* they left Him and **w** away.	Mk 12:12	565
w off to the chief priests in	Mk 14:10	565
The disciples **w** out and	Mk 14:16	1831
they **w** out to the Mount of Olives.	Mk 14:26	1831
And He **w** a little beyond *them,* and	Mk 14:35	4281
Again He **w** away and prayed,	Mk 14:39	565
coming, Judas immediately **w** to Him,	Mk 14:45	4334
And he **w** out onto the porch,	Mk 14:68	1831
The crowd **w** up and began	Mk 15:8	305
up courage and **w** in before Pilate,	Mk 15:43	1525
They **w** out and fled from the tomb,	Mk 16:8	1831
She **w** and reported to those who	Mk 16:10	4198
They **w** away and reported it to	Mk 16:13	565
w out and preached everywhere,	Mk 16:20	1831
were ended, he **w** back home.	Lk 1:23	565
Now at this time Mary arose and **w**	Lk 1:39	4198
decree **w** out from Caesar Augustus,	Lk 2:1	1831
Joseph also **w** up from Galilee,	Lk 2:4	305
The shepherds **w** back,	Lk 2:20	5290
Now His parents **w** to Jerusalem every	Lk 2:41	4198
they **w** up *there* according to the	Lk 2:42	305
the caravan, and **w** a day's journey;	Lk 2:44	2064
And He **w** down with them and came	Lk 2:51	2597
through their midst, He **w** His way.	Lk 4:30	4198
left and **w** to a secluded place;	Lk 4:42	4198
they **w** up on the roof and let him	Lk 5:19	305
lying on, and **w** home glorifying	Lk 5:25	565
After that He **w** out and	Lk 5:27	1831
He **w** off to the mountain to pray,	Lk 6:12	1831
of the people, He **w** to Capernaum.	Lk 7:1	1525
afterwards He **w** to a city called Nain;	Lk 7:11	4198
This report concerning Him **w** out	Lk 7:17	1831
"The sower **w** out to sow his seed;	Lk 8:5	1831
w out to see what had happened;	Lk 8:35	1831
So he **w** away, proclaiming	Lk 8:39	565
But as He **w**, the crowds were	Lk 8:42	5217
and **w** up on the mountain to pray.	Lk 9:28	305
and they **w** and entered a village	Lk 9:52	4198
And they **w** on to another village.	Lk 9:56	4198
and **w** away leaving him half dead.	Lk 10:30	565
and He **w** in, and reclined *at the*	Lk 11:37	1525
when He **w** into the house of one of	Lk 14:1	2064
And He also **w** on to say to the one	Lk 14:12	
w on a journey into a distant country,	Lk 15:13	589
"So he **w** and hired himself out to	Lk 15:15	4198
but on the day that Lot **w** out from	Lk 17:29	1831
men **w** up into the temple to pray,	Lk 18:10	305
this man **w** to his house	Lk 18:14	2597
things, Jesus **w** on to tell a parable,	Lk 19:11	4369
"A nobleman **w** to a	Lk 19:12	4198
So those who were sent **w** away and	Lk 19:32	565
w on a journey for a long time.	Lk 20:9	589
And he **w** away and discussed with	Lk 22:4	565
And he **w** out and wept bitterly.	Lk 22:62	1831
this man **w** to Pilate and asked for	Lk 23:52	4334
and he **w** away to his home,	Lk 24:12	565
those who were with us **w** to the tomb	Lk 24:24	565
So He **w** in to stay with them.	Lk 24:29	1525
After this He **w** down to Capernaum,	Jn 2:12	2597
near, and Jesus **w** up to Jerusalem.	Jn 2:13	305
He left Judea and **w** away again into	Jn 4:3	565
her waterpot, and **w** into the city and	Jn 4:28	565
They **w** out of the city, and were	Jn 4:30	1831
w forth from there into Galilee.	Jn 4:43	1831
themselves also **w** to the feast.	Jn 4:45	2064
Judea into Galilee, he **w** to Him and	Jn 4:47	565
Jews, and Jesus **w** up to Jerusalem.	Jn 5:1	305
for an angel of the Lord **w** down at	Jn 5:4	2597
The man **w** away, and told the Jews	Jn 5:15	565
After these things Jesus **w** away to	Jn 6:1	565
Then Jesus **w** up on the mountain,	Jn 6:3	424
His disciples **w** down to the sea,	Jn 6:16	2597
feast, then He Himself also **w** up,	Jn 7:10	305
feast Jesus **w** up into the temple,	Jn 7:14	305
[Everyone **w** to his home.	Jn 7:53	4198
Jesus **w** to the Mount of Olives.	Jn 8:1	4198
Himself and **w** out of the temple.	Jn 8:59	1831
So he **w** away and washed, and	Jn 9:7	565
so I **w** away and washed, and I	Jn 9:11	565
And He **w** away again beyond the	Jn 10:40	565
Jesus was coming, **w** to meet Him,	Jn 11:20	5221
she had said this, she **w** away and	Jn 11:28	565
Mary got up quickly and **w** out,	Jn 11:31	1831
But some of them **w** to the	Jn 11:46	565
but **w** away from there to the	Jn 11:54	565
and many **w** up to Jerusalem out of	Jn 11:55	305
palm trees and **w** out to meet Him,	Jn 12:13	1831
also the people **w** and met Him,	Jn 12:18	5221
and He **w** away and hid Himself from	Jn 12:36	565
the morsel he **w** out immediately;	Jn 13:30	1831
He **w** forth with His disciples over	Jn 18:1	1831
were coming upon Him, **w** forth and	Jn 18:4	1831
w out and spoke to the doorkeeper,	Jn 18:16	1831
Pilate **w** out to them	Jn 18:29	1831
this, he **w** out again to the Jews and	Jn 18:38	1831
Jesus, therefore, and He **w** out,	Jn 19:17	1831
So Peter and the other disciple **w** forth,	Jn 20:3	1831
disciples **w** away again to their own	Jn 20:10	565
They **w** out and got into the boat;	Jn 21:3	1831
Simon Peter **w** up and drew the net	Jn 21:11	305
Therefore this saying **w** out among	Jn 21:23	1831
they **w** up to the upper room where	Ac 1:13	305
Lord Jesus **w** in and out among us	Ac 1:21	1831
they **w** to their own *companions*	Ac 4:23	2064

Then the captain **w** along with the	Ac 5:26	565
So they **w** on their way from the	Ac 5:41	4198
"And Jacob **w** down to Egypt and	Ac 7:15	2597
They **w** on stoning Stephen as	Ac 7:59	3036
w about preaching the word.	Ac 8:4	1330
Philip **w** down to the city of	Ac 8:5	2718
So he got up and **w**;	Ac 8:27	4198
As they **w** along the road they	Ac 8:36	4198
they both **w** down into the water,	Ac 8:38	2597
him, but **w** on his way rejoicing.	Ac 8:39	4198
of the Lord, **w** to the high priest,	Ac 9:1	4334
So Peter arose and **w** with them.	Ac 9:39	4905
Peter **w** up on the housetop about	Ac 10:9	305
Peter **w** down to the men and said,	Ac 10:21	2597
day he got up and **w** away with them,	Ac 10:23	1831
and *how* He **w** about doing good and	Ac 10:38	1330
"You **w** to uncircumcised men and	Ac 11:3	1525
These six brethren also **w** with me	Ac 11:12	2064
he **w** out and continued to follow,	Ac 12:9	1831
w out and went along one street,	Ac 12:10	1831
went out and **w** along one street,	Ac 12:10	4281
this, he **w** to the house of Mary,	Ac 12:12	2064
left and **w** to another place.	Ac 12:17	4198
Then he **w** down from Judea to	Ac 12:19	2718
they **w** down to Seleucia and from	Ac 13:4	2718
and he **w** about seeking those who	Ac 13:11	4013
and on the Sabbath day they **w** into	Ac 13:14	2064
against them and **w** to Iconium.	Ac 13:51	2064
he **w** away with Barnabas to Derbe.	Ac 14:20	1831
in Perga, they **w** down to Attalia.	Ac 14:25	2597
sent away, they **w** down to Antioch;	Ac 15:30	2718
And on the Sabbath day we **w**	Ac 16:13	1831
They **w** out of the prison and	Ac 16:40	1831
to Paul's custom, he **w** to them,	Ac 17:2	1525
they **w** into the synagogue of the	Ac 17:10	549
So Paul **w** out of their midst.	Ac 17:33	1831
he left Athens and **w** to Corinth.	Ac 18:1	2064
and **w** to the house of a man	Ac 18:7	2064
he **w** up and greeted the church,	Ac 18:22	305
the church, and **w** down to Antioch.	Ac 18:22	2597
them and the evil spirits **w** out.	Ac 19:12	1607
who **w** from place to place,	Ac 19:13	4022
But Paul **w** down and fell upon him	Ac 20:10	2597
I **w** about preaching the kingdom,	Ac 20:25	1330
we **w** aboard and set sail.	Ac 21:2	1910
Then we **w** on board the ship, and	Ac 21:6	1684
day Paul **w** in with us to James,	Ac 21:18	1524
with them, **w** into the temple giving	Ac 21:26	1524
w to the commander and told him,	Ac 22:26	4334
I **w** up to Jerusalem to worship.	Ac 24:11	305
w up to Jerusalem from Caesarea.	Ac 25:1	305
among them, he **w** down to Caesarea,	Ac 25:6	2597
and Paul **w** in *to see* him and after	Ac 28:8	1525
the word of God *first* **w** forth?	1Co 14:36	1831
of them, I **w** on to Macedonia.	2Co 2:13	1831
but I **w** away to Arabia, and	Ga 1:17	565
Then three years later I **w** up to	Ga 1:18	424
Then I **w** into the regions of Syria	Ga 1:21	2064
I **w** up again to Jerusalem with	Ga 2:1	305
of a revelation that I **w** up;	Ga 2:2	305
and he **w** out, not knowing where he	Heb 11:8	1831
country from which they **w** out,	Heb 11:15	1544a
they **w** about in sheepskins, in	Heb 11:37	4022
in which also He **w** and made	1Pe 3:19	4198
They **w** out from us, but they were	1Jn 2:19	1831
but *they* **w** *out,* so that it would	1Jn 2:19	
w out for the sake of the Name,	3Jn 1:7	1831
and **w** after strange flesh,	Jude 1:7	565
and he **w** out conquering and to	Rv 6:2	1831
And another, a red horse, **w** out;	Rv 6:4	1831
w up before God out of the angel's	Rv 8:4	305
and smoke **w** up out of the pit,	Rv 9:2	305
So I **w** to the angel, telling him	Rv 10:9	565
they **w** up into heaven in the cloud,	Rv 11:12	305
and **w** off to make war with the	Rv 12:17	565
So the first *angel* **w** and poured	Rv 16:2	565

WEPT

and lifted up her voice and **w**.	Gn 21:16	1058
So Esau lifted his voice and **w**.	Gn 27:38	1058
and lifted his voice and **w**.	Gn 29:11	1058
neck and kissed him, and they **w**.	Gn 33:4	1058
So his father **w** for him.	Gn 37:35	1058
He turned away from them and **w**.	Gn 42:24	1058
entered his chamber and **w** there.	Gn 43:30	1058
He **w** so loudly that the	Gn 45:2	
		5414, 6963, 1065
his brother Benjamin's neck and **w**,	Gn 45:14	1058
and Benjamin **w** on his neck.	Gn 45:14	1058
all his brothers and **w** on them,	Gn 45:15	1058
and **w** on his neck a long time.	Gn 46:29	1058
and **w** over him and kissed him.	Gn 50:1	1058
Egyptians **w** for him seventy days.	Gn 50:3	1058
Joseph **w** when they spoke to him.	Gn 50:17	1058
sons of Israel **w** again and said,	Nu 11:4	1058
you have **w** in the ears of the LORD,	Nu 11:18	1058
among you and have **w** before Him,	Nu 11:20	1058
and the people **w** that night.	Nu 14:1	1058
of Israel **w** for Aaron thirty days.	Nu 20:29	1058
returned and **w** before the LORD;	Dt 1:45	1058
So the sons of Israel **w** for Moses	Dt 34:8	1058
lifted up their voices and **w**.	Jg 2:4	1058
and **w** on the mountains because of	Jg 11:38	1058
wife **w** before him and said,	Jg 14:16	1058
However she **w** before him seven	Jg 14:17	1058
w before the LORD until evening,	Jg 20:23	1058
went up and came to Bethel and **w**;	Jg 20:26	1058
lifted up their voices and **w** bitterly.	Jg 21:2	1058
they lifted up their voices and **w**.	Ru 1:9	1058
lifted up their voices and **w** again;	Ru 1:14	1058

her; so she **w** and would not eat. 1Sa 1:7 1058
prayed to the LORD and **w** bitterly. 1Sa 1:10 1058
lifted up their voices and **w**. 1Sa 11:4 1058
kissed each other and **w** together, 1Sa 20:41 1058
but David **w** the more. 1Sa 20:41 1058
Saul lifted up his voice and **w**. 1Sa 24:16 1058
w until there was no strength in them 1Sa 30:4 1058
They mourned and **w** and fasted 2Sa 1:12 1058
voice and **w** at the grave of Abner, 2Sa 3:32 1058
of Abner, and all the people **w**. 2Sa 3:32 1058
all the people **w** again over him. 2Sa 3:34 1058
child was alive, you fasted and **w**; 2Sa 12:21 1058
was *still* alive, I fasted and **w**; 2Sa 12:22 1058
and lifted their voices and **w**; 2Sa 13:36 1058
all his servants **w** very bitterly. 2Sa 13:36 1058
Mount of Olives, and **w** as he went, 2Sa 15:30 1058
the chamber over the gate and **w**. 2Sa 18:33 1058
was ashamed, and the man of God **w**. 2Ki 8:11 1058
to him and **w** over him and said, 2Ki 13:14 1058
And Hezekiah **w** bitterly. 2Ki 20:3 1058
torn your clothes and **w** before Me, 2Ki 22:19 1058
your clothes and **w** before Me, 2Ch 34:27 1058
w with a loud voice when the Ezr 3:12 1058
for the people **w** bitterly. Ezr 10:1 1058
down and **w** and mourned for days; Ne 1:4 1058
to the king, fell at his feet, **w** and Es 8:3 1058
they raised their voices and **w**. Jb 2:12 1058
"Have I not **w** for the one whose Jb 30:25 1058
When I **w** in my soul with fasting, Ps 69:10 1058
Babylon, There we sat down and **w**, Ps 137:1 1058
And Hezekiah **w** bitterly. Is 38:3 1058
He **w** and sought His favor. Hos 12:4 1058
And he went out and **w** bitterly. Mt 26:75 *2799*
He saw the city and **w** over it, Lk 19:41 *2799*
And he went out and **w** bitterly. Lk 22:62 *2799*
Jesus **w**. Jn 11:35 *1145*
and so, as she **w**, she stooped and Jn 20:11 *2799*

WEST

Bethel on the **w** and Ai on the east; Gn 12:8 3220
and you will spread out to the **w** Gn 28:14 3220
to the **w** side of the wilderness and Ex 3:1 310
a very strong **w** wind which took up Ex 10:19 3220
rear of the tabernacle, to the **w**, Ex 26:22 3220
for the rear *side* to the **w**. Ex 26:27 3220
court on the **w** side *shall be* hangings Ex 27:12 3220
rear of the tabernacle, to the **w**, Ex 36:27 3220
for the rear *side* to the **w**. Ex 36:32 3220
For the **w** side *there were* Ex 38:12 3220
"On the **w** side *shall be* the Nu 2:18 3220
this shall be your **w** border. Nu 34:6 3220
on the **w** side two thousand cubits, Nu 35:5 3220
w and north and south and east, Dt 3:27 3220
w of the way toward the sunset, Dt 11:30 310
were beyond the Jordan to the **w**, Jos 5:1 3220
and Ai, on the **w** side of Ai; Jos 8:9 3220
and Ai, on the **w** side of the city. Jos 8:12 3220
guard on the **w** side of the city, Jos 8:13 3220
on the heights of Dor on the **w** Jos 11:2 3220
on the east and on the **w**, Jos 11:3 3220
beyond the Jordan toward the **w**, Jos 12:7 3220
the valley of Hinnom to the **w**, Jos 15:8 3220
The **w** border *was* at the Great Sea, Jos 15:12 3220
round on the **w** side southward, Jos 18:14 3220
This *was* the **w** side. Jos 18:14 3220
went up to the **w** and to Maralah, Jos 19:11 3220
it reached to Carmel on the **w** and Jos 19:26 3220
south and touched Asher on the **w**, Jos 19:34 3220
behold, it is **w** of Kiriath-jearim. Jg 18:12 310
over everything **w** of the River, 1Ki 4:24 5676
over all the kings **w** of the River; 1Ki 4:24 5676
facing north, three facing **w**, 1Ki 7:25 3220
and to the **w** Gezer with its towns, 1Ch 7:28 4628
on the four sides, to the east, **w**, 1Ch 9:24 3220
both to the east and to the **w**. 1Ch 12:15 4628
Shuppim and Hosah *it was* to the **w**, 1Ch 26:16 4628
At the Parbar on the **w** *there were* 1Ch 26:18 4628
affairs of Israel **w** of the Jordan, 1Ch 26:30 4628
facing the north, three facing **w**, 2Ch 4:4 3220
the **w** side of the city of David. 2Ch 32:30 4628
of David on the **w** side of Gihon, 2Ch 33:14 4628
in the **w** are appalled at his fate, Jb 18:20 314
not from the east, nor from the **w**, Ps 75:6 4628
As far as the east is from the **w**, Ps 103:12 4628
From the east and from the **w**, Ps 107:3 4628
east and the Philistines on the **w**; Is 9:12 268
of the Philistines on the **w**; Is 11:14 3220
They cry out from the **w** concerning Is 24:14 3220
east, And gather you from the **w**. Is 43:5 4628
from the north and from the **w**, Is 49:12 3220
the name of the LORD from the **w** Is 59:19 4628
the **w** *was* seventy cubits wide; Ezk 41:12 3220
He turned to the **w** side Ezk 42:19 3220
on the **w** side toward the west and Ezk 45:7 3220
on the west side toward the **w** and Ezk 45:7 3220
the **w** border to the east border. Ezk 45:7 3220
at the extreme rear toward the **w**. Ezk 46:19 3220
The **w** side *shall be* the Great Sea, Ezk 47:20 3220
This is the **w** side. Ezk 47:20 3220
Hamath, running from east to **w**, Ezk 48:1 3220
from the east side to the **w** side, Ezk 48:2 3220
from the east side to the **w** side, Ezk 48:3 3220
from the east side to the **w** side, Ezk 48:4 3220
from the east side to the **w** side, Ezk 48:5 3220
from the east side to the **w** side, Ezk 48:6 3220
from the east side to the **w** side, Ezk 48:7 3220
from the east side to the **w** side; Ezk 48:8 3220
toward the **w** 10,000 in width, Ezk 48:10 3220
and the **w** side 4,500 *cubits*. Ezk 48:16 3220
cubits, and on the **w** 250 *cubits*. Ezk 48:17 3220
the east and 10,000 toward the **w**; Ezk 48:18 3220
of the 25,000 toward the **w** border, Ezk 48:21 3220
from the east side to the **w** side, Ezk 48:23 3220
from the east side to the **w** side, Ezk 48:24 3220
from the east side to the **w** side, Ezk 48:25 3220
from the east side to the **w** side, Ezk 48:26 3220
from the east side to the **w** side, Ezk 48:27 3220
"On the **w** side, 4,500 *cubits*, Ezk 48:34 3220
a male goat was coming from the **w** Da 8:5 4628
will come trembling from the **w**. Hos 11:10 3220
east and from the land of the **w**; Zch 8:7
3996, 8121
be split in its middle from east to **w** Zch 14:4 3220
many will come from east and **w**, Mt 8:11 *1424*
east and flashes even to the **w**, Mt 24:27 *1424*
sent out through them from east to **w** Mk 16:20
you see a cloud rising in the **w**, Lk 12:54 *1424*
they will come from east and **w** and Lk 13:29 *1424*
south and three gates on the **w**. Rv 21:13 *1424*

WESTERN

'As for the **w** border, you shall Nu 34:6 3220
Euphrates, as far as the **w** sea. Dt 11:24 314
land of Judah as far as the **w** sea, Dt 34:2 314
And its rear guard into the **w** sea. Jl 2:20 314
the other half toward the **w** sea; Zch 14:8 314

WESTWARD

and southward and eastward and **w**; Gn 13:14 3220
to camp behind the tabernacle **w**, Nu 3:23 3220
about from Baalah **w** to Mount Seir, Jos 15:10 3220
It went down **w** to the Jos 16:3 3220
the border went **w** at Michmethath Jos 16:6 3220
continued **w** to the brook of Kanah, Jos 16:8 3220
up through the hill country **w**, Jos 18:12 3220
and the border went **w** and went to Jos 18:15 3220
border turned **w** to Aznoth-tabor and Jos 19:34 3220
brothers **w** beyond the Jordan. Jos 22:7 3220
and **w** in front of the 25,000 toward Ezk 48:21 3220
I saw the ram butting **w**, Da 8:4 3220

WET

are **w** with the mountain rains And Jb 24:8 7372
to **w** His feet with her tears, Lk 7:38 *1026*
she has **w** My feet with her tears and Lk 7:44 *1026*

WHAT

man to see **w** he would call them; Gn 2:19 4100
"**W** is this you have done?" Gn 3:13 4100
He said, "**W** have you done? Gn 4:10 4100
he knew **w** his youngest son had Gn 9:24 834
And this is **w** they began to do, Gn 11:6
"**W** is this you have done to me? Gn 12:18 4100
except **w** the young men have eaten, Gn 14:24 834
"O Lord GOD, **w** will You give me, Gn 15:2 4100
to her **w** is good in your sight." Gn 16:6 2896a
from Abraham **w** I am about to do, Gn 18:17 834
w He has spoken about him." Gn 18:19 834
cities, and **w** grew on the ground. Gn 19:25 6780
"**W** have you done to us? Gn 20:9 4100
"**W** have you encountered, that you Gn 20:10 4100
"**W** is the matter with you, Hagar? Gn 21:17 4100
"**W** do these seven ewe lambs mean, Gn 21:29 4100
w is that between me and you? Gn 23:15 4100
"This is **w** the man said to me," Gn 24:30 3541
so of **w** *use* then is the birthright Gn 25:32 4100
"**W** is this you have done to us? Gn 26:10 4100
Now as for you then, **w** can I do, Gn 27:37 4100
and he forgets **w** you did to him. Gn 27:45 834
w good will my life be to me?" Gn 27:46 4100
have done **w** I have promised you." Gn 28:15 834
Tell me, **w** shall your wages be?" Gn 29:15 4100
"**W** is this you have done to me? Gn 29:25 4100
"**W** shall I give you?" Gn 30:31 4100
and from **w** belonged to our father Gn 31:1 834
"**W** have you done by deceiving me Gn 31:26 4100
point out **w** is yours among my Gn 31:32 4100
"**W** is my transgression? Gn 31:36 4100
W is my sin that you have hotly Gn 31:36 4100
w have you found of all your Gn 31:37 4100
But **w** can I do this day to these Gn 31:43 4100
Then he selected from **w** he had Gn 32:13
"**W** is your name?" Gn 32:27 4100
"**W** do you mean by all this Gn 33:8 4310
let **w** you have be your own." Gn 33:9 834
But he said, "**W** need is there? Gn 33:15 4100
"**W** is this dream that you have Gn 37:10 4100
"**W** are you looking for?" Gn 37:15 4100
see **w** will become of his dreams!" Gn 37:20 4100
"**W** profit is it for us to kill Gn 37:26 4100
But **w** he did was displeasing in Gn 38:10 834
"**W** will you give me, that you may Gn 38:16 4100
"**W** pledge shall I give you?" Gn 38:18 4100
"**W** a breach you have made for Gn 38:29 4100
"This is **w** your slave did to me," Gn 39:19 1697
to Pharaoh **w** He is about to do. Gn 41:25
853, 834
to Pharaoh **w** He is about to do. Gn 41:28 834
"**W** is this that God has done to Gn 42:28 4100
"**W** is this deed that you have Gn 44:15 4100
W can we say to my lord? Gn 44:16 4100
W can we speak? And how can we Gn 44:16 4100
'**W** is your occupation?' Gn 46:33 4100
"**W** is your occupation?" Gn 47:3 4100
that I may tell you **w** will befall you Gn 49:1 834
and this is **w** their father said to Gn 49:28 834
"**W** if Joseph bears a grudge Gn 50:15
to find out **w** would happen to him. Ex 2:4 4100
and **w** is more, he even drew the Ex 2:19 1571
they may say to me, '**W** is His name?' Ex 3:13 4100
W shall I say to them?" Ex 3:13 4100
w has been done to you in Egypt. Ex 3:16
They will pay heed to **w** you say; Ex 3:18 6963
"**W** if they will not believe me or Ex 4:1
believe me or listen to **w** I say? Ex 4:1 6963
"**W** is that in your hand?" Ex 4:2 4100
these two signs or heed **w** you say, Ex 4:9 6963
and teach you **w** you are to say." Ex 4:12 834
I will teach you **w** you are to do. Ex 4:15 834
shall see **w** I will do to Pharaoh; Ex 6:1 834
w is an abomination to the Egyptians. Ex 8:26
sacrifice **w** is an abomination to the Ex 8:26
also eat the rest of **w** has escaped Ex 10:5 6413
w is left to you from the hail Ex 10:5
LORD, for that is **w** you desire." Ex 10:11
with **w** we shall serve the LORD." Ex 10:26 4100
to **w** each man should eat, Ex 12:4
w must be eaten by every person, Ex 12:16 834
for whoever eats **w** is leavened, Ex 12:19 4263b
'**W** does this rite mean to you?' Ex 12:26 4100
'It is because of **w** the LORD did Ex 13:8 2088
'**W** is this?' then you shall say to him Ex 13:14 4100
"**W** is this we have done, that we Ex 14:5 4100
"**W** shall we drink?" Ex 15:24 4100
and do **w** is right in His sight, Ex 15:26
when they prepare **w** they bring in, Ex 16:5 834
and **w** are we, that you grumble Ex 16:7 4100
And **w** are we? Your grumblings are Ex 16:8 4100
they said to one another, "**W** is it?" Ex 16:15 4478b
For they did not know **w** it was. Ex 16:15 4100
"This is **w** the LORD has Ex 16:16
1697, 834
"This is **w** the LORD meant: Ex 16:23 834
Bake **w** you will bake and boil what Ex 16:23 834
bake and boil **w** you will boil, Ex 16:23 834
"This is **w** the LORD has Ex 16:32
1697, 834
"**W** shall I do to this people? Ex 17:4 4100
"**W** is this thing that you are Ex 18:14 4100
seen **w** I did to the Egyptians, Ex 19:4 834
or any likeness of **w** is in heaven Ex 20:4 834
"If **w** he stole is actually found Ex 22:4 1591
for **w** has been torn to pieces. Ex 22:13 2966
W else shall he sleep in? Ex 22:27 4100
from **w** you sow in the field; Ex 23:16 834
of **w** is left over in the length of Ex 26:13
"Now this is **w** you shall do to Ex 29:1
1697, 834
is **w** you shall offer on the altar: Ex 29:38 834
"This is **w** everyone who is Ex 30:13
do not know **w** has become of him." Ex 32:1 4100
"**W** did this people do to you, Ex 32:21 4100
do not know **w** has become of him.' Ex 32:23 4100
because of **w** they did with the Ex 32:35 834
may know **w** I shall do with you.' " Ex 33:5 4100
w I am commanding you this day: Ex 34:11 834
of Israel **w** he had been commanded, Ex 34:34 834
and brought **w** they had spun, Ex 35:25 4299
table and arrange **w** belongs on it; Ex 40:4 6187
or has found **w** was lost and lied Lv 6:3 9
restore **w** he took by robbery or Lv 6:4 834
robbery or **w** he got by extortion, Lv 6:4 834
'**W** is left of it Aaron and his Lv 6:16
you shall wash **w** was splashed on. Lv 6:27 834
day **w** is left of it may be eaten; Lv 7:16
but **w** is left over from the flesh Lv 7:17
So they took **w** Moses had commanded Lv 9:5 834
"It is **w** the LORD spoke, saying, Lv 10:3 834
"*He shall offer* **w** he can afford, Lv 14:31 834
'This is **w** the LORD has commanded, Lv 17:2
1697, 834
'You shall not do **w** is done in the Lv 18:3 4639
nor are you to do **w** is done in the Lv 18:3 4639
but **w** remains until the third day Lv 19:6
"**W** are we going to eat on the Lv 25:20 4100
buy back **w** his relative has sold. Lv 25:25 4465
then **w** he has sold shall remain in Lv 25:28 4465
'**W**, therefore, belongs to the Lv 25:33 834
addition to **w** *else* he can afford; Nu 6:21 834
"This is **w** *applies* to the Levites: Nu 8:24 834
and I will listen to **w** the LORD Nu 9:8 4100
"See **w** the land is like, and Nu 13:18 4100
declared **w** should be done to him. Nu 15:34 4100
and I will find out **w** else the Nu 22:19 4100
"**W** have I done to you, that you Nu 22:28 4100
"**W** have you done to me? Nu 23:11 4100
w the LORD puts in my mouth?" Nu 23:12 834
"**W** has the LORD spoken?" Nu 23:17 4100
And to Israel, **w** God has done! Nu 23:23 4100
W the LORD speaks, that I will Nu 24:13 834
w this people will do to your people Nu 24:14 834
to the LORD **w** each man found, Nu 31:50 834
"This is **w** your fathers did when Nu 32:8 3541
and do **w** you have promised." Nu 32:24
"This is **w** the LORD has commanded Nu 36:6
1697, 834
for **w** god is there in heaven or on Dt 3:24 4310
w the LORD has done in the case of Dt 4:3 853, 834
"For **w** great nation is there that Dt 4:7 4310
"Or **w** great nation is there that Dt 4:8 4310
or any likeness *of* **w** is in heaven Dt 5:8 834
"You shall do **w** is right and Dt 6:18
'**W** *do* the testimonies and the Dt 6:20 4100
you shall well remember **w** the LORD Dt 7:18 834
you, to know **w** was in your heart, Dt 8:2 834
w was evil in the sight of the LORD Dt 9:18 7451a
w does the LORD your God require Dt 10:12 4100
and **w** He did to Egypt's army, to Dt 11:4 834
and **w** He did to you in the Dt 11:5 834
and **w** He did to Dathan and Abiram, Dt 11:6 834

at all **w** we are doing here today,	**Dt 12:8**	834
for you will be doing **w** is right	**Dt 12:25**	3477
for you will be doing **w** is good	**Dt 12:28**	2896a
and doing **w** is right in the sight	**Dt 13:18**	3477
all the produce from **w** you sow,	**Dt 14:22**	2233
w he has loaned to his neighbor;	**Dt 15:2**	834
w is evil in the sight of the LORD	**Dt 17:2**	7451a
except **w** *they receive* from	**Dt 18:8**	
when you do **w** is right in the eyes	**Dt 21:9**	3477
day he wills **w** he has to his sons,	**Dt 21:16**	834
perform **w** goes out from your lips,	**Dt 23:23**	4161
your God, **w** you have promised.	**Dt 23:23**	834
"Remember **w** the LORD your God did	**Dt 24:9**	834
"Remember **w** Amalek did to you	**Dt 25:17**	834
mad by the sight of **w** you see.	**Dt 28:34**	834
I will see **w** their end *shall be;*	**Dt 32:20**	4100
'They have made Me jealous with **w**	**Dt 32:21**	
and **w** you did to the two kings of	**Jos 2:10**	834
'**W** do these stones mean to you?'	**Jos 4:6**	4100
'**W** are these stones?'	**Jos 4:21**	4100
"**W** has my lord to say to his	**Jos 5:14**	4100
w can I say since Israel has	**Jos 7:8**	4100
And **w** will You do for Your great	**Jos 7:9**	4100
and tell me now **w** you have done.	**Jos 7:19**	4100
of Israel, and this is **w** I did:	**Jos 7:20**	2088
heard **w** Joshua had done to Jericho	**Jos 9:3**	834
Caleb said to her, "**W** do you want?"	**Jos 15:18**	4100
'**W** is this unfaithful act which	**Jos 22:16**	4100
"**W** have you to do with the LORD,	**Jos 22:24**	4100
Egypt by **w** I did in its midst;	**Jos 24:5**	834
own eyes saw **w** I did in Egypt.	**Jos 24:7**	834
Caleb said to her, "**W** do you want?"	**Jg 1:14**	4100
w is this you have done?"	**Jg 2:2**	4100
The sons of Israel did **w** was	**Jg 3:7**	7451a
Then the sons of Israel did **w** was	**Jg 6:1**	7451a
and you will hear **w** they say;	**Jg 7:11**	4100
"**W** is this thing you have done to	**Jg 8:1**	4100
"**W** have I done now in comparison	**Jg 8:2**	4100
and **w** was I able to do in	**Jg 8:3**	4100
"**W** kind of men *were* they whom you	**Jg 8:18**	375
"**W** you have seen me do, hurry *and*	**Jg 9:48**	4100
"**W** is between you and me, that	**Jg 11:12**	4100
'Do you not possess **w** Chemosh your	**Jg 11:24**	834
he may teach us **w** to do for the boy	**Jg 13:8**	4100
w shall be the boy's mode of life	**Jg 13:12**	4100
"**W** is your name, so that when	**Jg 13:17**	4310
father or mother **w** he had done.	**Jg 14:6**	834
"**W** is sweeter than honey?	**Jg 14:18**	4100
And **w** is stronger than a lion?"	**Jg 14:18**	4100
W then is this that you have done	**Jg 15:11**	4100
did **w** was right in his own eyes.	**Jg 17:6**	3477
And **w** are you doing in this *place?*	**Jg 18:3**	4100
And **w** do you have here?"	**Jg 18:3**	4100
"**W** *do you report?*"	**Jg 18:8**	4100
consider **w** you should do."	**Jg 18:14**	4100
"**W** are you doing?"	**Jg 18:18**	4100
"**W** is *the matter* with you, that	**Jg 18:23**	4100
away, and **w** do I have besides?	**Jg 18:24**	4100
'**W** is *the matter* with you?' "	**Jg 18:24**	4100
Then they took **w** Micah had made	**Jg 18:27**	834
"**W** is this wickedness that has	**Jg 20:12**	4100
"**W** shall we do for wives for	**Jg 21:7**	4100
"**W** one is there of the tribes of	**Jg 21:8**	4310
"**W** shall we do for wives for	**Jg 21:16**	4310
did **w** was right in his own eyes.	**Jg 21:25**	3477
drink from **w** the servants draw."	**Ru 2:9**	834
she beat out **w** she had gleaned,	**Ru 2:17**	834
mother-in-law saw **w** she had gleaned.	**Ru 2:18**	834
gave Naomi **w** she had left after she	**Ru 2:18**	834
he will tell you **w** you shall do."	**Ru 3:4**	834
"Do **w** seems best to you.	**1Sa 1:23**	2896a
w is in My heart and in My soul;	**1Sa 2:35**	834
"**W** is the word that He spoke to	**1Sa 3:17**	4100
let Him do **w** seems good to Him."	**1Sa 3:18**	2896a
"**W** *does* the noise of this great	**1Sa 4:6**	4100
"**W** *does* the noise of this	**1Sa 4:14**	4100
"**W** shall we do with the ark of	**1Sa 5:8**	4100
"**W** shall we do with the ark of	**1Sa 6:2**	4100
"**W** shall be the guilt offering	**1Sa 6:4**	4100
we go, **w** shall we bring the man?	**1Sa 9:7**	4100
to the man of God. **W** do we have?"	**1Sa 9:7**	4100
cook took up the leg with **w** was on it	**1Sa 9:24**	
"Here is **w** has been reserved!	**1Sa 9:24**	
"**W** shall I do about my son?" '	**1Sa 10:2**	4100
yourself **w** the occasion requires,	**1Sa 10:7**	834
and show you **w** you should do."	**1Sa 10:8**	834
"**W** has happened to the son of	**1Sa 10:11**	4100
tell me **w** Samuel said to you."	**1Sa 10:15**	4100
"**W** is *the matter* with the people	**1Sa 11:5**	4100
for consider **w** great things He has	**1Sa 12:24**	834
"**W** have you done?"	**1Sa 13:11**	4100
kept **w** the LORD commanded you."	**1Sa 13:14**	834
"Do **w** seems good to you."	**1Sa 14:40**	2896a
"Tell me **w** you have done."	**1Sa 14:43**	4100
Amalek *for* **w** he did to Israel,	**1Sa 15:2**	834
"**W** then is this bleating of the	**1Sa 15:14**	4100
and let me tell you **w** the LORD	**1Sa 15:16**	834
and did **w** was evil in the sight of the	**1Sa 15:19**	7451a
I will show you **w** you shall do;	**1Sa 16:3**	834
So Samuel did **w** the LORD said, and	**1Sa 16:4**	834
"**W** will be done for the man who	**1Sa 17:26**	4100
"**W** have I done now?	**1Sa 17:29**	4100
Now **w** more can he have but the	**1Sa 18:8**	
and **w** is my life *or* my father's	**1Sa 18:18**	4310
said to Jonathan, "**W** have I done?	**1Sa 20:1**	4100
W is my iniquity?	**1Sa 20:1**	4100
w is my sin before your father,	**1Sa 20:1**	4100
he be put to death? **W** has he done?	**1Sa 20:32**	4100
therefore, **w** do you have on hand?	**1Sa 21:3**	4100

I know **w** God will do for me."	**1Sa 22:3**	4100
w you have done to me this day.	**1Sa 24:19**	834
know and consider **w** you should do,	**1Sa 25:17**	4100
her hand **w** she had brought him and	**1Sa 25:35**	834
For **w** have I done?	**1Sa 26:18**	4100
Or **w** evil is in my hand?	**1Sa 26:18**	4100
know **w** your servant can do."	**1Sa 28:2**	834
"Behold, you know **w** Saul has done,	**1Sa 28:9**	834
but **w** do you see?"	**1Sa 28:13**	4100
He said to her, "**W** is his form?"	**1Sa 28:14**	4100
make known to me **w** I should do."	**1Sa 28:15**	4100
"**W** *are* these Hebrews *doing here?*"	**1Sa 29:3**	4100
For with **w** could this *man* make	**1Sa 29:4**	4100
"But **w** have I done?	**1Sa 29:8**	4100
And **w** have you found in your	**1Sa 29:8**	4100
with **w** the LORD has given us,	**1Sa 30:23**	834
Jabesh-gilead heard **w** the Philistines	**1Sa 31:11**	834
"**W** have you done? Behold, Abner	**2Sa 3:24**	4100
I, O Lord GOD, and **w** is my house,	**2Sa 7:18**	4310
w more can David say to You?	**2Sa 7:20**	4100
"And **w** one nation on the earth is	**2Sa 7:23**	4310
"**W** is your servant, that you	**2Sa 9:8**	4100
LORD do **w** is good in His sight."	**2Sa 10:12**	2896a
"**W** is this thing that you have	**2Sa 12:21**	4100
"**W** is your trouble?"	**2Sa 14:5**	4100
"From **w** city are you?"	**2Sa 15:2**	
		2088, 335
"**W** have I to do with you, O sons	**2Sa 16:10**	4100
"Give your advice. **W** shall we do?"	**2Sa 16:20**	4100
and let us hear **w** he has to say."	**2Sa 17:5**	4100
"This is **w** Ahithophel counseled	**2Sa 17:15**	2088
and this is **w** I have counseled.	**2Sa 17:15**	2088
tell the king **w** you have seen."	**2Sa 18:21**	834
but I did not know **w** *it was.*"	**2Sa 18:29**	4100
and to do **w** was good in his sight.	**2Sa 19:18**	2896a
nor remember **w** your servant did	**2Sa 19:19**	834
"**W** have I to do with you, O sons	**2Sa 19:22**	4100
do **w** is good in your sight.	**2Sa 19:27**	2896a
W right do I have yet that I	**2Sa 19:28**	4100
taste **w** I eat or what I drink?	**2Sa 19:35**	834
taste what I eat or **w** I drink?	**2Sa 19:35**	834
for him **w** is good in your sight."	**2Sa 19:37**	834
for him **w** is good in your sight;	**2Sa 19:38**	2896a
"**W** should I do for you?	**2Sa 21:3**	4100
w Rizpah the daughter of Aiah,	**2Sa 21:11**	834
sinned greatly in **w** I have done.	**2Sa 24:10**	834
Now consider and see **w** answer I	**2Sa 24:13**	4100
but these sheep, **w** have they done?	**2Sa 24:17**	4100
offer up **w** is good in his sight.	**2Sa 24:22**	2896a
the king said, "**W** do you wish?"	**1Ki 1:16**	4100
according to **w** is written in the	**1Ki 2:3**	
"Now you also know **w** Joab the son	**1Ki 2:5**	834
w he did to the two commanders of	**1Ki 2:5**	834
know **w** you ought to do to him,	**1Ki 2:9**	834
"Ask **w** *you wish* me to give you."	**1Ki 3:5**	4100
given you **w** you have not asked,	**1Ki 3:13**	834
I will do **w** you desire concerning	**1Ki 5:8**	2656
"**W** are these cities which you	**1Ki 9:13**	4100
besides **w** he gave her according to	**1Ki 10:13**	834
Solomon did **w** was evil in the	**1Ki 11:6**	7451a
observe **w** the LORD had commanded.	**1Ki 11:10**	834
"But **w** have you lacked with me,	**1Ki 11:22**	4100
doing **w** is right in My sight and	**1Ki 11:33**	3477
and do **w** is right in My sight by	**1Ki 11:38**	3477
"**W** counsel do you give that we	**1Ki 12:9**	4100
"**W** portion do we have in David?	**1Ki 12:16**	4100
you **w** will happen to the boy."	**1Ki 14:3**	4100
because David did **w** was right in	**1Ki 15:5**	3477
Asa did **w** was right in the	**1Ki 15:11**	3477
Baasha and **w** he did and his might,	**1Ki 16:5**	834
"**W** do I have to do with you, O	**1Ki 17:18**	4100
"**W** sin have I committed, that you	**1Ki 18:9**	4100
Has it not been told to my master **w** I	**1Ki 18:13**	834
"**W** are you doing here, Elijah?"	**1Ki 19:9**	4100
"**W** are you doing here, Elijah?"	**1Ki 19:13**	4100
again, for **w** have I done to you?"	**1Ki 19:20**	4100
observe and see **w** you have to do;	**1Ki 20:22**	834
LORD lives, **w** the LORD says to me,	**1Ki 22:14**	
		3588, 834
"**W** kind of man was he who came up	**2Ki 1:7**	4100
"Ask **w** I shall do for you before	**2Ki 2:9**	4100
"**W** do I have to do with you?	**2Ki 3:13**	4100
"**W** shall I do for you?	**2Ki 4:2**	4100
me, **w** do you have in the house?"	**2Ki 4:2**	4100
you shall set aside **w** is full."	**2Ki 4:4**	4392
w can I do for you?	**2Ki 4:13**	4100
"**W** then is to be done for her?"	**2Ki 4:14**	4100
for they did not know **w** *they were.*	**2Ki 4:39**	
"**W**, will I set this before a	**2Ki 4:43**	4100
from his hands **w** he brought.	**2Ki 5:20**	834
"Alas, my master! **W** shall we do?"	**2Ki 6:15**	351a
"**W** is the matter with you?"	**2Ki 6:28**	4100
w the Arameans have done to us.	**2Ki 7:12**	834
"But **w** is your servant, *who is*	**2Ki 8:13**	4100
"**W** did Elisha say to you?"	**2Ki 8:14**	4100
"**W** have you to do with peace?	**2Ki 9:18**	4100
"**W** have you to do with peace?	**2Ki 9:19**	4100
"**W** peace, so long as the	**2Ki 9:22**	4100
do **w** is good in your sight."	**2Ki 10:5**	2896a
for the LORD has done **w** He spoke	**2Ki 10:10**	834
executing **w** is right in My eyes,	**2Ki 10:30**	3477
according to **w** is written in the	**2Ki 14:6**	
He did **w** was right in the	**2Ki 15:34**	3477
and he did not do **w** was right in	**2Ki 16:2**	3477
"**W** is this confidence that you	**2Ki 18:19**	4100
you have heard **w** the kings of	**2Ki 19:11**	834
eat this year **w** grows of itself,	**2Ki 19:29**	5599b
year **w** springs from the same,	**2Ki 19:29**	5501b
done **w** is good in Your sight."	**2Ki 20:3**	2896a

"**W** will be the sign that the LORD	**2Ki 20:8**	4100
"**W** did these men say, and from	**2Ki 20:14**	4100
"**W** have they seen in your house?"	**2Ki 20:15**	4100
you heard **w** I spoke against this place	**2Ki 22:19**	834
"**W** is this monument that I see?"	**2Ki 23:17**	4100
w was fine gold and what was fine	**2Ki 25:15**	834
fine gold and **w** was fine silver.	**2Ki 25:15**	834
God granted him **w** he requested.	**1Ch 4:10**	834
knowledge of **w** Israel should do,	**1Ch 12:32**	4100
and **w** is my house that You have	**1Ch 17:16**	4310
"**W** more can David still *say* to	**1Ch 17:18**	4100
"And **w** one nation in the earth is	**1Ch 17:21**	4310
LORD do **w** is good in His sight."	**1Ch 19:13**	2896a
consider **w** answer I shall return	**1Ch 21:12**	4100
but these sheep, **w** have they done?	**1Ch 21:17**	4100
king do **w** is good in his sight.	**1Ch 21:23**	2896a
not take **w** is yours for the LORD,	**1Ch 21:24**	834
or **w** *is baked* in the pan or what	**1Ch 23:29**	
in the pan or **w** is well-mixed,	**1Ch 23:29**	
"Ask **w** I shall give you."	**2Ch 1:7**	4100
godly ones rejoice in **w** is good.	**2Ch 6:41**	2896b
for **w** she had brought to the king.	**2Ch 9:12**	834
"**W** counsel do you give that we	**2Ch 10:9**	4100
"**W** portion do we have in David?	**2Ch 10:16**	4100
even he may become a priest of **w**	**2Ch 13:9**	
"As the LORD lives, **w** my God says,	**2Ch 18:13**	834
"Consider **w** you are doing, for	**2Ch 19:6**	4100
be very careful **w** you do, for the	**2Ch 19:7**	
nor do we know **w** to do, but our	**2Ch 20:12**	4100
Joash did **w** was right in the	**2Ch 24:2**	
"But **w** *shall we* do for the	**2Ch 25:9**	4100
rejoiced over **w** God had prepared for	**2Ch 29:36**	
Judah to give them one heart to do **w**	**2Ch 30:12**	4687
and he did **w** *was* good, right and	**2Ch 31:20**	2896a
'On **w** are you trusting that you	**2Ch 32:10**	4100
'Do you not know **w** I and my	**2Ch 32:13**	4100
"**W** have we to do with each other,	**2Ch 35:21**	4100
did, and **w** was found against him,	**2Ch 36:8**	
Then we told them accordingly **w**	**Ezr 5:4**	4479
I issue a decree concerning **w** you	**Ezr 6:8**	
		4101, 1768
and I told them **w** to say to Iddo	**Ezr 8:17**	1697
God, **w** shall we say after this?	**Ezr 9:10**	4100
"**W** would you request?"	**Ne 2:4**	4100
I did not tell anyone **w** my God was	**Ne 2:12**	4100
where I had gone or **w** I had done;	**Ne 2:16**	4100
"**W** is this thing you are doing?	**Ne 2:19**	4100
"**W** are these feeble Jews doing?	**Ne 4:2**	4100
"Even **w** they are building	**Ne 4:3**	834
"**W** is this evil thing you are	**Ne 13:17**	4100
w is to be done with Queen Vashti,	**Es 1:15**	4100
he remembered Vashti and **w** she had	**Es 2:1**	834
Vashti and what she had done and **w**	**Es 2:1**	834
request anything except **w** Hegai,	**Es 2:15**	834
for Esther did **w** Mordecai told her	**Es 2:20**	3982
learn **w** this *was* and why it *was.*	**Es 4:5**	4100
"**W** is *troubling* you, Queen Esther?	**Es 5:3**	4100
And **w** is your request?	**Es 5:3**	4100
"**W** is your petition, for it shall	**Es 5:6**	4100
And **w** is your request?	**Es 5:6**	4100
my petition and do **w** I request,	**Es 5:8**	1246
w Mordecai had reported concerning	**Es 6:2**	834
"**W** honor or dignity has been	**Es 6:3**	4100
"**W** is to be done for the man whom	**Es 6:6**	4100
"**W** is your petition, Queen Esther?	**Es 7:2**	4100
And **w** is your request?	**Es 7:2**	4100
had disclosed **w** he was to her.	**Es 8:1**	4100
and they did **w** they pleased to	**Es 9:5**	7522
W then have they done in the rest	**Es 9:12**	4100
Now **w** is your petition?	**Es 9:12**	4100
And **w** is your further request?	**Es 9:12**	4100
w they had started to do,	**Es 9:23**	834
w Mordecai had written to them.	**Es 9:23**	834
both **w** they had seen in this	**Es 9:26**	4100
regard and **w** had happened to them,	**Es 9:26**	4100
"For **w** I fear comes upon me, And	**Jb 3:25**	6343
upon me, And **w** I dread befalls me.	**Jb 3:25**	834
"According to **w** I have seen,	**Jb 4:8**	834
"**W** is my strength, that I should	**Jb 6:11**	4100
And **w** is my end, that I should	**Jb 6:11**	4100
But **w** does your argument prove?	**Jb 6:25**	4100
"**W** is man that You magnify	**Jb 7:17**	4100
W have I done to You, O watcher	**Jb 7:20**	4100
the Almighty pervert **w** is right?	**Jb 8:3**	6664
'**W** are You doing?'	**Jb 9:12**	4100
high as the heavens, **w** can you do?	**Jb 11:8**	4100
Deeper than Sheol, **w** can you know?	**Jb 11:8**	4100
"**W** you know I also know;	**Jb 13:2**	1847
you speak **w** is unjust for God,	**Jb 13:7**	5767b
And speak **w** is deceitful for Him?	**Jb 13:7**	7423a
Then let come on me **w** may.	**Jb 13:13**	4100
"**W** do you know that we do not	**Jb 15:9**	4100
W do you understand that we do	**Jb 15:9**	
"**W** is man, that he should be	**Jb 15:14**	4100
And **w** I have seen I will also	**Jb 15:17**	2088
W wise men have told, And have not	**Jb 15:18**	834
Or **w** plagues you that you answer?	**Jb 16:3**	4100
And if I hold back, **w** has left me?	**Jb 16:6**	4100
'**W** pretext for a case against him	**Jb 19:28**	
"He returns **w** he has attained And	**Jb 20:18**	3022
And **w** would we gain if we entreat	**Jb 21:15**	4100
"For **w** does he care for his	**Jb 21:21**	4100
will repay him for **w** he has done?	**Jb 21:31**	
"You say, '**W** does God know?	**Jb 22:13**	4100
'**W** can the Almighty do to them?'	**Jb 22:17**	4100
And perceive **w** He would say to me.	**Jb 23:5**	4100
And **w** His soul desires, that He	**Jb 23:13**	
He performs **w** is appointed for me,	**Jb 23:14**	2706
"**W** a help you are to the weak!	**Jb 26:2**	4100

“**W** counsel you have given to *one*	**Jb 26:3**	4100
W helpful insight you have	**Jb 26:3**	
“For **w** is the hope of the godless	**Jb 27:8**	4100
W is with the Almighty I will not	**Jb 27:11**	834
And **w** is hidden he brings out to	**Jb 28:11**	8587
w *good was* the strength of their	**Jb 30:2**	4100
“And **w** is the portion of God from	**Jb 31:2**	4100
W then could I do when God arises?	**Jb 31:14**	4100
to account, **w** will I answer Him?	**Jb 31:14**	4100
and afraid to tell you **w** I think.	**Jb 32:6**	1843
to me, I too will tell **w** I think.’	**Jb 32:10**	1843
While you pondered **w** to say.	**Jb 32:11**	4405
remind a man **w** is right for him,	**Jb 33:23**	3477
sinned and perverted **w** is right,	**Jb 33:27**	3477
choose for ourselves **w** is right;	**Jb 34:4**	4941
us know among ourselves **w** is good.	**Jb 34:4**	4100
“**W** man is like Job, Who drinks up	**Jb 34:7**	4310
Teach me **w** I do not see;	**Jb 34:32**	
Therefore declare **w** you know.	**Jb 34:33**	4100
‘**W** advantage will it be to You?	**Jb 35:3**	4100
W profit will I have, more than	**Jb 35:3**	4100
“If you have sinned, **w** do you	**Jb 35:6**	4100
are many, **w** do you do to Him?	**Jb 35:6**	4100
righteous, **w** do you give to Him,	**Jb 35:7**	4100
Or **w** does He receive from your	**Jb 35:7**	4100
also, concerning **w** is coming up.	**Jb 36:33**	
“Teach us **w** we shall say to Him;	**Jb 37:19**	4100
“On **w** were its bases sunk?	**Jb 38:6**	4100
w can I reply to You?	**Jb 40:4**	4100
you have not spoken of Me **w** is right	**Jb 42:7**	
have not spoken of Me **w** is right,	**Jb 42:8**	
How long will you love **w** is worthless	**Ps 4:2**	7385b
is nothing reliable in **w** they say;	**Ps 5:9**	6310
W is man that You take	**Ps 8:4**	4100
W can the righteous do?”	**Ps 11:3**	4100
“**W** profit is there in my blood,	**Ps 30:9**	4100
me, because I follow **w** is good.	**Ps 38:20**	2896b
And **w** is the extent of my days;	**Ps 39:4**	4100
“And now, Lord, for **w** do I wait?	**Ps 39:7**	4100
as a moth **w** is precious to him;	**Ps 39:11**	
“**W** right have you to tell of My	**Ps 50:16**	4100
And done **w** is evil in Your sight,	**Ps 51:4**	7451a
more than speaking **w** is right.	**Ps 52:3**	6664
W can *mere* man do to me?	**Ps 56:4**	4100
W can man do to me?	**Ps 56:11**	4100
And will consider **w** He has done.	**Ps 64:9**	4639
tell of **w** He has done for my soul.	**Ps 66:16**	834
W I did not steal, I then have to	**Ps 69:4**	834
W god is great like our God?	**Ps 77:13**	4310
will hear **w** God the LORD will say;	**Ps 85:8**	4100
the LORD will give **w** is good,	**Ps 85:12**	2896b
Remember **w** my span of life is;	**Ps 89:47**	4100
For **w** vanity You have created all	**Ps 89:47**	4100
W man can live and not see death?	**Ps 89:48**	4310
made me glad by **w** You have done,	**Ps 92:4**	6467
soul He has filled with **w** is good.	**Ps 107:9**	2896b
W ails you, O sea, that you flee?	**Ps 114:5**	4100
W shall I render to the LORD For	**Ps 116:12**	4100
W can man do to me?	**Ps 118:6**	4100
W shall be given to you, and what	**Ps 120:3**	4100
and **w** more shall be done to you,	**Ps 120:3**	4100
will accomplish **w** concerns me;	**Ps 138:8**	1157
O LORD, **w** is man, that You take	**Ps 144:3**	4100
do not know over **w** they stumble.	**Pr 4:19**	4100
W the wicked fears will come upon	**Pr 10:24**	4034
bring forth **w** is acceptable,	**Pr 10:32**	7522
of the wicked **w** is perverted.	**Pr 10:32**	8419
one who withholds **w** is justly due,	**Pr 11:24**	3476
who speaks truth tells **w** is right,	**Pr 12:17**	6664
W is desirable in a man is his	**Pr 19:22**	8378
carefully **w** is before you,	**Pr 23:1**	834
When your lips speak **w** is right.	**Pr 23:16**	4339
w will you do in the end,	**Pr 25:8**	4100
Eat *only* **w** you need,	**Pr 25:16**	1767
not know **w** a day may bring forth.	**Pr 27:1**	4100
W is His name or His son’s name?	**Pr 30:4**	4100
W, O my son? And what, O son of	**Pr 31:2**	4100
And **w**, O son of my womb?	**Pr 31:2**	4100
And **w**, O son of my vows?	**Pr 31:2**	4100
drink and forget **w** is decreed,	**Pr 31:5**	
W advantage does man have in all	**Ec 1:3**	4100
W is crooked cannot be	**Ec 1:15**	
w is lacking cannot be counted.	**Ec 1:15**	2642
“**W** does it accomplish?”	**Ec 2:2**	4100
until I could see **w** good there is	**Ec 2:3**	335, 2088
for **w** *will* the man *do* who will	**Ec 2:12**	4100
except **w** has already been done?	**Ec 2:12**	834
For **w** does a man get in all his	**Ec 2:22**	4100
and a time to uproot **w** is planted.	**Ec 3:2**	
W profit is there to the worker	**Ec 3:9**	4100
for God seeks **w** has passed by.	**Ec 3:15**	
him to see **w** will occur after him?	**Ec 3:22**	4100
no delight in fools. Pay **w** you vow!	**Ec 5:4**	834
So **w** is the advantage to their	**Ec 5:11**	4100
w is the advantage to him who	**Ec 5:16**	4100
Here is **w** I have seen to be good	**Ec 5:18**	834
For **w** advantage does the wise man	**Ec 6:8**	4100
W *advantage* does the poor man	**Ec 6:8**	4100
W the eyes see is better than what	**Ec 6:9**	4758
is better than **w** the soul desires.	**Ec 6:9**	
named, and it is known **w** man is;	**Ec 6:10**	834
W *then* is the advantage to a man?	**Ec 6:11**	4100
For who knows **w** is good for a man	**Ec 6:12**	4100
For who can tell a man **w** will be	**Ec 6:12**	4100
able to straighten **w** He has bent?	**Ec 7:13**	834
W has been is remote and	**Ec 7:24**	4100
“**W** are you doing?”	**Ec 8:4**	4100
If no one knows **w** will happen, who	**Ec 8:7**	4100
No man knows **w** will happen, and	**Ec 10:14**	4100

tell him **w** will come after him?	**Ec 10:14**	834
for you do not know **w** misfortune	**Ec 11:2**	4100
“**W** is this coming up from	**SS 3:6**	4310
As to **w** you will tell him:	**SS 5:8**	4100
W kind of beloved is your beloved,	**SS 5:9**	4100
W kind of beloved is your beloved,	**SS 5:9**	4100
W shall we do for our sister On	**SS 8:8**	4100
“**W** are your multiplied sacrifices	**Is 1:11**	4100
For **w** he deserves will be done to	**Is 3:11**	
		1576, 3027
“**W** do you mean by crushing My	**Is 3:15**	4100
“**W** more was there to do for My	**Is 5:4**	4100
w I am going to do to My vineyard	**Is 5:5**	834
And you are not to fear **w** they	**Is 8:12**	4172
They slice off **w** *is* on the right	**Is 9:20**	
And they eat **w** *is* on the left	**Is 9:20**	
Now **w** will you do in the day of	**Is 10:3**	4100
will not judge by **w** His eyes see,	**Is 11:3**	4758
a decision by **w** His ears hear;	**Is 11:3**	4926
And let them understand **w** the LORD	**Is 19:12**	4100
lookout, let him report **w** he sees.	**Is 21:6**	834
W I have heard from the LORD of	**Is 21:10**	834
W is the matter with you now, that	**Is 22:1**	4100
‘**W** right do you have here, And	**Is 22:16**	4100
terror to understand **w** it means.”	**Is 28:19**	8052
That **w** is made would say to its	**Is 29:16**	4639
Or **w** is formed say to him who	**Is 29:16**	3336
not prophesy to us **w** is right,	**Is 30:10**	5228
the needy one speaks **w** is right.	**Is 32:7**	4941
are far away, hear **w** I have done;	**Is 33:13**	834
“**W** is this confidence that you	**Is 36:4**	4100
you have heard **w** the kings of	**Is 37:11**	834
eat this year **w** grows of itself,	**Is 37:30**	5599b
year **w** springs from the same,	**Is 37:30**	5501b
done **w** is good in Your sight.”	**Is 38:3**	2896a
“**W** shall I say? For He has spoken	**Is 38:15**	4100
“**W** is the sign that I shall go up	**Is 38:22**	4100
“**W** did these men say, and from	**Is 39:3**	4100
“**W** have they seen in your house?”	**Is 39:4**	4100
“**W** shall I call out?”	**Is 40:6**	4100
Or **w** likeness will you compare	**Is 40:18**	4100
to us **w** is going to take place;	**Is 41:22**	834
events, declare **w** they *were,*	**Is 41:22**	4100
Or announce to us **w** is coming;	**Is 41:22**	
‘**W** are you doing?’	**Is 45:9**	4100
‘**W** are you begetting?’	**Is 45:10**	4100
‘To **w** are you giving birth?’ ”	**Is 45:10**	4100
you from **w** will come upon you.	**Is 47:13**	834
“Now therefore, **w** do I have here,”	**Is 52:5**	4100
For **w** had not been told them they	**Is 52:15**	834
And **w** they had not heard they will	**Is 52:15**	834
spend money for **w** is not bread,	**Is 55:2**	
your wages for **w** does not satisfy?	**Is 55:2**	7654
to Me, and eat **w** is good,	**Is 55:2**	2896b
Without accomplishing **w** I desire,	**Is 55:11**	834
sabbaths, And choose **w** pleases Me,	**Is 56:4**	834
and rejoice forever in **w** I create;	**Is 65:18**	834
And will bring on them **w** they dread.	**Is 66:4**	4034
“**W** do you see, Jeremiah?”	**Jer 1:11**	4100
second time saying, “**W** do you see?”	**Jer 1:13**	4100
“**W** injustice did your fathers	**Jer 2:5**	4100
“But now **w** are you doing on the	**Jer 2:18**	4100
Or **w** are you doing on the road to	**Jer 2:18**	4100
Know **w** you have done!	**Jer 2:23**	4100
you seen **w** faithless Israel did?	**Jer 3:6**	834
O desolate one, **w** will you do?	**Jer 4:30**	4100
Nor can you understand **w** they say.	**Jer 5:15**	4100
w will you do at the end of it?	**Jer 5:31**	4100
O congregation, **w** is among them.	**Jer 6:18**	834
“For **w** purpose does frankincense	**Jer 6:20**	4100
and see **w** I did to it because of	**Jer 7:12**	834
“Do you not see **w** they are doing	**Jer 7:17**	4100
“But this is **w** I commanded them,	**Jer 7:23**	1697
They have spoken **w** is not right;	**Jer 8:6**	3653a
wickedness, Saying, ‘**W** have I done?’	**Jer 8:6**	4100
And **w** kind of wisdom do they have?	**Jer 8:9**	4100
And **w** I have given them will pass	**Jer 8:13**	
For **w** *else* can I do, because of	**Jer 9:7**	349
“**W** right has My beloved in My	**Jer 11:15**	4100
“**W** will you say when He appoints	**Jer 13:21**	4100
Judah, for **w** he did in Jerusalem.	**Jer 15:4**	834
‘For **w** reason has the LORD	**Jer 16:10**	4100
And **w** is our iniquity, or what is	**Jer 16:10**	4100
or **w** is our sin which we have	**Jer 16:10**	4100
to **w** my opponents are saying!	**Jer 18:19**	6963
not that **w** it means to know Me?”	**Jer 22:16**	4100
“I have heard **w** the prophets have	**Jer 23:25**	834
W does straw have *in common* with	**Jer 23:28**	4100
‘**W** is the oracle of the LORD?’	**Jer 23:33**	4100
you shall say to them, ‘**W** oracle?’	**Jer 23:33**	4100
‘**W** has the LORD answered?’	**Jer 23:35**	4100
‘**W** has the LORD spoken?’	**Jer 23:35**	4100
‘**W** has the LORD answered you?’	**Jer 23:37**	4100
‘**W** has the LORD spoken?’	**Jer 23:37**	4100
“**W** do you see, Jeremiah?”	**Jer 24:3**	4100
and **w** You have spoken has come to	**Jer 32:24**	834
w this people have spoken,	**Jer 33:24**	4100
and done **w** is right in My sight,	**Jer 34:15**	3477
w *way* have I sinned against you,	**Jer 37:18**	4100
the LORD in **w** I am saying to you,	**Jer 38:20**	834
us now **w** you said to the king and	**Jer 38:25**	4100
king and **w** the king said to you;	**Jer 38:25**	4100
w I have built I am about to tear	**Jer 45:4**	834
and **w** I have planted I am about to	**Jer 45:4**	834
escapes *And* say, ‘**W** has happened?’	**Jer 48:19**	4100
purposed and performed **W** He spoke	**Jer 51:12**	834
I will make **w** he has swallowed	**Jer 51:44**	1105
w was fine gold and what was fine	**Jer 52:19**	834
fine gold and **w** was fine silver.	**Jer 52:19**	834

To **w** shall I compare you, O	**La 2:13**	4100
To **w** shall I liken you as I	**La 2:13**	4100
The LORD has done **w** He purposed;	**La 2:17**	834
O LORD, **w** has befallen us;	**La 5:1**	4100
listen to **w** I am speaking to you;	**Ezk 2:8**	834
mouth and eat **w** I am giving you.”	**Ezk 2:8**	834
“Son of man, eat **w** you find;	**Ezk 3:1**	834
I have never eaten **w** died of itself or	**Ezk 4:14**	5038
do among you **w** I have not done,	**Ezk 5:9**	834
the seller will not regain **w** he sold	**Ezk 7:13**	4465
man, do you see **w** they are doing,	**Ezk 8:6**	4100
do you see **w** the elders of the	**Ezk 8:12**	834
‘**W** are you doing?’	**Ezk 12:9**	4100
w is this proverb you *people* have	**Ezk 12:22**	4100
you not know **w** these things *mean?*’	**Ezk 17:12**	4100
“**W** do you mean by using this	**Ezk 18:2**	4100
w was not good among his people,	**Ezk 18:18**	834
‘**W** was your mother?	**Ezk 19:2**	4100
‘**W** is the high place to which you	**Ezk 20:29**	4100
“**W** comes into your mind will not	**Ezk 20:32**	
and **w** if even the rod which	**Ezk 21:13**	4100
“Will you not tell us **w** these	**Ezk 24:19**	4100
back **w** he has taken by robbery,	**Ezk 33:15**	1500
and hear **w** the message is which	**Ezk 33:30**	4100
w you tread down with your feet and	**Ezk 34:19**	4823
w you foul with your feet!’ ”	**Ezk 34:19**	4833
to us **w** you mean by these?’	**Ezk 37:18**	4100
servants according to **w** you see.”	**Da 1:13**	3512c
“For **w** reason is the decree from	**Da 2:15**	4101
He knows **w** is in the darkness, And	**Da 2:22**	4101
to me **w** we requested of You,	**Da 2:23**	1768
w will take place in the latter days.	**Da 2:28**	4101
to **w** would take place in the future;	**Da 2:29**	4101
known to you **w** will take place.	**Da 2:29**	4101
w will take place in the future;	**Da 2:45**	4101
and **w** god is there who can deliver	**Da 3:15**	4479
‘**W** have You done?’	**Da 4:35**	4101
I am going to let you know **w** will	**Da 8:19**	834
like **w** was done to Jerusalem.	**Da 9:12**	3512c
an understanding of **w** will happen to	**Da 10:14**	834
I will tell you **w** is inscribed in	**Da 10:21**	
w his fathers never did,	**Da 11:24**	834
w *will be* the outcome of these	**Da 12:8**	4100
of Israel I declare **w** is sure.	**Hos 5:9**	
W shall I do with you, O Ephraim?	**Hos 6:4**	4100
W shall I do with you, O Judah?	**Hos 6:4**	4100
W will you do on the day of the	**Hos 9:5**	4100
w will You give? Give them a	**Hos 9:14**	4100
the king, **w** can he do for us?”	**Hos 10:3**	4100
w more have I to do with idols?	**Hos 14:8**	4100
W the gnawing locust has left, the	**Jl 1:4**	3499a
w the swarming locust has left,	**Jl 1:4**	3499a
w the creeping locust has left,	**Jl 1:4**	3499a
“Moreover, **w** are you to Me, O	**Jl 3:4**	4100
not know how to do **w** is right,”	**Am 3:10**	5228
to man **w** are His thoughts,	**Am 4:13**	4100
For **w** purpose *will* the day of the	**Am 5:18**	4100
“**W** do you see, Amos?”	**Am 7:8**	4100
“**W** do you see, Amos?”	**Am 8:2**	4100
W is your occupation?	**Jon 1:8**	4100
W is your country?	**Jon 1:8**	4100
From **w** people are you?”	**Jon 1:8**	335, 2088
“**W** should we do to you that the	**Jon 1:11**	4100
was not this **w** I said while I was	**Jon 4:2**	1697
see **w** would happen in the city.	**Jon 4:5**	4100
W is the rebellion of Jacob?	**Mi 1:5**	4310
W is the high place of Judah?	**Mi 1:5**	4310
Hear now **w** the LORD is saying,	**Mi 6:1**	834
“My people, **w** have I done to you,	**Mi 6:3**	4100
remember now **W** Balak king of Moab	**Mi 6:5**	4100
And **w** Balaam son of Beor answered	**Mi 6:5**	4100
With **w** shall I come to the LORD	**Mi 6:6**	4100
He has told you, O man, **w** is good;	**Mi 6:8**	4100
And **w** does the LORD require of you	**Mi 6:8**	4100
And **w** you do preserve I will give	**Mi 6:14**	834
to see **w** He will speak to me,	**Hab 2:1**	4100
“Woe to him who increases **w** is not	**Hab 2:6**	
“**W** profit is the idol when its	**Hab 2:18**	4100
the oil, on **w** the ground produces,	**Hg 1:11**	834
and **w** they offer there is unclean.	**Hg 2:14**	834
“My lord, **w** are these?”	**Zch 1:9**	4100
“I will show you **w** these are.”	**Zch 1:9**	4100
“**W** are these?” And he answered me	**Zch 1:19**	4100
“**W** are these coming to do?”	**Zch 1:21**	4100
He said to me, “**W** do you see?”	**Zch 4:2**	4100
“**W** are these, my lord?”	**Zch 4:4**	4100
“Do you not know **w** these are?”	**Zch 4:5**	4100
‘**W** are you, O great mountain?	**Zch 4:7**	4310
“**W** are these two olive trees on	**Zch 4:11**	4100
“**W** are the two olive branches	**Zch 4:12**	4100
“Do you not know **w** these are?”	**Zch 4:13**	4100
And he said to me, “**W** do you see?”	**Zch 5:2**	4100
now your eyes and see **w** this is	**Zch 5:5**	4100
I said, “**W** is it?” And he said,	**Zch 5:6**	4100
“**W** are these, my lord?”	**Zch 6:4**	4100
for all these are **w** I hate,’	**Zch 8:17**	834
For **w** comeliness and beauty *will*	**Zch 9:17**	4100
W is to die, let it die, and what	**Zch 11:9**	
die, and **w** is to be annihilated,	**Zch 11:9**	
‘**W** are these wounds between your	**Zch 13:6**	4100
you bring **w** was taken by robbery and	**Mal 1:13**	
what was taken by robbery and **w** *is*	**Mal 1:13**	
“Yet you say, ‘For **w** reason?’	**Mal 2:14**	4100
And **w** did *that* one *do* while he was	**Mal 2:15**	4100
‘**W** have we spoken against You?’	**Mal 3:13**	4100
and **w** profit is it that we have	**Mal 3:14**	4100
w was spoken by the Lord through	**Mt 1:22**	*3588*
for this is **w** has been written by	**Mt 2:5**	*3704*
fulfill **w** had been spoken by the Lord	**Mt 2:15**	*3588*

Then **w** had been spoken through	Mt 2:17	3588
fulfill **w** was spoken through the	Mt 2:23	3588
This was to fulfill **w** was spoken	Mt 4:14	3588
who love you, **w** reward do you have?	Mt 5:46	5101
w more are you doing *than others?*	Mt 5:47	5101
know **w** your right hand is doing	Mt 6:3	5101
and your Father who sees **w** *is done*	Mt 6:4	
and your Father who sees **w** *is done*	Mt 6:6	
for your Father knows **w** you need before	Mt 6:8	3739
and your Father who sees **w** *is done*	Mt 6:18	
your life, *as to* **w** you will eat	Mt 6:25	5101
will eat or **w** you will drink;	Mt 6:25	5101
body, *as to* **w** you will put on.	Mt 6:25	5101
"Do not worry then, saying, '**W**	Mt 6:31	5101
'**W** will we drink?'	Mt 6:31	5101
or '**W** will we wear for clothing?'	Mt 6:31	5101
"Do not give **w** is holy to dogs,	Mt 7:6	3588
"Or **w** man is there among you who	Mt 7:9	5101
give **w** is good to those who ask Him	Mt 7:11	
to fulfill **w** was spoken through	Mt 8:17	3588
"**W** kind of a man is this, that	Mt 8:27	4217
"**W** business do we have with each	Mt 8:29	5101
including **w** had happened to	Mt 8:33	3588
"But go and learn **w** this means:	Mt 9:13	5101
about how or **w** you are to say;	Mt 10:19	5101
in that hour **w** you are to say.	Mt 10:19	5101
"**W** I tell you in the darkness,	Mt 10:27	3739
and **w** you hear *whispered* in *your*	Mt 10:27	3739
report to John **w** you hear and see:	Mt 11:4	3739
"**W** did you go out into the	Mt 11:7	5101
"But **w** did you go out to see?	Mt 11:8	5101
"But **w** did you go out to see? A	Mt 11:9	5101
"But to **w** shall I compare this	Mt 11:16	5101
Your disciples do **w** is not lawful	Mt 12:2	3739
"Have you not read **w** David did when	Mt 12:3	5101
"But if you had known **w** this means,	Mt 12:7	5101
"**W** man is there among you	Mt 12:11	5101
to fulfill **w** was spoken through	Mt 12:17	3588
you, being evil, speak **w** is good?	Mt 12:34	
out of *his* good treasure **w** is good;	Mt 12:35	
out of *his* evil treasure **w** is evil.	Mt 12:35	
even **w** he has shall be taken away	Mt 13:12	3739
men desired to see **w** you see,	Mt 13:17	3739
and to hear **w** you hear, and did	Mt 13:17	3739
away **w** has been sown in his heart.	Mt 13:19	3588
to fulfill **w** was spoken through the	Mt 13:35	3588
They picked up **w** was left over	Mt 14:20	3588
not **w** enters into the mouth	Mt 15:11	3588
but **w** proceeds out of the mouth,	Mt 15:11	3588
and they picked up **w** was left over	Mt 15:37	3588
"For **w** will it profit a man if	Mt 16:26	5101
Or **w** will a man give in exchange	Mt 16:26	5101
"**W** do you think, Simon?	Mt 17:25	5101
"**W** do you think? If any man has a	Mt 18:12	5101
'Pay back **w** you owe.'	Mt 18:28	5101
he should pay back **w** was owed.	Mt 18:30	3588
fellow slaves saw **w** had happened,	Mt 18:31	3588
W therefore God has joined	Mt 19:6	3739
w good thing shall I do that I may	Mt 19:16	5101
are you asking Me about **w** is good?	Mt 19:17	3588
w am I still lacking?"	Mt 19:20	5101
w then will there be for us?"	Mt 19:27	5101
'Take **w** is yours and go,	Mt 20:14	3588
do **w** I wish with what is my own?	Mt 20:15	3739
do what I wish with **w** is my own?	Mt 20:15	3588
He said to her, "**W** do you wish?"	Mt 20:21	5101
do not know **w** you are asking.	Mt 20:22	5101
"**W** do you want Me to do for you?"	Mt 20:32	5101
w was spoken through the prophet	Mt 21:4	3588
hear **w** these *children* are saying?"	Mt 21:16	5101
do **w** was done to the fig tree,	Mt 21:21	3588
"By **w** authority are You doing	Mt 21:23	4169
by **w** authority I do these things.	Mt 21:24	4169
baptism of John was from **w** *source,*	Mt 21:25	4159
by **w** authority I do these things.	Mt 21:27	4169
"But **w** do you think?	Mt 21:28	5101
w will he do to those vine-growers?"	Mt 21:40	5101
they might trap Him in **w** He said.	Mt 22:15	
"Tell us then, **w** do You think?	Mt 22:17	5101
have you not read **w** was spoken to you	Mt 22:31	3588
"**W** do you think about the Christ,	Mt 22:42	5101
and **w** *will be* the sign of Your	Mt 24:3	5101
known at **w** time of the night the thief	Mt 24:43	4169
See, you have **w** is yours.'	Mt 25:25	3588
even **w** he does have shall be taken	Mt 25:29	3739
w this woman has done will also	Mt 26:13	3739
"**W** are you willing to give me to	Mt 26:15	5101
"Friend, *do* **w** you have come for."	Mt 26:50	3739
W is it that these men are	Mt 26:62	5101
W further need do we have of	Mt 26:65	5101
w do you think?"	Mt 26:66	5101
know **w** you are talking about."	Mt 26:70	5101
But they said, "**W** is that to us?	Mt 27:4	5101
"Then **w** shall I do with Jesus who	Mt 27:22	5101
"Why, **w** evil has He done?"	Mt 27:23	5101
"**W** business do we have with each other,	Mk 1:24	5101
"**W** is this? A new teaching with	Mk 1:27	5101
for that is **w** I came for."	Mk 1:38	
your cleansing **w** Moses commanded,	Mk 1:44	3739
w is not lawful on the Sabbath?"	Mk 2:24	3739
"Have you never read **w** David did	Mk 2:25	5101
"Take care **w** you listen to.	Mk 4:24	5101
even **w** he has shall be taken away	Mk 4:25	3739
by **w** parable shall we present it?	Mk 4:30	5101
"**W** business do we have with each other,	Mk 5:7	5101
"**W** is your name?"	Mk 5:9	5101
to see **w** it was that had happened.	Mk 5:14	5101
report to them **w** great things the Lord	Mk 5:19	3745
w great things Jesus had done for him	Mk 5:20	3745

aware of **w** had happened to her,	Mk 5:33	3739
overhearing **w** was being spoken,	Mk 5:36	3588, 3056
and **w** is *this* wisdom given to Him,	Mk 6:2	5101
"**W** shall I ask for?"	Mk 6:24	5101
of the man are **w** defile the man.	Mk 7:15	
man, that is **w** defiles the man.	Mk 7:20	
baskets full of **w** was left over of the	Mk 8:8	4051
"For **w** does it profit a man to	Mk 8:36	5101
"For **w** will a man give in	Mk 8:37	5101
For he did not know **w** to answer;	Mk 9:6	5101
relate to anyone **w** they had seen,	Mk 9:9	3739
w rising from the dead meant.	Mk 9:10	5101
"**W** are you discussing with them?"	Mk 9:16	5101
"**W** were you discussing on the way?"	Mk 9:33	5101
w will you make it salty *again?*	Mk 9:50	5101
"**W** did Moses command you?"	Mk 10:3	5101
"**W** therefore God has joined	Mk 10:9	3739
w shall I do to inherit eternal life?	Mk 10:17	5101
them **w** was going to happen to Him,	Mk 10:32	3588
"**W** do you want Me to do for you?"	Mk 10:36	5101
do not know **w** you are asking.	Mk 10:38	5101
"**W** do you want Me to do for you?"	Mk 10:51	5101
"**W** are you doing, untying the	Mk 11:5	5101
that **w** he says is going to happen,	Mk 11:23	3739
"By **w** authority are You doing	Mk 11:28	4169
by **w** authority I do these things.	Mk 11:29	4169
by **w** authority I do these things."	Mk 11:33	4169
"**W** will the owner of the vineyard	Mk 12:9	5101
"**W** commandment is the foremost of	Mk 12:28	4169
so in **w** sense is He his son?"	Mk 12:37	4159
behold **w** wonderful stones and what	Mk 13:1	4217
and **w** wonderful buildings!"	Mk 13:1	4217
and **w** *will be* the sign when all	Mk 13:4	5101
beforehand about **w** you are to say,	Mk 13:11	5101
"**W** I say to you I say to all, 'Be	Mk 13:37	3739
"She has done **w** she could;	Mk 14:8	3739
w this woman has done will also be	Mk 14:9	3588
yet not **w** I will, but what You	Mk 14:36	5101
what I will, but **w** You will."	Mk 14:36	5101
they did not know **w** to answer Him.	Mk 14:40	5101
W is it that these men are	Mk 14:60	5101
"**W** further need do we have of	Mk 14:63	5101
w you are talking about."	Mk 14:68	5101
"Then **w** shall I do with Him whom	Mk 15:12	5101
"Why, **w** evil has He done?"	Mk 15:14	5101
to decide **w** each man should take.	Mk 15:24	5101
and kept pondering **w** kind of	Lk 1:29	4217
a fulfillment of **w** had been spoken to	Lk 1:45	
as to **w** he wanted him called.	Lk 1:62	5101, 302
"**W** then will this child *turn out*	Lk 1:66	5101
according to **w** was said in the Law	Lk 2:24	
"Then **w** shall we do?"	Lk 3:10	5101
"Teacher, **w** shall we do?"	Lk 3:12	5101
than **w** you have been ordered to."	Lk 3:13	
"And **w** *about* us, what shall we	Lk 3:14	
what about us, **w** shall we do?"	Lk 3:14	5101
W business do we have with each other,	Lk 4:34	5101
"**W** is this message?	Lk 4:36	5101
picked up **w** he had been lying on,	Lk 5:25	3739
w is not lawful on the Sabbath?"	Lk 6:2	3739
w David did when he was hungry,	Lk 6:3	3739
But He knew **w** they were thinking,	Lk 6:8	1261
together **w** they might do to Jesus.	Lk 6:11	5101, 302
and whoever takes away **w** is yours,	Lk 6:30	3588
love you, **w** credit is *that* to you?	Lk 6:32	4169
to you, **w** credit is *that* to you?	Lk 6:33	4169
receive, **w** credit is *that* to you?	Lk 6:34	4169
his heart brings forth **w** is good;	Lk 6:45	18
treasure brings forth **w** is evil;	Lk 6:45	4190
'Lord, Lord,' and do not do **w** I say?	Lk 6:46	3739
to John **w** you have seen and heard:	Lk 7:22	3739
"**W** did you go out into the	Lk 7:24	5101
"But **w** did you go out to see?	Lk 7:25	5101
"But **w** did you go out to see?	Lk 7:26	5101
"To **w** then shall I compare the	Lk 7:31	5101
generation, and **w** are they like?	Lk 7:31	5101
He would know who and **w** sort of	Lk 7:39	4217
Him as to **w** this parable meant.	Lk 8:9	5101
even **w** he thinks he has shall be	Lk 8:18	3739
"**W** business do we have with	Lk 8:28	5101
"**W** is your name?"	Lk 8:30	5101
the herdsmen saw **w** had happened,	Lk 8:34	
went out to see **w** had happened;	Lk 8:35	
w great things God has done for you.	Lk 8:39	3745
w great things Jesus had done for him.	Lk 8:39	3745
to tell no one **w** had happened.	Lk 8:56	
"For **w** is a man profited if he	Lk 9:25	5101
not realizing **w** he was saying.	Lk 9:33	3739
knowing **w** they were thinking in	Lk 9:47	1261
know **w** kind of spirit you are of;	Lk 9:55	4169
and drinking **w** they give you;	Lk 10:7	
you, eat **w** is set before you;	Lk 10:8	
w shall I do to inherit eternal life?	Lk 10:25	5101
"**W** is written in the Law?	Lk 10:26	5101
and **w** you have whispered in the	Lk 12:3	3739
worry about how or **w** you are	Lk 12:11	5101
your defense, or **w** you are to say;	Lk 12:11	5101
very hour **w** you ought to say."	Lk 12:12	3739
'**W** shall I do, since I have no	Lk 12:17	5101
'This is **w** I will do:	Lk 12:18	
who will own **w** you have prepared?'	Lk 12:20	3739
your life, *as to* **w** you will eat;	Lk 12:22	5101
body, *as to* **w** you will put on.	Lk 12:22	5101
"And do not seek **w** you will eat	Lk 12:29	5101
will eat and **w** you will drink,	Lk 12:29	5101
at **w** hour the thief was coming,	Lk 12:39	4169

own initiative judge **w** is right?	Lk 12:57	1342
"**W** is the kingdom of God like,	Lk 13:18	5101
like, and to **w** shall I compare it?	Lk 13:18	5101
"To **w** shall I compare the kingdom	Lk 13:20	5101
w you commanded has been done,	Lk 14:22	3739
"Or **w** king, when he sets out to	Lk 14:31	5101
with **w** will it be seasoned?	Lk 14:34	5101
"**W** man among you, if he has a	Lk 15:4	5101
"Or **w** woman, if she has ten	Lk 15:8	5101
inquiring **w** these things could be.	Lk 15:26	5101, 302
'**W** is this I hear about you?	Lk 16:2	5101
'**W** shall I do, since my master is	Lk 16:3	5101
'I know **w** I shall do, so that when	Lk 16:4	5101
"Hear **w** the unrighteous judge said;	Lk 18:6	5101
w shall I do to inherit eternal life?	Lk 18:18	5101
began to inquire **w** this was.	Lk 18:36	5101
"**W** do you want Me to do for you?"	Lk 18:41	5101
know **w** business they had done.	Lk 19:15	5101
take up **w** you did not lay down and	Lk 19:21	3739
down and reap **w** you did not sow.'	Lk 19:21	3739
taking up **w** I did not lay down and	Lk 19:22	3739
down and reaping **w** I did not sow?	Lk 19:22	3739
even **w** he does have shall be taken	Lk 19:26	3739
"Tell us by **w** authority You are	Lk 20:2	4169
w authority I do these things."	Lk 20:8	4169
of the vineyard said, '**W** shall I do?	Lk 20:13	5101
W, then, will the owner of	Lk 20:15	5101
"**W** then is this that is written:	Lk 20:17	5101
And **w** *will be* the sign when these	Lk 21:7	5101
Him saw **w** was going to happen,	Lk 22:49	
know **w** you are talking about."	Lk 22:60	3739
"**W** further need do we have of	Lk 22:71	5101
"Why, **w** evil has this man done?	Lk 23:22	5101
w will happen when it is dry?"	Lk 23:31	5101
do not know **w** they are doing."	Lk 23:34	5101
w we deserve for our deeds;	Lk 23:41	3739
the centurion saw **w** had happened,	Lk 23:47	
when they observed **w** had happened,	Lk 23:48	
marveling at **w** had happened.	Lk 24:12	3588
"**W** are these words that you are	Lk 24:17	5101
And He said to them, "**W** things?"	Lk 24:19	4169
"**W** then? Are you Elijah?"	Jn 1:21	5101
W do you say about yourself?"	Jn 1:22	5101
and said to them, "**W** do you seek?"	Jn 1:38	5101
w does that have to do with us?	Jn 2:4	5101
"**W** sign do You show us	Jn 2:18	5101
for He Himself knew **w** was in man.	Jn 2:25	5101
we speak of **w** we know and testify of	Jn 3:11	3754
of what we know and testify of **w** we	Jn 3:11	3739
"**W** He has seen and heard, of that	Jn 3:32	3739
"You worship **w** you do not know; we	Jn 4:22	3739
we worship **w** we know, for salvation	Jn 4:22	3739
yet no one said, "**W** do You seek?"	Jn 4:27	5101
"**W** you said that we believe,	Jn 4:42	
knew **w** He was intending to do.	Jn 6:6	5101
w are these for so many people?"	Jn 6:9	5101
"**W** shall we do, so that we may work	Jn 6:28	5101
"**W** then do You do for a sign,	Jn 6:30	5101
W work do You perform?	Jn 6:30	5101
"**W** then if you see the Son of	Jn 6:62	
"**W** is this statement that He	Jn 7:36	5101
from him and knows **w** he is doing,	Jn 7:51	5101
w then do You say?"	Jn 8:5	5101
"**W** have I been saying to you *from*	Jn 8:25	3739, 5101
you not understand **w** I am saying?	Jn 8:43	2981
"**W** do you say about Him, since He	Jn 9:17	5101
"**W** did He do to you?	Jn 9:26	5101
but they did not understand **w**	Jn 10:6	5101
to Mary, and saw **w** He had done,	Jn 11:45	3739
and were saying, "**W** are we doing?	Jn 11:47	5101
"**W** do you think; that He will not	Jn 11:56	5101
used to pilfer **w** was put into it.	Jn 12:6	
and **w** shall I say,	Jn 12:27	5101
the word I spoke is **w** will judge	Jn 12:48	1565
a commandment *as to* **w** to say	Jn 12:49	5101
what to say and **w** to speak.	Jn 12:49	5101
"**W** I do you do not realize now,	Jn 13:7	3739
"Do you know **w** I have done to you?	Jn 13:12	5101
"**W** you do, do quickly."	Jn 13:27	3739
knew for **w** purpose He had said this	Jn 13:28	5101
w then has happened that You are	Jn 14:22	5101
if you do **w** I command you.	Jn 15:14	3739
not know **w** his master is doing;	Jn 15:15	5101
will disclose to you **w** is to come.	Jn 16:13	
"**W** is this thing He is telling	Jn 16:17	5101
"**W** is this that He says,	Jn 16:18	5101
not know **w** He is talking about."	Jn 16:18	5101
who have heard **w** I spoke to them;	Jn 18:21	5101
they know **w** I said."	Jn 18:21	3739
"**W** accusation do you bring	Jn 18:29	5101
signifying by **w** kind of death He	Jn 18:32	4169
w have You done?"	Jn 18:35	5101
Pilate said to Him, "**W** is truth?"	Jn 18:38	5101
"**W** I have written I have written."	Jn 19:22	3739
signifying by **w** kind of death he	Jn 21:19	4169
"Lord, and **w** about this man?"	Jn 21:21	5101
until I come, **w** *is that* to you?	Jn 21:22	5101
until I come, **w** *is that* to you?"	Jn 21:23	5101
for **w** the Father had promised,	Ac 1:4	
"**W** does this mean?"	Ac 2:12	5101
but this is **w** was spoken of	Ac 2:16	
"Brethren, **w** shall we do?"	Ac 2:37	5101
but **w** I do have I give to you:	Ac 3:6	3739
at **w** had happened to him.	Ac 3:10	
"By **w** power, or in what name,	Ac 4:7	4169
"By what power, or in **w** name,	Ac 4:7	4169
"**W** shall we do with these men?	Ac 4:16	5101

w we have seen and heard." Ac 4:20 *3739*
glorifying God for **w** had happened; Ac 4:21
in, not knowing **w** had happened. Ac 5:7
them as to **w** would come of this. Ac 5:24 *5101*
take care **w** you propose to do with Ac 5:35 *5101*
But some men from **w** was called the Ac 6:9
DO NOT KNOW **W** HAPPENED TO HIM.' Ac 7:40 *5101*
W KIND OF HOUSE WILL YOU BUILD FOR Ac 7:49 *4169*
'OR **W** PLACE IS THERE FOR MY REPOSE? Ac 7:49 *5101*
attention to **w** was said by Philip, Ac 8:6
"This man is **w** is called the Ac 8:10
so that nothing of **w** you have said Ac 8:24 *3739*
understand **w** you are reading?" Ac 8:30 *3739*
W prevents me from being baptized?" Ac 8:36 *5101*
will be told you **w** you must do." Ac 9:6
3739, 5101
w was called the Italian cohort, Ac 10:1
"**W** is it, Lord?" Ac 10:4 *5101*
"**W** God has cleansed, no *longer* Ac 10:15 *3739*
perplexed in mind as to **w** the vision Ac 10:17 *5101*
w is the reason for which you have Ac 10:21 *5101*
w reason you have sent for me." Ac 10:29 *5101*
who fears Him and does **w** is right is Ac 10:35
'**W** God has cleansed, no longer Ac 11:9 *3739*
w was being done by the angel was Ac 12:9
to **w** could have become of Peter, Ac 12:18 *5101*
when he saw **w** had happened, Ac 13:12
'**W** do you suppose that I am? Ac 13:25 *5101*
crowds saw **w** Paul had done, Ac 14:11 *3739*
relating **w** signs and wonders God had Ac 15:12 *3745*
w is strangled and from blood. Ac 15:20
"Sirs, **w** must I do to be saved?" Ac 16:30 *5101*
"**W** would this idle babbler wish Ac 17:18 *5101*
"May we know **w** this new teaching Ac 17:19 *5101*
know **w** these things mean." Ac 17:20 *5101*
Therefore **w** you worship in Ac 17:23 *3739*
"Into **w** then were you baptized?" Ac 19:3 *5101*
for **w** reason they had come together. Ac 19:32 *5101*
w man is there after all who does Ac 19:35 *5101*
knowing **w** will happen to me there, Ac 20:22
"This is **w** the Holy Spirit says: Ac 21:11 *3592*
"**W** are you doing, weeping and Ac 21:13 *5101*
"**W**, then, is *to be done?* Ac 21:22 *5101*
from blood and from **w** is strangled Ac 21:25
who he was and **w** he had done. Ac 21:33 *5101*
'**W** shall I do, Lord?' Ac 22:10 *5101*
men of **w** you have seen and heard. Ac 22:15 *3739*
"**W** are you about to do? Ac 22:26 *5101*
"**W** is it that you have to report Ac 23:19 *5101*
he asked from **w** province he was, Ac 23:34 *4169*
these men themselves tell **w** misdeed Ac 24:20 *5101*
this is just **w** I did in Jerusalem; Ac 26:10 *3739*
stating nothing but **w** the Prophets Ac 26:22 *3739*
than by **w** was being said by Paul. Ac 27:11
to hear from you **w** your views are; Ac 28:22 *3739*
through **w** has been made, Ro 1:20 *4161*
Then **w** advantage has the Jew? Ro 3:1 *5101*
Or **w** is the benefit of Ro 3:1 *5101*
W then? If some did not believe, Ro 3:3 *5101*
of God, **w** shall we say? Ro 3:5 *5101*
W then? Are we better than they? Ro 3:9 *5101*
By **w** kind of law? Ro 3:27 *4169*
W then shall we say that Abraham, Ro 4:1 *5101*
For **w** does the Scripture say? Ro 4:3 *5101*
as a favor, but as **w** is due. Ro 4:4 *3783*
assured that **w** God had promised, Ro 4:21 *3739*
W shall we say then? Ro 6:1 *5101*
W then? Shall we sin because we are Ro 6:15 *5101*
Therefore **w** benefit were you then Ro 6:21 *5101*
W shall we say then? Ro 7:7 *5101*
For **w** I am doing, I do not Ro 7:15 *3739*
practicing **w** I *would* like to *do*, Ro 7:15 *3739*
For **w** the Law could not do, weak Ro 8:3 *102*
who hopes for **w** he *already* sees? Ro 8:24 *3739*
if we hope for **w** we do not see, Ro 8:25 *3739*
knows **w** the mind of the Spirit is, Ro 8:27 *5101*
W then shall we say to these Ro 8:31 *5101*
W shall we say then? Ro 9:14 *5101*
W if God, although willing to Ro 9:22 *1161*
W shall we say then? Ro 9:30 *5101*
But **w** does it say? Ro 10:8 *5101*
Or do you not know **w** the Scripture Ro 11:2 *5101*
w is the divine response to him? Ro 11:4 *5101*
W then? What Israel is seeking, it Ro 11:7 *5101*
What then? **W** Israel is seeking, it Ro 11:7 *5101*
w will *their* acceptance be but Ro 11:15 *5101*
For if you were cut off from **w** is Ro 11:24 *65*
may prove **w** the will of God is, Ro 12:2 *5101*
Abhor **w** is evil; cling to what is good Ro 12:9 *4190*
cling to **w** is good. Ro 12:9 *18*
Respect **w** is right in the sight of Ro 12:17 *2570*
Do **w** is good and you will have Ro 13:3 *18*
But if you do **w** is evil, be afraid; Ro 13:4 *2556*
Render to all **w** is due them: Ro 13:7 *3782*
Therefore do not let **w** is for you Ro 14:16 *18*
condemn himself in **w** he approves. Ro 14:22 *3739*
except **w** Christ has accomplished Ro 15:18 *3739*
want you to be wise in **w** is good and Ro 16:19 *18*
good and innocent in **w** is evil. Ro 16:19 *2556*
W then is Apollos? 1Co 3:5 *5101*
What then is Apollos? And **w** is Paul 1Co 3:5 *5101*
is holy, and that is **w** you are. 1Co 3:17 *3748*
learn not to exceed **w** is written, 1Co 4:6 *3739*
For who regards you as superior? **W** 1Co 4:7 *5101*
W do you desire? Shall I come to you 1Co 4:21 *5101*
For **w** have I to do with judging 1Co 5:12 *5101*
but **w** *matters is* the keeping of 1Co 7:19
you, but to promote **w** is appropriate 1Co 7:35 *2158*
be so, let him do **w** he wishes, 1Co 7:36 *3739*
W then is my reward? 1Co 9:18 *5101*
be tempted beyond **w** you are able, 1Co 10:13 *3739*
you judge **w** I say. 1Co 10:15 *3739*
W do I mean then? 1Co 10:19 *5101*
W! Do you not have houses in which 1Co 11:22 *1063*
W shall I say to you? 1Co 11:22 *5101*
in tongues, **w** will I profit you 1Co 14:6 *5101*
how will it be known **w** is played 1Co 14:7 *5101*
how will it be known **w** is spoken? 1Co 14:9 *5101*
W is *the outcome* then? 1Co 14:15 *5101*
he does not know **w** you are saying? 1Co 14:16 *5101*
W is *the outcome* then, brethren? 1Co 14:26 *5101*
importance **w** I also received, 1Co 15:3 *3739*
by the grace of God I am **w** I am, 1Co 15:10 *3739*
w will those do who are baptized 1Co 15:29 *5101*
at Ephesus, **w** does it profit me? 1Co 15:32 *5101*
w kind of body do they come?" 1Co 15:35 *4169*
w was lacking on your part. 1Co 16:17 *5303*
than **w** you read and understand, 2Co 1:13 *3739*
Or **w** I purpose, do I purpose 2Co 1:17 *3739*
for indeed **w** I have forgiven, if I 2Co 2:10 *3739*
For indeed **w** had glory, in this 2Co 3:10
at the end of **w** was fading away. 2Co 3:13
faith, according to **w** is written, 2Co 4:13
so that **w** is mortal will be 2Co 5:4 *2349*
body, according to **w** he has done, 2Co 5:10 *3739*
for **w** partnership have righteousness 2Co 6:14 *5101*
or **w** fellowship has light with 2Co 6:14 *5101*
Or **w** harmony has Christ with 2Co 6:15 *5101*
or **w** has a believer in common with 2Co 6:15 *5101*
Or **w** agreement has the temple of 2Co 6:16 *5101*
"AND DO NOT TOUCH **W** IS UNCLEAN 2Co 6:17
w earnestness this very thing, 2Co 7:11 *4214*
w vindication of yourselves, what 2Co 7:11 *235*
of yourselves, **w** indignation, 2Co 7:11 *235*
what indignation, **w** fear, 2Co 7:11 *235*
indignation, what fear, **w** longing, 2Co 7:11 *235*
what fear, what longing, **w** zeal, 2Co 7:11 *235*
what zeal, **w** avenging of wrong! 2Co 7:11 *235*
according to **w** *a person* has, 2Co 8:12
according to **w** he does not have. 2Co 8:12
we have regard for **w** is honorable, 2Co 8:21
that **w** we are in word by letters 2Co 10:11 *3634*
and not to boast in **w** has been 2Co 10:16 *2092*
But **w** I am doing I will continue 2Co 11:12 *3739*
W I am saying, I am not saying as 2Co 11:17 *3739*
boast of **w** pertains to my weakness 2Co 11:30 *769*
For in **w** respect were you treated 2Co 12:13 *5101*
for I do not seek **w** is yours, 2Co 12:14
I may find you to be not **w** I wish 2Co 12:20 *3634*
found by you to be not **w** you wish; 2Co 12:20 *3634*
but that you may do **w** is right, 2Co 13:7 *2570*
preach to you a gospel contrary to **w** Ga 1:8 *3739*
to you a gospel contrary to **w** you Ga 1:9 *3739*
(Now in **w** I am writing to you, I Ga 1:20 *3739*
w they were makes no difference to Ga 2:6 *3697*
I rebuild **w** I have *once* destroyed, Ga 2:18 *3739*
W I am saying is this: Ga 3:17
But **w** does the Scripture say? Ga 4:30 *5101*
See with **w** large letters I am Ga 6:11 *4080*
know **w** is the hope of His calling, Eph 1:18 *5101*
w are the riches of the glory of Eph 1:18 *5101*
and **w** is the surpassing greatness Eph 1:19 *5101*
and to bring to light **w** is the Eph 3:9 *5101*
w is the breadth and length and height Eph 3:18 *5101*
w does it mean except that He also Eph 4:9 *5101*
being fitted and held together by **w** Eph 4:16 *1223*
with his own hands **w** is good, Eph 4:28 *18*
learn **w** is pleasing to the Lord. Eph 5:10 *5101*
w the will of the Lord is. Eph 5:17 *5101*
W then? Only that in every way, Php 1:18 *5101*
risking his life to complete **w** was Php 2:30 *5303*
forgetting **w** *lies* behind and Php 3:13
reaching forward to **w** *lies* ahead, Php 3:13
from Epaphroditus **w** you have sent, Php 4:18
in filling up **w** is lacking in Col 1:24 *3588*
w is the riches of the glory of this Col 1:27 *5101*
are a *mere* shadow of **w** is to come; Col 2:17
just as you know **w** kind of men we 1Th 1:5 *3634*
w kind of a reception we had with you, 1Th 1:9 *3697*
of men, but *for* **w** it really is, 1Th 2:13 *2531a*
For **w** thanks can we render to God 1Th 3:9 *5101*
w is lacking in your faith? 1Th 3:10 *5303*
For you know **w** commandments we 1Th 4:2 *5101*
And you know **w** restrains him now, 2Th 2:6
they will believe **w** is false, 2Th 2:11 *5579*
will *continue to* do **w** we command. 2Th 3:4 *3739*
they do not understand either **w** they 1Tm 1:7 *3739*
guard **w** has been entrusted to you, 1Tm 6:20 *3866*
arguments of **w** is falsely called 1Tm 6:20 *5581*
He is able to guard **w** I have entrusted 2Tm 1:12 *3866*
w services he rendered at Ephesus. 2Tm 1:18 *3745*
Consider **w** I say, for the Lord 2Tm 2:7 *3739*
w persecutions I endured, and out 2Tm 3:11 *3634*
you would set in order **w** remains Ti 1:5
but hospitable, loving **w** is good, Ti 1:8 *5358*
to much wine, teaching **w** is good, Ti 2:3 *2567*
in Christ to order you *to do* **w** is Phm 1:8 *3588*
will do even more than **w** I say. Phm 1:21 *3739*
attention to **w** we have heard, Heb 2:1
"**W** IS MAN, THAT YOU REMEMBER Heb 2:6 *5101*
w further need *was there* for Heb 7:11 *5101*
point in **w** has been said *is this:* Heb 8:1
you may receive **w** was promised. Heb 10:36 *1860*
so that **w** is seen was not made out Heb 11:3
And **w** more shall I say? Heb 11:32 *5101*
did not receive **w** was promised, Heb 11:39 *1860*
for **w** son is there whom *his* father Heb 12:7 *5101*
being content with **w** you have; Heb 13:5
W WILL MAN DO TO ME?" Heb 13:6 *5101*
forgotten **w** kind of person he was. Jas 1:24 *3697*
man will be blessed in **w** he does. Jas 1:25 *4162*
W use is it, my brethren, if someone Jas 2:14 *5101*
w is necessary for *their* body, Jas 2:16 *2006*
for *their* body, **w** use is that? Jas 2:16 *5101*
does not stumble in **w** he says, Jas 3:2 *3056*
W is the source of quarrels and Jas 4:1 *4159*
Yet you do not know **w** your life Jas 4:14 *4169*
seeking to know **w** person or time 1Pe 1:11 *4169*
For **w** credit is there if, when you 1Pe 2:20 *4169*
But if when you do **w** is right and 1Pe 2:20
do **w** is right without being frightened 1Pe 3:6
you prove zealous for **w** is good? 1Pe 3:13 *18*
that you suffer for doing **w** is 1Pe 3:17
rather than for doing **w** is wrong. 1Pe 3:17
w *will be* the outcome for those 1Pe 4:17 *5101*
W WILL BECOME OF THE GODLESS MAN 1Pe 4:18 *4226*
Creator in doing **w** is right. 1Pe 4:19 *16*
(for by **w** he saw and heard *that* 2Pe 2:8 *990*
for by **w** a man is overcome, by 2Pe 2:19 *3739*
w sort of people ought you to be 2Pe 3:11 *4217*
W was from the beginning, what we 1Jn 1:1 *3739*
the beginning, **w** we have heard, 1Jn 1:1 *3739*
w we have seen with our eyes, 1Jn 1:1 *3739*
w we have looked at and touched with 1Jn 1:1 *3739*
w we have seen and heard we 1Jn 1:3 *3739*
If **w** you heard from the beginning 1Jn 2:24 *3739*
not appeared as yet **w** we will be. 1Jn 3:2 *5101*
And for **w** reason did he slay him? 1Jn 3:12 *5101*
not lose **w** we have accomplished, 2Jn 1:8 *3739*
them, does not accept **w** we say. 3Jn 1:9
Beloved, do not imitate **w** is evil, 3Jn 1:11 *2556*
what is evil, but **w** is good. 3Jn 1:11 *18*
"Write in a book **w** you see, and Rv 1:11 *3739*
let him hear **w** the Spirit says to Rv 2:7 *5101*
fear **w** you are about to suffer. Rv 2:10 *3739*
let him hear **w** the Spirit says to Rv 2:11 *5101*
let him hear **w** the Spirit says to Rv 2:17 *5101*
'Nevertheless **w** you have, hold Rv 2:25 *3739*
let him hear **w** the Spirit says to Rv 2:29 *5101*
w you have received and heard; Rv 3:3 *4459*
at **w** hour I will come to you. Rv 3:3 *4169*
let him hear **w** the Spirit says to Rv 3:6 *5101*
hold fast **w** you have, so Rv 3:11 *3739*
let him hear **w** the Spirit says to Rv 3:13 *5101*
let him hear **w** the Spirit says to Rv 3:22 *5101*
and I will show you **w** must take Rv 4:1 *3739*
'**W** *city* is like the great city?' Rv 18:18 *5101*
man according to **w** he has done. Rv 22:12 *2041*

WHATEVER

and **w** the man called a living Gn 2:19
3605, 834
to you, and do to them **w** you like; Gn 19:8
2896a, 5869
w Sarah tells you, listen to her, Gn 21:12
3605, 834
then, do **w** God has said to you." Gn 31:16
3605, 834
And he sent across **w** he had. Gn 32:23 834
then I will give **w** you say to me. Gn 34:11 834
so that **w** was done there, he was Gn 39:22
3605, 834
and **w** he did, the LORD made to Gn 39:23 834
w he says to you, you shall do." Gn 41:55 834
bring your livestock and **w** you Ex 9:19
3605, 834
but **w** is left of it until morning, Ex 12:10
of his life **w** is demanded of him. Ex 21:30
3605, 834
and **w** they leave the beast of the Ex 23:11
and **w** touches the altar shall be Ex 29:37 3605
w touches them shall be holy. Ex 30:29 3605
of **w** *sort* his uncleanness *may* be Lv 5:3 3605
in **w** matter a man may speak Lv 5:4 3605, 834
'**W** divides a hoof, thus making Lv 11:3 3605
you may eat, **w** is in the water: Lv 11:9
3605, 834
'But **w** is in the seas and in the Lv 11:10
3605, 834
'**W** in the water does not have fins Lv 11:12
3605, 834
'Also **w** walks on its paws, among Lv 11:27 3605
w is in it becomes unclean and you Lv 11:33
3605, 834
'**W** crawls on its belly, and Lv 11:42 3605
belly, and **w** walks on *all* fours, Lv 11:42 3605
on *all* fours, **w** has many feet, Lv 11:42 3605
w the purpose for which the Lv 13:51 3605
made unclean, **w** his uncleanness; Lv 22:5 3605
'**W** has a defect, you shall not Lv 22:20
3605, 834
or flock, **w** passes under the rod, Lv 27:32
3605, 834
w any man gives to the priest, it Nu 5:10 834
that **w** good the LORD does for us, Nu 10:32 834
and I will do **w** you say to me. Nu 22:17
3605, 834
w He shows me I will tell you." Nu 23:3
4100, 1697
'**W** the LORD speaks, that I must Nu 23:26
3605, 834
then **w** proceeds out of her lips Nu 30:12 3605
But **w** cannot stand the fire you Nu 31:23
3605, 834
doing **w** is right in his own eyes; Dt 12:8 3605
any of your gates, **w** you desire, Dt 12:15 3605
you may eat meat, **w** you desire. Dt 12:20 3605
within your gates **w** you desire. Dt 12:21 3605

“**W** I command you, you shall be — **Dt 12:32** 3605, 1697, 834
money for **w** your heart desires: — **Dt 14:26** 3605, 834
drink, or **w** your heart desires; — **Dt 14:26** 3605, 834
w of yours is with your brother. — **Dt 15:3** 834
for his need *in* **w** he lacks. — **Dt 15:8** 834
God will bless you in **w** you do. — **Dt 15:18** 3605, 834
you shall do to them **w** you can.” — **Jg 9:33** 3512c
do to us **w** seems good to You; — **Jg 10:15** 3605
So **w** the LORD our God has driven — **Jg 11:24** 3605, 834
then it shall be that **w** comes out — **Jg 11:31** 834
them and do to them **w** you wish. — **Jg 19:24** 834
I will do for you **w** you ask, — **Ru 3:11** 3605, 834
do to us **w** seems good to you.” — **1Sa 11:10** 3605
“Do **w** seems good to you.” — **1Sa 14:36** 3605
“**W** you say, I will do for you.” — **1Sa 20:4** 4100
of bread, or **w** can be found.” — **1Sa 21:3**
Please give **w** you find at hand to — **1Sa 25:8** 834
do **w** my lord the king chooses.” — **2Sa 15:15** 3605, 834
So it shall be that **w** you hear — **2Sa 15:35** 3605, 1697, 834
“**W** seems best to you I will do.” — **2Sa 18:4** 834
“But **w** happens, please let me — **2Sa 18:22** 4100
“But **w** happens,” *he said,* “I will run — **2Sa 18:23** 4100
and **w** you require of me, I will do — **2Sa 19:38** 3605, 834
“I will do for you **w** you say.” — **2Sa 21:4** 4100
land of their cities, **w** plague, — **1Ki 8:37** 3605
plague, **w** sickness *there is,* — **1Ki 8:37** 3605
w prayer or supplication is made — **1Ki 8:38** 3605, 834
by **w** way You shall send them, — **1Ki 8:44** 834
you shall reign over **w** you desire, — **1Ki 11:37** 3605, 834
the acts of Solomon and **w** he did, — **1Ki 11:41** 3605, 834
w is desirable in your eyes, — **1Ki 20:6** 3605
w you impose on me I will bear.” — **2Ki 18:14** 834
w timber you need from Lebanon and — **2Ch 2:16** 3605
w plague or whatever sickness — **2Ch 6:28** 3605
plague or **w** sickness *there is,* — **2Ch 6:28** 3605
w prayer or supplication is made — **2Ch 6:29** 3605, 834
by **w** way You shall send them, — **2Ch 6:34** 834
survivor, at **w** place he may live, — **Ezr 1:4** 3605, 834
“**W** is needed, both young bulls, — **Ezr 6:9** 4101
“**W** seems good to you and to your — **Ezr 7:18** 4101
the River, that **w** Ezra the priest, — **Ezr 7:21** 3606, 1768
“**W** is commanded by the God of — **Ezr 7:23** 3606, 1768
“At **w** place you hear the sound of — **Ne 4:20** 834
That it may do **w** He commands it On — **Jb 37:12** 3605, 834
W is under the whole heaven is — **Jb 41:11**
And in **w** he does, he prospers. — **Ps 1:3** 3605, 834
W passes through the paths of the — **Ps 8:8**
And **w** moves in the field feeds on — **Ps 80:13** 2123a
He does **w** He pleases. — **Ps 115:3** 3605, 834
W the LORD pleases, He does, In — **Ps 135:6** 3605, 834
W exists has already been named, — **Ec 6:10** 4100, 7945
for he will do **w** he pleases.” — **Ec 8:3** 3605, 834
W your hand finds to do, do — **Ec 9:10** 3605, 834
and **w** the LORD our God says, tell — **Jer 42:20** 3605, 834
in **w** He has sent me to *tell* you. — **Jer 42:21** 3605, 834
and **w** word I speak will be — **Ezk 12:25** 834
W word I speak will be performed, — **Ezk 12:28** 3605, 834
not done in vain **w** I did to it,” — **Ezk 14:23** 3605, 834
and no injury **w** was found on him, — **Da 6:23** 3606
W you devise against the LORD, He — **Na 1:9** 4100
And **w** city or village you enter, — **Mt 10:11** 3739, 302
an oath to give her **w** she asked. — **Mt 14:7** 3739, 1437
“**W** I have that would help you has — **Mt 15:5** 3739, 1437
and **w** you bind on earth — **Mt 16:19** 3739, 1437
and **w** you loose on earth — **Mt 16:19** 3739, 1437
him, but did to him **w** they wished. — **Mt 17:12** 3745
w you bind on earth shall have been — **Mt 18:18** 3745, 1437
and **w** you loose on earth shall have — **Mt 18:18** 3745, 1437
and **w** is right I will give you.’ — **Mt 20:4** 3739, 1437
men, and **w** blasphemies they utter; — **Mk 3:28** 3745, 1437
“Ask me for **w** you want and I will — **Mk 6:22** 3739, 1437
“**W** you ask of me, I will give it — **Mk 6:23** 3739, 1437
w I have that would help you is — **Mk 7:11** 3739, 1437
Do you not understand that **w** goes — **Mk 7:18** 3956
and they did to him **w** they wished, — **Mk 9:13** 3745
to do for us **w** we ask of You.” — **Mk 10:35** 3739, 1437
say **w** is given you in that hour; — **Mk 13:11** 3739, 1437
W we heard was done at Capernaum, — **Lk 4:23** 3745
“**W** house you enter, stay there — **Lk 9:4** 3739
“**W** house you enter, first say, — **Lk 10:5** 3739
“**W** city you enter and they receive — **Lk 10:8** 3739
“But **w** city you enter and they do — **Lk 10:10** 3739, 302
and **w** more you spend, when I — **Lk 10:35** 3739, 5100, 302
w you have said in the dark will — **Lk 12:3** 3745
“**W** He says to you, do it.” — **Jn 2:5** 3739, 5100, 302
stepped in was made well from **w** — **Jn 5:4** 3739, 1221
for **w** the Father does, these — **Jn 5:19** 3739, 302
now I know that **w** You ask of God, — **Jn 11:22** 3745, 302
“**W** you ask in My name, that will I — **Jn 14:13** 3739
abide in you, ask **w** you wish, — **Jn 15:7** 3739, 1437
that **w** you ask of the Father in My — **Jn 15:16** 3739, 5100, 302
own initiative, but **w** He hears, — **Jn 16:13** 3745
to do **w** Your hand and Your purpose — **Ac 4:28** 3745
“‘AND **W** NATION TO WHICH THEY — **Ac 7:7** 3739, 1437
Now we know that **w** the Law says, — **Ro 3:19** 3745
and **w** is not from faith is sin. — **Ro 14:23** 3956, 3739
For **w** was written in earlier times — **Ro 15:4** 3745
and that you help her in **w** matter — **Ro 16:2** 3739, 302
you eat or drink or **w** you do, — **1Co 10:31** 5100
in **w** respect anyone *else* is bold — **2Co 11:21** 3739, 302
for **w** a man sows, this he will — **Ga 6:7** 3739, 1437
that **w** good thing each one does, — **Eph 6:8** 1437, 5100
But **w** things were gain to me, — **Php 3:7** 3748
Finally, brethren, **w** is true, — **Php 4:8** 3745
whatever is true, **w** is honorable, — **Php 4:8** 3745
whatever is honorable, **w** is right, — **Php 4:8** 3745
whatever is right, **w** is pure, — **Php 4:8** 3745
whatever is pure, **w** is lovely, — **Php 4:8** 3745
is lovely, **w** is of good repute, — **Php 4:8** 3745
content in **w** circumstances I am. — **Php 4:11** 3739
W you do in word or deed, *do* all — **Col 3:17** 3956
W you do, do your work heartily, — **Col 3:23** 3739, 1437
and **w** else is contrary to sound — **1Tm 1:10** 1487, 5100
But **w** is becoming obsolete and — **Heb 8:13**
in **w** our heart condemns us; — **1Jn 3:20** 3739, 5100, 1437
and **w** we ask we receive from Him, — **1Jn 3:22** 3739, 1437
For **w** is born of God overcomes the — **1Jn 5:4** 3956
know that He hears us *in* **w** we ask, — **1Jn 5:15** 3739, 1437
you are acting faithfully in **w** you — **3Jn 1:5** 3739, 1437

WHEAT
Now in the days of **w** harvest — **Gn 30:14** 2406
w and the spelt were not ruined, — **Ex 9:32** 2406
shall make them of fine **w** flour. — **Ex 29:2** 2406
the first fruits of the **w** harvest, — **Ex 34:22** 2406
a land of **w** and barley, of vines — **Dt 8:8** 2406
With the finest of the **w** — **Dt 32:14** 2406
as his son Gideon was beating out **w** — **Jg 6:11** 2406
a while, in the time of **w** harvest, — **Jg 15:1** 2406
barley harvest and the **w** harvest. — **Ru 2:23** 2406
reaping their **w** harvest in the valley, — **1Sa 6:13** 2406
“Is it not the **w** harvest today? — **1Sa 12:17** 2406
of the house as if to get **w**, — **2Sa 4:6** 2406
brought beds, basins, pottery, **w**, — **2Sa 17:28** 2406
then gave Hiram 20,000 kors of **w** — **1Ki 5:11** 2406
And Ornan was threshing **w**. — **1Ch 21:20** 2406
and the **w** for the grain offering; — **1Ch 21:23** 2406
timber, 20,000 kors of crushed **w** and — **2Ch 2:10** 2406
send to his servants **w** and barley, — **2Ch 2:15** 2406
ten thousand kors of **w** and ten — **2Ch 27:5** 2406
to the God of heaven, and **w**, — **Ezr 6:9** 2591a
talents of silver, 100 kors of **w**, — **Ezr 7:22** 2591a
Let briars grow instead of **w**, — **Jb 31:40** 2406
feed you with the finest of the **w**, — **Ps 81:16** 2406
you with the finest of the **w**. — **Ps 147:14** 2406
a heap of **w** Fenced about with lilies. — **SS 7:2** 2406
cummin And plant **w** in rows, — **Is 28:25** 2406
sown **w** and have reaped thorns, — **Jer 12:13** 2406
for we have stores of **w**, — **Jer 41:8** 2406
“But as for you, take **w**, — **Ezk 4:9** 2406
with the **w** of Minnith, cakes, — **Ezk 27:17** 2406
of an ephah from a homer of **w**; — **Ezk 45:13** 2406
For the **w** and the barley; — **Jl 1:11** 2406
that we may open the **w** *market,* — **Am 8:5** 1250
we may sell the refuse of the **w**?” — **Am 8:6** 1250
will gather His **w** into the barn, — **Mt 3:12** 4621
and sowed tares among the **w**, — **Mt 13:25** 4621
the **w** sprouted and bore grain, — **Mt 13:26** 5528
you may uproot the **w** with them. — **Mt 13:29** 4621
gather the **w** into my barn. — **Mt 13:30** 4621
and to gather the **w** into His barn; — **Lk 3:17** 4621
‘A hundred measures of **w**.’ — **Lk 16:7** 4621
permission to sift you like **w**; — **Lk 22:31** 4621
w falls into the earth and dies, — **Jn 12:24** 4621
throwing out the **w** into the sea. — **Ac 27:38** 4621
perhaps of **w** or of something else. — **1Co 15:37** 4621
“A quart of **w** for a denarius, and — **Rv 6:6** 4621
flour and **w** and cattle and sheep, — **Rv 18:13** 4621

WHEEL
height of a **w** *was* a cubit and a half. — **1Ki 7:32** 212
the workmanship of a chariot **w**. — **1Ki 7:33** 212
drives the *threshing* **w** over them. — **Pr 20:26** 212
the **w** at the cistern is crushed; — **Ec 12:6** 1534
Because the **w** of *his* cart and his — **Is 28:28** 1536
he was, making something on the **w**. — **Jer 18:3** 70
there was one **w** on the earth — **Ezk 1:15** 212
as if one **w** were within another. — **Ezk 1:16** 212
he entered and stood beside a **w**. — **Ezk 10:6** 212
one **w** beside each cherub; — **Ezk 10:9** 212
if one **w** were within another wheel. — **Ezk 10:10** 212
if one wheel were within another **w**. — **Ezk 10:10** 212
noise of the rattling of the **w**, — **Na 3:2** 212

WHEELS
He caused their chariot **w** to swerve, — **Ex 14:25** 212
four bronze **w** with bronze axles, — **1Ki 7:30** 212
four **w** *were* underneath the borders, — **1Ki 7:32** 212
axles of the **w** *were* on the stand. — **1Ki 7:32** 212
The workmanship of the **w** *was* — **1Ki 7:33** 212
its *chariot* **w** like a whirlwind. — **Is 5:28** 1534
and the rumbling of his **w**, — **Jer 47:3** 1534
The appearance of the **w** and their — **Ezk 1:16** 212
moved, the **w** moved with them. — **Ezk 1:19** 212
from the earth, the **w** rose *also.* — **Ezk 1:19** 212
And the **w** rose close beside them; — **Ezk 1:20** 212
of the living beings *was* in the **w**. — **Ezk 1:20** 212
the **w** rose close beside them; — **Ezk 1:21** 212
of the living beings *was* in the **w**. — **Ezk 1:21** 212
the sound of the **w** beside them, — **Ezk 3:13** 212
the whirling **w** under the cherubim and — **Ezk 10:2** 1534
fire from between the whirling **w**, — **Ezk 10:6** 1534
four **w** beside the cherubim, — **Ezk 10:9** 212
and the appearance of the **w** *was* — **Ezk 10:9** 212
w were full of eyes all around, — **Ezk 10:12** 212
w belonging to all four of them. — **Ezk 10:12** 212
The **w** were called in my hearing, — **Ezk 10:13** 212
in my hearing, the whirling **w**. — **Ezk 10:13** 1534
moved, the **w** would go beside them; — **Ezk 10:16** 212
the **w** would not turn from beside — **Ezk 10:16** 212
still, the **w** would stand still; — **Ezk 10:17**
up, the **w** would rise with them, — **Ezk 10:17**
my sight with the **w** beside them; — **Ezk 10:19** 212
wings with the **w** beside them, — **Ezk 11:22** 212
flames, Its **w** *were* a burning fire. — **Da 7:9** 1535

WHELP
“Judah is a lion’s **w**; — **Gn 49:9** 1482
“Dan is a lion’s **w**, That leaps — **Dt 33:22** 1482

WHELPS
w of the lioness are scattered. — **Jb 4:11** 1121

WHEN
and the earth **w** they were created, — **Gn 2:4**
W the woman saw that the tree was — **Gn 3:6**
about **w** they were in the field, — **Gn 4:8**
“**W** you cultivate the ground, it — **Gn 4:12** 3588
In the day **w** God created man, He — **Gn 5:1**
in the day **w** they were created. — **Gn 5:2**
W Adam had lived one hundred and — **Gn 5:3**
w men began to multiply on the — **Gn 6:1** 3588
w the sons of God came in to the — **Gn 6:4** 834
w the flood of water came upon the — **Gn 7:6**
w I bring a cloud over the earth, — **Gn 9:14**
“**W** the bow is in the cloud, then — **Gn 9:16**
W Noah awoke from his wine, he — **Gn 9:24**
old **w** he departed from Haran. — **Gn 12:4**
about **w** he came near to Egypt, — **Gn 12:11** 3512c
and **w** the Egyptians see you, — **Gn 12:12** 3588
about **w** Abram came into Egypt, — **Gn 12:14**
W Abram heard that his relative had — **Gn 14:14**
Now **w** the sun was going down, a — **Gn 15:12**
It came about **w** the sun had set, — **Gn 15:17**
and **w** she saw that she had — **Gn 16:4**
but **w** she saw that she had — **Gn 16:5**
old **w** Hagar bore Ishmael to him. — **Gn 16:16**
Now **w** Abram was ninety-nine years — **Gn 17:1**
W He finished talking with him, God — **Gn 17:22**
w he was circumcised in the flesh of — **Gn 17:24**
w he was circumcised in the flesh of — **Gn 17:25**
W he lifted up his eyes and looked, — **Gn 18:2**
and **w** he saw *them,* he ran from the — **Gn 18:2**
bear *a child,* **w** I am *so* old?’ — **Gn 18:13**
W Lot saw *them,* he rose to meet — **Gn 19:1**
W morning dawned, the angels urged — **Gn 19:15** 3644
W they had brought them outside, one — **Gn 19:17**
over the earth **w** Lot came to Zoar. — **Gn 19:23**
w God destroyed the cities of the — **Gn 19:29**
w He overthrew the cities in which — **Gn 19:29**
and he did not know **w** she lay down — **Gn 19:33**
when she lay down or **w** she arose. — **Gn 19:33**
and he did not know **w** she lay down — **Gn 19:35**
when she lay down or **w** she arose. — **Gn 19:35**
w God caused me to wander from my — **Gn 20:13** 3512c
son Isaac **w** he was eight days old, — **Gn 21:4**
w his son Isaac was born to him. — **Gn 21:5**
W the water in the skin was used up, — **Gn 21:15**
time **w** women go out to draw water. — **Gn 24:11**
Now **w** she had finished giving him — **Gn 24:19**
W the camels had finished drinking, — **Gn 24:22** 3512c
W he saw the ring — **Gn 24:30**
and **w** he heard the words of — **Gn 24:30**
But **w** *food* was set before him to — **Gn 24:33**

oath, **w** you come to my relatives;	**Gn 24:41**	3588
W Abraham's servant heard their words,	**Gn 24:52**	3512c
W they arose in the morning, he	**Gn 24:54**	
and **w** she saw Isaac she dismounted	**Gn 24:64**	
forty years old **w** he took Rebekah,	**Gn 25:20**	
W her days to be delivered were	**Gn 25:24**	
old **w** she gave birth to them.	**Gn 25:26**	
W the boys grew up, Esau became a	**Gn 25:27**	
W Jacob had cooked stew, Esau came	**Gn 25:29**	
W the men of the place asked about	**Gn 26:7**	
w he had been there a long time,	**Gn 26:8**	3588
But **w** Isaac's servants dug in the	**Gn 26:19**	
W Esau was forty years old he married	**Gn 26:34**	
it came about, **w** Isaac was old and	**Gn 27:1**	3588
So **w** Esau went to the field to	**Gn 27:5**	
and **w** he smelled the smell of his	**Gn 27:27**	
W Esau heard the words of his	**Gn 27:34**	
come about **w** you become restless,	**Gn 27:40**	3512c
Now **w** the words of her elder son	**Gn 27:42**	
w he blessed him he charged him,	**Gn 28:6**	
W all the flocks were gathered	**Gn 29:3**	
W Jacob saw Rachel the daughter of	**Gn 29:10**	3512c
w Laban heard the news of Jacob	**Gn 29:13**	
Now **w** Rachel saw that she bore	**Gn 30:1**	
W Leah saw that she had stopped	**Gn 30:9**	
W Jacob came in from the field in	**Gn 30:16**	
about **w** Rachel had borne Joseph,	**Gn 30:25**	3512c
w shall I provide for my own	**Gn 30:30**	4970
w you come concerning my wages.	**Gn 30:33**	3588
they mated **w** they came to drink.	**Gn 30:38**	
but **w** the flock was feeble, he did	**Gn 30:42**	
at the time **w** the flock were mating	**Gn 31:10**	
W Laban had gone to shear his	**Gn 31:19**	
W it was told Laban on the third	**Gn 31:22**	
w we are absent one from the other.	**Gn 31:49**	3588
Jacob said **w** he saw them,	**Gn 32:2**	3512c
"**W** my brother Esau meets you and	**Gn 32:17**	3588
speak to Esau **w** you find him;	**Gn 32:19**	
W he saw that he had not prevailed	**Gn 32:25**	
Canaan, **w** he came from Paddan-aram,	**Gn 33:18**	
W Shechem the son of Hamor the	**Gn 34:2**	
in from the field **w** they heard *it;*	**Gn 34:7**	
third day, **w** they were in pain,	**Gn 34:25**	
who appeared to you **w** you fled	**Gn 35:1**	
him **w** he fled from his brother.	**Gn 35:7**	
again **w** he came from Paddan-aram,	**Gn 35:9**	
and **w** there was still some	**Gn 35:16**	
W she was in severe labor the midwife	**Gn 35:17**	
w he was pasturing the donkeys of his	**Gn 36:24**	
Joseph, **w** seventeen years of age,	**Gn 37:2**	
and **w** he told it to his brothers,	**Gn 37:5**	
W they saw him from a distance and	**Gn 37:18**	
w Joseph reached his brothers,	**Gn 37:23**	3512c
so **w** he went in	**Gn 38:9**	518
and **w** the time of mourning was	**Gn 38:12**	
W Judah saw her, he thought she	**Gn 38:15**	
W Judah sent the young goat by his	**Gn 38:20**	
W she saw that he had left his	**Gn 39:13**	
"**W** he heard that I raised my voice	**Gn 39:15**	
W his master heard the words of his	**Gn 39:19**	
W Joseph came to them in the	**Gn 40:6**	
custom **w** you were his cupbearer.	**Gn 40:13**	834
in mind **w** it goes well with you,	**Gn 40:14**	3512c
W the chief baker saw that he had	**Gn 40:16**	
and **w** he had shaved himself and	**Gn 41:14**	
that **w** you hear a dream you can	**Gn 41:15**	
"Yet **w** they had devoured them, it	**Gn 41:21**	
old **w** he stood before Pharaoh,	**Gn 41:46**	
W the seven years of plenty which	**Gn 41:53**	
So **w** all the land of Egypt was	**Gn 41:55**	
W the famine was *spread* over all	**Gn 41:56**	
W Joseph saw his brothers he	**Gn 42:7**	
of his soul **w** he pleaded with us,	**Gn 42:21**	
But **w** he returned to them and	**Gn 42:24**	
W they came to their father Jacob	**Gn 42:29**	
and **w** they and their father saw	**Gn 42:35**	
w they had finished eating the grain	**Gn 43:2**	3512c
W Joseph saw Benjamin with them,	**Gn 43:16**	
w we came to the lodging place,	**Gn 43:21**	3588
W Joseph came home, they brought	**Gn 43:26**	
w Joseph said to his house	**Gn 44:4**	
and **w** you overtake them, say to	**Gn 44:4**	
and **w** each man loaded his donkey,	**Gn 44:13**	
W Judah and his brothers came to	**Gn 44:14**	
"Thus it came about **w** we went up	**Gn 44:24**	3588
w I come to your servant my	**Gn 44:30**	
w he sees that the lad	**Gn 44:31**	
w Joseph made himself known to his	**Gn 45:1**	
Now **w** the news was heard in	**Gn 45:16**	
W they told him all the words of	**Gn 45:27**	
and **w** he saw the wagons that	**Gn 45:27**	
"**W** Pharaoh calls you and says,	**Gn 46:33**	3588
W the money was all spent in the land	**Gn 47:15**	
W that year was ended, they came to	**Gn 47:18**	
W the time for Israel to die drew	**Gn 47:29**	
but **w** I lie down with my fathers,	**Gn 47:30**	
W it was told to Jacob,	**Gn 48:2**	
as for me, **w** I came from Paddan,	**Gn 48:7**	
w there was still some distance to	**Gn 48:7**	
W Israel saw Joseph's sons, he	**Gn 48:8**	
W Joseph saw that his father laid	**Gn 48:17**	
"**W** he saw that a resting place	**Gn 49:15**	
said to them **w** he blessed them.	**Gn 49:28**	
W Jacob finished charging his	**Gn 49:33**	
W the days of mourning for him were	**Gn 50:4**	
W they came to the threshing floor	**Gn 50:10**	
Now **w** the inhabitants of the land,	**Gn 50:11**	
W Joseph's brothers saw that their	**Gn 50:15**	
Joseph wept **w** they spoke to him.	**Gn 50:17**	

"**W** you are helping the Hebrew	**Ex 1:16**	
w she saw that he was beautiful,	**Ex 2:2**	
w she could hide him no longer,	**Ex 2:3**	
W she opened *it,* she saw the	**Ex 2:6**	
those days, **w** Moses had grown up,	**Ex 2:11**	
and **w** he saw there was no one	**Ex 2:12**	
W Pharaoh heard of this matter, he	**Ex 2:15**	
W they came to Reuel their father,	**Ex 2:18**	
W the LORD saw that he turned	**Ex 3:4**	
w you have brought the people out	**Ex 3:12**	
and it shall be that **w** you go,	**Ex 3:21**	
his bosom, and **w** he took it out,	**Ex 4:6**	
and **w** he took it out of his bosom,	**Ex 4:7**	
w he sees you, he will be glad in	**Ex 4:14**	
"**W** you go back to Egypt see that	**Ex 4:21**	
and **w** they heard that the LORD was	**Ex 4:31**	
amount, just as **w** you had straw."	**Ex 5:13**	
W they left Pharaoh's presence,	**Ex 5:20**	
w the LORD spoke to Moses in the	**Ex 6:28**	
"**W** Pharaoh does not listen to	**Ex 7:4**	
w I stretch out My hand on Egypt	**Ex 7:5**	
w they spoke to Pharaoh.	**Ex 7:7**	
"**W** Pharaoh speaks to you, saying,	**Ex 7:9**	3588
w shall I entreat for you and your	**Ex 8:9**	4970
But **w** Pharaoh saw that there was	**Ex 8:15**	
w the hail comes down on them,	**Ex 9:19**	
But **w** Pharaoh saw that the rain	**Ex 9:34**	
and **w** it was morning, the east	**Ex 10:13**	
W he lets you go, he will surely	**Ex 11:1**	
and **w** I see the blood I will pass	**Ex 12:13**	
you **w** I strike the land of Egypt.	**Ex 12:13**	
and **w** He sees the blood on the	**Ex 12:23**	
"**W** you enter the land which the	**Ex 12:25**	3588
w your children say to you,	**Ex 12:26**	
in Egypt **w** He smote the Egyptians,	**Ex 12:27**	
w the LORD brings you to the land	**Ex 13:5**	3588
did for me **w** I came out of Egypt.'	**Ex 13:8**	
w the LORD brings you to the land	**Ex 13:11**	3588
"And it shall be **w** your son asks	**Ex 13:14**	3588
w Pharaoh was stubborn about	**Ex 13:15**	3588
w Pharaoh had let the people go,	**Ex 13:17**	
change their minds **w** they see war,	**Ex 13:17**	
W the king of Egypt was told that	**Ex 14:5**	
w I am honored through Pharaoh,	**Ex 14:18**	
W Israel saw the great power which	**Ex 14:31**	
W they came to Marah, they could not	**Ex 15:23**	
w we sat by the pots of meat,	**Ex 16:3**	
meat, **w** we ate bread to the full;	**Ex 16:3**	
w they prepare what they bring in,	**Ex 16:5**	
w the LORD gives you meat to eat in	**Ex 16:8**	
W the layer of dew evaporated,	**Ex 16:14**	
W the sons of Israel saw *it,* they	**Ex 16:15**	
W they measured it with an omer,	**Ex 16:18**	
but **w** the sun grew hot, it would	**Ex 16:21**	
W all the leaders of the	**Ex 16:22**	
w I brought you out of the land of	**Ex 16:32**	
about **w** Moses held his hand up,	**Ex 17:11**	3512c
and **w** he let his hand down,	**Ex 17:11**	3512c
it was proven **w** they dealt proudly	**Ex 18:11**	834
Now **w** Moses' father-in-law saw all	**Ex 18:14**	
"**W** they have a dispute, it comes	**Ex 18:16**	3588
W they set out from Rephidim, they	**Ex 19:2**	
may hear **w** I speak with you and	**Ex 19:9**	
W the ram's horn sounds a long	**Ex 19:13**	
the third day, **w** it was morning,	**Ex 19:16**	
W the sound of the trumpet grew	**Ex 19:19**	
and **w** the people saw *it,* they	**Ex 20:18**	
about that **w** he cries out to Me,	**Ex 22:27**	3588
at the end of the year **w** you gather in	**Ex 23:16**	
of the altar **w** it is carried.	**Ex 27:7**	
heart **w** he enters the holy place,	**Ex 28:29**	
w he goes in before the LORD;	**Ex 28:30**	
shall be on Aaron **w** he ministers;	**Ex 28:35**	
w he enters and leaves the holy	**Ex 28:35**	
w they enter the tent of meeting,	**Ex 28:43**	
or **w** they approach the altar to	**Ex 28:43**	
shall put them on **w** he enters the tent	**Ex 29:30**	834
altar **w** you make atonement for it,	**Ex 29:36**	
morning **w** he trims the lamps.	**Ex 30:7**	
"**W** Aaron trims the lamps at twilight,	**Ex 30:8**	
"**W** you take a census of the sons	**Ex 30:12**	3588
to the LORD, **w** you number them,	**Ex 30:12**	
among them **w** you number them.	**Ex 30:12**	
w you give the contribution to the	**Ex 30:15**	
w they enter the tent of meeting,	**Ex 30:20**	
or **w** they approach the altar to	**Ex 30:20**	
W He had finished speaking with him	**Ex 31:18**	
Now **w** the people saw that Moses	**Ex 32:1**	
Now **w** Aaron saw *this,* he built an	**Ex 32:5**	
Now **w** Joshua heard the sound of	**Ex 32:17**	
Now **w** Moses saw that the people	**Ex 32:25**	
in the day **w** I punish,	**Ex 32:34**	
W the people heard this sad word,	**Ex 33:4**	
W all the people saw the pillar of	**Ex 33:10**	
W Moses returned to the camp, his	**Ex 33:11**	
w you go up three times a year to	**Ex 34:24**	
It came about **w** Moses was	**Ex 34:29**	
So **w** Aaron and all the sons of	**Ex 34:30**	
W Moses had finished speaking with	**Ex 34:33**	
and a span wide **w** folded double.	**Ex 39:9**	
settings **w** they were mounted.	**Ex 39:13**	
W they entered the tent of	**Ex 40:32**	
and **w** they approached the altar,	**Ex 40:32**	
until the day **w** it was taken up.	**Ex 40:37**	
'**W** any man of you brings an	**Lv 1:2**	3588
'Now **w** anyone presents a grain	**Lv 2:1**	3588
'Now **w** you bring an offering of a	**Lv 2:4**	
'**W** you bring in the grain offering	**Lv 2:8**	
w the sin which they have	**Lv 4:14**	

'**W** a leader sins and	**Lv 4:22**	834
to testify **w** he is a witness,	**Lv 5:1**	
'So it shall be **w** he becomes	**Lv 5:5**	3588
'**W** a person sins and acts	**Lv 6:2**	3588
be, **w** he sins and becomes guilty,	**Lv 6:4**	3588
LORD on the day **w** he is anointed;	**Lv 6:20**	
W it is *well* stirred, you shall	**Lv 6:21**	
and **w** any of its blood splashes on	**Lv 6:27**	834
'**W** anyone touches anything unclean,	**Lv 7:21**	3588
in that day **w** he presented them to	**Lv 7:35**	
W the congregation was assembled	**Lv 8:4**	
W he had cut the ram into its	**Lv 8:20**	
W they came out and blessed the	**Lv 9:23**	
and **w** all the people saw *it,* they	**Lv 9:24**	
w you come into the tent of	**Lv 10:9**	
W things like these happened to	**Lv 10:19**	
W Moses heard *that,* it seemed	**Lv 10:20**	
whoever touches them **w** they are	**Lv 11:31**	
of them may fall **w** they are dead	**Lv 11:32**	
'**W** a woman gives birth and bears a	**Lv 12:2**	3588
'**W** the days of her purification are	**Lv 12:6**	
"**W** a man has on the skin of his	**Lv 13:2**	3588
w the priest has looked at him, he	**Lv 13:3**	
"**W** the infection of leprosy is on	**Lv 13:9**	3588
"**W** the body has a boil on its skin	**Lv 13:18**	3588
"**W** a man or a woman has bright spots	**Lv 13:38**	3588
"**W** a garment has a mark of	**Lv 13:47**	3588
mark has departed **w** you washed it,	**Lv 13:58**	
"**W** you enter the land of Canaan,	**Lv 14:34**	3588
to teach **w** they are unclean and	**Lv 14:57**	3117
are unclean and **w** they are clean.	**Lv 14:57**	3117
'**W** any man has a discharge from	**Lv 15:2**	3588
'Now **w** the man with the discharge	**Lv 15:13**	3588
'**W** a woman has a discharge, *if* her	**Lv 15:19**	3588
she is sitting, **w** he touches it,	**Lv 15:23**	
'**W** she becomes clean from her	**Lv 15:28**	518
w they had approached the presence	**Lv 16:1**	
"**W** he goes in to make atonement	**Lv 16:17**	
"**W** he finishes atoning for the	**Lv 16:20**	
on **w** he went into the holy place,	**Lv 16:23**	
"So **w** any man from the sons of	**Lv 17:13**	
"**W** any person eats *an animal*	**Lv 17:15**	
'Now **w** you offer a sacrifice of	**Lv 19:5**	3588
'Now **w** you reap the harvest of	**Lv 19:9**	
'**W** you enter the land and plant all	**Lv 19:23**	3588
'**W** a stranger resides with you in	**Lv 19:33**	3588
w he gives any of his offspring to	**Lv 20:4**	
'But **w** the sun sets, he will be	**Lv 22:7**	
'**W** a man offers a sacrifice of peace	**Lv 22:21**	3588
"**W** an ox or a sheep or a goat is	**Lv 22:27**	3588
"**W** you sacrifice a sacrifice of	**Lv 22:29**	3588
'**W** you enter the land which I am	**Lv 23:10**	3588
on the day **w** you wave the sheaf,	**Lv 23:12**	
from the day **w** you brought in the	**Lv 23:15**	
'**W** you reap the harvest of your	**Lv 23:22**	
w you have gathered in the crops	**Lv 23:39**	
w I brought them out from the land	**Lv 23:43**	
native, **w** he blasphemes the Name,	**Lv 24:16**	
'**W** you come into the land which I	**Lv 25:2**	3588
'**W** you are sowing the eighth year,	**Lv 25:22**	
ninth year **w** its crop comes in.	**Lv 25:22**	5704
the year **w** he sold himself to him	**Lv 25:50**	
flee **w** no one is pursuing you.	**Lv 26:17**	
and **w** you gather together into	**Lv 26:25**	
'**W** I break your staff of bread,	**Lv 26:26**	
and even **w** no one is pursuing they	**Lv 26:36**	
w they are in the land of their	**Lv 26:44**	
'**W** a man makes a difficult vow, he	**Lv 27:2**	3588
and **w** it reverts in the jubilee,	**Lv 27:21**	
"So **w** the tabernacle is to set	**Nu 1:51**	
and **w** the tabernacle encamps, the	**Nu 1:51**	
time **w** the LORD spoke with Moses on	**Nu 3:1**	
w they offered strange fire before the	**Nu 3:4**	
"**W** the camp sets out, Aaron and	**Nu 4:5**	
"**W** Aaron and his sons have finished	**Nu 4:15**	
w the camp is to set out,	**Nu 4:15**	
w they approach the most holy *objects*	**Nu 4:19**	
'**W** a man or woman commits any of	**Nu 5:6**	3588
wife **w** she has defiled herself,	**Nu 5:14**	
wife **w** she has not defiled herself,	**Nu 5:14**	
'**W** he has made her drink the	**Nu 5:27**	
w a wife, *being* under *the*	**Nu 5:29**	834
or **w** a spirit of jealousy comes	**Nu 5:30**	834
'**W** a man or woman makes a special	**Nu 6:2**	3588
or for his sister, **w** they die,	**Nu 6:7**	
on the day **w** he becomes clean;	**Nu 6:9**	
w the days of his separation are	**Nu 6:13**	3117
shall take the ram's shoulder **w** *it*	**Nu 6:19**	
W they brought their offering	**Nu 7:3**	
for the altar **w** it was anointed,	**Nu 7:10**	3117
of Israel **w** it was anointed:	**Nu 7:84**	3117
Now **w** Moses went into the tent of	**Nu 7:89**	
'**W** you mount the lamps, the seven	**Nu 8:2**	
Even **w** the cloud lingered over the	**Nu 9:19**	
w the cloud was lifted in the	**Nu 9:21**	
but **w** it was lifted, they did set	**Nu 9:22**	
"**W** both are blown, all	**Nu 10:3**	
"But **w** you blow an alarm, the	**Nu 10:5**	
"**W** you blow an alarm the second time,	**Nu 10:6**	
"**W** convening the assembly,	**Nu 10:7**	
"**W** you go to war in your land	**Nu 10:9**	3588
day **w** they set out from the camp.	**Nu 10:34**	
Then it came about **w** the ark set	**Nu 10:35**	
W it came to rest, he said,	**Nu 10:36**	
and **w** the LORD heard *it,* His anger	**Nu 11:1**	
W the dew fell on the camp at night,	**Nu 11:9**	
w the Spirit rested upon them,	**Nu 11:25**	
W they had both come forward,	**Nu 12:5**	
But **w** the cloud had withdrawn from	**Nu 12:10**	

whose flesh is half eaten away **w**	Nu 12:12	
W Moses sent them to spy out the	Nu 13:17	
W they had gone up into the Negev,	Nu 13:22	
W they returned from spying out	Nu 13:25	
W Moses spoke these words to all	Nu 14:39	
the LORD, **w** it will not succeed?	Nu 14:41	
'W you enter the land where you	Nu 15:2	3588
'W you prepare a bull as a burnt	Nu 15:8	3588
'W you enter the land where I	Nu 15:18	
that **w** you eat of the food of the	Nu 15:19	
'But **w** you unwittingly fail and do	Nu 15:22	3588
from the day **w** the LORD gave	Nu 15:23	834
astray **w** he sins unintentionally,	Nu 15:28	
W Moses heard *this,* he fell on his	Nu 16:4	
of all flesh, **w** one man sins,	Nu 16:22	
w the congregation had assembled	Nu 16:42	
'W you take from the sons of	Nu 18:26	3588
'W you have offered from it the	Nu 18:30	
w you have offered the best of it.	Nu 18:32	
is the law **w** a man dies in a tent:	Nu 19:14	3588
w our brothers perished before the	Nu 20:3	
'But **w** we cried out to the LORD,	Nu 20:16	
Now **w** they set out from Kadesh,	Nu 20:22	
W all the congregation saw that Aaron	Nu 20:29	
W the Canaanite, the king of Arad,	Nu 21:1	
who is bitten, **w** he looks at it,	Nu 21:8	
w he looked to the bronze serpent,	Nu 21:9	
W the donkey saw the angel of the	Nu 22:23	
W the donkey saw the angel of the	Nu 22:25	
W the donkey saw the angel of the	Nu 22:27	
W Balak heard that Balaam was	Nu 22:36	
W He has blessed, then I cannot	Nu 23:20	
W Balaam saw that it pleased the	Nu 24:1	
W Phinehas the son of Eleazar, the	Nu 25:7	
w they contended against the LORD,	Nu 26:9	
with Korah, **w** that company died,	Nu 26:10	
died, **w** the fire devoured 250 men,	Nu 26:10	
w they offered strange fire before the	Nu 26:61	
"W you have seen it, you too will	Nu 27:13	
w you present a new grain offering	Nu 28:26	
So **w** they saw the land of Jazer	Nu 32:1	
w I sent them from Kadesh-barnea	Nu 32:8	
'For **w** they went up to the valley	Nu 32:9	
years old **w** he died on Mount Hor.	Nu 33:39	
'W you cross over the Jordan into	Nu 33:51	3588
'W you enter the land of Canaan,	Nu 34:2	3588
'W you cross the Jordan into the	Nu 35:10	3588
put him to death **w** he meets him.	Nu 35:19	
murderer to death **w** he meets him.	Nu 35:21	
"W the jubilee of the sons of Israel	Nu 36:4	518
w all the men of war had finally	Dt 2:16	3512c
'W you come opposite the sons of	Dt 2:19	
w He destroyed the Horites from	Dt 2:22	834
w they hear the report of you,	Dt 2:25	
at Horeb, **w** the LORD said to me,	Dt 4:10	
"W you become the father of	Dt 4:25	3588
"W you are in distress and all	Dt 4:30	
w they came out from Egypt,	Dt 4:45	
w they came out from Egypt.	Dt 4:46	
w you heard the voice from the	Dt 5:23	
of your words **w** you spoke to me,	Dt 5:28	
talk of them **w** you sit in your house	Dt 6:7	
you sit in your house and **w** you	Dt 6:7	
w you lie down and when you rise up.	Dt 6:7	
you lie down and **w** you rise up.	Dt 6:7	
w the LORD your God brings you	Dt 6:10	3588
"W your son asks you in time to	Dt 6:20	3588
"W the LORD your God brings	Dt 7:1	3588
and **w** the LORD your God delivers	Dt 7:2	
"W you have eaten and are	Dt 8:10	
w you have eaten and are	Dt 8:12	
and **w** your herds and your flocks	Dt 8:13	
w the LORD your God has driven	Dt 9:4	
"W I went up to the mountain to	Dt 9:9	
"W the LORD sent you from	Dt 9:23	
w He made the water of the Red Sea	Dt 11:4	834
w the earth opened its mouth and	Dt 11:6	
talking of them **w** you sit in your	Dt 11:19	
you sit in your house and **w** you walk	Dt 11:19	
w you lie down and when you rise up.	Dt 11:19	
you lie down and **w** you rise up.	Dt 11:19	
w the LORD your God brings you	Dt 11:29	3588
"W you cross the Jordan and live	Dt 12:10	
"W the LORD your God extends your	Dt 12:20	3588
"W the LORD your God cuts off	Dt 12:29	3588
w the LORD your God blesses you,	Dt 14:24	3588
not be grieved **w** you give to him,	Dt 15:10	
"W you set him free, you shall not	Dt 15:13	3588
hard to you **w** you set him free,	Dt 15:18	
the day **w** you came out of the land	Dt 16:3	
"W you enter the land which the	Dt 17:14	3588
w he sits on the throne of his	Dt 17:18	
"W you enter the land which the	Dt 18:9	3588
"W a prophet speaks in the name	Dt 18:22	834
"W the LORD your God cuts off the	Dt 19:1	3588
w he kills his friend	Dt 19:4	834
as **w** *a man* goes into the forest	Dt 19:5	834
"W you go out to battle against	Dt 20:1	3588
"W you are approaching the battle,	Dt 20:2	
"W the officers have finished	Dt 20:9	
"W you approach a city to fight	Dt 20:10	3588
"W the LORD your God gives it	Dt 20:13	
"W you besiege a city a long	Dt 20:19	3588
w you do what is right in the eyes	Dt 21:9	3588
"W you go out to battle against	Dt 21:10	3588
mother, and **w** they chastise him,	Dt 21:18	
"W you build a new house, you	Dt 22:8	3588
this woman, *but* **w** I came near her,	Dt 22:14	
"W he found her in the field, the	Dt 22:27	3588
the way **w** you came out of Egypt,	Dt 23:4	
"W you go out as an army against	Dt 23:9	3588
it shall be **w** evening approaches,	Dt 23:11	
shall be **w** you sit down outside,	Dt 23:13	
"W you make a vow to the LORD	Dt 23:21	3588
"W you enter your neighbor's	Dt 23:24	3588
"W you enter your neighbor's	Dt 23:25	3588
"W a man takes a wife and marries	Dt 24:1	3588
"W a man takes a new wife, he	Dt 24:5	3588
"W you make your neighbor a loan	Dt 24:10	3588
"W the sun goes down you shall	Dt 24:13	
"W you reap your harvest in your	Dt 24:19	3588
"W you beat your olive tree, you	Dt 24:20	3588
"W you gather the grapes of your	Dt 24:21	3588
"W brothers live together and one	Dt 25:5	3588
the way **w** you came out from Egypt,	Dt 25:17	
rear **w** you were faint and weary;	Dt 25:18	
w the LORD your God has given you	Dt 25:19	
w you enter the land which the	Dt 26:1	3588
"W you have finished paying all	Dt 26:12	3588
w you cross the Jordan to the	Dt 27:2	834
of this law, **w** you cross over,	Dt 27:3	
shall be **w** you cross the Jordan,	Dt 27:4	
"W you cross the Jordan, these	Dt 27:12	
shall you *be* **w** you come in,	Dt 28:6	
blessed *shall* you *be* **w** you go out.	Dt 28:6	
"Cursed *shall* you *be* **w** you come in,	Dt 28:19	
cursed *shall* you *be* **w** you go out.	Dt 28:19	
"W you reached this place, Sihon	Dt 29:7	
"It shall be **w** he hears the	Dt 29:19	
w they see the plagues of the land	Dt 29:22	
w He brought them out of the land	Dt 29:25	
"So it shall be **w** all of these	Dt 30:1	3588
their land, **w** He destroyed them.	Dt 31:4	834
w all Israel comes to appear	Dt 31:11	
"For **w** I bring them into the land	Dt 31:20	
w many evils and troubles have	Dt 31:21	3588
w Moses finished writing the words	Dt 31:24	
"W the Most High gave the nations	Dt 32:8	
W He separated the sons of man,	Dt 32:8	
W He sees that *their* strength is	Dt 32:36	3588
W Moses had finished speaking all	Dt 32:45	
W the heads of the people were	Dt 33:5	
and twenty years old **w** he died,	Dt 34:7	
w *it was time* to shut the gate at	Jos 2:5	
you **w** you came out of Egypt,	Jos 2:10	
"W we heard *it,* our hearts	Jos 2:11	
w the LORD gives us the land	Jos 2:14	
unless, **w** we come into the land,	Jos 2:18	
"W you see the ark of the	Jos 3:3	
'W you come to the edge of the	Jos 3:8	
w the soles of the feet of the priests	Jos 3:13	
So **w** the people set out from	Jos 3:14	
and **w** those who carried the ark	Jos 3:15	
w all the nation had finished crossing	Jos 4:1	3512c
so that **w** your children ask later,	Jos 4:6	
w it crossed the Jordan, the	Jos 4:7	
w all the people had finished crossing	Jos 4:11	3512c
It came about **w** the priests	Jos 4:18	
"W your children ask their	Jos 4:21	834
Now it came about **w** all the kings	Jos 5:1	
w they had finished circumcising all	Jos 5:8	3512c
about **w** Joshua was by Jericho,	Jos 5:13	
"It shall be that **w** they make	Jos 6:5	
and **w** you hear the sound of the	Jos 6:5	
that **w** Joshua had spoken to the	Jos 6:8	
w the priests blew the trumpets,	Jos 6:16	
w the people heard the sound of	Jos 6:20	
w I saw among the spoil a	Jos 7:21	
And **w** they come out to meet us	Jos 8:5	3588
be **w** you have seized the city,	Jos 8:8	
about **w** the king of Ai saw *it,*	Jos 8:14	
w he had stretched out his hand,	Jos 8:19	
W the men of Ai turned back and	Jos 8:20	
W Joshua and all Israel saw that	Jos 8:21	
w Israel had finished killing all the	Jos 8:24	
Now it came about **w** all the kings	Jos 9:1	
W the inhabitants of Gibeon heard	Jos 9:3	
"This our bread *was* warm **w**	Jos 9:12	
w you are living within our land?	Jos 9:22	
Now it came about **w** Adoni-zedek	Jos 10:1	
w the LORD delivered up the Amorites	Jos 10:12	
w the LORD listened to the voice	Jos 10:14	
It came about **w** Joshua and the	Jos 10:20	
W they brought these kings out to	Jos 10:24	
w Jabin king of Hazor heard *of it,*	Jos 11:1	
in years **w** the LORD said to him,	Jos 13:1	
"I was forty years old **w** Moses	Jos 14:7	
w Israel walked in the wilderness;	Jos 14:10	834
came about that **w** she came *to him,*	Jos 15:18	
w the sons of Israel became strong,	Jos 17:13	3588
W they finished apportioning the	Jos 19:49	
So **w** Joshua sent them away to	Jos 22:7	3588
W they came to the region of	Jos 22:10	
W the sons of Israel heard *of it,*	Jos 22:12	
So **w** Phinehas the priest and the	Jos 22:30	
w the LORD had given rest to	Jos 23:1	310, 834
"W you transgress the covenant of	Jos 23:16	
'But **w** they cried out to the LORD,	Jos 24:7	
w I destroyed them before you.	Jos 24:8	
it came about **w** she came *to him,*	Jg 1:14	
came about **w** Israel became strong,	Jg 1:28	3588
but **w** the power of the house of	Jg 1:35	
W the angel of the LORD spoke	Jg 2:4	
W Joshua had dismissed the people,	Jg 2:6	
w the LORD raised up judges for	Jg 2:18	3588
it came about **w** the judge died,	Jg 2:19	
which Joshua left **w** he died,	Jg 2:21	
W the sons of Israel cried to the	Jg 3:9	
W he went out to war, the LORD	Jg 3:10	
But **w** the sons of Israel cried to	Jg 3:15	
w he had finished presenting the	Jg 3:18	3512c
W he had gone out, his servants	Jg 3:24	
It came about **w** he had arrived,	Jg 3:27	
w You went out from Seir,	Jg 5:4	
W You marched from the field	Jg 5:4	
For it was **w** Israel had sown, that	Jg 6:3	518
w the sons of Israel cried to the	Jg 6:7	3588
W Gideon saw that he was the angel	Jg 6:22	
W the men of the city arose early	Jg 6:28	
And **w** they searched about and	Jg 6:29	
W he arose early the next morning	Jg 6:38	
W Gideon came, behold, a man was	Jg 7:13	
W Gideon heard the account of	Jg 7:15	
w I come to the outskirts of the	Jg 7:17	
"W I and all who are with me blow	Jg 7:18	
w they had just posted the watch;	Jg 7:19	389
W the three companies blew the	Jg 7:20	
W they blew 300 trumpets, the LORD	Jg 7:22	
not calling us **w** you went to fight	Jg 8:1	3588
him subsided **w** he said that.	Jg 8:3	
w the LORD has given Zebah and	Jg 8:7	
"W I return safely, I will tear	Jg 8:9	
camp **w** the camp was unsuspecting.	Jg 8:11	
W Zebah and Zalmunna fled, he	Jg 8:12	
Now **w** they told Jotham, he went	Jg 9:7	
W Zebul the ruler of the city heard	Jg 9:30	
w he and the people who are with	Jg 9:33	
W Gaal saw the people, he said to	Jg 9:36	
w he looked and saw the people	Jg 9:43	
W all the leaders of the tower of	Jg 9:46	
W the men of Israel saw that	Jg 9:55	
"Also **w** the Sidonians, the	Jg 10:12	
and **w** his wife's sons grew up,	Jg 11:2	
W the sons of Ammon fought against	Jg 11:5	3512c
to me now **w** you are in trouble?"	Jg 11:7	3512c
my land **w** they came up from Egypt,	Jg 11:13	
'For **w** they came up from Egypt,	Jg 11:16	
w I return in peace from the sons of	Jg 11:31	
W Jephthah came to his house at	Jg 11:34	
w he saw her, he tore his clothes	Jg 11:35	
w I called you, you did not	Jg 12:2	
"W I saw that you would not deliver	Jg 12:3	
And it happened **w** *any of* the	Jg 12:5	3588
and **w** he came to the man he said	Jg 13:11	
"Now **w** your words come *to pass,*	Jg 13:12	
so that **w** your words come *to pass,*	Jg 13:17	
For it came about **w** the flame went	Jg 13:20	
W Manoah and his wife saw *this,*	Jg 13:20	
W he returned later to take her,	Jg 14:8	
W he came to his father and	Jg 14:9	
W they saw him, they brought thirty	Jg 14:11	
Philistines **w** I do them harm."	Jg 15:3	3588
W he had set fire to the torches,	Jg 15:5	
W he came to Lehi, the Philistines	Jg 15:14	
W he had finished speaking, he threw	Jg 15:17	
W he drank, his strength returned	Jg 15:19	
W *it was told* to the Gazites,	Jg 16:2	
of tow snaps **w** it touches fire.	Jg 16:9	
you,' **w** your heart is not with me?	Jg 16:15	
It came about **w** she pressed	Jg 16:16	3588
W Delilah saw that he had told her	Jg 16:18	
W the people saw him, they praised	Jg 16:24	
w they were in high spirits,	Jg 16:25	
So **w** he returned the silver to his	Jg 17:4	
W they were near the house of	Jg 18:3	
W they came back to their brothers	Jg 18:8	
"W you enter, you will come to a	Jg 18:10	
W these went into Micah's house	Jg 18:18	
W they had gone some distance from	Jg 18:22	
and **w** Micah saw that they were too	Jg 18:26	
w there was no king in Israel,	Jg 19:1	
and **w** the girl's father saw him,	Jg 19:3	
W the man arose to go along with	Jg 19:9	
W they *were* near Jebus, the day	Jg 19:11	
W they entered, they sat down in	Jg 19:15	
W her master arose in the morning	Jg 19:27	
W he entered his house, he took a	Jg 19:29	
the day **w** the sons of Israel came up	Jg 19:30	
that **w** they come to Gibeah of	Jg 20:10	
W ten thousand choice men from all	Jg 20:34	
W the men of Israel gave ground to	Jg 20:36	
But **w** the cloud began to rise from	Jg 20:40	
For **w** the people were numbered,	Jg 21:9	
w their fathers or their brothers	Jg 21:22	3588
in the days **w** the judges governed,	Ru 1:1	
W she saw that she was determined	Ru 1:18	
w they had come to Bethlehem,	Ru 1:19	
W you are thirsty, go to the water	Ru 2:9	
W she rose to glean, Boaz	Ru 2:15	
"It shall be **w** he lies down,	Ru 3:4	
W Boaz had eaten and drunk and his	Ru 3:7	
this night, and **w** morning comes,	Ru 3:13	
W she came to her mother-in-law, she	Ru 3:16	
W the day came that Elkanah	1Sa 1:4	
Now **w** she had weaned him, she took	1Sa 1:24	3512c
W any man was offering a	1Sa 2:13	
year **w** she would come up with her	1Sa 2:19	
w they were in Egypt *in bondage* to	1Sa 2:27	
the days are coming **w** I will break	1Sa 2:31	
W the battle spread, Israel was	1Sa 4:2	
W the people came into the camp,	1Sa 4:3	
W the Philistines heard the noise of	1Sa 4:6	
W he came, behold, Eli was sitting	1Sa 4:13	
W Eli heard the noise of the	1Sa 4:14	
W he mentioned the ark of God, Eli	1Sa 4:18	
and **w** she heard the news that the	1Sa 4:19	
W the Ashdodites arose early the	1Sa 5:3	

Context	Reference	No.
But **w** they arose early the next	**1Sa 5:4**	
W the men of Ashdod saw that it	**1Sa 5:7**	
W He had severely dealt with them,	**1Sa 6:6**	3512c
W the five lords of the Philistines	**1Sa 6:16**	
Now **w** the Philistines heard that	**1Sa 7:7**	
And **w** the sons of Israel heard it,	**1Sa 7:7**	
And it came about **w** Samuel was old	**1Sa 8:1**	3512c
the sight of Samuel **w** they said,	**1Sa 8:6**	3512c
W they came to the land of Zuph,	**1Sa 9:5**	
w a man went to inquire of God,	**1Sa 9:9**	
W Samuel saw Saul, the LORD said	**1Sa 9:17**	
W they came down from the high	**1Sa 9:25**	
"**W** you go from me today, then you	**1Sa 10:2**	
be **w** these signs come to you,	**1Sa 10:7**	3588
Then it happened **w** he turned his	**1Sa 10:9**	
W they came to the hill there,	**1Sa 10:10**	
w all who knew him previously saw	**1Sa 10:11**	
W he had finished prophesying, he	**1Sa 10:13**	
W we saw that they could not be	**1Sa 10:14**	
but **w** they looked for him, he	**1Sa 10:21**	
and **w** he stood among the people,	**1Sa 10:23**	
mightily **w** he heard these words,	**1Sa 11:6**	
"**W** Jacob went into Egypt and your	**1Sa 12:8**	3512c
"**W** you saw that Nahash the king	**1Sa 12:12**	
years old **w** he began to reign,	**1Sa 13:1**	
W the men of Israel saw that they	**1Sa 13:6**	
W both of them revealed themselves to	**1Sa 14:11**	
And **w** they had numbered, behold,	**1Sa 14:17**	
W all the men of Israel who had	**1Sa 14:22**	
W the people entered the forest,	**1Sa 14:26**	
But Jonathan had not heard **w** his	**1Sa 14:27**	
Now **w** Saul had taken the kingdom	**1Sa 14:47**	
and **w** Saul saw any mighty man or	**1Sa 14:52**	
w they came up from Egypt."	**1Sa 15:6**	
W Saul hears *of it,* he will kill	**1Sa 16:2**	
W they entered, he looked at Eliab	**1Sa 16:6**	
w the evil spirit from God is on you,	**1Sa 16:16**	
W Saul and all Israel heard these	**1Sa 17:11**	
W all the men of Israel saw the	**1Sa 17:24**	
heard **w** he spoke to the men;	**1Sa 17:28**	
W the words which David spoke were	**1Sa 17:31**	
W a lion or a bear came and took a	**1Sa 17:34**	
and **w** he rose up against me, I	**1Sa 17:35**	
W the Philistine looked and saw	**1Sa 17:42**	
Then it happened **w** the Philistine	**1Sa 17:48**	3588
W the Philistines saw that their	**1Sa 17:51**	
Now **w** Saul saw David going out	**1Sa 17:55**	
So **w** David returned from killing	**1Sa 17:57**	
w he had finished speaking to Saul,	**1Sa 18:1**	
w David returned from killing the	**1Sa 18:6**	
W Saul saw that he was prospering	**1Sa 18:15**	
it came about at the time **w** Merab,	**1Sa 18:19**	
W they told Saul, the thing was	**1Sa 18:20**	
W his servants told David these	**1Sa 18:26**	
W Saul saw and knew that the LORD	**1Sa 18:28**	
W there was war again, David went	**1Sa 19:8**	
W Saul sent messengers to take	**1Sa 19:14**	
W the messengers entered, behold,	**1Sa 19:16**	
but **w** they saw the company of the	**1Sa 19:20**	
W it was told Saul, he sent other	**1Sa 19:21**	
W I have sounded out my father	**1Sa 20:12**	3588
not even **w** the LORD cuts off every	**1Sa 20:15**	
"**W** you have stayed for three	**1Sa 20:19**	
and **w** the new moon came, the king	**1Sa 20:24**	
W the lad reached the place of the	**1Sa 20:37**	
W the lad was gone, David rose	**1Sa 20:41**	
kept from us as previously **w** I set out	**1Sa 21:5**	
in its place **w** it was taken away.	**1Sa 21:6**	3117
and **w** his brothers and all his	**1Sa 22:1**	
no one who discloses to me **w** my son	**1Sa 22:8**	
day, **w** Doeg the Edomite was there,	**1Sa 22:22**	3588
w Abiathar the son of Ahimelech	**1Sa 23:6**	
W it was told Saul that David had	**1Sa 23:7**	
W it was told Saul that David had	**1Sa 23:13**	
W Saul and his men went to seek	**1Sa 23:25**	
And **w** Saul heard *it,* he pursued	**1Sa 23:25**	
Now **w** Saul returned	**1Sa 24:1**	3512c
And **w** Saul looked behind him,	**1Sa 24:8**	
W David had finished speaking these	**1Sa 24:16**	
W David's young men came, they	**1Sa 25:9**	
W Abigail saw David, she hurried	**1Sa 25:23**	
w the LORD does for my lord	**1Sa 25:30**	3588
W the LORD deals well with my lord,	**1Sa 25:31**	
w the wine had gone out of Nabal,	**1Sa 25:37**	
W David heard that Nabal was dead,	**1Sa 25:39**	
W the servants of David came to	**1Sa 25:40**	
W he saw that Saul came after him	**1Sa 26:3**	
W Saul saw the camp of the	**1Sa 28:5**	
W Saul inquired of the LORD, the	**1Sa 28:6**	
W the woman saw Samuel, she cried	**1Sa 28:12**	
strength **w** you go on *your* way."	**1Sa 28:22**	3588
w I came before you to this day,	**1Sa 29:8**	834
W David and his men came to Ziklag	**1Sa 30:1**	
W David and his men came to the city,	**1Sa 30:3**	
w I fell sick three days ago.	**1Sa 30:13**	3588
W he had brought him down, behold,	**1Sa 30:16**	
W David came to the two hundred	**1Sa 30:21**	
Now **w** David came to Ziklag, he	**1Sa 30:26**	
W his armor bearer saw that Saul was	**1Sa 31:5**	
W the men of Israel who were on	**1Sa 31:7**	
w the Philistines came to strip the	**1Sa 31:8**	
Now **w** the inhabitants of	**1Sa 31:11**	
w David had returned from the	**2Sa 1:1**	
And it came about **w** he came to	**2Sa 1:2**	
"**W** he looked behind him, he saw me	**2Sa 1:7**	
old **w** he became king over Israel,	**2Sa 2:10**	
and **w** the sun was going down,	**2Sa 2:24**	
w he had gathered all the people	**2Sa 2:30**	
daughter, **w** you come to see me."	**2Sa 3:13**	
W Joab and all the army that was	**2Sa 3:23**	
W Joab came out from David, he	**2Sa 3:26**	
So **w** Abner returned to Hebron,	**2Sa 3:27**	
Afterward **w** David heard it, he	**2Sa 3:28**	
Now **w** Ish-bosheth, Saul's son,	**2Sa 4:1**	
He was five years old **w** the report	**2Sa 4:4**	
Now **w** they came into the house, as	**2Sa 4:7**	
w one told me, saying,	**2Sa 4:10**	3588
w wicked men have killed a	**2Sa 4:11**	3588
w Saul was king over us,	**2Sa 5:2**	
thirty years old **w** he became king,	**2Sa 5:4**	
W the Philistines heard that they	**2Sa 5:17**	
and **w** David heard *of it,* he went	**2Sa 5:17**	
W David inquired of the LORD, He	**2Sa 5:23**	
w you hear the sound of marching	**2Sa 5:24**	
But **w** they came to the threshing	**2Sa 6:6**	
that **w** the bearers of the ark of	**2Sa 6:13**	3588
W David had finished offering	**2Sa 6:18**	
But **w** David returned to bless his	**2Sa 6:20**	
w the king lived in his house,	**2Sa 7:1**	3588
"**W** your days are complete and you	**2Sa 7:12**	3588
w he commits iniquity, I will	**2Sa 7:14**	834
W the Arameans of Damascus came to	**2Sa 8:5**	
Now **w** Toi king of Hamath heard	**2Sa 8:9**	
w he returned from killing 18,000	**2Sa 8:13**	
But **w** David's servants came to the	**2Sa 10:2**	
W they told *it* to David, he sent	**2Sa 10:5**	
Now **w** the sons of Ammon saw that	**2Sa 10:6**	
W David heard *of it,* he sent Joab	**2Sa 10:7**	
Now **w** Joab saw that the battle was	**2Sa 10:9**	
W the sons of Ammon saw that the	**2Sa 10:14**	
W the Arameans saw that they had	**2Sa 10:15**	
Now **w** it was told David, he	**2Sa 10:17**	
W all the kings, servants of	**2Sa 10:19**	
the time **w** kings go out *to battle,*	**2Sa 11:1**	
Now **w** evening came David arose	**2Sa 11:2**	
took her, and **w** she came to him,	**2Sa 11:4**	
and **w** she had purified herself	**2Sa 11:4**	
W Uriah came to him, David asked	**2Sa 11:7**	
Now **w** they told David, saying,	**2Sa 11:10**	
"**W** you have finished telling all	**2Sa 11:19**	
Now **w** the wife of Uriah heard that	**2Sa 11:26**	
W the *time of* mourning was over,	**2Sa 11:27**	
But **w** David saw that his servants	**2Sa 12:19**	
his own house, and **w** he requested,	**2Sa 12:20**	
but **w** the child died, you arose	**2Sa 12:21**	3512c
w your father comes to see you,	**2Sa 13:5**	
w the king came to see him, Amnon	**2Sa 13:6**	
W she brought *them* to him to eat,	**2Sa 13:11**	
Now **w** King David heard of all	**2Sa 13:21**	
But **w** Absalom urged him, he let	**2Sa 13:27**	
w Amnon's heart is merry with	**2Sa 13:28**	
with wine, and **w** I say to you,	**2Sa 13:28**	
Now **w** the woman of Tekoa spoke to	**2Sa 14:4**	
W he cut the hair of his head	**2Sa 14:26**	
So **w** Joab came to the king and	**2Sa 14:33**	
and **w** any man had a suit	**2Sa 15:2**	
And **w** a man came near	**2Sa 15:5**	
Now **w** David had passed a little	**2Sa 16:1**	
W King David came to Bahurim,	**2Sa 16:5**	
Thus Shimei said **w** he cursed,	**2Sa 16:7**	
came about **w** Hushai the Archite,	**2Sa 16:16**	3512c
W Hushai had come to Absalom,	**2Sa 17:6**	3512c
and it will be **w** he falls on them	**2Sa 17:9**	3512c
And **w** they searched and could not	**2Sa 17:20**	3512c
Now **w** Ahithophel saw that his	**2Sa 17:23**	3512c
Now **w** David had come to Mahanaim,	**2Sa 17:27**	
heard **w** the king charged all the	**2Sa 18:5**	
W a certain man saw *it,* he told	**2Sa 18:10**	
"**W** Joab sent the king's servant,	**2Sa 18:29**	
steal away **w** they flee in battle.	**2Sa 19:3**	
W they told all the people,	**2Sa 19:8**	
w my lord the king came out from	**2Sa 19:19**	834
It was **w** he came from	**2Sa 19:25**	3588
W they were at the large stone	**2Sa 20:8**	
And **w** the man saw that all the	**2Sa 20:12**	
threw a garment over him **w** he saw	**2Sa 20:12**	3512c
W it was told David what Rizpah	**2Sa 21:11**	
Now **w** the Philistines were at war	**2Sa 21:15**	
W he defied Israel, Jonathan the son	**2Sa 21:21**	
Is as the light of the morning **w**	**2Sa 23:4**	
W the tender grass *springs*	**2Sa 23:4**	
w they defied the Philistines who	**2Sa 23:9**	
So **w** they had gone about through	**2Sa 24:8**	
W David arose in the morning, the	**2Sa 24:11**	
W the angel stretched out his hand	**2Sa 24:16**	
w he saw the angel who was striking	**2Sa 24:17**	
And **w** he came in before the king,	**1Ki 1:23**	
W Joab heard the sound of the	**1Ki 1:41**	
for they assisted me **w** I fled from	**1Ki 2:7**	
But **w** he came down to me at the	**1Ki 2:8**	
"**W** I rose in the morning to nurse my	**1Ki 3:21**	
but **w** I looked at him carefully in	**1Ki 3:21**	
W all Israel heard of the judgment	**1Ki 3:28**	
w he heard that they had anointed	**1Ki 5:1**	3588
W Hiram heard the words of Solomon,	**1Ki 5:7**	
w they came out of the land of	**1Ki 8:9**	
It happened that **w** the priests	**1Ki 8:10**	
W He brought them from the land	**1Ki 8:21**	
w they pray toward this place;	**1Ki 8:30**	834
"**W** Your people Israel are defeated	**1Ki 8:33**	
"**W** the heavens are shut up and	**1Ki 8:35**	
sin **w** You afflict them,	**1Ki 8:35**	3588
w he comes from a far country for	**1Ki 8:41**	
w he comes and prays toward this	**1Ki 8:42**	
"**W** Your people go out to battle	**1Ki 8:44**	3588
"**W** they sin against You	**1Ki 8:46**	3588
w You brought our fathers forth	**1Ki 8:53**	
W Solomon had finished praying this	**1Ki 8:54**	
Now it came about **w** Solomon had	**1Ki 9:1**	
Now **w** the queen of Sheba heard	**1Ki 10:1**	
W she came to Solomon, she spoke	**1Ki 10:2**	
W the queen of Sheba perceived all	**1Ki 10:4**	
w Solomon was old,	**1Ki 11:4**	6256
came about, **w** David was in Edom,	**1Ki 11:15**	
But **w** Hadad heard in Egypt that	**1Ki 11:21**	
and **w** Solomon saw that the young	**1Ki 11:28**	
w Jeroboam went out of Jerusalem,	**1Ki 11:29**	
w Jeroboam the son of Nebat heard	**1Ki 12:2**	
W all Israel *saw* that the king did	**1Ki 12:16**	
w all Israel heard that Jeroboam had	**1Ki 12:20**	
Now **w** Rehoboam had come to	**1Ki 12:21**	
Now **w** the king heard the saying	**1Ki 13:4**	
Now **w** he had gone, a lion met him	**1Ki 13:24**	
Now **w** the prophet who brought him	**1Ki 13:26**	
"**W** I die, bury me in the grave in	**1Ki 13:31**	
for it will be **w** she arrives that	**1Ki 14:5**	
W Ahijah heard the sound of her feet	**1Ki 14:6**	
W your feet enter the city the	**1Ki 14:12**	
years old **w** he became king,	**1Ki 14:21**	
W Baasha heard *of it,* he ceased	**1Ki 15:21**	
It came about **w** he became king,	**1Ki 16:11**	
W Zimri saw that the city was taken,	**1Ki 16:18**	
and **w** he came to the gate of the	**1Ki 17:10**	
w Jezebel destroyed the prophets	**1Ki 18:4**	
and **w** they said,	**1Ki 18:10**	
"It will come about **w** I leave	**1Ki 18:12**	
so **w** I come and tell Ahab and he	**1Ki 18:12**	
w Jezebel killed the prophets of the	**1Ki 18:13**	
W Ahab saw Elijah, Ahab said to him,	**1Ki 18:17**	
W midday was past, they raved until	**1Ki 18:29**	
W all the people saw it, they fell	**1Ki 18:39**	
W Elijah heard *it,* he wrapped	**1Ki 19:13**	
Damascus, and **w** you have arrived,	**1Ki 19:15**	
W *Ben-hadad* heard this message,	**1Ki 20:12**	
W Jezebel heard that Naboth had been	**1Ki 21:15**	
W Ahab heard that Naboth was dead,	**1Ki 21:16**	
about **w** Ahab heard these words,	**1Ki 21:27**	
W he came to the king, the king	**1Ki 22:15**	
w you enter an inner room to hide	**1Ki 22:25**	834
w the captains of the chariots saw	**1Ki 22:32**	
W the captains of the chariots saw	**1Ki 22:33**	
years old **w** he became king,	**1Ki 22:42**	
W the messengers returned to him	**2Ki 1:5**	
W the third captain of fifty went	**2Ki 1:13**	
w the LORD was about to take up	**2Ki 2:1**	
W they had crossed over, Elijah said	**2Ki 2:9**	
you see me **w** I am taken from you,	**2Ki 2:10**	
w he also had struck the waters,	**2Ki 2:14**	
Now **w** the sons of the prophets who	**2Ki 2:15**	
But **w** they urged him until he was	**2Ki 2:17**	
W he looked behind him and saw	**2Ki 2:24**	
But **w** Ahab died,	**2Ki 3:5**	
came about, **w** the minstrel played,	**2Ki 3:15**	
But **w** they came to the camp of	**2Ki 3:24**	
W the king of Moab saw that the	**2Ki 3:26**	
W the vessels were full, she said to	**2Ki 4:6**	
w Elisha passed over to Shunem,	**2Ki 4:8**	
and it shall be, **w** he comes to us,	**2Ki 4:10**	
And **w** he had called her, she stood	**2Ki 4:12**	
W he had called her,	**2Ki 4:15**	
W the child was grown, the day	**2Ki 4:18**	
W he had taken him and brought him	**2Ki 4:20**	
W the man of God saw her at a	**2Ki 4:25**	
W she came to the man of God to	**2Ki 4:27**	
W Elisha came into the house,	**2Ki 4:32**	
And **w** she came in to him, he said,	**2Ki 4:36**	
W Elisha returned to Gilgal, *there*	**2Ki 4:38**	
W the king of Israel read the letter,	**2Ki 5:7**	
It happened **w** Elisha the man	**2Ki 5:8**	
much more *then,* **w** he says to you,	**2Ki 5:13**	3588
W he returned to the man of God	**2Ki 5:15**	
w my master goes into the house of	**2Ki 5:18**	
w I bow myself in the house of	**2Ki 5:18**	
W Naaman saw one running after	**2Ki 5:21**	
W he came to the hill, he took	**2Ki 5:24**	
w the man turned from his chariot	**2Ki 5:26**	3512c
and **w** they came to the Jordan,	**2Ki 6:4**	
And **w** he showed him the place, he	**2Ki 6:6**	
Now **w** the attendant of the man of	**2Ki 6:15**	
W they came down to him, Elisha	**2Ki 6:18**	
W they had come into Samaria, Elisha	**2Ki 6:20**	
the king of Israel **w** he saw them,	**2Ki 6:21**	
and **w** they had eaten and drunk he	**2Ki 6:23**	
W the king heard the words of	**2Ki 6:30**	
Look, **w** the messenger comes, shut	**2Ki 6:32**	
w they came to the outskirts of	**2Ki 7:5**	
W these lepers came to the	**2Ki 7:8**	
"**W** they come out of the city, we	**2Ki 7:12**	3588
spoke **w** the king came down to him.	**2Ki 7:17**	
W the king asked the woman, she	**2Ki 8:6**	
years old **w** he became king,	**2Ki 8:17**	
years old **w** he became king,	**2Ki 8:26**	
w he fought against Hazael king of	**2Ki 8:29**	
"**W** you arrive there, search out	**2Ki 9:2**	
W he came, behold, the captains of	**2Ki 9:5**	
w he fought with Hazael king of Aram	**2Ki 9:15**	
W Joram saw Jehu, he said, "Is it	**2Ki 9:22**	
for I remember **w** you and I were	**2Ki 9:25**	
W Ahaziah the king of Judah saw	**2Ki 9:27**	
W Jehu came to Jezreel, Jezebel	**2Ki 9:30**	
W he came in, he ate and drank;	**2Ki 9:34**	
Now, **w** this letter comes to you,	**2Ki 10:2**	
W the letter came to them, they took	**2Ki 10:7**	
W the messenger came and told him,	**2Ki 10:8**	
Now **w** he had departed from there,	**2Ki 10:15**	
W he came to Samaria, he killed all	**2Ki 10:17**	
And **w** they went into the house of	**2Ki 10:21**	

W Athaliah the mother of Ahaziah	**2Ki 11:1**	
And be with the king **w** he goes out	**2Ki 11:8**	
he goes out and **w** he comes in."	**2Ki 11:8**	
W Athaliah heard the noise of the	**2Ki 11:13**	
and **w** she arrived at the horses'	**2Ki 11:16**	
seven years old **w** he became king.	**2Ki 11:21**	
W they saw that there was much money	**2Ki 12:10**	
W Elisha became sick with the	**2Ki 13:14**	
And **w** the man touched the bones of	**2Ki 13:21**	
W Hazael king of Aram died,	**2Ki 13:24**	
years old **w** he became king,	**2Ki 14:2**	
years old **w** he became king,	**2Ki 15:2**	
years old **w** he became king,	**2Ki 15:33**	
twenty years old **w** he became king,	**2Ki 16:2**	
W the king came from Damascus,	**2Ki 16:12**	
W He had torn Israel from the	**2Ki 17:21**	3588
years old **w** he became king,	**2Ki 18:2**	
And **w** they went up, they came and	**2Ki 18:17**	
W they called to the king, Eliakim	**2Ki 18:18**	
to Hezekiah **w** he misleads you,	**2Ki 18:32**	3588
And **w** King Hezekiah heard *it,* he	**2Ki 19:1**	
W he heard *them* say concerning	**2Ki 19:9**	
w men rose early in the morning,	**2Ki 19:35**	
w all that is in your house,	**2Ki 20:17**	
twelve years old **w** he became king,	**2Ki 21:1**	
years old **w** he became king,	**2Ki 21:19**	
eight years old **w** he became king,	**2Ki 22:1**	
W the king heard the words of	**2Ki 22:11**	
w you heard what I spoke against	**2Ki 22:19**	
Now **w** Josiah turned, he saw the	**2Ki 23:16**	
and **w** *Pharaoh Neco* saw him he	**2Ki 23:29**	
years old **w** he became king,	**2Ki 23:31**	
years old **w** he became king,	**2Ki 23:36**	
years old **w** he became king,	**2Ki 24:8**	
years old **w** he became king,	**2Ki 24:18**	
W all the captains of the forces,	**2Ki 25:23**	
W Bela died, Jobab the son of	**1Ch 1:44**	
W Jobab died, Husham of the land	**1Ch 1:45**	
W Husham died, Hadad the son of	**1Ch 1:46**	
W Hadad died, Samlah of Masrekah	**1Ch 1:47**	
W Samlah died, Shaul of Rehoboth	**1Ch 1:48**	
W Shaul died, Baal-hanan the son	**1Ch 1:49**	
W Baal-hanan died, Hadad became	**1Ch 1:50**	
W Azubah died, Caleb married	**1Ch 2:19**	
married **w** he was sixty years old;	**1Ch 2:21**	
w the LORD carried Judah and	**1Ch 6:15**	
w they brought them in and when	**1Ch 9:28**	
them in and **w** they took them out.	**1Ch 9:28**	
W his armor bearer saw that Saul was	**1Ch 10:5**	
W all the men of Israel who were	**1Ch 10:7**	
w the Philistines came to strip	**1Ch 10:8**	
W all Jabesh-gilead heard all that	**1Ch 10:11**	
times past, even **w** Saul was king,	**1Ch 11:2**	
w the Philistines were gathered	**1Ch 11:13**	
w it was overflowing all its banks	**1Ch 12:15**	
w he was about to go to battle	**1Ch 12:19**	
W they came to the threshing floor	**1Ch 13:9**	
W the Philistines heard that David	**1Ch 14:8**	
"It shall be **w** you hear the	**1Ch 14:15**	
It happened **w** the ark of the	**1Ch 15:29**	
W David had finished offering the	**1Ch 16:2**	
W they were only a few in number,	**1Ch 16:19**	
about, **w** David dwelt in his house,	**1Ch 17:1**	3512c
"**W** your days are fulfilled that you	**1Ch 17:11**	3588
W the Arameans of Damascus came to	**1Ch 18:5**	
Now **w** Tou king of Hamath heard	**1Ch 18:9**	
W the sons of Ammon saw that they	**1Ch 19:6**	
W David heard *of it,* he sent Joab	**1Ch 19:8**	
Now **w** Joab saw that the battle was	**1Ch 19:10**	
W the sons of Ammon saw that the	**1Ch 19:15**	
W the Arameans saw that they had	**1Ch 19:16**	
W it was told David, he gathered	**1Ch 19:17**	
And **w** David drew up in battle	**1Ch 19:17**	
So **w** the servants of Hadadezer saw	**1Ch 19:19**	
the time **w** kings go out *to battle,*	**1Ch 20:1**	
W he taunted Israel, Jonathan	**1Ch 20:7**	
w David saw that the LORD had	**1Ch 21:28**	
Now **w** David reached old age, he	**1Ch 23:1**	
w *they* came in to the house of the	**1Ch 24:19**	
Israel, **w** they came out of Egypt.	**2Ch 5:10**	
W the priests came forth from	**2Ch 5:11**	
in unison **w** the trumpeters and the	**2Ch 5:13**	
and **w** they lifted up their voice	**2Ch 5:13**	
and **w** they praised the LORD	**2Ch 5:13**	
w they pray toward this place;	**2Ch 6:21**	834
"**W** the heavens are shut up and	**2Ch 6:26**	
sin **w** You afflict them;	**2Ch 6:26**	3588
w he comes from a far country for	**2Ch 6:32**	
w they come and pray toward this	**2Ch 6:32**	
"**W** Your people go out to battle	**2Ch 6:34**	3588
"**W** they sin against You	**2Ch 6:36**	3588
w Solomon had finished praying,	**2Ch 7:1**	
Now **w** the queen of Sheba heard of	**2Ch 9:1**	
and **w** she came to Solomon, she	**2Ch 9:1**	
W the queen of Sheba had seen	**2Ch 9:3**	
W Jeroboam the son of Nebat heard	**2Ch 10:2**	
W Jeroboam and all Israel came,	**2Ch 10:3**	
W all Israel *saw* that the king	**2Ch 10:16**	
Now **w** Rehoboam had come to	**2Ch 11:1**	
W the kingdom of Rehoboam was	**2Ch 12:1**	
W the LORD saw that they humbled	**2Ch 12:7**	
And **w** he humbled himself, the	**2Ch 12:12**	
years old **w** he began to reign,	**2Ch 12:13**	
w he was young and timid and could	**2Ch 13:7**	
W Judah turned around, behold,	**2Ch 13:14**	
and **w** the men of Judah raised the	**2Ch 13:15**	
W the sons of Israel fled before	**2Ch 13:16**	
is with you **w** you are with Him.	**2Ch 15:2**	
Now **w** Asa heard these words and	**2Ch 15:8**	
defected to him from Israel **w** they saw	**2Ch 15:9**	
W Baasha heard *of it,* he ceased	**2Ch 16:5**	
W he came to the king, the king said	**2Ch 18:14**	
w you enter an inner room to hide	**2Ch 18:24**	834
w the captains of the chariots saw	**2Ch 18:31**	
W the captains of the chariots saw	**2Ch 18:32**	
is with you **w** you render judgment.	**2Ch 19:6**	
w they came out of the land of Egypt	**2Ch 20:10**	
and **w** they went out, Jehoshaphat	**2Ch 20:20**	
W he had consulted with the people,	**2Ch 20:21**	
W they began singing and praising,	**2Ch 20:22**	6256
and **w** they had finished with the	**2Ch 20:23**	
W Judah came to the lookout of the	**2Ch 20:24**	
W Jehoshaphat and his people came to	**2Ch 20:25**	
w they heard that the LORD had	**2Ch 20:29**	
years old **w** he became king,	**2Ch 20:31**	
Now **w** Jehoram had taken over the	**2Ch 21:4**	
years old **w** he became king,	**2Ch 21:5**	
years old **w** he became king,	**2Ch 21:20**	
years old **w** he became king,	**2Ch 22:2**	
w he fought against Hazael king of	**2Ch 22:6**	
For **w** he came, he went out with	**2Ch 22:7**	
It came about **w** Jehu was	**2Ch 22:8**	
Now **w** Athaliah the mother of	**2Ch 22:10**	
Thus be with the king **w** he comes	**2Ch 23:7**	
he comes in and **w** he goes out."	**2Ch 23:7**	
W Athaliah heard the noise of the	**2Ch 23:12**	
and **w** she arrived at the entrance	**2Ch 23:15**	
seven years old **w** he became king,	**2Ch 24:1**	
and **w** they saw that there was much	**2Ch 24:11**	
W they had finished, they brought	**2Ch 24:14**	
Now **w** Jehoiada reached a ripe old	**2Ch 24:15**	
W they had departed from him (for	**2Ch 24:25**	
years old **w** he became king,	**2Ch 25:1**	
years old **w** he became king,	**2Ch 26:3**	
But **w** he became strong, his heart	**2Ch 26:16**	
years old **w** he became king,	**2Ch 27:1**	
years old **w** he became king,	**2Ch 27:8**	
twenty years old **w** he became king,	**2Ch 28:1**	
w Ahaz gathered together the	**2Ch 28:24**	
Hezekiah became king **w** *he was*	**2Ch 29:1**	
W the burnt offering began, the	**2Ch 29:27**	6256
Now **w** all this was finished, all	**2Ch 31:1**	
W Hezekiah and the rulers came	**2Ch 31:8**	
Now **w** Hezekiah saw that	**2Ch 32:2**	
And **w** he had entered the temple of	**2Ch 32:21**	
twelve years old **w** he became king,	**2Ch 33:1**	
W he was in distress, he entreated	**2Ch 33:12**	
W he prayed to Him, He was moved	**2Ch 33:13**	
years old **w** he became king,	**2Ch 33:21**	
eight years old **w** he became king,	**2Ch 34:1**	
w he had purged the land and the	**2Ch 34:8**	
W they were bringing out the money	**2Ch 34:14**	
W the king heard the words of the law,	**2Ch 34:19**	
w you heard His words against this	**2Ch 34:27**	
w Josiah had set the temple in	**2Ch 35:20**	834
years old **w** he became king,	**2Ch 36:2**	
years old **w** he became king,	**2Ch 36:5**	
eight years old **w** he became king,	**2Ch 36:9**	
years old **w** he became king,	**2Ch 36:11**	
w they arrived at the house of the	**Ezr 2:68**	
Now **w** the seventh month came, and	**Ezr 3:1**	
Now **w** the builders had laid the	**Ezr 3:10**	
great shout **w** they praised the LORD	**Ezr 3:11**	
w the foundation of this house was	**Ezr 3:12**	
Now **w** the enemies of Judah and	**Ezr 4:1**	
W the prophets, Haggai the prophet	**Ezr 5:1**	
and **w** I observed the people and	**Ezr 8:15**	
Now **w** these things had been	**Ezr 9:1**	
W I heard about this matter, I tore	**Ezr 9:3**	
W I heard these words, I sat down	**Ne 1:4**	
my face not be sad **w** the city,	**Ne 2:3**	834
be, and **w** will you return?"	**Ne 2:6**	4970
W Sanballat the Horonite and Tobiah	**Ne 2:10**	
But **w** Sanballat the Horonite and	**Ne 2:19**	
w Sanballat heard that we were	**Ne 4:1**	3512c
Now **w** Sanballat,	**Ne 4:7**	3512c
W the Jews who lived near them came	**Ne 4:12**	3512c
W I saw *their fear,* I rose and	**Ne 4:14**	
W our enemies heard that it was known	**Ne 4:15**	3512c
Then I was very angry **w** I had	**Ne 5:6**	3512c
w it was reported to Sanballat,	**Ne 6:1**	3512c
W I entered the house of Shemaiah	**Ne 6:10**	
W all our enemies heard *of it,*	**Ne 6:16**	3512c
w the wall was rebuilt and I had set	**Ne 7:1**	3512c
And **w** the seventh month came, the	**Ne 7:73**	
and **w** he opened it, all the people	**Ne 8:5**	
people were weeping **w** they heard	**Ne 8:9**	
"Even **w** they made for themselves	**Ne 9:18**	3588
But **w** they cried to You in the	**Ne 9:27**	
W they cried again to You, You	**Ne 9:28**	
w the Levites receive tithes,	**Ne 10:38**	
w they heard the law,	**Ne 13:3**	
W these days were completed,	**Es 1:5**	
w the heart of the king was merry	**Es 1:10**	
"**W** the king's edict which he will	**Es 1:20**	
After these things **w** the anger of	**Es 2:1**	
and **w** her father and her mother	**Es 2:7**	
So it came about **w** the command and	**Es 2:8**	
Now **w** the turn of each young lady	**Es 2:12**	
Now **w** the turn of Esther, the	**Es 2:15**	
W the virgins were gathered together	**Es 2:19**	
as she had done **w** under his care.	**Es 2:20**	3512c
Now **w** the plot was investigated	**Es 2:23**	
Now it was **w** they had spoken daily	**Es 3:4**	
W Haman saw that Mordecai neither	**Es 3:5**	
W Mordecai learned all that had	**Es 4:1**	
W the king saw Esther the queen	**Es 5:2**	
but **w** Haman saw Mordecai in the	**Es 5:9**	
Now **w** the king returned from the	**Es 7:8**	
on the thirteenth day **w** the king's	**Es 9:1**	834
on the day **w** the enemies of the	**Es 9:1**	834
But **w** it came to the king's	**Es 9:25**	
W the days of feasting had completed	**Jb 1:5**	3588
w the sons of God came to present	**Jb 1:6**	
Now on the day **w** his sons and	**Jb 1:13**	
w the sons of God came to present	**Jb 2:1**	
Now **w** Job's three friends heard of	**Jb 2:11**	
W they lifted up their eyes at	**Jb 2:12**	
exult **w** they find the grave?	**Jb 3:22**	3588
night, **W** deep sleep falls on men,	**Jb 4:13**	
be afraid of violence **w** it comes.	**Jb 5:21**	3588
"**W** they become waterless, they	**Jb 6:17**	6256
they are silent, **W** it is hot,	**Jb 6:17**	
W the words of one in despair	**Jb 6:26**	
"**W** I lie down I say,	**Jb 7:4**	518
'**W** shall I arise?'	**Jb 7:4**	4970
"**W** a cloud vanishes, it is gone,	**Jb 7:9**	
W He overturns them in His anger;	**Jb 9:5**	834
W the foal of a wild donkey is born	**Jb 11:12**	
"Will it be well **w** He examines you?	**Jb 13:9**	3588
hope for a tree, **W** it is cut down,	**Jb 14:7**	518
"For **w** a few years are past, I	**Jb 16:22**	
"**W** he fills his belly, *God* will	**Jb 20:23**	
"Even **w** I remember, I am	**Jb 21:6**	518
W the number of his months is cut	**Jb 21:21**	
"**W** you are cast down, you will	**Jb 22:29**	3588
W He acts on the left, I cannot	**Jb 23:9**	
"But He knows the way I take; **W**	**Jb 23:10**	
W I consider, I am terrified of	**Jb 23:15**	
of the godless **w** he is cut off,	**Jb 27:8**	3588
cut off, **W** God requires his life?	**Jb 27:8**	3588
cry **W** distress comes upon him?	**Jb 27:9**	3588
"**W** He imparted weight to the	**Jb 28:25**	
W He set a limit for the rain And	**Jb 28:26**	
in the days **w** God watched over me;	**Jb 29:2**	
W His lamp shone over my head, *And*	**Jb 29:3**	
W the friendship of God *was* over	**Jb 29:4**	
W the Almighty was yet with me,	**Jb 29:5**	
W my steps were bathed in butter,	**Jb 29:6**	
"**W** I went out to the gate of the	**Jb 29:7**	
W I took my seat in the square,	**Jb 29:7**	
"For **w** the ear heard, it called	**Jb 29:11**	
And **w** the eye saw, it gave witness	**Jb 29:11**	
on them **w** they did not believe,	**Jb 29:24**	
"**W** I expected good, then evil	**Jb 30:26**	3588
W I waited for light, then	**Jb 30:26**	
W they filed a complaint against me,	**Jb 31:13**	
What then could I do **w** God arises?	**Jb 31:14**	3588
And **w** He calls me to account,	**Jb 31:14**	3588
have looked at the sun **w** it shone Or	**Jb 31:26**	3588
Or exulted **w** evil befell him?	**Jb 31:29**	3588
And **w** Elihu saw that there was no	**Jb 32:5**	
night, **W** sound sleep falls on men,	**Jb 33:15**	
nothing **W** he is pleased with God.'	**Jb 34:9**	
W He keeps quiet, who then can	**Jb 34:29**	
And **w** He hides His face, who then	**Jb 34:29**	
w you say you do not behold Him,	**Jb 35:14**	3588
not cry for help **w** He binds them.	**Jb 36:13**	3588
W people vanish in their place.	**Jb 36:20**	
lightnings **w** His voice is heard.	**Jb 37:4**	
W the land is still because of the	**Jb 37:17**	
w I laid the foundation of the earth	**Jb 38:4**	
W the morning stars sang together And	**Jb 38:7**	
W, bursting forth, it went out from	**Jb 38:8**	
W I made a cloud its garment And	**Jb 38:9**	
W the dust hardens into a mass And	**Jb 38:38**	
W they crouch in *their* dens *And*	**Jb 38:40**	3588
W its young cry to God And	**Jb 38:41**	3588
"**W** she lifts herself on high, She	**Jb 39:18**	6256
capture him **w** he is on watch,	**Jb 40:24**	
"**W** he raises himself up, the	**Jb 41:25**	4480
Job **w** he prayed for his friends,	**Jb 42:10**	
Answer me **w** I call, O God of my	**Ps 4:1**	
The LORD hears **w** I call to Him.	**Ps 4:3**	
More than **w** their grain and new	**Ps 4:7**	6256
W I consider Your heavens, the work	**Ps 8:3**	3588
W my enemies turn back, They	**Ps 9:3**	
w he draws him into his net.	**Ps 10:9**	
W vileness is exalted among the	**Ps 12:8**	
adversaries will rejoice **w** I am shaken.	**Ps 13:4**	3588
W the LORD restores His captive	**Ps 14:7**	
with Your likeness **w** I awake.	**Ps 17:15**	
You made me trust **w** upon my	**Ps 22:9**	
But **w** he cried to Him for help, He	**Ps 22:24**	
W evildoers came upon me to devour	**Ps 27:2**	
O LORD, **w** I cry with my voice,	**Ps 27:7**	
W *You said,* "Seek My face,"	**Ps 27:8**	
w I cry to You for help,	**Ps 28:2**	
W I lift up my hands toward Your	**Ps 28:2**	
supplications **W** I cried to You.	**Ps 31:22**	
W I kept silent *about my sin,* my	**Ps 32:3**	3588
in a time **w** You may be found;	**Ps 32:6**	
But as for me, **w** they were sick, my	**Ps 35:13**	
W he falls, he will not be hurled	**Ps 37:24**	3588
him be condemned **w** he is judged.	**Ps 37:33**	
W the wicked are cut off, you will	**Ps 37:34**	
over me, *Who,* **w** my foot slips,	**Ps 38:16**	
"**W** will he die, and his name	**Ps 41:5**	4970
And **w** he comes to see *me,* he	**Ps 41:6**	518
W he goes outside, he tells it.	**Ps 41:6**	
out upon him, That **w** he lies down,	**Ps 41:8**	834
W shall I come and appear before	**Ps 42:2**	4970
God will help her **w** morning dawns.	**Ps 46:5**	
W the iniquity of my foes	**Ps 49:5**	
be afraid **w** a man becomes rich,	**Ps 49:16**	3588
W the glory of his house is	**Ps 49:16**	3588
For **w** he dies he will carry	**Ps 49:17**	3588

you **w** you do well for yourself	Ps 49:18	3588
"**W** you see a thief, you are	Ps 50:18	518
So that You are justified **w** You speak	Ps 51:4	
And blameless **w** You judge.	Ps 51:4	
W God restores His captive people,	Ps 53:6	
W I am afraid, I will put my trust	Ps 56:3	3117
turn back in the day **w** I call;	Ps 56:9	
W he aims his arrows, let them	Ps 58:7	
The righteous will rejoice **w** he sees	Ps 58:10	3588
the end of the earth I call to You **w**	Ps 61:2	
W I remember You on my bed, I	Ps 63:6	518
mouth spoke **w** I was in distress.	Ps 66:14	
w You went forth before Your	Ps 68:7	
W You marched through the	Ps 68:7	
inheritance **w** it was parched.	Ps 68:9	
W you lie down among the	Ps 68:13	518
W the Almighty scattered the kings	Ps 68:14	
W I wept in my soul with fasting,	Ps 69:10	
W I made sackcloth my clothing, I	Ps 69:11	
And **w** they are in peace, *may it*	Ps 69:22	
forsake me **w** my strength fails.	Ps 71:9	
And even **w** *I am* old and gray, O	Ps 71:18	5704
for joy **w** I sing praises to You;	Ps 71:23	3588
the needy **w** he cries for help,	Ps 72:12	
W I pondered to understand this,	Ps 73:16	
Like a dream **w** one awakes, O Lord,	Ps 73:20	4480
one awakes, O Lord, **w** aroused,	Ps 73:20	
W my heart was embittered And I	Ps 73:21	3588
"**W** I select an appointed time, It	Ps 75:2	3588
presence **w** once You are angry?	Ps 76:7	4480
W God arose to judgment, To save	Ps 76:9	
W I remember God, then I am	Ps 77:3	
W I sigh, then my spirit grows	Ps 77:3	
W He rained meat upon them like	Ps 78:27	
W He killed them, then they sought	Ps 78:34	518
The day **w** He redeemed them from	Ps 78:42	834
W He performed His signs in Egypt	Ps 78:43	834
W God heard, He was filled with	Ps 78:59	
W he went throughout the land of	Ps 81:5	
count **w** He registers the peoples,	Ps 87:6	
W its waves rise, You still	Ps 89:9	
Are like yesterday **w** it passes by,	Ps 90:4	3588
That **w** the wicked sprouted up like	Ps 92:7	
And **w** will you understand, stupid	Ps 94:8	4970
W my anxious thoughts multiply	Ps 94:19	
"**W** your fathers tested Me, They	Ps 95:9	834
W will You come to me?	Ps 101:2	4970
In the day **w** I call answer me quickly.	Ps 102:2	
W the peoples are gathered	Ps 102:22	
W the wind has passed over it, it	Ps 103:16	3588
W the sun rises they withdraw	Ps 104:22	
W they were only a few men in	Ps 105:12	
Egypt was glad **w** they departed,	Ps 105:38	
W they became envious of Moses in	Ps 106:16	
distress **W** He heard their cry;	Ps 106:44	
W they are diminished and bowed	Ps 107:39	
W he is judged, let him come forth	Ps 109:7	
like a shadow **w** it lengthens;	Ps 109:23	
W they see me, they wag their head.	Ps 109:25	
W they arise, they shall be	Ps 109:28	
W Israel went forth from Egypt,	Ps 114:1	
I believed **w** I said,	Ps 116:10	3588
not be ashamed **W** I look upon all	Ps 119:6	
W I learn Your righteous judgments.	Ps 119:7	
"**W** will You comfort me?"	Ps 119:82	4970
W will You execute judgment on	Ps 119:84	4970
I am *for* peace, but **w** I speak,	Ps 120:7	3588
I was glad **w** they said to me,	Ps 122:1	
side **W** men rose up against us	Ps 124:2	
W their anger was kindled against	Ps 124:3	
W the LORD brought back the	Ps 126:1	
W they speak with their enemies in	Ps 127:5	3588
W you shall eat of the fruit of	Ps 128:2	3588
and wept, **W** we remembered Zion.	Ps 137:1	
W they have heard the words of Your	Ps 138:4	3588
w I sit down and when I rise up;	Ps 139:2	
when I sit down and **w** I rise up;	Ps 139:2	
from You, **W** I was made in secret,	Ps 139:15	834
W as yet there was not one of them.	Ps 139:16	
W I awake, I am still with You.	Ps 139:18	
ear to my voice **w** I call to You!	Ps 141:1	
As **w** one plows and breaks open the	Ps 141:7	
W my spirit was overwhelmed within	Ps 142:3	
I will mock **w** your dread comes,	Pr 1:26	
W your dread comes like a storm And	Pr 1:27	
W distress and anguish come upon you.	Pr 1:27	
W you lie down, you will not be	Pr 3:24	518
W you lie down, your sleep will be	Pr 3:24	
of the wicked **w** it comes;	Pr 3:25	3588
W it is in your power to do *it.*	Pr 3:27	
give *it,*" **W** you have it with you.	Pr 3:28	
W I was a son to my father, Tender	Pr 4:3	3588
W you walk, your steps will not be	Pr 4:12	
W your flesh and your body are	Pr 5:11	
W will you arise from your sleep?	Pr 6:9	4970
W you walk about, they will guide	Pr 6:22	
W you sleep, they will watch over	Pr 6:22	
And **w** you awake, they will talk to	Pr 6:22	
To satisfy himself **w** he is hungry;	Pr 6:30	3588
But **w** he is found, he must repay	Pr 6:31	
"**W** there were no depths I was	Pr 8:24	
W there were no springs abounding	Pr 8:24	
"**W** He established the heavens, I	Pr 8:27	
W He inscribed a circle on the	Pr 8:27	
W He made firm the skies above,	Pr 8:28	
W the springs of the deep became	Pr 8:28	
W He set for the sea its boundary So	Pr 8:29	
W He marked out the foundations of	Pr 8:29	
W there are many words,	Pr 10:19	
W the whirlwind passes, the wicked	Pr 10:25	
W pride comes, then comes	Pr 11:2	
W a wicked man dies, *his*	Pr 11:7	
W it goes well with the righteous,	Pr 11:10	
rejoices, And **w** the wicked perish,	Pr 11:10	
righteous has a refuge **w** he dies.	Pr 14:32	
face, But **w** the heart is sad,	Pr 15:13	
W a man's ways are pleasing to the	Pr 16:7	
to buy wisdom, **W** he has no sense?	Pr 17:16	
Even a fool, **w** he keeps silent, is	Pr 17:28	
W he closes his lips, he is	Pr 17:28	
W a wicked man comes, contempt	Pr 18:3	
But **w** he goes his way, then he	Pr 20:14	
Take his garment **w** he becomes	Pr 20:16	3588
W the scoffer is punished, the	Pr 21:11	
But **w** the wise is instructed, he	Pr 21:11	
w he brings it with evil intent!	Pr 21:27	3588
Even **w** he is old he will not	Pr 22:6	3588
W you sit down to dine with a	Pr 23:1	3588
W you set your eyes on it, it is	Pr 23:5	
W your lips speak what is right.	Pr 23:16	
despise your mother **w** she is old.	Pr 23:22	3588
not look on the wine **w** it is red,	Pr 23:31	3588
is red, **W** it sparkles in the cup,	Pr 23:31	3588
the cup, **W** it goes down smoothly;	Pr 23:31	
W shall I awake? I will seek another	Pr 23:35	4970
Do not rejoice **w** your enemy falls,	Pr 24:17	
your heart be glad **w** he stumbles;	Pr 24:17	
W I saw, I reflected upon it;	Pr 24:32	
W your neighbor humiliates you?	Pr 25:8	
W he speaks graciously, do not	Pr 26:25	3588
w he becomes surety for a stranger;	Pr 27:13	3588
W the grass disappears, the new	Pr 27:25	
wicked flee **w** no one is pursuing,	Pr 28:1	
W the righteous triumph, there is	Pr 28:12	
glory, But **w** the wicked rise,	Pr 28:12	
W the wicked rise, men hide	Pr 28:28	
But **w** they perish, the righteous	Pr 28:28	
W the righteous increase, the	Pr 29:2	
rejoice, But **w** a wicked man rules,	Pr 29:2	
W a wise man has a controversy	Pr 29:9	
W the wicked increase,	Pr 29:16	
Under a slave **w** he becomes king,	Pr 30:22	3588
fool **w** he is satisfied with food,	Pr 30:22	3588
woman **w** she gets a husband,	Pr 30:23	3588
w she supplants her mistress.	Pr 30:23	3588
which are stately **w** they walk:	Pr 30:29	
And a king **w** *his* army is with him.	Pr 30:31	
W he sits among the elders of the	Pr 31:23	
W there is a man who has labored	Ec 2:21	3588
w there is not another to lift him up.	Ec 4:10	
W you make a vow to God, do not be	Ec 5:4	3512c
W good things increase, those who	Ec 5:11	
W those riches were lost through a	Ec 5:14	
For **w** a face is sad a heart may be	Ec 7:3	
who can tell him **w** it will happen?	Ec 8:7	
		3588, 3512c
W I gave my heart to know wisdom	Ec 8:16	3512c
time **w** it suddenly falls on them.	Ec 9:12	
Even **w** the fool walks along the	Ec 10:3	7945
years draw near **w** you will say,	Ec 12:1	834
conclusion, **w** all has been heard,	Ec 12:13	
the day **w** the shadows flee away,	SS 2:17	
W I found him whom my soul loves	SS 3:4	
		5704, 7945
the day **W** the shadows flee away,	SS 4:6	
On the day **w** she is spoken for?	SS 8:8	7945
"**W** you come to appear before Me,	Is 1:12	3588
"So **w** you spread out your hands	Is 1:15	
W He arises to make the earth	Is 2:19	
W He arises to make the earth	Is 2:21	
W a man lays hold of his brother	Is 3:6	3588
W the Lord has washed away the	Is 4:4	518
w I expected *it* to produce *good*	Is 5:4	
stump remains **w** it is felled.	Is 6:13	834
W it was reported to the house of	Is 7:2	
W they say to you, "Consult	Is 8:19	3588
turn out that **w** they are hungry,	Is 8:21	3588
rejoice **w** they divide the spoil.	Is 9:3	
w the Lord has completed all His	Is 10:12	3588
be as **w** a sick man wastes away.	Is 10:18	
The sun will be dark **w** it rises And	Is 13:10	
Will be as **w** God overthrew Sodom	Is 13:19	
W the LORD will have compassion on	Is 14:1	3588
w the LORD gives you rest from your	Is 14:3	
over you to meet you **w** you come;	Is 14:9	
about **w** Moab presents himself,	Is 16:12	3588
W he wearies himself upon *his* high	Is 16:12	3588
w Sargon the king of Assyria sent	Is 20:1	
"**W** he sees riders, horsemen in	Is 21:7	
W he opens no one will shut,	Is 22:22	
shut, **W** he shuts no one will open.	Is 22:22	
W the report *reaches* Egypt, They	Is 23:5	3512c
w the grape harvest is over.	Is 24:13	518
For **w** the earth experiences Your	Is 26:9	3512c
W he makes all the altar stones	Is 27:9	
W Asherim and incense altars will	Is 27:9	
W its limbs are dry, they are	Is 27:11	
They totter **w** *rendering* judgment.	Is 28:7	
will not reach us **w** it passes by,	Is 28:15	3588
W the overwhelming scourge passes	Is 28:18	3588
It will be as **w** a hungry man	Is 29:8	3512c
But **w** he awakens, his hunger is	Is 29:8	
Or as **w** a thirsty man dreams	Is 29:8	3512c
he is drinking, But **w** he awakens,	Is 29:8	
which **w** they give it to the one	Is 29:11	
But **w** he sees his children, the	Is 29:23	3588
w He hears it, He will answer you.	Is 30:19	
slaughter, **w** the towers fall.	Is 30:25	
the night **w** you keep the festival,	Is 30:29	
And gladness of heart as **w** one	Is 30:29	
W He strikes with the rod.	Is 30:31	
will hail **w** the forest comes down,	Is 32:19	
And **w** have they delivered Samaria	Is 36:19	3588
And **w** King Hezekiah heard *it,* he	Is 37:1	
W he heard *them* say concerning	Is 37:9	
and **w** he heard *it* he sent	Is 37:9	
and **w** men arose early in the	Is 37:36	
w all that is in your house and	Is 39:6	
W the breath of the LORD blows	Is 40:7	3588
"But **w** I look, there is no one,	Is 41:28	
"**W** you pass through the waters, I	Is 43:2	3588
W you walk through the fire, you	Is 43:2	3588
W I call to them, they stand	Is 48:13	
They did not thirst **w** He led	Is 48:21	
"Why was there no man **w** I came?	Is 50:2	
W I called, *why* was there none to	Is 50:2	
W *he was but* one I called him, Then I	Is 51:2	3588
own eyes **W** the LORD restores Zion.	Is 52:8	
of *one's* youth **w** she is rejected,"	Is 54:6	3588
W I swore that the waters of Noah	Is 54:9	834
worried and fearful **W** you lied,	Is 57:11	3588
"**W** you cry out, let your	Is 57:13	
W you see the naked, to cover him;	Is 58:7	3588
W You did awesome things which	Is 64:3	
gods **W** they were not gods?	Jer 2:11	
your God **W** He led you in the way?	Jer 2:17	6256
is shamed **w** he is discovered,	Jer 2:26	3588
w you are multiplied and increased	Jer 3:16	3588
W I had fed them to the full, They	Jer 5:7	
It shall come about **w** they say,	Jer 5:19	3588
"**w** it will no longer be called	Jer 7:32	
W He utters His voice, *there is* a	Jer 10:13	
for I will not listen **w** they call	Jer 11:14	6256
W she has done many vile deeds?	Jer 11:15	3588
And **w** they say to you,	Jer 13:12	
"What will you say **w** He appoints	Jer 13:21	3588
"**W** they fast, I am not going to	Jer 14:12	3588
and **w** they offer burnt offering	Jer 14:12	3588
shall be that **w** they say to you,	Jer 15:2	3588
w you tell this people all these words	Jer 16:10	3588
"**w** it will no longer be said,	Jer 16:14	
will not see **w** prosperity comes,	Jer 17:6	3588
will not fear **w** the heat comes;	Jer 17:8	3588
W You suddenly bring raiders	Jer 18:22	3588
"**w** this place will no longer be	Jer 19:6	
W Pashhur the priest, the son of	Jer 20:1	
w Pashhur released Jeremiah from	Jer 20:3	
Cursed be the day **w** I was born;	Jer 20:14	834
be blessed **w** my mother bore me!	Jer 20:14	834
w King Zedekiah sent to him Pashhur	Jer 21:1	
will groan **w** pangs come upon you,	Jer 22:23	
"**W** I will raise up for David a	Jer 23:5	
"**w** they will no longer say,	Jer 23:7	
"Now **w** this people or the prophet	Jer 23:33	3588
w seventy years are completed I will	Jer 25:12	
W Jeremiah finished speaking all that	Jer 26:8	
W the officials of Judah heard these	Jer 26:10	
W King Jehoiakim and all his	Jer 26:21	
w he carried into exile Jeconiah the	Jer 27:20	
w the word of the prophet comes	Jer 28:9	
'**W** seventy years have been	Jer 29:10	3588
w you search for Me with all your	Jer 29:13	3588
'**w** I will restore the fortunes of	Jer 30:3	
W it went to find its rest."	Jer 31:2	
"For there will be a day **w**	Jer 31:6	
W I restore their fortunes,	Jer 31:23	
"**w** I will sow the house of Israel	Jer 31:27	
"**w** I will make a new covenant	Jer 31:31	
"**w** the city will be rebuilt for	Jer 31:38	
'**w** I will fulfill the good word	Jer 33:14	
w Nebuchadnezzar king of Babylon	Jer 34:1	
w the army of the king of Babylon	Jer 34:7	
w they cut the calf in two	Jer 34:18	
w Nebuchadnezzar king of Babylon	Jer 35:11	
Now **w** Micaiah the son of Gemariah,	Jer 36:11	
w Baruch read from the book to the	Jer 36:13	
W they had heard all the words, they	Jer 36:16	
W Jehudi had read three or four	Jer 36:23	
and **w** the Chaldeans who had been	Jer 37:5	
w the army of the Chaldeans had	Jer 37:11	
Now **w** Jerusalem was captured	Jer 39:1	3512c
W Zedekiah the king of Judah and all	Jer 39:4	3512c
w he had taken him bound in	Jer 40:1	
Gedaliah, **w** no one knew about *it,*	Jer 41:4	
w we listen to the voice of the LORD	Jer 42:6	3588
out on you **w** you enter Egypt.	Jer 42:18	
"**w** we were burning sacrifices to	Jer 44:19	3588
w he had written down these words	Jer 45:1	
W the LORD has given it an order?	Jer 47:7	
"**w** I will send to him those who	Jer 48:12	
The time **w** I will punish you.	Jer 50:31	
"As **w** God overthrew Sodom And	Jer 50:40	
W He utters His voice, *there is* a	Jer 51:16	
"**W** they become heated up, I will	Jer 51:39	
days are coming **W** I will punish	Jer 51:47	
"**W** I will punish her idols, And	Jer 51:52	
w he went with Zedekiah the king	Jer 51:59	
years old **w** he became king,	Jer 52:1	
W her people fell into the hand of the	La 1:7	
W little ones and infants faint In	La 2:11	
w I cry out and call for help,	La 3:8	3588
drew near **w** I called on You;	La 3:57	3117
faces did not turn **w** they moved,	Ezk 1:9	
And **w** I saw *it,* I fell on my face	Ezk 1:28	
W He spread it out before me, it	Ezk 2:10	
"**W** I say to the wicked,	Ezk 3:18	
w a righteous man turns away from	Ezk 3:20	

Context	Reference	Number
“But **w** I speak to you, I will	Ezk 3:27	
“**W** you have completed these, you	Ezk 4:6	
w the days of the siege are	Ezk 5:2	
have spoken in My zeal **w** I have	Ezk 5:13	
w I execute judgments against you	Ezk 5:15	
‘**W** I send against them the deadly	Ezk 5:16	
w you are scattered among the	Ezk 6:8	
w their slain are among their	Ezk 6:13	
‘Even **w** their survivors escape,	Ezk 7:16	
‘**W** anguish comes, they will seek	Ezk 7:25	
of the court, and **w** I looked,	Ezk 8:7	
of the temple **w** the man entered,	Ezk 10:3	
voice of God Almighty **w** He speaks.	Ezk 10:5	
It came about **w** He commanded	Ezk 10:6	
W they moved, they went in *any of*	Ezk 10:11	
Now **w** the cherubim moved, the	Ezk 10:16	
also **w** the cherubim lifted up	Ezk 10:16	
W the cherubim stood still, the	Ezk 10:17	
and **w** they rose up, the wheels	Ezk 10:17	
W the cherubim departed, they	Ezk 10:19	
“**W** they come there, they will	Ezk 11:18	
w I scatter them among the nations and	Ezk 12:15	
w the LORD has not sent them;	Ezk 13:6	
a lying divination **w** you said,	Ezk 13:7	
w there is no peace.	Ezk 13:10	
And **w** anyone builds a wall,	Ezk 13:10	
“Behold, **w** the wall has fallen,	Ezk 13:12	
and **w** it falls, you will be	Ezk 13:14	
peace for her **w** there is no peace,’	Ezk 13:16	
w I did not cause him grief,	Ezk 13:22	
“How much more **w** I send My four	Ezk 14:21	3588
w you see their conduct and actions,	Ezk 14:23	3588
w the fire has consumed it and it	Ezk 15:5	3588
w I set My face against them.	Ezk 15:7	3588
“**W** I passed by you and saw you	Ezk 16:6	
w you were naked and bare and	Ezk 16:22	
“**W** you built your shrine at the	Ezk 16:31	
I removed them **w** I saw *it.*	Ezk 16:50	3512c
w you become a consolation to them.	Ezk 16:54	
w you receive your sisters,	Ezk 16:61	
w I have forgiven you for all that	Ezk 16:63	
w they cast up ramps and build	Ezk 17:17	
W the son has practiced justice	Ezk 18:19	
“But **w** a righteous man turns away	Ezk 18:24	
“**W** a righteous man turns away	Ezk 18:26	
w a wicked man turns away from his	Ezk 18:27	
‘**W** she brought up one of her cubs,	Ezk 19:3	
‘**W** she saw, as she waited, *That*	Ezk 19:5	
“On the day **w** I chose Israel and	Ezk 20:5	
land of Egypt, **w** I swore to them,	Ezk 20:5	
“**W** I had brought them into the	Ezk 20:28	
“**W** you offer your gifts, when you	Ezk 20:31	
w you cause your sons to pass	Ezk 20:31	
will not come about, **w** you say:	Ezk 20:32	834
w I bring you out from the peoples	Ezk 20:41	
w I bring you into the land of	Ezk 20:42	
w I have dealt with you for My	Ezk 20:44	
w they say to you,	Ezk 21:7	3588
GOD,’ **w** the LORD has not spoken.	Ezk 22:28	
“**W** she saw them she lusted after	Ezk 23:16	
w she had been defiled by them,	Ezk 23:17	
w she played the harlot in the	Ezk 23:19	834
w the Egyptians handled your bosom	Ezk 23:21	
“For **w** they had slaughtered their	Ezk 23:39	
adultery with her **w** she is *thus?’*	Ezk 23:43	
w it comes, then you will know	Ezk 24:24	
will *it* not be on the day **w** I take	Ezk 24:25	
My sanctuary **w** it was profaned,	Ezk 25:3	3588
of Israel **w** it was made desolate,	Ezk 25:3	3588
of Judah **w** they went into exile,	Ezk 25:3	3588
w I lay My vengeance on them.” ’ ”	Ezk 25:17	
w he enters your gates as men	Ezk 26:10	
of your fall **w** the wounded groan,	Ezk 26:15	
w the slaughter occurs in your	Ezk 26:15	
“**W** I make you a desolate	Ezk 26:19	
w I bring up the deep over	Ezk 26:19	
‘**W** your wares went out from the	Ezk 27:33	
w I execute judgments in her,	Ezk 28:22	
“**W** I gather the house of Israel	Ezk 28:25	
w I execute judgments upon all who	Ezk 28:26	
“**W** they took hold of you with the	Ezk 29:7	
And **w** they leaned on you, You	Ezk 29:7	
W the slain fall in Egypt,	Ezk 30:4	
W I set a fire in Egypt And all	Ezk 30:8	
W I break there the yoke bars of	Ezk 30:18	
w I put My sword into the hand of	Ezk 30:25	
‘**W** I scatter the Egyptians among	Ezk 30:26	
“On the day **w** it went down to	Ezk 31:15	
w I made it go down to Sheol with	Ezk 31:16	
“And **w** *I* extinguish you, I will	Ezk 32:7	
w I bring your destruction among	Ezk 32:9	
w I brandish My sword before them;	Ezk 32:10	
“**W** I make the land of Egypt a	Ezk 32:15	
W I smite all those who live in	Ezk 32:15	
“**W** I say to the wicked,	Ezk 33:8	
in the day **w** he turns from	Ezk 33:12	
on the day **w** he commits sin.’	Ezk 33:12	
“**W** I say to the righteous he will	Ezk 33:13	
“But **w** I say to the wicked,	Ezk 33:14	
w it is their own way that is not	Ezk 33:17	
“**W** the righteous turns from his	Ezk 33:18	
“But **w** the wicked turns from his	Ezk 33:19	
w I make the land a desolation and	Ezk 33:29	
“So **w** it comes to pass	Ezk 33:33	
w he is among his scattered sheep,	Ezk 34:12	
w I have broken the bars of their	Ezk 34:27	
known among them **w** I judge you.	Ezk 35:11	3512c
w the house of Israel was living	Ezk 36:17	
“**W** they came to the nations where	Ezk 36:20	

Context	Reference	Number
“**w** I prove Myself holy among you	Ezk 36:23	
w I have opened your graves and	Ezk 37:13	
“**W** the sons of your people speak to	Ezk 37:18	3512c
w My sanctuary is in their midst	Ezk 37:28	
“On that day **w** My people Israel	Ezk 38:14	
may know Me **w** I am sanctified	Ezk 38:16	
w Gog comes against the land of	Ezk 38:18	3117
w they live securely on their *own*	Ezk 39:26	
“**W** I bring them back from the	Ezk 39:27	
“**W** the priests enter, then they	Ezk 42:14	
Now **w** he had finished measuring	Ezk 42:15	
saw **w** He came to destroy the city.	Ezk 43:3	
corpses of their kings **w** they die,	Ezk 43:7	
‘**W** you have finished cleansing *it,*	Ezk 43:23	
‘**W** they have completed the days, it	Ezk 43:27	
w you brought in foreigners,	Ezk 44:7	
My house, **w** you offered My food,	Ezk 44:7	
far from Me **w** Israel went astray,	Ezk 44:10	
w the sons of Israel went astray	Ezk 44:15	
w they enter at the gates of the inner	Ezk 44:17	
“**W** they go out into the outer court,	Ezk 44:19	
wine **w** they enter the inner court.	Ezk 44:21	
“And **w** you divide by lot	Ezk 45:1	
“**W** the prince enters, he shall go	Ezk 46:8	
“But **w** the people of the land	Ezk 46:9	
“**W** they go in, the prince shall go	Ezk 46:10	
and **w** they go out, he shall go out.	Ezk 46:10	
“**W** the prince provides a freewill	Ezk 46:12	3588
W the man went out toward the east	Ezk 47:3	
Now **w** I had returned, behold, on	Ezk 47:7	
w the sons of Israel went astray as	Ezk 48:11	
w all the peoples heard the sound	Da 3:7	1768
W Belshazzar tasted the wine, he	Da 5:2	
“But **w** his heart was lifted up	Da 5:20	1768
Now **w** Daniel knew that the	Da 6:10	1768
W he had come near the den to Daniel,	Da 6:20	
and the time arrived **w** the saints	Da 7:22	
W I, Daniel, had seen the vision,	Da 8:15	
and **w** he came I was frightened and	Da 8:17	
w the transgressors have run *their*	Da 8:23	
w he had spoken this word to me,	Da 10:11	
W he had spoken to me according to	Da 10:15	
“**W** the multitude is carried away,	Da 11:12	
“Now **w** they fall they will be	Da 11:34	
W the LORD first spoke through	Hos 1:2	
W she had weaned Lo-ruhamah, she	Hos 1:8	
her as on the day **w** she was born.	Hos 2:3	
W she used to offer sacrifices to them	Hos 2:13	834
As in the day **w** she came up from	Hos 2:15	
daughters **w** they play the harlot	Hos 4:14	3588
brides **w** they commit adultery,	Hos 4:14	3588
W Ephraim saw his sickness, And	Hos 5:13	
W I restore the fortunes of My	Hos 6:11	
W I would heal Israel, The	Hos 7:1	
W they go, I will spread My net	Hos 7:12	3512c
heart **W** they wail on their beds;	Hos 7:14	3588
them indeed **w** I depart from them!	Hos 9:12	
W it is My desire, I will chastise	Hos 10:10	
W they are bound for their double	Hos 10:10	
W mothers were dashed in pieces	Hos 10:14	
W Israel *was* a youth I loved him,	Hos 11:1	3588
W Ephraim spoke, *there was*	Hos 13:1	
W they burst through the defenses,	Jl 2:8	
W I restore the fortunes of Judah	Jl 3:1	834
down **w** filled with sheaves.	Am 2:13	
in the forest **w** he has no prey?	Am 3:4	
ground **w** there is no bait in it?	Am 3:5	
w it captures nothing at all?	Am 3:5	
W they will take you away with	Am 4:2	
As **w** a man flees from a lion And	Am 5:19	3512c
w the spring crop began to sprout	Am 7:1	
w it had finished eating the	Am 7:2	518
“**W** will the new moon be over, So	Am 8:5	4970
“**W** I will send a famine on the	Am 8:11	
“**W** the plowman will overtake the	Am 9:13	
W the mountains will drip sweet	Am 9:13	
W the word reached the king of	Jon 3:6	
W God saw their deeds, that they	Jon 3:10	
a worm **w** dawn came the next day and	Jon 4:7	
W the sun came up God appointed a	Jon 4:8	
W morning comes, they do it, For	Mi 2:1	
W they have *something* to bite with	Mi 3:5	
until the time **W** she who is in labor	Mi 5:3	
W the Assyrian invades our land,	Mi 5:5	3588
W he tramples on our citadels,	Mi 5:5	3588
the Assyrian **W** he attacks our land	Mi 5:6	3588
And **w** he tramples our territory.	Mi 5:6	3588
The day **w** you post your watchmen,	Mi 7:4	
It *will be* a day **w** they will come	Mi 7:12	
“As in the days **w** you came out	Mi 7:15	
steel **W** he is prepared *to march,*	Na 2:3	3117
W shaken, they fall into the eater’s	Na 3:12	518
Why are You silent **w** the wicked	Hab 1:13	
how I may reply **w** I am reproved.	Hab 2:1	5921
idol **w** its maker has carved it,	Hab 2:18	3588
W he fashions speechless idols.	Hab 2:18	
the day **w** I rise up as a witness.	Zph 3:8	
the time **w** I gather you together;	Zph 3:20	
W I restore your fortunes before	Zph 3:20	
w you bring *it* home, I blow it	Hg 1:9	
made you **w** you came out of Egypt,	Hg 2:5	
from that time **w** one came to a	Hg 2:16	
and **w** one came to the wine vat to	Hg 2:16	
from the day **w** the temple of the	Hg 2:18	834
w they see the plumb line in the	Zch 4:10	
and **w** it is prepared, she will be	Zch 5:11	
“**W** the strong ones went out, they	Zch 6:7	
‘**W** you fasted and mourned in the	Zch 7:5	3588
‘**W** you eat and drink, do you not	Zch 7:6	3588

Context	Reference	Number
w Jerusalem was inhabited and	Zch 7:7	
w your fathers provoked Me to wrath,	Zch 8:14	
“**W** I scatter them among the	Zch 10:9	
and **w** the siege is against	Zch 12:2	
him through **w** he prophesies.	Zch 13:3	
of his vision **w** he prophesies,	Zch 13:4	
w the spoil taken from you will be	Zch 14:1	
as **w** He fights on a day of battle.	Zch 14:3	3117
“But **w** you present the blind for	Mal 1:8	3588
w you present the lame and sick,	Mal 1:8	3588
And who can stand **w** He appears?	Mal 3:2	
w His mother Mary had been betrothed	Mt 1:18	
But **w** he had considered this,	Mt 1:20	
W Herod the king heard *this,* he	Mt 2:3	
and **w** you have found *Him,* report	Mt 2:8	*1875*
W they saw the star, they rejoiced	Mt 2:10	
Now **w** they had gone, behold,	Mt 2:13	
Then **w** Herod saw that he had been	Mt 2:16	
But **w** Herod died, behold, an	Mt 2:19	
But **w** he heard that Archelaus was	Mt 2:22	
referred to by Isaiah the prophet **w**	Mt 3:3	
But **w** he saw many of the Pharisees	Mt 3:7	
Now **w** Jesus heard that John had been	Mt 4:12	
W Jesus saw the crowds, He went up	Mt 5:1	
are you **w** *people* insult you	Mt 5:11	*3752*
“So **w** you give to the poor, do not	Mt 6:2	*3752*
“But **w** you give to the poor,	Mt 6:3	
“**W** you pray, you are not to be like	Mt 6:5	*3752*
“But you, **w** you pray, go into	Mt 6:6	*3752*
“And **w** you are praying, do not	Mt 6:7	
so that they will be noticed by men **w**	Mt 6:16	
“But you, **w** you fast, anoint your	Mt 6:17	
w his son asks for a loaf,	Mt 7:9	*3739*
W Jesus had finished these words,	Mt 7:28	*3753*
W Jesus came down from the mountain,	Mt 8:1	
And **w** Jesus entered Capernaum, a	Mt 8:5	
Now **w** Jesus heard *this,* He	Mt 8:10	
W Jesus came into Peter’s home, He	Mt 8:14	
W evening came, they brought to Him	Mt 8:16	
w Jesus saw a crowd around Him,	Mt 8:18	
W He got into the boat, His	Mt 8:23	
W He came to the other side into	Mt 8:28	
and **w** they saw Him, they implored	Mt 8:34	
But **w** the crowds saw *this,*	Mt 9:8	
W the Pharisees saw *this,* they	Mt 9:11	
But **w** Jesus heard *this,* He said,	Mt 9:12	
w the bridegroom is taken away	Mt 9:15	*3752*
W Jesus came into the official’s	Mt 9:23	
But **w** the crowd had been sent out,	Mt 9:25	*3753*
W He entered the house, the blind	Mt 9:28	*1161*
“But **w** they hand you over, do	Mt 10:19	*3752*
W Jesus had finished giving	Mt 11:1	*3753*
Now **w** John, while imprisoned, heard	Mt 11:2	
But **w** the Pharisees saw *this,* they	Mt 12:2	
David did **w** he became hungry,	Mt 12:3	*3753*
But **w** the Pharisees heard *this,* they	Mt 12:24	
“Now **w** the unclean spirit goes	Mt 12:43	*3752*
and **w** it comes, it finds	Mt 12:44	
“But **w** the sun had risen, they	Mt 13:6	
“**W** anyone hears the word of the	Mt 13:19	
and **w** affliction or persecution	Mt 13:21	
“But **w** the wheat sprouted and	Mt 13:26	*3753*
but **w** it is full grown, it is	Mt 13:32	*3752*
and **w** it was filled, they drew it	Mt 13:48	*3753*
W Jesus had finished these parables,	Mt 13:53	*3753*
For **w** Herod had John arrested, he	Mt 14:3	
But **w** Herod’s birthday came, the	Mt 14:6	
Now **w** Jesus heard *about John,*	Mt 14:13	
w the people heard *of this,*	Mt 14:13	
W He went ashore, He saw a large	Mt 14:14	
W it was evening, the disciples came	Mt 14:15	
and **w** it was evening, He was there	Mt 14:23	
W the disciples saw Him walking on	Mt 14:26	
W they got into the boat, the wind	Mt 14:32	
W they had crossed over, they came	Mt 14:34	
And **w** the men of that place	Mt 14:35	
their hands **w** they eat bread.”	Mt 15:2	*3752*
w they heard this statement?”	Mt 15:12	
“**W** it is evening, you say,	Mt 16:2	
Now **w** Jesus came into the district	Mt 16:13	
W the disciples heard *this,* they	Mt 17:6	
W they came to the crowd, a man came	Mt 17:14	
W they came to Capernaum, those who	Mt 17:24	
And **w** he came into the house,	Mt 17:25	
W Peter said, “From strangers,”	Mt 17:26	
and **w** you open its mouth, you will	Mt 17:27	
“**W** he had begun to settle *them,*	Mt 18:24	
“So **w** his fellow slaves saw what	Mt 18:31	
W Jesus had finished these words, He	Mt 19:1	*3753*
But **w** the young man heard this	Mt 19:22	
W the disciples heard *this,* they	Mt 19:25	
w the Son of Man will sit on His	Mt 19:28	*3752*
“**W** he had agreed with the laborers	Mt 20:2	
“**W** evening came, the owner of	Mt 20:8	
“**W** those *hired* about	Mt 20:9	*2532*
“**W** those *hired* first came, they	Mt 20:10	
“**W** they received it, they grumbled	Mt 20:11	
W they had approached Jerusalem	Mt 21:1	*3753*
W He had entered Jerusalem, all	Mt 21:10	
But **w** the chief priests and the	Mt 21:15	
w He was returning to the city,	Mt 21:18	
W He entered the temple, the chief	Mt 21:23	
“**W** the harvest time approached, he	Mt 21:34	*3753*
“But **w** the vine-growers saw the	Mt 21:38	
w the owner of the vineyard comes,	Mt 21:40	*3752*
W the chief priests and the Pharisees	Mt 21:45	
W they sought to seize Him, they	Mt 21:46	
“But **w** the king came in to look	Mt 22:11	
W the crowds heard *this,* they	Mt 22:33	

But **w** the Pharisees heard that Jesus	Mt 22:34	
and **w** he becomes one, you make him	Mt 23:15	3752
was going away **w** His disciples came	Mt 24:1	2532
"Tell us, **w** will these things happen,	Mt 24:3	4219
w you see the ABOMINATION OF	Mt 24:15	3752
w its branch has already become	Mt 24:32	3752
too, **w** you see all these things,	Mt 24:33	3752
hour **w** you do not think *He will.*	Mt 24:44	3739
master finds so doing **w** he comes.	Mt 24:46	
on a day **w** he does not expect *him*	Mt 24:50	3739
w the foolish took their lamps,	Mt 25:3	
"But **w** the Son of Man comes in	Mt 25:31	3752
'Lord, **w** did we see You hungry,	Mt 25:37	4219
'And **w** did we see You a stranger,	Mt 25:38	4219
'**W** did we see You sick, or in	Mt 25:39	4219
'Lord, **w** did we see You hungry, or	Mt 25:44	4219
W Jesus had finished all these words,	Mt 26:1	3753
Now **w** Jesus was in Bethany, at the	Mt 26:6	
were indignant **w** they saw *this,*	Mt 26:8	
"For **w** she poured this perfume	Mt 26:12	
Now **w** evening came, Jesus was	Mt 26:20	
And **w** He had taken a cup and given	Mt 26:27	
day **w** I drink it new with you in My	Mt 26:29	3752
W he had gone out to the gateway,	Mt 26:71	
Now **w** morning came, all the	Mt 27:1	
Then **w** Judas, who had betrayed	Mt 27:3	
So **w** the people gathered together,	Mt 27:17	
W Pilate saw that he was	Mt 27:24	
And **w** they came to a place	Mt 27:33	
And **w** they had crucified Him, they	Mt 27:35	
standing there, **w** they heard it,	Mt 27:47	
w they saw the earthquake and the	Mt 27:54	
W it was evening, there came a rich	Mt 27:57	
we remember that **w** He was still	Mt 27:63	
And **w** they had assembled with the	Mt 28:12	
W they saw Him, they worshiped *Him*	Mt 28:17	
W evening came, after the sun had	Mk 1:32	
W He had come back to Capernaum	Mk 2:1	
and **w** they had dug an opening,	Mk 2:4	
W the scribes of the Pharisees saw	Mk 2:16	
w the bridegroom is taken away	Mk 2:20	3752
what David did **w** he was in need and	Mk 2:25	3753
W His own people heard *of this,*	Mk 3:21	
and **w** they hear, immediately Satan	Mk 4:15	3752
places, who, **w** they hear the word,	Mk 4:16	3752
w affliction or persecution arises	Mk 4:17	
"But **w** the crop permits, he	Mk 4:29	3752
seed, which, **w** sown upon the soil,	Mk 4:31	3752
yet **w** it is sown, it grows up and	Mk 4:32	3752
On that day, **w** evening came,	Mk 4:35	
W He got out of the boat,	Mk 5:2	
W Jesus had crossed over again in	Mk 5:21	
W the Sabbath came, He began to	Mk 6:2	
But **w** Herod heard *of it,* he kept	Mk 6:16	
And **w** he heard him, he was very	Mk 6:20	
A strategic day came **w** Herod	Mk 6:21	3753
and **w** the daughter of Herodias	Mk 6:22	
W his disciples heard *about this,*	Mk 6:29	
W Jesus went ashore, He saw a large	Mk 6:34	
W it was already quite late, His	Mk 6:35	
And **w** they found out, they said,	Mk 6:38	
W it was evening, the boat was in	Mk 6:47	
But **w** they saw Him walking on the	Mk 6:49	
W they had crossed over they came to	Mk 6:53	
W they got out of the boat,	Mk 6:54	
w they had come from Jerusalem,	Mk 7:1	
and **w** *they come* from the market	Mk 7:4	
W he had left the crowd *and*	Mk 7:17	3753
And **w** He had entered a house, He	Mk 7:24	
w there was again a large crowd and	Mk 8:1	
w I broke the five loaves for the	Mk 8:19	3753
"**W** *I broke* the seven for	Mk 8:20	3753
w He comes in the glory of His Father	Mk 8:38	3752
W they came *back* to the disciples,	Mk 9:14	
w the entire crowd saw Him,	Mk 9:15	
They brought the boy to Him. **W** he	Mk 9:20	2532
W Jesus saw that a crowd was rapidly	Mk 9:25	
W He came into *the* house, His	Mk 9:28	
and **w** He has been killed, He will	Mk 9:31	
and **w** He was in the house, He	Mk 9:33	
But **w** Jesus saw this, He was	Mk 10:14	
W he heard that it was Jesus	Mk 10:47	
w they had left Bethany,	Mk 11:12	
and **w** He came to it, He found	Mk 11:13	
W evening came, they would go out of	Mk 11:19	3752
resurrection, **w** they rise again,	Mk 12:23	3752
"For **w** they rise from the dead,	Mk 12:25	3752
W Jesus saw that he had answered	Mk 12:34	
"Tell us, **w** will these things be,	Mk 13:4	4219
and what *will be* the sign **w** all	Mk 13:4	3752
"**W** you hear of wars and rumors of	Mk 13:7	3752
"**W** they arrest you and hand you over,	Mk 13:11	3752
"But **w** you see the ABOMINATION OF	Mk 13:14	3752
w its branch has already become	Mk 13:28	3752
w you see these things happening,	Mk 13:29	3752
know **w** the *appointed* time will come.	Mk 13:33	4219
w the master of the house is coming,	Mk 13:35	4219
w the rooster crows, or in the morning	Mk 13:35	4219
They were glad **w** they heard *this,*	Mk 14:11	
w the Passover *lamb* was being	Mk 14:12	3753
W it was evening He came with	Mk 14:17	
And **w** He had taken a cup *and*	Mk 14:23	
w I drink it new in the kingdom of	Mk 14:25	3752
third hour **w** they crucified Him.	Mk 15:25	2532
W the sixth hour came, darkness fell	Mk 15:33	
W some of the bystanders heard it,	Mk 15:35	
W the centurion, who was standing	Mk 15:39	
W He was in Galilee, they used to	Mk 15:41	3753
W evening had already come, because	Mk 15:42	

W the Sabbath was over, Mary	Mk 16:1	
to the tomb **w** the sun had risen.	Mk 16:2	
W they heard that He was alive	Mk 16:11	
w the Lord Jesus had spoken to	Mk 16:19	
was troubled **w** he saw *the*	Lk 1:12	
the day **w** these things take place,	Lk 1:20	3739
But **w** he came out, he was unable	Lk 1:22	
W the days of his priestly service	Lk 1:23	5613
w He looked *with favor* upon *me,*	Lk 1:25	3739
W Elizabeth heard Mary's greeting,	Lk 1:41	5613
w the sound of your greeting	Lk 1:44	5613
w the angels had gone away from them	Lk 2:15	5613
W they had seen this, they made	Lk 2:17	
And **w** eight days had passed,	Lk 2:21	3753
And **w** the days for their	Lk 2:22	3753
and **w** the parents brought in the	Lk 2:27	1722
W they had performed everything	Lk 2:39	5613
And **w** He became twelve, they went	Lk 2:42	3753
W they did not find Him, they	Lk 2:45	
W they saw Him, they were astonished;	Lk 2:48	
w Pontius Pilate was governor of	Lk 3:1	
But **w** Herod the tetrarch was	Lk 3:19	
w all the people were baptized,	Lk 3:21	1722
W He began His ministry, Jesus	Lk 3:23	
and **w** they had ended, He became	Lk 4:2	
W the devil had finished every	Lk 4:13	
w the sky was shut up for three	Lk 4:25	3753
w a great famine came over all the	Lk 4:25	5613
And **w** the demon had thrown him	Lk 4:35	
W day came, Jesus left and went to a	Lk 4:42	
W He had finished speaking, He said	Lk 5:4	5613
W they had done this, they enclosed	Lk 5:6	
But **w** Simon Peter saw *that,* he	Lk 5:8	
W they had brought their boats to	Lk 5:11	
and **w** he saw Jesus, he fell on his	Lk 5:12	
and **w** the bridegroom is taken away	Lk 5:35	3752
what David did **w** he was hungry,	Lk 6:3	3698
And **w** day came, He called His	Lk 6:13	3753
"Blessed are you **w** men hate you,	Lk 6:22	3752
you **w** all men speak well of you,	Lk 6:26	3752
w you yourself do not see the log	Lk 6:42	
and **w** a flood occurred, the torrent	Lk 6:48	
W He had completed all His	Lk 7:1	1894
W he heard about Jesus, he sent some	Lk 7:3	
W they came to Jesus, they earnestly	Lk 7:4	
and **w** He was not far from	Lk 7:6	
Now **w** Jesus heard this, He	Lk 7:9	
W those who had been sent returned to	Lk 7:10	
W the Lord saw her, He felt	Lk 7:13	
W the men came to Him, they said,	Lk 7:20	
W the messengers of John had left,	Lk 7:24	
W all the people and the tax	Lk 7:29	
and **w** she learned that He was	Lk 7:37	
Now **w** the Pharisee who had invited	Lk 7:39	
"**W** they were unable to repay, he	Lk 7:42	
W a large crowd was coming together,	Lk 8:4	
soil are those who, **w** they hear,	Lk 8:13	3752
w He came out onto the land,	Lk 8:27	
W the herdsmen saw what had	Lk 8:34	
W the woman saw that she had not	Lk 8:47	
But **w** Jesus heard *this,* He	Lk 8:50	
W He came to the house, He did not	Lk 8:51	
W the apostles returned, they gave	Lk 9:10	
him **w** He comes in His glory,	Lk 9:26	3752
but **w** they were fully awake, they	Lk 9:32	
And **w** the voice had spoken, Jesus	Lk 9:36	1722
w they came down from the mountain,	Lk 9:37	
W the days were approaching for His	Lk 9:51	1722
W His disciples James and John saw	Lk 9:54	
on that road, and **w** he saw him,	Lk 10:31	
w he came to the place and saw	Lk 10:32	
and **w** he saw him, he felt	Lk 10:33	
more you spend, **w** I return I	Lk 10:35	1722
"**W** you pray, say:	Lk 11:2	3752
w the demon had gone out,	Lk 11:14	
"**W** a strong *man,* fully armed,	Lk 11:21	3752
"But **w** someone stronger than he	Lk 11:22	1875
"**W** the unclean spirit goes out of	Lk 11:24	3752
"And **w** it comes, it finds it	Lk 11:25	
w your eye is clear, your whole	Lk 11:34	3752
but **w** it is bad, your body also is	Lk 11:34	1875
as **w** the lamp illumines you with	Lk 11:36	3752
Now **w** He had spoken, a Pharisee	Lk 11:37	1722
W the Pharisee saw it, he was	Lk 11:38	
"Teacher, **w** You say this, You	Lk 11:45	
W He left there, the scribes	Lk 11:53	
"**W** they bring you before	Lk 12:11	3752
for not *even* **w** one has an	Lk 12:15	1722
w he returns from the wedding feast,	Lk 12:36	4219
door to him **w** he comes and knocks.	Lk 12:36	
find on the alert **w** he comes;	Lk 12:37	
master finds so doing **w** he comes.	Lk 12:43	
on a day **w** he does not expect *him*	Lk 12:46	3739
"**W** you see a cloud rising in the	Lk 12:54	3752
w *you see* a south wind blowing,	Lk 12:55	3752
W Jesus saw her, He called her over	Lk 13:12	
w you see Abraham and Isaac and	Lk 13:28	3752
Me until *the time* comes **w** you say,	Lk 13:35	3753
It happened that **w** He went into	Lk 14:1	1722
a parable to the invited guests **w** He	Lk 14:7	
"**W** you are invited by someone to	Lk 14:8	3752
"But **w** you are invited, go and	Lk 14:10	3752
so that **w** the one who has invited	Lk 14:10	3752
"**W** you give a luncheon or a	Lk 14:12	3752
"But **w** you give a reception,	Lk 14:13	3752
W one of those who were reclining	Lk 14:15	
you, **w** he wants to build a tower,	Lk 14:28	
w he has laid a foundation and	Lk 14:29	4218
w he sets out to meet another king	Lk 14:31	

"**W** he has found it, he lays it on	Lk 15:5	
"And **w** he comes home, he calls	Lk 15:6	
"**W** she has found it, she calls	Lk 15:9	
"Now **w** he had spent everything, a	Lk 15:14	
"But **w** he came to his senses, he	Lk 15:17	
and **w** he came and approached the	Lk 15:25	5613
but **w** this son of yours came, who	Lk 15:30	3753
so that **w** I am removed from the	Lk 16:4	3752
that **w** it fails, they will receive	Lk 16:9	3752
w he has come in from the field,	Lk 17:7	
w you do all the things which are	Lk 17:10	3752
W He saw them, He said to them,	Lk 17:14	
w he saw that he had been healed,	Lk 17:15	
w the kingdom of God was coming,	Lk 17:20	4219
"The days will come **w** you will	Lk 17:22	3753
w it flashes out of one part of	Lk 17:24	
However, **w** the Son of Man comes,	Lk 18:8	
them, but **w** the disciples saw it,	Lk 18:15	
W Jesus heard *this,* He said to	Lk 18:22	
But **w** he had heard these things,	Lk 18:23	
and **w** he came near, He	Lk 18:40	
and **w** all the people saw it, they	Lk 18:43	
W Jesus came to the place, He looked	Lk 19:5	5613
W they saw it, they all *began* to	Lk 19:7	
"**W** he returned, after receiving	Lk 19:15	1722
W He approached Bethphage	Lk 19:29	5613
W He approached *Jerusalem,* He	Lk 19:41	5613
w your enemies will throw up a	Lk 19:43	2532
"But **w** the vine-growers saw him,	Lk 20:14	
W they heard it, they said, "May	Lk 20:16	1161
w therefore will these things happen?	Lk 21:7	4219
And what *will be* the sign **w** these	Lk 21:7	3752
"**W** you hear of wars and disturbances,	Lk 21:9	3752
"But **w** you see Jerusalem	Lk 21:20	3752
"But **w** these things begin to take	Lk 21:28	
w you see these things happening,	Lk 21:31	3752
And He said to them, "**W** you have	Lk 22:10	2400
W the hour had come, He reclined	Lk 22:14	3753
And **w** He had taken a cup *and* given	Lk 22:17	
And **w** He had taken *some* bread *and*	Lk 22:19	
you, **w** once you have turned again,	Lk 22:32	4218
"**W** I sent you out without money	Lk 22:35	3753
W He arrived at the place, He said	Lk 22:40	
W He rose from prayer, He came to	Lk 22:45	
W those who were around Him	Lk 22:49	
W it was day, the Council of elders	Lk 22:66	5613
W Pilate heard it, he asked whether	Lk 23:6	1161
And **w** he learned that He belonged	Lk 23:7	
was very glad **w** he saw Jesus;	Lk 23:8	
W they led Him away, they seized a	Lk 23:26	5613
days are coming **w** they will say,	Lk 23:29	
		1722, 3739
"For if they do these things **w**	Lk 23:31	1722
what will happen **w** it is dry?"	Lk 23:31	1722
W they came to the place called The	Lk 23:33	3753
me **w** You come in Your kingdom!"	Lk 23:42	3752
Now **w** the centurion saw what had	Lk 23:47	
w they observed what had happened,	Lk 23:48	
but **w** they entered, they did not	Lk 24:3	
W they were at the tomb early in	Lk 24:22	
W He had reclined *at the table*	Lk 24:30	1722
And **w** He had said this, He showed	Lk 24:40	
w the Jews sent to him priests and	Jn 1:19	3753
w you were under the fig tree,	Jn 1:48	
W the wine ran out, the mother of	Jn 2:3	
W the headwaiter tasted the water	Jn 2:9	5613
and **w** *the people* have drunk freely,	Jn 2:10	3752
So **w** He was raised from the dead,	Jn 2:22	3753
Now **w** He was in Jerusalem at the	Jn 2:23	5613
"How can a man be born **w** he is old?	Jn 3:4	
Therefore **w** the Lord knew that	Jn 4:1	5613
coming **w** neither in this mountain nor	Jn 4:21	3753
w the true worshipers will	Jn 4:23	3753
w that One comes, He will declare	Jn 4:25	3752
So **w** the Samaritans came to Jesus,	Jn 4:40	5613
So **w** He came to Galilee, the	Jn 4:45	3753
W he heard that Jesus had come out	Jn 4:47	
the hour **w** he began to get better.	Jn 4:52	
		1722, 3739
w He had come out of Judea into	Jn 4:54	
W Jesus saw him lying *there,* and	Jn 5:6	
pool **w** the water is stirred up,	Jn 5:7	3752
w the dead will hear the voice of	Jn 5:25	3753
w you receive glory from one	Jn 5:44	
W they were filled, He said to His	Jn 6:12	5613
Therefore **w** the people saw the sign	Jn 6:14	
Now **w** evening came, His disciples	Jn 6:16	5613
Then, **w** they had rowed about three	Jn 6:19	
So **w** the crowd saw that Jesus was not	Jn 6:24	3753
W they found Him on the other side of	Jn 6:25	4219
"Rabbi, **w** did You get here?"	Jn 6:25	4219
disciples, **w** they heard *this* said,	Jn 6:60	
w he himself seeks to be *known*	Jn 7:4	2532
But **w** His brothers had gone up to	Jn 7:10	5613
But **w** it was now the midst of the	Jn 7:14	
"**W** the Christ comes, He will	Jn 7:31	3752
w they heard these words,	Jn 7:40	
w they persisted in asking Him,	Jn 8:7	5613
W they heard it, they *began* to	Jn 8:9	
"**W** you lift up the Son of Man,	Jn 8:28	3752
is coming **w** no one can work.	Jn 9:4	3753
W He had said this, He spat on the	Jn 9:6	
on the day **w** Jesus made the clay and	Jn 9:14	3739
"**W** he puts forth all his own, he	Jn 10:4	3752
But **w** Jesus heard *this,* He said,	Jn 11:4	
So **w** He heard that he was sick, He	Jn 11:6	5613
So **w** Jesus came, He found that he	Jn 11:17	
w she heard that Jesus was coming,	Jn 11:20	5613
W she had said this, she went away	Jn 11:28	

And **w** she heard it, she got	**Jn 11:29**	*5613*
w they saw that Mary got up	**Jn 11:31**	
w Mary came where Jesus was,	**Jn 11:32**	*5613*
W Jesus therefore saw her weeping,	**Jn 11:33**	*5613*
W He had said these things, He cried	**Jn 11:43**	
w they heard that Jesus was coming	**Jn 12:12**	
but **w** Jesus was glorified, then	**Jn 12:16**	*3753*
w He called Lazarus out of the tomb and	**Jn 12:17**	*3753*
So **w** He had washed their feet,	**Jn 13:12**	*3753*
to pass, so that **w** it does occur,	**Jn 13:19**	*3752*
W Jesus had said this, He became	**Jn 13:21**	
So **w** He had dipped the morsel, He	**Jn 13:26**	
Therefore **w** he had gone out, Jesus	**Jn 13:31**	*3753*
it happens, so that **w** it happens,	**Jn 14:29**	*3752*
"**W** the Helper comes, whom I will	**Jn 15:26**	*3752*
to you, so that **w** their hour comes,	**Jn 16:4**	*3752*
"And He, **w** He comes, will convict	**Jn 16:8**	
"But **w** He, the Spirit of truth,	**Jn 16:13**	*3752*
w she gives birth to the child,	**Jn 16:21**	*3752*
an hour is coming **w** I will no	**Jn 16:25**	*3753*
W Jesus had spoken these words, He	**Jn 18:1**	
So **w** He said to them, "I am *He,*"	**Jn 18:6**	*5613*
W He had said this, one of	**Jn 18:22**	
And **w** he had said this, he went	**Jn 18:38**	
So **w** the chief priests	**Jn 19:6**	*3753*
Therefore **w** Pilate heard this	**Jn 19:8**	*3753*
Therefore **w** Pilate heard these words,	**Jn 19:13**	
w they had crucified Jesus,	**Jn 19:23**	*3753*
W Jesus then saw His mother,	**Jn 19:26**	
Therefore **w** Jesus had received	**Jn 19:30**	*3753*
w they saw that He was already	**Jn 19:33**	*5613*
W she had said this, she turned	**Jn 20:14**	
So **w** it was evening on that day,	**Jn 20:19**	
and **w** the doors were shut where	**Jn 20:19**	
And **w** He had said this, He showed	**Jn 20:20**	
rejoiced **w** they saw the Lord.	**Jn 20:20**	
And **w** He had said this, He	**Jn 20:22**	
was not with them **w** Jesus came.	**Jn 20:24**	*3753*
But **w** the day was now breaking,	**Jn 21:4**	
So **w** Simon Peter heard that it	**Jn 21:7**	
So **w** they got out on the land,	**Jn 21:9**	*5613*
So **w** they had finished breakfast,	**Jn 21:15**	*3753*
I say to you, **w** you were younger,	**Jn 21:18**	*3753*
but **w** you grow old, you will	**Jn 21:18**	*3752*
And **w** He had spoken this, He said	**Jn 21:19**	
until the day **w** He was taken up	**Ac 1:2**	
So **w** they had come together,	**Ac 1:6**	
receive power **w** the Holy Spirit has	**Ac 1:8**	
W they had entered *the city,*	**Ac 1:13**	*3753*
W the day of Pentecost had come,	**Ac 2:1**	*1722*
And **w** this sound occurred, the	**Ac 2:6**	
Now **w** they heard *this,* they were	**Ac 2:37**	
W he saw Peter and John about to go	**Ac 3:3**	
But **w** Peter saw *this,* he replied	**Ac 3:12**	
w he had decided to release Him.	**Ac 3:13**	
W they had placed them in the center,	**Ac 4:7**	
But **w** they had ordered them to leave	**Ac 4:15**	
And **w** they had summoned them, they	**Ac 4:18**	
W they had threatened them further,	**Ac 4:21**	
W they had been released, they went	**Ac 4:23**	
And **w** they heard *this,* they lifted	**Ac 4:24**	
And **w** they had prayed, the place	**Ac 4:31**	
pallets, so that **w** Peter came by at	**Ac 5:15**	
Now **w** the high priest and his	**Ac 5:21**	
but **w** we had opened up, we found	**Ac 5:23**	
Now **w** the captain of the temple	**Ac 5:24**	*5613*
W they had brought them, they stood	**Ac 5:27**	
But **w** they heard this, they were	**Ac 5:33**	
Abraham **w** he was in Mesopotamia,	**Ac 7:2**	
and *yet,* even **w** he had no child,	**Ac 7:5**	
"But **w** Jacob heard that there was	**Ac 7:12**	
"But **w** he was approaching the age	**Ac 7:23**	*5613*
"And **w** he saw one *of them* being	**Ac 7:24**	
"**W** Moses saw it, he marveled at	**Ac 7:31**	
Now **w** they heard this, they were	**Ac 7:54**	
W they had driven him out of the city,	**Ac 7:58**	
But **w** they believed Philip	**Ac 8:12**	*3753*
Now **w** the apostles in Jerusalem	**Ac 8:14**	
Now **w** Simon saw that the Spirit	**Ac 8:18**	
w they had solemnly testified and	**Ac 8:25**	
W they came up out of the water,	**Ac 8:39**	*3753*
W many days had elapsed, the Jews	**Ac 9:23**	*5613*
W he came to Jerusalem, he was	**Ac 9:26**	
But **w** the brethren learned *of it,*	**Ac 9:30**	
and **w** they had washed her body,	**Ac 9:37**	
So Peter arose and went with them. **W**	**Ac 9:39**	*3854*
her eyes, and **w** she saw Peter,	**Ac 9:40**	
W the angel who was speaking to him	**Ac 10:7**	*5613*
W Peter entered, Cornelius met him,	**Ac 10:25**	*5613*
any objection **w** I was sent for.	**Ac 10:29**	
And **w** Peter came up to Jerusalem,	**Ac 11:2**	*3753*
and **w** I had fixed my gaze on it	**Ac 11:6**	
W they heard this, they quieted down	**Ac 11:18**	
Then **w** he arrived and witnessed	**Ac 11:23**	
and **w** he had found him, he brought	**Ac 11:26**	
W he saw that it pleased the Jews,	**Ac 12:3**	
W he had seized him, he put him in	**Ac 12:4**	
On the very night **w** Herod was	**Ac 12:6**	*3753*
W they had passed the first	**Ac 12:10**	
W Peter came to himself, he said,	**Ac 12:11**	
And **w** he realized *this,* he went to	**Ac 12:12**	
W he knocked at the door of the gate,	**Ac 12:13**	
W she recognized Peter's voice,	**Ac 12:14**	
and **w** they had opened *the door,*	**Ac 12:16**	
Now **w** day came, there was no small	**Ac 12:18**	
W Herod had searched for him and had	**Ac 12:19**	
and Saul returned from Jerusalem **w**	**Ac 12:25**	
w they had fasted and prayed and	**Ac 13:3**	
W they reached Salamis, they *began*	**Ac 13:5**	
W they had gone through the whole	**Ac 13:6**	
w he saw what had happened,	**Ac 13:12**	
"**W** He had destroyed seven nations in	**Ac 13:19**	
"**W** they had carried out all that was	**Ac 13:29**	*5613*
Now **w** *the meeting of* the synagogue	**Ac 13:43**	
But **w** the Jews saw the crowds,	**Ac 13:45**	
W the Gentiles heard this, they	**Ac 13:48**	
And **w** an attempt was made by both	**Ac 14:5**	*5613*
w he had fixed his gaze on him	**Ac 14:9**	
W the crowds saw what Paul had done,	**Ac 14:11**	
But **w** the apostles Barnabas and	**Ac 14:14**	
W they had appointed elders for them	**Ac 14:23**	
W they had spoken the word in Perga,	**Ac 14:25**	
W they had arrived and gathered	**Ac 14:27**	
And **w** Paul and Barnabas had great	**Ac 15:2**	
W they arrived at Jerusalem, they	**Ac 15:4**	
So **w** they were sent away, they	**Ac 15:30**	
W they had read it, they rejoiced	**Ac 15:31**	
W he had seen the vision,	**Ac 16:10**	*5613*
And **w** she and her household had	**Ac 16:15**	*5613*
But **w** her masters saw that their	**Ac 16:19**	
and **w** they had brought them to the	**Ac 16:20**	
W they had struck them with many	**Ac 16:23**	
W the jailer awoke and saw the prison	**Ac 16:27**	
Now **w** day came, the chief	**Ac 16:35**	
w they heard that they were Romans,	**Ac 16:38**	
and **w** they had brought them out,	**Ac 16:39**	
and **w** they saw the brethren,	**Ac 16:40**	
Now **w** they had traveled through	**Ac 17:1**	
W they did not find them, they	**Ac 17:6**	
And **w** they had received a pledge	**Ac 17:9**	
and **w** they arrived, they went into	**Ac 17:10**	
But **w** the Jews of Thessalonica	**Ac 17:13**	*5613*
Now **w** they heard of the	**Ac 17:32**	
But **w** Silas and Timothy came down	**Ac 18:5**	*5613*
w they resisted and blasphemed,	**Ac 18:6**	
the Corinthians **w** they heard were	**Ac 18:8**	
But **w** Paul was about to open his	**Ac 18:14**	
W they asked him to stay for a longer	**Ac 18:20**	
W he had landed at Caesarea, he went	**Ac 18:22**	
But **w** Priscilla and Aquila heard	**Ac 18:26**	
And **w** he wanted to go across to	**Ac 18:27**	
and **w** he had arrived, he greatly	**Ac 18:27**	
the Holy Spirit **w** you believed?"	**Ac 19:2**	
W they heard this, they were	**Ac 19:5**	
And **w** Paul had laid his hands upon	**Ac 19:6**	
But **w** some were becoming hardened	**Ac 19:9**	*5613*
W they heard *this* and were filled	**Ac 19:28**	
And **w** Paul wanted to go into the	**Ac 19:30**	
But **w** they recognized that he was	**Ac 19:34**	
disciples, and **w** he had exhorted them	**Ac 20:1**	
W he had gone through those districts	**Ac 20:2**	
and **w** a plot was formed against	**Ac 20:3**	
w we were gathered together to	**Ac 20:7**	
W he had gone *back* up and had	**Ac 20:11**	
And **w** he met us at Assos, we took	**Ac 20:14**	*5613*
And **w** they had come to him, he	**Ac 20:18**	*5613*
W he had said these things, he knelt	**Ac 20:36**	
W we had parted from them and had set	**Ac 21:1**	*5613*
W we came in sight of Cyprus,	**Ac 21:3**	
W our days there were ended, we left	**Ac 21:5**	*3753*
W we had finished the voyage from	**Ac 21:7**	
W we had heard this, we as well as	**Ac 21:12**	*5613*
And **w** they heard it they *began*	**Ac 21:20**	
W the seven days were almost over,	**Ac 21:27**	*5613*
and **w** they saw the commander and	**Ac 21:32**	
and **w** he could not find out the	**Ac 21:34**	
W he got to the stairs, he was	**Ac 21:35**	*3753*
W he had given him permission, Paul,	**Ac 21:40**	
and **w** there was a great hush, he	**Ac 21:40**	
And **w** they heard that he was	**Ac 22:2**	
w I returned to Jerusalem and was	**Ac 22:17**	
'And **w** the blood of Your witness	**Ac 22:20**	*3753*
But **w** they stretched him out with	**Ac 22:25**	*5613*
W the centurion heard *this,* he	**Ac 22:26**	
w he found out that he was a Roman,	**Ac 22:29**	
W it was day, the Jews formed a	**Ac 23:12**	
"**W** this man was arrested by the	**Ac 23:27**	
"**W** I was informed that there would	**Ac 23:30**	
W these had come to Caesarea	**Ac 23:33**	
W he had read it, he asked from what	**Ac 23:34**	
and **w** he learned that he was from	**Ac 23:34**	
W the governor had nodded for him to	**Ac 24:10**	
w I stood before the Council,	**Ac 24:20**	
"**W** Lysias the commander comes	**Ac 24:22**	*3752*
the present, and **w** I find time I	**Ac 24:25**	
Then **w** Festus had conferred with	**Ac 25:12**	
Now **w** several days had elapsed,	**Ac 25:13**	
and **w** I was at Jerusalem, the	**Ac 25:15**	
"**W** the accusers stood up, they	**Ac 25:18**	
"But **w** Paul appealed to be held	**Ac 25:21**	
on the next day **w** Agrippa came	**Ac 25:23**	
but also **w** they were being put to	**Ac 26:10**	
"And **w** we had all fallen to the	**Ac 26:14**	
and **w** they had gone aside, they	**Ac 26:31**	
W it was decided that we would sail	**Ac 27:1**	*5613*
W we had sailed through the sea along	**Ac 27:5**	
W we had sailed slowly for a good	**Ac 27:7**	
W considerable time had passed	**Ac 27:9**	
W a moderate south wind came up,	**Ac 27:13**	
and **w** the ship was caught *in it*	**Ac 27:15**	
W they had gone a long time without	**Ac 27:21**	
w the fourteenth night came,	**Ac 27:27**	*5613*
W they had eaten enough, they	**Ac 27:38**	
W day came, they could not recognize	**Ac 27:39**	*3753*
W they had been brought safely	**Ac 28:1**	
But **w** Paul had gathered a bundle	**Ac 28:3**	
W the natives saw the creature	**Ac 28:4**	*5613*
and **w** we were setting sail, they	**Ac 28:10**	
brethren, **w** they heard about us,	**Ac 28:15**	
and **w** Paul saw them, he thanked	**Ac 28:15**	
W we entered Rome, Paul was allowed	**Ac 28:16**	*3753*
and **w** they came together,	**Ac 28:17**	
"And **w** they had examined me, they	**Ac 28:18**	
"But **w** the Jews objected, I was	**Ac 28:19**	
W they had set a day for Paul, they	**Ac 28:23**	
And **w** they did not agree with one	**Ac 28:25**	
[**W** he had spoken these words,	**Ac 28:29**	
w you pass judgment on those who	**Ro 2:3**	
For **w** Gentiles who do not have the	**Ro 2:14**	*3752*
on the day **w**, according to my	**Ro 2:16**	*3739*
PREVAIL **W** YOU ARE JUDGED."	**Ro 3:4**	*1722*
is not imputed **w** there is no law.	**Ro 5:13**	
Do you not know that **w** you present	**Ro 6:16**	*3739*
For **w** you were slaves of sin, you	**Ro 6:20**	*3753*
but **w** the commandment came, sin	**Ro 7:9**	
w she had conceived *twins* by one	**Ro 9:10**	
THEM, **W** I TAKE AWAY THEIR SINS."	**Ro 11:27**	*3752*
nearer to us than **w** we believed.	**Ro 13:11**	*3753*
w I have first enjoyed your	**Ro 15:24**	
Therefore, **w** I have finished this,	**Ro 15:28**	
I know that **w** I come to you, I	**Ro 15:29**	
And **w** I came to you, brethren, I	**1Co 2:1**	
For **w** one says, "I am of Paul,	**1Co 3:4**	*3752*
w we are reviled, we bless;	**1Co 4:12**	
w we are persecuted, we endure;	**1Co 4:12**	
w we are slandered, we try to	**1Co 4:13**	
Lord Jesus, **w** you are assembled,	**1Co 5:4**	
w he has a case against his	**1Co 6:1**	
Was any man called **w** *he was already*	**1Co 7:18**	
their conscience **w** it is weak,	**1Co 8:12**	
That, **w** I preach the gospel, I may	**1Co 9:18**	
w you come together as a church,	**1Co 11:18**	
Therefore **w** you meet together, it	**1Co 11:20**	
and **w** He had given thanks, He	**1Co 11:24**	
But **w** we are judged, we are	**1Co 11:32**	
w you come together to eat,	**1Co 11:33**	
matters I will arrange **w** I come.	**1Co 11:34**	*5613*
You know that **w** you were pagans,	**1Co 12:2**	*3753*
but **w** the perfect comes, the	**1Co 13:10**	*3752*
W I was a child, I used to speak	**1Co 13:11**	*3753*
w I became a man, I did away with	**1Co 13:11**	*3753*
W you assemble, each one has a	**1Co 14:26**	*3752*
w He hands over the kingdom to	**1Co 15:24**	*3752*
w He has abolished all rule and	**1Co 15:24**	*3752*
But **w** He says, "All things are put in	**1Co 15:27**	*3752*
W all things are subjected to Him,	**1Co 15:28**	*3752*
But **w** this perishable will have	**1Co 15:54**	*3752*
no collections be made **w** I come.	**1Co 16:2**	*3752*
W I arrive, whomever you may	**1Co 16:3**	*3752*
he will come **w** he has opportunity.	**1Co 16:12**	*3752*
w I intended to do this,	**2Co 1:17**	
thing I wrote you, so that **w** I came,	**2Co 2:3**	
Now **w** I came to Troas for the	**2Co 2:12**	
w a door was opened for me in the	**2Co 2:12**	
For even **w** we came into Macedonia	**2Co 7:5**	
am meek **w** face to face with you,	**2Co 10:1**	
you, but bold toward you **w** absent!	**2Co 10:1**	
I ask that **w** I am present I	**2Co 10:2**	
are in word by letters **w** absent,	**2Co 10:11**	
we are also in deed **w** present.	**2Co 10:11**	
but **w** they measure themselves by	**2Co 10:12**	
and **w** I was present with you and	**2Co 11:9**	
for **w** the brethren came from	**2Co 11:9**	
for **w** I am weak, then I am strong.	**2Co 12:10**	*3752*
w I come I may find you to be not	**2Co 12:20**	
I am afraid that **w** I come again my	**2Co 12:21**	
said **w** present the second time,	**2Co 13:2**	*5613*
we rejoice **w** we ourselves are weak	**2Co 13:9**	*3752*
so that **w** present I *need* not	**2Co 13:10**	
But **w** God, who had set me apart	**Ga 1:15**	*3753*
But **w** Cephas came to Antioch, I	**Ga 2:11**	*3753*
but **w** they came, he *began* to	**Ga 2:12**	*3753*
But **w** I saw that they were not	**Ga 2:14**	*3753*
yet **w** it has been ratified,	**Ga 3:15**	
w the fullness of the time came,	**Ga 4:4**	*3753*
that time, **w** you did not know God,	**Ga 4:8**	
not only **w** I am present with you.	**Ga 4:18**	*1722*
he is something **w** he is nothing,	**Ga 6:3**	
w He raised Him from the dead and	**Eph 1:20**	
even **w** we were dead in our	**Eph 2:5**	
w you read you can understand my	**Eph 3:4**	
"**W** HE ASCENDED ON HIGH, HE LED	**Eph 4:8**	
w they are exposed by the light,	**Eph 5:13**	
w I learn of your condition.	**Php 2:19**	
w you see him again you may rejoice	**Php 2:28**	
W you were dead in your	**Col 2:13**	
W He had disarmed the rulers and	**Col 2:15**	
W Christ, who is our life, is	**Col 3:4**	*3752*
walked, **w** you were living in them.	**Col 3:7**	*3753*
W this letter is read among you,	**Col 4:16**	*3752*
that **w** you received the word	**1Th 2:13**	
w we could endure *it* no longer,	**1Th 3:1**	
For indeed **w** we were with you, we	**1Th 3:4**	*3753*
w I could endure *it* no longer,	**1Th 3:5**	
w the Lord Jesus will be revealed	**2Th 1:7**	*1722*
w He comes to be glorified in His	**2Th 1:10**	*3752*
For even **w** we were with you, we	**2Th 3:10**	*3753*
for **w** they feel sensual desires in	**1Tm 5:11**	*3752*
w accompanied by contentment.	**1Tm 6:6**	
but **w** he was in Rome, he eagerly	**2Tm 1:17**	
able to teach, patient **w** wronged,	**2Tm 2:24**	*420*
w they will not endure sound	**2Tm 4:3**	*3753*
W you come bring the cloak which I	**2Tm 4:13**	
But **w** the kindness of God our	**Ti 3:4**	*3753*
W I send Artemas or Tychicus to	**Ti 3:12**	*3752*
W He had made purification of	**Heb 1:3**	
And **w** He again brings the	**Heb 1:6**	*3752*

YOUR HEARTS AS **W** THEY PROVOKED ME, **Heb 3:8** 1722
HEARTS, AS **W** THEY PROVOKED ME." **Heb 3:15** 1722
who provoked *Him* **w** they had heard? **Heb 3:16**
receives it **w** he is called by God, **Heb 5:4**
For **w** God made the promise to **Heb 6:13**
his father **w** Melchizedek met him. **Heb 7:10** 3753
For **w** the priesthood is changed, **Heb 7:12**
for all **w** He offered up Himself. **Heb 7:27**
just as Moses was warned *by God* **w** **Heb 8:5**
W I WILL EFFECT A NEW COVENANT **Heb 8:8** 2532
ON THE DAY **W** I TOOK THEM BY THE **Heb 8:9**
W He said, "A new *covenant*," **Heb 8:13** 1722
Now **w** these things have been so **Heb 9:6**
But **w** Christ appeared *as* a high **Heb 9:11**
is valid *only* **w** men are dead, **Heb 9:17**
For **w** every commandment had been **Heb 9:19**
w He comes into the world, **Heb 10:5**
But remember the former days, **w**, **Heb 10:32** 1722, 3739
w you have done the will of God, **Heb 10:36**
By faith Abraham, **w** he was called, **Heb 11:8**
By faith Abraham, **w** he was tested, **Heb 11:17**
By faith Joseph, **w** he was dying, **Heb 11:22**
By faith Moses, **w** he was born, was **Heb 11:23**
By faith Moses, **w** he had grown up, **Heb 11:24**
Egyptians, **w** they attempted it, **Heb 11:29**
FAINT **W** YOU ARE REPROVED BY HIM, **Heb 12:5**
w he desired to inherit the **Heb 12:17**
w they refused him who warned **Heb 12:25**
w you encounter various trials, **Jas 1:2** 3752
Let no one say **w** he is tempted, **Jas 1:13**
w he is carried away and enticed by **Jas 1:14**
Then **w** lust has conceived, it **Jas 1:15**
and **w** sin is accomplished, it **Jas 1:15**
w he offered up Isaac his son on **Jas 2:21**
w she received the messengers and **Jas 2:25**
sorrows **w** suffering unjustly. **1Pe 2:19**
w you sin and are harshly treated, **1Pe 2:20**
But if **w** you do what is right and **1Pe 2:20**
w the patience of God kept waiting **1Pe 3:20** 3753
And **w** the Chief Shepherd appears, **1Pe 5:4**
w we made known to you the power **2Pe 1:16**
For **w** He received honor and glory **2Pe 1:17**
from heaven **w** we were with Him **2Pe 1:18**
not spare angels **w** they sinned, **2Pe 2:4**
w He brought a flood upon the **2Pe 2:5**
w they revile angelic majesties, **2Pe 2:10**
For **w** they maintain this, it **2Pe 3:5**
in Him, so that **w** He appears, **1Jn 2:28** 1437
We know that **w** He appears, we **1Jn 3:2** 1437
w we love God and observe His **1Jn 5:2** 3752
w brethren came and testified **3Jn 1:3**
and especially **w** *they are* **3Jn 1:5**
w he disputed with the devil and **Jude 1:9** 3753
w they feast with you without fear, **Jude 1:12**
w it has been made to glow in a **Rv 1:15** 5613
W I saw Him, I fell at His feet like **Rv 1:17** 3753
And **w** the living creatures give **Rv 4:9** 3752
W He had taken the book, the four **Rv 5:8** 3753
Then I saw **w** the Lamb broke one of **Rv 6:1** 3753
W He broke the second seal, I heard **Rv 6:3** 3753
W He broke the third seal, I heard **Rv 6:5** 3753
W the Lamb broke the fourth seal, I **Rv 6:7** 3753
W the Lamb broke the fifth seal, I **Rv 6:9** 3753
looked **w** He broke the sixth seal, **Rv 6:12** 3753
figs **w** shaken by a great wind. **Rv 6:13**
like a scroll **w** it is rolled up, **Rv 6:14**
W the Lamb broke the seventh seal, **Rv 8:1** 3752
of a scorpion **w** it stings a man. **Rv 9:5** 3752
a loud voice, as **w** a lion roars; **Rv 10:3**
and **w** he had cried out, the seven **Rv 10:3** 3753
W the seven peals of thunder had **Rv 10:4** 3753
angel, **w** he is about to sound, **Rv 10:7** 3752
and **w** I had eaten it, my stomach **Rv 10:10** 3753
W they have finished their testimony, **Rv 11:7** 3752
so that **w** she gave birth he might **Rv 12:4** 3752
they did not love their life even **w** **Rv 12:11** 891
And **w** the dragon saw that he was **Rv 12:13** 3753
W I saw her, I wondered greatly. **Rv 17:6**
will wonder **w** they see the beast, **Rv 17:8**
and **w** he comes, he must remain a **Rv 17:10** 3752
w they see the smoke of her burning, **Rv 18:9** 3752
W the thousand years are completed, **Rv 20:7** 3752
And **w** I heard and saw, I fell down **Rv 22:8** 3753

WHENEVER

w the stronger of the flock were **Gn 30:41** 3605
w Moses went out to the tent, **Ex 33:8**
W Moses entered the tent, the pillar **Ex 33:9**
But **w** Moses went in before the **Ex 34:34**
and **w** he came out and spoke to the **Ex 34:34**
w the cloud was taken up from over **Ex 40:36**
"But **w** raw flesh appears on him, **Lv 13:14** 3117
W the cloud was lifted from over **Nu 9:17** 6310
at night, **w** the cloud was lifted, **Nu 9:21**
the LORD our God **w** we call on Him? **Dt 4:7** 3605
and comes **w** he desires to the **Dt 18:6** 3605
w the *evil* spirit from God came to **1Sa 16:23**
to them **w** they call to You. **1Ki 8:52** 3605
w he gave praise by their means, **2Ch 7:6**
"**W** any dispute comes to you from **2Ch 19:10** 834
w the chest was brought in to the **2Ch 24:11** 6256
w you turn to the right or to the **Is 30:21** 3588
W they moved, they moved in any of **Ezk 1:17**
W the living beings moved, **Ezk 1:19**
And **w** the living beings rose from **Ezk 1:19**
W those went, these went; **Ezk 1:21**
and **w** those stood still, these **Ezk 1:21**
And **w** those rose from the earth, **Ezk 1:21**
w they stood still, they dropped **Ezk 1:24**
w they stood still, they dropped **Ezk 1:25**
w you hear a word from My mouth, **Ezk 3:17**
"**W** you fast, do not put on a gloomy **Mt 6:16** 3752
"But **w** they persecute you in one **Mt 10:23** 3752
W the unclean spirits saw Him, they **Mk 3:11** 3752
and **w** it seizes him, it slams him **Mk 9:18** 3699
"**W** you stand praying, forgive, if **Mk 11:25** 3752
poor with you, and **w** you wish **Mk 14:7** 3752
but **w** the Christ may come, no one **Jn 7:27** 3752
W he speaks a lie, he speaks from **Jn 8:44** 3752
"**W** a woman is in labor she has **Jn 16:21** 3752
w I go to Spain **Ro 15:24** 5613, 1437
But to this day **w** Moses is read, a **2Co 3:15** 2259, 302
but **w** a person turns to the Lord, the **2Co 3:16** 2259, 1437
w your obedience is complete. **2Co 10:6** 3752

WHERE

land of Havilah, **w** there is gold. **Gn 2:11** 834, 8033
and said to him, "**W** are you?" **Gn 3:9** 335
"**W** is Abel your brother?" **Gn 4:9** 335
to the place **w** his tent had been **Gn 13:3** 834, 8033
and look from the place **w** you are, **Gn 13:14** 834, 8033
w they will be enslaved and **Gn 15:13**
w have you come from and where are **Gn 16:8** 335, 2088
come from and **w** are you going?" **Gn 16:8** 575
"**W** is Sarah your wife?" **Gn 18:9** 335
"**W** are the men who came to you **Gn 19:5** 346
w he had stood before the LORD; **Gn 19:27** 834, 8033
the voice of the lad **w** he is. **Gn 21:17** 834, 8033
but **w** is the lamb for the burnt **Gn 22:7** 346
to the land from **w** you came?" **Gn 24:5** 834, 8033
"My brothers, **w** are you from?" **Gn 29:4** 370
w the flocks came to drink; **Gn 30:38** 834
Bethel, **w** you anointed a pillar, **Gn 31:13** 834, 8033
a pillar, **w** you made a vow to Me; **Gn 31:13** 834, 8033
you belong, and **w** are you going, **Gn 32:17** 575
w he had pitched his tent from the **Gn 33:19** 834, 8033
place **w** He had spoken with him. **Gn 35:13** 834
place **w** He had spoken with him, **Gn 35:14** 834
place **w** God had spoken with him, **Gn 35:15** 834, 8033
w Abraham and Isaac had sojourned. **Gn 35:27** 834, 8033
and the land **w** they sojourned **Gn 36:7** 4033
land **w** his father had sojourned, **Gn 37:1** 4033
w they are pasturing *the flock*." **Gn 37:16** 375
as for me, **w** am I to go?" **Gn 37:30** 575
"**W** is the temple prostitute who **Gn 38:21** 346
the place **w** the king's prisoners **Gn 39:20** 834
place **w** Joseph was imprisoned. **Gn 40:3** 834, 8033
"**W** have you come from?" **Gn 42:7** 370
said to his daughters, "**W** is he then? **Ex 2:20** 335
of Goshen, **w** My people are living, **Ex 8:22** 834
Goshen, **w** the sons of Israel *were*, **Ex 9:26** 834, 8033
for you on the houses **w** you live; **Ex 12:13** 834, 8033
home **w** there was not someone dead. **Ex 12:30** 834, 8033
w there *were* twelve springs of water **Ex 15:27** 8033
in the wilderness **w** he was camped, **Ex 18:5** 834, 8033
the thick cloud **w** God *was*. **Ex 20:21** 834, 8033
in every place **w** I cause My name **Ex 20:24** 834
close to the place **w** it is joined, **Ex 28:27** 4225
the LORD, **w** I will meet with you, **Ex 29:42** 834, 8033
testimony, **w** I will meet with you. **Ex 30:6** 834, 8033
meeting **w** I will meet with you; **Ex 30:36** 834, 8033
now, lead the people **w** I told you. **Ex 32:34** 413, 834
close to the place **w** it joined, **Ex 39:20** 4225
camp **w** the ashes are poured out, **Lv 4:12** 413
w the ashes are poured out it **Lv 4:12** 5921
w they slay the burnt offering **Lv 4:24** 834
w they slay the burnt offering. **Lv 4:33** 834
in the place **w** the burnt offering **Lv 6:25** 834
'In the place **w** they slay the **Lv 7:2** 834
place **w** they slaughter the sin offering **Lv 14:13** 834
in the land of Egypt **w** you lived, **Lv 18:3** 834
of Canaan **w** I am bringing you; **Lv 18:3** 834, 8033
camp **w** I dwell in their midst." **Nu 5:3** 834
place **w** the cloud settled down, **Nu 9:17** 834, 8033
w we should camp in the wilderness, **Nu 10:31**
"**W** am I to get meat to give to **Nu 11:13** 4480, 370
they came to Hebron **w** Ahiman, **Nu 13:22** 8033
went in to the land **w** you sent us; **Nu 13:27** 834
enter the land **w** you are to live, **Nu 15:2** 4186
you enter the land **w** I bring you, **Nu 15:18** 834, 8033
the testimony, **w** I meet with you. **Nu 17:4** 834, 8033
the well **w** the LORD said to Moses, **Nu 21:16** 834
w there was no way to turn to the **Nu 22:26** 834
place from **w** you may see them, **Nu 23:13** 834, 8033
burned all their cities **w** they lived **Nu 31:10** 4186
'**W** can we go up? Our brethren have **Dt 1:28** 575
and in the wilderness **w** you saw **Dt 1:31** 834
the land **w** you are entering to possess **Dt 4:5** 834, 8033
in the land **w** you are going over to **Dt 4:14** 834, 8033
w you are going over the Jordan to **Dt 4:26** 834, 8033
w the LORD drives you. **Dt 4:27** 834, 8033
land **w** you are going over to possess **Dt 6:1** 834, 8033
land **w** you are entering to possess it **Dt 7:1** 834, 8033
a land **w** you will eat food **Dt 8:9** 834
ground **w** there was no water; **Dt 8:15** 834
w you used to sow your seed and **Dt 11:10** 834
land **w** you are entering to possess it **Dt 11:29** 834, 8033
destroy all the places **w** the nations **Dt 12:2** 834, 8033
at the place **w** He chooses to **Dt 14:23** 834, 8033
since the place **w** the LORD your **Dt 14:24** 834, 8033
in the place **w** the LORD chooses to **Dt 16:2** 834, 8033
but at the place **w** the LORD your **Dt 16:6** 834, 8033
in the place **w** the LORD your God **Dt 16:11** 834, 8033
throughout Israel **w** he resides, **Dt 18:6** 834, 8033
of your towns **w** it pleases him; **Dt 23:16**
go to the place **w** the LORD your God **Dt 26:2** 834, 8033
w you are entering to possess it. **Dt 28:21** 834, 8033
people **w** the LORD drives you. **Dt 28:37** 834, 8033
land **w** you are entering to possess it. **Dt 28:63** 834, 8033
w the LORD your God has banished **Dt 30:1** 834, 8033
w the LORD your God has scattered **Dt 30:3** 834, 8033
land **w** you are entering to possess it. **Dt 30:16** 834, 8033
w you are crossing the Jordan to **Dt 30:18** 834, 8033
'**W** are their gods, The rock in **Dt 32:37** 335
die on the mountain **w** you ascend, **Dt 32:50** 834, 8033
I did not know **w** they were from. **Jos 2:4** 370
I do not know **w** the men went. **Jos 2:5** 575
from the place **w** the priests' feet **Jos 4:3** 4673
w you will lodge tonight.'" **Jos 4:3** 4673
at the place **w** the feet of the priests **Jos 4:9** 4673
w you are standing is holy." **Jos 5:15** 834, 5921
wilderness **w** they pursued them, **Jos 8:24** 834
are you and **w** do you come from?" **Jos 9:8** 370
cave **w** they had hidden themselves, **Jos 10:27** 834, 8033
w the LORD's tabernacle stands, **Jos 22:19** 834, 8033
W he bowed, there he fell dead. **Jg 5:27** 834
And **w** are all His miracles which **Jg 6:13** 346
"**W** is your boasting now with **Jg 9:38** 346
I did not ask him **w** he *came* from, **Jg 13:6** 335
and see **w** his great strength *lies* **Jg 16:5** 4100
tell me **w** your great strength is and **Jg 16:6** 4100
me **w** your great strength is." **Jg 16:15** 4100
"**W** do you come from?" **Jg 17:9** 370
a place **w** there is no lack of **Jg 18:10** 834, 8033
"**W** are you going, and where do **Jg 19:17** 575
going, and **w** do you come from?" **Jg 19:17** 370
the man's house **w** her master was, **Jg 19:26** 834, 8033
place **w** they had arrayed themselves **Jg 20:22** 834, 8033
departed from the place **w** she was, **Ru 1:7** 834, 8033
for **w** you go, I will go, and where **Ru 1:16** 413, 834
and **w** you lodge, I will lodge. **Ru 1:16** 834
"**W** you die, I will die, and there **Ru 1:17** 834
"**W** did you glean today and where **Ru 2:19** 375
glean today and **w** did you work? **Ru 2:19** 575
shall notice the place **w** he lies, **Ru 3:4** 834, 8033
of the LORD **w** the ark of God *was*, **1Sa 3:3** 834, 8033
there **w** there *was* a large stone; **1Sa 6:14** 8033
to the city **w** the man of God was. **1Sa 9:10** 834, 8033
tell me **w** the seer's house is." **1Sa 9:18** 335
God **w** the Philistine garrison is; **1Sa 10:5** 834, 8033
"**W** did you go?" And he said, **1Sa 10:14** 575
w they have hidden themselves." **1Sa 14:11** 834, 8033
my father in the field **w** you are, **1Sa 19:3** 834, 8033
"**W** are Samuel and David?" **1Sa 19:22** 375
the place **w** you hid yourself on that **1Sa 20:19** 834, 8033

and see his place **w** his haunt is, 1Sa 23:22 834, 8033
hiding places **w** he hides himself and 1Sa 23:23 834, 8033
on the way, **w** there *was* a cave; 1Sa 24:3 8033
to the place **w** Saul had camped. 1Sa 26:5 834, 8033
David saw the place **w** Saul lay, 1Sa 26:5 834, 8033
And now, see **w** the king's spear is and 1Sa 26:16 335
"**W** have you made a raid today?" 1Sa 27:10 575
his place **w** you have assigned him, 1Sa 29:4 834, 8033
w those left behind remained. 1Sa 30:9
And **w** are you from?" 1Sa 30:13 335
and to all the places **w** David 1Sa 30:31 834, 8033
"From **w** do you come?" 2Sa 1:3 335
"**W** are you from?" 2Sa 1:13 335
"**W** shall I go up?" 2Sa 2:1 575
w Asahel had fallen and died, 2Sa 2:23 834, 8033
So the king said to him, "**W** is he?" 2Sa 9:4 375
w he knew there *were* valiant men. 2Sa 11:16 834, 8033
w could I get rid of my reproach? 2Sa 13:13 575
with us, while I go **w** I will? 2Sa 15:20 5921, 834
the summit, **w** God was worshiped, 2Sa 15:32 834, 8033
"And **w** is your master's son?" 2Sa 16:3 346
of the places **w** he can be found, 2Sa 17:12 834, 8033
"**W** are Ahimaaz and Jonathan?" 2Sa 17:20 346
w the Philistines had hanged them 2Sa 21:12 834, 8033
w there was a man of *great* stature 2Sa 21:20
w there was a plot of ground full 2Sa 23:11 8033
to the place **w** it should be, 1Ki 4:28 834, 8033
sea to the place **w** you direct me, 1Ki 5:9 834
of the throne **w** he was to judge, 1Ki 7:7 834, 8033
His house **w** he was to live, 1Ki 7:8 834, 8033
w the LORD made a covenant with 1Ki 8:9 834
w they have been taken captive, 1Ki 8:47 834, 8033
the city **w** I have chosen for 1Ki 11:36 834, 8033
w he had fled from the presence of 1Ki 12:2 834
the city **w** the old prophet lived. 1Ki 13:25 834
to the upper room **w** he was living, 1Ki 17:19 834, 8033
w my master has not sent to search 1Ki 18:10 834, 8033
will carry you **w** I do not know; 1Ki 18:12 5921, 834
w he has gone down to take 1Ki 21:18 834, 8033
"In the place **w** the dogs licked 1Ki 21:19 834
from the bed **w** you have gone up, 2Ki 1:4 834, 8033
from the bed **w** you have gone up, 2Ki 1:6 834, 8033
from the bed **w** you have gone up, 2Ki 1:16 834, 8033
"**W** is the LORD, the God of Elijah?" 2Ki 2:14 346
w there was a prominent woman, 2Ki 4:8 8033
"**W** have you been, Gehazi?" 2Ki 5:25 575
the place before you **w** we are 2Ki 6:1 834, 8033
for ourselves **w** we may live." 2Ki 6:2 8033
the man of God said, "**W** did it fall? 2Ki 6:6 575
"Go and see **w** he is, that I may 2Ki 6:13 351a
you, from **w** shall I help you? 2Ki 6:27 370
'**W** are the gods of Hamath and 2Ki 18:34 346
W are the gods of Sepharvaim, Hena 2Ki 18:34 346
'**W** is the king of Hamath, the king 2Ki 19:13 335
from **w** have they come to you?" 2Ki 20:14 370
w the women were weaving hangings 2Ki 23:7 834, 8033
w the priests had burned incense, 2Ki 23:8 834, 8033
cherubim, **w** His name is called. 1Ch 13:6 834
w I have walked with all Israel, 1Ch 17:6 834
w there was a man of *great* stature 1Ch 20:6
w *the* LORD had appeared to his 2Ch 3:1 834
w the LORD made a covenant with 2Ch 5:10 834
the land **w** they are taken captive, 2Ch 6:37 834, 8033
w they have been taken captive, 2Ch 6:38 834
w the ark of the LORD has entered 2Ch 8:11 834
he was in Egypt **w** he had fled from 2Ch 10:2 834
w he died and was buried in the 2Ch 35:24
w the treasures were stored in Ezr 6:1 1768, 8536
place **w** sacrifices are offered, Ezr 6:3 1768
Ahava, **w** we camped for three days; Ezr 8:15 8033
them to the place **w** I have chosen Ne 1:9 834, 8033
w I had gone or what I had done; Ne 2:16 575
from every place **w** you may turn," Ne 4:12 834
w formerly they put the grain Ne 13:5 8033
In each and every province **w** Es 4:3 4725, 834
w the king had magnified him and Es 5:11 834
"Who is he, and **w** is he, who Es 7:5 335
place **w** they were drinking wine, Es 7:8 4960
falling on the couch **w** Esther was. Es 7:8 834, 5921
"From **w** do you come?" Jb 1:7 370
"**W** have you come from?" Jb 2:2 335
Or **w** were the upright destroyed? Jb 4:7 375
Man expires, and **w** is he? Jb 14:10 335
about for food, saying, '**W** is it?' Jb 15:23 346
W now is my hope? Jb 17:15 346
Nor any survivor **w** he sojourned. Jb 18:19 4033
have seen him will say, '**W** is he?' Jb 20:7 335
'**W** is the house of the nobleman, Jb 21:28 346
the nobleman, And **w** is the tent, Jb 21:28 346
"Oh that I knew **w** I might find Jb 23:3
And a place **w** they refine gold. Jb 28:1
"But **w** can wisdom be found? Jb 28:12 370
w is the place of understanding? Jb 28:12 335
"**W** then does wisdom come from? Jb 28:20 370
w is the place of understanding? Jb 28:20 335
W the workers of iniquity may hide Jb 34:22 8033
'**W** is God my Maker, Who gives Jb 35:10 346
"**W** were you when I laid the Jb 38:4 375
"**W** is the way to the dwelling of Jb 38:19 335
And darkness, **w** is its place, Jb 38:19 335
"**W** is the way that the light is Jb 38:24 335
And **w** the slain are, there is he." Jb 39:30 834
down the wicked **w** they stand. Jb 40:12 8478
And the place **w** Your glory dwells. Ps 26:8 4908
to me all day long, "**W** is your God? Ps 42:3 346
to me all day long, "**W** is your God? Ps 42:10 346
There they were in great fear **w** Ps 53:5
weary land **w** there is no water. Ps 63:1
Mount Zion, **w** You have dwelt. Ps 74:2 2088
"**W** is their God?" Ps 79:10 346
herself, **w** she may lay her young, Ps 84:3 834
W are Your former lovingkindnesses, Ps 89:49 346
W the birds build their nests, *And* Ps 104:17 834, 8033
"**W**, now, is their God?" Ps 115:2 346
From **w** shall my help come? Ps 121:1 370
W can I go from Your Spirit? Ps 139:7 575
Or **w** can I flee from Your presence? Ps 139:7 575
In the way **w** I walk They have Ps 142:3 2098
beside the way, **W** the paths meet, Pr 8:2 1004
W there is no guidance the people Pr 11:14
W no oxen are, the manger is Pr 14:4
is a dish of vegetables **w** love is Than Pr 15:17 8033
out, And **w** there is no whisperer, Pr 26:20
W there is no vision, the people Pr 29:18
To the place **w** the rivers flow, Ec 1:7 7945
in the city **w** they did thus. Ec 8:10 834
wisdom in Sheol **w** you are going. Ec 9:10 834, 8033
W do you pasture *your flock*, SS 1:7 351a
W do you make *it* lie down at noon? SS 1:7 351a
"**W** has your beloved gone, O most SS 6:1 575
W has your beloved turned, That we SS 6:1 575
W will you be stricken again, *As* Is 1:5 5921, 4100
that every place **w** there used to Is 7:23 834, 8033
And **w** will you leave your wealth? Is 10:3 575
Well then, **w** are your wise men? Is 19:12 335
w we fled for help to be delivered Is 20:6 834, 8033
Woe, O Ariel, Ariel the city **w** Is 29:1
And from the dust **w** you are Is 29:4
From **w** *come* lioness and lion, Is 30:6 1992a
"**W** is he who counts? Is 33:18 346
W is he who weighs? Is 33:18 346
W is he who counts the towers?" Is 33:18 346
'**W** are the gods of Hamath and Is 36:19 346
W are the gods of Sepharvaim? Is 36:19 346
'**W** is the king of Hamath, the king Is 37:13 346
from **w** have they come to you?" Is 39:3 370
The settlements **w** Kedar inhabits. Is 42:11
From **w** did these come?' " Is 49:21 375
"**W** is the certificate of divorce By Is 50:1 335
w is the fury of the oppressor? Is 51:13 346
W is He who brought them up out of Is 63:11 346
W is He who put His Holy Spirit in Is 63:11 346
W are Your zeal and Your mighty Is 63:15 346
house, **W** our fathers praised You, Is 64:11 834
W then is a house you could build Is 66:1 335
And **w** is a place that I may rest? Is 66:1 335
"**W** is the LORD Who brought us up Jer 2:6 346
one crossed And **w** no man dwelt?' Jer 2:6 8033
priests did not say, '**W** is the LORD?' Jer 2:8 346
"But **w** are your gods Which you Jer 2:28 346
W have you not been violated? Jer 3:2 375
ancient paths, **W** the good way is, Jer 6:16 335
w I made My name dwell at the Jer 7:12 834, 8033
from the place **w** I had hidden it; Jer 13:7 834, 8033
W is the flock that was given you, Jer 13:20 346
they say to you, '**W** should we go?' Jer 15:2 575
countries **w** He had banished them.' Jer 16:15 834, 8033
"**W** is the word of the LORD? Jer 17:15 346
w the LORD had sent him to Jer 19:14 834, 8033
the place **w** they led him captive, Jer 22:12 834, 8033
country **w** you were not born, Jer 22:26 834, 8033
the countries **w** I have driven them Jer 23:3 834, 8033
countries **w** I had driven them.' Jer 23:8 834, 8033
all places **w** I will scatter them. Jer 24:9 834, 8033
city **w** I have sent you into exile, Jer 29:7 834, 8033
the places **w** I have driven you,' Jer 29:14 834, 8033
from **w** I sent you into exile.' Jer 29:14 834, 8033
the nations **w** I have driven them, Jer 29:18 834, 8033
nations **w** I have scattered you, Jer 30:11 834, 8033
w *people* have offered incense to Baal Jer 32:29 834
days in the land **w** you sojourn.' Jer 35:7 834, 8033
not let anyone know **w** you are." Jer 36:19 375
"**W** then are your prophets who Jer 37:19 346
w he is because of the famine, Jer 38:9 8478
w Ishmael had cast all the corpses Jer 41:9 834, 8033
w we will not see war or hear the Jer 42:14 834
place **w** you wish to go to reside. Jer 42:22 834, 8033
w you are entering to reside, Jer 44:8 834, 8033
all the places **w** you may go.' " Jer 45:5 834, 8033
the nations **W** I have driven you, Jer 46:28 834, 8033
"**W** is grain and wine?" La 2:12 346
seven days **w** they were living, Ezk 3:15 8033
nations **w** I will banish them." Ezk 4:13 834, 8033
places **w** they offered soothing aroma Ezk 6:13 834, 8033
w the seat of the idol of Ezk 8:3 834, 8033
the countries **w** they had gone." Ezk 11:16 834, 8033
among the nations **w** they go, Ezk 12:16 834, 8033
'**W** is the plaster with which you Ezk 13:12 346
from the beds **w** it was planted, Ezk 17:7 4302
on the beds **w** it grew? Ezk 17:10 6780
the lands **w** you are scattered, Ezk 20:34 834
out of the land **w** they sojourn, Ezk 20:38 4033
the lands **w** you are scattered; Ezk 20:41 834
In the place **w** you were created, Ezk 21:30 834
came to the nations **w** they went, Ezk 36:20 834, 8033
among the nations **w** they went. Ezk 36:21 834, 8033
among the nations **w** you went. Ezk 36:22 834, 8033
the nations **w** they have gone, Ezk 37:21 834, 8033
they are the holy chambers **w** the Ezk 42:13 834, 8033
w I will dwell among the sons of Ezk 43:7 834, 8033
the place **w** the priests shall boil Ezk 46:20 834, 8033
and **w** they shall bake the grain Ezk 46:20 834
"These are the boiling places **w** Ezk 46:24 834, 8033
in every place **w** the river goes, Ezk 47:9 834, 8033
will live **w** the river goes. Ezk 47:9 834, 8033
he came near to **w** I was standing, Da 8:17 5977
in the place **W** it is said to them, Hos 1:10 834
W now is your king That he may Hos 13:10 165
O Death, **w** are your thorns? Hos 13:14 165
O Sheol, **w** is your sting? Hos 13:14 165
'**W** is their God?' " Jl 2:17 346
the place **w** you have sold them, Jl 3:7 834, 8033
And **w** do you come from? Jon 1:8 370
"**W** is the LORD your God?" Mi 7:10 335
W is the den of the lions And the Na 2:11 346
of the young lions, **W** the lion, Na 2:11 834, 8033
W will I seek comforters for you?" Na 3:7 370
the place **w** they are is not known. Na 3:17 335
"Your fathers, **w** are they? Zch 1:5 346
"**W** are you going?" Zch 2:2 575
"**W** are they taking the ephah?" Zch 5:10 575
w they have arrived from Babylon. Zch 6:10 834
He will branch out from **w** He is; Zch 6:12 8478
if I am a father, **w** is My honor? Mal 1:6 346
I am a master, **w** is My respect?' Mal 1:6 346
"**W** is the God of justice?" Mal 2:17 346
"**W** is He who has been born King Mt 2:2 *4226*
them **w** the Messiah was to be born. Mt 2:4 *4226*
stood over *the place* **w** the Child was. Mt 2:9 *3757*
earth, **w** moth and rust destroy, Mt 6:19 *3699*
and **w** thieves break in and steal. Mt 6:19 *3699*
w neither moth nor rust destroys, Mt 6:20 *3699*
and **w** thieves do not break in or Mt 6:20 *3699*
for **w** your treasure is, there your Mt 6:21 *3699*
w they did not have much soil; Mt 13:5 *3699*
"**W** *did* this man *get* this wisdom and Mt 13:54 *4159*
W then *did* this man *get* all these Mt 13:56 *4159*
"**W** would we get so many loaves in Mt 15:33 *4159*
"For **w** two or three have gathered Mt 18:20 *3757*
man, reaping **w** you did not sow and Mt 25:24 *3699*
gathering **w** you scattered no *seed*. Mt 25:24 *3606*
knew that I reap **w** I did not sow and Mt 25:26 *3699*
and gather **w** I scattered no *seed*. Mt 25:26 *3606*
"**W** do You want us to prepare for Mt 26:17 *4226*
w the scribes and the elders were Mt 26:57 *3699*
see the place **w** He was lying. Mt 28:6 *3699*
w it did not have much soil; Mk 4:5 *3699*
the road **w** the word is sown; Mk 4:15 *3699*
entered *the room* **w** the child was. Mk 5:40 *3699*
"**W** did this man *get* these things, Mk 6:2 *4159*
"**W** will anyone be able *to find* Mk 8:4 *4159*
W THEIR WORM DOES NOT DIE, AND Mk 9:44 *3699*
W THEIR WORM DOES NOT DIE, AND Mk 9:46 *3699*

w THEIR WORM DOES NOT DIE, AND THE Mk 9:48 3699
standing w it should not be Mk 13:14 3699
"W do You want us to go and Mk 14:12 4226
"W is My guest room in which I Mk 14:14 4226
looking on *to see* w He was laid. Mk 15:47 4226
here is the place w they laid Him. Mk 16:6 3699
w He had been brought up; Lk 4:16 3757
found the place w it was written, Lk 4:17 3757
"W is your faith?" Lk 8:25 4226
w He Himself was going to come. Lk 10:1 3757
in heaven, w no thief comes near nor Lk 12:33 3699
"For w your treasure is, there Lk 12:34 3699
'I do not know w you are from.' Lk 13:25 4159
you, I do not know w you are from; Lk 13:27 4159
But the nine—w are they? Lk 17:17 4226
they said to Him, "W, Lord?" Lk 17:37 4226
"W the body *is,* there also the Lk 17:37 3699
they did not know w *it came* from. Lk 20:7 4159
w he calls the Lord THE GOD OF Lk 20:37 5613
"W do You want us to prepare it?" Lk 22:9 4226
"W is the guest room in which I Lk 22:11 4226
the rock, w no one had ever lain. Lk 23:53 3757
the village w they were going, Lk 24:28 3757
the Jordan, w John was baptizing. Jn 1:28 3699
w are You staying?" Jn 1:38 4226
and saw w He was staying; Jn 1:39 4226
and did not know w it came from Jn 2:9 4159
"The wind blows w it wishes and Jn 3:8 3699
but do not know w it comes from Jn 3:8 4159
it comes from and w it is going; Jn 3:8 4226
w then do You get that living water Jn 4:11 4159
place w men ought to worship." Jn 4:20 3699
w He had made the water wine. Jn 4:46 3699
"W are we to buy bread, so Jn 6:5 4159
to the place w they ate the bread Jn 6:23 3699
of Man ascending to w He was before? Jn 6:62 3699
feast and were saying, "W is He?" Jn 7:11 4226
we know w this man is from; Jn 7:27 4159
come, no one knows w He is from." Jn 7:27 4159
both know Me and know w I am from; Jn 7:28 4159
and w I am, you cannot come." Jn 7:34 3699
"W does this man intend to go Jn 7:35 4226
and w I am, you cannot come'?" Jn 7:36 3699
the village w David was?" Jn 7:42 3699
woman, w she was, in the center Jn 8:9
"Woman, w are they? Jn 8:10 4226
for I know w I came from and Jn 8:14 4159
I came from and w I am going; Jn 8:14 4226
but you do not know w I come from or Jn 8:14 4159
I come from or w I am going. Jn 8:14 4226
"W is Your Father?" Jn 8:19 4226
w I am going, you cannot come." Jn 8:21 3699
'W I am going, you cannot come'?" Jn 8:22 3699
They said to him, "W is He?" Jn 9:12 4226
we do not know w He is from." Jn 9:29 4159
that you do not know w He is from, Jn 9:30 4159
place w John was first baptizing, Jn 10:40 3699
days *longer* in the place w He was. Jn 11:6 3739
in the place w Martha met Him. Jn 11:30 3699
when Mary came w Jesus was, Jn 11:32 3699
"W have you laid him?" Jn 11:34 4226
that if anyone knew w He was, Jn 11:57 4226
came to Bethany w Lazarus was, Jn 12:1 3699
and w I am, there My servant Jn 12:26 3699
darkness does not know w he goes. Jn 12:35 4226
'W I am going, you cannot come.' Jn 13:33 3699
"Lord, w are You going?" Jn 13:36 4226
"W I go, you cannot follow Me now; Jn 13:36 3699
that w I am, *there* you may be also. Jn 14:3 3699
you know the way w I am going." Jn 14:4 3699
we do not know w You are going, Jn 14:5 4226
'W are You going?' Jn 16:5 4226
have given Me, be with Me w I am, Jn 17:24 3699
the Kidron, w there was a garden, Jn 18:1 3699
w all the Jews come together; Jn 18:20 3699
"W are You from?" Jn 19:9 4159
for the place w Jesus was crucified Jn 19:20 3699
in the place w He was crucified Jn 19:41 3699
not know w they have laid Him." Jn 20:2 4226
w the body of Jesus had been lying. Jn 20:12 3699
not know w they have laid Him." Jn 20:13 4226
away, tell me w you have laid Him, Jn 20:15 4226
were shut w the disciples were, Jn 20:19 3699
you w you do not wish to *go.*" Jn 21:18 3699
upper room w they were staying; Ac 1:13 3757
whole house w they were sitting. Ac 2:2 3757
the place w they had gathered Ac 4:31
1722, 3739
w he became the father of two sons. Ac 7:29 3757
w many were gathered together and Ac 12:12 3757
w we were supposing that there Ac 16:13 3757
w there was a synagogue of the Ac 17:1 3699
room w we were gathered together. Ac 20:8 3757
tribunal, w I ought to be tried. Ac 25:10 3757
striking a reef w two seas met, Ac 27:41 1337
W then is boasting? Ro 3:27 4226
wrath, but w there is no law, Ro 4:15 3757
but w sin increased, grace Ro 5:20 3757
THE PLACE W IT WAS SAID TO THEM, Ro 9:26 3757
not w Christ was *already* named, Ro 15:20 3699
W is the wise man? 1Co 1:20 4226
W is the scribe? Where is the debater 1Co 1:20 4226
W is the debater of this age? 1Co 1:20 4226
an eye, w would the hearing be? 1Co 12:17 4226
w would the sense of smell be? 1Co 12:17 4226
one member, w would the body be? 1Co 12:19 4226
"O DEATH, W IS YOUR VICTORY? 1Co 15:55 4226
O DEATH, W IS YOUR STING?" 1Co 15:55 4226
and w the Spirit of the Lord is, 2Co 3:17 3757
W then is that sense of blessing Ga 4:15 4226
the things above, w Christ is, Col 3:1 3757
W YOUR FATHERS TRIED *Me* BY TESTING Heb 3:9 3757
w Jesus has entered as a Heb 6:20 3699
For w a covenant is, there must of Heb 9:16 3699
Now w there is forgiveness of Heb 10:18 3699
out, not knowing w he was going. Heb 11:8 4226
For w jealousy and selfish Jas 3:16 3699
reviling w they have no knowledge, 2Pe 2:12
1722, 3739
"W is the promise of His coming? 2Pe 3:4 4226
and does not know w he is going 1Jn 2:11 4226
remember from w you have fallen, Rv 2:5 4159
'I know w you dwell, where Satan's Rv 2:13 4226
you dwell, w Satan's throne is; Rv 2:13 3699
killed among you, w Satan dwells. Rv 2:13 3699
they, and w have they come from?" Rv 7:13 4159
w also their Lord was crucified. Rv 11:8 3699
w she had a place prepared by God, Rv 12:6 3699
w she was nourished for a time and Rv 12:14 3699
which you saw w the harlot sits, Rv 17:15 3757
w the beast and the false prophet Rv 20:10 3699

WHEREAS

w you were as numerous as the stars Dt 28:62
8478, 834
'W my father loaded you with a 1Ki 12:11 6258
'W my father loaded you with a 2Ch 10:11 6258
"W you have been forsaken and Is 60:15 8478
w a sword touches the throat." Jer 4:10
w a righteous man will not be able Ezk 33:12
wpresentable members have no need 1Co 12:24 1161
w God is *only* one. Ga 3:20 1161
w angels who are greater in might 2Pe 2:11 3699

WHEREBY

w they have forsaken Me and have Jer 1:16 834

WHEREFORE

W, the LORD his God delivered him 2Ch 28:5
W I urge you to reaffirm *your* love 2Co 2:8 1352

WHEREIN

w a man has exercised authority over Ec 8:9 834

WHEREVER

settle w you please." Gn 20:15
you and will keep you w you go, Gn 28:15
3605, 834
LORD has blessed you w I turned. Gn 30:30
has been with me w I have gone." Gn 35:3
1870, 834
for yourselves w you can find *it,* Ex 5:11
4480, 834
W the lot falls to anyone, that Nu 33:54
413, 834, 8033
and w the LORD our God had Dt 2:37
3605, 834
you shall let her go w she wishes; Dt 21:14
you may have success w you go. Jos 1:7 3605, 834
your God is with you w you go." Jos 1:9 3605, 834
do, and w you send us we will go. Jos 1:16
413, 3605, 834
W they went, the hand of the LORD Jg 2:15
3605, 834
to stay w he might find *a place;* Jg 17:8 834
to stay w I may find *a place.*" Jg 17:9 834
and w he turned, he inflicted 1Sa 14:47
3605, 834
So David went out w Saul sent him, 1Sa 18:5
3605, 834
and they went w they could go. 1Sa 23:13 834
"W I have gone with all the sons 2Sa 7:7 3605, 834
been with you w you have gone 2Sa 7:9 3605, 834
the LORD helped David w he went. 2Sa 8:6 3605, 834
the LORD helped David w he went. 2Sa 8:14
3605, 834
surely w my lord the king may be, 2Sa 15:21
4725, 834, 8033
in all that you do and w you turn, 1Ki 2:3
3605, 834, 8033
and sojourn w you can sojourn; 2Ki 8:1 834
house w any damage may be found. 2Ki 12:5
3605, 834, 8033
w he went he prospered. 2Ki 18:7
3605, 834
been with you w you have gone, 1Ch 17:8
3605, 834
the LORD helped David w he went. 1Ch 18:6
3605, 834
the LORD helped David w he went. 1Ch 18:13
3605, 834
w the king's commandment and his Es 8:17
4725, 834
W he turns, he prospers. Pr 17:8
413, 3605, 834
He turns it w He wishes. Pr 21:1
5921, 3605, 834
the north, w the tree falls, Ec 11:3 4725
go w it seems good and right for Jer 40:4 8033
w the spirit was about to go, they Ezk 1:12
413, 834, 8033
W the spirit was about to go, they Ezk 1:20
5921, 834, 8033
left, w your edge is appointed. Ezk 21:16 575
and w the sons of men dwell, *or* Da 2:38
3606, 1768
I will follow You w You go." Mt 8:19
3699, 1437
"W the corpse is, there the Mt 24:28
3699, 1437
w this gospel is preached in the Mt 26:13
3699, 1437
"W you enter a house, stay there Mk 6:10
3699, 1437
W He entered villages, or cities, Mk 6:56 3699
w the gospel is preached in the Mk 14:9
3699, 1437
and w he enters, say to the owner Mk 14:14
3699, 1437
"I will follow You w You go." Lk 9:57
3699, 1437
yourself and walk w you wished; Jn 21:18 3699
may send me on my way w I may go. 1Co 16:6
3757, 1437
w the inclination of the pilot desires. Jas 3:4 3699
who follow the Lamb w He goes. Rv 14:4
3699, 302

WHETHER

to know w the LORD had made his Gn 24:21
w you are really my son Esau or Gn 27:21
You required it of my hand w Gn 31:39
w it is your son's tunic or not." Gn 37:32
tested, w there is truth in you. Gn 42:16
w you still had *another* brother?" Gn 43:6
even bark, w against man or beast, Ex 11:7 4480
w *he is* an alien or a native of Ex 12:19
w or not they will walk in My Ex 16:4
w beast or man, he shall not live.' Ex 19:13 518
w he sells him or he is found in Ex 21:16
"W it gores a son or a daughter, Ex 21:31 176
w an ox or a donkey or a sheep, Ex 22:4 4480
to determine w he laid his hands Ex 22:8
518, 3808
"For every breach of trust, w *it* Ex 22:9
out of the herd, w male or female, Lv 3:1 518
w he has seen or *otherwise* known, Lv 5:1 176
w a carcass of an unclean beast or Lv 5:2 176
unclean, w human uncleanness, Lv 7:21
w a male or a female. Lv 12:7
w it is a wool garment or a linen Lv 13:47
w in warp or woof, of linen or of Lv 13:48 176
w in leather or in any article Lv 13:48 176
w in the warp or in the woof, Lv 13:51 176
garment, w the warp or the woof, Lv 13:52 176
w an eating away has produced Lv 13:55
w from the warp or from the woof; Lv 13:56 176
w in the warp or in the woof, Lv 13:57 176
garment, w the warp or the woof, Lv 13:58 176
w in the warp or in the woof, Lv 13:59 176
w his body allows its discharge to Lv 15:3
or w his body obstructs its Lv 15:3
'W it be on the bed or on the Lv 15:23 518
a discharge, w a male or a female, Lv 15:33
w the native, or the alien who Lv 16:29
w he is a native or an alien, Lv 17:15
w born at home or born outside, Lv 18:9
w it is any of their votive or any Lv 22:18
"But, w it is an ox or a sheep, Lv 22:28
w ox or sheep, it is the LORD's. Lv 27:26 518
be concerned w *it is* good or bad, Lv 27:33 996
w made from wine or strong drink, Nu 6:3
W it was two days or a month or a Nu 9:22 176
w My word will come true for you Nu 11:23
and w the people who live in it Nu 13:18
or weak, w they are few or many. Nu 13:18
w he is native or an alien, Nu 15:30 4480
of all flesh, w man or animal, Nu 18:15
w you would keep His commandments Dt 8:2
w *he is* one of your countrymen or Dt 24:14 4480
w the gods which your fathers Jos 24:15 518
w they will keep the way of the Jg 2:22
that we may know w our way on Jg 18:5
after young men, w poor or rich. Ru 3:10 518
was missing, w small or great, 1Sa 30:19 4480
may be, w for death or for life, 2Sa 15:21 518
w I will recover from this 2Ki 1:2 518
be put to death, w small or great, 2Ch 15:13 4480
by divisions, w great or small, 2Ch 31:15
w they were of Israel: Ezr 2:59 518
w for death or for banishment or Ezr 7:26 2006
w they were of Israel: Ne 7:61 518
w Mordecai's reason would stand; Es 3:4
And who knows w you have not Es 4:14 518
"W for correction, or for His Jb 37:13 518
And who knows w he will be a wise Ec 2:19
w he eats little or much; Ec 5:12 518
know w *it will be* love or hatred; Ec 9:1 1571
and w a tree falls toward the Ec 11:3 518
w morning or evening sowing will Ec 11:6 335
or w both of them alike will be Ec 11:6 518
is hidden, w it is good or evil. Ec 12:14 518
To see w the vine had budded *Or* SS 6:11
Let us see w the vine has budded SS 7:12 518
And w the pomegranates have SS 7:12
"W *it* is pleasant or unpleasant, Jer 42:6 518
dwelling in it, w man or beast, Jer 51:62 4480
As for them, w they listen or not Ezk 2:5 518
to them w they listen or not, Ezk 2:7 518
tell them, w they listen or not, Ezk 3:11 518
w He will *not* turn and relent And Jl 2:14
You tell us w You are the Christ, Mt 26:63 1487
w Elijah will come to save Him." Mt 27:49 1487
w it was lawful for a man to divorce Mk 10:2 1487
house is coming, w in the evening, Mk 13:35 2228
"Let us see w Elijah will come to Mk 15:36 1487
him as to w He was already dead. Mk 15:44 1487
as to w he was the Christ, Lk 3:15 3379
"W he comes in the second watch, Lk 12:38 2579
consider w he is strong enough Lk 14:31 1487
he asked w the man was a Galilean. Lk 23:6 1487
of the teaching, w it is of God or Jn 7:17 4220

whether it is of God or **w** I speak **Jn 7:17**
"**W** He is a sinner, I do not know; **Jn 9:25** *1487*
"**W** it is right in the sight of **Ac 4:19** *1487*
"Tell me **w** you sold the land for **Ac 5:8** *1487*
out, they were asking **w** Simon, **Ac 10:18** *1487*
to see **w** these things were so. **Ac 17:11** *1487*
heard **w** there is a Holy Spirit." **Ac 19:2** *1487*
I asked **w** he was willing to go to **Ac 25:20** *1487*
that **w** in a short or long time, **Ac 26:29** *2532*
therefore **w** we live or die, we are **Ro 14:8**
1437, 5037
not know **w** I baptized any other. **1Co 1:16** *1487*
w Paul or Apollos or Cephas or the **1Co 3:22** *1535a*
w you will save your husband? **1Co 7:16** *1487*
w you will save your wife? **1Co 7:16** *1487*
gods **w** in heaven or on earth, **1Co 8:5** *1535a*
W, then, you eat or drink or **1Co 10:31** *1535a*
into one body, **w** Jews or Greeks, **1Co 12:13** *1535a*
Jews or Greeks, **w** slaves or free, **1Co 12:13** *1535a*
W then *it was* I or they, so we **1Co 15:11** *1535a*
w you are obedient in all things. **2Co 2:9** *1487*
our ambition, **w** at home or absent, **2Co 5:9** *1535a*
what he has done, **w** good or bad. **2Co 5:10** *1535a*
w in the body I do not know, **2Co 12:2** *1535a*
w in the body or apart from the body **2Co 12:3** *1535a*
from the Lord, **w** slave or free. **Eph 6:8** *1535a*
way, **w** in pretense or in truth, **Php 1:18** *1535a*
in my body, **w** by life or by death. **Php 1:20** *1535a*
so that **w** I come and see you or **Php 1:27** *1535a*
w thrones or dominions or rulers **Col 1:16** *1535a*
w things on earth or things in **Col 1:20** *1535a*
us, so that **w** we are awake or asleep, **1Th 5:10** *1535a*
w by word *of mouth* or by letter **2Th 2:15** *1535a*
w to a king as the one in **1Pe 2:13** *1535a*
to see **w** they are from God, **1Jn 4:1** *1487*

WHICH

and separated the waters **w** were **Gn 1:7** 834
waters **w** were above the expanse; **Gn 1:7** 834
with **w** the waters swarmed after **Gn 1:21** 834
tree **w** has fruit yielding seed; **Gn 1:29** 834
moves on the earth **w** has life, **Gn 1:30** 834
completed His work **w** He had done, **Gn 2:2** 834
from all His work **w** He had done. **Gn 2:2** 834
work **w** God had created and made. **Gn 2:3** 834
rib **w** He had taken from the man, **Gn 2:22** 834
the field **w** the LORD God had made. **Gn 3:1** 834
but from the fruit of the tree **w** **Gn 3:3** 834
of **w** I commanded you not to eat?" **Gn 3:11** 834
the tree about **w** I commanded you, **Gn 3:17** 834
the ground from **w** he was taken. **Gn 3:23** 834
sword **w** turned every direction to **Gn 3:24**
w has opened its mouth to receive **Gn 4:11** 834
ground **w** the LORD has cursed." **Gn 5:29** 834
flesh in **w** is the breath of life, **Gn 6:17** 834
some of all food **w** is edible, **Gn 6:21** 834
flesh in **w** was the breath of life. **Gn 7:15** 834
window of the ark **w** he had made; **Gn 8:6** 834
sign of the covenant **w** I am making **Gn 9:12** 834
w is between Me and you and every **Gn 9:15** 834
"This is the sign of the covenant **w** I **Gn 9:17** 834
(from **w** came the Philistines) **Gn 10:14** 834
tower **w** the sons of men had built. **Gn 11:5** 834
and now nothing **w** they purpose to **Gn 11:6** 834
To the land **w** I will show you; **Gn 12:1** 834
w they had accumulated, **Gn 12:5** 834
w they had acquired in Haran, **Gn 12:5** 834
w he had made there formerly; **Gn 13:4** 834
for all the land **w** you see, **Gn 13:15** 834
oaks of Mamre, **w** are in Hebron, **Gn 13:18** 834
El-paran, **w** is by the wilderness. **Gn 14:6** 834
as Hobah, **w** is north of Damascus. **Gn 14:15** 834
w passed between these pieces. **Gn 15:17** 834
is My covenant, **w** you shall keep, **Gn 17:10** 834
and the calf **w** he had prepared, **Gn 18:8** 834
the tent door, **w** was behind him. **Gn 18:10** 1931
to its outcry, **w** has come to Me; **Gn 18:21**
w you have shown me by saving my **Gn 19:19** 834
the town of **w** you have spoken. **Gn 19:21** 834
the cities in **w** Lot lived. **Gn 19:29** 834
kindness **w** you will show to me: **Gn 20:13** 834
time of **w** God had spoken to him. **Gn 21:2** 834
land in **w** you have sojourned." **Gn 21:23** 834
water **w** the servants of Abimelech **Gn 21:25** 834
w you have set by themselves?" **Gn 21:29** 834
mountains of **w** I will tell you." **Gn 22:2** 834
the place of **w** God had told him. **Gn 22:3** 834
the place of **w** God had told him; **Gn 22:9** 834
as the sand **w** is on the seashore; **Gn 22:17** 834
the cave of Machpelah **w** he owns, **Gn 23:9** 834
w is at the end of his field; **Gn 23:9** 834
weighed out for Ephron the silver **w** **Gn 23:16** 834
Ephron's field, **w** was in Machpelah, **Gn 23:17** 834
was in Machpelah, **w** faced Mamre, **Gn 23:17** 834
the field and cave **w** was in it, **Gn 23:17** 834
all the trees **w** were in the field, **Gn 23:17** 834
my journey on **w** I go successful; **Gn 24:42** 834
the field **w** Abraham purchased from **Gn 25:10** 834
Havilah to Shur **w** is east of Egypt **Gn 25:18** 834
in the land of **w** I shall tell you. **Gn 26:2** 834
and I will establish the oath **w** I **Gn 26:3** 834
Now all the wells **w** his father's **Gn 26:15** 834
Isaac dug again the wells of water **w** **Gn 26:18** 834
names **w** his father had given them. **Gn 26:18** 834
him about the well **w** they had dug, **Gn 26:32** 834
son, **w** were with her in the house, **Gn 27:15** 834
and the bread, **w** she had made, **Gn 27:17** 834
of a field **w** the LORD has blessed; **Gn 27:27** 834
with **w** his father had blessed him; **Gn 27:41** 834
w God gave to Abraham." **Gn 28:4** 834
the land on **w** you lie, I will give **Gn 28:13** 834
w I have set up as a pillar, **Gn 28:22** 834
the service **w** you shall serve with me **Gn 29:27** 834
service **w** I have rendered you." **Gn 30:26** 834
the white **w** *was* in the rods. **Gn 30:37** 834
He set the rods **w** he had **Gn 30:38** 834
goats **w** were mating *were* striped, **Gn 31:10**
goats **w** are mating are striped, **Gn 31:12**
"Surely all the wealth **w** God has **Gn 31:16** 834
his property **w** he had gathered, **Gn 31:18** 834
his acquired livestock **w** he had **Gn 31:18** 834
"That **w** was torn *of beasts* I did **Gn 31:39**
w I have set between you and me. **Gn 31:51** 834
company **w** is left will escape." **Gn 32:8**
the faithfulness **w** You have shown to **Gn 32:10** 834
w is too great to be numbered.' " **Gn 32:12** 834
w is on the socket of the thigh, **Gn 32:32** 834
all this company **w** I have met?" **Gn 33:8** 834
my gift **w** has been brought to you, **Gn 33:11** 834
w are nursing are a care to me. **Gn 33:13**
w is in the land of Canaan, **Gn 33:18** 834
and that **w** was in the city and **Gn 34:28** 834
city and that **w** was in the field; **Gn 34:28** 834
the foreign gods **w** are among you, **Gn 35:2** 834
all the foreign gods **w** they had and **Gn 35:4** 834
the rings **w** were in their ears, **Gn 35:4** 834
under the oak **w** was near Shechem. **Gn 35:4** 834
the cities **w** were around them, **Gn 35:5** 834
w is in the land of Canaan, he and **Gn 35:6** 834
w I gave to Abraham and Isaac, **Gn 35:12** 834
all his goods **w** he had acquired in the **Gn 36:6** 834
listen to this dream **w** I have had; **Gn 37:6** 834
Enaim, **w** is on the road to Timnah; **Gn 38:14** 834
anything except the food **w** he ate. **Gn 39:6** 834
of his wife, **w** she spoke to him, **Gn 39:19** 834
w *was* Pharaoh's birthday, that **Gn 40:20**
the seven years of famine **w** will occur **Gn 41:36** 834
w occurred in the land of Egypt and **Gn 41:48** 834
When the seven years of plenty **w** **Gn 41:53** 834
the dreams **w** he had about them, **Gn 42:9** 834
w they had brought from Egypt, **Gn 43:2** 834
to him the present **w** was in their hand **Gn 43:26** 834
the one from **w** my lord drinks and **Gn 44:5** 834
w he indeed uses for divination? **Gn 44:5**
the money **w** we found in the mouth **Gn 44:8** 834
in **w** there will be neither plowing **Gn 45:6** 834
is my mouth **w** is speaking to you. **Gn 45:12**
w Pharaoh had sent to carry him. **Gn 46:5** 834
w they had acquired in the land of **Gn 46:6** 834
for the grain **w** they bought, **Gn 47:14** 834
the allotment **w** Pharaoh gave them. **Gn 47:22** 834
w I took from the hand of the **Gn 48:22** 834
of Machpelah, **w** is before Mamre, **Gn 49:30** 834
w Abraham bought along with the **Gn 49:30** 834
in my grave **w** I dug for myself in **Gn 50:5** 834
of Atad, **w** is beyond the Jordan, **Gn 50:10** 834
w is beyond the Jordan. **Gn 50:11** 834
w Abraham had bought along with **Gn 50:13** 834
all the wrong **w** we did to him!" **Gn 50:15** 834
to the land **w** He promised on oath to **Gn 50:24** 834
all their labors **w** they rigorously **Ex 1:14** 834
for the place on **w** you are **Ex 3:5** 834
with **w** the Egyptians are oppressing **Ex 3:9** 834
w I shall do in the midst of it; **Ex 3:20** 834
and the water **w** you take from the **Ex 4:9** 834
w you shall perform the signs." **Ex 4:17** 834
w I have put in your power; **Ex 4:21** 834
the LORD with **w** He had sent him, **Ex 4:28** 834
w the LORD had spoken to Moses. **Ex 4:30** 834
w they were making previously, **Ex 5:8** 834
the land in **w** they sojourned. **Ex 6:4** 834
land **w** I swore to give to Abraham, **Ex 6:8** 834
w will come up and go into your **Ex 8:3**
w He had inflicted upon Pharaoh. **Ex 8:12** 834
also the ground on **w** they *dwell*. **Ex 8:21** 834
your livestock **w** are in the field, **Ex 9:3** 834
they will eat every tree **w** sprouts for **Ex 10:5**
something **w** neither your fathers **Ex 10:6** 834
west wind **w** took up the locusts and **Ex 10:19**
even a darkness **w** may be felt." **Ex 10:21**
of the houses in **w** they eat it. **Ex 12:7** 834
it in the blood **w** is in the basin, **Ex 12:22** 834
the land **w** the LORD will give you, **Ex 12:25** 834
They baked the dough **w** they **Ex 12:39** 834
day in **w** you went out from Egypt, **Ex 13:3** 834
w He swore to your fathers to give **Ex 13:5** 834
see the salvation of the LORD **w** He **Ex 14:13** 834
Israel saw the great power **w** the LORD **Ex 14:31** 834
w You have made for Your dwelling, **Ex 15:17**
w Your hands have established. **Ex 15:17**
you **w** I have put on the Egyptians; **Ex 15:26** 834
Sin, **w** is between Elim and Sinai, **Ex 16:1** 834
w you grumble against Him. **Ex 16:8** 834
w the LORD has given you to eat. **Ex 16:15** 834
staff with **w** you struck the Nile, **Ex 17:5** 834
w the LORD had done to Israel, **Ex 18:9** 834
the way in **w** they are to walk and **Ex 18:20**
w the LORD had commanded him. **Ex 19:7** 834
w the LORD your God gives you. **Ex 20:12** 834
w you are to set before them: **Ex 21:1** 834
you a place to **w** he may flee. **Ex 21:13** 834
any lost thing about **w** one says, **Ex 22:9** 834
everything **w** I have said to you, **Ex 23:13** 834
into the place **w** I have prepared. **Ex 23:20** 834
"All the words **w** the LORD has **Ex 24:3** 834
w the LORD has made with you in **Ex 24:8** 834
the commandment **w** I have written **Ex 24:12** 834
w you are to raise from them: **Ex 25:3** 834
the testimony **w** I shall give you. **Ex 25:16** 834
testimony **w** I will give to you. **Ex 25:21** 834
from between the two cherubim **w** **Ex 25:22** 834
corners **w** are on its four feet. **Ex 25:26** 834
bowls with **w** to pour drink offerings; **Ex 25:29** 834
w was shown to you on the mountain. **Ex 25:40** 834
the tabernacle according to its plan **w** **Ex 26:30** 834
veil **w** is before the testimony, **Ex 27:21** 834
the garments **w** they shall make: **Ex 28:4** 834
skillfully woven band, **w** is on it, **Ex 28:8** 834
w is toward the inner side of the **Ex 28:26** 834
w the sons of Israel consecrate, **Ex 28:38** 834
bread **w** is *set* before the LORD; **Ex 29:23** 834
the thigh of the heave offering **w** was **Ex 29:27** 834
and **w** was offered from the ram of **Ex 29:27** 834
from the one **w** was for Aaron and **Ex 29:27** 834
from the one **w** was for his sons. **Ex 29:27** 834
eat those things by **w** atonement was **Ex 29:33** 834
for poles with **w** to carry it. **Ex 30:4** 1992a
"The incense **w** you shall **Ex 30:37** 834
with **w** to carry on their **Ex 31:10**
w are in the ears of your wives, **Ex 32:2** 834
gold rings **w** were in their ears and **Ex 32:3** 834
from the way **w** I commanded them. **Ex 32:8** 834
and all this land of **w** I have **Ex 32:13** 834
the harm **w** He said He would do **Ex 32:14** 834
w were written on both sides; **Ex 32:15**
He took the calf **w** they had **Ex 32:20** 834
Your book **w** You have written!" **Ex 32:32** 834
with the calf **w** Aaron had made. **Ex 32:35** 834
the land of **w** I swore to Abraham, **Ex 33:1** 834
of meeting **w** was outside the camp. **Ex 33:7** 834
this thing of **w** you have spoken; **Ex 33:17** 834
former tablets **w** you shattered. **Ex 34:1** 834
I will perform miracles **w** have not **Ex 34:10** 834
of the land into **w** you are going, **Ex 34:12** 834
thing **w** the LORD has commanded, **Ex 35:4** 834
w the LORD had commanded through **Ex 35:29** 834
from Moses all the contributions **w** **Ex 36:3** 834
from the work **w** he was performing, **Ex 36:4** 834
work **w** the LORD commanded *us* to **Ex 36:5** 834
the utensils **w** were on the table, **Ex 37:16** 834
with **w** to pour out drink **Ex 37:16** 834
for poles with **w** to carry it. **Ex 37:27** 1992a
of the altar, with **w** to carry it. **Ex 38:7** 1992a
holy garments **w** were for Aaron, **Ex 39:1** 834
The skillfully woven band **w** **Ex 39:5** 834
edge **w** was next to the ephod. **Ex 39:19** 834
and the suet over the wood **w** is on **Lv 1:8** 834
on the wood **w** is on the fire that is **Lv 1:12** 834
on the wood **w** is on the fire; **Lv 1:17** 834
bring in the grain offering **w** is made **Lv 2:8** 834
offering, **w** you bring to the LORD, **Lv 2:11** 834
is on them, **w** is on the loins, **Lv 3:4** 834
w he shall remove with the kidneys. **Lv 3:4** 834
w is on the wood that is on the **Lv 3:5** 834
the entire fat tail **w** he shall **Lv 3:9**
is on them, **w** is on the loins, **Lv 3:10** 834
w he shall remove with the kidneys. **Lv 3:10** 834
is on them, **w** is on the loins, **Lv 3:15** 834
w he shall remove with the kidneys. **Lv 3:15** 834
things **w** the LORD has commanded **Lv 4:2** 834
fragrant incense **w** is before the LORD **Lv 4:7** 834
base of the altar of burnt offering **w** is **Lv 4:7** 834
all the fat **w** is on the entrails, **Lv 4:8** 834
is on them, **w** is on the loins, **Lv 4:9** 834
w he shall remove with the kidneys **Lv 4:9** 834
w the LORD has commanded not to be **Lv 4:13** 834
when the sin **w** they have committed **Lv 4:14** 834
the altar **w** is before the LORD in the **Lv 4:18** 834
base of the altar of burnt offering **w** **Lv 4:18** 834
w the LORD his God has commanded **Lv 4:22** 834
if his sin **w** he has committed is **Lv 4:23** 834
w the LORD has commanded not to be **Lv 4:27** 834
if his sin **w** he has committed **Lv 4:28** 834
for his sin **w** he has committed. **Lv 4:28** 834
to his sin **w** he has committed, **Lv 4:35** 834
may be with **w** he becomes unclean, **Lv 5:3** 834
confess that in **w** he has sinned. **Lv 5:5** 834
for his sin **w** he has committed, **Lv 5:6** 834
for that in **w** he has sinned, **Lv 5:7** 834
who shall offer first that **w** is **Lv 5:8** 834
for his sin **w** he has committed, **Lv 5:10** 834
offering for that **w** he has sinned, **Lv 5:11** 834
his sin **w** he has committed from one **Lv 5:13** 834
He shall make restitution for that **w** he **Lv 5:16** 834
does any of the things **w** the LORD **Lv 5:17** 834
concerning his error in **w** he sinned **Lv 5:18** 834
deposit **w** was entrusted to him or **Lv 6:4** 834
him or the lost thing **w** he found, **Lv 6:4** 834
anything about **w** he swore falsely; **Lv 6:5** 834
forgiven for any one of the things **w** **Lv 6:7** 834
he shall take up the ashes *to* **w** the fire **Lv 6:10** 834
"This is the offering **w** Aaron and **Lv 6:20** 834
w it was boiled shall be broken; **Lv 6:28** 834
'But no sin offering **w** any of **Lv 6:30** 834
is on them, **w** is on the loins, **Lv 7:4** 834
burnt offering **w** he has presented. **Lv 7:8** 834
peace offerings **w** shall be presented **Lv 7:11** 834
offerings **w** belong to the LORD, **Lv 7:20** 834
offerings **w** belong to the LORD, **Lv 7:21** 834
'Also the fat of *an animal* **w** dies and **Lv 7:24**
eats the fat of the animal from **w** an **Lv 7:25** 834
'This is that **w** is consecrated to **Lv 7:35** 4888b
consecrated to Aaron and that **w** is **Lv 7:35** 4888b
w the LORD commanded Moses at **Lv 7:38** 834
w the LORD has commanded to do." **Lv 8:5** 834
ephod, with **w** he tied *it* to him. **Lv 8:7**
of the blood **w** was on the altar and **Lv 8:30** 834
eat it there together with the bread **w** **Lv 8:31** 834

things **w** the LORD had commanded	Lv 8:36	834
"This is the thing **w** the LORD has	Lv 9:6	834
sin offering **w** was for himself.	Lv 9:8	834
sin offering **w** was for the people,	Lv 9:15	834
offerings **w** was for the people;	Lv 9:18	834
LORD, **w** He had not commanded them.	Lv 10:1	834
w the LORD has brought about.	Lv 10:6	834
the statutes **w** the LORD has spoken to	Lv 10:11	834
'These are the creatures **w** you may	Lv 11:2	834
these, among those **w** chew the cud,	Lv 11:4	
or among those **w** divide the hoof:	Lv 11:4	
insects **w** walk on *all* fours:	Lv 11:21	
those **w** have above their feet	Lv 11:21	834
legs with **w** to jump on the earth.	Lv 11:21	1992a
'But all other winged insects **w**	Lv 11:23	834
all the animals **w** divide the hoof but	Lv 11:26	834
split *hoof,* or **w** do not chew cud,	Lv 11:26	
things **w** swarm on the earth:	Lv 11:29	
'Also anything on **w** one of them	Lv 11:32	834
any article of **w** use is made	Lv 11:32	834
into **w** one of them may fall,	Lv 11:33	834
'Any of the food **w** may be eaten,	Lv 11:34	834
may be eaten, on **w** water comes,	Lv 11:34	834
and any liquid **w** may be drunk in	Lv 11:34	834
on **w** part of their carcass may	Lv 11:35	834
seed for sowing **w** is to be sown,	Lv 11:37	834
animals dies **w** you have for food.	Lv 11:39	834
the creature **w** is not to be eaten.	Lv 11:47	834
during **w** he has the infection;	Lv 13:46	834
purpose for **w** the leather is used,	Lv 13:51	834
of leather in **w** the mark occurs,	Lv 13:52	834
the thing in **w** the mark occurs and	Lv 13:54	834
or any article of leather from **w**	Lv 13:58	1992a
remaining oil **w** is in his palm,	Lv 14:17	834
pigeons **w** are within his means,	Lv 14:22	834
pigeons, **w** are within his means.	Lv 14:30	834
w I give you for a possession,	Lv 14:34	834
'Every bed on **w** the person with	Lv 15:4	834
on **w** he sits becomes unclean.	Lv 15:4	834
and whoever sits on the thing on **w**	Lv 15:6	834
'Every saddle on **w** the person	Lv 15:9	834
then touches any of the things **w** were	Lv 15:10	834
an earthenware vessel **w** the person	Lv 15:12	834
on **w** there is seminal emission,	Lv 15:17	834
'Everything also on **w** she lies	Lv 15:20	834
on **w** she sits shall be unclean.	Lv 15:20	834
Whoever touches any thing on **w** she	Lv 15:22	834
on the thing on **w** she is sitting,	Lv 15:23	834
bed on **w** he lies shall be unclean.	Lv 15:24	834
'Any bed on **w** she lies all the	Lv 15:26	834
on **w** she sits shall be unclean,	Lv 15:26	834
the mercy seat **w** is on the ark,	Lv 16:2	834
the sin offering **w** is for himself,	Lv 16:6	834
on **w** the lot for the LORD fell,	Lv 16:9	834
"But the goat on **w** the lot for	Lv 16:10	834
the sin offering **w** is for himself and	Lv 16:11	834
the sin offering **w** is for himself.	Lv 16:11	834
sin offering **w** is for the people,	Lv 16:15	834
tent of meeting **w** abides with them	Lv 16:16	
take off the linen garments **w** he put	Lv 16:23	834
of Israel may bring their sacrifices **w**	Lv 17:5	834
with **w** they play the harlot.	Lv 17:7	834
a beast or a bird **w** may be eaten,	Lv 17:13	834
any person eats *an animal* **w** dies or	Lv 17:15	5038
by **w** a man may live if he does	Lv 18:5	834
for by all these the nations **w** I	Lv 18:24	834
the nation **w** has been before you.	Lv 18:28	834
any of the abominable customs **w**	Lv 18:30	834
for his sin **w** he has committed,	Lv 19:22	834
and the sin **w** he has committed	Lv 19:22	834
so that the land to **w** I am	Lv 20:22	834
w I will drive out before you,	Lv 20:23	834
w I have separated for you as	Lv 20:25	834
of Israel, **w** they dedicate to Me,	Lv 22:2	834
holy *gifts* **w** the sons of Israel dedicate	Lv 22:3	834
things by **w** he is made unclean,	Lv 22:5	834
w dies or is torn *by beasts,*	Lv 22:8	5038
Israel **w** they offer to the LORD,	Lv 22:15	834
w they present to the LORD for a	Lv 22:18	834
'In respect to an ox or a lamb **w**	Lv 22:23	
'The LORD's appointed times **w** you	Lv 23:2	834
holy convocations **w** you shall	Lv 23:4	834
'When you enter the land **w** I am	Lv 23:10	834
appointed times of the LORD **w** you	Lv 23:37	834
offerings, **w** you give to the LORD.	Lv 23:38	834
into the land **w** I shall give you,	Lv 25:2	834
w have no surrounding wall shall	Lv 25:31	834
the cities **w** are their possession.	Lv 25:32	
w will bereave you of your	Lv 26:22	
a sword **w** will execute vengeance	Lv 26:25	
w it did not observe on your sabbaths,	Lv 26:35	834
w they committed against Me,	Lv 26:40	834
laws **w** the LORD established between	Lv 26:46	834
if it is an animal of the kind **w** men	Lv 27:9	834
of the kind **w** men do not present as	Lv 27:11	834
the LORD a field **w** he has bought,	Lv 27:22	
w is not a part of the field of	Lv 27:22	834
w as a firstborn belongs to the	Lv 27:26	834
anything **w** a man sets apart to the	Lv 27:28	834
These are the commandments **w** the	Lv 27:34	834
w the LORD had commanded Moses,	Nu 1:54	834
w is around the tabernacle and the	Nu 3:26	834
sanctuary with **w** they minister,	Nu 3:31	834
oil vessels, by **w** they serve it;	Nu 4:9	834
w they serve in the sanctuary,	Nu 4:12	834
also put on it all its utensils by **w** they	Nu 4:14	834
w the sons of Kohath are to carry.	Nu 4:15	
doorway of the gate of the court **w** is	Nu 4:26	834
his sins **w** he has committed,	Nu 5:7	834
the restitution **w** is made for the	Nu 5:8	
by **w** atonement is made for him.	Nu 5:8	834
w they offer to the priest,	Nu 5:9	834
w is the grain offering of	Nu 5:18	1931
so that the water **w** brings a curse	Nu 5:24	
that the water **w** brings a curse	Nu 5:27	
days are fulfilled for **w** he separated	Nu 6:5	834
and put *it* on the fire **w** is under the	Nu 6:18	834
according to his vow **w** he takes,	Nu 6:21	834
w they carried on the shoulder.	Nu 7:9	
w the LORD had shown Moses,	Nu 8:4	834
w *formed* the rear guard for all	Nu 10:25	
to the place of **w** the LORD said,	Nu 10:29	834
w we used to eat free in Egypt,	Nu 11:5	834
to the land **w** You swore to	Nu 11:12	834
in **w** we have acted foolishly and	Nu 12:11	834
foolishly and in **w** we have sinned.	Nu 12:11	834
w I am going to give to the sons	Nu 13:2	834
How is the land in **w** they live,	Nu 13:19	834
how are the cities in **w** they live,	Nu 13:19	834, 1992a
because of the cluster **w** the sons	Nu 13:24	834
of the land **w** they had spied out,	Nu 13:32	834
"The land through **w** we have gone,	Nu 13:32	834
"The land **w** we passed through to	Nu 14:7	834
land **w** flows with milk and honey.	Nu 14:8	834
despite all the signs **w** I have	Nu 14:11	834
land **w** He promised them by oath,	Nu 14:16	834
w I performed in Egypt and in the	Nu 14:22	834
land **w** I swore to their fathers,	Nu 14:23	834
bring into the land **w** he entered,	Nu 14:24	834
w they are making against Me.	Nu 14:27	834
land in **w** I swore to settle you,	Nu 14:30	834
know the land **w** you have rejected.	Nu 14:31	834
of days **w** you spied out the land,	Nu 14:34	834
place **w** the LORD has promised."	Nu 14:40	834
are to live, **w** I am giving you,	Nu 15:2	834
w the LORD has spoken to Moses,	Nu 15:22	834
after **w** you played the harlot,	Nu 15:39	834
the priest took the bronze censers **w**	Nu 16:39	834
w they shall render to Me,	Nu 18:9	834
of those **w** they give to the LORD,	Nu 18:12	834
land, **w** they bring to the LORD,	Nu 18:13	834
animal, **w** they offer to the LORD,	Nu 18:15	834
the sanctuary, **w** is twenty gerahs.	Nu 18:16	1931
w the sons of Israel offer to the	Nu 18:19	834
for their service **w** they perform,	Nu 18:21	834
w they offer as an offering to the	Nu 18:24	834
tithe **w** I have given you from them	Nu 18:26	834
w you receive from the sons of	Nu 18:28	834
the law **w** the LORD has commanded,	Nu 19:2	834
red heifer in **w** is no defect	Nu 19:2	834
on **w** a yoke has never been placed.	Nu 19:2	834
w has no covering tied down on it,	Nu 19:15	834
the land **w** I have given them."	Nu 20:12	834
not enter the land **w** I have given to	Nu 20:24	834
the wilderness **w** is opposite Moab,	Nu 21:11	834
w is in the wilderness that comes	Nu 21:13	834
"The well, **w** the leaders sank,	Nu 21:18	
W the nobles of the people dug,	Nu 21:18	
Pisgah **w** overlooks the wasteland.	Nu 21:20	
to Nophah, **W** *reaches* to Medeba."	Nu 21:30	834
at Pethor, **w** is near the River,	Nu 22:5	834
w I speak to you shall you do."	Nu 22:20	834
"Am I not your donkey on **w** you	Nu 22:30	834
the word **w** I tell you."	Nu 22:35	834
of Moab, **w** is on the Arnon border,	Nu 22:36	834
of Peor **w** overlooks the wasteland.	Nu 23:28	
with **w** they have deceived you in	Nu 25:18	834
and see the land **w** I have given to	Nu 27:12	834
like sheep **w** have no shepherd."	Nu 27:17	834
w you shall offer to the LORD:	Nu 28:3	834
'It is a continual burnt offering **w** was	Nu 28:6	
w is for a continual burnt	Nu 28:23	834
year old, **w** are without defect;	Nu 29:13	
the word **w** the LORD has commanded.	Nu 30:1	834
by **w** she has bound herself,	Nu 30:4	834
and every obligation by **w** she has	Nu 30:4	834
her vows or her obligations by **w** she	Nu 30:5	834
lips by **w** she has bound herself,	Nu 30:6	834
her obligations by **w** she has bound	Nu 30:7	834
then he shall annul her vow **w** she	Nu 30:8	834
lips by **w** she has bound herself;	Nu 30:8	834
by **w** she has bound herself,	Nu 30:9	834
w she bound herself shall stand.	Nu 30:11	834
all her obligations **w** are on her;	Nu 30:14	834
w the LORD commanded Moses,	Nu 30:16	834
w are by the Jordan	Nu 31:12	834
w the LORD has commanded Moses:	Nu 31:21	834
booty that remained from the spoil **w**	Nu 31:32	834
from **w** the LORD's levy was 72;	Nu 31:38	
from **w** the LORD's levy was 61;	Nu 31:39	
Moses gave the levy **w** *was* the	Nu 31:41	
w Moses separated from the men who	Nu 31:42	834
w they offered up to the LORD,	Nu 31:52	834
the land **w** the LORD conquered	Nu 32:4	834
land **w** the LORD has given them?	Nu 32:7	834
land **w** the LORD had given them.	Nu 32:9	834
see the land **w** I swore to Abraham,	Nu 32:11	834
names to the cities **w** they built.	Nu 32:38	834
by **w** they came out from the land	Nu 33:1	834
w is on the edge of the wilderness.	Nu 33:6	834
to Pi-hahiroth, **w** faces Baal-zephon,	Nu 33:7	834
you in the land in **w** you live.	Nu 33:55	834
w the LORD has commanded to give	Nu 34:13	834
The pasture lands of the cities **w** you	Nu 35:4	834
"The cities **w** you shall give	Nu 35:6	834
w you shall give for the manslayer	Nu 35:6	834
"All the cities **w** you shall give	Nu 35:7	834
"As for the cities **w** you shall	Nu 35:8	834
to his possession **w** he inherits."	Nu 35:8	834
'The cities **w** you are to give	Nu 35:13	834
in the hand, by **w** he will die,	Nu 35:17	834
in the hand, by **w** he might die,	Nu 35:18	834
his city of refuge to **w** he fled;	Nu 35:25	834
city of refuge to **w** he may flee,	Nu 35:26	834
not pollute the land in **w** you are;	Nu 35:33	834
not defile the land in **w** you live,	Nu 35:34	834
live, in the midst of **w** I dwell;	Nu 35:34	834
of the tribe to **w** they belong;	Nu 36:3	834
of the tribe to **w** they belong;	Nu 36:4	834
ordinances **w** the LORD commanded	Nu 36:13	834
These are the words **w** Moses spoke	Dt 1:1	834
the land **w** the LORD swore to give	Dt 1:8	834
w you have said to do is good.'	Dt 1:14	834
and terrible wilderness **w** you saw on	Dt 1:19	834
country of the Amorites **w** the LORD	Dt 1:20	834
of the way by **w** we should go up and	Dt 1:22	834
and the cities **w** we shall enter.'	Dt 1:22	834
'It is a good land **w** the LORD our	Dt 1:25	834
in all the way **w** you have walked until	Dt 1:31	834
you the way in **w** you should go.	Dt 1:33	834
w I swore to give your fathers,	Dt 1:35	834
the land on **w** he has set foot,	Dt 1:36	834
w the LORD gave to them.)	Dt 2:12	834
cross over the Jordan into the land **w**	Dt 2:29	834
of the cities **w** we had captured.	Dt 2:35	834
"From Aroer **w** is on the edge of	Dt 2:36	834
from the city **w** is in the valley,	Dt 2:36	834
city **w** we did not take from them:	Dt 3:4	834
w is by the valley of Arnon,	Dt 3:12	834
in your cities **w** I have given you,	Dt 3:19	834
and they also possess the land **w**	Dt 3:20	834
possession **w** I have given you.'	Dt 3:20	834
into **w** you are about to cross.	Dt 3:21	834
the land **w** you will see.'	Dt 3:28	834
w I am teaching you to perform,	Dt 4:1	834
possession of the land **w** the LORD,	Dt 4:1	834
to the word **w** I am commanding you,	Dt 4:2	834
the LORD your God **w** I command you.	Dt 4:2	834
w I am setting before you today?	Dt 4:8	834
the things **w** your eyes have seen and	Dt 4:9	834
w He commanded you to perform,	Dt 4:13	834
those **w** the LORD your God has	Dt 4:19	834
that I would not enter the good land **w**	Dt 4:21	834
LORD your God **w** He made with you,	Dt 4:23	834
in the form of anything *against* **w** the	Dt 4:23	834
and do that **w** is evil in the sight	Dt 4:25	7451a
w neither see nor hear nor eat nor	Dt 4:28	834
your fathers **w** He swore to them.	Dt 4:31	834
the former days **w** were before you,	Dt 4:32	834
w I am giving you today,	Dt 4:40	834
that you may live long on the land **w**	Dt 4:40	834
Now this is the law **w** Moses set	Dt 4:44	834
w Moses spoke to the sons of Israel,	Dt 4:45	834
w is on the edge of the valley of	Dt 4:48	834
statutes and the ordinances **w** I am	Dt 5:1	834
w the LORD your God gives you.	Dt 5:16	834
people **w** they have spoken to you.	Dt 5:28	834
judgments **w** you shall teach them,	Dt 5:31	834
land **w** I give them to possess.'	Dt 5:31	834
"You shall walk in all the way **w**	Dt 5:33	834
in the land **w** you will possess.	Dt 5:33	834
the statutes and the judgments **w**	Dt 6:1	834
His commandments **w** I command	Dt 6:2	834
w I am commanding you today,	Dt 6:6	834
land **w** He swore to your fathers,	Dt 6:10	834
cities **w** you did not build,	Dt 6:10	834
good things **w** you did not fill,	Dt 6:11	834
hewn cisterns **w** you did not dig,	Dt 6:11	834
olive trees **w** you did not plant,	Dt 6:11	834
statutes **w** He has commanded you.	Dt 6:17	834
go in and possess the good land **w** the	Dt 6:18	834
w the LORD our God commanded you?'	Dt 6:20	834
w He had sworn to our fathers.'	Dt 6:23	834
w He swore to your forefathers,	Dt 7:8	834
w I am commanding you today,	Dt 7:11	834
w He swore to your forefathers.	Dt 7:12	834
in the land **w** He swore to your	Dt 7:13	834
of Egypt **w** you have known,	Dt 7:15	834
the great trials **w** your eyes saw	Dt 7:19	834
the outstretched arm by **w** the LORD	Dt 7:19	834
and go in and possess the land **w**	Dt 8:1	834
remember all the way **w** the LORD	Dt 8:2	834
you with manna **w** you did not know,	Dt 8:3	834
in **w** you will not lack anything;	Dt 8:9	
the good land **w** He has given you.	Dt 8:10	834
w I am commanding you today;	Dt 8:11	834
manna **w** your fathers did not know,	Dt 8:16	834
w He swore to your fathers,	Dt 8:18	834
in order to confirm the oath **w** the	Dt 9:5	834
w the LORD had made with you,	Dt 9:9	834
and on them *were* all the words **w**	Dt 9:10	834
from the way **w** I commanded them;	Dt 9:12	834
way **w** the LORD had commanded you.	Dt 9:16	834
because of all your sin **w** you had	Dt 9:18	834
and hot displeasure with **w** the LORD	Dt 9:19	834
thing, the calf **w** you had made,	Dt 9:21	834
the land **w** I have given you,'	Dt 9:23	834
w I did because the LORD had said	Dt 9:25	834
w You brought us may say,	Dt 9:28	834
the land **w** He had promised them	Dt 9:28	834
former tablets **w** you shattered,	Dt 10:2	834
the Ten Commandments **w** the LORD	Dt 10:4	834
tablets in the ark **w** I had made;	Dt 10:5	834
may go in and possess the land **w** I	Dt 10:11	834
His statutes **w** I am commanding you	Dt 10:13	834
for you **w** your eyes have seen.	Dt 10:21	834

and His signs and His works **w** He	Dt 11:3	834
great work of the LORD **w** He did.	Dt 11:7	834
w I am commanding you today,	Dt 11:8	834
the land into **w** you are about to cross	Dt 11:8	834
may prolong *your* days on the land **w**	Dt 11:9	834
into **w** you are entering to possess	Dt 11:10	834
the land of Egypt from **w** you came,	Dt 11:10	834
"But the land into **w** you are	Dt 11:11	834
for **w** the LORD your God cares;	Dt 11:12	834
w I am commanding you today,	Dt 11:13	834
land **w** the LORD is giving you.	Dt 11:17	834
sons may be multiplied on the land **w**	Dt 11:21	834
commandment **w** I am commanding	Dt 11:22	834
"Every place on **w** the sole of	Dt 11:24	834
on all the land on **w** you set foot,	Dt 11:25	834
God, **w** I am commanding you today;	Dt 11:27	834
way **w** I am commanding you today,	Dt 11:28	834
other gods **w** you have not known.	Dt 11:28	834
Jordan to go in to possess the land **w**	Dt 11:31	834
w I am setting before you today.	Dt 11:32	834
the judgments **w** you shall carefully	Dt 12:1	834
observe in the land **w** the LORD,	Dt 12:1	834
seek *the LORD* at the place **w**	Dt 12:5	834
rejoice in all your undertakings in **w**	Dt 12:7	834
the inheritance **w** the LORD your God	Dt 12:9	834
live in the land **w** the LORD your God	Dt 12:10	834
in **w** the LORD your God will choose	Dt 12:11	834
w you will vow to the LORD.	Dt 12:11	834
but in the place **w** the LORD	Dt 12:14	834
LORD your God **w** He has given you;	Dt 12:15	834
your votive offerings **w** you vow,	Dt 12:17	834
w the LORD your God will choose,	Dt 12:18	834
"If the place **w** the LORD your God	Dt 12:21	834
flock **w** the LORD has given you,	Dt 12:21	834
"Only your holy things **w** you may	Dt 12:26	834
to the place **w** the LORD chooses.	Dt 12:26	834
all these words **w** I command you,	Dt 12:28	834
cuts off before you the nations **w** you	Dt 12:29	834
for every abominable act **w** the	Dt 12:31	834
concerning **w** he spoke to you,	Dt 13:2	834
to seduce you from the way in **w**	Dt 13:5	834
w the LORD your God is giving you	Dt 13:12	834
"Nothing from that **w** is put	Dt 13:17	2764a
w I am commanding you today,	Dt 13:18	834
are the animals **w** you may eat:	Dt 14:4	834
these among those **w** chew the cud,	Dt 14:7	834
are the ones **w** you shall not eat:	Dt 14:12	834
not eat anything **w** dies *of itself.*	Dt 14:21	5038
w comes out of the field every	Dt 14:22	834
place **w** the LORD your God chooses.	Dt 14:25	834
the work of your hand **w** you do.	Dt 14:29	834
will surely bless you in the land **w**	Dt 15:4	834
w I am commanding you today.	Dt 15:5	834
w the LORD your God is giving you,	Dt 15:7	834
in the place **w** the LORD chooses.	Dt 15:20	834
and none of the flesh **w** you	Dt 16:4	834
the Passover in any of your towns **w**	Dt 16:5	834
place **w** the LORD your God chooses.	Dt 16:7	834
w you shall give just as the LORD	Dt 16:10	834
in the place **w** the LORD chooses,	Dt 16:15	834
God in the place **w** He chooses,	Dt 16:16	834
LORD your God **w** He has given you.	Dt 16:17	834
all your towns **w** the LORD your God	Dt 16:18	834
possess the land **w** the LORD your	Dt 16:20	834
w you shall make for yourself.	Dt 16:21	834
pillar **w** the LORD your God hates.	Dt 16:22	834
w has a blemish *or* any defect,	Dt 17:1	834
w the LORD your God is giving you,	Dt 17:2	834
host, **w** I have not commanded,	Dt 17:3	834
place **w** the LORD your God chooses.	Dt 17:8	834
of the verdict **w** they declare to you	Dt 17:10	834
that place **w** the LORD chooses;	Dt 17:10	834
terms of the law **w** they teach you,	Dt 17:11	834
to the verdict **w** they tell you,	Dt 17:11	834
the word **w** they declare to you,	Dt 17:11	834
w the LORD your God gives you,	Dt 17:14	834
of **w** they shall give to the priest	Dt 18:3	834
to the place **w** the LORD chooses,	Dt 18:6	834
w the LORD your God gives you,	Dt 18:9	834
nations, **w** you shall dispossess,	Dt 18:14	834
words **w** he shall speak in My name,	Dt 18:19	834
My name **w** I have not commanded	Dt 18:20	834
or **w** he speaks in the name of	Dt 18:20	834
word **w** the LORD has not spoken?'	Dt 18:21	834
thing **w** the LORD has not spoken.	Dt 18:22	834
w the LORD your God gives you to	Dt 19:2	834
w the LORD your God will give you	Dt 19:3	834
and gives you all the land **w** He	Dt 19:8	834
w I command you today,	Dt 19:9	834
land **w** the LORD your God gives you	Dt 19:10	834
mark, **w** the ancestors have set,	Dt 19:14	834
in your inheritance **w** you will	Dt 19:14	834
or any sin **w** he has committed;	Dt 19:15	834
shall use the spoil of your enemies **w**	Dt 20:14	834
w are not of the cities of these	Dt 20:15	834
w they have done for their gods,	Dt 20:18	834
"Only the trees **w** you know are	Dt 20:20	834
land **w** the LORD your God gives you	Dt 21:1	834
cities **w** are around the slain one.	Dt 21:2	834
w is nearest to the slain man,	Dt 21:3	834
w has not been worked and which	Dt 21:3	834
and **w** has not pulled in a yoke;	Dt 21:3	834
w has not been plowed or sown,	Dt 21:4	834
that city **w** is nearest to the slain man	Dt 21:6	834
so that you do not defile your land **w**	Dt 21:23	834
w he has lost and you have found.	Dt 22:3	834
of the seed **w** you have sown and	Dt 22:9	834
garment with **w** you cover yourself.	Dt 22:12	834
in the place **w** he shall choose in	Dt 23:16	834

in the land **w** you are about to enter	Dt 23:20	834
you shall not bring sin on the land **w**	Dt 24:4	834
w the LORD your God gives you.	Dt 25:15	834
in the land **w** the LORD your God	Dt 25:19	834
when you enter the land **w** the LORD	Dt 26:1	834
of all the produce of the ground **w**	Dt 26:2	834
I have entered the land **w** the LORD	Dt 26:3	834
the produce of the ground **w** You,	Dt 26:10	834
you shall rejoice in all the good **w** the	Dt 26:11	834
w You have commanded me;	Dt 26:13	834
the ground **w** You have given us,	Dt 26:15	834
above all nations **w** He has made,	Dt 26:19	834
w I command you today.	Dt 27:1	834
w the LORD your God gives you,	Dt 27:2	834
w the LORD your God gives you,	Dt 27:3	834
statutes **w** I command you today."	Dt 27:10	834
w I command you today,	Dt 28:1	834
w the LORD your God gives you.	Dt 28:8	834
in the land **w** the LORD swore to	Dt 28:11	834
your God, **w** I charge you today,	Dt 28:13	834
the words **w** I command you today,	Dt 28:14	834
with **w** I charge you today,	Dt 28:15	834
"The heaven **w** is over your	Dt 28:23	834
and the earth **w** is under you,	Dt 28:23	834
itch, from **w** you cannot be healed.	Dt 28:27	834
from **w** you cannot be healed,	Dt 28:35	834
to a nation **w** neither you nor your	Dt 28:36	834
His statutes **w** He commanded you.	Dt 28:45	834
and fortified walls in **w** you trusted	Dt 28:52	834
your towns throughout your land **w**	Dt 28:52	834
by **w** your enemy will oppress you.	Dt 28:53	834
of his children **w** he will eat,	Dt 28:55	834
by **w** your enemy will oppress you	Dt 28:55	834
and toward her afterbirth **w** issues	Dt 28:57	834
by **w** your enemy will oppress you	Dt 28:57	834
law **w** are written in this book,	Dt 28:58	834
of Egypt of **w** you were afraid,	Dt 28:60	834
every sickness and every plague **w**,	Dt 28:61	834
w you or your fathers have not	Dt 28:64	834
dread of your heart **w** you dread,	Dt 28:67	834
of your eyes **w** you will see.	Dt 28:67	834
by the way about **w** I spoke to you,	Dt 28:68	834
the words of the covenant **w** the LORD	Dt 29:1	834
besides the covenant **w** He had made	Dt 29:1	834
trials **w** your eyes have seen,	Dt 29:3	834
and into His oath **w** the LORD your	Dt 29:12	834
the nations through **w** you passed;	Dt 29:16	834
and gold, **w** *they had* with them);	Dt 29:17	834
and every curse **w** is written in	Dt 29:20	834
curses of the covenant **w** are written	Dt 29:21	834
with **w** the LORD has afflicted it,	Dt 29:22	834
w the LORD overthrew in His anger	Dt 29:23	834
w He made with them when He	Dt 29:25	834
curse **w** is written in this book;	Dt 29:27	834
the curse **w** I have set before you,	Dt 30:1	834
the land **w** your fathers possessed,	Dt 30:5	834
w I command you today.	Dt 30:8	834
His statutes **w** are written in this book	Dt 30:10	834
"For this commandment **w** I command	Dt 30:11	834
that you may live in the land **w**	Dt 30:20	834
w I have commanded you.	Dt 31:5	834
into the land **w** the LORD has sworn	Dt 31:7	834
God at the place **w** He will choose,	Dt 31:11	834
as long as you live on the land **w** you	Dt 31:13	834
the midst of **w** they are going,	Dt 31:16	834
covenant **w** I have made with them.	Dt 31:16	834
of all the evil **w** they will do,	Dt 31:18	834
honey, **w** I swore to their fathers,	Dt 31:20	834
w they are developing today,	Dt 31:21	834
them into the land **w** I swore."	Dt 31:21	834
into the land **w** I swore to them,	Dt 31:23	834
the way **w** I have commanded you;	Dt 31:29	834
for you will do that **w** is evil in	Dt 31:29	7451a
The rock in **w** they sought refuge?	Dt 32:37	834
with **w** I am warning you today,	Dt 32:46	834
w you shall command your sons to	Dt 32:46	834
w you are about to cross the	Dt 32:47	834
w is in the land of Moab opposite	Dt 32:49	834
w I am giving to the sons of	Dt 32:49	834
into the land **w** I am giving the	Dt 32:52	834
Now this is the blessing with **w**	Dt 33:1	834
of Pisgah, **w** is opposite Jericho.	Dt 34:1	834
is the land **w** I swore to Abraham,	Dt 34:4	834
for all the signs and wonders **w**	Dt 34:11	834
the great terror **w** Moses performed	Dt 34:12	834
to the land **w** I am giving to them,	Jos 1:2	834
on **w** the sole of your foot treads,	Jos 1:3	834
land **w** I swore to their fathers to give	Jos 1:6	834
do according to all the law **w** Moses	Jos 1:7	834
to go in to possess the land **w** the	Jos 1:11	834
"Remember the word **w** Moses the	Jos 1:13	834
your cattle shall remain in the land **w**	Jos 1:14	834
and they also possess the land **w**	Jos 1:15	834
and possess that **w** Moses the	Jos 1:15	834
hidden them in the stalks of flax **w**	Jos 2:6	834
to you **w** you have made us swear,	Jos 2:17	834
window through **w** you let us down,	Jos 2:18	834
oath **w** you have made us swear."	Jos 2:20	834
know the way by **w** you shall go,	Jos 3:4	834
and the waters **w** are flowing down	Jos 3:13	834
the waters **w** were flowing	Jos 3:16	834
and those **w** were flowing down	Jos 3:16	834
Those twelve stones **w** they had	Jos 4:20	834
w He dried up before us until we	Jos 4:23	834
He would not let them see the land **w**	Jos 5:6	834
Jericho to Ai, **w** is near Beth-aven,	Jos 7:2	834
My covenant **w** I commanded them.	Jos 7:11	834
And it shall be that the tribe **w**	Jos 7:14	834
and the family **w** the LORD takes	Jos 7:14	834

and the household **w** the LORD takes	Jos 7:14	834
did not withdraw his hand with **w** he	Jos 8:26	834
LORD **w** He had commanded Joshua.	Jos 8:27	834
on **w** no man had wielded an iron	Jos 8:31	834
law of Moses, **w** he had written,	Jos 8:32	834
w Joshua did not read before all the	Jos 8:35	834
wineskins **w** we filled were new,	Jos 9:13	834
for the oath **w** we swore to them."	Jos 9:20	834
in the place **w** He would choose.	Jos 9:27	834
except Hazor alone, **w** Joshua burned.	Jos 11:13	834
There was not a city **w** made peace	Jos 11:19	834
w is on the edge of the valley of	Jos 12:2	834
Mount Halak, **w** rises toward Seir;	Jos 12:7	834
king of Ai, **w** is beside Bethel,	Jos 12:9	834
the Shihor **w** is east of Egypt,	Jos 13:3	834
Gadites received their inheritance **w**	Jos 13:8	834
w is on the edge of the valley of	Jos 13:9	834
with the city **w** is in the middle	Jos 13:9	834
w is on the edge of the valley of	Jos 13:16	834
with the city **w** is in the middle	Jos 13:16	834
all its cities **w** are on the plain:	Jos 13:17	834
far as Aroer **w** is before Rabbah;	Jos 13:25	834
towns of Jair, **w** are in Bashan,	Jos 13:30	834
These are *the territories* **w** Moses	Jos 13:32	834
Now these are *the territories* **w**	Jos 14:1	834
of Canaan, **w** Eleazar the priest,	Jos 14:1	834
"You know the word **w** the LORD	Jos 14:6	834
'Surely the land on **w** your foot	Jos 14:9	834
w the LORD spoke on that day,	Jos 14:12	834
Gilgal **w** is opposite the ascent of	Jos 15:7	834
w is on the south of the valley;	Jos 15:7	834
went up to the top of the mountain **w**	Jos 15:8	834
w is at the end of the valley of	Jos 15:8	834
together with the cities **w** were	Jos 16:9	834
Bashan, **w** is beyond the Jordan,	Jos 17:5	834
Michmethath **w** was east of Shechem;	Jos 17:7	834
possession of the land **w** the LORD,	Jos 18:3	834
w Moses the servant of the LORD	Jos 18:7	834
near the hill **w** *lies* on the south	Jos 18:13	834
from the hill **w** *lies* before	Jos 18:14	834
hill **w** is in the valley of Ben-hinnom,	Jos 18:16	834
w is in the valley of Rephaim	Jos 18:16	834
w is opposite the ascent of	Jos 18:17	834
and all the villages **w** *were* around	Jos 19:8	834
to Rimmon **w** stretches to Neah.	Jos 19:13	834
gave him the city for **w** he asked,	Jos 19:50	834
These are the inheritances **w**	Jos 19:51	834
of **w** I spoke to you through Moses,	Jos 20:2	834
to the city from **w** he fled.' "	Jos 20:6	834
They gave these cities **w** are	Jos 21:9	834
the LORD gave Israel all the land **w**	Jos 21:43	834
Not one of the good promises **w** the	Jos 21:45	834
w Moses the servant of the LORD	Jos 22:4	834
commandment and the law **w** Moses	Jos 22:5	834
Shiloh **w** is in the land of Canaan,	Jos 22:9	834
possession **w** they had possessed,	Jos 22:9	834
Jordan **w** is in the land of Canaan,	Jos 22:10	834
'What is this unfaithful act **w** you	Jos 22:16	834
from **w** we have not cleansed	Jos 22:17	834
of the LORD **w** our fathers made,	Jos 22:28	834
God **w** is before His tabernacle."	Jos 22:29	834
heard the words **w** the sons of	Jos 22:30	834
to destroy the land in **w** the sons	Jos 22:33	834
apportioned to you these nations **w**	Jos 23:4	834
all the nations **w** I have cut off,	Jos 23:4	834
nations, these **w** remain among you,	Jos 23:7	834
nations, these **w** remain among you,	Jos 23:12	834
you perish from off this good land **w**	Jos 23:13	834
words **w** the LORD your God spoke	Jos 23:14	834
words **w** the LORD your God spoke to	Jos 23:15	834
w the LORD your God has given you.	Jos 23:15	834
LORD your God, **w** He commanded you,	Jos 23:16	834
good land **w** He has given you."	Jos 23:16	834
a land on **w** you had not labored,	Jos 24:13	834
and cities **w** you had not built,	Jos 24:13	834
olive groves **w** you did not plant.'	Jos 24:13	834
and put away the gods **w** your	Jos 24:14	834
whether the gods **w** your fathers	Jos 24:15	834
served **w** were beyond the River,	Jos 24:15	834
us through all the way in **w** we went	Jos 24:17	834
foreign gods **w** are in your midst,	Jos 24:23	834
of the LORD **w** He spoke to us;	Jos 24:27	834
w is in the hill country of	Jos 24:30	834
the LORD **w** He had done for Israel.	Jos 24:31	834
w the sons of Israel brought up	Jos 24:32	834
in the piece of ground **w** Jacob had	Jos 24:32	834
w was given him in the hill	Jos 24:33	834
Judah **w** is in the south of Arad;	Jg 1:16	834
it Luz **w** is its name to this day.	Jg 1:26	1931
w I have sworn to your fathers;	Jg 2:1	834
the LORD **w** He had done for Israel.	Jg 2:7	834
the work **w** He had done for Israel.	Jg 2:10	834
the way in **w** their fathers had walked	Jg 2:17	834
w I commanded their fathers and	Jg 2:20	834
w Joshua left when he died,	Jg 2:21	834
are the nations **w** the LORD left,	Jg 3:1	834
w He had commanded their fathers	Jg 3:4	834
himself a sword **w** had two edges,	Jg 3:16	834
from the idols **w** were at Gilgal,	Jg 3:19	834
in Zaanannim, **w** is near Kedesh.	Jg 4:11	834
For this is the day in **w** the LORD	Jg 4:14	834
Israel made for themselves the dens **w**	Jg 6:2	834
w belonged to Joash the Abiezrite	Jg 6:11	834
w our fathers told us about,	Jg 6:13	834
of Baal **w** belongs to your father,	Jg 6:25	834
Asherah **w** you shall cut down."	Jg 6:26	834
w was beside it was cut down,	Jg 6:28	834
on the altar **w** had been built.	Jg 6:28	834
the Asherah **w** was beside it."	Jg 6:30	834

w were on their camels' necks. Jg 8:21 834
w *were* on the kings of Midian, Jg 8:26 7945
'W is better for you, that seventy Jg 9:2 4100
with w Abimelech hired worthless Jg 9:4 1992a
of the pillar w was in Shechem. Jg 9:6 834
with w God and men are honored, Jg 9:9 834
my new wine, w cheers God and men, Jg 9:13 834
your boasting now with w you said, Jg 9:38 834
w he had done to his father in Jg 9:56 834
out to the gods w you have chosen; Jg 10:14 834
the message w Jephthah sent him. Jg 11:28 834
to the vow w he had made; Jg 11:39 834
w is in Lehi to this day. Jg 15:19 834
the mountain w is opposite Hebron. Jg 16:3 834
new ropes w have not been used, Jg 16:11 834
the pillars on w the house rests, Jg 16:26 834
pillars on w the house rested, Jg 16:29 834
of silver w were taken from you, Jg 17:2 834
about w you uttered a curse in my Jg 17:2
our way on w we are going will be Jg 18:5 834
your way in w you are going has Jg 18:6 834
have taken away my gods w I made, Jg 18:24 834
in the valley w is near Beth-rehob. Jg 18:28 834
Micah's graven image w he had made, Jg 18:31 834
near Gibeah w belongs to Benjamin. Jg 19:14 834
at Gibeah w belongs to Benjamin. Jg 20:4 834
the thing w we will do to Gibeah: Jg 20:9 834
one of w goes up to Bethel and the Jg 20:31 834
fire all the cities w they found. Jg 20:48 834
w is in the land of Canaan. Jg 21:12 834
w is on the north side of Bethel, Jg 21:19 834
eyes be on the field w they reap, Ru 2:9 834
has to sell the piece of land w Ru 4:3 834
through the offspring w the LORD Ru 4:12 834
me my petition w I asked of Him. 1Sa 1:27 834
for the report is not good w I 1Sa 2:24 834
at My offering w I have commanded 1Sa 2:29 834
'This will be the sign to you w 1Sa 2:34 834
am about to do a thing in Israel at w 1Sa 3:11 834
for the iniquity w he knew, 1Sa 3:13 834
w we shall return to Him?" 1Sa 6:4 834
on w there has never been a yoke; 1Sa 6:7 834
and put the articles of gold w you 1Sa 6:8 834
in w were the articles of gold, 1Sa 6:15 834
These are the golden tumors w 1Sa 6:17 834
The large stone on w they set the 1Sa 6:18 834
The cities w the Philistines 1Sa 7:14 834
"Like all the deeds w they have 1Sa 8:8 834
journey on w we have set out." 1Sa 9:6 834
w were lost three days ago, 1Sa 9:20 834
you, concerning w I said to you, 1Sa 9:23 834
'The donkeys w you went to look 1Sa 10:2 834
w you will accept from their hand. 1Sa 10:4 834
kingdom w Samuel had mentioned. 1Sa 10:16 834
all the righteous acts of the LORD w 1Sa 12:7 834
see this great thing w the LORD will 1Sa 12:16 834
your wickedness is great w you have 1Sa 12:17 834
w can not profit or deliver, 1Sa 12:21 834
of w 2,000 were with Saul in 1Sa 13:2 834
and people like the sand w is on 1Sa 13:5 834
LORD your God, w He commanded you, 1Sa 13:13 834
company turned toward the border w 1Sa 13:18 834
pomegranate tree w is in Migron. 1Sa 14:2 834
Between the passes by w 1Sa 14:4 834
That first slaughter w 1Sa 14:14 834
spoil of their enemies w they found! 1Sa 14:30 834
go to Shur, w is east of Egypt. 1Sa 15:7 834
the lowing of the oxen w I hear?" 1Sa 15:14 834
the mission on w the LORD sent me, 1Sa 15:20 834
at Socoh w belongs to Judah, 1Sa 17:1 834
he was clothed with scale-armor w 1Sa 17:5 834
words w David spoke were heard, 1Sa 17:31 834
in the shepherd's bag w he had, 1Sa 17:40 834
to him according to these words w 1Sa 18:24 834
of w you and I have spoken, 1Sa 20:23 834
arrows w I am about to shoot." 1Sa 20:36 834
of the arrow w Jonathan had shot, 1Sa 20:37 834
the matter on w I am sending you 1Sa 21:2 834
with w I have commissioned you; 1Sa 21:2 834
bread of the Presence w was removed 1Sa 21:6 834
w is on the south of Jeshimon? 1Sa 23:19 834
the day of w the LORD said to you, 1Sa 24:4 834
"Now let this gift w your 1Sa 25:27 834
w *is* before Jeshimon?" 1Sa 26:1 834
of Hachilah, w is before Jeshimon, 1Sa 26:3 834
to your words w you spoke to me. 1Sa 28:21 834
by the spring w is in Jezreel. 1Sa 29:1 834
and on that w belongs to Judah, 1Sa 30:14 834
all the sheep and the cattle w 1Sa 30:20 834
And I took the crown w *was* on his 2Sa 1:10 834
and the bracelet w *was* on his arm, 2Sa 1:10 834
Helkath-hazzurim, w is in Gibeon. 2Sa 2:16 834
of the gazelles w is in the field. 2Sa 2:18 834
w is in front of Giah by the way 2Sa 2:24 834
father's tomb w was in Bethlehem. 2Sa 2:32 834
w was the reward I gave him for 2Sa 4:10 834
ark of God w is called by the Name, 2Sa 6:2 834
of Abinadab w was on the hill; 2Sa 6:3 834
of Abinadab, w was on the hill; 2Sa 6:4 834
tent w David had pitched for it; 2Sa 6:17 834
w I commanded to shepherd My 2Sa 7:7 834
David took the shields of gold w were 2Sa 8:7 834
all the nations w he had subdued: 2Sa 8:11 834
lamb W he bought and nourished; 2Sa 12:3 834
So Tamar took the cakes w she had 2Sa 13:10 834
for the hatred with w he hated her 2Sa 13:15 834
the love with w he had loved her. 2Sa 13:15 834
long-sleeved garment w *was* on her; 2Sa 13:19 834
in Baal-hazor, w is near Ephraim, 2Sa 13:23 834
will extinguish my coal w is left, 2Sa 14:7 834
w cannot be gathered up again. 2Sa 14:14 834
my vow w I have vowed to the LORD, 2Sa 15:7 834
w he gave in those days, 2Sa 16:23 834
a pillar w is in the King's Valley, 2Sa 18:18 834
set time w he had appointed him. 2Sa 20:5 834
at the large stone w is in Gibeon, 2Sa 20:8 834
the sword w was in Joab's hand 2Sa 20:10 834
of the LORD w was between them, 2Sa 21:7 834
of Bethlehem w is by the gate!" 2Sa 23:15 834
of Bethlehem w was by the gate, 2Sa 23:16 834
of them, w I will do to you. 2Sa 24:12
LORD my God w cost me nothing." 2Sa 24:24 2600
of Zoheleth, w is beside En-rogel; 1Ki 1:9 834
is the noise w you have heard. 1Ki 1:45 834
promise w He spoke concerning me, 1Ki 2:4 834
with w my father was afflicted." 1Ki 2:26 834
w He had spoken concerning the 1Ki 2:27 834
blood w Joab shed without cause. 1Ki 2:31 834
'The word w I have heard is good.' 1Ki 2:42
command w I have laid on you?" 1Ki 2:43 834
w you acknowledge in your heart, 1Ki 2:44 834
w you did to my father David; 1Ki 2:44 834
of Your people w You have chosen, 1Ki 3:8 834
w the king had handed down, 1Ki 3:28 834
and all Beth-shean w is beside 1Ki 4:12 834
Manasseh, w are in Gilead were 1Ki 4:13 834
region of Argob, w is in Bashan, 1Ki 4:13 834
of the wars w surrounded him, 1Ki 5:3 834
the message w you have sent me; 1Ki 5:8 834
of Ziv w is the second month, 1Ki 6:1 1931
As for the house w King Solomon 1Ki 6:2 834
this house w you are building, 1Ki 6:12 834
w I spoke to David your father. 1Ki 6:12 834
Also the whole altar w was by the 1Ki 6:22 834
of Bul, w is the eighth month, 1Ki 6:38 1931
chambers w were on the 45 pillars, 1Ki 7:3 834
the capitals w were on the top of the 1Ki 7:17 834
one network to cover the capitals w 1Ki 7:18 834
The capitals w *were* on the top 1Ki 7:19 834
w was beside the network; 1Ki 7:20 834
and on the borders w were between 1Ki 7:29 834
all the work w he performed for King 1Ki 7:40 834
the *two* bowls of the capitals w *were* 1Ki 7:41 834
the two bowls of the capitals w *were* 1Ki 7:41 834
the two bowls of the capitals w *were* 1Ki 7:42 834
even all these utensils w Hiram 1Ki 7:45 834
w *was in* the house of the LORD: 1Ki 7:48 834
w *was* the bread of the Presence; 1Ki 7:48 834
from the city of David, w is Zion. 1Ki 8:1 1931
Ethanim, w is the seventh month. 1Ki 8:2 1931
holy utensils, w were in the tent, 1Ki 8:4 834
stone w Moses put there at Horeb, 1Ki 8:9 834
of all the tribes of Israel *in* w 1Ki 8:16 834
has fulfilled His word w He spoke; 1Ki 8:20 834
in w is the covenant of the LORD, 1Ki 8:21 834
w He made with our fathers when He 1Ki 8:21 834
that w You have promised him; 1Ki 8:24 834
that w You have promised him, 1Ki 8:25 834
be confirmed w You have spoken to 1Ki 8:26 834
less this house w I have built! 1Ki 8:27 834
the prayer w Your servant prays before 1Ki 8:28 834
the place of w You have said, 1Ki 8:29 834
to listen to the prayer w Your 1Ki 8:29 834
and bring them back to the land w 1Ki 8:34 834
good way in w they should walk. 1Ki 8:36 834
w You have given Your people for 1Ki 8:36 834
land w You have given to our fathers. 1Ki 8:40 834
for w the foreigner calls to You, 1Ki 8:43 834
house w I have built is called by Your 1Ki 8:43 834
toward the city w You have chosen 1Ki 8:44 834
house w I have built for Your name, 1Ki 8:44 834
their land w You have given to their 1Ki 8:48 834
the city w You have chosen, 1Ki 8:48 834
house w I have built for Your name; 1Ki 8:48 834
all their transgressions w they have 1Ki 8:50 834
Your people and Your inheritance w 1Ki 8:51 834
w He promised through Moses His 1Ki 8:56 834
w He commanded our fathers. 1Ki 8:58 834
with w I have made supplication 1Ki 8:59 834
w he offered to the LORD, 1Ki 8:63 834
w you have made before Me; 1Ki 9:3 834
I have consecrated this house w 1Ki 9:3 834
My statutes w I have set before you 1Ki 9:6 834
from the land w I have given them, 1Ki 9:7 834
and the house w I have consecrated 1Ki 9:7 834
end of twenty years in w Solomon had 1Ki 9:10 834
cities w Solomon had given him, 1Ki 9:12 834
these cities w you have given me, 1Ki 9:13 834
forced labor w King Solomon levied 1Ki 9:15 834
the storage cities w Solomon had, 1Ki 9:19 834
house w *Solomon* had built for her, 1Ki 9:24 834
the altar w he built to the LORD, 1Ki 9:25 834
the altar w *was* before the LORD. 1Ki 9:25 834
w is near Eloth on the shore of 1Ki 9:26 834
king w he did not explain to her. 1Ki 10:3 834
and his stairway by w he went up 1Ki 10:5 834
"It was a true report w I heard 1Ki 10:6 834
prosperity the report w I heard. 1Ki 10:7 834
that w the queen of Sheba gave King 1Ki 10:10 834
Hiram, w brought gold from Ophir, 1Ki 10:11 834
all her desire w she requested, 1Ki 10:13 834
Now the weight of gold w came in 1Ki 10:14 834
wisdom w God had put in his heart. 1Ki 10:24 834
from the nations concerning w the 1Ki 11:2 834
mountain w is east of Jerusalem, 1Ki 11:7 834
statutes, w I have commanded you, 1Ki 11:11 834
of Jerusalem w I have chosen." 1Ki 11:13 834
of the new cloak w was on him and 1Ki 11:30 834
the city w I have chosen from all 1Ki 11:32 834
and his heavy yoke w he put on us, 1Ki 12:4 834
the elders w they had given him, 1Ki 12:8 834
yoke w your father put on us'?" 1Ki 12:9 834
the elders w they had given him, 1Ki 12:13 834
w the LORD spoke through Ahijah 1Ki 12:15 834
like the feast w is in Judah, 1Ki 12:32 834
to the calves w he had made. 1Ki 12:32 834
of the high places w he had made. 1Ki 12:32 834
Then he went up to the altar w he 1Ki 12:33 834
even in the month w he had devised 1Ki 12:33 834
is the sign w the LORD has spoken, 1Ki 13:3 834
w are on it shall be poured out.' " 1Ki 13:3 834
w he cried against the altar in 1Ki 13:4 834
But his hand w he stretched out 1Ki 13:4 834
according to the sign w the man of 1Ki 13:5 834
return by the way w you came.' " 1Ki 13:9 834
by the way w he came to Bethel. 1Ki 13:10 834
all the deeds w the man of God had 1Ki 13:11 834
words w he had spoken to the king, 1Ki 13:11 834
"W way did he go?" 1Ki 13:12 335, 2088
Now his sons had seen the way w 1Ki 13:12 834
by going the way w you came.' " 1Ki 13:17 834
commandment w the LORD your God 1Ki 13:21 834
in the place of w He said to you, 1Ki 13:22 834
w has torn him and killed him, 1Ki 13:26 834
of the LORD w He spoke to him." 1Ki 13:26 834
in w the man of God is buried; 1Ki 13:31 834
the thing shall surely come to pass w 1Ki 13:32 834
w are in the cities of Samaria." 1Ki 13:32 834
only that w was right in My sight; 1Ki 14:8 3477
land w He gave to their fathers, 1Ki 14:15 834
w he committed and with which he 1Ki 14:16 834
with w he made Israel to sin." 1Ki 14:16 834
to the word of the LORD w He spoke 1Ki 14:18 834
the city w the LORD had chosen 1Ki 14:21 834
with the sins w they committed. 1Ki 14:22 834
the nations w the LORD dispossessed 1Ki 14:24 834
of gold w Solomon had made. 1Ki 14:26 834
w he had committed before him; 1Ki 15:3 834
the idols w his fathers had made. 1Ki 15:12 834
Asa took all the silver and the gold w 1Ki 15:18 834
timber with w Baasha had built. 1Ki 15:22 834
he did and the cities w he built, 1Ki 15:23 834
in his sin w he made Israel sin. 1Ki 15:26 834
w belonged to the Philistines, 1Ki 15:27 834
w He spoke by His servant Ahijah 1Ki 15:29 834
the sins of Jeroboam w he sinned, 1Ki 15:30 834
sinned, and w he made Israel sin, 1Ki 15:30 834
because of his provocation with w he 1Ki 15:30 834
in his sin w he made Israel sin. 1Ki 15:34 834
both because of all the evil w he 1Ki 16:7 834
w He spoke against Baasha through 1Ki 16:12 834
w they sinned and which they made 1Ki 16:13 834
sinned and w they made Israel sin, 1Ki 16:13 834
w belonged to the Philistines. 1Ki 16:15 834
because of his sins w he sinned, 1Ki 16:19 834
Jeroboam, and in his sin w he did, 1Ki 16:19 834
his conspiracy w he carried out, 1Ki 16:20 834
named the city w he built Samaria, 1Ki 16:24 834
in his sins w he made Israel sin, 1Ki 16:26 834
the rest of the acts of Omri w he did 1Ki 16:27 834
he did and his might w he showed, 1Ki 16:27 834
of Baal w he built in Samaria. 1Ki 16:32 834
w He spoke by Joshua the son of 1Ki 16:34 834
Cherith, w is east of the Jordan. 1Ki 17:3 834
Cherith, w is east of the Jordan. 1Ki 17:5 834
to Zarephath, w belongs to Sidon, 1Ki 17:9 834
LORD w He spoke through Elijah. 1Ki 17:16 834
Then they took the ox w was given 1Ki 18:26 834
about the altar w they made. 1Ki 18:26 834
of the LORD w had been torn down. 1Ki 18:30 834
to Beersheba, w belongs to Judah, 1Ki 19:3 834
and the army w followed them. 1Ki 20:19 834
"The cities w my father took from 1Ki 20:34 834
had a vineyard w *was* in Jezreel 1Ki 21:1 834
vexed because of the word w Naboth 1Ki 21:4 834
the letters w she had sent them. 1Ki 21:11 834
w he refused to give you for money; 1Ki 21:15 834
w you have provoked *Me* to anger, 1Ki 21:22 834
Like sheep w have no shepherd. 1Ki 22:17 834
the word of the LORD w He spoke. 1Ki 22:38 834
the ivory house w he built and all the 1Ki 22:39 834
and all the cities w he built, 1Ki 22:39 834
w he showed and how he warred, 1Ki 22:45 834
upper chamber w *was* in Samaria, 2Ki 1:2 834
of the LORD w Elijah had spoken. 2Ki 1:17 834
of the acts of Ahaziah w he did, 2Ki 1:18 834
fire w separated the two of them. 2Ki 2:11 834
to the word of Elisha w he spoke. 2Ki 2:22 834
of Baal w his father had made. 2Ki 3:2 834
of Nebat, w he made Israel sin; 2Ki 3:3 834
"W way shall we go up?" 2Ki 3:8 335, 2088
w the man of God had told him; 2Ki 6:10 834
"Will you tell me w of us is for 2Ki 6:11 4310
take five of the horses w remain, 2Ki 7:13 834
remain, w are left in the city. 2Ki 7:13 834
w the Arameans had thrown away in 2Ki 7:15 834
wounds w the Arameans had inflicted 2Ki 8:29 834
"For w *one* of us?" 2Ki 9:5 4310
wounds w the Arameans had inflicted 2Ki 9:15 834
the ascent of Gur, w is at Ibleam. 2Ki 9:27 834
w He spoke by His servant Elijah 2Ki 9:36 834
w the LORD spoke concerning the 2Ki 10:10 834
of the LORD w He spoke to Elijah. 2Ki 10:17 834
of Nebat, w he made Israel sin, 2Ki 10:29 834
of Jeroboam, w he made Israel sin. 2Ki 10:31 834
w is by the valley of the Arnon, 2Ki 10:33 834

Now the time **w** Jehu reigned over	**2Ki 10:36**	834
w *were* in the house of the LORD.	**2Ki 11:10**	834
all his days in **w** Jehoiada the priest	**2Ki 12:2**	834
"All the money of the sacred things **w**	**2Ki 12:4**	834
and all the money **w** any man's heart	**2Ki 12:4**	834
put in it all the money **w** was brought	**2Ki 12:9**	
and counted the money **w** was found	**2Ki 12:10**	
They gave the money **w** was	**2Ki 12:11**	
or vessels of silver from the money **w**	**2Ki 12:13**	
Nebat, with **w** he made Israel sin;	**2Ki 13:2**	834
with **w** he made Israel sin,	**2Ki 13:6**	834
Nebat, with **w** he made Israel sin,	**2Ki 13:11**	834
his might with **w** he fought against	**2Ki 13:12**	834
the illness of **w** he was to die,	**2Ki 13:14**	834
the cities **w** he had taken in war from	**2Ki 13:25**	834
"The thorn bush **w** was in Lebanon	**2Ki 14:9**	834
to the cedar **w** was in Lebanon,	**2Ki 14:9**	834
Beth-shemesh, **w** belongs to Judah.	**2Ki 14:11**	834
gold and silver and all the utensils **w**	**2Ki 14:14**	
of the acts of Jehoash **w** he did,	**2Ki 14:15**	834
of Nebat, **w** he made Israel sin.	**2Ki 14:24**	834
w He spoke through His servant	**2Ki 14:25**	834
w *was* very bitter; for there was	**2Ki 14:26**	
w *had belonged* to Judah, are	**2Ki 14:28**	
of Nebat, **w** he made Israel sin.	**2Ki 15:9**	834
of the LORD **w** He spoke to Jehu,	**2Ki 15:12**	834
and his conspiracy **w** he made,	**2Ki 15:15**	834
of Nebat, **w** he made Israel sin.	**2Ki 15:18**	834
of Nebat, **w** he made Israel sin.	**2Ki 15:24**	834
of Nebat, **w** he made Israel sin.	**2Ki 15:28**	834
saw the altar **w** *was* at Damascus;	**2Ki 16:10**	834
altar, **w** *was* before the LORD,	**2Ki 16:14**	834
the bronze oxen **w** were under it and	**2Ki 16:17**	834
w they had built in the house,	**2Ki 16:18**	834
rest of the acts of Ahaz **w** he did,	**2Ki 16:19**	834
of Israel **w** they had introduced.	**2Ki 17:8**	834
things secretly **w** were not right against	**2Ki 17:9**	834
w the LORD had carried away to exile	**2Ki 17:11**	834
w the LORD had said to them,	**2Ki 17:12**	834
law **w** I commanded your fathers,	**2Ki 17:13**	834
and **w** I sent to you through My	**2Ki 17:13**	834
w He made with their fathers and	**2Ki 17:15**	834
warnings with **w** He warned them.	**2Ki 17:15**	834
the nations **w** surrounded them,	**2Ki 17:15**	834
concerning **w** the LORD had	**2Ki 17:15**	834
customs **w** Israel had introduced.	**2Ki 17:19**	834
all the sins of Jeroboam **w** he did;	**2Ki 17:22**	834
among them **w** killed some of them.	**2Ki 17:25**	
high places **w** the people of Samaria	**2Ki 17:29**	834
in their cities in **w** they lived.	**2Ki 17:29**	834
or the commandments **w** the LORD	**2Ki 17:34**	834
commandment **w** He wrote for you,	**2Ki 17:37**	834
w the LORD had commanded Moses.	**2Ki 18:6**	834
w was the seventh year of Hoshea	**2Ki 18:9**	1931
w was the ninth year of Hoshea	**2Ki 18:10**	1931
Hezekiah gave *him* all the silver **w**	**2Ki 18:15**	
and *from* the doorposts **w** Hezekiah	**2Ki 18:16**	834
w is on the highway of the	**2Ki 18:17**	834
on **w** if a man leans, it will go	**2Ki 18:21**	834
w the LORD your God has heard.	**2Ki 19:4**	834
with **w** the servants of the king of	**2Ki 19:6**	834
'Did the gods of those nations **w**	**2Ki 19:12**	834
w he has sent to reproach the	**2Ki 19:16**	834
you back by the way **w** you came.	**2Ki 19:28**	834
back ten steps by **w** it had gone down	**2Ki 20:11**	834
LORD **w** you have spoken is good."	**2Ki 20:19**	834
For he rebuilt the high places **w**	**2Ki 21:3**	834
the LORD, of **w** the LORD had said,	**2Ki 21:4**	834
in the house of **w** the LORD said to	**2Ki 21:7**	834
w I have chosen from all the	**2Ki 21:7**	834
the land **w** I gave their fathers,	**2Ki 21:8**	834
his sin with **w** he made Judah sin,	**2Ki 21:16**	834
he did and his sin **w** he committed,	**2Ki 21:17**	834
rest of the acts of Amon **w** he did,	**2Ki 21:25**	834
w the doorkeepers have gathered from	**2Ki 22:4**	834
book **w** the king of Judah has read.	**2Ki 22:16**	834
the words **w** you have heard,	**2Ki 22:18**	834
w I will bring on this place.	**2Ki 22:20**	834
w was found in the house of the	**2Ki 23:2**	
w *were* in the house of the LORD,	**2Ki 23:7**	834
w *were* at the entrance of the gate of	**2Ki 23:8**	834
w *were* on one's left at the city	**2Ki 23:8**	834
w is in the valley of the son of	**2Ki 23:10**	834
He did away with the horses **w**	**2Ki 23:11**	834
official, **w** *was* in the precincts;	**2Ki 23:11**	834
The altars **w** *were* on the roof,	**2Ki 23:12**	834
w the kings of Judah had made,	**2Ki 23:12**	834
and the altars **w** Manasseh had made	**2Ki 23:12**	834
places **w** *were* before Jerusalem,	**2Ki 23:13**	834
w *were* on the right of the mount	**2Ki 23:13**	834
w Solomon the king of Israel had built	**2Ki 23:13**	834
place **w** Jeroboam the son of Nebat,	**2Ki 23:15**	834
LORD **w** the man of God proclaimed,	**2Ki 23:16**	834
w you have done against the altar of	**2Ki 23:17**	834
w *were* in the cities of Samaria,	**2Ki 23:19**	834
w the kings of Israel had made	**2Ki 23:19**	834
confirm the words of the law **w** were	**2Ki 23:24**	
of His great wrath with **w** His anger	**2Ki 23:26**	834
with **w** Manasseh had provoked Him.	**2Ki 23:26**	834
this city **w** I have chosen,	**2Ki 23:27**	834
and the temple of **w** I said,	**2Ki 23:27**	834
w He had spoken through His	**2Ki 24:2**	834
for the innocent blood **w** he shed,	**2Ki 24:4**	834
cut in pieces all the vessels of gold **w**	**2Ki 24:13**	834
w was the nineteenth year of King	**2Ki 25:8**	1931
w were in the house of the LORD,	**2Ki 25:13**	834
w were in the house of the LORD,	**2Ki 25:13**	834
w were used in *temple* service.	**2Ki 25:14**	834
and the stands **w** Solomon had made	**2Ki 25:16**	834

from **w** the Philistines came,	**1Ch 1:12**	834
w Solomon built in Jerusalem),	**1Ch 6:10**	834
cities **w** are mentioned by name.	**1Ch 6:65**	834
the things **w** were baked in pans.	**1Ch 9:31**	
w he committed against the LORD,	**1Ch 10:13**	834
of the LORD **w** he did not keep;	**1Ch 10:13**	834
of Bethlehem, **w** is by the gate!"	**1Ch 11:17**	834
of Bethlehem **w** *was* by the gate,	**1Ch 11:18**	834
Kiriath-jearim, **w** belongs to Judah,	**1Ch 13:6**	834
place **w** he had prepared for it.	**1Ch 15:3**	834
tent **w** David had pitched for it,	**1Ch 16:1**	834
His wonderful deeds **w** He has done,	**1Ch 16:12**	834
The word **w** He commanded to a	**1Ch 16:15**	
covenant **w** He made with Abraham,	**1Ch 16:16**	834
in the high place **w** *was* at Gibeon,	**1Ch 16:39**	834
the LORD, **w** He commanded Israel.	**1Ch 16:40**	834
David took the shields of gold **w**	**1Ch 18:7**	834
with **w** Solomon made the bronze sea	**1Ch 18:8**	
and the gold **w** he had carried away	**1Ch 18:11**	834
w I will do to you." ' "	**1Ch 21:10**	
w he spoke in the name of the LORD.	**1Ch 21:19**	834
offering **w** costs me nothing."	**1Ch 21:24**	2600
w Moses had made in the	**1Ch 21:29**	834
ordinances **w** the LORD commanded	**1Ch 22:13**	834
w David made for giving praise.	**1Ch 23:5**	834
w King David and the heads of the	**1Ch 26:26**	834
the affairs of the divisions **w** came in	**1Ch 27:1**	
cattle **w** were grazing in Sharon;	**1Ch 27:29**	
property **w** belonged to King David.	**1Ch 27:31**	834
for **w** I have made provision."	**1Ch 29:19**	834
bestowed on him royal majesty **w** had	**1Ch 29:25**	834
The period **w** he reigned over	**1Ch 29:27**	834
the circumstances **w** came on him,	**1Ch 29:30**	834
to the high place **w** was at Gibeon,	**2Ch 1:3**	834
w Moses the servant of the LORD	**2Ch 1:3**	834
altar, **w** Bezalel the son of Uri,	**2Ch 1:5**	834
w *was* at the tent of meeting,	**2Ch 1:6**	834
the high place **w** was at Gibeon,	**2Ch 1:13**	834
"The house **w** I am about to	**2Ch 2:5**	834
for the house **w** I am about to	**2Ch 2:9**	834
design **w** may be assigned to him,	**2Ch 2:14**	834
oil and wine, of **w** he has spoken.	**2Ch 2:15**	834
w his father David had taken;	**2Ch 2:17**	834
Now these are the foundations **w**	**2Ch 3:3**	
The porch **w** was in front of	**2Ch 3:4**	834
also made ten basins in **w** to wash,	**2Ch 4:6**	1992a
Huram finished doing the work **w** he	**2Ch 4:11**	
w were on top of the pillars,	**2Ch 4:12**	834
capitals **w** were on the pillars.	**2Ch 4:13**	834
of the city of David, **w** is Zion.	**2Ch 5:2**	1931
holy utensils **w** *were* in the tent;	**2Ch 5:5**	
w Moses put *there* at Horeb,	**2Ch 5:10**	834
of all the tribes of Israel *in* **w**	**2Ch 6:5**	
has fulfilled His word **w** He spoke;	**2Ch 6:10**	834
in **w** is the covenant of the LORD,	**2Ch 6:11**	834
w He made with the sons of Israel."	**2Ch 6:11**	834
that **w** You have promised him;	**2Ch 6:15**	834
that **w** You have promised him,	**2Ch 6:16**	834
let Your word be confirmed **w** You	**2Ch 6:17**	834
less this house **w** I have built.	**2Ch 6:18**	834
w Your servant prays before You;	**2Ch 6:19**	834
toward the place of **w** You have	**2Ch 6:20**	834
to listen to the prayer **w** Your	**2Ch 6:20**	834
bring them back to the land **w** You	**2Ch 6:25**	834
good way in **w** they should walk.	**2Ch 6:27**	834
w You have given to Your people	**2Ch 6:27**	834
as long as they live in the land **w**	**2Ch 6:31**	834
for **w** the foreigner calls to You,	**2Ch 6:33**	834
know that this house **w** I have built	**2Ch 6:33**	834
this city **w** You have chosen and	**2Ch 6:34**	834
house **w** I have built for Your name,	**2Ch 6:34**	834
and pray toward their land **w** You	**2Ch 6:38**	834
and the city **w** You have chosen,	**2Ch 6:38**	834
house **w** I have built for Your name,	**2Ch 6:38**	834
w King David had made for giving	**2Ch 7:6**	834
because the bronze altar **w** Solomon	**2Ch 7:7**	834
commandments **w** I have set before	**2Ch 7:19**	834
from My land **w** I have given you,	**2Ch 7:20**	834
and this house **w** I have	**2Ch 7:20**	834
"As for this house, **w** was exalted,	**2Ch 7:21**	834
in **w** Solomon had built the house of	**2Ch 8:1**	834
cities **w** Huram had given to him,	**2Ch 8:2**	834
cities **w** he had built in Hamath.	**2Ch 8:4**	834
the house **w** he had built for her,	**2Ch 8:11**	834
w he had built before the porch;	**2Ch 8:12**	834
w he did not explain to her.	**2Ch 9:2**	834
Solomon, the house **w** he had built,	**2Ch 9:3**	834
and his stairway by **w** he went up	**2Ch 9:4**	834
"It was a true report **w** I heard	**2Ch 9:5**	834
there had never been spice like that **w**	**2Ch 9:9**	834
all her desire **w** she requested besides	**2Ch 9:12**	834
Now the weight of gold **w** came to	**2Ch 9:13**	834
besides that **w** the traders and	**2Ch 9:14**	
For the king had ships **w** went to	**2Ch 9:21**	
wisdom **w** God had put in his heart.	**2Ch 9:23**	834
and his heavy yoke **w** he put on us,	**2Ch 10:4**	834
the elders **w** they had given him,	**2Ch 10:8**	834
yoke **w** your father put on us'?"	**2Ch 10:9**	834
w He spoke through Ahijah the	**2Ch 10:15**	834
w are fortified cities in Judah	**2Ch 11:10**	834
and for the calves **w** he had made.	**2Ch 11:15**	834
golden shields **w** Solomon had made.	**2Ch 12:9**	834
the city **w** the LORD had chosen	**2Ch 12:13**	834
w is in the hill country of	**2Ch 13:4**	834
the golden calves **w** Jeroboam made	**2Ch 13:8**	834
the prophecy **w** Azariah the son of	**2Ch 15:8**	
and from the cities **w** he had captured	**2Ch 15:8**	834
then restored the altar of the LORD **w**	**2Ch 15:8**	834
with **w** Baasha had been building,	**2Ch 16:6**	834

They buried him in his own tomb **w** he	**2Ch 16:14**	834
they laid him in the resting place **w**	**2Ch 16:14**	834
w Asa his father had captured.	**2Ch 17:2**	834
of the lands **w** *were* around Judah,	**2Ch 17:10**	834
Like sheep **w** have no shepherd;	**2Ch 18:16**	834
to drive us out from Your possession **w**	**2Ch 20:11**	834
things **w** they took for themselves,	**2Ch 20:25**	
w is recorded in the Book of the	**2Ch 20:34**	834
covenant **w** He had made with David,	**2Ch 21:7**	834
be healed in Jezreel of the wounds **w**	**2Ch 22:6**	834
"This is the thing **w** you shall do:	**2Ch 23:4**	834
shields **w** had been King David's,	**2Ch 23:9**	834
w were in the house of God.	**2Ch 23:9**	834
kindness **w** his father Jehoiada had	**2Ch 24:22**	834
of Moses, **w** the LORD commanded,	**2Ch 25:4**	834
talents **w** I have given to the troops	**2Ch 25:9**	834
troops **w** came to him from Ephraim,	**2Ch 25:10**	834
"The thorn bush **w** was in Lebanon	**2Ch 25:18**	834
to the cedar **w** was in Lebanon,	**2Ch 25:18**	834
Beth-shemesh, **w** belonged to Judah.	**2Ch 25:21**	834
and all the utensils **w** were found	**2Ch 25:24**	
w entered combat by divisions according	**2Ch 26:11**	
the grave **w** belonged to the kings,	**2Ch 26:23**	834
and he went out to meet the army **w**	**2Ch 28:9**	
and you have slain them in a rage **w**	**2Ch 28:9**	
of Damascus **w** had defeated him,	**2Ch 28:23**	
and every unclean thing **w** they	**2Ch 29:16**	834
all the utensils **w** King Ahaz had	**2Ch 29:19**	834
offerings **w** the assembly brought was	**2Ch 29:32**	834
w He has consecrated forever,	**2Ch 30:8**	834
the altars **w** *were* in Jerusalem;	**2Ch 30:14**	834
the priests sprinkled the blood **w**	**2Ch 30:16**	
and the tithe of sacred gifts **w**	**2Ch 31:6**	
Every work **w** he began in the	**2Ch 31:21**	834
springs **w** *were* outside the city,	**2Ch 32:3**	834
w flowed through the region,	**2Ch 32:4**	
among all the gods of those nations **w**	**2Ch 32:14**	834
For he rebuilt the high places **w**	**2Ch 33:3**	834
the LORD of **w** the LORD had said,	**2Ch 33:4**	834
he put the carved image of the idol **w**	**2Ch 33:7**	834
of **w** God had said to David and to	**2Ch 33:7**	834
w I have chosen from all the	**2Ch 33:7**	834
from the land **w** I have appointed for	**2Ch 33:8**	834
as well as all the altars **w** he had	**2Ch 33:15**	834
and the sites on **w** he built high	**2Ch 33:19**	834
w his father Manasseh had made,	**2Ch 33:22**	834
the house of God, **w** the Levites,	**2Ch 34:9**	834
and to make beams for the houses **w**	**2Ch 34:11**	834
were bringing out the money **w** had	**2Ch 34:14**	
have also emptied out the money **w**	**2Ch 34:17**	
of the book **w** has been found;	**2Ch 34:21**	834
wrath of the LORD **w** is poured out on	**2Ch 34:21**	834
all the curses written in the book **w**	**2Ch 34:24**	834
the words **w** you have heard,	**2Ch 34:26**	834
your eyes will not see all the evil **w**	**2Ch 34:28**	834
book of the covenant **w** was found in	**2Ch 34:30**	
"Put the holy ark in the house **w**	**2Ch 35:3**	834
the house with **w** I am at war,	**2Ch 35:21**	
in the second chariot **w** he had,	**2Ch 35:24**	834
and the abominations **w** he did,	**2Ch 36:8**	834
they defiled the house of the LORD **w**	**2Ch 36:14**	834
house in Jerusalem, **w** is in Judah.	**2Ch 36:23**	834
house in Jerusalem, **w** is in Judah.	**Ezr 1:2**	834
go up to Jerusalem **w** is in Judah and	**Ezr 1:3**	834
of God **w** is in Jerusalem.' "	**Ezr 1:4**	834
of the LORD **w** is in Jerusalem.	**Ezr 1:5**	834
w Nebuchadnezzar had carried away	**Ezr 1:7**	834
of the LORD **w** is in Jerusalem,	**Ezr 2:68**	834
and the rest of the nations **w** the	**Ezr 4:10**	1768
of the letter **w** they sent to him:	**Ezr 4:11**	1768
the document **w** you sent to us has	**Ezr 4:18**	1768
house of God **w** is in Jerusalem;	**Ezr 5:2**	1768
the copy of the letter **w** Tattenai,	**Ezr 5:6**	1768
to him in **w** it was written thus:	**Ezr 5:7**	
w is being built with huge stones,	**Ezr 5:8**	1932
w a great king of Israel built and	**Ezr 5:11**	
silver utensils of the house of God **w**	**Ezr 5:14**	1768
house, **w** is there in Babylon,	**Ezr 5:17**	1768
w is in the province of Media,	**Ezr 6:2**	1768
w Nebuchadnezzar took from the	**Ezr 6:5**	1768
w the LORD God of Israel had given;	**Ezr 7:6**	834
w was in the seventh year of the	**Ezr 7:8**	1931
copy of the decree **w** King Artaxerxes	**Ezr 7:11**	834
law of your God **w** is in your hand,	**Ezr 7:14**	1768
w the king and his counselors have	**Ezr 7:15**	1768
with all the silver and gold **w** you	**Ezr 7:16**	1768
of their God **w** is in Jerusalem;	**Ezr 7:16**	1768
of your God **w** is in Jerusalem.	**Ezr 7:17**	1768
"Also the utensils **w** are given to	**Ezr 7:19**	1768
for **w** you may have occasion to	**Ezr 7:20**	1768
of your God **w** is in your hand,	**Ezr 7:25**	1768
of the LORD **w** is in Jerusalem,	**Ezr 7:27**	834
offering for the house of our God **w**	**Ezr 8:25**	
w You have commanded by Your	**Ezr 9:11**	834
'The land **w** you are entering to	**Ezr 9:11**	834
with their abominations **w** have	**Ezr 9:11**	834
w I am praying before You now,	**Ne 1:6**	834
w we have sinned against You;	**Ne 1:6**	834
nor the ordinances **w** You commanded	**Ne 1:7**	834
"Remember the word **w** You	**Ne 1:8**	834
the fortress **w** is by the temple,	**Ne 2:8**	834
for the house to **w** I will go."	**Ne 2:8**	834
the animal on **w** I was riding.	**Ne 2:12**	834
inspecting the walls of Jerusalem **w**	**Ne 2:13**	834
its gates **w** were consumed by fire.	**Ne 2:13**	
king's words **w** he had spoken to me.	**Ne 2:18**	834
w is by the court of the guard.	**Ne 3:25**	834
thing **w** you are doing is not good;	**Ne 5:9**	834
Now that **w** was prepared for each	**Ne 5:18**	834

in **w** I found the following record: Ne 7:5
That **w** the rest of the people Ne 7:72 834
gathered as one man at the square **w** Ne 8:1 834
w the LORD had given to Israel. Ne 8:1 834
He read from it before the square **w** Ne 8:3 834
w they had made for the purpose. Ne 8:4 834
w had been made known to them. Ne 8:12 834
them the way In **w** they were to go. Ne 9:12 834
w You swore to give them. Ne 9:15 834
not remember Your wondrous deeds **w** Ne 9:17 834
them the way in **w** they were to go. Ne 9:19 834
into the land **W** You had told their Ne 9:23 834
By **w** if a man observes them he Ne 9:29 834
before You, **W** has come upon us, Ne 9:32 834
with **w** You have admonished them. Ne 9:34 834
goodness **w** You gave them, Ne 9:35 834
land **w** You set before them, Ne 9:35 834
And as to the land **w** You gave Ne 9:36 834
law, **w** was given through Moses, Ne 10:29 834
and do not blot out my loyal deeds **w** Ne 13:14 834
throne **w** *was* at the citadel in Susa, Es 1:2 834
w belonged to King Ahasuerus. Es 1:9 834
"When the king's edict **w** he Es 1:20 834
tenth month **w** is the month Tebeth, Es 2:16 1931
first month, **w** is the month Nisan, Es 3:7 1931
month, **w** is the month Adar, Es 3:13 1931
the edict **w** had been issued in Susa Es 4:8 834
w is not according to the law; Es 4:16 834
golden scepter **w** *was* in his hand. Es 5:2 834
the banquet **w** Esther had prepared. Es 5:5 834
w I will prepare for them, Es 5:8 834
to the banquet **w** she had prepared; Es 5:12 834
gallows **w** he had prepared for him. Es 6:4 834
a royal robe **w** the king has worn, Es 6:8 834
horse on **w** the king has ridden, Es 6:8 834
the banquet **w** Esther had prepared. Es 6:14 834
w Haman made for Mordecai who Es 7:9 834
w he had prepared for Mordecai, Es 7:10 834
w he had taken away from Haman, Es 8:2 834
of Haman the Agagite and his plot **w** Es 8:3 834
w he wrote to destroy the Jews who Es 8:5 834
calamity **w** will befall my people, Es 8:6 834
for a decree **w** is written in the Es 8:8 834
provinces **w** *extended* from India to Es 8:9 834
or province **w** might attack them, Es 8:11
and *it was a* month **w** was turned Es 9:22 834
w he had devised against the Jews, Es 9:25 834
to **w** the king advanced him, Es 10:2 834
day perish on **w** I was to be born, Jb 3:3
And the night **w** said, 'A boy is Jb 3:3
like a miscarriage **w** is discarded, Jb 3:16
And to **w** of the holy ones will you Jb 5:1 4310
the torrents of wadis **w** vanish, Jb 6:15
W are turbid because of ice *And* Jb 6:16
of ice *And* into **w** the snow melts. Jb 6:16
And **w** shines as the darkness." Jb 10:22
with words **w** are not profitable? Jb 15:3
W are destined to become ruins. Jb 15:28 834
to the reproof **w** insults me, Jb 20:3
eye **w** saw him sees him no longer, Jb 20:9
seized a house **w** he has not built. Jb 20:19
chaff **w** the storm carries away? Jb 21:18
the plans by **w** you would wrong me. Jb 21:27
path **W** wicked men have trod, Jb 22:15 834
"I would learn the words **w** He Jb 23:5
Nor deep gloom **w** covers me. Jb 23:17
And the inheritance **w** tyrants Jb 27:13
Or as a hut **w** the watchman has Jb 27:18
the case **w** I did not know. Jb 29:16
w my adversary has written, Jb 31:35
bones **w** were not seen stick out. Jb 33:21
And that **w** was set on your table Jb 36:16 5183a
His work, Of **w** men have sung. Jb 36:24 834
W the clouds pour down, They drip Jb 36:28 834
things **w** we cannot comprehend. Jb 37:5
light **w** is bright in the skies; Jb 37:21 1931
W I have reserved for the time of Jb 38:23 834
Behemoth, **w** I made as well as you; Jb 40:15 834
that **w** I did not understand, Jb 42:3
for me, **w** I did not know." Jb 42:3
W yields its fruit in its season And Ps 1:3 834
like chaff **w** the wind drives away. Ps 1:4 834
And has fallen into the hole **w** he Ps 7:15
the stars, **W** You have ordained; Ps 8:3 834
down in the pit **w** they have made; Ps 9:15
In the net **w** they hid, their own Ps 9:15 2098
in the plots **w** they have devised. Ps 10:2 2098
in the safety for **w** he longs." Ps 12:5
w is not from deceitful lips. Ps 17:1
W is as a bridegroom coming out of Ps 19:5 1931
net **w** they have secretly laid for me, Ps 31:4 2098
W speak arrogantly against the Ps 31:18
W You have stored up for those Ps 31:19 834
W You have wrought for those who Ps 31:19
you in the way **w** you should go; Ps 32:8 2098
the mule **w** have no understanding, Ps 32:9
the net **w** he hid catch himself; Ps 35:8 834
are the wonders **w** You have done, Ps 40:5
bones **w** You have broken rejoice. Ps 51:8
my soul in peace from the battle **w** Ps 55:18
w melts away as it goes along, Ps 58:8
of a woman **w** never see the sun. Ps 58:8
of curses and lies **w** they utter. Ps 59:12
W my lips uttered And my mouth Ps 66:14 834
w God has desired for His abode? Ps 68:16
heavens, **w** are from ancient times; Ps 68:33
to **w** I may continually come; Ps 71:3
And my soul, **w** You have redeemed. Ps 71:23 834
w You have purchased of old, Ps 74:2
W You have redeemed to be the Ps 74:2
You **w** ascends continually. Ps 74:23
W we have heard and known, And our Ps 78:3 834
W He commanded our fathers That Ps 78:5 834
swarms of flies **w** devoured them, Ps 78:45
them, And frogs **w** destroyed them. Ps 78:45
w His right hand had gained. Ps 78:54
tent **w** He had pitched among men, Ps 78:60
of Judah, Mount Zion **w** He loved. Ps 78:68 834
earth **w** He has founded forever. Ps 78:69
the nations **w** do not know You, Ps 79:6 834
w do not call upon Your name. Ps 79:6 834
of Your servants **w** has been shed. Ps 79:10
with **w** they have reproached You, Ps 79:12 834
w Your right hand has planted, Ps 80:15 834
W You swore to David in Your Ps 89:49
With **w** Your enemies have Ps 89:51 834
With **w** they have reproached the Ps 89:51 834
are like grass **w** sprouts anew. Ps 90:5
One **w** devises mischief by decree? Ps 94:20
w You established for them. Ps 104:8 2088
And wine **w** makes man's heart glad, Ps 104:15
And food **w** sustains man's heart. Ps 104:15
cedars of Lebanon **w** He planted, Ps 104:16 834
In **w** all the beasts of the forest Ps 104:20
In **w** are swarms without number, Ps 104:25 8033
w You have formed to sport in it. Ps 104:26 2088
His wonders **w** He has done, Ps 105:5 834
The word **w** He commanded to a Ps 105:8
covenant **w** He made with Abraham, Ps 105:9 834
idols, **W** became a snare to them. Ps 106:36
W lifted up the waves of the sea. Ps 107:25
garment with **w** he covers himself, Ps 109:19
with **w** he constantly girds himself. Ps 109:19
The stone **w** the builders rejected Ps 118:22
is the day **w** the LORD has made; Ps 118:24
w produces reverence for You. Ps 119:38 834
Turn away my reproach **w** I dread, Ps 119:39 834
in Your commandments, **W** I love. Ps 119:47 834
to Your commandments, **W** I love; Ps 119:48 834
In **w** You have made me hope. Ps 119:49 834
To **w** the tribes go up, even the Ps 122:4 8033
as Mount Zion, **w** cannot be moved but Ps 125:1
W withers before it grows up; Ps 129:6 7945
With **w** the reaper does not fill Ps 129:7 7945
from **w** He will not turn back: Ps 132:11
My testimony **w** I will teach them, Ps 132:12 2097
with **w** you have repaid us. Ps 137:8 7945
deep pits from **w** they cannot rise. Ps 140:10
the trap **w** they have set for me, Ps 141:9
me the way in **w** I should walk; Ps 143:8 2098
And to the young ravens **w** cry. Ps 147:9 834
a decree **w** will not pass away. Ps 148:6
W, having no chief, Officer or Pr 6:7 834
are six things **w** the LORD hates, Pr 6:16
seven **w** are an abomination to Him: Pr 6:16
There is a way **w** *seems* right to a Pr 14:12
There is a way **w** *seems* right to a Pr 16:25
the stronghold in **w** they trust. Pr 21:22 4009
If you have nothing with **w** to pay, Pr 22:27
boundary **W** your fathers have set. Pr 22:28 834
of Solomon **w** the men of Hezekiah, Pr 25:1 834
Like the legs **w** are useless Pr 26:7
Like a thorn **w** falls into Pr 26:9
a driving rain **w** leaves no food. Pr 28:3
things **w** are too wonderful for me, Pr 30:18
me, Four **w** I do not understand: Pr 30:18
w are stately in *their* march, Pr 30:29
four **w** are stately when they walk: Pr 30:29
The lion **w** is mighty among beasts Pr 30:30
oracle **w** his mother taught him: Pr 31:1 834
ways to that **w** destroys kings. Pr 31:3
his work **W** he does under the sun? Ec 1:3 7945
That **w** has been is that which will Ec 1:9
4100, 7945
which has been is that **w** will be, Ec 1:9 7945
And that **w** has been done is that Ec 1:9
4100, 7945
been done is that **w** will be done. Ec 1:9 7945
there anything of **w** one might say, Ec 1:10 7945
existed for ages **W** were before us. Ec 1:10 834
of the later things **w** will occur, Ec 1:11 7945
It is a grievous task **w** God Ec 1:13
w have been done under the sun, Ec 1:14 7945
from **w** to irrigate a forest of growing Ec 2:6
all my activities **w** my hands had done Ec 2:11 7945
and the labor **w** I had exerted, Ec 2:11 7945
for the work **w** had been done under Ec 2:17 7945
for **w** I had labored under the sun, Ec 2:18 7945
over all the fruit of my labor for **w** I Ec 2:19 7945
for **w** I had labored under the sun. Ec 2:20 7945
with **w** he labors under the sun? Ec 2:22 7945
worker from that in **w** he toils? Ec 3:9 834
I have seen the task **w** God has Ec 3:10 834
men with **w** to occupy themselves. Ec 3:10
man will not find out the work **w** God Ec 3:11 834
That **w** is has been already and Ec 3:15
4100, 7945
that **w** will be has already been, Ec 3:15 834
w were being done under the sun. Ec 4:1 834
and every skill **w** is done is *the result of* Ec 4:4
There is a grievous evil **w** I have Ec 5:13
in all one's labor in **w** he toils under Ec 5:18 7945
of his life **w** God has given him; Ec 5:18 834
There is an evil **w** I have seen Ec 6:1 834
many words **w** increase futility. Ec 6:11
seriously all words **w** are spoken, Ec 7:21 834
w I am still seeking but have not Ec 7:28 834
futility **w** is done on the earth, Ec 8:14 834
days of his life **w** God has given him Ec 8:15 834
task **w** has been done on the earth Ec 8:16 834
w has been done under the sun. Ec 8:17 834
your fleeting life **w** He has given to Ec 9:9 834
and in your toil in **w** you have Ec 9:9 834
error **w** goes forth from the ruler Ec 10:5 7945
judgment, everything **w** is hidden, Ec 12:14
The Song of Songs, **w** is Solomon's. SS 1:1 834
W lies all night between my breasts. SS 1:13
crown With **w** his mother has crowned SS 3:11 7945
flock of *newly* shorn ewes **W** have SS 4:2 7945
washing, All of **w** bear twins, SS 4:2 7945
On **w** are hung a thousand shields, SS 4:4
gazelle **W** feed among the lilies. SS 4:5
Your teeth are like a flock of ewes **W** SS 6:6 7945
washing, All of **w** bear twins, SS 6:6 7945
goblet **W** never lacks mixed wine; SS 7:2
Lebanon, **W** faces toward Damascus. SS 7:4
old, **W** I have saved up for you, SS 7:13
w he saw during the reigns of Uzziah, Is 1:1 834
of the oaks **w** you have desired, Is 1:29 834
at the gardens **w** you have chosen. Is 1:29 834
The word **w** Isaiah the son of Amoz Is 2:1 834
That **w** their fingers have made. Is 2:8 834
W they made for themselves to Is 2:20 834
coal in his hand, **w** he had taken from Is 6:6
As for all the hills **w** used to Is 7:25 834
devastation **w** will come from afar? Is 10:3
w Isaiah the son of Amoz saw. Is 13:1 834
in **w** you have been enslaved, Is 14:3 834
W used to strike the peoples in Is 14:6
W subdued the nations in anger Is 14:6
Therefore the abundance **w** they Is 15:7
clusters **W** reached as far as Jazer Is 16:8
This is the word **w** the LORD spoke Is 16:13 834
to that **w** his fingers have made, Is 17:8 834
Or like branches **w** they abandoned Is 17:9 834
oh land of whirring wings **W** lies Is 18:1 834
W sends envoys by the sea, Even in Is 18:2
work for Egypt **W** *its* head or tail, Is 19:15 834
w He is going to wave over them. Is 19:16 834
w He is purposing against them. Is 19:17 834
Chaldeans—this is the people **w** Is 23:13
covering **w** is over all peoples, Is 25:7
w is stretched over all nations. Is 25:7
W is at the head of the fertile Is 28:1 834
W is at the head of the fertile Is 28:4 834
W one sees, *And* as soon as it is Is 28:4 834
is too short on **w** to stretch out, Is 28:20
ones like the chaff **w** blows away; Is 29:5
w when they give it to the one who Is 29:11 834
seed **w** you will sow in the ground, Is 30:23 834
Also the oxen and the donkeys **w** Is 30:24
w has been winnowed with shovel Is 30:24 834
torrent, **W** reaches to the neck, Is 30:28
the bridle **w** leads to ruin. Is 30:28
W the LORD will lay on him, Is 30:32 834
Against **w** a band of shepherds is Is 31:4 834
w your sinful hands have made for you Is 31:7 834
For the land of my people *in* **w** Is 32:13
thorns **w** are burned in the fire. Is 33:12
speech **w** no one comprehends, Is 33:19
tongue **w** no one understands. Is 33:19
A tent **w** will not be folded Is 33:20
On **w** no boat with oars will go, Is 33:21
on **w** no mighty ship will pass Is 33:21
on **w** if a man leans, it will go Is 36:6 834
w the LORD your God has heard. Is 37:4 834
with **w** the servants of the king of Is 37:6 834
'Did the gods of those nations **w** Is 37:12 834
you back by the way **w** you came. Is 37:29 834
w has gone down with the sun on Is 38:8 834
stairway on **w** it had gone down. Is 38:8 834
LORD **w** you have spoken is good." Is 39:8 834
into the ships in **w** they rejoice. Is 43:14
times things **w** have not been done, Is 46:10 834
"But evil will come on you **W** you Is 47:11
on you For **w** you cannot atone; Is 47:11
And destruction about **w** you do not Is 47:11
sorceries With **w** you have labored Is 47:12 834
things **w** you have not known. Is 48:6
By **w** I have sent your mother away? Is 50:1 834
to the rock from **w** you were hewn And Is 51:1
to the quarry from **w** you were dug. Is 51:1
w knows you not will run to you, Is 55:5
be **w** goes forth from My mouth; Is 55:11 834
in the matter for **w** I sent it. Is 55:11 834
sign **w** will not be cut off." Is 55:13
name **w** will not be cut off. Is 56:5 834
"Is it a fast like this **w** I choose, Is 58:5
"Is this not the fast **w** I choose, Is 58:6
of the streets in **w** to dwell. Is 58:12
And *from* that **w** is crushed a snake Is 59:5
W the wind of the LORD drives. Is 59:19
"My Spirit **w** is upon you, and My Is 59:21 834
words **w** I have put in your mouth shall Is 59:21 834
"For the nation and the kingdom **w** Is 60:12 834
W the mouth of the LORD will Is 62:2 834
wine for **w** you have labored." Is 62:8 834
W He has granted them according to Is 63:7 834
cattle **w** go down into the valley, Is 63:14
things **w** we did not expect, Is 64:3
nation **w** did not call on My name. Is 65:1
Who walk *in* the way **w** is not good, Is 65:2
that in **w** I did not delight." Is 65:12 834
that in **w** I did not delight." Is 66:4 834
W I make will endure before Me," Is 66:22 834
speak to them all **w** I command you. Jer 1:17 834
glory For that **w** does not profit. Jer 2:11

Context	Reference	No.
gods **W** you made for yourself?	**Jer 2:28**	834
fortified cities in **w** you trust.	**Jer 5:17**	834
house, **w** is called by My name,	**Jer 7:10**	834
house, **w** is called by My name,	**Jer 7:11**	834
now to My place **w** was in Shiloh,	**Jer 7:12**	834
the house **w** is called by My name,	**Jer 7:14**	834
called by My name, in **w** you trust,	**Jer 7:14**	834
w I gave you and your fathers,	**Jer 7:14**	834
in all the way **w** I command you,	**Jer 7:23**	834
done that **w** is evil in My sight,"	**Jer 7:30**	7451a
the house **w** is called by My name,	**Jer 7:30**	834
w is in the valley of the son of Hinnom,	**Jer 7:31**	834
in the fire, **w** I did not command,	**Jer 7:31**	834
host of heaven, **w** they have loved and	**Jer 8:2**	834
loved and **w** they have served,	**Jer 8:2**	834
and **w** they have gone after and	**Jer 8:2**	834
after and **w** they have sought,	**Jer 8:2**	834
sought, and **w** they have worshiped.	**Jer 8:2**	834
places to **w** I have driven them,"	**Jer 8:3**	834
Adders, for **w** there is no charm,	**Jer 8:17**	834
My law **w** I set before them,	**Jer 9:13**	834
the word **w** the LORD speaks to you,	**Jer 10:1**	834
The word **w** came to Jeremiah from	**Jer 11:1**	834
w I commanded your forefathers in	**Jer 11:4**	834
according to all **w** I command you;	**Jer 11:4**	834
w I swore to your forefathers,	**Jer 11:5**	834
w I commanded *them* to do,	**Jer 11:8**	834
w I made with their fathers."	**Jer 11:10**	834
disaster on them **w** they will not be	**Jer 11:11**	834
w they have done to provoke Me by	**Jer 11:17**	834
inheritance with **w** I have endowed	**Jer 12:14**	834
bought, **w** is around your waist,	**Jer 13:4**	834
w I commanded you to hide there."	**Jer 13:6**	834
waistband **w** is totally worthless.	**Jer 13:10**	834
That **w** came as the word of the	**Jer 14:1**	834
or what is our sin **w** we have	**Jer 16:10**	834
the land **w** you have not known,	**Jer 16:13**	834
land **w** I gave to their fathers.	**Jer 16:15**	834
In the land **w** you do not know;	**Jer 17:4**	834
in My anger **W** will burn forever.	**Jer 17:4**	
hatches eggs **w** it has not laid,	**Jer 17:11**	
through **w** the kings of Judah come	**Jer 17:19**	834
The word **w** came to Jeremiah from	**Jer 18:1**	834
that nation against **w** I have spoken	**Jer 18:8**	834
with **w** I had promised to bless it.	**Jer 18:10**	834
w is by the entrance of the	**Jer 19:2**	834
at **w** the ears of everyone that	**Jer 19:3**	834
w I never commanded or spoke of,	**Jer 19:5**	834
in the distress with **w** their enemies	**Jer 19:9**	834
w cannot again be repaired;	**Jer 19:11**	834
w was by the house of the LORD.	**Jer 20:2**	834
like the cities **W** the LORD overthrew	**Jer 20:16**	834
The word **w** came to Jeremiah from	**Jer 21:1**	834
of war **w** are in your hands,	**Jer 21:4**	834
with **w** you are warring against the	**Jer 21:4**	834
Like cities **w** are not inhabited.	**Jer 22:6**	
land to **w** they desire to return,	**Jer 22:27**	834
His name by **w** He will be called,	**Jer 23:6**	834
w they relate to one another,	**Jer 23:27**	834
like a hammer **w** shatters a rock?	**Jer 23:29**	
w I gave you and your fathers.	**Jer 23:39**	834
w will not be forgotten."	**Jer 23:40**	834
w could not be eaten due to	**Jer 24:2**	834
w cannot be eaten due to	**Jer 24:3**	834
'But like the bad figs **w** cannot be	**Jer 24:8**	834
destroyed from the land **w** I gave to	**Jer 24:10**	834
w Jeremiah the prophet spoke to	**Jer 25:2**	834
and dwell on the land **w** the LORD	**Jer 25:5**	834
w I have pronounced against it,	**Jer 25:13**	834
w Jeremiah has prophesied against	**Jer 25:13**	834
coastlands **w** are beyond the sea;	**Jer 25:22**	834
all the kingdoms of the earth **w** are	**Jer 25:26**	834
sword **w** I will send among you."	**Jer 25:27**	834
this city **w** is called by My name,	**Jer 25:29**	834
the calamity **w** I am planning to do	**Jer 26:3**	834
My law **w** I have set before you,	**Jer 26:4**	834
w He has pronounced against you.	**Jer 26:13**	834
the misfortune **w** He had pronounced	**Jer 26:19**	834
the men and the beasts **w** are on	**Jer 27:5**	834
the kingdom **w** will not serve him,	**Jer 27:8**	834
and **w** will not put its neck under	**Jer 27:8**	834
"But the nation **w** will bring its	**Jer 27:11**	834
the LORD has spoken to that nation **w**	**Jer 27:13**	834
that the vessels **w** are left in the	**Jer 27:18**	
w Nebuchadnezzar king of Babylon	**Jer 27:20**	834
w Nebuchadnezzar king of Babylon	**Jer 28:3**	834
your words **w** you have prophesied	**Jer 28:6**	834
"Yet hear now this word **w** I am	**Jer 28:7**	834
letter **w** Jeremiah the prophet sent	**Jer 29:1**	834
listen to the dreams **w** they dream.	**Jer 29:8**	834
'**w** I sent to them again and again	**Jer 29:19**	834
falsely, **w** I did not command them;	**Jer 29:23**	834
The word **w** came to Jeremiah from	**Jer 30:1**	834
'Write all the words **w** I have	**Jer 30:2**	834
Now these are the words **w** the LORD	**Jer 30:4**	834
path in **w** they will not stumble;	**Jer 31:9**	
highway, The way by **w** you went.	**Jer 31:21**	
not like the covenant **w** I made	**Jer 31:32**	834
Egypt, My covenant **w** they broke,	**Jer 31:32**	834
"But this is the covenant **w** I	**Jer 31:33**	834
w was the eighteenth year of	**Jer 32:1**	1931
w *was in* the house of the king of	**Jer 32:2**	834
my field **w** is at Anathoth,	**Jer 32:7**	834
w is in the land of Benjamin;	**Jer 32:8**	834
"I bought the field **w** was at	**Jer 32:9**	834
w You swore to their forefathers	**Jer 32:22**	834
w they have done to provoke Me to	**Jer 32:32**	834
the house **w** is called by My name,	**Jer 32:34**	834
w I had not commanded them nor had	**Jer 32:35**	834
concerning this city of **w** you say,	**Jer 32:36**	834
all the lands to **w** I have driven them	**Jer 32:37**	834
bought in this land of **w** you say,	**Jer 32:43**	834
mighty things, **w** you do not know.'	**Jer 33:3**	
w are broken down *to make a*	**Jer 33:4**	
by **w** they have sinned against Me,	**Jer 33:8**	834
by **w** they have sinned against Me	**Jer 33:8**	834
and by **w** they have transgressed	**Jer 33:8**	834
w will hear of all the good that	**Jer 33:9**	834
heard in this place, of **w** you say,	**Jer 33:10**	834
again be in this place **w** is waste,	**Jer 33:12**	
fulfill the good word **w** I have spoken	**Jer 33:14**	834
the name by **w** she will be called:	**Jer 33:16**	834
'The two families **w** the LORD chose,	**Jer 33:24**	834
The word **w** came to Jeremiah from	**Jer 34:1**	834
The word **w** came to Jeremiah from	**Jer 34:8**	834
the house **w** is called by My name.	**Jer 34:15**	834
covenant **w** they made before Me,	**Jer 34:18**	834
Babylon **w** has gone away from you.	**Jer 34:21**	
The word **w** came to Jeremiah from	**Jer 35:1**	834
w was near the chamber of the	**Jer 35:4**	834
w was above the chamber of	**Jer 35:4**	834
w he commanded his sons not to	**Jer 35:14**	834
dwell in the land **w** I have given to	**Jer 35:15**	834
their father **w** he commanded them,	**Jer 35:16**	834
and write on it all the words **w** I have	**Jer 36:2**	834
w I plan to bring on them,	**Jer 36:3**	834
the LORD **w** He had spoken to him	**Jer 36:4**	834
and read from the scroll **w** you have	**Jer 36:6**	834
the scroll from **w** you have read	**Jer 36:14**	834
and the words **w** Baruch had written	**Jer 36:27**	834
the first scroll **w** Jehoiakim the king	**Jer 36:28**	834
all the words of the book **w** Jehoiakim	**Jer 36:32**	834
words of the LORD **w** He spoke	**Jer 37:2**	834
Pharaoh's army **w** has come out for	**Jer 37:7**	
w they had made into the prison.	**Jer 37:15**	
w was in the court of the	**Jer 38:6**	834
the word **w** the LORD has shown me:	**Jer 38:21**	834
words **w** the king had commanded;	**Jer 38:27**	834
The word **w** came to Jeremiah from	**Jer 40:1**	834
the chains **w** are on your hands.	**Jer 40:4**	834
places to **w** they had been driven	**Jer 40:12**	834
Chimham, **w** is beside Bethlehem,	**Jer 41:17**	834
tell us the way in **w** we should walk	**Jer 42:3**	834
message **w** the LORD will answer you	**Jer 42:4**	834
message with **w** the LORD your God	**Jer 42:5**	834
w you are afraid of, will overtake	**Jer 42:16**	834
famine, about **w** you are anxious,	**Jer 42:16**	834
to **w** they had been driven away,	**Jer 43:5**	834
brick *terrace* **w** is at the entrance of	**Jer 43:9**	834
w is in the land of Egypt;	**Jer 43:13**	834
because of their wickedness **w** they	**Jer 44:3**	834
this abominable thing **w** I hate."	**Jer 44:4**	834
w they committed in the land of	**Jer 44:9**	834
w I have set before you and before	**Jer 44:10**	834
to **w** they are longing to return	**Jer 44:14**	834
abominations **w** you have committed;	**Jer 44:22**	834
is the message **w** Jeremiah the	**Jer 45:1**	834
That **w** came as the word of the	**Jer 46:1**	834
w was by the Euphrates River at	**Jer 46:2**	834
w Nebuchadnezzar king of Babylon	**Jer 46:2**	834
This is the message **w** the LORD	**Jer 46:13**	834
That **w** came as the word of the	**Jer 47:1**	834
w He has planned against Edom,	**Jer 49:20**	834
and His purposes **w** He has purposed	**Jer 49:20**	834
w Nebuchadnezzar king of Babylon	**Jer 49:28**	834
up against a nation **w** is at ease,	**Jer 49:31**	
is at ease, **W** lives securely,"	**Jer 49:31**	
That **w** came as the word of the	**Jer 49:34**	834
And there will be no nation To **w**	**Jer 49:36**	834
The word **w** the LORD spoke	**Jer 50:1**	834
hear the plan of the LORD **w** He has	**Jer 50:45**	834
and His purposes **w** He has purposed	**Jer 50:45**	834
desert, A land in **w** no man lives And	**Jer 51:43**	2004
through **w** no son of man passes.	**Jer 51:43**	2004
The message **w** Jeremiah the prophet	**Jer 51:59**	834
w would come upon Babylon,	**Jer 51:60**	834
all these words **w** have been	**Jer 51:60**	
walls **w** *was* by the king's garden,	**Jer 52:7**	834
w was the nineteenth year of King	**Jer 52:12**	1931
Now the bronze pillars **w** belonged	**Jer 52:17**	834
w were in the house of the LORD,	**Jer 52:17**	834
w were used in *temple* service.	**Jer 52:18**	834
w King Solomon had made for the	**Jer 52:20**	834
W was severely dealt out to me,	**La 1:12**	834
W the LORD inflicted on the day of	**La 1:12**	834
the day **w** You have proclaimed,	**La 1:21**	
"Is this the city of **w** they said,	**La 2:15**	7945
this is the day for **w** we waited;	**La 2:16**	7945
W He commanded from days of old.	**La 2:17**	834
W was overthrown as in a moment,	**La 4:6**	
W has consumed its foundations.	**La 4:11**	
of Mount Zion **w** lies desolate,	**La 5:18**	7945
and on that **w** resembled a throne,	**Ezk 1:26**	1823
this scroll **w** I am giving you."	**Ezk 3:3**	834
My words **w** I will speak to you	**Ezk 3:10**	834
and his righteous deeds **w** he has	**Ezk 3:20**	834
glory **w** I saw by the river Chebar,	**Ezk 3:23**	834
"Your food **w** you eat *shall be*	**Ezk 4:10**	834
w you will prepare your bread."	**Ezk 4:15**	
than the lands **w** surround her;	**Ezk 5:6**	834
than the nations **w** surround you	**Ezk 5:7**	834
of the nations **w** surround you,'	**Ezk 5:7**	834
like of **w** I will never do again.	**Ezk 5:9**	834
among the nations **w** surround you,	**Ezk 5:14**	834
the deadly arrows of famine **w** were	**Ezk 5:16**	834
to **w** they will be carried captive,	**Ezk 6:9**	834
hearts **w** turned away from Me,	**Ezk 6:9**	834
w played the harlot after their	**Ezk 6:9**	
the evils **w** they have committed,	**Ezk 6:9**	834
of Israel, **w** will fall by sword,	**Ezk 6:11**	834
jealousy, **w** provokes to jealousy,	**Ezk 8:3**	834
appearance **w** I saw in the plain.	**Ezk 8:4**	834
the great abominations **w** the house	**Ezk 8:6**	834
w they are committing."	**Ezk 8:13**	834
house **w** *was* toward the north;	**Ezk 8:14**	834
w they have committed here,	**Ezk 8:17**	834
of the upper gate **w** faces north,	**Ezk 9:2**	834
from the cherub on **w** it had been,	**Ezk 9:3**	834
abominations **w** are being committed	**Ezk 9:4**	
fire **w** was between the cherubim,	**Ezk 10:7**	834
in the direction **w** they faced,	**Ezk 10:11**	834
the LORD's house **w** faced eastward.	**Ezk 11:1**	
among **w** you have been scattered,	**Ezk 11:17**	834
mountain **w** is east of the city.	**Ezk 11:23**	834
with **w** you plastered *it?*' "	**Ezk 13:12**	834
"So I will tear down the wall **w**	**Ezk 13:14**	834
by **w** you hunt lives there as birds and	**Ezk 13:20**	834
the calamity **w** I have brought against	**Ezk 14:22**	834
w I have brought upon it.	**Ezk 14:22**	834
a branch **w** is among the trees	**Ezk 15:2**	834
from it on **w** to hang any vessel?	**Ezk 15:3**	
w I have given to the fire for	**Ezk 15:6**	834
My splendor **w** I bestowed on you,"	**Ezk 16:14**	834
w should never come about nor	**Ezk 16:16**	
of My silver, **w** I had given you,	**Ezk 16:17**	834
"Also My bread **w** I gave you, fine	**Ezk 16:19**	834
oil and honey with **w** I fed you,	**Ezk 16:19**	
of your sons **w** you gave to idols,	**Ezk 16:36**	834
abominations **w** you have committed.	**Ezk 16:51**	834
Because of your sins in **w** you	**Ezk 16:52**	834
surely My oath **w** he despised and	**Ezk 17:19**	834
and My covenant **w** he broke,	**Ezk 17:19**	834
act **w** he has committed against Me.	**Ezk 17:20**	834
his father's sins **w** he committed,	**Ezk 18:14**	834
wicked man turns from all his sins **w**	**Ezk 18:21**	834
"All his transgressions **w** he has	**Ezk 18:22**	834
righteousness **w** he has practiced,	**Ezk 18:22**	834
All his righteous deeds **w** he has	**Ezk 18:24**	834
for his treachery **w** he has committed	**Ezk 18:24**	834
and his sin **w** he has committed;	**Ezk 18:24**	834
w he has committed he will die.	**Ezk 18:26**	834
turns away from his wickedness **w**	**Ezk 18:27**	834
transgressions **w** he had committed,	**Ezk 18:28**	834
w you have committed and	**Ezk 18:31**	834
w is the glory of all lands.	**Ezk 20:6**	1931
them of My ordinances, by **w**,	**Ezk 20:11**	834
they rejected My ordinances, by **w**,	**Ezk 20:13**	834
into the land **w** I had given them,	**Ezk 20:15**	834
w is the glory of all lands,	**Ezk 20:15**	1931
to observe My ordinances, by **w**,	**Ezk 20:21**	834
by **w** they could not live;	**Ezk 20:25**	
land **w** I swore to give to them,	**Ezk 20:28**	834
is the high place to **w** you go?'	**Ezk 20:29**	834
into the land **w** I swore to give to	**Ezk 20:42**	834
w you have defiled yourselves;	**Ezk 20:43**	834
rod **w** despises will be no more?"	**Ezk 21:13**	
great one slain, **w** surrounds them,	**Ezk 21:14**	
Exalt that **w** is low and abase	**Ezk 21:26**	8217
is low and abase that **w** is high.	**Ezk 21:26**	1364
by the blood **w** you have shed,	**Ezk 22:4**	834
by your idols **w** you have made.	**Ezk 22:4**	834
dishonest gain **w** you have acquired	**Ezk 22:13**	834
at the bloodshed **w** is among you.	**Ezk 22:13**	834
sister's cup, **W** is deep and wide.	**Ezk 23:32**	
on **w** you had set My incense and My	**Ezk 23:41**	
To the pot in **w** there is rust And	**Ezk 24:6**	834
its cities **w** are on its frontiers,	**Ezk 25:9**	
city, **W** was mighty on the sea,	**Ezk 26:17**	834
the coastlands **w** are by the sea	**Ezk 26:18**	834
the cities **w** are not inhabited,	**Ezk 26:19**	834
w *were* among your merchandise.	**Ezk 27:24**	
land **w** I gave to My servant Jacob.	**Ezk 28:25**	834
for his labor **w** he performed,	**Ezk 29:20**	834
Eden, **w** were in the garden of God,	**Ezk 31:9**	834
"To **w** among the trees of Eden are	**Ezk 31:18**	4310
into lands **w** you have not known.	**Ezk 32:9**	834
is destitute of that **w** filled it,	**Ezk 32:15**	4393
w he has committed he will die.	**Ezk 33:13**	834
walks by the statutes **w** ensure	**Ezk 33:15**	
w they have committed."	**Ezk 33:29**	834
is **w** comes forth from the LORD.'	**Ezk 33:30**	
deliver them from all the places to **w**	**Ezk 34:12**	834
according to your envy **w** you showed	**Ezk 35:11**	834
have heard all your revilings **w**	**Ezk 35:12**	834
w have become a prey and a	**Ezk 36:4**	834
of the nations **w** are round about,	**Ezk 36:4**	834
surely the nations **w** are around you	**Ezk 36:7**	834
blood **w** they had shed on the land,	**Ezk 36:18**	834
w the house of Israel had profaned	**Ezk 36:21**	834
w you have profaned among the	**Ezk 36:22**	834
My great name **w** has been profaned	**Ezk 36:23**	
w you have profaned in their midst.	**Ezk 36:23**	834
and planted that **w** was desolate;	**Ezk 36:36**	
w is in the hand of Ephraim,	**Ezk 37:19**	834
"The sticks on **w** you write	**Ezk 37:20**	834
places in **w** they have sinned,	**Ezk 37:23**	834
servant, in **w** your fathers lived;	**Ezk 37:25**	834
w had been a continual waste;	**Ezk 38:8**	834
waste places **w** are *now* inhabited,	**Ezk 38:12**	
is the day of **w** I have spoken.	**Ezk 39:8**	834
My sacrifice **w** I am going to sacrifice	**Ezk 39:17**	834
w I have sacrificed for you.	**Ezk 39:19**	834
see My judgment **w** I have executed and	**Ezk 39:21**	834
and My hand **w** I have laid on them.	**Ezk 39:21**	834
w they perpetrated against Me,	**Ezk 39:26**	834
each of **w** *was* a cubit and a	**Ezk 40:5**	
he went to the gate **w** faced east,	**Ezk 40:6**	834

the outer court **w** faced the north, Ezk 40:20 834
the gate **w** faced toward the east; Ezk 40:22 834
on **w** to slaughter the burnt Ezk 40:39
on **w** they slaughter *sacrifices.* Ezk 40:41
on **w** they lay the instruments with Ezk 40:42
instruments with **w** they slaughter the Ezk 40:42 834
one of **w** was at the side of the Ezk 40:44 834
chamber **w** faces toward the south, Ezk 40:45 834
but the chamber **w** faces toward the Ezk 40:46 834
and at the stairway by **w** it was Ezk 40:49 834
the wall **w** *stood* on their inward side Ezk 41:6 834
chamber **w** *was* opposite the separate Ezk 42:1 834
Along the length, **w** *was* a Ezk 42:2
w belonged to the inner court, Ezk 42:3 834
w belonged to the outer court, Ezk 42:3 834
For the length of the chambers **w** Ezk 42:8 834
the chambers **w** *were* on the north, Ezk 42:11 834
the openings of the chambers **w** were Ezk 42:12 834
w are opposite the separate area, Ezk 42:13 834
their garments in **w** they minister, Ezk 42:14 834
that **w** is for the people." Ezk 42:14 834
the gate **w** faced toward the east and Ezk 42:15 834
appearance of the vision **w** I saw, Ezk 43:3 834
like the vision **w** I saw when He Ezk 43:3 834
w I saw by the river Chebar; Ezk 43:3 834
w they have committed. Ezk 43:8 834
the sanctuary, **w** faces the east; Ezk 44:1
w they have committed. Ezk 44:13 834
not gird themselves with *anything* **w** Ezk 44:18
their garments in **w** they have been Ezk 44:19 834
of a bath from *each* kor (**w** *is* Ezk 45:14
"The burnt offering **w** the Ezk 46:4 834
w shall be without blemish. Ezk 46:6
by way of the gate by **w** he entered Ezk 46:9 834
w *was* at the side of the gate, Ezk 46:19
for the priests, **w** faced north; Ezk 46:19
that every living creature **w** swarms Ezk 47:9 834
"This *shall be* the boundary by **w** Ezk 47:13 834
w is between the border of Ezk 47:16 834
w is by the border of Hauran. Ezk 47:16 834
the tribe with **w** the alien stays, Ezk 47:23 834
allotment **w** you shall set apart, Ezk 48:8 834
w are in the middle of that which Ezk 48:22
of that **w** belongs to the prince, Ezk 48:22 834
"This is the land **w** you shall Ezk 48:29 834
food and from the wine **w** he drank, Da 1:5 4960
at the end of **w** they were to enter Da 1:5
food or with the wine **w** he drank; Da 1:8 4960
Then at the end of the days **w** the Da 1:18 834
about **w** the king consulted them, Da 1:20 834
w the king demands is difficult, Da 2:11 1768
to make known to me the dream **w** I Da 2:26 1768
about **w** the king has inquired, Da 2:27 1768
w was large and of extraordinary Da 2:31 1768
w will rule over all the earth. Da 2:39 1768
kingdom **w** will never be destroyed, Da 2:44 1768
the height of **w** *was* sixty cubits Da 3:1
golden image **w** you have set up." Da 3:12 1768
to declare the signs and wonders **w** Da 4:2 1768
visions of my dream **w** I have seen, Da 4:9 1768
'This is the dream **w** I, King Da 4:18
w became large and grew strong, Da 4:20 1768
and in **w** *was* food for all, Da 4:21
under **w** the beasts of the field Da 4:21
w has come upon my lord the king: Da 4:24 1768
w I myself have built as a royal Da 4:30 1768
silver vessels **w** Nebuchadnezzar his Da 5:2 1768
of the temple **w** *was* in Jerusalem, Da 5:2 1768
house of God **w** *was* in Jerusalem; Da 5:3 1768
the grandeur **w** He bestowed on him, Da 5:19 1768
wood and stone, **w** do not see, Da 5:23 1768
Persians, **w** may not be revoked." Da 6:8 1768
Persians, **w** may not be revoked." Da 6:12 1768
or to the injunction **w** you signed, Da 6:13 1768
or statute **w** the king establishes may Da 6:15 1768
is one **w** will not be destroyed, Da 6:26 1768
w had on its back four wings of a Da 7:6 1768
words **w** the horn was speaking; Da 7:11 1768
dominion **w** will not pass away; Da 7:14 1768
is one **W** will not be destroyed. Da 7:14 1768
beasts, **w** are four *in number,* Da 7:17 1768
w was different from all the Da 7:19 1768
and **w** devoured, crushed Da 7:19
and the other *horn* **w** came up, Da 7:20 1768
and before **w** three *of them* fell, Da 7:20
that horn **w** had eyes and a mouth Da 7:20
and **w** was larger in appearance Da 7:20
w will be different from all the Da 7:23 1768
one **w** appeared to me previously. Da 8:1
w is in the province of Elam; Da 8:2 834
a ram **w** had two horns was standing Da 8:3
w I had seen standing in front of Da 8:6 834
small horn **w** grew exceedingly great Da 8:9
"The ram **w** you saw with the two Da 8:20 834
place *represent* four kingdoms **w** Da 8:22
mornings **W** has been told is true; Da 8:26 834
number of the years **w** was *revealed as* Da 9:2 834
to **w** You have driven them, Da 9:7 834
deeds **w** they have committed against Da 9:7 834
to walk in His teachings **w** He set Da 9:10 834
along with the oath **w** is written Da 9:11 834
His words **w** He had spoken against Da 9:12 834
to all His deeds **w** He has done, Da 9:14 834
the city **w** is called by Your name; Da 9:18 834
to his authority **w** he wielded, Da 11:4 834
peace **w** he will put into effect; Da 11:17
that **w** is decreed will be done. Da 11:36
The word of the LORD **w** came to Hos 1:1 834
W cannot be measured or numbered; Hos 1:10 834

W they used for Baal. Hos 2:8
and fig trees, Of **w** she said, Hos 2:12 834
wages **W** my lovers have given me.' Hos 2:12 834
like the dew **w** goes away early. Hos 6:4
a vessel in **w** no one delights. Hos 8:8
detestable as that **w** they loved. Hos 9:10 159
me No iniquity, **w** *would be* sin." Hos 12:8 834
And like dew **w** soon disappears, Hos 13:3
Like chaff **w** is blown away from Hos 13:3
My great army **w** I sent among you. Jl 2:25 834
their blood **w** I have not avenged, Jl 3:21 834
w he envisioned in visions Am 1:1 834
after **w** their fathers walked. Am 2:4 834
Hear this word **w** the LORD has Am 3:1 834
against the entire family **w** He Am 3:1 834
also from that **w** is leavened, Am 4:5 2557
w I take up for you as a dirge, Am 5:1 834
"The city **w** goes forth a thousand Am 5:3
And the one **w** goes forth a hundred Am 5:3
gods **w** you made for yourselves. Am 5:26 834
their land **W** I have given them," Am 9:15 834
a ship **w** was going to Tarshish, Jon 1:3
and they threw the cargo **w** was in Jon 1:5 834
That **w** I have vowed I will pay. Jon 2:9 834
w I am going to tell you." Jon 3:2 834
the violence **w** is in his hands. Jon 3:8 834
relented concerning the calamity **w** He Jon 3:10 834
the plant for **w** you did not work and Jon 4:10 834
for which you did not work and **w** Jon 4:10
w came up overnight and perished Jon 4:10 7945
the great city in **w** there are more Jon 4:11 834
The word of the LORD **w** came *to* Mi 1:1 834
w he saw concerning Samaria and Mi 1:1 834
w you cannot remove your necks; Mi 2:3 834
Like showers on vegetation **W** do Mi 5:7 834
lion among flocks of sheep, **W,** Mi 5:8 834
the nations **w** have not obeyed." Mi 5:15 834
Or a first-ripe fig **w** I crave. Mi 7:1
The flock of Your possession **W** Mi 7:14
W You swore to our forefathers Mi 7:20 834
W was situated by the waters of Na 3:8
oracle **w** Habakkuk the prophet saw. Hab 1:1 834
dwelling places **w** are not theirs. Hab 1:6
beasts by **w** you terrified them, Hab 2:17
The word of the LORD **w** came to Zph 1:1 834
With **w** they have taunted My people Zph 2:8 834
All beasts **w** range in herds; Zph 2:14
exultant city **W** dwells securely, Zph 2:15
By **w** you have rebelled against Me; Zph 3:11 834
of My house **w** *lies* desolate, Hg 1:9 834
'As for the promise **w** I made you Hg 2:5 834
w I commanded My servants the Zch 1:6 834
month, **w** is the month Shebat, Zch 1:7 1931
myrtle trees **w** were in the ravine, Zch 1:8 834
with **w** You have been indignant Zch 1:12 834
the horns **w** have scattered Judah, Zch 1:19 834
the horns **w** have scattered Judah so Zch 1:21 834
against the nations **w** plunder you, Zch 2:8
the lamps **w** are on the top of it; Zch 4:2 834
eyes of the LORD **w** range to and fro Zch 4:10 1992a
branches **w** are beside the two golden Zch 4:12 834
w empty the golden *oil* from Zch 4:12
with one of **w** the black horses are Zch 6:6 834
ninth month, **w** *is* Chislev. Zch 7:1
'Are not *these* the words **w** the Zch 7:7 834
words **w** the LORD of hosts had sent Zch 7:12 834
are the things **w** you should do: Zch 8:16 834
And Hamath also, **w** borders on it; Zch 9:2
to break my covenant **w** I had made Zch 11:10 834
price at **w** I was valued by them." Zch 11:13 834
'*Those* with **w** I was wounded in the Zch 13:6 834
w is in front of Jerusalem on the Zch 14:4 834
unique day **w** is known to the LORD, Zch 14:7 1931
the plague with **w** the LORD will strike Zch 14:12 834
it will be the plague with **w** the Zch 14:18 834
sanctuary of the LORD **w** He loves and Mal 2:11 834
on the day **w** I am preparing," Mal 4:3 834
and ordinances **w** I commanded him Mal 4:4 834
NAME IMMANUEL," **w** translated means, Mt 1:23 3739
star, **w** they had seen in the east, Mt 2:9 3739
according to the time **w** he had Mt 2:16 3739
in Capernaum, **w** is by the sea, Mt 4:13
w is *alive* today and tomorrow is Mt 6:30
"**W** is easier, to say, 'Your sins Mt 9:5 5101
denounce the cities in **w** most of His Mt 11:20 3739
Tyre and Sidon **w** occurred in you, Mt 11:21
in Sodom **w** occurred in you, Mt 11:23
w was not lawful for him to eat nor Mt 12:4 3739
out of that **w** fills the heart. Mt 12:34 4051
return to my house from **w** I came'; Mt 12:44 3606
Isaiah is being fulfilled, **w** says, Mt 13:14
w a man took and sowed in his Mt 13:31 3739
is like leaven, **w** a woman took and Mt 13:33 3739
the field, **w** a man found and hid Mt 13:44 3739
"Every plant **w** My heavenly Father Mt 15:13 3739
are the things **w** defile the man; Mt 15:20
the dogs feed on the crumbs **w** fall Mt 15:27
has come to save that **w** was lost. Mt 18:11
ninety-nine **w** have not gone astray. Mt 18:13
he said to Him, "**W** ones?" Mt 19:18 4169
one thing, **w** if you tell Me, Mt 21:24 3739
"**W** of the two did the will of his Mt 21:31 5101
'THE STONE **W** THE BUILDERS Mt 21:42 3739
w is the great commandment in the Mt 22:36 4169
"You fools and blind men! **W** is more Mt 23:17 5101
blind men, **w** is more important, Mt 23:19 5101
you are like whitewashed tombs **w** on Mt 23:27 3748
w will not be torn down." Mt 24:2 3739
the ABOMINATION OF DESOLATION **W** Mt 24:15

know **w** day your Lord is coming. Mt 24:42 4169
and at an hour **w** he does not know, Mt 24:50 3739
into the eternal fire **w** has been Mt 25:41
w is poured out for many for Mt 26:28
w *say* that it must happen this Mt 26:54
the word **w** Jesus had said, Mt 26:75
Then that **w** was spoken through Mt 27:9
"**W** of the two do you want me to Mt 27:21 5101
w means Place of a Skull, Mt 27:33 3739
the charge against Him **w** read, Mt 27:37
w he had hewn out in the rock; Mt 27:60 3739
mountain **w** Jesus had designated. Mt 28:16 3757
on **w** the paralytic was lying. Mk 2:4 3699
"**W** is easier, to say to the Mk 2:9 5101
w is not lawful for *anyone* to eat Mk 2:26 3739
gave the name Boanerges, **w** means, Mk 3:17 3739
the word **w** has been sown in them. Mk 4:15
"*It is* like a mustard seed, **w,** Mk 4:31 3739
(**w** translated means, Mk 5:41 3739
other things **w** they have received Mk 7:4 3739
tradition **w** you have handed down; Mk 7:13 3739
w can defile him if it goes into him; Mk 7:15
but the things **w** proceed out of Mk 7:15
"That **w** proceeds out of the man, Mk 7:20
with a spirit **w** makes him mute; Mk 9:17
w *of them was* the greatest. Mk 9:34 5101
baptism with **w** I am baptized?" Mk 10:38 3739
the baptism with **w** I am baptized. Mk 10:39 3739
on **w** no one yet has ever sat; Mk 11:2 3739
w they had cut from the fields. Mk 11:8
tree **w** You cursed has withered." Mk 11:21 3739
all things for **w** you pray and ask, Mk 11:24 3745
STONE **W** THE BUILDERS REJECTED, Mk 12:10 3739
again, **w** one's wife will she be? Mk 12:23 5101
copper coins, **w** amount to a cent. Mk 12:42 3739
another **w** will not be torn down." Mk 13:2 3739
of the creation **w** God created until Mk 13:19 3739
"Where is My guest room in **w** I Mk 14:14 3699
w is poured out for many. Mk 14:24 3588
place Golgotha, **w** is translated, Mk 15:22 3739
Scripture was fulfilled **w** says, Mk 15:28
w is translated, "MY GOD, MY GOD, Mk 15:34 3739
w had been hewn out in the rock; Mk 15:46 3739
w will be fulfilled in their Lk 1:20 3748
The oath **w** He swore to Abraham our Lk 1:73 3739
With **w** the Sunrise from on high Lk 1:78 3739
of David **w** is called Bethlehem, Lk 2:4 3748
joy **w** will be for all the people; Lk 2:10 3748
w the Lord has made known to us." Lk 2:15 3739
they made known the statement **w** Lk 2:17
wondered at the things **w** were told Lk 2:18
W You have prepared in the Lk 2:31 3739
w were being said about Him. Lk 2:33
statement **w** He had made to them. Lk 2:50 3739
wicked things **w** Herod had done, Lk 3:19 3739
w were falling from His lips; Lk 4:22
on **w** their city had been built, Lk 4:29 3739
one of the boats, **w** was Simon's, Lk 5:3 3739
catch of fish **w** they had taken; Lk 5:9 3739
"**W** is easier, to say, Lk 5:23 5101
bread **w** is not lawful for any to eat Lk 6:4 3739
no good tree **w** produces bad fruit, Lk 6:43
a bad tree **w** produces good fruit. Lk 6:43
from that **w** fills his heart. Lk 6:45 4051
So **w** of them will love him more?" Lk 7:42 5101
say to you, her sins, **w** are many, Lk 7:47
The *seed* **w** fell among the thorns, Lk 8:14
Gerasenes, **w** is opposite Galilee. Lk 8:26 3748
and the broken pieces **w** they had Lk 9:17
were speaking of His departure **w** Lk 9:31 3739
any of the things **w** they had seen. Lk 9:36 3739
w of them might be the greatest. Lk 9:46 5101
of your city **w** clings to our feet we Lk 10:11
Tyre and Sidon **w** occurred in you, Lk 10:13 3739
the eyes **w** see the things you see, Lk 10:23
to see the things **w** you see, Lk 10:24 3739
and to hear the things **w** you hear, Lk 10:24 3739
"**W** of these three do you think Lk 10:36 5101
w shall not be taken away from her." Lk 10:42 3748
all his armor on **w** he had relied and Lk 11:22 3739
return to my house from **w** I came.' Lk 11:24 3606
and the breasts at **w** You nursed." Lk 11:27 3739
give that **w** is within as charity, Lk 11:41
of the Pharisees, **w** is hypocrisy. Lk 12:1 3748
"And **w** of you by worrying Lk 12:25 5101
w is *alive* today and tomorrow is Lk 12:28
belts **w** do not wear out, Lk 12:33
"A man had a fig tree **w** Lk 13:6
six days in **w** work should be done; Lk 13:14 3739
w a man took and threw into his Lk 13:19 3739
w a woman took and hid in three Lk 13:21 3739
"**W** one of you will have a son or Lk 14:5 5101
"For **w** one of you, when he wants Lk 14:28 5101
and go after the one **w** is lost until Lk 15:4
I have found my sheep **w** was lost!' Lk 15:6
have found the coin **w** I had lost!' Lk 15:9 3739
in *the use of* that **w** is another's, Lk 16:12
will give you that **w** is your own? Lk 16:12
for that **w** is highly esteemed Lk 16:15
to be fed with the *crumbs* **w** were Lk 16:21
"**W** of you, having a slave plowing Lk 17:7 5101
did the things **w** were commanded, Lk 17:9
the things **w** are commanded you, Lk 17:10
that **w** we ought to have done.' " Lk 17:10 3739
and all things **w** are written Lk 18:31
and to save that **w** was lost." Lk 19:10
w I kept put away in a Lk 19:20 3739
on **w** no one yet has ever sat; Lk 19:30 3739
all the miracles **w** they had seen, Lk 19:37 3739

you, the things **w** make for peace!	Lk 19:42	
'THE STONE **W** THE BUILDERS	Lk 20:17	*3739*
w one's wife will she be?	Lk 20:33	*5101*
these things **w** you are looking at,	Lk 21:6	*3739*
the days will come in **w** there will	Lk 21:6	*3739*
another **w** will not be torn down."	Lk 21:6	*3739*
wisdom **w** none of your opponents	Lk 21:15	*3739*
w are written will be fulfilled.	Lk 21:22	
w are coming upon the world;	Lk 21:26	
Bread, **w** is called the Passover,	Lk 22:1	
on **w** the Passover *lamb* had to be	Lk 22:7	*3739*
"Where is the guest room in **w** I	Lk 22:11	*3699*
is My body **w** is given for you;	Lk 22:19	
"This cup **w** is poured out for you	Lk 22:20	
to discuss among themselves **w** one	Lk 22:23	*5101*
a dispute among them *as to* **w** one of	Lk 22:24	*5101*
that this **w** is written must be	Lk 22:37	
for that **w** refers to Me has *its*	Lk 22:37	
charges **w** you make against Him.	Lk 23:14	*3739*
the spices **w** they had prepared.	Lk 24:1	*3739*
w was about seven miles from	Lk 24:13	
these things **w** had taken place.	Lk 24:14	
the things **w** have happened here	Lk 24:18	
"These are My words **w** I spoke to	Lk 24:44	*3739*
that all things **w** are written	Lk 24:44	
There was the true Light **w**,	Jn 1:9	*3739*
"Rabbi (**w** translated means Teacher),	Jn 1:38	*3739*
(**w** translated means Christ).	Jn 1:41	*3739*
Cephas" (**w** is translated Peter).	Jn 1:42	*3739*
the water **w** had become wine,	Jn 2:9	
and the word **w** Jesus had spoken.	Jn 2:22	*3739*
His signs **w** He was doing.	Jn 2:23	*3739*
w is born of the flesh is flesh,	Jn 3:6	
and that **w** is born of the Spirit	Jn 3:6	
that for **w** you have not labored;	Jn 4:38	*3739*
that hour in **w** Jesus said to him,	Jn 4:53	*3739*
w is called in Hebrew Bethesda,	Jn 5:2	
disease with **w** he was afflicted.	Jn 5:4	*3739*
in **w** all who are in the tombs	Jn 5:28	*3739*
testimony **w** He gives about Me is true.	Jn 5:32	*3739*
testimony **w** I receive is not from man,	Jn 5:34	
"But the testimony **w** I have is	Jn 5:36	
for the works **w** the Father has	Jn 5:36	*3739*
saw the signs **w** He was performing	Jn 6:2	*3739*
w were left over by those who had	Jn 6:13	*3739*
saw the sign **w** He had performed,	Jn 6:14	*3739*
at the land to **w** they were going.	Jn 6:21	*3739*
not work for the food **w** perishes,	Jn 6:27	
food **w** endures to eternal life,	Jn 6:27	
w the Son of Man will give to	Jn 6:27	*3739*
that **w** comes down out of heaven,	Jn 6:33	
bread **w** comes down out of heaven,	Jn 6:50	
and the bread also **w** I will give	Jn 6:51	*3739*
bread **w** came down out of heaven;	Jn 6:58	*3588*
see Your works **w** You are doing.	Jn 7:3	*3739*
signs than those **w** this man has,	Jn 7:31	*3739*
"But this crowd **w** does not	Jn 7:49	
and the things **w** I heard from Him,	Jn 8:26	*3739*
w I have seen with *My* Father;	Jn 8:38	*3739*
w you heard from *your* father."	Jn 8:38	*3739*
you the truth, **w** I heard from God;	Jn 8:40	*3739*
"**W** one of you convicts Me of sin?	Jn 8:46	*5101*
pool of Siloam" (**w** is translated, Sent	Jn 9:7	*3739*
were **w** He had been saying to them.	Jn 10:6	*3739*
sheep, **w** are not of this fold;	Jn 10:16	*3739*
for **w** of them are you stoning Me?"	Jn 10:32	*4169*
them the things **w** Jesus had done.	Jn 11:46	*3739*
kind of death by **w** He was to die.	Jn 12:33	*4169*
word of Isaiah the prophet **w** he spoke:	Jn 12:38	*3739*
the towel with **w** He was girded.	Jn 13:5	*3739*
to know of **w** one He was speaking.	Jn 13:22	*5101*
the word **w** you hear is not Mine,	Jn 14:24	*3739*
the word **w** I have spoken to you.	Jn 15:3	*3739*
them the works **w** no one else did,	Jn 15:24	*3739*
work **w** You have given Me to do.	Jn 17:4	*3739*
with the glory **w** I had with You	Jn 17:5	*3739*
for the words **w** You gave Me I	Jn 17:8	*3739*
the name **w** You have given Me,	Jn 17:11	*3739*
in Your name **w** You have given Me;	Jn 17:12	*3739*
"The glory **w** You have given	Jn 17:22	*3739*
My glory **w** You have given Me	Jn 17:24	*3739*
so that the love with **w** You loved Me	Jn 17:26	*3739*
garden, in **w** He entered	Jn 18:1	*3739*
to fulfill the word **w** He spoke,	Jn 18:9	*3739*
the cup **w** the Father has given Me,	Jn 18:11	*3739*
fulfill the word of Jesus **w** He spoke,	Jn 18:32	*3739*
of a Skull, **w** is called in Hebrew,	Jn 19:17	*3739*
in **w** no one had yet been laid.	Jn 19:41	*3739*
face-cloth **w** had been on His head,	Jn 20:7	*3739*
"Rabboni!" (**w** means, Teacher).	Jn 20:16	*3739*
w are not written in this book;	Jn 20:30	*3739*
the fish **w** you have now caught."	Jn 21:10	*3739*
many other things **w** Jesus did,	Jn 21:25	*3739*
w if they were written in detail,	Jn 21:25	*3748*
"**W**," *He said,* "you heard of from Me	Ac 1:4	*3739*
times or epochs **w** the Father has fixed	Ac 1:7	*3739*
Olivet, **w** is near Jerusalem,	Ac 1:12	*3739*
w the Holy Spirit foretold by the	Ac 1:16	*3739*
show **w** one of these two You have	Ac 1:24	*3739*
apostleship from **w** Judas turned aside	Ac 1:25	*3739*
own language to **w** we were born?	Ac 2:8	*3739*
signs **w** God performed through Him	Ac 2:22	*3739*
again, to **w** we are all witnesses.	Ac 2:32	*3739*
this **w** you both see and hear.	Ac 2:33	*3739*
the temple **w** is called Beautiful,	Ac 3:2	
a fact to **w** we are witnesses.	Ac 3:15	*3739*
it is the name of Jesus **w** has	Ac 3:16	
and the faith **w** *comes* through Him	Ac 3:16	
"But the things **w** God announced	Ac 3:18	*3739*
all things about **w** God spoke	Ac 3:21	*3739*
w God made with your fathers,	Ac 3:25	*3739*
the STONE **W** WAS REJECTED by you,	Ac 4:11	
W BECAME THE CHIEF CORNER *stone.*	Ac 4:11	
men by **w** we must be saved."	Ac 4:12	*3739*
basis on **w** to punish them)	Ac 4:21	
w translated means Son of	Ac 4:36	*3739*
the Spirit with **w** he was speaking.	Ac 6:10	*3739*
w Moses handed down to us."	Ac 6:14	*3739*
country in **w** you are now living.	Ac 7:4	*3739*
WHATEVER NATION TO **W** THEY	Ac 7:7	*3739*
and laid in the tomb **w** Abraham had	Ac 7:16	*3739*
w God had assured to Abraham,	Ac 7:17	*3739*
FOR THE PLACE ON **W** YOU ARE	Ac 7:33	*3739*
IMAGES **W** YOU MADE TO WORSHIP.	Ac 7:43	*3739*
to the pattern **w** he had seen.	Ac 7:44	*3739*
MY HAND **W** MADE ALL THESE THINGS?'	Ac 7:50	
"**W** one of the prophets did your	Ac 7:52	*5101*
saw the signs **w** he was performing.	Ac 8:6	*3739*
w he was reading was this:	Ac 8:32	*3739*
on the road by **w** you were coming,	Ac 9:17	*3739*
w translated *in Greek* is called Dorcas	Ac 9:36	*3739*
charity **w** she continually did.	Ac 9:36	*3739*
the vision **w** he had seen might be,	Ac 10:17	*3739*
the reason for **w** you have come?"	Ac 10:21	*3739*
w He sent to the sons of Israel,	Ac 10:36	*3739*
you yourselves know the thing **w**	Ac 10:37	
the baptism **w** John proclaimed.	Ac 10:37	*3739*
the house in **w** we were *staying,*	Ac 11:11	*3739*
to you by **w** you will be saved,	Ac 11:14	*3739*
city, **w** opened for them by itself;	Ac 12:10	*3748*
work to **w** I have called them."	Ac 13:2	*3739*
as an inheritance—*all of* **w**	Ac 13:19	
prophets **w** are read every Sabbath,	Ac 13:27	
from **w** you could not be freed	Ac 13:39	*3739*
A WORK **W** YOU WILL NEVER BELIEVE,	Ac 13:41	*3739*
from **w** they had been commended to	Ac 14:26	*3606*
a yoke **w** neither our fathers nor we	Ac 15:10	*3739*
TABERNACLE OF DAVID **W** HAS FALLEN,	Ac 15:16	
city in **w** we proclaimed the word	Ac 15:36	*3739*
w had been decided upon by the	Ac 16:4	
w is a leading city of the	Ac 16:12	*3748*
and are proclaiming customs **w** it	Ac 16:21	*3739*
teaching is **w** you are proclaiming?	Ac 17:19	
because He has fixed a day in **w** He	Ac 17:31	*3739*
the *image* **w** fell down from heaven?	Ac 19:35	*1356*
tears and with trials **w** came upon me	Ac 20:19	
and the ministry **w** I received from	Ac 20:24	*3739*
among **w** the Holy Spirit has made	Ac 20:28	*3739*
to shepherd the church of God **w** He	Ac 20:28	*3739*
w is able to build *you* up and to	Ac 20:32	
over the word **w** he had spoken,	Ac 20:38	*3739*
the things **w** God had done among	Ac 21:19	*3739*
w they have been told about you,	Ac 21:24	*3739*
my defense **w** I now *offer* to you."	Ac 22:1	
for **w** they were accusing him,	Ac 23:28	*3739*
the things of **w** we accuse him."	Ac 24:8	*3739*
charges of **w** they now accuse me.	Ac 24:13	*3739*
that according to the Way **w** they	Ac 24:14	*3739*
w these men cherish themselves,	Ac 24:15	*3739*
in **w** they found me *occupied* in the	Ac 24:18	*3739*
this one statement **w** I shouted out	Ac 24:21	*3739*
him **w** they could not prove,	Ac 25:7	*3739*
is *true* of **w** these men accuse me,	Ac 25:11	*3739*
of **w** I am accused by the Jews,	Ac 26:2	*3739*
w from the beginning was spent	Ac 26:4	
the promise to **w** our twelve tribes	Ac 26:7	*3739*
to the things **w** you have seen,	Ac 26:16	*3739*
things in **w** I will appear to you;	Ac 26:16	*3739*
w was about to sail to the regions	Ac 27:2	
near **w** was the city of Lasea.	Ac 27:8	*3739*
ship **w** had wintered at the island,	Ac 28:11	
and **w** had the Twin Brothers for	Ac 28:11	
w He promised beforehand through	Ro 1:2	*3739*
because that **w** is known about God	Ro 1:19	*1110*
function for that **w** is unnatural,	Ro 1:26	
do those things **w** are not proper,	Ro 1:28	
for in that **w** you judge another, you	Ro 2:1	*3739*
that **w** is outward in the flesh.	Ro 2:28	
is that **w** is of the heart,	Ro 2:29	
redemption **w** is in Christ Jesus;	Ro 3:24	
w he had while uncircumcised,	Ro 4:11	
w he had while uncircumcised.	Ro 4:12	
into being that **w** does not exist.	Ro 4:17	
to that **w** had been spoken,	Ro 4:18	
into this grace in **w** we stand;	Ro 5:2	*3739*
The gift is not like *that* **w** *came*	Ro 5:16	
teaching to **w** you were committed,	Ro 6:17	*3739*
things of **w** you are now ashamed?	Ro 6:21	*3739*
w were *aroused* by the Law,	Ro 7:5	
died to that by **w** we were bound,	Ro 7:6	*3739*
w was to result in life,	Ro 7:10	
Therefore did that **w** is good	Ro 7:13	*18*
my death through that **w** is good,	Ro 7:13	*18*
doing it, but sin **w** dwells in me.	Ro 7:17	
doing it, but sin **w** dwells in me.	Ro 7:20	
the law of sin **w** is in my members.	Ro 7:23	
adoption as sons by **w** we cry out,	Ro 8:15	*3739*
w is in Christ Jesus our Lord.	Ro 8:39	
w He prepared beforehand for	Ro 9:23	*3739*
the righteousness **w** is by faith;	Ro 9:30	
the righteousness **w** is based on law	Ro 10:5	
word of faith **w** we are preaching,	Ro 10:8	*3739*
JEALOUS BY THAT **W** IS NOT A NATION,	Ro 10:19	
w *is* your spiritual service of	Ro 12:1	
that **w** is good and acceptable and	Ro 12:2	*18*
those **w** exist are established by God.	Ro 13:1	
pursue the things **w** make for peace	Ro 14:19	
by **w** your brother stumbles.	Ro 14:21	*3739*
The faith **w** you have, have as your	Ro 14:22	*3739*
of the church **w** is at Cenchrea;	Ro 16:1	
to the teaching **w** you learned,	Ro 16:17	*3739*
the mystery **w** has been kept secret	Ro 16:25	
the church of God **w** is at Corinth,	1Co 1:2	
w was given you in Christ Jesus,	1Co 1:4	
to shame the things **w** are strong,	1Co 1:27	*2478*
w God predestined before the ages	1Co 2:7	*3739*
the wisdom **w** none of the rulers of	1Co 2:8	*3739*
"THINGS **W** EYE HAS NOT SEEN AND	1Co 2:9	*3739*
AND **W** HAVE NOT ENTERED THE HEART	1Co 2:9	
spirit of the man **w** is in him?	1Co 2:11	
w things we also speak, not in	1Co 2:13	*3739*
grace of God **w** was given to me,	1Co 3:10	
other than the one **w** is laid,	1Co 3:11	
which is laid, **w** is Jesus Christ.	1Co 3:11	*3739*
w he has built on it remains,	1Co 3:14	*3739*
you of my ways **w** are in Christ,	1Co 4:17	
the things about **w** you wrote,	1Co 7:1	*3739*
that condition in **w** he was called.	1Co 7:20	*3739*
that *condition* in **w** he was called.	1Co 7:24	*3739*
a spiritual rock **w** followed them;	1Co 10:4	
Is not the cup of blessing **w** we	1Co 10:16	*3739*
Is not the bread **w** we break a	1Co 10:16	*3739*
things **w** the Gentiles sacrifice,	1Co 10:20	*3739*
that for **w** I give thanks?	1Co 10:30	*3739*
have houses in **w** to eat and drink?	1Co 11:22	
that **w** I also delivered to you,	1Co 11:23	*3739*
in the night in **w** He was betrayed	1Co 11:23	*3739*
"This is My body, **w** is for you;	1Co 11:24	
members of the body **w** seem to be	1Co 12:22	
body **w** we deem less honorable,	1Co 12:23	*3739*
honor to that *member* **w** lacked,	1Co 12:24	
things **w** I write to you are the Lord's	1Co 14:37	*3739*
the gospel **w** I preached to you,	1Co 15:1	*3739*
to you, **w** also you received,	1Co 15:1	*3739*
you received, in **w** also you stand,	1Co 15:1	*3739*
by **w** also you are saved, if you	1Co 15:2	*3739*
fast the word **w** I preached to you,	1Co 15:2	*5101*
w I have in Christ Jesus our Lord,	1Co 15:31	*3739*
That **w** you sow does not come to	1Co 15:36	*3739*
and that **w** you sow, you do not sow	1Co 15:37	*3739*
do not sow the body **w** is to be,	1Co 15:37	
To the church of God **w** is at	2Co 1:1	
the comfort with **w** we ourselves are	2Co 1:4	*3739*
w is effective in the patient	2Co 1:6	
same sufferings **w** we also suffer;	2Co 1:6	*3739*
affliction **w** came *to us* in Asia,	2Co 1:8	
love **w** I have especially for you.	2Co 2:4	*3739*
w *was inflicted* by the majority,	2Co 2:6	
that **w** fades away *was* with glory,	2Co 3:11	
more that **w** remains *is* in glory.	2Co 3:11	
that the grace **w** is spreading to	2Co 4:15	
look not at the things **w** are seen,	2Co 4:18	
but at the things **w** are not seen;	2Co 4:18	
things **w** are seen are temporal,	2Co 4:18	
things **w** are not seen are eternal.	2Co 4:18	
tent **w** is our house is torn down,	2Co 5:1	
with **w** he was comforted in you,	2Co 7:7	*3739*
the grace of God **w** has been given	2Co 8:1	
w is being administered by us for	2Co 8:19	
of **w** I boast about you to the	2Co 9:2	*3739*
w through us is producing	2Co 9:11	*3748*
the confidence with **w** I propose to be	2Co 10:2	*3739*
w the Lord gave for building you	2Co 10:8	*3739*
the sphere **w** God apportioned to us	2Co 10:13	*3739*
spirit **w** you have not received,	2Co 11:4	*3739*
gospel **w** you have not accepted,	2Co 11:4	*3739*
matter about **w** they are boasting.	2Co 11:12	*3739*
w a man is not permitted to speak.	2Co 12:4	*3739*
sensuality **w** they have practiced.	2Co 12:21	*3739*
the authority **w** the Lord gave me for	2Co 13:10	*3739*
w is *really* not another;	Ga 1:7	*3739*
that the gospel **w** was preached by	Ga 1:11	
of Judea **w** were in Christ;	Ga 1:22	
w he once tried to destroy."	Ga 1:23	*3739*
w I preach among the Gentiles,	Ga 2:2	*3739*
liberty **w** we have in Christ Jesus,	Ga 2:4	*3739*
and the *life* **w** I now live in the	Ga 2:20	*3739*
w came four hundred and thirty	Ga 3:17	
given **w** was able to impart life,	Ga 3:21	
faith **w** was later to be revealed.	Ga 3:23	
to those **w** by nature are no gods.	Ga 4:8	
to **w** you desire to be enslaved all	Ga 4:9	*3739*
and that **w** was a trial to you in	Ga 4:14	*3986*
of the flesh are evident, **w** are:	Ga 5:19	*3748*
of **w** I forewarn you, just as I have	Ga 5:21	*3739*
through **w** the world has been	Ga 6:14	*3739*
w He freely bestowed on us in the	Eph 1:6	*3739*
w He lavished on us.	Eph 1:8	*3739*
intention **w** He purposed in Him	Eph 1:9	*3739*
the Lord Jesus **w** *exists* among you and	Eph 1:15	
w He brought about in Christ, when	Eph 1:20	*3739*
w is His body, the fullness of Him	Eph 1:23	*3748*
in **w** you formerly walked according	Eph 2:2	*3739*
His great love with **w** He loved us,	Eph 2:4	*3739*
works, **w** God prepared beforehand so	Eph 2:10	*3739*
w *is* performed in the flesh by	Eph 2:11	
w *is* the Law of commandments	Eph 2:15	
grace **w** was given to me for you;	Eph 3:2	
w in other generations was not	Eph 3:5	*3739*
of **w** I was made a minister,	Eph 3:7	*3739*
gift of God's grace **w** was given to me	Eph 3:7	
mystery **w** for ages has been hidden in	Eph 3:9	
the eternal purpose **w** He carried out	Eph 3:11	*3739*
of Christ **w** surpasses knowledge,	Eph 3:19	
with **w** you have been called,	Eph 4:1	*3739*
to the measure of the stature **w**	Eph 4:13	
w is being corrupted in accordance	Eph 4:22	

w in *the likeness of* God has been Eph 4:24
coarse jesting, w are not fitting, Eph 5:4 3739
w are done by them in secret. Eph 5:12
w is the first commandment with a Eph 6:2 3748
taking up the shield of faith with w Eph 6:16 3739
the Spirit, w is the word of God. Eph 6:17 3739
w I am an ambassador in chains; Eph 6:20 3739
w *comes* through Jesus Christ, Php 1:11
and I do not know w to choose. Php 1:22 5101
w is a sign of destruction for them, Php 1:28 3748
the same conflict w you saw in me, Php 1:30 3634
w was also in Christ Jesus, Php 2:5 3739
the name w is above every name, Php 2:9
the righteousness w is in the Law, Php 3:6
that w is through faith in Christ, Php 3:9
the righteousness w *comes* from God Php 3:9
w also I was laid hold of by Christ Php 3:12 3739
standard to w we have attained. Php 3:16 3739
from w also we eagerly wait for a Php 3:20 3739
w surpasses all comprehension, Php 4:7
w increases to your account. Php 4:17
w you have for all the saints; Col 1:4 3739
of w you previously heard in the Col 1:5 3739
w has come to you, just as in all Col 1:6
w was proclaimed in all creation Col 1:23
of w I, Paul, was made a minister. Col 1:23 3739
of His body, w is the church, Col 1:24 3739
the mystery w has been hidden from Col 1:26
the Gentiles, w is Christ in you, Col 1:27 3739
power, w mightily works within me. Col 1:29
in w you were also raised up with Col 2:12 3739
us, w was hostile to us; Col 2:14 3739
things w are a *mere* shadow of what Col 2:17 3739
grows with a growth w is from God. Col 2:19
(w all *refer to* things destined to Col 2:22 3739
These are matters w have, Col 2:23 3748
and greed, w amounts to idolatry. Col 3:5 3748
a renewal in w there is no Col 3:11 3699
w is the perfect bond of unity. Col 3:14 3739
to w indeed you were called in one Col 3:15 3739
of the wrong w he has done, Col 3:25 3739
for w I have also been imprisoned; Col 4:3 3739
w you have received in the Lord, Col 4:17 3739
when you received the word of God w 1Th 2:13 3739
w also performs its work in you 1Th 2:13 3739
for all the joy with w we rejoice 1Th 3:9 3739
but always seek after that w is 1Th 5:15 18
hold fast to that w is good; 1Th 5:21 2570
and afflictions w you endure. 2Th 1:4 3739
for w indeed you are suffering. 2Th 1:5 3739
the traditions w you were taught, 2Th 2:15 3739
tradition w you received from us. 2Th 3:6 3739
w give rise to mere speculation 1Tm 1:4 3748
of God w is by faith. 1Tm 1:4
or the matters about w they make 1Tm 1:7 5101
God, with w I have been entrusted. 1Tm 1:11 3739
love w are *found* in Christ Jesus. 1Tm 1:14
w some have rejected and suffered 1Tm 1:19 3739
w is the church of the living God, 1Tm 3:15 3748
w God has created to be gratefully 1Tm 4:3 3739
w you have been following. 1Tm 4:6 3739
w was bestowed on you through 1Tm 4:14 3739
and those w are otherwise cannot 1Tm 5:25
about words, out of w arise envy, 1Tm 6:4 3739
harmful desires w plunge men into 1Tm 6:9 3748
eternal life to w you were called, 1Tm 6:12 3739
w He will bring about at the 1Tm 6:15 3739
hold of that w is life indeed. 1Tm 6:19
w some have professed and thus 1Tm 6:21 3739
w first dwelt in your grandmother 2Tm 1:5 3748
the gift of God w is in you through 2Tm 1:6 3739
and grace w was granted us in Christ 2Tm 1:9
for w I was appointed a preacher 2Tm 1:11 3739
words w you have heard from me, 2Tm 1:13 3739
and love w are in Christ Jesus. 2Tm 1:13
w has been entrusted to *you.* 2Tm 1:14
The things w you have heard 2Tm 2:2 3739
for w I suffer hardship even to 2Tm 2:9 3739
may obtain the salvation w is in Christ 2Tm 2:10
wrangle about words, w is useless 2Tm 2:14
sacred writings w are able to give you 2Tm 3:15
faith w is in Christ Jesus. 2Tm 3:15
of righteousness, w the Lord, 2Tm 4:8 3739
w I left at Troas with Carpus, 2Tm 4:13 3739
truth w is according to godliness, Ti 1:1
the hope of eternal life, w God, Ti 1:2 3739
in the proclamation with w I was Ti 1:3 3739
holding fast the faithful word w Ti 1:9
speak the things w are fitting for Ti 2:1 3739
in speech w is beyond reproach, Ti 2:8 176
w we have done in righteousness, Ti 3:5 3739
and of the faith w you have toward Phm 1:5 3739
w is in you for Christ's sake. Phm 1:6
w of the angels did He ever say, Heb 1:5 5101
But to w of the angels has He ever Heb 1:13 5101
concerning w we are speaking. Heb 2:5 3739
for w reason He is not ashamed to Heb 2:11 3739
tempted in that w He has suffered, Heb 2:18 3739
things w were to be spoken later; Heb 3:5
from the things w He suffered. Heb 5:8 3739
For ground that drinks the rain w Heb 6:7
work and the love w you have shown Heb 6:10 3739
in w it is impossible for God to Heb 6:18 3739
and one w enters within the veil, Heb 6:19
king of Salem, w is king of peace. Heb 7:2 3739
from w no one has officiated at Heb 7:13 3739
a tribe with reference to w Moses Heb 7:14 3739
through w we draw near to God. Heb 7:19 3739
of the oath, w came after the Law, Heb 7:28

tabernacle, w the Lord pitched, Heb 8:2 3739
W WAS SHOWN YOU ON THE MOUNTAIN." Heb 8:5
w has been enacted on better Heb 8:6 3748
NOT LIKE THE COVENANT W I MADE Heb 8:9 3739
in w *were* the lampstand and the Heb 9:2 3739
w is called the Holy of Holies, Heb 9:3
in w was a golden jar holding the Heb 9:4 3739
manna, and Aaron's rod w budded, Heb 9:4
w he offers for himself and for Heb 9:7 3739
w *is* a symbol for the present time. Heb 9:9 3748
w cannot make the worshiper perfect Heb 9:9
COVENANT W GOD COMMANDED YOU." Heb 9:20 3739
w they offer continually year by Heb 10:1 3739
w are offered according to the Law Heb 10:8 3748
w can never take away sins; Heb 10:11 3748
by a new and living way w He Heb 10:20 3739
W WILL CONSUME THE ADVERSARIES. Heb 10:27
covenant by w he was sanctified, Heb 10:29 3739
confidence, w has a great reward. Heb 10:35 3748
made out of things w are visible. Heb 11:3
through w he obtained the Heb 11:4 3739
by w he condemned the world, Heb 11:7 3739
w is according to faith. Heb 11:7
obeyed by going out to a place w Heb 11:8 3739
for the city w has foundations, Heb 11:10 3739
AS THE SAND W IS BY THE SEASHORE. Heb 11:12
that *country* from w they went out, Heb 11:15 3739
from w he also received him back Heb 11:19 3606
the sin w so easily entangles us, Heb 12:1
w is addressed to you as sons, Heb 12:5 3748
of w all have become partakers, Heb 12:8 3739
so that *the limb* w is lame may not Heb 12:13
w no one will see the Lord. Heb 12:14 3739
the sound of words w *sound was* Heb 12:19 3739
w speaks better than *the blood* of Heb 12:24
of those things w can be shaken, Heb 12:27
w cannot be shaken may remain. Heb 12:27
a kingdom w cannot be shaken, Heb 12:28
by w we may offer to God an Heb 12:28 3739
through w those who were so Heb 13:9 3739
from w those who serve the Heb 13:10 3739
are seeking *the city* w is to come. Heb 13:14
that w is pleasing in His sight, Heb 13:21 2101
w *the Lord* has promised to those Jas 1:12 3739
w is able to save your souls. Jas 1:21
heirs of the kingdom w He promised Jas 2:5 3739
name by w you have been called? Jas 2:7
Scripture was fulfilled w says, Jas 2:23
as that w defiles the entire body, Jas 3:6
not that w comes down from above, Jas 3:15
w He has made to dwell in us"? Jas 4:5 3739
miseries w are coming upon you. Jas 5:1
and w has been withheld by you, Jas 5:4
to *obtain* an inheritance w *is* 1Pe 1:4
than gold w is perishable, 1Pe 1:7
in these things w now have been 1Pe 1:12 3739
into w angels long to look. 1Pe 1:12 3739
be conformed to the former lusts w 1Pe 1:14
born again not of seed w is perishable 1Pe 1:23 5349
is the word w was preached to you. 1Pe 1:25
coming to Him as to a living stone w 1Pe 2:4
STONE W THE BUILDERS REJECTED, 1Pe 2:7 3739
w wage war against the soul. 1Pe 2:11 3748
w they slander you as evildoers, 1Pe 2:12 3739
w is precious in the sight of God. 1Pe 3:4 3739
the thing in w you are slandered, 1Pe 3:16 3739
in w also He went and made 1Pe 3:19 3739
of the ark, in w a few, 1Pe 3:20 3739
serving by the strength w God supplies; 1Pe 4:11 3739
w comes upon you for your testing, 1Pe 4:12
the truth w is present with *you.* 2Pe 1:12
to w you do well to pay attention 2Pe 1:19 3739
letter I am writing to you in w I am 2Pe 3:1 3739
through w the world at that time 2Pe 3:6 3739
in w the heavens will pass away 2Pe 3:10 3739
because of w the heavens will 2Pe 3:12 3739
earth, in w righteousness dwells. 2Pe 3:13 3739
in w are some things hard to 2Pe 3:16 3739
w the untaught and unstable 2Pe 3:16 3739
w was with the Father and was 1Jn 1:2 3748
but an old commandment w you have 1Jn 2:7 3739
is the word w you have heard. 1Jn 2:7 3739
you, w is true in Him and in you, 1Jn 2:8 3739
w you heard from the beginning. 1Jn 2:24 3739
promise w He Himself made to us: 1Jn 2:25 3739
the anointing w you received from 1Jn 2:27 3739
For this is the message w you have 1Jn 3:11 3739
of w you have heard that it is 1Jn 4:3 3739
the love w God has for us. 1Jn 4:16 3739
confidence w we have before Him, 1Jn 5:14 3739
requests w we have asked from Him. 1Jn 5:15 3739
for the sake of the truth w abides 2Jn 1:2
but the one w we have had from the 2Jn 1:5 3739
attention to his deeds w he does, 3Jn 1:10 3739
faith w was once for all handed down Jude 1:3
things w they do not understand; Jude 1:10 3745
things w they know by instinct, Jude 1:10 3745
of all their ungodly deeds w they have Jude 1:15 3739
and of all the harsh things w Jude 1:15 3739
w God gave Him to show to His Rv 1:1 3739
things w must soon take place; Rv 1:1 3739
the things w are written in it; Rv 1:3
and kingdom and perseverance w *are* Rv 1:9
the things w you have seen, Rv 1:19 3739
have seen, and the things w are, Rv 1:19 3739
and the things w will take place Rv 1:19 3739
stars w you saw in My right hand, Rv 1:20 3739
of the Nicolaitans, w I also hate. Rv 2:6 3739
w is in the Paradise of God.' Rv 2:7 3739

name written on the stone w no one Rv 2:17 3739
that remain, w were about to die; Rv 3:2 3739
an open door w no one can shut, Rv 3:8 3739
that *hour* w is about to come upon Rv 3:10
w comes down out of heaven from My Rv 3:12
and the first voice w I had heard, Rv 4:1 3739
w are the seven Spirits of God; Rv 4:5 3739
w are the seven Spirits of God, Rv 5:6 3739
w are the prayers of the saints. Rv 5:8 3739
And every created thing w is in Rv 5:13 3739
testimony w they had maintained; Rv 6:9 3739
multitude w no one could count, Rv 7:9 3739
altar w was before the throne. Rv 8:3
w were in the sea and had life, Rv 8:9 3588
heaven w had fallen to the earth; Rv 9:1
the golden altar w is before God, Rv 9:13
w proceeded out of their mouths. Rv 9:18
w can neither see nor hear nor Rv 9:20 3739
his hand a little book w was open. Rv 10:2
"Seal up the things w the seven Rv 10:4 3739
the voice w I heard from heaven, Rv 10:8 3739
take the book w is open in the Rv 10:8
the court w is outside the temple and Rv 11:2
city w mystically is called Sodom and Rv 11:8 3748
of God w is in heaven was opened; Rv 11:19
drank up the river w the dragon Rv 12:16 3739
beast w I saw was like a leopard, Rv 13:2 3739
signs w it was given him to perform Rv 13:14 3739
and the voice w I heard *was* like Rv 14:2 3739
w is mixed in full strength in the Rv 14:10
out of the temple w is in heaven, Rv 14:17 3588
w *are* the last, because in them Rv 15:1
w go out to the kings of the whole Rv 16:14 3739
gathered them together to the place w Rv 16:16
w has the seven heads and the ten Rv 17:7
"Here is the mind w has wisdom. Rv 17:9
mountains on w the woman sits, Rv 17:9 3699
"The beast w was and is not, Rv 17:11 3739
ten horns w you saw are ten kings who Rv 17:12 3739
w you saw where the harlot sits, Rv 17:15 3739
"And the ten horns w you saw, Rv 17:16 3739
w reigns over the kings of the Rv 17:18
in the cup w she has mixed, mix Rv 18:6 3739
in w all who had ships at sea Rv 18:19 3739
Him w no one knows except Himself. Rv 19:12 3739
And the armies w are in heaven, Rv 19:14
all the birds w fly in midheaven, Rv 19:17
by w he deceived those who had Rv 19:20 3739
of fire w burns with brimstone. Rv 19:20
sword w came from the mouth of Him Rv 19:21
the nations w are in the four corners Rv 20:8
was opened, w is *the book* of life; Rv 20:12 3739
w were written in the books, Rv 20:12
sea gave up the dead w were in it, Rv 20:13
gave up the dead w were in them; Rv 20:13
w is the second death." Rv 21:8 3739
w are *the names* of the twelve tribes Rv 21:12 3739
w are *also* angelic *measurements.* Rv 21:17 3739
things w must soon take place. Rv 22:6 3739
w are written in this book; Rv 22:18
city, w are written in this book. Rv 22:19

WHICHEVER

w of the families of the earth does Zch 14:17 834

WHILE

"W the earth remains, Seedtime Gn 8:22 5750
sustain them w dwelling together, Gn 13:6
w Lot settled in the cities of the Gn 13:12
w he was sitting at the tent door Gn 18:1
w Abraham was still standing Gn 18:22
gave gifts w he was still living, Gn 25:6
w Isaac spoke to his son Esau. Gn 27:5
W he was still speaking with them, Gn 29:9
w he himself spent that night in Gn 32:21
dislocated w he wrestled with him. Gn 32:25
w Israel was dwelling in that land, Gn 35:22
brothers w he was *still* a youth, Gn 37:2
It was w she was being brought out Gn 38:25
took place w she was giving birth, Gn 38:28
brother, w you remain confined, Gn 42:16
fight for you w you keep silent." Ex 14:14
w the Egyptians were fleeing right Ex 14:27
w Moses approached the thick cloud Ex 20:21
the thief is caught w breaking in and Ex 22:2
driven away w no one is looking, Ex 22:10
dies w its owner is not with it, Ex 22:14
about, w My glory is passing by, Ex 33:22
w the rest of the blood shall be Lv 5:9
w the rest of the oil that is in Lv 14:18
sister as a rival w she is alive, Lv 18:18
the LORD, w he has an uncleanness, Lv 22:3
w you are in your enemies' land; Lv 26:34
sabbaths, w you were living on it. Lv 26:35
w it is made desolate without them. Lv 26:43
W the meat was still between their Nu 11:33
eye, w Your cloud stands over them; Nu 14:14
Now w the sons of Israel were in Nu 15:32
w you and your sons with you are Nu 18:2
here beside your burnt offering w I Nu 23:15
W Israel performs valiantly. Nu 24:18
W Israel remained at Shittim, the Nu 25:1
w they were weeping at the doorway Nu 25:6
she should marry w under her vows Nu 30:6
w *she is* in her youth in her Nu 30:16
to war w you yourselves sit here? Nu 32:6
w our little ones live in the Nu 32:17
w your servants, everyone who is Nu 32:27
w the Egyptians were burying all Nu 33:4
w he was not his enemy nor seeking Nu 35:23

w I was standing between the Dt 5:5
w the mountain was burning with Dt 5:23
w the mountain was burning with fire, Dt 9:15
them w they were pursuing you, Dt 11:4
muzzle the ox w he is threshing. Dt 25:4
'I have not eaten of it w mourning, Dt 26:14
removed any of it w I was unclean, Dt 26:14
w your eyes look on and Dt 28:32
w I am still alive with you today, Dt 31:27
w all Israel crossed on dry ground, Jos 3:17
W the sons of Israel camped at Jos 5:10
w they continued to blow the Jos 6:9
w they continued to blow the Jos 6:13
As they fled from before Israel, w Jos 10:11
Ehud came to him w he was Jg 3:20
Ehud escaped w they were delaying, Jg 3:26 5704
of Zeeb, w they pursued Midian; Jg 7:25
It came about after a w that Jg 11:4 3117
'W Israel lived in Heshbon and its Jg 11:26
w Manoah and his wife looked on. Jg 13:19
seven days w their feast lasted. Jg 14:17 834
But after a w, in the time of Jg 15:1 3117
So w he slept, Delilah took the Jg 16:14
on w Samson was amusing *them.* Jg 16:27
w the priest stood by the entrance Jg 18:17
W they were celebrating, behold, Jg 19:22
but the battle overtook them w Jg 20:42 834
in the house for a little w." Ru 2:7 4592
would come w the meat was boiling, 1Sa 2:13
w the Philistines camped in Aphek. 1Sa 4:1
w 1,000 were with Jonathan at 1Sa 13:2
w the Philistines camped at Michmash 1Sa 13:16
W Saul talked to the priest, 1Sa 14:19 5704
way w he was coming up from Egypt. 1Sa 15:2
w Israel stood on the mountain on the 1Sa 17:3
w the army was going out in battle 1Sa 17:20
w he has been a warrior from his 1Sa 17:33
w David was playing *the harp* with 1Sa 18:10
w Jonathan went into the city. 1Sa 20:42
w David was in the wilderness of 1Sa 23:15
w Jonathan went to his house. 1Sa 23:18
W I have dealt wickedly with you. 1Sa 24:17
w he was shearing his sheep in 1Sa 25:2
behind David w two hundred stayed 1Sa 25:13
them, w we were in the fields. 1Sa 25:15
w the Israelites were camping by 1Sa 29:1
It came about w there was war 2Sa 3:6
to eat bread w it was still day; 2Sa 3:35
w he was taking his midday rest. 2Sa 4:5
w the Arameans of Zobah and of 2Sa 10:8
w the child was *still* alive, 2Sa 12:18
W the child was alive, you fasted 2Sa 12:21 5668
"W the child was *still* alive, I 2Sa 12:22
Now it was w they were on the way 2Sa 13:30
"For your servant vowed a vow w I 2Sa 15:8
w he was offering the sacrifices. 2Sa 15:12
with us, w I go where I will? 2Sa 15:20
W all the country was weeping with 2Sa 15:23
w he is weary and exhausted and 2Sa 17:2
w the mule that was under him kept 2Sa 18:9
heart of Absalom w he was yet alive 2Sa 18:14
the king w he stayed at Mahanaim, 2Sa 19:32
w the troop of the Philistines was 2Sa 23:13
w the garrison of the Philistines 2Sa 23:14
w the eyes of my lord the king 2Sa 24:3
your foes w they pursue you? 2Sa 24:13
w you are still there speaking 1Ki 1:14
w she was still speaking with the 1Ki 1:22
W he was still speaking, behold, 1Ki 1:42
today w my own eyes see *it.*'" 1Ki 1:48
w my father David did not know *it:* 1Ki 2:32
to a child w she *was* in the house. 1Ki 3:17 5973
me w your maidservant slept, 1Ki 3:20
The house, w it was being built, 1Ki 6:7
in the house w it was being built. 1Ki 6:7
w all the assembly of Israel was 1Ki 8:14
with him, w Hadad *was* a young boy. 1Ki 11:17
Solomon w he was still alive, 1Ki 12:6
w Jeroboam was standing by the 1Ki 13:1
w Nadab and all Israel were laying 1Ki 15:27
It happened after a w that 1Ki 17:7 3117
In a little w the sky grew black 1Ki 18:45
5704, 3541
w he was plowing with twelve pairs 1Ki 19:19
w Ben-hadad was drinking himself 1Ki 20:16
"W your servant was busy here 1Ki 20:40
one said this w another said that. 1Ki 22:20
w the two of them stood by the 2Ki 2:7
him w he was staying at Jericho; 2Ki 2:18
W he was still talking with them, 2Ki 6:33
On the way w he was at Beth-eked 2Ki 10:12
w Athaliah was reigning over the 2Ki 11:3
w Jotham the king's son was over 2Ki 15:5
w these nations feared the LORD, 2Ki 17:41
w his servants were besieging it. 2Ki 24:11
w the army of the Philistines was 1Ch 11:15
w the garrison of the Philistines 1Ch 11:16
w he was still restricted because 1Ch 12:1
house for a great w to come, 1Ch 17:17 7350
w the sword of your enemies 1Ch 21:12
w all the assembly of Israel was 2Ch 6:3
w the priests on the other side 2Ch 7:6
Solomon w he was still alive, 2Ch 10:6
w Jeroboam drew up in battle 2Ch 13:3
one said this w another said that. 2Ch 18:19
him w he was hiding in Samaria; 2Ch 22:9
w Athaliah reigned over the land. 2Ch 22:12
and w he was enraged with the 2Ch 26:19
W the whole assembly worshiped, 2Ch 29:28

w he *was* besieging Lachish with all 2Ch 32:9
his reign w he was still a youth, 2Ch 34:3
and w the priests sprinkled the 2Ch 35:11
w many shouted aloud for joy, Ezr 3:12
Now w Ezra was praying and making Ezr 10:1
year, w I was in Susa the capitol, Ne 1:1
w half of them held the spears, Ne 4:16
w the trumpeter *stood* near me. Ne 4:18
Why should the work stop w I leave Ne 6:3 3512c
and w they are standing *guard,* Ne 7:3 5704
w lifting up their hands; Ne 8:6
w the people *remained* in their place. Ne 8:7
W they stood in their place, they Ne 9:3
w nine-tenths *remained* in the Ne 11:1
w I followed them with half of the Ne 12:38
w Mordecai was sitting at the Es 2:21
w the decree was issued at the citadel Es 3:15
and w the king and Haman sat down Es 3:15
W they were still talking with Es 6:14
W he was still speaking, another Jb 1:16
W he was still speaking, another Jb 1:17
W he was still speaking, another Jb 1:18
took a potsherd to scrape himself w Jb 2:8
"W it is still green *and* not cut Jb 8:12
W I am decaying like a rotten Jb 13:28
W at peace the destroyer comes Jb 15:21
rain *it* on him w he is eating. Jb 20:23
W another dies with a bitter soul, Jb 21:25
"W he is carried to the grave, Jb 21:32
W countless ones *go* before him. Jb 21:33
"They are exalted a little w, Jb 24:24 4592
W you pondered what to say. Jb 32:11 5704
men, W they slumber in their beds, Jb 33:15
away, w there is none to deliver. Ps 7:2
W evil is in their hearts. Ps 28:3
W they took counsel together Ps 31:13
Yet a little w and the wicked man Ps 37:10 4592
W the wicked are in my presence." Ps 39:1 5750
W I was musing the fire burned; Ps 39:3
W *they* say to me all day long, Ps 42:3
me, W they say to me all day long, Ps 42:10
Though w he lives he congratulates Ps 49:18
My eyes fail w I wait for my God. Ps 69:3
them fear You w the sun *endures,* Ps 72:5 5973
W their food was in their mouths, Ps 78:30 5750
to my God w I have my being. Ps 104:33 5750
longing for Your word, W I say, Ps 119:82
own nets, W I pass by safely. Ps 141:10 5704
I will praise the LORD w I live; Ps 146:2
to my God w I have my being. Ps 146:2 5750
W he lives securely beside you. Pr 3:29
W He had not yet made the earth Pr 8:26 5704
W his words are like scorching Pr 16:27 5921
Discipline your son w there is hope, Pr 19:18 3588
W the righteous gives and does not Pr 21:26
rises also w it is still night And Pr 31:15
w my mind was guiding *me* wisely, Ec 2:3
w to the sinner He has given the Ec 2:26
W the mind of fools is in the Ec 7:4
w rich men sit in humble places. Ec 10:6
w the lips of a fool consume him; Ec 10:12
w mourners go about in the street. Ec 12:5
"W the king was at his table, My SS 1:12 5704
W our vineyards are in blossom." SS 2:15
w the temple was filling with Is 6:4
"For in a very little w My Is 10:25 5750
Indeed, w *following* the way of Is 26:8
Hide for a little w Until Is 26:20 7281
They reel w having visions, They Is 28:7
Is it not yet just a little w Is 29:17 4592
W you were not destroyed; Is 33:1
w *others* did not deal Is 33:1
Seek the LORD w He may be found; Is 55:6
Call upon Him w He is near. Is 55:6
taken away, w no one understands. Is 57:1
Your sanctuary for a little w, Is 63:18 4705
and w they are still speaking, I Is 65:24
And w you are hoping for light He Jer 13:16
Her sun has set w it was yet day; Jer 15:9
and w your eyes look on, they will Jer 20:4
w he was still confined in the Jer 33:1
'W *they* are coming to fight with Jer 33:5
W he was at the Gate of Benjamin, Jer 37:13
w he was in the king's palace, Jer 38:7
W your feet were sunk in the mire, Jer 38:22
w he was confined in the court Jer 39:15
W they were eating bread together Jer 41:1
W you yourself were not aware; Jer 50:24
Yet in a little w the time of Jer 51:33 4592
W they sought food to restore La 1:19 3588
w I was by the river Chebar among Ezk 1:1
w your abominations are in your Ezk 7:9
I was a sanctuary for them a little w Ezk 11:16 4592
"Behold, w it is intact, it is Ezk 15:5
I said to you w *you were* in your Ezk 16:6
I said to you w *you were* in your Ezk 16:6
"w you do all these things, the Ezk 16:30
w they see for you false visions, Ezk 21:29
w they divine lies for you Ezk 21:29
played the harlot w she was Mine; Ezk 23:5 8478
w a man was standing beside me. Ezk 43:6
w they are ministering in the gates Ezk 44:17
and the visions in your mind w on Da 2:28
"As for you, O king, w on your Da 2:29
w Daniel *was* at the king's court. Da 2:49
a w as his thoughts alarmed him. Da 4:19 8160
"W the word *was* in the king's Da 4:31 5751
"W I was contemplating the horns, Da 7:8
and w I was looking Da 8:2

W I was observing, behold, a male Da 8:5
w the transgression causes horror, Da 8:13
Now w he was talking with me, I Da 8:18
destroy many w *they are* at ease. Da 8:25
Now w I was speaking and praying, Da 9:20 5750
w I was still speaking in prayer, Da 9:21 5750
w I was by the bank of the great Da 10:4
w the men who were with me did not Da 10:7
for yet a little w, Hos 1:4 4592
W he stifled his compassion; Am 1:11
W *there were* still three months until Am 4:7
W the part not rained on would dry Am 4:7
W they anoint themselves with the Am 6:6
"W I was fainting away, I Jon 2:7
w I was still in my *own* country? Jon 4:2 5704
w this house *lies* desolate?" Hg 1:4
w each of you runs to his own Hg 1:9
'Once more in a little w, Hg 2:6 4592
for w I was only a little angry, Zch 1:15
w the angel of the LORD was Zch 3:5
w the dappled ones go forth to the Zch 6:6
w I strike every horse of the Zch 12:4
w the inhabitants of Jerusalem Zch 12:6
rot w they stand on their feet, Zch 14:12
w he was seeking a godly offspring Mal 2:15
and took the Child and His mother w Mt 2:14
law w you are with him on the way, Mt 5:25 *2193*
W He was saying these things to Mt 9:18
Now when John, w imprisoned, heard Mt 11:2 *1722*
W He was still speaking to the Mt 12:46
because w seeing they do not see, Mt 13:13
and w hearing they do not hear, Mt 13:13
"But w his men were sleeping, his Mt 13:25 *1722*
for w you are gathering up the Mt 13:29
w He sent the crowds away. Mt 14:22 *2193*
W he was still speaking, a Mt 17:5
And w they were gathering together Mt 17:22
elders of the people came to Him w He Mt 21:23
Now w the Pharisees were gathered Mt 22:41
"Now w the bridegroom was Mt 25:5
"And w they were going away to Mt 25:10
W they were eating, Jesus took Mt 26:26
here w I go over there and pray." Mt 26:36 *2193*
W He was still speaking, behold, Mt 26:47
And w He was being accused by the Mt 27:12 *1722*
W he was sitting on the judgment seat, Mt 27:19
who had followed Jesus from Galilee w Mt 27:55
Now w they were on their way, Mt 28:11
stole Him away w we were asleep.' Mt 28:13
morning, w it was still dark, Mk 1:35 *1773*
"W the bridegroom is with them, Mk 2:19
1722, 3739
w picking the heads *of grain.* Mk 2:23
so that W SEEING, THEY MAY Mk 4:12
AND W HEARING, THEY MAY HEAR AND Mk 4:12
W He was still speaking, they came Mk 5:35
to a secluded place and rest a w." Mk 6:31 *3641*
w He Himself was sending the Mk 6:45 *2193*
W He was in Bethany at the home of Mk 14:3
W they were eating, He took *some* Mk 14:22
w He was still speaking, Mk 14:43
And after a little w the Mk 14:70 *3398*
w they were mourning and weeping. Mk 16:10
w they were walking along on their Mk 16:12
w the Lord worked with them, Mk 16:20
w he was performing his priestly Lk 1:8 *1722*
Spirit w yet in his mother's womb. Lk 1:15
w Quirinius was governor of Syria. Lk 2:2
W they were there, the days were Lk 2:6 *1722*
Now w the people were in a state Lk 3:15
baptized, and w He was praying, Lk 3:21
W the sun was setting, all those who Lk 4:40
w the crowd was pressing Lk 5:1 *1722*
W He was in one of the cities, Lk 5:12 *1722*
w the bridegroom is with them, Lk 5:34
1722, 3739
they believe for a w, Lk 8:13 *2540*
And w they were all denying it, Lk 8:45
W He was still speaking, someone Lk 8:49
happened that w He was praying alone, Lk 9:18 *1722*
And w He was praying, the Lk 9:29 *1722*
W he was saying this, a cloud formed Lk 9:34
W he was still approaching, Lk 9:42
But w everyone was marveling at Lk 9:43
w Jesus was praying in a certain place, Lk 11:1 *1722*
W Jesus was saying these things, one Lk 11:27 *1722*
w you yourselves will not even Lk 11:46 *2532*
"For w you are going with your Lk 12:58 *5613*
w the other is still far away, Lk 14:32
But w he was still a long way off, Lk 15:20
clothe yourself and serve me w I Lk 17:8 *2193*
W He was on the way to Jerusalem, He Lk 17:11 *1722*
"For a w he was unwilling; Lk 18:4 *5550*
W they were listening to these things, Lk 19:11
w He was teaching the people in the Lk 20:1
w all the people were listening, Lk 20:45
And w some were talking about the Lk 21:5
W He was still speaking, behold, a Lk 22:47
"W I was with you daily in the Lk 22:53
w he was still speaking, Lk 22:60
W they were perplexed about this, Lk 24:4 *1722*
to you w He was still in Galilee, Lk 24:6
W they were talking and discussing, Lk 24:15 *1722*
w He was speaking to us on the road, Lk 24:32 *5613*
w He was explaining the Scriptures Lk 24:32 *5613*
W they were telling these things, He Lk 24:36
W they still could not believe *it* Lk 24:41
to you w I was still with you, Lk 24:44
W He was blessing them, He parted Lk 24:51 *1722*

is stirred up, but **w** I am coming, Jn 5:7 1722, 3739
w there was a crowd in *that* place. Jn 5:13
to rejoice for a **w** in his light. Jn 5:35 5610
a little **w** longer I am with you, Jn 7:33 5550
"**W** I am in the world, I am the Jn 9:5 3752
"**W** John performed no sign, yet Jn 10:41 3303a
For a little **w** longer the Light is Jn 12:35 5550
Walk **w** you have the Light, so that Jn 12:35 5613
"**W** you have the Light, believe in Jn 12:36 5613
I am with you a little **w** longer. Jn 13:33 3398
"After a little **w** the world will Jn 14:19 3398
spoken to you **w** abiding with you. Jn 14:25
"A little **w**, and you will no Jn 16:16 3398
and again a little **w**, Jn 16:16 3398
'A little **w**, and you will not Jn 16:17 3398
and again a little **w**, Jn 16:17 3398
What is this that He says, 'A little **w**' Jn 16:18 3398
'A little **w**, and you will not Jn 16:19 3398
see Me, and again a little **w**, Jn 16:19 3398
"**W** I was with them, I was keeping Jn 17:12 3753
to the tomb, **w** it was still dark, Jn 20:1
lifted up **w** they were looking on, Ac 1:9
into the sky **w** He was going, Ac 1:10
W he was clinging to Peter and John, Ac 3:11
w You extend Your hand to Ac 4:30 1722
"**W** it remained *unsold*, did it not Ac 5:4
Now at this time **w** the disciples Ac 6:1
used to make **w** she was with them. Ac 9:39 3745
w they were making preparations, Ac 10:10
Now **w** Peter was greatly perplexed Ac 10:17 5613
W Peter was reflecting on the vision, Ac 10:19
W Peter was still speaking these Ac 10:44
W they were ministering to the Lord Ac 13:2
"And **w** John was completing his Ac 13:25 5613
But **w** the disciples stood around Ac 14:20
Now **w** they were passing through Ac 16:4 5613
Now **w** Paul was waiting for them at Ac 17:16
"For **w** I was passing through and Ac 17:23
But **w** Gallio was proconsul of Ac 18:12
that **w** Apollos was at Corinth, Ac 19:1 1722
he himself stayed in Asia for a **w**. Ac 19:22 5550
he talked with them a long **w** until Ac 20:11 2425
on our journey, **w** they all, Ac 21:5
W they were seeking to kill him, a Ac 21:31
shouted out **w** standing among them, Ac 24:21
w Paul said in his own defense, Ac 25:8
W they were spending many days Ac 25:14 5613
"**W** so engaged as I was Ac 26:12 1722
W *Paul* was saying this in his Ac 26:24
they left them in the sea **w** at the Ac 27:40
be encouraged together with you **w** Ro 1:12
W he was circumcised, or Ro 4:10
Not **w** circumcised, but while Ro 4:10
circumcised, but **w** uncircumcised; Ro 4:10
which he had **w** uncircumcised, Ro 4:11
which he had **w** uncircumcised. Ro 4:12
For **w** we were still helpless, at Ro 5:6
us, in that **w** we were yet sinners, Ro 5:8
For if **w** we were enemies we were Ro 5:10
law to her husband **w** he is living; Ro 7:2
then, if **w** her husband is living Ro 7:3
For **w** we were in the flesh, the Ro 7:5 3753
enjoyed your company for a **w** Ro 15:24 3313
Were you called **w** a slave? 1Co 7:21
was called in the Lord **w** a slave, 1Co 7:22
likewise he who was called **w** free, 1Co 7:22
MUZZLE THE OX **W** HE IS THRESHING." 1Co 9:9
his head **w** praying or prophesying 1Co 11:4
w praying or prophesying disgraces 1Co 11:5
w we look not at the things which 2Co 4:18
For indeed **w** we are in this tent, 2Co 5:4
and knowing that **w** we are at home 2Co 5:6
you sorrow, though only for a **w** 2Co 7:8 5610
w they also, by prayer on your 2Co 9:14
am writing these things **w** absent, 2Co 13:10
w seeking to be justified in Ga 2:17
So also we, **w** we were children, Ga 4:3 3753
So then, **w** we have opportunity, Ga 6:10 5613
w making mention *of you* in my Eph 1:16
taken away from you for a short **w** 1Th 2:17 5610
W they are saying, 1Th 5:3 3752
that **w** I was still with you, 2Th 2:5
pleasure is dead even **w** she lives. 1Tm 5:6
MUZZLE THE OX **W** HE IS THRESHING," 1Tm 5:18
reason separated *from you* for a **w**, Phm 1:15 5610
A LITTLE **W** LOWER THAN THE ANGELS; Heb 2:7 1024
a little **w** lower than the angels, Heb 2:9 1024
w it is said, "TODAY IF YOU HEAR Heb 3:15 1722
w a promise remains of entering Heb 4:1
w the outer tabernacle is still Heb 9:8
force **w** the one who made it lives. Heb 9:17 3753
FOR YET IN A VERY LITTLE **W**, Heb 10:37 3745
a vapor that appears for a little **w** Jas 4:14 3641
even though now for a little **w**, 1Pe 1:6 3641
and **w** being reviled, He did not 1Pe 2:23
w suffering, He uttered no 1Pe 2:23
you have suffered for a little **w**, 1Pe 5:10 3641
man, **w** living among them, 2Pe 2:8
w they themselves are slaves of 2Pe 2:19
w I was making every effort to Jude 1:3
should rest for a little **w** longer, Rv 6:11 5550
comes, he must remain a little **w**. Rv 17:10 3641

WHIP
and a **w** on your sides and thorns Jos 23:13 7850
A **w** is for the horse, a bridle for Pr 26:3 7752
The noise of the **w**, Na 3:2 7752

WHIPS
my father disciplined you with **w**, 1Ki 12:11 7752
my father disciplined you with **w**, 1Ki 12:14 7752
my father disciplined you with **w**, 2Ch 10:11 7752
my father disciplined you with **w**, 2Ch 10:14 7752

WHIRL
sword will **w** against their cities, Hos 11:6 2342a

WHIRLING
my God, make them like the **w** dust, Ps 83:13 1534
Or like **w** dust before a gale. Is 17:13 1534
forth in wrath, Even a **w** tempest; Jer 23:19 2342a
the **w** wheels under the cherubim and Ezk 10:2 1534
fire from between the **w** wheels, Ezk 10:6 1534
in my hearing, the **w** wheels. Ezk 10:13 1534

WHIRLS
For it **w** him away from his place. Jb 27:21 8175a

WHIRLWIND
take up Elijah by a **w** to heaven, 2Ki 2:1 5591b
Elijah went up by a **w** to heaven. 2Ki 2:11 5591b
the LORD answered Job out of the **w** Jb 38:1 5591b
He will sweep them away with a **w**, Ps 58:9 8175a
sound of Your thunder was in the **w**; Ps 77:18 1534
your calamity comes like a **w**, Pr 1:27 5492a
When the **w** passes, the wicked is Pr 10:25 5492a
and its *chariot* wheels like a **w**. Is 5:28 5492a
With **w** and tempest and the flame Is 29:6 5492a
fire And His chariots like the **w**, Is 66:15 5492a
And his chariots like the **w**; Jer 4:13 5492a
sow the wind And they reap the **w**. Hos 8:7 5492a
In **w** and storm is His way, And Na 1:3 5492a
and to darkness and gloom and **w**, Heb 12:18 2366

WHIRRING
oh land of **w** wings Which lies Is 18:1 6767a

WHISPER
And my ear received a **w** of it. Jb 4:12 8102
who hate me **w** together against me; Ps 41:7 3907
the spiritists who **w** and mutter," Is 8:19 6850
They could only **w** a prayer, Your Is 26:16 3908
your speech will **w** from the dust. Is 29:4 6850

WHISPERED
and what you hear **w** in *your* Mt 10:27
and what you have **w** in the inner Lk 12:3 2980, 4314, 3775

WHISPERER
words of a **w** are like dainty morsels, Pr 18:8 7279
goes out, And where there is no **w**, Pr 26:20 7279
words of a **w** are like dainty morsels, Pr 26:22 7279

WHISPERING
that his servants were **w** together, 2Sa 12:19 3907
For I have heard the **w** of many, Jer 20:10 1681
lips of my assailants and their **w** La 3:62 1902
in the talk and the **w** of the people. Ezk 36:3 1681

WHISTLE
And will **w** for it from the ends of Is 5:26 8319
that day the LORD will **w** for the fly Is 7:18 8319
"I will **w** for them to gather them Zch 10:8 8319

WHITE
goats, every one with **w** in it, Gn 30:35 3836
and peeled **w** stripes in them, Gn 30:37 3836
the **w** which *was* in the rods. Gn 30:37 3836
baskets of **w** bread on my head; Gn 40:16 2751
wine, And his teeth **w** from milk. Gn 49:12 3836
and it was like coriander seed, **w**, Ex 16:31 3836
and the **w** owl and the pelican and Lv 11:18 8580
the hair in the infection has turned **w** Lv 13:3 3836
spot is **w** on the skin of his body, Lv 13:4 3836
the hair on it has not turned **w**, Lv 13:4 3836
there is a **w** swelling in the skin, Lv 13:10 3836
and it has turned the hair **w**, Lv 13:10 3836
has all turned **w** *and* he is clean. Lv 13:13 3836
turns again and is changed to **w**, Lv 13:16 3836
if the infection has turned to **w**, Lv 13:17 3836
is a **w** swelling or a reddish-white, Lv 13:19 3836
and the hair on it has turned **w**, Lv 13:20 3836
there are no **w** hairs in it and it Lv 13:21 3836
a bright spot, reddish-white, or **w**, Lv 13:24 3836
in the bright spot has turned **w** and Lv 13:25 3836
is no **w** hair in the bright spot and Lv 13:26 3836
of the body, *even* **w** bright spots, Lv 13:38 3836
of their bodies are a faint **w**, Lv 13:39 3836
as **w** *as* snow. As Aaron turned Nu 12:10
owl, the great owl, the **w** owl, Dt 14:16 8580
"You who ride on **w** donkeys, You Jg 5:10 6715
out from his presence a leper *as* **w** 2Ki 5:27
hangings of fine **w** and violet linen Es 1:6 2353
king in royal robes of blue and **w**, Es 8:15 2353
any taste in the **w** of an egg? Jb 6:6 2495
your clothes be **w** all the time, Ec 9:8 3836
They will be as **w** as snow; Is 1:18 3835a
the weavers of **w** cloth will be utterly Is 19:9 2360a
of the wine of Helbon and **w** wool. Ezk 27:18 6713
His vesture *was* like **w** snow And Da 7:9 2358
Their branches have become **w**. Jl 1:7 3835a
sorrel and **w** horses behind him. Zch 1:8 3836
with the third chariot **w** horses, Zch 6:3 3836
the **w** ones go forth after them, Zch 6:6 3836
cannot make one hair **w** or black. Mt 5:36 3022
His garments became as **w** as light. Mt 17:2 3022
and his clothing as **w** as snow Mt 28:3 3022
became radiant and exceedingly **w**, Mk 9:3 3022
at the right, wearing a **w** robe; Mk 16:5 3022
His clothing *became* **w** *and* gleaming. Lk 9:29 3022
that they are **w** for harvest. Jn 4:35 3022
saw two angels in **w** sitting, Jn 20:12 3022
two men in **w** clothing stood beside Ac 1:10 3022
His hair were **w** like white wool, Rv 1:14 3022
His hair were white like **w** wool, Rv 1:14 3022
and I will give him a **w** stone, Rv 2:17 3022
and they will walk with Me in **w**, Rv 3:4 3022
thus be clothed in **w** garments; Rv 3:5 3022
may become rich, and **w** garments so Rv 3:18 3022
sitting, clothed in **w** garments, Rv 4:4 3022
I looked, and behold, a **w** horse, Rv 6:2 3022
given to each of them a **w** robe; Rv 6:11 3022
the Lamb, clothed in **w** robes, Rv 7:9 3022
who are clothed in the **w** robes, Rv 7:13 3022
them **w** in the blood of the Lamb. Rv 7:14 3021
I looked, and behold, a **w** cloud, Rv 14:14 3022
and behold, a **w** horse, and He who Rv 19:11 3022
in fine linen, **w** *and* clean, Rv 19:14 3022
were following Him on **w** horses. Rv 19:14 3022
Then I saw a great **w** throne and Him Rv 20:11 3022

WHITEN
no launderer on earth can **w** them. Mk 9:3 3021

WHITER
me, and I shall be **w** than snow. Ps 51:7 3835a
than snow, They were **w** than milk; La 4:7 6705

WHITEWASH
they plaster it over with **w**; Ezk 13:10 8602b
those who plaster *it* over with **w**, Ezk 13:11 8602b
wall which you plastered over with **w** Ezk 13:14 8602b
who have plastered it over with **w**; Ezk 13:15 8602b
prophets have smeared **w** for them. Ezk 22:28 8602b

WHITEWASHED
For you are like **w** tombs which on Mt 23:27 2867
going to strike you, you **w** wall! Ac 23:3 2867

WHO
"**W** told you that you were naked? Gn 3:11 4310
he was the father of those **w** dwell Gn 4:20
those **w** play the lyre and pipe. Gn 4:21
were the mighty men **w** *were* of old, Gn 6:4 834
Now the sons of Noah **w** came out of Gn 9:18
I will bless those **w** bless you, Gn 12:3
the one **w** curses you I will curse. Gn 12:3
to the LORD **w** had appeared to him. Gn 12:7
Now Lot, **w** went with Abram, also Gn 13:5
Amorites, **w** lived in Hazazon-tamar. Gn 14:7
But those **w** survived fled to the Gn 14:10
and the kings **w** were with him, Gn 14:17 834
W has delivered your enemies into Gn 14:20 834
share of the men **w** went with me, Gn 14:24 834
but one **w** will come forth from Gn 15:4 834
"I am the LORD **w** brought you out Gn 15:7 834
name of the LORD **w** spoke to her, Gn 16:13
"You are a God **w** sees"; Gn 16:13 7210
"And every male among you **w** is Gn 17:12
a *servant* **w** is born in the house Gn 17:12 3211
w is bought with money from any Gn 17:12 4736
w is not of your descendants. Gn 17:12 834
"A *servant* **w** is born in your Gn 17:13 3211
or **w** is bought with your money Gn 17:13 4736
"But an uncircumcised male **w** is Gn 17:14 834
will Sarah, **w** is ninety years old, Gn 17:17
and all *the servants* **w** were born Gn 17:23 3211
all **w** were bought with his money, Gn 17:23 4736
w were born in the house or bought Gn 17:27 3211
the fifty righteous **w** are in it? Gn 18:24 834
are the men **w** came to you tonight? Gn 19:5 834
I have two daughters **w** have not Gn 19:8 834
They struck the men **w** were at Gn 19:11 834
w were to marry his daughters, Gn 19:14
your two daughters **w** are here, Gn 19:15
die, you and all **w** are yours." Gn 20:7 834
before all **w** are with you, Gn 20:16 834
name of his son **w** was born to him, Gn 21:3
everyone **w** hears will laugh with me Gn 21:6
"**W** would have said to Abraham Gn 21:7 4310
do not know **w** has done this thing; Gn 21:26 4310
even of all **w** went in at the gate Gn 23:10
before all **w** went in at the gate Gn 23:18
w had charge of all that he owned, Gn 24:2
w took me from my father's house Gn 24:7 834
of my birth, and **w** spoke to me and Gn 24:7 834
spoke to me and **w** swore to me, Gn 24:7 834
that I may drink,' and **w** answers, Gn 24:14
Rebekah **w** was born to Bethuel the Gn 24:15 834
w has not forsaken His Gn 24:27 834
feet of the men **w** were with him. Gn 24:32 834
the maiden **w** comes out to draw, Gn 24:43
w had guided me in the right way Gn 24:48 834
Then he and the men **w** were with Gn 24:54 834
The gate of those **w** hate them." Gn 24:60
"**W** is that man walking in the Gn 24:65 4310
"He **w** touches this man or his Gn 26:11
W are you, my son?" Gn 27:18 4310
Cursed be those **w** curse you, And Gn 27:29
blessed be those **w** bless you." Gn 27:29
his father said to him, "**W** are you?" Gn 27:32 4310
"**W** was he then that hunted game Gn 27:33 4310
w has withheld from you the fruit Gn 30:2 834
the people **w** were with him, Gn 32:7 834
Isaac, O LORD, **w** said to me, Gn 32:9
all those **w** followed the droves, Gn 32:19
"**W** are these with you?" Gn 33:5 4310
of the people **w** are with me." Gn 33:15 834
sister to one **w** is uncircumcised, Gn 34:14 834
All **w** went out of the gate of Gn 34:24
all **w** went out of the gate of his Gn 34:24
w appeared to you when you fled Gn 35:1
and to all **w** were with him, Gn 35:2 834
w answered me in the day of my Gn 35:3
all the people **w** were with him. Gn 35:6 834
These are the sons of Jacob **w** were Gn 35:26 834
These are the sons of Esau **w** were Gn 36:5 834
is the Anah **w** found the hot springs Gn 36:24 834

Now these are the kings **w** reigned	**Gn 36:31**	834
w defeated Midian in the field of	**Gn 36:35**	
w was by the road at Enaim?"	**Gn 38:21**	1931
w had the scarlet *thread* on his hand;	**Gn 38:30**	
w had taken him down there.	**Gn 39:1**	834
the prisoners **w** were in the jail;	**Gn 39:22**	834
of Egypt, **w** were confined in jail,	**Gn 40:5**	834
He asked Pharaoh's officials **w**	**Gn 40:7**	834
but there was no one **w** could	**Gn 41:8**	
no one **w** could explain it to me."	**Gn 41:24**	
grain among those **w** were coming,	**Gn 42:5**	
he was the one **w** sold to all the	**Gn 42:6**	
w put our money in our sacks."	**Gn 43:22**	4310
and the Egyptians **w** ate with him	**Gn 43:32**	
before all those **w** stood by him,	**Gn 45:1**	
it was not you **w** sent me here,	**Gn 45:8**	
and his sons, **w** went to Egypt:	**Gn 46:8**	
of Rachel, **w** were born to Jacob;	**Gn 46:22**	834
to Jacob, **w** came to Egypt,	**Gn 46:26**	
and the sons of Joseph, **w** were born	**Gn 46:27**	
house of Jacob, **w** came to Egypt,	**Gn 46:27**	
w *were* in the land of Canaan,	**Gn 46:31**	834
w were born to you in the land of	**Gn 48:5**	
Joseph's sons, he said, "**W** are these?"	**Gn 48:8**	4310
of Ephraim, **w** was the younger,	**Gn 48:14**	1931
The God **w** has been my shepherd all	**Gn 48:15**	
w has redeemed me from all evil,	**Gn 48:16**	
as a lion, **w** dares rouse him up?	**Gn 49:9**	4310
God of your father **w** helps you,	**Gn 49:25**	
And by the Almighty **w** blesses you	**Gn 49:25**	
and all **w** had gone up with him to	**Gn 50:14**	
Israel **w** came to Egypt with Jacob;	**Ex 1:1**	
All the persons **w** came from	**Ex 1:5**	
over Egypt, **w** did not know Joseph.	**Ex 1:8**	834
themselves to those **w** hate us,	**Ex 1:10**	834
"Every son **w** is born you are to	**Ex 1:22**	
"**W** made you a prince or a judge	**Ex 2:14**	4310
of My people **w** are in Egypt,	**Ex 3:7**	834
"**W** am I, that I should go to	**Ex 3:11**	4310
you that it is I **w** have sent you:	**Ex 3:12**	
God said to Moses, "I AM **W** I AM";	**Ex 3:14**	834
the woman **w** lives in her house,	**Ex 3:22**	
"**W** has made man's mouth?	**Ex 4:11**	4310
Or **w** makes *him* mute or deaf, or	**Ex 4:11**	4310
to my brethren **w** are in Egypt,	**Ex 4:18**	834
for all the men **w** were seeking	**Ex 4:19**	
"**W** is the LORD that I should obey	**Ex 5:2**	4310
w brought you out from under the	**Ex 6:7**	
They were the ones **w** spoke to	**Ex 6:27**	
servants of Pharaoh **w** feared the word	**Ex 9:20**	
but he **w** paid no regard to the	**Ex 9:21**	834
W are the ones that are going?"	**Ex 10:8**	4310
the Pharaoh **w** sits on his throne,	**Ex 11:5**	
girl **w** is behind the millstones;	**Ex 11:5**	834
and all the people **w** follow you,'	**Ex 11:8**	834
LORD **w** passed over the houses of	**Ex 12:27**	834
from the firstborn of Pharaoh **w**	**Ex 12:29**	
the captive **w** was in the dungeon,	**Ex 12:29**	834
stranger **w** sojourns among you."	**Ex 12:49**	
w had been going before the camp	**Ex 14:19**	
those **w** rise up against You;	**Ex 15:7**	
"**W** is like You among the gods, O	**Ex 15:11**	4310
W is like You, majestic in holiness,	**Ex 15:11**	4310
he **w** had gathered much had no	**Ex 16:18**	
he **w** had gathered little had no lack	**Ex 16:18**	
"Blessed be the LORD **w** delivered	**Ex 18:10**	834
and **w** delivered the people from	**Ex 18:10**	834
and these people **w** are with you,	**Ex 18:18**	834
the people able men **w** fear God,	**Ex 18:21**	
those **w** hate dishonest gain;	**Ex 18:21**	
w *were* in the camp trembled.	**Ex 19:16**	834
"Also let the priests **w** come	**Ex 19:22**	
w brought you out of the land of	**Ex 20:2**	834
generations of those **w** hate Me,	**Ex 20:5**	
to those **w** love Me and keep My	**Ex 20:6**	
w takes His name in vain.	**Ex 20:7**	834
your sojourner **w** stays with you.	**Ex 20:10**	834
w designated her for himself,	**Ex 21:8**	834
"He **w** strikes a man so that he	**Ex 21:12**	
"He **w** strikes his father or	**Ex 21:15**	
"He **w** kidnaps a man, whether	**Ex 21:16**	
"He **w** curses his father or	**Ex 21:17**	
then he **w** struck him shall go	**Ex 21:19**	
he **w** started the fire shall surely	**Ex 22:6**	
seduces a virgin **w** is not engaged,	**Ex 22:16**	834
"He **w** sacrifices to any god,	**Ex 22:20**	
"If you see the donkey of one **w**	**Ex 23:5**	
one of his sons **w** is priest in his stead	**Ex 29:30**	
God **w** brought them out of the land	**Ex 29:46**	834
everyone **w** is numbered shall give:	**Ex 30:13**	
"Everyone **w** is numbered, from	**Ex 30:14**	
w are skillful I have put skill,	**Ex 31:6**	2450
I am the LORD **w** sanctifies you.	**Ex 31:13**	
Everyone **w** profanes it shall	**Ex 31:14**	
make us a god **w** will go before us;	**Ex 32:1**	834
the man **w** brought us up from the	**Ex 32:1**	834
w brought you up from the land of	**Ex 32:4**	834
w brought you up from the land of	**Ex 32:8**	834
a god for us **w** will go before us;	**Ex 32:23**	834
the man **w** brought us up from the	**Ex 32:23**	834
And everyone **w** sought the LORD	**Ex 33:7**	
other people **w** are upon the face of	**Ex 33:16**	834
w keeps lovingkindness for	**Ex 34:7**	
thousands, **w** forgives iniquity,	**Ex 34:7**	
so *did* every man **w** presented an	**Ex 35:22**	834
w had in his possession blue and	**Ex 35:23**	834
Everyone **w** could make a	**Ex 35:24**	
w had in his possession acacia	**Ex 35:24**	834
And all the skillful men **w** were	**Ex 36:4**	
those **w** were performing the work	**Ex 36:8**	
women **w** served at the doorway of	**Ex 38:8**	834
the congregation **w** were numbered	**Ex 38:25**	
for each one **w** passed over to	**Ex 38:26**	
over to those **w** were numbered,	**Ex 38:26**	
w shall offer first that which is	**Lv 5:8**	
'The anointed priest **w** will	**Lv 6:22**	
'The priest **w** offers it for sin	**Lv 6:26**	
'Anyone **w** touches its flesh will	**Lv 6:27**	834
the priest **w** makes atonement with	**Lv 7:7**	834
'Also the priest **w** presents any	**Lv 7:8**	
to the priest **w** presents it.	**Lv 7:9**	
it shall belong to the priest **w**	**Lv 7:14**	
he **w** offers it will not be	**Lv 7:18**	
and the person **w** eats of it will	**Lv 7:18**	
w is clean may eat *such* flesh.	**Lv 7:19**	
'But the person **w** eats the flesh	**Lv 7:20**	834
even the person **w** eats shall be	**Lv 7:25**	
'Any person **w** eats any blood, even	**Lv 7:27**	834
'He **w** offers the sacrifice of his	**Lv 7:29**	
'The one among the sons of Aaron **w**	**Lv 7:33**	
'By those **w** come near Me I will be	**Lv 10:3**	
and the one **w** picks up their	**Lv 11:28**	
though the one **w** touches their	**Lv 11:36**	
the one **w** touches its carcass	**Lv 11:39**	
w eats some of its carcass shall	**Lv 11:40**	
and the one **w** picks up its carcass	**Lv 11:40**	
w brought you up from the land of	**Lv 11:45**	
the law for her **w** bears *a child,*	**Lv 12:7**	
then the priest shall isolate *him* **w**	**Lv 13:4**	
covers all the skin of *him* **w** *has*	**Lv 13:12**	
he shall pronounce clean *him* **w** *has*	**Lv 13:13**	
priest shall pronounce clean *him* **w**	**Lv 13:17**	
for the leper **w** has the infection,	**Lv 13:45**	834
for the one **w** is to be cleansed.	**Lv 14:4**	
w is to be cleansed from the leprosy and	**Lv 14:7**	
and the priest **w** pronounces him	**Lv 14:11**	
then the one **w** owns the house	**Lv 14:35**	834
w touches his bed shall wash his	**Lv 15:5**	834
discharge spits on one **w** is clean,	**Lv 15:8**	2889
and he **w** carries them shall wash	**Lv 15:10**	
'Anyone **w** touches her bed	**Lv 15:21**	
and for the man **w** has a seminal	**Lv 15:32**	834
and for the woman **w** is ill because	**Lv 15:33**	1739
and for the one **w** has a discharge,	**Lv 15:33**	
man **w** lies with an unclean woman.	**Lv 15:33**	834
of a man **w** *stands* in readiness.	**Lv 16:21**	
"The one **w** released the goat	**Lv 16:26**	
"Then the one **w** burns them shall	**Lv 16:28**	
or the alien **w** sojourns among you;	**Lv 16:29**	
"So the priest **w** is anointed and	**Lv 16:32**	834
of Israel **w** slaughters an ox or	**Lv 17:3**	834
or **w** slaughters it outside the	**Lv 17:3**	834
the aliens **w** sojourn among them,	**Lv 17:8**	834
w offers a burnt offering or	**Lv 17:8**	834
the aliens **w** sojourn among them,	**Lv 17:10**	
among them, **w** eats any blood,	**Lv 17:10**	834
against that person **w** eats blood and	**Lv 17:10**	
w sojourns among you eat blood.'	**Lv 17:12**	
the aliens **w** sojourn among them,	**Lv 17:13**	
the alien **w** sojourns among you	**Lv 18:26**	
(for the men of the land **w** have	**Lv 18:27**	834
those persons **w** do *so* shall be cut	**Lv 18:29**	
'Everyone **w** eats it will bear	**Lv 19:8**	
carnally with a woman **w** is a slave	**Lv 19:20**	1931
but **w** has in no way been redeemed nor	**Lv 19:20**	
'The stranger **w** resides with you	**Lv 19:34**	
w brought you out from the land of	**Lv 19:36**	834
w gives any of his offspring to	**Lv 20:2**	834
those **w** play the harlot after him,	**Lv 20:5**	
'As for the person **w** turns to	**Lv 20:6**	834
I am the LORD **w** sanctifies you.	**Lv 20:8**	
'If *there is* anyone **w** curses his	**Lv 20:9**	834
'If *there is* a man **w** commits	**Lv 20:10**	834
one **w** commits adultery with his	**Lv 20:10**	834
man **w** lies with his father's wife,	**Lv 20:11**	834
man **w** lies with his daughter-in-law,	**Lv 20:12**	834
'If *there is* a man **w** lies with a	**Lv 20:13**	834
male as those **w** lie with a woman,	**Lv 20:13**	
'If *there is* a man **w** marries a	**Lv 20:14**	834
is a man **w** lies with an animal,	**Lv 20:15**	834
'If *there is* a woman **w** approaches	**Lv 20:16**	834
there is a man **w** takes his sister,	**Lv 20:17**	834
'If *there is* a man **w** lies with a	**Lv 20:18**	834
'If *there is* a man **w** lies with his	**Lv 20:20**	834
a man **w** takes his brother's wife,	**Lv 20:21**	834
w has separated you from the	**Lv 20:24**	834
'Now a man or a woman **w** is a	**Lv 20:27**	
relatives **w** are nearest to him,	**Lv 21:2**	
w is near to him because she has	**Lv 21:3**	
a woman **w** is profaned by harlotry,	**Lv 21:7**	
for I the LORD, **w** sanctifies you,	**Lv 21:8**	
'The priest **w** is the highest	**Lv 21:10**	
and **w** has been consecrated to wear	**Lv 21:10**	
or one **w** is profaned by harlotry,	**Lv 21:14**	
am the LORD **w** sanctifies him.' "	**Lv 21:15**	
w has a defect shall approach to offer	**Lv 21:17**	834
one **w** has a defect shall approach:	**Lv 21:18**	834
or he **w** has a disfigured *face,*	**Lv 21:18**	
or a man **w** has a broken foot or	**Lv 21:19**	834
or *one* **w** *has* a defect in his eye	**Lv 21:20**	
Aaron the priest **w** has a defect	**Lv 21:21**	834
am the LORD **w** sanctifies them.' "	**Lv 21:23**	
w is a leper or who has a	**Lv 22:4**	1931
is a leper or **w** has a discharge,	**Lv 22:4**	
a person **w** touches any such shall	**Lv 22:6**	834
I am the LORD **w** sanctifies them.	**Lv 22:9**	
and those **w** are born in his house	**Lv 22:11**	3211
am the LORD **w** sanctifies them.' "	**Lv 22:16**	
in Israel **w** presents his offering,	**Lv 22:18**	834
I am the LORD **w** sanctifies you,	**Lv 22:32**	
w brought you out from the land of	**Lv 22:33**	
"If there is any person **w** will	**Lv 23:29**	834
"As for any person **w** does any	**Lv 23:30**	834
one **w** has cursed outside the camp,	**Lv 24:14**	
and let all **w** heard him lay their	**Lv 24:14**	
the one **w** blasphemes the name of	**Lv 24:16**	
'The one **w** takes the life of	**Lv 24:18**	
'Thus the one **w** kills an animal	**Lv 24:21**	
but the one **w** kills a man shall be	**Lv 24:21**	
and they brought the one **w** had	**Lv 24:23**	
those **w** live as aliens with you.	**Lv 25:6**	
w brought you out of the land of	**Lv 25:38**	834
sojourners **w** live as aliens among you	**Lv 25:45**	
of their families **w** are with you,	**Lv 25:45**	834
stranger **w** is sojourning with you,	**Lv 25:47**	
w brought you out of the land of	**Lv 26:13**	834
w hate you will rule over you,	**Lv 26:17**	
so that your enemies **w** settle in it	**Lv 26:32**	
'As for those of you **w** may be left,	**Lv 26:36**	
'So those of you **w** may be left	**Lv 26:39**	
to the means of the one **w** vowed,	**Lv 27:8**	
'Yet if the one **w** consecrates it	**Lv 27:15**	
'If the one **w** consecrates it	**Lv 27:19**	
'No one **w** may have been set apart	**Lv 27:29**	834
of the men **w** shall stand with you:	**Nu 1:5**	834
"These are they **w** were called of	**Nu 1:16**	7148
men **w** had been designated by name,	**Nu 1:17**	834
are the ones **w** were numbered,	**Nu 1:44**	
But the layman **w** comes near shall	**Nu 1:51**	
"Now those **w** camp on the east	**Nu 2:3**	
"Those **w** camp next to him	**Nu 2:5**	
"Those **w** camp next to him	**Nu 2:12**	
"Those **w** camp next to him	**Nu 2:27**	
but the layman **w** comes near shall	**Nu 3:10**	
and had the oversight of those **w**	**Nu 3:32**	
Now those **w** were to camp before	**Nu 3:38**	
w are in excess beyond the Levites,	**Nu 3:46**	
those **w** are in excess among them,	**Nu 3:48**	
money from those **w** were in excess,	**Nu 3:49**	
all **w** enter the service to do the	**Nu 4:3**	
all **w** enter to perform the service	**Nu 4:23**	
everyone **w** enters the service to	**Nu 4:30**	
everyone **w** entered the service for	**Nu 4:35**	
everyone **w** was serving in the tent	**Nu 4:37**	
everyone **w** entered the service for	**Nu 4:39**	
everyone **w** was serving in the tent	**Nu 4:41**	
everyone **w** entered the service for	**Nu 4:43**	
everyone **w** could enter to do the	**Nu 4:47**	
everyone **w** is unclean because of a	**Nu 5:2**	
law of the Nazirite **w** vows his offering	**Nu 6:21**	834
w were over the numbered men).	**Nu 7:2**	
Now the one **w** presented his	**Nu 7:12**	
But there were *some* men **w** were	**Nu 9:6**	834
'But the man **w** is clean and is not	**Nu 9:13**	834
the adversary **w** attacks you,	**Nu 10:9**	
w were carrying the tabernacle,	**Nu 10:17**	
those **w** hate You flee before You."	**Nu 10:35**	
like those **w** complain of adversity	**Nu 11:1**	
The rabble **w** were among them	**Nu 11:4**	834
"**W** will give us meat to eat?	**Nu 11:4**	4310
it I **w** conceived all this people?	**Nu 11:12**	
Was it I **w** brought them forth,	**Nu 11:12**	
take of the Spirit **w** is upon you,	**Nu 11:17**	834
rejected the LORD **w** is among you	**Nu 11:20**	834
and He took of the Spirit **w** was	**Nu 11:25**	834
among those **w** had been registered,	**Nu 11:26**	
he **w** gathered least gathered ten	**Nu 11:32**	
the people **w** had been greedy.	**Nu 11:34**	
w was on the face of the earth.)	**Nu 12:3**	834
all of them men **w** were heads of	**Nu 13:3**	
w live in it are strong *or* weak,	**Nu 13:18**	
w live in the land are strong,	**Nu 13:28**	
men **w** had gone up with him said,	**Nu 13:31**	834
of those **w** had spied out the land,	**Nu 14:6**	
then the nations **w** have heard of	**Nu 14:15**	834
"Surely all the men **w** have seen	**Nu 14:22**	
any of those **w** spurned Me see it.	**Nu 14:23**	
w are grumbling against Me?	**Nu 14:27**	834
w have grumbled against Me.	**Nu 14:29**	834
w are gathered together against Me.	**Nu 14:35**	
to spy out the land and **w** returned	**Nu 14:36**	
even those men **w** brought out the	**Nu 14:37**	
men **w** went to spy out the land.	**Nu 14:38**	
Canaanites **w** lived in that hill country	**Nu 14:45**	
'The one **w** presents his	**Nu 15:4**	
'All **w** are native shall do these	**Nu 15:13**	
or one **w** may be among you	**Nu 15:14**	834
for the alien **w** sojourns *with you,*	**Nu 15:15**	
the alien **w** sojourns with you.' "	**Nu 15:16**	
the alien **w** sojourns among them,	**Nu 15:26**	
person **w** goes astray when he sins	**Nu 15:28**	
w does *anything* unintentionally,	**Nu 15:29**	
for him **w** is native among the sons	**Nu 15:29**	
the alien **w** sojourns among them.	**Nu 15:29**	
person **w** does *anything* defiantly,	**Nu 15:30**	834
Those **w** found him gathering	**Nu 15:33**	
"I am the LORD your God **w** brought	**Nu 15:41**	834
the LORD will show **w** is His,	**Nu 16:5**	834
show who is His, and **w** is holy,	**Nu 16:5**	
shall be the one **w** is holy.	**Nu 16:7**	1931
w is he that you grumble against	**Nu 16:11**	4100
all the men **w** belonged to Korah with	**Nu 16:32**	834
All Israel **w** *were* around them	**Nu 16:34**	834
men **w** were offering the incense.	**Nu 16:35**	
men **w** have sinned at the cost of	**Nu 16:38**	2400
the men **w** were burned had offered,	**Nu 16:39**	
no layman **w** is not of the descendants	**Nu 16:40**	834

“You are the ones **w** have caused	**Nu 16:41**	
But those **w** died by the plague	**Nu 16:49**	
those **w** died on account of Korah.	**Nu 16:49**	
w are grumbling against you.”	**Nu 17:5**	834
“Everyone **w** comes near, who comes	**Nu 17:13**	
w comes near to the tabernacle of	**Nu 17:13**	
but the outsider **w** comes near	**Nu 18:7**	
household **w** is clean may eat it.	**Nu 18:11**	
household **w** is clean may eat it.	**Nu 18:13**	
‘The one **w** burns it shall also	**Nu 19:8**	
‘Now a man **w** is clean shall gather	**Nu 19:9**	
‘The one **w** gathers the ashes	**Nu 19:10**	
the alien **w** sojourns among them.	**Nu 19:10**	
‘The one **w** touches the corpse of	**Nu 19:11**	
‘Anyone **w** touches a corpse, the	**Nu 19:13**	
the body of a man **w** has died,	**Nu 19:13**	834
everyone **w** comes into the tent and	**Nu 19:14**	
everyone **w** is in the tent shall be	**Nu 19:14**	834
anyone **w** in the open field touches	**Nu 19:16**	834
touches one **w** has been slain with a	**Nu 19:16**	2491a
a sword or **w** has died *naturally,*	**Nu 19:16**	
and on the persons **w** were there,	**Nu 19:18**	834
and on the one **w** touched the bone	**Nu 19:18**	
‘But the man **w** is unclean and does	**Nu 19:20**	834
And he **w** sprinkles the water for	**Nu 19:21**	
and he **w** touches the water for	**Nu 19:21**	
and the person **w** touches *it* shall	**Nu 19:22**	
of Arad, **w** lived in the Negev,	**Nu 21:1**	
about, that everyone **w** is bitten,	**Nu 21:8**	
w had fought against the former	**Nu 21:26**	1931
those **w** use proverbs say,	**Nu 21:27**	
the Amorites **w** *were* there.	**Nu 21:32**	834
Amorites, **w** lived at Heshbon.”	**Nu 21:34**	834
“**W** are these men with you?”	**Nu 22:9**	4310
there is a people **w** came out of	**Nu 22:11**	
and the leaders **w** were with him.	**Nu 22:40**	834
a people **w** dwells apart,	**Nu 23:9**	
“**W** can count the dust of Jacob,	**Nu 23:10**	4310
of him **w** hears the words of God,	**Nu 24:4**	
W sees the vision of the Almighty,	**Nu 24:4**	834
He will devour the nations **w** *are*	**Nu 24:8**	
And as a lion, **w** dares rouse him?	**Nu 24:9**	4310
Blessed is everyone **w** blesses you,	**Nu 24:9**	
cursed is everyone **w** curses you.”	**Nu 24:9**	
of him **w** hears the words of God,	**Nu 24:16**	
W sees the vision of the Almighty,	**Nu 24:16**	
w can live except God has ordained	**Nu 24:23**	4310
“Each of you slay his men **w** have	**Nu 25:5**	
Those **w** died by the plague	**Nu 25:9**	
man of Israel **w** was slain with the	**Nu 25:14**	834
woman **w** was slain was Cozbi	**Nu 25:15**	
w was head of the people of a	**Nu 25:15**	1931
their sister **w** was slain on the	**Nu 25:18**	
Now the sons of Israel **w** came out	**Nu 26:4**	
and those **w** were numbered of them	**Nu 26:7**	
w were called by the congregation,	**Nu 26:9**	7148
w contended against Moses and	**Nu 26:9**	834
to those **w** were numbered of them,	**Nu 26:18**	
to those **w** were numbered of them,	**Nu 26:22**	
to those **w** were numbered of them,	**Nu 26:25**	
to those **w** were numbered of them,	**Nu 26:27**	
and those **w** were numbered of them	**Nu 26:34**	
to those **w** were numbered of them,	**Nu 26:37**	
and those **w** were numbered of them	**Nu 26:41**	
to those **w** were numbered of them,	**Nu 26:43**	
to those **w** were numbered of them,	**Nu 26:47**	
and those **w** were numbered of them	**Nu 26:50**	
These are those **w** were numbered of	**Nu 26:51**	
to those **w** were numbered of them.	**Nu 26:54**	
These are those **w** were	**Nu 26:57**	
Levi, **w** was born to Levi in Egypt;	**Nu 26:59**	834
Those **w** were numbered of them	**Nu 26:62**	
These are those **w** were numbered by	**Nu 26:63**	
W numbered the sons of Israel in	**Nu 26:63**	834
of those **w** were numbered by Moses	**Nu 26:64**	
w numbered the sons of Israel in	**Nu 26:64**	834
those **w** gathered themselves together	**Nu 27:3**	
w will go out and come in before	**Nu 27:17**	834
and **w** will lead them out and bring	**Nu 27:17**	834
w shall inquire for him by the	**Nu 27:21**	
w had come from service in the war.	**Nu 31:14**	
woman **w** has known man intimately.	**Nu 31:17**	
w have not known man intimately,	**Nu 31:18**	834
men of war **w** had gone to battle,	**Nu 31:21**	
the warriors **w** went out to battle	**Nu 31:27**	
men of war **w** went out to battle,	**Nu 31:28**	
and give them to the Levites **w**	**Nu 31:30**	
w had not known man intimately,	**Nu 31:35**	834
of those **w** went out to war,	**Nu 31:36**	
from the men **w** had gone to war	**Nu 31:42**	
w kept charge of the tabernacle of	**Nu 31:47**	
Then the officers **w** were over the	**Nu 31:48**	834
of men of war **w** are in our charge,	**Nu 31:49**	834
of the men **w** came up from Egypt,	**Nu 32:11**	
generation of those **w** had done evil	**Nu 32:13**	
everyone **w** is armed for war,	**Nu 32:27**	
everyone **w** is armed for battle,	**Nu 32:29**	
the Amorites **w** were in it.	**Nu 32:39**	834
the king of Arad **w** lived in the	**Nu 33:40**	1931
“These are the names of the men **w**	**Nu 34:17**	834
that the manslayer **w** has killed	**Nu 35:11**	
that anyone **w** kills a person	**Nu 35:15**	
the one **w** struck him shall surely	**Nu 35:21**	
the death of the high priest **w** was	**Nu 35:25**	834
a murderer **w** is guilty of death,	**Nu 35:31**	834
him **w** has fled to his city of refuge,	**Nu 35:32**	
by the blood of him **w** shed it.	**Nu 35:33**	
“Every daughter **w** comes into	**Nu 36:8**	
the Amorites, **w** lived in Heshbon,	**Dt 1:4**	834
w lived in Ashtaroth and Edrei.	**Dt 1:4**	834
or the alien **w** is with him.	**Dt 1:16**	
‘The LORD your God **w** goes before	**Dt 1:30**	
w goes before you on *your* way, to	**Dt 1:33**	
son of Nun, **w** stands before you,	**Dt 1:38**	
w you said would become a prey,	**Dt 1:39**	834
w this day have no knowledge of	**Dt 1:39**	834
“The Amorites **w** lived in that	**Dt 1:44**	
the sons of Esau **w** live in Seir;	**Dt 2:4**	
the sons of Esau, **w** live in Seir,	**Dt 2:8**	
the sons of Esau, **w** live in Seir,	**Dt 2:22**	
w lived in villages as far as	**Dt 2:23**	
the Caphtorim **w** came from Caphtor,	**Dt 2:23**	
everywhere under the heavens, **w**,	**Dt 2:25**	834
just as the sons of Esau **w** live in	**Dt 2:29**	
Moabites **w** live in Ar did for me,	**Dt 2:29**	
the Amorites, **w** lived at Heshbon.’	**Dt 3:2**	834
Amorites **w** were beyond the Jordan,	**Dt 3:8**	834
w can do such works and mighty acts	**Dt 3:24**	834
all the men **w** followed Baal-peor,	**Dt 4:3**	834
“But you **w** held fast to the LORD	**Dt 4:4**	
peoples **w** will hear all these statutes	**Dt 4:6**	834
w unintentionally slew his	**Dt 4:42**	834
the Amorites **w** lived at Heshbon,	**Dt 4:46**	834
w *were* across the Jordan to	**Dt 4:47**	
w brought you out of the land of	**Dt 5:6**	834
generations of those **w** hate Me,	**Dt 5:9**	
to those **w** love Me and keep My	**Dt 5:10**	
w takes His name in vain.	**Dt 5:11**	834
your sojourner **w** stays with you,	**Dt 5:14**	834
‘For **w** is there of all flesh who	**Dt 5:26**	4310
w has heard the voice of the	**Dt 5:26**	834
do not forget the LORD **w** brought	**Dt 6:12**	834
of the peoples **w** surround you,	**Dt 6:14**	834
w are on the face of the earth.	**Dt 7:6**	834
w keeps His covenant and His	**Dt 7:9**	
with those **w** love Him and keep His	**Dt 7:9**	
those **w** hate Him to their faces,	**Dt 7:10**	
not delay with him **w** hates Him,	**Dt 7:10**	
will lay them on all **w** hate you.	**Dt 7:15**	
until those **w** are left and hide	**Dt 7:20**	
your God **w** brought you out from	**Dt 8:14**	
for it is He **w** is giving you power	**Dt 8:18**	
‘**W** can stand before the sons of	**Dt 9:2**	4310
your God **w** is crossing over before	**Dt 9:3**	
God **w** does not show partiality nor	**Dt 10:17**	834
w has done these great and awesome	**Dt 10:21**	834
I *am* not *speaking* with your sons **w**	**Dt 11:2**	834
and **w** have not seen the discipline of	**Dt 11:2**	834
Canaanites **w** live in the Arabah,	**Dt 11:30**	
the Levite **w** is within your gates,	**Dt 12:12**	834
the Levite **w** is within your gates;	**Dt 12:18**	834
God **w** brought you from the land of	**Dt 13:5**	
your friend **w** is as your own soul,	**Dt 13:6**	834
of the peoples **w** are around you,	**Dt 13:7**	834
God **w** brought you out from the land	**Dt 13:10**	
w are on the face of the earth.	**Dt 14:2**	834
it to the alien **w** is in your town,	**Dt 14:21**	834
the Levite **w** is in your town,	**Dt 14:27**	834
and the widow **w** are in your town,	**Dt 14:29**	834
and the Levite **w** is in your town,	**Dt 16:11**	834
and the widow **w** are in your midst,	**Dt 16:11**	834
and the widow **w** are in your towns.	**Dt 16:14**	834
a man or a woman **w** does what is	**Dt 17:2**	834
woman **w** has done this evil deed to	**Dt 17:5**	834
he **w** is to die shall be put to	**Dt 17:6**	
w is *in office* in those days,	**Dt 17:9**	834
“The man **w** acts	**Dt 17:12**	834
by not listening to the priest **w** stands	**Dt 17:12**	
all the nations **w** are around me,’	**Dt 17:14**	834
w is not your countryman.	**Dt 17:15**	834
from those **w** offer a sacrifice,	**Dt 18:3**	
w stand there before the LORD.	**Dt 18:7**	
w makes his son or his daughter pass	**Dt 18:10**	
the fire, one **w** uses divination,	**Dt 18:10**	
one **w** practices witchcraft,	**Dt 18:10**	
or one **w** interprets omens,	**Dt 18:10**	
or one **w** casts a spell, or a	**Dt 18:11**	
or one **w** calls up the dead.	**Dt 18:11**	
listen to those **w** practice	**Dt 18:14**	
‘But the prophet **w** speaks a	**Dt 18:20**	834
w may flee there and live:	**Dt 19:4**	834
“But if there is a man **w** hates	**Dt 19:11**	
then both the men **w** have the	**Dt 19:17**	834
before the priests and the judges **w**	**Dt 19:17**	834
w brought you up from the land of	**Dt 20:1**	834
God is the one **w** goes with you,	**Dt 20:4**	
‘**W** is the man that has built a new	**Dt 20:5**	4310
‘**W** is the man that has planted a	**Dt 20:6**	4310
‘And **w** is the man that is engaged	**Dt 20:7**	4310
‘**W** is the man that is afraid and	**Dt 20:8**	4310
then all the people **w** are found in it	**Dt 20:11**	
it is not known **w** has struck him,	**Dt 21:1**	4310
the unloved, **w** is the firstborn.	**Dt 21:16**	
son **w** will not obey his father or his	**Dt 21:18**	
w is hanged is accursed of God),	**Dt 21:23**	
die, the man **w** lay with the woman,	**Dt 22:22**	
w is a virgin engaged to a man,	**Dt 22:23**	
man finds the girl **w** is engaged,	**Dt 22:25**	
the man **w** lies with her shall die.	**Dt 22:25**	834
a man finds a girl **w** is a virgin,	**Dt 22:28**	
who is a virgin, **w** is not engaged,	**Dt 22:28**	834
then the man **w** lay with her shall	**Dt 22:29**	
“No one **w** is emasculated or has	**Dt 23:1**	
third generation **w** are born to them	**Dt 23:8**	834
“If there is among you any man **w**	**Dt 23:10**	834
not hand over to his master a slave **w**	**Dt 23:15**	834
dies **w** took her to be his wife,	**Dt 24:3**	834
then her former husband **w** sent her	**Dt 24:4**	834
shall not oppress a hired servant **w**	**Dt 24:14**	
w is in your land in your towns.	**Dt 24:14**	834
‘Thus it is done to the man **w** does	**Dt 25:9**	834
hand of the one **w** is striking him,	**Dt 25:11**	
“For everyone **w** does these	**Dt 25:16**	834
everyone **w** acts unjustly is an	**Dt 25:16**	
w is in office at that time and	**Dt 26:3**	834
you and the Levite and the alien **w** is	**Dt 26:11**	834
‘Cursed is the man **w** makes an idol	**Dt 27:15**	834
‘Cursed is he **w** dishonors his	**Dt 27:16**	
‘Cursed is he **w** moves his	**Dt 27:17**	
‘Cursed is he **w** misleads a blind	**Dt 27:18**	
‘Cursed is he **w** distorts the	**Dt 27:19**	
he **w** lies with his father’s wife,	**Dt 27:20**	
is he **w** lies with any animal.’	**Dt 27:21**	
is he **w** lies with his sister,	**Dt 27:22**	
he **w** lies with his mother-in-law.’	**Dt 27:23**	
‘Cursed is he **w** strikes his	**Dt 27:24**	
‘Cursed is he **w** accepts a bribe to	**Dt 27:25**	
‘Cursed is he **w** does not confirm	**Dt 27:26**	834
“The LORD shall cause your enemies **w**	**Dt 28:7**	
“The alien **w** is among you shall	**Dt 28:43**	834
a nation of fierce countenance **w**	**Dt 28:50**	834
w also leaves you no grain,	**Dt 28:51**	834
“The man **w** is refined and very	**Dt 28:54**	
the rest of his children **w** remain,	**Dt 28:54**	834
w would not venture to set the	**Dt 28:56**	834
the alien **w** is within your camps,	**Dt 29:11**	834
from the one **w** chops your wood to	**Dt 29:11**	
to the one **w** draws your water,	**Dt 29:11**	
but both with those **w** stand here	**Dt 29:15**	834
and with those **w** are not with	**Dt 29:15**	834
your sons **w** rise up after you and	**Dt 29:22**	834
w comes from a distant land,	**Dt 29:22**	834
enemies and on those **w** hate you,	**Dt 30:7**	
who hate you, **w** persecuted you.	**Dt 30:7**	834
‘**W** will go up to heaven for us to	**Dt 30:12**	4310
‘**W** will cross the sea for us to	**Dt 30:13**	4310
God **w** will cross ahead of you;	**Dt 31:3**	
the one **w** will cross ahead of you,	**Dt 31:3**	
God is the one **w** goes with you.	**Dt 31:6**	
is the one **w** goes ahead of you;	**Dt 31:8**	
the sons of Levi **w** carried the ark	**Dt 31:9**	
and the alien **w** is in your town,	**Dt 31:12**	834
Their children, **w** have not known,	**Dt 31:13**	834
the Levites **w** carried the ark of the	**Dt 31:25**	
He your Father **w** has bought you?	**Dt 32:6**	
Then he forsook God **w** made him,	**Dt 32:15**	
to demons **w** were not God,	**Dt 32:17**	
not known, New *gods* **w** came lately,	**Dt 32:17**	
neglected the Rock **w** begot you,	**Dt 32:18**	
forgot the God **w** gave you birth.	**Dt 32:18**	
will make them jealous with *those* **w**	**Dt 32:21**	
‘**W** ate the fat of their	**Dt 32:38**	834
is I **w** put to death and give life.	**Dt 32:39**	
have wounded and it is I **w** heal	**Dt 32:39**	
no one **w** can deliver from My hand.	**Dt 32:39**	
And I will repay those **w** hate Me.	**Dt 32:41**	
W said of his father and his	**Dt 33:9**	
of those **w** rise up against him,	**Dt 33:11**	
against him, And those **w** hate him,	**Dt 33:11**	
by Him, **W** shields him all the day,	**Dt 33:12**	
favor of Him **w** dwelt in the bush.	**Dt 33:16**	
“Blessed is the one **w** enlarges Gad;	**Dt 33:20**	
W rides the heavens to your help,	**Dt 33:26**	
W is like you, a people saved by	**Dt 33:29**	4310
W is the shield of your help And	**Dt 33:29**	
“Anyone **w** rebels against your	**Jos 1:18**	834
out the men **w** have come to you,	**Jos 2:3**	
to you, **w** have entered your house,	**Jos 2:3**	834
and as soon as those **w** were	**Jos 2:7**	
Amorites **w** were beyond the Jordan,	**Jos 2:10**	834
with all **w** belong to them,	**Jos 2:13**	834
that anyone **w** goes out of the doors	**Jos 2:19**	834
anyone **w** is with you in the house,	**Jos 2:19**	834
command the priests **w** are carrying	**Jos 3:8**	
w carry the ark of the LORD,	**Jos 3:13**	
and when those **w** carried the ark	**Jos 3:15**	
And the priests **w** carried the ark	**Jos 3:17**	
place where the feet of the priests **w**	**Jos 4:9**	
For the priests **w** carried the ark	**Jos 4:10**	
“Command the priests **w** carry the	**Jos 4:16**	
when the priests **w** carried the ark of	**Jos 4:18**	
when all the kings of the Amorites **w**	**Jos 5:1**	834
the Canaanites **w** *were* by the sea,	**Jos 5:1**	834
all the people **w** came out of Egypt	**Jos 5:4**	
came out of Egypt **w** were males,	**Jos 5:4**	
For all the people **w** came out	**Jos 5:5**	
but all the people **w** were born in	**Jos 5:5**	
men of war **w** came out of Egypt,	**Jos 5:6**	
the priests **w** blew the trumpets,	**Jos 6:9**	
and all **w** are with her in the house	**Jos 6:17**	834
two men **w** had spied out the land,	**Jos 6:22**	
So the young men **w** were spies went	**Jos 6:23**	
Cursed before the LORD is the man **w**	**Jos 6:26**	834
‘It shall be that the one **w** is	**Jos 7:15**	
“Then I and all the people **w** are	**Jos 8:5**	834
Then all the people of war **w** *were*	**Jos 8:11**	834
And all the people **w** were in the	**Jos 8:16**	834
w had not gone out after Israel,	**Jos 8:17**	834
for the people **w** had been fleeing	**Jos 8:20**	
of those **w** survived or escaped.	**Jos 8:22**	8300
All **w** fell that day, both men	**Jos 8:25**	
the Levitical priests **w** carried the ark	**Jos 8:33**	
w were living among them.	**Jos 8:35**	
kings **w** were beyond the Jordan,	**Jos 9:1**	834
“**W** are you and where do you come	**Jos 9:8**	4310
Amorites **w** were beyond the Jordan,	**Jos 9:10**	834
king of Bashan **w** was at Ashtaroth.	**Jos 9:10**	834

there were more **w** died from the	**Jos 10:11**	834
and the survivors **w** remained of	**Jos 10:20**	834
men of war **w** had gone with him,	**Jos 10:24**	
it and every person **w** was in it.	**Jos 10:28**	834
he struck it and every person **w** *was*	**Jos 10:30**	834
and struck it and every person **w**	**Jos 10:32**	834
that day every person **w** *was* in it,	**Jos 10:35**	834
and all the persons **w** *were* in it with	**Jos 10:37**	834
it and every person **w** *was* in it.	**Jos 10:37**	834
utterly destroyed every person **w**	**Jos 10:39**	
utterly destroyed all **w** breathed,	**Jos 10:40**	5397
and to the kings **w** were of the	**Jos 11:2**	834
They struck every person **w** was	**Jos 11:11**	834
there was no one left **w** breathed.	**Jos 11:11**	5397
They left no one **w** breathed.	**Jos 11:14**	5397
the Amorites, **w** lived in Heshbon,	**Jos 12:2**	
w lived at Ashtaroth and at Edrei,	**Jos 12:4**	
Amorites, **w** reigned in Heshbon,	**Jos 13:10**	834
w reigned in Ashtaroth and in	**Jos 13:12**	834
the Amorites **w** reigned in Heshbon,	**Jos 13:21**	834
of Sihon, **w** lived in the land.	**Jos 13:21**	
"Nevertheless my brethren **w** went	**Jos 14:8**	834
"The one **w** attacks Kiriath-sepher	**Jos 15:16**	834
the Canaanites **w** lived in Gezer,	**Jos 16:10**	
and all the Canaanites **w** live in	**Jos 17:16**	
both those **w** are in Beth-shean and	**Jos 17:16**	834
and those **w** are in the valley of	**Jos 17:16**	834
seven tribes **w** had not divided their	**Jos 18:2**	834
those **w** went to describe the land,	**Jos 18:8**	
that the manslayer **w** kills any	**Jos 20:3**	
w is high priest in those days.	**Jos 20:6**	834
stranger **w** sojourns among them,	**Jos 20:9**	
the priest, **w** were of the Levites,	**Jos 21:4**	
of Israel **w** *were* with him,	**Jos 22:30**	834
is He **w** has been fighting for you.	**Jos 23:3**	
your God is He **w** fights for you,	**Jos 23:10**	
w lived beyond the Jordan,	**Jos 24:8**	
for the LORD our God is He **w**	**Jos 24:17**	
and **w** did these great signs in our	**Jos 24:17**	834
the Amorites **w** lived in the land.	**Jos 24:18**	
of the elders **w** survived Joshua,	**Jos 24:31**	834
"**W** shall go up first for us	**Jg 1:1**	4310
the Canaanites **w** lived in Hebron	**Jg 1:10**	
"The one **w** attacks Kiriath-sepher	**Jg 1:12**	834
Jebusites **w** lived in Jerusalem;	**Jg 1:21**	
Canaanites **w** were living in Gezer;	**Jg 1:29**	
of the elders **w** survived Joshua,	**Jg 2:7**	834
w had seen all the great work of	**Jg 2:7**	834
them **w** did not know the LORD,	**Jg 2:10**	834
w had brought them out of the land	**Jg 2:12**	
of the peoples **w** were around them,	**Jg 2:12**	834
of plunderers **w** plundered them;	**Jg 2:14**	
Then the LORD raised up judges **w**	**Jg 2:16**	
hands of those **w** plundered them.	**Jg 2:16**	
w oppressed and afflicted them.	**Jg 2:18**	
all **w** had not experienced any of	**Jg 3:1**	834
those **w** had not experienced it	**Jg 3:2**	834
Hivites **w** lived in Mount Lebanon,	**Jg 3:3**	
people **w** had carried the tribute.	**Jg 3:18**	
And all **w** attended him left him.	**Jg 3:19**	
w struck down six hundred	**Jg 3:31**	
of Canaan, **w** reigned in Hazor;	**Jg 4:2**	834
Sisera, **w** lived in Harosheth-hagoyim.	**Jg 4:2**	834
all the people **w** *were* with him,	**Jg 4:13**	834
"You **w** ride on white donkeys, You	**Jg 5:10**	
You **w** sit on *rich* carpets,	**Jg 5:10**	
And you **w** travel on the road—sing!	**Jg 5:10**	
"At the sound of those **w** divide	**Jg 5:11**	
those **w** wield the staff of office.	**Jg 5:14**	
"Zebulun *was* a people **w** despised	**Jg 5:18**	
But let those **w** love Him be like	**Jg 5:31**	
was I **w** brought you up from Egypt	**Jg 6:8**	
it is You **w** speak with me.	**Jg 6:17**	
"**W** did this thing?"	**Jg 6:29**	4310
said to all **w** stood against him,	**Jg 6:31**	834
all the people **w** were with him,	**Jg 7:1**	834
"The people **w** are with you are	**Jg 7:2**	834
"You shall separate everyone **w**	**Jg 7:5**	834
as everyone **w** kneels to drink."	**Jg 7:5**	834
Now the number of those **w** lapped,	**Jg 7:6**	
I will deliver you with the 300 men **w**	**Jg 7:7**	
w are with me blow the trumpet,	**Jg 7:18**	834
So Gideon and the hundred men **w**	**Jg 7:19**	834
Then Gideon and the 300 men **w** were	**Jg 8:4**	834
to the people **w** are following me,	**Jg 8:5**	834
all **w** were left of the entire army	**Jg 8:10**	
by the way of those **w** lived in tents	**Jg 8:11**	
bread to your men **w** are weary?' "	**Jg 8:15**	
w were his direct descendants,	**Jg 8:30**	
His concubine **w** was in Shechem	**Jg 8:31**	834
w had delivered them from the	**Jg 8:34**	
their brother, **w** killed them,	**Jg 9:24**	834
w strengthened his hands to kill	**Jg 9:24**	834
and they robbed all **w** might pass	**Jg 9:25**	834
"**W** is Abimelech, and who is	**Jg 9:28**	4310
is Abimelech, and **w** is Shechem,	**Jg 9:28**	4310
you and the people **w** are with you,	**Jg 9:32**	834
when he and the people **w** are with	**Jg 9:33**	834
So Abimelech and all the people **w**	**Jg 9:34**	834
and Abimelech and the people **w**	**Jg 9:35**	834
'**W** is Abimelech that we should	**Jg 9:38**	4310
Then Abimelech and the company **w**	**Jg 9:44**	834
dashed against all **w** *were* in the field	**Jg 9:44**	834
killed the people **w** *were* in it;	**Jg 9:45**	834
all the people **w** *were* with him;	**Jg 9:48**	834
to the people **w** *were* with him,	**Jg 9:48**	834
sons **w** rode on thirty donkeys,	**Jg 10:4**	
they *afflicted* all the sons of Israel **w**	**Jg 10:8**	834
"**W** is the man who will begin to	**Jg 10:18**	4310
"Who is the man **w** will begin to	**Jg 10:18**	834
you are among those **w** trouble me;	**Jg 11:35**	
w did to her according to the vow	**Jg 11:39**	
w rode on seventy donkeys;	**Jg 12:14**	
do for the boy **w** is to be born."	**Jg 13:8**	
the man **w** came the *other* day has	**Jg 13:10**	834
the man **w** spoke to the woman?"	**Jg 13:11**	834
to those **w** told the riddle.	**Jg 14:19**	
companion **w** had been his friend.	**Jg 14:20**	834
the Philistines said, "**W** did this?"	**Jg 15:6**	4310
country, **W** has slain many of us."	**Jg 16:24**	834
to the boy **w** was holding his hand,	**Jg 16:26**	
and all the people **w** were in it.	**Jg 16:30**	834
gave them to the silversmith **w** made	**Jg 17:4**	
family of Judah, **w** was a Levite;	**Jg 17:7**	1931
"**W** brought you here?	**Jg 18:3**	4310
w were in it living in security,	**Jg 18:7**	834
Then the five men **w** went to spy	**Jg 18:14**	
of war, **w** were of the sons of Dan,	**Jg 18:16**	834
Now the five men **w** went to spy out	**Jg 18:17**	
the men **w** *were* in the houses near	**Jg 18:22**	834
w turned around and said to Micah,	**Jg 18:23**	
the priest **w** had belonged to him,	**Jg 18:27**	834
their father **w** was born in Israel;	**Jg 18:29**	834
w took a concubine for himself	**Jg 19:1**	
w are not of the sons of Israel;	**Jg 19:12**	834
young man **w** is with your servants;	**Jg 19:19**	
"Bring out the man **w** came into	**Jg 19:22**	834
All **w** saw it said,	**Jg 19:30**	
foot soldiers **w** drew the sword.	**Jg 20:2**	
of the woman **w** was murdered,	**Jg 20:4**	
26,000 men **w** draw the sword,	**Jg 20:15**	
of Gibeah **w** were numbered,	**Jg 20:15**	
400,000 men **w** draw the sword;	**Jg 20:17**	
"**W** shall go up first for us to	**Jg 20:18**	4310
that day, all **w** drew the sword.	**Jg 20:35**	428
while those **w** came out of the cities	**Jg 20:42**	834
So all of Benjamin **w** fell that day	**Jg 20:46**	
were 25,000 men **w** draw the sword;	**Jg 20:46**	
"**W** is there among all the tribes	**Jg 21:5**	4310
w did not come up in the assembly	**Jg 21:5**	834
taken a great oath concerning him **w**	**Jg 21:5**	834
do for wives for those **w** are left,	**Jg 21:7**	
w did not come up to the LORD at	**Jg 21:8**	834
woman **w** has lain with a man."	**Jg 21:11**	
of Jabesh-gilead 400 young virgins **w**	**Jg 21:12**	834
w were at the rock of Rimmon,	**Jg 21:13**	834
do for wives for those **w** are left,	**Jg 21:16**	
he **w** gives a wife to Benjamin."	**Jg 21:18**	
their number from those **w** danced,	**Jg 21:23**	
w returned from the land of Moab.	**Ru 1:22**	
w was of the family of Elimelech.	**Ru 2:3**	834
w was in charge of the reapers,	**Ru 2:5**	
"She is the young Moabite woman **w**	**Ru 2:6**	
w took notice of you be blessed."	**Ru 2:19**	
"May he be blessed of the LORD **w**	**Ru 2:20**	834
He said, "**W** are you?"	**Ru 3:9**	4310
w has come back from the land of	**Ru 4:3**	
before those **w** are sitting *here*,	**Ru 4:4**	
the people **w** were in the court,	**Ru 4:11**	834
May the LORD make the woman **w** is	**Ru 4:11**	
"Blessed is the LORD **w** has not	**Ru 4:14**	834
w loves you and is better to you	**Ru 4:15**	834
the woman **w** stood here beside you,	**1Sa 1:26**	
"Those **w** were full hire	**1Sa 2:5**	
those **w** were hungry cease *to hunger*.	**1Sa 2:5**	
she **w** has many children languishes.	**1Sa 2:5**	
"Those **w** contend with the LORD	**1Sa 2:10**	
all the Israelites **w** came there.	**1Sa 2:14**	
say to the man **w** was sacrificing,	**1Sa 2:15**	
and how they lay with the women **w**	**1Sa 2:22**	
LORD, **w** can intercede for him?"	**1Sa 2:25**	4310
those **w** honor Me I will honor,	**1Sa 2:30**	
and those **w** despise Me will be	**1Sa 2:30**	
faithful priest **w** will do according to	**1Sa 2:35**	
'Everyone **w** is left in your house will	**1Sa 2:36**	
everyone **w** hears it will tingle.	**1Sa 3:11**	
was defeated before the Philistines **w**	**1Sa 4:2**	
hosts **w** sits *above* the cherubim;	**1Sa 4:4**	
W shall deliver us from the hand	**1Sa 4:8**	4310
These are the gods **w** smote the	**1Sa 4:8**	
one **w** came from the battle line.	**1Sa 4:16**	
Then the one **w** brought the news	**1Sa 4:17**	
women **w** stood by her said to her,	**1Sa 4:20**	
nor all **w** enter Dagon's house tread	**1Sa 5:5**	
And the men **w** did not die were	**1Sa 5:12**	834
"**W** is able to stand before the	**1Sa 6:20**	4310
the king **w** will reign over them."	**1Sa 8:9**	834
people **w** had asked of him a king.	**1Sa 8:10**	
of the king **w** will reign over you:	**1Sa 8:11**	834
to his servant **w** was with him,	**1Sa 9:5**	834
for *he* **w** *is called* a prophet now	**1Sa 9:9**	
those **w** are invited will eat.	**1Sa 9:13**	
the head of those **w** were invited,	**1Sa 9:22**	
invited, **w** were about thirty men.	**1Sa 9:22**	1992a
when all **w** knew him previously saw	**1Sa 10:11**	
"Now, **w** is their father?"	**1Sa 10:12**	4310
w delivers you from all your	**1Sa 10:19**	834
said to the messengers **w** had come,	**1Sa 11:9**	
Those **w** survived were scattered,	**1Sa 11:11**	
"**W** is he that said,	**1Sa 11:12**	4310
"It is the LORD **w** appointed Moses	**1Sa 12:6**	834
and **w** brought your fathers up from	**1Sa 12:6**	834
w brought your fathers out of Egypt	**1Sa 12:8**	
and also the king **w** reigns over you	**1Sa 12:14**	834
people **w** were present with him,	**1Sa 13:15**	
Jonathan and the people **w** were	**1Sa 13:16**	
w *were* with Saul and Jonathan,	**1Sa 13:22**	834
man **w** was carrying his armor,	**1Sa 14:1**	
And the people **w** *were* with him	**1Sa 14:2**	834
man **w** was carrying his armor,	**1Sa 14:6**	
to the people **w** *were* with him,	**1Sa 14:17**	834
now and see **w** has gone from us."	**1Sa 14:17**	4310
Then Saul and all the people **w**	**1Sa 14:20**	834
Now the Hebrews **w** were with	**1Sa 14:21**	
w went up with them all around in	**1Sa 14:21**	834
w *were* with Saul and Jonathan.	**1Sa 14:21**	834
When all the men of Israel **w** had	**1Sa 14:22**	
man **w** eats food before evening,	**1Sa 14:24**	834
be the man **w** eats food today.' "	**1Sa 14:28**	834
the LORD lives, **w** delivers Israel,	**1Sa 14:39**	
w has brought about this great	**1Sa 14:45**	834
hands of those **w** plundered them.	**1Sa 14:48**	
neighbor, **w** is better than you.	**1Sa 15:28**	
your servants **w** are before you.	**1Sa 16:16**	
Let them seek a man **w** is a	**1Sa 16:16**	
for me now a man **w** can play well and	**1Sa 16:17**	
w is a skillful musician,	**1Sa 16:18**	
son David **w** is with the flock."	**1Sa 16:19**	834
the names of his three sons **w** went to	**1Sa 17:13**	834
you seen this man **w** is coming up?	**1Sa 17:25**	
king will enrich the man **w** kills him	**1Sa 17:25**	834
to the men **w** were standing by him,	**1Sa 17:26**	
the man **w** kills this Philistine and	**1Sa 17:26**	834
For **w** is this uncircumcised	**1Sa 17:26**	4310
be done for the man **w** kills him."	**1Sa 17:27**	834
"The LORD **w** delivered me from the	**1Sa 17:37**	834
"**W** am I, and what is my life *or*	**1Sa 18:18**	4310
"**W** will tell me if your father	**1Sa 20:10**	4310
Everyone **w** was in distress,	**1Sa 22:2**	
and everyone **w** was in debt,	**1Sa 22:2**	834
everyone **w** was discontented gathered	**1Sa 22:2**	
David and the men **w** were with him	**1Sa 22:6**	834
his servants **w** stood around him,	**1Sa 22:7**	
that there is no one **w** discloses to me	**1Sa 22:8**	
and there is none of you **w** is	**1Sa 22:8**	
w was standing by the servants of	**1Sa 22:9**	1931
the priests **w** were in Nob;	**1Sa 22:11**	834
"And **w** among all your servants is	**1Sa 22:14**	4310
w is captain over your guard,	**1Sa 22:14**	
the guards **w** were attending him,	**1Sa 22:17**	
men **w** wore the linen ephod.	**1Sa 22:18**	
w seeks my life seeks your life,	**1Sa 22:23**	834
is, *and* **w** has seen him there;	**1Sa 23:22**	4310
"**W** is David? And who is the son of	**1Sa 25:10**	4310
And **w** is the son of Jesse?	**1Sa 25:10**	4310
There are many servants today **w**	**1Sa 25:10**	
one male of any **w** belong to him."	**1Sa 25:22**	834
those **w** seek evil against my lord,	**1Sa 25:26**	
the young men **w** accompany my lord.	**1Sa 25:27**	
w sent you this day to meet me,	**1Sa 25:32**	834
w have kept me this day from	**1Sa 25:33**	834
w has restrained me from harming	**1Sa 25:34**	834
w has pleaded the cause of my	**1Sa 25:39**	834
her five maidens **w** attended her;	**1Sa 25:42**	
son of Laish, **w** was from Gallim.	**1Sa 25:44**	834
"**W** will go down with me to Saul	**1Sa 26:6**	4310
for **w** can stretch out his hand	**1Sa 26:9**	4310
"**W** are you who calls to the king?"	**1Sa 26:14**	4310
"Who are you **w** calls to the king?"	**1Sa 26:14**	
And **w** is like you in Israel?	**1Sa 26:15**	4310
six hundred men **w** were with him,	**1Sa 27:2**	834
w were mediums and spiritists.	**1Sa 28:3**	
"Seek for me a woman **w** is a medium,	**1Sa 28:7**	
a woman **w** is a medium at En-dor."	**1Sa 28:7**	
how he has cut off those **w** are	**1Sa 28:9**	
w has been with me these days,	**1Sa 29:3**	834
servants of your lord **w** have come	**1Sa 29:10**	834
the women *and all* **w** were in it,	**1Sa 30:2**	834
Then David and the people **w** were	**1Sa 30:4**	834
six hundred men **w** were with him,	**1Sa 30:9**	834
for two hundred **w** were too	**1Sa 30:10**	834
men **w** rode on camels and fled.	**1Sa 30:17**	834
men **w** were too exhausted to follow	**1Sa 30:21**	834
w had also been left at the brook	**1Sa 30:21**	
meet the people **w** were with him,	**1Sa 30:21**	834
men among those **w** went with David	**1Sa 30:22**	834
w has kept us and delivered into	**1Sa 30:23**	
"And **w** will listen to you in this	**1Sa 30:24**	4310
is **w** goes down to the battle,	**1Sa 30:24**	
share be **w** stays by the baggage;	**1Sa 30:24**	
to those **w** were in Bethel, and to	**1Sa 30:27**	834
w were in Ramoth of the Negev,	**1Sa 30:27**	834
and to those **w** were in Jattir,	**1Sa 30:27**	834
and to those **w** were in Aroer, and	**1Sa 30:28**	834
and to those **w** were in Siphmoth,	**1Sa 30:28**	834
and to those **w** were in Eshtemoa,	**1Sa 30:28**	834
and to those **w** were in Racal, and	**1Sa 30:29**	834
and to those **w** were in the cities	**1Sa 30:29**	834
and to those **w** were in the cities	**1Sa 30:29**	834
and to those **w** were in Hormah, and	**1Sa 30:30**	834
and to those **w** were in Bor-ashan,	**1Sa 30:30**	834
and to those **w** were in Athach,	**1Sa 30:30**	834
and to those **w** were in Hebron, and	**1Sa 30:31**	834
When the men of Israel **w** were	**1Sa 31:7**	834
those **w** were beyond the Jordan,	**1Sa 31:7**	834
said to the young man **w** told him,	**2Sa 1:5**	
The young man **w** told him said,	**2Sa 1:6**	
"He said to me, '**W** are you?'	**2Sa 1:8**	4310
did all the men **w** *were* with him.	**2Sa 1:11**	834
said to the young man **w** told him,	**2Sa 1:13**	
W clothed you luxuriously in	**2Sa 1:24**	
w put ornaments of gold on your	**2Sa 1:24**	
up his men **w** *were* with him,	**2Sa 2:3**	834
men of Jabesh-gilead **w** buried Saul.	**2Sa 2:4**	834
And it came about that all **w** came	**2Sa 2:23**	
Abner and the men **w** were with him.	**2Sa 3:20**	834
of Joab one **w** has a discharge,	**2Sa 3:29**	

has a discharge, or **w** is a leper, 2Sa 3:29
or **w** takes hold of a distaff, 2Sa 3:29
distaff, or **w** falls by the sword, 2Sa 3:29
by the sword, or **w** lacks bread." 2Sa 3:29
to all the people **w** were with him, 2Sa 3:31 834
men **w** were commanders of bands; 2Sa 4:2
your enemy, **w** sought your life; 2Sa 4:8 834
w has redeemed my life from all 2Sa 4:9 834
the one **w** led Israel out and in. 2Sa 5:2
blind, **w** are hated by David's soul, 2Sa 5:8
w were born to him in Jerusalem: 2Sa 5:14 3209
w were with him to Baale-judah, 2Sa 6:2 834
w is enthroned *above* the cherubim. 2Sa 6:2
w chose me above your father and 2Sa 6:21 834
"Are you the one **w** should build 2Sa 7:5
the great men **w** are on the earth. 2Sa 7:9 834
you, **w** will come forth from you, 2Sa 7:12 834
"**W** am I, O Lord GOD, and what is 2Sa 7:18 4310
w is crippled in both feet." 2Sa 9:3
And all **w** lived in the house of 2Sa 9:12
So Joab and the people **w** were with 2Sa 10:13 834
Arameans **w** were beyond the River, 2Sa 10:16 834
'**W** struck down Abimelech the son 2Sa 11:21 4310
the wayfarer **w** had come to him; 2Sa 12:4
for the man **w** had come to him." 2Sa 12:4
w has done this deserves to die. 2Sa 12:5
'It is I **w** anointed you king over 2Sa 12:7
and it is I **w** delivered you from the 2Sa 12:7
'**W** knows, the LORD may be gracious 2Sa 12:22 4310
out the people **w** were in it, 2Sa 12:31 834
young man **w** attended him and said, 2Sa 13:17
And the young man **w** was the 2Sa 13:34
but be like a woman **w** has been 2Sa 14:2
over the one **w** struck his brother, 2Sa 14:7
the king is as one **w** is guilty, 2Sa 14:13 818
w would destroy both me and my son 2Sa 14:16
your servant Joab **w** commanded me, 2Sa 14:19 1931
and it was he **w** put all these 2Sa 14:19
then every man **w** has any suit or 2Sa 15:4 834
w came to the king for judgment; 2Sa 15:6 834
w were invited and went 2Sa 15:11 834
w were with him at Jerusalem, 2Sa 15:14 834
men **w** had come with him from Gath, 2Sa 15:18 834
the little ones **w** *were* with him. 2Sa 15:22 834
Then all the people **w** were with 2Sa 15:30 834
'Curse David,' then **w** shall say, 2Sa 16:10 4310
my son **w** came out from me seeks my 2Sa 16:11 834
The king and all the people **w** 2Sa 16:14 834
The hands of all **w** are with you 2Sa 16:21 834
people **w** are with him will flee. 2Sa 17:2 834
the people **w** follow Absalom.' 2Sa 17:9 834
"And even the one **w** is valiant, 2Sa 17:10
w are with him are valiant men. 2Sa 17:10 834
and of all the men **w** are with him, 2Sa 17:12 834
w are with him will be destroyed.'" 2Sa 17:16 834
w had a well in his courtyard, 2Sa 17:18
Then David and all the people **w** 2Sa 17:22 834
w had not crossed the Jordan. 2Sa 17:22 834
w went in to Abigail the daughter 2Sa 17:25 834
for the people **w** *were* with him, 2Sa 17:29 834
Then David numbered the people **w** 2Sa 18:1 834
said to the man **w** had told him, 2Sa 18:11
And ten young men **w** carried Joab's 2Sa 18:15
w has delivered up the men who 2Sa 18:28 834
who has delivered up the men **w** 2Sa 18:28 834
all those **w** rose up against you." 2Sa 18:31
w rise up against you for evil, 2Sa 18:32 834
as people **w** are humiliated steal 2Sa 19:3
w today have saved your life and 2Sa 19:5
by loving those **w** hate you, and by 2Sa 19:6
and by hating those **w** love you. 2Sa 19:6
the Benjamite **w** was from Bahurim, 2Sa 19:16 834
those **w** ate at your own table. 2Sa 19:28
w came by him stood still. 2Sa 20:12
and all the people **w** were with 2Sa 20:15 834
"I am of those **w** are peaceable 2Sa 20:19
"The man **w** consumed us and who 2Sa 21:5 834
and **w** planned to exterminate us 2Sa 21:5 834
w had stolen them from the open 2Sa 21:12 834
bones of those **w** had been hanged. 2Sa 21:13
w was among the descendants of the 2Sa 21:16 834
w was among the descendants of the 2Sa 21:18 834
man of *great* stature **w** had six fingers 2Sa 21:20
LORD, **w** is worthy to be praised, 2Sa 22:4
enemy, From those **w** hated me, 2Sa 22:18
to all **w** take refuge in Him. 2Sa 22:31
"For **w** is God, besides the LORD? 2Sa 22:32 4310
And **w** is a rock, besides our God? 2Sa 22:32 4310
me those **w** rose up against me. 2Sa 22:40
And I destroyed those **w** hated me. 2Sa 22:41
God **w** executes vengeance for me, 2Sa 22:48
W also brings me out from my 2Sa 22:49
above those **w** rise up against me; 2Sa 22:49
man **w** was raised on high declares, 2Sa 23:1
'He **w** rules over men righteously, 2Sa 23:3
W rules in the fear of God, 2Sa 23:3
But the man **w** touches them Must be 2Sa 23:7
defied the Philistines **w** were gathered 2Sa 23:9
Shall I drink the blood of the men **w** 2Sa 23:17
Kabzeel, **w** had done mighty deeds, 2Sa 23:20
of the army **w** was with him, 2Sa 24:2 834
valiant men **w** drew the sword, 2Sa 24:9
I shall return to Him **w** sent me." 2Sa 24:13
the angel **w** destroyed the people, 2Sa 24:16
w was striking down the people, 2Sa 24:17
"Behold, it is I **w** have sinned, 2Sa 24:17
and it is I **w** have done wrong; 2Sa 24:17
mighty men **w** belonged to David, 1Ki 1:8 834
to tell them **w** shall sit on the 1Ki 1:20 4310
w should sit on the throne of my lord 1Ki 1:27 4310
w has redeemed my life from all 1Ki 1:29 834
guests **w** *were* with him heard *it* 1Ki 1:41 834
w has granted one to sit on my 1Ki 1:48 834
among those **w** eat at your table; 1Ki 2:7 834
now it was he **w** cursed me with a 1Ki 2:8
w has established me and set me on 1Ki 2:24 834
and **w** has made me a house as He 1Ki 2:24 834
a great people **w** are too many to be 1Ki 3:8 834
For **w** is able to judge this great 1Ki 3:9 4310
Then two women **w** were harlots came 1Ki 3:16
'This is my son **w** is living, and 1Ki 3:23
w provided for the king and his 1Ki 4:7
the only deputy **w** *was* in the land. 1Ki 4:19 834
all **w** came to King Solomon's table, 1Ki 4:27
earth **w** had heard of his wisdom. 1Ki 4:34 834
w knows how to cut timber like the 1Ki 5:6
w has given to David a wise son 1Ki 5:7 834
chief deputies **w** *were* over the project 1Ki 5:16 834
who *were* over the project *and* **w** ruled 1Ki 5:16
the people **w** were doing the work. 1Ki 5:16
Israel, **w** were assembled to him, 1Ki 8:5
w spoke with His mouth to my 1Ki 8:15 834
your son **w** will be born to you, 1Ki 8:19
to Your servants **w** walk before You 1Ki 8:23
w have kept with Your servant, my 1Ki 8:24 834
w is not of Your people Israel, 1Ki 8:41 834
there is no man **w** does not sin) 1Ki 8:46 834
those **w** have taken them captive, 1Ki 8:47
enemies **w** have taken them captive, 1Ki 8:48 834
and forgive Your people **w** have 1Ki 8:50
those **w** have taken them captive, 1Ki 8:50
w has given rest to His people 1Ki 8:56 834
everyone **w** passes by will be 1Ki 9:8
w brought their fathers out of the 1Ki 9:9 834
Canaanites **w** lived in the city, 1Ki 9:16
w were left of the Amorites, 1Ki 9:20
w were not of the sons of Israel, 1Ki 9:20 834
their descendants **w** were left 1Ki 9:21 834
w *were* over Solomon's work, 1Ki 9:23 834
w ruled over the people doing the 1Ki 9:23
the fleet, sailors **w** knew the sea, 1Ki 9:27
how blessed are these your servants **w** 1Ki 10:8
"Blessed be the LORD your God **w** 1Ki 10:9 834
w burned incense and sacrificed to 1Ki 11:8
w had appeared to him twice, 1Ki 11:9
w gave him a house and assigned 1Ki 11:18
w had fled from his lord Hadadezer 1Ki 11:23 834
w observed My commandments and 1Ki 11:34 834
consulted with the elders **w** had served 1Ki 12:6 834
the young men **w** grew up with him 1Ki 12:8 834
this people **w** have spoken to me, 1Ki 12:9 834
w grew up with him spoke to him, 1Ki 12:10 834
say to this people **w** spoke to you, 1Ki 12:10 834
w lived in the cities of Judah, 1Ki 12:17
w was over the forced labor, 1Ki 12:18 834
chosen men **w** were warriors, 1Ki 12:21
w were not of the sons of Levi. 1Ki 12:31 834
high places **w** burn incense on you, 1Ki 13:2
of God **w** came from Judah had gone. 1Ki 13:12 834
man of God **w** came from Judah?" 1Ki 13:14 834
prophet **w** had brought him back; 1Ki 13:20 834
the man of God **w** came from Judah, 1Ki 13:21 834
Now when the prophet **w** brought him 1Ki 13:26 834
w disobeyed the command of the 1Ki 13:26 834
any **w** would, he ordained, to be 1Ki 13:33
w spoke concerning me *that I would* 1Ki 14:2 1931
w kept My commandments and who 1Ki 14:8 834
who kept My commandments and **w** 1Ki 14:8 834
evil than all **w** were before you, 1Ki 14:9 834
"Anyone belonging to Jeroboam **w** 1Ki 14:11
And he **w** dies in the field the 1Ki 14:11
a king over Israel **w** will cut off the 1Ki 14:14 834
the guard **w** guarded the doorway of 1Ki 14:27
king of Aram, **w** lived in Damascus, 1Ki 15:18
"Anyone of Baasha **w** dies in the 1Ki 16:4
and anyone of his **w** dies in the 1Ki 16:4
w *was* over the household at Tirzah. 1Ki 16:9 834
w were camped heard it said, 1Ki 16:16
But the people **w** followed Omri 1Ki 16:22 834
over the people **w** followed Tibni the 1Ki 16:22 834
than all **w** *were* before him. 1Ki 16:25 834
more than all **w** were before him. 1Ki 16:30 834
kings of Israel **w** were before him. 1Ki 16:33 834
w was of the settlers of Gilead, 1Ki 17:1
Obadiah **w** *was* over the household. 1Ki 18:3 834
w eat at Jezebel's table." 1Ki 18:19
and the God **w** answers by fire, 1Ki 18:24 834
the one **w** escapes from the sword 1Ki 19:17
and the one **w** escapes from the 1Ki 19:17
for all the people **w** follow me." 1Ki 20:10 834
'Let not him **w** girds on *his armor* 1Ki 20:11
boast like him **w** takes *it* off.'" 1Ki 20:11
"**W** shall begin the battle?" 1Ki 20:14 4310
the thirty-two kings **w** helped him. 1Ki 20:16
fell on 27,000 men **w** were left. 1Ki 20:30
w were living with Naboth in his city. 1Ki 21:8 834
the nobles **w** lived in his city, 1Ki 21:11 834
king of Israel, **w** is in Samaria; 1Ki 21:18 834
to Ahab, **w** dies in the city, 1Ki 21:24
and the one **w** dies in the field 1Ki 21:24
Ahab **w** sold himself to do evil in the 1Ki 21:25 834
Then the messenger **w** went to 1Ki 22:13 834
'**W** will entice Ahab to go up and 1Ki 22:20 4310
remnant of the sodomites **w** remained 1Ki 22:46 834
of Nebat, **w** caused Israel to sin. 1Ki 22:52 834
king **w** sent you and say to him, 2Ki 1:6 834
"What kind of man was he **w** came 2Ki 1:7 834
Then the sons of the prophets **w** 2Ki 2:3 834
The sons of the prophets **w** 2Ki 2:5 834
sons of the prophets **w** *were* at Jericho 2Ki 2:15 834
w used to pour water on the hands 2Ki 3:11 834
And all **w** were able to put on 2Ki 3:21
with him 700 men **w** drew swords, 2Ki 3:26
son **w** was to reign in his place, 2Ki 3:27 834
with the prophet **w** is in Samaria! 2Ki 5:3 834
w is from the land of Israel." 2Ki 5:4 834
the prophet **w** is in Israel, 2Ki 6:12 834
for those **w** are with us are more 2Ki 6:16 834
more than those **w** are with them." 2Ki 6:16 834
of Israel **w** are left in it; 2Ki 7:13 834
of Israel **w** have already perished, 2Ki 7:13 834
w spoke when the king came down to 2Ki 7:17 834
to life the one **w** was dead, 2Ki 8:5
w *is but* a dog, that he should 2Ki 8:13
to his master, **w** said to him, 2Ki 8:14
the Edomites **w** had surrounded him 2Ki 8:21
horseman, **w** came to them and said, 2Ki 9:19
and said, "**W** is on my side? 2Ki 9:32 4310
"Who is on my side? **W**?" 2Ki 9:32 4310
the one **w** *was* over the household, 2Ki 10:5 834
and he **w** *was* over the city, 2Ki 10:5 834
of the city, **w** were rearing them. 2Ki 10:6
him, but **w** killed all these? 2Ki 10:9 4310
So Jehu killed all **w** remained of 2Ki 10:11
"**W** are you?" And they answered, 2Ki 10:13 4310
all **w** remained to Ahab in Samaria, 2Ki 10:17
was not a man left **w** did not come. 2Ki 10:21 834
w *was* in charge of the wardrobe, 2Ki 10:22 834
"The one **w** permits any of the men 2Ki 10:24 834
sons **w** were being put to death, 2Ki 11:2
w come in on the sabbath and keep 2Ki 11:5
even all **w** go out on the sabbath, 2Ki 11:7
each one of them took his men **w** 2Ki 11:9
w were to go out on the sabbath, 2Ki 11:9
w were appointed over the army and 2Ki 11:15
and the priests **w** guarded the 2Ki 12:9
the hands of those **w** did the work, 2Ki 12:11
w had the oversight of the house 2Ki 12:11
w worked on the house of the LORD; 2Ki 12:11
gave that to those **w** did the work, 2Ki 12:14
to pay to those **w** did the work, 2Ki 12:15
w had slain the king his father. 2Ki 14:5
Azariah, **w** *was* sixteen years old, 2Ki 14:21 1931
the prophet, **w** was of Gath-hepher. 2Ki 14:25 834
struck Tiphsah and all **w** were in it 2Ki 15:16 834
all its women **w** were with child. 2Ki 15:16
w are rising up against me." 2Ki 16:7
kings of Israel **w** were before him. 2Ki 17:2 834
w had sent messengers to So king 2Ki 17:4 834
w had brought them up from the 2Ki 17:7
w did not believe in the LORD 2Ki 17:14 834
w acted for them in the houses of 2Ki 17:32
w brought you up from the land of 2Ki 17:36 834
nor *among those* **w** were before him. 2Ki 18:5 834
Hilkiah, **w** was over the household, 2Ki 18:18 834
of Egypt to all **w** rely on him. 2Ki 18:21
of the people **w** are on the wall." 2Ki 18:26 834
not to the men **w** sit on the wall, 2Ki 18:27
'**W** among all the gods of the lands 2Ki 18:35 4310
Hilkiah, **w** was over the household, 2Ki 18:37 834
Then he sent Eliakim **w** was over 2Ki 19:2 834
sons of Eden **w** *were* in Telassar? 2Ki 19:12 834
w are enthroned *above* the 2Ki 19:15
your sons **w** shall issue from you, 2Ki 20:18 834
Amorites did **w** *were* before him, 2Ki 21:11 834
people of the land killed all those **w** 2Ki 21:24
workmen **w** have the oversight of the 2Ki 22:5
let them give it to the workmen **w** are 2Ki 22:5 834
the book to Shaphan **w** read it. 2Ki 22:8
workmen **w** have the oversight of the 2Ki 22:9
'Tell the man **w** sent you to me, 2Ki 22:15 834
"But to the king of Judah **w** sent 2Ki 22:18
those **w** burned incense to Baal, 2Ki 23:5
son of Nebat, **w** made Israel sin, 2Ki 23:15 834
w proclaimed these things. 2Ki 23:16 834
the grave of the man of God **w** came 2Ki 23:17 834
the prophet **w** came from Samaria. 2Ki 23:18 834
priests of the high places **w** *were* there 2Ki 23:20 834
of the judges **w** judged Israel, 2Ki 23:22 834
no king like him **w** turned to the LORD 2Ki 23:25 834
all the army of the Chaldeans **w** *were* 2Ki 25:10 834
Then the rest of the people **w** were 2Ki 25:11 834
w had deserted to the king of Babylon 2Ki 25:11 834
one official **w** was overseer of the men 2Ki 25:19 834
advisers **w** were found in the city; 2Ki 25:19 834
w mustered the people of the land; 2Ki 25:19
the land **w** were found in the city. 2Ki 25:19
Now *as for* the people **w** were left 2Ki 25:22
w were with him at Mizpah, 2Ki 25:25 834
kings **w** *were* with him in Babylon. 2Ki 25:28 834
Now these are the kings **w** reigned 1Ch 1:43 834
w defeated Midian in the field of 1Ch 1:46
of Israel, **w** violated the ban. 1Ch 2:7 834
w were born to him *were* Jerahmeel, 1Ch 2:9 834
married Ephrath, **w** bore him Hur. 1Ch 2:19
w had twenty-three cities in the 1Ch 2:22
w was the father of Ziph; 1Ch 2:42 1931
The families of scribes **w** 1Ch 2:55
the Kenites **w** came from Hammath, 1Ch 2:55
w were born to him in Hebron: 1Ch 3:1 834
Mehir, **w** was the father of Eshton. 1Ch 4:11 1931
Joash, Saraph, **w** ruled in Moab, 1Ch 4:22 834
for those **w** lived there formerly 1Ch 4:40
the Meunites **w** were found there, 1Ch 4:41 834
of the Amalekites **w** escaped, 1Ch 4:43 6413
the son of Joel, **w** lived in Aroer, 1Ch 5:8 1931
Hagrites, **w** fell by their hand, 1Ch 5:10

men **w** bore shield and sword and **1Ch 5:18**
were 44,760, **w** went to war. **1Ch 5:18**
and the Hagrites and all **w** *were* **1Ch 5:20**
he **w** served as the priest in the house **1Ch 6:10** 834
those **w** served with their sons: **1Ch 6:33**
w were ready to go out with the **1Ch 7:11**
w were born in the land killed, **1Ch 7:21**
w built lower and upper **1Ch 7:24**
w was the father of Birzaith. **1Ch 7:31** 1931
and Shemed, **w** built Ono and Lod, **1Ch 8:12** 1931
w were heads of fathers' **1Ch 8:13** 1992a
w put to flight the inhabitants of **1Ch 8:13** 1992a
chief men **w** lived in Jerusalem. **1Ch 8:28** 428
Now the first **w** lived in their **1Ch 9:2** 834
w lived in the villages of the **1Ch 9:16**
All these **w** were chosen to be **1Ch 9:22**
chief gatekeepers **w** *were* Levites, **1Ch 9:26** 1992a
w was the firstborn of Shallum **1Ch 9:31** 1931
w *lived* in the chambers *of* **1Ch 9:33**
chief men, **w** lived in Jerusalem. **1Ch 9:34** 428
When all the men of Israel **w** were **1Ch 10:7** 834
w led out and brought in Israel; **1Ch 11:2**
w gave him strong support in his **1Ch 11:10**
w *was* one of the three mighty men. **1Ch 11:12** 1931
I drink the blood of these men **w** **1Ch 11:19**
ones **w** came to David at Ziklag, **1Ch 12:1**
mighty men **w** helped *him* in war. **1Ch 12:1**
w could handle shield and spear, **1Ch 12:8**
he **w** was least was equal to a **1Ch 12:14**
These are the ones **w** crossed the **1Ch 12:15** 834
w was the chief of the thirty, **1Ch 12:18**
you, And peace to him **w** helps you; **1Ch 12:18**
thousands **w** belonged to Manasseh. **1Ch 12:20** 834
war, **w** came to David at Hebron, **1Ch 12:23**
The sons of Judah **w** bore shield **1Ch 12:24**
w were designated by name to come **1Ch 12:31** 834
men **w** understood the times, **1Ch 12:32**
50,000 **w** went out in the army, **1Ch 12:33**
w could draw up in battle **1Ch 12:33**
Of the Danites **w** could draw up **1Ch 12:35**
Of Asher *there were* 40,000 **w** **1Ch 12:36**
w could draw up in battle **1Ch 12:38**
those **w** were near to them, **1Ch 12:40**
to our kinsmen **w** remain in all the **1Ch 13:2**
to the priests and Levites **w** are with **1Ch 13:2**
the LORD **w** is enthroned *above* the **1Ch 13:6**
w went to bring up the ark of the **1Ch 15:25**
the Levites **w** were carrying the ark **1Ch 15:26**
Levites **w** were carrying the ark, **1Ch 15:27**
of those **w** seek the LORD be glad. **1Ch 16:10**
and the rest **w** were chosen, **1Ch 16:41**
chosen, **w** were designated by name, **1Ch 16:41** 834
for those **w** should sound aloud, **1Ch 16:42**
the great ones **w** are in the earth. **1Ch 17:8** 834
you, **w** will be of your sons; **1Ch 17:11** 834
took it from him **w** was before you. **1Ch 17:13** 834
"**W** am I, O LORD God, and what is **1Ch 17:16** 4310
w came and camped before Medeba. **1Ch 19:7**
and the kings **w** had come were by **1Ch 19:9** 834
So Joab and the people **w** were with **1Ch 19:14** 834
Arameans **w** were beyond the River, **1Ch 19:16** 834
out the people **w** *were* in it, **1Ch 20:3** 834
w had twenty-four fingers and toes **1Ch 20:6**
1,100,000 men **w** drew the sword; **1Ch 21:5**
was 470,000 men **w** drew the sword. **1Ch 21:5**
I shall return to Him **w** sent me." **1Ch 21:12**
I **w** commanded to count the people? **1Ch 21:17**
I am the one **w** has sinned and done **1Ch 21:17** 834
and his four sons **w** *were* with him **1Ch 21:20**
w were in the land of Israel, **1Ch 22:2** 834
to you, **w** shall be a man of rest; **1Ch 22:9** 1931
and all men **w** are skillful in **1Ch 22:15**
of those of them **w** were counted, **1Ch 23:24**
Eleazar, **w** had no sons. **1Ch 24:28**
w *were* to prophesy with lyres, **1Ch 25:1**
w performed their service was: **1Ch 25:1**
w prophesied under the direction **1Ch 25:2**
w prophesied in giving thanks and **1Ch 25:3**
Their number **w** were trained in **1Ch 25:7**
relatives, all **w** were skillful, **1Ch 25:7**
sons were born **w** ruled over the house **1Ch 26:6**
everyone **w** had dedicated *anything,* **1Ch 26:28**
and their officers **w** served the **1Ch 27:1**
workers **w** tilled the soil. **1Ch 27:26**
'Your son Solomon is the one **w** **1Ch 28:6** 1931
W then is willing to consecrate **1Ch 29:5** 4310
"But **w** am I and who are my people **1Ch 29:14** 4310
"But who am I and **w** are my people **1Ch 29:14** 4310
Your people, **w** are present here, **1Ch 29:17**
for **w** can rule this great people **2Ch 1:10** 4310
or the life of those **w** hate you, **2Ch 1:11**
w were before you has possessed nor **2Ch 1:12** 834
nor those **w** will come after you." **2Ch 1:12**
"But **w** is able to build a house **2Ch 2:6** 4310
So **w** am I, that I should build a **2Ch 2:6** 4310
w knows how to make engravings, **2Ch 2:7**
the woodsmen **w** cut the timber, **2Ch 2:10**
w has made heaven and earth, **2Ch 2:12** 834
w has given King David a wise son, **2Ch 2:12** 834
w will build a house for the LORD **2Ch 2:12** 834
w knows how to work in gold, **2Ch 2:14**
and **w** *knows how* to make all kinds **2Ch 2:14**
w *were* in the land of Israel, **2Ch 2:17** 834
all the congregation of Israel **w** were **2Ch 5:6**
priests **w** were present had sanctified **2Ch 5:11**
w spoke with His mouth to my **2Ch 6:4** 834
your son **w** will be born to you, **2Ch 6:9**
to Your servants **w** walk before You **2Ch 6:14**
w has kept with Your servant David, **2Ch 6:15** 834

w is not from Your people Israel, **2Ch 6:32** 834
there is no man **w** does not sin) **2Ch 6:36** 834
people **w** have sinned against You. **2Ch 6:39** 834
a very great assembly **w** *came* from **2Ch 7:8**
My people **w** are called by My name **2Ch 7:14** 834
everyone **w** passes by it will be **2Ch 7:21**
w brought them from the land of **2Ch 7:22** 834
w were left of the Hittites, **2Ch 8:7**
Jebusites, **w** were not of Israel, **2Ch 8:7** 834
from their descendants **w** were left **2Ch 8:8** 834
and fifty **w** ruled over the people. **2Ch 8:10**
ships and servants **w** knew the sea; **2Ch 8:18**
your servants **w** stand before you **2Ch 9:7**
LORD your God **w** delighted in you, **2Ch 9:8** 834
Solomon **w** brought gold from Ophir, **2Ch 9:10** 834
consulted with the elders **w** had served **2Ch 10:6** 834
men **w** grew up with him and served **2Ch 10:8** 834
this people, **w** have spoken to me, **2Ch 10:9** 834
w grew up with him spoke to him, **2Ch 10:10** 834
say to the people **w** spoke to you, **2Ch 10:10** 834
w lived in the cities of Judah, **2Ch 10:17**
w was over the forced labor, **2Ch 10:18** 834
chosen men **w** were warriors, **2Ch 11:1**
the priests and the Levites **w** were **2Ch 11:13** 834
w set their hearts on seeking the LORD **2Ch 11:16**
And the people **w** came with him **2Ch 12:3** 834
the princes of Judah **w** had gathered **2Ch 12:5** 834
w guarded the door of the king's **2Ch 12:10**
800,000 chosen men **w** *were* valiant **2Ch 13:3**
w proved too strong for Rehoboam, **2Ch 13:7**
and those **w** have no strength; **2Ch 14:11**
Asa and the people **w** *were* with **2Ch 14:13** 834
down those **w** owned livestock, **2Ch 14:15**
there was no peace to him **w** went out **2Ch 15:5**
who went out or to him **w** came in, **2Ch 15:5**
and Simeon **w** resided with them, **2Ch 15:9**
king of Aram, **w** lived in Damascus, **2Ch 16:2**
w volunteered for the LORD, **2Ch 17:16**
These are they **w** served the king, **2Ch 17:19**
and the people **w** were with him, **2Ch 18:2** 834
Then the messenger **w** went to **2Ch 18:12** 834
'**W** will entice Ahab king of Israel **2Ch 18:19** 4310
and love those **w** hate the LORD **2Ch 19:2**
for the LORD **w** is with you when you **2Ch 19:6**
brethren **w** live in their cities, **2Ch 19:10**
multitude **w** are coming against us; **2Ch 20:12**
he appointed those **w** sang to the **2Ch 20:21**
and those **w** praised *Him* in holy **2Ch 20:21**
Seir, **w** had come against Judah; **2Ch 20:22**
and struck down the Edomites **w** were **2Ch 21:9**
family, **w** were better than you, **2Ch 21:13**
Arabs **w** bordered the Ethiopians; **2Ch 21:16** 834
for the band of men **w** came with **2Ch 22:1**
w sought the LORD with all his **2Ch 22:9** 834
sons **w** were being put to death, **2Ch 22:11**
Levites **w** come in on the sabbath, **2Ch 23:4**
took his men **w** were to come in on **2Ch 23:8**
w were to go out on the sabbath, **2Ch 23:8**
w were appointed over the army and **2Ch 23:14**
so that no one would enter **w** *was* **2Ch 23:19**
gave it to those **w** did the work of the **2Ch 24:12**
are those **w** conspired against him: **2Ch 24:26**
w had slain his father the king. **2Ch 25:3**
sent him a prophet **w** said to him, **2Ch 25:15**
the gods of the people **w** have not **2Ch 25:15** 834
Uzziah, **w** *was* sixteen years old, **2Ch 26:1** 1931
w had understanding through the **2Ch 26:5**
the Arabians **w** lived in Gur-baal, **2Ch 26:7**
w could wage war with great power, **2Ch 26:13**
the sons of Aaron **w** are **2Ch 26:18**
w inflicted him with heavy **2Ch 28:5**
w were coming from the battle, **2Ch 28:12**
w were designated by name arose, **2Ch 28:15** 834
the king and all **w** were present **2Ch 29:29**
and all those **w** were willing **2Ch 29:31**
may return to those of you **w** escaped **2Ch 30:6** 6413
w were unfaithful to the LORD God **2Ch 30:7** 834
before those **w** led them captive and **2Ch 30:9**
w had not consecrated themselves; **2Ch 30:17** 834
lambs for everyone **w** *was* unclean, **2Ch 30:17**
everyone **w** prepares his heart to **2Ch 30:19**
Levites **w** showed good insight *in the* **2Ch 30:22**
both the sojourners **w** came from **2Ch 30:25**
all Israel **w** were present went out **2Ch 31:1**
Also he commanded the people **w** **2Ch 31:4**
w lived in the cities of Judah also **2Ch 31:6**
everyone **w** entered the house of the **2Ch 31:16**
as well as the priests **w** were **2Ch 31:17**
for the sons of Aaron the priests **w** **2Ch 31:19**
there were men **w** were designated **2Ch 31:19** 834
all Judah **w** *were* at Jerusalem, **2Ch 32:9** 834
'**W** *was there* among all the gods of **2Ch 32:14** 4310
w could deliver his people out of my **2Ch 32:14** 834
of Jerusalem **w** were on the wall, **2Ch 32:18** 834
And the LORD sent an angel **w** **2Ch 32:21**
It was Hezekiah **w** stopped the **2Ch 32:30**
w sent to him to inquire of the **2Ch 32:31**
and the words of the seers **w** spoke **2Ch 33:18**
of those **w** had sacrificed to them. **2Ch 34:4**
workmen **w** had the oversight of the **2Ch 34:10**
and the workmen **w** were working in **2Ch 34:10** 834
all **w** were skillful with musical **2Ch 34:12**
those **w** are left in Israel and in Judah **2Ch 34:21**
'Tell the man **w** sent you to Me, **2Ch 34:23** 834
"But to the king of Judah **w** sent **2Ch 34:26**
he made all **w** were present in **2Ch 34:32**
and made all **w** were present in **2Ch 34:33**
He also said to the Levites **w** **2Ch 35:3**
and **w** were holy to the LORD, **2Ch 35:3**

lay people, to all **w** were present, **2Ch 35:7**
Thus the sons of Israel **w** were **2Ch 35:17**
Judah and Israel **w** were present, **2Ch 35:18**
interfering with God **w** is with me, **2Ch 35:21** 834
the prophet **w** spoke for the LORD. **2Ch 36:12**
against King Nebuchadnezzar **w** had **2Ch 36:13** 834
Chaldeans **w** slew their young men **2Ch 36:17**
Those **w** had escaped from the **2Ch 36:20**
He is the God **w** is in Jerusalem. **Ezr 1:3** 834
exiles **w** went up from Babylon **Ezr 1:11**
people of the province **w** came up **Ezr 2:1**
are those **w** came up from Tel-melah, **Ezr 2:59**
w took a wife from the daughters **Ezr 2:61** 834
female servants **w** numbered 7,337; **Ezr 2:65** 428
and from everyone **w** offered a **Ezr 3:5**
and all **w** came from the captivity **Ezr 3:8**
men **w** had seen the first temple, **Ezr 3:12** 834
Assyria, **w** brought us up here." **Ezr 4:2**
that the Jews **w** came up from you **Ezr 4:12** 1768
of their colleagues **w** live in Samaria **Ezr 4:17** 1768
w were in Judah and Jerusalem in **Ezr 5:1** 1768
God of Israel, **w** was over them, **Ezr 5:1**
"**W** issued you a decree to rebuild **Ezr 5:3** 4479
men were **w** were reconstructing this **Ezr 5:4** 1768
w were beyond the River, **Ezr 5:6** 1768
'**W** issued you a decree to rebuild **Ezr 5:9** 4479
of the men **w** were at their head. **Ezr 5:10** 1768
w destroyed this temple **Ezr 5:12**
any man **w** violates this edict, **Ezr 6:11** 1768
"May the God **w** has caused His **Ezr 6:12** 1768
or people **w** attempts to change *it,* **Ezr 6:12** 1768
The sons of Israel **w** returned **Ezr 6:21**
all those **w** had separated themselves **Ezr 6:21**
w are willing to go to Jerusalem, **Ezr 7:13** 1768
w offered willingly for the house **Ezr 7:16**
the treasurers **w** are *in the provinces* **Ezr 7:21** 1768
all the people **w** are in *the province* **Ezr 7:25** 1768
those **w** know the laws of your God; **Ezr 7:25**
anyone **w** is ignorant *of them.* **Ezr 7:25** 1768
w has put *such a thing* as this in **Ezr 7:27** 834
those **w** went up with me from **Ezr 8:1**
of the sons of Shecaniah **w** *was* of **Ezr 8:3**
Zechariah and with him 150 males **w** **Ezr 8:3**
disposed to all those **w** seek Him, **Ezr 8:22**
against all those **w** forsake Him." **Ezr 8:22**
The exiles **w** had come from the **Ezr 8:35**
Then everyone **w** trembled at the **Ezr 9:4**
w commit these abominations? **Ezr 9:14**
is no remnant nor any **w** escape? **Ezr 9:14**
those **w** tremble at the commandment **Ezr 10:3**
all those in our cities **w** have married **Ezr 10:14**
And Ezra the priest selected men **w** **Ezr 10:16**
men **w** had married foreign wives by **Ezr 10:17**
the sons of the priests **w** had married **Ezr 10:18** 834
concerning the Jews **w** had escaped **Ne 1:2**
w survived the captivity are in great **Ne 1:3** 834
w preserves the covenant and **Ne 1:5**
lovingkindness for those **w** love Him **Ne 1:5**
though those of you **w** have been **Ne 1:9**
w delight to revere Your name, **Ne 1:11**
or the rest **w** did the work. **Ne 2:16**
When the Jews **w** lived near them **Ne 4:12**
the Lord **w** is great and awesome, **Ne 4:14**
Those **w** were rebuilding the wall **Ne 4:17**
and those **w** carried burdens took **Ne 4:17**
men of the guard **w** followed me, **Ne 4:23** 834
For there were those **w** said, **Ne 5:2** 834
There were others **w** said, **Ne 5:3** 834
Also there were those **w** said, **Ne 5:4** 834
w were sold to the nations; **Ne 5:8**
w does not fulfill this promise; **Ne 5:13** 834
But the former governors **w** were **Ne 5:15** 834
besides those **w** came to us from **Ne 5:17**
Mehetabel, **w** was confined at home, **Ne 6:10** 1931
w were *trying* to frighten me. **Ne 6:14** 834
genealogy of those **w** came up first **Ne 7:5**
the people of the province **w** came up **Ne 7:6**
and **w** returned to Jerusalem and **Ne 7:6**
w came with Zerubbabel, Jeshua, **Ne 7:7**
were they **w** came up from Tel-melah, **Ne 7:61**
w took a wife of the daughters of **Ne 7:63** 834
and all **w** *could* listen with **Ne 8:2**
women, those **w** could understand; **Ne 8:3**
Then Nehemiah, **w** was the governor, **Ne 8:9** 1931
and the Levites **w** taught the **Ne 8:9**
to him **w** has nothing prepared; **Ne 8:10**
assembly of those **w** had returned **Ne 8:17**
W chose Abram And brought him out **Ne 9:7** 834
God **W** brought you up from Egypt,' **Ne 9:18** 834
killed Your prophets **w** had admonished **Ne 9:26** 834
their oppressors **w** oppressed them, **Ne 9:27**
deliverers **w** delivered them from the **Ne 9:27**
w keeps covenant and **Ne 9:32**
and all those **w** had separated **Ne 10:28**
all those **w** had knowledge and **Ne 10:28**
As for the peoples of the land **w** **Ne 10:31**
for the priests **w** are ministering **Ne 10:36**
for the Levites are they **w** receive **Ne 10:37**
the priests **w** are ministering, **Ne 10:39**
w volunteered to live in Jerusalem. **Ne 11:2**
provinces **w** lived in Jerusalem, **Ne 11:3** 834
All the sons of Perez **w** lived in **Ne 11:6**
and their kinsmen **w** performed the **Ne 11:12**
w were in charge of the outside **Ne 11:16**
w was the leader in beginning the **Ne 11:17**
w kept watch at the gates, **Ne 11:19**
w were the singers for the service **Ne 11:22**
Levites **w** came up with Zerubbabel **Ne 12:1** 834
and Mattaniah **w** *was* in charge **Ne 12:8**

the priests and Levites **w** served.	**Ne 12:44**	
w was appointed over the chambers	**Ne 13:4**	
Levites and the singers **w** performed	**Ne 13:10**	
some **w** were treading wine presses	**Ne 13:15**	
men of Tyre were living there **w**	**Ne 13:16**	
the Ahasuerus **w** reigned from India	**Es 1:1**	
people **w** were present at the citadel	**Es 1:5**	
the seven eunuchs **w** served in the	**Es 1:10**	
the wise men **w** understood the times	**Es 1:13**	
before all **w** knew law and justice	**Es 1:13**	
w had access to the king's presence	**Es 1:14**	
and all the peoples **w** are in all	**Es 1:16**	834
ladies of Persia and Media **w** have	**Es 1:18**	834
another **w** is more worthy than she.	**Es 1:19**	
one **w** speaks in the language of his	**Es 1:22**	
king's attendants, **w** served him,	**Es 2:2**	
w is in charge of the women;	**Es 2:3**	
"Then let the young lady **w**	**Es 2:4**	834
w had been taken into exile from	**Es 2:6**	834
with the captives **w** had been exiled	**Es 2:6**	834
w was in charge of the women.	**Es 2:8**	
the king's eunuch **w** was in charge	**Es 2:14**	
w had taken her as his daughter,	**Es 2:15**	834
w was in charge of the women,	**Es 2:15**	
in the eyes of all **w** saw her.	**Es 2:15**	
from those **w** guarded the door,	**Es 2:21**	
all the princes **w** *were* with him.	**Es 3:1**	834
All the king's servants **w** were	**Es 3:2**	834
Then the king's servants **w** were at	**Es 3:3**	834
for they had told him **w**	**Es 3:6**	
w *were* throughout the whole	**Es 3:6**	834
w carry on the *king's* business,	**Es 3:9**	
w were over each province and	**Es 3:12**	834
man or woman **w** comes to the king	**Es 4:11**	834
the inner court **w** is not summoned,	**Es 4:11**	834
And **w** knows whether you have not	**Es 4:14**	4310
all the Jews **w** are found in Susa,	**Es 4:16**	
king's eunuchs **w** were doorkeepers,	**Es 6:2**	
servants **w** attended him said,	**Es 6:3**	
"**W** is in the court?"	**Es 6:4**	4310
w is sitting at the king's gate;	**Es 6:10**	
"**W** is he, and where is he, who	**Es 7:5**	4310
he, **w** would presume to do thus?"	**Es 7:5**	834
w *were* before the king said,	**Es 7:9**	
which Haman made for Mordecai **w**	**Es 7:9**	834
to destroy the Jews **w** are in all the	**Es 8:5**	834
Jews **w** were in each and every city	**Es 8:11**	834
mastery over those **w** hated them.	**Es 9:1**	
on those **w** sought their harm;	**Es 9:2**	
and those **w** were doing the king's	**Es 9:3**	
pleased to those **w** hated them.	**Es 9:5**	
On that day the number of those **w**	**Es 9:11**	
be granted to the Jews **w** are in Susa	**Es 9:13**	834
The Jews **w** were in Susa	**Es 9:15**	834
Now the rest of the Jews **w** *were* in	**Es 9:16**	834
kill 75,000 of those **w** hated them;	**Es 9:16**	
But the Jews **w** were in Susa	**Es 9:18**	834
areas, **w** live in the rural towns,	**Es 9:19**	
he sent letters to all the Jews **w** were	**Es 9:20**	834
w allied themselves with them,	**Es 9:27**	
one **w** sought the good of his	**Es 10:3**	
one **w** spoke for the welfare of his	**Es 10:3**	
those curse it **w** curse the day,	**Jb 3:8**	
W are prepared to rouse Leviathan.	**Jb 3:8**	
W rebuilt ruins for themselves;	**Jb 3:14**	
Or with princes **w** had gold, Who	**Jb 3:15**	
W were filling their houses *with*	**Jb 3:15**	
is light given to him **w** suffers,	**Jb 3:20**	6001a
W long for death, but there is	**Jb 3:21**	
W rejoice greatly, *And* exult when they	**Jb 3:22**	
But **w** can refrain from speaking?	**Jb 4:2**	4310
w *ever* perished being innocent?	**Jb 4:7**	4310
those **w** plow iniquity And those	**Jb 4:8**	
those **w** sow trouble harvest it.	**Jb 4:8**	
those **w** dwell in houses of clay,	**Jb 4:19**	
W are crushed before the moth!	**Jb 4:19**	
is there anyone **w** will answer you?	**Jb 5:1**	
W does great and unsearchable	**Jb 5:9**	
He sets on high those **w** are lowly,	**Jb 5:11**	
And those **w** mourn are lifted to	**Jb 5:11**	
"As a slave **w** pants for the	**Jb 7:2**	
man **w** eagerly waits for his wages,	**Jb 7:2**	
"The eye of him **w** sees me will	**Jb 7:8**	
So he **w** goes down to Sheol does	**Jb 7:9**	
are the paths of all **w** forget God;	**Jb 8:13**	7911
"Those **w** hate you will be clothed	**Jb 8:22**	
W has defied Him without harm?	**Jb 9:4**	4310
"*It is God* **w** removes the	**Jb 9:5**	
W shakes the earth out of its	**Jb 9:6**	
W commands the sun not to shine,	**Jb 9:7**	
W alone stretches out the heavens And	**Jb 9:8**	
W makes the Bear, Orion and the	**Jb 9:9**	
W does great things, unfathomable,	**Jb 9:10**	
snatch away, **w** could restrain Him?	**Jb 9:12**	4310
W could say to Him,	**Jb 9:12**	4310
of justice, **w** can summon Him?	**Jb 9:19**	4310
If *it is* not *He*, then **w** is it?	**Jb 9:24**	4310
W may lay his hand upon us both.	**Jb 9:33**	
an assembly, **w** can restrain Him?	**Jb 11:10**	4310
And **w** does not know such things as	**Jb 12:3**	4310
The one **w** called on God and He	**Jb 12:4**	
"He **w** is at ease holds calamity	**Jb 12:5**	
those **w** provoke God are secure,	**Jb 12:6**	
"**W** among all these does not know	**Jb 12:9**	4310
"**W** will contend with me?	**Jb 13:19**	4310
"Man, **w** is born of woman, Is	**Jb 14:1**	
"**W** can make the clean out of the	**Jb 14:4**	4310
Or he **w** is born of a woman,	**Jb 15:14**	
one **w** is detestable and corrupt,	**Jb 15:16**	
Man, **w** drinks iniquity like water!	**Jb 15:16**	
W is there that will be my	**Jb 17:3**	4310
"He **w** informs against friends for	**Jb 17:5**	
And he **w** has clean hands will	**Jb 17:9**	
And **w** regards my hope?	**Jb 17:15**	4310
"O you **w** tear yourself in your	**Jb 18:4**	
of him **w** does not know God."	**Jb 18:21**	
"Those **w** live in my house and my	**Jb 19:15**	
Those **w** have seen him will say,	**Jb 20:7**	
w suffers will come *against* him.	**Jb 20:22**	6001a
'**W** is the Almighty, that we should	**Jb 21:15**	4100
"**W** will confront him with his	**Jb 21:31**	4310
And **w** will repay him for what he	**Jb 21:31**	4310
W were snatched away before their	**Jb 22:16**	834
deliver one **w** is not innocent,	**Jb 22:30**	
He is unique and **w** can turn Him?	**Jb 23:13**	4310
"*It is* God **w** has made my	**Jb 23:16**	
And the Almighty **w** has dismayed	**Jb 23:16**	
those **w** know Him not see His days?	**Jb 24:1**	
those **w** rebel against the light;	**Jb 24:13**	
So does Sheol *those* **w** have	**Jb 24:19**	
is not so, **w** can prove me a liar,	**Jb 24:25**	4310
"Dominion and awe belong to Him **W**	**Jb 25:2**	
he be clean **w** is born of woman?	**Jb 25:4**	
thunder, **w** can understand?"	**Jb 26:14**	4310
"As God lives, **w** has taken away my	**Jb 27:2**	
w has embittered my soul,	**Jb 27:2**	
the poor **w** cried for help,	**Jb 29:12**	
And the orphan **w** had no helper.	**Jb 29:12**	
As one **w** comforted the mourners.	**Jb 29:25**	3512c
W gnaw the dry ground by night	**Jb 30:3**	
W pluck mallow by the bushes, And	**Jb 30:4**	
to the sound of those **w** weep.	**Jb 30:31**	
disaster to those **w** work iniquity?	**Jb 31:3**	
He **w** made me in the womb make	**Jb 31:15**	
'**W** can find one who has not been	**Jb 31:31**	4310
'Who can find one **w** has not been	**Jb 31:31**	
there was no one **w** refuted Job,	**Jb 32:12**	
one of you **w** answered his words.	**Jb 32:12**	
his life to those **w** bring death.	**Jb 33:22**	
men, And listen to me, you **w** know.	**Jb 34:2**	
W drinks up derision like water,	**Jb 34:7**	4310
W goes in company with the workers	**Jb 34:8**	
"**W** gave Him authority over the	**Jb 34:13**	4310
And **w** has laid *on Him* the whole	**Jb 34:13**	4310
"Shall one **w** hates justice rule?	**Jb 34:17**	
W says to a king,	**Jb 34:18**	
W shows no partiality to princes Nor	**Jb 34:19**	834
keeps quiet, **w** then can condemn?	**Jb 34:29**	4310
His face, **w** then can behold Him,	**Jb 34:29**	4310
to me, And a wise man **w** hears me,	**Jb 34:34**	
Maker, **W** gives songs in the night,	**Jb 35:10**	
W teaches us more than the beasts	**Jb 35:11**	
One **w** is perfect in knowledge is	**Jb 36:4**	8549
W is a teacher like Him?	**Jb 36:22**	4310
"**W** has appointed Him His way, And	**Jb 36:23**	4310
Him His way, And **w** has said,	**Jb 36:23**	4310
regard any **w** are wise of heart."	**Jb 37:24**	
"**W** is this that darkens counsel	**Jb 38:2**	4310
W set its measurements? Since you	**Jb 38:5**	4310
Or **w** stretched the line on it?	**Jb 38:5**	4310
Or **w** laid its cornerstone,	**Jb 38:6**	4310
"Or **w** enclosed the sea with	**Jb 38:8**	
"**W** has cleft a channel for the	**Jb 38:25**	4310
w has begotten the drops of dew?	**Jb 38:28**	4310
of heaven, **w** has given it birth?	**Jb 38:29**	4310
"**W** has put wisdom in the	**Jb 38:36**	4310
"**W** can count the clouds by	**Jb 38:37**	4310
"**W** prepares for the raven its	**Jb 38:41**	4310
"**W** sent out the wild donkey free?	**Jb 39:5**	4310
And **w** loosed the bonds of the	**Jb 39:5**	4310
Let him **w** reproves God answer it."	**Jb 40:2**	
And look on everyone **w** is proud,	**Jb 40:11**	1343
"Look on everyone **w** is proud,	**Jb 40:12**	1343
W then is he that can stand before	**Jb 41:10**	4310
"**W** has given to Me that I should	**Jb 41:11**	4310
"**W** can strip off his outer armor?	**Jb 41:13**	4310
W can come within his double mail?	**Jb 41:13**	4310
"**W** can open the doors of his face?	**Jb 41:14**	4310
'**W** is this that hides counsel	**Jb 42:3**	4310
and all **w** had known him before came	**Jb 42:11**	
How blessed is the man **w** does not	**Ps 1:1**	834
He **w** sits in the heavens laughs,	**Ps 2:4**	
are all **w** take refuge in Him!	**Ps 2:12**	
and the One **w** lifts my head.	**Ps 3:3**	
W have set themselves against me	**Ps 3:6**	834
"**W** will show us *any* good?"	**Ps 4:6**	4310
w takes pleasure in wickedness;	**Ps 5:4**	
You hate all **w** do iniquity.	**Ps 5:5**	
destroy those **w** speak falsehood;	**Ps 5:6**	
all **w** take refuge in You be glad,	**Ps 5:11**	
That those **w** love Your name may	**Ps 5:11**	
w blesses the righteous man,	**Ps 5:12**	
In Sheol **w** will give You thanks?	**Ps 6:5**	4310
from me, all you **w** do iniquity,	**Ps 6:8**	
me from all those **w** pursue me,	**Ps 7:1**	
Or have plundered him **w** without	**Ps 7:4**	
God, **W** saves the upright in heart.	**Ps 7:10**	
a God **w** has indignation every day.	**Ps 7:11**	
W have displayed Your splendor	**Ps 8:1**	834
And those **w** know Your name will put	**Ps 9:10**	
not forsaken those **w** seek You.	**Ps 9:10**	
to the LORD, **w** dwells in Zion;	**Ps 9:11**	
w requires blood remembers them;	**Ps 9:12**	
affliction from those **w** hate me,	**Ps 9:13**	
You **w** lift me up from the	**Ps 9:13**	
Even all the nations **w** forget God.	**Ps 9:17**	7913
So that man **w** is of the earth will	**Ps 10:18**	
w loves violence His soul hates.	**Ps 11:5**	
W have said, "With our tongue we	**Ps 12:4**	834
w is lord over us?"	**Ps 12:4**	4310
There is no one **w** does good.	**Ps 14:1**	
see if there are any **w** understand,	**Ps 14:2**	
who understand, **W** seek after God.	**Ps 14:2**	
There is no one **w** does good, not	**Ps 14:3**	
W eat up my people *as* they eat	**Ps 14:4**	
O Lord, **w** may abide in Your tent?	**Ps 15:1**	4310
W may dwell on Your holy hill?	**Ps 15:1**	4310
He **w** walks with integrity, and	**Ps 15:2**	
But **w** honors those who fear the	**Ps 15:4**	
who honors those **w** fear the LORD;	**Ps 15:4**	
He **w** does these things will never	**Ps 15:5**	
for the saints **w** are in the earth,	**Ps 16:3**	834
The sorrows of those **w** have	**Ps 16:4**	
bless the LORD **w** has counseled me;	**Ps 16:7**	834
O Savior of those **w** take refuge at	**Ps 17:7**	
From those **w** rise up *against them.*	**Ps 17:7**	
From the wicked **w** despoil me, My	**Ps 17:9**	
My deadly enemies **w** surround me.	**Ps 17:9**	
LORD, **w** is worthy to be praised,	**Ps 18:3**	
enemy, And from those **w** hated me,	**Ps 18:17**	
to all **w** take refuge in Him.	**Ps 18:30**	
For **w** is God, but the LORD?	**Ps 18:31**	4310
And **w** is a rock, except our God,	**Ps 18:31**	4310
The God **w** girds me with strength And	**Ps 18:32**	
me those **w** rose up against me.	**Ps 18:39**	
And I destroyed those **w** hated me.	**Ps 18:40**	
God **w** executes vengeance for me,	**Ps 18:47**	
above those **w** rise up against me;	**Ps 18:48**	
W can discern *his* errors?	**Ps 19:12**	4310
will find out those **w** hate you.	**Ps 21:8**	
O You **w** are enthroned upon the	**Ps 22:3**	
All **w** see me sneer at me;	**Ps 22:7**	
Yet You are He **w** brought me	**Ps 22:9**	
You **w** fear the LORD, praise Him;	**Ps 22:23**	
my vows before those **w** fear Him.	**Ps 22:25**	
w seek Him will praise the LORD.	**Ps 22:26**	
All those **w** go down to the dust	**Ps 22:29**	
he **w** cannot keep his soul alive.	**Ps 22:29**	
To a people **w** will be born,	**Ps 22:31**	
world, and those **w** dwell in it.	**Ps 24:1**	
W may ascend into the hill of the	**Ps 24:3**	4310
And **w** may stand in His holy place?	**Ps 24:3**	4310
He **w** has clean hands and a pure	**Ps 24:4**	
W has not lifted up his soul to	**Ps 24:4**	834
generation of those **w** seek Him,	**Ps 24:6**	
who seek Him, **W** seek Your face	**Ps 24:6**	
W is the King of glory?	**Ps 24:8**	4310
W is this King of glory?	**Ps 24:10**	4310
w wait for You will be ashamed;	**Ps 25:3**	
Those **w** deal treacherously without	**Ps 25:3**	
To those **w** keep His covenant and	**Ps 25:10**	
W is the man who fears the LORD?	**Ps 25:12**	4310
Who is the man **w** fears the LORD?	**Ps 25:12**	
the LORD is for those **w** fear Him,	**Ps 25:14**	
like those **w** go down to the pit.	**Ps 28:1**	
And with those **w** work iniquity,	**Ps 28:3**	
W speak peace with their	**Ps 28:3**	
I hate those **w** regard vain idols,	**Ps 31:6**	
Those **w** see me in the street flee	**Ps 31:11**	
and from those **w** persecute me.	**Ps 31:15**	
stored up for those **w** fear You,	**Ps 31:19**	
for those **w** take refuge in You,	**Ps 31:19**	
All you **w** hope in the LORD.	**Ps 31:24**	
let everyone **w** is godly pray to	**Ps 32:6**	
But he **w** trusts in the LORD,	**Ps 32:10**	
all you **w** are upright in heart.	**Ps 32:11**	
He **w** fashions the hearts of them	**Ps 33:15**	
He **w** understands all their works.	**Ps 33:15**	
the LORD is on those **w** fear Him,	**Ps 33:18**	
On those **w** hope for His	**Ps 33:18**	
the LORD encamps around those **w**	**Ps 34:7**	
is the man **w** takes refuge in Him!	**Ps 34:8**	
For to those **w** fear Him there is	**Ps 34:9**	
But they **w** seek the LORD shall not	**Ps 34:10**	
W is the man who desires life And	**Ps 34:12**	4310
Who is the man **w** desires life And	**Ps 34:12**	
those **w** are crushed in spirit.	**Ps 34:18**	1793a
And those **w** hate the righteous	**Ps 34:21**	
And none of those **w** take refuge in	**Ps 34:22**	
with those **w** contend with me;	**Ps 35:1**	
against those **w** fight against me.	**Ps 35:1**	
to meet those **w** pursue me;	**Ps 35:3**	
and dishonored **w** seek my life;	**Ps 35:4**	
w devise evil against me.	**Ps 35:4**	
"LORD, **w** is like You, Who	**Ps 35:10**	4310
W delivers the afflicted from him	**Ps 35:10**	
from him **w** is too strong for him,	**Ps 35:10**	2389
the needy from him **w** robs him?"	**Ps 35:10**	
as one **w** sorrows for a mother.	**Ps 35:14**	57
Do not let those **w** are wrongfully	**Ps 35:19**	
Nor let those **w** hate me	**Ps 35:19**	
those **w** are quiet in the land.	**Ps 35:20**	7282
w rejoice at my distress;	**Ps 35:26**	
w magnify themselves over me.	**Ps 35:26**	
rejoice, **w** favor my vindication;	**Ps 35:27**	2655
W delights in the prosperity of His	**Ps 35:27**	2655
to those **w** know You,	**Ps 36:10**	
of him **w** prospers in his way,	**Ps 37:7**	
man **w** carries out wicked schemes.	**Ps 37:7**	
But those **w** wait for the LORD,	**Ps 37:9**	
those **w** are upright in conduct.	**Ps 37:14**	3477
LORD is the One **w** holds his hand.	**Ps 37:24**	
Those **w** seek my life lay snares	**Ps 38:12**	
And those **w** seek to injure me have	**Ps 38:12**	
man **w** does not open his mouth.	**Ps 38:13**	
I am like a man **w** does not hear,	**Ps 38:14**	834
W, when my foot slips, would	**Ps 38:16**	

are those **w** hate me wrongfully.	Ps 38:19	
And those **w** repay evil for good,	Ps 38:20	
does not know **w** will gather them.	Ps 39:6	4310
Because it is You **w** have done *it.*	Ps 39:9	
man **w** has made the LORD his trust,	Ps 40:4	834
to those **w** lapse into falsehood.	Ps 40:4	
W seek my life to destroy it;	Ps 40:14	
dishonored **W** delight in my hurt.	Ps 40:14	2655
of their shame **W** say to me,	Ps 40:15	
Let all **w** seek You rejoice and be	Ps 40:16	
Let those **w** love Your salvation say	Ps 40:16	
is he **w** considers the helpless;	Ps 41:1	
All **w** hate me whisper together	Ps 41:7	
in whom I trusted, **W** ate my bread,	Ps 41:9	
down those **w** rise up against us.	Ps 44:5	
have put to shame those **w** hate us.	Ps 44:7	
And those **w** hate us have taken	Ps 44:10	
of him **w** reproaches and reviles,	Ps 44:16	
her companions **w** follow her,	Ps 45:14	
W has wrought desolations in the	Ps 46:8	834
those **w** trust in their wealth And	Ps 49:6	
is the way of those **w** are foolish,	Ps 49:13	
after them **w** approve their words.	Ps 49:13	
Those **w** have made a covenant with	Ps 50:5	
consider this, you **w** forget God,	Ps 50:22	
"He **w** offers a sacrifice of	Ps 50:23	
And to him **w** orders *his* way *aright*	Ps 50:23	
w would not make God his refuge,	Ps 52:7	
There is no one **w** does good.	Ps 53:1	
if there is anyone **w** understands,	Ps 53:2	
understands, **W** seeks after God.	Ps 53:2	
There is no one **w** does good, not	Ps 53:3	
W eat up My people *as though* they	Ps 53:4	
of him **w** encamped against you;	Ps 53:5	
is not an enemy **w** reproaches me,	Ps 55:12	
Nor is it one **w** hates me who has	Ps 55:12	
Nor is it one who hates me **w** has	Ps 55:12	
w had sweet fellowship together	Ps 55:14	834
For they are many **w** *strive* with	Ps 55:18	
the one **w** sits enthroned from of old	Ps 55:19	
no change, And **w** do not fear God.	Ps 55:19	
those **w** were at peace with him;	Ps 55:20	7965
many **w** fight proudly against me.	Ps 56:2	
To God **w** accomplishes *all things*	Ps 57:2	
reproaches him **w** tramples upon me.	Ps 57:3	
among those **w** breathe forth fire,	Ps 57:4	
These **w** speak lies go astray from	Ps 58:3	
is a God **w** judges on earth!"	Ps 58:11	
from those **w** rise up against me.	Ps 59:1	
me from those **w** do iniquity And	Ps 59:2	
Do not be gracious to any **w** *are*	Ps 59:5	
For, *they say,* "**W** hears?"	Ps 59:7	4310
the God **w** shows me lovingkindness.	Ps 59:17	
a banner to those **w** fear You,	Ps 60:4	
W will bring me into the besieged	Ps 60:9	4310
W will lead me to Edom?	Ps 60:9	4310
And it is He **w** will tread down our	Ps 60:12	
of those **w** fear Your name.	Ps 61:5	
But those **w** seek my life to	Ps 63:9	
w swears by Him will glory,	Ps 63:11	
w speak lies will be stopped.	Ps 63:11	
the tumult of those **w** do iniquity,	Ps 64:2	
W have sharpened their tongue like	Ps 64:3	834
"**W** can see them?"	Ps 64:5	4310
w see them will shake the head.	Ps 64:8	
O You **w** hear prayer, To You	Ps 65:2	
You **w** are the trust of all the	Ps 65:5	4009
W establishes the mountains by	Ps 65:6	
W stills the roaring of the seas,	Ps 65:7	
They **w** dwell in the ends *of*	Ps 65:8	
Come and see the works of God, **W**	Ps 66:5	
W keeps us in life And does not	Ps 66:9	
Come *and* hear, all **w** fear God,	Ps 66:16	
W has not turned away my prayer Nor	Ps 66:20	834
those **w** hate Him flee before Him.	Ps 68:1	
Him **w** rides through the deserts,	Ps 68:4	
The women **w** proclaim the *good*	Ps 68:11	
And she **w** remains at home will	Ps 68:12	5116b
Lord, **w** daily bears our burden,	Ps 68:19	
The God **w** is our salvation.	Ps 68:19	
him **w** goes on in his guilty deeds.	Ps 68:21	
you **w** *are* of the fountain of	Ps 68:26	
O God, **w** have acted on our behalf.	Ps 68:28	2098
the peoples **w** delight in war.	Ps 68:30	
To Him **w** rides upon the highest	Ps 68:33	
Those **w** hate me without a cause	Ps 69:4	
Those **w** would destroy me are	Ps 69:4	
it is You **w** knows my folly,	Ps 69:5	
May those **w** wait for You not be	Ps 69:6	
May those **w** seek You not be	Ps 69:6	
And the reproaches of those **w**	Ps 69:9	
w sit in the gate talk about me,	Ps 69:12	
You **w** seek God, let your heart	Ps 69:32	
needy And does not despise His **w**	Ps 69:33	
And those **w** love His name will	Ps 69:36	
and humiliated **W** seek my life;	Ps 70:2	
dishonored **W** delight in my hurt.	Ps 70:2	
back because of their shame **W** say,	Ps 70:3	
Let all **w** seek You rejoice and be	Ps 70:4	
And let those **w** love Your salvation	Ps 70:4	
w took me from my mother's womb;	Ps 71:6	
And those **w** watch for my life have	Ps 71:10	
Let those **w** are adversaries of my	Ps 71:13	
and dishonor, **w** seek to injure me.	Ps 71:13	
Your power to all **w** are to come.	Ps 71:18	
You **w** have done great things;	Ps 71:19	834
O God, **w** is like You?	Ps 71:19	4310
w have shown me many troubles and	Ps 71:20	834
are humiliated **w** seek my hurt.	Ps 71:24	
also, and him **w** has no helper.	Ps 72:12	
of Israel, **W** alone works wonders.	Ps 72:18	
To those **w** are pure in heart!	Ps 73:1	1249
those **w** are far from You will	Ps 73:27	
those **w** are unfaithful to You.	Ps 73:27	
any among us **w** knows how long.	Ps 74:9	
W works deeds of deliverance in	Ps 74:12	
The uproar of those **w** rise against	Ps 74:23	
time, It is I **w** judge with equity.	Ps 75:2	
earth and all **w** dwell in it melt;	Ps 75:3	
It is I **w** have firmly set its pillars.	Ps 75:3	
And **w** may stand in Your presence	Ps 76:7	4310
Let all **w** are around Him bring	Ps 76:11	
gifts to Him **w** is to be feared.	Ps 76:11	4172
are the God **w** works wonders;	Ps 77:14	
those **w** are doomed to die.	Ps 79:11	1121
You **w** lead Joseph like a flock;	Ps 80:1	
You **w** are enthroned *above* the	Ps 80:1	
w pass *that* way pick its *fruit?*	Ps 80:12	
W brought you up from the land of	Ps 81:10	
"Those **w** hate the LORD would	Ps 81:15	
w possesses all the nations.	Ps 82:8	
And those **w** hate You have exalted	Ps 83:2	
W were destroyed at En-dor, Who	Ps 83:10	
W became as dung for the ground.	Ps 83:10	
W said, "Let us possess for ourselves	Ps 83:12	834
are those **w** dwell in Your house!	Ps 84:4	
from those **w** walk uprightly.	Ps 84:11	
is the man **w** trusts in You!	Ps 84:12	
is near to those **w** fear Him,	Ps 85:9	
save Your servant **w** trusts in You.	Ps 86:2	
to all **w** call upon You.	Ps 86:5	
That those **w** hate me may see *it* and	Ps 86:17	
Babylon among those **w** know Me;	Ps 87:4	
Then those **w** sing as well as those	Ps 87:7	
those **w** play the flutes *shall say,*	Ps 87:7	
among those **w** go down to the pit;	Ps 88:4	
Like the slain **w** lie in the grave,	Ps 88:5	
For **w** in the skies is comparable	Ps 89:6	4310
W among the sons of the mighty is	Ps 89:6	
above all those **w** are around Him?	Ps 89:7	
LORD God of hosts, **w** is like You,	Ps 89:8	4310
crushed Rahab like one **w** is slain;	Ps 89:10	
people **w** know the joyful sound!	Ps 89:15	
given help to one **w** is mighty;	Ps 89:19	1368
him, And strike those **w** hate him.	Ps 89:23	
All **w** pass along the way plunder	Ps 89:41	
W understands the power of Your	Ps 90:11	4310
He **w** dwells in the shelter of the	Ps 91:1	
For it is He **w** delivers you from	Ps 91:3	
And all **w** did iniquity flourished,	Ps 92:7	
w do iniquity will be scattered.	Ps 92:9	
evildoers **w** rise up against me.	Ps 92:11	
All **w** do wickedness vaunt	Ps 94:4	
He **w** planted the ear, does He not	Ps 94:9	
He **w** formed the eye, does He not	Ps 94:9	
He **w** chastens the nations, will He	Ps 94:10	
Even He **w** teaches man knowledge?	Ps 94:10	
W will stand up for me against	Ps 94:16	4310
W will take his stand for me	Ps 94:16	4310
me against those **w** do wickedness?	Ps 94:16	
is His, for it was He **w** made it,	Ps 95:5	
are a people **w** err in their heart,	Ps 95:10	
be ashamed **w** serve graven images,	Ps 97:7	
W boast themselves of idols;	Ps 97:7	
Hate evil, you **w** love the LORD,	Ps 97:10	
W preserves the souls of His godly	Ps 97:10	
The world and those **w** dwell in it.	Ps 98:7	
among those **w** called on His name;	Ps 99:6	
It is He **w** has made us, and not we	Ps 100:3	
the work of those **w** fall away;	Ps 101:3	7846
No one **w** has a haughty look and an	Ps 101:5	
He **w** walks in a blameless way is	Ps 101:6	
is the one **w** will minister to me.	Ps 101:6	
He **w** practices deceit shall not	Ps 101:7	
He **w** speaks falsehood shall not	Ps 101:7	
the LORD all those **w** do iniquity.	Ps 101:8	
Those **w** deride me have used my	Ps 102:8	
free those **w** were doomed to death,	Ps 102:20	1121
W pardons all your iniquities,	Ps 103:3	
W heals all your diseases;	Ps 103:3	
W redeems your life from the pit,	Ps 103:4	
W crowns you with lovingkindness	Ps 103:4	
W satisfies your years with good	Ps 103:5	
judgments for all **w** are oppressed.	Ps 103:6	
toward those **w** fear Him.	Ps 103:11	
compassion on those **w** fear Him.	Ps 103:13	
everlasting on those **w** fear Him,	Ps 103:17	
To those **w** keep His covenant And	Ps 103:18	
in strength, **w** perform His word,	Ps 103:20	
you His hosts, You **w** serve Him,	Ps 103:21	
of those **w** seek the LORD be glad.	Ps 105:3	
w was sold as a slave.	Ps 105:17	
there was not one **w** stumbled.	Ps 105:37	
W can speak of the mighty deeds of	Ps 106:2	4310
blessed are those **w** keep justice,	Ps 106:3	
W practice righteousness at all	Ps 106:3	
the hand of the one **w** hated *them,*	Ps 106:10	
W had done great things in Egypt,	Ps 106:21	
w hated them ruled over them.	Ps 106:41	
There were those **w** dwelt in	Ps 107:10	
w go down to the sea in ships,	Ps 107:23	
W do business on great waters;	Ps 107:23	
wickedness of those **w** dwell in it.	Ps 107:34	
W is wise? Let him give heed to	Ps 107:43	4310
W will bring me into the besieged	Ps 108:10	4310
W will lead me to Edom?	Ps 108:10	4310
And it is He **w** shall tread down our	Ps 108:13	
w speak evil against my soul.	Ps 109:20	
him from those **w** judge his soul.	Ps 109:31	
studied by all **w** delight in them.	Ps 111:2	
given food to those **w** fear Him;	Ps 111:5	
all those **w** do *His commandments;*	Ps 111:10	
is the man **w** fears the LORD,	Ps 112:1	
W greatly delights in His	Ps 112:1	
the man **w** is gracious and lends;	Ps 112:5	
W is like the LORD our God, Who is	Ps 113:5	4310
our God, **W** is enthroned on high,	Ps 113:5	
W humbles Himself to behold *The*	Ps 113:6	
W turned the rock into a pool of	Ps 114:8	
Those **w** make them will become like	Ps 115:8	
them, Everyone **w** trusts in them.	Ps 115:8	834
You **w** fear the LORD, trust in the	Ps 115:11	
will bless those **w** fear the LORD,	Ps 115:13	
Nor *do* any **w** go down into silence;	Ps 115:17	
Oh let those **w** fear the LORD say,	Ps 118:4	
is for me among those **w** help me;	Ps 118:7	
satisfaction on those **w** hate me.	Ps 118:7	
w comes in the name of the LORD;	Ps 118:26	
W walk in the law of the LORD.	Ps 119:1	
those **w** observe His testimonies,	Ps 119:2	
W seek Him with all *their* heart.	Ps 119:2	
W wander from Your commandments.	Ps 119:21	
an answer for him **w** reproaches me,	Ps 119:42	
of the wicked, **W** forsake Your law.	Ps 119:53	
of all those **w** fear You,	Ps 119:63	834
And of those **w** keep Your precepts.	Ps 119:63	
w fear You see me and be glad,	Ps 119:74	
May those **w** fear You turn to me,	Ps 119:79	
Even those **w** know Your testimonies.	Ps 119:79	
judgment on those **w** persecute me?	Ps 119:84	
Men **w** are not in accord with Your	Ps 119:85	834
I hate those **w** are double-minded,	Ps 119:113	5588
those **w** wander from Your statutes,	Ps 119:118	
manner with those **w** love Your name.	Ps 119:132	
Those **w** follow after wickedness	Ps 119:150	
word, As one **w** finds great spoil.	Ps 119:162	
w love Your law have great peace,	Ps 119:165	
dwelling With those **w** hate peace.	Ps 120:6	
the LORD, **W** made heaven and earth.	Ps 121:2	
He **w** keeps you will not slumber.	Ps 121:3	
He **w** keeps Israel Will neither	Ps 121:4	
"May they prosper **w** love you.	Ps 122:6	
w are enthroned in the heavens!	Ps 123:1	
scoffing of those **w** are at ease,	Ps 123:4	7600
been the LORD **w** was on our side,"	Ps 124:1	7945
been the LORD **w** was on our side When	Ps 124:2	7945
W has not given us to be torn by	Ps 124:6	7945
the LORD, **W** made heaven and earth.	Ps 124:8	
Those **w** trust in the LORD Are as	Ps 125:1	
good, O LORD, to those **w** are good And	Ps 125:4	2896a
And to those **w** are upright in	Ps 125:4	2896a
But as for those **w** turn aside to	Ps 125:5	
Zion, We were like those **w** dream.	Ps 126:1	
Those **w** sow in tears shall reap	Ps 126:5	
He **w** goes to and fro weeping,	Ps 126:6	
They labor in vain **w** build it;	Ps 127:1	
is everyone **w** fears the LORD,	Ps 128:1	
the LORD, **W** walks in His ways.	Ps 128:1	
man be blessed **W** fears the LORD.	Ps 128:4	
May all **w** hate Zion Be put to	Ps 129:5	
Nor do those **w** pass by say,	Ps 129:8	
iniquities, O Lord, **w** could stand?	Ps 130:3	4310
W serve by night in the house of	Ps 134:1	
Zion, He **w** made heaven and earth.	Ps 134:3	
You **w** stand in the house of the	Ps 135:2	7945
W makes lightnings for the rain,	Ps 135:7	
W brings forth the wind from His	Ps 135:7	
w make them will be like them,	Ps 135:18	
Yes, everyone **w** trusts in them.	Ps 135:18	834
You **w** revere the LORD, bless the	Ps 135:20	
from Zion, **W** dwells in Jerusalem.	Ps 135:21	
To Him **w** alone does great wonders,	Ps 136:4	
Him **w** made the heavens with skill,	Ps 136:5	
To Him **w** spread out the earth	Ps 136:6	
To Him **w** made *the* great lights,	Ps 136:7	
To Him **w** smote the Egyptians in	Ps 136:10	
Him **w** divided the Red Sea asunder,	Ps 136:13	
To Him **w** led His people through	Ps 136:16	
To Him **w** smote great kings, For	Ps 136:17	
W remembered us in our low estate,	Ps 136:23	7945
W gives food to all flesh, For His	Ps 136:25	
Edom The day of Jerusalem, **W** said,	Ps 137:7	
How blessed will be the one **w**	Ps 137:8	7945
How blessed will be the one **w**	Ps 137:9	7945
Do I not hate those **w** hate You,	Ps 139:21	
those **w** rise up against You?	Ps 139:21	
W devise evil things in *their*	Ps 140:2	834
W have purposed to trip up my feet.	Ps 140:4	834
the head of those **w** surround me,	Ps 140:9	
wickedness With men **w** do iniquity;	Ps 141:4	
the snares of those **w** do iniquity.	Ps 141:9	
For there is no one **w** regards me;	Ps 142:4	
like those **w** have long been dead.	Ps 143:3	
like those **w** go down to the pit.	Ps 143:7	
all those **w** afflict my soul,	Ps 143:12	
rock, **W** trains my hands for war,	Ps 144:1	
W subdues my people under me.	Ps 144:2	
W gives salvation to kings,	Ps 144:10	
W rescues David His servant	Ps 144:10	
are the people **w** are so situated;	Ps 144:15	7945
The LORD sustains all **w** fall And	Ps 145:14	
raises up all **w** are bowed down.	Ps 145:14	
is near to all **w** call upon Him,	Ps 145:18	
To all **w** call upon Him in truth.	Ps 145:18	834
the desire of those **w** fear Him;	Ps 145:19	
The LORD keeps all **w** love Him,	Ps 145:20	
W made heaven and earth, The sea	Ps 146:6	

W keeps faith forever; Ps 146:6
W executes justice for the Ps 146:7
W gives food to the hungry. Ps 146:7
raises up those **w** are bowed down; Ps 146:8
W covers the heavens with clouds, Ps 147:8
W provides rain for the earth, Ps 147:8
W makes grass to grow on the Ps 147:8
The LORD favors those **w** fear Him, Ps 147:11
w wait for His lovingkindness. Ps 147:11
W can stand before His cold? Ps 147:17 4310
as those **w** go down to the pit; Pr 1:12
of everyone **w** gains by violence; Pr 1:19
"But he **w** listens to me shall Pr 1:33
to those **w** walk in integrity, Pr 2:7
the man **w** speaks perverse things; Pr 2:12
From those **w** leave the paths of Pr 2:13
W delight in doing evil And Pr 2:14 8056
And **w** are devious in their ways; Pr 2:15
w flatters with her words; Pr 2:16
None **w** go to her return again, Nor Pr 2:19
blessed is the man **w** finds wisdom Pr 3:13
And the man **w** gains understanding. Pr 3:13
life to those **w** take hold of her, Pr 3:18
And happy are all **w** hold her fast. Pr 3:18
are life to those **w** find them And Pr 4:22
one **w** walks with a perverse mouth, Pr 6:12
W winks with his eyes, who signals Pr 6:13
his eyes, **w** signals with his feet, Pr 6:13
feet, **W** points with his fingers; Pr 6:13
W *with* perversity in his heart Pr 6:14
evil, **W** spreads strife. Pr 6:14
A false witness **w** utters lies, Pr 6:19
w spreads strife among brothers. Pr 6:19
So is the one **w** goes in to his Pr 6:29
The one **w** commits adultery with a Pr 6:32
w would destroy himself does it. Pr 6:32
w flatters with her words. Pr 7:5
to him **w** understands, Pr 8:9
right to those **w** find knowledge. Pr 8:9
and nobles, All **w** judge rightly. Pr 8:16
"I love those **w** love me; Pr 8:17
And those **w** diligently seek me Pr 8:17
endow those **w** love me with wealth, Pr 8:21
blessed are they **w** keep my ways. Pr 8:32
is the man **w** listens to me, Pr 8:34
"For he **w** finds me finds life And Pr 8:35
"But he **w** sins against me injures Pr 8:36
All those **w** hate me love death." Pr 8:36
w lacks understanding she says, Pr 9:4 2638
He **w** corrects a scoffer gets Pr 9:7
And he **w** reproves a wicked man Pr 9:7
Calling to those **w** pass by, Pr 9:15
W are making their paths straight: Pr 9:15
w lacks understanding she says, Pr 9:16 2638
he **w** works with a negligent hand, Pr 10:4
He **w** gathers in summer is a son Pr 10:5
in summer is a son **w** acts wisely, Pr 10:5
But he **w** sleeps in harvest is a Pr 10:5
is a son **w** acts shamefully. Pr 10:5
He **w** walks in integrity walks Pr 10:9
But he **w** perverts his ways will be Pr 10:9
He **w** winks the eye causes trouble, Pr 10:10
back of him **w** lacks understanding. Pr 10:13 2638
path of life **w** heeds instruction, Pr 10:17
he **w** ignores reproof goes astray. Pr 10:17
He **w** conceals hatred *has* lying Pr 10:18
he **w** spreads slander is a fool. Pr 10:18
he **w** restrains his lips is wise. Pr 10:19
the lazy one to those **w** send him. Pr 10:26
He **w** despises his neighbor lacks Pr 11:12
He **w** goes about as a talebearer Pr 11:13
But he **w** is trustworthy conceals a Pr 11:13
He **w** is guarantor for a stranger will Pr 11:15
he **w** hates being a guarantor is secure. Pr 11:15
But he **w** sows righteousness *gets* a Pr 11:18
He **w** is steadfast in righteousness Pr 11:19 3653a
And he **w** pursues evil *will bring* Pr 11:19
woman **w** lacks discretion. Pr 11:22
There is one **w** scatters, and Pr 11:24
And there is one **w** withholds Pr 11:24
And he **w** waters will himself be Pr 11:25
He **w** withholds grain, the people Pr 11:26
be on the head of him **w** sells *it.* Pr 11:26
He **w** diligently seeks good seeks Pr 11:27
But he **w** seeks evil, Pr 11:27
He **w** trusts in his riches will Pr 11:28
He **w** troubles his own house will Pr 11:29
life, And he **w** is wise wins souls. Pr 11:30
But he **w** hates reproof is stupid. Pr 12:1
will condemn a man **w** devises evil. Pr 12:2
But she **w** shames *him* is like Pr 12:4
Better is he **w** is lightly esteemed Pr 12:9
Than he **w** honors himself and lacks Pr 12:9
He **w** tills his land will have Pr 12:11
he **w** pursues worthless *things* lacks Pr 12:11
man is he **w** listens to counsel. Pr 12:15
He **w** speaks truth tells what is Pr 12:17
There is one **w** speaks rashly like Pr 12:18
the heart of those **w** devise evil, Pr 12:20
But those **w** deal faithfully are Pr 12:22
The one **w** guards his mouth Pr 13:3
The one **w** opens wide his lips Pr 13:3
is one **w** pretends to be rich, Pr 13:7
wisdom is with those **w** receive Pr 13:10
w gathers by labor increases *it.* Pr 13:11
The one **w** despises the word will Pr 13:13
But the one **w** fears the Pr 13:13
come to him **w** neglects discipline, Pr 13:18
But he **w** regards reproof will be Pr 13:18

He **w** walks with wise men will be Pr 13:20
He **w** withholds his rod hates his son, Pr 13:24
But he **w** loves him disciplines him Pr 13:24
He **w** walks in his uprightness Pr 14:2
But he **w** is devious in his ways Pr 14:2
easy to one **w** has understanding. Pr 14:6
those **w** love the rich are many. Pr 14:20
He **w** despises his neighbor sins, Pr 14:21
is he **w** is gracious to the poor. Pr 14:21
they not go astray **w** devise evil? Pr 14:22
will be to those **w** devise good. Pr 14:22
he **w** utters lies is treacherous. Pr 14:25
He **w** is slow to anger has great Pr 14:29 750
But he **w** is quick-tempered exalts Pr 14:29 7116
He **w** oppresses the poor taunts Pr 14:31
But he **w** is gracious to the needy Pr 14:31
heart of one **w** has understanding, Pr 14:33
is toward a servant **w** acts wisely, Pr 14:35
is toward him **w** acts shamefully. Pr 14:35
he **w** regards reproof is sensible. Pr 15:5
loves one **w** pursues righteousness. Pr 15:9
is for him **w** forsakes the way; Pr 15:10
He **w** hates reproof will die. Pr 15:10
does not love one **w** reproves him, Pr 15:12
Folly is joy to him **w** lacks sense, Pr 15:21 2638
He **w** profits illicitly troubles Pr 15:27
But he **w** hates bribes will live. Pr 15:27
He **w** neglects discipline despises Pr 15:32
But he **w** listens to reproof Pr 15:32
Everyone **w** is proud in heart is an Pr 16:5
And he **w** speaks right is loved. Pr 16:13
He **w** watches his way preserves his Pr 16:17
He **w** gives attention to the word Pr 16:20
is he **w** trusts in the LORD. Pr 16:20
fountain of life to one **w** has it, Pr 16:22 1167
He **w** winks his eyes *does so* to Pr 16:30
He **w** compresses his lips brings Pr 16:30
He **w** is slow to anger is better Pr 16:32 750
mighty, And he **w** rules his spirit, Pr 16:32
spirit, than he **w** captures a city. Pr 16:32
A servant **w** acts wisely will rule Pr 17:2
rule over a son **w** acts shamefully, Pr 17:2
He **w** mocks the poor taunts his Pr 17:5
He **w** rejoices at calamity will not Pr 17:5
He **w** conceals a transgression seeks Pr 17:9
But he **w** repeats a matter Pr 17:9
A rebuke goes deeper into one **w** Pr 17:10
He **w** returns evil for good, Evil Pr 17:13
He **w** justifies the wicked and he Pr 17:15
and he **w** condemns the righteous, Pr 17:15
He **w** loves transgression loves Pr 17:19
He **w** raises his door seeks Pr 17:19
He **w** has a crooked mind finds no Pr 17:20 6141
And he **w** is perverted in his Pr 17:20
He **w** sires a fool *does so* to his Pr 17:21
of the one **w** has understanding, Pr 17:24
And bitterness to her **w** bore him. Pr 17:25
He **w** restrains his words has Pr 17:27
And he **w** has a cool spirit is a Pr 17:27 7119
He **w** separates himself seeks *his* Pr 18:1
He also **w** is slack in his work Is Pr 18:9
work Is brother to him **w** destroys. Pr 18:9
He **w** gives an answer before he Pr 18:13
a broken spirit **w** can bear it? Pr 18:14 4310
w love it will eat its fruit. Pr 18:21
He **w** finds a wife finds a good Pr 18:22
w sticks closer than a brother. Pr 18:24 1695
Better is a poor man **w** walks in Pr 19:1
Than he **w** is perverse in speech and Pr 19:1 6141
And he **w** hurries his footsteps errs. Pr 19:2
he **w** tells lies will not escape. Pr 19:5
is a friend to him **w** gives gifts. Pr 19:6
He **w** gets wisdom loves his own Pr 19:8
He **w** keeps understanding will find Pr 19:8
And he **w** tells lies will perish. Pr 19:9
He **w** keeps the commandment keeps Pr 19:16
But he **w** is careless of conduct Pr 19:16
One **w** is gracious to a poor man Pr 19:17
But reprove one **w** has Pr 19:25
He **w** assaults *his* father *and* Pr 19:26
He **w** provokes him to anger Pr 20:2
But **w** can find a trustworthy man? Pr 20:6 4310
A righteous man **w** walks in his Pr 20:7
A king **w** sits on the throne of Pr 20:8
W can say, "I have cleansed my Pr 20:9 4310
He **w** goes about as a slanderer Pr 20:19
He **w** curses his father or his Pr 20:20
But everyone **w** is hasty *comes* Pr 21:5
He **w** shuts his ear to the cry of Pr 21:13
A man **w** wanders from the way of Pr 21:16
He **w** loves pleasure *will become* a Pr 21:17
He **w** loves wine and oil will not Pr 21:17
He **w** pursues righteousness and Pr 21:21
He **w** guards his mouth and his Pr 21:23
names, **W** acts with insolent pride. Pr 21:24
But the man **w** listens *to the truth* Pr 21:28
He **w** guards himself will be far Pr 22:5
He **w** sows iniquity will reap Pr 22:8
He **w** is generous will be blessed, Pr 22:9
He **w** loves purity of heart *And* Pr 22:11
He **w** is cursed of the LORD will Pr 22:14
He **w** oppresses the poor to make Pr 22:16
himself Or **w** gives to the rich, Pr 22:16
answer him **w** sent you? Pr 22:21
take the life of those **w** rob them. Pr 22:23
not be among those **w** give pledges, Pr 22:26
those **w** become guarantors for debts. Pr 22:26
Listen to your father **w** begot you, Pr 23:22
And he **w** sires a wise son will be Pr 23:24

her rejoice **w** gave birth to you. Pr 23:25
W has woe? Who has sorrow? Pr 23:29 4310
Who has woe? **W** has sorrow? Pr 23:29 4310
W has contentions? Who has Pr 23:29 4310
W has complaining? Who has Pr 23:29 4310
W has wounds without cause? Pr 23:29 4310
W has redness of eyes? Pr 23:29 4310
Those **w** linger long over wine, Pr 23:30
Those **w** go to taste mixed wine. Pr 23:30
And you will be like one **w** lies Pr 23:34
Or like one **w** lies down on the top Pr 23:34
One **w** plans to do evil, Men will Pr 24:8
w are being taken away to death, Pr 24:11
w are staggering to slaughter, Pr 24:11
consider *it* **w** weighs the hearts? Pr 24:12
He not know *it* **w** keeps your soul? Pr 24:12
with those **w** are given to change, Pr 24:21
And **w** knows the ruin *that comes* Pr 24:22 4310
He **w** says to the wicked, Pr 24:24
But to those **w** rebuke the *wicked* Pr 24:25
the lips **W** gives a right answer. Pr 24:26
Or he **w** hears *it* will reproach you, Pr 25:10
messenger to those **w** send him, Pr 25:13
man **w** boasts of his gifts falsely. Pr 25:14
Is a man **w** bears false witness against Pr 25:18
Like one **w** takes off a garment on Pr 25:20
Is he **w** sings songs to a troubled Pr 25:20
man **w** gives way before the wicked. Pr 25:26
man **w** has no control over his spirit. Pr 25:28 834
W sends a message by the hand of a Pr 26:6
one **w** binds a stone in a sling, Pr 26:8
So is he **w** gives honor to a fool. Pr 26:8
Like an archer **w** wounds everyone, Pr 26:10
So is he **w** hires a fool or who Pr 26:10
fool or **w** hires those who pass by. Pr 26:10
fool or who hires those **w** pass by. Pr 26:10
Is a fool **w** repeats his folly. Pr 26:11
men **w** can give a discreet answer. Pr 26:16
Like one **w** takes a dog by the ears Pr 26:17
Is he **w** passes by *and* meddles with Pr 26:17
Like a madman **w** throws Firebrands, Pr 26:18
the man **w** deceives his neighbor, Pr 26:19
He **w** hates disguises *it* with his Pr 26:24
He **w** digs a pit will fall into it, Pr 26:27
into it, And he **w** rolls a stone, Pr 26:27
But **w** can stand before jealousy? Pr 27:4 4310
is a man **w** wanders from his home. Pr 27:8
Better is a neighbor **w** is near Pr 27:10
may reply to him **w** reproaches me. Pr 27:11
He **w** blesses his friend with a Pr 27:14
He **w** would restrain her restrains Pr 27:16
He **w** tends the fig tree will eat Pr 27:18
And he **w** cares for his master will Pr 27:18
A poor man **w** oppresses the lowly Pr 28:3
Those **w** forsake the law praise the Pr 28:4
w keep the law strive with them. Pr 28:4
But those **w** seek the LORD Pr 28:5
the poor **w** walks in his integrity Than Pr 28:6
he **w** is crooked though he be rich. Pr 28:6
He **w** keeps the law is a discerning Pr 28:7
But he **w** is a companion of Pr 28:7
He **w** increases his wealth by Pr 28:8
for him **w** is gracious to the poor. Pr 28:8
He **w** turns away his ear from Pr 28:9
He **w** leads the upright astray in Pr 28:10
But the poor **w** has understanding Pr 28:11
He **w** conceals his transgressions Pr 28:13
But he **w** confesses and forsakes Pr 28:13
blessed is the man **w** fears always, Pr 28:14
But he **w** hardens his heart will Pr 28:14
A leader **w** is a great oppressor Pr 28:16
But he **w** hates unjust gain will Pr 28:16
A man **w** is laden with the guilt of Pr 28:17
He **w** walks blamelessly will be Pr 28:18
But he **w** is crooked will fall all Pr 28:18
He **w** tills his land will have Pr 28:19
But he **w** follows empty *pursuits* Pr 28:19
But he **w** makes haste to be rich Pr 28:20
He **w** rebukes a man will afterward Pr 28:23
he **w** flatters with the tongue. Pr 28:23
He **w** robs his father or his mother And Pr 28:24
the companion of a man **w** destroys. Pr 28:24
But he **w** trusts in the LORD will Pr 28:25
He **w** trusts in his own heart is a Pr 28:26
But he **w** walks wisely will be Pr 28:26
He **w** gives to the poor will never Pr 28:27
But he **w** shuts his eyes will have Pr 28:27
A man **w** hardens *his* neck after Pr 29:1
A man **w** loves wisdom makes his Pr 29:3
But he **w** keeps company with Pr 29:3
man **w** takes bribes overthrows it. Pr 29:4 8641
A man **w** flatters his neighbor Is Pr 29:5
But a child **w** gets his own way Pr 29:15
But happy is he **w** keeps the law. Pr 29:18
see a man **w** is hasty in his words? Pr 29:20
He **w** pampers his slave from Pr 29:21
He **w** is a partner with a thief Pr 29:24
But he **w** trusts in the LORD will Pr 29:25
And he **w** is upright in the way is Pr 29:27 3477
W has ascended into heaven and Pr 30:4 4310
W has gathered the wind in His Pr 30:4 4310
W has wrapped the waters in His Pr 30:4 4310
W has established all the ends of Pr 30:4 4310
to those **w** take refuge in Him. Pr 30:5
deny *You* and say, "**W** is the LORD? Pr 30:9 4310
a kind of *man* **w** curses his father And Pr 30:11
a kind **w** is pure in his own eyes, Pr 30:12
drink to him **w** is perishing, Pr 31:6
An excellent wife, **w** can find? Pr 31:10 4310

But a woman **w** fears the LORD,	**Pr 31:30**	
those **w** will come later *still.*	**Ec 1:11**	7945
w were over Jerusalem before me;	**Ec 1:16**	834
all **w** preceded me in Jerusalem.	**Ec 2:7**	7945
all **w** preceded me in Jerusalem.	**Ec 2:9**	7945
for what *will* the man *do* **w** will	**Ec 2:12**	7945
to the man **w** will come after me.	**Ec 2:18**	7945
And **w** knows whether he will be a	**Ec 2:19**	4310
a man **w** has labored with wisdom,	**Ec 2:21**	7945
one **w** has not labored with them.	**Ec 2:21**	7945
For **w** can eat and who can have	**Ec 2:25**	4310
For who can eat and **w** can have	**Ec 2:25**	4310
For to a person **w** is good in His	**Ec 2:26**	7945
to one **w** is good in God's sight.	**Ec 2:26**	2896a
that every man **w** eats and drinks	**Ec 3:13**	7945
W knows that the breath of man	**Ec 3:21**	4310
For **w** will bring him to see what	**Ec 3:22**	4310
So I congratulated the dead **w** are	**Ec 4:2**	7945
the living **w** are still living.	**Ec 4:2**	834
is the one **w** has never existed,	**Ec 4:3**	834
w has never seen the evil activity	**Ec 4:3**	834
But woe to the one **w** falls when	**Ec 4:10**	7945
one can overpower him **w** is alone,	**Ec 4:12**	259
foolish king **w** no longer knows *how*	**Ec 4:13**	834
of the second lad **w** replaces him.	**Ec 4:15**	834
people, to all **w** were before them,	**Ec 4:16**	834
and even the ones **w** will come	**Ec 4:16**	314
a king **w** cultivates the field is	**Ec 5:9**	
He **w** loves money will not be	**Ec 5:10**	
nor he **w** loves abundance *with its*	**Ec 5:10**	4310
those **w** consume them increase.	**Ec 5:11**	
to him **w** toils for the wind?	**Ec 5:16**	7945
with him **w** is stronger than he is.	**Ec 6:10**	7945
For **w** knows what is good for a man	**Ec 6:12**	4310
For **w** can tell a man what will be	**Ec 6:12**	4310
advantage to those **w** see the sun.	**Ec 7:11**	
For **w** is able to straighten what	**Ec 7:13**	4310
a righteous man **w** perishes in his	**Ec 7:15**	
and there is a wicked man **w**	**Ec 7:15**	
for the one **w** fears God comes	**Ec 7:18**	
than ten rulers **w** are in a city.	**Ec 7:19**	834
man on earth **w** *continually* does good	**Ec 7:20**	834
does good and **w** never sins.	**Ec 7:20**	
W can discover it?	**Ec 7:24**	4310
One **w** is pleasing to God will	**Ec 7:26**	2896a
W is like the wise man and who	**Ec 8:1**	4310
Who is like the wise man and **w**	**Ec 8:1**	4310
authoritative, **w** will say to him,	**Ec 8:4**	4310
He **w** keeps a *royal* command	**Ec 8:5**	
w can tell him when it will happen?	**Ec 8:7**	4310
not deliver those **w** practice it.	**Ec 8:8**	1167
those **w** used to go in and out from	**Ec 8:10**	
will be well for those **w** fear God,	**Ec 8:12**	
who fear God, **w** fear Him openly.	**Ec 8:12**	834
for the man **w** offers a sacrifice	**Ec 9:2**	
for the one **w** does not sacrifice.	**Ec 9:2**	834
is the one **w** is afraid to swear.	**Ec 9:2**	
He **w** digs a pit may fall into it,	**Ec 10:8**	
bite him **w** breaks through a wall.	**Ec 10:8**	
He **w** quarries stones may be hurt	**Ec 10:9**	
and he **w** splits logs may be	**Ec 10:9**	
and **w** can tell him what will come	**Ec 10:14**	4310
He **w** watches the wind will not sow	**Ec 11:4**	
he **w** looks at the clouds will not reap.	**Ec 11:4**	
of God **w** makes all things.	**Ec 11:5**	834
w look through windows grow dim;	**Ec 12:3**	
spirit will return to God **w** gave it.	**Ec 12:7**	834
For why should I be like one **w**	**SS 1:7**	
"The watchmen **w** make the rounds	**SS 3:3**	
the room of her **w** conceived me."	**SS 3:4**	
"The watchmen **w** make the rounds	**SS 5:7**	
He **w** pastures *his flock* among the	**SS 6:3**	
pure *child* of the one **w** bore her.	**SS 6:9**	
'**W** is this that grows like the	**SS 6:10**	4310
the lips of those **w** fall asleep.	**SS 7:9**	3463
me **W** nursed at my mother's breasts.	**SS 8:1**	
my mother, **w** used to instruct me;	**SS 8:2**	
"**W** is this coming up from the	**SS 8:5**	4310
in his eyes as one **w** finds peace.	**SS 8:10**	
those **w** take care of its fruit."	**SS 8:12**	
"O you **w** sit in the gardens, *My*	**SS 8:13**	
evildoers, Sons **w** act corruptly!	**Is 1:4**	
W requires of you this trampling	**Is 1:12**	4310
She **w** was full of justice!	**Is 1:21**	
And those **w** forsake the LORD will	**Is 1:28**	
everyone **w** is proud and lofty And	**Is 2:12**	1343
against everyone **w** is lifted up,	**Is 2:12**	
Those **w** guide you lead *you* astray And	**Is 3:12**	
you **w** have devoured the vineyard;	**Is 3:14**	
he **w** is left in Zion and remains in	**Is 4:3**	
everyone **w** is recorded for life in	**Is 4:3**	
Woe to those **w** add house to house	**Is 5:8**	
Woe to those **w** rise early in the	**Is 5:11**	
W stay up late in the evening that	**Is 5:11**	
Woe to those **w** drag iniquity with	**Is 5:18**	
W say, "Let Him make speed,	**Is 5:19**	
Woe to those **w** call evil good, and	**Is 5:20**	
W substitute darkness for light	**Is 5:20**	
W substitute bitter for sweet and	**Is 5:20**	
w are wise in their own eyes And	**Is 5:21**	2450
w are heroes in drinking wine And	**Is 5:22**	
W justify the wicked for a bribe,	**Is 5:23**	
of the ones **w** are in the right!	**Is 5:23**	6662
at the voice of him **w** called out,	**Is 6:4**	
I send, and **w** will go for Us?"	**Is 6:8**	4310
And I will wait for the LORD **w** is	**Is 8:17**	
of hosts, **w** dwells on Mount Zion.	**Is 8:18**	
spiritists **w** whisper and mutter,"	**Is 8:19**	
gloom for her **w** was in anguish;	**Is 9:1**	834

The people **w** walk in darkness Will	**Is 9:2**	
Those **w** live in a dark land, The	**Is 9:2**	
turn back to Him **w** struck them,	**Is 9:13**	
w teaches falsehood is the tail.	**Is 9:15**	
For those **w** guide this people are	**Is 9:16**	
And those **w** are guided by them are	**Is 9:16**	
to those **w** enact evil statutes And	**Is 10:1**	
And to those **w** constantly record	**Is 10:1**	
over the one **w** chops with it?	**Is 10:15**	
itself over the one **w** wields it?	**Is 10:15**	
a club wielding those **w** lift it,	**Is 10:15**	
Or like a rod lifting *him* **w**	**Is 10:15**	
the house of Jacob **w** have escaped,	**Is 10:20**	6413
rely on the one **w** struck them,	**Is 10:20**	
"O My people **w** dwell in Zion, do	**Is 10:24**	
do not fear the Assyrian **w** strikes	**Is 10:24**	
Those also **w** are tall in stature	**Is 10:33**	
those **w** are lofty will be abased.	**Is 10:33**	1364
W will stand as a signal for the	**Is 11:10**	834
of His people, **w** will remain,	**Is 11:11**	834
w harass Judah will be cut off;	**Is 11:13**	
of His people **w** will be left,	**Is 11:16**	834
Anyone **w** is found will be thrust	**Is 13:15**	
And anyone **w** is captured will fall	**Is 13:15**	
W will not value silver or take	**Is 13:17**	834
You **w** have weakened the nations!	**Is 14:12**	
"Those **w** see you will gaze at	**Is 14:16**	
the man **w** made the earth tremble,	**Is 14:16**	
earth tremble, **W** shook kingdoms,	**Is 14:16**	
W made the world like a wilderness	**Is 14:17**	
W did not allow his prisoners to	**Is 14:17**	
slain **w** are pierced with a sword,	**Is 14:19**	
W go down to the stones of the	**Is 14:19**	
planned, and **w** can frustrate *it?*	**Is 14:27**	4310
hand, **w** can turn it back?"	**Is 14:27**	4310
w are most helpless will eat,	**Is 14:30**	
As those **w** are utterly stricken.	**Is 16:7**	5218a
the uproar of many peoples **W** roar	**Is 17:12**	
And the rumbling of nations **W** rush	**Is 17:12**	
the portion of those **w** plunder us And	**Is 17:14**	
And the lot of those **w** pillage us.	**Is 17:14**	
And all those **w** cast a line into	**Is 19:8**	
And those **w** spread nets on the	**Is 19:8**	
Those **w** *are* the cornerstone of	**Is 19:13**	
You **w** were full of noise, You	**Is 22:2**	4392
All of you **w** were found were taken	**Is 22:3**	
did not depend on Him **w** made it,	**Is 22:11**	
Him **w** planned it long ago.	**Is 22:11**	
w is in charge of the *royal*	**Is 22:15**	834
You **w** hew a tomb on the height,	**Is 22:16**	
You **w** carve a resting place for	**Is 22:16**	
W has planned this against Tyre,	**Is 23:8**	4310
w dwell in the presence of the LORD.	**Is 23:18**	
w live in it are held guilty.	**Is 24:6**	
is bitter to those **w** drink it.	**Is 24:9**	
Then it will be that he **w** flees	**Is 24:18**	
And he **w** climbs out of the pit	**Is 24:18**	
brought low those **w** dwell on high,	**Is 26:5**	
You **w** lie in the dust, awake and	**Is 26:19**	
the dragon **w** *lives* in the sea.	**Is 27:1**	834
striking of Him **w** has struck them,	**Is 27:7**	
and those **w** were perishing in the	**Is 27:13**	
w were scattered in the land of Egypt	**Is 27:13**	
Of those **w** are overcome with wine!	**Is 28:1**	
for him **w** sits in judgment,	**Is 28:6**	
A strength to those **w** repel the	**Is 28:6**	
He **w** said to them,	**Is 28:12**	834
W rule this people who are in	**Is 28:14**	
this people **w** are in Jerusalem,	**Is 28:14**	834
He **w** believes *in it* will not be	**Is 28:16**	
W has made *His* counsel	**Is 28:29**	
nations **w** wage war against Ariel,	**Is 29:7**	
Even all **w** wage war against her	**Is 29:7**	
stronghold, and **w** distress her,	**Is 29:7**	
be **W** wage war against Mount Zion.	**Is 29:8**	
give it to the one **w** is literate,	**Is 29:11**	
given to the one **w** is illiterate,	**Is 29:12**	834
Woe to those **w** deeply hide their	**Is 29:15**	
"**W** sees us?" or "Who knows us?"	**Is 29:15**	4310
"Who sees us?" or "**W** knows us?"	**Is 29:15**	4310
is formed say to him **w** formed it,	**Is 29:16**	
Indeed all **w** are intent on doing	**Is 29:20**	
W cause a person to be indicted by	**Is 29:21**	
him **w** adjudicates at the gate,	**Is 29:21**	
says the LORD, **w** redeemed Abraham,	**Is 29:22**	834
"Those **w** err in mind will	**Is 29:24**	
And those **w** criticize will accept	**Is 29:24**	
"**W** execute a plan, but not Mine,	**Is 30:1**	
W proceed down to Egypt Without	**Is 30:2**	
of a people **w** cannot profit them,	**Is 30:5**	
W *are* not for help or profit,	**Is 30:5**	
To a people **w** cannot profit *them;*	**Is 30:6**	
"Rahab **w** has been exterminated."	**Is 30:7**	1992a
Sons **w** refuse to listen To the	**Is 30:9**	
W say to the seers,	**Is 30:10**	834
those **w** pursue you shall be swift.	**Is 30:16**	
are all those **w** long for Him.	**Is 30:18**	
those **w** go down to Egypt for help	**Is 31:1**	
And he **w** helps will stumble And he	**Is 31:3**	
And he **w** is helped will fall,	**Is 31:3**	
those **w** see will not be blinded,	**Is 32:3**	
ears of those **w** hear will listen.	**Is 32:3**	
Rise up, you women **w** are at ease,	**Is 32:9**	7600
Tremble, you *women* **w** are at ease;	**Is 32:11**	7600
be, you **w** sow beside all waters,	**Is 32:20**	
W let out freely the ox and the	**Is 32:20**	
And he **w** is treacherous, while	**Is 33:1**	
"You **w** are far away, hear what I	**Is 33:13**	7350
And you **w** are near, acknowledge My	**Is 33:13**	7138

"**W** among us can live with the	**Is 33:14**	4310
W among us can live with continual	**Is 33:14**	4310
He **w** walks righteously and speaks	**Is 33:15**	
He **w** rejects unjust gain And	**Is 33:15**	
He **w** stops his ears from hearing	**Is 33:15**	
"Where is he **w** counts?	**Is 33:18**	
Where is he **w** weighs?	**Is 33:18**	
Where is he **w** counts the towers?"	**Is 33:18**	
The people **w** dwell there will be	**Is 33:24**	
will be for him **w** walks *that* way,	**Is 35:8**	
Hilkiah, **w** was over the household,	**Is 36:3**	834
of Egypt to all **w** rely on him.	**Is 36:6**	
of the people **w** are on the wall."	**Is 36:11**	834
not to the men **w** sit on the wall,	**Is 36:12**	
'**W** among all the gods of these	**Is 36:20**	4310
Hilkiah, **w** was over the household,	**Is 36:22**	834
Then he sent Eliakim **w** was over	**Is 37:2**	834
sons of Eden **w** *were* in Telassar?	**Is 37:12**	834
w is enthroned *above* the	**Is 37:16**	
w sent *them* to reproach the living	**Is 37:17**	
It is You **w** has kept my soul	**Is 38:17**	
Those **w** go down to the pit cannot	**Is 38:18**	
the living **w** give thanks to You,	**Is 38:19**	
your sons **w** will issue from you,	**Is 39:7**	834
W has measured the waters in the	**Is 40:12**	4310
W has directed the Spirit of the	**Is 40:13**	4310
With whom did He consult and **w**	**Is 40:14**	
And **w** taught Him in the path of	**Is 40:14**	
He **w** is too impoverished for *such*	**Is 40:20**	
It is He **w** sits above the circle of	**Is 40:22**	
W stretches out the heavens like a	**Is 40:22**	
it is **w** reduces rulers to nothing,	**Is 40:23**	
W makes the judges of the earth	**Is 40:23**	
And see **w** has created these *stars,*	**Is 40:26**	4310
The One **w** leads forth their host	**Is 40:26**	
And to *him* **w** lacks might He	**Is 40:29**	
Yet those **w** wait for the LORD Will	**Is 40:31**	
"**W** has aroused one from the east	**Is 41:2**	4310
"**W** has performed and accomplished	**Is 41:4**	4310
And he **w** smooths *metal* with the	**Is 41:7**	
encourages him **w** beats the anvil,	**Is 41:7**	
all those **w** are angered at you	**Is 41:11**	
Those **w** contend with you will be	**Is 41:11**	376
seek those **w** quarrel with you,	**Is 41:12**	376
Those **w** war with you will be as	**Is 41:12**	376
God, **w** upholds your right hand,	**Is 41:13**	
your right hand, **W** says to you,	**Is 41:13**	
He **w** chooses you is an abomination.	**Is 41:24**	
W has declared *this* from the	**Is 41:26**	4310
there was no one **w** declared,	**Is 41:26**	
there was no one **w** proclaimed,	**Is 41:26**	
was no one **w** heard your words.	**Is 41:26**	
is no counselor among them **W**,	**Is 41:28**	
W created the heavens and	**Is 42:5**	
W spread out the earth and its	**Is 42:5**	
W gives breath to the people on	**Is 42:5**	
And spirit to those **w** walk in it,	**Is 42:5**	
And those **w** dwell in darkness from	**Is 42:7**	
You **w** go down to the sea, and all	**Is 42:10**	
islands, and those **w** dwell on them.	**Is 42:10**	
put to shame, **W** trust in idols,	**Is 42:17**	
in idols, **W** say to molten images,	**Is 42:17**	
W is blind but My servant, Or so	**Is 42:19**	4310
W is so blind as he that is at	**Is 42:19**	4310
W among you will give ear to this?	**Is 42:23**	4310
W will give heed and listen	**Is 42:23**	
W gave Jacob up for spoil, and	**Is 42:24**	4310
O Jacob, And He **w** formed you,	**Is 43:1**	
Everyone **w** is called by My name,	**Is 43:7**	
Bring out the people **w** are blind,	**Is 43:8**	5787
W among them can declare this And	**Is 43:9**	4310
"It is I **w** have declared and	**Is 43:12**	
none **w** can deliver out of My hand;	**Is 43:13**	
I act and **w** can reverse it?"	**Is 43:13**	4310
W makes a way through the sea And	**Is 43:16**	
W brings forth the chariot and the	**Is 43:17**	
am the one **w** wipes out your	**Is 43:25**	
Thus says the LORD **w** made you And	**Is 44:2**	
from the womb, **w** will help you,	**Is 44:2**	
'**W** is like Me? Let him proclaim	**Is 44:7**	4310
Those **w** fashion a graven image are	**Is 44:9**	
W has fashioned a god or cast an	**Is 44:10**	4310
one **w** formed you from the womb,	**Is 44:24**	
It is I **w** says of Jerusalem,	**Is 44:26**	
I **w** says to the depth of the sea,	**Is 44:27**	
"*It is I* **w** says of Cyrus,	**Is 44:28**	
Israel, **w** calls you by your name.	**Is 45:3**	
I am the LORD **w** does all these.	**Is 45:7**	
"Woe to *the one* **w** quarrels with	**Is 45:9**	
"Woe to him **w** says to a father,	**Is 45:10**	
"It is I **w** made the earth, and	**Is 45:12**	
You are a God **w** hides Himself,	**Is 45:15**	
the LORD, **w** created the heavens	**Is 45:18**	
w formed the earth and made it,	**Is 45:18**	
W carry about their wooden idol And	**Is 45:20**	
And pray to a god **w** cannot save.	**Is 45:20**	
W has announced this from of old?	**Is 45:21**	4310
W has long since declared it?	**Is 45:21**	
And all **w** were angry at Him will	**Is 45:24**	
You **w** have been borne by Me from	**Is 46:3**	
"Those **w** lavish gold from the	**Is 46:6**	
W are far from righteousness.	**Is 46:12**	
sensual one, **W** dwells securely,	**Is 47:8**	
securely, **W** says in your heart,	**Is 47:8**	
Those **w** prophesy by the stars,	**Is 47:13**	
Those **w** predict by the new moons,	**Is 47:13**	
W have trafficked with you from	**Is 47:15**	
w are named Israel And who came	**Is 48:1**	
who are named Israel And **w** came	**Is 48:1**	

W swear by the name of the LORD	**Is 48:1**	
W among them has declared these	**Is 48:14**	4310
your God, **w** teaches you to profit,	**Is 48:17**	
W leads you in the way you should go.	**Is 48:17**	
w formed Me from the womb to be	**Is 49:5**	
Because of the LORD **w** is faithful,	**Is 49:7**	834
One of Israel **w** has chosen You."	**Is 49:7**	
Saying to those **w** are bound,	**Is 49:9**	
forth,' To those **w** are in darkness,	**Is 49:9**	834
For He **w** has compassion on them	**Is 49:10**	
And those **w** swallowed you will be	**Is 49:19**	
'**W** has begotten these for me,	**Is 49:21**	4310
And **w** has reared these?	**Is 49:21**	4310
Those **w** hopefully wait for Me will	**Is 49:23**	834
with the one **w** contends with you,	**Is 49:25**	3401
gave My back to those **w** strike *Me,*	**Is 50:6**	
to those **w** pluck out the beard;	**Is 50:6**	
He **w** vindicates Me is near;	**Is 50:8**	
W will contend with Me?	**Is 50:8**	4310
W has a case against Me?	**Is 50:8**	4310
W is he who condemns Me?	**Is 50:9**	4310
Who is he **w** condemns Me?	**Is 50:9**	
W is among you that fears the	**Is 50:10**	4310
Behold, all you **w** kindle a fire,	**Is 50:11**	
W encircle yourselves with	**Is 50:11**	
to me, you **w** pursue righteousness,	**Is 51:1**	
righteousness, **W** seek the LORD:	**Is 51:1**	
Sarah **w** gave birth to you in pain;	**Is 51:2**	
to Me, you **w** know righteousness,	**Is 51:7**	
it not You **w** cut Rahab in pieces,	**Is 51:9**	
in pieces, **W** pierced the dragon?	**Is 51:9**	
it not You **w** dried up the sea,	**Is 51:10**	
W made the depths of the sea a	**Is 51:10**	
"I, even I, am He **w** comforts you.	**Is 51:12**	
W are you that you are afraid of	**Is 51:12**	4310
that you are afraid of man **w** dies And	**Is 51:12**	
son of man **w** is made like grass,	**Is 51:12**	
W stretched out the heavens And	**Is 51:13**	
w stirs up the sea and its waves	**Is 51:15**	
You **w** have drunk from the LORD's	**Is 51:17**	834
W will mourn for you?	**Is 51:19**	4310
this, you afflicted, **W** are drunk,	**Is 51:21**	
God **W** contends for His people,	**Is 51:22**	
tormentors, **W** have said to you,	**Is 51:23**	834
street for those **w** walk over *it.*"	**Is 51:23**	
"Those **w** rule over them howl, and	**Is 52:5**	
day I am the one **w** is speaking,	**Is 52:6**	
feet of him **w** brings good news,	**Is 52:7**	
W announces peace And brings good	**Is 52:7**	
happiness, **W** announces salvation,	**Is 52:7**	
w carry the vessels of the LORD.	**Is 52:11**	
W has believed our message?	**Is 53:1**	4310
w considered That He was cut off	**Is 53:8**	4310
one, you **w** have borne no *child;*	**Is 54:1**	
aloud, you **w** have not travailed;	**Is 54:1**	
W is called the God of all the	**Is 54:5**	
the LORD **w** has compassion on you.	**Is 54:10**	
smith **w** blows the fire of coals And	**Is 54:16**	
Every one **w** thirsts, come to the	**Is 55:1**	
And you **w** have no money come, buy	**Is 55:1**	834
blessed is the man **w** does this,	**Is 56:2**	
the son of man **w** takes hold of it;	**Is 56:2**	
W keeps from profaning the	**Is 56:2**	
Let not the foreigner **w** has joined	**Is 56:3**	
"To the eunuchs **w** keep My	**Is 56:4**	834
w join themselves to the LORD,	**Is 56:6**	
every one **w** keeps from profaning	**Is 56:6**	
w gathers the dispersed of Israel,	**Is 56:8**	
lying down, **w** love to slumber;	**Is 56:10**	
shepherds **w** have no understanding;	**Is 56:11**	
one **w** walked in his upright way.	**Is 57:2**	
W inflame yourselves among	**Is 57:5**	
W slaughter the children in the	**Is 57:5**	
But he **w** takes refuge in Me will	**Is 57:13**	
and exalted One **W** lives forever,	**Is 57:15**	
w is far and to him who is near,"	**Is 57:19**	
who is far and to him **w** is near,"	**Is 57:19**	
He **w** eats of their eggs dies, And	**Is 59:5**	
grope like those **w** have no eyes;	**Is 59:10**	
Among those **w** are vigorous *we are*	**Is 59:10**	820
And he **w** turns aside from evil	**Is 59:15**	
And to those **w** turn from	**Is 59:20**	
"**W** are these who fly like a	**Is 60:8**	4310
"Who are these **w** fly like a	**Is 60:8**	
"The sons of those **w** afflicted you	**Is 60:14**	
And all those **w** despised you will	**Is 60:14**	
To comfort all **w** mourn,	**Is 61:2**	
To grant those **w** mourn *in* Zion,	**Is 61:3**	
All **w** see them will recognize them	**Is 61:9**	
You **w** remind the LORD, take no	**Is 62:6**	
But those **w** garner it will eat it and	**Is 62:9**	
And those **w** gather it will drink	**Is 62:9**	
W is this who comes from Edom,	**Is 63:1**	4310
Who is this **w** comes from Edom,	**Is 63:1**	
One **w** is majestic in His apparel,	**Is 63:1**	
"It is I **w** speak in	**Is 63:1**	
one **w** treads in the wine press?	**Is 63:2**	
Sons **w** will not deal falsely."	**Is 63:8**	
Where is He **w** brought them up out	**Is 63:11**	
Where is He **w** put His Holy Spirit	**Is 63:11**	
W caused His glorious arm to go at	**Is 63:12**	
W divided the waters before them	**Is 63:12**	
W led them through the depths?	**Is 63:13**	
w were not called by Your name.	**Is 63:19**	
W acts in behalf of the one who	**Is 64:4**	
behalf of the one **w** waits for Him.	**Is 64:4**	
You meet him **w** rejoices in	**Is 64:5**	
W remembers You in Your ways.	**Is 64:5**	
have become like one **w** is unclean,	**Is 64:6**	
is no one **w** calls on Your name,	**Is 64:7**	
W arouses himself to take hold of	**Is 64:7**	
by those **w** did not ask *for Me;*	**Is 65:1**	
found by those **w** did not seek Me.	**Is 65:1**	
W walk *in* the way which is not	**Is 65:2**	
A people **w** continually provoke Me	**Is 65:3**	
W sit among graves and spend the	**Is 65:4**	
W eat swine's flesh, And the broth	**Is 65:4**	
"**W** say, 'Keep to yourself,	**Is 65:5**	
herds, For My people **w** seek Me.	**Is 65:10**	834
"But you **w** forsake the LORD, Who	**Is 65:11**	
LORD, **W** forget My holy mountain,	**Is 65:11**	7913
W set a table for Fortune,	**Is 65:11**	7913
And **w** fill *cups* with mixed wine	**Is 65:11**	
"Because he **w** is blessed in the	**Is 65:16**	
And he **w** swears in the earth will	**Is 65:16**	
will there be in it an infant **w**	**Is 65:20**	
man **w** does not live out his days;	**Is 65:20**	834
the one **w** does not reach the age of	**Is 65:20**	
To him **w** is humble and contrite of	**Is 66:2**	6041
spirit, and **w** trembles at My word.	**Is 66:2**	2730a
"*But* he **w** kills an ox is *like* one	**Is 66:3**	
an ox is *like* one **w** slays a man;	**Is 66:3**	
He **w** sacrifices a lamb is *like* the	**Is 66:3**	
like the one **w** breaks a dog's neck;	**Is 66:3**	
He **w** offers a grain offering *is*	**Is 66:3**	
a grain offering *is like one* **w**	**Is 66:3**	
He **w** burns incense is *like* the one	**Is 66:3**	
is *like* the one **w** blesses an idol.	**Is 66:3**	
LORD, you **w** tremble at His word:	**Is 66:5**	2730a
"Your brothers **w** hate you, who	**Is 66:5**	
w exclude you for My name's sake,	**Is 66:5**	
The voice of the LORD **w** is	**Is 66:6**	
"**W** has heard such a thing?	**Is 66:8**	4310
W has seen such things?	**Is 66:8**	4310
I **w** gives delivery shut *the womb?*"	**Is 66:9**	
for her, all you **w** love her;	**Is 66:10**	
her, all you **w** mourn over her,	**Is 66:10**	
"Those **w** sanctify and purify	**Is 66:17**	
in the center, **W** eat swine's flesh,	**Is 66:17**	
W have transgressed against Me.	**Is 66:24**	
of the priests **w** were in Anathoth	**Jer 1:1**	834
All **w** ate of it became guilty;	**Jer 2:3**	
'Where is the LORD **W** brought us up	**Jer 2:6**	
W led us through the wilderness,	**Jer 2:6**	
And those **w** handle the law did not	**Jer 2:8**	
of her heat **w** can turn her away?	**Jer 2:24**	4310
All **w** seek her will not become	**Jer 2:24**	
W say to a tree,	**Jer 2:27**	
w will feed you on knowledge and	**Jer 3:15**	
If there is one **w** does justice,	**Jer 5:1**	
who does justice, **w** seeks truth,	**Jer 5:1**	
Everyone **w** goes out of them will	**Jer 5:6**	
And sworn by those **w** are not gods.	**Jer 5:7**	
and senseless people, **W** have eyes but	**Jer 5:21**	
W have ears but do not hear.	**Jer 5:21**	
God, **W** gives rain in its season,	**Jer 5:24**	
W keeps for us The appointed weeks	**Jer 5:24**	
shall fall among those **w** fall;	**Jer 6:15**	
w enter by these gates to worship	**Jer 7:2**	
shall fall among those **w** fall;	**Jer 8:12**	
W is the wise man that may	**Jer 9:12**	4310
And **w** *is* he to whom the mouth of	**Jer 9:12**	
let him **w** boasts boast of this,	**Jer 9:24**	
LORD **w** exercises lovingkindness,	**Jer 9:24**	
"that I will punish all **w** are	**Jer 9:25**	
w clip the hair on their temples	**Jer 9:26**	
W would not fear You, O King of	**Jer 10:7**	4310
He **w** made the earth by His power,	**Jer 10:12**	
W established the world by His	**Jer 10:12**	
ground, You **w** dwell under siege!	**Jer 10:17**	
a man **w** walks to direct his steps.	**Jer 10:23**	
"Cursed is the man **w** does not	**Jer 11:3**	834
w refused to hear My words,	**Jer 11:10**	834
The LORD of hosts, **w** planted you,	**Jer 11:17**	
of hosts, **w** judges righteously,	**Jer 11:20**	
W tries the feelings and the heart,	**Jer 11:20**	
men of Anathoth, **w** seek your life,	**Jer 11:21**	
those **w** deal in treachery at ease?	**Jer 12:1**	
wickedness of those **w** dwell in it,	**Jer 12:4**	
all My wicked neighbors **w** strike at	**Jer 12:14**	
w refuse to listen to My words,	**Jer 13:10**	3987
w walk in the stubbornness of	**Jer 13:10**	
good **W** are accustomed to doing evil.	**Jer 13:23**	
like a traveler **w** has pitched his *tent*	**Jer 14:8**	
Like a mighty man **w** cannot save?	**Jer 14:9**	
w are prophesying in My name,	**Jer 14:15**	
although it was not I **w** sent	**Jer 14:15**	
idols of the nations **w** give rain?	**Jer 14:22**	
one **w** has done all these things.	**Jer 14:22**	
"Indeed, **w** will have pity on you,	**Jer 15:5**	4310
Or **w** will mourn for you,	**Jer 15:5**	4310
Or **w** will turn aside to ask about	**Jer 15:5**	4310
"You **w** have forsaken Me,"	**Jer 15:6**	
"She **w** bore seven *sons* pines away;	**Jer 15:9**	
You **w** know, O LORD, Remember	**Jer 15:15**	
their mothers **w** bear them,	**Jer 16:3**	
fathers **w** beget them in this land:	**Jer 16:3**	
w brought up the sons of Israel	**Jer 16:14**	834
w brought up the sons of Israel	**Jer 16:15**	834
"Cursed is the man **w** trusts in	**Jer 17:5**	834
"Blessed is the man **w** trusts in	**Jer 17:7**	834
W can understand it?	**Jer 17:9**	4310
laid, *So* is he **w** makes a fortune,	**Jer 17:11**	
All **w** forsake You will be put to	**Jer 17:13**	
Those **w** turn away on earth will be	**Jer 17:13**	
w persecute me be put to shame,	**Jer 17:18**	
w come in through these gates:	**Jer 17:20**	
W ever heard the like of this?	**Jer 18:13**	4310
Everyone **w** passes by it will be	**Jer 18:16**	
hand of those **w** seek their life;	**Jer 19:7**	
everyone **w** passes by it will be	**Jer 19:8**	
enemies and those **w** seek their life	**Jer 19:9**	
sight of the men **w** accompany you	**Jer 19:10**	
w was chief officer in the house	**Jer 20:1**	1931
and all **w** live in your house will	**Jer 20:6**	
You **w** test the righteous,	**Jer 20:12**	
W see the mind and the heart;	**Jer 20:12**	
w brought the news To my father,	**Jer 20:15**	834
the Chaldeans **w** are besieging you	**Jer 21:4**	
even those **w** survive in this city	**Jer 21:7**	
hand of those **w** seek their lives;	**Jer 21:7**	
"He **w** dwells in this city will	**Jer 21:9**	
but he **w** goes out and falls away	**Jer 21:9**	
w are besieging you will live,	**Jer 21:9**	
And deliver the *person* **w** has been	**Jer 21:12**	
"You men **w** say,	**Jer 21:13**	
'**W** will come down against us?	**Jer 21:13**	4310
Or **w** will enter into our	**Jer 21:13**	4310
of Judah, **w** sits on David's throne,	**Jer 22:2**	
your people **w** enter these gates.	**Jer 22:2**	
and deliver the one **w** has been	**Jer 22:3**	
for the one **w** goes away;	**Jer 22:10**	
w became king in the place of	**Jer 22:11**	
w went forth from this place,	**Jer 22:11**	834
"Woe to him **w** builds his house	**Jer 22:13**	
W uses his neighbor's services	**Jer 22:13**	
W says, 'I will build myself a roomy	**Jer 22:14**	
"You **w** dwell in Lebanon, Nested	**Jer 22:23**	
of those **w** are seeking your life,	**Jer 22:25**	
hurl you and your mother **w** bore you	**Jer 22:26**	834
w will not prosper in his days;	**Jer 22:30**	
"Woe to the shepherds **w** are	**Jer 23:1**	
shepherds **w** are tending My people:	**Jer 23:2**	
w brought up the sons of Israel	**Jer 23:7**	834
w brought up and led back the	**Jer 23:8**	834
prophets **w** are prophesying to you.	**Jer 23:16**	
keep saying to those **w** despise Me,	**Jer 23:17**	
And as for everyone **w** walks in the	**Jer 23:17**	
"But **w** has stood in the council	**Jer 23:18**	4310
W has given heed to His word and	**Jer 23:18**	4310
"Am I a God **w** is near,"	**Jer 23:23**	
w prophesy falsely in My name,	**Jer 23:25**	
the prophets **w** prophesy falsehood,	**Jer 23:26**	
w intend to make My people forget	**Jer 23:27**	
"The prophet **w** has a dream may	**Jer 23:28**	834
but let him **w** has My word speak My	**Jer 23:28**	834
"**w** steal My words from each other.	**Jer 23:30**	
"**w** use their tongues and declare,	**Jer 23:31**	
w have prophesied false dreams,"	**Jer 23:32**	
or the priest or the people **w** say,	**Jer 23:34**	834
Jerusalem **w** remain in this land and	**Jer 24:8**	
ones **w** dwell in the land of Egypt.	**Jer 24:8**	
w cut the corners *of their hair;*	**Jer 25:23**	
people **w** dwell in the desert;	**Jer 25:24**	
like those **w** tread *the grapes,*	**Jer 25:30**	
w have come to worship *in* the	**Jer 26:2**	
there was also a man **w** prophesied	**Jer 26:20**	
w slew him with a sword and	**Jer 26:23**	
the messengers **w** come to Jerusalem	**Jer 27:3**	
the one **w** is pleasing in My sight.	**Jer 27:5**	834
or your sorcerers **w** speak to you,	**Jer 27:9**	834
of the prophets **w** speak to you,	**Jer 27:14**	
the prophets **w** prophesy to you."	**Jer 27:15**	
your prophets **w** prophesy to you,	**Jer 27:16**	
the prophet, **w** was from Gibeon,	**Jer 28:1**	834
exiles of Judah **w** went to Babylon,'	**Jer 28:4**	
people **w** were standing in the house	**Jer 28:5**	
"The prophets **w** were before me	**Jer 28:8**	834
"The prophet **w** prophesies of	**Jer 28:9**	834
'Do not let your prophets **w** are in	**Jer 29:8**	834
w sits on the throne of David,	**Jer 29:16**	
the people **w** dwell in this city,	**Jer 29:16**	
your brothers **w** did not go with	**Jer 29:16**	834
w are prophesying to you falsely	**Jer 29:21**	
from Judah **w** are in Babylon,	**Jer 29:22**	834
and I am He **w** knows and am a	**Jer 29:23**	
all the people **w** are in Jerusalem,	**Jer 29:25**	834
over every madman **w** prophesies,	**Jer 29:26**	
of Anathoth **w** prophesies to you?	**Jer 29:27**	
all **w** devour you will be devoured;	**Jer 30:16**	
And those **w** plunder you will be	**Jer 30:16**	
And all **w** prey upon you I will	**Jer 30:16**	
the voice of those **w** celebrate;	**Jer 30:19**	
For **w** would dare to risk his life	**Jer 30:21**	4310
"The people **w** survived the sword	**Jer 31:2**	8300
and she **w** is in labor with child,	**Jer 31:8**	
"He **w** scattered Israel will	**Jer 31:10**	
of him **w** was stronger than he.	**Jer 31:11**	2389
and they **w** go about with flocks.	**Jer 31:24**	
refresh everyone **w** languishes."	**Jer 31:25**	
each man **w** eats the sour grapes,	**Jer 31:30**	
W gives the sun for light by day And	**Jer 31:35**	
W stirs up the sea so that its	**Jer 31:35**	
w signed the deed of purchase,	**Jer 32:12**	
before all the Jews **w** were sitting	**Jer 32:12**	
w shows lovingkindness to	**Jer 32:18**	
w has set signs and wonders in	**Jer 32:20**	834
the Chaldeans **w** fight against it,	**Jer 32:24**	
"The Chaldeans **w** are fighting	**Jer 32:29**	
says the LORD **w** made *the earth,*	**Jer 33:2**	
LORD **w** formed it to establish it,	**Jer 33:2**	
bride, the voice of those **w** say,	**Jer 33:11**	
and of those **w** bring a thank offering	**Jer 33:11**	
of shepherds **w** rest their flocks.	**Jer 33:12**	
hands of the one **w** numbers them,'	**Jer 33:13**	
the Levites **w** minister to Me.' "	**Jer 33:22**	
former kings **w** were before you,	**Jer 34:5**	834

all the people w were in Jerusalem	Jer 34:8	834
w had entered into the covenant	Jer 34:10	834
w has been sold to you and has	Jer 34:14	834
w have transgressed My covenant,	Jer 34:18	
w have not fulfilled the words of	Jer 34:18	834
w passed between the parts of the	Jer 34:19	
hand of those w seek their life.	Jer 34:20	
hand of those w seek their life,	Jer 34:21	
of Judah w come from their cities.	Jer 36:6	
all the people w came from the cities	Jer 36:9	
officials w stood beside the king.	Jer 36:21	
the king and all his servants w heard	Jer 36:24	
and when the Chaldeans w had been	Jer 37:5	
w sent you to Me to inquire of Me:	Jer 37:7	
w were fighting against you,	Jer 37:10	
your prophets w prophesied to you,	Jer 37:19	834
'He w stays in this city will die	Jer 38:2	
but he w goes out to the Chaldeans	Jer 38:2	
the men of war w are left in this city	Jer 38:4	
lives, w made this life for us,	Jer 38:16	834
men w are seeking your life."	Jer 38:16	834
"I dread the Jews w have gone	Jer 38:19	834
all of the women w have been left	Jer 38:22	834
people w were left in the city,	Jer 39:9	
the deserters w had gone over to	Jer 39:9	834
the rest of the people w remained,	Jer 39:9	
the poorest people w had nothing,	Jer 39:10	834
w were being exiled to Babylon.	Jer 40:1	
people w were left in the land.	Jer 40:6	
w had not been exiled to Babylon.	Jer 40:7	834
before the Chaldeans w come to us;	Jer 40:10	834
Likewise, also all the Jews w were	Jer 40:11	834
and w were in all the *other*	Jer 40:11	834
so that all the Jews w are	Jer 40:15	
the ten men w were with him	Jer 41:2	834
down all the Jews w were with him,	Jer 41:3	834
the Chaldeans w were found there,	Jer 41:3	834
But ten men w were found among	Jer 41:8	
of the people w were in Mizpah,	Jer 41:10	834
the people w were left in Mizpah,	Jer 41:10	
as soon as all the people w were	Jer 41:13	834
that is, the men w were soldiers,	Jer 41:16	
"So all the men w set their mind	Jer 42:17	834
w sent me to the LORD your God,	Jer 42:20	
remnant of Judah w had returned	Jer 43:5	834
those w are *meant* for death *will*	Jer 43:11	834
those w were living in Migdol,	Jer 44:1	
remnant of Judah w have set their	Jer 44:12	834
those w live in the land of Egypt,	Jer 44:13	
the remnant of Judah w have entered	Jer 44:14	
Then all the men w were aware that	Jer 44:15	
all the women w were standing by,	Jer 44:15	
including all the people w were	Jer 44:15	
even to all the people w were giving	Jer 44:20	
Judah w are in the land of Egypt,	Jer 44:24	834
all Judah w are living in the land	Jer 44:26	
and all the men of Judah w are in	Jer 44:27	834
'Those w escape the sword will	Jer 44:28	6412a
Then all the remnant of Judah w	Jer 44:28	
the hand of those w seek his life,	Jer 44:30	
w *was* his enemy and was seeking	Jer 44:30	
W is this that rises like the	Jer 46:7	4310
"Surely one shall come w *looms up*	Jer 46:18	
Pharaoh and those w trust in him.	Jer 46:25	
those w are seeking their lives,	Jer 46:26	
The city and those w live in it;	Jer 47:2	
"Cursed be the one w does the	Jer 48:10	
And cursed be the one w restrains	Jer 48:10	
send to him those w tip *vessels,*	Jer 48:12	
him, all you w *live* around him,	Jer 48:17	
Even all of you w know his name;	Jer 48:17	
Ask him w flees and her who	Jer 48:19	
flees and her w escapes *And* say,	Jer 48:19	
"the one w offers *sacrifice* on	Jer 48:35	
one w burns incense to his gods.	Jer 48:35	
"The one w flees from the terror	Jer 48:44	
And the one w climbs up out of the	Jer 48:44	
W trusts in her treasures,	Jer 49:4	
'W will come against me?'	Jer 49:4	4310
those w were not sentenced to	Jer 49:12	834
w will be completely acquitted?	Jer 49:12	
O you w live in the clefts of the	Jer 49:16	
W occupy the height of the hill.	Jer 49:16	
everyone w passes by it will be	Jer 49:17	
For w is like Me, and who will	Jer 49:19	4310
and w will summon Me *into court?*	Jer 49:19	4310
And w then is the shepherd who can	Jer 49:19	4310
shepherd w can stand against Me?"	Jer 49:19	834
w cut the corners *of their hair;*	Jer 49:32	
before those w seek their lives;	Jer 49:37	
"All w came upon them have	Jer 50:7	
have sinned against the LORD w	Jer 50:7	
W does not return empty-handed.	Jer 50:9	
w plunder her will have enough,"	Jer 50:10	
O you w pillage My heritage,	Jer 50:11	
She w gave you birth will be	Jer 50:12	
Everyone w passes by Babylon will	Jer 50:13	
side, All you w bend the bow;	Jer 50:14	
And the one w wields the sickle at	Jer 50:16	
The first one w devoured him was	Jer 50:17	
and this last one w has broken	Jer 50:17	
Babylon, All those w bend the bow:	Jer 50:29	
And all w took them captive have	Jer 50:33	
w are in the midst of her,	Jer 50:37	834
For w is like Me, and who will	Jer 50:44	4310
and w will summon Me *into court?*	Jer 50:44	4310
And w then is the shepherd who can	Jer 50:44	4310
shepherd w can stand before Me?"	Jer 50:44	834
not him w bends his bow bend *it,*	Jer 51:3	
O you w dwell by many waters,	Jer 51:13	
He w made the earth by His power,	Jer 51:15	
W established the world by His	Jer 51:15	
W destroys the whole earth,"	Jer 51:25	
You w have escaped the sword,	Jer 51:50	6412b
w was in the service of the king	Jer 52:12	
all the army of the Chaldeans w *were*	Jer 52:14	834
people w were left in the city,	Jer 52:15	
the deserters w had deserted to	Jer 52:15	834
one official w was overseer of the men	Jer 52:25	834
advisers w were found in the city,	Jer 52:25	834
commander of the army w mustered	Jer 52:25	
w were found in the midst of the city.	Jer 52:25	834
kings w *were* with him in Babylon.	Jer 52:32	834
like a widow W was *once* great	La 1:1	7227a
She w was a princess among the	La 1:1	
All w honored her despise her	La 1:8	
to all you w pass this way?	La 1:12	
comforter, One w restores my soul.	La 1:16	
W can heal you?	La 2:13	4310
All w pass along the way Clap	La 2:15	
ones W are faint because of hunger	La 2:19	
little ones w were born healthy?	La 2:20	2949
And there was no one w escaped or	La 2:22	6412a
I am the man w has seen affliction	La 3:1	
Like those w have long been dead.	La 3:6	
is good to those w wait for Him,	La 3:25	
Him, To the person w seeks Him.	La 3:25	
W is there who speaks and it comes	La 3:37	4310
w speaks and it comes to pass,	La 3:37	
Those w ate delicacies Are	La 4:5	
W have shed in her midst The blood	La 4:13	
Edom, W dwells in the land of Uz;	La 4:21	
we w have borne their iniquities.	La 5:7	
people w have rebelled against Me;	Ezk 2:3	834
them w are stubborn and obstinate	Ezk 2:4	
to them w should listen to you;	Ezk 3:6	
Then I came to the exiles w lived	Ezk 3:15	
cannot be a man w rebukes them,	Ezk 3:26	
He w hears, let him hear;	Ezk 3:27	
and he w refuses, let him refuse;	Ezk 3:27	
in the sight of all w pass by.	Ezk 5:14	
to the nations w surround you when	Ezk 5:15	834
for you will have those w escaped	Ezk 6:8	6412a
"Then those of you w escape will	Ezk 6:9	6412a
"He w is far off will die by the	Ezk 6:12	7350
and he w is near will fall by the	Ezk 6:12	7138
and he w remains and is besieged	Ezk 6:12	
He w is in the field will die by	Ezk 7:15	834
men w sigh and groan over all the	Ezk 9:4	
elders w *were* before the temple.	Ezk 9:6	834
in linen, w took *it* and went out.	Ezk 10:7	
these are the men w devise	Ezk 11:2	
w say, *'The time* is not near to build	Ezk 11:3	
w have eyes to see but do not see,	Ezk 12:2	834
house of Israel w are in it."	Ezk 12:10	834
"The prince w is among them	Ezk 12:12	834
every wind all w are around him,	Ezk 12:14	834
the violence of all w live in it.	Ezk 12:19	
the prophets of Israel w prophesy,	Ezk 13:2	
and say to those w prophesy from	Ezk 13:2	
"Woe to the foolish prophets w	Ezk 13:3	834
and lying divination w are saying,	Ezk 13:6	
it is not I w have spoken?	Ezk 13:7	
against the prophets w see false visions	Ezk 13:9	
so tell those w plaster *it* over	Ezk 13:11	
and on those w have plastered it over	Ezk 13:15	
of Israel w prophesy to Jerusalem,	Ezk 13:16	
and w see visions of peace for her	Ezk 13:16	
w are prophesying from their own	Ezk 13:17	
w sew *magic* bands on all wrists and	Ezk 13:18	
to put to death some w should not die	Ezk 13:19	834
others alive w should not live,	Ezk 13:19	834
My people w listen to lies.	Ezk 13:19	
"Any man of the house of Israel w	Ezk 14:4	834
the hearts of the house of Israel w are	Ezk 14:5	834
or of the immigrants w stay in Israel	Ezk 14:7	834
w separates himself from Me,	Ezk 14:7	
w have prevailed upon that	Ezk 14:9	
left in it w will be brought out,	Ezk 14:22	
every passer-by w might be *willing.*	Ezk 16:15	
to the desire of those w hate you,	Ezk 16:27	
w are ashamed of your lewd conduct.	Ezk 16:27	
w takes strangers instead of her	Ezk 16:32	
like women w commit adultery or	Ezk 16:38	
everyone w quotes proverbs will	Ezk 16:44	
w loathed her husband and children.	Ezk 16:45	
w loathed their husbands and	Ezk 16:45	834
w lives north of you with her	Ezk 16:46	
sister, w lives south of you,	Ezk 16:46	
Edom and of all w are around her,	Ezk 16:57	
surrounding *you* w despise you.	Ezk 16:57	
you w have despised the oath by	Ezk 16:59	834
Will he w does such things escape?	Ezk 17:15	
the king w put him on the throne,	Ezk 17:16	
The soul w sins will die.	Ezk 18:4	
have a violent son w sheds blood and	Ezk 18:10	
and w does any of these things to	Ezk 18:10	
he has a son w has observed all	Ezk 18:14	
"The person w sins will die.	Ezk 18:20	
in the death of anyone w dies,"	Ezk 18:32	
I am the LORD w sanctifies them.	Ezk 20:12	
and those w transgress against Me;	Ezk 20:38	
necks of the wicked w are slain,	Ezk 21:29	2491a
"Those w are near and those who	Ezk 22:5	7138
those w are far from you will mock	Ezk 22:5	7350
in you they have humbled her w was	Ezk 22:10	2931
I searched for a man among them w	Ezk 22:30	
w were clothed in purple,	Ezk 23:6	
sent for men w come from afar,	Ezk 23:40	
her w was worn out by adulteries,	Ezk 23:43	
judgment of women w shed blood,	Ezk 23:45	
that on that day he w escapes will	Ezk 24:26	6412a
will be opened to him w escaped,	Ezk 24:27	6412a
'Also her daughters w are on the	Ezk 26:6	834
W imposed her terror On all her	Ezk 26:17	834
with those w go down to the pit,	Ezk 26:20	
with those w go down to the pit,	Ezk 26:20	
w dwells at the entrance to the	Ezk 27:3	
all your men of war w are in you,	Ezk 27:27	834
"All w handle the oar, The	Ezk 27:29	
'W is like Tyre, Like her who is	Ezk 27:32	4310
Like her w is silent in the midst	Ezk 27:32	1822
will die the death of those w are slain	Ezk 28:8	
In the hands of those w wound you?	Ezk 28:9	
were the anointed cherub w covers,	Ezk 28:14	
In the eyes of all w see you.	Ezk 28:18	
"All w know you among the peoples	Ezk 28:19	
round about them w scorned them;	Ezk 28:24	
all w scorn them round about them.	Ezk 28:26	
those w support Egypt will fall And	Ezk 30:6	
with those w go down to the pit."	Ezk 31:14	
with those w go down to the pit;	Ezk 31:16	
those w were slain by the sword;	Ezk 31:17	
and those w were its strength	Ezk 31:17	
those w were slain by the sword.	Ezk 31:18	
I smite all those w live in it,	Ezk 32:15	
with those w go down to the pit;	Ezk 32:18	
of those w are slain by the sword.	Ezk 32:20	
w spread terror in the land of the	Ezk 32:23	834
w went down uncircumcised to the	Ezk 32:24	834
w instilled their terror in the	Ezk 32:24	834
with those w went down to the pit.	Ezk 32:24	
with those w go down to the pit;	Ezk 32:25	
w went down to Sheol with their	Ezk 32:27	834
w for *all* their might are laid	Ezk 32:29	834
with those w go down to the pit.	Ezk 32:29	
w in spite of the terror resulting	Ezk 32:30	834
with those w go down to the pit.	Ezk 32:30	
then he w hears the sound of the	Ezk 33:4	
they w live in these waste places	Ezk 33:24	
so to us w are many the land has	Ezk 33:24	7227a
surely those w are in the waste	Ezk 33:27	834
and those w are in the strongholds	Ezk 33:27	834
your fellow citizens w talk about	Ezk 33:30	
song by one w has a beautiful voice	Ezk 33:32	
w have been feeding themselves!	Ezk 34:2	834
"Those w are sickly you have not	Ezk 34:4	
the hand of those w enslaved them.	Ezk 34:27	
one w passes through and returns.	Ezk 35:7	
w appropriated My land for	Ezk 36:5	834
the sight of everyone w passes by.	Ezk 36:34	
I am the LORD w sanctifies Israel,	Ezk 37:28	
go against those w are at rest,	Ezk 38:11	
w are gathered from the nations,	Ezk 38:12	
w have acquired cattle and goods,	Ezk 38:12	
w live at the center of the world.'	Ezk 38:12	
w prophesied in those days for	Ezk 38:17	
and all the men w are on the face	Ezk 38:20	834
the many peoples w are with him,	Ezk 38:22	834
and the peoples w are with you;	Ezk 39:4	834
for it is I w have spoken,"	Ezk 39:5	
and those w inhabit the coastlands	Ezk 39:6	
"Then those w inhabit the cities	Ezk 39:9	
spoil of those w despoiled them and	Ezk 39:10	
of those w plundered them,"	Ezk 39:10	
those w pass by east of the sea,	Ezk 39:11	
and it will block off those w would	Ezk 39:11	
"They will set apart men w	Ezk 39:14	
those w were passing through,	Ezk 39:14	
"As those w pass through the	Ezk 39:15	
w keep charge of the temple;	Ezk 40:45	
w keep charge of the altar.	Ezk 40:46	
w from the sons of Levi come near	Ezk 40:46	
the priests w are near to the LORD	Ezk 42:13	834
Levitical priests w are from the	Ezk 43:19	834
w draw near to Me to minister to	Ezk 43:19	
w are among the sons of Israel,	Ezk 44:9	834
the Levites w went far from Me when	Ezk 44:10	834
w went astray from Me after their	Ezk 44:10	834
w kept charge of My sanctuary when	Ezk 44:15	834
widow w is the widow of a priest.	Ezk 44:22	834
a sister w has not had a husband,	Ezk 44:25	834
w come near to minister to the	Ezk 45:4	
w goes astray or is naive;	Ezk 45:20	
he w enters by way of the north	Ezk 46:9	
And he w enters by way of the	Ezk 46:9	
the aliens w stay in your midst,	Ezk 47:22	
w bring forth sons in your midst.	Ezk 47:22	834
"It shall be for the priests w	Ezk 48:11	
of Zadok, w have kept My charge,	Ezk 48:11	834
w did not go astray when the sons	Ezk 48:11	834
was no defect, w were good-looking,	Da 1:4	
and w had ability for serving in	Da 1:4	834
w has appointed your food and your	Da 1:10	834
the youths w are your own age?	Da 1:10	834
youths w are eating the king's choice	Da 1:13	834
they were fatter than all the youths w	Da 1:15	834
conjurers w *were* in all his realm.	Da 1:20	834
"There is not a man on earth w	Da 2:10	1768
and there is no one else w could	Da 2:11	1768
w had gone forth to slay the wise	Da 2:14	1768
"It is He w changes the times	Da 2:21	
"It is He w reveals the profound	Da 2:22	
w can make the interpretation known	Da 2:25	1768
God in heaven w reveals mysteries,	Da 2:28	1768
and He w reveals mysteries has	Da 2:29	
man w hears the sound of the horn,	Da 3:10	1768

and what god is there **w** can	**Da 3:15**	1768
valiant warriors **w** *were* in his army	**Da 3:20**	1768
those men **w** carried up Shadrach,	**Da 3:22**	1768
w has sent His angel and delivered	**Da 3:28**	1768
servants **w** put their trust in Him,	**Da 3:28**	1768
is no other god **w** is able to deliver	**Da 3:29**	1768
dream applied to those **w** hate you and	**Da 4:19**	
and honored Him **w** lives forever;	**Da 4:34**	2417
to humble those **w** walk in pride."	**Da 4:37**	1768
"Any man **w** can read this	**Da 5:7**	1768
"Are you that Daniel **w** is one of	**Da 5:13**	1768
anyone **w** makes a petition to any god	**Da 6:7**	1768
that any man **w** makes a petition to	**Da 6:12**	1768
w is one of the exiles from Judah,	**Da 6:13**	1768
and they brought those men **w** had	**Da 6:24**	1768
w were living in all the land:	**Da 6:25**	1768
W has *also* delivered Daniel from	**Da 6:27**	1768
"I approached one of those **w** were	**Da 7:16**	
are four kings **w** will arise	**Da 7:17**	
particular one **w** was speaking,	**Da 8:13**	
me was one **w** looked like a man.	**Da 8:15**	4758
w was made king over the kingdom	**Da 9:1**	834
w keeps His covenant and	**Da 9:4**	
for those **w** love Him and keep His	**Da 9:4**	
w spoke in Your name to our kings,	**Da 9:6**	834
those **w** are nearby and those who	**Da 9:7**	
those who are nearby and those **w**	**Da 9:7**	
and against our rulers **w** ruled us,	**Da 9:12**	834
w have brought Your people out of	**Da 9:15**	834
and the people of the prince **w** is	**Da 9:26**	
will come one **w** makes desolate,	**Da 9:27**	
out on the one **w** makes desolate."	**Da 9:27**	
Daniel, **w** was named Belteshazzar;	**Da 10:1**	834
while the men **w** were with me did	**Da 10:7**	834
one **w** resembled a human being was	**Da 10:16**	1823
to him **w** was standing before me,	**Da 10:16**	
Yet there is no one **w** stands	**Da 10:21**	
along with *one* of his princes **w**	**Da 11:5**	
along with those **w** brought her in and	**Da 11:6**	
her in and the one **w** sired her	**Da 11:6**	
he **w** supported her in *those* times.	**Da 11:6**	
"But he **w** comes against him will	**Da 11:16**	
one will arise **w** will send an oppressor	**Da 11:20**	
"Those **w** eat his choice food	**Da 11:26**	
those **w** forsake the holy covenant.	**Da 11:30**	
he will turn to godlessness those **w** act	**Da 11:32**	
but the people **w** know their God	**Da 11:32**	
"Those **w** have insight among	**Da 11:33**	
of those **w** have insight will fall,	**Da 11:35**	
honor to those **w** acknowledge *him*	**Da 11:39**	834
the great prince **w** stands *guard*	**Da 12:1**	
w is found written in the book,	**Da 12:1**	
"Many of those **w** sleep in the	**Da 12:2**	3463
"Those **w** have insight will	**Da 12:3**	
and those **w** lead the many to	**Da 12:3**	
w was above the waters of the	**Da 12:6**	834
w was above the waters of the	**Da 12:7**	834
and swore by Him **w** lives forever	**Da 12:7**	2416a
w have insight will understand.	**Da 12:10**	
"How blessed is he **w** keeps	**Da 12:12**	
She **w** conceived them has acted	**Hos 2:5**	
W give *me* my bread and my water,	**Hos 2:5**	
it was I **w** gave her the grain,	**Hos 2:8**	
her **w** had not obtained compassion,	**Hos 2:23**	
say to those **w** were not My people,	**Hos 2:23**	
love a woman **w** is loved by *her*	**Hos 3:1**	
And everyone **w** lives in it	**Hos 4:3**	
those **w** contend with the priest.	**Hos 4:4**	
like those **w** move a boundary;	**Hos 5:10**	
W ceases to stir up *the fire* From	**Hos 7:4**	
All **w** eat of it will be defiled,	**Hos 9:4**	
it is I **w** taught Ephraim to walk,	**Hos 11:3**	
And I became to them as one **w**	**Hos 11:4**	
the Holy One **w** is faithful.	**Hos 11:12**	
men **w** sacrifice kiss the calves!"	**Hos 13:2**	
Those **w** live in his shadow Will	**Hos 14:7**	
is I **w** answer and look after you.	**Hos 14:8**	
is he **w** carries out His word.	**Jl 2:11**	
very awesome, And **w** can endure it?	**Jl 2:11**	
W knows whether He will *not* turn	**Jl 2:14**	4310
W has dealt wondrously with you;	**Jl 2:26**	834
There will be those **w** escape,	**Jl 2:32**	
w was among the sheepherders from	**Am 1:1**	834
Aven, And him **w** holds the scepter,	**Am 1:5**	
And him **w** holds the scepter,	**Am 1:8**	
"These **w** pant after the *very* dust	**Am 2:7**	
wine of those **w** have been fined.	**Am 2:8**	
"Yet it was I **w** destroyed the	**Am 2:9**	
"It was I **w** brought you up	**Am 2:10**	
"He **w** grasps the bow will not	**Am 2:15**	
w rides the horse save his life.	**Am 2:15**	
A lion has roared! **W** will not fear?	**Am 3:8**	4310
W can but prophesy?	**Am 3:8**	4310
"these **w** hoard up violence and	**Am 3:10**	
you cows of Bashan **w** are on the	**Am 4:1**	834
of Samaria, **W** oppress the poor,	**Am 4:1**	
the poor, **w** crush the needy,	**Am 4:1**	
the needy, **W** say to your husbands,	**Am 4:1**	
He **w** forms mountains and creates	**Am 4:13**	
He **w** makes dawn into darkness And	**Am 4:13**	
For those **w** turn justice into	**Am 5:7**	
He **w** made the Pleiades and Orion	**Am 5:8**	
W also darkens day *into* night,	**Am 5:8**	
W calls for the waters of the sea	**Am 5:8**	
It is He **w** flashes forth *with*	**Am 5:9**	
hate him **w** reproves in the gate,	**Am 5:10**	
abhor him **w** speaks *with* integrity.	**Am 5:10**	
You **w** distress the righteous *and*	**Am 5:12**	
you **w** are longing for the day of	**Am 5:18**	
to those **w** are at ease in Zion And	**Am 6:1**	
And to those **w** *feel* secure in the	**Am 6:1**	
Those **w** recline on beds of ivory	**Am 6:4**	
W improvise to the sound of the	**Am 6:5**	
W drink wine from sacrificial	**Am 6:6**	
and he will say to the one **w** is in	**Am 6:10**	834
You **w** rejoice in Lodebar, And	**Am 6:13**	
this, you **w** trample the needy,	**Am 8:4**	
And everyone **w** dwells in it mourn?	**Am 8:8**	
w swear by the guilt of Samaria,	**Am 8:14**	
by the guilt of Samaria, **W** say,	**Am 8:14**	
not have a fugitive **w** will flee,	**Am 9:1**	
flee, Or a refugee **w** will escape.	**Am 9:1**	
The One **w** touches the land so that	**Am 9:5**	
And all those **w** dwell in it mourn,	**Am 9:5**	
The One **w** builds His upper	**Am 9:6**	
He **w** calls for the waters of the	**Am 9:6**	
die by the sword, Those **w** say,	**Am 9:10**	
nations **w** are called by My name,"	**Am 9:12**	834
Declares the LORD **w** does this.	**Am 9:12**	
treader of grapes him **w** sows seed;	**Am 9:13**	
You **w** live in the clefts of the	**Ob 1:3**	
place, **W** say in your heart,	**Ob 1:3**	
'**W** will bring me down to earth?'	**Ob 1:3**	4310
They **w** *eat* your bread Will set an	**Ob 1:7**	
Zion there will be those **w** escape,	**Ob 1:17**	6413
W are *among* the Canaanites as far	**Ob 1:20**	834
And the exiles of Jerusalem **w** are	**Ob 1:20**	834
w made the sea and the dry land."	**Jon 1:9**	834
"Those **w** regard vain idols	**Jon 2:8**	
"**W** knows, God may turn and	**Jon 3:9**	4310
one **w** relents concerning calamity.	**Jon 4:2**	
persons **w** do not know *the difference*	**Jon 4:11**	834
on you The one **w** takes possession,	**Mi 1:15**	
Woe to those **w** scheme iniquity,	**Mi 2:1**	
W work out evil on their beds!	**Mi 2:1**	
"You **w** hate good and love evil,	**Mi 3:2**	
W tear off their skin from them	**Mi 3:2**	
W eat the flesh of my people, Strip	**Mi 3:3**	834
prophets **W** lead my people astray;	**Mi 3:5**	
W puts nothing in their mouths They	**Mi 3:5**	834
W abhor justice And twist	**Mi 3:9**	
W build Zion with bloodshed And	**Mi 3:10**	
been assembled against you **W** say,	**Mi 4:11**	
w is in labor has borne a child.	**Mi 5:3**	
W has appointed its time?	**Mi 6:9**	4310
From her **w** lies in your bosom	**Mi 7:5**	
shame will cover her **w** said to me,	**Mi 7:10**	
W is a God like You, who pardons	**Mi 7:18**	4310
w pardons iniquity And passes over	**Mi 7:18**	
W can stand before His indignation?	**Na 1:6**	4310
W can endure the burning of His	**Na 1:6**	4310
knows those **w** take refuge in Him.	**Na 1:7**	
w are drunken with their drink,	**Na 1:10**	
w plotted evil against the LORD,	**Na 1:11**	
feet of him **w** brings good news,	**Na 1:15**	
good news, **W** announces peace!	**Na 1:15**	
The one **w** scatters has come up	**Na 2:1**	4650
W sells nations by her harlotries	**Na 3:4**	
all **w** see you Will shrink from you	**Na 3:7**	
W will grieve for her?'	**Na 3:7**	4310
All **w** hear about you Will clap	**Na 3:19**	
people **W** march throughout the earth	**Hab 1:6**	
On those **w** deal treacherously?	**Hab 1:13**	
That the one **w** reads it may run.	**Hab 2:2**	
'Woe to him **w** increases what is	**Hab 2:6**	
those **w** collect from you awaken?	**Hab 2:7**	
"Woe to him **w** gets evil gain for	**Hab 2:9**	
"Woe to him **w** builds a city with	**Hab 2:12**	
you **w** make your neighbors drink,	**Hab 2:15**	
W mix in your venom even to make	**Hab 2:15**	
to him **w** says to a *piece of* wood,	**Hab 2:19**	
like those **w** devour the oppressed	**Hab 3:14**	
For the people to arise **w** will	**Hab 3:16**	
"And those **w** bow down on the	**Zph 1:5**	
And those **w** bow down *and* swear to	**Zph 1:5**	
And those **w** have turned back from	**Zph 1:6**	
And those **w** have not sought the	**Zph 1:6**	834
And all **w** clothe themselves with	**Zph 1:8**	
w leap on the *temple* threshold,	**Zph 1:9**	
W fill the house of their lord	**Zph 1:9**	
All **w** weigh out silver will be cut	**Zph 1:11**	
the men **W** are stagnant in spirit,	**Zph 1:12**	
in spirit, **W** say in their hearts,	**Zph 1:12**	
All you humble of the earth **W** have	**Zph 2:3**	834
securely, **W** says in her heart,	**Zph 2:15**	
Everyone **w** passes by her will hiss	**Zph 2:15**	
her **w** is rebellious and defiled,	**Zph 3:1**	
"I will gather those **w** grieve	**Zph 3:18**	
and he **w** earns, earns wages *to put*	**Hg 1:6**	
'**W** is left among you who saw this	**Hg 2:3**	4310
'Who is left among you **w** saw this	**Hg 2:3**	834
"If one **w** is unclean from a	**Hg 2:13**	
And the angel **w** was speaking with	**Zch 1:9**	
And the man **w** was standing among	**Zch 1:10**	
angel of the LORD **w** was standing	**Zch 1:11**	
The LORD answered the angel **w**	**Zch 1:13**	
So the angel **w** was speaking with	**Zch 1:14**	
with the nations **w** are at ease;	**Zch 1:15**	
the angel **w** was speaking with me,	**Zch 1:19**	
nations **w** have lifted up *their* horns	**Zch 1:21**	
the angel **w** was speaking with me	**Zch 2:3**	
you **w** are living with the daughter	**Zch 2:7**	
plunder you, for he **w** touches you,	**Zch 2:8**	
the LORD **w** has chosen Jerusalem	**Zch 3:2**	
He spoke and said to those **w**	**Zch 3:4**	
among these **w** are standing *here.*	**Zch 3:7**	
you and your friends **w** are sitting	**Zch 3:8**	
they are men **w** are a symbol,	**Zch 3:8**	
w was speaking with me returned and	**Zch 4:1**	
man **w** is awakened from his sleep.	**Zch 4:1**	834
w was speaking with me saying,	**Zch 4:4**	
So the angel **w** was speaking with	**Zch 4:5**	
"For **w** has despised the day of	**Zch 4:10**	4310
w are standing by the Lord of the	**Zch 4:14**	
surely everyone **w** steals will be	**Zch 5:3**	
and everyone **w** swears will be	**Zch 5:3**	
one **w** swears falsely by My name;	**Zch 5:4**	
w was speaking with me went out and	**Zch 5:5**	
the angel **w** was speaking with me,	**Zch 5:10**	
the angel **w** was speaking with me,	**Zch 6:4**	
those **w** are going to the land of	**Zch 6:8**	
it is He **w** will build the temple	**Zch 6:13**	
and He **w** will bear the honor and	**Zch 6:13**	
"Those **w** are far off will	**Zch 6:15**	7350
speaking to the priests **w** belong	**Zch 7:3**	834
you **w** are listening in these days	**Zch 8:9**	
those **w** *spoke* in the day that the	**Zch 8:9**	834
and for him **w** went out or came in	**Zch 8:10**	
of him **w** passes by and returns;	**Zch 9:8**	
O prisoners **w** have the hope;	**Zch 9:12**	
The LORD **w** makes the storm clouds;	**Zch 10:1**	
"Those **w** buy them slay them and	**Zch 11:5**	834
each of those **w** sell them says,	**Zch 11:5**	
and let those **w** are left eat one	**Zch 11:9**	
afflicted of the flock **w** were watching	**Zch 11:11**	
land **w** will not care for the perishing,	**Zch 11:16**	
shepherd **W** leaves the flock!	**Zch 11:17**	
LORD **w** stretches out the heavens,	**Zch 12:1**	
all **w** lift it will be severely	**Zch 12:3**	
and the one **w** is feeble among them	**Zch 12:8**	
then his father and mother **w** gave	**Zch 13:3**	
and his father and mother **w** gave	**Zch 13:3**	
all the peoples **w** have gone to war	**Zch 14:12**	834
any **w** are left of all the nations that	**Zch 14:16**	
the LORD smites the nations **w** do not	**Zch 14:18**	834
nations **w** do not go up to celebrate	**Zch 14:19**	834
and all **w** sacrifice will come and	**Zch 14:21**	
you, O priests **w** despise My name.	**Mal 1:6**	
among you **w** would shut the gates,	**Mal 1:10**	
w has a male in his flock and	**Mal 1:14**	
"*As* for the man **w** does this, may	**Mal 2:12**	834
everyone **w** awakes and answers,	**Mal 2:12**	
or **w** presents an offering to the	**Mal 2:12**	
so **w** has a remnant of the Spirit.	**Mal 2:15**	
w covers his garment with wrong,"	**Mal 2:16**	
"Everyone **w** does evil is good in	**Mal 2:17**	
"But **w** can endure the day of His	**Mal 3:2**	4310
And **w** can stand when He appears?	**Mal 3:2**	4310
and against those **w** swear falsely,	**Mal 3:5**	
and against those **w** oppress the	**Mal 3:5**	
and those **w** turn aside the alien and	**Mal 3:5**	
Then those **w** feared the LORD spoke	**Mal 3:16**	
for those **w** fear the LORD and who	**Mal 3:16**	
the LORD and **w** esteem His name.	**Mal 3:16**	
spares his own son **w** serves him."	**Mal 3:17**	
between one **w** serves God and one	**Mal 3:18**	
God and one **w** does not serve Him.	**Mal 3:18**	834
"But for you **w** fear My name,	**Mal 4:2**	
the father of Solomon by Bathsheba **w**	**Mt 1:6**	
Jesus was born, **w** is called the Messiah.	**Mt 1:16**	
for the Child **w** has been conceived in	**Mt 1:20**	*3588*
"Where is He **w** has been born King	**Mt 2:2**	
W WILL SHEPHERD MY PEOPLE ISRAEL.	**Mt 2:6**	*3748*
slew all the male children **w** were in	**Mt 2:16**	
for those **w** sought the Child's	**Mt 2:20**	
w warned you to flee from the	**Mt 3:7**	*5101*
but He **w** is coming after me is	**Mt 3:11**	
PEOPLE **W** WERE SITTING IN DARKNESS	**Mt 4:16**	
AND THOSE **W** WERE SITTING IN THE	**Mt 4:16**	
Simon **w** was called Peter,	**Mt 4:18**	
brought to Him all **w** were ill,	**Mt 4:24**	
"Blessed are those **w** mourn,	**Mt 5:4**	
"Blessed are those **w** hunger and	**Mt 5:6**	
"Blessed are those **w** have been	**Mt 5:10**	
the prophets **w** were before you.	**Mt 5:12**	
light to all **w** are in the house.	**Mt 5:15**	
your Father **w** is in heaven.	**Mt 5:16**	
"But I say to you that everyone **w**	**Mt 5:22**	
that everyone **w** looks at a woman	**Mt 5:28**	
that everyone **w** divorces his wife,	**Mt 5:32**	
"Give to him **w** asks of you, and	**Mt 5:42**	
him **w** wants to borrow from you.	**Mt 5:42**	
pray for those **w** persecute you	**Mt 5:44**	
of your Father **w** is in heaven;	**Mt 5:45**	*3588*
"For if you love those **w** love you,	**Mt 5:46**	
with your Father **w** is in heaven.	**Mt 6:1**	*3588*
w sees *what is done* in secret	**Mt 6:4**	
to your Father **w** is in secret,	**Mt 6:6**	*3588*
and your Father **w** sees *what is*	**Mt 6:6**	*3588*
'Our Father **w** is in heaven,	**Mt 6:9**	*3588*
but by your Father **w** is in secret;	**Mt 6:18**	*3588*
your Father **w** sees *what is*	**Mt 6:18**	*3588*
"And **w** of you by being worried can	**Mt 6:27**	*5101*
"For everyone **w** asks receives,	**Mt 7:8**	
receives, and he **w** seeks finds,	**Mt 7:8**	
him **w** knocks it will be opened.	**Mt 7:8**	
"Or what man is there among you **w**,	**Mt 7:9**	*3739*
your Father **w** is in heaven give what	**Mt 7:11**	
what is good to those **w** ask Him!	**Mt 7:11**	
and there are many **w** enter through it.	**Mt 7:13**	
life, and there are few **w** find it.	**Mt 7:14**	
w come to you in sheep's clothing,	**Mt 7:15**	*3748*
"Not everyone **w** says to Me,	**Mt 7:21**	
but he **w** does the will of My	**Mt 7:21**	
will of My Father **w** is in heaven	**Mt 7:21**	
YOU **W** PRACTICE LAWLESSNESS.'	**Mt 7:23**	
w hears these words of Mine and	**Mt 7:24**	*3748*

w built his house on the rock.	**Mt 7:24**	*3748*
w hears these words of Mine and	**Mt 7:26**	
w built his house on the sand.	**Mt 7:26**	*3748*
said to those **w** were following,	**Mt 8:10**	
to Him many **w** were demon-possessed;	**Mt 8:16**	
a word, and healed all **w** were ill	**Mt 8:16**	
two men **w** were demon-possessed	**Mt 8:28**	
w had given such authority to men.	**Mt 9:8**	
"*It is* not those **w** are healthy	**Mt 9:12**	
are healthy **w** need a physician,	**Mt 9:12**	
a physician, but those **w** are sick.	**Mt 9:12**	
a woman **w** had been suffering from	**Mt 9:20**	
first, Simon, **w** is called Peter,	**Mt 10:2**	
Iscariot, the one **w** betrayed Him.	**Mt 10:4**	
enter, inquire **w** is worthy in it,	**Mt 10:11**	*5101*
"For it is not you **w** speak,	**Mt 10:20**	
of your Father **w** speaks in you.	**Mt 10:20**	
but it is the one **w** has endured to	**Mt 10:22**	
to the end **w** will be saved.	**Mt 10:22**	
Do not fear those **w** kill the body	**Mt 10:28**	
but rather fear Him **w** is able to	**Mt 10:28**	
w confesses Me before men,	**Mt 10:32**	*3748*
before My Father **w** is in heaven.	**Mt 10:32**	
before My Father **w** is in heaven.	**Mt 10:33**	
"He **w** loves father or mother more	**Mt 10:37**	
and he **w** loves son or daughter	**Mt 10:37**	
"And he **w** does not take his cross	**Mt 10:38**	*3739*
"He **w** has found his life will	**Mt 10:39**	
and he **w** has lost his life for My	**Mt 10:39**	
"He **w** receives you receives Me,	**Mt 10:40**	
and he **w** receives Me receives Him	**Mt 10:40**	
Me receives Him **w** sent Me.	**Mt 10:40**	
"He **w** receives a prophet in *the*	**Mt 10:41**	
and he **w** receives a righteous man	**Mt 10:41**	
w does not take offense at Me."	**Mt 11:6**	*3739*
Those **w** wear soft *clothing* are in	**Mt 11:8**	
and one **w** is more than a prophet.	**Mt 11:9**	
W WILL PREPARE YOUR WAY BEFORE	**Mt 11:10**	*3739*
Yet the one **w** is least in the kingdom	**Mt 11:11**	
himself is Elijah **w** was to come.	**Mt 11:14**	
"He **w** has ears to hear, let him	**Mt 11:15**	
w call out to the other *children,*	**Mt 11:16**	*3739*
all **w** are weary and heavy-laden,	**Mt 11:28**	
among you **w** has a sheep,	**Mt 12:11**	*3739*
and warned them not to tell **w** He was.	**Mt 12:16**	*846*
demon-possessed man **w** *was* blind	**Mt 12:22**	
"He **w** is not with Me is against Me;	**Mt 12:30**	
and he **w** does not gather with Me	**Mt 12:30**	
one **w** was telling Him and said,	**Mt 12:48**	
"**W** is My mother and who are My	**Mt 12:48**	*5101*
My mother and **w** are My brothers?"	**Mt 12:48**	*5101*
will of My Father **w** is in heaven,	**Mt 12:50**	
"He **w** has ears, let him hear."	**Mt 13:9**	
this is the man **w** hears the word and	**Mt 13:20**	
this is the man **w** hears the word,	**Mt 13:22**	
this is the man **w** hears the word	**Mt 13:23**	
w indeed bears fruit and brings	**Mt 13:23**	*3739*
w sowed good seed in his field.	**Mt 13:24**	
"The one **w** sows the good seed is	**Mt 13:37**	
enemy **w** sowed them is the devil,	**Mt 13:39**	
and those **w** commit lawlessness,	**Mt 13:41**	
He **w** has ears, let him hear.	**Mt 13:43**	
"Therefore every scribe **w** has	**Mt 13:52**	
w brings out of his treasure	**Mt 13:52**	*3748*
about five thousand men **w** ate,	**Mt 14:21**	
And those **w** were in the boat	**Mt 14:33**	
brought to Him all **w** were sick;	**Mt 14:35**	
'HE **W** SPEAKS EVIL OF FATHER OR	**Mt 15:4**	
bringing with them *those* **w** *were*	**Mt 15:30**	
w ate were four thousand men,	**Mt 15:38**	
"**W** do people say that the Son of	**Mt 16:13**	*5101*
"But **w** do you say that I am?"	**Mt 16:15**	*5101*
you, but My Father **w** is in heaven.	**Mt 16:17**	*3588*
there are some of those **w** are	**Mt 16:28**	
w will not taste death until they see	**Mt 16:28**	*3748*
those **w** collected the two-drachma	**Mt 17:24**	
"**W** then is greatest in the	**Mt 18:1**	*5101*
ones **w** believe in Me to stumble,	**Mt 18:6**	
face of My Father **w** is in heaven.	**Mt 18:10**	
the will of your Father **w** is in heaven	**Mt 18:14**	
them by My Father **w** is in heaven.	**Mt 18:19**	
king **w** wished to settle accounts with	**Mt 18:23**	*3739*
w owed him ten thousand talents was	**Mt 18:24**	
w owed him a hundred denarii;	**Mt 18:28**	*3739*
that He **w** created *them* from the	**Mt 19:4**	
"For there are eunuchs **w** were	**Mt 19:12**	*3748*
w were made eunuchs by men;	**Mt 19:12**	*3748*
and there are *also* eunuchs **w** made	**Mt 19:12**	*3748*
He **w** is able to accept *this,* let	**Mt 19:12**	
There is *only* One **w** is good;	**Mt 19:17**	
he was one **w** owned much property.	**Mt 19:22**	
"Then **w** can be saved?"	**Mt 19:25**	*5101*
you, that you **w** have followed Me,	**Mt 19:28**	
"And everyone **w** has left houses	**Mt 19:29**	*3748*
"But many **w** *are* first will be	**Mt 19:30**	
a landowner **w** went out early in the	**Mt 20:1**	*3748*
equal to us **w** have borne the burden	**Mt 20:12**	*3588*
and those **w** followed, were	**Mt 21:9**	
W COMES IN THE NAME OF THE LORD;	**Mt 21:9**	
city was stirred, saying, "**W** is this?"	**Mt 21:10**	*5101*
drove out all those **w** were buying and	**Mt 21:12**	
of those **w** were selling doves.	**Mt 21:12**	
and the children **w** were shouting	**Mt 21:15**	
and **w** gave You this authority?"	**Mt 21:23**	*5101*
There was a landowner **W** PLANTED A	**Mt 21:33**	*3748*
w will pay him the proceeds at the	**Mt 21:41**	*3748*
"And he **w** falls on this stone	**Mt 21:44**	
w gave a wedding feast for his son.	**Mt 22:2**	*3748*
to call those **w** had been invited	**Mt 22:3**	
'Tell those **w** have been invited,	**Mt 22:4**	
w were invited were not worthy.	**Mt 22:8**	
he saw a man there **w** was not dressed	**Mt 22:11**	
(**w** say there is no resurrection)	**Mt 22:23**	
is your Father, He **w** is in heaven.	**Mt 23:9**	
those **w** are entering to go in.	**Mt 23:13**	
"Woe to you, blind guides, **w** say,	**Mt 23:16**	
and by Him **w** dwells within it.	**Mt 23:21**	
of God and by Him **w** sits upon it.	**Mt 23:22**	
w strain out a gnat and swallow a	**Mt 23:24**	
of those **w** murdered the prophets.	**Mt 23:31**	
w kills the prophets and stones	**Mt 23:37**	
stones those **w** are sent to her!	**Mt 23:37**	
W COMES IN THE NAME OF THE LORD!	**Mt 23:39**	
"But the one **w** endures to the end,	**Mt 24:13**	
then those **w** are in Judea must flee	**Mt 24:16**	*3588*
"But woe to those **w** are pregnant	**Mt 24:19**	
w are nursing babies in those days!	**Mt 24:19**	
"**W** then is the faithful and	**Mt 24:45**	*5101*
ten virgins, **w** took their lamps and	**Mt 25:1**	*3748*
and those **w** were ready went in	**Mt 25:10**	
journey, **w** called his own slaves and	**Mt 25:14**	
one **w** had received the five talents	**Mt 25:16**	
the one **w** *had received* the two *talents*	**Mt 25:17**	
"But he **w** received the one *talent*	**Mt 25:18**	
"The one **w** had received the	**Mt 25:20**	
"Also the one **w** *had received* the	**Mt 25:22**	*3588*
"And the one also **w** had received	**Mt 25:24**	
to the one **w** has the ten talents.'	**Mt 25:28**	
w has, *more* shall be given,	**Mt 25:29**	
but from the one **w** does not have,	**Mt 25:29**	
you **w** are blessed of My Father,	**Mt 25:34**	
"He **w** dipped his hand with Me in	**Mt 26:23**	
bowl is the one **w** will betray Me.	**Mt 26:23**	
And Judas, **w** was betraying Him,	**Mt 26:25**	
the one **w** betrays Me is at hand!"	**Mt 26:46**	
w *came* from the chief priests	**Mt 26:47**	
Now he **w** was betraying Him gave	**Mt 26:48**	
one of those **w** were with Jesus	**Mt 26:51**	*3588*
for all those **w** take up the sword	**Mt 26:52**	
Those **w** had seized Jesus led	**Mt 26:57**	
w is the one who hit You?"	**Mt 26:68**	*5101*
who is the one **w** hit You?"	**Mt 26:68**	
and said to those **w** were there,	**Mt 26:71**	*3588*
when Judas, **w** had betrayed Him,	**Mt 27:3**	
or Jesus **w** is called Christ?"	**Mt 27:17**	
with Jesus **w** is called Christ?"	**Mt 27:22**	
"You **w** *are going to* destroy the	**Mt 27:40**	
The robbers **w** had been	**Mt 27:44**	
of those **w** were standing there,	**Mt 27:47**	
w had fallen asleep were raised;	**Mt 27:52**	
and those **w** were with him keeping	**Mt 27:54**	
w had followed Jesus from Galilee	**Mt 27:55**	*3748*
w himself had also become a	**Mt 27:57**	*3739*
for Jesus **w** has been crucified.	**Mt 28:5**	
YOU, **W** WILL PREPARE YOUR WAY;	**Mk 1:2**	*3739*
is coming **w** is mightier than I,	**Mk 1:7**	
w were also in the boat mending	**Mk 1:19**	*846*
w You are—the Holy One of God!"	**Mk 1:24**	*5101*
they *began* bringing to Him all **w**	**Mk 1:32**	
and those **w** were demon-possessed.	**Mk 1:32**	
And He healed many **w** were ill with	**Mk 1:34**	
speak, because they knew **w** He was.	**Mk 1:34**	
w can forgive sins but God alone?"	**Mk 2:7**	*5101*
"*It is* not those **w** are healthy	**Mk 2:17**	
are healthy **w** need a physician,	**Mk 2:17**	
a physician, but those **w** are sick;	**Mk 2:17**	
it to those **w** were with him?"	**Mk 2:26**	
with the result that all those **w**	**Mk 3:10**	*3745*
earnestly warned them not to tell **w**	**Mk 3:12**	*846*
Iscariot, **w** betrayed Him.	**Mk 3:19**	*3739*
The scribes **w** came down from	**Mk 3:22**	
"**W** are My mother and My brothers?"	**Mk 3:33**	*5101*
those **w** were sitting around Him,	**Mk 3:34**	
"He **w** has ears to hear, let him	**Mk 4:9**	*3739*
but those **w** are outside get	**Mk 4:11**	
"These are the ones **w** are	**Mk 4:15**	*3588*
was sown on the rocky *places,* **w**,	**Mk 4:16**	*3739*
the ones **w** have heard the word,	**Mk 4:18**	
a man **w** casts seed upon the soil;	**Mk 4:26**	
"**W** then is this, that even the	**Mk 4:41**	*5101*
the man **w** had been demon-possessed	**Mk 5:15**	
mind, the very man **w** had had the	**Mk 5:15**	
Those **w** had seen it described	**Mk 5:16**	
the man **w** had been demon-possessed	**Mk 5:18**	
A woman **w** had had a hemorrhage	**Mk 5:25**	
"**W** touched My garments?"	**Mk 5:30**	*5101*
'**W** touched Me?' "	**Mk 5:31**	*5101*
to see the woman **w** had done this.	**Mk 5:32**	
thousand men **w** ate the loaves.	**Mk 6:44**	
their pallets those **w** were sick,	**Mk 6:55**	
'HE **W** SPEAKS EVIL OF FATHER OR	**Mk 7:10**	
They brought to Him one **w** was	**Mk 7:32**	*2974*
"**W** do people say that I am?"	**Mk 8:27**	*5101*
"But **w** do you say that I am?"	**Mk 8:29**	*5101*
there are some of those **w** are	**Mk 9:1**	
w will not taste death until they see	**Mk 9:1**	*3748*
are possible to him **w** believes."	**Mk 9:23**	
receive Me, but Him **w** sent Me."	**Mk 9:37**	
for there is no one **w** will	**Mk 9:39**	*3739*
he **w** is not against us is for us.	**Mk 9:40**	*3739*
little ones **w** believe to stumble,	**Mk 9:42**	
he was one **w** owned much property.	**Mk 10:22**	
"How hard it will be for those **w**	**Mk 10:23**	
"Then **w** can be saved?"	**Mk 10:26**	*5101*
there is no one **w** has left house	**Mk 10:29**	*3739*
"But many **w** *are* first will be	**Mk 10:31**	
and those **w** followed were fearful.	**Mk 10:32**	
"You know that those **w** are	**Mk 10:42**	
Those **w** went in front and those	**Mk 11:9**	
and those **w** followed were	**Mk 11:9**	
W COMES IN THE NAME OF THE LORD;	**Mk 11:9**	
to drive out those **w** were buying and	**Mk 11:15**	
of those **w** were selling doves;	**Mk 11:15**	
so that your Father **w** is in	**Mk 11:25**	*3588*
neither will your Father **w** is in	**Mk 11:26**	*3588*
or **w** gave You this authority to do	**Mk 11:28**	*5101*
w say that there is no resurrection	**Mk 12:18**	*3748*
"Beware of the scribes **w** like to	**Mk 12:38**	
w devour widows' houses, and for	**Mk 12:40**	
for it is not you **w** speak,	**Mk 13:11**	
but the one **w** endures to the end,	**Mk 13:13**	
then those **w** are in Judea must flee	**Mk 13:14**	*3588*
"The one **w** is on the housetop	**Mk 13:15**	*3588*
the one **w** is in the field must not	**Mk 13:16**	*3588*
"But woe to those **w** are pregnant	**Mk 13:17**	
w are nursing babies in those days!	**Mk 13:17**	
w upon leaving his house	**Mk 13:34**	
Iscariot, **w** was one of the twelve,	**Mk 14:10**	*3588*
one **w** is eating with Me."	**Mk 14:18**	
one **w** dips with Me in the bowl.	**Mk 14:20**	
the one **w** betrays Me is at hand!"	**Mk 14:42**	
w *were* from the chief priests	**Mk 14:43**	
Now he **w** was betraying Him had	**Mk 14:44**	
those **w** stood by drew his sword,	**Mk 14:47**	
the insurrectionists **w** had committed	**Mk 15:7**	*3748*
You **w** *are going to* destroy the	**Mk 15:29**	
Those **w** were crucified with	**Mk 15:32**	
w was standing right in front of	**Mk 15:39**	
women **w** came up with Him	**Mk 15:41**	
w himself was waiting for the	**Mk 15:43**	*3739*
"**W** will roll away the stone for	**Mk 16:3**	*5101*
Nazarene, **w** has been crucified.	**Mk 16:6**	
to those **w** had been with Him,	**Mk 16:10**	
w had seen Him after He had risen.	**Mk 16:14**	
"He **w** has believed and has been	**Mk 16:16**	
but he **w** has disbelieved shall be	**Mk 16:16**	
accompany those **w** have believed:	**Mk 16:17**	
by those **w** from the beginning	**Lk 1:2**	
"It is he **w** will go *as a*	**Lk 1:17**	
w stands in the presence of God,	**Lk 1:19**	
and she **w** was called barren is now	**Lk 1:36**	
"And blessed *is* she **w** believed	**Lk 1:45**	
TOWARD THOSE **W** FEAR HIM.	**Lk 1:50**	
He has scattered *those* **w** *were*	**Lk 1:51**	
has exalted those **w** were humble.	**Lk 1:52**	
w is called by that name."	**Lk 1:61**	*3739*
w heard them kept them in mind,	**Lk 1:66**	
FROM THE HAND OF ALL **W** HATE US;	**Lk 1:71**	
TO SHINE UPON THOSE **W** SIT IN	**Lk 1:79**	
with Mary, **w** was engaged to him,	**Lk 2:5**	
a Savior, **w** is Christ the Lord.	**Lk 2:11**	*3739*
And all **w** heard it wondered at the	**Lk 2:18**	
to speak of Him to all those **w** were	**Lk 2:38**	
And all **w** heard Him were amazed at	**Lk 2:47**	
the crowds **w** were going out to be	**Lk 3:7**	
w warned you to flee from the	**Lk 3:7**	*5101*
"The man **w** has two tunics	**Lk 3:11**	
to share with him **w** has none;	**Lk 3:11**	
he **w** has food is to do likewise."	**Lk 3:11**	
is coming **w** is mightier than I,	**Lk 3:16**	
SET FREE THOSE **W** ARE OPPRESSED,	**Lk 4:18**	
Sidon, to a woman **w** was a widow.	**Lk 4:26**	
w You are—the Holy One of God!"	**Lk 4:34**	*5101*
all those **w** had any *who were* sick	**Lk 4:40**	*3745*
all those who had any **w** *were* sick	**Lk 4:40**	
w were partners with Simon.	**Lk 5:10**	*3739*
w had come from every village of	**Lk 5:17**	*3739*
on a bed a man **w** was paralyzed;	**Lk 5:18**	*3739*
"**W** is this *man* who speaks	**Lk 5:21**	*5101*
is this *man* **w** speaks blasphemies?	**Lk 5:21**	*3739*
W can forgive sins, but God alone?"	**Lk 5:21**	*5101*
tax collectors and other *people* **w** were	**Lk 5:29**	*3739*
"*It is* not those **w** are well who	**Lk 5:31**	
who are well **w** need a physician,	**Lk 5:31**	
a physician, but those **w** are sick.	**Lk 5:31**	
he and those **w** were with him,	**Lk 6:3**	
and Simon **w** was called the Zealot;	**Lk 6:15**	
Iscariot, **w** became a traitor.	**Lk 6:16**	*3739*
w had come to hear Him and to be	**Lk 6:18**	*3739*
and those **w** were troubled with	**Lk 6:18**	
"Blessed *are* you **w** *are* poor,	**Lk 6:20**	
"Blessed *are* you **w** hunger now,	**Lk 6:21**	
Blessed *are* you **w** weep now, for	**Lk 6:21**	
"But woe to you **w** are rich, for	**Lk 6:24**	
"Woe to you **w** are well-fed now,	**Lk 6:25**	
Woe *to you* **w** laugh now, for you	**Lk 6:25**	
"But I say to you **w** hear,	**Lk 6:27**	
do good to those **w** hate you,	**Lk 6:27**	
bless those **w** curse you, pray for	**Lk 6:28**	
pray for those **w** mistreat you.	**Lk 6:28**	
"Give to everyone **w** asks of you,	**Lk 6:30**	
"If you love those **w** love you,	**Lk 6:32**	
sinners love those **w** love them.	**Lk 6:32**	
do good to those **w** do good to you,	**Lk 6:33**	
"Everyone **w** comes to Me and	**Lk 6:47**	
w dug deep and laid a foundation	**Lk 6:48**	*3739*
"But the one **w** has heard and has	**Lk 6:49**	
is like a man **w** built a house on	**Lk 6:49**	
w was highly regarded by him,	**Lk 7:2**	*3739*
was he **w** built us our synagogue."	**Lk 7:5**	
When those **w** had been sent	**Lk 7:10**	
and He gave sight to many **w** *were*	**Lk 7:21**	
w does not take offense at Me."	**Lk 7:23**	*3739*
Those **w** are splendidly clothed and	**Lk 7:25**	
and one **w** is more than a prophet.	**Lk 7:26**	
W WILL PREPARE YOUR WAY BEFORE	**Lk 7:27**	*3739*
yet he **w** is least in the kingdom	**Lk 7:28**	

"They are like children **w** sit in	**Lk 7:32**	
woman in the city **w** was a sinner;	**Lk 7:37**	*3748*
w had invited Him saw this,	**Lk 7:39**	
He would know **w** and what sort of	**Lk 7:39**	*5101*
this woman is **w** is touching Him,	**Lk 7:39**	*3748*
but he **w** is forgiven little, loves	**Lk 7:47**	*3739*
Those **w** were reclining *at the*	**Lk 7:49**	
"**W** is this *man* who even forgives	**Lk 7:49**	*5101*
this *man* **w** even forgives sins?"	**Lk 7:49**	*3739*
and *also* some women **w** had been	**Lk 8:2**	*3739*
Mary **w** was called Magdalene, from	**Lk 8:2**	
and many others **w** were	**Lk 8:3**	*3748*
"He **w** has ears to hear, let him	**Lk 8:8**	
the road are those **w** have heard;	**Lk 8:12**	
w, when they hear, receive the word	**Lk 8:13**	*3739*
these are the ones **w** have heard,	**Lk 8:14**	
these are the ones **w** have heard	**Lk 8:15**	*3748*
those **w** come in may see the light.	**Lk 8:16**	
and My brothers are these **w** hear the	**Lk 8:21**	
"**W** then is this, that He commands	**Lk 8:25**	*5101*
city **w** was possessed with demons;	**Lk 8:27**	
and **w** had not put on any clothing	**Lk 8:27**	
Those **w** had seen it reported	**Lk 8:36**	
how the man **w** was demon-possessed	**Lk 8:36**	
And a woman **w** had a hemorrhage for	**Lk 8:43**	
"**W** is the one who touched Me?"	**Lk 8:45**	*5101*
"Who is the one **w** touched Me?"	**Lk 8:45**	
as for those **w** do not receive you,	**Lk 9:5**	
but **w** is this man about whom I	**Lk 9:9**	*5101*
those **w** had need of healing.	**Lk 9:11**	
"**W** do the people say that I	**Lk 9:18**	*5101*
"But **w** do you say that I am?"	**Lk 9:20**	*5101*
he is the one **w** will save it.	**Lk 9:24**	
w will not taste death until they see	**Lk 9:27**	*3739*
w, appearing in glory, were	**Lk 9:31**	*3739*
Me receives Him **w** sent Me;	**Lk 9:48**	
for the one **w** is least among all	**Lk 9:48**	
you, this is the one **w** is great."	**Lk 9:48**	
w is not against you is for you."	**Lk 9:50**	*3739*
and heal those in it **w** are sick,	**Lk 10:9**	
"The one **w** listens to you listens	**Lk 10:16**	
the one **w** rejects you rejects Me;	**Lk 10:16**	
and he **w** rejects Me rejects the	**Lk 10:16**	
Me rejects the One **w** sent Me."	**Lk 10:16**	
w the Son is except the Father,	**Lk 10:22**	*5101*
w the Father is except the Son,	**Lk 10:22**	*5101*
"And **w** is my neighbor?"	**Lk 10:29**	*5101*
Samaritan, **w** was on a journey,	**Lk 10:33**	
w fell into the robbers' *hands?*"	**Lk 10:36**	
one **w** showed mercy toward him."	**Lk 10:37**	
w was seated at the Lord's feet,	**Lk 10:39**	*3739*
everyone **w** is indebted to us.	**Lk 11:4**	
"For everyone **w** asks, receives;	**Lk 11:10**	
and he **w** seeks, finds;	**Lk 11:10**	
and to him **w** knocks, it will be	**Lk 11:10**	
Holy Spirit to those **w** ask Him?"	**Lk 11:13**	
"He **w** is not with Me is against Me;	**Lk 11:23**	
and he **w** does not gather with Me,	**Lk 11:23**	
are those **w** hear the word of God and	**Lk 11:28**	
those **w** enter may see the light.	**Lk 11:33**	
did not He **w** made the outside make	**Lk 11:40**	
and the people **w** walk over *them*	**Lk 11:44**	
and *it was* your fathers **w**	**Lk 11:47**	
because it was they **w** killed them,	**Lk 11:48**	
w was killed between the altar and	**Lk 11:51**	
you hindered those **w** were entering."	**Lk 11:52**	
afraid of those **w** kill the body and	**Lk 12:4**	
fear the One **w**, after He has killed	**Lk 12:5**	
w confesses Me before men,	**Lk 12:8**	*3739*
but he **w** denies Me before men	**Lk 12:9**	
"And everyone **w** speaks a word	**Lk 12:10**	*3739*
but he **w** blasphemes against the	**Lk 12:10**	
w appointed Me a judge or arbitrator	**Lk 12:14**	*5101*
and *now* **w** will own what you have	**Lk 12:20**	*5101*
w stores up treasure for himself,	**Lk 12:21**	
"Be like men **w** are waiting	**Lk 12:36**	
"**W** then is the faithful and	**Lk 12:42**	*5101*
"And that slave **w** knew his	**Lk 12:47**	
but the one **w** did not know *it,* and	**Lk 12:48**	
From everyone **w** has been given	**Lk 12:48**	*3739*
were some present **w** reported to Him	**Lk 13:1**	
all the men **w** live in Jerusalem?	**Lk 13:4**	
there was a woman **w** for eighteen	**Lk 13:11**	
just a few **w** are being saved?"	**Lk 13:23**	
some are last **w** will be first and	**Lk 13:30**	*3739*
some are first **w** will be last."	**Lk 13:30**	*3739*
W COMES IN THE NAME OF THE LORD!'"	**Lk 13:35**	
and he **w** invited you both will	**Lk 14:9**	
the one **w** has invited you comes,	**Lk 14:10**	
all **w** are at the table with you.	**Lk 14:10**	
"For everyone **w** exalts himself	**Lk 14:11**	
and he **w** humbles himself will be	**Lk 14:11**	
say to the one **w** had invited Him,	**Lk 14:12**	
When one of those **w** were	**Lk 14:15**	
"Blessed is everyone **w** will eat	**Lk 14:15**	*3748*
say to those **w** had been invited,	**Lk 14:17**	
none of those men **w** were invited	**Lk 14:24**	
all **w** observe it begin to ridicule	**Lk 14:29**	
My disciple **w** does not give up all his	**Lk 14:33**	*3739*
He **w** has ears to hear, let him	**Lk 14:35**	
heaven over one sinner **w** repents than	**Lk 15:7**	
persons **w** need no repentance.	**Lk 15:7**	*3748*
God over one sinner **w** repents."	**Lk 15:10**	
w has devoured your wealth with	**Lk 15:30**	
rich man **w** had a manager,	**Lk 16:1**	*3739*
"He **w** is faithful in a very	**Lk 16:10**	
and he **w** is unrighteous in a very	**Lk 16:10**	
w will entrust the true *riches* to	**Lk 16:11**	*5101*
w will give you that which is your	**Lk 16:12**	*5101*

Pharisees, **w** were lovers of money,	**Lk 16:14**	
"You are those **w** justify	**Lk 16:15**	
"Everyone **w** divorces his wife and	**Lk 16:18**	
and he **w** marries one who is	**Lk 16:18**	
and he who marries one **w** is	**Lk 16:18**	
so that those **w** wish to come	**Lk 16:26**	
men **w** stood at a distance met Him;	**Lk 17:12**	*3739*
"Was no one found **w** returned	**Lk 17:18**	
the one **w** is on the housetop	**Lk 17:31**	*3739*
one **w** is in the field must not turn	**Lk 17:31**	*3739*
was a judge **w** did not fear God	**Lk 18:2**	
elect **w** cry to Him day and night,	**Lk 18:7**	
some people **w** trusted in themselves	**Lk 18:9**	
for everyone **w** exalts himself	**Lk 18:14**	
but he **w** humbles himself will be	**Lk 18:14**	
"How hard it is for those **w** are	**Lk 18:24**	
They **w** heard it said,	**Lk 18:26**	
"Then **w** can be saved?"	**Lk 18:26**	*5101*
there is no one **w** has left house	**Lk 18:29**	*3739*
w will not receive many times as	**Lk 18:30**	*3739*
Those **w** led the way were	**Lk 18:39**	
Zaccheus was trying to see **w** Jesus	**Lk 19:3**	*5101*
guest of a man **w** is a sinner."	**Lk 19:7**	
to the one **w** has the ten minas.'	**Lk 19:24**	
w has, more shall be given,	**Lk 19:26**	
but from the one **w** does not have,	**Lk 19:26**	
w did not want me to reign over	**Lk 19:27**	
So those **w** were sent went away	**Lk 19:32**	
W COMES IN THE NAME OF THE LORD;	**Lk 19:38**	
to drive out those **w** were selling,	**Lk 19:45**	
or **w** is the one who gave You this	**Lk 20:2**	*5101*
one **w** gave You this authority?"	**Lk 20:2**	
"Everyone **w** falls on that stone	**Lk 20:18**	
spies **w** pretended to be righteous,	**Lk 20:20**	
w say that there is no resurrection	**Lk 20:27**	
but those **w** are considered worthy	**Lk 20:35**	
w like to walk around in long	**Lk 20:46**	
w devour widows' houses, and for	**Lk 20:47**	*3739*
"Then those **w** are in Judea	**Lk 21:21**	*3588*
and those **w** are in the midst	**Lk 21:21**	*3588*
and those **w** are in the country	**Lk 21:21**	*3588*
"Woe to those **w** are pregnant	**Lk 21:23**	
those **w** are nursing babies in those	**Lk 21:23**	
for it will come upon all those **w**	**Lk 21:35**	
into Judas **w** was called Iscariot,	**Lk 22:3**	
be **w** was going to do this thing.	**Lk 22:23**	
and those **w** have authority over	**Lk 22:25**	
but the one **w** is the greatest	**Lk 22:26**	
"For **w** is greater, the one who	**Lk 22:27**	*5101*
the one **w** reclines *at the table*	**Lk 22:27**	
at the table or the one **w** serves?	**Lk 22:27**	
the one **w** reclines *at the table?*	**Lk 22:27**	
am among you as the one **w** serves.	**Lk 22:27**	
w have stood by Me in My trials;	**Lk 22:28**	
When those **w** were around Him	**Lk 22:49**	*3588*
and elders **w** had come against Him,	**Lk 22:52**	
Now the men **w** were holding Jesus	**Lk 22:63**	
w is the one who hit You?"	**Lk 22:64**	*5101*
who is the one **w** hit You?"	**Lk 22:64**	
w himself also was in Jerusalem at	**Lk 23:7**	
one **w** incites the people to rebellion,	**Lk 23:14**	
(He was one **w** had been thrown into	**Lk 23:19**	*3748*
w had been thrown into prison for	**Lk 23:25**	
and of women **w** were mourning and	**Lk 23:27**	*3739*
Two others also, **w** were criminals,	**Lk 23:32**	
One of the criminals **w** were	**Lk 23:39**	
And all the crowds **w** came	**Lk 23:48**	
w accompanied Him from Galilee were	**Lk 23:49**	
w was a member of the Council,	**Lk 23:50**	
w was waiting for the kingdom of	**Lk 23:51**	*3739*
Now the women **w** had come with Him	**Lk 23:55**	*3748*
w was a prophet mighty in deed and	**Lk 24:19**	*3739*
He **w** was going to redeem Israel.	**Lk 24:21**	
angels **w** said that He was alive.	**Lk 24:23**	*3739*
"Some of those **w** were with us	**Lk 24:24**	
eleven and those **w** were with them,	**Lk 24:33**	*3588*
and those **w** were His own did not	**Jn 1:11**	
to those **w** believe in His name,	**Jn 1:12**	
w were born, not of blood nor of	**Jn 1:13**	*3739*
'He **w** comes after me has a higher	**Jn 1:15**	
w is in the bosom of the Father,	**Jn 1:18**	
Jerusalem to ask him, "**W** are you?"	**Jn 1:19**	*5101*
"**W** are you, so that we may give	**Jn 1:22**	*5101*
give an answer to those **w** sent us?	**Jn 1:22**	
"*It is* He **w** comes after me, the	**Jn 1:27**	
the Lamb of God **w** takes away the	**Jn 1:29**	
a Man **w** has a higher rank than I,	**Jn 1:30**	*3739*
but He **w** sent me to baptize in	**Jn 1:33**	
w baptizes in the Holy Spirit.'	**Jn 1:33**	
One of the two **w** heard John *speak*	**Jn 1:40**	
w had drawn the water knew),	**Jn 2:9**	
those **w** were selling oxen and sheep	**Jn 2:14**	
and to those **w** were selling the	**Jn 2:16**	
w is born of the Spirit."	**Jn 3:8**	
but He **w** descended from heaven:	**Jn 3:13**	
w believes in Him is not judged;	**Jn 3:18**	
he **w** does not believe has been	**Jn 3:18**	
w does evil hates the Light,	**Jn 3:20**	
"But he **w** practices the truth	**Jn 3:21**	
He **w** was with you beyond the	**Jn 3:26**	*3739*
"He **w** has the bride is the	**Jn 3:29**	
w stands and hears him,	**Jn 3:29**	
"He **w** comes from above is above	**Jn 3:31**	
he **w** is of the earth is from the	**Jn 3:31**	
He **w** comes from heaven is above	**Jn 3:31**	
"He **w** has received His testimony	**Jn 3:33**	
"He **w** believes in the Son has	**Jn 3:36**	
but he **w** does not obey the Son	**Jn 3:36**	
God, and **w** it is who says to you,	**Jn 4:10**	*5101*

God, and who it is **w** says to you,	**Jn 4:10**	
are You, **w** gave us the well,	**Jn 4:12**	*3739*
"Everyone **w** drinks of this water	**Jn 4:13**	
and those **w** worship Him must	**Jn 4:24**	
is coming (He **w** is called Christ);	**Jn 4:25**	
"I **w** speak to you am *He.*"	**Jn 4:26**	
see a man **w** told me all the things	**Jn 4:29**	*3739*
to do the will of Him **w** sent Me and	**Jn 4:34**	
he **w** reaps is receiving wages and	**Jn 4:36**	
that he **w** sows and he who reaps	**Jn 4:36**	
he **w** reaps may rejoice together.	**Jn 4:36**	
the word of the woman **w** testified,	**Jn 4:39**	
a multitude of those **w** were sick,	**Jn 5:3**	
w had been ill for thirty-eight years.	**Jn 5:5**	
were saying to the man **w** was cured,	**Jn 5:10**	
"He **w** made me well was the one	**Jn 5:11**	
me well was the one **w** said to me,	**Jn 5:11**	
"**W** is the man who said to you,	**Jn 5:12**	*5101*
"Who is the man **w** said to you,	**Jn 5:12**	
But the man **w** was healed did not know	**Jn 5:13**	
was healed did not know **w** it was,	**Jn 5:13**	*5101*
it was Jesus **w** had made him well.	**Jn 5:15**	
He **w** does not honor the Son does	**Jn 5:23**	
not honor the Father **w** sent Him.	**Jn 5:23**	
I say to you, he **w** hears My word,	**Jn 5:24**	
word, and believes Him **w** sent Me,	**Jn 5:24**	
and those **w** hear will live.	**Jn 5:25**	
in which all **w** are in the tombs	**Jn 5:28**	*3588*
those **w** did the good *deeds* to a	**Jn 5:29**	
those **w** committed the evil *deeds*	**Jn 5:29**	
but the will of Him **w** sent Me.	**Jn 5:30**	
is another **w** testifies of Me,	**Jn 5:32**	
"And the Father **w** sent Me, He has	**Jn 5:37**	
the one **w** accuses you is Moses, in	**Jn 5:45**	
performing on those **w** were sick.	**Jn 6:2**	
"There is a lad here **w** has five	**Jn 6:9**	*3739*
to those **w** were seated;	**Jn 6:11**	
left over by those **w** had eaten.	**Jn 6:13**	
w is to come into the world."	**Jn 6:14**	
it is not Moses **w** has given you	**Jn 6:32**	
but it is My Father **w** gives you	**Jn 6:32**	
he **w** comes to Me will not hunger,	**Jn 6:35**	
and he **w** believes in Me will	**Jn 6:35**	
and the one **w** comes to Me I will	**Jn 6:37**	
but the will of Him **w** sent Me.	**Jn 6:38**	
This is the will of Him **w** sent Me,	**Jn 6:39**	
that everyone **w** beholds the Son	**Jn 6:40**	
the Father **w** sent Me draws him;	**Jn 6:44**	
Everyone **w** has heard and learned	**Jn 6:45**	
except the One **w** is from God;	**Jn 6:46**	
he **w** believes has eternal life.	**Jn 6:47**	
"He **w** eats My flesh and drinks My	**Jn 6:54**	
"He **w** eats My flesh and drinks My	**Jn 6:56**	
of the Father, so he **w** eats Me,	**Jn 6:57**	
he **w** eats this bread will live	**Jn 6:58**	
w can listen to it?"	**Jn 6:60**	*5101*
"It is the Spirit **w** gives life;	**Jn 6:63**	
some of you **w** do not believe."	**Jn 6:64**	*3739*
w they were who did not believe,	**Jn 6:64**	*5101*
who they were **w** did not believe,	**Jn 6:64**	
w it was that would betray Him.	**Jn 6:64**	*5101*
is not Mine, but His **w** sent Me.	**Jn 7:16**	
"He **w** speaks from himself seeks	**Jn 7:18**	
but He **w** is seeking the glory of	**Jn 7:18**	
the glory of the One **w** sent Him,	**Jn 7:18**	
W seeks to kill You?"	**Jn 7:20**	*5101*
Myself, but He **w** sent Me is true,	**Jn 7:28**	
you, then I go to Him **w** sent Me.	**Jn 7:33**	
"He **w** believes in Me, as the	**Jn 7:38**	
whom those **w** believed in Him were	**Jn 7:39**	
(he **w** came to Him before,	**Jn 7:50**	
"He **w** is without sin among you,	**Jn 8:7**	
he **w** follows Me will not walk in	**Jn 8:12**	
but I and the Father **w** sent Me.	**Jn 8:16**	
"I am He **w** testifies about	**Jn 8:18**	
w sent Me testifies about Me."	**Jn 8:18**	
were saying to Him, "**W** are You?"	**Jn 8:25**	*5101*
you, but He **w** sent Me is true;	**Jn 8:26**	
"And He **w** sent Me is with Me;	**Jn 8:29**	
to those Jews **w** had believed Him,	**Jn 8:31**	
everyone **w** commits sin is the	**Jn 8:34**	
a man **w** has told you the truth,	**Jn 8:40**	*3739*
"He **w** is of God hears the words	**Jn 8:47**	
there is One **w** seeks and judges.	**Jn 8:50**	
than our father Abraham, **w** died?	**Jn 8:53**	*3748*
it is My Father **w** glorifies Me, of	**Jn 8:54**	
"Rabbi, **w** sinned, this man or his	**Jn 9:2**	*5101*
work the works of Him **w** sent Me as	**Jn 9:4**	
and those **w** previously saw him as	**Jn 9:8**	
the one **w** used to sit and beg?"	**Jn 9:8**	
man **w** is called Jesus made clay,	**Jn 9:11**	
man **w** was formerly blind.	**Jn 9:13**	
"How can a man **w** is a sinner	**Jn 9:16**	
very one **w** had received his sight,	**Jn 9:18**	
son, **w** you say was born blind?	**Jn 9:19**	*3739*
or **w** opened his eyes, we do not	**Jn 9:21**	*5101*
called the man **w** had been blind,	**Jn 9:24**	*3739*
He answered, "**W** is He, Lord, that	**Jn 9:36**	*5101*
the one **w** is talking with you."	**Jn 9:37**	
that those **w** do not see may see,	**Jn 9:39**	
those **w** see may become blind."	**Jn 9:39**	
Those of the Pharisees **w** were with	**Jn 9:40**	
he **w** does not enter by the door	**Jn 10:1**	
"But he **w** enters by the door is a	**Jn 10:2**	
"All **w** came before Me are thieves	**Jn 10:8**	*3745*
"He **w** is a hired hand, and not a	**Jn 10:12**	
w is not the owner of the sheep,	**Jn 10:12**	*3739*
"My Father, **w** has given *them* to	**Jn 10:29**	*3739*
It was the Mary **w** anointed the	**Jn 11:2**	

Thomas, **w** is called Didymus, **Jn 11:16**
he **w** believes in Me will live **Jn 11:25**
and everyone **w** lives and believes **Jn 11:26**
even He **w** comes into the world." **Jn 11:27**
Jews **w** were with her in the house, **Jn 11:31**
and the Jews **w** came with her **Jn 11:33**
w opened the eyes of the blind man, **Jn 11:37**
man **w** had died came forth, bound **Jn 11:44**
w came to Mary, and saw what **Jn 11:45**
w was high priest that year, **Jn 11:49**
of God **w** are scattered abroad. **Jn 11:52**
w was intending to betray Him, **Jn 12:4**
crowd **w** had come to the feast, **Jn 12:12**
W COMES IN THE NAME OF THE LORD, **Jn 12:13**
So the people, **w** were with **Jn 12:17**
those **w** were going up to worship **Jn 12:20**
w was from Bethsaida of Galilee, **Jn 12:21** *3588*
"He **w** loves his life loses it, **Jn 12:25**
and he **w** hates his life in this **Jn 12:25**
w stood by and heard it were **Jn 12:29**
W is this Son of Man?" **Jn 12:34** *5101*
he **w** walks in the darkness does **Jn 12:35**
"LORD, **W** HAS BELIEVED OUR REPORT? **Jn 12:38** *5101*
"He **w** believes in Me, does not **Jn 12:44**
in Me but in Him **w** sent Me. **Jn 12:44**
"He **w** sees Me sees the **Jn 12:45**
Me sees the One **w** sent Me. **Jn 12:45**
that everyone **w** believes in Me will **Jn 12:46**
"He **w** rejects Me and does not **Jn 12:48**
My sayings, has one **w** judges him; **Jn 12:48**
but the Father Himself **w** sent Me **Jn 12:49**
loved His own **w** were in the world, **Jn 13:1** *3588*
"He **w** has bathed needs only to **Jn 13:10**
knew the one **w** was betraying Him; **Jn 13:11**
nor *is* one **w** is sent greater **Jn 13:16**
greater than the one **w** sent him. **Jn 13:16**
'HE **W** EATS MY BREAD HAS LIFTED UP **Jn 13:18**
he **w** receives whomever I send **Jn 13:20**
and he **w** receives Me receives Him **Jn 13:20**
Me receives Him **w** sent Me." **Jn 13:20**
w it is of whom He is speaking." **Jn 13:24** *5101*
said to Him, "Lord, **w** is it?" **Jn 13:25** *5101*
He **w** has seen Me has seen the **Jn 14:9**
I say to you, he **w** believes in Me, **Jn 14:12**
"He **w** has My commandments and **Jn 14:21**
keeps them is the one **w** loves Me; **Jn 14:21**
and he **w** loves Me will be loved **Jn 14:21**
"He **w** does not love Me does not **Jn 14:24**
Mine, but the Father's **w** sent Me. **Jn 14:24**
he **w** abides in Me and I in him, **Jn 15:5**
do not know the One **w** sent Me. **Jn 15:21**
w hates Me hates My Father also. **Jn 15:23**
truth **w** proceeds from the Father, **Jn 15:26** *3739*
an hour is coming for everyone **w** kills **Jn 16:2**
now I am going to Him **w** sent Me; **Jn 16:5**
but for those also **w** believe in Me **Jn 17:20**
Judas also, **w** was betraying Him, **Jn 18:2**
Judas also, **w** was betraying Him, **Jn 18:5**
w was high priest that year. **Jn 18:13** *3739*
Now Caiaphas was the one **w** had **Jn 18:14**
w was known to the high priest, **Jn 18:16**
w kept the door said to Peter, **Jn 18:17**
Question those **w** have heard what I **Jn 18:21**
Everyone **w** is of the truth hears **Jn 18:37**
for this reason he **w** delivered Me **Jn 19:11**
everyone **w** makes himself out *to be* **Jn 19:12**
other **w** was crucified with Him; **Jn 19:32**
he **w** has seen has testified, **Jn 19:35**
w had first come to Him by night, **Jn 19:39**
So the other disciple **w** had first **Jn 20:8**
Blessed *are* they **w** did not see, **Jn 20:29**
to question Him, "**W** are You?" **Jn 21:12** *5101*
the one **w** also had leaned back on **Jn 21:20** *3739*
w is the one who betrays You?" **Jn 21:20** *5101*
who is the one **w** betrays You?" **Jn 21:20**
w is testifying to these things **Jn 21:24**
w has been taken up from you into **Ac 1:11**
w became a guide to those who **Ac 1:16**
a guide to those **w** arrested Jesus. **Ac 1:16**
to all **w** were living in Jerusalem; **Ac 1:19**
of the men **w** have accompanied us **Ac 1:21**
(**w** was also called Justus), **Ac 1:23** *3739*
w know the hearts of all men, **Ac 1:24** *2589*
these **w** are speaking Galileans? **Ac 2:7**
and all you **w** live in Jerusalem, **Ac 2:14**
EVERYONE **W** CALLS ON THE NAME **Ac 2:21** *3739*
not David **w** ascended into heaven, **Ac 2:34**
and for all **w** are far off, **Ac 2:39** *3588*
those **w** had received his word were **Ac 2:41**
w had believed were together and **Ac 2:44**
by day those **w** were being saved. **Ac 2:47**
And a man **w** had been lame **Ac 3:2**
those **w** were entering the temple. **Ac 3:2**
of him as being the one **w** used to sit **Ac 3:10**
all the prophets **w** have spoken, **Ac 3:24** *3745*
w are the sons of the prophets and **Ac 3:25**
But many of those **w** had heard the **Ac 4:4**
w were of high-priestly descent. **Ac 4:6** *3745*
And seeing the man **w** had been **Ac 4:14**
to all **w** live in Jerusalem, **Ac 4:16**
it is You **W** MADE THE HEAVEN **Ac 4:24**
w by the Holy Spirit, *through* the **Ac 4:25**
And the congregation of those **w** **Ac 4:32**
for all **w** were owners of land or **Ac 4:34** *3745*
w was also called Barnabas by the **Ac 4:36**
and **w** owned a tract of land, sold **Ac 4:37**
fear came over all **w** heard of it. **Ac 5:5**
the feet of those **w** have buried **Ac 5:9**
over all **w** heard of these things. **Ac 5:11**

bringing people **w** were sick or **Ac 5:16**
But the officers **w** came did not **Ac 5:22**
has given to those **w** obey Him." **Ac 5:32**
and all **w** followed him were **Ac 5:36** *3745*
w followed him were scattered. **Ac 5:37** *3745*
forward false witnesses **w** said, **Ac 6:13**
all **w** were sitting in the Council **Ac 6:15**
W KNEW NOTHING ABOUT JOSEPH. **Ac 7:18** *3739*
"It was he **w** took shrewd **Ac 7:19**
"But the one **w** was injuring his **Ac 7:27**
'**W** MADE YOU A RULER AND JUDGE **Ac 7:27** *5101*
'**W** MADE YOU A RULER AND A JUDGE?' **Ac 7:35** *5101*
help of the angel **w** appeared to him **Ac 7:35**
w said to the sons of Israel, **Ac 7:37**
"This is the one **w** was in the **Ac 7:38**
the angel **w** was speaking to him on **Ac 7:38**
and **w** *was* with our fathers; **Ac 7:38**
FOR US GODS **W** WILL GO BEFORE US; **Ac 7:40** *3739*
FOR THIS MOSES **W** LED US OUT OF THE **Ac 7:40** *3739*
just as He **w** spoke to Moses **Ac 7:44**
Solomon **w** built a house for Him. **Ac 7:47**
"You men **w** are stiff-necked and **Ac 7:51**
They killed those **w** had **Ac 7:52**
you **w** received the law as ordained **Ac 7:53** *3748*
those **w** had been scattered went **Ac 8:4**
of many **w** had unclean spirits, **Ac 8:7**
and many **w** had been paralyzed and **Ac 8:7**
w formerly was practicing magic in **Ac 8:9**
w came down and prayed for them that **Ac 8:15** *3748*
w was in charge of all her **Ac 8:27** *3739*
W WILL RELATE HIS GENERATION? **Ac 8:33** *5101*
"**W** are You, Lord?" **Ac 9:5** *5101*
The men **w** traveled with him **Ac 9:7**
bind all **w** call on Your name." **Ac 9:14**
w appeared to you on the road by **Ac 9:17**
the disciples **w** were at Damascus, **Ac 9:19**
"Is this not he **w** in Jerusalem **Ac 9:21**
those **w** called on this name, **Ac 9:21**
and **w** had come here for **Ac 9:21**
and confounding the Jews **w** lived at **Ac 9:22**
to the saints **w** lived at Lydda. **Ac 9:32**
w had been bedridden eight years, **Ac 9:33**
And all **w** lived at Lydda and **Ac 9:35**
and one **w** feared God with all his **Ac 10:2**
of God **w** had *just* come in **Ac 10:3**
Simon, **w** is also called Peter; **Ac 10:5** *3739*
When the angel **w** was speaking **Ac 10:7**
those **w** were his personal attendants, **Ac 10:7**
men **w** had been sent by Cornelius, **Ac 10:17**
Simon, **w** was also called Peter, **Ac 10:18**
unlawful it is for a man **w** is a Jew to **Ac 10:28**
Simon, **w** is also called Peter, **Ac 10:32** *3739*
but in every nation the man **w** **Ac 10:35**
all **w** were oppressed by the devil, **Ac 10:38**
w were chosen beforehand by God, **Ac 10:41**
w ate and drank with Him after He **Ac 10:41** *3748*
this is the One **w** has been appointed **Ac 10:42**
everyone **w** believes in Him receives **Ac 10:43**
w were listening to the message. **Ac 10:44**
believers **w** came with Peter were **Ac 10:45** *3745*
w have received the Holy Spirit **Ac 10:47** *3748*
brethren **w** were throughout Judea **Ac 11:1**
those **w** were circumcised took **Ac 11:2**
Simon, **w** is also called Peter, **Ac 11:13**
w was I that I could stand in **Ac 11:17** *5101*
So then those **w** were scattered **Ac 11:19**
w came to Antioch and *began* **Ac 11:20** *3748*
w believed turned to the Lord. **Ac 11:21**
on some **w** belonged to the church in **Ac 12:1** *3588*
of John **w** was also called Mark, **Ac 12:12**
them John, **w** was also called Mark. **Ac 12:25**
and Simeon **w** was called Niger, **Ac 13:1**
and Manaen **w** had been brought up **Ac 13:1**
w was with the proconsul, Sergius **Ac 13:7** *3739*
Saul, **w** was also *known as* Paul, **Ac 13:9** *3588*
"You **w** are full of all deceit and **Ac 13:10**
w would lead him by the hand. **Ac 13:11** *5497*
"Men of Israel, and you **w** fear God, **Ac 13:16**
MY HEART, **w** will do all My will.' **Ac 13:22** *3739*
and those among you **w** fear God, **Ac 13:26**
"For those **w** live in Jerusalem, **Ac 13:27**
He appeared to those **w** came up **Ac 13:31**
the very ones **w** are now His **Ac 13:31** *3748*
and through Him everyone **w** **Ac 13:39**
followed Paul and Barnabas, **w**, **Ac 13:43** *3748*
But the Jews **w** disbelieved stirred **Ac 14:2**
w was testifying to the word **Ac 14:3**
At Lystra a man was sitting **w** had no **Ac 14:8** *3739*
mother's womb, **w** had never walked. **Ac 14:8** *3739*
listening to Paul as he spoke, **w**, **Ac 14:9** *3739*
W MADE THE HEAVEN AND THE EARTH **Ac 14:15** *3739*
of the Pharisees **w** had believed stood **Ac 15:5**
"And God, **w** knows the heart, testified **Ac 15:8** *2589*
GENTILES **W** ARE CALLED BY MY NAME,' **Ac 15:17** *3739*
W MAKES THESE THINGS KNOWN FROM **Ac 15:18**
we do not trouble those **w** are turning **Ac 15:19**
in every city those **w** preach him, **Ac 15:21**
and the brethren **w** are elders, **Ac 15:23**
Cilicia **w** are from the Gentiles, **Ac 15:23** *3588*
men **w** have risked their lives for **Ac 15:26**
w themselves will also report the **Ac 15:27**
to those **w** had sent them out. **Ac 15:33**
not take him along **w** had deserted **Ac 15:38**
a Jewish woman **w** was a believer, **Ac 16:1**
w were in Lystra and Iconium. **Ac 16:2**
of the Jews **w** were in those parts, **Ac 16:3**
and elders **w** were in Jerusalem, **Ac 16:4** *3588*
to the women **w** had assembled. **Ac 16:13**
w was bringing her masters much **Ac 16:16** *3748*

w are proclaiming to you the way **Ac 16:17** *3748*
with all **w** were in his house. **Ac 16:32** *3588*
without trial, men **w** are Romans, **Ac 16:37**
"These men **w** have upset the world **Ac 17:6**
authorities **w** heard these things. **Ac 17:8**
Now those **w** escorted Paul brought **Ac 17:15**
those **w** happened to be present. **Ac 17:17**
"The God **w** made the world and all **Ac 17:24**
w had believed through grace, **Ac 18:27**
in Him **w** was coming after him, **Ac 19:4**
so that all **w** lived in Asia heard **Ac 19:10**
w went from place to place, **Ac 19:13**
attempted to name over those **w** had **Ac 19:13**
know about Paul, but **w** are you?" **Ac 19:15** *5101*
and Greeks, **w** lived in Ephesus; **Ac 19:17**
those **w** had believed kept coming, **Ac 19:18**
And many of those **w** practiced **Ac 19:19**
two of those **w** ministered to him, **Ac 19:22**
w made silver shrines of Artemis, **Ac 19:24**
Also some of the Asiarchs **w** **Ac 19:31**
what man is there after all **w** does **Ac 19:35** *3739*
w are neither robbers of temples **Ac 19:37**
if Demetrius and the craftsmen **w** **Ac 19:38**
among all those **w** are sanctified. **Ac 20:32**
and to the men **w** were with me. **Ac 20:34**
w was one of the seven, **Ac 21:8**
daughters **w** were prophetesses. **Ac 21:9**
will bind the man **w** owns this belt **Ac 21:11** *3739*
the Jews of those **w** have believed, **Ac 21:20**
all the Jews **w** are among the Gentiles **Ac 21:21**
have four men **w** are under a vow; **Ac 21:23**
the Gentiles **w** have believed, **Ac 21:25**
This is the man **w** preaches to all **Ac 21:28**
w he was and what he had done. **Ac 21:33** *5101*
"Then you are not the Egyptian **w** **Ac 21:38**
those **w** were there to Jerusalem as **Ac 22:5**
'**W** are You, Lord?' **Ac 22:8** *5101*
w were with me saw the light, **Ac 22:9** *5101*
of the One **w** was speaking to me. **Ac 22:9**
the hand by those **w** were with me and **Ac 22:11**
a man **w** was devout by the standard **Ac 22:12**
of by all the Jews **w** lived there, **Ac 22:12**
and beat those **w** believed in You. **Ac 22:19**
of those **w** were slaying him.' **Ac 22:20**
the centurion **w** was standing by, **Ac 22:25**
w is a Roman and uncondemned?" **Ac 22:25**
Therefore those **w** were about to **Ac 22:29**
than forty **w** formed this plot. **Ac 23:13**
are lying in wait for him **w** have **Ac 23:21** *3748*
pest and a fellow **w** stirs up dissension **Ac 24:5**
w ought to have been present **Ac 24:19** *3739*
Drusilla, his wife **w** was a Jewess, **Ac 24:24**
the Jews **w** had come down from **Ac 25:7**
"There is a man **w** was left as a **Ac 25:14**
those **w** were journeying with me. **Ac 26:13**
'**W** are You, Lord?' **Ac 26:15** *5101*
w have been sanctified by faith in Me. **Ac 26:18**
but also all **w** hear me this day, **Ac 26:29**
those **w** were sitting with them, **Ac 26:30**
all those **w** are sailing with you.' **Ac 27:24**
and commanded that those **w** could **Ac 27:43**
w welcomed us and entertained us **Ac 28:7** *3739*
w had diseases were coming to him **Ac 28:9**
the soldier **w** was guarding him. **Ac 28:16**
w were the leading men of the Jews, **Ac 28:17**
was welcoming all **w** came to him, **Ac 28:30**
w was born of a descendant of **Ro 1:3**
w was declared the Son of God with **Ro 1:4**
all **w** are beloved of God in Rome, **Ro 1:7**
gospel to you also **w** are in Rome. **Ro 1:15** *3588*
salvation to everyone **w** believes, **Ro 1:16**
w suppress the truth in **Ro 1:18**
the Creator, **w** is blessed forever. **Ro 1:25** *3739*
that those **w** practice such things **Ro 1:32**
approval to those **w** practice them. **Ro 1:32**
everyone of you **w** passes judgment, **Ro 2:1**
for you **w** judge practice the same **Ro 2:1**
upon those **w** practice such things. **Ro 2:2**
pass judgment on those **w** practice **Ro 2:3**
W WILL RENDER TO EACH PERSON **Ro 2:6** *3739*
to those **w** by perseverance in **Ro 2:7**
but to those **w** are selfishly **Ro 2:8**
for every soul of man **w** does evil, **Ro 2:9**
peace to everyone **w** does good, **Ro 2:10**
For all **w** have sinned without the **Ro 2:12** *3745*
and all **w** have sinned under the **Ro 2:12** *3745*
is not the hearers of the Law **w** **Ro 2:13**
For when Gentiles **w** do not have **Ro 2:14**
light to those **w** are in darkness, **Ro 2:19**
you, therefore, **w** teach another, **Ro 2:21**
You **w** preach that one shall not **Ro 2:21**
You **w** say that one should not **Ro 2:22**
You **w** abhor idols, do you rob **Ro 2:22**
You **w** boast in the Law, through **Ro 2:23** *3739*
he **w** is physically uncircumcised, **Ro 2:27**
will he not judge you **w** though **Ro 2:27** *3588*
is not a Jew **w** is one outwardly, **Ro 2:28** *3588*
But he is a Jew **w** is one inwardly; **Ro 2:29** *3588*
The God **w** inflicts wrath is not **Ro 3:5**
THERE IS NONE **W** UNDERSTANDS, **Ro 3:11**
THERE IS NONE **W** SEEKS FOR GOD; **Ro 3:11**
THERE IS NONE **W** DOES GOOD, **Ro 3:12**
to those **w** are under the Law, **Ro 3:19**
Christ for all those **w** believe; **Ro 3:22**
of the one **w** has faith in Jesus. **Ro 3:26**
since indeed God **w** will justify **Ro 3:30** *3739*
Now to the one **w** works, his wage **Ro 4:4**
But to the one **w** does not work, **Ro 4:5**
in Him **w** justifies the ungodly, **Ro 4:5**

might be the father of all **w** believe	Ro 4:11	
w not only are of the circumcision,	Ro 4:12	
but **w** also follow in the steps of	Ro 4:12	
those **w** are of the Law are heirs,	Ro 4:14	
only to those **w** are of the Law,	Ro 4:16	
also to those **w** are of the faith	Ro 4:16	
w is the father of us all,	Ro 4:16	3739
w gives life to the dead and calls	Ro 4:17	
as those **w** believe in Him who	Ro 4:24	
as those who believe in Him **w**	Ro 4:24	
He **w** was delivered over because of	Ro 4:25	3739
the Holy Spirit **w** was given to us.	Ro 5:5	
even over those **w** had not sinned	Ro 5:14	
w is a type of Him who was to come.	Ro 5:14	3739
is a type of Him **w** was to come.	Ro 5:14	
came through the one **w** sinned;	Ro 5:16	
much more those **w** receive the	Ro 5:17	
we **w** died to sin still live in it?	Ro 6:2	3748
us **w** have been baptized into Christ	Ro 6:3	3745
he **w** has died is freed from sin.	Ro 6:7	
speaking to those **w** know the law),	Ro 7:1	
to Him **w** was raised from the dead,	Ro 7:4	
me, the one **w** wants to do good.	Ro 7:21	
W will set me free from the body	Ro 7:24	5101
for those **w** are in Christ Jesus.	Ro 8:1	
w do not walk according to the	Ro 8:4	
For those **w** are according to the	Ro 8:5	
but those **w** are according to the	Ro 8:5	
and those **w** are in the flesh	Ro 8:8	
But if the Spirit of Him **w** raised	Ro 8:11	
He **w** raised Christ Jesus from the	Ro 8:11	
through His Spirit **w** dwells in you.	Ro 8:11	
For all **w** are being led by the	Ro 8:14	3745
but because of Him **w** subjected it,	Ro 8:20	
for **w** hopes for what he *already*	Ro 8:24	5100
and He **w** searches the hearts knows	Ro 8:27	
for good to those **w** love God,	Ro 8:28	
to those **w** are called according to	Ro 8:28	
If God *is* for us, **w** *is* against us?	Ro 8:31	5101
He **w** did not spare His own Son,	Ro 8:32	3739
W will bring a charge against	Ro 8:33	5101
God is the one **w** justifies;	Ro 8:33	
w is the one who condemns?	Ro 8:34	5101
who is the one **w** condemns?	Ro 8:34	
Christ Jesus is He **w** died,	Ro 8:34	
died, yes, rather **w** was raised,	Ro 8:34	
w is at the right hand of God,	Ro 8:34	3739
of God, **w** also intercedes for us.	Ro 8:34	3739
W will separate us from the love	Ro 8:35	5101
conquer through Him **w** loved us.	Ro 8:37	
w are Israelites, to whom belongs	Ro 9:4	3748
to the flesh, **w** is over all,	Ro 9:5	
w are *descended* from Israel;	Ro 9:6	3588
the flesh **w** are children of God,	Ro 9:8	3778
works but because of Him **w** calls,	Ro 9:11	
man **w** wills or the man who runs,	Ro 9:16	
man who wills or the man **w** runs,	Ro 9:16	
who runs, but on God **w** has mercy.	Ro 9:16	
For **w** resists His will?"	Ro 9:19	5101
On the contrary, **w** are you,	Ro 9:20	5101
you, O man, **w** answers back to God?	Ro 9:20	
CALL THOSE **W** WERE NOT MY PEOPLE,	Ro 9:25	
AND HER **W** WAS NOT BELOVED,	Ro 9:25	
w did not pursue righteousness,	Ro 9:30	
AND HE **W** BELIEVES IN HIM WILL NOT	Ro 9:33	
to everyone **w** believes.	Ro 10:4	
For Moses writes that the man **w**	Ro 10:5	
'**W** WILL ASCEND INTO HEAVEN?'	Ro 10:6	5101
'**W** WILL DESCEND INTO THE ABYSS?'	Ro 10:7	5101
in riches for all **w** call on Him;	Ro 10:12	
FEET OF THOSE **W** BRING GOOD NEWS	Ro 10:15	
"LORD, **W** HAS BELIEVED OUR REPORT?"	Ro 10:16	5101
FOUND BY THOSE **W** DID NOT SEEK ME,	Ro 10:20	
TO THOSE **W** DID NOT ASK FOR ME."	Ro 10:20	
MEN **W** HAVE NOT BOWED THE KNEE TO	Ro 11:4	3748
those **w** were chosen obtained it,	Ro 11:7	
am speaking to you **w** are Gentiles.	Ro 11:13	
it is not you **w** supports the root,	Ro 11:18	
to those **w** fell, severity, but to	Ro 11:22	
how much more will these **w** are	Ro 11:24	3588
For **W** HAS KNOWN THE MIND OF THE	Ro 11:34	5101
LORD, OR **W** BECAME HIS COUNSELOR?	Ro 11:34	5101
Or **W** HAS FIRST GIVEN TO HIM THAT	Ro 11:35	5101
so we, **w** are many, are one body in	Ro 12:5	
or he **w** teaches, in his teaching;	Ro 12:7	
or he **w** exhorts, in his	Ro 12:8	
he **w** gives, with liberality;	Ro 12:8	
he **w** leads, with diligence;	Ro 12:8	
he **w** shows mercy, with	Ro 12:8	
Bless those **w** persecute you;	Ro 12:14	
Rejoice with those **w** rejoice,	Ro 12:15	
and weep with those **w** weep.	Ro 12:15	
and they **w** have opposed will	Ro 13:2	
an avenger **w** brings wrath on the	Ro 13:4	
on the one **w** practices evil.	Ro 13:4	
for he **w** loves his neighbor has	Ro 13:8	
accept the one **w** is weak in faith,	Ro 14:1	
he **w** is weak eats vegetables *only*.	Ro 14:2	
The one **w** eats is not to regard	Ro 14:3	
with contempt the one **w** does not eat,	Ro 14:3	
and the one **w** does not eat	Ro 14:3	
not to judge the one **w** eats,	Ro 14:3	
W are you to judge the servant of	Ro 14:4	5101
He **w** observes the day, observes it	Ro 14:6	
it for the Lord, and he **w** eats,	Ro 14:6	
and he **w** eats not, for the Lord he	Ro 14:6	
w thinks anything to be unclean,	Ro 14:14	
For he **w** in this *way* serves Christ	Ro 14:18	
the man **w** eats and gives offense.	Ro 14:20	
Happy is he **w** does not condemn	Ro 14:22	
But he **w** doubts is condemned if he	Ro 14:23	
Now we **w** are strong ought to bear	Ro 15:1	
W REPROACHED YOU FELL ON ME."	Ro 15:3	
Now may the God **w** gives	Ro 15:5	
AND HE **W** ARISES TO RULE OVER THE	Ro 15:12	
W HAD NO NEWS OF HIM SHALL SEE,	Ro 15:21	3739
AND THEY **W** HAVE NOT HEARD SHALL	Ro 15:21	
those **w** are disobedient in Judea,	Ro 15:31	
w is a servant of the church which	Ro 16:1	
w for my life risked their own	Ro 16:4	3748
w is the first convert to Christ	Ro 16:5	3739
Mary, **w** has worked hard for you.	Ro 16:6	3748
w are outstanding among the	Ro 16:7	3748
w also were in Christ before me.	Ro 16:7	3739
Greet those **w** are of the *household*	Ro 16:10	3588
of Narcissus, **w** are in the Lord.	Ro 16:11	
w has worked hard in the Lord.	Ro 16:12	3748
all the saints **w** are with them.	Ro 16:15	
keep your eye on those **w** cause	Ro 16:17	
I, Tertius, **w** write this letter,	Ro 16:22	
Now to Him **w** is able to establish	Ro 16:25	
to those **w** have been sanctified in	1Co 1:2	
with all **w** in every place call	1Co 1:2	
w will also confirm you to the	1Co 1:8	3739
those **w** are perishing,	1Co 1:18	
but to us **w** are being saved it is	1Co 1:18	
preached to save those **w** believe.	1Co 1:21	
but to those **w** are the called,	1Co 1:24	
w became to us wisdom from God,	1Co 1:30	3739
"LET HIM **W** BOASTS, BOAST IN THE	1Co 1:31	
wisdom among those **w** are mature;	1Co 2:6	
of this age, **w** are passing away;	1Co 2:6	
ALL THAT GOD HAS PREPARED FOR THOSE **W**	1Co 2:9	
For **w** among men knows the *thoughts*	1Co 2:11	5101
but the Spirit **w** is from God,	1Co 2:12	3588
But he **w** is spiritual appraises	1Co 2:15	
For **W** HAS KNOWN THE MIND OF THE	1Co 2:16	5101
So then neither the one **w** plants	1Co 3:7	
nor the one **w** waters is anything,	1Co 3:7	
but God **w** causes the growth.	1Co 3:7	
Now he **w** plants and he who waters	1Co 3:8	
plants and he **w** waters are one;	1Co 3:8	
"*He is* THE ONE **W** CATCHES THE WISE	1Co 3:19	
the one **w** examines me is the Lord.	1Co 4:4	
but wait until the Lord comes **w**	1Co 4:5	3739
For **w** regards you as superior?	1Co 4:7	5101
w is my beloved and faithful child	1Co 4:17	3739
the words of those **w** are arrogant but	1Co 4:19	
so that the one **w** had done	1Co 5:2	
him **w** has so committed this,	1Co 5:3	
those **w** are within *the church?*	1Co 5:12	3588
But those **w** are outside, God	1Co 5:13	3588
do you appoint them as judges **w**	1Co 6:4	
one wise man **w** will be able to decide	1Co 6:5	3739
Or do you not know that the one **w**	1Co 6:16	
But the one **w** joins himself to the	1Co 6:17	
of the Holy Spirit **w** is in you,	1Co 6:19	
has a wife **w** is an unbeliever,	1Co 7:12	
w has an unbelieving husband,	1Co 7:13	3748
For he **w** was called in the Lord	1Co 7:22	
he **w** was called while free,	1Co 7:22	
but I give an opinion as one **w** by	1Co 7:25	
so that from now on those **w** have	1Co 7:29	
and those **w** weep, as though they	1Co 7:30	
and those **w** rejoice, as though	1Co 7:30	
and those **w** buy, as though they	1Co 7:30	
and those **w** use the world, as	1Co 7:31	
One **w** is unmarried is concerned	1Co 7:32	
but one **w** is married is concerned	1Co 7:33	
The woman **w** is unmarried, and	1Co 7:34	
but one **w** is married is concerned	1Co 7:34	
But he **w** stands firm in his heart,	1Co 7:37	3739
So then both he **w** gives his own	1Co 7:38	
and he **w** does not give her in	1Co 7:38	
sees you, **w** have knowledge,	1Co 8:10	
knowledge he **w** is weak is ruined,	1Co 8:11	
to those **w** examine me is this:	1Co 9:3	
W at any time serves as a soldier	1Co 9:7	5101
W plants a vineyard and does not	1Co 9:7	5101
Or **w** tends a flock and does not	1Co 9:7	5101
those **w** perform sacred services eat	1Co 9:13	
and those **w** attend regularly to	1Co 9:13	
So also the Lord directed those **w**	1Co 9:14	
to those **w** are under the Law, as	1Co 9:20	3588
win those **w** are under the Law;	1Co 9:20	3588
to those **w** are without law, as	1Co 9:21	
might win those **w** are without law.	1Co 9:21	
those **w** run in a race all run,	1Co 9:24	
Everyone **w** competes in the	1Co 9:25	
Therefore let him **w** thinks he	1Co 10:12	
w will not allow you to be tempted	1Co 10:13	3739
bread, we **w** are many are one body;	1Co 10:17	
are not those **w** eat the sacrifices	1Co 10:18	
sake of the one **w** informed *you,*	1Co 10:28	
Every man **w** has *something* on his	1Co 11:4	
But every woman **w** has her head	1Co 11:5	
so that those **w** are approved	1Co 11:19	
and shame those **w** have nothing?	1Co 11:22	
For he **w** eats and drinks, eats and	1Co 11:29	
but the same God **w** works all	1Co 12:6	
For one **w** speaks in a tongue does	1Co 14:2	
But one **w** prophesies speaks to men	1Co 14:3	
One **w** speaks in a tongue edifies	1Co 14:4	
w prophesies edifies the church.	1Co 14:4	
and greater is one **w** prophesies	1Co 14:5	
than one **w** speaks in tongues,	1Co 14:5	
w will prepare himself for battle?	1Co 14:8	5101
to the one **w** speaks a barbarian,	1Co 14:11	
and the one **w** speaks will be a	1Co 14:11	
Therefore let one **w** speaks in a	1Co 14:13	
how will the one **w** fills the place	1Co 14:16	
a sign, not to those **w** believe but	1Co 14:22	
but to those **w** believe.	1Co 14:22	
is made to another **w** is seated,	1Co 14:30	
Then those also **w** have fallen	1Co 15:18	
fruits of those **w** are asleep.	1Co 15:20	
those **w** are Christ's at His coming,	1Co 15:23	3588
He is excepted **w** put all things in	1Co 15:27	
One **w** subjected all things to Him,	1Co 15:28	
do **w** are baptized for the dead?	1Co 15:29	
so also are those **w** are earthy;	1Co 15:48	
so also are those **w** are heavenly.	1Co 15:48	
w gives us the victory through our	1Co 15:57	
w helps in the work and labors.	1Co 16:16	
saints **w** are throughout Achaia:	2Co 1:1	
w comforts us in all our	2Co 1:4	
comfort those **w** are in any affliction	2Co 1:4	
but in God **w** raises the dead;	2Co 1:9	
w delivered us from so great a	2Co 1:10	3739
w was preached among you by us	2Co 1:19	
Now He **w** establishes us with you	2Co 1:21	
w also sealed us and gave *us* the	2Co 1:22	
w then makes me glad but the one	2Co 2:2	5101
those **w** ought to make me rejoice;	2Co 2:3	3739
w always leads us in triumph	2Co 2:14	
among those **w** are being saved	2Co 2:15	
and among those **w** are perishing;	2Co 2:15	
w is adequate for these things?	2Co 2:16	5101
w also made us adequate *as*	2Co 3:6	3739
and *are* not like Moses, **w**	2Co 3:13	
veiled to those **w** are perishing,	2Co 4:3	
of Christ, **w** is the image of God.	2Co 4:4	3739
For God, **w** said,	2Co 4:6	
is the One **w** has shone in our	2Co 4:6	3739
For we **w** live are constantly being	2Co 4:11	
knowing that He **w** raised the Lord	2Co 4:14	
Now He **w** prepared us for this very	2Co 5:5	
w gave to us the Spirit as a	2Co 5:5	
those **w** take pride in appearance and	2Co 5:12	
that they **w** live might no longer	2Co 5:15	
but for Him **w** died and rose again	2Co 5:15	
w reconciled us to Himself through	2Co 5:18	3588
He made Him **w** knew no sin *to be*	2Co 5:21	
But God, **w** comforts the depressed,	2Co 7:6	
w were the first to begin a year	2Co 8:10	3748
"HE **W** *gathered* MUCH DID NOT HAVE	2Co 8:15	
HE **W** *gathered* LITTLE HAD NO LACK."	2Co 8:15	
w puts the same earnestness on	2Co 8:16	
he **w** sows sparingly will also	2Co 9:6	
and he **w** sows bountifully will	2Co 9:6	
Now He **w** supplies seed to the	2Co 9:10	
I **w** am meek when face to face with	2Co 10:1	3739
w regard us as if we walked	2Co 10:2	
of those **w** commend themselves;	2Co 10:12	
But HE **W** BOASTS IS TO BOAST IN	2Co 10:17	
w commends himself that is approved,	2Co 10:18	
from those **w** desire an opportunity	2Co 11:12	
W is weak without my being weak?	2Co 11:29	5101
W is led into sin without my	2Co 11:29	5101
Jesus, He **w** is blessed forever,	2Co 11:31	
I know a man in Christ **w** fourteen	2Co 12:2	
those **w** have sinned in the past	2Co 12:21	
to those **w** have sinned in the past	2Co 13:2	
of the Christ **w** speaks in me,	2Co 13:3	
me, and **w** is not weak toward you,	2Co 13:3	3739
Father, **w** raised Him from the dead	Ga 1:1	
all the brethren **w** are with me,	Ga 1:2	
w gave Himself for our sins so that	Ga 1:4	
so quickly deserting Him **w** called you	Ga 1:6	
are some **w** are disturbing you and	Ga 1:7	
But when God, **w** had set me apart	Ga 1:15	
those **w** were apostles before me;	Ga 1:17	
"He **w** once persecuted us is now	Ga 1:23	
to those **w** were of reputation,	Ga 2:2	
But not even Titus, **w** was with me,	Ga 2:3	3588
w had sneaked in to spy	Ga 2:4	
those **w** were of high reputation	Ga 2:6	
those **w** were of reputation	Ga 2:6	
(for He **w** effectually worked for	Ga 2:8	
w were reputed to be pillars,	Ga 2:9	
and it is no longer I **w** live,	Ga 2:20	
in the Son of God, **w** loved me and	Ga 2:20	
Galatians, **w** has bewitched you,	Ga 3:1	5101
w provides you with the Spirit and	Ga 3:5	
those **w** are of faith who are sons of	Ga 3:7	
of faith **w** are sons of Abraham.	Ga 3:7	3778
So then those **w** are of faith are	Ga 3:9	
"CURSED IS EVERYONE **W** DOES NOT	Ga 3:10	3739
"HE **W** PRACTICES THEM SHALL LIVE	Ga 3:12	
IS EVERYONE **W** HANGS ON A TREE"	Ga 3:13	
might be given to those **w** believe.	Ga 3:22	
For all of you **w** were baptized	Ga 3:27	3745
redeem those **w** were under the Law,	Ga 4:5	
me, you **w** want to be under law,	Ga 4:21	
children **w** are to be slaves;	Ga 4:24	
BARREN WOMAN **W** DOES NOT BEAR;	Ga 4:27	
AND SHOUT, YOU **W** ARE NOT IN LABOR;	Ga 4:27	
THAN OF THE ONE **W** HAS A HUSBAND."	Ga 4:27	
But as at that time he **w** was born	Ga 4:29	
to the flesh persecuted him **w** *was*	Ga 4:29	
every man **w** receives circumcision,	Ga 5:3	
you **w** are seeking to be justified	Ga 5:4	3748
w hindered you from obeying the	Ga 5:7	5101
did not come from Him **w** calls you.	Ga 5:8	
but the one **w** is disturbing you	Ga 5:10	
wish that those **w** are troubling	Ga 5:12	
those **w** practice such things will not	Ga 5:21	

Now those **w** belong to Christ Jesus	**Ga 5:24**	
any trespass, you **w** are spiritual,	**Ga 6:1**	
The one **w** is taught the	**Ga 6:6**	
good things with the one **w** teaches	**Ga 6:6**	
For the one **w** sows to his own	**Ga 6:8**	
but the one **w** sows to the Spirit	**Ga 6:8**	
and especially to those **w** are of	**Ga 6:10**	*3609b*
Those **w** desire to make a good	**Ga 6:12**	*3745*
For those **w** are circumcised do not	**Ga 6:13**	
those **w** will walk by this rule,	**Ga 6:16**	*3745*
To the saints **w** are at Ephesus	**Eph 1:1**	
the saints who are at Ephesus and **w**	**Eph 1:1**	
w has blessed us with every	**Eph 1:3**	
according to His purpose **w** works all	**Eph 1:11**	
to the end that we **w** were the	**Eph 1:12**	
w is given as a pledge of our	**Eph 1:14**	*3739*
of His power toward us **w** believe.	**Eph 1:19**	
fullness of Him **w** fills all in all.	**Eph 1:23**	
in the flesh, **w** are called	**Eph 2:11**	
you **w** formerly were far off	**Eph 2:13**	*3739*
w made both *groups into* one and	**Eph 2:14**	
PEACE TO YOU **W** WERE FAR AWAY,	**Eph 2:17**	*3588*
AND PEACE TO THOSE **W** WERE NEAR;	**Eph 2:17**	
in God **w** created all things;	**Eph 3:9**	
Now to Him **w** is able to do	**Eph 3:20**	
one God and Father of all **w** is	**Eph 4:6**	*3588*
He **w** descended is Himself also He	**Eph 4:10**	
also He **w** ascended far above all	**Eph 4:10**	
aspects into Him **w** is the head,	**Eph 4:15**	*3739*
He **w** steals must steal no longer;	**Eph 4:28**	
to share with one **w** has need.	**Eph 4:28**	
it will give grace to those **w** hear.	**Eph 4:29**	
or covetous man, **w** is an idolater,	**Eph 5:5**	*3739*
He **w** loves his own wife loves	**Eph 5:28**	
be obedient to those **w** are your	**Eph 6:5**	
Grace be with all those **w** love our	**Eph 6:24**	
in Christ Jesus **w** are in Philippi,	**Php 1:1**	
that He **w** began a good work in you	**Php 1:6**	
w, although He existed in the form	**Php 2:6**	*3739*
BOW, of those **w** are in heaven	**Php 2:10**	
for it is God **w** is at work in you,	**Php 2:13**	
spirit **w** will genuinely be concerned	**Php 2:20**	*3748*
w is also your messenger and	**Php 2:25**	
w worship in the Spirit of God and	**Php 3:3**	
and observe those **w** walk according	**Php 3:17**	
w set their minds on earthly	**Php 3:19**	
w will transform the body of our	**Php 3:21**	*3739*
to help these women **w** have shared	**Php 4:3**	*3748*
through Him **w** strengthens me.	**Php 4:13**	
brethren **w** are with me greet you.	**Php 4:21**	
and faithful brethren in Christ **w**	**Col 1:2**	
w is a faithful servant of Christ	**Col 1:7**	*3739*
w has qualified us to share in the	**Col 1:12**	
and for those **w** are at Laodicea,	**Col 2:1**	*3588*
and for all those **w** have not	**Col 2:1**	*3745*
God, **w** raised Him from the dead.	**Col 2:12**	
When Christ, **w** is our life, is	**Col 3:4**	
and have put on the new self **w** is	**Col 3:10**	
image of the One **w** created him	**Col 3:10**	
those **w** have been chosen of God,	**Col 3:12**	
those **w** are your masters on earth,	**Col 3:22**	
as those **w** *merely* please men,	**Col 3:22**	*441*
For he **w** does wrong will receive	**Col 3:25**	
brother, **w** is one of your *number*.	**Col 4:9**	*3739*
and *also* Jesus **w** is called Justus;	**Col 4:11**	
God **w** are from the circumcision,	**Col 4:11**	
Epaphras, **w** is one of your number,	**Col 4:12**	*3588*
and for those **w** are in Laodicea and	**Col 4:13**	
Greet the brethren **w** are in	**Col 4:15**	
w rescues us from the wrath to	**1Th 1:10**	
but God **w** examines our hearts.	**1Th 2:4**	
worthy of the God **w** calls you into	**1Th 2:12**	
its work in you **w** believe.	**1Th 2:13**	
w both killed the Lord Jesus and	**1Th 2:15**	
For **w** is our hope or joy or crown	**1Th 2:19**	*5101*
the Gentiles **w** do not know God;	**1Th 4:5**	
he **w** rejects *this* is not rejecting	**1Th 4:8**	
w gives His Holy Spirit to you.	**1Th 4:8**	
brethren **w** are in all Macedonia.	**1Th 4:10**	*3588*
about those **w** are asleep,	**1Th 4:13**	
as do the rest **w** have no hope.	**1Th 4:13**	
w have fallen asleep in Jesus.	**1Th 4:14**	
of the Lord, that we **w** are alive and	**1Th 4:15**	
those **w** have fallen asleep.	**1Th 4:15**	
Then we **w** are alive and remain	**1Th 4:17**	
For those **w** sleep do their	**1Th 5:7**	
and those **w** get drunk get drunk at	**1Th 5:7**	
w died for us, so that whether we are	**1Th 5:10**	
w diligently labor among you,	**1Th 5:12**	
Faithful is He **w** calls you, and He	**1Th 5:24**	
affliction those **w** afflict you,	**2Th 1:6**	
and *to give* relief to you **w** are	**2Th 1:7**	
retribution to those **w** do not know	**2Th 1:8**	
and to those **w** do not obey the gospel	**2Th 1:8**	
marveled at among all **w** have believed	**2Th 1:10**	
w opposes and exalts himself above	**2Th 2:4**	
only he **w** now restrains *will do so*	**2Th 2:7**	
of wickedness for those **w** perish,	**2Th 2:10**	
w did not believe the truth,	**2Th 2:12**	
w has loved us and given us	**2Th 2:16**	
every brother **w** leads an unruly life	**2Th 3:6**	
Christ Jesus, **w** *is* our hope,	**1Tm 1:1**	
w are lawless and rebellious,	**1Tm 1:9**	
w kill their fathers or mothers,	**1Tm 1:9**	
our Lord, **w** has strengthened me,	**1Tm 1:12**	
as an example for those **w** would	**1Tm 1:16**	
kings and all **w** are in authority,	**1Tm 2:2**	
w desires all men to be saved and	**1Tm 2:4**	*3739*
w gave Himself as a ransom for	**1Tm 2:6**	
it was Adam **w** was first created,	**1Tm 2:13**	
And *it was* not Adam **w** was	**1Tm 2:14**	
He must be one **w** manages his own	**1Tm 3:4**	
For those **w** have served well as	**1Tm 3:13**	
He **w** was revealed in the flesh,	**1Tm 3:16**	*3739*
men **w** forbid marriage *and advocate*	**1Tm 4:3**	
w believe and know the truth.	**1Tm 4:3**	
God, **w** is the Savior of all men,	**1Tm 4:10**	*3739*
an example of those **w** believe.	**1Tm 4:12**	
yourself and for those **w** hear you.	**1Tm 4:16**	
Honor widows **w** are widows indeed;	**1Tm 5:3**	
Now she **w** is a widow indeed and	**1Tm 5:5**	
and **w** has been left alone,	**1Tm 5:5**	
But she **w** gives herself to wanton	**1Tm 5:6**	
If any woman **w** is a believer has	**1Tm 5:16**	
assist those **w** are widows indeed.	**1Tm 5:16**	
The elders **w** rule well are to be	**1Tm 5:17**	
especially those **w** work hard at	**1Tm 5:17**	
Those **w** continue in sin, rebuke in	**1Tm 5:20**	
All **w** are under the yoke as	**1Tm 6:1**	*3745*
Those **w** have believers as	**1Tm 6:2**	
because those **w** partake of the	**1Tm 6:2**	
w suppose that godliness is a	**1Tm 6:5**	
But those **w** want to get rich fall	**1Tm 6:9**	
God, **w** gives life to all things,	**1Tm 6:13**	
w testified the good confession before	**1Tm 6:13**	
He **w** is the blessed and only Sovereign	**1Tm 6:15**	
w alone possesses immortality and	**1Tm 6:16**	
Instruct those **w** are rich in this	**1Tm 6:17**	
w richly supplies us with all	**1Tm 6:17**	
w has saved us and called us with	**2Tm 1:9**	
Christ Jesus, **w** abolished death and	**2Tm 1:10**	
the Holy Spirit **w** dwells in us,	**2Tm 1:14**	
all **w** are in Asia turned away from	**2Tm 1:15**	
w will be able to teach others	**2Tm 2:2**	*3748*
one **w** enlisted him as a soldier.	**2Tm 2:4**	
the sake of those **w** are chosen,	**2Tm 2:10**	
w does not need to be ashamed,	**2Tm 2:15**	
men **w** have gone astray from the	**2Tm 2:18**	*3748*
"The Lord knows those **w** are His,"	**2Tm 2:19**	
"Everyone **w** names the name of	**2Tm 2:19**	
with those **w** call on the Lord from	**2Tm 2:22**	
those **w** are in opposition,	**2Tm 2:25**	
For among them are those **w** enter	**2Tm 3:6**	
all **w** desire to live godly in	**2Tm 3:12**	
w is to judge the living and the	**2Tm 4:1**	
to all **w** have loved His appearing.	**2Tm 4:8**	
life, which God, **w** cannot lie,	**Ti 1:2**	*893*
wife, having children **w** believe,	**Ti 1:6**	*4103*
and to refute those **w** contradict.	**Ti 1:9**	
w must be silenced because they	**Ti 1:11**	*3739*
of men **w** turn away from the truth.	**Ti 1:14**	
w are defiled and unbelieving,	**Ti 1:15**	
w gave Himself for us	**Ti 2:14**	*3739*
so that those **w** have believed God	**Ti 3:8**	
All **w** are with me greet you.	**Ti 3:15**	*3588*
those **w** love us in *the* faith.	**Ti 3:15**	
w formerly was useless to you, but	**Phm 1:11**	
"**W** MAKES HIS ANGELS WINDS, AND	**Heb 1:7**	
of those **w** will inherit salvation?	**Heb 1:14**	
confirmed to us by those **w** heard,	**Heb 2:3**	
But we do see Him **w** was made	**Heb 2:9**	
For both He **w** sanctifies and those	**Heb 2:11**	
those **w** are sanctified are all from one	**Heb 2:11**	
him **w** had the power of death,	**Heb 2:14**	
and might free those **w** through	**Heb 2:15**	*3745*
to the aid of those **w** are tempted.	**Heb 2:18**	
faithful to Him **w** appointed Him,	**Heb 3:2**	
For **w** provoked *Him* when they had	**Heb 3:16**	*5101*
did not all those **w** came out of	**Heb 3:16**	*5101*
Was it not with those **w** sinned,	**Heb 3:17**	*5101*
but to those **w** were disobedient?	**Heb 3:18**	*5101*
united by faith in those **w** heard.	**Heb 4:2**	*5101*
w have believed enter that rest,	**Heb 4:3**	*5101*
and those **w** formerly had good news	**Heb 4:6**	*5101*
For the one **w** has entered His rest	**Heb 4:10**	*5101*
great high priest **w** has passed through	**Heb 4:14**	*5101*
high priest **w** cannot sympathize with	**Heb 4:15**	*5101*
but One **w** has been tempted in all	**Heb 4:15**	*5101*
high priest, but He **w** said to Him,	**Heb 5:5**	*5101*
He became to all those **w** obey Him	**Heb 5:9**	
For everyone **w** partakes *only* of	**Heb 5:13**	
w because of practice have their	**Heb 5:14**	
For in the case of those **w** have	**Heb 6:4**	
but imitators of those **w** through	**Heb 6:12**	
we **w** have taken refuge	**Heb 6:18**	
w met Abraham as he was returning	**Heb 7:1**	
the sons of Levi **w** receive the priest's	**Heb 7:5**	
the one **w** had the promises.	**Heb 7:6**	
even Levi, **w** received tithes,	**Heb 7:9**	
w has become *such* not on the basis	**Heb 7:16**	*3739*
through the One **w** said to Him,	**Heb 7:21**	
w draw near to God through Him,	**Heb 7:25**	
w does not need daily, like those	**Heb 7:27**	*3739*
men as high priests **w** are weak,	**Heb 7:28**	
w has taken His seat at the right	**Heb 8:1**	*3739*
since there are those **w** offer the	**Heb 8:4**	
w serve a copy and shadow of the	**Heb 8:5**	*3748*
those **w** have been defiled sanctify	**Heb 9:13**	
w through the eternal Spirit	**Heb 9:14**	*3739*
those **w** have been called may	**Heb 9:15**	
be the death of the one **w** made it.	**Heb 9:16**	
while the one **w** made it lives.	**Heb 9:17**	
sin, to those **w** eagerly await Him.	**Heb 9:28**	
make perfect those **w** draw near.	**Heb 10:1**	
all time those **w** are sanctified.	**Heb 10:14**	
for He **w** promised is faithful;	**Heb 10:23**	
Anyone **w** has set aside the Law of	**Heb 10:28**	
w has trampled under foot the Son of	**Heb 10:29**	
For we know Him **w** said,	**Heb 10:30**	
with those **w** were so treated.	**Heb 10:33**	
HE **W** IS COMING WILL COME,	**Heb 10:37**	
those **w** shrink back to destruction,	**Heb 10:39**	
but of those **w** have faith to the	**Heb 10:39**	
for he **w** comes to God must believe	**Heb 11:6**	
is a rewarder of those **w** seek Him.	**Heb 11:6**	
Him faithful **w** had promised.	**Heb 11:11**	
For those **w** say such things make	**Heb 11:14**	
and he **w** had received the promises	**Heb 11:17**	
as seeing Him **w** is unseen.	**Heb 11:27**	
so that he **w** destroyed the	**Heb 11:28**	
with those **w** were disobedient,	**Heb 11:31**	
w by faith conquered kingdoms,	**Heb 11:33**	*3739*
w for the joy set before Him	**Heb 12:2**	*3739*
For consider Him **w** has endured	**Heb 12:3**	
those **w** have been trained by it,	**Heb 12:11**	
w sold his own birthright for a	**Heb 12:16**	*3739*
sound was such that those **w** heard	**Heb 12:19**	
w are enrolled in heaven,	**Heb 12:23**	
do not refuse Him **w** is speaking.	**Heb 12:25**	
him **w** warned *them* on earth,	**Heb 12:25**	
much less *will* we *escape* **w** turn	**Heb 12:25**	
away from Him **w** *warns* from heaven.	**Heb 12:25**	
them, *and* those **w** are ill-treated,	**Heb 13:3**	
Remember those **w** led you, who	**Heb 13:7**	
w spoke the word of God to you;	**Heb 13:7**	*3748*
through which those **w** were so	**Heb 13:9**	
from which those **w** serve the	**Heb 13:10**	
as those **w** will give an account.	**Heb 13:17**	
w brought up from the dead the	**Heb 13:20**	
tribes **w** are dispersed abroad:	**Jas 1:1**	*3588*
w gives to all generously and	**Jas 1:5**	
for the one **w** doubts is like the	**Jas 1:6**	
is a man **w** perseveres under trial;	**Jas 1:12**	*3739*
has promised to those **w** love Him.	**Jas 1:12**	
hearers **w** delude themselves.	**Jas 1:22**	
he is like a man **w** looks at his	**Jas 1:23**	
But one **w** looks intently at the	**Jas 1:25**	
one **w** is wearing the fine clothes,	**Jas 2:3**	
He promised to those **w** love Him?	**Jas 2:5**	
Is it not the rich **w** oppress you	**Jas 2:6**	
For He **w** said, "DO NOT COMMIT	**Jas 2:11**	
as those **w** are to be judged by *the*	**Jas 2:12**	
to one **w** has shown no mercy;	**Jas 2:13**	
w have been made in the likeness	**Jas 3:9**	
W among you is wise and	**Jas 3:13**	*5101*
in peace by those **w** make peace.	**Jas 3:18**	
He **w** speaks against a brother or	**Jas 4:11**	
the One **w** is able to save and to	**Jas 4:12**	
but **w** are you who judge your	**Jas 4:12**	*5101*
who are you **w** judge your neighbor?	**Jas 4:12**	
Come now, you **w** say,	**Jas 4:13**	
one **w** knows *the* right thing to do and	**Jas 4:17**	
the laborers **w** mowed your fields,	**Jas 5:4**	
and the outcry of those **w** did the	**Jas 5:4**	
w spoke in the name of the Lord.	**Jas 5:10**	*3739*
We count those blessed **w** endured.	**Jas 5:11**	
will restore the one **w** is sick,	**Jas 5:15**	
let him know that he **w** turns a	**Jas 5:20**	
To those **w** reside as aliens,	**1Pe 1:1**	
Asia, and Bithynia, **w** are chosen	**1Pe 1:1**	
w according to His great mercy has	**1Pe 1:3**	
w are protected by the power of	**1Pe 1:5**	
the prophets **w** prophesied of the	**1Pe 1:10**	
through those **w** preached the gospel	**1Pe 1:12**	
like the Holy One **w** called you,	**1Pe 1:15**	
One **w** impartially judges according	**1Pe 1:17**	
w through Him are believers in God,	**1Pe 1:21**	
w raised Him from the dead and	**1Pe 1:21**	
HE **W** BELIEVES IN HIM WILL NOT	**1Pe 2:6**	
value, then, is for you **w** believe;	**1Pe 2:7**	
but for those **w** disbelieve,	**1Pe 2:7**	
Him **w** has called you out of darkness	**1Pe 2:9**	
the praise of those **w** do right.	**1Pe 2:14**	
to those **w** are good and gentle,	**1Pe 2:18**	
also to those **w** are unreasonable.	**1Pe 2:18**	
W COMMITTED NO SIN, NOR WAS ANY	**1Pe 2:22**	*3739*
to Him **w** judges righteously;	**1Pe 2:23**	
holy women also, **w** hoped in God,	**1Pe 3:5**	
"THE ONE **W** DESIRES LIFE, TO LOVE AND	**1Pe 3:10**	
LORD IS AGAINST THOSE **W** DO EVIL."	**1Pe 3:12**	
W is there to harm you if you prove	**1Pe 3:13**	*5101*
to make a defense to everyone **w** asks	**1Pe 3:15**	
those **w** revile your good behavior	**1Pe 3:16**	
w once were disobedient, when the	**1Pe 3:20**	
w is at the right hand of God,	**1Pe 3:22**	*3739*
because he **w** has suffered in the	**1Pe 4:1**	
to Him **w** is ready to judge the living	**1Pe 4:5**	
preached even to those **w** are dead,	**1Pe 4:6**	
is to do so as one **w** is speaking	**1Pe 4:11**	
serves *is to do so* as one **w**	**1Pe 4:11**	
w do not obey the gospel of God?	**1Pe 4:17**	
those also **w** suffer according	**1Pe 4:19**	
your brethren **w** are in the world.	**1Pe 5:9**	
w called you to His eternal glory	**1Pe 5:10**	
She **w** is in Babylon, chosen	**1Pe 5:13**	
be to you all **w** are in Christ.	**1Pe 5:14**	*3588*
To those **w** have received a faith	**2Pe 1:1**	
true knowledge of Him **w** called us	**2Pe 1:3**	
For he **w** lacks these *qualities* is	**2Pe 1:9**	*3739*
w will secretly introduce	**2Pe 2:1**	*3748*
denying the Master **w** bought them,	**2Pe 2:1**	
w would live ungodly	**2Pe 2:6**	
and especially those **w** indulge the	**2Pe 2:10**	
whereas angels **w** are greater in	**2Pe 2:11**	
w loved the wages of	**2Pe 2:15**	*3739*
those **w** barely escape from the	**2Pe 2:18**	
from the ones **w** live in error,	**2Pe 2:18**	

w says, "I have come to know Him," **1Jn 2:4**
the one **w** says he abides in Him **1Jn 2:6**
The one **w** says he is in the Light **1Jn 2:9**
The one **w** loves his brother abides **1Jn 2:10**
But the one **w** hates his brother is **1Jn 2:11**
Him **w** has been from the beginning. **1Jn 2:13**
Him **w** has been from the beginning. **1Jn 2:14**
but the one **w** does the will of God **1Jn 2:17**
W is the liar but the one who **1Jn 2:22** *5101*
Who is the liar but the one **w** **1Jn 2:22**
one **w** denies the Father and the Son. **1Jn 2:22**
the one **w** confesses the Son has **1Jn 2:23**
those **w** are trying to deceive you. **1Jn 2:26**
you know that everyone also **w** **1Jn 2:29**
And everyone **w** has this hope *fixed* **1Jn 3:3**
Everyone **w** practices sin also **1Jn 3:4**
No one **w** abides in Him sins; **1Jn 3:6**
no one **w** sins has seen Him or **1Jn 3:6**
the one **w** practices righteousness **1Jn 3:7**
w practices sin is of the devil; **1Jn 3:8**
w is born of God practices sin, **1Jn 3:9**
anyone **w** does not practice **1Jn 3:10**
one **w** does not love his brother. **1Jn 3:10**
not as Cain, **w** was of the evil **1Jn 3:12**
w does not love abides in death. **1Jn 3:14**
Everyone **w** hates his brother is a **1Jn 3:15**
The one **w** keeps His **1Jn 3:24**
because greater is He **w** is in you **1Jn 4:4**
in you than he **w** is in the world. **1Jn 4:4**
he **w** knows God listens to us; **1Jn 4:6**
he **w** is not from God does not **1Jn 4:6** *3739*
and everyone **w** loves is born of **1Jn 4:7**
The one **w** does not love does not **1Jn 4:8**
w abides in love abides in God, **1Jn 4:16**
and the one **w** fears is not **1Jn 4:18**
for the one **w** does not love his **1Jn 4:20**
that the one **w** loves God should **1Jn 4:21**
W is the one who overcomes the world, **1Jn 5:5** *5101*
is the one **w** overcomes the world, **1Jn 5:5**
but he **w** believes that Jesus is **1Jn 5:5**
the One **w** came by water and blood, **1Jn 5:6**
It is the Spirit **w** testifies, **1Jn 5:6**
The one **w** believes in the Son of **1Jn 5:10**
the one **w** does not believe God has **1Jn 5:10**
He **w** has the Son has the life; **1Jn 5:12**
he **w** does not have the Son of God **1Jn 5:12**
you **w** believe in the name of the Son **1Jn 5:13**
give life to those **w** commit sin **1Jn 5:16**
that no one **w** is born of God sins; **1Jn 5:18**
but He **w** was born of God keeps him **1Jn 5:18**
that we may know Him **w** is true **1Jn 5:20** *228*
true; and we are in Him **w** is true, **1Jn 5:20** *228*
I, but also all **w** know the truth, **2Jn 1:1**
those **w** do not acknowledge Jesus **2Jn 1:7**
Anyone **w** goes too far and does not **2Jn 1:9**
the one **w** abides in the teaching, **2Jn 1:9**
for the one **w** gives him a greeting **2Jn 1:11**
w loves to be first among them, **3Jn 1:9**
forbids those **w** desire *to do so* **3Jn 1:10**
The one **w** does good is of God; **3Jn 1:11**
one **w** does evil has not seen God. **3Jn 1:11**
James, To those **w** are the called, **Jude 1:1**
those **w** were long beforehand **Jude 1:4**
ungodly persons **w** turn the grace **Jude 1:4**
destroyed those **w** did not believe. **Jude 1:5**
w did not keep their own domain, **Jude 1:6**
These are the men **w** are hidden **Jude 1:12**
are the ones **w** cause divisions, **Jude 1:19**
mercy on some, **w** are doubting; **Jude 1:22**
Now to Him **w** is able to keep you **Jude 1:24**
w testified to the word of God **Rv 1:2** *3739*
Blessed is he **w** reads and those **Rv 1:3**
w hear the words of the prophecy, **Rv 1:3**
from Him **w** is and who was and who **Rv 1:4**
is and **w** was and who is to come, **Rv 1:4**
is and who was and **w** is to come, **Rv 1:4**
Spirits **w** are before His throne, **Rv 1:4** *3739*
To Him **w** loves us and released us **Rv 1:5**
see Him, even those **w** pierced Him; **Rv 1:7** *3748*
"**w** is and who was and who is to **Rv 1:8**
is and **w** was and who is to come, **Rv 1:8** *3588*
is and who was and **w** is to come, **Rv 1:8**
The One **w** holds the seven stars in **Rv 2:1**
the One **w** walks among the seven **Rv 2:1**
those **w** call themselves apostles, **Rv 2:2**
'He **w** has an ear, let him hear **Rv 2:7**
To him **w** overcomes, I will grant **Rv 2:7**
first and the last, **w** was dead, **Rv 2:8** *3739*
w say they are Jews and are not, **Rv 2:9**
'He **w** has an ear, let him hear **Rv 2:11**
He **w** overcomes will not be hurt **Rv 2:11**
The One **w** has the sharp two-edged **Rv 2:12**
one, **w** was killed among you, **Rv 2:13** *3739*
w hold the teaching of Balaam, **Rv 2:14**
w kept teaching Balak to put a **Rv 2:14** *3739*
w in the same way hold the teaching **Rv 2:15**
'He **w** has an ear, let him hear **Rv 2:17**
To him **w** overcomes, to him I will **Rv 2:17**
one knows but he **w** receives it.' **Rv 2:17**
w has eyes like a flame of fire, **Rv 2:18**
w calls herself a prophetess, **Rv 2:20**
and those **w** commit adultery with **Rv 2:22**
w searches the minds and hearts; **Rv 2:23**
you, the rest **w** are in Thyatira, **Rv 2:24**
w do not hold this teaching, **Rv 2:24** *3745*
w have not known the deep things **Rv 2:24** *3748*
'He **w** overcomes, and he who **Rv 2:26**
he **w** keeps My deeds until the end, **Rv 2:26**
'He **w** has an ear, let him hear **Rv 2:29**

He **w** has the seven Spirits of God and **Rv 3:1**
people in Sardis **w** have not soiled **Rv 3:4** *3739*
'He **w** overcomes will thus be **Rv 3:5**
'He **w** has an ear, let him hear **Rv 3:6**
He **w** is holy, who is true, who has **Rv 3:7**
He who is holy, **w** is true, who has **Rv 3:7**
is true, **w** has the key of David, **Rv 3:7**
w opens and no one will shut, **Rv 3:7**
and **w** shuts and no one opens, **Rv 3:7**
Satan, **w** say that they are Jews and **Rv 3:9**
test those **w** dwell on the earth. **Rv 3:10**
'He **w** overcomes, I will make him a **Rv 3:12**
'He **w** has an ear, let him hear **Rv 3:13**
'He **w** overcomes, I will grant to **Rv 3:21**
'He **w** has an ear, let him hear **Rv 3:22**
And He **w** was sitting *was* like a **Rv 4:3**
W WAS AND WHO IS AND WHO IS TO COME." **Rv 4:8** *3588*
WAS AND **W** IS AND WHO IS TO COME." **Rv 4:8**
WAS AND WHO IS AND **W** IS TO COME." **Rv 4:8**
to Him **w** sits on the throne, **Rv 4:9**
to Him **w** lives forever and ever, **Rv 4:9**
before Him **w** sits on the throne, **Rv 4:10**
Him **w** lives forever and ever, **Rv 4:10**
I saw in the right hand of Him **w** sat **Rv 5:1**
"**W** is worthy to open the book and **Rv 5:2** *5101*
hand of Him **w** sat on the throne. **Rv 5:7**
"To Him **w** sits on the throne, and **Rv 5:13**
and he **w** sat on it had a bow; **Rv 6:2**
and to him **w** sat on it, it was **Rv 6:4**
and he **w** sat on it had a pair of **Rv 6:5**
he **w** sat on it had the name Death; **Rv 6:8**
the souls of those **w** had been slain **Rv 6:9**
on those **w** dwell on the earth?" **Rv 6:10**
and their brethren **w** were to be killed **Rv 6:11**
of Him **w** sits on the throne, **Rv 6:16**
and **w** is able to stand?" **Rv 6:17** *5101*
the number of those **w** were sealed, **Rv 7:4**
to our God **w** sits on the throne, **Rv 7:10**
"These **w** are clothed in the white **Rv 7:13**
in the white robes, **w** are they, **Rv 7:13** *5101*
"These are the ones **w** come out of **Rv 7:14**
and He **w** sits on the throne will **Rv 7:15**
seven angels **w** stand before God, **Rv 8:2** *3739*
And the seven angels **w** had the **Rv 8:6**
to those **w** dwell on the earth, **Rv 8:13**
angels **w** are about to sound!" **Rv 8:13**
but only the men **w** do not have the **Rv 9:4** *3748*
the sixth angel **w** had the trumpet, **Rv 9:14**
"Release the four angels **w** are **Rv 9:14**
w had been prepared for the hour **Rv 9:15**
horses and those **w** sat on them: **Rv 9:17**
w were not killed by these **Rv 9:20** *3739*
by Him **w** lives forever and ever, **Rv 10:6**
W CREATED HEAVEN AND THE THINGS **Rv 10:6** *3739*
the angel **w** stands on the sea and on **Rv 10:8**
altar, and those **w** worship in it. **Rv 11:1**
And those **w** dwell on the earth **Rv 11:10**
those **w** dwell on the earth. **Rv 11:10**
upon those **w** were watching them. **Rv 11:11**
w sit on their thrones before God, **Rv 11:16**
the Almighty, **w** are and who were, **Rv 11:17**
the Almighty, who are and **w** were, **Rv 11:17** *3588*
and those **w** fear Your name, **Rv 11:18**
those **w** destroy the earth." **Rv 11:18**
woman **w** was about to give birth, **Rv 12:4**
w is to rule all the nations with **Rv 12:5** *3739*
w is called the devil and Satan, **Rv 12:9**
Satan, **w** deceives the whole world; **Rv 12:9**
w accuses them before our God day **Rv 12:10**
O heavens and you **w** dwell in them. **Rv 12:12**
w gave birth to the male *child.* **Rv 12:13** *3748*
w keep the commandments of God **Rv 12:17**
"**W** is like the beast, and who is **Rv 13:4** *5101*
w is able to wage war with him?" **Rv 13:4** *5101*
that is, those **w** dwell in heaven. **Rv 13:6**
All **w** dwell on the earth will **Rv 13:8**
life of the Lamb **w** has been slain. **Rv 13:8**
he makes the earth and those **w** dwell **Rv 13:12**
And he deceives those **w** dwell on **Rv 13:14**
telling those **w** dwell on the earth **Rv 13:14**
beast **w** had the wound of the sword **Rv 13:14** *3739*
except the one **w** has the mark, **Rv 13:17**
Let him **w** has understanding **Rv 13:18**
w had been purchased from the earth. **Rv 14:3**
ones **w** have not been defiled **Rv 14:4**
These *are* the ones **w** follow the **Rv 14:4**
to those **w** live on the earth, **Rv 14:6**
worship Him **w** made the heaven **Rv 14:7**
she **w** has made all the nations **Rv 14:8** *3739*
those **w** worship the beast and his **Rv 14:11**
the perseverance of the saints **w** keep **Rv 14:12**
w die in the Lord from now on!' " **Rv 14:13**
voice to Him **w** sat on the cloud, **Rv 14:15**
Then He **w** sat on the cloud swung **Rv 14:16**
the one **w** has power over fire, **Rv 14:18**
to him **w** had the sharp sickle, **Rv 14:18**
seven angels **w** had seven plagues, **Rv 15:1**
and those **w** had been victorious **Rv 15:2**
"**W** will not fear, O Lord, and **Rv 15:4** *5101*
and the seven angels **w** had the **Rv 15:6**
of God, **w** lives forever and ever. **Rv 15:7**
the people **w** had the mark of the beast **Rv 16:2**
beast and **w** worshiped his image. **Rv 16:2**
are You, **w** are and who were, **Rv 16:5**
are You, who are and **w** were, **Rv 16:5** *3588*
name of God **w** has the power over **Rv 16:9**
Blessed is the one **w** stays awake **Rv 16:15**
Then one of the seven angels **w** had **Rv 17:1**
harlot **w** sits on many waters, **Rv 17:1**

and those **w** dwell on the earth **Rv 17:2**
And those **w** dwell on the earth **Rv 17:8**
w have not yet received a kingdom, **Rv 17:12** *3748*
and those **w** are with Him *are the* **Rv 17:14** *3588*
Lord God **w** judges her is strong. **Rv 18:8**
w committed *acts of* immorality and **Rv 18:9**
things, **w** became rich from her, **Rv 18:15**
she **w** was clothed in fine linen **Rv 18:16**
in which all **w** had ships at sea **Rv 18:19**
w have been slain on the earth." **Rv 18:24**
harlot **w** was corrupting the earth **Rv 19:2** *3748*
God **w** sits on the throne saying, **Rv 19:4**
His bond-servants, you **w** fear Him, **Rv 19:5**
'Blessed are those **w** are invited **Rv 19:9**
w hold the testimony of Jesus; **Rv 19:10**
and He **w** sat on it *is* called **Rv 19:11**
the flesh of horses and of those **w** sit **Rv 19:18**
against Him **w** sat on the horse **Rv 19:19**
and with him the false prophet **w** **Rv 19:20**
by which he deceived those **w** had **Rv 19:20**
and those **w** worshiped his image; **Rv 19:20**
mouth of Him **w** sat on the horse, **Rv 19:21**
of old, **w** is the devil and Satan, **Rv 20:2** *3739*
And I *saw* the souls of those **w** had **Rv 20:4**
and those **w** had not worshiped the **Rv 20:4** *3748*
Blessed and holy is the one **w** has **Rv 20:6**
And the devil **w** deceived them was **Rv 20:10**
throne and Him **w** sat upon it, **Rv 20:11**
And He **w** sits on the throne said, **Rv 21:5**
I will give to the one **w** thirsts **Rv 21:6**
"He **w** overcomes will inherit **Rv 21:7**
Then one of the seven angels **w** had **Rv 21:9**
The one **w** spoke with me had a **Rv 21:15**
and nothing unclean, and no one **w** **Rv 21:27**
Blessed is he **w** heeds the words of **Rv 22:7**
one **w** heard and saw these things. **Rv 22:8**
angel **w** showed me these things. **Rv 22:8**
w heed the words of this book. **Rv 22:9**
"Let the one **w** does wrong, still **Rv 22:11**
and the one **w** is filthy, still be **Rv 22:11** *4508*
and let the one **w** is righteous, still **Rv 22:11** *3588*
and the one **w** is holy, still keep **Rv 22:11** *40*
are those **w** wash their robes, **Rv 22:14**
w loves and practices lying. **Rv 22:15**
And let the one **w** hears say, **Rv 22:17**
And let the one **w** is thirsty come; **Rv 22:17**
let the one **w** wishes take the **Rv 22:17**
I testify to everyone **w** hears the **Rv 22:18**
He **w** testifies to these things **Rv 22:20**

WHOEVER

and **w** finds me will kill me." **Gn 4:14** 3605
"Therefore **w** kills Cain, **Gn 4:15** 3605
"**W** sheds man's blood, By man his **Gn 9:6**
for **w** eats anything leavened from **Ex 12:15** 3605
for **w** eats what is leavened, that **Ex 12:19** 3605
w touches the mountain shall **Ex 19:12** 3605
"**W** lies with an animal shall **Ex 22:19** 3605
w has a legal matter, let him **Ex 24:14** 4310
'**W** shall mix *any* like it or **Ex 30:33**
376, 834
or **w** puts any of it on a layman shall **Ex 30:33** 834
"**W** shall make *any* like it, to use **Ex 30:38**
376, 834
for **w** does any work on it, that **Ex 31:14** 3605
w does any work on the sabbath day **Ex 31:15** 3605
"**W** has any gold, let them tear it **Ex 32:24** 4310
"**W** is for the LORD, *come* to me!" **Ex 32:26** 4310
"**W** has sinned against Me, I will **Ex 32:33**
4310, 834
w does any work on it shall be put **Ex 35:2** 3605
w is of a willing heart, let him **Ex 35:5** 3605
W touches them will become **Lv 6:18**
3605, 834
'For **w** eats the fat of the animal **Lv 7:25** 3605
w touches their carcasses becomes **Lv 11:24** 3605
and **w** picks up any of their **Lv 11:25** 3605
w touches them becomes unclean. **Lv 11:26** 3605
w touches their carcasses becomes **Lv 11:27** 3605
w touches them when they are dead **Lv 11:31** 3605
w goes into the house during the **Lv 14:46**
w lies down in the house shall **Lv 14:47**
and **w** eats in the house shall wash **Lv 14:47**
and **w** sits on the thing on which **Lv 15:6**
'Also **w** touches the person with **Lv 15:7**
'**W** then touches any of the things **Lv 15:10** 3605
and **w** touches her shall be unclean **Lv 15:19** 3605
'**W** touches any thing on which she **Lv 15:22** 3605
w touches them shall be unclean **Lv 15:27** 3605
w eats it shall be cut off.' **Lv 17:14** 3605
'For **w** does any of these **Lv 18:29**
3605, 834
w *is able to* go out to war in **Nu 1:3** 3605
w *was able to* go out to war, **Nu 1:20** 3605
w *was able to* go out to war, **Nu 1:22** 3605
w *was able to* go out to war, **Nu 1:24** 3605
w *was able to* go out to war, **Nu 1:26** 3605
w *was able to* go out to war, **Nu 1:28** 3605
w *was able to* go out to war, **Nu 1:30** 3605
w *was able to* go out to war, **Nu 1:32** 3605
w *was able to* go out to war, **Nu 1:34** 3605
w *was able to* go out to war, **Nu 1:36** 3605
w *was able to* go out to war, **Nu 1:38** 3605
w *was able to* go out to war, **Nu 1:40** 3605
w *was able to* go out to war, **Nu 1:42** 3605
w *was able to* go out to war in **Nu 1:45** 3605
w is able to go out to war in **Nu 26:2** 3605
w has killed any person and **Nu 31:19** 3605
and **w** has touched any slain, **Nu 31:19** 3605
"For **w** does these things is **Dt 18:12** 3605

w will not listen to My words which Dt 18:19 376, 834
for **w** does these things is an Dt 22:5 3605
that **w** kills any person Jos 20:9 3605
W will plead for him shall be put Jg 6:31 834
'**W** is afraid and trembling, let Jg 7:3 4310
"**W** does not come out after Saul 1Sa 11:7 834
"**W** would strike the Jebusites, 2Sa 5:8 3605
"**W** speaks to you, bring him to 2Sa 14:10
for **w** is faint in the wilderness 2Sa 16:2 3287
attack, that **w** hears *it* will say, 2Sa 17:9
"**W** favors Joab and whoever is for 2Sa 20:11 4310, 834
favors Joab and **w** is for David, 2Sa 20:11 4310, 834
w is missing shall not live." 2Ki 10:19 3605, 834
and **w** comes within the ranks shall 2Ki 11:8
and **w** follows her put to death 2Ki 11:15
and Judah, that **w** hears of it, 2Ki 21:12 3605
"**W** strikes down a Jebusite first 1Ch 11:6 3605
W possessed *precious* stones gave 1Ch 29:8
W comes to consecrate himself with 2Ch 13:9 3605
and **w** would not seek the LORD God 2Ch 15:13 834, 3605
and **w** enters the house, let him be 2Ch 23:7
and **w** follows her, put to death 2Ch 23:14
W there is among you of all His 2Ch 36:23 4310
'**W** there is among you of all His Ezr 1:3 4310
"**W** will not observe the law of your Ezr 7:26 3605
and that **w** would not come within Ezr 10:8 3605, 834
W secretly slanders his neighbor, Ps 101:5
W touches her will not go Pr 6:29 3605
"**W** is naive, let him turn in here!" Pr 9:4 4310
"**W** is naive, let him turn in Pr 9:16 4310
W loves discipline loves Pr 12:1
And **w** is intoxicated by it is not Pr 20:1 3605
For **w** is joined with all the living, Ec 9:4 4310, 834
W assails you will fall because of Is 54:15 4310
W treads on them does not know Is 59:8 3605
and **w** is chosen I shall appoint Jer 49:19 4310
and **w** is chosen I will appoint Jer 50:44 4310
and **w** is in the open field I will Ezk 33:27 834
"But **w** does not fall down and Da 3:6 4479
"But **w** does not fall down and Da 3:11 4479
W is wise, let him understand Hos 14:9 4310
W is discerning, let him know Hos 14:9
w calls on the name of the LORD Jl 2:32 3605, 834
"**W** then annuls one of the least Mt 5:19 3739, 1437
but **w** keeps and teaches *them,* he Mt 5:19 3739, 302
'**W** commits murder shall be liable Mt 5:21 3739, 302
and **w** says to his brother, Mt 5:22 3739, 302
and **w** says, 'You fool,' Mt 5:22 3739, 302
'**W** SENDS HIS WIFE AWAY, LET HIM Mt 5:31 3739, 302
and **w** marries a divorced woman Mt 5:32 3739, 1437
w slaps you on your right cheek, Mt 5:39 3748
"**W** forces you to go one mile, go Mt 5:41 3748
"**W** does not receive you, nor heed Mt 10:14 3739
"But **w** denies Me before men, Mt 10:33 3748, 302
"And **w** in the name of a disciple Mt 10:42 3739, 1437
"**W** speaks a word against Mt 12:32 3739, 1437
w speaks against the Holy Spirit, Mt 12:32 3739, 302
"For **w** does the will of My Father Mt 12:50 3748, 302
"For **w** has, to him *more* shall be Mt 13:12 3748
but **w** does not have, even what he Mt 13:12 3748
'**W** says to *his* father or Mt 15:5 3739, 302
"For **w** wishes to save his life Mt 16:25 3739, 1437
but **w** loses his life for My sake Mt 16:25 3739, 302
"**W** then humbles himself as this Mt 18:4 3748
"And **w** receives one such child in Mt 18:5 3739, 1437
but **w** causes one of these little Mt 18:6 3739, 302
I say to you, **w** divorces his wife, Mt 19:9 3739, 302
but **w** wishes to become great among Mt 20:26 3739, 1437
and **w** wishes to be first among you Mt 20:27 3739, 1437
"**W** exalts himself shall be humbled; Mt 23:12 3748
and **w** humbles himself shall be Mt 23:12 3748
'**W** swears by the temple, *that* is Mt 23:16 3739, 302
but **w** swears by the gold of the Mt 23:16 3739, 302
'**W** swears by the altar, *that* is Mt 23:18 3739, 302
but **w** swears by the offering on Mt 23:18 3739, 302
"Therefore, **w** swears by the altar, Mt 23:20 3588
"And **w** swears by the temple, swears Mt 23:21 3588
"And **w** swears by heaven, swears Mt 23:22 3588
"**W** is on the housetop must not Mt 24:17 3588
"**W** is in the field must not turn back Mt 24:18 3588
w blasphemes against the Holy Spirit Mk 3:29 3739, 302
"For **w** does the will of God Mk 3:35 3739, 302
"For **w** has, to him *more* shall be Mk 4:25 3739
and **w** does not have, even what he Mk 4:25 3739
"For **w** wishes to save his life Mk 8:35 3739, 1437
but **w** loses his life for My sake Mk 8:35 3739, 302
"For **w** is ashamed of Me and My Mk 8:38 3739, 1437
"**W** receives one child like this Mk 9:37 3739, 302
and **w** receives Me does not receive Mk 9:37 3739, 302
"For **w** gives you a cup of water Mk 9:41 3739, 302
"**W** causes one of these little ones Mk 9:42 3739
"**W** divorces his wife and marries Mk 10:11 3739, 302
w does not receive the kingdom of Mk 10:15 3739, 302
but **w** wishes to become great among Mk 10:43 3739, 302
and **w** wishes to be first among you Mk 10:44 3739, 302
to you, **w** says to this mountain, Mk 11:23 3739, 302
"**W** hits you on the cheek, offer Lk 6:29
and **w** takes away your coat, do not Lk 6:29
and **w** takes away what is yours, Lk 6:30
for **w** has, to him *more* shall be Lk 8:18 3739, 302
and **w** does not have, even what he Lk 8:18 3739, 302
"For **w** wishes to save his life Lk 9:24 3739, 1437
but **w** loses his life for My sake, Lk 9:24 3739, 302
w is ashamed of Me and My words, Lk 9:26 3739, 302
"**W** receives this child in My name Lk 9:48 3739, 1437
and **w** receives Me receives Him who Lk 9:48 3739, 302
"**W** does not carry his own cross Lk 14:27 3748
"**W** seeks to keep his life will Lk 17:33 3739, 1437
and **w** loses *his life* will Lk 17:33 3739, 302
w does not receive the kingdom of Lk 18:17 3739, 302
And He said to them, "But now, **w** Lk 22:36 3588
and **w** has no sword is to sell his Lk 22:36 3588
that **w** believes will in Him have Jn 3:15 3956
that **w** believes in Him shall not Jn 3:16 3956
but **w** drinks of the water that I Jn 4:14 3739, 302
w then first, after the stirring Jn 5:4
"**W** BELIEVES IN HIM WILL NOT BE Ro 10:11 3956
"**W** WILL CALL ON THE NAME OF THE Ro 10:13 3956
Therefore **w** resists authority has Ro 13:2 3588
Therefore **w** eats the bread or 1Co 11:27 3739, 302
will bear his judgment, **w** he is. Ga 5:10 3748, 1437
w has a complaint against anyone; Col 3:13 1437, 5100
For **w** keeps the whole law and yet Jas 2:10 3748
Therefore **w** wishes to be a friend Jas 4:4 3739, 1437
W speaks, *is to do so* as 1Pe 4:11 1487, 5100
w serves *is to do so* as 1Pe 4:11 1487, 5100
but **w** keeps His word, in him the 1Jn 2:5 3739, 302
W denies the Son does not have the 1Jn 2:23 3956
But **w** has the world's goods, and 1Jn 3:17 3739, 302
W confesses that Jesus is the Son 1Jn 4:15 3739, 1437
W believes that Jesus is the Christ 1Jn 5:1 3956
and **w** loves the Father loves the 1Jn 5:1 3956
w receives the mark of his name." Rv 14:11 1487, 5100

WHOLE

water the **w** surface of the ground. Gn 2:6 3605
around the **w** land of Havilah, Gn 2:11 3605
flows around the **w** land of Cush. Gn 2:13 3605
these the **w** earth was populated. Gn 9:19 3605
Now the **w** earth used the same Gn 11:1 3605
over the face of the **w** earth." Gn 11:4 3605
over the face of the **w** earth; Gn 11:8 3605
the language of the **w** earth; Gn 11:9 3605
over the face of the **w** earth. Gn 11:9 3605
"Is not the **w** land before you? Gn 13:9 3605
the **w** place on their account." Gn 18:26 3605
will You destroy the **w** city because Gn 18:28 3605
smite your **w** territory with frogs. Ex 8:2 3605
covered the surface of the **w** land, Ex 10:15 3605
then the **w** assembly of the Ex 12:6 3605
The **w** congregation of the sons Ex 16:2 3605
to kill this **w** assembly with hunger." Ex 16:3 3605
as Aaron spoke to the **w** congregation Ex 16:10 3605
the **w** mountain quaked violently. Ex 19:18 3605
in smoke the **w** ram on the altar; Ex 29:18 3605
the **w** of it *was* a single hammered Ex 37:22 3605
'Now if the **w** congregation of Israel Lv 4:13 3605
Moses offered up the **w** ram Lv 8:21 3605
and the **w** congregation came near Lv 9:5 3605
kinsmen, the **w** house of Israel, Lv 10:6 3605
for him and for the **w** congregation Nu 3:7 3605
use a razor over their **w** body and Nu 8:7 3605
w congregation of the sons of Israel, Nu 8:9 3605
but a **w** month, until it comes out Nu 11:20 3117
that they may eat for a **w** month.' Nu 11:21 3117
the **w** congregation said to them, Nu 14:2 3605
of Israel, the **w** congregation, Nu 20:1 3605
of Israel, the **w** congregation, Nu 20:22 3605
judgments as righteous as this **w** law Dt 4:8 3605
the peoples under the **w** heaven. Dt 4:19 3605
as a **w** burnt offering to the LORD Dt 13:16 3632
priests, the **w** tribe of Levi, Dt 18:1 3605
And **w** burnt offerings on Your Dt 33:10 3632
And the **w** congregation grumbled Jos 9:18 3605
said to the **w** congregation, Jos 9:19 3605
of water for the **w** congregation, Jos 9:21 3605
to go *down* for about a **w** day. Jos 10:13 8549
So Joshua took the **w** land, Jos 11:23 3605
w congregation of the sons of Israel Jos 18:1 3605
the **w** congregation of the sons of Jos 22:12 3605
the **w** congregation of the LORD, Jos 22:16 3605
with the **w** congregation of Israel Jos 22:18 3605
even throughout the **w** army; Jg 7:22 3605
Zalmunna, and routed the **w** army. Jg 8:12 3605
and to the **w** clan of the household Jg 9:1 3605
five men out of their **w** number, Jg 18:2 7098
the **w** city was going up *in smoke* Jg 20:40 3632
Then the **w** congregation sent *word* Jg 21:13 3605
a **w** burnt offering to the LORD; 1Sa 7:9 3632
sacrifice there for the **w** family.' 1Sa 20:6 3605
nothing at all of this **w** affair." 1Sa 22:15 3605
and to the **w** house of Benjamin. 2Sa 3:19 3605
the **w** family has risen against 2Sa 14:7 3605
was spread over the **w** countryside, 2Sa 18:8 3605
was over the **w** army of Israel, 2Sa 20:23 3605
had gone about through the **w** land, 2Sa 24:8 3605
the stories against the **w** house, 1Ki 6:10 3605
He overlaid the **w** house with gold, 1Ki 6:22 3605
Also the **w** altar which was by the 1Ki 6:22 3605
the **w** kingdom out of his hand, 1Ki 11:34 3605
the **w** house of Ahab shall perish, 2Ki 9:8 3605
king of Assyria invaded the **w** land 2Ki 17:5 3605
You in truth and with a **w** heart and 2Ki 20:3 8003
with a **w** heart and a willing mind; 1Ch 28:9 8003
to the LORD with a **w** heart, 1Ch 29:9 8003
they had sworn with their **w** heart 2Ch 15:15 3605
the LORD, yet not with a **w** heart. 2Ch 25:2 8003
cleansed the **w** house of the LORD, 2Ch 29:18 3605
While the **w** assembly worshiped, 2Ch 29:28 3605
Then the **w** assembly decided to 2Ch 30:23 3605
daughters, for the **w** assembly, 2Ch 31:18 3605
The **w** assembly numbered 42,360, Ezr 2:64 3605
find in the **w** province of Babylon, Ezr 7:16 3606
our leaders represent the **w** assembly Ezr 10:14 3605
w wall was joined together to half its Ne 4:6 3605
were behind the **w** house of Judah. Ne 4:16 3605
w assembly together *was* 42,360, Ne 7:66 3605
the **w** kingdom of Ahasuerus. Es 3:6 3605
for the welfare of his **w** nation. Es 10:3 3605
who has laid *on Him* the **w** world? Jb 34:13 3605
Under the **w** heaven He lets it loose, Jb 37:3 3605
Whatever is under the **w** heaven is Jb 41:11 3605
elevation, the joy of the **w** earth, Ps 48:2 3605
offering and **w** burnt offering; Ps 51:19 3632
the **w** earth be filled with His glory. Ps 72:19 3605
of the Lord of the **w** earth. Ps 97:5 3605
He broke the **w** staff of bread. Ps 105:16 3605
them alive like Sheol, Even **w**, Pr 1:12 8549
The **w** head is sick And the whole Is 1:5 3605
is sick And the **w** heart is faint. Is 1:5 3605
support, the **w** supply of bread And Is 3:1 3605
bread And the **w** supply of water; Is 3:1 3605
the LORD will create over the **w** area Is 4:5 3605
w earth is full of His glory." Is 6:3 3605
in the midst of the **w** land. Is 10:23 3605
To destroy the **w** land. Is 13:5 3605
w earth is at rest *and* is quiet; Is 14:7 3605
plan devised against the **w** earth; Is 14:26 3605
will fill the **w** world with fruit. Is 27:6 6440
You in truth and with a **w** heart, Is 38:3 8003
and the precious oil and his **w** armory Is 39:2 3605
of bronze against the **w** land, Jer 1:18 3605
For the **w** land is devastated; Jer 4:20 3605
"The **w** land shall be a Jer 4:27 3605
his stallions The **w** land quakes; Jer 8:16 3605
The **w** land has been made desolate, Jer 12:11 3605
so I made the **w** household of Israel Jer 13:11 3605
the **w** household of Judah cling to Me Jer 13:11 3605
return to Me with their **w** heart. Jer 24:7 3605
'This **w** land will be a Jer 25:11 3605
"And the **w** valley of the dead Jer 31:40 3605
and the **w** house of the Rechabites, Jer 35:3 3605
Look, the **w** land is before you; Jer 40:4 3605
I will tell you the **w** message Jer 42:4 3605
the **w** message with which the LORD Jer 42:5 3605
to uproot, that is, the **w** land." Jer 45:4 3605
"How the hammer of the **w** earth Jer 50:23 3605
Who destroys the **w** earth," Jer 51:25 3605
praise of the **w** earth been seized! Jer 51:41 3605
her **w** land will be put to shame And Jer 51:47 3605
Surely the **w** house of Israel is Ezk 3:7 3605
Are You destroying the **w** remnant Ezk 9:8 3605
Their **w** body, their backs, Ezk 10:12 3605
exiles and the **w** house of Israel, Ezk 11:15 3605

"there the **w** house of Israel, all **Ezk 20:40** 3605
and the **w** surface from south to **Ezk 20:47** 3605
beasts of the **w** earth with you. **Ezk 32:4** 3605
bones are the **w** house of Israel; **Ezk 37:11** 3605
mercy on the **w** house of Israel; **Ezk 39:25** 3605
its **w** design and all its statutes and **Ezk 43:11** 3605
be for the **w** house of Israel. **Ezk 45:6** 3605
The **w** length *shall be* 25,000 **Ezk 48:13** 3605
"The **w** allotment *shall be* 25,000 **Ezk 48:20** 3605
mountain and filled the **w** earth. **Da 2:35** 3606
ruler over the **w** province of Babylon **Da 2:48** 3606
visible to the end of the **w** earth. **Da 4:11** 3606
be in charge of the **w** kingdom, **Da 6:1** 3606
and will devour the **w** earth and **Da 7:23** 3606
all the kingdoms under the **w** heaven **Da 7:27** 3606
over the surface of the **w** earth **Da 8:5** 3605
for under the **w** heaven there has **Da 9:12** 3605
he will arouse the **w** *empire* **Da 11:2** 3605
with the power of his **w** kingdom, **Da 11:17** 3605
Also anguish is in the **w** body And **Na 2:10** 3605
by the Lord of the **w** earth." **Zch 4:14** 3605
forth over the face of the **w** land; **Zch 5:3** 3605
robbing Me, the **w** nation *of you!* **Mal 3:9** 3605
the **w** tithe into the storehouse, **Mal 3:10** 3605
w body to be thrown into hell. **Mt 5:29** *3650*
for your **w** body to go into hell. **Mt 5:30** *3650*
your **w** body will be full of light. **Mt 6:22** *3650*
w body will be full of darkness. **Mt 6:23** *3650*
the **w** herd rushed down the steep **Mt 8:32** *3956*
the **w** city came out to meet Jesus; **Mt 8:34** *3956*
and the **w** crowd was standing **Mt 13:2** *3956*
profit a man if he gains the **w** world **Mt 16:26** *3650*
the **w** Law and the Prophets." **Mt 22:40** *3650*
preached in the **w** world as a testimony **Mt 24:14** *3650*
gospel is preached in the **w** world, **Mt 26:13** *3650*
w Council kept trying to obtain false **Mt 26:59** *3650*
the **w** *Roman* cohort around Him. **Mt 27:27** *3650*
w city had gathered at the door. **Mk 1:33** *3650*
and the **w** crowd was by the sea **Mk 4:1** *3956*
Him and told Him the **w** truth. **Mk 5:33** *3956*
and ran about that **w** country and **Mk 6:55** *3650*
profit a man to gain the **w** world, **Mk 8:36** *3650*
for the **w** crowd was astonished at His **Mk 11:18** *3956*
gospel is preached in the **w** world, **Mk 14:9** *3650*
the **w** Council kept trying to obtain **Mk 14:55** *3650*
and scribes and the **w** Council, **Mk 15:1** *3650*
together the **w** *Roman* cohort. **Mk 15:16** *3650*
the **w** land until the ninth hour. **Mk 15:33** *3650*
And the **w** multitude of the people **Lk 1:10** *3956*
the **w** night in prayer to God. **Lk 6:12** *1273*
proclaiming throughout the **w** city **Lk 8:39** *3650*
profited if he gains the **w** world, **Lk 9:25** *3650*
your **w** body also is full of light; **Lk 11:34** *3650*
your **w** body is full of light, **Lk 11:36** *3650*
the **w** crowd of the disciples **Lk 19:37** *537a*
Then the **w** body of them got up and **Lk 23:1** *537a*
the **w** land until the ninth hour, **Lk 23:44** *3650*
believed and his **w** household. **Jn 4:53** *3650*
the **w** nation not perish." **Jn 11:50** *3650*
w house where they were sitting. **Ac 2:2** *3650*
great fear came over the **w** church, **Ac 5:11** *3650*
the **w** message of this Life." **Ac 5:20** *3956*
approval with the **w** congregation; **Ac 6:5** *3956*
the **w** island as far as Paphos, **Ac 13:6** *3650*
w city assembled to hear the word **Ac 13:44** *3956*
being spread through the **w** region. **Ac 13:49** *3650*
and the elders, with the **w** church, **Ac 15:22** *3650*
in God with his **w** household. **Ac 16:34** *3832*
how I was with you the **w** time, **Ac 20:18** *3956*
to you the **w** purpose of God. **Ac 20:27** *3956*
proclaimed throughout the **w** world. **Ro 1:8** *3650*
the **w** creation groans and suffers **Ro 8:22** *3956*
THROUGHOUT THE **W** EARTH." **Ro 9:17** *3956*
host to me and to the **w** church, **Ro 16:23** *3650*
leavens the **w** lump *of dough?* **1Co 5:6** *3650*
If the **w** body were an eye, where **1Co 12:17** *3650*
If the **w** were hearing, where would **1Co 12:17** *3650*
Therefore if the **w** church **1Co 14:23** *3650*
obligation to keep the **w** Law. **Ga 5:3** *3650*
leavens the **w** lump *of dough.* **Ga 5:9** *3650*
w Law is fulfilled in one word, **Ga 5:14** *3956*
in whom the **w** building, being **Eph 2:21** *3956*
from whom the **w** body, being fitted **Eph 4:16** *3956*
throughout the **w** praetorian guard **Php 1:13** *3650*
you about the **w** situation here. **Col 4:9** *3956*
they are upsetting **w** families, **Ti 1:11** *3650*
IN **W** BURNT OFFERINGS AND **Heb 10:6** *3646*
OFFERINGS AND **W** BURNT OFFERINGS **Heb 10:8** *3646*
For whoever keeps the **w** law and **Jas 2:10** *3650*
able to bridle the **w** body as well. **Jas 3:2** *3650*
but also for *those of* the **w** world. **1Jn 2:2** *3650*
and that the **w** world lies in *the power* **1Jn 5:19** *3650*
is about to come upon the **w** world, **Rv 3:10** *3650*
and the **w** moon became like blood; **Rv 6:12** *3650*
Satan, who deceives the **w** world; **Rv 12:9** *3650*
And the **w** earth was amazed *and* **Rv 13:3** *3650*
out to the kings of the **w** world, **Rv 16:14** *3650*

WHOLEHEARTED
with **w** joy *and* with scorn of soul, **Ezk 36:5** 3605, 3824

WHOLEHEARTEDLY
of the LORD, faithfully and **w**. **2Ch 19:9** 3824, 8003

WHOLLY
they are **w** given to him from among **Nu 3:9** 5414
for they are **w** given to Me from **Nu 8:16** 5414
"I **w** dedicate the silver from my **Jg 17:3** 6942
be **w** devoted to the LORD our God, **1Ki 8:61** 8003
not **w** devoted to the LORD his God, **1Ki 11:4** 8003
not **w** devoted to the LORD his God, **1Ki 15:3** 8003
Asa was **w** devoted to the LORD **1Ki 15:14** 8003
Being **w** at ease and satisfied; **Jb 21:23** 3605
And he is **w** desirable. **SS 5:16** 3605
into exile, **W** carried into exile. **Jer 13:19** 7965
in it, it will be **w** illumined, **Lk 11:36** *3650*

WHOM
He placed the man **w** He had formed. **Gn 2:8** 834
woman **w** You gave *to be* with me, **Gn 3:12** 834
"I will blot out man **w** I have **Gn 6:7** 834
the nation **w** they will serve, **Gn 15:14** 834
the name of his son, **w** Hagar bore, **Gn 16:15** 834
w Sarah will bear to you at this **Gn 17:21** 834
"**W** else have you here? **Gn 19:12** 4310
of the woman **w** you have taken, **Gn 20:3** 834
born to him, **w** Sarah bore to him, **Gn 21:3** 834
w she had borne to Abraham, **Gn 21:9** 834
son, your only son, **w** you love, **Gn 22:2** 834
of the Canaanites, among **w** I live, **Gn 24:3** 834
it be that the girl to **w** I say, **Gn 24:14** 834
she *be the one* **w** You have **Gn 24:14**
of Milcah, **w** she bore to Nahor." **Gn 24:24** 834
'The LORD, before **w** I have walked, **Gn 24:40** 834
comes out to draw, and to **w** I say, **Gn 24:43**
let her be the woman **w** the LORD **Gn 24:44** 834
Nahor's son, **w** Milcah bore to him'; **Gn 24:47** 834
son, **w** Hagar the Egyptian, **Gn 25:12** 834
children for **w** I have served you, **Gn 30:26** 834
"The one with **w** you find your **Gn 31:32** 834
their children **w** they have borne? **Gn 31:43** 834
'To **w** do you belong, and where are **Gn 32:17** 4310
and to **w** do these *animals* in front **Gn 32:17** 4310
"The children **w** God has **Gn 33:5** 834
of Leah, **w** she had borne to Jacob, **Gn 34:1** 834
man to **w** these things belong." **Gn 38:25** 834
Hebrew slave, **w** you brought to us, **Gn 39:17** 834
this, in **w** is a divine spirit?" **Gn 41:38** 834
were born to Joseph, **w** Asenath, **Gn 41:50** 834
old father well, of **w** you spoke? **Gn 43:27** 834
brother, of **w** you spoke to me?" **Gn 43:29** 834
w it is found shall be my slave, **Gn 44:10** 834
Joseph, **w** you sold into Egypt. **Gn 45:4** 834
w she bore to Jacob in **Gn 46:15** 834
w Laban gave to his daughter Leah; **Gn 46:18** 834
Manasseh and Ephraim, **w** Asenath, **Gn 46:20** 834
w Laban gave to his daughter **Gn 46:25** 834
sons, **w** God has given me here." **Gn 48:9** 834
"The God before **w** my fathers **Gn 48:15** 834
one of **w** was named Shiphrah and **Ex 1:15** 834
w Pharaoh's taskmasters had set **Ex 5:14** 834
and Moses to **w** the LORD said, **Ex 6:26** 834
Egyptians **w** you have seen today, **Ex 14:13** 834
the people **w** You have redeemed; **Ex 15:13** 2098
pass over **w** You have purchased. **Ex 15:16** 2098
sons, of **w** one was named Gershom, **Ex 18:3** 834
he **w** the judges condemn shall pay **Ex 22:9** 834
all the people among **w** you come, **Ex 23:27** 834
skillful persons **w** I have endowed **Ex 28:3** 834
w you brought up from the land of **Ex 32:7** 834
Your people **w** You have brought out **Ex 32:11** 834
to **w** You swore by Yourself, **Ex 32:13** 834
you and the people **w** you have **Ex 33:1** 834
me know **w** You will send with me. **Ex 33:12** 834
gracious to **w** I will be gracious, **Ex 33:19** 834
on **w** I will show compassion." **Ex 33:19** 834
and all the people among **w** you **Ex 34:10** 834
and every skillful person in **w** the **Ex 36:1** 834
in **w** the LORD had put skill, **Ex 36:2** 834
He shall give it to the one to **w** **Lv 6:5** 834
"This is the law *for him* in **w** **Lv 14:32** 834
any man by **w** he is made unclean, **Lv 22:5** 834
to the man to **w** he sold it, **Lv 25:27** 834
'For they are My servants **w** I **Lv 25:42** 834
and female slaves **w** you may have **Lv 25:44** 834
w they will have produced in your **Lv 25:45** 834
they are My servants **w** I brought **Lv 25:55** 834
w I brought out of the land of **Lv 26:45** 834
to the one from **w** he bought it, **Lv 27:24** 834
to **w** the possession of the land **Lv 27:24** 834
w Moses and Aaron numbered, **Nu 1:44** 834
of **w** was of his father's household. **Nu 1:44** 259
w he ordained to serve as priests. **Nu 3:3** 834
w Moses and Aaron numbered at the **Nu 3:39** 834
w Moses and Aaron numbered **Nu 4:37** 834
w Moses and Aaron numbered **Nu 4:41** 834
w Moses and Aaron numbered **Nu 4:45** 834
w Moses and Aaron and the leaders **Nu 4:46** 834
give *it* to him **w** he has wronged. **Nu 5:7** 834
to **w** restitution may be made **Nu 5:8**
w you know to be the elders of the **Nu 11:16** 834
"The people, among **w** I am, **Nu 11:21** 834
Cushite woman **w** he had married **Nu 12:1** 834
These are the names of the men **w** **Nu 13:16** 834
and all the people **w** we saw in it **Nu 13:32** 834
w you said would become a prey **Nu 14:31** 834
As for the men **w** Moses sent to spy **Nu 14:36** 834
even the one **w** He will choose, He **Nu 16:5** 834
and the man **w** the LORD chooses **Nu 16:7** 834
of the man **w** I choose will sprout. **Nu 17:5** 834
that he **w** you bless is blessed, **Nu 22:6** 834
and he **w** you curse is cursed." **Nu 22:6** 834
I curse **w** God has not cursed? **Nu 23:8**
w the LORD has not denounced? **Nu 23:8**
messengers **w** you had sent to me, **Nu 24:12** 834
of Nun, a man in **w** is the Spirit, **Nu 27:18** 834
from **w** the LORD's levy was 32 **Nu 31:40**
firstborn **w** the LORD had struck **Nu 33:4** 834
those **w** you let remain of them *will* **Nu 33:55** 834
These are those **w** the LORD **Nu 34:29** 834
'Let them marry **w** they wish; **Nu 36:6**
w Moses and the sons of Israel **Dt 4:46** 834
consume all the peoples **w** the LORD **Dt 7:16** 834
the peoples of **w** you are afraid. **Dt 7:19** 834
w you know and of whom you have **Dt 9:2** 834
and of **w** you have heard *it said,* **Dt 9:2** 834
for your people **w** you brought out **Dt 9:12** 834
w You have redeemed through Your **Dt 9:26** 834
w You have brought out of Egypt **Dt 9:26** 834
w You have brought out by Your **Dt 9:29** 834
nations **w** you shall dispossess serve **Dt 12:2** 834
other gods (**w** you have not known) **Dt 13:2** 834
w neither you nor your fathers have **Dt 13:6** 834
other gods' (**w** you have not known), **Dt 13:13** 834
you **w** the LORD your God chooses, **Dt 17:15** 834
Israel **w** You have redeemed, **Dt 21:8** 834
to his wife **w** he has taken. **Dt 24:5** 834
and the man to **w** you make the loan **Dt 24:11** 834
shall be that the firstborn **w** she bears **Dt 25:6** 834
"A people **w** you do not know shall **Dt 28:33** 834
king, **w** you set over you, **Dt 28:36** 834
w the LORD will send against you, **Dt 28:48** 834
your daughters **w** the LORD your God **Dt 28:53** 834
toward her children **w** she bears; **Dt 28:57** 834
gods **w** they have not known and **Dt 29:26** 834
and **w** He had not allotted to them. **Dt 29:26**
To gods **w** they have not known, **Dt 32:17**
W your fathers did not dread. **Dt 32:17**
Sons in **w** is no faithfulness. **Dt 32:20**
man, **W** You proved at Massah, **Dt 33:8** 834
With **w** You contended at the **Dt 33:8**
w the LORD knew face to face, **Dt 34:10** 834
and Og, **w** you utterly destroyed. **Jos 2:10** 834
So Joshua called the twelve men **w** **Jos 4:4** 834
to **w** the LORD had sworn that He **Jos 5:6** 834
w He raised up in their place, **Jos 5:7**
she hid the messengers **w** we sent. **Jos 6:17** 834
for she hid the messengers **w** **Jos 6:25** 834
those **w** the sons of Israel killed with **Jos 10:11** 834
your enemies with **w** you fight." **Jos 10:25** 834
w the sons of Israel defeated, **Jos 12:1** 834
the kings of the land **w** Joshua and **Jos 12:7** 834
w Moses struck with the chiefs of **Jos 13:21** 834
w the LORD has thus far blessed?" **Jos 17:14** 834
yourselves today **w** you will serve: **Jos 24:15** 4310
you the man **w** you are seeking." **Jg 4:22** 834
be that he of **w** I say to you, **Jg 7:4** 834
but everyone of **w** I say to you, **Jg 7:4** 834
concerning **w** you taunted me, **Jg 8:15** 834
were they **w** you killed at Tabor?" **Jg 8:18** 834
not the people **w** you despised? **Jg 9:38** 834
and thirty daughters **w** he gave in **Jg 12:9**
please let the man of God **w** You **Jg 13:8** 834
So the dead **w** he killed at his **Jg 16:30** 834
those **w** he killed in his life. **Jg 16:30** 834
w they had set against Gibeah, **Jg 20:36** 834
and they gave them the women **w** **Jg 21:14** 834
who danced, **w** they carried away. **Jg 21:23** 834
with **w** she had worked and said, **Ru 2:19** 834
with **w** I worked today is Boaz." **Ru 2:19** 834
of **w** Boaz spoke was passing by, **Ru 4:1** 834
of **w** built the house of Israel; **Ru 4:11** 834
of Perez **w** Tamar bore to Judah, **Ru 4:12** 834
And to **w** shall He go up from us?" **1Sa 6:20** 4310
your king **w** you have chosen **1Sa 8:18** 834
the man of **w** I spoke to you! **1Sa 9:17** 834
And for **w** is all that is desirable **1Sa 9:20** 4310
you see him **w** the LORD has chosen? **1Sa 10:24** 834
I taken, or **w** have I defrauded? **1Sa 12:3** 4310
W have I oppressed, or from whose **1Sa 12:3** 4310
is the king **w** you have chosen, **1Sa 12:13** 4310
have chosen, **w** you have asked for, **1Sa 12:13** 4310
Me the one **w** I designate to you." **1Sa 16:3** 834
And with **w** have you left those few **1Sa 17:28** 4310
of Israel, **w** you have taunted. **1Sa 17:45** 834
w you killed in the valley of **1Sa 21:9** 834
"After **w** has the king of Israel **1Sa 24:14** 4310
W are you pursuing? **1Sa 24:14** 4310
young men of my lord **w** you sent. **1Sa 25:25** 834
up for me **w** I shall name to you." **1Sa 28:8** 834
"**W** shall I bring up for you?" **1Sa 28:11** 4310
of **w** they sing in the dances, **1Sa 29:5** 834
"To **w** do you belong? **1Sa 30:13** 4310
to **w** I was betrothed for a hundred **2Sa 3:14** 834
the maids of **w** you have spoken, **2Sa 6:22** 834
Saul, **w** I removed from before you. **2Sa 7:15** 834
w God went to redeem for Himself **2Sa 7:23** 834
before Your people **w** You have **2Sa 7:23** 834
to **w** I may show the kindness of God **2Sa 9:3**
life of his brother **w** he killed, **2Sa 14:7** 834
For **w** the LORD, this people, and **2Sa 16:18** 834
"Besides, **w** should I serve? **2Sa 16:19** 4310
w he has left to keep the house; **2Sa 16:21** 834
Absalom, **w** we anointed over us, **2Sa 19:10** 834
w he had left to keep the house, **2Sa 20:3** 834
w she had borne to Saul, **2Sa 21:8** 834
w she had borne to Adriel the son **2Sa 21:8** 834
God, my rock, in **w** I take refuge, **2Sa 22:3**
But Your eyes are on the haughty **w** **2Sa 22:28**
people **w** I have not known serve me. **2Sa 22:44**
of the mighty men **w** David had: **2Sa 23:8** 834
the son of Jether, **w** he killed; **1Ki 2:5**
was not my son, **w** I had borne." **1Ki 3:21** 834
w I will set on your throne in **1Ki 5:5** 834
daughter, **w** Solomon had married. **1Ki 7:8** 834
w the sons of Israel were unable to **1Ki 9:21** 834
w Tahpenes weaned in Pharaoh's **1Ki 11:20**
of My servant David **w** I chose, **1Ki 11:34** 834

Context	Reference	Number
the prophet **w** he had brought back.	1Ki 13:23	834
of Israel lives, before **w** I stand,	1Ki 17:1	834
to the widow with **w** I am staying,	1Ki 17:20	834
of hosts lives, before **w** I stand,	1Ki 18:15	834
w the word of the LORD had come,	1Ki 18:31	834
Ahab said, "By **w**?"	1Ki 20:14	4310
w I had devoted to destruction,	1Ki 20:42	834
w the LORD cast out before the	1Ki 21:26	834
by **w** we may inquire of the LORD,	1Ki 22:8	834
of hosts lives, before **w** I stand,	2Ki 3:14	834
the LORD lives, before **w** I stand,	2Ki 5:16	834
bring you to the man **w** you seek."	2Ki 6:19	834
son, **w** Elisha restored to life."	2Ki 8:5	834
the men **w** I bring into your hands	2Ki 10:24	834
nations **w** the LORD had driven out	2Ki 16:3	834
nations **w** the LORD had driven out	2Ki 17:8	834
"The nations **w** you have carried	2Ki 17:26	834
w you carried away into exile and	2Ki 17:27	834
So one of the priests **w** they had	2Ki 17:28	834
nations from among **w** they had been	2Ki 17:33	834
sons of Jacob, **w** He named Israel;	2Ki 17:34	834
with **w** the LORD made a covenant	2Ki 17:35	834
Now on **w** do you rely, that you	2Ki 18:20	4310
w his master the king of Assyria	2Ki 19:4	834
in **w** you trust deceive you saying,	2Ki 19:10	834
'**W** have you reproached and	2Ki 19:22	4310
w have you raised *your* voice,	2Ki 19:22	4310
issue from you, **w** you will beget,	2Ki 20:18	834
the nations **w** the LORD dispossessed	2Ki 21:2	834
the nations **w** the LORD destroyed	2Ki 21:9	834
idolatrous priests **w** the kings of Judah	2Ki 23:5	834
w Nebuchadnezzar king of Babylon	2Ki 25:22	834
w she bore, *were* Zimran,	1Ch 1:32	
w he married when he was sixty	1Ch 2:21	
daughter of Pharaoh, **w** Mered took)	1Ch 4:17	834
w Tilgath-pilneser king of Assyria	1Ch 5:6	834
w God had destroyed before them.	1Ch 5:25	834
Now these are those **w** David	1Ch 6:31	834
w his Aramean concubine bore;	1Ch 7:14	834
and Ezer and Elead **w** the men of	1Ch 7:21	
w David and Samuel the seer	1Ch 9:22	1992a
of the mighty men **w** David had,	1Ch 11:10	834
of the mighty men **w** David had:	1Ch 11:11	834
hundred **w** he killed at one time.	1Ch 11:11	
w I commanded to shepherd My	1Ch 17:6	834
w God went to redeem for Himself	1Ch 17:21	834
w You redeemed out of Egypt?	1Ch 17:21	834
Solomon, **w** alone God has chosen,	1Ch 29:1	
over **w** I have made you king,	2Ch 1:11	834
w I have in Judah and Jerusalem,	2Ch 2:7	834
w David my father provided.	2Ch 2:7	834
w the sons of Israel had not destroyed,	2Ch 8:8	834
apart from those **w** the king put in	2Ch 17:19	834
by **w** we may inquire of the LORD,	2Ch 18:7	
w You did not let Israel invade	2Ch 20:10	834
w the LORD had anointed to cut off	2Ch 22:7	834
w David had assigned over the	2Ch 23:18	834
But the troops **w** Amaziah sent back	2Ch 25:13	834
the nations **w** the LORD had driven	2Ch 28:3	834
return the captives **w** you captured	2Ch 28:11	834
the nations **w** the LORD dispossessed	2Ch 33:2	834
the nations **w** the LORD destroyed	2Ch 33:9	834
So Hilkiah and *those* **w** the king	2Ch 34:22	834
the exiles **w** Nebuchadnezzar the king	Ezr 2:1	834
w he had appointed governor.	Ezr 5:14	1768
w David and the princes had given	Ezr 8:20	7945
and some of them had wives *by* **w**	Ezr 10:44	
Your people **w** You redeemed by	Ne 1:10	834
the exiles **w** Nebuchadnezzar the king	Ne 7:6	834
servants, of **w** *there were* 7,337;	Ne 7:67	428
the kings **W** You have set over us	Ne 9:37	834
w Nebuchadnezzar the king of	Es 2:6	834
w the king had appointed to attend	Es 4:5	834
man **w** the king desires to honor?"	Es 6:6	834
"**W** would the king desire to honor	Es 6:6	4310
man **w** the king desires to honor,	Es 6:7	834
the man **w** the king desires to honor	Es 6:9	834
the man **w** the king desires to honor	Es 6:9	834
man **w** the king desires to honor."	Es 6:11	834
before **w** you have begun to fall,	Es 6:13	834
hidden, And **w** God has hedged in?	Jb 3:23	834
happy is the man **w** God reproves,	Jb 5:17	
W God brings into their power.	Jb 12:6	834
To **w** alone the land was given, And	Jb 15:19	1992a
And I am one at **w** men spit.	Jb 17:6	
W I myself shall behold, And whom	Jb 19:27	834
And **w** my eyes will see and not	Jb 19:27	
upon **w** does His light not rise?	Jb 25:3	4310
"To **w** have you uttered words?	Jb 26:4	4310
To **w** I gave the wilderness for a	Jb 39:6	834
ones in **w** is all my delight.	Ps 16:3	
God, my rock, in **w** I take refuge;	Ps 18:2	
w I have not known serve me.	Ps 18:43	
and my salvation; **W** shall I fear?	Ps 27:1	4310
defense of my life; **W** shall I dread?	Ps 27:1	4310
How blessed is the man to **w** the	Ps 32:2	
The people **w** He has chosen for His	Ps 33:12	
The smiters **w** I did not know	Ps 35:15	
my close friend in **w** I trusted,	Ps 41:9	834
The glory of Jacob **w** He loves.	Ps 47:4	834
With **w** there is no change, And who	Ps 55:19	834
is the one **w** You choose	Ps 65:4	
him **w** You Yourself have smitten,	Ps 69:26	834
pain of those **w** You have wounded.	Ps 69:26	
W have I in heaven *but You?*	Ps 73:25	4310
And on the son **w** You have	Ps 80:15	
Upon the son of man **w** You made	Ps 80:17	
All nations **w** You have made shall	Ps 86:9	834
W You remember no more,	Ps 88:5	834
With **w** My hand will be established;	Ps 89:21	834
fortress, My God, in **w** I trust!"	Ps 91:2	
is the man **w** You chasten,	Ps 94:12	834
And **w** You teach out of Your law;	Ps 94:12	
And Aaron, **w** He had chosen.	Ps 105:26	834
W they sacrificed to the idols of	Ps 106:38	834
W He has redeemed from the hand of	Ps 107:2	834
shield and He in **w** I take refuge,	Ps 144:2	
man, in **w** there is no salvation.	Ps 146:3	7945
For **w** the LORD loves He reproves,	Pr 3:12	834
father *corrects* the son in **w** he delights.	Pr 3:12	
good from those to **w** it is due,	Pr 3:27	
the prince, **W** your eyes have seen.	Pr 25:7	834
"And for **w** am I laboring and	Ec 4:8	4310
as for every man to **w** God has	Ec 5:19	834
a man to **w** God has given riches	Ec 6:2	834
there are righteous men to **w** it	Ec 8:14	834
there are evil men to **w** it happens	Ec 8:14	7945
Enjoy life with the woman **w** you	Ec 9:9	834
"Tell me, O you **w** my soul loves,	SS 1:7	7945
I sought him **W** my soul loves;	SS 3:1	7945
I must seek him **w** my soul loves.'	SS 3:2	7945
you seen him **w** my soul loves?'	SS 3:3	7945
When I found him **w** my soul loves;	SS 3:4	7945
"**W** shall I send, and who will go	Is 6:8	4310
hosts **w** you should regard as holy.	Is 8:13	
I and the children **w** the LORD has	Is 8:18	834
To **w** will you flee for help?	Is 10:3	4310
everyone to **w** it is mentioned will	Is 19:17	834
w the LORD of hosts has blessed,	Is 19:25	834
have here, And **w** do you have here,	Is 22:16	4310
this is our God for **w** we have	Is 25:9	
is the LORD for **w** we have waited;	Is 25:9	
"To **w** would He teach knowledge,	Is 28:9	4310
And to **w** would He interpret the	Is 28:9	4310
from **w** you have deeply defected,	Is 31:6	834
w I have devoted to destruction.	Is 34:5	
nobles—there is no one there **W**	Is 34:12	
Now on **w** do you rely, that you	Is 36:5	4310
w his master the king of Assyria	Is 37:4	834
God in **w** you trust deceive you,	Is 37:10	834
"**W** have you reproached and	Is 37:23	4310
against **w** have you raised *your* voice	Is 37:23	4310
issue from you, **w** you will beget,	Is 39:7	834
With **w** did He consult and *who* gave	Is 40:14	4310
To **w** then will you liken God?	Is 40:18	4310
"To **w** then will you liken Me That	Is 40:25	4310
W He calls in righteousness to His	Is 41:2	
My servant, Jacob **w** I have chosen,	Is 41:8	834
You **w** I have taken from the ends	Is 41:9	834
"Behold, My Servant, **w** I uphold;	Is 42:1	
My chosen one *in* **w** My soul	Is 42:1	
so deaf as My messenger **w** I send?	Is 42:19	
LORD, against **w** we have sinned,	Is 42:24	2098
And **w** I have created for My glory,	Is 43:7	
for My glory, **W** I have formed,	Is 43:7	
have formed, even **w** I have made."	Is 43:7	
"And My servant **w** I have chosen,	Is 43:10	834
"The people **w** I formed for	Is 43:21	2098
And Israel, **w** I have chosen:	Is 44:1	
And you Jeshurun **w** I have chosen.	Is 44:2	
W I have taken by the right hand,	Is 45:1	834
"To **w** would you liken Me And	Is 46:5	4310
to you with **w** you have labored,	Is 47:15	834
O Jacob, even Israel **w** I called;	Is 48:12	
In **W** I will show My glory."	Is 49:3	834
"The children of **w** you were	Is 49:20	
Or to **w** of My creditors did I sell	Is 50:1	4310
And to **w** has the arm of the LORD	Is 53:1	4310
one from **w** men hide their face He	Is 53:3	
my people, to **w** the stroke *was due?*	Is 53:8	
"Against **w** do you jest?	Is 57:4	4310
Against **w** do you open wide your	Is 57:4	4310
"Of **w** were you worried and	Is 57:11	4310
And the breath *of those* **w** I have	Is 57:16	
Because they are the offspring **w**	Is 61:9	
over **w** You have never ruled,	Is 63:19	
"As one **w** his mother comforts, so	Is 66:13	834
to **w** the word of the LORD came in	Jer 1:2	834
has rejected those in **w** you trust,	Jer 2:37	4009
To **w** shall I speak and give	Jer 6:10	4310
And *who is* he to **w** the mouth of	Jer 9:12	834
w neither they nor their fathers	Jer 9:16	834
the gods to **w** they burn incense,	Jer 11:12	834
"The people also to **w** they are	Jer 14:16	834
to **w** you have falsely prophesied.	Jer 20:6	834
the hand of those **w** you dread,	Jer 22:25	834
w I have sent out of this place	Jer 24:5	834
all the nations to **w** I send you	Jer 25:15	834
to **w** the LORD sent me drink it:	Jer 25:17	834
w I have been sending to you again	Jer 26:5	834
one **w** the LORD has truly sent."	Jer 28:9	834
w Nebuchadnezzar had taken into	Jer 29:1	834
w Zedekiah king of Judah sent to	Jer 29:3	834
to all the exiles **w** I have sent	Jer 29:4	834
w I have sent away from Jerusalem	Jer 29:20	834
w the king of Babylon roasted in	Jer 29:22	834
king, **w** I will raise up for them.	Jer 30:9	834
men **w** I have slain in My anger and	Jer 33:5	834
servants **w** they had set free,	Jer 34:11	834
w you had set free according to	Jer 34:16	834
Now Zedekiah the son of Josiah **w**	Jer 37:1	834
Jeremiah the prophet **w** they have cast	Jer 38:9	834
the hand of the men **w** you dread.	Jer 39:17	834
w the king of Babylon has	Jer 40:5	834
put to death the one **w** the king of	Jer 41:2	834
corpses of the men **w** he had struck	Jer 41:9	834
w Nebuzaradan the captain of the	Jer 41:10	834
So all the people **w** Ishmael had	Jer 41:14	834
the people **w** he had recovered	Jer 41:16	834
w he had brought back from Gibeon.	Jer 41:16	834
w the king of Babylon had	Jer 41:18	834
our God to **w** we are sending you,	Jer 42:6	834
to **w** you sent me to present your	Jer 42:9	834
of Babylon, **w** you are *now* fearing;	Jer 42:11	834
w the LORD their God had sent,	Jer 43:1	834
other gods **w** they had not known,	Jer 44:3	834
those **w** I leave as a remnant.'	Jer 50:20	834
w Nebuchadnezzar carried away into	Jer 52:28	834
The ones **w** You commanded That	La 1:10	834
into the hands Of *those against* **w**	La 1:14	
With **w** have You dealt thus?	La 2:20	4310
Those **w** I bore and reared, My	La 2:22	834
in their pits, Of **w** we had said,	La 4:20	834
w I will send to destroy you,	Ezk 5:16	834
touch any man on **w** is the mark;	Ezk 9:6	834
"Your slain **w** you have laid in	Ezk 11:7	834
are those to **w** the inhabitants of	Ezk 11:15	834
those lives **w** you hunt as birds.	Ezk 13:20	834
daughters **w** you had borne to Me and	Ezk 16:20	834
lovers with **w** you took pleasure,	Ezk 16:37	834
even all those **w** you loved *and* all	Ezk 16:37	834
loved *and* all those **w** you hated.	Ezk 16:37	834
of the nations among **w** they *lived,*	Ezk 20:9	834
all of **w** *were* the choicest men of	Ezk 23:7	
and with all **w** she lusted after,	Ezk 23:7	834
the Assyrians, after **w** she lusted.	Ezk 23:9	834
you, from **w** you were alienated,	Ezk 23:22	834
into the hand of those **w** you hate,	Ezk 23:28	834
those from **w** you were alienated.	Ezk 23:28	834
their sons, **w** they bore to Me,	Ezk 23:37	834
afar, to **w** a messenger was sent;	Ezk 23:40	834
for **w** you bathed, painted your eyes	Ezk 23:40	834
daughters **w** you have left behind	Ezk 24:21	834
among **w** they are scattered,	Ezk 28:25	834
among **w** they were scattered.	Ezk 29:13	834, 8033
'**W** are you like in your greatness?	Ezk 31:2	413, 4310
'**W** do you surpass in beauty?	Ezk 32:19	4310
"Are you the one of **w** I spoke in	Ezk 38:17	834
youths in **w** was no defect, who	Da 1:4	834
But Daniel said to the overseer **w**	Da 1:11	834
w the king had appointed to	Da 2:24	1768
to **w** the God of heaven has given	Da 2:37	1768
"There are certain Jews **w** you	Da 3:12	1768
our God **w** we serve is able to	Da 3:17	1768
in **w** is a spirit of the holy gods;	Da 4:8	1768
And bestows it on **w** He wishes And	Da 4:17	1768, 4479
in **w** is a spirit of the holy gods;	Da 5:11	1768
w the king named Belteshazzar.	Da 5:12	1768
w my father the king brought from	Da 5:13	1768
(of **w** Daniel was one),	Da 6:2	1768
"Your God **w** you constantly serve	Da 6:16	1768
your God, **w** you constantly serve,	Da 6:20	1768
w I had seen in the vision	Da 9:21	834
on **w** the honor of kingship has not	Da 11:21	
a god **w** his fathers did not know;	Da 11:38	834
your judges of **w** you requested,	Hos 13:10	834
the survivors **w** the LORD calls.	Jl 2:32	834
W they have scattered among the	Jl 3:2	834
To **w** the house of Israel comes.	Am 6:1	1992a
Even those **w** I have afflicted.	Mi 4:6	834
For on **w** has not your evil passed	Na 3:19	4310
to **w** the former prophets	Zch 1:4	834
"These are those **w** the LORD has	Zch 1:10	834
the nations **w** they have not known.	Zch 7:14	834
look on Me **w** they have pierced;	Zch 12:10	834
toward **w** the LORD is indignant	Mal 1:4	834
w you have dealt treacherously,	Mal 2:14	834
And the Lord, **w** you seek, will	Mal 3:1	834
of the covenant, in **w** you delight,	Mal 3:1	834
Mary, by **w** Jesus was born,	Mt 1:16	*3739*
Son, in **w** I am well-pleased."	Mt 3:17	*3739*
is the one about **w** it is written,	Mt 11:10	*3739*
to **w** the Son wills to reveal *Him.*	Mt 11:27	*3739*
MY SERVANT **W** I HAVE CHOSEN;	Mt 12:18	*3739*
IN **W** MY SOUL IS WELL-PLEASED;	Mt 12:18	*3739*
by **w** do your sons cast *them* out?	Mt 12:27	*5101*
on **w** seed was sown beside the road.	Mt 13:19	
"The one on **w** seed was sown	Mt 13:20	
"And the one on **w** seed was sown	Mt 13:22	
"And the one on **w** seed was sown	Mt 13:23	
Son, with **w** I am well-pleased;	Mt 17:5	*3739*
From **w** do the kings of the earth	Mt 17:25	*5101*
w the stumbling block comes!	Mt 18:7	*3739*
only those to **w** it has been given.	Mt 19:11	*3739*
but it is for those for **w** it has	Mt 20:23	*3739*
w you murdered between the temple	Mt 23:35	*3739*
slave **w** his master put in charge of	Mt 24:45	*3739*
"Blessed is that slave **w** his	Mt 24:46	*3739*
by **w** the Son of Man is betrayed!	Mt 26:24	*3739*
any one prisoner **w** they wanted.	Mt 27:15	*3739*
"**W** do you want me to release for	Mt 27:17	*5101*
w they pressed into service to	Mt 27:32	*3778*
those **w** He Himself wanted,	Mk 3:13	*3739*
(to **w** He gave the name Peter),	Mk 3:16	
these are the ones on **w** seed was sown	Mk 4:16	
"And others are the ones on **w**	Mk 4:18	
"And those are the ones on **w** seed	Mk 4:20	
"John, **w** I beheaded, has risen!"	Mk 6:16	*3739*
for **w** it has been prepared."	Mk 10:40	*3739*
the sake of the elect, **w** He chose,	Mk 13:20	*3739*
by **w** the Son of Man is betrayed!	Mk 14:21	*3739*
any one prisoner **w** they requested.	Mk 15:6	*3739*
w you call the King of the Jews?"	Mk 15:12	*3739*
among **w** *were* Mary Magdalene,	Mk 15:40	*3739*

w He had cast out seven demons. Mk 16:9 *3739*
among men with **w** He is pleased." Lk 2:14 *3739*
them, **w** He also named as apostles: Lk 6:13 *3739*
Simon, **w** He also named Peter, and Lk 6:14 *3739*
from **w** you expect to receive, Lk 6:34 *3739*
I will show you **w** he is like: Lk 6:47 *5101*
is the one about **w** it is written, Lk 7:27 *3739*
the one **w** he forgave more." Lk 7:43 *3739*
from **w** seven demons had gone out, Lk 8:2 *3739*
from **w** the demons had gone out, Lk 8:35 *3739*
But the man from **w** the demons had Lk 8:38 *3739*
man about **w** I hear such things?" Lk 9:9 *3739*
w the Son wills to reveal *Him*." Lk 10:22 *3739*
by **w** do your sons cast them out? Lk 11:19 *5101*
"But I will warn you **w** to fear: Lk 12:5 *5101*
"Blessed are those slaves **w** the Lk 12:37 *3739*
w his master will put in charge of Lk 12:42 *3739*
"Blessed is that slave **w** his Lk 12:43 *3739*
and to **w** they entrusted much, of Lk 12:48 *3739*
eighteen on **w** the tower in Siloam fell Lk 13:4 *3739*
w Satan has bound for eighteen Lk 13:16 *3739*
woe to him through **w** they come! Lk 17:1 *3739*
to **w** he had given the money, Lk 19:15 *3739*
to that man by **w** He is betrayed!" Lk 22:22 *3739*
"This was He of **w** I said, Jn 1:15 *3739*
you stands One **w** you do not know. Jn 1:26 *3739*
"This is He on behalf of **w** I said, Jn 1:30 *3739*
'He upon **w** you see the Spirit Jn 1:33 *3739*
"We have found Him of **w** Moses in Jn 1:45 *3739*
indeed, in **w** there is no deceit!" Jn 1:47 *3739*
to **w** you have testified, Jn 3:26 *3739*
"For He **w** God has sent speaks the Jn 3:34 *3739*
and the one **w** you now have is not Jn 4:18 *3739*
also gives life to **w** He wishes. Jn 5:21 *3739*
you do not believe Him **w** He sent. Jn 5:38 *3739*
in **w** you have set your hope. Jn 5:45 *3739*
believe in Him **w** He has sent." Jn 6:29 *3739*
"Lord, to **w** shall we go? Jn 6:68 *5101*
man **w** they are seeking to kill? Jn 7:25 *3739*
Me is true, **w** you do not know. Jn 7:28 *3739*
w those who believed in Him were Jn 7:39 *3739*
w do You make Yourself out *to be*?" Jn 8:53 *5101*
who glorifies Me, of **w** you say, Jn 8:54 *3739*
gods, to **w** the word of God came Jn 10:35 *3739*
w the Father sanctified and sent Jn 10:36 *3739*
behold, he **w** You love is sick." Jn 11:3 *3739*
w Jesus had raised from the dead. Jn 12:1 *3739*
w He raised from the dead. Jn 12:9 *3739*
AND TO **W** HAS THE ARM OF THE LORD Jn 12:38 *5101*
of His disciples, **w** Jesus loved. Jn 13:23 *3739*
who it is of **w** He is speaking." Jn 13:24 *3739*
for **w** I shall dip the morsel and give Jn 13:26 *3739*
truth, **w** the world cannot receive, Jn 14:17 *3739*
w the Father will send in My name, Jn 14:26 *3739*
w I will send to you from the Jn 15:26 *3739*
that to all **w** You have given Him, Jn 17:2 *3739*
and Jesus Christ **w** You have sent. Jn 17:3 *3739*
to the men **w** You gave Me Jn 17:6 *3739*
but of those **w** You have given Me; Jn 17:9 *3739*
they also, **w** You have given Me, Jn 17:24 *3739*
and said to them, "**W** do you seek?" Jn 18:4 *5101*
again asked them, "**W** do you seek?" Jn 18:7 *5101*
"Of those **w** You have given Me I Jn 18:9 *3739*
w He loved standing nearby, Jn 19:26 *3739*
LOOK ON HIM **W** THEY PIERCED." Jn 19:37 *3739*
the other disciple **w** Jesus loved, Jn 20:2 *3739*
W are you seeking?" Jn 20:15 *5101*
Therefore that disciple **w** Jesus loved Jn 21:7 *3739*
saw the disciple **w** Jesus loved Jn 21:20 *3739*
to the apostles **w** He had chosen. Ac 1:2 *3739*
Jesus **w** you crucified." Ac 2:36 *3739*
w they used to set down every day Ac 3:2 *3739*
Jesus, *the one* **w** you delivered and Ac 3:13 *3739*
one **w** God raised from the dead, Ac 3:15 *3739*
this man **w** you see and know; Ac 3:16 *3739*
w heaven must receive until *the* Ac 3:21 *3739*
the Nazarene, **w** you crucified, Ac 4:10 *3739*
w God raised from the dead Ac 4:10 *3739*
on **w** this miracle of healing had been Ac 4:22 *3739*
Jesus, **w** You anointed. Ac 4:27 *3739*
The men **w** you put in prison are Ac 5:25 *3739*
w you had put to death by hanging Ac 5:30 *3739*
"He is the one **w** God exalted to Ac 5:31
w God has given to those who obey Ac 5:32 *3739*
w we may put in charge of this Ac 6:3 *3739*
"This Moses **w** they disowned, Ac 7:35 *3739*
is the one **w** God sent *to be* both a Ac 7:35 *3778*
nations **w** God drove out before our Ac 7:45 *3739*
everyone on **w** I lay my hands may Ac 8:19 *3739*
of **w** does the prophet say this? Ac 8:34 *5101*
"I am Jesus **w** you are persecuting, Ac 9:5 *3739*
w He also testified and said, Ac 13:22 *3739*
but He **w** God raised did not Ac 13:37 *3739*
the Lord in **w** they had believed. Ac 14:23 *3739*
number to **w** we gave no instruction Ac 15:24 *3739*
"This Jesus **w** I am proclaiming to Ac 17:3 *3739*
through a Man **w** He has appointed, Ac 17:31 *3739*
among **w** also were Dionysius the Ac 17:34 *3739*
you by Jesus **w** Paul preaches." Ac 19:13 *3739*
the man, in **w** was the evil spirit, Ac 19:16 *3739*
w all of Asia and the world worship Ac 19:27 *3739*
among **w** I went about preaching the Ac 20:25 *3739*
standing with **w** we were to lodge. Ac 21:16 *3739*
Nazarene, **w** you are persecuting.' Ac 22:8 *3739*
Jesus, **w** Paul asserted to be alive. Ac 25:19 *3739*
you see this man about **w** all Ac 25:24 *3739*
'I am Jesus **w** you are persecuting. Ac 26:15 *3739*
Gentiles, to **w** I am sending you, Ac 26:17 *3739*
an angel of the God to **w** I belong Ac 27:23 *3739*
and **w** I serve stood before me, Ac 27:23 *3739*
through **w** we have received grace Ro 1:5 *3739*
among **w** you also are the called of Ro 1:6 *3739*
w I serve in my spirit in the Ro 1:9 *3739*
w God displayed publicly as a Ro 3:25 *3739*
man to **w** God credits righteousness Ro 4:6 *3739*
in the presence of Him **w** he believed, Ro 4:17 *3739*
also, to **w** it will be credited, Ro 4:24 *3739*
through **w** also we have obtained Ro 5:2 *3739*
through **w** we have now received the Ro 5:11 *3739*
are slaves of the one **w** you obey, Ro 6:16 *3739*
For those **w** He foreknew, He also Ro 8:29 *3739*
and these **w** He predestined, Ro 8:30 *3739*
and these **w** He called, He also Ro 8:30 *3739*
and these **w** He justified, He also Ro 8:30 *3739*
to **w** belongs the adoption as sons Ro 9:4 *3739*
and from **w** is the Christ according Ro 9:5 *3739*
WILL HAVE MERCY ON **W** I HAVE MERCY, Ro 9:15 *3739*
ON **W** I HAVE COMPASSION." Ro 9:15 *3739*
then He has mercy on **w** He desires, Ro 9:18 *3739*
and He hardens **w** He desires. Ro 9:18 *3739*
even us, **w** He also called, not Ro 9:24 *3739*
Him in **w** they have not believed? Ro 10:14 *3739*
in Him **w** they have not heard? Ro 10:14 *3739*
rejected His people **w** He foreknew. Ro 11:2 *3739*
tax to **w** tax *is due* Ro 13:7 *3588*
custom to **w** custom; Ro 13:7 *3588*
fear to **w** fear; honor to whom honor. Ro 13:7 *3588*
honor to **w** honor. Ro 13:7 *3588*
your food him for **w** Christ died. Ro 14:15 *3739*
to **w** not only do I give thanks, Ro 16:4 *3739*
through **w** you were called into 1Co 1:9 *3739*
Servants through **w** you believed, 1Co 3:5 *3739*
is in you, **w** you have from God, 1Co 6:19 *3739*
to be married to **w** she wishes, 1Co 7:39 *3739*
the Father, from **w** are all things and 1Co 8:6 *3739*
Jesus Christ, by **w** are all things, 1Co 8:6 *3739*
upon **w** the ends of the ages have 1Co 10:11 *3739*
time, most of **w** remain until now, 1Co 15:6 *3739*
raised Christ, **w** He did not raise, 1Co 15:15 *3739*
us, He on **w** we have set our hope. 2Co 1:10 *3739*
but the one **w** I made sorrowful? 2Co 2:2
But one **w** you forgive anything, I 2Co 2:10 *3739*
w we have often tested and found 2Co 8:22 *3739*
but he **w** the Lord commends. 2Co 10:18 *3739*
Jesus **w** we have not preached, 2Co 11:4 *3739*
any of those **w** I have sent to you, 2Co 12:17 *3739*
to **w** *be* the glory forevermore. Ga 1:5 *3739*
to **w** the promise had been made. Ga 3:19 *3739*
with **w** I am again in labor until Ga 4:19 *3739*
in **w** the whole building, being Eph 2:21 *3739*
in **w** you also are being built Eph 2:22 *3739*
in **w** we have boldness and Eph 3:12 *3739*
from **w** every family in heaven and Eph 3:15 *3739*
from **w** the whole body, being Eph 4:16 *3739*
by **w** you were sealed for the day Eph 4:30 *3739*
among **w** you appear as lights in Php 2:15 *3739*
for **w** I have suffered the loss of Php 3:8 *3739*
many walk, of **w** I often told you, Php 3:18 *3739*
beloved brethren **w** I long *to see,* Php 4:1 *1973*
in **w** we have redemption, the Col 1:14 *3739*
to **w** God willed to make known what Col 1:27 *3739*
in **w** are hidden all the treasures Col 2:3 *3739*
the head, from **w** the entire body, Col 2:19 *3739*
It is the Lord Christ **w** you serve. Col 3:24
(about **w** you received instructions; Col 4:10 *3739*
heaven, **w** He raised from the dead, 1Th 1:10 *3739*
w the Lord will slay with the breath 2Th 2:8 *3739*
among **w** I am foremost *of all.* 1Tm 1:15 *3739*
w I have handed over to Satan, 1Tm 1:20 *3739*
w no man has seen or can see. 1Tm 6:16 *3739*
w I serve with a clear conscience 2Tm 1:3 *3739*
for I know **w** I have believed and I 2Tm 1:12 *3739*
w are Phygelus and Hermogenes. 2Tm 1:15 *3739*
from **w** you have learned *them,* 2Tm 3:14 *5101*
w He poured out upon us richly Ti 3:6 *3739*
w I have begotten in my Phm 1:10 *3739*
w I wished to keep with me, so Phm 1:13 *3739*
w He appointed heir of all things, Heb 1:2 *3739*
through **w** also He made the world. Heb 1:2 *3739*
for Him, for **w** are all things, Heb 2:10 *3739*
and through **w** are all things, Heb 2:10 *3739*
THE CHILDREN **W** GOD HAS GIVEN ME." Heb 2:13 *3739*
with **w** was He angry for forty years? Heb 3:17 *5101*
And to **w** did He swear that they Heb 3:18 *5101*
eyes of Him with **w** we have to do. Heb 4:13 *3739*
to **w** also Abraham apportioned a Heb 7:2 *3739*
great this man was to **w** Abraham, Heb 7:4 *3739*
of **w** it is witnessed that he lives Heb 7:8
For the one concerning **w** these Heb 7:13 *3739*
it was he to **w** it was said, Heb 11:18 *3739*
of **w** the world was not worthy), Heb 11:38 *3739*
W THE LORD LOVES HE DISCIPLINES, Heb 12:6 *3739*
EVERY SON **W** HE RECEIVES." Heb 12:6 *3739*
for what son is there **w** *his* father Heb 12:7 *3739*
w *be* the glory forever and ever. Heb 13:21 *3739*
with **w**, if he comes soon, I will see Heb 13:23 *3739*
with **w** there is no variation or Jas 1:17 *3739*
to **w** belongs the glory and 1Pe 4:11 *3739*
Son with **w** I am well-pleased" 2Pe 1:17 *3739*
for **w** the black darkness has been 2Pe 2:17 *3739*
by the Spirit **w** He has given us. 1Jn 3:24 *3739*
love his brother **w** he has seen, 1Jn 4:20 *3739*
cannot love God **w** he has not seen. 1Jn 4:20 *3739*
her children, **w** I love in truth; 2Jn 1:1 *3739*
beloved Gaius, **w** I love in truth. 3Jn 1:1 *3739*
for **w** the black darkness has been Jude 1:13 *3739*
'Those **w** I love, I reprove and Rv 3:19 *3745*
to **w** it was granted to harm the earth Rv 7:2 *3739*
Then the angel **w** I saw standing on Rv 10:5 *3739*
with **w** the kings of the earth Rv 17:2 *3739*
woman **w** you saw is the great city, Rv 17:18 *3739*

WHOMEVER

for themselves, **w** they chose. Gn 6:2 3605, 834
and **w** you have in the city, Gn 19:12 3605, 834
With **w** of your servants it is found, Gn 44:9 834
send *the message* by **w** You will." Ex 4:13
w the one with the discharge Lv 15:11 3605, 834
and bestows it on **w** He wishes. Da 4:25 4479, 1768
and bestows it on **w** He wishes.' Da 4:32 4479, 1768
w he wished he killed and Da 5:19 1768
and **w** he wished he spared alive; Da 5:19 1768
and **w** he wished he elevated and Da 5:19 1768
and **w** he wished he humbled. Da 5:19 1768
that He sets over it **w** He wishes. Da 5:21 4479, 1768
but on **w** it falls, it will scatter Mt 21:44 *3739, 302*
"**W** I kiss, He is the one; Mt 26:48 *3739, 302*
"**W** I kiss, He is the one; Mk 14:44 *3739, 302*
to me, and I give it to **w** I wish. Lk 4:6 *3739, 1437*
but on **w** it falls, it will scatter Lk 20:18 *3739, 302*
who receives **w** I send receives Me; Jn 13:20 *302, 5100*
When I arrive, **w** you may approve, 1Co 16:3 *3739, 1437*

WHOSE

all in **w** nostrils was the breath Gn 7:22 834
w top *will reach* into heaven, Gn 11:4
an Egyptian maid **w** name was Hagar. Gn 16:1
His concubine, **w** name was Reumah, Gn 22:24
"**W** daughter are you? Gn 24:23 4310
had a brother **w** name was Laban; Gn 24:29
the Canaanites, in **w** land I live; Gn 24:37 834
'**W** daughter are you?' Gn 24:47 4310
another wife, **w** name was Keturah. Gn 25:1
Adullamite, **w** name was Hirah. Gn 38:1
certain Canaanite **w** name was Shua; Gn 38:2
w signet ring and cords and staff Gn 38:25 4310
one in **w** possession the cup has been Gn 44:16 834
The man in **w** possession the cup Gn 44:17 834
from every man **w** heart moves him Ex 25:2 834
for the LORD, **w** name is Jealous, Ex 34:14
Everyone **w** heart stirred him Ex 35:21 834
everyone **w** spirit moved him came Ex 35:21 834
Then all **w** hearts moved them, both Ex 35:22
All the women **w** heart stirred Ex 35:26 834
w heart moved them to bring Ex 35:29 834
everyone **w** heart stirred him, Ex 36:2 834
w means are limited for his Lv 14:32 834
w blood was brought in to make Lv 16:27 834
on **w** head the anointing oil has Lv 21:10 834
woman, **w** father was an Egyptian, Lv 24:10
silver dish **w** weight *was* one hundred Nu 7:13
his offering one silver dish **w** weight Nu 7:19
silver dish **w** weight *was* one hundred Nu 7:25
silver dish **w** weight *was* one hundred Nu 7:31
silver dish **w** weight *was* one hundred Nu 7:37
silver dish **w** weight *was* one hundred Nu 7:43
silver dish **w** weight *was* one hundred Nu 7:49
silver dish **w** weight *was* one hundred Nu 7:55
silver dish **w** weight *was* one hundred Nu 7:61
silver dish **w** weight *was* one hundred Nu 7:67
silver dish **w** weight *was* one hundred Nu 7:73
silver dish **w** weight *was* one hundred Nu 7:79
w flesh is half eaten away when he Nu 12:12 834
oracle of the man **w** eye is opened; Nu 24:3
oracle of the man **w** eye is opened, Nu 24:15
a land **w** stones are iron, and out Dt 8:9 834
out of **w** hills you can dig copper. Dt 8:9
w land the LORD your God gives Dt 19:1 834
w neck was broken in the valley; Dt 21:6
house of him **w** sandal is removed.' Dt 25:10
a nation **w** language you shall not Dt 28:49 834
w heart turns away today from the Dt 29:18 834
of a harlot **w** name was Rahab, Jos 2:1
and **w** land they possessed beyond Jos 12:1
Amorites in **w** land you are living; Jos 24:15 834
peoples through **w** midst we passed. Jos 24:17 834
w root is in Amalek *came down,* Jg 5:14
the Amorites in **w** land you live. Jg 6:10 834
of the Danites, **w** name was Manoah; Jg 13:2
of Sorek, **w** name was Delilah. Jg 16:4
of Ephraim **w** name was Micah. Jg 17:1
of Elimelech, **w** name was Boaz. Ru 2:1
one in **w** sight I may find favor." Ru 2:2 834
"**W** young woman is this?" Ru 2:5 4310
under **w** wings you have come to Ru 2:12 834
kinsman, with **w** maids you were? Ru 3:2 834
w name was Kish the son of Abiel, 1Sa 9:1
He had a son **w** name was Saul, 1Sa 9:2
and the valiant *men* **w** hearts God 1Sa 10:26 834
W ox have I taken, or whose donkey 1Sa 12:3 4310
I taken, or **w** donkey have I taken, 1Sa 12:3 4310
or from **w** hand have I taken a 1Sa 12:3 4310
w height was six cubits and a span. 1Sa 17:4
in Judah, **w** name was Jesse, 1Sa 17:12
"Abner, **w** son is this young man?" 1Sa 17:55 4310
"You inquire **w** son the youth is." 1Sa 17:56 4310

“**W** son are you, young man?” 1Sa 17:58 4310
in Maon **w** business was in Carmel; 1Sa 25:2
to men **w** origin I do not know?” 1Sa 25:11 834
had a concubine **w** name was Rizpah, 2Sa 3:7
in his place, saying, “**W** is the land? 2Sa 3:12 4310
the house of Saul **w** name was Ziba, 2Sa 9:2
had a young son **w** name was Mica. 2Sa 9:12
beautiful sister **w** name was Tamar, 2Sa 13:1
had a friend **w** name was Jonadab, 2Sa 13:3
and one daughter **w** name was Tamar; 2Sa 14:27
house of Saul **w** name was Shimei, 2Sa 16:5
Saul, in **w** place you have reigned; 2Sa 16:8 834
w heart is like the heart of a 2Sa 17:10 834
w name was Ithra the Israelite, 2Sa 17:25
to be there **w** name was Sheba, 2Sa 20:1
the weight of **w** spear was three 2Sa 21:16
the shaft of **w** spear was like a 2Sa 21:19
Then the woman **w** child *was* the 1Ki 3:26 834
his ways, **w** heart You know, 1Ki 8:39 834
w mother’s name was Zeruah, 1Ki 11:26
The royal officer on **w** hand 2Ki 7:2 834
the royal officer on **w** hand he leaned 2Ki 7:17 834
w son he had restored to life, 2Ki 8:1 834
w son he had restored to life appealed 2Ki 8:5 834
men into **w** hand they gave the money 2Ki 12:15 834
is it not He **w** high places and 2Ki 18:22 834
w altars Hezekiah has taken away, 2Ki 18:22
another wife, **w** name was Atarah; 1Ch 2:26
Egyptian servant **w** name was Jarha. 1Ch 2:34
w sister’s name was Maacah. 1Ch 7:15
had six sons **w** names are these: 1Ch 9:44
and **w** faces were like the faces of 1Ch 12:8
the shaft of **w** spear *was* like a 1Ch 20:5
Obed and Elzabad, **w** brothers, 1Ch 26:7
w heart You know for You 2Ch 6:30 834
those **w** heart is completely His. 2Ch 16:9
LORD was there, **w** name *was* Oded; 2Ch 28:9
even everyone **w** spirit God had Ezr 1:5
to one **w** name was Sheshbazzar, Ezr 5:14
w dwelling is in Jerusalem, Ezr 7:15 1768
a Jew **w** name was Mordecai, Es 2:5
and on **w** head a royal crown has Es 6:8 834
in the land of Uz **w** name was Job Jb 1:1
given to a man **w** way is hidden, Jb 3:23 834
clay, **W** foundation is in the dust, Jb 4:19 834
W confidence is fragile, And whose Jb 8:14 834
And **w** trust a spider’s web. Jb 8:14
As prepared for those **w** feet slip. Jb 12:5
In **w** hand is the life of every Jb 12:10 834
W foundations were washed away by Jb 22:16
And **w** spirit was expressed through Jb 26:4 4310
W fathers I disdained to put with Jb 30:1 834
And **w** food is the root of the Jb 30:4
wept for the one **w** life is hard? Jb 30:25
You **w** garments are hot, When the Jb 37:17 834
“From **w** womb has come the ice? Jb 38:29 4310
In **w** eyes a reprobate is despised, Ps 15:4
world, **w** portion is in *this* life, Ps 17:14
And **w** belly You fill with Ps 17:14
In **w** hands is a wicked scheme, And Ps 26:10 834
w right hand is full of bribes. Ps 26:10
is he **w** transgression is forgiven, Ps 32:1
is forgiven, **W** sin is covered! Ps 32:1
in **w** spirit there is no deceit! Ps 32:2
W trappings include bit and bridle Ps 32:9
is the nation **w** God is the LORD, Ps 33:12 834
And in **w** mouth are no arguments. Ps 38:14
There is a river **w** streams make Ps 46:4
In God, **w** word I praise, In God I Ps 56:4
In God, **w** word I praise, Ps 56:10
w word I praise, Ps 56:10
w teeth are spears and arrows And Ps 57:4
the deserts, **W** name is the LORD, Ps 68:4
And **w** spirit was not faithful to Ps 78:8
You alone, **w** name is the LORD, Ps 83:18
is the man **w** strength is in You, Ps 84:5
In **w** heart are the highways *to* Ps 84:5
In **w** hand are the depths of the Ps 95:4 834
stork, **w** home is the fir trees. Ps 104:17
are those **w** way is blameless, Ps 119:1
the man **w** quiver is full of them; Ps 127:5 834
W mouths speak deceit, And whose Ps 144:8 834
And **w** right hand is a right hand Ps 144:8
of aliens, **W** mouth speaks deceit And Ps 144:11 834
And **w** right hand is a right hand Ps 144:11
are the people **w** God is the LORD! Ps 144:15 7945
is he **w** help is the God of Jacob, Ps 146:5 7945
W hope is in the LORD his God, Ps 146:5
W paths are crooked, And who are Pr 2:15 834
guards the one **w** way is blameless, Pr 13:6
He **w** ear listens to the Pr 15:31
of heart *And* **w** speech is gracious, Pr 22:11
of *man* **w** teeth are *like* swords And Pr 30:14
And wine to him **w** life is bitter. Pr 31:6
woman **w** heart is snares and nets, Ec 7:26 834
and nets, **w** hands are chains. Ec 7:26
w king is a lad and whose princes Ec 10:16 7945
w princes feast in the morning. Ec 10:16
w king is of nobility and whose Ec 10:17 7945
whose king is of nobility and **w** Ec 10:17
be like an oak **w** leaf fades away Or Is 1:30
w breath *of life* is in his Is 2:22 834
Like a terebinth or an oak **W** stump Is 6:13 834
the land **w** two kings you dread Is 7:16 834
in **w** hands is My indignation, Is 10:5
W graven images *were* greater than Is 10:10
nation **W** land the rivers divide. Is 18:2 834
nation, **W** land the rivers divide Is 18:7 834
city, **W** origin is from antiquity, Is 23:7

W feet used to carry her to Is 23:7
crowns, **W** merchants were princes, Is 23:8 834
w traders were the honored of the Is 23:8 834
And **w** deeds are *done* in a dark Is 29:15
Egypt, **w** help is vain and empty. Is 30:7
W collapse comes suddenly in an Is 30:13 834
W collapse is like the smashing of Is 30:14
w fire is in Zion and whose Is 31:9 834
and **w** furnace is in Jerusalem. Is 31:9
is it not He **w** high places and Is 36:7 834
w altars Hezekiah has taken away and Is 36:7
And in **w** ways they were not Is 42:24
walk, And **w** law they did not obey? Is 42:24
A people in **w** heart is My law; Is 51:7
W name is the LORD of hosts; Is 54:5
Who lives forever, **w** name is Holy, Is 57:15
of water **w** waters do not fail. Is 58:11 834
nation **w** language you do not know, Jer 5:15
In **w** midst there is only Jer 6:6
And **w** heart turns away from the Jer 17:5
the LORD And **w** trust is the LORD. Jer 17:7
on **w** rooftops they burned sacrifices Jer 19:13 834
w eyes are open to all the ways of Jer 32:19 834
of the guard **w** name was Irijah, Jer 37:13
there will know **w** word will stand, Jer 44:28 4310
the rivers **w** waters surge about? Jer 46:7
the rivers **w** waters surge about; Jer 46:8
King **W** name is the LORD of hosts, Jer 46:18
King, **W** name is the LORD of hosts. Jer 48:15
King, **w** name is the LORD of hosts. Jer 51:57
w words you cannot understand. Ezk 3:6 834
at **w** loins was the writing case. Ezk 9:3 834
at **w** loins was the writing case Ezk 9:11 834
w appearance I had seen by the river Ezk 10:22 834
“But as for those **w** hearts go Ezk 11:21
on the throne, **w** oath he despised and Ezk 17:16 834
despised and **w** covenant he broke, Ezk 17:16 834
in **w** sight I made Myself known to Ezk 20:9 834
w sight I had brought them out. Ezk 20:14 834
in **w** sight I had brought them out. Ezk 20:22 834
prince of Israel, **w** day has come, Ezk 21:25 834
until He comes **w** right it is, Ezk 21:27 834
who are slain, **w** day has come, Ezk 21:29 834
w flesh is *like* the flesh of Ezk 23:20 834
and **w** issue is *like* the issue of horses. Ezk 23:20
And **w** rust has not gone out of it! Ezk 24:6
w graves are set in the remotest Ezk 32:23 834
and **w** swords were laid under their Ezk 32:27
w *inhabitants* have been gathered Ezk 38:8
there was a man **w** appearance was Ezk 40:3
w dwelling place is not with Da 2:11 1768
Daniel, **w** name was Belteshazzar, Da 2:26 1768
w name is Belteshazzar according Da 4:8 1768
Daniel, **w** name is Belteshazzar, Da 4:19 1768
w height reached to the sky and Da 4:20
and **w** foliage *was* beautiful and Da 4:21
in **w** branches the birds of the sky Da 4:21
But the God in **w** hand are your Da 5:23 1768
w waist was girded with *a belt of* Da 10:5
in **w** hands are false balances, Hos 12:7
In **w** land they have shed innocent Jl 3:19 834
LORD, **w** name is the God of hosts. Am 5:27
on **w** account this calamity *has struck* Jon 1:7 4310
On **w** account *has* this calamity Jon 1:8 4310
her, **W** rampart *was* the sea, Na 3:8 834
sea, **W** wall *consisted* of the sea? Na 3:8
They **w** strength is their god.” Hab 1:11 2098
“Behold, a man **w** name is Branch, Zch 6:12
And a man *was there* **w** hand was Mt 12:10
“**W** likeness and inscription is Mt 22:20 *5101*
w wife of the seven will she be? Mt 22:28 *5101*
about the Christ, **w** son is He?” Mt 22:42 *5101*
THE PRICE OF THE ONE **W** PRICE HAD Mt 27:9 *3739*
and a man was there **w** hand was Mk 3:1
a woman **w** little daughter had an Mk 7:25 *3739*
“**W** likeness and inscription is Mk 12:16 *5101*
to a man **w** name was Joseph, Lk 1:27 *3739*
in Jerusalem **w** name was Simeon; Lk 2:25 *3739*
there **w** right hand was withered. Lk 6:6 *2532, 846*
w blood Pilate had mixed with Lk 13:1 *3739*
and **w** goods are in the house Lk 17:31 *846*
W likeness and inscription does it Lk 20:24 *5101*
sent from God, **w** name was John. Jn 1:6 *846*
the thong of **w** sandal I am not Jn 1:27 *3739*
w son was sick at Capernaum. Jn 4:46 *3739*
w father and mother we know? Jn 6:42 *3739*
hair, **w** brother Lazarus was sick. Jn 11:2 *3739*
of the one **w** ear Peter cut off, Jn 18:26 *3739*
for it, *to decide* **w** it shall be”; Jn 19:24 *5101*
w betrayers and murderers you have Ac 7:52 *3739*
Simon, **w** house is by the sea.” Ac 10:6 *3739*
false prophet **w** name was Bar-Jesus, Ac 13:6 *3739*
w feet I am not worthy to untie.’ Ac 13:25 *3739*
w *temple* was just outside the Ac 14:13
w house was next to the synagogue. Ac 18:7 *3739*
“**W** MOUTH IS FULL OF CURSING AND Ro 3:14 *3739*
“BLESSED ARE THOSE **W** LAWLESS Ro 4:7 *3739*
AND **W** SINS HAVE BEEN COVERED. Ro 4:7 *3739*
“BLESSED IS THE MAN **W** SIN THE Ro 4:8 *3739*
w are the fathers, and from whom Ro 9:5 *3739*
brother for **w** sake Christ died. 1Co 8:11 *3739*
same as the woman **w** head is shaved. 1Co 11:5
in **w** case the god of this world 2Co 4:4 *3739*
the brother **w** fame in *the things of* 2Co 8:18 *3739*
w end will be according to their 2Co 11:15 *3739*
before **w** eyes Jesus Christ was Ga 3:1 *3739*
w end is destruction, whose god is Php 3:19 *3739*
w god is *their* appetite, Php 3:19 *3739*
and **w** glory is in their shame, Php 3:19

w names are in the book of life. Php 4:3 *3739*
the one **w** coming is in accord with 2Th 2:9 *3739*
Son over His house—**w** house we are, Heb 3:6 *3739*
w bodies fell in the wilderness? Heb 3:17 *3739*
for **w** sake it is also tilled, Heb 6:7 *3739*
But the one **w** genealogy is not Heb 7:6
w architect and builder is God. Heb 11:10 *3739*
w blood is brought into the holy Heb 13:11 *3739*
And the seed **w** fruit is righteousness Jas 3:18
everyone **w** name has not been Rv 13:8 *3739*
beast, **w** fatal wound was healed. Rv 13:12 *3739*
w name has not been written in the Rv 17:8 *3739*
from **w** presence earth and heaven Rv 20:11 *3739*
but only those **w** names are written Rv 21:27

WHY

LORD said to Cain, “**W** are you angry? Gn 4:6 4100
And **w** has your countenance fallen? Gn 4:6 4100
W did you not tell me that she was Gn 12:18 4100
“**W** did you say, Gn 12:19 4100
“**W** did Sarah laugh, saying, Gn 18:13 4100
W do you stand outside since I Gn 24:31 4100
it is so, **w** then am I *this way?*” Gn 25:22 4100
“**W** have you come to me, since you Gn 26:27 4069
W should I be bereaved of you both Gn 27:45 4100
W then have you deceived me?” Gn 29:25 4100
“**W** did you flee secretly and Gn 31:27 4100
but **w** did you steal my gods?” Gn 31:30 4100
“**W** is it that you ask my name?” Gn 32:29 4100
“**W** are your faces so sad today?” Gn 40:7 4069
“**W** are you staring at one another?” Gn 42:1 4100
“**W** did you treat me so badly by Gn 43:6 4100
W have you repaid evil for good? Gn 44:4 4100
“**W** does my lord speak such words Gn 44:7 4100
for **w** should we die in your Gn 47:15 4100
“**W** should we die before your Gn 47:19 4100
“**W** have you done this thing, and Ex 1:18 4069
“**W** are you striking your Ex 2:13 4100
“**W** have you come *back* so soon Ex 2:18 4069
W is it that you have left the man Ex 2:20 4100
w the bush is not burned up.” Ex 3:3 4069
w do you draw the people away from Ex 5:4 4100
“**W** have you not completed your Ex 5:14 4069
“**W** do you deal this way with your Ex 5:15 4100
w have You brought harm to this Ex 5:22 4100
W did You ever send me? Ex 5:22 4100
W have you dealt with us in this Ex 14:11 4100
“**W** are you crying out to Me? Ex 14:15 4100
“**W** do you quarrel with me? Ex 17:2 4100
W do you test the LORD?” Ex 17:2 4100
“**W**, now, have you brought us up Ex 17:3 4100
W do you alone sit *as judge* and Ex 18:14 4069
w does Your anger burn against Ex 32:11 4100
“**W** should the Egyptians speak, Ex 32:12 4100
“**W** did you not eat the sin Lv 10:17 4069
w are we restrained from Nu 9:7 4100
“**W** have You been so hard on Your Nu 11:11 4100
And **w** have I not found favor in Nu 11:11 4100
“**W** did we ever leave Egypt?” Nu 11:20 4100
W then were you not afraid To Nu 12:8 4069
“**W** is the LORD bringing us into Nu 14:3 4100
“**W** then are you transgressing the Nu 14:41 4100
so **w** do you exalt yourselves above Nu 16:3 4069
“**W** then have you brought the Nu 20:4 4100
“**W** have you made us come up from Nu 20:5 4100
“**W** have you brought us up out of Nu 21:5 4100
“**W** have you struck your donkey Nu 22:32 5921, 4100
W did you not come to me? Nu 22:37 4100
“**W** should the name of our father Nu 27:4 4100
“Now **w** are you discouraging the Nu 32:7 4100
‘Now then **w** should we die? Dt 5:25 4100
‘**W** has the LORD done thus to this Dt 29:24 5921, 4100
W this great outburst of anger?’ Dt 29:24 4100
reason **w** Joshua circumcised them: Jos 5:4 834
w did You ever bring this Jos 7:7 4100
W is it that you have fallen on Jos 7:10 4100
“**W** have you troubled us? Jos 7:25 4100
“**W** have you deceived us, saying, Jos 9:22 4100
“**W** have you given me only one lot Jos 17:14 4069
“**W** did you sit among the Jg 5:16 4100
And **w** did Dan stay in ships? Jg 5:17 4100
‘**W** does his chariot delay in Jg 5:28 4069
W do the hoofbeats of his chariots Jg 5:28 4069
w then has all this happened to us? Jg 6:13 4100
but **w** should we serve him? Jg 9:28 4069
So **w** have you come to me now when Jg 11:7 4069
w did you not recover them within Jg 11:26 4069
“**W** did you cross over to fight Jg 12:1 4069
W then have you come up to me this Jg 12:3 4100
“**W** do you ask my name, seeing it Jg 13:18 4100
“**W** have you come up against us?” Jg 15:10 4100
“**W**, O LORD, God of Israel, has Jg 21:3 4100
W should you go with me? Ru 1:11 4100
W do you call me Naomi, since the Ru 1:21 4100
“**W** have I found favor in your Ru 2:10 4069
w do you weep and why do you not 1Sa 1:8 4100
and **w** do you not eat and why 1Sa 1:8 4100
not eat and **w** is your heart sad? 1Sa 1:8 4100
“**W** do you do such things, the 1Sa 2:23 4100
“**W** do you kick at My sacrifice and 1Sa 2:29 4100
“**W** has the LORD defeated us today 1Sa 4:3 4100
w His hand is not removed from you 1Sa 6:3 4100
“**W** then do you harden your hearts 1Sa 6:6 4100
W then do you speak to me in this 1Sa 9:21 4100
“**W** then did you not obey the 1Sa 15:19 4100
“**W** do you come out to draw up in 1Sa 17:8 4100
“**W** have you come down? 1Sa 17:28 4100
W then will you sin against 1Sa 19:5 4100

"**W** have you deceived me like this	1Sa 19:17	4100
W should I put you to death?'"	1Sa 19:17	4100
So **w** should my father hide this	1Sa 20:2	4069
for **w** then should you bring me to	1Sa 20:8	4100
"**W** has the son of Jesse not come	1Sa 20:27	4069
"**W** should he be put to death?	1Sa 20:32	4100
"**W** are you alone and no one with	1Sa 21:1	4069
W do you bring him to me?	1Sa 21:14	4100
"**W** have you and the son of Jesse	1Sa 22:13	4100
"**W** do you listen to the words of	1Sa 24:9	4100
W then have you not guarded your	1Sa 26:15	4100
"**W** then is my lord pursuing his	1Sa 26:18	4100
for **w** should your servant live in	1Sa 27:5	4100
W are you then laying a snare for	1Sa 28:9	4100
"**W** have you deceived me?	1Sa 28:12	4100
"**W** have you disturbed me by	1Sa 28:15	4100
"**W** then do you ask me, since the	1Sa 28:16	4100
W should I strike you to the	2Sa 2:22	4100
"**W** have you gone in to my	2Sa 3:7	4069
w then have you sent him away and	2Sa 3:24	4100
'**W** have you not built Me a house	2Sa 7:7	4100
W did you not go down to your	2Sa 11:10	4069
'**W** did you go so near to the city	2Sa 11:20	4069
W did you go so near the wall?	2Sa 11:21	4100
'**W** have you despised the word of	2Sa 12:9	4069
now he has died, **w** should I fast?	2Sa 12:23	4100
w are you so depressed morning	2Sa 13:4	4069
"**W** should he go with you?"	2Sa 13:26	4100
"**W** then have you planned such a	2Sa 14:13	4100
"**W** have your servants set my	2Sa 14:31	4100
"**W** have I come from Geshur?	2Sa 14:32	4100
"**W** will you also go with us?	2Sa 15:19	4100
"**W** do you have these?"	2Sa 16:2	4100
"**W** should this dead dog curse my	2Sa 16:9	4100
'**W** have you done so?'"	2Sa 16:10	4069
"**W** did you not go with your friend?"	2Sa 16:17	4100
W then did you not strike him	2Sa 18:11	4069
"**W** would you run, my son, since	2Sa 18:22	
		4100, 2088
w are you silent about bringing	2Sa 19:10	4100
'**W** are you the last to bring the	2Sa 19:11	4100
W then should you be the last to	2Sa 19:12	4100
"**W** did you not go with me,	2Sa 19:25	4100
"**W** do you still speak of your	2Sa 19:29	4100
W then should your servant be an	2Sa 19:35	4100
W should the king compensate me	2Sa 19:36	4100
"**W** had our brothers the men of	2Sa 19:41	4069
W then are you angry about this	2Sa 19:42	4100
W then did you treat us with	2Sa 19:43	4069
W would you swallow up the	2Sa 20:19	4100
but **w** does my lord the king	2Sa 24:3	4100
"**W** has my lord the king come to	2Sa 24:21	4069
"**W** have you done so?"	1Ki 1:6	4069
W then has Adonijah become king?'	1Ki 1:13	4069
"**W** is the city making such an	1Ki 1:41	4069
"And **w** are you asking Abishag the	1Ki 2:22	4100
"**W** then have you not kept the	1Ki 2:43	4069
'**W** has the LORD done thus to this	1Ki 9:8	
		5921, 4100
w he rebelled against the king:	1Ki 11:27	834
w do you pretend to be another	1Ki 14:6	4100
"**W** have you returned?"	2Ki 1:5	4100
"**W** will you go to him today?	2Ki 4:23	4069
"**W** have you torn your clothes?	2Ki 5:8	4100
w should I wait for the LORD any	2Ki 6:33	4100
"**W** do we sit here until we die?	2Ki 7:3	4100
"**W** does my lord weep?"	2Ki 8:12	4069
W did this mad fellow come to you?"	2Ki 9:11	4069
"**W** do you not repair the damages	2Ki 12:7	4069
for **w** should you provoke trouble	2Ki 14:10	4100
'**W** have you not built for Me a	1Ch 17:6	4100
W does my lord seek this thing?	1Ch 21:3	4100
W should he be a cause of guilt to	1Ch 21:3	4100
'**W** has the LORD done thus to this	2Ch 7:21	4100
"**W** have you not required the	2Ch 24:6	4069
'**W** do you transgress the	2Ch 24:20	4100
"**W** have you sought the gods of	2Ch 25:15	4100
W should you be struck down?"	2Ch 25:16	4100
for **w** should you provoke trouble	2Ch 25:19	4100
"**W** should the kings of Assyria	2Ch 32:4	4100
w should damage increase to the	Ezr 4:22	4101
"**W** is your face sad though you	Ne 2:2	4069
W should my face not be sad when	Ne 2:3	4069
W should the work stop while I	Ne 6:3	4100
"**W** is the house of God forsaken?"	Ne 13:11	4069
"**W** do you spend the night in	Ne 13:21	4069
"**W** are you transgressing the	Es 3:3	4069
learn what this *was* and **w** it *was*.	Es 4:5	4100
"**W** did I not die at birth, Come	Jb 3:11	4100
"**W** did the knees receive me, And	Jb 3:12	4069
w the breasts, that I should suck?	Jb 3:12	4100
"**W** is light given to him who	Jb 3:20	4100
"**W** *is light given* to a man whose	Jb 3:23	4100
W have You set me as Your target,	Jb 7:20	4100
"**W** then do You not pardon my	Jb 7:21	4100
W then should I toil in vain?	Jb 9:29	4100
know **w** You contend with me.	Jb 10:2	
		5921, 4100
'**W** then have You brought me out	Jb 10:18	4100
"**W** should I take my flesh in my	Jb 13:14	
		5921, 4100
"**W** do You hide Your face And	Jb 13:24	4100
"**W** does your heart carry you away?	Jb 15:12	4100
And **w** do your eyes flash,	Jb 15:12	4100
"**W** are we regarded as beasts, As	Jb 18:3	4069
"**W** do you persecute me as God	Jb 19:22	4100
And **w** should I not be impatient?	Jb 21:4	4069
"**W** do the wicked *still* live,	Jb 21:7	4069
"**W** are times not stored up by the	Jb 24:1	4069
And **w** do those who know Him not	Jb 24:1	
W then do you act foolishly?	Jb 27:12	4100
"**W** do you complain against Him That	Jb 33:13	4069
W are the nations in an uproar And	Ps 2:1	4100
W do You stand afar off,	Ps 10:1	4100
W do You hide *Yourself* in times	Ps 10:1	
W has the wicked spurned God?	Ps 10:13	
		5921, 4100
my God, **w** have You forsaken me?	Ps 22:1	4100
W are you in despair, O my soul?	Ps 42:5	4100
And **w** have you become disturbed	Ps 42:5	4100
"**W** have You forgotten me?	Ps 42:9	4100
W do I go mourning because of the	Ps 42:9	4100
W are you in despair, O my soul?	Ps 42:11	4100
And **w** have you become disturbed	Ps 42:11	4100
w have You rejected me?	Ps 43:2	4100
W do I go mourning because of the	Ps 43:2	4100
W are you in despair, O my soul?	Ps 43:5	4100
And **w** are you disturbed within me?	Ps 43:5	4100
Arouse Yourself, **w** do You sleep,	Ps 44:23	4100
W do You hide Your face *And*	Ps 44:24	4100
W should I fear in days of	Ps 49:5	4100
W do you boast in evil, O mighty	Ps 52:1	4100
W do you look with envy, O	Ps 68:16	4100
w have You rejected *us* forever?	Ps 74:1	4100
W does Your anger smoke against	Ps 74:1	
W do You withdraw Your hand,	Ps 74:11	4100
W should the nations say,	Ps 79:10	4100
W have You broken down its	Ps 80:12	4100
LORD, **w** do You reject my soul?	Ps 88:14	4100
W do You hide Your face from me?	Ps 88:14	
W should the nations say,	Ps 115:2	4100
For **w** should you, my son, be	Pr 5:20	4100
W is there a price in the hand of	Pr 17:16	
		4100, 2088
W should he take your bed from	Pr 22:27	4100
W then have I been extremely wise?"	Ec 2:15	4100
W should God be angry on account	Ec 5:6	4100
"**W** is it that the former days	Ec 7:10	4100
W should you ruin yourself?	Ec 7:16	4100
W should you die before your time?	Ec 7:17	4100
For **w** should I be like one who	SS 1:7	4100
"**W** should you gaze at the	SS 6:13	4100
For **w** should he be esteemed?	Is 2:22	4100
W, when I expected *it* to produce	Is 5:4	4069
W do you say, O Jacob, and assert,	Is 40:27	4100
"**W** was there no man when I came?	Is 50:2	4069
w was there none to answer?	Is 50:2	
"**W** do you spend money for what is	Is 55:2	4100
'**W** have we fasted and You do	Is 58:3	4100
W have we humbled ourselves	Is 58:3	
W is Your apparel red, And Your	Is 63:2	4069
W, O LORD, do You cause us to	Is 63:17	4100
W has he become a prey?	Jer 2:14	4069
"**W** do you contend with Me?	Jer 2:29	4100
W do My people say,	Jer 2:31	4069
"**W** do you go around so much	Jer 2:36	4100
"**W** should I pardon you?	Jer 5:7	335
"**W** has the LORD our God done all	Jer 5:19	
		8478, 4100
"**W** then has this people,	Jer 8:5	4069
W are we sitting still?	Jer 8:14	
		5921, 4100
"**W** have they provoked Me with	Jer 8:19	4069
W then has not the health of the	Jer 8:22	4069
W is the land ruined, laid waste	Jer 9:12	
		5921, 4100
W has the way of the wicked	Jer 12:1	4069
W are all those who deal in	Jer 12:1	
'**W** have these things happened to	Jer 13:22	4069
W are You like a stranger in the	Jer 14:8	4100
"**W** are You like a man dismayed,	Jer 14:9	4100
W have You stricken us so that we	Jer 14:19	4069
W has my pain been perpetual And	Jer 15:18	4100
W did I ever come forth from the	Jer 20:18	4100
'**W** has the LORD done thus to this	Jer 22:8	
		5921, 4100
W have he and his descendants been	Jer 22:28	4069
"**W** have you prophesied in the	Jer 26:9	4069
"**W** will you die, you and your	Jer 27:13	4100
W should this city become a ruin?	Jer 27:17	4100
w have you not rebuked Jeremiah of	Jer 29:27	4100
W do I see every man *With* his	Jer 30:6	4069
And **w** have all faces turned pale?	Jer 30:6	
"**W** do you cry out over your injury?	Jer 30:15	4100
"**W** do you prophesy, saying,	Jer 32:3	4069
"**W** have you written on it that the	Jer 36:29	4069
W should he take your life, so	Jer 40:15	4100
"**W** are you doing great harm to	Jer 44:7	4100
"**W** have I seen *it*?	Jer 46:5	4069
"**W** have your mighty ones become	Jer 46:15	4069
W then has Malcam taken possession	Jer 49:1	4069
W should *any* living mortal, or *any*	La 3:39	4100
W do You forget us forever?	La 5:20	4100
W do You forsake us so long?	La 5:20	
'**W** should the son not bear the	Ezk 18:19	4069
For **w** will you die, O house of	Ezk 18:31	4100
they say to you, '**W** do you groan?'	Ezk 21:7	
		5921, 4100
W then will you die, O house of	Ezk 33:11	4100
for **w** should he see your faces	Da 1:10	4100
"Do you understand **w** I came to you?	Da 10:20	4100
W should they among the peoples	Jl 2:17	4100
"Now, **w** do you cry out loudly?	Mi 4:9	4100
W do You make me see iniquity,	Hab 1:3	4100
W do You look with favor On	Hab 1:13	4100
W are You silent when the wicked	Hab 1:13	
W have You made men like the fish	Hab 1:14	
blow it *away*. **W**?" declares the LORD	Hg 1:9	
		3282, 4100
W not offer it to your governor?	Mal 1:8	
W do we deal treacherously each	Mal 2:10	4069
"And **w** are you worried about	Mt 6:28	*5101*
"**W** do you look at the speck that is	Mt 7:3	*5101*
"**W** are you afraid, you men of	Mt 8:26	*5101*
"**W** are you thinking evil in your	Mt 9:4	*2444*
"**W** is your Teacher eating with	Mt 9:11	
		1223, 5101
"**W** do we and the Pharisees fast,	Mt 9:14	
		1223, 5101
"**W** do You speak to them in	Mt 13:10	
		1223, 5101
w miraculous powers are at work in	Mt 14:2	*1223*
little faith, **w** did you doubt?"	Mt 14:31	
		1519, 5101
"**W** do Your disciples break	Mt 15:2	
		1223, 5101
"**W** do you yourselves transgress	Mt 15:3	*1223*
w do you discuss among yourselves	Mt 16:8	*5101*
"**W** then do the scribes say that	Mt 17:10	*5101*
"**W** could we not drive it out?"	Mt 17:19	
		1223, 5101
"**W** then did Moses command to GIVE	Mt 19:7	*5101*
"**W** are you asking Me about what	Mt 19:17	*5101*
'**W** have you been standing here	Mt 20:6	*5101*
'Then **w** did you not believe him?'	Mt 21:25	
		1223, 5101
"**W** are you testing Me, you	Mt 22:18	*5101*
saw *this*, and said, "**W** this waste?	Mt 26:8	
		1519, 5101
"**W** do you bother the woman?	Mt 26:10	*5101*
"**W**, what evil has He done?"	Mt 27:23	*1063*
GOD, **W** HAVE YOU FORSAKEN ME?"	Mt 27:46	*2444*
"**W** does this man speak that way?	Mk 2:7	*5101*
"**W** are you reasoning about these	Mk 2:8	*5101*
"**W** is He eating and drinking with	Mk 2:16	*5101*
"**W** do John's disciples and the	Mk 2:18	
		1223, 5101
w are they doing what is not	Mk 2:24	*5101*
"**W** are you afraid?	Mk 4:40	*5101*
w trouble the Teacher anymore?"	Mk 5:35	*5101*
"**W** make a commotion and weep?	Mk 5:39	*5101*
w these miraculous powers are at	Mk 6:14	*1223*
"**W** do Your disciples not walk	Mk 7:5	
		1223, 5101
"**W** does this generation seek for	Mk 8:12	*5101*
"**W** do you discuss *the fact* that	Mk 8:17	*5101*
They asked Him, saying, "**W** *is it*	Mk 9:11	
"**W** could we not drive it out?"	Mk 9:28	
		3739, 5101
"**W** do you call Me good?	Mk 10:18	*5101*
'**W** are you doing this?'	Mk 11:3	*5101*
'Then **w** did you not believe him?'	Mk 11:31	
		1223, 5101
"**W** are you testing Me?	Mk 12:15	*5101*
"**W** has this perfume been wasted?	Mk 14:4	
		1519, 5101
w do you bother her?	Mk 14:6	*5101*
"**W**, what evil has He done?"	Mk 15:14	*1063*
MY GOD, **W** HAVE YOU FORSAKEN ME	Mk 15:34	
		1519, 5101
w have You treated us this way?	Lk 2:48	*5101*
"**W** is it that you were looking	Lk 2:49	*5101*
"**W** are you reasoning in your	Lk 5:22	*5101*
"**W** do you eat and drink with the	Lk 5:30	
		1223, 5101
"**W** do you do what is not lawful	Lk 6:2	*5101*
"**W** do you look at the speck that is	Lk 6:41	*5101*
"**W** do you call Me, 'Lord, Lord,'	Lk 6:46	*5101*
the reason **w** she had touched Him,	Lk 8:47	
		1223, 3739
w do you worry about other	Lk 12:26	*5101*
but **w** do you not analyze this	Lk 12:56	*4459*
"And **w** do you not even on your	Lk 12:57	*5101*
W does it even use up the ground?'	Lk 13:7	*2444*
"**W** do you call Me good?	Lk 18:19	*5101*
'Then **w** did you not put my money	Lk 19:23	
		1223, 5101
'**W** are you untying it?'	Lk 19:31	
		1223, 5101
"**W** are you untying the colt?"	Lk 19:33	*5101*
'**W** did you not believe him?'	Lk 20:5	
		1223, 5101
"**W** are you sleeping?	Lk 22:46	*5101*
"**W**, what evil has this man done?	Lk 23:22	*1063*
"**W** do you seek the living One	Lk 24:5	*5101*
"**W** are you troubled, and why do	Lk 24:38	*5101*
and **w** do doubts arise in your	Lk 24:38	
		1223, 5101
"**W** then are you baptizing, if you	Jn 1:25	*5101*
W do You speak with her?"	Jn 4:27	*5101*
W do you seek to kill Me?"	Jn 7:19	*5101*
"**W** did you not bring Him?"	Jn 7:45	
		1223, 5101
"**W** do you not understand what I	Jn 8:43	
		1223, 5101
truth, **w** do you not believe Me?	Jn 8:46	
		1223, 5101
w do you want to hear *it* again?	Jn 9:27	*5101*
W do you listen to Him?"	Jn 10:20	*5101*
"**W** was this perfume not sold for	Jn 12:5	
		1223, 5101
w can I not follow You right now?	Jn 13:37	
		1223, 5101
"**W** do you question Me?	Jn 18:21	*5101*
if rightly, **w** do you strike Me?"	Jn 18:23	*5101*
"Woman, **w** are you weeping?"	Jn 20:13	*5101*

“Woman, w are you weeping? Jn 20:15 *5101*
w do you stand looking into the Ac 1:11 *5101*
“W, are not all these who are Ac 2:7 *2400*
Israel, w are you amazed at this, Ac 3:12 *5101*
at this, or w do you gaze at us, Ac 3:12 *5101*
‘W DID THE GENTILES RAGE, AND THE Ac 4:25
2443, 5101
w has Satan filled your heart to Ac 5:3
1223, 5101
W is it that you have conceived Ac 5:4 *5101*
“W is it that you have agreed Ac 5:9 *5101*
w do you injure one another?’ Ac 7:26
2443, 5101
Saul, w are you persecuting Me?” Ac 9:4 *5101*
“That is w I came without even Ac 10:29 *1352*
“Men, w are you doing these things? Ac 14:15 *5101*
w do you put God to the test by Ac 15:10 *5101*
Saul, w are you persecuting Me?’ Ac 22:7 *5101*
‘Now w do you delay? Ac 22:16 *5101*
w they were shouting against him Ac 22:24
1223, 3739
w he had been accused by the Jews, Ac 22:30 *5101*
“W is it considered incredible Ac 26:8 *5101*
Saul, w are you persecuting Me? Ac 26:14 *5101*
w am I also still being judged as Ro 3:7 *5101*
And w not *say* Ro 3:8
“W does He still find fault? Ro 9:19 *5101*
“W did you make me like this,” Ro 9:20 *5101*
W? Because *they did* not *pursue it* by Ro 9:32
1223, 5101
w do you judge your brother? Ro 14:10 *5101*
w do you regard your brother with Ro 14:10 *5101*
w do you boast as if you had not 1Co 4:7 *5101*
W not rather be wronged? 1Co 6:7
1223, 5101
W not rather be defrauded? 1Co 6:7
1223, 5101
for w is my freedom judged by 1Co 10:29
2443, 5101
w am I slandered concerning that 1Co 10:30 *5101*
w then are they baptized for them? 1Co 15:29 *5101*
W are we also in danger every hour? 1Co 15:30 *5101*
W? Because I do not love you? 2Co 11:11
1223, 5101
W the Law then? It was added Ga 3:19 *5101*
w am I still persecuted? Ga 5:11 *5101*
principles of the world, w, Col 2:20 *5101*
angel said to me, “W do you wonder? Rv 17:7
1223, 5101

WICK

burning w He will not extinguish; Is 42:3 6594
and extinguished like a w): Is 43:17 6594
SMOLDERING W HE WILL NOT PUT OUT, Mt 12:20 *3043*

WICKED

Now the men of Sodom were w Gn 13:13 7451a
sweep away the righteous with the w? Gn 18:23 7563
to slay the righteous with the w, Gn 18:25 7563
and the w are *treated* alike. Gn 18:25 7563
I and my people are the w ones. Ex 9:27 7563
do not join your hand with a w man Ex 23:1 7563
now from the tents of these w men, Nu 16:26 7563
again do such a w thing among you. Dt 13:11 7451a
the righteous and condemn the w, Dt 25:1 7563
the w man deserves to be beaten, Dt 25:2 7563
w ones are silenced in darkness; 1Sa 2:9 7563
Out of the w comes forth wickedness 1Sa 24:13 7563
Then all the w and worthless men 1Sa 30:22 7451a
As one falls before the w, 2Sa 3:34
5767b, 1121
when w men have killed a righteous 2Sa 4:11 7563
nor will the w afflict them any 2Sa 7:10
5767b, 1121
condemning the w by bringing his 1Ki 8:32 7563
was w in the sight of the LORD, 1Ch 2:3 7451a
the w will not waste them 1Ch 17:9
5767b, 1121
punishing the w by bringing his 2Ch 6:23 7563
face and turn from their w ways, 2Ch 7:14 7451a
“Should you help the w and love 2Ch 19:2 7563
For the sons of the w Athaliah had 2Ch 24:7 4849
and an enemy is this w Haman!” Es 7:6 7451a
his w scheme which he had devised Es 9:25 7451a
“There the w cease from raging, Jb 3:17 7563
tent of the w will be no longer.” Jb 8:22 7563
destroys the guiltless and the w.’ Jb 9:22 7563
is given into the hand of the w; Jb 9:24 7563
“I am accounted w, Why then Jb 9:29 7561
favorably on the schemes of the w? Jb 10:3 7563
‘If I am w, woe to me! Jb 10:15 7561
“But the eyes of the w will fail, Jb 11:20 7563
“The w man writhes in pain all Jb 15:20 7563
tosses me into the hands of the w. Jb 16:11 7563
the light of the w goes out, Jb 18:5 7563
such are the dwellings of the w, Jb 18:21 5767a
the triumphing of the w is short, Jb 20:5 7563
is the w man’s portion from God, Jb 20:29 7563
“Why do the w *still* live, Jb 21:7 7563
counsel of the w is far from me. Jb 21:16 7563
is the lamp of the w put out, Jb 21:17 7563
the dwelling places of the w?’ Jb 21:28 7563
“For the w is reserved for the Jb 21:30 7451a
path Which w men have trod, Jb 22:15 205
counsel of the w is far from me. Jb 22:18 7563
And glean the vineyard of the w. Jb 24:6 7563
“May my enemy be as the w And Jb 27:7 7563
the portion of a w man from God, Jb 27:13 7563
“I broke the jaws of the w And Jb 29:17 5767a
of iniquity, And walks with w men? Jb 34:8 7562
‘Worthless one,’ To nobles, ‘W ones’; Jb 34:18 7563
them like the w In a public place, Jb 34:26 7563
Because he answers like w men. Jb 34:36 205
“He does not keep the w alive, Jb 36:6 7563
were full of judgment on the w; Jb 36:17 7563
And the w be shaken out of it? Jb 38:13 7563
From the w their light is withheld, Jb 38:15 7563
tread down the w where they stand. Jb 40:12 7563
not walk in the counsel of the w, Ps 1:1 7563
The w are not so, But they are Ps 1:4 7563
the w will not stand in the judgment, Ps 1:5 7563
But the way of the w will perish. Ps 1:6 7563
have shattered the teeth of the w. Ps 3:7 7563
the evil of the w come to an end, Ps 7:9 7563
You have destroyed the w; Ps 9:5 7563
of his own hands the w is snared. Ps 9:16 7563
The w will return to Sheol, *Even* Ps 9:17 7563
the w hotly pursue the afflicted; Ps 10:2 7563
the w boasts of his heart’s desire, Ps 10:3 7563
The w, in the haughtiness of his Ps 10:4 7563
Why has the w spurned God? Ps 10:13 7563
the arm of the w and the evildoer, Ps 10:15 7563
For, behold, the w bend the bow, Ps 11:2 7563
tests the righteous and the w, Ps 11:5 7563
Upon the w He will rain snares; Ps 11:6 7563
The w strut about on every side When Ps 12:8 7563
From the w who despoil me, My Ps 17:9 7563
my soul from the w with Your sword, Ps 17:13 7563
And I will not sit with the w. Ps 26:5 7563
In whose hands is a w scheme, Ps 26:10 2154
Do not drag me away with the w And Ps 28:3 7563
Let the w be put to shame, let Ps 31:17 7563
Many are the sorrows of the w, Ps 32:10 7563
Evil shall slay the w, Ps 34:21 7563
the hand of the w drive me away. Ps 36:11 7563
the man who carries out w schemes. Ps 37:7 4209
and the w man will be no more; Ps 37:10 7563
The w plots against the righteous And Ps 37:12 7563
The w have drawn the sword and Ps 37:14 7563
Than the abundance of many w. Ps 37:16 7563
the arms of the w will be broken, Ps 37:17 7563
But the w will perish; Ps 37:20 7563
w borrows and does not pay back, Ps 37:21 7563
descendants of the w will be cut off. Ps 37:28 7563
The w spies upon the righteous And Ps 37:32 7563
When the w are cut off, you will Ps 37:34 7563
I have seen a w, violent man Ps 37:35 7563
The posterity of the w will be cut off Ps 37:38 7563
He delivers them from the w and Ps 37:40 7563
While the w are in my presence.” Ps 39:1 7563
“A w thing is poured out upon Ps 41:8 1100
But to the w God says, Ps 50:16 7563
Because of the pressure of the w; Ps 55:3 7563
The w are estranged from the womb; Ps 58:3 7563
wash his feet in the blood of the w. Ps 58:10 7563
So let the w perish before God. Ps 68:2 7563
my God, out of the hand of the w, Ps 71:4 7563
As I saw the prosperity of the w. Ps 73:3 7563
Behold, these are the w; Ps 73:12 7563
to the w, ‘Do not lift up the horn; Ps 75:4 7563
Surely all the w of the earth must Ps 75:8 7563
horns of the w He will cut off, Ps 75:10 7563
And show partiality to the w? Ps 82:2 7563
them out of the hand of the w. Ps 82:4 7563
And see the recompense of the w. Ps 91:8 7563
when the w sprouted up like grass And Ps 92:7 7563
How long shall the w, Ps 94:3 7563
LORD, How long shall the w exult? Ps 94:3 7563
Until a pit is dug for the w. Ps 94:13 7563
them from the hand of the w. Ps 97:10 7563
destroy all the w of the land, Ps 101:8 7563
earth And let the w be no more. Ps 104:35 7563
The flame consumed the w. Ps 106:18 7563
opened the w and deceitful mouth Ps 109:2 7563
Appoint a w man over him, Ps 109:6 7563
The w will see it and be vexed, Ps 112:10 7563
The desire of the w will perish. Ps 112:10 7563
has seized me because of the w, Ps 119:53 7563
cords of the w have encircled me, Ps 119:61 7563
The w wait for me to destroy me; Ps 119:95 7563
The w have laid a snare for me, Ps 119:110 7563
all the w of the earth *like* dross; Ps 119:119 7563
Salvation is far from the w, Ps 119:155 7563
has cut in two the cords of the w. Ps 129:4 7563
O that You would slay the w, Ps 139:19 7563
O LORD, from the hands of the w; Ps 140:4 7563
O LORD, the desires of the w; Ps 140:8 7563
prayer is against their w deeds. Ps 141:5 7463a
the w fall into their own nets, Ps 141:10 7563
But all the w He will destroy. Ps 145:20 7563
But He thwarts the way of the w. Ps 146:9 7563
brings down the w to the ground. Ps 147:6 7563
w will be cut off from the land And Pr 2:22 7563
onslaught of the w when it comes; Pr 3:25 7563
the LORD is on the house of the w, Pr 3:33 7563
Do not enter the path of the w And Pr 4:14 7563
The way of the w is like darkness; Pr 4:19 7563
own iniquities will capture the w, Pr 5:22 7563
A worthless person, a w man, Pr 6:12 205
A heart that devises w plans, Pr 6:18 205
a w man *gets* insults for himself. Pr 9:7 7563
reject the craving of the w. Pr 10:3 7563
mouth of the w conceals violence. Pr 10:6 7563
But the name of the w will rot. Pr 10:7 7563
mouth of the w conceals violence. Pr 10:11 7563
The income of the w, punishment. Pr 10:16 7563
heart of the w is *worth* little. Pr 10:20 7563
the w fears will come upon him, Pr 10:24 7563
passes, the w is no more, Pr 10:25 7563
years of the w will be shortened. Pr 10:27 7563
the expectation of the w perishes. Pr 10:28 7563
the w will not dwell in the land. Pr 10:30 7563
mouth of the w what is perverted. Pr 10:32 7563
But the w will fall by his own Pr 11:5 7563
When a w man dies, *his* expectation Pr 11:7 7563
But the w takes his place. Pr 11:8 7563
rejoices, And when the w perish, Pr 11:10 7563
by the mouth of the w it is torn Pr 11:11 7563
The w earns deceptive wages, But Pr 11:18 7563
the expectation of the w is wrath. Pr 11:23 7563
much more the w and the sinner! Pr 11:31 7563
counsels of the w are deceitful. Pr 12:5 7563
words of the w lie in wait for blood, Pr 12:6 7563
The w are overthrown and are no Pr 12:7 7563
the compassion of the w is cruel. Pr 12:10 7563
w man desires the booty of evil men, Pr 12:12 7563
But the w are filled with trouble. Pr 12:21 7563
way of the w leads them astray. Pr 12:26 7563
But a w man acts disgustingly and Pr 13:5 7563
But the lamp of the w goes out. Pr 13:9 7563
A w messenger falls into Pr 13:17 7563
the stomach of the w is in need. Pr 13:25 7563
house of the w will be destroyed, Pr 14:11 7563
w at the gates of the righteous. Pr 14:19 7563
The w is thrust down by his Pr 14:32 7563
trouble is in the income of the w. Pr 15:6 7563
sacrifice of the w is an abomination Pr 15:8 7563
The way of the w is an abomination Pr 15:9 7563
mouth of the w pours out evil things. Pr 15:28 7563
The LORD is far from the w, Pr 15:29 7563
Even the w for the day of evil. Pr 16:4 7563
an abomination for kings to commit w Pr 16:12 7562
An evildoer listens to w lips; Pr 17:4 205
He who justifies the w and Pr 17:15 7563
A w man receives a bribe from the Pr 17:23 7563
When a w man comes, contempt also Pr 18:3 7563
partiality to the w is not good, Pr 18:5 7563
mouth of the w spreads iniquity. Pr 19:28 7563
A wise king winnows the w, Pr 20:26 7563
a proud heart, The lamp of the w, Pr 21:4 7563
The violence of the w will drag them Pr 21:7 7563
The soul of the w desires evil; Pr 21:10 7563
one considers the house of the w, Pr 21:12 7563
the wicked, Turning the w to ruin. Pr 21:12 7563
w is a ransom for the righteous, Pr 21:18 7563
sacrifice of the w is an abomination, Pr 21:27 7563
A w man displays a bold face, But as Pr 21:29 7563
Do not lie in wait, O w man, Pr 24:15 7563
the w stumble in *time of* calamity. Pr 24:16 7563
evildoers Or be envious of the w; Pr 24:19 7563
The lamp of the w will be put out. Pr 24:20 7563
He who says to the w, Pr 24:24 7563
But to those who rebuke the w Pr 24:25
away the w before the king, Pr 25:5 7563
man who gives way before the w. Pr 25:26 7563
Are burning lips and a w heart. Pr 26:23 7451a
w flee when no one is pursuing, Pr 28:1 7563
who forsake the law praise the w, Pr 28:4 7563
great glory, But when the w rise, Pr 28:12 7563
Is a w ruler over a poor people. Pr 28:15 7563
When the w rise, men hide Pr 28:28 7563
when a w man rules, people groan. Pr 29:2 7563
The w does not understand *such* Pr 29:7 7563
All his ministers *become* w. Pr 29:12 7563
When the w increase, transgression Pr 29:16 7563
in the way is abominable to the w. Pr 29:27 7563
the righteous man and the w man,” Ec 3:17 7563
and there is a w man who prolongs Ec 7:15 7563
Do not be excessively w and Ec 7:17 7561
So then, I have seen the w buried, Ec 8:10 7563
according to the deeds of the w. Ec 8:14 7563
for the righteous and for the w; Ec 9:2 7563
and the end of it is w madness. Ec 10:13 7463a
Woe to the w! *It will go* badly *with* Is 3:11 7563
Who justify the w for a bribe, And Is 5:23 7563
of His lips He will slay the w. Is 11:4 7563
And the w for their iniquity; Is 13:11 7563
has broken the staff of the w, Is 14:5 7563
Though the w is shown favor, He Is 26:10 7563
He devises w schemes To destroy Is 32:7 2154
“There is no peace for the w,” Is 48:22 7563
His grave was assigned with w men, Is 53:9 7563
Let the w forsake his way And the Is 55:7 7563
the w are like the tossing sea, Is 57:20 7563
no peace,” says my God, “for the w.” Is 57:21 7563
and to strike with a w fist. Is 58:4 7562
Therefore even the w women You Jer 2:33 7451a
your w thoughts Lodge within you? Jer 4:14 205
w men are found among My people, Jer 5:26 7563
on, But the w are not separated. Jer 6:29 7451a
has the way of the w prospered? Jer 12:1 7563
LORD concerning all My w neighbors Jer 12:14 7451a
‘This w people, who refuse to Jer 13:10 7451a
you from the hand of the w, Jer 15:21 7451a
swirl down on the head of the w. Jer 23:19 7563
As for the w, He has given them to Jer 25:31 7563
will burst on the head of the w. Jer 30:23 7563
“When I say to the w, Ezk 3:18 7563
to warn the w from his wicked way Ezk 3:18 7563
from his w way that he may live, Ezk 3:18 7563
w man shall die in his iniquity, Ezk 3:18 7563
“Yet if you have warned the w and Ezk 3:19 7563
his wickedness or from his w way, Ezk 3:19 7563

to the w of the earth as spoil,	Ezk 7:21	7563
"Go in and see the w abominations	Ezk 8:9	7451a
have encouraged the w not to turn	Ezk 13:22	7563
wicked not to turn from his w way	Ezk 13:22	7451a
the wickedness of the w will be upon	Ezk 18:20	7563
"But if the w man turns from all	Ezk 18:21	7563
pleasure in the death of the w,"	Ezk 18:23	7563
abominations that a w man does,	Ezk 18:24	7563
when a w man turns away from his	Ezk 18:27	7563
from you the righteous and the w.	Ezk 21:3	7563
from you the righteous and the w,	Ezk 21:4	7563
'And you, O slain, w one,	Ezk 21:25	7563
the necks of the w who are slain,	Ezk 21:29	7563
"When I say to the w,	Ezk 33:8	7563
'O w man, you will surely die,'	Ezk 33:8	7563
speak to warn the w from his way,	Ezk 33:8	7563
w man shall die in his iniquity,	Ezk 33:8	7563
warn a w man to turn from his way and	Ezk 33:9	7563
no pleasure in the death of the w,	Ezk 33:11	7563
the w turn from his way and live.	Ezk 33:11	7563
as for the wickedness of the w,	Ezk 33:12	7563
"But when I say to the w,	Ezk 33:14	7563
if a w man restores a pledge, pays	Ezk 33:15	7563
"But when the w turns from his	Ezk 33:19	7563
we have sinned, we have been w.	Da 9:15	7561
but the w will act wickedly; and	Da 12:10	7563
and none of the w will understand,	Da 12:10	7563
that each may turn from his w way	Jon 3:8	7463a
that they turned from their w way,	Jon 3:10	7463a
"Is there yet a man in the w house,	Mi 6:10	7563
"Can I justify w scales And a bag	Mi 6:11	7562
against the LORD, A w counselor.	Na 1:11	1100
will the w one pass through you;	Na 1:15	1100
For the w surround the righteous;	Hab 1:4	7563
w swallow up Those more righteous	Hab 1:13	7563
And the ruins along with the w;	Zph 1:3	7563
will call them the w territory,	Mal 1:4	7562
between the righteous and the w,	Mal 3:18	7563
"You will tread down the w,	Mal 4:3	7563
other spirits more w than itself,	Mt 12:45	*4190*
the w from among the righteous,	Mt 13:49	*4190*
'You w slave, I forgave you all	Mt 18:32	*4190*
'You w, lazy slave, you knew that	Mt 25:26	*4190*
the w things which Herod had done,	Lk 3:19	*4190*
"This generation is a w generation;	Lk 11:29	*4190*
one *of you* from your w ways."	Ac 3:26	*4189*
some w men from the market place,	Ac 17:5	*4190*
of both the righteous and the w.	Ac 24:15	*94*
THE W MAN FROM AMONG YOURSELVES.	1Co 5:13	*4190*
unjustly accusing us with w words;	3Jn 1:10	*4190*

WICKEDLY

"Please, my brothers, do not act w.	Gn 19:7	7489a
fellows, please do not act so w;	Jg 19:23	7489a
"But if you still do w,	1Sa 12:25	7489a
me, while I have dealt w with you.	1Sa 24:17	7463a
have not acted w against my God.	2Sa 22:22	7561
iniquity, we have acted w';	1Ki 8:47	7561
acted more w than all who *were*	1Ki 16:25	7489a
having done w more than all the	2Ki 21:11	7489a
who has sinned and done very w,	1Ch 21:17	7489a
iniquity and have acted w';	2Ch 6:37	7561
He acted w in so doing.	2Ch 20:35	7561
mother was his counselor to do w.	2Ch 22:3	7561
faithfully, but we have acted w.	Ne 9:33	7561
"Surely, God will not act w,	Jb 34:12	7561
have not w departed from my God.	Ps 18:21	7561
mock and w speak of oppression;	Ps 73:8	7451b
iniquity, we have behaved w.	Ps 106:6	7561
For they speak against You w,	Ps 139:20	4209
these men have acted w in all that	Jer 38:9	7489a
against My ordinances more w than	Ezk 5:6	7564
committed iniquity, acted w and	Da 9:5	7561
who act w toward the covenant,	Da 11:32	7561
but the wicked will act w;	Da 12:10	7561

WICKEDNESS

w of man was great on the earth,	Gn 6:5	7463a
because of the w of these nations	Dt 9:4	7564
because of the w of these nations	Dt 9:5	7564
people or at their w or their sin.	Dt 9:27	7562
God repaid the w of Abimelech,	Jg 9:56	7463a
all the w of the men of Shechem	Jg 9:57	7463a
us, how did this w take place?"	Jg 20:3	7463a
"What is this w that has taken	Jg 20:12	7463a
and remove *this* w from Israel."	Jg 20:13	7463a
will know and see that your w is great	1Sa 12:17	7463a
insolence and the w of your heart;	1Sa 17:28	7455
'Out of the wicked comes forth w'	1Sa 24:13	7562
but if w is found in him, he will	1Ki 1:52	7463a
do not let w dwell in your tents;	Jb 11:14	5767b
"Is not your w great, And your	Jb 22:5	7463a
And w will be broken like a tree.	Jb 24:20	5767b
Far be it from God to do w,	Jb 34:10	7562
"Your w is for a man like	Jb 35:8	7562
not a God who takes pleasure in w;	Ps 5:4	7562
Behold, he travails with w,	Ps 7:14	205
his tongue is mischief and w.	Ps 10:7	205
Seek out his w until You find	Ps 10:15	7562
Do all the workers of w not know,	Ps 14:4	205
words of his mouth are w and deceit	Ps 36:3	205
He plans w upon his bed;	Ps 36:4	205
His heart gathers w to itself;	Ps 41:6	205
loved righteousness and hated w;	Ps 45:7	7562
the workers of w no knowledge,	Ps 53:4	205
Because of w, cast them forth, In	Ps 56:7	205
If I regard w in my heart, The	Ps 66:18	205
God Than dwell in the tents of w.	Ps 84:10	7562
him, Nor the son of w afflict him.	Ps 89:22	5767b
All who do w vaunt themselves.	Ps 94:4	205
for me against those who do w?	Ps 94:16	205
brought back their w upon them And	Ps 94:23	205
Because of the w of those who dwell	Ps 107:34	7463a
who follow after w draw near;	Ps 119:150	2154
For the scepter of w shall not	Ps 125:3	7562
To practice deeds of w With men	Ps 141:4	7562
For they eat the bread of w And	Pr 4:17	7562
w is an abomination to my lips.	Pr 8:7	7562
Doing w is like sport to a fool,	Pr 10:23	2154
the wicked will fall by his own w.	Pr 11:5	7564
man will not be established by w,	Pr 12:3	7562
But w subverts the sinner.	Pr 13:6	7564
His w will be revealed before the	Pr 26:26	7463a
the place of justice there is w and	Ec 3:16	7562
place of righteousness there is w.	Ec 3:16	7562
who prolongs *his life* in his w.	Ec 7:15	7463a
For w burns like a fire;	Is 9:18	7564
And his heart inclines toward w:	Is 32:6	205
felt secure in your w and said,	Is 47:10	7463a
choose, To loosen the bonds of w,	Is 58:6	7562
of the finger and speaking w,	Is 58:9	205
falsehood, Your tongue mutters w.	Is 59:3	5767b
on them concerning all their w,	Jer 1:16	7463a
"Your own w will correct you, And	Jer 2:19	7463a
your harlotry and with your w.	Jer 3:2	7463a
proclaims w from Mount Ephraim.	Jer 4:15	205
They also excel in deeds of w;	Jer 5:28	7451b
fresh, So she keeps fresh her w.	Jer 6:7	7463a
of the w of My people Israel.	Jer 7:12	7463a
No man repented of his w,	Jer 8:6	7463a
the w of those who dwell in it,	Jer 12:4	7463a
pour out their *own* w on them.	Jer 14:16	7463a
We know our w, O LORD, The	Jer 14:20	7562
humiliated Because of all your w.	Jer 22:22	7463a
My house I have found their w,"	Jer 23:11	7463a
no one has turned back from his w.	Jer 23:14	7463a
this city because of all their w:	Jer 33:5	7463a
because of their w which they	Jer 44:3	7463a
their ears to turn from their w,	Jer 44:5	7463a
forgotten the w of your fathers,	Jer 44:9	7463a
the w of the kings of Judah,	Jer 44:9	7463a
Judah, and the w of their wives,	Jer 44:9	7463a
of their wives, your own w,	Jer 44:9	7463a
and the w of your wives,	Jer 44:9	7463a
"Let all their w come before You;	La 1:22	7463a
from his w or from his wicked way,	Ezk 3:19	7562
has grown into a rod of w.	Ezk 7:11	7562
it came about after all your w	Ezk 16:23	7463a
before your w was uncovered, so	Ezk 16:57	7463a
and the w of the wicked will be	Ezk 18:20	7564
wicked man turns away from his w	Ezk 18:27	7564
According to its w I have driven it	Ezk 31:11	7562
and as for the w of the wicked,	Ezk 33:12	7564
the day when he turns from his w;	Ezk 33:12	7562
when the wicked turns from his w	Ezk 33:19	7564
That I remember all their w.	Hos 7:2	7463a
With their w they make the king glad	Hos 7:3	7463a
Because of the w of their deeds I	Hos 9:15	7455
You have plowed w, you have reaped	Hos 10:13	7562
at Bethel because of your great w.	Hos 10:15	7463a
overflow, for their w is great.	Jl 3:13	7463a
their w has come up before Me."	Jon 1:2	7463a
house, *Along with* treasures of w And	Mi 6:10	7562
And cause *me* to look on w?	Hab 1:3	5999
can not look on w *with favor.*	Hab 1:13	5999
Then he said, "This is W!"	Zch 5:8	7564
only are the doers of w built up but	Mal 3:15	7564
deeds of coveting *and* w,	Mk 7:22	*4189*
you are full of robbery and w.	Lk 11:39	*4189*
a field with the price of his w,	Ac 1:18	*93*
repent of this w of yours,	Ac 8:22	*2549*
with all unrighteousness, w,	Ro 1:29	*4189*
with the leaven of malice and w,	1Co 5:8	*4189*
against the spiritual *forces* of w in	Eph 6:12	*4189*
and with all the deception of w for	2Th 2:10	*93*
the truth, but took pleasure in w.	2Th 2:12	*93*
name of the Lord is to abstain from w."	2Tm 2:19	*93*
and *all* that remains of w,	Jas 1:21	*2549*

WICKER

she got him a w basket and covered	Ex 2:3	1573

WIDE

long, and one and a half cubits w,	Ex 25:10	7341
long and one and a half cubits w.	Ex 25:17	7341
two cubits long and one cubit w	Ex 25:23	7341
cubits long and five cubits w;	Ex 27:1	7341
long and one and a half cubits w.	Ex 37:6	7341
two cubits long and a cubit w and	Ex 37:10	7341
a cubit long and a cubit w,	Ex 37:25	7341
cubits long, and five cubits w,	Ex 38:1	7341
and a span w when folded double.	Ex 39:9	7341
lowest story *was* five cubits w,	1Ki 6:6	7341
and the middle *was* six cubits w,	1Ki 6:6	7341
and the third *was* seven cubits w;	1Ki 6:6	7341
five cubits long, five cubits w and	2Ch 6:13	7341
"As *through* a w breach they come,	Jb 30:14	7342
They open w their mouth at me, As	Ps 22:13	6475
opened their mouth w against me;	Ps 35:21	7337
Open your mouth w and I will fill it.	Ps 81:10	7337
I opened my mouth w and panted,	Ps 119:131	6473
one who opens w his lips comes to	Pr 13:3	6589
To a people feared far and w,	Is 18:2	1973
from a people feared far and w,	Is 18:7	1973
us A place of rivers *and* w canals On	Is 33:21	7342
Against whom do you open w your	Is 57:4	7337
have gone up and made your bed w.	Is 57:8	7337
opened their mouths w against you;	La 2:16	6475
sister's cup, Which is deep and w.	Ezk 23:32	7342
was one rod long and one rod w;	Ezk 40:7	7341
a barrier *wall* one cubit w	Ezk 40:12	
long and twenty-five cubits w.	Ezk 40:29	7341
cubits long and five cubits w.	Ezk 40:30	7341
long and twenty-five cubits w.	Ezk 40:33	7341
a half long, a cubit and a half w and	Ezk 40:42	7341
long and a hundred cubits w;	Ezk 40:47	7341
six cubits w on each side *was* the	Ezk 41:1	7341
the west *was* seventy cubits w;	Ezk 41:12	7341
was an inner walk ten cubits w,	Ezk 42:4	7341
be twelve *cubits* long by twelve w,	Ezk 43:16	7341
by fourteen w in its four sides,	Ezk 43:17	7341
5,000 *cubits* w and 25,000 *cubits* long	Ezk 45:6	7341
forty *cubits* long and thirty w;	Ezk 46:22	7341
gates of your land are opened w to	Na 3:13	6605a
see how w it is and how long it is."	Zch 2:2	7341
for the gate is w and the way is	Mt 7:13	*4116*
for a w door for effective *service*	1Co 16:9	*3173*
our heart is opened w.	2Co 6:11	*4115*
open w *to us* also.	2Co 6:13	*4115*

WIDELY

story was w spread among the Jews,	Mt 28:15	*1310*
w they continued to proclaim it.	Mk 7:36	*4053*

WIDER

were w at each successive story.	Ezk 41:7	7337

WIDOW

"Remain a w in your father's	Gn 38:11	490
shall not afflict any w or orphan.	Ex 22:22	490
'A w, or a divorced woman, or one	Lv 21:14	490
daughter becomes a w or divorced,	Lv 22:13	490
vow of a w or of a divorced woman,	Nu 30:9	490
justice for the orphan and the w,	Dt 10:18	490
and the w who are in your town,	Dt 14:29	490
and the w who are in your midst,	Dt 16:11	490
and the w who are in your towns.	Dt 16:14	490
for the orphan, and for the w,	Dt 24:19	490
for the orphan, and for the w.	Dt 24:20	490
for the orphan, and for the w.	Dt 24:21	490
to the orphan and to the w,	Dt 26:12	490
the alien, the orphan and the w,	Dt 26:13	490
due an alien, orphan, and w.'	Dt 27:19	490
Moabitess, the w of the deceased,	Ru 4:5	802
the Moabitess, the w of Mahlon,	Ru 4:10	802
Abigail the Carmelitess, Nabal's w.	1Sa 27:3	802
the w of Nabal the Carmelite.	1Sa 30:5	802
the w of Nabal the Carmelite.	2Sa 2:2	802
the w of Nabal the Carmelite;	2Sa 3:3	802
child that Uriah's w bore to David,	2Sa 12:15	802
"Truly I am a w, for my husband	2Sa 14:5	490
mother's name was Zeruah, a w,	1Ki 11:26	490
I have commanded a w there to	1Ki 17:9	490
a w was there gathering sticks;	1Ki 17:10	490
You also brought calamity to the w	1Ki 17:20	490
woman And does no good for the w.	Jb 24:21	490
caused the eyes of the w to fail,	Jb 31:16	490
They slay the w and the stranger And	Ps 94:6	490
be fatherless And his wife a w.	Ps 109:9	490
supports the fatherless and the w,	Ps 146:9	490
establish the boundary of the w.	Pr 15:25	490
the orphan, Plead for the w.	Is 1:17	490
I will not sit as a w,	Is 47:8	490
the alien, the orphan, or the w,	Jer 7:6	490
stranger, the orphan, or the w;	Jer 22:3	490
She has become like a w Who was	La 1:1	490
the w they have wronged in you.	Ezk 22:7	490
"And they shall not marry a w or	Ezk 44:22	490
a w who is the widow of a priest.	Ezk 44:22	490
a widow who is the w of a priest.	Ezk 44:22	490
not oppress the w or the orphan,	Zch 7:10	490
his wages, the w and the orphan,	Mal 3:5	490
A poor w came and put in two	Mk 12:42	*5503*
this poor w put in more than all	Mk 12:43	*5503*
as a w to the age of eighty-four.	Lk 2:37	*5503*
of Sidon, to a woman who was a w.	Lk 4:26	*5503*
of his mother, and she was a w;	Lk 7:12	*5503*
"There was a w in that city,	Lk 18:3	*5503*
yet because this w bothers me,	Lk 18:5	*5503*
And He saw a poor w	Lk 21:2	*5503*
poor w put in more than all *of them;*	Lk 21:3	*5503*
any w has children or grandchildren,	1Tm 5:4	*5503*
Now she who is a w indeed and	1Tm 5:5	*5503*
A w is to be put on the list	1Tm 5:9	*5503*
as A QUEEN AND I AM NOT A W,	Rv 18:7	*5503*

WIDOWED

wives become childless and w.	Jer 18:21	490

WIDOWHOOD

Loss of children and w.	Is 47:9	489
the reproach of your w you will	Is 54:4	491

WIDOW'S

So she removed her w garments and	Gn 38:14	491
veil and put on her w garments.	Gn 38:19	491
nor take a w garment in pledge.	Dt 24:17	490
He was a w son from the tribe of	1Ki 7:14	490
They take the w ox for a pledge.	Jb 24:3	490
I made the w heart sing for joy.	Jb 29:13	490
does the w plea come before them.	Is 1:23	490

WIDOWS

and your wives shall become w and	Ex 22:24	490
day of their death, living as w.	2Sa 20:3	491
"You have sent w away empty, And	Jb 22:9	490
their w will not be able to weep.	Jb 27:15	490
fatherless and a judge for the w,	Ps 68:5	490
And His w could not weep.	Ps 78:64	490
pity on their orphans or their w;	Is 9:17	490
So that w may be their spoil	Is 10:2	490
"Their w will be more numerous	Jer 15:8	490
And let your w trust in Me."	Jer 49:11	490
a father, Our mothers are like w.	La 5:3	490

made many w in the midst of her. Ezk 22:25 490
there were many w in Israel in the Lk 4:25 5503
because their w were being Ac 6:1 5503
the w stood beside him, Ac 9:39 5503
and calling the saints and w, Ac 9:41 5503
But I say to the unmarried and to w 1Co 7:8 5503
Honor w who are widows indeed; 1Tm 5:3 5503
Honor widows who are w indeed; 1Tm 5:3 5503
refuse *to put* younger w *on the list,* 1Tm 5:11 5503
Therefore, I want younger w to 1Tm 5:14
who is a believer has *dependent* w, 1Tm 5:16 5503
may assist those who are w indeed. 1Tm 5:16 5503
visit orphans and w in their distress, Jas 1:27 5503

WIDOWS'

because you devour w houses, Mt 23:14 5503
who devour w houses, and for Mk 12:40 5503
who devour w houses, and for Lk 20:47 5503

WIDTH

the w of each curtain four cubits; Ex 26:2 7341
the w of each curtain four cubits; Ex 26:8 7341
a half cubits the w of each board. Ex 26:16 7341
"*For* the w of the court on Ex 27:12 7341
"The w of the court on the Ex 27:13 7341
and the w fifty throughout, Ex 27:18 7341
a span in length and a span in w. Ex 28:16 7341
be a cubit, and its w a cubit, Ex 30:2 7341
the w of each curtain four cubits; Ex 36:9 7341
four cubits the w of each curtain; Ex 36:15 7341
a half cubits the w of each board. Ex 36:21 7341
and its w one and a half cubits, Ex 37:1 7341
its w four cubits by ordinary cubit.) Dt 3:11 7341
its w twenty *cubits* and its height 1Ki 6:2 7341
to the w of the house, 1Ki 6:3 7341
in length, twenty cubits in w, 1Ki 6:20 7341
its length was 100 cubits and its w 50 1Ki 7:2 7341
was 50 cubits and its w 30 cubits, 1Ki 7:6 7341
was four cubits and its w four cubits 1Ki 7:27 7341
cubits, and the w twenty cubits. 2Ch 3:3 7341
was as long as the w of the house, 2Ch 3:4 7341
length across the w of the house 2Ch 3:8 7341
and its w *was* twenty cubits; 2Ch 3:8 7341
twenty cubits in w and ten cubits in 2Ch 4:1 7341
60 cubits and its w 60 cubits; Ezr 6:3 6613
of the gate, one rod in w; Ezk 40:6 7341
other threshold *was* one rod in w. Ezk 40:6 7341
he measured the w of the gateway, Ezk 40:11 7341
a w of twenty-five cubits from *one* Ezk 40:13 7341
Then he measured the w from the Ezk 40:19 7341
he measured its length and its w. Ezk 40:20 7341
and the w twenty-five cubits. Ezk 40:21 7341
and the w twenty-five cubits. Ezk 40:25 7341
and the w twenty-five cubits. Ezk 40:36 7341
and the w of the gate was three Ezk 40:48 7341
cubits and the w eleven cubits; Ezk 40:49 7341
side *was* the w of the side pillar. Ezk 41:1 7341
The w of the entrance *was* ten Ezk 41:2 7341
the nave, forty cubits, and the w, Ezk 41:2 7341
and the w of the doorway, seven Ezk 41:3 7341
length, twenty cubits, and the w, Ezk 41:4 7341
and the w of the side chambers, Ezk 41:5 7341
therefore the w of the temple Ezk 41:7 7341
was twenty cubits in w all around Ezk 41:10 7341
and the w of the free space Ezk 41:11 7341
Also the w of the front of the Ezk 41:14 7341
the w *was* fifty cubits. Ezk 42:2 7341
to their length so was their w, Ezk 42:11 7341
hundred and the w five hundred, Ezk 42:20 7341
be a cubit and the w a cubit, Ezk 43:13 7341
two cubits and the w one cubit; Ezk 43:14 7341
four cubits and the w one cubit. Ezk 43:14 7341
cubits, and the w shall be 20,000. Ezk 45:1 7341
cubits and a w of 10,000 *cubits;* Ezk 45:3 7341
cubits in length and 10,000 in w Ezk 45:5 7341
set apart, 25,000 *cubits* in w, Ezk 48:8 7341
cubits in length and 10,000 in w. Ezk 48:9 7341
toward the west 10,000 in w, Ezk 48:10 7341
toward the east 10,000 in w, Ezk 48:10 7341
cubits in length and 10,000 in w. Ezk 48:13 7341
be 25,000 *cubits* and the w 10,000. Ezk 48:13 7341
5,000 *cubits* in w and 25,000 in Ezk 48:15 7341
sixty cubits *and* its w six cubits; Da 3:1 6613
cubits and its w ten cubits." Zch 5:2 7341
its length is as great as the w; Rv 21:16 4114
length and w and height are equal. Rv 21:16 4114

WIELD

for if you w your tool on it, Ex 20:25 5130
but you shall not w a sickle in Dt 23:25 5130
shall not w an iron *tool* on them. Dt 27:5 5130
those who w the staff of office. Jg 5:14 4900

WIELDED

which no man had w an iron *tool;* Jos 8:31 5130
to his authority which he w, Da 11:4 4910

WIELDERS

"All of them are w of the sword, SS 3:8 270

WIELDING

bearing shields and w bows; 2Ch 14:8 1869
like a club w those who lift it, Is 10:15 5130
and shield, all of them w swords; Ezk 38:4 8610

WIELDS

itself over the one who w it? Is 10:15 5130
And the one who w the sickle at Jer 50:16 8610

WIFE

mother, and be joined to his w; Gn 2:24 802
the man and his w were both naked Gn 2:25 802
and the man and his w hid Gn 3:8 802
listened to the voice of your w, Gn 3:17 802
of skin for Adam and his w, Gn 3:21 802
man had relations with his w Eve, Gn 4:1 802
Cain had relations with his w and Gn 4:17 802
had relations with his w again; Gn 4:25 802
you and your sons and your w, Gn 6:18 802
Then Noah and his sons and his w Gn 7:7 802
and Noah's w and the three wives Gn 7:13 802
you and your w and your sons and Gn 8:16 802
his w and his sons' wives with him. Gn 8:18 802
The name of Abram's w was Sarai; Gn 11:29 802
the name of Nahor's w was Milcah, Gn 11:29 802
daughter-in-law, his son Abram's w; Gn 11:31 802
Sarai his w and Lot his nephew, Gn 12:5 802
that he said to Sarai his w, Gn 12:11 802
they will say, 'This is his w'; and they Gn 12:12 802
because of Sarai, Abram's w. Gn 12:17 802
not tell me that she was your w? Gn 12:18 802
so that I took her for my w? Gn 12:19 802
Now then, here is your w, Gn 12:19 802
his w and all that belonged to him. Gn 12:20 802
his w and all that belonged to him, Gn 13:1 802
w had borne him no *children,* Gn 16:1 802
w Sarai took Hagar the Egyptian, Gn 16:3 802
her to her husband Abram as his w. Gn 16:3 802
"As for Sarai your w, Gn 17:15 802
Sarah your w will bear you a son, Gn 17:19 802
"Where is Sarah your w?" Gn 18:9 802
Sarah your w will have a son." Gn 18:10 802
your w and your two daughters who Gn 19:15 802
seized his hand and the hand of his w Gn 19:16 802
But his w, from behind him, looked Gn 19:26 802
Abraham said of Sarah his w, Gn 20:2 802
"Now therefore, restore the man's w, Gn 20:7 802
they will kill me because of my w. Gn 20:11 802
of my mother, and she became my w; Gn 20:12 802
and restored his w Sarah to him. Gn 20:14 802
Abimelech and his w and his maids, Gn 20:17 802
because of Sarah, Abraham's w. Gn 20:18 802
and his mother took a w for him Gn 21:21 802
Abraham buried Sarah his w in the Gn 23:19 802
that you shall not take a w for my Gn 24:3 802
and take a w for my son Isaac." Gn 24:4 802
take a w for my son from there. Gn 24:7 802
the w of Abraham's brother Nahor, Gn 24:15 802
'Now Sarah my master's w bore a Gn 24:36 802
'You shall not take a w for my son Gn 24:37 802
and take a w for my son.' Gn 24:38 802
a w for my son from my relatives and Gn 24:40 802
her be the w of your master's son, Gn 24:51 802
Rebekah, and she became his w, Gn 24:67 802
Now Abraham took another w, Gn 25:1 802
was buried with Sarah his w. Gn 25:10 802
of Laban the Aramean, to be his w. Gn 25:20 802
to the LORD on behalf of his w, Gn 25:21 802
him and Rebekah his w conceived. Gn 25:21 802
of the place asked about his w, Gn 26:7 802
for he was afraid to say, "my w," Gn 26:7 802
Isaac was caressing his w Rebekah. Gn 26:8 802
"Behold, certainly she is your w! Gn 26:9 802
easily have lain with your w, Gn 26:10 802
his w shall surely be put to death." Gn 26:11 802
a w from the daughters of Heth, Gn 27:46 802
a w from the daughters of Canaan. Gn 28:1 802
and from there take to yourself a w Gn 28:2 802
to take to himself a w from there, Gn 28:6 802
"You shall not take a w from the Gn 28:6 802
"Give *me* my w, for my time is Gn 29:21 802
him his daughter Rachel as his w. Gn 29:28 802
gave him her maid Bilhah as a w, Gn 30:4 802
and gave her to Jacob as a w. Gn 30:9 802
"Get me this young girl for a w." Gn 34:4 802
Eliphaz the son of Esau's w Adah, Gn 36:10 802
Reuel the son of Esau's w Basemath. Gn 36:10 802
are the sons of Esau's w Adah. Gn 36:12 802
were the sons of Esau's w Basemath. Gn 36:13 802
the sons of Esau's w Oholibamah, Gn 36:14 802
are the sons of Esau's w Basemath. Gn 36:17 802
the sons of Esau's w Oholibamah: Gn 36:18 802
descended from Esau's w Oholibamah, Gn 36:18 802
Judah took a w for Er his firstborn, Gn 38:6 802
"Go in to your brother's w, Gn 38:8 802
when he went in to his brother's w, Gn 38:9 802
Shua's daughter, the w of Judah, Gn 38:12 802
had not been given to him as a w. Gn 38:14 802
his master's w looked with desire at Gn 39:7 802
refused and said to his master's w, Gn 39:8 802
except you, because you are his w. Gn 39:9 802
master heard the words of his w, Gn 39:19 802
Potiphera priest of On, as his w. Gn 41:45 802
know that my w bore me two sons; Gn 44:27 802
The sons of Jacob's w Rachel: Gn 46:19 802
buried Abraham and his w Sarah, Gn 49:31 802
buried Isaac and his w Rebekah, Gn 49:31 802
So Moses took his w and his sons Ex 4:20 802
took Moses' w Zipporah, Ex 18:2 802
came with his sons and his w to Ex 18:5 802
your w and her two sons with her." Ex 18:6 802
you shall not covet your neighbor's w Ex 20:17 802
if he is the husband of a w, Ex 21:3 802
then his w shall go out with him. Ex 21:3 802
"If his master gives him a w, Ex 21:4 802
the w and her children shall Ex 21:4 802
my master, my w and my children; Ex 21:5 802
pay a dowry for her *to be* his w. Ex 22:16 802
the nakedness of your father's w; Lv 18:8 802
you shall not approach his w, Lv 18:14 802
she is your son's w, Lv 18:15 802
the nakedness of your brother's w; Lv 18:16 802
intercourse with your neighbor's w, Lv 18:20 802
adultery with another man's w, Lv 20:10 802
adultery with his friend's w, Lv 20:10 802
a man who lies with his father's w, Lv 20:11 802
is a man who lies with his uncle's w Lv 20:20 1733
is a man who takes his brother's w, Lv 20:21 802
shall take a w in her virginity. Lv 21:13 802
'If any man's w goes astray and is Nu 5:12 802
he is jealous of his w when she has Nu 5:14 802
he is jealous of his w when she has not Nu 5:14 802
then bring his w to the priest, Nu 5:15 802
when a w, *being under the* Nu 5:29 802
a man and he is jealous of his w, Nu 5:30 802
The name of Amram's w was Jochebed, Nu 26:59 802
Moses, *as* between a man and his w, Nu 30:16 802
shall be w to one of the family of Nu 36:8 802
shall not covet your neighbor's w, Dt 5:21 802
or daughter, or the w you cherish, Dt 13:6 802
take her as a w for yourself, Dt 21:11 802
husband and she shall be your w. Dt 21:13 802
"If any man takes a w and goes in Dt 22:13 802
my daughter to this man for a w, Dt 22:16 802
And she shall remain his w; Dt 22:19 802
he has violated his neighbor's w. Dt 22:24 802
she shall become his w because he Dt 22:29 802
"A man shall not take his father's w Dt 22:30 802
a man takes a w and marries her, Dt 24:1
goes and becomes another man's w, Dt 24:2 802
dies who took her to be his w, Dt 24:3 802
to take her again to be his w, Dt 24:4 802
"When a man takes a new w, Dt 24:5 802
to his w whom he has taken. Dt 24:5 802
the w of the deceased shall not be Dt 25:5 802
in to her and take her to himself as w Dt 25:5 802
not desire to take his brother's w, Dt 25:7 2994
then his brother's w shall go up Dt 25:7 2994
then his brother's w shall come to Dt 25:9 2994
and the w of one comes near to Dt 25:11 802
is he who lies with his father's w, Dt 27:20 802
"You shall betroth a w, Dt 28:30 802
and toward the w he cherishes and Dt 28:54 802
him Achsah my daughter as a w." Jos 15:16 802
him Achsah his daughter as a w. Jos 15:17 802
him my daughter Achsah for a w." Jg 1:12 802
him his daughter Achsah for a w. Jg 1:13 802
a prophetess, the w of Lappidoth, Jg 4:4 802
of Jael the w of Heber the Kenite, Jg 4:17 802
But Jael, Heber's w, Jg 4:21 802
Jael, The w of Heber the Kenite; Jg 5:24 802
Gilead's w bore him sons; Jg 11:2 802
and his w was barren and had borne Jg 13:2 802
Manoah arose and followed his w, Jg 13:11 802
while Manoah and his w looked on. Jg 13:19 802
When Manoah and his w saw *this,* Jg 13:20 802
not appear to Manoah or his w again. Jg 13:21 802
So Manoah said to his w, Jg 13:22 802
But his w said to him, Jg 13:23 802
get her for me as a w." Jg 14:2 802
that you go to take a w from the Jg 14:3 802
day that they said to Samson's w, Jg 14:15 802
Samson's w wept before him and Jg 14:16 802
But Samson's w was *given* to his Jg 14:20 802
Samson visited his w with a young Jg 15:1 802
"I will go in to my w in *her* room." Jg 15:1 802
he took his w and gave her to his Jg 15:6 802
is he who gives a w to Benjamin." Jg 21:18 802
w from the daughters of Shiloh, Jg 21:21 802
take for each man *of Benjamin* a w Jg 21:22 802
Moab with his w and his two sons. Ru 1:1 802
Elimelech, and the name of his w, Ru 1:2 802
to be my w in order to raise up Ru 4:10 802
took Ruth, and she became his w, Ru 4:13 802
give portions to Peninnah his w 1Sa 1:4 802
had relations with Hannah his w, 1Sa 1:19 802
bless Elkanah and his w and say, 1Sa 2:20 802
Now his daughter-in-law, Phinehas' w, 1Sa 4:19 802
The name of Saul's w was 1Sa 14:50 802
I will give her to you as a w, 1Sa 18:17 802
to Adriel the Meholathite for a w. 1Sa 18:19 802
him Michal his daughter for a w. 1Sa 18:27 802
But Michal, David's w, 1Sa 19:11 802
young men told Abigail, Nabal's w, 1Sa 25:14 802
his w told him these things, 1Sa 25:37 802
to Abigail, to take her as his w. 1Sa 25:39 802
us to you to take you as his w." 1Sa 25:40 802
of David and became his w. 1Sa 25:42 802
Michal his daughter, David's w, 1Sa 25:44 802
every man his w and his children, 1Sa 30:22 802
sixth, Ithream, by David's w Eglah. 2Sa 3:5 802
"Give me my w Michal, to whom I 2Sa 3:14 802
the w of Uriah the Hittite?" 2Sa 11:3 802
and to drink and to lie with my w? 2Sa 11:11 802
Now when the w of Uriah heard that 2Sa 11:26 802
to his house and she became his w; 2Sa 11:27 802
have taken his w to be your wife, 2Sa 12:9 802
have taken his wife to be your w, 2Sa 12:9 802
have taken the w of Uriah the Hittite 2Sa 12:10 802
Uriah the Hittite to be your w.' 2Sa 12:10 802
David comforted his w Bathsheba, 2Sa 12:24 802
Abishag the Shunammite as a w." 1Ki 2:17 802
to Adonijah your brother as a w." 1Ki 2:21 802
daughter of Solomon was his w); 1Ki 4:11 802
dowry to his daughter, Solomon's w. 1Ki 9:16 802
marriage the sister of his own w, 1Ki 11:19 802
Jeroboam said to his w, 1Ki 14:2 802
that you are the w of Jeroboam, 1Ki 14:2 802
Jeroboam's w did so, and arose 1Ki 14:4 802
the w of Jeroboam is coming to 1Ki 14:5 802
"Come in, w of Jeroboam, why do 1Ki 14:6 802
Then Jeroboam's w arose and 1Ki 14:17 802
his w came to him and said to him, 1Ki 21:5 802

Jezebel his **w** said to him,	**1Ki 21:7**	802
because Jezebel his **w** incited him.	**1Ki 21:25**	802
and she waited on Naaman's **w**.	**2Ki 5:2**	802
the daughter of Ahab became his **w**;	**2Ki 8:18**	802
w of Shallum the son of Tikvah,	**2Ki 22:14**	802
Hezron had sons by Azubah *his* **w**,	**1Ch 2:18**	802
Caleb-ephrathah, Abijah, Hezron's **w**,	**1Ch 2:24**	802
Jerahmeel had another **w**,	**1Ch 2:26**	802
name of Abishur's **w** *was* Abihail,	**1Ch 2:29**	802
sixth *was* Ithream, by his **w** Eglah.	**1Ch 3:3**	802
His Jewish **w** bore Jered the	**1Ch 4:18**	802
The sons of the **w** of Hodiah,	**1Ch 4:19**	802
took a **w** for Huppim and Shuppim,	**1Ch 7:15**	802
Maacah the **w** of Machir bore a son,	**1Ch 7:16**	802
Then he went in to his **w**,	**1Ch 7:23**	802
By Hodesh his **w** he became the	**1Ch 8:9**	802
"My **w** shall not dwell in the	**2Ch 8:11**	802
Then Rehoboam took as a **w** Mahalath	**2Ch 11:18**	802
(for Ahab's daughter was his **w**),	**2Ch 21:6**	802
the **w** of Jehoiada the priest	**2Ch 22:11**	802
w of Shallum the son of Tokhath,	**2Ch 34:22**	802
who took a **w** from the daughters of	**Ezr 2:61**	802
who took a **w** of the daughters of	**Ne 7:63**	802
for his friends and his **w** Zeresh.	**Es 5:10**	802
Zeresh his **w** and all his friends said	**Es 5:14**	802
Haman recounted to Zeresh his **w**	**Es 6:13**	802
men and Zeresh his **w** said to him,	**Es 6:13**	802
Then his **w** said to him,	**Jb 2:9**	802
"My breath is offensive to my **w**,	**Jb 19:17**	802
May my **w** grind for another, And	**Jb 31:10**	802
be fatherless And his **w** a widow.	**Ps 109:9**	802
Your **w** shall be like a fruitful vine	**Ps 128:3**	802
rejoice in the **w** of your youth.	**Pr 5:18**	802
who goes in to his neighbor's **w**;	**Pr 6:29**	802
An excellent **w** is the crown of her	**Pr 12:4**	802
He who finds a **w** finds a good thing	**Pr 18:22**	802
the contentions of a **w** are a constant	**Pr 19:13**	802
But a prudent **w** is from the LORD.	**Pr 19:14**	802
An excellent **w**, who can find?	**Pr 31:10**	802
a **w** forsaken and grieved in spirit,	**Is 54:6**	802
Even like a **w** of *one's* youth when	**Is 54:6**	802
"If a husband divorces his **w** And	**Jer 3:1**	802
neighing after his neighbor's **w**.	**Jer 5:8**	802
both husband and **w** shall be taken,	**Jer 6:11**	802
"You shall not take a **w** for	**Jer 16:2**	802
"You adulteress **w**, who takes	**Ezk 16:32**	802
Israel, or defile his neighbor's **w** or	**Ezk 18:6**	802
and defiles his neighbor's **w**,	**Ezk 18:11**	802
Israel, or defile his neighbor's **w**,	**Ezk 18:15**	802
abomination with his neighbor's **w** and	**Ezk 22:11**	802
and in the evening my **w** died.	**Ezk 24:18**	802
of you defiles his neighbor's **w**.	**Ezk 33:26**	802
take to yourself a **w** of harlotry and	**Hos 1:2**	802
contend, For she is not my **w**,	**Hos 2:2**	802
Aram, And Israel worked for a **w**,	**Hos 12:12**	802
a wife, And for a **w** he kept *sheep.*	**Hos 12:12**	802
'Your **w** will become a harlot in	**Am 7:17**	802
you and the **w** of your youth,	**Mal 2:14**	802
companion and your **w** by covenant.	**Mal 2:14**	802
against the **w** of your youth.	**Mal 2:15**	802
by Bathsheba who had been the **w** of	**Mt 1:6**	*1135*
be afraid to take Mary as your **w**;	**Mt 1:20**	*1135*
him, and took *Mary* as his **w**,	**Mt 1:24**	*1135*
'WHOEVER SENDS HIS **W** AWAY,	**Mt 5:31**	*1135*
that everyone who divorces his **w**,	**Mt 5:32**	*1135*
the **w** of his brother Philip.	**Mt 14:3**	*1135*
along with his **w** and children and	**Mt 18:25**	*1135*
man to divorce his **w** for any reason	**Mt 19:3**	*1135*
MOTHER AND BE JOINED TO HIS **W**,	**Mt 19:5**	*1135*
to you, whoever divorces his **w**,	**Mt 19:9**	*1135*
the man with his **w** is like this,	**Mt 19:10**	*1135*
AS NEXT OF KIN SHALL MARRY HIS **W**,	**Mt 22:24**	*1135*
left his **w** to his brother;	**Mt 22:25**	*1135*
whose **w** of the seven will she be?	**Mt 22:28**	*1135*
judgment seat, his **w** sent him	**Mt 27:19**	*1135*
the **w** of his brother Philip,	**Mk 6:17**	*1135*
for you to have your brother's **w**."	**Mk 6:18**	*1135*
lawful for a man to divorce a **w**.	**Mk 10:2**	*1135*
"Whoever divorces his **w** and	**Mk 10:11**	*1135*
DIES and leaves behind a **w**	**Mk 12:19**	*1135*
HIS BROTHER SHOULD MARRY THE **W**	**Mk 12:19**	*1135*
and the first took a **w**,	**Mk 12:20**	*1135*
again, which one's **w** will she be?	**Mk 12:23**	*1135*
a **w** from the daughters of Aaron,	**Lk 1:5**	*1135*
your **w** Elizabeth will bear you a son	**Lk 1:13**	*1135*
and my **w** is advanced in years."	**Lk 1:18**	*1135*
Elizabeth his **w** became pregnant,	**Lk 1:24**	*1135*
of Herodias, his brother's **w**,	**Lk 3:19**	*1135*
and Joanna the **w** of Chuza, Herod's	**Lk 8:3**	*1135*
'I have married a **w**,	**Lk 14:20**	*1135*
his own father and mother and **w**	**Lk 14:26**	*1135*
"Everyone who divorces his **w** and	**Lk 16:18**	*1135*
"Remember Lot's **w**.	**Lk 17:32**	*1135*
no one who has left house or **w** or	**Lk 18:29**	*1135*
A MAN'S BROTHER DIES, having a **w**,	**Lk 20:28**	*1135*
HIS BROTHER SHOULD MARRY THE **W** AND	**Lk 20:28**	*1135*
and the first took a **w** and	**Lk 20:29**	*1135*
which one's **w** will she be?	**Lk 20:33**	*1135*
Mary the **w** of Clopas, and Mary	**Jn 19:25**	*1135*
Ananias, with his **w** Sapphira,	**Ac 5:1**	*1135*
three hours, and his **w** came in,	**Ac 5:7**	*1135*
from Italy with his **w** Priscilla,	**Ac 18:2**	*1135*
Drusilla, his **w** who was a Jewess,	**Ac 24:24**	*1135*
that someone has his father's **w**.	**1Co 5:1**	*1135*
each man is to have his own **w**,	**1Co 7:2**	*1135*
husband must fulfill his duty to his **w**,	**1Co 7:3**	*1135*
also the **w** to her husband.	**1Co 7:3**	*1135*
The **w** does not have authority over	**1Co 7:4**	*1135*
over his own body, but the **w** *does.*	**1Co 7:4**	*1135*
w should not leave her husband	**1Co 7:10**	*1135*
should not divorce his **w**.	**1Co 7:11**	*1135*
has a **w** who is an unbeliever,	**1Co 7:12**	*1135*
is sanctified through his **w**,	**1Co 7:14**	*1135*
unbelieving **w** is sanctified through	**1Co 7:14**	*1135*
For how do you know, O **w**,	**1Co 7:16**	*1135*
whether you will save your **w**?	**1Co 7:16**	*1135*
Are you bound to a **w**?	**1Co 7:27**	*1135*
Are you released from a **w**?	**1Co 7:27**	*1135*
from a wife? Do not seek a **w**.	**1Co 7:27**	*1135*
world, how he may please his **w**,	**1Co 7:33**	*1135*
A **w** is bound as long as her	**1Co 7:39**	*1135*
right to take along a believing **w**,	**1Co 9:5**	*1135*
the husband is the head of the **w**,	**Eph 5:23**	*1135*
who loves his own **w** loves himself;	**Eph 5:28**	*1135*
MOTHER AND SHALL BE JOINED TO HIS **W**,	**Eph 5:31**	*1135*
love his own **w** even as himself,	**Eph 5:33**	*1135*
and the **w** must *see to it* that she	**Eph 5:33**	*1135*
reproach, the husband of one **w**,	**1Tm 3:2**	*1135*
must be husbands of *only* one **w**,	**1Tm 3:12**	*1135*
old, *having been* the **w** of one man,	**1Tm 5:9**	*1135*
reproach, the husband of one **w**,	**Ti 1:6**	*1135*
the bride, the **w** of the Lamb."	**Rv 21:9**	*1135*

WIFE'S

Now the man called his **w** name Eve,	**Gn 3:20**	802
and his **w** name was Mehetabel, the	**Gn 36:39**	802
of your father's **w** daughter,	**Lv 18:11**	802
and when his **w** sons grew up, they	**Jg 11:2**	802
Nabal, and his **w** name was Abigail.	**1Sa 25:3**	802
Pai, and his **w** name was Mehetabel,	**1Ch 1:50**	802
lived, and his **w** name was Maacah;	**1Ch 8:29**	802
lived, and his **w** name was Maacah,	**1Ch 9:35**	802
with his **w** full knowledge,	**Ac 5:2**	*1135*

WILD

He will be a **w** donkey of a man,	**Gn 16:12**	6501
'A **w** beast devoured him.'	**Gn 37:20**	7451a
A **w** beast has devoured him;	**Gn 37:33**	7451a
them like the horns of the **w** ox.	**Nu 23:22**	7214
him like the horns of the **w** ox.	**Nu 24:8**	7214
for the **w** beasts would grow too	**Dt 7:22**	7704
gazelle, the roebuck, the **w** goat,	**Dt 14:5**	689
horns are the horns of the **w** ox;	**Dt 33:17**	7214
sky and the **w** beasts of the earth,	**1Sa 17:46**	2421b
front of the Rocks of the **W** Goats.	**1Sa 24:2**	3277
and found a **w** vine and gathered	**2Ki 4:39**	7704
from it his lap full of **w** gourds,	**2Ki 4:39**	7704
by a **w** beast that was in Lebanon,	**2Ki 14:9**	7704
by a **w** beast that was in Lebanon and	**2Ch 25:18**	7704
branches and **w** olive branches,	**Ne 8:15**	6086, 8081
will not be afraid of **w** beasts.	**Jb 5:22**	776
the **w** donkey bray over *his* grass,	**Jb 6:5**	6501
foal of a **w** donkey is born a man.	**Jb 11:12**	6501
as **w** donkeys in the wilderness	**Jb 24:5**	6501
"Who sent out the **w** donkey free?	**Jb 39:5**	6501
the **w** ox consent to serve you,	**Jb 39:9**	7214
"Can you bind the **w** ox in a furrow	**Jb 39:10**	7214
that a **w** beast may trample them.	**Jb 39:15**	7704
From the horns of the **w** oxen	**Ps 22:21**	7214
And Sirion like a young **w** ox.	**Ps 29:6**	7214
of Your turtledove to the **w** beast;	**Ps 74:19**	2421b
my horn like *that of* the **w** ox;	**Ps 92:10**	7214
The **w** donkeys quench their thirst.	**Ps 104:11**	6501
mountains are for the **w** goats;	**Ps 104:18**	3277
forever, A delight for **w** donkeys,	**Is 32:14**	6501
W oxen will also fall with them	**Is 34:7**	7214
A **w** donkey accustomed to the	**Jer 2:24**	6501
"The **w** donkeys stand on the	**Jer 14:6**	6501
I have given him also the **w** animals	**Jer 27:6**	2421b
send on you famine and **w** beasts,	**Ezk 5:17**	7451a
"If I were to cause **w** beasts to	**Ezk 14:15**	7451a
sword, famine, **w** beasts and	**Ezk 14:21**	7451a
place *was* with the **w** donkeys.	**Da 5:21**	6167
Like a **w** donkey all alone;	**Hos 8:9**	6501
As a **w** beast would tear them.	**Hos 13:8**	7704
his food was locusts and **w** honey.	**Mt 3:4**	*66*
his diet was locusts and **w** honey.	**Mk 1:6**	*66*
and He was with the **w** beasts,	**Mk 1:13**	*2342*
w beasts and the crawling creatures	**Ac 11:6**	*2342*
off, and you, being a **w** olive,	**Ro 11:17**	*65*
what is by nature a **w** olive tree,	**Ro 11:24**	*65*
I fought with **w** beasts at Ephesus,	**1Co 15:32**	*2341*
w waves of the sea, casting up	**Jude 1:13**	*66*
and by the **w** beasts of the earth.	**Rv 6:8**	*2342*

WILDERNESS

far as El-paran, which is by the **w**.	**Gn 14:6**	4057b
her by a spring of water in the **w**,	**Gn 16:7**	4057b
about in the **w** of Beersheba.	**Gn 21:14**	4057b
and he lived in the **w** and	**Gn 21:20**	4057b
He lived in the **w** of Paran,	**Gn 21:21**	4057b
who found the hot springs in the **w**	**Gn 36:24**	4057b
into this pit that is in the **w**,	**Gn 37:22**	4057b
flock to the west side of the **w** and	**Ex 3:1**	4057b
a three days' journey into the **w**,	**Ex 3:18**	4057b
"Go to meet Moses in the **w**."	**Ex 4:27**	4057b
may celebrate a feast to Me in the **w**.	**Ex 5:1**	4057b
go a three days' journey into the **w**	**Ex 5:3**	4057b
that they may serve Me in the **w**.	**Ex 7:16**	4057b
go a three days' journey into the **w**	**Ex 8:27**	4057b
to the LORD your God in the **w**;	**Ex 8:28**	4057b
the way of the **w** to the Red Sea;	**Ex 13:18**	4057b
in Etham on the edge of the **w**.	**Ex 13:20**	4057b
the **w** has shut them in.'	**Ex 14:3**	4057b
taken us away to die in the **w**?	**Ex 14:11**	4057b
Egyptians than to die in the **w**."	**Ex 14:12**	4057b
they went out into the **w** of Shur;	**Ex 15:22**	4057b
they went three days in the **w** and	**Ex 15:22**	4057b
of Israel came to the **w** of Sin,	**Ex 16:1**	4057b
against Moses and Aaron in the **w**.	**Ex 16:2**	4057b
you have brought us out into this **w**	**Ex 16:3**	4057b
that they looked toward the **w**,	**Ex 16:10**	4057b
on the surface of the **w** there was	**Ex 16:14**	4057b
the bread that I fed you in the **w**,	**Ex 16:32**	4057b
by stages from the **w** of Sin,	**Ex 17:1**	4057b
in the **w** where he was camped,	**Ex 18:5**	4057b
day they came into the **w** of Sinai.	**Ex 19:1**	4057b
they came to the **w** of Sinai and	**Ex 19:2**	4057b
of Sinai and camped in the **w**;	**Ex 19:2**	4057b
from the **w** to the River *Euphrates;*	**Ex 23:31**	4057b
to the LORD in the **w** of Sinai.	**Lv 7:38**	4057b
it into the **w** as the scapegoat.	**Lv 16:10**	4057b
the goat and send *it* away into the **w**	**Lv 16:21**	4057b
shall release the goat in the **w**.	**Lv 16:22**	4057b
spoke to Moses in the **w** of Sinai,	**Nu 1:1**	4057b
numbered them in the **w** of Sinai.	**Nu 1:19**	4057b
before the LORD in the **w** of Sinai;	**Nu 3:4**	4057b
spoke to Moses in the **w** of Sinai,	**Nu 3:14**	4057b
spoke to Moses in the **w** of Sinai,	**Nu 9:1**	4057b
at twilight, in the **w** of Sinai;	**Nu 9:5**	4057b
journeys from the **w** of Sinai.	**Nu 10:12**	4057b
settled down in the **w** of Paran.	**Nu 10:12**	4057b
where we should camp in the **w**,	**Nu 10:31**	4057b
and camped in the **w** of Paran.	**Nu 12:16**	4057b
sent them from the **w** of Paran	**Nu 13:3**	4057b
from the **w** of Zin as far as Rehob,	**Nu 13:21**	4057b
sons of Israel in the **w** of Paran,	**Nu 13:26**	4057b
would that we had died in this **w**!	**Nu 14:2**	4057b
He slaughtered them in the **w**.'	**Nu 14:16**	4057b
I performed in Egypt and in the **w**,	**Nu 14:22**	4057b
the **w** by the way of the Red Sea."	**Nu 14:25**	4057b
your corpses will fall in this **w**,	**Nu 14:29**	4057b
your corpses will fall in this **w**.	**Nu 14:32**	4057b
for forty years in the **w**,	**Nu 14:33**	4057b
until your corpses lie in the **w**.	**Nu 14:33**	4057b
In this **w** they shall be destroyed,	**Nu 14:35**	4057b
the sons of Israel were in the **w**,	**Nu 15:32**	4057b
and honey to have us die in the **w**,	**Nu 16:13**	4057b
came to the **w** of Zin in the first	**Nu 20:1**	4057b
the LORD's assembly into this **w**,	**Nu 20:4**	4057b
up out of Egypt to die in the **w**?	**Nu 21:5**	4057b
in the **w** which is opposite Moab,	**Nu 21:11**	4057b
which is in the **w** that comes out	**Nu 21:13**	4057b
from the **w** *they continued* to	**Nu 21:18**	4057b
went out against Israel in the **w**,	**Nu 21:23**	4057b
but he set his face toward the **w**.	**Nu 24:1**	4057b
sons of Israel in the **w** of Sinai.	**Nu 26:64**	4057b
"They shall surely die in the **w**."	**Nu 26:65**	4057b
"Our father died in the **w**,	**Nu 27:3**	4057b
for in the **w** of Zin, during the	**Nu 27:14**	4057b
of Kadesh in the **w** of Zin.)	**Nu 27:14**	4057b
them wander in the **w** forty years,	**Nu 32:13**	4057b
once more abandon them in the **w**,	**Nu 32:15**	4057b
which is on the edge of the **w**.	**Nu 33:6**	4057b
the midst of the sea into the **w**;	**Nu 33:8**	4057b
days' journey in the **w** of Etham and	**Nu 33:8**	4057b
Sea and camped in the **w** of Sin.	**Nu 33:11**	4057b
They journeyed from the **w** of Sin	**Nu 33:12**	4057b
and camped in the **w** of Sinai.	**Nu 33:15**	4057b
journeyed from the **w** of Sinai and	**Nu 33:16**	4057b
and camped in the **w** of Zin,	**Nu 33:36**	4057b
w of Zin along the side of Edom,	**Nu 34:3**	4057b
Israel across the Jordan in the **w**,	**Dt 1:1**	4057b
and terrible **w** which you saw on	**Dt 1:19**	4057b
and in the **w** where you saw how the	**Dt 1:31**	4057b
the **w** by the way to the Red Sea.'	**Dt 1:40**	4057b
the **w** by the way to the Red Sea,	**Dt 2:1**	4057b
wanderings through this great **w**.	**Dt 2:7**	4057b
by the way of the **w** of Moab.	**Dt 2:8**	4057b
"So I sent messengers from the **w**	**Dt 2:26**	4057b
Bezer in the **w** on the plateau for	**Dt 4:43**	4057b
LORD your God has led you in the **w**	**Dt 8:2**	4057b
through the great and terrible **w**,	**Dt 8:15**	4057b
"In the **w** He fed you manna which	**Dt 8:16**	4057b
LORD your God to wrath in the **w**;	**Dt 9:7**	4057b
them out to slay them in the **w**."	**Dt 9:28**	4057b
what He did to you in the **w** until	**Dt 11:5**	4057b
will be from the **w** to Lebanon,	**Dt 11:24**	4057b
I have led you forty years in the **w**;	**Dt 29:5**	4057b
And in the howling waste of a **w**;	**Dt 32:10**	3452
of Meribah-kadesh, in the **w** of Zin,	**Dt 32:51**	4057b
"From the **w** and this Lebanon,	**Jos 1:4**	4057b
war, died in the **w** along the way after	**Jos 5:4**	4057b
all the people who were born in the **w**	**Jos 5:5**	4057b
walked forty years in the **w**,	**Jos 5:6**	4057b
and fled by the way of the **w**.	**Jos 8:15**	4057b
who had been fleeing to the **w**	**Jos 8:20**	4057b
in the **w** where they pursued them,	**Jos 8:24**	4057b
on the slopes, and in the **w**,	**Jos 12:8**	4057b
when Israel walked in the **w**;	**Jos 14:10**	4057b
the **w** of Zin at the extreme south.	**Jos 15:1**	4057b
In the **w**: Beth-arabah, Middin and	**Jos 15:61**	4057b
of Jericho on the east into the **w**,	**Jos 16:1**	4057b
and it ended at the **w** of Beth-aven.	**Jos 18:12**	4057b
they designated Bezer in the **w** on	**Jos 20:8**	4057b
lived in the **w** for a long time.	**Jos 24:7**	4057b
to the **w** of Judah which is in the	**Jg 1:16**	4057b
thorns of the **w** and with briers."	**Jg 8:7**	4057b
and thorns of the **w** and briers,	**Jg 8:16**	4057b
and Israel went through the **w** to	**Jg 11:16**	4057b
'Then they went through the **w** and	**Jg 11:18**	4057b
from the **w** as far as the Jordan.	**Jg 11:22**	4057b
toward the direction of the **w**,	**Jg 20:42**	4057b
the **w** to the rock of Rimmon,	**Jg 20:45**	4057b
the **w** to the rock of Rimmon,	**Jg 20:47**	4057b
all *kinds of* plagues in the **w**.	**1Sa 4:8**	4057b
the valley of Zeboim toward the **w**.	**1Sa 13:18**	4057b
you left those few sheep in the **w**?	**1Sa 17:28**	4057b

in the **w** in the strongholds, 1Sa 23:14 4057b
the hill country in the **w** of Ziph. 1Sa 23:14 4057b
was in the **w** of Ziph at Horesh. 1Sa 23:15 4057b
and his men were in the **w** of Maon, 1Sa 23:24 4057b
rock and stayed in the **w** of Maon. 1Sa 23:25 4057b
he pursued David in the **w** of Maon. 1Sa 23:25 4057b
David is in the **w** of Engedi." 1Sa 24:1 4057b
and went down to the **w** of Paran. 1Sa 25:1 4057b
that David heard in the **w** that 1Sa 25:4 4057b
David sent messengers from the **w** 1Sa 25:14 4057b
all that this *man* has in the **w**, 1Sa 25:21 4057b
and went down to the **w** of Ziph, 1Sa 26:2 4057b
search for David in the **w** of Ziph. 1Sa 26:2 4057b
and David was staying in the **w**. 1Sa 26:3 4057b
Saul came after him into the **w**, 1Sa 26:3 4057b
by the way of the **w** of Gibeon. 2Sa 2:24 4057b
over toward the way of the **w**. 2Sa 15:23 4057b
going to wait at the fords of the **w** 2Sa 15:28 4057b
is faint in the **w** to drink." 2Sa 16:2 4057b
the night at the fords of the **w**, 2Sa 17:16 4057b
and weary and thirsty in the **w**." 2Sa 17:29 4057b
buried at his own house in the **w**. 1Ki 2:34 4057b
and Baalath and Tamar in the **w**, 1Ki 9:18 4057b
went a day's journey into the **w**, 1Ki 19:4 4057b
on your way to the **w** of Damascus, 1Ki 19:15 4057b
"The way of the **w** of Edom." 2Ki 3:8 4057b
as far as the entrance of the **w** 1Ch 5:9 4057b
Bezer in the **w** with its pasture lands, 1Ch 6:78 4057b
David in the stronghold in the **w**, 1Ch 12:8 4057b
which Moses had made in the **w**, 1Ch 21:29 4057b
of the LORD had made in the **w**. 2Ch 1:3 4057b
He built Tadmor in the **w** and 2Ch 8:4 4057b
in front of the **w** of Jeruel. 2Ch 20:16 4057b
and went out to the **w** of Tekoa; 2Ch 20:20 4057b
Judah came to the lookout of the **w**, 2Ch 20:24 4057b
servant of God on Israel in the **w**. 2Ch 24:9 4057b
He built towers in the **w** and hewed 2Ch 26:10 4057b
Did not forsake them in the **w**; Ne 9:19 4057b
provided for them in the **w** Ne 9:21 4057b
a great wind came from across the **w** Jb 1:19 4057b
as wild donkeys in the **w** They go Jb 24:5 4057b
To whom I gave the **w** for a home Jb 39:6 6160
voice of the LORD shakes the **w**; Ps 29:8 4057b
The LORD shakes the **w** of Kadesh. Ps 29:8 4057b
I would lodge in the **w**. Ps 55:7 4057b
The pastures of the **w** drip, Ps 65:12 4057b
You marched through the **w**, Ps 68:7 3452
food for the creatures of the **w**. Ps 74:14 6716b
He split the rocks in the **w** And Ps 78:15 4057b
"Can God prepare a table in the **w**? Ps 78:19 4057b
rebelled against Him in the **w** And Ps 78:40 4057b
guided them in the **w** like a flock; Ps 78:52 4057b
As in the day of Massah in the **w**, Ps 95:8 4057b
I resemble a pelican of the **w**; Ps 102:6 4057b
the deeps, as through the **w**. Ps 106:9 4057b
But craved intensely in the **w**, Ps 106:14 4057b
He would cast them down in the **w**, Ps 106:26 4057b
in the **w** in a desert region; Ps 107:4 4057b
He changes rivers into a **w** And Ps 107:33 4057b
He changes a **w** into a pool of water Ps 107:35 4057b
who led His people through the **w**, Ps 136:16 4057b
"What is this coming up from the **w** SS 3:6 4057b
"Who is this coming up from the **w** SS 8:5 4057b
Who made the world like a **w** Is 14:17 4057b
From Sela by way of the **w** to the Is 16:1 4057b
oracle concerning the **w** of the sea. Is 21:1 4057b
sweep on, It comes from the **w**, Is 21:1 4057b
And the **w** becomes a fertile field Is 32:15 4057b
Then justice will dwell in the **w** And Is 32:16 4057b
The **w** and the desert will be glad, Is 35:1 4057b
For waters will break forth in the **w** Is 35:6 4057b
Clear the way for the LORD in the **w**; Is 40:3 4057b
I will make the **w** a pool of water And Is 41:18 4057b
"I will put the cedar in the **w**, Is 41:19 4057b
Let the **w** and its cities lift up Is 42:11 4057b
will even make a roadway in the **w**, Is 43:19 4057b
I have given waters in the **w** And Is 43:20 4057b
My rebuke, I make the rivers a **w**; Is 50:2 4057b
And her **w** He will make like Eden, Is 51:3 4057b
Like the horse in the **w**, Is 63:13 4057b
Your holy cities have become a **w**, Is 64:10 4057b
a wilderness, Zion has become a **w**, Is 64:10 4057b
Your following after Me in the **w**, Jer 2:2 4057b
Egypt, Who led us through the **w**, Jer 2:6 4057b
A wild donkey accustomed to the **w**, Jer 2:24 4057b
Have I been a **w** to Israel, Or a Jer 2:31 4057b
wind from the bare heights in the **w** Jer 4:11 4057b
behold, the fruitful land was a **w**, Jer 4:26 4057b
for the pastures of the **w** a dirge, Jer 9:10 4057b
My pleasant field A desolate **w**. Jer 12:10 4057b
"On all the bare heights in the **w** Jer 12:12 4057b
live in stony wastes in the **w**, Jer 17:6 4057b
I will make you like a **w**, Jer 22:6 4057b
pastures of the **w** have dried up. Jer 23:10 4057b
Found grace in the **w** Jer 31:2 4057b
may be like a juniper in the **w**. Jer 48:6 4057b
A **w**, a parched land and a desert. Jer 50:12 4057b
cruel Like ostriches in the **w**. La 4:3 4057b
waited in ambush for us in the **w**. La 4:19 4057b
Because of the sword in the **w**. La 5:9 4057b
waste than the **w** toward Diblah; Ezk 6:14 4057b
'And now it is planted in the **w**, Ezk 19:13 4057b
Egypt and brought them into the **w**. Ezk 20:10 4057b
rebelled against Me in the **w**. Ezk 20:13 4057b
out My wrath on them in the **w**, Ezk 20:13 4057b
I swore to them in the **w** that I would Ezk 20:15 4057b
not cause their annihilation in the **w**. Ezk 20:17 4057b
I said to their children in the **w**, Ezk 20:18 4057b
My anger against them in the **w**. Ezk 20:21 4057b
"Also I swore to them in the **w** Ezk 20:23 4057b
bring you into the **w** of the peoples, Ezk 20:35 4057b
in the **w** of the land of Egypt, Ezk 20:36 4057b
drunkards were brought from the **w** Ezk 23:42 4057b
"I will abandon you to the **w**, Ezk 29:5 4057b
that they may live securely in the **w** Ezk 34:25 4057b
I will also make her like a **w**, Hos 2:3 4057b
allure her, Bring her into the **w** And Hos 2:14 4057b
found Israel like grapes in the **w**; Hos 9:10 4057b
I cared for you in the **w**, Hos 13:5 4057b
of the LORD coming up from the **w**; Hos 13:15 4057b
devoured the pastures of the **w** And Jl 1:19 4057b
devoured the pastures of the **w**. Jl 1:20 4057b
But a desolate **w** behind them, Jl 2:3 4057b
pastures of the **w** have turned green, Jl 2:22 4057b
And Edom will become a desolate **w**, Jl 3:19 4057b
And I led you in the **w** forty years Am 2:10 4057b
in the **w** for forty years, Am 5:25 4057b
a desolation, Parched like the **w**. Zph 2:13 4057b
for the jackals of the **w**." Mal 1:3 4057b
came, preaching in the **w** of Judea, Mt 3:1 *2048*
"THE VOICE OF ONE CRYING IN THE **W**, Mt 3:3 *2048*
was led up by the Spirit into the **w** Mt 4:1 *2048*
you go out into the **w** to see? Mt 11:7 *2048*
'Behold, He is in the **w**,' Mt 24:26 *2048*
THE VOICE OF ONE CRYING IN THE **W**, Mk 1:3 *2048*
John the Baptist appeared in the **w** Mk 1:4 *2048*
impelled Him *to go* out into the **w**. Mk 1:12 *2048*
And He was in the **w** forty days Mk 1:13 *2048*
the son of Zacharias, in the **w**. Lk 3:2 *2048*
"THE VOICE OF ONE CRYING IN THE **W** Lk 3:4 *2048*
led around by the Spirit in the **w** Lk 4:1 *2048*
often slip away to the **w** and pray. Lk 5:16 *2048*
you go out into the **w** to see? Lk 7:24 *2048*
am A VOICE OF ONE CRYING IN THE **W**, Jn 1:23 *2048*
lifted up the serpent in the **w**, Jn 3:14 *2048*
fathers ate the manna in the **w**; Jn 6:31 *2048*
fathers ate the manna in the **w**, Jn 6:49 *2048*
there to the country near the **w**, Jn 11:54 *2048*
TO HIM IN THE **W** OF MOUNT Sinai, Ac 7:30 *2048*
Sea and in the **w** for forty years. Ac 7:36 *2048*
who was in the congregation in the **w** Ac 7:38 *2048*
SACRIFICES FORTY YEARS IN THE **W**, Ac 7:42 *2048*
tabernacle of testimony in the **w**, Ac 7:44 *2048*
He put up with them in the **w**. Ac 13:18 *2048*
of the Assassins out into the **w**?" Ac 21:38 *2048*
for they were laid low in the **w**. 1Co 10:5 *2048*
in the city, dangers in the **w**, 2Co 11:26 *2047*
AS IN THE DAY OF TRIAL IN THE **W**, Heb 3:8 *2048*
whose bodies fell in the **w**? Heb 3:17 *2048*
Then the woman fled into the **w** Rv 12:6 *2048*
could fly into the **w** to her place, Rv 12:14 *2048*
me away in the Spirit into a **w**; Rv 17:3 *2048*

WILDLY

They rush **w** in the squares, Na 2:4 8264

WILL

eat from it you **w** surely die." Gn 2:17
I **w** make him a helper suitable for Gn 2:18
or you **w** die.'" Gn 3:3
"You surely **w** not die! Gn 3:4
eat from it your eyes **w** be opened, Gn 3:5
be opened, and you **w** be like God, Gn 3:5
On your belly you **w** go, And dust you Gn 3:14
And dust you **w** eat All the days of Gn 3:14
And I **w** put enmity Between you and Gn 3:15
"I **w** greatly multiply Your pain Gn 3:16
In pain you **w** bring forth children; Gn 3:16
Yet your desire **w** be for your husband, Gn 3:16
And he **w** rule over you." Gn 3:16
In toil you **w** eat of it All the days Gn 3:17
And you **w** eat the plants of the field; Gn 3:18
By the sweat of your face You **w** eat Gn 3:19
w not *your countenance* be lifted Gn 4:7
it **w** no longer yield its strength to Gn 4:12
you **w** be a vagrant and a wanderer on Gn 4:12
and from Your face I **w** be hidden, Gn 4:14
and I **w** be a vagrant and a wanderer Gn 4:14
and whoever finds me **w** kill me." Gn 4:14
vengeance **w** be taken on him Gn 4:15
"This one **w** give us rest from our Gn 5:29
"I **w** blot out man whom I have Gn 6:7
"But I **w** establish My covenant Gn 6:18
two of every *kind* **w** come to you Gn 6:20
I **w** send rain on the earth forty Gn 7:4
and I **w** blot out from the face of Gn 7:4
"I **w** never again curse the ground Gn 8:21
and I **w** never again destroy every Gn 8:21
terror of you **w** be on every beast Gn 9:2
Surely I **w** require your lifeblood; Gn 9:5
from every beast I **w** require it. Gn 9:5
I **w** require the life of man. Gn 9:5
that the bow **w** be seen in the cloud, Gn 9:14
and I **w** remember My covenant, Gn 9:15
the cloud, then I **w** look upon it, Gn 9:16
and a tower whose top **w** *reach* Gn 11:4
otherwise we **w** be scattered abroad Gn 11:4
to do **w** be impossible for them. Gn 11:6
so that they **w** not understand one Gn 11:7
To the land which I **w** show you; Gn 12:1
And I **w** make you a great nation, Gn 12:2
a great nation, And I **w** bless you, Gn 12:2
And I **w** bless those who bless you, Gn 12:3
the one who curses you I **w** curse. Gn 12:3
families of the earth **w** be blessed." Gn 12:3
descendants I **w** give this land." Gn 12:7
see you, they **w** say, Gn 12:12
and they **w** kill me, but they will Gn 12:12
kill me, but they **w** let you live. Gn 12:12
left, then I **w** go to the right; Gn 13:9
right, then I **w** go to the left." Gn 13:9
I **w** give it to you and to your Gn 13:15
"I **w** make your descendants as Gn 13:16
for I **w** give it to you." Gn 13:17
that I **w** not take a thread or a Gn 14:23
"I **w** take nothing except what the Gn 14:24
"O Lord GOD, what **w** You give me, Gn 15:2
"This man **w** not be your heir; Gn 15:4
but one who **w** come forth from your Gn 15:4
how may I know that I **w** possess it?" Gn 15:8
your descendants **w** be strangers in a Gn 15:13
where they **w** be enslaved and Gn 15:13
"But I **w** also judge the nation Gn 15:14
the nation whom they **w** serve, Gn 15:14
and afterward they **w** come out with Gn 15:14
you **w** be buried at a good old age. Gn 15:15
"Then in the fourth generation they **w** Gn 15:16
perhaps I **w** obtain children through Gn 16:2
"I **w** greatly multiply your Gn 16:10
your descendants so that they **w** be Gn 16:10
And you **w** bear a son; And you shall Gn 16:11
He **w** be a wild donkey of a man, Gn 16:12
His hand **w** *be* against everyone, Gn 16:12
And everyone's hand **w** *be* against Gn 16:12
And he **w** live to the east of all Gn 16:12
"I **w** establish My covenant Gn 17:2
I **w** multiply you exceedingly." Gn 17:2
And you **w** be the father of a Gn 17:4
I **w** make you exceedingly fruitful, Gn 17:6
and I **w** make nations of you, Gn 17:6
and kings **w** come forth from you. Gn 17:6
"I **w** establish My covenant Gn 17:7
"I **w** give to you and to your Gn 17:8
and I **w** be their God." Gn 17:8
"I **w** bless her, and indeed I Gn 17:16
indeed I **w** give you a son by her. Gn 17:16
Then I **w** bless her, and she shall Gn 17:16
kings of peoples **w** come from her." Gn 17:16
"**W** a child be born to a man one Gn 17:17
And **w** Sarah, who is ninety years Gn 17:17
but Sarah your wife **w** bear you a son, Gn 17:19
and I **w** establish My covenant with Gn 17:19
behold, I **w** bless him, and will Gn 17:20
him, and **w** make him fruitful and Gn 17:20
and **w** multiply him exceedingly. Gn 17:20
and I **w** make him a great nation. Gn 17:20
covenant I **w** establish with Isaac, Gn 17:21
whom Sarah **w** bear to you at this Gn 17:21
and I **w** bring a piece of bread, Gn 18:5
"I **w** surely return to you at this Gn 18:10
Sarah your wife **w** have a son." Gn 18:10
appointed time I **w** return to you, Gn 18:14
and Sarah **w** have a son." Gn 18:14
since Abraham **w** surely become a Gn 18:18
nations of the earth **w** be blessed? Gn 18:18
"I **w** go down now, and see if they Gn 18:21
and if not, I **w** know." Gn 18:21
"**W** You indeed sweep away the Gn 18:23
w You indeed sweep *it* away and Gn 18:24
then I **w** spare the whole place on Gn 18:26
w You destroy the whole city Gn 18:28
"I **w** not destroy *it* if I find Gn 18:28
"I **w** not do *it* on account of the Gn 18:29
"I **w** not do *it* if I find thirty Gn 18:30
"I **w** not destroy *it* on account of Gn 18:31
"I **w** not destroy *it* on account of Gn 18:32
we **w** treat you worse than them." Gn 19:9
for the LORD **w** destroy the city." Gn 19:14
or you **w** be swept away in Gn 19:15
or you **w** be swept away." Gn 19:17
for the disaster **w** overtake me and I Gn 19:19
disaster will overtake me and I **w** die; Gn 19:19
"Lord, **w** You slay a nation, even Gn 20:4
a prophet, and he **w** pray for you and Gn 20:7
will pray for you and you **w** live. Gn 20:7
they **w** kill me because of my wife. Gn 20:11
kindness which you **w** show to me: Gn 20:13
who hears **w** laugh with me." Gn 21:6
the maid I **w** make a nation also, Gn 21:13
I **w** make a great nation of him." Gn 21:18
you **w** not deal falsely with me or Gn 21:23
mountains of which I **w** tell you." Gn 22:2
and I and the lad **w** go over Gn 22:5
we **w** worship and return to you." Gn 22:5
"God **w** provide for Himself the Gn 22:8
of that place The LORD **W** Provide, Gn 22:14
of the LORD it **w** be provided." Gn 22:14
indeed I **w** greatly bless you, and Gn 22:17
and I **w** greatly multiply your seed Gn 22:17
none of us **w** refuse you his grave Gn 23:6
"If you **w** only please listen to me; Gn 23:13
I **w** give the price of the field, Gn 23:13
I **w** make you swear by the LORD, Gn 24:3
but you **w** go to my country and to my Gn 24:4
descendants I **w** give this land,' Gn 24:7
He **w** send His angel before you, Gn 24:7
and you **w** take a wife for my son Gn 24:7
you **w** be free from this my oath; Gn 24:8
and I **w** water your camels also' Gn 24:14
and by this I **w** know that You have Gn 24:14
"I **w** draw also for your camels Gn 24:19
"I **w** not eat until I have told my Gn 24:33
w send His angel with you to make Gn 24:40
and you **w** take a wife for my son Gn 24:40
then you **w** be free from my oath, Gn 24:41
you, you **w** be free from my oath.' Gn 24:41
if now You **w** make my journey on Gn 24:42

and she **w** say to me, **Gn 24:44**
I **w** draw for your camels also"; **Gn 24:44**
and I **w** water your camels also'; **Gn 24:46**
"We **w** call the girl and consult **Gn 24:57**
"**W** you go with this man?" **Gn 24:58**
And she said, "I **w** go." **Gn 24:58**
And two peoples **w** be separated from **Gn 25:23**
and I **w** be with you and bless you, **Gn 26:3**
I **w** give all these lands, **Gn 26:3**
and I **w** establish the oath which I **Gn 26:3**
"I **w** multiply your **Gn 26:4**
and **w** give your descendants all **Gn 26:4**
and we **w** be fruitful in the land." **Gn 26:22**
I **w** bless you, and multiply your **Gn 26:24**
that you **w** do us no harm, just as **Gn 26:29**
"Perhaps my father **w** feel me, **Gn 27:12**
then I **w** be as a deceiver in his **Gn 27:12**
and I **w** bring upon myself a curse **Gn 27:12**
me, and I **w** eat of my son's game, **Gn 27:25**
That you **w** break his yoke from your **Gn 27:40**
then I **w** kill my brother Jacob." **Gn 27:41**
Then I **w** send and get you from there. **Gn 27:45**
what good **w** my life be to me?" **Gn 27:46**
I **w** give it to you and to your **Gn 28:13**
"Your descendants **w** also be like **Gn 28:14**
and you **w** spread out to the west **Gn 28:14**
and **w** keep you wherever you go, **Gn 28:15**
and **w** bring you back to this land; **Gn 28:15**
for I **w** not leave you until I have **Gn 28:15**
"If God **w** be with me and will **Gn 28:20**
"If God will be with me and **w** keep me **Gn 28:20**
and **w** give me food to eat and **Gn 28:20**
safety, then the LORD **w** be my God. **Gn 28:21**
up as a pillar, **w** be God's house, **Gn 28:22**
I **w** surely give a tenth to You." **Gn 28:22**
"I **w** serve you seven years for **Gn 29:18**
and we **w** give you the other also **Gn 29:27**
surely now my husband **w** love me." **Gn 29:32**
husband **w** become attached to me, **Gn 29:34**
"This time I **w** praise the LORD." **Gn 29:35**
For women **w** call me happy." **Gn 30:13**
now my husband **w** dwell with me, **Gn 30:20**
me your wages, and I **w** give it." **Gn 30:28**
If you **w** do this *one* thing for me, **Gn 30:31**
I **w** again pasture *and* keep your **Gn 30:31**
my honesty **w** answer for me later, **Gn 30:33**
with me, **w** be considered stolen." **Gn 30:33**
relatives, and I **w** be with you." **Gn 31:3**
that I **w** not pass by this heap to **Gn 31:52**
and you **w** not pass by this heap **Gn 31:52**
company which is left **w** escape." **Gn 32:8**
relatives, and I **w** prosper you,' **Gn 32:9**
that he **w** come and attack me *and* **Gn 32:11**
'I **w** surely prosper you and make **Gn 32:12**
"I **w** appease him with the present **Gn 32:20**
Then afterward I **w** see his face; **Gn 32:20**
perhaps he **w** accept me." **Gn 32:20**
"I **w** not let you go unless you **Gn 32:26**
and go, and I **w** go before you." **Gn 33:12**
one day, all the flocks **w** die. **Gn 33:13**
and I **w** proceed at my leisure, **Gn 33:14**
I **w** give whatever you say to me. **Gn 34:11**
and I **w** give according as you say **Gn 34:12**
condition **w** we consent to you: **Gn 34:15**
if you **w** become like us, in that **Gn 34:15**
we **w** give our daughters to you, **Gn 34:16**
and we **w** take your daughters for **Gn 34:16**
and we **w** live with you and become **Gn 34:16**
"But if you **w** not listen to us to **Gn 34:17**
we **w** take our daughter and go." **Gn 34:17**
on this *condition* **w** the men consent **Gn 34:22**
"**W** not their livestock and their **Gn 34:23**
them, and they **w** live with us." **Gn 34:23**
they **w** gather together against me **Gn 34:30**
attack me and I **w** be destroyed, **Gn 34:30**
I **w** make an altar there to God, **Gn 35:3**
and Isaac, I **w** give it to you, **Gn 35:12**
And I **w** give the land to your **Gn 35:12**
Come, and I **w** send you to them." **Gn 37:13**
And he said to him, "I **w** go." **Gn 37:13**
we **w** say, 'A wild beast devoured **Gn 37:20**
see what **w** become of his dreams!" **Gn 37:20**
"Surely I **w** go down to Sheol in **Gn 37:35**
"What **w** you give me, that you may **Gn 38:16**
w send you a young goat from the **Gn 38:17**
"**W** you give a pledge until you **Gn 38:17**
we **w** become a laughingstock. **Gn 38:23**
within three more days Pharaoh **w** **Gn 40:13**
and you **w** put Pharaoh's cup into **Gn 40:13**
Pharaoh **w** lift up your head from **Gn 40:19**
from you and **w** hang you on a tree, **Gn 40:19**
birds **w** eat your flesh off you." **Gn 40:19**
God **w** give Pharaoh a favorable **Gn 41:16**
ears scorched by the east wind **w** be **Gn 41:27**
them seven years of famine **w** come, **Gn 41:30**
and all the abundance **w** be **Gn 41:30**
and the famine **w** ravage the land. **Gn 41:30**
"So the abundance **w** be unknown in **Gn 41:31**
for it **w** *be* very severe. **Gn 41:31**
and God **w** quickly bring it about. **Gn 41:32**
w occur in the land of Egypt, **Gn 41:36**
so that the land **w** not perish during **Gn 41:36**
throne I **w** be greater than you." **Gn 41:40**
by this you **w** be tested: **Gn 42:15**
be verified, and you **w** not die." **Gn 42:20**
'By this I **w** know that you are **Gn 42:33**
I **w** give your brother to you, and **Gn 42:34**
care, and I **w** return him to you." **Gn 42:37**
then you **w** bring my gray hair down **Gn 42:38**

us, we **w** go down and buy you food. **Gn 43:4**
do not send *him*, we **w** not go down; **Gn 43:5**
'You **w** not see my face unless your **Gn 43:5**
with me and we **w** arise and go, **Gn 43:8**
"I myself **w** be surety for him; **Gn 43:9**
so that he **w** release to you your **Gn 43:14**
we also **w** be my lord's slaves." **Gn 44:9**
you **w** not see my face again.' **Gn 44:23**
is with us, then we **w** go down; **Gn 44:26**
you **w** bring my gray hair down to **Gn 44:29**
lad is not *with us*, he **w** die. **Gn 44:31**
Thus your servants **w** bring the **Gn 44:31**
in which there **w** be neither plowing **Gn 45:6**
"There I **w** also provide for you, **Gn 45:11**
and I **w** give you the best of the **Gn 45:18**
of the land of Egypt and you **w** eat **Gn 45:18**
I **w** go and see him before I die." **Gn 45:28**
I **w** make you a great nation there. **Gn 46:3**
"I **w** go down with you to Egypt, **Gn 46:4**
and I **w** also surely bring you up **Gn 46:4**
and Joseph **w** close your eyes." **Gn 46:4**
"I **w** go up and tell Pharaoh, and **Gn 46:31**
tell Pharaoh, and **w** say to him, **Gn 46:31**
and I **w** give you *food* for your **Gn 47:16**
"We **w** not hide from my lord that **Gn 47:18**
our land **w** be slaves to Pharaoh. **Gn 47:19**
and we **w** be Pharaoh's slaves." **Gn 47:25**
"I **w** do as you have said." **Gn 47:30**
I **w** make you fruitful and **Gn 48:4**
I **w** make you a company of peoples, **Gn 48:4**
and **w** give this land to your **Gn 48:4**
he also **w** become a people and he also **Gn 48:19**
a people and he also **w** be great. **Gn 48:19**
"By you Israel **w** pronounce blessing, **Gn 48:20**
to die, but God **w** be with you, **Gn 48:21**
that I may tell you what **w** befall **Gn 49:1**
I **w** disperse them in Jacob, And **Gn 49:7**
"Zebulun **w** dwell at the seashore; **Gn 49:13**
But he **w** raid *at* their heels. **Gn 49:19**
And he **w** yield royal dainties. **Gn 49:20**
then I **w** return.'" **Gn 50:5**
I **w** provide for you and your **Gn 50:21**
but God **w** surely take care of you and **Gn 50:24**
"God **w** surely take care of you, **Gn 50:25**
or else they **w** multiply and in **Ex 1:10**
they **w** also join themselves to those **Ex 1:10**
and nurse him for me and I **w** give **Ex 2:9**
now, and I **w** send you to Pharaoh, **Ex 3:10**
"Certainly I **w** be with you, and **Ex 3:12**
and I **w** say to them, 'The God of **Ex 3:13**
I **w** bring you up out of the affliction **Ex 3:17**
They **w** pay heed to what you say; **Ex 3:18**
w come to the king of Egypt and **Ex 3:18**
of Egypt and you **w** say to him, **Ex 3:18**
of Egypt **w** not permit you to go, **Ex 3:19**
"So I **w** stretch out My hand and **Ex 3:20**
and after that he **w** let you go. **Ex 3:20**
"I **w** grant this people favor **Ex 3:21**
you go, you **w** not go empty-handed. **Ex 3:21**
and you **w** put them on your sons **Ex 3:22**
you **w** plunder the Egyptians." **Ex 3:22**
"What if they **w** not believe me or **Ex 4:1**
If they **w** not believe you or heed the **Ex 4:8**
"But if they **w** not believe **Ex 4:9**
w become blood on the dry ground." **Ex 4:9**
I, even I, **w** be with your mouth, **Ex 4:12**
the message by whomever You **w**." **Ex 4:13** 7971
you, he **w** be glad in his heart. **Ex 4:14**
w be with your mouth and his **Ex 4:15**
I **w** teach you what you are to do. **Ex 4:15**
and he **w** be as a mouth for you **Ex 4:16**
and you **w** be as God to him **Ex 4:16**
but I **w** harden his heart so that **Ex 4:21**
that he **w** not let the people go. **Ex 4:21**
Behold, I **w** kill your son, your **Ex 4:23**
besides, I **w** not let Israel go." **Ex 5:2**
otherwise He **w** fall upon us with **Ex 5:3**
them work at it so that they **w** pay **Ex 5:9**
of your labor **w** be reduced.'" **Ex 5:11**
go now *and* work; for you **w** be **Ex 5:18**
shall see what I **w** do to Pharaoh; **Ex 6:1**
for under compulsion he **w** let them go, **Ex 6:1**
and under compulsion he **w** drive them **Ex 6:1**
and I **w** bring you out from under **Ex 6:6**
and I **w** deliver you from their **Ex 6:6**
I **w** also redeem you with an **Ex 6:6**
'Then I **w** take you for My people, **Ex 6:7**
My people, and I **w** be your God; **Ex 6:7**
'I **w** bring you to the land **Ex 6:8**
and I **w** give it to you *for* a **Ex 6:8**
how then **w** Pharaoh listen to me, **Ex 6:12**
how then **w** Pharaoh listen to me?" **Ex 6:30**
"But I **w** harden Pharaoh's heart **Ex 7:3**
then I **w** lay My hand on Egypt and **Ex 7:4**
I **w** strike the water that is in **Ex 7:17**
and it **w** be turned to blood. **Ex 7:17**
fish that are in the Nile **w** die, **Ex 7:18**
die, and the Nile **w** become foul, **Ex 7:18**
and the Egyptians **w** find **Ex 7:18**
and there **w** be blood throughout all **Ex 7:19**
I **w** smite your whole territory **Ex 8:2**
"The Nile **w** swarm with frogs, **Ex 8:3**
which **w** come up and go into your **Ex 8:3**
"So the frogs **w** come up on you **Ex 8:4**
and I **w** let the people go, that **Ex 8:8**
"The frogs **w** depart from you **Ex 8:11**
they **w** be left only in the Nile." **Ex 8:11**
I **w** send swarms of insects on you **Ex 8:21**
and the houses of the Egyptians **w** be **Ex 8:21**

I **w** set apart the land of Goshen, **Ex 8:22**
no swarms of insects **w** be there, **Ex 8:22**
"I **w** put a division between **Ex 8:23**
Tomorrow this sign **w** occur."'" **Ex 8:23**
for we **w** sacrifice to the LORD **Ex 8:26**
eyes, **w** they not then stone us? **Ex 8:26**
"I **w** let you go, that you may **Ex 8:28**
the hand of the LORD **w** come *with* a **Ex 9:3**
"But the LORD **w** make a **Ex 9:4**
so that nothing **w** die of all that **Ex 9:4**
w do this thing in the land." **Ex 9:5**
"It **w** become fine dust over **Ex 9:9**
and **w** become boils breaking out **Ex 9:9**
"For this time I **w** send all My **Ex 9:14**
I **w** send a very heavy hail, **Ex 9:18**
comes down on them, **w** die. **Ex 9:19**
and I **w** let you go, and you shall **Ex 9:28**
I **w** spread out my hands to the **Ex 9:29**
the thunder **w** cease and there **Ex 9:29**
and there **w** be hail no longer, **Ex 9:29**
'How long **w** you refuse to humble **Ex 10:3**
tomorrow I **w** bring locusts into **Ex 10:4**
so that no one **w** be able to see **Ex 10:5**
They **w** also eat the rest of what has **Ex 10:5**
from the hail—and they **w** eat **Ex 10:5**
"How long **w** this man be a snare to **Ex 10:7**
I **w** bring on Pharaoh and on Egypt; **Ex 11:1**
that he **w** let you go from here. **Ex 11:1**
he **w** surely drive you out from **Ex 11:1**
any of the sons of Israel a dog **w** not **Ex 11:7**
All these your servants **w** come down **Ex 11:8**
you,' and after that I **w** go out." **Ex 11:8**
"Pharaoh **w** not listen to you, so **Ex 11:9**
so that My wonders **w** be multiplied **Ex 11:9**
'For I **w** go through the land of **Ex 12:12**
and **w** strike down all the **Ex 12:12**
gods of Egypt I **w** execute judgments **Ex 12:12**
I see the blood I **w** pass over you, **Ex 12:13**
and no plague **w** befall you to **Ex 12:13**
this day **w** be a memorial to you, **Ex 12:14**
"For the LORD **w** pass through to **Ex 12:23**
the LORD **w** pass over the door and **Ex 12:23**
w not allow the destroyer to come in **Ex 12:23**
land which the LORD **w** give you, **Ex 12:25**
"We **w** all be dead." **Ex 12:33**
"God **w** surely take care of you, **Ex 13:19**
Pharaoh **w** say of the sons of Israel, **Ex 14:3**
"Thus I **w** harden Pharaoh's heart, **Ex 14:4**
heart, and he **w** chase after them; **Ex 14:4**
and I **w** be honored through Pharaoh **Ex 14:4**
w know that I am the LORD." **Ex 14:4**
He **w** accomplish for you today; **Ex 14:13**
w never see them again forever. **Ex 14:13**
"The LORD **w** fight for you while **Ex 14:14**
I **w** harden the hearts of the **Ex 14:17**
so that they **w** go in after them; **Ex 14:17**
and I **w** be honored through Pharaoh **Ex 14:17**
w know that I am the LORD, **Ex 14:18**
"I **w** sing to the LORD, for He is **Ex 15:1**
is my God, and I **w** praise Him; **Ex 15:2**
My father's God, and I **w** extol Him. **Ex 15:2**
'I **w** pursue, I will overtake, I **Ex 15:9**
'I will pursue, I **w** overtake, **Ex 15:9**
overtake, I **w** divide the spoil; **Ex 15:9**
I **w** draw out my sword, my hand **Ex 15:9**
my hand **w** destroy them.' **Ex 15:9**
"You **w** bring them and plant them **Ex 15:17**
"If you **w** give earnest heed to **Ex 15:26**
I **w** put none of the diseases on **Ex 15:26**
I **w** rain bread from heaven for you; **Ex 16:4**
not they **w** walk in My instruction. **Ex 16:4**
it **w** be twice as much as they **Ex 16:5**
"At evening you **w** know that the **Ex 16:6**
you **w** see the glory of the LORD, **Ex 16:7**
Moses said, "*This* **w** *happen* when **Ex 16:8**
Bake what you **w** bake and boil what **Ex 16:23**
bake and boil what you **w** boil, **Ex 16:23**
you **w** not find it in the field. **Ex 16:25**
the sabbath, there **w** be none." **Ex 16:26**
little more and they **w** stone me." **Ex 17:4**
I **w** stand before you there on the **Ex 17:6**
rock, and water **w** come out of it, **Ex 17:6**
Tomorrow I **w** station myself on the **Ex 17:9**
that I **w** utterly blot out the **Ex 17:14**
the LORD **w** have war against Amalek **Ex 17:16**
"You **w** surely wear out, both **Ex 18:18**
"Now listen to me: I **w** give you **Ex 18:19**
major dispute they **w** bring to you, **Ex 18:22**
dispute they themselves **w** judge. **Ex 18:22**
So it **w** be easier for you, and **Ex 18:22**
they **w** bear *the burden* with you. **Ex 18:22**
you, then you **w** be able to endure, **Ex 18:23**
w go to their place in peace." **Ex 18:23**
if you **w** indeed obey My voice and **Ex 19:5**
the LORD has spoken we **w** do!" **Ex 19:8**
I **w** come to you in a thick cloud, so **Ex 19:9**
LORD **w** come down on Mount Sinai **Ex 19:11**
or else the LORD **w** break out **Ex 19:22**
or He **w** break forth upon them." **Ex 19:24**
for the LORD **w** not leave him **Ex 20:7**
to us yourself and we **w** listen; **Ex 20:19**
or we **w** die." **Ex 20:19**
I **w** come to you and bless you. **Ex 20:24**
your tool on it, you **w** profane it. **Ex 20:25**
so that your nakedness **w** not be **Ex 20:26**
I **w** not go out as a free man,' **Ex 21:5**
"If he **w** not do these three **Ex 21:11**
then I **w** appoint you a place to **Ex 21:13**
there **w** be no bloodguiltiness on **Ex 22:2**

there **w** be bloodguiltiness on his Ex 22:3
to Me, I **w** surely hear his cry; Ex 22:23
and My anger **w** be kindled, and I Ex 22:24
and I **w** kill you with the sword, Ex 22:24
he cries out to Me, I **w** hear *him,* Ex 22:27
for I **w** not acquit the guilty. Ex 23:7
w not pardon your transgression, Ex 23:21
then I **w** be an enemy to your Ex 23:22
"For My angel **w** go before you and Ex 23:23
and I **w** completely destroy them. Ex 23:23
and He **w** bless your bread and your Ex 23:25
and I **w** remove sickness from your Ex 23:25
I **w** fulfill the number of your Ex 23:26
"I **w** send My terror ahead of you, Ex 23:27
and I **w** make all your enemies turn Ex 23:27
"I **w** send hornets ahead of Ex 23:28
ahead of you so that they **w** drive Ex 23:28
"I **w** not drive them out before Ex 23:29
"I **w** drive them out before you Ex 23:30
"I **w** fix your boundary from Ex 23:31
for I **w** deliver the inhabitants of Ex 23:31
you **w** drive them out before you. Ex 23:31
because they **w** make you sin against Ex 23:33
it **w** surely be a snare to you." Ex 23:33
the LORD has spoken we **w** do!" Ex 24:3
that the LORD has spoken we **w** do, Ex 24:7
will do, and we **w** be obedient!" Ex 24:7
and I **w** give you the stone tablets Ex 24:12
put the testimony which I **w** give Ex 25:21
"There I **w** meet with you; Ex 25:22
I **w** speak to you about all that I Ex 25:22
speak to you about all that I **w** give Ex 25:22
clasps so that the tabernacle **w** be Ex 26:6
the tent together so that it **w** be Ex 26:11
so that the net **w** reach halfway up Ex 27:5
so that it **w** be on the skillfully Ex 28:28
and that the breastpiece **w** not come Ex 28:28
so that it **w** not be torn. Ex 28:32
so that he **w** not die. Ex 28:35
the LORD, where I **w** meet with you, Ex 29:42
"I **w** meet there with the sons Ex 29:43
"I **w** consecrate the tent of Ex 29:44
I **w** also consecrate Aaron and his Ex 29:44
"I **w** dwell among the sons of Ex 29:45
sons of Israel and **w** be their God. Ex 29:45
where I **w** meet with you. Ex 30:6
so that there **w** be no plague among Ex 30:12
so that they **w** not die; or when they Ex 30:20
so that they **w** not die; and it shall Ex 30:21
in the tent of meeting where I **w** meet Ex 30:36
make us a god who **w** go before us; Ex 32:1
I **w** make of you a great nation." Ex 32:10
"I **w** multiply your descendants as Ex 32:13
I **w** give to your descendants, Ex 32:13
a god for us who **w** go before us; Ex 32:23
"But now, if You **w**, Ex 32:32
Me, I **w** blot him out of My book. Ex 32:33
I **w** punish them for their sin." Ex 32:34
'To your descendants I **w** give it.' Ex 33:1
"I **w** send an angel before you Ex 33:2
and I **w** drive out the Canaanite, Ex 33:2
for I **w** not go up in your midst, Ex 33:3
me know whom You **w** send with me. Ex 33:12
with you, and I **w** give you rest." Ex 33:14
"I **w** also do this thing of which Ex 33:17
"I Myself **w** make all My goodness Ex 33:19
and **w** proclaim the name of the Ex 33:19
and I **w** be gracious to whom I will Ex 33:19
gracious to whom I **w** be gracious, Ex 33:19
and **w** show compassion on whom I Ex 33:19
on whom I **w** show compassion." Ex 33:19
and it **w** come about, while My Ex 33:22
that I **w** put you in the cleft of Ex 33:22
"Then I **w** take My hand away and Ex 33:23
and I **w** write on the tablets the Ex 34:1
yet He **w** by no means leave *the* Ex 34:7
Before all your people I **w** perform Ex 34:10
w see the working of the LORD, Ex 34:10
or it **w** become a snare in your midst. Ex 34:12
"For I **w** drive out nations before Ex 34:24
and their anointing **w** qualify them Ex 40:15
and they **w** be forgiven. Lv 4:20
and he **w** be forgiven. Lv 4:26
and he **w** be forgiven. Lv 4:31
and he **w** be forgiven. Lv 4:35
tell *it,* then he **w** bear his guilt. Lv 5:1
is unclean, then he **w** be guilty. Lv 5:2
comes to know *it,* he **w** be guilty. Lv 5:3
he **w** be guilty in one of these. Lv 5:4
and it **w** be forgiven him. Lv 5:10
and it **w** be forgiven him; then Lv 5:13
and it **w** be forgiven him. Lv 5:16
and it **w** be forgiven him. Lv 5:18
and he **w** be forgiven for any one of Lv 6:7
Whoever touches them **w** become Lv 6:18
"The anointed priest who **w** be Lv 6:22
who touches its flesh **w** become Lv 6:27
he who offers it **w** not be accepted, Lv 7:18
and it **w** not be reckoned to his Lv 7:18
and the person who eats of it **w** bear Lv 7:18
w ordain you through seven days. Lv 8:33
so that you **w** not die, for so I Lv 8:35
for today the LORD **w** appear to Lv 9:4
near Me I **w** be treated as holy, Lv 10:3
all the people I **w** be honored.'" Lv 10:3
so that you **w** not die and that He Lv 10:6
you will not die and that He **w** not Lv 10:6
or you **w** die; for the LORD's Lv 10:7
so that you **w** not die—it is a Lv 10:9

moreover, you **w** be made unclean: Lv 11:24
and she **w** be clean.'" Lv 12:8
then be washed a second time and **w** be Lv 13:58
"It **w** be on the seventh day Lv 14:9
and he **w** be clean. Lv 14:20
and it **w** be clean." Lv 14:53
body in running water and **w** become Lv 15:13
and afterward she **w** be clean. Lv 15:28
so that they **w** not die in their Lv 15:31
or he **w** die; for I will appear in Lv 16:2
for I **w** appear in the cloud over Lv 16:2
otherwise he **w** die. Lv 16:13
you **w** be clean from all your sins Lv 16:30
I **w** set My face against that Lv 17:10
and **w** cut him off from among his Lv 17:10
then he **w** become clean. Lv 17:15
so that the land **w** not spew you out, Lv 18:28
it **w** not be accepted. Lv 19:7
who eats it **w** bear his iniquity, Lv 19:8
the sin which he has committed **w** be Lv 19:22
so that the land **w** not fall to Lv 19:29
'I **w** also set My face against that Lv 20:3
w cut him off from among his people, Lv 20:3
then I Myself **w** set My face Lv 20:5
and I **w** cut off from among their Lv 20:5
I **w** also set My face against that Lv 20:6
w cut him off from among his people. Lv 20:6
so that there **w** be no immorality in Lv 20:14
they **w** bear their guilt. Lv 20:19
they **w** bear their sin. They will die Lv 20:20
They **w** die childless. Lv 20:20
They **w** be childless. Lv 20:21
you to live **w** not spew you out. Lv 20:22
of the nation which I **w** drive Lv 20:23
I Myself **w** give it to you to possess Lv 20:24
so that he **w** not profane his Lv 21:15
so that he **w** not profane My Lv 21:23
'But when the sun sets, he **w** be Lv 22:7
so that they **w** not bear sin because Lv 22:9
for it **w** not be accepted for you. Lv 22:20
but for a vow it **w** not be accepted. Lv 22:23
but I **w** be sanctified among the Lv 22:32
"If there is any person who **w** not Lv 23:29
I **w** destroy from among his people. Lv 23:30
then he **w** bear his sin. Lv 24:15
'Then the land **w** yield its Lv 25:19
then I **w** so order My blessing for Lv 25:21
w bring forth the crop for three years. Lv 25:21
they **w** have produced in your land; Lv 25:45
so that the land **w** yield its Lv 26:4
of the field **w** bear their fruit. Lv 26:4
your threshing **w** last for you Lv 26:5
grape gathering **w** last until sowing Lv 26:5
You **w** thus eat your food to the Lv 26:5
no sword **w** pass through your land. Lv 26:6
'But you **w** chase your enemies and Lv 26:7
w fall before you by the sword; Lv 26:7
five of you **w** chase a hundred, and Lv 26:8
hundred of you **w** chase ten thousand, Lv 26:8
your enemies **w** fall before you by Lv 26:8
'So I **w** turn toward you and make Lv 26:9
I **w** confirm My covenant with you. Lv 26:9
'You **w** eat the old supply and Lv 26:10
I **w** make My dwelling among you, Lv 26:11
you, and My soul **w** not reject you. Lv 26:11
'I **w** also walk among you and be Lv 26:12
I, in turn, **w** do this to you: Lv 26:16
I **w** appoint over you a sudden Lv 26:16
consumption and fever that **w** waste Lv 26:16
you **w** sow your seed uselessly, for Lv 26:16
for your enemies **w** eat it up. Lv 26:16
'I **w** set My face against you Lv 26:17
My face against you so that you **w** be Lv 26:17
and those who hate you **w** rule over Lv 26:17
and you **w** flee when no one is Lv 26:17
then I **w** punish you seven times Lv 26:18
'I **w** also break down your Lv 26:19
I **w** also make your sky like iron Lv 26:19
'Your strength **w** be spent uselessly, Lv 26:20
for your land **w** not yield its produce Lv 26:20
and the trees of the land **w** not Lv 26:20
I **w** increase the plague on you Lv 26:21
'I **w** let loose among you the Lv 26:22
which **w** bereave you of your children Lv 26:22
then I **w** act with hostility Lv 26:24
I, even I, **w** strike you seven times Lv 26:24
'I **w** also bring upon you a sword Lv 26:25
a sword which **w** execute vengeance Lv 26:25
I **w** send pestilence among you, Lv 26:25
w bake your bread in one oven, Lv 26:26
and they **w** bring back your bread Lv 26:26
you **w** eat and not be satisfied. Lv 26:26
then I **w** act with wrathful Lv 26:28
w punish you seven times for your Lv 26:28
'Further, you **w** eat the flesh of Lv 26:29
the flesh of your daughters you **w** eat. Lv 26:29
'I then **w** destroy your high Lv 26:30
'I **w** lay waste your cities as Lv 26:31
and **w** make your sanctuaries Lv 26:31
and I **w** not smell your soothing Lv 26:31
'I **w** make the land desolate so Lv 26:32
your enemies who settle in it **w** be Lv 26:32
I **w** scatter among the nations and Lv 26:33
and **w** draw out a sword after you, Lv 26:33
'Then the land **w** enjoy its Lv 26:34
land **w** rest and enjoy its sabbaths. Lv 26:34
the days of *its* desolation it **w** observe Lv 26:35
I **w** also bring weakness into their Lv 26:36
sound of a driven leaf **w** chase them Lv 26:36

they **w** flee as though from the Lv 26:36
from the sword, and they **w** fall. Lv 26:36
'They **w** therefore stumble over Lv 26:37
and you **w** have *no strength* to Lv 26:37
you **w** perish among the nations, Lv 26:38
your enemies' land **w** consume you. Lv 26:38
those of you who may be left **w** rot Lv 26:39
they **w** rot away with them. Lv 26:39
then I **w** remember My covenant with Lv 26:42
and I **w** remember also My covenant Lv 26:42
well, and I **w** remember the land. Lv 26:42
'For the land **w** be abandoned by them, Lv 26:43
and **w** make up for its sabbaths while Lv 26:43
w be making amends for their iniquity, Lv 26:43
enemies, I **w** not reject them, Lv 26:44
nor **w** I so abhor them as to Lv 26:44
'But I **w** remember for them the Lv 26:45
'Yet if he **w** not redeem the field, Lv 27:20
so that there **w** be no wrath on Nu 1:53
so that they **w** not touch the holy Nu 4:15
or they **w** die." Nu 4:20
so that they **w** not defile their camp Nu 5:3
the water which brings a curse **w** go Nu 5:24
the water which brings a curse **w** go Nu 5:27
and her abdomen **w** swell and her Nu 5:27
swell and her thigh **w** waste away, Nu 5:27
and the woman **w** become a curse Nu 5:27
she **w** then be free and conceive Nu 5:28
'Moreover, the man **w** be free from Nu 5:31
but the former days **w** be void because Nu 6:12
Israel, and I *then* **w** bless them." Nu 6:27
the seven lamps **w** give light in Nu 8:2
and they **w** be clean. Nu 8:7
so that there **w** be no plague among Nu 8:19
and I **w** listen to what the LORD Nu 9:8
LORD **w** command concerning you." Nu 9:8
That man **w** bear his sin. Nu 9:13
'I **w** give it to you'; Nu 10:29
come with us and we **w** do you good, Nu 10:29
"I **w** not come, but rather will go Nu 10:30
but rather **w** go to my *own* land and Nu 10:30
and you **w** be as eyes for us. Nu 10:31
"So it **w** be, if you go with us, Nu 10:32
does for us, we **w** do for you." Nu 10:32
"Who **w** give us meat to eat? Nu 11:4
"Then I **w** come down and speak Nu 11:17
and I **w** take of the Spirit who is Nu 11:17
upon you, and **w** put *Him* upon them; Nu 11:17
so that you **w** not bear *it all* Nu 11:17
Therefore the LORD **w** give you meat Nu 11:18
'I **w** give them meat, so that Nu 11:21
word **w** come true for you or not." Nu 11:23
for we **w** surely overcome it." Nu 13:30
our little ones **w** become plunder; Nu 14:3
then He **w** bring us into this land and Nu 14:8
for they **w** be our prey. Their Nu 14:9
"How long **w** this people spurn Me? Nu 14:11
how long **w** they not believe in Me, Nu 14:11
"I **w** smite them with pestilence Nu 14:12
and I **w** make you into a nation Nu 14:12
"Then the Egyptians **w** hear of it, Nu 14:13
and they **w** tell *it* to the Nu 14:14
who have heard of Your fame **w** say, Nu 14:15
He **w** by no means clear *the guilty,* Nu 14:18
all the earth **w** be filled with the Nu 14:21
I **w** bring into the land which he Nu 14:24
hearing, so I **w** surely do to you; Nu 14:28
your corpses **w** fall in this Nu 14:29
I **w** bring them in, and they will Nu 14:31
and they **w** know the land which you Nu 14:31
as for you, your corpses **w** fall Nu 14:32
and they **w** suffer *for* your Nu 14:33
and you **w** know *My* opposition. Nu 14:34
surely this I **w** do to all this Nu 14:35
and there they **w** die.'" Nu 14:35
but we **w** go up to the place which Nu 14:40
the LORD, when it **w** not succeed? Nu 14:41
"Do not go up, or you **w** be struck Nu 14:42
w be there in front of you, Nu 14:43
you, and you **w** fall by the sword, Nu 14:43
And the LORD **w** not be with you." Nu 14:43
and they **w** be forgiven; for it was Nu 15:25
the sons of Israel **w** be forgiven, Nu 15:26
his guilt **w** *be* on him.'" Nu 15:31
the LORD **w** show who is His, Nu 16:5
and **w** bring *him* near to Himself; Nu 16:5
even the one whom He **w** choose, Nu 16:5
He **w** bring near to Himself. Nu 16:5
"We **w** not come up. Nu 16:12
We **w** not come up!" Nu 16:14
w You be angry with the entire Nu 16:22
or you **w** be swept away in all their Nu 16:26
then you **w** understand that these Nu 16:30
so that he **w** not become like Korah Nu 16:40
"It **w** come about that the rod Nu 17:5
of the man whom I choose **w** sprout. Nu 17:5
Thus I **w** lessen from upon Myself Nu 17:5
so that they **w** not die." Nu 17:10
or both they and you **w** die. Nu 18:3
so that there **w** no longer be wrath on Nu 18:5
or they **w** bear sin and die. Nu 18:22
'You **w** bear no sin by reason of it Nu 18:32
of Israel, or you **w** die.'" Nu 18:32
and then he **w** be clean; but if Nu 19:12
he **w** not be clean. Nu 19:12
We **w** not pass through field or Nu 20:17
we **w** not even drink water from a well. Nu 20:17
We **w** go along the king's highway, Nu 20:17
or I **w** come out with the sword Nu 20:18

“We **w** go up by the highway, and if Nu 20:19
water, then I **w** pay its price. Nu 20:19
“Aaron **w** be gathered to his people; Nu 20:24
Aaron **w** be gathered *to his people,* Nu 20:26
to his people, and **w** die there.” Nu 20:26
“If You **w** indeed deliver this Nu 21:2
w utterly destroy their cities.” Nu 21:2
looks at it, he **w** live.” Nu 21:8
We **w** not turn off into field or Nu 21:22
we **w** not drink water from wells. Nu 21:22
We **w** go by the king’s highway Nu 21:22
w lick up all that is around us, Nu 22:4
and I **w** bring word back to you as Nu 22:8
for I **w** indeed honor you richly, Nu 22:17
and I **w** do whatever you say to me. Nu 22:17
and I **w** find out what else the Nu 22:19
else the LORD **w** speak to me.” Nu 22:19
to you, I **w** turn back.” Nu 22:34
your burnt offering, and I **w** go; Nu 23:3
perhaps the LORD **w** come to meet me Nu 23:3
He shows me I **w** tell you.” Nu 23:3
And **w** not be reckoned among Nu 23:9
although you **w** only see the Nu 23:13
them and **w** not see all of them; Nu 23:13
Has He said, and **w** He not do it? Nu 23:19
spoken, and **w** He not make it good? Nu 23:19
It **w** not lie down until it devours Nu 23:24
I **w** take you to another place; Nu 23:27
perhaps it **w** be agreeable with God Nu 23:27
“Water **w** flow from his buckets, Nu 24:7
And his seed **w** *be* by many waters, Nu 24:7
He **w** devour the nations *who are* Nu 24:8
And **w** crush their bones in pieces, Nu 24:8
the LORD speaks, that I **w** speak’? Nu 24:13
and I **w** advise you what this Nu 24:14
what this people **w** do to your people Nu 24:14
also **w** be a possession, While Israel Nu 24:18
And **w** destroy the remnant from Nu 24:19
“Nevertheless Kain **w** be consumed; Nu 24:22
How long **w** Asshur keep you captive?” Nu 24:22
shall afflict Asshur and **w** afflict Nu 24:24
So they also **w** *come* to Nu 24:24
you have seen it, you too **w** be Nu 27:13
who **w** go out and come in before Nu 27:17
and who **w** lead them out and bring Nu 27:17
congregation of the LORD **w** not Nu 27:17
It **w** be to you a day for blowing Nu 29:1
and the LORD **w** forgive her because Nu 30:5
and the LORD **w** forgive her. Nu 30:8
them, and the LORD **w** forgive her. Nu 30:12
w be gathered to your people.” Nu 31:2
He **w** once more abandon them in the Nu 32:15
you **w** destroy all these people.” Nu 32:15
“We **w** build here sheepfolds for Nu 32:16
but we ourselves **w** be armed ready Nu 32:17
“We **w** not return to our homes Nu 32:18
“For we **w** not have an inheritance Nu 32:19
“If you **w** do this, if you will Nu 32:20
if you **w** arm yourselves before the Nu 32:20
“But if you **w** not do so, behold, Nu 32:23
be sure your sin **w** find you out. Nu 32:23
w do just as my lord commands. Nu 32:25
w cross over in the presence of Nu 32:27
w cross with you over the Jordan Nu 32:29
w not cross over with you armed, Nu 32:30
said to your servants, so we **w** do. Nu 32:31
“We ourselves **w** cross over armed Nu 32:32
you let remain of them **w** *become* Nu 33:55
and they **w** trouble you in the land in Nu 33:55
do to them, so I **w** do to you.’ Nu 33:56
so that the manslayer **w** not die until Nu 35:12
by which he **w** die, and *as a result* Nu 35:17
he **w** not be guilty of blood Nu 35:27
their inheritance **w** be withdrawn Nu 36:3
and **w** be added to the inheritance of Nu 36:3
thus it **w** be withdrawn from our Nu 36:3
then their inheritance **w** be added Nu 36:4
so their inheritance **w** be Nu 36:4
I **w** appoint them as your heads.’ Dt 1:13
bring to me, and I **w** hear it.’ Dt 1:17
w Himself fight on your behalf, Dt 1:30
and to his sons I **w** give the land Dt 1:36
for he **w** cause Israel to inherit it. Dt 1:38
there, and I **w** give it to them and Dt 1:39
we **w** indeed go up and fight, just Dt 1:41
otherwise you **w** be defeated before Dt 1:42
“You **w** pass through the territory Dt 2:4
and they **w** be afraid of you. Dt 2:4
for I **w** not give you any of their Dt 2:5
for I **w** not give you any of their Dt 2:9
for I **w** not give you any of the Dt 2:19
‘This day I **w** begin to put the Dt 2:25
w tremble and be in anguish because Dt 2:25
I **w** travel only on the highway; Dt 2:27
I **w** not turn aside to the right or Dt 2:27
‘You **w** sell me food for money so Dt 2:28
God **w** give them beyond the Jordan. Dt 3:20
and he **w** give them as an inheritance Dt 3:28
the land which you **w** see.’ Dt 3:28
peoples who **w** hear all these statutes Dt 4:6
“For I **w** die in this land, I shall Dt 4:22
that you **w** surely perish quickly from Dt 4:26
but **w** be utterly destroyed. Dt 4:26
w scatter you among the peoples, Dt 4:27
and you **w** be left few in number among Dt 4:27
“There you **w** serve gods, the Dt 4:28
you **w** seek the LORD your God, Dt 4:29
and you **w** find *Him* if you search Dt 4:29
you **w** return to the LORD your God Dt 4:30
He **w** not fail you nor destroy you Dt 4:31
for the LORD **w** not leave him Dt 5:11
For this great fire **w** consume us; Dt 5:25
longer, then we **w** die. Dt 5:25
to you, and we **w** hear and do *it.’* Dt 5:27
your days in the land which you **w** Dt 5:33
anger of the LORD your God **w** be Dt 6:15
and He **w** wipe you off the face of Dt 6:15
“It **w** be righteousness for us Dt 6:25
“For they **w** turn your sons away Dt 7:4
the anger of the LORD **w** be kindled Dt 7:4
you and He **w** quickly destroy you. Dt 7:4
He **w** not delay with him who hates Dt 7:10
Him, He **w** repay him to his face. Dt 7:10
that the LORD your God **w** keep with Dt 7:12
“He **w** love you and bless you Dt 7:13
He **w** also bless the fruit of your Dt 7:13
there **w** be no male or female barren Dt 7:14
w remove from you all sickness; Dt 7:15
and He **w** not put on you any of the Dt 7:15
He **w** lay them on all who hate you. Dt 7:15
LORD your God **w** deliver to you; Dt 7:16
w send the hornet against them, Dt 7:20
“The LORD your God **w** clear Dt 7:22
you **w** not be able to put an end to Dt 7:22
“But the LORD your God **w** deliver Dt 7:23
and **w** throw them into great Dt 7:23
“He **w** deliver their kings Dt 7:24
into your hand so that you **w** make Dt 7:24
no man **w** be able to stand before Dt 7:24
or you **w** be snared by it, for it is Dt 7:25
a land where you **w** eat food without Dt 8:9
in which you **w** not lack anything; Dt 8:9
then your heart **w** become proud Dt 8:14
become proud and you **w** forget Dt 8:14
against you today that you **w** surely Dt 8:19
He **w** destroy them and He will Dt 9:3
and He **w** subdue them before you, Dt 9:3
and I **w** make of you a nation Dt 9:14
‘I **w** write on the tablets the Dt 10:2
that He **w** give the rain for your Dt 11:14
“He **w** give grass in your Dt 11:15
and you **w** eat and be satisfied. Dt 11:15
anger of the LORD **w** be kindled Dt 11:17
and He **w** shut up the heavens so Dt 11:17
there **w** be no rain and the ground Dt 11:17
the ground **w** not yield its fruit; Dt 11:17
and you **w** perish quickly from the Dt 11:17
then the LORD **w** drive out all Dt 11:23
and you **w** dispossess nations Dt 11:23
your border **w** be from the wilderness Dt 11:24
“No man **w** be able to stand before Dt 11:25
the LORD your God **w** lay the dread Dt 11:25
the LORD your God **w** choose Dt 12:5
the LORD your God **w** choose Dt 12:11
which you **w** vow to the LORD. Dt 12:11
which the LORD your God **w** choose, Dt 12:18
‘I **w** eat meat,’ because you desire Dt 12:20
so you **w** eat it; the unclean Dt 12:22
for you **w** be doing what is right Dt 12:25
for you **w** be doing what is good Dt 12:28
all Israel **w** hear and be afraid, Dt 13:11
and **w** never again do such a wicked Dt 13:11
if you **w** listen to the voice of Dt 13:18
“However, there **w** be no poor among Dt 15:4
since the LORD **w** surely bless you Dt 15:4
“For the LORD your God **w** bless Dt 15:6
and you **w** lend to many nations, Dt 15:6
nations, but you **w** not borrow; Dt 15:6
and you **w** rule over many nations, Dt 15:6
but they **w** not rule over you. Dt 15:6
you, and it **w** be a sin in you. Dt 15:9
God **w** bless you in all your work Dt 15:10
poor **w** never cease *to be* in the land; Dt 15:11
‘I **w** not go out from you,’ because Dt 15:16
the LORD your God **w** bless you in Dt 15:18
because the LORD your God **w** bless Dt 16:15
so that you **w** be altogether joyful. Dt 16:15
and they **w** declare to you the Dt 17:9
the people **w** hear and be afraid, Dt 17:13
w not act presumptuously again. Dt 17:13
‘I **w** set a king over me like all Dt 17:14
or else his heart **w** turn away; nor Dt 17:17
God **w** drive them out before you. Dt 18:12
“The LORD your God **w** raise up for Dt 18:15
anymore, or I **w** die.’ Dt 18:16
‘I **w** raise up a prophet from among Dt 18:18
and I **w** put My words in his mouth, Dt 18:18
whoever **w** not listen to My words Dt 18:19
I Myself **w** require *it* of him. Dt 18:19
may say in your heart, ‘How **w** we Dt 18:21
God **w** give you as a possession, Dt 19:3
“So innocent blood **w** not be shed Dt 19:10
in your inheritance which you **w** Dt 19:14
who **w** be *in office* in those days. Dt 19:17
“The rest **w** hear and be Dt 19:20
and **w** never again do such an evil Dt 19:20
and rebellious son who **w** not obey Dt 21:18
him, he **w** not even listen to them, Dt 21:18
and rebellious, he **w** not obey us, Dt 21:20
and all Israel **w** hear *of it* Dt 21:21
so that you **w** not bring bloodguilt on Dt 22:8
increase of the vineyard **w** become Dt 22:9
his father’s wife so that he **w** not Dt 22:30
indecent among you or He **w** turn Dt 23:14
God **w** surely require it of you. Dt 23:21
and it **w** be righteousness for you Dt 24:13
so that he **w** not cry against you to Dt 24:15
so that his name **w** not be blotted out Dt 25:6
and that He **w** set you high above all Dt 26:19
the LORD your God **w** set you high Dt 28:1
“All these blessings **w** come upon you Dt 28:2
they **w** come out against you one way Dt 28:7
out against you one way and **w** flee Dt 28:7
“The LORD **w** command the blessing Dt 28:8
and He **w** bless you in the land Dt 28:8
“The LORD **w** establish you as a Dt 28:9
all the peoples of the earth **w** see Dt 28:10
and they **w** be afraid of you. Dt 28:10
w make you abound in prosperity, Dt 28:11
“The LORD **w** open for you His good Dt 28:12
“The LORD **w** make you the head Dt 28:13
and you only **w** be above, and you Dt 28:13
and you **w** not be underneath, if you Dt 28:13
that all these curses **w** come upon you Dt 28:15
“The LORD **w** send upon you curses, Dt 28:20
“The LORD **w** make the pestilence Dt 28:21
“The LORD **w** smite you with Dt 28:22
and they **w** pursue you until you Dt 28:22
“The LORD **w** make the rain of your Dt 28:24
you **w** go out one way against them, Dt 28:25
but you **w** flee seven ways before them, Dt 28:25
and you **w** be *an example of* terror Dt 28:25
“Your carcasses **w** be food to all Dt 28:26
and there **w** be no one to frighten Dt 28:26
“The LORD **w** smite you with the Dt 28:27
“The LORD **w** smite you with Dt 28:28
and you **w** grope at noon, as Dt 28:29
and you **w** not prosper in your ways; Dt 28:29
but another man **w** violate her; Dt 28:30
but you **w** not live in it; Dt 28:30
but you **w** not use its fruit. Dt 28:30
but you **w** not eat of it; Dt 28:31
and **w** not be restored to you; Dt 28:31
and you **w** have none to save you. Dt 28:31
but there **w** be nothing you can do. Dt 28:32
and you **w** never be anything but Dt 28:33
“The LORD **w** strike you on the Dt 28:35
LORD **w** bring you and your king, Dt 28:36
seed to the field but you **w** gather Dt 28:38
for the locust **w** consume it. Dt 28:38
but you **w** neither drink of the wine Dt 28:39
for the worm **w** devour them. Dt 28:39
your territory but you **w** not Dt 28:40
for your olives **w** drop off. Dt 28:40
sons and daughters but they **w** not Dt 28:41
for they **w** go into captivity. Dt 28:41
but you **w** go down lower and lower. Dt 28:43
shall lend to you, but you **w** not Dt 28:44
and you **w** be the tail. Dt 28:44
your enemies whom the LORD **w** send Dt 28:48
and He **w** put an iron yoke on your Dt 28:48
“The LORD **w** bring a nation Dt 28:49
of fierce countenance who **w** have Dt 28:50
by which your enemy **w** oppress Dt 28:53
so that he **w** not give *even* one of Dt 28:55
flesh of his children which he **w** eat, Dt 28:55
by which your enemy **w** oppress Dt 28:55
for she **w** eat them secretly for lack Dt 28:57
by which your enemy **w** oppress Dt 28:57
then the LORD **w** bring Dt 28:59
“He **w** bring back on you all Dt 28:60
and they **w** cling to you. Dt 28:60
the LORD **w** bring on you until you Dt 28:61
so the LORD **w** delight over you to Dt 28:63
and you **w** be torn from the land where Dt 28:63
w scatter you among all peoples, Dt 28:64
and there **w** be no resting place for Dt 28:65
LORD **w** give you a trembling heart, Dt 28:65
and you **w** be in dread night and day, Dt 28:66
sight of your eyes which you **w** see. Dt 28:67
“The LORD **w** bring you back to Dt 28:68
‘You **w** never see it again!’ Dt 28:68
And there you **w** offer yourselves Dt 28:68
slaves, but there **w** be no buyer.” Dt 28:68
so that there **w** not be among you a Dt 29:18
that there **w** not be among you a root Dt 29:18
of this curse, that he **w** boast, Dt 29:19
jealousy **w** burn against that man, Dt 29:20
in this book **w** rest on him, Dt 29:20
and the LORD **w** blot out his name Dt 29:20
“Then the LORD **w** single him out Dt 29:21
the LORD has afflicted it, **w** say, Dt 29:22
“All the nations **w** say, ‘Why has Dt 29:24
“Then *men* **w** say, ‘Because they Dt 29:25
God **w** restore you from captivity, Dt 30:3
and **w** gather you again from all Dt 30:3
the LORD your God **w** gather you, Dt 30:4
from there He **w** bring you back. Dt 30:4
“The LORD your God **w** bring Dt 30:5
and He **w** prosper you and multiply Dt 30:5
your God **w** circumcise your heart Dt 30:6
“The LORD your God **w** inflict Dt 30:7
“Then the LORD your God **w** prosper Dt 30:9
for the LORD **w** again rejoice over Dt 30:9
‘Who **w** go up to heaven for us to Dt 30:12
‘Who **w** cross the sea for us to get Dt 30:13
turns away and you **w** not obey, Dt 30:17
You **w** not prolong *your* days in Dt 30:18
your God who **w** cross ahead of you; Dt 31:3
He **w** destroy these nations before Dt 31:3
the one who **w** cross ahead of you, Dt 31:3
“The LORD **w** do to them just Dt 31:4
LORD **w** deliver them up before you, Dt 31:5
w not fail you or forsake you.” Dt 31:6
He **w** be with you. Dt 31:8
He **w** not fail you or forsake you. Dt 31:8
at the place which He **w** choose, Dt 31:11

w hear and learn to fear the LORD Dt 31:13
and this people **w** arise and play Dt 31:16
and **w** forsake Me and break My Dt 31:16
"Then My anger **w** be kindled Dt 31:17
and I **w** forsake them and hide My Dt 31:17
and they **w** be consumed, and many Dt 31:17
and many evils and troubles **w** come Dt 31:17
so that they **w** say in that day, Dt 31:17
"But I **w** surely hide My face in Dt 31:18
of all the evil which they **w** do, Dt 31:18
do, for they **w** turn to other gods. Dt 31:18
then they **w** turn to other gods and Dt 31:20
that this song **w** testify before Dt 31:21
to them, and I **w** be with you." Dt 31:23
after my death you **w** act corruptly Dt 31:29
evil **w** befall you in the latter days, Dt 31:29
for you **w** do that which is evil in Dt 31:29
your father, and he **w** inform you, Dt 32:7
Your elders, and they **w** tell you. Dt 32:7
'I **w** hide My face from them, I Dt 32:20
I **w** see what their end *shall be;* Dt 32:20
So I **w** make them jealous with Dt 32:21
I **w** provoke them to anger with a Dt 32:21
'I **w** heap misfortunes on them; Dt 32:23
I **w** use My arrows on them. Dt 32:23
'They **w** *be* wasted by famine, Dt 32:24
of beasts I **w** send upon them, Dt 32:24
'Outside the sword **w** bereave, Dt 32:25
"I **w** cut them to pieces, I will Dt 32:26
I **w** remove the memory of them from Dt 32:26
In due time their foot **w** slip; Dt 32:35
the LORD **w** vindicate His people, Dt 32:36
And **w** have compassion on His Dt 32:36
And He **w** say, 'Where are their gods Dt 32:37
I **w** render vengeance on My Dt 32:41
And I **w** repay those who hate Me. Dt 32:41
'I **w** make My arrows drunk with Dt 32:42
And My sword **w** devour flesh, Dt 32:42
For He **w** avenge the blood of His Dt 32:43
And **w** render vengeance on His Dt 32:43
And **w** atone for His land *and* His Dt 32:43
And by this word you **w** prolong your Dt 32:47
so that they **w** not rise *again.*" Dt 33:11
With them he **w** push the peoples, All Dt 33:17
"They **w** call peoples *to* Dt 33:19
There they **w** offer righteous Dt 33:19
For they **w** draw out the abundance of Dt 33:19
"Your locks **w** be iron and bronze, Dt 33:25
so **w** your leisurely walk be. Dt 33:25
So your enemies **w** cringe before you, Dt 33:29
And you **w** tread upon their high Dt 33:29
'I **w** give it to your descendants'; Dt 34:4
of the sun **w** be your territory. Jos 1:4
"No man **w** *be able to* stand before Jos 1:5
been with Moses, I **w** be with you; Jos 1:5
I **w** not fail you or forsake you. Jos 1:5
you **w** make your way prosperous, Jos 1:8
and then you **w** have success. Jos 1:8
rest and **w** give you this land.' Jos 1:13
you have commanded us we **w** do, Jos 1:16
and wherever you send us we **w** go. Jos 1:16
in all things, so we **w** obey you; Jos 1:17
for you **w** overtake them." Jos 2:5
that you also **w** deal kindly with Jos 2:12
we **w** deal kindly and faithfully with Jos 2:14
so that the pursuers **w** not happen Jos 2:16
the LORD **w** do wonders among you." Jos 3:5
"This day I **w** begin to exalt you Jos 3:7
been with Moses, I **w** be with you. Jos 3:7
and that He **w** assuredly dispossess Jos 3:10
the waters of the Jordan **w** be cut off, Jos 3:13
are flowing down from above **w** stand Jos 3:13
where you **w** lodge tonight.' " Jos 4:3
wall of the city **w** fall down flat, Jos 6:5
and the people **w** go up every man Jos 6:5
of the land **w** hear of it, Jos 7:9
and they **w** surround us and cut off Jos 7:9
w You do for Your great name?" Jos 7:9
I **w** not be with you anymore unless Jos 7:12
The LORD **w** trouble you this day." Jos 7:25
are with me **w** approach the city. Jos 8:5
first, we **w** flee before them. Jos 8:5
"They **w** come out after us Jos 8:6
from the city, for they **w** say, Jos 8:6
So we **w** flee before them. Jos 8:6
God **w** deliver it into your hand. Jos 8:7
"Then it **w** be when you have Jos 8:8
for I **w** give it into your hand." Jos 8:18
"This we **w** do to them, even let Jos 9:20
so that wrath **w** not be upon us for Jos 9:20
for thus the LORD **w** do to all your Jos 10:25
for tomorrow at this time I **w** Jos 11:6
I **w** drive them out from before the Jos 13:6
on which your foot has trodden **w** be Jos 14:9
perhaps the LORD **w** be with me, Jos 14:12
and I **w** drive them out as the LORD Jos 14:12
I **w** give him Achsah my daughter as Jos 15:16
"How long **w** you put off entering Jos 18:3
I **w** cast lots for you here Jos 18:6
then I **w** cast lots for you here Jos 18:8
He **w** be angry with the whole Jos 22:18
so that your sons **w** not say to our Jos 22:27
"The LORD your God, He **w** thrust Jos 23:5
and you **w** possess their land, just Jos 23:5
so that you **w** not associate with Jos 23:7
the LORD your God **w** not continue to Jos 23:13
but they **w** be a snare and a trap to Jos 23:13
so the LORD **w** bring upon you all Jos 23:15
then the anger of the LORD **w** burn Jos 23:16
and you **w** perish quickly from off Jos 23:16
yourselves today whom you **w** serve: Jos 24:15
my house, we **w** serve the LORD." Jos 24:15
We also **w** serve the LORD, for He Jos 24:18
w not be able to serve the LORD, Jos 24:19
He **w** not forgive your Jos 24:19
then He **w** turn and do you harm and Jos 24:20
"No, but we **w** serve the LORD." Jos 24:21
"We **w** serve the LORD our God and Jos 24:24
our God and we **w** obey His voice." Jos 24:24
and I in turn **w** go with you into Jg 1:3
I **w** even give him my daughter Jg 1:12
city and we **w** treat you kindly." Jg 1:24
'I **w** never break My covenant with Jg 2:1
'I **w** not drive them out before you; Jg 2:3
but they **w** become *as thorns* in Jg 2:3
in your sides and their gods **w** be a Jg 2:3
I also **w** no longer drive out Jg 2:21
whether they **w** keep the way of the Jg 2:22
'I **w** draw out to you Sisera, Jg 4:7
I **w** give him into your hand.' " Jg 4:7
"If you **w** go with me, then I will Jg 4:8
you will go with me, then I **w** go; Jg 4:8
but if you **w** not go with me, I Jg 4:8
will not go with me, I **w** not go." Jg 4:8
"I **w** surely go with you; Jg 4:9
for the LORD **w** sell Sisera into Jg 4:9
and I **w** show you the man whom you Jg 4:22
I **w** sing, I will sing praise to the Jg 5:3
sing, I **w** sing praise to the LORD, Jg 5:3
"Surely I **w** be with you, and you Jg 6:16
"I **w** remain until you return." Jg 6:18
"**W** you contend for Baal, or will Jg 6:31
for Baal, or **w** you deliver him? Jg 6:31
Whoever **w** plead for him shall be Jg 6:31
You **w** deliver Israel through me, Jg 6:36 3426
I **w** put a fleece of wool on the Jg 6:37
then I **w** know that You will Jg 6:37
You **w** deliver Israel through me, Jg 6:37
and I **w** test them for you there. Jg 7:4
"I **w** deliver you with the 300 men Jg 7:7
w give the Midianites into your hands Jg 7:7
and you **w** hear what they say; Jg 7:11
your hands **w** be strengthened Jg 7:11
then I **w** thrash your bodies with Jg 8:7
I **w** tear down this tower." Jg 8:9
"I **w** not rule over you, nor shall Jg 8:23
"We **w** surely give *them.*" Jg 8:25
so that it **w** not be said of me, Jg 9:54
therefore I **w** no longer deliver you. Jg 10:13
"Who is the man who **w** begin to Jg 10:18
up to me, **w** I become your head?" Jg 11:9
surely we **w** do as you have said." Jg 11:10
out before us, we **w** possess it. Jg 11:24
"If You **w** indeed give the sons Jg 11:30
and I **w** offer it up as a burnt Jg 11:31
w burn your house down on you." Jg 12:1
detain me, I **w** not eat your food, Jg 13:16
said to his wife, "We **w** surely Jg 13:22
if you **w** indeed tell it to me Jg 14:12
then I **w** give you thirty linen Jg 14:12
so that he **w** tell us the riddle, Jg 14:15
or we **w** burn you and your father's Jg 14:15
w go in to my wife in *her* room." Jg 15:1
I **w** surely take revenge on you, Jg 15:7
on you, but after that I **w** quit." Jg 15:7
to me that you **w** not kill me." Jg 15:12
but we **w** bind you fast and give Jg 15:13
yet surely we **w** not kill you." Jg 15:13
light, then we **w** kill him." Jg 16:2
Then we **w** each give you eleven Jg 16:5
then I **w** become weak and be like any Jg 16:7
then I **w** become weak and be like any Jg 16:11
then I **w** become weak and be like any Jg 16:13
then my strength **w** leave me and I Jg 16:17
will leave me and I **w** become Jg 16:17
"I **w** go out as at other times and Jg 16:20
I **w** return them to you." Jg 17:3
and I **w** give you ten *pieces* of Jg 17:10
I know that the LORD **w** prosper me, Jg 17:13
we are going **w** be prosperous." Jg 18:5
And **w** you sit still? Jg 18:9
"When you enter, you **w** come to a Jg 18:10
or else fierce men **w** fall upon you Jg 18:25
men will fall upon you and you **w** lose Jg 18:25
"We **w** not turn aside into the Jg 19:12
but we **w** go on as far as Gibeah." Jg 19:12
and we **w** spend the night in Gibeah Jg 19:13
no man **w** take me into his house. Jg 19:18
"Not one of us **w** go to his tent, Jg 20:8
w any of us return to his house. Jg 20:8
the thing which we **w** do to Gibeah; Jg 20:9
we **w** *go up* against it by lot. Jg 20:9
"And we **w** take 10 men out of 100 Jg 20:10
I **w** deliver them into your hand." Jg 20:28
so that a tribe **w** not be blotted out Jg 21:17
but we **w** surely return with you to Ru 1:10
for where you go, I **w** go, Ru 1:16
and where you lodge, I **w** lodge. Ru 1:16
"Where you die, I **w** die, Ru 1:17
will die, and there I **w** be buried. Ru 1:17
he **w** tell you what you shall do." Ru 3:4
"All that you say I **w** do." Ru 3:5
I **w** do for you whatever you ask, Ru 3:11
morning comes, if he **w** redeem you, Ru 3:13
redeem you, then I **w** redeem you, Ru 3:13
for the man **w** not rest until he Ru 3:18
If you **w** redeem *it,* redeem *it;* Ru 4:4
And he said, "I **w** redeem *it.*" Ru 4:4
the name of the deceased **w** not Ru 4:10
which the LORD **w** give Ru 4:12
if You **w** indeed look on the 1Sa 1:11
but **w** give Your maidservant a son, 1Sa 1:11
then I **w** give him to the LORD all 1Sa 1:11
long **w** you make yourself drunk? 1Sa 1:14
"I **w** *not go up* until the child 1Sa 1:22
then I **w** bring him, that he may 1Sa 1:22
with the LORD **w** be shattered; 1Sa 2:10
them He **w** thunder in the heavens, 1Sa 2:10
LORD **w** judge the ends of the earth; 1Sa 2:10
He **w** give strength to His king, 1Sa 2:10
And **w** exalt the horn of His 1Sa 2:10
w not take boiled meat from you, 1Sa 2:15
if not, I **w** take it by force." 1Sa 2:16
another, God **w** mediate for him; 1Sa 2:25
those who honor Me I **w** honor, 1Sa 2:30
despise Me **w** be lightly esteemed. 1Sa 2:30
the days are coming when I **w** break 1Sa 2:31
so that there **w** not be an old man in 1Sa 2:31
'You **w** see the distress of *My* 1Sa 2:32
an old man **w** not be in your house 1Sa 2:32
'Yet I **w** not cut off every man of 1Sa 2:33
My altar so that your eyes **w** fail 1Sa 2:33
house **w** die in the prime of life. 1Sa 2:33
'This **w** be the sign to you 1Sa 2:34
will be the sign to you which **w** come 1Sa 2:34
on the same day both of them **w** die. 1Sa 2:34
'But I **w** raise up for Myself a 1Sa 2:35
a faithful priest who **w** do according 1Sa 2:35
I **w** build him an enduring house, 1Sa 2:35
and he **w** walk before My anointed 1Sa 2:35
who is left in your house **w** come 1Sa 2:36
of everyone who hears it **w** tingle. 1Sa 3:11
"In that day I **w** carry out 1Sa 3:12
w become slaves to the Hebrews, 1Sa 4:9
so that it **w** not kill us and our 1Sa 5:11
Then you **w** be healed and it will be 1Sa 6:3
Then you will be healed and it **w** be 1Sa 6:3
He **w** ease His hand from you, 1Sa 6:5
then we **w** know that it was not His 1Sa 6:9
and He **w** deliver you from the hand 1Sa 7:3
I **w** pray to the LORD for you." 1Sa 7:5
the king who **w** reign over them." 1Sa 8:9
"This **w** be the procedure of the 1Sa 8:11
of the king who **w** reign over you: 1Sa 8:11
he **w** take your sons and place *them* 1Sa 8:11
they **w** run before his chariots. 1Sa 8:11
"He **w** appoint for himself 1Sa 8:12
"He **w** also take your daughters 1Sa 8:13
"He **w** take the best of your 1Sa 8:14
"He **w** take a tenth of your 1Sa 8:15
"He **w** also take your male 1Sa 8:16
"He **w** take a tenth of your 1Sa 8:17
yourselves **w** become his servants. 1Sa 8:17
"Then you **w** cry out in that day 1Sa 8:18
LORD **w** not answer you in that day. 1Sa 8:18
or else my father **w** cease *to be* 1Sa 9:5
concerned about the donkeys and **w** 1Sa 9:5
I **w** give *it* to the man of God and 1Sa 9:8
of God and he **w** tell us our way." 1Sa 9:8
as you enter the city you **w** find him 1Sa 9:13
people **w** not eat until he comes, 1Sa 9:13
those who are invited **w** eat. 1Sa 9:13
up for you **w** find him at once." 1Sa 9:13
I **w** send you a man from the land 1Sa 9:16
and he **w** deliver My people from 1Sa 9:16
and in the morning I **w** let you go, 1Sa 9:19
and **w** tell you all that is on your 1Sa 9:19
then you **w** find two men close to 1Sa 10:2
and they **w** say to you, 1Sa 10:2
you **w** go on further from there, 1Sa 10:3
and you **w** come as far as the oak 1Sa 10:3
up to God at Bethel **w** meet you, 1Sa 10:3
and they **w** greet you and give you 1Sa 10:4
you **w** accept from their hand. 1Sa 10:4
"Afterward you **w** come to the hill 1Sa 10:5
that you **w** meet a group of 1Sa 10:5
them, and they **w** be prophesying. 1Sa 10:5
the LORD **w** come upon you mightily, 1Sa 10:6
I **w** come down to you to offer 1Sa 10:8
with us and we **w** serve you." 1Sa 11:1
"I **w** make *it* with you on this 1Sa 11:2
that I **w** gouge out the right eye 1Sa 11:2
thus I **w** make it a reproach on all 1Sa 11:2
us, we **w** come out to you." 1Sa 11:3
you **w** have deliverance.' " So 1Sa 11:9
'Tomorrow we **w** come out to you, 1Sa 11:10
I **w** restore *it* to you." 1Sa 12:3
our enemies, and we **w** serve You.' 1Sa 12:10
you **w** fear the LORD and serve Him, 1Sa 12:14
you **w** follow the LORD your God. 1Sa 12:14
"If you **w** not listen to the 1Sa 12:15
hand of the LORD **w** be against you, 1Sa 12:15
the LORD **w** do before your eyes. 1Sa 12:16
I **w** call to the LORD, that He may 1Sa 12:17
Then you **w** know and see that your 1Sa 12:17
"For the LORD **w** not abandon His 1Sa 12:22
but I **w** instruct you in the good 1Sa 12:23
both you and your king **w** be swept 1Sa 12:25
'Now the Philistines **w** come down 1Sa 13:12
the Hebrews **w** make swords 1Sa 13:19
perhaps the LORD **w** work for us, 1Sa 14:6
we **w** cross over to the men and 1Sa 14:8
then we **w** stand in our place and 1Sa 14:9
'Come up to us,' then we **w** go up, 1Sa 14:10
us and we **w** tell you something." 1Sa 14:12
W You give them into the hand of 1Sa 14:37
my son **w** be on the other side." 1Sa 14:40

'I w punish Amalek *for* what he did 1Sa 15:2
"I w not return with you; 1Sa 15:26
w not lie or change His mind; 1Sa 15:29
"How long w you grieve over Saul, 1Sa 16:1
I w send you to Jesse the 1Sa 16:1
Saul hears *of it,* he w kill me." 1Sa 16:2
I w show you what you shall do; 1Sa 16:3
for we w not sit down until he 1Sa 16:11
his hand, and you w be well." 1Sa 16:16
then we w become your servants; 1Sa 17:9
And it w be that the king will 1Sa 17:25
the king w enrich the man who kills 1Sa 17:25
w give him his daughter and make his 1Sa 17:25
"What w be done for the man who 1Sa 17:26
"Thus it w be done for the man 1Sa 17:27
your servant w go and fight with 1Sa 17:32
Philistine w be like one of them, 1Sa 17:36
He w deliver me from the hand of 1Sa 17:37
and I w give your flesh to the 1Sa 17:44
w deliver you up into my hands, 1Sa 17:46
and I w strike you down and remove 1Sa 17:46
And I w give the dead bodies of 1Sa 17:46
He w give you into our hands." 1Sa 17:47
"I w pin David to the wall." 1Sa 18:11
I w give her to you as a wife, 1Sa 18:17
"I w give her to him that she may 1Sa 18:21
"I w go out and stand beside 1Sa 19:3
and I w speak with my father about 1Sa 19:3
then I w tell you." 1Sa 19:3
Why then w you sin against 1Sa 19:5
tomorrow you w be put to death." 1Sa 19:11
or he w be grieved.' But truly as 1Sa 20:3
you say, I w do for you." 1Sa 20:4
your servant w *be* safe; but if 1Sa 20:7
"Who w tell me if your father 1Sa 20:10
w you not show me the 1Sa 20:14
and you w be missed because your 1Sa 20:18
because your seat w be empty. 1Sa 20:18
"I w shoot three arrows to 1Sa 20:20
"And behold, I w send the lad, 1Sa 20:21
nor your kingdom w be established. 1Sa 20:31
'The LORD w be between me and you, 1Sa 20:42
today w their vessels *be holy?*" 1Sa 21:5
I know what God w do for me." 1Sa 22:3
W the son of Jesse also give to 1Sa 22:7
W he make you all commanders of 1Sa 22:7
for I w give the Philistines into 1Sa 23:4
"W the men of Keilah surrender me 1Sa 23:11
W Saul come down just as Your 1Sa 23:11
"He w come down." 1Sa 23:11
"W the men of Keilah surrender me 1Sa 23:12
"They w surrender you." 1Sa 23:12
the hand of Saul my father w not 1Sa 23:17
and you w be king over Israel and 1Sa 23:17
Israel and I w be next to you; 1Sa 23:17
certainty, and I w go with you; 1Sa 23:23
I w search him out among all the 1Sa 23:23
'I w not stretch out my hand 1Sa 24:10
w he let him go away safely? 1Sa 24:19
"Now, behold, I know that you w 1Sa 24:20
and that the kingdom of Israel w be 1Sa 24:20
that you w not cut off my descendants 1Sa 24:21
and that you w not destroy my name 1Sa 24:21
young men and they w tell you. 1Sa 25:8
for the LORD w certainly make for 1Sa 25:28
and evil w not be found in you all 1Sa 25:28
lives of your enemies He w sling out 1Sa 25:29
this w not cause grief or a 1Sa 25:31
"Who w go down with me to Saul in 1Sa 26:6
"I w go down with you." 1Sa 26:6
and I w not strike him the second 1Sa 26:8
surely the LORD w strike him, 1Sa 26:10
or his day w come that he dies, 1Sa 26:10
or he w go down into battle and 1Sa 26:10
"W you not answer, Abner?" 1Sa 26:14
for I w not harm you again because 1Sa 26:21
"The LORD w repay each man 1Sa 26:23
you w both accomplish much and 1Sa 26:25
"Now I w perish one day by the 1Sa 27:1
Saul then w despair of searching 1Sa 27:1
and I w escape from his hand." 1Sa 27:1
"Otherwise they w tell about us, 1Sa 27:11
he w become my servant forever." 1Sa 27:12
you w go out with me in the camp, 1Sa 28:1
I w make you my bodyguard for life." 1Sa 28:2
"Moreover the LORD w also give 1Sa 28:19
you and your sons w be with me. 1Sa 28:19
Indeed the LORD w give over the 1Sa 28:19
he refused and said, "I w not eat." 1Sa 28:23
for you w surely overtake them, 1Sa 30:8
and you w surely rescue *all.*" 1Sa 30:8
"W you bring me down to this band?" 1Sa 30:15
you w not kill me or deliver me into 1Sa 30:15
I w bring you down to this band." 1Sa 30:15
we w not give them any of the 1Sa 30:22
w listen to you in this matter? 1Sa 30:24
otherwise these uncircumcised w come 1Sa 31:4
Or the daughters of the Philistines w 2Sa 1:20
of the uncircumcised w exult. 2Sa 1:20
also w show this goodness to you, 2Sa 2:6
that it w be bitter in the end? 2Sa 2:26
How long w you refrain from 2Sa 2:26
I w make a covenant with you, but 2Sa 3:13
I w save My people Israel from the 2Sa 3:18
that day that it had not been *the* w 2Sa 3:37
'You w shepherd My people Israel, 2Sa 5:2
you w be a ruler over Israel.' " 2Sa 5:2
but the blind and lame w turn you 2Sa 5:6
W You give them into my hand?" 2Sa 5:19

for I w certainly give the 2Sa 5:19
for then the LORD w have gone out 2Sa 5:24
I w celebrate before the LORD. 2Sa 6:21
"I w be more lightly esteemed 2Sa 6:22
and w be humble in my own eyes, 2Sa 6:22
with them I w be distinguished." 2Sa 6:22
and I w make you a great name, 2Sa 7:9
"I w also appoint a place for My 2Sa 7:10
My people Israel and w plant them, 2Sa 7:10
nor w the wicked afflict them any 2Sa 7:10
and I w give you rest from all 2Sa 7:11
the LORD w make a house for you. 2Sa 7:11
I w raise up your descendant after 2Sa 7:12
you, who w come forth from you, 2Sa 7:12
and I w establish his kingdom. 2Sa 7:12
and I w establish the throne of 2Sa 7:13
"I w be a father to him and he 2Sa 7:14
to him and he w be a son to Me; 2Sa 7:14
I w correct him with the rod of 2Sa 7:14
'I w build you a house'; 2Sa 7:27
for I w surely show kindness to 2Sa 9:7
and w restore to you all the land 2Sa 9:7
servant so your servant w do." 2Sa 9:11
"I w show kindness to Hanun the 2Sa 10:2
you, then I w come to help you. 2Sa 10:11
soul, I w not do this thing." 2Sa 11:11
and tomorrow I w let you go." 2Sa 11:12
I w raise up evil against you from 2Sa 12:11
I w even take your wives before 2Sa 12:11
and he w lie with your wives in broad 2Sa 12:11
but I w do this thing before all 2Sa 12:12
I w go to him, but he will not 2Sa 12:23
him, but he w not return to me." 2Sa 12:23
or I w capture the city myself and it 2Sa 12:28
capture the city myself and it w be 2Sa 12:28
W you not tell me?" 2Sa 13:4
you w be like one of the fools in 2Sa 13:13
he w not withhold me from you." 2Sa 13:13
for we w be burdensome to you." 2Sa 13:25
Thus they w extinguish my coal 2Sa 14:7
I w give orders concerning you." 2Sa 14:8
and he w not touch you anymore." 2Sa 14:10
that the avenger of blood w not 2Sa 14:11
otherwise they w destroy my son." 2Sa 14:11
"For we w surely die and are like 2Sa 14:14
ways so that the banished one w not 2Sa 14:14
perhaps the king w perform the 2Sa 14:15
'For the king w hear and deliver 2Sa 14:16
now, I w surely do this thing; 2Sa 14:21
then I w serve the LORD.' " 2Sa 15:8
for *otherwise* none of us w escape 2Sa 15:14
or he w overtake us quickly and bring 2Sa 15:14
"Why w you also go with us? 2Sa 15:19
with us, while I go where I w? 2Sa 15:20
there also your servant w be." 2Sa 15:21
then He w bring me back again and 2Sa 15:25
me, then you w be a burden to me. 2Sa 15:33
'I w be your servant, O king; 2Sa 15:34
past, so I w now be your servant,' 2Sa 15:34
'Today the house of Israel w restore 2Sa 16:3
"Perhaps the LORD w look on my 2Sa 16:12
of Israel have chosen, his I w be, 2Sa 16:18
I will be, and with him I w remain. 2Sa 16:18
so I w be in your presence." 2Sa 16:19
then all Israel w hear that you 2Sa 16:21
with you w also be strengthened." 2Sa 16:21
"I w come upon him while he 2Sa 17:2
people who are with him w flee. 2Sa 17:2
I w strike down the king alone, 2Sa 17:2
and I w bring back all the people 2Sa 17:3
then all the people w be at peace." 2Sa 17:3
and w not spend the night with the 2Sa 17:8
and it w be when he falls on them 2Sa 17:9
that whoever hears *it* w say, 2Sa 17:9
a lion, w completely lose heart; 2Sa 17:10
and we w fall on him as the dew 2Sa 17:12
with him, not even one w be left. 2Sa 17:12
and we w drag it into the valley 2Sa 17:13
all the people who are with him w be 2Sa 17:16
w surely go out with you also." 2Sa 18:2
flee, they w not care about us; 2Sa 18:3
us die, they w not care about us. 2Sa 18:3
seems best to you I w do." 2Sa 18:4
"I w not waste time here with you." 2Sa 18:14
you w have no reward for going?" 2Sa 18:22
whatever happens," *he said,* "I w run. 2Sa 18:23
a man w pass the night with you, 2Sa 19:7
and this w be worse for you than 2Sa 19:7
if you w not be commander of the 2Sa 19:13
'I w saddle a donkey for myself 2Sa 19:26
I w sustain you in Jerusalem with 2Sa 19:33
and I w do for him what is good in 2Sa 19:38
require of me, I w do for you." 2Sa 19:38
w do us more harm than Absalom; 2Sa 20:6
'They w surely ask *advice* at 2Sa 20:18
and I w depart from the city." 2Sa 20:21
his head w be thrown to you over 2Sa 20:21
"I w do for you whatever you say." 2Sa 21:4
and we w hang them before the LORD 2Sa 21:6
And the king said, "I w give *them.*" 2Sa 21:6
"Therefore I w give thanks to 2Sa 22:50
And I w sing praises to Your name. 2Sa 22:50
W He not indeed make *it* grow? 2Sa 23:5
them w be thrust away like thorns, 2Sa 23:6
And they w be completely burned 2Sa 23:7
which I w do to you." ' " 2Sa 24:12
Or w you flee three months before 2Sa 24:13
but I w surely buy *it* from you for 2Sa 24:24
for I w not offer burnt offerings 2Sa 24:24

exalted himself, saying, "I w be king. 1Ki 1:5
I w come in after you and confirm 1Ki 1:14
"Otherwise it w come about, as 1Ki 1:21
w be considered offenders." 1Ki 1:21
I w indeed do so this day." 1Ki 1:30
that he w not put his servant to death 1Ki 1:51
of his hairs w fall to the ground; 1Ki 1:52
is found in him, he w die." 1Ki 1:52
'I w not put you to death with the 1Ki 2:8
and you w know what you ought to 1Ki 2:9
and you w bring his gray hair down 1Ki 2:9
the king, for he w not refuse you, 1Ki 2:17
I w speak to the king for you." 1Ki 2:18
mother, for I w not refuse you." 1Ki 2:20
but I w not put you to death at 1Ki 2:26
"No, for I w die here." 1Ki 2:30
"The LORD w return his blood 1Ki 2:32
you w know for certain that you 1Ki 2:37
has said, so your servant w do." 1Ki 2:38
'You w know for certain that on 1Ki 2:42
so that there w not be any among 1Ki 3:13
then I w prolong your days." 1Ki 3:14
whom I w set on your throne in 1Ki 5:5
he w build the house for My name.' 1Ki 5:5
servants w be with your servants; 1Ki 5:6
and I w give you wages for your 1Ki 5:6
I w do what you desire concerning 1Ki 5:8
"My servants w bring *them* down 1Ki 5:9
and I w make them into rafts *to go* 1Ki 5:9
and I w have them broken up there, 1Ki 5:9
if you w walk in My statutes and 1Ki 6:12
then I w carry out My word with 1Ki 6:12
"I w dwell among the sons of 1Ki 6:13
w not forsake My people Israel." 1Ki 6:13
but your son who w be born to you, 1Ki 8:19
he w build the house for My name.' 1Ki 8:19
w God indeed dwell on the earth? 1Ki 8:27
(for they w hear of Your great name 1Ki 8:42
My heart w be there perpetually. 1Ki 9:3
if you w walk before Me as your 1Ki 9:4
you *and* w keep My statutes and My 1Ki 9:4
then I w establish the throne of 1Ki 9:5
then I w cut off Israel from the 1Ki 9:7
My name, I w cast out of My sight. 1Ki 9:7
So Israel w become a proverb and a 1Ki 9:7
house w become a heap of ruins; 1Ki 9:8
everyone who passes by w be 1Ki 9:8
"And they w say, 1Ki 9:9
for they w surely turn your heart 1Ki 11:2
I w surely tear the kingdom from 1Ki 11:11
and w give it to your servant. 1Ki 11:11
"Nevertheless I w not do it in 1Ki 11:12
but I w tear it out of the hand of 1Ki 11:12
I w not tear away all the kingdom, 1Ki 11:13
but I w give one tribe to your son 1Ki 11:13
I w tear the kingdom out of the 1Ki 11:31
(but he w have one tribe, for the 1Ki 11:32
'Nevertheless I w not take the 1Ki 11:34
but I w make him ruler all the 1Ki 11:34
but I w take the kingdom from his 1Ki 11:35
'But to his son I w give one tribe, 1Ki 11:36
'I w take you, and you shall 1Ki 11:37
'Then it w be, that if you listen 1Ki 11:38
then I w be with you and build you 1Ki 11:38
David, and I w give Israel to you. 1Ki 11:38
'Thus I w afflict the descendants 1Ki 11:39
put on us, and we w serve you." 1Ki 12:4
"If you w be a servant to this 1Ki 12:7
this people today, and w serve them 1Ki 12:7
they w be your servants forever." 1Ki 12:7
heavy yoke, I w add to your yoke; 1Ki 12:11
but I w discipline you with 1Ki 12:11
heavy, but I w add to your yoke; 1Ki 12:14
I w discipline you with scorpions." 1Ki 12:14
w return to the house of David. 1Ki 12:26
people w return to their lord, 1Ki 12:27
and they w kill me and return to 1Ki 12:27
and I w give you a reward." 1Ki 13:7
nor w I eat bread or drink water 1Ki 13:16
disguise yourself so that they w not 1Ki 14:2
He w tell you what will happen to 1Ki 14:3
you what w happen to the boy." 1Ki 14:3
for it w be when she arrives that 1Ki 14:5
w pretend to be another woman." 1Ki 14:5
and w cut off from Jeroboam every 1Ki 14:10
and I w make a clean sweep of the 1Ki 14:10
dies in the city the dogs w eat. 1Ki 14:11
the birds of the heavens w eat; 1Ki 14:11
enter the city the child w die. 1Ki 14:12
of Jeroboam's *family* w come 1Ki 14:13
the LORD w raise up for Himself a 1Ki 14:14
Himself a king over Israel who w cut 1Ki 14:14
"For the LORD w strike Israel, as 1Ki 14:15
and He w uproot Israel from this 1Ki 14:15
and w scatter them beyond the 1Ki 14:15
"He w give up Israel on 1Ki 14:16
so that he w withdraw from me." 1Ki 15:19
I w consume Baasha and his house, 1Ki 16:3
and I w make your house like the 1Ki 16:3
who dies in the city the dogs w eat, 1Ki 16:4
the birds of the heavens w eat." 1Ki 16:4
"It shall be that you w drink of 1Ki 17:4
and I w send rain on the face of 1Ki 18:1
perhaps we w find grass and keep 1Ki 18:5
"It w come about when I leave 1Ki 18:12
the Spirit of the LORD w carry you 1Ki 18:12
he cannot find you, he w kill me, 1Ki 18:12
he w then kill me." 1Ki 18:14
I w surely show myself to him 1Ki 18:15

"How long **w** you hesitate between 1Ki 18:21
and I **w** prepare the other ox and 1Ki 18:23
and I **w** not put a fire *under it.* 1Ki 18:23
I **w** call on the name of the LORD, 1Ki 18:24
"Yet I **w** leave 7,000 in Israel, 1Ki 19:18
my mother, then I **w** follow you." 1Ki 19:20
I **w** send my servants to you, 1Ki 20:6
and they **w** search your house and 1Ki 20:6
they **w** take in their hand and 1Ki 20:6
your servant at the first I **w** do, 1Ki 20:9
if the dust of Samaria **w** suffice for 1Ki 20:10
I **w** deliver them into your hand 1Ki 20:13
of Aram **w** come up against you." 1Ki 20:22
and surely we **w** be stronger than 1Ki 20:23
Then we **w** fight against them in 1Ki 20:25
and surely we **w** be stronger than they." 1Ki 20:25
therefore I **w** give all this great 1Ki 20:28
perhaps he **w** save your life." 1Ki 20:31
took from your father I **w** restore, 1Ki 20:34
"And I **w** let you go with 1Ki 20:34
from me, a lion **w** kill you." 1Ki 20:36
and I **w** give you a better vineyard 1Ki 21:2
I **w** give you the price of it in 1Ki 21:2
"I **w** not give you the inheritance 1Ki 21:4
I **w** give you a vineyard in its 1Ki 21:6
'I **w** not give you my vineyard.' " 1Ki 21:6
I **w** give you the vineyard of 1Ki 21:7
blood of Naboth the dogs **w** lick 1Ki 21:19
"Behold, I **w** bring evil upon you, 1Ki 21:21
you, and **w** utterly sweep you away, 1Ki 21:21
and **w** cut off from Ahab every 1Ki 21:21
and I **w** make your house like the 1Ki 21:22
'The dogs **w** eat Jezebel in 1Ki 21:23
the dogs **w** eat, and the one who dies 1Ki 21:24
field the birds of heaven **w** eat." 1Ki 21:24
I **w** not bring the evil in his 1Ki 21:29
but I **w** bring the evil upon his 1Ki 21:29
"**W** you go with me to battle at 1Ki 22:4
for the Lord **w** give *it* into the 1Ki 22:6
'With these you **w** gore 1Ki 22:11
for the LORD **w** give *it* into the 1Ki 22:12
and the LORD **w** give *it* into the 1Ki 22:15
'Who **w** entice Ahab to go up and 1Ki 22:20
the LORD and said, 'I **w** entice him.' 1Ki 22:21
'I **w** go out and be a deceiving 1Ki 22:22
"I **w** disguise myself and go into 1Ki 22:30
whether I **w** recover from this 2Ki 1:2
live, I **w** not leave you." 2Ki 2:2
"Do you know that the LORD **w** take 2Ki 2:3
live, I **w** not leave you." 2Ki 2:4
"Do you know that the LORD **w** take 2Ki 2:5
live, I **w** not leave you." 2Ki 2:6
W you go with me to fight against 2Ki 3:7
And he said, "I **w** go up; 2Ki 3:7
He **w** also give the Moabites into 2Ki 3:18
next year you **w** embrace a son. 2Ki 4:16
"Why **w** you go to him today? 2Ki 4:23
"*It* **w** *be* well." 2Ki 4:23
live, I **w** not leave you." 2Ki 4:30
His attendant said, "What, **w** I set 2Ki 4:43
and I **w** send a letter to the king 2Ki 5:5
and your flesh **w** be restored to you 2Ki 5:10
will be restored to you and *you* **w** 2Ki 5:10
'He **w** surely come out to me and 2Ki 5:11
whom I stand, I **w** take nothing." 2Ki 5:16
for your servant **w** no longer offer 2Ki 5:17
nor **w** he sacrifice to other gods, 2Ki 5:17
I **w** run after him and take 2Ki 5:20
"**W** you tell me which of us is for 2Ki 6:11
follow me and I **w** bring you to the 2Ki 6:19
and we **w** eat my son tomorrow.' 2Ki 6:28
time a measure of fine flour **w** be 2Ki 7:1
you **w** see it with your own eyes, 2Ki 7:2
but you **w** not eat of it." 2Ki 7:2
'We **w** enter the city,' then the 2Ki 7:4
famine is in the city and we **w** die 2Ki 7:4
we **w** live; and if they kill us, we 2Ki 7:4
we **w** but die." 2Ki 7:4
light, punishment **w** overtake us. 2Ki 7:9
"I **w** now tell you what the 2Ki 7:12
we **w** capture them alive and get into 2Ki 7:12
they **w** *be in any case* like all 2Ki 7:13
they **w** *be in any case* like all 2Ki 7:13
w be *sold* tomorrow about this 2Ki 7:18
you **w** see it with your own eyes, 2Ki 7:19
but you **w** not eat of it." 2Ki 7:19
and it **w** even come on the land for 2Ki 8:1
'**W** I recover from this sickness?' " 2Ki 8:8
'**W** I recover from this sickness?' " 2Ki 8:9
say to him, 'You **w** surely recover,' 2Ki 8:10
me that he **w** certainly die." 2Ki 8:10
you **w** do to the sons of Israel: 2Ki 8:12
strongholds you **w** set on fire, 2Ki 8:12
men you **w** kill with the sword, 2Ki 8:12
little ones you **w** dash in pieces, 2Ki 8:12
women with child you **w** rip up." 2Ki 8:12
me that you **w** be king over Aram." 2Ki 8:13
and I **w** cut off from Ahab every 2Ki 9:8
'I **w** make the house of Ahab 2Ki 9:9
I **w** repay you in this property,' 2Ki 9:26
and the corpse of Jezebel **w** be as 2Ki 9:37
all that you say to us we **w** do, 2Ki 10:5
do, we **w** not make any man king; 2Ki 10:5
and you **w** listen to my voice, 2Ki 10:6
Jehu **w** serve him much. 2Ki 10:18
for you **w** defeat the Arameans at 2Ki 13:17
and He **w** deliver you from the hand 2Ki 17:39
you impose on me I **w** bear." 2Ki 18:14
it **w** go into his hand and pierce 2Ki 18:21

I **w** give you two thousand horses, 2Ki 18:23
for he **w** not be able to deliver 2Ki 18:29
"The LORD **w** surely deliver us, 2Ki 18:30
and this city **w** not be given into 2Ki 18:30
"The LORD **w** deliver us." 2Ki 18:32
'Perhaps the LORD your God **w** hear 2Ki 19:4
and **w** rebuke the words which the 2Ki 19:4
I **w** put a spirit in him so that he 2Ki 19:7
put a spirit in him so that he **w** hear 2Ki 19:7
And I **w** make him fall by the sword 2Ki 19:7
"Jerusalem **w** not be given into 2Ki 19:10
So **w** you be spared? 2Ki 19:11
I **w** put My hook in your nose, 2Ki 19:28
And I **w** turn you back by the way 2Ki 19:28
you **w** eat this year what grows of 2Ki 19:29
remnant of the house of Judah **w** again 2Ki 19:30
'For out of Jerusalem **w** go forth a 2Ki 19:31
The zeal of the LORD **w** perform 2Ki 19:31
"He **w** not come to this city or shoot 2Ki 19:32
and he **w** not come before it with a 2Ki 19:32
by the same he **w** return, and he 2Ki 19:33
'For I **w** defend this city to save 2Ki 19:34
behold, I **w** heal you. 2Ki 20:5
"I **w** add fifteen years to 2Ki 20:6
and I **w** deliver you and this city 2Ki 20:6
and I **w** defend this city for My 2Ki 20:6
"What **w** be the sign that the LORD 2Ki 20:8
the sign that the LORD **w** heal me, 2Ki 20:8
that the LORD **w** do the thing that 2Ki 20:9
laid up in store to this day **w** be 2Ki 20:17
whom you **w** beget, will be taken away; 2Ki 20:18
w be taken away; and they will 2Ki 20:18
and they **w** become officials in 2Ki 20:18
if there **w** be peace and truth in my 2Ki 20:19
"In Jerusalem I **w** put My name." 2Ki 21:4
Israel, I **w** put My name forever. 2Ki 21:7
"And I **w** not make the feet of 2Ki 21:8
if only they **w** observe to do 2Ki 21:8
both his ears **w** tingle. 2Ki 21:12
'I **w** stretch over Jerusalem 2Ki 21:13
and I **w** wipe Jerusalem as one 2Ki 21:13
'I **w** abandon the remnant of My 2Ki 21:14
and they **w** become as plunder 2Ki 21:14
I **w** gather you to your fathers, 2Ki 22:20
and you **w** be gathered to your grave 2Ki 22:20
and your eyes **w** not see all the evil 2Ki 22:20
I **w** bring on this place. 2Ki 22:20
"I **w** remove Judah also from My 2Ki 23:27
And I **w** cast off Jerusalem, this 2Ki 23:27
and it **w** be well with you." 2Ki 25:24
otherwise these uncircumcised **w** come 1Ch 10:4
w You give them into my hand?" 1Ch 14:10
I **w** give them into your hand." 1Ch 14:10
for God **w** have gone out before you 1Ch 14:15
you I **w** give the land of Canaan, 1Ch 16:18
established, it **w** not be moved. 1Ch 16:30
w sing for joy before the LORD; 1Ch 16:33
and I **w** make you a name like the 1Ch 17:8
"I **w** appoint a place for My 1Ch 17:9
people Israel, and **w** plant them, 1Ch 17:9
and the wicked **w** not waste them 1Ch 17:9
And I **w** subdue all your enemies. 1Ch 17:10
the LORD **w** build a house for you. 1Ch 17:10
that I **w** set up *one of* your 1Ch 17:11
who **w** be of your sons; and I will 1Ch 17:11
and I **w** establish his kingdom. 1Ch 17:11
I **w** establish his throne forever. 1Ch 17:12
"I **w** be his father and he shall 1Ch 17:13
and I **w** not take My lovingkindness 1Ch 17:13
"But I **w** settle him in My house 1Ch 17:14
that You **w** build for him a house; 1Ch 17:25
"I **w** show kindness to Hanun the 1Ch 19:2
strong for you, then I **w** help you. 1Ch 19:12
which I **w** do to you." ' " 1Ch 21:10
I **w** give the oxen for burnt 1Ch 21:23
I **w** give *it* all." 1Ch 21:23
but I **w** surely buy *it* for the full 1Ch 21:24
for I **w** not take what is yours for 1Ch 21:24
I **w** make preparation for it." 1Ch 22:5
'Behold, a son **w** be born to you, 1Ch 22:9
and I **w** give him rest from all his 1Ch 22:9
and I **w** give peace and quiet to 1Ch 22:9
be My son and I **w** be his father; 1Ch 22:10
and I **w** establish the throne of 1Ch 22:10
"Then you **w** prosper, if you are 1Ch 22:13
the Levites **w** no longer need to 1Ch 23:26
to Me, and I **w** be a father to him. 1Ch 28:6
I **w** establish his kingdom forever if 1Ch 28:7
seek Him, He **w** let you find Him; 1Ch 28:9
Him, He **w** reject you forever. 1Ch 28:9
He **w** not fail you nor forsake you 1Ch 28:20
man of any skill **w** be with you in all 1Ch 28:21
w be entirely at your command." 1Ch 28:21
And I **w** give you riches and wealth 2Ch 1:12
nor those who **w** come after you." 2Ch 1:12
which I am about to build **w** *be* 2Ch 2:5
and indeed my servants **w** *work* 2Ch 2:8
which I am about to build **w** *be* 2Ch 2:9
behold, I **w** give to your servants, 2Ch 2:10
who **w** build a house for the LORD 2Ch 2:12
"We **w** cut whatever timber you 2Ch 2:16
but your son who **w** be born to you, 2Ch 6:9
"But **w** God indeed dwell with 2Ch 6:18
ways, then I **w** hear from heaven, 2Ch 7:14
from heaven, **w** forgive their sin and 2Ch 7:14
their sin and **w** heal their land. 2Ch 7:14
"Now My eyes **w** be open and My ears 2Ch 7:15
My heart **w** be there perpetually. 2Ch 7:16
and **w** keep My statutes and My 2Ch 7:17

then I **w** establish your royal 2Ch 7:18
then I **w** uproot you from My land 2Ch 7:20
My name I **w** cast out of My sight and 2Ch 7:20
and I **w** make it a proverb and a 2Ch 7:20
by it **w** be astonished and say, 2Ch 7:21
"And they **w** say, 2Ch 7:22
put on us, and we **w** serve you." 2Ch 10:4
"If you **w** be kind to this people 2Ch 10:7
they **w** be your servants forever." 2Ch 10:7
heavy yoke, I **w** add to your yoke; 2Ch 10:11
but I **w** *discipline you* with 2Ch 10:11
yoke heavy, but I **w** add to it; 2Ch 10:14
but I **w** *discipline you* with 2Ch 10:14
so I **w** not destroy them, 2Ch 12:7
but I **w** grant them some *measure* of 2Ch 12:7
"But they **w** become his slaves so 2Ch 12:8
fathers, for you **w** not succeed." 2Ch 13:12
seek Him, He **w** let you find Him; 2Ch 15:2
you forsake Him, He **w** forsake you. 2Ch 15:2
so that he **w** withdraw from me." 2Ch 16:3
now on you **w** surely have wars." 2Ch 16:9
"**W** you go with me *against* 2Ch 18:3
and *we* **w** *be* with you in 2Ch 18:3
for God **w** give *it* into the hand of 2Ch 18:5
for the LORD **w** give *it* into the 2Ch 18:11
my God says, that I **w** speak." 2Ch 18:13
they **w** be given into your hand." 2Ch 18:14
'Who **w** entice Ahab king of Israel 2Ch 18:19
the LORD and said, 'I **w** entice him.' 2Ch 18:20
'I **w** go and be a deceiving spirit 2Ch 18:21
Micaiah said, "Behold, you **w** see 2Ch 18:24
"I **w** disguise myself and go into 2Ch 18:29
for the LORD our God **w** have no 2Ch 19:7
shall do and you **w** not be guilty. 2Ch 19:10
Amariah the chief priest **w** be over 2Ch 19:11
we **w** stand before this house and 2Ch 20:9
and You **w** hear and deliver *us.*' 2Ch 20:9
"O our God, **w** You not judge them? 2Ch 20:12
w come up by the ascent of Ziz, 2Ch 20:16
and you **w** find them at the end of 2Ch 20:16
God and you **w** be established. 2Ch 20:20
and you **w** suffer severe sickness, 2Ch 21:15
The Levites **w** surround the king, 2Ch 23:7
yet God **w** bring you down before 2Ch 25:8
and **w** have no honor from the LORD 2Ch 26:18
I **w** sacrifice to them that they 2Ch 28:23
brothers and your sons **w** *find* 2Ch 30:9
and **w** return to this land. 2Ch 30:9
and **w** not turn *His* face away from 2Ch 30:9
"The LORD our God **w** deliver us 2Ch 32:11
How much less **w** your God deliver you 2Ch 32:15
so the God of Hezekiah **w** not deliver 2Ch 32:17
Israel, I **w** put My name forever; 2Ch 33:7
and I **w** not again remove the foot 2Ch 33:8
if only they **w** observe to do all 2Ch 33:8
wrath **w** be poured out on this place and 2Ch 34:25
the LORD, thus you **w** say to him, 2Ch 34:26
I **w** gather you to your fathers and 2Ch 34:28
so your eyes **w** not see all the evil 2Ch 34:28
not see all the evil which I **w** bring on 2Ch 34:28
it **w** be a burden on *your* shoulders 2Ch 35:3
so that He **w** not destroy you." 2Ch 35:21
but we ourselves **w** together build Ezr 4:3
finished, they **w** not pay tribute, Ezr 4:13
and it **w** damage the revenue of the Ezr 4:13
w discover in the record books and Ezr 4:15
as a result you **w** have no Ezr 4:16
do according to the **w** of your God. Ezr 7:18 7466b
so that there **w** not be wrath against Ezr 7:23
"Whoever **w** not observe the Ezr 7:26
but we **w** be with you; Ezr 10:4
God of your fathers and do His **w**; Ezr 10:11 7522
I **w** scatter you among the peoples; Ne 1:8
I **w** gather them from there and Ne 1:9
w bring them to the place where I Ne 1:9
"How long **w** your journey be, and Ne 2:6
be, and when **w** you return?" Ne 2:6
for the house to which I **w** go." Ne 2:8
the wall of Jerusalem so that we **w** no Ne 2:17
God of heaven **w** give us success; Ne 2:20
we His servants **w** arise and build, Ne 2:20
"They **w** not know or see until we Ne 4:11
"They **w** come up against us from Ne 4:12
Our God **w** fight for us." Ne 4:20
"We **w** give *it* back and will Ne 5:12
and **w** require nothing from them; Ne 5:12
we **w** do exactly as you say." Ne 5:12
And now it **w** be reported to the Ne 6:7
"They **w** become discouraged with Ne 6:9
the work and it **w** not be done." Ne 6:9
temple to save his life? I **w** not go in. Ne 6:11
and that we **w** not give our Ne 10:30
we **w** not buy from them on the Ne 10:31
and we **w** forego *the crops* the Ne 10:31
We **w** also bring the first of our Ne 10:37
Thus we **w** not neglect the house of Ne 10:39
I **w** use force against you." Ne 13:21
"For the queen's conduct **w** become Es 1:17
heard of the queen's conduct **w** speak Es 1:18
and there **w** be plenty of contempt Es 1:18
the king's edict which he **w** make Es 1:20
w give honor to their husbands, Es 1:20
and I **w** pay ten thousand talents Es 3:9
relief and deliverance **w** arise for Es 4:14
and your father's house **w** perish. Es 4:14
also **w** fast in the same way. Es 4:16
And thus I **w** go in to the king, Es 4:16
to the banquet which I **w** prepare Es 5:8
I **w** do as the king says." Es 5:8

origin, you **w** not overcome him, Es 6:13
but **w** surely fall before him." Es 6:13
"**W** he even assault the queen with Es 7:8
to see the calamity which **w** befall Es 8:6
w surely curse You to Your face." Jb 1:11
a man has he **w** give for his life. Jb 2:4
he **w** curse You to Your face." Jb 2:5
with you, **w** you become impatient? Jb 4:2
is there anyone who **w** answer you? Jb 5:1
which of the holy ones **w** you turn? Jb 5:1
six troubles He **w** deliver you, Jb 5:19
in seven evil **w** not touch you. Jb 5:19
famine He **w** redeem you from death, Jb 5:20
"You **w** be hidden from the scourge Jb 5:21
And you **w** not be afraid of Jb 5:21
w laugh at violence and famine, Jb 5:22
w not be afraid of wild beasts. Jb 5:22
"For you **w** be in league with the Jb 5:23
the beasts of the field **w** be at peace Jb 5:23
w know that your tent is secure, Jb 5:24
For you **w** visit your abode and Jb 5:24
"You **w** know also that your Jb 5:25
that your descendants **w** be many, Jb 5:25
"You **w** come to the grave in full Jb 5:26
"Teach me, and I **w** be silent; Jb 6:24
My eye **w** not again see good. Jb 7:7
who sees me **w** behold me no longer; Jb 7:8
Your eyes **w** *be* on me, but I will Jb 7:8
will be on me, but I **w** not be. Jb 7:8
w not return again to his house, Jb 7:10
Nor **w** his place know him anymore. Jb 7:10
I **w** not restrain my mouth; Jb 7:11
I **w** speak in the anguish of my Jb 7:11
I **w** complain in the bitterness of Jb 7:11
'My bed **w** comfort me, My couch Jb 7:13
me, My couch **w** ease my complaint,' Jb 7:13
I **w** not live forever. Jb 7:16
"**W** You never turn Your gaze away Jb 7:19
For now I **w** lie down in the dust; Jb 7:21
And You **w** seek me, but I will not Jb 7:21
will seek me, but I **w** not be." Jb 7:21
"How long **w** you say these things, Jb 8:2
Yet your end **w** increase greatly. Jb 8:7
"**W** they not teach you *and* tell Jb 8:10
the hope of the godless **w** perish, Jb 8:13
his place, Then it **w** deny him, Jb 8:18
out of the dust others **w** spring. Jb 8:19
w not reject *a man of* integrity, Jb 8:20
Nor **w** He support the evildoers. Jb 8:20
"He **w** yet fill your mouth with Jb 8:21
hate you **w** be clothed with shame, Jb 8:22
tent of the wicked **w** be no longer." Jb 8:22
"God **w** not turn back His anger; Jb 9:13
w not allow me to get my breath, Jb 9:18
righteous, my mouth **w** condemn me; Jb 9:20
guiltless, He **w** declare me guilty. Jb 9:20
'I **w** forget my complaint, I will Jb 9:27
I **w** leave off my *sad* countenance Jb 9:27
I know that You **w** not acquit me. Jb 9:28
I **w** give full vent to my complaint; Jb 10:1
I **w** speak in the bitterness of my Jb 10:1
"I **w** say to God, Jb 10:2
"An idiot **w** become Jb 11:12
"But the eyes of the wicked **w** fail, Jb 11:20
And there **w** be no escape for them; Jb 11:20
people, And with you wisdom **w** die! Jb 12:2
"**W** you speak what is unjust for Jb 13:7
"**W** you show partiality for Him? Jb 13:8
W you contend for God? Jb 13:8
"**W** it be well when He examines Jb 13:9
Or **w** you deceive Him as one Jb 13:9
"He **w** surely reprove you If you Jb 13:10
"**W** not His majesty terrify you, Jb 13:11
He slay me, I **w** hope in Him. Jb 13:15
I **w** argue my ways before Him. Jb 13:15
"This also **w** be my salvation, For Jb 13:16
I know that I **w** be vindicated. Jb 13:18
"Who **w** contend with me? Jb 13:19
Then I **w** not hide from Your face: Jb 13:20
"Then call, and I **w** answer; Jb 13:22
"**W** You cause a driven leaf to Jb 13:25
Or **w** You pursue the dry chaff? Jb 13:25
cut down, that it **w** sprout again, Jb 14:7
again, And its shoots **w** not fail. Jb 14:7
At the scent of water it **w** flourish Jb 14:9
He **w** not awake nor be aroused out Jb 14:12
"If a man dies, **w** he live *again?* Jb 14:14
the days of my struggle I **w** wait Until Jb 14:14
"You **w** call, and I will answer Jb 14:15
will call, and I **w** answer You; Jb 14:15
You **w** long for the work of Your Jb 14:15
"I **w** tell you, listen to me; Jb 15:17
what I have seen I **w** also declare; Jb 15:17
that he **w** return from darkness, Jb 15:22
"He **w** not become rich, nor will Jb 15:29
rich, nor **w** his wealth endure; Jb 15:29
his grain **w** not bend down to the Jb 15:29
"He **w** not escape from darkness; Jb 15:30
The flame **w** wither his shoots, And Jb 15:30
breath of His mouth he **w** go away. Jb 15:30
For emptiness **w** be his reward. Jb 15:31
"It **w** be accomplished before his Jb 15:32
his palm branch **w** not be green. Jb 15:32
"He **w** drop off his unripe grape Jb 15:33
And **w** cast off his flower like the Jb 15:33
is there that **w** be my guarantor? Jb 17:3
Therefore You **w** not exalt *them.* Jb 17:4
The eyes of his children also **w** Jb 17:5
"The upright **w** be appalled at this, Jb 17:8

And the innocent **w** stir up himself Jb 17:8
"Nevertheless the righteous **w** hold Jb 17:9
And he who has clean hands **w** grow Jb 17:9
"**W** it go down with me to Sheol? Jb 17:16
"How long **w** you hunt for words? Jb 18:2
"How long **w** you torment me And Jb 19:2
He **w** take His stand on the earth. Jb 19:25
And whom my eyes **w** see and not Jb 19:27
Those who have seen him **w** say, Jb 20:7
he desires it and **w** not let it go, Jb 20:13
riches, But **w** vomit them up; Jb 20:15
God **w** expel them from his belly. Jb 20:15
of his plenty he **w** be cramped; Jb 20:22
who suffers **w** come *against* him. Jb 20:22
God **w** send His fierce anger on him Jb 20:23
w rain *it* on him while he is eating. Jb 20:23
But the bronze bow **w** pierce him. Jb 20:24
And unfanned fire **w** devour him; Jb 20:26
It **w** consume the survivor in his Jb 20:26
"The heavens **w** reveal his Jb 20:27
the earth **w** rise up against him. Jb 20:27
increase of his house **w** depart; Jb 20:28
His possessions **w** flow away in the Jb 20:28
They **w** be led forth at the day of Jb 21:30
w confront him with his actions, Jb 21:31
And who **w** repay him for what he Jb 21:31
Men **w** keep watch over *his* tomb. Jb 21:32
of the valley **w** gently cover him; Jb 21:33
all men **w** follow after him, Jb 21:33
"How then **w** you vainly comfort Jb 21:34
"**W** you keep to the ancient path Jb 22:15
Thereby good **w** come to you. Jb 22:21
the Almighty, you **w** be restored; Jb 22:23
Then the Almighty **w** be your gold Jb 22:25
you **w** delight in the Almighty And Jb 22:26
"You **w** pray to Him, and He will Jb 22:27
pray to Him, and He **w** hear you; Jb 22:27
And you **w** pay your vows. Jb 22:27
"You **w** also decree a thing, and Jb 22:28
and it **w** be established for you; Jb 22:28
And light **w** shine on your ways. Jb 22:28
you **w** speak with confidence, Jb 22:29
And the humble person He **w** save. Jb 22:29
"He **w** deliver one who is not Jb 22:30
And he **w** be delivered through the Jb 22:30
'No eye **w** see me.' Jb 24:15
"A mother **w** forget him; Jb 24:20
wickedness **w** be broken like a tree. Jb 24:20
lips certainly **w** not speak unjustly, Jb 27:4
Nor **w** my tongue mutter deceit. Jb 27:4
Till I die I **w** not put away my Jb 27:5
righteousness and **w** not let it go. Jb 27:6
"**W** God hear his cry When Jb 27:9
"**W** he take delight in the Jb 27:10
W he call on God at all times? Jb 27:10
"I **w** instruct you in the power of Jb 27:11
with the Almighty I **w** not conceal. Jb 27:11
w not be satisfied with bread. Jb 27:14
"His survivors **w** be buried Jb 27:15
widows **w** not be able to weep. Jb 27:15
it, but the just **w** wear *it* Jb 27:17
the innocent **w** divide the silver. Jb 27:17
w hurl at him without sparing; Jb 27:22
He **w** surely try to flee from its Jb 27:22
'*Men* **w** clap their hands at him And Jb 27:23
And **w** hiss him from his place. Jb 27:23
"For I know that You **w** bring me Jb 30:23
to account, what **w** I answer Him? Jb 31:14
to me, I too **w** tell what I think.' Jb 32:10
God **w** rout him, not man.' Jb 32:13
Nor **w** I reply to him with your Jb 32:14
"I too **w** answer my share, I also Jb 32:17
share, I also **w** tell my opinion. Jb 32:17
Then he **w** pray to God, and He will Jb 33:26
pray to God, and He **w** accept him, Jb 33:26
"He **w** sing to men and say, Jb 33:27
and I **w** teach you wisdom." Jb 33:33
"Surely, God **w** not act wickedly, Jb 34:12
Almighty **w** not pervert justice. Jb 34:12
And **w** you condemn the righteous Jb 34:17
I **w** not offend *anymore;* Jb 34:31
done iniquity, I **w** not do it again'? Jb 34:32
"Men of understanding **w** say to me, Jb 34:34
'What advantage **w** it be to You? Jb 35:3
What profit **w** I have, more than if I Jb 35:3
"I **w** answer you, And your friends Jb 35:4
God **w** not listen to an empty *cry,* Jb 35:13
cry, Nor **w** the Almighty regard it. Jb 35:13
and I **w** show you That there is yet Jb 36:2
"I **w** fetch my knowledge from Jb 36:3
And I **w** ascribe righteousness to Jb 36:3
They **w** end their days in prosperity Jb 36:11
perish by the sword And they **w** die Jb 36:12
"**W** your riches keep you from Jb 36:19
And He **w** not do violence to Jb 37:23
loins like a man, And I **w** ask you, Jb 38:3
So that an abundance of water **w** cover Jb 38:34
"**W** the wild ox consent to serve Jb 39:9
Or **w** he spend the night at your Jb 39:9
Or **w** he harrow the valleys after Jb 39:10
"**W** you trust him because his Jb 39:11
"**W** you have faith in him that he Jb 39:12
him that he **w** return your grain And Jb 39:12
"**W** the faultfinder contend with Jb 40:2
I have spoken, and I **w** not answer; Jb 40:5
Even twice, and I **w** add nothing more." Jb 40:5
I **w** ask you, and you instruct Me. Jb 40:7
"**W** you really annul My judgment? Jb 40:8
W you condemn Me that you may be Jb 40:8

"Then I **w** also confess to you, Jb 40:14
"**W** he make many supplications to Jb 41:3
Or **w** he speak to you soft words? Jb 41:3
"**W** he make a covenant with you? Jb 41:4
W you take him for a servant Jb 41:4
"**W** you play with him as with a Jb 41:5
w you bind him for your maidens? Jb 41:5
"**W** the traders bargain over him? Jb 41:6
W they divide him among the Jb 41:6
you **w** not do it again! Jb 41:8
W you be laid low even at the Jb 41:9
"I **w** not keep silence concerning Jb 41:12
'Hear, now, and I **w** speak; Jb 42:4
I **w** ask You, and You instruct Jb 42:4
and My servant Job **w** pray for you. Jb 42:8
For I **w** accept him so that I may Jb 42:8
He **w** be like a tree *firmly* Ps 1:3
wicked **w** not stand in the judgment, Ps 1:5
the way of the wicked **w** perish. Ps 1:6
Then He **w** speak to them in His Ps 2:5
"I **w** surely tell of the decree of Ps 2:7
and I **w** surely give the nations as Ps 2:8
I **w** not be afraid of ten thousands Ps 3:6
long **w** my honor become a reproach? Ps 4:2
How long **w** you love what is Ps 4:2
"Who **w** show us *any* good?" Ps 4:6
peace I **w** both lie down and sleep, Ps 4:8
O LORD, You **w** hear my voice; Ps 5:3
In the morning I **w** order *my prayer* Ps 5:3
I **w** enter Your house, Ps 5:7
I **w** bow in reverence for You. Ps 5:7
In Sheol who **w** give You thanks? Ps 6:5
All my enemies **w** be ashamed Ps 6:10
they **w** suddenly be ashamed. Ps 6:10
Or he **w** tear my soul like a lion, Ps 7:2
repent, He **w** sharpen His sword; Ps 7:12
w return upon his own head, Ps 7:16
w descend upon his own pate. Ps 7:16
I **w** give thanks to the LORD Ps 7:17
And **w** sing praise to the name of Ps 7:17
I **w** give thanks to the LORD with Ps 9:1
I **w** tell of all Your wonders. Ps 9:1
I **w** be glad and exult in You; Ps 9:2
I **w** sing praise to Your name, O Ps 9:2
And He **w** judge the world in Ps 9:8
He **w** execute judgment for the Ps 9:8
The LORD also **w** be a stronghold Ps 9:9
name **w** put their trust in You, Ps 9:10
The wicked **w** return to Sheol, *Even* Ps 9:17
needy **w** not always be forgotten, Ps 9:18
He says to himself, "I **w** not be Ps 10:6
Throughout all generations I **w** not be Ps 10:6
He **w** never see it." Ps 10:11
"You **w** not require *it.*" Ps 10:13
You **w** strengthen their heart, Ps 10:17
heart, You **w** incline Your ear Ps 10:17
So that man who is of the earth **w** no Ps 10:18
Upon the wicked He **w** rain snares; Ps 11:6
w be the portion of their cup. Ps 11:6
The upright **w** behold His face. Ps 11:7
"With our tongue we **w** prevail; Ps 12:4
of the needy, Now I **w** arise," Ps 12:5
"I **w** set him in the safety for Ps 12:5
You, O LORD, **w** keep them; Ps 12:7
You **w** preserve him from this Ps 12:7
W You forget me forever? Ps 13:1
long **w** You hide Your face from me? Ps 13:1
w my enemy be exalted over me? Ps 13:2
or I **w** sleep the *sleep of* death, Ps 13:3
And my enemy **w** say, "I have Ps 13:4
And my adversaries **w** rejoice when Ps 13:4
I **w** sing to the LORD, Because He Ps 13:6
captive people, Jacob **w** rejoice, Ps 14:7
will rejoice, Israel **w** be glad. Ps 14:7
these things **w** never be shaken. Ps 15:5
for another *god* **w** be multiplied; Ps 16:4
Nor **w** I take their names upon my lips. Ps 16:4
I **w** bless the LORD who has Ps 16:7
my right hand, I **w** not be shaken. Ps 16:8
My flesh also **w** dwell securely. Ps 16:9
w not abandon my soul to Sheol; Ps 16:10
Nor **w** You allow Your Holy One Ps 16:10
You **w** make known to me the path Ps 16:11
that my mouth **w** not transgress. Ps 17:3
upon You, for You **w** answer me, Ps 17:6
I **w** be satisfied with Your likeness Ps 17:15
Therefore I **w** give thanks to You Ps 18:49
And I **w** sing praises to Your name. Ps 18:49
Then I **w** be blameless, And I shall Ps 19:13
We **w** sing for joy over your Ps 20:5
our God we **w** set up our banners. Ps 20:5
He **w** answer him from His holy Ps 20:6
w boast in the name of the LORD, Ps 20:7
Your strength the king **w** be glad, Ps 21:1
how greatly he **w** rejoice! Ps 21:1
the Most High he **w** not be shaken. Ps 21:7
hand **w** find out all your enemies; Ps 21:8
Your right hand **w** find out those Ps 21:8
You **w** make them as a fiery oven in Ps 21:9
w swallow them up in His wrath, Ps 21:9
His wrath, And fire **w** devour them. Ps 21:9
You **w** destroy from the earth, Ps 21:10
a plot, They **w** not succeed. Ps 21:11
You **w** make them turn their back; Ps 21:12
You **w** aim with Your bowstrings at Ps 21:12
We **w** sing and praise Your power. Ps 21:13
I **w** tell of Your name to my Ps 22:22
of the assembly I **w** praise You. Ps 22:22
The afflicted **w** eat and be satisfied; Ps 22:26

who seek Him **w** praise the LORD.	Ps 22:26
w remember and turn to the LORD,	Ps 22:27
the nations **w** worship before You.	Ps 22:27
of the earth **w** eat and worship,	Ps 22:29
down to the dust **w** bow before Him,	Ps 22:29
Posterity **w** serve Him;	Ps 22:30
It **w** be told of the Lord to the	Ps 22:30
They **w** come and will declare His	Ps 22:31
They will come and **w** declare His	Ps 22:31
To a people who **w** be born,	Ps 22:31
and lovingkindness **w** follow me all	Ps 23:6
And I **w** dwell in the house of the	Ps 23:6
who wait for You **w** be ashamed;	Ps 25:3
without cause **w** be ashamed.	Ps 25:3
He **w** instruct him in the way he	Ps 25:12
His soul **w** abide in prosperity,	Ps 25:13
descendants **w** inherit the land.	Ps 25:13
He **w** make them know His covenant.	Ps 25:14
He **w** pluck my feet out of the net.	Ps 25:15
men, Nor **w** I go with pretenders.	Ps 26:4
And I **w** not sit with the wicked.	Ps 26:5
And I **w** go about Your altar,	Ps 26:6
against me, My heart **w** not fear;	Ps 27:3
He **w** conceal me in His tabernacle;	Ps 27:5
place of His tent He **w** hide me;	Ps 27:5
He **w** lift me up on a rock.	Ps 27:5
And now my head **w** be lifted up	Ps 27:6
And I **w** offer in His tent	Ps 27:6
I **w** sing, yes, I will sing praises	Ps 27:6
yes, I **w** sing praises to the LORD.	Ps 27:6
me, But the LORD **w** take me up.	Ps 27:10
I **w** become like those who go down to	Ps 28:1
He **w** tear them down and not build	Ps 28:5
w give strength to His people;	Ps 29:11
w bless His people with peace.	Ps 29:11
I **w** extol You, O LORD, for You	Ps 30:1
"I **w** never be moved."	Ps 30:6
W the dust praise You?	Ps 30:9
W it declare Your faithfulness?	Ps 30:9
I **w** give thanks to You forever.	Ps 30:12
sake You **w** lead me and guide me.	Ps 31:3
You **w** pull me out of the net	Ps 31:4
I **w** rejoice and be glad in Your	Ps 31:7
"I **w** confess my transgressions to	Ps 32:5
in a flood of great waters they **w** not	Ps 32:6
I **w** instruct you and teach you in	Ps 32:8
I **w** counsel you with My eye upon	Ps 32:8
they **w** not come near to you.	Ps 32:9
I **w** bless the LORD at all times;	Ps 34:1
My soul **w** make its boast in the	Ps 34:2
The humble **w** hear it and rejoice.	Ps 34:2
And their faces **w** never be ashamed.	Ps 34:5
I **w** teach you the fear of the LORD.	Ps 34:11
hate the righteous **w** be condemned.	Ps 34:21
take refuge in Him **w** be condemned.	Ps 34:22
All my bones **w** say,	Ps 35:10
Lord, how long **w** You look on?	Ps 35:17
I **w** give You thanks in the great	Ps 35:18
I **w** praise You among a mighty	Ps 35:18
w wither quickly like the grass And	Ps 37:2
And He **w** give you the desires of	Ps 37:4
Trust also in Him, and He **w** do it.	Ps 37:5
He **w** bring forth your	Ps 37:6
For evildoers **w** be cut off, But	Ps 37:9
the LORD, they **w** inherit the land.	Ps 37:9
and the wicked man **w** be no more;	Ps 37:10
w look carefully for his place and	Ps 37:10
his place and he **w** not be *there.*	Ps 37:10
But the humble **w** inherit the land And	Ps 37:11
And **w** delight themselves in	Ps 37:11
sword **w** enter their own heart,	Ps 37:15
heart, And their bows **w** be broken.	Ps 37:15
arms of the wicked **w** be broken,	Ps 37:17
their inheritance **w** be forever.	Ps 37:18
They **w** not be ashamed in the time	Ps 37:19
of famine they **w** have abundance.	Ps 37:19
But the wicked **w** perish;	Ps 37:20
And the enemies of the LORD **w** be	Ps 37:20
blessed by Him **w** inherit the land,	Ps 37:22
those cursed by Him **w** be cut off.	Ps 37:22
When he falls, he **w** not be hurled	Ps 37:24
do good, So you **w** abide forever.	Ps 37:27
of the wicked **w** be cut off.	Ps 37:28
The righteous **w** inherit the land And	Ps 37:29
LORD **w** not leave him in his hand Or	Ps 37:33
He **w** exalt you to inherit the land;	Ps 37:34
wicked are cut off, you **w** see it.	Ps 37:34
man of peace **w** have a posterity.	Ps 37:37
w be altogether destroyed;	Ps 37:38
posterity of the wicked **w** be cut off.	Ps 37:38
You **w** answer, O Lord my God.	Ps 38:15
"I **w** guard my ways That I may	Ps 39:1
I **w** guard my mouth as with a	Ps 39:1
does not know who **w** gather them.	Ps 39:6
Many **w** see and fear And will	Ps 40:3
and fear And **w** trust in the LORD.	Ps 40:3
I delight to do Your **w**,	Ps 40:8 7522
Behold, I **w** not restrain my lips,	Ps 40:9
w not withhold Your compassion from	Ps 40:11
truth **w** continually preserve me.	Ps 40:11
The LORD **w** deliver him in a day of	Ps 41:1
The LORD **w** protect him and keep	Ps 41:2
w sustain him upon his sickbed;	Ps 41:3
"When **w** he die, and his name	Ps 41:5
down, he **w** not rise up again."	Ps 41:8
The LORD **w** command His	Ps 42:8
song **w** be with me in the night,	Ps 42:8
I **w** say to God my rock,	Ps 42:9
Then I **w** go to the altar of God,	Ps 43:4
we **w** push back our adversaries;	Ps 44:5
Through Your name we **w** trample	Ps 44:5
For I **w** not trust in my bow, Nor	Ps 44:6
in my bow, Nor **w** my sword save me.	Ps 44:6
And we **w** give thanks to Your name	Ps 44:8
the King **w** desire your beauty.	Ps 45:11
The daughter of Tyre **w** *come* with	Ps 45:12
the people **w** seek your favor.	Ps 45:12
She **w** be led to the King in	Ps 45:14
follow her, **W** be brought to You.	Ps 45:14
They **w** be led forth with gladness	Ps 45:15
They **w** enter into the King's	Ps 45:15
of your fathers **w** be your sons;	Ps 45:16
I **w** cause Your name to be	Ps 45:17
Therefore the peoples **w** give You	Ps 45:17
Therefore we **w** not fear, though	Ps 46:2
midst of her, she **w** not be moved;	Ps 46:5
God **w** help her when morning dawns.	Ps 46:5
I **w** be exalted among the nations,	Ps 46:10
I **w** be exalted in the earth."	Ps 46:10
God **w** establish her forever.	Ps 48:8
He **w** guide us until death.	Ps 48:14
My mouth **w** speak wisdom,	Ps 49:3
And the meditation of my heart **w** *be*	Ps 49:3
I **w** incline my ear to a proverb;	Ps 49:4
I **w** express my riddle on the harp.	Ps 49:4
But man in *his* pomp **w** not endure;	Ps 49:12
But God **w** redeem my soul from the	Ps 49:15
For He **w** receive me.	Ps 49:15
he dies he **w** carry nothing away;	Ps 49:17
His glory **w** not descend after him.	Ps 49:17
They **w** never see the light.	Ps 49:19
"Hear, O My people, and I **w** speak;	Ps 50:7
O Israel, I **w** testify against you;	Ps 50:7
rescue you, and you **w** honor Me."	Ps 50:15
I **w** reprove you and state *the*	Ps 50:21
Or I **w** tear *you* in pieces,	Ps 50:22
and there **w** be none to deliver.	Ps 50:22
part You **w** make me know wisdom.	Ps 51:6
I **w** teach transgressors Your ways,	Ps 51:13
sinners **w** be converted to You.	Ps 51:13
Then my tongue **w** joyfully sing of	Ps 51:14
heart, O God, You **w** not despise.	Ps 51:17
Then You **w** delight in righteous	Ps 51:19
bulls **w** be offered on Your altar.	Ps 51:19
But God **w** break you down forever;	Ps 52:5
He **w** snatch you up and tear you	Ps 52:5
The righteous **w** see and fear,	Ps 52:6
see and fear, And **w** laugh at him,	Ps 52:6
I **w** give You thanks forever,	Ps 52:9
done *it,* And I **w** wait on Your name,	Ps 52:9
He **w** recompense the evil to my	Ps 54:5
Willingly I **w** sacrifice to You;	Ps 54:6
I **w** give thanks to Your name, O	Ps 54:6
upon God, And the LORD **w** save me.	Ps 55:16
at noon, I **w** complain and murmur,	Ps 55:17
murmur, And He **w** hear my voice.	Ps 55:17
He **w** redeem my soul in peace from	Ps 55:18
God **w** hear and answer them	Ps 55:19
the LORD and He **w** sustain you;	Ps 55:22
He **w** never allow the righteous to	Ps 55:22
w bring them down to the pit of	Ps 55:23
w not live out half their days.	Ps 55:23
But I **w** trust in You.	Ps 55:23
afraid, I **w** put my trust in You.	Ps 56:3
Then my enemies **w** turn back in the	Ps 56:9
I **w** render thank offerings to You.	Ps 56:12
of Your wings I **w** take refuge Until	Ps 57:1
I **w** cry to God Most High, To God	Ps 57:2
He **w** send from heaven and save me;	Ps 57:3
God **w** send forth His	Ps 57:3
I **w** sing, yes, I will sing praises!	Ps 57:7
will sing, yes, I **w** sing praises!	Ps 57:7
and lyre! I **w** awaken the dawn.	Ps 57:8
I **w** give thanks to You, O Lord,	Ps 57:9
I **w** sing praises to You among the	Ps 57:9
He **w** sweep them away with a	Ps 58:9
The righteous **w** rejoice when he	Ps 58:10
He **w** wash his feet in the blood of	Ps 58:10
men **w** say, "Surely there is a reward	Ps 58:11
his strength I **w** watch for You,	Ps 59:9
in His lovingkindness **w** meet me;	Ps 59:10
God **w** let me look *triumphantly*	Ps 59:10
Do not slay them, or my people **w**	Ps 59:11
I **w** sing praises to You;	Ps 59:17
"I **w** exult, I will portion out	Ps 60:6
I **w** portion out Shechem and	Ps 60:6
Who **w** bring me into the besieged	Ps 60:9
Who **w** lead me to Edom?	Ps 60:9
And **w** You not go forth with our	Ps 60:10
who **w** tread down our adversaries.	Ps 60:12
You **w** prolong the king's life;	Ps 61:6
years **w** be as many generations.	Ps 61:6
He **w** abide before God forever;	Ps 61:7
So I **w** sing praise to Your name	Ps 61:8
How long **w** you assail a man, That	Ps 62:3
than life, My lips **w** praise You.	Ps 63:3
I **w** bless You as long as I live;	Ps 63:4
I **w** lift up my hands in Your name.	Ps 63:4
W go into the depths of the earth.	Ps 63:9
They **w** be delivered over to the	Ps 63:10
They **w** be a prey for foxes.	Ps 63:10
But the king **w** rejoice in God;	Ps 63:11
who swears by Him **w** glory,	Ps 63:11
those who speak lies **w** be stopped.	Ps 63:11
God **w** shoot at them with an arrow;	Ps 64:7
Suddenly they **w** be wounded.	Ps 64:7
So they **w** make him stumble;	Ps 64:8
All who see them **w** shake the head.	Ps 64:8
Then all men **w** fear, And they	Ps 64:9
And they **w** declare the work of God,	Ps 64:9
And **w** consider what He has done.	Ps 64:9
man **w** be glad in the LORD and	Ps 64:10
LORD and **w** take refuge in Him;	Ps 64:10
all the upright in heart **w** glory.	Ps 64:10
There **w** be silence before You,	Ps 65:1
to You the vow **w** be performed.	Ps 65:1
We **w** be satisfied with the	Ps 65:4
w give feigned obedience to You.	Ps 66:3
"All the earth **w** worship You,	Ps 66:4
You, And **w** sing praises to You;	Ps 66:4
They **w** sing praises to Your name.	Ps 66:4
And I **w** tell of what He has done	Ps 66:16
in my heart, The Lord **w** not hear;	Ps 66:18
For You **w** judge the peoples with	Ps 67:4
at home **w** divide the spoil!"	Ps 68:12
the LORD **w** dwell *there* forever.	Ps 68:16
Surely God **w** shatter the head of	Ps 68:21
"I **w** bring *them* back from Bashan.	Ps 68:22
I **w** bring *them* back from the	Ps 68:22
Kings **w** bring gifts to You.	Ps 68:29
Envoys **w** come out of Egypt;	Ps 68:31
Ethiopia **w** quickly stretch out her	Ps 68:31
I **w** praise the name of God with	Ps 69:30
And it **w** please the LORD better	Ps 69:31
For God **w** save Zion and build the	Ps 69:35
of His servants **w** inherit it,	Ps 69:36
who love His name **w** dwell in it.	Ps 69:36
as for me, I **w** hope continually,	Ps 71:14
w praise You yet more and more.	Ps 71:14
I **w** come with the mighty deeds of	Ps 71:16
I **w** make mention of Your	Ps 71:16
and distresses **W** revive me again,	Ps 71:20
And **w** bring me up again from the	Ps 71:20
I **w** also praise You with a harp,	Ps 71:22
I **w** sing praises with the lyre,	Ps 71:22
My lips **w** shout for joy when I	Ps 71:23
My tongue also **w** utter Your	Ps 71:24
For he **w** deliver the needy when he	Ps 72:12
He **w** have compassion on the poor	Ps 72:13
the lives of the needy he **w** save.	Ps 72:13
He **w** rescue their life from	Ps 72:14
blood **w** be precious in his sight;	Ps 72:14
Its fruit **w** wave like *the cedars*	Ps 72:16
"I **w** speak thus,"	Ps 73:15
You **w** despise their form.	Ps 73:20
With Your counsel You **w** guide me,	Ps 73:24
who are far from You **w** perish;	Ps 73:27
O God, **w** the adversary revile,	Ps 74:10
as for me, I **w** declare *it* forever;	Ps 75:9
I **w** sing praises to the God of	Ps 75:9
horns of the wicked He **w** cut off,	Ps 75:10
horns of the righteous **w** be lifted up.	Ps 75:10
With a remnant of wrath You **w** gird	Ps 76:10
w cut off the spirit of princes;	Ps 76:12
rises to God, and I **w** cry aloud;	Ps 77:1
rises to God, and He **w** hear me.	Ps 77:1
I **w** remember my song in the night;	Ps 77:6
I **w** meditate with my heart,	Ps 77:6
W the Lord reject forever?	Ps 77:7
And **w** He never be favorable again?	Ps 77:7
I **w** remember Your wonders of old.	Ps 77:11
I **w** meditate on all Your work And	Ps 77:12
I **w** open my mouth in a parable;	Ps 78:2
I **w** utter dark sayings of old,	Ps 78:2
We **w** not conceal them from their	Ps 78:4
W He provide meat for His people?"	Ps 78:20
W You be angry forever?	Ps 79:5
W Your jealousy burn like fire?	Ps 79:5
W give thanks to You forever;	Ps 79:13
we **w** tell of Your praise.	Ps 79:13
shine *upon us,* and we **w** be saved.	Ps 80:3
How long **w** You be angry with the	Ps 80:4
shine *upon us,* and we **w** be saved.	Ps 80:7
us, and we **w** call upon Your name.	Ps 80:18
shine *upon us,* and we **w** be saved.	Ps 80:19
O My people, and I **w** admonish you;	Ps 81:8
your mouth wide and I **w** fill it.	Ps 81:10
How long **w** you judge unjustly And	Ps 82:2
"Nevertheless you **w** die like men And	Ps 82:7
W You be angry with us forever?	Ps 85:5
W You prolong Your anger to all	Ps 85:5
W You not Yourself revive us	Ps 85:6
I **w** hear what God the LORD will	Ps 85:8
will hear what God the LORD **w** say;	Ps 85:8
He **w** speak peace to His people,	Ps 85:8
the LORD **w** give what is good,	Ps 85:12
And our land **w** yield its produce.	Ps 85:12
Righteousness **w** go before Him And	Ps 85:13
w make His footsteps into a way.	Ps 85:13
upon You, For You **w** answer me.	Ps 86:7
I **w** walk in Your truth;	Ps 86:11
I **w** give thanks to You, O Lord my	Ps 86:12
And **w** glorify Your name forever.	Ps 86:12
Most High Himself **w** establish her.	Ps 87:5
The LORD **w** count when He	Ps 87:6
W You perform wonders for the	Ps 88:10
W the departed spirits rise *and*	Ps 88:10
W Your lovingkindness be declared	Ps 88:11
W Your wonders be made known in the	Ps 88:12
I **w** sing of the lovingkindness of	Ps 89:1
To all generations I **w** make known	Ps 89:1
Lovingkindness **w** be built up forever	Ps 89:2
w establish Your faithfulness."	Ps 89:2
I **w** establish your seed forever And	Ps 89:4
The heavens **w** praise Your wonders,	Ps 89:5
whom My hand **w** be established;	Ps 89:21
My arm also **w** strengthen him.	Ps 89:21

"The enemy w not deceive him, Nor Ps 89:22
My lovingkindness w be with him, Ps 89:24
in My name his horn w be exalted. Ps 89:24
"He w cry to Me, Ps 89:26
I w keep for him forever, Ps 89:28
"So I w establish his descendants Ps 89:29
Then I w punish their transgression Ps 89:32
"But I w not break off My Ps 89:33
"My covenant I w not violate, Nor Ps 89:34
Nor w I alter the utterance of My Ps 89:34
I w not lie to David. Ps 89:35
W You hide Yourself forever? Ps 89:46
W Your wrath burn like fire? Ps 89:46
return, O LORD; how long w *it* Ps 90:13
W abide in the shadow of the Ps 91:1
I w say to the LORD, Ps 91:2
He w cover you with His pinions, Ps 91:4
You w not be afraid of the terror Ps 91:5
You w only look on with your eyes And Ps 91:8
No evil w befall you, Nor will any Ps 91:10
Nor w any plague come near your Ps 91:10
For He w give His angels charge Ps 91:11
They w bear you up in their hands, Ps 91:12
w tread upon the lion and cobra, Ps 91:13
the serpent you w trample down. Ps 91:13
Me, therefore I w deliver him; Ps 91:14
I w set him *securely* on high, Ps 91:14
"He w call upon Me, and I will Ps 91:15
call upon Me, and I w answer him; Ps 91:15
I w be with him in trouble; Ps 91:15
I w rescue him and honor him. Ps 91:15
"With a long life I w satisfy him And Ps 91:16
I w sing for joy at the works of Ps 92:4
behold, Your enemies w perish; Ps 92:9
All who do iniquity w be scattered. Ps 92:9
man w flourish like the palm tree, Ps 92:12
He w grow like a cedar in Lebanon. Ps 92:12
They w flourish in the courts of Ps 92:13
w still yield fruit in old age; Ps 92:14
established, it w not be moved. Ps 93:1
And when w you understand, stupid Ps 94:8
the nations, w He not rebuke, Ps 94:10
the LORD w not abandon His people, Ps 94:14
Nor w He forsake His inheritance. Ps 94:14
For judgment w again be righteous, Ps 94:15
the upright in heart w follow it. Ps 94:15
Who w stand up for me against Ps 94:16
Who w take his stand for me Ps 94:16
O LORD, w hold me up. Ps 94:18
And w destroy them in their evil; Ps 94:23
The LORD our God w destroy them. Ps 94:23
established, it w not be moved; Ps 96:10
He w judge the peoples with equity." Ps 96:10
the trees of the forest w sing for joy Ps 96:12
He w judge the world in Ps 96:13
He w judge the world with Ps 98:9
I w sing of lovingkindness and Ps 101:1
To You, O LORD, I w sing praises. Ps 101:1
I w give heed to the blameless way. Ps 101:2
When w You come to me? Ps 101:2
I w walk within my house in the Ps 101:2
I w set no worthless thing before Ps 101:3
I w know no evil. Ps 101:4
his neighbor, him I w destroy; Ps 101:5
and an arrogant heart w I endure. Ps 101:5
is the one who w minister to me. Ps 101:6
Every morning I w destroy all the Ps 101:8
You w arise *and* have compassion Ps 102:13
nations w fear the name of the LORD Ps 102:15
This w be written for the Ps 102:18
"Even they w perish, but You Ps 102:26
of them w wear out like a garment; Ps 102:26
Like clothing You w change them and Ps 102:26
them and they w be changed. Ps 102:26
Your years w not come to an end. Ps 102:27
children of Your servants w continue, Ps 102:28
w be established before You." Ps 102:28
He w not always strive *with us,* Ps 103:9
Nor w He keep *His anger* forever. Ps 103:9
You who serve Him, doing His w. Ps 103:21 7522
it w not totter forever and ever. Ps 104:5
So that they w not return to cover Ps 104:9
I w sing to the LORD as long as I Ps 104:33
I w sing praise to my God while I Ps 104:33
"To you I w give the land of Ps 105:11
To imprison his princes at w, Ps 105:22 5315
I w sing, I will sing praises, Ps 108:1
I will sing, I w sing praises, Ps 108:1
I w awaken the dawn! Ps 108:2
I w give thanks to You, O LORD, Ps 108:3
And I w sing praises to You among Ps 108:3
"I w exult, I will portion out Ps 108:7
exult, I w portion out Shechem And Ps 108:7
Over Philistia I w shout aloud." Ps 108:9
Who w bring me into the besieged Ps 108:10
Who w lead me to Edom? Ps 108:10
And w You not go forth with our Ps 108:11
Through God we w do valiantly, Ps 108:13
With my mouth I w give thanks Ps 109:30
the midst of many I w praise Him. Ps 109:30
The LORD w stretch forth Your Ps 110:2
Your people w volunteer freely in Ps 110:3
sworn and w not change His mind, Ps 110:4
He w shatter kings in the day of Ps 110:5
He w judge among the nations, He Ps 110:6
He w fill *them* with corpses, Ps 110:6
He w shatter the chief men over a Ps 110:6
He w drink from the brook by the Ps 110:7
Therefore He w lift up *His* head. Ps 110:7

I w give thanks to the LORD with Ps 111:1
w remember His covenant forever. Ps 111:5
descendants w be mighty on earth; Ps 112:2
of the upright w be blessed. Ps 112:2
He w maintain his cause in Ps 112:5
For he w never be shaken; Ps 112:6
righteous w be remembered forever. Ps 112:6
He w not fear evil tidings; Ps 112:7
heart is upheld, he w not fear, Ps 112:8
His horn w be exalted in honor. Ps 112:9
The wicked w see it and be vexed, Ps 112:10
w gnash his teeth and melt away; Ps 112:10
The desire of the wicked w perish. Ps 112:10
who make them w become like them, Ps 115:8
been mindful of us; He w bless *us;* Ps 115:12
He w bless the house of Israel; Ps 115:12
He w bless the house of Aaron. Ps 115:12
w bless those who fear the LORD, Ps 115:13
we w bless the LORD From this time Ps 115:18
The LORD is for me; I w not fear; Ps 118:6
Therefore I w look *with* Ps 118:7
the LORD I w surely cut them off. Ps 118:10
the LORD I w surely cut them off. Ps 118:11
the LORD I w surely cut them off. Ps 118:12
I w not die, but live, And tell of Ps 118:17
The righteous w enter through it. Ps 118:20
I w meditate on Your precepts And Ps 119:15
So I w meditate on Your wonders. Ps 119:27
For You w enlarge my heart. Ps 119:32
So I w have an answer for him who Ps 119:42
So I w keep Your law continually, Ps 119:44
And I w walk at liberty, For I Ps 119:45
I w also speak of Your testimonies Ps 119:46
And I w meditate on Your statutes. Ps 119:48
my heart I w observe Your precepts. Ps 119:69
So that I w not be ashamed. Ps 119:80
"When w You comfort me?" Ps 119:82
When w You execute judgment on Ps 119:84
I w never forget Your precepts, For Ps 119:93
I have sworn and I w confirm it, Ps 119:106
I w keep Your righteous ordinances. Ps 119:106
I w observe Your statutes. Ps 119:145
I w lift up my eyes to the Ps 121:1
He w not allow your foot to slip; Ps 121:3
He who keeps you w not slumber. Ps 121:3
W neither slumber nor sleep. Ps 121:4
The sun w not smite you by day, Ps 121:6
LORD w protect you from all evil; Ps 121:7
He w keep your soul. Ps 121:7
The LORD w guard your going out Ps 121:8
and my friends, I w now say, Ps 122:8
LORD our God, I w seek your good. Ps 122:9
So that the righteous w not put forth Ps 125:3
The LORD w lead them away with the Ps 125:5
w not be ashamed When they speak Ps 127:5
You w be happy and it will be well Ps 128:2
happy and it w be well with you. Ps 128:2
And He w redeem Israel From all Ps 130:8
"Surely I w not enter my house, Ps 132:3
I w not give sleep to my eyes Or Ps 132:4
from which He w not turn back: Ps 132:11
body I w set upon your throne. Ps 132:11
"If your sons w keep My covenant And Ps 132:12
My testimony which I w teach them, Ps 132:12
Here I w dwell, for I have desired Ps 132:14
"I w abundantly bless her Ps 132:15
I w satisfy her needy with bread. Ps 132:15
also I w clothe with salvation, Ps 132:16
godly ones w sing aloud for joy. Ps 132:16
"There I w cause the horn of Ps 132:17
"His enemies I w clothe with shame, Ps 132:18
For the LORD w judge His people And Ps 135:14
And w have compassion on His Ps 135:14
who make them w be like them, Ps 135:18
How blessed w be the one who Ps 137:8
How blessed w be the one who Ps 137:9
I w give You thanks with all my Ps 138:1
I w sing praises to You before Ps 138:1
I w bow down toward Your holy Ps 138:2
the earth w give thanks to You, Ps 138:4
w sing of the ways of the LORD, Ps 138:5
of trouble, You w revive me; Ps 138:7
You w stretch forth Your hand Ps 138:7
And Your right hand w save me. Ps 138:7
w accomplish what concerns me; Ps 138:8
Even there Your hand w lead me, Ps 139:10
Your right hand w lay hold of me. Ps 139:10
the darkness w overwhelm me, Ps 139:11
the light around me w be night," Ps 139:11
I w give thanks to You, for I am Ps 139:14
I know that the LORD w maintain Ps 140:12
w give thanks to Your name; Ps 140:13
upright w dwell in Your presence. Ps 140:13
The righteous w surround me, For Ps 142:7
You w deal bountifully with me." Ps 142:7
Or I w become like those who go down Ps 143:7
Teach me to do Your w, Ps 143:10
I w sing a new song to You, O God; Ps 144:9
strings I w sing praises to You, Ps 144:9
I w extol You, my God, O King, Ps 145:1
And I w bless Your name forever and Ps 145:1
Every day I w bless You, And I Ps 145:2
And I w praise Your name forever Ps 145:2
Your wonderful works, I w meditate. Ps 145:5
And I w tell of Your greatness. Ps 145:6
abundant goodness And w shout Ps 145:7
He w fulfill the desire of those Ps 145:19
He w also hear their cry and will Ps 145:19
hear their cry and w save them. Ps 145:19

But all the wicked He w destroy. Ps 145:20
w speak the praise of the LORD, Ps 145:21
And all flesh w bless His holy Ps 145:21
I w praise the LORD while I live; Ps 146:2
I w sing praises to my God while I Ps 146:2
The LORD w reign forever, Your God, Ps 146:10
a decree which w not pass away. Ps 148:6
He w beautify the afflicted ones Ps 149:4
A wise man w hear and increase in Pr 1:5
w acquire wise counsel, Pr 1:5
We w find all *kinds* of precious Pr 1:13
We w fill our houses with spoil; Pr 1:13
w you love being simple-minded? Pr 1:22
I w pour out my spirit on you; Pr 1:23
I w make my words known to you. Pr 1:23
I w also laugh at your calamity; Pr 1:26
I w mock when your dread comes, Pr 1:26
"Then they w call on me, but I Pr 1:28
call on me, but I w not answer; Pr 1:28
They w seek me diligently but Pr 1:28
seek me diligently but they w not Pr 1:28
the waywardness of the naive w kill Pr 1:32
And the complacency of fools w Pr 1:32
to me shall live securely And w be at Pr 1:33
son, if you w receive my words Pr 2:1
w discern the fear of the LORD And Pr 2:5
Then you w discern righteousness Pr 2:9
For wisdom w enter your heart And Pr 2:10
w be pleasant to your soul; Pr 2:10
Discretion w guard you, Pr 2:11
Understanding w watch over you, Pr 2:11
you w walk in the way of good men And Pr 2:20
the upright w live in the land And Pr 2:21
And the blameless w remain in it; Pr 2:21
wicked w be cut off from the land And Pr 2:22
treacherous w be uprooted from it. Pr 2:22
life And peace they w add to you. Pr 3:2
So you w find favor and good Pr 3:4
And He w make your paths straight. Pr 3:6
It w be healing to your body And Pr 3:8
barns w be filled with plenty And Pr 3:10
vats w overflow with new wine. Pr 3:10
So they w be life to your soul And Pr 3:22
you w walk in your way securely And Pr 3:23
And your foot w not stumble. Pr 3:23
you lie down, you w not be afraid; Pr 3:24
lie down, your sleep w be sweet. Pr 3:24
For the LORD w be your confidence And Pr 3:26
And w keep your foot from being Pr 3:26
back, And tomorrow I w give *it,*" Pr 3:28
The wise w inherit honor, But Pr 3:35
forsake her, and she w guard you; Pr 4:6
her, and she w watch over you. Pr 4:6
"Prize her, and she w exalt you; Pr 4:8
w honor you if you embrace her. Pr 4:8
"She w place on your head a Pr 4:9
She w present you with a crown of Pr 4:9
the years of your life w be many. Pr 4:10
walk, your steps w not be impeded; Pr 4:12
And if you run, you w not stumble. Pr 4:12
all your ways w be established. Pr 4:26
Or you w give your vigor to others Pr 5:9
And strangers w be filled with your Pr 5:10
And your hard-earned goods w *go* Pr 5:10
iniquities w capture the wicked, Pr 5:22
And he w be held with the cords of Pr 5:22
He w die for lack of instruction, Pr 5:23
of his folly he w go astray. Pr 5:23
How long w you lie down, O Pr 6:9
When w you arise from your sleep? Pr 6:9
poverty w come in like a vagabond And Pr 6:11
his calamity w come suddenly; Pr 6:15
Instantly he w be broken and Pr 6:15
broken and there w be no healing. Pr 6:15
you walk about, they w guide you; Pr 6:22
you sleep, they w watch over you; Pr 6:22
you awake, they w talk to you. Pr 6:22
touches her w not go unpunished. Pr 6:29
Wounds and disgrace he w find, Pr 6:33
his reproach w not be blotted out. Pr 6:33
And he w not spare in the day of Pr 6:34
He w not accept any ransom, Nor Pr 6:35
Nor w he be satisfied though you Pr 6:35
At the full moon he w come home." Pr 7:20
So he does not know that it w *cost* Pr 7:23
"Listen, for I w speak noble things; Pr 8:6
And the opening of my lips w *reveal* Pr 8:6
"For my mouth w utter truth; Pr 8:7
who diligently seek me w find me. Pr 8:17
reprove a scoffer, or he w hate Pr 9:8
a wise man and he w love you. Pr 9:8
wise man and he w be still wiser, Pr 9:9
and he w increase *his* learning. Pr 9:9
by me your days w be multiplied, Pr 9:11
years of life w be added to you. Pr 9:11
if you scoff, you alone w bear it. Pr 9:12
The LORD w not allow the righteous Pr 10:3
But He w reject the craving Pr 10:3
But the name of the wicked w rot. Pr 10:7
wise of heart w receive commands, Pr 10:8
a babbling fool w be ruined. Pr 10:8
perverts his ways w be found out. Pr 10:9
a babbling fool w be ruined. Pr 10:10
the wicked fears w come upon him, Pr 10:24
desire of the righteous w be granted. Pr 10:24
years of the wicked w be shortened. Pr 10:27
The righteous w never be shaken, Pr 10:30
wicked w not dwell in the land. Pr 10:30
the perverted tongue w be cut out. Pr 10:31

integrity of the upright **w** guide them	Pr 11:3	
of the treacherous **w** destroy them.	Pr 11:3	
of the blameless **w** smooth his way,	Pr 11:5	
wicked **w** fall by his own wickedness	Pr 11:5	
of the upright **w** deliver them,	Pr 11:6	
w be caught by *their own* greed.	Pr 11:6	
dies, *his* expectation **w** perish,	Pr 11:7	
the righteous **w** be delivered.	Pr 11:9	
a stranger **w** surely suffer for it,	Pr 11:15	
who is steadfast in righteousness **w**	Pr 11:19	
And he who pursues evil **w** *bring*	Pr 11:19	
the evil man **w** not go unpunished,	Pr 11:21	
of the righteous **w** be delivered.	Pr 11:21	
The generous man **w** be prosperous,	Pr 11:25	
who waters **w** himself be watered.	Pr 11:25	
grain, the people **w** curse him,	Pr 11:26	
But blessing **w** be on the head of	Pr 11:26	
evil, evil **w** come to him.	Pr 11:27	
who trusts in his riches **w** fall,	Pr 11:28	
w flourish like the *green* leaf.	Pr 11:28	
his own house **w** inherit wind,	Pr 11:29	
w be servant to the wisehearted.	Pr 11:29	
w be rewarded in the earth,	Pr 11:31	
man **w** obtain favor from the LORD,	Pr 12:2	
But He **w** condemn a man who devises	Pr 12:2	
A man **w** not be established by	Pr 12:3	
of the righteous **w** not be moved.	Pr 12:3	
of the upright **w** deliver them.	Pr 12:6	
house of the righteous **w** stand.	Pr 12:7	
A man **w** be praised according to	Pr 12:8	
of perverse mind **w** be despised.	Pr 12:8	
his land **w** have plenty of bread,	Pr 12:11	
righteous **w** escape from trouble.	Pr 12:13	
A man **w** be satisfied with good by	Pr 12:14	
of a man's hands **w** return to him.	Pr 12:14	
lips **w** be established forever,	Pr 12:19	
The hand of the diligent **w** rule,	Pr 12:24	
slack *hand* **w** be put to forced labor.	Pr 12:24	
one who despises the word **w** be in	Pr 13:13	
the commandment **w** be rewarded.	Pr 13:13	
Poverty and shame **w** *come* to him	Pr 13:18	
who regards reproof **w** be honored.	Pr 13:18	
who walks with wise men **w** be wise,	Pr 13:20	
companion of fools **w** suffer harm.	Pr 13:20	
w be rewarded with prosperity.	Pr 13:21	
lips of the wise **w** protect them.	Pr 14:3	
A trustworthy witness **w** not lie,	Pr 14:5	
Or you **w** not discern words of	Pr 14:7	
among the upright there is good **w**.	Pr 14:9	7522
house of the wicked **w** be destroyed,	Pr 14:11	
tent of the upright **w** flourish.	Pr 14:11	
w have his fill of his own ways,	Pr 14:14	
good man **w** *be satisfied* with his.	Pr 14:14	
evil **w** bow down before the good,	Pr 14:19	
W they not go astray who devise	Pr 14:22	
But kindness and truth **w** *be to*	Pr 14:22	
And his children **w** have refuge.	Pr 14:26	
He who hates reproof **w** die.	Pr 15:10	
him, He **w** not go to the wise.	Pr 15:12	
The LORD **w** tear down the house of	Pr 15:25	
But He **w** establish the boundary of	Pr 15:25	
But he who hates bribes **w** live.	Pr 15:27	
reproof **W** dwell among the wise.	Pr 15:31	
And your plans **w** be established.	Pr 16:3	
Assuredly, he **w** not be unpunished.	Pr 16:5	
But a wise man **w** appease it.	Pr 16:14	
gives attention to the word **w** find	Pr 16:20	
wise in heart **w** be called understanding,	Pr 16:21	
A servant who acts wisely **w** rule	Pr 17:2	
And **w** share in the inheritance	Pr 17:2	
at calamity **w** not go unpunished.	Pr 17:5	
messenger **w** be sent against him.	Pr 17:11	
Evil **w** not depart from his house.	Pr 17:13	
mouth his stomach **w** be satisfied;	Pr 18:20	
He **w** be satisfied *with* the product	Pr 18:20	
those who love it **w** eat its fruit.	Pr 18:21	
false witness **w** not go unpunished,	Pr 19:5	
he who tells lies **w** not escape.	Pr 19:5	
Many **w** seek the favor of a	Pr 19:6	
keeps understanding **w** find good.	Pr 19:8	
false witness **w** not go unpunished,	Pr 19:9	
And he who tells lies **w** perish.	Pr 19:9	
And an idle man **w** suffer hunger.	Pr 19:15	
who is careless of conduct **w** die.	Pr 19:16	
He **w** repay him for his good deed.	Pr 19:17	
A man of great anger **w** bear	Pr 19:19	
you **w** only have to do it again.	Pr 19:19	
counsel of the LORD **w** stand.	Pr 19:21	
But **w** not even bring it back to	Pr 19:24	
and he **w** gain knowledge.	Pr 19:25	
And you **w** stray from the words of	Pr 19:27	
for a man, But any fool **w** quarrel.	Pr 20:3	
Do not love sleep, or you **w** become	Pr 20:13	
and you **w** be satisfied with food.	Pr 20:13	
his mouth **w** be filled with gravel.	Pr 20:17	
lamp **w** go out in time of darkness.	Pr 20:20	
W not be blessed in the end.	Pr 20:21	
"I **w** repay evil";	Pr 20:22	
for the LORD, and He **w** save you.	Pr 20:22	
violence of the wicked **w** drag them	Pr 21:7	
W also cry himself and not be	Pr 21:13	
W rest in the assembly of the dead.	Pr 21:16	
He who loves pleasure **w** *become*	Pr 21:17	
wine and oil **w** not become rich.	Pr 21:17	
A false witness **w** perish, But the	Pr 21:28	
man who listens *to the truth* **w** speak	Pr 21:28	
guards himself **w** be far from them.	Pr 22:5	
he is old he **w** not depart from it.	Pr 22:6	
who sows iniquity **w** reap vanity,	Pr 22:8	
And the rod of his fury **w** perish.	Pr 22:8	
He who is generous **w** be blessed,	Pr 22:9	
scoffer, and contention **w** go out,	Pr 22:10	
Even strife and dishonor **w** cease.	Pr 22:10	
I **w** be killed in the streets!"	Pr 22:13	
cursed of the LORD **w** fall into it.	Pr 22:14	
The rod of discipline **w** remove it far	Pr 22:15	
w only *come to* poverty.	Pr 22:16	
For it **w** be pleasant if you keep	Pr 22:18	
For the LORD **w** plead their case And	Pr 22:23	
Or you **w** learn his ways And find a	Pr 22:25	
He **w** stand before kings;	Pr 22:29	
He **w** not stand before obscure men.	Pr 22:29	
You **w** vomit up the morsel you have	Pr 23:8	
For he **w** despise the wisdom of	Pr 23:9	
He **w** plead their case against you.	Pr 23:11	
him with the rod, he **w** not die.	Pr 23:13	
wise, My own heart also **w** be glad;	Pr 23:15	
And my inmost being **w** rejoice When	Pr 23:16	
And your hope **w** not be cut off.	Pr 23:18	
and the glutton **w** come to poverty,	Pr 23:21	
drowsiness **w** clothe *one* with rags.	Pr 23:21	
the righteous **w** greatly rejoice,	Pr 23:24	
a wise son **w** be glad in him.	Pr 23:24	
Your eyes **w** see strange things And	Pr 23:33	
your mind **w** utter perverse things.	Pr 23:33	
And you **w** be like one who lies	Pr 23:34	
I **w** seek another drink."	Pr 23:35	
by wise guidance you **w** wage war,	Pr 24:6	
do evil, Men **w** call a schemer.	Pr 24:8	
And **w** He not render to man	Pr 24:12	
find *it,* then there **w** be a future,	Pr 24:14	
And your hope **w** not be cut off.	Pr 24:14	
Or the LORD **w** see *it* and be	Pr 24:18	
w be no future for the evil man;	Pr 24:20	
lamp of the wicked **w** be put out.	Pr 24:20	
their calamity **w** rise suddenly,	Pr 24:22	
righteous," Peoples **w** curse him,	Pr 24:24	
curse him, nations **w** abhor him;	Pr 24:24	
rebuke the *wicked* **w** be delight,	Pr 24:25	
a good blessing **w** come upon them.	Pr 24:25	
I **w** render to the man according to	Pr 24:29	
your poverty **w** come *as* a robber And	Pr 24:34	
And his throne **w** be established in	Pr 25:5	
what **w** you do in the end,	Pr 25:8	
Or he who hears *it* **w** reproach you,	Pr 25:10	
And the evil report about you **w** not	Pr 25:10	
Or he **w** become weary of you and hate	Pr 25:17	
For you **w** heap burning coals on	Pr 25:22	
head, And the LORD **w** reward you.	Pr 25:22	
Or you **w** also be like him.	Pr 26:4	
His wickedness **w** be revealed	Pr 26:26	
He who digs a pit **w** fall into it,	Pr 26:27	
a stone, it **w** come back on him.	Pr 26:27	
It **w** be reckoned a curse to him.	Pr 27:14	
He who tends the fig tree **w** eat its	Pr 27:18	
cares for his master **w** be honored.	Pr 27:18	
his foolishness **w** not depart from him.	Pr 27:22	
The lambs **w** *be* for your clothing,	Pr 27:26	
And the goats **w** *bring* the price	Pr 27:26	
And *there* **w** *be* goats' milk	Pr 27:27	
W himself fall into his own pit,	Pr 28:10	
But the blameless **w** inherit good.	Pr 28:10	
his transgressions **w** not prosper,	Pr 28:13	
forsakes *them* **w** find compassion.	Pr 28:13	
he who hardens his heart **w** fall into	Pr 28:14	
he who hates unjust gain **w** prolong	Pr 28:16	
blood **W** be a fugitive until death;	Pr 28:17	
walks blamelessly **w** be delivered,	Pr 28:18	
who is crooked **w** fall all at once.	Pr 28:18	
He who tills his land **w** have plenty	Pr 28:19	
pursuits **w** have poverty in plenty.	Pr 28:19	
man **w** abound with blessings,	Pr 28:20	
to be rich **w** not go unpunished.	Pr 28:20	
piece of bread a man **w** transgress.	Pr 28:21	
know that want **w** come upon him.	Pr 28:22	
He who rebukes a man **w** afterward	Pr 28:23	
who trusts in the LORD **w** prosper.	Pr 28:25	
who walks wisely **w** be delivered.	Pr 28:26	
gives to the poor **w** never want,	Pr 28:27	
shuts his eyes **w** have many curses.	Pr 28:27	
W suddenly be broken beyond remedy	Pr 29:1	
throne **w** be established forever.	Pr 29:14	
the righteous **w** see their fall.	Pr 29:16	
son, and he **w** give you comfort;	Pr 29:17	
He **w** also delight your soul.	Pr 29:17	
A slave **w** not be instructed by	Pr 29:19	
there **w** be no response.	Pr 29:19	
W in the end find him to be a son.	Pr 29:21	
A man's pride **w** bring him low, But	Pr 29:23	
a humble spirit **w** obtain honor.	Pr 29:23	
trusts in the LORD **w** be exalted.	Pr 29:25	
Do not add to His words Or He **w**	Pr 30:6	
and you **w** be proved a liar.	Pr 30:6	
Or he **w** curse you and you will be	Pr 30:10	
Or he will curse you and you **w** be	Pr 30:10	
things that **w** not be satisfied,	Pr 30:15	
be satisfied, Four that **w** not say,	Pr 30:15	
ravens of the valley **w** pick it out,	Pr 30:17	
And the young eagles **w** eat it.	Pr 30:17	
For they **w** drink and forget what is	Pr 31:5	
And he **w** have no lack of gain.	Pr 31:11	
which has been is that which **w** be,	Ec 1:9	
been done is that which **w** be done.	Ec 1:9	
of the later things which **w** occur,	Ec 1:11	
There **w** be for them no remembrance	Ec 1:11	
those who **w** come later *still.*	Ec 1:11	
now, I **w** test you with pleasure.	Ec 2:1	
for what **w** the man *do* who	Ec 2:12	
for what *will* the man *do* who **w**	Ec 2:12	
of the fool, it **w** also befall me.	Ec 2:15	
coming days all **w** be forgotten.	Ec 2:16	
it to the man who **w** come after me.	Ec 2:18	
he **w** be a wise man or a fool?	Ec 2:19	
Yet he **w** have control over all the	Ec 2:19	
yet so that man **w** not find out the	Ec 3:11	
God does **w** remain forever;	Ec 3:14	
that which **w** be has already been,	Ec 3:15	
"God **w** judge both the righteous	Ec 3:17	
For who **w** bring him to see what	Ec 3:22	
him to see what **w** occur after him?	Ec 3:22	
the one **w** lift up his companion.	Ec 4:10	
and even the ones who **w** come later	Ec 4:16	
later **w** not be happy with him,	Ec 4:16	
w not be satisfied with money,	Ec 5:10	
womb, so **w** he return as he came.	Ec 5:15	
He **w** take nothing from the fruit	Ec 5:15	
as a man is born, thus **w** he die.	Ec 5:16	
For he **w** not often consider the	Ec 5:20	
He **w** spend them like a shadow.	Ec 6:12	
what **w** be after him under the sun?	Ec 6:12	
as the other So that man **w** not	Ec 7:14	
not discover anything *that* **w** *be*	Ec 7:14	
so that you **w** not hear your servant	Ec 7:21	
and I said, "I **w** be wise,"	Ec 7:23	
pleasing to God **w** escape from her,	Ec 7:26	
the sinner **w** be captured by her.	Ec 7:26	
for he **w** do whatever he pleases."	Ec 8:3	
authoritative, who **w** say to him,	Ec 8:4	
If no one knows what **w** happen,	Ec 8:7	
who can tell him when it **w** happen?	Ec 8:7	
and evil **w** not deliver those who	Ec 8:8	
still I know that it **w** be well for	Ec 8:12	
But it **w** not be well for the evil	Ec 8:13	
w not lengthen his days like a shadow	Ec 8:13	
and this **w** stand by him in his	Ec 8:15	
laboriously, he **w** not discover;	Ec 8:17	
Man does not know whether *it* **w** *be*	Ec 9:1	
For the living know they **w** die;	Ec 9:5	
and they **w** no longer have a share	Ec 9:6	
No man knows what **w** happen,	Ec 10:14	
tell him what **w** come after him?	Ec 10:14	
of the heavens **w** carry the sound and	Ec 10:20	
creature **w** make the matter known.	Ec 10:20	
for you **w** find it after many days.	Ec 11:1	
He who watches the wind **w** not sow	Ec 11:4	
looks at the clouds **w** not reap.	Ec 11:4	
or evening sowing **w** succeed,	Ec 11:6	
both of them alike **w** be good.	Ec 11:6	
for they **w** be many. Everything that	Ec 11:8	
Everything that is to come **w** *be*	Ec 11:8	
Yet know that God **w** bring you to	Ec 11:9	
years draw near when you **w** say,	Ec 12:1	
and one **w** arise at the sound of	Ec 12:4	
daughters of song **w** sing softly.	Ec 12:4	
w return to the earth as it was,	Ec 12:7	
w return to God who gave it.	Ec 12:7	
God **w** bring every act to judgment,	Ec 12:14	
"We **w** rejoice in you and be glad;	SS 1:4	
We **w** extol your love more than	SS 1:4	
"We **w** make for you ornaments of	SS 1:11	
w not arouse or awaken *my* love Until	SS 3:5	
I **w** go my way to the mountain of	SS 4:6	
As to what you **w** tell him:	SS 5:8	
'I **w** climb the palm tree, I will	SS 7:8	
w take hold of its fruit stalks.'	SS 7:8	
There I **w** give you my love.	SS 7:12	
love, Nor **w** rivers overflow it;	SS 8:7	
"If she is a wall, We **w** build on	SS 8:9	
We **w** barricade her with planks of	SS 8:9	
Where **w** you be stricken again, *As*	Is 1:5	
prayer, I **w** hide My eyes from you	Is 1:15	
multiply prayers, I **w** not listen.	Is 1:15	
They **w** be as white as snow;	Is 1:18	
like crimson, They **w** be like wool.	Is 1:18	
You **w** eat the best of the land;	Is 1:19	
You **w** be devoured by the sword."	Is 1:20	
I **w** be relieved of My adversaries And	Is 1:24	
"I **w** also turn My hand against	Is 1:25	
And **w** smelt away your dross as	Is 1:25	
lye And **w** remove all your alloy.	Is 1:25	
"Then I **w** restore your judges as	Is 1:26	
After that you **w** be called the	Is 1:26	
Zion **w** be redeemed with justice And	Is 1:27	
and sinners **w** be crushed together,	Is 1:28	
who forsake the LORD **w** come	Is 1:28	
you **w** be ashamed of the oaks which	Is 1:29	
And you **w** be embarrassed at the	Is 1:29	
For you **w** be like an oak whose	Is 1:30	
The strong man **w** become tinder,	Is 1:31	
there **w** be none to quench *them.*	Is 1:31	
Now it **w** come about that In the last	Is 2:2	
house of the LORD **W** be established	Is 2:2	
And **w** be raised above the hills;	Is 2:2	
all the nations **w** stream to it.	Is 2:2	
And many peoples **w** come and say,	Is 2:3	
For the law **w** go forth from Zion And	Is 2:3	
He **w** judge between the nations,	Is 2:4	
And **w** render decisions for many	Is 2:4	
And they **w** hammer their swords	Is 2:4	
Nation **w** not lift up sword against	Is 2:4	
And never again **w** they learn war.	Is 2:4	
The proud look of man **w** be abased	Is 2:11	
the loftiness of man **w** be humbled,	Is 2:11	
alone **w** be exalted in that day.	Is 2:11	
For the LORD of hosts **w** have a day	Is 2:12	
And *it* **w** *be* against all	Is 2:13	
The pride of man **w** be humbled And	Is 2:17	

the loftiness of men w be abased;	Is 2:17
LORD alone w be exalted in that day,	Is 2:17
But the idols w completely vanish.	Is 2:18
Men w go into caves of the rocks	Is 2:19
In that day men w cast away to the	Is 2:20
And I w make mere lads their	Is 3:4
children w rule over them,	Is 3:4
And the people w be oppressed,	Is 3:5
youth w storm against the elder And	Is 3:5
ruins w be under your charge,"	Is 3:6
He w protest on that day, saying,	Is 3:7
"I w not be *your* healer, For in	Is 3:7
Say to the righteous that *it* w *go*	Is 3:10
For they w eat the fruit of their	Is 3:10
Woe to the wicked! *It* w *go* badly	Is 3:11
what he deserves w be done to him.	Is 3:11
Therefore the Lord w afflict the	Is 3:17
w make their foreheads bare."	Is 3:17
In that day the Lord w take away	Is 3:18
Now it w come about that instead	Is 3:24
perfume there w be putrefaction;	Is 3:24
Your men w fall by the sword And	Is 3:25
And her gates w lament and mourn,	Is 3:26
deserted she w sit on the ground.	Is 3:26
For seven women w take hold of one	Is 4:1
"We w eat our own bread and wear	Is 4:1
LORD w be beautiful and glorious,	Is 4:2
and the fruit of the earth w *be*	Is 4:2
It w come about that he who is	Is 4:3
remains in Jerusalem w be called holy	Is 4:3
then the LORD w create over the	Is 4:5
over all the glory w be a canopy.	Is 4:5
There w be a shelter to *give*	Is 4:6
I w remove its hedge and it will	Is 5:5
its hedge and it w be consumed;	Is 5:5
I w break down its wall and it	Is 5:5
and it w become trampled ground.	Is 5:5
"I w lay it waste;	Is 5:6
It w not be pruned or hoed, But	Is 5:6
But briars and thorns w come up.	Is 5:6
I w also charge the clouds to rain	Is 5:6
w yield *only* one bath *of wine,*	Is 5:10
w yield *but* an ephah of grain."	Is 5:10
So the *common* man w be humbled and	Is 5:15
of the proud also w be abased.	Is 5:15
of hosts w be exalted in judgment,	Is 5:16
And the holy God w show Himself	Is 5:16
lambs w graze as in their pasture,	Is 5:17
And strangers w eat in the waste	Is 5:17
So their root w become like rot	Is 5:24
He w also lift up a standard to	Is 5:26
And w whistle for it from the ends	Is 5:26
it w come with speed swiftly.	Is 5:26
And it w growl over it in that day	Is 5:30
I send, and who w go for Us?"	Is 6:8
there w be a tenth portion in it,	Is 6:13
it w again be *subject* to burning,	Is 6:13
65 years Ephraim w be shattered,	Is 7:8
If you w not believe, you surely	Is 7:9
"I w not ask, nor will I test the	Is 7:12
not ask, nor w I test the LORD!"	Is 7:12
that you w try the patience of my	Is 7:13
Lord Himself w give you a sign:	Is 7:14
w be with child and bear a son,	Is 7:14
and she w call His name Immanuel.	Is 7:14
"He w eat curds and honey at the	Is 7:15
"For before the boy w know *enough*	Is 7:16
two kings you dread w be forsaken.	Is 7:16
"The LORD w bring on you, on your	Is 7:17
that day the LORD w whistle for the	Is 7:18
They w all come and settle on	Is 7:19
day the Lord w shave with a razor,	Is 7:20
and it w also remove the beard.	Is 7:20
the milk produced he w eat curds,	Is 7:22
the land w eat curds and honey.	Is 7:22
And it w come about in that day,	Is 7:23
w become briars and thorns.	Is 7:23
People w come there with bows and	Is 7:24
the land w be briars and thorns.	Is 7:24
you w not go there for fear of	Is 7:25
but they w become a place for	Is 7:25
"And I w take to Myself faithful	Is 8:2
spoil of Samaria w be carried away	Is 8:4
And it w rise up over all its	Is 8:7
"Then it w sweep on into Judah,	Is 8:8
it w overflow and pass through,	Is 8:8
It w reach even to the neck;	Is 8:8
w fill the breadth of your land,	Is 8:8
a plan, but it w be thwarted;	Is 8:10
a proposal, but it w not stand,	Is 8:10
"Many w stumble over them,	Is 8:15
Then they w fall and be broken;	Is 8:15
w even be snared and caught."	Is 8:15
And I w wait for the LORD who is	Is 8:17
I w even look eagerly for Him.	Is 8:17
They w pass through the land	Is 8:21
and it w turn out that when they	Is 8:21
they w be enraged and curse their	Is 8:21
Then they w look to the earth, and	Is 8:22
and *they* w *be* driven away into	Is 8:22
But there w be no *more* gloom for	Is 9:1
in darkness W see a great light;	Is 9:2
land, The light w shine on them.	Is 9:2
They w be glad in Your presence As	Is 9:3
rolled in blood, w be for burning,	Is 9:5
For a child w be born to us, a son	Is 9:6
to us, a son w be given to us;	Is 9:6
government w rest on His shoulders;	Is 9:6
w be called Wonderful Counselor,	Is 9:6
There w be no end to the increase	Is 9:7
LORD of hosts w accomplish this.	Is 9:7
we w rebuild with smooth stones;	Is 9:10
we w replace *them* with cedars."	Is 9:10
Now what w you do in the day of	Is 10:3
which w come from afar?	Is 10:3
To whom w you flee for help?	Is 10:3
And where w you leave your wealth?	Is 10:3
So it w be that when the Lord has	Is 10:12
He w *say,* "I will punish	Is 10:12
"I w punish the fruit of the	Is 10:12
w send a wasting disease among his	Is 10:16
And under his glory a fire w be	Is 10:16
And the light of Israel w become a	Is 10:17
And it w burn and devour his	Is 10:17
And He w destroy the glory of his	Is 10:18
And it w be as when a sick man	Is 10:18
trees of his forest w be so small in	Is 10:19
w never again rely on the one who	Is 10:20
but w truly rely on the LORD,	Is 10:20
A remnant w return, the remnant of	Is 10:21
a remnant within them w return;	Is 10:22
the Lord GOD of hosts w execute in	Is 10:23
indignation *against you* w be spent and	Is 10:25
you will be spent and My anger w	Is 10:25
The LORD of hosts w arouse a	Is 10:26
and His staff w be over the sea and	Is 10:26
and He w lift it up the way *He did*	Is 10:26
So it w be in that day, that his	Is 10:27
that his burden w be removed from	Is 10:27
w be broken because of fatness.	Is 10:27
"Geba w be our lodging place."	Is 10:29
Yet today he w halt at Nob;	Is 10:32
w lop off the boughs with a	Is 10:33
are tall in stature w be cut down And	Is 10:33
those who are lofty w be abased.	Is 10:33
He w cut down the thickets of	Is 10:34
Lebanon w fall by the Mighty One.	Is 10:34
w spring from the stem of Jesse,	Is 11:1
from his roots w bear fruit.	Is 11:1
Spirit of the LORD w rest on Him,	Is 11:2
And He w delight in the fear of	Is 11:3
And He w not judge by what His	Is 11:3
righteousness He w judge the poor,	Is 11:4
And He w strike the earth with the	Is 11:4
of His lips He w slay the wicked.	Is 11:4
w be the belt about His loins,	Is 11:5
the wolf w dwell with the lamb,	Is 11:6
leopard w lie down with the young goat,	Is 11:6
And a little boy w lead them.	Is 11:6
Also the cow and the bear w graze,	Is 11:7
Their young w lie down together,	Is 11:7
the lion w eat straw like the ox.	Is 11:7
The nursing child w play by the	Is 11:8
And the weaned child w put his	Is 11:8
They w not hurt or destroy in all	Is 11:9
For the earth w be full of the	Is 11:9
w resort to the root of Jesse,	Is 11:10
Who w stand as a signal for the	Is 11:10
His resting place w be glorious.	Is 11:10
Then it w happen on that day that	Is 11:11
Lord W again recover the second time	Is 11:11
of His people, who w remain,	Is 11:11
And He w lift up a standard for	Is 11:12
And w gather the dispersed of	Is 11:12
the jealousy of Ephraim w depart,	Is 11:13
who harass Judah w be cut off;	Is 11:13
Ephraim w not be jealous of Judah,	Is 11:13
And Judah w not harass Ephraim.	Is 11:13
They w swoop down on the	Is 11:14
w plunder the sons of the east;	Is 11:14
They w possess Edom and Moab,	Is 11:14
of Ammon w be subject to them.	Is 11:14
And the LORD w utterly destroy The	Is 11:15
And He w wave His hand over the	Is 11:15
He w strike it into seven streams And	Is 11:15
And there w be a highway from	Is 11:16
of His people who w be left,	Is 11:16
Then you w say on that day,	Is 12:1
"I w give thanks to You, O LORD;	Is 12:1
I w trust and not be afraid;	Is 12:2
Therefore you w joyously draw	Is 12:3
And in that day you w say,	Is 12:4
It w come as destruction from the	Is 13:6
Therefore all hands w fall limp,	Is 13:7
limp, And every man's heart w melt.	Is 13:7
They w be terrified, Pains and	Is 13:8
and anguish w take hold of *them;*	Is 13:8
w writhe like a woman in labor,	Is 13:8
They w look at one another in	Is 13:8
And He w exterminate its sinners	Is 13:9
W not flash forth their light;	Is 13:10
The sun w be dark when it rises And	Is 13:10
And the moon w not shed its light.	Is 13:10
I w punish the world for its evil And	Is 13:11
I w also put an end to the	Is 13:11
I w make mortal man scarcer than	Is 13:12
Therefore I w make the heavens	Is 13:13
And the earth w be shaken from its	Is 13:13
w be that like a hunted gazelle,	Is 13:14
w each turn to his own people,	Is 13:14
who is found w be thrust through,	Is 13:15
is captured w fall by the sword.	Is 13:15
Their little ones also w be dashed	Is 13:16
Their houses w be plundered And	Is 13:16
Who w not value silver or take	Is 13:17
bows w mow down the young men,	Is 13:18
They w not even have compassion on	Is 13:18
Nor w their eye pity children.	Is 13:18
W be as when God overthrew Sodom	Is 13:19
It w never be inhabited or lived	Is 13:20
Nor w the Arab pitch *his* tent there,	Is 13:20
Nor w shepherds make *their flocks*	Is 13:20
desert creatures w lie down there,	Is 13:21
their houses w be full of owls;	Is 13:21
owls; Ostriches also w live there,	Is 13:21
and shaggy goats w frolic there.	Is 13:21
Hyenas w howl in their	Is 13:22
Her *fateful* time also w soon come	Is 13:22
And her days w not be prolonged.	Is 13:22
LORD w have compassion on Jacob and	Is 14:1
then strangers w join them and	Is 14:1
The peoples w take them along	Is 14:2
and the house of Israel w possess	Is 14:2
they w take their captors captive and	Is 14:2
and w rule over their oppressors.	Is 14:2
And it w be in the day when the	Is 14:3
that you w take up this taunt	Is 14:4
"They w all respond and say to	Is 14:10
'I w ascend to heaven;	Is 14:13
I w raise my throne above the	Is 14:13
And I w sit on the mount of	Is 14:13
'I w ascend above the heights of	Is 14:14
I w make myself like the Most High.'	Is 14:14
you w be thrust down to Sheol,	Is 14:15
"Those who see you w gaze at you,	Is 14:16
at you, They w ponder over you,	Is 14:16
"You w not be united with them in	Is 14:20
"I w rise up against them,"	Is 14:22
"and w cut off from Babylon name	Is 14:22
"I w also make it a possession	Is 14:23
and I w sweep it with the broom of	Is 14:23
as I have planned so it w stand,	Is 14:24
I w trample him on My mountains.	Is 14:25
his yoke w be removed from them and	Is 14:25
serpent's root a viper w come out,	Is 14:29
its fruit w be a flying serpent.	Is 14:29
Those who are most helpless w eat,	Is 14:30
the needy w lie down in security;	Is 14:30
I w destroy your root with famine,	Is 14:30
And it w kill off your survivors.	Is 14:30
"How then w one answer the	Is 14:32
His people w seek refuge in it."	Is 14:32
I w bring added *woes* upon Dimon,	Is 15:9
w be at the fords of the Arnon.	Is 16:2
A throne w even be established in	Is 16:5
And a judge w sit on it in	Is 16:5
he w seek justice And be prompt in	Is 16:5
Therefore Moab w wail; everyone of	Is 16:7
everyone of Moab w wail. You will	Is 16:7
You w moan for the raisin cakes of	Is 16:7
I w weep bitterly for Jazer,	Is 16:9
I w drench you with my tears, O	Is 16:9
In the vineyards also there w be	Is 16:10
So it w come about when Moab	Is 16:12
to pray, That he w not prevail.	Is 16:12
the glory of Moab w be degraded	Is 16:14
his remnant w be very small *and*	Is 16:14
And w become a fallen ruin.	Is 17:1
w be for flocks to lie down in,	Is 17:2
w be no one to frighten *them.*	Is 17:2
city w disappear from Ephraim,	Is 17:3
They w be like the glory of the	Is 17:3
that day the glory of Jacob w fade,	Is 17:4
fatness of his flesh w become lean.	Is 17:4
It w be even like the reaper	Is 17:5
Or it w be like one gleaning ears	Is 17:5
Yet gleanings w be left in it like	Is 17:6
man w have regard for his Maker And	Is 17:7
And his eyes w look to the Holy	Is 17:7
He w not have regard for the	Is 17:8
Nor w he look to that which his	Is 17:8
In that day their strong cities w	Is 17:9
And the land w be a desolation.	Is 17:9
But the harvest w *be* a heap In a	Is 17:11
But He w rebuke them and they will	Is 17:13
them and they w flee far away,	Is 17:13
Such w *be* the portion of those	Is 17:14
on the mountains, you w see *it,*	Is 18:3
trumpet is blown, you w hear *it.*	Is 18:3
"I w look from My dwelling place	Is 18:4
Then He w cut off the sprigs with	Is 18:5
They w be left together for	Is 18:6
And the birds of prey w spend the	Is 18:6
w spend harvest time on them.	Is 18:6
At that time a gift of homage w be	Is 18:7
Egypt w tremble at His presence,	Is 19:1
the Egyptians w melt within them.	Is 19:1
"So I w incite Egyptians against	Is 19:2
And they w each fight against his	Is 19:2
w be demoralized within them;	Is 19:3
And I w confound their strategy,	Is 19:3
So that they w resort to idols and	Is 19:3
I w deliver the Egyptians into the	Is 19:4
a mighty king w rule over them,"	Is 19:4
The waters from the sea w dry up,	Is 19:5
the river w be parched and dry.	Is 19:5
The canals w emit a stench,	Is 19:6
of Egypt w thin out and dry up;	Is 19:6
The reeds and rushes w rot away.	Is 19:6
fields by the Nile W become dry,	Is 19:7
And the fishermen w lament,	Is 19:8
cast a line into the Nile w mourn,	Is 19:8
nets on the waters w pine away.	Is 19:8
white cloth w be utterly dejected.	Is 19:9
the pillars *of Egypt* w be crushed;	Is 19:10
laborers w be grieved in soul.	Is 19:10
There w be no work for Egypt	Is 19:15

the Egyptians **w** become like women, Is 19:16
and they **w** tremble and be in dread Is 19:16
Judah **w** become a terror to Egypt; Is 19:17
is mentioned **w** be in dread of it, Is 19:17
w be speaking the language of Canaan Is 19:18
one **w** be called the City of Is 19:18
In that day there **w** be an altar to Is 19:19
It **w** become a sign and a Is 19:20
for they **w** cry to the LORD because Is 19:20
and He **w** send them a Savior and a Is 19:20
a Champion, and He **w** deliver them. Is 19:20
w make Himself known to Egypt, Is 19:21
w know the LORD in that day. Is 19:21
They **w** even worship with sacrifice Is 19:21
and **w** make a vow to the LORD and Is 19:21
The LORD **w** strike Egypt, Is 19:22
so they **w** return to the LORD, and Is 19:22
and He **w** respond to them and will Is 19:22
respond to them and **w** heal them. Is 19:22
In that day there **w** be a highway Is 19:23
and the Assyrians **w** come into Is 19:23
w worship with the Assyrians. Is 19:23
In that day Israel **w** be the third Is 19:24
so the king of Assyria **w** lead away Is 20:4
"Then they **w** be dismayed and ashamed Is 20:5
this coastland **w** say in that day, Is 20:6
the splendor of Kedar **w** terminate; Is 21:16
of the sons of Kedar, **w** be few; Is 21:17
There you **w** die And there your Is 22:18
there your splendid chariots **w** be, Is 22:18
I **w** depose you from your office, Is 22:19
And I **w** pull you down from your Is 22:19
"Then it **w** come about in that Is 22:20
That I **w** summon My servant Is 22:20
I **w** clothe him with your tunic And Is 22:21
I **w** entrust him with your Is 22:21
And he **w** become a father to the Is 22:21
"Then I **w** set the key of the Is 22:22
When he opens no one **w** shut, Is 22:22
shut, When he shuts no one **w** open. Is 22:22
"I **w** drive him *like* a peg in Is 22:23
And he **w** become a throne of glory Is 22:23
"So they **w** hang on him all the Is 22:24
driven in a firm place **w** give way; Is 22:25
it **w** even break off and fall, and Is 22:25
load hanging on it **w** be cut off, Is 22:25
They **w** be in anguish at the report Is 23:5
even there you **w** find no rest." Is 23:12
Tyre **w** be forgotten for seventy years Is 23:15
it **w** happen to Tyre as *in* the song Is 23:15
It **w** come about at the end of Is 23:17
years that the LORD **w** visit Tyre. Is 23:17
w go back to her harlot's wages and Is 23:17
and **w** play the harlot with all the Is 23:17
wages **w** be set apart to the LORD; Is 23:18
it **w** not be stored up or hoarded, Is 23:18
but her gain **w** become sufficient Is 23:18
the people **w** be like the priest, Is 24:2
The earth **w** be completely laid Is 24:3
For thus it **w** be in the midst of Is 24:13
Then it **w** be that he who flees the Is 24:18
of disaster **w** fall into the pit, Is 24:18
the pit **w** be caught in the snare; Is 24:18
is heavy upon it, And it **w** fall, Is 24:20
So it **w** happen in that day, That Is 24:21
LORD **w** punish the host of heaven on Is 24:21
They **w** be gathered together Is 24:22
And **w** be confined in prison; Is 24:22
many days they **w** *be* punished. Is 24:22
Then the moon **w** be abashed and the Is 24:23
For the LORD of hosts **w** reign on Is 24:23
His glory **w** be before His elders. Is 24:23
I **w** exalt You, I will give thanks Is 25:1
You, I **w** give thanks to Your name; Is 25:1
no more, It **w** never be rebuilt. Is 25:2
a strong people **w** glorify You; Is 25:3
of ruthless nations **w** revere You. Is 25:3
The LORD of hosts **w** prepare a Is 25:6
And on this mountain He **w** swallow Is 25:7
He **w** swallow up death for all Is 25:8
And the Lord GOD **w** wipe tears away Is 25:8
And He **w** remove the reproach of Is 25:8
And it **w** be said in that day, Is 25:9
the LORD **w** rest on this mountain, Is 25:10
And Moab **w** be trodden down in his Is 25:10
And he **w** spread out his hands in Is 25:11
But *the Lord* **w** lay low his pride Is 25:11
of your walls He **w** bring down, Is 25:12
w be sung in the land of Judah: Is 26:1
mind You **w** keep in perfect peace, Is 26:3
"The foot **w** trample it, The feet Is 26:6
fire **w** devour Your enemies. Is 26:11
You **w** establish peace for us, Is 26:12
The dead **w** not live, the departed Is 26:14
the departed spirits **w** not rise; Is 26:14
Your dead **w** live; Is 26:19
Their corpses **w** rise. Is 26:19
And the earth **w** give birth to the Is 26:19
the earth **w** reveal her bloodshed And Is 26:21
And **w** no longer cover her slain. Is 26:21
In that day the LORD **w** punish Is 27:1
And He **w** kill the dragon who *lives* Is 27:1
So that no one **w** damage it, I guard Is 27:3
days to come Jacob **w** take root, Is 27:6
root, Israel **w** blossom and sprout, Is 27:6
And they **w** fill the whole world Is 27:6
Jacob's iniquity **w** be forgiven; Is 27:9
And this **w** be the full price of Is 27:9
and incense altars **w** not stand. Is 27:9

There the calf **w** graze, And there Is 27:10
And there it **w** lie down and feed Is 27:10
w not have compassion on them. Is 27:11
Creator **w** not be gracious to them. Is 27:11
that day the LORD **w** start *His* Is 27:12
you **w** be gathered up one by one, Is 27:12
It **w** come about also in that day Is 27:13
that a great trumpet **w** be blown, Is 27:13
w come and worship the LORD in the Is 27:13
W be like the first-ripe fig prior Is 28:4
In that day the LORD of hosts **w** Is 28:5
He **w** speak to this people Through Is 28:11
the word of the LORD to them **w** be, Is 28:13
The overwhelming scourge **w** not Is 28:15
believes *in it* **w** not be disturbed. Is 28:16
"I **w** make justice the Is 28:17
Then hail **w** sweep away the refuge of Is 28:17
of lies And the waters **w** overflow Is 28:17
"Your covenant with death **w** be Is 28:18
And your pact with Sheol **w** not stand; Is 28:18
it passes through, it **w** seize you; Is 28:19
after morning it **w** pass through, Is 28:19
And it **w** be sheer terror to Is 28:19
w rise up as *at* Mount Perazim, Is 28:21
He **w** be stirred up as in the Is 28:21
Or your fetters **w** be made stronger; Is 28:22
I **w** bring distress to Ariel, Is 29:2
And she **w** be *a city of* lamenting Is 29:2
And she **w** be like an Ariel to me. Is 29:2
I **w** camp against you Is 29:3
I **w** set siegeworks against you, Is 29:3
And I **w** raise up battle towers Is 29:3
Then you **w** be brought low; Is 29:4
From the earth you **w** speak, And from Is 29:4
are prostrate Your words **w** *come.* Is 29:4
Your voice **w** also be like that of a Is 29:4
And your speech **w** whisper from Is 29:4
multitude of your enemies **w** become Is 29:5
And it **w** happen instantly, suddenly. Is 29:5
From the LORD of hosts you **w** be Is 29:6
W be like a dream, a vision of Is 29:7
It **w** be as when a hungry man Is 29:8
the multitude of all the nations **w** be Is 29:8
The entire vision **w** be to you like Is 29:11
"Please read this," he **w** say, Is 29:11
Then the book **w** be given to the Is 29:12
And he **w** say, "I cannot read." Is 29:12
I **w** once again deal marvelously Is 29:14
wisdom of their wise men **w** perish, Is 29:14
of their discerning men **w** be Is 29:14
Lebanon **w** be turned into a fertile Is 29:17
field **w** be considered as a forest? Is 29:17
On that day the deaf **w** hear words of Is 29:18
darkness the eyes of the blind **w** see. Is 29:18
The afflicted also **w** increase their Is 29:19
And the needy of mankind **w** rejoice Is 29:19
For the ruthless **w** come to an end and Is 29:20
and the scorner **w** be finished, Is 29:20
intent on doing evil **w** be cut off; Is 29:20
midst, They **w** sanctify My name; Is 29:23
they **w** sanctify the Holy One of Is 29:23
And **w** stand in awe of the God of Is 29:23
who err in mind **w** know the truth, Is 29:24
criticize **w** accept instruction. Is 29:24
safety of Pharaoh **w** be your shame And Is 30:3
"Everyone **w** be ashamed because of Is 30:5
Therefore this iniquity **w** be to Is 30:13
That a sherd **w** not be found among Is 30:14
"In repentance and rest you **w** be Is 30:15
"No, for we **w** flee on horses," Is 30:16
"And we **w** ride on swift *horses,*" Is 30:16
One thousand **w** *flee* at the threat Is 30:17
You **w** flee at the threat of five, Is 30:17
Jerusalem, you **w** weep no longer. Is 30:19
He surely **w** be gracious to you at Is 30:19
when He hears it, He **w** answer you. Is 30:19
Teacher **w** no longer hide Himself, Is 30:20
your eyes **w** behold your Teacher. Is 30:20
ears **w** hear a word behind you, Is 30:21
you **w** defile your graven images Is 30:22
You **w** scatter them as an impure Is 30:22
Then He **w** give *you* rain for the Is 30:23
which you **w** sow in the ground, Is 30:23
and it **w** be rich and plenteous; Is 30:23
w graze in a roomy pasture. Is 30:23
the ground **w** eat salted fodder, Is 30:24
on every high hill there **w** be streams Is 30:25
moon **w** be as the light of the sun, Is 30:26
the sun **w** be seven times *brighter,* Is 30:26
You **w** have songs as in the night Is 30:29
And the LORD **w** cause His voice of Is 30:30
Assyria **w** be terrified, Is 30:31
Which the LORD **w** lay on him, Is 30:32
W be with *the music of* tambourines Is 30:32
weapons, He **w** fight them. Is 30:32
also is wise and **w** bring disaster And Is 31:2
But **w** arise against the house of Is 31:2
the LORD **w** stretch out His hand, Is 31:3
And he who helps **w** stumble And he Is 31:3
And he who is helped **w** fall, Is 31:3
of them **w** come to an end together. Is 31:3
And he **w** not be terrified at Is 31:4
So **w** the LORD of hosts come down Is 31:4
LORD of hosts **w** protect Jerusalem. Is 31:5
He **w** protect and deliver *it;* Is 31:5
He **w** pass over and rescue *it.* Is 31:5
For in that day every man **w** cast Is 31:7
w fall by a sword not of man, Is 31:8
a sword not of man **w** devour him. Is 31:8

So he **w** not escape the sword, And Is 31:8
men **w** become forced laborers. Is 31:8
rock **w** pass away because of panic, Is 31:9
w be terrified at the standard," Is 31:9
a king **w** reign righteously And Is 32:1
And princes **w** rule justly. Is 32:1
Each **w** be like a refuge from Is 32:2
of those who see **w** not be blinded, Is 32:3
ears of those who hear **w** listen. Is 32:3
of the hasty **w** discern the truth, Is 32:4
w hasten to speak clearly. Is 32:4
No longer **w** the fool be called noble Is 32:5
and *a few* days You **w** be troubled, Is 32:10
the *fruit* gathering **w** not come. Is 32:10
justice **w** dwell in the wilderness And Is 32:16
w abide in the fertile field. Is 32:16
work of righteousness **w** be peace, Is 32:17
w live in a peaceful habitation, Is 32:18
And it **w** hail when the forest Is 32:19
the city **w** be utterly laid low. Is 32:19
How blessed **w** you be, you who sow Is 32:20
you **w** be destroyed; As soon as you Is 33:1
others **w** deal treacherously with Is 33:1
And He **w** be the stability of your Is 33:6
"Now I **w** arise," says the LORD, Is 33:10
"Now I **w** be exalted, now I will Is 33:10
be exalted, now I **w** be lifted up. Is 33:10
you **w** give birth to stubble; Is 33:11
breath **w** consume you like a fire. Is 33:11
The peoples **w** be burned to lime, Is 33:12
He **w** dwell on the heights, Is 33:16
refuge **w** be the impregnable rock; Is 33:16
His bread **w** be given *him,* Is 33:16
His water **w** be sure. Is 33:16
eyes **w** see the King in His beauty; Is 33:17
They **w** behold a far-distant land. Is 33:17
Your heart **w** meditate on terror: Is 33:18
w no longer see a fierce people, Is 33:19
Your eyes **w** see Jerusalem, an Is 33:20
A tent which **w** not be folded; Is 33:20
Its stakes **w** never be pulled up, Nor Is 33:20
w be for us A place of rivers Is 33:21
On which no boat with oars **w** go, Is 33:21
which no mighty ship **w** pass Is 33:21
The LORD is our king; He **w** save us Is 33:22
of an abundant spoil **w** be divided; Is 33:23
The lame **w** take the plunder. Is 33:23
And no resident **w** say, Is 33:24
w be forgiven *their* iniquity. Is 33:24
So their slain **w** be thrown out, Is 34:3
corpses **w** give off their stench, Is 34:3
w be drenched with their blood. Is 34:3
the host of heaven **w** wear away, Is 34:4
sky **w** be rolled up like a scroll; Is 34:4
All their hosts **w** also wither away Is 34:4
Wild oxen **w** also fall with them Is 34:7
Thus their land **w** be soaked with Is 34:7
Its streams **w** be turned into pitch, Is 34:9
And its land **w** become burning pitch. Is 34:9
It **w** not be quenched night or day; Is 34:10
Its smoke **w** go up forever. Is 34:10
From generation to generation it **w** be Is 34:10
None **w** pass through it forever Is 34:10
But pelican and hedgehog **w** possess it, Is 34:11
And owl and raven **w** dwell in it; Is 34:11
And He **w** stretch over it the line of Is 34:11
king—And all its princes **w** be Is 34:12
Thorns **w** come up in its fortified Is 34:13
It **w** also be a haunt of jackals *And* Is 34:13
The desert creatures **w** meet with Is 34:14
The hairy goat also **w** cry to its kind; Is 34:14
the night monster **w** settle there And Is 34:14
monster will settle there And **w** find Is 34:14
The tree snake **w** make its nest Is 34:15
And it **w** hatch and gather *them* Is 34:15
the hawks **w** be gathered there, Every Is 34:15
Not one of these **w** be missing; Is 34:16
None **w** lack its mate. Is 34:16
to generation they **w** dwell Is 34:17
and the desert **w** be glad, Is 35:1
the Arabah **w** rejoice and blossom; Is 35:1
It **w** blossom profusely And rejoice Is 35:2
glory of Lebanon **w** be given to it, Is 35:2
They **w** see the glory of the LORD, Is 35:2
your God **w** come *with* vengeance; Is 35:4
The recompense of God **w** come, Is 35:4
will come, But He **w** save you." Is 35:4
the eyes of the blind **w** be opened And Is 35:5
ears of the deaf **w** be unstopped. Is 35:5
Then the lame **w** leap like a deer, Is 35:6
tongue of the mute **w** shout for joy. Is 35:6
For waters **w** break forth in the Is 35:6
The scorched land **w** become a pool Is 35:7
A highway **w** be there, a Is 35:8
And it **w** be called the Highway of Is 35:8
The unclean **w** not travel on it, Is 35:8
But it **w** be for him who walks Is 35:8
way, And fools **w** not wander *on it.* Is 35:8
No lion **w** be there, Nor will any Is 35:9
Nor **w** any vicious beast go up on it; Is 35:9
These **w** not be found there. Is 35:9
But the redeemed **w** walk *there,* Is 35:9
the ransomed of the LORD **w** return And Is 35:10
They **w** find gladness and joy, And Is 35:10
sorrow and sighing **w** flee away. Is 35:10
it **w** go into his hand and pierce Is 36:6
I **w** give you two thousand horses, Is 36:8
he **w** not be able to deliver you; Is 36:14
"The LORD **w** surely deliver us, Is 36:15

this city **w** not be given into Is 36:15
"The LORD **w** deliver us." Is 36:18
God **w** hear the words of Rabshakeh, Is 37:4
and **w** rebuke the words which the Is 37:4
I **w** put a spirit in him so that he Is 37:7
put a spirit in him so that he **w** hear Is 37:7
And I **w** make him fall by the sword Is 37:7
"Jerusalem **w** not be given into Is 37:10
So **w** you be spared? Is 37:11
And I **w** go to its highest peak, Is 37:24
I **w** put My hook in your nose And Is 37:29
And I **w** turn you back by the way Is 37:29
you **w** eat this year what grows of Is 37:30
remnant of the house of Judah **w** again Is 37:31
"For out of Jerusalem **w** go forth a Is 37:32
of the LORD of hosts **w** perform Is 37:32
'He **w** not come to this city or shoot Is 37:33
and he **w** not come before it with a Is 37:33
by the same he **w** return, and he will Is 37:34
and he **w** not come to this city,' Is 37:34
'For I **w** defend this city to save Is 37:35
I **w** add fifteen years to your life. Is 38:5
"I **w** deliver you and this Is 38:6
and I **w** defend this city." Is 38:6
that the LORD **w** do this thing that Is 38:7
I **w** cause the shadow on the Is 38:8
I said, "I **w** not see the LORD, Is 38:11
I **w** look on man no more among Is 38:11
I **w** wander about all my years because Is 38:15
"The LORD **w** surely save me; Is 38:20
So we **w** play my songs on stringed Is 38:20
laid up in store to this day **w** be Is 39:6
nothing **w** be left,' says the LORD. Is 39:6
'And *some* of your sons who **w** Is 39:7
whom you **w** beget, will be taken away, Is 39:7
w be taken away, and they will Is 39:7
and they **w** become officials in Is 39:7
w be peace and truth in my days." Is 39:8
glory of the LORD **w** be revealed, Is 40:5
And all flesh **w** see *it* together; Is 40:5
the Lord GOD **w** come with might, Is 40:10
a shepherd He **w** tend His flock, Is 40:11
In His arm He **w** gather the lambs And Is 40:11
He **w** gently lead the nursing *ewes.* Is 40:11
To whom then **w** you liken God? Is 40:18
likeness **w** you compare with Him? Is 40:18
prepare an idol that **w** not totter. Is 40:20
'To whom then **w** you liken Me That Is 40:25
for the LORD **W** gain new strength; Is 40:31
They **w** mount up *with* wings like Is 40:31
They **w** run and not get tired, Is 40:31
They **w** walk and not become weary. Is 40:31
So that it **w** not totter. Is 41:7
I **w** strengthen you, surely I will Is 41:10
you, surely I **w** help you, Is 41:10
Surely I **w** uphold you with My Is 41:10
at you **w** be shamed and dishonored; Is 41:11
contend with you **w** be as nothing and Is 41:11
will be as nothing and **w** perish. Is 41:11
"You **w** seek those who quarrel Is 41:12
with you, but **w** not find them, Is 41:12
who war with you **w** be as nothing and Is 41:12
'Do not fear, I **w** help you.' Is 41:13
I **w** help you," declares the LORD, Is 41:14
You **w** thresh the mountains and Is 41:15
And **w** make the hills like chaff. Is 41:15
"You **w** winnow them, and the wind Is 41:16
and the wind **w** carry them away, Is 41:16
And the storm **w** scatter them; Is 41:16
But you **w** rejoice in the LORD, You Is 41:16
You **w** glory in the Holy One of Is 41:16
I, the LORD, **w** answer them Myself, Is 41:17
of Israel I **w** not forsake them. Is 41:17
"I **w** open rivers on the bare Is 41:18
I **w** make the wilderness a pool of Is 41:18
"I **w** put the cedar in the Is 41:19
I **w** place the juniper in the Is 41:19
of the sun he **w** call on My name; Is 41:25
And he **w** come upon rulers as *upon* Is 41:25
w give a messenger of good news.' Is 41:27
He **w** bring forth justice to the Is 42:1
"He **w** not cry out or raise *His* Is 42:2
"A bruised reed He **w** not break And Is 42:3
burning wick He **w** not extinguish; Is 42:3
He **w** faithfully bring forth Is 42:3
"He **w** not be disheartened or Is 42:4
w wait expectantly for His law." Is 42:4
I **w** also hold you by the hand and Is 42:6
And I **w** appoint you as a covenant Is 42:6
I **w** not give My glory to another, Is 42:8
LORD **w** go forth like a warrior, Is 42:13
He **w** arouse *His* zeal like a man of Is 42:13
He **w** utter a shout, yes, He will Is 42:13
shout, yes, He **w** raise a war cry. Is 42:13
He **w** prevail against His enemies. Is 42:13
like a woman in labor I **w** groan, Is 42:14
groan, I **w** both gasp and pant. Is 42:14
"I **w** lay waste the mountains and Is 42:15
I **w** make the rivers into Is 42:15
"I **w** lead the blind by a way Is 42:16
they do not know I **w** guide them. Is 42:16
I **w** make darkness into light Is 42:16
These are the things I **w** do, Is 42:16
And I **w** not leave them undone." Is 42:16
They **w** be turned back *and* be Is 42:17
Who among you **w** give ear to this? Is 42:23
Who **w** give heed and listen Is 42:23
the waters, I **w** be with you; Is 43:2
rivers, they **w** not overflow you. Is 43:2

the fire, you **w** not be scorched, Is 43:2
Nor **w** the flame burn you. Is 43:2
I **w** give *other* men in your place Is 43:4
I **w** bring your offspring from the Is 43:5
"I **w** say to the north, Is 43:6
And there **w** be none after Me. Is 43:10
And **w** bring them all down as Is 43:14
They **w** lie down together *and* not rise Is 43:17
"Behold, I **w** do something new, Is 43:19
new, Now it **w** spring forth; Is 43:19
W you not be aware of it? Is 43:19
I **w** even make a roadway in the Is 43:19
beasts of the field **w** glorify Me, Is 43:20
for Myself **W** declare My praise. Is 43:21
And I **w** not remember your sins. Is 43:25
"So I **w** pollute the princes of Is 43:28
And I **w** consign Jacob to the ban and Is 43:28
you from the womb, who **w** help you, Is 44:2
'For I **w** pour out water on the Is 44:3
I **w** pour out My Spirit on your Is 44:3
And they **w** spring up among the Is 44:4
"This one **w** say, Is 44:5
one **w** call on the name of Jacob; Is 44:5
And another **w** write *on* his hand, Is 44:5
w name Israel's name with honor. Is 44:5
so that they **w** be put to shame. Is 44:9
his companions **w** be put to shame, Is 44:11
you **w** not be forgotten by Me. Is 44:21
And I **w** raise up her ruins *again.* Is 44:26
And I **w** make your rivers dry. Is 44:27
And he **w** perform all My desire.' Is 44:28
'She **w** be built,' And of the Is 44:28
'Your foundation **w** be laid.' " Is 44:28
him so that gates **w** not be shut: Is 45:1
"I **w** go before you and make the Is 45:2
I **w** shatter the doors of bronze and Is 45:2
"I **w** give you the treasures Is 45:3
I **w** gird you, though you have not Is 45:5
W the clay say to the potter, Is 45:9
And I **w** make all his ways smooth; Is 45:13
He **w** build My city and will let Is 45:13
city and **w** let My exiles go free, Is 45:13
W come over to you and will be Is 45:14
come over to you and **w** be yours; Is 45:14
They **w** walk behind you, they will Is 45:14
they **w** come over in chains And Is 45:14
in chains And **w** bow down to you; Is 45:14
They **w** make supplication to you: Is 45:14
They **w** be put to shame and even Is 45:16
The manufacturers of idols **w** go Is 45:16
You **w** not be put to shame or Is 45:17
righteousness And **w** not turn back, Is 45:23
back, That to Me every knee **w** bow, Is 45:23
every tongue **w** swear *allegiance.* Is 45:23
"They **w** say of Me, Is 45:24
Men **w** come to Him, And all who Is 45:24
And all who were angry at Him **w** be Is 45:24
of Israel **W** be justified and Is 45:25
Will be justified and **w** glory." Is 45:25
Even to *your* old age I **w** be Is 46:4
to *your* graying years I **w** bear Is 46:4
and I **w** carry *you;* And I will Is 46:4
And I **w** bear *you* and I will Is 46:4
And I will bear *you* and I **w** Is 46:4
'My purpose **w** be established, And Is 46:10
And I **w** accomplish all My good Is 46:10
truly I **w** bring it to pass. Is 46:11
have planned *it, surely* I **w** do it. Is 46:11
And My salvation **w** not delay. Is 46:13
And I **w** grant salvation in Zion, Is 46:13
"Your nakedness **w** be uncovered, Is 47:3
Your shame also **w** be exposed; Is 47:3
I **w** take vengeance and will not Is 47:3
vengeance and **w** not spare a man." Is 47:3
For you **w** no longer be called The Is 47:5
"Yet you said, 'I **w** be a queen Is 47:7
I **w** not sit as a widow, Nor know Is 47:8
"But these two things **w** come on you Is 47:9
They **w** come on you in full measure In Is 47:9
"But evil **w** come on you Which you Is 47:11
you **w** not know how to charm away; Is 47:11
And disaster **w** fall on you For Is 47:11
not know **W** come on you suddenly. Is 47:11
Perhaps you **w** be able to profit, Is 47:12
you from what **w** come upon you. Is 47:13
There **w** be no coal to warm by *Nor* Is 47:14
And you, **w** you not declare it? Is 48:6
So that you **w** not say, 'Behold, I Is 48:7
sake, For My own sake, I **w** act; Is 48:11
My glory I **w** not give to another. Is 48:11
he **w** carry out His good pleasure on Is 48:14
And His arm **w** *be against* Is 48:14
and He **w** make his ways successful. Is 48:15
In Whom I **w** show My glory." Is 49:3
I **w** also make You a light of the Is 49:6
"Kings **w** see and arise, Princes Is 49:7
Princes **w** also bow down, Because of Is 49:7
And I **w** keep You and give You for Is 49:8
Along the roads they **w** feed, Is 49:9
pasture **w** *be* on all bare heights. Is 49:9
"They **w** not hunger or thirst, Is 49:10
Nor **w** the scorching heat or Is 49:10
compassion on them **w** lead them And Is 49:10
And **w** guide them to springs of Is 49:10
I **w** make all My mountains a road, Is 49:11
And My highways **w** be raised up. Is 49:11
"Behold, these **w** come from afar; Is 49:12
these **w** *come* from the north Is 49:12
And **w** have compassion on His Is 49:13

forget, but I **w** not forget you. Is 49:15
and devastators **W** depart from you. Is 49:17
"You **w** surely put on all of them Is 49:18
Surely now you **w** be too cramped Is 49:19
who swallowed you **w** be far away. Is 49:19
bereaved **w** yet say in your ears, Is 49:20
"Then you **w** say in your heart, Is 49:21
I **w** lift up My hand to the Is 49:22
And they **w** bring your sons in Is 49:22
w be carried on *their* shoulders. Is 49:22
"Kings **w** be your guardians, Is 49:23
They **w** bow down to you with their Is 49:23
And *you* **w** know that I am the LORD; Is 49:23
wait for Me **w** not be put to shame. Is 49:23
of the mighty man **w** be taken away, Is 49:25
prey of the tyrant **w** be rescued; Is 49:25
For I **w** contend with the one who Is 49:25
with you, And I **w** save your sons. Is 49:25
"I **w** feed your oppressors Is 49:26
And they **w** become drunk with their Is 49:26
And all flesh **w** know that I, the Is 49:26
And I know that I **w** not be ashamed. Is 50:7
Who **w** contend with Me? Is 50:8
w all wear out like a garment; Is 50:9
The moth **w** eat them. Is 50:9
This you **w** have from My hand: Is 50:11
You **w** lie down in torment. Is 50:11
Indeed, the LORD **w** comfort Zion; Is 51:3
He **w** comfort all her waste places. Is 51:3
wilderness He **w** make like Eden, Is 51:3
and gladness **w** be found in her, Is 51:3
For a law **w** go forth from Me, And Is 51:4
And I **w** set My justice for a light Is 51:4
And My arms **w** judge the peoples; Is 51:5
The coastlands **w** wait for Me, And Is 51:5
My arm they **w** wait expectantly. Is 51:5
For the sky **w** vanish like smoke, Is 51:6
earth **w** wear out like a garment And Is 51:6
inhabitants **w** die in like manner; Is 51:6
But My salvation **w** be forever, Is 51:6
And My righteousness **w** not wane. Is 51:6
moth **w** eat them like a garment, Is 51:8
And the grub **w** eat them like wool. Is 51:8
But My righteousness **w** be forever, Is 51:8
the ransomed of the LORD **w** return And Is 51:11
And everlasting joy **w** *be* on their Is 51:11
They **w** obtain gladness and joy, Is 51:11
sorrow and sighing **w** flee away. Is 51:11
"The exile **w** soon be set free, Is 51:14
and **w** not die in the dungeon, Is 51:14
nor **w** his bread be lacking. Is 51:14
Who **w** mourn for you? Is 51:19
anger; You **w** never drink it again. Is 51:22
"I **w** put it into the hand of Is 51:23
unclean **W** no longer come into you. Is 52:1
you **w** be redeemed without money." Is 52:3
For they **w** see with their own eyes Is 52:8
But you **w** not go out in haste, Nor Is 52:12
haste, Nor **w** you go as fugitives; Is 52:12
For the LORD **w** go before you, And Is 52:12
And the God of Israel **w** *be* your Is 52:12
Behold, My servant **w** prosper, Is 52:13
He **w** be high and lifted up and Is 52:13
Thus He **w** sprinkle many nations, Is 52:15
Kings **w** shut their mouths on Is 52:15
had not been told them they **w** see, Is 52:15
had not heard they **w** understand. Is 52:15
offering, He **w** see *His* offspring, Is 53:10
offspring, He **w** prolong *His* days, Is 53:10
of the LORD **w** prosper in His hand. Is 53:10
He **w** see *it and* be satisfied; Is 53:11
My Servant, **w** justify the many, Is 53:11
As He **w** bear their iniquities. Is 53:11
I **w** allot Him a portion with the Is 53:12
And He **w** divide the booty with the Is 53:12
the sons of the desolate one **w** *be* Is 54:1
"For you **w** spread abroad to the Is 54:3
descendants **w** possess nations And Is 54:3
w resettle the desolate cities. Is 54:3
for you **w** not be put to shame; Is 54:4
for you **w** not be disgraced; Is 54:4
But you **w** forget the shame of your Is 54:4
widowhood you **w** remember no more. Is 54:4
great compassion I **w** gather you. Is 54:7
I **w** have compassion on you," Is 54:8
that I **w** not be angry with you Nor Is 54:9
with you Nor **w** I rebuke you. Is 54:9
w not be removed from you, Is 54:10
covenant of peace **w** not be shaken," Is 54:10
I **w** set your stones in antimony, Is 54:11
foundations I **w** lay in sapphires. Is 54:11
I **w** make your battlements of Is 54:12
your sons **w** be taught of the LORD; Is 54:13
well-being of your sons **w** be great. Is 54:13
you **w** be established; Is 54:14
You **w** be far from oppression, for Is 54:14
oppression, for you **w** not fear; Is 54:14
for it **w** not come near you. Is 54:14
assails *you* it **w** not be from Me. Is 54:15
assails you **w** fall because of you. Is 54:15
is formed against you **w** prosper; Is 54:17
you in judgment you **w** condemn. Is 54:17
And I **w** make an everlasting Is 55:3
w call a nation you do not know, Is 55:5
which knows you not **w** run to you, Is 55:5
And He **w** have compassion on him, Is 55:7
God, For He **w** abundantly pardon. Is 55:7
So **w** My word be which goes forth from Is 55:11
It **w** not return to Me empty, Without Is 55:11

"For you w go out with joy And Is 55:12
hills w break forth into shouts of joy Is 55:12
of the field w clap *their* hands. Is 55:12
thorn bush the cypress w come up, Is 55:13
the nettle the myrtle w come up, Is 55:13
it w be a memorial to the LORD, Is 55:13
sign which w not be cut off." Is 55:13
"The LORD w surely separate me Is 56:3
To them I w give in My house and Is 56:5
I w give them an everlasting name Is 56:5
name which w not be cut off. Is 56:5
I w bring to My holy mountain And Is 56:7
w be acceptable on My altar; Is 56:7
For My house w be called a house Is 56:7
"Yet *others* I w gather to them, Is 56:8
And tomorrow w be like today, only Is 56:12
"I w declare your righteousness Is 57:12
deeds, But they w not profit you. Is 57:12
the wind w carry all of them up, Is 57:13
up, *And* a breath w take *them away*. Is 57:13
But he who takes refuge in Me w Is 57:13
in Me will inherit the land And w Is 57:13
And it w be said, "Build up, build Is 57:14
"For I w not contend forever, Is 57:16
Nor w I always be angry; Is 57:16
seen his ways, but I w heal him; Is 57:18
I w lead him and restore comfort Is 57:18
"and I w heal him." Is 57:19
W you call this a fast, even an Is 58:5
light w break out like the dawn, Is 58:8
recovery w speedily spring forth; Is 58:8
righteousness w go before you; Is 58:8
of the LORD w be your rear guard. Is 58:8
"Then you w call, and the LORD Is 58:9
will call, and the LORD w answer; Is 58:9
You w cry, and He will say, Is 58:9
You will cry, and He w say, Is 58:9
your light w rise in darkness And Is 58:10
darkness And your gloom w *become* Is 58:10
the LORD w continually guide you, Is 58:11
you w be like a watered garden, Is 58:11
you w rebuild the ancient ruins; Is 58:12
You w raise up the age-old Is 58:12
And you w be called the repairer Is 58:12
you w take delight in the LORD, Is 58:14
And I w make you ride on the Is 58:14
And I w feed you *with* the heritage Is 58:14
Their webs w not become clothing, Is 59:6
Nor w they cover themselves with Is 59:6
to *their* deeds, so He w repay, Is 59:18
coastlands He w make recompense. Is 59:18
So they w fear the name of the Is 59:19
He w come like a rushing stream Which Is 59:19
"A Redeemer w come to Zion, Is 59:20
darkness w cover the earth And Is 60:2
But the LORD w rise upon you And Is 60:2
And His glory w appear upon you. Is 60:2
"Nations w come to your Is 60:3
Your sons w come from afar, And Is 60:4
daughters w be carried in the arms. Is 60:4
"Then you w see and be radiant, Is 60:5
your heart w thrill and rejoice; Is 60:5
of the sea w be turned to you, Is 60:5
of the nations w come to you. Is 60:5
"A multitude of camels w cover you, Is 60:6
All those from Sheba w come; Is 60:6
w bring gold and frankincense, Is 60:6
And w bear good news of the Is 60:6
w be gathered together to you, Is 60:7
of Nebaioth w minister to you; Is 60:7
They w go up with acceptance on My Is 60:7
the coastlands w wait for Me; Is 60:9
And the ships of Tarshish w *come* Is 60:9
Foreigners w build up your walls, Is 60:10
And their kings w minister to you; Is 60:10
Your gates w be open continually; Is 60:11
They w not be closed day or night, Is 60:11
which w not serve you will perish, Is 60:12
which will not serve you w perish, Is 60:12
the nations w be utterly ruined. Is 60:12
glory of Lebanon w come to you, Is 60:13
you w come bowing to you, Is 60:14
all those who despised you w bow Is 60:14
w call you the city of the LORD, Is 60:14
I w make you an everlasting pride, Is 60:15
w also suck the milk of nations And Is 60:16
Then you w know that I, the LORD, Is 60:16
"Instead of bronze I w bring gold, Is 60:17
instead of iron I w bring silver, Is 60:17
And I w make peace your Is 60:17
"Violence w not be heard again in Is 60:18
you w call your walls salvation, Is 60:18
"No longer w you have the sun for Is 60:19
w the moon give you light; Is 60:19
But you w have the LORD for an Is 60:19
"Your sun w no longer set, Nor Is 60:20
no longer set, Nor w your moon wane; Is 60:20
For you w have the LORD for an Is 60:20
days of your mourning w be over Is 60:20
"Then all your people w *be* Is 60:21
They w possess the land forever, Is 60:21
"The smallest one w become a clan, Is 60:22
LORD, w hasten it in its time." Is 60:22
So they w be called oaks of Is 61:3
they w rebuild the ancient ruins, Is 61:4
They w raise up the former Is 61:4
they w repair the ruined cities, Is 61:4
w stand and pasture your flocks, Is 61:5
And foreigners w be your farmers Is 61:5

But you w be called the priests of Is 61:6
You w be spoken of *as* ministers of Is 61:6
You w eat the wealth of nations, Is 61:6
And in their riches you w boast. Is 61:6
Instead of your shame *you w have a* Is 61:7
they w shout for joy over their portion Is 61:7
Therefore they w possess a double Is 61:7
land, Everlasting joy w be theirs. Is 61:7
And I w faithfully give them their Is 61:8
w be known among the nations, Is 61:9
All who see them w recognize them Is 61:9
I w rejoice greatly in the LORD, Is 61:10
LORD, My soul w exult in my God; Is 61:10
So the Lord GOD w cause Is 61:11
Zion's sake I w not keep silent, Is 62:1
sake I w not keep quiet, Is 62:1
nations w see your righteousness, Is 62:2
you w be called by a new name Is 62:2
the mouth of the LORD w designate. Is 62:2
You w also be a crown of beauty in Is 62:3
It w no longer be said to you, Is 62:4
your land w it any longer be said, Is 62:4
But you w be called, Is 62:4
And *to Him* your land w be married. Is 62:4
virgin, *So* your sons w marry you; Is 62:5
So your God w rejoice over you. Is 62:5
night they w never keep silent. Is 62:6
"I w never again give your grain Is 62:8
Nor w foreigners drink your new Is 62:8
But those who garner it w eat it and Is 62:9
And those who gather it w drink it Is 62:9
And they w call them, Is 62:12
And you w be called, Is 62:12
Sons who w not deal falsely." Is 63:8
W You restrain Yourself at these Is 64:12
W You keep silent and afflict us Is 64:12
before Me, I w not keep silent, Is 65:6
not keep silent, but I w repay; Is 65:6
I w even repay into their bosom, Is 65:6
Therefore I w measure their former Is 65:7
So I w act on behalf of My Is 65:8
"I w bring forth offspring Is 65:9
And My servants w dwell there. Is 65:9
"Sharon w be a pasture land for Is 65:10
I w destine you for the sword, And Is 65:12
And all of you w bow down to Is 65:12
My servants w eat, but you will be Is 65:13
but you w be hungry. Behold, My Is 65:13
My servants w drink, but you will be Is 65:13
but you w be thirsty. Behold, My Is 65:13
My servants w rejoice, but you will Is 65:13
but you w be put to shame. Is 65:13
"Behold, My servants w shout Is 65:14
But you w cry out with a heavy heart, Is 65:14
And you w wail with a broken spirit. Is 65:14
"You w leave your name for a Is 65:15
ones, And the Lord GOD w slay you. Is 65:15
w be called by another name. Is 65:15
he who is blessed in the earth w be Is 65:16
who swears in the earth w swear Is 65:16
And the former things w not be Is 65:17
"I w also rejoice in Jerusalem and Is 65:19
And there w no longer be heard in Is 65:19
"No longer w there be in it an Is 65:20
For the youth w die at the age of Is 65:20
not reach the age of one hundred w be Is 65:20
"They w build houses and inhabit Is 65:21
They w also plant vineyards and eat Is 65:21
"They w not build and another Is 65:22
They w not plant and another eat; Is 65:22
so w be the days of My people, Is 65:22
And My chosen ones w wear out Is 65:22
"They w not labor in vain, Or bear Is 65:23
"It w also come to pass that Is 65:24
that before they call, I w answer; Is 65:24
they are still speaking, I w hear. Is 65:24
"The wolf and the lamb w graze Is 65:25
and the lion w eat straw like the ox; Is 65:25
and dust w be the serpent's food. Is 65:25
They w do no evil or harm in all My Is 65:25
"But to this one I w look, Is 66:2
So I w choose their punishments And Is 66:4
And w bring on them what they dread. Is 66:4
But they w be put to shame. Is 66:5
And you w be nursed, you will be Is 66:12
you w be carried on the hip Is 66:12
comforts, so I w comfort you; Is 66:13
And you w be comforted in Jerusalem." Is 66:13
Then you w see *this*, and your Is 66:14
and your heart w be glad, And your Is 66:14
And your bones w flourish like Is 66:14
And the hand of the LORD w be Is 66:14
But He w be indignant toward His Is 66:14
the LORD w come in fire And His Is 66:15
For the LORD w execute judgment by Is 66:16
those slain by the LORD w be many. Is 66:16
W come to an end altogether," Is 66:17
"I w set a sign among them Is 66:19
and w send survivors from them to Is 66:19
And they w declare My glory among Is 66:19
"I w also take some of them for Is 66:21
Which I make w endure before Me," Is 66:22
offspring and your name w endure. Is 66:22
w come to bow down before Me," Is 66:23
"Then they w go forth and look On Is 66:24
For their worm w not die And their Is 66:24
will not die And their fire w not Is 66:24
And they w be an abhorrence to all Is 66:24
"Out of the north the evil w Jer 1:14

"and they w come and they will Jer 1:15
and they w set each one his throne Jer 1:15
"I w pronounce My judgments Jer 1:16
or I w dismay you before them. Jer 1:17
"They w fight against you, Jer 1:19
you, but they w not overcome you, Jer 1:19
I w yet contend with you," Jer 2:9
with your sons' sons I w contend. Jer 2:9
"Your own wickedness w correct you, Jer 2:19
And your apostasies w reprove you; Jer 2:19
But you said, 'I w not serve!' Jer 2:20
who seek her w not become weary; Jer 2:24
In her month they w find her. Jer 2:24
And after them I w walk.' Jer 2:25
time of their trouble they w say, Jer 2:27
We w no longer come to You'? Jer 2:31
I w enter into judgment with you Jer 2:35
you w be put to shame by Egypt As you Jer 2:36
"From this *place* also you w go Jer 2:37
And you w not prosper with them." Jer 2:37
man, W he still return to her? Jer 3:1
W not that land be completely Jer 3:1
'W He be angry forever? Jer 3:5
W He be indignant to the end?' Jer 3:5
these things she w return to Me'; Jer 3:7
'I w not look upon you in anger. Jer 3:12
'I w not be angry forever. Jer 3:12
And I w take you one from a city Jer 3:14
And I w bring you to Zion.' Jer 3:14
"Then I w give you shepherds Jer 3:15
who w feed you on knowledge and Jer 3:15
"they w no longer say, 'The ark Jer 3:16
And it w not come to mind, nor Jer 3:16
nor w they remember it, nor will Jer 3:16
nor w they miss *it*, nor will it Jer 3:16
nor w it be made again. Jer 3:16
"At that time they w call Jerusalem Jer 3:17
the nations w be gathered to it, Jer 3:17
nor w they walk anymore after Jer 3:17
w walk with the house of Israel, Jer 3:18
and they w come together from the Jer 3:18
I w heal your faithlessness." Jer 3:22
"If you w return, O Israel," Jer 4:1
And if you w put away your Jer 4:1
from My presence, And w not waver, Jer 4:1
And you w swear, Jer 4:2
nations w bless themselves in Him, Jer 4:2
in Him, And in Him they w glory." Jer 4:2
Or else My wrath w go forth like fire Jer 4:4
w be ruins Without inhabitant. Jer 4:7
the heart of the princes w fail; Jer 4:9
and the priests w be appalled and Jer 4:9
and the prophets w be astounded." Jer 4:9
'You w have peace'; Jer 4:10
In that time it w be said to this Jer 4:11
w come at My command; Jer 4:12
now I w also pronounce judgments Jer 4:12
How long w your wicked thoughts Jer 4:14
Yet I w not execute a complete Jer 4:27
And I w not change My mind, Jer 4:28
My mind, nor w I turn from it." Jer 4:28
O desolate one, what w you do? Jer 4:30
seeks truth, Then I w pardon her. Jer 5:1
"I w go to the great And will Jer 5:5
to the great And w speak to them, Jer 5:5
a lion from the forest w slay Jer 5:6
A wolf of the deserts w destroy them, Jer 5:6
Everyone who goes out of them w be Jer 5:6
Misfortune w not come on us, Jer 5:12
And we w not see sword or famine. Jer 5:12
Thus it w be done to them!" Jer 5:13
wood, and it w consume them. Jer 5:14
"They w devour your harvest Jer 5:17
They w devour your sons and your Jer 5:17
They w devour your flocks and your Jer 5:17
They w devour your vines and your Jer 5:17
They w demolish with the sword Jer 5:17
"I w not make you a complete Jer 5:18
so you w serve strangers in a land Jer 5:19
what w you do at the end of it? Jer 5:31
the daughter of Zion, I w cut off. Jer 6:2
and their flocks w come to her, Jer 6:3
w pitch *their* tents around her, Jer 6:3
They w pasture each in his place. Jer 6:3
"They w thoroughly glean as the Jer 6:9
For I w stretch out My hand Jer 6:12
And you w find rest for your souls. Jer 6:16
'We w not walk *in it*.' Jer 6:16
'We w not listen.' Jer 6:17
And they w stumble against them, Jer 6:21
Neighbor and friend w perish." Jer 6:21
And a great nation w be aroused Jer 6:22
the destroyer W come upon us. Jer 6:26
I w let you dwell in this place. Jer 7:3
I w let you dwell in this place, Jer 7:7
"W you steal, murder, and commit Jer 7:9
I w do to the house which is Jer 7:14
"I w cast you out of My Jer 7:15
wrath w be poured out on this place, Jer 7:20
it w burn and not be quenched." Jer 7:20
My voice, and I w be your God, Jer 7:23
your God, and you w be My people; Jer 7:23
and you w walk in all the way Jer 7:23
but they w not listen to you; Jer 7:27
them, but they w not answer you. Jer 7:27
it w no longer be called Topheth, Jer 7:32
for they w bury in Topheth because Jer 7:32
dead bodies of this people w be food Jer 7:33
and no one w frighten *them away*. Jer 7:33

“Then I **w** make to cease from the **Jer 7:34**
for the land **w** become a ruin. **Jer 7:34**
“they **w** bring out the bones of **Jer 8:1**
They **w** spread them out to the sun, **Jer 8:2**
They **w** not be gathered or buried; **Jer 8:2**
they **w** be as dung on the face of **Jer 8:2**
“And death **w** be chosen rather **Jer 8:3**
I **w** give their wives to others, **Jer 8:10**
“I **w** surely snatch them away,” **Jer 8:13**
“There **w** be no grapes on the **Jer 8:13**
And the leaf **w** wither; And what I **Jer 8:13**
And what I have given them **w** pass **Jer 8:13**
no charm, And they **w** bite you,” **Jer 8:17**
I **w** refine them and assay them; **Jer 9:7**
I **w** take up a weeping and wailing, **Jer 9:10**
“I **w** make Jerusalem a heap of **Jer 9:11**
And I **w** make the cities of Judah a **Jer 9:11**
“behold, I **w** feed them, this **Jer 9:15**
“I **w** scatter them among the **Jer 9:16**
and I **w** send the sword after them **Jer 9:16**
‘The corpses of men **w** fall like **Jer 9:22**
But no one **w** gather *them.*’ ” **Jer 9:22**
“that I **w** punish all who are **Jer 9:25**
hammers So that it **w** not totter. **Jer 10:4**
the heavens and the earth **w** perish **Jer 10:11**
of their punishment they **w** perish. **Jer 10:15**
time, And **w** cause them distress, **Jer 10:18**
or You **w** bring me to nothing. **Jer 10:24**
be My people, and I **w** be your God,’ **Jer 11:4**
they **w** not be able to escape; **Jer 11:11**
though they **w** cry to Me, yet I **Jer 11:11**
to Me, yet I **w** not listen to them. **Jer 11:11**
inhabitants of Jerusalem **w** go and cry **Jer 11:12**
but they surely **w** not save them in **Jer 11:12**
for I **w** not listen when they call **Jer 11:14**
so that you **w** not die at our hand”; **Jer 11:21**
The young men **w** die by the sword, **Jer 11:22**
and daughters **w** die by famine; **Jer 11:22**
a remnant **w** not be left to them, **Jer 11:23**
for I **w** bring disaster on the men **Jer 11:23**
“He **w** not see our latter ending.” **Jer 12:4**
How **w** you do in the thicket of the **Jer 12:5**
w uproot the house of Judah from **Jer 12:14**
“And it **w** come about that after I **Jer 12:15**
I **w** again have compassion on them; **Jer 12:15**
and I **w** bring them back, each one **Jer 12:15**
if they **w** really learn the ways of **Jer 12:16**
they **w** be built up in the **Jer 12:16**
“But if they **w** not listen, then I **Jer 12:17**
then I **w** uproot that nation, **Jer 12:17**
‘Just so **w** I destroy the pride of **Jer 13:9**
I **w** dash them against each other, **Jer 13:14**
“I **w** not show pity nor be sorry **Jer 13:14**
But if you **w** not listen to it, My **Jer 13:17**
w sob in secret for *such* pride; **Jer 13:17**
And my eyes **w** bitterly weep And **Jer 13:17**
“What **w** you say when He appoints **Jer 13:21**
W not pangs take hold of you Like **Jer 13:21**
“Therefore I **w** scatter them like **Jer 13:24**
How long **w** you remain unclean?” **Jer 13:27**
now He **w** remember their iniquity **Jer 14:10**
‘You **w** not see the sword nor will **Jer 14:13**
the sword nor **w** you have famine, **Jer 14:13**
but I **w** give you lasting peace in **Jer 14:13**
‘There **w** be no sword or famine in **Jer 14:15**
w be thrown out into the streets of **Jer 14:16**
and there **w** be no one to bury **Jer 14:16**
nor their daughters—for I **w** pour **Jer 14:16**
“You **w** say this word to them, **Jer 14:17**
“I **w** appoint over them four kinds **Jer 15:3**
“I **w** make them an object of horror **Jer 15:4**
“Indeed, who **w** have pity on you, **Jer 15:5**
Jerusalem, Or who **w** mourn for you, **Jer 15:5**
Or who **w** turn aside to ask about **Jer 15:5**
So I **w** stretch out My hand against **Jer 15:6**
“I **w** winnow them with a **Jer 15:7**
I **w** bereave *them* of children, I **Jer 15:7**
children, I **w** destroy My people; **Jer 15:7**
“Their widows **w** be more numerous **Jer 15:8**
I **w** bring against them, against **Jer 15:8**
I **w** suddenly bring down on her **Jer 15:8**
So I **w** give over their survivors to **Jer 15:9**
“Surely I **w** set you free for **Jer 15:11**
Surely I **w** cause the enemy to make **Jer 15:11**
I **w** give for booty without cost, **Jer 15:13**
“Then I **w** cause your enemies to **Jer 15:14**
in My anger, It **w** burn upon you.” **Jer 15:14**
W You indeed be to me like a **Jer 15:18**
“If you return, then I **w** restore you **Jer 15:19**
Before Me you **w** stand; **Jer 15:19**
You **w** become My spokesman. **Jer 15:19**
“Then I **w** make you to this people **Jer 15:20**
you, They **w** not prevail over you; **Jer 15:20**
“So I **w** deliver you from the hand **Jer 15:21**
And I **w** redeem you from the grasp **Jer 15:21**
“They **w** die of deadly diseases, **Jer 16:4**
they **w** not be lamented or buried; **Jer 16:4**
they **w** be as dung on the surface **Jer 16:4**
and their carcasses **w** become food **Jer 16:4**
men and small **w** die in this land; **Jer 16:6**
they **w** not be buried, they will **Jer 16:6**
be buried, they **w** not be lamented, **Jer 16:6**
nor **w** anyone gash himself or shave **Jer 16:6**
“Men **w** not break *bread* in **Jer 16:7**
words, they **w** say to you, **Jer 16:10**
‘So I **w** hurl you out of this land **Jer 16:13**
and there you **w** serve other gods **Jer 16:13**
for I **w** grant you no favor.’ **Jer 16:13**
“when it **w** no longer be said, **Jer 16:14**

For I **w** restore them to their own **Jer 16:15**
“and they **w** fish for them; **Jer 16:16**
and afterwards I **w** send for many **Jer 16:16**
and they **w** hunt them from every **Jer 16:16**
“I **w** first doubly repay their **Jer 16:18**
To You the nations **w** come From **Jer 16:19**
I **w** make them know My power **Jer 16:21**
I **w** give over your wealth and all **Jer 17:3**
And you **w**, even of yourself, let **Jer 17:4**
And I **w** make you serve your **Jer 17:4**
in My anger Which **w** burn forever. **Jer 17:4**
“For he **w** be like a bush in the **Jer 17:6**
w not see when prosperity comes, **Jer 17:6**
But **w** live in stony wastes in the **Jer 17:6**
“For he **w** be like a tree planted **Jer 17:8**
w not fear when the heat comes; **Jer 17:8**
But its leaves **w** be green, And it **Jer 17:8**
And it **w** not be anxious in a year **Jer 17:8**
of his days it **w** forsake him, **Jer 17:11**
And in the end he **w** be a fool.” **Jer 17:11**
forsake You **w** be put to shame. **Jer 17:13**
away on earth **w** be written down, **Jer 17:13**
me, O LORD, and I **w** be healed; **Jer 17:14**
Save me and I **w** be saved, For You **Jer 17:14**
“But it **w** come about, if you **Jer 17:24**
then there **w** come in through the **Jer 17:25**
this city **w** be inhabited forever **Jer 17:25**
‘They **w** come in from the cities **Jer 17:26**
then I **w** kindle a fire in its gates **Jer 17:27**
and it **w** devour the palaces of **Jer 17:27**
and there I **w** announce My words to **Jer 18:2**
I **w** relent concerning the calamity **Jer 18:8**
then I **w** think better of the good **Jer 18:10**
“But they **w** say, ‘It’s hopeless! **Jer 18:12**
and each of us **w** act according to **Jer 18:12**
Everyone who passes by it **w** be **Jer 18:16**
I **w** scatter them Before the enemy; **Jer 18:17**
I **w** show them My back and not *My* **Jer 18:17**
that hears of it **w** tingle. **Jer 19:3**
“when this place **w** no longer be **Jer 19:6**
“I **w** make void the counsel of Judah **Jer 19:7**
and I **w** cause them to fall by **Jer 19:7**
and I **w** give over their carcasses as **Jer 19:7**
“I **w** also make this city a **Jer 19:8**
everyone who passes by it **w** be **Jer 19:8**
“I **w** make them eat the flesh of **Jer 19:9**
and they **w** eat one another’s flesh **Jer 19:9**
their life **w** distress them.” **Jer 19:9**
“Just so **w** I break this people **Jer 19:11**
and they **w** bury in Topheth because **Jer 19:11**
“This is how I **w** treat this place **Jer 19:12**
Judah **w** be defiled like the place **Jer 19:13**
they **w** fall by the sword of their **Jer 20:4**
So I **w** give over all Judah to **Jer 20:4**
and he **w** carry them away as exiles **Jer 20:4**
and **w** slay them with the sword. **Jer 20:4**
‘I **w** also give over all the wealth **Jer 20:5**
of the kings of Judah I **w** give **Jer 20:5**
enemies, and they **w** plunder them, **Jer 20:5**
all who live in your house **w** go into **Jer 20:6**
and you **w** enter Babylon, and there **Jer 20:6**
Babylon, and there you **w** die and **Jer 20:6**
die and there you **w** be buried, **Jer 20:6**
“I **w** not remember Him Or speak **Jer 20:9**
“Perhaps he **w** be deceived, so **Jer 20:10**
w stumble and not prevail. **Jer 20:11**
They **w** be utterly ashamed, because **Jer 20:11**
disgrace that **w** not be forgotten. **Jer 20:11**
perhaps the LORD **w** deal with us **Jer 21:2**
so that *the enemy* **w** withdraw from **Jer 21:2**
and I **w** gather them into the center **Jer 21:4**
“I Myself **w** war against you with an **Jer 21:5**
“I **w** also strike down **Jer 21:6**
they **w** die of a great pestilence. **Jer 21:6**
“I **w** give over Zedekiah king of **Jer 21:7**
and he **w** strike them down with the **Jer 21:7**
He **w** not spare them nor have pity **Jer 21:7**
“He who dwells in this city **w** die **Jer 21:9**
who are besieging you **w** live, **Jer 21:9**
he **w** have his own life as booty. **Jer 21:9**
“It **w** be given into the hand of **Jer 21:10**
and he **w** burn it with fire.” **Jer 21:10**
‘Who **w** come down against us? **Jer 21:13**
who **w** enter into our habitations?’ **Jer 21:13**
“But I **w** punish you according to **Jer 21:14**
“And I **w** kindle a fire in its **Jer 21:14**
men **w** indeed perform this thing, **Jer 22:4**
w enter the gates of this house, **Jer 22:4**
“But if you **w** not obey these **Jer 22:5**
this house **w** become a desolation. **Jer 22:5**
Yet most assuredly I **w** make you like **Jer 22:6**
“For I **w** set apart destroyers **Jer 22:7**
And they **w** cut down your choicest **Jer 22:7**
Many nations **w** pass by this city; **Jer 22:8**
and they **w** say to one another, **Jer 22:8**
“Then they **w** answer, **Jer 22:9**
For he **w** never return Or see his **Jer 22:10**
“He **w** never return there; **Jer 22:11**
there he **w** die and not see this **Jer 22:12**
‘I **w** build myself a roomy house **Jer 22:14**
“They **w** not lament for him: **Jer 22:18**
They **w** not lament for him: **Jer 22:18**
“He **w** be buried with a donkey’s **Jer 22:19**
But you said, ‘I **w** not listen!’ **Jer 22:21**
w sweep away all your shepherds, **Jer 22:22**
your lovers **w** go into captivity; **Jer 22:22**
Then you **w** surely be ashamed and **Jer 22:22**
How you **w** groan when pangs come **Jer 22:23**
and I **w** give you over into the hand **Jer 22:25**

“I **w** hurl you and your mother who **Jer 22:26**
not born, and there you **w** die. **Jer 22:26**
return, they **w** not return to it. **Jer 22:27**
man who **w** not prosper in his days; **Jer 22:30**
For no man of his descendants **w** **Jer 22:30**
“Then I Myself **w** gather the remnant **Jer 23:3**
they **w** be fruitful and multiply. **Jer 23:3**
“I **w** also raise up shepherds over **Jer 23:4**
over them and they **w** tend them; **Jer 23:4**
they **w** not be afraid any longer, **Jer 23:4**
terrified, nor **w** any be missing,” **Jer 23:4**
“When I **w** raise up for David a **Jer 23:5**
And He **w** reign as king and act **Jer 23:5**
“In His days Judah **w** be saved, **Jer 23:6**
And Israel **w** dwell securely; **Jer 23:6**
His name by which He **w** be called, **Jer 23:6**
“when they **w** no longer say, **Jer 23:7**
they **w** live on their own soil.” **Jer 23:8**
“Therefore their way **w** be like **Jer 23:12**
They **w** be driven away into the **Jer 23:12**
For I **w** bring calamity upon them, **Jer 23:12**
“You **w** have peace” **Jer 23:17**
‘Calamity **w** not come upon you.’ **Jer 23:17**
It **w** swirl down on the head of the **Jer 23:19**
“The anger of the LORD **w** not turn **Jer 23:20**
days you **w** clearly understand it. **Jer 23:20**
‘I **w** abandon you,’ **Jer 23:33**
I **w** bring punishment upon that **Jer 23:34**
“Thus **w** each of you say to his **Jer 23:35**
“For you **w** no longer remember the **Jer 23:36**
man’s own word **w** become the oracle, **Jer 23:36**
“Thus you **w** say to *that* prophet, **Jer 23:37**
“Therefore behold, I **w** surely **Jer 23:39**
“I **w** put an everlasting **Jer 23:40**
which **w** not be forgotten.” **Jer 23:40**
so I **w** regard as good the captives **Jer 24:5**
I **w** set My eyes on them for good, **Jer 24:6**
I **w** bring them again to this land; **Jer 24:6**
and I **w** build them up and not **Jer 24:6**
and I **w** plant them and not pluck **Jer 24:6**
I **w** give them a heart to know Me, **Jer 24:7**
and they **w** be My people, and I **Jer 24:7**
My people, and I **w** be their God, **Jer 24:7**
for they **w** return to Me with their **Jer 24:7**
I **w** abandon Zedekiah king of Judah **Jer 24:8**
‘I **w** make them a terror *and an* **Jer 24:9**
and a curse in all places where I **w** **Jer 24:9**
‘I **w** send the sword, the **Jer 24:10**
hands, and I **w** do you no harm.’ **Jer 25:6**
I **w** send and take all the families **Jer 25:9**
‘and *I* **w** *send* to **Jer 25:9**
w bring them against this land and **Jer 25:9**
and I **w** utterly destroy them and **Jer 25:9**
I **w** take from them the voice of **Jer 25:10**
‘This whole land **w** be a desolation **Jer 25:11**
and these nations **w** serve the king of **Jer 25:11**
‘Then it **w** be when seventy years **Jer 25:12**
I **w** punish the king of Babylon and **Jer 25:12**
and I **w** make it an everlasting **Jer 25:12**
‘I **w** bring upon that land all **Jer 25:13**
‘(For many nations and great kings **w** **Jer 25:14**
and I **w** recompense them according **Jer 25:14**
“They **w** drink and stagger and go mad **Jer 25:16**
sword that I **w** send among them.” **Jer 25:16**
which I **w** send among you.” **Jer 25:27**
“And it **w** be, if they refuse to **Jer 25:28**
to drink, then you **w** say to them, **Jer 25:28**
You **w** not be free from punishment; **Jer 25:29**
‘The LORD **w** roar from on high And **Jer 25:30**
He **w** roar mightily against His **Jer 25:30**
He **w** shout like those who tread **Jer 25:30**
by the LORD on that day **w** be **Jer 25:33**
They **w** not be lamented, gathered or **Jer 25:33**
they **w** be like dung on the face of **Jer 25:33**
And you **w** fall like a choice vessel. **Jer 25:34**
“Flight **w** perish from the shepherds, **Jer 25:35**
‘Perhaps they **w** listen and **Jer 26:3**
everyone **w** turn from his evil way, **Jer 26:3**
“And you **w** say to them, **Jer 26:4**
“If you **w** not listen to Me, to **Jer 26:4**
I **w** make this house like Shiloh, **Jer 26:6**
and this city I **w** make a curse to **Jer 26:6**
‘This house **w** be like Shiloh and **Jer 26:9**
and this city **w** be desolate, **Jer 26:9**
and the LORD **w** change His mind **Jer 26:13**
you **w** bring innocent blood on **Jer 26:15**
“Zion **w** be plowed *as* a field, And **Jer 26:18**
And Jerusalem **w** become ruins, **Jer 26:18**
and I **w** give it to the one who is **Jer 27:5**
kings **w** make him their servant. **Jer 27:7**
“It **w** be, *that* the nation or **Jer 27:8**
the kingdom which **w** not serve him, **Jer 27:8**
and which **w** not put its neck under **Jer 27:8**
I **w** punish that nation with the **Jer 27:8**
‘You **w** not serve the king of Babylon.’ **Jer 27:9**
and I **w** drive you out and you **Jer 27:10**
drive you out and you **w** perish. **Jer 27:10**
“But the nation which **w** bring its **Jer 27:11**
him, I **w** let remain on its land,” **Jer 27:11**
w till it and dwell in it. **Jer 27:11**
“Why **w** you die, you and your **Jer 27:13**
w not serve the king of Babylon? **Jer 27:13**
‘You **w** not serve the king of Babylon,’ **Jer 27:14**
the vessels of the LORD’s house **w** **Jer 27:16**
‘They **w** be carried to Babylon **Jer 27:22**
be carried to Babylon and they **w** be **Jer 27:22**
‘Then I **w** bring them back and **Jer 27:22**
‘for I **w** break the yoke of the **Jer 28:4**
then that prophet **w** be known *as* **Jer 28:9**

w I break within two full years the Jer 28:11
and they **w** serve him. And I have Jer 28:14
its welfare you **w** have welfare.' Jer 29:7
I **w** visit you and fulfill My good Jer 29:10
'Then you **w** call upon Me and come Jer 29:12
pray to Me, and I **w** listen to you. Jer 29:12
'You **w** seek Me and find *Me* Jer 29:13
'I **w** be found by you,' Jer 29:14
'and I **w** restore your fortunes and Jer 29:14
and **w** gather you from all the nations Jer 29:14
'and I **w** bring you back to the Jer 29:14
and I **w** make them like split-open Jer 29:17
I **w** pursue them with the sword, Jer 29:18
and I **w** make them a terror to all Jer 29:18
I **w** deliver them into the hand of Jer 29:21
and he **w** slay them before your eyes. Jer 29:21
'Because of them a curse **w** be used Jer 29:22
'*The exile* **w** be long; Jer 29:28
he **w** not have anyone living among Jer 29:32
and he **w** not see the good that I am Jer 29:32
'when I **w** restore the fortunes of Jer 30:3
'I **w** also bring them back to the Jer 30:3
But he **w** be saved from it. Jer 30:7
'that I **w** break his yoke from off Jer 30:8
neck and **w** tear off their bonds; Jer 30:8
and strangers **w** no longer make them Jer 30:8
king, whom I **w** raise up for them. Jer 30:9
behold, I **w** save you from afar And Jer 30:10
And Jacob **w** return and will be quiet Jer 30:10
And Jacob will return and **w** be quiet Jer 30:10
And no one **w** make him afraid. Jer 30:10
For I **w** destroy completely all the Jer 30:11
I **w** not destroy you completely. Jer 30:11
But I **w** chasten you justly And Jer 30:11
And **w** by no means leave you Jer 30:11
'Therefore all who devour you **w** be Jer 30:16
w go into captivity; And those who Jer 30:16
And those who plunder you **w** be for Jer 30:16
prey upon you I **w** give for prey. Jer 30:16
'For I **w** restore you to health And Jer 30:17
And I **w** heal you of your wounds,' Jer 30:17
I **w** restore the fortunes of the Jer 30:18
And the city **w** be rebuilt on its ruin, Jer 30:18
And the palace **w** stand on its Jer 30:18
'From them **w** proceed thanksgiving Jer 30:19
And I **w** multiply them and they Jer 30:19
I will multiply them and they **w** not Jer 30:19
I **w** also honor them and they Jer 30:19
I will also honor them and they **w** not Jer 30:19
'Their children also **w** be as Jer 30:20
I **w** punish all their oppressors. Jer 30:20
And I **w** bring him near and he Jer 30:21
people, And I **w** be your God.' " Jer 30:22
It **w** burst on the head of the Jer 30:23
anger of the LORD **w** not turn back Until Jer 30:24
latter days you **w** understand this. Jer 30:24
"I **w** be the God of all the Jer 31:1
"Again I **w** build you and you Jer 31:4
"Again I will build you and you **w** be Jer 31:4
Again you **w** take up your tambourines, Jer 31:4
"Again you **w** plant vineyards On Jer 31:5
The planters **w** plant And will enjoy Jer 31:5
The planters will plant And **w** enjoy Jer 31:5
"For there **w** be a day when watchmen Jer 31:6
And I **w** gather them from the Jer 31:8
they **w** return here. Jer 31:8
"With weeping they **w** come, And by Jer 31:9
And by supplication I **w** lead them; Jer 31:9
I **w** make them walk by streams of Jer 31:9
straight path in which they **w** not Jer 31:9
who scattered Israel **w** gather him And Jer 31:10
"They **w** come and shout for joy on Jer 31:12
And they **w** be radiant over the bounty Jer 31:12
And their life **w** be like a watered Jer 31:12
And they **w** never languish again. Jer 31:12
"Then the virgin **w** rejoice in Jer 31:13
I **w** turn their mourning into joy And Jer 31:13
into joy And **w** comfort them Jer 31:13
"I **w** fill the soul of the Jer 31:14
And My people **w** be satisfied with My Jer 31:14
For your work **w** be rewarded," Jer 31:16
"And they **w** return from the land Jer 31:16
"And *your* children **w** return to Jer 31:17
I **w** surely have mercy on him," Jer 31:20
"How long **w** you go here and Jer 31:22
A woman **w** encompass a man." Jer 31:22
"Once again they **w** speak this Jer 31:23
its cities **w** dwell together in it, Jer 31:24
"when I **w** sow the house of Israel Jer 31:27
so I **w** watch over them to build Jer 31:28
those days they **w** not say again, Jer 31:29
w die for his own iniquity; Jer 31:30
his teeth **w** be set on edge. Jer 31:30
"when I **w** make a new covenant Jer 31:31
this is the covenant which I **w** make Jer 31:33
"I **w** put My law within them and Jer 31:33
and on their heart I **w** write it; Jer 31:33
and I **w** be their God, and they Jer 31:33
"They **w** not teach again, each man Jer 31:34
for they **w** all know Me, from Jer 31:34
"for I **w** forgive their iniquity, Jer 31:34
their sin I **w** remember no more." Jer 31:34
the offspring of Israel also **w** cease Jer 31:36
Then I **w** also cast off all the Jer 31:37
"when the city **w** be rebuilt for Jer 31:38
"The measuring line **w** go out farther Jer 31:39
then it **w** turn to Goah. Jer 31:39
it **w** not be plucked up or Jer 31:40
king of Babylon, and he **w** take it; Jer 32:3
and Zedekiah king of Judah **w** not Jer 32:4
but he **w** surely be given into Jer 32:4
and he **w** speak with him face to face Jer 32:4
and he **w** take Zedekiah to Babylon, Jer 32:5
and he **w** be there until I visit him," Jer 32:5
you **w** not succeed" '?" Jer 32:5
and fields and vineyards **w** again Jer 32:15
and he **w** take it. Jer 32:28
fighting against this city **w** enter Jer 32:29
I **w** gather them out of all the Jer 32:37
and I **w** bring them back to this Jer 32:37
My people, and I **w** be their God; Jer 32:38
and I **w** give them one heart and Jer 32:39
"I **w** make an everlasting Jer 32:40
that I **w** not turn away from them, Jer 32:40
and I **w** put the fear of Me in Jer 32:40
that they **w** not turn away from Me. Jer 32:40
"I **w** rejoice over them to do Jer 32:41
and **w** faithfully plant them in Jer 32:41
'Fields **w** be bought in this land of Jer 32:43
'Men **w** buy fields for money, sign Jer 32:44
for I **w** restore their fortunes,' Jer 32:44
'Call to Me and I **w** answer you, Jer 33:3
and I **w** tell you great and mighty Jer 33:3
I **w** bring to it health and Jer 33:6
and healing, and I **w** heal them; Jer 33:6
and I **w** reveal to them an Jer 33:6
'I **w** restore the fortunes of Jer 33:7
and **w** rebuild them as they were Jer 33:7
'I **w** cleanse them from all Jer 33:8
and I **w** pardon all their Jer 33:8
'It **w** be to Me a name of joy, Jer 33:9
nations of the earth which **w** hear Jer 33:9
and they **w** fear and tremble because Jer 33:9
'Yet again there **w** be heard in Jer 33:10
For I **w** restore the fortunes of Jer 33:11
'There **w** again be in this place Jer 33:12
the flocks **w** again pass under Jer 33:13
'when I **w** fulfill the good word Jer 33:14
w cause a righteous Branch of David Jer 33:15
'In those days Judah **w** be saved Jer 33:16
will be saved and Jerusalem **w** dwell Jer 33:16
is *the name* by which she **w** be Jer 33:16
so that day and night **w** not be at Jer 33:20
David My servant so that he **w** not Jer 33:21
so I **w** multiply the descendants of Jer 33:22
But I **w** restore their fortunes and Jer 33:26
and **w** have mercy on them.' " Jer 33:26
and he **w** burn it with fire. Jer 34:2
You **w** not escape from his hand, Jer 34:3
for you **w** surely be captured and Jer 34:3
and you **w** see the king of Babylon Jer 34:3
he **w** speak with you face to face, Jer 34:3
and you **w** go to Babylon. Jer 34:3
'You **w** not die by the sword. Jer 34:4
'You **w** die in peace; Jer 34:5
so they **w** burn *spices* for you; Jer 34:5
and they **w** lament for you, Jer 34:5
and I **w** make you a terror to all Jer 34:17
'I **w** give the men who have Jer 34:18
I **w** give them into the hand of Jer 34:20
And their dead bodies **w** be food for Jer 34:20
w give into the hand of their enemies Jer 34:21
I **w** bring them back to this city; Jer 34:22
and they **w** fight against it and take Jer 34:22
and I **w** make the cities of Judah a Jer 34:22
"We **w** not drink wine, for Jonadab Jer 35:6
"**W** you not receive instruction by Jer 35:13
Then you **w** dwell in the land which I Jer 35:15
"Perhaps the house of Judah **w** Jer 36:3
man **w** turn from his evil way; Jer 36:3
then I **w** forgive their iniquity Jer 36:3
w come before the LORD, Jer 36:7
everyone **w** turn from his evil way, Jer 36:7
"We **w** surely report all these Jer 36:16
on it that the king of Babylon **w** Jer 36:29
and **w** make man and beast to cease Jer 36:29
"I **w** also punish him and his Jer 36:31
and I **w** bring on them Jer 36:31
"The Chaldeans **w** also return and Jer 37:8
and they **w** capture it and burn it Jer 37:8
Chaldeans **w** surely go away from us Jer 37:9
away from us," for they **w** not go. Jer 37:9
"You **w** be given into the hand of Jer 37:17
'The king of Babylon **w** not come Jer 37:19
'He who stays in this city **w** die Jer 38:2
who goes out to the Chaldeans **w** live Jer 38:2
'This city **w** certainly be given Jer 38:3
Babylon and he **w** capture it.' " Jer 38:3
and he **w** die right where he is Jer 38:9
w you not certainly put me to Jer 38:15
advice, you **w** not listen to me." Jer 38:15
surely I **w** not put you to death Jer 38:16
I will not put you to death nor **w** I Jer 38:16
'If you **w** indeed go out to the Jer 38:17
king of Babylon, then you **w** live, Jer 38:17
city **w** not be burned with fire, Jer 38:17
you and your household **w** survive. Jer 38:17
'But if you **w** not go out to the Jer 38:18
then this city **w** be given over to Jer 38:18
and they **w** burn it with fire, and Jer 38:18
w not escape from their hand.' " Jer 38:18
into their hand and they **w** abuse Jer 38:19
"They **w** not give you over. Jer 38:20
and those women **w** say, Jer 38:22
'They **w** also bring out all your Jer 38:23
w not escape from their hand, Jer 38:23
but **w** be seized by the hand of the Jer 38:23
city **w** be burned with fire.' " Jer 38:23
these words and you **w** not die. Jer 38:24
us and we **w** not put you to death,' Jer 38:25
and they **w** take place before you Jer 39:16
"But I **w** deliver you on that day," Jer 39:17
"and you **w** not be given into Jer 39:17
"For I **w** certainly rescue you, Jer 39:18
and you **w** not fall by the sword; Jer 39:18
you **w** have your *own* life as booty, Jer 39:18
along, and I **w** look after you; Jer 40:4
Nethaniah, and not a man **w** know! Jer 40:15
I **w** tell you the whole message Jer 42:4
message which the LORD **w** answer you. Jer 42:4
w not keep back a word from you." Jer 42:4
LORD your God **w** send you to us. Jer 42:5
we **w** listen to the voice of the Jer 42:6
'If you **w** indeed stay in this Jer 42:10
then I **w** build you up and not tear Jer 42:10
I **w** plant you and not uproot you; Jer 42:10
for I **w** relent concerning Jer 42:10
'I **w** also show you compassion, so Jer 42:12
so that he **w** have compassion on Jer 42:12
"We **w** not stay in this land," Jer 42:13
but we **w** go to the land of Egypt, Jer 42:14
where we **w** not see war or hear Jer 42:14
for bread, and we **w** stay there"; Jer 42:14
which you are afraid of, **w** overtake Jer 42:16
w follow closely after you there *in* Jer 42:16
and you **w** die there. Jer 42:16
reside there **w** die by the sword, Jer 42:17
and they **w** have no survivors or Jer 42:17
so My wrath **w** be poured out on you Jer 42:18
And you **w** become a curse, an Jer 42:18
you **w** see this place no more." Jer 42:18
tell us so, and we **w** do it." Jer 42:20
that you **w** die by the sword, Jer 42:22
so they **w** put us to death or exile us Jer 43:3
he **w** spread his canopy over them. Jer 43:10
"He **w** also come and strike the Jer 43:11
who are *meant* for death **w** *be* Jer 43:11
and he **w** burn them and take them Jer 43:12
So he **w** wrap himself with the land Jer 43:12
and he **w** depart from there safely. Jer 43:12
"He **w** also shatter the obelisks Jer 43:13
Egypt he **w** burn with fire. Jer 43:13
'And I **w** take away the remnant of Jer 44:12
and they **w** all meet their end in Jer 44:12
they **w** fall by the sword *and* meet Jer 44:12
w die by the sword and famine; Jer 44:12
and they **w** become a curse, an Jer 44:12
'And I **w** punish those who live in Jer 44:13
'So there **w** be no refugees or Jer 44:14
none **w** return except *a few* refugees. Jer 44:14
"But rather we **w** certainly carry Jer 44:17
"We **w** certainly perform our vows Jer 44:25
w meet their end by the sword and Jer 44:27
'Those who escape the sword **w** Jer 44:28
w know whose word will stand, Jer 44:28
will know whose word **w** stand, Jer 44:28
'This **w** be the sign to you,' Jer 44:29
My words **w** surely stand against you Jer 44:29
'but I **w** give your life to you as Jer 45:5
"I **w** rise and cover *that* land; Jer 46:8
I **w** surely destroy the city and Jer 46:8
And the sword **w** devour and be Jer 46:10
For there **w** be a slaughter for the Jer 46:10
For Memphis **w** become a desolation; Jer 46:19
It **w** even be burned down *and* Jer 46:19
"Surely it **w** no *more* be found, Jer 46:23
it **w** be inhabited as in the days Jer 46:26
And Jacob **w** return and be undisturbed Jer 46:27
For I **w** make a full end of all Jer 46:28
Yet I **w** not make a full end of you; Jer 46:28
But I **w** correct you properly And by Jer 46:28
And the men **w** cry out, And every Jer 47:2
every inhabitant of the land **w** wail. Jer 47:2
How long **w** you gash yourself? Jer 47:5
LORD, How long **w** you not be quiet? Jer 47:6
You too, Madmen, **w** be silenced; Jer 48:2
The sword **w** follow after you. Jer 48:2
w ascend with continual weeping; Jer 48:5
Even you yourself **w** be captured; Jer 48:7
And Chemosh **w** go off into exile Jer 48:7
A destroyer **w** come to every city, Jer 48:8
city, So that no city **w** escape; Jer 48:8
The valley also **w** be ruined And Jer 48:8
And the plateau **w** be destroyed, Jer 48:8
to Moab, For she **w** flee away; Jer 48:9
her cities **w** become a desolation, Jer 48:9
"when I **w** send to him those who Jer 48:12
vessels, and they **w** tip him over, Jer 48:12
and they **w** empty his vessels and Jer 48:12
"And Moab **w** be ashamed of Jer 48:13
"The disaster of Moab **w** soon come, Jer 48:16
so Moab **w** wallow in his vomit, and Jer 48:26
he also **w** become a laughingstock. Jer 48:26
"Therefore I **w** wail for Moab, Even Jer 48:31
Even for all Moab **w** I cry out; Jer 48:31
I **w** moan for the men of Kir-heres. Jer 48:31
than the weeping for Jazer I **w** weep Jer 48:32
No one **w** tread *them* with shouting, Jer 48:33
shouting **w** not be shouts *of joy.* Jer 48:33
waters of Nimrim **w** become desolate Jer 48:34
"I **w** make an end of Moab," Jer 48:35
So Moab **w** become a laughingstock Jer 48:39
one **w** fly swiftly like an eagle And Jer 48:40
men of Moab in that day **W** be like Jer 48:41
"Moab **w** be destroyed from Jer 48:42
the terror **W** fall into the pit, Jer 48:44
the pit **W** be caught in the snare; Jer 48:44

"Yet I **w** restore the fortunes of	Jer 48:47
"That I **w** cause a trumpet blast of	Jer 49:2
And it **w** become a desolate heap,	Jer 49:2
And her towns **w** be set on fire.	Jer 49:2
Then Israel **w** take possession of	Jer 49:2
For Malcam **w** go into exile	Jer 49:3
'Who **w** come against me?'	Jer 49:4
of you **w** be driven out headlong,	Jer 49:5
"But afterward I **w** restore The	Jer 49:6
For I **w** bring the disaster of Esau	Jer 49:8
he **w** not be able to conceal himself;	Jer 49:10
behind, I **w** keep *them* alive;	Jer 49:11
the cup **w** certainly drink *it,*	Jer 49:12
one who **w** be completely acquitted?	Jer 49:12
You **w** not be acquitted, but you	Jer 49:12
but you **w** certainly drink *it.*	Jer 49:12
w become an object of horror,	Jer 49:13
cities **w** become perpetual ruins."	Jer 49:13
I **w** bring you down from there,"	Jer 49:16
Edom **w** become an object of horror;	Jer 49:17
everyone who passes by it **w** be	Jer 49:17
and **w** hiss at all its wounds.	Jer 49:17
"no one **w** live there, nor will a	Jer 49:18
nor **w** a son of man reside in it.	Jer 49:18
one **w** come up like a lion from the	Jer 49:19
for in an instant I **w** make him run	Jer 49:19
and who **w** summon Me *into court?*	Jer 49:19
surely they **w** drag them off, *even*	Jer 49:20
surely He **w** make their pasture	Jer 49:20
He **w** mount up and swoop like an	Jer 49:22
men of Edom in that day **w** be like	Jer 49:22
young men **w** fall in her streets,	Jer 49:26
war **w** be silenced in that day,"	Jer 49:26
"I **w** set fire to the wall of	Jer 49:27
And it **w** devour the fortified	Jer 49:27
"They **w** take away their tents and	Jer 49:29
They **w** carry off for themselves	Jer 49:29
they **w** call out to one another,	Jer 49:29
"Their camels **w** become plunder,	Jer 49:32
And I **w** scatter to all the winds	Jer 49:32
And I **w** bring their disaster from	Jer 49:32
Hazor **w** become a haunt of jackals,	Jer 49:33
No one **w** live there, Nor will a	Jer 49:33
Nor **w** a son of man reside in it."	Jer 49:33
'I **w** bring upon Elam the four winds	Jer 49:36
And **w** scatter them to all these winds;	Jer 49:36
And there **w** be no nation To which	Jer 49:36
the outcasts of Elam **w** not go.	Jer 49:36
'So I **w** shatter Elam before their	Jer 49:37
And I **w** bring calamity upon them,	Jer 49:37
'And I **w** send out the sword after	Jer 49:37
'Then I **w** set My throne in Elam	Jer 49:38
'But it **w** come about in the last	Jer 49:39
in the last days That I **w** restore	Jer 49:39
it **w** make her land an object of	Jer 50:3
there **w** be no inhabitant in it.	Jer 50:3
"the sons of Israel **w** come,	Jer 50:4
w go along weeping as they go,	Jer 50:4
and it **w** be the LORD their God	Jer 50:4
be the LORD their God they **w** seek.	Jer 50:4
"They **w** ask for the way to Zion,	Jer 50:5
they **w** come that they may join	Jer 50:5
covenant that **w** not be forgotten.	Jer 50:5
And they **w** draw up *their* battle	Jer 50:9
From there she **w** be taken captive.	Jer 50:9
Their arrows **w** be like an expert	Jer 50:9
"Chaldea **w** become plunder;	Jer 50:10
who plunder her **w** have enough,"	Jer 50:10
Your mother **w** be greatly ashamed,	Jer 50:12
gave you birth **w** be humiliated.	Jer 50:12
*she **w** be* the least of the nations,	Jer 50:12
the LORD she **w** not be inhabited,	Jer 50:13
But she **w** be completely desolate;	Jer 50:13
Everyone who passes by Babylon **w**	Jer 50:13
And **w** hiss because of all her wounds.	Jer 50:13
w each turn back to his own people And	Jer 50:16
they **w** each flee to his own land.	Jer 50:16
'And I **w** bring Israel back to his	Jer 50:19
he **w** graze on Carmel and Bashan,	Jer 50:19
and his desire **w** be satisfied in	Jer 50:19
'search **w** be made for the iniquity	Jer 50:20
of Israel, but there **w** be none;	Jer 50:20
of Judah, but they **w** not be found;	Jer 50:20
for I **w** pardon those whom I leave as	Jer 50:20
young men **w** fall in her streets,	Jer 50:30
war **w** be silenced in that day,"	Jer 50:30
The time when I **w** punish you.	Jer 50:31
"The arrogant one **w** stumble	Jer 50:32
And I **w** set fire to his cities And it	Jer 50:32
it **w** devour all his environs."	Jer 50:32
He **w** vigorously plead their case So	Jer 50:34
priests, and they **w** become fools!	Jer 50:36
men, and they **w** be shattered!	Jer 50:36
of her, And they **w** become women!	Jer 50:37
and they **w** be plundered!	Jer 50:37
waters, and they **w** be dried up!	Jer 50:38
the desert creatures **w** live *there*	Jer 50:39
The ostriches also **w** live in it,	Jer 50:39
And it **w** never again be inhabited	Jer 50:39
"No man **w** live there, Nor will a	Jer 50:40
Nor **w** *any* son of man reside in it.	Jer 50:40
many kings **w** be aroused from the	Jer 50:41
one **w** come up like a lion from the	Jer 50:44
for in an instant I **w** make them run	Jer 50:44
and whoever is chosen I **w** appoint	Jer 50:44
and who **w** summon Me *into court?*	Jer 50:44
surely they **w** drag them off, *even*	Jer 50:45
surely He **w** make their pasture	Jer 50:45
"I **w** dispatch foreigners to Babylon	Jer 51:2
on every side they **w** be opposed to	Jer 51:2
"They **w** fall down slain in	Jer 51:4
"Surely I **w** fill you with a	Jer 51:14
And they **w** cry out with shouts of	Jer 51:14
of their punishment they **w** perish.	Jer 51:18
"But I **w** repay Babylon and all	Jer 51:24
"And I **w** stretch out My hand	Jer 51:25
I **w** make you a burnt out mountain.	Jer 51:25
"They **w** not take from you	Jer 51:26
But you **w** be desolate forever,"	Jer 51:26
time of harvest **w** come for her."	Jer 51:33
The inhabitant of Zion **w** say;	Jer 51:35
of Chaldea," Jerusalem **w** say.	Jer 51:35
And I **w** dry up her sea And make her	Jer 51:36
Babylon **w** become a heap *of ruins,*	Jer 51:37
"They **w** roar together like young	Jer 51:38
They **w** growl like lions' cubs.	Jer 51:38
they become heated up, I **w** serve	Jer 51:39
"I **w** bring them down like lambs to	Jer 51:40
"I **w** punish Bel in Babylon, And I	Jer 51:44
And I **w** make what he has swallowed	Jer 51:44
nations **w** no longer stream to him.	Jer 51:44
not afraid at the report that **w** *be*	Jer 51:46
For the report **w** come one year,	Jer 51:46
And violence **w** *be* in the land	Jer 51:46
days are coming When I **w** punish	Jer 51:47
her whole land **w** be put to shame And	Jer 51:47
all her slain **w** fall in her midst.	Jer 51:47
all that is in them **W** shout for joy	Jer 51:48
the destroyers **w** come to her from	Jer 51:48
"When I **w** punish her idols,	Jer 51:52
the mortally wounded **w** groan	Jer 51:52
Me destroyers **w** come to her,"	Jer 51:53
And He **w** make *her* loud noise	Jer 51:55
waves **w** roar like many waters;	Jer 51:55
And her mighty men **w** be captured,	Jer 51:56
of recompense, He **w** fully repay.	Jer 51:56
"I **w** make her princes and her wise	Jer 51:57
of Babylon **w** be completely razed And	Jer 51:58
her high gates **w** be set on fire;	Jer 51:58
So the peoples **w** toil for nothing,	Jer 51:58
there **w** be nothing dwelling in it,	Jer 51:62
it **w** be a perpetual desolation.'	Jer 51:62
you **w** tie a stone to it and throw	Jer 51:63
and they **w** become exhausted.'"	Jer 51:64
For the Lord **w** not reject forever,	La 3:31
Then He **w** have compassion	La 3:32
You **w** recompense them, O LORD,	La 3:64
w give them hardness of heart,	La 3:65
of heart, Your curse **w** be on them.	La 3:65
You **w** pursue them in anger and	La 3:66
He **w** not continue to regard them;	La 4:16
cup **w** come around to you as well,	La 4:21
You **w** become drunk and make	La 4:21
He **w** exile you no longer.	La 4:22
But He **w** punish your iniquity, O	La 4:22
He **w** expose your sins!	La 4:22
they **w** know that a prophet has been	Ezk 2:5
yet the house of Israel **w** not be	Ezk 3:7
all My words which I **w** speak	Ezk 3:10
"When I say to the wicked, 'You **w**	Ezk 3:18
blood I **w** require at your hand.	Ezk 3:18
he **w** die; since you have not warned	Ezk 3:20
blood I **w** require at your hand.	Ezk 3:20
and there I **w** speak to you."	Ezk 3:22
they **w** put ropes on you and bind	Ezk 3:25
I **w** make your tongue stick to the	Ezk 3:26
your mouth so that you **w** be mute and	Ezk 3:26
speak to you, I **w** open your mouth and	Ezk 3:27
your mouth and you **w** say to them,	Ezk 3:27
I **w** put ropes on you so that you	Ezk 4:8
Then the LORD said, "Thus **w**	Ezk 4:13
among the nations where I **w** banish	Ezk 4:13
Then He said to me, "See, I **w** give	Ezk 4:15
which you **w** prepare your bread."	Ezk 4:15
and they **w** eat bread by weight and	Ezk 4:16
bread and water **w** be scarce;	Ezk 4:17
and they **w** be appalled with one	Ezk 4:17
I **w** unsheathe a sword behind them.	Ezk 5:2
from it a fire **w** spread to all the	Ezk 5:4
and I **w** execute judgments among	Ezk 5:8
I **w** do among you what I have not	Ezk 5:9
like of which I **w** never do again.	Ezk 5:9
fathers **w** eat *their* sons among you,	Ezk 5:10
you, and sons **w** eat their fathers;	Ezk 5:10
for I **w** execute judgments on you and	Ezk 5:10
therefore I **w** also withdraw,	Ezk 5:11
and My eye **w** have no pity and I will	Ezk 5:11
have no pity and I **w** not spare.	Ezk 5:11
'One third of you **w** die by plague	Ezk 5:12
w fall by the sword around you,	Ezk 5:12
third I **w** scatter to every wind,	Ezk 5:12
I **w** unsheathe a sword behind them.	Ezk 5:12
'Thus My anger **w** be spent and I	Ezk 5:13
and I **w** satisfy My wrath on them,	Ezk 5:13
and I **w** be appeased; then they will	Ezk 5:13
then they **w** know that I, the LORD,	Ezk 5:13
I **w** make you a desolation and a	Ezk 5:14
'So it **w** be a reproach, a	Ezk 5:15
destruction of those whom I **w** send	Ezk 5:16
then I **w** also intensify the famine	Ezk 5:16
I **w** send on you famine and wild	Ezk 5:17
they **w** bereave you of children;	Ezk 5:17
bloodshed also **w** pass through you,	Ezk 5:17
and I **w** bring the sword on you.	Ezk 5:17
and I **w** destroy your high places.	Ezk 6:3
"So your altars **w** become	Ezk 6:4
your incense altars **w** be smashed;	Ezk 6:4
and I **w** make your slain fall in front	Ezk 6:4
"I **w** also lay the dead bodies of	Ezk 6:5
and I **w** scatter your bones around	Ezk 6:5
cities **w** become waste and the high	Ezk 6:6
and the high places **w** be desolate,	Ezk 6:6
"The slain **w** fall among you,	Ezk 6:7
and you **w** know that I am the LORD.	Ezk 6:7
"However, I **w** leave a remnant, for	Ezk 6:8
for you **w** have those who escaped	Ezk 6:8
you who escape **w** remember Me	Ezk 6:9
which they **w** be carried captive,	Ezk 6:9
and they **w** loathe themselves in	Ezk 6:9
they **w** know that I am the LORD;	Ezk 6:10
of Israel, which **w** fall by sword,	Ezk 6:11
"He who is far off **w** die by the	Ezk 6:12
who is near **w** fall by the sword,	Ezk 6:12
is besieged **w** die by the famine.	Ezk 6:12
Thus **w** I spend My wrath on them.	Ezk 6:12
you **w** know that I am the LORD,	Ezk 6:13
all their habitations I **w** stretch	Ezk 6:14
w know that I am the LORD.	Ezk 6:14
the end is upon you, and I **w** send	Ezk 7:3
I **w** judge you according to your ways	Ezk 7:3
'For My eye **w** have no pity on you,	Ezk 7:4
nor **w** I spare *you,* but I will	Ezk 7:4
but I **w** bring your ways upon you,	Ezk 7:4
your abominations **w** be among you;	Ezk 7:4
you **w** know that I am the LORD!'	Ezk 7:4
'Now I **w** shortly pour out My wrath	Ezk 7:8
'My eye **w** show no pity nor	Ezk 7:9
will show no pity nor **w** I spare.	Ezk 7:9
I **w** repay you according to your	Ezk 7:9
then you **w** know that I, the LORD,	Ezk 7:9
the seller **w** not regain what he	Ezk 7:13
their multitude **w** not be averted,	Ezk 7:13
nor **w** any of them maintain his	Ezk 7:13
He who is in the field **w** die by the	Ezk 7:15
the plague **w** also consume those in	Ezk 7:15
they **w** be on the mountains like	Ezk 7:16
'All hands **w** hang limp and all	Ezk 7:17
and all knees **w** become *like* water.	Ezk 7:17
'They **w** gird themselves with	Ezk 7:18
and shuddering **w** overwhelm them;	Ezk 7:18
and shame **w** *be* on all faces	Ezk 7:18
'They **w** fling their silver into	Ezk 7:19
streets and their gold **w** become	Ezk 7:19
their silver and their gold **w** not be	Ezk 7:19
therefore I **w** make it an abhorrent	Ezk 7:20
'I **w** give it into the hands of	Ezk 7:21
as spoil, and they **w** profane it.	Ezk 7:21
'I **w** also turn My face from them,	Ezk 7:22
they **w** profane My secret place;	Ezk 7:22
robbers **w** enter and profane it.	Ezk 7:22
'Therefore, I **w** bring the worst of	Ezk 7:24
and they **w** possess their houses.	Ezk 7:24
I **w** also make the pride of the strong	Ezk 7:24
their holy places **w** be profaned.	Ezk 7:24
anguish comes, they **w** seek peace,	Ezk 7:25
seek peace, but there **w** be none.	Ezk 7:25
'Disaster **w** come upon disaster and	Ezk 7:26
and rumor **w** be *added* to rumor;	Ezk 7:26
w seek a vision from a prophet,	Ezk 7:26
but the law **w** be lost from the	Ezk 7:26
'The king **w** mourn, the prince will	Ezk 7:27
prince **w** be clothed with horror,	Ezk 7:27
the people of the land **w** tremble.	Ezk 7:27
According to their conduct I **w** deal	Ezk 7:27
and by their judgments I **w** judge them.	Ezk 7:27
w know that I am the LORD.'"	Ezk 7:27
you **w** see still greater abominations.	Ezk 8:6
"Yet you **w** see still greater	Ezk 8:13
Yet you **w** see still greater	Ezk 8:15
"Therefore, I indeed **w** deal in	Ezk 8:18
My eye **w** have no pity nor will I	Ezk 8:18
My eye will have no pity nor **w** I	Ezk 8:18
yet I **w** not listen to them."	Ezk 8:18
My eye **w** have no pity nor will I	Ezk 9:10
My eye will have no pity nor **w** I	Ezk 9:10
but I **w** bring their conduct upon	Ezk 9:10
but I **w** bring you out of it.	Ezk 11:7
so I **w** bring a sword upon you,"	Ezk 11:8
"And I **w** bring you out of the midst	Ezk 11:9
"You **w** fall by the sword.	Ezk 11:10
"You will fall by the sword. I **w**	Ezk 11:10
"This *city* **w** not be a pot for	Ezk 11:11
nor **w** you be flesh in the midst of	Ezk 11:11
but I **w** judge you to the border	Ezk 11:11
you **w** know that I am the LORD;	Ezk 11:12
W You bring the remnant of Israel	Ezk 11:13
"I **w** gather you from the peoples	Ezk 11:17
and I **w** give you the land of Israel."'	Ezk 11:17
they **w** remove all its detestable	Ezk 11:18
"And I **w** give them one heart,	Ezk 11:19
And I **w** take the heart of stone out	Ezk 11:19
Then they **w** be My people, and I	Ezk 11:20
I **w** bring their conduct down on their	Ezk 11:21
Perhaps they **w** understand though	Ezk 12:3
Then you **w** go out at evening in	Ezk 12:4
done, so it **w** be done to them;	Ezk 12:11
they **w** go into exile, into	Ezk 12:11
The prince who is among them **w** load	Ezk 12:12
They **w** dig a hole through the wall	Ezk 12:12
He **w** cover his face so that he can	Ezk 12:12
"I **w** also spread My net over him,	Ezk 12:13
and he **w** be caught in My snare.	Ezk 12:13
And I **w** bring him to Babylon in	Ezk 12:13
yet he **w** not see it, though he	Ezk 12:13
not see it, though he **w** die there.	Ezk 12:13
"I **w** scatter to every wind all who	Ezk 12:14
and I **w** draw out a sword after them.	Ezk 12:14

“So they **w** know that I am the Ezk 12:15
“But I **w** spare a few of them from Ezk 12:16
“They **w** eat their bread with Ezk 12:19
because their land **w** be stripped Ezk 12:19
inhabited cities **w** be laid waste and Ezk 12:20
and the land **w** be a desolation. Ezk 12:20
w know that I am the LORD. Ezk 12:20
“I **w** make this proverb cease so Ezk 12:23
they **w** no longer use it as a proverb Ezk 12:23
“For there **w** no longer be any Ezk 12:24
“For I the LORD **w** speak, Ezk 12:25
word I speak **w** be performed. Ezk 12:25
It **w** no longer be delayed, for in Ezk 12:25
I **w** speak the word and perform it,” Ezk 12:25
My words **w** be delayed any longer. Ezk 12:28
I speak **w** be performed, Ezk 12:28
“So My hand **w** be against the Ezk 13:9
They **w** have no place in the Ezk 13:9
nor **w** they be written down in the Ezk 13:9
nor **w** they enter the land of Ezk 13:9
with whitewash, that it **w** fall. Ezk 13:11
A flooding rain **w** come, and you, O Ezk 13:11
and you, O hailstones, **w** fall; Ezk 13:11
and a violent wind **w** break out. Ezk 13:11
has fallen, **w** you not be asked, Ezk 13:12
“I **w** make a violent wind break Ezk 13:13
There **w** also be in My anger a Ezk 13:13
“So I **w** tear down the wall which you Ezk 13:14
you **w** be consumed in its midst. Ezk 13:14
And you **w** know that I am the LORD. Ezk 13:14
“Thus I **w** spend My wrath on the wall Ezk 13:15
and I **w** say to you, ‘The wall is Ezk 13:15
W you hunt down the lives of My Ezk 13:18
and I **w** tear them from your arms; Ezk 13:20
and I **w** let them go, even those Ezk 13:20
“I **w** also tear off your veils and Ezk 13:21
and they **w** no longer be in your Ezk 13:21
and you **w** know that I am the LORD. Ezk 13:21
you women **w** no longer see false Ezk 13:23
and I **w** deliver My people out of Ezk 13:23
you **w** know that I am the LORD.” Ezk 13:23
I the LORD **w** be brought to give Ezk 14:4
I the LORD **w** be brought to answer Ezk 14:7
“I **w** set My face against that man Ezk 14:8
and I **w** cut him off from among My Ezk 14:8
So you **w** know that I am the LORD. Ezk 14:8
and I **w** stretch out My hand Ezk 14:9
“They **w** bear *the punishment* Ezk 14:10
the iniquity of the prophet **w** be, Ezk 14:10
Thus they **w** be My people, and I Ezk 14:11
survivors **w** be left in it who will Ezk 14:22
left in it who **w** be brought out, Ezk 14:22
you **w** see their conduct and actions; Ezk 14:22
then you **w** be comforted for the Ezk 14:22
“Then they **w** comfort you when you Ezk 14:23
for you **w** know that I have not Ezk 14:23
fire, yet the fire **w** consume them. Ezk 15:7
you **w** know that I am the LORD, Ezk 15:7
‘Thus I **w** make the land desolate, Ezk 15:8
therefore, behold, I **w** gather all Ezk 16:37
So I **w** gather them against you from Ezk 16:37
“Thus I **w** judge you like women who Ezk 16:38
and I **w** bring on you the blood of Ezk 16:38
“I **w** also give you into the hands of Ezk 16:39
and they **w** tear down your shrines, Ezk 16:39
and **w** leave you naked and bare. Ezk 16:39
“They **w** incite a crowd against Ezk 16:40
and they **w** stone you and cut you Ezk 16:40
“They **w** burn your houses with Ezk 16:41
Then I **w** stop you from playing Ezk 16:41
and you **w** also no longer pay your Ezk 16:41
“So I **w** calm My fury against you Ezk 16:42
and My jealousy **w** depart from you, Ezk 16:42
and I **w** be pacified and angry no more. Ezk 16:42
I in turn **w** bring your conduct Ezk 16:43
“so that you **w** not commit this Ezk 16:43
everyone who quotes proverbs **w** Ezk 16:44
I **w** restore their captivity, Ezk 16:53
w return to their former state, Ezk 16:55
and you with your daughters **w** *also* Ezk 16:55
“I **w** also do with you as you have Ezk 16:59
I **w** remember My covenant with you Ezk 16:60
and I **w** establish an everlasting Ezk 16:60
“Then you **w** remember your ways Ezk 16:61
I **w** give them to you as daughters, Ezk 16:61
“Thus I **w** establish My covenant Ezk 16:62
“**W** it thrive? Will he not pull up its Ezk 17:9
W he not pull up its roots and cut Ezk 17:9
though it is planted, **w** it thrive? Ezk 17:10
W it not completely wither as soon Ezk 17:10
W he succeed? Will he who does Ezk 17:15
W he who does such things escape? Ezk 17:15
company **w** not help him in the war, Ezk 17:17
he broke, I **w** inflict on his head. Ezk 17:19
“I **w** spread My net over him, Ezk 17:20
and he **w** be caught in My snare. Ezk 17:20
Then I **w** bring him to Babylon and Ezk 17:20
his troops **w** fall by the sword, Ezk 17:21
w be scattered to every wind; Ezk 17:21
and you **w** know that I, the LORD, Ezk 17:21
says the Lord GOD, “I **w** also Ezk 17:22
I **w** pluck from the topmost of its Ezk 17:22
twigs a tender one and I **w** plant Ezk 17:22
“On the high mountain of Israel I **w** Ezk 17:23
of every kind **w** nest under it; Ezk 17:23
they **w** nest in the shade of its Ezk 17:23
field **w** know that I am the LORD; Ezk 17:24
have spoken, and I **w** perform *it*.” Ezk 17:24
The soul who sins **w** die. Ezk 18:4

is righteous *and* **w** surely live,” Ezk 18:9
w he live? He will not live! Ezk 18:13
will he live? He **w** not live! Ezk 18:13
he **w** surely be put to death; Ezk 18:13
his blood **w** be on his own head. Ezk 18:13
he **w** not die for his father’s Ezk 18:17
iniquity, he **w** surely live. Ezk 18:17
behold, he **w** die for his iniquity. Ezk 18:18
“The person who sins **w** die. Ezk 18:20
The son **w** not bear the punishment Ezk 18:20
nor **w** the father bear the Ezk 18:20
the righteous **w** be upon himself, Ezk 18:20
of the wicked **w** be upon himself. Ezk 18:20
w not be remembered against him; Ezk 18:22
which he has practiced, he **w** live. Ezk 18:22
that a wicked man does, **w** he live? Ezk 18:24
w not be remembered for his treachery Ezk 18:24
for them he **w** die. Ezk 18:24
which he has committed he **w** die. Ezk 18:26
righteousness, he **w** save his life. Ezk 18:27
“Therefore I **w** judge you, O house Ezk 18:30
For why **w** you die, O house of Ezk 18:31
“I **w** not be inquired of by you.” Ezk 20:3
“**W** you judge them, will you judge Ezk 20:4
you judge them, **w** you judge them, Ezk 20:4
if a man observes them, he **w** live. Ezk 20:11
if a man observes them, he **w** live; Ezk 20:13
if a man observes them, he **w** live; Ezk 20:21
“**W** you defile yourselves after Ezk 20:30
“I **w** not be inquired of by you. Ezk 20:31
into your mind **w** not come about, Ezk 20:32
‘We **w** be like the nations, like Ezk 20:32
“I **w** bring you out from the peoples Ezk 20:34
and I **w** bring you into the wilderness Ezk 20:35
and there I **w** enter into judgment Ezk 20:35
w enter into judgment with you,” Ezk 20:36
“I **w** make you pass under the rod, Ezk 20:37
and I **w** bring you into the bond of Ezk 20:37
and I **w** purge from you the rebels Ezk 20:38
I **w** bring them out of the land where Ezk 20:38
w not enter the land of Israel. Ezk 20:38
you **w** know that I am the LORD. Ezk 20:38
later you **w** surely listen to Me, Ezk 20:39
and My holy name you **w** profane no Ezk 20:39
of them, **w** serve Me in the land; Ezk 20:40
there I **w** accept them and there I Ezk 20:40
I will accept them and there I **w** seek Ezk 20:40
“As a soothing aroma I **w** accept you Ezk 20:41
and I **w** prove Myself holy among you Ezk 20:41
“And you **w** know that I am the Ezk 20:42
“There you **w** remember your Ezk 20:43
and you **w** loathe yourselves in Ezk 20:43
“Then you **w** know that I am the Ezk 20:44
and it **w** consume every green tree in Ezk 20:47
blazing flame **w** not be quenched and Ezk 20:47
south to north **w** be burned by it. Ezk 20:47
“All flesh **w** see that I, the Ezk 20:48
and I **w** draw My sword out of its Ezk 21:3
“Because I **w** cut off from you Ezk 21:4
therefore My sword **w** go forth from Ezk 21:4
“Thus all flesh **w** know that I, Ezk 21:5
It **w** not return *to its sheath* Ezk 21:5
and every heart **w** melt, all hands Ezk 21:7
will melt, all hands **w** be feeble, Ezk 21:7
be feeble, every spirit **w** faint and Ezk 21:7
and all knees **w** be weak as water. Ezk 21:7
Behold, it comes and it **w** happen,’ Ezk 21:7
rod which despises **w** be no more?” Ezk 21:13
“I **w** also clap My hands together, Ezk 21:17
and I **w** appease My wrath; I, the Ezk 21:17
both of them **w** go out of one land. Ezk 21:19
“And it **w** be to them like a false Ezk 21:23
you **w** be seized with the hand. Ezk 21:24
this **w** no longer *be* the same. Ezk 21:26
‘A ruin, a ruin, a ruin, I **w** make Ezk 21:27
This also **w** be no more until He Ezk 21:27
and I **w** give it *to Him*.’ Ezk 21:27
I **w** judge you. Ezk 21:30
‘I **w** pour out My indignation on you; Ezk 21:31
I **w** blow on you with the fire of My Ezk 21:31
and I **w** give you into the hand of Ezk 21:31
‘You **w** be fuel for the fire; Ezk 21:32
your blood **w** be in the midst of the Ezk 21:32
You **w** not be remembered, for I, Ezk 21:32
“And you, son of man, **w** you judge, Ezk 22:2
w you judge the bloody city? Ezk 22:2
midst, so that her time **w** come, Ezk 22:3
who are far from you **w** mock you, Ezk 22:5
be strong in the days that I **w** deal Ezk 22:14
have spoken and **w** act. Ezk 22:14
“I **w** scatter you among the nations Ezk 22:15
among the nations and I **w** disperse Ezk 22:15
and I **w** consume your uncleanness from Ezk 22:15
“You **w** profane yourself in Ezk 22:16
w know that I am the LORD. Ezk 22:16
so I **w** gather *you* in My anger Ezk 22:20
My anger and in My wrath and I **w** lay Ezk 22:20
‘I **w** gather you and blow on you with Ezk 22:21
w be melted in the midst of it. Ezk 22:21
you **w** be melted in the midst of Ezk 22:22
and you **w** know that I, the LORD, Ezk 22:22
‘Behold I **w** arouse your lovers Ezk 23:22
and I **w** bring them against you Ezk 23:22
w come against you with weapons, Ezk 23:24
They **w** set themselves against you Ezk 23:24
and I **w** commit the judgment to them, Ezk 23:24
and they **w** judge you according to Ezk 23:24
I **w** set My jealousy against you, Ezk 23:25
They **w** remove your nose and your Ezk 23:25

survivors **w** fall by the sword. Ezk 23:25
They **w** take your sons and your Ezk 23:25
survivors **w** be consumed by the fire. Ezk 23:25
‘They **w** also strip you of your Ezk 23:26
‘Thus I **w** make your lewdness Ezk 23:27
so that you **w** not lift up your Ezk 23:27
I **w** give you into the hand of Ezk 23:28
They **w** deal with you in hatred, Ezk 23:29
the nakedness of your harlotries **w** be Ezk 23:29
‘These things **w** be done to you Ezk 23:30
I **w** give her cup into your hand.’ Ezk 23:31
‘You **w** drink your sister’s cup, Ezk 23:32
You **w** be laughed at and held in Ezk 23:32
‘You **w** be filled with drunkenness Ezk 23:33
‘You **w** drink it and drain it. Ezk 23:34
Then you **w** gnaw its fragments And Ezk 23:34
w you judge Oholah and Oholibah? Ezk 23:36
‘**W** they now commit adultery with Ezk 23:43
w judge them with the judgment of Ezk 23:45
‘The company **w** stone them with Ezk 23:47
they **w** slay their sons and their Ezk 23:47
‘Thus I **w** make lewdness cease from Ezk 23:48
lewdness **w** be requited upon you, Ezk 23:49
and you **w** bear the penalty of Ezk 23:49
you **w** know that I am the Lord Ezk 23:49
I also **w** make the pile great. Ezk 24:9
You **w** not be cleansed from your Ezk 24:13
it is coming and I **w** act. I will not Ezk 24:14
I **w** not relent, and I will not pity Ezk 24:14
and I **w** not pity and I will not be Ezk 24:14
and I will not pity and I **w** not be Ezk 24:14
according to your deeds I **w** judge Ezk 24:14
“**W** you not tell us what these Ezk 24:19
left behind **w** fall by the sword. Ezk 24:21
‘You **w** do as I have done; Ezk 24:22
you **w** not cover *your* mustache and Ezk 24:22
and you **w** not eat the bread of men. Ezk 24:22
‘Your turbans **w** be on your Ezk 24:23
You **w** not mourn and you will not Ezk 24:23
not mourn and you **w** not weep Ezk 24:23
you **w** rot away in your iniquities and Ezk 24:23
and you **w** groan to one another. Ezk 24:23
‘Thus Ezekiel **w** be a sign to you; Ezk 24:24
to all that he has done you **w** do; Ezk 24:24
you **w** know that I am the Lord Ezk 24:24
w *it* not be on the day when I take Ezk 24:25
he who escapes **w** come to you with Ezk 24:26
your mouth **w** be opened to him Ezk 24:27
you **w** speak and be mute no longer. Ezk 24:27
Thus you **w** be a sign to them, and Ezk 24:27
w know that I am the LORD.’ ” Ezk 24:27
and they **w** set their encampments Ezk 25:4
they **w** eat your fruit and drink Ezk 25:4
“I **w** make Rabbah a pasture for Ezk 25:5
you **w** know that I am the LORD.” Ezk 25:5
out My hand against you and I **w** give Ezk 25:7
And I **w** cut you off from the peoples Ezk 25:7
I **w** destroy you. Thus you will know Ezk 25:7
you **w** know that I am the LORD.” Ezk 25:7
and I **w** give it for a possession along Ezk 25:10
so that the sons of Ammon **w** not be Ezk 25:10
I **w** execute judgments on Moab, Ezk 25:11
they **w** know that I am the LORD.” Ezk 25:11
“I **w** also stretch out My hand Ezk 25:13
And I **w** lay it waste; Ezk 25:13
to Dedan they **w** fall by the sword. Ezk 25:13
“I **w** lay My vengeance on Edom Ezk 25:14
they **w** act in Edom according to My Ezk 25:14
thus they **w** know My vengeance,” Ezk 25:14
I **w** stretch out My hand against Ezk 25:16
“I **w** execute great vengeance Ezk 25:17
and they **w** know that I am the LORD Ezk 25:17
and I **w** bring up many nations Ezk 26:3
‘They **w** destroy the walls of Ezk 26:4
and I **w** scrape her debris from her Ezk 26:4
‘She **w** be a place for the Ezk 26:5
w become spoil for the nations. Ezk 26:5
mainland **w** be slain by the sword, Ezk 26:6
w know that I am the LORD.’ ” Ezk 26:6
I **w** bring upon Tyre from the north Ezk 26:7
“He **w** slay your daughters on the Ezk 26:8
he **w** make siege walls against you, Ezk 26:8
he **w** direct against your walls, Ezk 26:9
axes he **w** break down your towers. Ezk 26:9
dust *raised by* them **w** cover you; Ezk 26:10
your walls **w** shake at the noise of Ezk 26:10
he **w** trample all your streets. Ezk 26:11
He **w** slay your people with the Ezk 26:11
pillars **w** come down to the ground. Ezk 26:11
“Also they **w** make a spoil of your Ezk 26:12
“So I **w** silence the sound of your Ezk 26:13
sound of your harps **w** be heard no Ezk 26:13
“I **w** make you a bare rock; Ezk 26:14
you **w** be a place for the spreading Ezk 26:14
You **w** be built no more, for I the Ezk 26:14
sea **w** go down from their thrones, Ezk 26:16
They **w** clothe themselves with Ezk 26:16
they **w** sit on the ground, tremble Ezk 26:16
“They **w** take up a lamentation Ezk 26:17
‘Now the coastlands **w** tremble On Ezk 26:18
which are by the sea **W** be terrified Ezk 26:18
then I **w** bring you down with those Ezk 26:20
and I **w** make you dwell in the lower Ezk 26:20
so that you **w** not be inhabited; Ezk 26:20
but I **w** set glory in the land of Ezk 26:20
“I **w** bring terrors on you and you Ezk 26:21
on you and you **w** be no more; Ezk 26:21
though you **w** be sought, you will Ezk 26:21
you **w** never be found again,” Ezk 26:21

W fall into the heart of the seas	Ezk 27:27
pilots The pasture lands **w** shake.	Ezk 27:28
sea **W** come down from their ships;	Ezk 27:29
They **w** stand on the land,	Ezk 27:29
And they **w** make their voice heard	Ezk 27:30
heard over you And **w** cry bitterly.	Ezk 27:30
They **w** cast dust on their heads,	Ezk 27:30
heads, They **w** wallow in ashes.	Ezk 27:30
"Also they **w** make themselves bald	Ezk 27:31
And they **w** weep for you in	Ezk 27:31
in their wailing they **w** take up a	Ezk 27:32
And you **w** cease to be forever.' " ' "	Ezk 27:36
I **w** bring strangers upon you,	Ezk 28:7
And they **w** draw their swords	Ezk 28:7
'They **w** bring you down to the pit,	Ezk 28:8
And you **w** die the death of those	Ezk 28:8
'**W** you still say,	Ezk 28:9
'You **w** die the death of the	Ezk 28:10
And you **w** cease to be forever." ' "	Ezk 28:19
And I **w** be glorified in your midst.	Ezk 28:22
they **w** know that I am the LORD when	Ezk 28:22
And I **w** manifest My holiness in her.	Ezk 28:22
"For I **w** send pestilence to her And	Ezk 28:23
And the wounded **w** fall in her	Ezk 28:23
they **w** know that I am the LORD.	Ezk 28:23
"And there **w** be no more for the	Ezk 28:24
w know that I am the Lord GOD."	Ezk 28:24
and **w** manifest My holiness in them in	Ezk 28:25
then they **w** live in their land	Ezk 28:25
"They **w** live in it securely;	Ezk 28:26
and they **w** build houses, plant	Ezk 28:26
Then they **w** know that I am the	Ezk 28:26
"I **w** put hooks in your jaws And make	Ezk 29:4
And I **w** bring you up out of the midst	Ezk 29:4
rivers **w** cling to your scales.	Ezk 29:4
"I **w** abandon you to the wilderness,	Ezk 29:5
You **w** fall on the open field;	Ezk 29:5
you **w** not be brought together or	Ezk 29:5
Egypt **w** know that I am the LORD,	Ezk 29:6
I **w** bring upon you a sword and I will	Ezk 29:8
bring upon you a sword and I **w** cut	Ezk 29:8
Egypt **w** become a desolation and	Ezk 29:9
they **w** know that I am the LORD.	Ezk 29:9
and I **w** make the land of Egypt an	Ezk 29:10
"A man's foot **w** not pass through	Ezk 29:11
foot of a beast **w** not pass through it,	Ezk 29:11
and it **w** not be inhabited for	Ezk 29:11
"So I **w** make the land of Egypt a	Ezk 29:12
waste, **w** be desolate forty years;	Ezk 29:12
and I **w** scatter the Egyptians among	Ezk 29:12
"At the end of forty years I **w**	Ezk 29:13
"I **w** turn the fortunes of Egypt	Ezk 29:14
there they **w** be a lowly kingdom.	Ezk 29:14
w be the lowest of the kingdoms,	Ezk 29:15
and it **w** never again lift itself	Ezk 29:15
And I **w** make them so small that they	Ezk 29:15
they **w** not rule over the nations.	Ezk 29:15
"And it **w** never again be the	Ezk 29:16
w know that I am the Lord GOD.	Ezk 29:16
I **w** give the land of Egypt to	Ezk 29:19
And he **w** carry off her wealth and	Ezk 29:19
and it **w** be wages for his army.	Ezk 29:19
"On that day I **w** make a horn sprout	Ezk 29:21
and I **w** open your mouth in their	Ezk 29:21
they **w** know that I am the LORD."	Ezk 29:21
It **w** be a day of clouds, A time *of*	Ezk 30:3
"A sword **w** come upon Egypt,	Ezk 30:4
And anguish **w** be in Ethiopia;	Ezk 30:4
w fall with them by the sword."	Ezk 30:5
those who support Egypt **w** fall And	Ezk 30:6
pride of her power **w** come down;	Ezk 30:6
w fall within her by the sword,"	Ezk 30:6
"They **w** be desolate In the	Ezk 30:7
And her cities **w** be In the midst	Ezk 30:7
they **w** know that I am the LORD,	Ezk 30:8
"On that day messengers **w** go	Ezk 30:9
and anguish **w** be on them as on the	Ezk 30:9
"I **w** also make the hordes of	Ezk 30:10
W be brought in to destroy the	Ezk 30:11
And they **w** draw their swords	Ezk 30:11
I **w** make the Nile canals dry And	Ezk 30:12
And I **w** make the land desolate And	Ezk 30:12
"I **w** also destroy the idols And	Ezk 30:13
And there **w** no longer be a prince	Ezk 30:13
I **w** put fear in the land of Egypt.	Ezk 30:13
"I **w** make Pathros desolate,	Ezk 30:14
"I **w** pour out My wrath on	Ezk 30:15
I **w** also cut off the hordes of	Ezk 30:15
"I **w** set a fire in Egypt;	Ezk 30:16
Sin **w** writhe in anguish, Thebes	Ezk 30:16
in anguish, Thebes **w** be breached And	Ezk 30:16
will be breached And Memphis **w** *have*	Ezk 30:16
of Pi-beseth **W** fall by the sword,	Ezk 30:17
And the women **w** go into captivity.	Ezk 30:17
"In Tehaphnehes the day **w** be	Ezk 30:18
pride of her power **w** cease in her;	Ezk 30:18
A cloud **w** cover her, And her	Ezk 30:18
her daughters **w** go into captivity.	Ezk 30:18
I **w** execute judgments on Egypt,	Ezk 30:19
w know that I am the LORD.	Ezk 30:19
of Egypt and **w** break his arms,	Ezk 30:22
and I **w** make the sword fall from	Ezk 30:22
'I **w** scatter the Egyptians	Ezk 30:23
'For I **w** strengthen the arms of	Ezk 30:24
and I **w** break the arms of Pharaoh,	Ezk 30:24
so that he **w** groan before him with	Ezk 30:24
'Thus I **w** strengthen the arms of	Ezk 30:25
but the arms of Pharaoh **w** fall.	Ezk 30:25
they **w** know that I am the LORD,	Ezk 30:25
w know that I am the LORD.' "	Ezk 30:26
I **w** give it into the hand of a	Ezk 31:11
he **w** thoroughly deal with it.	Ezk 31:11
the birds of the heavens **w** dwell,	Ezk 31:13
all the beasts of the field **w** be on its	Ezk 31:13
Yet you **w** be brought down with the	Ezk 31:18
you **w** lie in the midst of the	Ezk 31:18
'Now I **w** spread My net over you	Ezk 32:3
"I **w** leave you on the land;	Ezk 32:4
I **w** cast you on the open field.	Ezk 32:4
And I **w** cause all the birds of the	Ezk 32:4
And I **w** satisfy the beasts of the	Ezk 32:4
"I **w** lay your flesh on the	Ezk 32:5
"I **w** also make the land drink the	Ezk 32:6
And the ravines **w** be full of you.	Ezk 32:6
you, I **w** cover the heavens and	Ezk 32:7
I **w** cover the sun with a cloud And	Ezk 32:7
sun with a cloud And the moon **w** not	Ezk 32:7
lights in the heavens I **w** darken over	Ezk 32:8
And **w** set darkness on your land,"	Ezk 32:8
"I **w** also trouble the hearts of	Ezk 32:9
"I **w** make many peoples	Ezk 32:10
and their kings **w** be horribly afraid	Ezk 32:10
and they **w** tremble every moment,	Ezk 32:10
sword of the king of Babylon **w** come	Ezk 32:11
I **w** cause your hordes to fall;	Ezk 32:12
And they **w** devastate the pride of	Ezk 32:12
And all its hordes **w** be destroyed.	Ezk 32:12
"I **w** also destroy all its cattle	Ezk 32:13
And the foot of man **w** not muddy them	Ezk 32:13
anymore And the hoofs of beasts **w** not	Ezk 32:13
"Then I **w** make their waters	Ezk 32:14
And **w** cause their rivers to run	Ezk 32:14
you **w** be broken and lie with those	Ezk 32:28
they **w** lie with the uncircumcised and	Ezk 32:29
"These Pharaoh **w** see, and he will	Ezk 32:31
and he **w** be comforted for all his	Ezk 32:31
yet he **w** be made to lie down among	Ezk 32:32
his blood **w** be on his *own* head.	Ezk 33:4
his blood **w** be on himself.	Ezk 33:5
but his blood I **w** require from the	Ezk 33:6
w hear a message from My mouth and	Ezk 33:7
you **w** surely die,' and you do not	Ezk 33:8
blood I **w** require from your hand.	Ezk 33:8
his way, he **w** die in his iniquity,	Ezk 33:9
Why then **w** you die, O house of	Ezk 33:11
a righteous man **w** not deliver	Ezk 33:12
he **w** not stumble because of it in	Ezk 33:12
whereas a righteous man **w** not be	Ezk 33:12
to the righteous he **w** surely live,	Ezk 33:13
righteous deeds **w** be remembered;	Ezk 33:13
which he has committed he **w** die.	Ezk 33:13
'You **w** surely die,' and he turns	Ezk 33:14
w be remembered against him.	Ezk 33:16
righteousness, he **w** live by them.	Ezk 33:19
I **w** judge each of you according to	Ezk 33:20
waste places **w** fall by the sword,	Ezk 33:27
whoever is in the open field I **w** give	Ezk 33:27
in the caves **w** die of pestilence.	Ezk 33:27
"I **w** make the land a desolation	Ezk 33:28
the pride of her power **w** cease;	Ezk 33:28
mountains of Israel **w** be desolate so	Ezk 33:28
so that no one **w** pass through.	Ezk 33:28
they **w** know that I am the LORD,	Ezk 33:29
when it comes to pass—as surely it **w**	Ezk 33:33
they **w** know that a prophet has been	Ezk 33:33
and I **w** demand My sheep from them	Ezk 34:10
w not feed themselves anymore,	Ezk 34:10
but I **w** deliver My flock from their	Ezk 34:10
so that they **w** not be food for them." ' "	Ezk 34:10
I Myself **w** search for My sheep and	Ezk 34:11
so I **w** care for My sheep and will	Ezk 34:12
I will care for My sheep and **w** deliver	Ezk 34:12
"I **w** bring them out from the	Ezk 34:13
and I **w** feed them on the mountains	Ezk 34:13
"I **w** feed them in a good pasture,	Ezk 34:14
and their grazing ground **w** be on	Ezk 34:14
There they **w** lie down on good	Ezk 34:14
"I **w** feed My flock and I will	Ezk 34:15
flock and I **w** lead them to rest,"	Ezk 34:15
"I **w** seek the lost, bring back	Ezk 34:16
fat and the strong I **w** destroy.	Ezk 34:16
I **w** feed them with judgment.	Ezk 34:16
I **w** judge between one sheep and	Ezk 34:17
w judge between the fat sheep and	Ezk 34:20
therefore, I **w** deliver My flock,	Ezk 34:22
and they **w** no longer be a prey;	Ezk 34:22
and I **w** judge between one sheep	Ezk 34:22
I **w** set over them one shepherd,	Ezk 34:23
servant David, and he **w** feed them;	Ezk 34:23
he **w** feed them himself and be	Ezk 34:23
"And I, the LORD, **w** be their God,	Ezk 34:24
David **w** be prince among them;	Ezk 34:24
"I **w** make a covenant of peace	Ezk 34:25
"I **w** make them and the places	Ezk 34:26
And I **w** cause showers to come down	Ezk 34:26
they **w** be showers of blessing.	Ezk 34:26
of the field **w** yield its fruit and	Ezk 34:27
the earth **w** yield its increase,	Ezk 34:27
they **w** be secure on their land.	Ezk 34:27
they **w** know that I am the LORD,	Ezk 34:27
"They **w** no longer be a prey	Ezk 34:28
of the earth **w** not devour them;	Ezk 34:28
but they **w** live securely, and no	Ezk 34:28
and no one **w** make *them* afraid.	Ezk 34:28
"I **w** establish for them a	Ezk 34:29
and they **w** not again be victims of	Ezk 34:29
and they **w** not endure the insults	Ezk 34:29
"Then they **w** know that I, the	Ezk 34:30
And I **w** stretch out My hand	Ezk 35:3
"I **w** lay waste your cities And	Ezk 35:4
And you **w** become a desolation.	Ezk 35:4
you **w** know that I am the LORD.	Ezk 35:4
"I **w** give you over to bloodshed,	Ezk 35:6
and bloodshed **w** pursue you;	Ezk 35:6
therefore bloodshed **w** pursue you.	Ezk 35:6
"I **w** make Mount Seir a waste	Ezk 35:7
and I **w** cut off from it the one	Ezk 35:7
"I **w** fill its mountains with	Ezk 35:8
those slain by the sword **w** fall.	Ezk 35:8
"I **w** make you an everlasting	Ezk 35:9
your cities **w** not be inhabited.	Ezk 35:9
you **w** know that I am the LORD.	Ezk 35:9
and these two lands **w** be mine,	Ezk 35:10
be mine, and we **w** possess them,'	Ezk 35:10
"I **w** deal *with you* according to	Ezk 35:11
so I **w** make Myself known among	Ezk 35:11
"Then you **w** know that I, the	Ezk 35:12
I **w** make you a desolation.	Ezk 35:14
it was desolate, so I **w** do to you.	Ezk 35:15
You **w** be a desolation, O Mount	Ezk 35:15
w know that I am the LORD."	Ezk 35:15
the nations which are around you **w**	Ezk 36:7
you **w** put forth your branches and	Ezk 36:8
for they **w** soon come.	Ezk 36:8
I am for you, and I **w** turn to you,	Ezk 36:9
and you **w** be cultivated and sown.	Ezk 36:9
'I **w** multiply men on you, all	Ezk 36:10
and the cities **w** be inhabited and	Ezk 36:10
and the waste places **w** be rebuilt.	Ezk 36:10
I **w** multiply on you man and beast;	Ezk 36:11
they **w** increase and be fruitful;	Ezk 36:11
and I **w** cause you to be inhabited	Ezk 36:11
w treat you better than at the first.	Ezk 36:11
you **w** know that I am the LORD.	Ezk 36:11
'Yes, I **w** cause men	Ezk 36:12
so that you **w** become their	Ezk 36:12
you **w** no longer devour men and	Ezk 36:14
"I **w** not let you hear insults	Ezk 36:15
nor **w** you bear disgrace from the	Ezk 36:15
nor **w** you cause your nation to	Ezk 36:15
"I **w** vindicate the holiness	Ezk 36:23
w know that I am the LORD,"	Ezk 36:23
"For I **w** take you from the	Ezk 36:24
I **w** sprinkle clean water on you,	Ezk 36:25
water on you, and you **w** be clean;	Ezk 36:25
I **w** cleanse you from all your	Ezk 36:25
I **w** give you a new heart and put a	Ezk 36:26
and I **w** remove the heart of stone	Ezk 36:26
"I **w** put My Spirit within you	Ezk 36:27
and you **w** be careful to observe My	Ezk 36:27
"You **w** live in the land that	Ezk 36:28
so you **w** be My people, and I will	Ezk 36:28
be My people, and I **w** be your God.	Ezk 36:28
I **w** save you from all your	Ezk 36:29
and I **w** call for the grain and	Ezk 36:29
and I **w** not bring a famine on you.	Ezk 36:29
"I **w** multiply the fruit of	Ezk 36:30
so that you **w** not receive again	Ezk 36:30
"Then you **w** remember your evil	Ezk 36:31
and you **w** loathe yourselves in	Ezk 36:31
I **w** cause the cities to be	Ezk 36:33
and the waste places **w** be rebuilt.	Ezk 36:33
The desolate land **w** be cultivated	Ezk 36:34
"They **w** say,	Ezk 36:35
round about you **w** know that I,	Ezk 36:36
LORD, have spoken and **w** do it."	Ezk 36:36
"This also I **w** let the house of	Ezk 36:37
I **w** increase their men like a	Ezk 36:37
so **w** the waste cities be filled	Ezk 36:38
w know that I am the LORD.	Ezk 36:38
I **w** cause breath to enter you that	Ezk 37:5
'I **w** put sinews on you, make	Ezk 37:6
you **w** know that I am the LORD.' "	Ezk 37:6
I **w** open your graves and cause you	Ezk 37:12
and I **w** bring you into the land of	Ezk 37:12
you **w** know that I am the LORD,	Ezk 37:13
"I **w** put My Spirit within	Ezk 37:14
you and you **w** come to life,	Ezk 37:14
I **w** place you on your own land.	Ezk 37:14
Then you **w** know that I, the LORD,	Ezk 37:14
'**W** you not declare to us what you	Ezk 37:18
I **w** take the stick of Joseph,	Ezk 37:19
and I **w** put them with it, with the	Ezk 37:19
and they **w** be one in My hand."	Ezk 37:19
The sticks on which you write **w** be in	Ezk 37:20
I **w** take the sons of Israel from	Ezk 37:21
and I **w** gather them from every	Ezk 37:21
and I **w** make them one nation in	Ezk 37:22
king **w** be king for all of them;	Ezk 37:22
and they **w** no longer be two	Ezk 37:22
"They **w** no longer defile	Ezk 37:23
but I **w** deliver them from all	Ezk 37:23
have sinned, and **w** cleanse them.	Ezk 37:23
And they **w** be My people, and I	Ezk 37:23
My people, and I **w** be their God.	Ezk 37:23
servant David **w** be king over them,	Ezk 37:24
and they **w** all have one shepherd;	Ezk 37:24
and they **w** walk in My ordinances and	Ezk 37:24
"They **w** live on the land that I gave	Ezk 37:25
and they **w** live on it, they, and	Ezk 37:25
and David My servant **w** be their	Ezk 37:25
"I **w** make a covenant of peace	Ezk 37:26
it **w** be an everlasting covenant	Ezk 37:26
I **w** place them and multiply them,	Ezk 37:26
and **w** set My sanctuary in their	Ezk 37:26
place also **w** be with them;	Ezk 37:27
and I **w** be their God, and they	Ezk 37:27

God, and they **w** be My people.	Ezk 37:27
"And the nations **w** know that I am	Ezk 37:28
"I **w** turn you about and put	Ezk 38:4
your jaws, and I **w** bring you out,	Ezk 38:4
"After many days you **w** be summoned;	Ezk 38:8
in the latter years you **w** come	Ezk 38:8
"You **w** go up, you will come	Ezk 38:9
go up, you **w** come like a storm;	Ezk 38:9
you **w** be like a cloud covering the	Ezk 38:9
"It **w** come about on that day,	Ezk 38:10
thoughts **w** come into your mind and	Ezk 38:10
and you **w** devise an evil plan,	Ezk 38:10
and you **w** say, 'I will go up against the	Ezk 38:11
'I **w** go up against the land of	Ezk 38:11
I **w** go against those who are at	Ezk 38:11
all its villages **w** say to you,	Ezk 38:13
securely, **w** you not know *it?*	Ezk 38:14
"You **w** come from your place	Ezk 38:15
and you **w** come up against My	Ezk 38:16
in the last days that I **w** bring	Ezk 38:16
"It **w** come about on that day,	Ezk 38:18
My fury **w** mount up in My anger.	Ezk 38:18
there **w** surely be a great earthquake	Ezk 38:19
the earth **w** shake at My presence;	Ezk 38:20
mountains also **w** be thrown down,	Ezk 38:20
the steep pathways **w** collapse and	Ezk 38:20
every wall **w** fall to the ground.	Ezk 38:20
"I **w** call for a sword against him on	Ezk 38:21
sword **w** be against his brother.	Ezk 38:21
pestilence and with blood I **w** enter	Ezk 38:22
and I **w** rain on him and on his troops,	Ezk 38:22
"I **w** magnify Myself, sanctify	Ezk 38:23
w know that I am the LORD."	Ezk 38:23
and I **w** turn you around, drive you	Ezk 39:2
"I **w** strike your bow from your left	Ezk 39:3
"You **w** fall on the mountains of	Ezk 39:4
I **w** give you as food to every kind of	Ezk 39:4
"You **w** fall on the open field;	Ezk 39:5
"And I **w** send fire upon Magog	Ezk 39:6
they **w** know that I am the LORD.	Ezk 39:6
"My holy name I **w** make known in	Ezk 39:7
and I **w** not let My holy name be	Ezk 39:7
nations **w** know that I am the LORD,	Ezk 39:7
the cities of Israel **w** go out and	Ezk 39:9
years they **w** make fires of them.	Ezk 39:9
"They **w** not take wood from	Ezk 39:10
they **w** make fires with the weapons;	Ezk 39:10
and they **w** take the spoil of those	Ezk 39:10
"On that day I **w** give Gog a burial	Ezk 39:11
w block off those who would pass by.	Ezk 39:11
So they **w** bury Gog there with all	Ezk 39:11
and they **w** call *it* the valley of	Ezk 39:11
Israel **w** be burying them in order to	Ezk 39:12
people of the land **w** bury *them;*	Ezk 39:13
and it **w** be to their renown *on* the	Ezk 39:13
"They **w** set apart men who	Ezk 39:14
men who **w** constantly pass through	Ezk 39:14
seven months they **w** make a search.	Ezk 39:14
then he **w** set up a marker by it	Ezk 39:15
the name of *the* city **w** be Hamonah.	Ezk 39:16
So they **w** cleanse the land."	Ezk 39:16
"You **w** eat the flesh of mighty men	Ezk 39:18
w eat fat until you are glutted,	Ezk 39:19
"You **w** be glutted at My table	Ezk 39:20
"And I **w** set My glory among	Ezk 39:21
and all the nations **w** see My	Ezk 39:21
"And the house of Israel **w** know	Ezk 39:22
"The nations **w** know that the	Ezk 39:23
"Now I **w** restore the fortunes of	Ezk 39:25
and I **w** be jealous for My holy name.	Ezk 39:25
"They **w** forget their disgrace	Ezk 39:26
"Then they **w** know that I am the	Ezk 39:28
and I **w** leave none of them there	Ezk 39:28
"I **w** not hide My face from	Ezk 39:29
for I **w** have poured out My Spirit on	Ezk 39:29
where I **w** dwell among the sons of	Ezk 43:7
house of Israel **w** not again defile	Ezk 43:7
and I **w** dwell among them forever.	Ezk 43:9
and I **w** accept you,' declares the	Ezk 43:27
but they **w** bear their shame and their	Ezk 44:13
"Yet I **w** appoint them to keep	Ezk 44:14
on other garments so that they **w** not	Ezk 44:19
so that the bath **w** contain a tenth of	Ezk 45:11
possession so that My people **w** not	Ezk 46:18
"It **w** come about that every	Ezk 47:9
where the river goes, **w** live.	Ezk 47:9
And there **w** be very many fish, for	Ezk 47:9
w live where the river goes.	Ezk 47:9
"And it **w** come about that	Ezk 47:10
that fishermen **w** stand beside it;	Ezk 47:10
from Engedi to Eneglaim there **w** be	Ezk 47:10
w be according to their kinds,	Ezk 47:10
and marshes **w** not become fresh;	Ezk 47:11
they **w** be left for salt.	Ezk 47:11
w grow all *kinds of* trees for food.	Ezk 47:12
Their leaves **w** not wither and	Ezk 47:12
and their fruit **w** not fail.	Ezk 47:12
They **w** bear every month because	Ezk 47:12
and their fruit **w** be for food and	Ezk 47:12
we **w** declare the interpretation."	Da 2:4
you **w** be torn limb from limb and	Da 2:5
houses **w** be made a rubbish heap.	Da 2:5
you **w** receive from me gifts and a	Da 2:6
we **w** declare the interpretation."	Da 2:7
and I **w** declare the interpretation	Da 2:24
w take place in the latter days.	Da 2:28
known to you what **w** take place.	Da 2:29
"This *was* the dream; now we **w**	Da 2:36
"After you there **w** arise	Da 2:39
which **w** rule over all the earth.	Da 2:39
"Then there **w** be a fourth kingdom	Da 2:40
it **w** crush and break all these in	Da 2:40
iron, it **w** be a divided kingdom;	Da 2:41
but it **w** have in it the toughness	Da 2:41
so some of the kingdom **w** be strong	Da 2:42
and part of it **w** be brittle.	Da 2:42
they **w** combine with one another in	Da 2:43
they **w** not adhere to one another,	Da 2:43
God of heaven **w** set up a kingdom	Da 2:44
which **w** never be destroyed,	Da 2:44
and *that* kingdom **w** not be left for	Da 2:44
it **w** crush and put an end to all	Da 2:44
but it **w** itself endure forever.	Da 2:44
what **w** take place in the future;	Da 2:45
you **w** immediately be cast into the	Da 3:15
He **w** deliver us out of your hand,	Da 3:17
periods of time **w** pass over you,	Da 4:25
your kingdom **w** be assured to you	Da 4:26
you **w** be driven away from mankind,	Da 4:32
and your dwelling place **w** *be* with	Da 4:32
You **w** be given grass to eat like	Da 4:32
periods of time **w** pass over you until	Da 4:32
But He does according to His **w** in	Da 4:35
6634	
he **w** declare the interpretation."	Da 5:12
you **w** be clothed with purple and	Da 5:16
and you **w** have authority as the	Da 5:16
I **w** read the inscription to the	Da 5:17
Then these men said, "We **w** not find	Da 6:5
serve **w** Himself deliver you."	Da 6:16
is one which **w** not be destroyed,	Da 6:26
And His dominion **w** *be* forever.	Da 6:26
dominion Which **w** not pass away;	Da 7:14
is one Which **w** not be destroyed.	Da 7:14
kings *who* **w** arise from the earth.	Da 7:17
saints of the Highest One **w** receive	Da 7:18
'The fourth beast **w** be a fourth	Da 7:23
which **w** be different from all the	Da 7:23
and **w** devour the whole earth	Da 7:23
of this kingdom ten kings **w** arise;	Da 7:24
and another **w** arise after them,	Da 7:24
and he **w** be different from the	Da 7:24
ones and **w** subdue three kings.	Da 7:24
'He **w** speak out against the	Da 7:25
and he **w** intend to make	Da 7:25
and they **w** be given into his hand	Da 7:25
'But the court **w** sit *for judgment,*	Da 7:26
and his dominion **w** be taken away,	Da 7:26
w be given to the people of the saints	Da 7:27
His kingdom **w** *be* an everlasting	Da 7:27
dominions **w** serve and obey Him.'	Da 7:27
the host **w** be given over *to the horn*	Da 8:12
and it **w** fling truth to the ground	Da 8:12
to the ground and perform *its* **w**	Da 8:12
"How long **w** the vision *about* the	Da 8:13
place **w** be properly restored."	Da 8:14
what **w** occur at the final period of	Da 8:19
which **w** arise from *his* nation,	Da 8:22
A king **w** arise, Insolent and	Da 8:23
"His power **w** be mighty, but	Da 8:24
And he **w** destroy to an	Da 8:24
And prosper and perform *his* **w**;	Da 8:24
He **w** destroy mighty men and the	Da 8:24
He **w** cause deceit to succeed by his	Da 8:25
he **w** magnify *himself* in his heart,	Da 8:25
And he **w** destroy many while *they*	Da 8:25
He **w** even oppose the Prince of	Da 8:25
But he **w** be broken without human	Da 8:25
until Messiah the Prince *there* **w** *be*	Da 9:25
it **w** be built again, with plaza	Da 9:25
w be cut off and have nothing,	Da 9:26
w destroy the city and the sanctuary.	Da 9:26
And its end **w** *come* with a flood;	Da 9:26
even to the end there **w** be war;	Da 9:26
"And he **w** make a firm covenant	Da 9:27
he **w** put a stop to sacrifice and grain	Da 9:27
the wing of abominations **w** *come*	Da 9:27
what **w** happen to your people in the	Da 10:14
I **w** tell you what is inscribed in	Da 10:21
"And now I **w** tell you the truth.	Da 11:2
Then a fourth **w** gain far more	Da 11:2
he **w** arouse the whole *empire*	Da 11:2
"And a mighty king **w** arise,	Da 11:3
and he **w** rule with great authority	Da 11:3
his kingdom **w** be broken up and	Da 11:4
for his sovereignty **w** be uprooted	Da 11:4
king of the South **w** grow strong,	Da 11:5
princes who **w** gain ascendancy over	Da 11:5
his domain **w** *be* a great dominion	Da 11:5
years they **w** form an alliance,	Da 11:6
daughter of the king of the South **w**	Da 11:6
But she **w** not retain her position	Da 11:6
nor **w** he remain with his power,	Da 11:6
his power, but she **w** be given up,	Da 11:6
of her line **w** arise in his place,	Da 11:7
and he **w** come against *their* army	Da 11:7
and he **w** deal with them and	Da 11:7
he **w** take into captivity to Egypt,	Da 11:8
and he on his part **w** refrain from	Da 11:8
"Then the latter **w** enter the	Da 11:9
but **w** return to his *own* land.	Da 11:9
"His sons **w** mobilize and	Da 11:10
and one of them **w** keep on coming	Da 11:10
The king of the South **w** be enraged	Da 11:11
latter **w** raise a great multitude,	Da 11:11
but *that* multitude **w** be given into	Da 11:11
away, his heart **w** be lifted up,	Da 11:12
and he **w** cause tens of thousands	Da 11:12
yet he **w** not prevail.	Da 11:12
the king of the North **w** again raise	Da 11:13
he **w** press on with a great army and	Da 11:13
"Now in those times many **w** rise	Da 11:14
violent ones among your people **w**	Da 11:14
the vision, but they **w** fall down.	Da 11:14
"Then the king of the North **w** come,	Da 11:15
South **w** not stand *their ground,*	Da 11:15
for there **w** be no strength to make	Da 11:15
against him **w** do as he pleases,	Da 11:16
no one **w** *be able to* withstand him;	Da 11:16
he **w** also stay *for a time* in the	Da 11:16
"He **w** set his face to come	Da 11:17
peace which he **w** put into effect;	Da 11:17
he **w** also give him the daughter of	Da 11:17
But she **w** not take a stand *for him*	Da 11:17
"Then he **w** turn his face to the	Da 11:18
But a commander **w** put a stop to	Da 11:18
he **w** repay him for his scorn.	Da 11:18
"So he **w** turn his face toward the	Da 11:19
but he **w** stumble and fall and be	Da 11:19
"Then in his place one **w** arise	Da 11:20
in his place one will arise who **w** send	Da 11:20
a few days he **w** be shattered,	Da 11:20
place a despicable person **w** arise,	Da 11:21
but he **w** come in a time of	Da 11:21
The overflowing forces **w** be flooded	Da 11:22
with him he **w** practice deception,	Da 11:23
and he **w** go up and gain power with	Da 11:23
he **w** enter the richest *parts* of the	Da 11:24
and he **w** accomplish what his	Da 11:24
he **w** distribute plunder, booty and	Da 11:24
and he **w** devise his schemes	Da 11:24
"He **w** stir up his strength	Da 11:25
the king of the South **w** mobilize an	Da 11:25
but he **w** not stand, for schemes	Da 11:25
schemes **w** be devised against him.	Da 11:25
eat his choice food **w** destroy him,	Da 11:26
him, and his army **w** overflow,	Da 11:26
but many **w** fall down slain.	Da 11:26
their hearts **w** be *intent* on evil,	Da 11:27
and they **w** speak lies *to each*	Da 11:27
but it **w** not succeed, for the end	Da 11:27
"Then he **w** return to his land	Da 11:28
but his heart **w** be *set* against the	Da 11:28
and he **w** take action and *then*	Da 11:28
"At the appointed time he **w** return	Da 11:29
but this last time it **w** not turn	Da 11:29
of Kittim **w** come against him;	Da 11:30
therefore he **w** be disheartened and	Da 11:30
and **w** return and become enraged at	Da 11:30
so he **w** come back and show regard	Da 11:30
"Forces from him **w** arise,	Da 11:31
And they **w** set up the abomination	Da 11:31
"By smooth *words* he **w** turn to	Da 11:32
people who know their God **w** display	Da 11:32
w give understanding to the many;	Da 11:33
they **w** fall by sword and by flame,	Da 11:33
they **w** be granted a little help,	Da 11:34
w join with them in hypocrisy.	Da 11:34
of those who have insight **w** fall,	Da 11:35
"Then the king **w** do as he	Da 11:36
and he **w** exalt and magnify himself	Da 11:36
and **w** speak monstrous things	Da 11:36
and he **w** prosper until the	Da 11:36
that which is decreed **w** be done.	Da 11:36
"He **w** show no regard for the	Da 11:37
nor **w** he show regard for any *other*	Da 11:37
for he **w** magnify himself above	Da 11:37
he **w** honor a god of fortresses,	Da 11:38
he **w** honor *him* with gold, silver,	Da 11:38
"He **w** take action against the	Da 11:39
he **w** give great honor to those who	Da 11:39
and **w** cause them to rule over	Da 11:39
and **w** parcel out land for a price.	Da 11:39
of the South **w** collide with him,	Da 11:40
and the king of the North **w** storm	Da 11:40
and he **w** enter countries, overflow	Da 11:40
w also enter the Beautiful Land,	Da 11:41
Land, and many *countries* **w** fall;	Da 11:41
w be rescued out of his hand:	Da 11:41
"Then he **w** stretch out his hand	Da 11:42
the land of Egypt **w** not escape.	Da 11:42
"But he **w** gain control over the	Da 11:43
and Libyans and Ethiopians **w** *follow*	Da 11:43
and from the North **w** disturb him,	Da 11:44
and he **w** go forth with great wrath	Da 11:44
"He **w** pitch the tents of his	Da 11:45
yet he **w** come to his end, and no	Da 11:45
to his end, and no one **w** help him.	Da 11:45
the sons of your people, **w** arise.	Da 12:1
And there **w** be a time of distress	Da 12:1
written in the book, **w** be rescued.	Da 12:1
in the dust of the ground **w** awake,	Da 12:2
Those who have insight **w** shine	Da 12:3
many **w** go back and forth, and	Da 12:4
forth, and knowledge **w** increase."	Da 12:4
"How long **w** *it be* until the end	Da 12:6
all these *events* **w** be completed.	Da 12:7
what **w** *be* the outcome of these	Da 12:8
"Many **w** be purged, purified and	Da 12:10
but the wicked **w** act wickedly; and	Da 12:10
none of the wicked **w** understand,	Da 12:10
who have insight **w** understand.	Da 12:10
there **w** *be* 1,290 days.	Da 12:11
then you **w** enter into rest and	Da 12:13
and I **w** punish the house of Jehu	Hos 1:4
and I **w** put an end to the kingdom	Hos 1:4
that day I **w** break the bow of Israel	Hos 1:5
for I **w** no longer have compassion	Hos 1:6

"But I w have compassion on the	Hos 1:7
and w not deliver them by bow,	Hos 1:7
W be like the sand of the sea,	Hos 1:10
My people," It w be said to them,	Hos 1:10
of Israel w be gathered together,	Hos 1:11
And they w appoint for themselves	Hos 1:11
And they w go up from the land,	Hos 1:11
For great w be the day of Jezreel.	Hos 1:11
Or I w strip her naked And expose her	Hos 2:3
I w also make her like a	Hos 2:3
I w have no compassion on her	Hos 2:4
'I w go after my lovers, Who give	Hos 2:5
I w hedge up her way with thorns,	Hos 2:6
And I w build a wall against her	Hos 2:6
"She w pursue her lovers, but	Hos 2:7
but she w not overtake them;	Hos 2:7
And she w seek them, but will not	Hos 2:7
seek them, but w not find *them.*	Hos 2:7
she w say, 'I will go back to my first	Hos 2:7
'I w go back to my first husband,	Hos 2:7
I w take back My grain at harvest	Hos 2:9
I w also take away My wool and My	Hos 2:9
"And then I w uncover her	Hos 2:10
no one w rescue her out of My hand	Hos 2:10
"I w also put an end to all her	Hos 2:11
"I w destroy her vines and	Hos 2:12
And I w make them a forest, And	Hos 2:12
beasts of the field w devour them.	Hos 2:12
"I w punish her for the days	Hos 2:13
"Therefore, behold, I w allure her,	Hos 2:14
"Then I w give her her vineyards	Hos 2:15
And she w sing there as in the	Hos 2:15
"It w come about in that day,"	Hos 2:16
"That you w call Me Ishi And will	Hos 2:16
And w no longer call Me Baali.	Hos 2:16
"For I w remove the names of the	Hos 2:17
So that they w be mentioned by	Hos 2:17
"In that day I w also make a	Hos 2:18
And I w abolish the bow, the	Hos 2:18
w make them lie down in safety.	Hos 2:18
"I w betroth you to Me forever;	Hos 2:19
I w betroth you to Me in	Hos 2:19
And I w betroth you to Me in	Hos 2:20
Then you w know the LORD.	Hos 2:20
"It w come about in that day	Hos 2:21
in that day that I w respond,"	Hos 2:21
"I w respond to the heavens, and	Hos 2:21
and they w respond to the earth,	Hos 2:21
the earth w respond to the grain,	Hos 2:22
And they w respond to Jezreel.	Hos 2:22
"I w sow her for Myself in	Hos 2:23
I w also have compassion on her	Hos 2:23
And I w say to those who were not	Hos 2:23
And they w say, '*You are* my God!'	Hos 2:23
so I w also be toward you."	Hos 3:3
For the sons of Israel w remain	Hos 3:4
the sons of Israel w return and seek	Hos 3:5
and they w come trembling to the	Hos 3:5
So you w stumble by day, And the	Hos 4:5
the prophet also w stumble with you	Hos 4:5
And I w destroy your mother.	Hos 4:5
I also w reject you from being My	Hos 4:6
I also w forget your children.	Hos 4:6
I w change their glory into shame.	Hos 4:7
And it w be, like people, like	Hos 4:9
So I w punish them for their ways And	Hos 4:9
They w eat, but not have	Hos 4:10
They w play the harlot, but not	Hos 4:10
I w not punish your daughters when	Hos 4:14
And they w be ashamed because of	Hos 4:19
But I w chastise all of them.	Hos 5:2
Their deeds w not allow them To	Hos 5:4
They w go with their flocks and	Hos 5:6
the LORD, but they w not find *Him;*	Hos 5:6
the new moon w devour them with	Hos 5:7
Ephraim w become a desolation in	Hos 5:9
I w pour out My wrath like water.	Hos 5:10
For I w *be* like a lion to Ephraim	Hos 5:14
I, w tear to pieces and go away,	Hos 5:14
and go away, I w carry away,	Hos 5:14
and there w be none to deliver.	Hos 5:14
I w go away *and* return to My place	Hos 5:15
they w earnestly seek Me.	Hos 5:15
He has torn *us,* but He w heal us;	Hos 6:1
wounded *us,* but He w bandage us.	Hos 6:1
"He w revive us after two days;	Hos 6:2
He w raise us up on the third day,	Hos 6:2
And He w come to us like the rain,	Hos 6:3
go, I w spread My net over them;	Hos 7:12
I w bring them down like the birds	Hos 7:12
I w chastise them in accordance	Hos 7:12
Their princes w fall by the sword	Hos 7:16
This w *be* their derision in	Hos 7:16
The enemy w pursue him.	Hos 8:3
How long w they be incapable of	Hos 8:5
the calf of Samaria w be broken to	Hos 8:6
nations, Now I w gather them up;	Hos 8:10
And they w begin to diminish	Hos 8:10
Now He w remember their iniquity,	Hos 8:13
They w return to Egypt.	Hos 8:13
But I w send a fire on its cities	Hos 8:14
and wine press w not feed them,	Hos 9:2
And the new wine w fail them.	Hos 9:2
w not remain in the LORD's land,	Hos 9:3
But Ephraim w return to Egypt,	Hos 9:3
Assyria they w eat unclean *food.*	Hos 9:3
They w not pour out drink offerings of	Hos 9:4
Their sacrifices w not please Him.	Hos 9:4
Their bread w *be* like	Hos 9:4
All who eat of it w be defiled,	Hos 9:4
bread w be for themselves *alone;*	Hos 9:4
It w not enter the house of the	Hos 9:4
What w you do on the day of the	Hos 9:5
they w go because of destruction;	Hos 9:6
Egypt w gather them up, Memphis	Hos 9:6
them up, Memphis w bury them.	Hos 9:6
Weeds w take over their treasures	Hos 9:6
Thorns w *be* in their tents.	Hos 9:6
He w remember their iniquity, He	Hos 9:9
iniquity, He w punish their sins.	Hos 9:9
their glory w fly away like a	Hos 9:11
Yet I w bereave them until not a	Hos 9:12
But Ephraim w bring out his	Hos 9:13
O LORD—what w You give?	Hos 9:14
I w drive them out of My house!	Hos 9:15
I w love them no more;	Hos 9:15
is dried up, They w bear no fruit.	Hos 9:16
I w slay the precious ones of	Hos 9:16
My God w cast them away Because	Hos 9:17
And they w be wanderers among the	Hos 9:17
The LORD w break down their altars	Hos 10:2
Surely now they w say,	Hos 10:3
The inhabitants of Samaria w fear	Hos 10:5
Indeed, its people w mourn for it,	Hos 10:5
priests w cry out over it,	Hos 10:5
The thing itself w be carried to	Hos 10:6
Ephraim w be seized with shame And	Hos 10:6
Israel w be ashamed of its own	Hos 10:6
Samaria w be cut off *with* her king Like	Hos 10:7
the sin of Israel, w be destroyed;	Hos 10:8
thistle w grow on their altars;	Hos 10:8
Then they w say to the mountains,	Hos 10:8
W not the battle against the sons	Hos 10:9
is My desire, I w chastise them;	Hos 10:10
And the peoples w be gathered	Hos 10:10
But I w come over her fair neck	Hos 10:11
I w harness Ephraim, Judah will	Hos 10:11
harness Ephraim, Judah w plow,	Hos 10:11
plow, Jacob w harrow for himself.	Hos 10:11
tumult w arise among your people,	Hos 10:14
your fortresses w be destroyed,	Hos 10:14
Thus it w be done to you at Bethel	Hos 10:15
of Israel w be completely cut off.	Hos 10:15
They w not return to the land of	Hos 11:5
But Assyria—he w be their king	Hos 11:5
w whirl against their cities,	Hos 11:6
And w demolish their gate bars And	Hos 11:6
I w not execute My fierce anger;	Hos 11:9
I w not destroy Ephraim again.	Hos 11:9
midst, And I w not come in wrath.	Hos 11:9
They w walk after the LORD, He	Hos 11:10
the LORD, He w roar like a lion;	Hos 11:10
Indeed He w roar And *His* sons	Hos 11:10
His sons w come trembling from the	Hos 11:10
They w come trembling like birds	Hos 11:11
I w settle them in their houses,	Hos 11:11
And w punish Jacob according to	Hos 12:2
He w repay him according to his	Hos 12:2
they w find in me No iniquity,	Hos 12:8
I w make you live in tents again,	Hos 12:9
Lord w leave his bloodguilt on him	Hos 12:14
they w be like the morning cloud And	Hos 13:3
So I w be like a lion to them;	Hos 13:7
I w lie in wait by the wayside.	Hos 13:7
I w encounter them like a bear	Hos 13:8
And I w tear open their chests;	Hos 13:8
There I w also devour them like a	Hos 13:8
Compassion w be hidden from My	Hos 13:14
the reeds, An east wind w come,	Hos 13:15
And his fountain w become dry And	Hos 13:15
dry And his spring w be dried up;	Hos 13:15
It w plunder *his* treasury of every	Hos 13:15
Samaria w be held guilty, For she	Hos 13:16
They w fall by the sword, Their	Hos 13:16
little ones w be dashed in pieces,	Hos 13:16
pregnant women w be ripped open.	Hos 13:16
"Assyria w not save us, We will	Hos 14:3
save us, We w not ride on horses;	Hos 14:3
Nor w we say again,	Hos 14:3
I w heal their apostasy, I will	Hos 14:4
apostasy, I w love them freely,	Hos 14:4
I w be like the dew to Israel;	Hos 14:5
He w blossom like the lily, And he	Hos 14:5
And he w take root like *the cedars*	Hos 14:5
His shoots w sprout, And his	Hos 14:6
beauty w be like the olive tree And	Hos 14:6
in his shadow W again raise grain,	Hos 14:7
And they w blossom like the vine.	Hos 14:7
His renown w *be* like the wine of	Hos 14:7
And the righteous w walk in them,	Hos 14:9
transgressors w stumble in them.	Hos 14:9
And it w come as destruction from	Jl 1:15
Nor w there be again after it To	Jl 2:2
whether He w *not* turn and relent And	Jl 2:14
LORD w be zealous for His land And	Jl 2:18
And w have pity on His people.	Jl 2:18
w answer and say to His people,	Jl 2:19
And you w be satisfied *in full*	Jl 2:19
And I w never again make you a	Jl 2:19
"But I w remove the northern *army*	Jl 2:20
And I w drive it into a parched	Jl 2:20
And its stench w arise and its	Jl 2:20
and its foul smell w come up,	Jl 2:20
floors w be full of grain,	Jl 2:24
And the vats w overflow with the	Jl 2:24
"Then I w make up to you for the	Jl 2:25
"You w have plenty to eat and be	Jl 2:26
My people w never be put to shame.	Jl 2:26
"Thus you w know that I am in the	Jl 2:27
My people w never be put to shame.	Jl 2:27
"It w come about after this	Jl 2:28
w pour out My Spirit on all mankind;	Jl 2:28
sons and daughters w prophesy,	Jl 2:28
Your old men w dream dreams,	Jl 2:28
Your young men w see visions.	Jl 2:28
I w pour out My Spirit in those days.	Jl 2:29
"I w display wonders in the	Jl 2:30
"The sun w be turned into	Jl 2:31
"And it w come about that whoever	Jl 2:32
name of the LORD W be delivered;	Jl 2:32
There w be those who escape,	Jl 2:32
I w gather all the nations And	Jl 3:2
Then I w enter into judgment with	Jl 3:2
swiftly and speedily I w return	Jl 3:4
"Also I w sell your sons and your	Jl 3:8
they w sell them to the Sabeans,	Jl 3:8
For there I w sit to judge All the	Jl 3:12
Then you w know that I am the LORD	Jl 3:17
So Jerusalem w be holy, And	Jl 3:17
strangers w pass through it no more.	Jl 3:17
mountains w drip with sweet wine,	Jl 3:18
And the hills w flow with milk,	Jl 3:18
brooks of Judah w flow with water;	Jl 3:18
And a spring w go out from the	Jl 3:18
Egypt w become a waste, And Edom	Jl 3:19
And Edom w become a desolate	Jl 3:19
But Judah w be inhabited forever And	Jl 3:20
And I w avenge their blood which I	Jl 3:21
I w not revoke its *punishment,*	Am 1:3
"So I w send fire upon the house	Am 1:4
And it w consume the citadels of	Am 1:4
"I w also break the *gate* bar of	Am 1:5
people of Aram w go exiled to Kir,"	Am 1:5
I w not revoke its *punishment,*	Am 1:6
"So I w send fire upon the wall	Am 1:7
And it w consume her citadels.	Am 1:7
"I w also cut off the inhabitant	Am 1:8
I w even unleash My power upon	Am 1:8
remnant of the Philistines w perish,"	Am 1:8
I w not revoke its *punishment,*	Am 1:9
"So I w send fire upon the wall	Am 1:10
And it w consume her citadels."	Am 1:10
I w not revoke its *punishment,*	Am 1:11
"So I w send fire upon Teman And	Am 1:12
And it w consume the citadels of	Am 1:12
I w not revoke its *punishment,*	Am 1:13
"So I w kindle a fire on the wall	Am 1:14
And it w consume her citadels Amid	Am 1:14
"Their king w go into exile, He	Am 1:15
I w not revoke its *punishment,*	Am 2:1
"So I w send fire upon Moab And	Am 2:2
And it w consume the citadels of	Am 2:2
And Moab w die amid tumult, With	Am 2:2
"I w also cut off the judge from	Am 2:3
I w not revoke its *punishment,*	Am 2:4
"So I w send fire upon Judah And	Am 2:5
And it w consume the citadels of	Am 2:5
I w not revoke its *punishment,*	Am 2:6
"Flight w perish from the swift,	Am 2:14
stalwart w not strengthen his power,	Am 2:14
the bow w not stand *his ground,*	Am 2:15
The swift of foot w not escape,	Am 2:15
Nor w he who rides the horse save	Am 2:15
warriors w flee naked in that day,"	Am 2:16
I w punish you for all your	Am 3:2
a city w not the people tremble?	Am 3:6
A lion has roared! Who w not fear?	Am 3:8
W pull down your strength from you	Am 3:11
And your citadels w be looted."	Am 3:11
So w the sons of Israel dwelling	Am 3:12
I w also punish the altars of	Am 3:14
horns of the altar w be cut off And	Am 3:14
And they w fall to the ground.	Am 3:14
"I w also smite the winter house	Am 3:15
The houses of ivory w also perish	Am 3:15
great houses w come to an end,"	Am 3:15
w take you away with meat hooks,	Am 4:2
"You w go out *through* breaches *in*	Am 4:3
And you w be cast to Harmon,"	Am 4:3
"Therefore thus I w do to you,	Am 4:12
Because I w do this to you, Prepare	Am 4:12
She has fallen, she w not rise again	Am 5:2
strong W have a hundred left,	Am 5:3
W have ten left to the house of Israel	Am 5:3
Gilgal w certainly go into captivity And	Am 5:5
And Bethel w come to trouble.	Am 5:5
Or He w break forth like a fire,	Am 5:6
And it w consume with none to quench	Am 5:6
stone, Yet you w not live in them;	Am 5:11
yet you w not drink their wine.	Am 5:11
Because I w pass through the midst of	Am 5:17
For what purpose w the day of	Am 5:18
It w *be* darkness and not light;	Am 5:18
W not the day of the LORD	Am 5:20
offerings, I w not accept *them;*	Am 5:22
And I w not *even* look at the peace	Am 5:22
I w not even listen to the sound	Am 5:23
I w make you go into exile beyond	Am 5:27
they w now go into exile at the	Am 6:7
sprawlers' banqueting w pass away.	Am 6:7
I w deliver up *the* city and all it	Am 6:8
And it w be, if ten men are left	Am 6:9
are left in one house, they w die.	Am 6:9
w lift him up to carry out *his*	Am 6:10
and he w say to the one who is in	Am 6:10
And that one w say,	Am 6:10
Then he w answer,	Am 6:10

“And they **w** afflict you from the **Am 6:14**
I **w** spare them no longer. **Am 7:8**
“The high places of Isaac **w** be **Am 7:9**
Then I **w** rise up against the house of **Am 7:9**
‘Jeroboam **w** die by the sword and **Am 7:11**
Israel **w** certainly go from its land **Am 7:11**
w become a harlot in the city, **Am 7:17**
daughters **w** fall by the sword, **Am 7:17**
your land **w** be parceled up by a **Am 7:17**
yourself **w** die upon unclean soil. **Am 7:17**
Israel **w** certainly go from its **Am 7:17**
I **w** spare them no longer. **Am 8:2**
w turn to wailing in that day,” **Am 8:3**
“Many **w** *be* the corpses; in **Am 8:3**
w cast them forth in silence.” **Am 8:3**
“When **w** the new moon be over, So **Am 8:5**
I **w** never forget any of their **Am 8:7**
Because of this **w** not the land quake **Am 8:8**
all of it **w** rise up like the Nile, **Am 8:8**
Nile, And it **w** be tossed about And **Am 8:8**
“It **w** come about in that day,” **Am 8:9**
“That I **w** make the sun go down at **Am 8:9**
“Then I **w** turn your festivals into **Am 8:10**
And I **w** bring sackcloth on **Am 8:10**
And I **w** make it like *a time of* **Am 8:10**
end of it **w** be like a bitter day. **Am 8:10**
I **w** send a famine on the land, **Am 8:11**
People **w** stagger from sea to sea **Am 8:12**
They **w** go to and fro to seek the **Am 8:12**
the LORD, But they **w** not find *it.* **Am 8:12**
the young men **w** faint from thirst. **Am 8:13**
They **w** fall and not rise again.” **Am 8:14**
so that the thresholds **w** shake, **Am 9:1**
Then I **w** slay the rest of them **Am 9:1**
They **w** not have a fugitive who **Am 9:1**
not have a fugitive who **w** flee, **Am 9:1**
flee, Or a refugee who **w** escape. **Am 9:1**
From there **w** My hand take them; **Am 9:2**
From there **w** I bring them down. **Am 9:2**
I **w** search them out and take them **Am 9:3**
From there I **w** command the serpent **Am 9:3**
the serpent and it **w** bite them. **Am 9:3**
From there I **w** command the sword **Am 9:4**
And I **w** set My eyes against them **Am 9:4**
And I **w** destroy it from the face **Am 9:8**
I **w** not totally destroy the house **Am 9:8**
And I **w** shake the house of Israel **Am 9:9**
not a kernel **w** fall to the ground. **Am 9:9**
of My people **w** die by the sword, **Am 9:10**
w not overtake or confront us.’ **Am 9:10**
“In that day I **w** raise up the **Am 9:11**
I **w** also raise up its ruins And **Am 9:11**
“When the plowman **w** overtake the **Am 9:13**
the mountains **w** drip sweet wine And **Am 9:13**
And all the hills **w** be dissolved. **Am 9:13**
“Also I **w** restore the captivity **Am 9:14**
And they **w** rebuild the ruined **Am 9:14**
They **w** also plant vineyards and **Am 9:14**
“I **w** also plant them on their **Am 9:15**
And they **w** not again be rooted out **Am 9:15**
I **w** make you small among the **Ob 1:2**
‘Who **w** bring me down to earth?’ **Ob 1:3**
From there I **w** bring you down,” **Ob 1:4**
O how you **w** be ruined! **Ob 1:5**
“O how Esau **w** be ransacked, **Ob 1:6**
W send you forth to the border, **Ob 1:7**
W deceive you and overpower you. **Ob 1:7**
bread **W** set an ambush for you. **Ob 1:7**
“**W** I not on that day,” **Ob 1:8**
your mighty men **w** be dismayed, **Ob 1:9**
You **w** be covered *with* shame, **Ob 1:10**
And you **w** be cut off forever. **Ob 1:10**
have done, it **w** be done to you. **Ob 1:15**
w return on your own head. **Ob 1:15**
the nations **w** drink continually. **Ob 1:16**
They **w** drink and swallow And **Ob 1:16**
Zion there **w** be those who escape, **Ob 1:17**
who escape, And it **w** be holy. **Ob 1:17**
Jacob **w** possess their possessions. **Ob 1:17**
“Then the house of Jacob **w** be a **Ob 1:18**
But the house of Esau **w** *be* as **Ob 1:18**
And they **w** set them on fire and **Ob 1:18**
So that there **w** be no survivor of **Ob 1:18**
w possess the mountain of Esau, **Ob 1:19**
And Benjamin **w** *possess* Gilead. **Ob 1:19**
W possess the cities of the Negev. **Ob 1:20**
The deliverers **w** ascend Mount Zion **Ob 1:21**
And the kingdom **w** be the LORD’s. **Ob 1:21**
Perhaps *your* god **w** be concerned **Jon 1:6**
us so that we **w** not perish.” **Jon 1:6**
the sea **w** become calm for you, **Jon 1:12**
Nevertheless I **w** look again toward **Jon 2:4**
But I **w** sacrifice to You With the **Jon 2:9**
That which I have vowed I **w** pay. **Jon 2:9**
and Nineveh **w** be overthrown.” **Jon 3:4**
His burning anger so that we **w** not **Jon 3:9**
He **w** come down and tread on the **Mi 1:3**
The mountains **w** melt under Him And **Mi 1:4**
Him And the valleys **w** be split, **Mi 1:4**
For I **w** make Samaria a heap of **Mi 1:6**
I **w** pour her stones down into the **Mi 1:6**
And **w** lay bare her foundations. **Mi 1:6**
All of her idols **w** be smashed, **Mi 1:7**
earnings **w** be burned with fire And **Mi 1:7**
of her images I **w** make desolate, **Mi 1:7**
of a harlot they **w** return. **Mi 1:7**
“He **w** take from you its support.” **Mi 1:11**
you **w** give parting gifts On behalf **Mi 1:14**
The houses of Achzib **w** become a **Mi 1:14**

I **w** bring on you The one who takes **Mi 1:15**
glory of Israel **w** enter Adullam. **Mi 1:15**
For they **w** go from you into exile. **Mi 1:16**
And you **w** not walk haughtily, For **Mi 2:3**
For it **w** be an evil time. **Mi 2:3**
“On that day they **w** take up **Mi 2:4**
you **w** have no one stretching a **Mi 2:5**
Reproaches **w** not be turned back. **Mi 2:6**
‘I **w** speak out to you concerning **Mi 2:11**
“I **w** surely assemble all of you, **Mi 2:12**
I **w** surely gather the remnant of **Mi 2:12**
I **w** put them together like sheep **Mi 2:12**
pasture They **w** be noisy with men. **Mi 2:12**
Then they **w** cry out to the LORD, **Mi 3:4**
LORD, But He **w** not answer them. **Mi 3:4**
He **w** hide His face from them at **Mi 3:4**
Therefore *it* **w** *be* night for you **Mi 3:6**
The sun **w** go down on the prophets, **Mi 3:6**
the day **w** become dark over them. **Mi 3:6**
The seers **w** be ashamed And the **Mi 3:7**
And the diviners **w** be embarrassed. **Mi 3:7**
they **w** all cover *their* mouths **Mi 3:7**
Calamity **w** not come upon us.” **Mi 3:11**
you Zion **w** be plowed as a field, **Mi 3:12**
w become a heap of ruins, **Mi 3:12**
mountain of the temple **w** *become* **Mi 3:12**
And it **w** come about in the last **Mi 4:1**
house of the LORD **W** be established **Mi 4:1**
It **w** be raised above the hills, **Mi 4:1**
And the peoples **w** stream to it. **Mi 4:1**
Many nations **w** come and say, **Mi 4:2**
For from Zion **w** go forth the law, **Mi 4:2**
And He **w** judge between many **Mi 4:3**
Then they **w** hammer their swords **Mi 4:3**
Nation **w** not lift up sword against **Mi 4:3**
never again **w** they train for war. **Mi 4:3**
Each of them **w** sit under his **Mi 4:4**
we **w** walk In the name of the LORD **Mi 4:5**
“I **w** assemble the lame And **Mi 4:6**
“I **w** make the lame a remnant And **Mi 4:7**
And the LORD **w** reign over them in **Mi 4:7**
daughter of Zion, To you it **w** come **Mi 4:8**
Even the former dominion **w** come, **Mi 4:8**
For now you **w** go out of the city, **Mi 4:10**
There you **w** be rescued; **Mi 4:10**
There the LORD **w** redeem you From **Mi 4:10**
For your horn I **w** make iron And **Mi 4:13**
And your hoofs I **w** make bronze, **Mi 4:13**
With a rod they **w** smite the judge **Mi 5:1**
From you One **w** go forth for Me to **Mi 5:2**
He **w** give them *up* until the time **Mi 5:3**
W return to the sons of Israel. **Mi 5:3**
And He **w** arise and shepherd *His* **Mi 5:4**
And they **w** remain, Because at that **Mi 5:4**
Because at that time He **w** be great **Mi 5:4**
This One **w** be *our* peace. **Mi 5:5**
Then we **w** raise against him Seven **Mi 5:5**
They **w** shepherd the land of **Mi 5:6**
And He **w** deliver *us* from the **Mi 5:6**
Then the remnant of Jacob **W** be **Mi 5:7**
of Jacob **W** be among the nations, **Mi 5:8**
Your hand **w** be lifted up against **Mi 5:9**
And all your enemies **w** be cut off. **Mi 5:9**
“It **w** be in that day,” **Mi 5:10**
“That I **w** cut off your horses **Mi 5:10**
“I **w** also cut off the cities of **Mi 5:11**
“I **w** cut off sorceries from your **Mi 5:12**
you **w** have fortune-tellers no more. **Mi 5:12**
“I **w** cut off your carved images **Mi 5:13**
So that you **w** no longer bow down **Mi 5:13**
“I **w** root out your Asherim from **Mi 5:14**
“And I **w** execute vengeance in **Mi 5:15**
Even with Israel He **w** dispute. **Mi 6:2**
The voice of the LORD **w** call to **Mi 6:9**
“So also I **w** make *you* sick, **Mi 6:13**
“You **w** eat, but you will not be **Mi 6:14**
eat, but you **w** not be satisfied, **Mi 6:14**
your vileness **w** be in your midst. **Mi 6:14**
You **w** *try to* remove *for* **Mi 6:14**
But you **w** not preserve *anything,* **Mi 6:14**
do preserve I **w** give to the sword. **Mi 6:14**
“You **w** sow but you will not reap. **Mi 6:15**
“You will sow but you **w** not reap. **Mi 6:15**
You **w** tread the olive but will not **Mi 6:15**
w not anoint yourself with oil; **Mi 6:15**
grapes, but you **w** not drink wine. **Mi 6:15**
I **w** give you up for destruction **Mi 6:16**
And you **w** bear the reproach of My **Mi 6:16**
watchmen, Your punishment **w** come. **Mi 7:4**
Then their confusion **w** occur. **Mi 7:4**
I **w** watch expectantly for the LORD; **Mi 7:7**
I **w** wait for the God of my **Mi 7:7**
My God **w** hear me. **Mi 7:7**
Though I fall I **w** rise; **Mi 7:8**
I **w** bear the indignation of the **Mi 7:9**
He **w** bring me out to the light, **Mi 7:9**
And I **w** see His righteousness. **Mi 7:9**
Then my enemy **w** see, And shame **Mi 7:10**
shame **w** cover her who said to me, **Mi 7:10**
My eyes **w** look on her; **Mi 7:10**
that time she **w** be trampled down Like **Mi 7:10**
It **w** be a day for building your **Mi 7:11**
day **w** your boundary be extended. **Mi 7:11**
It **w** *be* a day when they will come **Mi 7:12**
It *will be* a day when they **w** come **Mi 7:12**
And the earth **w** become desolate **Mi 7:13**
of Egypt, I **w** show you miracles.” **Mi 7:15**
Nations **w** see and be ashamed Of **Mi 7:16**
w put *their* hand on *their* mouth, **Mi 7:16**

their mouth, Their ears **w** be deaf. **Mi 7:16**
w lick the dust like a serpent, **Mi 7:17**
They **w** come trembling out of their **Mi 7:17**
LORD our God they **w** come in dread **Mi 7:17**
And they **w** be afraid before You. **Mi 7:17**
He **w** again have compassion on us; **Mi 7:19**
He **w** tread our iniquities under **Mi 7:19**
You **w** cast all their sins Into **Mi 7:19**
You **w** give truth to Jacob *And* **Mi 7:20**
And the LORD **w** by no means leave **Na 1:3**
He **w** make a complete end of its site, **Na 1:8**
And **w** pursue His enemies into **Na 1:8**
He **w** make a complete end of it. **Na 1:9**
Distress **w** not rise up twice. **Na 1:9**
they **w** be cut off and pass away. **Na 1:12**
you, I **w** afflict you no longer. **Na 1:12**
I **w** break his yoke bar from upon **Na 1:13**
And I **w** tear off your shackles.” **Na 1:13**
name **w** no longer be perpetuated. **Na 1:14**
I **w** cut off idol and image From **Na 1:14**
I **w** prepare your grave, For you **Na 1:14**
For never again **w** the wicked one **Na 1:15**
For the LORD **w** restore the **Na 2:2**
“I **w** burn up her chariots in **Na 2:13**
a sword **w** devour your young lions; **Na 2:13**
I **w** cut off your prey from the **Na 2:13**
and no longer **w** the voice of your **Na 2:13**
“And I **w** lift up your skirts over **Na 3:5**
“I **w** throw filth on you And make **Na 3:6**
“And it **w** come about that all who **Na 3:7**
all who see you **W** shrink from you **Na 3:7**
Who **w** grieve for her?’ **Na 3:7**
w I seek comforters for you?” **Na 3:7**
You too **w** become drunk, You will **Na 3:11**
become drunk, You **w** be hidden. **Na 3:11**
You too **w** search for a refuge from **Na 3:11**
There fire **w** consume you, The **Na 3:15**
you, The sword **w** cut you down; **Na 3:15**
It **w** consume you as the locust **Na 3:15**
you **W** clap *their* hands over you, **Na 3:19**
long, O LORD, **w** I call for help, **Hab 1:2**
for help, And You **w** not hear? **Hab 1:2**
“Then they **w** sweep through *like* **Hab 1:11**
But they **w** be held guilty, They **Hab 1:11**
We **w** not die. You, O LORD, have **Hab 1:12**
W they therefore empty their net **Hab 1:17**
I **w** stand on my guard post **Hab 2:1**
And I **w** keep watch to see what He **Hab 2:1**
to see what He **w** speak to me, **Hab 2:1**
the goal and it **w** not fail. **Hab 2:3**
For it **w** certainly come, it will **Hab 2:3**
certainly come, it **w** not delay. **Hab 2:3**
the righteous **w** live by his faith. **Hab 2:4**
“**W** not all of these take up a **Hab 2:6**
“**W** not your creditors rise up **Hab 2:7**
you **w** become plunder for them. **Hab 2:7**
remainder of the peoples **w** loot you **Hab 2:8**
the stone **w** cry out from the wall, **Hab 2:11**
w answer it from the framework. **Hab 2:11**
“For the earth **w** be filled With **Hab 2:14**
“You **w** be filled with disgrace **Hab 2:16**
right hand **w** come around to you, **Hab 2:16**
And utter disgrace **w** *come* upon **Hab 2:16**
done to Lebanon **w** overwhelm you, **Hab 2:17**
people to arise *who* **w** invade us. **Hab 3:16**
Yet I **w** exult in the LORD, I will **Hab 3:18**
I **w** rejoice in the God of my **Hab 3:18**
“I **w** completely remove all *things* **Zph 1:2**
“I **w** remove man and beast; **Zph 1:3**
I **w** remove the birds of the sky **Zph 1:3**
And I **w** cut off man from the face **Zph 1:3**
“So I **w** stretch out My hand **Zph 1:4**
And I **w** cut off the remnant of **Zph 1:4**
“Then it **w** come about on the day **Zph 1:8**
That I **w** punish the princes, **Zph 1:8**
“And I **w** punish on that day all **Zph 1:9**
“There **w** be the sound of a cry **Zph 1:10**
people of Canaan **w** be silenced; **Zph 1:11**
who weigh out silver **w** be cut off. **Zph 1:11**
“It **w** come about at that time **Zph 1:12**
I **w** search Jerusalem with lamps, **Zph 1:12**
And I **w** punish the men Who are **Zph 1:12**
‘The LORD **w** not do good or evil!’ **Zph 1:12**
their wealth **w** become plunder And **Zph 1:13**
they **w** build houses but not **Zph 1:13**
I **w** bring distress on men So **Zph 1:17**
that they **w** walk like the blind, **Zph 1:17**
blood **w** be poured out like dust And **Zph 1:17**
nor their gold **W** be able to deliver **Zph 1:18**
And all the earth **w** be devoured In **Zph 1:18**
For He **w** make a complete end, **Zph 1:18**
Perhaps you **w** be hidden In the day **Zph 2:3**
For Gaza **w** be abandoned And **Zph 2:4**
Ashdod **w** be driven out at noon And **Zph 2:4**
at noon And Ekron **w** be uprooted. **Zph 2:4**
And I **w** destroy you So that there **Zph 2:5**
So that there **w** be no inhabitant. **Zph 2:5**
So the seacoast **w** be pastures, **Zph 2:6**
And the coast **w** be For the remnant **Zph 2:7**
of Judah, They **w** pasture on it. **Zph 2:7**
they **w** lie down at evening; **Zph 2:7**
For the LORD their God **w** care for **Zph 2:7**
“Surely Moab **w** be like Sodom And **Zph 2:9**
of My people **w** plunder them And **Zph 2:9**
of My nation **w** inherit them.” **Zph 2:9**
This they **w** have in return for **Zph 2:10**
The LORD **w** be terrifying to them, **Zph 2:11**
for He **w** starve all the gods of **Zph 2:11**
of the nations **w** bow down to Him, **Zph 2:11**

w be slain by My sword." Zph 2:12
And He w stretch out His hand Zph 2:13
He w make Nineveh a desolation, Zph 2:13
Flocks w lie down in her midst, Zph 2:14
and the hedgehog W lodge in the tops Zph 2:14
Birds w sing in the window, Zph 2:14
Desolation w *be* on the threshold; Zph 2:14
Everyone who passes by her w hiss Zph 2:15
He w do no injustice. Zph 3:5
'Surely you w revere Me, Accept Zph 3:7
So her dwelling w not be cut off Zph 3:7
For all the earth w be devoured By Zph 3:8
"For then I w give to the peoples Zph 3:9
ones, W bring My offerings. Zph 3:10
"In that day you w feel no shame Zph 3:11
For then I w remove from your Zph 3:11
And you w never again be haughty Zph 3:11
"But I w leave among you A humble Zph 3:12
And they w take refuge in the name Zph 3:12
w do no wrong And tell no lies, Zph 3:13
Nor w a deceitful tongue Be found Zph 3:13
For they w feed and lie down With no Zph 3:13
You w fear disaster no more. Zph 3:15
day it w be said to Jerusalem: Zph 3:16
He w exult over you with joy, He Zph 3:17
joy, He w be quiet in His love, Zph 3:17
He w rejoice over you with shouts Zph 3:17
"I w gather those who grieve Zph 3:18
I w save the lame And gather the Zph 3:19
And I w turn their shame into Zph 3:19
"At that time I w bring you in, Zph 3:20
I w give you renown and praise Zph 3:20
'I w shake all the nations; Hg 2:7
and they w come with the wealth of Hg 2:7
I w fill this house with glory,' Hg 2:7
w be greater than the former,' Hg 2:9
'and in this place I w give peace,' Hg 2:9
other food, w it become holy?" Hg 2:12
w *the latter* become unclean?" Hg 2:13
"It w become unclean." Hg 2:13
this day on I w bless *you.*'" Hg 2:19
'I w overthrow the thrones of Hg 2:22
and I w overthrow the chariots and Hg 2:22
horses and their riders w go down, Hg 2:22
'I w take you, Zerubbabel, son of Hg 2:23
I w make you like a signet *ring,* Hg 2:23
"I w show you what these are." Zch 1:9
how long w You have no compassion Zch 1:12
"I w return to Jerusalem with Zch 1:16
My house w be built in it," Zch 1:16
w be stretched over Jerusalem." Zch 1:16
"My cities w again overflow with Zch 1:17
and the LORD w again comfort Zion Zch 1:17
w be inhabited without walls because Zch 2:4
'w be a wall of fire around her, Zch 2:5
I w be the glory in her midst.'" Zch 2:5
I w wave My hand over them so Zch 2:9
w be plunder for their slaves. Zch 2:9
Then you w know that the LORD of Zch 2:9
and I w dwell in your midst," Zch 2:10
"Many nations w join Zch 2:11
that day and w become My people. Zch 2:11
Then I w dwell in your midst, and Zch 2:11
and you w know that the LORD of Zch 2:11
"The LORD w possess Judah as Zch 2:12
and w again choose Jerusalem. Zch 2:12
w clothe you with festal robes." Zch 3:4
'If you w walk in My ways and if Zch 3:7
and if you w perform My service, Zch 3:7
then you w also govern My house Zch 3:7
and I w grant you free access Zch 3:7
I w engrave an inscription on it,' Zch 3:9
'and I w remove the iniquity of Zch 3:9
'every one of you w invite his Zch 3:10
Before Zerubbabel *you w become* Zch 4:7
and he w bring forth the top stone Zch 4:7
house, and his hands w finish *it.* Zch 4:9
Then you w know that the LORD of Zch 4:9
But these seven w be glad when Zch 4:10
surely everyone who steals w be Zch 5:3
and everyone who swears w be Zch 5:3
"I w make it go forth," Zch 5:4
"and it w enter the house of the Zch 5:4
and it w spend the night within Zch 5:4
she w be set there on her own Zch 5:11
He w branch out from where He is; Zch 6:12
He w build the temple of the LORD. Zch 6:12
who w build the temple of the LORD, Zch 6:13
and He who w bear the honor and Zch 6:13
He w be a priest on His throne, Zch 6:13
the counsel of peace w be between Zch 6:13
"Now the crown w become a Zch 6:14
"Those who are far off w come Zch 6:15
Then you w know that the LORD of Zch 6:15
And it w take place if you Zch 6:15
'I w return to Zion and will dwell Zch 8:3
'I will return to Zion and w dwell Zch 8:3
Jerusalem w be called the City of Zch 8:3
of the LORD of hosts w *be* Zch 8:3
'Old men and old women w again sit Zch 8:4
'And the streets of the city w be Zch 8:5
w it also be too difficult in My Zch 8:6
and I w bring them *back* and they Zch 8:8
and they w live in the midst of Zch 8:8
be My people, and I w be their God Zch 8:8
'But now I w not treat the remnant Zch 8:11
'For *there* w *be* peace for Zch 8:12
the vine w yield its fruit, the Zch 8:12
the land w yield its produce and Zch 8:12
and the heavens w give their dew; Zch 8:12
and I w cause the remnant of this Zch 8:12
'It w come about that just as Zch 8:13
so I w save you that you may Zch 8:13
of the tenth *months* w become joy, Zch 8:19
'*It* w yet *be* that peoples Zch 8:20
will yet *be* that peoples w come, Zch 8:20
of one w go to another, Zch 8:21
seek the LORD of hosts; I w also go. Zch 8:21
nations w come to seek the LORD of Zch 8:22
ten men from all the nations w grasp Zch 8:23
the Lord w dispossess her And cast Zch 9:4
And she w be consumed with fire. Zch 9:4
Ashkelon w see *it* and be afraid. Zch 9:5
Gaza too w writhe in great pain; Zch 9:5
the king w perish from Gaza, Zch 9:5
And Ashkelon w not be inhabited. Zch 9:5
a mongrel race w dwell in Ashdod, Zch 9:6
And I w cut off the pride of the Zch 9:6
And I w remove their blood from Zch 9:7
also w be a remnant for our God, Zch 9:7
But I w camp around My house Zch 9:8
w pass over them anymore, Zch 9:8
I w cut off the chariot from Zch 9:10
And the bow of war w be cut off. Zch 9:10
He w speak peace to the nations; Zch 9:10
His dominion w be from sea to sea, Zch 9:10
that I w restore double to you. Zch 9:12
For I w bend Judah as My bow, I Zch 9:13
I w fill the bow with Ephraim. Zch 9:13
And I w stir up your sons, O Zion, Zch 9:13
And I w make you like a warrior's Zch 9:13
Then the LORD w appear over them, Zch 9:14
arrow w go forth like lightning; Zch 9:14
the Lord GOD w blow the trumpet, Zch 9:14
And w march in the storm winds of Zch 9:14
The LORD of hosts w defend them. Zch 9:15
And they w devour and trample on Zch 9:15
And they w drink *and* be Zch 9:15
And they w be filled like a Zch 9:15
And the LORD their God w save them Zch 9:16
For what comeliness and beauty w *be* Zch 9:17
w make the young men flourish, Zch 9:17
He w give them showers of rain, Zch 10:1
And I w punish the male goats; Zch 10:3
And w make them like His majestic Zch 10:3
"From them w come the Zch 10:4
"They w be as mighty men, Zch 10:5
And they w fight, for the LORD Zch 10:5
for the LORD w *be* with them; Zch 10:5
on horses w be put to shame. Zch 10:5
"I w strengthen the house of Judah, Zch 10:6
And I w save the house of Joseph, Zch 10:6
And I w bring them back, Because I Zch 10:6
And they w be as though I had not Zch 10:6
their God and I w answer them. Zch 10:6
Ephraim w be like a mighty man, Zch 10:7
heart w be glad as if *from* wine; Zch 10:7
children w see *it* and be glad, Zch 10:7
Their heart w rejoice in the LORD. Zch 10:7
"I w whistle for them to gather Zch 10:8
And they w be as numerous as they Zch 10:8
w remember Me in far countries, Zch 10:9
children w live and come back. Zch 10:9
"I w bring them back from the Zch 10:10
And I w bring them into the land Zch 10:10
"And they w pass through the sea *of* Zch 10:11
the depths of the Nile w dry up; Zch 10:11
of Assyria w be brought down And Zch 10:11
And the scepter of Egypt w depart. Zch 10:11
"And I w strengthen them in the Zch 10:12
And in His name they w walk," Zch 10:12
"For I w no longer have pity on Zch 11:6
I w cause the men to fall, each into Zch 11:6
and they w strike the land, and I Zch 11:6
and I w not deliver *them* from Zch 11:6
"I w not pasture you. Zch 11:9
who w not care for the perishing, Zch 11:16
but w devour the flesh of the fat Zch 11:16
A sword w be on his arm And on his Zch 11:17
His arm w be totally withered And Zch 11:17
And his right eye w be blind." Zch 11:17
it w also be against Judah. Zch 12:2
"It w come about in that day Zch 12:3
I w make Jerusalem a heavy stone Zch 12:3
who lift it w be severely injured. Zch 12:3
earth w be gathered against it. Zch 12:3
"I w strike every horse with Zch 12:4
I w watch over the house of Judah, Zch 12:4
of Judah w say in their hearts, Zch 12:5
"In that day I w make the clans Zch 12:6
so they w consume on the right Zch 12:6
"The LORD also w save the tents Zch 12:7
of the inhabitants of Jerusalem w not Zch 12:7
"In that day the LORD w defend Zch 12:8
them in that day w be like David, Zch 12:8
and the house of David w *be* like Zch 12:8
I w set about to destroy all the nations Zch 12:9
"I w pour out on the house of Zch 12:10
so that they w look on Me whom Zch 12:10
and they w mourn for Him, as one Zch 12:10
and they w weep bitterly over Him like Zch 12:10
"In that day there w be great Zch 12:11
"The land w mourn, every Zch 12:12
"In that day a fountain w be Zch 13:1
"It w come about in that day," Zch 13:2
"that I w cut off the names of Zch 13:2
they w no longer be remembered; Zch 13:2
and I w also remove the prophets Zch 13:2
gave birth to him w say to him, Zch 13:3
mother who gave birth to him w pierce Zch 13:3
"Also it w come about in that day Zch 13:4
w each be ashamed of his vision Zch 13:4
and they w not put on a hairy robe Zch 13:4
but he w say, 'I am not a prophet; Zch 13:5
"And one w say to him, Zch 13:6
Then he w say, '*Those* with which I Zch 13:6
And I w turn My hand against the Zch 13:7
It w come about in all the land," Zch 13:8
in it w be cut off *and* perish; Zch 13:8
But the third w be left in it. Zch 13:8
"And I w bring the third part Zch 13:9
They w call on My name, And I will Zch 13:9
on My name, And I w answer them; Zch 13:9
I w say, 'They are My people,' Zch 13:9
are My people,' And they w say, Zch 13:9
from you w be divided among you. Zch 14:1
For I w gather all the nations Zch 14:2
and the city w be captured, Zch 14:2
rest of the people w not be cut off Zch 14:2
Then the LORD w go forth and fight Zch 14:3
w stand on the Mount of Olives, Zch 14:4
and the Mount of Olives w be split Zch 14:4
that half of the mountain w move Zch 14:4
You w flee by the valley of My Zch 14:5
of the mountains w reach to Azel; Zch 14:5
you w flee just as you fled before Zch 14:5
Then the LORD, my God, w come, Zch 14:5
that day there w be no light; Zch 14:6
the luminaries w dwindle. Zch 14:6
For it w be a unique day which is Zch 14:7
but it w come about that at Zch 14:7
at evening time there w be light. Zch 14:7
waters w flow out of Jerusalem, Zch 14:8
it w be in summer as well as in Zch 14:8
LORD w be king over all the earth; Zch 14:9
day the LORD w be *the only* one, Zch 14:9
All the land w be changed into a Zch 14:10
but Jerusalem w rise and remain on Zch 14:10
People w live in it, and there Zch 14:11
it, and there w no longer be a curse, Zch 14:11
for Jerusalem w dwell in security. Zch 14:11
Now this w be the plague with Zch 14:12
plague with which the LORD w strike Zch 14:12
their flesh w rot while they stand Zch 14:12
their eyes w rot in their sockets, Zch 14:12
their tongue w rot in their mouth. Zch 14:12
It w come about in that day Zch 14:13
from the LORD w fall on them; Zch 14:13
they w seize one another's hand, Zch 14:13
and the hand of one w be lifted Zch 14:13
Judah also w fight at Jerusalem; Zch 14:14
surrounding nations w be gathered, Zch 14:14
w be the plague on the horse, Zch 14:15
cattle that w be in those camps. Zch 14:15
Then it w come about that any who Zch 14:16
w go up from year to year to worship Zch 14:16
And it w be that whichever of the Zch 14:17
hosts, there w be no rain on them. Zch 14:17
then no *rain* w *fall* on them; it Zch 14:18
it w be the plague with which the Zch 14:18
This w be the punishment of Egypt, Zch 14:19
In that day there w *be inscribed* Zch 14:20
pots in the LORD's house w be like Zch 14:20
w be holy to the LORD of hosts; Zch 14:21
and all who sacrifice w come and Zch 14:21
And there w no longer be a Zch 14:21
w return and build up the ruins"; Mal 1:4
"They may build, but I w tear down; Mal 1:4
and *men* w call them the wicked Mal 1:4
eyes w see this and you will say, Mal 1:5
eyes will see this and you w say, Mal 1:5
now w you not entreat God's favor, Mal 1:9
w He receive any of you kindly?" Mal 1:9
w I accept an offering from you. Mal 1:10
My name w *be* great among Mal 1:11
for My name w *be* great among Mal 1:11
"then I w send the curse upon Mal 2:2
you and I w curse your blessings; Mal 2:2
I w spread refuse on your faces, Mal 2:3
and you w be taken away with it. Mal 2:3
"Then you w know that I have sent Mal 2:4
and he w clear the way before Me. Mal 3:1
w suddenly come to His temple; Mal 3:1
"He w sit as a smelter and Mal 3:3
and He w purify the sons of Levi Mal 3:3
Jerusalem w be pleasing to the LORD Mal 3:4
I w draw near to you for judgment; Mal 3:5
and I w be a swift witness against Mal 3:5
to Me, and I w return to you," Mal 3:7
"W a man rob God? Yet you are Mal 3:8
"if I w not open for you the Mal 3:10
I w rebuke the devourer for you, Mal 3:11
so that it w not destroy the fruits Mal 3:11
nor w your vine in the field cast Mal 3:11
the nations w call you blessed, Mal 3:12
"They w be Mine," Mal 3:17
and I w spare them as a man spares Mal 3:17
So you w again distinguish between Mal 3:18
and every evildoer w be chaff; Mal 4:1
day that is coming w set them ablaze Mal 4:1
"so that it w leave them neither Mal 4:1
of righteousness w rise with healing Mal 4:2
and you w go forth and skip about Mal 4:2
"You w tread down the wicked, Mal 4:3
for they w be ashes under the soles Mal 4:3
"He w restore the hearts of Mal 4:6
so that I w not come and smite Mal 4:6

"She **w** bear a Son;	Mt 1:21	
for He **w** save His people	Mt 1:21	
WHO **W** SHEPHERD MY PEOPLE ISRAEL	Mt 2:6	
He **w** baptize you with the Holy	Mt 3:11	
and He **w** thoroughly clear His	Mt 3:12	
and He **w** gather His wheat into the	Mt 3:12	
but He **w** burn up the chaff with	Mt 3:12	
'HE **W** COMMAND HIS ANGELS	Mt 4:6	
'ON *their* HANDS THEY **W** BEAR YOU UP,	Mt 4:6	
SO THAT YOU **W** NOT STRIKE YOUR FOOT	Mt 4:6	
"All these things I **w** give You,	Mt 4:9	
and I **w** make you fishers of men."	Mt 4:19	
you **w** not enter the kingdom of heaven.	Mt 5:20	
"Truly I say to you, you **w** not come	Mt 5:26	
your giving **w** be in secret;	Mt 6:4	
what is done in secret **w** reward	Mt 6:4	
what is done in secret **w** reward	Mt 6:6	
w be heard for their many words.	Mt 6:7	
Your **w** be done, On earth as it is	Mt 6:10	*2307*
Father **w** also forgive you.	Mt 6:14	
then your Father **w** not forgive	Mt 6:15	
their appearance so that they **w** be	Mt 6:16	
your fasting **w** not be noticed	Mt 6:18	
sees *what is done* in secret **w** reward	Mt 6:18	
is, there your heart **w** be also.	Mt 6:21	
whole body **w** be full of light.	Mt 6:22	
whole body **w** be full of darkness.	Mt 6:23	
for either he **w** hate the one and	Mt 6:24	
or he **w** be devoted to one and despise	Mt 6:24	
as to what you **w** eat or what you	Mt 6:25	
to what you will eat or what you **w**	Mt 6:25	
as to what you **w** put on. Is not	Mt 6:25	
w *He* not much more *clothe* you?	Mt 6:30	
'What **w** we eat?' or 'What will we	Mt 6:31	
or 'What **w** we drink?' or 'What	Mt 6:31	
or 'What **w** we wear for clothing?'	Mt 6:31	
and all these things **w** be added to	Mt 6:33	
for tomorrow **w** care for itself.	Mt 6:34	
"Do not judge so that you **w** not be	Mt 7:1	
way you judge, you **w** be judged;	Mt 7:2	
measure, it **w** be measured to you.	Mt 7:2	
and then you **w** see clearly to take	Mt 7:5	
or they **w** trample them under their	Mt 7:6	
"Ask, and it **w** be given to you;	Mt 7:7	
and you **w** find; knock, and it will	Mt 7:7	
and it **w** be opened to you.	Mt 7:7	
and to him who knocks it **w** be opened.	Mt 7:8	
for a loaf, **w** give him a stone?	Mt 7:9	
a fish, he **w** not give him a snake,	Mt 7:10	
will not give him a snake, **w** he?	Mt 7:10	
how much more **w** your Father who	Mt 7:11	
"You **w** know them by their fruits.	Mt 7:16	
you **w** know them by their fruits.	Mt 7:20	
w enter the kingdom of heaven,	Mt 7:21	
w of My Father who is in heaven	Mt 7:21	*2307*
of My Father who is in heaven **w**	Mt 7:21	
"Many **w** say to Me on that day,	Mt 7:22	
"And then I **w** declare to them,	Mt 7:23	
them, **w** be like a foolish man who	Mt 7:26	
"I **w** come and heal him."	Mt 8:7	
word, and my servant **w** be healed.	Mt 8:8	
"I say to you that many **w** come from	Mt 8:11	
but the sons of the kingdom **w** be cast	Mt 8:12	
in that place there **w** be weeping	Mt 8:12	
I **w** follow You wherever You go."	Mt 8:19	
But the days **w** come when the	Mt 9:15	
from them, and then they **w** fast.	Mt 9:15	
hand on her, and she **w** live."	Mt 9:18	
I **w** get well."	Mt 9:21	
it **w** be more tolerable for *the*	Mt 10:15	
w hand you over to *the* courts	Mt 10:17	
and you **w** even be brought before	Mt 10:18	
for it **w** be given you in that hour	Mt 10:19	
w betray brother to death,	Mt 10:21	
children **w** rise up against parents and	Mt 10:21	
"You **w** be hated by all because	Mt 10:22	
endured to the end who **w** be saved.	Mt 10:22	
you **w** not finish *going through*	Mt 10:23	
how much more **w** *they malign*	Mt 10:25	
concealed that **w** not be revealed,	Mt 10:26	
or hidden that **w** not be known.	Mt 10:26	
And *yet* not one of them **w** fall to	Mt 10:29	
I **w** also confess him before My	Mt 10:32	
I **w** also deny him before My Father	Mt 10:33	
and A MAN'S ENEMIES **W** BE THE	Mt 10:36	
"He who has found his life **w** lose it,	Mt 10:39	
lost his life for My sake **w** find	Mt 10:39	
W PREPARE YOUR WAY BEFORE YOU.'	Mt 11:10	
"Nevertheless I say to you, it **w** be	Mt 11:22	
w not be exalted to heaven,	Mt 11:23	
not be exalted to heaven, **w** you?	Mt 11:23	
You **w** descend to Hades; for if	Mt 11:23	
I say to you that it **w** be	Mt 11:24	
heavy-laden, and I **w** give you rest.	Mt 11:28	
and YOU **W** FIND REST FOR YOUR SOULS.	Mt 11:29	
Sabbath, **w** he not take hold of it and	Mt 12:11	
I **W** PUT MY SPIRIT UPON HIM, AND HE	Mt 12:18	
"HE **W** NOT QUARREL, NOR CRY OUT;	Mt 12:19	
NOR **W** ANYONE HEAR HIS VOICE IN THE	Mt 12:19	
BATTERED REED HE **W** NOT BREAK OFF,	Mt 12:20	
SMOLDERING WICK HE **W** NOT PUT OUT,	Mt 12:20	
IN HIS NAME THE GENTILES **W** HOPE."	Mt 12:21	
or house divided against itself **w** not	Mt 12:25	
how then **w** his kingdom stand?	Mt 12:26	
For this reason they **w** be your judges.	Mt 12:27	
And then he **w** plunder his house.	Mt 12:29	
"For by your words you **w** be	Mt 12:37	
your words you **w** be condemned."	Mt 12:37	
and *yet* no sign **w** be given to it	Mt 12:39	
so **w** the Son of Man be three days	Mt 12:40	
"The men of Nineveh **w** stand up with	Mt 12:41	
and **w** condemn it because they	Mt 12:41	
"*The* Queen of *the* South **w**	Mt 12:42	
at the judgment and **w** condemn	Mt 12:42	
'I **w** return to my house from which	Mt 12:44	
That is the way it **w** also be with	Mt 12:45	
w of My Father who is in heaven,	Mt 12:50	*2307*
and he **w** have an abundance; but	Mt 13:12	
'YOU **W** KEEP ON HEARING, BUT WILL	Mt 13:14	
ON HEARING, BUT **W** NOT UNDERSTAND;	Mt 13:14	
YOU **W** KEEP ON SEEING, BUT WILL NOT	Mt 13:14	
ON SEEING, BUT **W** NOT PERCEIVE;	Mt 13:14	
harvest I **w** say to the reapers,	Mt 13:30	
"I **W** OPEN MY MOUTH IN PARABLES;	Mt 13:35	
I **W** UTTER THINGS HIDDEN SINCE THE	Mt 13:35	
Son of Man **w** send forth His angels,	Mt 13:41	
and they **w** gather out of His	Mt 13:41	
and **w** throw them into the furnace	Mt 13:42	
in that place there **w** be weeping	Mt 13:42	
"Then THE RIGHTEOUS **W** SHINE FORTH	Mt 13:43	
"So it **w** be at the end of the age;	Mt 13:49	
the angels **w** come forth and take out	Mt 13:49	
and **w** throw them into the furnace	Mt 13:50	
in that place there **w** be weeping	Mt 13:50	
man, both **w** fall into a pit."	Mt 15:14	
'*It* **w** *be* fair weather, for	Mt 16:2	
"And in the morning, '*There* **w** *be*	Mt 16:3	
and a sign **w** not be given it,	Mt 16:4	
this rock I **w** build My church;	Mt 16:18	
and the gates of Hades **w** not	Mt 16:18	
"I **w** give you the keys of the	Mt 16:19	
whoever wishes to save his life **w** lose	Mt 16:25	
loses his life for My sake **w** find	Mt 16:25	
"For what **w** it profit a man if	Mt 16:26	
Or what **w** a man give in exchange	Mt 16:26	
and **W** THEN REPAY EVERY MAN	Mt 16:27	
who are standing here who **w** not	Mt 16:28	
I **w** make three tabernacles here,	Mt 17:4	
coming and **w** restore all things;	Mt 17:11	
you **w** say to this mountain, 'Move	Mt 17:20	
and it **w** move; and nothing will be	Mt 17:20	
and nothing **w** be impossible to you.	Mt 17:20	
and they **w** kill Him, and He will	Mt 17:23	
He **w** be raised on the third day."	Mt 17:23	
its mouth, you **w** find a shekel.	Mt 17:27	
you **w** not enter the kingdom of heaven.	Mt 18:3	
it is not *the* **w** of your Father who	Mt 18:14	*2307*
me and I **w** repay you everything.'	Mt 18:26	
with me and I **w** repay you.'	Mt 18:29	
"My heavenly Father **w** also do	Mt 18:35	
and you **w** have treasure in heaven;	Mt 19:21	
what then **w** there be for us?"	Mt 19:27	
Man **w** sit on His glorious throne,	Mt 19:28	
w receive many times as much,	Mt 19:29	
and **w** inherit eternal life.	Mt 19:29	
"But many *who are* first **w** be last;	Mt 19:30	
whatever is right I **w** give you.'	Mt 20:4	
and the Son of Man **w** be delivered	Mt 20:18	
and they **w** condemn Him to death,	Mt 20:18	
and **w** hand Him over to the Gentiles	Mt 20:19	
the third day He **w** be raised up."	Mt 20:19	
and immediately you **w** find a	Mt 21:2	
and immediately he **w** send them."	Mt 21:3	
you **w** not only do what was done to	Mt 21:21	
it **w** happen.	Mt 21:21	
you **w** receive."	Mt 21:22	
"I **w** also ask you one thing, which	Mt 21:24	
I **w** also tell you by what	Mt 21:24	
'From heaven,' He **w** say to us,	Mt 21:25	
"Neither **w** I tell you by what	Mt 21:27	
he answered, 'I **w** not';	Mt 21:29	
'I **w**, sir'; but he did not go.	Mt 21:30	*2309*
the two did the **w** of his father?"	Mt 21:31	*2307*
tax collectors and prostitutes **w** get into	Mt 21:31	
'They **w** respect my son.'	Mt 21:37	
w he do to those vine-growers?"	Mt 21:40	
"He **w** bring those wretches to a	Mt 21:41	
and **w** rent out the vineyard to	Mt 21:41	
who **w** pay him the proceeds at the	Mt 21:41	
of God **w** be taken away from you and	Mt 21:43	
this stone **w** be broken to pieces;	Mt 21:44	
it **w** scatter him like dust."	Mt 21:44	
in that place there **w** be weeping	Mt 22:13	
whose wife of the seven **w** she be?	Mt 22:28	
therefore you **w** receive greater	Mt 23:14	
how **w** you escape the sentence of hell?	Mt 23:33	
of them you **w** kill and crucify,	Mt 23:34	
you **w** scourge in your synagogues,	Mt 23:34	
all these things **w** come upon this	Mt 23:36	
from now on you **w** not see Me until	Mt 23:39	
not one stone here **w** be left upon	Mt 24:2	
which **w** not be torn down."	Mt 24:2	
"Tell us, when **w** these things happen,	Mt 24:3	
and what **w** *be* the sign of Your	Mt 24:3	
"For many **w** come in My name,	Mt 24:5	
am the Christ,' and **w** mislead many.	Mt 24:5	
"You **w** be hearing of wars and	Mt 24:6	*3195*
"For nation **w** rise against	Mt 24:7	
w be famines and earthquakes.	Mt 24:7	
they **w** deliver you to tribulation,	Mt 24:9	
to tribulation, and **w** kill you,	Mt 24:9	
and you **w** be hated by all nations	Mt 24:9	
"At that time many **w** fall	Mt 24:10	
many will fall away and **w** betray	Mt 24:10	
"Many false prophets **w** arise and	Mt 24:11	
will arise and **w** mislead many.	Mt 24:11	
most people's love **w** grow cold.	Mt 24:12	
he **w** be saved.	Mt 24:13	
and then the end **w** come.	Mt 24:14	
"But pray that your flight **w** not be	Mt 24:20	
there **w** be a great tribulation,	Mt 24:21	
nor ever **w**.	Mt 24:21	
the sake of the elect those days **w** be	Mt 24:22	
false Christs and false prophets **w**	Mt 24:24	
w show great signs and wonders,	Mt 24:24	
so **w** the coming of the Son of Man be.	Mt 24:27	
is, there the vultures **w** gather.	Mt 24:28	
those days THE SUN **W** BE DARKENED,	Mt 24:29	
AND THE MOON **W** NOT GIVE ITS LIGHT,	Mt 24:29	
AND THE STARS **W** FALL from the sky,	Mt 24:29	
powers of the heavens **w** be shaken.	Mt 24:29	
Son of Man **w** appear in the sky,	Mt 24:30	
the tribes of the earth **w** mourn,	Mt 24:30	
and they **w** see the SON OF MAN	Mt 24:30	
"And He **w** send forth His angels	Mt 24:31	
THEY **W** GATHER TOGETHER His elect	Mt 24:31	
this generation **w** not pass away	Mt 24:34	
"Heaven and earth **w** pass away,	Mt 24:35	
but My words **w** not pass away.	Mt 24:35	
w be just like the days of Noah.	Mt 24:37	
so **w** the coming of the Son of Man be.	Mt 24:39	
"Then there **w** be two men in	Mt 24:40	
one **w** be taken and one will be	Mt 24:40	
will be taken and one **w** be left.	Mt 24:40	
"Two women **w** *be* grinding at	Mt 24:41	
one **w** be taken and one will be	Mt 24:41	
will be taken and one **w** be left.	Mt 24:41	
an hour when you do not think *He* **w**.	Mt 24:44	
that he **w** put him in charge of all	Mt 24:47	
the master of that slave **w** come on	Mt 24:50	
and **w** cut him in pieces and assign	Mt 24:51	
in that place there **w** be weeping	Mt 24:51	
w be comparable to ten virgins,	Mt 25:1	
there **w** not be enough for us and	Mt 25:9	
I **w** put you in charge of many	Mt 25:21	
I **w** put you in charge of many	Mt 25:23	
and he **w** have an abundance; but from	Mt 25:29	
in that place there **w** be weeping	Mt 25:30	
He **w** sit on His glorious throne.	Mt 25:31	
nations **w** be gathered before Him;	Mt 25:32	
and He **w** separate them from one	Mt 25:32	
He **w** put the sheep on His right,	Mt 25:33	
King **w** say to those on His right,	Mt 25:34	
"Then the righteous **w** answer Him,	Mt 25:37	
The King **w** answer and say to them,	Mt 25:40	
He **w** also say to those on His left,	Mt 25:41	
they themselves also **w** answer,	Mt 25:44	
"Then He **w** answer them, '	Mt 25:45	
"These **w** go away into eternal	Mt 25:46	
what this woman has done **w** also be	Mt 26:13	
you that one of you **w** betray Me."	Mt 26:21	
bowl is the one who **w** betray Me.	Mt 26:23	
I **w** not drink of this fruit of the	Mt 26:29	
"You **w** all fall away because of	Mt 26:31	
'I **W** STRIKE DOWN THE SHEPHERD, AND	Mt 26:31	
I **w** go ahead of you to Galilee."	Mt 26:32	
of You, I **w** never fall away."	Mt 26:33	
you **w** deny Me three times."	Mt 26:34	
die with You, I **w** not deny You."	Mt 26:35	
yet not as I **w**, but as You will."	Mt 26:39	*2309*
not as I will, but as You **w**."	Mt 26:39	
I drink it, Your **w** be done."	Mt 26:42	*2307*
and He **w** at once put at My	Mt 26:53	
"How then **w** the Scriptures be	Mt 26:54	
hereafter you **w** see THE SON OF MAN	Mt 26:64	
you **w** deny Me three times."	Mt 26:75	
and we **w** believe in Him.	Mt 27:42	
Elijah **w** come to save Him."	Mt 27:49	
the last deception **w** be worse than	Mt 27:64	
into Galilee, there you **w** see Him;	Mt 28:7	
and there they **w** see Me."	Mt 28:10	
we **w** win him over and keep you out	Mt 28:14	
WHO **W** PREPARE YOUR WAY;	Mk 1:2	
but He **w** baptize you with the Holy	Mk 1:8	
and I **w** make you become fishers of	Mk 1:17	
"But the days **w** come when the	Mk 2:20	
and then they **w** fast in that day.	Mk 2:20	
the wine **w** burst the skins,	Mk 2:22	
that house **w** not be able to stand.	Mk 3:25	
and then he **w** plunder his house.	Mk 3:27	
For whoever does the **w** of God	Mk 3:35	*2307*
How **w** you understand all the	Mk 4:13	
By your standard of measure it **w** be	Mk 4:24	
and more **w** be given you besides.	Mk 4:24	
so that she **w** get well and live."	Mk 5:23	
touch His garments, I **w** get well."	Mk 5:28	
you want and I **w** give it to you."	Mk 6:22	
you ask of me, I **w** give it to you;"	Mk 6:23	
homes, they **w** faint on the way;	Mk 8:3	
"Where **w** anyone be able *to find*	Mk 8:4	
no sign **w** be given to this generation."	Mk 8:12	
whoever wishes to save his life **w** lose	Mk 8:35	
for My sake and the gospel's **w** save	Mk 8:35	
"For what **w** a man give in exchange	Mk 8:37	
the Son of Man **w** also be ashamed	Mk 8:38	
who are standing here who **w** not	Mk 9:1	
of the Son of Man that He **w** suffer	Mk 9:12	
hands of men, and they **w** kill Him;	Mk 9:31	
He **w** rise three days later."	Mk 9:31	
for there is no one who **w** perform a	Mk 9:39	
he **w** not lose his reward.	Mk 9:41	
everyone **w** be salted with fire.	Mk 9:49	
what **w** you make it salty *again?*	Mk 9:50	
the kingdom of God like a child **w** not	Mk 10:15	
and you **w** have treasure in heaven;	Mk 10:21	
"How hard it **w** be for those who	Mk 10:23	
but that he **w** receive a hundred times	Mk 10:30	

"But many *who are* first **w** be last	Mk 10:31	
and the Son of Man **w** be delivered	Mk 10:33	
and they **w** condemn Him to death and	Mk 10:33	
and **w** hand Him over to the Gentiles.	Mk 10:33	
"They **w** mock Him and spit on Him,	Mk 10:34	
days later He **w** rise again."	Mk 10:34	
it, you **w** find a colt tied *there,*	Mk 11:2	
he **w** send it back here."	Mk 11:3	
it **w** be *granted* him.	Mk 11:23	
and they **w** be *granted* you.	Mk 11:24	
your Father who is in heaven **w** also	Mk 11:25	
neither **w** your Father who is in	Mk 11:26	
"I **w** ask you one question, and	Mk 11:29	
and *then* I **w** tell you by what	Mk 11:29	
'From heaven,' He **w** say,	Mk 11:31	
"Nor **w** I tell you by what	Mk 11:33	
'They **w** respect my son.'	Mk 12:6	
and the inheritance **w** be ours!'	Mk 12:7	
w the owner of the vineyard do?	Mk 12:9	
He **w** come and destroy the	Mk 12:9	
and **w** give the vineyard to others.	Mk 12:9	
again, which one's wife **w** she be?	Mk 12:23	
w receive greater condemnation."	Mk 12:40	
Not one stone **w** be left upon another	Mk 13:2	
which **w** not be torn down."	Mk 13:2	
"Tell us, when **w** these things be,	Mk 13:4	
and what **w** *be* the sign when all	Mk 13:4	
"Many **w** come in My name, saying,	Mk 13:6	
and **w** mislead many.	Mk 13:6	
"For nation **w** rise up against	Mk 13:8	
there **w** be earthquakes in various	Mk 13:8	
there **w** *also* be famines.	Mk 13:8	
they **w** deliver you to *the* courts,	Mk 13:9	
you **w** be flogged in *the* synagogues,	Mk 13:9	
and you **w** stand before governors	Mk 13:9	
w betray brother to death,	Mk 13:12	
children **w** rise up against parents	Mk 13:12	
"You **w** be hated by all because	Mk 13:13	
he **w** be saved.	Mk 13:13	
"For those days **w** be a *time of*	Mk 13:19	
and never **w**.	Mk 13:19	
and false prophets **w** arise,	Mk 13:22	
and **w** show signs and wonders,	Mk 13:22	
THE SUN **W** BE DARKENED AND	Mk 13:24	
AND THE MOON **W** NOT GIVE ITS LIGHT,	Mk 13:24	
STARS **W** BE FALLING from heaven,	Mk 13:25	
are in the heavens **w** be shaken.	Mk 13:25	
they **w** see THE SON OF MAN COMING	Mk 13:26	
then He **w** send forth the angels,	Mk 13:27	
and **w** gather together His elect	Mk 13:27	
this generation **w** not pass away	Mk 13:30	
"Heaven and earth **w** pass away,	Mk 13:31	
but My words **w** not pass away.	Mk 13:31	
when the *appointed* time **w** come.	Mk 13:33	
what this woman has done **w** also be	Mk 14:9	
and a man **w** meet you carrying a	Mk 14:13	
"And he himself **w** show you a	Mk 14:15	
that one of you **w** betray Me	Mk 14:18	
"Truly I say to you, I **w** never	Mk 14:25	
"You **w** all fall away, because it	Mk 14:27	
'I **W** STRIKE DOWN THE SHEPHERD, AND	Mk 14:27	
I **w** go ahead of you to Galilee."	Mk 14:28	
all may fall away, yet I **w** not."	Mk 14:29	
you yourself **w** deny Me three times."	Mk 14:30	
die with You, I **w** not deny You!"	Mk 14:31	
yet not what I **w**, but what You	Mk 14:36	2309
what I will, but what You **w**."	Mk 14:36	
'I **w** destroy this temple made with	Mk 14:58	
and in three days I **w** build	Mk 14:58	
you **w** deny Me three times."	Mk 14:72	
Elijah **w** come to take Him down."	Mk 15:36	
"Who **w** roll away the stone for us	Mk 16:3	
there you **w** see Him, just as He	Mk 16:7	
"These signs **w** accompany	Mk 16:17	
in My name they **w** cast out demons,	Mk 16:17	
they **w** speak with new tongues;	Mk 16:17	
they **w** pick up serpents, and if	Mk 16:18	
it **w** not hurt them; they will lay	Mk 16:18	
they **w** lay hands on the sick, and	Mk 16:18	
on the sick, and they **w** recover."	Mk 16:18	
wife Elizabeth **w** bear you a son,	Lk 1:13	
and you **w** give him the name John.	Lk 1:13	
"You **w** have joy and gladness,	Lk 1:14	
and many **w** rejoice at his birth.	Lk 1:14	
"For he **w** be great in the sight	Lk 1:15	
and he **w** drink no wine or liquor,	Lk 1:15	
and he **w** be filled with the Holy	Lk 1:15	
"And he **w** turn many of the	Lk 1:16	
"It is he who **w** go *as a*	Lk 1:17	
said to the angel, "How **w** I	Lk 1:18	
which **w** be fulfilled in their proper	Lk 1:20	
you **w** conceive in your womb and	Lk 1:31	
"He **w** be great and will be	Lk 1:32	
and **w** be called the Son of the	Lk 1:32	
and the Lord God **w** give Him the	Lk 1:32	
and He **w** reign over the house of	Lk 1:33	
and His kingdom **w** have no end."	Lk 1:33	
"The Holy Spirit **w** come upon you,	Lk 1:35	
of the Most High **w** overshadow you;	Lk 1:35	
nothing **w** be impossible with God."	Lk 1:37	
generations **w** count me blessed.	Lk 1:48	
w this child *turn out to* be?"	Lk 1:66	
w be called the prophet of the	Lk 1:76	
For you **w** go on BEFORE THE LORD TO	Lk 1:76	
the Sunrise from on high **w** visit	Lk 1:78	
you good news of great joy which **w** be	Lk 2:10	
"This **w** *be* a sign for you:	Lk 2:12	
w find a baby wrapped in cloths and	Lk 2:12	
and a sword **w** pierce even your own	Lk 2:35	
'EVERY RAVINE **W** BE FILLED, AND	Lk 3:5	
AND EVERY MOUNTAIN AND HILL **W** BE	Lk 3:5	
THE CROOKED **W** BECOME STRAIGHT, AND	Lk 3:5	
AND ALL FLESH **W** SEE THE SALVATION	Lk 3:6	
He **w** baptize you with the Holy	Lk 3:16	
but He **w** burn up the chaff with	Lk 3:17	
"I **w** give You all this domain and	Lk 4:6	
'HE **W** COMMAND HIS ANGELS	Lk 4:10	
'ON *their* HANDS THEY **W** BEAR YOU UP,	Lk 4:11	
SO THAT YOU **W** NOT STRIKE YOUR FOOT	Lk 4:11	
you **w** quote this proverb to Me,	Lk 4:23	
but I **w** do as You say *and* let	Lk 5:5	
now on you **w** be catching men."	Lk 5:10	
"But *the* days **w** come;	Lk 5:35	
then they **w** fast in those days."	Lk 5:35	
otherwise he **w** both tear the new,	Lk 5:36	
from the new **w** not match the old.	Lk 5:36	
the new wine **w** burst the skins and	Lk 5:37	
skins and it **w** be spilled out,	Lk 5:37	
out, and the skins **w** be ruined.	Lk 5:37	
and your reward **w** be great, and	Lk 6:35	
you **w** be sons of the Most High;	Lk 6:35	
not judge, and you **w** not be judged;	Lk 6:37	
and you **w** not be condemned;	Lk 6:37	
pardon, and you **w** be pardoned.	Lk 6:37	
"Give, and it **w** be given to you.	Lk 6:38	
They **w** pour into your lap	Lk 6:38	
For by your standard of measure it **w**	Lk 6:38	
W they not both fall into a pit?	Lk 6:39	
trained, **w** be like his teacher.	Lk 6:40	
and then you **w** see clearly to take	Lk 6:42	
I **w** show you whom he is like:	Lk 6:47	
word, and my servant **w** be healed.	Lk 7:7	
W PREPARE YOUR WAY BEFORE YOU.'	Lk 7:27	
them **w** love him more?"	Lk 7:42	
so that they **w** not believe and be	Lk 8:12	
"For nothing is hidden that **w** not	Lk 8:17	
nor *anything* secret that **w** not be	Lk 8:17	
and she **w** be made well."	Lk 8:50	
whoever wishes to save his life **w** lose	Lk 9:24	
sake, he is the one who **w** save it.	Lk 9:24	
the Son of Man **w** be ashamed of him	Lk 9:26	
some of those standing here who **w** not	Lk 9:27	
"I **w** follow You wherever You go."	Lk 9:57	
"I **w** follow You, Lord;	Lk 9:61	
there, your peace **w** rest on him;	Lk 10:6	
but if not, it **w** return to you.	Lk 10:6	
it **w** be more tolerable in that day	Lk 10:12	
"But it **w** be more tolerable for	Lk 10:14	
"And you, Capernaum, **w** not be exalted	Lk 10:15	
not be exalted to heaven, **w** you?	Lk 10:15	
You **w** be brought down to Hades!	Lk 10:15	
and nothing **w** injure you.	Lk 10:19	
DO THIS AND YOU **W** LIVE."	Lk 10:28	
when I return I **w** repay you.'	Lk 10:35	
even though he **w** not get up and	Lk 11:8	
because of his persistence he **w** get up	Lk 11:8	
"So I say to you, ask, and it **w** be	Lk 11:9	
and you **w** find; knock, and it will	Lk 11:9	
and it **w** be opened to you.	Lk 11:9	
it **w** be opened.	Lk 11:10	
he **w** not give him a snake instead	Lk 11:11	
a snake instead of a fish, **w** he?	Lk 11:11	
egg, he **w** not give him a scorpion,	Lk 11:12	
not give him a scorpion, **w** he?	Lk 11:12	
how much more **w** *your* heavenly	Lk 11:13	
how **w** his kingdom stand? For you say	Lk 11:18	
So they **w** be your judges.	Lk 11:19	
'I **w** return to my house from which	Lk 11:24	
and *yet* no sign **w** be given to it	Lk 11:29	
so **w** the Son of Man be to this	Lk 11:30	
"The Queen of the South **w** rise up	Lk 11:31	
"The men of Nineveh **w** stand up with	Lk 11:32	
it **w** be wholly illumined, as when	Lk 11:36	
while you yourselves **w** not even	Lk 11:46	
'I **w** send to them prophets and	Lk 11:49	
and *some* of them they **w** kill and	Lk 11:49	
kill and *some* they **w** persecute,	Lk 11:49	
covered up that **w** not be revealed,	Lk 12:2	
and hidden that **w** not be known.	Lk 12:2	
you have said in the dark **w** be	Lk 12:3	
whispered in the inner rooms **w** be	Lk 12:3	
"But I **w** warn you whom to fear:	Lk 12:5	
the Son of Man **w** confess him also	Lk 12:8	
but he who denies Me before men **w** be	Lk 12:9	
it **w** be forgiven him; but he who	Lk 12:10	
it **w** not be forgiven him.	Lk 12:10	
for the Holy Spirit **w** teach you in	Lk 12:12	
'This is what I **w** do:	Lk 12:18	
I **w** tear down my barns and build	Lk 12:18	
and there I **w** store all my grain	Lk 12:18	
'And I **w** say to my soul,	Lk 12:19	
who **w** own what you have prepared?'	Lk 12:20	
as to what you **w** eat; nor for	Lk 12:22	
as to what you **w** put on.	Lk 12:22	
how much more **w** *He clothe* you?	Lk 12:28	
"And do not seek what you **w** eat	Lk 12:29	
you will eat and what you **w** drink,	Lk 12:29	
and these things **w** be added to you.	Lk 12:31	
is, there your heart **w** be also.	Lk 12:34	
slaves whom the master **w** find	Lk 12:37	
that he **w** gird himself *to serve,*	Lk 12:37	
and **w** come up and wait on them.	Lk 12:37	
w put in charge of his servants,	Lk 12:42	
that he **w** put him in charge of all	Lk 12:44	
master **w** be a long time in coming,'	Lk 12:45	
the master of that slave **w** come on	Lk 12:46	
not know, and **w** cut him in pieces,	Lk 12:46	
that slave who knew his master's **w**	Lk 12:47	2307
ready or act in accord with his **w**,	Lk 12:47	2307
w receive many lashes,	Lk 12:47	2307
of a flogging, **w** receive but few.	Lk 12:48	
much **w** be required; and to whom they	Lk 12:48	
of him they **w** ask all the more.	Lk 12:48	
in one household **w** be divided,	Lk 12:52	
"They **w** be divided, father	Lk 12:53	
'It **w** be a hot day,' and it turns	Lk 12:55	
"I say to you, you **w** not get out of	Lk 12:59	
repent, you **w** all likewise perish.	Lk 13:3	
you **w** all likewise perish."	Lk 13:5	
w seek to enter and will not be	Lk 13:24	
seek to enter and **w** not be able.	Lk 13:24	
then He **w** answer and say to you,	Lk 13:25	
"Then you **w** begin to say,	Lk 13:26	
He **w** say, 'I tell you, I do not know	Lk 13:27	
there **w** be weeping and gnashing	Lk 13:28	
they **w** come from east and west and	Lk 13:29	
and **w** recline *at the table* in the	Lk 13:29	
some are last who **w** be first and	Lk 13:30	
some are first who **w** be last."	Lk 13:30	
you **w** not see Me until *the time*	Lk 13:35	
"Which one of you **w** have a son or an	Lk 14:5	
and **w** not immediately pull him out	Lk 14:5	
and he who invited you both **w** come	Lk 14:9	
then you **w** have honor in the sight	Lk 14:10	
everyone who exalts himself **w** be	Lk 14:11	
and he who humbles himself **w** be	Lk 14:11	
you in return and *that* **w** be	Lk 14:12	
and you **w** be blessed, since they	Lk 14:14	
for you **w** be repaid at the	Lk 14:14	
"Blessed is everyone who **w** eat bread	Lk 14:15	
w not first sit down and consider	Lk 14:31	
with what **w** it be seasoned?	Lk 14:34	
there **w** be *more* joy in heaven over	Lk 15:7	
'I **w** get up and go to my father,	Lk 15:18	
go to my father, and **w** say to him,	Lk 15:18	
w welcome me into their homes.'	Lk 16:4	
they **w** receive you into the eternal	Lk 16:9	
who **w** entrust the true *riches* to	Lk 16:11	
who **w** give you that which is your	Lk 16:12	
for either he **w** hate the one and	Lk 16:13	
or else he **w** be devoted to one	Lk 16:13	
to come over from here to you **w** not	Lk 16:26	
so that they **w** not also come to this	Lk 16:28	
from the dead, they **w** repent!'	Lk 16:30	
they **w** not be persuaded even if	Lk 16:31	
w say to him when he has come in	Lk 17:7	
"But **w** he not say to him,	Lk 17:8	
nor **w** they say, 'Look, here *it is!*'	Lk 17:21	
"The days **w** come when you will	Lk 17:22	
"The days will come when you **w**	Lk 17:22	
Son of Man, and you **w** not see it.	Lk 17:22	
"They **w** say to you,	Lk 17:23	
so **w** the Son of Man be in His day.	Lk 17:24	
so it **w** be also in the days of	Lk 17:26	
"It **w** be just the same on the day	Lk 17:30	
seeks to keep his life **w** lose	Lk 17:33	
loses *his life* **w** preserve	Lk 17:33	
there **w** be two in one bed;	Lk 17:34	
one **w** be taken and the other will	Lk 17:34	
be taken and the other **w** be left.	Lk 17:34	
"There **w** be two women grinding at	Lk 17:35	
one **w** be taken and the other will	Lk 17:35	
be taken and the other **w** be left.	Lk 17:35	
"Two men **w** be in the field;	Lk 17:36	
one **w** be taken and the other will	Lk 17:36	
taken and the other **w** be left."	Lk 17:36	
also the vultures **w** be gathered."	Lk 17:37	
me, I **w** give her legal protection,	Lk 18:5	
by continually coming she **w** wear	Lk 18:5	
now, **w** not God bring about justice	Lk 18:7	
and **w** He delay long over them?	Lk 18:7	
"I tell you that He **w** bring about	Lk 18:8	
w He find faith on the earth?"	Lk 18:8	
for everyone who exalts himself **w** be	Lk 18:14	
but he who humbles himself **w** be	Lk 18:14	
the kingdom of God like a child **w** not	Lk 18:17	
who **w** not receive many times as much	Lk 18:30	
the Son of Man **w** be accomplished.	Lk 18:31	
He **w** be handed over to the Gentiles,	Lk 18:32	
and **w** be mocked and mistreated and	Lk 18:32	
scourged Him, they **w** kill Him;	Lk 18:33	
the third day He **w** rise again."	Lk 18:33	
possessions I **w** give to the poor,	Lk 19:8	
w give back four times as much."	Lk 19:8	
'By your own words I **w** judge you,	Lk 19:22	
you enter, you **w** find a colt tied	Lk 19:30	
silent, the stones **w** cry out!"	Lk 19:40	
"For the days **w** come upon you when	Lk 19:43	
your enemies **w** throw up a barricade	Lk 19:43	
and they **w** level you to the ground and	Lk 19:44	
and they **w** not leave in you one	Lk 19:44	
"I **w** also ask you a question,	Lk 20:3	
'From heaven,' He **w** say,	Lk 20:5	
the people **w** stone us to death,	Lk 20:6	
"Nor **w** I tell you by what	Lk 20:8	
I **w** send my beloved son;	Lk 20:13	
perhaps they **w** respect him.'	Lk 20:13	
kill him so that the inheritance **w** be	Lk 20:14	
w the owner of the vineyard do to	Lk 20:15	
"He **w** come and destroy these	Lk 20:16	
w give the vineyard to others."	Lk 20:16	
that stone **w** be broken to pieces;	Lk 20:18	
it **w** scatter him like dust."	Lk 20:18	
which one's wife **w** she be?	Lk 20:33	
w receive greater condemnation."	Lk 20:47	
the days **w** come in which there	Lk 21:6	
w not be left one stone upon another	Lk 21:6	

which **w** not be torn down."	**Lk 21:6**	
when therefore **w** these things happen?	**Lk 21:7**	
And what **w** *be* the sign when these	**Lk 21:7**	
for many **w** come in My name,	**Lk 21:8**	
"Nation **w** rise against nation and	**Lk 21:10**	
and there **w** be great earthquakes,	**Lk 21:11**	
and there **w** be terrors and great	**Lk 21:11**	
they **w** lay their hands on you and	**Lk 21:12**	
hands on you and **w** persecute you,	**Lk 21:12**	
"It **w** lead to an opportunity for	**Lk 21:13**	
for I **w** give you utterance and	**Lk 21:15**	
w be able to resist or refute.	**Lk 21:15**	
"But you **w** be betrayed even	**Lk 21:16**	
they **w** put *some* of you to death,	**Lk 21:16**	
and you **w** be hated by all because	**Lk 21:17**	
not a hair of your head **w** perish.	**Lk 21:18**	
endurance you **w** gain your lives.	**Lk 21:19**	
all things which are written **w** be	**Lk 21:22**	
for there **w** be great distress upon	**Lk 21:23**	
w fall by the edge of the sword,	**Lk 21:24**	
and **w** be led captive into all the	**Lk 21:24**	
and Jerusalem **w** be trampled under	**Lk 21:24**	
"There **w** be signs in sun and	**Lk 21:25**	
powers of the heavens **w** be shaken.	**Lk 21:26**	
"Then they **w** see THE SON OF	**Lk 21:27**	
this generation **w** not pass away	**Lk 21:32**	
"Heaven and earth **w** pass away,	**Lk 21:33**	
but My words **w** not pass away.	**Lk 21:33**	
on guard, so that your hearts **w** not	**Lk 21:34**	
and that day **w** not come on you	**Lk 21:34**	
for it **w** come upon all those who	**Lk 21:35**	
a man **w** meet you carrying a	**Lk 22:10**	
"And he **w** show you a large,	**Lk 22:12**	
I **w** not drink of the fruit of the	**Lk 22:18**	
and you **w** sit on thrones judging	**Lk 22:30**	
the rooster **w** not crow today until	**Lk 22:34**	
yet not My **w**, but Yours be done."	**Lk 22:42**	*2307*
you **w** deny Me three times."	**Lk 22:61**	
"If I tell you, you **w** not believe;	**Lk 22:67**	
ask a question, you **w** not answer.	**Lk 22:68**	
THE SON OF MAN **W** BE SEATED AT	**Lk 22:69**	
"Therefore I **w** punish Him and	**Lk 23:16**	
I **w** punish Him and	**Lk 23:22**	
but he delivered Jesus to their **w**.	**Lk 23:25**	*2307*
days are coming when they **w** say,	**Lk 23:29**	
w begin TO SAY TO THE MOUNTAINS,	**Lk 23:30**	
what **w** happen when it is dry?"	**Lk 23:31**	
blood nor of the **w** of the flesh	**Jn 1:13**	*2307*
of the flesh nor of the **w** of man,	**Jn 1:13**	*2307*
"Come, and you **w** see."	**Jn 1:39**	
You **w** see greater things than these."	**Jn 1:50**	
you **w** see the heavens opened	**Jn 1:51**	
"ZEAL FOR YOUR HOUSE **W** CONSUME ME."	**Jn 2:17**	
in three days I **w** raise it up."	**Jn 2:19**	
w You raise it up in three days?"	**Jn 2:20**	
how **w** you believe if I tell you	**Jn 3:12**	
so that whoever believes **w** in Him	**Jn 3:15**	
Light for fear that his deeds **w** be	**Jn 3:20**	
he who does not obey the Son **w** not	**Jn 3:36**	
who drinks of this water **w** thirst	**Jn 4:13**	
drinks of the water that I **w** give	**Jn 4:14**	
but the water that I **w** give him will	**Jn 4:14**	
water that I will give him **w** become	**Jn 4:14**	
this water, so I **w** not be thirsty nor	**Jn 4:15**	
mountain nor in Jerusalem **w** you	**Jn 4:21**	
when the true worshipers **w** worship	**Jn 4:23**	
He **w** declare all things to us."	**Jn 4:25**	
is to do the **w** of Him who sent Me and	**Jn 4:34**	*2307*
you *simply* **w** not believe."	**Jn 4:48**	
w show Him greater works than these,	**Jn 5:20**	
so that you **w** marvel.	**Jn 5:20**	
so that all **w** honor the Son even as	**Jn 5:23**	
when the dead **w** hear the voice of	**Jn 5:25**	
and those who hear **w** live.	**Jn 5:25**	
all who are in the tombs **w** hear	**Jn 5:28**	
and **w** come forth; those who did	**Jn 5:29**	
because I do not seek My own **w**,	**Jn 5:30**	*2307*
but the **w** of Him who sent Me.	**Jn 5:30**	*2307*
his own name, you **w** receive him.	**Jn 5:43**	
I **w** accuse you before the Father;	**Jn 5:45**	
how **w** you believe My words?"	**Jn 5:47**	
fragments so that nothing **w** be	**Jn 6:12**	
which the Son of Man **w** give to you,	**Jn 6:27**	
he who comes to Me **w** not hunger,	**Jn 6:35**	
and he who believes in Me **w** never	**Jn 6:35**	
"All that the Father gives Me **w** come	**Jn 6:37**	
to Me I **w** certainly not cast out.	**Jn 6:37**	
from heaven, not to do My own **w**,	**Jn 6:38**	*2307*
but the **w** of Him who sent Me.	**Jn 6:38**	*2307*
This is the **w** of Him who sent Me,	**Jn 6:39**	*2307*
"For this is the **w** of My Father,	**Jn 6:40**	*2307*
the Son and believes in Him **w** have	**Jn 6:40**	
w raise him up on the last day."	**Jn 6:40**	
I **w** raise him up on the last day.	**Jn 6:44**	
he **w** live forever; and the bread	**Jn 6:51**	
and the bread also which I **w** give for	**Jn 6:51**	
I **w** raise him up on the last day.	**Jn 6:54**	
he also **w** live because of Me.	**Jn 6:57**	
he who eats this bread **w** live forever."	**Jn 6:58**	
"If anyone is willing to do His **w**,	**Jn 7:17**	*2307*
he **w** know of the teaching, whether	**Jn 7:17**	
so that the Law of Moses **w** not	**Jn 7:23**	
He **w** not perform more signs than	**Jn 7:31**	
those which this man has, **w** He?"	**Jn 7:31**	
"You **w** seek Me, and will not find	**Jn 7:34**	
"You will seek Me, and **w** not find	**Jn 7:34**	
this man intend to go that we **w** not	**Jn 7:35**	
'You **w** seek Me, and will not find	**Jn 7:36**	
will seek Me, and **w** not find Me;	**Jn 7:36**	
'From his innermost being **w** flow	**Jn 7:38**	
he who follows Me **w** not walk in	**Jn 8:12**	
but **w** have the Light of life."	**Jn 8:12**	
and you **w** seek Me, and will die in	**Jn 8:21**	
and **w** die in your sin; where I am	**Jn 8:21**	
"Surely He **w** not kill Himself,	**Jn 8:22**	
He will not kill Himself, **w** He,	**Jn 8:22**	
I said to you that you **w** die	**Jn 8:24**	
you **w** die in your sins."	**Jn 8:24**	
Man, then you **w** know that I am *He,*	**Jn 8:28**	
and you **w** know the truth,	**Jn 8:32**	
and the truth **w** make you free."	**Jn 8:32**	
'You **w** become free'?"	**Jn 8:33**	
you **w** be free indeed.	**Jn 8:36**	
if anyone keeps My word he **w** never	**Jn 8:51**	
he **w** never taste of death.'	**Jn 8:52**	
I **w** be a liar like you, but I do	**Jn 8:55**	
he **w** speak for himself."	**Jn 9:21**	
is God-fearing and does His **w**,	**Jn 9:31**	*2307*
stranger they simply **w** not follow,	**Jn 10:5**	
not follow, but **w** flee from him,	**Jn 10:5**	
he **w** be saved, and will go in	**Jn 10:9**	
and **w** go in and out and find pasture.	**Jn 10:9**	
and they **w** hear My voice; and they	**Jn 10:16**	
and they **w** become one flock *with*	**Jn 10:16**	
long **w** You keep us in suspense?	**Jn 10:24**	
and they **w** never perish; and no one	**Jn 10:28**	
and no one **w** snatch them out of My	**Jn 10:28**	
has fallen asleep, he **w** recover."	**Jn 11:12**	
You ask of God, God **w** give You."	**Jn 11:22**	
said to her, "Your brother **w** rise	**Jn 11:23**	
"I know that he **w** rise again in	**Jn 11:24**	
he who believes in Me **w** live even if	**Jn 11:25**	
who lives and believes in Me **w** never	**Jn 11:26**	
by this time there **w** be a stench,	**Jn 11:39**	
you **w** see the glory of God?"	**Jn 11:40**	
this, all men **w** believe in Him,	**Jn 11:48**	
and the Romans **w** come and take	**Jn 11:48**	
He **w** not come to the feast at all?"	**Jn 11:56**	
hates his life in this world **w** keep	**Jn 12:25**	
there My servant **w** be also; if	**Jn 12:26**	
serves Me, the Father **w** honor him.	**Jn 12:26**	
it, and **w** glorify it again."	**Jn 12:28**	
now the ruler of this world **w** be cast	**Jn 12:31**	
earth, **w** draw all men to Myself."	**Jn 12:32**	
so that darkness **w** not overtake you;	**Jn 12:35**	
everyone who believes in Me **w** not	**Jn 12:46**	
what **w** judge him at the last day.	**Jn 12:48**	
but you **w** understand hereafter."	**Jn 13:7**	
that one of you **w** betray Me."	**Jn 13:21**	
God **w** also glorify Him in Himself,	**Jn 13:32**	
and **w** glorify Him immediately.	**Jn 13:32**	
You **w** seek Me; and as I said to	**Jn 13:33**	
"By this all men **w** know that you	**Jn 13:35**	
but you **w** follow later."	**Jn 13:36**	
I **w** lay down my life for You."	**Jn 13:37**	
"**W** you lay down your life for Me?	**Jn 13:38**	
a rooster **w** not crow until you deny	**Jn 13:38**	
a place for you, I **w** come again and	**Jn 14:3**	
he **w** do also; and greater *works*	**Jn 14:12**	
greater *works* than these he **w** do;	**Jn 14:12**	
you ask in My name, that **w** I do,	**Jn 14:13**	
Me anything in My name, I **w** do *it.*	**Jn 14:14**	
Me, you **w** keep My commandments.	**Jn 14:15**	
"I **w** ask the Father, and He	**Jn 14:16**	
and He **w** give you another Helper,	**Jn 14:16**	
abides with you and **w** be in you.	**Jn 14:17**	
"I **w** not leave you as orphans;	**Jn 14:18**	
you as orphans; I **w** come to you.	**Jn 14:18**	
the world **w** no longer see Me,	**Jn 14:19**	
but you **w** see Me; because I live,	**Jn 14:19**	
you **w** live also.	**Jn 14:19**	
"In that day you **w** know that I am in	**Jn 14:20**	
and he who loves Me **w** be loved by My	**Jn 14:21**	
by My Father, and I **w** love him and	**Jn 14:21**	
and **w** disclose Myself to him."	**Jn 14:21**	
loves Me, he **w** keep My word;	**Jn 14:23**	
and My Father **w** love him, and We	**Jn 14:23**	
love him, and We **w** come to him and	**Jn 14:23**	
whom the Father **w** send in My name,	**Jn 14:26**	
name, He **w** teach you all things,	**Jn 14:26**	
'I go away, and I **w** come to you.'	**Jn 14:28**	
"I **w** not speak much more with	**Jn 14:30**	
and it **w** be done for you.	**Jn 15:7**	
you **w** abide in My love;	**Jn 15:10**	
Me, they **w** also persecute you;	**Jn 15:20**	
My word, they **w** keep yours also.	**Jn 15:20**	
w do to you for My name's sake,	**Jn 15:21**	
I **w** send to you from the Father,	**Jn 15:26**	
Father, He **w** testify about Me,	**Jn 15:26**	
and you **w** testify also, because	**Jn 15:27**	
"They **w** make you outcasts from	**Jn 16:2**	
"These things they **w** do because	**Jn 16:3**	
the Helper **w** not come to you; but if	**Jn 16:7**	
but if I go, I **w** send Him to you.	**Jn 16:7**	
w convict the world concerning	**Jn 16:8**	
He **w** guide you into all the truth;	**Jn 16:13**	
for He **w** not speak on His own	**Jn 16:13**	
but whatever He hears, He **w** speak;	**Jn 16:13**	
and He **w** disclose to you what is	**Jn 16:13**	
"He **w** glorify Me, for He will take	**Jn 16:14**	
"He will glorify Me, for He **w** take	**Jn 16:14**	
for He will take of Mine and **w**	**Jn 16:14**	
of Mine and **w** disclose *it* to you.	**Jn 16:15**	
and you **w** no longer see Me;	**Jn 16:16**	
little while, and you **w** see Me."	**Jn 16:16**	
while, and you **w** not see Me;	**Jn 16:17**	
a little while, and you **w** see Me';	**Jn 16:17**	
while, and you **w** not see Me,	**Jn 16:19**	
a little while, and you **w** see Me'?	**Jn 16:19**	
you, that you **w** weep and lament,	**Jn 16:20**	
lament, but the world **w** rejoice;	**Jn 16:20**	
you **w** grieve, but your	**Jn 16:20**	
your grief **w** be turned into joy.	**Jn 16:20**	
but I **w** see you again, and your	**Jn 16:22**	
again, and your heart **w** rejoice,	**Jn 16:22**	
and no one **w** take your joy away	**Jn 16:22**	
that day you **w** not question Me	**Jn 16:23**	
in My name, He **w** give it to you.	**Jn 16:23**	
ask and you **w** receive, so that your	**Jn 16:24**	
an hour is coming when I **w** no	**Jn 16:25**	
but **w** tell you plainly of the	**Jn 16:25**	
"In that day you **w** ask in My name,	**Jn 16:26**	
and I do not say to you that I **w**	**Jn 16:26**	
to them, and **w** make it known,	**Jn 17:26**	
laid Him, and I **w** take Him away."	**Jn 20:15**	
into His side, I **w** not believe."	**Jn 20:25**	
"We **w** also come with you."	**Jn 21:3**	
boat and you **w** find *a catch.*"	**Jn 21:6**	
old, you **w** stretch out your hands and	**Jn 21:18**	
and someone else **w** gird you,	**Jn 21:18**	
but you **w** be baptized with the Holy	**Ac 1:5**	
but you **w** receive power when the Holy	**Ac 1:8**	
w come in just the same way as you	**Ac 1:11**	
'THAT I **W** POUR FORTH OF MY SPIRIT	**Ac 2:17**	
I **W** IN THOSE DAYS POUR FORTH OF MY	**Ac 2:18**	
'AND I **W** GRANT WONDERS IN THE SKY	**Ac 2:19**	
'THE SUN **W** BE TURNED INTO DARKNESS	**Ac 2:20**	
CALLS ON THE NAME OF THE LORD **W** BE	**Ac 2:21**	
SO THAT I **W** NOT BE SHAKEN.	**Ac 2:25**	
MY FLESH ALSO **W** LIVE IN HOPE;	**Ac 2:26**	
W NOT ABANDON MY SOUL TO HADES,	**Ac 2:27**	
YOU **W** MAKE ME FULL OF GLADNESS	**Ac 2:28**	
and you **w** receive the gift of	**Ac 2:38**	
as many as the Lord our God **w** call to	**Ac 2:39**	
said, 'THE LORD GOD **W** RAISE	**Ac 3:22**	
'And it **w** be that every soul that	**Ac 3:23**	
"But so that it **w** not spread any	**Ac 4:17**	
and they **w** carry you out *as well.*"	**Ac 5:9**	
is of men, it **w** be overthrown;	**Ac 5:38**	
w not be able to overthrow them;	**Ac 5:39**	
we **w** devote ourselves to prayer and	**Ac 6:4**	
w destroy this place and alter the	**Ac 6:14**	
INTO THE LAND THAT I **W** SHOW YOU.'	**Ac 7:3**	
"'AND WHATEVER NATION TO WHICH THEY **W**	**Ac 7:7**	
BE IN BONDAGE I MYSELF **W** JUDGE,'	**Ac 7:7**	
'AND AFTER THAT THEY **W** COME OUT	**Ac 7:7**	
NOW, AND I **W** SEND YOU TO EGYPT.'	**Ac 7:34**	
'GOD **W** RAISE UP FOR YOU A PROPHET	**Ac 7:37**	
FOR US GODS WHO **W** GO BEFORE US;	**Ac 7:40**	
ALSO I **W** REMOVE YOU BEYOND BABYLON.'	**Ac 7:43**	
KIND OF HOUSE **W** YOU BUILD FOR ME?'	**Ac 7:49**	
WHO **W** RELATE HIS GENERATION? FOR HIS	**Ac 8:33**	
and it **w** be told you what you must do."	**Ac 9:6**	
for I **w** show him how much he must	**Ac 9:16**	
and he **w** speak words to you by which	**Ac 11:14**	
to you by which you **w** be saved,	**Ac 11:14**	
but you **w** be baptized with the Holy	**Ac 11:16**	
w you not cease to make crooked	**Ac 13:10**	
and you **w** be blind and not see the	**Ac 13:11**	
MY HEART, who **w** do all My will.'	**Ac 13:22**	
MY HEART, who will do all My **w**.'	**Ac 13:22**	*2307*
'I **W** GIVE YOU THE HOLY *and* SURE	**Ac 13:34**	
'YOU **W** NOT ALLOW YOUR HOLY ONE	**Ac 13:35**	
A WORK WHICH YOU **W** NEVER BELIEVE,	**Ac 13:41**	
'AFTER THESE THINGS I **W** return,	**Ac 15:16**	
AND I **W** REBUILD THE TABERNACLE OF	**Ac 15:16**	
FALLEN, AND I **W** REBUILD ITS RUINS,	**Ac 15:16**	
ITS RUINS, AND I **W** RESTORE IT,	**Ac 15:16**	
who themselves **w** also report the	**Ac 15:27**	
from such things, you **w** do well.	**Ac 15:29**	
and you **w** be saved, you and your	**Ac 16:31**	
He **w** judge the world in righteousness	**Ac 17:31**	*3195*
From now on I **w** go to the Gentiles."	**Ac 18:6**	
and no man **w** attack you in order	**Ac 18:10**	
"I **w** return to you again if God	**Ac 18:21**	
Asia and the world worship **w** even	**Ac 19:27**	
and in this connection we **w** be unable	**Ac 19:40**	
knowing what **w** happen to me there,	**Ac 20:22**	
kingdom, **w** no longer see my face.	**Ac 20:25**	
savage wolves **w** come in among you,	**Ac 20:29**	
among your own selves men **w** arise,	**Ac 20:30**	
w bind the man who owns this belt	**Ac 21:11**	
"The **w** of the Lord be done!"	**Ac 21:14**	*2307*
They **w** certainly hear that you	**Ac 21:22**	
and all **w** know that there is	**Ac 21:24**	
and there you **w** be told of all	**Ac 22:10**	
has appointed you to know His **w** and	**Ac 22:14**	*2307*
'For you **w** be a witness for Him to	**Ac 22:15**	
because they **w** not accept your	**Ac 22:18**	
For I **w** send you far away to the	**Ac 22:21**	
"I **w** give you a hearing after	**Ac 23:35**	
you **w** be able to ascertain the	**Ac 24:8**	
down, I **w** decide your case."	**Ac 24:22**	
I find time I **w** summon you."	**Ac 24:25**	
things in which I **w** appear to you;	**Ac 26:16**	
"In a short time you **w** persuade	**Ac 26:28**	
I perceive that the voyage **w**	**Ac 27:10**	*3195*
for there **w** be no loss of life among	**Ac 27:22**	
that it **w** turn out exactly as I	**Ac 27:25**	
a hair from the head of any of you **w**	**Ac 27:34**	
"YOU **W** KEEP ON HEARING, BUT WILL	**Ac 28:26**	
ON HEARING, BUT **W** NOT UNDERSTAND;	**Ac 28:26**	
AND YOU **W** KEEP ON SEEING, BUT WILL	**Ac 28:26**	
ON SEEING, BUT **W** NOT PERCEIVE;	**Ac 28:26**	
they **w** also listen."	**Ac 28:28**	
if perhaps now at last by the **w** of	**Ro 1:10**	*2307*
you **w** escape the judgment of God?	**Ro 2:3**	

Context	Reference	No.
who **w** RENDER TO EACH PERSON	Ro 2:6	
There **w** *be* tribulation	Ro 2:9	
Law **w** also perish without the Law,	Ro 2:12	
the Law **w** be judged by the Law;	Ro 2:12	
doers of the Law **w** be justified.	Ro 2:13	
God **w** judge the secrets of men	Ro 2:16	
and know *His* **w** and approve the	Ro 2:18	2307
w not his uncircumcision be	Ro 2:26	
w he not judge you who though	Ro 2:27	
their unbelief **w** not nullify the	Ro 3:3	
the faithfulness of God, **w** it?	Ro 3:3	
how **w** God judge the world?	Ro 3:6	
no flesh **w** be justified in His sight;	Ro 3:20	
since indeed God who **w** justify the	Ro 3:30	
LORD **W** NOT TAKE INTO ACCOUNT."	Ro 4:8	
so that the promise **w** be guaranteed	Ro 4:16	
also, to whom it **w** be credited,	Ro 4:24	3195
For one **w** hardly die for a	Ro 5:7	
w reign in life through the One,	Ro 5:17	
One the many **w** be made righteous.	Ro 5:19	
Who **w** set me free from the body of	Ro 7:24	
w also give life to your mortal bodies	Ro 8:11	
the deeds of the body, you **w** live.	Ro 8:13	
that the creation itself also **w** be	Ro 8:21	
the saints according to *the* **w** *of*	Ro 8:27	
how **w** He not also with Him freely	Ro 8:32	
Who **w** bring a charge against God's	Ro 8:33	
Who **w** separate us from the love of	Ro 8:35	
W tribulation, or distress, or	Ro 8:35	
w be able to separate us from	Ro 8:39	
YOUR DESCENDANTS **W** BE NAMED."	Ro 9:7	
"AT THIS TIME I **W** COME, AND SARAH	Ro 9:9	
"THE OLDER **W** SERVE THE YOUNGER."	Ro 9:12	
"I **W** HAVE MERCY ON WHOM I HAVE	Ro 9:15	
AND I **W** HAVE COMPASSION ON WHOM I	Ro 9:15	
You **w** say to me then,	Ro 9:19	
For who resists His **w**?"	Ro 9:19	1013
molded **w** not say to the molder,	Ro 9:20	
did you make me like this," **w** it?	Ro 9:20	
"I **W** CALL THOSE WHO WERE NOT MY	Ro 9:25	
IT IS THE REMNANT THAT **W** BE SAVED;	Ro 9:27	
FOR THE LORD **W** EXECUTE HIS WORD	Ro 9:28	
IN HIM **W** NOT BE DISAPPOINTED."	Ro 9:33	
'WHO **W** ASCEND INTO HEAVEN?'	Ro 10:6	
'WHO **W** DESCEND INTO THE ABYSS?'	Ro 10:7	
you **w** be saved;	Ro 10:9	
IN HIM **W** NOT BE DISAPPOINTED."	Ro 10:11	
"WHOEVER **W** CALL ON THE NAME OF	Ro 10:13	
THE NAME OF THE LORD **W** BE SAVED."	Ro 10:13	
How then **w** they call on Him in whom	Ro 10:14	
How **w** they believe in Him whom they	Ro 10:14	
And how **w** they hear without a	Ro 10:14	
How **w** they preach unless they are	Ro 10:15	
"I **W** MAKE YOU JEALOUS BY THAT WHICH	Ro 10:19	
UNDERSTANDING **W** I ANGER YOU."	Ro 10:19	
much more **w** their fulfillment be!	Ro 11:12	
what **w** *their* acceptance be but	Ro 11:15	
You **w** say then, "Branches were	Ro 11:19	
branches, He **w** not spare you, either.	Ro 11:21	
otherwise you also **w** be cut off.	Ro 11:22	
their unbelief, **w** be grafted in,	Ro 11:23	
how much more **w** these who are	Ro 11:24	
mystery—so that you **w** not	Ro 11:25	
and so all Israel **w** be saved;	Ro 11:26	
"THE DELIVERER **W** COME FROM ZION,	Ro 11:26	
W REMOVE UNGODLINESS FROM JACOB."	Ro 11:26	
may prove what the **w** of God is,	Ro 12:2	2307
"VENGEANCE IS MINE, I **W** REPAY,"	Ro 12:19	
IN SO DOING YOU **W** HEAP BURNING	Ro 12:20	
and they who have opposed **w**	Ro 13:2	
you **w** have praise from the same;	Ro 13:3	
and he **w** stand, for the Lord is	Ro 14:4	
For we **w** all stand before	Ro 14:10	
So then each one of us **w** give an	Ro 14:12	
"THEREFORE I **W** GIVE PRAISE TO	Ro 15:9	
AND I **W** SING TO YOUR NAME."	Ro 15:9	
so that you **w** abound in hope by	Ro 15:13	
For I **w** not presume to speak of	Ro 15:18	
I **w** go on by way of you to Spain.	Ro 15:28	
I **w** come in the fullness of the	Ro 15:29	
come to you in joy by the **w** of God	Ro 15:32	2307
The God of peace **w** soon crush	Ro 16:20	
of Jesus Christ by the **w** of God,	1Co 1:1	2307
who **w** also confirm you to the end,	1Co 1:8	
"I **W** DESTROY THE WISDOM OF THE	1Co 1:19	
OF THE CLEVER I **W** SET ASIDE."	1Co 1:19	
THAT HE **W** INSTRUCT HIM? But we	1Co 2:16	
but each **w** receive his own reward	1Co 3:8	
each man's work **w** become evident;	1Co 3:13	
for the day **w** show it because it	1Co 3:13	
and the fire itself **w** test the	1Co 3:13	
he **w** receive a reward.	1Co 3:14	
If any man's work is burned up, he **w**	1Co 3:15	
but he himself **w** be saved, yet so as	1Co 3:15	
temple of God, God **w** destroy him,	1Co 3:17	
Lord comes who **w** both bring to light	1Co 4:5	
praise **w** come to him from God.	1Co 4:5	
so that no one of you **w** become	1Co 4:6	
and he **w** remind you of my ways	1Co 4:17	
But I **w** come to you soon, if the	1Co 4:19	
that the saints **w** judge the world?	1Co 6:2	
Do you not know that we **w** judge	1Co 6:3	
one wise man who **w** be able to decide	1Co 6:5	
not know that the unrighteous **w** not	1Co 6:9	
w inherit the kingdom of God.	1Co 6:10	
I **w** not be mastered by anything.	1Co 6:12	
God **w** do away with both of them.	1Co 6:13	
but **w** also raise us up through His	1Co 6:14	
together again so that Satan **w** not	1Co 7:5	
whether you **w** save your husband?	1Co 7:16	
whether you **w** save your wife?	1Co 7:16	
such **w** have trouble in this life,	1Co 7:28	
but has authority over his own **w**,	1Co 7:37	2307
own virgin *daughter,* he **w** do well.	1Co 7:37	
give her in marriage **w** do better.	1Co 7:38	
But food **w** not commend us to God;	1Co 8:8	
temple, **w** not his conscience,	1Co 8:10	
stumble, I **w** never eat meat again,	1Co 8:13	
so that I **w** not cause my brother to	1Co 8:13	
endure all things so that we **w** cause	1Co 9:12	
writing these things so that it **w** be	1Co 9:15	
but if against my **w**,	1Co 9:17	210
I myself **w** not be disqualified.	1Co 9:27	
who **w** not allow you to be tempted	1Co 10:13	
but with the temptation **w** provide	1Co 10:13	
so that you **w** be able to endure it.	1Co 10:13	
In this I **w** not praise you.	1Co 11:22	
by the Lord so that we **w** not	1Co 11:32	
so that you **w** not come together for	1Co 11:34	
The remaining matters I **w** arrange	1Co 11:34	
of prophecy, they **w** be done away;	1Co 13:8	
there are tongues, they **w** cease;	1Co 13:8	
is knowledge, it **w** be done away.	1Co 13:8	
comes, the partial **w** be done away.	1Co 13:10	
but then I **w** know fully just as I	1Co 13:12	
what **w** I profit you unless I speak to	1Co 14:6	
how **w** it be known what is played	1Co 14:7	
who **w** prepare himself for battle?	1Co 14:8	
how **w** it be known what is spoken?	1Co 14:9	
you **w** be speaking into the air.	1Co 14:9	
I **w** be to the one who speaks a	1Co 14:11	
who speaks **w** be a barbarian to me.	1Co 14:11	
is *the outcome* then? I **w** pray	1Co 14:15	
pray with the spirit and I **w** pray	1Co 14:15	
I **w** sing with the spirit and I will	1Co 14:15	
sing with the spirit and I **w** sing	1Co 14:15	
how **w** the one who fills the place	1Co 14:16	
I **W** SPEAK TO THIS PEOPLE,	1Co 14:21	
EVEN SO THEY **W** NOT LISTEN TO ME,"	1Co 14:21	
w they not say that you are mad?	1Co 14:23	
and so he **w** fall on his face and	1Co 14:25	
so also in Christ all **w** be made alive.	1Co 15:22	
that **w** be abolished is death.	1Co 15:26	
then the Son Himself also **w** be	1Co 15:28	
what **w** those do who are baptized	1Co 15:29	
But someone **w** say,	1Co 15:35	
we **w** also bear the image of	1Co 15:49	
Behold, I tell you a mystery; we **w**	1Co 15:51	
but we **w** all be changed,	1Co 15:51	
for the trumpet **w** sound, and the	1Co 15:52	
the dead **w** be raised imperishable,	1Co 15:52	
and we **w** be changed.	1Co 15:52	
w have put on the imperishable,	1Co 15:54	
mortal **w** have put on immortality,	1Co 15:54	
then **w** come about the saying that	1Co 15:54	
I **w** send them with letters to carry	1Co 16:3	
come to go also, they **w** go with me.	1Co 16:4	
But I **w** come to you after I go	1Co 16:5	
and perhaps I **w** stay with you, or	1Co 16:6	
But I **w** remain in Ephesus until	1Co 16:8	
he **w** come when he has opportunity.	1Co 16:12	
of Christ Jesus by the **w** of God,	2Co 1:1	2307
in all our affliction so that we **w** be	2Co 1:4	
peril of death, and **w** deliver *us,*	2Co 1:10	
And He **w** yet deliver us,	2Co 1:10	
you **w** understand until the end;	2Co 1:13	
so that with me there **w** be yes, yes	2Co 1:17	
how **w** the ministry of the Spirit fail	2Co 3:8	
greatness of the power **w** be	2Co 4:7	
He who raised the Lord Jesus **w** raise	2Co 4:14	
Jesus and **w** present us with you.	2Co 4:14	
as we, having put it on, **w** not	2Co 5:3	
so that what is mortal **w** be swallowed	2Co 5:4	
so that you **w** have *an answer* for	2Co 5:12	
so that the ministry **w** not be	2Co 6:3	
"I **W** DWELL IN THEM AND WALK AMONG	2Co 6:16	
AND I **W** BE THEIR GOD, AND THEY	2Co 6:16	
And I **w** welcome you.	2Co 6:17	
"And I **w** be a father to you,	2Co 6:18	
sorrowful according to *the* **w** *of*	2Co 7:9	
sorrow that is according to *the* **w**	2Co 7:10	
Lord and to us by the **w** of God.	2Co 8:5	2307
so that no one **w** discredit	2Co 8:20	
we—not to speak of you—**w** be	2Co 9:4	
he who sows sparingly **w** also reap	2Co 9:6	
and he who sows bountifully **w** also	2Co 9:6	
w supply and multiply your seed	2Co 9:10	
you **w** be enriched in everything	2Co 9:11	
they **w** glorify God for *your* obedience	2Co 9:13	
I **w** not be put to shame,	2Co 10:8	
we **w** not boast beyond *our* measure,	2Co 10:13	
we **w** be, within our sphere,	2Co 10:15	
your minds **w** be led astray from	2Co 11:3	
to you, and **w** continue to do so.	2Co 11:9	
this boasting of mine **w** not be	2Co 11:10	
I am doing I **w** continue to do,	2Co 11:12	
whose end **w** be according to their	2Co 11:15	
to the flesh, I **w** boast also.	2Co 11:18	
I **w** boast of what pertains to my	2Co 11:30	
but I **w** go on to visions and	2Co 12:1	
On behalf of such a man I **w** boast;	2Co 12:5	
on my own behalf I **w** not boast,	2Co 12:5	
For if I do wish to boast I **w** not be	2Co 12:6	
for I **w** be speaking the truth; but I	2Co 12:6	
so that no one **w** credit me with	2Co 12:6	
I **w** rather boast about my	2Co 12:9	
and I **w** not be a burden to you;	2Co 12:14	
I **w** most gladly spend and be	2Co 12:15	
that perhaps *there* **w** *be* strife,	2Co 12:20	
come again I **w** not spare *anyone,*	2Co 13:2	
yet we **w** live with Him because of	2Co 13:4	
But I trust that you **w** realize	2Co 13:6	
and the God of love and peace **w** be	2Co 13:11	
to the **w** of our God and Father,	Ga 1:4	2307
by the works of the Law no flesh **w** be	Ga 2:16	
"ALL THE NATIONS **W** BE BLESSED IN	Ga 3:8	
to shut you out so that you **w** seek	Ga 4:17	
Christ **w** be of no benefit to you.	Ga 5:2	
that you **w** adopt no other view;	Ga 5:10	
one who is disturbing you **w** bear	Ga 5:10	
and you **w** not carry out the desire	Ga 5:16	
those who practice such things **w** not	Ga 5:21	
so that you too **w** not be tempted.	Ga 6:1	
and then he **w** have *reason for*	Ga 6:4	
For each one **w** bear his own load.	Ga 6:5	
a man sows, this he **w** also reap.	Ga 6:7	
who sows to his own flesh **w** from	Ga 6:8	
one who sows to the Spirit **w** from	Ga 6:8	
for in due time we **w** reap if we do	Ga 6:9	
simply so that they **w** not be	Ga 6:12	
And those who **w** walk by this rule,	Ga 6:16	
of Christ Jesus by the **w** of God,	Eph 1:1	2307
to the kind intention of His **w**,	Eph 1:5	
known to us the mystery of His **w**,	Eph 1:9	
things after the counsel of His **w**,	Eph 1:11	
so that you **w** know what is the hope	Eph 1:18	
so that he **w** have *something* to	Eph 4:28	
so that it **w** give grace to those	Eph 4:29	
And Christ **w** shine on you."	Eph 5:14	
what the **w** of the Lord is.	Eph 5:17	2307
doing the **w** of God from the heart.	Eph 6:6	2307
With good **w** render service, as to	Eph 6:7	2133
he **w** receive back from the Lord,	Eph 6:8	
so that you **w** be able to stand firm	Eph 6:11	
so that you **w** be able to resist in	Eph 6:13	
shield of faith with which you **w** be	Eph 6:16	
w make everything known to you.	Eph 6:21	
w perfect it until the day of Christ	Php 1:6	
strife, but some also from good **w**;	Php 1:15	2107
I rejoice. Yes, and I **w** rejoice,	Php 1:18	
for I know that this **w** turn out for	Php 1:19	
that I **w** not be put to shame in	Php 1:20	
Christ **w** even now, as always, be	Php 1:20	
this **w** *mean* fruitful labor for me;	Php 1:22	
of this, I know that I **w** remain	Php 1:25	
I **w** hear of you that you are standing	Php 1:27	
name of Jesus EVERY KNEE **W** BOW,	Php 2:10	
and that every tongue **w** confess that	Php 2:11	
both to **w** and to work for *His* good	Php 2:13	2309
so that you **w** prove yourselves to be	Php 2:15	
so that in the day of Christ I **w** have	Php 2:16	
of kindred spirit who **w** genuinely be	Php 2:20	
in the Lord that I myself also **w** be	Php 2:24	
God **w** reveal that also to you;	Php 3:15	
who **w** transform the body of our	Php 3:21	
again I **w** say, rejoice!	Php 4:4	
w guard your hearts and your minds in	Php 4:7	
and the God of peace **w** be with you.	Php 4:9	
And my God **w** supply all your needs	Php 4:19	
of Jesus Christ by the **w** of God,	Col 1:1	2307
be filled with the knowledge of His **w**	Col 1:9	2307
so that you **w** walk in a manner worthy	Col 1:10	
so that He Himself **w** come to have	Col 1:18	
I say this so that no one **w** delude	Col 2:4	
w be revealed with Him in glory.	Col 3:4	
that the wrath of God **w** come upon	Col 3:6	
so that they **w** not lose heart.	Col 3:21	
knowing that from the Lord you **w**	Col 3:24	
For he who does wrong **w** receive	Col 3:25	
that God **w** open up to us a door for	Col 4:3	
so that you **w** know how you should	Col 4:6	
the Lord, **w** bring you information.	Col 4:7	
They **w** inform you about the whole	Col 4:9	
fully assured in all the **w** of God.	Col 4:12	2307
For this is the **w** of God, your	1Th 4:3	2307
so that you **w** behave properly toward	1Th 4:12	
so that you **w** not grieve as do	1Th 4:13	
even so God **w** bring with Him those	1Th 4:14	
w not precede those who have fallen	1Th 4:15	
For the Lord Himself **w** descend	1Th 4:16	
and the dead in Christ **w** rise first.	1Th 4:16	
Then we who are alive and remain **w** be	1Th 4:17	
w come just like a thief in the night.	1Th 5:2	
then destruction **w** come upon them	1Th 5:3	
and they **w** not escape.	1Th 5:3	
we **w** live together with Him.	1Th 5:10	
is God's **w** for you in Christ Jesus.	1Th 5:18	2307
And He also **w** bring it to pass.	1Th 5:24	
righteous judgment so that you **w** be	2Th 1:5	
us as well when the Lord Jesus **w** be	2Th 1:7	
These **w** pay the penalty of	2Th 1:9	
that our God **w** count you worthy of	2Th 1:11	
that the name of our Lord Jesus **w** be	2Th 1:12	
for *it* **w** *not come* unless	2Th 2:3	
so that in his time he **w** be revealed.	2Th 2:6	
only he who now restrains **w** *do so*	2Th 2:7	
Then that lawless one **w** be	2Th 2:8	
be revealed whom the Lord **w** slay	2Th 2:8	
For this reason God **w** send	2Th 2:11	
influence so that they **w** believe	2Th 2:11	
for us that the word of the Lord **w**	2Th 3:1	
and that we **w** be rescued from	2Th 3:2	
and He **w** strengthen and protect	2Th 3:3	
that you are doing and **w** *continue to*	2Th 3:4	
so that he **w** be put to shame.	2Th 3:14	
so that they **w** be taught not to	1Tm 1:20	
But *women* **w** be preserved through	1Tm 2:15	

how **w** he take care of the church 1Tm 3:5
so that he **w** not become conceited 1Tm 3:6
so that he **w** not fall into reproach 1Tm 3:7
I write so that you **w** know how 1Tm 3:15
some **w** fall away from the faith, 1Tm 4:1
you **w** be a good servant of Christ 1Tm 4:6
so that your progress **w** be evident to 1Tm 4:15
for as you do this you **w** ensure 1Tm 4:16
so that the rest also **w** be fearful 1Tm 5:20
of God and *our* doctrine **w** not 1Tm 6:1
which He **w** bring about at the 1Tm 6:15
of Christ Jesus by the **w** of God, 2Tm 1:1 *2307*
w be able to teach others also. 2Tm 2:2
for the Lord **w** give you 2Tm 2:7
we **w** also live with Him; 2Tm 2:11
If we endure, we **w** also reign with 2Tm 2:12
If we deny Him, He also **w** deny us; 2Tm 2:12
it **w** lead to further ungodliness, 2Tm 2:16
their talk **w** spread like gangrene. 2Tm 2:17
he **w** be a vessel for honor, 2Tm 2:21
held captive by him to do his **w**. 2Tm 2:26 *2307*
last days difficult times **w** come. 2Tm 3:1
For men **w** be lovers of self, 2Tm 3:2
they **w** not make further progress; 2Tm 3:9
their folly **w** be obvious to all, 2Tm 3:9
in Christ Jesus **w** be persecuted. 2Tm 3:12
w proceed *from bad* to worse, 2Tm 3:13
For the time **w** come when they will 2Tm 4:3
they **w** not endure sound doctrine; 2Tm 4:3
they **w** accumulate for themselves 2Tm 4:3
and **w** turn away their ears from 2Tm 4:4
truth and **w** turn aside to myths. 2Tm 4:4
Judge, **w** award to me on that day; 2Tm 4:8
the Lord **w** repay him according to 2Tm 4:14
The Lord **w** rescue me from every 2Tm 4:18
and **w** bring me safely to His 2Tm 4:18
so that he **w** be able both to exhort Ti 1:9
so that the word of God **w** not be Ti 2:5
so that the opponent **w** be put to Ti 2:8
all good faith so that they **w** adorn Ti 2:10
that those who have believed God **w** be Ti 3:8
so that they **w** not be unfruitful. Ti 3:14
but of your own free **w**. Phm 1:14 *1595*
with my own hand, I **w** repay it Phm 1:19
w do even more than what I say. Phm 1:21
that through your prayers I **w** be Phm 1:22
"I **W** BE A FATHER TO HIM AND HE Heb 1:5
THEY **W** PERISH, BUT YOU REMAIN; Heb 1:11
ALL **W** BECOME OLD LIKE A GARMENT, Heb 1:11
LIKE A MANTLE YOU **W** ROLL THEM UP; Heb 1:12
A GARMENT THEY **W** ALSO BE CHANGED. Heb 1:12
YOUR YEARS **W** NOT COME TO AN END." Heb 1:12
of those who **w** inherit salvation? Heb 1:14 *3195*
how **w** we escape if we neglect so Heb 2:3
Spirit according to His own **w**. Heb 2:4 *2308*
"I **W** PROCLAIM YOUR NAME TO MY Heb 2:12
I **W** SING YOUR PRAISE." Heb 2:12
"I **W** PUT MY TRUST IN HIM." Heb 2:13
so that none of you **w** be hardened by Heb 3:13
so that no one **w** fall, through Heb 4:11
And this we **w** do, if God permits. Heb 6:3
so that you **w** not be sluggish, but Heb 6:12
saying, "I **W** SURELY BLESS YOU Heb 6:14
AND I **W** SURELY MULTIPLY YOU." Heb 6:14
SWORN AND **W** NOT CHANGE HIS MIND, Heb 7:21
WHEN I **W** EFFECT A NEW COVENANT Heb 8:8
THIS IS THE COVENANT THAT I **W** MAKE Heb 8:10
I **W** PUT MY LAWS INTO THEIR MINDS, Heb 8:10
I **W** WRITE THEM ON THEIR HEARTS. Heb 8:10
AND I **W** BE THEIR GOD, AND THEY Heb 8:10
FOR ALL **W** KNOW ME, FROM THE LEAST Heb 8:11
"FOR I **W** BE MERCIFUL TO THEIR Heb 8:12
I **W** REMEMBER THEIR SINS NO MORE." Heb 8:12
much more **w** the blood of Christ, Heb 9:14
w appear a second time for salvation Heb 9:28
TO DO YOUR **W**, O GOD.'" Heb 10:7 *2307*
"BEHOLD, I HAVE COME TO DO YOUR **W**." Heb 10:9 *2307*
By this **w** we have been sanctified Heb 10:10 *2307*
"THIS IS THE COVENANT THAT I **W** Heb 10:16
I **W** PUT MY LAWS UPON THEIR HEART, Heb 10:16
ON THEIR MIND I **W** WRITE THEM," Heb 10:16
DEEDS I **W** REMEMBER NO MORE." Heb 10:17
WHICH **W** CONSUME THE ADVERSARIES. Heb 10:27 *3195*
he **w** deserve who has trampled under Heb 10:29
"VENGEANCE IS MINE, I **W** REPAY." Heb 10:30
"THE LORD **W** JUDGE HIS PEOPLE." Heb 10:30
when you have done the **w** of God, Heb 10:36 *2307*
WHILE, HE WHO IS COMING **W** COME, Heb 10:37
COMING WILL COME, AND **W** NOT DELAY. Heb 10:37
w fail me if I tell of Gideon, Heb 11:32
so that you **w** not grow weary and lose Heb 12:3
which no one **w** see the Lord. Heb 12:14
THE MOUNTAIN, IT **W** BE STONED." Heb 12:20
much less **w** we *escape* who Heb 12:25
MORE I **W** SHAKE NOT ONLY THE EARTH, Heb 12:26
and adulterers God **w** judge. Heb 13:4
"I **W** NEVER DESERT YOU, NOR WILL I Heb 13:5
YOU, NOR **W** I EVER FORSAKE YOU," Heb 13:5
IS MY HELPER, I **W** NOT BE AFRAID. Heb 13:6
WHAT **W** MAN DO TO ME?" Heb 13:6
as those who **w** give an account. Heb 13:17
in every good thing to do His **w**, Heb 13:21 *2307*
I **w** see you. Heb 13:23
and it **w** be given to him. Jas 1:5
man ought not to expect that he **w** Jas 1:7
flowering grass he **w** pass away. Jas 1:10
midst of his pursuits **w** fade away. Jas 1:11
he **w** receive the crown of life which Jas 1:12
In the exercise of His **w** He Jas 1:18 *1014*
this man **w** be blessed in what he does. Jas 1:25
For judgment **w** *be* merciless to Jas 2:13
w show you my faith by my works." Jas 2:18
knowing that as such we **w** incur a Jas 3:1
the horses' mouths so that they **w** Jas 3:3
the devil and he **w** flee from you. Jas 4:7
to God and He **w** draw near to you. Jas 4:8
of the Lord, and He **w** exalt you. Jas 4:10
"Today or tomorrow we **w** go to such Jas 4:13
what your life **w** be like tomorrow. Jas 4:14
we **w** live and also do this or that." Jas 4:15
and their rust **w** be a witness Jas 5:3
w consume your flesh like fire. Jas 5:3
w restore the one who is sick, Jas 5:15
sick, and the Lord **w** raise him up, Jas 5:15
sins, they **w** be forgiven him. Jas 5:15
way **w** save his soul from death and Jas 5:20
and **w** cover a multitude of sins. Jas 5:20
and undefiled and **w** not fade away, 1Pe 1:4
AND HE WHO BELIEVES IN HIM **W** NOT BE 1Pe 2:6
For such is the **w** of God that by 1Pe 2:15 *2307*
so that your prayers **w** not be 1Pe 3:7
your good behavior in Christ **w** be 1Pe 3:16
is better, if God should **w** it so, 1Pe 3:17 *2309*
of men, but for the **w** of God. 1Pe 4:2 *2307*
but they **w** give account to Him who is 1Pe 4:5
spirit according to *the* **w** *of* 1Pe 4:6
what **w** *be* the outcome for those 1Pe 4:17
WHAT **W** BECOME OF THE GODLESS MAN 1Pe 4:18
who suffer according to the **w** of God 1Pe 4:19 *2307*
according to *the* **w** *of* God; 1Pe 5:2
you **w** receive the unfading crown 1Pe 5:4
in Christ, **w** Himself perfect, 1Pe 5:10
these things, you **w** never stumble; 2Pe 1:10
w be abundantly supplied to you. 2Pe 1:11
Therefore, I **w** always be ready to 2Pe 1:12
And I **w** also be diligent that at 2Pe 1:15
any time after my departure you **w** be 2Pe 1:15
ever made by an act of human **w**, 2Pe 1:21 *2307*
there **w** also be false teachers among 2Pe 2:1
who **w** secretly introduce 2Pe 2:1
Many **w** follow their sensuality, 2Pe 2:2
way of the truth **w** be maligned; 2Pe 2:2
w exploit you with false words; 2Pe 2:3
w in the destruction of those 2Pe 2:12
mockers **w** come with *their* mocking, 2Pe 3:3
of the Lord **w** come like a thief, 2Pe 3:10
in which the heavens **w** pass away 2Pe 3:10
elements **w** be destroyed with intense 2Pe 3:10
and its works **w** be burned up. 2Pe 3:10
heavens **w** be destroyed by burning, 2Pe 3:12
elements **w** melt with intense heat! 2Pe 3:12
does the **w** of God lives forever. 1Jn 2:17 *2307*
you also **w** abide in the Son and in 1Jn 2:24
has not appeared as yet what we **w** be. 1Jn 3:2
we **w** be like Him, because we will 1Jn 3:2
because we **w** see Him just as He is. 1Jn 3:2
We **w** know by this that we are of 1Jn 3:19
and **w** assure our heart before Him 1Jn 3:19
ask anything according to His **w**, 1Jn 5:14 *2307*
he shall ask and *God* **w** for him 1Jn 5:16
in us and **w** be with us forever: 2Jn 1:2
mercy *and* peace **w** be with us, 2Jn 1:3
You **w** do well to send them on 3Jn 1:6
I **w** call attention to his deeds 3Jn 1:10
and we **w** speak face to face. Peace 3Jn 1:14
"In the last time there **w** be mockers, Jude 1:18
CLOUDS, and every eye **w** see Him, Rv 1:7
of the earth **w** mourn over Him. Rv 1:7
and the things which **w** take place Rv 1:19
and **w** remove your lampstand out of Rv 2:5
I **w** grant to eat of the tree of Rv 2:7
so that you **w** be tested, and you Rv 2:10
you **w** have tribulation for ten days. Rv 2:10
I **w** give you the crown of life. Rv 2:10
He who overcomes **w** not be hurt by Rv 2:11
and I **w** make war against them with Rv 2:16
I **w** give *some* of the hidden manna, Rv 2:17
and I **w** give him a white stone, Rv 2:17
I **w** throw her on a bed *of* Rv 2:22
'And I **w** kill her children with Rv 2:23
and all the churches **w** know that I Rv 2:23
and I **w** give to each one of you Rv 2:23
TO HIM I **W** GIVE AUTHORITY OVER THE Rv 2:26
and I **w** give him the morning star. Rv 2:28
wake up, I **w** come like a thief, Rv 3:3
and you **w** not know at what hour I Rv 3:3
at what hour I **w** come to you. Rv 3:3
and they **w** walk with Me in white, Rv 3:4
'He who overcomes **w** thus be clothed Rv 3:5
and I **w** not erase his name from Rv 3:5
and I **w** confess his name before My Rv 3:5
who opens and no one **w** shut, Rv 3:7
I **w** cause *those* of the synagogue Rv 3:9
I **w** make them come and bow down Rv 3:9
I also **w** keep you from the hour of Rv 3:10
so that no one **w** take your crown. Rv 3:11
I **w** make him a pillar in the Rv 3:12
he **w** not go out from it anymore; Rv 3:12
and I **w** write on him the name of Rv 3:12
I **w** spit you out of My mouth. Rv 3:16 *3195*
that the shame of your nakedness **w** Rv 3:18
the door, I **w** come in to him and Rv 3:20
in to him and **w** dine with him, Rv 3:20
I **w** grant to him to sit down with Rv 3:21
and I **w** show you what must take Rv 4:1
the twenty-four elders **w** fall down Rv 4:10
and **w** worship Him who lives Rv 4:10
and **w** cast their crowns before the Rv 4:10
and because of Your **w** they existed, Rv 4:11 *2307*
and they **w** reign upon the earth." Rv 5:10
w You refrain from judging and Rv 6:10
and He who sits on the throne **w** Rv 7:15
"They **w** hunger no longer, nor Rv 7:16
nor **w** the sun beat down on them, nor Rv 7:16
Lamb in the center of the throne **w** be Rv 7:17
and **w** guide them to springs of Rv 7:17
and God **w** wipe every tear from their Rv 7:17
And in those days men **w** seek death Rv 9:6
will seek death and **w** not find it; Rv 9:6
they **w** long to die, and death Rv 9:6
that there **w** be delay no longer, Rv 10:6
it **w** make your stomach bitter, Rv 10:9
mouth it **w** be sweet as honey." Rv 10:9
and they **w** tread under foot the Rv 11:2
"And I **w** grant *authority* to my Rv 11:3
and they **w** prophesy for twelve Rv 11:3
so that rain **w** not fall during Rv 11:6
of the abyss **w** make war with them, Rv 11:7
And their dead bodies **w** *lie* in Rv 11:8
tribes and tongues and nations **w** Rv 11:9
and **w** not permit their dead bodies Rv 11:9
And those who dwell on the earth **w** Rv 11:10
they **w** send gifts to one another, Rv 11:10
and He **w** reign forever and ever." Rv 11:15
dwell on the earth **w** worship him, Rv 13:8
and *he provides* that no one **w** be Rv 13:17
he also **w** drink of the wine of the Rv 14:10
and he **w** be tormented with fire Rv 14:10
"Who **w** not fear, O Lord, and Rv 15:4
W COME AND WORSHIP BEFORE YOU, Rv 15:4
so that he **w** not walk about naked Rv 16:15
not walk about naked and men **w** not Rv 16:15
I **w** show you the judgment of Rv 17:1
I **w** tell you the mystery of the woman Rv 17:7
w wonder when they see the beast, Rv 17:8
that he was and is not and **w** come. Rv 17:8
"These **w** wage war against the Rv 17:14
and the Lamb **w** overcome them, Rv 17:14
these **w** hate the harlot and will Rv 17:16
and **w** make her desolate and naked, Rv 17:16
and **w** eat her flesh and will burn Rv 17:16
flesh and **w** burn her up with fire. Rv 17:16
until the words of God **w** be fulfilled. Rv 17:17
so that you **w** not participate in her Rv 18:4
and **w** never see mourning.' Rv 18:7
in one day her plagues **w** come, Rv 18:8
and she **w** be burned up with fire; Rv 18:8
w weep and lament over her when Rv 18:9
you and *men* **w** no longer find them. Rv 18:14
w stand at a distance because of Rv 18:15
"So **w** Babylon, the great city, Rv 18:21
and **w** not be found any longer. Rv 18:21
and trumpeters **w** not be heard in you Rv 18:22
w be found in you any longer; Rv 18:22
and the sound of a mill **w** not be Rv 18:22
w not shine in you any longer; Rv 18:23
and bride **w** not be heard in you any Rv 18:23
He **w** rule them with a rod of iron; Rv 19:15
but they **w** be priests of God and Rv 20:6
w reign with Him for a thousand years. Rv 20:6
w be released from his prison, Rv 20:7
and **w** come out to deceive the Rv 20:8
and they **w** be tormented day and Rv 20:10
and He **w** dwell among them, and they Rv 21:3
and God Himself **w** be among them, Rv 21:3
and He **w** wipe away every tear from Rv 21:4
and there **w** no longer be *any* Rv 21:4
there **w** no longer be *any* mourning, Rv 21:4
I **w** give to the one who thirsts Rv 21:6
"He who overcomes **w** inherit these Rv 21:7
and I **w** be his God and he will be Rv 21:7
be his God and he **w** be My son. Rv 21:7
their part **w** *be* in the lake that Rv 21:8
I **w** show you the bride, the wife of Rv 21:9
The nations **w** walk by its light, Rv 21:24
and the kings of the earth **w** bring Rv 21:24
In the daytime (for there **w** be no Rv 21:25
no night there) its gates **w** never Rv 21:25
and they **w** bring the glory Rv 21:26
There **w** no longer be any curse; Rv 22:3
throne of God and of the Lamb **w** be Rv 22:3
and His bond-servants **w** serve Him; Rv 22:3
they **w** see His face, and His name Rv 22:4
and His name **w** *be* on their Rv 22:4
And there **w** no longer be *any* Rv 22:5
and they **w** not have need of the light Rv 22:5
because the Lord God **w** illumine them; Rv 22:5
and they **w** reign forever and ever. Rv 22:5
God **w** add to him the plagues which Rv 22:18
God **w** take away his part from Rv 22:19

WILLED
to whom God **w** to make known what Col 1:27 *2309*

WILLFULLY
For if we go on sinning **w** after Heb 10:26 *1596*

WILLING
woman is not **w** to follow me Gn 24:5 14
the woman is not **w** to follow you, Gn 24:8 14
Moses was **w** to dwell with the man, Ex 2:21 2974
and he was not **w** to let them go. Ex 10:27 14
whoever is of a **w** heart, let him Ex 35:5 5081
"Yet you were not **w** to go up, Dt 1:26 14
not **w** for us to pass through his land; Dt 2:30 14
the LORD was not **w** to destroy you. Dt 10:10 14
God was not **w** to listen to Balaam, Dt 23:5 14
he is not **w** to perform the duty of Dt 25:7 14
shall never be **w** to forgive him, Dt 29:20 14

been w to dwell beyond the Jordan! Jos 7:7 2974
I was not w to listen to Balaam. Jos 24:10 14
"Please be w to spend the night, Jg 19:6 2974
man was not w to spend the night, Jg 19:10 14
not w to destroy them utterly; 1Sa 15:9 14
the servants of the king were not w to 1Sa 22:17 14
But Asahel was not w to turn aside 2Sa 2:21 14
But Jehoshaphat was not w. 1Ki 22:49 14
be w to go with your servants." 2Ki 6:3 2974
LORD was not w to destroy Judah, 2Ki 8:19 14
the Arameans were not w to help 1Ch 19:19 14
with a whole heart and a w mind; 1Ch 28:9 2655
and every w man of any skill will 1Ch 28:21 5081
Who then is w to consecrate 1Ch 29:5 5068
Yet the LORD was not w to destroy 2Ch 21:7 14
were w *brought* burnt offerings. 2Ch 29:31 5081
who are w to go to Jerusalem, Ezr 7:13 5069
"Would that God were w to crush me, Jb 6:9 2974
And sustain me with a w spirit. Ps 51:12 5082
But you were not w, Is 30:15 14
ways they were not w to walk, Is 42:24 14
will not be w to listen to you, Ezk 3:7 14
they are not w to listen to Me. Ezk 3:7 14
on every passer-by who might be w. Ezk 16:15
Me and were not w to listen to Me; Ezk 20:8 14
"Lord, if You are w, Mt 8:2 2309
saying, "I am w; be cleansed." Mt 8:3 2309
"And if you are w to accept *it*, Mt 11:14 2309
"What are you w to give me to Mt 26:15 2309
the spirit is w, but the flesh is Mt 26:41 4289
"If You are w, You can make me Mk 1:40 2309
said to him, "I am w; be cleansed." Mk 1:41 2309
the spirit is w, but the flesh is Mk 14:38 4289
"Lord, if You are w, Lk 5:12 2309
saying, "I am w; be cleansed." Lk 5:13 2309
angry and was not w to go in; Lk 15:28 2309
"Father, if You are w, Lk 22:42 1014
and you were w to rejoice for a while Jn 5:35 2309
So they were w to receive Jn 6:21 2309
"If anyone is w to do His will, Jn 7:17 2309
"Are you w to go up to Jerusalem Ac 25:9 2309
I asked whether he was w to go to Ac 25:20 1014
if they are w to testify, Ac 26:5 2309
they were w to release me because Ac 28:18 1014
for the w is present in me, but Ro 7:18 2309
although w to demonstrate His Ro 9:22 2309
if anyone is not w to work, then he 2Th 3:10 2309
But are you w to recognize, you Jas 2:20 2309
but I am not w to write *them* to 3Jn 1:13 2309

WILLINGLY
over the king's work, offered w; 1Ch 29:6 5068
because they had offered so w, 1Ch 29:9 5068
have w offered all these *things;* 1Ch 29:17 5068
make *their* offerings w to You. 1Ch 29:17 5068
offered w for the house of God to Ezr 2:68 5068
who offered w for the house of Ezr 7:16 5069
W I will sacrifice to You; Ps 54:6 5071
For He does not afflict w Or La 3:33 4480, 3820
not w, but because of Him who Ro 8:20 1635

WILLOW
he set it *like* a w. Ezk 17:5 6851

WILLOWS
of leafy trees and w of the brook, Lv 23:40 6155
The w of the brook surround him. Jb 40:22 6155
Upon the w in the midst of it We Ps 137:2 6155

WILLS
day he w what he has to his sons, Dt 21:16 5157
to whom the Son w to reveal *Him.* Mt 11:27 1014
to whom the Son w to reveal *Him.*" Lk 10:22 1014
return to you again if God w," Ac 18:21 2309
the man who w or the man who runs, Ro 9:16 2309
come to you soon, if the Lord w, 1Co 4:19 2309
one individually just as He w. 1Co 12:11 1014
"If the Lord w, we will live and Jas 4:15 2309

WILTED
the field w away on account of it. Ezk 31:15 5968

WIN
we will w him over and keep you Mt 28:14 3982
to all, so that I may w more. 1Co 9:19 2770
as a Jew, so that I might w Jews; 1Co 9:20 2770
that I might w those who are under 1Co 9:20 2770
might w those who are without law. 1Co 9:21 2770
weak, that I might w the weak; 1Co 9:22 2770
Run in such a way that you may w. 1Co 9:24 2638
he does not w the prize unless he 2Tm 2:5 4737

WIND
caused a w to pass over the earth, Gn 8:1 7307
thin and scorched by the east w, Gn 41:6 6921
thin, *and* scorched by the east w, Gn 41:23 6921
seven thin ears scorched by the east w Gn 41:27 6921
and the LORD directed an east w on Ex 10:13 7307
the east w brought the locusts. Ex 10:13 7307
So the LORD shifted *the* w to Ex 10:19
west w which took up the locusts and Ex 10:19 7307
back by a strong east w all night and Ex 14:21 7307
"You blew with Your w, Ex 15:10 7307
went forth a w from the LORD and Nu 11:31 7307
He appeared on the wings of the w. 2Sa 22:11 7307
sky grew black with clouds and w, 1Ki 18:45 7307
And a great and strong w was 1Ki 19:11 7307
but the LORD *was* not in the w. 1Ki 19:11 7307
And after the w an earthquake, *but* 1Ki 19:11 7307
not see w nor shall you see rain; 2Ki 3:17 7307
a great w came from across the Jb 1:19 7307
"The paths of their course w along, Jb 6:18 3943
of one in despair belong to the w? Jb 6:26 7307
words of your mouth be a mighty w? Jb 8:2 7307
And fill himself with the east w? Jb 15:2 6921
"Are they as straw before the w, Jb 21:18 7307
"The east w carries him away, and Jb 27:21 6921
"When He imparted weight to the w Jb 28:25 7307
me; They pursue my honor as the w, Jb 30:15 7307
"You lift me up to the w *and* Jb 30:22 7307
is still because of the south w? Jb 37:17
the w has passed and cleared them. Jb 37:21 7307
the east w scattered on the earth? Jb 38:24 6921
chaff which the w drives away. Ps 1:4 7307
Fire and brimstone and burning w Ps 11:6 7307
He sped upon the wings of the w. Ps 18:10 7307
fine as the dust before the w; Ps 18:42 7307
them be like chaff before the w, Ps 35:5 7307
With the east w You break Ps 48:7 7307
From the stormy w *and* tempest." Ps 55:8 7307
the east w to blow in the heavens And Ps 78:26 6921
His power He directed the south w. Ps 78:26 8486
A w that passes and does not Ps 78:39 7307
Like chaff before the w. Ps 83:13 7307
When the w has passed over it, it Ps 103:16 7307
He walks upon the wings of the w; Ps 104:3 7307
He spoke and raised up a stormy w, Ps 107:25 7307
forth the w from His treasuries. Ps 135:7 7307
He causes His w to blow and the Ps 147:18 7307
Stormy w, fulfilling His word; Ps 148:8 7307
his own house will inherit w, Pr 11:29 7307
Like clouds and w without rain Is Pr 25:14 7307
The north w brings forth rain, And Pr 25:23 7307
restrain her restrains the w, Pr 27:16 7307
has gathered the w in His fists? Pr 30:4 7307
The w continues swirling along; Ec 1:6 7307
circular courses the w returns. Ec 1:6 7307
is vanity and striving after w. Ec 1:14 7307
this also is striving after w. Ec 1:17 7307
all was vanity and striving after w Ec 2:11 7307
is futility and striving after w. Ec 2:17 7307
is vanity and striving after w. Ec 2:26 7307
is vanity and striving after w. Ec 4:4 7307
of labor and striving after w. Ec 4:6 7307
is vanity and striving after w. Ec 4:16 7307
to him who toils for the w? Ec 5:16 7307
futility and a striving after w. Ec 6:9 7307
to restrain the w with the wind, Ec 8:8 7307
to restrain the wind with the w, Ec 8:8 7307
He who watches the w will not sow Ec 11:4 7307
as you do not know the path of the w Ec 11:5 7307
"Awake, O north w, And come, SS 4:16
w *of* the south; Make my garden SS 4:16
trees of the forest shake with the w. Is 7:2 7307
the River With His scorching w; Is 11:15 7307
in the mountains before the w, Is 17:13 7307
gave birth, as it seems, *only* to w. Is 26:18 7307
With His fierce w He has expelled Is 27:8 7307
them on the day of the east w. Is 27:8 6921
will be like a refuge from the w And Is 32:2 7307
and the w will carry them away, Is 41:16 7307
molten images are w and emptiness. Is 41:29 7307
the w will carry all of them up, Is 57:13 7307
Which the w of the LORD drives. Is 59:19 7307
And our iniquities, like the w, Is 64:6 7307
That sniffs the w in her passion. Jer 2:24 7307
"A scorching w from the bare Jer 4:11 7307
a w too strong for this Jer 4:12 7307
"The prophets are *as* w, Jer 5:13 7307
out the w from His storehouses. Jer 10:13 7307
drifting straw To the desert w. Jer 13:24 7307
'Like an east w I will scatter Jer 18:17 7307
"The w will sweep away all your Jer 22:22 7307
forth the w from His storehouses. Jer 51:16 7307
storm w was coming from the north, Ezk 1:4 7307
third you shall scatter to the w; Ezk 5:2 7307
all your remnant to every w. Ezk 5:10 7307
third I will scatter to every w, Ezk 5:12 7307
I will scatter to every w all who are Ezk 12:14 7307
and a violent w will break out. Ezk 13:11 7307
I will make a violent w break out Ezk 13:13 7307
wither as soon as the east w strikes it Ezk 17:10 7307
will be scattered to every w; Ezk 17:21 7307
And the east w dried up its fruit. Ezk 19:12 7307
The east w has broken you In the Ezk 27:26 7307
and the w carried them away so Da 2:35 7308
The w wraps them in its wings, And Hos 4:19 7307
For they sow the w And Hos 8:7 7307
Ephraim feeds on w, Hos 12:1 7307
pursues the east w continually; Hos 12:1 6921
the reeds, An east w will come, Hos 13:15 6921
The w of the LORD coming up from Hos 13:15 7307
"I smote you with scorching w Am 4:9
forms mountains and creates the w Am 4:13 7307
The LORD hurled a great w on Jon 1:4 7307
God appointed a scorching east w, Jon 4:8 7307
"If a man walking after w and Mi 2:11 7307
they will sweep through *like* the w Hab 1:11 7307
of your hands with blasting w, Hg 2:17 7711b
out with the w in their wings; Zch 5:9 7307
"but I scattered them with a storm w Zch 7:14 5590
A reed shaken by the w? Mt 11:7 417
for the w was contrary. Mt 14:24 417
But seeing the w, he became Mt 14:30 417
got into the boat, the w stopped. Mt 14:32 417
there arose a fierce gale of w, Mk 4:37 417
rebuked the w and said to the sea, Mk 4:39 417
And the w died down and it became Mk 4:39 417
even the w and the sea obey Him?" Mk 4:41 417
oars, for the w was against them, Mk 6:48 417
boat with them, and the w stopped; Mk 6:51 417
A reed shaken by the w? Lk 7:24 417
gale of w descended on the lake, Lk 8:23 417
and rebuked the w and the surging Lk 8:24 417
when *you see* a south w blowing, Lk 12:55 3558
"The w blows where it wishes and Jn 3:8 4151
up because a strong w was blowing. Jn 6:18 417
a noise like a violent rushing w, Ac 2:2 4157
since the w did not permit us *to* Ac 27:7 417
When a moderate south w came up, Ac 27:13 3558
down from the land a violent w, Ac 27:14 417
in it and could not face the w, Ac 27:15 417
hoisting the foresail to the w, Ac 27:40 4154
a day later a south w sprang up, Ac 28:13 3558
about by every w of doctrine, Eph 4:14 417
sea, driven and tossed by the w. Jas 1:6 4494
the sun rises with a scorching w and Jas 1:11 2742
figs when shaken by a great w. Rv 6:13 417
so that no w would blow on the Rv 7:1 417

WIND-DRIVEN
As the w chaff with his bow. Is 41:2

WINDING
by w stairs to the middle *story,* 1Ki 6:8 3883

WINDOW
"You shall make a w for the ark, Gn 6:16 6672b
Noah opened the w of the ark which Gn 8:6 2474
looked out through a w, Gn 26:8 2474
them down by a rope through the w, Jos 2:15 2474
this cord of scarlet thread in the w Jos 2:18 2474
tied the scarlet cord in the w. Jos 2:21 2474
"Out of the w she looked and Jg 5:28 2474
Michal let David down through a w, 1Sa 19:12 2474
daughter of Saul looked out of the w 2Sa 6:16 2474
There were artistic w frames in 1Ki 7:4
and w was opposite window in three 1Ki 7:4 4237
was opposite w in three ranks. 1Ki 7:4 4237
and w was opposite window in three 1Ki 7:5 4237
was opposite w in three ranks. 1Ki 7:5 4237
her head and looked out the w. 2Ki 9:30 2474
Then he lifted up his face to the w 2Ki 9:32 2474
"Open the w toward the east," 2Ki 13:17 2474
daughter of Saul looked out of the w 1Ch 15:29 2474
For at the w of my house I looked Pr 7:6 2474
Birds will sing in the w, Zph 2:14 2474
Eutychus sitting on the w sill, Ac 20:9 2376
a basket through a w in the wall, 2Co 11:33 2376

WINDOWS
he made w with *artistic* frames. 1Ki 6:4 2474
the LORD should make w in heaven, 2Ki 7:2 699
the LORD should make w in heaven, 2Ki 7:19 699
those who look through w grow dim; Ec 12:3 699
wall, He is looking through the w, SS 2:9 2474
For the w above are opened, and Is 24:18 699
death has come up through our w; Jer 9:21 2474
upper rooms, And cut out its w, Jer 22:14 2474
w *looking* toward the guardrooms, Ezk 40:16 2474
there were w all around inside; Ezk 40:16 2474
Its w and its porches and Ezk 40:22 2474
The gate and its porches had w Ezk 40:25 2474
all around like those other w; Ezk 40:25 2474
and its porches had w all around; Ezk 40:29 2474
and its porches had w all around; Ezk 40:33 2474
And the gate had w all around; Ezk 40:36 2474
The thresholds, the latticed w and Ezk 41:16 2474
and *from* the ground to the w Ezk 41:16 2474
windows (but the w were covered), Ezk 41:16 2474
There were latticed w and palm Ezk 41:26 2474
he had w open toward Jerusalem); Da 6:10 3551
enter through the w like a thief. Jl 2:9 2474
not open for you the w of heaven and Mal 3:10 699

WINDS
He makes the w His messengers, Ps 104:4 7307
And I will scatter to all the w Jer 49:32 7307
I will bring upon Elam the four w Jer 49:36 7307
will scatter them to all these w; Jer 49:36 7307
"Come from the four w, Ezk 37:9 7307
the four w of heaven were stirring Da 7:2 7308
horns toward the four w of heaven. Da 8:8 7307
as the four w of the heavens," Zch 2:6 7307
march in the storm w of the south. Zch 9:14 5591b
the floods came, and the w blew and Mt 7:25 417
the floods came, and the w blew and Mt 7:27 417
and rebuked the w and the sea, Mt 8:26 417
even the w and the sea obey Him?" Mt 8:27 417
His elect from the four w, Mt 24:31 417
His elect from the four w, Mk 13:27 417
commands even the w and the water, Lk 8:25 417
because the w were contrary. Ac 27:4 417
"WHO MAKES HIS ANGELS W, Heb 1:7 4151
great and are driven by strong w, Jas 3:4 417
without water, carried along by w; Jude 1:12 417
back the four w of the earth, Rv 7:1 417

WINDSTORMS
As w in the Negev sweep on, It Is 21:1 5492a

WINDY
wise man answer with w knowledge Jb 15:2 7307
"Is there *no* limit to w words? Jb 16:3 7307

WINE
drank of the w and became drunk, Gn 9:21 3196
When Noah awoke from his w, Gn 9:24 3196
of Salem brought out bread and w; Gn 14:18 3196
let us make our father drink w, Gn 19:32 3196
So they made their father drink w Gn 19:33 3196
let us make him drink w tonight also Gn 19:34 3196
So they made their father drink w Gn 19:35 3196
also brought him w and he drank. Gn 27:25 3196
an abundance of grain and new w; Gn 27:28 8492
and with grain and new w I have Gn 27:37 8492
He washes his garments in w, Gn 49:11 3196

"His eyes are dull from w, Gn 49:12 3196
and one-fourth of a hin of w for a Ex 29:40 3196
"Do not drink w or strong drink, Lv 10:9 3196
drink offering, a fourth of a hin of w. Lv 23:13 3196
abstain from w and strong drink; Nu 6:3 3196
made from w or strong drink, Nu 6:3 3196
the Nazirite may drink w.' Nu 6:20 3196
shall prepare w for the drink offering, Nu 15:5 3196
you shall offer one-third of a hin of w Nu 15:7 3196
a hin of w as an offering by fire, Nu 15:10 3196
of the fresh w and of the grain, Nu 18:12 8492
the full produce from the w vat. Nu 18:27 3342
and as the product of the w vat. Nu 18:30 3342
drink offerings shall be half a hin of w Nu 28:14 3196
grain and your new w and your oil, Dt 7:13 8492
grain and your new w and your oil. Dt 11:14 8492
the tithe of your grain or new w Dt 12:17 8492
tithe of your grain, your new w, Dt 14:23 8492
desires: for oxen, or sheep, or w, Dt 14:26 3196
floor and from your w vat; Dt 15:14 3342
threshing floor and your w vat; Dt 16:13 3342
fruits of your grain, your new w, Dt 18:4 8492
you will neither drink of the w nor Dt 28:39 3196
also leaves you no grain, new w, Dt 28:51 8492
have you drunk w or strong drink, Dt 29:6 3196
the blood of grapes you drank w. Dt 32:14 2561
"Their w is the venom of Dt 32:33 3196
And drank the w of their drink offering? Dt 32:38 3196
In a land of grain and new w; Dt 33:28 8492
was beating out wheat in the w press Jg 6:11 1660
Zeeb at the w press of Zeeb, Jg 7:25 3342
'Shall I leave my new w, Jg 9:13 8492
not to drink w or strong drink, Jg 13:4 3196
and now you shall not drink w or Jg 13:7 3196
vine nor drink w or strong drink, Jg 13:14 3196
and also bread and w for me, Jg 19:19 3196
Put away your w from you." 1Sa 1:14 3196
drunk neither w nor strong drink, 1Sa 1:15 3196
one ephah of flour and a jug of w, 1Sa 1:24 3196
and another carrying a jug of w; 1Sa 10:3 3196
and a jug of w and a young goat, 1Sa 16:20 3196
loaves of bread and two jugs of w 1Sa 25:18 3196
when the w had gone out of Nabal, 1Sa 25:37 3196
when Amnon's heart is merry with w, 2Sa 13:28 3196
summer fruits, and a jug of w. 2Sa 16:1 3196
the young men to eat, and the w, 2Sa 16:2 3196
floor, or from the w press?" 2Ki 6:27 3342
land, a land of grain and new w, 2Ki 18:32 8492
and over the fine flour and the w 1Ch 9:29 3196
cakes and bunches of raisins, w, 1Ch 12:40 3196
vineyards *stored* in the w cellars. 1Ch 27:27 3196
of barley, and 20,000 baths of w and 2Ch 2:10 3196
wheat and barley, oil and w, 2Ch 2:15 3196
and stores of food, oil and w. 2Ch 11:11 3196
the first fruits of grain, new w, 2Ch 31:5 8492
the produce of grain, w and oil, 2Ch 32:28 8492
God of heaven, and wheat, salt, w and Ezr 6:9 2562
100 kors of wheat, 100 baths of w, Ezr 7:22 2562
Artaxerxes, that w *was* before him, Ne 2:1 3196
I took up the w and gave it to the Ne 2:1 3196
money and of the grain, the new w and Ne 5:11 8492
and took from them bread and w Ne 5:15 3196
all sorts of w *were furnished* in Ne 5:18 3196
the new w and the oil to the Ne 10:37 8492
the grain, the new w and the oil to Ne 10:39 8492
w and oil prescribed for the Ne 13:5 8492
brought the tithe of the grain, w and Ne 13:12 8492
treading w presses on the sabbath, Ne 13:15 1660
them on donkeys, as well as w, Ne 13:15 3196
and the royal w was plentiful Es 1:7 3196
of the king was merry with w, Es 1:10 3196
they drank their w at the banquet, Es 5:6 3196
the king and Haman came to drink w Es 7:1 3196
they drank their w at the banquet, Es 7:2 3196
arose in his anger from drinking w Es 7:7 3196
place where they were drinking w, Es 7:8 3196
daughters were eating and drinking w Jb 1:13 3196
daughters were eating and drinking w Jb 1:18 3196
They tread w presses but thirst. Jb 24:11 3342
my belly is like unvented w, Jb 32:19 3196
when their grain and new w abound. Ps 4:7 8492
You have given us w to drink that Ps 60:3 3196
hand of the LORD, and the w foams; Ps 75:8 3196
Like a warrior overcome by w. Ps 78:65 3196
And w which makes man's heart Ps 104:15 3196
vats will overflow with new w. Pr 3:10 8492
And drink the w of violence. Pr 4:17 3196
her food, she has mixed her w; Pr 9:2 3196
And drink of the w I have mixed. Pr 9:5 3196
W is a mocker, strong drink a Pr 20:1 3196
He who loves w and oil will not Pr 21:17 3196
not be with heavy drinkers of w, Pr 23:20 3196
Those who linger long over w, Pr 23:30 3196
Those who go to taste mixed w. Pr 23:30 4469
not look on the w when it is red, Pr 23:31 3196
It is not for kings to drink w, Pr 31:4 3196
And w to him whose life is bitter. Pr 31:6 3196
how to stimulate my body with w Ec 2:3 3196
drink your w with a cheerful heart; Ec 9:7 3196
enjoyment, and w makes life merry, Ec 10:19 3196
For your love is better than w. SS 1:2 3196
will extol your love more than w. SS 1:4 3196
much better is your love than w, SS 4:10 3196
I have drunk my w and my milk. SS 5:1 3196
goblet Which never lacks mixed w; SS 7:2 4197
And your mouth like the best w!" SS 7:9 3196
I would give you spiced w to drink SS 8:2 3196
And also hewed out a w vat in it; Is 5:2 3342
will yield *only* one bath *of* w, Is 5:10

evening that w may inflame them! Is 5:11 3196
by tambourine and flute, and by w; Is 5:12 3196
who are heroes in drinking w And Is 5:22 3196
treads out w in the presses, Is 16:10 3196
Eating of meat and drinking of w: Is 22:13 3196
The new w mourns, The vine decays, Is 24:7 8492
They do not drink w with song; Is 24:9 3196
in the streets concerning the w; Is 24:11 3196
A banquet of aged w, Is 25:6 8105
with marrow, *And* refined, aged w. Is 25:6 8105
"A vineyard of w, sing of it! Is 27:2 2561
Of those who are overcome with w! Is 28:1 3196
these also reel with w and stagger Is 28:7 3196
drink, They are confused by w, Is 28:7 3196
They become drunk, but not with w, Is 29:9 3196
land, a land of grain and new w, Is 36:17 8492
their own blood as with sweet w; Is 49:26 6071
Who are drunk, but not with w: Is 51:21 3196
buy w and milk Without money and Is 55:1 3196
"let us get w, and let us drink Is 56:12 3196
will foreigners drink your new w for Is 62:8 8492
the one who treads in the w press? Is 63:2 1660
"I have trodden the w trough alone, Is 63:3 6333b
the new w is found in the cluster, Is 65:8 8492
cups with mixed w for Destiny, Is 65:11 4469
"Every jug is to be filled with w." Jer 13:12 3196
every jug is to be filled with w?' Jer 13:12 3196
Even like a man overcome with w, Jer 23:9 3196
"Take this cup of the w of wrath Jer 25:15 3196
Over the grain and the new w Jer 31:12 8492
and give them w to drink." Jer 35:2 3196
the Rechabites pitchers full of w and Jer 35:5 3196
and I said to them, "Drink w!" Jer 35:5 3196
"We will not drink w, Jer 35:6 3196
'You shall not drink w, Jer 35:6 3196
us, not to drink w all our days, Jer 35:8 3196
commanded his sons not to drink w, Jer 35:14 3196
So they do not drink w to this Jer 35:14
gather in w and summer fruit and oil Jer 40:10 3196
and gathered in w and summer fruit Jer 40:12 3196
like w on its dregs, And he has Jer 48:11
And I have made the w to cease Jer 48:33 3196
wine to cease from the w presses; Jer 48:33 3342
The nations have drunk of her w; Jer 51:7 3196
Lord has trodden *as in* a w press La 1:15 1660
"Where is grain and w?" La 2:12 3196
of the w of Helbon and white wool. Ezk 27:18 3196
"Nor shall any of the priests drink w Ezk 44:21 3196
and from the w which he drank, Da 1:5 3196
food or with the w which he drank; Da 1:8 3196
food and the w they were to drink, Da 1:16 3196
and he was drinking w in the Da 5:1 2562
When Belshazzar tasted the w, Da 5:2 2562
They drank the w and praised the Da 5:4 2562
have been drinking w from them; Da 5:23 2562
nor did meat or w enter my mouth, Da 10:3 3196
who gave her the grain, the new w and Hos 2:8 8492
time And My new w in its season. Hos 2:9 8492
to the grain, to the new w and Hos 2:22 8492
Harlotry, w and new wine take Hos 4:11 3196
new w take away the understanding. Hos 4:11 8492
became sick with the heat of w; Hos 7:5 3196
For the sake of grain and new w Hos 7:14 8492
and w press will not feed them, Hos 9:2 3342
And the new w will fail them. Hos 9:2 8492
out drink offerings of w to the LORD, Hos 9:4 3196
will be like the w of Lebanon. Hos 14:7 3196
And wail, all you w drinkers, Jl 1:5 3196
On account of the sweet w That is Jl 1:5 6071
is ruined, The new w dries up, Jl 1:10 8492
am going to send you grain, new w and Jl 2:19 8492
overflow with the new w and oil. Jl 2:24 8492
sold a girl for w that they may drink Jl 3:3 3196
tread, for the w press is full; Jl 3:13 1660
mountains will drip with sweet w, Jl 3:18 6071
w of those who have been fined. Am 2:8 3196
you made the Nazirites drink w, Am 2:12 3196
yet you will not drink their w. Am 5:11 3196
Who drink w from sacrificial bowls Am 6:6 3196
the mountains will drip sweet w And Am 9:13 6071
plant vineyards and drink their w, Am 9:14 3196
to you concerning w and liquor,' Mi 2:11 3196
grapes, but you will not drink w. Mi 6:15 3196
w betrays the haughty man, Hab 2:5 3196
vineyards but not drink their w." Zph 1:13 3196
on the grain, on the new w, Hg 1:11 8492
with this fold, or cooked food, w, Hg 2:12 3196
one came to the w vat to draw fifty Hg 2:16 3342
and be boisterous as with w; Zch 9:15 3196
flourish, and new w the virgins. Zch 9:17 8492
heart will be glad as if *from* w; Zch 10:7 3196
of Hananel to the king's w presses. Zch 14:10 3342
people put new w into old wineskins; Mt 9:17 *3631*
burst, and the w pours out and Mt 9:17 *3631*
put new w into fresh wineskins, Mt 9:17 *3631*
AROUND IT AND DUG A W PRESS IN IT, Mt 21:33 *3025b*
Him w to drink mixed with gall; Mt 27:34 *3631*
sponge, he filled it with sour w and Mt 27:48 *3690*
one puts new w into old wineskins; Mk 2:22 *3631*
the w will burst the skins, Mk 2:22 *3631*
the skins, and the w is lost and Mk 2:22 *3631*
puts new w into fresh wineskins." Mk 2:22 *3631*
AND DUG A VAT UNDER THE W PRESS Mk 12:1 *5276*
to give Him w mixed with myrrh; Mk 15:23 *3631*
and filled a sponge with sour w, Mk 15:36 *3690*
and he will drink no w or liquor, Lk 1:15 *3631*
one puts new w into old wineskins; Lk 5:37 *3631*
the new w will burst the skins and Lk 5:37 *3631*
"But new w must be put into fresh Lk 5:38 *3631*

"And no one, after drinking old w Lk 5:39
eating no bread and drinking no w, Lk 7:33 *3631*
wounds, pouring oil and w on *them* Lk 10:34 *3631*
up to Him, offering Him sour w, Lk 23:36 *3690*
When the w ran out, the Jn 2:3 *3631*
"They have no w." Jn 2:3 *3631*
the water which had become w, Jn 2:9 *3631*
"Every man serves the good w first, Jn 2:10 *3631*
then he serves the poorer w; Jn 2:10
have kept the good w until now." Jn 2:10 *3631*
where He had made the water w. Jn 4:46 *3631*
jar full of sour w was standing there Jn 19:29 *3690*
sour w upon *a branch of* hyssop Jn 19:29 *3690*
Jesus had received the sour w, Jn 19:30 *3690*
"They are full of sweet w." Ac 2:13 *1098*
not to eat meat or to drink w, Ro 14:21 *3631*
And do not get drunk with w, Eph 5:18 *3631*
not addicted to w or pugnacious, 1Tm 3:3 *3943*
or addicted to much w or fond of 1Tm 3:8 *3631*
but use a little w for the sake of 1Tm 5:23 *3631*
quick-tempered, not addicted to w, Ti 1:7 *3943*
gossips nor enslaved to much w, Ti 2:3 *3631*
do not damage the oil and the w." Rv 6:6 *3631*
w of the passion of her immorality. Rv 14:8 *3631*
drink of the w of the wrath of God, Rv 14:10 *3631*
great w press of the wrath of God. Rv 14:19 *3025b*
And the w press was trodden Rv 14:20 *3025b*
blood came out from the w press, Rv 14:20 *3025b*
cup of the w of His fierce wrath. Rv 16:19 *3631*
drunk with the w of her immorality. Rv 17:2 *3631*
w of the passion of her immorality, Rv 18:3 *3631*
and perfume and frankincense and w Rv 18:13 *3631*
w press of the fierce wrath of God, Rv 19:15 *3025b, 3631*

WINESKIN
have become like a w in the smoke, Ps 119:83 4997

WINESKINS
sacks on their donkeys, and w worn-out Jos 9:4 4997
These w which we filled were new, Jos 9:13 4997
Like new w it is about to burst. Jb 32:19 178
do *people* put new wine into old w; Mt 9:17 *779*
otherwise the w burst, and the Mt 9:17 *779*
pours out and the w are ruined; Mt 9:17 *779*
they put new wine into fresh w, Mt 9:17 *779*
No one puts new wine into old w; Mk 2:22 *779*
one puts new wine into fresh w." Mk 2:22 *779*
no one puts new wine into old w; Lk 5:37 *779*
new wine must be put into fresh w. Lk 5:38 *779*

WING
cubits *was* the one w of the cherub 1Ki 6:24 3671
cubits the other w of the cherub; 1Ki 6:24 3671
from the end of one w to the end 1Ki 6:24 3671
to the end of the other w *were* ten 1Ki 6:24 3671
so that the w of the one was 1Ki 6:27 3671
and the w of the other cherub was 1Ki 6:27 3671
the w of one, of five cubits, 2Ch 3:11 3671
of the house, and *its* other w, 2Ch 3:11 3671
touched the w of the other cherub. 2Ch 3:11 3671
The w of the other cherub, of 2Ch 3:12 3671
and *its* other w of five cubits was 2Ch 3:12 3671
to the w of the first cherub. 2Ch 3:12 3671
there was not one that flapped its w Is 10:14 3671
and on the w of abominations *will* Da 9:27 3671

WINGED
and every w bird after its kind; Gn 1:21 3671
'All the w insects that walk on Lv 11:20 5775
you may eat among all the w insects Lv 11:21 5775
'But all other w insects which are Lv 11:23 5775
any w bird that flies in the sky, Dt 4:17 3671
Even w fowl like the sand of the Ps 78:27 3671
Creeping things and w fowl; Ps 148:10 3671
and the w creature will make the Ec 10:20 3671

WINGS
and *how* I bore you on eagles' w, Ex 19:4 3671
shall have *their* w spread upward, Ex 25:20 3671
covering the mercy seat with their w Ex 25:20 3671
cherubim had *their* w spread upward Ex 37:9 3671
covering the mercy seat with their w Ex 37:9 3671
'Then he shall tear it by its w, Lv 1:17 3671
And all the teeming life with w are Dt 14:19 5775
He spread His w and caught them, Dt 32:11 3671
under whose w you have come to Ru 2:12 3671
He appeared on the w of the wind. 2Sa 22:11 3671
and the w of the cherubim were 1Ki 6:27 3671
So their w were touching each 1Ki 6:27 3671
under the w of the cherubim. 1Ki 8:6 3671
their w over the place of the ark, 1Ki 8:7 3671
cherubim that spread out *their* w 1Ch 28:18
The w of these cherubim extended 2Ch 3:13 3671
under the w of the cherubim. 2Ch 5:7 3671
their w over the place of the ark, 2Ch 5:8 3671
"The ostriches' w flap joyously Jb 39:13 3671
Stretching his w toward the south? Jb 39:26 3671
Hide me in the shadow of Your w Ps 17:8 3671
He sped upon the w of the wind. Ps 18:10 3671
refuge in the shadow of Your w. Ps 36:7 3671
"Oh, that I had w like a dove! Ps 55:6 83
in the shadow of Your w I will take Ps 57:1 3671
refuge in the shelter of Your w. Ps 61:4 3671
in the shadow of Your w I sing for Ps 63:7 3671
w of a dove covered with silver, Ps 68:13 3671
under His w you may seek refuge; Ps 91:4 3671
He walks upon the w of the wind; Ps 104:3 3671
If I take the w of the dawn, If I Ps 139:9 3671
wealth certainly makes itself w Like Pr 23:5 3671
above Him, each having six w: Is 6:2 3671
And the spread of its w will fill Is 8:8 3671
oh land of whirring w Which lies Is 18:1 3671

will mount up *with* **w** like eagles, **Is 40:31** 83
"Give **w** to Moab, For she will **Jer 48:9** 6731a
And spread out his **w** against Moab. **Jer 48:40** 3671
spread out His **w** against Bozrah; **Jer 49:22** 3671
of them had four faces and four **w**. **Ezk 1:6** 3671
Under their **w** on their four sides **Ezk 1:8** 3671
faces and **w** of the four of them, **Ezk 1:8** 3671
their **w** touched one another; **Ezk 1:9** 3671
Their **w** were spread out above; **Ezk 1:11** 3671
w *were stretched out* straight, **Ezk 1:23** 3671
each one also had two **w** covering **Ezk 1:23**
I also heard the sound of their **w** **Ezk 1:24** 3671
stood still, they dropped their **w**. **Ezk 1:24** 3671
stood still, they dropped their **w**. **Ezk 1:25** 3671
sound of the **w** of the living beings **Ezk 3:13** 3671
the sound of the **w** of the cherubim **Ezk 10:5** 3671
form of a man's hand under their **w**. **Ezk 10:8** 3671
their backs, their hands, their **w** and **Ezk 10:12** 3671
when the cherubim lifted up their **w** **Ezk 10:16** 3671
they lifted their **w** and rose up **Ezk 10:19** 3671
four faces and each one four **w**, **Ezk 10:21** 3671
beneath their **w** *was* the form of **Ezk 10:21** 3671
Then the cherubim lifted up their **w** **Ezk 11:22** 3671
"A great eagle with great **w**, **Ezk 17:3** 3671
with great **w** and much plumage; **Ezk 17:7** 3671
a lion and had *the* **w** of an eagle. **Da 7:4** 1611
looking until its **w** were plucked, **Da 7:4** 1611
had on its back four **w** of a bird; **Da 7:6** 1611
The wind wraps them in its **w**, **Hos 4:19** 3671
out with the wind in their **w**; **Zch 5:9** 3671
had **w** like the wings of a stork, **Zch 5:9** 3671
had wings like the **w** of a stork, **Zch 5:9** 3671
will rise with healing in its **w**; **Mal 4:2** 3671
gathers her chicks under her **w**, **Mt 23:37** *4420*
hen *gathers* her brood under her **w**, **Lk 13:34** *4420*
each one of them having six **w**, **Rv 4:8** *4420*
and the sound of their **w** was like **Rv 9:9** *4420*
But the two **w** of the great eagle **Rv 12:14** *4420*

WINGSPAN

The **w** of the cherubim *was* **2Ch 3:11** 3671

WINK

me without cause **w** maliciously. **Ps 35:19** 7169

WINKS

Who **w** with his eyes, who signals **Pr 6:13** 7169
He who **w** the eye causes trouble, **Pr 10:10** 7169
He who **w** his eyes *does so* to **Pr 16:30** 6095

WINNOW

"You will **w** them, and the wind **Is 41:16** 2219
not to **w** and not to cleanse, **Jer 4:11** 2219
"I will **w** them with a **Jer 15:7** 2219
to Babylon that they may **w** her **Jer 51:2** 2219

WINNOWED

has been **w** with shovel and fork. **Is 30:24** 2219

WINNOWING

a **w** fork At the gates of the land; **Jer 15:7** 2219
"His **w** fork is in His hand, **Mt 3:12** *4425*
"His **w** fork is in His hand to **Lk 3:17** *4425*

WINNOWS

he **w** barley at the threshing floor **Ru 3:2** 2219
A wise king **w** the wicked, And **Pr 20:26** 2219

WINS

life, And he who is wise **w** souls. **Pr 11:30** 3947

WINTER

cold and heat, And summer and **w**, **Gn 8:22** 2779
You have made summer and **w**. **Ps 74:17** 2779
'For behold, the **w** is past, The **SS 2:11** 5638
the king was sitting in the **w** house **Jer 36:22** 2779
"I will also smite the **w** house **Am 3:15** 2779
will be in summer as well as in **w**. **Zch 14:8** 2779
your flight will not be in the **w**, **Mt 24:20** *5494*
that it may not happen in the **w**. **Mk 13:18** *5494*
it was **w**, and Jesus was walking in **Jn 10:23** *5494*
northwest, and spend the **w** *there*. **Ac 27:12** *3914*
with you, or even spend the **w**, **1Co 16:6** *3914*
every effort to come before **w**. **2Tm 4:21** *5494*
have decided to spend the **w** there. **Ti 3:12** *3914*

WINTERED

ship which had **w** at the island, **Ac 28:11** *3914*

WINTERING

the harbor was not suitable for **w**, **Ac 27:12** *3915*

WIPE

w you off the face of the earth. **Dt 6:15** 8045
w Jerusalem as one wipes a dish, **2Ki 21:13** 4229a
and let us **w** them out as a nation, **Ps 83:4** 3582
GOD will **w** tears away from all faces **Is 25:8** 4229a
we **w** off *in protest* against you; **Lk 10:11** *631*
and to **w** them with the towel with **Jn 13:5** *1591*
w every tear from their eyes." **Rv 7:17** *1813*
and He will **w** away every tear **Rv 21:4** *1813*

WIPED

w out all remembrance of them. **Is 26:14** 6
"I have **w** out your transgressions **Is 44:22** 4229a
tears and **w** them with her hair. **Lk 7:44** *1591*
and **w** His feet with her hair, **Jn 11:2** *1591*
and **w** His feet with her hair; **Jn 12:3** *1591*
that your sins may be **w** away, **Ac 3:19** *1813*

WIPES

wipe Jerusalem as one **w** a dish, **2Ki 21:13** 4229a
She eats and **w** her mouth, And **Pr 30:20** 4229a
one who **w** out your transgressions **Is 43:25** 4229a

WIPING

w it and turning it upside down. **2Ki 21:13** 4229a
and kept **w** them with the hair of **Lk 7:38** *1591*

WISDOM

have endowed with the spirit of **w**, **Ex 28:3** 2451
him with the Spirit of God in **w**, **Ex 31:3** 2451
him with the Spirit of God, in **w**, **Ex 35:31** 2451
for that is your **w** and your **Dt 4:6** 2451
was filled with the spirit of **w**, **Dt 34:9** 2451
like the **w** of the angel of God, **2Sa 14:20** 2451
"So act according to your **w**, **1Ki 2:6** 2451
for they saw that the **w** of God was **1Ki 3:28** 2451
Now God gave Solomon **w** and very **1Ki 4:29** 2451
Solomon's **w** surpassed the **1Ki 4:30** 2451
the **w** of all the sons of the east **1Ki 4:30** 2451
the east and all the **w** of Egypt. **1Ki 4:30** 2451
peoples to hear the **w** of Solomon, **1Ki 4:34** 2451
the earth who had heard of his **w**. **1Ki 4:34** 2451
The LORD gave **w** to Solomon, **1Ki 5:12** 2451
and he was filled with **w** and **1Ki 7:14** 2451
perceived all the **w** of Solomon, **1Ki 10:4** 2451
land about your words and your **w**. **1Ki 10:6** 2451
You exceed *in* **w** and prosperity the **1Ki 10:7** 2451
you continually *and* hear your **w**. **1Ki 10:8** 2451
of the earth in riches and in **w**. **1Ki 10:23** 2451
to hear his **w** which God had put in **1Ki 10:24** 2451
and whatever he did, and his **w**, **1Ki 11:41** 2451
"Give me now **w** and knowledge, **2Ch 1:10** 2451
for yourself **w** and knowledge that **2Ch 1:11** 2451
w and knowledge have been granted **2Ch 1:12** 2451
Sheba had seen the **w** of Solomon, **2Ch 9:3** 2451
land about your words and your **w**. **2Ch 9:5** 2451
the half of the greatness of your **w** **2Ch 9:6** 2451
you continually and hear your **w** **2Ch 9:7** 2451
of the earth in riches and **w**. **2Ch 9:22** 2451
to hear his **w** which God had put in **2Ch 9:23** 2451
according to the **w** of your God **Ezr 7:25** 2452
They die, yet without **w**.' **Jb 4:21** 2451
And show you the secrets of **w**! **Jb 11:6** 2451
For sound **w** has two sides. **Jb 11:6** 8454
people, And with you **w** will die! **Jb 12:2** 2451
"**W** is with aged men, *With* long **Jb 12:12** 2451
"With Him are **w** and might; **Jb 12:13** 2451
"With Him are strength and sound **w**, **Jb 12:16** 8454
And that it would become your **w**! **Jb 13:5** 2451
of God, And limit **w** to yourself? **Jb 15:8** 2451
you have given to *one* without **w**! **Jb 26:3** 2451
"But where can **w** be found? **Jb 28:12** 2451
the acquisition of **w** is above *that of* **Jb 28:18** 2451
"Where then does **w** come from? **Jb 28:20** 2451
the fear of the Lord, that is **w**; **Jb 28:28** 2451
increased years should teach **w**. **Jb 32:7** 2451
Do not say, 'We have found **w**; **Jb 32:13** 2451
silent, and I will teach you **w**." **Jb 33:33** 2451
And his words are without **w**. **Jb 34:35** 7919a
has put **w** in the innermost being Or **Jb 38:36** 2451
"Who can count the clouds by **w**, **Jb 38:37** 2451
Because God has made her forget **w**, **Jb 39:17** 2451
mouth of the righteous utters **w**, **Ps 37:30** 2451
My mouth will speak **w**; **Ps 49:3** 2451
part You will make me know **w**. **Ps 51:6** 2451
may present to You a heart of **w**. **Ps 90:12** 2451
In **w** You have made them all; **Ps 104:24** 2451
That he might teach his elders **w**. **Ps 105:22** 2449
of the LORD is the beginning of **w**; **Ps 111:10** 2451
To know **w** and instruction, To **Pr 1:2** 2451
Fools despise **w** and instruction. **Pr 1:7** 2451
W shouts in the street, She lifts **Pr 1:20** 2451
Make your ear attentive to **w**, **Pr 2:2** 2451
For the LORD gives **w**; **Pr 2:6** 2451
stores up sound **w** for the upright; **Pr 2:7** 8454
For **w** will enter your heart And **Pr 2:10** 2451
blessed is the man who finds **w** And **Pr 3:13** 2451
The LORD by **w** founded the earth, **Pr 3:19** 2451
Keep sound **w** and discretion, **Pr 3:21** 8454
Acquire **w**! Acquire understanding! **Pr 4:5** 2451
"The beginning of **w** *is:* **Pr 4:7** 2451
beginning of wisdom *is:* Acquire **w**; **Pr 4:7** 2451
have directed you in the way of **w**; **Pr 4:11** 2451
My son, give attention to my **w**, **Pr 5:1** 2451
Say to **w**, "You are my sister," **Pr 7:4** 2451
Does not **w** call, And understanding **Pr 8:1** 2451
And, O fools, understand **w**. **Pr 8:5** 3820
"For **w** is better than jewels; **Pr 8:11** 2451
"I, **w**, dwell with prudence, And I **Pr 8:12** 2451
"Counsel is mine and sound **w**; **Pr 8:14** 8454
W has built her house, She has **Pr 9:1** 2451
of the LORD is the beginning of **w**, **Pr 9:10** 2451
of the discerning, **w** is found, **Pr 10:13** 2451
so is **w** to a man of understanding. **Pr 10:23** 2451
mouth of the righteous flows with **w**, **Pr 10:31** 2451
But with the humble is **w**. **Pr 11:2** 2451
w is with those who receive counsel. **Pr 13:10** 2451
A scoffer seeks **w** and *finds* none, **Pr 14:6** 2451
The **w** of the sensible is to **Pr 14:8** 2451
W rests in the heart of one who **Pr 14:33** 2451
the LORD is the instruction for **w**, **Pr 15:33** 2451
better it is to get **w** than gold! **Pr 16:16** 2451
in the hand of a fool to buy **w**, **Pr 17:16** 2451
W is in the presence of the one **Pr 17:24** 2451
He quarrels against all sound **w**. **Pr 18:1** 8454
fountain of **w** is a bubbling brook. **Pr 18:4** 2451
He who gets **w** loves his own soul; **Pr 19:8** 3820
There is no **w** and no understanding **Pr 21:30** 2451
he will despise the **w** of your words. **Pr 23:9** 7922
Get **w** and instruction and **Pr 23:23** 2451
By **w** a house is built, And by **Pr 24:3** 2451
W is *too* exalted for a fool, He does **Pr 24:7** 2451
Know *that* **w** is thus for your soul; **Pr 24:14** 2451
who loves **w** makes his father glad, **Pr 29:3** 2451
The rod and reproof give **w**, **Pr 29:15** 2451
Neither have I learned **w**, **Pr 30:3** 2451
She opens her mouth in **w**, **Pr 31:26** 2451
set my mind to seek and explore by **w** **Ec 1:13** 2451
I have magnified and increased **w** **Ec 1:16** 2451
a wealth of **w** and knowledge." **Ec 1:16** 2451
And I set my mind to know **w** and **Ec 1:17** 2451
in much **w** there is much grief, **Ec 1:18** 2451
My **w** also stood by me. **Ec 2:9** 2451
So I turned to consider **w**, **Ec 2:12** 2451
And I saw that **w** excels folly as **Ec 2:13** 2451
is a man who has labored with **w**, **Ec 2:21** 2451
has given **w** and knowledge and joy, **Ec 2:26** 2451
from **w** that you ask about this. **Ec 7:10** 2451
W along with an inheritance is **Ec 7:11** 2451
For **w** is protection *just as* money **Ec 7:12** 2451
w preserves the lives of its possessors. **Ec 7:12** 2451
W strengthens a wise man more than **Ec 7:19** 2451
I tested all this with **w**, **Ec 7:23** 2451
and to seek **w** and an explanation, **Ec 7:25** 2451
A man's **w** illumines him and causes **Ec 8:1** 2451
When I gave my heart to know **w** and **Ec 8:16** 2451
activity or planning or knowledge or **w** **Ec 9:10** 2451
I came to see as **w** under the sun, **Ec 9:13** 2451
he delivered the city by his **w**. **Ec 9:15** 2451
"**W** is better than strength." **Ec 9:16** 2451
But the **w** of the poor man is **Ec 9:16** 2451
W is better than weapons of war, **Ec 9:18** 2451
is weightier than **w** *and* honor. **Ec 10:1** 2451
W has the advantage of giving **Ec 10:10** 2451
of my hand and by my **w** I did *this*, **Is 10:13** 2451
The spirit of **w** and understanding, **Is 11:2** 2451
counsel wonderful and *His* **w** great. **Is 28:29** 8454
And the **w** of their wise men will **Is 29:14** 2451
times, A wealth of salvation, **w** and **Is 33:6** 2451
me,' Your **w** and your knowledge, **Is 47:10** 2451
And what kind of **w** do they have? **Jer 8:9** 2451
"Let not a wise man boast of his **w**, **Jer 9:23** 2451
established the world by His **w**; **Jer 10:12** 2451
"Is there no longer any **w** in Teman? **Jer 49:7** 2451
Has their **w** decayed? **Jer 49:7** 2451
established the world by His **w**, **Jer 51:15** 2451
"By your **w** and understanding You **Ezk 28:4** 2451
"By your great **w**, by your trade **Ezk 28:5** 2451
Against the beauty of your **w** **Ezk 28:7** 2451
Full of **w** and perfect in beauty. **Ezk 28:12** 2451
You corrupted your **w** by reason of **Ezk 28:17** 2451
intelligence in every *branch of* **w**, **Da 1:4** 2451
every *branch of* literature and **w**; **Da 1:17** 2451
As for every matter of **w** and **Da 1:20** 2451
For **w** and power belong to Him. **Da 2:20** 2452
He gives **w** to wise men And **Da 2:21** 2452
You have given me **w** and power; **Da 2:23** 2452
for any **w** residing in me more than **Da 2:30** 2452
and **w** like the wisdom of the gods **Da 5:11** 2452
w of the gods were found in him. **Da 5:11** 2452
w have been found in you. **Da 5:14** 2452
it is sound **w** to fear Your name: **Mi 6:9** 8454
w is vindicated by her deeds." **Mt 11:19** *4678*
earth to hear the **w** of Solomon; **Mt 12:42** *4678*
"Where *did* this man *get* this **w** and **Mt 13:54** *4678*
and what is *this* **w** given to Him, **Mk 6:2** *4678*
become strong, increasing in **w**; **Lk 2:40** *4678*
kept increasing in **w** and stature, **Lk 2:52** *4678*
"Yet **w** is vindicated by all her **Lk 7:35** *4678*
earth to hear the **w** of Solomon; **Lk 11:31** *4678*
reason also the **w** of God said, **Lk 11:49** *4678*
for I will give you utterance and **w** **Lk 21:15** *4678*
full of the Spirit and of **w**, **Ac 6:3** *4678*
they were unable to cope with the **w** **Ac 6:10** *4678*
and **w** in the sight of Pharaoh, **Ac 7:10** *4678*
of the **w** and knowledge of God! **Ro 11:33** *4678*
"I WILL DESTROY THE **W** OF THE WISE, **1Co 1:19** *4678*
God made foolish the **w** of the world **1Co 1:20** *4678*
For since in the **w** of God the **1Co 1:21** *4678*
the world through its **w** did not **1Co 1:21** *4678*
signs and Greeks search for **w**; **1Co 1:22** *4678*
the power of God and the **w** of God. **1Co 1:24** *4678*
who became to us **w** from God, **1Co 1:30** *4678*
superiority of speech or of **w**, **1Co 2:1** *4678*
were not in persuasive words of **w**, **1Co 2:4** *4678*
would not rest on the **w** of men, **1Co 2:5** *4678*
w among those who are mature; **1Co 2:6** *4678*
a **w**, however, not of this age nor **1Co 2:6** *4678*
but we speak God's **w** in a mystery, **1Co 2:7** *4678*
the hidden **w** which God **1Co 2:7**
the **w** which none of the rulers of **1Co 2:8**
not in words taught by human **w**, **1Co 2:13** *4678*
For the **w** of this world is foolishness **1Co 3:19** *4678*
the word of **w** through the Spirit, **1Co 12:8** *4678*
not in fleshly **w** but in the grace of **2Co 1:12** *4678*
In all **w** and insight **Eph 1:8** *4678*
may give to you a spirit of **w** and **Eph 1:17** *4678*
the manifold **w** of God might now **Eph 3:10** *4678*
all spiritual **w** and understanding, **Col 1:9** *4678*
and teaching every man with all **w**, **Col 1:28** *4678*
the treasures of **w** and knowledge. **Col 2:3** *4678*
the appearance of **w** in self-made **Col 2:23** *4678*
with all **w** teaching and **Col 3:16** *4678*
Conduct yourselves with **w** toward **Col 4:5** *4678*
w that leads to salvation through faith **2Tm 3:15** *4679*
But if any of you lacks **w**, **Jas 1:5** *4678*
his deeds in the gentleness of **w**. **Jas 3:13** *4678*
This **w** is not that which comes **Jas 3:15** *4678*
the **w** from above is first pure, **Jas 3:17** *4678*
according to the **w** given him, **2Pe 3:15** *4678*
to receive power and riches and **w** **Rv 5:12** *4678*
blessing and glory and **w** and **Rv 7:12** *4678*
Here is **w**. Let him who has **Rv 13:18** *4678*
"Here is the mind which has **w**. **Rv 17:9** *4678*

WISE

tree was desirable to make *one* **w**, **Gn 3:6** 7919a
of Egypt, and all its **w** men. **Gn 41:8** 2450
look for a man discerning and **w**, **Gn 41:33** 2450

so discerning and w as you are. Gn 41:39 2450
for the w men and the sorcerers, Ex 7:11 2450
'Choose w and discerning and Dt 1:13 2450
tribes, w and experienced men, Dt 1:15 2450
is a w and understanding people.' Dt 4:6 2450
for a bribe blinds the eyes of the w Dt 16:19 2450
"Would that they were w, Dt 32:29 2449
"Her w princesses would answer Jg 5:29 2450
to Tekoa and brought a w woman 2Sa 14:2 2450
But my lord is w, like the wisdom 2Sa 14:20 2450
a w woman called from the city, 2Sa 20:16 2450
unpunished, for you are a w man; 1Ki 2:9 2450
given you a w and discerning heart, 1Ki 3:12 2450
a w son over this great people." 1Ki 5:7 2450
who has given King David a w son, 2Ch 2:12 2450
Then the king said to the w men Es 1:13 2450
Then his w men and Zeresh his wife Es 6:13 2450
"He captures the w by their own Jb 5:13 2450
"W in heart and mighty in Jb 9:4 2450
"Should a w man answer with windy Jb 15:2 2450
What w men have told, And have not Jb 15:18 2450
I do not find a w man among you. Jb 17:10 2450
Or a w man be useful to himself? Jb 22:2 7919a
abundant *in years* may not be w, Jb 32:9 2449
"Hear my words, you w men, Jb 34:2 2450
to me, And a w man who hears me, Jb 34:34 2450
regard any who are w of heart." Jb 37:24 2450
LORD is sure, making w the simple. Ps 19:7 2449
has ceased to be w *and* to do good. Ps 36:3 7919a
For he sees *that even* w men die; Ps 49:10 2450
Who is w? Let him give heed Ps 107:43 2450
receive instruction in w behavior, Pr 1:3 7919a
A w man will hear and increase in Pr 1:5 2450
will acquire w counsel, Pr 1:5 8458
words of the w and their riddles. Pr 1:6 2450
Do not be w in your own eyes; Pr 3:7 2450
The w will inherit honor, But Pr 3:35 2450
Observe her ways and be w, Pr 6:6 2449
"Heed instruction and be w, Pr 8:33 2449
or he will hate you, Reprove a w man Pr 9:8 2450
Give *instruction* to a w man and Pr 9:9 2450
If you are w, you are wise for Pr 9:12 2449
are wise, you are w for yourself, Pr 9:12 2449
A w son makes a father glad, But a Pr 10:1 2450
The w of heart will receive Pr 10:8 2450
W men store up knowledge, But with Pr 10:14 2450
he who restrains his lips is w. Pr 10:19 7919a
life, And he who is w wins souls. Pr 11:30 2450
But a w man is he who listens to Pr 12:15 2450
tongue of the w brings healing." Pr 12:18 2450
A w son *accepts his* father's Pr 13:1 2450
The teaching of the w is a fountain Pr 13:14 2450
who walks with w men will be wise, Pr 13:20 2450
who walks with wise men will be w, Pr 13:20 2449
The w woman builds her house, But Pr 14:1 2450
lips of the w will protect them. Pr 14:3 2450
A w man is cautious and turns away Pr 14:16 2450
crown of the w is their riches, Pr 14:24 2450
tongue of the w makes knowledge Pr 15:2 2450
lips of the w spread knowledge, Pr 15:7 2450
him, He will not go to the w. Pr 15:12 2450
A w son makes a father glad, But a Pr 15:20 2450
of life *leads* upward for the w That Pr 15:24 7919a
reproof Will dwell among the w. Pr 15:31 2450
But a w man will appease it. Pr 16:14 2450
The w in heart will be called Pr 16:21 2450
heart of the w instructs his mouth Pr 16:23 2450
he keeps silent, is considered w; Pr 17:28 2450
the ear of the w seeks knowledge. Pr 18:15 2450
may be w the rest of your days. Pr 19:20 2449
is intoxicated by it is not w. Pr 20:1 2449
And make war by w guidance. Pr 20:18 8458
A w king winnows the wicked, And Pr 20:26 2450
is punished, the naive becomes w; Pr 21:11 7919a
But when the w is instructed, he Pr 21:11 2449
and oil in the dwelling of the w, Pr 21:20 2450
A w man scales the city of the Pr 21:22 2450
ear and hear the words of the w, Pr 22:17 2450
My son, if your heart is w, Pr 23:15 2449
Listen, my son, and be w, Pr 23:19 2449
he who sires a w son will be glad Pr 23:24 2450
A w man is strong, And a man of Pr 24:5 2450
by w guidance you will wage war, Pr 24:6 8458
These also are sayings of the w. Pr 24:23 2450
a w reprover to a listening ear. Pr 25:12 2450
That he not be w in his own eyes. Pr 26:5 2450
you see a man w in his own eyes? Pr 26:12 2450
Be w, my son, and make my heart Pr 27:11 2449
The rich man is w in his own eyes, Pr 28:11 2450
aflame, But w men turn away anger. Pr 29:8 2450
When a w man has a controversy Pr 29:9 2450
temper, But a w man holds it back. Pr 29:11 2450
earth, But they are exceedingly w: Pr 30:24 2450
The w man's eyes are in his head, Ec 2:14 2450
then have I been extremely w?" Ec 2:15 2449
lasting remembrance of the w man Ec 2:16 2450
the w man and the fool alike die! Ec 2:16 2450
he will be a w man or a fool? Ec 2:19 2450
yet w lad is better than an old Ec 4:13 2450
does the w man have over the fool? Ec 6:8 2450
the w is in the house of mourning, Ec 7:4 2450
to listen to the rebuke of a w man Ec 7:5 2450
For oppression makes a w man mad, Ec 7:7 2450
righteous and do not be overly w. Ec 7:16 2449
Wisdom strengthens a w man more Ec 7:19 2450
and I said, "I will be w," Ec 7:23 2449
Who is like the w man and who Ec 8:1 2450
for a w heart knows the proper Ec 8:5 2450
and though the w man should say, Ec 8:17 2450
it that righteous men, w men, Ec 9:1 2450
and neither is bread to the w nor Ec 9:11 2450
there was found in it a poor w man Ec 9:15 2450
The words of the w heard in Ec 9:17 2450
A w man's heart *directs him* toward Ec 10:2 2450
the mouth of a w man are gracious, Ec 10:12 2450
In addition to being a w man, Ec 12:9 2450
The words of w men are like goads, Ec 12:11 2450
those who are w in their own eyes And Is 5:21 2450
"I am a son of the w, Is 19:11 2450
Well then, where are your w men? Is 19:12 2450
wisdom of their w men will perish, Is 29:14 2450
He also is w and will bring disaster And Is 31:2 2450
Causing w men to draw back And Is 44:25 2450
'We are w, And the law of the LORD Jer 8:8 2450
"The w men are put to shame, They Jer 8:9 2450
w man that may understand this? Jer 9:12 2450
not a w man boast of his wisdom, Jer 9:23 2450
all the w men of the nations And Jer 10:7 2450
her officials and her w men! Jer 50:35 2450
her princes and her w men drunk, Jer 51:57 2450
Your w men, O Tyre, were aboard; Ezk 27:8 2450
"The elders of Gebal and her w men Ezk 27:9 2450
destroy all the w men of Babylon. Da 2:12 2445
that the w men should be slain; Da 2:13 2445
to slay the w men of Babylon; Da 2:14 2445
the rest of the w men of Babylon. Da 2:18 2445
He gives wisdom to w men And Da 2:21 2445
to destroy the w men of Babylon; Da 2:24 2445
not destroy the w men of Babylon! Da 2:24 2445
king has inquired, neither w men, Da 2:27 2445
over all the w men of Babylon. Da 2:48 2445
presence all the w men of Babylon, Da 4:6 2445
none of the w men of my kingdom Da 4:18 2445
and said to the w men of Babylon, Da 5:7 2445
Then all the king's w men came in, Da 5:8 2445
"Just now the w men *and* the Da 5:15 2445
He is not a w son, For it is not Hos 13:13 2450
Whoever is w, let him understand Hos 14:9 2450
"Destroy w men from Edom And Ob 1:8 2450
and Sidon, though they are very w. Zch 9:2 2449
them, may be compared to a w man who Mt 7:24 5429
have hidden these things from *the* w Mt 11:25 4680
prophets and w men and scribes; Mt 23:34 4680
have hidden these things from *the* w Lk 10:21 4680
both to the w and to the foolish. Ro 1:14 4680
Professing to be w, Ro 1:22 4680
not be w in your own estimation Ro 11:25 5429
not be w in your own estimation. Ro 12:16 5429
want you to be w in what is good and Ro 16:19 4680
to the only w God, through Jesus Ro 16:27 4680
WILL DESTROY THE WISDOM OF THE W, 1Co 1:19 4680
Where is the w man? 1Co 1:20 4680
not many w according to the flesh, 1Co 1:26 4680
of the world to shame the w, 1Co 1:27 4680
like a w master builder I laid a 1Co 3:10 4680
thinks that he is w in this age, 1Co 3:18 4680
so that he may become w. 1Co 3:18 4680
CATCHES THE W IN THEIR CRAFTINESS 1Co 3:19 4680
KNOWS THE REASONINGS of the w, 1Co 3:20 4680
there is not among you one w man 1Co 6:5 4680
I speak as to w men; 1Co 10:15 5429
For you, being *so* w, 2Co 11:19 5429
walk, not as unwise men but as w, Eph 5:15 4680
among you is w and understanding? Jas 3:13 4680

WISEHEARTED

foolish will be servant to the w. Pr 11:29 2450

WISELY

"Come, let us deal w with them, Ex 1:10 2449
more w than all the servants of Saul. 1Sa 18:30 7919a
woman w came to all the people. 2Sa 20:22 2451
He acted w and distributed 2Ch 11:23 995
in summer is a son who acts w, Pr 10:5 7919a
is toward a servant who acts w, Pr 14:35 7919a
A servant who acts w will rule Pr 17:2 7919a
he who walks w will be delivered. Pr 28:26 2451
while my mind was guiding *me* w, Ec 2:3 2451
labored by acting w under the sun. Ec 2:19 2449
And He will reign as king and act w Jer 23:5 7919a

WISER

For he was w than all men, than 1Ki 4:31 2449
w than the birds of the heavens?' Jb 35:11 2449
make me w than my enemies, Ps 119:98 2449
wise man and he will be still w, Pr 9:9 2449
The sluggard is w in his own eyes Pr 26:16 2450
Behold, you are w than Daniel; Ezk 28:3 2450
foolishness of God is w than men, 1Co 1:25 4680

WISEST

advice of Pharaoh's w advisers has Is 19:11 2450

WISH

"If it is your w *for me* to bury Gn 23:8 5315
'But if he should ever w *to* Lv 27:13
the one who consecrates it should w Lv 27:15
should ever w to redeem the field, Lv 27:19
'Let them marry whom they w; Nu 36:6 2896a, 5869
and do to them whatever you w. Jg 19:24 2896a, 5869
if he does not w to redeem you, Ru 3:13 2654a
the king said, "What do you w?" 1Ki 1:16
"Ask what *you* w me to give you." 1Ki 3:5
"I w that my master were with the 2Ki 5:3 305
place where you w to go to reside. Jer 42:22 2654a
be done for you as you w." Mt 15:28 2309
if You w, I will make three Mt 17:4 2309
but if you w to enter into life, Mt 19:17 2309
"If you w to be complete, go *and* Mt 19:21 2309
but I w to give to this last man Mt 20:14 2309
do what I w with what is my own? Mt 20:15 2309
He said to her, "What do you w?" Mt 20:21 2309
poor with you, and whenever you w Mk 14:7 2309
me, and I give it to whomever I w. Lk 4:6 2309
how I w it were already kindled! Lk 12:49 2309
so that those who w to come Lk 16:26 2309
"Do you w to get well?" Jn 5:6 2309
"Sir, we w to see Jesus." Jn 12:21 2309
abide in you, ask whatever you w, Jn 15:7 2309
do you w then that I release for Jn 18:39 1014
you where you do not w to *go*." Jn 21:18 2309
this idle babbler w to say?" Ac 17:18 2309
And Paul *said*, "I would w to Ac 26:29 2172
could w that I myself were accursed, Ro 9:3 2172
I w that you had become kings so 1Co 4:8 3785
Yet I w that all men were even as 1Co 7:7 2309
I w that you all spoke in tongues, 1Co 14:5 2309
For I do not w to see you now *just* 1Co 16:7 2309
Now, brethren, we w *to* make 2Co 8:1
for I do not w to seem as if I 2Co 10:9
I w that you would bear with me in 2Co 11:1 3785
For if I do w to boast I will not 2Co 12:6 2309
I may find you to be not what I w 2Co 12:20 2309
found by you to be not what you w; 2Co 12:20 2309
but they w to shut you out so Ga 4:17 2309
but I could w to be present with Ga 4:20 2309
I w that those who are troubling you Ga 5:12 3785
I w that you were cold or hot. Rv 3:15 3785

WISHED

"If one w to dispute with Him, He Jb 9:3 2654a
whomever he w he killed and Da 5:19 6634
and whomever he w he spared alive; Da 5:19 6634
and whomever he w he elevated and Da 5:19 6634
and whomever he w he humbled. Da 5:19 6634
but did to him whatever they w. Mt 17:12 2309
a king who w to settle accounts Mt 18:23 2309
they did to him whatever they w, Mk 9:13 2309
many prophets and kings w to see Lk 10:24 2309
knew that they w to question Him, Jn 16:19 2309
yourself and walk wherever you w; Jn 21:18 2309
from the stern and w for daybreak. Ac 27:29 2172
God gives it a body just as He w, 1Co 15:38 2309
whom I w to keep with me, so that Phm 1:13 1014

WISHES

call the girl and consult her w." Gn 24:57 6310
man w to redeem part of his tithe, Lv 27:31 1350
and he w *to* make an offering by Nu 15:14
shall let her go wherever she w; Dt 21:14 5315
apart, *Even* the w of my heart. Jb 17:11 4180
He turns it wherever He w. Pr 21:1 2654a
And bestows it on whom He w And Da 4:17 6634
and bestows it on whomever He w. Da 4:25 6634
and bestows it on whomever He w.' Da 4:32 6634
He sets over it whomever He w. Da 5:21 6634
"If anyone w to come after Me, Mt 16:24 2309
"For whoever w to save his life Mt 16:25 2309
but whoever w to become great Mt 20:26 2309
and whoever w to be first among Mt 20:27 2309
"If anyone w to come after Me, Mk 8:34 2309
"For whoever w to save his life Mk 8:35 2309
but whoever w to become great Mk 10:43 2309
and whoever w to be first among Mk 10:44 2309
after drinking old *wine* w for new; Lk 5:39 2309
"If anyone w to come after Me, Lk 9:23 2309
"For whoever w to save his life Lk 9:24 2309
"The wind blows where it w and Jn 3:8 2309
Son also gives life to whom He w. Jn 5:21 2309
must be so, let him do what he w, 1Co 7:36 2309
free to be married to whom she w, 1Co 7:39 2309
Therefore whoever w to be a friend Jas 4:4 1014
let the one who w take the water Rv 22:17 2309

WISHING

W to satisfy the crowd, Pilate Mk 15:15 1014
standing outside, w to see You." Lk 8:20 2309
But w to justify himself, he said Lk 10:29 2309
w to know for certain why he had Ac 22:30 1014
and w to do the Jews a favor, Ac 24:27 2309
Festus, w to do the Jews a favor, Ac 25:9 2309
not w for any to perish but for 2Pe 3:9 1014

WISTFULLY

My eyes look w to the heights; Is 38:14 1809

WITCHCRAFT

divination, one who practices w, Dt 18:10 6049a
listen to those who practice w and Dt 18:14 6049a
practiced w and used divination, 2Ki 21:6 6049a
and he practiced w, 2Ch 33:6 6049a

WITCHCRAFTS

Jezebel and her w are so many?" 2Ki 9:22 3785

WITHDRAW

For Joshua did not w his hand with Jos 8:26 7725
Saul said to the priest, "W your hand 1Sa 14:19 622
fiercest battle and w from him, 2Sa 11:15 7725
so that he will w from me." 1Ki 15:19 5927
I have done wrong. W from me; 2Ki 18:14 7725
so that he will w from me." 2Ch 16:3 5927
W from me that I may have a little Jb 10:20 7896
not w His eyes from the righteous; Jb 36:7 1639
Why do You w Your hand, even Your Ps 74:11 7725
When the sun rises they w And Ps 104:22 622
that *the enemy* will w from us." Jer 21:2 5927
W into your sheath; Jer 47:6 622
therefore I will also w, Ezk 5:11 1639
and w His burning anger so that we Jon 3:9 7725
began to w and hold himself aloof, Ga 2:12 5288

WITHDRAWN

cloud had w from over the tent, Nu 12:10 5493
should the name of our father be w Nu 27:4 1639

their inheritance will be **w** from	Nu 36:3	1639
thus it will be **w** from our	Nu 36:3	1639
so their inheritance will be **w**	Nu 36:4	1639
blessed of the LORD who has not **w**	Ru 2:20	5800a
and the men of Israel had **w**.	2Sa 23:9	5927
has He in anger **w** His compassion?	Ps 77:9	7092
w My peace from this people,"	Jer 16:5	622
He has **w** from them.	Hos 5:6	2502a

WITHDRAWS

"If he **w** into a city, then	2Sa 17:13	622

WITHDREW

of Israel **w** from following David	2Sa 20:2	5927
You **w** all Your fury; You turned away	Ps 85:3	622
"But I **w** My hand and acted for	Ezk 20:22	7725
into custody, He **w** into Galilee;	Mt 4:12	*402*
aware of *this,* **w** from there.	Mt 12:15	*402*
He **w** from there in a boat	Mt 14:13	*402*
and **w** into the district of Tyre	Mt 15:21	*402*
Jesus **w** to the sea with His disciples;	Mk 3:7	*402*
He **w** by Himself to a city called	Lk 9:10	*5298*
And He **w** from them about a stone's	Lk 22:41	*645*
w again to the mountain by Himself	Jn 6:15	*402*
of this many of His disciples **w** and	Jn 6:66	*3694, 565*
he **w** from them and took away the	Ac 19:9	*868*

WITHER

The flame will **w** his shoots, And	Jb 15:30	3001
season And its leaf does not **w**;	Ps 1:3	5034b
will **w** quickly like the grass And	Ps 37:2	4448c
And I **w** away like grass.	Ps 102:11	3001
All their hosts will also **w** away	Is 34:4	5034b
merely blows on them, and they **w**,	Is 40:24	3001
hills And **w** all their vegetation;	Is 42:15	3001
And all of us **w** like a leaf, And	Is 64:6	5034b
fig tree, And the leaf will **w**;	Jer 8:13	5034b
vegetation of the countryside to **w**?	Jer 12:4	3001
that all its sprouting leaves **w**?	Ezk 17:9	3001
Will it not completely **w** as soon	Ezk 17:10	3001
w on the beds where it grew?	Ezk 17:10	3001
Their leaves will not **w** and	Ezk 47:12	5034b
Bashan and Carmel **w**;	Na 1:4	535
The blossoms of Lebanon **w**.	Na 1:4	535
"How did the fig tree **w** *all* at once?"	Mt 21:20	*3583*

WITHERED

and lo, seven ears, **w**,	Gn 41:23	6798
smitten like grass and has **w** away,	Ps 102:4	3001
Surely the grass is **w**,	Is 15:6	3001
For the fields of Heshbon have **w**,	Is 16:8	535
shriveled on their bones, It is **w**,	La 4:8	3001
branch was torn off So that it **w**;	Ezk 19:12	3001
it attacked the plant and it **w**.	Jon 4:7	3001
consumed As stubble completely **w**.	Na 1:10	3002
His arm will be totally **w** And	Zch 11:17	3001
a man *was there* whose hand was **w**.	Mt 12:10	*3584*
they had no root, they **w** away.	Mt 13:6	*3583*
And at once the fig tree **w**.	Mt 21:19	*3583*
a man was there whose hand was **w**.	Mk 3:1	*3583*
said to the man with the **w** hand,	Mk 3:3	*3584*
because it had no root, it **w** away.	Mk 4:6	*3583*
the fig tree **w** from the roots *up.*	Mk 11:20	*3583*
fig tree which You cursed has **w**."	Mk 11:21	*3583*
man there whose right hand was **w**.	Lk 6:6	*3584*
said to the man with the **w** hand,	Lk 6:8	*3584*
as soon as it grew up, it **w** away,	Lk 8:6	*3583*
who were sick, blind, lame, and **w**,	Jn 5:3	*3584*

WITHERS

Yet it **w** before any *other* plant.	Jb 8:12	3001
Like a flower he comes forth and **w**.	Jb 14:2	4448c
evening it fades and **w** away.	Ps 90:6	3001
Which **w** before it grows up;	Ps 129:6	3001
The earth mourns *and* **w**,	Is 24:4	5034b
withers, the world fades *and* **w**,	Is 24:4	5034b
away, Lebanon is shamed *and* **w**;	Is 33:9	7060
away As a leaf **w** from the vine,	Is 34:4	5034b
Or as *one* **w** from the fig tree.	Is 34:4	5034b
The grass **w**, the flower fades,	Is 40:7	3001
The grass **w**, the flower fades, But	Is 40:8	3001
and cut off its fruit, so that it **w**	Ezk 17:9	3001
a scorching wind and **w** the grass;	Jas 1:11	*3583*
THE GRASS **W**, AND THE FLOWER FALLS	1Pe 1:24	*3583*

WITHHELD

since you have not **w** your son,	Gn 22:12	2820
thing and have not **w** your son,	Gn 22:16	2820
who has **w** from you the fruit of	Gn 30:2	4513
has **w** nothing from me except you,	Gn 39:9	2820
from the hungry you have **w** bread.	Jb 22:7	4513
From the wicked their light is **w**,	Jb 38:15	4513
have not **w** the request of his lips.	Ps 21:2	4513
"Therefore the showers have been **w**,	Jer 3:3	4513
your sins have **w** good from you.	Jer 5:25	4513
offering and the drink offering Are **w**	Jl 1:13	4513
I **w** the rain from you While *there were*	Am 4:7	4513
of you the sky has **w** its dew and	Hg 1:10	3607
and the earth has **w** its produce.	Hg 1:10	3607
and which has been **w** by you,	Jas 5:4	*879b*

WITHHOLD

for he will not **w** me from you."	2Sa 13:13	4513
You did not **w** from their mouth,	Ne 9:20	4513
You, O LORD, will not **w** Your	Ps 40:11	3607
No good thing does He **w** from	Ps 84:11	4513
Do not **w** good from those to whom	Pr 3:27	4513
not **w** my heart from any pleasure,	Ec 2:10	4513
And to **w** drink from the thirsty.	Is 32:6	2637
So the overseer continued to **w**	Da 1:16	5375
not **w** your shirt from him either.	Lk 6:29	*2967*

WITHHOLDS

is one who **w** what is justly due,	Pr 11:24	2820
He who **w** grain, the people will	Pr 11:26	4513
He who **w** his rod hates his son,	Pr 13:24	2820

WITHIN

are fifty righteous **w** the city;	Gn 18:24	8432
Sodom fifty righteous **w** the city,	Gn 18:26	8432
that were **w** all the confines of	Gn 23:17	
children struggled together **w** her;	Gn 25:22	7130
w three more days Pharaoh will	Gn 40:13	
w three more days Pharaoh will	Gn 40:19	
sacrifice to your God **w** the land."	Ex 8:25	
of the testimony there **w** the veil;	Ex 26:33	1004
pigeons which are **w** his means,	Lv 14:22	5381
pigeons, which are **w** his means.	Lv 14:30	5381
him **w** the space of a full year,	Lv 25:30	5704
only they must marry **w** the family	Nu 36:6	
of war perished from **w** the camp,	Dt 2:14	7130
to destroy them from **w** the camp until	Dt 2:15	7130
from **w** *another* nation by trials,	Dt 4:34	7130
the Levite who is **w** your gates,	Dt 12:12	
and eat meat **w** any of your gates,	Dt 12:15	
are not allowed to eat **w** your gates	Dt 12:17	
the Levite who is **w** your gates;	Dt 12:18	
and you may eat **w** your gates	Dt 12:21	
"You shall eat it **w** your gates;	Dt 15:22	
and the alien who is **w** your camps,	Dt 29:11	7130
for **w** three days you are to cross	Jos 1:11	5750
"Perhaps you are living **w** our land;	Jos 9:7	7130
they were living **w** their land.	Jos 9:16	7130
when you are living **w** our land?	Jos 9:22	7130
with Israel and were **w** their land,	Jos 10:1	7130
you not recover them **w** that time?	Jg 11:26	
me **w** the seven days of the feast,	Jg 14:12	
anymore **w** the border of Israel.	1Sa 7:13	
did not come **w** the appointed days,	1Sa 13:11	
twenty men **w** about half a furrow in	1Sa 14:14	
And Nabal's heart was merry **w** him,	1Sa 25:36	5921
and his heart died **w** him so that	1Sa 25:37	7130
of God dwells **w** tent curtains."	2Sa 7:2	8432
men of Judah for me **w** three days,	2Sa 20:4	
remaining **w** any border of Israel,	2Sa 21:5	
There was cedar on the house **w**,	1Ki 6:18	6441
an inner sanctuary **w** the house	1Ki 6:19	8432
for her soul is troubled **w** her;	2Ki 4:27	
and told *it* **w** the king's household.	2Ki 7:11	6441
and whoever comes **w** the ranks	2Ki 11:8	413
to their camps **w** their borders.	1Ch 6:54	
incited revolt **w** it in past days;	Ezr 4:15	1459
would not come **w** three days,	Ezr 10:8	
at Jerusalem **w** the three days.	Ezr 10:9	
spend the night **w** Jerusalem so that	Ne 4:22	8432
in the house of God, **w** the temple,	Ne 6:10	8432
angry and his wrath burned **w** him.	Es 1:12	
their tent-cord plucked up **w** them?	Jb 4:21	
arrows of the Almighty are **w** me,	Jb 6:4	5973
"Is it that my help is not **w** me,	Jb 6:13	
I know that this is **w** You:	Jb 10:13	5973
My heart faints **w** me!	Jb 19:27	2436
To the venom of cobras **w** him.	Jb 20:14	7130
"Because he knew no quiet **w** him	Jb 20:20	990
"**W** the walls they produce oil;	Jb 24:11	996
now my soul is poured out **w** me;	Jb 30:16	5921
"At night it pierces my bones **w** me,	Jb 30:17	4480, 5921
"I am seething **w** and cannot	Jb 30:27	4578
The spirit **w** me constrains me.	Jb 32:18	990
Who can come **w** his double mail?	Jb 41:13	
It is melted **w** me.	Ps 22:14	8432
speaks to the ungodly **w** his heart;	Ps 36:1	7130
My heart was hot **w** me,	Ps 39:3	7130
Your Law is **w** my heart."	Ps 40:8	8432
Your righteousness **w** my heart;	Ps 40:10	8432
and I pour out my soul **w** me.	Ps 42:4	5921
have you become disturbed **w** me?	Ps 42:5	5921
God, my soul is in despair **w** me;	Ps 42:6	5921
have you become disturbed **w** me?	Ps 42:11	5921
And why are you disturbed **w** me?	Ps 43:5	5921
King's daughter is all glorious **w**;	Ps 45:13	6441
And renew a steadfast spirit **w** me.	Ps 51:10	7130
My heart is in anguish **w** me,	Ps 55:4	7130
embittered And I was pierced **w**,	Ps 73:21	3629
everything **w** the sanctuary.	Ps 74:3	
From **w** Your bosom, destroy *them!*	Ps 74:11	7130
my anxious thoughts multiply **w** me,	Ps 94:19	7130
I will walk **w** my house in the	Ps 101:2	7130
deceit shall not dwell **w** my house;	Ps 101:7	7130
And all that is **w** me, *bless* His	Ps 103:1	7130
Their soul fainted **w** them.	Ps 107:5	
And my heart is wounded **w** me.	Ps 109:22	7130
feet are standing **W** your gates,	Ps 122:2	
"May peace be **w** your walls, And	Ps 122:7	
And prosperity **w** your palaces."	Ps 122:7	
"May peace be **w** you."	Ps 122:8	
a fruitful vine **W** your house,	Ps 128:3	3411
soul is like a weaned child **w** me.	Ps 131:2	5921
my spirit was overwhelmed **w** me,	Ps 142:3	5921
my spirit is overwhelmed **w** me;	Ps 143:4	5921
My heart is appalled **w** me.	Ps 143:4	8432
He has blessed your sons **w** you.	Ps 147:13	7130
treasure my commandments **w** you,	Pr 2:1	854
treasure my commandments **w** you.	Pr 7:1	854
pleasant if you keep them **w** you,	Pr 22:18	990
For as he thinks **w** himself,	Pr 23:7	
revelry and the jubilant **w** her,	Is 5:14	
w another 65 years Ephraim will be	Is 7:8	
everyone that is left **w** the land will	Is 7:22	7130
Only a remnant **w** them will return;	Is 10:22	
His soul trembles **w** him.	Is 15:4	
"**W** three years, as a hired man	Is 16:14	
of the Egyptians will melt **w** them.	Is 19:1	7130
will be demoralized **w** them;	Is 19:3	7130
mixed **w** her a spirit of distortion;	Is 19:14	7130
my spirit **w** me seeks You diligently;	Is 26:9	7130
in its place and rye **w** its area?	Is 28:25	
W a year and *a few* days You will	Is 32:10	5921
house and **w** My walls a memorial,	Is 56:5	
or destruction **w** your borders;	Is 60:18	
your wicked thoughts Lodge **w** you?	Jer 4:14	7130
My heart is faint **w** *me!*	Jer 8:18	
Is her King not **w** her?"	Jer 8:19	
your sins And **w** all your borders.	Jer 15:13	
My heart is broken **w** me,	Jer 23:9	7130
"**W** two years I am going to bring	Jer 28:3	5750
so will I break **w** two full years the	Jer 28:11	5750
"I will put My law **w** them and	Jer 31:33	7130
My heart is overturned **w** me,	La 1:20	7130
remembers And is bowed down **w** me.	La 3:20	5921
W it there were figures resembling	Ezk 1:5	8432
as if one wheel were **w** another.	Ezk 1:16	8432
looked like fire all around **w** it,	Ezk 1:27	1004
the plague and the famine are **w**.	Ezk 7:15	1004
if one wheel were **w** another wheel.	Ezk 10:10	8432
and put a new spirit **w** them.	Ezk 11:19	7130
divination **w** the house of Israel.	Ezk 12:24	8432
father and mother lightly **w** you.	Ezk 22:7	
"Her princes **w** her are like	Ezk 22:27	7130
and lo, thus they did **w** My house.	Ezk 23:39	8432
will fall **w** her by the sword,"	Ezk 30:6	
heart and put a new spirit **w** you;	Ezk 36:26	7130
"I will put My Spirit **w** you	Ezk 36:27	7130
"I will put My Spirit **w** you and	Ezk 37:14	
pillars **w** the gate all around,	Ezk 40:16	6441
w all its boundary round about.	Ezk 45:1	
my spirit was distressed **w** me,	Da 7:15	1459
yet **w** a few days he will be	Da 11:20	
a spirit of harlotry is **w** them,	Hos 5:4	7130
My heart is turned over **w** Me,	Hos 11:8	5921
and see *the* great tumults **w** her	Am 3:9	8432
one, His soul is not right **w** him;	Hab 2:4	
princes **w** her are roaring lions,	Zph 3:3	7130
The LORD is righteous **w** her;	Zph 3:5	7130
multitude of men and cattle **w** it.	Zch 2:4	8432
it will spend the night **w** that house	Zch 5:4	8432
and forms the spirit of man **w** him,	Zch 12:1	7130
temple and by Him who dwells **w** it.	Mt 23:21	*2730*
reasoning that way **w** themselves,	Mk 2:8	*1722*
"For from **w**, out of the heart of	Mk 7:21	*2081*
All these evil things proceed from **w**	Mk 7:23	*2081*
w the region of Decapolis.	Mk 7:31	*303, 3319*
give that which is **w** as charity,	Lk 11:41	*1751*
ground and your children **w** you,	Lk 19:44	*1722*
"Were not our hearts burning **w** us	Lk 24:32	*1722*
again being deeply moved **w**,	Jn 11:38	*1722, 1438*
his spirit was being provoked **w** him	Ac 17:16	*1722*
came to them at Troas **w** five days;	Ac 20:6	*891*
known about God is evident **w** them;	Ro 1:19	*1722*
has been poured out **w** our hearts	Ro 5:5	*1722*
we ourselves groan **w** ourselves,	Ro 8:23	*1722*
judge those who are **w** *the church?*	1Co 5:12	*2080*
the sentence of death **w** ourselves	2Co 1:9	*1722*
conflicts without, fears **w**.	2Co 7:5	*2081*
him consider this again **w** himself,	2Co 10:7	*1909*
but **w** the measure of the sphere	2Co 10:13	*2596*
grows, we will be, **w** our sphere,	2Co 10:15	*2596*
to the power that works **w** us,	Eph 3:20	*1722*
power, which mightily works **w** me.	Col 1:29	*1722*
word of Christ richly dwell **w** you,	Col 3:16	*1722*
neglect the spiritual gift **w** you,	1Tm 4:14	*1722*
mindful of the sincere faith **w** you,	2Tm 1:5	*1722*
and one which enters **w** the veil,	Heb 6:19	*2082*
the Spirit of Christ **w** them was	1Pe 1:11	*1722*
are full of eyes around and **w**;	Rv 4:8	*2081*

WITHOUT

pit was empty, **w** any water in it.	Gn 37:24	369
yet **w** your permission no one shall	Gn 41:44	1107
go out as a free man **w** payment.	Ex 21:2	2600
for nothing, **w** *payment of* money.	Ex 21:11	369
young bull and two rams **w** blemish,	Ex 29:1	8549
shall offer it, a male **w** defect;	Lv 1:3	8549
he shall offer it a male **w** defect.	Lv 1:10	8549
offer it **w** defect before the LORD.	Lv 3:1	8549
it, male or female, **w** defect.	Lv 3:6	8549
offer to the LORD a bull **w** defect	Lv 4:3	8549
offering a goat, a male **w** defect.	Lv 4:23	8549
a goat, a female **w** defect,	Lv 4:28	8549
shall bring it, a female **w** defect.	Lv 4:32	8549
a ram **w** defect from the flock,	Lv 5:15	8549
a ram **w** defect from the flock,	Lv 5:18	8549
a ram **w** defect from the flock,	Lv 6:6	8549
a burnt offering, *both* **w** defect,	Lv 9:2	8549
lamb, both one year old, **w** defect,	Lv 9:3	8549
to take two male lambs **w** defect,	Lv 14:10	8549
and a yearling ewe lamb **w** defect,	Lv 14:10	8549
touches **w** having rinsed his hands in	Lv 15:11	3808
a male **w** defect from the cattle,	Lv 22:19	8549
a male lamb one year old **w** defect	Lv 23:12	8549
one year old male lambs **w** defect,	Lv 23:18	8549
while it is made desolate **w** them.	Lv 26:43	4480
one male lamb a year old **w** defect	Nu 6:14	8549
one ewe-lamb a year old **w** defect	Nu 6:14	8549
ram **w** defect for a peace offering,	Nu 6:14	8549
shall blow **w** sounding an alarm.	Nu 10:7	3808
w the knowledge of the congregation	Nu 15:24	4480
male lambs one year old **w** defect	Nu 28:3	8549
male lambs one year old **w** defect,	Nu 28:9	8549
male lambs one year old **w** defect;	Nu 28:11	8549
year old, having them **w** defect.	Nu 28:19	8549

They shall be **w** defect. **Nu 28:31** 8549
male lambs one year old **w** defect; **Nu 29:2** 8549
year old, having them **w** defect; **Nu 29:8** 8549
one year old, which are **w** defect; **Nu 29:13** 8549
male lambs one year old **w** defect; **Nu 29:17** 8549
male lambs one year old **w** defect; **Nu 29:20** 8549
male lambs one year old **w** defect; **Nu 29:23** 8549
male lambs one year old **w** defect; **Nu 29:26** 8549
male lambs one year old **w** defect; **Nu 29:29** 8549
male lambs one year old **w** defect; **Nu 29:32** 8549
male lambs one year old **w** defect; **Nu 29:36** 8549
he pushed him suddenly **w** enmity, **Nu 35:22** 3808
something at him **w** lying in wait, **Nu 35:22** 3808
and **w** seeing it dropped on him so **Nu 35:23** 3808
slew his neighbor **w** having enmity **Dt 4:42** 3808
you will eat food **w** scarcity, **Dt 8:9** 3808
A God of faithfulness and **w** injustice, **Dt 32:4** 369
unintentionally, **w** premeditation, **Jos 20:3** 1097
struck his neighbor **w** premeditation **Jos 20:5** 1097
and their camels were **w** number, **Jg 7:12** 369
Ammon **w** calling us to go with you? **Jg 12:1** 3808
pursued them **w** rest *and* trod them **Jg 20:43**
not left you **w** a redeemer today, **Ru 4:14** 7673a
David to death **w** a cause?" **1Sa 19:5** 2600
or small **w** disclosing it to me. **1Sa 20:2** 3808
both by having shed blood **w** cause **1Sa 25:31** 2600
LORD'S anointed and be **w** guilt?" **1Sa 26:9** 5352
small and great, **w** killing anyone, **1Sa 30:2** 3808
the sun rises, A morning **w** clouds, **2Sa 23:4** 3808
the blood which Joab shed **w** cause. **1Ki 2:31** 2600
w war between Aram and Israel. **1Ki 22:1** 369
until he left him **w** a survivor. **2Ki 10:11** 1115
now come up **w** the LORD's approval **2Ki 18:25** 1107
and Appaim, and Seled died **w** sons. **1Ch 2:30** 3808
Jonathan, and Jether died **w** sons. **1Ch 2:32** 3808
w regard to divisions), **2Ch 5:11** 369
with him from Egypt were **w** number: **2Ch 12:3** 369
Israel was **w** the true God and **2Ch 15:3** 3808
w a teaching priest and without law. **2Ch 15:3** 3808
a teaching priest and **w** law. **2Ch 15:3** 3808
w regard to their genealogical **2Ch 31:16**
4480, 905
the River, and that **w** delay. **Ezr 6:8** 3809
to be given to them daily **w** fail, **Ezr 6:9** 3809
him to ruin him **w** cause." **Jb 2:3** 2600
They die, yet **w** wisdom.' **Jb 4:21** 3808
things, Wonders **w** number. **Jb 5:9** 5704, 369
tasteless be eaten **w** salt, **Jb 6:6** 1097
And come to an end **w** hope. **Jb 7:6** 657
"Can the papyrus grow up **w** a marsh? **Jb 8:11** 3808
Can the rushes grow **w** water? **Jb 8:11** 1097
Who has defied Him **w** harm? **Jb 9:4** 7999a
And wondrous works **w** number. **Jb 9:10**
5704, 369
And multiplies my wounds **w** cause. **Jb 9:17** 2600
itself, Of deep shadow **w** order, **Jb 10:22** 3808
He sees iniquity **w** investigating. **Jb 11:11** 3808
lift up your face **w** *moral* defect, **Jb 11:15** 4480
W mercy He splits my kidneys open; **Jb 16:13** 3808
"His ox mates **w** fail; **Jb 21:10** 3808
great, And your iniquities **w** end? **Jb 22:5** 369
pledges of your brothers **w** cause, **Jb 22:6** 2600
spend the night naked, **w** clothing, **Jb 24:7** 1097
poor to go about naked **w** clothing, **Jb 24:10** 1097
you have saved the arm **w** strength! **Jb 26:2** 3808
you have given to *one* **w** wisdom! **Jb 26:3** 3808
"For it will hurl at him **w** sparing; **Jb 27:22** 3808
"Fools, even those **w** a name, **Jb 30:8** 1097
"I go about mourning **w** comfort; **Jb 30:28** 3808
If I have eaten its fruit **w** money, **Jb 31:39** 1097
'I am pure, **w** transgression; **Jb 33:9** 1097
though I am **w** transgression.' **Jb 34:6** 1097
mighty are taken away **w** a hand. **Jb 34:20** 3808
in pieces mighty men **w** inquiry, **Jb 34:24** 3808
'Job speaks **w** knowledge, And his **Jb 34:35** 3808
And his words are **w** wisdom. **Jb 34:35** 3808
He multiplies words **w** knowledge." **Jb 35:16** 1097
And they will die **w** knowledge. **Jb 36:12** 1097
counsel By words **w** knowledge? **Jb 38:2** 1097
To bring rain on a land **w** people, **Jb 38:26** 3808
people, *On* a desert **w** a man in it, **Jb 38:26** 3808
to God And wander about **w** food? **Jb 38:41** 1097
is like him, One made **w** fear. **Jb 41:33** 1097
that hides counsel **w** knowledge?' **Jb 42:3** 1097
him who **w** cause was my adversary, **Ps 7:4** 7387
who deal treacherously **w** cause **Ps 25:3** 7387
trusted in the LORD **w** wavering. **Ps 26:1** 3808
For **w** cause they hid their net for **Ps 35:7** 2600
W cause they dug a pit for my soul. **Ps 35:7** 2600
me, They slandered me **w** ceasing. **Ps 35:15** 3808
let those who hate me **w** cause wink **Ps 35:19** 2600
in *his* pomp, yet **w** understanding, **Ps 49:20** 3808
Those who hate me **w** a cause are **Ps 69:4** 2600
was stretched out **w** weariness; **Ps 77:2** 3808
have become like a man **w** strength, **Ps 88:4** 369
In which are swarms **w** number, **Ps 104:25** 369
And young locusts, even **w** number, **Ps 105:34** 369
And fought against me **w** cause. **Ps 109:3** 2600
flesh has grown lean, **w** fatness. **Ps 109:24** 4480
Princes persecute me **w** cause, **Ps 119:161** 2600
bear **W** mishap and without loss, **Ps 144:14** 369
bear Without mishap and **w** loss, **Ps 144:14** 369
us ambush the innocent **w** cause; **Pr 1:11** 2600
Do not contend with a man **w** cause, **Pr 3:30** 2600
W consultation, plans are **Pr 15:22** 369
for a person to be **w** knowledge, **Pr 19:2** 3808
Who has wounds **w** cause? **Pr 23:29** 2600
against your neighbor **w** cause, **Pr 24:28** 2600
Like clouds and wind **w** rain Is a **Pr 25:14** 369

a city that is broken into *and* **w** walls **Pr 25:28** 369
a curse **w** cause does not alight. **Pr 26:2** 2600
and who can have enjoyment **w** Him? **Ec 2:25**
2351, 4480
was a certain man **w** a dependent, **Ec 4:8** 369
concubines, And maidens **w** number; **SS 6:8** 369
great and fine ones, **w** occupants. **Is 5:9** 369
and opened its mouth **w** measure; **Is 5:14** 1097
are devastated *and* **w** inhabitant, **Is 6:11** 369
inhabitant, Houses are **w** people And **Is 6:11** 369
And have been captured **w** the bow; **Is 22:3** 4480
is destroyed, **w** house *or* harbor; **Is 23:1** 4480
vomit, **w** a *single clean* place. **Is 28:8** 1097
down to Egypt **W** consulting Me, **Is 30:2** 3808
now come up **w** the LORD'S approval **Is 36:10** 1107
free, **W** any payment or reward," **Is 45:13** 3808
Sit on the ground **w** a throne, **Is 47:1** 369
you will be redeemed **w** money." **Is 52:3** 3808
Assyrian oppressed them **w** cause. **Is 52:4** 657
have been taken away **w** cause?" **Is 52:5** 2600
and milk **W** money and without cost. **Is 55:1** 3808
and milk Without money and **w** cost. **Is 55:1** 3808
return there **w** watering the earth And **Is 55:10**
3588, 518
W accomplishing what I desire, **Is 55:11**
3588, 518
And **w** succeeding *in the matter* for **Is 55:11**
have been destroyed, **w** inhabitant. **Jer 2:15** 1097
have forgotten Me Days **w** number. **Jer 2:32** 369
cities will be ruins **W** inhabitant. **Jer 4:7** 369
a desolation, **w** inhabitant." **Jer 9:11** 1097
I will give for booty **w** cost, **Jer 15:13** 3808
own evil heart, **w** listening to Me. **Jer 16:12** 1115
A land of salt **w** inhabitant. **Jer 17:6** 3808
the LORD overthrew **w** relenting, **Jer 20:16** 3808
who builds his house **w** righteousness **Jer 22:13** 3808
And his upper rooms **w** justice, **Jer 22:13** 3808
uses his neighbor's services **w** pay **Jer 22:13** 2600
will be desolate, **w** inhabitant'?" **Jer 26:9** 369
is a desolation, **w** man or beast; **Jer 32:43** 369
waste, **w** man and without beast," **Jer 33:10** 369
waste, without man and **w** beast," **Jer 33:10** 369
w man and without inhabitant **Jer 33:10** 369
w inhabitant and without beast, **Jer 33:10** 369
without inhabitant and **w** beast, **Jer 33:10** 369
which is waste, **w** man or beast, **Jer 33:12**
4480, 369
a desolation **w** inhabitant.' " **Jer 34:22** 369
leaving yourselves **w** remnant, **Jer 44:7** 1115
was it **w** our husbands that we made **Jer 44:19**
4480, 1107
and a curse, **w** an inhabitant, **Jer 44:22** 369
refuge in flight, **W** facing back; **Jer 46:5** 3808
than locusts And are **w** number. **Jer 46:23** 369
desolation, **W** inhabitants in them. **Jer 48:9** 369
The fugitives stand **w** strength; **Jer 48:45** 4480
A desolation **w** inhabitants. **Jer 51:29** 369
horror and hissing, **w** inhabitants. **Jer 51:37** 369
fled **w** strength Before the pursuer. **La 1:6** 3808
He has thrown down **w** sparing, **La 2:17** 3808
pour down unceasingly, **W** stopping, **La 3:49** 369
My enemies **w** cause Hunted me down **La 3:52** 2600
We have become orphans **w** a father, **La 5:3** 369
would go, **w** turning as they went. **Ezk 1:12** 3808
w turning as they moved. **Ezk 1:17** 3808
directions **w** turning as they went; **Ezk 10:11** 3808
faced, **w** turning as they went. **Ezk 10:11** 3808
oppressed the sojourner **w** justice. **Ezk 22:29** 3808
after piece, **W** making a choice. **Ezk 24:6** 3808
ensure life **w** committing iniquity, **Ezk 33:15** 1115
the fat *sheep* **w** feeding the flock. **Ezk 34:3** 3808
all of them living **w** walls and **Ezk 38:11** 369
from the sanctuary **w** laying there **Ezk 42:14**
goat **w** blemish for a sin offering, **Ezk 43:22** 8549
present a young bull **w** blemish and **Ezk 43:23** 8549
a ram **w** blemish from the flock. **Ezk 43:23** 8549
a ram from the flock, **w** blemish, **Ezk 43:25** 8549
shall take a young bull **w** blemish **Ezk 45:18** 8549
seven rams **w** blemish on every day **Ezk 45:23** 8549
shall be six lambs **w** blemish and **Ezk 46:4** 8549
blemish and a ram **w** blemish; **Ezk 46:4** 8549
offer a young bull **w** blemish, **Ezk 46:6** 8549
a ram, *which* shall be **w** blemish. **Ezk 46:6** 8549
provide a lamb a year old **w** blemish **Ezk 46:13** 8549
until a stone was cut out **w** hands, **Da 2:34** 3809
was cut out of the mountain **w** hands **Da 2:45** 3809
in the midst of the fire **w** harm, **Da 3:25** 3809
whole earth **w** touching the ground; **Da 8:5** 369
he will be broken **w** human agency. **Da 8:25** 657
for many days **w** king or prince, **Hos 3:4** 369
w sacrifice or *sacred* pillar and **Hos 3:4** 369
and **w** ephod or household idols. **Hos 3:4** 369
people **w** understanding are ruined. **Hos 4:14** 3808
become like a silly dove, **w** sense; **Hos 7:11** 369
my land, Mighty and **w** number; **Jl 1:6** 369
it will be night for you—**w** vision, **Mi 3:6** 4480
And darkness for you—**w** divination. **Mi 3:6** 4480
might, And Egypt too, **w** limits. **Na 3:9** 369
things **w** a ruler over them? **Hab 1:14** 3808
slay nations **w** sparing? **Hab 1:17** 3808
yes, gather, O nation **w** shame, **Zph 2:1** 3808
cities are laid waste, **W** a man, **Zph 3:6**
4480, 1097
Without a man, **w** an inhabitant. **Zph 3:6** 4480, 369
will be inhabited **w** walls because **Zch 2:4** 6519
dispirited like sheep **w** a shepherd. **Mt 9:36**
3361, 2192
did not speak to them **w** a parable. **Mt 13:34** *5565*
"A prophet is not **w** honor except in **Mt 13:57** *820*

come in here **w** wedding clothes?' **Mt 22:12**
3361, 2192
have done **w** neglecting the others. **Mt 23:23** *3361*
did not speak to them **w** a parable; **Mk 4:34** *5565*
"A prophet is not **w** honor except in **Mk 6:4** *820*
they were like sheep **w** a shepherd; **Mk 6:34**
3361, 2192
I will build another made **w** hands. **Mk 14:58** *886*
enemies, Might serve Him **w** fear, **Lk 1:74** *870*
out of him **w** doing him any harm. **Lk 4:35** *3367*
on the ground **w** any foundation; **Lk 6:49** *5565*
have done **w** neglecting the others. **Lk 11:42** *3361*
on this fig tree **w** finding any. **Lk 13:7**
2532, 3756
I sent you out **w** money belt and bag **Lk 22:35** *817*
for He gives the Spirit **w** measure. **Jn 3:34**
3756, 1537
"He who is **w** sin among you, let **Jn 8:7** *361*
'THEY HATED ME **W** A CAUSE.' **Jn 15:25** *1431*
to bring them *back* **w** violence **Ac 5:26**
3756, 3326
And he was three days **w** sight, **Ac 9:9** *3361*
and accompany them **w** misgivings, **Ac 10:20** *3367*
I came **w** even raising any objection **Ac 10:29** *369*
me to go with them **w** misgivings. **Ac 11:12** *3367*
did not leave Himself **w** witness, **Ac 14:17** *267*
have beaten us in public **w** trial, **Ac 16:37** *178*
purified, **w** *any* crowd or uproar. **Ac 24:18**
3326, 3756
they had gone a long time **w** food, **Ac 27:21** *776*
watching and going **w** eating, **Ac 27:33** *777*
made, so that they are **w** excuse. **Ro 1:20** *379*
w understanding, untrustworthy, **Ro 1:31** *801*
For all who have sinned **w** the Law **Ro 2:12** *460*
Law will also perish **w** the Law, **Ro 2:12** *460*
who believe **w** being circumcised, **Ro 4:11** *203*
W becoming weak in faith he **Ro 4:19** *3361*
how will they hear **w** a preacher? **Ro 10:14** *5565*
BY A NATION **W** UNDERSTANDING **Ro 10:19** *801*
Let love *be* **w** hypocrisy. **Ro 12:9** *505*
the weaknesses of those **w** strength **Ro 15:1** *102*
rich, you have become kings **w** us; **1Co 4:8** *5565*
distinguished, but we are **w** honor. **1Co 4:10** *820*
I may offer the gospel **w** charge, **1Co 9:18** *77*
to those who are **w** law, **1Co 9:21** *459*
who are without law, as **w** law, **1Co 9:21** *459*
though not being **w** the law of God **1Co 9:21** *459*
I might win those who are **w** law. **1Co 9:21** *459*
I run in such a way, as not **w** aim; **1Co 9:26** *84*
w asking questions for conscience' **1Co 10:25** *3367*
w asking questions for conscience' **1Co 10:27** *3367*
world, and no *kind* is **w** meaning. **1Co 14:10** *880*
is with you **w** cause to be afraid, **1Co 16:10** *870*
conflicts **w**, fears within. **2Co 7:5** *1855*
produces a repentance **w** regret, **2Co 7:10** *278*
they are **w** understanding. **2Co 10:12** *3756*
the gospel of God to you **w** charge? **2Co 11:7** *1431*
beaten times **w** number, **2Co 11:23** *5234*
hunger and thirst, often **w** food, **2Co 11:27** *3521*
Who is weak **w** my being weak? **2Co 11:29**
2532, 3756
led into sin **w** my intense concern? **2Co 11:29**
2532, 3756
no hope and **w** God in the world. **Eph 2:12** *112*
to speak the word of God **w** fear. **Php 1:14** *870*
things **w** grumbling or disputing; **Php 2:14** *5565*
with a circumcision made **w** hands, **Col 2:11** *886*
inflated **w** cause by his fleshly mind, **Col 2:18** *1500*
has done, and that **w** partiality. **Col 3:25** *3756*
that He may establish your hearts **w** **1Th 3:13** *273*
pray **w** ceasing; **1Th 5:17** *89*
w blame at the coming of our Lord **1Th 5:23** *274*
eat anyone's bread **w** paying for it, **2Th 3:8** *1431*
hands, **w** wrath and dissension. **1Tm 2:8** *5565*
maintain these *principles* **w** bias, **1Tm 5:21** *5565*
commandment **w** stain or reproach **1Tm 6:14** *784, 423*
malicious gossips, **w** self-control, **2Tm 3:3** *193*
but **w** your consent I did not want **Phm 1:14** *5565*
all things as *we are, yet* **w** sin. **Heb 4:15** *5565*
W father, without mother, without **Heb 7:3** *540*
Without father, **w** mother, without **Heb 7:3** *282*
without mother, **w** genealogy, **Heb 7:3** *35*
But **w** any dispute the lesser is **Heb 7:7** *5565*
inasmuch as *it was* not **w** an oath **Heb 7:20** *5565*
indeed became priests **w** an oath, **Heb 7:21** *5565*
once a year, not **w** *taking* blood, **Heb 9:7** *5565*
offered Himself **w** blemish to God, **Heb 9:14** *299b*
was not inaugurated **w** blood. **Heb 9:18** *5565*
and **w** shedding of blood there is **Heb 9:22** *5565*
for salvation **w** *reference to* sin, **Heb 9:28** *5565*
confession of our hope **w** wavering, **Heb 10:23** *186*
dies **w** mercy on *the testimony of* two **Heb 10:28** *5565*
And **w** faith it is impossible to **Heb 11:6** *5565*
faith, **w** receiving the promises, **Heb 11:13** *3361*
But if you are **w** discipline, of **Heb 12:8** *5565*
and the sanctification **w** which no **Heb 12:14** *5565*
entertained angels **w** knowing it. **Heb 13:2** *2990*
all generously and **w** reproach, **Jas 1:5** *3361*
must ask in faith **w** any doubting, **Jas 1:6** *3367*
If a brother or sister is **w** clothing **Jas 2:15** *1131*
show me your faith **w** the works, **Jas 2:18** *5565*
that faith **w** works is useless? **Jas 2:20** *5565*
as the body **w** *the* spirit is dead, **Jas 2:26** *5565*
so also faith **w** works is dead. **Jas 2:26** *5565*
fruits, unwavering, **w** hypocrisy. **Jas 3:17** *505*
they may be won **w** a word by the **1Pe 3:1** *427*
w being frightened by any fear. **1Pe 3:6**
2532, 3361
to one another **w** complaint. **1Pe 4:9** *427*

These are springs **w** water and	**2Pe 2:17**	*504*
when they feast with you **w** fear,	**Jude 1:12**	*870*
clouds **w** water, carried along by	**Jude 1:12**	*504*
autumn trees **w** fruit, doubly dead,	**Jude 1:12**	*175*
of the water of life **w** cost.	**Rv 21:6**	*1431*
take the water of life **w** cost.	**Rv 22:17**	*1431*

WITHSTAND

the ram had no strength to **w** him.	**Da 8:7**	5975
and no one will *be able to* **w** him;	**Da 11:16**	6440, 5975

WITHSTANDING

was **w** me for twenty-one days;	**Da 10:13**	5975

WITNESS

so that it may be a **w** to me,	**Gn 21:30**	5713a
it be a **w** between you and me."	**Gn 31:44**	5707
a **w** between you and me this day."	**Gn 31:48**	5707
God is **w** between you and me."	**Gn 31:50**	5707
"This heap is a **w**, and the pillar	**Gn 31:52**	5707
a witness, and the pillar is a **w**,	**Gn 31:52**	5713a
or heed the **w** of the first sign,	**Ex 4:8**	6963
believe the **w** of the last sign.	**Ex 4:8**	6963
"You shall not bear false **w** against	**Ex 20:16**	5707
a wicked man to be a malicious **w**.	**Ex 23:1**	5707
to testify when he is a **w**,	**Lv 5:1**	5707
and there is no **w** against her and	**Nu 5:13**	5707
death on the testimony of one **w**.	**Nu 35:30**	5707
and earth to **w** against you today,	**Dt 4:26**	5749b
'You shall not bear false **w** against	**Dt 5:20**	5707
to death on the evidence of one **w**.	**Dt 17:6**	5707
"A single **w** shall not rise up	**Dt 19:15**	5707
"If a malicious **w** rises up	**Dt 19:16**	5707
and if the **w** is a false witness	**Dt 19:18**	5707
and if the witness is a false **w**	**Dt 19:18**	5707
and earth to **w** against you today,	**Dt 30:19**	5749b
that this song may be a **w** for Me	**Dt 31:19**	5707
will testify before them as a **w**	**Dt 31:21**	5707
remain there as a **w** against you.	**Dt 31:26**	5707
and the earth to **w** against them.	**Dt 31:28**	5749b
rather it shall be a **w** between us	**Jos 22:27**	5707
it is a **w** between us and you."	**Jos 22:28**	5707
the sons of Gad called the altar **W**;	**Jos 22:34**	
"it is a **w** between us that the	**Jos 22:34**	5707
stone shall be for a **w** against us,	**Jos 24:27**	5713a
it shall be for a **w** against you,	**Jos 24:27**	5713a
"The LORD is **w** between us;	**Jg 11:10**	8085
set the ark of the LORD *is a* **w**	**1Sa 6:18**	
bear **w** against me before the LORD	**1Sa 12:3**	6030a
"The LORD is **w** against you, and	**1Sa 12:5**	5707
and His anointed is **w** this day	**1Sa 12:5**	5707
And they said, "*He is* **w**."	**1Sa 12:5**	5707
be **w**! When I have sounded out my	**1Sa 20:12**	
me up, It has become a **w**;	**Jb 16:8**	5707
now, behold, my **w** is in heaven,	**Jb 16:19**	5707
And do you not recognize their **w**?	**Jb 21:29**	226
when the eye saw, it gave **w** of me,	**Jb 29:11**	5749b
And the **w** in the sky is faithful.	**Ps 89:37**	5707
A false **w** *who* utters lies, And one	**Pr 6:19**	5707
what is right, But a false **w**, deceit.	**Pr 12:17**	5707
A trustworthy **w** will not lie, But a	**Pr 14:5**	5707
lie, But a false **w** utters lies.	**Pr 14:5**	5707
A truthful **w** saves lives, But he	**Pr 14:25**	5707
A false **w** will not go unpunished,	**Pr 19:5**	5707
A false **w** will not go unpunished,	**Pr 19:9**	5707
w makes a mockery of justice,	**Pr 19:28**	5707
A false **w** will perish, But the man	**Pr 21:28**	5707
Do not be a **w** against your neighbor	**Pr 24:28**	5707
bears false **w** against his neighbor.	**Pr 25:18**	5707
their faces bears **w** against them,	**Is 3:9**	6030a
It will become a sign and a **w**	**Is 19:20**	5707
the time to come As a **w** forever.	**Is 30:8**	
have made him a **w** to the peoples,	**Is 55:4**	5707
I am He who knows and am a **w**,"	**Jer 29:23**	5707
a true and faithful **w** against us if	**Jer 42:5**	5707
the Lord GOD be a **w** against you,	**Mi 1:2**	5707
"For the day when I rise up as a **w**.	**Zph 3:8**	5707
Because the LORD has been a **w**	**Mal 2:14**	5749b
and I will be a swift **w** against	**Mal 3:5**	5707
fornications, thefts, false **w**,	**Mt 15:19**	*5577a*
YOU SHALL NOT BEAR FALSE **W**;	**Mt 19:18**	*5576*
DO NOT STEAL, DO NOT BEAR FALSE **W**,	**Mk 10:19**	*5576*
DO NOT STEAL, DO NOT BEAR FALSE **W**,	**Lk 18:20**	*5576*
He came as a **w**,	**Jn 1:7**	*3141*
one of these *must* become a **w**	**Ac 1:22**	*3144*
"Of Him all the prophets bear **w**	**Ac 10:43**	*3140*
did not leave Himself without **w**,	**Ac 14:17**	*267*
'For you will be a **w** for Him to	**Ac 22:15**	*3144*
blood of Your **w** Stephen was being	**Ac 22:20**	*3144*
so you must **w** at Rome also."	**Ac 23:11**	*3140*
to appoint you a minister and a **w**	**Ac 26:16**	*3144*
is my **w** *as to* how unceasingly I	**Ro 1:9**	*3144*
their conscience bearing **w** and	**Ro 2:15**	*4828*
But I call God as **w** to my soul,	**2Co 1:23**	*3144*
For I bear you **w** that, if	**Ga 4:15**	*3140*
For God is my **w**, how I long for	**Php 1:8**	*3144*
God is **w**	**1Th 2:5**	*3144*
for he obtained the **w** that before	**Heb 11:5**	*3140*
and their rust will be a **w** against	**Jas 5:3**	*3142*
and **w** of the sufferings of Christ,	**1Pe 5:1**	*3144*
from Jesus Christ, the faithful **w**,	**Rv 1:5**	*3144*
even in the days of Antipas, My **w**,	**Rv 2:13**	*3144*
The Amen, the faithful and true **W**,	**Rv 3:14**	*3144*

WITNESSED

since the LORD has **w** against me	**Ru 1:21**	6030a
arrived and the grace of God,	**Ac 11:23**	*3708*
w to My cause at Jerusalem,	**Ac 23:11**	*1263*
w by the Law and the Prophets,	**Ro 3:21**	*3140*
of whom it is **w** that he lives on.	**Heb 7:8**	*3140*

WITNESSES

put to death at the evidence of **w**,	**Nu 35:30**	5707
evidence of two **w** or three witnesses,	**Dt 17:6**	5707
evidence of two witnesses or three **w**,	**Dt 17:6**	5707
"The hand of the **w** shall be first	**Dt 17:7**	5707
on the evidence of two or three **w**	**Dt 19:15**	5707
"You are **w** against yourselves	**Jos 24:22**	5707
And they said, "We are **w**."	**Jos 24:22**	5707
"You are **w** today that I have	**Ru 4:9**	5707
you are **w** today."	**Ru 4:10**	5707
and the elders, said, "*We are* **w**.	**Ru 4:11**	5707
'You renew Your **w** against me	**Jb 10:17**	5707
For false **w** have risen against me,	**Ps 27:12**	5707
Malicious **w** rise up;	**Ps 35:11**	5707
Myself faithful **w** for testimony,	**Is 8:2**	5707
Let them present their **w** that they	**Is 43:9**	5707
"You are My **w**," declares the LORD,	**Is 43:10**	5707
So you are My **w**,"	**Is 43:12**	5707
And you are My **w**.	**Is 44:8**	5707
their own **w** fail to see or know,	**Is 44:9**	5707
sealed the deed, and called in **w**,	**Jer 32:10**	5707
and in the sight of the **w** who	**Jer 32:12**	5707
the field with money and call in **w**	**Jer 32:25**	5707
call in **w** in the land of Benjamin,	**Jer 32:44**	5707
BY THE MOUTH OF TWO OR THREE **W**	**Mt 18:16**	*3144*
though many false **w** came forward.	**Mt 26:60**	*5577b*
What further need do we have of **w**?	**Mt 26:65**	*3144*
"What further need do we have of **w**?	**Mk 14:63**	*3144*
you are **w** and approve the deeds of	**Lk 11:48**	*3144*
"You are **w** of these things.	**Lk 24:48**	*3144*
"You yourselves are my **w** that I said,	**Jn 3:28**	*3140*
shall be My **w** both in Jerusalem,	**Ac 1:8**	*3144*
up again, to which we are all **w**.	**Ac 2:32**	*3144*
dead, *a fact* to which we are **w**.	**Ac 3:15**	*3144*
"And we are **w** of these things;	**Ac 5:32**	*3144*
They put forward false **w** who said,	**Ac 6:13**	*3144*
and the **w** laid aside their robes	**Ac 7:58**	*3144*
"We are **w** of all the things	**Ac 10:39**	*3144*
but to **w** who were chosen	**Ac 10:41**	*3144*
who are now His **w** to the people.	**Ac 13:31**	*3144*
even found *to be* false **w** of God,	**1Co 15:15**	*5577b*
THE TESTIMONY OF TWO OR THREE **W**.	**2Co 13:1**	*3144*
You are **w**, and *so is* God, how	**1Th 2:10**	*3144*
on the basis of two or three **w**.	**1Tm 5:19**	*3144*
in the presence of many **w**.	**1Tm 6:12**	*3144*
from me in the presence of many **w**,	**2Tm 2:2**	*3144*
the testimony of two or three **w**.	**Heb 10:28**	*3144*
great a cloud of **w** surrounding us,	**Heb 12:1**	*3144*
will grant *authority* to my two **w**,	**Rv 11:3**	*3144*
with the blood of the **w** of Jesus.	**Rv 17:6**	*3144*

WITS'

And were at their **w** end.	**Ps 107:27**	2451

WIVES

Lamech took to himself two **w**:	**Gn 4:19**	802
Lamech said to his **w**,	**Gn 4:23**	802
to my voice, You **w** of Lamech,	**Gn 4:23**	802
and they took **w** for themselves,	**Gn 6:2**	802
wife, and your sons' **w** with you.	**Gn 6:18**	802
his sons' **w** with him entered the ark	**Gn 7:7**	802
the three **w** of his sons with them,	**Gn 7:13**	802
sons and your sons' **w** with you.	**Gn 8:16**	802
his wife and his sons' **w** with him.	**Gn 8:18**	802
Abram and Nahor took **w** for	**Gn 11:29**	802
besides the **w** that he had,	**Gn 28:9**	802
"Give *me* my **w** and my children for	**Gn 30:26**	802
children and his **w** upon camels;	**Gn 31:17**	802
you take **w** besides my daughters,	**Gn 31:50**	802
that same night and took his two **w**	**Gn 32:22**	802
all their little ones and their **w**,	**Gn 34:29**	802
w from the daughters of Canaan:	**Gn 36:2**	802
Then Esau took his **w** and his sons	**Gn 36:6**	802
the sons of Zilpah, his father's **w**.	**Gn 37:2**	802
your little ones and for your **w**,	**Gn 45:19**	802
and their little ones and their **w** in	**Gn 46:5**	802
not including the **w** of Jacob's sons,	**Gn 46:26**	802
and your **w** shall become widows and	**Ex 22:24**	802
which are in the ears of your **w**,	**Ex 32:2**	802
Our **w** and our little ones will	**Nu 14:3**	802
along with their **w** and their sons	**Nu 16:27**	802
"Our little ones, our **w**,	**Nu 32:26**	802
'But your **w** and your little ones	**Dt 3:19**	802
shall not multiply **w** for himself,	**Dt 17:17**	802
"If a man has two **w**,	**Dt 21:15**	802
your little ones, your **w**,	**Dt 29:11**	802
"Your **w**, your little ones, and	**Jos 1:14**	802
daughters for themselves as **w**,	**Jg 3:6**	802
descendants, for he had many **w**.	**Jg 8:30**	802
do for **w** for those who are left,	**Jg 21:7**	802
do for **w** for those who are left,	**Jg 21:16**	802
give them **w** of our daughters."	**Jg 21:18**	802
and took **w** according to their	**Jg 21:23**	802
for themselves Moabite women *as* **w**;	**Ru 1:4**	802
He had two **w**:	**1Sa 1:2**	802
and they both became his **w**.	**1Sa 25:43**	802
even David with his two **w**,	**1Sa 27:3**	802
and their **w** and their sons and	**1Sa 30:3**	802
two **w** had been taken captive,	**1Sa 30:5**	802
had taken, and rescued his two **w**.	**1Sa 30:18**	802
went up there, and his two **w** also,	**2Sa 2:2**	802
concubines and **w** from Jerusalem,	**2Sa 5:13**	802
and your master's **w** into your care,	**2Sa 12:8**	802
even take your **w** before your eyes and	**2Sa 12:11**	802
lie with your **w** in broad daylight.	**2Sa 12:11**	802
daughters, the lives of your **w**,	**2Sa 19:5**	802
He had seven hundred **w**,	**1Ki 11:3**	802
and his **w** turned his heart away.	**1Ki 11:3**	802
his **w** turned his heart away after	**1Ki 11:4**	802
also he did for all his foreign **w**,	**1Ki 11:8**	802
w and children are also mine.' "	**1Ki 20:3**	802
and your **w** and your children,"	**1Ki 20:5**	802
for he sent to me for my **w** and my	**1Ki 20:7**	802
the **w** of the sons of the prophets	**2Ki 4:1**	802
the king's mother and the king's **w**	**2Ki 24:15**	802
the father of Tekoa, had two **w**,	**1Ch 4:5**	802
war, for they had many **w** and sons.	**1Ch 7:4**	802
sent away Hushim and Baara his **w**.	**1Ch 8:8**	802
David took more **w** at Jerusalem,	**1Ch 14:3**	802
took them *as* **w**.	**1Ch 23:22**	
all his *other* **w** and concubines.	**2Ch 11:21**	802
For he had taken eighteen **w** and	**2Ch 11:21**	802
And he sought many **w** *for them.*	**2Ch 11:23**	802
and took fourteen **w** to himself,	**2Ch 13:21**	802
LORD, with their infants, their **w** and	**2Ch 20:13**	802
your people, your sons, your **w** and	**2Ch 21:14**	802
together with his sons and his **w**,	**2Ch 21:17**	802
Jehoiada took two **w** for him,	**2Ch 24:3**	802
our **w** are in captivity for this.	**2Ch 29:9**	802
their little children, their **w**,	**2Ch 31:18**	802
taken some of their daughters *as* **w**	**Ezr 9:2**	
put away all the **w** and their children	**Ezr 10:3**	802
married foreign **w** adding to the guilt	**Ezr 10:10**	802
the land and from the foreign **w**."	**Ezr 10:11**	802
who have married foreign **w**	**Ezr 10:14**	802
the men who had married foreign **w**	**Ezr 10:17**	802
priests who had married foreign **w**	**Ezr 10:18**	802
They pledged to put away their **w**,	**Ezr 10:19**	802
All these had married foreign **w**,	**Ezr 10:44**	802
had **w** *by whom* they had children.	**Ezr 10:44**	802
your sons, your daughters, your **w** and	**Ne 4:14**	802
w against their Jewish brothers.	**Ne 5:1**	802
lands to the law of God, their **w**,	**Ne 10:28**	802
be plundered And their **w** ravished.	**Is 13:16**	802
Their fields and their **w** together;	**Jer 6:12**	802
I will give their **w** to others,	**Jer 8:10**	802
neither them, *nor* their **w**, nor their	**Jer 14:16**	802
w become childless and widowed.	**Jer 18:21**	802
'Take **w** and become the fathers of	**Jer 29:6**	802
and take **w** for your sons and give	**Jer 29:6**	802
adultery with their neighbors' **w** and	**Jer 29:23**	802
wine all our days, we, our **w**,	**Jer 35:8**	802
'They will also bring out all your **w**	**Jer 38:23**	802
and the wickedness of their **w**,	**Jer 44:9**	802
and the wickedness of your **w**,	**Jer 44:9**	802
that their **w** were burning sacrifices to	**Jer 44:15**	802
'As for you and your **w**,	**Jer 44:25**	802
the king and his nobles, his **w** and	**Da 5:2**	7695
the king and his nobles, his **w** and	**Da 5:3**	7695
your **w** and your concubines have	**Da 5:23**	7695
and their **w** into the lions' den;	**Da 6:24**	5389
itself and their **w** by themselves;	**Zch 12:12**	802
itself and their **w** by themselves;	**Zch 12:12**	802
itself and their **w** by themselves;	**Zch 12:13**	802
itself and their **w** by themselves;	**Zch 12:13**	802
itself and their **w** by themselves.	**Zch 12:14**	802
permitted you to divorce your **w**;	**Mt 19:8**	*1135*
they all, with **w** and children,	**Ac 21:5**	*1135*
that from now on those who have **w**	**1Co 7:29**	*1135*
W, *be subject* to your own	**Eph 5:22**	*1135*
the **w** *ought to be* to their husbands	**Eph 5:24**	*1135*
Husbands, love your **w**,	**Eph 5:25**	*1135*
ought also to love their own **w** as	**Eph 5:28**	*1135*
W, be subject to your husbands, as	**Col 3:18**	*1135*
Husbands, love your **w** and	**Col 3:19**	*1135*
you **w**, be submissive to your own	**1Pe 3:1**	*1135*
a word by the behavior of their **w**,	**1Pe 3:1**	*1135*
live with *your* **w** in an	**1Pe 3:7**	

WOE

"**W** to you, O Moab!	**Nu 21:29**	188
"**W** to us! For nothing like this has	**1Sa 4:7**	188
"**W** to us! Who shall deliver us from	**1Sa 4:8**	188
'If I am wicked, **w** to me!	**Jb 10:15**	480
W is me, for I sojourn in Meshech,	**Ps 120:5**	190
Who has **w**? Who has sorrow?	**Pr 23:29**	188
But **w** to the one who falls when	**Ec 4:10**	337
W to you, O land, whose king is a	**Ec 10:16**	337
W to them! For they have brought	**Is 3:9**	188
W to the wicked! *It will go* badly	**Is 3:11**	188
W to those who add house to house	**Is 5:8**	1945
W to those who rise early in the	**Is 5:11**	1945
W to those who drag iniquity with	**Is 5:18**	1945
W to those who call evil good, and	**Is 5:20**	1945
W to those who are wise in their	**Is 5:21**	1945
W to those who are heroes in	**Is 5:22**	1945
"**W** is me, for I am ruined!	**Is 6:5**	188
W to those who enact evil	**Is 10:1**	1945
W to Assyria, the rod of My anger	**Is 10:5**	1945
"**W** to me! Woe to me! Alas for me!	**Is 24:16**	7334
Woe to me! **W** to me! Alas for me!	**Is 24:16**	7334
W to the proud crown of the	**Is 28:1**	1945
W, O Ariel, Ariel the city *where*	**Is 29:1**	1945
W to those who deeply hide their	**Is 29:15**	1945
"**W** to the rebellious children,"	**Is 30:1**	1945
W to those who go down to Egypt	**Is 31:1**	1945
W to you, O destroyer, While you	**Is 33:1**	1945
"**W** to *the one* who quarrels with	**Is 45:9**	1945
"**W** to him who says to a father,	**Is 45:10**	1945
W to us, for we are ruined!"	**Jer 4:13**	188
"Ah, **w** is me, for I faint before	**Jer 4:31**	188
W to us, for the day declines, For	**Jer 6:4**	188
W is me, because of my injury!	**Jer 10:19**	188
W to you, O Jerusalem!	**Jer 13:27**	188
W to me, my mother, that you have	**Jer 15:10**	188
"**W** to him who builds his house	**Jer 22:13**	1945
"**W** to the shepherds who are	**Jer 23:1**	1945
to set My face against you for **w**,	**Jer 44:11**	7463a
w is me! For the LORD has added	**Jer 45:3**	188
"**W** to Nebo, for it has been	**Jer 48:1**	1945

“**W** to you, Moab! **Jer 48:46** 188
W be upon them, for their day has **Jer 50:27** 1945
W to us, for we have sinned! **La 5:16** 188
were lamentations, mourning and **w**. **Ezk 2:10** 1958
“**W** to the foolish prophets who **Ezk 13:3** 1945
“**W** to the women who sew *magic* **Ezk 13:18** 1945
(‘**W**, woe to you!’ **Ezk 16:23** 188
Woe, **w** to you!’ declares the Lord **Ezk 16:23** 188
“**W** to the bloody city, To the pot **Ezk 24:6** 188
“**W** to the bloody city! **Ezk 24:9** 188
“**W**, shepherds of Israel who have **Ezk 34:2** 1945
W to them, for they have strayed **Hos 7:13** 188
w to them indeed when I depart **Hos 9:12** 188
W to those who are at ease in **Am 6:1** 1945
W to those who scheme iniquity, **Mi 2:1** 1945
W is me! For I am Like the fruit **Mi 7:1** 480
W to the bloody city, completely **Na 3:1** 1945
‘**W** to him who increases what is **Hab 2:6** 1945
“**W** to him who gets evil gain for **Hab 2:9** 1945
“**W** to him who builds a city with **Hab 2:12** 1945
“**W** to you who make your neighbors **Hab 2:15** 1945
“**W** to him who says to a *piece of* **Hab 2:19** 1945
W to the inhabitants of the **Zph 2:5** 1945
W to her who is rebellious and **Zph 3:1** 1945
“**W** to the worthless shepherd Who **Zch 11:17** 1945
“**W** to you, Chorazin! **Mt 11:21** *3759*
W to you, Bethsaida! **Mt 11:21** *3759*
“**W** to the world because of *its* **Mt 18:7** *3759*
but **w** to that man through whom the **Mt 18:7** *3759*
“But **w** to you, scribes and **Mt 23:13** *3759*
“**W** to you, scribes and **Mt 23:14** *3759*
“**W** to you, scribes and Pharisees, **Mt 23:15** *3759*
“**W** to you, blind guides, who say, **Mt 23:16** *3759*
“**W** to you, scribes and Pharisees, **Mt 23:23** *3759*
“**W** to you, scribes and Pharisees, **Mt 23:25** *3759*
“**W** to you, scribes and Pharisees, **Mt 23:27** *3759*
“**W** to you, scribes and Pharisees, **Mt 23:29** *3759*
“But **w** to those who are pregnant **Mt 24:19** *3759*
but **w** to that man by whom the Son **Mt 26:24** *3759*
“But **w** to those who are pregnant **Mk 13:17** *3759*
but **w** to that man by whom the Son **Mk 14:21** *3759*
“But **w** to you who are rich, for **Lk 6:24** *3759*
“**W** to you who are well-fed now, **Lk 6:25** *3759*
W *to you* who laugh now, for you **Lk 6:25** *3759*
“**W** *to you* when all men speak well **Lk 6:26** *3759*
“**W** to you, Chorazin! **Lk 10:13** *3759*
W to you, Bethsaida! **Lk 10:13** *3759*
“But **w** to you Pharisees! **Lk 11:42** *3759*
“**W** to you Pharisees! **Lk 11:43** *3759*
“**W** to you! For you are like **Lk 11:44** *3759*
“**W** to you lawyers as well! **Lk 11:46** *3759*
“**W** to you! For you build the tombs **Lk 11:47** *3759*
“**W** to you lawyers! **Lk 11:52** *3759*
w to him through whom they come! **Lk 17:1** *3759*
“**W** to those who are pregnant **Lk 21:23** *3759*
but **w** to that man by whom He is **Lk 22:22** *3759*
for **w** is me if I do not preach the **1Co 9:16** *3759*
W to them! For they have gone the **Jude 1:11** *3759*
“**W**, woe, woe to those who dwell **Rv 8:13** *3759*
“Woe, **w**, woe to those who dwell **Rv 8:13** *3759*
“Woe, woe, **w** to those who dwell **Rv 8:13** *3759*
The first **w** is past; **Rv 9:12** *3759*
The second **w** is past; **Rv 11:14** *3759*
the third **w** is coming quickly. **Rv 11:14** *3759*
W to the earth and the sea, **Rv 12:12** *3759*
‘**W**, woe, the great city, Babylon, **Rv 18:10** *3759*
‘Woe, **w**, the great city, Babylon, **Rv 18:10** *3759*
‘**W**, woe, the great city, she who **Rv 18:16** *3759*
‘Woe, **w**, the great city, she who **Rv 18:16** *3759*
‘**W**, woe, the great city, in which **Rv 18:19** *3759*
‘Woe, **w**, the great city, in which **Rv 18:19** *3759*

WOEFUL

Nor have I longed for the **w** day; **Jer 17:16** 605

WOES

Surely I will bring added **w** upon **Is 15:9**
two **w** are still coming after these **Rv 9:12** *3759*

WOKE

And they came to *Him* and **w** Him, **Mt 8:25** *1453*
and they **w** Him and said to Him, **Mk 4:38** *1453*
They came to Jesus and **w** Him up, **Lk 8:24** *1326*
and he struck Peter’s side and **w** him **Ac 12:7** *1453*

WOLF

“Benjamin is a ravenous **w**; **Gn 49:27** 2061
the **w** will dwell with the lamb, **Is 11:6** 2061
“The **w** and the lamb will graze **Is 65:25** 2061
A **w** of the deserts will destroy **Jer 5:6** 2061
the sheep, sees the **w** coming, **Jn 10:12** *3074*
flees, and the **w** snatches them and **Jn 10:12** *3074*

WOLVES

creatures will meet with the **w**, **Is 34:14** 338
her are like **w** tearing the prey, **Ezk 22:27** 2061
And keener than **w** in the evening. **Hab 1:8** 2061
Her judges are **w** at evening; **Zph 3:3** 2061
but inwardly are ravenous **w**. **Mt 7:15** *3074*
out as sheep in the midst of **w**; **Mt 10:16** *3074*
out as lambs in the midst of **w**. **Lk 10:3** *3074*
savage **w** will come in among you, **Ac 20:29** *3074*

WOMAN

God fashioned into a **w** the rib which **Gn 2:22** 802
She shall be called **W**, **Gn 2:23** 802
And he said to the **w**, **Gn 3:1** 802
The **w** said to the serpent, **Gn 3:2** 802
The serpent said to the **w**, **Gn 3:4** 802
When the **w** saw that the tree was **Gn 3:6** 802
“The **w** whom You gave *to be* **Gn 3:12** 802
Then the LORD God said to the **w**, **Gn 3:13** 802
the **w** said, “The serpent deceived me **Gn 3:13** 802
put enmity Between you and the **w**, **Gn 3:15** 802
To the **w** He said, **Gn 3:16** 802
I know that you are a beautiful **w**; **Gn 12:11** 802
saw that the **w** was very beautiful. **Gn 12:14** 802
and the **w** was taken into Pharaoh’s **Gn 12:15** 802
of the **w** whom you have taken, **Gn 20:3** 802
“Suppose the **w** is not **Gn 24:5** 802
w is not willing to follow you, **Gn 24:8** 802
‘Suppose the **w** does not follow me.’ **Gn 24:39** 802
let her be the **w** whom the LORD has **Gn 24:44** 802
Shaul the son of a Canaanite **w**. **Gn 46:10**
The **w** conceived and bore a son; **Ex 2:2** 802
w took the child and nursed him. **Ex 2:9** 802
“But every **w** shall ask of her **Ex 3:22** 802
and the **w** who lives in her house, **Ex 3:22**
Shaul the son of a Canaanite **w**; **Ex 6:15** 3669a
each **w** from her neighbor for articles **Ex 11:2** 802
do not go near a **w**.” **Ex 19:15** 802
“If he takes to himself another **w**, **Ex 21:10** 312
and strike a **w** with child so that she **Ex 21:22** 802
an ox gores a man or a **w** to death, **Ex 21:28** 802
it and it kills a man or a **w**, **Ex 21:29** 802
“Let no man or **w** any longer **Ex 36:6** 802
‘When a **w** gives birth and bears a **Lv 12:2** 802
“Now if a man or **w** has an **Lv 13:29** 802
“When a man or a **w** has bright **Lv 13:38** 802
‘If a man lies with a **w** *so that* **Lv 15:18** 802
‘When a **w** has a discharge, *if* her **Lv 15:19** 802
‘Now if a **w** has a discharge of her **Lv 15:25** 802
and for the **w** who is ill because **Lv 15:33** 1739
a man who lies with an unclean **w**. **Lv 15:33** 2931
not uncover the nakedness of a **w** **Lv 18:17** 802
‘You shall not marry a **w** in **Lv 18:18** 802
‘Also you shall not approach a **w** **Lv 18:19** 802
nor shall any **w** stand before an **Lv 18:23** 802
lies carnally with a **w** who is a slave **Lv 19:20** 802
a male as those who lie with a **w**, **Lv 20:13** 802
who marries a **w** and her mother, **Lv 20:14** 802
‘If *there is* a **w** who approaches **Lv 20:16** 802
shall kill the **w** and the animal; **Lv 20:16** 802
man who lies with a menstruous **w** **Lv 20:18** 802
‘Now a man or a **w** who is a medium **Lv 20:27** 802
a **w** who is profaned by harlotry, **Lv 21:7** 802
a **w** divorced from her husband; **Lv 21:7** 802
‘A widow, or a divorced **w**, **Lv 21:14**
Now the son of an Israelite **w**, **Lv 24:10** 802
The son of the Israelite **w** **Lv 24:11** 802
‘When a man or **w** commits any of **Nu 5:6** 802
have the **w** stand before the LORD **Nu 5:18** 802
an oath and shall say to the **w**, **Nu 5:19** 802
shall have the **w** swear with the oath **Nu 5:21** 802
the priest shall say to the **w**), **Nu 5:21** 802
And the **w** shall say, **Nu 5:22** 802
‘Then he shall make the **w** drink **Nu 5:24** 802
shall make the **w** drink the water. **Nu 5:26** 802
and the **w** will become a curse **Nu 5:27** 802
‘But if the **w** has not defiled herself **Nu 5:28** 802
make the **w** stand before the LORD, **Nu 5:30** 802
that **w** shall bear her guilt.’ ” **Nu 5:31** 802
a man or **w** makes a special vow, **Nu 6:2** 802
the Cushite **w** whom he had married **Nu 12:1** 802
(for he had married a Cushite **w**); **Nu 12:1** 802
to his relatives a Midianite **w**, **Nu 25:6** 4084
the man of Israel and the **w**, **Nu 25:8** 802
was slain with the Midianite **w**, **Nu 25:14** 4084
The name of the Midianite **w** **Nu 25:15** 802
if a **w** makes a vow to the LORD, **Nu 30:3** 802
vow of a widow or of a divorced **w**, **Nu 30:9**
w who has known man intimately. **Nu 31:17** 802
your kinsman, a Hebrew man or **w**, **Dt 15:12** 5680
a man or a **w** who does what is evil **Dt 17:2** 802
w who has done this evil deed to **Dt 17:5** 802
gates, *that is,* the man or the **w**, **Dt 17:5** 802
is the man that is engaged to a **w** **Dt 20:7** 802
among the captives a beautiful **w**, **Dt 21:11** 802
“A **w** shall not wear man’s **Dt 22:5** 802
‘I took this **w**, *but* when I came **Dt 22:14** 802
is found lying with a married **w**, **Dt 22:22** 802
die, the man who lay with the **w**, **Dt 22:22** 802
who lay with the woman, and the **w**; **Dt 22:22** 802
refined and delicate **w** among you, **Dt 28:56** 6028
not be among you a man or **w**, **Dt 29:18** 802
But the **w** had taken the two men **Jos 2:4** 802
in the city, both man and **w**, **Jos 6:21** 802
bring the **w** and all she has out of **Jos 6:22** 802
Sisera into the hands of a **w**.” **Jg 4:9** 802
certain **w** threw an upper millstone **Jg 9:53** 802
‘A **w** slew him.’ ” **Jg 9:54** 802
you are the son of another **w**.” **Jg 11:2** 802
of the LORD appeared to the **w** and **Jg 13:3** 802
the **w** came and told her husband, **Jg 13:6** 802
the angel of God came again to the **w** **Jg 13:9** 802
So the **w** ran quickly and told her **Jg 13:10** 802
you the man who spoke to the **w**?” **Jg 13:11** 802
“Let the **w** pay attention to all **Jg 13:13** 802
Then the **w** gave birth to a son and **Jg 13:24** 802
to Timnah and saw a **w** in Timnah, **Jg 14:1** 802
“I saw a **w** in Timnah, *one* of the **Jg 14:2** 802
“Is there no **w** among the **Jg 14:3** 802
he went down and talked to the **w**; **Jg 14:7** 802
his father went down to the **w**; **Jg 14:10** 802
loved a **w** in the valley of Sorek, **Jg 16:4** 802
the **w** came and fell down at the **Jg 19:26** 802
husband of the **w** who was murdered, **Jg 20:4** 802
every **w** who has lain with a man.” **Jg 21:11** 802
and the **w** was bereft of her two **Ru 1:5** 802
“Whose young **w** is this?” **Ru 2:5** 5291
“She is the young Moabite **w** who **Ru 2:6** 5291
behold, a **w** was lying at his feet. **Ru 3:8** 802
that you are a **w** of excellence. **Ru 3:11** 802
w came to the threshing floor.” **Ru 3:14** 802
the **w** who is coming into your home **Ru 4:11** 802
LORD will give you by this young **w** **Ru 4:12** 5291
I am a **w** oppressed in spirit; **1Sa 1:15** 802
your maidservant as a worthless **w**, **1Sa 1:16** 1323
So the **w** went her way and ate, and **1Sa 1:18** 802
So the **w** remained and nursed her **1Sa 1:23** 802
the **w** who stood here beside you, **1Sa 1:26** 802
LORD give you children from this **w** **1Sa 2:20** 802
but put to death both man and **w**, **1Sa 15:3** 802
son of a perverse, rebellious **w**! **1Sa 20:30**
And the **w** was intelligent and **1Sa 25:3** 802
did not leave a man or a **w** alive, **1Sa 27:9** 802
did not leave a man or a **w** alive to **1Sa 27:11** 802
“Seek for me a **w** who is a medium, **1Sa 28:7** 802
is a **w** who is a medium at En-dor.” **1Sa 28:7** 802
and they came to the **w** by night; **1Sa 28:8** 802
But the **w** said to him, **1Sa 28:9** 802
Then the **w** said, **1Sa 28:11** 802
When the **w** saw Samuel, she cried **1Sa 28:12** 802
and the **w** spoke to Saul, saying, **1Sa 28:12** 802
And the **w** said to Saul, **1Sa 28:13** 802
The **w** came to Saul and saw **1Sa 28:21** 802
servants together with the **w** urged **1Sa 28:23** 802
The **w** had a fattened calf in **1Sa 28:24** 802
me with a guilt concerning the **w**. **2Sa 3:8** 802
from the roof he saw a **w** bathing; **2Sa 11:2** 802
and the **w** was very beautiful in **2Sa 11:2** 802
sent and inquired about the **w**. **2Sa 11:3** 802
The **w** conceived; **2Sa 11:5** 802
w throw an upper millstone on him **2Sa 11:21** 802
throw this **w** out of my *presence,* **2Sa 13:17** 2088
brought a wise **w** from there and **2Sa 14:2** 802
a **w** who has been mourning for the **2Sa 14:2** 802
the **w** of Tekoa spoke to the king, **2Sa 14:4** 802
Then the king said to the **w**, **2Sa 14:8** 802
The **w** of Tekoa said to the king, **2Sa 14:9** 802
Then the **w** said, **2Sa 14:12** 802
w said, “Why then have you planned **2Sa 14:13** 802
king answered and said to the **w**, **2Sa 14:18** 802
the **w** said, “Let my lord the king **2Sa 14:18** 802
And the **w** replied, **2Sa 14:19** 802
was a **w** of beautiful appearance. **2Sa 14:27** 802
And the **w** took a covering and **2Sa 17:19** 802
Absalom’s servants came to the **w** **2Sa 17:20** 802
And the **w** said to them, **2Sa 17:20** 802
a wise **w** called from the city, **2Sa 20:16** 802
he approached her, and the **w** said, **2Sa 20:17** 802
And the **w** said to Joab, **2Sa 20:21** 802
w wisely came to all the people. **2Sa 20:22** 802
The one **w** said, **1Ki 3:17** 802
this **w** and I live in the same house; **1Ki 3:17** 802
this **w** also gave birth to a child, **1Ki 3:18** 802
Then the other **w** said, **1Ki 3:22** 802
But the first **w** said, **1Ki 3:22** 2088
Then the **w** whose child *was* the **1Ki 3:26** 802
“Give the first **w** the living **1Ki 3:27**
will pretend to be another **w**.” **1Ki 14:5** 5235a
do you pretend to be another **w**? **1Ki 14:6** 5235a
things that the son of the **w**, **1Ki 17:17** 802
Then the **w** said to Elijah, **1Ki 17:24** 802
a certain **w** of the wives of the sons **2Ki 4:1** 802
where there was a prominent **w**, **2Ki 4:8** 802
The **w** conceived and bore a son **2Ki 4:17** 802
on the wall a **w** cried out to him, **2Ki 6:26** 802
“This **w** said to me, **2Ki 6:28** 802
the king heard the words of the **w**, **2Ki 6:30** 802
Now Elisha spoke to the **w** whose **2Ki 8:1** 802
So the **w** arose and did according **2Ki 8:2** 802
the **w** returned from the land **2Ki 8:3** 802
the **w** whose son he had restored to **2Ki 8:5** 802
this is the **w** and this is her son, **2Ki 8:5** 802
When the king asked the **w**, **2Ki 8:6** 802
now to this cursed **w** and bury her, **2Ki 9:34** 779
of Israel, both man and **w**, **1Ch 16:3** 802
the son of a Danite **w** and a Tyrian **2Ch 2:14** 802
whether small or great, man or **w**. **2Ch 15:13** 802
any man or **w** who comes to the king **Es 4:11** 802
“Man, who is born of **w**, **Jb 14:1** 802
be pure, Or he who is born of a **w**, **Jb 15:14** 802
“He wrongs the barren **w** And **Jb 24:21** 6135
can he be clean who is born of **w**? **Jb 25:4** 802
my heart has been enticed by a **w**, **Jb 31:9** 802
Anguish, as of a **w** in childbirth. **Ps 48:6**
miscarriages of a **w** which never see **Ps 58:8** 802
He makes the barren **w** abide in the **Ps 113:9** 6135
To deliver you from the strange **w**, **Pr 2:16** 802
To keep you from the evil **w**, **Pr 6:24** 802
one who commits adultery with a **w** **Pr 6:32** 802
And behold, a **w** *comes* to meet him, **Pr 7:10** 802
The **w** of folly is boisterous, *She* **Pr 9:13** 802
A gracious **w** attains honor, And **Pr 11:16** 802
beautiful **w** who lacks discretion. **Pr 11:22** 802
The wise **w** builds her house, But **Pr 14:1** 802
house shared with a contentious **w**. **Pr 21:9** 802
with a contentious and vexing **w**. **Pr 21:19** 802
an adulterous **w** is a narrow well. **Pr 23:27** 5237
house shared with a contentious **w**. **Pr 25:24** 802
adulterous **w** hold him in pledge. **Pr 27:13** 5237
And a contentious **w** are alike; **Pr 27:15** 802
is the way of an adulterous **w**: **Pr 30:20** 802
unloved **w** when she gets a husband, **Pr 30:23**
vain, *But* a **w** who fears the LORD, **Pr 31:30** 802
the **w** whose heart is snares and nets, **Ec 7:26** 802
not found a **w** among all these. **Ec 7:28** 802
Enjoy life with the **w** whom you **Ec 9:9** 802
in the womb of the pregnant **w**, **Ec 11:5** 4392
will writhe like a **w** in labor, **Is 13:8**
me like the pains of a **w** in labor. **Is 21:3**

As the pregnant **w** approaches *the*	**Is 26:17**	2030
like a **w** in labor I will groan,	**Is 42:14**	
to a **w**, 'To what are you giving birth?'	**Is 45:10**	802
"Can a **w** forget her nursing child And	**Is 49:15**	802
Than the sons of the married **w**,"	**Is 54:1**	
as a **w** treacherously departs from	**Jer 3:20**	802
I heard a cry as of a **w** in labor,	**Jer 4:31**	
us, Pain as of a **w** in childbirth.	**Jer 6:24**	
of you Like a **w** in childbirth?	**Jer 13:21**	802
you, Pain like a **w** in childbirth!	**Jer 22:23**	
his loins, as a **w** in childbirth?	**Jer 30:6**	
The **w** with child and she who is in	**Jer 31:8**	2030
A **w** will encompass a man."	**Jer 31:22**	5347
a Hebrew man or a Hebrew **w**;	**Jer 34:9**	5680
as to cut off from you man and **w**,	**Jer 44:7**	802
be like the heart of a **w** in labor.	**Jer 48:41**	802
be like the heart of a **w** in labor.	**Jer 49:22**	802
of her Like a **w** in childbirth.	**Jer 49:24**	
him, Agony like a **w** in childbirth.	**Jer 50:43**	
And with you I shatter man and **w**,	**Jer 51:22**	802
a **w** during her menstrual period	**Ezk 18:6**	802
uncleanness of a **w** in her impurity.	**Ezk 36:17**	
not marry a widow or a divorced **w**	**Ezk 44:22**	
a **w** *who* is loved by *her* husband,	**Hos 3:1**	802
you like a **w** in childbirth?	**Mi 4:9**	
of Zion, Like a **w** in childbirth.	**Mi 4:10**	
is a **w** sitting inside the ephah."	**Zch 5:7**	802
that everyone who looks at a **w** with	**Mt 5:28**	*1135*
and whoever marries a divorced **w**	**Mt 5:32**	*1135*
a **w** who had been suffering from a	**Mt 9:20**	*1135*
At once the **w** was made well.	**Mt 9:22**	*1135*
is like leaven, which a **w** took and	**Mt 13:33**	*1135*
w from that region came out	**Mt 15:22**	*1135*
"O **w**, your faith is great;	**Mt 15:28**	*1135*
another **w** commits adultery."	**Mt 19:9**	*243*
"Last of all, the **w** died.	**Mt 22:27**	*1135*
a **w** came to Him with an alabaster	**Mt 26:7**	*1135*
"Why do you bother the **w**?	**Mt 26:10**	*1135*
what this **w** has done will also be	**Mt 26:13**	*3778*
A **w** who had had a hemorrhage	**Mk 5:25**	*1135*
to see the **w** who had done this.	**Mk 5:32**	
But the **w** fearing and trembling,	**Mk 5:33**	*1135*
a **w** whose little daughter had an	**Mk 7:25**	*1135*
Now the **w** was a Gentile, of the	**Mk 7:26**	*1135*
his wife and marries another **w**	**Mk 10:11**	*243*
Last of all the **w** died also.	**Mk 12:22**	*1135*
there came a **w** with an alabaster	**Mk 14:3**	*1135*
what this **w** has done will also	**Mk 14:9**	*3778*
of Sidon, to a **w** who was a widow.	**Lk 4:26**	*1135*
a **w** in the city who was a sinner;	**Lk 7:37**	*1135*
this **w** is who is touching Him,	**Lk 7:39**	*1135*
Turning toward the **w**,	**Lk 7:44**	*1135*
"Do you see this **w**?	**Lk 7:44**	*1135*
And He said to the **w**,	**Lk 7:50**	*1135*
And a **w** who had a hemorrhage for	**Lk 8:43**	*1135*
When the **w** saw that she had	**Lk 8:47**	*1135*
and a **w** named Martha welcomed Him	**Lk 10:38**	*1135*
there was a **w** who for eighteen	**Lk 13:11**	*1135*
"**W**, you are freed from your	**Lk 13:12**	*1135*
"And this **w**, a daughter of	**Lk 13:16**	*3778*
which a **w** took and hid in three	**Lk 13:21**	*1135*
"Or what **w**, if she has ten silver	**Lk 15:8**	*1135*
"Finally the **w** died also.	**Lk 20:32**	*1135*
"**W**, I do not know Him."	**Lk 22:57**	*1135*
"**W**, what does that have to do with us?	**Jn 2:4**	*1135*
came a **w** of Samaria to draw water.	**Jn 4:7**	*1135*
Samaritan **w** said to Him,	**Jn 4:9**	*1135*
drink since I am a Samaritan **w**?"	**Jn 4:9**	*1135*
The **w** said to Him,	**Jn 4:15**	*1135*
The **w** answered and said,	**Jn 4:17**	*1135*
The **w** said to Him,	**Jn 4:19**	*1135*
"**W**, believe Me, an hour is coming	**Jn 4:21**	*1135*
The **w** said to Him,	**Jn 4:25**	*1135*
He had been speaking with a **w**,	**Jn 4:27**	*1135*
So the **w** left her waterpot, and	**Jn 4:28**	*1135*
the word of the **w** who testified,	**Jn 4:39**	*1135*
and they were saying to the **w**,	**Jn 4:42**	*1135*
brought a **w** caught in adultery,	**Jn 8:3**	*1135*
w has been caught in adultery,	**Jn 8:4**	*1135*
and He was left alone, and the **w**,	**Jn 8:9**	*1135*
"**W**, where are they?	**Jn 8:10**	*1135*
"Whenever a **w** is in labor she has	**Jn 16:21**	*1135*
"**W**, behold, your son!"	**Jn 19:26**	*1135*
"**W**, why are you weeping?"	**Jn 20:13**	*1135*
"**W**, why are you weeping?	**Jn 20:15**	*1135*
this **w** was abounding with deeds of	**Ac 9:36**	*3778*
the son of a Jewish **w** who was a	**Ac 16:1**	*1135*
A **w** named Lydia, from	**Ac 16:14**	*1135*
and a **w** named Damaris and others	**Ac 17:34**	*1135*
the natural function of the **w** and	**Ro 1:27**	*2338*
For the married **w** is bound by law	**Ro 7:2**	*1135*
good for a man not to touch a **w**.	**1Co 7:1**	*1135*
each **w** is to have her own husband.	**1Co 7:2**	*1135*
w who has an unbelieving husband,	**1Co 7:13**	*1135*
The **w** who is unmarried, and	**1Co 7:34**	*1135*
and the man is the head of a **w**,	**1Co 11:3**	*1135*
every **w** who has her head uncovered	**1Co 11:5**	*1135*
for she is one and the same as the **w**	**1Co 11:5**	*1135*
if a **w** does not cover her head,	**1Co 11:6**	*1135*
for a **w** to have her hair cut off or	**1Co 11:6**	*1135*
but the **w** is the glory of man.	**1Co 11:7**	*1135*
For man does not originate from **w**,	**1Co 11:8**	*1135*
from woman, but **w** from man;	**1Co 11:8**	*1135*
sake, but **w** for the man's sake.	**1Co 11:9**	*1135*
Therefore the **w** ought to have *a*	**1Co 11:10**	*1135*
neither is **w** independent of man,	**1Co 11:11**	*1135*
man, nor is man independent of **w**.	**1Co 11:11**	*1135*
as the **w** originates from the man,	**1Co 11:12**	*1135*
man *has his birth* through the **w**;	**1Co 11:12**	*1135*
is it proper for a **w** to pray to	**1Co 11:13**	*1135*
but if a **w** has long hair, it is a	**1Co 11:15**	*1135*
for a **w** to speak in church.	**1Co 14:35**	*1135*
sent forth His Son, born of a **w**,	**Ga 4:4**	*1135*
bondwoman and one by the free **w**.	**Ga 4:22**	*1658*
the son by the free **w** through the	**Ga 4:23**	*1658*
BARREN **W** WHO DOES NOT BEAR;	**Ga 4:27**	*4723*
HEIR WITH THE SON OF THE FREE **W**."	**Ga 4:30**	*1658*
of a bondwoman, but of the free **w**.	**Ga 4:31**	*1658*
labor pains upon a **w** with child,	**1Th 5:3**	
A **w** must quietly receive instruction	**1Tm 2:11**	*1135*
But I do not allow a **w** to teach or	**1Tm 2:12**	*1135*
but the **w** being deceived,	**1Tm 2:14**	*1135*
If any **w** who is a believer has	**1Tm 5:16**	*5100*
someone weaker, since she is a **w**;	**1Pe 3:7**	*1134*
that you tolerate the **w** Jezebel,	**Rv 2:20**	*1135*
a **w** clothed with the sun, and the	**Rv 12:1**	*1135*
the **w** who was about to give birth,	**Rv 12:4**	*1135*
Then the **w** fled into the wilderness	**Rv 12:6**	*1135*
he persecuted the **w** who gave birth	**Rv 12:13**	*1135*
great eagle were given to the **w**,	**Rv 12:14**	*1135*
out of his mouth after the **w**,	**Rv 12:15**	*1135*
But the earth helped the **w**,	**Rv 12:16**	*1135*
the dragon was enraged with the **w**,	**Rv 12:17**	*1135*
a **w** sitting on a scarlet beast,	**Rv 17:3**	*1135*
The **w** was clothed in purple	**Rv 17:4**	*1135*
And I saw the **w** drunk with the	**Rv 17:6**	*1135*
I will tell you the mystery of the **w**	**Rv 17:7**	*1135*
mountains on which the **w** sits,	**Rv 17:9**	*1135*
"The **w** whom you saw is the	**Rv 17:18**	*1135*

WOMAN'S

to receive the pledge from the **w** hand,	**Gn 38:20**	802
surely be fined as the **w** husband	**Ex 21:22**	802
and the Israelite **w** son and a man of	**Lv 24:10**	3481
and let *the hair of* the **w** head	**Nu 5:18**	802
offering of jealousy from the **w** hand,	**Nu 5:25**	802
nor shall a man put on a **w** clothing;	**Dt 22:5**	802
"This **w** son died in the night,	**1Ki 3:19**	802
man was not created for the **w** sake,	**1Co 11:9**	*1135*

WOMB

"Two nations are in your **w**; And two	**Gn 25:23**	990
there were twins in her **w**.	**Gn 25:24**	990
and He opened her **w**, but Rachel was	**Gn 29:31**	7358
withheld from you the fruit of the **w**?"	**Gn 30:2**	990
God gave heed to her and opened her **w**.	**Gn 30:22**	7358
there were twins in her **w**.	**Gn 38:27**	990
Blessings of the breasts and of the **w**.	**Gn 49:25**	7358
the first offspring of every **w** among	**Ex 13:2**	7358
LORD the first offspring of every **w**,	**Ex 13:12**	7358
the first offspring of every **w**,	**Ex 13:15**	7358
"The first offspring from every **w**	**Ex 34:19**	7358
the first issue of the **w** among	**Nu 3:12**	7358
instead of every first issue of the **w**,	**Nu 8:16**	7358
when he comes from his mother's **w**!"	**Nu 12:12**	7358
"Every first issue of the **w** of all	**Nu 18:15**	7358
will also bless the fruit of your **w**	**Dt 7:13**	990
shall be a Nazirite to God from the **w**;	**Jg 13:5**	990
shall be a Nazirite to God from the **w**	**Jg 13:7**	990
a Nazirite to God from my mother's **w**.	**Jg 16:17**	990
Have I yet sons in my **w**, that they	**Ru 1:11**	4578
but the LORD had closed her **w**.	**1Sa 1:5**	7358
because the LORD had closed her **w**.	**1Sa 1:6**	7358
"Naked I came from my mother's **w**,	**Jb 1:21**	990
shut the opening of my *mother's* **w**,	**Jb 3:10**	990
Come forth from the **w** and expire?	**Jb 3:11**	990
have You brought me out of the **w**?	**Jb 10:18**	7358
Carried from **w** to tomb.'	**Jb 10:19**	990
"Did not He who made me in the **w**	**Jb 31:15**	990
And the same one fashion us in the **w**?	**Jb 31:15**	990
it went out from the **w**;	**Jb 38:8**	7358
"From whose **w** has come the ice?	**Jb 38:29**	990
He who brought me forth from the **w**;	**Ps 22:9**	990
been my God from my mother's **w**.	**Ps 22:10**	990
The wicked are estranged from the **w**;	**Ps 58:3**	7358
He who took me from my mother's **w**;	**Ps 71:6**	990
from the **w** of the dawn, Your youth	**Ps 110:3**	7358
The fruit of the **w** is a reward.	**Ps 127:3**	990
You wove me in my mother's **w**.	**Ps 139:13**	990
Sheol, and the barren **w**, Earth that	**Pr 30:16**	7358
O son of my **w**? And what, O son of	**Pr 31:2**	990
had come naked from his mother's **w**,	**Ec 5:15**	990
and how bones *are formed* in the **w**	**Ec 11:5**	990
have compassion on the fruit of the **w**,	**Is 13:18**	990
made you And formed you from the **w**,	**Is 44:2**	990
the one who formed you from the **w**,	**Is 44:24**	990
And have been carried from the **w**;	**Is 46:3**	7358
The LORD called Me from the **w**;	**Is 49:1**	990
who formed Me from the **w** to be His	**Is 49:5**	990
no compassion on the son of her **w**?	**Is 49:15**	990
I who gives delivery shut *the* **w**?"	**Is 66:9**	
"Before I formed you in the **w** I knew	**Jer 1:5**	990
And her **w** ever pregnant.	**Jer 20:17**	7358
Why did I ever come forth from the **w**	**Jer 20:18**	7358
Give them a miscarrying **w** and dry	**Hos 9:14**	7358
slay the precious ones of their **w**.	**Hos 9:16**	990
In the **w** he took his brother by	**Hos 12:3**	990
should delay at the opening of the **w**.	**Hos 13:13**	4866
born that way from their mother's **w**;	**Mt 19:12**	*2836*
Spirit while yet in his mother's **w**.	**Lk 1:15**	*2836*
you will conceive in your **w** and bear	**Lk 1:31**	*1064*
the baby leaped in her **w**;	**Lk 1:41**	*2836*
blessed *is* the fruit of your **w**!	**Lk 1:42**	*2836*
the baby leaped in my **w** for joy.	**Lk 1:44**	*2836*
before He was conceived in the **w**.	**Lk 2:21**	*2836*
firstborn MALE THAT OPENS THE **W**	**Lk 2:23**	*3388*
"Blessed is the **w** that bore You	**Lk 11:27**	*2836*
a second time into his mother's **w**	**Jn 3:4**	*2836*
had been lame from his mother's **w**	**Ac 3:2**	*2836*
lame from his mother's **w**, who had	**Ac 14:8**	*2836*
and the deadness of Sarah's **w**;	**Ro 4:19**	*3388*
me apart *even* from my mother's **w**	**Ga 1:15**	*2836*

WOMBS

LORD had closed fast all the **w** of	**Gn 20:18**	7358
and the **w** that never bore,	**Lk 23:29**	*2836*

WOMEN

and also the **w**, and the people.	**Gn 14:16**	802
the time when **w** go out to draw water.	**Gn 24:11**	
Then Leah said, "Happy am I! For **w**	**Gn 30:13**	1323
for the manner of **w** is upon me." So	**Gn 31:35**	802
He lifted his eyes and saw the **w**	**Gn 33:5**	802
"When you are helping the Hebrew **w**	**Ex 1:16**	5680
"Because the Hebrew **w** are not as	**Ex 1:19**	5680
women are not as the Egyptian **w**; for	**Ex 1:19**	802
a nurse for you from the Hebrew **w**	**Ex 2:7**	5680
and all the **w** went out after her with	**Ex 15:20**	802
both men and **w**, came *and* brought	**Ex 35:22**	802
All the skilled **w** spun with their	**Ex 35:25**	802
All the **w** whose heart stirred with a	**Ex 35:26**	802
The Israelites, all the men and **w**,	**Ex 35:29**	802
from the mirrors of the serving **w** who	**Ex 38:8**	
ten **w** will bake your bread in one	**Lv 26:26**	802
The sons of Israel captured the **w** of	**Nu 31:9**	802
"Have you spared all the **w**?	**Nu 31:15**	5347
and of human beings, of the **w** who	**Nu 31:35**	802
w and children of every city.	**Dt 2:34**	802
w and children of every city.	**Dt 3:6**	802
"Only the **w** and the children	**Dt 20:14**	802
the men and the **w** and children	**Dt 31:12**	802
both men and **w**, were 12,000—all	**Jos 8:25**	802
all the assembly of Israel with the **w**	**Jos 8:35**	802
"Most blessed of **w** is Jael,	**Jg 5:24**	802
Most blessed is she of **w** in the tent.	**Jg 5:24**	802
about a thousand men and **w**.	**Jg 9:49**	802
and all the men and **w** with all	**Jg 9:51**	802
Now the house was full of men and **w**,	**Jg 16:27**	802
men and **w** were on the roof looking	**Jg 16:27**	802
with the **w** and the little ones.	**Jg 21:10**	802
and they gave them the **w** whom they	**Jg 21:14**	802
whom they had kept alive from the **w**	**Jg 21:14**	802
since the **w** are destroyed out of	**Jg 21:16**	802
They took for themselves Moabite **w**	**Ru 1:4**	802
and the **w** said, "Is this Naomi?"	**Ru 1:19**	
Then the **w** said to Naomi, "Blessed	**Ru 4:14**	802
The neighbor **w** gave him a name,	**Ru 4:17**	7934
and how they lay with the **w** who	**1Sa 2:22**	802
And about the time of her death the **w**	**1Sa 4:20**	
they found young **w** going out to draw	**1Sa 9:11**	5291
"As your sword has made **w** childless,	**1Sa 15:33**	802
your mother be childless among **w**."	**1Sa 15:33**	802
that the **w** came out of all the cities	**1Sa 18:6**	802
The **w** sang as they played, and said,	**1Sa 18:7**	802
men have kept themselves from **w**."	**1Sa 21:4**	802
"Surely **w** have been kept from us as	**1Sa 21:5**	802
both men and **w**, children and infants;	**1Sa 22:19**	802
and they took captive the **w** *and all*	**1Sa 30:2**	802
more wonderful Than the love of **w**.	**2Sa 1:26**	802
both to men and **w**, a cake of bread	**2Sa 6:19**	802
the voice of singing men and **w**?	**2Sa 19:35**	
and the king took the ten **w**,	**2Sa 20:3**	802
Then two **w** who were harlots came to	**1Ki 3:16**	802
King Solomon loved many foreign **w**	**1Ki 11:1**	802
Edomite, Sidonian, and Hittite **w**,	**1Ki 11:1**	802
and their **w** with child you will rip	**2Ki 8:12**	2030
struck *it* and ripped up all its **w**	**2Ki 15:16**	2030
where the **w** were weaving hangings	**2Ki 23:7**	802
w, sons and daughters; and they	**2Ch 28:8**	802
and they had 200 singing men and **w**.	**Ezr 2:65**	
w and children, gathered to him from	**Ezr 10:1**	802
to our God and have married foreign **w**	**Ezr 10:2**	802
w and all who *could* listen with	**Ne 8:2**	802
in the presence of men and **w**, those	**Ne 8:3**	802
even the **w** and children rejoiced, so	**Ne 12:43**	802
also saw that the Jews had married **w**	**Ne 13:23**	802
nevertheless the foreign **w** caused	**Ne 13:26**	802
our God by marrying foreign **w**?"	**Ne 13:27**	802
Vashti also gave a banquet for the **w**	**Es 1:9**	802
will become known to all the **w**	**Es 1:17**	802
then all **w** will give honor to their	**Es 1:20**	802
who is in charge of the **w**;	**Es 2:3**	802
who was in charge of the **w**.	**Es 2:8**	802
under the regulations for the **w**	**Es 2:12**	802
with spices and the cosmetics for **w**	**Es 2:12**	802
eunuch who was in charge of the **w**,	**Es 2:15**	802
king loved Esther more than all the **w**,	**Es 2:17**	802
w and children, in one day,	**Es 3:13**	802
men and **w**, I would have remained	**Es 7:4**	8198
including children and **w**, and to	**Es 8:11**	802
"You speak as one of the foolish **w**	**Jb 2:10**	5036
In all the land no **w** were found so	**Jb 42:15**	802
The Lord gives the command; The **w**	**Ps 68:11**	
Do not give your strength to **w**,	**Pr 31:3**	802
Most beautiful among **w**, Go forth on	**SS 1:8**	802
O most beautiful among **w**? What kind	**SS 5:9**	802
O most beautiful among **w**? Where has	**SS 6:1**	802
And **w** rule over them. O My people!	**Is 3:12**	802
For seven **w** will take hold of one man	**Is 4:1**	802
day the Egyptians will become like **w**,	**Is 19:16**	802
W come *and* make a fire with them,	**Is 27:11**	802
Rise up, you **w** who are at ease,	**Is 32:9**	802
Tremble, you **w** who are at ease;	**Is 32:11**	
Therefore even the wicked **w** You have	**Jer 2:33**	7451a
and the **w** knead dough to make cakes	**Jer 7:18**	802
"Consider and call for the mourning **w**,	**Jer 9:17**	6969
And send for the wailing **w**, that	**Jer 9:17**	2450
O you **w**, And let your ear receive	**Jer 9:20**	802
'Then behold, all of the **w** who have	**Jer 38:22**	802

and those w will say, "Your close Jer 38:22 802
w and children, those of the poorest Jer 40:7 802
the w, *the* children, and Jer 41:16 802
the men, the w, the children, Jer 43:6 802
along with all the w who were Jer 44:15 802
"And," *said the* w, "when we Jer 44:19 802
to the men and w—even to all Jer 44:20 802
including all the w, "Hear the word Jer 44:24 802
And they will become w! A sword Jer 50:37 802
They are becoming *like* w; Jer 51:30 802
Should w eat their offspring, La 2:20 802
The hands of compassionate w Boiled La 4:10 802
They ravished the w in Zion, La 5:11 802
w were sitting there weeping for Ezk 8:14 802
and w, but do not touch any man on Ezk 9:6 802
"Woe to the w who sew *magic* Ezk 13:18
therefore, you w will no longer see Ezk 13:23
"Thus you are different from those w Ezk 16:34 802
"Thus I will judge you like w who Ezk 16:38
on you in the sight of many w. Then Ezk 16:41 802
"Son of man, there were two w, Ezk 23:2 802
Thus she became a byword among w, Ezk 23:10 802
put bracelets on the hands of the w Ezk 23:42
and to Oholibah, the lewd w. Ezk 23:44 802
and with the judgment of w who shed Ezk 23:45
that all w may be admonished and not Ezk 23:48 802
And the w will go into captivity. Ezk 30:17 1992a
will also give him the daughter of w Da 11:17 802
of his fathers or for the desire of w, Da 11:37 802
And their pregnant w will be ripped Hos 13:16 2030
they ripped open the pregnant w of Am 1:13 2030
"The w of My people you evict, Each Mi 2:9 802
Behold, your people are w in your Na 3:13 802
and there two w were coming out with Zch 5:9 802
'Old men and old w will again sit in Zch 8:4 2205
the w ravished and half of the city Zch 14:2 802
among those born of w there has not Mt 11:11 *1135*
besides w and children. Mt 14:21 *1135*
besides w and children. Mt 15:38 *1135*
"Two w *will be* grinding at Mt 24:41
Many w were there looking on from a Mt 27:55 *1135*
The angel said to the w, "Do not be Mt 28:5 *1135*
There were also *some* w looking on Mk 15:40 *1135*
and *there were* many other w who Mk 15:41 *243*
"Blessed *are* you among w, Lk 1:42 *1135*
among those born of w there is no one Lk 7:28 *1135*
and *also* some w who had been Lk 8:2 *1135*
one of the w in the crowd raised her Lk 11:27 *1135*
both men and w, and to eat Lk 12:45 *3814*
"There will be two w grinding at Lk 17:35
and of w who were mourning Lk 23:27 *1135*
And all His acquaintances and the w Lk 23:49 *1135*
Now the w who had come with Him out Lk 23:55 *1135*
and as *the* w were terrified Lk 24:5
also the other w with them were Lk 24:10 *3062*
"But also some w among us amazed us. Lk 24:22 *1135*
and found it just exactly as the w Lk 24:24 *1135*
Moses commanded us to stone such w; Jn 8:5 *5108*
along with *the* w, and Mary Ac 1:14 *1135*
BOTH MEN AND W, I WILL IN THOSE Ac 2:18 *1401*
multitudes of men and w, were Ac 5:14 *1135*
and dragging off men and w, he would Ac 8:3 *1135*
men and w alike. Ac 8:12 *1135*
both men and w, he might bring them Ac 9:2 *1135*
But the Jews incited the devout w of Ac 13:50 *1135*
sat down and began speaking to the w Ac 16:13 *1135*
Greeks and a number of the leading w. Ac 17:4 *1135*
with a number of prominent Greek w Ac 17:12 *1135*
binding and putting both men and w Ac 22:4 *1135*
for their w exchanged the natural Ro 1:26 *2338*
The w are to keep silent in 1Co 14:34 *1135*
for these w are two covenants: Ga 4:24
I ask you also to help these w who Php 4:3 *846*
Likewise, *I want* w to adorn 1Tm 2:9 *1135*
as is proper for w making a claim to 1Tm 2:10 *1135*
But w will be preserved through 1Tm 2:15
W *must* likewise *be* dignified, 1Tm 3:11 *1135*
worldly fables fit only for old w. 1Tm 4:7 *1126*
the older w as 1Tm 5:2 *4245*
and the younger w as sisters, in 1Tm 5:2 *4245*
into households and captivate weak w 2Tm 3:6 *1133*
Older w likewise are to be reverent Ti 2:3 *4247*
that they may encourage the young w Ti 2:4 *3501b*
W received *back* their dead by Heb 11:35 *1135*
this way in former times the holy w 1Pe 3:5 *1135*
They had hair like the hair of w, Rv 9:8 *1135*
ones who have not been defiled with w, Rv 14:4 *1135*

WON

They dedicated part of the spoil w in 1Ch 26:27
brother offended *is harder to be* w Pr 18:19
you have w your brother. Mt 18:15 *2770*
and having w over Blastus the king's Ac 12:20 *3982*
and having w over the crowds, they Ac 14:19 *3982*
they may be w without a word by 1Pe 3:1 *2770*

WONDER

among you and gives you a sign or a w, Dt 13:1 4159
and the sign or the w comes true, Dt 13:2 4159
"They shall become a sign and a w on Dt 28:46 4159
who sent to him to inquire of the w 2Ch 32:31 4159
W! Because *I am* doing something Hab 1:5 8539
and they were filled with w Ac 3:10 *2285*
No w, for even Satan disguises 2Co 11:14 *2295*
"Why do you w? I will tell you Rv 17:7 *2296*
will w when they see the beast, that Rv 17:8 *2296*

WONDERED

And He w at their unbelief. Mk 6:6 *2296*
Pilate w if He was dead by this time, Mk 15:44 *2296*
And all who heard it w at the things Lk 2:18 *2296*
I w greatly. Rv 17:6 *2296*

WONDERFUL

seeing it is w?" Jg 13:18 6383
Your love to me was more w Than 2Sa 1:26 6381
Remember His w deeds which He has 1Ch 16:12 6381
His w deeds among all the peoples. 1Ch 16:24 6381
to build *will be* great and w. 2Ch 2:9 6381
Things too w for me, which I did not Jb 42:3 6381
sinned And did not believe in His w Ps 78:32 6381
His w deeds among all the peoples. Ps 96:3 6381
For He has done w things, His right Ps 98:1 6381
Open my eyes, that I may behold W Ps 119:18 6381
Your testimonies are w; Therefore my Ps 119:129 6382
Such knowledge is too w for me; Ps 139:6 6383
W are Your works, And my soul knows Ps 139:14 6381
of Your majesty And on Your w works, Ps 145:5 6381
are three things which are too w for Pr 30:18 6381
And His name will be called W Is 9:6 6382
Who has made *His* counsel w Is 28:29 6381
deal with us according to all His w Jer 21:2 6381
priests and the scribes saw the w Mt 21:15 *2297*
behold what w stones and what Mk 13:1 *4217*
what wonderful stones and what w Mk 13:1 *4217*

WONDERFULLY

for I am fearfully and w made; Ps 139:14 6395

WONDERING

and were w at his delay in the temple. Lk 1:21 *2296*
a state of expectation and all were w Lk 3:15 *1260*
and w at the gracious words which Lk 4:22 *2296*

WONDERS

you perform before Pharaoh all the w Ex 4:21 4159
that I may multiply My signs and My w Ex 7:3 4159
so that My w will be multiplied in Ex 11:9 4159
Moses and Aaron performed all these w Ex 11:10 4159
in praises, working w? Ex 15:11 6382
by signs and w and by war and by a Dt 4:34 4159
great and distressing signs and w Dt 6:22 4159
your eyes saw and the signs and the w Dt 7:19 4159
great terror and with signs and w; Dt 26:8 4159
those great signs and w. Dt 29:3 4159
for all the signs and w which the Dt 34:11 4159
for tomorrow the LORD will do w Jos 3:5 6381
and He performed w while Manoah Jg 13:19 6381
Speak of all His w. 1Ch 16:9 6381
"Then You performed signs and w Ne 9:10 4159
things, W without number. Jb 5:9 6381
Stand and consider the w of God. Jb 37:14 6381
The w of one perfect in knowledge, Jb 37:16 4652
I will tell of all Your w. Ps 9:1 6381
thanksgiving And declare all Your w. Ps 26:7 6381
Many, O LORD my God, are the w Ps 40:5 6381
Who alone works w. Ps 72:18 6381
Surely I will remember Your w of Ps 77:11 6382
You are the God who works w; You Ps 77:14 6382
He wrought w before their fathers In Ps 78:12 6382
Will You perform w for the dead? Ps 88:10 6382
Will Your w be made known in Ps 88:12 6382
The heavens will praise Your w, O Ps 89:5 6382
Speak of all His w. Ps 105:2 6381
Remember His w which He has done, Ps 105:5 4159
in Egypt did not understand Your w; Ps 106:7 6381
W in the land of Ham *And* awesome Ps 106:22 6381
And for His w to the sons of men! Ps 107:8 6381
And for His w to the sons of men! Ps 107:15 6381
And for His w to the sons of men! Ps 107:21 6381
And His w in the deep. Ps 107:24 6381
And for His w to the sons of men! Ps 107:31 6381
He has made His w to be remembered; Ps 111:4 6381
So I will meditate on Your w. Ps 119:27 6381
He sent signs and w into your midst, Ps 135:9 4159
To Him who alone does great w, For Ps 136:4 6381
has given me are for signs and w in Is 8:18 4159
For You have worked w, Plans Is 25:1 6382
who has set signs and w in the land Jer 32:20 4159
land of Egypt with signs and with w, Jer 32:21 4159
good to me to declare the signs and w Da 4:2 8540
His signs And how mighty are His w! Da 4:3 8540
and rescues and performs signs and w Da 6:27 8540
it be until the end of *these* w?" Da 12:6 6382
"I will display w in the sky and on Jl 2:30 4159
arise and will show great signs and w, Mt 24:24 *5059*
and will show signs and w, in order Mk 13:22 *5059*
"Unless you *people* see signs and w, Jn 4:48 *5059*
'AND I WILL GRANT W IN THE SKY Ac 2:19 *5059*
to you by God with miracles and w Ac 2:22 *5059*
and many w and signs were taking Ac 2:43 *5059*
and signs and w take place through Ac 4:30 *5059*
of the apostles many signs and w were Ac 5:12 *5059*
was performing great w and signs Ac 6:8 *5059*
performing w and signs in the land of Ac 7:36 *5059*
granting that signs and w be done by Ac 14:3 *5059*
they were relating what signs and w Ac 15:12 *5059*
in the power of signs and w, Ro 15:19 *5059*
by signs and w and miracles. 2Co 12:12 *5059*
with all power and signs and false w, 2Th 2:9 *5059*
both by signs and w and by various Heb 2:4 *5059*

WONDROUS

And did not remember Your w deeds Ne 9:17 6381
And w works without number. Jb 9:10 6381
And I still declare Your w deeds. Ps 71:17 6381
Men declare Your w works. Ps 75:1 6381
And His strength and His w works Ps 78:4 6381
For You are great and do w deeds; Ps 86:10 6381
They performed His w acts among Ps 105:27 226

WONDROUSLY

"God thunders with His voice w, Jb 37:5 6381
W show Your lovingkindness, O Savior Ps 17:7 6395
w marvelous; And the wisdom of their Is 29:14 6381
Who has dealt w with you; Then My Jl 2:26 6381

WOOD

"Make for yourself an ark of gopher w; Gn 6:14 6086
and he split w for the burnt offering, Gn 22:3 6086
Abraham took the w of the burnt Gn 22:6 6086
the fire and the w, but where is Gn 22:7 6086
the altar there and arranged the w, Gn 22:9 6086
on top of the w. Gn 22:9 6086
both in *vessels of* w and in Ex 7:19 6086
skins, acacia w, Ex 25:5 6086
shall construct an ark of acacia w Ex 25:10 6086
"You shall make poles of acacia w Ex 25:13 6086
"You shall make a table of acacia w, Ex 25:23 6086
"You shall make the poles of acacia w Ex 25:28 6086
boards for the tabernacle of acacia w, Ex 26:15 6086
"Then you shall make bars of acacia w, Ex 26:26 6086
you shall make the altar of acacia w, Ex 27:1 6086
poles of acacia w, and overlay them Ex 27:6 6086
you shall make it of acacia w. Ex 30:1 6086
"You shall make the poles of acacia w Ex 30:5 6086
and in the carving of w, that he may Ex 31:5 6086
skins, and acacia w, Ex 35:7 6086
who had in his possession acacia w Ex 35:24 6086
for settings and in the carving of w, Ex 35:33 6086
boards for the tabernacle of acacia w, Ex 36:20 6086
Then he made bars of acacia w, five Ex 36:31 6086
Now Bezalel made the ark of acacia w; Ex 37:1 6086
He made poles of acacia w Ex 37:4 6086
Then he made the table of acacia w, Ex 37:10 6086
He made the poles of acacia w Ex 37:15 6086
made the altar of incense of acacia w: Ex 37:25 6086
He made the poles of acacia w Ex 37:28 6086
altar of burnt offering of acacia w, Ex 38:1 6086
He made the poles of acacia w Ex 38:6 6086
put fire on the altar and arrange w Lv 1:7 6086
the head and the suet over the w Lv 1:8 6086
priest shall arrange them on the w Lv 1:12 6086
it up in smoke on the altar on the w Lv 1:17 6086
which is on the w that is on the fire; Lv 3:5 6086
and burn it on w with fire; where Lv 4:12 6086
but the priest shall burn w on it Lv 6:12 6086
take two live clean birds and cedar w Lv 14:4 6086
take it together with the cedar w Lv 14:6 6086
he shall take two birds and cedar w Lv 14:49 6086
"Then he shall take the cedar w Lv 14:51 6086
the live bird and with the cedar w Lv 14:52 6086
they found a man gathering w on Nu 15:32 6086
Those who found him gathering w Nu 15:33 6086
"The priest shall take cedar w Nu 19:6 6086
and all articles of w." Nu 31:20 6086
w and stone, which neither see nor Dt 4:28 6086
and make an ark of w for yourself. Dt 10:1 6086
"So I made an ark of acacia w Dt 10:3 6086
the forest with his friend to cut w, Dt 19:5 6086
serve other gods, w and stone. Dt 28:36 6086
w and stone, which you or your Dt 28:64 6086
from the one who chops your w to Dt 29:11 2404
abominations and their idols *of* w, Dt 29:17 6086
So they became hewers of w Jos 9:21 2404
both hewers of w and drawers of water Jos 9:23 2404
Joshua made them that day hewers of w Jos 9:27 2404
and offer a burnt offering with the w Jg 6:26 6086
and they split the w of the cart 1Sa 6:14 6086
of *instruments made of* fir w, 2Sa 6:5 6086
and the yokes of the oxen for the w. 2Sa 24:22 6086
the walls on the inside with w, 1Ki 6:15 6086
he made two cherubim of olive w, 1Ki 6:23 6086
sanctuary he made doors of olive w, 1Ki 6:31 6086
So *he made* two doors of olive w, 1Ki 6:32 6086
nave four-sided doorposts of olive w 1Ki 6:33 6086
and two doors of cypress w; 1Ki 6:34 6086
and place it on the w, but put no 1Ki 18:23 6086
the other ox and lay it on the w; 1Ki 18:23 6086
Then he arranged the w and cut the ox 1Ki 18:33 6086
ox in pieces and laid *it* on the w. 1Ki 18:33 6086
on the burnt offering and on the w." 1Ki 18:34 6086
consumed the burnt offering and the w 1Ki 18:38 6086
w and stone. So they have destroyed 2Ki 19:18 6086
and the threshing sledges for w 1Ch 21:23 6086
and w for the *things of* wood, 1Ch 29:2 6086
and wood for the *things of* w, 1Ch 29:2 6086
stone and w, *and* in purple, 2Ch 2:14 6086
overlaid the main room with cypress w 2Ch 3:5 6086
to bring cedar w from Lebanon to Ezr 3:7 6086
we cast lots for the supply of w Ne 10:34 6086
I arranged for the supply of w at Ne 13:31 6086
Bronze as rotten w. Jb 41:27 6086
For lack of w the fire goes out, Pr 26:20 6086
Like charcoal to hot embers and w Pr 26:21 6086
a rod lifting *him who* is not w. Is 10:15 6086
A pyre of fire with plenty of w; Is 30:33 6086
w and stone. So they have destroyed Is 37:19 6086
Another shapes w, he extends a Is 44:13 6086
I fall down before a block of w!" Is 44:19 6086
And instead of w, bronze, Is 60:17 6086
in your mouth fire And this people w, Jer 5:14 6086
"The children gather w, Jer 7:18 6086
Because it is w cut from the forest, Jer 10:3 6086
of delusion—their idol is w! Jer 10:8 6086
"You have broken the yokes of w, Jer 28:13 6086
it has become like w. La 4:8 6086
Our w comes *to us* at a price. La 5:4 6086
youths stumbled under *loads* of w. La 5:13 6086
"Son of man, how is the w of Ezk 15:2 6086
of the vine *better* than any w of Ezk 15:2 6086
"Can w be taken from it to make Ezk 15:3 6086
'As the w of the vine among Ezk 15:6 6086
of the lands, serving w and stone.' Ezk 20:32 6086
And also pile w under the pot. Make Ezk 24:5 6106

“Heap on the **w**, kindle the fire, **Ezk 24:10** 6086
“They will not take **w** from the field **Ezk 39:10** 6086
were paneled with **w** all around, **Ezk 41:16** 6086
The altar *was* of **w**, three cubits **Ezk 41:22** 6086
its base and its sides *were* of **w**. **Ezk 41:22** 6086
and *there was* a threshold of **w** on **Ezk 41:25** 6086
bronze, iron, **w** and stone. **Da 5:4** 636
w and stone, which do not see, hear **Da 5:23** 636
to him who says to a *piece of* **w**, **Hab 2:19** 6086
“Go up to the mountains, bring **w** **Hg 1:8** 6086
like a firepot among pieces of **w** **Zch 12:6** 6086
stones, **w**, hay, straw, **1Co 3:12** *3586*
but also vessels of **w** and of **2Tm 2:20** *3585*
and of brass and of stone and of **w**, **Rv 9:20** *3585*
and every *kind of* citron **w** **Rv 18:12** *3586*
article *made* from very costly **w** **Rv 18:12** *3586*

WOODCUTTERS
on like an army And come to her as **w** **Jer 46:22** 2404

WOODED
built fortresses and towers on the **w** **2Ch 27:4** 2793

WOODEN
including any **w** article, or clothing, **Lv 11:32** 6086
and every **w** vessel shall be rinsed in **Lv 15:12** 6086
‘Or if he struck him with a **w** object **Nu 35:18** 6086
Ezra the scribe stood at a **w** podium **Ne 8:4** 6086
Who carry about their **w** idol And pray **Is 45:20** 6086
My people consult their **w** idol, **Hos 4:12** 6086

WOODLAND
Which dwells by itself in the **w**, In **Mi 7:14** 3293a

WOODS
two female bears came out of the **w** **2Ki 2:24** 3293a
in the wilderness and sleep in the **w**. **Ezk 34:25** 3293a

WOODSMEN
the **w** who cut the timber, 20,000 kors **2Ch 2:10** 2404

WOOF
whether in warp or **w**, of linen or of **Lv 13:48** 6154b
or in the warp or in the **w**, or in **Lv 13:49** 6154b
whether in the warp or in the **w**, **Lv 13:51** 6154b
whether the warp or the **w**, in wool **Lv 13:52** 6154b
either in the warp or in the **w**, **Lv 13:53** 6154b
whether from the warp or from the **w**; **Lv 13:56** 6154b
whether in the warp or in the **w**, or **Lv 13:57** 6154b
whether the warp or the **w**, or any **Lv 13:58** 6154b
whether in the warp or in the **w**, **Lv 13:59** 6154b

WOOL
whether it is a **w** garment or a linen **Lv 13:47** 6785
of linen or of **w**, whether in leather **Lv 13:48** 6785
in **w** or in linen, or any article of **Lv 13:52** 6785
the mark of leprosy in a garment of **w** **Lv 13:59** 6785
shall not wear a material mixed of **w** **Dt 22:11** 6785
behold, I will put a fleece of **w** on **Jg 6:37** 6785
lambs and the **w** of 100,000 rams. **2Ki 3:4** 6785
He gives snow like **w**; He scatters **Ps 147:16** 6785
She looks for **w** and flax And works **Pr 31:13** 6785
They will be like **w**. **Is 1:18** 6785
And the grub will eat them like **w**. **Is 51:8** 6785
of the wine of Helbon and white **w**. **Ezk 27:18** 6785
fat and clothe yourselves with the **w**, **Ezk 34:3** 6785
and **w** shall not be on them while they **Ezk 44:17** 6785
And the hair of His head like pure **w**. **Da 7:9** 6015
My **w** and my flax, my oil and my **Hos 2:5** 6785
I will also take away My **w** and My **Hos 2:9** 6785
with water and scarlet **w** and hyssop, **Heb 9:19** *2053*
and His hair were white like white **w**, **Rv 1:14** *2053*

WORD
After these things the **w** of the **Gn 15:1** 1697
Then behold, the **w** of the LORD **Gn 15:4** 1697
let it be according to your **w**.” **Gn 30:34** 1697
and bring **w** back to me.” So he sent **Gn 37:14** 1697
may your servant please speak a **w** in **Gn 44:18** 1697
“*May it be* according to your **w**, **Ex 8:10** 1697
The LORD did according to the **w** **Ex 8:13** 1697
servants of Pharaoh who feared the **w** **Ex 9:20** 1697
but he who paid no regard to the **w** of **Ex 9:21** 1697
of Israel had done according to the **w** **Ex 12:35** 1697
“Is this not the **w** that we spoke to **Ex 14:12** 1697
He sent **w** to Moses, “I, your **Ex 18:6** 559
When the people heard this sad **w**, **Ex 33:4** 1697
So they did according to the **w** of **Lv 10:7** 1697
numbered them according to the **w** of **Nu 3:16** 6310
Now you shall see whether My **w** will **Nu 11:23** 1697
and they brought back **w** to them **Nu 13:26** 1697
pardoned *them* according to your **w**; **Nu 14:20** 1697
‘Because he has despised the **w** of **Nu 15:31** 1697
and I will bring **w** back to you as **Nu 22:8** 1697
king of Moab, has sent **w** to me, **Nu 22:10**
but only the **w** which I speak to you **Nu 22:20** 1697
but you shall speak only the **w** which **Nu 22:35** 1697
The **w** that God puts in my mouth, **Nu 22:38** 1697
Then the LORD put a **w** in Balaam’s **Nu 23:5** 1697
the LORD met Balaam and put a **w** **Nu 23:16** 1697
“This is the **w** which the LORD **Nu 30:1** 1697
he shall not violate his **w**; he shall **Nu 30:2** 1697
the sons of Israel according to the **w** **Nu 36:5** 6310
and bring back to us **w** of the way by **Dt 1:22** 1697
“You shall not add to the **w** which I **Dt 4:2** 1697
to declare to you the **w** of the LORD; **Dt 5:5** 1697
you shall not turn aside from the **w** **Dt 17:11** 1697
‘But the prophet who speaks a **w** **Dt 18:20** 1697
‘How will we know the **w** which the **Dt 18:21** 1697
“But the **w** is very near you, in **Dt 30:14** 1697
“For it is not an idle **w** for you; **Dt 32:47** 1697
And by this **w** you will prolong your **Dt 32:47** 1697
For they observed Your **w**, And kept **Dt 33:9** 565a
according to the **w** of the LORD. **Dt 34:5** 6310
“Remember the **w** which Moses **Jos 1:13** 1697
And the king of Jericho sent **w** to **Jos 2:3**
let your voice be heard nor let a **w** **Jos 6:10** 1697
shall do *it* according to the **w** of **Jos 8:8** 1697
according to the **w** of the LORD **Jos 8:27** 1697
There was not a **w** of all that Moses **Jos 8:35** 1697
king of Jerusalem sent **w** to Hoham **Jos 10:3**
Then the men of Gibeon sent **w** to **Jos 10:6**
No one uttered a **w** against any of **Jos 10:21** 3956
“You know the **w** which the LORD **Jos 14:6** 1697
and I brought **w** back to him as *it* **Jos 14:7** 1697
time that the LORD spoke this **w** **Jos 14:10** 1697
and brought back **w** to them. **Jos 22:32** 1697
The **w** pleased the sons of Israel, **Jos 22:33** 1697
and in all your souls that not one **w** **Jos 23:14** 1697
for I have given my **w** to the LORD, **Jg 11:35** 6310
you have given your **w** to the LORD; **Jg 11:36** 6310
Then the whole congregation sent **w** **Jg 21:13**
only may the LORD confirm His **w**.” **1Sa 1:23** 1697
And **w** from the LORD was rare in **1Sa 3:1** 1697
nor had the **w** of the LORD yet **1Sa 3:7** 1697
He said, “What is the **w** that He **1Sa 3:17** 1697
Himself to Samuel at Shiloh by the **w** **1Sa 3:21** 1697
Thus the **w** of Samuel came to all **1Sa 4:1** 1697
that I may proclaim the **w** of God to **1Sa 9:27** 1697
Then the **w** of the LORD came to **1Sa 15:10** 1697
Because you have rejected the **w** of **1Sa 15:23** 1697
for you have rejected the **w** of the **1Sa 15:26** 1697
answered him in accord with this **w**, **1Sa 17:27** 1697
he could no longer answer Abner a **w**, **2Sa 3:11** 1697
But in the same night the **w** of the **2Sa 7:4** 1697
did I speak a **w** with one of **2Sa 7:7** 1697
“For the sake of Your **w**, **2Sa 7:21** 1697
the **w** that You have spoken concerning **2Sa 7:25** 1697
‘Why have you despised the **w** of **2Sa 12:9** 1697
and sent **w** through Nathan **2Sa 12:25**
according to your servant’s **w**, so it **2Sa 13:35** 1697
“Please let your maidservant speak a **w** **2Sa 14:12** 1697
For in speaking this **w** the king is as **2Sa 14:13** 1697
reason I have come to speak this **w** to **2Sa 14:15** 1697
‘Please let the **w** of my lord **2Sa 14:17** 1697
the fords of the wilderness until **w** **2Sa 15:28** 1697
was as if one inquired of the **w** **2Sa 16:23** 1697
since the **w** of all Israel has come to **2Sa 19:11** 1697
so that they sent **w** to the king, **2Sa 19:14** 1697
The **w** of the LORD is tested; **2Sa 22:31** 565a
And His **w** was on my tongue. **2Sa 23:2** 4405
Nevertheless, the king’s **w** prevailed **2Sa 24:4** 1697
the **w** of the LORD came to **2Sa 24:11** 1697
David went up according to the **w** of **2Sa 24:19** 1697
if Adonijah has not spoken this **w** **1Ki 2:23** 1697
in order to fulfill the **w** of the **1Ki 2:27** 1697
And Benaiah brought the king **w** again, **1Ki 2:30** 1697
“The **w** is good. As my lord the king **1Ki 2:38** 1697
‘The **w** which I have heard is good.’ **1Ki 2:42** 1697
Then Solomon sent **w** to Hiram, **1Ki 5:2**
So Hiram sent **w** to Solomon, **1Ki 5:8**
Now the **w** of the LORD came to **1Ki 6:11** 1697
then I will carry out My **w** with you **1Ki 6:12** 1697
“Now the LORD has fulfilled His **w** **1Ki 8:20** 1697
let Your **w**, I pray, be confirmed **1Ki 8:26** 1697
not one **w** has failed of all His good **1Ki 8:56** 1697
that He might establish His **w**, **1Ki 12:15** 1697
But the **w** of God came to Shemaiah **1Ki 12:22** 1697
So they listened to the **w** of the **1Ki 12:24** 1697
went *their way* according to the **w** **1Ki 12:24** 1697
of God from Judah to Bethel by the **w** **1Ki 13:1** 1697
He cried against the altar by the **w** **1Ki 13:2** 1697
the man of God had given by the **w** of **1Ki 13:5** 1697
“For so it was commanded me by the **w** of **1Ki 13:9** 1697
“For a command *came* to me by the **w** **1Ki 13:17** 1697
and an angel spoke to me by the **w** of **1Ki 13:18** 1697
that the **w** of the LORD came to **1Ki 13:20** 1697
according to the **w** of the LORD **1Ki 13:26** 1697
come to pass which he cried by the **w** **1Ki 13:32** 1697
according to the **w** of the LORD **1Ki 14:18** 1697
according to the **w** of the LORD, **1Ki 15:29** 1697
Now the **w** of the LORD came to **1Ki 16:1** 1697
Moreover, the **w** of the LORD **1Ki 16:7** 1697
according to the **w** of the LORD, **1Ki 16:12** 1697
according to the **w** of the LORD, **1Ki 16:34** 1697
these years, except by my **w**.” **1Ki 17:1** 1697
The **w** of the LORD came to him, **1Ki 17:2** 1697
So he went and did according to the **w** **1Ki 17:5** 1697
Then the **w** of the LORD came to **1Ki 17:8** 1697
she went and did according to the **w** **1Ki 17:15** 1697
according to the **w** of the LORD **1Ki 17:16** 1697
you are a man of God and that the **w** **1Ki 17:24** 1697
after many days that the **w** of **1Ki 18:1** 1697
But the people did not answer him a **w**. **1Ki 18:21** 1697
to whom the **w** of the LORD had **1Ki 18:31** 1697
have done all these things at Your **w**. **1Ki 18:36** 1697
the **w** of the LORD *came* to him, **1Ki 19:9** 1697
“It is according to your **w**, my lord, **1Ki 20:4** 1697
messengers departed and brought him **w** **1Ki 20:9** 1697
and quickly catching his **w** said, **1Ki 20:33**
the prophets said to another by the **w** **1Ki 20:35** 1697
sullen and vexed because of the **w** **1Ki 21:4** 1697
did as Jezebel had sent **w** to them, **1Ki 21:11**
Then they sent **w** to Jezebel, **1Ki 21:14**
Then the **w** of the LORD came to **1Ki 21:17** 1697
Then the **w** of the LORD came to **1Ki 21:28** 1697
“Please inquire first for the **w** of **1Ki 22:5** 1697
Please let your **w** be like the word of **1Ki 22:13** 1697
Please let your word be like the **w** of **1Ki 22:13** 1697
hear the **w** of the LORD. **1Ki 22:19** 1697
according to the **w** of the LORD **1Ki 22:38** 1697
God in Israel to inquire of His **w**? **2Ki 1:16** 1697
So Ahaziah died according to the **w** of **2Ki 1:17** 1697
according to the **w** of Elisha which he **2Ki 2:22** 1697
Then he went and sent **w** to **2Ki 3:7**
Jehoshaphat said, “The **w** of the **2Ki 3:12** 1697
according to the **w** of the LORD. **2Ki 4:44** 1697
that this man is sending **w** to me **2Ki 5:7**
that he sent **w** to the king, **2Ki 5:8**
according to the **w** of the man of God; **2Ki 5:14** 1697
The man of God sent **w** to the king **2Ki 6:9**
with blindness according to the **w** of **2Ki 6:18** 1697
Then Elisha said, “Listen to the **w** **2Ki 7:1** 1697
according to the **w** of the LORD. **2Ki 7:16** 1697
arose and did according to the **w** of **2Ki 8:2** 1697
“I have a **w** for you, O captain.” **2Ki 9:5** 1697
according to the **w** of the LORD.” **2Ki 9:26** 1697
“This is the **w** of the LORD, **2Ki 9:36** 1697
sent **w** to Jehu, saying, **2Ki 10:5**
fall to the earth nothing of the **w** of **2Ki 10:10** 1697
according to the **w** of the LORD **2Ki 10:17** 1697
according to the **w** of the LORD, **2Ki 14:25** 1697
This is the **w** of the LORD which **2Ki 15:12** 1697
“Hear the **w** of the great king, **2Ki 18:28** 1697
were silent and answered him not a **w**, **2Ki 18:36** 1697
“This is the **w** that the LORD has **2Ki 19:21** 1697
the **w** of the LORD came to him, **2Ki 20:4** 1697
“Hear the **w** of the LORD. **2Ki 20:16** 1697
“The **w** of the LORD which you **2Ki 20:19** 1697
came to the king and brought back **w** **2Ki 22:9** 1697
So they brought back **w** to the king. **2Ki 22:20** 1697
and defiled it according to the **w** of **2Ki 23:16** 1697
according to the **w** of the LORD **2Ki 24:2** 1697
because of the **w** of the LORD **1Ch 10:13** 1697
according to the **w** of the LORD **1Ch 11:3** 1697
according to the **w** of the LORD **1Ch 11:10** 1697
according to the **w** of the LORD. **1Ch 12:23** 6310
had commanded according to the **w** of **1Ch 15:15** 1697
Remember His covenant forever, The **w** **1Ch 16:15** 1697
came about the same night that the **w** **1Ch 17:3** 1697
have I spoken a **w** with any of **1Ch 17:6** 1697
“Now, O LORD, let the **w** that **1Ch 17:23** 1697
and bring me **w** that I may know **1Ch 21:2** 1697
Nevertheless, the king’s **w** prevailed **1Ch 21:4** 1697
So David went up at the **w** of Gad, **1Ch 21:19** 1697
“But the **w** of the LORD came to **1Ch 22:8** 1697
Then Solomon sent **w** to Huram **2Ch 2:3**
“Now the LORD has fulfilled His **w** **2Ch 6:10** 1697
let Your **w** be confirmed which You **2Ch 6:17** 1697
the LORD might establish His **w**, **2Ch 10:15** 1697
But the **w** of the LORD came to **2Ch 11:2** 1697
the **w** of the LORD came to **2Ch 12:7** 1697
“Please inquire first for the **w** of **2Ch 18:4** 1697
So please let your **w** be like one of **2Ch 18:12** 1697
hear the **w** of the LORD. I saw **2Ch 18:18** 1697
and the princes commanded by the **w** of **2Ch 30:12** 1697
to the king and reported further **w** to **2Ch 34:16** 1697
our fathers have not observed the **w** **2Ch 34:21** 1697
And they brought back **w** to the king. **2Ch 34:28** 1697
brethren to do according to the **w** of **2Ch 35:6** 1697
sent **w** to them again and again by **2Ch 36:15**
to fulfill the **w** of the LORD by **2Ch 36:21** 1697
Persia—in order to fulfill the **w** **2Ch 36:22** 1697
in order to fulfill the **w** of the **Ezr 1:1** 1697
the **w** which You commanded **Ne 1:8** 1697
were silent and could not find a **w** **Ne 5:8** 1697
This **w** pleased the king **Es 1:21** 1697
As the **w** went out of the king’s mouth, **Es 7:8** 1697
seven nights with no one speaking a **w** **Jb 2:13** 1697
“If one ventures a **w** with you, will **Jb 4:2** 1697
“Now a **w** was brought to me **Jb 4:12** 1697
Even the **w** *spoken* gently with you? **Jb 15:11** 1697
And how faint a **w** we hear of Him! **Jb 26:14** 1697
As for the deeds of men, by the **w** of **Ps 17:4** 1697
The **w** of the LORD is tried; **Ps 18:30** 565a
For the **w** of the LORD is upright, **Ps 33:4** 1697
By the **w** of the LORD the heavens **Ps 33:6** 1697
In God, whose **w** I praise, In God I **Ps 56:4** 1697
In God, *whose* **w** I praise, In **Ps 56:10** 1697
whose **w** I praise, **Ps 56:10** 1697
who perform His **w**, Obeying the voice **Ps 103:20** 1697
Obeying the voice of His **w**! **Ps 103:20** 1697
The **w** which He commanded to a **Ps 105:8** 1697
Until the time that his **w** came to **Ps 105:19** 1697
The **w** of the LORD tested him. **Ps 105:19** 1697
For He remembered His holy **w** *With* **Ps 105:42** 1697
They did not believe in His **w**, **Ps 106:24** 1697
He sent His **w** and healed them, **Ps 107:20** 1697
By keeping *it* according to Your **w**. **Ps 119:9** 1697
Your **w** I have treasured in my heart, **Ps 119:11** 565a
I shall not forget Your **w**. **Ps 119:16** 1697
That I may live and keep Your **w**. **Ps 119:17** 1697
Revive me according to Your **w**. **Ps 119:25** 1697
Strengthen me according to Your **w**. **Ps 119:28** 1697
Establish Your **w** to Your servant, As **Ps 119:38** 565a
Your salvation according to Your **w**; **Ps 119:41** 565a
For I trust in Your **w**. **Ps 119:42** 1697
And do not take the **w** of truth **Ps 119:43** 1697
Remember the **w** to Your servant, In **Ps 119:49** 1697
That Your **w** has revived me. **Ps 119:50** 565a
Be gracious to me according to Your **w**. **Ps 119:58** 565a
according to Your **w**. **Ps 119:65** 1697
But now I keep Your **w**. **Ps 119:67** 565a
Because I wait for Your **w**. **Ps 119:74** 1697
According to Your **w** to Your servant. **Ps 119:76** 565a
I wait for Your **w**. **Ps 119:81** 1697
eyes fail *with longing* for Your **w**, **Ps 119:82** 565a
Forever, O LORD, Your **w** is **Ps 119:89** 1697
That I may keep Your **w**. **Ps 119:101** 1697
Your **w** is a lamp to my feet And a **Ps 119:105** 1697
according to Your **w**. **Ps 119:107** 1697
I wait for Your **w**. **Ps 119:114** 1697
Sustain me according to Your **w**, that **Ps 119:116** 565a
salvation And for Your righteous **w**. **Ps 119:123** 565a

Establish my footsteps in Your **w**,	Ps 119:133	565a
Your **w** is very pure, Therefore Your	Ps 119:140	565a
That I may meditate on Your **w**.	Ps 119:148	565a
Revive me according to Your **w**.	Ps 119:154	565a
Because they do not keep Your **w**.	Ps 119:158	565a
The sum of Your **w** is truth,	Ps 119:160	1697
I rejoice at Your **w**, As one who	Ps 119:162	565a
me understanding according to Your **w**.	Ps 119:169	1697
Deliver me according to Your **w**.	Ps 119:170	565a
Let my tongue sing of Your **w**,	Ps 119:172	565a
And in His **w** do I hope.	Ps 130:5	1697
For You have magnified Your **w**	Ps 138:2	565a
Even before there is a **w** on my tongue,	Ps 139:4	4405
His **w** runs very swiftly.	Ps 147:15	1697
He sends forth His **w** and melts them;	Ps 147:18	1697
Stormy wind, fulfilling His **w**;	Ps 148:8	1697
But a good **w** makes it glad.	Pr 12:25	1697
The one who despises the **w** will be in	Pr 13:13	1697
But a harsh **w** stirs up anger.	Pr 15:1	1697
And how delightful is a timely **w**!	Pr 15:23	1697
He who gives attention to the **w** will	Pr 16:20	1697
of gold in settings of silver Is a **w**	Pr 25:11	1697
Every **w** of God is tested; He is a	Pr 30:5	565a
Do not be hasty in **w** or impulsive in	Ec 5:2	6310
Since the **w** of the king is	Ec 8:4	1697
Hear the **w** of the LORD, You	Is 1:10	1697
The **w** which Isaiah the son of Amoz	Is 2:1	1697
law will go forth from Zion And the **w**	Is 2:3	1697
LORD of hosts And despised the **w**	Is 5:24	565a
they do not speak according to this **w**,	Is 8:20	1697
This is the **w** which the LORD	Is 16:13	1697
for the LORD has spoken this **w**.	Is 24:3	1697
So the **w** of the LORD to them will	Is 28:13	1697
Therefore, hear the **w** of the LORD,	Is 28:14	1697
cause a person to be indicted by a **w**,	Is 29:21	1697
"Since you have rejected this **w**	Is 30:12	1697
Your ears will hear a **w** behind you,	Is 30:21	1697
Give ear to my **w**, You complacent	Is 32:9	565a
were silent and answered him not a **w**;	Is 36:21	1697
Then Isaiah the son of Amoz sent **w**	Is 37:21	
this is the **w** that the LORD has	Is 37:22	1697
Then the **w** of the LORD came to	Is 38:4	1697
"Hear the **w** of the LORD of hosts,	Is 39:5	1697
"The **w** of the LORD which you	Is 39:8	1697
But the **w** of our God stands forever.	Is 40:8	1697
Confirming the **w** of His servant And	Is 44:26	1697
"I have sworn by Myself, The **w** has	Is 45:23	1697
how to sustain the weary one with a **w**.	Is 50:4	1697
So will My **w** be which goes forth from	Is 55:11	1697
pleasure And speaking *your own* **w**,	Is 58:13	1697
and who trembles at My **w**.	Is 66:2	1697
Hear the **w** of the LORD, you who	Is 66:5	1697
you who tremble at His **w**: "Your	Is 66:5	1697
to whom the **w** of the LORD came in	Jer 1:2	1697
Now the **w** of the LORD came to me	Jer 1:4	1697
The **w** of the LORD came to me	Jer 1:11	1697
for I am watching over My **w** to	Jer 1:12	1697
The **w** of the LORD came to me a	Jer 1:13	1697
Now the **w** of the LORD came to me	Jer 2:1	1697
Hear the **w** of the LORD, O house	Jer 2:4	1697
"O generation, heed the **w** of the	Jer 2:31	1697
And the **w** is not in them. Thus it	Jer 5:13	1699b
"Because you have spoken this **w**,	Jer 5:14	1697
the **w** of the LORD has become a	Jer 6:10	1697
The **w** that came to Jeremiah from	Jer 7:1	1697
house and proclaim there this **w**	Jer 7:2	1697
'Hear the **w** of the LORD, all	Jer 7:2	1697
they have rejected the **w** of the	Jer 8:9	1697
Now hear the **w** of the LORD, O	Jer 9:20	1697
And let your ear receive the **w** of His	Jer 9:20	1697
Hear the **w** which the LORD speaks	Jer 10:1	1697
The **w** which came to Jeremiah from	Jer 11:1	1697
waistband in accordance with the **w** of	Jer 13:2	1697
Then the **w** of the LORD came to me	Jer 13:3	1697
Then the **w** of the LORD came to me,	Jer 13:8	1697
"Therefore you are to speak this **w**	Jer 13:12	1697
That which came as the **w** of the	Jer 14:1	1697
"You will say this **w** to them, 'Let	Jer 14:17	1697
The **w** of the LORD also came to me	Jer 16:1	1697
"Where is the **w** of the LORD?	Jer 17:15	1697
and say to them, 'Listen to the **w**	Jer 17:20	1697
The **w** which came to Jeremiah from	Jer 18:1	1697
Then the **w** of the LORD came to me	Jer 18:5	1697
nor the *divine* **w** to the prophet!	Jer 18:18	1697
and say, 'Hear the **w** of the LORD,	Jer 19:3	1697
Because for me the **w** of the LORD	Jer 20:8	1697
The **w** which came to Jeremiah from	Jer 21:1	1697
'Hear the **w** of the LORD,	Jer 21:11	1697
of Judah, and there speak this **w**	Jer 22:1	1697
and say, 'Hear the **w** of the LORD,	Jer 22:2	1697
"O land, land, land, Hear the **w**	Jer 22:29	1697
That he should see and hear His **w**?	Jer 23:18	1697
Who has given heed to His **w**	Jer 23:18	1697
but let him who has My **w** speak My	Jer 23:28	1697
who has My word speak My **w** in	Jer 23:28	1697
"Is not My **w** like fire?" declares	Jer 23:29	1697
because every man's own **w** will	Jer 23:36	1697
'Because you said this **w**,	Jer 23:38	1697
Then the **w** of the LORD came to me,	Jer 24:4	1697
The **w** that came to Jeremiah	Jer 25:1	1697
these twenty-three years the **w** of	Jer 25:3	1697
this **w** came from the LORD,	Jer 26:1	1697
Do not omit a **w**!	Jer 26:2	1697
this **w** came to Jeremiah from the	Jer 27:1	1697
and send **w** to the king of Edom, to	Jer 27:3	
and if the **w** of the LORD is with	Jer 27:18	1697
"Yet hear now this **w** which I am	Jer 28:7	1697
when the **w** of the prophet comes to	Jer 28:9	1697
The **w** of the LORD came to	Jer 28:12	1697
will visit you and fulfill My good **w**	Jer 29:10	1697
"You, therefore, hear the **w** of	Jer 29:20	1697
Then came the **w** of the LORD to	Jer 29:30	1697
The **w** which came to Jeremiah from	Jer 30:1	1697
Hear the **w** of the LORD, O	Jer 31:10	1697
"Once again they will speak this **w**	Jer 31:23	1697
The **w** that came to Jeremiah from	Jer 32:1	1697
And Jeremiah said, "The **w** of the	Jer 32:6	1697
court of the guard according to the **w**	Jer 32:8	1697
Then I knew that this was the **w** of	Jer 32:8	1697
Then the **w** of the LORD came to	Jer 32:26	1697
Then the **w** of the LORD came to	Jer 33:1	1697
'when I will fulfill the good **w**	Jer 33:14	1697
The **w** of the LORD came to	Jer 33:19	1697
And the **w** of the LORD came to	Jer 33:23	1697
The **w** which came to Jeremiah from	Jer 34:1	1697
"Yet hear the **w** of the LORD, O	Jer 34:4	1697
For I have spoken the **w**,"	Jer 34:5	1697
The **w** which came to Jeremiah from	Jer 34:8	1697
Then the **w** of the LORD came to	Jer 34:12	1697
The **w** which came to Jeremiah from	Jer 35:1	1697
Then the **w** of the LORD came to	Jer 35:12	1697
this **w** came to Jeremiah from the	Jer 36:1	1697
Then the **w** of the LORD came to	Jer 36:27	1697
Then the **w** of the LORD came to	Jer 37:6	1697
"Is there a **w** from the LORD?"	Jer 37:17	1697
this is the **w** which the LORD has	Jer 38:21	1697
the captain of the bodyguard sent **w**,	Jer 39:13	
Now the **w** of the LORD had come to	Jer 39:15	1697
The **w** which came to Jeremiah from	Jer 40:1	1697
I will not keep back a **w** from you."	Jer 42:4	1697
Now at the end of ten days the **w** of	Jer 42:7	1697
then in that case listen to the **w** of	Jer 42:15	1697
Then the **w** of the LORD came to	Jer 43:8	1697
The **w** that came to Jeremiah for all	Jer 44:1	1697
we will certainly carry out every **w**	Jer 44:17	1697
"Hear the **w** of the LORD, all	Jer 44:24	1697
"Nevertheless hear the **w** of the	Jer 44:26	1697
to reside there will know whose **w**	Jer 44:28	1697
That which came as the **w** of the	Jer 46:1	1697
That which came as the **w** of the	Jer 47:1	1697
That which came as the **w** of the	Jer 49:34	1697
The **w** which the LORD spoke	Jer 50:1	1697
He has accomplished His **w** Which He	La 2:17	565b
the **w** of the LORD came expressly	Ezk 1:3	1697
At the end of seven days the **w** of	Ezk 3:16	1697
whenever you hear a **w** from My mouth,	Ezk 3:17	1697
And the **w** of the LORD came to me	Ezk 6:1	1697
listen to the **w** of the Lord GOD!	Ezk 6:3	1697
Moreover, the **w** of the LORD came	Ezk 7:1	1697
Then the **w** of the LORD came to me,	Ezk 11:14	1697
Then the **w** of the LORD came to me,	Ezk 12:1	1697
In the morning the **w** of the LORD	Ezk 12:8	1697
Moreover, the **w** of the LORD came	Ezk 12:17	1697
Then the **w** of the LORD came to me,	Ezk 12:21	1697
and whatever **w** I speak will be	Ezk 12:25	1697
I will speak the **w** and perform it,"	Ezk 12:25	1697
Furthermore, the **w** of the LORD	Ezk 12:26	1697
w I speak will be performed,"'"	Ezk 12:28	1697
Then the **w** of the LORD came to me	Ezk 13:1	1697
'Listen to the **w** of the LORD!	Ezk 13:2	1697
for the fulfillment of *their* **w**.	Ezk 13:6	1697
And the **w** of the LORD came to me,	Ezk 14:2	1697
is prevailed upon to speak a **w**, it	Ezk 14:9	1697
Then the **w** of the LORD came to me	Ezk 14:12	1697
Then the **w** of the LORD came to me,	Ezk 15:1	1697
Then the **w** of the LORD came to me,	Ezk 16:1	1697
Therefore, O harlot, hear the **w** of	Ezk 16:35	1697
Now the **w** of the LORD came to me	Ezk 17:1	1697
Moreover, the **w** of the LORD came	Ezk 17:11	1697
Then the **w** of the LORD came to me,	Ezk 18:1	1697
And the **w** of the LORD came to me	Ezk 20:2	1697
Now the **w** of the LORD came to me,	Ezk 20:45	1697
'Hear the **w** of the LORD: thus	Ezk 20:47	1697
And the **w** of the LORD came to me	Ezk 21:1	1697
Again the **w** of the LORD came to	Ezk 21:8	1697
The **w** of the LORD came to me	Ezk 21:18	1697
Then the **w** of the LORD came to me,	Ezk 22:1	1697
And the **w** of the LORD came to me,	Ezk 22:17	1697
And the **w** of the LORD came to me,	Ezk 22:23	1697
The **w** of the LORD came to me	Ezk 23:1	1697
And the **w** of the LORD came to me	Ezk 24:1	1697
And the **w** of the LORD came to me	Ezk 24:15	1697
Then I said to them, "The **w** of	Ezk 24:20	1697
And the **w** of the LORD came to me	Ezk 25:1	1697
'Hear the **w** of the Lord GOD!	Ezk 25:3	1697
the **w** of the LORD came to me	Ezk 26:1	1697
Moreover, the **w** of the LORD came	Ezk 27:1	1697
The **w** of the LORD came again to	Ezk 28:1	1697
Again the **w** of the LORD came to	Ezk 28:11	1697
And the **w** of the LORD came to me	Ezk 28:20	1697
the **w** of the LORD came to me	Ezk 29:1	1697
the **w** of the LORD came to me	Ezk 29:17	1697
The **w** of the LORD came again to	Ezk 30:1	1697
the **w** of the LORD came to me	Ezk 30:20	1697
the **w** of the LORD came to me	Ezk 31:1	1697
the **w** of the LORD came to me	Ezk 32:1	1697
the **w** of the LORD came to me	Ezk 32:17	1697
And the **w** of the LORD came to me,	Ezk 33:1	1697
Then the **w** of the LORD came to me	Ezk 33:23	1697
Then the **w** of the LORD came to me	Ezk 34:1	1697
hear the **w** of the LORD:	Ezk 34:7	1697
hear the **w** of the LORD:	Ezk 34:9	1697
Moreover, the **w** of the LORD came	Ezk 35:1	1697
hear the **w** of the LORD.	Ezk 36:1	1697
hear the **w** of the Lord GOD. Thus	Ezk 36:4	1697
Then the **w** of the LORD came to me	Ezk 36:16	1697
hear the **w** of the LORD.'	Ezk 37:4	1697
The **w** of the LORD came again to	Ezk 37:15	1697
And the **w** of the LORD came to me	Ezk 38:1	1697
Then Nebuchadnezzar the king sent **w**	Da 3:2	
"While the **w** *was* in the king's	Da 4:31	4406
"Immediately the **w** concerning	Da 4:33	4406
years which was *revealed as* the **w**	Da 9:2	1697
And when he had spoken this **w** to me,	Da 10:11	1697
The **w** of the LORD which came to	Hos 1:1	1697
Listen to the **w** of the LORD, O	Hos 4:1	1697
The **w** of the LORD that came to	Jl 1:1	1697
strong is he who carries out His **w**.	Jl 2:11	1697
Hear this **w** which the LORD has	Am 3:1	1697
Hear this **w**, you cows of Bashan who	Am 4:1	1697
Hear this **w** which I take up for you	Am 5:1	1697
sent **w** to Jeroboam king of Israel,	Am 7:10	
"Now hear the **w** of the LORD:	Am 7:16	1697
They will go to and fro to seek the **w**	Am 8:12	1697
The **w** of the LORD came to Jonah	Jon 1:1	1697
Now the **w** of the LORD came to	Jon 3:1	1697
went to Nineveh according to the **w** of	Jon 3:3	1697
When the **w** reached the king of	Jon 3:6	1697
The **w** of the LORD which came *to*	Mi 1:1	1697
Even the **w** of the LORD from	Mi 4:2	1697
The **w** of the LORD which came to	Zph 1:1	1697
The **w** of the LORD is against you,	Zph 2:5	1697
the **w** of the LORD came by	Hg 1:1	1697
Then the **w** of the LORD came by	Hg 1:3	1697
the **w** of the LORD came by Haggai	Hg 2:1	1697
the **w** of the LORD came to Haggai	Hg 2:10	1697
Then the **w** of the LORD came a	Hg 2:20	1697
the **w** of the LORD came to	Zch 1:1	1697
the **w** of the LORD came to	Zch 1:7	1697
Then he said to me, "This is the **w**	Zch 4:6	1697
Also the **w** of the LORD came to me,	Zch 4:8	1697
The **w** of the LORD also came to me,	Zch 6:9	1697
the **w** of the LORD came to	Zch 7:1	1697
Then the **w** of the LORD of hosts	Zch 7:4	1697
Then the **w** of the LORD came to	Zch 7:8	1697
Then the **w** of the LORD of hosts	Zch 8:1	1697
Then the **w** of the LORD of hosts	Zch 8:18	1697
The burden of the **w** of the LORD	Zch 9:1	1697
me realized that it was the **w** of	Zch 11:11	1697
The burden of the **w** of the LORD	Zch 12:1	1697
The oracle of the **w** of the LORD	Mal 1:1	1697
BUT ON EVERY **W** THAT PROCEEDS OUT OF	Mt 4:4	*4487*
but just say the **w**, and my servant	Mt 8:8	*3056*
and He cast out the spirits with a **w**,	Mt 8:16	*3056*
he sent **w** by his disciples	Mt 11:2	
"Whoever speaks a **w** against the Son	Mt 12:32	*3056*
"But I tell you that every careless **w**	Mt 12:36	*4487*
"When anyone hears the **w** of	Mt 13:19	*3056*
this is the man who hears the **w**	Mt 13:20	*3056*
persecution arises because of the **w**,	Mt 13:21	*3056*
this is the man who hears the **w**,	Mt 13:22	*3056*
deceitfulness of wealth choke the **w**,	Mt 13:22	*3056*
this is the man who hears the **w**	Mt 13:23	*3056*
they sent **w** into all that	Mt 14:35	
And *by this* you invalidated the **w**	Mt 15:6	*3056*
But He did not answer her a **w**. And	Mt 15:23	*3056*
No one was able to answer Him a **w**,	Mt 22:46	*3056*
And Peter remembered the **w** which	Mt 26:75	*4487*
go and take **w** to My brethren to leave	Mt 28:10	*518*
and He was speaking the **w** to them.	Mk 2:2	*3056*
and standing outside they sent **w**	Mk 3:31	
"The sower sows the **w**.	Mk 4:14	*3056*
who are beside the road where the **w**	Mk 4:15	*3056*
Satan comes and takes away the **w**	Mk 4:15	*3056*
when they hear the **w**, immediately	Mk 4:16	*3056*
persecution arises because of the **w**,	Mk 4:17	*3056*
are the ones who have heard the **w**,	Mk 4:18	*3056*
other things enter in and choke the **w**,	Mk 4:19	*3056*
and they hear the **w** and accept it	Mk 4:20	*3056*
such parables He was speaking the **w**	Mk 4:33	*3056*
thus invalidating the **w** of God by	Mk 7:13	*3056*
and confirmed the **w** by the signs that	Mk 16:20	*3056*
eyewitnesses and servants of the **w**,	Lk 1:2	*3056*
it be done to me according to your **w**."	Lk 1:38	*4487*
According to Your **w**;	Lk 2:29	*4487*
the **w** of God came to John, the son	Lk 3:2	*4487*
listening to the **w** of God,	Lk 5:1	*3056*
but *just* say the **w**, and my	Lk 7:7	*3056*
the seed is the **w** of God.	Lk 8:11	*3056*
the devil comes and takes away the **w**	Lk 8:12	*3056*
receive the **w** with joy; and these	Lk 8:13	*3056*
are the ones who have heard the **w** in	Lk 8:15	*3056*
My brothers are these who hear the **w**	Lk 8:21	*3056*
listening to His **w**.	Lk 10:39	*3056*
blessed are those who hear the **w** of	Lk 11:28	*3056*
"And everyone who speaks a **w** against	Lk 12:10	*3056*
the people were hanging on to every **w**	Lk 19:48	
And Peter remembered the **w** of	Lk 22:61	*3056*
was a prophet mighty in deed and **w** in	Lk 24:19	*3056*
In the beginning was the **W**,	Jn 1:1	*3056*
and the **W** was with God, and the Word	Jn 1:1	*3056*
and the **W** was God.	Jn 1:1	*3056*
And the **W** became flesh, and dwelt	Jn 1:14	*3056*
they believed the Scripture and the **w**	Jn 2:22	*3056*
believed in Him because of the **w** of	Jn 4:39	*3056*
Many more believed because of His **w**;	Jn 4:41	*3056*
The man believed the **w** that Jesus	Jn 4:50	*3056*
he who hears My **w**, and believes Him	Jn 5:24	*3056*
"You do not have His **w** abiding in	Jn 5:38	*3056*
"If you continue in My **w**, *then*	Jn 8:31	*3056*
because My **w** has no place in you.	Jn 8:37	*3056*
It is because you cannot hear My **w**.	Jn 8:43	*3056*
if anyone keeps My **w** he will never	Jn 8:51	*3056*
'If anyone keeps My **w**, he will	Jn 8:52	*3056*
but I do know Him and keep His **w**.	Jn 8:55	*3056*
to whom the **w** of God came	Jn 10:35	*3056*
So the sisters sent **w** to Him,	Jn 11:3	

Context	Reference	Strong's
This was to fulfill the **w** of	Jn 12:38	3056
the **w** I spoke is what will judge him	Jn 12:48	3056
he will keep My **w**; and My Father	Jn 14:23	3056
and the **w** which you hear is not Mine,	Jn 14:24	3056
are already clean because of the **w**	Jn 15:3	3056
"Remember the **w** that I said to you,	Jn 15:20	3056
if they kept My **w**, they will keep	Jn 15:20	3056
have done this to fulfill the **w**	Jn 15:25	3056
and they have kept Your **w**.	Jn 17:6	3056
"I have given them Your **w**;	Jn 17:14	3056
"Sanctify them in the truth; Your **w**	Jn 17:17	3056
who believe in Me through their **w**;	Jn 17:20	3056
to fulfill the **w** which He spoke,	Jn 18:9	3056
to fulfill the **w** of Jesus which He	Jn 18:32	3056
those who had received his **w** were	Ac 2:41	3056
Your bond-servants may speak Your **w**	Ac 4:29	3056
Spirit and *began* to speak the **w**	Ac 4:31	3056
not desirable for us to neglect the **w**	Ac 6:2	3056
prayer and to the ministry of the **w**."	Ac 6:4	3056
The **w** of God kept on spreading;	Ac 6:7	3056
"Then Joseph sent **w** and invited	Ac 7:14	
scattered went about preaching the **w**.	Ac 8:4	3056
heard that Samaria had received the **w**	Ac 8:14	3056
solemnly testified and spoken the **w**	Ac 8:25	3056
"The **w** which He sent to the sons of	Ac 10:36	3056
the Gentiles also had received the **w**	Ac 11:1	3056
"And I remembered the **w** of the Lord,	Ac 11:16	4487
speaking the **w** to no one except to	Ac 11:19	3056
But the **w** of the Lord continued to	Ac 12:24	3056
they *began* to proclaim the **w** of	Ac 13:5	3056
and Saul and sought to hear the **w** of	Ac 13:7	3056
if you have any **w** of exhortation for	Ac 13:15	3056
whole city assembled to hear the **w** of	Ac 13:44	3056
"It was necessary that the **w** of God	Ac 13:46	3056
rejoicing and glorifying the **w** of	Ac 13:48	3056
And the **w** of the Lord was being	Ac 13:49	3056
who was testifying to the **w** of His	Ac 14:3	3056
When they had spoken the **w** in Perga,	Ac 14:25	3056
mouth the Gentiles would hear the **w**	Ac 15:7	3056
will also report the same things by **w**	Ac 15:27	3056
the **w** of the Lord.	Ac 15:35	3056
city in which we proclaimed the **w** of	Ac 15:36	3056
by the Holy Spirit to speak the **w** in	Ac 16:6	3056
And they spoke the **w** of the Lord to	Ac 16:32	3056
for they received the **w** with great	Ac 17:11	3056
of Thessalonica found out that the **w**	Ac 17:13	3056
devoting himself completely to the **w**,	Ac 18:5	3056
teaching the **w** of God among them.	Ac 18:11	3056
all who lived in Asia heard the **w** of	Ac 19:10	3056
So the **w** of the Lord was growing	Ac 19:20	3056
now I commend you to God and to the **w**	Ac 20:32	3056
grieving especially over the **w** which	Ac 20:38	3056
Paul had spoken one *parting* **w**,	Ac 28:25	4487
But *it is* not as though the **w** of	Ro 9:6	3056
For this is the **w** of promise: "AT	Ro 9:9	3056
FOR THE LORD WILL EXECUTE HIS **W** ON	Ro 9:28	3056
But what does it say? "THE **W** IS	Ro 10:8	4487
the **w** of faith which we are preaching,	Ro 10:8	4487
and hearing by the **w** of Christ.	Ro 10:17	4487
in the obedience of the Gentiles by **w**	Ro 15:18	3056
For the **w** of the cross is foolishness	1Co 1:18	3056
For to one is given the **w** of wisdom	1Co 12:8	3056
and to another the **w** of knowledge	1Co 12:8	3056
Was it from you that the **w** of God	1Co 14:36	3056
if you hold fast the **w** which I	1Co 15:2	3056
But as God is faithful, our **w** to you	2Co 1:18	3056
peddling the **w** of God, but as from	2Co 2:17	3056
in craftiness or adulterating the **w**	2Co 4:2	3056
and He has committed to us the **w** of	2Co 5:19	3056
in the **w** of truth, in the power of	2Co 6:7	3056
that what we are in **w** by letters when	2Co 10:11	3056
the whole Law is fulfilled in one **w**,	Ga 5:14	3056
The one who is taught the **w** is to	Ga 6:6	3056
Let no unwholesome **w** proceed from	Eph 4:29	3056
but only such *a* **w** as is good for	Eph 4:29	
by the washing of water with the **w**,	Eph 5:26	4487
which is the **w** of God.	Eph 6:17	4487
have far more courage to speak the **w**	Php 1:14	3056
holding fast the **w** of life, so that	Php 2:16	3056
which you previously heard in the **w**	Col 1:5	3056
carry out the *preaching of* the **w**	Col 1:25	3056
Let the **w** of Christ richly dwell	Col 3:16	3056
Whatever you do in **w** or deed, *do*	Col 3:17	3056
will open up to us a door for the **w**,	Col 4:3	3056
our gospel did not come to you in **w**	1Th 1:5	3056
having received the **w** in much	1Th 1:6	3056
For the **w** of the Lord has sounded	1Th 1:8	3056
God that when you received the **w** of	1Th 2:13	3056
you accepted *it* not *as* the **w**	1Th 2:13	3056
the **w** of God, which also performs	1Th 2:13	3056
For this we say to you by the **w** of	1Th 4:15	3056
whether by **w** *of mouth* or by	2Th 2:15	3056
your hearts in every good work and **w**.	2Th 2:17	3056
pray for us that the **w** of the Lord	2Th 3:1	3056
it is sanctified by means of the **w** of	1Tm 4:5	3056
but the **w** of God is not imprisoned.	2Tm 2:9	3056
accurately handling the **w** of truth.	2Tm 2:15	3056
preach the **w**; be ready in season	2Tm 4:2	3056
even His **w**, in the proclamation	Ti 1:3	3056
holding fast the faithful **w** which is	Ti 1:9	3056
so that the **w** of God will not be	Ti 2:5	3056
and upholds all things by the **w** of	Heb 1:3	4487
For if the **w** spoken through angels	Heb 2:2	3056
but the **w** they heard did not profit	Heb 4:2	3056
For the **w** of God is living and active	Heb 4:12	3056
of milk is not accustomed to the **w**	Heb 5:13	3056
and have tasted the good **w** of God	Heb 6:5	4487
but the **w** of the oath, which came	Heb 7:28	3056
the worlds were prepared by the **w** of	Heb 11:3	4487
who heard begged that no further **w** be	Heb 12:19	3056
who spoke the **w** of God to you;	Heb 13:7	3056
bear with this **w** of exhortation, for	Heb 13:22	3056
His will He brought us forth by the **w**	Jas 1:18	3056
in humility receive the **w** implanted,	Jas 1:21	3056
But prove yourselves doers of the **w**,	Jas 1:22	3056
For if anyone is a hearer of the **w**	Jas 1:23	3056
through the living and enduring **w**	1Pe 1:23	3056
BUT THE **W** OF THE LORD ENDURES	1Pe 1:25	4487
And this is the **w** which was preached	1Pe 1:25	4487
long for the pure milk of the **w**, so	1Pe 2:2	3050
because they are disobedient to the **w**,	1Pe 2:8	3056
of them are disobedient to the **w**,	1Pe 3:1	3056
they may be won without a **w** by	1Pe 3:1	3056
So we have the prophetic **w** *made*	2Pe 1:19	3056
it escapes their notice that by the **w**	2Pe 3:5	3056
But by His **w** the present heavens	2Pe 3:7	3056
concerning the **W** of Life	1Jn 1:1	3056
we make Him a liar and His **w** is not	1Jn 1:10	3056
but whoever keeps His **w**, in him	1Jn 2:5	3056
the old commandment is the **w** which	1Jn 2:7	3056
and the **w** of God abides in you,	1Jn 2:14	3056
let us not love with **w** or with tongue,	1Jn 3:18	3056
who testified to the **w** of God and to	Rv 1:2	3056
island called Patmos because of the **w**	Rv 1:9	3056
and have kept My **w**, and have not	Rv 3:8	3056
'Because you have kept the **w** of My	Rv 3:10	3056
who had been slain because of the **w**	Rv 6:9	3056
of the Lamb and because of the **w** of	Rv 12:11	3056
and His name is called The **W** of God.	Rv 19:13	3056
of Jesus and because of the **w** of God,	Rv 20:4	3056
WORDS		
used the same language and the same **w**.	Gn 11:1	1697
and when he heard the **w** of Rebekah	Gn 24:30	1697
When Abraham's servant heard their **w**,	Gn 24:52	1697
When Esau heard the **w** of his father,	Gn 27:34	1697
Now when the **w** of her elder son Esau	Gn 27:42	1697
Now Jacob heard the **w** of Laban's sons,	Gn 31:1	1697
Now their **w** seemed reasonable to	Gn 34:18	1697
more for his dreams and for his **w**.	Gn 37:8	1697
Then she spoke to him with these **w**,	Gn 39:17	1697
Now when his master heard the **w** of	Gn 39:19	1697
that your **w** may be tested, whether	Gn 42:16	1697
so your **w** may be verified, and you	Gn 42:20	1697
So he overtook them and spoke these **w**	Gn 44:6	1697
"Why does my lord speak such **w** as	Gn 44:7	1697
let it also be according to your **w**;	Gn 44:10	1697
we told him the **w** of my lord.	Gn 44:24	1697
When they told him all the **w** of	Gn 45:27	1697
He gives beautiful **w**.	Gn 49:21	561
"You are to speak to him and put the **w**	Ex 4:15	1697
Moses told Aaron all the **w** of the	Ex 4:28	1697
and Aaron spoke all the **w** which the	Ex 4:30	1697
they will pay no attention to false **w**."	Ex 5:9	1697
These are the **w** that you shall	Ex 19:6	1697
and set before them all these **w** which	Ex 19:7	1697
And Moses brought back the **w** of	Ex 19:8	1697
Then Moses told the **w** of the people	Ex 19:9	1697
Then God spoke all these **w**, saying,	Ex 20:1	1697
and recounted to the people all the **w**	Ex 24:3	1697
"All the **w** which the LORD has	Ex 24:3	1697
Moses wrote down all the **w** of the	Ex 24:4	1697
you in accordance with all these **w**."	Ex 24:8	1697
and I will write on the tablets the **w**	Ex 34:1	1697
"Write down these **w**, for in	Ex 34:27	1697
for in accordance with these **w** I have	Ex 34:27	1697
And he wrote on the tablets the **w** of	Ex 34:28	1697
went out and told the people the **w** of	Nu 11:24	1697
He said, "Hear now My **w**: If there	Nu 12:6	1697
When Moses spoke these **w** to all	Nu 14:39	1697
As he finished speaking all these **w**,	Nu 16:31	1697
came to Balaam and repeated Balak's **w**	Nu 22:7	1697
The oracle of him who hears the **w** of	Nu 24:4	561
The oracle of him who hears the **w** of	Nu 24:16	561
These are the **w** which Moses spoke to	Dt 1:1	1697
LORD heard the sound of your **w**,	Dt 1:34	1697
to Sihon king of Heshbon with **w** of	Dt 2:26	1697
that I may let them hear My **w** so they	Dt 4:10	1697
you heard the sound of **w**, but you	Dt 4:12	1697
and you heard His **w** from the midst of	Dt 4:36	1697
"These **w** the LORD spoke to all	Dt 5:22	1697
LORD heard the voice of your **w**	Dt 5:28	1697
'I have heard the voice of the **w** of	Dt 5:28	1697
"These **w**, which I am commanding you	Dt 6:6	1697
and on them *were* all the **w** which	Dt 9:10	1697
'I will write on the tablets the **w**	Dt 10:2	1697
"You shall therefore impress these **w**	Dt 11:18	1697
"Be careful to listen to all these **w**	Dt 12:28	1697
you shall not listen to the **w** of that	Dt 13:3	1697
eyes of the wise and perverts the **w**	Dt 16:19	1697
by carefully observing all the **w** of	Dt 17:19	1697
and I will put My **w** in his mouth,	Dt 18:18	1697
that whoever will not listen to My **w**	Dt 18:19	1697
and write on them all the **w** of this	Dt 27:3	1697
shall write on the stones all the **w**	Dt 27:8	1697
is he who does not confirm the **w** of	Dt 27:26	1697
do not turn aside from any of the **w**	Dt 28:14	1697
are not careful to observe all the **w**	Dt 28:58	1697
These are the **w** of the covenant which	Dt 29:1	1697
"So keep the **w** of this covenant to	Dt 29:9	1697
"It shall be when he hears the **w** of	Dt 29:19	1697
that we may observe all the **w** of this	Dt 29:29	1697
So Moses went and spoke these **w** to	Dt 31:1	1697
and be careful to observe all the **w**	Dt 31:12	1697
when Moses finished writing the **w** of	Dt 31:24	1697
that I may speak these **w** in their	Dt 31:28	1697
of all the assembly of Israel the **w** of	Dt 31:30	1697
And let the earth hear the **w** of my	Dt 32:1	561
Then Moses came and spoke all the **w**	Dt 32:44	1697
had finished speaking all these **w** to	Dt 32:45	1697
"Take to your heart all the **w** with	Dt 32:46	1697
even all the **w** of this law.	Dt 32:46	1697
Everyone receives of Your **w**.	Dt 33:3	1703
command and does not obey your **w**	Jos 1:18	1697
She said, "According to your **w**, so	Jos 2:21	1697
and hear the **w** of the LORD your	Jos 3:9	1697
Then afterward he read all the **w** of	Jos 8:34	1697
heard the **w** which the sons of Reuben	Jos 22:30	1697
that not one word of all the good **w**	Jos 23:14	1697
about that just as all the good **w**	Jos 23:15	1697
And Joshua wrote these **w** in the book	Jos 24:26	1697
for it has heard all the **w** of the	Jos 24:27	561
angel of the LORD spoke these **w**	Jg 2:4	1697
Indeed she repeats her **w** to herself,	Jg 5:29	561
mother's relatives spoke all these **w**	Jg 9:3	1697
the ruler of the city heard the **w** of	Jg 9:30	1697
and Jephthah spoke all his **w** before	Jg 11:11	1697
Manoah said, "Now when your **w** come	Jg 13:12	1697
so that when your **w** come *to pass*,	Jg 13:17	1697
when she pressed him daily with her **w**	Jg 16:16	1697
hide anything from me of all the **w**	1Sa 3:17	1697
was with him and let none of his **w**	1Sa 3:19	1697
So Samuel spoke all the **w** of the	1Sa 8:10	1697
Now after Samuel had heard all the **w**	1Sa 8:21	1697
to Gibeah of Saul and spoke these **w**	1Sa 11:4	1697
So they related to him the **w** of	1Sa 11:5	1697
Saul mightily when he heard these **w**,	1Sa 11:6	1697
listen to the **w** of the LORD.	1Sa 15:1	1697
command of the LORD and your **w**,	1Sa 15:24	1697
Saul and all Israel heard these **w** of	1Sa 17:11	1697
and he spoke these same **w**;	1Sa 17:23	1697
When the **w** which David spoke were	1Sa 17:31	1697
So Saul's servants spoke these **w** to	1Sa 18:23	1697
reported to him according to these **w**	1Sa 18:24	1697
When his servants told David these **w**,	1Sa 18:26	1697
and Jonathan told him all these **w**.	1Sa 19:7	1697
David took these **w** to heart	1Sa 21:12	1697
persuaded his men with *these* **w**	1Sa 24:7	1697
"Why do you listen to the **w** of men,	1Sa 24:9	1697
David had finished speaking these **w**	1Sa 24:16	1697
to Nabal according to all these **w** in	1Sa 25:9	1697
and told him according to all these **w**.	1Sa 25:12	1697
and listen to the **w** of your	1Sa 25:24	1697
let my lord the king listen to the **w**	1Sa 26:19	1697
and was very afraid because of the **w**	1Sa 28:20	1697
my hand and have listened to your **w**	1Sa 28:21	1697
Then Abner was very angry over the **w**	2Sa 3:8	1697
In accordance with all these **w**	2Sa 7:17	1697
and Your **w** are truth, and You have	2Sa 7:28	1697
So Joab put the **w** in her mouth.	2Sa 14:3	1697
and it was he who put all these **w** in	2Sa 14:19	1697
Yet the **w** of the men of Judah were	2Sa 19:43	1697
men of Judah were harsher than the **w**	2Sa 19:43	1697
"Listen to the **w** of your maidservant."	2Sa 20:17	1697
And David spoke the **w** of this song to	2Sa 22:1	1697
Now these are the last **w** of David.	2Sa 23:1	1697
come in after you and confirm your **w**."	1Ki 1:14	1697
I have done according to your **w**.	1Ki 3:12	1697
When Hiram heard the **w** of Solomon,	1Ki 5:7	1697
"And may these **w** of mine, with	1Ki 8:59	1697
I heard in my own land about your **w**	1Ki 10:6	1697
and speak good **w** to them, then they	1Ki 12:7	1697
the **w** which he had spoken to the king,	1Ki 13:11	1697
It came about when Ahab heard these **w**,	1Ki 21:27	1697
the **w** of the prophets are uniformly	1Ki 22:13	1697
came up to meet you and spoke these **w**	2Ki 1:7	1697
tells the king of Israel the **w** that	2Ki 6:12	1697
When the king heard the **w** of	2Ki 6:30	1697
say (but *they are* only empty **w**),	2Ki 18:20	1697
master and to you to speak these **w**,	2Ki 18:27	1697
their clothes torn and told him the **w**	2Ki 18:37	1697
LORD your God will hear all the **w**	2Ki 19:4	1697
and will rebuke the **w** which the	2Ki 19:4	1697
"Do not be afraid because of the **w**	2Ki 19:6	1697
and listen to the **w** of Sennacherib,	2Ki 19:16	1697
When the king heard the **w** of the book	2Ki 22:11	1697
people and all Judah concerning the **w**	2Ki 22:13	1697
fathers have not listened to the **w** of	2Ki 22:13	1697
even all the **w** of the book which	2Ki 22:16	1697
"*Regarding* the **w** which you have	2Ki 22:18	1697
he read in their hearing all the **w** of	2Ki 23:2	1697
to carry out the **w** of this covenant	2Ki 23:3	1697
that he might confirm the **w** of	2Ki 23:24	1697
According to all these **w**	1Ch 17:15	1697
For by the last **w** of David the sons	1Ch 23:27	1697
seer to exalt him according to the **w**	1Ch 25:5	1697
I heard in my own land about your **w**	2Ch 9:5	1697
and please them and speak good **w** to	2Ch 10:7	1697
So they listened to the **w** of the	2Ch 11:4	1697
and his ways and his **w** are written in	2Ch 13:22	1697
Now when Asa heard these **w**	2Ch 15:8	1697
the **w** of the prophets are uniformly	2Ch 18:12	1697
the commandment of the king by the **w**	2Ch 29:15	1697
praises to the LORD with the **w** of	2Ch 29:30	1697
And the people relied on the **w** of	2Ch 32:8	1697
and the **w** of the seers who spoke to	2Ch 33:18	1697
When the king heard the **w** of the law,	2Ch 34:19	1697
concerning the **w** of the book which	2Ch 34:21	1697
God of Israel *regarding* the **w**	2Ch 34:26	1697
before God when you heard His **w**	2Ch 34:27	1697
he read in their hearing all the **w** of	2Ch 34:30	1697
to perform the **w** of the covenant	2Ch 34:31	1697
nor did he listen to the **w** of Neco	2Ch 35:22	1697
despised His **w** and scoffed at His	2Ch 36:16	1697
learned in the **w** of the commandments	Ezr 7:11	1697
Then everyone who trembled at the **w**	Ezr 9:4	1697
The **w** of Nehemiah the son of Hacaliah.	Ne 1:1	1697
When I heard these **w**, I sat down	Ne 1:4	1697

to me and also about the king's w	Ne 2:18	1697
I had heard their outcry and these w.	Ne 5:6	1697
in my presence and reported my w to	Ne 6:19	1697
were weeping when they heard the w of	Ne 8:9	1697
because they understood the w which	Ne 8:12	1697
they might gain insight into the w of	Ne 8:13	1697
came back and related Mordecai's w to	Es 4:9	1697
They related Esther's w to Mordecai.	Es 4:12	1697
namely, w of peace and truth,	Es 9:30	1697
"Your w have helped the tottering to	Jb 4:4	4405
Therefore my w have been rash.	Jb 6:3	1697
That I have not denied the w of	Jb 6:10	561
"How painful are honest w! But what	Jb 6:25	561
"Do you intend to reprove *my* w,	Jb 6:26	561
When the w of one in despair belong	Jb 6:26	561
And the w of your mouth be a mighty	Jb 8:2	561
And bring forth w from their minds?	Jb 8:10	4405
And choose my w before Him?	Jb 9:14	1697
"Shall a multitude of w go	Jb 11:2	1697
"Does not the ear test w,	Jb 12:11	4405
Or with w which are not profitable?	Jb 15:3	4405
against God And allow *such* w to	Jb 15:13	4405
"Is there *no* limit to windy w?	Jb 16:3	1697
I could compose w against you And	Jb 16:4	4405
"How long will you hunt for w?	Jb 18:2	4405
you torment me And crush me with w?	Jb 19:2	4405
"Oh that my w were written! Oh that	Jb 19:23	4405
from His mouth And establish His w in	Jb 22:22	561
"I would learn the w *which* He	Jb 23:5	4405
I have treasured the w of His mouth	Jb 23:12	561
"To whom have you uttered w?	Jb 26:4	4405
"After my w they did not speak again,	Jb 29:22	1697
The w of Job are ended.	Jb 31:40	1697
"Behold, I waited for your w, I	Jb 32:11	1697
Not one of you who answered his w.	Jb 32:12	561
"For he has not arranged *his* w	Jb 32:14	4405
W have failed them.	Jb 32:15	4405
"For I am full of w; The spirit	Jb 32:18	4405
And listen to all my w.	Jb 33:1	1697
"My w are *from* the uprightness	Jb 33:3	561
I have heard the sound of *your* w:	Jb 33:8	4405
"Hear my w, you wise men,	Jb 34:2	4405
"For the ear tests w As the palate	Jb 34:3	4405
Listen to the sound of my w.	Jb 34:16	4405
And his w are without wisdom.	Jb 34:35	1697
And multiplies his w against God.' "	Jb 34:37	561
He multiplies w without knowledge."	Jb 35:16	4405
"For truly my w are not false; One	Jb 36:4	4405
"Who is this that darkens counsel By w	Jb 38:2	4405
Or will he speak to you soft w?	Jb 41:3	1697
after the LORD had spoken these w	Jb 42:7	1697
Give ear to my w, O LORD,	Ps 5:1	561
The w of the LORD are pure words;	Ps 12:6	565a
The words of the LORD are pure w;	Ps 12:6	565a
There is no speech, nor are there w;	Ps 19:3	561
Let the w of my mouth	Ps 19:14	561
Far from my deliverance are the w of	Ps 22:1	1697
But they devise deceitful w against	Ps 35:20	1697
The w of his mouth are wickedness	Ps 36:3	1697
those after them who approve their w.	Ps 49:13	6310
And you cast My w behind you.	Ps 50:17	1697
You love all w that devour, O	Ps 52:4	1697
Give ear to the w of my mouth.	Ps 54:2	561
His w were softer than oil, Yet they	Ps 55:21	1697
All day long they distort my w; All	Ps 56:5	1697
the sin of their mouth *and the* w	Ps 59:12	1697
Incline your ears to the w of my	Ps 78:1	561
They pour forth w, they speak	Ps 94:4	
And they did not rebel against His w.	Ps 105:28	1697
Then they believed His w; They sang	Ps 106:12	1697
they had rebelled against the w of	Ps 107:11	561
They have also surrounded me with w	Ps 109:3	1697
I have promised to keep Your w.	Ps 119:57	1697
How sweet are Your w to my taste!	Ps 119:103	565a
The unfolding of Your w gives light;	Ps 119:130	1697
my adversaries have forgotten Your w.	Ps 119:139	1697
I wait for Your w.	Ps 119:147	1697
But my heart stands in awe of Your w.	Ps 119:161	1697
When they have heard the w of Your	Ps 138:4	561
And they hear my w, for they are	Ps 141:6	561
He declares His w to Jacob, His	Ps 147:19	1697
The w of the wise and their riddles.	Pr 1:6	1697
I will make my w known to you.	Pr 1:23	1697
My son, if you will receive my w	Pr 2:1	561
adulteress who flatters with her w;	Pr 2:16	561
"Let your heart hold fast my w;	Pr 4:4	1697
not forget nor turn away from the w	Pr 4:5	561
My son, give attention to my w;	Pr 4:20	1697
to me And do not depart from the w of	Pr 5:7	561
If you have been snared with the w	Pr 6:2	561
Have been caught with the w of your	Pr 6:2	561
My son, keep my w And treasure my	Pr 7:1	561
the foreigner who flatters with her w.	Pr 7:5	561
And pay attention to the w of my	Pr 7:24	561
When there are many w, transgression	Pr 10:19	1697
The w of the wicked lie in wait for	Pr 12:6	1697
with good by the fruit of his w,	Pr 12:14	6310
Or you will not discern w of	Pr 14:7	8193
But pleasant w are pure.	Pr 15:26	561
Pleasant w are a honeycomb, Sweet to	Pr 16:24	561
While his w are like scorching fire.	Pr 16:27	8193
He who restrains his w has knowledge,	Pr 17:27	561
The w of a man's mouth are deep	Pr 18:4	1697
The w of a whisperer are like dainty	Pr 18:8	1697
He pursues *them with* w, *but*	Pr 19:7	561
And you will stray from the w of	Pr 19:27	561
But He overthrows the w of	Pr 22:12	1697
Incline your ear and hear the w of	Pr 22:17	1697
make you know the certainty of the w	Pr 22:21	561
he will despise the wisdom of your w.	Pr 23:9	4405
to discipline And your ears to w of	Pr 23:12	561
The w of a whisperer are like dainty	Pr 26:22	1697
A slave will not be instructed by w	Pr 29:19	1697
you see a man who is hasty in his w?	Pr 29:20	1697
The w of Agur the son of Jakeh,	Pr 30:1	1697
Do not add to His w Or He will	Pr 30:6	1697
The w of King Lemuel, the oracle	Pr 31:1	1697
The w of the Preacher, the son of	Ec 1:1	1697
therefore let your w be few.	Ec 5:2	1697
the voice of a fool through many w.	Ec 5:3	1697
For in many dreams and in many w	Ec 5:7	1697
For there are many w which increase	Ec 6:11	1697
Also, do not take seriously all w	Ec 7:21	1697
of the poor man is despised and his w	Ec 9:16	1697
The w of the wise heard in quietness	Ec 9:17	1697
W from the mouth of a wise man are	Ec 10:12	1697
Yet the fool multiplies w. No man	Ec 10:14	1697
Preacher sought to find delightful w	Ec 12:10	1697
find delightful words and to write w	Ec 12:10	1697
The w of wise men are like goads,	Ec 12:11	1697
Listen and hear my w.	Is 28:23	565a
where you are prostrate Your w	Is 29:4	565a
vision will be to you like the w of a	Is 29:11	1697
this people draw near with their w	Is 29:13	6310
On that day the deaf will hear w of a	Is 29:18	1697
Speak to us pleasant w, Prophesy	Is 30:10	2513b
disaster And does not retract His w,	Is 31:2	1697
strength for the war are only empty w.'	Is 36:5	1697
master and to you to speak these w,	Is 36:12	1697
"Hear the w of the great king,	Is 36:13	1697
their clothes torn and told him the w	Is 36:22	1697
the LORD your God will hear the w	Is 37:4	1697
and will rebuke the w which the	Is 37:4	1697
"Do not be afraid because of the w	Is 37:6	1697
and listen to all the w of	Is 37:17	1697
there was no one who heard your w.	Is 41:26	561
"I have put My w in your mouth	Is 51:16	1697
and uttering from the heart lying w.	Is 59:13	1697
and My w which I have put in your	Is 59:21	1697
The w of Jeremiah the son of Hilkiah,	Jer 1:1	1697
I have put My w in your mouth.	Jer 1:9	1697
"Go and proclaim these w toward	Jer 3:12	1697
I am making My w in your mouth fire	Jer 5:14	1697
they have not listened to My w,	Jer 6:19	1697
"Do not trust in deceptive w,	Jer 7:4	1697
you are trusting in deceptive w to no	Jer 7:8	1697
"You shall speak all these w to them,	Jer 7:27	1697
"Hear the w of this covenant,	Jer 11:2	1697
is the man who does not heed the w of	Jer 11:3	1697
"Proclaim all these w in the cities	Jer 11:6	1697
'Hear the w of this covenant and do	Jer 11:6	1697
therefore I brought on them all the w	Jer 11:8	1697
ancestors who refused to hear My w	Jer 11:10	1697
who refuse to listen to My w, who	Jer 13:10	1697
Your w were found and I ate them,	Jer 15:16	1697
And Your w became for me a joy	Jer 15:16	1697
when you tell this people all these w,	Jer 16:10	1697
and there I will announce My w to you."	Jer 18:2	1697
let us give no heed to any of his w."	Jer 18:18	1697
and proclaim there the w that I tell	Jer 19:2	1697
their necks so as not to heed My w.' "	Jer 19:15	1697
"But if you will not obey these w,	Jer 22:5	1697
LORD And because of His holy w.	Jer 23:9	1697
"Do not listen to the w of	Jer 23:16	1697
Then they would have announced My w	Jer 23:22	1697
"who steal My w from each other.	Jer 23:30	1697
and you have perverted the w of	Jer 23:36	1697
'Because you have not obeyed My w,	Jer 25:8	1697
'I will bring upon that land all My w	Jer 25:13	1697
prophesy against them all these w,	Jer 25:30	1697
in the LORD's house all the w	Jer 26:2	1697
to listen to the w of My servants	Jer 26:5	1697
heard Jeremiah speaking these w in	Jer 26:7	1697
house and against this city all the w	Jer 26:12	1697
sent me to you to speak all these w	Jer 26:15	1697
this city and against this land w	Jer 26:20	1697
men and all the officials heard his w,	Jer 26:21	1697
I spoke w like all these to Zedekiah	Jer 27:12	1697
"So do not listen to the w of	Jer 27:14	1697
Do not listen to the w of your	Jer 27:16	1697
may the LORD confirm your w which	Jer 28:6	1697
Now these are the w of the letter	Jer 29:1	1697
they have not listened to My w,'	Jer 29:19	1697
neighbors' wives and have spoken w	Jer 29:23	1697
'Write all the w which I have spoken	Jer 30:2	1697
Now these are the w which the LORD	Jer 30:4	1697
the prophet spoke all these w to	Jer 34:6	1697
who have not fulfilled the w of	Jer 34:18	1697
instruction by listening to My w?"	Jer 35:13	1697
"The w of Jonadab the son of Rechab,	Jer 35:14	1697
a scroll and write on it all the w	Jer 36:2	1697
the dictation of Jeremiah all the w	Jer 36:4	1697
have written at my dictation the w of	Jer 36:6	1697
reading from the book the w of the	Jer 36:8	1697
Then Baruch read from the book the w	Jer 36:10	1697
had heard all the w of the LORD	Jer 36:11	1697
Micaiah declared to them all the w	Jer 36:13	1697
When they had heard all the w, they	Jer 36:16	1697
"We will surely report all these w	Jer 36:16	1697
how did you write all these w? *Was*	Jer 36:17	1697
"He dictated all these w to me,	Jer 36:18	1697
and they reported all the w to	Jer 36:20	1697
his servants who heard all these w	Jer 36:24	1697
king had burned the scroll and the w	Jer 36:27	1697
and write on it all the former w that	Jer 36:28	1697
the dictation of Jeremiah all the w	Jer 36:32	1697
and many similar w were added to them.	Jer 36:32	1697
people of the land listened to the w	Jer 37:2	1697
the son of Malchijah heard the w that	Jer 38:1	1697
by speaking such w to them; for this	Jer 38:4	1697
"Let no man know about these w	Jer 38:24	1697
them in accordance with all these w	Jer 38:27	1697
I am about to bring My w on this city	Jer 39:16	1697
your God in accordance with your w;	Jer 42:4	1697
telling all the people all the w of	Jer 43:1	1697
all these w	Jer 43:1	1697
so that you may know that My w will	Jer 44:29	1697
when he had written down these w in a	Jer 45:1	1697
all these w which have been written	Jer 51:60	1697
then see that you read all these w	Jer 51:61	1697
Thus far are the w of Jeremiah.	Jer 51:64	1697
neither fear them nor fear their w,	Ezk 2:6	1697
neither fear their w nor be dismayed	Ezk 2:6	1697
"But you shall speak My w to them	Ezk 2:7	1697
house of Israel and speak with My w	Ezk 3:4	1697
whose w you cannot understand. But I	Ezk 3:6	1697
take into your heart all My w which I	Ezk 3:10	1697
"None of My w will be delayed any	Ezk 12:28	1697
you *as* My people and hear your w,	Ezk 33:31	1697
for they hear your w but they do not	Ezk 33:32	1697
against Me and have multiplied your w	Ezk 35:13	1697
together to speak lying and corrupt w	Da 2:9	4406
the banquet hall because of the w of	Da 5:10	4406
of the sound of the boastful w which	Da 7:11	4406
"Thus He has confirmed His w which	Da 9:12	1697
and the sound of his w like the sound	Da 10:6	1697
But I heard the sound of his w;	Da 10:9	1697
as soon as I heard the sound of his w,	Da 10:9	1697
understand the w that I am about to	Da 10:11	1697
your w were heard, and I have come	Da 10:12	1697
and I have come in response to your w.	Da 10:12	1697
had spoken to me according to these w,	Da 10:15	1697
"By smooth w he will turn to	Da 11:32	
conceal these w and seal up the book	Da 12:4	1697
for *these* w are concealed	Da 12:9	1697
I have slain them by the w of My	Hos 6:5	561
They speak *mere* w, With	Hos 10:4	1697
Take w with you and return to the	Hos 14:2	1697
The w of Amos, who was among	Am 1:1	1697
land is unable to endure all his w.	Am 7:10	1697
But rather for hearing the w of the	Am 8:11	1697
Do not My w do good To the one	Mi 2:7	1697
of the LORD their God and the w	Hg 1:12	1697
"But did not My w and My statutes,	Zch 1:6	1697
was speaking with me with gracious w,	Zch 1:13	1697
with gracious words, comforting w.	Zch 1:13	1697
'Are not *these* the w which the	Zch 7:7	1697
they could not hear the law and the w	Zch 7:12	1697
listening in these days to these w	Zch 8:9	1697
have wearied the LORD with your w.	Mal 2:17	1697
"Your w have been arrogant against	Mal 3:13	1697
they will be heard for their many w.	Mt 6:7	*4180*
"Therefore everyone who hears these w	Mt 7:24	*3056*
"Everyone who hears these w of Mine	Mt 7:26	*3056*
When Jesus had finished these w,	Mt 7:28	*3056*
nor heed your w, as you go out of	Mt 10:14	*3056*
"For by your w you will be	Mt 12:37	*3056*
your w you will be condemned."	Mt 12:37	*3056*
When Jesus had finished these w, He	Mt 19:1	*3056*
but My w will not pass away.	Mt 24:35	*3056*
When Jesus had finished all these w,	Mt 26:1	*3056*
also insulting Him with the same w.	Mt 27:44	
whoever is ashamed of Me and My w	Mk 8:38	*3056*
But at these w he was saddened,	Mk 10:22	*3056*
The disciples were amazed at His w.	Mk 10:24	*3056*
but My w will not pass away.	Mk 13:31	*3056*
saying the same w.	Mk 14:39	*3056*
because you did not believe my w,	Lk 1:20	*3056*
as it is written in the book of the w	Lk 3:4	*3056*
and wondering at the gracious w which	Lk 4:22	*3056*
who comes to Me and hears My w	Lk 6:47	*3056*
whoever is ashamed of Me and My w,	Lk 9:26	*3056*
"Let these w sink into your ears;	Lk 9:44	*3056*
"He said to him, 'By your own w I	Lk 19:22	*4750*
but My w will not pass away.	Lk 21:33	*3056*
And they remembered His w,	Lk 24:8	*4487*
But these w appeared to them as	Lk 24:11	*4487*
"What are these w that you are	Lk 24:17	*3056*
"These are My w which I spoke to you	Lk 24:44	*3056*
He whom God has sent speaks the w	Jn 3:34	*4487*
how will you believe My w?"	Jn 5:47	*4487*
the w that I have spoken to you are	Jn 6:63	*4487*
You have w of eternal life.	Jn 6:68	*4487*
when they heard these w, were saying,	Jn 7:40	*3056*
These w He spoke in the treasury, as	Jn 8:20	*4487*
"He who is of God hears the w of God;	Jn 8:47	*4487*
among the Jews because of these w.	Jn 10:19	*3056*
The w that I say to you I do not	Jn 14:10	*4487*
does not love Me does not keep My w;	Jn 14:24	*3056*
"If you abide in Me, and My w abide	Jn 15:7	*4487*
for the w which You gave Me I have	Jn 17:8	*4487*
When Jesus had spoken these w, He	Jn 18:1	
Therefore when Pilate heard these w,	Jn 19:13	*3056*
be known to you and give heed to my w.	Ac 2:14	*4487*
"Men of Israel, listen to these w:	Ac 2:22	*3056*
And with many other w he solemnly	Ac 2:40	*3056*
And as he heard these w, Ananias	Ac 5:5	*3056*
and the chief priests heard these w,	Ac 5:24	*3056*
heard him speak blasphemous w	Ac 6:11	*4487*
and he was a man of power in w	Ac 7:22	*3056*
Peter was still speaking these w,	Ac 10:44	*4487*
and he will speak w to you by which	Ac 11:14	*4487*
"With this the w of the Prophets	Ac 15:15	*3056*
have disturbed you with *their* w,	Ac 15:24	*3056*
And the jailer reported these w to	Ac 16:36	*3056*
The policemen reported these w to	Ac 16:38	*4487*
but if there are questions about w	Ac 18:15	*3056*

must help the weak and remember the **w** Ac 20:35 *3056*
but I utter **w** of sober truth. Ac 26:25 *4487*
[When he had spoken these **w**, Ac 28:29
"THAT YOU MAY BE JUSTIFIED IN YOUR **W**, Ro 3:4 *3056*
us with groanings too deep for **w**; Ro 8:26 *215*
THEIR **W** TO THE ENDS OF THE WORLD." Ro 10:18 *4487*
my preaching were not in persuasive **w** 1Co 2:4 *3056*
which things we also speak, not in **w** 1Co 2:13 *3056*
thoughts with spiritual **w**. 1Co 2:13
not the **w** of those who are arrogant 1Co 4:19 *3056*
kingdom of God does not consist in **w** 1Co 4:20 *3056*
the church I desire to speak five **w** 1Co 14:19 *3056*
rather than ten thousand **w** in a 1Co 14:19 *3056*
Paradise and heard inexpressible **w**, 2Co 12:4 *4487*
Let no one deceive you with empty **w**, Eph 5:6 *3056*
comfort one another with these **w**. 1Th 4:18 *3056*
constantly nourished on the **w** of 1Tm 4:6 *3056*
and does not agree with sound **w**, 1Tm 6:3 *3056*
questions and disputes about **w**, out 1Tm 6:4 *3055*
Retain the standard of sound **w** which 2Tm 1:13 *3056*
of God not to wrangle about **w**, which 2Tm 2:14 *3054*
blast of a trumpet and the sound of **w** Heb 12:19 *4487*
they will exploit you with false **w**; 2Pe 2:3 *3056*
For speaking out arrogant **w** of 2Pe 2:18
that you should remember the **w** spoken 2Pe 3:2 *4487*
unjustly accusing us with wicked **w**; 3Jn 1:10 *3056*
ought to remember the **w** that were Jude 1:17 *4487*
he who reads and those who hear the **w** Rv 1:3 *3056*
to him a mouth speaking arrogant **w** Rv 13:5
until the **w** of God will be fulfilled. Rv 17:17 *3056*
"These are true **w** of God." Rv 19:9 *3056*
for these **w** are faithful and true." Rv 21:5 *3056*
And he said to me, "These **w** are Rv 22:6 *3056*
Blessed is he who heeds the **w** of Rv 22:7 *3056*
prophets and of those who heed the **w** Rv 22:9 *3056*
"Do not seal up the **w** of Rv 22:10 *3056*
I testify to everyone who hears the **w** Rv 22:18 *3056*
and if anyone takes away from the **w** Rv 22:19 *3056*

WORE

men who **w** the linen ephod. 1Sa 22:18 5375
David also **w** an ephod of linen. 1Ch 15:27 5921
As for the builders, each **w** his Ne 4:18
was clothed with camel's hair and **w** Mk 1:6

WORK

completed His **w** which He had done, Gn 2:2 4399
from all His **w** which He had done. Gn 2:2 4399
He rested from all His **w** which God Gn 2:3 4399
"This one will give us rest from our **w** Gn 5:29 4639
went into the house to do his **w**, Gn 39:11 4399
draw the people away from their **w**? Ex 5:4 4639
let them **w** at it so that they will Ex 5:9 6213a
"Complete your **w** quota, *your* Ex 5:13 4639
"So go now *and* **w**; for you will be Ex 5:18 5647
'**W** a miracle,' then you shall say Ex 7:9 5414
no **w** at all shall be done on them, Ex 12:16 4399
to walk and the **w** they are to do. Ex 18:20 4639
you shall labor and do all your **w**, Ex 20:9 4399
in it you shall not do any **w**, Ex 20:10 4399
"Six days you are to do your **w**, Ex 23:12 4639
make them of hammered **w** at the two Ex 25:18 4749
are to be made of hammered **w**; Ex 25:31 4749
piece of hammered **w** of pure gold. Ex 25:36 4749
the **w** of a skillful workman. Ex 26:1 4639
the **w** of a skillful workman. Ex 26:31 4639
twisted linen, the **w** of a weaver. Ex 26:36 4639
twisted linen, the **w** of a weaver, Ex 27:16 4639
a robe and a tunic of checkered **w**, Ex 28:4 8665
the **w** of the skillful workman. Ex 28:6 4639
make them of twisted cordage **w**, Ex 28:14 4639
the **w** of a skillful workman; Ex 28:15 4639
like the **w** of the ephod you shall Ex 28:15 4639
of twisted cordage **w** in pure gold. Ex 28:22 4639
shall be a binding of woven **w**, Ex 28:32 4639
of checkered **w** of fine linen, Ex 28:39 7760
make a sash, the **w** of a weaver. Ex 28:39 4639
mixture, the **w** of a perfumer; Ex 30:25 7660
a perfume, the **w** of a perfumer, Ex 30:35 7660
artistic designs for **w** in gold, Ex 31:4 6213a
w in all *kinds of* craftsmanship. Ex 31:5 6213a
for whoever does any **w** on it, Ex 31:14 4399
'For six days **w** may be done, but Ex 31:15 4399
whoever does any **w** on the sabbath Ex 31:15 4399
The tablets were God's **w**, Ex 32:16 4639
"You shall **w** six days, but on the Ex 34:21 5647
"For six days **w** may be done, but Ex 35:2 4399
whoever does any **w** on it shall be Ex 35:2 4399
for the **w** of the tent of meeting Ex 35:21 4399
wood for any **w** of the service brought Ex 35:24 4399
to bring *material* for all the **w**, Ex 35:29 4399
to perform in every inventive **w**. Ex 35:33 4399
to perform every **w** of an engraver Ex 35:35 4399
performers of every **w** and makers Ex 35:35 4399
to know how to perform all the **w** in Ex 36:1 4399
to come to the **w** to perform it. Ex 36:2 4399
to perform the **w** in the construction Ex 36:3 4399
all the **w** of the sanctuary came, Ex 36:4 4399
the **w** which he was performing, Ex 36:4 4399
the construction **w** which the LORD Ex 36:5 5656
or woman any longer perform **w** for Ex 36:6 4399
more than enough for all the **w**, Ex 36:7 4399
those who were performing the **w** Ex 36:8 4399
the **w** of a skillful workman, Ex 36:8 4639
the **w** of a skillful workman. Ex 36:35 4639
twisted linen, the **w** of a weaver; Ex 36:37 4639
he made them of hammered **w** at Ex 37:7 4749
made the lampstand of hammered **w**, Ex 37:17 4749
a single hammered **w** of pure gold. Ex 37:22 4749
of spices, the **w** of a perfumer. Ex 37:29 4639

the court was the **w** of the weaver, Ex 38:18 4639
the gold that was used for the **w**, Ex 38:24 4399
in all the **w** of the sanctuary, Ex 38:24 4399
the **w** of a skillful workman. Ex 39:3 4639
the **w** of a skillful workman, Ex 39:8 4639
of twisted cordage **w** in pure gold. Ex 39:15 4639
the robe of the ephod of woven **w**, Ex 39:22 4639
material, the **w** of the weaver, Ex 39:29 4639
Thus all the **w** of the tabernacle Ex 39:32 5656
sons of Israel did all the **w** according Ex 39:42 5656
And Moses examined all the **w** and Ex 39:43 4399
Thus Moses finished the **w**. Ex 40:33 4399
your souls and not do any **w**, Lv 16:29 4399
'For six days **w** may be done, Lv 23:3 4399
You shall not do any **w**; Lv 23:3 4399
you shall not do any laborious **w**. Lv 23:7 4399
you shall not do any laborious **w** Lv 23:8 4399
You shall do no laborious **w**. Lv 23:21 4399
'You shall not do any laborious **w**, Lv 23:25 4399
not do any **w** on this same day, Lv 23:28 4399
who does any **w** on this same day, Lv 23:30 4399
"You shall do no **w** at all. Lv 23:31 4399
do no laborious **w** of any kind. Lv 23:35 4399
You shall do no laborious **w**. Lv 23:36 4399
do the **w** in the tent of meeting. Nu 4:3 4399
"This is the **w** of the descendants Nu 4:4 5656
of them to his **w** and to his load; Nu 4:19 5656
do the **w** in the tent of meeting. Nu 4:23 5656
their loads and in all their **w**, Nu 4:27 5656
do the **w** of the tent of meeting. Nu 4:30 5656
for **w** in the tent of meeting. Nu 4:35 5656
for **w** in the tent of meeting. Nu 4:39 5656
for **w** in the tent of meeting. Nu 4:43 5656
who could enter to do the **w** of service Nu 4:47 5647
work of service and the **w** of carrying Nu 4:47 5656
the lampstand, hammered **w** of gold; Nu 8:4 4749
to its flowers it was hammered **w**; Nu 8:4 4749
in the **w** of the tent of meeting. Nu 8:24 5656
in the **w** and not work any more. Nu 8:25 5656
in the work and not **w** any more. Nu 8:25 5647
but they *themselves* shall do no **w**. Nu 8:26 5656
of hammered **w** you shall make them; Nu 10:2 4749
you shall do no laborious **w**. Nu 28:18 4399
you shall do no laborious **w**. Nu 28:25 4399
you shall do no laborious **w**. Nu 28:26 4399
you shall do no laborious **w**. Nu 29:1 4399
you shall not do any **w**. Nu 29:7 4399
you shall do no laborious **w**, Nu 29:12 4399
you shall do no laborious **w**. Nu 29:35 4399
and all the **w** of goats' *hair,* Nu 31:20 4639
serve gods, the **w** of man's hands, Dt 4:28 4639
you shall labor and do all your **w**, Dt 5:13 4399
in it you shall not do any **w**, Dt 5:14 4399
great **w** of the LORD which He did. Dt 11:7 4639
the **w** of your hand which you do. Dt 14:29 4639
God will bless you in all your **w** Dt 15:10 4639
you shall not **w** with the Dt 15:19 5647
you shall do no **w** *on it.* Dt 16:8 4399
and in all the **w** of your hands, Dt 16:15 4639
you in all the **w** of your hands. Dt 24:19 4639
w of the hands of the craftsman, Dt 27:15 4639
to bless all the **w** of your hand; Dt 28:12 4639
in all the **w** of your hand, Dt 30:9 4639
anger with the **w** of your hands." Dt 31:29 4639
His **w** is perfect, For all His ways Dt 32:4 6467
And accept the **w** of his hands; Dt 33:11 6467
had seen all the great **w** of the LORD Jg 2:7 4639
w which He had done for Israel. Jg 2:10 4639
To Sisera a spoil of dyed **w**, Jg 5:30 6648
A spoil of dyed **w** embroidered, Jg 5:30 6648
Dyed **w** of double embroidery on the Jg 5:30 6648
the field from his **w** at evening. Jg 19:16 4639
"May the LORD reward your **w**, Ru 2:12 6467
glean today and where did you **w**? Ru 2:19 6213a
donkeys and use *them* for his **w**. 1Sa 8:16 4399
perhaps the LORD will **w** for us, 1Sa 14:6 6213a
the people who were doing the **w**. 1Ki 5:16 4399
evenly applied on the engraved **w**. 1Ki 6:35
skill for doing any **w** in bronze. 1Ki 7:14 4399
Solomon and performed all his **w**. 1Ki 7:14 4399
the **w** of the pillars was finished. 1Ki 7:22 4399
oxen *were* wreaths of hanging **w**. 1Ki 7:29 4639
So Hiram finished doing all the **w** 1Ki 7:40 4399
Thus all the **w** that King Solomon 1Ki 7:51 4399
officers who *were* over Solomon's **w**, 1Ki 9:23 4399
ruled over the people doing the **w**. 1Ki 9:23 4399
to anger with the **w** of his hands, 1Ki 16:7 4639
the hands of those who did the **w**, 2Ki 12:11 4399
gave that to those who did the **w**, 2Ki 12:14 4399
to pay to those who did the **w**, 2Ki 12:15 4399
not gods but the **w** of men's hands, 2Ki 19:18 4639
with all the **w** of their hands, 2Ki 22:17 4639
there with the king for his **w**. 1Ch 4:23 4399
all the **w** of the most holy place, 1Ch 6:49 4399
w of the service of the house of God. 1Ch 9:13 4399
were over the **w** of the service, 1Ch 9:19 4399
engaged in their **w** day and night. 1Ch 9:33 4399
as every day's **w** required; 1Ch 16:37 1697
are skillful in every kind of **w**. 1Ch 22:15 4399
Arise and **w**, and may the LORD be 1Ch 22:16 6213a
the **w** of the house of the LORD; 1Ch 23:4 4399
w for the service of the house of the 1Ch 23:24 4399
w of the service of the house of God, 1Ch 23:28 4399
for all the **w** of the LORD and the 1Ch 26:30 4399
w of the service of the house 1Ch 28:13 4399
w for the service of the house of the 1Ch 28:20 4399
the **w** for all kinds of service. 1Ch 28:21 4399
inexperienced and the **w** is great; 1Ch 29:1 4399
all the **w** done by the craftsmen. 1Ch 29:5 4399

the overseers over the king's **w**, 1Ch 29:6 4399
me a skilled man to **w** in gold, 2Ch 2:7 6213a
to **w** with the skilled men whom I 2Ch 2:7
and indeed my servants *will* **w** 2Ch 2:8
who knows how to **w** in gold, 2Ch 2:14 6213a
to **w** with your skilled men 2Ch 2:14
supervisors to make the people **w**. 2Ch 2:18 5647
So Huram finished doing the **w** 2Ch 4:11 4399
Thus all the **w** that Solomon 2Ch 5:1 4399
did not make slaves for his **w** from 2Ch 8:9 4399
Thus all the **w** of Solomon was 2Ch 8:16 4399
and the Levites attend to their **w**. 2Ch 13:10 4399
for there is reward for your **w**." 2Ch 15:7 6468
Ramah and stopped his **w**. 2Ch 16:5 4399
w of the service of the house of the 2Ch 24:12 4399
w progressed in their hands, 2Ch 24:13 4399
them until the **w** was completed and 2Ch 29:34 4399
for their **w** in their duties according 2Ch 31:16 5656
Every **w** which he began in the 2Ch 31:21 4639
of the earth, the **w** of men's hands. 2Ch 32:19 4639
The men did the **w** faithfully 2Ch 34:12 4399
for the **w** 61,000 gold drachmas and Ezr 2:69 4399
began *the* **w** and appointed Ezr 3:8
the **w** of the house of the LORD. Ezr 3:8 4399
a decree to make these men stop **w**, Ezr 4:21
Then **w** on the house of God in Ezr 4:24 5673
and this **w** is going on with great Ezr 5:8 5673
this **w** on the house of God alone; Ezr 6:7 5673
them in the **w** of the house of God, Ezr 6:22 4399
or the rest who did the **w**. Ne 2:16 4399
they put their hands to the good **w**. Ne 2:18
support the **w** of their masters. Ne 3:5 5656
for the people had a mind to **w**. Ne 4:6 6213a
them and put a stop to the **w**." Ne 4:11 4399
to the wall, each one to his **w**. Ne 4:15 4399
half of my servants carried on the **w** Ne 4:16 4399
one hand doing the **w** and the other Ne 4:17 4399
"The **w** is great and extensive, Ne 4:19 4399
So we carried on the **w** with half Ne 4:21 4399
myself to the **w** on this wall; Ne 5:16 4399
were gathered there for the **w**. Ne 5:16 4399
"I am doing a great **w** and I cannot Ne 6:3 4399
Why should the **w** stop while I Ne 6:3 4399
will become discouraged with the **w** Ne 6:9 4399
for they recognized that this **w** Ne 6:16 4399
fathers' *households* gave to the **w**. Ne 7:70 4399
gave into the treasury of the **w** Ne 7:71 4399
all the **w** of the house of our God. Ne 10:33 4399
who performed the **w** of the temple, Ne 11:12 4399
the outside **w** of the house of God; Ne 11:16 4399
have blessed the **w** of his hands, Jb 1:10 4639
will long for the **w** of Your hands. Jb 14:15 4639
disaster to those who **w** iniquity? Jb 31:3 6466
He pays a man according to his **w**, Jb 34:11 6467
they all are the **w** of His hands? Jb 34:19 4639
their **w** And their transgressions, Jb 36:9 6467
that you should exalt His **w**, Jb 36:24 6467
man, That all men may know His **w**. Jb 37:7 4639
Your heavens, the **w** of Your fingers, Ps 8:3 4639
In the **w** of his own hands the Ps 9:16 6467
is declaring the **w** of His hands. Ps 19:1 4639
And with those who **w** iniquity, Ps 28:3 6466
Requite them according to their **w** Ps 28:4 6467
all His **w** is *done* in faithfulness. Ps 33:4 4639
w that You did in their days, Ps 44:1 6467
led to the King in embroidered **w**; Ps 45:14 7553
in heart you **w** unrighteousness; Ps 58:2 6466
a man according to his **w**. Ps 62:12 4639
And they will declare the **w** of God, Ps 64:9 6467
And now all its carved **w** They Ps 74:6 6603
I will meditate on all Your **w** And Ps 77:12 6467
Let Your **w** appear to Your servants Ps 90:16 6467
confirm for us the **w** of our hands; Ps 90:17 4639
Yes, confirm the **w** of our hands. Ps 90:17 4639
Me, though they had seen My **w**. Ps 95:9 6467
I hate the **w** of those who fall away; Ps 101:3 6213a
heavens are the **w** of Your hands. Ps 102:25 4639
Man goes forth to his **w** And to his Ps 104:23 6467
Splendid and majestic is His **w**, Ps 111:3 6467
and gold, The **w** of man's hands. Ps 115:4 4639
and gold, The **w** of man's hands. Ps 135:15 4639
I muse on the **w** of Your hands. Ps 143:5 4639
He also who is slack in his **w** Is Pr 18:9 4399
death, For his hands refuse to **w**; Pr 21:25 6213a
Do you see a man skilled in his **w**? Pr 22:29 4399
render to man according to his **w**? Pr 24:12 6467
Prepare your **w** outside And make Pr 24:27 4399
to the man according to his **w**." Pr 24:29 6467
his **w** Which he does under the sun? Ec 1:3 5999
for the **w** which had been done Ec 2:17 4639
so that man will not find out the **w** Ec 3:11 4639
and destroy the **w** of your hands? Ec 5:6 4639
Consider the **w** of God, For who is Ec 7:13 4639
and I saw every **w** of God, *I* Ec 8:17 4639
man cannot discover the **w** which has Ec 8:17 4639
The **w** of the hands of an artist. SS 7:1 4639
become tinder, His **w** also a spark. Is 1:31 6467
They worship the **w** of their hands, Is 2:8 4639
they consider the **w** of His hands. Is 5:12 4639
make speed, let Him hasten His **w**, Is 5:19 4639
completed all His **w** on Mount Zion Is 10:12 4639
the altars, the **w** of his hands, Is 17:8 4639
There will be no **w** for Egypt Is 19:15 4639
and Assyria the **w** of My hands, Is 19:25 4639
unusual task, And to **w** His work, Is 28:21 5647
unusual task, And to work His **w**, Is 28:21 5656
His work, His extraordinary **w**. Is 28:21 5656
his children, the **w** of My hands, Is 29:23 4639
and the donkeys which **w** the ground Is 30:24 5647

And the **w** of righteousness will be Is 32:17 4639
not gods but the **w** of men's hands, Is 37:19 4639
And your **w** amounts to nothing; Is 41:24 6467
and does his **w** over the coals, Is 44:12 6466
commit to Me the **w** of My hands. Is 45:11 6467
And brings out a weapon for its **w**; Is 54:16 4639
of My planting, The **w** of My hands, Is 60:21 4639
all of us are the **w** of Your hand. Is 64:8 4639
their former **w** into their bosom." Is 65:7 6468
wear out the **w** of their hands. Is 65:22 4639
The **w** of the hands of a craftsman Jer 10:3 4639
The **w** of a craftsman and of the Jer 10:9 4639
They are all the **w** of skilled men. Jer 10:9 4639
are worthless, a **w** of mockery; Jer 10:15 4639
on the sabbath day nor do any **w**, Jer 17:22 4399
day holy by doing no **w** on it, Jer 17:24 4399
to anger with the **w** of your hands, Jer 25:6 4639
to anger with the **w** of your hands Jer 25:7 4639
to the **w** of their hands.)' " Jer 25:14 4639
I am beginning to **w** calamity in Jer 25:29 7489a
For your **w** will be rewarded," Jer 31:16 6468
to anger by the **w** of their hands," Jer 32:30 4639
who does the LORD's **w** negligently, Jer 48:10 4399
it is a **w** of the Lord GOD of hosts Jer 50:25 4399
Repay her according to her **w**; Jer 50:29 6467
in Zion The **w** of the LORD our God! Jer 51:10 4639
are worthless, a **w** of mockery; Jer 51:18 4639
According to the **w** of their hands. La 3:64 4639
jars, The **w** of a potter's hands! La 4:2 4639
emeralds, purple, embroidered **w**, Ezk 27:16 7553
clothes of blue and embroidered **w**, Ezk 27:24 7553
All of them the **w** of craftsmen. Hos 13:2 4639
'Our god,' To the **w** of our hands; Hos 14:3 4639
the plant for which you did not **w** and Jon 4:10 5998
Who **w** out evil on their beds! Mi 2:1 6466
bow down To the **w** of your hands. Mi 5:13 4639
revive Your **w** in the midst of the Hab 3:2 6467
For He has laid bare the cedar **w**. Zph 2:14 731
'and **w**; for I am with you,' Hg 2:4 6213a
'and so is every **w** of their hands; Hg 2:14 4639
every **w** of your hands with blasting Hg 2:17 4639
powers are at **w** in him." Mt 14:2 *1754*
'Son, go **w** today in the vineyard.' Mt 21:28 *2038b*
powers are at **w** in Him." Mk 6:14 *1754*
days in which **w** should be done; Lk 13:14 *2038b*
sent Me and to accomplish His **w**. Jn 4:34 *2041*
not **w** for the food which perishes, Jn 6:27 *2038b*
that we may **w** the works of God?" Jn 6:28 *2038b*
"This is the **w** of God, that you Jn 6:29 *2041*
What **w** do You perform? Jn 6:30 *2038b*
w the works of Him who sent Me as Jn 9:4 *2038b*
is coming when no one can **w**. Jn 9:4 *2038b*
"For a good **w** we do not stone Jn 10:33 *2041*
having accomplished the **w** which Jn 17:4 *2041*
on (for he was stripped *for* **w**), Jn 21:7
w to which I have called them." Ac 13:2 *2041*
AM ACCOMPLISHING A **W** IN YOUR DAYS Ac 13:41 *2041*
A **W** WHICH YOU WILL NEVER BELIEVE, Ac 13:41 *2041*
the **w** that they had accomplished. Ac 14:26 *2041*
had not gone with them to the **w**. Ac 15:38 *2041*
in that they show the **w** of the Law Ro 2:15 *2041*
But to the one who does not **w**, Ro 4:5 *2038b*
were at **w** in the members of our Ro 7:5 *1754*
God causes all things to **w** together Ro 8:28 *4903*
Do not tear down the **w** of God for Ro 14:20 *2041*
each man's **w** will become evident; 1Co 3:13 *2041*
test the quality of each man's **w**. 1Co 3:13 *2041*
If any man's **w** which he has built 1Co 3:14 *2041*
If any man's **w** is burned up, he 1Co 3:15 *2041*
Are you not my **w** in the Lord? 1Co 9:1 *2041*
abounding in the **w** of the Lord, 1Co 15:58 *2041*
for he is doing the Lord's **w**, 1Co 16:10 *2041*
who helps in the **w** and labors. 1Co 16:16 *4903*
complete in you this gracious **w** 2Co 8:6 *5485*
abound in this gracious **w** also. 2Co 8:7 *5485*
travel with us in this gracious **w**, 2Co 8:19 *5485*
each one must examine his own **w**, Ga 6:4 *2041*
the saints for the **w** of service, Eph 4:12 *2041*
that He who began a good **w** in you Php 1:6 *2041*
w out your salvation with fear and Php 2:12 *2716*
for it is God who is at **w** in you, Php 2:13 *1754*
and to **w** for *His* good pleasure. Php 2:13 *1754*
to death for the **w** of Christ, Php 2:30 *2041*
bearing fruit in every good **w** and Col 1:10 *2041*
you do, do your **w** heartily, Col 3:23 *2038b*
your **w** of faith and labor of love 1Th 1:3 *2041*
performs its **w** in you who believe. 1Th 2:13 *1754*
business and **w** with your hands, 1Th 4:11 *2038b*
highly in love because of their **w**. 1Th 5:13 *2041*
and the **w** of faith with power, 2Th 1:11 *2041*
of lawlessness is already at **w**; 2Th 2:7 *1754*
hearts in every good **w** and word. 2Th 2:17 *2041*
if anyone is not willing to **w**, then 2Th 3:10 *2038b*
life, doing no **w** at all, 2Th 3:11 *2038b*
to **w** in quiet fashion and eat their 2Th 3:12 *2038b*
it is a fine **w** he desires *to do.* 1Tm 3:1 *2041*
devoted herself to every good **w**. 1Tm 5:10 *2041*
especially those who **w** hard at 1Tm 5:17 *2872*
Master, prepared for every good **w**. 2Tm 2:21 *2041*
equipped for every good **w**. 2Tm 3:17 *2041*
do the **w** of an evangelist, 2Tm 4:5 *2041*
is not unjust so as to forget your **w** Heb 6:10 *2041*
the sanctifying **w** of the Spirit, 1Pe 1:2 *38*
judges according to each one's **w**, 1Pe 1:17 *2041*

WORKED

which has not been **w** and which has Dt 21:3 5647
with whom she had **w** and said, Ru 2:19 6213a
man with whom I **w** today is Boaz." Ru 2:19 6213a
for he has **w** with God this day." 1Sa 14:45 6213a
who **w** on the house of the LORD; 2Ki 12:11 6213a
linen, and he **w** cherubim on it. 2Ch 3:14 5927
God has *so* **w** that men should fear Ec 3:14 6213a
For You have **w** wonders, Plans Is 25:1 6213a
Young men **w** at the grinding mill, La 5:13 5375
of Aram, And Israel **w** for a wife, Hos 12:12 5647
and they came and **w** on the house Hg 1:14 6213a
last men have **w** *only* one hour, Mt 20:12 *4160*
while the Lord **w** with them, Mk 16:20 *4903*
we **w** hard all night and caught Lk 5:5 *2872*
Mary, who has **w** hard for you. Ro 16:6 *2872*
who has **w** hard in the Lord. Ro 16:12 *2872*
(for He who effectually **w** for Peter Ga 2:8 *1754*
effectually **w** for me also to the Gentiles Ga 2:8 *1754*

WORKER

was a man of Tyre, a **w** in bronze; 1Ki 7:14 2790a
Like a sharp razor, O **w** of deceit. Ps 52:2 6213a
What profit is there to the **w** from Ec 3:9 6213a
the **w** is worthy of his support. Mt 10:10 *2040*
Urbanus, our fellow **w** in Christ, Ro 16:9 *4904*
Timothy my fellow **w** greets you, Ro 16:21 *4904*
my partner and fellow **w** among you; 2Co 8:23 *4904*
and fellow **w** and fellow soldier, Php 2:25 *4904*
fellow **w** in the gospel of Christ, 1Th 3:2 *4904*
our beloved *brother* and fellow **w**, Phm 1:1 *4904*

WORKER'S

A **w** appetite works for him, For Pr 16:26 6001a

WORKERS

families of the house of the linen **w** 1Ch 4:21 5656
agricultural **w** who tilled the soil. 1Ch 27:26 4399
and also **w** in iron and bronze to 2Ch 24:12 2796
in company with the **w** of iniquity, Jb 34:8 6466
Where the **w** of iniquity may hide Jb 34:22 6466
all the **w** of wickedness not know, Ps 14:4 6466
the **w** of wickedness no knowledge, Ps 53:4 6466
But ruin to the **w** of iniquity. Pr 10:29 6466
is terror to the **w** of iniquity. Pr 21:15 6466
the help of the **w** of iniquity. Is 31:2 6466
desire, And drive hard all your **w**. Is 58:3 6092
be food for the **w** of the city. Ezk 48:18 5647
"The **w** of the city, out of Ezk 48:19 5647
is plentiful, but the **w** are few. Mt 9:37 *2040*
to send out **w** into His harvest." Mt 9:38 *2040*
my fellow **w** in Christ Jesus, Ro 16:3 *4904*
and Tryphosa, **w** in the Lord. Ro 16:12 *2872*
For we are God's fellow **w**; 1Co 3:9 *4904*
All are not **w** *of* miracles, are 1Co 12:29
but are **w** with you for your joy; 2Co 1:24 *4904*
are false apostles, deceitful **w**, 2Co 11:13 *2040*
of the dogs, beware of the evil **w**, Php 3:2 *2040*
also and the rest of my fellow **w**, Php 4:3 *4904*
these are the only fellow **w** for Col 4:11 *4904*
to be sensible, pure, **w** at home, Ti 2:5 *3626*
Demas, Luke, my fellow **w**. Phm 1:24 *4904*
we may be fellow **w** with the truth. 3Jn 1:8 *4904*

WORKING

Awesome in praises, **w** wonders? Ex 15:11 6213a
live will see the **w** of the LORD, Ex 34:10 4639
to make designs for **w** in gold and Ex 35:32 6213a
and the workmen who were **w** in the 2Ch 34:10 6213a
sleep of the **w** man is pleasant, Ec 5:12 5647
and **w** it with his strong arm. Is 44:12 6466
east shall be shut the six **w** days; Ezk 46:1 4639
"My Father is **w** until now, and I Jn 5:17 *2038b*
until now, and I Myself am **w**." Jn 5:17 *2038b*
stayed with them and they were **w**, Ac 18:3 *2038b*
by **w** hard in this manner you must Ac 20:35 *2872*
and we toil, **w** with our own hands; 1Co 4:12 *2038b*
have a right to refrain from **w**? 1Co 9:6 *2038b*
And **w** together *with Him,* we also 2Co 6:1 *4903*
but faith **w** through love. Ga 5:6 *1754*
w of the strength of His might Eph 1:19 *1753b*
now **w** in the sons of disobedience. Eph 2:2 *1754*
according to the **w** of His power. Eph 3:7 *1753b*
proper **w** of each individual part, Eph 4:16 *1753b*
Him through faith in the **w** of God, Col 2:12 *1753b*
how **w** night and day so as not to 1Th 2:9 *2038b*
with labor and hardship we *kept* **w** 2Th 3:8 *2038b*
w in us that which is pleasing in Heb 13:21 *4160*
that faith was **w** with his works, Jas 2:22 *4903*

WORKMAN

the work of a skillful **w**. Ex 26:1 2803
the work of a skillful **w**. Ex 26:31 2803
linen, the work of the skillful **w**. Ex 28:6 2803
the work of a skillful **w**; Ex 28:15 2803
the work of a skillful **w**, Ex 36:8 2803
the work of a skillful **w**. Ex 36:35 2803
an engraver and a skillful **w** and a Ex 38:23 2803
linen, the work of a skillful **w**. Ex 39:3 2803
the work of a skillful **w**, Ex 39:8 2803
I was beside Him, *as* a master **w**; Pr 8:30 525
a **w** who does not need to be ashamed 2Tm 2:15 *2040*

WORKMANSHIP

is on it, shall be like its **w**, Ex 28:8 4639
which was on it was like its **w**, Ex 39:5 4639
workman, like the **w** of the ephod: Ex 39:8 4639
this was the **w** of the lampstand, Nu 8:4 4639
from the hall, was of the same **w**. 1Ki 7:8 4639
The **w** of the wheels *was* like 1Ki 7:33 4639
was like the **w** of a chariot wheel. 1Ki 7:33 4639
its model, according to all its **w**. 2Ki 16:10 4639
their **w** *was* like sparkling beryl, Ezk 1:16 4639
their appearance and **w** *being* as if Ezk 1:16 4639
w of your settings and sockets, Ezk 28:13 4399
For we are His **w**, created in Eph 2:10 *4161*

WORKMEN

deliver it into the hand of the **w** 2Ki 22:5 4399
and let them give it to the **w** who 2Ki 22:5 4399
delivered it into the hand of the **w** 2Ki 22:9 4399
there are many **w** with you, 1Ch 22:15 4399, 6213a
So the **w** labored, and the repair 2Ch 24:13 4399, 6213a
they gave *it* into the hands of the **w** 2Ch 34:10 4399, 6213a
and the **w** who were working in the 2Ch 34:10 4399
supervised all the **w** from job to job; 2Ch 34:13 6213a, 4399
hands of the supervisors and the **w**." 2Ch 34:17 4399, 6213a
oversee the **w** in the temple of God. Ezr 3:9 4399
with the **w** of similar *trades,* Ac 19:25 *2040*

WORKMEN'S

her right hand for the **w** hammer. Jg 5:26 6001a

WORKS

such **w** and mighty acts as Yours? Dt 3:24 4639
and His signs and His **w** which He Dt 11:3 4639
the LORD has destroyed your **w**." 2Ch 20:37 4639
with all the **w** of their hands; 2Ch 34:25 4639
according to these **w** of theirs, Ne 6:14 4639
And wondrous **w** without number. Jb 9:10 6381
"Therefore He knows their **w**, Jb 34:25 4566
to rule over the **w** of Your hands; Ps 8:6 4639
integrity, and **w** righteousness, Ps 15:2 6466
Because they do not regard the **w** Ps 28:5 6468
He who understands all their **w**. Ps 33:15 4639
Come, behold the **w** of the LORD, Ps 46:8 4659b
"How awesome are Your **w**! Ps 66:3 4639
Come and see the **w** of God, Ps 66:5 4659b
of Israel, Who alone **w** wonders. Ps 72:18 6213a
That I may tell of all Your **w**. Ps 73:28 4399
Who **w** deeds of deliverance in the Ps 74:12 6466
Men declare Your wondrous **w**. Ps 75:1 6381
You are the God who **w** wonders; Ps 77:14 6213a
His wondrous **w** that He has done. Ps 78:4 6381
God And not forget the **w** of God, Ps 78:7 4611
not believe in His wonderful **w**. Ps 78:32 6381
Nor are there any **w** like Yours. Ps 86:8 4639
sing for joy at the **w** of Your hands. Ps 92:4 4639
How great are Your **w**, O LORD! Ps 92:5 4639
Bless the LORD, all you **w** of His, Ps 103:22 4639
satisfied with the fruit of His **w**. Ps 104:13 4639
O LORD, how many are Your **w**! Ps 104:24 4639
Let the LORD be glad in His **w**; Ps 104:31 4639
They quickly forgot His **w**; Ps 106:13 4639
tell of His **w** with joyful singing. Ps 107:22 4639
They have seen the **w** of the LORD, Ps 107:24 4639
Great are the **w** of the LORD; Ps 111:2 4639
to His people the power of His **w**, Ps 111:6 4639
The **w** of His hands are truth and Ps 111:7 4639
And tell of the **w** of the LORD. Ps 118:17 4639
Do not forsake the **w** of Your hands. Ps 138:8 4639
Wonderful are Your **w**, Ps 139:14 4639
shall praise Your **w** to another, Ps 145:4 4639
on Your wonderful **w**, I will meditate. Ps 145:5 6381
His mercies are over all His **w**. Ps 145:9 4639
Your **w** shall give thanks to You, Ps 145:10 4639
of His way, Before His **w** of old. Pr 8:22 4659a
is he who **w** with a negligent hand, Pr 10:4 6213a
Commit your **w** to the LORD And Pr 16:3 4639
A worker's appetite **w** for him, Pr 16:26 5998
And a flattering mouth **w** ruin. Pr 26:28 6213a
And **w** with her hands in delight. Pr 31:13 6213a
let her **w** praise her in the gates. Pr 31:31 4639
I have seen all the **w** which have Ec 1:14 4639
I enlarged my **w**: I built houses for Ec 2:4 4639
God has already approved your **w**. Ec 9:7 4639
also performed for us all our **w**. Is 26:12 4639
Their **w** are worthless, Their Is 41:29 4639
He **w** it with planes and outlines Is 44:13 6213a
cover themselves with their **w**; Is 59:6 4639
Their **w** are works of iniquity, And Is 59:6 4639
Their works are **w** of iniquity, And Is 59:6 4639
I know their **w** and their thoughts; Is 66:18 4639
worshiped the **w** of their own hands. Jer 1:16 4639
to anger with the **w** of your hands, Jer 44:8 4639
and your **w** may be blotted out. Ezk 6:6 4639
His **w** are true and His ways just, Da 4:37 4567
w of the house of Ahab are observed; Mi 6:16 4639
way that they may see your good **w**, Mt 5:16 *2041*
heard of the **w** of Christ, Mt 11:2 *2041*
will show Him greater **w** than these, Jn 5:20 *2041*
for the **w** which the Father has Jn 5:36 *2041*
accomplish—the very **w** that I do Jn 5:36 *2041*
that we may work the **w** of God?" Jn 6:28 *2041*
see Your **w** which You are doing. Jn 7:3 *2041*
the **w** of God might be displayed in Jn 9:3 *2041*
work the **w** of Him who sent Me as Jn 9:4 *2041*
w that I do in My Father's name, Jn 10:25 *2041*
you many good **w** from the Father; Jn 10:32 *2041*
"If I do not do the **w** of My Father, Jn 10:37 *2041*
do not believe Me, believe the **w**, Jn 10:38 *2041*
Father abiding in Me does His **w**. Jn 14:10 *2041*
because of the **w** themselves. Jn 14:11 *2041*
the **w** that I do, he will do also; Jn 14:12 *2041*
and greater **w** than these he will Jn 14:12
them the **w** which no one else did, Jn 15:24 *2041*
rejoicing in the **w** of their hands. Ac 7:41 *2041*
because by the **w** of the Law no Ro 3:20 *2041*
By what kind of law? Of **w**? Ro 3:27 *2041*
by faith apart from **w** of the Law. Ro 3:28 *2041*
For if Abraham was justified by **w**, Ro 4:2 *2041*
Now to the one who **w**, Ro 4:4 *2038b*
righteousness apart from **w**: Ro 4:6 *2041*
would stand, not because of **w** Ro 9:11 *2041*

faith, but as though *it were* by **w**. Ro 9:32 *2041*
it is no longer on the basis of **w**, Ro 11:6 *2041*
God who **w** all things in all *persons.* 1Co 12:6 *1754*
same Spirit **w** all these things, 1Co 12:11 *1754*
So death **w** in us, but life in you. 2Co 4:12 *1754*
is not justified by the **w** of the Law Ga 2:16 *2041*
and not by the **w** of the Law; Ga 2:16 *2041*
since by the **w** of the Law no Ga 2:16 *2041*
the Spirit by the **w** of the Law, Ga 3:2 *2041*
Spirit and **w** miracles among you, Ga 3:5 *1754*
you, do it by the **w** of the Law, Ga 3:5 *2041*
as many as are of the **w** of the Law Ga 3:10 *2041*
according to His purpose who **w** all Eph 1:11 *1754*
not as a result of **w**, Eph 2:9 *2041*
in Christ Jesus for good **w**, Eph 2:10 *2041*
to the power that **w** within us, Eph 3:20 *1754*
power, which mightily **w** within me. Col 1:29 *1754*
but rather by means of good **w**, 1Tm 2:10 *2041*
having a reputation for good **w**; 1Tm 5:10 *2041*
to do good, to be rich in good **w**, 1Tm 6:18 *2041*
calling, not according to our **w**, 2Tm 1:9 *2041*
HEAVENS ARE THE **W** OF YOUR HANDS; Heb 1:10 *2041*
HIM OVER THE **W** OF YOUR HANDS; Heb 2:7 *2041*
Me, AND SAW MY **W** FOR FORTY YEARS. Heb 3:9 *2041*
although His **w** were finished from Heb 4:3 *2041*
THE SEVENTH DAY FROM ALL HIS **W**"; Heb 4:4 *2041*
himself also rested from his **w**, Heb 4:10 *2041*
repentance from dead **w** and of faith Heb 6:1 *2041*
cleanse your conscience from dead **w** Heb 9:14 *2041*
he has faith but he has no **w**? Jas 2:14 *2041*
Even so faith, if it has no **w**, Jas 2:17 *2041*
"You have faith and I have **w**; Jas 2:18 *2041*
show me your faith without the **w**, Jas 2:18 *2041*
will show you my faith by my **w**." Jas 2:18 *2041*
that faith without **w** is useless? Jas 2:20 *2041*
Abraham our father justified by **w** when Jas 2:21 *2041*
that faith was working with his **w**, Jas 2:22 *2041*
works, and as a result of the **w**, Jas 2:22 *2041*
see that a man is justified by **w** and Jas 2:24 *2041*
the harlot also justified by **w** when Jas 2:25 *2041*
so also faith without **w** is dead. Jas 2:26 *2041*
earth and its **w** will be burned up. 2Pe 3:10 *2041*
to destroy the **w** of the devil. 1Jn 3:8 *2041*
not repent of the **w** of their hands, Rv 9:20 *2041*
"Great and marvelous are Your **w**, Rv 15:3 *2041*

WORLD

LORD'S, And He set the **w** on them. 1Sa 2:8 8398
foundations of the **w** were laid bare By 2Sa 22:16 8398
the **w** is firmly established, 1Ch 16:30 8398
And chased from the inhabited **w**. Jb 18:18 8398
who has laid *on Him* the whole **w**? Jb 34:13 8398
for correction, or for His **w**, Jb 37:13 776
He will judge the **w** in righteousness; Ps 9:8 8398
hand, O LORD, From men of the **w**, Ps 17:14 2465
foundations of the **w** were laid bare Ps 18:15 8398
utterances to the end of the **w**. Ps 19:4 8398
The **w**, and those who dwell in it. Ps 24:1 8398
inhabitants of the **w** stand in awe Ps 33:8 8398
ear, all inhabitants of the **w**, Ps 49:1 2465
For the **w** is Mine, and all it Ps 50:12 8398
The lightnings lit up the **w**; Ps 77:18 8398
The **w** and all it contains, You Ps 89:11 8398
gave birth to the earth and the **w**, Ps 90:2 8398
the **w** is firmly established, Ps 93:1 8398
the **w** is firmly established, Ps 96:10 8398
He will judge the **w** in righteousness Ps 96:13 8398
His lightnings lit up the **w**; Ps 97:4 8398
The **w** and those who dwell in it. Ps 98:7 8398
judge the **w** with righteousness And Ps 98:9 8398
Nor the first dust of the **w**. Pr 8:26 8398
Rejoicing in the **w**, His earth, Pr 8:31 8398
I will punish the **w** for its evil And Is 13:11 8398
Who made the **w** like a wilderness Is 14:17 8398
the face of the **w** with cities." Is 14:21 8398
All you inhabitants of the **w** and Is 18:3 8398
withers, the **w** fades *and* withers, Is 24:4 8398
The inhabitants of the **w** learn Is 26:9 8398
were inhabitants of the **w** born. Is 26:18 8398
will fill the whole **w** with fruit. Is 27:6 8398
w and all that springs from it. Is 34:1 8398
among the inhabitants of the **w**. Is 38:11 2465
established the **w** by His wisdom, Jer 10:12 8398
established the **w** by His wisdom; Jer 51:15 8398
any of the inhabitants of the **w**, La 4:12 8398
powerful nations, to the nether **w**, Ezk 32:18 776
who live at the center of the **w**.' Ezk 38:12 776
w and all the inhabitants in it. Na 1:5 8398
Him all the kingdoms of the **w** and Mt 4:8 *2889*
"You are the light of the **w**. Mt 5:14 *2889*
the word, and the worry of the **w** and Mt 13:22 *165*
SINCE THE FOUNDATION OF THE **W**." Mt 13:35 *2889*
and the field is the **w**; Mt 13:38 *2889*
profit a man if he gains the whole **w** Mt 16:26 *2889*
"Woe to the **w** because of *its* Mt 18:7 *2889*
preached in the whole **w** as a testimony Mt 24:14 *3625*
the beginning of the **w** until now, Mt 24:21 *2889*
you from the foundation of the **w**. Mt 25:34 *2889*
gospel is preached in the whole **w**, Mt 26:13 *2889*
but the worries of the **w**, Mk 4:19 *165*
profit a man to gain the whole **w**, Mk 8:36 *2889*
gospel is preached in the whole **w**, Mk 14:9 *2889*
"Go into all the **w** and preach the Mk 16:15 *2889*
all the kingdoms of the **w** in a Lk 4:5 *3625*
profited if he gains the whole **w**, Lk 9:25 *2889*
since the foundation of the **w**, Lk 11:50 *2889*
the nations of the **w** eagerly seek; Lk 12:30 *2889*
which are coming upon the **w**; Lk 21:26 *3625*
Light which, coming into the **w**, Jn 1:9 *2889*
He was in the **w**, and the world was Jn 1:10 *2889*
and the **w** was made through Him, Jn 1:10 *2889*
Him, and the **w** did not know Him. Jn 1:10 *2889*
who takes away the sin of the **w**! Jn 1:29 *2889*
"For God so loved the **w**, Jn 3:16 *2889*
not send the Son into the **w** to judge Jn 3:17 *2889*
Son into the world to judge the **w**, Jn 3:17 *2889*
the **w** might be saved through Him. Jn 3:17 *2889*
that the Light has come into the **w**, Jn 3:19 *2889*
is indeed the Savior of the **w**." Jn 4:42 *2889*
who is to come into the **w**." Jn 6:14 *2889*
heaven, and gives life to the **w**." Jn 6:33 *2889*
the life of the **w** is My flesh." Jn 6:51 *2889*
things, show Yourself to the **w**." Jn 7:4 *2889*
"The **w** cannot hate you, Jn 7:7 *2889*
"I am the Light of the **w**; Jn 8:12 *2889*
you are of this **w**, I am not of Jn 8:23 *2889*
of this world, I am not of this **w**. Jn 8:23 *2889*
Him, these I speak to the **w**." Jn 8:26 *2889*
"While I am in the **w**, Jn 9:5 *2889*
world, I am the Light of the **w**." Jn 9:5 *2889*
"For judgment I came into this **w**, Jn 9:39 *2889*
sanctified and sent into the **w**, Jn 10:36 *2889*
he sees the light of this **w**. Jn 11:9 *2889*
even He who comes into the **w**." Jn 11:27 *2889*
look, the **w** has gone after Him." Jn 12:19 *2889*
and he who hates his life in this **w** Jn 12:25 *2889*
"Now judgment is upon this **w**; Jn 12:31 *2889*
ruler of this **w** will be cast out. Jn 12:31 *2889*
"I have come *as* Light into the **w**, Jn 12:46 *2889*
for I did not come to judge the **w**, Jn 12:47 *2889*
the world, but to save the **w**. Jn 12:47 *2889*
that He would depart out of this **w** Jn 13:1 *2889*
loved His own who were in the **w**, Jn 13:1 *2889*
truth, whom the **w** cannot receive, Jn 14:17 *2889*
the **w** will no longer see Me, Jn 14:19 *2889*
to us and not to the **w**?" Jn 14:22 *2889*
not as the **w** gives do I give to Jn 14:27 *2889*
for the ruler of the **w** is coming, Jn 14:30 *2889*
but so that the **w** may know that I Jn 14:31 *2889*
"If the **w** hates you, you know Jn 15:18 *2889*
"If you were of the **w**, Jn 15:19 *2889*
world, the **w** would love its own; Jn 15:19 *2889*
but because you are not of the **w**, Jn 15:19 *2889*
but I chose you out of the **w**, Jn 15:19 *2889*
because of this the **w** hates you. Jn 15:19 *2889*
will convict the **w** concerning sin and Jn 16:8 *2889*
ruler of this **w** has been judged. Jn 16:11 *2889*
lament, but the **w** will rejoice; Jn 16:20 *2889*
a child has been born into the **w**. Jn 16:21 *2889*
Father and have come into the **w**; Jn 16:28 *2889*
I am leaving the **w** again and Jn 16:28 *2889*
In the **w** you have tribulation, but Jn 16:33 *2889*
I have overcome the **w**." Jn 16:33 *2889*
I had with You before the **w** was. Jn 17:5 *2889*
whom You gave Me out of the **w**; Jn 17:6 *2889*
I do not ask on behalf of the **w**, Jn 17:9 *2889*
"I am no longer in the **w**; Jn 17:11 *2889*
yet they themselves are in the **w**, Jn 17:11 *2889*
and these things I speak in the **w** so Jn 17:13 *2889*
and the **w** has hated them, because Jn 17:14 *2889*
because they are not of the **w**, Jn 17:14 *2889*
world, even as I am not of the **w**. Jn 17:14 *2889*
You to take them out of the **w**, Jn 17:15 *2889*
"They are not of the **w**, Jn 17:16 *2889*
world, even as I am not of the **w**. Jn 17:16 *2889*
"As You sent Me into the **w**, Jn 17:18 *2889*
I also have sent them into the **w**. Jn 17:18 *2889*
that the **w** may believe that You Jn 17:21 *2889*
that the **w** may know that You Jn 17:23 *2889*
Me before the foundation of the **w**. Jn 17:24 *2889*
although the **w** has not known You, Jn 17:25 *2889*
"I have spoken openly to the **w**; Jn 18:20 *2889*
"My kingdom is not of this **w**. Jn 18:36 *2889*
If My kingdom were of this **w**, Jn 18:36 *2889*
for this I have come into the **w**, Jn 18:37 *2889*
I suppose that even the **w** itself Jn 21:25 *2889*
be a great famine all over the **w**. Ac 11:28 *3625*
"These men who have upset the **w** Ac 17:6 *3625*
made the **w** and all things in it, Ac 17:24 *2889*
a day in which He will judge the **w** Ac 17:31 *3625*
whom all of Asia and the **w** worship Ac 19:27 *3625*
all the Jews throughout the **w**, Ac 24:5 *3625*
proclaimed throughout the whole **w**. Ro 1:8 *2889*
For since the creation of the **w** His Ro 1:20 *2889*
how will God judge the **w**? Ro 3:6 *2889*
w may become accountable to God; Ro 3:19 *2889*
that he would be heir of the **w** Ro 4:13 *2889*
one man sin entered into the **w**, Ro 5:12 *2889*
until the Law sin was in the **w**, Ro 5:13 *2889*
WORDS TO THE ENDS OF THE **W**." Ro 10:18 *3625*
their transgression is riches for the **w** Ro 11:12 *2889*
is the reconciliation of the **w**, Ro 11:15 *2889*
And do not be conformed to this **w**, Ro 12:2 *165*
made foolish the wisdom of the **w**? 1Co 1:20 *2889*
w through its wisdom did not *come* 1Co 1:21 *2889*
chosen the foolish things of the **w** 1Co 1:27 *2889*
has chosen the weak things of the **w** 1Co 1:27 *2889*
the base things of the **w** and the 1Co 1:28 *2889*
received, not the spirit of the **w**, 1Co 2:12 *2889*
the wisdom of this **w** is foolishness 1Co 3:19 *2889*
Paul or Apollos or Cephas or the **w** 1Co 3:22 *2889*
have become a spectacle to the **w**, 1Co 4:9 *2889*
have become as the scum of the **w**, 1Co 4:13 *2889*
with the immoral people of this **w**, 1Co 5:10 *2889*
you would have to go out of the **w**. 1Co 5:10 *2889*
that the saints will judge the **w**? 1Co 6:2 *2889*
If the **w** is judged by you, are 1Co 6:2 *2889*
and those who use the **w**, 1Co 7:31 *2889*
form of this **w** is passing away. 1Co 7:31 *2889*
about the things of the **w**, 1Co 7:33 *2889*
about the things of the **w**, 1Co 7:34 *2889*
no such thing as an idol in the **w**, 1Co 8:4 *2889*
not be condemned along with the **w**. 1Co 11:32 *2889*
many kinds of languages in the **w**, 1Co 14:10 *2889*
have conducted ourselves in the **w**, 2Co 1:12 *2889*
god of this **w** has blinded the minds 2Co 4:4 *165*
God was in Christ reconciling the **w** 2Co 5:19 *2889*
sorrow of the **w** produces death. 2Co 7:10 *2889*
the elemental things of the **w**. Ga 4:3 *2889*
the **w** has been crucified to me, Ga 6:14 *2889*
crucified to me, and I to the **w**. Ga 6:14 *2889*
before the foundation of the **w**, Eph 1:4 *2889*
according to the course of this **w**, Eph 2:2 *2889*
no hope and without God in the **w**. Eph 2:12 *2889*
the **w** forces of this darkness, Eph 6:12 *2888*
you appear as lights in the **w**, Php 2:15 *2889*
just as in all the **w** also it is Col 1:6 *2889*
elementary principles of the **w**, Col 2:8 *2889*
elementary principles of the **w**, Col 2:20 *2889*
as if you were living in the **w**, Col 2:20 *2889*
Jesus came into the **w** to save sinners 1Tm 1:15 *2889*
the nations, Believed on in the **w**, 1Tm 3:16 *2889*
have brought nothing into the **w**, 1Tm 6:7 *2889*
those who are rich in this present **w** 1Tm 6:17 *165*
having loved this present **w**, 2Tm 4:10 *165*
through whom also He made the **w**. Heb 1:2 *165*
brings the firstborn into the **w**, Heb 1:6 *3625*
not subject to angels the **w** to come, Heb 2:5 *3625*
from the foundation of the **w**. Heb 4:3 *2889*
since the foundation of the **w**; Heb 9:26 *2889*
when He comes into the **w**, Heb 10:5 *2889*
by which he condemned the **w**, Heb 11:7 *2889*
(*men* of whom the **w** was not worthy), Heb 11:38 *2889*
keep oneself unstained by the **w**. Jas 1:27 *2889*
did not God choose the poor of this **w** Jas 2:5 *2889*
is a fire, the *very* **w** of iniquity; Jas 3:6 *2889*
friendship with the **w** is hostility Jas 4:4 *2889*
wishes to be a friend of the **w** Jas 4:4 *2889*
before the foundation of the **w**, 1Pe 1:20 *2889*
by your brethren who are in the **w**. 1Pe 5:9 *2889*
that is in the **w** by lust. 2Pe 1:4 *2889*
and did not spare the ancient **w**, 2Pe 2:5 *2889*
a flood upon the **w** of the ungodly; 2Pe 2:5 *2889*
have escaped the defilements of the **w** 2Pe 2:20 *2889*
the **w** at that time was destroyed, 2Pe 3:6 *2889*
but also for *those of* the whole **w**. 1Jn 2:2 *2889*
Do not love the **w** nor the things 1Jn 2:15 *2889*
world nor the things in the **w**. 1Jn 2:15 *2889*
If anyone loves the **w**, 1Jn 2:15 *2889*
For all that is in the **w**, 1Jn 2:16 *2889*
the Father, but is from the **w**. 1Jn 2:16 *2889*
The **w** is passing away, and 1Jn 2:17 *2889*
reason the **w** does not know us, 1Jn 3:1 *2889*
brethren, if the **w** hates you. 1Jn 3:13 *2889*
prophets have gone out into the **w**. 1Jn 4:1 *2889*
and now it is already in the **w**. 1Jn 4:3 *2889*
is in you than he who is in the **w**. 1Jn 4:4 *2889*
They are from the **w**; 1Jn 4:5 *2889*
they speak *as* from the **w**, 1Jn 4:5 *2889*
world, and the **w** listens to them. 1Jn 4:5 *2889*
sent His only begotten Son into the **w** 1Jn 4:9 *2889*
the Son *to be* the Savior of the **w**. 1Jn 4:14 *2889*
He is, so also are we in this **w**. 1Jn 4:17 *2889*
is born of God overcomes the **w**; 1Jn 5:4 *2889*
the victory that has overcome the **w** 1Jn 5:4 *2889*
is the one who overcomes the **w**, 1Jn 5:5 *2889*
and that the whole **w** lies in *the power* 1Jn 5:19 *2889*
have gone out into the **w**, 2Jn 1:7 *2889*
is about to come upon the whole **w**, Rv 3:10 *3625*
"The kingdom of the **w** has become Rv 11:15 *2889*
Satan, who deceives the whole **w**; Rv 12:9 *3625*
written from the foundation of the **w** Rv 13:8 *2889*
out to the kings of the whole **w**, Rv 16:14 *3625*
life from the foundation of the **w**, Rv 17:8 *2889*

WORLDLY

w fables fit only for old women. 1Tm 4:7 *952*
avoiding **w** *and* empty chatter *and* 1Tm 6:20 *952*
But avoid **w** *and* empty chatter, for 2Tm 2:16 *952*
to deny ungodliness and **w** desires Ti 2:12 *2886*

WORLDLY-MINDED

the ones who cause divisions, **w**, Jude 1:19 *5591*

WORLD'S

But whoever has the **w** goods, 1Jn 3:17 *2889*

WORLDS

w were prepared by the word of God Heb 11:3 *165*

WORM

foul nor was there any **w** in it. Ex 16:24 7415
for the **w** will devour them. Dt 28:39 8439b
To the **w**, 'my mother and my sister'; Jb 17:14 7415
The **w** feeds sweetly till he is Jb 24:20 7415
And the son of man, *that* **w**!" Jb 25:6 8439b
But I am a **w** and not a man, A Ps 22:6 8439b
"Do not fear, you **w** Jacob, Is 41:14 8439b
For their **w** will not die And Is 66:24 8439b
God appointed a **w** when dawn Jon 4:7 8439b
where THEIR **W** DOES NOT DIE, AND Mk 9:44 *4663*
where THEIR **W** DOES NOT DIE, AND Mk 9:46 *4663*
where THEIR **W** DOES NOT DIE, AND Mk 9:48 *4663*

WORMS

and it bred **w** and became foul; Ex 16:20 8438
"My flesh is clothed with **w** and a Jb 7:5 7415
in the dust, And **w** cover them. Jb 21:26 7415
you And **w** are your covering.' Is 14:11 8439b
and he was eaten by **w** and died. Ac 12:23 *4662*

WORMWOOD

bearing poisonous fruit and **w**. Dt 29:18 3939

But in the end she is bitter as **w**, Pr 5:4 3939
with **w** and give them poisoned Jer 9:15 3939
I am going to feed them **w** And make Jer 23:15 3939
He has made me drunk with **w**. La 3:15 3939
wandering, the **w** and bitterness. La 3:19 3939
For those who turn justice into **w** Am 5:7 3939
the fruit of righteousness into **w**, Am 6:12 3939
The name of the star is called **W**; Rv 8:11 *894*
a third of the waters became **w**, Rv 8:11 *894*

WORN
clothes have not **w** out on you, Dt 29:5 1086
sandal has not **w** out on your foot. Dt 29:5 1086
our clothes and our sandals are **w** out Jos 9:13 1086
a royal robe which the king has **w**, Es 6:8 3847
We are **w** out, there is no rest for La 5:5 3021
her who was **w** out by adulteries, Ezk 23:43 1087

WORN-OUT
and took **w** sacks on their donkeys, Jos 9:4 1087
wineskins **w** and torn and mended, Jos 9:4 1087
and **w** and patched sandals on their Jos 9:5 1087
feet, and **w** clothes on themselves; Jos 9:5 1087
and took from there **w** clothes and Jer 38:11 1094
worn-out clothes and **w** rags and Jer 38:11 1094
"Now put these **w** clothes and rags Jer 38:12 1094

WORRIED
"Of whom were you **w** and fearful Is 57:11 1672
do not be **w** about your life, *as to* Mt 6:25 *3309*
"And who of you by being **w** can add a Mt 6:27 *3309*
"And why are you **w** about clothing? Mt 6:28 *3309*
you are **w** and bothered about so Lk 10:41 *3309*

WORRIES
but the **w** of the world, and the Mk 4:19 *3308*
they are choked with **w** and riches Lk 8:14 *3308*
and drunkenness and the **w** of life, Lk 21:34 *3308*

WORRY
"Do not **w** then, saying, 'What Mt 6:31 *3309*
"So do not **w** about tomorrow; Mt 6:34 *3309*
do not **w** about how or what you are to Mt 10:19 *3309*
the word, and the **w** of the world and Mt 13:22 *3308*
do not **w** beforehand about what you Mk 13:11 *4305*
do not **w** about how or what you are to Lk 12:11 *3309*
do not **w** about *your* life, *as* Lk 12:22 *3309*
why do you **w** about other matters? Lk 12:26 *3309*
Do not **w** about it; 1Co 7:21 *3199*

WORRYING
"And which of you by **w** can add a Lk 12:25 *3309*
will drink, and do not keep **w**. Lk 12:29 *3349*

WORSE
we will treat you **w** than them." Gn 19:9 7489a
Thus may the LORD do to me, and **w**, Ru 1:17 3541, 3254
and this will be **w** for you than 2Sa 19:7 7489a
And my sorrow grew **w**. Ps 39:2 5916
the garment, and a **w** tear results. Mt 9:16 *5501*
that man becomes **w** than the first. Mt 12:45 *5501*
will be **w** than the first." Mt 27:64 *5501*
the old, and a **w** tear results. Mk 2:21 *5501*
at all, but rather had grown **w** Mk 5:26 *5501*
man becomes **w** than the first." Lk 11:26 *5501*
Siloam fell and killed them were **w** Lk 13:4
that nothing **w** happens to you." Jn 5:14 *5501*
neither the **w** if we do not eat, 1Co 8:8 *5302*
not for the better but for the **w**. 1Co 11:17 *2269b*
and is **w** than an unbeliever. 1Tm 5:8 *5501*
will proceed *from bad* to **w**, 2Tm 3:13 *5501*
last state has become **w** for them 2Pe 2:20 *5501*

WORSHIP
and we will **w** and return to you." Gn 22:5 7812
Then Israel bowed *in* **w** at Gn 47:31 7812
shall **w** God at this mountain." Ex 3:12 5647
and go, **w** the LORD, as you have Ex 12:31 5647
You shall not **w** them or serve them; Ex 20:5 7812
"You shall not **w** their gods, nor Ex 23:24 7812
and you shall **w** at a distance. Ex 24:1 7812
all the people would arise and **w**, Ex 33:10 7812
to bow low toward the earth and **w**. Ex 34:8 7812
for you shall not **w** any other god, Ex 34:14 7812
away and **w** them and serve them, Dt 4:19 7812
You shall not **w** them or serve them; Dt 5:9 7812
and you shall **w** Him and swear by Dt 6:13 5647
gods and serve them and **w** them, Dt 8:19 7812
and serve other gods and **w** them. Dt 11:16 7812
and **w** before the LORD your God; Dt 26:10 7812
and **w** other gods and serve them, Dt 30:17 7812
he bowed in **w**. Jg 7:15 7812
would go up from his city yearly to **w** 1Sa 1:3 7812
with me, that I may **w** the LORD." 1Sa 15:25 7812
that I may **w** the LORD your God." 1Sa 15:30 7812
and serve other gods and **w** them, 1Ki 9:6 7812
for the people went *to* **w** before 1Ki 12:30 7812
the house of Rimmon to **w** there, 2Ki 5:18 7812
'You shall **w** before this altar in 2Ki 18:22 7812
W the LORD in holy array. 1Ch 16:29 7812
and serve other gods and **w** them, 2Ch 7:19 7812
"You shall **w** before one altar, 2Ch 32:12 7812
they performed the **w** of their God Ne 12:45 4931
W the LORD with reverence And Ps 2:11 5647
all the families of the nations will **w** Ps 22:27 7812
of the earth will eat and **w**, Ps 22:29 7812
W the LORD in holy array. Ps 29:2 7812
"All the earth will **w** You, Ps 66:4 7812
Nor shall you **w** any foreign god. Ps 81:9 7812
made shall come and **w** before You, Ps 86:9 7812
Come, let us **w** and bow down, Ps 95:6 7812
W the LORD in holy attire; Ps 96:9 7812
W Him, all you gods. Ps 97:7 7812
our God And **w** at His footstool; Ps 99:5 7812
our God And **w** at His holy hill Ps 99:9 7812
Let us **w** at His footstool. Ps 132:7 7812
They **w** the work of their hands, Is 2:8 7812
they made for themselves to **w**, Is 2:20 7812
w with sacrifice and offering, Is 19:21 5647
Egyptians will **w** with the Assyrians. Is 19:23 5647
w the LORD in the holy mountain at Is 27:13 7812
'You shall **w** before this altar'? Is 36:7 7812
They bow down, indeed they **w** it. Is 46:6 7812
enter by these gates to **w** the LORD! Jer 7:2 7812
gods to serve them and to **w** them, Jer 25:6 7812
have come to **w** *in* the LORD's house all Jer 26:2 7812
not go after other gods to **w** them. Jer 35:15 5647
and he shall **w** at the threshold of Ezk 46:2 7812
people of the land shall also **w** at the Ezk 46:3 7812
enters by way of the north gate to **w** Ezk 46:9 7812
you are to fall down and **w** the Da 3:5 5457
whoever does not fall down and **w** Da 3:6 5457
fall down and **w** the golden image. Da 3:10 5457
whoever does not fall down and **w** Da 3:11 5457
they do not serve your gods or **w** Da 3:12 5457
or **w** the golden image that I have set Da 3:14 5457
and **w** the image that I have made, Da 3:15 5457
But if you do not **w**, Da 3:15 5457
or **w** the golden image that you have Da 3:18 5457
or **w** any god except their own God. Da 3:28 5457
from year to year to **w** the King, Zch 14:16 7812
go up to Jerusalem to **w** the King, Zch 14:17 7812
east and have come to **w** Him." Mt 2:2 *4352*
that I too may come and **w** Him." Mt 2:8 *4352*
You, if You fall down and **w** me." Mt 4:9 *4352*
'YOU SHALL **W** THE LORD YOUR GOD, Mt 4:10 *4352*
'BUT IN VAIN DO THEY **W** ME, Mt 15:9 *4576*
'BUT IN VAIN DO THEY **W** ME, Mk 7:7 *4576*
"Therefore if You **w** before me, Lk 4:7 *4352*
'YOU SHALL **W** THE LORD YOUR GOD Lk 4:8 *4352*
the place where men ought to **w**." Jn 4:20 *4352*
Jerusalem will you **w** the Father. Jn 4:21 *4352*
"You **w** what you do not know; Jn 4:22 *4352*
we **w** what we know, for Jn 4:22 *4352*
true worshipers will **w** the Father Jn 4:23 *4352*
and those who **w** Him must worship Jn 4:24 *4352*
Him must **w** in spirit and truth." Jn 4:24 *4352*
were going up to **w** at the feast; Jn 12:20 *4352*
IMAGES WHICH YOU MADE TO **W**. Ac 7:43 *4352*
and he had come to Jerusalem to **w**, Ac 8:27 *4352*
examining the objects of your **w**, Ac 17:23 *4574*
Therefore what you **w** in ignorance, Ac 17:23 *2151*
to **w** God contrary to the law." Ac 18:13 *4576*
she whom all of Asia and the world **w** Ac 19:27 *4576*
ago I went up to Jerusalem to **w**. Ac 24:11 *4352*
is your spiritual service of **w**. Ro 12:1 *2999*
will fall on his face and **w** God, 1Co 14:25 *4352*
who **w** in the Spirit of God and Php 3:3 *3000*
and the **w** of the angels, Col 2:18 *2356*
every so-called god or object of **w**, 2Th 2:4 *4574*
LET ALL THE ANGELS OF GOD **W** HIM." Heb 1:6 *4352*
had regulations of divine **w** and Heb 9:1 *2999*
performing the divine **w**, Heb 9:6 *2999*
and will **w** Him who lives forever Rv 4:10 *4352*
hands, so as not to **w** demons, Rv 9:20 *4352*
the altar, and those who **w** in it. Rv 11:1 *4352*
who dwell on the earth will **w** him, Rv 13:8 *4352*
dwell in it to **w** the first beast, Rv 13:12 *4352*
as do not **w** the image of the beast to Rv 13:15 *4352*
w Him who made the heaven and Rv 14:7 *4352*
who **w** the beast and his image, Rv 14:11 *4352*
WILL COME AND **W** BEFORE YOU, Rv 15:4 *4352*
Then I fell at his feet to **w** him. Rv 19:10 *4352*
hold the testimony of Jesus; **w** God. Rv 19:10 *4352*
I fell down to **w** at the feet of Rv 22:8 *4352*
of this book. **W** God." Rv 22:9 *4352*

WORSHIPED
the man bowed low and **w** the LORD. Gn 24:26 7812
"And I bowed low and **w** the LORD, Gn 24:48 7812
then they bowed low and **w**. Ex 4:31 7812
And the people bowed low and **w**. Ex 12:27 7812
a molten calf, and have **w** it and Ex 32:8 7812
and served other gods and **w** them, Dt 17:3 7812
and served other gods and **w** them, Dt 29:26 7812
the morning and **w** before the LORD, 1Sa 1:19 7812
And he **w** the LORD there. 1Sa 1:28 7812
Saul, and Saul **w** the LORD. 1Sa 15:31 7812
into the house of the LORD and **w**. 2Sa 12:20 7812
to the summit, where God was **w**, 2Sa 15:32 7812
gods and **w** them and served them, 1Ki 9:9 7812
and have **w** Ashtoreth the goddess 1Ki 11:33 7812
and went to serve Baal and **w** him. 1Ki 16:31 7812
So he served Baal and **w** him and 1Ki 22:53 7812
and made an Asherah and **w** all the 2Ki 17:16 7812
and **w** all the host of heaven and 2Ki 21:3 7812
his father had served and **w** them. 2Ki 21:21 7812
w and gave praise to the LORD, 2Ch 7:3 7812
gods and **w** them and served them; 2Ch 7:22 7812
While the whole assembly **w**, 2Ch 29:28 7812
present with him bowed down and **w**. 2Ch 29:29 7812
with joy, and bowed down and **w**. 2Ch 29:30 7812
and **w** all the host of heaven and 2Ch 33:3 7812
then they bowed low and **w** the LORD Ne 8:6 7812
and **w** the LORD their God. Ne 9:3 7812
and he fell to the ground and **w**. Jb 1:20 7812
in Horeb And **w** a molten image. Ps 106:19 7812
w the works of their own hands. Jer 1:16 7812
sought, and which they have **w**. Jer 8:2 7812
fell down *and* **w** the golden image Da 3:7 5457
fell to the ground and **w** Him. Mt 2:11 *4352*
those who were in the boat **w** Him, Mt 14:33 *4352*
took hold of His feet and **w** Him. Mt 28:9 *4352*
When they saw Him, they **w** *Him;* Mt 28:17 *4352*
"Our fathers **w** in this mountain, Jn 4:20 *4352*
"Lord, I believe." And he **w** Him. Jn 9:38 *4352*
and fell at his feet and **w** *him.* Ac 10:25 *4352*
and **w** and served the creature Ro 1:25 *4573*
w, *leaning* on the top of his staff. Heb 11:21 *4352*
And the elders fell down and **w**. Rv 5:14 *4352*
faces before the throne and **w** God, Rv 7:11 *4352*
fell on their faces and **w** God, Rv 11:16 *4352*
they **w** the dragon because he Rv 13:4 *4352*
and they **w** the beast, saying, Rv 13:4 *4352*
of the beast and who **w** his image. Rv 16:2 *4352*
living creatures fell down and **w** God Rv 19:4 *4352*
beast and those who **w** his image; Rv 19:20 *4352*
had not **w** the beast or his image, Rv 20:4 *4352*

WORSHIPER
of purple fabrics, a **w** of God, Ac 16:14 *4576*
named Titius Justus, a **w** of God, Ac 18:7 *4576*
make the **w** perfect in conscience, Heb 9:9 *3000*

WORSHIPERS
all his **w** and all his priests; 2Ki 10:19 5647
he might destroy the **w** of Baal. 2Ki 10:19 5647
Israel and all the **w** of Baal came, 2Ki 10:21 5647
garments for all the **w** of Baal." 2Ki 10:22 5647
and he said to the **w** of Baal, 2Ki 10:23 5647
LORD, but only the **w** of Baal." 2Ki 10:23 5647
the rivers of Ethiopia My **w**, Zph 3:10 6282a
when the true **w** will worship the Jn 4:23 *4353*
the Father seeks to be His **w**. Jn 4:23 *4352*
to be offered, because the **w**, Heb 10:2 *3000*

WORSHIPING
as he was **w** in the house of Nisroch 2Ki 19:37 7812
down before the LORD, **w** the LORD. 2Ch 20:18 7812
as he was **w** in the house of Nisroch Is 37:38 7812
and you will bear the penalty of **w** Ezk 23:49
And they, after **w** Him, returned to Lk 24:52 *4352*

WORSHIPS
He also makes a god and **w** it; Is 44:15 7812
He falls down before it and **w**; Is 44:17 7812
anyone **w** the beast and his image, Rv 14:9 *4352*

WORST
I will bring the **w** of the nations, Ezk 7:24 7451a

WORTH
a piece of land **w** four hundred Gn 23:15
But you are **w** ten thousand of us; 2Sa 18:3
and silver utensils **w** 100 talents, Ezr 8:26
and 20 gold bowls **w** 1,000 Ezr 8:27
The heart of the wicked is **w** Pr 10:20
For her **w** is far above jewels. Pr 31:10 4377
Are you not **w** much more than they? Mt 6:26 *1308*
"Two hundred denarii **w** of bread Jn 6:7
But you know of his proven **w**, Php 2:22 *1382*

WORTHLESS
some **w** men have gone out from Dt 13:13 1100
hired **w** and reckless fellows, Jg 9:4 7386
and **w** fellows gathered themselves Jg 11:3 7386
of the city, certain **w** fellows, Jg 19:22 1100
the men, the **w** fellows in Gibeah, Jg 20:13 1100
your maidservant as a **w** woman, 1Sa 1:16 1100
Now the sons of Eli were **w** men; 1Sa 2:12 1100
But certain **w** men said, 1Sa 10:27 1100
but everything despised and **w**, 1Sa 15:9 4549
and he is such a **w** man that no one 1Sa 25:17 1100
lord pay attention to this **w** man, 1Sa 25:25 1100
Then all the wicked and **w** men 1Sa 30:22 1100
man of bloodshed, and **w** fellow! 2Sa 16:7 1100
Now a **w** fellow happened to be 2Sa 20:1 1100
"But the **w**, every one of them 2Sa 23:6 1100
and seat two **w** men before him, and 1Ki 21:10 1100
Then the two **w** men came in and sat 1Ki 21:13 1100
the **w** men testified against him, 1Ki 21:13 1100
and **w** men gathered about him, 2Ch 13:7 7386
You are all **w** physicians. Jb 13:4 457
me a liar, And make my speech **w**?" Jb 24:25 408
Who says to a king, '**W** one,' Jb 34:18 1100
How long will you love what is **w** Ps 4:2 7385b
I will set no **w** thing before my eyes; Ps 101:3 1100
A **w** person, a wicked man, Is the Pr 6:12 1100
But he who pursues **w** *things* lacks Pr 12:11 7386
A **w** man digs up evil, While his Pr 16:27 1100
"Bring your **w** offerings no Is 1:13 7723
But it produced *only* **w** ones. Is 5:2 891
good grapes did it produce **w** ones? Is 5:4 891
Their works are **w**, Their molten Is 41:29 657
They are **w**, a work of mockery; Jer 10:15 1892
on it, And its branches are **w**. Jer 11:16 7489b
was ruined, it was totally **w**. Jer 13:7 3808, 6743b
waistband which is totally **w**. Jer 13:10 3808, 6743b
extract the precious from the **w**, Jer 15:19 2151b
They burn incense to **w** gods And Jer 18:15 7723
They are **w**, a work of mockery; Jer 51:18 1892
With **w** oaths they make covenants; Hos 10:4 7723
Surely they are **w**. Hos 12:11 7723
w shepherd Who leaves the flock! Zch 11:17 457
Throw out the **w** slave into the outer Mt 25:30 *888*
I will judge you, you **w** slave. Lk 19:22 *4190*
goddess Artemis be regarded as **w** Ac 19:27 *3762*
not been raised, your faith is **w**; 1Co 15:17 *3152*
the weak and **w** elemental things, Ga 4:9 *4434*
and **w** for any good deed. Ti 1:16 *96b*
for they are unprofitable and **w**. Ti 3:9 *3152*
it is **w** and close to being cursed, Heb 6:8 *96b*
heart, this man's religion is **w**. Jas 1:26 *3152*

WORTHY
has committed a sin **w** of death and Dt 21:22 4941
is no sin in the girl **w** of death, Dt 22:26

the LORD, who is w to be praised, 2Sa 22:4
"If he is a w man, not one 1Ki 1:52 2428
to another who is more w than she. Es 1:19 2896a
the LORD, who is w to be praised, Ps 18:3
w for You to come under my roof, Mt 8:8 2425
the worker is w of his support. Mt 10:10 514
you enter, inquire who is w in it, Mt 10:11 514
"If the house is w, Mt 10:13 514
But if it is not w, Mt 10:13 514
more than Me is not w of Me; Mt 10:37 514
more than Me is not w of Me. Mt 10:37 514
follow after Me is not w of Me. Mt 10:38 514
those who were invited were not w. Mt 22:8 514
is w for You to grant this to him; Lk 7:4 514
w for You to come under my roof; Lk 7:6 2425
consider myself w to come to You, Lk 7:7 515
for the laborer is w of his wages. Lk 10:7 514
committed deeds w of a flogging, Lk 12:48 514
no longer w to be called your son; Lk 15:19 514
no longer w to be called your son.' Lk 15:21 514
but those who are considered w to Lk 20:35 2661
sandal I am not w to untie." Jn 1:27 514
w to suffer shame for *His* name. Ac 5:41 2661
whose feet I am not w to untie.' Ac 13:25 514
committed anything w of death, Ac 25:11 514
had committed nothing w of death; Ac 25:25 514
w of death or imprisonment." Ac 26:31 514
such things are w of death, Ro 1:32 514
not w to be compared with the glory Ro 8:18 514
Lord in a manner w of the saints, Ro 16:2 516
to walk in a manner w of the calling Eph 4:1 516
manner w of the gospel of Christ, Php 1:27 516
and if anything w of praise, Php 4:8 1868
walk in a manner w of the Lord, Col 1:10 516
walk in a manner w of the God who 1Th 2:12 516
w of the kingdom of God, 2Th 1:5 2661
will count you w of your calling, 2Th 1:11 515
be considered w of double honor, 1Tm 5:17 515
"The laborer is w of his wages." 1Tm 5:18 514
their own masters as w of all honor 1Tm 6:1 514
w of more glory than Moses, Heb 3:3 515
(*men* of whom the world was not w), Heb 11:38 514
on their way in a manner w of God. 3Jn 1:6 516
with Me in white, for they are w. Rv 3:4 514
"W are You, our Lord and our Rv 4:11 514
"Who is w to open the book and to Rv 5:2 514
one was found w to open the book or Rv 5:4 514
"W are You to take the book and Rv 5:9 514
"W is the Lamb that was slain to Rv 5:12 514

WOULD

man to see what he w call them; Gn 2:19
so that no one finding him w slay him. Gn 4:15
for fear you w say, 'I have made Gn 14:23
"Who w have said to Abraham that Gn 21:7
that Sarah w nurse children? Gn 21:7
w have brought guilt upon us." Gn 26:10
they w then roll the stone from Gn 29:3
And w you take my son's mandrakes Gn 30:15
Jacob w place the rods in the Gn 30:41
that you w take your daughters Gn 31:31
surely now you w have sent me away Gn 31:42
for that w be a disgrace to us. Gn 34:14
that the offspring w not be his; Gn 38:9
"I w make mention today of my *own* Gn 41:9
with us, yet we w not listen; Gn 42:21
and you w not listen? Gn 42:22
no more, and you w take Benjamin; Gn 42:36
we possibly know that he w say, Gn 43:7
his father, his father w die.' Gn 44:22
evil that w overtake my father?" Gn 44:34
household and all that you have w be Gn 45:11
to find out what w happen to him. Ex 2:4
and you w have them cease from Ex 5:5
you w then have been cut off from Ex 9:15
nor w there be so *many* again. Ex 10:14
that He w only remove this death Ex 10:17
For it w have been better for us Ex 14:12
"W that we had died by the LORD's Ex 16:3
4310, 5414
when the sun grew hot, it w melt. Ex 16:21
dispute they w bring to Moses, Ex 18:26
dispute they themselves w judge. Ex 18:26
He said He w do to His people. Ex 32:14
for one moment, I w destroy you. Ex 33:5
everyone who sought the LORD w go Ex 33:7
all the people w arise and stand, Ex 33:8
the pillar of cloud w descend and Ex 33:9
and the LORD w speak with Moses. Ex 33:9
the people w arise and worship, Ex 33:10
man, w not depart from the tent. Ex 33:11
of the land and they w play Ex 34:15
he w take off the veil until he Ex 34:34
of Israel w see the face of Moses, Ex 34:35
So Moses w replace the veil over Ex 34:35
the tent together so that it w be Ex 36:18
so that it w be on the woven band of Ex 39:21
and that the breastpiece w not come Ex 39:21
so that it w not be torn. Ex 39:23
the sons of Israel w set out; Ex 40:36
w it have been good in the sight Lv 10:19
land of Egypt so that *you* w not Lv 26:13
the cloud w cover it *by day,* and Nu 9:16
the sons of Israel w then set out; Nu 9:17
there the sons of Israel w camp. Nu 9:17
LORD the sons of Israel w set out, Nu 9:18
command of the LORD they w camp; Nu 9:18
the sons of Israel w keep the Nu 9:19
in the morning, they w move out; Nu 9:21
cloud was lifted, they w set out. Nu 9:21

The people w go about and gather Nu 11:8
night, the manna w fall with it. Nu 11:9
someone w give us meat to eat! Nu 11:18
W that all the LORD's people were Nu 11:29
4310, 5414
LORD w put His Spirit upon them!" Nu 11:29
w she not bear her shame for seven Nu 12:14
"W that we had died in the land Nu 14:2 3863
Or w that we had died in this Nu 14:2 3863
w it not be better for us to Nu 14:3
whom you said w become a prey Nu 14:31
but you w also lord it over us? Nu 16:13
W you put out the eyes of these Nu 16:14
But Sihon w not permit Israel to Nu 21:23
I w have killed you by now." Nu 22:29
I w surely have killed you just Nu 22:33
I said I w honor you greatly, but Nu 24:11
ones who you said w become a prey, Dt 1:39
to you, but you w not listen. Dt 1:43
account, and w not listen to me; Dt 3:26
and swore that I w not cross Dt 4:21
and that I w not enter the good land Dt 4:21
in them, that they w fear Me and Dt 5:29
for that w *be* a snare to you. Dt 7:16
for the wild beasts w grow too Dt 7:22
w keep His commandments or not. Dt 8:2
because you w not listen to the Dt 8:20
you that He w have destroyed you. Dt 9:8
LORD had said He w destroy you. Dt 9:25
die in the battle and another man w Dt 20:5
the battle and another man w begin Dt 20:6
the battle and another man w marry Dt 20:7
w sin against the LORD your God. Dt 20:18
w take her as a wife for yourself, Dt 21:11
to pay it, for it w be sin in you, Dt 23:21
vowing, it w not be sin in you. Dt 23:22
he w be taking a life in pledge. Dt 24:6
and that you w walk in His ways Dt 26:17
because you w not obey the LORD Dt 28:45
who w not venture to set the sole Dt 28:56
'W that it were evening!' Dt 28:67
4310, 5414
'W that it were morning!' Dt 28:67
4310, 5414
'I have said, "I will cut them to Dt 32:26
That their adversaries w misjudge, Dt 32:27
That they w say, "Our hand is Dt 32:27
"W that they were wise, that they Dt 32:29 3863
That they w discern their future! Dt 32:29
that He w not let them see the land Jos 5:6
in the place which He w choose. Jos 9:27
that they w turn back and act more Jg 2:19
to find out if they w obey the Jg 3:4
"Her wise princesses w answer her, Jg 5:29
that the Midianites w come up with Jg 6:3
So they w camp against them and Jg 6:4
For they w come up with their Jg 6:5
they w come in like locusts for Jg 6:5
for Israel w become boastful, saying, Jg 7:2
let them live, I w not kill you." Jg 8:19
"I w request of you, that each of Jg 8:24
"W, therefore, that this people Jg 9:29
4310, 5414
Then I w remove Abimelech." Jg 9:29
but the king of Edom w not listen. Jg 11:17
of Moab, but he w not consent. Jg 11:17
I saw that you w not deliver *me,* Jg 12:3
the men of Gilead w say to him, Jg 12:5
then they w say to him, Jg 12:6
He w not have accepted a burnt Jg 13:23
nor w He have shown us all these Jg 13:23
nor w He have let us hear *things* Jg 13:23
w not have found out my riddle." Jg 14:18
But the men w not listen to him. Jg 19:25 14
But the sons of Benjamin w not Jg 20:13 14
men in ambush was that they w make Jg 20:38
else you w now be guilty.'" Jg 21:22
w you therefore wait until they Ru 1:13
W you therefore refrain from Ru 1:13
because I w jeopardize my own Ru 4:6
Now this man w go up from his city 1Sa 1:3
he w give portions to Peninnah his 1Sa 1:4
Hannah he w give a double portion, 1Sa 1:5
w provoke her bitterly to irritate 1Sa 1:6
of the LORD, she w provoke her; 1Sa 1:7
her; so she wept and w not eat. 1Sa 1:7
the priest's servant w come while 1Sa 2:13
Then he w thrust it into the pan, 1Sa 2:14
up the priest w take for himself. 1Sa 2:14
the priest's servant w come and 1Sa 2:15
much as you desire," then he w say, 1Sa 2:16
And his mother w make him a little 1Sa 2:19
she w come up with her husband to 1Sa 2:19
Then Eli w bless Elkanah and his 1Sa 2:20
But they w not listen to the voice 1Sa 2:25
for *then you* w *go* after futile 1Sa 12:21
for now the LORD w have 1Sa 13:13
David w take the harp and play *it* 1Sa 16:23
Saul w be refreshed and be well, 1Sa 16:23
the evil spirit w depart from him. 1Sa 16:23
then w I not tell you about it?" 1Sa 20:9
if you w take it for yourself, 1Sa 21:9
so that he w rise up against me by 1Sa 22:13
there, that he w surely tell Saul. 1Sa 22:22
surely there w not have been left 1Sa 25:34
driven me out today so that I w have 1Sa 26:19
W it not *be* with the heads of 1Sa 29:4
But his armor bearer w not, 1Sa 31:4 14
w have gone away in the morning, 2Sa 2:27

"Whoever w strike the Jebusites, 2Sa 5:8
that they w shoot from the wall? 2Sa 11:20
It w eat of his bread and drink of 2Sa 12:3
I w have added to you many more 2Sa 12:8
and w not eat food with them. 2Sa 12:17
However, he w not listen to her; 2Sa 13:14 14
Yet he w not listen to her. 2Sa 13:16 14
he urged him, he w not go, 2Sa 13:25 14
the man who w destroy both me and 2Sa 14:16
king, but he w not come to him. 2Sa 14:29 14
a second time, but he w not come. 2Sa 14:29 14
It w be better for me still to be 2Sa 14:32
Absalom w call to him and say, 2Sa 15:2
And he w say, "Your servant is from 2Sa 15:2
Then Absalom w say to him, 2Sa 15:3
Moreover, Absalom w say, 2Sa 15:4
w appoint me judge in the land, 2Sa 15:4
to me and I w give him justice." 2Sa 15:4
he w put out his hand and take 2Sa 15:5
a maidservant w go and tell them, 2Sa 17:17
and they w go and tell King David, 2Sa 17:17
And I w have given you ten *pieces* 2Sa 18:11
I w not put out my hand against 2Sa 18:12
you yourself w have stood aloof." 2Sa 18:13
"Why w you run, my son, since you 2Sa 18:22
W I had died instead of you, O 2Sa 18:33
4310, 5414
dead today, then you w be pleased. 2Sa 19:6
so that the king w take *it* to 2Sa 19:19
"Your servant w merely cross over 2Sa 19:36
Why w you swallow up the 2Sa 20:19
"Oh that someone w give me water 2Sa 23:15
Nevertheless he w not drink it, 2Sa 23:16 14
Therefore he w not drink it. 2Sa 23:17 14
Solomon w give Hiram year by year. 1Ki 5:11
in order that *the beams* w not 1Ki 6:6
and they w go up by winding stairs 1Ki 6:8
He w dwell in the thick cloud. 1Ki 8:12
your house I w not go with you, 1Ki 13:8
nor w I eat bread or drink water 1Ki 13:8
any who w, he ordained, to be 1Ki 13:33 2655
who spoke concerning me *that I* w *be* 1Ki 14:2
that the guards w carry them and 1Ki 14:28
w bring them back into the guards' 1Ki 14:28
and he w drink from the brook. 1Ki 17:6
"Did I not tell you that he w not 1Ki 22:18
I w not look at you nor see you. 2Ki 3:14
W you be spoken for to the king or 2Ki 4:13 3426
he w cure him of his leprosy." 2Ki 5:3
thing, w you not have done *it?* 2Ki 5:13
W you kill those you have taken 2Ki 6:22
me that you w surely recover." 2Ki 8:14
that they w be the LORD's people, 2Ki 11:17
priests agreed that they w take 2Ki 12:8
then you w have struck Aram until 2Ki 13:19
until you w have destroyed *it.* 2Ki 13:19
the bands of the Moabites w invade 2Ki 13:20
and w not destroy them or cast 2Ki 13:23 14
w fall, and Judah with you?" 2Ki 14:10
But Amaziah w not listen. 2Ki 14:11
LORD did not say that He w blot out 2Ki 14:27
they w neither listen nor do *it.* 2Ki 18:12
and the LORD w not forgive. 2Ki 24:4 14
"Oh that You w bless me indeed and 1Ch 4:10
and that You w keep *me* from harm that 1Ch 4:10
But his armor bearer w not, 1Ch 10:4 14
"Oh that someone w give me water 1Ch 11:17
nevertheless David w not drink it, 1Ch 11:18 14
Therefore he w not drink it. 1Ch 11:19 14
assembly said that they w do so, 1Ch 13:4
because the LORD had said He w 1Ch 27:23
He w dwell in the thick cloud. 2Ch 6:1
of which You have said that *You* w 2Ch 6:20
and whoever w not seek the LORD 2Ch 15:13
"Did I not tell you that he w not 2Ch 18:17
that she w not put him to death. 2Ch 22:11
that they w be the LORD's people. 2Ch 23:16
so that no one w enter *who was* 2Ch 23:19
the chief priest's officer w come, 2Ch 24:11
against them, they w not listen. 2Ch 24:19
w fall and Judah with you?" 2Ch 25:19
But Amaziah w not listen, for it 2Ch 25:20
Josiah w not turn away from him, 2Ch 35:22
W You not be angry with us to the Ezr 9:14
w do according to this proposal; Ezr 10:5
w not come within three days, Ezr 10:8
"What w you request?" Ne 2:4
w break their stone wall down!" Ne 4:3
now w you even sell your brothers Ne 5:8
w do according to this promise. Ne 5:12
They became stubborn and w not Ne 9:16
their neck, and w not listen. Ne 9:29
prophets, Yet they w not give ear. Ne 9:30
gates *so that* no load w enter Ne 13:19
w go in to the king in this way: Es 2:13
In the evening she w go in and in Es 2:14
she w return to the second harem, Es 2:14
She w not again go in to the king Es 2:14
him and he w not listen to them, Es 3:4
whether Mordecai's reason w stand; Es 3:4
"Whom w the king desire to honor Es 6:6
women, I w have remained silent, Es 7:4
for the trouble w not be Es 7:4
is he, who w presume to do thus?" Es 7:5
so that the Jews w be ready for this Es 8:13
so that they w not fail to celebrate Es 9:27
and they w send and invite their Jb 1:4
Job w send and consecrate them, Jb 1:5
I w have lain down and been quiet; Jb 3:13

I w have slept then, I would have Jb 3:13
slept then, I w have been at rest, Jb 3:13
which is discarded, I w not be, Jb 3:16
"But as for me, I w seek God, Jb 5:8
And I w place my cause before God; Jb 5:8
"For then it w be *heavier* than Jb 6:3
And that God w grant my longing! Jb 6:8
"W that God were willing to crush Jb 6:9
He w loose His hand and cut me off! Jb 6:9
"You w even cast *lots* for the Jb 6:27
that my soul w choose suffocation, Jb 7:15
"If you w seek God And implore Jb 8:5
Surely now He w rouse Himself for Jb 8:6
He to pass by me, I w not see Him; Jb 9:11
past *me*, I w not perceive Him. Jb 9:11
I w have to implore the mercy of Jb 9:15
Yet You w plunge me into the pit, Jb 9:31
And my own clothes w abhor me. Jb 9:31
"*Then* I w speak and not fear Him; Jb 9:35
altogether, And w You destroy me? Jb 10:8
w You turn me into dust again? Jb 10:9
sin, then You w take note of me, Jb 10:14
And w not acquit me of my guilt. Jb 10:14
up, You w hunt me like a lion; Jb 10:16
You w show Your power against me. Jb 10:16
W that I had died and no eye had Jb 10:18
"W He not let my few days alone? Jb 10:20
"But w that God might speak, And Jb 11:5
4310, 5414
"If you w direct your heart Jb 11:13
you w be steadfast and not fear. Jb 11:15
"For you w forget *your* trouble, Jb 11:16
have passed by, you w remember *it.* Jb 11:16
life w be brighter than noonday; Jb 11:17
Darkness w be like the morning. Jb 11:17
"Then you w trust, because there Jb 11:18
w look around and rest securely. Jb 11:18
"You w lie down and none would Jb 11:19
lie down and none w disturb *you,* Jb 11:19
And many w entreat your favor. Jb 11:19
"But I w speak to the Almighty, Jb 13:3
"O that you w be completely silent, Jb 13:5
And that it w become your wisdom! Jb 13:5
For then I w be silent and die. Jb 13:19
"Oh that You w hide me in Sheol, Jb 14:13
That You w conceal me until Your Jb 14:13
That You w set a limit for me and Jb 14:13
In houses no one w inhabit, Jb 15:28
what w we gain if we entreat Him?' Jb 21:15
the plans by which you w wrong me. Jb 21:27
"I w present *my* case before Him Jb 23:4
"I w learn the words *which* He Jb 23:5
learn the words *which* He w answer, Jb 23:5
And perceive what He w say to me. Jb 23:5
"W He contend with me by the Jb 23:6
surely He w pay attention to me. Jb 23:6
the upright w reason with Him; Jb 23:7
And I w be delivered forever from Jb 23:7
I w be dismayed at His presence; Jb 23:15
"For that w be a lustful crime; Jb 31:11
it w be an iniquity *punishable by* Jb 31:11
"For it w be fire that consumes Jb 31:12
And w uproot all my increase. Jb 31:12
That too w have been an iniquity Jb 31:28
For I w have denied God above. Jb 31:28
I w carry it on my shoulder, Jb 31:36
I w bind it to myself like a crown. Jb 31:36
"I w declare to Him the number of Jb 31:37
Like a prince I w approach Him. Jb 31:37
Else my Maker w soon take me away. Jb 32:22
All flesh w perish together, And Jb 34:15
And man w return to dust. Jb 34:15
So that godless men w not rule Nor be Jb 34:30
it be told Him that I w speak? Jb 37:20
man say that he w be swallowed up? Jb 37:20
One w think the deep to be Jb 41:32
You w put to shame the counsel of Ps 14:6
that the salvation of Israel w come Ps 14:7
I w have despaired unless I had Ps 27:13
that I w see the goodness of the LORD Ps 27:13
that I w not go down to the pit. Ps 30:3
w magnify themselves against me." Ps 38:16
If I w declare and speak of them, Ps 40:5
They w be too numerous to count. Ps 40:5
W not God find this out? Ps 44:21
I were hungry I w not tell you Ps 50:12
sacrifice, otherwise I w give it; Ps 51:16
man who w not make God his refuge, Ps 52:7
that the salvation of Israel w come Ps 53:6
I w fly away and be at rest. Ps 55:6
"Behold, I w wander far away, I Ps 55:7
I w lodge in the wilderness. Ps 55:7
"I w hasten to my place of refuge Ps 55:8
who w destroy me are powerful, Ps 69:4
I w have betrayed the generation of Ps 73:15
O Israel, if you w listen to Me! Ps 81:8
"Oh that My people w listen to Me, Ps 81:13
Me, That Israel w walk in My ways! Ps 81:13
"I w quickly subdue their Ps 81:14
Those who hate the LORD w pretend Ps 81:15
time *of punishment* w be forever. Ps 81:15
"But I w feed you with the finest Ps 81:16
from the rock I w satisfy you." Ps 81:16
I w rather stand at the threshold Ps 84:10
My soul w soon have dwelt in *the* Ps 94:17
Today, if you w hear His voice, Ps 95:7
He said that He w destroy them, Ps 106:23
That He w cast them down in the Ps 106:26
And that He w cast their seed Ps 106:27
Many times He w deliver them; Ps 106:43
Then I w have perished in my Ps 119:92
they w have swallowed us alive, Ps 124:3
the waters w have engulfed us, Ps 124:4
stream w have swept over our soul; Ps 124:4
w have swept over our soul." Ps 124:5
them, they w outnumber the sand. Ps 139:18
O that You w slay the wicked, O Ps 139:19
"They w not accept my counsel, Pr 1:30 14
He who w destroy himself does it. Pr 6:32
its boundary So that the water w not Pr 8:29
He who w restrain her restrains Pr 27:16
on to him and w not let him go Until SS 3:4
found you outdoors, I w kiss you; SS 8:1
No one w despise me, either. SS 8:1
"I w lead you *and* bring you Into SS 8:2
I w give you spiced wine to drink SS 8:2
love, It w be utterly despised." SS 8:7
few survivors, We w be like Sodom, Is 1:9
like Sodom, We w be like Gomorrah. Is 1:9
That w be like a club wielding Is 10:15
as a hired man w count them, Is 16:14
If you w inquire, inquire; Is 21:12
a year, as a hired man w count it, Is 21:16
in battle, *Then* I w step on them, Is 27:4
on them, I w burn them completely. Is 27:4
"To whom w He teach knowledge, Is 28:9
whom w He interpret the message? Is 28:9
is repose," but they w not listen. Is 28:12 14
That what is made w say to its maker, Is 29:16
that the LORD w deliver Jerusalem Is 36:20
then will you liken Me That I w be Is 40:25
"To whom w you liken Me And make Is 46:5
That we w be alike? Is 46:5
So that you w not say, 'My idol has Is 48:5
you w deal very treacherously; Is 48:8
well-being w have been like a river, Is 48:18
Your descendants w have been like Is 48:19
Their name w never be cut off or Is 48:19
If He w render Himself *as* a guilt Is 53:10
I swore that the waters of Noah W not Is 54:9
the spirit w grow faint before Me, Is 57:16
that You w rend the heavens *and* Is 64:1
'How I w set you among My sons Jer 3:19
Who w not fear You, O King of the Jer 10:7
that I w plead *my* case with You; Jer 12:1
Indeed I w discuss matters of justice Jer 12:1
My heart w not be with this people; Jer 15:1
my mother w have been my grave, Jer 20:17
right hand, yet I w pull you off; Jer 22:24
Then they w have announced My Jer 23:22
And w have turned them back from Jer 23:22
For who w dare to risk his life to Jer 30:21
they w not listen and receive Jer 32:33
then I w reject the descendants of Jer 33:26
scroll, he w not listen to them. Jer 36:25
they w rise up and burn this city Jer 37:10
yet he w not listen to him. Jer 37:14
If you w prefer to come with me to Jer 40:4
but if you w prefer not to come Jer 40:4
the Jews who are gathered to you w be Jer 40:15
and the remnant of Judah w perish?" Jer 40:15
you, W they not leave gleanings? Jer 49:9
They w destroy *only* until they had Jer 49:9
which w come upon Babylon, Jer 51:60
that You w bring the day which La 1:21
spirit was about to go, they w go, Ezk 1:12
go, they w go in that direction. Ezk 1:20
w inflict this disaster on them." Ezk 6:10
so that I w be far from My sanctuary? Ezk 8:6
the wheels w go beside them; Ezk 10:16
wheels w not turn from beside them. Ezk 10:16
still, the wheels w stand still; Ezk 10:17
up, the wheels w rise with them, Ezk 10:17
no one w pass through it because of Ezk 14:15
They alone w be delivered, but the Ezk 14:16
but the country w be desolate. Ezk 14:16
but they alone w be delivered. Ezk 14:18
They w deliver only themselves by Ezk 14:20
you w offer before them for a Ezk 16:19
hunting nets So that his voice w be Ezk 19:9
that I w not bring them into the land Ezk 20:15
I w scatter them among the nations Ezk 20:23
searched for a man among them who w Ezk 22:30
so that I w not destroy it; but I Ezk 22:30
her as they w go in to a harlot. Ezk 23:44
Because I w have cleansed you, Ezk 24:13
he w have delivered his life. Ezk 33:5
that you w become a possession of Ezk 36:3
that I w bring you against them? Ezk 38:17
will block off those who w pass Ezk 39:11
Daniel made up his mind that he w Da 1:8
Then you w make me forfeit my head Da 1:10
the king that he w give him time, Da 2:16
so that Daniel and his friends w not Da 2:18
what w take place in the future; Da 2:29
that they w be in charge of the whole Da 6:1
so that nothing w be changed in Da 6:17
forever that it w be for a time, Da 12:7
that I w ever forgive them. Hos 1:6
When I w heal Israel, The iniquity Hos 7:1
I w redeem them, but they speak Hos 7:13
yield, strangers w swallow it up. Hos 8:7
No iniquity, which w *be* sin." Hos 12:8
As a wild beast w tear them. Hos 13:8
Then I w send rain on one city And Am 4:7
on another city I w not send rain; Am 4:7
One part w be rained on, While the Am 4:7
the part not rained on w dry up. Am 4:7
"So two or three cities w stagger Am 4:8
water, But w not be satisfied; Am 4:8
And w you bring near the seat of Am 6:3
W they not steal *only* until they Ob 1:5
W they not leave *some* gleanings? Ob 1:5
had declared He w bring upon them. Jon 3:10
see what w happen in the city. Jon 4:5
He w be spokesman to this people. Mi 2:11
w not believe if you were told. Hab 1:5
measures, there w be only ten; Hg 2:16
measures, there w be *only* twenty. Hg 2:16
He called and they w not listen, Zch 7:13
they called and I w not listen," Zch 7:13
W he be pleased with you? Mal 1:8
Or w he receive you kindly?" Mal 1:8
among you who w shut the gates, Mal 1:10
they w have repented long ago in Mt 11:21
it w have remained to this day. Mt 11:23
you w not have condemned the Mt 12:7
OTHERWISE THEY W SEE WITH THEIR EYES, Mt 13:15
AND I W HEAL THEM.' Mt 13:15
"Whatever I have that w help you has Mt 15:5
"Where w we get so many loaves in Mt 15:33
it w be better for him to have a Mt 18:6
thought that they w receive more; Mt 20:10
we w not have been partners with Mt 23:30
short, no life w have been saved; Mt 24:22
he w have been on the alert and Mt 24:43
w not have allowed his house to be Mt 24:43
and on my arrival I w have Mt 25:27
It w have been good for that man Mt 26:24
and clubs to arrest Me as *you* w Mt 26:55
if He w heal him on the Sabbath, Mk 3:2
so that they w not crowd Him; Mk 3:9
they w fall down before Him and Mk 3:11
so that they w be with Him and that Mk 3:14
but that it w come to light. Mk 4:22
whatever I have that w help you is Mk 7:11
it w be better for him if, Mk 9:42
perhaps He w find anything on it; Mk 11:13
and He w not permit anyone to Mk 11:16
came, they w go out of the city. Mk 11:19
no one w venture to ask Him any Mk 12:34
days, no life w have been saved; Mk 13:20
It w have been good for that man Mk 14:21
as *you* w against a robber? Mk 14:48
that the mother of my Lord w come to Lk 1:43
believed that there w be a fulfillment Lk 1:45
that he w not see death before he had Lk 2:26
And he w answer and say to them, Lk 3:11
He w not allow them to speak, Lk 4:41
But Jesus Himself w *often* slip away Lk 5:16
He w know who and what sort of Lk 7:39
said these things, He w call out, Lk 8:8
and *yet* he w break his bonds and Lk 8:29
from them so that they w not Lk 9:45
they w have repented long ago, Lk 10:13
he w not have allowed his house to Lk 12:39
for it cannot be that a prophet w Lk 13:33
her wings, and you w not *have it!* Lk 13:34 2309
"And he w have gladly filled his Lk 15:16
"It w be better for him if a Lk 17:2
than that he w cause one of these Lk 17:2
you w say to this mulberry tree, Lk 17:6
and it w obey you. Lk 17:6
babies to Him so that He w touch Lk 18:15
I w have collected it with Lk 19:23
so that they w give him *some* of Lk 20:10
but at evening He w go out and Lk 21:37
And all the people w get up early Lk 21:38
swords and clubs as you w against Lk 22:52
and they w not believe them. Lk 24:11
that the Christ w suffer and rise Lk 24:46
for forgiveness of sins w be Lk 24:47
Me a drink,' you w have asked Him, Jn 4:10
w have given you living water." Jn 4:10
believed Moses, you w believe Me, Jn 5:46
and who it was that w betray Him. Jn 6:64
Me, you w know My Father also." Jn 8:19
were your Father, you w love Me, Jn 8:42
that he w be born blind?" Jn 9:2
you were blind, you w have no sin; Jn 9:41
here, my brother w not have died. Jn 11:21
my brother w not have died." Jn 11:32
SO THAT THEY W NOT SEE WITH THEIR Jn 12:40
for fear that they w be put out of Jn 12:42
hour had come that He w depart Jn 13:1
it were not so, I w have told you; Jn 14:2
you w have known My Father also; Jn 14:7
you loved Me, you w have rejoiced Jn 14:28
and appointed you that you w go Jn 15:16
and *that* your fruit w remain, so Jn 15:16
world, the world w love its own; Jn 15:19
to them, they w not have sin, Jn 15:22
one else did, they w not have sin; Jn 15:24
so that the Scripture w be fulfilled. Jn 17:12
the Praetorium so that they w not Jn 18:28
we w not have delivered Him to Jn 18:30
then My servants w be fighting so Jn 18:36
would be fighting so that I w not be Jn 18:36
"You w have no authority over Me, Jn 19:11
so that the bodies w not remain on Jn 19:31
kind of death he w glorify God. Jn 21:19
that that disciple w not die; Jn 21:23
not say to him that he w not die, Jn 21:23
world itself w not contain the books Jn 21:25
would not contain the books that w be Jn 21:25
that His Christ w suffer, He has Ac 3:18
owners of land or houses w sell them Ac 4:34

turn away His **w** from destroying Ps 106:23 2534
They also provoked *Him* to **w** at Ps 106:32 7107
shatter kings in the day of His **w**. Ps 110:5 639
hand against the **w** of my enemies, Ps 138:7 639
Riches do not profit in the day of **w**, Pr 11:4 5678
expectation of the wicked is **w**. Pr 11:23 5678
A gentle answer turns away **w**, Pr 15:1 2534
king's **w** is like the roaring of a lion, Pr 19:12 2197
a bribe in the bosom, strong **w**. Pr 21:14 2534
W is fierce and anger is a flood, Pr 27:4 2534
"I have no **w**. Should someone give Is 27:4 2534
His **w** against all their armies; Is 34:2 2534
the sake of My name I delay My **w**, Is 48:9 639
a net, Full of the **w** of the LORD, Is 51:20 2534
will repay, **W** to His adversaries, Is 59:18 2534
For in My **w** I struck you, And in Is 60:10 7110a
anger And trampled them in My **w**; Is 63:3 2534
And My **w** upheld Me. Is 63:5 2534
And made them drunk in My **w**, Is 63:6 2534
Or else My **w** will go forth like fire Jer 4:4 2534
I am full of the **w** of the LORD; Jer 6:11 2534
My anger and My **w** will be poured Jer 7:20 2534
forsaken The generation of His **w**.' Jer 7:29 5678
At His **w** the earth quakes, And the Jer 10:10 7110a
Pour out Your **w** on the nations Jer 10:25 2534
as to turn away Your **w** from them. Jer 18:20 2534
anger and **w** and great indignation. Jer 21:5 2534
That My **w** may not go forth like Jer 21:12 2534
of the LORD has gone forth in **w**, Jer 23:19 2534
cup of the wine of **w** from My hand and Jer 25:15 2534
W has gone forth, A sweeping Jer 30:23 2534
a provocation of My anger and My **w** Jer 32:31 2534
driven them in My anger, in My **w** and Jer 32:37 2534
slain in My anger and in My **w**, Jer 33:5 2534
for great is the anger and the **w** Jer 36:7 2534
"As My anger and **w** have been Jer 42:18 2534
so My **w** will be poured out on you Jer 42:18 2534
'Therefore My **w** and My anger were Jer 44:6 2534
In His **w** He has thrown down The La 2:2 5678
He has poured out His **w** like fire. La 2:4 2534
Because of the rod of His **w**. La 3:1 5678
The LORD has accomplished His **w**, La 4:11 2534
and I will satisfy My **w** on them, Ezk 5:13 2534
when I have spent My **w** upon them. Ezk 5:13 2534
judgments against you in anger, **w** and Ezk 5:15 2534
Thus will I spend My **w** on them. Ezk 6:12 2534
will shortly pour out My **w** on you and Ezk 7:8 2534
for **w** is against all their Ezk 7:12 2740
for My **w** is against all their Ezk 7:14 2740
in the day of the **w** of the LORD. Ezk 7:19 5678
I indeed will deal in **w**. Ezk 8:18 2534
pouring out Your **w** on Jerusalem?" Ezk 9:8 2534
a violent wind break out in My **w**. Ezk 13:13 2534
and hailstones to consume *it* in **w**. Ezk 13:13 2534
"Thus I will spend My **w** on the Ezk 13:15 2534
and pour out My **w** in blood on it to Ezk 14:19 2534
you the blood of **w** and jealousy. Ezk 16:38 2534
resolved to pour out My **w** on them, Ezk 20:8 2534
Then I resolved to pour out My **w** Ezk 20:13 2534
resolved to pour out My **w** on them, Ezk 20:21 2534
arm and with **w** poured out, Ezk 20:33 2534
arm and with **w** poured out; Ezk 20:34 2534
and I will appease My **w**; Ezk 21:17 2534
blow on you with the fire of My **w**, Ezk 21:31 5678
you in My anger and in My **w** and Ezk 22:20 2534
blow on you with the fire of My **w**, Ezk 22:21 5678
have poured out My **w** on you.'" Ezk 22:22 2534
them with the fire of My **w**; Ezk 22:31 5678
that they may deal with you in **w**. Ezk 23:25 2534
w to come up to take vengeance, Ezk 24:8 2534
Until I have spent My **w** on you. Ezk 24:13 2534
to My anger and according to My **w**; Ezk 25:14 2534
"I will pour out My **w** on Sin, Ezk 30:15 2534
spoken in My jealousy and in My **w** Ezk 36:6 2534
I poured out My **w** on them for the Ezk 36:18 2534
In My zeal and in My blazing **w** I Ezk 38:19 5678
Nebuchadnezzar was filled with **w**, Da 3:19 2528
and rushed at him in his mighty **w**. Da 8:6 2534
let now Your anger and Your **w** turn Da 9:16 2534
will go forth with great **w** to destroy Da 11:44 2534
I will pour out My **w** like water. Hos 5:10 5678
midst, And I will not come in **w**. Hos 11:9 5892a
anger And took him away in My **w**. Hos 13:11 5678
will execute vengeance in anger and **w** Mi 5:15 2534
And He reserves **w** for His enemies. Na 1:2 2534
His **w** is poured out like fire And Na 1:6 2534
In **w** remember mercy. Hab 3:2 7267
Or *was* Your **w** against the sea, Hab 3:8 5678
A day of **w** is that day, A day of Zph 1:15 5678
them On the day of the LORD's **w**; Zph 1:18 5678
My **w** in the land of the north." Zch 6:8 7307
w came from the LORD of hosts. Zch 7:12 7110a
with great **w** I am jealous for her.' Zch 8:2 2534
your fathers provoked Me to **w**,' Zch 8:14 7107
you to flee from the **w** to come? Mt 3:7 *3709*
you to flee from the **w** to come? Lk 3:7 *3709*
the land and **w** to this people Lk 21:23 *3709*
but the **w** of God abides on him." Jn 3:36 *3709*
For the **w** of God is revealed from Ro 1:18 *3709*
storing up **w** for yourself in the day Ro 2:5 *3709*
in the day of **w** and revelation Ro 2:5 *3709*
unrighteousness, **w** and indignation. Ro 2:8 *3709*
who inflicts **w** is not unrighteous, Ro 3:5 *3709*
for the Law brings about **w**, Ro 4:15 *3709*
we shall be saved from the **w** *of God* Ro 5:9 *3709*
willing to demonstrate His **w** and Ro 9:22 *3709*
vessels of **w** prepared for destruction Ro 9:22 *3709*
but leave room for the **w** *of God,* Ro 12:19 *3709*
an avenger who brings **w** on the Ro 13:4 *3709*
subjection, not only because of **w**, Ro 13:5 *3709*
and were by nature children of **w**, Eph 2:3 *3709*
Let all bitterness and **w** and anger Eph 4:31 *2372*
because of these things the **w** of God Eph 5:6 *3709*
that the **w** of God will come upon Col 3:6 *3709*
anger, **w**, malice, slander, *and* Col 3:8 *2372*
rescues us from the **w** to come. 1Th 1:10 *3709*
But **w** has come upon them to the 1Th 2:16 *3709*
For God has not destined us for **w**, 1Th 5:9 *3709*
hands, without **w** and dissension. 1Tm 2:8 *3709*
AS I SWORE IN MY **W**, Heb 3:11 *3709*
"AS I SWORE IN MY **W**, Heb 4:3 *3709*
not fearing the **w** of the king; Heb 11:27 *2372*
and from the **w** of the Lamb; Rv 6:16 *3709*
the great day of their **w** has come, Rv 6:17 *3709*
were enraged, and Your **w** came, Rv 11:18 *3709*
come down to you, having great **w**, Rv 12:12 *2372*
drink of the wine of the **w** of God, Rv 14:10 *2372*
great wine press of the **w** of God. Rv 14:19 *2372*
in them the **w** of God is finished. Rv 15:1 *2372*
golden bowls full of the **w** of God, Rv 15:7 *2372*
the seven bowls of the **w** of God Rv 16:1 *2372*
cup of the wine of His fierce **w**. Rv 16:19 *3709*
wine press of the fierce **w** of God, Rv 19:15 *3709*

WRATHFUL
that He will not become **w** against Lv 10:6 7107
act with **w** hostility against you, Lv 26:28 2534
the LORD was **w** against you in order Dt 9:19 7107
vengeance on them with **w** rebukes; Ezk 25:17 2534
The LORD is avenging and **w**. Na 1:2 1167, 2534

WREAKING
with Joab were **w** destruction in order 2Sa 20:15 7843

WREATH
are a graceful **w** to your head And Pr 1:9 3880
do it to receive a perishable **w**, 1Co 9:25 *4735*

WREATHS
and oxen *were* **w** of hanging work. 1Ki 7:29 3914
cast supports with **w** at each side. 1Ki 7:30 3914
space on each, with **w** *all* around. 1Ki 7:36 3914

WRESTLED
I have **w** with my sister, Gn 30:8 6617
a man **w** with him until daybreak. Gn 32:24 79
dislocated while he **w** with him. Gn 32:25 79
he **w** with the angel and prevailed; Hos 12:4 8280

WRESTLINGS
"With mighty **w** I have wrestled Gn 30:8 5319

WRETCHED
to bring us in to this **w** place? Nu 20:5 7451a
attention, Laishah *and* **w** Anathoth! Is 10:30 6041
bring those wretches to a **w** end, Mt 21:41 *2560*
W man that I am! Who will set me Ro 7:24 *5005*
you do not know that you are **w** and Rv 3:17 *5005*

WRETCHEDNESS
and do not let me see my **w**." Nu 11:15 7463a

WRETCHES
bring those **w** to a wretched end, Mt 21:41 *2556*

WRING
to the altar, and **w** off its head Lv 1:15 4454

WRINKLE
no spot or **w** or any such thing; Eph 5:27 *4512*

WRISTS
two bracelets for her **w** weighing Gn 24:22 3027
the bracelets on his sister's **w**, Gn 24:30 3027
nose, and the bracelets on her **w**. Gn 24:47 3027
who sew *magic* bands on all **w** and Ezk 13:18 3027, 679

WRIT
away and given her a **w** of divorce, Jer 3:8 5612

WRITE
"**W** this in a book as a memorial and Ex 17:14 3789
and I will **w** on the tablets the Ex 34:1 3789
"**W** down these words, for in Ex 34:27 3789
then **w** these curses on a scroll, Nu 5:23 3789
You shall **w** each name on his rod, Nu 17:2 3789
and **w** Aaron's name on the rod of Nu 17:3 3789
"You shall **w** them on the Dt 6:9 3789
'I will **w** on the tablets the Dt 10:2 3789
"You shall **w** them on the Dt 11:20 3789
he shall **w** for himself a copy of Dt 17:18 3789
and **w** on them all the words of Dt 27:3 3789
"You shall **w** on the stones Dt 27:8 3789
w this song for yourselves, Dt 31:19 3789
and **w** a description of it according to Jos 18:4 3789
and that we might **w** down the names Ezr 5:10 3790
you **w** to the Jews as you see fit, Es 8:8 3789
You **w** bitter things against me Jb 13:26 3789
W them on the tablet of your heart. Pr 3:3 3789
W them on the tablet of your heart. Pr 7:3 3789
and to **w** words of truth correctly. Ec 12:10 3789
and **w** on it in ordinary letters: Is 8:1 3789
That a child could **w** them down. Is 10:19 3789
w it on a tablet before them And Is 30:8 3789
And another will **w** *on* his hand, Is 44:5 3789
'**W** this man down childless, A man Jer 22:30 3789
'**W** all the words which I have Jer 30:2 3789
and on their heart I will **w** it; Jer 31:33 3789
'Take a scroll and **w** on it all Jer 36:2 3789
how did you **w** all these words? Jer 36:17 3789
and **w** on it all the former words Jer 36:28 3789
"Son of man, **w** the name of the Ezk 24:2 3789
yourself one stick and **w** on it, Ezk 37:16 3789
take another stick and **w** on it, Ezk 37:16 3789
"The sticks on which you **w** Ezk 37:20 3789
And **w** *it* in their sight, so that Ezk 43:11 3789
TO **W** A CERTIFICATE OF DIVORCE AND Mk 10:4 *1125*
to **w** *it* out for you in consecutive Lk 1:3 *1125*
and sit down quickly and **w** fifty.' Lk 16:6 *1125*
'Take your bill, and **w** eighty.' Lk 16:7 *1125*
"Do not **w**, 'The King of the Jews'; Jn 19:21 *1125*
but that we **w** to them that they Ac 15:20 *1989*
about him to **w** to my lord. Ac 25:26 *1125*
place, I may have something to **w**. Ac 25:26 *1125*
I, Tertius, who **w** this letter, Ro 16:22 *1125*
not **w** these things to shame you, 1Co 4:14 *1125*
recognize that the things which I **w** 1Co 14:37 *1125*
For we **w** nothing else to you than 2Co 1:13 *1125*
For it is superfluous for me to **w** 2Co 9:1 *1125*
To **w** the same things *again* is no Php 3:1 *1125*
w this greeting with my own hand. Col 4:18 *1125*
no need for *anyone* to **w** to you, 1Th 4:9 *1125*
w this greeting with my own hand, 2Th 3:17 *1125*
this is the way I **w**. 2Th 3:17 *1125*
but in case I am delayed, *I* **w** so 1Tm 3:15 *1125*
in your obedience, I **w** to you, Phm 1:21 *1125*
I WILL **W** THEM ON THEIR HEARTS. Heb 8:10 *1924*
ON THEIR MIND I WILL **W** THEM," Heb 10:16 *1924*
These things we **w**, 1Jn 1:4 *1125*
have many things to **w** to you, 2Jn 1:12 *1125*
I had many things to **w** to you, 3Jn 1:13 *1125*
to **w** *them* to you with pen and ink; 3Jn 1:13 *1125*
while I was making every effort to **w** Jude 1:3 *1125*
I felt the necessity to **w** to you Jude 1:3 *1125*
"**W** in a book what you see, and Rv 1:11 *1125*
"Therefore **w** the things which you Rv 1:19 *1125*
angel of the church in Ephesus **w**: Rv 2:1 *1125*
angel of the church in Smyrna **w**: Rv 2:8 *1125*
angel of the church in Pergamum **w**: Rv 2:12 *1125*
angel of the church in Thyatira **w**: Rv 2:18 *1125*
angel of the church in Sardis **w**: Rv 3:1 *1125*
of the church in Philadelphia **w**: Rv 3:7 *1125*
w on him the name of My God, Rv 3:12 *1125*
angel of the church in Laodicea **w**: Rv 3:14 *1125*
had spoken, I was about to **w**; Rv 10:4 *1125*
have spoken and do not **w** them." Rv 10:4 *1125*
"**W**, 'Blessed are the dead who die Rv 14:13 *1125*
"**W**, 'Blessed are those who are Rv 19:9 *1125*
"**W**, for these words are faithful Rv 21:5 *1125*

WRITER
My tongue is the pen of a ready **w**. Ps 45:1 5613b

WRITES
and he **w** her a certificate of Dt 24:1 3789
and **w** her a certificate of divorce Dt 24:3 3789
For Moses **w** that the man who Ro 10:5 *1125*

WRITHE
They will **w** like a woman in labor, Is 13:8 2342a
Sin will **w** in anguish, Thebes will Ezk 30:16 2342a
"**W** and labor to give birth, Mi 4:10 2342a
Gaza too will **w** in great pain; Zch 9:5 2342a

WRITHED
and the queen **w** in great anguish. Es 4:4 2342a
We were pregnant, we **w** *in labor,* Is 26:18 2342a

WRITHES
wicked man **w** in pain all *his* days, Jb 15:20 2342a
She **w** *and* cries out in her labor Is 26:17 2342a
So the land quakes and **w**, Jer 51:29 2342a

WRITING
and the **w** was God's writing Ex 32:16 4385
God's **w** engraved on the tablets. Ex 32:16 4385
on the tablets, like the former **w**, Dt 10:4 4385
when Moses finished **w** the words of Dt 31:24 3789
in **w** by His hand upon me, 1Ch 28:19 3791
according to the **w** of David king 2Ch 35:4 3791
to the **w** of his son Solomon. 2Ch 35:4 4385
his kingdom, and also *put it* in **w**, 2Ch 36:22 4385
his kingdom, and also *put it* in **w**, Ezr 1:1 4385
We are making an agreement in **w**; Ne 9:38 3772
the **w** of many books is endless, Ec 12:12 6213a
A **w** of Hezekiah king of Judah after Is 38:9 4385
linen with a **w** case at his loins. Ezk 9:2 5613b
at whose loins was the **w** case. Ezk 9:3 5613b
loins was the **w** case reported, Ezk 9:11 7083
a man's hand emerged and began **w** Da 5:5 3790
back of the hand that did the **w**. Da 5:5 3790
is inscribed in the **w** of truth. Da 10:21 3791
according to the **w** on one side, Zch 5:3
to the **w** on the other side. Zch 5:3
And I am not **w** these things so 1Co 9:15 *1125*
I am **w** these things while absent, 2Co 13:10 *1125*
(Now in what I am **w** to you, Ga 1:20 *1125*
I am **w** to you with my own hand. Ga 6:11 *1125*
I am **w** these things to you, hoping 1Tm 3:14 *1125*
Paul, am **w** this with my own hand, Phm 1:19 *1125*
the second letter I am **w** to you in 2Pe 3:1 *1125*
I am **w** these things to you so 1Jn 2:1 *1125*
I am not **w** a new commandment to 1Jn 2:7 *1125*
I am **w** a new commandment to you, 1Jn 2:8 *1125*
I am **w** to you, little children, 1Jn 2:12 *1125*
I am **w** to you, fathers, because 1Jn 2:13 *1125*
I am **w** to you, young men, because 1Jn 2:13 *1125*
not as though *I were* **w** to you 2Jn 1:5 *1125*

WRITINGS
"But if you do not believe his **w**, Jn 5:47 *1121*
you have known the sacred **w** which 2Tm 3:15 *1121*

WRITTEN
I have **w** for their instruction." Ex 24:12 3789
of stone, **w** by the finger of God. Ex 31:18 3789
which were **w** on both sides; Ex 32:15 3789
were **w** on one *side* and the other. Ex 32:15 3789
from Your book which You have **w**!" Ex 32:32 3789
of stone **w** by the finger of God; Dt 9:10 3789
this law which are **w** in this book, Dt 28:58 3789
not **w** in the book of this law, Dt 28:61 3789

w in this book will rest on him,	**Dt 29:20**	3789
are **w** in this book of the law.	**Dt 29:21**	3789
curse which is **w** in this book;	**Dt 29:27**	3789
are **w** in this book of the law,	**Dt 30:10**	3789
according to all that is **w** in it;	**Jos 1:8**	3789
as it is **w** in the book of the law	**Jos 8:31**	3789
the law of Moses, which he had **w**,	**Jos 8:32**	3789
that is **w** in the book of the law.	**Jos 8:34**	3789
Is it not **w** in the book of Jashar?	**Jos 10:13**	3789
to keep and do all that is **w** in	**Jos 23:6**	3789
it is **w** in the book of Jashar.	**2Sa 1:18**	3789
He had **w** in the letter,	**2Sa 11:15**	3789
to what is **w** in the Law of Moses,	**1Ki 2:3**	3789
are they not **w** in the book of the	**1Ki 11:41**	3789
they are **w** in the Book of the	**1Ki 14:19**	3789
are they not **w** in the Book of the	**1Ki 14:29**	3789
are they not **w** in the Book of the	**1Ki 15:7**	3789
are they not **w** in the Book of the	**1Ki 15:23**	3789
are they not **w** in the Book of the	**1Ki 15:31**	3789
are they not **w** in the Book of the	**1Ki 16:5**	3789
are they not **w** in the Book of the	**1Ki 16:14**	3789
are they not **w** in the Book of the	**1Ki 16:20**	3789
are they not **w** in the Book of the	**1Ki 16:27**	3789
just as it was **w** in the letters	**1Ki 21:11**	3789
are they not **w** in the Book of the	**1Ki 22:39**	3789
are they not **w** in the Book of the	**1Ki 22:45**	3789
are they not **w** in the Book of the	**2Ki 1:18**	3789
are they not **w** in the Book of the	**2Ki 8:23**	3789
are they not **w** in the Book of the	**2Ki 10:34**	3789
are they not **w** in the Book of the	**2Ki 12:19**	3789
are they not **w** in the Book of the	**2Ki 13:8**	3789
are they not **w** in the Book of the	**2Ki 13:12**	3789
according to what is **w** in the book	**2Ki 14:6**	3789
are they not **w** in the Book of the	**2Ki 14:15**	3789
are they not **w** in the Book of the	**2Ki 14:18**	3789
are they not **w** in the Book of the	**2Ki 14:28**	3789
are they not **w** in the Book of the	**2Ki 15:6**	3789
behold they are **w** in the Book of	**2Ki 15:11**	3789
behold they are **w** in the Book of	**2Ki 15:15**	3789
are they not **w** in the Book of the	**2Ki 15:21**	3789
behold they are **w** in the Book of	**2Ki 15:26**	3789
they are **w** in the Book of the	**2Ki 15:31**	3789
are they not **w** in the Book of the	**2Ki 15:36**	3789
are they not **w** in the Book of the	**2Ki 16:19**	3789
are they not **w** in the Book of the	**2Ki 20:20**	3789
are they not **w** in the Book of the	**2Ki 21:17**	3789
are they not **w** in the Book of the	**2Ki 21:25**	3789
to all that is **w** concerning us."	**2Ki 22:13**	3789
covenant that were **w** in this book.	**2Ki 23:3**	3789
w in this book of the covenant."	**2Ki 23:21**	3789
w in the book that Hilkiah the priest	**2Ki 23:24**	3789
are they not **w** in the Book of the	**2Ki 23:28**	3789
are they not **w** in the Book of the	**2Ki 24:5**	3789
they are **w** in the Book of the	**1Ch 9:1**	3789
that is **w** in the law of the LORD,	**1Ch 16:40**	3789
are **w** in the chronicles of Samuel	**1Ch 29:29**	3789
are they not **w** in the records of	**2Ch 9:29**	3789
are they not **w** in the records of	**2Ch 12:15**	3789
and his ways and his words are **w**	**2Ch 13:22**	3789
they are **w** in the Book of the	**2Ch 16:11**	3789
they are **w** in the annals of Jehu	**2Ch 20:34**	3789
as it is **w** in the law of Moses	**2Ch 23:18**	3789
they are **w** in the treatise of the	**2Ch 24:27**	3789
but *did* as it is **w** in the law in	**2Ch 25:4**	3789
are they not **w** in the Book of the	**2Ch 25:26**	3789
Isaiah, the son of Amoz, has **w**.	**2Ch 26:22**	3789
they are **w** in the Book of the	**2Ch 27:7**	3789
they are **w** in the Book of the	**2Ch 28:26**	3789
as it is **w** in the law of the LORD.	**2Ch 31:3**	3789
are **w** in the vision of Isaiah	**2Ch 32:32**	3789
are **w** in the records of the Hozai.	**2Ch 33:19**	3789
to all that is **w** in this book."	**2Ch 34:21**	3789
even all the curses **w** in the book	**2Ch 34:24**	3789
of the covenant **w** in this book.	**2Ch 34:31**	3789
as it is **w** in the book of Moses.	**2Ch 35:12**	3789
are also **w** in the Lamentations.	**2Ch 35:25**	3789
as **w** in the law of the LORD,	**2Ch 35:26**	3789
are they not **w** in the Book of the	**2Ch 35:27**	3789
they are **w** in the Book of the	**2Ch 36:8**	3789
as it is **w** in the law of Moses,	**Ezr 3:2**	3789
the Feast of Booths, as it is **w**,	**Ezr 3:4**	3789
and the text of the letter was **w**	**Ezr 4:7**	3789
and then a **w** reply be returned	**Ezr 5:5**	5407
to him in which it was **w** thus:	**Ezr 5:7**	3790
and there was **w** in it as follows:	**Ezr 6:2**	3790
as it is **w** in the book of Moses.	**Ezr 6:18**	3792
In it was **w**, "It is reported among	**Ne 6:6**	3789
They found **w** in the law how	**Ne 8:14**	3789
to make booths, as it is **w**."	**Ne 8:15**	3789
our God, as it is **w** in the law;	**Ne 10:34**	3789
our flocks as it is **w** in the law,	**Ne 10:36**	3789
and there was found **w** in it that	**Ne 13:1**	3789
let it be **w** in the laws of Persia and	**Es 1:19**	3789
and it was **w** in the Book of the	**Es 2:23**	3789
and it was **w** just as Haman	**Es 3:12**	3789
being **w** in the name of King	**Es 3:12**	3789
It was found **w** what Mordecai	**Es 6:2**	3789
let it be **w** to revoke the letters	**Es 8:5**	3789
for a decree which is **w** in the	**Es 8:8**	3789
and it was **w** according to all that	**Es 8:9**	3789
and what Mordecai had **w** to them.	**Es 9:23**	3789
Purim, and it was **w** in the book.	**Es 9:32**	3789
are they not **w** in the Book of the	**Es 10:2**	3789
"Oh that my words were **w**!	**Jb 19:23**	3789
which my adversary has **w**,	**Jb 31:35**	3789
scroll of the book it is **w** of me.	**Ps 40:7**	3789
be **w** for the generation to come,	**Ps 102:18**	3789
And in Your book were all **w**	**Ps 139:16**	3789
To execute on them the judgment **w**;	**Ps 149:9**	3789
Have I not **w** to you excellent	**Pr 22:20**	3789
"Behold, it is **w** before Me, I	**Is 65:6**	3789
is **w** down with an iron stylus;	**Jer 17:1**	3789
turn away on earth will be **w** down,	**Jer 17:13**	3789
it, all that is **w** in this book which	**Jer 25:13**	3789
the scroll which you have **w** at my	**Jer 36:6**	3789
w at the dictation of Jeremiah,	**Jer 36:27**	3789
'Why have you **w** on it that the	**Jer 36:29**	3789
when he had **w** down these words in	**Jer 45:1**	3789
have been **w** concerning Babylon.	**Jer 51:60**	3789
it was **w** on the front and back,	**Ezk 2:10**	3789
and **w** on it were lamentations,	**Ezk 2:10**	3789
nor will they be **w** down in the	**Ezk 13:9**	3789
and this inscription was **w** out.	**Da 5:24**	7560
is the inscription that was **w** out:	**Da 5:25**	7560
along with the oath which is **w** in	**Da 9:11**	3789
"As it is **w** in the law of Moses,	**Da 9:13**	3789
who is found **w** in the book,	**Da 12:1**	3789
and a book of remembrance was **w**	**Mal 3:16**	3789
what has been **w** by the prophet:	**Mt 2:5**	*1125*
"It is **w**, 'MAN SHALL NOT LIVE ON	**Mt 4:4**	*1125*
for it is **w**, 'HE WILL COMMAND HIS ANGELS	**Mt 4:6**	*1125*
"On the other hand, it is **w**,	**Mt 4:7**	*1125*
For it is **w**, 'YOU SHALL WORSHIP THE	**Mt 4:10**	*1125*
is the one about whom it is **w**,	**Mt 11:10**	*1125*
It is **w**, 'MY HOUSE SHALL BE CALLED	**Mt 21:13**	*1125*
is to go, just as it is **w** of Him;	**Mt 26:24**	*1125*
of Me this night, for it is **w**,	**Mt 26:31**	*1125*
As it is **w** in Isaiah the prophet:	**Mk 1:2**	*1125*
of you hypocrites, as it is **w**:	**Mk 7:6**	*1125*
And *yet* how is it **w** of the Son of	**Mk 9:12**	*1125*
wished, just as it is **w** of him."	**Mk 9:13**	*1125*
"Is it not **w**, 'MY HOUSE SHALL BE	**Mk 11:17**	*1125*
is to go just as it is **w** of Him;	**Mk 14:21**	*1125*
all fall away, because it is **w**,	**Mk 14:27**	*1125*
(as it is **w** in the Law of the	**Lk 2:23**	*1125*
as it is **w** in the book of the	**Lk 3:4**	*1125*
"It is **w**, 'MAN SHALL NOT LIVE ON	**Lk 4:4**	*1125*
"It is **w**, 'YOU SHALL WORSHIP THE	**Lk 4:8**	*1125*
it is **w**, 'HE WILL COMMAND HIS ANGELS	**Lk 4:10**	*1125*
found the place where it was **w**,	**Lk 4:17**	*1125*
is the one about whom it is **w**,	**Lk 7:27**	*1125*
"What is **w** in the Law?	**Lk 10:26**	*1125*
and all things which are **w** through	**Lk 18:31**	*1125*
"It is **w**, 'AND MY HOUSE SHALL BE	**Lk 19:46**	*1125*
"What then is this that is **w**:	**Lk 20:17**	*1125*
things which are **w** will be fulfilled.	**Lk 21:22**	*1125*
this which is **w** must be fulfilled in	**Lk 22:37**	*1125*
that all things which are **w** about	**Lk 24:44**	*1125*
"Thus it is **w**, that the Christ	**Lk 24:46**	*1125*
disciples remembered that it was **w**,	**Jn 2:17**	*1125*
as it is **w**, 'HE GAVE THEM BREAD	**Jn 6:31**	*1125*
"It is **w** in the prophets,	**Jn 6:45**	*1125*
"Even in your law it has been **w** that	**Jn 8:17**	*1125*
"Has it not been **w** in your Law,	**Jn 10:34**	*1125*
a young donkey, sat on it; as it is **w**,	**Jn 12:14**	*1125*
that these things were **w** of Him,	**Jn 12:16**	*1125*
word that is **w** in their Law,	**Jn 15:25**	*1125*
It was **w**, "JESUS THE	**Jn 19:19**	*1125*
and it was **w** in Hebrew, Latin *and*	**Jn 19:20**	*1125*
"What I have **w** I have written."	**Jn 19:22**	*1125*
"What I have written I have **w**."	**Jn 19:22**	*1125*
which are not **w** in this book;	**Jn 20:30**	*1125*
but these have been **w** so that you may	**Jn 20:31**	*1125*
which if they were **w** in detail,	**Jn 21:25**	*1125*
contain the books that would be **w**.	**Jn 21:25**	*1125*
"For it is **w** in the book of Psalms,	**Ac 1:20**	*1125*
is **w** in the book of the prophets,	**Ac 7:42**	*1125*
out all that was **w** concerning Him,	**Ac 13:29**	*1125*
it is also **w** in the second Psalm,	**Ac 13:33**	*1125*
Prophets agree, just as it is **w**,	**Ac 15:15**	*1125*
it is **w**, 'YOU SHALL NOT SPEAK EVIL	**Ac 23:5**	*1125*
and that is **w** in the Prophets;	**Ac 24:14**	*1125*
as it is **w**, "BUT THE RIGHTEOUS *man*	**Ro 1:17**	*1125*
work of the Law **w** in their hearts,	**Ro 2:15**	*1123*
BECAUSE OF YOU," just as it is **w**.	**Ro 2:24**	*1125*
man *be found* a liar, as it is **w**,	**Ro 3:4**	*1125*
it is **w**, "THERE IS NONE RIGHTEOUS,	**Ro 3:10**	*1125*
it is **w**, "A FATHER OF MANY NATIONS	**Ro 4:17**	*1125*
not for his sake only was it **w** that	**Ro 4:23**	*1125*
Just as it is **w**,	**Ro 8:36**	*1125*
Just as it is **w**,	**Ro 9:13**	*1125*
just as it is **w**,	**Ro 9:33**	*1125*
Just as it is **w**,	**Ro 10:15**	*1125*
just as it is **w**,	**Ro 11:8**	*1125*
just as it is **w**,	**Ro 11:26**	*1125*
for it is **w**, "VENGEANCE IS MINE,	**Ro 12:19**	*1125*
it is **w**, "AS I LIVE, SAYS THE LORD,	**Ro 14:11**	*1125*
but as it is **w**, "THE REPROACHES OF	**Ro 15:3**	*1125*
For whatever was **w** in earlier times	**Ro 15:4**	*4270*
times was **w** for our instruction,	**Ro 15:4**	*1125*
as it is **w**, "THEREFORE I WILL GIVE	**Ro 15:9**	*1125*
But I have **w** very boldly to you on	**Ro 15:15**	*1125*
as it is **w**, "THEY WHO HAD NO NEWS	**Ro 15:21**	*1125*
For it is **w**, "I WILL DESTROY THE	**1Co 1:19**	*1125*
that, just as it is **w**,	**1Co 1:31**	*1125*
but just as it is **w**,	**1Co 2:9**	*1125*
it is **w**, "*He is* THE ONE WHO CATCHES	**1Co 3:19**	*1125*
learn not to exceed what is **w**,	**1Co 4:6**	*1125*
For it is **w** in the Law of Moses,	**1Co 9:9**	*1125*
Yes, for our sake it was **w**,	**1Co 9:10**	*1125*
as it is **w**, "THE PEOPLE SAT DOWN	**1Co 10:7**	*1125*
they were **w** for our instruction,	**1Co 10:11**	*1125*
In the Law it is **w**,	**1Co 14:21**	*1125*
So also it is **w**,	**1Co 15:45**	*1125*
come about the saying that is **w**,	**1Co 15:54**	*1125*
are our letter, **w** in our hearts,	**2Co 3:2**	*1449*
cared for by us, **w** not with ink but	**2Co 3:3**	*1449*
of faith, according to what is **w**,	**2Co 4:13**	*1125*
as it is **w**, "HE WHO *gathered* MUCH	**2Co 8:15**	*1125*
as it is **w**, "HE SCATTERED ABROAD,	**2Co 9:9**	*1125*
for it is **w**, "CURSED IS EVERYONE	**Ga 3:10**	*1125*
THINGS **W** IN THE BOOK OF THE LAW,	**Ga 3:10**	*1125*
for it is **w**, "CURSED IS EVERYONE	**Ga 3:13**	*1125*
it is **w** that Abraham had two sons,	**Ga 4:22**	*1125*
it is **w**, "REJOICE, BARREN WOMAN	**Ga 4:27**	*1125*
need of anything to be **w** to you.	**1Th 5:1**	*1125*
SCROLL OF THE BOOK IT IS **W** OF ME)	**Heb 10:7**	*1125*
for I have **w** to you briefly.	**Heb 13:22**	*1989*
because it is **w**,	**1Pe 1:16**	*1125*
I have **w** to you briefly, exhorting	**1Pe 5:12**	*1125*
I have **w** to you, children, because	**1Jn 2:13**	*1125*
I have **w** to you, fathers, because	**1Jn 2:14**	*1125*
I have **w** to you, young men,	**1Jn 2:14**	*1125*
I have not **w** to you because you do	**1Jn 2:21**	*1125*
These things I have **w** to you	**1Jn 2:26**	*1125*
These things I have **w** to you who	**1Jn 5:13**	*1125*
heed the things which are **w** in it;	**Rv 1:3**	*1125*
and a new name **w** on the stone	**Rv 2:17**	*1125*
a book **w** inside and on the back,	**Rv 5:1**	*1125*
everyone whose name has not been **w**	**Rv 13:8**	*1125*
His Father **w** on their foreheads.	**Rv 14:1**	*1125*
on her forehead a name *was* **w**,	**Rv 17:5**	*1125*
whose name has not been **w** in the	**Rv 17:8**	*1125*
and He has a name **w** *on Him* which	**Rv 19:12**	*1125*
and on His thigh He has a name **w**,	**Rv 19:16**	*1125*
things which were **w** in the books,	**Rv 20:12**	*1125*
not found **w** in the book of life,	**Rv 20:15**	*1125*
and names *were* **w** on them, which	**Rv 21:12**	*1924*
are **w** in the Lamb's book of life.	**Rv 21:27**	*1125*
plagues which are **w** in this book;	**Rv 22:18**	*1125*
city, which are **w** in this book.	**Rv 22:19**	*1125*

WRONG

"May the **w** done me be upon you.	**Gn 16:5**	2555
You have done **w** in doing this.' "	**Gn 44:5**	7489a
all the **w** which we did to him!"	**Gn 50:15**	7463a
their sin, for they did you **w**."	**Gn 50:17**	7463a
not **w** a stranger or oppress him,	**Ex 22:21**	3238
your land, you shall not do him **w**.	**Lv 19:33**	3238
'You shall do no **w** in judgment, in	**Lv 19:35**	5766
hand, you shall not **w** one another.	**Lv 25:14**	3238
'So you shall not **w** one another,	**Lv 25:17**	3238
restitution in full for his **w** and	**Nu 5:7**	817
restitution may be made for the **w**,	**Nu 5:8**	817
restitution which is made for the **w**	**Nu 5:8**	817
me **w** by making war against me;	**Jg 11:27**	7463a
because this **w** in sending me away	**2Sa 13:16**	7463a
what your servant did **w** on the day	**2Sa 19:19**	5753b
and it is I who have done **w**;	**2Sa 24:17**	5753b
"I have done **w**. Withdraw from me;	**2Ki 18:14**	2398
since there is no **w** in my hands,	**1Ch 12:17**	2555
me; You are not ashamed to **w** me.	**Jb 19:3**	1970
the plans by which you would **w** me.	**Jb 21:27**	2554
And from the Almighty to do **w**.	**Jb 34:10**	5766
'You have done **w**'?	**Jb 36:23**	5767b
not put forth their hands to do **w**.	**Ps 125:3**	5767b
"I have done no **w**."	**Pr 30:20**	205
through Baal he did **w** and died.	**Hos 13:1**	816
will do no **w** And tell no lies,	**Zph 3:13**	5767b
who covers his garment with **w**,"	**Mal 2:16**	2555
'Friend, I am doing you no **w**;	**Mt 20:13**	*91*
but this man has done nothing **w**."	**Lk 23:41**	*824*
testify of the **w**; but if rightly,	**Jn 18:23**	*2556*
a matter of **w** or of vicious crime,	**Ac 18:14**	*92*
"We find nothing **w** with this man;	**Ac 23:9**	*2556*
there is anything **w** about the man,	**Ac 25:5**	*824*
I have done no **w** to *the* Jews, as	**Ac 25:10**	*91*
Love does no **w** to a neighbor;	**Ro 13:10**	*2556*
you yourselves **w** and defraud.	**1Co 6:8**	*91*
take into account a **w** *suffered*,	**1Co 13:5**	*2556*
what zeal, what avenging of **w**!	**2Co 7:11**	*1557*
Forgive me this **w**!	**2Co 12:13**	*93*
we pray to God that you do no **w**;	**2Co 13:7**	*2556*
You have done me no **w**;	**Ga 4:12**	*91*
For he who does **w** will receive the	**Col 3:25**	*91*
receive the consequences of the **w**	**Col 3:25**	*91*
because you ask with **w** motives,	**Jas 4:3**	*2560*
rather than for doing what is **w**.	**1Pe 3:17**	*2554*
w as the wages of doing wrong.	**2Pe 2:13**	*91*
wrong as the wages of doing **w**.	**2Pe 2:13**	*93*
"Let the one who does **w**,	**Rv 22:11**	*91*
one who does wrong, still do **w**;	**Rv 22:11**	*91*

WRONGDOER

grasp of the **w** and ruthless man,	**Ps 71:4**	5765
"If, then, I am a **w** and have	**Ac 25:11**	*91*

WRONGDOERS

Be not envious toward **w**.	**Ps 37:1**	5767b
Gilead is a city of **w**,	**Hos 6:8**	205

WRONGDOING

against a man to accuse him of **w**,	**Dt 19:16**	5627
wicked is thrust down by his **w**,	**Pr 14:32**	7463a

WRONGED

and give *it* to him whom he has **w**.	**Nu 5:7**	816
"Queen Vashti has **w** not only the	**Es 1:16**	5753b
Know then that God has **w** me And	**Jb 19:6**	5791
and the widow they have **w** in you.	**Ezk 22:7**	3238
and they have **w** the poor and needy	**Ezk 22:29**	3238
Why not rather be **w**?	**1Co 6:7**	*91*
we **w** no one, we corrupted no one,	**2Co 7:2**	*91*
able to teach, patient when **w**,	**2Tm 2:24**	*420*
But if he has **w** you in any way or	**Phm 1:18**	*91*

WRONGFULLY

not let those who are **w** my enemies	**Ps 35:19**	8267
And many are those who hate me **w**.	**Ps 38:19**	8267
are powerful, being **w** my enemies	**Ps 69:4**	8267

WRONGLY
"If I have spoken **w**, Jn 18:23 *2560*

WRONGS
"He **w** the barren woman And does Jb 24:21 7462a
And my **w** are not hidden from You. Ps 69:5 819

WROTE
Moses **w** down all the words of Ex 24:4 3789
And he **w** on the tablets the words Ex 34:28 3789
He **w** them on two tablets of stone. Dt 4:13 3789
He **w** them on two tablets of Dt 5:22 3789
"He **w** on the tablets, like Dt 10:4 3789
So Moses **w** this law and gave it to Dt 31:9 3789
So Moses **w** this song the same day, Dt 31:22 3789
He **w** there on the stones a Jos 8:32 3789
And Joshua **w** these words in the Jos 24:26 3789
Then *the youth* **w** down for him the Jg 8:14 3789
and **w** *them* in the book and placed 1Sa 10:25 3789
morning David **w** a letter to Joab 2Sa 11:14 3789
So she **w** letters in Ahab's name 1Ki 21:8 3789
Now she **w** in the letters, saying, 1Ki 21:9 3789
And Jehu **w** letters and sent *them* 2Ki 10:1 3789
Then he **w** a letter to them a 2Ki 10:6 3789
commandment which He **w** for you, 2Ki 17:37 3789
and **w** letters also to Ephraim and 2Ch 30:1 3789
He also **w** letters to insult the 2Ch 32:17 3789
they **w** an accusation against the Ezr 4:6 3789
w to Artaxerxes king of Persia; Ezr 4:7 3789
Shimshai the scribe **w** a letter against Ezr 4:8 3790
then **w** Rehum the commander Ezr 4:9
which he **w** to destroy the Jews who Es 8:5 3789
w in the name of King Ahasuerus, Es 8:10 3789
w with full authority to confirm Es 9:29 3789
and Baruch **w** on a scroll Jer 36:4 3789
I **w** them with ink on the book." Jer 36:18 3789
and he **w** on it at the dictation of Jer 36:32 3789
So Jeremiah **w** in a single scroll Jer 51:60 3789
the king **w** to all the peoples, Da 6:25 3790
then he **w** the dream down *and* Da 7:1 3790
Though I **w** for him ten thousand Hos 8:12 3789
heart he **w** you this commandment. Mk 10:5 *1125*
Moses **w** for us that IF A MAN'S Mk 12:19 *1125*
for a tablet and **w** as follows, Lk 1:63 *1125*
Moses **w** for us that IF A MAN'S Lk 20:28 *1125*
the Law and *also* the Prophets **w** Jn 1:45 *1125*
would believe Me, for he **w** about Me. Jn 5:46 *1125*
with His finger **w** on the ground. Jn 8:6 *2608b*
stooped down and **w** on the ground. Jn 8:8 *1125*
Pilate also **w** an inscription Jn 19:19 *1125*
these things and **w** these things Jn 21:24 *1125*
w to the disciples to welcome him; Ac 18:27 *1125*
Gentiles who have believed, we **w**, Ac 21:25 *1989*
he **w** a letter having this form: Ac 23:25 *1125*
I **w** you in my letter not to 1Co 5:9 *1125*
I **w** to you not to associate with 1Co 5:11 *1125*
the things about which you **w**, 1Co 7:1 *1125*
This is the very thing I **w** you, 2Co 2:3 *1125*
heart I **w** to you with many tears; 2Co 2:4 *1125*
For to this end also I **w**, so that 2Co 2:9 *1125*
So although I **w** to you, *it was* not 2Co 7:12 *1125*
mystery, as I **w** before in brief. Eph 3:3 *4270*
to the wisdom given him, **w** to you, 2Pe 3:15 *1125*
I **w** something to the church; 3Jn 1:9 *1125*

WROUGHT
them, all kinds of **w** articles. Nu 31:51 4639
You have **w** all this greatness, 1Ch 17:19 6213a
Which You have **w** for those who Ps 31:19 6466
has **w** desolations in the earth. Ps 46:8 7760
He **w** wonders before their fathers In Ps 78:12 6213a
w in the depths of the earth; Ps 139:15 7551
w iron, cassia and sweet cane Ezk 27:19 6219
as having been **w** in God." Jn 3:21 *2038b*

Y

YARDS
but about one hundred **y** away, Jn 21:8 *4083*
measured its wall, seventy-two **y**, Rv 21:17 *4083*

YEA
Y, for all the joyful houses Is 32:13 3588

YEAR
the six hundredth **y** of Noah's life, Gn 7:11 8141
in the six hundred and first **y**, Gn 8:13 8141
the thirteenth **y** they rebelled. Gn 14:4 8141
In the fourteenth **y** Gn 14:5 8141
"Bring Me a three **y** old heifer, Gn 15:9 8027
and a three **y** old female goat, Gn 15:9 8027
goat, and a three **y** old ram, Gn 15:9 8027
to you at this season next **y**." Gn 17:21 8141
return to you at this time next **y**; Gn 18:10 2416a
to you, at this time next **y**, Gn 18:14 2416a
in the same **y** a hundredfold. Gn 26:12 8141
Now before the **y** of famine came, Gn 41:50 8141
for all their livestock that **y**. Gn 47:17 8141
When that **y** was ended, they Gn 47:18 8141
they came to him the next **y** and said Gn 47:18 8141
the first month of the **y** to you. Ex 12:2 8141
be an unblemished male a **y** old; Ex 12:5 8141
its appointed time from **y** to year. Ex 13:10 3117
its appointed time from year to **y**. Ex 13:10 3117
but *on* the seventh **y** you shall let Ex 23:11 7637
"Three times a **y** you shall Ex 23:14 8141
Ingathering at the end of the **y** when Ex 23:16 8141
"Three times a **y** all your males Ex 23:17 8141
them out before you in a single **y**, Ex 23:29 8141
two one **y** old lambs each day, Ex 29:38 8141
atonement on its horns once a **y**; Ex 30:10 8141
sin offering of atonement once a **y** Ex 30:10 8141
Ingathering at the turn of the **y**. Ex 34:22 8141
"Three times a **y** all your males Ex 34:23 8141
you go up three times a **y** to appear Ex 34:24 8141
the first month of the second **y**, Ex 40:17 8141
a calf and a lamb, both one **y** old, Lv 9:3 8141
y old lamb for a burnt offering and Lv 12:6 8141
for all their sins once every **y**." Lv 16:34 8141
in the fourth **y** all its fruit shall be Lv 19:24 8141
In the fifth **y** you are to eat of its Lv 19:25 8141
you shall offer a male lamb one **y** old Lv 23:12 8141
y old male lambs without defect, Lv 23:18 8141
and two male lambs one **y** old for a Lv 23:19 8141
the LORD for seven days in the **y**. Lv 23:41 8141
but during the seventh **y** the land Lv 25:4 8141
land shall have a sabbatical **y**. Lv 25:5 8141
shall thus consecrate the fiftieth **y** Lv 25:10 8141
have the fiftieth **y** as a jubilee; Lv 25:11 8141
'On this **y** of jubilee each of you Lv 25:13 8141
are we going to eat on the seventh **y** Lv 25:20 8141
My blessing for you in the sixth **y** Lv 25:21 8141
'When you are sowing the eighth **y**, Lv 25:22 8141
eating *the old* until the ninth **y** Lv 25:22 8141
purchaser until the **y** of jubilee; Lv 25:28 8141
until a full **y** from its sale; Lv 25:29 8141
of redemption lasts a full **y**. Lv 25:29 3117
him within the space of a full **y**, Lv 25:30 8141
with you until the **y** of jubilee. Lv 25:40 8141
calculate from the **y** when he sold Lv 25:50 8141
to him up to the **y** of jubilee; Lv 25:50 8141
remain until the **y** of jubilee, Lv 25:52 8141
y by year he shall be with him; Lv 25:53 8141
year by **y** he shall be with him; Lv 25:53 8141
still go out in the **y** of jubilee, Lv 25:54 8141
his field as of the **y** of jubilee, Lv 27:17 8141
are left until the **y** of jubilee; Lv 27:18 8141
valuation up to the **y** of jubilee; Lv 27:23 8141
'In the **y** of jubilee the field Lv 27:24 8141
in the second **y** after they had Nu 1:1 8141
lamb a **y** old for a guilt offering; Nu 6:12 8141
one male lamb a **y** old without Nu 6:14 8141
one ewe-lamb a **y** old without defect Nu 6:14 8141
one ram, one male lamb one **y** old, Nu 7:15 8141
goats, five male lambs one **y** old. Nu 7:17 8141
one ram, one male lamb one **y** old, Nu 7:21 8141
goats, five male lambs one **y** old. Nu 7:23 8141
one ram, one male lamb one **y** old, Nu 7:27 8141
goats, five male lambs one **y** old. Nu 7:29 8141
one ram, one male lamb one **y** old, Nu 7:33 8141
goats, five male lambs one **y** old. Nu 7:35 8141
one ram, one male lamb one **y** old, Nu 7:39 8141
goats, five male lambs one **y** old. Nu 7:41 8141
one ram, one male lamb one **y** old, Nu 7:45 8141
goats, five male lambs one **y** old. Nu 7:47 8141
one ram, one male lamb one **y** old, Nu 7:51 8141
goats, five male lambs one **y** old. Nu 7:53 8141
one ram, one male lamb one **y** old, Nu 7:57 8141
goats, five male lambs one **y** old. Nu 7:59 8141
one ram, one male lamb one **y** old, Nu 7:63 8141
goats, five male lambs one **y** old. Nu 7:65 8141
one ram, one male lamb one **y** old, Nu 7:69 8141
goats, five male lambs one **y** old. Nu 7:71 8141
one ram, one male lamb one **y** old, Nu 7:75 8141
goats, five male lambs one **y** old. Nu 7:77 8141
one ram, one male lamb one **y** old, Nu 7:81 8141
goats, five male lambs one **y** old. Nu 7:83 8141
the male lambs one **y** old with Nu 7:87 8141
60, the male lambs one **y** old 60. Nu 7:88 8141
in the first month of the second **y** Nu 9:1 8141
or a **y** that the cloud lingered over Nu 9:22 3117
Now in the second **y**, Nu 10:11 8141
day you shall bear your guilt a **y**, Nu 14:34 8141
shall offer a one **y** old female goat Nu 15:27 8141
two male lambs one **y** old without Nu 28:3 8141
lambs one **y** old without defect, Nu 28:9 8141
lambs one **y** old without defect; Nu 28:11 8141
throughout the months of the **y**. Nu 28:14 8141
and seven male lambs one **y** old, Nu 28:19 8141
ram, seven male lambs one **y** old; Nu 28:27 8141
lambs one **y** old without defect; Nu 29:2 8141
ram, seven male lambs one **y** old, Nu 29:8 8141
fourteen male lambs one **y** old, Nu 29:13 8141
lambs one **y** old without defect; Nu 29:17 8141
lambs one **y** old without defect; Nu 29:20 8141
lambs one **y** old without defect; Nu 29:23 8141
lambs one **y** old without defect; Nu 29:26 8141
lambs one **y** old without defect; Nu 29:29 8141
lambs one **y** old without defect; Nu 29:32 8141
lambs one **y** old without defect; Nu 29:36 8141
in the fortieth **y** after the sons Nu 33:38 8141
In the fortieth **y**, Dt 1:3 8141
even to the end of the **y**. Dt 11:12 8141
comes out of the field every **y**. Dt 14:22 8141
"At the end of every third **y** you Dt 14:28 8141
tithe of your produce in that **y**, Dt 14:28 8141
'The seventh **y**, the year of Dt 15:9 8141
seventh year, the **y** of remission, Dt 15:9 8141
seventh **y** you shall set him free. Dt 15:12 8141
your household shall eat it every **y** Dt 15:20 8141
"Three times in a **y** all your Dt 16:16 8141
he shall be free at home one **y** and Dt 24:5 8141
of your increase in the third **y**, Dt 26:12 8141
the third year, the **y** of tithing, Dt 26:12 8141
time of the **y** of remission of debts, Dt 31:10 8141
the land of Canaan during that **y**. Jos 5:12 8141
crushed the sons of Israel that **y**; Jg 10:8 8141
the Gileadite four days in the **y**. Jg 11:40 8141
give you ten *pieces* of silver a **y**, Jg 17:10 3117
a feast of the LORD from **y** to year Jg 21:19 3117
a feast of the LORD from year to **y** Jg 21:19 3117
It happened **y** after year, as 1Sa 1:7 8141
It happened year after **y**, 1Sa 1:7 8141
little robe and bring it to him from **y** 1Sa 2:19 3117
year to **y** when she would come up 1Sa 2:19 3117
was a **y** and four months. 1Sa 27:7 3117
the end of every **y** that he cut *it*, 2Sa 14:26 3117
for three years, **y** after year; 2Sa 21:1 8141
for three years, year after **y**; 2Sa 21:1 8141
to provide for a month in the **y**. 1Ki 4:7 8141
would give Hiram **y** by year. 1Ki 5:11 8141
would give Hiram year by **y**. 1Ki 5:11 8141
in the four hundred and eightieth **y** 1Ki 6:1 8141
in the fourth **y** of Solomon's reign 1Ki 6:1 8141
In the fourth **y** the foundation of 1Ki 6:37 8141
In the eleventh **y**, 1Ki 6:38 8141
Now three times in a **y** Solomon 1Ki 9:25 8141
which came in to Solomon in one **y** 1Ki 10:14 8141
and mules, so much **y** by year. 1Ki 10:25 8141
and mules, so much year by **y**. 1Ki 10:25 8141
in the fifth **y** of King Rehoboam, 1Ki 14:25 8141
the eighteenth **y** of King Jeroboam, 1Ki 15:1 8141
So in the twentieth **y** of Jeroboam 1Ki 15:9 8141
the second **y** of Asa king of Judah, 1Ki 15:25 8141
the third **y** of Asa king of Judah and 1Ki 15:28 8141
the third **y** of Asa king of Judah, 1Ki 15:33 8141
twenty-sixth **y** of Asa king of Judah, 1Ki 16:8 8141
y of Asa king of Judah, 1Ki 16:10 8141
y of Asa king of Judah, 1Ki 16:15 8141
thirty-first **y** of Asa king of Judah, 1Ki 16:23 8141
thirty-eighth **y** of Asa king of Judah, 1Ki 16:29 8141
came to Elijah in the third **y**, 1Ki 18:1 8141
for at the turn of the **y** the king 1Ki 20:22 8141
At the turn of the **y**, 1Ki 20:26 8141
In the third **y** 1Ki 22:2 8141
fourth **y** of Ahab king of Israel. 1Ki 22:41 8141
in the seventeenth **y** of Jehoshaphat 1Ki 22:51 8141
his place in the second **y** of Jehoram 2Ki 1:17 8141
in the eighteenth **y** of Jehoshaphat 2Ki 3:1 8141
next **y** you will embrace a son." 2Ki 4:16 6256
a son at that season the next **y**, 2Ki 4:17 6256
Now in the fifth **y** of Joram the 2Ki 8:16 8141
In the twelfth **y** of Joram the son 2Ki 8:25 8141
and he reigned one **y** in Jerusalem. 2Ki 8:26 8141
Now in the eleventh **y** of Joram, 2Ki 9:29 8141
Now in the seventh **y** Jehoiada sent 2Ki 11:4 8141
In the seventh **y** of Jehu, Jehoash 2Ki 12:1 8141
the twenty-third **y** of King Jehoash 2Ki 12:6 8141
In the twenty-third **y** of Joash 2Ki 13:1 8141
In the thirty-seventh **y** of Joash 2Ki 13:10 8141
the land in the spring of the **y**. 2Ki 13:20 8141
In the second **y** of Joash son of 2Ki 14:1 8141
In the fifteenth **y** of Amaziah the 2Ki 14:23 8141
In the twenty-seventh **y** of Jeroboam 2Ki 15:1 8141
In the thirty-eighth **y** of Azariah 2Ki 15:8 8141
in the thirty-ninth **y** of Uzziah 2Ki 15:13 8141
In the thirty-ninth **y** of Azariah 2Ki 15:17 8141
In the fiftieth **y** of Azariah 2Ki 15:23 8141
In the fifty-second **y** of Azariah 2Ki 15:27 8141
in the twentieth **y** of Jotham 2Ki 15:30 8141
In the second **y** of Pekah the son 2Ki 15:32 8141
In the seventeenth **y** of Pekah 2Ki 16:1 8141
twelfth **y** of Ahaz king of Judah, 2Ki 17:1 8141
Assyria, as *he had done* **y** by year; 2Ki 17:4 8141
Assyria, as *he had done* year by **y**; 2Ki 17:4 8141
In the ninth **y** of Hoshea, the king 2Ki 17:6 8141
about in the third **y** of Hoshea, 2Ki 18:1 8141
in the fourth **y** of King Hezekiah, 2Ki 18:9 8141
which was the seventh **y** of Hoshea 2Ki 18:9 8141
in the sixth **y** of Hezekiah, which 2Ki 18:10 8141
ninth **y** of Hoshea king of Israel, 2Ki 18:10 8141
the fourteenth **y** of King Hezekiah, 2Ki 18:13 8141
eat this **y** what grows of itself, 2Ki 19:29 8141
in the second **y** what springs from 2Ki 19:29 8141
and in the third **y** sow, reap, plant 2Ki 19:29 8141
in the eighteenth **y** of King Josiah 2Ki 22:3 8141
the eighteenth **y** of King Josiah, 2Ki 23:23 8141
in the eighth **y** of his reign. 2Ki 24:12 8141
Now in the ninth **y** of his reign, 2Ki 25:1 8141
the eleventh **y** of King Zedekiah. 2Ki 25:2 8141
y of King Nebuchadnezzar, 2Ki 25:8 8141
in the thirty-seventh **y** of the exile 2Ki 25:27 8141
in the **y** that he became king, 2Ki 25:27 8141
in the fortieth **y** of David's reign, 1Ch 26:31 8141
all the months of the **y**, 1Ch 27:1 8141
of the fourth **y** of his reign. 2Ch 3:2 8141
which came to Solomon in one **y** 2Ch 9:13 8141
and mules, so much **y** by year. 2Ch 9:24 8141
and mules, so much year by **y**. 2Ch 9:24 8141
about in King Rehoboam's fifth **y**, 2Ch 12:2 8141
the eighteenth **y** of King Jeroboam, 2Ch 13:1 8141
of the fifteenth **y** of Asa's reign. 2Ch 15:10 8141
the thirty-fifth **y** of Asa's reign. 2Ch 15:19 8141
In the thirty-sixth **y** of Asa's reign 2Ch 16:1 8141
In the thirty-ninth **y** of his reign 2Ch 16:12 8141
in the forty-first **y** of his reign. 2Ch 16:13 8141
Then in the third **y** of his reign 2Ch 17:7 8141
and he reigned one **y** in Jerusalem. 2Ch 22:2 8141
Now in the seventh **y** Jehoiada 2Ch 23:1 8141
at the turn of the **y** that the army of 2Ch 24:23 8141
Ammonites gave him during that **y** 2Ch 27:5 8141
in the second and in the third **y**. 2Ch 27:5 8141
In the first **y** of his reign, in 2Ch 29:3 8141
For in the eighth **y** of his reign 2Ch 34:3 8141
and in the twelfth **y** he began to 2Ch 34:3 8141
in the eighteenth **y** of his reign, 2Ch 34:8 8141
In the eighteenth **y** of Josiah's reign 2Ch 35:19 8141
At the turn of the **y** King 2Ch 36:10 8141

Now in the first **y** of Cyrus king **2Ch 36:22** 8141
first **y** of Cyrus king of Persia, **Ezr 1:1** 8141
Now in the second **y** of their coming **Ezr 3:8** 8141
the second **y** of the reign of Darius **Ezr 4:24** 8140
first **y** of Cyrus king of Babylon, **Ezr 5:13** 8140
"In the first **y** of King Cyrus, **Ezr 6:3** 8140
sixth **y** of the reign of King Darius. **Ezr 6:15** 8140
the seventh **y** of King Artaxerxes. **Ezr 7:7** 8141
was in the seventh **y** of the king. **Ezr 7:8** 8141
month Chislev, *in* the twentieth **y**, **Ne 1:1** 8141
twentieth **y** of King Artaxerxes, **Ne 2:1** 8141
from the twentieth **y** to the **Ne 5:14** 8141
thirty-second **y** of King Artaxerxes, **Ne 5:14** 8141
we will forego *the crops* the seventh **y** **Ne 10:31** 8141
in the thirty-second **y** of Artaxerxes **Ne 13:6** 8141
in the third **y** of his reign he **Es 1:3** 8141
in the seventh **y** of his reign. **Es 2:16** 8141
the twelfth **y** of King Ahasuerus, **Es 3:7** 8141
rejoice among the days of the **y**; **Jb 3:6** 8141
crowned the **y** with Your bounty, **Ps 65:11** 8141
In the **y** of King Uzziah's death I **Is 6:1** 8141
In the **y** that King Ahaz died this **Is 14:28** 8141
In the **y** that the commander came **Is 20:1** 8141
"In a **y**, as a hired man would **Is 21:16** 8141
Add **y** to year, observe *your* feasts **Is 29:1** 8141
Add year to **y**, observe *your* feasts **Is 29:1** 8141
Within a **y** and *a few* days You **Is 32:10** 8141
A **y** of recompense for the cause of **Is 34:8** 8141
the fourteenth **y** of King Hezekiah, **Is 36:1** 8141
eat this **y** what grows of itself, **Is 37:30** 8141
in the second **y** what springs from **Is 37:30** 8141
in the third **y** sow, reap, plant **Is 37:30** 8141
the favorable **y** of the LORD And **Is 61:2** 8141
And My **y** of redemption has come. **Is 63:4** 8141
in the thirteenth **y** of his reign. **Jer 1:2** 8141
end of the eleventh **y** of Zedekiah the **Jer 1:3** 8141
y of their punishment." **Jer 11:23** 8141
will not be anxious in a **y** of drought **Jer 17:8** 8141
them, The **y** of their punishment," **Jer 23:12** 8141
in the fourth **y** of Jehoiakim the **Jer 25:1** 8141
was the first **y** of Nebuchadnezzar **Jer 25:1** 8141
"From the thirteenth **y** of Josiah **Jer 25:3** 8141
Now in the same **y**, **Jer 28:1** 8141
king of Judah, in the fourth **y**, **Jer 28:1** 8141
This **y** you are going to die, **Jer 28:16** 8141
the same **y** in the seventh month. **Jer 28:17** 8141
tenth **y** of Zedekiah king of Judah, **Jer 32:1** 8141
eighteenth **y** of Nebuchadnezzar. **Jer 32:1** 8141
In the fourth **y** of Jehoiakim **Jer 36:1** 8141
in the fifth **y** of Jehoiakim **Jer 36:9** 8141
ninth **y** of Zedekiah king of Judah, **Jer 39:1** 8141
in the eleventh **y** of Zedekiah, in **Jer 39:2** 8141
in the fourth **y** of Jehoiakim the **Jer 45:1** 8141
defeated in the fourth **y** of Jehoiakim **Jer 46:2** 8141
Moab, The **y** of their punishment," **Jer 48:44** 8141
For the report will come one **y**, **Jer 51:46** 8141
that another report in another **y**, **Jer 51:46** 8141
in the fourth **y** of his reign. **Jer 51:59** 8141
about in the ninth **y** of his reign, **Jer 52:4** 8141
the eleventh **y** of King Zedekiah. **Jer 52:5** 8141
y of King Nebuchadnezzar, **Jer 52:12** 8141
in the seventh **y** 3,023 Jews; **Jer 52:28** 8141
the eighteenth **y** of Nebuchadnezzar **Jer 52:29** 8141
twenty-third **y** of Nebuchadnezzar, **Jer 52:30** 8141
in the thirty-seventh **y** of the exile of **Jer 52:31** 8141
in the *first* **y** of his reign, **Jer 52:31** 8141
it came about in the thirtieth **y**, **Ezk 1:1** 8141
fifth **y** of King Jehoiachin's exile, **Ezk 1:2** 8141
for forty days, a day for each **y**. **Ezk 4:6** 8141
It came about in the sixth **y**, **Ezk 8:1** 8141
in the seventh **y**, **Ezk 20:1** 8141
LORD came to me in the ninth **y**, **Ezk 24:1** 8141
in the eleventh **y**, **Ezk 26:1** 8141
In the tenth **y**, in the tenth **Ezk 29:1** 8141
Now in the twenty-seventh **y**, **Ezk 29:17** 8141
In the eleventh **y**, **Ezk 30:20** 8141
In the eleventh **y**, **Ezk 31:1** 8141
In the twelfth **y**, **Ezk 32:1** 8141
In the twelfth **y**, **Ezk 32:17** 8141
in the twelfth **y** of our exile, **Ezk 33:21** 8141
In the twenty-fifth **y** of our exile, **Ezk 40:1** 8141
exile, at the beginning of the **y**, **Ezk 40:1** 8141
in the fourteenth **y** after the city was **Ezk 40:1** 8141
a lamb a **y** old without blemish **Ezk 46:13** 8141
be his until the **y** of liberty; **Ezk 46:17** 8141
In the third **y** of the reign of Jehoiakim **Da 1:1** 8141
the first **y** of Cyrus the king. **Da 1:21** 8141
Now in the second **y** of the reign **Da 2:1** 8141
In the first **y** of Belshazzar king **Da 7:1** 8140
third **y** of the reign of Belshazzar **Da 8:1** 8141
In the first **y** of Darius the son **Da 9:1** 8141
in the first **y** of his reign, **Da 9:2** 8141
In the third **y** of Cyrus king of **Da 10:1** 8141
In the first **y** of Darius the Mede, **Da 11:1** 8141
the second **y** of Darius the king, **Hg 1:1** 8141
the second **y** of Darius the king. **Hg 1:15** 8141
month, in the second **y** of Darius, **Hg 2:10** 8141
month of the second **y** of Darius, **Zch 1:1** 8141
Shebat, in the second **y** of Darius, **Zch 1:7** 8141
In the fourth **y** of King Darius, **Zch 7:1** 8141
will go up from **y** to year to worship **Zch 14:16** 8141
will go up from year to **y** to worship **Zch 14:16** 8141
went to Jerusalem every **y** **Lk 2:41** *2094*
fifteenth **y** of the reign of Tiberius **Lk 3:1** *2094*
THE FAVORABLE **Y** OF THE LORD." **Lk 4:19** *1763*
'Let it alone, sir, for this **y** too, **Lk 13:8** *2094*
and if it bears fruit next **y**, **Lk 13:9**
who was high priest that **y**, **Jn 11:49** *1763*
but being high priest that **y**, **Jn 11:51** *1763*
who was high priest that **y**. **Jn 18:13** *1763*
an entire **y** they met with the church **Ac 11:26** *1763*
settled *there* a **y** and six months, **Ac 18:11** *1763*
begin a **y** ago not only to do *this,* **2Co 8:10** *4070*
has been prepared since last **y**, **2Co 9:2** *4070*
the high priest *enters* once a **y**, **Heb 9:7** *1763*
priest enters the holy place **y** by year **Heb 9:25** *1763*
priest enters the holy place year by **y** **Heb 9:25** *1763*
which they offer continually **y** by **Heb 10:1** *1763*
they offer continually year by **y**, **Heb 10:1** *1763*
is a reminder of sins **y** by year. **Heb 10:3** *1763*
is a reminder of sins year by **y**. **Heb 10:3** *1763*
and spend a **y** there and engage in **Jas 4:13** *1763*
the hour and day and month and **y**, **Rv 9:15** *1763*

YEARLING
and a **y** ewe lamb without defect, **Lv 14:10** 8141
burnt offerings, With **y** calves? **Mi 6:6** 8141

YEARLY
that the daughters of Israel went **y** to **Jg 11:40** 3117
this man would go up from his city **y** **1Sa 1:3** 3117
to offer to the LORD the **y** sacrifice **1Sa 1:21** 3117
husband to offer the **y** sacrifice. **1Sa 2:19** 3117
because it is the **y** sacrifice **1Sa 20:6** 3117
to contribute **y** one third of a shekel **Ne 10:32** 8141

YEARN
on and **y** for them continually; **Dt 28:32** 3616
y for you because of the **2Co 9:14** *1971*

YEARNED
even **y** for the courts of the LORD; **Ps 84:2** 3615

YEARNS
for You, my flesh **y** for You, **Ps 63:1** 3642
Therefore My heart **y** for him; **Jer 31:20** 1993

YEARS
for seasons and for days and **y**; **Gn 1:14** 8141
lived one hundred and thirty **y**, **Gn 5:3** 8141
of Seth were eight hundred **y**, **Gn 5:4** 8141
were nine hundred and thirty **y**, **Gn 5:5** 8141
Seth lived one hundred and five **y**, **Gn 5:6** 8141
Seth lived eight hundred and seven **y** **Gn 5:7** 8141
were nine hundred and twelve **y**, **Gn 5:8** 8141
Enosh lived ninety **y**, **Gn 5:9** 8141
lived eight hundred and fifteen **y** **Gn 5:10** 8141
were nine hundred and five **y**, **Gn 5:11** 8141
Kenan lived seventy **y**, **Gn 5:12** 8141
Kenan lived eight hundred and forty **y** **Gn 5:13** 8141
Kenan were nine hundred and ten **y**, **Gn 5:14** 8141
Mahalalel lived sixty-five **y**, **Gn 5:15** 8141
lived eight hundred and thirty **y** after **Gn 5:16** 8141
eight hundred and ninety-five **y**, **Gn 5:17** 8141
lived one hundred and sixty-two **y**, **Gn 5:18** 8141
Then Jared lived eight hundred **y** **Gn 5:19** 8141
were nine hundred and sixty-two **y**, **Gn 5:20** 8141
Enoch lived sixty-five **y**, **Gn 5:21** 8141
walked with God three hundred **y** **Gn 5:22** 8141
three hundred and sixty-five **y**. **Gn 5:23** 8141
one hundred and eighty-seven **y**, **Gn 5:25** 8141
lived seven hundred and eighty-two **y** **Gn 5:26** 8141
were nine hundred and sixty-nine **y**, **Gn 5:27** 8141
lived one hundred and eighty-two **y**, **Gn 5:28** 8141
lived five hundred and ninety-five **y** **Gn 5:30** 8141
seven hundred and seventy-seven **y**, **Gn 5:31** 8141
Noah was five hundred **y** old, **Gn 5:32** 8141
be one hundred and twenty **y**." **Gn 6:3** 8141
Now Noah was six hundred **y** old **Gn 7:6** 8141
and fifty **y** after the flood. **Gn 9:28** 8141
were nine hundred and fifty **y**, **Gn 9:29** 8141
Shem was one hundred **y** old, **Gn 11:10** 8141
Arpachshad two **y** after the flood; **Gn 11:10** 8141
and Shem lived five hundred **y** **Gn 11:11** 8141
Arpachshad lived thirty-five **y**, **Gn 11:12** 8141
lived four hundred and three **y** after **Gn 11:13** 8141
Shelah lived thirty **y**, **Gn 11:14** 8141
Shelah lived four hundred and three **y** **Gn 11:15** 8141
Eber lived thirty-four **y**, **Gn 11:16** 8141
Eber lived four hundred and thirty **y** **Gn 11:17** 8141
Peleg lived thirty **y**, **Gn 11:18** 8141
Peleg lived two hundred and nine **y** **Gn 11:19** 8141
Reu lived thirty-two **y**, **Gn 11:20** 8141
Reu lived two hundred and seven **y** **Gn 11:21** 8141
Serug lived thirty **y**, **Gn 11:22** 8141
and Serug lived two hundred **y** **Gn 11:23** 8141
Nahor lived twenty-nine **y**, **Gn 11:24** 8141
lived one hundred and nineteen **y** **Gn 11:25** 8141
Terah lived seventy **y**, **Gn 11:26** 8141
Terah were two hundred and five **y**; **Gn 11:32** 8141
Now Abram was seventy-five **y** old **Gn 12:4** 8141
y they had served Chedorlaomer, **Gn 14:4** 8141
and oppressed four hundred **y**. **Gn 15:13** 8141
Abram had lived ten **y** in the land **Gn 16:3** 8141
Abram was eighty-six **y** old **Gn 16:16** 8141
when Abram was ninety-nine **y** old, **Gn 17:1** 8141
born to a man one hundred **y** old? **Gn 17:17** 8141
will Sarah, who is ninety **y** old, **Gn 17:17** 8141
Now Abraham was ninety-nine **y** old **Gn 17:24** 8141
Ishmael his son was thirteen **y** old **Gn 17:25** 8141
Now Abraham was one hundred **y** old **Gn 21:5** 8141
one hundred and twenty-seven **y**; **Gn 23:1** 8141
were the **y** of the life of Sarah. **Gn 23:1** 8141
These are all the **y** of Abraham's life **Gn 25:7** 8141
one hundred and seventy-five **y**. **Gn 25:7** 8141
are the **y** of the life of Ishmael, **Gn 25:17** 8141
one hundred and thirty-seven **y**; **Gn 25:17** 8141
Isaac was forty **y** old when he took **Gn 25:20** 8141
and Isaac was sixty **y** old when she **Gn 25:26** 8141
When Esau was forty **y** old he **Gn 26:34** 8141
"I will serve you seven **y** for **Gn 29:18** 8141
So Jacob served seven **y** for Rachel **Gn 29:20** 8141
with me for another seven **y**." **Gn 29:27** 8141
with Laban for another seven **y**. **Gn 29:30** 8141
twenty **y** I *have been* with you; **Gn 31:38** 8141
twenty **y** I have been in your house; **Gn 31:41** 8141
I served you fourteen **y** for your two **Gn 31:41** 8141
and six **y** for your flock, **Gn 31:41** 8141
were one hundred and eighty **y**. **Gn 35:28** 8141
Joseph, when seventeen **y** of age, **Gn 37:2** 8141
it happened at the end of two full **y** **Gn 41:1** 8141
"The seven good cows are seven **y**; **Gn 41:26** 8141
the seven good ears are seven **y**; **Gn 41:26** 8141
came up after them are seven **y**, **Gn 41:27** 8141
wind will be seven **y** of famine. **Gn 41:27** 8141
seven **y** of great abundance are **Gn 41:29** 8141
them seven **y** of famine will come, **Gn 41:30** 8141
Egypt in the seven **y** of abundance. **Gn 41:34** 8141
gather all the food of these good **y** **Gn 41:35** 8141
seven **y** of famine which will occur **Gn 41:36** 8141
Now Joseph was thirty **y** old when **Gn 41:46** 8141
During the seven **y** of plenty **Gn 41:47** 8141
gathered all the food of *these* seven **y** **Gn 41:48** 8141
When the seven **y** of plenty which **Gn 41:53** 8141
seven **y** of famine began to come, **Gn 41:54** 8141
has been in the land these two **y**, **Gn 45:6** 8141
and there are still five **y** in **Gn 45:6** 8141
still five **y** of famine *to come,* **Gn 45:11** 8141
"How many **y** have you lived?" **Gn 47:8** 8141
"The **y** of my sojourning are one **Gn 47:9** 8141
have been the **y** of my life, **Gn 47:9** 8141
nor have they attained the **y** that **Gn 47:9** 8141
in the land of Egypt seventeen **y**; **Gn 47:28** 8141
was one hundred and forty-seven **y**. **Gn 47:28** 8141
Joseph lived one hundred and ten **y**. **Gn 50:22** 8141
the age of one hundred and ten **y**; **Gn 50:26** 8141
was one hundred and thirty-seven **y**. **Ex 6:16** 8141
was one hundred and thirty-three **y**. **Ex 6:18** 8141
was one hundred and thirty-seven **y**. **Ex 6:20** 8141
Moses was eighty **y** old and **Ex 7:7** 8141
was four hundred and thirty **y**. **Ex 12:40** 8141
end of four hundred and thirty **y**, **Ex 12:41** 8141
of Israel ate the manna forty **y**, **Ex 16:35** 8141
slave, he shall serve for six **y**; **Ex 21:2** 8141
You shall sow your land for six **y** **Ex 23:10** 8141
from twenty **y** old and over, **Ex 30:14** 8141
from twenty **y** old and upward, **Ex 38:26** 8141
Three **y** it shall be forbidden to you; **Lv 19:23** 8141
'Six **y** you shall sow your field, **Lv 25:3** 8141
and six **y** you shall prune your **Lv 25:3** 8141
seven sabbaths of **y** for yourself, **Lv 25:8** 8141
for yourself, seven times seven **y**, **Lv 25:8** 8141
time of the seven sabbaths of **y**, **Lv 25:8** 8141
of years, *namely,* forty-nine **y**. **Lv 25:8** 8141
the number of **y** after the jubilee, **Lv 25:15** 8141
to the number of **y** of crops. **Lv 25:15** 8141
In proportion to the extent of the **y** **Lv 25:16** 8141
to the fewness of the **y** you **Lv 25:16** 8141
bring forth the crop for three **y**. **Lv 25:21** 8141
then he shall calculate the **y** **Lv 25:27** 8141
correspond to the number of **y**. **Lv 25:50** 8141
'If there are still many **y**, **Lv 25:51** 8141
and if few **y** remain until the year **Lv 25:52** 8141
In proportion to his **y** he is to **Lv 25:52** 8141
twenty **y** even to sixty years old, **Lv 27:3** 8141
twenty years even to sixty **y** old, **Lv 27:3** 8141
'If it be from five **y** even to **Lv 27:5** 8141
from five years even to twenty **y** old **Lv 27:5** 8141
a month even up to five **y** old, **Lv 27:6** 8141
are from sixty **y** old and upward, **Lv 27:7** 8141
price for him proportionate to the **y** **Lv 27:18** 8141
from twenty **y** old and upward, **Nu 1:3** 8141
from twenty **y** old and upward, **Nu 1:18** 8141
male from twenty **y** old and upward, **Nu 1:20** 8141
male from twenty **y** old and upward, **Nu 1:22** 8141
from twenty **y** old and upward, **Nu 1:24** 8141
from twenty **y** old and upward, **Nu 1:26** 8141
from twenty **y** old and upward, **Nu 1:28** 8141
from twenty **y** old and upward, **Nu 1:30** 8141
from twenty **y** old and upward, **Nu 1:32** 8141
from twenty **y** old and upward, **Nu 1:34** 8141
from twenty **y** old and upward, **Nu 1:36** 8141
from twenty **y** old and upward, **Nu 1:38** 8141
from twenty **y** old and upward, **Nu 1:40** 8141
from twenty **y** old and upward, **Nu 1:42** 8141
from twenty **y** old and upward, **Nu 1:45** 8141
from thirty **y** and upward, even to **Nu 4:3** 8141
and upward, even to fifty **y** old, **Nu 4:3** 8141
y and upward to fifty years old, **Nu 4:23** 8141
years and upward to fifty **y** old, **Nu 4:23** 8141
from thirty **y** and upward even to **Nu 4:30** 8141
and upward even to fifty **y** old, **Nu 4:30** 8141
from thirty **y** and upward even to **Nu 4:35** 8141
and upward even to fifty **y** old, **Nu 4:35** 8141
from thirty **y** and upward even to **Nu 4:39** 8141
and upward even to fifty **y** old, **Nu 4:39** 8141
from thirty **y** and upward even to **Nu 4:43** 8141
and upward even to fifty **y** old, **Nu 4:43** 8141
from thirty **y** and upward even to **Nu 4:47** 8141
and upward even to fifty **y** old, **Nu 4:47** 8141
from twenty-five **y** old and upward **Nu 8:24** 8141
"But at the age of fifty **y** they **Nu 8:25** 8141
seven **y** before Zoan in Egypt.) **Nu 13:22** 8141
from twenty **y** old and upward, **Nu 14:29** 8141
for forty **y** in the wilderness, **Nu 14:33** 8141
your guilt a year, *even* forty **y**, **Nu 14:34** 8141
from twenty **y** old and upward, **Nu 26:2** 8141
from twenty **y** old and upward, **Nu 26:4** 8141
from twenty **y** old and upward, **Nu 32:11** 8141
wander in the wilderness forty **y**, **Nu 32:13** 8141
was one hundred twenty-three **y** old **Nu 33:39** 8141
These forty **y** the LORD your God **Dt 2:7** 8141

Context	Ref	No.
brook Zered was thirty-eight y	Dt 2:14	8141
in the wilderness these forty y,	Dt 8:2	8141
did your foot swell these forty y.	Dt 8:4	8141
"At the end of *every* seven y you	Dt 15:1	8141
then he shall serve you six y,	Dt 15:12	8141
for he has given you six y *with*	Dt 15:18	8141
led you forty y in the wilderness;	Dt 29:5	8141
a hundred and twenty y old today;	Dt 31:2	8141
"At the end of *every* seven y,	Dt 31:10	8141
Consider the y of all generations.	Dt 32:7	8141
was one hundred and twenty y old	Dt 34:7	8141
For the sons of Israel walked forty y	Jos 5:6	8141
Joshua was old *and* advanced in y	Jos 13:1	3117
"You are old *and* advanced in y,	Jos 13:1	3117
"I was forty y old when Moses the	Jos 14:7	8141
as He spoke, these forty-five y,	Jos 14:10	8141
I am eighty-five y old today.	Jos 14:10	8141
and Joshua was old, advanced in y,	Jos 23:1	3117
"I am old, advanced in y.	Jos 23:2	3117
being one hundred and ten y old.	Jos 24:29	8141
served Cushan-rishathaim eight y.	Jg 3:8	8141
Then the land had rest forty y.	Jg 3:11	8141
Eglon the king of Moab eighteen y.	Jg 3:14	8141
land was undisturbed for eighty y.	Jg 3:30	8141
of Israel severely for twenty y.	Jg 4:3	8141
land was undisturbed for forty y.	Jg 5:31	8141
into the hands of Midian seven y.	Jg 6:1	8141
and a second bull seven y old,	Jg 6:25	8141
the land was undisturbed for forty y	Jg 8:28	8141
Abimelech ruled over Israel three y.	Jg 9:22	8141
He judged Israel twenty-three y.	Jg 10:2	8141
and judged Israel twenty-two y.	Jg 10:3	8141
for eighteen y they *afflicted* all	Jg 10:8	8141
of the Arnon, three hundred y,	Jg 11:26	8141
Jephthah judged Israel six y.	Jg 12:7	8141
And he judged Israel seven y.	Jg 12:9	8141
and he judged Israel ten y.	Jg 12:11	8141
and he judged Israel eight y.	Jg 12:14	8141
hands of the Philistines forty y.	Jg 13:1	8141
So he judged Israel twenty y in	Jg 15:20	8141
he had judged Israel twenty y.	Jg 16:31	8141
And they lived there about ten y.	Ru 1:4	8141
Now Eli was ninety-eight y old,	1Sa 4:15	8141
Thus he judged Israel forty y.	1Sa 4:18	8141
was long, for it was twenty y;	1Sa 7:2	8141
Saul was *thirty* y old when he began	1Sa 13:1	8141
reigned *forty* two y over Israel.	1Sa 13:1	8141
advanced *in* y among men.	1Sa 17:12	8141
me these days, or *rather* these y,	1Sa 29:3	8141
was forty y old when he became	2Sa 2:10	8141
Israel, and he was king for two y.	2Sa 2:10	8141
Judah was seven y and six months.	2Sa 2:11	8141
He was five y old when the report	2Sa 4:4	8141
David was thirty y old when he	2Sa 5:4	8141
king, *and* he reigned forty y.	2Sa 5:4	8141
over Judah seven y and six months,	2Sa 5:5	8141
he reigned thirty-three y over all	2Sa 5:5	8141
Now it came about after two full y	2Sa 13:23	8141
to Geshur, and was there three y.	2Sa 13:38	8141
Now Absalom lived two full y in	2Sa 14:28	8141
it came about at the end of forty y	2Sa 15:7	8141
was very old, being eighty y old;	2Sa 19:32	8141
"I am now eighty y old.	2Sa 19:35	8141
in the days of David for three y,	2Sa 21:1	8141
"Shall seven y of famine come to	2Sa 24:13	8141
reigned over Israel *were* forty y:	1Ki 2:11	8141
seven y he reigned in Hebron and	1Ki 2:11	8141
and thirty-three y he reigned in	1Ki 2:11	8141
came about at the end of three y,	1Ki 2:39	8141
So he was seven y in building it.	1Ki 6:38	8141
building his own house thirteen y,	1Ki 7:1	8141
It came about at the end of twenty y	1Ki 9:10	8141
once every three y the ships of	1Ki 10:22	8141
over all Israel was forty y.	1Ki 11:42	8141
Jeroboam reigned *was* twenty-two y;	1Ki 14:20	8141
Rehoboam was forty-one y old when	1Ki 14:21	8141
reigned seventeen y in Jerusalem,	1Ki 14:21	8141
He reigned three y in Jerusalem;	1Ki 15:2	8141
reigned forty-one y in Jerusalem;	1Ki 15:10	8141
and he reigned over Israel two y.	1Ki 15:25	8141
Tirzah, *and reigned* twenty-four y.	1Ki 15:33	8141
at Tirzah, *and reigned* two y.	1Ki 16:8	8141
over Israel *and reigned* twelve y;	1Ki 16:23	8141
he reigned six y at Tirzah.	1Ki 16:23	8141
Israel in Samaria twenty-two y.	1Ki 16:29	8141
be neither dew nor rain these y,	1Ki 17:1	8141
Three y passed without war	1Ki 22:1	8141
Jehoshaphat was thirty-five y old	1Ki 22:42	8141
reigned twenty-five y in Jerusalem.	1Ki 22:42	8141
and he reigned two y over Israel.	1Ki 22:51	8141
of Judah, and reigned twelve y.	2Ki 3:1	8141
come on the land for seven y."	2Ki 8:1	8141
land of the Philistines seven y.	2Ki 8:2	8141
the end of seven y,	2Ki 8:3	8141
He was thirty-two y old when he	2Ki 8:17	8141
he reigned eight y in Jerusalem.	2Ki 8:17	8141
Ahaziah *was* twenty-two y old when	2Ki 8:26	8141
in Samaria *was* twenty-eight y.	2Ki 10:36	8141
in the house of the LORD six y,	2Ki 11:3	8141
Jehoash was seven y old when	2Ki 11:21	8141
he reigned forty y in Jerusalem;	2Ki 12:1	8141
and he reigned seventeen y.	2Ki 13:1	8141
in Samaria, *and reigned* sixteen y.	2Ki 13:10	8141
He was twenty-five y old when he	2Ki 14:2	8141
reigned twenty-nine y in Jerusalem.	2Ki 14:2	8141
king of Judah lived fifteen y after the	2Ki 14:17	8141
Azariah, who was sixteen y old,	2Ki 14:21	8141
Samaria, *and reigned* forty-one y.	2Ki 14:23	8141
sixteen y old when he became king,	2Ki 15:2	8141
reigned fifty-two y in Jerusalem;	2Ki 15:2	8141
and reigned ten y in Samaria.	2Ki 15:17	8141
in Samaria, *and reigned* two y.	2Ki 15:23	8141
in Samaria, *and reigned* twenty y.	2Ki 15:27	8141
He was twenty-five y old when he	2Ki 15:33	8141
he reigned sixteen y in Jerusalem;	2Ki 15:33	8141
Ahaz *was* twenty y old when he	2Ki 16:2	8141
he reigned sixteen y in Jerusalem;	2Ki 16:2	8141
in Samaria, *and reigned* nine y.	2Ki 17:1	8141
Samaria and besieged it three y.	2Ki 17:5	8141
He was twenty-five y old when he	2Ki 18:2	8141
reigned twenty-nine y in Jerusalem;	2Ki 18:2	8141
At the end of three y they captured	2Ki 18:10	8141
I will add fifteen y to your life,	2Ki 20:6	8141
Manasseh was twelve y old when he	2Ki 21:1	8141
reigned fifty-five y in Jerusalem;	2Ki 21:1	8141
Amon was twenty-two y old when	2Ki 21:19	8141
and he reigned two y in Jerusalem;	2Ki 21:19	8141
Josiah was eight y old when he	2Ki 22:1	8141
reigned thirty-one y in Jerusalem;	2Ki 22:1	8141
Jehoahaz was twenty-three y old	2Ki 23:31	8141
Jehoiakim was twenty-five y old	2Ki 23:36	8141
he reigned eleven y in Jerusalem;	2Ki 23:36	8141
became his servant *for* three y;	2Ki 24:1	8141
Jehoiachin was eighteen y old when	2Ki 24:8	8141
Zedekiah was twenty-one y old	2Ki 24:18	8141
he reigned eleven y in Jerusalem;	2Ki 24:18	8141
married when he was sixty y old;	1Ch 2:21	8141
he reigned seven y and six months.	1Ch 3:4	8141
he reigned thirty-three y.	1Ch 3:4	8141
either three y of famine, or three	1Ch 21:12	8141
from thirty y old and upward,	1Ch 23:3	8141
from twenty y old and upward.	1Ch 23:24	8141
from twenty y old and upward.	1Ch 23:27	8141
those twenty y of age and under,	1Ch 27:23	8141
reigned over Israel *was* forty y;	1Ch 29:27	8141
he reigned in Hebron seven y and	1Ch 29:27	8141
and in Jerusalem thirty-three y.	1Ch 29:27	
twenty y in which Solomon had built	2Ch 8:1	8141
once every three y the ships of	2Ch 9:21	8141
Solomon reigned forty y in	2Ch 9:30	8141
the son of Solomon for three y,	2Ch 11:17	8141
of David and Solomon for three y.	2Ch 11:17	8141
Now Rehoboam was forty-one y old	2Ch 12:13	8141
reigned seventeen y in Jerusalem,	2Ch 12:13	8141
He reigned three y in Jerusalem;	2Ch 13:2	8141
The land was undisturbed for ten y	2Ch 14:1	8141
at war with him during those y,	2Ch 14:6	8141
Some y later he went down to	2Ch 18:2	8141
He *was* thirty-five y old when he	2Ch 20:31	8141
reigned in Jerusalem twenty-five y.	2Ch 20:31	8141
Jehoram *was* thirty-two y old when	2Ch 21:5	8141
he reigned eight y in Jerusalem.	2Ch 21:5	8141
of time, at the end of two y,	2Ch 21:19	3117
He was thirty-two y old when he	2Ch 21:20	8141
he reigned in Jerusalem eight y;	2Ch 21:20	8141
Ahaziah *was* twenty-two y old when	2Ch 22:2	8141
with them in the house of God six y	2Ch 22:12	8141
Joash *was* seven y old when he	2Ch 24:1	8141
he reigned forty y in Jerusalem;	2Ch 24:1	8141
he was one hundred and thirty y old	2Ch 24:15	8141
Amaziah was twenty-five y old when	2Ch 25:1	8141
reigned twenty-nine y in Jerusalem.	2Ch 25:1	8141
from twenty y old and upward and	2Ch 25:5	8141
lived fifteen y after the death of Joash	2Ch 25:25	8141
Uzziah, who *was* sixteen y old,	2Ch 26:1	8141
Uzziah was sixteen y old when he	2Ch 26:3	8141
reigned fifty-two y in Jerusalem;	2Ch 26:3	8141
Jotham was twenty-five y old when	2Ch 27:1	8141
he reigned sixteen y in Jerusalem.	2Ch 27:1	8141
He was twenty-five y old when he	2Ch 27:8	8141
he reigned sixteen y in Jerusalem.	2Ch 27:8	8141
Ahaz *was* twenty y old when he	2Ch 28:1	8141
he reigned sixteen y in Jerusalem;	2Ch 28:1	8141
king *when he was* twenty-five y old;	2Ch 29:1	8141
reigned twenty-nine y in Jerusalem.	2Ch 29:1	8141
to the males from thirty y old and	2Ch 31:16	8141
from twenty y old and upwards,	2Ch 31:17	8141
Manasseh was twelve y old when he	2Ch 33:1	8141
reigned fifty-five y in Jerusalem.	2Ch 33:1	8141
Amon *was* twenty-two y old when	2Ch 33:21	8141
and he reigned two y in Jerusalem.	2Ch 33:21	8141
Josiah *was* eight y old when he	2Ch 34:1	8141
reigned thirty-one y in Jerusalem.	2Ch 34:1	8141
Joahaz was twenty-three y old when	2Ch 36:2	8141
Jehoiakim was twenty-five y old	2Ch 36:5	8141
he reigned eleven y in Jerusalem;	2Ch 36:5	8141
Jehoiachin was eight y old when he	2Ch 36:9	8141
Zedekiah was twenty-one y old	2Ch 36:11	8141
he reigned eleven y in Jerusalem.	2Ch 36:11	8141
until seventy y were complete.	2Ch 36:21	8141
appointed the Levites from twenty y	Ezr 3:8	8141
temple that was built many y ago,	Ezr 5:11	8140
of King Artaxerxes, *for* twelve y,	Ne 5:14	8141
forty y You provided for	Ne 9:21	8141
bore with them for many y,	Ne 9:30	8141
a mortal, Or Your y as man's years,	Jb 10:5	8141
a mortal, Or Your years as man's y,	Jb 10:5	3117
the y stored up for the ruthless.	Jb 15:20	8141
"For when a few y are past, I	Jb 16:22	8141
because they were y older than he.	Jb 32:4	3117
"I am young in y and you are old;	Jb 32:6	3117
increased y should teach wisdom.	Jb 32:7	8141
"The abundant *in* y may not be	Jb 32:9	
And their y in pleasures.	Jb 36:11	8141
number of His y is unsearchable.	Jb 36:26	8141
After this, Job lived 140 y,	Jb 42:16	8141
sorrow And my y with sighing;	Ps 31:10	8141
His y will be as many generations.	Ps 61:6	8141
days of old, The y of long ago.	Ps 77:5	8141
And their y in sudden terror.	Ps 78:33	8141
For a thousand y in Your sight Are	Ps 90:4	8141
have finished our y like a sigh.	Ps 90:9	8141
our life, they contain seventy y,	Ps 90:10	8141
Or if due to strength, eighty y,	Ps 90:10	8141
us, *And* the y we have seen evil.	Ps 90:15	8141
forty y I loathed *that* generation,	Ps 95:10	8141
Your y are throughout all generations	Ps 102:24	8141
And Your y will not come to an end.	Ps 102:27	8141
satisfies your y with good things,	Ps 103:5	5716
For length of days and y of life And	Pr 3:2	8141
the y of your life will be many.	Pr 4:10	8141
And your y to the cruel one;	Pr 5:9	8141
y of life will be added to you.	Pr 9:11	8141
But the y of the wicked will be	Pr 10:27	8141
heaven the few y of their lives.	Ec 2:3	3117
toils under the sun *during* the few y	Ec 5:18	3117
often consider the y of his life,	Ec 5:20	3117
hundred *children* and lives many y,	Ec 6:3	8141
other man lives a thousand y twice	Ec 6:6	8141
the few y of his futile life?	Ec 6:12	3117
if a man should live many y,	Ec 11:8	8141
the y draw near when you will say,	Ec 12:1	8141
within another 65 y Ephraim will be	Is 7:8	8141
"Within three y, as a hired man	Is 16:14	8141
has gone naked and barefoot three y	Is 20:3	8141
Tyre will be forgotten for seventy y	Is 23:15	8141
At the end of seventy y it will	Is 23:15	8141
come about at the end of seventy y	Is 23:17	8141
I will add fifteen y to your life.	Is 38:5	8141
be deprived of the rest of my y."	Is 38:10	8141
I will wander about all my y	Is 38:15	8141
to *your* graying y I will bear *you!*	Is 46:4	7872
these twenty-three y the word of	Jer 25:3	8141
serve the king of Babylon seventy y.	Jer 25:11	8141
when seventy y are completed I will	Jer 25:12	8141
'Within two y I am going to bring	Jer 28:3	8141
so will I break within two full y the	Jer 28:11	8141
'When seventy y have been	Jer 29:10	8141
"At the end of seven y each of	Jer 34:14	8141
to you and has served you six y,	Jer 34:14	8141
Zedekiah was twenty-one y old	Jer 52:1	8141
he reigned eleven y in Jerusalem;	Jer 52:1	8141
to the y of their iniquity,	Ezk 4:5	8141
vision that he sees is for many y	Ezk 12:27	3117
day near and have come to your y;	Ezk 22:4	8141
will not be inhabited for forty y.	Ezk 29:11	8141
waste, will be desolate forty y;	Ezk 29:12	8141
"At the end of forty y I will	Ezk 29:13	8141
in the latter y you will come into	Ezk 38:8	8141
prophesied in those days for *many* y	Ezk 38:17	8141
for seven y they will make fires of	Ezk 39:9	8141
they should be educated three y,	Da 1:5	8141
number of the y which was *revealed*	Da 9:2	8141
of Jerusalem, *namely*, seventy y.	Da 9:2	8141
"After some y they will form an	Da 11:6	8141
the king of the North for *some* y.	Da 11:8	8141
and after an interval of some y he	Da 11:13	8141
it To the y of many generations.	Jl 2:2	8141
I will make up to you for the y That	Jl 2:25	8141
two y before the earthquake.	Am 1:1	8141
I led you in the wilderness forty y	Am 2:10	8141
in the wilderness for forty y,	Am 5:25	8141
Your work in the midst of the y,	Hab 3:2	8141
In the midst of the y make it known;	Hab 3:2	8141
been indignant these seventy y?"	Zch 1:12	8141
as I have done these many y?"	Zch 7:3	8141
seventh months these seventy y,	Zch 7:5	8141
days of old and as in former y.	Mal 3:4	8141
from two y old and under,	Mt 2:16	*1332*
from a hemorrhage for twelve y,	Mt 9:20	*2094*
had had a hemorrhage for twelve y,	Mk 5:25	*2094*
for she was twelve y old.	Mk 5:42	*2094*
and they were both advanced in y.	Lk 1:7	*2250*
and my wife is advanced in y."	Lk 1:18	*2250*
She was advanced in y and	Lk 2:36	*2250*
lived with *her* husband seven y	Lk 2:36	*2250*
Himself was about thirty y of age,	Lk 3:23	*2094*
up for three y and six months,	Lk 4:25	*2094*
only daughter, about twelve y old,	Lk 8:42	*2094*
who had a hemorrhage for twelve y,	Lk 8:43	*2094*
goods laid up for many y *to come*	Lk 12:19	*2094*
for three y I have come looking	Lk 13:7	*2094*
for eighteen y had had a sickness	Lk 13:11	*2094*
has bound for eighteen long y,	Lk 13:16	*2094*
so many y I have been serving you and	Lk 15:29	*2094*
forty-six y to build this temple,	Jn 2:20	*2094*
ill for thirty-eight y.	Jn 5:5	*2094*
"You are not yet fifty y old,	Jn 8:57	*2094*
the man was more than forty y old	Ac 4:22	*2094*
AND MISTREATED FOR FOUR HUNDRED Y.	Ac 7:6	*2094*
"After forty y had passed, AN	Ac 7:30	*2094*
and in the wilderness for forty y.	Ac 7:36	*2094*
FORTY Y IN THE WILDERNESS,	Ac 7:42	*2094*
who had been bedridden eight y,	Ac 9:33	*2094*
about forty y He put up with them	Ac 13:18	*5066a*
about four hundred and fifty y.	Ac 13:19	*2094*
tribe of Benjamin, for forty y.	Ac 13:21	*2094*
This took place for two y,	Ac 19:10	*2094*
night and day for a period of three y	Ac 20:31	*5148*
"Knowing that for many y you have	Ac 24:10	*2094*
"Now after several y I came to	Ac 24:17	*2094*
But after two y had passed, Felix	Ac 24:27	*1333*
And he stayed two full y in his own	Ac 28:30	*1333*
he was about a hundred y old,	Ro 4:19	*1541*
I have had for many y a longing to	Ro 15:23	*2094*
a man in Christ who fourteen y ago	2Co 12:2	*2094*
Then three y later I went up to	Ga 1:18	*2094*

after an interval of fourteen **y** I went Ga 2:1 *2094*
four hundred and thirty **y** later, Ga 3:17 *2094*
days and months and seasons and **y**. Ga 4:10 *1763*
she is not less than sixty **y** old, 1Tm 5:9 *2094*
YOUR **Y** WILL NOT COME TO AN END." Heb 1:12 *2094*
Me, AND SAW MY WORKS FOR FORTY **Y**. Heb 3:9 *2094*
whom was He angry for forty **y**? Heb 3:17 *2094*
earth for three **y** and six months. Jas 5:17 *1763*
Lord one day is like a thousand **y**, 2Pe 3:8 *2094*
and a thousand **y** like one day. 2Pe 3:8 *2094*
and bound him for a thousand **y**; Rv 20:2 *2094*
the thousand **y** were completed; Rv 20:3 *2094*
with Christ for a thousand **y**. Rv 20:4 *2094*
the thousand **y** were completed. Rv 20:5 *2094*
reign with Him for a thousand **y**. Rv 20:6 *2094*
When the thousand **y** are completed, Rv 20:7 *2094*

YELLOWISH

and there is thin **y** hair in it, Lv 13:30 6669
and no **y** hair has grown in it, Lv 13:32 6669
need not seek for the **y** hair; Lv 13:36 6669

YES

"**Y**, I know that in the integrity Gn 20:6 1571
Y, and he shall be blessed." Gn 27:33 1571
"**Y**, the men came to me, but I did Jos 2:4 3653a
the LORD. **Y**, I cried to my God; 2Sa 22:7
And he said, "**Y**, I know; be still." 2Ki 2:3 1571
he answered, "**Y**, I know; be still." 2Ki 2:5 1571
Y, all that a man has he will give Jb 2:4
than gold, **y**, than much fine gold; Ps 19:10
I will sing, **y**, I will sing Ps 27:6
Y, wait for the LORD. Ps 27:14
Y, the LORD breaks in pieces the Ps 29:5
Y, the LORD sits as King forever. Ps 29:10
Y, I am like a man who does not Ps 38:14
I will sing, **y**, I will sing Ps 57:7
Y, I shall joyfully sing of Your Ps 59:16
They shout for joy, **y**, they sing. Ps 65:13 637
Y, let them rejoice with gladness. Ps 68:3
Y, confirm the work of our hands. Ps 90:17
Y, our God is compassionate. Ps 116:5
y, they surrounded me; Ps 118:11 1571
Y, *sweeter* than honey to my Ps 119:103
Above gold, **y**, above fine gold. Ps 119:127
Y, everyone who trusts in them. Ps 135:18
Y, seven which are an abomination Pr 6:16
Y, the honey from the comb is sweet Pr 24:13
I will hide My eyes from you; **Y**, Is 1:15 1571
Y, the night monster will settle Is 34:14 389
Y, the hawks will be gathered Is 34:15 389
a shout, **y**, He will raise a war cry. Is 42:13 637
Y, let him recount it to Me in Is 44:7
Y, truth is lacking; Is 59:15
y, let us denounce him!" Jer 20:10
y, into the hand of those whom you Jer 22:25
"**Y**, thus says the LORD of hosts, Jer 27:21 3588
Y, I said to you *while you were* Ezk 16:6
Y, be also ashamed and bear your Ezk 16:52 1571
Y, the coastlands which are by the Ezk 26:18
"**Y**, I will cause men Ezk 36:12
Y, I will betroth you to Me in Hos 2:19
Y, woe to them indeed when I Hos 9:12 3588
Y, he wrestled with the angel and Hos 12:4
Y, their altars are like the stone Hos 12:11 1571
Y, do not boast In the day of Ob 1:12
Y, you, do not gloat over their Ob 1:13 1571
Y, You will cast all their sins Mi 7:19
Y, she is desolate and waste! Na 2:10
Y, destruction and violence are Hab 1:3
Y, the perpetual mountains were Hab 3:6
Y, they will build houses but not Zph 1:13
y, gather, O nation without shame, Zph 2:1
"**Y**, it is He who will build the Zch 6:13
y, with great wrath I am jealous for Zch 8:2
y, you will flee just as you fled Zch 14:5
But let your statement be, '**Y**, yes' *or* Mt 5:37 *3483a*
But let your statement be, 'Yes, **y**' Mt 5:37 *3483a*
They said to Him, "**Y**, Lord." Mt 9:28 *3483a*
Y, I tell you, and one who is Mt 11:9 *3483a*
"**Y**, Father, for this way was Mt 11:26 *3483a*
They said to Him, "**Y**." Mt 13:51 *3483a*
"**Y**, Lord; but even the dogs feed on Mt 15:27 *3483a*
He said, "**Y**." And when he came Mt 17:25 *3483a*
And Jesus said to them, "**Y**; Mt 21:16 *3483a*
"**Y**, Lord, *but* even the dogs under Mk 7:28 *3483a*
Y, I say to you, and one who is Lk 7:26 *3483a*
Y, Father, for this way was Lk 10:21 *3483a*
y, I tell you, it shall be charged Lk 11:51 *3483a*
y, I tell you, fear Him! Lk 12:5 *3483a*
and sisters, **y**, and even his own life, Lk 14:26 *2089*
And He said to them, "**Y**, I am." Lk 22:70 *3483a*
"**Y**, Lord; I have believed that You Jn 11:27 *3483a*
Y, Lord; You know that I love You. Jn 21:15 *3483a*
"**Y**, Lord; You know that I love You. Jn 21:16 *3483a*
"**Y**, that was the price." Ac 5:8 *3483a*
And he said, "**Y**." Ac 22:27 *3483a*
Y, of Gentiles also, Ro 3:29 *3483a*
who died, **y**, rather who was raised, Ro 8:34 *1161*
Y, they were pleased *to do so,* and Ro 15:27 *1063*
Y, for our sake it was written, 1Co 9:10 *1063*
that with me there will be **y**, yes 2Co 1:17 *3483a*
there will be yes, **y** and no, no 2Co 1:17 *3483a*
our word to you is not **y** and no. 2Co 1:18 *3483a*
was not **y** and no, but is yes in Him. 2Co 1:19 *3483a*
not yes and no, but is **y** in Him. 2Co 1:19 *3483a*
of God, in Him they are **y**; 2Co 1:20 *3483a*
Y, and I will rejoice, Php 1:18 *235*
Y, brother, let me benefit from Phm 1:20 *3483a*
y, also chains and imprisonment. Heb 11:36 *2089*
but your **y** is to be yes, and your no, Jas 5:12 *3483a*
but your yes is to be **y**, and your no, Jas 5:12 *3483a*
"**Y**," says the Spirit, "so that they may Rv 14:13 *3483a*
"**Y**, O Lord God, the Almighty, Rv 16:7 *3483a*
"**Y**, I am coming quickly." Rv 22:20 *3483a*

YESTERDAY

required amount either **y** or today Ex 5:14 8543
to the meal, either **y** or today?" 1Sa 20:27 8543
"You came *only* **y**, and shall I 2Sa 15:20 8543
'Surely I have seen **y** the blood of 2Ki 9:26 570
we are *only* of **y** and know nothing, Jb 8:9 8543
Are like **y** when it passes by, Ps 90:4
3117, 8543
"**Y** at the seventh hour the fever Jn 4:52 *2189a*
ME AS YOU KILLED THE EGYPTIAN **Y**, Ac 7:28 *2189a*
Jesus Christ *is* the same **y** and today and Heb 13:8 *2189a*

YET

shrub of the field was **y** in the earth, Gn 2:5 2962
plant of the field had **y** sprouted, Gn 2:5 2962
Y your desire will be for your Gn 3:16
So he waited **y** another seven days; Gn 8:10 5750
he waited **y** another seven days, Gn 8:12 5750
the Amorite is not **y** complete." Gn 15:16
5704, 2008
He spoke to Him **y** again and said, Gn 18:29 5750
Y he urged them strongly, so they Gn 19:3
Y I have borne him a son in his Gn 21:7 3588
"**Y** your father has cheated me and Gn 31:7
y my life has been preserved." Gn 32:30
Y the chief cupbearer did not Gn 40:23
"**Y** when they had devoured them, Gn 41:21
y without your permission no one Gn 41:44
Y he said to them, Gn 42:12
with us, **y** we would not listen; Gn 42:21
fire, **y** the bush was not consumed. Ex 3:2
y they keep saying to us, Ex 5:16
y you must deliver the quota of Ex 5:18
Y Pharaoh's heart was hardened, Ex 7:13
you do not **y** fear the LORD God." Ex 9:30 2962
y the LORD hardened Pharaoh's Ex 11:10
y it gave light at night. Ex 14:20
y there is no injury, Ex 21:22
warned, **y** he does not confine it and Ex 21:29
y its owner has not confined it, Ex 21:36
Y He did not stretch out His hand Ex 24:11
y He will by no means leave *the* Ex 34:7
'**Y** these you may eat among all the Lv 11:21 389
'**Y** if in spite of this you do not Lv 26:27
'**Y** in spite of this, when they are Lv 26:44
'**Y** if the one who consecrates it Lv 27:15
'**Y** if he will not redeem the Lv 27:20
and **y** neglects to observe the Nu 9:13
"**Y** if *only* one is blown, then the Nu 10:4
y You have said, Nu 11:21
y have put Me to the test these Nu 14:22
down, **y** having his eyes uncovered, Nu 24:4
down, **y** having his eyes uncovered. Nu 24:16
y he was not among the company of Nu 27:3
"**Y** you were not willing to go up, Dt 1:26
God speaks with man, **y** he lives. Dt 5:24
'**Y** they are Your people, even Your Dt 9:29
"**Y** on your fathers did the LORD Dt 10:15 7534
for you have not as **y** come to the Dt 12:9 6258
"**Y** to this day the LORD has not Dt 29:4
y the Amorites persisted in living Jg 1:35
nor **y** the work which He had done Jg 2:10 1571
Y they did not listen to their judges, Jg 2:17 1571
crossed over, weary **y** pursuing. Jg 8:4
Y Gideon said to them, Jg 8:24
"**Y** you have forsaken Me and Jg 10:13
y surely we will not kill you." Jg 15:13
"**Y** there is both straw and fodder Jg 19:19
"Shall I **y** again go out to battle Jg 20:28 5750
y they were not enough for them. Jg 21:14
Have I **y** sons in my womb, that Ru 1:11 5750
'**Y** I will not cut off every man of 1Sa 2:33
lamp of God had not **y** gone out, 1Sa 3:3 2962
The LORD called **y** again, 1Sa 3:6 5750
Samuel did not **y** know the LORD, 1Sa 3:7 2962
word of the LORD **y** been revealed 1Sa 3:7 2962
y you have said, 1Sa 10:19
"Has the man come here **y**?" 1Sa 10:22 5750
y do not turn aside from following 1Sa 12:20 389
"There remains **y** the youngest, 1Sa 16:11 5750
Y David vowed again, saying, 1Sa 20:3
delivered me into your hand and **y** 1Sa 24:18
"**Y** the men were very good to us, 1Sa 25:15
and **y** today you charge me with a 2Sa 3:8
"And **y** this was insignificant in 2Sa 7:19 5750
"Is there **y** anyone left of the 2Sa 9:1 5750
"Is there not **y** anyone of the 2Sa 9:3 5750
Y he would not listen to her. 2Sa 13:16
Y God does not take away life, but 2Sa 14:14
y alive in the midst of the oak. 2Sa 18:14 5750
y you set your servant among those 2Sa 19:28
What right do I have **y** that I 2Sa 19:28 5750
"How long have I **y** to live, that 2Sa 19:34
Y the words of the men of Judah 2Sa 19:43
David, **y** I am but a little child; 1Ki 3:7
"**Y** have regard to the prayer of 1Ki 8:28
he was **y** in Egypt, where he had fled 1Ki 12:2 5750
"**y** you have not been like My servant 1Ki 14:8
"**Y** I will leave 7,000 in Israel, 1Ki 19:18
not **y** a prophet of the LORD here that 1Ki 22:7 5750
"There is **y** one man by whom we 1Ki 22:8 5750
y that valley shall be filled with 2Ki 3:17
LORD, **y** not like David his father; 2Ki 14:3 7534
Y the LORD warned Israel and 2Ki 17:13
y the birthright belonged to 1Ch 5:2
The Philistines made **y** another raid 1Ch 14:13 5750
"**Y**, the LORD, the God of Israel, 1Ch 28:4
"**Y** have regard to the prayer of 2Ch 6:19
"**Y** Jeroboam the son of Nebat, the 2Ch 13:6
Y because you relied on the LORD, 2Ch 16:8
y even in his disease he did not 2Ch 16:12
"Is there not **y** a prophet of the 2Ch 18:6 5750
"There is **y** one man by whom we 2Ch 18:7 5750
the people had not **y** directed 2Ch 20:33 5750
Y the LORD was not willing to 2Ch 21:7
Y He sent prophets to them to 2Ch 24:19
y the LORD delivered a very great 2Ch 24:24
LORD, **y** not with a whole heart. 2Ch 25:2 7534
y God will bring you down before 2Ch 25:8
y more unfaithful to the LORD. 2Ch 28:22 3254
y they ate the Passover otherwise 2Ch 30:18 3588
Y many of the priests and Levites Ezr 3:12
under construction and it is not **y** Ezr 5:16
y in our bondage our God has not Ezr 9:9
y now there is hope for Israel in Ezr 10:2
nor had I as **y** told the Jews, the Ne 2:16 3651
failing, **Y** there is much rubbish; Ne 4:10
Y behold, we are forcing our sons Ne 5:5
Y for all this I did not demand Ne 5:18
Y they acted arrogantly and did Ne 9:29
Y they would not give ear. Ne 9:30
Y you are adding to the wrath on Ne 13:18
Y among the many nations there was Ne 13:26
Esther had not **y** made known her Es 2:20
"**Y** all of this does not satisfy Es 5:13
They die, **y** without wisdom.' Jb 4:21
my righteousness is **y** in it. Jb 6:29 5750
Y your end will increase greatly. Jb 8:7
Y it withers before any *other* Jb 8:12
y fill your mouth with laughter And Jb 8:21 5704
Y You would plunge me into the Jb 9:31 227
Y there is no deliverance from Your Jb 10:7
'**Y** these things You have Jb 10:13
Y from my flesh I shall see God; Jb 19:26
Y his food in his stomach is Jb 20:14
"**Y** He filled their houses with Jb 22:18
Y God does not pay attention to Jb 24:12
When the Almighty was **y** with me, Jb 29:5 5750
"**Y** does not one in a heap of Jb 30:24 389
answer, and **y** had condemned Job. Jb 32:3
y no one notices it. Jb 33:14
y more to be said in God's behalf. Jb 36:2 5750
Y You have made him a little Ps 8:5
Y You are holy, O You who are Ps 22:3
Y You are He who brought me Ps 22:9 3588
Y a little while and the wicked Ps 37:10 5750
Y I have not seen the righteous Ps 37:25
in God, for I shall **y** praise Him, Ps 42:11 5750
Y You have rejected *us* and Ps 44:9 637
Y You have crushed us in a place Ps 44:19 3588
his pomp, **y** without understanding, Ps 49:20
oil, **Y** they were drawn swords. Ps 55:21
Y You brought us out into *a* Ps 66:12
will praise You **y** more and more. Ps 71:14 3254
Y God is my king from of old, Who Ps 74:12
even the children **y** to be Ps 78:6
Y they turned back in the day of Ps 78:9
Y they still continued to sin Ps 78:17
Y He commanded the clouds above Ps 78:23
Y they tempted and rebelled Ps 78:56
Y their pride is *but* labor and Ps 90:10
And **y** an avenger of their *evil* Ps 99:8
That a people **y** to be created may Ps 102:18
The arrogant utterly deride me, **Y** Ps 119:51
hand, **Y** I do not forget Your law. Ps 119:109
Y I have not gone astray from Your Ps 119:110
I am small and despised, **Y** I do Ps 119:141
Y Your commandments are my Ps 119:143
Y I do not turn aside from Your Ps 119:157
Y they have not prevailed against Ps 129:2 1571
exalted, **Y** He regards the lowly, Ps 138:6
as **y** there was not one of them. Ps 139:16
Y He gives grace to the afflicted. Pr 3:34
While He had not **y** made the earth Pr 8:26
There is one who scatters, and **y** Pr 11:24
and **y** *it results* only in want. Pr 11:24
Y his foolishness will not depart Pr 27:22
Y is not washed from his Pr 30:12
Y they make their houses in the Pr 30:26
Y all of them go out in ranks; Pr 30:27
hands, **Y** it is in kings' palaces. Pr 30:28
the sea, **Y** the sea is not full. Ec 1:7
And **y** I know that one fate befalls Ec 2:14 1571
Y he will have control over all Ec 2:19
y so that man will not find out Ec 3:11 1097
y there was no end to all his Ec 4:8
A poor **y** wise lad is better than an Ec 4:13
y God has not empowered him to eat Ec 6:2
y the appetite is not satisfied. Ec 6:7 1571
Y no one remembered that poor man. Ec 9:15
Y the fool multiplies words. Ec 10:14
Y know that God will bring you to Ec 11:9
"**Y** there will be a tenth portion Is 6:13 5750
Gird yourselves, **y** be shattered; Is 8:9
Gird yourselves, **y** be shattered. Is 8:9
Y the people do not turn back to Is 9:13
Y it does not so intend, Nor does Is 10:7
Y today he will halt at Nob; Is 10:32 5750
Y gleanings will be left in it Is 17:6
Your hand is lifted up **y** they Is 26:11
Is it not **y** just a little while Is 29:17 5750
Y He also is wise and will bring Is 31:2
Y those who wait for the LORD Will Is 40:31

around, **Y** he did not recognize *it;* Is 42:25
"**Y** you have not called on Me, O Is 43:22
"**Y** you said, 'I will be a queen Is 47:7
Y surely the justice *due* to Me is Is 49:4
bereaved will **y** say in your ears, Is 49:20 5750
Y we ourselves esteemed Him Is 53:4
Y He did not open His mouth; Is 53:7
Y He was with a rich man in His Is 53:9
Y He Himself bore the sin of many, Is 53:12
"**Y** *others* I will gather to them, Is 56:8 5750
Y you did not say, 'It is Is 57:10
"**Y** they seek Me day by day and Is 58:2
I will **y** contend with you," Jer 2:9 5750
"**Y** I planted you a choice vine, A Jer 2:21
Y My people have forgotten Me Jer 2:32
Y you said, 'I am innocent; Surely Jer 2:35
Y you turn to Me," Jer 3:1
Y you had a harlot's forehead; Jer 3:3
y her treacherous sister Judah did Jer 3:8
"**Y** in spite of all this her Jer 3:10 1571
Y I will not execute a complete Jer 4:27
"**Y** even in those days," Jer 5:18
waves toss, **y** they cannot prevail; Jer 5:22
roar, **y** they cannot cross over it. Jer 5:22
"**Y** they did not obey or incline Jer 7:24
"**Y** they did not listen to Me or Jer 7:26
circumcised and **y** uncircumcised Jer 9:25
'**Y** they did not obey or incline Jer 11:8
Me, **y** I will not listen to them. Jer 11:11
Y You are in our midst, O LORD, Jer 14:9
y they keep saying, 'There will be no Jer 14:15
sun has set while it was **y** day; Jer 15:9 5750
Y everyone curses me. Jer 15:10
Y they are not gods! Jer 16:20
"**Y** they did not listen or incline Jer 17:23
Y You, O LORD, know All their Jer 18:23
Y, O LORD of hosts, You who test Jer 20:12
Y most assuredly I will make you Jer 22:6
hand, **y** I would pull you off; Jer 22:24 3588
y I did not send them or command Jer 23:32
"**Y** you have not listened to Me," Jer 25:7
"**Y** hear now this word which I am Jer 28:7 389
"**Y** again there will be heard in Jer 33:10 5750
"**Y** hear the word of the LORD, O Jer 34:4 389
"**Y** you turned and profaned My Jer 34:16
y you have not listened to Me. Jer 35:14
Y the king and all his servants Jer 36:24
Y King Zedekiah sent Jehucal the Jer 37:3
for they had not **y** put him in Jer 37:4
y he would not listen to him. Jer 37:14
Y it turned out that as soon as Jer 41:7
'**Y** I sent you all My servants the Jer 44:4
Y I will not make a full end of Jer 46:28
"**Y** I will restore the fortunes of Jer 48:47
Y in a little while the time of Jer 51:33 5750
Y our eyes failed, La 4:17 5750
y the house of Israel will not be Ezk 3:7
"**Y** if you have warned the wicked and Ezk 3:19
But **y** you will see still greater Ezk 8:6 5750
"**Y** you will see still greater Ezk 8:13 5750
Y you will see still greater Ezk 8:15 5750
y I will not listen to them." Ezk 8:18
y I was a sanctuary for them a Ezk 11:16
y he will not see it, though he Ezk 12:13
y they hope for the fulfillment of Ezk 13:6
"**Y**, behold, survivors will be Ezk 14:22
y the fire will consume them. Ezk 15:7
Y you were naked and bare. Ezk 16:7
y even with this you were not Ezk 16:29
"**Y** you have not merely walked in Ezk 16:47
y did all these things; Ezk 17:18
Y you say, 'Why should the son not Ezk 18:19
"**Y** you say, 'The way of the Lord is Ezk 18:25
"**Y** My eye spared them rather than Ezk 20:17
"**Y** in this your fathers have Ezk 20:27 5750
y she was more corrupt in her lust Ezk 23:11
"**Y** she multiplied her harlotries, Ezk 23:19
Y her great rust has not gone from Ezk 24:12
cleansed you, **Y** you are not clean, Ezk 24:13
Y you are a man and not God, Ezk 28:2
Y you will be brought down with Ezk 31:18
Y you are like the monster in the Ezk 32:2
y he will be made to lie down Ezk 32:32
"**Y** your fellow citizens say, Ezk 33:17
"**Y** you say, 'The way of the Lord is Ezk 33:20
only one, **y** he possessed the land; Ezk 33:24
y they have come out of His land.' Ezk 36:20
"**Y** they shall be ministers in My Ezk 44:11
"**Y** I will appoint them to keep Ezk 44:14
y they shall not let their locks Ezk 44:20
"**Y** leave the stump with its roots Da 4:15 1297
y leave the stump with its roots Da 4:23 1297
"**Y** you, his son, Belshazzar, have Da 5:22
y we have not sought the favor of Da 9:13
y no strength was left in me, for Da 10:8
pertains to the days **y** *future.*" Da 10:14 5750
Y there is no one who stands Da 10:21
y he will not prevail. Da 11:12
y within a few days he will be Da 11:20
y they will fall by sword and by Da 11:33
y he will come to his end, and no Da 11:45
for **y** a little while, and I will Hos 1:4 5750
Y the number of the sons of Israel Hos 1:10
by *her* husband, **y** an adulteress, Hos 3:1
Y let no one find fault, and let Hos 4:4 389
strength, **Y** he does not know *it;* Hos 7:9
on him, **Y** he does not know *it.* Hos 7:9
Y they have not returned to Hos 7:10
Y they devise evil against Me. Hos 7:15
Y the snare of a bird catcher is Hos 9:8
Y I will bereave them until not a Hos 9:12
Y it is I who taught Ephraim to Hos 11:3
Y I *have been* the LORD your God Hos 13:4
"**Y** even now," declares the LORD, Jl 2:12
"**Y** it was I who destroyed the Am 2:9
Y you have not returned to Me," Am 4:6
Y you have not returned to Me," Am 4:8
Y you have not returned to Me," Am 4:9
Y you have not returned to Me," Am 4:10
Y you have not returned to Me," Am 4:11
Y you will not live in them; Am 5:11
y you will not drink their wine. Am 5:11
Y they have not grieved over the Am 6:6
Y you have turned justice into Am 6:12 3588
"**Y** forty days and Nineveh will be Jon 3:4 5750
Y they lean on the LORD saying, Mi 3:11
there **y** a man in the wicked house, Mi 6:10 5750
Y she became an exile, She went Na 3:10 1571
Y You do not save. Hab 1:2
vision is **y** for the appointed time; Hab 2:3 5750
Y I will exult in the LORD, I will Hab 3:18
and swear to the LORD and **y** Zph 1:5
y you *did* not *come back* to Me,' Hg 2:17
Y from this day on I will bless Hg 2:19
will **y** *be* that peoples will come, Zch 8:20 5750
"**Y** I have loved Jacob; Mal 1:2
"**Y** you say, 'For what reason?' Mal 2:14
Y you say, "How have we wearied Mal 2:17
Y you are robbing Me! Mal 3:8 3588
"**Y** you say, 'What have we spoken Mal 3:13
and **y** your heavenly Father feeds Mt 6:26
y I say to you that not even Solomon Mt 6:29 1161
and **y** it did not fall, for it Mt 7:25
And **y** not one of them will fall Mt 10:29
Y the one who is least in the kingdom Mt 11:11 1161
Y wisdom is vindicated by her Mt 11:19 2532
and **y** no sign will be given to it Mt 12:39
y he has no *firm* root in himself, Mt 13:21 1161
"Do you not **y** understand or Mt 16:9 3768
place, but *that* is not **y** the end. Mt 24:6 3768
y not as I will, but as You will." Mt 26:39 4133
y when it is sown, it grows up and Mk 4:32 2532
y because of his oaths Mk 6:26
y He could not escape notice. Mk 7:24 2532
Do you not **y** see or understand? Mk 8:17 3768
"Do you not **y** understand?" Mk 8:21 3768
And **y** how is it written of Mk 9:12
on which no one **y** has ever sat; Mk 11:2 3768
and **y** they feared the people, Mk 12:12
but *that is* not **y** the end. Mk 13:7 3768
all may fall away, **y** I will not." Mk 14:29 235
y not what I will, but what You Mk 14:36 235
while **y** in his mother's womb. Lk 1:15 2089
and **y** Elijah was sent to none of Lk 4:26
y he who is least in the kingdom Lk 7:28 1161
"**Y** wisdom is vindicated by all Lk 7:35 2532
and **y** he would break his bonds Lk 8:29
y be sure of this, that the Lk 10:11 4133
y because of his persistence he Lk 11:8 1065
and **y** no sign will be given to it Lk 11:29
and **y** disregard justice Lk 11:42
Y not one of them is forgotten Lk 12:6
and **y** God feeds them; how much Lk 12:24
and **y** you have never given me a Lk 15:29
y because this widow bothers me, I Lk 18:5 1065
on which no one **y** has ever sat; Lk 19:30 4455
"**Y** not a hair of your head will Lk 21:18 2532
y not My will, but Yours be done." Lk 22:42 4133
My hour has not **y** come." Jn 2:4 3768
John had not **y** been thrown into Jn 3:24 3768
y no one said, "What do You seek?" Jn 4:27 3305
'There are **y** four months, and *then* Jn 4:35 2089
and Jesus had not **y** come to them. Jn 6:17 3768
seen Me, and **y** do not believe. Jn 6:36
and **y** one of you is a devil?" Jn 6:70
"My time is not **y** here, but Jn 7:6 3768
My time has not **y** fully come." Jn 7:8 3768
Y no one was speaking openly of Jn 7:13 3305
and **y** none of you carries out Jn 7:19
because His hour had not **y** come. Jn 7:30 3768
for the Spirit was not **y** *given,* Jn 7:39 3768
because Jesus was not **y** glorified. Jn 7:39 3764
because His hour had not **y** come. Jn 8:20 3768
never **y** been enslaved to anyone; Jn 8:33 4455
y you seek to kill Me, because My Jn 8:37 235
"You are not **y** fifty years old, Jn 8:57 3768
and **y** He opened my eyes. Jn 9:30
y everything John said about this Jn 10:41 1161
Now Jesus had not **y** come into the Jn 11:30 3768
y they were not believing in Him. Jn 12:37
and **y** you have not come to know Jn 14:9
and **y** I am not alone, because Jn 16:32
and **y** they themselves are in Jn 17:11
known You, **y** I have known You; Jn 17:25 1161
in which no one had **y** been laid. Jn 19:41 3764
For as **y** they did not understand Jn 20:9 3764
have not **y** ascended to the Father; Jn 20:17 3768
did not see, and **y** believed." Jn 20:29
y the disciples did not know that Jn 21:4 3305
y Jesus did not say to him that he Jn 21:23 1161
and **y**, you have filled Jerusalem Ac 5:28 2400
and **y**, even when he had no child, Ac 7:5
Y God was with him, Ac 7:9
and **y** did not keep it." Ac 7:53
had not **y** fallen upon any of them; Ac 8:16 3764
and **y** God has shown me that I Ac 10:28
and **y** He did not leave Himself Ac 14:17 2543
for him to be kept in custody and **y** Ac 24:23
"**Y** I have nothing definite about Ac 25:26
"**Y** now I urge you to keep up Ac 27:22
y I was delivered as a prisoner from Ac 28:17
y, with respect to the promise of Ro 4:20 1161
in that while we were **y** sinners, Ro 5:8 2089
y the spirit is alive because of Ro 8:10 1161
though *the twins* were not **y** born and Ro 9:11 3380b
Y we do speak wisdom among those 1Co 2:6 1161
y he himself is appraised by no 1Co 2:15 1161
you were not **y** able *to receive it.* 1Co 3:2 3768
even now you are not **y** able, 1Co 3:2 2089
be saved, **y** so as through fire. 1Co 3:15 1161
y I am not by this acquitted; 1Co 4:4 235
y *you would* not *have* many fathers, 1Co 4:15 235
Y the body is not for immorality, 1Co 6:13 1161
Y I wish that all men were even as 1Co 7:7 1161
Y if the unbelieving one leaves, 1Co 7:15 1161
Y such will have trouble in this 1Co 7:28 1161
not **y** known as he ought to know; 1Co 8:2 3768
y for us there is *but* one God, the 1Co 8:6 235
For even as the body is one and **y** 1Co 12:12
y desire earnestly spiritual 1Co 14:1 1161
Y *even* lifeless things, either 1Co 14:7 3676
y in evil be infants, but in your 1Co 14:20 235
y not I, but the grace of God with 1Co 15:10 1161
And He will **y** deliver us, 2Co 1:10 2089
y our inner man is being renewed 2Co 4:16 235
y now we know *Him in this way* 2Co 5:16 235
regarded as deceivers and **y** true; 2Co 6:8
as unknown **y** well-known, as dying 2Co 6:9 2532
as dying **y** behold, we live; 2Co 6:9 2532
as punished **y** not put to death, 2Co 6:9 2532
as sorrowful **y** always rejoicing, 2Co 6:10 1161
as poor **y** making many rich, 2Co 6:10 1161
nothing **y** possessing all things. 2Co 6:10 2532
y for your sake He became poor, 2Co 8:9
y I am not *so* in knowledge; 2Co 11:6 235
y He lives because of the power of 2Co 13:4 235
y we will live with Him because 2Co 13:4 235
y when it has been ratified, Ga 3:15 3676
BE ANGRY, AND **Y** DO NOT SIN; Eph 4:26
y to remain on in the flesh is Php 1:24 1161
as having laid hold of *it* **y**; Php 3:13 3768
y He has now reconciled you in His Col 1:22 1161
more than once—and **y** Satan 1Th 2:18
Y do not regard him as an enemy, 2Th 3:15
Y I was shown mercy because I acted 1Tm 1:13 235
Y for this reason I found mercy, so 1Tm 1:16 235
y for love's sake I rather appeal Phm 1:9
But now we do not **y** see all things Heb 2:8 3768
we are, **y** without sin. Heb 4:15
holy place has not **y** been disclosed Heb 9:8 3380b
FOR **Y** IN A VERY LITTLE WHILE, HE Heb 10:37 2089
by God about things not **y** seen, Heb 11:7 3369
You have not **y** resisted to the Heb 12:4 3768
y to those who have been trained Heb 12:11 1161
"**Y** ONCE MORE I WILL SHAKE NOT Heb 12:26 2089
expression, "**Y** once more," denotes Heb 12:27 2089
and **y** does not bridle his tongue Jas 1:26
law and **y** stumbles in one *point,* Jas 2:10 1161
and **y** you do not give them what is Jas 2:16 1161
and **y** it boasts of great things. Jas 3:5
Y you do not know what your life Jas 4:14 3748
y with gentleness and reverence; 1Pe 3:15 235
nor **y** as lording it over those 1Pe 5:3
we have fellowship with Him and **y** 1Jn 1:6
who says he is in the Light and **y** 1Jn 2:9
appeared as **y** what we will be. 1Jn 3:2 3768
Y in the same way these men, Jude 1:8 3305
'**Y** this you do have, that you hate Rv 2:6 235
one is, the other has not **y** come; Rv 17:10 3768
who have not **y** received a kingdom, Rv 17:12 3768

YIELD

no longer **y** its strength to you; Gn 4:12 5414
And he will **y** royal dainties. Gn 49:20 5414
for six years and gather in its **y**, Ex 23:10 8393
that its **y** may increase for you; Lv 19:25 8393
'Then the land will **y** its produce, Lv 25:19 5414
so that the land will **y** its produce Lv 26:4 5414
for your land will not **y** its produce Lv 26:20 5414
the trees of the land will not **y** their Lv 26:20 5414
eyes, that it may **y** its water. Nu 20:8 5414
the ground will not **y** its fruit; Dt 11:17 5414
not **y** to him or listen to him; Dt 13:8 14
And consumes the earth with its **y**, Dt 32:22 2981
And with the choice **y** of the sun, Dt 33:14 8393
some of the **y** of the land of Canaan Jos 5:12 8393
but **y** to the LORD and enter His 2Ch 30:8 5414, 3027
"**Y** now and be at peace with Him; Jb 22:21 5532a
And our land will **y** its produce. Ps 85:12 5414
will still **y** fruit in old age; Ps 92:14 5107
And my **y** *better* than choicest silver. Pr 8:19 8393
ten acres of vineyard will **y** *only* one Is 5:10 6213a
a homer of seed will **y** *but* an ephah Is 5:10 6213a
bread *from* the **y** of the ground, Is 30:23 8393
of drought Nor cease to **y** fruit. Jer 17:8 6213a
might **y** branches and bear fruit Ezk 17:8 6213a
the tree of the field will **y** its fruit and Ezk 34:27 5414
and the earth will **y** its increase, Ezk 34:27 5414
Should it **y**, strangers would swallow Hos 8:7 6213a
the **y** of the olive should fail And Hab 3:17 4639
the vine will **y** its fruit, the Zch 8:12 5414
the land will **y** its produce and Zch 8:12 5414
But we did not **y** in subjection to Ga 2:5 1502

YIELDED

The earth has **y** its produce; Ps 67:6 5414
y shoots and sent out branches. Ezk 17:6 6213a

and **y** up their bodies so as not to **Da 3:28** 3052
fig tree and the vine have **y** in full. **Jl 2:22** 5414
on the good soil and **y** a crop, **Mt 13:8** *1325*
a loud voice, and **y** up His spirit. **Mt 27:50** *863*
and choked it, and it **y** no crop. **Mk 4:7** *1325*
they **y** a crop and produced thirty, **Mk 4:8** *1325*

YIELDING
sprout vegetation, plants **y** seed, **Gn 1:11** 2232
plants **y** seed after their kind, **Gn 1:12** 2232
I have given you every plant **y** seed **Gn 1:29** 2232
every tree which has fruit **y** seed; **Gn 1:29** 2232
of fruit, **y** its fruit every month; **Rv 22:2** *591*

YIELDS
Which **y** its fruit in its season And **Ps 1:3** 5414
the root of the righteous **y** *fruit.* **Pr 12:12** 5414
grain has no heads; It **y** no grain. **Hos 8:7** 6213a
but if it **y** thorns and thistles, **Heb 6:8** *1627*
afterwards it **y** the peaceful fruit **Heb 12:11** *591*

YIRON
and **Y** and Migdal-el, Horem and **Jos 19:38** 3375

YOKE
break his **y** from your neck." **Gn 27:40** 5923
and I broke the bars of your **y** and **Lv 26:13** 5923
on which a **y** has never been placed. **Nu 19:2** 5923
and which has not pulled in a **y**; **Dt 21:3** 5923
and He will put an iron **y** on your **Dt 28:48** 5923
on which there has never been a **y**; **1Sa 6:7** 5923
He took a **y** of oxen and cut **1Sa 11:7** 6776
"Your father made our **y** hard; **1Ki 12:4** 5923
his heavy **y** which he put on us, **1Ki 12:4** 5923
y which your father put on us'?" **1Ki 12:9** 5923
'Your father made our **y** heavy, **1Ki 12:10** 5923
father loaded you with a heavy **y**, **1Ki 12:11** 5923
heavy yoke, I will add to your **y**; **1Ki 12:11** 5923
"My father made your **y** heavy, **1Ki 12:14** 5923
heavy, but I will add to your **y**; **1Ki 12:14** 5923
"Your father made our **y** hard; **2Ch 10:4** 5923
his heavy **y** which he put on us, **2Ch 10:4** 5923
y which your father put on us'?" **2Ch 10:9** 5923
'Your father made our **y** heavy, **2Ch 10:10** 5923
father loaded you with a heavy **y**, **2Ch 10:11** 5923
heavy yoke, I will add to your **y**; **2Ch 10:11** 5923
"My father made your **y** heavy, **2Ch 10:14** 5923
3,000 camels, 500 **y** of oxen, **Jb 1:3** 6776
6,000 camels and 1,000 **y** of oxen **Jb 42:12** 6776
shall break the **y** of their burden **Is 9:4** 5923
and his **y** from your neck, **Is 10:27** 5923
and the **y** will be broken because **Is 10:27** 5923
his **y** will be removed from them and **Is 14:25** 5923
aged you made your **y** very heavy. **Is 47:6** 5923
To undo the bands of the **y**, **Is 58:6** 4133
go free And break every **y**? **Is 58:6** 4133
you remove the **y** from your midst, **Is 58:9** 4133
long ago I broke your **y** *And* tore off **Jer 2:20** 5923
broken the **y** *And* burst the bonds. **Jer 5:5** 5923
the **y** of the king of Babylon, **Jer 27:8** 5923
under the **y** of the king of Babylon **Jer 27:11** 5923
the **y** of the king of Babylon and **Jer 27:12** 5923
broken the **y** of the king of Babylon. **Jer 28:2** 5923
break the **y** of the king of Babylon. **Jer 28:4** 5923
Hananiah the prophet took the **y** **Jer 28:10** 4133
the **y** of Nebuchadnezzar king of **Jer 28:11** 5923
the prophet had broken the **y** from **Jer 28:12** 4133
"I have put a **y** of iron on the **Jer 28:14** 5923
break his **y** from off their neck and **Jer 30:8** 5923
y of my transgressions is bound; **La 1:14** 5923
he should bear The **y** in his youth. **La 3:27** 5923
I break there the **y** bars of Egypt. **Ezk 30:18** 4133
I have broken the bars of their **y** and **Ezk 34:27** 5923
come over her fair neck *with a* **y**; **Hos 10:11**
who lifts the **y** from their jaws; **Hos 11:4** 5923
break his **y** bar from upon you, **Na 1:13** 4132
"Take My **y** upon you and learn **Mt 11:29** *2218*
"For My **y** is easy and My burden is **Mt 11:30** *2218*
'I have bought five **y** of oxen, **Lk 14:19** *2201*
upon the neck of the disciples a **y** **Ac 15:10** *2218*
subject again to a **y** of slavery. **Ga 5:1** *2218*
All who are under the **y** as slaves **1Tm 6:1** *2218*

YOKES
the **y** of the oxen for the wood. **2Sa 24:22** 3627
and **y** and put them on your neck, **Jer 27:2** 4133
"You have broken the **y** of wood, **Jer 28:13** 4133
made instead of them **y** of iron." **Jer 28:13** 4133

YOUNG
except what the **y** men have eaten, **Gn 14:24** 5288
a turtledove, and a **y** pigeon." **Gn 15:9** 1469
the house, both **y** and old, **Gn 19:4** 5288
and took two of his **y** men with him **Gn 22:3** 5288
Abraham said to his **y** men, **Gn 22:5** 5288
So Abraham returned to his **y** men, **Gn 22:19** 5288
and bring me two choice **y** goats **Gn 27:9** 1423, 5795
And she put the skins of the **y** goats **Gn 27:16** 1423, 5795
"Get me this **y** girl for a wife." **Gn 34:4** 3207
The **y** man did not delay to do **Gn 34:19** 5288
"I will send you a **y** goat from **Gn 38:17** 1423, 5795
When Judah sent the **y** goat by his **Gn 38:20** 1423, 5795
I sent this **y** goat, but you did not **Gn 38:23** 1423
shall go with our **y** and our old; **Ex 10:9** 5288
"You are not to boil a **y** goat in **Ex 23:19** 1423
sent **y** men of the sons of Israel, **Ex 24:5** 5288
sacrificed **y** bulls as peace offerings **Ex 24:5** 6499
take one **y** bull and two rams **Ex 29:1** 1121
Joshua, the son of Nun, a **y** man, **Ex 33:11** 5288
"You shall not boil a **y** goat in its **Ex 34:26** 1423
slay the **y** bull before the LORD; **Lv 1:5** 1121
the turtledoves or from **y** pigeons. **Lv 1:14** 1121
two turtledoves or two **y** pigeons, **Lv 5:7** 1121
two turtledoves or two **y** pigeons, **Lv 5:11** 1121
and a **y** pigeon or a turtledove for **Lv 12:6** 1121
two turtledoves or two **y** pigeons, **Lv 12:8** 1121
two turtledoves or two **y** pigeons **Lv 14:22** 1121
of the turtledoves or **y** pigeons, **Lv 14:30** 1121
two turtledoves or two **y** pigeons, **Lv 15:14** 1121
two turtledoves or two **y** pigeons and **Lv 15:29** 1121
kill *both* it and its **y** in one day. **Lv 22:28** 1121
or two **y** pigeons to the priest, **Nu 6:10** 1121
one **y** bull, one ram, one male lamb **Nu 7:27** 1121
So a **y** man ran and told Moses and **Nu 11:27** 5288
aroma to the LORD: two **y** bulls, **Nu 28:27** 1121
your herd and the **y** of your flock, **Dt 7:13** 6251
You shall not boil a **y** goat in its **Dt 14:21** 1423
the ground, with **y** ones or eggs, **Dt 22:6** 667
sitting on the **y** or on the eggs, **Dt 22:6** 667
not take the mother with the **y**; **Dt 22:6** 1121
the **y** you may take for yourself, **Dt 22:7** 1121
your herd and the **y** of your flock. **Dt 28:4** 6251
your herd and the **y** of your flock. **Dt 28:18** 6251
the old, nor show favor to the **y**. **Dt 28:50** 5288
of your herd or the **y** of your flock **Dt 28:51** 6251
its nest, That hovers over its **y**, **Dt 32:11** 1469
Both **y** man and virgin, **Dt 32:25** 970
both man and woman, **y** and old, **Jos 6:21** 5288
So the **y** men who were spies went **Jos 6:23** 5288
Gideon went in and prepared a **y** goat **Jg 6:19** 1423, 5795
he called quickly to the **y** man, **Jg 9:54** 5288
So the **y** man pierced him through, **Jg 9:54** 5288
so that we may prepare a **y** goat **Jg 13:15** 1423, 5795
So Manoah took the **y** goat with **Jg 13:19** 1423, 5795
a **y** lion *came* roaring toward him. **Jg 14:5** 3715
he tore him as one tears a **y** goat **Jg 14:6** 1423
the **y** men customarily did this. **Jg 14:10** 970
visited his wife with a **y** goat, **Jg 15:1** 1423
a **y** man from Bethlehem in Judah, **Jg 17:7** 5288
and the **y** man became to him like **Jg 17:11** 5288
and the **y** man became his priest **Jg 17:12** 5288
recognized the voice of the **y** man, **Jg 18:3** 5288
came to the house of the **y** man, **Jg 18:15** 5288
y man who is with your servants; **Jg 19:19** 5288
400 **y** virgins who had not known a **Jg 21:12** 5291
"Whose **y** woman is this?" **Ru 2:5** 5291
"She is the **y** Moabite woman who **Ru 2:6** 5291
first by not going after **y** men, **Ru 3:10** 970
will give you by this **y** woman." **Ru 4:12** 5291
Shiloh, although the child was **y**. **1Sa 1:24** 5288
Thus the sin of the **y** men was very **1Sa 2:17** 5288
men of the city, both **y** and old, **1Sa 5:9** 6996b
your best **y** men and your donkeys and **1Sa 8:16** 970
y women going out to draw water and **1Sa 9:11** 5291
one carrying three **y** goats, another **1Sa 10:3** 1423
said to the **y** man who was carrying **1Sa 14:1** 5288
Then Jonathan said to the **y** man **1Sa 14:6** 5288
one of the **y** men said, **1Sa 16:18** 5288
and a jug of wine and a **y** goat, **1Sa 16:20** 1423
"Abner, whose son is this **y** man?" **1Sa 17:55** 5288
"Whose son are you, **y** man?" **1Sa 17:58** 5288
and I have directed the **y** men to a **1Sa 21:2** 5288
if only the **y** men have kept **1Sa 21:4** 5288
vessels of the **y** men were holy, **1Sa 21:5** 5288
So David sent ten **y** men; **1Sa 25:5** 5288
men; and David said to the **y** men, **1Sa 25:5** 5288
'Ask your **y** men and they will tell **1Sa 25:8** 5288
my **y** men find favor in your eyes, **1Sa 25:8** 5288
When David's **y** men came, they **1Sa 25:9** 5288
So David's **y** men retraced their **1Sa 25:12** 5288
But one of the **y** men told Abigail, **1Sa 25:14** 5288
She said to her **y** men, **1Sa 25:19** 5288
y men of my lord whom you sent. **1Sa 25:25** 5288
the **y** men who accompany my lord. **1Sa 25:27** 5288
the **y** men come over and take it. **1Sa 26:22** 5288
"I am a **y** man of Egypt, a servant **1Sa 30:13** 5288
except four hundred **y** men who rode **1Sa 30:17** 5288
said to the **y** man who told him, **2Sa 1:5** 5288
The **y** man who told him said, **2Sa 1:6** 5288
said to the **y** man who told him, **2Sa 1:13** 5288
called one of the **y** men and said, **2Sa 1:15** 5288
"Now let the **y** men arise and hold **2Sa 2:14** 5288
take hold of one of the **y** men for **2Sa 2:21** 5288
Then David commanded the **y** men, **2Sa 4:12** 5288
had a **y** son whose name was Mica. **2Sa 9:12** 6996a
called his **y** man who attended him **2Sa 13:17** 5288
have put to death all the **y** men, **2Sa 13:32** 5288
And the **y** man who was the watchman **2Sa 13:34** 5288
bring back the **y** man Absalom." **2Sa 14:21** 5288
summer fruit for the **y** men to eat, **2Sa 16:2** 5288
my sake with the **y** man Absalom." **2Sa 18:5** 5288
'Protect for me the **y** man Absalom!' **2Sa 18:12** 5288
And ten **y** men who carried Joab's **2Sa 18:15** 5288
it well with the **y** man Absalom?" **2Sa 18:29** 5288
it well with the **y** man Absalom?" **2Sa 18:32** 5288
you for evil, be as that **y** man!" **2Sa 18:32** 5288
stood by him one of Joab's **y** men, **2Sa 20:11** 5288
a **y** virgin for my lord the king, **1Ki 1:2** 5291
with him, while Hadad *was* a **y** boy. **1Ki 11:17** 6996a
that the **y** man was industrious, **1Ki 11:28** 5288
and consulted with the **y** men who **1Ki 12:8** 3206
The **y** men who grew up with him **1Ki 12:10** 3206
to the advice of the **y** men, **1Ki 12:14** 3206
'By the **y** men of the rulers of the **1Ki 20:14** 5288
y men of the rulers of the provinces **1Ki 20:15** 5288
The **y** men of the rulers of the **1Ki 20:17** 5288
the **y** men of the rulers of the **1Ki 20:19** 5288
y lads came out from the city and **2Ki 2:23** 6996a
y men of the sons of the prophets **2Ki 5:22** 5288
and their **y** men you will kill with **2Ki 8:12** 970
So the **y** man, the servant of the **2Ki 9:4** 5288
Zadok, a **y** man mighty of valor, **1Ch 12:28** 5288
Solomon is **y** and inexperienced, **1Ch 22:5** 5288
is still **y** and inexperienced and **1Ch 29:1** 5288
and consulted with the **y** men who **2Ch 10:8** 3206
The **y** men who grew up with him **2Ch 10:10** 3206
to the advice of the **y** men, **2Ch 10:14** 3206
when he was **y** and timid and could **2Ch 13:7** 5288
with a **y** bull and seven rams, **2Ch 13:9** 1121
flocks of lambs and **y** goats, all for **2Ch 35:7** 1121, 5795
the Chaldeans who slew their **y** men **2Ch 36:17** 970
no compassion on **y** man or virgin, **2Ch 36:17** 970
Whatever is needed, both **y** bulls, **Ezr 6:9** 1123
"Let beautiful **y** virgins be **Es 2:2** 5291
may gather every beautiful **y** virgin **Es 2:3** 5291
"Then let the **y** lady who pleases **Es 2:4** 5291
Now the **y** lady was beautiful of **Es 2:7** 5291
many **y** ladies were gathered to the **Es 2:8** 5291
Now the **y** lady pleased him and **Es 2:9** 5291
Now when the turn of each **y** lady **Es 2:12** 5291
the **y** lady would go in to the king **Es 2:13** 5291
all the Jews, both **y** and old, **Es 3:13** 5288
it fell on the **y** people and they died, **Jb 1:19** 5288
teeth of the **y** lions are broken. **Jb 4:10** 3715
"Even **y** children despise me; **Jb 19:18** 5759
y men saw me and hid themselves, **Jb 29:8** 5288
"I am **y** in years and you are old; **Jb 32:6** 6810
the appetite of the **y** lions, **Jb 38:39** 3715
When its **y** cry to God And **Jb 38:41** 3206
down, they bring forth their **y**, **Jb 39:3** 3206
"She treats her **y** cruelly, as if **Jb 39:16** 1121
"His **y** ones also suck up blood; **Jb 39:30** 667
a **y** lion lurking in hiding places. **Ps 17:12** 3715
calf, And Sirion like a **y** wild ox. **Ps 29:6** 1121
The **y** lions do lack and suffer **Ps 34:10** 3715
I have been **y** and now I am old **Ps 37:25** 5288
take no **y** bull out of your house Nor **Ps 50:9** 6499
Then **y** bulls will be offered on **Ps 51:19** 6499
Break out the fangs of the **y** lions, **Ps 58:6** 3715
Or a **y** bull with horns and hoofs. **Ps 69:31** 6499
Fire devoured His **y** men, **Ps 78:63** 970
herself, where she may lay her **y**, **Ps 84:3** 667
The **y** lion and the serpent you **Ps 91:13** 3715
The **y** lions roar after their prey And **Ps 104:21** 3715
and locusts came, And **y** locusts, **Ps 105:34** 3218
How can a **y** man keep his way pure? **Ps 119:9** 5288
And to the **y** ravens which cry. **Ps 147:9** 1121
Both **y** men and virgins; **Ps 148:12** 970
the youths A **y** man lacking sense, **Pr 7:7** 5288
glory of **y** men is their strength, **Pr 20:29** 970
out, And the **y** eagles will eat it. **Pr 30:17** 1121
Rejoice, **y** man, during your **Ec 11:9** 970
during the days of **y** manhood. **Ec 11:9** 979
And pasture your **y** goats By the **SS 1:8** 1429
So is my beloved among the **y** men. **SS 2:3** 1121
beloved is like a gazelle or a **y** stag. **SS 2:9** 6082
and be like a gazelle Or a **y** stag **SS 2:17** 6082
not one among them has lost her **y**. **SS 4:2** 7909b
not one among them has lost her **y**. **SS 6:6** 7909b
And be like a gazelle or a **y** stag **SS 8:14** 6082
and it roars like **y** lions; **Is 5:29** 3715
not take pleasure in their **y** men, **Is 9:17** 970
will lie down with the **y** goat, **Is 11:6** 1423
y lion and the fatling together; **Is 11:6** 3715
Their **y** will lie down together, **Is 11:7** 3206
bows will mow down the **y** men, **Is 13:18** 5288
and the exiles of Cush, **y** and old, **Is 20:4** 5288
I have neither brought up **y** men *nor* **Is 23:4** 970
their riches on the backs of **y** donkeys **Is 30:6** 5895
the **y** lion growls over his prey, **Is 31:4** 3715
And his **y** men will become forced **Is 31:8** 970
And **y** bulls with strong ones; **Is 34:7** 6499
And vigorous **y** men stumble badly, **Is 40:30** 970
The **y** camels of Midian and Ephah; **Is 60:6** 1072
For *as* a **y** man marries a virgin, **Is 62:5** 970
"The **y** lions have roared at him, **Jer 2:15** 3715
swift **y** camel entangling her ways, **Jer 2:23** 1072
the gathering of **y** men together; **Jer 6:11** 970
The **y** men from the town squares. **Jer 9:21** 970
The **y** men will die by the sword, **Jer 11:22** 970
given birth only to abandon *her* **y**, **Jer 14:5**
against the mother of a **y** man, **Jer 15:8** 970
Their **y** men struck down by the **Jer 18:21** 970
the **y** of the flock and the herd; **Jer 31:12** 1121
dance, And the **y** men and the old, **Jer 31:13** 970
His choicest **y** men have also gone **Jer 48:15** 970
y men will fall in her streets, **Jer 49:26** 970
Put all her **y** bulls to the sword; **Jer 50:27** 6499
y men will fall in her streets, **Jer 50:30** 970
So do not spare her **y** men; **Jer 51:3** 970
you I shatter **y** man and virgin, **Jer 51:22** 970
will roar together like **y** lions, **Jer 51:38** 3715
time against me To crush my **y** men; **La 1:15** 970
my **y** men Have gone into captivity. **La 1:18** 970
in the streets Lie **y** and old; **La 2:21** 5288
my **y** men Have fallen by the sword. **La 2:21** 970
the breast, They nurse their **y**; **La 4:3** 1482
Y men worked at the grinding mill, **La 5:13** 970
the gate, **Y** men from their music. **La 5:14** 970
"Utterly slay old men, **y** men, **Ezk 9:6** 970
plucked off the topmost of its **y** twigs **Ezk 17:4** 3242
from the topmost of its **y** twigs **Ezk 17:22** 3127
She lay down among **y** lions, **Ezk 19:2** 3715
of her cubs And made him a **y** lion. **Ezk 19:5** 3715

He became a y lion, He learned to Ezk 19:6 3715
all of them desirable y men, Ezk 23:6 970
all of them desirable y men. Ezk 23:12 970
desirable y men, governors and Ezk 23:23 970
"The y men of On and of Pi-beseth Ezk 30:17 970
to a y lion of the nations, Ezk 32:2 3715
and a y lion's face toward the Ezk 41:19 3715
'a y bull for a sin offering. Ezk 43:19 1121
you shall present a y bull without Ezk 43:23 1121
a y bull and a ram from the flock, Ezk 43:25 1121
you shall take a y bull without Ezk 45:18 1121
offer a y bull without blemish, Ezk 46:6 1121
a y lion to the house of Judah. Hos 5:14 3715
Your y men will see visions. Jl 2:28 970
some of your y men to be Nazirites. Am 2:11 970
Does a y lion growl from his den Am 3:4 3715
I slew your y men by the sword Am 4:10 970
the y men will faint from thirst. Am 8:13 970
a y lion among flocks of sheep, Mi 5:8 3715
the feeding place of the y lions, Na 2:11 3715
a sword will devour your y lions; Na 2:13 3715
"Run, speak to that y man, Zch 2:4 5288
Grain will make the y men flourish, Zch 9:17 970
is a sound of the y lions' roar, Zch 11:3 3715
The y man said to Him, Mt 19:20 *3495*
the y man heard this statement, Mt 19:22 *3495*
A y man was following Him, Mk 14:51 *3495*
saw a y man sitting at the right, Mk 16:5 *3495*
TURTLEDOVES OR TWO Y PIGEONS." Lk 2:24 *3556b*
"Y man, I say to you, arise!" Lk 7:14 *3495*
have never given me a y goat, Lk 15:29 *2056*
Jesus, finding a y donkey, Jn 12:14 *3678*
AND YOUR Y MEN SHALL SEE VISIONS, Ac 2:17 *3495*
y men got up and covered him up, Ac 5:6 *3501b*
and the y men came in and found Ac 5:10 *3495*
at the feet of a y man named Saul. Ac 7:58 *3494*
And there was a y man Ac 20:9 *3494*
"Lead this y man to the Ac 23:17 *3494*
asked me to lead this y man to you Ac 23:18 *3495*
the commander let the y man go, Ac 23:22 *3495*
y women to love their husbands, Ti 2:4 *3501b*
urge the y men to be sensible; Ti 2:6 *3501b*
I am writing to you, y men, 1Jn 2:13 *3495*
I have written to you, y men, 1Jn 2:14 *3495*

YOUNGER

Then the firstborn said to the y, Gn 19:31 6810
the firstborn said to the y, Gn 19:34 6810
and the y arose and lay with him; Gn 19:35 6810
As for the y, she also bore a Gn 19:38 6810
And the older shall serve the y." Gn 25:23 6810
and put them on Jacob her y son. Gn 27:15 6996a
sent and called her y son Jacob, Gn 27:42 6996a
and the name of the y was Rachel. Gn 29:16 6996a
for your y daughter Rachel." Gn 29:18 6996a
marry off the y before the firstborn. Gn 29:26 6810
head of Ephraim, who was the y, Gn 48:14 6810
his y brother shall be greater Gn 48:19 6996b
son of Kenaz, Caleb's y brother, Jg 1:13 6996b
son of Kenaz, Caleb's y brother. Jg 3:9 6996b
Is not her y sister more beautiful Jg 15:2 6996a
and the name of the y Michal. 1Sa 14:49 6996a
as well as those of his y brother. 1Ch 24:31 6996a
"But now those y than I mock me, Jb 30:1 6810
and your y sister, who lives south Ezk 16:46 6996a
both your older and your y; Ezk 16:61 6996a
"The y of them said to his father, Lk 15:12 *3501b*
the y son gathered everything Lk 15:13 *3501b*
when you were y, you used to gird Jn 21:18 *3501b*
"THE OLDER WILL SERVE THE Y." Ro 9:12 *1640*
father, *to* the y men as brothers, 1Tm 5:1 *3501b*
and the y women as sisters, 1Tm 5:2 *3501b*
refuse *to put* y widows *on the list,* 1Tm 5:11 *3501b*
I want y *widows* to get married, 1Tm 5:14 *3501b*
You y men, likewise, be subject to 1Pe 5:5 *3501b*

YOUNGEST

what his y son had done to him. Gn 9:24 6996a
the y is with our father today, Gn 42:13 6996b
unless your y brother comes here! Gn 42:15 6996b
and bring your y brother to me, so Gn 42:20 6996b
and the y is with our father today Gn 42:32 6996b
'But bring your y brother to me Gn 42:34 6996b
"Is this your y brother, of whom Gn 43:29 6996b
and the y according to his youth, Gn 43:33 6810
in the mouth of the sack of the y, Gn 44:2 6996b
the oldest and ending with the y, Gn 44:12 6996b
y brother comes down with you, Gn 44:23 6996b
If our y brother is with us, then Gn 44:26 6996b
unless our y brother is with us.' Gn 44:26 6996b
with *the loss of* his y son he shall set Jos 6:26 6810
I am the y in my father's house." Jg 6:15 6810
the y son of Jerubbaal was left, Jg 9:5 6996b
"There remains yet the y, 1Sa 16:11 6996a
David was the y. 1Sa 17:14 6996a
with the *loss of* his y son Segub, 1Ki 16:34 6810
Jehoahaz, the y of his sons. 2Ch 21:17 6996b
Jerusalem made Ahaziah, his y son, 2Ch 22:1 6996b
There is Benjamin, the y, Ps 68:27 6810
among you must become like the y, Lk 22:26 *3501b*

YOURS

thong or anything that is y, Gn 14:23
die, you and all who are y." Gn 20:7
point out what is y among my Gn 31:32
of all the land of Egypt is y.'" Gn 45:20
been born after them shall be y; Gn 48:6
'The honor is y to tell me: Ex 8:9
'Every grain offering of y, Lv 2:13
for their nakedness is y. Lv 18:10
'If a fellow countryman of y Lv 25:25
'Now in case a countryman of y Lv 25:35
'If a countryman of y becomes Lv 25:39
and a countryman of y becomes so Lv 25:47
'Every valuation of y, Lv 27:25
be y from the most holy *gifts reserved* Nu 18:9
'This also is y, the offering of Nu 18:11
bring to the LORD, shall be y; Nu 18:13
thing in Israel shall be y. Nu 18:14
offer to the LORD, shall be y; Nu 18:15
"Their meat shall be y; Nu 18:18
it shall be y like the breast of a Nu 18:18
and this land shall be y for a Nu 32:22
do such works and mighty acts as Y? Dt 3:24
your foot treads shall be y; Dt 11:24
hand shall release whatever of y Dt 15:3
daughters but they will not be y, Dt 28:41
"Our life for y if you do not Jos 2:14
but the hill country shall be y. Jos 17:18
farthest borders it shall be y; Jos 17:18
the honor shall not be y on the Jg 4:9
Please let her be y instead." Jg 15:2
I will not cut off every man of y 1Sa 2:33
belongs to Mephibosheth is y." 2Sa 16:4
able to judge this great people of Y?" 1Ki 3:9
"He shall be neither mine nor y; 1Ki 3:26
I am y, and all that I have." 1Ki 20:4
lick up your blood, even y. 1Ki 21:19 859
the lives of these fifty servants of y 2Ki 1:13
"*We are* y, O David, And with you, 1Ch 12:18
not take what is y for the LORD, 1Ch 21:24
"Y, O LORD, is the greatness 1Ch 29:11
Y is the dominion, O LORD, 1Ch 29:11
from Your hand, and all is Y. 1Ch 29:16
who can rule this great people of Y?" 2Ch 1:10
for the battle is not y but God's. 2Ch 20:15
"The silver is y, and the people Es 3:11 5414
And that no purpose of Y can be Jb 42:2
And lovingkindness is Y, O Lord, Ps 62:12
Your righteousness, Y alone. Ps 71:16
Y is the day, Yours also is Ps 74:16
Yours is the day, Y also is Ps 74:16
Nor are there any works like Y. Ps 86:8
The heavens are Y, the earth also is Ps 89:11
the earth also is Y; The world Ps 89:11
I am Y, save me; For I have sought Ps 119:94
Let them be y alone And not for Pr 5:17
come over to you and will be y; Is 45:14
in a land that is not y.' Jer 5:19
and the redemption is y; Jer 32:8
is their territory greater than y? Am 6:2
[For Y is the kingdom and the power Mt 6:13 *4771*
'Take what is y and go, Mt 20:14 *4674*
See, you have what is y.' Mt 25:25 *4674*
before me, it shall all be Y." Lk 4:7 *4674*
but Y eat and drink." Lk 5:33 *4674*
poor, for y is the kingdom of God. Lk 6:20 *5212*
and whoever takes away what is y, Lk 6:30 *4674*
never neglected a command of y; Lk 15:29 *4771*
but when this son of y came, Lk 15:30 *4771*
me, and all that is mine is y. Lk 15:31 *4674*
for this brother of y was dead and Lk 15:32 *4771*
but Y be done." Lk 22:42 *4674*
and the power of darkness are y." Lk 22:53 *4771*
My word, they will keep y also. Jn 15:20 *5212*
they were Y and You gave them to Me, Jn 17:6 *4771*
for they are Y; Jn 17:9 *4771*
and all things that are Mine are Y, Jn 17:10 *4674*
and Y are Mine; and I have been Jn 17:10 *4674*
repent of this wickedness of y, Ac 8:22 *4771*
the other's faith, both y and mine. Ro 1:12 *4771*
But take care that this liberty of y 1Co 8:9 *4771*
have refreshed my spirit and y. 1Co 16:18 *4771*
for I do not seek what is y, 2Co 12:14 *4771*
their Master and y is in heaven, Eph 6:9 *4771*
and peace be y in the fullest measure. 1Pe 1:2 *4771*
to the former lusts *which were* y 1Pe 1:14
For if these *qualities* are y and are 2Pe 1:8 *4771*
I am a fellow servant of y and Rv 19:10 *4771*
I am a fellow servant of y and of Rv 22:9 *4771*

YOURSELF

"Make for y an ark of gopher wood; Gn 6:14
take for y some of all food which Gn 6:21
is edible, and gather *it* to y; Gn 6:21
to me and take the goods for y." Gn 14:21
and submit y to her authority." Gn 16:9
and from there take to y a wife Gn 28:2
for you y know my service which I Gn 30:26 859
"You y know how I have served you Gn 30:29 859
my belongings and take *it* for y." Gn 31:32
a breach you have made for y!" Gn 38:29
and station y to meet him on the Ex 7:15 5324
and present y before Pharaoh, Ex 8:20 3320
"Still you exalt y against My Ex 9:17
you refuse to humble y before Me? Ex 10:3
both y and these people who are Ex 18:18 859
"You shall not make for y an idol, Ex 20:4
"Speak to us y and we will listen; Ex 20:19 859
bring near to y Aaron your brother, Ex 28:1
Take also for y the finest of spices: Ex 30:23
"Take for y spices, stacte and Ex 30:34
servants to whom You swore by Y, Ex 32:13
you know the people y, Ex 32:22 859
But You Y have not let me know Ex 33:12 859
"Cut out for y two stone tablets Ex 34:1
and present y there to Me on the Ex 34:2 5324
"Watch y that you make no Ex 34:12
shall make for y no molten gods. Ex 34:17
"Take for y a calf, a bull, for a Lv 9:2
that you may make atonement for y Lv 9:7
you shall love your neighbor as y; Lv 19:18
you, and you shall love him as y, Lv 19:34
y, and your male and female Lv 25:6
off seven sabbaths of years for y, Lv 25:8
and if you have defiled y and a Nu 5:20
"Make y two trumpets of silver, Nu 10:2
"Send out for y men so that they Nu 13:2
give heed to y and keep your soul Dt 4:9
'You shall not make for y an idol, Dt 5:8
then watch y, that you do not forget the Dt 6:12
'Cut out for y two tablets of Dt 10:1
and make an ark of wood for y. Dt 10:1
"You shall count seven weeks for y; Dt 16:9
"You shall appoint for y judges Dt 16:18
"You shall not plant for y an Dt 16:21
God, which you shall make for y. Dt 16:21
"You shall not set up for y a Dt 16:22
you shall set aside three cities for y Dt 19:2
"You shall prepare the roads for y, Dt 19:3
set aside three cities for y.' Dt 19:7
shall add three more cities for y, Dt 19:9
you shall take as booty for y; Dt 20:14
would take her as a wife for y, Dt 21:11
but the young you may take for y, Dt 22:7
"You shall make y tassels on the Dt 22:12
garment with which you cover y. Dt 22:12
keep y from every evil thing. Dt 23:9
shall set up for y large stones and Dt 27:2
will not anoint y with the oil, Dt 28:40
and gather to y into the house Jos 2:18
"Make for y flint knives and Jos 5:2
to the forest and clear a place for y Jos 17:15
"Rise up y, and fall on us; Jg 8:21 859
"Sustain y with a piece of bread, Jg 19:5 3820
"Please sustain y, and wait until Jg 19:8 3824
"Wash y therefore, and anoint Ru 3:3
anoint y and put on your *best* Ru 3:3
but do not make y known to the man Ru 3:3
Redeem *it* for y; you *may have* my Ru 4:6
relative said to Boaz, "Buy *it* for y." Ru 4:8
"How long will you make y drunk? 1Sa 1:14
do for y what the occasion requires, 1Sa 10:7
turn y, *and* here I am with you 1Sa 14:7
stay in a secret place and hide y. 1Sa 19:2
iniquity in me, put me to death y; 1Sa 20:8 859
you hid y on that eventful day, 1Sa 20:19
if you would take it for y, 1Sa 21:9
from avenging y by your own hand, 1Sa 25:26
of one of the young men for y, 2Sa 2:21
and take for y his spoil." 2Sa 2:21
people whom You have redeemed for Y 2Sa 7:23
"For You have established for Y Your 2Sa 7:24
now, and do not anoint y with oil, 2Sa 14:2
have made y odious to your father. 2Sa 16:21
you y would have stood aloof." 2Sa 18:13 859
days, and be present here y." 2Sa 20:4 859
"With the kind You show Y kind, 2Sa 22:26
With the blameless You show Y 2Sa 22:26
With the pure You show Y pure, 2Sa 22:27
And with the perverted You show Y 2Sa 22:27
choose for y one of them, which I 2Sa 24:12
therefore, and show y a man. 1Ki 2:2
"Build for y a house in Jerusalem 1Ki 2:36
have not asked for y long life, 1Ki 3:11
life, nor have asked riches for y, 1Ki 3:11
but have asked for y discernment 1Ki 3:11
"Take for y ten pieces; 1Ki 11:31
"Come home with me and refresh y, 1Ki 13:7
and disguise y so that they will 1Ki 14:2
made for y other gods and molten 1Ki 14:9
and hide y by the brook Cherith, 1Ki 17:3
make *one* for y and for your son. 1Ki 17:13
"Go, show y to Ahab, and I will 1Ki 18:1
strengthen y and observe and see 1Ki 20:22
make streets for y in Damascus, 1Ki 20:34
you y have decided *it*." 1Ki 20:40 859
because you have sold y to do evil 1Ki 21:20
enter an inner room to hide y." 1Ki 22:25
the LORD lives and as you y live, 2Ki 2:2 5315
the LORD lives, and as you y live, 2Ki 2:4 5315
the LORD lives, and as you y live, 2Ki 2:6 5315
"Go, borrow vessels at large for y 2Ki 4:3
the LORD lives and as you y live, 2Ki 4:30 5315
"Take it up for y." 2Ki 6:7
and you humbled y before the LORD 2Ki 22:19 3665
choose for y one of them, which I 1Ch 21:10
"Thus says the LORD, 'Take for y 1Ch 21:11
Ornan said to David, "Take *it* for y; 1Ch 21:23
and You exalt Y as head over all. 1Ch 29:11
asked for y wisdom and knowledge that 2Ch 1:11
enter an inner room to hide y." 2Ch 18:24
so *bring* wrath on y from the LORD? 2Ch 19:2
you have allied y with Ahaziah, 2Ch 20:37
and you humbled y before God when 2Ch 34:27 3665
because you humbled y before Me, 2Ch 34:27 3665
And made a name for Y as *it is* Ne 9:10
Hear it, and know for y." Jb 5:27
And bring him into judgment with Y. Jb 14:3
of God, And limit wisdom to y? Jb 15:8
a pledge for me with Y; Who is there Jb 17:3
"O you who tear y in your anger Jb 18:4 5315
wickedness is for a man like y, Jb 35:8
"Adorn y with eminence and dignity, Jb 40:10 5710b
clothe y with honor and majesty. Jb 40:10 3847
Lift up Y against the rage of my Ps 7:6
And arouse Y for me; You have Ps 7:6
Why do You hide Y in times of Ps 10:1
With the kind You show Y kind; With Ps 18:25
With the blameless You show Y Ps 18:25

With the pure You show **Y** pure,	**Ps 18:26**	
And with the crooked You show **Y**	**Ps 18:26**	
"Commit **y** to the LORD; let	**Ps 22:8**	
Stir up **Y**, and awake to my right	**Ps 35:23**	
Delight **y** in the LORD;	**Ps 37:4**	
Arouse **Y**, why do You sleep, O Lord?	**Ps 44:23**	
praise you when you do well for **y**	**Ps 49:18**	
And do not hide **Y** from my	**Ps 55:1**	
Arouse **Y** to help me, and see!	**Ps 59:4**	
Have not You **Y**, O God, rejected us?	**Ps 60:10**	859
Show **Y** strong, O God, who have	**Ps 68:28**	
they have persecuted him whom You **Y**	**Ps 69:26**	859
a remnant of wrath You will gird **Y**.	**Ps 76:10**	
son whom You have strengthened for **Y**.	**Ps 80:15**	
of man whom You made strong for **Y**.	**Ps 80:17**	
Will You not **Y** revive us again,	**Ps 85:6**	859
You **Y** crushed Rahab like one who is	**Ps 89:10**	859
Will You hide **Y** forever? Will Your	**Ps 89:46**	
Covering **Y** with light as with a cloak,	**Ps 104:2**	
Have not You **Y**, O God, rejected us?	**Ps 108:11**	
For You **Y** have taught me.	**Ps 119:102**	859
this then, my son, and deliver **y**;	**Pr 6:3**	5337
of your neighbor, Go, humble **y**,	**Pr 6:3**	
Deliver **y** like a gazelle from *the*	**Pr 6:5**	5337
you are wise, you are wise for **y**,	**Pr 9:12**	
his ways And find a snare for **y**.	**Pr 22:25**	5315
Do not weary **y** to gain wealth,	**Pr 23:4**	
make it ready for **y** in the field;	**Pr 24:27**	
you have been foolish in exalting **y**	**Pr 30:32**	
test you with pleasure. So enjoy **y**."	**Ec 2:1**	
Why should you ruin **y**?	**Ec 7:16**	
"If you **y** do not know, Most	**SS 1:8**	
"Ask a sign for **y** from the LORD	**Is 7:11**	
"Take for **y** a large tablet and	**Is 8:1**	
you have hewn a tomb for **y** here,	**Is 22:16**	
who carve a resting place for **y** in	**Is 22:16**	
At the lifting up of **Y** nations	**Is 33:3**	
Get **y** up on a high mountain, O	**Is 40:9**	
Rouse **y**! Rouse yourself! Arise, O	**Is 51:17**	5782
Rouse **y**! Arise, O Jerusalem,	**Is 51:17**	5782
awake, Clothe **y** in your strength,	**Is 52:1**	3847
Clothe **y** in your beautiful garments,	**Is 52:1**	3847
Shake **y** from the dust, rise up, O	**Is 52:2**	
Loose **y** from the chains around	**Is 52:2**	
good, And delight **y** in abundance.	**Is 55:2**	5315
from Me, you have uncovered **y**,	**Is 57:8**	
And you have made an agreement for **y**	**Is 57:8**	
not to hide **y** from your own flesh?	**Is 58:7**	
And if you give **y** to the hungry And	**Is 58:10**	5315
To make for **Y** a glorious name.	**Is 63:14**	
Will You restrain **Y** at these things,	**Is 64:12**	
'Keep to **y**, do not come near me,	**Is 65:5**	
"Have you not done this to **y** By	**Jer 2:17**	
How then have you turned **y** before	**Jer 2:21**	
wash **y** with lye And use much soap,	**Jer 2:22**	
your gods Which you made for **y**?	**Jer 2:28**	
Although you decorate **y** *with*	**Jer 4:30**	
In vain you make **y** beautiful.	**Jer 4:30**	
"Go and buy **y** a linen waistband and	**Jer 13:1**	
And you **y** had taught them	**Jer 13:21**	855b
"You shall not take a wife for **y**	**Jer 16:2**	
And you will, even of **y**,	**Jer 17:4**	
You **Y** know that the utterance of my	**Jer 17:16**	859
am going to make you a terror to **y**	**Jer 20:4**	
Make for **y** bonds and yokes and put	**Jer 27:2**	
"Set up for **y** roadmarks, Place	**Jer 31:21**	
roadmarks, Place for **y** guideposts;	**Jer 31:21**	
"Buy for **y** my field which is at	**Jer 32:7**	
redemption is yours; buy *it* for **y**.'	**Jer 32:8**	
And you have made a name for **Y**, as	**Jer 32:20**	
"Buy for **y** the field with money and	**Jer 32:25**	
"Go, hide **y**, you and Jeremiah,	**Jer 36:19**	
and you **y** will not escape from	**Jer 38:18**	859
and you **y** will not escape from	**Jer 38:23**	859
you seeking great things for **y**?	**Jer 45:5**	
'Take your stand and get **y** ready,	**Jer 46:14**	
valley, How long will you gash **y**?	**Jer 47:5**	
Even you **y** will be captured;	**Jer 48:7**	855b
While you **y** were not aware;	**Jer 50:24**	855b
Give **y** no relief,	**La 2:18**	
You have covered **Y** with anger	**La 3:43**	
You have covered **Y** with a cloud So	**La 3:44**	
become drunk and make **y** naked.	**La 4:21**	
but you have delivered **y**.	**Ezk 3:19**	5315
and you have delivered **y**."	**Ezk 3:21**	5315
"Go, shut **y** up in your house.	**Ezk 3:24**	
"Now you son of man, get **y** a brick,	**Ezk 4:1**	
"Then get **y** an iron plate and set	**Ezk 4:3**	
and make them into bread for **y**;	**Ezk 4:9**	
prepare for **y** baggage for exile	**Ezk 12:3**	
made for **y** high places of various	**Ezk 16:16**	
and made for **y** male images that	**Ezk 16:17**	
that you built **y** a shrine and made	**Ezk 16:24**	
made **y** a high place in every square.	**Ezk 16:24**	
"You built **y** a high place at the	**Ezk 16:25**	
"Show **y** sharp, go to the right;	**Ezk 21:16**	
go to the right; set **y**; go to the left,	**Ezk 21:16**	
profane **y** in the sight of the nations,	**Ezk 22:16**	
have defiled **y** with their idols.	**Ezk 23:30**	
You have acquired riches for **y** And	**Ezk 28:4**	
'You compared **y** to a young lion of	**Ezk 32:2**	
take for **y** one stick and write on it,	**Ezk 37:16**	
join them for **y** one to another into	**Ezk 37:17**	
"Be prepared, and prepare **y**,	**Ezk 38:7**	
"Keep your gifts for **y** or	**Da 5:17**	
exalted **y** against the Lord of heaven;	**Da 5:23**	
hand and have made a name for **Y**, as	**Da 9:15**	
and on humbling **y** before your God,	**Da 10:12**	
"Go, take to **y** a wife of harlotry and	**Hos 1:2**	
you **y** will die upon unclean soil.	**Am 7:17**	859
Beth-le-aphrah roll **y** in the dust.	**Mi 1:10**	
Make **y** bald and cut off your hair,	**Mi 1:16**	
but will not anoint **y** with oil;	**Mi 6:15**	
Draw for **y** water for the siege!	**Na 3:14**	
Multiply **y** like the creeping locust,	**Na 3:15**	
Multiply **y** like the swarming locust.	**Na 3:15**	
So you are sinning against **y**.	**Hab 2:10**	5315
Now you **y** drink and expose your	**Hab 2:16**	859
"Take again for **y** the equipment	**Zch 11:15**	
are the Son of God, throw **Y** down;	**Mt 4:6**	4572
but go, show **y** to the priest and	**Mt 8:4**	4572
SHALL LOVE YOUR NEIGHBOR AS **Y**."	**Mt 19:19**	4572
YOU HAVE PREPARED PRAISE FOR **Y**'?"	**Mt 21:16**	
SHALL LOVE YOUR NEIGHBOR AS **Y**.'	**Mt 22:39**	4572
"You have said *it* **y**."	**Mt 26:25**	4771
"You have said it **y**;	**Mt 26:64**	
"What is that to us? See *to that* **y**!"	**Mt 27:4**	4771
rebuild it in three days, save **Y**!	**Mt 27:40**	4572
show **y** to the priest and offer for	**Mk 1:44**	4572
SHALL LOVE YOUR NEIGHBOR AS **Y**.'	**Mk 12:31**	4572
before a rooster crows twice, you **y**	**Mk 14:30**	4771
save **Y**, and come down from the	**Mk 15:30**	4572
of God, throw **Y** down from here;	**Lk 4:9**	4572
'Physician, heal **y**!	**Lk 4:23**	4572
"But go and show **y** to the priest and	**Lk 5:14**	4572
when you **y** do not see the log that	**Lk 6:42**	846
"Lord, do not trouble **Y** further,	**Lk 7:6**	
AND YOUR NEIGHBOR AS **Y**."	**Lk 10:27**	4572
and *properly* clothe **y** and serve me	**Lk 17:8**	
the King of the Jews, save **Y**!"	**Lk 23:37**	4572
You not the Christ? Save **Y** and us!"	**Lk 23:39**	4572
What do you say about **y**?"	**Jn 1:22**	4572
things, show **Y** to the world."	**Jn 7:4**	4572
"You are testifying about **Y**;	**Jn 8:13**	4572
whom do You make **Y** out *to be?*"	**Jn 8:53**	4572
a man, make **Y** out *to be* God."	**Jn 10:33**	4572
You are going to disclose **Y** to us and	**Jn 14:22**	4572
glorify Me together with **Y**, with	**Jn 17:5**	4572
were younger, you used to gird **y** and	**Jn 21:18**	4572
"Gird **y** and put on your sandals."	**Ac 12:8**	
"Do not harm **y**, for we are all	**Ac 16:28**	4572
them and purify **y** along with them,	**Ac 21:24**	
but that you **y** also walk orderly,	**Ac 21:24**	846
By examining him **y** concerning all	**Ac 24:8**	846
are permitted to speak for **y**."	**Ac 26:1**	4572
you judge another, you condemn **y**;	**Ro 2:1**	4572
such things and do the same **y**,	**Ro 2:3**	
you are storing up wrath for **y** in the	**Ro 2:5**	4572
you **y** are a guide to the blind,	**Ro 2:19**	4572
another, do you not teach **y**?	**Ro 2:21**	4572
SHALL LOVE YOUR NEIGHBOR AS **Y**."	**Ro 13:9**	4572
SHALL LOVE YOUR NEIGHBOR AS **Y**."	**Ga 5:14**	4572
each one looking to **y**,	**Ga 6:1**	4572
world, do you submit **y** to decrees,	**Col 2:20**	
discipline **y** for the purpose of	**1Tm 4:7**	4572
show **y** an example of those who	**1Tm 4:12**	
Pay close attention to **y** and to your	**1Tm 4:16**	4572
you will ensure salvation both for **y**	**1Tm 4:16**	4572
keep **y** free from sin.	**1Tm 5:22**	4572
Be diligent to present **y** approved	**2Tm 2:15**	4572
Be on guard against him **y**,	**2Tm 4:15**	4771
in all things show **y** to be an	**Ti 2:7**	4572
SHALL LOVE YOUR NEIGHBOR AS **Y**,"	**Jas 2:8**	4572
garments so that you may clothe **y**,	**Rv 3:18**	

YOURSELVES

feet, and rest **y** under the tree;	**Gn 18:4**	8172
of bread, that you may refresh **y**;	**Gn 18:5**	3820
us and take our daughters for **y**.	**Gn 34:9**	
which are among you, and purify **y** and	**Gn 35:2**	
do not be grieved or angry with **y**,	**Gn 45:5**	5869
Do not concern **y** with your goods,	**Gn 45:20**	5869
"Assemble **y** that I may tell you	**Gn 49:1**	
go *and* get straw for **y** wherever	**Ex 5:11**	
"Take for **y** handfuls of soot from a	**Ex 9:8**	
"Go and take for **y** lambs	**Ex 12:21**	
'You **y** have seen what I did to the	**Ex 19:4**	864b
'You **y** have seen that I have	**Ex 20:22**	864b
of gold, you shall not make for **y**.	**Ex 20:23**	864b
since you **y** know the feelings of a	**Ex 23:9**	864b
the LORD to make atonement for **y**.	**Ex 30:15**	5315
LORD, to make atonement for **y**."	**Ex 30:16**	5315
in the same proportions for **y**;	**Ex 30:37**	
"Dedicate **y** today to the LORD	**Ex 32:29**	3027
"You **y** have committed a great sin;	**Ex 32:30**	864b
'Do not render **y** detestable	**Lv 11:43**	5315
and you shall not make **y** unclean	**Lv 11:43**	
Consecrate **y** therefore, and be holy	**Lv 11:44**	
And you shall not make **y** unclean	**Lv 11:44**	5315
not defile **y** by any of these things;	**Lv 18:24**	
so as not to defile **y** with them;	**Lv 18:30**	
idols or make for **y** molten gods;	**Lv 19:4**	
nor make any tattoo marks on **y**:	**Lv 19:28**	
'You shall consecrate **y** therefore	**Lv 20:7**	
you shall not make **y** detestable by	**Lv 20:25**	5315
'You shall also count for **y** from	**Lv 23:15**	
take for **y** the foliage of beautiful trees	**Lv 23:40**	
'You shall not make for **y** idols,	**Lv 26:1**	
nor shall you set up for **y** an image	**Lv 26:1**	
'Consecrate **y** for tomorrow, and	**Nu 11:18**	
so why do you exalt **y** above the	**Nu 16:3**	
take censers for **y**,	**Nu 16:6**	
"Separate **y** from among this	**Nu 16:21**	
and you shall humble **y**;	**Nu 29:7**	5315
known man intimately, spare for **y**.	**Nu 31:18**	
has touched any slain, purify **y**,	**Nu 31:19**	
"You shall purify for **y** every	**Nu 31:20**	
go to war while you **y** sit here?	**Nu 32:6**	864b
arm **y** before the LORD for the war,	**Nu 32:20**	
"Build **y** cities for your little ones,	**Nu 32:24**	
then you shall select for **y** cities	**Nu 35:11**	
and cross over the brook Zered **y**.'	**Dt 2:13**	
"So watch **y** carefully, since you	**Dt 4:15**	5315
and make a graven image for **y** in	**Dt 4:16**	
"So watch **y**, that you do not forget the	**Dt 4:23**	
and make for **y** a graven image in	**Dt 4:23**	
is on them, nor take it for **y**,	**Dt 7:25**	
You had made for **y** a molten calf;	**Dt 9:16**	
you shall not cut **y** nor shave your	**Dt 14:1**	
you shall set as king over **y**;	**Dt 17:15**	
you may not put a foreigner over **y**	**Dt 17:15**	
And there you will offer **y** for	**Dt 28:68**	
present **y** at the tent of meeting,	**Dt 31:14**	
therefore, write this song for **y**,	**Dt 31:19**	
'Prepare provisions for **y**,	**Jos 1:11**	
and hide **y** there for three days until	**Jos 2:16**	
"Consecrate **y**, for tomorrow the	**Jos 3:5**	
take for **y** twelve men from the	**Jos 3:12**	
"Take for **y** twelve men from the	**Jos 4:2**	
'Take up for **y** twelve stones from	**Jos 4:3**	
only keep **y** from the things under	**Jos 6:18**	
'Consecrate **y** for tomorrow, for	**Jos 7:13**	
and its cattle as plunder for **y**.	**Jos 8:2**	
but do not stay *there* **y**;	**Jos 10:19**	864b
"Provide for **y** three men from	**Jos 18:4**	
this day, by building **y** an altar,	**Jos 22:16**	
us by building an altar for **y**,	**Jos 22:19**	
take diligent heed to **y** to love the	**Jos 23:11**	5315
choose for **y** today whom you will	**Jos 24:15**	
"You are witnesses against **y** that	**Jos 24:22**	
you have chosen for **y** the LORD,	**Jos 24:22**	
by making **y** fat with the choicest	**1Sa 2:29**	
you **y** will become his servants.	**1Sa 8:17**	864b
king whom you have chosen for **y**,	**1Sa 8:18**	
present **y** before the LORD by your	**1Sa 10:19**	
the LORD by asking for **y** a king."	**1Sa 12:17**	
"Disperse **y** among the people and	**1Sa 14:34**	6327a
Consecrate **y** and come with me to	**1Sa 16:5**	
Choose a man for **y** and let him	**1Sa 17:8**	
"Choose one ox for **y** and prepare	**1Ki 18:25**	
"Station **y**." So they stationed	**1Ki 20:12**	
nor bow down **y** to them nor serve	**2Ki 17:35**	
and to Him you shall bow **y** down,	**2Ki 17:36**	
consecrate **y** both you and your	**1Ch 15:12**	
and made for **y** priests like the	**2Ch 13:9**	
station **y**, stand and see the	**2Ch 20:17**	
subjugate for **y** the people of Judah	**2Ch 28:10**	
Consecrate **y** now, and consecrate	**2Ch 29:5**	
have consecrated **y** to the LORD,	**2Ch 29:31**	3027
misleading you to give **y** over to die	**2Ch 32:11**	
y by your fathers' households	**2Ch 35:4**	
the Passover *animals,* sanctify **y** and	**2Ch 35:6**	
and separate **y** from the peoples of	**Ezr 10:11**	
daughters for your sons or for **y**.	**Ne 13:25**	
"If indeed you vaunt **y** against me And	**Jb 19:5**	
Then be afraid of the sword for **y**,	**Jb 19:29**	
Array **y** before me, take your stand.	**Jb 33:5**	
take for **y** seven bulls and seven	**Jb 42:8**	
offer up a burnt offering for **y**,	**Jb 42:8**	
"Wash **y**, make yourselves clean;	**Is 1:16**	
"Wash yourselves, make **y** clean;	**Is 1:16**	
Gird **y**, yet be shattered;	**Is 8:9**	
Gird **y**, yet be shattered.	**Is 8:9**	
Blind **y** and be blind;	**Is 29:9**	
"Gather **y** and come;	**Is 45:20**	
those who are in darkness, 'Show **y**.'	**Is 49:9**	
Who encircle **y** with firebrands,	**Is 50:11**	
out of the midst of her, purify **y**,	**Is 52:11**	
Who inflame **y** among the oaks,	**Is 57:5**	
the LORD, take no rest for **y**;	**Is 62:6**	
"Circumcise **y** to the LORD And	**Jer 4:4**	
'Assemble **y**, and let us go Into	**Jer 4:5**	
Assemble **y**, and let us go into the	**Jer 8:14**	
"Take heed for **y**, and do not	**Jer 17:21**	5315
will bring innocent blood on **y**,	**Jer 26:15**	
'Do not deceive **y**, saying,	**Jer 37:9**	5315
For you have *only* deceived **y**;	**Jer 42:20**	5315
'You **y** have seen all the calamity	**Jer 44:2**	864b
"Why are you doing great harm to **y**,	**Jer 44:7**	5315
Judah, leaving **y** without remnant,	**Jer 44:7**	
Gird **y** with sackcloth and lament,	**Jer 49:3**	2296
Gather **y** together and come against	**Jer 49:14**	
And each of you save **y** From the	**Jer 51:45**	5315
the lives *of others* for **y**?	**Ezk 13:18**	
make **y** a new heart and a new spirit	**Ezk 18:31**	
not defile **y** with the idols of Egypt;	**Ezk 20:7**	
or defile **y** with their idols.	**Ezk 20:18**	
"Will you defile **y** after the	**Ezk 20:30**	
you are defiling **y** with all your	**Ezk 20:31**	
with which you have defiled **y**;	**Ezk 20:43**	
and you will loathe **y** in your own	**Ezk 20:43**	
and decorated **y** with ornaments;	**Ezk 23:40**	5710b
fat and clothe **y** with the wool,	**Ezk 34:3**	3847
and you will loathe **y** in your own	**Ezk 36:31**	
kept charge of My holy things **y**,	**Ezk 44:8**	
you shall divide this land among **y**	**Ezk 47:21**	
it by lot for an inheritance among **y**	**Ezk 47:22**	
Gird **y** *with sackcloth* And lament,	**Jl 1:13**	2296
nations, And gather **y** there.	**Jl 3:11**	
"Assemble **y** on the mountains of	**Am 3:9**	
of your gods which you made for **y**.	**Am 5:26**	
"Now muster **y** in troops, daughter	**Mi 5:1**	
Gather **y** together, yes, gather, O	**Zph 2:1**	7917b
"Is it time for you **y** to dwell in	**Hg 1:4**	864b
do you not eat for **y** and do you	**Zch 7:6**	
and do you not drink for **y**?	**Zch 7:6**	
not suppose that you can say to **y**,	**Mt 3:9**	1438
not store up for **y** treasures on earth,	**Mt 6:19**	4771

store up for **y** treasures in heaven, Mt 6:20 *4771*
"Why do you **y** transgress the Mt 15:3 *4771*
why do you discuss among **y** that Mt 16:8 *1438*
for you do not enter in **y**, Mt 23:13 *4771*
twice as much a son of hell as **y**. Mt 23:15 *4771*
you testify against **y**, Mt 23:31 *1438*
the dealers and buy *some* for **y**.' Mt 25:9 *1438*
of this Man's blood; see *to that* **y**." Mt 27:24 *4771*
"Come away by **y** to a secluded place Mk 6:31 *4771, 846*
Have salt in **y**, and be at peace Mk 9:50 *1438*
and do not begin to say to **y**, Lk 3:8 *1438*
while you **y** will not even touch Lk 11:46 *846*
you **y** did not enter, Lk 11:52 *846*
make **y** money belts which do not wear Lk 12:33 *1438*
of God, but **y** being thrown out. Lk 13:28 *4771*
make friends for **y** by means of the Lk 16:9 *1438*
who justify **y** in the sight of men, Lk 16:15 *1438*
"Go and show **y** to the priests." Lk 17:14 *1438*
to prepare beforehand to defend **y**; Lk 21:14
know for **y** that summer is now near Lk 21:30 *1438*
"Take this and share it among **y**; Lk 22:17 *1438*
weep for **y** and for your children. Lk 23:28 *1438*
"You **y** are my witnesses that I Jn 3:28 *846*
do not have the love of God in **y**. Jn 5:42 *1438*
"Do not grumble among **y**. Jn 6:43 *240*
His blood, you have no life in **y**. Jn 6:53 *1438*
"Go up to the feast **y**; Jn 7:8 *4771*
"Take Him **y**, and judge Him Jn 18:31 *4771*
"Take Him **y** and crucify Him, for Jn 19:6 *4771*
in your midst, just as you **y** know Ac 2:22 *846*
"Pray to the Lord for me **y**, Ac 8:24 *4771*
"You **y** know how unlawful it is Ac 10:28 *4771*
you **y** know the thing which took Ac 10:37 *4771*
judge **y** unworthy of eternal life, Ac 13:46 *1438*
you keep **y** free from such things, Ac 15:29 *1438*
and your own law, look after it **y**; Ac 18:15 *846*
"You **y** know, from the first day Ac 20:18 *4771*
guard for **y** and for all the flock, Ac 20:28 *1438*
"You **y** know that these hands Ac 20:34 *846*
the ship, you **y** cannot be saved." Ac 27:31 *4771*
so consider **y** to be dead to sin, Ro 6:11 *1438*
but present **y** to God as those Ro 6:13 *1438*
when you present **y** to someone *as* Ro 6:16 *1438*
that you **y** are full of goodness, Ro 15:14 *846*
THE WICKED MAN FROM AMONG **Y**. 1Co 5:13 *4771, 846*
contrary, you **y** wrong and defraud. 1Co 6:8 *4771*
that you may devote **y** to prayer, 1Co 7:5 *4980*
Judge for **y**: is it proper for a woman 1Co 11:13 *4771, 846*
what vindication of **y**, 2Co 7:11
you demonstrated **y** to be innocent 2Co 7:11 *1438*
you **y** compelled me. 2Co 12:11 *4771*
Test **y** *to see* if you are in the 2Co 13:5 *1438*
if you are in the faith; examine **y**! 2Co 13:5 *1438*
do you not recognize this about **y**, 2Co 13:5 *1438*
Christ have clothed **y** with Christ. Ga 3:27
and that not of **y**, *it is* the gift Eph 2:8 *4771*
Only conduct **y** in a manner worthy Php 1:27
one another as more important than **y**; Php 2:3 *1438*
Have this attitude in **y** which was Php 2:5 *4771*
you will prove **y** to be blameless Php 2:15
You **y** also know, Philippians, Php 4:15 *4771*
Devote **y** to prayer, keeping alert Col 4:2 *4342*
Conduct **y** with wisdom toward Col 4:5 *4043*
For you **y** know, brethren, that our 1Th 2:1 *846*
for you **y** know that we have been 1Th 3:3 *846*
for you **y** are taught by God to 1Th 4:9 *846*
For you **y** know full well that the 1Th 5:2 *846*
For you **y** know how you ought to 2Th 3:7 *846*
knowing that you have for **y** a Heb 10:34 *1438*
since you **y** also are in the body. Heb 13:3 *846*
But prove **y** doers of the word, and Jas 1:22
you not made distinctions among **y**, Jas 2:4 *1438*
Humble **y** in the presence of the Jas 4:10
that you **y** may not be judged; Jas 5:9
be holy **y** also in all *your* behavior; 1Pe 1:15 *846*
conduct **y** in fear during the time 1Pe 1:17
Submit **y** for the Lord's sake to 1Pe 2:13
arm **y** also with the same purpose, 1Pe 4:1
clothe **y** with humility toward one 1Pe 5:5
Therefore humble **y** under the 1Pe 5:6
children, guard **y** from idols. 1Jn 5:21 *1438*
Watch **y**, that you do not lose 2Jn 1:8 *1438*
building **y** up on your most holy Jude 1:20 *1438*
keep **y** in the love of God, waiting Jude 1:21 *1438*

YOUTH

of man's heart is evil from his **y**; Gn 8:21 5271
brothers while he was *still* a **y**, Gn 37:2 5288
"Now a Hebrew **y** *was* with us Gn 41:12 5288
the youngest according to his **y**, Gn 43:33 6812
from our **y** even until now, Gn 46:34 5271
to her father's house as in her **y**, Lv 22:13 5271
the attendant of Moses from his **y**, Nu 11:28 979
in her father's house in her **y**, Nu 30:3 5271
is in her **y** in her father's house. Nu 30:16 5271
And he captured a **y** from Succoth Jg 8:14 5288
Then *the* **y** wrote down for him Jg 8:14
But the **y** did not draw his sword, Jg 8:20 5288
afraid, because he was still a **y**. Jg 8:20 5288
you from my **y** even to this day. 1Sa 12:2 5271
for you are *but* a **y** while he has 1Sa 17:33 5271
has been a warrior from his **y**." 1Sa 17:33 5271
for he was *but* a **y**, 1Sa 17:42 5288
"You inquire whose son the **y** is." 1Sa 17:56 5958
"But if I say to the **y**, 1Sa 20:22 5958
upon you from your **y** until now." 2Sa 19:7 5271
have feared the LORD from my **y**. 1Ki 18:12 5271
his reign while he was still a **y**, 2Ch 34:3 5288
to inherit the iniquities of my **y**. Jb 13:26 5271
(But from my **y** he grew up with me Jb 31:18 5271
flesh become fresher than in **y**, Jb 33:25 5290
"They die in **y**, And their life Jb 36:14 5290
Do not remember the sins of my **y** Ps 25:7 5271
You are my confidence from my **y**. Ps 71:5 5271
You have taught me from my **y**, Ps 71:17 5271
and about to die from my **y** on; Ps 88:15 5290
have shortened the days of his **y**; Ps 89:45 5934
your **y** is renewed like the eagle. Ps 103:5 5271
Your **y** are to You *as* the dew. Ps 110:3 3208
So are the children of one's **y**. Ps 127:4 5271
have persecuted me from my **y** up," Ps 129:1 5271
have persecuted me from my **y** up; Ps 129:2 5271
Let our sons in their **y** be as Ps 144:12 5271
To the **y** knowledge and discretion, Pr 1:4 5288
leaves the companion of her **y** And Pr 2:17 5271
And rejoice in the wife of your **y**. Pr 5:18 5271
Creator in the days of your **y**, Ec 12:1 979
y will storm against the elder And Is 3:5 5288
you have labored from your **y**; Is 47:12 5271
trafficked with you from your **y**; Is 47:15 5271
will forget the shame of your **y**, Is 54:4 5934
like a wife of *one's* **y** when she is Is 54:6 5271
For the **y** will die at the age of Is 65:20 5288
how to speak, Because I am a **y**." Jer 1:6 5288
'I am a **y**,' Because everywhere I Jer 1:7 5288
you the devotion of your **y**, Jer 2:2 5271
You are the friend of my **y**? Jer 3:4 5271
labor of our fathers since our **y**, Jer 3:24 5271
from our **y** even to this day. Jer 3:25 5271
been your practice from your **y**, Jer 22:21 5271
I bore the reproach of my **y**.' Jer 31:19 5271
evil in My sight from their **y**; Jer 32:30 5272a
"Moab has been at ease since his **y**; Jer 48:11 5271
with you I shatter old man and **y**, Jer 51:22 5288
he should bear The yoke in his **y**. La 3:27 5271
for from my **y** until now I have Ezk 4:14 5271
not remember the days of your **y**, Ezk 16:22 5271
not remembered the days of your **y** Ezk 16:43 5271
with you in the days of your **y**, Ezk 16:60 5271
They played the harlot in their **y**; Ezk 23:3 5271
in her **y** men had lain with her, Ezk 23:8 5271
remembering the days of her **y**, Ezk 23:19 5271
longed for the lewdness of your **y**, Ezk 23:21 5271
because of the breasts of your **y**. Ezk 23:21 5271
there as in the days of her **y**, Hos 2:15 5271
When Israel *was* a **y** I loved him, Hos 11:1 5288
For the bridegroom of her **y**. Jl 1:8 5271
a man sold me as a slave in my **y**.' Zch 13:5 5271
you and the wife of your **y**, Mal 2:14 5271
against the wife of your **y**. Mal 2:15 5271
all these things from my **y** up." Mk 10:20 *3503*
things I have kept from *my* **y**." Lk 18:21 *3503*
my manner of life from my **y** up, Ac 26:4 *3503*
if she is past her **y**, and if it 1Co 7:36 *5230*

YOUTHFUL

"His bones are full of his **y** vigor, Jb 20:11 5934
return to the days of his **y** vigor; Jb 33:25 5934
Now flee from **y** lusts and pursue 2Tm 2:22 *3512*

YOUTHFULNESS

Let no one look down on your **y**, 1Tm 4:12 *3503*

YOUTHS

naive, *And* discerned among the **y** Pr 7:7 1121
Though **y** grow weary and tired, And Is 40:30 5288
y stumbled under *loads* of wood. La 5:13 5288
y in whom was no defect, who were Da 1:4 3206
than the **y** who are your own age? Da 1:10 3206
and the appearance of the **y** who Da 1:13 3206
they were fatter than all the **y** who Da 1:15 3206
As for these four **y**, Da 1:17 3206

Z

ZAANAN

inhabitant of **Z** does not escape. Mi 1:11 6630

ZAANANNIM

in **Z** and Adami-nekeb and Jabneel, Jos 19:33 6815
tent as far away as the oak in **Z**, Jg 4:11 6815

ZAAVAN

Bilhan and **Z** and Akan. Gn 36:27 2190
of Ezer *were* Bilhan, **Z** and Jaakan. 1Ch 1:42 2190

ZABAD

and Nathan became the father of **Z**, 1Ch 2:36 2066
and **Z** became the father of Ephlal, 1Ch 2:37 2066
Z his son, Shuthelah his son, and 1Ch 7:21 2066
the Hittite, **Z** the son of Ahlai, 1Ch 11:41 2066
Z the son of Shimeath the 2Ch 24:26 2066
Eliashib, Mattaniah, Jeremoth, **Z** and Ezr 10:27 2066
Mattenai, Mattattah, **Z**, Ezr 10:33 2066
there were Jeiel, Mattithiah, **Z**, Ezr 10:43 2066

ZABBAI

Jehohanan, Hananiah, **Z** Ezr 10:28 2079
After him Baruch the son of **Z** Ne 3:20 2079

ZABBUD

and **Z**, and 70 males with them. Ezr 8:14 2072

ZABDI

the son of Carmi, the son of **Z**, Jos 7:1 2067
near man by man, and **Z** was taken. Jos 7:17 2067
and Achan, son of Carmi, son of **Z**, Jos 7:18 2067
Jakim, Zichri, **Z**, 1Ch 8:19 2067
and **Z** the Shiphmite had charge of 1Ch 27:27 2067
the son of Mica, the son of **Z**, Ne 11:17 2067

ZABDIEL

Jashobeam the son of **Z** had charge 1Ch 27:2 2068
And their overseer was **Z**, Ne 11:14 2068

ZABUD

and **Z** the son of Nathan, a priest, 1Ki 4:5 2071

ZACCAI

the sons of **Z**, 760; Ezr 2:9 2140
the sons of **Z**, 760; Ne 7:14 2140

ZACCHEUS

was a man called by the name of **Z**; Lk 19:2 *2195*
Z was trying to see who Jesus was, Lk 19:3
"**Z**, hurry and come down, for Lk 19:5 *2195*
Z stopped and said to the Lord, Lk 19:8 *2195*

ZACCUR

of Reuben, Shammua the son of **Z**; Nu 13:4 2139
were Hammuel his son, **Z** his son, 1Ch 4:26 2139
by Jaaziah *were* Beno, Shoham, **Z** and 1Ch 24:27 2139
Z, Joseph, Nethaniah and 1Ch 25:2 2139
the third to **Z**, his sons and his 1Ch 25:10 2139
to them **Z** the son of Imri built. Ne 3:2 2139
Z, Sherebiah, Shebaniah, Ne 10:12 2139
the son of Micaiah, the son of **Z**, Ne 12:35 2139
to them was Hanan the son of **Z**, Ne 13:13 2139

ZACHARIAS

was a priest named **Z**, Lk 1:5 *2197*
Z was troubled when he saw *the* Lk 1:12 *2197*
"Do not be afraid, **Z**, Lk 1:13 *2197*
Z said to the angel, Lk 1:18 *2197*
The people were waiting for **Z**, Lk 1:21 *2197*
entered the house of **Z** and greeted Lk 1:40 *2197*
and they were going to call him **Z**, Lk 1:59 *2197*
And his father **Z** was filled with Lk 1:67 *2197*
of God came to John, the son of **Z**, Lk 3:2 *2197*

ZADOK

Z the son of Ahitub and 2Sa 8:17 6659
Now behold, **Z** also *came,* and all 2Sa 15:24 6659
The king said to **Z**, 2Sa 15:25 6659
king said also to **Z** the priest, 2Sa 15:27 6659
Therefore **Z** and Abiathar returned 2Sa 15:29 6659
"Are not **Z** and Abiathar the 2Sa 15:35 6659
report to **Z** and Abiathar the priests. 2Sa 15:35 6659
to **Z** and to Abiathar the priests, 2Sa 17:15 6659
Then Ahimaaz the son of **Z** said, 2Sa 18:19 6659
son of **Z** said once more to Joab, 2Sa 18:22 6659
running of Ahimaaz the son of **Z**." 2Sa 18:27 6659
King David sent to **Z** and Abiathar 2Sa 19:11 6659
and **Z** and Abiathar were priests; 2Sa 20:25 6659
But **Z** the priest, Benaiah the son 1Ki 1:8 6659
and **Z** the priest and Benaiah the 1Ki 1:26 6659
"Call to me **Z** the priest, Nathan 1Ki 1:32 6659
"Let **Z** the priest and Nathan 1Ki 1:34 6659
So **Z** the priest, Nathan the 1Ki 1:38 6659
Z the priest then took the horn of 1Ki 1:39 6659
also sent with him **Z** the priest, 1Ki 1:44 6659
"**Z** the priest and Nathan the 1Ki 1:45 6659
and the king appointed **Z** the 1Ki 2:35 6659
the son of **Z** *was* the priest; 1Ki 4:2 6659
and **Z** and Abiathar *were* priests; 1Ki 4:4 6659
was Jerusha the daughter of **Z**. 2Ki 15:33 6659
and Ahitub became the father of **Z**, 1Ch 6:8 6659
Z became the father of Ahimaaz, 1Ch 6:8 6659
and Ahitub became the father of **Z**, 1Ch 6:12 6659
Z became the father of Shallum, 1Ch 6:12 6659
Z his son, Ahimaaz his son. 1Ch 6:53 6659
son of Meshullam, the son of **Z**, 1Ch 9:11 6659
also **Z**, a young man mighty of 1Ch 12:28 6659
David called for **Z** and Abiathar 1Ch 15:11 6659
He left **Z** the priest and his 1Ch 16:39 6659
and **Z** the son of Ahitub and 1Ch 18:16 6659
with **Z** of the sons of Eleazar and 1Ch 24:3 6659
king, the princes, **Z** the priest, 1Ch 24:6 6659
the presence of David the king, **Z**, 1Ch 24:31 6659
the son of Kemuel; for Aaron, **Z**; 1Ch 27:17 6659
for the LORD and **Z** as priest. 1Ch 29:22 6659
was Jerushah the daughter of **Z**. 2Ch 27:1 6659
chief priest of the house of **Z** said 2Ch 31:10 6659
son of Shallum, son of **Z**, Ezr 7:2 6659
And next to him **Z** the son of Baana Ne 3:4 6659
After them **Z** the son of Immer Ne 3:29 6659
Meshezabel, **Z**, Jaddua, Ne 10:21 6659
son of Meshullam, the son of **Z**, Ne 11:11 6659
the priest, **Z** the scribe, Ne 13:13 6659
These are the sons of **Z**, Ezk 40:46 6659
who are from the offspring of **Z**, Ezk 43:19 6659
Levitical priests, the sons of **Z**, Ezk 44:15 6659
are sanctified of the sons of **Z**, Ezk 48:11 6659
Azor was the father of **Z**, Mt 1:14 *4524*
Azor was the father of Zadok, **Z** Mt 1:14 *4524*

ZADOK'S

Ahimaaz, **Z** son and Jonathan, 2Sa 15:36 6659

ZAHAM

Jeush, Shemariah and **Z**. 2Ch 11:19 2093

ZAIR

Then Joram crossed over to **Z**, 2Ki 8:21 6811

ZALAPH

and Hanun the sixth son of **Z**, Ne 3:30 6764

ZALMON

So Abimelech went up to Mount **Z**, Jg 9:48 6756a
Z the Ahohite, Maharai the 2Sa 23:28 6756b
kings there, It was snowing in **Z**. Ps 68:14 6756a

ZALMONAH

from Mount Hor and camped at **Z**. Nu 33:41 6758
They journeyed from **Z** and Nu 33:42 6758

ZALMUNNA

and I am pursuing Zebah and **Z**, Jg 8:5 6759
Zebah and **Z** already in your hands, Jg 8:6 6759

given Zebah and Z into my hand, Jg 8:7 6759
Now Zebah and Z were in Karkor, Jg 8:10 6759
When Zebah and Z fled, he pursued Jg 8:12 6759
two kings of Midian, Zebah and Z, Jg 8:12 6759
"Behold Zebah and Z, Jg 8:15 6759
'Are the hands of Zebah and Z Jg 8:15 6759
Then he said to Zebah and Z, Jg 8:18 6759
Then Zebah and Z said, Jg 8:21 6759
arose and killed Zebah and Z, Jg 8:21 6759
their princes like Zebah and Z, Ps 83:11 6759

ZAMZUMMIN
it, but the Ammonites call them Z, Dt 2:20 2157

ZANOAH
and Z and En-gannim, Tappuah and Jos 15:34 2182
and Jezreel and Jokdeam and Z, Jos 15:56 2182
and Jekuthiel the father of Z. 1Ch 4:18 2182
inhabitants of Z repaired the Valley Ne 3:13 2182
Z, Adullam, and their villages, Ne 11:30 2182

ZAPHENATH-PANEAH
Then Pharaoh named Joseph Z; Gn 41:45 6847

ZAPHON
and Beth-nimrah and Succoth and Z, Jos 13:27 6829
crossed to Z and said to Jephthah, Jg 12:1 6829

ZAREPHATH
"Arise, go to Z, which belongs to 1Ki 17:9 6886
So he arose and went to Z, 1Ki 17:10 6886
among the Canaanites as far as Z, Ob 1:20 6886
to none of them, but only to Z, Lk 4:26 *4558*

ZARETHAN
Adam, the city that is beside Z; Jos 3:16 6891
which is beside Z below Jezreel, 1Ki 4:12 6891
clay ground between Succoth and Z. 1Ki 7:46 6891

ZATTU
the sons of Z, 945; Ezr 2:8 2240
of the sons of Z, Shecaniah, Ezr 8:5 2240
and of the sons of Z: Ezr 10:27 2240
the sons of Z, 845; Ne 7:13 2240
Parosh, Pahath-moab, Elam, Z, Ne 10:14 2240

ZAZA
sons of Jonathan *were* Peleth and Z. 1Ch 2:33 2117

ZEAL
Saul had sought to kill them in his z 2Sa 21:2 7065
me and see my z for the LORD." 2Ki 10:16 7068
The z of the LORD will perform 2Ki 19:31 7068
let it be done with z for the Ezr 7:23 149
z for Your house has consumed me, Ps 69:9 7068
My z has consumed me, Because my Ps 119:139 7068
and their z have already perished, Ec 9:6 7068
The z of the LORD of hosts will Is 9:7 7068
They see *Your* z for the people and Is 26:11 7068
The z of the LORD of hosts will Is 37:32 7068
arouse *His* z like a man of war. Is 42:13 7068
wrapped Himself with z as a mantle. Is 59:17 7068
are Your z and Your mighty deeds? Is 63:15 7068
have spoken in My z when I have Ezk 5:13 7068
"In My z and in My blazing Ezk 38:19 7068
be devoured By the fire of My z. Zph 3:8 7068
Z FOR YOUR HOUSE WILL CONSUME ME Jn 2:17 *2205b*
that they have a z for God, Ro 10:2 *2205b*
your mourning, your z for me; 2Co 7:7 *2205b*
what fear, what longing, what z, 2Co 7:11 *2205b*
your z has stirred up most of them. 2Co 9:2 *2205b*
as to z, a persecutor of the church; Php 3:6 *2205b*

ZEALOT
Simon the Z, and Judas Iscariot, Mt 10:4 *2581*
and Thaddaeus, and Simon the Z; Mk 3:18 *2581*
and Simon who was called the Z; Lk 6:15 *2208*
son of Alphaeus, and Simon the Z, Ac 1:13 *2208*

ZEALOUS
"I have been very z for the LORD, 1Ki 19:10 7065
"I have been very z for the LORD, 1Ki 19:14 7065
the LORD will be z for His land And Jl 2:18 7065
and they are all z for the Law; Ac 21:20 *2207*
of our fathers, being z for God just Ac 22:3 *2207*
you are z of spiritual *gifts,* 1Co 14:12 *2207*
z for my ancestral traditions. Ga 1:14 *2207*
own possession, z for good deeds. Ti 2:14 *2207*
if you prove z for what is good? 1Pe 3:13 *2207*
therefore be z and repent. Rv 3:19 *2205a*

ZEALOUSLY
Zabbai z repaired another section, Ne 3:20 2734

ZEBADIAH
Z, Arad, Eder, 1Ch 8:15 2069
Z, Meshullam, Hizki, Heber, 1Ch 8:17 2069
and Joelah and Z, the sons of 1Ch 12:7 2069
Jediael the second, Z the third, 1Ch 26:2 2069
of Joab, and Z his son after him; 1Ch 27:7 2069
Levites, Shemaiah, Nethaniah, Z, 2Ch 17:8 2069
and Z the son of Ishmael, the 2Ch 19:11 2069
Z the son of Michael and 80 males Ezr 8:8 2069
of Immer *there were* Hanani and Z; Ezr 10:20 2069

ZEBAH
and I am pursuing Z and Zalmunna, Jg 8:5 2078
"Are the hands of Z and Zalmunna Jg 8:6 2078
given Z and Zalmunna into my hand, Jg 8:7 2078
Now Z and Zalmunna were in Karkor, Jg 8:10 2078
When Z and Zalmunna fled, he Jg 8:12 2078
kings of Midian, Z and Zalmunna, Jg 8:12 2078
"Behold Z and Zalmunna, Jg 8:15 2078
'Are the hands of Z and Zalmunna Jg 8:15 2078
Then he said to Z and Zalmunna, Jg 8:18 2078
Then Z and Zalmunna said, Jg 8:21 2078
arose and killed Z and Zalmunna, Jg 8:21 2078
their princes like Z and Zalmunna, Ps 83:11 2078

ZEBEDEE
brothers, James the *son* of Z, Mt 4:21 *2199*
in the boat with Z their father, Mt 4:21 *2199*
and James the son of Z, Mt 10:2 *2199*
the mother of the sons of Z came to Mt 20:20 *2199*
Him Peter and the two sons of Z, Mt 26:37 *2199*
and the mother of the sons of Z. Mt 27:56 *2199*
He saw James the son of Z, Mk 1:19 *2199*
and they left their father Z in Mk 1:20 *2199*
and James, the *son* of Z, Mk 3:17 *2199*
James and John, the two sons of Z, Mk 10:35 *2199*
so also *were* James and John, sons of Z, Lk 5:10 *2199*
in Galilee, and the *sons* of Z, Jn 21:2 *2199*

ZEBIDAH
and his mother's name *was* Z the 2Ki 23:36 2080

ZEBINA
were Jeiel, Mattithiah, Zabad, Z, Ezr 10:43 2081

ZEBOIIM
and Gomorrah and Admah and Z, Gn 10:19 6636
of Admah, and Shemeber king of Z, Gn 14:2 6636
king of Z and the king of Bela Gn 14:8 6636
Sodom and Gomorrah, Admah and Z, Dt 29:23 6636
How can I treat you like Z? Hos 11:8 6636

ZEBOIM
which overlooks the valley of Z 1Sa 13:18 6650
Hadid, Z, Neballat, Ne 11:34 6650

ZEBUL
and *is* Z *not* his lieutenant? Jg 9:28 2083
When Z the ruler of the city Jg 9:30 2083
Gaal saw the people, he said to Z, Jg 9:36 2083
But Z said to him, Jg 9:36 2083
Then Z said to him, Jg 9:38 2083
but Z drove out Gaal and his Jg 9:41 2083

ZEBULUN
So she named him Z. Gn 30:20 2074
Levi and Judah and Issachar and Z; Gn 35:23 2074
The sons of Z: Gn 46:14 2074
"Z will dwell at the seashore; Gn 49:13 2074
Issachar, Z and Benjamin; Ex 1:3 2074
of Z, Eliab the son of Helon; Nu 1:9 2074
Of the sons of Z, their Nu 1:30 2074
numbered men of the tribe of Z Nu 1:31 2074
"*Then comes* the tribe of Z, Nu 2:7 2074
and the leader of the sons of Z: Nu 2:7 2074
of Helon, leader of the sons of Z; Nu 7:24 2074
the tribal army of the sons of Z. Nu 10:16 2074
from the tribe of Z, Nu 13:10 2074
of Z according to their families: Nu 26:26 2074
tribe of the sons of Z a leader, Nu 34:25 2074
Reuben, Gad, Asher, Z, Dt 27:13 2074
Of Z he said, Dt 33:18 2074
"Rejoice, Z, in your going forth, Dt 33:18 2074
sons of Z according to their families. Jos 19:10 2074
sons of Z according to their families, Jos 19:16 2074
to Beth-dagon and reached to Z, Jos 19:27 2074
and it reached to Z on the south Jos 19:34 2074
of Gad and from the tribe of Z, Jos 21:7 2074
they gave from the tribe of Z, Jos 21:34 2074
Z did not drive out the Jg 1:30 2074
Naphtali and from the sons of Z. Jg 4:6 2074
Barak called Z and Naphtali Jg 4:10 2074
And from Z those who wield the Jg 5:14 2074
"Z *was* a people who despised Jg 5:18 2074
he sent messengers to Asher, Z, Jg 6:35 2074
at Aijalon in the land of Z. Jg 12:12 2074
Simeon, Levi, Judah, Issachar, Z, 1Ch 2:1 2074
tribe of Gad and the tribe of Z, 1Ch 6:63 2074
were given, from the tribe of Z: 1Ch 6:77 2074
Of Z, there were 50,000 who went 1Ch 12:33 2074
as Issachar and Z and Naphtali, 1Ch 12:40 2074
for Z, Ishmaiah the son of Obadiah; 1Ch 27:19 2074
and Manasseh, and as far as Z, 2Ch 30:10 2074
and Z humbled themselves and came 2Ch 30:11 2074
and Manasseh, Issachar and Z, 2Ch 30:18 2074
in their throng, The princes of Z, Ps 68:27 2074
He treated the land of Z and the land Is 9:1 2074
the east side to the west side, Z, Ezk 48:26 2074
"Beside the border of Z, Ezk 48:27 2074
the gate of Z, one. Ezk 48:33 2074
in the region of Z and Naphtali. Mt 4:13 *2194*
OF Z AND THE LAND OF NAPHTALI, Mt 4:15 *2194*
the tribe of Z twelve thousand, Rv 7:8 *2194*

ZEBULUNITE
the Z judged Israel after him; Jg 12:11 2075
Then Elon the Z died and was Jg 12:12 2075

ZEBULUNITES
These are the families of the Z Nu 26:27 2075

ZECHARIAH
and Z his son became king in his 2Ki 14:29 2148a
Z the son of Jeroboam became king 2Ki 15:8 2148a
Now the rest of the acts of Z, 2Ki 15:11 2148a
name was Abi the daughter of Z. 2Ki 18:2 2148a
were Jeiel the chief, then Z 1Ch 5:7 2148a
Z the son of Meshelemiah was 1Ch 9:21 2148a
Gedor, Ahio, Z and Mikloth. 1Ch 9:37 2148a
relatives of the second rank, Z, 1Ch 15:18 2148a
and Z, Aziel, Shemiramoth, Jehiel, 1Ch 15:20 2148a
Joshaphat, Nethanel, Amasai, Z, 1Ch 15:24 2148a
the chief, and second to him Z, 1Ch 16:5 2148a
of the sons of Isshiah, Z. 1Ch 24:25 2148a
Z the firstborn, Jediael the 1Ch 26:2 2148a
Tebaliah the third, Z the fourth; 1Ch 26:11 2148a
Then they cast lots *for* his son Z, 1Ch 26:14 2148a
in Gilead, Iddo the son of Z; 1Ch 27:21 2148a
officials, Ben-hail, Obadiah, Z, 2Ch 17:7 2148a
came upon Jahaziel the son of Z, 2Ch 20:14 2148a
Azariah, Jehiel, Z, 2Ch 21:2 2148a
Then the Spirit of God came on Z 2Ch 24:20 2148a
to seek God in the days of Z, 2Ch 26:5 2148a
was Abijah, the daughter of Z. 2Ch 29:1 2148a
sons of Asaph, Z and Mattaniah; 2Ch 29:13 2148a
Z and Meshullam of the sons of the 2Ch 34:12 2148a
Hilkiah and Z and Jehiel, the 2Ch 35:8 2148a
the prophet and Z the son of Iddo, Ezr 5:1 2148b
the prophet and Z the son of Iddo. Ezr 6:14 2148b
Z and with him 150 males *who were* Ezr 8:3 2148a
Z the son of Bebai and 28 males Ezr 8:11 2148a
Jarib, Elnathan, Nathan, Z and Ezr 8:16 2148a
Mattaniah, Z, Jehiel, Abdi, Ezr 10:26 2148a
Hashum, Hashbaddanah, Z, Ne 8:4 2148a
the son of Uzziah, the son of Z, Ne 11:4 2148a
the son of Joiarib, the son of Z, Ne 11:5 2148a
the son of Amzi, the son of Z, Ne 11:12 2148a
of Iddo, Z; of Ginnethon, Meshullam Ne 12:16 2148a
and Z the son of Jonathan, the son Ne 12:35 2148a
Miniamin, Micaiah, Elioenai, Z and Ne 12:41 2148a
and Z the son of Jeberechiah." Is 8:2 2148a
of the LORD came to Z the prophet, Zch 1:1 2148a
of the LORD came to Z the prophet, Zch 1:7 2148a
the word of the LORD came to Z on Zch 7:1 2148a
word of the LORD came to Z saying, Zch 7:8 2148a
righteous Abel to the blood of Z, Mt 23:35 *2197*
blood of Abel to the blood of Z, Lk 11:51 *2197*

ZECHER
Gedor, Ahio and Z. 1Ch 8:31 2144

ZEDAD
of the border shall be at Z; Nu 34:8 6657
of Hethlon, to the entrance of Z; Ezk 47:15 6657

ZEDEKIAH
Then Z the son of Chenaanah made 1Ki 22:11 6667
Then Z the son of Chenaanah came 1Ki 22:24 6667
place, and changed his name to Z. 2Ki 24:17 6667
Z was twenty-one years old when he 2Ki 24:18 6667
And Z rebelled against the king of 2Ki 24:20 6667
until the eleventh year of King Z. 2Ki 25:2 6667
They slaughtered the sons of Z 2Ki 25:7 6667
then put out the eyes of Z and 2Ki 25:7 6667
second *was* Jehoiakim, the third Z, 1Ch 3:15 6667
were Jeconiah his son, Z his son. 1Ch 3:16 6667
Z the son of Chenaanah made 2Ch 18:10 6667
Then Z the son of Chenaanah came 2Ch 18:23 6667
he made his kinsman Z king over 2Ch 36:10 6667
Z was twenty-one years old when he 2Ch 36:11 6667
the son of Hacaliah, and Z, Ne 10:1 6667
the end of the eleventh year of Z the Jer 1:3 6667
King Z sent to him Pashhur the son Jer 21:1 6667
"You shall say to Z as follows: Jer 21:3 6667
"I will give over Z king of Judah Jer 21:7 6667
so I will abandon Z king of Judah Jer 24:8 6667
the reign of Z the son of Josiah, Jer 27:1 6667
to Jerusalem to Z king of Judah. Jer 27:3 6667
like all these to Z king of Judah, Jer 27:12 6667
of the reign of Z king of Judah, Jer 28:1 6667
whom Z king of Judah sent to Jer 29:3 6667
concerning Z the son of Maaseiah, Jer 29:21 6667
make you like Z and like Ahab, Jer 29:22 6667
the tenth year of Z king of Judah, Jer 32:1 6667
Z king of Judah had shut him up, Jer 32:3 6667
and Z king of Judah will not Jer 32:4 6667
and he will take Z to Babylon, Jer 32:5 6667
'Go and speak to Z king of Judah Jer 34:2 6667
of the LORD, O Z king of Judah! Jer 34:4 6667
prophet spoke all these words to Z Jer 34:6 6667
after King Z had made a covenant Jer 34:8 6667
'Z king of Judah and his Jer 34:21 6667
and Z the son of Hananiah, Jer 36:12 6667
Now Z the son of Josiah whom Jer 37:1 6667
Yet King Z sent Jehucal the son of Jer 37:3 6667
Now King Z sent and took him *out;* Jer 37:17 6667
Moreover Jeremiah said to King Z, Jer 37:18 6667
Then King Z gave commandment, and Jer 37:21 6667
King Z said, "Behold, he is in your Jer 38:5 6667
Then King Z sent and had Jeremiah Jer 38:14 6667
Then Jeremiah said to Z, Jer 38:15 6667
But King Z swore to Jeremiah in Jer 38:16 6667
Then Jeremiah said to Z, Jer 38:17 6667
Then King Z said to Jeremiah, Jer 38:19 6667
Then Z said to Jeremiah, Jer 38:24 6667
the ninth year of Z king of Judah, Jer 39:1 6667
in the eleventh year of Z, Jer 39:2 6667
When Z the king of Judah and all Jer 39:4 6667
overtook Z in the plains of Jericho; Jer 39:5 6667
king of Babylon slew the sons of Z Jer 39:6 6667
just as I gave over Z king of Jer 44:30 6667
at the beginning of the reign of Z Jer 49:34 6667
when he went with Z the king of Jer 51:59 6667
Z was twenty-one years old when he Jer 52:1 6667
And Z rebelled against the king of Jer 52:3 6667
until the eleventh year of King Z. Jer 52:5 6667
overtook Z in the plains of Jericho, Jer 52:8 6667
slaughtered the sons of Z before his Jer 52:10 6667
Then he blinded the eyes of Z; Jer 52:11 6667

ZEDEKIAH'S
He then blinded Z eyes and bound Jer 39:7 6667

ZEEB
two leaders of Midian, Oreb and Z, Jg 7:25 2062
killed Z at the wine press of Zeeb, Jg 7:25 2062
killed Zeeb at the wine press of Z, Jg 7:25 2062
brought the heads of Oreb and Z to Jg 7:25 2062
Oreb and Z into your hands; Jg 8:3 2062
Make their nobles like Oreb and Z And Ps 83:11 2062

ZELA
in the country of Benjamin in Z, 2Sa 21:14 6762

ZELAH
and Z, Haeleph and the Jebusite Jos 18:28 6762

ZELEK
Z the Ammonite, Naharai the 2Sa 23:37 6768
Z the Ammonite, Naharai the 1Ch 11:39 6768

ZELOPHEHAD
Z the son of Hepher had no sons, Nu 26:33 6765
of the daughters of Z were Mahlah, Nu 26:33 6765
Then the daughters of Z, Nu 27:1 6765
The daughters of Z are right in *their* Nu 27:7 6765
to give the inheritance of Z our Nu 36:2 6765
concerning the daughters of Z, Nu 36:6 6765
Moses, so the daughters of Z did: Nu 36:10 6765
daughters of Z married their uncles' Nu 36:11 6765
However, Z, the son of Hepher, the Jos 17:3 6765
And the name of the second was Z, 1Ch 7:15 6765
Zelophehad, and Z had daughters. 1Ch 7:15 6765

ZELZAH
in the territory of Benjamin at Z; 1Sa 10:2 6766

ZEMARAIM
and Beth-arabah and Z and Bethel, Jos 18:22 6787
Then Abijah stood on Mount Z, 2Ch 13:4 6787

ZEMARITE
and the Z and the Hamathite; Gn 10:18 6786

ZEMARITES
the Arvadites, the Z and 1Ch 1:16 6786

ZEMIRAH
The sons of Becher *were* Z, 1Ch 7:8 2160

ZENAN
Z and Hadashah and Migdal-gad, Jos 15:37 6799

ZENAS
Diligently help Z the lawyer and Ti 3:13 *2211*

ZEPHANIAH
priest and Z the second priest, 2Ki 25:18 6846
the son of Azariah, the son of Z, 1Ch 6:36 6846
of Malchijah, and Z the priest, Jer 21:1 6846
and to Z the son of Maaseiah, Jer 29:25 6846
Z the priest read this letter Jer 29:29 6846
and Z the son of Maaseiah, Jer 37:3 6846
priest and Z the second priest, Jer 52:24 6846
LORD which came to Z son of Cushi, Zph 1:1 6846
the house of Josiah the son of Z, Zch 6:10 6846
Jedaiah and Hen the son of Z. Zch 6:14 6846

ZEPHATH
struck the Canaanites living in Z, Jg 1:17 6857

ZEPHATHAH
in the valley of Z at Mareshah. 2Ch 14:10 6859

ZEPHI
of Eliphaz *were* Teman, Omar, Z, 1Ch 1:36 6825

ZEPHO
Omar, Z and Gatam and Kenaz. Gn 36:11 6825
chief Teman, chief Omar, chief Z, Gn 36:15 6825

ZEPHON
of Z, the family of the Zephonites; Nu 26:15 6827

ZEPHONITES
of Zephon, the family of the Z; Nu 26:15 6831

ZER
cities *were* Ziddim, Z and Hammath, Jos 19:35 6863

ZERAH
Nahath and Z, Shammah and Mizzah. Gn 36:13 2226
chief Nahath, chief Z, Gn 36:17 2226
and Jobab the son of Z of Bozrah Gn 36:33 2226
and he was named Z. Gn 38:30 2226
Onan and Shelah and Perez and Z Gn 46:12 2226
of Z, the family of the Zerahites; Nu 26:13 2226
of Z, the family of the Zerahites. Nu 26:20 2226
the son of Zabdi, the son of Z, Jos 7:1 2226
of Carmi, son of Zabdi, son of Z, Jos 7:18 2226
with him, took Achan the son of Z, Jos 7:24 2226
'Did not Achan the son of Z act Jos 22:20 2226
The sons of Reuel *were* Nahath, Z, 1Ch 1:37 2226
Jobab the son of Z of Bozrah 1Ch 1:44 2226
bore him Perez and Z. 1Ch 2:4 2226
The sons of Z *were* Zimri, 1Ch 2:6 2226
were Nemuel and Jamin, Jarib, Z, 1Ch 4:24 2226
his son, Iddo his son, Z his son, 1Ch 6:21 2226
the son of Ethni, the son of Z, 1Ch 6:41 2226
From the sons of Z *were* Jeuel 1Ch 9:6 2226
Now Z the Ethiopian came out 2Ch 14:9 2226
of the sons of Z the son of Judah, Ne 11:24 2226
was the father of Perez and Z by Tamar, Mt 1:3 *2196*

ZERAHIAH
and Uzzi became the father of Z, 1Ch 6:6 2228
Z became the father of Meraioth, 1Ch 6:6 2228
his son, Uzzi his son, Z his son, 1Ch 6:51 2228
son of Z, son of Uzzi, son of Ezr 7:4 2228
son of Z and 200 males with him; Ezr 8:4 2228

ZERAHITES
of Zerah, the family of the Z; Nu 26:13 2227
of Zerah, the family of the Z. Nu 26:20 2227
and he took the family of the Z; Jos 7:17 2227
he brought the family of the Z near Jos 7:17 2227
Sibbecai the Hushathite of the Z; 1Ch 27:11 2227
Maharai the Netophathite of the Z; 1Ch 27:13 2227

ZERED
they set out and camped in Wadi Z. Nu 21:12 2218
cross over the brook Z yourselves.' Dt 2:13 2218
So we crossed over the brook Z. Dt 2:13 2218
until we crossed over the brook Z was Dt 2:14 2218

ZEREDAH
son of Nebat, an Ephraimite of Z, 1Ki 11:26 6868a
clay ground between Succoth and Z. 2Ch 4:17 6868b

ZERERAH
as far as Beth-shittah toward Z, Jg 7:22 6888

ZERESH
for his friends and his wife Z. Es 5:10 2238
Then Z his wife and all his Es 5:14 2238
Haman recounted to Z his wife Es 6:13 2238
men and Z his wife said to him, Es 6:13 2238

ZERETH
The sons of Helah *were* Z, 1Ch 4:7 6889

ZERETH-SHAHAR
and Z on the hill of the valley, Jos 13:19 6890

ZERI
Gedaliah, Z, Jeshaiah, Shimei, 1Ch 25:3 6874

ZEROR
the son of Abiel, the son of Z, 1Sa 9:1 6872c

ZERUAH
servant, whose mother's name was Z, 1Ki 11:26 6871

ZERUBBABEL
sons of Pedaiah *were* Z and Shimei. 1Ch 3:19 2216
of Z *were* Meshullam and Hananiah, 1Ch 3:19 2216
These came with Z, Jeshua, Ezr 2:2 2216
and Z the son of Shealtiel and Ezr 3:2 2216
Z the son of Shealtiel and Jeshua Ezr 3:8 2216
they approached Z and the heads of Ezr 4:2 2216
But Z and Jeshua and the rest of Ezr 4:3 2216
then Z the son of Shealtiel and Ezr 5:2 2217
who came with Z, Jeshua, Nehemiah, Ne 7:7 2216
came up with Z the son of Shealtiel, Ne 12:1 2216
Israel in the days of Z and Nehemiah Ne 12:47 2216
Haggai to Z the son of Shealtiel, Hg 1:1 2216
Then Z the son of Shealtiel, and Hg 1:12 2216
spirit of Z the son of Shealtiel, Hg 1:14 2216
now to Z the son of Shealtiel, Hg 2:2 2216
'But now take courage, Z,' Hg 2:4 2216
"Speak to Z governor of Judah, Hg 2:21 2216
'I will take you, Z, Hg 2:23 2216
the word of the LORD to Z saying, Zch 4:6 2216
Before Z *you will become* a plain; Zch 4:7 2216
"The hands of Z have laid the Zch 4:9 2216
see the plumb line in the hand of Z Zch 4:10 2216
and Shealtiel the father of Z. Mt 1:12 *2216*
Z was the father of Abihud, Mt 1:13 *2216*
the son of Rhesa, the son of Z, Lk 3:27 *2216*

ZERUIAH
and to Abishai the son of Z, 1Sa 26:6 6870
And Joab the son of Z and the 2Sa 2:13 6870
the three sons of Z were there, 2Sa 2:18 6870
sons of Z are too difficult for me. 2Sa 3:39 6870
the son of Z *was* over the army, 2Sa 8:16 6870
Now Joab the son of Z perceived 2Sa 14:1 6870
the son of Z said to the king, 2Sa 16:9 6870
I to do with you, O sons of Z? 2Sa 16:10 6870
daughter of Nahash, sister of Z, 2Sa 17:25 6870
command of Abishai the son of Z, 2Sa 18:2 6870
the son of Z said, 2Sa 19:21 6870
I to do with you, O sons of Z, 2Sa 19:22 6870
Abishai the son of Z helped him, 2Sa 21:17 6870
the brother of Joab, the son of Z, 2Sa 23:18 6870
bearers of Joab the son of Z, 2Sa 23:37 6870
conferred with Joab the son of Z 1Ki 1:7 6870
what Joab the son of Z did to me, 1Ki 2:5 6870
and for Joab the son of Z!" 1Ki 2:22 6870
their sisters *were* Z and Abigail. 1Ch 2:16 6870
the three sons of Z *were* Abshai, 1Ch 2:16 6870
Joab the son of Z went up first, 1Ch 11:6 6870
armor bearer of Joab the son of Z, 1Ch 11:39 6870
Moreover Abishai the son of Z 1Ch 18:12 6870
the son of Z *was* over the army, 1Ch 18:15 6870
son of Ner and Joab the son of Z, 1Ch 26:28 6870
son of Z had begun to count *them,* 1Ch 27:24 6870

ZETHAM
Jehiel the first and Z and Joel, 1Ch 23:8 2241
Jehieli, Z and Joel his brother, 1Ch 26:22 2241

ZETHAN
Benjamin, Ehud, Chenaanah, Z, 1Ch 7:10 2133

ZETHAR
Harbona, Bigtha, Abagtha, Z and Es 1:10 2242

ZEUS
they *began* calling Barnabas, Z, Ac 14:12 *2203*
The priest of Z, Ac 14:13 *2203*

ZIA
Meshullam, Sheba, Jorai, Jacan, Z and 1Ch 5:13 2127

ZIBA
house of Saul whose name was Z, 2Sa 9:2 6717
the king said to him, "Are you Z?" 2Sa 9:2 6717
And Z said to the king, 2Sa 9:3 6717
And Z said to the king, 2Sa 9:4 6717
the king called Saul's servant Z and 2Sa 9:9 6717
Now Z had fifteen sons and twenty 2Sa 9:10 6717
Then Z said to the king, 2Sa 9:11 6717
all who lived in the house of Z 2Sa 9:12 6717
Z the servant of Mephibosheth met 2Sa 16:1 6717
The king said to Z, 2Sa 16:2 6717
And Z said, "The donkeys are for 2Sa 16:2 6717
And Z said to the king, 2Sa 16:3 6717
So the king said to Z, 2Sa 16:4 6717
And Z said, "I prostrate myself; 2Sa 16:4 6717
with Z the servant of the house of 2Sa 19:17 6717
'You and Z shall divide the land.' 2Sa 19:29 6717

ZIBEON
the granddaughter of Z the Hivite; Gn 36:2 6649
Anah and the granddaughter of Z: Gn 36:14 6649
Lotan and Shobal and Z and Anah, Gn 36:20 6649
These are the sons of Z: Gn 36:24 6649
the donkeys of his father Z. Gn 36:24 6649
Lotan, chief Shobal, chief Z, Gn 36:29 6649
of Seir *were* Lotan, Shobal, Z, 1Ch 1:38 6649
the sons of Z *were* Aiah and Anah. 1Ch 1:40 6649

ZIBIA
he became the father of Jobab, Z, 1Ch 8:9 6644

ZIBIAH
mother's name was Z of Beersheba. 2Ki 12:1 6645
mother's name *was* Z from Beersheba. 2Ch 24:1 6645

ZICHRI
Korah and Nepheg and Z. Ex 6:21 2147
Jakim, Z, Zabdi, 1Ch 8:19 2147
Abdon, Z, Hanan, 1Ch 8:23 2147
and Z *were* the sons of Jeroham. 1Ch 8:27 2147
the son of Mica, the son of Z, 1Ch 9:15 2147
his son, Joram his son, Z his son and 1Ch 26:25 2147
was Eliezer the son of Z; 1Ch 27:16 2147
next to him Amasiah the son of Z, 2Ch 17:16 2147
and Elishaphat the son of Z, 2Ch 23:1 2147
And Z, a mighty man of Ephraim, 2Ch 28:7 2147
the son of Z was their overseer, Ne 11:9 2147
Abijah, Z; of Miniamin, of Moadiah, Ne 12:17 2147

ZIDDIM
The fortified cities *were* Z, Jos 19:35 6661

ZIHA
the sons of Z, the sons of Ezr 2:43 6727
the sons of Z, the sons of Ne 7:46 6727
and Z and Gishpa were in charge of Ne 11:21 6727

ZIKLAG
and Z and Madmannah and Sansannah, Jos 15:31 6860
and Z and Beth-marcaboth and Jos 19:5 6860
So Achish gave him Z that day; 1Sa 27:6 6860
therefore Z has belonged to the 1Sa 27:6 6860
men came to Z on the third day, 1Sa 30:1 6860
made a raid on the Negev and on Z, 1Sa 30:1 6860
had overthrown Z and burned it 1Sa 30:1 6860
and we burned Z with fire." 1Sa 30:14 6860
Now when David came to Z, 1Sa 30:26 6860
that David remained two days in Z. 2Sa 1:1 6860
I seized him and killed him in Z, 2Sa 4:10 6860
Bethuel, Hormah, Z, 1Ch 4:30 6860
the ones who came to David at Z, 1Ch 12:1 6860
As he went to Z there defected to 1Ch 12:20 6860
and in Z, in Meconah and in its Ne 11:28 6860

ZILLAH
and the name of the other, Z. Gn 4:19 6741
As for Z, she also gave birth to Gn 4:22 6741
"Adah and Z, Listen to my voice, Gn 4:23 6741

ZILLETHAI
Elienai, Z, Eliel, 1Ch 8:20 6769
Michael, Jozabad, Elihu and Z, 1Ch 12:20 6769

ZILPAH
Laban also gave his maid Z to his Gn 29:24 2153
she took her maid Z and gave her Gn 30:9 2153
Leah's maid Z bore Jacob a son. Gn 30:10 2153
maid Z bore Jacob a second son. Gn 30:12 2153
and the sons of Z, Leah's maid: Gn 35:26 2153
sons of Bilhah and the sons of Z, Gn 37:2 2153
These are the sons of Z, Gn 46:18 2153

ZIMMAH
son, Jahath his son, Z his son, 1Ch 6:20 2155
the son of Ethan, the son of Z, 1Ch 6:42 2155
son of Z and Eden the son of Joah; 2Ch 29:12 2155

ZIMRAN
She bore to him Z and Jokshan Gn 25:2 2175
concubine, *whom* she bore, *were* Z, 1Ch 1:32 2175

ZIMRI
woman, was Z the son of Salu, Nu 25:14 2174a
His servant Z, commander of 1Ki 16:9 2174a
Then Z went in and struck him and 1Ki 16:10 2174a
Thus Z destroyed all the household 1Ki 16:12 2174a
Z reigned seven days at Tirzah. 1Ki 16:15 2174a
"Z has conspired and has also 1Ki 16:16 2174a
Z saw that the city was taken, 1Ki 16:18 2174a
Now the rest of the acts of Z and 1Ki 16:20 2174a
"Is it well, Z, your master's 2Ki 9:31 2174a
The sons of Zerah *were* Z, 1Ch 2:6 2174a
of Alemeth, Azmaveth and Z; 1Ch 8:36 2174a
and Z became the father of Moza. 1Ch 8:36 2174a
of Alemeth, Azmaveth and Z; 1Ch 9:42 2174a
and Z became the father of Moza, 1Ch 9:42 2174a
and all the kings of Z, Jer 25:25 2174b

ZIN
wilderness of Z as far as Rehob, Nu 13:21 6790
came to the wilderness of Z in the Nu 20:1 6790
for in the wilderness of Z, Nu 27:14 6790
of Kadesh in the wilderness of Z.) Nu 27:14 6790
and camped in the wilderness of Z, Nu 33:36 6790
of Z along the side of Edom, Nu 34:3 6790
of Akrabbim and continue to Z, Nu 34:4 6790
in the wilderness of Z, Dt 32:51 6790
of Z at the extreme south. Jos 15:1 6790
of Akrabbim and continued to Z, Jos 15:3 6790

ZINA
The sons of Shimei *were* Jahath, Z, 1Ch 23:10 2126

ZION
captured the stronghold of Z, 2Sa 5:7 6726
the city of David, which is Z. 1Ki 8:1 6726
you, The virgin daughter of Z; 2Ki 19:21 6726
and out of Mount Z survivors. 2Ki 19:31 6726
captured the stronghold of Z 1Ch 11:5 6726
of the city of David, which is Z. 2Ch 5:2 6726
I have installed My King Upon Z, Ps 2:6 6726
to the LORD, who dwells in Z; Ps 9:11 6726
That in the gates of the daughter of Z Ps 9:14 6726
of Israel would come out of Z! Ps 14:7 6726
sanctuary And support you from Z! Ps 20:2 6726
Is Mount Z *in* the far north, Ps 48:2 6726
Let Mount Z be glad, Let the Ps 48:11 6726
Walk about Z and go around her; Ps 48:12 6726
Out of Z, the perfection of Ps 50:2 6726
By Your favor do good to Z; Ps 51:18 6726

of Israel would come out of **Z**! Ps 53:6 6726
before You, *and* praise in **Z**, Ps 65:1 6726
Z and build the cities of Judah, Ps 69:35 6726
Mount **Z**, where You have dwelt. Ps 74:2 6726
His dwelling place also is in **Z**. Ps 76:2 6726
of Judah, Mount **Z** which He loved. Ps 78:68 6726
whose heart are the highways *to* **Z**! Ps 84:5 6726
of them appears before God in **Z**. Ps 84:7 6726
The LORD loves the gates of **Z** More Ps 87:2 6726
But of **Z** it shall be said, Ps 87:5 6726
Z heard *this* and was glad, And the Ps 97:8 6726
The LORD is great in **Z**, Ps 99:2 6726
arise *and* have compassion on **Z**; Ps 102:13 6726
For the LORD has built up **Z**; Ps 102:16 6726
tell of the name of the LORD in **Z** And Ps 102:21 6726
forth Your strong scepter from **Z**, Ps 110:2 6726
trust in the LORD Are as Mount **Z**, Ps 125:1 6726
back the captive ones of **Z**, Ps 126:1 6726
The LORD bless you from **Z**, Ps 128:5 6726
May all who hate **Z** Be Ps 129:5 6726
For the LORD has chosen **Z**; Ps 132:13 6726
down upon the mountains of **Z**; Ps 133:3 6726
May the LORD bless you from **Z**, Ps 134:3 6726
Blessed be the LORD from **Z**, Ps 135:21 6726
and wept, When we remembered **Z**. Ps 137:1 6726
"Sing us one of the songs of **Z**." Ps 137:3 6726
will reign forever, Your God, O **Z**, Ps 146:10 6726
Praise your God, O **Z**! Ps 147:12 6726
sons of **Z** rejoice in their King. Ps 149:2 6726
"Go forth, O daughters of **Z**, SS 3:11 6726
The daughter of **Z** is left like Is 1:8 6726
Z will be redeemed with justice And Is 1:27 6726
For the law will go forth from **Z** And Is 2:3 6726
the daughters of **Z** are proud And Is 3:16 6726
the scalp of the daughters of **Z** Is 3:17 6726
he who is left in **Z** and remains in Is 4:3 6726
the filth of the daughters of **Z** and Is 4:4 6726
over the whole area of Mount **Z** Is 4:5 6726
of hosts, who dwells on Mount **Z**. Is 8:18 6726
work on Mount **Z** and on Jerusalem, Is 10:12 6726
"O My people who dwell in **Z**, Is 10:24 6726
the mountain of the daughter of **Z**, Is 10:32 6726
shout for joy, O inhabitant of **Z**, Is 12:6 6726
That the LORD has founded **Z**, Is 14:32 6726
the mountain of the daughter of **Z**. Is 16:1 6726
the LORD of hosts, *even* Mount **Z**. Is 18:7 6726
LORD of hosts will reign on Mount **Z** Is 24:23 6726
"Behold, I am laying in **Z** a stone, Is 28:16 6726
be Who wage war against Mount **Z**. Is 29:8 6726
O people in **Z**, inhabitant in Is 30:19 6726
war on Mount **Z** and on its hill." Is 31:4 6726
whose fire is in **Z** and whose Is 31:9 6726
He has filled **Z** with justice and Is 33:5 6726
Sinners in **Z** are terrified; Is 33:14 6726
Look upon **Z**, the city of our Is 33:20 6726
of recompense for the cause of **Z**. Is 34:8 6726
come with joyful shouting to **Z**, Is 35:10 6726
you, The virgin daughter of **Z**; Is 37:22 6726
and out of Mount **Z** survivors. Is 37:32 6726
up on a high mountain, O **Z**, Is 40:9 6726
"Formerly *I said* to **Z**, Is 41:27 6726
And I will grant salvation in **Z**, Is 46:13 6726
Z said, "The LORD has forsaken me, Is 49:14 6726
Indeed, the LORD will comfort **Z**; Is 51:3 6726
come with joyful shouting to **Z**, Is 51:11 6726
found the earth, and to say to **Z**, Is 51:16 6726
yourself in your strength, O **Z**; Is 52:1 6726
your neck, O captive daughter of **Z**. Is 52:2 6726
salvation, *And* says to **Z**, Is 52:7 6726
own eyes When the LORD restores **Z**. Is 52:8 6726
"A Redeemer will come to **Z**, Is 59:20 6726
The **Z** of the Holy One of Israel. Is 60:14 6726
To grant those who mourn *in* **Z**, Is 61:3 6726
earth, Say to the daughter of **Z**, Is 62:11 6726
Z has become a wilderness, Is 64:10 6726
As soon as **Z** travailed, she also Is 66:8 6726
And I will bring you to **Z**.' Jer 3:14 6726
"Lift up a standard toward **Z**! Jer 4:6 6726
daughter of **Z** gasping for breath, Jer 4:31 6726
and dainty one, the daughter of **Z**, Jer 6:2 6726
Against you, O daughter of **Z**!" Jer 6:23 6726
"Is the LORD not in **Z**? Jer 8:19 6726
voice of wailing is heard from **Z**, Jer 9:19 6726
Or have You loathed **Z**? Jer 14:19 6726
"**Z** will be plowed *as* a field, And Jer 26:18 6726
saying: "It *is* **Z**; no one cares for her Jer 30:17 6726
'Arise, and let us go up *to* **Z**, Jer 31:6 6726
shout for joy on the height of **Z**, Jer 31:12 6726
"They will ask for the way to **Z**, Jer 50:5 6726
To declare in **Z** the vengeance of Jer 50:28 6726
let us recount in **Z** The work of the Jer 51:10 6726
have done in **Z** before your eyes," Jer 51:24 6726
The inhabitant of **Z** will say; Jer 51:35 6726
The roads of **Z** are in mourning La 1:4 6726
departed from the daughter of **Z**; La 1:6 6726
Z stretches out her hands; La 1:17 6726
Lord has covered the daughter of **Z** La 2:1 6726
In the tent of the daughter of **Z** La 2:4 6726
appointed feast and sabbath in **Z**, La 2:6 6726
The wall of the daughter of **Z**, La 2:8 6726
daughter of **Z** Sit on the ground, La 2:10 6726
you, O virgin daughter of **Z**? La 2:13 6726
"O wall of the daughter of **Z**, La 2:18 6726
The precious sons of **Z**, La 4:2 6726
And He has kindled a fire in **Z** La 4:11 6726
been completed, O daughter of **Z**; La 4:22 6726
They ravished the women in **Z**, La 5:11 6726
of Mount **Z** which lies desolate, La 5:18 6726
Blow a trumpet in **Z**, Jl 2:1 6726
Blow a trumpet in **Z**, Jl 2:15 6726
So rejoice, O sons of **Z**, Jl 2:23 6726
For on Mount **Z** and in Jerusalem Jl 2:32 6726
The LORD roars from **Z** And Jl 3:16 6726
Dwelling in **Z**, My holy mountain. Jl 3:17 6726
avenged, For the LORD dwells in **Z**. Jl 3:21 6726
"The LORD roars from **Z** And Am 1:2 6726
Woe to those who are at ease in **Z** And Am 6:1 6726
"But on Mount **Z** there will be Ob 1:17 6726
The deliverers will ascend Mount **Z** Ob 1:21 6726
beginning of sin To the daughter of **Z** Mi 1:13 6726
Who build **Z** with bloodshed And Mi 3:10 6726
Z will be plowed as a field, Mi 3:12 6726
For from **Z** will go forth the law, Mi 4:2 6726
will reign over them in Mount **Z** Mi 4:7 6726
flock, Hill of the daughter of **Z**, Mi 4:8 6726
to give birth, Daughter of **Z**, Mi 4:10 6726
And let our eyes gloat over **Z**.' Mi 4:11 6726
"Arise and thresh, daughter of **Z**, Mi 4:13 6726
Shout for joy, O daughter of **Z**! Zph 3:14 6726
"Do not be afraid, O **Z**; Zph 3:16 6726
O **Z**; *The* reproach *of exile* Zph 3:18 6726
jealous for Jerusalem and **Z**. Zch 1:14 6726
the LORD will again comfort **Z** and Zch 1:17 6726
"Ho, **Z**! Escape, you who are living Zch 2:7 6726
joy and be glad, O daughter of **Z**; Zch 2:10 6726
'I am exceedingly jealous for **Z**, Zch 8:2 6726
'I will return to **Z** and will dwell Zch 8:3 6726
Rejoice greatly, O daughter of **Z**! Zch 9:9 6726
And I will stir up your sons, O **Z**, Zch 9:13 6726
"SAY TO THE DAUGHTER OF **Z**, Mt 21:5 *4622*
"FEAR NOT, DAUGHTER OF **Z**; Jn 12:15 *4622*
I LAY IN **Z** A STONE OF STUMBLING Ro 9:33 *4622*
"THE DELIVERER WILL COME FROM **Z**, Ro 11:26 *4622*
But you have come to Mount **Z** and Heb 12:22 *4622*
"BEHOLD, I LAY IN **Z** A CHOICE STONE, 1Pe 2:6 *4622*
the Lamb *was* standing on Mount **Z**, Rv 14:1 *4622*

ZION'S
For **Z** sake I will not keep silent, Is 62:1 6726

ZIOR
and **Z**; nine cities with their villages. Jos 15:54 6730

ZIPH
Z and Telem and Bealoth, Jos 15:24 2128
Maon, Carmel and **Z** and Juttah, Jos 15:55 2128
country in the wilderness of **Z**. 1Sa 23:14 2128
in the wilderness of **Z** at Horesh. 1Sa 23:15 2128
arose and went to **Z** before Saul. 1Sa 23:24 2128
went down to the wilderness of **Z**, 1Sa 26:2 2128
for David in the wilderness of **Z**. 1Sa 26:2 2128
who was the father of **Z**; 1Ch 2:42 2128
of Jehallelel *were* **Z** and Ziphah, 1Ch 4:16 2128
Gath, Mareshah, **Z**, 2Ch 11:8 2128

ZIPHAH
of Jehallelel *were* Ziph and **Z**, 1Ch 4:16 2129

ZIPHION
Z and Haggi, Shuni and Ezbon, Eri Gn 46:16 6837

ZIPHITES
Then **Z** came up to Saul at Gibeah, 1Sa 23:19 2130
Then the **Z** came to Saul at Gibeah, 1Sa 26:1 2130

ZIPHRON
and the border shall proceed to **Z**, Nu 34:9 2202

ZIPPOR
Now Balak the son of **Z** saw all Nu 22:2 6834
And Balak the son of **Z** was king of Nu 22:4 6834
"Balak the son of **Z**, Nu 22:10 6834
"Thus says Balak the son of **Z**, Nu 22:16 6834
Give ear to me, O son of **Z**! Nu 23:18 6834
'Then Balak the son of **Z**, Jos 24:9 6834
better than Balak the son of **Z**, Jg 11:25 6834

ZIPPORAH
he gave his daughter **Z** to Moses. Ex 2:21 6855
Then **Z** took a flint and cut off Ex 4:25 6855
father-in-law, took Moses' wife **Z**, Ex 18:2 6855

ZIV
of **Z** which is the second month, 1Ki 6:1 2099
LORD was laid, in the month of **Z**. 1Ki 6:37 2099

ZIZ
will come up by the ascent of **Z**, 2Ch 20:16 6732

ZIZA
Z the son of Shiphi, the son of 1Ch 4:37 2124
and she bore him Abijah, Attai, **Z** and 2Ch 11:20 2124

ZIZAH
was the first and **Z** the second; 1Ch 23:11 2125

ZOAN
seven years before **Z** in Egypt.) Nu 13:22 6814
land of Egypt, in the field of **Z**. Ps 78:12 6814
And His marvels in the field of **Z**, Ps 78:43 6814
The princes of **Z** are mere fools; Is 19:11 6814
princes of **Z** have acted foolishly, Is 19:13 6814
'For their princes are at **Z** And Is 30:4 6814
Pathros desolate, Set a fire in **Z** And Ezk 30:14 6814

ZOAR
the land of Egypt as you go to **Z**. Gn 13:10 6820
and the king of Bela (that is, **Z**). Gn 14:2 6820
and the king of Bela (that is, **Z**) Gn 14:8 6820
the name of the town was called **Z**. Gn 19:22 6820
over the earth when Lot came to **Z**. Gn 19:23 6820
Lot went up from **Z**, Gn 19:30 6820
for he was afraid to stay in **Z**; Gn 19:30 6820
city of palm trees, as far as **Z**. Dt 34:3 6820
as far as **Z** *and* Eglath-shelishiyah, Is 15:5 6820
from **Z** even to Horonaim *and to* Jer 48:34 6820

ZOBAH
of Ammon, Edom, the kings of **Z**, 1Sa 14:47 6678
the son of Rehob king of **Z**, 2Sa 8:3 6678
came to help Hadadezer, king of **Z**, 2Sa 8:5 6678
son of Rehob, king of **Z**. 2Sa 8:12 6678
Beth-rehob and the Arameans of **Z**, 2Sa 10:6 6678
while the Arameans of **Z** and of 2Sa 10:8 6678
Igal the son of Nathan of **Z**, 2Sa 23:36 6678
from his lord Hadadezer king of **Z**. 1Ki 11:23 6678
after David slew them of **Z**; 1Ki 11:24
king of **Z** *as far as* Hamath, 1Ch 18:3 6678
came to help Hadadezer king of **Z**, 1Ch 18:5 6678
the army of Hadadezer king of **Z**, 1Ch 18:9 6678
from Aram-maacah and from **Z**, 1Ch 19:6 6678

ZOBEBAH
became the father of Anub and **Z**, 1Ch 4:8 6637

ZOHAR
approach Ephron the son of **Z** for Gn 23:8 6714
Ephron the son of **Z** the Hittite, Gn 25:9 6714
Jamin and Ohad and Jachin and **Z** Gn 46:10 6714
Z and Shaul the son of a Canaanite Ex 6:15 6714

ZOHELETH
and fatlings by the stone of **Z**, 1Ki 1:9 2120

ZOHETH
sons of Ishi *were* **Z** and Ben-zoheth. 1Ch 4:20 2105

ZOPHAH
sons of his brother Helem *were* **Z**, 1Ch 7:35 6690
The sons of **Z** *were* Suah, 1Ch 7:36 6690

ZOPHAI
were **Z** his son and Nahath his son, 1Ch 6:26 6689

ZOPHAR
the Shuhite and **Z** the Naamathite; Jb 2:11 6691
Then **Z** the Naamathite answered, Jb 11:1 6691
Then **Z** the Naamathite answered, Jb 20:1 6691
Z the Naamathite went and did as Jb 42:9 6691

ZOPHIM
So he took him to the field of **Z**, Nu 23:14 6839

ZORAH
Eshtaol and **Z** and Ashnah, Jos 15:33 6881
was **Z** and Eshtaol and Ir-shemesh, Jos 19:41 6881
There was a certain man of **Z**, Jg 13:2 6881
Mahaneh-dan, between **Z** and Eshtaol. Jg 13:25 6881
and buried him between **Z** and Jg 16:31 6881
valiant men from **Z** and Eshtaol, Jg 18:2 6881
their brothers at **Z** and Eshtaol, Jg 18:8 6881
Danites, from **Z** and from Eshtaol, Jg 18:11 6881
Z, Aijalon and Hebron, which are 2Ch 11:10 6881
in En-rimmon, in **Z** and in Jarmuth, Ne 11:29 6881

ZORATHITES
came the **Z** and the Eshtaolites. 1Ch 2:53 6882
These *were* the families of the **Z**. 1Ch 4:2 6882

ZORITES
half of the Manahathites, the **Z**. 1Ch 2:54 6882

ZUAR
Issachar, Nethanel the son of **Z**; Nu 1:8 6686
Nethanel the son of **Z**, Nu 2:5 6686
second day Nethanel the son of **Z**, Nu 7:18 6686
offering of Nethanel the son of **Z**. Nu 7:23 6686
and Nethanel the son of **Z**, Nu 10:15 6686

ZUPH
the son of Tohu, the son of **Z**, 1Sa 1:1 6689
When they came to the land of **Z**, 1Sa 9:5 6689
the son of **Z**, the son of Elkanah, 1Ch 6:35 6689

ZUR
slain was Cozbi the daughter of **Z**, Nu 25:15 6698
and Rekem and **Z** and Hur and Reba, Nu 31:8 6698
and Rekem and **Z** and Hur and Reba, Jos 13:21 6698
firstborn son *was* Abdon, then **Z**, 1Ch 8:30 6698
firstborn son *was* Abdon, then **Z**, 1Ch 9:36 6698

ZURIEL
Merari *was* **Z** the son of Abihail. Nu 3:35 6700

ZURISHADDAI
of Simeon, Shelumiel the son of **Z**; Nu 1:6 6701a
Shelumiel the son of **Z**, Nu 2:12 6701a
day *it was* Shelumiel the son of **Z**, Nu 7:36 6701a
of Shelumiel the son of **Z**. Nu 7:41 6701a
and Shelumiel the son of **Z** over Nu 10:19 6701a

ZUZIM
and the **Z** in Ham and the Emim Gn 14:5 2104

NUMBERS

10
"And we will take # men out of 100 Jg 20:10 6235

12
for all Israel # male goats, Ezr 6:17 8648, 6236
bulls for all Israel, 96 rams, 77 Ezr 8:35 8147, 6240
male goats for a sin offering, Ezr 8:35 8147, 6240

13
sons and relatives of Hosah *were* #. 1Ch 26:11 7969, 6240

15
on the 45 pillars, # in each row. 1Ki 7:3 2568, 6240

18
sons and relatives, # valiant men. 1Ch 26:9 8083, 6240
and his sons and brothers, # men; Ezr 8:18 8083, 6240

20
his brothers and their sons, # men; Ezr 8:19 6242
and # gold bowls *worth* 1,000 Ezr 8:27 6242

24
sacrifice of peace offerings # bulls, **Nu 7:88** 6242, 702

28
son of Bebai and # males with him; **Ezr 8:11** 6242, 8083

29
was # talents and 730 shekels, **Ex 38:24** 8672, 6242
1,000 silver dishes, # duplicates; **Ezr 1:9** 8672, 6242

30
50 cubits and its height # cubits, **1Ki 7:2** 7970
50 cubits and its width # cubits, **1Ki 7:6** 7970
gold dishes, 1,000 silver dishes, **Ezr 1:9** 7970
gold bowls, 410 silver bowls of a **Ezr 1:10** 7970

32
whom the LORD's levy was # persons. **Nu 31:40** 8147, 7970

42
the sons of Azmaveth, #; **Ezr 2:24** 705, 8147
the men of Beth-azmaveth, #; **Ne 7:28** 705, 8147

45
which were on the # pillars, **1Ki 7:3** 705, 2568

50
and its width # cubits and its height **1Ki 7:2** 2572
its length was # cubits and its **1Ki 7:6** 2572
of Jonathan and # males with him; **Ezr 8:6** 2572
1,000 gold drachmas, # basins, **Ne 7:70** 2572

52
the sons of Nebo, #; **Ezr 2:29** 2572, 8147
the men of the other Nebo, #; **Ne 7:33** 2572, 8147

56
the men of Netophah, #; **Ezr 2:22** 2572, 8337a

60
offerings 24 bulls, *all* the rams #, **Nu 7:88** 8346
all the rams 60, the male goats #, **Nu 7:88** 8346
60, the male lambs one year old #. **Nu 7:88** 8346
its height being # cubits and its **Ezr 6:3** 8361
60 cubits and its width # cubits; **Ezr 6:3** 8361
and Shemaiah, and # males with them; **Ezr 8:13** 8346

61
from which the LORD's levy was #; **Nu 31:39** 259, 8346

62
for the service, # from Obed-edom. **1Ch 26:8** 8346, 8147

65
within another # years Ephraim will **Is 7:8** 8346, 2568

67
minas and # priests' garments. **Ne 7:72** 8346, 7651

68
and Obed-edom with his # relatives; **1Ch 16:38** 8346, 8083

70
of the wave offering was # talents and **Ex 38:29** 7657
the assembly brought was # bulls, **2Ch 29:32** 7657
of Athaliah and # males with him; **Ezr 8:7** 7657
and Zabbud, and # males with them. **Ezr 8:14** 7657

72
from which the LORD's levy was #; **Nu 31:38** 8147, 7657

74
of the sons of Hodaviah, #. **Ezr 2:40** 7657, 702
Kadmiel, of the sons of Hodevah, #. **Ne 7:43** 7657, 702

77
for all Israel, 96 rams, # lambs, **Ezr 8:35** 7657, 7651

80
the chief, and # of his relatives; **1Ch 15:9** 8084
of Michael and # males with him; **Ezr 8:8** 8084

95
the sons of Gibbar, #; **Ezr 2:20** 8673, 2568
the sons of Gibeon, #; **Ne 7:25** 8673, 2568

96
12 bulls for all Israel, # rams, **Ezr 8:35** 8673, 8337a

98
the sons of Ater of Hezekiah, #; **Ezr 2:16** 8673, 8083
the sons of Ater, of Hezekiah, #; **Ne 7:21** 8673, 8083

100
was # talents and 1,775 shekels, **Ex 38:25** 3967
"And we will take 10 men out of # **Jg 20:10** 3967
of Israel, and # out of 1,000, **Jg 20:10** 3967
enough of them for # chariots. **2Sa 8:4** 3967
its length was # cubits and its **1Ki 7:2** 3967
enough of them for # chariots. **1Ch 18:4** 3967
brought was 70 bulls, # rams, **2Ch 29:32** 3967
minas and # priestly garments. **Ezr 2:69** 3967
of this temple of God # bulls, **Ezr 6:17** 3969
even up to # talents of silver, 100 **Ezr 7:22** 3967
talents of silver, # kors of wheat, **Ezr 7:22** 3967
100 kors of wheat, # baths of wine, **Ezr 7:22** 3967
100 baths of wine, # baths of oil, **Ezr 7:22** 3967
silver utensils *worth* # talents, **Ezr 8:26** 3967
worth 100 talents, *and* # talents, **Ezr 8:26** 3967

110
of Hakkatan and # males with him; **Ezr 8:12** 3967, 6235

112
the chief, and # of his relatives. **1Ch 15:10** 3967, 8147, 6240
the sons of Jorah, #; **Ezr 2:18** 3967, 8147, 6240
the sons of Hariph, #; **Ne 7:24** 3967, 8147, 6240

120
all the gold of the pans # *shekels;* **Nu 7:86** 6242, 3967
sent to the king # talents of gold. **1Ki 9:14** 3967, 6242
the chief, and # of his relatives; **1Ch 15:5** 3967, 6242
twenty cubits, and the height #; **2Ch 3:4** 3967, 6242
appoint # satraps over the kingdom, **Da 6:1** 3969, 6243

122
the men of Michmas, #; **Ezr 2:27** 3967, 6242, 8147
the men of Michmas, #; **Ne 7:31** 3967, 6242, 8147

123
the men of Bethlehem, #; **Ezr 2:21** 3967, 6242, 7969
the men of Bethel and Ai, #; **Ne 7:32** 3967, 6242, 7969

127
India to Ethiopia over # provinces, **Es 1:1** 7651, 6242, 3967
India to Ethiopia, # provinces, **Es 8:9** 7651, 6242, 3967
to the # provinces of the kingdom **Es 9:30** 7651, 6242, 3967

128
the men of Anathoth, #; **Ezr 2:23** 3967, 6242, 8083
the sons of Asaph, #. **Ezr 2:41** 3967, 6242, 8083
the men of Anathoth, #; **Ne 7:27** 3967, 6242, 8083
their brothers, valiant warriors, #. **Ne 11:14** 3967, 6242, 8083

130
the chief, and # of his relatives; **1Ch 15:7** 3967, 7970

138
of Hatita, the sons of Shobai, #. **Ne 7:45** 3967, 7970, 8083

139
the sons of Shobai, in all #. **Ezr 2:42** 3967, 7970, 8672

140
After this, Job lived # years, **Jb 42:16** 3967, 705

148
the sons of Asaph, #. **Ne 7:44** 3967, 705, 8083

150
of silver, and a horse for #; **1Ki 10:29** 2572, 3967
many sons and grandsons, # *of them.* **1Ch 8:40** 3967, 2572
apiece and horses for # apiece, **2Ch 1:17** 2572, 3967
Zechariah and with him # males *who* **Ezr 8:3** 3967, 2572

156
the sons of Magbish, #; **Ezr 2:30** 3967, 2572, 8337a

160
of Josiphiah and # males with him; **Ezr 8:10** 3967, 8346

172
kept watch at the gates, *were* #. **Ne 11:19** 3967, 7657, 8147

180
majesty for many days, # days. **Es 1:4** 8084, 3967

188
men of Bethlehem and Netophah, #; **Ne 7:26** 3967, 8084, 8083

200
at # shekels by the king's weight. **2Sa 14:26** 3967
large shields of beaten gold, **1Ki 10:16** 3967
the chief, and # of his relatives; **1Ch 15:8** 3967
large shields of beaten gold, **2Ch 9:15** 3967
70 bulls, 100 rams, and # lambs; **2Ch 29:32** 3967
they had # singing men and women. **Ezr 2:65** 3967
temple of God 100 bulls, # rams, **Ezr 6:17** 3969
of Zerahiah and # males with him; **Ezr 8:4** 3967

212
at the thresholds were #. **1Ch 9:22** 3967, 8147, 6240

218
son of Jehiel and # males with him; **Ezr 8:9** 3967, 8083, 6240

220
the chief, and # of his relatives; **1Ch 15:6** 3967, 6242
and # of the temple servants, whom **Ezr 8:20** 3967, 6242

223
the sons of Hashum, #; **Ezr 2:19** 3967, 6242, 7969
the men of Bethel and Ai, #; **Ezr 2:28** 3967, 6242, 7969

232
of the provinces, and there were #; **1Ki 20:15** 3967, 8147, 7970

242
heads of fathers' *households,* #; **Ne 11:13** 3967, 705, 8147

245
horses were 736; their mules, #; **Ezr 2:66** 3967, 705, 2568
they had # male and female singers. **Ne 7:67** 3967, 705, 2568
horses were 736; their mules, #; **Ne 7:68** 3967, 705, 2568

250
died, when the fire devoured # men, **Nu 26:10** 2572, 3967
on the north # *cubits,* on the south **Ezk 48:17** 2572, 3967
250 *cubits,* on the south # *cubits,* **Ezk 48:17** 2572, 3967
250 *cubits,* on the east # *cubits,* **Ezk 48:17** 2572, 3967
cubits, and on the west # *cubits.* **Ezk 48:17** 2572, 3967

273
ransom of the # of the firstborn **Nu 3:46** 7969, 7657, 3967

284
Levites in the holy city *were* #. **Ne 11:18** 3967, 8084, 702

288
all who were skillful, *was* #. **1Ch 25:7** 3967, 8084, 8083

300
hand to their mouth, was # men; **Jg 7:6** 7969, 3967
"I will deliver you with the # men **Jg 7:7** 7969, 3967
So the # men took the people's **Jg 7:8**
his tent, but retained the # men; **Jg 7:8** 7969, 3967
the # men into three companies, **Jg 7:16** 7969, 3967
When they blew # trumpets, **Jg 7:22** 7969, 3967
Then Gideon and the # men who were **Jg 8:4** 7969, 3967
He made # shields of beaten gold, **1Ki 10:17** 7969, 3967
He made # shields of beaten gold, **2Ch 9:16** 7969, 3967
of a million men and # chariots, **2Ch 14:9** 7969, 3967
2,600 *from the flocks* and # bulls. **2Ch 35:8** 7969, 3967
of Jahaziel and # males with him; **Ezr 8:5** 7969, 3967

320
the sons of Harim, #; **Ezr 2:32** 7969, 3967, 6242
the sons of Harim, #; **Ne 7:35** 7969, 3967, 6242

323
the sons of Bezai, #; **Ezr 2:17** 7969, 3967, 6242, 7969

324
the sons of Bezai, #; **Ne 7:23** 7969, 3967, 6242, 702

328
the sons of Hashum, #; **Ne 7:22** 7969, 3967, 6242, 8083

345
the men of Jericho, #; **Ezr 2:34** 7969, 3967, 705, 2568
the men of Jericho, #; **Ne 7:36** 7969, 3967, 705, 2568

372
the sons of Shephatiah, #; **Ezr 2:4** 7969, 3967, 7657, 8147
the sons of Shephatiah, #; **Ne 7:9** 7969, 3967, 7657, 8147

392
sons of Solomon's servants were #. **Ezr 2:58** 7969, 3967, 8673, 8147
sons of Solomon's servants *were* #. **Ne 7:60** 7969, 3967, 8673, 8147

400
of Jabesh-gilead # young virgins **Jg 21:12** 702, 3967
Baal and # prophets of the Asherah, **1Ki 18:19** 702, 3967

to the Corner Gate, # cubits. **2Ki 14:13** 702, 3967

to the Corner Gate, # cubits. **2Ch 25:23** 702, 3967

God 100 bulls, 200 rams, # lambs, **Ezr 6:17** 702, 3967

410

silver bowls of a second *kind and* **Ezr 1:10** 702, 3967, 6235

435

their camels, #; *their* donkeys, 6,720 **Ezr 2:67** 702, 3967, 7970, 2568

their camels, #; *their* donkeys, 6,720 **Ne 7:69** 702, 3967, 7970, 2568

450

together with # prophets of Baal **1Ki 18:19** 702, 3967, 2572

LORD, but Baal's prophets are # men. **1Ki 18:22** 702, 3967, 2572

454

the sons of Adin, #; **Ezr 2:15** 702, 3967, 2572, 702

468

lived in Jerusalem were # able men. **Ne 11:6** 702, 3967, 8346, 8083

500

5,000 *from the flocks* and # bulls. **2Ch 35:9** 2568, 3967

3,000 camels, # yoke of oxen, **Jb 1:3** 2568, 3967

500 yoke of oxen, # female donkeys, **Jb 1:3** 2568, 3967

530

50 basins, # priests' garments. **Ne 7:70** 7970, 2568, 3967

600

But # men turned and fled toward **Jg 20:47** 8337a, 3967

using # *shekels of* gold on each **1Ki 10:16** 8337a, 3967

from Egypt for # *shekels* of silver, **1Ki 10:29** 8337a, 3967

David gave Ornan # shekels of gold **1Ch 21:25** 8337a, 3967

for # *shekels* of silver apiece and **2Ch 1:17** 8337a, 3967

fine gold, *amounting* to # talents. **2Ch 3:8** 8337a, 3967

using # *shekels of* beaten gold on **2Ch 9:15** 8337a, 3967

were # bulls and 3,000 sheep. **2Ch 29:33** 8337a, 3967

621

the sons of Ramah and Geba, #; **Ezr 2:26** 8337a, 3967, 6242, 259

the men of Ramah and Geba, #; **Ne 7:30** 8337a, 3967, 6242, 259

623

the sons of Bebai, #; **Ezr 2:11** 8337a, 3967, 6242, 7969

628

the sons of Bebai, #; **Ne 7:16** 8337a, 3967, 6242, 8083

642

the sons of Bani, #; **Ezr 2:10** 8337a, 3967, 705, 8147

of Tobiah, the sons of Nekoda, #. **Ne 7:62** 8337a, 3967, 705, 8147

648

the sons of Binnui, #; **Ne 7:15** 8337a, 3967, 705, 8083

650

their hands # talents of silver, **Ezr 8:26** 8337a, 3967, 2572

652

of Tobiah, the sons of Nekoda, #. **Ezr 2:60** 8337a, 3967, 2572, 8147

the sons of Arah, #; **Ne 7:10** 8337a, 3967, 2572, 8147

655

the sons of Adin, #; **Ne 7:20** 8337a, 3967, 2572, 2568

666

in one year was # talents of gold, **1Ki 10:14** 8337a, 3967, 8346, 8337a

in one year was # talents of gold, **2Ch 9:13** 8337a, 3967, 8346, 8337a

the sons of Adonikam, #; **Ezr 2:13** 8337a, 3967, 8346, 8337a

667

the sons of Adonikam, #; **Ne 7:18** 8337a, 3967, 8346, 7651

675

the LORD's levy of the sheep was #; **Nu 31:37** 8337a, 3967, 2568, 7657

690

and their relatives, # *of them.* **1Ch 9:6** 8337a, 3967, 8673

700

who were numbered, # choice men. **Jg 20:15** 7651, 3967

choice men were left-handed; **Jg 20:16** 7651, 3967

and David killed # charioteers of **2Sa 10:18** 7651, 3967

with him # men who drew swords, **2Ki 3:26** 7651, 3967

to the LORD that day # oxen **2Ch 15:11** 7651, 3967

721

the sons of Lod, Hadid and Ono, #; **Ne 7:37** 7651, 3967, 6242, 259

725

the sons of Lod, Hadid and Ono, #; **Ezr 2:33** 7651, 3967, 6242, 2568

730

was 29 talents and # shekels, **Ex 38:24** 7651, 3967, 7970

736

Their horses were #; **Ezr 2:66** 7651, 3967, 7970, 8337a

Their horses were #; **Ne 7:68** 7651, 3967, 7970, 8337a

743

Chephirah and Beeroth, #; **Ezr 2:25** 7651, 3967, 705, 7969

Chephirah and Beeroth, #; **Ne 7:29** 7651, 3967, 705, 7969

745

carried into exile # Jewish people; **Jer 52:30** 7651, 3967, 705, 2568

760

the sons of Zaccai, #; **Ezr 2:9** 7651, 3967, 8346

the sons of Zaccai, #; **Ne 7:14** 7651, 3967, 8346

775

the sons of Arah, #; **Ezr 2:5** 7651, 3967, 2568, 7657

822

the work of the temple, #; **Ne 11:12** 8083, 3967, 6242, 8147

832

persons from Jerusalem; **Jer 52:29** 8083, 3967, 7970, 8147

845

the sons of Zattu, #; **Ne 7:13** 8083, 3967, 705, 2568

928

and after him Gabbai *and* Sallai, #. **Ne 11:8** 8672, 3967, 6242, 8083

945

the sons of Zattu, #; **Ezr 2:8** 8672, 3967, 705, 2568

956

according to their generations, #. **1Ch 9:9** 8672, 3967, 2572, 8337a

973

Jedaiah of the house of Jeshua, #; **Ezr 2:36** 8672, 3967, 7657, 7969

Jedaiah of the house of Jeshua, #; **Ne 7:39** 8672, 3967, 7657, 7969

1,000

#, and 1,000 out of 10,000 to **Jg 20:10** 505

out of 10,000 to supply food for **Jg 20:10** 505

were with Jonathan at Gibeah of **1Sa 13:2** 505

men, and the men of Tob **2Sa 10:6** 505

Of Naphtali *there were* # **1Ch 12:34** 505

David took from him # chariots **1Ch 18:4** 505

talents of silver to hire for **1Ch 19:6** 505

bulls, 1,000 rams *and* 1,000 **1Ch 29:21** 505

rams *and* 1,000 lambs, with **1Ch 29:21** 505

lambs, with their drink offerings **1Ch 29:21** 505

bulls and 7,000 sheep, **2Ch 30:24** 505

bulls and 10,000 sheep; and a **2Ch 30:24** 505

silver dishes, 29 duplicates; **Ezr 1:9** 505

other articles. **Ezr 1:10** 505

gold bowls *worth* # darics, **Ezr 8:27** 505

gold drachmas, 50 basins, 530 **Ne 7:70** 505

yoke of oxen and 1,000 female **Jb 42:12** 505

oxen and # female donkeys. **Jb 42:12** 505

1,005

and his songs were #. **1Ki 4:32** 2568, 505

1,017

the sons of Harim, #. **Ezr 2:39** 505, 7651, 6240

the sons of Harim, #. **Ne 7:42** 505, 7651, 6240

1,052

the sons of Immer, #; **Ezr 2:37** 505, 2572, 8147

the sons of Immer, #; **Ne 7:40** 505, 2572, 8147

1,200

with # chariots and 60,000 **2Ch 12:3** 505, 3967

1,222

the sons of Azgad, #; **Ezr 2:12** 505, 3967, 6242, 8147

1,247

the sons of Pashhur, #; **Ezr 2:38** 505, 3967, 705, 7651

the sons of Pashhur, #; **Ne 7:41** 505, 3967, 705, 7651

1,254

the sons of Elam, #; **Ezr 2:7** 505, 3967, 2572, 702

the sons of the other Elam, #; **Ezr 2:31** 505, 3967, 2572, 702

the sons of Elam, #; **Ne 7:12** 505, 3967, 2572, 702

the sons of the other Elam, #; **Ne 7:34** 505, 3967, 2572, 702

1,290

there will be # days. **Da 12:11** 505, 3967, 8673

1,335

attains to the # days! **Da 12:12** 505, 7969, 3967, 7970, 2568

1,365

shekel of the sanctuary, #. **Nu 3:50** 2568, 8346, 7969, 3067, 505

1,400

chariots and 12,000 horsemen, **1Ki 10:26** 505, 702, 3967

chariots and 12,000 horsemen, **2Ch 1:14** 505, 702, 3967

1,700

shekels of gold, besides **Jg 8:26** 505, 7651, 3967

David captured from him # **2Sa 8:4** 505, 7651, 3967

capable men, had charge of **1Ch 26:30** 505, 7651, 3967

1,760

very able men for the work of **1Ch 9:13** 505, 7651, 3967, 8346

1,775

shekels, according to the shekel **Ex 38:25** 505, 7651, 3967, 2568, 7657

Of the # *shekels,* he made **Ex 38:28** 505, 7651, 3967, 2568, 7657

2,000

of about # cubits by measure. **Jos 3:4** 505

and killed # of them. **Jg 20:45** 505

were with Saul in Michmash and in **1Sa 13:2** 505

donkeys; and 100,000 men. **1Ch 5:21** 505

silver minas and 67 priests' **Ne 7:72** 505

2,056

the sons of Bigvai, #; **Ezr 2:14** 505, 2572, 8337a

2,067

the sons of Bigvai, #; **Ne 7:19** 505, 8346, 7651

2,172

the sons of Parosh, #; **Ezr 2:3** 505, 3967, 7657, 8147

the sons of Parosh, #; **Ne 7:8** 505, 3967, 7667, 8147

2,200

drachmas and # silver minas. **Ne 7:71** 505, 3967

2,300

He said to me, "For # evenings **Da 8:14** 505, 7969, 3967

2,322

the sons of Azgad, #; **Ne 7:17** 505, 7969, 3967, 6242, 8147

2,400

was 70 talents and # shekels. **Ex 38:29** 505, 702, 3967

shekels, according to **Nu 7:85** 505, 702, 3967

2,600

of valiant warriors, was #. **2Ch 26:12** 505, 8337a, 3967

from the flocks and 300 bulls. **2Ch 35:8** 505, 8337a, 3967

2,630

fathers' households, were #. **Nu 4:40** 505, 8337a, 3967, 7970

2,700

in number, heads of **1Ch 26:32** 505, 7651, 3967

2,750

by their families were #. **Nu 4:36** 505, 7651, 3967, 2572

2,812

sons of Jeshua *and* Joab, #; **Ezr 2:6** 505, 8083, 3967, 8147, 6240

2,818

the sons of Jeshua and Joab, #; **Ne 7:11** 505, 8083, 3967, 8083, 6240

3,000

Then # men of Judah went down to **Jg 15:11** 7969, 505

men and women were on the roof **Jg 16:27** 7969, 505

Now Saul chose for himself # men **1Sa 13:2** 7969, 505

He also spoke # proverbs, **1Ki 4:32** 7969, 505

#; for until now the greatest part **1Ch 12:29** 7969, 505

namely, # talents of gold, **1Ch 29:4** 7969, 505

could hold # baths. **2Ch 4:5** 7969, 505

struck down # of them **2Ch 25:13** 7969, 505

things were 600 bulls and # sheep. **2Ch 29:33** 7969, 505

bulls; these were from the king's **2Ch 35:7** 7969, 505

camels, 500 yoke of oxen, 500 **Jb 1:3** 7969, 505

3,023
seventh year # Jews; **Jer 52:28** 7969, 505, 6242, 7969

3,200
by their families were #. **Nu 4:44** 7969, 505, 3967

3,300
Solomon's # chief deputies **1Ki 5:16** 7969, 505, 7969, 3967

3,600
to supervise them. **2Ch 2:2** 7969, 505, 8337a, 3967
supervisors to make the people work. **2Ch 2:18** 7969, 505, 8337a, 3967

3,630
the sons of Senaah, #. **Ezr 2:35** 7969, 505, 8337a, 3967, 7970

3,700
Aaron, and with him were #, **1Ch 12:27** 7969, 505, 7651, 3967

3,930
the sons of Senaah, #. **Ne 7:38** 7969, 505, 8672, 3967, 7970

4,000
were gatekeepers, **1Ch 23:5** 702, 505
were praising the LORD with **1Ch 23:5** 702, 505
Now Solomon had # stalls for **2Ch 9:25** 702, 505

4,500
cubits, the south side 4,500 **Ezk 48:16** 2568, 3967, 702, 505
cubits, the east side 4,500 **Ezk 48:16** 2568, 3967, 702, 505
cubits, and the west side **Ezk 48:16** 2568, 3967, 702, 505
west side # *cubits*. **Ezk 48:16** 2568, 3967, 702, 505
side, # *cubits* by measurement, **Ezk 48:30** 2568, 3967, 702, 505
the east side, # *cubits*, **Ezk 48:32** 2568, 3967, 702, 505
the south side, # *cubits* **Ezk 48:33** 2568, 3967, 702, 505
the west side, # *cubits*, **Ezk 48:34** 2568, 3967, 702, 505

4,600
Of the sons of Levi #. **1Ch 12:26** 702, 505, 8337a, 3967
persons in all. **Jer 52:30** 702, 505, 8337a, 3967

5,000
And he took about # men and set **Jos 8:12** 2568, 505
# of them on the highways **Jg 20:45** 2568, 505
talents and 10,000 darics of gold, **1Ch 29:7** 2568, 505
from the flocks and 500 bulls. **2Ch 35:9** 2568, 505
silver minas and 100 priestly **Ezr 2:69** 2568, 505
cubits wide and 25,000 **Ezk 45:6** 2568, 505
"The remainder, # *cubits* in **Ezk 48:15** 2568, 505

5,400
#. Sheshbazzar brought them all up **Ezr 1:11** 2568, 505, 702, 3967

6,000
horsemen, and people like the sand **1Sa 13:5** 8337a, 505
were officers and judges, **1Ch 23:4** 8337a, 505
camels and 1,000 yoke of oxen **Jb 42:12** 8337a, 505

6,200
month old and upward, *were* #. **Nu 3:34** 8337a, 505, 3967

6,720
their donkeys, #. **Ezr 2:67** 8337a, 505, 7651, 3967, 6242
their donkeys, #. **Ne 7:69** 8337a, 505, 7651, 3967, 6242

6,800
#, equipped for war. **1Ch 12:24** 8337a, 505, 8083, 3967

7,000
I will leave # in Israel, **1Ki 19:18** 7651, 505
all the sons of Israel, #. **1Ki 20:15** 7651, 505
horsemen and 20,000 foot soldiers, **1Ch 18:4** 7651, 505
charioteers and 40,000 foot **1Ch 19:18** 7651, 505
talents of refined silver, to **1Ch 29:4** 7651, 505
sheep from the spoil they had **2Ch 15:11** 7651, 505
sheep , and the princes had **2Ch 30:24** 7651, 505
His possessions also were # sheep, **Jb 1:3** 7651, 505

7,100
men of valor for war, #. **1Ch 12:25** 7651, 505, 3967

7,337
#; and they had 200 singing men **Ezr 2:65** 7651, 505, 7969, 3967, 7970, 7651
#; and they had 245 male and **Ne 7:67** 7651, 505, 7969, 3967, 7970, 7651

7,500
even their numbered men *were* #. **Nu 3:22** 7651, 505, 2568, 3967

7,700
rams and 7,700 male goats. **2Ch 17:11** 7651, 505, 7651, 3967
rams and # male goats. **2Ch 17:11** 7651, 505, 7651, 3967

8,580
Their numbered men were #. **Nu 4:48** 8083, 505, 2568, 3967, 8084

8,600
were #, performing the duties of **Nu 3:28** 8083, 505, 8337a, 3967

10,000
returned, but # remained. **Jg 7:3** 6235, 505
to supply food for the people, **Jg 20:10** 6235, 505
men of Judah. **1Sa 15:4** 6235, 505
He sent them to Lebanon, # **1Ki 5:14** 6235, 505
footmen, for the king of Aram had **2Ki 13:7** 6235, 505
and took Sela by war, and named it **2Ki 14:7** 6235, 505
darics of gold, and 10,000 **1Ch 29:7** 6235, 505
talents of silver, and 18,000 **1Ch 29:7** 6235, 505
struck down # of the sons **2Ch 25:11** 6235, 505
captured # alive and brought them to **2Ch 25:12** 6235, 505
sheep; and a large number of **2Ch 30:24** 6235, 505
cubits; and in it shall **Ezk 45:3** 6235, 505
in width shall be for the Levites, **Ezk 45:5** 6235, 505
length and # in width. **Ezk 48:9** 6235, 505
in width, toward the east 10,000 **Ezk 48:10** 6235, 505
in width, and toward the south **Ezk 48:10** 6235, 505
in width. The whole length *shall* **Ezk 48:13** 6235, 505
cubits and the width #. **Ezk 48:13** 6235, 505
cubits toward the east **Ezk 48:18** 6235, 505
toward the west; and it **Ezk 48:18** 6235, 505

12,000
were #—all the people of Ai. **Jos 8:25** 8147, 6240, 505
And the congregation sent # of **Jg 21:10** 8147, 6240, 505
the men of Tob with # men. **2Sa 10:6** 8147, 6240, 505
men that I may arise and pursue **2Sa 17:1** 8147, 6240, 505
his chariots, and # horsemen. **1Ki 4:26** 8147, 6240, 505
horsemen, and he stationed them in **1Ki 10:26** 8147, 6240, 505
horsemen, and he stationed them in **2Ch 1:14** 8147, 6240, 505
horsemen, and he stationed them in **2Ch 9:25** 8147, 6240, 505

14,000
sheep and 6,000 camels **Jb 42:12** 702, 6240, 505

14,700
#, besides those who died on account **Nu 16:49** 702, 6240, 505, 7651, 3967

15,000
about # men, all who were left of **Jg 8:10** 2568, 6240, 505

16,000
and the human beings were #, **Nu 31:40** 8337a, 6240, 505
and the human beings were # **Nu 31:46** 8337a, 6240, 505

16,750
captains of hundreds, was # shekels. **Nu 31:52** 8337a, 6240, 505, 7651, 3967, 2572

17,200
mighty men of valor, who were **1Ch 7:11** 7651, 6240, 505, 3967

18,000
men of the sons of Israel; all **Jg 20:25** 8083, 6240, 505
Thus # men of Benjamin fell; **Jg 20:44** 8083, 6240, 505
Arameans in the Valley of Salt. **2Sa 8:13** 8083, 6240, 505
Of the half-tribe of Manasseh #, **1Ch 12:31** 8083, 6240, 505
Edomites in the Valley of Salt. **1Ch 18:12** 8083, 6240, 505
talents of brass, and 100,000 **1Ch 29:7** 8083, 7239, 505
"*The city shall be* # **Ezk 48:35** 8083, 6240, 505

20,000
foot soldiers; and David hamstrung **2Sa 8:4** 6242, 505
foot soldiers, and the king of **2Sa 10:6** 6242, 505
there that day was great, # men. **2Sa 18:7** 6242, 505
Solomon then gave Hiram # kors **1Ki 5:11** 6242, 505
foot soldiers, and David hamstrung **1Ch 18:4** 6242, 505
kors of crushed wheat and 20,000 **2Ch 2:10** 6242, 505
kors of barley, and 20,000 baths **2Ch 2:10** 6242, 505
baths of wine and 20,000 baths of **2Ch 2:10** 6242, 505
wine and # baths of **2Ch 2:10** 6242, 505
gold drachmas and 2,200 silver **Ne 7:71** 8147, 7239
gold drachmas and 2,000 silver **Ne 7:72** 8147, 7239
#. It shall be holy within all its **Ezk 45:1** 6235, 505

20,200
mighty men of valor. **1Ch 7:9** 6242, 505, 3967

20,800
Of the sons of Ephraim #, **1Ch 12:30** 6242, 505, 8083, 3967

22,000
month old and upward, *were* #. **Nu 3:39** 8147, 6242, 505
people returned, but 10,000 **Jg 7:3** 6242, 8147, 505
that day # men of Israel. **Jg 20:21** 8147, 6242, 505
David killed # Arameans. **2Sa 8:5** 6242, 8147, 505
oxen and 120,000 sheep. **1Ki 8:63** 6242, 8147, 505
men of the Arameans. **1Ch 18:5** 6242, 8147, 505
oxen and 120,000 sheep. **2Ch 7:5** 6242, 8147, 505

22,034
enrolled by genealogy. **1Ch 7:7** 6242, 8147, 505, 7970, 702

22,200
families of the Simeonites, #. **Nu 26:14** 8147, 6242, 505, 3967

22,273
for their numbered men were #. **Nu 3:43** 8147, 6242, 505, 7969, 7657, 3967

22,600
in the days of David was #. **1Ch 7:2** 6242, 8083, 505, 8337a, 3967

23,000
#, every male from a month old **Nu 26:62** 7969, 6242, 505

24,000
died by the plague were #. **Nu 25:9** 6242, 702, 505
Of these , # were to oversee **1Ch 23:4** 702, 6242, 505
each division *numbering* #: **1Ch 27:1** 6242, 702, 505
in his division *were* #. **1Ch 27:2** 6242, 702, 505
in his division *were* #. **1Ch 27:4** 6242, 702, 505
in his division *were* #. **1Ch 27:5** 6242, 702, 505
in his division *were* #. **1Ch 27:7** 6242, 702, 505
in his division *were* #. **1Ch 27:8** 6242, 702, 505
in his division *were* #. **1Ch 27:9** 6242, 702, 505
in his division *were* #. **1Ch 27:10** 6242, 702, 505
in his division *were* #. **1Ch 27:11** 6242, 702, 505
in his division *were* #. **1Ch 27:12** 6242, 702, 505
in his division *were* #. **1Ch 27:13** 6242, 702, 505
in his division *were* #. **1Ch 27:14** 6242, 702, 505
in his division *were* #. **1Ch 27:15** 6242, 702, 505

25,000
men who draw the sword; all these **Jg 20:46** 2568, 6242, 505
cubits, and the width shall be **Ezk 45:1** 2568, 6242, 505
cubits and a width of **Ezk 45:3** 2568, 6242, 505
area # *cubits* in **Ezk 45:5** 2568, 6242, 505

cubits long, alongside Ezk 45:6
2568, 6242, 505
cubits in width, and in length Ezk 48:8
6242, 2568, 505
cubits in length and 10,000 Ezk 48:9
2568, 6242, 505
the north # *cubits in length,* toward Ezk 48:10
2568, 6242, 505
in length; and the sanctuary of Ezk 48:10
2568, 6242, 505
cubits in length and 10,000 Ezk 48:13
2568, 6242, 505
cubits and the width 10,000. Ezk 48:13
2568, 6242, 505
in length, shall be for common use Ezk 48:15
2568, 6242, 505
by 25,000 *cubits;* you shall Ezk 48:20
2568, 6242, 505
cubits; you shall set apart Ezk 48:20
2568, 6242, 505
cubits of the allotment toward Ezk 48:21
2568, 6242, 505
toward the west border, alongside Ezk 48:21
2568, 6242, 505

25,100
men of Benjamin that day, all who Jg 20:35
6242, 2568, 505, 3967

26,000
men who draw the sword, besides Jg 20:15
6242, 8337a, 505
war was # men. 1Ch 7:40
6242, 8337a, 505

27,000
men who were left. And Ben-hadad 1Ki 20:30
6242, 7651, 505

28,600
battle formation, *there were* #. 1Ch 12:35
6242, 8083, 505, 8337a, 3967

30,000
men, valiant warriors, and sent Jos 8:3 7970, 505
the men of Judah #. 1Sa 11:8
7970, 505
chariots and 6,000 horsemen, 1Sa 13:5
7970, 505
laborers numbered # men. 1Ki 5:13
7970, 505
numbering # plus 3,000 bulls; 2Ch 35:7
7970, 505

30,500
and the donkeys were #, from Nu 31:39
7970, 505, 2568, 3967
and # donkeys, Nu 31:45
7970, 505, 2568, 3967

32,000
all the persons were #. Nu 31:35
8147, 7970, 505
So they hired for themselves # 1Ch 19:7
8147, 7970, 505

32,200
tribe of Manasseh *were* #. Nu 1:35
8147, 7970, 505, 3967
even their numbered men, #. Nu 2:21
8147, 7970, 505, 3967

32,500
#. These are the sons of Joseph Nu 26:37
8147, 7970, 505, 2568, 3967

35,400
tribe of Benjamin *were* #. Nu 1:37
2568, 7970, 505, 702, 3967
even their numbered men, #. Nu 2:23
2568, 7970, 505, 702, 3967

36,000
and the cattle were #, from Nu 31:38
7970, 8337a, 505
and # cattle, Nu 31:44
8337a, 7970, 505
troops of the army for war, for 1Ch 7:4
8337a, 7970, 505

37,000
with shield and spear. 1Ch 12:34
7970, 7651, 505

38,000
by census of men was #. 1Ch 23:3
7970, 8083, 505

40,000
about # equipped for war, Jos 4:13 705, 505
horsemen and struck down Shobach 2Sa 10:18
705, 505
Solomon had # stalls of horses 1Ki 4:26 705, 505
Of Asher *there were* # who 1Ch 12:36
705, 505
foot soldiers, and put to death 1Ch 19:18
705, 505

40,500
tribe of Ephraim *were* #. Nu 1:33
705, 505, 2568, 3967
even their numbered men, #. Nu 2:19
705, 505, 2568, 3967
were numbered of them, #. Nu 26:18
705, 505, 2568, 3967

41,500
tribe of Asher *were* #. Nu 1:41
259, 705, 505, 2568, 3967
even their numbered men, #. Nu 2:28
259, 705, 505, 2568, 3967

42,000
that time # of Ephraim. Jg 12:6
705, 8147, 505

42,360
whole assembly numbered #, Ezr 2:64
702, 7239, 505, 7969, 3967, 8346
assembly together *was* #, Ne 7:66
702, 7239, 505, 7969, 3967, 8346

43,730
numbered of them were #. Nu 26:7
7969, 705, 505, 7651, 3967, 7970

44,760
#, who went to war. 1Ch 5:18
705, 702, 505, 7651, 3967, 8346

45,400
were numbered of them were #. Nu 26:50
2568, 705, 505, 702, 3967

45,600
were numbered of them were #. Nu 26:41
2568, 705, 505, 8337a, 3967

45,650
tribe of Gad *were* #. Nu 1:25
2568, 705, 505, 8337a, 3967, 2572
even their numbered men, #. Nu 2:15
2568, 705, 505, 8337a, 3967, 2572

46,500
tribe of Reuben *were* #. Nu 1:21
8337a, 705, 505, 2568, 3967
even their numbered men, #. Nu 2:11
8337a, 705, 505, 2568, 3967

50,000
camels, 250,000 sheep, 2,000 1Ch 5:21
2572, 505
Of Zebulun, there were # who 1Ch 12:33
2572, 505

50,070
men, and the people mourned 1Sa 6:19
7657, 2572, 505

52,700
were numbered of them were #. Nu 26:34
8147, 2572, 505, 7651, 3967

53,400
tribe of Naphtali *were* #. Nu 1:43
7969, 2572, 505, 702, 3967
even their numbered men, #. Nu 2:30
7969, 2572, 505, 702, 3967
were numbered of them, #. Nu 26:47
7969, 2572, 505, 702, 3967

54,400
tribe of Issachar *were* #. Nu 1:29
702, 7657, 505, 8337a, 3967
even their numbered men, #. Nu 2:6
702, 2572, 505, 702, 3967

57,400
tribe of Zebulun *were* #. Nu 1:31
7651, 2572, 505, 702, 3967
even his numbered men, #. Nu 2:8
7651, 2572, 505, 702, 3967

59,300
tribe of Simeon *were* #. Nu 1:23
8672, 2572, 505, 7969, 3967
even their numbered men, #. Nu 2:13
8672, 2572, 505, 7969, 3967

60,000
with 1,200 chariots and # 2Ch 12:3
8346, 505

60,500
were numbered of them, #. Nu 26:27
8346, 505, 2568, 3967

61,000
and # donkeys, Nu 31:34
259, 8346, 505
gold drachmas and 5,000 silver Ezr 2:69
8337a, 7239, 505

62,700
tribe of Dan *were* #. Nu 1:39
8147, 8346, 505, 7651, 3967
even their numbered men, #. Nu 2:26
8147, 8346, 505, 7651, 3967

64,300
were numbered of them, #. Nu 26:25
702, 8346, 505, 7969, 3967

64,400
were numbered of them, were #. Nu 26:43
702, 8346, 505, 702, 3967

70,000
Now Solomon had # transporters, 1Ki 5:15
7657, 505
men of Israel fell. 1Ch 21:14
7657, 505
So Solomon assigned # men to 2Ch 2:2 7657, 505
He appointed # of them to carry 2Ch 2:18
7657, 505

72,000
and # cattle, Nu 31:33
8147, 7657, 505

74,600
tribe of Judah *were* #. Nu 1:27
702, 7657, 505, 8337a, 3967
even their numbered men, #. Nu 2:4
702, 7657, 505, 8337a, 3967

75,000
# of those who hated them; Es 9:16
2568, 7657, 505

76,500
were numbered of them, #. Nu 26:22
8337a, 7657, 505, 2658, 3967

80,000
hewers *of stone* in 1Ki 5:15
8084, 505
men to quarry *stone* in 2Ch 2:2 8084, 505
to quarry *stones* in 2Ch 2:18
8084, 505

87,000
by genealogy, in all #. 1Ch 7:5
8084, 7651, 505

100,000
foot soldiers in one day. 1Ki 20:29
3967, 505
lambs and the wool of 100,000 2Ki 3:4 3967, 505
wool of # rams. 2Ki 3:4 3967, 505
2,000 donkeys; and # men. 1Ch 5:21
3967, 505
talents of gold and 1,000,000 1Ch 22:14
3967, 505
and # talents of iron. 1Ch 29:7
3967, 505
hired also # valiant warriors 2Ch 25:6
3967, 505

108,100
#, by their armies. And they shall Nu 2:24
3967, 505, 8083, 505, 3967

120,000
fallen were # swordsmen. Jg 8:10
3967, 6242, 505
sheep. So the king and all 1Ki 8:63
3967, 6242, 505
with all *kinds* of weapons of 1Ch 12:37
3967, 6242, 505
sheep. Thus the king and all 2Ch 7:5
3967, 6242, 505
in one day, all valiant men, 2Ch 28:6
3967, 6242, 505
persons who do not know Jon 4:11
8147, 6240, 7239

151,450
by their armies. And they shall Nu 2:16
3967, 505, 259, 2572, 505, 702, 3967, 2572

153,600
and # were found. 2Ch 2:17
3967, 2572, 505, 7969, 505, 8337a, 3967

157,600
#. They shall set out last by their Nu 2:31
3967, 505, 7651, 2572, 505, 8337a, 3967

180,000
chosen men who were warriors, to 1Ki 12:21
3967, 8084, 505
chosen men who were warriors, to 2Ch 11:1
3967, 8084, 505
with him # equipped for war. 2Ch 17:18
3967, 8084, 505

185,000
in the camp of the Assyrians; 2Ki 19:35
3967, 8084, 2568, 505
in the camp of the Assyrians; Is 37:36
3967, 8084, 2568, 505

186,400
#, by their armies. They shall set Nu 2:9
3967, 505, 8084, 505, 8337a, 505, 702, 3967

200,000
foot soldiers and 10,000 men of 1Sa 15:4
3967, 505
with him # valiant warriors; 2Ch 17:16
3967, 505
with him # armed with bow and shield; 2Ch 17:17
3967, 505
women, sons and daughters; 2Ch 28:8
3967, 505

250,000
sheep, 2,000 donkeys; and 100,000 1Ch 5:21
3967, 2572, 505

280,000
from Benjamin, bearing shields 2Ch 14:8
3967, 8084, 505
the commander, and with him #; 2Ch 17:15
3967, 8084, 505

300,000
#, and the men of Judah 30,000. 1Sa 11:8
7969, 3967, 505
Now Asa had an army of # from 2Ch 14:8
7969, 3967, 505
with him # valiant warriors; 2Ch 17:14
7969, 3967, 505
choice men, *able* to go 2Ch 25:5
7969, 3967, 505

307,500
army of #, who could wage war 2Ch 26:13
7969, 3967, 505, 7651, 505, 2568, 3967

337,500
the number of sheep was #, Nu 31:36
7969, 3967, 505, 7970, 505, 7651, 505, 2568, 3967
congregation's half was # sheep, Nu 31:43
7969, 3967, 505, 7970, 505, 7651, 505, 2568, 3967

400,000
foot soldiers who drew the sword. Jg 20:2
702, 3967, 505
men who draw the sword; all these Jg 20:17
702, 3967, 505

chosen men, while Jeroboam drew up 2Ch 13:3
702, 3967, 505

470,000
men who drew the sword. 1Ch 21:5
702, 3967, 7657, 505

500,000
chosen men of Israel fell slain. 2Ch 13:17
2568, 3967, 505

600,000
on foot; yet You have said, Nu 11:21
8337a, 3967, 505

601,730
the sons of Israel, #. Nu 26:51
8337a, 3967, 505, 505, 7651, 3967, 7970

603,550
twenty years old and upward, for # men. Ex 38:26
8337a, 3967, 505, 7969, 505, 2568, 3967, 2572
the numbered men were #. Nu 1:46
8337a, 3967, 505, 7969, 505, 2568, 3967, 2572
camps by their armies, #. Nu 2:32
3967, 505, 7651, 2572, 505, 8337a, 3967

675,000
war had plundered was # sheep, Nu 31:32
8337a, 3967, 505, 7657, 505, 2568, 505

800,000
chosen men *who were* valiant 2Ch 13:3
8083, 3967, 505

1,000,000
talents of silver, 1Ch 22:14
505, 505

1,100,000
men who drew the sword; 1Ch 21:5
505, 505, 3967, 505

HEBREW—ARAMAIC DICTIONARY

OF THE
NEW AMERICAN STANDARD EXHAUSTIVE CONCORDANCE

Updated Edition

HOW TO USE THE HEBREW–ARAMAIC DICTIONARY

The first four items in each entry are standard:

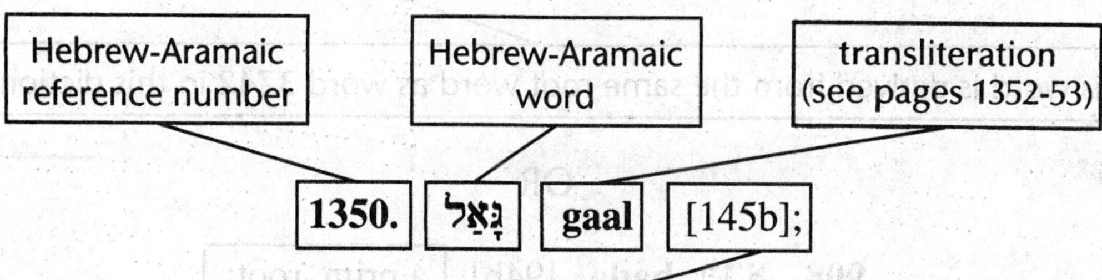

Page and quadrant indicator. This number refers to a page in *A Hebrew and English Lexicon of the Old Testament* by Brown, Driver and Briggs (Oxford University Press). The lower case letter refers to the quadrant on that page containing the article that discusses this Hebrew or Aramaic word.

The *a* quadrant is the upper left part of the page, the *b* quadrant is lower left, the *c* quadrant is upper right and the *d* quadrant is the lower right.

ORIGIN OR DERIVATION

Next, the word's origin or derivation is given on the basis of the lexicon by Brown, Driver and Briggs. This information is presented in the following ways:

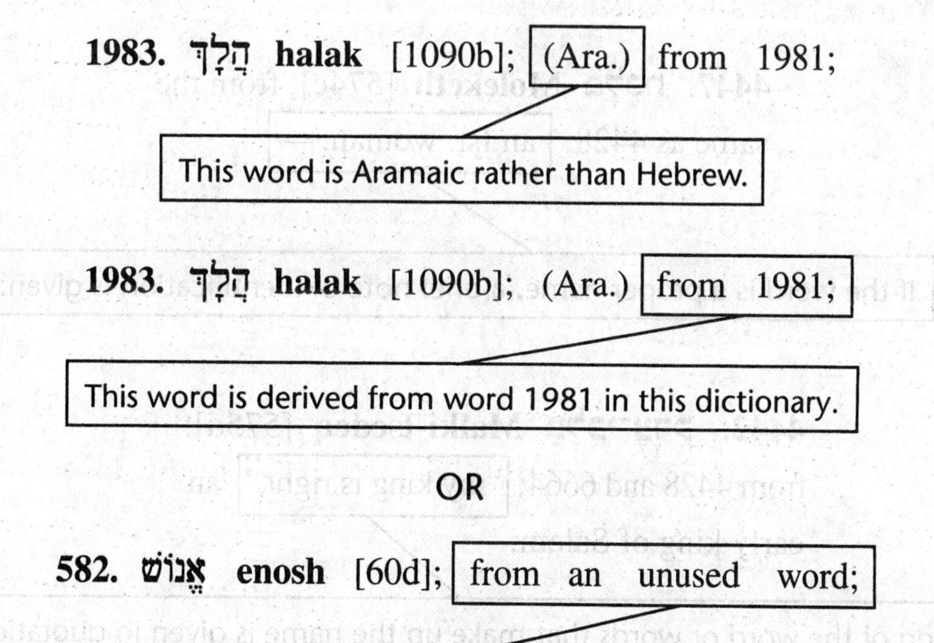

OR

3743. כְּרוּב **Kerub** [500c]; from the same as 3742;

This word is derived from the same root word as word 3742 in this dictionary.

OR

908. בָּדָא **bada** [94b]; a prim. root;

This word is called primitive because it is not derived from any other known word in the Hebrew language. This is also true for Aramaic words that are not derived from other known words in the Aramaic language.

MEANINGS

General Meanings: Following the second semicolon in each entry is the section that gives the general meaning of the Hebrew or Aramaic word.

1350. גָּאַל **gaal** [145b]; a prim. root; *to redeem, act as kinsman:—*

4447. מֹלֶכֶת **Moleketh** [574c]; from the same as 4428; an Isr. woman:—

If the word is a proper name, a brief note of identification is given.

4442. מַלְכִּי־צֶדֶק **Malki-tsedeq** [575d]; from 4428 and 6664; "my king is right," an early king of Salem:—

The meaning of the word or words that make up the name is given in quotation marks for some proper names.

Specific Meanings: Specific meanings of words are dependent upon the context in which the words are found. Following the colon-dash (:—) in each entry is a list of NEW AMERICAN STANDARD BIBLE translations of the Hebrew or Aramaic word.

1350. גָּאַל **gaal** [145b]; a prim. root; *to redeem, act as kinsman:*— avenger(13), bought back(1), buy back(1), claim(1), close relative(3), closest relative(3), closest relatives(1), ever redeem(2), kinsman(2), redeem(22), redeemed(25), Reedeemer(18), redeemer(1), redeems(1), relative(2), relatives(1), rescue(1), wishes to redeem(1).

The number in parentheses gives the number of times that English key word was used to translate the Hebrew or Aramaic word in the NEW AMERICAN STANDARD BIBLE Updated Edition.

SPECIAL SIGNS

An asterisk (*) indicates that the key word represents two or more Hebrew or Aramaic words. Refer to the English concordance listing of the key word for the additional Hebrew or Aramaic word numbers.

913. בְּדִיל **bedil** [95d]; from 914; *alloy, tin, dross:*—alloy(1), plumb line*(1), tin (4).

The proper or special name of God, YHWH, has been translated LORD.

THE HEBREW ALPHABET

Name	Hebrew Letter	(Final form[1])	Sound	Transliteration
Aleph	א		*silent*	*none*
Beth	ב		v	b
	בּ[2]		b	
Gimel	ג		**g** in growl	g
	גּ[2]		**g** in **g**o	
Daleth	ד		**th** in **th**is	d
	דּ[2]		d	
He[3]	ה		h	h
Waw or Vav	ו		w or v	v
Zayin	ז		z	z
Heth or Cheth	ח		**ch** in Ba**ch**	ch
Teth	ט		t	t
Yod	י		**y** in **y**et	y
Kaph	כ	ך	**ch** in Ba**ch**	k
	כּ[2]		k	
Lamed	ל		l	l
Mem	מ	ם	m	m
Nun	נ	ן	n	n
Samek	ס		s	s
Ayin	ע		*silent*	*none*
Pe	פ	ף	f	ph
	פּ[2]		p	p
Tsade	צ	ץ	**ts** in **ts**etse fly	ts
Qoph	ק		q	q
Resh	ר		r	r
Sin	שׂ		s	s
Shin	שׁ		**sh** in **sh**ine	sh
Taw	ת		**th** in **th**in	th
	תּ[2]		t	

---

[1] I.e. a special form of the letter, which must be used if the letter occurs at the end of a word.

[2] A dot used within a letter is called a *dagesh*. It can be of two kinds : *dagesh lene* ("weak dagesh") and *dagesh forte* ("strong dagesh"). These two uses are explained here:

1) There are six Hebrew letters which have alternate forms designated by a *dagesh lene*. The dot, *dagesh lene*, hardens these letters (designating them as a 'stop', like the English 'p' and 'b'; a short stopping of air). Letters without the dot are soft (designating them as a 'spirant', like the English 'f' or 'v'; the friction of air passing through some part of the oral passage). These six letters are designated by the mnemonic **begadkephat** (**b**et, **g**imel **d**alet, **k**ap, **p**e **t**sade).

2) The dagesh forte indicates that the letter should be doubled (e.g., מּ = mm; צּ = tsts). Some letters cannot be doubled: guttural letters (אהחע), spirants (בגדכפת), and ר. There are special rules that help to identify whether the dagesh in the *begadkephat* letters is "strong" (to designate doubling) or "weak" (to designate stops). One great advantage of the transliteration in the *New American Standard Exhaustive Concordance* is that it applies these rules for you.

[3] Pronounced like the word *hay*.

VOWEL SIGNS

Name	Symbol	Placement	Sound	Transliteration
Qamets	ָ	בָ	a in father	a
Qamets-he	ָה	בָה	a in father	ah
Pathach	ַ	בַ	a in bad	a
Chateph-pathach	ֲ	הֲ	a in bad	a
Tsere	ֵ	בֵ	e in they	e
Tsere Yod	ֵי	בֵי	e in they	e
Segol	ֶ	הֶ	e in set	e
Chateph-segol	ֱ	הֱ	e in set	e
Chireq	ִ	בִ	i in hit	i
Chireq-yod	ִי	בִי	i in machine	i
Cholem	ֹ	דֹ	o in pole	o
Cholem-waw or Cholem-vav	וֹ	בוֹ	o in pole	o
Qamets-chatuph[4]	ָ	בָ	o in top	o
Chateph-qamets	ֳ	הֳ	o in top	o
Qibbuts	ֻ	בֻ	u in pull	u
Shureq	וּ	בוּ	u in rule	u
Shewa	ְ	בְ	e in met or *silent*	e or *none*

[4] There are special rules for distinguishing between qamets (a) and qamets-chatuph (o).

ABBREVIATIONS USED IN THE HEBREW-ARAMAIC DICTIONARY

abb.	abbreviated, abbreviation
act.	active
adj.	adjective
adv.	adverb, adverbial
appar.	apparent, apparently
Ara.	Aramaic
Assyr.	Assyrian
Bab.	Babylon, Babylonian
card.	cardinal
conjunc.	conjunction
contr.	contracted, contraction
corr.	corresponding
denom.	denominative
der.	derivation, derivative, derived
desc.	descended, descendant(s)
E.	east, eastern
Eg.	Egypt, Egyptian
equiv.	equivalent
fem.	feminine
for.	foreign
Heb.	Hebrew
i.e.	id est, that is
inhab.	inhabited, inhabitant
intens.	intensive
interj.	interjection
Isr.	Israel, Israelite
Jer.	Jerusalem
masc.	masculine
N.	north, northern
neg.	negative
or.	origin
ord.	ordinal
orth.	orthographic
Pal.	Palestine
part.	participle
pass.	passive
perh.	perhaps
Pers.	Persian
pl.	plural
pref.	prefix
prep.	preposition, prepositional
prim.	primary, primitive
prob.	probably
prol.	prolongated, prolongation
pron.	pronoun
q.v.	quod vide, which see
redupl.	reduplicated, reduplication
rel.	relative
S.	south, southern
short.	shortened
sing.	singular
suff.	suffix
transp.	transposition
unc.	uncertain
var.	variation
vb.	verb
W.	west, western

The Hebraica II font used to print this work is available from Linguist's Software, Inc., PO Box 580, Edmonds, WA 98020-0580 USA tel (206) 775-1130.

א

1. אָב ab (3a); from an unused word; *father:*— ancestors(1), family*(1), father(571), Father(8), father's(137), fathers(333), fathers'(120), fathers' households(1), forefather(1), forefathers(27), grandfather(1), grandfathers(1), households(5), Huram-abi*(2), sons(1).

2. אַב ab (1078b); (Ara.) corr. to 1; *father:*— father(6), fathers(3).

3. אֵב eb (1a); from the same as 24; *freshness, fresh green:*— blossoms(1), green(1).

4. אֵב eb (1078a); (Ara.) corr. to 3; *fruit:*— fruit(3).

5. אֲבַגְתָא Abagtha (1b); of for. or.; a eunuch of Ahasuerus:— Abagtha(1).

6. אָבַד abad (1b), a prim. root; *to perish:*— annihilate(2), annihilated(1), been lost(1), broken(1), corrupts(1), destroy(33), destroyed(15), destroying(2), destroys(2), destruction(2), dying(2), fail(1), fails(1), give up as lost(1), lacking(1), lost(12), make vanish(1), makes to perish(1), no(2), obliterate(1), perish(61), perished(16), perishes(7), perishing(2), ruined(4), surely perish(3), take(1), utterly destroy(1), wandering(1), wastes(1), wiped(1).

7. אֲבַד abad (1078b); (Ara.) corr. to 6; *to perish:*— destroy(3), destroyed(3), perish(1).

8. אֹבֵד obed (2b); act. part. of 6; *destruction:*— destruction(2).

9. אֲבֵדָה abedah (2b); from 6; *a lost thing:*— lost(1), lost thing(2), what was lost(1).

10. אֲבַדֹּה abaddoh (2b); the same as 11, q.v.

11. אֲבַדּוֹן abaddon (2b); from 6; (place of) *destruction* or *ruin, Abaddon:*— Abaddon(6).

12. אַבְדָן abdan (2b); from 6; *destruction:*— destroying(1), destruction(1).

13. אָבְדַן obdan (2b); the same as 12, q.v.

14. אָבָה abah (2c); a prim. root; *to be willing, to consent:*— consent(5), obey(1), refuse*(1), refused*(1), satisfied(1), unwilling*(3), want(1), willing(23), would(16), would...accept(1), yield(1).

15. אָבֶה abeh (106b); see 994b.

16. אֵבֶה ebeh (3a); from 14; *reed, papyrus:*— reed(1).

17. אֲבוֹי aboy (5a); a prim. interj.; *Oh!:*— sorrow(1).

18. אֵבוּס ebus (7b); from 75; *a crib, feeding trough:*— manger(3).

19. אִבְחָה ibchah (5b); from an unused word; *slaughter:*— glittering(1).

20. אֲבַטִּיחַ abattich (105c); of unc. der.; *watermelon:*— melons(1).

21. אֲבִי Abi (4a); from the same as 1; "my father," Hezekiah's mother:— Abi(1).

22. אֲבִיאֵל Abiel (3d); from 1 and 410; "El is my father," an Isr. name:— Abiel(3).

23. אֲבִיאָסָף Abiasaph (4a); from 1 and 622; "my father has gathered," an Isr. name:— Abiasaph(1).

24. אָבִיב abib (1b); from an unused word; *fresh, young ears,* also Canaanite name for the first month of the Jewish calendar:— Abib(6), ear(1), fresh heads(1), fresh heads of grain(1).

25. אֲבִי גִבְעוֹן Abi Gibon (149c); from 1 and 1391, q.v.

26. אֲבִיגַיִל Abigayil (4a); from 1 and 1524a; "my father is joy," two Isr. women:— Abigail(17).

27. אֲבִידָן Abidan (4a); from 1 and 1777; "my father is judge," a Benjamite leader:— Abidan(5).

28. אֲבִידָע Abida (4a); from 1 and 3045; "my father took knowledge," a son of Midian:— Abida(2).

29. אֲבִיָּה Abiyyah (4a); from 1 and 3050; "Yah is my father," an Isr. name:— Abijah(25).

30. אֲבִיהוּא Abihu (4b); from 1 and 1931; "he is father," a son of Aaron:— Abihu(12).

31. אֲבִיהוּד Abihud (4b); from 1 and 1935; "my father is majesty," a Benjamite:— Abihud(1).

32. אֲבִיהַיִל Abihayil or **אֲבִיחַיִל Abichayil** (4b); from 1 and 2428; "my father is might," an Isr. name:— Abihail(6).

33. אֲבִי הָעֶזְרִי Abi Haezri (4c); from 44; a desc. of Abiezer:— Abiezrite(1), Abiezrites(2).

34. אֶבְיוֹן ebyon (2d); from 14; *in want, needy, poor:*— needy(45), needy one(2), poor(12), poor man(1).

35. אֲבִיּוֹנָה abiyyonah (2d); from 14; *the caperberry:*— caperberry(1).

36. אֲבִיטוּב Abitub (4b); from 1 and 2898; "my father is goodness," a Benjamite:— Abitub(1).

37. אֲבִיטַל Abital (4b); from 1 and 2919; "my father is (the) dew," a wife of David:— Abital(2).

38. אֲבִיָּם Abiyyam (4a); from 1 and 3220; "father of (the) sea," an Isr. name:— Abijam(5).

39. אֲבִימָאֵל Abimael (4b); from 1 and an unused word; "a father is El," a son of Joktan, also his desc.:— Abimael(2).

40. אֲבִימֶלֶךְ Abimelek (4b); from 1 and 4428; "father is king," a Philistine name, also an Isr. name:— Abimelech(65), Abimelech's(1).

41. אֲבִינָדָב Abinadab (4c); from 1 and 5068; "my father is noble," three Isr.:— Abinadab(12).

42. אֲבִינֹעַם Abinoam (4c); from 1 and 5278; "my father is delight," the father of Barak:— Abinoam(4).

43. אֶבְיָסָף Ebyasaph (4a); contr. from 23, q.v.:— Ebiasaph(3).

44. אֲבִיעֶזֶר Abiezer (4c); from 1 and 5829; "my father is help," a Manassite, also a Benjamite:— Abiezer(6), Abiezrites(1).

45. אֲבִי־עַלְבוֹן Abi-albon (3d); from 1 and an unused word; "father of strength," one of David's heroes:— Abi-albon(1).

46. אָבִיר abir (7d); from the same as 82; *strong:*— Mighty One(6).

47. אַבִּיר abbir (7d); from the same as 82; *mighty, valiant:*— angels(1), bulls(2), chief(1), man(1), mighty(1), mighty ones(1), stallions(3), stout-hearted*(1), strong(1), strong men(1), strong ones(1), stubborn-minded*(1), valiant(1), valiant steeds(1).

48. אֲבִירָם Abiram (4d); from 1 and 7311; "exalted father," an Isr. name:— Abiram(11).

49. אֲבִישַׁג Abishag (4d); from 1 and 7686; "my father is a wanderer," an Isr. woman:— Abishag(5).

50. אֲבִישׁוּעַ Abishua (4d); from 1 and 7771a; "my father is rescue," two Isr.:— Abishua(5).

51. אֲבִישׁוּר Abishur (4d); from 1 and 7791; "my father is a wall," an Isr.:— Abishur(1), Abishur's(1).

52. אֲבִישַׁי Abishay (5a); from 1 and 7862; "my father is Jesse," an Isr. name:— Abishai(21), Abshai(4).

53. אֲבִישָׁלוֹם Abishalom (5a); from 1 and 7965; "my father is peace," two Isr.:— Abishalom(2), Absalom(104), Absalom's(4).

54. אֶבְיָתָר Ebyathar (5a); from 1 and 3498; "the great one is father," an Isr. priest:— Abiathar(29), Abiathar's(1).

55. אָבַךְ abak (5b); a prim. root; *to turn:*— roll upward(1).

56. אָבַל abal (5b); a prim. root; *to mourn:*— caused lamentations(1), grieve(1), grieved(1), lament(1), mourn(13), mourned(7), mourning(3), mourns(10), pretend to be a mourner(1), went into mourning(1).

57. אָבֵל abel (5d); from 56; *mourning:*— mourn(2), mourners(2), mourning(3), one who sorrows(1).

58. אָבֵל abel (5d); from an unused word; "meadow," part of a place name, see 64.

59. אָבֵל Abel (5d); from the same as 58; "meadow," two places in Pal.:— Abel(2).

60. אֵבֶל ebel (5c); from 56; *mourning:*— mourn(1), mourning(23).

61. אֲבָל abal (6a); a prim. root; *verily, of a truth:*— however(2), nevertheless(2), no(2), truly(3).

62. אָבֵל בֵּית־מַעֲכָה Abel Beth-maakah (5d); from 58, 1004 and 4601; a city in N. Isr.:— Abel(1), Abel-beth-maacah(2).

63. אָבֵל הַשִּׁטִּים Abel Hashshittim (5d); from 58 and the pl. of 7848; a place in the lowlands of Moab:— Abel-shittim(1).

64. אָבֵל כְּרָמִים Abel Keramim (5d); from 58 and the pl. of 3754; a place in Ammon:— Abel-keramim(1).

65. אָבֵל מְחוֹלָה Abel Mecholah (5d); from 58 and 4246; Elisha's birthplace in Pal.:— Abel-meholah(3).

66. אָבֵל מַיִם Abel Mayim (5d); from 58 and 4325; "meadow of water," same location as 62:— Abel-maim(1).

67. אָבֵל מִצְרַיִם Abel Mitsrayim (5d); from 58 and 4714; "meadow of Egypt," a place E. of the Jordan:— Abel-mizraim(1).

68. אֶבֶן eben (6b); a prim. root; *a stone:*— another(1), charm*(1), cornerstone*(1), death(1), differing weights(3), hailstones*(4), jeweler*(1), lapis lazuli*(1), line*(1), plumb line(1), plumb*(1), rock(2), rocks(1), slingstones*(1), stone(106), stonecutters*(1), stonemasons*(1), stones(125), weight(4), weights(3).

69. אֶבֶן eben (1078b); (Ara.) corr. to 68; *a stone:*— stone(6), stones(2).

70. אֹבֶן oben (7a); from 68; *a wheel, disk:*— birthstool(1), wheel(1).

71. אֲבָנָה Abanah (53d); see 549; a river near Damascus:— Abanah(1).

72. אֶבֶן הָעֵזֶר Eben Haezer (6b); from 68 and 5828; "stone of the help," a place of unc. location, also a commemorative stone:— Ebenezer(3).

73. אַבְנֵט abnet (126a); of unc. der.; *a girdle:*— sash(6), sashes(3).

74. אַבְנֵר Abner (4c); from 1 and 5216; "my father is a lamp," an Isr. name:— Abner(62), Abner's(1).

75. אָבַס abas (7b); a prim. root; *to feed, fatten:*— fattened(2).

76. אֲבַעְבֻּעָה ababuah (101b); from an unused word; *blisters, boils:*— sores(2).

77. אֶבֶץ Ebets (7b); from an unused word; a city in Issachar:— Ebez(1).

78. אִבְצָן Ibtsan (7b); from the same as 77; a judge of Isr.:— Ibzan(2).

79. אָבַק abaq (7c); from an unused word; *to wrestle:*— wrestled(2).

80. אָבָק abaq (7b); from the same as 79; *dust:*— dust(5), powder(1).

81. אֲבָקָה abaqah (7c); fem. of 80; *powder:*— scented powders(1).

82. אָבַר abar (7d); from an unused word; *to fly:*— soars(1).

83. אֵבֶר eber (7c); from the same as 82; *pinions:*— pinions(1), wings(2).

84. אֶבְרָה ebrah (7c); fem. of 83; *a pinion:*— pinion(1), pinions(3).

85. אַבְרָהָם Abraham (4d); from 1 and an unused word, see 87; "exalted father," the father of the Jewish nation:— Abraham(162), Abraham's(12).

86. אַבְרֵךְ abrek (7d); prob. of for. or.; *to kneel:*— bow the knee(1).

87. אַבְרָם Abram (4d); from the same as 48, see 85; "exalted father," the original name of Abraham:— Abram(53), Abram's(7).

88. אֹבֹת Oboth (15c); pl. of 178; "waterskins," a place in Edom:— Oboth(4).

89. אָגֵא Age (8a); from an unused word; the father of one of David's heroes:— Agee(1).

90. אֲגַג Agag (8a); from the same as 89; king of Amalek:— Agag(8).

91. אֲגָגִי Agagi (8a); from 90; a descriptive term for Haman:— Agagite(5).

92. אֲגֻדָּה aguddah (8a); from an unused word; *a band:*— band(1), bands(1), bunch(1), vaulted dome(1).

93. אֱגוֹז egoz (8b); of unc. der.; *nuts:*— nut trees(1).

94. אָגוּר Agur (8d); from an unused word; "hired," an author of proverbs:— Agur(1).

95. אֲגוֹרָה agorah (8d); from the same as 94; *payment:*— piece(1).

96. אֶגֶל egel (8b); from an unused word; *a drop:*— drops(1).

97. אֶגְלַיִם Eglayim (8b); from the same as 96; a city in Moab:— Eglaim(1).

98. אֲגַם agam (8b); from an unused word; *a marsh, muddy pool:*— marshes(1), ponds(1), pool(4), pools(2), swamps(1).

99. אָגֵם agem (8c); from the same as 98; *sad:*— grieved(1).

100. אַגְמוֹן agmon (8c); from the same as 98; *a rush, bulrush:*— bulrush(2), reed(1), rope(1), rushes(1).

101. אַגָּן aggan (8c); from an unused word; *a bowl, basin:*— basins(1), bowls*(1), goblet(1).

102. אֲגַף agaph (8d); from an unused word; *a band, army:*— troops(7).

103. אָגַר agar (8d); a prim. root; *to gather:*— gather(1), gathers(2).

104. אִגְּרָה iggerah (1078b); (Ara.) corr. to 107; *a letter:*— letter(3).

105. אֲגַרְטָל agartal (173d); of unc. der.; *a basin, basket:*— dishes(2).

106. אֶגְרֹף egroph (175d); from 1640; *a fist:*— fist(2).

107. אִגֶּרֶת iggereth (8d); from the same as 94; *a letter:*— letter(4), letters(6).

108. אֵד ed (15d); from the same as 181; *a mist:*— mist(2).

109. אָדַב adab (9a); a prim. root; *to grieve:*— grieve(1).

110. אַדְבְּאֵל Adbeel (9a); from 109 and 410; "disciplined of God," the third son of Ishmael:— Adbeel(2).

111. אֲדַד Adad (212d); prob. an orth. var. for 1908, q.v.

112a. אִדּוֹ Iddo (9a); of unc. der.; an Isr. leader:— Iddo(2).

112b. אֱדוֹם Edom (10b); from the same as 119; another name for Esau, older son of Isaac, also his desc. and their territory:— Edom(94), Edomites(7).

113. אָדוֹן adon (10d); from an unused word; *lord:*— husbands(1), Lord(5), lord(172), lord's(9), lords(2), master(91), master's(24), masters(5), owner(1).

114. אַדּוֹן Addon (11d); prob. intens. for 113; "powerful," appar. a place in Bab.:— Addon(1).

115. אֲדוֹרַיִם Adorayim (12a); from 142; perh. "two hills," a city in Judah:— Adoraim(1).

116. אֱדַיִן edayin (1078c); (Ara.) of unc. der.; *then, thereupon:*— then(57).

117. אַדִּיר addir (12b); from 142; *majestic:*— glorious(1), leader(1), magnificent(1), majestic(4), majestic ones(1), masters(3), mighty(6), Mighty One(1), nobles(7), powerful(1), stately(1).

118. אֲדַלְיָא Adalya (9a); of for. or.; the fifth son of Haman:— Adalia(1).

119. אָדֹם adom (10a); from an unused word; *to be red:*— dyed red(6), red(3), ruddy(1).

120. אָדָם adam (9a); from an unused word; *man, mankind:*— any man(2), anyone(4), anyone's(1), being*(1), common sort*(1), human(19), infantry(1), low degree*(1), low*(1), man(363), man's(20), man*(1), mankind(9), men(104), men of low degree*(1), men's(3), men*(4), mortal(1), one(3), people(1), person(5), person*(1), persons(3), population(1), someone(1).

121. אָדָם Adam (9a); from the same as 120; the first man, also a city in the Jordan Valley:— Adam(12).

122. אָדֹם adom (10b); from the same as 119; *red:*— red(7), ruddy(1).

123. אֱדֹם edom (10b); from the same as 119; the name of a condiment:— stuff(1).

אֱדֹם Edom; see also 112b.

124. אֹדֶם odem (10b); from the same as 119; *a carnelian:*— ruby(3).

125. אֲדַמְדָּם adamdam (10c); from the same as 119; *reddish:*— reddish(2), reddish-white(4).

126. אַדְמָה Admah (10a); from the same as 120; a city near Sodom and Gomorrah:— Admah(5).

127. אֲדָמָה adamah (9c); from the same as 120; *ground, land:*— country(1), dirt(1), dust(3), earth(32), farming*(1), fields(1), ground(64), land(112), lands(2), soil(7).

128. אֲדָמָה Adamah (9c); from the same as 127; a city in Naphtali:— Adamah(1).

129. אֲדָמִי הַנֶּקֶב Adami Hanneqeb (10a); from 127 and 5346; a place on the border of Naphtali:— Adami-nekeb(1).

130. אֱדֹמִי Adomi (10c); from 112b; a desc. of Edom:— Arameans(1), Edomite(7), Edomites(3).

131. אֲדֻמִּים Adummim (10c); from the same as 119; a place between Jer. and Jericho:— Adummim(2).

132. אַדְמֹנִי admoni (10c); from the same as 119; *red, ruddy:*— red(1), ruddy(2).

133. אַדְמָתָא Admatha (10d); of for. or.; a prince of Pers. and Media:— Admatha(1).

134. אֶדֶן eden (10d); from the same as 113; *a base, pedestal:*— bases(1), pedestals(1), socket(1), sockets(52).

135. אַדָּן Addan (11d); from the same as 113; a place in Bab.:— Addan(1).

136. אֲדֹנָי Adonay (10d); an emphatic form of 113; *Lord:*— Lord(456), lord(1), lords(2).

137. אֲדֹנִי־בֶזֶק Adoni-bezeq (11d); from 113 and 966; "lord of Bezek," a ruler in Canaan:— Adoni-bezek(3).

138. אֲדֹנִיָּהוּ Adoniyyahu (11d); from 113 and 3050; "my Lord is Yahweh," the name of several Isr.:— Adonijah(26).

139. אֲדֹנִי־צֶדֶק Adoni-tsedeq (11d); from 113 and 6664; "Lord of righteousness," king of Jer.:— Adoni-zedek(2).

140. אֲדֹנִיקָם Adoniqam (12a); from 113 and 6965; "my Lord has arisen," head of an Isr. family:— Adonikam(3).

141. אֲדֹנִירָם Adoniram (12a); from 113 and 7311; "my Lord is exalted," one of Solomon's leaders:— Adoniram(2).

142. אָדַר adar (12a); a prim. root; *wide, great:*— glorious(1), majestic(2).

143. אֲדָר Adar (12c); of for. or.; the twelfth month in the Jewish calendar:— Adar(8).

144. אֲדָר Adar (1078d); (Ara.) corr. to 143; the twelfth month in the Jewish calendar:— Adar(1).

145. אֶדֶר eder (12a); from 142; *glory, magnificence, a mantle, cloak:*— magnificent(1), robe*(1).

146. אַדָּר Addar (12b); from 142; a desc. of Benjamin, also a city in Judah:— Addar(2).

147. אִדַּר iddar (1078d); (Ara.) of for. or.; *a threshing floor:*— threshing floors(1).

148. אֲדַרְגָּזַר adargazar (1078d); (Ara.) of for. or.; *a counselor:*— counselors(2).

149. אַדְרַזְדָּא adrazda (1079a); (Ara.) of for. or.; *correctly, exactly:*— zeal(1).

150. אֲדַרְכֹּן adarkon (204b); of for. or.; *a drachma:*— darics(2).

151. אֲדֹרָם Adoram (12a); contr. for 141; an Isr. leader:— Adoram(2).

152. אַדְרַמֶּלֶךְ Adrammelek (12c); from 142 and 4428; "Adar is prince," an Assyr. idol, also a son of Sennacherib:— Adrammelech(3).

153. אֶדְרָע edra (1089b); (Ara.) from the same as 1872; *a force:*— force(1).

154. אֶדְרֶעִי Edrei (204c); from an unused word; a chief city of Bashan, also a place in Naphtali:— Edrei(8).

155. אַדֶּרֶת addereth (12b); from 142; *glory, a cloak:*— garment(1), glory(1), mantle(7), robe(2), splendid(1).

156. אָדַשׁ adash (190b); the same as 1758, q.v.

157. אָהֵב aheb (12d); a prim. root; *to love:*— beloved(1), dearly love(1), friend(5), friends(6), love(88), loved(53), lover(1), lovers(16), loves(42), loving(2), show your love(1), shows love(1).

158. אַהַב ahab (13b); from 157; *love* (noun):— lovers(1), loving(1).

159. אֹהַב ohab (13b); from 157; *love* (noun):— caresses(1), which(1).

160. אַהֲבָה ahabah (13b); from 157; *love* (noun):— love(28), lovesick*(2), lovingly(1).

161. אֹהַד Ohad (13c); of unc. der.; an Isr.:— Ohad(2).

162. אֲהָהּ ahah (13c); a prim. interj.; *alas!*:— Ah(5), alas(10).

163. אַהֲוָא Ahava (13c); prob. of for. or.; a place and a stream in Bab.:— Ahava(3).

164. אֵהוּד Ehud (13c); from the same as 161; the name of several Isr.:— Ehud(9).

165. אֱהִי ehi (13c); a prim. adv.; *where?*:— where(3).

166. אָהַל ahal (14c); a prim. root; *to be clear, shine*:— has...brightness(1).

167. אָהַל ahal (14b); denom. vb. from the same as 168; *to move a tent* (from place to place):— moved tent(1), moved tents(1), pitch tent(1).

168. אֹהֶל ohel (13d); from an unused word; *a tent*:— home(1), owned(1), side pillar(1), tent(285), tents(56).

169. אֹהֶל Ohel (14b); from the same as 168; an Isr.:— Ohel(1).

170. אָהֳלָה Oholah (14b); from the same as 168; "she who has a tent," a symbolic name for Samaria:— Oholah(5).

171. אָהֳלִיאָב Oholiab (14b); from 168 and 1; "father's tent," an assistant of Bezalel:— Oholiab(5).

172. אָהֳלִיבָה Oholibah (14c); from the same as 168; "tent in her," a symbolic name for Jer.:— Oholibah(6).

173. אָהֳלִיבָמָה Oholibamah (14c); from 168 and 1116; "tent of the high place," wife of Esau, also an Edomite leader:— Oholibamah(8).

174. אֲהָלִים ahalim (14c); a prim. root; *the aloe* (a tree):— aloes(4).

175. אַהֲרוֹן Aharon (14d); of unc. der.; an elder brother of Moses:— Aaron(318), Aaron's(29).

176. אוֹ o (14d); a prim. root; *or*:— also(1), either(1), if(2), if*(1), nor(1), or(294), otherwise(1), say(1), whether(8).

177a. אַו av (16b); from the same as 183; *desire*:— desire(1).

177b. אוּאֵל Uel (15a); of unc. der.; "will of God," a Judean:— Uel(1).

178. אוֹב ob (15b); from an unused word; *a bottle* (made from animal skin), *a necromancer*:— medium(2), medium*(3), mediums(9), spirit(1), wineskins(1).

179. אוֹבִיל Obil (6b); from an unused word; overseer of David's camels:— Obil(1).

180. אוּבָל ubal (385c); from 2986; *a stream, river*:— Canal(1), canal(2).

181. אוּד ud (15c); from an unused word; *a brand, firebrand*:— brand(1), firebrand(1), firebrands(1).

182. אוֹדוֹת odoth (15c); from the same as 181; *a cause*:— about*(1), account(1), because(1), because*(4), concerning*(1), sake*(1).

183. אָוָה avah (16a); from an unused word; *to incline, desire*:— been greedy(1), crave(1), craved(1), craves(1), craving(1), desire(8), desired(2), desires(5), desires*(1), had(1), had a craving(2), longed(1), longing(1), longs(1).

184. אָוָה avah (16c); a prim. root; *to sign, mark, describe with a mark*:— draw(1).

185. אַוָּה avvah (16b); from the same as 183; *desire*:— desire(5), desires(1), passion*(1).

186. אוּזַי Uzay (17a); of unc. der.; a Judean:— Uzai(1).

187. אוּזָל Uzal (23d); from 235; a son of Joktan, also his desc., also a place of unc. location:— Uzal(3).

188. אוֹי oy (17a); a prim. interj.; *woe!*:— alas(2), woe(21).

189. אֱוִי Evi (16c); from the same as 183; one of five chiefs of Midian:— Evi(2).

190. אוֹיָה oyah (17a); from 188; *woe!*:— woe(2).

191. אֱוִיל evil (17b); from an unused word; *foolish*:— fool(11), fool's(1), foolish(6), foolish man(1), fools(7).

192. אֱוִיל מְרֹדַךְ Evil Merodak (17b); of for. or.; "man of Merodach," son and successor of Nebuchadnezzar:— Evil-merodach(2).

193a. אוּל ul (17c); from an unused word; *the body, belly*:— body(1).

193b. אוּל ul (17c); from the same as 193a; *a leading man, noble*:— leading men(1).

194. אוּלַי ulay (19c); a prim. root; *perhaps*:— if(1), perhaps(35), should(1), suppose(8).

195. אוּלַי Ulay (19c); of for. or.; a river of Elam:— Ulai(2).

196. אֱוִלִי evili (17c); from the same as 191; *foolish*:— foolish(1).

197. אוּלָם ulam (17c); from the same as 193a; *a porch*:— hall(5), porch(28), porches(1).

198. אוּלָם Ulam (17d); from the same as 193a; two Isr.:— Ulam(4).

199. אוּלָם ulam (19d); a prim. root; *but, but indeed*:— however(5), indeed(2), nevertheless(1), other hand(1), rather(1), truly(1).

200. אִוֶּלֶת ivveleth (17c); from the same as 191; *folly*:— folly(17), foolish(1), foolishly(1), foolishness(6).

201. אוֹמָר Omar (57b); from 559; a grandson of Esau:— Omar(3).

202. אוֹן on (20b); from an unused word; *vigor, wealth*:— maturity(1), might(2), power(1), strength(3), strong men(1), vigor(1), vigorous(1), virility(1), wealth(2).

203. אוֹן On (20b); from the same as 202; a chief of the tribe of Reuben.

204. אוֹן On (58a); of for. or.; a city in N. Eg.

205. אָוֶן aven (19d); from an unused word; *trouble, sorrow, wickedness*:— affliction(1), distress(1), evil(4), false(1), harm(1), idol(1), iniquity(37), misfortune(1), mourners'(1), mourning(1), sorrow(1), trouble(2), unrighteous(1), vanity(1), wicked(6), wickedness(15), wrong(1), wrongdoers(1).

206. אָוֶן Aven (19d); from the same as 205; "wickedness," a contemptuous synonym for two places:— Aven(2).

207. אוֹנוֹ Ono (20c); from the same as 202; "vigorous," a city in Benjamin:— Ono(5).

208. אוֹנָם Onam (20c); from the same as 202; "vigorous," the name of an Edomite and of an Isr.:— Onam(4).

209. אוֹנָן Onan (20c); from the same as 202; "vigorous," a son of Judah:— Onan(8).

210. אוּפָז Uphaz (20c); of unc. der.; a region where gold is found:— Uphaz(2).

211. אוֹפִיר Ophir (20c); of unc. der.; a son of Joktan, also his desc., also a region from which gold comes:— Ophir(13).

212. אוֹפָן ophan (66d); of unc. der.; *a wheel*:— another(1), wheel(9), wheel(1), wheels(22).

213. אוּץ uts (21a); a prim. root; *to press, be pressed, make haste*:— hasten(1), hasty(2), hurried(1), hurries(1), makes haste(1), narrow(1), pressed(1), try(1), urged(1).

214. אוֹצָר otsar (69d); from 686; *treasure, store, a treasury, storehouse*:— armory(1), cellars(1), gains(1), storehouse(3), storehouses(13), storeroom(1), stores(3), treasure(3), treasures(26), treasuries(19), treasury(7), treasury*(1).

215. אוֹר or (21a); a prim. root; *to be* or *become light*:— bright(1), brightened(2), dawned(1), enlighten(2), enlightened(1), enlightening(1), gave light(1), give(1), give light(5), given us light(1), gives light(2), illumine(1), illumines(1), kindle(1), light(5), lit(2), make a fire(1), make shine(1), resplendent(1), shed light(1), shine(9), shines(1), shone(1).

216. אוֹר or (21c); from 215; *a light*:— broad(1), dawn(1), dawn*(1), daylight(1), daylight*(1), early morning(1), light(105), lightning(5), lights(2), sun(1), sunlight(1), sunshine(1).

217. אוּר ur (22a); from 215; *a flame*:— fire(4), light(1).

218a. אוּר Ur (22d); from 215; a city in S. Bab.:— Ur(4).

218b. אוּר Ur (22b); from 215; "flame," the father of one of David's heroes:— Ur(1).

219a. אוֹרָה orah (21d); fem. of 216; *a light*:— dawn(1), light(2).

219b. אוֹרָה orah (21d); from 215; *an herb*:— herbs(1).

220. אֲוֵרָה averah (71d, 1120d); by transp. for 723a, q.v.

221. אוּרִי Uri (22b); from 215; "fiery," three Isr.:— Uri(8).

222. אוּרִיאֵל Uriel (22b); from 217 and 410; "flame of God," two Isr.:— Uriel(4).

223a. אוּרִיָּה Uriyyah (22c); from 217 and 3050; "flame of Yah," the name of a Hittite and of two Isr.:— Uriah(30), Uriah's(1), Urijah(5).

223b. אוּרִיָּהוּ Uriyyahu (22c); from 217 and 3050; "flame of Yah," a prophet slain by Jehoiakim:— Uriah(3).

224. אוּרִים Urim (22a); pl. of 217; part of the high priest's breastplate:— Urim(7).

225. אוּת uth (22d); a prim. root; *to consent, agree*:— agreed(1), consent(3).

226. אוֹת oth (16d); from 184; *a sign*:— banners(1), omens(1), pledge(1), sign(43), signs(30), standards(1), witness(1), wondrous(1).

227. אָז az (23a); of unc. der.; *at that time*:— if(1), now(1), once(1), rather*(1), since*(1), so(1), then(113), time(5), yet(1).

228. אֲזָא aza (1079a); (Ara.) a prim. root; *to make hot, heat*:— heat(1), heated(1), made...hot(1).

229. אֶזְבַּי Ezbay (23c); of unc. der.; the father of one of David's men:— Ezbai(1).

230. אָזְדָא azda (1079b); (Ara.) of unc. der.; *sure, assured*:— firm(2).

231. אֵזוֹב ezob (23c); of for. or.; *hyssop:*— hyssop(10).

232. אֵזוֹר ezor (25b); from 247; *a waist cloth:*— belt(3), belts(1), girdle(2), waistband(8).

233. אֲזַי azay (23b); prob. from 227; *then, in that case:*— then(3).

234. אַזְכָּרָה azkarah (272b); from 2142; *a memorial offering:*— memorial offering(2), memorial portion(5).

235. אָזַל azal (23c); a prim. root; *to go:*— evaporates(1), go(1), goes his way(1), gone(2).

236. אֲזַל azal (1079b); (Ara.) corr. to 235; *to go, go off:*— go(1), gone(1), went(4), went off(1).

237. אֶזֶל Ezel (23d); from 235; a memorial stone in Pal.:— Ezel(1).

238. אָזַן azan (24b); a denom. vb. from the same as 241; *to give ear, listen:*— give ear(24), give heed(2), hear(3), listen(8), listened(1), listening(1), pays attention(1), perceived by ear(1).

239. אָזַן azan (24d); a prim. root; *to weigh, test, prove:*— pondered(1).

240. אָזֵן azen (24c); from the same as 241; *implements, tools:*— tools(1).

241. אֹזֶן ozen (23d); from an unused word; *an ear:*— attentive(1), closely(1), ear(60), ears(58), hear*(2), hearing(39), inform*(1), known*(2), recite*(1), reported*(1), reveal*(1), revealed*(2), revelation*(1).

242. אֻזֵּן שֶׁאֱרָה Uzzen Sheerah (25a); from 239 and 7609; "portion of Sheerah," a place in Pal.:— Uzzen-sheerah(1).

243. אַזְנוֹת תָּבוֹר Aznoth Tabor (24d); from 238 and 8396; a place in Naphtali:— Aznoth-tabor(1).

244a. אָזְנִי Ozni (24c); from the same as 241; "my hearing," a son of Gad:— Ozni(1).

244b. אָזְנִי Ozni (24d); from 244a; a desc. of Ozni:— Oznites(1).

245. אֲזַנְיָה Azanyah (24d); from 238 and 3050; "Yah has heard," a Levite:— Azaniah(1).

246. אֲזִק azeq (279b); from the same as 2203b; *a manacle:*— chains(2).

247. אָזַר azar (25a); a prim. root; *to gird, encompass, equip:*— binds(1), bound(1), encircle(1), gird(7), girded(5), girds(1).

248. אֶזְרוֹעַ ezroa (284b); from the same as 2220; *the arm:*— arm(1).

249. אֶזְרָח ezrach (280c); from 2224; *a native:*— native(14), native-born(2), tree in its native(1).

250. אֶזְרָחִי Ezrachi (280d); from 2224; a desc. of Zerah:— Ezrahite(1).

251. אָח ach (26b); from an unused word; *a brother:*— alike(1), another(16), brethren(17), brother(218), brother with his brothers(1), brother's(21), brotherhood(1), brothers(195), brothers'(1), companions(1), countryman(10), countryman's(2), countrymen(10), fellow(2), fellow countryman(3), fellow countrymen(2), fellows(1), kinsman(3), kinsmen(27), nephew*(2), other(7), relative(7), relatives(80).

252. אַח ach (1079c); (Ara.) corr. to 251; *a brother:*— brothers(1).

253. אָהּ ach (25b); of unc. der.; *ah!, alas!:*— Ah(1), alas(1).

254. אָח ach (28d); of unc. der.; *a firepot, brazier:*— brazier(3).

255. אֹחַ oach (28d); from an unused word; *owl:*— owls(1).

256. אַחְאָב Achab (26c); from 251 and 1; "father's brother," a king of Isr., also a false prophet:— Ahab(91), Ahab's(2).

257. אַחְבָּן Achban (26c); from 251 and 995; "brother of an intelligent one," an Isr.:— Ahban(1).

258. אָחַד achad (292b, 1119d); the same as 2300, q.v.

259. אֶחָד echad (25c); a prim. card. number; *one:*— 151,450*(1), 41,500*(2), 61*(1), 61,000*(1), 621*(2), 721*(1), alike(1), all at once(1), alone(2), altogether(1), another(23), another into one(1), any(15), any one(2), any*(1), anyone*(1), apiece(1), certain(11), certain man(1), each(48), each one(4), each other(1), each*(4), eleven*(9), eleventh*(4), every(1), everyone(1), few(3), first(38), forty-first*(1), forty-one*(4), numbered(1), once(14), once*(4), one(586), one and on another(1), one and the other(2), one at the other(1), one can him who(1), one the other(1), one to another(1), one will to another(1), one another(4), one thing(2), one thing to another(1), one-tenth(1), one-tenth for each(1), only(2), other(27), other was one(1), outermost*(1), same(25), same one(1), single(15), some(2), thirty-first*(1), thirty-one*(3), together(3), twenty-first*(4), twenty-one*(4), uniformly*(2), unique(4), unison(1), unit(4), united(1), whom(1).

260. אָחוּ achu (28a); of for. or.; *reeds, rushes:*— marsh grass(2), reeds(1), rushes(1).

261. אֵחוּד Echud (26a); from 259; "union," a Benjamite:— Ehud(1).

262. אַחְוָה achvah (296a); from 2331a; *a declaration:*— declaration(1).

263. אַחֲוָה achavah or

אַחֲוָיָה achavayah (1092b); (Ara.) corr. to 262; *a declaring:*— explanation(1).

264. אַחֲוָה achavah (27d); from the same as 251; *brotherhood:*— brotherhood(1).

265. אֲחוֹחַ Achoach (29a); of unc. der.; a Benjamite:— Ahoah(1).

266. אֲחוֹחִי Achochi (29a); from 265; a desc. of Ahoah:— Ahohite(5).

267. אֲחוּמַי Achumay (26c); from 251 and 4325; a desc. of Judah:— Ahumai(1).

268. אָחוֹר achor (30c); from 309; *the hind side, back part:*— afterward(1), away(1), back(22), backs(1), backward(7), behind(1), hereafter(1), hindquarters(1), rear(3), rear parts(1), west(1).

269. אָחוֹת achoth (27d); from the same as 251; *sister:*— another(2), other(1), sister(89), sister of your sisters(1), sister's(5), sisters(10).

270. אָחַז achaz (28a); a prim. root; *to grasp, take hold, take possession:*— acquire property(1), acquired property(1), attached(1), bolt(1), catch(1), caught(3), drawn(2), fastened(3), grasp(2), grasped(1), grasps(1), gripped(1), grips(1), handle(1), have possessions(1), held(4), held fast(1), hold(3), holding(1), inserted(1), lay hold(1), obscures(1), possessed(1), seized(10), seizes(3), take hold(6), take possession(1), taken(2), taken hold(3), takes hold(2), took(1), took hold(3), trapped(1), wielders(1).

271. אָחָז Achaz (28c); from 270; "he has grasped," two Isr.:— Ahaz(41).

272. אֲחֻזָּה achuzzah (28c); from 270; *a possession:*— possession(40), possessions(2), property(19), site(5).

273. אַחְזַי Achzay (28d); from 270 and 3050; "Yah has grasped," an Isr. name:— Ahzai(1).

274. אֲחַזְיָה Achazyah (28d); from 270 and 3050; "Yah has grasped," the name of several Isr.:— Ahaziah(36), Ahaziah's to Ahaziah(1).

275. אֲחֻזָּם Achuzzam (28d); from 270; "possessor," a man of Judah:— Ahuzzam(1).

276. אֲחֻזַּת Achuzzath (28d); from 270; "possession," a friend of Abimelech:— Ahuzzath(1).

277. אֲחִי Achi (26d); from 251 and 3050; "brother of Yah," an Isr. name:— Ahi(2).

278. אֵחִי Echi (29a); of unc. der.; a son of Benjamin:— Ehi(1).

279. אֲחִיאָם Achiam (26c); from 251 and 517; "brother of mother," one of David's men:— Ahiam(2).

280. אֲחִידָה achidah (1092b); (Ara.) corr. to 2420; *a riddle:*— enigmas(1).

281. אֲחִיָּה Achiyyah (26d); from 251 and 3050; "brother of Yah," an Isr. name:— Ahiah(1), Ahijah(22).

282. אֲחִיהוּד Achihud (26d); from 251 and 1935; "brother of majesty," a leader of Asher:— Ahihud(1).

283. אַחְיוֹ Achyo (26d); from the same as 251; "brotherly," the name of several Isr.:— Ahio(6).

284. אֲחִיחֻד Achichud (26d); from 251 and 2330; "brother of a riddle," a Benjamite:— Ahihud(1).

285. אֲחִיטוּב Achitub (26d); from 251 and 2898; "my brother is goodness," two Isr.:— Ahitub(15).

286. אֲחִילוּד Achilud (27a); from 251 and 3205; "child's brother," two Isr.:— Ahilud(5).

287. אֲחִימוֹת Achimoth (27a); from 251 and 4191; "my brother is death," a Levite:— Ahimoth(1).

288. אֲחִימֶלֶךְ Achimelek (27a); from 251 and 4428; "brother of a king," an Isr. name, also a Hittite name:— Ahimelech(16).

289. אֲחִימַן Achiman (27a); from the same as 251; a Levite, also a son of Anak:— Ahiman(4).

290. אֲחִימַעַץ Achimaats (27b); from 251 and the equiv. of 4619; "my brother is wrath," two Isr.:— Ahimaaz(15).

291. אַחְיָן Achyan (27b); from the same as 251; "brotherly," a Manassite:— Ahian(1).

292. אֲחִינָדָב Achinadab (27b); from 251 and 5068; "my brother is noble," an official of Solomon:— Ahinadab(1).

293. אֲחִינֹעַם Achinoam (27b); from 251 and 5278; "my brother is delight," two Isr. women:— Ahinoam(7).

294. אֲחִיסָמָךְ Achisamak (27b); from 251 and 5564; "my brother has supported," an Isr.:— Ahisamach(3).

295. אֲחִיעֶזֶר Achiezer (27b); from 251 and 5828; "my brother is help," two Isr.:— Ahiezer(6).

296. אֲחִיקָם Achiqam (27b); from 251 and 6965; "my brother has arisen," an Isr.:— Ahikam(20).

297. אֲחִירָם Achiram (27b); from 251 and 7311; "brother of (the) lofty," a son of Benjamin:— Ahiram(1).

298. אֲחִירָמִי Achirami (27c); from 297; desc. of Ahiram:— Ahiramites(1).

299. אֲחִירַע Achira (27c); from 251 and 7451b; "my brother is evil," a leader of Naphtali:— Ahira(5).

300. אֲחִישַׁחַר Achishachar (27c); from 251 and 7837; "brother of (the) dawn," a Benjamite:— Ahishahar(1).

301. אֲחִישָׁר Achishar (27c); from 251 and 7891; "my brother has sung," one of Solomon's officials:— Ahishar(1).

302. אֲחִיתֹפֶל Achithophel (27d); from 251 and perh. 8602a; an adviser of David:— Ahithophel(20).

303. אַחְלָב Achlab (317b); from the same as 2459; a city assigned to Asher:— Ahlab(1).

304. אַחְלַי Achlay (29a); of unc. der.; an Isr. name:— Ahlai(2).

305. אַחֲלַי achalay (25b); of unc. der.; *O! would that!:*— Oh(1), wish(1).

306. אַחְלָמָה achlamah (29a); of unc. der.; *amethyst:*— amethyst(2), GOD(1).

307. אַחְמְתָא Achmetha (1079c); (Ara.) of for. or.; the capital of Media:— Ecbatana(1).

308. אֲחַסְבַּי Achasbay (29b); of unc. der.; an Isr.:— Ahasbai(1).

309. אָחַר achar (29b); a prim. root; *to remain behind, tarry:*— delay(11), delayed(1), late(2), linger(1), stay up late(1), stayed(1), tarry(1).

310. אַחַר achar (29d); from 309; *the hind* or *following part:*— according(1), after(363), after*(6), afterward(30), afterward*(18), afterwards(3), afterwards*(5), again(4), away(1), back(2), behind(49), behind*(9), besides(1), butt end(1), care(1), follow(11), follow*(16), followed(16), followed*(24), following(35), following and followed(1), following*(5), follows*(3), forsaking*(1), later(1), long*(1), pursuing(4), rear(3), since(3), since*(4), subsequent(2), succeeded(1), survived*(2), then(1), thereafter*(1), west(2), west side(1), when*(1).

311. אַחַר achar (1079d); (Ara.) corr. to 310; *after:*— after(1), future(2).

312. אַחֵר acher (29c); from 309; *another:*— another(59), another woman(1), any(1), any other(1), different(1), first(1), following(1), foreign(1), next(3), other(89), others(11).

313. אַחֵר Acher (31b); of unc. der.; an Isr.:— Aher(1).

314. אַחֲרוֹן acharon (30d); from 309; *coming after* or *behind:*— afterward(2), afterwards(1), come(5), come later(1), end(1), future*(1), last(23), last one(1), last ones(1), last time(1), later(2), later things(1), latter(3), next(2), ones who(1), rear(1), west(1), western(4).

315. אַחְרַח Acharach (31b); from 309; a son of Benjamin:— Aharah(1).

316. אֲחַרְחֵל Acharchel (31c); from 309; a desc. of Judah:— Aharhel(1).

317. אָחֳרִי ochori (1079d); fem. of 321, q.v.

318a. אַחֲרַי acharay (30c); from 309; (a man) *that turns backward:*— afterward(1).

318b. אָחֳרֵין ochoren (1079d); (Ara.) from 311; *last:*— finally(1).

319. אַחֲרִית acharith (31a); from 309; *the after-part, end:*— come(2), descendants(1), end(20), final end(1), final period(1), future(7), last(8), latter(7), latter ending(1), latter period(1), least(1), outcome(3), posterity(3), remotest part(1), rest(2), survivors(2).

320. אַחֲרִית acharith (1079d); (Ara.) from 311; *the end:*— latter(1).

321. אָחֳרָן ochoran (1079d); (Ara.) from 311; *another:*— another(6), one else(1), other(2), someone else(1).

322. אֲחֹרַנִּית achorannith (30d); prol. from 268; *backwards:*— back(2), back again(1), backward(3), turned away(1).

323. אֲחַשְׁדַּרְפַּן achashdarpan (31c); of for. or.; *satraps:*— satraps(4).

324. אֲחַשְׁדַּרְפְּנִין achashdarpenin (1080a); (Ara.) corr. to 323; *satraps:*— satraps(9).

325. אֲחַשְׁוֵרוֹשׁ Achashverosh (31c); of for. or.; king of Persia:— Ahasuerus(31).

326. אֲחַשְׁתָּרִי Achashtari (31c); prob. of for. or.; "belonging to the realm," an Isr.:— Haahashtari(1).

327. אֲחַשְׁתְּרָן achashteran (31c); of for. or.; *royal:*— royal(1).

328. אַט at (31d); from an unused word; *gentleness:*— despondently(1), gently(3), leisure(1).

329. אָטָד atad (31d); from an unused word; *a bramble, buckthorn,* also a city in Canaan:— Atad(2), bramble(3), thorns(1).

330a. אֵטוּן etun (32a); from 331; *thread, yarn:*— linens(1).

330b. אִטִּי itti (31d); from the same as 328; *a mutterer:*— ghosts of the dead(1).

331. אָטַם atam (31d); a prim. root; *to shut, shut up:*— closes(1), latticed(2), shuts(1), shuttered(1), stops(2).

332. אָטַר atar (32a); a prim. root; *to shut up, close, bind:*— shut(1).

333. אָטֵר Ater (32a); from 332; a leader in Isr.:— Ater(5).

334. אִטֵּר itter (32a); from 332; *shut up, bound:*— left-handed*(2).

335. אַי ay (32b); a prim. adv.; *where?:*— how*(2), origin*(1), what*(3), where(28), where*(1), whether(1), which*(2), why(1).

336. אִי i (33a); a prim. adv.; *not.*

337. אִי i (33a); a prim. interj.; *alas!:*— woe(2).

338. אִי i (17b); from 188; *a jackal:*— Hyenas(1), jackals(1), wolves(1).

339. אִי i (15d); from an unused word; *coast, region:*— coastland(4), coastlands(26), islands(6).

340. אָיַב ayab (33b); a prim. root; *to be hostile to:*— enemies(196), enemies'(2), enemy(79), enemy to your enemies(1), enemy's(1), foes(2).

341. אֹיֵב oyeb (33b); act. part. of 340, q.v.

342. אֵיבָה ebah (33c); from 340; *enmity:*— enmity(5).

343. אֵיד ed (15c); from the same as 182; *distress, calamity:*— calamity(17), destruction(1), disaster(6).

344. אַיָּה ayyah (17b); of unc. der.; *a hawk, falcon, kite:*— falcon(2), falcon's(1).

345. אַיָּה Ayyah (17b); from 344; "falcon," the name of a Horite, also of an Isr.:— Aiah(6).

346. אַיֵּה ayyeh (32c); from 335; *where?:*— where(44).

347. אִיּוֹב Iyyob (33c); of unc. der.; a patriarch:— Job(56), Job's(2).

348. אִיזֶבֶל Izebel (33b); of unc. der.; queen of Isr. with King Ahab:— Jezebel(21), Jezebel's(1).

349. אֵיךְ ek (32c); from 335; *how?:*— how(60), what(1).

350. אִי־כָבוֹד I-kabod (33b); from 338 and 3519b; "inglorious," a son of Phinehas:— Ichabod(1), Ichabod's(1).

351a. אֵיכֹה ekoh or
אֵיכָה ekah (32d); from 349 and 3541; *in what manner? how? where?:*— how(14), what(1), where(3).

351b. אֵיכוֹ eko (32d); another form for 351a, q.v.

351c. אֵיכָכָה ekakah (32d); from 335 and 3602; *how?:*— how(4).

352a. אַיִל ayil (17d); from the same as 197; *a ram:*— ram(87), ram's(1), rams(60), rams'(6).

352b. אַיִל ayil (18a); from the same as 197; *a projecting pillar* or *pilaster:*— lintel(1), side pillar(4), side pillars(17).

352c. אַיִל ayil (18b); from the same as 197; *a leader, chief:*— despot(1), leaders(1), mighty(2), ram(1).

352d. אַיִל ayil (18b); from the same as 197; *a terebinth:*— oaks(3).

353. אֱיָל eyal (33d); of Ara. or.; *help:*— strength(1).

354. אַיָּל ayyal (19b); from the same as 197; *a hart, stag, deer:*— deer(8), stag(3).

355. אַיָּלָה ayyalah (19b); fem. of 354; *a hind, doe:*— deer(2), doe(2), hind(1), hinds(2), hinds'(3).

356. אֵילוֹן Elon (19a); from 352d; "terebinth," an Isr. name, also a Hittite, also a city in Dan:— Elon(7).

357. אַיָּלוֹן Ayyalon (19c); from 354; "deer," the name of several cities in Pal.:— Aijalon(10).

358. אֵילוֹן בֵּית חָנָן Elon Beth Chanan (19a, 111c); from 356, 1004 and 2603a; "terebinth of (the) house of favor," a place in Dan:— Elonbeth-hanan(1).

359. אֵילוֹת Eloth (19a); from 352d; "grove of lofty trees," the same location as 365a:— Elath(1), Eloth(3).

360. אֱיָלוּת eyaluth (33d); fem. of 353; *my help:*— help(1).

361. אֵילָם elam (19a); from 352d; *a porch:*— porch(1), porches(14).

362. אֵילִם Elim (18c); pl. of 352d; "terebinths," a place in the desert:— Elim(6).

363. אִילָן ilan (1079a); (Ara.) corr. to 356; *a tree:*— tree(6).

364. אֵיל פָּארָן El Paran (18c); from 352d and 6290; "terebinth of Paran," a city and harbor on the Red Sea:— El-paran(1).

365a. אֵילַת Elath (19a); from 352d; "lofty tree," a city and harbor on the Red Sea:— Elath(4).

365b. אַיֶּלֶת ayyeleth or
אַיָּלָה ayyalah (19b); the same as 355, q.v.

366. אָיֹם ayom (33d); from an unused word; *terrible, dreadful:*— awesome(2), dreaded(1).

367. אֵימָה emah (33d); from the same as 366; *terror, dread:*— dread(2), fear(1), fearsome(1), terrible(1), terrified(1), terror(8), terrors(3).

368a. אֵימִים Emim (34a); pl. of 367; "terrors," an inhab. of Moab:— Emim(3).

368b. אֵימְתָן emethan (1080a); (Ara.) corr. to 366; *terrible:*— terrifying(1).

369. אַיִן ayin (34a); a prim. root; *nothing, nought:*— almost(1), bereft*(1), beyond(5), beyond*(1), cease(2), countless*(2), else*(1), endless*(1), fails(1), found(1), gone(6), had(2), had no(11), had no one(2), has(2), has he no(1), has no(23), has none(1), has nothing(1), have(5), have i no(1), have no(24), have none(2), have nothing(2), having a nor(1), having no(2), helpless*(1), incurable*(1), infinite*(1), infrequent*(1), innumerable*(1), inscrutable*(1), lack(4), lacks(1), leaves no(1), neither(2), neither*(1), neither...nor(2), never(2), no(43), no account(1), no longer(3), no more(16), no one(101), no*(1), no...have(1), none(18), none other(1), none*(1), nor(12), nor are there(2), nor is there(3), nor is there one(1), nor was there(2), nor have(1), nor*(1), nothing(19), nothing*(10), one(3), one should never(1), or(1), powerless*(1), senseless*(1), surely*(1), there(15), there are no(2), there be no(2), there is not one(1), there is no(108), there is no one(31), there is no...nor(2), there is none(22), there is nothing(11), there was not(1), there was not one(1), there was no(38), there was no one(15), there was none(5), there was nothing(2), there were no(3), there will be neither(1), there will be no(9), there will be no one(3), there will be none(5), there will be nothing(1), there no(6), there none(1), there one(1), undesirable*(2), unfathomable*(1), unless(1), unsearchable*(3), waterless*(1), without(46), without and having no(1), without*(4).

370. אַיִן ayin (32d); from 335; *whence?:*— where(15), where*(1).

371. אִין in (35b); appar. a short. form of 369; *not.*

372. אִיעֶזֶר Iezer (4c); from 336 and 5828; "region of help," two Isr. (the same as 44):— Iezer(1).

373. אִיעֶזְרִי Iezri (4c); from 372; a desc. of Iezer (the same as 33):— Iezerites(1).

374. אֵיפָה ephah (35b); of for. or.; *an ephah* (a measure of grain):— bushel(1), differing measures(2), ephah(33), measure(2).

375. אֵיפֹה ephoh (33a); from 335 and 6311; *where?:*— what kind(1), where(9).

376. אִישׁ ish (35d); from an unused word; *man:*— adulteress*(1), all(1), another(2), any(6), any man(21), any man's(4), any one(3), anyone(16), anyone*(1), archers*(1), Benjamite*(3), certain(6), champion*(2), counselor*(1), counselors*(1), deserve(1), each(148), each had another(1), each his man(1), each man(1), each man(37), each man's(3), each one(37), each one by another(1), each person(1), each*(5), eloquent*(1), every(1), every man(38), every man's(7), every one(8), everyone(16), everyone*(3), expert(1), farming*(1), father*(1), fellow(3), fellows(2), friend*(1), friends*(1), high*(1), himself(1), hunter*(1), husband(65), husband's(1), husbands(4), idiot*(1), Ishi(1), keepers(2), liar*(1), male(2), man(746), man against another(1), man of each(1), man the men(1), man your husband(1), man's(21), man's are the men(1), manchild(1), mankind*(1), marry*(1), marrying*(1), men(669), men at one(1), men's(1), men*(1), no*(1), none*(10), one(89), one of men(1), one's(1), oppressor*(1), ordinary(1), own(1), people(3), person(5), persons(2), prime(1), rank(1), respective(1), sailors*(1), slanderer*(1), soldiers(1), soldiers*(3), some(8), son*(1), steward*(1), swordsmen*(1), this one(1), this one and that one(1), those(1), those who(3), tiller*(1), together*(1), traders*(2), tradition*(1), traveler*(1), troop(1), warriors(3), whoever*(3).

377. אִישׁ ish (not included); a denom. vb. from 376, q.v.

378. אִישׁ־בֹּשֶׁת Ish-bosheth (36b); from 376 and 1322; "man of shame," a son of Saul and king of Isr.:— Ish-bosheth(11).

379. אִישְׁהוֹד Ishhod (36b); from 376 and 1935; "man of majesty," a man of Manasseh:— Ishhod(1).

380. אִישׁוֹן ishon (36b); from 376; *the pupil* (of the eye):— apple(2), middle(1), pupil(1), time(1).

381. אִישׁ־חַיִל ish-chayil (298c); from 376 and 2428, q.v.

382a. אִישׁ־טוֹב ish-Tob (35d, 376a); from 376 and 2897; "men of Tob," inhab. of a region E. of the Jordan:— men of Tob(2).

382b. אִיתוֹן ithon (87c); from 857; *an entrance:*— entrance(1).

383. אִיתַי ithay (1080a); (Ara.) corr. to 3426; *there is, are:*— do(1), has(1), have(1), residing(1), there(6).

384. אִיתִיאֵל Ithiel (87b); perh. from 854 and 410; "with me is God," an Isr. name:— Ithiel(3), this(193).

385. אִיתָמָר Ithamar (16a); from 339 and 8558; "land of palms," a son of Aaron:— Ithamar(21).

386. אֵיתָן ethan (450d); from an unused word; *perennial, ever-flowing, permanence:*— enduring(3), ever-flowing(2), firm(1), hard(1), normal state(1), perennially(2), running water(1), secure ones(1), unceasing(1).

387. אֵיתָן Ethan (451a); from the same as 386; "permanence," an Isr. name:— Ethan(7).

388. אֵיתָנִים Ethanim (450d); pl. of 386; (month of) "steady flowings," the seventh month in the Jewish calendar:— Ethanim(1).

389. אַךְ ak (36c); of unc. der., see 403; *surely, howbeit:*— altogether(1), certainly(1), completely(1), exactly(2), except(1), hardly*(1), however(9), indeed(3), just(1), just*(1), mere(1), nevertheless(13), nothing(1), only(52), only*(1), rather(1), soon(1), surely(37), surely*(1), truly(1), utterly(1), when they had just(1), yes(2), yet(6).

390. אַכַּד Akkad (37a); of for. or.; the name of a city in N. Bab.:— Accad(1).

391. אַכְזָב akzab (469d); from 3576; *deceptive, disappointing:*— deception(1), deceptive(1).

392. אַכְזִיב Akzib (469d); from 3576; "deceptive," two places in Pal.:— Achzib(4).

393. אַכְזָר akzar (470a); from an unused word; *cruel, fierce:*— cruel(2), deadly(1), fierce(1).

394. אַכְזָרִי akzari (470a); from 393; *cruel:*— cruel(5), cruel man(1), cruel one(1), cruel one(1).

395. אַכְזְרִיּוּת akzeriyyuth (470a); from the same as 393; *cruelty, fierceness:*— fierce(1).

396. אֲכִילָה akilah (38b); from 398; *an eating, a meal:*— food(1).

397. אָכִישׁ Akish (37a); of unc. der.; king of Gath:— Achish(21).

398. אָכַל akal (37a); a prim. root; *to eat:*— ate(76), certainly have eaten(1), certainly not eat(1), consume(30), consumed(30), consumes(9), consuming(9), devour(38), devour you will be devoured(1), devoured(30), devourer(2), devouring(3), devours(7), dine(1), eat(398), eat freely(1), eaten(66), eaten at all(2), eaten freely(1), eater(2), eater's(1), eating(25), eats(29), edible(2), enjoys(2), entirely consumed(1), feast(1), fed(8), feed(10), food(4), give him to eat(1), had(2), has enough(1), lived off(1), meal*(1), moth-eaten*(1), plenty to eat(1), reduces(1), shared*(1), tasting(1), took space away(1), use(1).

399. אֲכַל akal (1080b); (Ara.) corr. to 398; *to eat, devour:*— brought(1), devour(2), devoured(2), eating(1), maliciously accused*(1).

400. אֹכֶל okel (38a); from 398; *food:*— food(34), food supply(1), mealtime*(1), prey(1).

401. אֻכָל Ukal (38b); from 398; an Isr. name:— Ucal(1).

402. אָכְלָה oklah (38a); fem. of 400; *food, eating:*— eat(1), food(13), fuel(3).

403. אָכֵן aken (38c); a prim. root; *surely:*— certainly(1), nevertheless(2), surely(11), truly(1).

404. אָכַף akaph (38c); a prim. root; *to press, urge:*— urges(1).

405. אֶכֶף ekeph (38d); from 404; *pressure:*— pressure(1).

406. אִכָּר ikkar (38d); from an unused word; *a plowman, husbandman:*— farmer(3), farmers(3), plowmen(1).

407. אַכְשָׁף Akshaph (506d); of unc. der.; a place in N. Canaan:— Achshaph(3).

408. אַל al (39a); a prim. particle; *not* (a subjective neg.):— neither(1), neither their nor(1), neither them nor(1), never(2), never*(2), no(46), none(2), none*(4), nor(36), nothing(3), nothing*(4), rather(1), so(1), worthless(1).

409. אַל al (1080b); (Ara.) corr. to 408; *not.*

410. אֵל el (41d); a prim. root; *God,* in pl. *gods:*— El-berith*(1), God(204), god(16), God's(2), gods(3), helpless*(1), mighty(3), Mighty One(3), power(1), strong(1).

411. אֵל el (41b); a prim. pron.; *these:*— these(8), those(1).

412. אֵל el (1080b); another reading for 429, q.v.

413. אֶל el (39b); a prim. particle; *to, into, towards:*— about(12), above(1), according(4), addition(2), adjacent*(1), after(4), after*(1), against(162), along(1), along*(1), among(3), among*(1), because(5), before(11), before*(4), behind*(2), beside(3), beside*(3), between*(2), carried(1), concerning(31), corresponding*(1), defied*(1), everywhere*(1), faced(1), facing*(3), far(1), greatly*(1), inside*(1), next(1), next*(1), nor(1), onto(1), opposite(1), opposite*(2), outside*(12), over(23), recalls*(1), regard(2), regarding(1), straight*(3), through(1), together*(2), toward(75), toward*(2), visit*(1), where(1), where*(2), wherever*(4), whom*(1), within(1).

414. אֵלָא Ela (41d); of unc. der.; an Isr.:— Ela(1).

415. אֵל אֱלֹהֵי יִשְׂרָאֵל El Elohe Yisrael (41d); from 410, 430 and 3478; "the mighty God of Israel," an altar of Jacob:— El-Elohe-Israel(1).

416. אֵל בֵּית־אֵל El Beth-el (41d); from 410 and 1008; "the God of Bethel," an altar of Jacob:— El-bethel(1).

417. אֶלְגָּבִישׁ elgabish (38d); of for. or.; *hail:*— hailstones*(2).

418. אַלְגּוּמִּים algummim (38d); of for. or.; perh. *a sandalwood tree:*— algum(2), algum trees(1).

419. אֶלְדָּד Eldad (44d); from 410 and 1730; "God has loved," an Isr. name:— Eldad(2).

420. אֶלְדָּעָה Eldaah (44d); from 410 and 3045; "God has called," a son of Midian:— Eldaah(2).

421. אָלָה alah (46d); a prim. root; *to wail:*— wail(1).

422. אָלָה alah (46d); a prim. root; *to swear, curse:*— oaths(1), put the under oath(1), swearing(1), take(2), takes an oath(2), under oath(1), uttered a curse(1).

423. אָלָה alah (46d); from 422; *an oath:*— adjuration(1), curse(12), curses(6), oath(13).

424. אֵלָה elah (18c); fem. of 352d; *a terebinth:*— Elah(3), oak(11), terebinth(2).

425. אֵלָה Elah (18d); from 424; "terebinth," an Isr. name, also an Edomite name:— Elah(13).

426. אֱלָהּ elah (1080c); (Ara.) corr. to 433; *God, god:*— God(74), god(6), gods(15).

427. אַלָּה allah (47c); of unc. der.; *an oak:*— oak(1).

428. אֵלֶּה elleh (41c); a prim. pron.; *these:*— former(1), one(1), one as the other(1), one the other(1), others(3), same(1), some(4), such(7), such things(1), these(627), these men(1), these same(1), these things(51), this(14), this manner(1), this*(1), those(15), who(4), whom(1).

429. אֵלֶּה elleh (1080c); (Ara.) corr. to 428; *these:*— these(1).

430. אֱלֹהִים elohim (43b); pl. of 433; *God, god:*— divine(1), divine being(1), exceedingly(1), God(2326), god(45), God's(14), goddess(2), godly(1), gods(204), great(2), judges(3), mighty(2), rulers(1), shrine*(1).

431. אֲלוּ alu (1080d); (Ara.) a prim. interj.; *lo!:*— behold(5).

432. אִלּוּ illu (47a); of unc. der.; *if, though:*— if(2).

433. אֱלוֹהַּ eloah (43a); prol. from 410; *God, god:*— God(50), god(6), God's(1).

434. אֱלוּל elul (47b); see 457.

435. אֱלוּל Elul (47a); of unc. der.; the sixth Jewish month:— Elul(1).

436. אֵלוֹן elon (18d); prol. from 352d; *a terebinth:*— oak(6), oaks(4).

437. אַלּוֹן allon (47c); from the same as 427; *an oak:*— oak(4), oaks(4).

438. אַלּוֹן Allon (47d); from the same as 427; a Simeonite:— Allon(1).

439. אַלּוֹן בָּכוּת Allon Bakuth (47c, 113d); from 437 and 1058; "oak of weeping," a tree near the grave of Rebekah's nurse:— Allon-bacuth(1).

440. אֵלֹנִי Eloni (19a); from 356; a desc. of Elon:— Elonites(1).

441a. אַלּוּף alluph (48d); from 502; *tame:*— cattle(1), companion(2), companions(1), friend(1), gentle(1), intimate friends(2).

441b. אַלּוּף alluph (49b); from 505; *a chief, chiliarch:*— chief(43), chiefs(14), clan(1), clans(2).

442. אָלוּשׁ Alush (47a); of unc. der.; a place in the wilderness:— Alush(2).

443. אֶלְזָבָד Elzabad (44d); from 410 and 2064; "God has given," two Isr.:— Elzabad(2).

444. אָלַח alach (47a); a prim. root; *to be corrupt* (morally):— become corrupt(2), corrupt(1).

445. אֶלְחָנָן Elchanan (44d); from 410 and 2603a; "God has been gracious," two of David's leaders:— Elhanan(4).

446. אֱלִיאָב Eliab (45a); from 410 and 1; "God is father," the name of several Isr.:— Eliab(20), Eliab's(1).

447. אֱלִיאֵל Eliel (45a); from 410 repeated; "my God is God," the name of several Isr.:— Eliel(10).

448. אֱלִיאָתָה Eliathah (45a); from 410 and 857; "God has come," an Isr.:— Eliathah(2).

449. אֱלִידָד Elidad (44d); from the same as 419; "God has loved," an Isr. name:— Elidad(1).

450. אֶלְיָדָע Elyada (45b); from 410 and 3045; "God knows," three Isr.:— Eliada(4).

451. אַלְיָה alyah (46d); from 421; *the fat tail* (of sheep):— fat tail(5).

452. אֵלִיָּה Eliyyah (45b); from 410 and 3050; "Yah is God," a well-known prophet of Isr., also three other Isr.:— Elijah(71).

453. אֱלִיהוּ Elihu (45b); from 410 and 1931; "He is (my) God," five Isr.:— Elihu(11).

454a. אֶלְיְהוֹעֵינַי Elyehoenay (41b); from 413, 3068 and 5869; "toward Yah (are) my eyes," two Isr.:— Eliehoenai(2).

454b. אֶלְיוֹעֵינַי Elyoenay (41b); from 413, 3068 and 5869; "to Yah (are) my eyes," the name of several Isr.:— Elioenai(7).

455. אֶלְיַחְבָּא Elyachba (45b); from 410 and 2244; "God hides," one of David's leaders:— Eliahba(2).

456. אֱלִיחֹרֶף Elichoreph (45b); from 410 and 2779; "God of autumn," one of Solomon's scribes:— Elihoreph(1).

457. אֱלִיל elil (47b); of unc. der.; *insufficiency, worthlessness:*— futility(1), idols(16), images(1), worthless(2).

458. אֱלִימֶלֶךְ Elimelek (45b); from 410 and 4428; "God is king," the husband of Naomi:— Elimelech(6).

459. אִלֵּין illen (1080d); (Ara.) prol. from 412; *these:*— these(5).

460. אֶלְיָסָף Elyasaph (45b); from 410 and 3254; "God has added," two Isr.:— Eliasaph(6).

461. אֱלִיעֶזֶר Eliezer (45c); from 410 and 5828; "God is help," the name of several Isr., also of a Damascene:— Eliezer(14).

462. אֱלִיעֵינַי Elienay (not included); prob. a contr. for 454b; an Isr.:— Elienai(1).

463. אֱלִיעָם Eliam (45c); from 410 and 5971b; "God is kinsman," an Isr. name:— Eliam(2).

464. אֱלִיפַז Eliphaz (45c); from 410 and 6337; "God is fine gold," a son of Esau, also a friend of Job:— Eliphaz(15).

465. אֱלִיפַל Eliphal (45c); from 410 and 6419; "God has judged," one of David's heroes:— Eliphal(1).

466. אֱלִיפְלֵהוּ Eliphelehu (45c); from 410 and 6395; "may God distinguish him," a doorkeeper:— Eliphelehu(2).

467. אֱלִיפֶלֶט Eliphelet (45d); from 410 and 6405; "God is deliverance," the name of several Isr.:— Eliphelet(8), Elpelet(1).

468. אֱלִיצוּר Elitsur (45d); from 410 and 6697; "God of (the) rock," a Reubenite leader:— Elizur(5).

469. אֱלִיצָפָן Elitsaphan or

אֶלְצָפָן Eltsaphan (45d); from 410 and 6845; "God has protected," two Isr.:— Elizaphan(4), Elzaphan(2).

470. אֱלִיקָא Eliqa (45d); from 410 and 7006a; "God of rejection," one of David's heroes:— Elika(1).

471. אֶלְיָקִים Elyaqim (45d); from 410 and 6965; "God sets up," three Isr.:— Eliakim(12).

472. אֱלִישֶׁבַע Elisheba (45d); from 410 and 7650; "God is an oath," the wife of Aaron:— Elisheba(1).

473. אֱלִישָׁה Elishah (47a); of for. or.; a son of Javan, also his desc. and their land:— Elishah(3).

474. אֱלִישׁוּעַ Elishua (46a); from 410 and 3467; "God is salvation," a son of David:— Elishua(2).

475. אֶלְיָשִׁיב Elyashib (46a); from 410 and 7725; "God restores," the name of several Isr.:— Eliashib(15), Eliashib's(1).

476. אֱלִישָׁמָע Elishama (46a); from 410 and 8085; "God has heard," the name of several Isr.:— Elishama(17).

477. אֱלִישָׁע Elisha (46a); contr. from 474; "God is salvation," a well-known Isr. prophet:— Elisha(58).

478. אֱלִישָׁפָט Elishaphat (46a); from 410 and 8199; "God has judged," an Isr.:— Elishaphat(1).

479. אִלֵּךְ illek (1080d); (Ara.) prol. from 412; *these:*— these(11), those(3).

480. אַלְלַי alelay (47d); a prim. interj.; *alas! woe!:*— woe(2).

481. אָלַם alam (47d); of unc. der.; *to bind:*— became speechless(1), become mute(1), binding(1), mute(4), silent(1), speechless(1).

482. אֵלֶם elem (48a); from the same as 481; *silence.*

483. אִלֵּם illem (48a); from the same as 481; *mute* (unable to speak):— mute(4), mute man(1), speechless(1).

484. אַלְמֻגִּים almuggim (38d); of for. or.; perh. *the sandalwood tree:*— almug(3).

485. אֲלֻמָּה alummah (48a); from the same as 481; *a sheaf:*— sheaf(2), sheaves(3).

486. אַלְמוֹדָד Almodad (38d); prob. of for. or.; a son of Joktan, also his desc.:— Almodad(2).

487. אַלַּמֶּלֶךְ Allammelek (47d); from 427 and 4428; "an oak of (the) king," a place in Asher:— Allammelech(1).

488. אַלְמָן alman (48a); from 481; *widowed:*— forsaken(1).

489. אַלְמֹן almon (48a); from 481; *widowhood:*— widowhood(1).

490. אַלְמָנָה almanah (48b); fem. of 488; *a widow:*— fortified(2), widow(37), widow's(5), widowed(1), widows(11).

491. אַלְמָנוּת almanuth (48b); fem. of 488; *widowhood:*— widow's(2), widowhood(1), widows(1).

492. אַלְמֹנִי almoni (48c); from 481; *someone, a certain* (one):— certain*(1), friend*(1), such(1).

493. אֶלְנַעַם Elnaam (46b); from 410 and 5276; "God is pleasantness," the father of two of David's heroes:— Elnaam(1).

494. אֶלְנָתָן Elnathan (46b); from 410 and 5414; "God has given," the name of several Isr.:— Elnathan(7).

495. אֶלָּסָר Ellasar (48c); of for. or.; a country of unknown location:— Ellasar(2).

496. אֶלְעָד Elad (46b); from 410 and 5749b; "God has testified," an Ephraimite:— Elead(1).

497. אֶלְעָדָה Eladah (46b); from 410 and 5710b; "God has adorned," an Ephraimite:— Eleadah(1).

498. אֶלְעוּזַי Eluzay (46b); from 410 and 5756; "God is my strength," one of David's heroes:— Eluzai(1).

499. אֶלְעָזָר Elazar (46b); from 410 and 5826; "God has helped," six Isr.:— Eleazar(72).

500. אֶלְעָלֵא Elale (46c); from 410 and 5927; "God ascends," four Isr.:— Elealeh(5).

501. אֶלְעָשָׂה Elasah (46c); from 410 and 6213a; "God has made," the name of several Isr.:— Elasah(2), Eleasah(4).

502. אָלַף alaph (48c); a prim. root; *to learn:*— learn(1), teach(1), teaches(2).

503. אָלַף alaph (49b, 1120b); denom. vb. from 505; *to produce thousands:*— bring forth(1).

504. אֶלֶף eleph (48c); from 502; *cattle:*— herd(4), oxen(3).

505. אֶלֶף eleph (48d); a prim. root; *a thousand:*— 1,000(18), 1,000,000*(2), 1,005*(1), 1,017*(2), 1,052*(2), 1,100,000*(3), 1,200*(1), 1,222*(1), 1,247*(2), 1,254*(4), 1,290*(1), 1,335*(1), 1,365*(1), 1,400*(2), 1,700*(3), 1,760*(1), 1,775*(2), 10,000*(20), 100,000*(7), 108,100*(2), 12,000*(8), 120,000*(5), 14,000*(1), 14,700*(1), 15,000*(1), 151,450*(2), 153,600*(2), 157,600*(2), 16,000*(2), 16,750*(1), 17,200*(1), 18,000*(7), 180,000*(3), 185,000*(2), 186,400*(3), 2,000(5), 2,056*(1), 2,067*(1), 2,172*(2), 2,200*(1), 2,300*(1), 2,322*(1), 2,400*(2), 2,600*(2), 2,630*(1), 2,700*(1), 2,750*(1), 2,812*(1), 2,818*(1), 20,000*(10), 20,200*(1), 20,800*(1), 200,000*(4), 22,000*(7), 22,034*(1), 22,200*(1), 22,273*(1), 22,600*(1), 23,000*(1), 24,000*(15), 25,000*(16), 25,100*(1), 250,000*(1), 26,000*(2), 27,000*(1), 28,600*(1), 280,000*(2), 3,000*(11), 3,023*(1), 3,200*(1), 3,300*(1), 3,600*(2), 3,630*(1), 3,700*(1), 3,930*(1), 30,000*(5), 30,500*(2), 300,000*(4), 307,500*(2), 32,000*(2), 32,200*(2), 32,500*(1), 337,500*(6), 35,400*(2), 36,000*(3), 37,000*(1), 38,000*(1), 4,000*(3), 4,500*(8), 4,600*(2), 40,000*(5), 40,500*(3), 400,000*(3), 41,500*(2), 42,000*(1), 42,360*(2), 43,730*(1), 44,760*(1), 45,400*(1), 45,600*(1), 45,650*(2), 46,500*(2), 470,000*(1), 5,000*(7), 5,400*(1), 50,000*(2), 50,070*(1), 500,000*(1), 52,700*(1), 53,400*(3), 54,400*(2), 57,400*(2), 59,300*(2), 6,000*(3), 6,200*(1), 6,720*(2), 6,800*(1), 60,000*(1), 60,500*(1), 600,000*(1), 601,730*(2), 603,550*(6), 61,000*(2), 62,700*(2), 64,300*(1), 64,400*(1), 675,000*(3), 7,000*(8), 7,100*(1), 7,337*(2), 7,500*(1), 7,700*(2), 70,000*(4), 72,000*(1), 74,600*(2), 75,000*(1), 76,500*(1), 8,580*(1), 8,600*(1), 80,000*(3), 800,000*(1), 87,000*(1), clan(1), clans(2), divisions(2), eleven*(3), families(2), family(1), million(1), thousand(78), thousand-fold*(1), thousands(41), thousandth(1).

506. אֲלַף alaph (1081a); (Ara.) corr. to 505; *a thousand:*— thousand(2), thousands(2).

507. אֶלֶף Eleph (49b); from 505; a city in Benjamin:— Haeleph(1).

508. אֶלְפַּעַל Elpaal (46c); from 410 and 6466; perh. "God of doing," a Benjamite:— Elpaal(3).

509. אָלַץ alats (49b); a prim. root; *to urge:*— urged(1).

510. אַלְקוּם alqum (39a); of unc. der.; *a band of soldiers:*— army(1).

511. אֶלְקָנָה Elqanah (46c); from 410 and 7069; "God has created," or "God has taken possession," the name of several Isr.:— Elkanah(21).

512. אֶלְקֹשִׁי Elqoshi (49b); of unc. der.; a native of Elkosh:— Elkoshite(1).

513. אֶלְתּוֹלַד Eltolad (39a); from 410 and 3205; "God is generator," a city in S. Judah:— Eltolad(2).

514. אֶלְתְּקֵא Elteqe or

אֶלְתְּקֵה Elteqeh (49c); of unc. der.; a city in Pal.:— Elteke(1), Eltekeh(1).

515. אֶלְתְּקֹן Elteqon (49c); of unc. der.; a city in Pal.:— Eltekon(1).

516. אַל־תַּשְׁחֵת al-tashcheth (1007d); from 408 and 7843; "destroy not," a phrase in Psalm titles.

517. אֵם em (51c); from an unused word; *a mother:*— infancy*(1), mother(145), mother's(67), mothers(5), mothers'(1), parting(1).

518. אִם im (49c); a prim. conjunc.; *if:*— although(2), although*(1), certainly(1), either(1), either an or(1), either their or(2), else*(1), except*(22), however*(1), if(588), if*(1), indeed(1), less than*(1), more of her than*(1), more than*(1), most assuredly*(1), never(2), never*(1), nevertheless*(1), no(6), no means(1), none(1), nor(7), nothing(1), O(1), Oh(2), only(4), only*(7), or(75), rather*(11), should(1), since(4), surely(6), surely there shall be neither(1), surely*(35), than*(2), though(35), though*(2), truly(1), truly*(2), unless*(16), until*(7), when(17), whether(16), whether for or(1), whether it is or(1), whether they or(3), whether*(1), without*(2).

519. אָמָה amah (51a); of unc. der.; *a maid, handmaid:*— female(15), female servant(4), female slave(2), handmaid(2), handmaids(1), maid(8), maids(5), maidservant(19), servant*(1), servants*(6), slave*(4), slaves*(4).

520. אַמָּה ammah (52a); from the same as 517; *an ell, a cubit:*— cubit(25), cubits(204), cubits and a cubit(1), cubits and one cubit(1), cubits by cubit(1), measure(1).

521. אַמָּה ammah (1081a); (Ara.) corr. to 520; *a cubit:*— cubits(4).

522a. אַמָּה Ammah (52c); from the same as 517; a hill in Pal.:— Ammah(1).

522b. אַמָּה ammah (52a); from the same as 517; *a mother city:*— chief city(1).

522c. אַמָּה ammah (52c); perh. from the same as 517; perh. *a holder:*— foundations(1).

523. אֻמָּה ummah (52c); from the same as 517; *a tribe, people:*— people(1), peoples(1), tribes(1).

524. אֻמָּה ummah (1081a); (Ara.) corr. to 523; *a nation:*— nation(1), nations(7).

525. אָמוֹן amon (54c); from 539; *an artificer, architect, master workman:*— artisans(1), master workman(1).

526. אָמוֹן Amon (54c); from 539; "master-workman," three Isr.:— Amon(17).

527. אָמוֹן amon (54c); the same as 525, q.v.

528. אָמוֹן Amon (51b); of for. or.; an Eg. god:— Amon(1), No-amon*(1).

529. אֵמוּן emun or

אֵמֻן emun (53c); from 539; *faithfulness:*— faithful(2), faithfulness(1), trustworthy(2).

530. אֱמוּנָה emunah (53c); from 539; *firmness, steadfastness, fidelity:*— faith(1), faithful(3), faithfully(8), faithfulness(25), honestly(1), responsibility(1), stability(1), steady(1), trust(2), truth(5).

531. אָמוֹץ Amots (55b); from 553; "strong," the father of Isaiah:— Amoz(13).

532a. אָמִי Ami (51b); of unc. der.; an Isr. (the same as 526):— Ami(1).

532b. אֲמִינוֹן Aminon (54c); the same as 550, q.v.

533. אַמִּיץ ammits (55c); from 553; *mighty:*— bravest*(1), mighty(2), strength(1), strong(1), strong one(1).

534. אָמִיר amir (57b); from 559; *the top, summit:*— bough(1), branches(1), topmost*(1).

535. אָמַל amal (51b); a prim. root; *to be weak, languish:*— decays(1), fade away(1), fades(1), fails(2), languish(1), languished(1), languishes(2), languishing(1), pine away(1), pines away(2), wither(2), withered(1).

536. אֻמְלַל umlal (51c); from 535; *feeble:*— pining away(1).

537. אֲמֵלָל amelal (51c); from 535; *feeble:*— feeble(1).

538. אֲמָם Amam (52d); from the same as 517; a place in S. Judah:— Amam(1).

539. אָמַן aman (52d); a prim. root; *to confirm, support:*— believe(26), believed(11), believes(2), bringing(1), carried(1), chronic(1), confirmed(5), doorposts(1), endure(1), enduring(3), established(3), faithful(21), firm(2), fulfilled(1), guardians(3), has assurance(1), have faith(1), have...assurance(1), last(1), lasting(1), nurse(3), put your trust(2), puts...trust(2), reared(1), reliable(1), stand still(1), sure(4), trust(4), trusted(1), trustworthy*(1), unreliable*(1), verified(1).

540. אֲמַן aman (1081a); (Ara.) corr. to 539; *to trust:*— faithful(1), trusted(1), trustworthy(1).

541. אָמַן aman (54d); the same as 3231, q.v.

542. אָמָּן omman (53b); from 539; *a master-workman, artist:*— artist(1).

543. אָמֵן amen (53b); from 539; *verily, truly:*— Amen(28), truth(2).

544. אֹמֶן omen (53b); from 539; *faithfulness:*— perfect faithfulness(1).

545. אָמְנָה omnah (53d); from 539; *bringing up, nourishment:*— care(1).

546. אָמְנָה omnah (53d); from 539; *verily, truly, indeed:*— actually(1), truly(1).

547. אֹמְנָה omnah (52d); part. of 539, q.v.

548. אֲמָנָה amanah (53d); from 539; *faith, support:*— agreement(1), firm regulation(1).

549. אֲמָנָה Amanah (53d); from 539; a river near Damascus (the same as 71), also the region from which it flows:— Amana(1).

550. אַמְנוֹן Amnon (54c); from 539; "faithful," two Isr.:— Amnon(25), Amnon's(3).

551. אָמְנָם omnam (53d); from 539; *verily, truly:*— indeed(1), surely*(1), true(1), truly(5), truth(1).

552. אֻמְנָם umnam (53d); from 539; *verily, truly, indeed:*— indeed(3), indeed*(1), really(1).

553. אָמֵץ amets (54d); a prim. root; *to be stout, strong, bold, alert:*— conquered(1), courageous(11), determined(1), harden(1), hardened(1), increases(1), made his obstinate(1), made firm(1), made haste(2), made strong(1), makes her strong(1), mighty(1), proved...strong(1), raises(1), strengthen(6), strengthened(3), strong(2), stronger(1), summon(1), supported(1), take courage(2).

554. אָמֹץ amots (55b); from 553; *strong:*— strong(1), strong ones(1).

555. אֹמֶץ omets (55b); from 553; *strength:*— stronger(1).

556. אַמְצָה amtsah (55b); from 553; *strength:*— strong support(1).

557. אַמְצִי Amtsi (55c); from 553; two Isr.:— Amzi(2).

558. אֲמַצְיָהוּ Amatsyahu or

אֲמַצְיָה Amatsyah (55c); from 553 and 3050; "Yah is mighty," the name of several Isr.:— Amaziah(40).

559. אָמַר amar (55c); a prim. root; *to utter, say:*— address(1), advised(1), answer(2), answered(50), answers(1), ask(2), asked(4), asking(1), Asserting(1), assigned(1), call(2), called(4), command(1), commanded(14), commanded to say(1), commands(3), consider(1), continued(2), decided(2), declare*(1), declared(2), declared*(1), declares(1), demonstrates(1), designate(1), desired(1), follows(2), gave an order(2), gave the order(2), gave orders(2), indeed say(1), informed(1), intend(2), intended(1), intending(1), meditate(1), mentioned(1), name(1), namely(2), news(1), ordered(6), plainly says(1), promised(6), proposing(2), really thought(1), repeated*(1), replied*(1), requested(1), resolved(3), responded*(7), said(2766), said*(2), say(601), saying(862), saying*(1), says(594), sent word(1), speak(29), speak to you saying(1), speaking(2), speaks(2), specifically say(1), specified(1), spoke(77), spoken(15), still say(1), suppose(1), tell(23), telling(2), tells(1), think(1), thinking(2), thought(17), told(25), utters(1), vaunt(1).

560. אֲמַר amar (1081a); (Ara.) corr. to 559; *to say, tell, command:*— command is given(1), commanded(2), declared(1), gave orders(8), giving orders(1), related(3), said(27), said*(1), say(2), saying(2), speak(1), speaks(1), spoke(7), tell(6), told(2).

561. אֵמֶר emer (56d); from 559; *speech, word:*— arguments(1), chastisement(1), command(1), decreed(1), promise(1), sayings(4), slander*(1), speech(2), thing(1), utterances(1), words(43).

562. אֹמֶר omer (56d); see 561.

563. אִמַּר immar (1081b); (Ara.) perh. from 560; *a lamb:*— lambs(3).

564. אִמֵּר Immer (57b); from 559; the name of several Isr., perh. also a place in Bab.:— Immer(10).

565a. אִמְרָה imrah (57a); from 559; *utterance, speech, word:*— command(1), speech(4), word(25), words(5).

565b. אֶמְרָה emrah (57b); from 559; *utterance, speech, word:*— word(1).

566. אִמְרִי Imri (57c); from 559; perh. "tall" or "eloquent," an Isr. name:— Imri(2).

567. אֱמֹרִי Emori (57b); from 559; perh. "mountain dwellers," a Canaanite tribe:— Amorite(24), Amorites(63).

568. אֲמַרְיָהוּ Amaryahu or

אֲמַרְיָה Amaryah (57c); from 559 and 3050; "Yah has promised," the name of several Isr.:— Amariah(16).

569. אַמְרָפֶל Amraphel (57d); of unc. der.; king of Shinar:— Amraphel(2).

570. אֶמֶשׁ emesh (57d); of unc. der.; *yesterday:*— last night(3), night(1), yesterday(1).

571. אֱמֶת emeth (54a); from 539; *firmness, faithfulness, truth:*— faith(1), faithful(2), faithfully(6), faithfulness(10), lasting(1), nor*(1), right(1), true(18), truly(4), truth(80), truth that you may correctly(1), truthful(2).

572. אַמְתַּחַת amtachath (607d); from 4969; *a sack:*— sack(8), sacks(7).

573. אֲמִתַּי Amittay (54c); from 571; "true," the father of Jonah:— Amittai(2).

574. אֵמְתָן emthan (1080a); the same as 368b, q.v.

575. אָן an (33a); from 370; *where? whither?:*— any place(1), anywhere(1), how(14), nowhere*(1), where(22), wherever(1).

576. אֲנָה anah (1081b); (Ara.) corr. to 589; *I:*— myself(1), personally(1).

577. אָנָּה annah or

אָנָּא anna (58a); of unc. der.; *ah, now! I (we) beseech you!:*— alas(2), beg(1), beseech(7), earnestly pray(1), O(7), please(1).

578. אָנָה anah (58b); a prim. root; *to mourn:*— lament(2).

579. אָנָה anah (58c); a prim. root; *to be opportune, to meet, encounter opportunely:*— befall(1), befalls(1), let him fall(1), seeking a quarrel(1).

580. אֲנוּ anu (59a); a prim. pron.; *we.*

581. אִנּוּן innun (1081c); (Ara.) corr. to 1992a; *they, those:*— those(1).

582. אֱנוֹשׁ enosh (60d); from an unused word; *man, mankind:*— advisers*(2), friends*(1), life(1), man(26), man's(4), mankind(1), men(6), mortal(1), mortal man(1), ordinary(1), scoffers*(1), scorners*(1), soldiers*(3).

583. אֱנוֹשׁ Enosh (60d); from an unused word; "man," a son of Seth:— Enosh(7).

584. אָנַח anach (58d); a prim. root; *to sigh, groan:*— groan(7), groaning(1), groans(1), sigh(2), sighed(1).

585. אֲנָחָה anachah (58d); from 584; *a sighing, groaning:*— groaning(3), groans(1), sighing(5).

586. אֲנַחְנָא anachna (1081c); (Ara.) corr. to 587; *we.*

587. אֲנַחְנוּ anachnu (59d); a prim. pron.; *we:*— ourselves(7).

588. אֲנָחֲרַת Anacharath (58d); of unc. der.; a city in Issachar:— Anaharath(1).

589. אֲנִי ani (58d); a prim. pron.; *I:*— alone(1), Myself(12), myself(5).

590. אֳנִי oni (58b); from an unused word; *ships, a fleet:*— boat(1), fleet(1), fleet of ships(1), ships(4).

591. אֳנִיָּה oniyyah (58b); from the same as 590; *a ship:*— boats(1), sailors*(1), ship(4), ships(25).

592. אֲנִיָּה aniyyah (58b); from 578; *mourning:*— mourning(1), mourning and moaning(1).

593. אֲנִיעָם Aniam (58b); from 578 and 5971a; "lament of people," an Isr. name:— Aniam(1).

594. אֲנָךְ anak (59d); of unc. der.; *to plummet:*— plumb line(3), vertical with a plumb(1).

595. אָנֹכִי anoki (59a); a prim. pron.; *I:*— Myself(2), myself(4).

596. אָנַן anan (59d); a prim. root; *to complain, murmur:*— complain(1), offer complaint(1).

597. אָנַס anas (60a); a prim. root; *to compel, constrain:*— compulsion(1).

598. אֲנַס anas (1081c); (Ara.) a prim. root; *to oppress:*— baffles(1).

599. אָנַף anaph (60a); a prim. root; *to be angry:*— angry(12), become angry(1), been angry(1).

600. אֲנַף anaph (1081d); (Ara.) corr. to 639; *a face:*— face(1), facial(1).

601. אֲנָפָה anaphah (60b); from 599; a ceremonially unclean bird:— heron(2).

602. אָנַק anaq (60b); a prim. root; *to cry, groan:*— groan(4).

603. אֲנָקָה anaqah (60c); from 602; *a crying, groaning:*— groaning(6).

604. אֲנָקָה anaqah (60c); from 602; *a ferret, shrewmouse:*— gecko(1).

605. אָנַשׁ anash (60c); a prim. root; *to be weak, sick:*— desperately sick(1), incurable(6), sick(1), woeful(1).

606. אֱנָשׁ enash (1081d); (Ara.) corr. to 582; *man, mankind:*— human(1), man(11), man's(1), mankind(8), men(4).

607. אַנְתָּה antah (1082a); (Ara.) corr. to 859; *you* (sing.).

608. אַנְתּוּן antun (1082a); (Ara.) corr. to 864b; *you* (pl.).

609. אָסָא Asa (61d); from an unused word; perh. "healer," an Isr. name:— Asa(54), Asa's(4).

610. אָסוּךְ asuk (692a); from 5480a; *a flask:*— jar(1).

611. אָסוֹן ason (62a); from an unused word; *mischief, evil, harm:*— harm(3), injury(2).

612. אֵסוּר esur (64a); from 631; *a band, bond:*— bonds(1), chains(1), jail*(1).

613. אֱסוּר esur (1082b); (Ara.) corr. to 612; *a band, bond:*— band(2), imprisonment(1).

614. אָסִיף asiph (63b); from 622; *ingathering, harvest:*— ingathering(2).

615. אָסִיר asir (64a); from 631; *a bondman, prisoner:*— prisoner(2), prisoners(10).

616. אַסִּיר assir (64b); from 631; *prisoners:*— captives(1), prisoner(1), prisoners(2).

617. אַסִּיר Assir (64b); from 631; an Isr. name:— Assir(4).

618. אָסָם asam (62a); from an unused word; *a storehouse:*— barns(2).

619. אַסְנָה Asnah (62a); of unc. der.; perh. "thornbush," one of the Nethinim:— Asnah(1).

620. אָסְנַפַּר Asenappar (1082a); (Ara.) of for. or.; an Assyr. king:— Osnappar(1).

621. אָסְנַת Asenath (62a); of for. or.; perh. "belonging to Neith," the wife of Joseph:— Asenath(3).

622. אָסַף asaph (62a); a prim. root; *to gather, remove:*— again(1), all together(1), amassed(1), assemble(9), assembled(12), assembling(1), attached(1), bring(1), brought(2), brought together(1), collect(1), collected(2), collects(1), cure(4), destroy(1), disappear(1), drew(1), garner(1), gather(33), gathered(81), gathering(1), gathers(3), lose(3), pick(1), put(1), put them all together(1), reaper(1), rear guard(5), received(2), returned(1), surely assemble(1), surely gathered(1), take(3), take my away(1), take away(2), taken away(5), took(1), victims(1), wane(1), withdraw(3), withdrawn(1), withdraws(1), withdrew(1).

623. אָסָף Asaph (63a); from 622; "gatherer," the name of several Isr.:— Asaph(34).

624. אָסֹף asoph (63b); from 622; *a store* (i.e. a supply of provisions):— storehouse(2), storehouses(1).

625. אֹסֶף oseph (63a); from 622; *a gathering:*— gathering(1), gathers(1), pickers(1).

626. אֲסֵפָה asephah (63b); from 622; *a collecting, gathering:*— together(1).

627. אֲסֻפָּה asuppah (63b); from 622; *a collection:*— collections(1).

628. אֲסַפְסֻף asaphsuph (63c); from 622; *a collection, rabble:*— rabble(1).

629. אָסְפַּרְנָא osparna (1082a); (Ara.) of for. or.; *thoroughly, with* (all) *diligence:*— all diligence(2), diligently(2), full(1), great care(1), strictly(1).

630. אַסְפָּתָא Aspatha (63c); of for. or.; a son of Haman:— Aspatha(1).

631. אָסַר asar (63c); a prim. root; *to tie, bind, imprison:*— began(1), begin(1), bind(8), bind me tightly(1), bind you fast(1), binds(3), bound(28), captivated(1), captured(1), confined(4), get ready(1), girded(1), harness(1), hitch(1), hitched(1), imprison(1), imprisoned(2), made his ready(2), prepare(1), prepared(1), prison*(3), prisoners(2), taken captive(1), tied(2), ties(1).

632. אִסָּר issar (64b); from 631; *a bond, binding obligation:*— binding(1), binding obligation(1), obligation(6), obligations(3).

633. אֱסָר esar (1082b); (Ara.) from the same as 613; *an interdict:*— injunction(7).

634. אֵסַר־חַדֹּן Esarchaddon (64d); of for. or.; "Ashur has given a brother," an Assyr. king:— Esarhaddon(3).

635. אֶסְתֵּר Ester (64d); of for. or.; "star," Ahasuerus' queen who delivered Isr.:— Esther(52), Esther's(3).

636. אָע a (1082b); (Ara.) corr. to 6086; *wood:*— beams(1), timber(1), timbers(1), wood(2).

637. אַף aph (64d); a prim. conjunc.; *also, yea:*— all(1), also(42), even(10), furthermore(2), how(9), how much(1), how much less(7), how much more(4), indeed(20), indeed*(2), less(2), more(1), more*(1), much more*(8), much*(10), no(1), really(1), scarcely*(3), so(2), spite*(1), surely(9), surely*(1), then*(1), though(1), too(2), truly(2), turn(1), well(2), yes(2), yet(1).

638. אַף aph (1082b); (Ara.) corr. to 637; *also:*— also(4).

639. אַף aph (60a); from 599; *a nostril, nose, face, anger:*— anger(205), angry(2), angry*(5), before(2), breath(1), countenance(1), double(1), face(15), faces(4), forbearance*(1), ground(1), nose(10), noses(1), nostril(1), nostrils(13), quick-tempered*(1), snout(1), wrath(8), wrath with his anger(1).

640. אָפַד aphad (65d); a denom. vb. from the same as 646; *to gird on the ephod:*— gird(1), tied(1).

641. אֵפֹד Ephod (65d); from the same as 646; an Isr.:— ephod(1).

642. אֲפֻדָּה aphuddah (65d); from the same as 646; *an ephod:*— plated(1).

643. אַפֶּדֶן appeden (66a); of for. or.; *a palace:*— royal pavilion(1).

644. אָפָה aphah (66a); a prim. root; *to bake:*— anger(1), bake(6), baked(8), baker(8), bakers(1), bakers'(1).

645. אֵפוֹ epho (66b); a prim. particle; *then:*— now(4), so(1), then(8), well then(1).

646. אֵפוֹד ephod (65b); from an unused word; *an ephod:*— ephod(49).

647a. אֲפוּנָה aphunah (67a); from the same as 212; perh. *helpless:*— overcome(1).

647b. אֲפִיחַ Aphiach (66c); of unc. der.; an Isr.:— Aphiah(1).

648. אָפִיל aphil (66d); from the same as 652; *late:*— late(1).

649. אַפַּיִם Appayim (60b); from 599; an Isr.:— Appaim(2).

650. אָפִיק aphiq (67d); from 662; *a channel:*— brooks(3), channels(3), ravines(6), streams(3), strong(1), torrents(1), tubes(1).

651. אָפֵל aphel (66c); from the same as 652; *gloomy:*— gloom(1).

652. אֹפֶל ophel (66c); from an unused word; *darkness, gloom:*— darkness(6), gloom(3).

653. אֲפֵלָה aphelah (66c); from the same as 652; *darkness, gloominess, calamity:*— darkness(4), gloom(5), thick(1).

654. אֶפְלָל Ephlal (813d); from 6419; an Isr.:— Ephlal(2).

655. אֹפֶן ophen (67a); from the same as 212; *circumstance, condition:*— circumstances(1).

656. אָפֵס aphes (67a); a prim. root; *to cease, fail, come to an end:*— ceased(1), come to an end(2), gone(2).

657. אֶפֶס ephes (67a); from 656; *a ceasing:*— dearth(1), ends(14), however(2), lack(1), less...nothing(1), neither(1), nevertheless*(3), no more(1), no one(6), no other(1), non-existent(1), nor(1), nothing(2), only(2), there(1), there is no one(3), there is none(1), without(2), without cause(1), worthless(1).

658a. אֹפֶס ophes (67b); from 656; *the two extremities* (i.e. the soles of the feet or the ankles):— ankles(1).

658b. אֶפֶס דַּמִּים Ephes Dammim (67c); from 657 and 1818; a place in Judah:— Ephes-dammim(1).

659. אֶפַע epha (67c); of unc. der., perh. for 657, q.v.

660. אֶפְעֶה epheh (821b); from 6463; (a kind of) *viper:*— snake(1), viper(1), viper's(1).

661. אָפַף aphaph (67c); a prim. root; *to surround, encompass:*— encompassed(4), surrounded(1).

662. אָפַק aphaq (67c); a prim. root; *to hold, be strong:*— control(1), controlled(2), forced(1), restrain(1), restrained(2).

663. אֲפֵק Apheq (67d); from 662; perh. "fortress," the name of several places in Pal.:— Aphek(8), Aphik(1).

664. אֲפֵקָה Apheqah (68a); from 663; perh. "fortress," a city in Pal.:— Aphekah(1).

665. אֵפֶר epher (68a); from an unused word; *ashes:*— ashes(21), dust(1).

666. אֲפֵר apher (68b); from an unused word; *a covering, bandage:*— bandage(2).

667. אֶפְרֹחַ ephroach (827b); from 6524a; *a young one:*— young(2), young ones(2).

668. אַפִּרְיוֹן appiryon (68b); of for. or.; *a sedan, litter, palanquin:*— sedan chair(1).

669. אֶפְרַיִם Ephrayim (68b); from the same as 666; a son of Joseph, also his desc. and their territory:— Ephraim(176), Ephraim's(4).

670. אֲפָרְסָיֵא apharesaye (1082b); (Ara.) of for. or.; *official:*— secretaries(1).

671a. אֲפָרְסְכָיֵא Apharesekaye (1082b); (Ara.) from the same as 670; *official:*— officials(2).

671b. אֲפַרְסַתְכָיֵא apharesattekaye (1082c); (Ara.) from the same as 670; *official:*— lesser governors(1).

672. אֶפְרָת Ephrath or **אֶפְרָתָה Ephrathah** (68c); from the same as 666; an Isr. woman, also the name of several places in Pal.:— Ephrath(5), Ephrathah(5).

673. אֶפְרָתִי Ephrathi (68d); from the same as 666; a desc. of Ephraim, also an inhab. of Ephrath:— Ephraimite(3), Ephrathite(1), Ephrathites(1).

674. אַפְּתֹם appethom (1082c); (Ara.) of for. or.; perh. *treasury:*— revenue(1).

675. אֶצְבּוֹן Etsbon (69a); of unc. der.; two Isr.:— Ezbon(2).

676. אֶצְבַּע etsba (840c); from an unused word; *a finger:*— finger(19), fingers(10), fingers and toes(1), toes(1).

677. אֶצְבַּע etsba (1109c); (Ara.) corr. to 676; *a finger, toe:*— fingers(1), toes(2).

678. אָצִיל atsil (69c); from the same as 681a; *a side, corner, a chief:*— nobles(1), remotest parts(1).

679. אַצִּיל atstsil (69c); from the same as 681a; *a joining, joint:*— armpits*(1), long(1), wrists*(1).

680. אָצַל atsal (69b); a denom. vb. from the same as 681a; *to lay aside, reserve, withdraw, withhold:*— refuse(1), reserved(1), set back(1), take(1), took(1).

681a. אֵצֶל etsel (69a); from an unused word; *a joining together, proximity:*— away*(1), beside(39), near(8), side(1).

681b. אָצֵל Etsel (69b); part of the proper name 1018, q.v.

682a. אָצֵל Atsel (69b); from the same as 681a; a desc. of Jonathan:— Azel(6).

682b. אָצֵל Atsel (69c); from the same as 681a; a place in Judah:— Azel(1).

683. אֲצַלְיָהוּ Atsalyahu (69d); from 680 and 3050; "Yah has reserved," an Isr.:— Azaliah(2).

684. אֹצֶם Otsem (69d); of unc. der.; two Isr.:— Ozem(2).

685. אֶצְעָדָה etsadah (858a); from the same as 6807b; *an armlet:*— armlets(1), bracelet(1).

686. אָצַר atsar (69d); a prim. root; *to lay up, store up:*— appointed(1), hoard(1), laid up in store(2), stored(1).

687. אֵצֶר Etser (69d); from 686; "treasure," a chief of the Horites:— Ezer(5).

688. אֶקְדָּח eqdach (869b); from 6919; *a fiery glow, sparkle:*— crystal(1).

689. אַקּוֹ aqqo (70a); of unc. der.; perh. *a wild goat:*— wild goat(1).

690. אֲרָא Ara (70b); of unc. der.; a desc. of Asher:— Ara(1).

691. אֶרְאֵל erel (72a); of unc. der.; perh. *a hero:*— brave men(1).

692. אַרְאֵלִי Areli (72a); of unc. der.; a son of Gad, also his desc.:— Areli(2), Arelites(1).

693. אָרַב arab (70b); a prim. root; *to lie in wait:*— ambush(15), ambushes(2), lay in wait(3), lie in ambush(1), lie in wait(7), lies in wait(1), lurked(1), lurks(4), lying in ambush(1), lying in wait(3), set an ambush(2), waited in ambush(1).

694. אֲרָב Arab (70c); from 693; a city in Pal.:— Arab(1).

695. אֶרֶב ereb (70c); from 693; *a lying in wait, a covert, lair:*— lair(1), lie in wait(1).

696. אֹרֶב oreb (70c); from 693; *an ambuscade:*— ambush(1), plotting(1).

697. אַרְבֶּה arbeh (916a); from 7235a; (a kind of) *locust:*— locust(8), locusts(11), swarming locust(5).

698. אָרְבָּה orbah (70c); from 693; *an artifice:*— trickery(1).

699. אֲרֻבָּה arubbah (70c); from 693; *a lattice, window, sluice:*— chimney(1), floodgates(2), lattices(1), windows(5).

700. אֲרֻבּוֹת Arubboth (70d); from 693; a place in Pal.:— Arubboth(1).

701. אַרְבִּי Arbi (70c); of unc. der.; a native of Arab:— Arbite(1).

702. אַרְבַּע arba (916d); of unc. der.; *four:*— 1,254*(4), 1,400*(2), 14,000*(1), 14,700*(1), 151,450*(1), 186,400*(1), 2,400*(2), 22,034*(1), 24*(1), 24,000*(15), 284*(1), 324*(1), 35,400*(2), 4,000*(3), 4,500*(8), 4,600*(2), 400*(5), 400,000*(3), 410*(1), 42,360*(2), 435*(2), 44,760*(1), 45,400*(1), 450*(2), 454*(2), 468*(1), 470,000*(1), 5,400*(1), 53,400*(3), 54,400*(3), 57,400*(2), 64,300*(1), 64,400*(2), 74*(2), 74,600*(2), any of their four(1), four(167), four things(1), four-fifths*(1), four-footed*(1), fours(4), fourteen*(17), fourteenth*(23), fourth(4), thirty-four*(1), twenty-four*(3), twenty-fourth*(9).

703. אַרְבַּע arba (1112c); (Ara.) corr. to 702; *four:*— four(7).

704. אַרְבַּע Arba (917b); part of the place name 7153, q.v.

705. אַרְבָּעִים arbaim (917b); from the same as 702; *forty:*— 1,247*(2), 140*(1), 148*(1), 242*(1), 245*(3), 345*(2), 40,000*(5), 40,500*(3), 41,500*(2), 42*(2), 42,000*(1), 43,730*(1), 44,760*(1), 45*(1), 45,400*(1), 45,600*(1), 45,650*(2), 46,500*(2), 642*(2), 648*(1), 743*(2), 745*(1), 845*(1), 945*(1), fortieth(3), forty(73), forty times(1), forty-eight*(2), forty-first*(1), forty-five*(2), forty-nine*(1), forty-one*(4), forty-seven*(1), forty-two*(3), twenty-two*(1).

706. אַרְבַּעְתַּיִם arbatayim (917a); from 702; *fourfold:*— fourfold(1).

707. אָרַג arag (70d); a prim. root; *to weave:*— weave(2), weaver(2), weaver's(4), weavers(1), weaving(1), woven(3).

708. אֶרֶג ereg (71a); from 707; *a loom:*— loom(1), weaver's shuttle(1).

709a. אַרְגָּב argab (918d); an incorrect reading found in some sources.

709b. אַרְגֹּב Argob (918d); from the same as 7263; "heap," a district of Bashan, also an Isr.:— Argob(5).

710. אַרְגְּוָן argevan (71a); of unc. der.; *purple:*— purple(1).

711. אַרְגְּוָן argevan (1082c); (Ara.) of unc. der.; *purple, red-purple:*— purple(3).

712. אַרְגַּז argaz (919c); from 7264; *a box, chest:*— box(3).

713. אַרְגָּמָן argaman (71a); of unc. der.; *purple, red-purple:*— purple(36), purple fabric(1), purple threads(1).

714. אַרְדְּ Ard (71b); of unc. der.; a desc. of Benjamin:— Ard(2).

715. אַרְדּוֹן Ardon (71b); of unc. der.; a son of Caleb:— Ardon(1).

716. אַרְדִּי Ardi (71b); from 714; a desc. of Ard:— Ardites(1).

717. אָרָה arah (71c); a prim. root; *to gather, pluck:*— gathered(1), pick(1).

718. אֲרוּ aru (1082d); (Ara.) of unc. der.; *lo!:*— behold(5).

719. אַרְוַד Arvad (71c); of unc. der.; a city of Phoenicia:— Arvad(2).

720. אֲרוֹד Arod (71b); of unc. der.; a son of Gad:— Arod(1).

721. אַרְוָדִי Arvadi (71c); from 719; inhab. of Arvad:— Arvadite(1), Arvadites(1).

722. אֲרוֹדִי Arodi (71b); of unc. der.; a son of Gad, also desc. of Arod:— Arodi(1), Arodites(1).

723a. אֻרְוָה urvah (71d); from 717, see 745b; *a manger, crib:*— pens(1), sheepfolds(1), stalls(2).

723b. אָרוּז aruz (72d); from the same as 730; *firm, strong:*— tightly(1).

724. אֲרוּכָה arukah (74a); from 748; *healing, restoration:*— health(3), recovery(1), repair(2).

725. אֲרוּמָה Arumah (72b); of unc. der.; a place near Shechem:— Arumah(1).

726. אֲרוֹמִים Aromim (10c); scribal error for 130, q.v.

727. אָרוֹן aron (75b); of unc. der.; *a chest, ark:*— ark(194), chest(6), coffin(1).

728. אֲרַוְנָה Aravnah (72b); of unc. der.; a Jebusite:— Araunah(9).

729. אָרַז araz (72d); see 723b.

730. אֶרֶז erez (72c); from an unused word (729); *a cedar:*— cedar(48), cedars(25).

731. אַרְזָה arzah (72d); fem. of 730; *cedar panels, cedar work:*— cedar work(1).

732. אָרַח arach (72d); a prim. root; *to wander, journey, go:*— goes(1), traveler(1), traveler*(1), wayfarer(1), wayfarers'(1).

733. אָרַח Arach (73b); from 732; perh. "traveler," an Isr. name:— Arah(4).

734. אֹרַח orach (73a); from 732; *a way, path:*— caravans(1), childbearing*(1), course(1), highways(1), path(13), paths(19), traveler(1), way(15), ways(6).

735. אֹרַח orach (1082d); (Ara.) corr. to 734; *a way:*— ways(2).

736. אֹרְחָה orechah (73c); act. part. of 732; *a traveling company, caravan:*— caravan(1), caravans(1).

737. אֲרֻחָה aruchah (73c); pass. part. of 732; *a meal, allowance:*— allowance(4), dish(1), ration(1).

738. אֲרִי ari (71c); from 717; *a lion:*— lion(14), lion's(1), lions(15), lions'(1).

739. אֲרִיאֵל Ariel (72a); from 738 and 410; "lioness of El," an Isr. name, also a man of Moab:— Ariel(3).

740. אֲרִיאֵל Ariel (72a); from 738 and 410; "lioness of El," a symbolic name for Jer.:— Ariel(5).

741. אֲרִאֵיל ariel (72b); from an unused word; *hearth, altar-hearth:*— altar hearth(3).

742. אֲרִידַי Ariday (71c); of for. or.; a son of Haman:— Aridai(1).

743a. אֲרִידָתָא Aridatha (71c); of for. or.; a son of Haman:— Aridatha(1).

743b. אַרְיֵה aryeh (71d); from 717; *a lion:*— lion(41), lion's(4), lions(2).

744. אַרְיֵה aryeh (1082c); (Ara.) corr. to 738; *a lion:*— lion(1), lions(3), lions'(6).

745a. אַרְיֵה Aryeh (72a); from 717; "lion," an Isr.:— Arieh(1).

745b. אֻרְיָה uryah (71d); the same as 723a, q.v.

746a. אַרְיוֹךְ Aryok (73c); of for. or.; king of Ellasar:— Arioch(2).

746b. אַרְיוֹךְ Aryok (1082d); (Ara.) of for. or.; a Bab. name:— Arioch(5).

747a. אֻרִים urim (22a); from 215; *region of light:*— east(1).

747b. אֲרִיסַי Arisay (73c, 1120d); of for. or.; a son of Haman:— Arisai(1).

748. אָרַךְ arak (73c); a prim. root; *to be long:*— continue(1), delay(1), endure*(1), endures(1), lengthen(3), lengthened(1), lingered(2), live(2), long(5), long*(3), makes him slow(1), prolong(8), prolonged(4), prolongs(1), stick(1), survived*(2).

749. אֲרַךְ arak or

אֲרִיךְ arik (1082d); (Ara.) of unc. der.; *fitting, proper:*— fitting(1).

750. אָרֵךְ arek (74a); from 748; *long:*— long(1), patience(2), slow(10), who is slow(2).

751. אֶרֶךְ Erek (74b); of for. or.; a city in Bab.:— Erech(1).

752. אָרֹךְ arok (74a); from 748; *long:*— long(2), longer(1).

753. אֹרֶךְ orek (73d); from 748; *length:*— base(1), forbearance*(1), forever*(1), forevermore*(1), high(1), length(59), long(29), so long*(1).

754. אַרְכָּא arka (not included); see 755b:— extension(1), prolonging(1).

755a. אַרְכֻבָּה arkubbah (1085c); (Ara.) from 1289; *the knee:*— knees(1).

755b. אַרְכָה arkah (1082d); (Ara.) of unc. der.; *a lengthening, prolonging.*

756. אַרְכְּוָיֵ Arkevaye (1083a); (Ara.) from 751; inhab. of Erech:— men of Erech(1).

757. אַרְכִּי Arki (74b); of unc. der.; a native of a place in Pal.:— Archite(5), Archites(1).

758. אֲרָם Aram (74b); of unc. der.; Syria and its inhab., also the names of a son of Shem, a grandson of Nahor, and an Isr.:— Aram(65), Aram-maacah*(1), Arameans(64).

759. אַרְמוֹן armon (74d); of unc. der.; *a citadel:*— castle(1), citadel(2), citadels(13), fortified buildings(1), fortified towers(1), palace(3), palaces(9), palatial dwellings(1), towers(2).

760. אֲרָם צוֹבָה Aram Tsobah (74b, 844b); see 758 and 6678.

761. אֲרַמִּי Arammi (74c); from 758; an inhab. of Aram (Syria):— Aramean(8), Arameans(4).

762. אֲרָמִית Aramith (74c); fem. of 761; the language of Aram (Syria):— Aramaic(5).

763. אֲרַם נַהֲרַיִם Aram Naharayim (74c); from 758 and 5104; "Aram of (the) two rivers," a district of Aram (Syria):— Mesopotamia(5).

764. אַרְמֹנִי Armoni (74d); from the same as 759; a son of Saul:— Armoni(1).

765. אֲרָן Aran (75a); of unc. der.; an Edomite:— Aran(2).

766. אֹרֶן oren (75a); from the same as 765; *fir, cedar:*— fir(1).

767. אֹרֶן Oren (75a); from the same as 765; "fir tree," a desc. of Judah:— Oren(1).

768. אַרְנֶבֶת arnebeth (58a); from an unused word; *a hare:*— rabbit(2).

769. אַרְנוֹן Arnon (75a); from the same as 765; "a roaring stream," a wadi and stream in Moab:— Arnon(25).

770. אַרְנָן Arnan (75a); from the same as 765; a desc. of David:— Arnan(1).

771. אָרְנָן Ornan (75a); from the same as 765; a Jebusite:— Ornan(12).

772. אֲרַע ara (1083a); (Ara.) corr. to 776; *the earth:*— earth(15), ground(3), inferior(1), land(1).

773. אַרְעִי ari (1083a); (Ara.) from 772; *the bottom:*— bottom(1).

774. אַרְפָּד Arpad (75d); of for. or.; a city in Aram (Syria):— Arpad(6).

775. אַרְפַּכְשַׁד Arpakshad (75d); of unc. der.; third son of Shem, also the region settled by him:— Arpachshad(9).

776. אֶרֶץ erets (75d); a prim. root; *earth, land:*— common(1), countries(15), countries and their lands(1), country(44), countryside(1), distance*(3), dust(1), earth(655), earth the ground(1), earth's(1), fail*(1), floor(1), ground(119), land(1581), lands(57), lands have their land(2), open(1), other*(2), piece(1), plateau*(1), region(1), territories(1), wild(1), world(3).

777. אַרְצָא Artsa (76c); from 776; an Isr.:— Arza(1).

778. אֲרַק araq (1083a); (Ara.) a form of 772; *the earth:*— earth(2).

779. אָרַר arar (76c); a prim. root; *to curse:*— brings a curse(6), curse(8), curse is cursed(1), cursed(40), cursed be those who curse(1), cursed is everyone who curses(1), cursed woman(1), utterly curse(1).

780. אֲרָרַט Ararat (76d); of for. or.; a district in E. Armenia:— Ararat(4).

781. אָרַשׂ aras (76d); a prim. root; *to betroth:*— betroth(4), betrothed(1), engaged(6).

782. אֲרֶשֶׁת aresheth (77a); from an unused word; *a desire, request:*— request(1).

783a. אַרְתַּחְשַׁשְׂתָּא Artachshasta (77a); of for. or.; a son and successor of Xerxes, king of Persia:— Artaxerxes(9).

783b. אַרְתַּחְשַׁשְׂתָּא Artachshast (1083a); (Ara.) of for. or.; a son and successor of Xerxes, king of Persia:— Artaxerxes(5), Artaxerxes'(1).

784. אֵשׁ esh (77b); a prim. root; *a fire:*— blazing(1), burned*(1), burning(1), burning coals(1), fiery(1), fire(362), fires(2), flame(1), flaming(3), flashing(1), man(1).

785. אֵשׁ esh or
אֶשָּׁא eshsha (1083b); (Ara.) corr. to 784; *a fire:*— fire(1).

786. אִשׁ ish (78a); corr. to 3426; a questionable reading found in Masoretic text.

787. אֹשׁ osh (1083b); (Ara.) prob. of for. or.; *a foundation:*— foundations(3).

788. אַשְׁבֵּל Ashbel (78a); of unc. der.; the second son of Benjamin:— Ashbel(3).

789. אַשְׁבֵּלִי Ashbeli (78b); from 788; desc. of Ashbel:— Ashbelites(1).

790. אֶשְׁבָּן Eshban (78b); of unc. der.; son of an Edomite leader:— Eshban(2).

791. אַשְׁבֵּעַ Ashbea (990a); from the same as 7650; "adjurer," an Isr.:— Beth-ashbea*(1).

792. אֶשְׁבַּעַל Eshbaal (36b); from 376 and 1168a; "man of Baal," a son of Saul:— Eshbaal(2).

793. אֶשֶׁד eshed (78b); from an unused word; *a foundation, bottom, lower part:*— slope(1).

794. אֲשֵׁדָה ashedah (78b); fem. of 793; *a foundation,* (mountain) *slope:*— slopes(6).

795. אַשְׁדּוֹד Ashdod (78b); of for. or.; a city of the Philistines:— Ashdod(17).

796. אַשְׁדּוֹדִי Ashdodi (78c); from 795; an inhab. of Ashdod:— Ashdod(1), Ashdodite(1), Ashdodites(3).

797. אַשְׁדּוֹדִית Ashdodith (78c); fem. of 796; *in the language of Ashdod:*— language of Ashdod(1).

798. אַשְׁדּוֹת הַפִּסְגָּה Ashdoth Happisgah (78b); see 794 and 6449.

799. אֵשׁ דָּת esh dath (77d); from 784 and 1881; *fire of a law:*— flashing lightning(1).

800. אֶשָּׁה eshshah (77d); fem. of 784; *a fire:*— fire(1).

801. אִשֶּׁה ishsheh (77d); from 784; *an offering made by fire:*— fire(5), offering by fire(45), offerings(3), offerings by fire(15).

802. אִשָּׁה ishshah (61a); from an unused word; *woman, wife, female:*— adulteress*(2), any woman(1), childbearing*(1), each(3), each one(1), each woman(1), every(1), everyone(1), female(3), girls*(1), harem*(5), harlot's*(2), harlot*(3), marriage(9), married(3), married*(6), marry*(3), none*(1), one(8), widow(7), wife(274), wife and his wives(2), wife and the wives(1), wife or a woman(1), wife's(8), wives(100), woman(203), woman of the wives(1), woman's(6), women(104), women as wives(1).

803. אֲשׁוּיָה ashuyah (78c); see 806b.

804a. אָשׁוּר ashur (81a); from 833; *step, going:*— footsteps(1), path(1), steps(5).

804b. אַשּׁוּר Ashshur (78d); of unc. der.; the second son of Shem, also the people of Asshur, also the land of Assyr.:— Asshur(5), Assyria(132), Assyrian(5), Assyrians(6), Assyrians*(3).

805a. אֲשׁוּרִי Ashuri (79a); from 804b; desc. of Asshur, also a region of Isr.:— Ashurites(1).

805b. אַשּׁוּרִם Ashshurim (78d); of unc. der.; an Arab tribe:— Asshurim(1).

806a. אַשְׁחוּר Ashchur (1007b); from 7835; "black," an Isr.:— Ashhur(2).

806b. אָשְׁיָה asheyah (78c); from an unused word; *a buttress:*— pillars(1).

807. אֲשִׁימָא Ashima (79a); of for. or.; a god of Hamath:— Ashima(1).

808. אָשִׁישׁ ashish (84b); see 809.

809. אֲשִׁישָׁה ashishah (84b); from 847a; *a raisin cake:*— cakes(1), raisin cake(1), raisin cakes(2), raisin*(1), raisins(1).

810. אֶשֶׁךְ eshek (79a); of unc. der.; *a testicle:*— testicles(1).

811. אֶשְׁכּוֹל eshkol (79a); of unc. der.; *a cluster:*— cluster(5), clusters(4).

812. אֶשְׁכֹּל Eshkol (79b); from the same as 811; an Amorite, also a region of Hebron:— Eshcol(6).

813. אַשְׁכְּנַז Ashkenaz (79b); of unc. der.; a son of Gomer, also his desc. and their land:— Ashkenaz(3).

814. אֶשְׁכָּר eshkar (1016d); of unc. der.; *a gift:*— gifts(1), payment(1).

815. אֵשֶׁל eshel (79b); from an unused word; *a tamarisk tree:*— tamarisk tree(3).

816. אָשַׁם asham (79c); a prim. root; *to offend, be guilty:*— acknowledge their guilt(1), bear their guilt(1), became guilty(1), become guilty(3), becomes guilty(4), certainly guilty(1), condemned(2), desolate(1), did wrong(1), found guilty(1), go(1), guilty(9), held guilty(3), hold them guilty(1), incurred grievous guilt(1), suffer(1), unpunished*(1), wronged(1).

817. אָשָׁם asham (79d); from 816; *offense, guilt:*— guilt(2), guilt offering(38), guilt offerings(1), guilty deeds(1), sin(1), wrong(3).

818. אָשֵׁם ashem (79d); from 816; *guilty:*— guilty(2), offense(1), one who(1), one who is guilty(1).

819. אַשְׁמָה ashmah (80a); fem. of 817; *wrongdoing, guiltiness:*— bring guilt(1), cause of guilt(1), guilt(12), guilt offering(1), incur guilt(1), transgressions(1), wrongs(1).

820. אַשְׁמַנִּים ashmannim (1032c); from 8080; perh. *stout:*— who are vigorous(1).

821. אַשְׁמֹרֶת ashmoreth or
אַשְׁמוּרָה ashmurah (1038a); from 8104; *a watch:*— watch(4), watches(3).

822. אֶשְׁנָב eshnab (1039d); of unc. der.; *a window lattice:*— lattice(2).

823. אַשְׁנָה Ashnah (80b); from an unused word; two cities in Judah:— Ashnah(2).

824. אֶשְׁעָן Eshan (1043d); from 8172; "support," a place in Judah:— Eshan(1).

825. אַשָּׁף ashshaph (80b); a prim. root; *a conjurer, necromancer:*— conjurers(2).

826. אָשַׁף ashaph (1083b); (Ara.) corr. to 825; *a conjurer, enchanter:*— conjurer(1), conjurers(5).

827. אַשְׁפָּה ashpah (80c); of unc. der.; *a quiver* (for arrows):— quiver(6).

828. אַשְׁפְּנַז Ashpenaz (80c); of for. or.; a Bab. eunuch:— Ashpenaz(1).

829. אֶשְׁפָּר eshpar (80c); of unc. der.; perh. *cake* or *roll:*— dates(1), portion(1).

830. אַשְׁפֹּת ashpoth (1046b); from the same as 8239; *an ash heap, refuse heap, dunghill:*— ash(2), ash pits(1), refuse(4).

831. אַשְׁקְלוֹן Ashqelon (80c); of for. or.; a city of the Philistines:— Ashkelon(12).

832. אֶשְׁקְלוֹנִי Eshqeloni (80d); from 831; inhab. of Ashkelon:— Ashkelonite(1).

833. אָשַׁר ashar (80d); of prim. root; *to go straight, go on, advance:*— bless(1), call him blessed(1), call the blessed(1), call you blessed(1), called her blessed(1), called me blessed(1), called blessed(1), direct(1), guide(2), guided(1), happy(2), proceed(2), reprove(1).

834. אֲשֶׁר asher (81c); a prim. pron.; *who, which, that:*— although(1), anyone(1), because(45), because*(73), before*(3), concerning*(1), deadly*(1), everything*(2), everywhere*(2), how(24), how*(6), if(8), inasmuch(1), inasmuch*(2), just(1), just*(6), much(1), powder*(1), reason(1), set(1), since(3), since*(5), so(9), so*(1), steward*(4), storehouses(1), such(8), such*(2), than*(1), therefore(1), these(2), this(1), though*(1), unless*(1), until*(35), what(166), what*(8), whatever(16), whatever*(40), when(44), when*(1), whenever(1), where(49), where you how(1), where*(136), whereas*(1), whereby(1), wherein(1), wherever(4), wherever*(27), which(1925), which he and how(1), which*(1), whichever(1), while(1), while those who(1), who(1), who(850), whoever(4), whoever*(13), whom(345), whom*(1), whomever(1), whomever*(3), whose(80), whose remains when(1), why(2).

835. אֶשֶׁר **esher** (80d); from 833; *happiness, blessedness:*— blessed(41), happy(4).

836. אָשֵׁר **Asher** (81a); from 833; "happy one," a son of Jacob, also the tribe descended from him, also perh. a city in Pal.:— Asher(43).

837. אֹשֶׁר **osher** (81a); from 833; *happiness:*— happy(1).

838. אַשֻּׁר **ashshur** (81a); from 833; *step, going:*— step(1), steps(1).

839. אֲשֻׁר **ashur** or

אֲשֻׁרִים **ashurim** (81b); from 833; perh. *boxwood* (a kind of wood):— boxwood(1).

840. אֲשַׂרְאֵל **Asarel** (77b); of unc. der.; a desc. of Judah:— Asarel(1).

841. אֲשַׂרְאֵלָה **Asarelah** (77b); of unc. der.; a son of Asaph:— Asharelah(1).

842. אֲשֵׁרָה **Asherah** (81b); of for. or.; a Phoenician goddess, also an image of the same:— Asherah(18), Asherim(20), Asheroth(2).

843. אָשֵׁרִי **Asheri** (81b); from 836; desc. of Asher:— Asherites(1).

844. אַשְׂרִיאֵל **Asriel** (77b); of unc. der.; a Manassite:— Asriel(3).

845. אַשְׂרִאֵלִי **Asrieli** (77b); from 844; desc. of Asriel:— Asrielites(1).

846. אֻשַּׁרְנָא **ushsharna** (1083b); (Ara.) of unc. der.; perh. *a wall:*— structure(2).

847a. אָשַׁשׁ **ashash** (84b); a prim. root; *to found, establish:*— assured(1).

847b. אֶשְׁתָּאוֹל **Eshtaol** or

אֶשְׁתָּאֹל **Eshtaol** (84b); of unc. der.; a city in Judah:— Eshtaol(7).

848. אֶשְׁתָּאֻלִי **Eshtauli** (84b); from 847b; inhab. of Eshtaol:— Eshtaolites(1).

849. אֶשְׁתַּדּוּר **eshtaddur** (1114c); (Ara.) from 7712; *a revolt:*— revolt(2).

850. אֶשְׁתּוֹן **Eshton** (84c); of unc. der.; an Isr.:— Eshton(2).

851. אֶשְׁתְּמוֹעַ **Eshtemoa** or

אֶשְׁתְּמֹעַ **Eshtemoa** or

אֶשְׁתְּמֹה **Eshtemoh** (84c); of unc. der.; a man of Judah, also a city in Judah:— Eshtemoa(5), Eshtemoh(1).

852. אָת **ath** (1079a); (Ara.) corr. to 226; *a sign:*— signs(3).

853. אֵת **eth** (84c); a prim. particle; untranslatable mark of the accusative case.

854. אֵת **eth** (85c); a prim. prep.; *with* (denoting proximity):— accompany*(1), against(36), all alone*(1), along(2), among(7), before(3), beside(2), besides(2), concerning(1), doing*(1), has(2), have(1), help*(1), how*(6), including(1), know(1), near(2), part*(1), possession(2), presence*(1), side(1), together(1), toward(2), within(2).

855a. אֵת **eth** (88c); of unc. der.; *a plowshare:*— mattock(1), mattocks(1), plowshares(3).

855b. אַתְּ **at** (61d); short. from 862b; *you* (fem. sing.):— yourself(3).

856. אֶתְבַּעַל **Ethbaal** (87a); from 854 and 1168a; "with Baal," a king of Sidon:— Ethbaal(1).

857. אָתָה **athah** (87b); a prim. root; *to come:*— bring(2), came(2), come(10), comes(4), past(1), things(1), things that are coming(1), things to come(1).

858. אֲתָה **athah** or

אֲתָא **atha** (1083c); (Ara.) corr. to 857; *to come:*— bring(2), brought(7), came(3), come(3), coming(1).

859. אַתָּה **attah** (61c); from an unused word; *you* (masc. sing.):— part(1), yours(1), yourself(21).

860. אָתוֹן **athon** (87d); from an unused word; *a female donkey:*— donkey(16), donkey's(1), donkeys(12), female donkeys(5).

861. אַתּוּן **attun** (1083c); (Ara.) of unc. der.; *a furnace:*— furnace(10).

862a. אַתּוּק **attuq** (87d); of unc. der.; *a gallery, porch:*— gallery(1).

862b. אַתִּי **atti** (61c); from the same as 859; *you* (fem. sing.).

863a. אִתַּי **Ittay** (87b); from 854; perh. "companionable," an Isr., also a Philistine:— Ithai(1), Ittai(8).

863b. אַתִּיק **attiq** (87d); from the same as 862a; *a gallery, porch:*— galleries(2), gallery(2).

864a. אֵתָם **Etham** (87c); of for. or.; a place in Eg.:— Etham(4).

864b. אַתֶּם **attem** (61d); from the same as 859; *you* (masc. pl.):— yourselves(10).

865a. אֶתְמוֹל **ethmol** or

אִתְּמוֹל **ittemol** or

אֶתְמוּל **ethmul** (1069d); of unc. der.; *yesterday, recently, formerly:*— formerly*(1), long(1), previously*(3), recently(1).

865b. אַתֵּן **atten** (61d); from the same as 859; *you* (fem. pl.).

866. אֶתְנָה **ethnah** (1071d); from 8566; *the wages* (of a harlot):— wages(1).

867. אֶתְנִי **Ethni** (87d); of unc. der.; an Isr.:— Ethni(1).

868. אֶתְנַן **ethnan** (1072c); from an unused word; *the wages* (of a harlot):— earnings(4), harlot's wages(2), hire(1), lovers(1), money(3).

869. אֶתְנָן **Ethnan** (87d); of unc. der.; an Isr.:— Ethnan(1).

870. אֲתַר **athar** (1083d); (Ara.) a prim. root; *a place:*— after(3), place(2), places(1), site(1), trace(1).

871. אֲתָרִים **Atharim** (87d); of unc. der.; a caravan route in the Negev:— Atharim(1).

ב

872. בִּאָה **biah** (99d); from 935; *an entrance, entry:*— entrance(1).

873. בִּאישׁ **bish** (1084a); (Ara.) from 888; *bad:*— evil(1).

874. בָּאַר **baar** (91b); a prim. root; *to make distinct* or *plain:*— distinctly(1), expound(1), inscribe(1).

875. בְּאֵר **beer** (91c); from 874; *a well, pit:*— pit(2), pits(1), well(29), well's(1), wells(3).

876. בְּאֵר **Beer** (91d); from the same as 875; "well," a place in the desert, also one in Pal.:— Beer(2).

877. בֹּאר **bor** (92b); from 874; *a cistern, pit, well:*— cisterns(2), pit(1), well(2).

878. בְּאֵרָא **Beera** (92a); from 875; "well," an Asherite:— Beera(1).

879. בְּאֵר אֵילִים **Beer Elim** (91d); from 875 and 410; "well of heroes," a city of Moab:— Beer-elim(1).

880. בְּאֵרָה **Beerah** (92a); from 875; "well," a Reubenite:— Beerah(1).

881. בְּאֵרוֹת **Beeroth** (92a); pl. of 875; "wells," a place in Pal.:— Beeroth(5).

882. בְּאֵרִי **Beeri** (92b); from 875; "my well," the name of a Hittite, also of Hosea's father:— Beeri(2).

883. בְּאֵר לַחַי רֹאִי **Beer Lachay Roi** (91d); from 875, 2416a and 7203a; "well of the living One that sees me," a place in the desert:— Beer-lahai-roi(3).

884. בְּאֵר שֶׁבַע **Beer Sheba** (92a); from 875 and 7651; "well of seven," a place in the Negev:— Beersheba(34).

885. בְּאֵרֹת בְּנֵי־יַעֲקָן **Beeroth Bene-yaaqan** (92b); from 875, 1121 and 3292; "wells of (the) sons of Jaakan," a place in the desert:— Beeroth Bene-jaakan(1).

886. בְּאֵרֹתִי **Beerothi** (92b); from 881; inhab. of Beeroth:— Beerothite(4), Beerothites(1).

887. בָּאַשׁ **baash** (92d); a prim. root; *to have a bad smell, to stink:*— acts disgustingly(1), became foul(3), become foul(2), become odious(2), grow foul(1), made(1), made themselves odious(1), made yourself odious(1), making me odious(1), odious*(1), stink(2), surely made(1), surely made himself odious(1).

888. בְּאֵשׁ **beesh** (1084a); (Ara.) corr. to 887; *to be evil, bad:*— distressed(1).

889. בְּאֹשׁ **beosh** (93b); from 887; *stench:*— stench(3).

890. בָּאְשָׁה **boshah** (93b); fem. of 889; *stinking* or *noxious weeds:*— stinkweed(1).

891. בְּאֻשִׁים **beushim** (93b); pl. of 889; *stinking* or *worthless* (things), *wild grapes:*— worthless ones(2).

892. בָּבָה **babah** (93b); of unc. der.; *the apple* (of the eye):— apple(1).

893. בֵּבַי **Bebay** (93c); prob. of for. or.; an Isr.:— Bebai(6).

894. בָּבֶל **Babel** (93c); perh. from 1101a; an E. Mediterranean empire and its capital city:— Babel(2), Babylon(257), Babylonians*(3).

895. בָּבֶל **Babel** (1084a); (Ara.) corr. to 894; an E. Mediterranean empire and its capital city:— Babylon(25).

896. בָּבְלָי **Babelay** (1084a); (Ara.) from 895; inhab. of Bab.:— Babylonians(1).

897. בַּג **bag** (93c, 103a); scribal error for 957, q.v.

898. בָּגַד **bagad** (93d); a prim. root; *to act* or *deal treacherously:*— acted deceitfully(1), acted treacherously(2), betrayed(1), betrays(1), deal(1), deal treacherously(10), deal very treacherously(1), deals treacherously(1), dealt treacherously(8), dealt very treacherously(1), faithless(2), treacherous(15), treacherous one still deals treacherously(1), treacherous deal(1), treacherously(1), unfairness(1).

899a. בֶּגֶד **beged** (93d); from 898; *treachery:*— treachery(1), very(1).

899b. בֶּגֶד **beged** (93d); from 898; *a garment, covering:*— cloth(8), clothes(81), clothing(6), garment(39), garments(72), lap(1), robes(5), saddlecloths*(1), wardrobe(2).

900. בֹּגְדוֹת **bogedoth** (93d); from 898; *treachery:*— treacherous(1).

901. בָּגוֹד **bagod** (93d); from 898; *treacherous:*— treacherous(2).

902. בִּגְוַי Bigvay (94a); prob. of for. or.; perh. "happy," an Isr. name:— Bigvai(6).

903. בִּגְתָא Bigtha (94a); of for. or.; a eunuch of Ahasuerus:— Bigtha(1).

904. בִּגְתָן Bigthan or

בִּגְתָנָא Bigthana (94b); of for. or.; a eunuch of Ahasuerus:— Bigthan(1), Bigthana(1).

905. בַּד bad (94c); from 909; *separation, a part:*— addition*(1), alone(58), alone*(4), apart(2), aside(2), bars(1), besides*(40), disease(1), except(1), except*(1), himself(6), including(1), itself(7), limbs(2), Myself(1), only(11), part of each(1), poles(37), separate(1), themselves(15), unless*(1), without*(1).

906. בַּד bad (94b); of unc. der.; *white linen:*— linen(22).

907. בַּד bad (95a); from an unused word; *empty, idle talk:*— boasters(1), boasts(1), idle boasts(2), oracle priests(1).

908. בָּדָא bada (94b); a prim. root; *to devise, invent:*— devised(1), inventing(1).

909. בָּדַד badad (94b); a prim. root; *to be separate, isolated:*— alone(1), lonely(1), shoots(2), straggler(1).

910. בָּדָד badad (94d); from 909; *isolation, separation:*— alone(6), apart(1), isolated(1), itself(1), lonely(1), secluded(1).

911. בְּדַד Bedad (95a); from the same as 907; an Edomite:— Bedad(2).

912. בֵּדְיָה Bedeyah (95a); short. from 5662; "servant of Yah," an Isr.:— Bedeiah(1).

913. בְּדִיל bedil (95d); from 914; *alloy, tin, dross:*— alloy(1), line*(1), plumb*(1), tin(4).

914. בָּדַל badal (95a); a prim. root; *to be divided, separate:*— came over(1), dismissed(1), divide(1), excluded(2), made a separation(1), made...distinction(1), make a distinction(3), partition(1), selected(1), separate(6), separated(10), serve(1), set you apart(1), set apart(6), set aside(2), sever(2), single(1), surely separate(1).

915. בָּדָל badal (95d); from 914; *a piece, severed piece:*— piece(1).

916. בְּדֹלַח bedolach (95d); of unc. der.; prob. *bdellium:*— bdellium(2).

917. בְּדָן Bedan (96a); perh. from 5658; an Isr. name:— Bedan(2).

918. בָּדַק badaq (96a); denom. vb. from 919; *to mend, repair:*— restore(1).

919. בֶּדֶק bedeq (96a); from an unused word; *a fissure, rent, breach:*— damage(1), damages(7), seams(2).

920. בִּדְקַר Bidqar (96a); of unc. der.; an Isr.:— Bidkar(1).

921. בְּדַר bedar (1084a); (Ara.) corr. to 967; *to scatter:*— scatter(1).

922. בֹּהוּ bohu (96a); from an unused word; *emptiness:*— emptiness(1), void(2).

923. בַּהַט bahat (96b); of unc. der.; perh. *porphyry:*— porphyry(1).

924. בְּהִילוּ behilu (1084b); (Ara.) from 927; *haste:*— haste(1).

925. בָּהִיר bahir (97c); from the same as 934; *bright, brilliant:*— bright(1).

926. בָּהַל bahal (96b); a prim. root; *to disturb, terrify:*— dismayed(12), disturb(1), disturbed(2), eager(1), hastened(1), hastens(1), hastily(1), hasty(1), hurried(1), hurriedly(1), hurry(2), quickly(1), terrified(7), terrifies(1), terrify(3), terrifying(1), tremble(1).

927. בְּהַל behal (1084b); (Ara.) corr. to 926; *to alarm, dismay:*— alarm(2), alarmed(3), alarming(2), haste(2), hurriedly(1), kept alarming(1).

928. בֶּהָלָה behalah (96d); from 926; *dismay, sudden terror* or *ruin:*— calamity(1), dismay(1), sudden terror(2).

929. בְּהֵמָה behemah (96d); from an unused word; *a beast, animal, cattle:*— animal(33), animals(27), beast(44), beasts(31), cattle(49), cattle*(1), herd(1), kinds of cattle(1), mount(1).

930. בְּהֵמוֹת Behemoth (97a); prob. pl. of 929; a kind of animal:— Behemoth(1).

931. בֹּהֶן bohen (97b); from an unused word; *thumb, great toe:*— big toe(6), big toes(1), thumb(6), thumbs(1), thumbs and their big(1), thumbs and big(1), toes*(2).

932. בֹּהַן Bohan (97b); from the same as 931; "closing," a desc. of Reuben:— Bohan(2).

933. בֹּהַק bohaq (97b); from an unused word; *tetter:*— eczema(1).

934. בַּהֶרֶת bahereth (97b); from an unused word; *brightness, bright spot:*— bright spot(9), bright spots(3).

935. בּוֹא bo (97c); a prim. root; *to come in, come, go in, go:*— actually come(1), advanced(8), alight(1), apply(1), approach(1), arrival(1), arrive(3), arrived(11), arrives(1), associate(4), attacks(1), attain(4), befalls(1), border(1), born(1), bring(246), bring it to pass(1), bringing(21), brings(9), brought(255), brought it to pass(2), came(590), came and brought(2), came and invaded(1), came to pass(3), came*(1), can get(1), carried(2), carry(1), certainly come(2), come(511), come and let us go(1), come from going(1), come to pass(3), comes(90), comes to pass(2), coming(106), departed(1), devoured*(2), enter(127), enter and go(1), entered(74), entering(14), enters(16), entrance(10), extended(1), fall(1), fallen(1), far*(1), followed(1), follows*(2), fulfilled(2), gave(1), get(2), give(1), go(147), go through(1), go*(2), goes(17), going(8), gone(7), granted(1), had(2), harbor(1), harvest(1), imported(1), indeed come(1), inserted(2), invade(1), invade when they came(1), invaded(1), invades(1), keep on coming(1), laid(1), Lebo-hamath(6), led(3), lifted(1), mentioned(1), migration(1), now(1), once(1), planned*(1), present(1), presented(1), presenting(1), press(1), proceed*(1), put(8), putting(1), reach(1), reached(4), reached the age(1), reenter*(2), replace*(1), reported(1), return(2), return*(1), returned(1), returned*(1), runs(1), set(6), sets(4), shedding(1), spring(1), stand(2), sundown*(1), sunset*(5), support*(1), surely comes(1), take(2), take place(1), takes(1), taking(1), threatened*(1), took(1), took place(1), traversing(1), visit*(1), went(109), went through(1).

936. בּוּז buz (100b); a prim. root; *to despise:*— despise(5), despised(1), despises(3), scorns*(1), utterly despised(1).

937. בּוּז buz (100b); from 936; *contempt:*— contempt(9), despised(1), laughingstock(1).

938. בּוּז Buz (100c); from 936; two Isr.:— Buz(3).

939. בּוּזָה buzah (100c); pass. part. of 936; *contempt:*— despised(1).

940. בּוּזִי Buzi (100c); from 938; a desc. of Buz:— Buzite(2).

941. בּוּזִי Buzi (100c); from 936; the father of Ezekiel:— Buzi(1).

942. בַּוַּי Bavvai (100c); perh. of for. or.; an Isr.:— Bavvai(1).

943. בּוּךְ buk (100c); a prim. root; *to perplex, confuse:*— confusion(1), wander aimlessly(1), wandering aimlessly(1).

944. בּוּל bul (385b); from 2986; *produce, outgrowth:*— block(1), food(1).

945. בּוּל Bul (100d); of unc. der.; the eighth month of the Jewish calendar:— Bul(1).

946. בּוּנָה Bunah (107b); from 995; "intelligence," a man of Judah:— Bunah(1).

947. בּוּס bus (100d); a prim. root; *to tread down, trample:*— loathes(1), squirming(2), trample(1), trample down(1), trampled(1), trampled down(1), tread down(2), treading down(1), trod down(1), trodden it down(1).

948. בּוּץ buts (101b); from an unused word; *byssus:*— fine linen(5), fine...linen(1), linen(2).

949. בּוֹצֵץ Botsets (130d); from the same as 1207; a rock near Michmash:— Bozez(1).

950. בּוּקָה buqah (101c); from an unused word; *emptiness:*— emptied(1).

951. בּוֹקֵר boqer (133c); from 1239; *a herdsman:*— herdsman(1).

952. בּוּר bur (101c); a prim. root; *to make clear, clear up, explain:*— explain(1).

953a. בּוֹר bor (92b); from 874; *a pit, cistern, well:*— cistern(14), cisterns(3), death(1), dungeon(3), dungeon*(2), pit(35), pits(2), quarry*(1), well(5).

953b. בּוֹר עָשָׁן Bor Ashan (92c); from 953a and 6227; "smoking pit," a place in Judah:— Bor-ashan(1).

954. בּוֹשׁ bosh (101d); a prim. root; *to be ashamed:*— acted shamefully(1), acts shamefully(3), ashamed(60), ashamed at all(1), became anxious(1), become dry(1), been confounded(1), been put(8), been put to shame(8), been shamed(1), brings shame(1), covered with shame(1), delayed(1), disappointed(2), feel...shame(1), put me to shame(1), put them to shame(1), put to shame(32), shame(1), shamed(3), shameful(1), shames(1), utterly dejected(1), utterly put(1), utterly put to shame(1).

955. בּוּשָׁה bushah (102a); pass. part. of 954; *shame:*— shame(4).

956. בּוּת buth (not included); see 1006b.

957. בַּז baz (103a); from 962; *spoiling, robbery, spoil, booty:*— booty(2), plunder(10), prey(11), spoil(4).

958. בָּזָא baza (102b); a prim. root; *to divide, cut through:*— divide(2).

959. בָּזָה bazah (102b); a prim. root; *to despise:*— careless(1), contempt(1), despicable(1), despise(5), despised(32), despises(2), disdained(1), disdained*(1).

960. בָּזֹה bazoh or

בְּזֹה bezoh (102b); infinitive construct of 959; *to despise:*— despised(1).

961. בִּזָּה bizzah (103a); fem. of 957; *spoil, booty:*— plunder(8), spoil(1).

962. בָּזַז bazaz (102d); a prim. root; *to spoil, plunder:*— booty(1), completely despoiled(1), despoiled(1), looted(3), pillage(1), plunder(11), plunder of those who plundered(1), plundered(6), plunderers(1), prey(2), seize(4), seize the plunder(1), seize their as plunder(1), take(3), take as booty(1), take spoil(1), taken booty(1), taking(1), took(3), took as our booty(1), took as their plunder(1).

963. בִּזָּיוֹן bizzayon (102c); from 959; *contempt:*— contempt(1).

964. בִּזְיוֹתְיָה Bizyothyah (103b); from 959 and 3050; "contempts of the LORD," a place near Beersheba:— Biziothiah(1).

965. בָּזָק bazaq (103b); from an unused word; *a lightning flash:*— bolts of lightning(1).

966. בֶּזֶק Bezeq (103b); from the same as 965; a place in Pal.:— Bezek(3).

967. בָּזַר bazar (103b); a prim. root; *to scatter:*— distribute(1), scattered(1).

968. בִּזְּתָא Bizzetha (103b); of for. or.; a eunuch of Ahasuerus:— Biztha(1).

969a. בָּחוּן bachun (103d); from 974; *a tower:*— siege towers(1).

969b. בָּחוֹן bachon (103d); from 974; *an assayer:*— assayer(1).

970. בָּחוּר bachur (104c); pass. part. of 977; *a young man:*— choice(4), vigorous young men(1), young man(6), young men(35).

971. בַּחִין bachin (103d); see 969a.

972. בָּחִיר bachir (104c); from 977; *chosen:*— chosen(6), chosen ones(7).

973a. בָּחַל bachel (103b); a prim. root; *to feel a loathing:*— weary(1).

973b. בָּחַל bachel (103c); a prim. root; *to get by greed:*— gained(1).

974. בָּחַן bachan (103c); a prim. root; *to examine, try:*— assay(2), examine(2), proved(1), test(7), tested(3), tests(3), tried(5), tries(2), try(3).

975. בַּחַן bachan (103d); from 974; *a watchtower:*— watch-tower(1).

976. בֹּחַן bochan (103d); from 974; *a testing:*— tested(1), testing(1).

977. בָּחַר bachar (103d); a prim. root; *to choose:*— choice(6), choicest(2), choose(40), chooses(22), choosing(1), chose(21), chosen(67), desired(2), men(1), preferred(1), require(1), select(1), selected(1), selected from the choice(1), selects(1), tested(1).

978. בַּחֲרוּמִי Bacharumi (104d); prob. from 980; inhab. of Bacharum:— Baharumite(1), Barhumite(1).

979. בְּחֻרִים bechurim or
בְּחֻרוֹת **bechuroth** or
בְּחוּרוֹת **bechuroth** (104c); masc. and fem. pl. of 970; *youth:*— young manhood(1), youth(2).

980. בַּחֻרִים Bachurim (104c); masc. pl. of 970; "young men's village," a city in Benjamin:— Bahurim(5).

981. בָּטָא bata or
בָּטָה **batah** (104d); of unc. der.; *to speak rashly* or *thoughtlessly:*— speak thoughtlessly(1), speaks rashly(1), spoke rashly(1), thoughtlessly(1).

982. בָּטַח batach (105a); a prim. root; *to trust:*— bold(1), careless(1), complacent(3), confident(2), fall down(1), felt secure(1), have(2), have confidence(1), put my trust(3), put their trust(2), put your trust(1), relied(1), rely(8), secure(5), trust(51), trusted(15), trusting(3), trusts(19).

983. בֶּטַח betach (105b); from 982; *security:*— confidence(1), safely(1), safety(6), secure(2), securely(21), security(8), unawares(1), unsuspecting(2).

984. בֶּטַח Betach (105c); from 982; a place in Aram (Syria):— Betah(1).

985. בִּטְחָה bitchah (105c); fem. of 983; *a trust:*— trust(1).

986. בִּטָּחוֹן bittachon (105c); from 982; *trust:*— confidence(2), hope(1).

987. בַּטֻּחוֹת battuchoth (105c); from 982; *security, safety:*— secure(1).

988. בָּטַל batal (105d); a prim. root; *to cease:*— stand idle(1).

989. בְּטֵל betel (1084b); (Ara.) corr. to 988; *to cease:*— ceased(1), delay(1), stop(2), stopped(2).

990. בֶּטֶן beten (105d); from an unused word; *belly, body, womb:*— abdomen(3), being(1), belly(8), birth(4), body(11), brothers*(1), depth(1), himself(1), infancy*(1), inward parts(1), mind(1), parts(1), pregnancy(1), rounded projection(1), stomach(3), within(3), womb(32).

991. בֶּטֶן Beten (106b); from the same as 990; "depression," a city in Asher:— Beten(1).

992. בָּטְנִים botnim (106b); from an unused word; *pistachio:*— pistachio nuts(1).

993. בְּטֹנִים Betonim (106b); from the same as 992; a city of Gad:— Betonim(1).

994a. בִּי bi (106c); from 994b; *I pray, excuse me:*— beg(1), O(4), Oh(6), please(2), please*(1).

994b. בָּיַי bayay (106b); a prim. root; *to entreat:*— ought(1).

995. בִּין bin (106c); a prim. root; *to discern:*— acted wisely(1), cared(1), clever(1), consider(8), consider carefully(1), considers(1), diligently consider(1), discern(9), discerned(2), discerning(9), discernment(1), explain(1), explained(1), feel(1), gain understanding(1), gave him understanding(1), gave me instruction(1), gaze(1), get understanding(1), give man an understanding(1), give me understanding(5), give you an understanding(1), give heed(1), give understanding(1), gives them understanding(1), gives understanding(1), has understanding(6), have understanding(1), have...understanding(1), intelligent(1), interpret(1), investigating(1), learned(1), look carefully(1), looked at him carefully(1), observe(1), observed(2), observing(1), paid close attention(1), pay heed(2), perceive(5), perceived(2), ponder(2), prudent(4), regard(1), show(1), show regard(2), show understanding(1), show...regard(1), skilled(1), skillful(4), taught(2), teacher(1), teachers(1), turn your attention(1), understand(35), understanding(14), understanding and he will gain(1), understanding and discerning(1), understands(6), understood(7).

996. בַּיִן bayin (107b); from 995; *an interval, space between:*— above*(1), among(30), among*(1), between(204), champion*(2), either(2), forehead*(5), midst(3), once(1), or(1), whether(1), within(1).

997. בֵּין ben (1084b); (Ara.) corr. to 996; *between:*— among(1), between(1).

998. בִּינָה binah (108a); from 995; *an understanding:*— clearly(1), consideration(1), discernment(3), truth(1), understand(1), understanding(29), understands(1), understood(1).

999. בִּינָה binah (1084b); (Ara.) corr. to 998; *an understanding:*— understanding(1).

1000. בֵּיצָה betsah (101b); from the same as 948; *an egg:*— eggs(6).

1001. בִּירָא bira (not included); see 1003b.

1002. בִּירָה birah (108b); of for. or.; *a castle, palace:*— capitol(1), citadel(11), fortress(2), temple(2).

1003a. בִּירָנִית biranith (108c); from 1002; *a fortress, fortified place:*— fortresses(2).

1003b. בִּירְתָא biretha (1084c); (Ara.) corr. to 1002; *a castle:*— fortress(1).

1004. בַּיִת bayith (108c); a prim. root; *a house:*— armory*(1), beneath(1), Beth-ashbea*(1), Beth-togarmah*(2), between*(2), boxes(1), buildings(2), daughter(1), dungeon*(2), faced inward(1), family(2), family*(1), guard*(1), hall(1), hangings(1), harem*(5), holders(7), home(33), homeborn*(2), homes(2), house(1534), house and the houses(2), household(125), household was inside(1), households(73), houses(101), houses while house(1), inner(2), inside*(13), inward(5), inward*(1), jail*(6), jailer*(3), large enough to hold(1), palace(22), palace and the houses(1), perfume*(1), place(2), places(1), prison*(15), residence(1), room(6), rooms(1), shrine*(1), temple(36), temple to the house(1), temples(2), tomb(1), treasury*(1), turned inwards(1), web(1), where(1), within(3).

1005. בַּיִת bayith (1084c); (Ara.) corr. to 1004; *a house:*— archives*(1), hall(1), house(30), houses(2), residence(1), temple(7), treasury(1).

1006a. בַּיִת Bayith (110c); from 1004, q.v.

1006b. בִּית bith (1084c); (Ara.) denom. vb. from 1005; *to pass the night:*— spent the night(1).

1007a. בֵּית beth (108a); from 995; *between:*— between(1), meet(1).

1007b. בֵּית אָוֶן Beth Aven (110c); from 1004 and 205; "house of iniquity," a place in Benjamin:— Beth-aven(7).

1008. בֵּיתְאֵל Betheel (110d); from 1004 and 410; "house of God," a city in Ephraim, also a place in S. Judah:— Bethel(71).

1009. בֵּית אַרְבֵאל Beth Arebel (111a); from 1004, 695 and 410; "house of God's ambush," a place in Pal.:— Beth-arbel(1).

1010. בֵּית בַּעַל מְעוֹן Beth Baal Meon (111a); from 1004, 1168a, and 4583; "house of Baal of (the) habitation," a place E. of the Jordan:— Beth-baal-meon(1), Beth-meon(1).

1011. בֵּית בִּרְאִי Beth Biri (111b); from 1004 and 1254a; "house of a creative one," a place in Pal.:— Beth-biri(1).

1012. בֵּית בָּרָה Beth Barah (111b); from 1004 and 5679; "place of ford," a place in Pal.:— Beth-barah(2).

1013. בֵּית גָּדֵר Beth Gader (111b); from 1004 and 1444; "place of a wall," a place in Judah:— Beth-gader(1).

1014. בֵּית גָּמוּל Beth Gamul (111b); from 1004 and pass. part. of 1580; "place of recompense," a place in Moab:— Beth-gamul(1).

1015. בֵּית דִּבְלָתַיִם Beth Diblathayim (111b); from 1004 and a word from the same as 1690; a place in Moab (the same as 5963):— Beth-diblathaim(1).

1016. בֵּית־דָּגוֹן Beth-dagon (111b); from 1004 and 1712; "house of Dagon," two places in Pal.:— Beth-dagon(2).

1017. בֵּית הָאֱלִי Beth Haeli (111a); from 1008; an inhab. of Bethel:— Bethelite(1).

1018. בֵּית הָאֵצֶל Beth Haetsel (111a); from 1004 and perh. 681a; a place in Judah:— Beth-ezel(1).

1019. בֵּית הַגִּלְגָּל Beth Haggilgal (111b); from 1004 and 1537; "house of the Gilgal," a place in Pal.:— Beth-gilgal(1).

1020. בֵּית הַיְשִׁימוֹת Beth Hayshimoth (111d); from 1004 and 3451; "place of the desert," a place E. of the Jordan in Moab:— Beth-jeshimoth(4).

1021. בֵּית הַכֶּרֶם **Beth Hakkerem** (111d); from 1004 and 3754; "vineyard place," a place in Judah:— Beth-haccerem(1), Beth-haccherem(1).

1022. בֵּית הַלַּחְמִי **Beth Hallachmi** (112a); from 1035; an inhab. of Bethlehem:— Bethlehemite(4).

1023. בֵּית הַמֶּרְחָק **beth hammerchaq** (112a); see 1004 and 4801.

1024. בֵּית־הַמַּרְכָּבֹת **Beth Hammarkaboth** or בֵּית מַרְכָּבוֹת **Beth Markaboth** (112b); from 1004 and 4818; "place of chariots," a place in Simeon:— Beth-marcaboth(2).

1025. בֵּית הָעֵמֶק **Beth Haemeq** (112b); from 1004 and 6010; "valley house," a place on the border of Asher:— Beth-emek(1).

1026. בֵּית הָעֲרָבָה **Beth Haarabah** (112c); from 1004 and 6160; "place of the depression," a place near the Dead Sea:— Beth-arabah(3).

1027. בֵּית הָרָם **Beth Haram** (111b); from 1004 and perh. 7311; "house of the height," a place E. of the Jordan:— Beth-haram(1), Beth-haran(1).

1028. בֵּית הָרָן **Beth Haran** (111c); the same as 1027, q.v.

1029. בֵּית הַשִּׁטָּה **Beth Hashshittah** (112d); from 1004 and 7848; "place of the acacia," a place in Pal.:— Beth-shittah(1).

1030. בֵּית־הַשִּׁמְשִׁי **Beth-hashshimshi** (113a); from 1053; an inhab. of Bethshemesh:— Beth-shemite(2).

1031. בֵּית חָגְלָה **Beth Choglah** (111c); from 1004 and a word from the same as 2295; "place of partridge," a place in Benjamin:— Beth-hoglah(3).

1032. בֵּית חוֹרֹן **Beth Choron** (111c); from 1004 and 2356; "place of a hollow," two adjoining cities in Pal.:— Beth-horon(14).

1033. בֵּית כָּר **Beth Kar** (111d); from 1004 and 3733c; "place of a lamb," a place in Pal.:— Beth-car(1).

1034. בֵּית לְבָאוֹת **Beth Lebaoth** (111d); from 1004 and 3833b; perh. "place of lionesses," a place in Simeon:— Beth-lebaoth(1).

1035. בֵּית לֶחֶם **Beth Lechem** (111d); from 1004 and 3899; "place of bread," a city in Judah, also a city in Zebulun:— Bethlehem(41).

1036. בֵּית לְעַפְרָה **Beth Leaphrah** (112a); from 1004 and 6083; "house to dust," a place in Pal.:— Beth-le-aphrah(1).

1037. בֵּית מִלּוֹא **Beth Millo** (571c); from 1004 and 4407; "house of earthwork," a place near Shechem, also a citadel in Jer.:— Beth-millo(3).

1038. בֵּית מַעֲכָה **Beth Maakah** (112a); from 1004 and 4601; "house of Maakah," a place in N. Isr.:— Beth-maacah(2).

1039. בֵּית נִמְרָה **Beth Nimrah** (112b); from 1004 and fem. of 5246; "place of a leopard," a place E. of the Jordan:— Beth-nimrah(2).

1040. בֵּית עֶדֶן **Beth Eden** (112b); from 1004 and 5730a; "house of pleasure," a place in Aram (Syria):— Beth-eden(1).

1041. בֵּית־עַזְמָוֶת **Beth-azmaveth** (112b); from 1004 and 5820b; "house of Azmaveth," a place near Jer.:— Beth-azmaveth(1).

1042. בֵּית־עֲנוֹת **Beth-anoth** (112b); from 1004 and a word of unc. der.; perh. "temple of Anat," a place in Judah:— Beth-anoth(1).

1043. בֵּית־עֲנָת **Beth-anath** (112c); from 1004 and a word from the same as 6067; "temple of Anat," a place in Naphtali:— Beth-anath(3).

1044. בֵּית־עֵקֶד **Beth-eqed** (112c); from 1004 and 6123; "house of binding," a place in Pal.:— Beth-eked(2).

1045. בֵּית עַשְׁתָּרוֹת **beth Ashtaroth** (108c, 800a); see 1004 and 6252b.

1046. בֵּית פֶּלֶט **Beth Palet** (112c); from 1004 and 6412a; "place of escape," a place in S. Judah:— Beth-pelet(2).

1047. בֵּית פְּעוֹר **Beth Peor** (112c); from 1004 and 6465; "house of Peor," a place E. of the Jordan:— Beth-peor(4).

1048. בֵּית פַּצֵּץ **Beth Patstsets** (112d); from 1004 and a der. of 6327a; "place of dispersion," a place in Issachar:— Beth-pazzez(1).

1049. בֵּית־צוּר **Beth-tsur** (112d); from 1004 and 6697; "house of a rock," a place in Judah:— Beth-zur(3), Bethzur(1).

1050. בֵּית־רְחוֹב **Beth-rechob** (112d); from 1004 and 7339; "place of a street," a place near Dan:— Beth-rehob(2).

1051. בֵּית רָפָא **Beth Rapha** (112d); from 1004 and 7497; an Isr. name:— Beth-rapha(1).

1052. בֵּית שְׁאָן **Beth Shean** (112d); from 1004 and 7599; "place of quiet," a place in Manasseh, W. of the Jordan:— Beth-shan(3), Beth-shean(6).

1053. בֵּית שֶׁמֶשׁ **Beth Shemesh** (112d); from 1004 and 8121; "sun temple," three places in Pal., also a place in Eg.:— Beth-shemesh(20), Heliopolis(1).

1054. בֵּית־תַּפּוּחַ **Beth-tappuach** (113a); from 1004 and 8598; "place of apples," a place in Judah:— Beth-tappuah(1).

1055. בִּיתָן **bithan** (113a); prob. from 1004; *house, palace:*— palace(3).

1056. בָּכָא **Baka** (113a); of unc. der.; a valley in Pal.:— Baca(1).

1057. בָּכָא **baka** (113a); from the same as 1056; *balsam tree:*— balsam trees(4).

1058. בָּכָה **bakah** (113b); a prim. root; *to weep, bewail:*— bewail(1), crying(1), mourn(1), sob(1), weep(27), weep not at all(1), weep continually(1), weep...longer(1), weeping(12), weeps bitterly(1), wept(60), wept bitterly(1).

1059. בֶּכֶה **bekeh** (113d); from 1058; *a weeping:*— bitterly*(1).

1060. בְּכוֹר **bekor** (114a); from 1069; *first-born:*— firstborn(118), firstlings(1), most(1), oldest(3).

1061. בִּכּוּרִים **bikkurim** (114c); from 1069; *first fruits:*— early ripened things(2), first fruits(12), first ripe(1), first ripe fruits(1), ripe fruit(1).

1062. בְּכוֹרָה **bekorah** or בְּכֹרָה **bekorah** (114c); fem. of 1069; *the right of first- born:*— birthright(9), firstborn(1).

1063. בִּכּוּרָה **bikkurah** (114c); from 1069; *the first ripe fig, early fig:*— earliest fruit(1), first-ripe(1), first-ripe fig(2).

1064. בְּכוֹרַת **Bekorath** (114c); from 1069; "first-born," a Benjamite:— Becorath(1).

1065. בֶּכִי **beki** (113d); from 1058; *a weeping:*— bitterly(1), bitterly*(3), continual weeping(1), flowing(1), tears(1), weep(2), weeping(19), wept*(1).

1066. בֹּכִים **Bokim** (114a); act. part. of 1058; "weepers," a place in Pal.:— Bochim(2).

1067. בְּכִירָה **bekirah** (114c); from 1069; *first-born* (always of women):— firstborn(6).

1068. בְּכִית **bekith** (114a); from 1058; *a weeping:*— mourning(1).

1069. בָּכַר **bakar** (114a); a prim. root; *to bear new fruit, to constitute as first-born:*— bear(1), first child(1), firstborn(2), giving birth(1), make(1).

1070. בֶּכֶר **beker** (not included); see 1072.

1071. בֶּכֶר **Beker** (114b); from 1069; "young camel," two Isr.:— Becher(5).

1072. בִּכְרָה **bikrah** (114c); from 1069; *a young camel, dromedary:*— young camel(1), young camels(1).

1073. בַּכֻּרָה **bakkurah** (not included); see 1063.

1074. בֹּכְרוּ **Bokeru** (114b); from 1069; a Benjamite:— Bocheru(2).

1075. בִּכְרִי **Bikri** (114b); from 1069; "youthful," a Benjamite, perh. also his desc.:— Bichri(8).

1076. בַּכְרִי **Bakri** (114b); from 1071; desc. of Becher:— Becherites(1).

1077. בַּל **bal** (115b); from 1086; *not:*— cannot(2), fail(1), immovable*(1), never(1), never*(4), no(5), none(2), nor(5), nothing(1), nothing*(1), scarcely*(3), untouched*(1).

1078. בֵּל **Bel** (128c); short. form of 1168a; a chief Bab. deity:— Bel(3).

1079. בָּל **bal** (1084b); (Ara.) from an unused word; *the mind:*— mind(1).

1080. בְּלָא **bela** (1084c); (Ara.) corr. to 1086; *to wear away* or *out:*— wear down(1).

1081. בַּלְאֲדָן **Baladan** (114d); of for. or.; "he has given a son," father of a Bab. king:— Baladan(2).

1082. בָּלַג **balag** (114d); a prim. root; *to gleam, smile:*— cheerful(1), flashes forth(1), have a cheer(1), smile(1).

1083. בִּלְגָּה **Bilgah** (114d); from 1082; "cheerfulness," two Isr.:— Bilgah(3).

1084. בִּלְגַּי **Bilgay** (114d); from 1082; an Isr.:— Bilgai(1).

1085. בִּלְדַּד **Bildad** (115a); of unc. der.; perh. "Bel has loved," one of Job's friends:— Bildad(5).

1086. בָּלָה **balah** (115a); a prim. root; *to become old, wear out:*— become old(1), consume(1), decaying(1), spend(1), waste(1), waste away(1), wasted away(1), wear(6), worn(3).

1087. בָּלֶה **baleh** (115b); from 1086; *worn-out:*— worn(1), worn-out(4).

1088. בָּלָה **Balah** (115a); of unc. der.; a place in Simeon:— Balah(1).

1089. בָּלַהּ **balah** (117a); a prim. root; *to be troubled:*— frightened(1).

1090a. בִּלְהָה **Bilhah** (117b); of unc. der.; a concubine of Jacob:— Bilhah(10).

1090b. בִּלְהָה **Bilhah** (117b); of unc. der.; a city in Simeon:— Bilhah(1).

1091. בַּלָּהָה **ballahah** (117a); from 1089; *terror, dreadful event, calamity, destruction:*— sudden terrors(1), terrified(2), terror(1), terrors(6).

1092. בִּלְהָן **Bilhan** (117b); of unc. der.; the name of an Edomite, also of an Isr.:— Bilhan(4).

1093. בְּלוֹ belo (1084c); (Ara.) of for. or.; *tribute:*— custom(2).

1094. בְּלוֹא belo (115b); from 1086; *worn-out things, rags:*— worn-out(3).

1095. בֵּלְטְשַׁאצַּר Belteshatstsar (117b); of for. or.; Bab. name of Daniel:— Belteshazzar(2).

1096. בֵּלְטְשַׁאצַּר Belteshatstsar (1084d); (Ara.) corr. to 1095; Bab. name of Daniel:— Belteshazzar(8).

1097. בְּלִי beli (115c); from 1086; *a wearing out:*— because*(6), cannot(1), lack(4), no(6), no more(1), no one(3), nor(1), nothing(1), nothing*(1), nothingness(1), one(2), overflows*(1), so*(3), unconcerned*(1), unintentionally*(2), unobserved*(1), unrestrained*(1), want(1), without(20), without*(1), yet so(1).

1098. בְּלִיל belil (117d); from 1101a; *fodder:*— fodder(3).

1099. בְּלִימָה belimah (116a); from 1097 and 4100; *nothingness:*— nothing(1).

1100. בְּלִיַּעַל beliyyaal (116a); from 1097 and 3276; *worthlessness:*— base(1), destruction(1), rascally(1), scoundrels*(1), ungodliness(1), wicked(3), worthless(18), worthless one(1).

1101a. בָּלַל balal (117b); a prim. root; *to mingle, mix, confuse, confound:*— anointed(1), confuse(1), confused(1), mixed(38), mixes(1).

1101b. בָּלַל balal (117d); denom. vb. from 1098; *to give provender:*— gave the fodder(1).

1102. בָּלַם balam (117d); a prim. root; *to curb, hold in:*— hold them in check(1).

1103. בָּלַס balas (118a); denom. vb. from an unused word; *to gather figs:*— grower of figs(1).

1104. בָּלַע bala (118a); a prim. root; *to swallow down, swallow up, engulf:*— brought to confusion(1), confound(1), confuse(2), confused(1), consume(1), destroy(1), destroyed(1), destroying(1), end(1), moment(1), removed(1), ruin(1), spreads(1), swallow(13), swallowed(18), swallows(4).

1105. בֶּלַע bela (118c); from 1104; *a swallowing, devouring, a thing swallowed:*— devour(1), what he has swallowed(1).

1106a. בֶּלַע Bela (118c); from 1104; an Edomite, also two Isr.:— Bela(12).

1106b. בֶּלַע Bela (118d); from 1104; another name for Zoar:— Bela(2).

1107. בִּלְעֲדֵי bilade (116b); from 1077 and 5704; *apart from, except, without:*— besides(3), besides*(5), nothing except(1), other than(1), without(3), without*(1).

1108. בַּלְעִי Bali (118c); from 1106a; desc. of Bela:— Belaites(1).

1109a. בִּלְעָם Bilam (118d); from 1104; a prophet:— Balaam(58), Balaam's(2).

1109b. בִּלְעָם Bilam (118d); from 1104; a city in Manasseh:— Bileam(1).

1110. בָּלַק balaq (118d); a prim. root; *to waste, lay waste:*— devastates(1), waste(1).

1111. בָּלָק Balaq (118d); from 1110; "devastator," a Moabite king:— Balak(40), Balak's(3).

1112. בֵּלְשַׁאצַּר Beleshatstsar or

בֵּלְאשַׁצַּר Beleshatstsar (128d); of for. or.; "Bel, protect the king," a Bab. king:— Belshazzar(1).

1113. בֵּלְשַׁאצַּר Belshatstsar (1084d); (Ara.) corr. to 1112; a Bab. king:— Belshazzar(7).

1114. בִּלְשָׁן Bilshan (119a); of unc. der.; perh. "inquirer," an Isr.:— Bilshan(2).

1115. בִּלְתִּי bilti (116c); from 1086; *not, except:*— besides(2), except(3), except*(1), less than*(1), moreover(1), neither(1), no(15), no longer(1), no*(1), nor(2), nothing(3), other than(1), prevent*(2), so(3), stop(1), unceasing*(1), unless(3), unless*(1), until(1), without(4).

1116. בָּמָה bamah (119a); of unc. der.; *a high place:*— heights(3), high place(19), high places(76), places(1), waves(1).

1117. בָּמָה Bamah (119a); from 1116; a high place (for idols) in Isr.:— Bamah(1).

1118. בִּמְהָל Bimhal (119d); perh. from 1121 and 4107; perh. "son of circumcision," a desc. of Asher:— Bimhal(1).

1119. בְּמוֹ bemo (91b); poetic form of a prep. pref.; *in:*— through(1).

1120. בָּמוֹת Bamoth (119d); from the same as 1116; "high place," a place in Moab:— Bamoth(2), Bamoth-baal*(1).

1121. בֵּן ben (119d); a prim. root; *son:*— afflicted(1), afflicted*(1), age(7), aliens*(2), Ammonites*(7), anointed*(1), arrow(1), arrows(1), Assyrians*(3), baby(1), Babylonians*(3), beasts(1), being*(1), Ben-hinnom*(7), bough(2), breed(1), brothers*(1), builders(1), bull*(21), bulls*(5), calf*(2), calves(2), calves*(1), child(2), children(111), children and on the grandchildren(1), children and their grandchildren(1), children and your children's(1), children and children's(1), children's(2), children's children(5), colt(1), colts(1), common(2), descendants(14), descendants of the son(1), deserves(2), exiles*(5), father*(1), fellow*(3), fellows(2), fertile*(1), foal(1), fools*(1), foreigner*(6), foreigners(1), foreigners*(10), Gileadites*(1), grandchildren(1), granddaughters*(1), grandson(6), heir*(1), high*(1), homeborn*(1), Israelites*(1), lambs*(2), lay(4), Levites*(1), low degree*(1), low*(1), man(5), man one old(1), man*(1), men(19), men of low degree*(1), men*(4), mortal(1), must(1), must surely(1), nephew*(2), nobility*(1), offspring(1), old(167), old when his son(1), one(1), one(2), one born(1), ones(1), ones*(1), opening*(1), overnight*(2), people(5), public*(1), revelers*(1), satellites(1), scoundrels*(1), sired(1), slaves(1), son(1876), son and his grandson(1), son and your grandson(1), son of and grandson(1), son was old(1), son's(16), son's son(1), sons(2369), sons and his grandsons(2), sons and his sons'(1), sons and on his sons'(1), sons and their sons'(1), sons and your grandsons(1), sons and your sons'(1), sons and grandsons(2), sons of the son(14), sons'(7), sons' sons(2), sparks*(1), those(1), those who(2), those who are doomed(1), those who were doomed(1), troops*(1), unfortunate*(1), valiant*(3), warriors(1), whelps(1), wicked*(3), young(28), young goats*(1), young men(1), youths(1).

1122. בֵּן Ben (122a); from 1121; a Levite:— Ben(1).

1123. בֵּן ben (1085b); (Ara.) corr. to 1121, see 1247; *son:*— among*(1), children(1), exiles*(4), sons(4), young(1).

1124. בְּנָא bena or

בְּנָה benah (1084d); (Ara.) corr. to 1129; *to build:*— building(2), built(4), rebuild(6), rebuilding(3), rebuilt(5), reconstructing(1), under construction(1).

1125. בֶּן־אֲבִינָדָב Ben-abinadab (122a); from 1121 and 41; "son of Abinadab," one of Solomon's leaders:— Ben-abinadab(1).

1126. בֶּן־אוֹנִי Ben-oni (122b); from 1121 and 205; "son of my sorrow," Rachel's name for Benjamin:— Ben-oni(1).

1127. בֶּן־גֶּבֶר Ben-geber (122b); from 1121 and 1397; "son of a man," one of Solomon's leaders:— Ben-geber(1).

1128. בֶּן־דֶּקֶר Ben-deqer (122b); from 1121 and 1856; "son of Deker," one of Solomon's leaders:— Ben-deker(1).

1129. בָּנָה banah (124a); a prim. root; *to build:*— besieged*(1), build(112), build*(1), builders(10), building(16), builds(8), built(177), construct(1), constructed(1), fashioned(1), fortified(3), fortifying(2), have children(1), made(1), obtain children(1), rebuild(13), rebuilding(3), rebuilt(17), rebuilt*(2), restored(1), set(1), surely built(1).

1130. בֶּן־הֲדַד Ben-hadad (122b); from 1121 and 1908; "son of Hadad," the name of several Aramean (Syrian) kings:— Ben-hadad(25).

1131a. בְּנוֹ Beno (122b); from 1121; "his son," an Isr.:— Beno(2).

1131b. בִּנּוּי Binnuy (125a); from 1129; several postexilic Isr.:— Binnui(7).

1132. בֶּן־זוֹחֵת Ben-zocheth (122b); from 1121 and 2105; "son of Zoheth," a man of Judah:— Ben-zoheth(1).

1133. בֶּן־חוּר Ben-chur (122b); from 1121 and 2354; "son of Hur," one of Solomon's leaders:— Ben-hur(1).

1134. בֶּן־חַיִל Ben-chayil (122c); from 1121 and 2428; "son of might," one of Jehoshaphat's leaders:— Ben-hail(1).

1135. בֶּן־חָנָן Ben-chanan (122c); from 1121 and 2605; "son of Hanan," a man of Judah:— Benhanan(1).

1136. בֶּן־חֶסֶד Ben-chesed (122c); from 1121 and 2617a; "son of mercy," one of Solomon's leaders:— Ben-hesed(1).

1137. בָּנִי Bani (125b); from 1129; the name of several Isr.:— Bani(16).

1138. בֻּנִּי Bunni (125b); from 1129; the name of several Isr.:— Bunni(3).

1139. בְּנֵי־בְרַק Bene-beraq (122c); from 1121 and 1300; "sons of lightning," a city in Dan:— Bene-berak(1).

1140. בִּנְיָה binyah (125b); from 1129; *a structure, building:*— building(1).

1141. בְּנָיָהוּ Benayahu or

בְּנָיָה Benayah (125c); from 1129 and 3050; "Yah has built up," the name of several Isr.:— Benaiah(42).

1142. בְּנֵי יַעֲקָן Bene Yaaqan (122c); from 1121 and 3292; "sons of Jaakan," a place in the desert:— Bene-jaakan(2).

1143. בֵּנַיִם benayim (107b); a form of 996, q.v.

1144. בִּנְיָמִין Binyamin (122c); from 1121 and 3225; "son of (the) right hand," youngest son of Jacob, also the name of two other Isr .:— Benjamin(162), Benjamin's(4).

1145. בֶּן־יְמִינִי Ben-yemini (122d); from 1144; a desc. of Benjamin:— Benjamite(5), Benjamites(4).

1146. בִּנְיָן binyan (125c); from 1129; *a structure:*— building(6).

1147. בִּנְיָן binyan (1084d); (Ara.) corr. to 1146; *a building:*— building(1).

1148. בְּנִינוּ Beninu (123a); prob. from 1121; perh. "our son," a Levite:— Beninu(1).

1149. בְּנַס benas (1084d); (Ara.) a prim. root; *to be angry:*— became indignant(1).

1150. בִּנְעָא Bina (126a); of unc. der.; a desc. of Jonathan:— Binea(2).

1151. בֶּן־עַמִּי Ben-ammi (122c); from 1121 and 5971a; "son of my people," a son of Lot:— Ben-ammi(1).

1152. בְּסוֹדְיָה Besodeyah (126a); of unc. der.; an Isr.:— Besodeiah(1).

1153. בֵּסַי Besay (126a); of unc. der.; one of the Nethinim:— Besai(2).

1154. בֶּסֶר beser (not included); see 1155.

1155. בֹּסֶר boser (126a); from an unused word; *unripe* or *sour grapes:*— grape(1), sour grapes(3), unripe grape(1).

1156. בְּעָא bea (1085a); (Ara.) corr. to 1158; *to ask, seek:*— asking(1), looked(1), made request(1), makes(1), makes a petition(1), making(1), making petition(1), request(1), requested(2), seeking(1), trying(1).

1157. בְּעַד baad (126b); from an unused word; *away from, behind, about, on behalf of:*— about(2), account(1), around(2), because(1), behalf(4), behind(7), behind*(3), over(1), sake(2), through(9), what concerns(1).

1158. בָּעָה baah (126d); a prim. root; *to inquire, cause to swell* or *boil up:*— boil(1), bulge(1), inquire(2), searched(1).

1159. בָּעוּ bau (1085a); (Ara.) from 1156; *a petition:*— petition(2).

1160. בְּעוֹר Beor (129d); from 1197a; "a burning," father of an Edomite king, also the father of Balaam:— Beor(10).

1161. בִּעוּתִים biuthim (130a); from 1204; *terrors, alarms:*— terrors(2).

1162. בֹּעַז Boaz (126d); from an unused word; "quickness," an ancestor of David, also a pillar before the temple:— Boaz(24).

1163. בָּעַט baat (127a); a prim. root; *to kick:*— kick(1), kicked(1).

1164. בְּעִי bei (730d); see 5856.

1165. בְּעִיר beir (129c); from 1197a; *beasts, cattle:*— animal(1), beasts(4), cattle(1).

1166. בָּעַל baal (127a); a prim. root; *to marry, rule over:*— gets a husband(1), high(1), husband(3), married(4), married*(2), marries(2), marry(1), marrying*(1), master(1), ruled(2).

1167. בַּעַל baal (127b); from 1166; *owner, lord:*— allies*(1), archers*(1), bird*(1), bound(1), bridegroom(1), captain(1), case*(1), charmer*(1), citizens(1), creditor*(1), dominant(1), dreamer*(1), due(1), husband(8), husbands(2), leaders(6), lords(1), man(3), married*(2), master's(1), masters(1), men(14), owner(15), owners(2), possessors(2), relative by marriage(1), schemer*(1), who has(1), who practice(1), wrathful*(1).

1168a. בַּעַל Baal (127c); from 1166; a heathen god:— Baal(58), Baal's(1), Baals(18), Bamoth-baal*(1).

1168b. בַּעַל Baal (127d); from 1166; the name of a city in Simeon, also two Isr.:— Baal(4).

1169. בְּעֵל beel (1085a); (Ara.) corr. to 1167; *owner, lord:*— commander*(3).

1170. בַּעַל בְּרִית Baal Berith (127d); from 1168a and 1285; "Baal of (the) covenant," a Shechemite god:— Baal-berith(2).

1171. בַּעַל גָּד Baal Gad (128a); from 1168a and 1409; "Baal of fortune," a place near Mt. Hermon:— Baal-gad(3).

1172. בַּעֲלָה baalah (128b); fem. of 1167; *a mistress:*— medium*(2), mistress(2).

1173. בַּעֲלָה Baalah (128b); fem. of 1167; the name of several places in Isr.:— Baalah(5).

1174. בַּעַל הָמוֹן Baal Hamon (128a); from 1167 and 1995; "possessor of abundance," a place in Pal.:— Baal-hamon(1).

1175. בְּעָלוֹת Bealoth (128c); pl. of 1172; "mistresses," a city in S. Judah, also a city of unc. location:— Bealoth(2).

1176. בַּעַל זְבוּב Baal Zebub (127d); from 1168a and 2070; "Baal of flies," a Philistine god:— Baal-zebub(4).

1177. בַּעַל חָנָן Baal Chanan (128a); from 1168a and 2603a; "Baal is gracious," a king of Edom, also an Isr.:— Baal-hanan(5).

1178. בַּעַל חָצוֹר Baal Chatsor (128a); from 1167 and 2691a; "possessor of a court," a city between Ephraim and Benjamin:— Baal-hazor(1).

1179. בַּעַל חֶרְמוֹן Baal Chermon (128a); from 1168a and 2768; "Baal of Hermon," the center of Baal worship on Mt. Hermon:— Baal-hermon(2).

1180. בַּעֲלִי Bali (127b); from 1167 with pron. suff.; "my Baal," a symbolic name for Yah:— Baali(1).

1181. בַּעֲלֵי בָּמוֹת baale bamoth (119a, 127b); from 1168a and 1116; *lords of (the) high places:*— heights(1).

1182. בְּעֶלְיָדָע Beelyada (128c); from 1168a and 3045; "Baal knows," a son of David:— Beeliada(1).

1183. בְּעַלְיָה Baalyah (128c); from 1167 and 3050; "Yah is lord," one of David's heroes:— Bealiah(1).

1184. בַּעֲלֵי יְהוּדָה Baale Yehudah (128b); from 1168a and 3063; "Baal of Judah," the center of Baal worship in Judah:— Baale-judah(1).

1185. בַּעֲלִיס Baalis (128d); of unc. der.; perh. "son of delight," an Ammonite king:— Baalis(1).

1186. בַּעַל מְעוֹן Baal Meon (128b); from 1168a and 4583; "Baal of (the) habitation," a place E. of the Jordan:— Baal-meon(3).

1187. בַּעַל פְּעוֹר Baal Peor (128b); from 1168a and 6465; "Baal of Peor," a Moabite god:— Baal of Peor(2), Baal-peor(4).

1188. בַּעַל פְּרָצִים Baal Peratsim (128b); from 1167 and 6556; "possessor of breaches," a place in Pal.:— Baal-perazim(4).

1189. בַּעַל צְפוֹן Baal Tsephon (128b); from 1168a and perh. 6828; "Baal of winter," a place in Eg.:— Baal-zephon(3).

1190. בַּעַל שָׁלִשָׁה Baal Shalishah (128b); from 1168a and 8031; "Baal of Shalishah," a place in Pal.:— Baal-shalishah(1).

1191. בַּעֲלָת Baalath (128c); prob. from 1172; a city in Dan:— Baalath(3).

1192. בַּעֲלַת בְּאֵר Baalath Beer (128c); from 1172 and 875; "mistress of a well," a city in Simeon:— Baalath-beer(1).

1193. בַּעַל תָּמָר Baal Tamar (128b); from 1167 and 8558; "possessor of palms," a place near Gibeah:— Baal-tamar(1).

1194. בְּעֹן Beon (111a); prob. a short. form of 1010; a place E. of the Jordan:— Beon(1).

1195. בַּעֲנָא Baana (128d); from the same as 1196; the name of several Isr.:— Baana(3).

1196. בַּעֲנָה Baanah (128d); of unc. der.; the name of several Isr.:— Baanah(9).

1197a. בָּעַר baar (128d); a prim. root; *to burn, consume:*— blazed(1), burn(15), burned(12), burning(13), burns(3), clean sweep(1), consume(1), consumed(2), destroy(1), devoured(1), expelled(1), heated(1), kindle(2), kindled(5), light(1), make(2), make a clean sweep(1), make fires(1), purge(9), remove(3), removed(4), set(1), set ablaze(1), sets it afire(1), started(1), sweeps away(1), utterly sweep(1), utterly sweep you away(1).

1197b. בָּעַר baar (129c); denom. vb. from 1165; *to be brutish:*— become stupid(2), brutal(1), grazed(1), grazes(1), senseless(1), stupid(3).

1198. בַּעַר baar (129d); from 1197b; *brutishness:*— senseless(3), stupid(2).

1199. בַּעֲרָא Baara (129d); from 1197b; an Isr. woman:— Baara(1).

1200. בְּעֵרָה beerah (129c); from 1197a; *a burning:*— fire(1).

1201. בַּעְשָׁא Basha (129d); of unc. der.; a king of Isr.:— Baasha(28).

1202. בַּעֲשֵׂיָה Baaseyah (129d); of unc. der.; a Levite:— Baaseiah(1).

1203. בְּעֶשְׁתְּרָה Beeshterah (129d); perh. from 1004 and 6252b; perh. "house of Ashtoreth," a Levitical city in Manasseh:— Beeshterah(1).

1204. בָּעַת baath (129d); a prim. root; *to fall upon, startle, terrify:*— frighten(1), frightened(1), overwhelmed(1), overwhelms(1), terrified(3), terrify(7), terrorized(1), terrorizing(1).

1205. בְּעָתָה beathah (130a); from 1204; *terror, dismay:*— terror(2).

1206. בֹּץ bots (130c); from an unused word; *mire:*— mire(1).

1207. בִּצָּה bitstsah (130c); from the same as 1206; *a swamp:*— marsh(2), swamps and marshes(1).

1208. בָּצוֹר batsor (130d); see 1219.

1209. בֵּצַי Betsay (130a); of unc. der.; an Isr. name:— Bezai(3).

1210. בָּצִיר batsir (131b); from 1219; *a vintage:*— grape(1), grape gathering(2), grape harvest(2), vintage(2).

1211. בָּצָל batsal (130b); from an unused word; *an onion:*— onions(1).

1212. בְּצַלְאֵל Betsalel (130b); prob. from 6738 and 410; "in the shadow (protection) of El," two Isr.:— Bezalel(9).

1213. בַּצְלוּת Batsluth (130b); from the same as 1211; "stripping," an Isr.:— Bazlith(1), Bazluth(1).

1214. בָּצַע batsa (130b); a prim. root; *to cut off, break off, gain by violence:*— accomplished(1), break(1), break ranks(1), completed(1), cut me off(1), cut off(1), cuts me off(1), finish(1), gains by violence(1), get dishonest(1), gets(1), greedy(2), greedy man(1), injured your for gain(1), profits(1).

1215. בֶּצַע betsa (130c); from 1214; *gain made by violence, unjust gain, profit:*— dishonest gain(4), end(1), gain(7), illicitly(1), plunder(1), profit(4), unjust gain(4), unjust*(1).

1216. בָּצֵק batseq (130d); of unc. der.; *to swell:*— swell(2).

1217. בָּצֵק batseq (130d); of unc. der.; *dough* (for cooking):— dough(5).

1218. בָּצְקַת Botsqath (130d); from the same as 1216; a city in Judah:— Bozkath(2).

1219. בָּצַר batsar (130d); a prim. root; *to cut off, make inaccessible, enclose:*— cut off(1), fortified(24), fortify(2), gather(3), gathered(1), gatherer(1), gatherers(2), impenetrable(1), impossible(1), mighty things(1), thwarted(1).

1220. בֶּצֶר betser (131a); from 1219; *precious ore, an ingot:*— gold(2).

1221. בֶּצֶר Betser (131a); from 1219; "fortress," a city in Reuben, also a desc. of Asher:— Bezer(5).

1222. בְּצַר betsar (865a); another reading for 6862b, q.v.

1223. בָּצְרָה botsrah (131b); from 1219; *an enclosure, a fold* (for sheep):— fold(1).

1224a. בָּצְרָה Botsrah (131b); from 1219; "fortress," a city in Edom, also one in Moab:— Bozrah(8).

1224b. בַּצָּרָה batstsarah (131b); from 1219; *dearth, destitution:*— drought(1).

1225. בִּצָּרוֹן bitstsaron (131b); from 1219; *a stronghold:*— stronghold(1).

1226. בַּצֹּרֶת batstsoreth (131b); from 1219; *a dearth:*— drought(1).

1227. בַּקְבּוּק Baqbuq (132d); from 1238b; one of the Nethinim:— Bakbuk(2).

1228. בַּקְבֻּק baqbuq (132d); from 1238b; *a flask:*— jar(3).

1229. בַּקְבֻּקְיָה Baqbuqyah (132d); from 1228 and 3050; "emptying of Yah," a Levite:— Bakbukiah(3).

1230. בַּקְבַּקַּר Baqbaqqar (131c); of unc. der.; a Levite:— Bakbakkar(1).

1231. בֻּקִּי Buqqi (131c); short. form of 1232; two Isr.:— Bukki(5).

1232. בֻּקִּיָּהוּ Buqqiyyahu (131c); from an unused word and 3050; "proved of Yah," a Levite:— Bukkiah(2).

1233. בְּקִיעַ beqia or

בָּקִיעַ baqia (132c); from 1234; *fissure, breach:*— breaches(1), fragments(1).

1234. בָּקַע baqa (131d); a prim. root; *to cleave, break open* or *through:*— breached(3), break(4), break forth(1), break through(1), breaks forth(1), breaks open(1), broke open(1), broke through(2), broken(3), burst(2), burst open(1), cleaved(1), dashed to pieces(1), divide(1), divided(4), forth(1), hatch(2), hews(1), invaded(1), make for ourselves a breach(1), rip(1), ripped(1), ripped open(2), shook(1), split(7), split open(1), splits(1), tear(1), tore(2), torn(2).

1235. בֶּקַע beqa (132b); from 1234; *half:*— beka(1), half-shekel(1).

1236. בִּקְעָא biqa (1085a); (Ara.) corr. to 1237; *a plain:*— plain(1).

1237. בִּקְעָה biqah (132c); from 1234; *a valley, plain:*— broad valley(1), plain(7), valley(8), valleys(4).

1238a. בָּקַק baqaq (132c); a prim. root; *to be luxuriant:*— luxuriant(1).

1238b. בָּקַק baqaq (132d); a prim. root; *to empty:*— completely laid waste(1), demoralized(1), devastate(1), devastators have devastated(1), lays the waste(1), make void(1).

1239. בָּקַר baqar (133a); a prim. root; *to inquire, seek:*— care(1), concerned(1), inquire(1), make inquiry(1), meditate(1), seek(2).

1240. בְּקַר beqar (1085a); (Ara.) corr. to 1239; *to inquire, seek:*— inquire(1), search(1), search be conducted(1), search has been made(1), search was made(1).

1241. בָּקָר baqar (133a); from 1239; *cattle, herd, an ox:*— bull(1), bull*(21), bulls(9), bulls*(5), calf*(2), calves*(1), cattle(13), cow's(1), cows(1), herd(20), herds(27), ox(3), oxen(68).

1242. בֹּקֶר boqer (133c); from 1239; *morning:*— dawn(1), dawn*(2), day(1), daybreak(1), every morning(5), morning(195), mornings(2), soon(1), tomorrow morning(1).

1243. בַּקָּרָה baqqarah (134c); from 1239; *a seeking:*— cares(1).

1244. בִּקֹּרֶת biqqoreth (134c); from 1239; *punishment:*— punishment(1).

1245. בָּקַשׁ baqash (134c); a prim. root; *to seek:*— aim(1), beg(1), begging(1), concerned(1), consulted(1), demand(1), desire(1), eager(1), hold*(1), inquired(2), investigated(1), look(3), looked(1), looking(3), plead(1), pursuit(1), request(2), require(7), required(1), requires(1), search(8), search will be made(1), searched(8), searching(1), seek(94), seeking(24), seeks(16), set about(1), sought(38), tried(2).

1246. בַּקָּשָׁה baqqashah (135a); from 1245; *request, entreaty:*— request(6), requested(1), what i request(1).

1247. בַּר bar (1085b); (Ara.) corr. to 1121; *son:*— age*(1), son(7).

1248. בַּר bar (135a); from 1247; *son:*— son(4).

1249. בַּר bar (141a); from 1305; *pure, clean:*— clean(1), innocent(1), pure(4), who are pure(1).

1250. בַּר bar (141b); from 1305; *grain, corn:*— grain(11), wheat(2).

1251. בַּר bar (1085c); (Ara.) corr. to 1250; (an open) *field:*— field(8).

1252. בֹּר bor (141b); from 1305; *cleanness, pureness:*— cleanness(5).

1253a. בֹּר bor (141b); from 1305; *lye, potash:*— lye(2).

1253b. בָּר bor (141b); of for. or.; *a field:*— open field(1).

1254a. בָּרָא bara (135b); a prim. root; *to shape, create:*— brings about(1), clear(2), create(6), created(32), creates(1), creating(3), Creator(4), cut them down(1), make(2), produced(1).

1254b. בָּרָא bara (135d); a prim. root; *to be fat:*— making yourselves fat(1).

1255. בְּרֹאדַךְ בַּלְאֲדָן Berodak Baladan (114d, 597d); of for. or.; "he has given a son," a Bab. king (the same as 4757):— Berodach-baladan(1).

1256. בְּרָאיָה Berayah (135c); from 1254a and 3050; "Yah has created," a Benjamite:— Beraiah(1).

1257. בַּרְבֻּרִים barburim (141b); from 1305; *capons* or *geese, fowl:*— fowl(1).

1258. בָּרַד barad (136a); denom. vb. from 1259; *to hail:*— hail(1).

1259. בָּרָד barad (135d); from an unused word; *hail:*— hail(23), hailstones(4), hailstones*(2).

1260. בֶּרֶד Bered (136a); from the same as 1259; a place near Kadesh, also an Ephraimite:— Bered(2).

1261. בָּרֹד barod (136a); from the same as 1259; *spotted, marked:*— dappled(1), dappled ones(1), mottled(2).

1262. בָּרָה barah (136a); a prim. root; *to eat:*— choose(1), eat(5), food(1).

1263. בָּרוּךְ Baruk (140a); pass. part. from 1288; "blessed," three Isr.:— Baruch(26).

1264. בְּרוֹם berom (140b); from an unused word; *variegated cloth:*— many colors(1).

1265. בְּרוֹשׁ berosh (141b); of unc. der.; *cypress* or *fir:*— cypress(11), cypress trees(1), cypresses(3), fir(1), fir trees(2), juniper(2).

1266. בְּרוֹת beroth (141c); an Ara. form of 1265; *cypress* or *fir:*— cypresses(1).

1267. בָּרוּת baruth (136a); from 1262; *food:*— food(1).

1268. בֵּרוֹתָה Berothah (92d); of unc. der.; a place near Hamath:— Berothah(1).

1269. בִּרְזוֹת Birzoth (137b); from an unused word; a desc. of Asher:— Birzaith(1).

1270. בַּרְזֶל barzel (137b); from the same as 1269; *iron:*— axe(1), axe head(1), chains(1), iron(71), irons(1).

1271. בַּרְזִלַּי Barzillay (137d); from 1270; "man of iron," three Isr.:— Barzillai(12).

1272. בָּרַח barach (137d); a prim. root; *to go through, flee:*— drives his away(1), drove him away(1), fled(34), flee(11), flee away(1), fleeing(4), flees(2), gone away(1), hurry(1), pass through(2), put to flight(2), ran away(2), surely try to flee(1).

1273. בַּרְחֻמִי Barchumi (138c); by transp. for 978, q.v.

1274. בְּרִי beri (138c); see 7377.

1275. בֵּרִי Beri (92d); from 874; a desc. of Asher:— Beri(1).

1276. בֵּרִי Beri (138c); of unc. der.; perh. a place in Pal.:— Berites(1).

1277. בָּרִיא bari (135d); adj. from 1254b; *fat:*— fat(10), fatter*(1), plentiful(1), plump(2).

1278. בְּרִיאָה beriah (135c); from 1254a; *a creation, thing created:*— entirely new thing(1).

1279. בִּרְיָה biryah (136a); from 1262; *food:*— food(3).

1280. בְּרִיחַ beriach (138b); from 1272; *a bar:*— bar(3), bars(36), bolt(1).

1281. בָּרִיחַ bariach (138a); adj. from 1272; *fleeing:*— fleeing(2), fugitives(2).

1282. בָּרִיחַ Bariach (138a); from 1272; an Isr.:— Bariah(1).

1283. בְּרִיעָה Beriah (140b); of unc. der.; four Isr.:— Beriah(11).

1284. בְּרִיעִי Berii (140b); from 1283; desc. of Beriah:— Beriites(1).

1285. בְּרִית berith (136b); from an unused word; *a covenant:*— allied(1), allies*(1), covenant(275), covenants(1), El-berith*(1), league(2), treaty(4).

1286. בְּרִית Berith (127b); short. form of 1170; a Shechemite deity.

1287. בֹּרִית borith (141b); fem. of 1252; *lye, alkali, potash, soap:*— soap(2).

1288. בָּרַךְ barak (138c); a prim. root; *to kneel, bless:*— abundantly bless(1), actually blessed(1), bless(111), bless is blessed(1), bless me indeed(1), bless them at all(1), blessed(167), blessed be those who bless(1), blessed is everyone who blesses(1), blesses(10), blessing(1), boast(1), congratulates(1), curse(3), cursed(3), curses(1), greatly bless(1), greet(2), greeted(1), had to bless(1), kneel(1), kneel down(1), knelt(1), persisted in blessing(1), pronounce blessing(1), salute(1), salutes(1), surely bless(1), thanked(1).

1289. בְּרַךְ berak (1085b); (Ara.) corr. to 1288; *to kneel, bless:*— blessed(4), kneeling(1).

1290. בֶּרֶךְ berek (139c); from 1288; *the knee:*— feeble*(1), knee(1), kneeled*(1), kneels*(1), knees(20), lap(1).

1291. בְּרַךְ berak (1085c); (Ara.) corr. to 1290; *the knee:*— knees(1).

1292. בָּרַכְאֵל Barakel (140a); from 1288 and 410; "El does bless," the father of one of Job's friends:— Barachel(2).

1293. בְּרָכָה berakah (139c); from 1288; *a blessing:*— benefit(1), blessed(1), blessing(48), blessings(11), generous(1), gift(3), most blessed(1), peace(2), present(1).

1294. בְּרָכָה Berakah (139d); from 1288; an Isr., also a valley in Judah:— Beracah(3).

1295. בְּרֵכָה berekah (140a); from 1288; *a pool, pond:*— ponds(1), pool(15), pools(1).

1296. בֶּרֶכְיָה Berekyah or

בֶּרֶכְיָהוּ Berekyahu (140a); from 1288 and 3050, see 3000; "Yah blesses," the name of several Isr.:— Berechiah(11).

1297. בְּרַם beram (1085c); (Ara.) of unc. der.; *only, nevertheless:*— however(3), yet(2).

1298. בֶּרַע Bera (140b); of unc. der.; a king of Sodom:— Bera(1).

1299. בָּרַק baraq (140b); a prim. root; *to flash* (of lightning):— flash forth(1).

1300. בָּרָק baraq (140c); from 1299; *lightning:*— flash like lightning(1), flashing(1), gleaming(2), glittering point(1), lightning(9), lightning flashes(3), lightnings(4).

1301. בָּרָק Baraq (140c); from 1299; "flash of lightning," an Isr. leader:— Barak(13).

1302. בַּרְקוֹס Barqos (140d); of unc. der.; one of the Nethinim:— Barkos(2).

1303. בַּרְקָנִים barqanim (140d); of unc. der.; *briars:*— briers(2).

1304a. בָּרֶקֶת bareqeth (140c); from 1299; *an emerald:*— emerald(2).

1304b. בָּרְקַת bareqath (140d); from 1299; *an emerald:*— emerald(1).

1305. בָּרַר barar (140d); a prim. root; *to purify, select:*— choice(2), chosen(2), cleanse(1), pure you show(2), purge(2), purged(1), purified(1), purify(1), select(1), sharpen(1), show yourself pure(2), sincerely(1), tested(1).

1306. בִּרְשַׁע Birsha (141d); of unc. der.; a king of Gomorrah:— Birsha(1).

1307a. בֵּרֹתַי Berothay (92d); perh. from the same as 1268; a city in Aram (Syria):— Berothai(1).

1307b. בֵּרֹתִי Berothi (92d); from 1268, see 886; inhab. of Berothah:— Berothite(1).

1308. בְּשׂוֹר Besor (143a); perh. from 1319; a stream in Pal.:— Besor(3).

1309. בְּשׂוֹרָה besorah or

בְּשֹׂרָה besorah (142d); from 1319; *tidings:*— carry news(1), news(4), reward(2).

1310. בָּשַׁל bashal (143a); a prim. root; *to boil, seethe, grow ripe:*— baked(1), boil(12), boiled(7), boiled at all(1), boiling(2), cook(1), produced ripe(1), ripe(1), roasted(1), seethe(1).

1311. בָּשֵׁל bashel (143b); from 1310; *cooked, boiled:*— boiled(1).

1312. בִּשְׁלָם Bishlam (143b); perh. from 1121 and 7965; perh. "son of peace," a Pers.:— Bishlam(1).

1313. בָּשָׂם basam (141d); the same as 1314, q.v.

1314. בֹּשֶׂם bosem (141d); from an unused word; *spice, balsam, the balsam tree:*— balsam(3), fragrant(2), spice(2), spices(22), sweet perfume(1).

1315. בָּשְׂמַת Basemath (142a); from the same as 1314; "perfume," a wife of Esau (or perh. two wives with the same name), also a daughter of Solomon:— Basemath(7).

1316. בָּשָׁן Bashan (143b); from an unused word; "smooth," a region E. of the Jordan:— Bashan(60).

1317. בָּשְׁנָה boshnah (102a); fem. noun from 954; *shame:*— shame(1).

1318. בָּשַׁס bashas (143c); a prim. root; *to trample:*— impose heavy rent(1).

1319. בָּשַׂר basar (142a); a prim. root; *to bear tidings:*— bear good news(1), bearer of good news(2), bring good news(1), bring the news(1), bring...news(1), bringing good news(2), brings good news(3), brought the news(2), carry the good news(2), carry news(1), carry...news(1), messenger of good news(1), proclaim(1), proclaim good tidings(2), proclaim the good tidings(1), proclaimed glad tidings(1), receive good news(1).

1320. בָּשָׂר basar (142b); from 1319; *flesh:*— anyone*(1), bodies(2), body(39), fatter*(1), flesh(176), gaunt*(3), lustful*(1), man(1), mankind(3), mankind*(1), meat(34), men(1), person(1).

1321. בְּשַׂר besar (1085c); (Ara.) corr. to 1320; *flesh:*— flesh(1), living creatures(1), meat(1).

1322. בֹּשֶׁת bosheth (102a); from 954; *shame, shameful thing:*— humiliation*(1), shame(21), shame*(2), shameful(1), shameful thing(3).

1323. בַּת bath (123a); from 1121; *daughter:*— branches(1), Danite*(1), daughter(265), daughter or her daughter's(1), daughter your daughter's(1), daughter's(1), daughter's daughter(2), daughters(241), dispersed*(1), granddaughter(4), granddaughters*(1), maidens(2), old(3), ostriches*(1), towns(28), villages(17), woman(1), women(1).

1324. בַּת bath (144c); from an unused word; *a bath* (a Heb. measure):— bath(6), baths(7).

1325. בַּת bath (1085d); (Ara.) corr. to 1324; *a bath* (a liquid measure):— baths(2).

1326. בָּתָה bathah (144d); from the same as 1324; *end, destruction:*— waste(1).

1327. בַּתָּה battah (144c); from the same as 1324; *a precipice:*— steep(1).

1328a. בְּתוּאֵל Bethuel (143d); perh. from 4962 and 410; perh. "man of God," a nephew of Abraham:— Bethuel(9).

1328b. בְּתוּאֵל Bethuel (143d); from the same as 1328a; a place in Simeon:— Bethuel(1).

1329. בְּתוּל Bethul (143d); short. from 1328b; a place in Simeon:— Bethul(1).

1330. בְּתוּלָה bethulah (143d); from an unused word; *a virgin:*— maidens(1), virgin(32), virgins(17).

1331. בְּתוּלִים bethulim (144a); from the same as 1330; *virginity:*— evidence of my virginity(1), virgin(5), virginity(4).

1332. בִּתְיָה Bithyah (124a); perh. from 1323 and 3050; "daughter (i.e. worshiper) of Yah," an Eg. woman:— Bithia(1).

1333. בָּתַק bathaq (144a); a prim. root; *to cut, cut off, cut down:*— cut you to pieces(1).

1334. בָּתַר bathar (144a); a prim. root; *to cut in two:*— cut(2).

1335. בֶּתֶר bether (144a); from 1334; *a part, piece:*— half(1), parts(2).

1336. בֶּתֶר Bether (144b); from 1334; "cutting," a place of unc. location in Isr.:— Bether(1).

1337. בַּת־רַבִּים Bath-rabbim (123d); from 1323 and 7227a; "daughter of multitudes," a name for Heshbon or its gate:— Bath-rabbim(1).

1338. בִּתְרוֹן bithron (144c); from 1334; *forenoon:*— morning(1).

1339. בַּת־שֶׁבַע Bath-sheba (124a); from 1323 and perh. 7650; perh. "daughter of oath," the mother of Solomon:— Bathsheba(10).

1340. בַּת־שׁוּעַ Bath-shua (124a); from 1323 and perh. 7770b; perh. "daughter of opulence," an Isr. woman, also a Canaanite woman:— Bath-shua(2).

ג

1341. גֵּא ge (144b); scribal error for 1343, q.v.

1342. גָּאָה gaah (144b); a prim. root; *to rise up:*— grow(1), highly exalted(2), lifted(1), risen(1).

1343. גֵּאֶה geeh (144b); from 1342; *proud:*— pride(1), proud(5), who is proud(3).

1344. גֵּאָה geah (144d); from 1342; *pride:*— pride and arrogance(1).

1345. גְּאוּאֵל Geuel (145b); from 1342 and 410; "majesty of El," a Gadite spy:— Geuel(1).

1346. גַּאֲוָה gaavah (144d); from 1342; *majesty, pride:*— arrogance(2), back(1), haughtiness(1), majesty(3), pride(8), proud(2), proudly(1), swelling pride(1).

1347a. גְּאוּלִים geulim (145d); from 1350; *redemption:*— redemption(1).

1347b. גָּאוֹן gaon (144d); from 1342; *exaltation:*— arrogance(3), eminence(1), excellence(1), glory(1), majestic(1), majesty(5), pomp(1), pride(29), proud(1), splendor(2), thicket(2), thickets(1).

1348. גֵּאוּת geuth (145a); from 1342; *majesty:*— column(1), excellent things(1), majesty(2), proud(2), proudly(1), swelling(1).

1349. גַּאֲיוֹן gaayon (145b); from 1342; *proud:*— proud(1).

1350. גָּאַל gaal (145b); a prim. root; *to redeem, act as kinsman:*— avenger(13), bought back(1), buy back(1), claim(1), close relative(3), closest relative(3), closest relatives(1), ever wish to redeem(2), kinsman(2), redeem(22), redeemed(25), redeemer(1), Redeemer(18), redeems(1), relative(2), relatives(1), rescue(1), wishes to redeem(1).

1351. גָּאַל gaal (146a); a prim. root; *to defile:*— defile(2), defiled(6), stained(1), unclean(2).

1352. גֹּאַל goel (146a); from 1351; *defiling, defilement:*— defiled(1).

1353. גְּאֻלָּה **geullah** (145d); pass. part. of 1350; *redemption,* perh. *kin:*— redemption(7), redemption right(2), redemption rights(1), right of redemption(3).

1354. גַּב **gab** (146b); from an unused word; *a back:*— back(1), backs(1), base(1), defenses(2), eyebrows*(1), massive*(1), rims(3), shrine(2), shrines(1).

1355. גַּב **gab** (1085d); (Ara.) corr. to 1354; *back* or *side:*— back(1).

1356a. גֵּב **geb** (155d); from 1461; *a pit, trench, ditch:*— cisterns(1), full of trenches(1).

1356b. גֵּב **geb** (155d); from 1461; *a beam, rafter:*— beams(1).

1357. גֵּב **geb** (146d); see 1361a.

1358. גֹּב **gob** (1085d); (Ara.) corr. to 1356a; *a pit, den:*— den(10).

1359. גֹּב **Gob** (146c); from the same as 1354; a place in Pal.:— Gob(2).

1360. גֶּבֶא **gebe** (146b); from an unused word; *a cistern, pool:*— cistern(1).

1361a. גֵּבֶה **gebeh** (146d); from an unused word; *locust:*— locusts(1).

1361b. גָּבַהּ **gabah** (146d); a prim. root; *to be high, exalted:*— build high(1), exalt(2), exalted(4), haughty(4), high(4), higher(3), lifted(3), loftier(1), made it high(1), make your as high(1), mounts(1), pride*(1), proud(4), raised(1), raises(1), taller(1), took great(1), upward(1).

1362. גָּבֹהַּ **gabah** (147a); the same as 1364, q.v.

1363. גֹּבַהּ **gobah** (147b); from 1361b; *height:*— dignity(1), haughtiness(1), haughty(1), height(6), high(2), loftiness(1), lofty(1), pride(1), raised platform(1).

1364. גָּבֹהַּ **gaboah** (147a); from 1361b; *high, exalted:*— haughtiness(1), haughty(2), high(22), higher officials(1), lofty(1), long(1), longer(1), longer one(1), official(2), proud(2), taller(1), very proudly(1), which is high(1), who are lofty(1).

1365. גַּבְהוּת **gabhuth** (147b); from 1361b; *haughtiness:*— pride(1), proud(1).

1366. גְּבוּל **gebul** (147d); from an unused word; *border, boundary, territory:*— area(1), barrier(1), border(144), borders(10), boundary(13), coastline(3), districts(1), land(1), line(1), territories(1), territory(61), wall(1).

1367. גְּבוּלָה **gebulah** (148b); fem. of 1366; *border, boundary:*— area(1), borders(4), boundaries(3), landmarks(1), territories(1).

1368. גִּבּוֹר **gibbor** (150a); from 1396; *strong, mighty:*— champion(2), great(1), helpers(1), heroes(3), men(3), men of outstanding(1), Mighty(1), mighty(27), mighty man(15), mighty men(57), Mighty One(1), mighty one(2), mighty ones(3), mighty warrior(1), mighty warriors(2), strong(1), strong man(1), valiant warriors(1), valiant*(1), warrior(14), warrior has over another(1), warrior's(1), warriors(17), who is mighty(1).

1369. גְּבוּרָה **geburah** (150b); pass. part. from 1396; *strength, might:*— courage(1), might(26), mighty(1), mighty acts(3), mighty deeds(4), mighty ones(1), mighty strength(1), power(9), strength(13), strong(1), triumph(1).

1370. גְּבוּרָה **geburah** (1086a); (Ara.) corr. to 1369; *might:*— power(2).

1371. גִּבֵּחַ **gibbeach** (147c); from an unused word; *having a bald forehead:*— bald on the forehead(1).

1372. גַּבַּחַת **gabbachath** (147c); from the same as 1371; *a bald forehead:*— bald(1), bald forehead(3), bareness*(1), front(1).

1373a. גַּבַּי **Gabbay** (146c); from the same as 1354; a Benjamite:— Gabbai(1).

1373b. גֹּבַי **gobay** or

גּוֹבַי **gobay** (146d); from the same as 1361a; *locusts:*— locust-swarm(1).

1374. גֵּבִים **Gebim** (155d); pl. of 1356a; "trenches," a place N. of Jer.:— Gebim(1).

1375. גָּבִיעַ **gabia** (149b); from the same as 1387; *a cup, bowl:*— cup(5), cups(8), pitchers(1).

1376. גְּבִיר **gebir** (150c); from 1396; *lord:*— master(2).

1377. גְּבִירָה **gebirah** (150c); fem. of 1376; *lady, queen:*— queen(1), queen mother(5).

1378. גָּבִישׁ **gabish** (150d); from an unused word; *crystal:*— crystal(1).

1379. גָּבַל **gabal** (148b); denom. vb. from 1366; *to bound, border:*— border(1), borders(1), set(1), set bounds(2).

1380. גְּבַל **Gebal** (148b); from the same as 1366; a city in Phoenicia:— Gebal(1).

1381. גְּבָל **Gebal** (148c); from the same as 1366; a region S. of the Dead Sea:— Gebal(1).

1382. גִּבְלִי **Gibli** (148c); from 1380; inhab. of Gebal:— Gebalite(1), Gebalites(1).

1383. גַּבְלֻת **gabluth** (148b); from the same as 1366; *a twisting:*— twisted(2).

1384. גִּבֵּן **gibben** (148c); from an unused word; *crookbacked, humpbacked:*— hunchback(1).

1385. גְּבִנָה **gebinah** (148c); from the same as 1384; *curd, cheese:*— cheese(1).

1386. גַּבְנֹן **gabnon** (148d); from the same as 1384; *a peak, rounded summit:*— peaks(2).

1387. גֶּבַע **Geba** (148d); from an unused word; a Levitical city of Benjamin:— Geba(17), Maareh-geba*(1).

1388. גִּבְעָא **Giba** (148d); from the same as 1387; a desc. of Caleb:— Gibea(1).

1389. גִּבְעָה **gibah** (148d); fem. from the same as 1387; *a hill:*— Gibeath-haaraloth*(1), hill(30), hills(39).

1390. גִּבְעָה **Gibah** (149b); from the same as 1387; "hill," three cities in Pal.:— Gibeah(45).

1391. גִּבְעוֹן **Gibon** (149c); from the same as 1387; a Levitical city in Benjamin:— Gibeon(37).

1392. גִּבְעֹל **gibol** (149c); prol. of 1375; *a bud:*— bud(1).

1393. גִּבְעֹנִי **Giboni** (149c); from 1391; inhab. of Gibeon:— Gibeonite(2), Gibeonites(6).

1394. גִּבְעַת **Gibath** (149b); the same as 1390, q.v.

1395. גִּבְעָתִי **Gibathi** (149b); from 1390; an inhab. of Gibath (or Gibeah):— Gibeathite(1).

1396. גָּבַר **gabar** (149c); a prim. root; *to be strong, mighty:*— become(1), conducts himself arrogantly(1), exert(1), great(2), magnified(1), make a firm(1), prevail(5), prevailed(9), strengthen(2), stronger(1), surpassed(1).

1397. גֶּבֶר **geber** (149d); from 1396; *man:*— boy(1), everyone(1), man(54), man's(3), men(8), warrior(1).

1398. גֶּבֶר **Geber** (150a); from 1396; an Isr. name:— Geber(1).

1399. גְּבַר **gebar** (149d); the same as 1397, q.v.

1400. גְּבַר **gebar** (1086a); (Ara.) corr. to 1397; *man:*— certain(3), man(2), men(15), people(1).

1401. גִּבָּר **gibbar** (1086a); (Ara.) from the same as 1400; *mighty one:*— warriors(1).

1402. גִּבָּר **Gibbar** (150a); from 1396; "hero," an Isr.:— Gibbar(1).

1403. גַּבְרִיאֵל **Gabriel** (150c); from 1397 and 410; "man of El," an archangel:— Gabriel(2).

1404. גְּבֶרֶת **gebereth** (150c); from 1396; *lady, queen, mistress:*— mistress(7), queen(2).

1405. גִּבְּתוֹן **Gibbethon** (146d); from the same as 1354; "mound," a city in Dan:— Gibbethon(6).

1406. גָּג **gag** (150d); of unc. der.; *a roof, a top:*— housetop(1), housetops(7), roof(18), roofs(1), rooftops(1), top(2).

1407. גַּד **gad** (151b); perh. from 1413; *coriander:*— coriander(2).

1408. גַּד **Gad** (151c); perh. of for. or.; "fortune," a Bab. god.

1409. גָּד **gad** (151c); perh. of for. or.; *fortune, good fortune:*— fortunate(1), fortune(1).

1410. גָּד **Gad** (151c); perh. from 1408; a son of Jacob, also his tribe and its territory, also a prophet:— Dibon-gad*(2), Gad(71).

1411. גְּדָבְרַיָּא **gedaberayya** (1086a); (Ara.) of unc. der., perh. corr. to 1489; perh. *treasurer:*— treasurers(2).

1412. גֻּדְגֹּדָה **Gudgodah** (151d); perh. from 1413; a place in the desert:— Gudgodah(2).

1413. גָּדַד **gadad** (151a); a prim. root; *to penetrate, cut:*— cut(2), gash(2), gashed(1), muster yourselves in troops(1), together(1), trooped(1).

1414. גְּדַד **gedad** (1086a); (Ara.) corr. to 1413; *to hew down:*— chop down(2).

1415. גָּדָה **gadah** (152a); from an unused word; *bank* (of a river):— banks(4).

1416. גְּדוּד **gedud** (151b); from 1413; *a band, troop:*— band(6), band of raiders(1), Bandits(1), bands(7), divisions(1), marauding band(2), marauding bands(1), raid(1), raiders(3), troop(2), troops(7), troops*(1).

1417. גְּדוּד **gedud** or

גְּדוּדָה **gedudah** (151b); from 1413; *a furrow, cutting:*— gashes(1), ridges(1).

1418. גְּדוּדָה **gedudah** (151b); the same as 1417, q.v.

1419. גָּדוֹל **gadol** (152d); from 1431; *great:*— all*(2), bigger(1), bitterly(1), bitterly*(3), deep(1), elder(3), exceedingly(2), extremely*(2), far more(1), Great(12), great(340), great man(2), great men(7), great one(1), great ones(1), great things(7), greater(18), greatest(9), greatly(3), greatness(1), hard(1), heavy(2), high(21), highest(1), impressed(1), large(30), larger(1), loud(22), loudly(1), main(1), major(1), many(1), marvelous(1), mighty(1), mighty and great(1), more*(1), much(1), nobles(1), old(1), older(8), oldest(3), prominent(1), rich(1), screamed*(1), severe(1), spacious(1), vast(1), very*(2), violently*(1).

1420. גְּדוּלָּה **gedullah** (153c); from 1431; *greatness:*— dignity(1), great(1), great majesty(1), great thing(1), great things(1), greatness(7).

1421. גִּדּוּף **gidduph** (154d); from 1442; *revilings, reviling words:*— revilement(1), revilings(2).

1422. גְּדוּפָה geduphah (154d); fem. part. of 1442; *a taunt:*— reviling(1).

1423. גְּדִי gedi (152a); from the same as 1415; *a kid* (a young goat):— young(2), young goat(6), young goat*(5), young goats(1), young goats*(2).

1424. גָּדִי Gadi (151d); from 1409; an Isr.:— Gadi(2).

1425. גָּדִי Gadi (151d); from 1410; desc. of Gad:— Gadite(1), Gadites(14).

1426. גַּדִּי Gaddi (151d); from 1409; "my fortune," a Manassite:— had(1).

1427. גַּדִּיאֵל Gaddiel (151d); from 1409 and 410; "El is my fortune," an Isr.:— Gaddiel(1).

1428. גִּדְיָה gidyah (152a); the same as 1415, q.v.

1429. גְּדִיָּה gediyyah (152a); fem. of 1423; *a kid* (a young goat):— young goats(1).

1430a. גָּדִישׁ gadish (155c); from an unused word; *a heap, stack:*— grain(1), shocks(1), stacked(1).

1430b. גָּדִישׁ gadish (155c); from an unused word; *a tomb:*— tomb(1).

1431. גָּדַל gadal (152a); a prim. root; *to grow up, become great:*— advanced(1), arrogantly(1), became great(1), became greater(2), became rich(1), became tall(1), became...wealthy(1), become arrogant(4), become great(1), become rich(1), become so great(1), bigger(1), boast*(1), bring(1), brought(1), educated(1), enlarged(1), exalt(2), exalted(4), great(10), great things(5), great things he has done(1), greater(4), grew(15), grew...great(1), grow(2), grow long(1), grown(5), grown-up(1), grows(1), highly valued(2), increase(1), lifted(1), magnificent(1), magnified(15), magnify(9), make his greater(1), make the great(2), make your great(1), make great(1), makes it grow(1), more(1), promoted(1), reared(3), rearing(1), spoken*(1), vaunt(1).

1432. גָּדֵל gadel (152d); from 1431; *becoming great, growing up:*— greater(1), grow richer(1), growing*(1), lustful*(1), stature(1).

1433. גֹּדֶל godel (152d); from 1431; *greatness:*— arrogance(1), arrogant(1), greatness(11).

1434. גְּדִל gedil (152d); from 1431; *twisted threads:*— tassels(1), twisted threads(1).

1435. גִּדֵּל Giddel (153c); from 1431; "very great," one of the Nethinim, also one of Solomon's servants:— Giddel(4).

1436a. גְּדַלְיָה Gedalyah (153d); from 1431 and 3050; "Yah is great," three Isr.:— Gedaliah(5).

1436b. גְּדַלְיָהוּ Gedalyahu (153d); from 1431 and 3050; "Yah is great," three Isr.:— Gedaliah(27).

1437. גִּדַּלְתִּי Giddalti (153d); from 1431; "I magnify (God)," an Isr.:— Giddalti(2).

1438. גָּדַע gada (154b); a prim. root; *to hew, hew down* or *off:*— break(1), break off(1), chopped down(2), cut in pieces(1), cut it in pieces(1), cut of asunder(1), cut down(7), cut off(6), cut through(1), hew down(1).

1439. גִּדְעוֹן Gidon (154c); from 1438; a judge of Isr.:— Gideon(38).

1440. גִּדְעֹם Gidom (154c); from 1438; a place in Benjamin:— Gidom(1).

1441. גִּדְעֹנִי Gidoni (154c); from 1438; a Benjamite:— Gideoni(5).

1442. גָּדַף gadaph (154c); a prim. root; *to revile, blaspheme:*— blasphemed(5), blaspheming(1), reviles(1).

1443. גָּדַר gadar (154d); a prim. root; *to wall up* or *off, to build a wall:*— blocked(1), build(2), build the wall(1), masons(2), repairer(1), wall(1), walled(2).

1444. גֶּדֶר geder (154d); the same as 1447, q.v.

1445. גֶּדֶר Geder (155a); from 1443; a city in Canaan:— Geder(1).

1446. גְּדֹר Gedor or

גְּדוֹר Gedor (155b); from 1443; "wall," three cities in Isr., also a Benjamite:— Gedor(7).

1447. גָּדֵר gader (154d); from 1443; *a wall:*— fence(1), hedges(1), wall(11), walls(1).

1448. גְּדֵרָה gederah or

גְּדֶרֶת gedereth (155a); from 1443; *a wall:*— folds(1), Gederah(1), sheepfolds(2), sheepfolds*(2), wall(1), walls(3).

1449. גְּדֵרָה Gederah (155b); from 1448; "wall," a city in Judah:— Gederah(1).

1450. גְּדֵרוֹת Gederoth (155b); from 1443; "walls," a place in Judah:— Gederoth(2).

1451. גְּדֵרִי Gederi (155b); from 1445; inhab. of Geder:— Gederite(1).

1452. גְּדֵרָתִי Gederathi (155b); from 1449; inhab. of Gederah:— Gederathite(1).

1453. גְּדֵרֹתַיִם Gederothayim (155b); dual of 1448; "double wall," a place in Judah:— Gederothaim(1).

1454. גֵּה geh (155c); prob. a scribal error for 2088, q.v.

1455. גָּהָה gahah (155c); a prim. root; *to depart, be cured* or *healed:*— cure(1).

1456. גֵּהָה gehah (155c); from 1455; *a healing, cure:*— medicine(1).

1457. גָּהַר gahar (155c); a prim. root; *to bend, crouch:*— crouched down(1), stretched(2).

1458. גַּו gav (156a); from an unused word; *the back:*— back(2), backs(1).

1459. גַּו gav (1086a); (Ara.) corr. to 1460b; *midst, middle:*— midst(9), within(2).

1460a. גֵּו gev (156a); from the same as 1458; *the back:*— back(6).

1460b. גֵּו gev (156b); of for. or.; *midst, middle:*— community(1).

1461. גּוּב gub (155c); another reading for 3009, q.v.

1462. גּוֹב gob (146d); from the same as 1361a; *locusts:*— hordes of grasshoppers(1).

1463. גּוֹג Gog (155d); of unc. der.; the name of an Isr., also leader of a northern nation:— Gog(10).

1464. גּוּד gud (156a); a prim. root; *to invade, attack:*— invade(1), raid(2).

1465. גֵּוָה gevah (156b); fem. of 1460a; *the back:*— back(1).

1466. גֵּוָה gevah (145b); from 1342; *pride:*— confidence(1), pride(2).

1467. גֵּוָה gevah (1085d); (Ara.) corr. to 1344; *pride:*— pride(1).

1468. גּוּז guz (156d); a prim. root; *to pass over* or *away:*— brought(1), gone(1).

1469. גּוֹזָל gozal (160a); from an unused word; *young birds:*— young(1), young pigeon(1).

1470. גּוֹזָן Gozan (157a); of unc. der.; a city and area in Mesopotamia:— Gozan(5).

1471. גּוֹי goy (156c); from the same as 1458; *nation, people:*— every nation(2), Gentiles(1), Goiim(1), Harosheth-hagoyim*(3), herds(1), nation(120), nations(425), people(4).

1472a. גְּוִיָּה geviyyah (156b); from the same as 1458; *a body, corpse:*— bodies(4), body(6), corpses(1), dead bodies(2).

1472b. גּוֹיִם Goyim (157a); prob. of for. or.; a kingdom N.E. of Bab., prob. also a place in Gilgal:— Goiim(2).

1473. גּוֹלָה golah (163c); fem. part. of 1540; *exiles, exile:*— captives(1), exile(19), exiled*(1), exiles(16), exiles*(5).

1474. גּוֹלָן Golan (157b); of unc. der.; a city and a region E. of the Jordan in Manasseh:— Golan(4).

1475. גּוּמָּץ gummats (170a); from an unused word; *a pit:*— pit(1).

1476. גּוּנִי Guni (157b); from an unused word; two Isr.:— Guni(4).

1477. גּוּנִי Guni (157b); from 1476; desc. of Guni:— Gunites(1).

1478. גָּוַע gava (157b); a prim. root; *to expire, perish, die:*— breathed his last(4), die(5), died(2), expire(2), expires(1), perish(6), perished(4).

1479. גּוּף guph (157c); a prim. root; *to shut, close:*— shut(1).

1480. גּוּפָה guphah (157c); from 1479; *a body, corpse:*— bodies(1), body(1).

1481a. גּוּר gur (157c); a prim. root; *to sojourn:*— abide*(1), alien(1), aliens(1), assemble(1), colonize(1), dwell(3), dwells(1), habitation(1), live(4), live as aliens(2), lives(1), reside(13), resided(1), resides(3), sojourn(11), sojourned(9), sojourning(1), sojourns(13), stay(6), staying(4), stays(1), strangers(3).

1481b. גּוּר gur (158d); a prim. root; *to stir up strife, quarrel:*— assails(1), attack(1), band(1), fiercely assails(1), launch an attack(1), stir(1).

1481c. גּוּר gur (158d); a prim. root; *to dread:*— afraid(2), dreaded(1), fear(4), feared(1), stand in awe(2).

1482. גּוּר gur (158d); from 1481b; *a whelp:*— cub(1), cubs(3), whelp(2), young(1).

1483. גּוּר Gur (158a); from 1481a; "sojourning, dwelling," a place in Pal.:— Gur(1).

1484. גּוֹר gor (158d); from 1481b; *a whelp:*— cubs(2).

1485. גּוּר־בַּעַל Gur-baal (158a); from 1481a and 1168a; "dwelling of Baal," a place in Arabia:— Gur-baal(1).

1486. גּוֹרָל goral (174a); from an unused word; *a lot* (for casting):— allotted(2), allotted portion(1), choice(1), land(1), lot(53), lots(15), lots and the lot(1), territory allotted(2).

1487. גּוּשׁ gush (159a); from an unused word; *a clod, lump:*— crust(1).

1488. גֵּז gez (159c); from 1494; *a shearing, mowing:*— fleece(1), mowing(1), mown(1), shearing(1).

1489. גִּזְבָּר gizbar (159b); of for. or.; *treasurer:*— treasurer(1).

1490. גִּזְבָּר gizbar (1086b); (Ara.) corr. to 1489; *treasurer:*— treasurers(1).

1491. גָּזָה gazah (159b); a prim. root; *to cut:*— took(1).

1492. גִּזָּה gizzah (159c); from 1494; *a fleece:*— fleece(7).

1493. גִּזוֹנִי Gizoni (159b); from an unused place name; inhab. of Gizon:— Gizonite(1).

1494. גָּזַז gazaz (159c); a prim. root; *to shear:*— cut off(3), cut off your hair(1), shaved(1), shear(3), shearers(3), shearing(2), sheepshearers(2), sheepshearers*(1).

1495. גָּזֵז Gazez (159d); from 1494; two Isr.:— Gazez(2).

1496. גָּזִית gazith (159b); from 1491; *a cutting, hewing:*— cut(1), cut stone(2), cut stones(1), hewn(1), hewn stone(1), smooth stones(1), stone cut(2), well-hewn stone(1).

1497. גָּזַל gazal (159d); a prim. root; *to tear away, seize, rob:*— carried away(1), commit(2), commits(1), committed(1), consume(1), force(1), rob(3), robbed(6), robs(2), seize(2), seized(2), snatch(1), snatched(2), steal(1), take(1), taken by robbery(1), tear off(1), took by robbery(1), torn away(1).

1498. גָּזֵל gazel (160a); from 1497; *robbery:*— denial(1), robbery(4).

1499. גֵּזֶל gezel (160a); the same as 1498, q.v.

1500. גְּזֵלָה gezelah (160a); fem. of 1498; *plunder, spoil:*— plunder(1), robbery(3), taken by robbery(1), what he has taken(1).

1501. גָּזָם gazam (160b); from an unused word; *locusts:*— caterpillar(1), gnawing locust(2).

1502. גַּזָּם Gazzam (160b); from the same as 1501; "devourer," an Isr.:— Gazzam(2).

1503. גֶּזַע geza (160b); from an unused word; *a stock, stem:*— stem(1), stock(1), stump(1).

1504. גָּזַר gazar (160b); a prim. root; *to cut, divide:*— cut down(1), cut off(6), decree(1), decreed(1), divide(2), divided(1), slice off(1).

1505. גְּזַר gezar (1086b); (Ara.) corr. to 1504; *to cut, determine:*— cut(2), diviners(4).

1506. גֶּזֶר gezer (160c); from 1504; *part:*— asunder(1), pieces(1).

1507. גֶּזֶר Gezer (160c); from 1504; "portion," a Levitical city on the border of Ephraim:— Gezer(15).

1508. גִּזְרָה gizrah (160d); fem. of 1506; *a cutting, separation:*— polishing(1), separate area(6), separate areas(1).

1509. גְּזֵרָה gezerah (160c); from 1504; *separation:*— solitary(1).

1510. גְּזֵרָה gezerah (1086b); (Ara.) from 1505; *a decree:*— decree(2).

1511. גִּזְרִי Gizri (160c); another reading for 1629b, q.v.

גִּחוֹן **Gichon**; see 1521.

1512. גָּחוֹן gachon (161a); from an unused word; *belly* (of reptiles):— belly(2).

גֵּחֲזִי **Gechazi**; see 1522.

גָּחֹל **gachol**; see 1513.

1513. גֶּחֶל gechel or

גַּחֶלֶת **gacheleth** (160d); from an unused word; *coal:*— coal(2), coals(15), hot embers(1).

1514. גַּחַם Gacham (161a); from an unused word; perh. "flame," a son of Nahor:— Gaham(1).

1515. גַּחַר Gachar (161a); from an unused word; "lurker," an Isr.:— Gahar(2).

גֹּי **goy**; see 1471.

1516. גַּיְא gay or

גַּי **gay** (161a); of unc. der.; *a valley:*— Geharashim*(1), Valley(8), valley(43), valleys(7).

1517. גִּיד gid (161c); from an unused word; *sinew:*— sinew(3), sinews(4).

1518. גִּיחַ giach (161d); a prim. root; *to burst forth:*— broke(1), brought me forth(1), burst forth(1), bursting forth(1), give birth(1), labor to give birth(1), rushes(1).

1519. גִּיחַ giach (1127c); (Ara.) corr. to 1518; *to break forth:*— stirring(1).

1520. גִּיחַ Giach (161d); from 1518; perh. "a spring," a place in Benjamin:— Giah(1).

1521. גִּיחוֹן Gichon (161d); from 1518; "a bursting forth," one of the rivers of Eden, also a spring near Jer.:— Gihon(6).

1522. גֵּיחֲזִי Gechazi or

גֵּחֲזִי **Gechazi** (161c); perh. from 1516 and 2372; perh. "valley of vision," servant of Elisha:— Gehazi(12).

1523. גִּיל gil (162a); a prim. root; *to rejoice:*— cry(1), exult(1), glad(3), rejoice(38), rejoiced(1), rejoices(1).

1524a. גִּיל gil (162b); from 1523; *a rejoicing:*— exultation(1), greatly(1), greatly*(1), joy(3), rejoicing(2).

1524b. גִּיל gil (162b); from 1523; *a circle, age:*— age(1).

1525. גִּילָה gilah (162b); fem. of 1524a; *a rejoicing:*— rejoicing(2).

גִּילֹה **Giloh**; see 1542.

1526. גִּילֹנִי Giloni (162b); from 1542; an inhab. of Giloh:— Gilonite(2).

1527. גִּינַת Ginath (171b); from 1598; an Isr.:— Ginath(2).

1528. גִּיר gir (1086b); (Ara.) corr. to 1615; *chalk, plaster:*— plaster(1).

גֵּיר **ger**; see 1616.

1529. גֵּישָׁן Geshan (162c); of unc. der.; a desc. of Judah:— Geshan(1).

1530. גַּל gal (164c); from 1556; *a heap, wave, billow:*— billows(1), heap(13), heaps(2), rock garden(1), rock pile(1), ruins(1), stone heaps(1), waves(14).

1531. גֹּל gol (165a); the same as 1543, q.v.

גְּלָא **gela**; see 1541.

1532. גַּלָּב gallab (162c); from an unused word; *a barber:*— barber's(1).

1533. גִּלְבֹּעַ Gilboa (162c); of unc. der.; a mountain in N. Isr.:— Gilboa(8).

1534. גַּלְגַּל galgal (165d); from 1556; *a wheel, whirl, whirlwind:*— wagons(2), wheel(1), wheels(2), whirling dust(2), whirling wheels(3), whirlwind(1).

1535. גַּלְגַּל galgal (1086c); (Ara.) corr. to 1534; *a wheel:*— wheels(1).

1536. גִּלְגָּל gilgal (166a); var. of 1534; *a wheel:*— wheel(1).

1537. גִּלְגָּל Gilgal (166a); from the same as 1536; "circle (of stones)," the name of several places in Pal.:— Gilgal(40).

1538. גֻּלְגֹּלֶת gulgoleth (166b); from 1556; *a skull, head, poll* (of persons):— apiece(2), census(2), head(11), skull(2).

1539. גֶּלֶד geled (162d); from an unused word; *skin:*— skin(1).

1540. גָּלָה galah (162d); a prim. root; *to uncover, remove:*— away into exile(2), banished(1), betray(1), captives(1), captivity(1), carried(1), carried and away(1), carried into exile(4), carried them into exile(3), carried them away into exile(2), carried them captive(1), carried away(14), carried away into exile(10), carried away to exile(1), carried away captive(1), carried...away into exile(4), carry them away as exiles(2), certainly go(3), certainly go into captivity(1), committed(1), depart(1), departed(3), deported(1), disappears(1), discloses(2), disclosing(1), exile(8), exiled(4), exiles(1), expose(2), exposed(3), go from you into exile(1), go into exile(6), go exiled(1), gone into exile(1), indeed reveal(1), inform*(1), known*(2), laid bare(3), lay bare(1), led him captive(1), led away(3), led away into exile(3), led...away into exile(2), lift(1), made(1), make(2), open(4), opened(1), opens(3), published(2), remove(1), removed(3), reported(1), reveal(5), reveal*(1), revealed(12), revealed*(2), revealing(1), reveals(4), revelation*(1), sent into exile(1), sent you into exile(2), set forth(1), shamelessly uncovers(1), show(1), strip off(1), stripped(1), taken(1), taken into exile(1), things revealed(1), uncover(22), uncovered(22), uncovers(1), went into exile(1).

1541. גְּלָה gelah or

גְּלָא **gela** (1086c); (Ara.) corr. to 1540; *to reveal:*— deported(2), reveal(1), revealed(2), revealer(1), reveals(3).

גּוֹלָה **golah**; see 1473.

1542. גִּלֹה Giloh (162b); from 1523; a city in Judah:— Giloh(2).

1543. גֻּלָּה gullah (165a); from 1556; *a basin, bowl:*— bowl(3), bowls(6), springs(6).

1544. גִּלּוּל gillul (165c); from 1556; *an idol:*— idols(48).

1545. גְּלוֹם gelom (166b); from 1563; *a wrapping, garment:*— clothes(1).

1546. גָּלוּת galuth (163d); from 1540; *an exile:*— captives(1), exile(5), exiles(8), population(2).

1547. גָּלוּת galuth or

גָּלוּ **galu** (1086c); (Ara.) corr. to 1546; *an exile:*— exiles*(4).

1548. גָּלַח galach (164a); a prim. root; *to be bald, shave, shave off:*— cut(3), shave(9), shave off(4), shaved(4), shaved off(3).

1549. גִּלָּיוֹן gillayon (163d); from 1540; *a table, tablet:*— hand mirrors(1), tablet(1).

1550. גָּלִיל galil (165b); from 1556; *a turning, folding:*— turned on pivots(2).

1551. גָּלִיל galil (165b); from 1556; *a cylinder, rod, circuit, district,* also a district in Pal.:— Galilee(5), rings(1), rods(1).

1552. גְּלִילָה gelilah (165b); from 1556; *a circuit, boundary, territory,* also a district in Pal.:— Galilee(1), region(3), regions(2).

1553. גְּלִילוֹת Geliloth (165c); pl. of 1552; "circles," a Pal. place name:— Geliloth(1).

1554. גַּלִּים Gallim (164d); pl. of 1530; "heaps," a place near Jer.:— Gallim(2).

1555. גָּלְיָת Golyath (163d); from 1540; a Philistine giant:— Goliath(6).

1556. גָּלַל galal (164b); a prim. root; *to roll, roll away:*— commit(3), lay wallowing(1), roll(5), roll you down(1), roll down(1), rolled(3), rolled away(1), rolls(1), seek occasion(1), take away(1).

1557. גָּלָל galal (165b); from 1556; *dung:*— dung(2).

1558. גָּלָל galal (164b); from an unused word; *an account:*— account(6), because(3), because*(1).

1559. גָּלָל **Galal** (165b); from 1556; two Levites:— Galal(3).

1560. גְּלָל **gelal** (1086c); (Ara.) from a word corr. to 1556; *a rolling:*— huge(2).

1561. גֶּלֶל **gelel** or

גֵּל **gel** (165a); from 1556; *dung:*— dung(1), dung*(1), refuse(1).

1562. גִּלֲלַי **Gilalay** (165b); from 1556; a Levitical musician:— Gilalai(1).

1563. גָּלַם **galam** (166b); a prim. root; *to wrap up, fold, fold together:*— folded it together(1).

1564. גֹּלֶם **golem** (166b); from 1563; *an embryo:*— unformed substance(1).

1565. גַּלְמוּד **galmud** (166c); prob. from 1563; *hard, barren:*— barren(3), gaunt(1).

1566. גָּלַע **gala** (166c); a prim. root; *to expose, lay bare:*— breaks(1), quarrel(1), quarrels(1).

1567. גַּלְעֵד **Galed** (165a); from 1530 and 5707; "witness-pile," a memorial of stones E. of the Jordan River:— Galeed(2).

1568. גִּלְעָד **Gilad** (166d); from 1566; a region in Pal., also the name of several Isr.:— Gilead(99), Gilead's(1), Gileadites(2), Jabesh-gilead*(12).

1569. גִּלְעָדִי **Giladi** (167c); from 1568; a desc. of Gilead, also an inhab. of Gilead:— Gileadite(9), Gileadites(1), Gileadites*(1).

1570. גָּלַשׁ **galash** (167c); a prim. root; *to recline:*— descended(2).

1571. גַּם **gam** (168d); from an unused word; *also, moreover, yea:*— addition(1), alike(1), all(1), all*(1), also(364), although(1), any(3), besides(4), bitterly*(1), both(28), both you and also(1), both*(6), certainly(2), either(6), either by or(1), even(114), even they also(2), even they too(1), furthermore(15), however(1), indeed(21), itself(1), likewise(5), merely(1), moreover(17), moreover*(1), neither*(5), neither(1), nevertheless(1), nor(4), nor yet(1), nor*(4), now(3), now*(2), only(1), or(4), part also(1), previously*(1), so(1), spite*(1), still(1), still*(1), then(1), therefore(1), though(2), times*(2), together(2), too(30), truly(2), turn(2), very(1), well(6), what is more(1), whether(1), yes(9), yet(6).

1572. גָּמָא **gama** (167c); a prim. root; *to swallow* (liquids):— drink(1), races(1).

1573. גֹּמֶא **gome** (167d); from 1572; *a rush, reed, papyrus:*— papyrus(2), rushes(1), wicker(1).

1574. גֹּמֶד **gomed** (167d); from an unused word; *a short cubit* (from elbow to knuckles of clenched fist):— cubit(1).

1575. גַּמָּדִים **Gammadim** (167d); from the same as 1574; "men of valor," defenders of Tyre:— Gammadim(1).

1576. גְּמוּל **gemul** (168b); from 1580; *a dealing, recompense, benefit:*— benefit(1), benefits(1), dealings(1), deeds(1), deserved*(1), good deed(1), recompense(11), recompense*(1), what he deserves*(1).

1577. גָּמוּל **Gamul** (168c); from 1580; "weaned," a Levite:— Gamul(1).

1578. גְּמוּלָה **gemulah** (168c); fem. of 1576; *a dealing, recompense:*— deeds(1), recompense(1), reward(1).

1579. גִּמְזוֹ **Gimzo** (168a); of unc. der.; a city in Judah:— Gimzo(1).

1580. גָּמַל **gamal** (168a); a prim. root; *to deal fully* or *adequately with, deal out to, wean, ripen:*— bore ripe(1), brought(1), compensate(1), deal bountifully(2), dealt(2), dealt bountifully(2), did(2), does(2), done(1), granted(2), recompense(1), repaid(1), repay(1), rewarded(4), rewarding(1), ripening(1), weaned(12).

1581. גָּמָל **gamal** (168c); from 1580; *a camel:*— camel(5), camel's(1), camels(44), camels'(4).

1582. גְּמַלִּי **Gemalli** (168d); from 1580; a Danite:— Gemalli(1).

1583. גַּמְלִיאֵל **Gamliel** (168c); from 1580 and 410; a Manassite:— Gamaliel(5).

1584. גָּמַר **gamar** (170a); a prim. root; *to end, come to an end, complete:*— accomplish(1), accomplishes(1), ceases(1), come to an end(2).

1585. גְּמַר **gemar** (1086c); (Ara.) corr. to 1584; *to complete:*— perfect(1).

1586. גֹּמֶר **Gomer** (170a); from 1584; a son of Japheth, also his desc., also the wife of Hosea:— Gomer(6).

1587. גְּמַרְיָה **Gemaryah** or

גְּמַרְיָהוּ **Gemaryahu** (170b); from 1584 and 3050; "Yah has accomplished," two Isr.:— Gemariah(5).

1588. גַּן **gan** (171a); from 1598; *an enclosure, garden:*— garden(40), gardens(2).

1589. גָּנַב **ganab** (170b); a prim. root; *to steal:*— actually stolen(1), brought to me stealthily(1), carries away(1), deceive(1), deceived(1), deceiving(1), fact kidnapped(1), kidnapping(1), kidnaps(1), steal(9), steal away(1), stealing(1), steals(3), steals him away(1), stealth(1), stole(3), stole away(1), stolen(8), stolen you away(1).

1590. גַּנָּב **gannab** (170c); from 1589; *a thief:*— thief(13), thieves(4).

1591. גְּנֵבָה **genebah** (170c); from 1589; *a thing stolen:*— theft(1), what he stole(1).

1592. גְּנֻבַת **Genubath** (170c); from 1589; son of an Edomite:— Genubath(2).

1593. גַּנָּה **gannah** (171b); fem. of 1588; *a garden:*— garden(6), gardens(9), orchard(1).

1594. גִּנָּה **ginnah** (171b); the same as 1593, q.v.

1595. גֶּנֶז **genez** (170d); from an unused word; *treasury,* perh. *chests:*— carpets(1), treasuries(2).

1596. גְּנַז **genaz** (1086d); (Ara.) corr. to 1595; *a treasure:*— treasure(1), treasures(1), treasury(1).

1597. גַּנְזַךְ **ganzak** (170d); from the same as 1595; *treasury:*— storehouses(1).

1598. גָּנַן **ganan** (170d); a prim. root; *to cover, surround, defend:*— defend(6), protect(2).

1599. גִּנְּתוֹן **Ginnethon** or

גִּנְּתוֹי **Ginnethoy** (171b); from 1598; an Isr. priest:— Ginnethoi(1), Ginnethon(2).

1600. גָּעָה **gaah** (171d); a prim. root; *to low:*— low(1), lowing(1).

1601. גֹּעָה **Goah** (171d); from 1600; a place near Jer.:— Goah(1).

1602. גָּעַל **gaal** (171d); a prim. root; *to abhor, loathe:*— abhor(2), abhorred(1), abhors(1), defiled(1), fail(1), loathed(3), reject(1).

1603. גַּעַל **Gaal** (172a); from 1602; prob. a Canaanite:— Gaal(9).

1604. גֹּעַל **goal** (172a); from 1602; *a loathing:*— abhorred(1).

1605. גָּעַר **gaar** (172a); a prim. root; *to rebuke:*— rebuke(9), rebuked(4), rebukes(1).

1606. גְּעָרָה **gearah** (172a); from 1605; *a rebuke:*— rebuke(13), threat(2).

1607. גָּעַשׁ **gaash** (172b); a prim. root; *to shake, quake:*— shaken(3), shook(2), stagger(1), surge(2), toss(1).

1608. גַּעַשׁ **Gaash** (172b); from 1607; a mountain in Ephraim:— Gaash(4).

1609. גַּעְתָּם **Gatam** (172b); of unc. der.; an Edomite:— Gatam(3).

1610. גַּף **gaph** (172d); from an unused word; *body, self, height, elevation:*— alone(3), tops(1).

1611. גַּף **gaph** (1086d); (Ara.) corr. to 1610; *wing* (of a bird):— wings(3).

1612. גֶּפֶן **gephen** (172b); of unc. der.; *a vine:*— vine(45), vines(10).

1613. גֹּפֶר **gopher** (172d); of unc. der.; *gopher* (a kind of tree or wood):— gopher(1).

1614. גָּפְרִית **gophrith** (172d); from the same as 1613; *brimstone:*— brimstone(7).

1615. גִּר **gir** (162c); from an unused word; *chalk, lime:*— chalk(1).

1616. גֵּר **ger** (158a); from 1481a; *a sojourner:*— alien(40), aliens(11), foreigners(1), immigrants(1), sojourner(5), sojourners(2), stranger(25), stranger's(1), strangers(6).

גֻּר **gur**; see 1482.

1617. גֵּרָא **Gera** (173a); of unc. der.; the name of several Isr., also a Benjamite family:— Gera(9).

1618. גָּרָב **garab** (173a); from an unused word; *an itch, a scab:*— eczema(2), scab(1).

1619. גָּרֵב **Gareb** (173a); from the same as 1618; one of David's heroes, also a hill near Jer.:— Gareb(3).

1620. גַּרְגַּר **gargar** (176b); from 1641; *a berry:*— olives(1).

1621. גַּרְגְּרוֹת **gargeroth** (176b); from 1641; *neck:*— neck(4).

1622. גִּרְגָּשִׁי **Girgashi** (173a); of unc. der.; a native tribe of Canaan:— Girgashite(5), Girgashites(2).

1623. גָּרַד **garad** (173b); a prim. root; *to scrape, scratch:*— scrape(1).

1624. גָּרָה **garah** (173b); a prim. root; *to stir up* (strife), *engage in strife:*— contend(1), engaged in conflict(1), mobilize(2), provoke(5), stirs(3), strive(1), wage war(1).

1625. גֵּרָה **gerah** (176a); from 1641; *cud:*— cud(11).

1626. גֵּרָה **gerah** (176a); from 1641; *a gerah* (one-twentieth of a shekel):— gerahs(5).

גֹּרָה **gorah**; see 1484.

1627. גָּרוֹן **garon** (173c); perh. from 1624; *neck, throat:*— heads(1), loudly(1), mouth(1), neck(1), throat(4).

1628. גֵּרוּת **Geruth** (158c); from 1481a; "lodging place," a place near Bethlehem:— Geruth(1).

1629a. גָּרַז **garaz** (173d); a prim. root; *to cut, cut off:*— cut off(1).

1629b. גִּרְזִי **Girzi** (173d); from 1630; member of a native tribe in Pal:— Girzites(1).

1630. גְּרִזִּים **Gerizim** (173d); from 1629a; a mountain in N. Isr.:— Gerizim(4).

1631. גַּרְזֶן **garzen** (173d); from 1629a; *an axe:*— axe(4).

1632. גָּרֹל **garol** (175a); another reading for 1419, q.v.

גֹּרָל **goral**; see 1486.

1633a. גָּרַם **garam** (175a); a prim. root; *to cut off, reserve:*— leave(1).

1633b. גָּרַם **garam** (175a); denom. vb. from 1634; *to break bones, break:*— crush(1), gnaw(1).

1634. גֶּרֶם **gerem** (175a); from 1633a; *a bone, strength:*— bare(1), bone(1), bones(1), limbs(1), strong(1).

1635. גְּרַם **geram** (1086d); (Ara.) corr. to 1634; *a bone:*— bones(1).

1636. גַּרְמִי **Garmi** (175a); from 1633a; "bony," a name applied to Keilah:— Garmite(1).

1637. גֹּרֶן **goren** (175b); from an unused word; *threshing floor:*— threshing floor(34), threshing floors(2).

גָּרֹן **garon**; see 1627.

1638. גָּרַס **garas** (176b); a prim. root; *to be crushed:*— broken(1), crushed(1).

1639. גָּרַע **gara** (175c); a prim. root; *to diminish, restrain, withdraw:*— cut off(1), cut short(1), deducted(1), diminished(1), draws(1), hinder(1), limit(1), omit(1), reduce(3), reduced(1), restrained(1), take(1), take away(2), withdraw(2), withdrawn(4).

1640. גָּרַף **garaph** (175d); a prim. root; *to sweep away:*— swept them away(1).

1641. גָּרַר **garar** (176a); a prim. root; *to drag, drag away:*— chew(1), drag them away(2), sawed(1), sweeping(1).

1642. גְּרָר **Gerar** (176b); from 1641; a place S. of Gaza:— Gerar(10).

1643. גֶּרֶשׂ **geres** (176c); from an unused word; *a crushing:*— grits(2).

1644. גָּרַשׁ **garash** (176c); a prim. root; *to drive out, cast out:*— dismissed(1), dispossessed(1), divorced(5), drive(16), driven(6), driven it away(1), driving(1), drove(8), drove them away(1), evict(1), expelled(1), surely drive(1), toss(1), tossed about(1), tossing(1).

1645. גֶּרֶשׁ **geresh** (177a); from 1644; *a thing thrust, a thing put forth:*— produce(1).

1646. גְּרֻשָׁה **gerushah** or

גְּרוּשָׁה **gerushah** (177a); from 1644; *expulsion, violence:*— expropriations(1).

1647. גֵּרְשֹׁם **Gereshom** (177a); from 1644; three Isr.:— Gershom(14).

1648. גֵּרְשׁוֹן **Gereshon** or

גֵּרְשׁוֹם **Gereshom** (177b); from 1644; a son of Levi:— Gershon(17).

1649. גֵּרְשֻׁנִּי **Gereshunni** (177b); from 1648; desc. of Gershon:— Gershonite(2), Gershonites(11).

1650. גְּשׁוּר **Geshur** (178a); from an unused word; a territory E. of the upper Jordan, also inhab. of Geshur:— Geshur(9).

1651. גְּשׁוּרִי **Geshuri** (178c); from 1650; inhab. of Geshur, also a people S. of Philistia:— Geshurites(6).

1652. גָּשַׁם **gasham** (177d); denom. vb. from 1653; *to rain:*— give rain(1), rained(1).

1653. גֶּשֶׁם **geshem** (177c); from an unused word; *rain, shower:*— downpour and the rain*(1), rain(24), rains(1), rainy(2), shower(3), showers(2), showers of rain(1).

1654. גֶּשֶׁם **Geshem** or

גַּשְׁמוּ **Gashmu** (177c); from the same as 1653; an opponent of Nehemiah:— Gashmu(1), Geshem(3).

1655. גְּשֵׁם **geshem** (1086d); (Ara.) corr. to 1653; *the body:*— bodies(2), body(3).

1656. גֹּשֶׁם **goshem** (177d); another reading for 1652, q.v.

גַּשְׁמוּ **Gashmu**; see 1654.

1657. גֹּשֶׁן **Goshen** (177d); of for. or.; a district in Eg., also a city in S. Judah:— Goshen(15).

1658. גִּשְׁפָּא **Gishpa** (177d); of unc. der.; one of the Nethinim:— Gishpa(1).

1659. גָּשַׁשׁ **gashash** (178c); a prim. root; *to feel with the hand, feel, stroke:*— grope(2).

1660. גַּת **gath** (387c); from an unused word; *a wine press:*— wine press(4), wine presses(1).

1661. גַּת **Gath** (387d); from the same as 1660; "wine press," a Philistine city:— Gath(32).

1662. גַּת־הַחֵפֶר **Gath-hachepher** (387d); from 1660 and 2658; "wine press of digging," home of Jonah:— Gath-hepher(2).

1663. גִּתִּי **Gitti** (388a); from 1661; an inhab. of Gath:— Gittite(9), Gittites(1).

1664. גִּתַּיִם **Gittayim** (388a); from the same as 1660; a city in Benjamin:— Gittaim(2).

1665. גִּתִּית **Gittith** (388a); fem. of 1663; a musical term of unc. meaning.

1666. גֶּתֶר **Gether** (178c); of unc. der.; a desc. of Shem:— Gether(2).

1667. גַּת־רִמּוֹן **Gath-rimmon** (387d); from 1660 and 7416; "wine press of a pomegranate," two places in Pal.:— Gath-rimmon(4).

ד

1668. דָּא **da** (1086d); (Ara.) corr. to 2088; *this:*— one another(1), this(2), together(1).

1669. דָּאַב **daeb** (178b); a prim. root; *to become faint, languish:*— languish(1), languishes(1), wasted away(1).

1670. דְּאָבָה **deabah** (178b); from 1669; *faintness, dismay:*— dismay(1).

1671. דְּאָבוֹן **deabon** (178b); from 1669; *faintness, languishing:*— despair(1).

1672. דָּאַג **daag** (178b); a prim. root; *to be anxious* or *concerned, to fear:*— anxious(3), become anxious(1), dread(1), full of anxiety(1), worried(1).

1673. דֹּאֵג **Doeg** or

דּוֹאֵג **Doeg** (178c); from 1672; an Edomite:— Doeg(5).

1674. דְּאָגָה **deagah** (178c); from 1672; *anxiety, anxious care:*— anxiety(5), concern(1).

1675. דָּאָה **daah** (178d); a prim. root; *to fly swiftly, dart through the air:*— fly swiftly(1), sped(1), swoop(1), swoops down(1).

1676. דָּאָה **daah** (178d); from 1675; perh. *kite* (a bird of prey):— kite(3).

1677. דֹּב **dob** or

דּוֹב **dob** (179a); from 1680; *a bear:*— bear(10), bears(2).

1678. דֹּב **dob** (1087a); (Ara.) corr. to 1677; *a bear:*— bear(1).

1679. דֹּבֶא **dobe** (179a); of unc. der.; perh. *rest:*— leisurely walk(1).

1680. דָּבַב **dabab** (179a); a prim. root; *to move gently, glide, glide over:*— flowing gently(1).

1681. דִּבָּה **dibbah** (179b); from 1680; *whispering, defamation, evil report:*— bad report(2), bad*(2), evil report(1), report(2), slander(2), whispering(2).

1682. דְּבוֹרָה **deborah** (184b); from 1696; *a bee:*— bee(1), bees(3).

1683. דְּבוֹרָה **Deborah** (184b); from 1696; two Isr. women:— Deborah(10).

1684. דְּבַח **debach** (1087a); (Ara.) corr. to 2076; *to sacrifice:*— offered(1).

1685. דְּבַח **debach** (1087a); (Ara.) from 1684; *a sacrifice:*— sacrifices(1).

1686. דִּבְיוֹנִים **dibyonim** (179b); of unc. der., prob. *dove's dung:*— dung(1).

1687. דְּבִיר **debir** (184b); perh. from 1696; perh. (a place of) *speaking* (the innermost room of Solomon's temple):— inner sanctuary(15), sanctuary(1).

1688. דְּבִיר **Debir** (184c); from the same as 1687; an Amorite king, also the name of several places in Pal.:— Debir(14).

1689. דִּבְלָה **Diblah** (179c); from the same as 1690; a place in Aram (Syria) or N. Isr.:— Diblah(1).

1690. דְּבֵלָה **debelah** (179b); from an unused word; *a lump* (of pressed figs), *a pressed* (fig) *cake:*— cake(2), cakes of figs(1), fig cake(1), fig cakes(1).

1691a. דִּבְלַיִם **Diblayim** (179c); from the same as 1690; the father-in-law of Hosea:— Diblaim(1).

1691b. דִּבְלָתַיִם **Diblathayim** (179c); see 1015 and 5963.

1692. דָּבַק **dabaq** (179c); a prim. root; *to cling, cleave, keep close:*— cleaves(4), cling(14), clings(3), closely pursued(1), closer(1), clung(4), deeply attracted(1), fasten its grip(1), follow closely(1), held fast(1), hold(2), hold fast(2), holding fast(1), joined(2), joined together(1), overtake(1), overtook(5), pursued him closely(1), pursued them closely(1), remained steadfast(1), stay(1), stay close(1), stayed close(1), stick(1), stick together(1), stuck(2).

1693. דְּבַק **debeq** (1087a); (Ara.) corr. to 1692; *to cling:*— adhere(1).

1694. דֶּבֶק **debeq** (180a); from 1692; *a joining, soldering, appendage:*— joint(2), soldering(1).

1695. דָּבֵק **dabeq** (180a); from 1692; *a clinging, cleaving:*— attached(1), held fast(1), who sticks(1).

1696. דָּבַר **dabar** (180b); a prim. root; *to speak:*— again(2), assert(1), boast*(1), commanded(1), counseled(2), declare(2), declared(5), declared*(1), directed(2), discuss(1), made(1), meant(1), named(1), passed sentence(3), preached(1), proclaimed(2), promised(34), promising(1), pronounce(3), pronounced(6), proposal(1), repeated(2), said(50), say(18), saying(1), saying*(1), says(4), sing(1), speak(297), speaking(61), speaks(34), speaks fluently(1), spoke(333), spoken(188), state(2), statements(2), subdues(2), talk(7), talked(7), talking(9), tell(18), telling(4), tells(2), threatened(1), told(16), utter(1), uttered(1), utters(1).

1697. דָּבָר **dabar** (182a); from 1696; *speech, word:*— account(2), account*(2), act(1), acts(52), advice(3), affair(3), affairs(3), agreement(1), amount*(2), annals(1), answer(6), answer*(5), anything(12), anything*(4), asked(1), because*(10), business(3), case(9), cases(1), cause(3), charge(2), Chronicles(3), Chronicles*(38), claims(1), command(11), commandment(1), commandments(1), Commandments(2), commands(1), compliments*(1), concerned(1), concerning(1), concerning*(3), conclusion*(1), conditions(1), conduct(2), conferred(1), consultation(1), conversation(1), counsel(1), custom(1), customs(1), dealings(2), decree(2), deed(2), deeds(3), defect*(1), desires(1), dispute(5), disputes(1), doings(1), duty(1), edict(1), eloquent*(1), event(3), events(5), fulfillment(1), harm(1), harm*(1), idea(1), instructed(1), instructions(2), manner(7), matter(45), matters(2), message(18), nothing*(21), oath(1), obligations(1), one of the promises(1), order(1), parts(1), pertains(2), plan(2), plot(2), portion(3), promise(8), proposal(3), proposed(1), proven(1), purpose(2), question(1), questions(3), ration(1), reason(4), records(5), regard(1), render(1), reply*(1), report(4), reported*(1), reports(4), request(3), required(2), requires(1), rule(2), said(5), same thing(1), saying(3), says(1), so much(2), some(1), something(4), songs*(1), speak(2), speech(2), talk(2), talking*(1), task(1), theme(1), thing(96), things(36), things at your word(1), things the word(1), this*(1), thought(1), thoughts(1), threats*(1), thus*(1), told*(1), trouble*(1), verdict(2), way(3), what(4), what*(5), whatever*(3), word(454), words(375), work required(1).

1698. דֶּבֶר deber (184a); from 1696; *pestilence:*— pestilence(38), plague(10), thorns(1).

1699a. דֹּבֶר dober (184a); from 1696; *a pasture:*— pasture(2).

דְּבִר debir or **Debir**; see 1687, 1688.

1699b. דִּבֵּר dibber (184c); from 1696; *a speaking:*— word(1).

1700. דִּבְרָה dibrah (184a); from 1696; *a cause, reason, manner:*— cause(1), concerning*(1), order(1), so*(1).

1701. דִּבְרָה dibrah (1087a); (Ara.) corr. to 1700; *a cause, reason:*— order*(1), purpose(1).

דְּבוֹרָה deborah or **Deborah**; see 1682, 1683.

1702. דֹּבְרָה doberah (184a); from 1696; *floats, rafts:*— rafts(1).

1703. דַּבָּרָה dabbarah or

דַּבֶּרֶת dabbereth (184c); from 1696; *a word:*— words(1).

1704. דִּבְרִי Dibri (184c); from 1696; a Danite:— Dibri(1).

1705. דָּבְרַת Daberath (184b); from 1696; a Levitical city in Issachar:— Daberath(3).

1706. דְּבַשׁ debash (185a); from an unused word; *honey:*— honey(52), honeycomb*(2).

1707. דַּבֶּשֶׁת dabbesheth (185c); from the same as 1706; *a hump:*— humps(1).

1708. דַּבֶּשֶׁת Dabbesheth (185c); from the same as 1706; "hump," a place in Zebulun:— Dabbesheth(1).

1709. דָּג dag (185c); from 1711; *a fish:*— fish(17), fishing(1).

1710. דָּגָה dagah (185d); fem. of 1709; *a fish:*— fish(16).

1711. דָּגָה dagah (185c); a prim. root; *to multiply, increase:*— grow(1).

1712. דָּגוֹן Dagon (186a); from 1709; a god and an idol of the Philistines:— Dagon(12), Dagon's(1).

1713a. דָּגַל dagal (186a); a prim. root; *to look, behold:*— outstanding(1).

1713b. דָּגַל dagal (186b); denom. vb. from 1714; *to carry* or *set up a standard* or *banner:*— army with banners(2), set up our banners(1).

1714. דֶּגֶל degel (186b); from 1713a; *a standard, banner:*— banner(1), standard(10), standards(3).

1715. דָּגָן dagan (186b); from an unused word; *corn, grain* (of cereals):— food(1), grain(38).

1716. דָּגַר dagar (186c); a prim. root; *to gather together as a brood:*— gather(1), hatches eggs(1).

1717. דַּד dad (186d); of unc. der.; *breast, teat, nipple:*— bosom(3), breasts(1).

1718. דָּדָה dadah (186d); a prim. root; perh. *to move slowly:*— lead them in procession(1), wander(1).

1719. דְּדָן Dedan or

דְּדָנֶה Dedaneh (186d); of unc. der.; a desc. of Ham, also a desc. of Abraham, also the tribes desc. from them:— Dedan(11).

1720. דְּדָנִי Dedani (187a); pl. of 1719; desc. or inhab. of Dedan:— Dedanites(1).

1721. דֹּדָנִים Dodanim (187a); of unc. der., see also 7290c; a son of Javan, also his desc.:— Dodanim(1).

1722. דְּהַב dehab (1087a); (Ara.) corr. to 2091; *gold:*— gold(17), golden(6).

1723. דְּהָוא dahava (1087a); (Ara.) of unc. der.; *that is.*

1724. דָּהַם daham (187b); a prim. root; *to astonish, astound:*— dismayed(1).

1725. דָּהַר dahar (187b); a prim. root; *to rush, dash* (of a horse):— galloping(1).

1726. דַּהֲרָה daharah (187b); from 1725; *a rushing, dashing:*— dashing(2).

דּוֹאֵג Doeg; see 1673.

1727. דּוּב dub (187b); a prim. root; *to pine away:*— pine away(1).

דֹּב dob; see 1677.

1728. דַּוָּג davvag (186a); from 1709; *a fisherman:*— fishermen(3).

1729. דּוּגָה dugah (186a); from 1709; *fishing, fishery:*— fish(1).

1730. דּוֹד dod (187c); from an unused word; *beloved, love, uncle:*— beloved(31), beloved's(1), beloved's and my beloved(1), love(8), lovers(1), uncle(11), uncle's(6), uncles'(1).

1731. דּוּד dud (188b); from the same as 1730; *a pot, jar:*— basket(3), baskets(2), kettle(1), kettles(1), pot(1).

1732. דָּוִד David or

דָּוִיד David (187d); from the same as 1730; perh. "beloved one," a son of Jesse:— David(941), David's(55).

1733. דּוֹדָה dodah or

דֹּדָה dodah (187d); fem. of 1730; *aunt:*— aunt(1), father's sister(1), uncle's wife(1).

1734. דּוֹדוֹ Dodo (187d); from the same as 1730; "his beloved," three Isr.:— Dodo(5).

1735. דּוֹדָוָהוּ Dodavahu (187d); from 1730 and 3050; "beloved of Yah," an Isr. name:— Dodavahu(1).

1736. דּוּדַי duday (188b); from the same as 1730; *mandrake:*— mandrakes(6).

1737. דּוֹדַי Doday (187d); from the same as 1730; an Isr.:— Dodai(1).

1738. דָּוָה davah (188c); a prim. root; *to be ill, unwell:*— menstruation*(1).

1739. דָּוֶה daveh (188c); from 1738; *faint, unwell:*— faint(2), impure thing(1), menstruous(1), woman who(1), woman who is ill(1).

1740. דּוּחַ duach (188d); a prim. root; *to rinse, cleanse away by rinsing* or *washing:*— purged(1), rinse(2), washed me away(1).

1741. דְּוַי devay (188c); from 1738; *illness:*— loathsome(1), sickbed*(1).

1742. דַּוָּי davvay (188d); adj. from 1738; *faint:*— faint(3).

דָּוִיד David; see 1732.

1743. דּוּךְ duk (188d); of unc. der.; *to pound, beat:*— beat(1).

1744. דּוּכִיפַת dukiphath (189a); from the same as 1743; perh. *hoopoe* (a ceremonially unclean bird):— hoopoe(2).

1745. דּוּמָה dumah (189a); from an unused word; *a silence:*— silence(2).

1746. דּוּמָה Dumah (189a); from the same as 1745; a son of Ishmael, also a city in Judah and a name of Edom:— Dumah(3).

1747. דּוּמִיָּה dumiyyah (189b); from the same as 1745; *a silence, a quiet waiting, repose:*— rest(1), silence(2), silent(1).

1748. דּוּמָם dumam (189b); from the same as 1745; *a silence, in silence, silently:*— mute(1), silently(2).

דּוּמֶשֶׂק dumesheq; see 1833.

1749. דּוֹנַג donag (200a); from an unused word; *wax* (as melting):— wax(4).

1750. דּוּץ duts (189b); a prim. root; *to spring, leap, dance:*— leaps(1).

1751. דּוּק duq (1089a); (Ara.) the same as 1855, q.v.

1752. דּוּר dur (189c); a prim. root; *to heap up, pile, dwell:*— dwell(1).

1753. דּוּר dur (1087b); (Ara.) corr. to 1752; *to dwell:*— dwell(1), dwelt(2), inhabitants(2), live(1), living(1).

1754. דּוּר dur (189c); from 1752; *a circle, ball:*— ball(1), encircling(1), pile(1).

1755. דּוֹר dor or

דֹּר dor (189c); from 1752; *period, generation, dwelling:*— age-old(1), all generations(20), another(1), dwelling(1), every generation(1), forever(1), generation(53), generations(52), kind(4), many generations(3), nor(1), time(2).

1756. דּוֹר Dor or

דֹּאר Dor (190b); from 1752; a city in Pal.:— Dor(7).

1757. דּוּרָא Dura (1087b); (Ara.) from 1753; a place near Bab.:— Dura(1).

1758. דּוּשׁ dush or

דִּישׁ dish (190b); a prim. root; *to tread, thresh:*— continue to thresh(1), thrash(1), thresh(3), threshed(2), threshing(4), trample(1), trampled(1), trodden down(2).

1759. דּוּשׁ dush (1087c); (Ara.) corr. to 1758; *to tread down:*— tread it down(1).

1760. דָּחָה dachah (190d); a prim. root; *to push, thrust:*— away(1), driving(1), pushed me violently(1), thrust down(2), tottering(1), trip(1).

1761a. דַּחֲוָה dachavah (1087c); (Ara.) from the equiv. of 1760; perh. a musical instrument:— entertainment(1).

1761b. דָּחַח dachach (191a); another reading for 1760, q.v:— driven(1).

1762. דְּחִי dechi (191a); from 1760; *a stumbling:*— stumbling(2).

1763. דְּחַל dechal (1087c); (Ara.) a prim. root; *to fear:*— awesome(1), dreadful(2), fear(1), feared(1), made me fearful(1).

1764. דֹּחַן dochan (191a); from an unused word; *millet:*— millet(1).

1765. דָּחַף dachaph (191b); a prim. root; *to drive, hasten:*— hastened(1), hurried(1), impelled(2).

1766. דָּחַק dachaq (191b); a prim. root; *to thrust, crowd, oppress:*— afflicted(1), crowd(1).

1767. דַּי day (191b); a prim. root; *sufficiency, enough:*— ability(1), according(1), annually*(2), each time(2), enough(6), had enough(1), nothing*(1), often(8), overflows*(1), plenty(1), sufficient(4), sufficient numbers(1), what you need(1).

1768. דִּי di (1087c); (Ara.) a prim. particle; *who, which, that, because:*— after*(1), against(1), because(1), because*(5), before*(1), even(1), forasmuch*(1), inasmuch*(9), since(2), so(6), soon(1), soon*(1), surely*(1), than*(1), until*(11), what(1), what*(1), whatever*(2), when(3), where(1), where*(1), wherever*(1), which(46), who(34), whom(12), whom*(1), whomever(4), whomever*(3), whose(6).

1769. דִּיבֹן Dibon or

דִּיבוֹן Dibon (192a); of unc. der.; a city in Moab, also a place in Judah:— Dibon(9), Dibon-gad*(2).

1770. דִּיג dig (185d); denom. vb. from 1709; *to fish for, catch:*— fish(1).

1771. דַּוָּג davvag or

דַּיָּג diyyag (186a); from 1709, see 1728.

1772. דַּיָּה dayyah (178d); from 1675; perh. *a kite* (a bird of prey):— hawks(1).

1773. דְּיוֹ deyo (188d); noun from 1738; *ink:*— ink(1).

1774. דִּי זָהָב Di Zahab (191d); from 1767 and 2091; prob. a place in the desert:— Dizahab(1).

1775. דִּימוֹן Dimon (192a); of unc. der., see also 1769; a city in Moab:— Dimon(2).

1776. דִּימוֹנָה Dimonah (192a); of unc. der., see also 1769; a place in Judah:— Dimonah(1).

1777. דִּין din (192a); a prim. root; *to judge:*— administer(1), defend(1), dispute(1), execute judgment(1), govern(1), judge(9), judges(2), plead(2), pled(1), quarreling(1), strive(1), vindicate(2), vindicated(1).

1778. דִּין din (1088b); (Ara.) corr. to 1777; *to judge:*— judge*(1).

1779. דִּין din (192c); from 1777; *judgment:*— case(1), cause(6), judgment(4), justice(3), lawsuit or another(1), rights(4), strife(1).

1780. דִּין din (1088b); (Ara.) from 1778; *judgment:*— court(2), judgment(2), just(1).

1781. דַּיָּן dayyan (193a); from 1777; *a judge:*— judge(2).

1782. דַּיָּן dayyan (1088c); (Ara.) from 1778; *a judge:*— judges(1).

1783. דִּינָה Dinah (192d); from 1777; daughter of Jacob:— Dinah(7), Dinah's(1).

1784a. דִּינָיֵא dinaye (1088c); (Ara.) from 1778; *judges:*— judges(1).

1784b. דִּיפַת Diphath (193d); of unc. der.; a son of Gomer:— Diphath(1).

1785. דָּיֵק dayeq (189b); from an unused word; *bulwark, siege wall:*— siege wall(4), siege walls(2).

1786. דַּיִשׁ dayish (190c); from 1758; *a threshing:*— threshing(1).

1787. דִּישׁוֹן Dishon (190d); from 1788; two Edomites:— Dishon(7).

1788. דִּישֹׁן dishon (190d); from 1758; *mountain goat* (a cermonially clean animal):— ibex(1).

1789. דִּישָׁן Dishan (190d); from 1788; an Edomite:— Dishan(5).

1790. דַּךְ dak (194c); from an unused word; *crushed, oppressed:*— crushes(1), oppressed(3).

1791. דֵּךְ dek (1088c); (Ara.) a prim. pron.; *this:*— this(7).

1792. דָּכָא daka (193d); a prim. root; *to crush:*— become contrite(1), contrite(1), crush(7), crushed(7), crushing(1), oppressed(1).

1793a. דַּכָּא dakka (194b); from 1792; *contrite:*— contrite(1), who are crushed(1).

1793b. דַּכָּא dakka (194b); from 1792; *dust* (as pulverized):— dust(1).

1794. דָּכָה dakah (194b); a prim. root; *to crush:*— broken(1), contrite(1), crouches(1), crushed(2).

1795. דַּכָּה dakkah (194c); from the same as 1790; *a crushing:*— emasculated*(1).

1796. דֳּכִי doki (194b); from 1794; *a pounding* (of waves):— pounding waves(1).

1797. דִּכֵּן dikken (1088c); (Ara.) from 1791; *this, that.*

1798. דְּכַר dekar (1088d); (Ara.) corr. to 2145; *a ram:*— rams(3).

1799a. דִּכְרוֹן dikron (1088d); (Ara.) corr. to 2146; *memorandum, record:*— memorandum(1).

1799b. דָּכְרָן dokran (1088d); (Ara.) corr. to 2146; *memorandum, record:*— record(2).

1800a. דַּל dal (194d); from 1802a; *a door:*— door(1).

1800b. דַּל dal (195d); from 1809; *low, weak, poor, thin:*— depressed(1), helpless(7), least(1), lowly(2), needy(1), poor(29), poor man(3), poorest(1), weak(2), weaker(1).

1801. דָּלַג dalag (194c); a prim. root; *to leap:*— climbing(1), leap(4).

1802a. דָּלָה dalah (194c); a prim. root; *to draw* (water):— draw water(1), draws(1), drew the water(1), lifted(1), useless(1).

1802b. דָּלָה dalah (194d); from 1802a; *a door:*— doors(1).

1803a. דַּלָּה dallah (195d); from 1809; *hair, thrum:*— flowing locks(1), loom(1).

1803b. דַּלָּה dallah (195d); from 1809; *the poor:*— poorest(5).

1804. דָּלַח dalach (195c); a prim. root; *to make turbid:*— muddied(1), muddy(2).

1805. דְּלִי deli (194d); from 1802a; *a bucket:*— bucket(1), buckets(1).

1806. דְּלָיָה Delayah or

דְּלָיָהוּ Delayahu (195b); from 1802a and 3050; "Yah has drawn," five Isr.:— Delaiah(7).

1807. דְּלִילָה Delilah (196a); from 1809; Philistine mistress of Samson:— Delilah(6).

1808. דָּלִית dalith (194d); from 1802a; *a branch, bough:*— branches(8).

1809. דָּלַל dalal (195c); a prim. root; *to hang, be low, languish:*— brought low(1), brought...low(3), fade(1), hang(1), look wistfully(1), thin(1).

1810. דִּלְעָן Dilan (196a); from 1807; a city in Judah:— Dilean(1).

1811. דָּלַף dalaph (196a); a prim. root; *to drip, drop:*— leaks(1), weeps(2).

1812. דֶּלֶף deleph (196a); from 1811; *a dropping:*— dripping(2).

1813. דַּלְפוֹן Dalphon (196a); from 1811; a son of Haman:— Dalphon(1).

1814. דָּלַק dalaq (196a); a prim. root; *to burn, hotly pursue:*— burning(1), chased(1), chasing(1), fiery shafts(1), hotly pursue(1), hotly pursued(1), inflame(1), kindle(1), set them on fire(1).

1815. דְּלַק delaq (1088d); (Ara.) corr. to 1814; *to burn:*— burning(1).

1816. דַּלֶּקֶת dalleqeth (196b); from 1814; *inflammation:*— inflammation(1).

1817. דֶּלֶת deleth (195a); from 1802a; *a door:*— columns(1), door(21), door and leaves(1), doors(45), doors had leaves(1), gates(11), gateway(1), leaves(1), lid(1), opening(1).

1818. דָּם dam (196b); a prim. root; *blood:*— blood(303), bloodguilt(2), bloodguiltiness(12), bloodshed(27), bloody(7), death(1), guilt of blood(2), homicide or another(1), life(1), lifeblood*(2).

1819. דָּמָה damah (197d); a prim. root; *to be like, resemble:*— alike(1), compare(3), compared(1), equal(1), gave parables(1), imagine(1), intend(1), intended(2), like(9), liken(3), make myself like(1), plan(1), planned(1), resemble(1), thought(2).

1820. דָּמָה damah (198c); a prim root; *to cease, cause to cease, cut off, destroy:*— cease(1), completely cut off(1), cut off(2), destroy(1), destroyed(1), perish(2), ruined(5), silenced(1), unceasingly*(1).

1821. דְּמָה demah (1088d); (Ara.) corr. to 1819; *to be like:*— like(1), resembling(1).

1822. דֻּמָּה dummah (199a); from 1826a; *one silenced* or *brought to silence:*— who is silent(1).

1823. דְּמוּת demuth (198b); from 1819; *likeness, similitude:*— figure(1), figures like(1), figures resembling(1), form(4), like(4), likeness(8), pattern(1), resembling(1), something resembling(1), which resembled(1), who resembled(1).

1824. דֳּמִי domi (198c); from 1820; *cessation, a pause, a quiet, a rest:*— middle(1), quiet(1), rest(2).

1825. דִּמְיוֹן dimyon (198b); from 1819; *likeness:*— like(1).

1826a. דָּמַם damam (198d); a prim. root; *to be* or *grow dumb, silent* or *still:*— ceasing(1), destroyed(1), doomed(1), have...rest(1), keeps silent(1), kept silent(3), made silent(1), motionless(1), perish(1), quieted(1), relax(1), rest(1), silenced(4), silent(5), silently(1), stand still(1), stay still(1), still(1), stood still(1), wait(1), wait in silence(1).

1826b. דָּמַם damam (199b); a verb meaning *to wail,* spelled like 1826a, q.v.

1827. דְּמָמָה demamah (199a); from 1826a; *a whisper:*— silence(1), still(1).

1828. דֹּמֶן domen (199b); from an unused word; *dung:*— dung(6).

1829. דִּמְנָה Dimnah (199b); from the same as 1828; a Levitical city in Zebulun:— Dimnah(1).

1830. דָּמַע dama (199c); a prim. root; *to weep:*— bitterly weep(1).

1831. דֶּמַע dema (199c); from 1830; *juice:*— vintage(1).

1832. דִּמְעָה dimah (199c); from 1830; *tears* (of one weeping):— tears(23).

1833. דְּמֶשֶׁק demesheq (200a); of for. or.; perh. *silk:*— cover(1).

1834. דַּמֶּשֶׂק Dammeseq (199d); of for. or.; a city in Aram (Syria):— Damascus(45).

1835. דָּן Dan (192d); from 1777; "judge," a son of Jacob, also his desc. and their territory, also a place in N. Isr.:— Dan(68), Danite*(1).

1836. דְּנָה denah (1088d); (Ara.) a prim. pron.; *this:*— one another*(1), therefore*(6), this(42), thus(2).

1837. דַּנָּה Dannah (200a); of unc. der.; a city in Judah:— Dannah(1).

1838. דִּנְהָבָה Dinhabah (200b); of unc. der.; a city in Edom:— Dinhabah(2).

1839. דָּנִי Dani (193a); from 1835; desc. of Dan:— Danites(5).

1840. דָּנִיֵּאל Daniyyel or

דָּנִאֵל Daniel (193a); from 1777 and 410; "God is my judge," the name of several Isr.:— Daniel(29).

1841. דָּנִיֵּאל Daniyyel (1088c); (Ara.) corr. to 1840; "God is my judge," an Isr. leader in Bab.:— Daniel(52).

1842. דָּן יַעַן Dan Yaan (193a); from 1835 and perh. 3282; a place in Pal.:— Dan-jaan(1).

1843. דֵּעַ dea (395b); from 3045; *knowledge, opinion:*— knowledge(2), opinion(1), what i think(2).

1844. דֵּעָה deah (395c); from 3045; *knowledge:*— knowledge(6).

1845. דְּעוּאֵל Deuel (396a); from 3045 and 410; "known of God," a Gadite:— Deuel(5).

1846. דָּעַךְ daak (200b); a prim. root; *to go out, be extinguished:*— extinguished(1), go(1), goes(3), put(2), vanish(1).

1847. דַּעַת daath (395c); from 3045; *knowledge:*— concern(1), know(3), knowledge(81), premeditation(2), skill(1), truth(1), unintentionally*(2), what(1).

1848. דֳּפִי dophi (200c); from an unused word; *a blemish, fault:*— slander*(1).

1849. דָּפַק daphaq (200c); a prim. root; *to beat, knock:*— driven hard(1), knocking(1), pounding(1).

1850. דָּפְקָה Dophqah (200c); from 1849; a place in the desert:— Dophkah(2).

1851. דַּק daq (201a); from 1854; *thin, small, fine:*— dwarf(1), fine(3), fine dust(1), finely ground(1), gaunt*(2), gentle blowing(1), thin(5).

1852. דֹּק doq (201a); from 1854; *a veil, curtain:*— curtain(1).

1853. דִּקְלָה Diqlah (200c); from an unused word; a son of Joktan, also the S. Arabian tribe desc. from him:— Diklah(2).

1854. דָּקַק daqaq (200d); a prim. root; *to crush, pulverize, thresh:*— crushed(3), fine(1), ground(2), ground to powder(1), powder(1), powder*(1), pulverize(2), thresh(1), very fine(1).

1855. דְּקַק deqaq (1089a); (Ara.) corr. to 1854; *to be shattered, fall to pieces:*— crush(3), crushed(6), crushes(1).

1856. דָּקַר daqar (201a); a prim. root; *to pierce, pierce through:*— pierce him through(1), pierce me through(2), pierced(1), pierced him through(1), pierced of them through(1), pierced through(1), stricken(1), thrust me through(1), thrust through(1), wounded(1).

1857. דֶּקֶר Deqer (201b); see 1128.

1858. דַּר dar (204d); from the same as 1865; perh. *pearl* or *mother-of-pearl:*— mother-of-pearl(1).

1859. דָּר dar (1087b); (Ara.) from 1753; *a generation:*— generation(4).

1860. דְּרָאוֹן deraon (201b); from an unused word; *aversion, abhorrence:*— abhorrence(1), contempt(1).

1861a. דָּרְבָן dorban (201c); from an unused word; *a goad:*— hoes(1).

1861b. דָּרְבֹנָה darebonah (201c); from the same as 1861a; *a goad:*— goads(1).

1862. דַּרְדַּע Darda (201c); from an unused word; an Isr.:— Darda(1).

1863. דַּרְדַּר dardar (205a); from the same as 1865; *thistles:*— thistle(1), thistles(1).

1864. דָּרוֹם darom (204d); from the same as 1865; *the south:*— south(17).

1865. דְּרוֹר deror (204d); from an unused word; *a flowing, free run, liberty:*— flowing(1), liberty(2), release(5).

1866. דְּרוֹר deror (204d); from the same as 1865; *swallow* (a kind of bird):— swallow(2).

1867. דָּרְיָוֶשׁ Dareyavesh (201d); of for. or.; the name of several Pers. kings:— Darius(10).

1868. דָּרְיָוֶשׁ Dareyavesh (1089a); (Ara.) corr. to 1867; two Pers. kings:— Darius(15).

1869. דָּרַךְ darak (201d); a prim. root; *to tread, march:*— aimed(1), aims(1), archers*(1), bend(6), bends his bend(1), bent(6), come(1), guide(1), lead(1), leads(2), led(2), march(1), set foot(2), shot(1), stamped firm(1), trampled(1), tramples(2), tramples down(1), tread(8), treader(1), treader treads(1), treading(1), treads(5), trod(3), trod them down(1), trodden(4), walk(3), wielding(1).

1870. דֶּרֶךְ derek (202c); from 1869; *way, road, distance, journey, manner:*— actions(1), acts(1), conduct(11), course(2), crooked*(2), direction(4), distance(1), example(1), favors(1), highway(4), highway*(1), impulses(1), journey(37), line(1), manner(4), mission(2), path(4), pathless*(2), pathway(1), pathway*(1), practice(1), road(30), roads(5), roadway(2), safely*(1), street(2), toward(33), toward*(1), walk(1), way(382), way in the direction(1), way toward(1), ways(150), wayside(2), wherever*(1).

1871. דַּרְכְּמוֹן darkemon or

אֲדַרְכּוֹן adarkon (204b); of for. or.; (a unit of value), perh. *a drachma:*— drachmas(4).

1872. דְּרָע dera (1089a); (Ara.) corr. to 2220; *an arm:*— arms(1).

1873. דָּרַע Dara (201c); prob. contr. from 1862; an Isr.:— Dara(1).

1874. דַּרְקוֹן Darqon (204c); from an unused word; one of the Nethinim:— Darkon(2).

1875. דָּרַשׁ darash (205a); a prim. root; *to resort to, seek:*— ask(1), avenge(1), calls(1), care(1), cares(3), comes the reckoning(1), consult(2), consulted by them at all(1), demand(1), inquire(33), inquired(5), inquirer(1), investigate(3), investigated(1), looks(2), making inquiry(1), questioned(1), require(7), required(1), requires(1), resort(3), search(6), searched(1), searched carefully(1), searches(2), seek(53), seek after(1), seeking(2), seeks(3), sought(18), studied(1), study(1), surely require(1).

1876. דָּשָׁא dasha (205d); a prim. root; *to sprout, shoot, grow green:*— sprout(1), turned green(1).

1877. דֶּשֶׁא deshe (206a); from 1876; *grass:*— fresh grass(1), grass(3), green(1), herb(3), new grass(1), new growth(1), tender grass(2), vegetation(2).

1878. דָּשֵׁן dashen (206a); a prim. root; *to be fat, grow fat:*— anointed(1), become greasy(1), become prosperous(1), find your acceptable(1), made fat(1), prosper(1), prosperous(1), puts fat(1), removing its ashes(1), sated(1), take away(1), take away the ashes(1).

1879. דָּשֵׁן dashen (206c); adj. from 1878; *fat:*— full of sap(1), prosperous(1), rich(1).

1880. דֶּשֶׁן deshen (206b); from 1878; *fatness, ashes of fat:*— abundance(3), ashes(8), fatness(4).

1881. דָּת dath (206c); of for. or.; *decree, law:*— decree(5), edict(4), edicts(1), law(7), laws(3), regulations(1).

1882. דָּת dath (1089b); (Ara.) corr. to 1881; *decree, law:*— decree(3), law(10), laws(1).

1883. דֶּתֶא dethe (1089b); (Ara.) corr. to 1877; *grass:*— new grass(2).

1884. דְּתָבַר dethabar (1089b); (Ara.) of for. or.; *a judge:*— judges(2).

1885. דָּתָן Dathan (206d); of unc. der.; a Reubenite:— Dathan(10).

1886. דֹּתָן Dothan (206d); of unc. der.; a place N. of Samaria:— Dothan(3).

ה

1887. הֵא he (210c); a prim. interj.; *lo! behold!:*— behold(1), now(1).

1888. הָא ha (1089c); (Ara.) corr. to 1887; *lo! behold!:*— even(1), look(1).

1889. הֶאָח heach (210c); a prim. interj.; *aha!:*— aha(12).

1890. הַבְהָב habhab (396d); from 3051; *a gift:*— gifts(1).

1891. הָבַל habal (211a); denom. vb. from 1892; *to act emptily, become vain:*— act foolishly(1), became empty(1), became vain(1), leading you into futility(1), vainly hope(1).

1892. הֶבֶל hebel (210c); a prim. root; *vapor, breath:*— breath(5), delusion(2), emptily(1), emptiness(2), fleeting(2), fraud(1), futile(1), futility(13), idols(7), mere breath(2), nothing(1), useless(1), vain(3), vainly(1), vanity(19), vanity of vanities(3), vapor(1), worthless(2).

1893. הֶבֶל Hebel or

הָבֶל Habel (211a); a prim. root; the second son of Adam:— Abel(8).

1894. **הָבְנִי** **hobni** (211b); from 1893; *ebony* (a kind of wood):— ebony(1).

1895. **הָבַר** **habar** (211b); a prim. root; prob. *divide:*— astrologers*(1).

1896a. **הֵגֶא** **Hege** (211b); of for. or.; eunuch of Ahasuerus:— Hegai(4).

1896b. **הַגְּדוֹלִים** **Haggedolim** (153c); from 1431; an Isr.:— Haggedolim(1).

1897. **הָגָה** **hagah** (211c); a prim. root; *to moan, growl, utter, speak, muse:*— declare(1), devise(2), devising(1), growls(1), make a sound(1), meditate(5), meditates(1), moan(3), moan sadly(1), mutter(2), mutters(1), ponders(1), utter(2), uttering(1), utters(1).

1898. **הָגָה** **hagah** (212a); a prim. root; *to remove:*— expelled(1), take away(2).

1899. **הֶגֶה** **hegeh** (211d); from 1897; *a rumbling, growling, moaning:*— mourning(1), rumbling(1), sigh(1).

1900. **הָגוּת** **haguth** (212a); from 1897; *meditation, a musing:*— meditation(1).

1901. **הָגִיג** **hagig** (211c); from an unused word; *a whisper, musing, murmuring:*— groaning(1), musing(1).

1902. **הִגָּיוֹן** **higgayon** (212a); from 1897; *resounding music, meditation, musing:*— Higgaion(1), meditation(1), resounding music(1), whispering(1).

1903. **הָגִין** **hagin** (212b); from an unused word; perh. *appropriate, suitable.*

1904. **הָגָר** **Hagar** (212b); from an unused word; Sarah's Eg. maid, the mother of Ishmael:— Hagar(12).

1905. **הַגְרִי** **Hagri** (212b); from 1904; a tribe E. of the Jordan, also a member of the tribe, also an Isr.:— Hagri(1), Hagrite(1), Hagrites(4).

1906. **הֵד** **hed** (212d); from the same as 1959; *a shout, shouting, cheer:*— joyful shouting(1).

1907. **הַדָּבַר** **haddabar** (1089c); (Ara.) of for. or.; *counselor, minister:*— counselors(1), high officials(3).

1908. **הֲדַד** **Hadad** (212d); from the same as 1959; three Edomites:— Hadad(13).

1909. **הֲדַדְעֶזֶר** **Hadadezer** (212d); from 1908 and 5828; "Hadad is help(er)," an Aramean (Syrian) king:— Hadadezer(21).

1910. **הֲדַדְרִמּוֹן** **Hadadrimmon** (213a); from 1908 and 7417a; prob. a heathen god:— Hadadrimmon(1).

1911. **הָדָה** **hadah** (213a); a prim. root; *stretch out* (the hand):— put(1).

1912. **הֹדּוּ** **Hoddu** (213a); of for. or.; *India:*— India(2).

1913. **הֲדוֹרָם** **Hadoram** (213b); of for. or.; a son of Joktan and his desc., also son of the king of Hamath, perh. also an official of Rehoboam:— Hadoram(4).

1914. **הִדַּי** **Hidday** (213b); of unc. der.; one of David's heroes:— Hiddai(1).

1915. **הָדַךְ** **hadak** (213b); a prim. root; *to cast* or *tread down:*— tread down(1).

1916. **הֲדֹם** **hadom** (213b); from an unused word; *a stool, footstool:*— footstool*(6).

1917. **הַדָּם** **haddam** (1089d); (Ara.) of for. or.; *a member, limb:*— limb(2).

1918. **הֲדַס** **hadas** (213c); from the same as 1916; *myrtle* (tree):— myrtle(3), myrtle trees(3).

1919. **הֲדַסָּה** **Hadassah** (213c); from 1918; "myrtle," Esther's Jewish name:— Hadassah(1).

1920. **הָדַף** **hadaph** (213c); a prim. root; *to thrust, drive, push:*— depose(1), driven(2), driving(1), push(1), push her away(1), pushed(2), reject(1), thrust(2), thrust them down(1).

1921. **הָדַר** **hadar** (213d); a prim. root; *to honor, adorn,* perh. *to swell:*— claim honor(1), defer*(1), honor(1), majestic(1), partial(1), respected(1), rough places(1).

1922. **הֲדַר** **hadar** (1089d); (Ara.) corr. to 1921; *to glorify* (God):— glorified(1), honor(1), honored(1).

1923. **הֲדַר** **hadar** (1089d); (Ara.) from 1922; *an honor, majesty:*— majesty(3).

1924. **הֲדַר** **Hadar** (214c); from 1921; an Edomite king:— Hadar(1).

1925. **הֶדֶר** **heder** (214a); from 1921; *an ornament, adornment, splendor:*— Jewel(1).

1926. **הָדָר** **hadar** (214a); from 1921; *an ornament, honor, splendor:*— array(1), beautiful(1), dignity(1), honor(2), majestic(2), majesty(15), splendor(8).

1927a. **הֲדָרָה** **hadarah** (214c); from 1921; *adornment, glory:*— array(2), attire(2), glory(1).

1927b. **הֲדֹרָם** **Hadoram** (214c); perh. the same as 1913, q.v.

1928. **הֲדַרְעֶזֶר** **Hadarezer** (214c); another spelling for 1909, q.v.

1929. **הָהּ** **hah** (214c); a prim. interj.; *alas!:*— alas(1).

1930. **הוֹ** **ho** (214d); a prim. interj.; *ah!:*— alas(2).

1931. **הוּא** **hu** or

הִיא **hi** (214d); a prim. pron.; *he, she, it:*— anyone(1), far*(2), herself(4), Himself(11), himself(20), itself(2), one(6), part(1), same(28), such(3), these(2), this(33), this same(1), those(1), which(24), who(26).

1932. **הוּא** **hu** or

הִיא **hi** (1090a); (Ara.) corr. to 1931; *he, she, it:*— Himself(1), itself(1), this(1), which(1).

1933a. **הָוָא** **hava** (216d); a prim. root; *to fall:*— fall(1).

1933b. **הָוָה** **havah** (217c); a prim. root; *to become:*— get(1).

1934. **הֲוָא** **hava** or

הֲוָה **havah** (1089d); (Ara.) corr. to 1933b; *to become, come to pass, be:*— became(2), beware(1), continued(1), had(1), have(1), judge*(1), kept(8), ruled(1), take place(4).

1935. **הוֹד** **hod** (217a); from an unused word; *splendor, majesty, vigor:*— authority(2), beauty(1), glory(1), honor(3), majestic(2), majesty(4), natural color(1), splendid(1), splendor(8), vigor(1).

1936. **הוֹד** **Hod** (217b); from the same as 1935; "splendor, vigor," an Asherite:— Hod(1).

1937. **הוֹדְוָה** **Hodevah** or

הוֹדְיָה **Hodeyah** (217b); from the same as 1935; a Levitical family:— Hodevah(1).

1938. **הוֹדַוְיָה** **Hodavyah** (1124a); from 3034; an Isr. name:— Hodaviah(3).

1939. **הוֹדַוְיָהוּ** **Hodavyahu** (1124a); from 3034; an Isr. name:— Hodaviah(1).

1940. **הוֹדִיָּה** **Hodiyyah** (217c); the same as 1941, q.v.

1941. **הוֹדִיָּה** **Hodiyyah** (217c); from the same as 1935 and from 3050; "my splendor is Yah," the name of several Isr.:— Hodiah(6).

1942. **הַוָּה** **havvah** (217c); from 1933b; *desire, chasm, destruction:*— calamities(1), calamity(1), craving(1), deadly(1), desire(2), destruction(8), destructive(1), greed(1).

1943. **הֹוָה** **hovah** (217d); from 1933b; *a ruin, disaster:*— disaster(3).

1944. **הוֹהָם** **Hoham** (222d); of unc. der.; an Amorite king of Hebron:— Hoham(1).

1945. **הוֹי** **hoy** (222d); a prim. interj.; *ah! alas! ha!:*— Ah(2), alas(11), ho(2), ho there(1), woe(34).

1946. **הוּךְ** **huk** (1090b); (Ara.) the same as 1981, q.v.

1947. **הוֹלֵלָה** **holelah** (239c); from 1984b; *madness:*— insanity(1), madness(3).

1948. **הוֹלֵלוּת** **holeluth** (239c); from 1984b; *madness:*— madness(1).

1949. **הוּם** **hum** or

הִים **him** (223a); a prim. root; *to murmur, roar, defeat in battle:*— noisy(1), resounded(1), stirred(1), surely distracted(1), throw(1), uproar(1).

1950. **הוֹמָם** **Homam** (243a); from 2000; a Horite:— Hemam(1), Homam(1).

1951. **הוּן** **hun** (223b); a prim. root; *to be easy:*— regarded it as easy(1).

1952. **הוֹן** **hon** (223c); from 1951; *wealth, sufficiency:*— cheaply*(1), enough(2), possession(1), riches(4), substance(1), wealth(17).

1953. **הוֹשָׁמָע** **Hoshama** or

יְהוֹשָׁמָע **Yehoshama** (221d); from 3068 and 8085; "Yah has heard," a desc. of the royal family of Judah:— Hoshama(1).

1954. **הוֹשֵׁעַ** **Hoshea** (448a); from 3467; "salvation," the name of several Isr.:— Hosea(3), Hoshea(12), Joshua(1).

1955. **הוֹשַׁעְיָה** **Hoshayah** (448a); from 3467 and 3050; "Yah has saved," two Isr.:— Hoshaiah(3).

1956a. **הוּת** **huth** (223d); a prim. root; *to shout at:*— assail(1).

1956b. **הוֹתִיר** **Hothir** (452d); from 3498; "abundance, superabundance," a son of Homam:— Hothir(2).

1957. **הָזָה** **hazah** (223d); a prim. root; *to dream, rave:*— dreamers(1).

1958. **הִי** **hi** (223d); of unc. der.; *lamentation, wailing:*— woe(1).

1959. **הֵידָד** **hedad** (212c); from an unused word; *a shout, shouting, cheer:*— shout(1), shouting(3), shouting will not be shouts(1), shouts(1).

1960. **הֻיְּדוֹת** **huyyedoth** (392d); from 3034; *songs of praise:*— songs of thanksgiving(1).

1961. **הָיָה** **hayah** (224a); a prim. root; *to fall out, come to pass, become, be:*— act(1), administered*(1), allotted(1), am(13), appeared*(1), apply(1), became(85), became his and lived(1), became*(1), become(221), becomes(13), becoming(1), been(90), been done(2), befall(1), befallen(2), being(7), belong(9), belonged(4), belongs(2), brought(1), came(358), came into being(1), came expressly(1), cause(1), caused(1), come(86), come to pass(3), comes(2), comes to pass(1), committed(1), consists(1), continue(6), continued(3), correspond(1), decided*(1), done(4), done*(1), ended*(13), endure(3), event*(1), exhausted(1), existed(3), exists(2), extend(3), extended(3), fall(4), fallen(1), fared(1), fell(1), follow*(1), followed*(1), form(1), gave(1), give(1), go(4), gone(1), grown(1), had(80), had not been(2), had been(1), had belonged(1), had...been(2), happen(11), happened(48), happens(4), has(19), has become(1), has had(1), have(90), have become(6), have...place(1), having(2), held(1), help*(1), indeed(1), keep*(1), lasted(1), lasts(1), lay(2), left(2), lies(1), lived*(1), lives(1), made(3), marry*(4), marrying*(1), numbered(1), occur(7), occurred(3), occurs(3), own(3), placed(1), possessed*(1), present(1), pressed*(1), qualify(2), ran(1), reach(3), reached(1), realized(1), receive(1), received(1), remain(9), remain*(1), remained(6), remained*(1), remains(1), rest(1), rested(1), resulted(1), running(1), seemed*(1), serve(3), show(1), sold(1), surely become(1), surely come(1), surely come to pass(1), sustains(1), take(1), take place(3), taken(1), taken place(1), time(1), took place(4), turn(1), turn*(1), turned(4), use(1), used(3), waited(1), wear(1), went(1).

1962. הַיָּה **hayyah** (217d); see 1942.

1963. הֵיךְ **hek** (228a); a prim. adv.; *how?:*— how(2).

1964. הֵיכָל **hekal** (228a); a prim. root; *a palace, temple:*— court(1), nave(14), palace(7), palaces(4), temple(53), temples(1).

1965. הֵיכַל **hekal** (1090b); (Ara.) of for. or.; *a palace, temple:*— palace(5), temple(8).

1966. הֵילֵל **helel** (237d); from 1984a; *a shining one:*— star of the morning(1).

1967. הֵימָם **Hemam** (243a); a form of 1950, q.v.

1968. הֵימָן **Heman** (54c); from 539; an Isr. name:— Heman(16).

1969. הִין **hin** (228d); of for. or.; *a hin* (a liquid measure):— hin(22).

1970. הָכַר **hakar** (229a); a prim. root; perh. *to wrong:*— wrong(1).

1971. הַכָּרָה **hakkarah** (648b); from 5234; *a look:*— expression(1).

1972. הָלָא **hala** (229c); denom. vb. from 1973; *to be removed far off:*— outcasts(1).

1973. הָלְאָה **haleah** (229b); a prim. adv.; *out there, onwards, further:*— abroad(1), aside(1), beyond(1), beyond*(5), further(1), onward(3), wide(2).

1974. הִלּוּל **hillul** (239b); from 1984b; *a rejoicing, praise:*— festival(1), praise(1).

1975. הַלָּז **hallaz** (229c); a prim. pron.; *this:*— there(1), this(4).

1976. הַלָּזֶה **hallazeh** (229d); a prim. pron.; *this:*— this(2).

1977. הַלֵּזוּ **hallezu** (229d); the same as 1976, q.v.

1978. הָלִיךְ **halik** (237b); from 1980; *a step:*— steps(1).

1979. הֲלִיכָה **halikah** (237b); from 1980; *a going, way, traveling company:*— march(1), procession(2), travelers(1), ways(2).

1980. הָלַךְ **halak** (229d); a prim. root; *to go, come, walk:*— access(1), accompany*(2), act(5), acting(2), already gone(1), am(1), am about(1), attended*(1), became greater(3), become(1), becoming(1), becoming increasingly(1), blowing(1), brighter(2), bring(4), brought(5), came(13), came nearer(1), carry(2), come(82), come and let us go(1), coming(3), continually(1), continued(5), continues...along(1), continuing(1), continuing*(1), crawls(1), darting back(1), depart(14), departed(55), departs(1), desires(1), die(1), disappears(1), down(2), down*(1), enter(2), extended(2), flashed(1), fled(1), floated(1), flow(6), flowed(1), flowing(1), flows(1), follow(2), follow*(14), followed(2), followed*(21), following(1), following*(5), follows*(1), get(1), get away(2), get rid(1), go(426), go and walk(1), go at once(1), go my way(1), go to patrol(1), go back(1), go*(4), goes(22), goes to and fro(1), goes down(1), going(30), gone(39), grew(2), grew steadily(1), grew...continually(1), grow(1), growing*(1), indeed gone(1), involve(1), lead(2), leads(1), leave(1), leave*(3), led(14), left(2), live(1), living(1), march(4), marches(1), move(2), moved(8), moves(1), moving(1), once the went forth(1), parades(1), passes(1), passing(1), patrol(2), patrolled(2), pressed heavier(1), proceed(2), proceed*(1), proceeded(4), prowl(1), prowled(1), ran(3), resort(1), return*(1), robber(1), run(1), runs off(1), set(3), set*(1), spent(1), spread(1), sprout(1), stalks(1), steadily(2), steps(1), strut(1), surely go(2), swept(1), take(6), taking(2), throng(1), took(1), took for us to come(1), travel(3), traveled(1), travelers*(1), vagabond(1), vanished(1), walk(142), walked(84), walked around(1), walked back(1), walking(14), walking around(2), walks(31), walks around(1), wandered(2), wanderings(1), way(1), weak(1), went(309), went along continually(1), went on his way(1), went on continually(1), went they could go(1), went forth(1), went*(1).

1981. הֲלַךְ **halak** (1090b); (Ara.) corr. to 1980; *to go:*— brought(1), come(1), go(2), walk(1), walking(2).

1982. הֵלֶךְ **helek** (237a); from 1980; *traveler:*— flow(1), traveler(1).

1983. הֲלָךְ **halak** (1090b); (Ara.) from 1981; *a toll:*— toll(3).

1984a. הָלַל **halal** (237c); a prim. root; *to shine:*— flash forth(2), shone(2).

1984b. הָלַל **halal** (237d); a prim. root; *to be boastful, to priase:*— acted insanely(1), arrogant(1), boast(9), boasted(1), boastful(3), boasts(3), boasts boast(1), deride(1), drive madly(1), give praise(1), giving praise(1), glory(8), go mad(1), going mad(1), mad(1), madness(1), make its boast(1), makes a mad(1), makes fools(1), making fools(1), offers praises(1), praise(90), praised(20), praises(1), praising(5), race madly(1), renowned(1), sang praises(1), sing praises(1), wedding songs(1).

1985. הִלֵּל **Hillel** (239b); from 1984b; "he has praised," father of a judge of Isr.:— Hillel(2).

1986. הָלַם **halam** (240c); a prim. root; *to smite, hammer, strike down:*— beat(2), beats(1), overcome(1), smash(1), smite(1), struck(1), trampled down(1).

1987. הֵלֶם **Helem** (240c); from 1986; an Asherite:— Helem(1).

1988. הֲלֹם **halom** (240d); a prim. adv.; *hither:*— here(9), this far(2), this place(1).

1989. הַלְמוּת **halmuth** (240d); from 1986; *a hammer, mallet:*— hammer(1).

1990. הָם **Ham** (241a); of unc. der.; a place in Pal.:— Ham(1).

1991. הֵם **hem** (241a); of unc. der.; perh. *a moaning, wailing, wealth:*— wealth(1).

1992a. הֵם **hem** or

הֵמָּה **hemmah** (241a); a prim. pron.; *they:*— both(1), both*(1), ones(1), others(1), part(1), places(1), same(1), side(1), such(1), theirs(8), theirs*(3), themselves(9), there(5), these(13), things(1), this(2), those(65), very(1), where(1), which(8), which*(1), who(5), whom(3), women(1).

1992b. הַמְּדָתָא **Hammedatha** (241a); of for. or.; father of Haman:— Hammedatha(5).

1993. הָמָה **hamah** (242a); a prim. root; *to murmur, growl, roar, be boisterous:*— aroused(1), become disturbed(2), boisterous(4), brawler(1), disturbed(2), growl(1), howl(2), intones(1), made an uproar(1), make an uproar(2), making such an uproar(1), mourning(1), murmur(1), noisy(1), pounding(1), roar(5), roar like the roaring(1), roars(2), wails(2), yearns(1).

1994. הִמּוֹ **himmo** or

הִמּוֹן **himmon** (1090b); (Ara.) corr. to 1992a; *they:*— these(1).

1995. הָמוֹן **hamon** (242b); from 1993; *a sound, murmur, roar, crowd, abundance:*— abundance(4), commotion(2), great quantity(1), horde(2), hordes(14), many(3), multitude(31), multitudes(2), noise(2), people(1), populated(1), population(1), roar(1), rumbling(1), sound(1), stirrings(1), tumult(9), tumultuous(1), uproar(1), wealth(2).

1996. הֲמוֹן גּוֹג **Hamon Gog** (242b); from 1995 and 1463; a valley in which Gog will be buried:— Hamon-gog(2).

1997. הֲמוֹנָה **Hamonah** (242d); from 1995; a city where Gog will be defeated:— Hamonah(1).

1998. הֶמְיָה **hemyah** (242d); from 1995; *a sound, music:*— music(1).

1999. הֲמֻלָּה **hamullah** or

הֲמוּלָּה **hamullah** (242d); from an unused word; perh. *rainstorm, a rushing* or *roaring sound:*— tumult(2).

2000. הָמַם **hamam** (243a); a prim. root; *to make a noise, move noisily, confuse, discomfit:*— brought(1), confounded(1), confuse(1), confused(1), confusion(1), crushed(1), damage(1), destroy(1), disturb(1), routed(3), throw into confusion(1), troubled(1).

2001a. הָמַן **haman** (243a); denom. vb. from an unused word; *to rage, be turbulent:*— turmoil(1).

2001b. הָמָן **Haman** (243b); of for. or.; a Pers. leader serving under Ahasuerus:— Haman(50), Haman's(4).

2002. הַמְנִיכָא **hamnika** (1090c); (Ara.) of for. or.; *a chain, necklace:*— necklace(3).

2003. הֶמֶס **hemes** (243b); of unc. der.; *brushwood:*— brushwood(1).

2004. הֵן **hen** (243b); fem. pl. pron. from 1931; *they:*— likewise(1), which(2).

2005. הֵן **hen** (243b); a prim. interj.; *lo! behold!:*— behold(79), even(1), good(1), here(1), if(12), lo(1), look(1), see(1), since(1), though(1).

2006. הֵן **hen** (1090c); (Ara.) corr. to 2005; *if, whether:*— case(1), if(12), or(1), whether for or(1).

2007. הֵנָּה **hennah** (244d); prol. of 2004; *they:*— such(1), these(4), those(1).

2008. הֵנָּה **hennah** (244c); perh. from 2005; *hither:*— back and forth(1), direction(1), here(22), here and there(3), here*(2), nearby(1), now(5), other(1), since*(1), still*(1), this(2), this side(1), thus(3), way(1), yet*(1).

2009. הִנֵּה **hinneh** (243d); prol. of 2005; *lo! behold!:*— after all(1), behold(938), go(1), here(41), how(5), if(18), if he sees(1), if the has indeed(1), indeed(11), lo(16), look(3), now(3), now*(1), see(4), surely(2), there(2), unless(1).

2010. הֲנָחָה **hanachah** (629c); from 5117; *a giving of rest:*— holiday(1).

2011. הִנֹּם Hinnom (244d); of unc. der.; a valley S.W. of Jer.:— Ben-hinnom*(7), Hinnom(6).

2012. הֵנַע Hena (245a); of unc. der.; a city in Aram (Syria) or Mesopotamia:— Hena(3).

2013. הַס has or

הָס has (245a); a prim. interj.; *hush! keep silence!:*— keep quiet(1), keep silence(1), quieted(1), silence(1), silent(3), still(1).

2014. הֲפֻגָה haphugah (806b); from 6313; *benumbing, cessation:*— stopping(1).

2015. הָפַךְ haphak (245b); a prim. root; *to turn, overturn:*— become(1), came(1), change(1), changed(6), changes(1), come(1), drained(1), give(1), had a change(1), inundate(1), overthrew(5), overthrow(5), overthrown(3), overthrows(1), overturned(1), overturns(2), perverted(2), reined about*(1), restore(1), retraced(1), shifted(1), tumbling(1), turn(6), turned(44), turned aside(1), turned back(1), turned over(1), turning(1), turning around(1).

2016. הֶפֶךְ hephek (246b); from 2015; *the contrary, contrariness, perversity:*— different(2), turn things around(1).

2017. הֹפֶךְ hophek (246b); the same as 2016, q.v.

2018. הֲפֵכָה haphekah (246b); fem. of 2016; *an overthrow:*— overthrow(1).

2019. הֲפַכְפַּךְ haphakpak (246b); from 2015; *crooked:*— crooked(1).

2020. הַצָּלָה hatstsalah (665a); from 5337; *deliverance:*— deliverance(1).

2021. הֹצֶן hotsen (246c); of unc. der.; perh. *a weapon* (of war):— weapons(1).

2022. הַר har (249a); of unc. der.; *mountain, hill, hill country:*— hill(16), hill country(91), hills(8), hillside*(1), mount(118), Mount(5), mountain(156), Mountain(2), mountains(161).

2023. הֹר Hor (246d); of unc. der.; two mountains in Pal.:— Hor(12).

2024. הָרָא Hara (246d); of unc. der.; a region of N. Mesopotamia:— Hara(1).

2025. הַרְאֵל harel (246d, 72b); another reading for 741, q.v.

2026. הָרַג harag (246d); a prim. root; *to kill, slay:*— destroyed(1), kill(44), kill me as you killed(1), kill me at once(1), killed(58), killing(3), kills(2), murdered(2), murderer(1), murderers(1), occurs(1), slain(16), slaughter(1), slay(14), slayer(2), slays(2), slew(11), smitten(1), surely kill(1).

2027. הֶרֶג hereg (247c); from 2026; *a slaughter:*— killing(1), slaughter(3).

2028. הֲרֵגָה haregah (247c); fem. of 2027; *a slaughter:*— carnage(1), slaughter(4).

2029. הָרָה harah (247d); a prim. root; *to conceive, become pregnant:*— am(1), ancestors(1), child(1), conceive(3), conceived(35), conceives(1), conceiving(1), pregnant(1).

2030. הָרֶה harah (248a); from 2029; *pregnant:*— child(5), conceive(2), pregnant(3), pregnant woman(1), pregnant women(1), woman with child(1), women(1), women who were with child(1), women with child(1).

2031. הַרְהֹר harhor (1090d); (Ara.) from a root corr. to 2029; *fancy, imagining:*— fantasies(1).

2032. הֵרוֹן heron or

הֵרָיוֹן herayon (248a); from 2029; *conception, pregnancy:*— childbirth(1), conceive(1), conception(1).

2033. הֲרוֹרִי Harori (248b); prob. a scribal error for 2733, see 5878; an inhab. of Harod:— Harorite(1).

2034a. הָרִיָּה hariyyah (248a); from 2029; *pregnant:*— pregnant(1).

2034b. הֲרִיסָה harisah (249a); from 2040; *a ruin:*— ruins(1).

2035. הֲרִיסוּת harisuth (249a); from 2040; *an overthrow, destruction, ruin:*— destroyed(1).

2036. הֹרָם Horam (248b); of unc. der.; a Canaanite king:— Horam(1).

2037. הָרֻם Harum (248b); of unc. der.; a desc. of Judah:— Harum(1).

2038. הַרְמוֹן Harmon (248b); of unc. der.; a place name:— Harmon(1).

2039. הָרָן Haran (248c); perh. from 2022; "mountaineer," a brother of Abram, also an Isr.:— Haran(7).

2040. הָרַס haras (248c); a prim. root; *to throw down, break* or *tear down:*— break down(2), break through(2), broken down(1), destroyed(2), destroyers(1), overthrew(2), overthrow(5), overthrown(1), overthrows(1), pull you down(1), pull down(1), ruined(2), shatter(1), tear them down(1), tear you down(1), tear down(5), tears it down(1), tears down(1), thrown down(3), torn down(7), utterly overthrow(1).

2041. הֶרֶס heres (249a); from 2040; *an overthrow, destruction:*— destruction(1).

2042. הָרַר harar (249a); the same as 2022, q.v.

2043. הֲרָרִי Harari or

הָרָרִי Harari (251b); appar. from the same as 2022; "mountain dweller," descriptive of two of David's heroes:— Ararite(1), Hararite(4).

2044. הָשֵׁם Hashem (251c); of unc. der.; father of one of David's heroes:— Hashem(1).

2045. הַשְׁמָעוּת hashmauth (1036a); from 8085; *a causing to hear:*— information(1).

2046. הִתּוּךְ hittuk (678a); from 5413; *a melting:*— melted(1).

2047. הֲתָךְ Hathak (251c); prob. of for. or.; a Pers. official:— Hathach(4).

2048. הָתַל hathal (251c); a prim. root; *to deceive, mock:*— mocked(1).

2049. הֲתֻלִּים hathulim (251d); from 2048; *mockery:*— mockers(1).

2050. הָתַת hathath (223d); the same as 1956a, q.v.

ו

2051. וְדָן Vedan (255a); of unc. der.; a place of unknown location:— Vedan(1).

2052. וָהֵב Vaheb (255b); of unc. der., perh. a place in Moab:— Waheb(1).

2053. וָו vav (255b); of unc. der.; *a hook, pin, peg:*— hooks(13).

2054. וָזָר vazar (255c); from an unused word; *criminal, guilty:*— guilty(1).

2055. וַיְזָתָא Vayzatha (255c); of for. or.; a son of Haman:— Vaizatha(1).

2056. וָלָד valad (409b); from 3205; *offspring, child:*— child(1).

2057. וַנְיָה Vanyah (255c); of unc. der.; an Isr.:— Vaniah(1).

2058. וָפְסִי Vophsi (255c); of unc. der.; a Naphtalite:— Vophsi(1).

2059. וַשְׁנִי Vashni (255d); another reading for 8145, q.v.

2060. וַשְׁתִּי Vashti (255d); of for. or.; queen of Pers.:— Vashti(10).

ז

2061. זְאֵב zeeb (255b); from an unused word; *a wolf:*— wolf(4), wolves(3).

2062. זְאֵב Zeeb (255d); from the same as 2061; "wolf," a leader in Midian:— Zeeb(6).

2063. זֹאת zoth (260a); fem. of 2088, q.v.

2064. זָבַד zabad (256b); a prim. root; *bestow upon, endow with:*— endowed(1).

2065. זֶבֶד zebed (256b); from 2064; *endowment, gift:*— gift(1).

2066. זָבָד Zabad (256b); from 2064; "he has given," the name of several Isr.:— Zabad(8).

2067. זַבְדִּי Zabdi (256c); from 2065; "gift," four Isr.:— Zabdi(6).

2068. זַבְדִּיאֵל Zabdiel (256c); from 2065 and 410; "my gift is God," two Isr.:— Zabdiel(2).

2069. זְבַדְיָה Zebadyah or

זְבַדְיָהוּ Zebadyahu (256c); from 2064 and 3050; "Yah has bestowed," the name of several Isr.:— Zebadiah(9).

2070. זְבוּב zebub (256a); from an unused word; *a fly:*— flies(1), fly(1).

2071. זָבוּד Zabud (256b); from 2064; "bestowed," an officer of Solomon:— Zabud(1).

2072. זַבּוּד Zabbud (256b); a form of 2071; "bestowed," an Isr.:— Zabbud(1).

2073. זְבוּל zebul or

זְבֻל zebul (259c); from 2082; *elevation, height, lofty abode:*— habitation(2), lofty(2), places(1).

2074. זְבוּלוּן Zebulun or

זְבֻלוּן Zebulun or

זְבוּלֻן Zebulun (259d); from 2082; a son of Jacob, also his desc. and their territory:— Zebulun(45).

2075. זְבוּלֹנִי Zebuloni (259d); from 2074; desc. of Zebulun:— Zebulunite(2), Zebulunites(1).

2076. זָבַח zabach (256d); a prim. root; *to slaughter for sacrifice:*— made(1), offer(12), offer a sacrifice(2), offer to a sacrifice(1), offer sacrifices(3), offered(11), offered sacrifice(1), offering(2), offering sacrifices(1), offers a sacrifice(2), sacrifice(47), sacrificed(33), sacrifices(3), sacrificing(9), slaughter(3), slaughtered(3).

2077. זֶבַח zebach (257b); from 2076; *a sacrifice:*— feasting(1), offer(2), sacrifice(98), sacrifices(54), sacrificial(1), slaughter(1).

2078. זֶבַח Zebach (258a); from 2076; a Midianite king:— Zebah(12).

2079. זַבַּי Zabbay (256a); from the same as 2070; an Isr.:— Zabbai(2).

2080. זְבִידָה Zebiddah (256b); from 2064; mother of Jehoiakim:— Zebidah(1).

2081. זְבִינָא Zebina (259b); an Aramaism from 2084; "bought," an Isr.:— Zebina(1).

2082. זָבַל zabal (259c); a prim. root; prob. *to dwell:*— dwell(1).

2083. זְבֻל Zebul (259d); from 2082; an officer of Abimelech:— Zebul(6).

2084. זְבַן zeban (1091a); (Ara.) a prim. root; *to buy, gain:*— bargaining(1).

2085. זָג zag (260a); from an unused word; *skin* (of the grape):— skin(1).

2086. זֵד zed (267d); from 2102; *insolent, presumptuous:*— arrogant(9), arrogant men(1), presumptuous(1), proud(2).

2087. זָדוֹן zadon (268a); from 2102; *insolence, presumptuousness:*— arrogance(3), arrogant(2), insolence(2), insolent pride(1), presumptuously(2), pride(1).

2088. זֶה zeh (260a); a prim. pron.; *this, here:*— another(5), both sides*(1), both*(1), completely*(1), daylight*(1), each side(1), either side(1), ever(3), first woman(1), follows(1), here(29), how*(3), itself(1), just(1), morning(1), now(1), now*(1), one(12), one and another(1), one as well as another(1), one out to another(1), one side and the other(1), one while another(2), one side(11), one thing(1), origin*(1), other(12), other on the other side(1), other side(2), purpose(2), really(2), same(10), side(4), side and on the other(6), similarly(1), so(3), such(13), such a thing(2), then(9), there(4), therefore*(1), these(40), these to this(1), this(1230), this and these(1), this is what(3), this one(22), this side(2), this thing(1), this way(2), this woman(1), those(1), thus(7), thus*(1), today*(1), what(2), what*(3), where(1), where*(1), which(2), which*(2), why*(2).

2089. זֶה zeh (262b); typographical error for 7716, q.v.

2090. זֹה zoh (262b); a prim. pron.; *this:*— this(7), thus(2).

2091. זָהָב zahab (262c); of unc. der.; *gold:*— gold(354), golden(33).

2092. זָהַם zaham (263d); a prim. root; *to be foul, loathsome:*— loathes(1).

2093. זַהַם Zaham (263d); from 2092; "loathing," a son of Rehoboam:— Zaham(1).

2094a. זָהַר zahar (263d); a prim. root; *to be light* or *shining:*— shine brightly(1).

2094b. זָהַר zahar (264a); a prim. root; *to warn:*— give them warning(1), receive instruction(1), take warning(2), taken warning(1), teach(1), took warning(1), warn(6), warned(7), warns(1).

2095. זְהַר zehar (1091a); (Ara.) corr. to 2094b; *to warn.*

2096. זֹהַר zohar (264a); from 2094a; *shining, brightness:*— brightness(2).

2097. זוֹ zo (262b); from 2090; *this:*— this(1), which(1).

2098. זוּ zu (262b); from 2090; *this, which, who:*— this(2), where(1), which(5), who(1), whom(4), whose(1).

2099. זִו Ziv (264c); of unc. der.; the second month of the Jewish calendar:— Ziv(2).

2100. זוּב zub (264c); a prim. root; *to flow, gush:*— discharge(14), flow(1), flowed(1), flowing(19), flows(1), gushed(2), has(1), has a discharge(1), pine away(1).

2101. זוֹב zob (264d); from 2100; *an issue* (of fluid):— discharge(13).

2102. זוּד zud or

זִיד zid (267c); a prim. root; *to boil up, seethe, act proudly* or *presumptuously* or *rebelliously:*— act presumptuously(1), acted arrogantly(3), acted presumptuously(1), acts presumptuously(1), become arrogant(1), cooked(1), dealt proudly(1), presumptuously(1).

2103. זוּד zud (1091b); (Ara.) corr. to 2102; *to be presumptuous:*— behaved arrogantly(1).

2104. זוּזִים Zuzim (265c); from the same as 2123b; a people E. of the Jordan:— Zuzim(1).

2105. זוֹחֵת Zocheth (265d); of unc. der.; a desc. of Judah:— Zoheth(1).

2106. זָוִית zavith (265a); from an unused word; *a corner:*— corner(1), corners(1).

2107. זוּל zul (266a); a prim. root; *to lavish:*— lavish(1).

2108. זוּלָה zulah (265d); from an unused word; *except, only:*— besides(5), except(7), only(2).

2109. זוּן zun (266a); a prim. root; *to feed:*— well-fed(1).

2110. זוּן zun (1091b); (Ara.) corr. to 2109; *to feed:*— fed(1).

2111. זוּעַ zua (266a); a prim. root; *to tremble, quake:*— collect(1), tremble(2).

2112. זוּעַ zua (1091b); (Ara.) corr. to 2111; *to tremble:*— tremble(1), trembled(1).

2113. זְוָעָה zevaah (266b); from 2111; *a trembling, an object of trembling* or *terror:*— object of horror(1), object of terror(1), terror(6).

2114a. זוּר zur (266b); a prim. root; *to be a stranger:*— adulteress(3), adulteress*(1), alien(2), aliens(2), another(2), enemies(1), estranged(4), foreign(2), foreigners(2), illegitimate(1), layman(9), outsider(2), satisfied(1), strange(11), strange thing(1), strange things(1), stranger(7), strangers(22), turned away(1), unusual(1).

2114b. זוּר zur or

זִיר zir (266d); a prim. root; *to be loathsome:*— offensive(1).

2115. זוּר zur (266d); a prim. root; *to press down and out:*— crush(1), crushed(1), pressed(1), squeezed(1).

2116. זוּרֶה zureh (266d); the same as 2115, q.v.

2117. זָזָא Zaza (265b); perh. from the same as 2123a; a desc. of Judah:— Zaza(1).

2118. זָחַח zachach (267b); a prim. root; *to remove, displace:*— come loose(2).

2119a. זָחַל zachal (267b); a prim. root; *to shrink back, crawl away:*— crawling things(1), reptiles(1).

2119b. זָחַל zachal (267c); a prim. root; *to fear, be afraid:*— shy(1).

2120. זֹחֶלֶת zocheleth (267b); fem. act. part. of 2119a; *a crawling thing, serpent:*— Zoheleth(1).

2121. זֵידוֹן zedon (268a); from 2102; *insolent, raging:*— raging(1).

2122. זִיו ziv (1091b); (Ara.) corr. to 2099; *brightness, splendor:*— face(4), splendor(2).

2123a. זִיז ziz (265a); from an unused word; *moving things* (i.e. beasts):— everything that moves(1), whatever moves(1).

2123b. זִיז ziz (265c); from an unused word; *abundance, fulness:*— bountiful(1).

2124. זִיזָא Ziza (265b); from the same as 2123a; two Isr.:— Ziza(2).

2125. זִיזָה Zizah (265b); from the same as 2123a; a Levite:— Zizah(1).

2126. זִינָא Zina (268b); of unc. der., see 2125; a Levite:— Zina(1).

2127. זִיעַ Zia (266b); from 2111; a Gadite:— Zia(1).

2128. זִיף Ziph (268b); of unc. der.; a son of Judah, also a city S.E. of Hebron and a city in S. Judah:— Ziph(10).

2129. זִיפָה Ziphah (268b); fem. of 2128; an Isr.:— Ziphah(1).

2130. זִיפִי Ziphi (268b); from 2128; inhab. of Ziph:— Ziphites(2).

2131. זִיקָה ziqah or

זֵק zeq (278a); of unc. der.; *a missile, spark:*— brands(1), firebrands(2).

2132. זַיִת zayith (268b); of unc. der.; *olive tree, olive:*— groves(1), olive(10), olive grove(1), olive groves(5), olive tree(9), olive trees(6), Olives(3), olives(3).

2133. זֵיתָן Zethan (268d); from 2132; "olive tree," a Benjamite:— Zethan(1).

2134. זַךְ zak (269b); from 2141; *pure, clean:*— clean(1), clear(2), pure(8).

2135. זָכָה zakah (269a); a prim. root; *to be clear, clean* or *pure:*— blameless(1), clean(1), cleansed(1), justify(1), keep his pure(1), kept my pure(1), make yourselves clean(1), pure(1).

2136. זָכוּ zaku (1091b); (Ara.) corr. to 2135; *purity, innocence:*— innocent(1).

2137. זְכוֹכִית zekokith (269b); from 2141; *glass:*— glass(1).

2138. זָכוּר zakur (271d); from 2142; *a male:*— males(3), men(1).

2139. זַכּוּר Zakkur (271d); from 2142; the name of several Isr.:— Zaccur(9).

2140. זַכַּי Zakkay (269b); from 2141; an Isr.:— Zaccai(2).

2141. זָכַךְ zakak (269a); a prim. root; *to be bright, clean* or *pure:*— cleanse(1), pure(2), purer(1).

2142. זָכַר zakar (269c); a prim. root; *remember:*— been mindful(1), boast(1), bring my to remembrance(1), bringing to mind(1), brings to remembrance(1), burns(1), call to mind(1), celebrate(1), certainly still remember(1), come to remembrance(1), confess(1), consider(2), extol(1), invoke(1), invoked(1), keep(1), make mention(2), mention(4), mentioned(5), mentioning(1), mindful(1), named*(1), preserve(1), put me in remembrance(1), recorder(9), remember(132), remembered(42), remembering(1), remembers(4), remind(1), reminder(1), report(1), surely my remembers(1), take thought(1), well remember(1).

2143. זֵכֶר zeker (271b); from 2142; *remembrance, memorial:*— memorial-name(1), memory(12), mention(1), name(4), remembered(2), remembrance(2), renown(1).

2144. זֶכֶר Zeker (271b); from 2142; an Isr.:— Zecher(1).

2145. זָכָר zakar (271b); from 2142; *male:*— boy(2), intimately*(3), male(56), males(19), man(4).

2146. זִכָּרוֹן zikkaron (272a); from 2142; *memorial, remembrance:*— memorable sayings(1), memorial(12), records(1), remembrance(4), reminder(5), sign(1).

2147. זִכְרִי Zikri (271d); from 2142; the name of several Isr.:— Zichri(12).

2148a. זְכַרְיָה Zekaryah or

זְכַרְיָהוּ Zekaryahu (272a); from 2142 and 3050; the name of a number of Isr.:— Zechariah(41).

2148b. זְכַרְיָה Zekaryah (1091c); (Ara.) corr. to 2148a; a Heb. prophet:— Zechariah(2).

2149. זֻלּוּת zulluth (273a); from 2151b; *worthlessness:*— vileness(1).

2150. זַלְזַל zalzal (272d); from 2151a; *tendrils:*— sprigs(1).

2151a. זָלַל zalal (272d); a prim. root; *to shake:*— quake(1), quaked(1).

2151b. זָלַל zalal (272d); a prim. root; *to be light* or *worthless, make light of:*— despise(1), despised(1), glutton(2), gluttonous eaters(1), gluttons(1), worthless(1).

2152. זַלְעָפָה zalaphah (273a); of unc. der.; *raging heat:*— burning(1), burning heat(1), burning indignation(1).

2153. זִלְפָּה Zilpah (273a); from an unused word; one of Jacob's wives:— Zilpah(7).

2154. זִמָּה zimmah (273b); from 2161; *a plan, device, wickedness:*— acts of lewdness(1), crime(1), devising(1), evil intent(1), immorality(2), lewd(3), lewdly(1), lewdness(13), lustful crime(1), plans(1), wicked scheme(1), wicked schemes(1), wickedness(2).

2155. זִמָּה Zimmah (273c); from 2161; an Isr. name:— Zimmah(3).

2156. זְמוֹרָה zemorah (274d); from 2168; *branch, twig, shoot:*— branch(2), twig(1), vine branches(1), vine slips(1).

2157. זַמְזֻמִּים Zamzummim (273d); from 2161; another name for the Rephaim:— Zamzummin(1).

2158. זָמִיר zamir (274b); from 2167; *song:*— psalmist(1), psalms(1), song(1), songs(1), songs(2).

2159. זָמִיר zamir (274d); from 2168; *trimming, pruning:*— pruning(1).

2160. זְמִירָה Zemirah (275b); of unc. der.; a Benjamite:— Zemirah(1).

2161. זָמַם zamam (273b); a prim. root; *to consider, purpose, devise:*— considers(1), intended(1), plots(1), plotted(1), purpose(1), purposed(7), schemed(1).

2162. זָמָם zamam (273b); from 2161; *a plan, device:*— device(1).

2163. זָמַן zaman (273d); from 2161; *to be fixed, appointed:*— appointed(4), fixed(1).

2164. זְמַן zeman (1091c); (Ara.) corr. to 2163; *to agree together:*— agreed together(1).

2165. זְמָן zeman (273d); from 2163; *appointed time, time:*— appointed time(1), definite time(1), time(1), times(1).

2166. זְמָן zeman (1091c); (Ara.) corr. to 2165; *time:*— appointed period(1), epochs(1), time(6), times(3).

2167. זָמַר zamar (274a); a prim. root; *to make music* (in praise of God):— praise(1), praise the in song(1), sing(3), sing praise(7), sing praises(35).

2168. זָמַר zamar (274d); a prim. root; *to trim, prune:*— prune(2), pruned(1).

2169. זֶמֶר zemer (275a); of unc. der.; perh. *a mountain sheep* or *goat:*— mountain sheep(1).

2170. זְמָר zemar (1091c); (Ara.) corr. to 2167; *music:*— music(4).

2171. זַמָּר zammar (1091c); (Ara.) from the same as 2170; *singer:*— singers(1).

2172. זִמְרָה zimrah (274b); from 2167; *melody, song* (in praise of Yah):— melody(2), song(3), sound(1).

2173. זִמְרָה zimrah (275a); from an unused word; perh. *choice products:*— best products(1).

2174a. זִמְרִי Zimri (275b); of unc. der.; four Isr.:— Zimri(14).

2174b. זִמְרִי Zimri (275b); of unc. der.; perh. a place in Ethiopia:— Zimri(1).

2175. זִמְרָן Zimran (275b); of unc. der.; a son of Abraham:— Zimran(2).

2176. זִמְרָת zimrath (274b); the same as 2172, q.v.:— song(1).

2177. זַן zan (275b); of unc. der.; *kind, sort:*— every kind(1), kinds(1).

2178. זַן zan (1091c); (Ara.) corr. to 2177; *kind, sort:*— kinds(4).

2179. זָנַב zinneb (275c); denom. vb. from 2180, *to cut off* or *smite the tail:*— attack them in the rear(1), attacked(1).

2180. זָנָב zanab (275b); of unc. der.; *tail, end, stump:*— stubs(1), tail(9), tails(1).

2181. זָנָה zanah (275c); a prim. root; *to commit fornication, be a harlot:*— adulterous(1), become a harlot(1), commit adultery(1), commits flagrant harlotry(1), fall to harlotry(1), harlot(22), harlot continually(1), harlot's(2), harlot's*(2), harlot*(3), harlotry(3), harlots(5), making her a harlot(1), play the harlot(18), play the harlot continually(1), played the harlot(24), playing the harlot(3), plays the harlot(1), prostitute(1), unfaithful(1).

2182. זָנוֹחַ Zanoach (276c); from 2186b; two cities in Judah:— Zanoah(5).

2183. זְנוּנִים zenunim (276a); from 2181; *fornication:*— harlotries(5), harlotry(8).

2184. זְנוּת zenuth (276a); from 2181; *fornication:*— harlotry(6), prostitution(1), unfaithfulness(1).

2185. זֹנוֹת zonoth (275c); fem. pl. part. of 2181, q.v.

2186a. זָנַח zanach (276b); a prim. root; *to reject, spurn:*— been rejected(1), cast off(1), discarded(1), excluded(1), reject(5), rejected(10).

2186b. זָנַח zanach (276c); a prim. root; *to stink, emit a stench:*— emit a stench(1).

2187. זָנַק zanaq (276c); a prim. root; *to leap:*— leaps(1).

2188. זֵעָה zeah (402c); from the same as 3154; *sweat:*— sweat(1).

2189. זַעֲוָה zaavah (266b); by transp. for 2113, q.v.

2190. זַעֲוָן Zaavan (266b, 276c); of unc. der.; a desc. of Seir:— Zaavan(2).

2191. זְעֵיר zeer (277d); from an unused word; *a little:*— little(5).

2192. זְעֵיר zeer (1091d); (Ara.) corr. to 2191; *little, small:*— little one(1).

2193. זָעַךְ zaak (276c); a prim. root; *to extinguish:*— extinguished(1).

2194. זָעַם zaam (276d); a prim. root; *to be indignant:*— abhor(1), angry(1), become enraged(1), been indignant(1), cursed(2), denounce(2), denounced(1), indignant(2), indignation(1).

2195. זַעַם zaam (276d); from 2194; *indignation:*— indignation(21), insolence(1).

2196. זָעַף zaaph (277a); a prim. root; *to be vexed, be enraged:*— dejected(1), enraged(2), looking...haggard(1), rages(1).

2197. זַעַף zaaph (277a); from 2196; *a storming, raging, rage:*— enraged(1), fierce(1), indignation(1), rage(1), raging(1), wrath(1).

2198. זָעֵף zaeph (277a); from 2196; *vexed:*— vexed(2).

2199. זָעַק zaaq (277a); a prim. root; *to cry, cry out, call:*— assembled(1), assembled together(1), call(2), called(1), called and together(1), called together(4), complain(1), cried(28), cries(3), cry(25), cry aloud(2), crying aloud(1), issued a proclamation(1), rallied(1), shouting(1), wailed(1).

2200. זְעִק zeiq (1091d); (Ara.) corr. to 2199; *to cry, call:*— cried(1).

2201. זְעָקָה zeaqah (277c); from 2199; *a cry, outcry:*— cry(5), cry of distress(2), crying(1), lamentations(1), outcry(7).

2202. זִפְרֹן Ziphron (277d); of unc. der.; a place on N. boundary of the promised land:— Ziphron(1).

2203a. זֶפֶת zepheth (278a); perh. of for. or.; *pitch:*— pitch(3).

2203b. זֵק zeq (279b); from an unused word; *a fetter:*— chains(2), fetters(2).

2204. זָקֵן zaqen (278b); from the same as 2206; *to be* or *become old:*— am so old(1), am old(3), am...old(1), being old(1), grow old(1), grown old(1), old(17), reached a old(1), reached old(1).

2205. זָקֵן zaqen (278c); from the same as 2206; *old:*— aged(3), aged*(1), elder(3), elders(132), old(21), old man(7), old men(7), old women(1), older(1), oldest(1), senior(1).

2206. זָקָן zaqan (278b); from an unused word; *beard, chin:*— beard(14), beards(5).

2207. זֹקֶן zoqen (279a); from the same as 2206; *old age:*— age(1).

2208. זְקֻנִים zaqun (279a); pass. part. of 2204; *old age:*— old age(4).

2209. זִקְנָה ziqnah (279a); fem. of 2207; *old age:*— old(2), old age(4).

2210. זָקַף zaqaph (279a); a prim. root; *to raise up:*— raises(2).

2211. זְקַף zeqaph (1091d); (Ara.) corr. to 2210; *to raise, lift up:*— impaled*(1).

2212. זָקַק zaqaq (279b); a prim. root; *to refine, purify:*— distill(1), refine(2), refined(4).

2213. זֵר zer (267a); from 2115; *circlet, border:*— border(2), molding(8).

2214. זָרָא zara (266d); from 2114b; *loathsome thing:*— loathsome(1).

2215. זָרַב zarab (279c); a prim. root; *to burn, scorch:*— become waterless(1).

2216. זְרֻבָּבֶל Zerubbabel (279c); perh. from 2215 and 894; "begotten in Babylon," a leader of returning Isr. exiles:— Zerubbabel(21).

2217. זְרֻבָּבֶל Zerubbabel (1091d); (Ara.) corr. to 2216; "begotten in Babylon," leader of returning Isr. exiles:— Zerubbabel(1).

2218. זֶרֶד Zered (279d); of unc. der.; a wadi E. of the Dead Sea:— Zered(4).

2219. זָרָה zarah (279d); a prim. root; *to scatter, fan, winnow:*— disperse(5), dispersed(1), disperses(1), north(1), scatter(13), scattered(7), scrutinize(1), spread(4), winnow(3), winnow them with a winnowing(1), winnowed(1), winnows(2).

2220. זְרוֹעַ zeroa (283d); from an unused word; *arm, shoulder, strength:*— arm(53), arms(19), forces(3), help(1), mighty(1), position(1), power(4), shoulder(2), strength(8).

2221. זֵרוּעַ zerua (283b); from 2232; *a sowing, thing sown:*— sowing(1), things sown(1).

2222. זַרְזִיף zarziph (284b); from an unused word; *a drop, dripping:*— water(1).

2223. זַרְזִיר zarzir (267a); from 2115; *girded:*— strutting*(1).

2224. זָרַח zarach (280b); a prim. root; *to rise, come forth:*— arises(1), broke(1), came(1), dawned(1), rise(3), risen(2), rises(5), rose(1), shine(1), shone(1).

2225. זֶרַח zerach (280b); from 2224; *a dawning, shining:*— rising(1).

2226. זֶרַח Zerach (280b); from 2224; three Isr., also an Edomite, also an Ethiopian:— Zerah(21).

2227. זַרְחִי Zarchi (280c); from 2226; desc. of Zerah:— Zerahites(6).

2228. זְרַחְיָה Zerachyah (280c); from 2224 and 3050; "Yah has risen," two Isr.:— Zerahiah(5).

2229. זָרַם zaram (281a); a prim. root; *to pour forth in floods, flood away:*— away like(1), away like a flood(1), poured(1), swept them away like(1).

2230. זֶרֶם zerem (281b); from 2229; *a flood of rain, rainstorm, downpour:*— downpour(2), rains(1), storm(6).

2231. זִרְמָה zirmah (281b); fem. of 2230; *an issue* (a fluid):— issue(2).

2232. זָרַע zara (281b); a prim. root; *to sow, scatter seed:*— conceive(1), gives birth(1), perpetuated(1), plant seed(1), scatter(1), set(1), sow(28), sowed(2), sower(2), sowing(2), sown(10), sows(2), unsown*(1), yielding(4).

2233. זֶרַע zera (282a); from 2232; *a sowing, seed, offspring:*— carnally*(1), child(1), children(3), descendant(3), descendants(105), descent(1), family(6), fertile(1), grain(3), intercourse*(2), line(1), nation(1), offspring(38), offspring's offspring(1), origin(1), posterity(1), race(1), seed(48), seedtime(1), seminal(4), seminal*(1), son*(1), time(1), what you sow(1).

2234. זְרַע zera (1091d); (Ara.) corr. to 2233; *a seed:*— seed(1).

2235a. זֵרֹעַ zeroa (283b); from 2232; *vegetable:*— vegetables(1).

2235b. זֵרְעֹן zereon (283b); from 2232; *vegetable:*— vegetables(1).

2236a. זָרַף zaraph (284b); another reading for 2222, q.v.

2236b. זָרַק zaraq (284c); a prim. root; *to toss* or *throw, scatter abundantly:*— scatter(2), scattered(1), sprinkle(13), sprinkled(15), sprinkles(1), threw(2), throw(1).

2237. זָרַר zarar (284d); a prim. root; *to sneeze:*— sneezed(1).

2238. זֶרֶשׁ Zeresh (284d); of for. or.; wife of Haman:— Zeresh(4).

2239. זֶרֶת zereth (284d); of unc. der.; *a span:*— span(7).

2240. זַתּוּא Zattu (285c); of unc. der.; an Isr.:— Zattu(5).

2241. זֵתָם Zetham (285c); of unc. der.; a Levite:— Zetham(2).

2242. זֵתַר Zethar (285c); of for. or.; a eunuch of Ahasuerus:— Zethar(1).

ח

2243. חֹב chob (285c); from 2245; *bosom:*— bosom(1).

2244. חָבָא chaba (285a); a prim. root; *to withdraw, hide:*— becomes hard(1), concealed(1), hid(10), hidden(11), hide(5), hides(1), hiding(2), hushed(1), secretly(1).

2245. חָבַב chabab (285c); a prim. root; *to love:*— loves(1).

2246. חֹבָב Chobab (285d); from 2245; father-in-law of Moses:— Hobab(2).

2247. חָבָה chabah (285d); a prim. root; *to withdraw, hide:*— conceal(1), hide(4).

2248. חֲבוּלָא chabula (1092a); (Ara.) from 2255; *a hurtful act, crime:*— crime(1).

2249. חָבוֹר Chabor (289c); from 2266; a river of Assyr.:— Habor(3).

2250. חַבּוּרָה chabburah or
חַבֻּרָה **chabburah** or
חֲבֻרָה **chaburah** (289a); from 2266; *a stripe, blow:*— bruise(2), scourging(1), striking(1), stripes(1), welts(1), wounds(1).

2251. חָבַט chabat (286a); a prim. root; *to beat off, beat out:*— beat(2), beaten(1), beating(1), threshing(1).

2252. חֲבַיָה Chabayah (285d); from 2247 and 3050; "Yah has hidden," an Isr.:— Habaiah(1), Hobaiah(1).

2253. חֶבְיוֹן chebyon (285d); from 2247; *a hiding, hiding place:*— hiding(1).

2254a. חָבַל chabal (286b); a prim. root; *to bind, pledge:*— debt(1), ever take(1), hold him in pledge(2), labor(2), pledge(4), retain(1), take(3), take a pledge(1), taken as pledges(1), taken pledges(1), taking a in pledge(1), travails(1).

2254b. חָבַל chabal (287b); a prim. root; *to act corruptly:*— acted very corruptly(1), brings on destruction(1), broken(2), destroy(3), offend(1), ruin(1), ruining(1).

2255. חֲבַל chabal (1091d); (Ara.) corr. to 2254b; *to destroy, hurt:*— destroy(2), destroyed(3), harmed(1).

2256a. חֶבֶל chebel (286c); from 2254a; *cord, territory, band:*— allotment(1), coast(1), cord(2), cords(13), group(2), line(4), lines(2), measurement(1), measuring line(1), noose(1), portion(3), portions(2), region(5), rope(1), ropes(7), seacoast*(2), tackle(1).

2256b. חֵבֶל chebel (286d); from 2254a; *a pain, pang:*— anguish(1), destruction(1), labor pains(2), pain(1), pains(1), pangs(3).

2256c. חֶבֶל chebel (287c); from 2254b; *destruction:*— destruction(1).

2257. חֲבָל chabal (1092a); (Ara.) from 2255; *a hurt, injury:*— damage(1), harm(1), injury(1).

2258. חֲבֹל chabol (287a); from 2254a; *a pledge:*— pledge(3).

2259. חֹבֵל chobel (287a); from 2256a; *sailor:*— captain*(1), pilots(4).

2260a. חִבֵּל chibbel (287a); from 2256a; prob. *a mast:*— mast(1).

2260b. חֲבֹלָה chabolah (287a); from 2254a; *a pledge:*— pledge(1).

2260c. חֹבְלִים chobelim (287a); from 2254a; *union:*— Union(2).

2261. חֲבַצֶּלֶת chabatstseleth (287c); of unc. der.; *meadow saffron* or *crocus:*— crocus(1), rose(1).

2262. חֲבַצִּנְיָה Chabatstsanyah (287d); of unc. der.; a Rechabite:— Habazziniah(1).

2263. חָבַק chabaq (287d); a prim. root; *to clasp, embrace:*— embrace(7), embraced(3), embracing(1), folds(1), hug(1).

2264. חִבֻּק chibbuq (287d); from 2263; *a clasping, folding* (of the hands):— folding(2).

2265. חֲבַקּוּק Chabaqquq (287d); from 2263; a Heb. prophet:— Habakkuk(2).

2266. חָבַר chabar (287d); a prim. root; *to unite, be joined, to tie a magic knot* or *spell, to charm:*— alliance is made(1), allied(4), attached(1), attaching(1), came as allies(1), caster(1), casts(1), compact(1), compose(1), form an alliance(1), join(2), join the together(2), joined(10), touched(1), touching(1).

2267. חֶבֶר cheber (288c); from 2266; *company, association, spell:*— band(1), shared(2), spell(1), spells(3).

2268. חֶבֶר Cheber or
חֵבֶר **Cheber** (288c); from 2266; a Kenite, also several Isr.:— Heber(10), Heber's(1).

2269. חֲבַר chabar (1092a); (Ara.) corr. to 2266; *fellow, comrade:*— friends(3).

2270. חָבֵר chaber (288d); from 2266; *united, associate, companion:*— companion(3), companions(7), fellows(1), united(1).

2271. חַבָּר chabbar (289a); from 2266; *associate, partner* (in a trade):— traders(1).

2272. חֲבַרְבֻּרָה chabarburah (289a); from 2266; *stripe, mark:*— spots(1).

2273. חַבְרָה chabrah (1092a); (Ara.) fem. of 2269; *a fellow:*— associates(1).

2274. חֶבְרָה chebrah (288d); fem. of 2267; *association, company:*— company(1).

2275a. חֶבְרוֹן Chebron (289b); from 2266; "association, league," a city in S. Judah:— Hebron(62).

2275b. חֶבְרוֹן Chebron (289b); from 2266; two Isr.:— Hebron(9).

2276. חֶבְרוֹנִי Chebroni or
חֶבְרֹנִי **Chebroni** (289c); from 2275b; inhab. of Hebron:— Hebronites(6).

2277. חֶבְרִי Chebri (288d); from 2268; desc. of Heber:— Heberites(1).

2278. חֲבֶרֶת chabereth (289a); fem. of 2270; *consort:*— companion(1).

2279. חֹבֶרֶת chobereth (289a); fem. part. of 2266; *a thing that joins or is joined:*— set(4).

2280. חָבַשׁ chabash (289d); a prim. root; *to bind, bind on, bind up:*— bandage(1), bandaged(1), bind(5), binds(2), bound(3), dams(1), gives relief(1), healer(1), rule(1), saddle(3), saddled(10), wound(1), wrapped(3).

2281. חֲבִתִּים chabittim (290a); from an unused word; *flat cakes, bread wafers:*— baked in pans(1).

2282. חַג chag (290d); from 2287; *a festival gathering, feast, pilgrim feast:*— feast(52), feasts(5), festival(1), festival sacrifice(1), festivals(3).

2283. חָגָּא chagga (291b); of unc. der.; *a reeling:*— terror(1).

2284. חָגָב chagab (290b); from an unused word; *locust, grasshopper:*— grasshopper(2), grasshoppers(2), locust(1).

2285. חָגָב Chagab (290c); from the same as 2284; an Isr.:— Hagab(1).

2286a. חֲגָבָא Chagaba (290c); from the same as 2284; an Isr.:— Hagaba(1).

2286b. חָגָבָה Chagabah (290c); from the same as 2284; an Isr.:— Hagabah(1).

2287. חָגַג chagag (290c); a prim. root; *to make a pilgrimage, keep a pilgrim feast:*— celebrate(9), celebrate a feast(3), dancing(1), keeping festival(1), observe(1), reeled(1).

2288. חֲגָוִים chagavim (291c); from an unused word; *places of concealment, retreats:*— clefts(3).

2289. חָגוֹר chagor (292a); from 2296; *girded:*— girded(1).

2290a. חֲגוֹר chagor or

חֲגֹר chagor (292a); from 2296; *a belt, girdle:*— belt(2), belts(1).

2290b. חֲגוֹרָה chagorah or

חֲגֹרָה chagorah (292a); from 2296; *a girdle, loin covering, belt:*— armor(1), belt(3), loin coverings(1).

2291. חַגִּי Chaggi (291b); from 2282; "festal," a son of Gad, also his desc.:— Haggi(2), Haggites(1).

2292a. חַגַּי Chaggay (291b); from 2282; "festal," a Heb. prophet:— Haggai(9).

2292b. חַגַּי Chaggay (1092a); (Ara.) corr. to 2292a; a Heb. prophet:— Haggai(2).

2293. חַגִּיָּה Chaggiyyah (291b); from 2282 and 3050; "feast of Yah," a Levite:— Haggiah(1).

2294. חַגִּית Chaggith (291b); fem. of 2291; "festal," a wife of David:— Haggith(5).

2295. חָגְלָה Choglah (291c); from an unused word; "partridge," a female desc. of Manasseh:— Hoglah(4).

2296. חָגַר chagar (291c); a prim. root; *to gird, gird on, gird oneself:*— armed(3), bound(1), come trembling(1), dressed*(1), gird(11), gird yourselves(2), girded(15), girds(3), put(4), wearing(3).

2297. חַד chad (26a); short form of 259; *one:*— one(1).

2298. חַד chad (1079c); (Ara.) corr. to 2297 and 259; *one:*— first(3), one(4), same time(1), single(1), times(1).

2299. חַד chad (292b); from 258; *sharp:*— sharp(4).

2300. חָדַד chadad (292b, 1119d); a prim. root; *to be sharp, keen:*— keener(1), sharpened(3), show yourself sharp(1).

2301. חֲדַד Chadad (292c); from 2300; a son of Ishmael:— Hadad(2).

2302a. חָדָה chadah (292c); a prim. root; *to be* or *grow sharp:*— sharpens(2).

2302b. חָדָה chadah (292d); a prim. root; *to rejoice:*— make him joyful(1), rejoice(1), rejoiced(1).

2303. חַדּוּד chaddud (292c); from 2300; *sharpened, sharp, pointed:*— sharp(1).

2304. חֶדְוָה chedvah (292d); from 2302b; *joy:*— joy(2).

2305. חֶדְוָה chedvah (1092a); (Ara.) corr. to 2304; *joy:*— joy(1).

2306. חֲדִי chadi (1092a); (Ara.) corr. to 2373; *breast:*— breast(1).

2307. חָדִיד Chadid (292c); from 2300; a place in Benjamin:— Hadid(3).

2308. חָדַל chadal (292d); a prim. root; *to cease:*— cease(10), ceased(8), ceasing(1), deserted(1), fail(1), failed(1), gave(1), hold back(1), leave(5), let my alone(1), neglects(1), never mind(2), no(1), past(1), quit(1), refrain(6), refrained(1), refuse(1), regarding*(1), rest(1), stop(4), stopped(4), stops(1), unavoidable*(1).

2309. חֶדֶל chedel (293b); another reading for 2465, q.v.

2310. חָדֵל chadel (293b); from 2308; *forbearing, lacking:*— forsaken(1), refuses(1), transient(1).

2311. חַדְלָי Chadlay (293b); from 2309; an Ephraimite:— Hadlai(1).

2312. חֵדֶק chedeq (293b); from an unused word; *a briar:*— briar(1), thorns(1).

2313. חִדֶּקֶל Chiddeqel (293c); prob. of for. or.; *Hiddekel,* ancient name of a Mesopotamian river:— Tigris(2).

2314. חָדַר chadar (293c); a prim. root; *to surround, enclose:*— surrounds(1).

2315. חֶדֶר cheder (293c); from 2314; *a chamber, room:*— bedroom(3), bedroom*(5), chamber(1), chambers(4), inner chamber(1), inner room(5), innermost(1), innermost parts(3), inside*(1), room(5), rooms(4), south(1).

2316. חֲדַר Chadar (not included); a scribal error for 1924, q.v.

2317. חַדְרָךְ Chadrak (293d); of unc. der.; a region in Aram (Syria):— Hadrach(1).

2318. חָדַשׁ chadash (293d); a prim. root; *to renew, repair:*— renew(5), renewed(1), repair(1), restore(3), restored(1).

2319. חָדָשׁ chadash (294a); from 2318; *new:*— new(47), New(2), new thing(1), new things(2), something new(1).

2320. חֹדֶשׁ chodesh (294b); from 2318; *new moon, a month:*— month(204), month and months(1), month throughout the months(2), months(33), new moon(17), new moons(9).

2321. חֹדֶשׁ Chodesh (295a); from 2318; an Isr. woman:— Hodesh(1).

2322a. חֲדָשָׁה Chadashah (295a); fem. of 2319; "new," a city in Judah:— Hadashah(1).

2322b. חָדְשִׁי Chodshi (295a); see 8483.

2323. חֲדָת chadath (1092a); an optional reading not chosen in NASB.

2324. חֲוָא chava (1092b); see 2331b.

2325. חוּב chub (295a); a prim. root; *to be guilty:*— forfeit(1).

2326. חוֹב chob (295b); from 2325; *debt:*— debtor(1).

2327. חוֹבָה Chobah (295b); from 2325; a place N. of Damascus:— Hobah(1).

2328. חוּג chug (295b); a prim. root; *to draw around, make a circle:*— inscribed a circle(1).

2329. חוּג chug (295b); from 2328; *vault, horizon:*— circle(2), vault(1).

2330. חוּד chud (295c); denom. vb. from the same as 2420; *to propound a riddle:*— propound(3), propounded(1).

2331a. חָוָה chavah (296a); a prim. root; *to tell, declare:*— reveals(1), show(1), tell(4).

2331b. חֲוָה chavah (1092b); (Ara.) corr. to 2331a; *to declare:*— declare(13), explain(1).

2332. חַוָּה Chavvah (295d); from an unused word; "life," the first woman:— Eve(2).

2333. חַוָּה chavvah (295d); from an unused word; *a tent village:*— towns(4).

2334. חַוּוֹת יָאִיר Chavvoth Yair (295d); from 2333 and 2971; "tent villages of Jair," an area E. of the Jordan:— Havvoth-jair(3).

2335. חוֹזָי Chozay (302c); from 2372; "seer," a keeper of records:— Hozai(1).

2336. חוֹחַ choach (296b); of unc. der.; *briar, bramble, hook, ring, fetter:*— briars(1), hook(1), hooks(1), thickets(1), thistles(1), thorn(1), thorn bush(4), thorns(2).

2337. חָוָח chavach (296b); the same as 2336, q.v.

2338. חוּט chut (1092b); (Ara.) corr. to the root of 2339; *to repair* (foundations):— repairing(1).

2339. חוּט chut (296c); from an unused word; *thread, cord, line:*— circumference*(1), cord(1), line(1), thread(4).

2340. חִוִּי Chivvi (295d); prob. from the same as 2333; prob. "villagers," a Canaanite tribe:— Hivite(14), Hivites(11).

2341. חֲוִילָה Chavilah (296c); of unc. der.; a son of Cush, also a son of Joktan, also territories of unc. location:— Havilah(7).

2342a. חוּל chul or

חִיל chil (296d); a prim. root; *to whirl, dance, writhe:*— anguish(6), becomes weak waiting(1), birth to you in pain(1), born(1), brings forth(1), brought forth(4), burst(1), calve(1), calving(1), danced(1), fall(1), gave you birth(1), gave birth(2), giving birth(1), labor(1), quaked(1), shakes(2), swirl down(1), take part(1), travailed(4), tremble(5), trembled(1), turned(1), wait(1), wait patiently(1), waited(2), whirl(1), whirling(1), wounded(2), wounds(1), writhe(2), writhe in anguish(1), writhe in pain(1), writhed(2), writhes(2), writhes in pain(1).

2342b. חוּל chul or

חִיל chil (298c); a prim. root; *to be firm, strong:*— endure(1), prosper(1).

2343. חוּל Chul (299a); from 2342b; a son of Aram:— Hul(2).

2344. חוֹל chol (297c); from 2342a; *sand:*— sand(23).

2345. חוּם chum (299b); from an unused word; *darkened, dark brown* or *black:*— black(3), black ones(1).

2346. חוֹמָה chomah (327b); from the same as 2524; *a wall:*— two walls(1), Wall(2), wall(93), walled(2), walls(36).

2347. חוּס chus (299b); from the same as 2345; *to pity, look upon with compassion:*— concern*(1), had compassion(1), have compassion(3), have pity(1), have...pity(4), looked with pity(1), pity(6), show pity(2), show...pity(1), sorry(1), spare(2), spared(1).

2348. חוֹף choph (342b); from 2653; *shore, coast:*— coast(1), haven(1), seacoast*(3), seashore*(2).

2349. חוּפָם Chupham (299c); of unc. der.; a Benjamite:— Hupham(1).

2350. חוּפָמִי Chuphami (299c); from 2349; desc. of Hupham:— Huphamites(1).

2351. חוּץ chuts (299c); of unc. der.; *the outside, a street:*— abroad(2), abroad*(1), exterior(1), fields(3), large(1), open(1), outdoors(1), outer(3), outside(35), outside to the outer(1), outside*(52), outward(1), street(13), streets(37), without*(1).

חֵוק chevq (300c); see 2436.

2352a. חוּקֹק **Chuqoq** (301a); from the same as 2436; a city in Asher:— Hukok(1).

חוּקֹק **Chuqoq** (350c); see 2520.

2352b. חוּר **chur** (359d); from the same as 2356; *a hole:*— caves(1), hole(1).

2353. חוּר **chur** (301a); from 2357; *white stuff:*— white(2).

2354. חוּר **Chur** (301b); from 2357; four Isr., also a Midianite:— Hur(15).

2355. חוֹר **chor** (301a); see 2360a.

2356. חוֹר **chor** (359d); from an unused word; *a hole:*— hole(2), holes(2), lairs(1), opening(1), sockets(1).

2357. חָוַר **chavar** (301a); a prim. root; *to be* or *grow white* or *pale:*— turn pale(1).

2358. חִוָּר **chivvar** (1092c); (Ara.) corr. to 2357; *white:*— white(1).

2359. חוּרִי **Churi** (301b); from 2357; a Gadite:— Huri(1).

2360a. חֹרָי **choray** (301a); from 2357; *white stuff:*— white cloth(1).

2360b. חוּרַי **Churay** (301b); from 2357; one of David's heroes:— Hurai(1).

2361. חוּרָם **Churam** (27c); short. from 297; a Benjamite, also two Arameans (Syrians):— Huram(10), Huram-abi*(2).

2362. חַוְרָן **Chavran** (301c); of unc. der.; a district S.E. of Mount Hermon:— Hauran(2).

2363a. חוּשׁ **chush** (301c); a prim. root; *to hasten, make haste:*— agitation(1), disturbed(1), hasten(8), hastened(2), hastening(1), hurried(1), make haste(2), quick(1), ready(1), speedy(1), swooping(1).

2363b. חוּשׁ **chush** (301d); a prim. root; *to feel, enjoy:*— have enjoyment(1).

2364. חוּשָׁה **Chushah** (302a); from 2363b; perh. a place in Judah:— Hushah(1).

2365. חוּשַׁי **Chushay** (302a); from 2363b; two Isr.:— Hushai(14).

2366a. חוּשִׁים **Chushim** or

חֻשִׁים **Chushim** (302a); from 2363b; an Isr. woman:— Hushim(2).

2366b. חוּשִׁים **Chushim** or

חֻשִׁים **Chushim** (302a); from 2363b; a Danite:— Hushim(2).

2367. חוּשָׁם **Chusham** or

חֻשָׁם **Chusham** (302a); from 2363b; a king of Edom:— Husham(4).

2368. חוֹתָם **chotham** or

חֹתָם **chotham** (368a); from 2856; *a seal, signet ring:*— seal(8), signet(7).

2369. חוֹתָם **Chotham** (368b); from 2856; two Isr.:— Hotham(2).

2370. חֲזָה **chazah** (1092c); (Ara.) corr. to 2372; *see, behold:*— looking(13), saw(10), see(2), seen(4), usually(1).

2371. חֲזָאֵל **Chazael** or

חֲזָהאֵל **Chazahel** (303c); from 2372 and 410; "God sees," a king of Aram (Syria):— Hazael(23).

2372. חָזָה **chazah** (302b); a prim. root; *see, behold:*— behold(7), envisioned in visions(1), gaze(2), gloat(1), look(3), looked(1), prophesy(3), saw(7), see(12), seeing(1), seen(7), sees(4), select(1).

2373. חָזֶה **chazeh** (303d); from an unused word; *breast* (of animals):— breast(11), breasts(2).

2374. חֹזֶה **chozeh** (302d); act. part. of 2372; *a seer:*— pact(1), prophets(1), seer(12), seers(3).

2375. חֲזוֹ **Chazo** (303d); from the same as 2373; a son of Nahor:— Hazo(1).

2376. חֵזוּ **chezu** (1092c); (Ara.) from 2370; *vision, appearance:*— appearance(1), vision(2), visions(9).

2377. חָזוֹן **chazon** (302d); from 2372; *vision:*— vision(31), visions(4).

2378. חָזוֹת **chazoth** (303a); from 2372; *vision:*— visions(1).

2379. חֲזוֹת **chazoth** (1092d); (Ara.) from 2370; *sight, visibility:*— visible(2).

2380. חָזוּת **chazuth** (303b); from 2372; *vision, conspicuousness:*— conspicuous(2), pact(1), vision(2).

2381. חֲזִיאֵל **Chaziel** (303c); from 2372 and 410; "vision of God," a Levite:— Haziel(1).

2382. חֲזָיָה **Chazayah** (303c); from 2372 and 3050; "Yah has seen," a desc. of Judah:— Hazaiah(1).

2383. חֶזְיוֹן **Chezyon** (303c); from 2372; "vision," an Aramean (Syrian):— Hezion(1).

2384. חִזָּיוֹן **chizzayon** (303b); from 2372; *vision:*— vision(6), visions(3).

2385. חֲזִיז **chaziz** (304a); from an unused word; *a thunderbolt, lightning flash:*— storm clouds(1), thunderbolt*(2).

2386. חֲזִיר **chazir** (306b); from an unused word; *swine, boar:*— boar(1), pig(2), swine's(4).

2387. חֵזִיר **Chezir** (306c); from the same as 2386; two Isr.:— Hezir(2).

2388. חָזַק **chazaq** (304a); a prim. root; *to be* or *grow firm* or *strong, strengthen:*— adopted(2), applied(1), became(1), became mighty(1), became powerful(1), became strong(2), became...strong(1), been arrogant(1), captured(1), carried out repairs(12), caught(1), caught fast(1), caught hold(1), collected his strength(1), courageous(3), detained(1), devote(1), display great strength(1), display strength(1), encourage(4), encourage*(1), encouraged(2), encouraged*(3), encouragement(1), encourages(1), established himself securely(1), fasten(1), fastens(1), fierce(1), firm(2), firmly(2), firmly in his grasp(1), forces(1), fortified(1), gain ascendancy(1), gave him strong support(1), grasp(1), gripped(3), grow strong(1), harden(4), hardened(9), held(2), held them fast(1), help*(1), helped(1), hold(4), hold his own(1), hold fast(5), holding(3), holds fast(3), joining(1), laid hold(1), louder(1), made(1), made himself secure(1), made their harder(1), made repairs(12), made stronger(1), maintain(1), make(1), make an effort(1), making himself strong(1), overcome(1), persuaded(1), post a strong(1), prevailed(4), prevailed over(1), put(1), received strength(1), recovered(1), rely(1), repair(12), repaired(14), repairers(1), repairing(1), resist(1), resolutely(2), retain(1), retained(1), seize(4), seized(6), seizes(2), severe(5), show ourselves courageous(2), snaps shut(1), stands firmly(1), strengthen(12), strengthened(19), strengthening(1), strong(31), strong support(1), stronger(6), strongly support(1), support*(1), supported(1), sure(1), sustain(1), take(1), take courage(6), take courage and be courageous(1), take hold(7), taken(2), taken hold(1), takes(1), takes hold(2), tie your securely(1), took(2), took courage(2), took hold(5), upholds(1), urged*(1).

2389. חָזָק **chazaq** (305c); from 2388; *strong, stout, mighty:*— compulsion*(3), fiercest(1), hard(2), harder(1), loud(1), might(1), mighty(20), obstinate*(1), powerful(1), severe(3), stalwart(1), strong(19), stubborn*(1), who is strong(1), who was stronger(1).

2390. חָזֵק **chazeq** (305d); part. from 2388, q.v.

2391. חֵזֶק **chezeq** (305d); from 2388; *strength:*— strength(1).

2392. חֹזֶק **chozeq** (305d); from 2388; *strength:*— power(1), powerful(3), strength(1).

2393. חֶזְקָה **chezqah** (305d); fem. of 2391; *strength, force:*— mighty(1), strong(3).

2394. חָזְקָה **chozqah** (306a); fem. of 2392; *strength, force, violence:*— earnestly(1), force(2), severely(1), vigorously(1).

2395. חִזְקִי **Chizqi** (306a); from 2388; a Benjamite:— Hizki(1).

2396. חִזְקִיָּה **Chizqiyyah** or

חִזְקִיָּהוּ **Chizqiyyahu** or

יְחִזְקִיָּה **Yechizqiyyah** or

יְחִזְקִיָּהוּ **Yechizqiyyahu** (306a); from 2388 and 3050; "Yah has strengthened," a king of Judah, also several other Isr.:— Hezekiah(127), Hizkiah(1).

2397. חָח **chach** (296b); from the same as 2336; *hook, ring, fetter:*— brooches(1), hook(2), hooks(4).

2398. חָטָא **chata** (306c); a prim. root; *to miss, go wrong, sin:*— bear the blame(2), bewildered(1), bore the loss(1), bring sin(1), cleanse(5), cleansed(1), cleansing(1), commit(2), commits sin(1), committed(21), done wrong(1), errs(1), fault(1), fear...loss(1), forfeits(1), indicted(1), miss(1), offended(1), offered it for sin(1), offers it for sin(1), purged(1), purified(2), purified themselves from sin(1), purify(6), purify him from uncleanness(1), purify himself from uncleanness(2), reach(1), sin(55), sin have i committed(1), sinful(1), sinned(87), sinner(7), sinning(4), sins(23).

2399. חֵטְא **chet** (307d); from 2398; *a sin:*— greatly(1), offenses(2), penalty(1), sin(22), sins(7).

2400. חַטָּא **chatta** (308b); from 2398; *sinful, sinners:*— men*(1), offenders(1), sinful(2), sinners(15), who have sinned(1).

2401. חֲטָאָה **chataah** (308b); from 2398; *sin, sin offering:*— sin(7), sin offering(1).

2402. חַטָּאָה **chattaah** (not included); the same as 2409, q.v.

2403a. חַטָּאָה **chattaah** (308b); from 2398; *sinful thing, sin:*— sin(2).

2403b. חַטָּאת **chattath** (308b); from 2398; *sin, sin offering:*— offering for the sin(1), punishment(3), purification from sin(2), sin(93), sin offering(117), sin offerings(2), sinful(1), sinned(1), sinner(1), sins(70).

2404. חָטַב **chatab** (310a); a prim. root; *to cut* or *gather wood:*— chops your wood(1), cut(1), fashioned(1), gather firewood(1), hewers of wood(3), woodcutters(1), woodsmen(1).

2405. חֲטֻבוֹת **chatuboth** (310b); from an unused word; *dark-hued stuffs:*— colored(1).

2406. חִטָּה **chittah** (334d); from 2590; *wheat:*— wheat(30).

2407. חַטּוּשׁ **Chattush** (310d); of unc. der.; three Isr.:— Hattush(5).

2408. חֲטָי **chatay** (1092d); (Ara.) from a root corr. to 2398; *a sin:*— sins(1).

2409. חַטָּיָא **chattaya** (1092d); (Ara.) corr. to 2401; *sin offering:*— sin offering(1).

2410. חֲטִיטָא Chatita (310b); from an unused word; a Levite:— Hatita(2).

2411. חַטִּיל Chattil (310b); from an unused word; an Isr.:— Hattil(2).

2412. חֲטִיפָא Chatipha (310c); from 2414; one of the Nethinim:— Hatipha(2).

2413. חָטַם chatam (310c); a prim. root; *to hold in, restrain:*— restrain(1).

2414. חָטַף chataph (310c); a prim. root; *to catch, seize:*— catch(2), catches(1).

2415. חֹטֶר choter (310d); from an unused word; *branch* or *twig, a rod:*— rod(1), shoot(1).

2416a. חַי chay (311d); from 2421a; *alive, living:*— alive(38), flowing(2), fresh(1), green(1), life(7), live(44), lives(54), living(63), living one(4), living thing(6), man living(1), next(2), next year(2), raw(6), renewed(1), running(6), next year(1), vigorous(1), who lives(1).

2416b. חַי chay (312c); another reading for 2416a, q.v.

2417. חַי chay (1092d); (Ara.) corr. to 2416a; *living:*— life(2), living(3), living man(1), who lives(1).

2418. חֲיָא chaya (1092d); (Ara.) corr. to 2421a; *to live:*— live(5), spared alive(1).

2419. חִיאֵל Chiel (27d, 313c); prob. from 251 and 410; prob. "brother of God," a rebuilder of Jericho:— Hiel(1).

2420. חִידָה chidah (295b); from an unused word; *a riddle, an enigmatic, perplexing saying* or *question:*— dark sayings(2), difficult questions(2), insinuations(1), intrigue(1), riddle(10), riddles(1).

2421a. חָיָה chayah (310d); a prim. root; *to live:*— alive(3), alive should not live(1), came to life(1), come to life(3), come alive(1), give life(2), gives me life(1), healed(1), keep(1), keep him alive(1), keep his alive(1), keep the alive(1), keep them alive(4), keep you alive(1), keep alive(3), keep...alive(2), kept me alive(1), kept alive(1), leave(2), leave alive(1), live(120), lived(42), lives(5), make alive(1), makes alive(1), nourished(1), preserve(3), preserve his life(1), preserve...alive(1), preserves the lives(1), raise(1), recover(4), recovered(1), recovery(1), remained alive(1), repaired(1), restored to life(4), revive(20), revived(6), save(2), save his life(1), saved(1), saved our lives(1), saving(1), spare(3), spared(2), stay alive(1), surely live(9), surely recover(2), survival(1), survive(2), survived(1).

2421b. חַיָּה chayyah (312c); from 2421a; *living thing, animal:*— animals(2), appetite(1), beast(27), beasts(43), creature(2), creatures(3), life(9), life*(1), live*(1), living beings(15), living thing(1), wild animals(1), wild beast(1), wild beasts(1).

2422a. חַיָּה chayyah (312d); from 2421a; *community:*— troop(2).

2422b. חָיֶה chayeh (313a); from 2421a; *having the vigor of life, lively:*— vigorous(1).

2423. חֵיוָא cheva or

חֵיוָה chevah (1092d); (Ara.) corr. to 2421b; *beast:*— beast(6), beast's(1), beasts(13).

2424. חַיּוּת chayyuth (313c); from 2421a; *living:*— living(1).

2425a. חַיַּי chayay (not included); the same as 2416a, q.v.

2425b. חַיִּים chayyim (313a); from 2421a; *life:*— alive(1), life(124), life-giving(1), lifetime(4), live(5), live*(1), lived(2), lived*(1), lives(4), living(1), sustenance(1).

2426. חֵיל chel or

חֵל chel (298a); from 2342a; *rampart, fortress:*— district(1), host(1), rampart(3), ramparts(2), walls(1).

2427. חִיל chil (297d); from 2342a; *a writhing, anguish:*— agony(2), anguish(2), pain(2).

2428. חַיִל chayil (298c); from 2342b; *strength, efficiency, wealth, army:*— able(5), armies(3), army(82), army*(1), capability(1), capable(3), elite army(1), excellence(1), excellent(2), forces(12), full(1), goods(1), great(1), might(1), mighty(1), nobly(1), power(2), retinue(2), riches(9), strength(10), strong(2), substance(1), troops(2), valiant(41), valiant*(4), valiantly(6), valor(18), very powerful(1), warriors(1), wealth(25), wealthy(1), worthy(1).

2429. חַיִל chayil (1093a); (Ara.) corr. to 2428; *power, strength, army:*— aloud(1), arms(1), army(1), host(1), loudly(1), valiant(1).

2430a. חֵילָה chelah (298a); the same as 2426, q.v.

2430b. חִילָה chilah (297d); from 2342a; *anguish:*— pain(1).

2431. חֵילָם Chelam (298a); from 2342a; a place E. of the Jordan:— Helam(2).

2432. חִילֵן Chilen (298b); from 2342a; a place in Judah:— Hilen(1).

2433. חִין chin (336d); from 2603a; perh. *beauty:*— orderly(1).

2434. חַיִץ chayits (300c); from an unused word; *a party wall:*— wall(1).

2435. חִיצוֹן chitson (300b); from the same as 2351; *outer, external:*— outer(22), outside(3).

2436. חֵיק cheq or

חֵק cheq or

חוֹק choq (300d); from an unused word; *bosom:*— arms(1), base(3), bosom(26), bottom(1), care(1), cherish(1), cherishes(2), lap(2), within(1).

2437. חִירָה Chirah (301b); from 2357; a friend of Judah:— Hirah(2).

2438. חִירָם Chiram (27c); short. from 297; a Benjamite, also two Arameans (Syrians):— Hiram(22), Hiram's(1).

2439. חִישׁ chish (301c); the same as 2363a, q.v.

2440. חִישׁ chish (301d); from 2363a; *quickly:*— soon(1).

2441. חֵךְ chek (335a); of unc. der.; *palate, roof of the mouth, gums:*— lips(1), mouth(6), palate(4), roof of its mouth(1), roof of my mouth(1), roof of your mouth(1), speech(1), taste(3).

2442. חָכָה chakah (314a); a prim. root; *to wait, await:*— long(2), longs(1), wait(7), waited(1), waiting(1), waits(3).

2443. חַכָּה chakkah (335c); from the same as 2441; *a hook, fishhook:*— fishhook(1), hook(1), line(1).

2444. חֲכִילָה Chakilah (314b); from an unused word; "dark," a hill in S. Judah:— Hachilah(3).

2445. חַכִּים chakkim (1093a); (Ara.) from a root corr. to 2449; *a wise man:*— wise men(14).

2446. חֲכַלְיָה Chakalyah (314b); perh. from the same as 2444 and from 3050; perh. "wait for Yah," father of Nehemiah:— Hacaliah(2).

2447. חַכְלִילִי chaklili (314b); from the same as 2444; *dull:*— dull(1).

2448. חַכְלִלוּת chakliluth (314b); from the same as 2444; *dullness:*— redness(1).

2449. חָכַם chakam (314b); a prim. root; *to be wise:*— acting wisely(1), becomes(1), been...wise(1), deal wisely(1), exceedingly(1), make me wiser(1), makes us wiser(1), making wise(1), skillful(1), teach his wisdom(1), wise(16), wiser(2).

2450. חָכָם chakam (314c); from 2449; *wise:*— expert(1), men who are skillful(1), sage(1), shrewd(2), skilled(2), skilled men(3), skilled men and with those(1), skilled*(1), skillful(1), skillful man*(1), skillful men(1), skillful men*(1), skillful persons*(1), skillful*(3), unwise*(1), wailing women(1), who(1), who are wise(1), wise(64), wise man(21), wise man's(2), wise men(22), wise son(1), wisehearted(1), wiser(2), wisest(1).

2451. חָכְמָה chokmah (315b); from 2449; *wisdom:*— skill(5), skill*(1), wisdom(143), wisely(3), wits'(1).

2452. חָכְמָה chokmah (1093a); (Ara.) corr. to 2451; *wisdom:*— wisdom(8).

2453. חַכְמוֹנִי Chakmoni (315d); from 2449; "wise," two Isr.:— Hachmoni(1), Hachmonite(1).

2454. חָכְמוֹת chokmoth (315b); the same as 2451, q.v.

2455. חֹל chol (320d); from 2490c; *profaneness, commonness:*— common use(1), ordinary(2), profane(8).

2456. חָלָא chala (316a); a prim. root; *to be sick* or *diseased:*— became diseased(1).

2457. חֶלְאָה chelah (316a); from an unused word; *rust:*— rust(5).

2458. חֶלְאָה Chelah (316a); from the same as 2457; an Isr. woman:— Helah(2).

2459. חֵלֶב cheleb (316d); from an unused word; *fat:*— best(5), fat(74), fat portions(2), fatness(1), finest(2), finest*(1), marrow(1), portions of fat(5), unfeeling(1).

2460. חֵלֶב Cheleb (317a); from the same as 2459; one of David's heroes:— Heleb(1).

2461. חָלָב chalab (316b); of unc. der.; *milk:*— cheese(1), milk(41), suckling(1).

2462. חֶלְבָּה Chelbah (317a); fem. of 2459; a city in Asher:— Helbah(1).

2463. חֶלְבּוֹן Chelbon (317a); from the same as 2459; a place in Aram (Syria):— Helbon(1).

2464. חֶלְבְּנָה chelbenah (317b); from the same as 2459; *gum* (a type used in incense):— galbanum(1).

2465. חֶלֶד cheled (317b); from an unused word; *duration, world:*— life(1), lifetime(1), span of life(1), world(3).

2466. חֵלֶד Cheled (317c); from the same as 2467; one of David's heroes:— Heled(1).

2467. חֹלֶד choled (317c); from an unused word; *weasel:*— mole(1).

2468. חֻלְדָּה Chuldah (317c); fem. of 2467; an Isr. prophetess:— Huldah(2).

2469. חֶלְדַּי Chelday (317c); from the same as 2467; two Isr.:— Heldai(2).

2470a. חָלָה chalah (317c); a prim. root; *to be weak* or *sick:*— afflicted(1), am severely wounded(2), became ill(1), became sick(4), became...ill(3), become ill(1), become weak(3), been sick(2), diseased(2), faint(1), fell sick(1), grief(1), grieved(1), grievous(2), incurable(2), infected(1), lovesick*(2), made himself ill(1), made weak(1), make you sick(1), makes the sick(1), pretend to be ill(1), pretended to be ill(1), putting him to grief(1), serious(1), sick(13), sickliness(1), sickly(1), sorry(1), strained(1), weak(3), weaken(1), wounded(1).

2470b. חָלָה chalah (318c); from 2470a; *to mollify, appease, entreat the favor of:*— asked(1), entreat(6), entreated(4), favor*(3), seek(2), seek the favor(1), sought(2).

2471. חַלָּה challah (319c); from 2490a; *a cake* (a type used in offerings):— cake(7), cakes(7).

2472. חֲלוֹם chalom (321c); from 2492b; *a dream:*— dream(41), dreamer*(1), dreamers(1), dreams(22).

2473. חֹלוֹן Cholon (298b); prob. from 2426; a place in Moab, also a city in Judah:— Holon(3).

2474. חַלּוֹן challon (319d); from 2490a; *a window:*— window(14), windows(17).

2475. חֲלוֹף chaloph (322b); from 2498; *a passing away, vanishing:*— unfortunate*(1).

2476. חֲלוּשָׁה chalushah (325d); fem. pass. part. of 2522; *weakness, prostration:*— defeat(1).

2477. חֲלַח Chalach (318d); prob. of for. or.; an area under Assyr. control:— Halah(3).

2478. חַלְחוּל Chalchul (319a); of unc. der.; a city in Judah:— Halhul(1).

2479. חַלְחָלָה chalchalah (298b); from 2342a; *anguish:*— anguish(4).

2480. חָלַט chalat (319a); a prim. root; *to catch:*— catching(1).

2481. חֲלִי chali (318d); from an unused word; *an ornament:*— jewels(1), ornament(1).

2482. חֲלִי Chali (318d); from the same as 2481; a place in Asher:— Hali(1).

2483. חֳלִי choli (318b); from 2470a; *sickness:*— affliction(1), disease(2), grief(1), griefs(1), illness(3), sick(1), sickness(14), sicknesses(1).

2484. חֶלְיָה chelyah (318d); from the same as 2481; *jewelry:*— jewelry(1).

2485. חָלִיל chalil (319d); from 2490a; *flute, pipe:*— flute(3), flutes(3).

2486. חָלִילָה chalilah (321a); from 2490c; *far be it!:*— far(19), forbid(2).

2487. חֲלִיפָה chaliphah (322b); from 2498; *a change:*— change(2), changes(8), hardship(1), relays(1).

2488. חֲלִיצָה chalitsah (322d); from 2502a; *what is stripped off* (a person):— spoil(2).

2489. חֵלְכָה chelekah (319a); from an unused word; *hapless, unfortunate:*— unfortunate(3).

2490a. חָלַל chalal (319b); a prim. root; *to bore, pierce:*— kill(1), pierced(2), pierced through(1), slain(1), wound(1), wounded(1).

2490b. חָלַל chalal (320a); denom. vb. from 2485; *to play the pipe, to pipe:*— play the flutes(1), playing(1).

2490c. חָלַל chalal (320a); a prim. root; *to pollute, defile, profane:*— became*(1), began(30), begin(10), begin to use its fruit(2), beginning(3), begun(7), begun to use its fruit(2), cast you as profane(1), defile(2), defiled(3), desecrate(1), enjoy(1), first(1), pollute(1), polluted(1), profane(21), profaned(29), profanes(3), profaning(5), start(1), started(2), use its fruit(1), violate(3), violated(1).

2491a. חָלָל chalal (319c); from 2490a; *pierced:*— kill*(1), killed(3), mortally(1), one slain(1), one who(1), one who has been slain(1), slain(71), slain man(2), slain one(1), victims(1), who are slain(1), wounded(6), wounded man(2).

2491b. חָלָל chalal (321a); from 2490c; *profaned:*— profaned(2).

2492a. חָלַם chalam (321b); a prim. root; *to be healthy* or *strong:*— become strong(1), restore me to health(1).

2492b. חָלַם chalam (321b); a prim. root; *to dream:*— dream(3), dreamed(2), dreamer(3), dreams(2), had(13), had a dream(4).

2493. חֵלֶם chelem (1093a); (Ara.) corr. to 2472; *a dream:*— dream(21), dreams(1).

2494. חֵלֶם Chelem (321b); from 2492a; "strength," an Isr.:— Helem(1).

2495. חַלָּמוּת challamuth (321d); from 2492b; (a plant), prob. *a purslane:*— white of an egg(1).

2496. חַלָּמִישׁ challamish (321d); of unc. der.; *flint:*— flint(4), flinty(1).

2497. חֵלֹן Chelon (298b); from 2342a; a man of Zebulon:— Helon(5).

2498. חָלַף chalaph (322a); a prim. root; *to pass on* or *away, pass through:*— change(2), changed(5), gain new(2), go(1), move past(1), over(1), passed(1), passes(1), pierce(1), pierced(1), renewed(1), replace(2), slip(1), sprout(1), sprouts anew(2), sweep(2), sweep through(1), vanish(1), violated(1).

2499. חֲלַף chalaph (1093a); (Ara.) corr. to 2498; *to pass* (over):— pass(4).

2500. חֵלֶף cheleph (322b); from 2498; *an exchange:*— return(2).

2501. חֶלֶף Cheleph (322b); from 2498; a place in Naphtali:— Heleph(1).

2502a. חָלַץ chalats (322c); a prim. root; *to draw off* or *out, withdraw:*— delivered(4), delivers(1), offer(1), plundered(1), pull(1), removed(1), rescue(5), rescued(4), rescues(1), take(1), tear(1), torn(1), withdrawn(1).

2502b. חָלַץ chalats (323a); a prim. root; *to equip* (for war):— arm(2), armed(13), army(1), equipped(4), give strength(1).

2503. חֶלֶץ Chelets (323b); from 2502b; two Isr.:— Helez(5).

2504. חָלָץ chalats (323b); from 2502b; *loins:*— born*(2), loins(5), waist(3).

2505a. חָלַק chalaq (323c); a prim. root; *to divide, share:*— allot him a portion(1), allotted(3), apportion(2), apportions(1), assigned(1), disperse(1), distribute(1), distributed(2), divide(12), divided(18), divides(1), dividing(2), given her a share(1), parcel(1), parceled(1), partner(1), portion(2), scattered(1), share(2), take possession(1), take possession of some property(1), took a portion(1).

2505b. חָלַק chalaq (325a); a prim. root; *to be smooth, slippery:*— faithless(1), flatter(1), flatters(5), smoother(1), smooths(1).

2506. חֵלֶק cheleq (324a); from 2505a; *portion, tract, territory:*— associate(1), catch(1), divisions(2), equal portions(1), farm land(1), inheritance(1), land(1), legacy(1), lot(1), portion(36), portions(4), property(2), reward(4), share(9), territory(1).

2507a. חֵלֶק Cheleq (324c); from 2505a; a Gileadite:— Helek(2).

2507b. חֵלֶק cheleq (325b); from 2505b; *smoothness, seductiveness:*— flattering(1).

2508. חֲלָק chalaq (1093b); (Ara.) from a root corr. to 2505a; *portion, possession:*— possession(1), share(2).

2509. חָלָק chalaq (325b); from 2505b; *smooth:*— flattering(2), smooth(2), smoother(1).

2510. חָלָק Chalaq (325b); from 2505b; "smooth," a mountain S. of the Dead Sea:— Halak(2).

2511. חַלָּק challaq (325b); the same as 2509, q.v.

2512. חַלֻּק challuq (325c); from 2505b; *smooth:*— smooth(1).

2513a. חֶלְקָה chelqah (324c); from 2505a; *a portion* (of ground):— field(5), part(2), piece(2), piece of land(3), plot(4), portion(3), property(4).

2513b. חֶלְקָה chelqah (325c); from 2505b; *smooth part, smoothness, flattery:*— flattering(2), pleasant words(1), slippery places(1), smooth(1), smooth part(1).

2514. חֲלַקָּה chalaqqah (325c); from 2505b; *smoothness, flattery:*— smooth(1).

2515. חֲלֻקָּה chaluqqah (324c); from 2505a; *part, portion:*— division(1).

2516. חֶלְקִי Chelqi (324c); from 2505a; desc. of Helek:— Helekites(1).

2517. חֶלְקַי Chelqay (324d); from 2505a; an Isr. priest:— Helkai(1).

2518. חִלְקִיָּהוּ Chilqiyyahu or

חִלְקִיָּה Chilqiyyah (324d); from 2506 and 3050; "my portion is Yah," the name of several Isr.:— Hilkiah(34).

2519. חֲלַקְלַקּוֹת chalaqlaqqoth (325c); by redupl. from 2505b; *smoothness:*— hypocrisy(1), intrigue(1), slippery(1), slippery paths(1).

2520. חֶלְקַת Chelqath (324d); from 2505a; "portion, possession," a city in Asher:— Helkath(2).

2521. חֶלְקַת הַצֻּרִים Chelqath Hatstsurim (324d); from 2520 and the pl. of 6697; a place near the pool of Gibeon:— Helkath-hazzurim(1).

2522. חָלַשׁ chalash (325d); a prim. root; *to be weak* or *prostrate:*— lies prostrate(1), overwhelmed(1), weakened(1).

2523. חַלָּשׁ challash (325d); from 2522; *weak:*— weak(1).

2524. חָם cham (327a); from an unused word; *husband's father:*— father-in-law(4).

2525. חָם cham (328d); from 2552; *hot:*— hot(1), warm(1).

2526. חָם Cham (325d); of unc. der.; a son of Noah, also his desc., also a name for Egyptians:— Ham(15), Hamites*(1).

2527. חֹם chom (328d); from 2552; *heat:*— heat(8), hot(1).

2528. חֱמָא chema (1095c); (Ara.) corr. to 2534; *a rage:*— anger(1), wrath(1).

2529. חֶמְאָה chemah (326a); from an unused word; *curd:*— butter(2), curds(8).

2530. חָמַד chamad (326b); a prim. root; *to desire, take pleasure in:*— attracted(1), covet(6), coveted(1), delight(1), desirable(2), desire(1), desired(2), desires(2), pleasing(1), precious(2), precious things(1), took great delight(1).

2531. חֶמֶד chemed (326c); from 2530; *desire, delight:*— desirable(3), pleasant(2).

2532. חֶמְדָּה chemdah (326c); fem. of 2531; *desire, delight:*— beautiful(1), choice(1), desirable(2), desire(1), pleasant(5), precious(2), regret(1), valuable(2), wealth(1).

2533. חֶמְדָּן Chemdan (326d); from 2530; an Edomite:— Hemdan(1).

2534. חֵמָה chemah (404b); from 3179; *heat, rage:*— anger(7), angry(1), burning anger(1), enrages(1), fury(9), heat(2), hot displeasure(1), hot-tempered(3), poison(2), rage(3), venom(5), wrath(86), wrath and raging(1), wrathful(2), wrathful*(1).

חֶמְאָה chemah (326a); see 2529.

2535. חַמָּה chammah (328d); from 2525; *heat, sun:*— heat(1), sun(4).

2536a. חַמּוּאֵל Chammuel (329b); from 2535 and 410; "anger of God," a Simeonite:— Hammuel(1).

2536b. חֲמוּדָה chamudah (326d); from 2530; *desirableness, preciousness:*— best(1), high esteem(2), highly esteemed(1), precious(1), precious things(1), tasty(1), treasures(1), valuable(1).

2537. חֲמוּטַל Chamutal (327d); perh. from 2524 and 2919; perh. "my husband's father is the dew," mother of two kings of Judah:— Hamutal(3).

2538. חָמוּל Chamul (328b); from 2550; "spared," grandson of Judah:— Hamul(3).

2539. חָמוּלִי Chamuli (328b); from 2538; desc. of Hamul:— Hamulites(1).

2540. חַמּוֹן Chammon (329a); from 2552; "hot (spring)," two cities, one in Asher and one in Naphtali:— Hammon(2).

2541. חָמוֹץ chamots (330b); from 2556c; *the ruthless* (ones):— ruthless(1).

2542. חַמּוּק chammuq (330b); from 2559; *curving, curve:*— curves(1).

2543. חֲמוֹר chamor (331a); from 2560c; *a male ass:*— donkey(53), donkey's(2), donkeys(41).

2544. חֲמוֹר Chamor (331c); from 2560c; father of Shechem:— Hamor(12), Hamor's(1).

2545. חָמוֹת chamoth (327b); fem. of 2524; *husband's mother:*— mother-in-law(11).

2546. חֹמֶט chomet (328a); from an unused word; (a kind of) *lizard:*— sand reptile(1).

2547. חֻמְטָה Chumtah (328a); fem. of 2546; a city in Judah:— Humtah(1).

2548. חָמִיץ chamits (330a); from 2556a; *seasoned* (with salt):— salted(1).

2549. חֲמִישִׁי chamishi (332c); ord. from 2568; *fifth:*— fifth(36), fifth part(1), five-sided(1), one-fifth(7).

2550. חָמַל chamal (328a); a prim. root; *to spare:*— concern(1), desires(1), had compassion(2), had pity(1), had...compassion(2), have compassion(1), have pity(4), have...pity(1), mercy(1), ruthlessly*(1), show pity(1), spare(11), spared(5), spares(2), sparing(5), unsparing*(1), unwilling(1).

2551. חֶמְלָה chemlah (328b); from 2550; *compassion, mercy:*— compassion(1), mercy(1).

2552. חָמַם chamam (328c); a prim. root; *to be* or *become warm:*— became warm(1), become heated(1), grew hot(1), heat(1), hot(6), inflame(1), keep warm(3), mated(2), warm(4), warmed(1), warms(3).

2553. חַמָּן chamman (329a); from 2552; *a sun pillar:*— incense altars(7), incense stands(1).

2554. חָמַס chamas (329b); a prim. root; *to treat violently* or *wrong:*— do violence(1), done violence(2), drop off(1), exposed(1), injures(1), violently treated(1), wrong(1).

2555. חָמָס chamas (329c); from 2554; *violence, wrong:*— malicious(3), violence(48), violent(6), wrong(3).

2556a. חָמֵץ chamets (329d); a prim. root; *to be sour* or *leavened:*— become leavened(1), embittered(1), leavened(2).

2556b. חָמַץ chamats (330a); a prim. root; *to be red:*— glowing colors(1).

2556c. חָמַץ chamats (330a); a prim. root; *to be ruthless:*— ruthless man(1).

2557. חָמֵץ chamets (329d); from 2556a; *that which is leavened:*— leaven(3), leavened(4), leavened bread(3), which is leavened(1).

2558. חֹמֶץ chomets (330a); from 2556a; *vinegar:*— vinegar(5).

2559. חָמַק chamaq (330b); a prim. root; *to turn away:*— go here(1), go here and there(1), turned away(1).

2560a. חָמַר chamar (330b); a prim. root; *to ferment, boil* or *foam up:*— foam(1), foams(1), greatly troubled(2).

2560b. חָמַר chamar (330d); denom. vb. from 2563a; *to cover* or *smear with asphalt:*— covered(1).

2560c. חָמַר chamar (331a); a prim. root; *to be red:*— flushed(1).

2561. חֶמֶר chemer (330c); from 2560a; *wine:*— wine(2).

2562. חֲמַר chamar (1093b); (Ara.) corr. to 2561; *wine:*— wine(6).

2563a. חֹמֶר chomer (330c); from 2560a; *cement, mortar, clay:*— clay(12), mire(1), mortar(4), mud(1).

2563b. חֹמֶר chomer (330d); from an unused word; *a heap:*— heaps(1), surge(1).

2563c. חֹמֶר chomer (330d); from the same as 2563b; *homer* (a dry measure):— homer(10), homers(1).

2564. חֵמָר chemar (330c); from 2560a; *bitumen, asphalt:*— tar(3).

2565. חֲמֹרָה chamorah or

חֲמוֹר chamor (331a); from the same as 2563b; *a heap:*— heaps(2).

2566. חַמְרָן Chamran (331c); from 2560c; a desc. of Esau:— Hamran(1).

2567. חָמַשׁ chamash (332b); denom. vb. from 2568; *to take the fifth part:*— exact a fifth(1).

2568. חָמֵשׁ chamesh or

חֲמִשָּׁה chamishshah (331d); of unc. der.; *five:*— 1,005*(1), 1,335*(1), 1,365*(1), 1,775*(2), 15*(1), 15,000*(1), 185,000*(2), 245*(3), 25,000*(16), 25,100*(1), 30,500*(2), 307,500*(1), 32,500*(1), 337,500*(2), 345*(2), 35,400*(2), 4,500*(8), 40,500*(3), 41,500*(2), 435*(2), 45*(1), 45,400*(1), 45,600*(1), 45,650*(2), 46,500*(2), 5,000*(7), 5,400*(1), 500*(3), 500,000*(1), 530*(1), 60,500*(1), 603,550*(2), 65*(1), 655*(1), 675*(1), 675,000*(1), 7,500*(1), 725*(1), 745*(1), 75,000*(1), 775*(1), 8,580*(1), 845*(1), 945*(1), 95*(2), fifteen*(15), fifteenth*(17), fifth(5), five(168), forty-five*(2), ninety-five*(2), sixty-five*(3), thirty-fifth*(1), thirty-five*(4), twenty-fifth*(3), twenty-five*(22).

2569. חֹמֶשׁ chomesh (332b); from the same as 2568; *fifth part:*— fifth(1).

2570. חֹמֶשׁ chomesh (332d); of unc. der.; *belly:*— belly(4).

2571. חֲמֻשִׁים chamushim (332d); from an unused word; *in battle array:*— army(1), battle array(2), martial array(1).

2572. חֲמִשִּׁים chamishshim (332b); multiple of 2568; *fifty:*— 1,052*(2), 1,254*(4), 150*(4), 151,450*(2), 153,600*(1), 156*(1), 157,600*(1), 16,750*(1), 2,056*(1), 2,750*(1), 250*(5), 250,000*(1), 45,650*(2), 450*(2), 454*(1), 50(4), 50,000*(2), 50,070*(1), 52*(2), 52,700*(1), 53,400*(3), 54,400*(1), 56*(1), 57,400*(2), 59,300*(2), 603,550*(3), 650*(1), 652*(2), 655*(1), 956*(1), fifties(6), fiftieth(3), fifty(87), fifty with their fifties(1), fifty-five(2), fifty-second(1), fifty-two(3).

2573. חֵמֶת chemeth (332d); from an unused word; *a water skin:*— skin(3).

2574. חֲמָת Chamath (333a); from the same as 2573; a place N. of Damascus:— Hamath(30).

2575a. חַמַּת Chammath (329a); from 2552; "hot (spring)," a city in Naphtali:— Hammath(1).

2575b. חַמַּת Chammath (329a); from 2552; perh. "hot (spring)," father of the house of Rechab:— Hammath(1).

2576. חַמֹּת דֹּאר Chammoth Dor (329b); from 2535 and 1756; a Levitical city in Naphtali:— Hammoth-dor(1).

2577. חֲמָתִי Chamathi (333b); from 2574; desc. of Canaan:— Hamathite(1), Hamathites(1).

2578. חֲמַת צוֹבָה Chamath Tsobah (333a); from 2574 and 6678; a place N. of Damascus:— Hamath-zobah(1).

2579. חֲמַת רַבָּה Chamath Rabbah (333a); from 2574 and 7227a, see 2574 and 7227a.

2580. חֵן chen (336b); from 2603a; *favor, grace:*— adornment(1), charm(1), charm*(1), charming*(1), favor(51), grace(8), graceful(2), gracious(3), pleases*(1).

2581. חֵן Chen (336d); from 2603a; "favor," a contemporary of Zerubbabel:— Hen(1).

2582. חֵנָדָד Chenadad (337b); prob. from 2580 and 1908; a Levite:— Henadad(4).

2583. חָנָה chanah (333b); a prim. root; *to decline, bend down, encamp:*— besieged*(2), camp(25), camped(96), camping(5), coming to an end(1), encamp(3), encamped(3), encamps(2), pitched(2), remained camped(3), Settling(1).

2584. חַנָּה Channah (336d); from 2603a; mother of Samuel:— Hannah(13).

2585. חֲנוֹךְ Chanok (335c); from the same as 2441; four Isr., sons of Cain, Jered, Midian and Reuben:— Enoch(10), Hanoch(6).

2586. חָנוּן Chanun (337a); from 2603a; "favored," two contemporaries of Nehemiah, also an Ammonite king:— Hanun(11).

2587. חַנּוּן channun (337a); from 2603a; *gracious:*— gracious(13).

2588. חָנוּת chanuth (333d); from 2583; *a cell, vault:*— vaulted cell(1).

2589. חַנּוֹת channoth (335d); infinitive construct of 2603a, q.v.

2590. חָנַט chanat (334c); a prim. root; *to spice, make spicy, embalm:*— embalm(1), embalmed(2), ripened(1).

2591a. חִנְטָה chintah (1093b); (Ara.) corr. to 2406; *wheat:*— wheat(2).

2591b. חֲנֻטִים chanutim (334d); from 2590; *an embalming:*— embalming(1).

2592. חַנִּיאֵל Channiel (337a); from 2603a and 410; "favor of God," a Manassite, also an Asherite:— Hanniel(2).

2593. חָנִיךְ chanik (335c); from the same as 2441; *trained, tried, experienced:*— trained men(1).

2594. חֲנִינָה chaninah (337a); from 2603a; *favor:*— favor(1).

2595. חֲנִית chanith (333d); from 2583; *a spear:*— spear(40), spears(7).

2596. חָנַךְ chanak (335b); denom. vb. from 2441; *to train up, dedicate:*— dedicate(1), dedicated(3), train(1).

2597. חֲנֻכָּה chanukkah (1093b); (Ara.) corr. to 2598; *dedication:*— dedication(4).

2598. חֲנֻכָּה chanukkah (335c); from the same as 2441; *dedication, consecration:*— dedication(7).

2599. חֲנֹכִי Chanoki (335c); from 2585; desc. of Enoch:— Hanochites(1).

2600. חִנָּם chinnam (336c); from 2603a; *out of favor:*— free(1), nothing(4), useless(1), uselessly(1), vain(2), which cost(1), which cost me nothing(1), which costs(1), which costs me nothing(1), without a cause(2), without cause(17), without pay(1), without payment(1).

2601. חֲנַמְאֵל Chanamel (335d); perh. from 2606; Jeremiah's cousin:— Hanamel(4).

2602. חֲנָמַל chanamel (335d); of unc. der.; perh. *frost:*— frost(1).

2603a. חָנַן chanan (335d); a prim. root; *to show favor, be gracious:*— begged(1), dealt graciously(1), favor(1), feel pity(1), finds...favor(1), give them to us voluntarily(1), gracious(45), graciously(1), graciously given(1), graciously grant(1), groan(1), implore(1), implore his favor(1), implore the compassion(1), implore the mercy(1), implored(1), made(1), made supplication(2), make supplication(5), pity(2), pleaded(2), show favor(1), show...favor(1), shown favor(1), sought his favor(1), surely be gracious(1).

2603b. חָנַן chanan (337d); a prim. root; *to be loathsome:*— loathsome(1).

2604. חֲנַן chanan (1093b); (Ara.) corr. to 2603a; *to show favor:*— showing mercy(1), supplication(1).

2605. חָנָן Chanan (336d); from 2603a; "gracious," the name of several Isr.:— Hanan(12).

2606. חֲנַנְאֵל Chananel (337a); from 2603a and 410; "God is gracious," a tower in Jer.:— Hananel(4).

2607. חֲנָנִי Chanani (337b); from 2603a; the name of several Isr.:— Hanani(11).

2608a. חֲנַנְיָה Chananyah or

חֲנַנְיָהוּ Chananyahu (337b); from 2603a and 3050; "Yah has been gracious," the name of a number of Isr.:— Hananiah(29).

2608b. חֲנַנְיָה Chananyah (1093b); (Ara.) from 2604 and 3050; an Isr. captive in Bab.

2609. חָנֵס Chanes (337d); of for. or.; a place in Eg.:— Hanes(1).

2610. חָנֵף chaneph (337d); a prim. root; *to be polluted* or *profane:*— completely polluted(1), pollute(1), polluted(6), pollutes(1), turn to godlessness(1).

2611. חָנֵף chaneph (338a); from 2610; *profane, irreligious:*— godless(11), godless man(2).

2612. חֹנֶף choneph (338a); from 2610; *profaneness:*— ungodliness(1).

2613. חֲנֻפָּה chanuppah (338b); from 2610; *profaneness, pollution:*— pollution(1).

2614. חָנַק chanaq (338b); a prim. root; *to strangle:*— killed(1), strangled(1).

2615. חַנָּתֹן Channathon (337b); from 2603a; a place in Zebulun:— Hannathon(1).

2616a. חָסַד chasad (338b); a prim. root; *to be good, kind:*— show yourself kind(2).

2616b. חָסַד chasad (340a); a prim. root; *to be reproached* or *ashamed:*— reproach(1).

2617a. חֶסֶד chesed (338c); from 2616a; *goodness, kindness:*— deeds of devotion(2), devotion(1), devout(1), faithfulness(1), favor(2), good(1), kindly(7), kindness(32), kindnesses(1), loveliness(1), lovingkindness(176), lovingkindnesses(7), loyal deeds(1), loyalty(6), mercies(1), merciful(2), mercy(1), righteousness(1), unchanging love(2).

2617b. חֶסֶד chesed (340a); from 2616b; *shame, reproach:*— disgrace(2).

2618. חֶסֶד Chesed (122c); see 1136.

2619. חֲסַדְיָה Chasadyah (339d); from 2617a and 3050; "Yah is kind," a son of Zerubbabel:— Hasadiah(1).

2620. חָסָה chasah (340a); a prim. root; *to seek refuge:*— has a refuge(1), seek refuge(3), seek shelter(1), sought refuge(1), take refuge(25), taken refuge(3), takes refuge(3).

2621. חֹסָה Chosah (340b); from 2620; a Levite, also a place in Asher:— Hosah(5).

2622. חָסוּת chasuth (340b); from 2620; *refuge:*— shelter(1).

2623. חָסִיד chasid (339c); from 2616a; *kind, pious:*— godly(2), godly man(3), godly ones(20), godly person(1), gracious(1), Holy One(1), kind(3), love(1), ungodly*(1).

2624. חֲסִידָה chasidah (339d); fem. of 2623; *stork:*— stork(5).

2625. חָסִיל chasil (340c); from 2628; (a kind of) *locust:*— caterpillar(1), grasshopper(3), stripping locust(2).

2626. חֲסִין chasin (340d); from the same as 2633; *strong, mighty:*— mighty(1).

2627. חַסִּיר chassir or

חַסִּר chassir (1093c); (Ara.) from a root corr. to 2637; *lacking, wanting, deficient:*— deficient(1).

2628. חָסַל chasal (340c); a prim. root; *to finish off, consume:*— consume(1).

2629. חָסַם chasam (340c); a prim. root; *to stop up, muzzle:*— block off(1), muzzle(1).

2630. חָסַן chasan (340d, 1123c); denom. vb. from 2633; *to be treasured up* or *hoarded:*— hoarded(1).

2631. חֲסַן chasan (1093c); (Ara.) corr. to 2630; *to take possession of:*— possess(1), took possession(1).

2632. חֵסֶן chesen (1093c); (Ara.) from 2631; (royal) *power:*— power(2).

2633. חֹסֶן chosen (340d); from an unused word; *wealth, treasure:*— riches(1), treasure(1), wealth(3).

2634. חָסֹן chason (340d); from the same as 2633; *strong:*— strong(1), strong man(1).

2635. חֲסַף chasaph (1093c); (Ara.) from a root corr. to that of 2636; *clay, potsherd:*— clay(7), pottery(2).

2636. חַסְפַּס chaspas (341a); from an unused word; *scale-like:*— flake-like thing(1).

2637. חָסֵר chaser (341a); a prim. root; *to lack, need, be lacking, decrease:*— become empty(1), decreased(2), depriving(1), empty(1), have...lack(1), lack(2), lacked(2), lacking(4), lacks(2), made him a lower(1), need(1), scarce(1), want(3), withhold(1).

2638. חָסֵר chaser (341c); from 2637; *needy, lacking, in want of:*— lack(2), lacked(1), lacking(4), lacks(6), who lacks(4).

2639. חֶסֶר cheser (341c); from 2637; *want, poverty:*— want(2).

2640. חֹסֶר choser (341c); from 2637; *want, lack:*— lack(3).

2641. חַסְרָה Chasrah (341c); from 2637; an Isr.:— Hasrah(1).

2642. חֶסְרוֹן chesron (341c); from 2637; *a thing lacking, deficiency:*— what is lacking(1).

2643. חַף chaph (342c); from an unused word; *clean:*— innocent(1).

2644. חָפָא chapha (341d); a prim. root; *to do secretly:*— did...secretly(1).

2645. חָפָה chaphah (341d); a prim. root; *to cover:*— cover(1), covered(6), overlaid(5).

2646. חֻפָּה chuppah (342c); from 2653; *a canopy, chamber:*— canopy(1), chamber(2).

2647. חֻפָּה Chuppah (342c); from 2653; an Isr. priest:— Huppah(1).

2648. חָפַז chaphaz (342a); a prim. root; *to be in trepidation, hurry* or *alarm:*— alarm(2), alarmed(1), fled in alarm(1), haste(1), hurried away(1), hurry(1), hurrying(1), panic(1).

2649. חִפָּזוֹן chippazon (342a); from 2648; *trepidation, hurried flight:*— haste(3).

2650. חֻפִּים Chuppim (342c); from 2653; a son of Benjamin:— Huppim(3).

2651. חֹפֶן chophen (342b); from an unused word; *the hollow of the hand:*— fists(2), handfuls*(2), hands(2).

2652. חָפְנִי Chophni (342b); from the same as 2651; a son of Eli:— Hophni(5).

2653. חָפַף chaphaph (342b); a prim. root; *to enclose, surround, cover:*— shields(1).

2654a. חָפֵץ chaphets (342c); a prim. root; *to delight in:*— delight(15), delighted(7), delights(8), desire(9), desired(3), desired*(1), desires(5), favors(1), have any pleasure(1), have...delight(2), have...pleasure(1), pleased(6), pleases(7), take pleasure(1), take...pleasure(2), wish(2), wished(1), wishes(1).

2654b. חָפֵץ chaphats (343c); a prim. root; *to bend down:*— bends(1).

2655. חָפֵץ chaphets (343a); from 2654a; *delighting in, having pleasure in:*— delight(4), desires(1), pleases(1), takes pleasure(1), who delight(1), who delights(1), who favor(1), willing(1), would(1).

2656. חֵפֶץ chephets (343a); from 2654a; *delight, pleasure:*— care(1), delight(8), delightful(2), delights(1), desirable things(1), desire(10), desired(2), event(1), good pleasure(3), matter(1), pleased(1), pleasure(3), precious(1), sight(1), undesirable*(2), what you desire(1).

2657. חֶפְצִי־בָהּ Chephtsi-bah (343b); from 2656; "my delight is in her," a name for Zion, also the mother of King Manasseh:— Hephzibah(1).

2658. חָפַר chaphar (343c); a prim. root; *to dig, search for:*— 76,500*(1), dig(2), digs(1), dug(11), hollowed(1), look around(1), paws(1), sank(1), search(3), spies(1).

2659. חָפֵר chapher (344a); a prim. root; *to be abashed* or *ashamed:*— abashed(1), ashamed(1), confounded(1), disgraced(1), disgraceful(1), embarrassed(2), humiliated(6), shamed(1), shamefully(1).

2660a. חֵפֶר Chepher (343d); from 2658; three Isr.:— Hepher(7).

2660b. חֵפֶר Chepher (343d); from 2658; a Canaanite city, also a place in Judah:— Hepher(2).

2661. חֲפֹר chaphor (344a); see 2663c.

2662. חֶפְרִי Chephri (343d); from 2660a; desc. of Hepher:— Hepherites(1).

2663a. חֲפָרַיִם Chapharayim (343d); from 2658; a place in Issachar:— Hapharaim(1).

2663b. חָפְרַע Chophra (344b); see 6548.

2663c. חֲפַרְפָּרָה chapharparah (344a); from 2658; *a mole:*— moles(1).

2664. חָפַשׂ chaphas (344b); a prim. root; *to search:*— devise(1), disguise(2), disguised(5), distorted(1), examine(1), hide(1), ponders(1), ransacked(1), search(6), searched(2), searching(1), well-conceived(1).

2665. חֵפֶשׂ chephes (344c); from 2664; *a device, plot:*— plot(1).

2666. חָפַשׁ chaphash (344d); a prim. root; *to be free:*— free(1).

2667. חֹפֶשׁ chophesh (344d); from 2666; perh. *a spread:*— saddlecloths*(1).

2668. חֻפְשָׁה chuphshah (344d); from 2666; *freedom:*— freedom(1).

2669. חָפְשׁוּת chophshuth or **חָפְשִׁית chophshith** (345a); from 2666; *freedom, separateness:*— separate(2).

2670. חָפְשִׁי chophshi (344d); from 2666; *free:*— forsaken(1), free(14), free man(2).

2671. חֵץ chets (346b); from 2686a; *arrow:*— archers*(1), arrow(14), arrows(36), shaft(1), wound(1).

2672. חָצַב chatsab or **חָצֵב chatseb** (345a); a prim. root; *to hew, hew out, cleave:*— chops(1), cut in pieces(1), dig(2), engraved(1), hew(2), hewed(2), hewers(1), hewn(5), hewn them in pieces(1), hews(1), masons(2), quarry(2), stonecutters(1), stonecutters to hew(1), stonecutters*(1).

2673. חָצָה chatsah (345b); a prim. root; *to divide:*— divide(4), divided(7), live out half(1), parceled(1), reaches(1), separated(1).

2674. חָצוֹר Chatsor (347d); from the same as 2691b; the name of several places in Pal., also one in Arabia:— Hazor(18).

2675. חָצוֹר חֲדַתָּה Chatsor Chadattah (347d); from 2674 and 2319; a place in the desert of Judah:— Hazor-hadattah(1).

2676. חָצוֹת chatsoth (345c); from 2673; *division, middle:*— midnight*(3).

2677. חֲצִי chatsi (345c); from 2673; *half:*— half(76), half-tribe(1), half-tribe*(32), halfway(2), middle(6), midnight*(3), midst(2), two parts(1).

2678. חֵצִי chetsi (345d); from 2673; *arrow:*— arrow(5).

2679. חֲצִי הַמְּנֻחוֹת chatsi Hammenuchoth (345d, 630a); from 2677 and 4506c, q.v.

2680. חֲצִי הַמְּנַחְתִּי chatsi Hammanachti (345c, 630a); from 2677 and 4506c, q.v.

2681. חָצִיר chatsir (347d); from the same as 2691b; *a settled abode, haunt:*— abode(1).

2682. חָצִיר chatsir (348b); from an unused word; *green grass, herbage:*— grass(19), leeks(1), plant(1).

2683. חֵצֶן chetsen (346a); from an unused word; *bosom* (of a garment):— bosom(1).

2684. חֹצֶן chotsen (346a); from the same as 2683; *bosom:*— bosom(1), front of my garment(1).

2685. חֲצַף chatsaph (1093c); (Ara.) a prim. root; *to show insolence* or *harshness:*— urgent(2).

2686a. חָצַץ chatsats (346b); a prim. root; *to divide:*— cut off(1), ranks(1).

2686b. חָצַץ chatsats (346d); denom. vb. from 2671; *to shoot arrows:*— divide(1).

2687. חָצָץ chatsats (346b); from 2686a; *gravel:*— gravel(2).

2688. חַצְצוֹן תָּמָר Chatsatson Tamar or **חַצֲצֹן תָּמָר Chatsatson Tamar** (346c); from 2686a and 8558; a place on the W. side of the Dead Sea, the same as 5872:— Hazazon-tamar(2).

2689. חֲצֹצְרָה chatsotsrah (348c); from an unused word; (an ancient) *trumpet:*— trumpet(1), trumpeters(3), trumpets(26).

2690. חָצַר chatsar or **חֲצֹצֵר chatsotser** (348d); denom. vb. from 2689; *to sound a trumpet:*— blew(2), blew trumpets(1), blowing(1), sounded(1).

2691a. חָצֵר chatser (346d); from an unused word; *enclosure, court:*— court(112), court there were courts(1), court*(1), courts(24), courtyard(2).

2691b. חָצֵר chatser (347b); from an unused word; *settled abode, settlement, village:*— settlements(1), villages(47).

2692. חֲצַר־אַדָּר Chatsar-addar (347b); from 2691b and 146; a place on the S. border of Canaan:— Hazaraddar(1).

2693. חֲצַר גַּדָּה Chatsar Gaddah (347c); from 2691b and 1409; a place in S. Judah:— Hazar-gaddah(1).

2694. חָצֵר הַתִּיכוֹן Chatser Hattikon (347c); from 2691b and 8484; a place near the border of Hauran:— Hazer-hatticon(1).

2695. חֶצְרוֹ Chetsro (347d); from the same as 2691b; one of David's heroes:— Hezro(2).

2696. חֶצְרוֹן Chetsron (348a); from the same as 2691b; two Isr., also two places in Judah:— Hezron(16), Hezron's(1), Kerioth-hezron*(1).

2697. חֶצְרוֹנִי Chetsroni (348a); from 2696; desc. of Hezron:— Hezronites(2).

2698. חֲצֵרוֹת Chatseroth (348a); pl. of 2691b; a place in the wilderness:— Hazeroth(6).

2699. חֲצֵרִים chatserim (347b); masc. pl. of 2691b, q.v.

2700. חֲצַרְמָוֶת Chatsarmaveth (348a); from 2691b and 4194; a son of Joktan, also his desc.:— Hazarmaveth(2).

2701. חֲצַר סוּסָה Chatsar Susah (347c); from 2691b and 5484; "village of cavalry," a place in Simeon:— Hazar-susah(1).

2702. חֲצַר סוּסִים Chatsar Susim (347c); from 2691b and 5483b; "village of horses," a place in Simeon:— Hazar-susim(1).

2703. חֲצַר עֵינוֹן Chatsar Enon (347c); from 2691b and a der. of 5869; a place on the N.E. border of Canaan:— Hazar-enan(1).

2704. חֲצַר עֵינָן Chatsar Enan (347c); from 2691b and 5881; a place on the N.E. border of Canaan:— Hazar-enan(3).

2705. חֲצַר שׁוּעָל Chatsar Shual (347c); from 2691b and 7776; "village of the fox," a place in S. Judah:— Hazar-shual(4).

2706. חֹק choq (349b); from 2710; *something prescribed* or *owed, a statute:*— allotment(5), boundaries(1), boundary(2), conditions(1), custom(1), decree(5), due(5), fixed order(1), limit(2), limits(1), measure(1), necessary food(1), ordinance(4), portion(3), portions(1), prescribed portion(1), rations(1), required amount(1), resolves(1), statute(9), statutes(79), thing...due(1), what is appointed(1).

2707. חָקָה chaqah (348d); a prim. root; *to cut in, carve:*— carved(1), engraved(1), portrayed(1), set a limit(1).

2708. חֻקָּה chuqqah (349d); fem. of 2706; *something prescribed, an enactment, statute:*— appointed(1), customs(5), due(1), fixed order(1), fixed patterns(1), ordinance(5), ordinances(1), statute(25), statutes(62), statutory(2).

2709. חֲקוּפָא Chaqupha (349a); of unc. der.; an Isr.:— Hakupha(2).

2710. חָקַק chaqaq (349a); a prim. root; *to cut in, inscribe, decree:*— carve(1), commanders(2), decree(1), decreed(1), enact(1), inscribe(2), inscribed(3), lawgiver(1), marked(1), portrayed(1), ruler's(1), ruler's staff(1), scepter(3).

2711. חֵקֶק cheqeq (349b); the same as 2706, q.v.

2712. חֻקֹּק Chuqoq or **חוּקֹק Chuqoq** (350c); from 2710; a place in Naphtali:— Hukkok(1).

2713. חָקַר chaqar (350c); a prim. root; *to search:*— ascertained(1), examines(2), find(1), found(2), investigated(2), make a search(1), pondered(1), probe(1), search(8), searched(4), searches(1), sees through(1), sounded(1), taste(1).

2714. חֵקֶר cheqer (350d); from 2713; *a searching, a thing* (to be) *searched out:*— depths(1), inquiry(1), inscrutable*(1), recesses(1), search(1), searchings(1), things(1), things searched(1), unfathomable*(1), unsearchable*(4).

2715. חֹר chor (359d); from an unused word; *a noble:*— nobility*(1), nobles(12).

2716. חֶרֶא chere (351a); of unc. der.; *dung:*— dung(2).

2717a. חָרֵב chareb (351a); a prim. root; *to be dry* or *dried up:*— becomes parched(1), dried(10), dries(1), dry(3), parched(1).

2717b. חָרֵב chareb (351c); a prim. root; *to be waste* or *desolate:*— become waste(2), desolate(4), destroyer(1), devastated(3), devastators(1), laid waste(5), lay waste(1), made their desolate(1), utterly ruined(1).

2717c. חָרַב charab (352b); a prim. root; *to attack, smite down:*— put(1), slay(1), surely fought together(1), sword(1).

2718. חֲרַב charab (1093d); (Ara.) a root corr. to 2717b; *to be a waste:*— laid waste(1).

2719. חֶרֶב chereb (352b); from 2717c; *a sword:*— axes(1), knives(2), sword(390), swords(18), swordsmen*(1), tool(1).

2720a. חָרֵב chareb (351b); from 2717a; *dry:*— dry(2).

2720b. חָרֵב chareb (351d); from 2717b; *waste, desolate:*— desolate(4), waste(4).

2721a. חֹרֶב **choreb** (351b); from 2717a; *dryness, drought, heat:*— drought(2), dry(3), fever(1), heat(6).

2721b. חֹרֶב **choreb** (351d); from 2717b; *desolation:*— desolation(1), ruin(1), ruined(1), utter waste(1).

2722. חֹרֵב **Choreb** (352a); from 2717b; "waste," a mountain in Sinai:— Horeb(17).

2723. חָרְבָּה **chorbah** (352a); from 2717b; *waste, desolation, ruin:*— deserts(1), desolation(4), desolations(1), ruin(6), ruined homes(1), ruins(11), waste(7), waste places(10), wastes(1).

2724. חָרָבָה **charabah** (351c); from 2717a; *dry ground:*— dry(1), dry ground(4), dry land(3).

2725. חֲרָבוֹן **cherabon** (351c); from 2717a; *drought:*— fever heat(1).

2726. חַרְבוֹנָא **Charbona** or
חַרְבוֹנָה **Charbonah** (353a); of for. or.; eunuch of Ahasuerus:— Harbona(1), Harbonah(1).

2727. חָרַג **charag** (353a); a prim. root; *to quake:*— come trembling(1).

2728. חַרְגֹּל **chargol** (353b); from an unused word; (a kind of) *locust:*— cricket(1).

2729. חָרַד **charad** (353b); a prim. root; *to tremble, be terrified:*— been careful(1), came trembling(2), come trembling(2), disturb(2), frighten(3), frighten them away(1), make him afraid(1), make them afraid(3), quaked(1), routed(1), startled(1), terrified(2), terrify(2), tremble(10), trembled(4), trembles(1), trembling(2).

2730a. חָרֵד **chared** (353d); from 2729; *trembling:*— tremble(1), trembled(1), trembling(2), who tremble(1), who trembles(1).

2730b. חֲרֹד **Charod** (353d); from 2729; a spring by which Gideon camped:— Harod(1).

2731. חֲרָדָה **charadah** (353d); fem. of 2730a; *trembling, fear, anxiety:*— care(1), dread(1), fear(1), terror(1), trembling(4), violently*(1).

2732. חֲרָדָה **Charadah** (354a); from 2729; a place in the S. desert:— Haradah(2).

2733. חֲרֹדִי **Charodi** (353d); from 2730b; inhab. of Harod:— Harodite(2).

2734. חָרָה **charah** (354a); a prim. root; *to burn* or *be kindled with anger:*— angered(1), angry(18), angry*(5), became(1), became angry(4), became furious(1), became...angry(3), burn(5), burned(29), burns(1), compete(1), competing(1), distressed(1), fret(4), kindled(15), rage(1), very angry(1), zealously(1).

2735. חֹר הַגִּדְגָּד **Chor Haggidgad** (301b); from an unused word and a collateral form of 1412; "hollow of Gidgad," a place in the S. desert:— Hor-haggidgad(2).

2736. חַרְהֲיָה **Charhayah** (354d); see 2744b.

2737. חָרוּז **charuz** (354d); from an unused word; *string of beads:*— strings of beads(1).

2738. חָרוּל **charul** (355b); of unc. der.; (a kind of weed), perh. *chickpea:*— nettles(3).

2739. חֲרוּמַף **Charumaph** (354d); of unc. der.; an Isr.:— Harumaph(1).

2740. חָרוֹן **charon** (354c); from 2734; (burning of) *anger:*— burning(17), burning anger(2), fierce(15), fierceness(3), fury(1), wrath(3).

2741. חֲרוּפִי **Charuphi** (358b); from the same as 2779; desc. of Hariph:— Haruphite(1).

2742a. חָרוּץ **charuts** (358d); pass. part. of 2782; *sharp, diligent:*— diligence(1), diligent(4), sharp(2), threshing sledge(2).

2742b. חָרוּץ **charuts** (358d); pass. part. of 2782; *strict decision:*— decision(2).

2742c. חָרוּץ **charuts** (358d); pass. part. of 2782; *a trench, moat:*— moat(1).

2742d. חָרוּץ **charuts** (359a); from an unused word; *gold:*— gold(6).

2743. חָרוּץ **Charuts** (358d); pass. part. of 2782; grandfather of King Amon:— Haruz(1).

2744a. חַרְחוּר **Charchur** (359c); a form of 2746; an Isr.:— Harhur(2).

2744b. חַרְהֲיָה **Charchayah** (354d); of unc. der.; an Isr.:— Harhaiah(1).

2745. חַרְחַס **Charchas** (354d); of unc. der.; an Isr.:— Harhas(1).

2746. חַרְחֻר **charchur** (359c); from 2787; *violent heat, fever:*— fiery heat(1).

2747. חֶרֶט **cheret** (354d); from an unused word; *engraving tool, stylus:*— graving tool(1), letters(1).

2748. חַרְטֹם **chartom** (355a); from the same as 2747; *an engraver, writer:*— magicians(11).

2749. חַרְטֹם **chartom** (1093d); (Ara.) corr. to 2748; *magician:*— magician(1), magicians(4).

2750. חֳרִי **chori** (354c); from 2734; *burning:*— fierce(4), hot(1), outburst(1).

2751. חֹרִי **chori** (301b); from 2357; *white* (bread):— white bread(1).

2752. חֹרִי **Chori** (360a); from the same as 2356; inhab. of Edom, also the name of an Edomite, also the name of a Simeonite:— Hori(3), Horite(1), Horites(6).

2753. חֹרִי **Chori** or
חוֹרִי **Chori** (360a); the same as 2752, q.v.

2754. חָרִיט **charit** (355a); from an unused word; *bag, purse:*— bags(1), money purses(1).

2755. חֲרֵי יוֹנִים **chare yonim** (351a); see 2716 and 3123.

2756. חָרִיף **Chariph** (358b); from 2778a; an Isr.:— Hariph(2).

2757. חָרִיץ **charits** (358d); from 2782; *a cut, thing cut, sharp instrument:*— cuts(1), sharp instruments(1), sharp...instruments(1).

2758. חָרִישׁ **charish** (361a); from 2790a; *a plowing, plowing time:*— plowing(2), plowing time(1).

2759. חֲרִישִׁי **charishi** (362a); perh. from the same as 2791b; perh. *sultry:*— scorching(1).

2760. חָרַךְ **charak** (355b); a prim. root; perh. *to scorch, parch:*— roast(1).

2761. חֲרַךְ **charak** (1093d); (Ara.) a root prob. corr. to 2787; *to singe:*— singed(1).

2762. חֲרַכִּים **charakkim** (355b); of unc. der.; *a lattice:*— lattice(1).

2763a. חָרַם **charam** (355c); a prim. root; *to ban, devote, exterminate:*— annihilate(1), covet(1), destroy them utterly(1), destroy utterly(1), destroyed them utterly(1), destroying(1), destroying them completely(2), destruction(2), devote(2), forfeited(1), set apart(1), sets apart(1), utterly destroy(11), utterly destroyed(22), utterly destroying(3).

2763b. חָרַם **charam** (356d); a prim. root; *to slit:*— disfigured(1).

2764a. חֵרֶם **cherem** (356a); from 2763a; *devoted thing, devotion, ban:*— accursed(2), ban(2), curse(2), devoted(2), devoted to destruction(1), devoted thing(2), set apart(1), something banned(1), things devoted(1), things devoted to destruction(1), things under(10), things under the ban(10), under the ban(3), which is put under(1).

2764b. חֵרֶם **cherem** (357a); from 2763b; *a net:*— net(5), nets(4).

2765. חֹרֵם **Chorem** (356c); from 2763a; "sacred," a place in Naphtali:— Horem(1).

2766. חָרִם **Charim** (356c); from 2763a; "consecrated," the name of several Isr.:— Harim(11).

2767. חָרְמָה **Chormah** (356c); from 2763a; "asylum," a place in Simeon:— Hormah(9).

2768. חֶרְמוֹן **Chermon** (356d); from 2763a; "sacred (mountain)," a mountain in S. Aram (Syria) and N. Isr.:— Hermon(13).

2769. חֶרְמוֹנִים **Chermonim** (356d); pl. of 2768, q.v.:— Hermon(1).

2770. חֶרְמֵשׁ **chermesh** (357a); from 2763b; *a sickle:*— sickle(2).

2771a. חָרָן **Charan** (357a); of unc. der.; "crossroads," a city in N. Mesopotamia:— Haran(10).

2771b. חָרָן **Charan** (357b); from the same as 2771a; son of Caleb:— Haran(2).

2772. חֹרֹנִי **Choroni** (357b); from 1032 (in part); inhab. of Beth-horon:— Horonite(3).

2773. חֹרֹנַיִם **Choronayim** (357b); from the same as 1032 (in part); "two hollows," a place in Moab:— Horonaim(4).

2774. חַרְנֶפֶר **Charnepher** (357b); of unc. der.; an Asherite:— Harnepher(1).

2775a. חֶרֶס **cheres** (357b); of unc. der.; *the sun:*— sun(2).

2775b. חֶרֶס **cheres** (360b); from the same as 2789; (an eruptive disease) *itch:*— itch(1).

2776. חֶרֶס **Cheres** (357c); from the same as 2775a; a mountain E. of the Jordan, also dwelling place of the Amorites:— Heres(2).

2777. חַרְסוּת **charsuth** (360b); from the same as 2789; *potsherd:*— potsherd(1).

2778a. חָרַף **charaph** (357c); a prim. root; *to reproach:*— defied(2), defy(2), despised(1), insult(1), reproach(7), reproached(8), reproaches(5), revile(2), reviled(1), scorned(1), taunt(1), taunted(6), taunts(2).

2778b. חָרַף **charaph** (358b); denom. vb. from 2779; *to remain in harvest time:*— spend harvest time(1).

2778c. חָרַף **charaph** (358b); a prim. root; *to acquire:*— acquired(1).

2779. חֹרֶף **choreph** (358a); from an unused word; *harvest time, autumn:*— autumn(1), prime(1), winter(5).

2780. חָרֵף **Chareph** (358b); perh. from the same as 2779; a leader in Judah:— Hareph(1).

2781. חֶרְפָּה **cherpah** (357d); from 2778a; *a reproach:*— contempt(1), disgrace(5), reproach(60), reproaches(2), scorn(3), shame(1), taunting(1).

2782. חָרַץ **charats** (358c); a prim. root; *to cut, sharpen, decide:*— act promptly(1), bark*(1), decided(1), decisive(1), decreed(3), determined(3), maimed(1), uttered(1).

2783. חֲרַץ **charats** (1093d); (Ara.) from a root corr. to 2782; *loin:*— hip(1).

2784. חַרְצֻבָּה **chartsubbah** (359b); from an unused word; *bond, fetter, pang:*— bonds(1), pains(1).

2785. חַרְצַנִּים **chartsannim** (359a); from 2782; prob. *grape kernels, grape stones:*— seeds(1).

2786. חָרַק charaq (359b); a prim. root; *to gnash* or *grind:*— gnash(2), gnashed(2), gnashes(1).

2787. חָרַר charar (359b); a prim. root; *to be hot* or *scorched, to burn:*— been charred(1), blow fiercely(1), burn(1), burned(2), charred(1), glow(1), kindle(1), parched(1), scorched(1).

2788. חָרֵר charer (359c); from 2787; *a parched place:*— stony wastes(1).

2789. חֶרֶשׂ cheres (360a); from an unused word; *earthenware, earthen vessel, sherd, potsherd:*— earthen(1), earthen vessel(1), earthenware(8), earthenware vessel(1), earthenware vessel the vessels(1), fragments(1), potsherd(2), potsherds(1), sherd(1).

2790a. חָרַשׁ charash (360b); a prim. root; *to cut in, engrave, plow, devise:*— devise(4), devises(2), do(1), engraved(1), farmer plow(1), implements(1), plotting(1), plow(5), plowed(4), plowers plowed(1), plowing(2), plowman(1), worker(1).

2790b. חָרַשׁ charash (361a); a prim. root; *to be silent, dumb, speechless,* or *deaf:*— cease(1), ceased speaking(1), completely silent(1), deaf(2), indeed says nothing(1), keep silence(2), keep silent(5), keeps silent(2), kept silence(1), kept silent(4), quiet(1), remain silent(1), remained silent(1), said nothing(2), says nothing(2), silence(3), silent(13), still(1).

2791a. חֶרֶשׁ cheresh (361c); from 2790b; *silently, secretly:*— secretly(1).

2791b. חֶרֶשׁ cheresh (361d); see 2796.

2792. חֶרֶשׁ Cheresh (361d); from the same as 2791b; a Levite:— Heresh(1).

2793. חֹרֶשׁ choresh (361c); of unc. der.; *wood, wooded height:*— forest(2), Horesh(4), wooded(1).

2794. חֹרֵשׁ choresh (360b); act. part. of 2790a, q.v.

2795. חֵרֵשׁ cheresh (361b); from 2790b; *deaf:*— deaf(7), deaf man(2).

2796. חָרָשׁ charash (360d); from 2790a; *engraver, artificer:*— artisan(1), blacksmith(1), carpenters(4), carpenters*(4), craftsman(7), craftsmen(10), engraver(2), jeweler*(1), manufacturers(1), masons(1), masons*(1), shapes(2), skilled(1), smith(1), stonemasons*(1), workers(1).

2797. חַרְשָׁא Charsha (361d); from the same as 2791b; an Isr.:— Harsha(2).

2798. חֲרָשִׁים Charashim (360d); pl. of 2796; "craftsmen," a man of Judah:— Ge-harashim*(1).

2799. חֲרֹשֶׁת charosheth (360d); from 2790a; *a carving, skillful working:*— carving(2), cutting(2).

2800. חֲרֹשֶׁת Charosheth (361d); from the same as 2791b; a place in Pal.:— Harosheth-hagoyim*(3).

2801. חָרַת charath (362a); a prim. root; *to grave, engrave:*— engraved(1).

2802. חֶרֶת Chereth (362a); from 2801; a forest in Judah:— Hereth(1).

2803. חָשַׁב chashab (362d); a prim. root; *to think, account:*— accounting(1), calculate(5), composed(1), consider(3), considered(13), counted(1), counts(1), designer(1), determined(1), devise(13), devised(8), devises(1), devising(1), esteem(2), esteemed(2), execute(1), have(1), impute(1), intend(2), make(2), makers(1), meant(2), mindful(1), plan(2), planned(3), planning(5), plans(4), plotted(1), pondered(1), purposed(3), reckoned(10), regard(1), regarded(8), regards(1), require an accounting(1), scheme(1), schemed(1), seem(1), skillful(1), skillful workman(9), think(3), thought(2), value(1).

2804. חֲשַׁב chashab (1093d); (Ara.) corr. to 2803; *to think, account:*— accounted(1).

2805. חֵשֶׁב chesheb (363d); from 2803; *ingenious work:*— artistic band(1), skillfully woven band(5), woven band(2).

2806. חַשְׁבַּדָּנָה Chashbaddanah (364c); of unc. der.; an Isr.:— Hashbaddanah(1).

2807. חֲשֻׁבָה Chashubah (363d); from 2803; "consideration," son of Zerubbabel:— Hashubah(1).

2808. חֶשְׁבּוֹן cheshbon (363d); from 2803; *a reckoning, account:*— explanation(2).

2809. חֶשְׁבּוֹן Cheshbon (363d); from 2803; a place E. of the Jordan:— Heshbon(38).

2810. חִשָּׁבוֹן chishshabon (364a); from 2803; *device, invention:*— devices(1), engines(1).

2811. חֲשַׁבְיָהוּ Chashabyahu or
חֲשַׁבְיָה **Chashabyah** (364a); from 2803 and 3050; "Yah has taken account," the name of a number of Isr.:— Hashabiah(15).

2812. חֲשַׁבְנָה Chashabnah (364b); from 2803; an Isr. leader in Nehemiah's time:— Hashabnah(1).

2813. חֲשַׁבְנְיָה Chashabneyah (364b); from 2803 and 3050; "Yah has accounted," two Isr.:— Hashabneiah(2).

2814. חָשָׁה chashah (364c); a prim. root; *to be silent, inactive,* or *still:*— calmed(1), hushed(1), keep silent(4), keeping silent(1), kept(1), kept silent(1), refrained(1), silent(3), sit still(1), still(2), still doing nothing(1).

2815. חַשּׁוּב Chashshub (363d); from 2803; the name of several Isr.:— Hasshub(5).

2816. חֲשׁוֹךְ chashok (1094a); (Ara.) from a root corr. to 2821; *darkness:*— darkness(1).

2817. חֲשׂוּפָא Chasupha or
חֲשֻׂפָא **Chasupha** (362d); from 2834; an Isr.:— Hasupha(2).

חָשֻׁק **chashuq**; see 2838.

חִשֻּׁק **chishshuq**; see 2839.

חִשֻּׁר **chishshur**; see 2840.

2818. חֲשַׁח chashach (1093d); (Ara.) a prim. root; *to need:*— need(1).

2819a. חַשְׁחָה chashchah (1093d); (Ara.) from 2818; *things needed:*— needed(1).

2819b. חַשְׁחוּ chashchu (1093d); (Ara.) from 2818; *things needed, requirement:*— needs(1).

2820. חָשַׂךְ chasak (362a); a prim. root; *to withhold, refrain:*— hold them back(1), hold back(2), keep back(1), keeps back(1), kept(1), kept their in check(1), kept back(1), lessen(1), lessened(1), refrain(1), requited(1), reserved(2), restrain(1), restrained(1), restrains(2), spare(2), spared(1), unrestrained*(1), withheld(3), withholds(2).

2821. חָשַׁךְ chashak (364d); a prim. root; *to be* or *grow dark:*— blacker(1), brings darkness(1), dark(3), darkened(5), darkens(2), dim(1), grow dim(2), made it dark(1), make the dark(1).

2822. חֹשֶׁךְ choshek (365a); from 2821; *darkness, obscurity:*— dark(5), darkness(73), obscurity(2).

2823. חָשֹׁךְ chashok (365b); from 2821; *obscure, low:*— obscure men(1).

2824. חֶשְׁכָה cheshkah (365b); the same as 2825, q.v.

2825. חֲשֵׁכָה chashekah (365b); from 2821; *darkness:*— darkness(7).

2826. חָשַׁל chashal (365b); a prim. root; *to shatter:*— stragglers(1).

2827. חֲשַׁל chashal (1094a); (Ara.) corr. to 2826; *to shatter:*— shatters(1).

2828. חָשֻׁם Chashum (365c); of unc. der.; an Isr.:— Hashum(5).

2829. חֶשְׁמוֹן Cheshmon (365c); from the same as 2831; a city in S. Judah:— Heshmon(1).

2830. חַשְׁמַל chashmal (365c); of unc. der.; perh. *amber:*— glowing metal(3).

2831. חַשְׁמַן chashman (365c); of unc. der.; *ambassador:*— envoys(1).

2832. חַשְׁמֹנָה Chashmonah (365d); fem. of 2831; a place in the S. desert:— Hashmonah(2).

2833. חֹשֶׁן choshen (365d); from an unused word; *breastpiece, sacred pouch:*— breastpiece(25).

2834. חָשַׂף chasaph (362c); a prim. root; *to strip off, strip, make bare:*— bared(2), draw(1), scoop(1), strip off(1), stripped them bare(1), stripped your off(1), stripped...bare(1), strips the bare(1), uncovered(1).

2835. חָשִׂף chasiph or
חֲשִׂיף **chasiph** (362c); from 2834; *little flock:*— little flocks(1).

2836a. חָשַׁק chashaq (365d); a prim. root; *to be attached to, love:*— have a desire(1), kept(1), longs(1), loved(1), pleased*(2), set his affection(1), set his love(1).

2836b. חָשַׁק chashaq (366a); denom. vb. from 2838; *to furnish with fillets* or *rings:*— furnished with bands(2), made bands(1).

2837. חֵשֶׁק chesheq (366a); from 2836a; *desire:*— all(1), desired*(1), longed(1), pleased*(2).

2838. חָשֻׁק chashuq or
חָשׁוּק **chashuq** (366a); pass. part. of 2836a; *a fillet* or *ring:*— bands(8).

2839. חִשֻּׁק chishshuq or
חִשּׁוּק **chishshuq** (366b); from 2836a; *spoke* (of a wheel):— spokes(1).

2840. חִשֻּׁר chishshur or
חִשּׁוּר **chishshur** (366b); from the same as 2841; *a nave, hub* (of a wheel):— hubs(1).

2841. חַשְׁרָה chashrah (366b); from an unused word; *collection, mass:*— mass(1).

2842. חֲשַׁשׁ chashash (366b); from an unused word; *chaff:*— chaff(1), dry grass(1).

2843. חֻשָׁתִי Chushathi (302a); from 2364; perh. an inhab. of Hushah:— Hushathite(5).

2844a. חַת chath (369c); from 2865; *terror, fear:*— fear(1), terror(1).

2844b. חַת chath (369c); from 2865; *shattered, dismayed:*— shattered(1), terrified(1).

2845. חֵת Cheth (366c); of unc. der.; a son of Canaan and probably ancestor of the Hittites:— Heth(14).

2846. חָתָה chathah (367a); a prim. root; *to snatch up:*— heap(1), snatch(1), take(2).

2847. חִתָּה chittah (369d); from 2865; *terror:*— terror(1).

2848. חִתּוּל chittul (367c); from 2853; *a bandage:*— bandage(1).

2849. חַתְחַת chathchath (369d); from 2865; *terror:*— terrors(1).

2850. חִתִּי Chitti (366c); from 2845; desc. of Heth:— Hittite(35), Hittites(13).

2851. חִתִּית chittith (369d); from 2865; *terror:*— terror(8).

2852. חָתַךְ chathak (367b); a prim. root; *to divide, determine:*— decreed(1).

2853. חָתַל chathal (367c); a prim. root; perh. *entwine, enwrap:*— wrapped in cloths(1).

2854. חֲתֻלָּה chathullah (367c); from 2853; *swaddling band:*— swaddling band(1).

2855. חֶתְלֹן Chethlon (367c); from 2853; a place in N. Pal.:— Hethlon(2).

2856. חָתַם chatham (367c); a prim. root; *to seal, affix a seal, seal up:*— obstructs(1), seal(6), sealed(15), seals(2), sets a seal(1), shut(1).

2857. חֲתַם chatham (1094a); (Ara.) corr. to 2856; *to seal:*— sealed(1).

2858. חֹתֶמֶת chothemeth (368b); from 2856; *signet ring:*— ring(1).

2859. חָתַן chathan (368d); denom. vb. from 2860a; *make oneself a daughter's husband:*— allied himself by marriage(1), become the son-in-law(4), formed a marriage alliance(1), intermarry(4), marriage alliance(1), son-in-law(1).

2860a. חָתָן chathan (368c); from an unused word; *daughter's husband, bridegroom:*— bridegroom(9), groom(1), son-in-law(8), sons-in-law(2).

2860b. חֹתֵן chothen (368c); from the same as 2860a; *wife's father* or *mother:*— father-in-law(21), mother-in-law(1).

2861. חֲתֻנָּה chathunnah (368d); from the same as 2860a; *a marriage, wedding:*— wedding(1).

2862. חָתַף chathaph (368d); a prim. root; *to seize, snatch away:*— snatch away(1).

2863. חֶתֶף chetheph (369a); from 2862; *prey:*— robber(1).

2864. חָתַר chathar (369a); a prim. root; *to dig, row:*— dig(5), dug(2), rowed(1).

2865. חָתַת chathath (369a); a prim. root; *to be shattered* or *dismayed:*— been shattered(3), break(1), cracked(1), dismay(1), dismayed(26), frighten(1), shatter(1), shattered(9), stood in awe(1), terrified(8), wane(1).

2866. חֲתַת chathath (369d); from 2865; *terror:*— terror(1).

2867. חֲתַת Chathath (369d); from 2865; an Isr.:— Hathath(1).

ט

2868. טְאֵב teeb (1094a); (Ara.) corr. to 2895; *to be good:*— pleased(1).

2869. טָב tab (1094a); (Ara.) from 2868; *good:*— fine(1), pleases(1).

2870a. טָבְאַל Tabeal (370b); from 2895 and 408; "good for nothing," an Aramean (Syrian):— Tabeel(1).

2870b. טָבְאֵל Tabeel (370b); perh. from 2895 and 410; perh. "God is good," a Pers. officer:— Tabeel(1).

2871. טְבוּל tebul (371b); from an unused word; *a turban:*— turbans(1).

2872. טַבּוּר tabbur (371d); of unc. der.; *highest part, center:*— center(1), highest part(1).

2873. טָבַח tabach (370b); a prim. root; *to slaughter, butcher, slay:*— make(1), prepared(1), slaughter(3), slaughtered(3), slaughters(1), slay(2).

2874. טֶבַח tebach (370d); from 2873; *slaughtering, slaughter:*— animal(1), food(1), slaughter(10).

2875. טֶבַח Tebach (370d); from 2873; son of Nahor:— Tebah(1).

2876. טַבָּח tabbach (371a); from 2873; *cook, guardsman:*— bodyguard(16), cook(2), guard(14).

2877. טַבָּח tabbach (1094b); (Ara.) corr. to 2876; *guardsman:*— bodyguard(1).

2878. טִבְחָה tibchah (370d); fem. of 2874; *thing slaughtered, slaughtered meat, slaughter:*— meat(1), slaughter(1), slaughtered(1).

2879. טַבָּחָה tabbachah (371a); fem. of 2876; *female cook:*— cooks(1).

2880. טִבְחַת Tibchath (371a); from 2873; an Aramean (Syrian) city:— Tibhath(1).

2881. טָבַל tabal (371a); a prim. root; *to dip:*— dip(9), dipped(6), plunge(1).

2882. טְבַלְיָהוּ Tebalyahu (371b); from 2881 and 3050; "Yah has dipped," an Isr.:— Tebaliah(1).

2883. טָבַע taba (371c); a prim. root; *to sink, sink down:*— drowned(1), sank(2), settled(1), sink(1), sunk(4), sunk down(1).

2884. טַבָּעוֹת Tabbaoth (371d); pl. of 2885; an Isr.:— Tabbaoth(2).

2885. טַבַּעַת tabbaath (371c); from 2883; *signet ring, ring, signet:*— finger rings(1), ring(2), rings(37), signet ring(7), signet rings(2).

2886. טַבְרִמּוֹן Tabrimmon (372a); perh. from 2895 and 7417a; perh. "Rimmon is good," father of Benhaddad, king of Aram (Syria):— Tabrimmon(1).

2887. טֵבֵת Tebeth (372a); of for. or.; tenth Heb. month:— Tebeth(1).

2888. טַבַּת Tabbath (372a); of unc. der.; a place of refuge of the Midianites:— Tabbath(1).

2889. טָהוֹר tahor (373a); from 2891; *clean, pure:*— clean(51), pure(40), purity(1), unclean*(2), who is clean(1).

2890. טְהוֹר tahor (373a); the same as 2889, q.v.

2891. טָהֵר taher (372a); a prim. root; *to be clean* or *pure:*— become clean(2), becomes clean(2), becomes cleansed(1), clean(25), cleanse(15), cleansed(19), cleansing(1), cleared(1), pronounce him clean(6), pronounce the clean(1), pronounce clean(2), pronounces him clean(1), pronouncing it clean(1), pure(2), purge(1), purged(2), purified(5), purifier(1), purify(5), purifying(1), remain(1), unclean*(1).

2892a. טֹהַר tohar (372d); from 2891; *purity, purifying:*— clear(1), purification(2).

2892b. טְהָר tohar (372d); from 2891; *clearness, luster:*— splendor(1).

2893. טָהֳרָה tahorah (372d); from 2891; *purifying, cleansing:*— becomes clean(1), cleansed(1), cleansing(6), purification(4), purifying(1).

2894. טוּא tu or

טֵאטֵא tete (370a); a prim. root; *to sweep:*— sweep(1).

2895. טוֹב tob (373b); a prim. root; *to be pleasing* or *good:*— any(1), did well(2), done well(1), fair(1), go well(1), good(1), good(5), high(1), merry(3), please(2), pleased*(2), pleases(4), pleases*(2), pleasing(1), well(8), well-off(1).

2896a. טוֹב tob (373c); from 2895; *pleasant, agreeable, good:*— beautiful(11), beneficial(1), best(7), better(75), better a good(1), charming*(1), cheerful(3), choice(2), delightful(1), fair(1), favor(1), favorable(3), favorably(3), festive(1), fine(3), fine ones(1), fit(1), generous*(1), glad(1), good(196), good and to those who(1), good is better(1), good man(3), good men(1), good-looking*(1), gracious(1), handsome(3), handsome*(1), happy(1), holiday*(3), intelligent*(1), kind(1), like*(1), man(1), more*(2), one(1), one who(1), one who(1), one who is good(1), one who is pleasing(1), pleasant(2), please*(2), pleased(1), pleases(1), pleasing(5), precious(3), pure(1), right(1), ripe(3), safely*(1), sound(1), splendid(1), sweet(1), upright(1), very well(1), well(6), well off(1), what is good(11), what seems best(1), what seems good(2), what was good(2), whatever you like*(1), who are good(1), wish*(2), worthy(1).

2896b. טוֹב tob (375a); from 2895; *a good thing, benefit, welfare:*— enjoy*(1), good(66), good thing(3), good things(2), goodness(1), graciously(1), happiness(1), happy(1), pleasant(1), prosperity(8), richer(1), well(1), what is good(1), what is good(4).

2897. טוֹב Tob (376a); from 2895; a region E. of the Jordan:— Tob(2).

2898. טוּב tub (375c); from 2895; *good things, goods, goodness:*— best(3), best things(1), bounty(2), comeliness(1), fair(1), glad(2), good(2), good thing(2), good things(3), goodness(10), goodness'(1), prosperity(3), well(1).

2899a. טוֹב אֲדֹנִיָּהוּ Tob Adoniyyahu (375b); from 2896b and 138; "good is my LORD," a Levite:— Tobadonijah(1).

2899b. טוֹבָה tobah (375c); from 2895; *welfare, benefit, good things, good:*— bounty(1), enjoy*(2), favorably disposed(1), good(34), good deeds(1), good thing(2), good things(3), goodness(5), happiness(1), kindly(2), nice things(1), pleasure(1), prosperity(6), welfare(2), well(3).

2900. טוֹבִיָּהוּ Tobiyyahu or

טוֹבִיָּה Tobiyyah (375d); from 2896b and 3050; "Yah is my good," three Isr., also an Ammonite:— Tobiah(13), Tobiah's(2), Tobijah(3).

2901. טָוָה tavah (376a); a prim. root; *to spin:*— spun(2).

2902. טוּחַ tuach (376b); a prim. root; *to overspread, overlay, coat, besmear:*— overlay(1), plaster it over(2), plastered(1), plastered it over(1), plastered over(1), plasterers(1), replaster(1), replastered(2), smeared(1).

2903. טוֹטָפוֹת totaphoth (377d); from an unused word; *bands:*— frontals(2), phylacteries(1).

2904. טוּל tul (376c); a prim. root; *to hurl, cast:*— cast(2), hurl(3), hurled(4), hurled headlong(1), laid low(1), threw(2), throw(1).

2905. טוּר tur (377a); from an unused word; *a row:*— row(14), rows(12).

2906. טוּר tur (1094b); (Ara.) corr. to 6697; *mountain:*— mountain(2).

2907. טוּשׂ tus (377b); a prim. root; *to rush, dart:*— swoops(1).

2908. טְוָת tevath (1094b); (Ara.) from a root corr. to 2901; *hungrily:*— fasting(1).

2909. טָחָה tachah (377b); a prim. root; *to hurl, shoot:*— bowshot*(1).

2910. טֻחָה tuchah (376b); from 2902; *inward parts:*— innermost being(2).

2911a. טְחוֹן techon (377c); from 2912; *grinding mill, hand mill:*— grinding mill(1).

2911b. טָחַח tachach (377c); a prim. root; *to be besmeared:*— smeared over(1).

2912. טָחַן tachan (377c); a prim. root; *to grind:*— grind(3), grinder(1), grinding(3), ground(1).

2913. טַחֲנָה tachanah (377d); from 2912; *a mill:*— grinding mill(1).

2914. טְחֹר techor (377d); from an unused word; *tumors* (a result of dysentery):— tumors(2).

2915. טִיחַ tiach (376b); from 2902; *a coating:*— plaster(1).

2916. טִיט tit (376c); of unc. der.; *mud, mire, clay:*— clay(2), mire(7), mud(3).

2917. טִין tin (1094b); (Ara.) perh. corr. to 2916; *clay:*— common(2).

2918. טִירָה tirah (377a); from the same as 2905; *encampment, battlement:*— battlement(1), camp(1), camps(3), encampments(1), rows(1).

2919. טַל tal (378b); from an unused word; *night mist, dew:*— dew(31).

2920. טַל tal (1094b); (Ara.) corr. to 2919; *dew:*— dew(5).

2921. טָלָא tala (378a); a prim. root; *to patch, spot:*— patched(1), spotted(6), various colors(1).

2922. טְלָא tela (378b); the same as 2924, q.v.

2923. טְלָאִים Telaim (378a); from 2921; a place where Saul mustered his forces:— Telaim(1).

2924. טָלֶה taleh (378b); from an unused word; *a lamb:*— lamb(2), lambs(1).

2925. טַלְטֵלָה taltelah (376d); from 2904; *a hurling:*— headlong(1).

2926. טָלַל talal (378d); a prim. root; *to cover over, roof:*— covered(1).

2927. טְלַל telal (1094b); (Ara.) corr. to 2926; *to have shade:*— found shade(1).

2928. טֶלֶם Telem (378d); from an unused word; an Isr., also a place in the desert of Judah:— Telem(2).

2929. טַלְמוֹן Talmon (379a); from the same as 2728; an Isr. name:— Talmon(5).

2930. טָמֵא tame (379a); a prim. root; *to be* or *become unclean:*— became unclean(1), become defiled(3), become unclean(6), becomes unclean(13), becoming unclean(1), been defiled(2), defile(25), defiled(38), defilement(1), defiles(5), defiling(2), made unclean(3), make himself unclean(1), make yourselves unclean(1), make...unclean(1), pronounce him unclean(9), pronounced them unclean(1), remain unclean(2), surely pronounce(1), surely pronounce him unclean(1), unclean(44).

2931. טָמֵא tame (379d); from 2930; *unclean:*— defiled(1), ill(1), unclean(83), unclean thing(1), unclean woman(1), who was unclean(1).

2932a. טֻמְאָה tumah (380a); from 2930; *uncleanness:*— filthiness(4), impure(2), impurities(3), impurity(3), unclean(1), unclean thing(3), uncleanness(20).

2932b. טָמְאָה tomah (380a); from 2930; *uncleanness:*— uncleanness(1).

2933. טָמָה tamah (380b); a prim. root; *to be stopped up, stupid:*— stupid(1).

2934. טָמַן taman (380b); a prim. root; *to hide, conceal:*— buries(2), concealed(2), discarded(1), held in reserve(1), hid(8), hidden(9), hide(5), hiding(1), laying...secretly(1), secretly laid(1).

2935. טֶנֶא tene (380d); from an unused word; *a basket:*— basket(4).

2936. טָנַף tanaph (380d); a prim. root; *to soil, defile:*— dirty(1).

2937. טָעָה taah (380d); a prim. root; *to wander, stray:*— misled(1).

2938. טָעַם taam (380d); a prim. root; *to taste, perceive:*— indeed tasted(1), senses(1), taste(4), tasted(2), tastes(2).

2939. טְעֵם teem (1094b); (Ara.) corr. to 2938; *to feed:*— given to eat(3).

2940. טַעַם taam (381a); from 2938; *taste, judgment:*— decree(1), discernment(3), discreet(1), discretion(1), flavor(1), sanity(1), taste(4).

2941. טַעַם taam (1094c); (Ara.) the same as 2942, q.v.

2942. טְעֵם teem (1094c); (Ara.) from 2939; *taste, judgment, command:*— accountable(1), command(1), commanded*(1), commander*(3), decree(18), discernment(1), disregarded*(1), orders(1), report(1), tasted(1).

2943. טָעַן taan (381b); a prim. root; *to load:*— load(1).

2944. טָעַן taan (381b); a prim. root; *to pierce:*— pierced(1).

2945. טַף taph (381d); from 2952; *children:*— children(11), girls*(1), infants(1), little children(2), little ones(27).

2946. טָפַח taphach (381b); a prim. root; *to extend, spread:*— bore(1), spread(1).

2947. טֶפַח tephach (381c); from 2946; *a span, handbreadth, coping:*— coping(1), handbreadth(2), handbreadths(1).

2948. טֹפַח tophach (381c); from 2946; *a span, handbreadth:*— handbreadth(5).

2949. טִפֻּחִים tippuchim (381c); from 2946; *tenderly cared for:*— born healthy(1), who were born healthy(1).

2950. טָפַל taphal (381c); a prim. root; *to smear, plaster over, stick, glue:*— forged(1), smear(1), wrap(1).

2951. טִפְסַר tiphsar (381d); of for. or.; *a scribe, marshal:*— marshal(1), marshals(1).

2952. טָפַף taphaph (381d); a prim. root; *to trip, take small quick steps:*— mincing steps(1).

2953. טְפַר tephar (1094c); (Ara.) from a root corr. to 6852; *a nail, claw:*— claws(1), nails(1).

2954. טָפַשׁ taphash (382a); a prim. root; *to be gross:*— covered(1).

2955. טָפַת Taphath (382a); of unc. der.; daughter of Solomon:— Taphath(1).

2956. טָרַד tarad (382a); a prim. root; *to pursue, chase, be continuous:*— constant(2).

2957. טְרַד terad (1094c); (Ara.) corr. to 2956; *to chase away:*— driven away(4).

2958. טְרוֹם terom (382c); the same as 2962, q.v.

2959. טָרַח tarach (382b); a prim. root; *to toil, be burdened:*— loads(1).

2960. טֹרַח torach (382b); from 2959; *a burden:*— burden(1), load(1).

2961. טָרִי tari (382b); from an unused word; *fresh:*— fresh(1), raw(1).

2962. טֶרֶם terem (382c); a prim. adv.; *not yet, ere, before that:*— before(45), before*(3), no*(2), nor(1), prior(1), yet(6).

2963. טָרַף taraph (382d); a prim. root; *to tear, rend, pluck:*— feed(1), ravening(1), ravenous(1), surely been torn to pieces(2), tear(7), tearing(2), tears(2), tore(2), torn(2), torn in pieces(2), torn to pieces(1).

2964. טֶרֶף tereph (383a); from 2963; *prey, food, a leaf:*— food(4), leaves(1), prey(17), torn(1).

2965. טָרָף taraph (383a); from 2963; *fresh-plucked:*— freshly picked(1).

2966. טְרֵפָה terephah (383c); fem. of 2964; *torn animal, torn flesh:*— animal torn(1), torn(4), torn by beasts(1), torn to pieces(1), torn flesh(1), what has been torn(1).

2967. טַרְפְּלָיֵא tarpelaye (1094c); (Ara.) of for. or.; *official* (a Pers. title):— officials(1).

י

2968. יָאַב yaab (383b); a prim. root; *to long, desire:*— longed(1).

2969. יָאָה yaah (383b); a prim. root; *to befit, be befitting:*— due(1).

2970. יַאֲזַנְיָהוּ Yaazanyahu or

יַאֲזַנְיָה Yaazanyah (24d); from 238 and 3050; "Yah hears," the name of several Isr.:— Jaazaniah(4).

2971. יָאִיר Yair (22c); from 215; "he enlightens," three Isr.:— Jair(9).

2972. יָאִירִי Yairi or

יָאִרִי Yairi (22c); from 2971; desc. of Jair:— Jairite(1).

2973. יָאַל yaal (383b); a prim. root; *to be foolish:*— acted foolishly(2), become fools(1), foolish(1).

2974. יָאַל yaal (383d); a prim. root; *to show willingness, be pleased, determine, undertake* (to do anything):— agreed(1), determined(1), persisted(3), please(2), pleased(2), pleased*(1), tried(1), undertook(1), ventured(2), willing(5).

2975. יְאֹר yeor (384b); of for. or.; *stream* (of the Nile), *stream, canal:*— canals(1), channels(1), Nile(44), Nile canals(1), river(5), rivers(10), streams(3).

2976. יָאַשׁ yaash (384c); a prim. root; *to despair:*— despair(2), despaired(1), hopeless(3).

2977. יֹאשִׁיָּה Yoshiyyah or

יֹאשִׁיָּהוּ Yoshiyyahu (78c); from 3050 and 806b; "Yah supports," two Isr.:— Josiah(52), Josiah's(1).

2978. יְאִתוֹן yeithon (87c); see 382b.

2979. יְאָתְרַי Yeatheray (384d); of unc. der.; an ancestor of Asaph:— Jeatherai(1).

2980. יָבַב yabab (384d); a prim. root; *to cry in a shrill voice:*— lamented(1).

2981. יְבוּל yebul (385b); from 2986; *produce* (of the soil):— crops(1), fruit(2), increase(2), produce(7), yield(1).

2982. יְבוּס Yebus (101a); from 947; an early name of Jer.:— Jebus(4).

2983. יְבוּסִי Yebusi (101a); from 2982; inhab. of Jebus:— Jebusite(25), Jebusites(16).

2984. יִבְחָר Yibchar (104d); from 977; "He chooses," a son of David:— Ibhar(3).

2985. יָבִין Yabin (108a); from 995; "one who is intelligent," two Canaanite kings:— Jabin(7), Jabin's(1).

2986. יָבַל yabal (384d); a prim. root; *to conduct, bear along:*— bring(5), brought(1), carried(4), carry(1), lead(1), led(3), led forth(3).

2987. יְבַל yebal (1094d); (Ara.) corr. to 2986; *to bear along, carry:*— bring(1), brought(2).

2988. יָבָל yabal (385a); from 2986; *water-course, stream:*— running(1), streams(1).

2989. יָבָל Yabal (385b); from 2986; a son of Lamech:— Jabal(1).

2990. יַבֶּל yabbal (385c); from 2986; *a running, suppurating:*— running sore(1).

2991. יִבְלְעָם Yibleam (385d); of unc. der.; a city of Manasseh:— Ibleam(3).

2992. יָבַם yabam (386a); denom. vb. from 2993; *to perform the duty of a husband's brother:*— duty as a brother-in-law(1), husband's brother(2), perform the duty(2), perform your duty(1).

2993. יָבָם yabam (386a); of unc. der.; *husband's brother:*— husband's brother(2).

2994. יְבֵמֶת yebemeth (386a); from the same as 2993; *sister-in-law:*— brother's wife(2), sister-in-law(2), wife(1).

2995. יַבְנְאֵל Yabneel (125c); from 1129 and 410; "El causes to build," two cities in Isr.:— Jabneel(2).

2996. יַבְנֶה Yabneh (125c); from 1129; "he causes to build," a Philistine city:— Jabneh(1).

2997. יִבְנְיָה Yibneyah (125d); from 1129 and 3050; "Yah builds up," a Benjamite:— Ibneiah(1).

2998. יִבְנִיָּה Yibniyyah (125d); from 1129 and 3050; "Yah builds up," a Benjamite:— Ibnijah(1).

2999. יַבֹּק Yabboq (132d); prob. from 1238b; a river E. of the Jordan:— Jabbok(7).

3000. יְבֶרֶכְיָהוּ Yeberekyahu (140a); from 1288 and 3050; "Yah blesses," the name of several Isr.:— Jeberechiah(1).

3001. יָבֵשׁ yabesh (386b); a prim. root; *to be dry, dried up,* or *withered:*— become dry(1), completely wither(1), dried(18), dries(5), dry(11), make her dry(1), make your dry(1), makes it dry(1), totally withered(1), wither(7), withered(5), withers(6).

3002. יָבֵשׁ yabesh (386d); from 3001; *dry, dried:*— dried(1), dry(6), gone(1), withered(1).

3003. יָבֵשׁ Yabesh or

יָבֵישׁ Yabesh (386d); from 3001; a place in Gilead, also an Isr.:— Jabesh(12), Jabesh-gilead*(12).

3004. יַבָּשָׁה yabbashah (387a); from 3001; *dry land, dry ground:*— dry ground(4), dry land(9), land(1).

3005. יִבְשָׂם Yibsam (142a); from the same as 1314; a desc. of Issachar:— Ibsam(1).

3006. יַבֶּשֶׁת yabbesheth (387a); from 3001; *dry land, dry ground:*— dry ground(1), dry land(1).

3007. יַבֶּשֶׁת yabbesheth (1094d); (Ara.) corr. to 3006; *earth:*— earth(1).

3008. יִגְאָל Yigal (145d); from 1350; "He redeems," three Isr.:— Igal(3).

3009. יָגַב yagab (387a); a prim. root; *to till, be a husbandman:*— plowmen(2).

3010. יָגֵב yageb (387a); from 3009; *a field:*— fields(1).

3011. יָגְבְּהָה Yogbehah (147b); from 1361b; perh. "exalted," a place in Gad:— Jogbehah(2).

3012. יִגְדַּלְיָהוּ Yigdalyahu (153d); from 1431 and 3050; "Yah is great," an Isr. prophet:— Igdaliah(1).

3013. יָגָה yagah (387b); a prim. root; *to suffer:*— afflicted(1), caused her grief(1), causes grief(1), grieve(2), inflicted(1), torment(1), tormentors(1).

3014. יָגָה yagah (387c); a prim. root; *to thrust away:*— removed(1).

3015. יָגוֹן yagon (387b); from 3013; *grief, sorrow:*— sorrow(14).

3016. יָגוֹר yagor (388d); from 3025; *fearing:*— dread(2).

3017. יָגוּר Yagur (158c); from 1481a; a city in S. Judah:— Jagur(1).

3018. יְגִיעַ yegia (388c); from 3021; *toil, product:*— fruit(1), labor(5), labors(2), possessions(1), produce(1), product of his labor(1), product of their labor(1), products(1), property(1), toil(1), wages(1).

3019. יָגִיעַ yagia (388c); from 3021; *weary:*— weary(1).

3020. יָגְלִי Yogli (163d); from 1540; perh. "led into exile," a Danite:— Jogli(1).

3021. יָגַע yaga or

יָגֵעַ yagea (388a); a prim. root; *to toil, grow* or *be weary:*— become weary(1), get tired(1), labor(1), labored(4), tired(3), toil(4), toiled(1), wearied(4), wearies(1), weary(5), worn(1).

3022. יָגָע yaga (388b); from 3021; *a gain:*— what he has attained(1).

3023. יָגֵעַ yagea (388b); from 3021; *weary, wearisome:*— wearisome(1), weary(2).

3024. יְגִעָה yegiah (388b); from 3021; *wearying:*— wearying(1).

3025. יָגֹר yagor (388c); a prim. root; *to be afraid, fear:*— afraid(3), dread(2).

3026. יְגַר שָׂהֲדוּתָא Yegar Sahadutha (1094d, 1113c); (Ara.) from an unused word and one corr. to 7717; "heap (of stones) of the testimony, " a memorial of Jacob and Laban:— Jegar-sahadutha(1).

3027. יַד yad (388d); a prim. root; *hand:*— abandon*(1), able(1), able*(1), addition*(1), afford*(4), against*(3), allegiance(1), allegiance*(1), along(1), alongside*(1), armpits*(1), arms(5), around(2), assist(1), assuredly(2), authority(9), axles(2), bank(1), banks(1), because(1), become*(1), beside(3), beside*(8), boldly*(2), bordered*(1), borders(1), bounty(3), care(7), charge(7), close*(1), coast(1), command(3), compulsion*(3), consecrate*(3), consecrated*(4), control(1), courage*(1), creditor*(1), custody(4), debt(1), defiantly*(1), delivered(1), deserved*(1), direction(10), directions(1), discouraged*(2), discouraging*(1), do(1), done(2), encourage*(1), encouraged*(3), enough(1), entrust*(1), entrusted(1), entrusted*(1), exhausted*(2), fist(1), force(1), four-fifths*(1), guarantor*(1), had(1), hand(859), handed(1), hands(303), hands*(1), have*(1), help*(1), helpless*(1), herself(1), himself(1), hold*(1), human agency(1), idle*(1), influence(1), jaws(1), labor(1), large*(2), leadership(1), left-handed*(2), let go*(1), lose courage*(1), manhood(1), means(11), means*(3), memorial(1), monument(2), much(1), much as he is able(1), much as one is able(1), next(2), next*(13), occasion(1), ordain*(4), ordained*(4), order(1), ordination*(1), part(1), parts(2), paw(2), place(4), pledged*(1), possess*(1), possession(4), power(44), prepared(1), prevailed*(1), reached*(1), rebelled*(2), reined about*(1), representative(1), responsible*(1), rule(5), seized*(2), service(1), side(5), sides(1), signpost(1), slackness*(1), some(1), spacious*(1), stays(2), strength(5), submitted*(1), support(1), support*(1), swore*(12), sworn*(4), tenons(6), through(60), times(2), undertake*(2), undertakings*(3), what he deserves*(1), wrists(3), wrists*(1), yield*(1), yourselves(2).

3028. יַד yad (1094d); (Ara.) corr. to 3027; *hand:*— attempts*(1), hand(12), hands(4), power(1).

3029. יְדָא yeda (1095a); (Ara.) corr. to 3034; *to praise:*— give thanks(1), giving thanks(1).

3030. יִדְאֲלָה Yidalah (391d); of unc. der.; a place in Zebulun:— Idalah(1).

3031. יִדְבָּשׁ Yidbash (185c); from the same as 1706; an Isr.:— Idbash(1).

3032. יָדַד yadad (391d); a prim. root; *to cast a lot:*— cast(3).

3033. יְדִדוּת yediduth (392a); from the same as 3039; *love:*— beloved(1).

3034. יָדָה yadah (392a); a prim. root; *to throw, cast:*— confess(10), confessed(3), confesses(1), confessing(2), gave(1), gave praise(1), give you thanks(5), give thanks(59), giving praise(1), giving thanks(3), glorify(1), hymns of thanksgiving(1), making confession(1), placed(1), praise(17), shoot(1), thank(5), thanksgiving(1), throw down(1).

3035. יִדּוֹ Yiddo (392a); from the same as 3039; two Isr.:— Iddo(1), Jaddai(1).

3036. יָדוֹן Yadon (193d); of unc. der.; a builder of the Jer. wall:— Jadon(1).

3037. יַדּוּעַ Yaddua (396a); from 3045; two Isr.:— Jaddua(3).

3038. יְדוּתוּן Yeduthun or

יְדֻתוּן Yeduthun (393a); from 3034; leader of a choir of the temple:— Jeduthun(14).

יַדַּי Yadday; see 3035.

3039. יָדִיד yadid (391d); from an unused word; *beloved:*— beloved(5), lovely(1), well-beloved(2).

3040. יְדִידָה Yedidah (392a); from the same as 3039; "beloved," mother of King Josiah:— Jedidah(1).

3041. יְדִידְיָה Yedideyah (392a); from 3039 and 3050; "beloved of Yah," a name of Solomon:— Jedidiah(1).

3042. יְדָיָה Yedayah (393a); from 3034 and 3050; perh. "praised by Yah," two Isr.:— Jedaiah(2).

3043. יְדִיעֲאֵל Yediael (396a); from 3045 and 410; "knowing God," three Isr.:— Jediael(6).

3044. יִדְלָף Yidlaph (393b); of unc. der.; a son of Nahor:— Jidlaph(1).

3045. יָדַע yada (393b); a prim. root; *to know:*— ability(1), acknowledge(4), acknowledged(2), acquaintances(5), acquainted(1), aware(6), becomes known(1), bring forth(1), cared(1), chosen(2), clearly understand(2), cohabit(1), comprehend(1), concern(2), concerned(1), consider(3), declare(1), detected(1), directed(1), discern(2), disciplined(1), discovered(3), distinguish(1), endowed(3), experienced(4), experiences(1), familiar friend(1), find(5), found(1), gain(1), had knowledge(1), had relations(6), had...relations(1), has(1), has regard(1), has...knowledge(1), have(4), have relations(3), have...knowledge(2), ignorant*(1), illiterate*(1), indeed learn(1), inform(1), informed(4), instruct(3), instructed(1), intimate friends(1), investigate(2), knew(38), know(542), know for certain(4), know with certainty(1), know assuredly(1), know well(1), knowing(5), knowledge(4), known(65), knows(54), knows well(1), lain*(1), leading(1), learn(7), learned(1), literate*(1), made himself known(2), made it known(1), made myself known(2), made known(10), make himself known(1), make his known(1), make it known(1), make my known(1), make myself known(4), make them known(1), make your known(1), make yourself known(1), make known(14), notice(2), observe(2), perceive(1), perceived(1), possibly know(1), predict(1), professional mourners(1), provided(1), raped(1), read*(1), realize(1), realized(5), recognize(2), recognized(1), regard(1), satisfied*(1), seems(1), show(3), shown(1), skillful(3), sure(1), take knowledge(1), take note(1), take notice(1), taught(2), teach(6), tell(3), tells(1), took notice(1), unaware*(1), unawares*(1), understand(10), understands(1), understood(3), unknown*(1), very well know(1), well aware(1).

3046. יְדַע yeda (1095a); (Ara.) corr. to 3045; *to know:*— ignorant*(1), inform(3), informed(3), knew(2), know(5), known(4), knows(1), learn(1), made known(6), make its known(3), make the known(3), make known(5), making the known(1), recognize(4), recognized(1), teach(1), understand(2).

3047. יָדָע Yada (395b); from 3045; "the shrewd one," a man of Judah:— Jada(2).

3048. יְדַעְיָה Yedayah (396a); from 3045 and 3050; "Yah has known," the name of several Isr.:— Jedaiah(11).

3049. יִדְּעֹנִי yiddeoni (396b); from 3045; *familiar spirit:*— spiritist(2), spiritists(9).

3050. יָהּ Yah (219c); contr. from 3068; the name of the God of Israel:— GOD(1), LORD(49).

3051. יָהַב yahab (396c); a prim. root; *to give:*— ascribe(10), choose(1), come(4), give(15), here(1), place(1), provide(1).

3052. יְהַב yehab (1095b); (Ara.) corr. to 3051; *to give:*— bestowed(1), gave(2), give(1), given(14), gives(1), granted(2), laid(1), paid(3), passed(1), yielded(1).

3053. יְהָב yehab (396d); from 3051; *a lot, what is given:*— burden(1).

3054. יָהַד yahad (397d); denom. vb. from 3063; *to become a Jew:*— became Jews(1).

3055. יְהֻד Yehud (397a); of unc. der.; a place in Dan:— Jehud(1).

3056. יֶהְדַּי Yahday (213a); from 1911; member of Caleb's family:— Jahdai(1).

3057. יְהֻדִיָּה Yehudiyyah (397c); fem. of 3064; *a Jewess:*— Jewish(1).

3058. יֵהוּא Yehu (219d); from 3068 and 1931; "the LORD is He," the name of several Isr.:— Jehu(58).

3059. יְהוֹאָחָז Yehoachaz (219d); from 3068 and 270; "Yah has grasped," the name of several Isr.:— Jehoahaz(19), Joahaz(1).

3060. יְהוֹאָשׁ Yehoash (219d); from 3068 and perh. 784; "Yah is strong," the name of several Isr.:— Jehoash(17), Joash(47).

3061. יְהוּד Yehud (1095c); (Ara.) corr. to 3063; the S. kingdom, named for one of the twelve tribes:— Judah(7).

3062. יְהוּדָאִין Yehudain (1095c); (Ara.) from 3061; an inhab. of Judah:— Jews(9), Judah(1).

3063. יְהוּדָה Yehudah (397a); prob. from 3034; prob. "praised," a son of Jacob, also his desc., the S. kingdom, also four Isr.:— Jews(1), Judah(815), Judah's(2).

3064. יְהוּדִי Yehudi (397c); from 3063; *Jewish:*— Jew(10), Jewish(4), Jews(59), Jews'(1), Judeans(1).

3065. יְהוּדִי Yehudi (397c); from the same as 3064; "Jewish," an officer of Jehoiakim:— Jehudi(4).

3066. יְהוּדִית Yehudith (397c); fem. of 3064; *Jewish:*— Judean(4), language of Judah(2).

3067. יְהוּדִית Yehudith (397c); from the same as 3066; Esau's wife:— 1,365*(1), Judith(1).

3068. יהוה Yhvh (i.e. יְהֹוָה **Yehovah** or יַהְוֶה **Yahveh**) [217d]; from 1933b; the proper name of the God of Israel:— GOD(314), LORD(6399), LORD'S(111).

3069. יהוה Yhvh (217d); the same as 3068, q.v.

3070. יהוה יִרְאֶה Yhvh Yireh (217d); see 3068 and 7200.

3071. יהוה נִסִּי Yhvh Nissi (217d); see 3068 and 5251.

3072. יהוה צִדְקֵנוּ Yhvh Tsidqenu (217d); from 3068 and 6664; "the LORD is our righteousness," a symbolic name for Jer. and for Messiah.

3073. יהוה שָׁלוֹם Yhvh Shalom (217d); see 3068 and 7965.

3074. יהוה שָׁמָּה Yhvh Shammah (217d); see 3068 and 8033.

3075. יְהוֹזָבָד Yehozabad (220a); from 3068 and 2064; "the LORD has bestowed," name of a number of Isr.:— Jehozabad(4).

3076. יְהוֹחָנָן Yehochanan (220b); from 3068 and 2603a; "the LORD has been gracious," the name of a number of Isr., a lso a son of Tobiah:— Jehohanan(5), Johanan(28).

3077. יְהוֹיָדָע Yehoyada (220b); from 3068 and 3045; "the LORD knows," the name of several Isr.:— Jehoiada(51), Joiada(5).

3078. יְהוֹיָכִין Yehoyakin (220c); from 3068 and 3559; "the LORD appoints," a king of Judah:— Coniah(3), Jehoiachin(10), Jehoiachin's(1).

3079. יְהוֹיָקִים Yehoyaqim (220c); from 3068 and 6965; "the LORD raises up," three Isr.:— Jehoiakim(36), Joiakim(4).

3080. יְהוֹיָרִיב Yehoyarib (220d); from 3068 and 7378; "the LORD contends," two Isr., also a priestly family:— Jehoiarib(2), Joiarib(5).

3081. יְהוּכַל Yehukal (220d); from 3068 and 3201; "the LORD is able," a courtier of King Zedekiah:— Jehucal(1), Jucal(1).

3082. יְהוֹנָדָב Yehonadab (220d); from 3068 and 5068; "the LORD is noble," a Rechabite, also a nephew of David:— Jehonadab(3), Jonadab(12).

3083. יְהוֹנָתָן Yehonathan (220d); from 3068 and 5414; "the LORD has given," the name of a number of Isr.:— Jehonathan(2), Jonathan(120), Jonathan's(2).

3084. יְהוֹסֵף Yehoseph (415c); the same as 3130, q.v.

3085. יְהוֹעַדָּה Yehoaddah (221a); from 3068 and 5710b; "the LORD has adorned," a desc. of Saul:— Jehoaddah(2).

3086. יְהוֹעַדִּין Yehoaddin or

יְהוֹעַדָּן Yehoaddan (221b); from 3068 and perh. 5727; perh. "the LORD delights," mother of King Amaziah:— Jehoaddan(1), Jehoaddin(1).

3087. יְהוֹצָדָק Yehotsadaq (221b); from 3068 and 6664; "the LORD is righteous," father of Joshua the high priest:— Jehozadak(8), Jozadak(4).

3088. יְהוֹרָם Yehoram (221b); from 3068 and 7311; "the LORD is exalted," the name of several Isr., also a king of H amath:— Jehoram(22), Joram(7).

3089. יְהוֹשֶׁבַע Yehosheba (221b); from 3068 and 7650; "the LORD is an oath," wife of Jehoiada the priest:— Jehosheba(1).

3090. יְהוֹשַׁבְעַת Yehoshabath (221c); alternate spelling of 3089, q.v.:— Jehoshabeath(2).

3091. יְהוֹשׁוּעַ Yehoshua or

יְהוֹשֻׁעַ Yehoshua (221c); from 3068 and 3467; "the LORD is salvation," Moses' successor, also the name of a number of Isr.:— Jeshua(28), Joshua(219).

3092. יְהוֹשָׁפָט Yehoshaphat (221d); from 3068 and 8199; "the LORD has judged," the name of a number of Isr.:— Jehoshaphat(84), Joshaphat(2).

3093. יָהִיר yahir (397d); from an unused word; *proud, haughty:*— haughty(2).

3094. יְהַלֶּלְאֵל Yehallelel (239c); from 1984b and 410; "he shall praise God," two Isr.:— Jehallelel(2).

3095. יַהֲלֹם yahalom (240d); from 1986; (a precious stone) perh. *jasper* or *onyx:*— diamond(3).

3096. יַהַץ Yahats (397d); from an unused word; a place in Moab:— Jahaz(7), Jahzah(2).

3097. יוֹאָב Yoab (222a); from 3068 and 1; "the LORD is father," three Isr.:— Joab(136), Joab's(8).

3098. יוֹאָח Yoach (222a); from 3068 and 251; "the LORD is brother," the name of several Isr.:— Joah(11).

3099. יוֹאָחָז Yoachaz (219d); a form of 3059, q.v.:— Joahaz(4).

3100. יוֹאֵל Yoel (222a); from 3068 and 410; prob. "the LORD is God," the name of a number of Isr.:— Joel(20).

3101. יוֹאָשׁ Yoash (219d); the same as 3060, q.v.

3102. יוֹב Yob (398a); of unc. der.; a son of Issachar:— Iob(1).

3103. יוֹבָב Yobab (384d); from 2980; a son of Joktan, also his desc., also two non-Isr. kings, also two Benjamites:— Jobab(9).

3104. יוֹבֵל yobel or

יֹבֵל yobel (385c); from 2986; *a ram, ram's horn* (a wind instrument):— jubilee(21), ram's(1), ram's horn(1), rams' horns(4).

3105. יוּבַל yubal (385b); from 2986; *a stream:*— stream(1).

3106. יוּבָל Yubal (385b); from 2986; a son of Lamech:— Jubal(1).

3107. יוֹזָבָד Yozabad (220a); the same as 3075, q.v.:— Jozabad(10).

3108. יוֹזָכָר Yozakar (222b); from 3068 and 2142; "the LORD has remembered," murderer of King Joash:— Jozacar(1).

3109. יוֹחָא Yocha (398a); of unc. der.; two Isr.:— Joha(2).

3110. יוֹחָנָן Yochanan (220b); the same as 3076, q.v.

3111. יוֹיָדָע Yoyada (220b); the same as 3077, q.v.

3112. יוֹיָכִין Yoyakin (220c); the same as 3078, q.v.

3113. יוֹיָקִים Yoyaqim (220c); the same as 3079, q.v.

3114. יוֹיָרִיב Yoyarib (220d); the same as 3080, q.v.

3115. יוֹכֶבֶד Yokebed (222c); from 3068 and 3513; "the LORD is glory," mother of Moses:— Jochebed(2).

3116. יוּכַל Yukal (220d); the same as 3081, q.v.

3117. יוֹם yom (398a); a prim. root; *day:*— afternoon*(1), age(8), age*(1), all(1), always*(14), amount*(2), battle(1), birthday*(1), Chronicles*(38), completely*(1), continually*(14), course*(1), daily(22), daily the days(1), day(1115), day of the days(1), day that the period(1), day's(6), day's every day(1), daylight*(1), days(635), days on the day(1), days to day(1), days you shall daily(1), days ago(1), days'(11), each(1), each day(4), entire(2), eternity(1), evening*(1), ever in your life*(1), every day(2), fate(1), first(5), forever*(11), forevermore*(1), full(5), full year(1), future*(1), holiday*(3), later*(2), length(1), life(12), life*(1), lifetime(2), lifetime*(1), live(1), long(2), long as i live(1), long*(11), midday*(1), now(5), older*(1), once(2), period(3), perpetually*(2), present(1), recently(1), reigns(1), ripe*(1), short-lived*(1), so long*(1), some time(1), survived*(2), time(45), time*(1), times*(2), today(172), today*(1), usual(1), very old*(1), when(10), when the days(1), whenever(1), while(3), whole(2), year(10), yearly(5), years(13), yesterday*(1).

3118. יוֹם yom (1095c); (Ara.) corr. to 3117; *day:*— daily(1), day(3), days(10), period(1).

3119. יוֹמָם yomam (401b); from 3117; *daytime, by day:*— daily(1), day(48), daytime(2).

3120. יָוָן Yavan (402a); from the same as 3123; a son of Japheth, also his desc. and their land:— Greece(4), Javan(7).

3121. יָוֵן yaven (401c); of unc. der.; *mire:*— mire(1), miry(1).

3122. יוֹנָדָב Yonadab (220d); the same as 3082, q.v.

3123. יוֹנָה yonah (401d); from an unused word; *dove:*— dove(13), dove's(1), doves(8), pigeon(1), pigeons(9).

3124. יוֹנָה Yonah (402a); from the same as 3123; an Isr. prophet:— Jonah(18), Jonah's(1).

3125. יְוָנִי Yevani (402b); from 3120; desc. of Javan:— Greeks(1).

3126. יוֹנֵק yoneq (413c); act. part. of 3243; *a young plant, sapling:*— tender shoot(1).

3127. יוֹנֶקֶת yoneqeth (413c); fem. of 3126; *a young shoot, twig:*— shoots(5), young twigs(1).

3128. יוֹנַת אֵלֶם רְחֹקִים Yonath Elem Rechoqim (401d); from 3123, 482 and 7350; "dove of distant silences," prob. the name of a melody.

3129. יוֹנָתָן Yonathan (220d); the same as 3083, q.v.

3130. יוֹסֵף Yoseph (415c); from 3254; "he increases," a son of Jacob, also the name of several Isr.:— Joseph(194), Joseph's(19).

3131. יוֹסִפְיָה Yosiphyah (415d); from act. part. of 3254 and from 3050; "Yah adds," an Isr.:— Josiphiah(1).

3132. יוֹעֵאלָה Yoelah (418d); from 3276; "may He avail," one of David's heroes:— Joelah(1).

3133. יוֹעֵד Yoed (222c); from 3068 and 5707; "the LORD is a witness," a Benjamite:— Joed(1).

3134. יוֹעֶזֶר Yoezer (222c); from 3068 and 5828; "the LORD is a help," one of David's mighty men:— Joezer(1).

3135. יוֹעָשׁ Yoash (222c); from 3068 and 5789; "the LORD has aided," two Isr.:— Joash(2).

3136a. יוֹצָדָק Yotsadaq (221b); the same as 3087, q.v.

3136b. יוֹצָדָק Yotsadaq (1095c); (Ara.) corr. to 3136a; an Isr.:— Jozadak(1).

3137. יוֹקִים Yoqim (220c); the same as 3079, q.v.:— Jokim(1).

3138. יוֹרֶה yoreh (435c); act. part. of 3384; *the early rain:*— autumn rain(1), early(1), rain*(1).

3139. יוֹרָה Yorah (435c); from 3384; an Isr. family:— Jorah(1).

3140. יוֹרַי Yoray (436c); from 3384; "He teaches," a Gadite:— Jorai(1).

3141. יוֹרָם Yoram (221b); the same as 3088, q.v.:— Joram(20).

3142. יוּשַׁב חֶסֶד Yushab Chesed (1000b); from 7725 and 2617a; a son of Zerubbabel:— Jushab-hesed(1).

3143. יוֹשִׁבְיָה Yoshibyah (444a); from 3427 and 3050; "Yah causes to dwell," a Simeonite:— Joshibiah(1).

3144. יוֹשָׁה Yoshah (444d); from 8454; a Simeonite:— Joshah(1).

3145. יוֹשַׁוְיָה Yoshavyah (444d); from 3050 and the same as 8454; one of David's heroes:— Joshaviah(1).

3146. יוֹשָׁפָט Yoshaphat (221d); the same as 3092, q.v.

3147. יוֹתָם Yotham (222d); from 3068 and 8535; "the LORD is perfect," three Isr.:— Jotham(24).

3148. יוֹתֵר yother (452c); act. part. of 3498; *superiority, advantage, excess:*— addition(1), advantage(3), beyond(1), extremely(1), more(1), overly(1).

3149. יְזִוְאֵל Yezivel or

יְזִיאֵל Yeziel (402b); from an unused word; one of David's heroes:— Jeziel(1).

3150. יִזִּיָּה Yizziyyah (633c); from 5137a and 3050; "may Yah sprinkle," an Isr.:— Izziah(1).

3151. יָזִיז Yaziz (265c); from the same as 2123a; an officer of David:— Jaziz(1).

3152a. יִזְלִיאָה Yizliah (272c); of unc. der.; a Benjamite:— Izliah(1).

3152b. יָזַן yazan (402c); another reading for 2109, q.v.

3153. יְזַנְיָה Yezanyah or

יְזַנְיָהוּ Yezanyahu (24d); the same as 2970, q.v.:— Jezaniah(2).

3154. יֶזַע yeza (402c); from an unused word; *sweat:*— sweat(1).

3155. יִזְרָח Yizrach (280d); from 2224; a descriptive title for one of David's men:— Izrahite(1).

3156. יִזְרַחְיָה Yizrachyah (280d); from 2224 and 3050; "Yah will shine," two Isr.:— Izrahiah(2), Jezrahiah(1).

3157. יִזְרְעֶאל Yizreel (283b); from 2232 and 410; "God sows," two Isr., also two cities in Isr., also a valley in N. Isr.:— Jezreel(36).

3158. יִזְרְעֵאלִי Yizreeli (283c); from 3157; an inhab. of Jezreel:— Jezreelite(8).

3159. יִזְרְעֵאלִית Yizreelith (283c); fem. of 3158, q.v.:— Jezreelitess(5).

3160. יְחֻבָּה Yechubbah (285d); from 2245; a desc. of Asher:— Jehubbah(1).

3161. יָחַד yachad (402d); a prim. root; *to be united:*— unite(1), united(2).

3162. יַחַד yachad (403a); from 3161; *unitedness:*— alike(1), all(4), altogether(2), altogether*(1), both(4), completely(2), each other(1), one accord(1), safely(1), together(26), together in unity(1), united(1).

3163. יַחְדּוֹ Yachdo (403c); from 3161; a Gileadite:— Jahdo(1).

3164a. יַחְדָּו yachdav (403b); from 3161; *together:*— alike(3), all(1), all at once(1), altogether(4), same(1), together(78), well(3).

3164b. יַחְדִּיאֵל Yachdiel (292d); from 2302b and 410; "God gives joy," a Manassite:— Jahdiel(1).

3165. יֶחְדְּיָהוּ Yechdeyahu (292d); from 2302b and 3050; "may Yah give joy," two Isr.:— Jehdeiah(2).

3166. יַחֲזִיאֵל Yachaziel (303c); from 2372 and 410; "God sees," the name of several Isr.:— Jahaziel(6).

3167. יַחְזְיָה Yachzeyah (303c); from 2372 and 3050; "Yah sees," an Isr.:— Jahzeiah(1).

3168. יְחֶזְקֵאל Yechezqel (306b); from 2388 and 410; "God strengthens," two Isr.:— Ezekiel(2), Jehezkel(1).

3169. יְחִזְקִיָּה Yechizqiyyah or

יְחִזְקִיָּהוּ Yechizqiyyahu (306a); the same as 2396, q.v.:— Jehizkiah(1).

3170. יַחְזֵרָה Yachzerah (306c, 403d); from the same as 2386; an Isr. priest:— Jahzerah(1).

3171. יְחִיאֵל Yechiel or

יְחִוְאֵל Yechavel (313c); from 2421a and 410; "may God live," the name of a number of Isr.:— Jehiel(14).

3172. יְחִיאֵלִי Yechieli (313d); from 3171; desc. of Jehiel:— Jehieli(1), Jehielites(1).

3173. יָחִיד yachid (402d); from 3161; *only, only one, solitary:*— lonely(2), one and child(1), only(5), only son(4).

3174. יְחִיָּה Yechiyyah (313d); from 2421a and 3050; "may Yah live," an Isr.:— Jehiah(1).

3175. יָחִיל yachil (404a); from 3176; *waiting:*— waits(1).

3176. יָחַל yachal (403d); a prim. root; *to wait, await:*— delay(1), have hope(2), hope(13), hoped(1), wait(13), wait expectantly(2), waited(7), waste time(1).

3177. יַחְלְאֵל Yachleel (404b); from 3176 and 410; "wait for God," a Zebulunite:— Jahleel(2).

3178. יַחְלְאֵלִי Yachleeli (404b); from 3177; desc. of Jahleel:— Jahleelites(1).

3179. יָחַם yacham (404b); a prim. root; *to be hot, to conceive:*— conceived(1), mate(1), mating(2).

3180. יַחְמוּר yachmur (331c); from 2560c; *a roebuck:*— roebuck(1), roebucks(1).

3181. יַחְמַי Yachmay (327d); from the same as 2524; "may He protect," a man of Issachar:— Jahmai(1).

3182. יָחֵף yacheph (405a); from an unused word; *barefoot:*— barefoot(4), unshod(1).

3183. **יַחְצְאֵל Yachtseel** (345d); from 2673 and 410; "God apportions," a son of Naphtali:— Jahzeel(2).

3184. **יַחְצְאֵלִי Yachtseeli** (345d); from 3183; desc. of Jahzeel:— Jahzeelites(1).

3185. **יַחְצִיאֵל Yachtsiel** (345d); the same as 3183, q.v.:— Jahziel(1).

3186. **יָחַר yachar** (29b); the same as 309, q.v.

3187. **יָחַשׂ yachas** (405b); from the same as 3188; *to enroll oneself* or *be enrolled by genealogy:*— ancestral(2), enrolled by genealogies(2), enrolled by genealogy(5), enrolled in the genealogies(1), enrolled in the genealogy(1), enrolled genealogically(1), genealogical enrollment(4), genealogical list(1), genealogically enrolled(1), genealogy(2), registration*(2).

3188. **יַחַשׂ yachas** (405b); from an unused word; *genealogy:*— genealogy(1).

3189. **יַחַת Yachath** (367a); from 2846; "He will snatch up," the name of several Isr.:— Jahath(8).

3190. **יָטַב yatab** (405c); a prim. root; *to be good, well, glad,* or *pleasing:*— adorned(1), amend(3), better(3), better he made(1), bless(1), celebrating*(1), deals well(1), do(1), do it well(1), do them good(1), do them good(1), do you good(1), do good(1), do good(12), do well(3), do...good(1), does(1), does...good(1), done good(1), done well(1), found favor(1), glad(1), go well(6), goes well(1), good(1), good(2), good that i do(1), good reason(3), happy(1), joyful(1), make(1), makes a cheerful(1), makes...acceptable(1), merry(3), pleasant(1), please(1), please the better(1), pleased(2), pleased*(9), pleases*(1), pleasing(2), prosper(4), reform(1), seemed good(2), seemed reasonable(1), seems(1), seems best(1), seems good(1), shown(1), skillfully(2), stately(2), surely prosper(1), thoroughly(4), treat you better(1), treated...well(1), trims(1), truly amend(1), very(1), very small(1), well(13), well you prepare(1).

3191. **יְטַב yetab** (1095d); (Ara.) corr. to 3190; *to be good* or *pleasing:*— good(1).

3192. **יָטְבָה Yotbah** (406a); from 3190; "pleasantness," a city prob. in Judah:— Jotbah(1).

3193. **יָטְבָתָה Yotbathah** (406a); from 3190; "pleasantness," a place in the desert:— Jotbathah(3).

3194. **יֻטָּה Yuttah** or

יוּטָה Yutah (641b); from 5186; a city in Judah:— Juttah(2).

3195. **יְטוּר Yetur** (377b); from the same as 2905; a son of Ishmael, also his desc. and the region where they lived:— Jetur(3).

3196. **יַיִן yayin** (406b); from an unused word; *wine:*— banquet(1), grape(1), wine(136).

3197. **יַךְ yak** (406d); scribal error for 3027, q.v.

יְכוֹנְיָה Yekoneyah; see 3204.

3198. **יָכַח yakach** (406d); a prim. root; *to decide, adjudge, prove:*— adjudicates(1), appointed(2), argue(3), argument prove(1), chastened(1), cleared(1), complained(1), correct(2), decide(3), dispute(1), make a decision(1), offer reproof(1), plead(1), prove(1), reason(2), rebuke(6), rebukes(2), refuted(1), render decisions(2), rendered judgment(1), reprove(9), reproved(2), reprover(1), reproves(7), surely reprove(2), umpire(1).

3199. **יָכִין Yakin** (467c); from 3559; "He will establish," an Isr. name:— Jachin(8).

3200. **יָכִינִי Yakini** (467c); from 3199; desc. of Jachin:— Jachinites(1).

3201. **יָכֹל yakol** or

יָכוֹל yakol (407b); a prim. root; *to be able, have power:*— able(41), able at all(1), allowed(4), can(15), can i endure(2), can do(1), cannot*(47), could(41), endure(3), had your way(1), incapable*(1), may(1), overcome(3), overpower(2), overpowered(1), prevail(8), prevailed(6), succeed(1), surely overcome(1), surely prevail(1), unable*(10).

3202. **יְכֵל yekel** or

יְכִיל yekil (1095d); (Ara.) corr. to 3201; *to be able:*— able(7), been able(2), could(2), overpowering(1).

3203. **יְכָלְיָה Yekolyah** or

יְכָלְיָהוּ Yekolyahu or

יְכִילְיָה Yekileyah (408a); from 3201 and 3050; "Yah has been able," mother of King Azariah:— Jechiliah(1), Jecoliah(1).

3204. **יְכָנְיָה Yekonyah** or

יְכָנְיָהוּ Yekonyahu or

יְכוֹנְיָה Yekoneyah (220c); the same as 3078, q.v.:— Jeconiah(7).

3205. **יָלַד yalad** (408b); a prim. root; *to bear, bring forth, beget:*— bear(13), bearing(3), bears(6), became(1), became the father(144), become the father(2), become the fathers(1), beget(3), begetting(1), begot(2), begotten(3), birth(2), birthday*(1), bore(85), born(73), borne(20), bring forth(5), brings forth(1), brought them forth(1), brought forth(6), child(2), childbirth(10), children(1), children born(1), deliver(1), delivered(1), descended(2), father(1), fathered(2), fathers(1), gave me birth(1), gave you birth(2), gave birth(25), gave birth to a child(2), give birth(13), give birth the midwife(1), give delivery(1), given it birth(1), given birth(4), gives birth(2), gives delivery(1), giving birth(2), had(17), had sons(1), has(1), have(2), labor(5), labor has borne(1), labor the midwife(1), laid(1), midwife(1), midwives(6), produced(1), registered by ancestry(1), sired(1), sires(2), takes effect(1).

3206. **יֶלֶד yeled** (409b); from 3205; *child, son, boy, youth:*— boy(7), boys(3), child(32), child's(2), children(27), lad(2), lads(1), young(3), young men(6), youths(5).

3207. **יַלְדָּה yaldah** (409c); fem. of 3206; *girl, maiden:*— girl(1), girls(1), young girl(1).

3208. **יַלְדוּת yalduth** (409c); from 3205; *childhood, youth:*— childhood(2), youth(1).

3209. **יִלּוֹד yillod** (409c); from 3205; *born:*— born(4), who were born(1).

3210. **יָלוֹן Yalon** (410a, 1124a); of unc. der.; an Isr.:— Jalon(1).

3211. **יָלִיד yalid** (409d); from 3205; *born:*— born(1), children(1), descendants(5), homeborn*(1), who are born(1), who is born(2), who were born(2).

3212. **יָלַךְ yalak** (229d); the same as 1980, q.v.

3213. **יָלַל yalal** (410b); a prim. root; *to howl, make a howling:*— howl(1), turn to wailing(1), wail(25), wailed(1), wailing(2), wails(1).

3214. **יְלֵל yelel** (410b); from 3213; *a howling:*— howling(1).

3215. **יְלָלָה yelalah** (410b); fem. of 3214; *a howling:*— wail(3), wailing(1).

3216. **יָלַע yala** (534b); the same as 3886a, q.v.

3217. **יַלֶּפֶת yallepheth** (410c); from an unused word; *scab, scurf* (an eruptive disease):— scabs(2).

3218. **יֶלֶק yeleq** (410c); from an unused word; (a kind of) *locust:*— creeping locust(5), locust(1), locusts(2), young locusts(1).

3219. **יַלְקוּט yalqut** (545a); from 3950; *receptacle,* perh. *a wallet:*— pouch(1).

3220. **יָם yam** (410d); of unc. der.; *sea:*— red*(24), sea(278), seacoast*(5), seas(27), seashore(1), seashore*(9), south(1), west(59), west side(4), western(1), westward(12).

3221. **יָם yam** (1095d); (Ara.) corr. to 3220; *sea:*— sea(2).

3222. **יֵם yem** or

יֵמִם yemim (411b); from the same as 3220; perh. *hot springs:*— hot springs(1).

3223. **יְמוּאֵל Yemuel** (410c); of unc. der.; a son of Simeon:— Jemuel(2).

3224. **יְמִימָה Yemimah** (410d); of unc. der.; a daughter of Job:— Jemimah(1).

3225. **יָמִין yamin** (411c); from an unused word; *right hand:*— left-handed*(2), right(49), right hand(75), right side(8), south(4), southward(1).

3226. **יָמִין Yamin** (412c); from the same as 3225; three Isr.:— Jamin(6).

3227. **יְמִינִי yemini** (412a); another reading for 3233, q.v.

3228. **יְמִינִי Yamini** (412c); from 3226; desc. of Jamin:— Benjamite*(3), Jaminites(1).

3229. **יִמְלָא Yimla** or

יִמְלָה Yimlah (571c); from 4390; father of the prophet Micaiah:— Imla(1), Imla's(1), Imlah(2).

3230. **יַמְלֵךְ Yamlek** (576a); from the same as 4428; a Simeonite:— Jamlech(1).

3231. **יָמַן yaman** (412b); denom. vb. from 3225; *to go to* or *choose the right, to use the right hand:*— go to the right(2), right hand(1), turn to the right(2).

3232. **יִמְנָה Yimnah** (412c); from the same as 3225; "good fortune," two Isr.:— Imnah(4), Imnites(1).

3233. **יְמָנִי yemani** (412b); from the same as 3225; *right hand, right:*— right(30), right-hand(2), south(1).

3234. **יִמְנָע Yimna** (586b); from 4513; "He will restrain," an Asherite:— Imna(1).

3235. **יָמַר yamar** (413a); a prim. root; perh. *to exchange:*— boast(1).

3236. **יִמְרָה Yimrah** (598c); from 4784; an Asherite:— Imrah(1).

3237. **יָמַשׁ yamash** (413a); another reading for 4184, q.v.

3238. **יָנָה yanah** (413a); a prim. root; *to oppress, maltreat,* perh. *suppress:*— do him wrong(1), mistreat(2), oppress(3), oppresses(1), oppressing(1), oppressor(2), oppressors(1), subdue(1), thrusting(1), tyrannical(1), wrong(3), wronged(2).

3239a. **יָנוֹחַ Yanoach** (629c); from 5117; a place in N. Isr.:— Janoah(1).

3239b. **יָנוֹחָה Yanochah** (629c); from 5117; a place on the border of Ephraim:— Janoah(2).

3240. **יָנַח yanach** (628a); the same as 5117, q.v.

3241. **יָנִים Yanim** or

יָנוּם Yanum (630b); from 5123; a city in Judah:— Janum(1).

3242. **יְנִיקָה yeniqah** (413d); from 3243; *a young shoot, twig:*— young twigs(1).

3243. **יָנַק yanaq** (413b); a prim. root; *to suck:*— draw(1), infant(3), infants(2), milking(1), nurse(11), nursed(3), nurses(1), nursing(1), nursing babes(1), nursing infant(1), nursing infants*(1), nursling(1), suck(4), sucks(1).

3244. **יַנְשׁוּף yanshuph** or

יַנְשׁוֹף yanshoph (676b); from 5398; (a ceremonially unclean bird) perh. *an owl:*— great owl(2), owl(1).

3245. **יָסַד yasad** (413d); a prim. root; *to establish, found, fix:*— appointed(2), established(4), firmly placed(1), found(1), foundation(6), foundation will be laid(1), foundations i will lay(1), foundations which laid(1), founded(11), given orders(1), laid(5), laid its foundations(1), laid the foundation(3), laid the foundations(1), lay its foundation(1), lay the foundation(1), laying(1), lays the foundation(1), make(1), rebuilding(1), set(1), take counsel(1), took counsel(1).

3246. **יְסֻד yesud** (414b); from 3245; *foundation, beginning:*— began(1).

3247. **יְסוֹד yesod** (414b); from 3245; *foundation, base:*— base(9), foundation(5), foundations(4), thigh(1).

3248. **יְסוּדָה yesudah** (414b); fem. of 3246; *foundation:*— foundation(1).

3249. **יָסוּר yasur** (693b); the same as 5493, q.v.

3250. **יִסּוֹר yissor** (416b); from 3256; *one who reproves, faultfinder:*— faultfinder(1).

3251. **יָסַךְ yasak** (691d); the same as 5480a, q.v.

3252. **יִסְכָּה Yiskah** (414d); of unc. der.; a daughter of Haran:— Iscah(1).

3253. **יִסְמַכְיָהוּ Yismakyahu** (702b); from 5564 and 3050; "Yah has sustained," a Korahite:— Ismachiah(1).

3254. **יָסַף yasaph** (414d); a prim. root; *to add:*— add(26), add to it more(1), added(8), added...more(1), adding(3), adds(4), again(58), again*(9), another(3), another*(1), any more(1), anymore(4), anymore*(1), continue(5), continued(2), continued*(1), did(3), did not again(1), do it again(4), else(1), even(1), exceed(1), farther(1), further(2), give(1), give you increase(1), grow(1), increase(4), increase you a more(1), increased(6), increases(3), increasing(2), intensify(1), join(1), longer(9), longer*(7), more(18), more shall be done(1), more also(1), more*(5), once more*(3), once*(1), prolong(1), prolongs(1), repeated*(1), surpass(1), worse*(1), yet more(2), yet more and more(1).

3255. **יְסַף yesaph** (1095d); (Ara.) corr. to 3254; *to add:*— added(1).

3256. **יָסַר yasar** (415d); a prim. root; *to discipline, chasten, admonish:*— admonished(2), chasten(5), chastens(1), chastise(4), chastised(2), correct(4), corrects(1), discipline(4), disciplined(4), disciplined me severely(1), disciplines(1), disciplining(1), gave instruction(1), instructed(2), instructs(2), punish(2), take warning(1), taught(1), trained(1), turned(1), warned(1).

3257. **יָע ya** (418b); from 3261; *a shovel:*— shovels(9).

3258. **יַעְבֵּץ Yabets** (716d); of unc. der.; a desc. of Judah, also a place in Judah:— Jabez(4).

3259. **יָעַד yaad** (416d); a prim. root; *to appoint:*— agreed to meet(1), appointed(3), assemble(1), assembled(3), assigned(1), designated(1), designates(1), gather(1), gathered(3), made an appointment(2), meet(7), meet together(1), set(1), summon(3).

3260. **יֶעְדִּי Yedi** or

יֶעְדּוֹ Yedo (418a); of unc. der.; an Isr.:— Iddo(1).

3261. **יָעָה yaah** (418a); a prim. root; *to sweep together:*— sweep away(1).

3262. **יְעוּאֵל Yeuel** (418b); from 3261 and 410; "carried away by God," the name of several Isr.:— Jeiel(12), Jeuel(2).

3263. **יְעוּץ Yeuts** (734b); from 5779; a Benjamite:— Jeuz(1).

3264. **יָעוֹר yaor** (420c); the same as 3293a, q.v.

3265. **יָעוּר Yaor** (735d); from 5782; an Isr.:— Jair(1).

3266. **יְעוּשׁ Yeush** (736b); from 5789; "he comes to help," an Edomite, also the name of several Isr.:— Jeush(9).

3267. **יָעַז yaaz** (418b); a prim. root; perh. *barbarous:*— fierce(1).

3268. **יַעֲזִיאֵל Yaaziel** (739d); from 5810 and 410; a Levite:— Jaaziel(1).

3269. **יַעֲזִיָּהוּ Yaaziyyahu** (739d); from 5810 and 3050; a Levite:— Jaaziah(2).

3270. **יַעְזֵיר Yazer** or

יַעְזֵר Yazer (741b); from 5826; a place E. of the Jordan:— Jazer(14).

3271. **יָעַט yaat** (418c); another reading for 5844a, q.v.

3272a. **יְעַט yaet** (1096a); (Ara.) from 3272b; *counselor:*— counselors(2).

3272b. **יְעַט yeat** (1095d); (Ara.) corr. to 3289; *to advise:*— consulted together(1).

3273. **יְעִיאֵל Yeiel** (418b); the same as 3262, q.v.

3274. **יְעִישׁ Yeish** (736b); the same as 3266, q.v.

3275. **יַעְכָּן Yakan** (747c); from the same as 5912; a Gadite:— Jacan(1).

3276. **יָעַל yaal** (418c); a prim. root; *to confer* or *gain profit* or *benefit:*— avail(1), furnish the slightest(1), gain(1), profit(17), profitable(1), slightest benefit(1), things of profit(1).

3277. **יָעֵל yael** (418d); from an unused word; *mountain goat:*— mountain goats*(1), wild goats(1), Wild Goats(1).

3278. **יָעֵל Yael** (418d); from the same as 3277; a Canaanite woman:— Jael(6).

3279. **יַעְלָא Yaala** or

יַעֲלָה Yaalah (419a); from the same as 3277; an Isr.:— Jaala(1), Jaalah(1).

3280. **יַעֲלָה yaalah** (418d); fem. of 3277; *female mountain goat:*— doe(1).

3281. **יַעְלָם Yalam** (761c); from 5956; an Edomite:— Jalam(4).

3282. **יַעַן yaan** (774d); from 6030a; *on account of, because:*— because(54), because*(35), definitely because(1), inasmuch*(2), reason(1), since(1), so*(1), why*(1).

3283. **יָעֵן yaen** (419a); from an unused word; *ostrich:*— ostriches(1).

3284. **יַעֲנָה yaanah** (419a); fem. of 3283; perh. *greed:*— ostrich(2), ostriches(5), ostriches*(1).

3285. **יַעֲנַי Yaanay** (775a); from 6030a; an Isr.:— Janai(1).

3286. **יָעֵף yaeph** (419b); a prim. root; *to be weary, faint:*— become exhausted(2), become weary(3), becomes weary(1), extreme(1), grow weary(2).

3287. **יָעֵף yaeph** (419b); from 3286; *weary, faint:*— weary(2), weary one(1), whoever is faint(1).

3288. **יְעָף yeaph** (419b); from 3286; *weariness, faintness:*— weariness(1).

3289. **יָעַץ yaats** (419c); a prim. root; *to advise, counsel:*— advise(1), advisers(1), conspire(1), conspired(1), consult(2), consulted(8), counsel(4), counsel do you give(2), counsel you have given(1), counseled(7), Counselor(1), counselor(10), counselors(11), decided(3), devised(2), devises(2), formed(1), gave(1), give(2), give you advice(1), give you counsel(1), given(4), planned(8), purposed(1), purposing(1), receive counsel(1), take counsel(1), took counsel(1).

3290. **יַעֲקֹב Yaaqob** (784d); from the same as 6119; a son of Isaac, also his desc.:— Jacob(331), Jacob's(18).

3291. **יַעֲקֹבָה Yaaqobah** (785b); from the same as 6119; a Simeonite:— Jaakobah(1).

3292. **יַעֲקָן Yaaqan** (785c); the same as 6130, q.v.:— Jaakan(1).

3293a. **יַעַר yaar** (420c); from an unused word; *wood, forest, thicket:*— forest(51), forests(2), Jaar(1), thickets(1), woodland(1), woods(2).

3293b. **יַעַר yaar** (421a); from an unused word; *honeycomb:*— honeycomb(1).

3294. **יַעְרָה Yarah** (421a); from the same as 3293b; a desc. of Saul:— Jarah(2).

3295. **יַעְרָה yarah** (421a); fem. of 3293b; *honeycomb:*— honeycomb*(1).

3296. **יַעְרֵי אֹרְגִים Yaare Oregim** (421b); from 3293b and 707; father of Elhanan:— Jaare-oregim(1).

3297. **יְעָרִים Yearim** (421b); from the same as 3293b; a mountain in Pal.:— Jearim(1).

3298. **יַעֲרֶשְׁיָה Yaareshyah** (793b); of unc. der.; a Benjamite:— Jaareshiah(1).

3299. **יַעֲשָׂו Yaasav** (795c); from 6213a; an Isr.:— Jaasu(1).

3300. **יַעֲשִׂיאֵל Yaasiel** (795c); from 6213a and 410; "made by God," two Isr.:— Jaasiel(2).

3301. **יִפְדְּיָה Yiphdeyah** (804c); from 6299 and 3050; "Yah will ransom," an Isr.:— Iphdeiah(1).

3302. **יָפָה yaphah** (421b); a prim. root; *to be fair* or *beautiful:*— beautiful(5), decorate(1), fairer(1), make yourself beautiful(1).

3303. **יָפֶה yapheh** [421c]; from 3302; *fair, beautiful:*— appropriate(1), beautiful(28), beautiful one(2), fair(1), fitting(1), handsome(4), sleek(3).

3304. **יְפֵה־פִיָּה yepheh-phiyyah** (421d); from 3302; *pretty:*— pretty(1).

3305. **יָפוֹ Yapho** or

יָפוֹא Yapho (421d); from 3302; a seaport city of Pal.:— Joppa(4).

3306. **יָפַח yaphach** (422a); a prim. root; *to breathe, puff:*— gasping for breath(1).

3307. יָפֵחַ yapheach (422a); from 3306; *breathing* or *puffing out:*— breathe(1).

3308. יֳפִי yophi (421d); from 3302; *beauty:*— beauty(19).

3309. יָפִיעַ Yaphia (422b); from 3313; a king of Lachish, also a son of David, also a place on the border of Zebulun:— Japhia(5).

3310. יַפְלֵט Yaphlet (812d); from 6403; an Asherite:— Japhlet(3).

3311. יַפְלֵטִי Yaphleti (812d); from 3310; desc. of Japhlet:— Japhletites(1).

3312. יְפֻנֶּה Yephunneh (819c); from 6437; father of Caleb, also an Asherite:— Jephunneh(16).

3313. יָפַע yapha (422a); a prim. root; *to shine out* or *forth, to send out beams, cause to shine:*— look favorably(1), shine(2), shine forth(2), shines(1), shone forth(2).

3314. יִפְעָה yiphah (422b); from 3313; *brightness, splendor:*— splendor(2).

3315. יֶפֶת Yepheth (834d); from 6601b; a son of Noah:— Japheth(11).

3316. יִפְתָּח Yiphtach (836b); from 6605a; "He opens," a Gileadite, also a city of Judah:— Iphtah(1), Jephthah(29).

3317. יִפְתַּח־אֵל Yiphtach-el (836b); from 6605a and 410; "God opens," a valley between Zebulun and Asher:— Iphtahel(2).

3318. יָצָא yatsa (422b); a prim. root; *to go* or *come out:*— any time goes beyond(1), appeared(1), become known(1), beyond*(1), born*(3), breaks(1), bring(58), bring forth(12), bringing(6), brings(6), brings forth(5), brought(121), brought me forth(2), brought our forth(1), brought about(1), brought forth(6), bulges(1), came(97), came forth(7), came forward(2), carried(1), carried away(1), carry(5), clear(1), come(53), come forth(14), come forward(1), comes(17), comes forth(4), coming(12), coming forth(2), defamed*(1), defames*(1), depart(3), departed(12), departing(1), departs(1), departure(1), descendants(2), do(1), draw(1), drawn(1), end(1), entered(1), escape(3), escaped(2), exacted(1), exiled*(1), exported(2), expressed(1), extract(1), falls(1), fell(5), flashing(1), flee away(1), flew here(1), flow(2), flowed(1), flowing(1), flowing forth(1), flows(1), gave(1), get(7), go(138), go forth(32), go free(1), go off(1), go outside(2), go straight(1), goes(10), goes forth(9), going(20), going forth(8), gone(23), gone forth(10), grow(1), grows(1), hardly*(1), has(3), imported*(2), indeed go(1), issue(2), issued(2), issues(1), laid(1), lay(1), lead(1), lead forth(1), leads(1), leads forth(1), leave(2), leave*(2), leaves(2), led(2), left(4), loses(1), loss(1), march forward(1), originate(1), paid(1), passing(1), pluck(1), prematurely(1), proceed(4), proceeded(11), proceeds(1), produces(3), projecting(3), promised*(1), publicly(2), pull(1), pursuit(1), put away(2), put forth(1), reach(1), released(1), reported(1), revert(3), reverts(2), risen(1), rises(1), rising(1), said*(1), sank(1), send(1), sent(2), set(2), set*(1), spread(3), spreads(1), spring(1), started(1), surely come(1), surely go(1), take(6), taken(1), took(9), upheld(1), went(176), went forth(11), went forward(1), went through(1).

3319. יְצָא yetsa (1115a); (Ara.) corr. to 3318; *to bring out, finish:*— completed(1).

3320. יָצַב yatsab (426b); a prim. root; *to set* or *station oneself, take one's stand:*— present(5), present yourself(1), presented(2), remaining(1), sets(1), stand(14), stand forth(1), standing(1), station(2), stood(7), take his stand(1), take their stand(2), take your stand(5), took his stand(3), took their stand(2).

3321. יְצַב yetsab (1096a); (Ara.) corr. to 3320; *to make certain, gain certainty:*— exact meaning(1), know the exact meaning(1).

3322. יָצַג yatsag (426c); a prim. root; *to set, place:*— detained(1), establish(1), expose(1), leave(1), made(1), placed(2), presented*(1), put(1), set(5), set me down(1).

3323. יִצְהָר yitshar (844a); from the same as 6672a; *fresh oil:*— anointed*(1), fresh oil(2), oil(19).

3324. יִצְהָר Yitshar (844b); from the same as 6672a; a Levite:— Izhar(9).

3325. יִצְהָרִי Yitshari (844b); from 3324; desc. of Izhar:— Izharites(4).

3326. יָצוּעַ yatsua (426d); pass. part. of 3331; *a couch, bed:*— bed(3), bed*(1), couch(1).

3327. יִצְחָק Yitschaq (850c); from 6711; "he laughs," son of Abraham and Sarah:— Isaac(109), Isaac's(3).

3328. יִצְחַר Yitschar (850d); the same as 6714, q.v.:— Izhar(1).

3329. יָצִיא yatsi (425c); from 3318; *coming forth:*— children*(1).

3330a. יַצִּיב yatstsib (1096a); (Ara.) from 3321; *certain, true:*— certain(1), certainly(1), exact meaning(1), true(2).

3330b. יָצִיעַ yatsia (427a); from 3331; *flat surface:*— stories(2), story(1).

3331. יָצַע yatsa (426d); a prim. root; *to lay, spread:*— lay(1), make my bed(1), spread(1), spreading(1).

3332. יָצַק yatsaq (427a); a prim. root; *to pour, cast, flow:*— cast(14), casting(1), dished(1), firm(1), hard(2), hardens(1), molten(2), pour(14), poured(13), ran(1), set down(1), steadfast(1), washed away(1).

3333. יְצֻקָה yetsuqah (427c); from 3332; *a casting:*— rest(1).

3334. יָצַר yatsar (864c); the same as 6887a, q.v.

3335. יָצַר yatsar (427c); a prim. root; *to form, fashion:*— Creator(1), devises(1), earthenware*(1), fashion(1), fashioned(1), fashioning(2), fashions(1), formed(20), forming(2), forms(2), made(1), Maker(2), maker(4), ordained(1), planned(4), potter(9), potter's(7), potters(1).

3336. יֵצֶר yetser (428a); from 3335; *a form, framing, purpose:*— formed(1), frame(1), handiwork(1), intent(4), intentions*(1), mind(1), what(1).

3337. יֵצֶר Yetser (428a); from 3335; a son of Naphtali:— Jezer(3).

3338. יָצֻר yatsur (428b); from 3335; *form, member:*— members(1).

3339. יִצְרִי Yitsri (428b); from 3335; a Levite:— Izri(1).

3340. יִצְרִי Yitsri (428b); from 3337; desc. of Jezer:— Jezerites(1).

3341. יָצַת yatsath (428b); a prim. root; *to kindle, burn:*— aflame(1), burn(1), burned(3), burned down(1), burns(2), kindle(4), kindled(2), set(12), set on fire(1), sets(1).

3342. יֶקֶב yeqeb (428c); from an unused word; *wine vat:*— presses(1), vats(3), wine press(3), wine presses(3), wine vat(6).

3343. יְקַבְצְאֵל Yeqabtseel (868b); the same as 6909, q.v.

3344. יָקַד yaqad (428d); a prim. root; *to be kindled, to burn:*— burn(2), burning(3), burns(2), hearth(1), kindled(1).

3345. יְקַד yeqad (1096a); (Ara.) corr. to 3344; *to burn:*— blazing(8).

3346. יְקֵדָה yeqedah (1096a); (Ara.) from 3345; *a burning:*— burning(1).

3347. יָקְדְעָם Yoqdeam (429a); from 3344 and 5971a; a city in Judah:— Jokdeam(1).

3348. יָקֶה Yaqeh (429a); from an unused word; father of Agur:— Jakeh(1).

3349. יִקְּהָה yiqhah (429b); from an unused word; *obedience:*— obedience(1), scorns*(1).

3350. יְקוֹד yeqod (428d); from 3344; *a burning:*— burning(1), fire(1).

3351. יְקוּם yequm (879c); from 6965; *substance, existence:*— living thing(3).

3352. יָקוֹשׁ yaqosh (430c); from 3369; *a fowler, trapper:*— bird catcher(1).

3353. יָקוּשׁ yaqush (430c); pass. part. of 3369; *a fowler, trapper:*— fowler(1), fowlers(1), trapper(1).

3354. יְקוּתִיאֵל Yequthiel (429a); from the same as 3348 and from 410; a man of Judah:— Jekuthiel(1).

3355. יָקְטָן Yoqtan (429b); of unc. der.; a desc. of Shem and ancestor of several Arabian tribes:— Joktan(6).

3356. יָקִים Yaqim (879c); from 6965; "He lifts up," two Isr.:— Jakim(2).

3357. יַקִּיר yaqqir (430b); from 3365; *very precious, dear:*— dear(1).

3358. יַקִּיר yaqqir (1096a); (Ara.) corr. to 3357; *honorable, difficult:*— difficult(1), honorable(1).

3359. יְקַמְיָה Yeqamyah (880c); from 6965 and 3050; "Yah will rise," two Isr.:— Jekamiah(3).

3360. יְקַמְעָם Yeqamam (880c); from 6965 and 5971b; "may kinsman establish," a Levite:— Jekameam(2).

3361. יָקְמְעָם Yoqmeam (880c); from 6965 and 5971b; "let the people be established," a city in N. Isr.:— Jokmeam(2).

3362. יָקְנְעָם Yoqneam (429b); of unc. der.; a city of Canaan:— Jokneam(3).

3363. יָקַע yaqa (429b); a prim. root; *to be dislocated* or *alienated:*— alienated(1), became disgusted(2), dislocated(1), execute(1), hang(1), hanged(2).

3364. יָקַץ yaqats (429c); a prim. root; *to awake:*— awaken(1), awakened(1), awoke(9), wake(2).

3365. יָקַר yaqar (429c); a prim. root; *to be precious, prized* or *appraised:*— costly(1), esteemed(1), make...scarcer(1), precious(6), rarely(1), valued(1).

3366. יְקָר yeqar (430b); from 3365; *preciousness, price, honor:*— costly things(1), honor(9), pomp(2), precious(2), precious things(1), price(1), splendor(1).

3367. יְקָר yeqar (1096a); (Ara.) corr. to 3366; *honor:*— glory(6), honor(1).

3368. יָקָר yaqar (429d); from 3365; *precious, rare, splendid, weighty:*— costly(6), glory(1), luminaries(1), noble(1), precious(23), rare(1), splendor(1), weightier(1).

3369. יָקֹשׁ yaqosh (430b); a prim. root; *to lay a bait* or *lure:*— ensnared(1), set(1), set a snare(1), snared(4), trapper(1).

3370. יָקְשָׁן Yoqshan (430d); from 3369; a son of Abraham and Keturah:— Jokshan(4).

3371. יָקְתְאֵל Yoqtheel (430d); of unc. der.; a city in Judah, also a city in Edom (the same as 5554):— Joktheel(2).

3372a. יָרֵא yare (431a); a prim. root; *to fear:*— afraid(100), awesome(21), awesome acts(1), awesome things(4), became afraid(1), became...frightened(2), become frightened(1), cautious(1), dismayed(1), fear(165), fear and awesome(1), feared(36), fearful(1), fearful thing(1), fearfully(1), fearing(5), fears(9), frighten(4), frightened(1), have...fear(1), made me afraid(1), revere(10), revered(3), reverence(3), showed reverence(1), stand in awe(1), terrible(3), terrible things(1), terrifying(2).

3372b. יָרָא yara (432b); a prim. root; *to shoot, pour:*— archers shot(1), shooting(1), watered(1).

3373. יָרֵא yare (431a); the same as 3372a, q.v.

3374. יִרְאָה yirah (432a); from 3372a; *a fear:*— awesome(1), extremely*(1), fear(35), fearing(1), reverence(5).

3375. יִרְאוֹן Yiron (432a); from 3372a; a city in Naphtali:— Yiron(1).

3376. יִרְאִיָּה Yiriyyah or

יִרְאִיָּיהּ Yiriyyayh (909d); from 7200 and 3050; "Yah sees," an Isr. of Jeremiah's time:— Irijah(2).

3377. יָרֵב Yareb (937a); from 7378; "let him contend," the name of an Assyr. king:— Jareb(2).

3378. יְרֻבַּעַל Yerubbaal (937c); from 7378 and 1168a; "let Baal contend," a name of Gideon:— Jerubbaal(14).

3379. יָרָבְעָם Yarobam (914c); from 7231 and 5971a; "the people increase," the name of two Isr. kings:— Jeroboam(100), Jeroboam's(3).

3380. יְרֻבֶּשֶׁת Yerubbesheth (937c); from 7378 and 1322; "shame will contend," a name of Gideon:— Jerubbesheth(1).

3381. יָרַד yarad (432c); a prim. root; *to come* or *go down, descend:*— alighted(1), bowed(1), bring(1), bring him down(2), bring his down(1), bring it down(1), bring me down(2), bring my down(3), bring the down(1), bring them down(10), bring you down(5), bring your down(1), brings(1), brings down(3), brought him down(4), brought it down(1), brought the down(3), brought them down(1), brought down(5), came(1), came down(35), carry down(1), come(1), come down(48), comes down(3), coming down(10), departed(1), descend(7), descended(4), descending(2), descends(1), dismounted(1), dissolved(1), do so(1), down(5), down*(2), fall(2), fallen(1), falls(1), fell(1), flow down(2), flowing down(4), go(1), go down(81), go*(2), goes down(2), going down(3), gone below(1), gone down(9), indeed came down(1), let them down(1), let us down(1), let...down(1), lowered(3), once(1), poured(1), poured down(1), pull down(1), put down(1), put off(1), run down(5), sank down(1), shed(2), stepped down(1), take it down(1), take down(1), taken him down(1), taken down(2), thrust down(1), took his down(1), took them down(1), took down(2), tread(1), went(2), went down(70).

3382. יֶרֶד Yered (434b); from 3381; a desc. of Seth, also a man of Judah:— Jared(6), Jered(1).

3383. יַרְדֵּן Yarden (434c); from 3381; the principal river of Pal.:— Jordan(182).

3384. יָרָה yarah or

יָרָא yara (434d); a prim. root; *to throw, shoot:*— archers(2), archers shot(1), archers*(2), cast(3), cast them down(1), directed(1), instruct(4), instructed(1), instruction(1), instructs(1), laid(1), point(1), points(1), rain(1), set(1), shoot(10), shot(3), shot through(1), showed(1), taught(3), teach(27), teacher(2), teaches(2), teaching(1), throws(1), watering(1).

3385a. יָרָה yarah (436c); a prim. root; perh. *to be stupefied:*— afraid(1).

3385b. יְרוּאֵל Yeruel (436c); from 3384 and 410; "founded by God," a location prob. in the wilderness of Judah:— Jeruel(1).

3386. יָרוֹחַ Yaroach (437b); from the same as 3394; a Gadite:— Jaroah(1).

3387. יָרוֹק yaroq (438d); from the same as 3418; *a green thing:*— green thing(1).

3388. יְרוּשָׁא Yerusha or

יְרוּשָׁה Yerushah (440b); from 3423; "taken possession of," mother of King Jotham:— Jerusha(1), Jerushah(1).

3389. יְרוּשָׁלַםִ Yerushalaim or

יְרוּשָׁלַיִם Yerushalayim (436c); from 3385a and 7999a; prob. "foundation of peace," capital city of all Isr.:— Jerusalem(642), Jerusalem's(1).

3390. יְרוּשְׁלֶם Yerushalem (1096b); (Ara.) corr. to 3389; the capital city of all Isr.:— Jerusalem(26).

3391. יֶרַח yerach (437b); from the same as 3394; *month:*— month(6), months(6).

3392. יֶרַח Yerach (437b); from the same as 3394; a son of Joktan, also his desc.:— Jerah(2).

3393. יְרַח yerach (1096b); (Ara.) corr. to 3391; *month:*— month(1), months(1).

3394. יָרֵחַ yareach (437a); from an unused word; *moon:*— moon(27).

3395. יְרֹחָם Yerocham (934a); from 7355; "may He be compassionate," the name of several Isr.:— Jeroham(10).

3396. יְרַחְמְאֵל Yerachmeel (934a); from 7355 and 410; "may God have compassion," an Isr. name:— Jerahmeel(8).

3397. יְרַחְמְאֵלִי Yerachmeeli (934a); from 3396; desc. of Jerahmeel:— Jerahmeelites(2).

3398. יַרְחָע Yarcha (437c); of for. or.; an Eg. slave:— Jarha(2).

3399. יָרַט yarat (437c); a prim. root; *to be precipitate, to precipitate:*— contrary(1), tosses(1).

3400. יְרִיאֵל Yeriel (436c); from 3384 and 410; "thrown by God," a man of Issachar:— Jeriel(1).

3401. יָרִיב yarib (937a); from 7378; *opponent, adversary:*— contend(1), one who contends(1), opponents(1).

3402. יָרִיב Yarib (937b); from 7378; "He contends," an Isr. name:— Jarib(3).

3403. יְרִיבַי Yeribay (937b); from 7378; one of David's heroes:— Jeribai(1).

3404. יְרִיָּה Yeriyyah or

יְרִיָּהוּ Yeriyyahu (436c); from 3384 and 3050; "Yah will throw," a Levite:— Jeriah(2), Jerijah(1).

3405. יְרִיחוֹ Yericho or

יְרֵחוֹ Yerecho or

יְרִיחֹה Yerichoh (437c); of unc. der.; a city in the Jordan Valley captured by Joshua:— Jericho(57).

3406. יְרִימוֹת Yerimoth or

יְרֵימוֹת Yeremoth or

יְרֵמוֹת Yeremoth (438b); of unc. der.; the name of a number of Isr.:— Jeremoth(8), Jerimoth(6).

3407. יְרִיעָה yeriah (438c); from 3415; *curtain:*— curtain(23), curtains(28), tent curtains(3).

3408. יְרִיעוֹת Yerioth (438c); pl. of 3407; an Isr. woman:— Jerioth(1).

3409. יָרֵךְ yarek (437d); of unc. der.; *thigh, loin, side, base:*— base(3), direct(2), hips(1), loins(1), ruthlessly*(1), side(7), thigh(18), thighs(1).

3410. יַרְכָה yarkah (1096b); (Ara.) corr. to 3411; *thigh, loin:*— thighs(1).

3411. יְרֵכָה yerekah (438a); fem. of 3409; *flank, side, extreme parts, recesses:*— extreme rear(1), far(1), flank(1), hold(1), inner recesses(1), innermost part(1), rear(6), rear part(1), recesses(2), remote part(2), remote parts(5), remotest parts(5), within(1).

3412. יַרְמוּת Yarmuth (438b); of unc. der.; a Canaanite city in Judah, also a city in Issachar:— Jarmuth(7).

3413. יְרֵמַי Yeremay (438b); of unc. der.; an Isr.:— Jeremai(1).

3414. יִרְמְיָה Yirmeyah or

יִרְמְיָהוּ Yirmeyahu (941c); from the same as 7423b and from 3050; "Yah loosens," the name of a number of Isr.:— Jeremiah(146), Jeremiah's(1).

3415. יָרַע yara (438c); a prim. root; *to quiver:*— trembles(1).

3416. יִרְפְּאֵל Yirpeel (951b); from 7495 and 410; "God will heal," a place in Benjamin:— Irpeel(1).

3417. יָרַק yaraq (439a); a prim. root; *to spit:*— spit(2).

3418. יֶרֶק yereq (438d); from an unused word; *green, greenness:*— grass(1), green(4), green thing(1).

3419. יָרָק yaraq (438d); from the same as 3418; *herbs, herbage:*— green(2), vegetable(2), vegetables(1).

3420. יֵרָקוֹן yeraqon (439a); from the same as 3418; *mildew, paleness, lividness:*— mildew(5), pale(1).

3421. יָרְקְעָם Yorqeam (439a); from 7324 and 5971a; an Isr.:— Jorkeam(1).

3422. יְרַקְרַק yeraqraq (439a); from the same as 3418; *greenish, pale green:*— glistening(1), greenish(2).

3423. יָרַשׁ yarash or

יָרֵשׁ yaresh (439a); a prim. root; *to take possession of, inherit, dispossess:*— assuredly dispossess(1), become poor(1), cast(1), come to poverty(1), comes into possession(1), destroy(1), dispossess(12), dispossessed(9), dispossessing(1), drive(22), drive them out completely(2), driven(6), driving(3), drove(4), expel(1), given us as an inheritance(1), gives you to possess(1), heir(6), heirs(1), impoverish(1), impoverished(1), inherit(8), leave it as an inheritance(1), makes poor(1), new owners(1), occupy(1), possess(88), possessed(13), possession(2), receive(1), ruler*(1), seize(1), supplants(1), take over(1), take possession(19), take possession of his possessors(1), taken possession(2), takes possession(1), took possession(8), want(1).

3424. יְרֵשָׁה yereshah (440b); from 3423; *possession.*

3425. יְרֻשָּׁה yerushshah (440b); from 3423; *possession, inheritance:*— inheritance(2), own(1), possession(11).

3426. יֵשׁ yesh (441b); of unc. der.; *being, substance, existence, is:*— any(1), Gaddi(1), going(1), had(1), has(4), have(17), owned(3), owns(1), sometimes(2), there(70), there are any(1), there is any(1), there any(5), there had been(1), wealth(1), will(1), would(1).

3427. יָשַׁב yashab (442a); a prim. root; *to sit, remain, dwell:*— abide(5), abides(2), abode(1), convened(1), dwell(61), dweller(1), dwelling(20), dwells(12), dwelt(9), enthroned(9), had(1), inhabit(6), inhabitant(27), inhabitants(202), inhabitants of dwell(1), inhabited(25), inhabiting(1), inhabits(1), left(1), live(118), lived(137), lives(7), living(44), lurking(1), makes(1), married(6), marrying(1), occupants(1), occupied(1), passed(1), peaceful(1), placed(1), remain(21), remained(27), remaining(1), reposed(1), resettle(1), residents(1), retire(1), rule(1), sat(42), sat down(21), seat(2), seated(3), set(3), settle(6), settled(23), sit(68), sit down(7), sits(20), sits enthroned(1), sitting(48), sitting down(3), sitting still(1), situated(1), spent(1), stand(1), stay(29), stayed(25), staying(6), stays(2), take a seat(1), taken his seat(1), wait(2).

3428. יֶשֶׁבְאָב Yeshebab (444a); from 3427 and 1; "seat of (his) father," a Levite:— Jeshebeab(1).

3429. יֹשֵׁב בַּשֶּׁבֶת Yosheb Bashshebeth (444a); from 3427, a prep. prefix, the article, and 7674; "sitting in the seat," one of David's heroes:— Josheb-basshebeth(1).

3430. יִשְׁבּוֹ בְּנֹב Yishbo Benob (444a); from 3427 and 5011; "his dwelling (is) in Nob," a Philistine:— Ishbi-benob(1).

3431. יִשְׁבַּח Yishbach (986d); from 7623b; a man of Judah:— Ishbah(1).

3432. יָשֻׁבִי Yashubi (1000b); from 3437; desc. of Jashub:— Jashubites(1).

3433. יָשֻׁבִי לֶחֶם Yashubi Lechem (1000b); from 7725 and 3899; "returner of bread," a man of Judah:— Jashubi-lehem(1).

3434. יָשָׁבְעָם Yashobam (1000b); from 7725 and 5971a; "people will return," one of David's heroes:— Jashobeam(3).

3435. יִשְׁבָּק Yishbaq (990b); from the same as 7733; a son of Abraham and Keturah:— Ishbak(2).

3436. יָשְׁבְּקָשָׁה Yoshbeqashah (444a); from 3427 and 7186; "a hard seat," a son of Heman:— Joshbekashah(2).

3437. יָשׁוּב Yashub or

יָשִׁיב Yashib (1000b); from 7725; "He will return," two Isr.:— Jashub(3).

3438. יִשְׁוָה Yishvah (1001a); from 7737a; an Asherite:— Ishvah(2).

3439. יְשׁוֹחָיָה Yeshochayah (1006a); from 7817 and 3050; a Simeonite:— Jeshohaiah(1).

3440. יִשְׁוִי Yishvi (1001a); from 7737a; two Isr.:— Ishvi(4).

3441. יִשְׁוִי Yishvi (1001a); from 3440; a desc. of Ishvi:— Ishvites(1).

3442. יֵשׁוּעַ Yeshua (221c); the same as 3091, q.v.

3443. יֵשׁוּעַ Yeshua (1096b); (Ara.) corr. to 3442 and 3091; a high priest after the Bab. captivity:— Jeshua(1).

3444. יְשׁוּעָה yeshuah (447b); from 3467; *salvation:*— deeds of deliverance(1), deliverance(6), help(4), prosperity(1), salvation(61), save(1), saving(1), security(1), victories(1), victory(1).

3445. יֶשַׁח yeshach (445a); of unc. der.; perh. *emptiness:*— vileness(1).

3446. יִשְׂחָק Yischaq (850c); the same as 3327, q.v.

3447. יָשַׁט yashat (445a); a prim. root; *to extend, hold out:*— extended(2), holds(1).

3448. יִשַׁי Yishay (445a); of unc. der.; father of David:— Jesse(42).

3449. יִשִּׁיָּה Yishshiyyah or

יִשִּׁיָּהוּ Yishshiyyahu (674d); from 5382 and 3050; the name of several Isr.:— Isshiah(6), Isshijah(1).

3450. יְשִׂימִאֵל Yesimiel (964d); from 7760 and 410; a Simeonite:— Jesimiel(1).

3451. יְשִׁימָה yeshimah (445b); another reading for 4194, q.v.

3452. יְשִׁימוֹן yeshimon (445b); from 3456; *waste, wilderness:*— desert(4), desert region(1), Jeshimon(4), wasteland(2), wilderness(2).

3453. יָשִׁישׁ yashish (450a); from the same as 3486; *aged:*— aged(1), aged men(1), old(1), old men(1).

3454. יְשִׁישַׁי Yeshishay (450b); from the same as 3486; a Gileadite:— Jeshishai(1).

3455. יָשַׂם yasam (962c); the same as 7760, q.v.

3456. יָשַׁם yasham (445b); a prim. root; *to be desolate:*— appalled(1), desolate(1), stripped(1).

3457. יִשְׁמָא Yishma (445c); from 3456; "desolate," a man of Judah:— Ishma(1).

3458. יִשְׁמָעֵאל Yishmael (1035d); from 8085 and 410; "God hears," the name of several Isr.:— Ishmael(47), Ishmael's(1).

3459. יִשְׁמְעֵאלִי Yishmeeli (1035d); from 3458; desc. of Ishmael:— Ishmaelite(2), Ishmaelites(6).

3460. יִשְׁמַעְיָה Yishmayah or

יִשְׁמַעְיָהוּ Yishmayahu (1036a); from 8085 and 3050; "Yah hears," two Isr.:— Ishmaiah(2).

3461. יִשְׁמְרַי Yishmeray (1038b); from 8104; "preserver," a Benjamite:— Ishmerai(1).

3462. יָשֵׁן yashen (445c); a prim. root; *to sleep:*— chronic(1), fell asleep(1), remained long(1), sleep(10), sleeps(1), slept(5), supply(1).

3463. יָשֵׁן yashen (445d); from 3462; *sleeping:*— asleep(3), sleep(1), sleeping(1), slept(1), smolders(1), who fall asleep(1), who sleep(1).

3464. יָשֵׁן Yashen (445d); from 3462; one of David's heroes:— Jashen(1).

3465. יָשָׁן yashan (445d); from 3462; *old:*— old(6), old things(1).

3466. יְשָׁנָה Yeshanah (446a); fem. of 3465; a city near Bethel:— Jeshanah(1).

3467. יָשַׁע yasha (446b); a prim. root; *to deliver:*— avenged(1), avenging(2), brought salvation(2), deliver(27), delivered(8), deliverer(3), deliverers(1), deliverers who delivered(1), delivers(2), endowed with salvation(1), gained the victory(1), help(9), helped(5), preserve(1), safe(1), save(85), saved(33), saves(5), savior(13), surely will not save(1), victorious(1).

3468. יֶשַׁע yesha or

יֵשַׁע yesha (447a); from 3467; *deliverance, rescue, salvation, safety, welfare:*— safety(3), salvation(31), saving(2).

3469. יִשְׁעִי Yishi (447d); from 3467; "saving," four Isr.:— Ishi(5).

3470a. יְשַׁעְיָה Yeshayah (447d); from 3467 and 3050; "salvation of Yah," four Isr.:— Jeshaiah(4).

3470b. יְשַׁעְיָהוּ Yeshayahu (447d); from 3467 and 3050; "salvation of Yah," three Isr.:— Isaiah(32), Jeshaiah(3).

3471. יָשְׁפֵה yashepheh (448c); of for. or.; *jasper:*— jasper(3).

3472. יִשְׁפָּה Yishpah (1046a); from 8192; "He sweeps," a Benjamite:— Ishpah(1).

3473. יִשְׁפָּן Yishpan (1051a); from the same as 8227a; a Benjamite:— Ishpan(1).

3474. יָשַׁר yashar (448c); a prim. root; *to be smooth, straight,* or *right:*— agreeable(2), directed(1), esteem right(1), evenly applied(1), fixed straight(1), good(2), looked*(1), looks*(1), make his smooth(1), make the smooth(1), make your straight(2), make smooth(1), making their straight(1), please*(1), pleased*(4), pleasing(1), right(4), smooth(1), straight(1), took the straight(1).

3475. יֵשֶׁר Yesher (449c); from 3474; "uprightness," a son of Caleb:— Jesher(1).

3476. יֹשֶׁר yosher (449c); from 3474; *straightness, uprightness:*— correctly(1), honest(1), integrity(1), justly due(1), right(1), upright(1), uprightness(8), what is justly due(1).

3477. יָשָׁר yashar (449a); from 3474; *straight, right:*— conscientious*(1), fittest(1), Jashar(2), just(1), proposal of peace(1), right(35), safe(1), straight(5), upright(51), Upright One(1), uprightly(1), uprightness(1), what(2), what is right(7), what was right(6), which was right(1), who are upright(1), who is upright(1).

3478. יִשְׂרָאֵל Yisrael (975b); from 8280 and 410; "God strives," another name of Jacob and his desc.:— Israel(2485), Israel's(13), Israelites(5), Israelites*(1).

3479. יִשְׂרָאֵל Yisrael (1096b); (Ara.) corr. to 3478; desc. of Jacob:— Israel(8).

3480. יְשַׂרְאֵלָה Yesarelah (441a); of unc. der.; a son of Asaph:— Jesharelah(1).

3481. יִשְׂרְאֵלִי Yisreeli (976a); from 3478; desc. of Isr.:— Israel(1), Israelite(1), woman's(1).

3482. יִשְׂרְאֵלִית Yisreelith (976a); fem. of 3481; female desc. of Isr.:— Israelite(3).

3483. יִשְׁרָה yesharah (449c); fem. of 3477; *uprightness:*— uprightness(1).

3484. יְשֻׁרוּן Yeshurun (449c); from 3474; "upright one," poetic name for Isr.:— Jeshurun(4).

3485. יִשָּׂשכָר Yissaskar (441a); of unc. der.; perh. "there is recompense," a son of Jacob and Leah, also a son of Obed-edom:— Issachar(43).

3486. יָשֵׁשׁ yashesh (450a); from an unused word; *aged, decrepit:*— infirm(1).

3487. יָת yath (1096b); (Ara.) corr. to 853; mark of the accusative.

3488. יְתִב yethib (1096b); (Ara.) corr. to 3427; *to sit, dwell:*— live(1), sat(1), settled(1), sit(1), took his seat(1).

3489. יָתֵד yathed (450b); from an unused word; *a peg, pin:*— peg(6), pegs(11), pin(3), spade(1), stakes(1), tent peg(3).

3490. יָתוֹם yathom (450c); from an unused word; *an orphan:*— fatherless(7), fatherless children(1), orphan(26), orphans(8).

3491. יְתוּר yethur (1064d); another reading for 8446, q.v.

3492. יַתִּיר Yattir (452d); from 3498; a city in Judah:— Jattir(4).

3493. יַתִּיר yattir (1096c); (Ara.) corr. to 3492; *preeminent, surpassing:*— exceedingly(1), extraordinary(4), extremely(2), surpassing(1).

3494. יִתְלָה Yithlah (1068b); from 8518; "it will hang," a place in Dan:— Ithlah(1).

3495. יִתְמָה Yithmah (450d); from the same as 3490; one of David's valiant men:— Ithmah(1).

3496. יַתְנִיאֵל Yathniel (1072a); from 8566 and 410; "God hires," a Levite:— Jathniel(1).

3497. יִתְנָן Yithnan (451a); from the same as 386; a city in the desert of Judah:— Ithnan(1).

3498. יָתַר yathar (451b); a prim. root; *to remain over:*— abound(1), had some left(1), had left(1), have preeminence(1), leave(3), leave a remnant(1), leave of it over(1), leaving(1), left(47), left behind(1), left over(6), let remain(1), more than enough(1), preserve(1), prosper you abundantly(1), remain(2), remainder(7), remained(2), remaining(2), remains(3), reserved(2), rest(18), spare(1), surviving(2).

3499a. יֶתֶר yether (451d); from 3498; *remainder, excess, preeminence:*— abundance(2), exceedingly(1), excellent(1), fully*(1), leave(1), left(3), more*(1), preeminent(2), remainder(5), remained*(1), remaining(1), remnant(5), rest(71), what(3).

3499b. יֶתֶר yether (452a); from 3498; *a cord:*— bowstring(1), cords(3), string(1), tent-cord(1).

3500. יֶתֶר Yether (452b); from 3498; Moses' father-in-law (see 3503), also the name of several Isr.:— Jether(8), Jethro(1).

3501. יִתְרָא Yithra (452b); from 3498; father of Amasa:— Ithra(1).

3502. יִתְרָה yithrah (452b); fem. of 3499a; *abundance, riches:*— abundance(2).

3503. יִתְרוֹ Yithro (452b); from 3498; Moses' father-in-law:— Jethro(9).

3504. יִתְרוֹן yithron (452c); from 3498; *advantage, profit:*— advantage(5), excels(2), profit(3).

3505. יִתְרִי Yithri (452b); from 3500; desc. of Jethro:— Ithrite(4), Ithrites(1).

3506. יִתְרָן Yithran (452d); from 3498; an Edomite, also an Asherite:— Ithran(3).

3507. יִתְרְעָם Yithream (453c); from 3499a and 5971a; a son of David:— Ithream(2).

3508. יֹתֶרֶת yothereth (452c); from 3498; *appendage:*— lobe(11).

3509. יְתֵת Yetheth (453c); of unc. der.; an Edomite:— Jetheth(2).

כ

3510. כָּאַב kaab (456a); a prim. root; *to be in pain:*— cause him grief(1), inflicts pain(1), mar(1), pain(3), painful(1), pains(1).

3511. כְּאֵב keeb (456b); from 3510; *a pain:*— heavy(1), pain(4), sorrow(1).

3512a. כָּאָה kaah (456c); a prim. root; *to be disheartened* or *timid:*— despondent(1), disheartened(2).

3512b. כָּאֶה kaeh (456c); another reading for 2489, q.v.

3512c. כַּאֲשֶׁר kaasher (455b); from a prep. prefix and 834; *according as, as, when:*— according(1), accordingly(1), after(1), even(5), ever(1), if(2), just(172), just*(1), more(1), much(2), same(1), since(2), soon(8), such(3), though(2), what(2), whatever(1), when(57), when*(1), while(1), who(1).

3513. כָּבַד kabad or

כָּבֵד kabed (457a); a prim. root; *to be heavy, weighty,* or *burdensome:*— abounding(1), achieve honor(1), became fierce(1), became heavy(1), boasting(1), burdensome(1), dim(1), distinguished(3), dull(2), enjoy your glory(1), glorified(4), glorify(7), glorious(2), glorious things(1), grave(1), grew strong(1), harden(1), hardened(6), heavier(2), heavy(6), held in honor(1), honor(17), honor you greatly(1), honorable(4), honored(19), honoring(2), honors(5), indeed honor(1), laid burdens(1), made my heavy(1), made our heavy(2), made your heavy(3), make(1), make it glorious(1), makes himself rich(1), multiply(2), nobles(1), respected(1), stopped(1), weigh(1), weigh heavily(1), went heavily(1).

3514. כֹּבֶד kobed (458c); from 3513; *heaviness, mass:*— dense(1), heavy(1), mass(1), press(1).

3515. כָּבֵד kabed (458a); from 3513; *heavy:*— burdensome(1), difficult(2), great(4), grievous(1), heavier(1), heavy(11), huge(1), large(4), large number(1), much(1), numerous(1), rich(1), severe(7), slow(2), sorrowful(1), stubborn(1), thick(1), weighed down(1).

3516. כָּבֵד kabed (458b); from 3513; *liver:*— heart(1), liver(13).

3517. כְּבֵדֻת kebeduth (459c); from 3513; *heaviness:*— difficulty(1).

3518. כָּבָה kabah (459c); a prim. root; *to be quenched* or *extinguished, to go out:*— extinguish(5), go(3), goes(1), gone(1), put(1), quench(4), quenched(8), quenched and extinguished(1).

3519a. כָּבוֹד kabod (458c); from 3513; *glorious:*— glorious(1), splendid(1).

3519b. כָּבוֹד kabod or

כָּבֹד kabod (458c); from 3513; *abundance, honor, glory:*— bosom(1), glorious(8), glory(147), honor(33), honorable(1), honored(1), riches(1), soul(2), splendid(1), splendor(2), wealth(3).

3520. כְּבוּדָּה kebuddah (459c); from 3513; *abundance, riches:*— valuables(1).

3521. כָּבוּל Kabul (459d); of unc. der.; a city in Asher, also a region in Galilee:— Cabul(2).

3522. כַּבּוֹן Kabbon (460a); from an unused word; a place in Judah:— Cabbon(1).

3523. כְּבִיר kabir (460d); from an unused word; (something woven) perh. *a quilt* or *net:*— quilt(2).

3524. כַּבִּיר kabbir (460b); from 3527; *great, mighty, much:*— impotent*(1), mighty(6), mighty men(1), mighty one(1), much(1), older*(1).

3525. כֶּבֶל kebel (459d); from an unused word; *a fetter:*— fetters(2).

3526. כָּבַס kabas (460a); a prim. root; *to wash:*— fuller's(3), fullers'(1), wash(38), washed(8), washes(1).

3527. כָּבַר kabar (460b); a prim. root; *to be much* or *many:*— abundance(1), multiplies(1).

3528. כְּבָר kebar (460c); from 3527; *already:*— already(8).

3529. כְּבָר Kebar (460c); from 3527; a river of Bab.:— Chebar(8).

3530. כִּבְרָה kibrah (460c); from 3527; *distance:*— distance*(3), some(3).

3531. כְּבָרָה kebarah (460d); from the same as 3523; *a sieve:*— sieve(1).

3532. כֶּבֶשׂ kebes (461a); of unc. der.; *a lamb:*— lamb(21), lambs(28), male(1), male lamb(18), male lambs(32), sheep(2).

3533. כָּבַשׁ kabash (461b); a prim. root; *to subdue, bring into bondage:*— assault(1), brought them into subjection(2), forced into bondage(1), forcing(1), subdue(1), subdued(5), subjugate(1), trample(1), tread our under foot(1), under foot(1).

3534. כֶּבֶשׁ kebesh (461c); from 3533; *footstool:*— footstool(1).

3535. כִּבְשָׂה kibsah or

כַּבְשָׂה kabsah (461a); from the same as 3532; *ewe lamb:*— ewe lamb(3), ewe lambs(3), ewe-lamb(1), lamb(1).

3536. כִּבְשָׁן kibshan (461c); from 3533; *a kiln:*— furnace(2), kiln(2).

3537. כַּד kad (461c); from an unused word; *a jar:*— bowl(3), jar(9), pitcher(1), pitchers(5).

3538a. כְּדַב kedab (1096c); (Ara.) from a root corr. to 3576; *false:*— lying(1).

3538b. כִּדּוּר kaddur (462a); another reading for 1754, q.v.

3539. כַּדְכֹּד kadkod (461d); from the same as 3537; (a precious stone) perh. *ruby:*— rubies(2).

3540. כְּדָרְלָעֹמֶר Kedorlaomer (462a); of for. or.; a king of Elam:— Chedorlaomer(5).

3541. כֹּה koh (462a); a prim. adv.; *thus, here:*— also(9), even(1), follows(1), here(4), little while*(1), now(1), other side(1), over there(1), over there*(1), same(1), so(17), such(1), this(2), this is what(2), this side(1), this way(2), thus(518), worse*(1).

3542. כָּה kah (1096d); (Ara.) corr. to 3541; *here:*— this point(1).

3543a. כָּהָה kahah (462c); a prim. root; *to be* or *grow dim* or *faint:*— blind(1), dim(2), disheartened(1), faint(1), grown dim(1).

3543b. כָּהָה kahah (462d); a prim. root; *to rebuke:*— rebuke(1).

3544. כֵּהֶה keheh (462d); from 3543a; *dim, dull, faint:*— dim(3), dimly(1), faded(3), faint(1), fainting(1).

3545. כֵּהָה kehah (462d); from 3543a; *lessening, alleviation:*— relief(1).

3546. כְּהַל kehal (1096d); (Ara.) a root corr. to 3201 and 3557; *to be able:*— able(2), could(2).

3547. כָּהַן kahan (464c); denom. vb. from 3548; *to act as a priest:*— carry on their priesthood(1), decks(1), minister as a priest(1), minister as priest(3), minister as priests(6), ministered as priest(1), priest(1), serve as a priest(1), serve as priest(1), serve as priests(2), serve me as priests(1), served as the priest(1), served as priests(2), serving as priests(1).

3548. **כֹּהֵן** **kohen** (463a); from an unused word; *priest:*— chief ministers(1), priest(425), priest and the priests(2), priest's(9), priestly(2), priests(301), priests'(5).

3549. **כָּהֵן** **kahen** (1096d); (Ara.) corr. to 3548; *priest:*— priest(2), priests(6).

3550. **כְּהֻנָּה** **kehunnah** (464d); from the same as 3548; *priesthood:*— priest's offices(1), priesthood(13).

3551. **כַּו** **kav** or

כַּוָּה **kavvah** (1096d); (Ara.) from a root corr. to 3554; *window:*— windows(1).

3552. **כּוּב** **Kub** (464d); another reading for 3864, q.v.

3553. **כּוֹבַע** **koba** (464d); of unc. der.; *helmet:*— helmet(4), helmets(2).

3554. **כָּוָה** **kavah** (464d); a prim. root; *to burn, scorch, brand:*— scorched(2).

3555. **כְּוִיָּה** **keviyyah** (465a); from 3554; *a burning:*— burn(2).

3556. **כּוֹכָב** **kokab** (456d); from an unused word; *a star:*— star(2), stars(35).

3557. **כּוּל** **kul** (465a); a prim. root; *to comprehend, contain:*— calculated(1), contain(4), contains(1), endure(5), had to provide(1), held(1), hold(4), holding(2), maintain(1), provide(4), provided(6), provided them with sustenance(1), provisioned(1), sustain(3), sustained(1), sustainer(1).

3558. **כּוּמָז** **kumaz** (484d); from an unused word; (a golden ornament) perh. *a bracelet:*— bracelets(1), necklaces(1), though(1).

3559. **כּוּן** **kun** (465c); a prim. root; *to be firm:*— aim(1), appointed(1), carried(1), certain(2), certainty(1), confirm(2), confirmed(1), consider(1), could(1), counted(1), definitely(1), determined(1), direct(3), direct your right(1), directed(1), directs(1), establish(15), established(52), establishes(2), fashion(1), fashioned(1), firm(1), firmly established(3), formed(1), founds(1), full(1), get yourself ready(1), installed(1), made it ready(1), made preparations(1), made provision(1), made...preparations(1), made...ready(1), maintain his position(1), make preparation(1), make ready(2), make...sure(1), makes his sure(1), makes ready(1), making my firm(1), ordained(1), ordered(1), place(1), prepare(21), prepared(37), prepares(5), provide(1), provided(5), provides(1), ready(7), reliable(1), rested(1), rests(1), right(3), set(10), set the in order(1), steadfast(6), strengthen(1), took(1).

3560. **כּוּן** **Kun** (467b); from 3559; a city in Aram (Syria):— Cun(1).

3561. **כַּוָּן** **kavvan** (467d); from 3559; *a cake, sacrificial cake:*— cakes(2).

3562. **כּוֹנַנְיָהוּ** **Konanyahu** (467b); from 3559 and 3050; "Yah has sustained," two Levites:— Conaniah(3).

3563a. **כּוֹס** **kos** (468a); of unc. der.; *a cup:*— chalice*(2), cup(28), cups(1).

3563b. **כּוֹס** **kos** (468a); from the same as 3563a; (a kind of) *owl:*— little owl(2), owl(1).

3564a. **כּוּר** **kur** (468b); from an unused word; *smelting pot* or *furnace:*— furnace(9).

3564b. **כּוּר** **kur** (468c); a prim. root; perh. *to bore, dig* or *hew:*— pierced(1).

3565. **כּוֹר עָשָׁן** **Kor Ashan** (92d); the same as 953b, q.v.

3566. **כּוֹרֶשׁ** **Koresh** or

כֹּרֶשׁ **Koresh** (468d); of for. or.; a Pers. king:— Cyrus(15).

3567. **כּוֹרֶשׁ** **Koresh** (1096d); (Ara.) corr. to 3566; a Pers. king:— Cyrus(8).

3568a. **כּוּשׁ** **Kush** (468d); prob. of for. or.; a son of Ham, also his desc., also a land in the S. Nile Valley:— Cush(16), Ethiopia(13).

3568b. **כּוּשִׁי** **Kushi** (469a); prob. of for. or.; a Benjamite.

3569. **כּוּשִׁי** **Kushi** (469a); from 3568a; desc. of Cush:— Cushite(8), Ethiopia(1), Ethiopian(6), Ethiopians(8).

3570. **כּוּשִׁי** **Kushi** (469b); from the same as 3568a; two Isr.:— Cushi(2).

3571. **כּוּשִׁית** **Kushith** (469a); the same as 3569, q.v.:— Cushite(2).

3572. **כּוּשָׁן** **Kushan** (469b); from the same as 3568a; a region of Arabia:— Cushan(1).

3573. **כּוּשַׁן רִשְׁעָתַיִם** **Kushan Rishathayim** (469b); appar. from 3572 and 7564; king of Aram-naharaim:— Cushan-rishathaim(4).

3574. **כּוֹשָׁרָה** **kosharah** (507a); from 3787; *prosperity:*— prosperity(1).

3575. **כּוּת** **Kuth** or

כּוּתָה **Kuthah** (469b); of for. or.; a city of Assyr.:— Cuth(1), Cuthah(1).

3576. **כָּזַב** **kazab** (469b); a prim. root; *to lie, be a liar:*— fail(2), false(1), liars(1), lie(6), lied(2), lying(1), prove me a liar(1), proved a liar(1), told lies(1).

3577. **כָּזָב** **kazab** (469c); from 3576; *a lie, falsehood, deceptive thing:*— deception(1), deceptive(1), false(1), falsehood(4), liar*(1), lie(2), lies(18), lying(3).

3578. **כֹּזֵבָא** **Kozeba** (469d); from 3576; a city in Judah:— Cozeba(1).

3579. **כָּזְבִּי** **Kozbi** (469d); from 3576; a woman of Midian:— Cozbi(2).

3580. **כְּזִיב** **Kezib** (469d); from 3576; a place in the plain of Judah:— Chezib(1).

3581a. **כֹּחַ** **koach** or

כּוֹחַ **koach** (470b); of unc. der.; *a small reptile* (of unknown species):— crocodile(1).

3581b. **כֹּחַ** **koach** (470c); from an unused word; *strength, power:*— ability(3), able(1), able*(2), force(1), fruit(1), might(4), mightily(1), mighty(1), power(40), powerful(1), powerless*(1), strength(65), strong(1), wealth(1).

3582. **כָּחַד** **kachad** (470b); a prim. root; *to hide:*— annihilated(3), blot(1), completely destroy(1), conceal(4), concealed(2), cut off(2), denied(1), desolate(1), destroyed(2), hid(1), hidden(4), hide(7), hides(1), perishing(1), wipe(1).

3583. **כָּחַל** **kachal** (471a); a prim. root; *to paint:*— painted(1).

3584. **כָּחַשׁ** **kachash** (471a); a prim. root; *to disappoint, deceive, fail, grow lean:*— cringe(1), deceive(1), deceived(1), deceives(1), deception(1), denied(2), deny(3), denying(1), fail(2), give feigned obedience(1), grown lean(1), lied(3), pretend obedience(2), submit(1).

3585. **כַּחַשׁ** **kachash** (471c); from 3584; *lying, leanness:*— leanness(1), lies(5).

3586. **כֶּחָשׁ** **kechash** (471c); from 3584; *deceptive, false:*— false(1).

3587. **כִּי** **ki** (465a); from 3554; *a burning, branding:*— branding(1).

3588. **כִּי** **ki** (471c); a prim. conjunc.; *that, for, when:*— also(1), although(11), although*(1), because(409), because*(18), case(2), certainly(1), either(1), even(3), even though(3), event*(1), except(1), except*(21), how(12), however*(1), if(169), if*(2), inasmuch*(6), indeed(61), indeed*(1), last*(1), more of her than*(1), more than*(1), more*(1), moreover*(1), much more*(8), much*(10), nevertheless(1), nevertheless*(4), nor*(1), now(3), only*(7), or(1), rather(5), rather i indeed(1), rather*(12), seeing(1), since(38), since*(1), so(2), soon(1), still*(1), surely(63), surely*(8), than(1), than*(2), then(2), then*(1), though(37), though*(2), truly(5), unless*(10), until*(5), what*(1), when(241), when*(1), whenever(1), while(2), without*(2), Yea(1), yes(2), yet(7).

3589. **כִּיד** **kid** (475d); of unc. der.; prob. *misfortune:*— decay(1).

3590. **כִּידוֹד** **kidod** (461d); from the same as 3537; *a spark:*— sparks(1).

3591. **כִּידוֹן** **kidon** (475d); from an unused word; *a dart, javelin:*— javelin(8), spear(1).

3592. **כִּידוֹן** **Kidon** or

כִּידֹן **Kidon** (475d); from the same as 3591; a place in Pal.:— Chidon(1).

3593. **כִּידוֹר** **kidor** (461d); from an unused word; *onset:*— attack(1).

3594. **כִּיּוּן** **Kiyyun** (475d); of unc. der.; a heathen god:— Kiyyun(1).

3595. **כִּיּוֹר** **kiyyor** or

כִּיֹּר **kiyyor** (468c); from the same as 3564a; *pot, basin:*— basin(6), basins(5), firepot(1), laver(9), pan(1), platform(1).

3596. **כִּילַי** **kilay** or

כֵּלַי **kelay** (647d); from 5230; *a rascal:*— rogue(2).

3597. **כֵּילַפּוֹת** **kelappoth** (476a); of for. or.; *an axe:*— hammers(1).

3598. **כִּימָה** **Kimah** (465b); from an unused word; *a cluster of stars:*— Pleiades(3).

3599. **כִּיס** **kis** (476a); of unc. der.; *bag, purse:*— bag(3), purse(2).

3600. **כִּיר** **kir** (468c); from the same as 3564a; *cooking furnace:*— stove(1).

3601. **כִּישׁוֹר** **kishor** (507a); from 3787; *a distaff:*— distaff(1).

3602. **כָּכָה** **kakah** (462b); from 3541; *thus:*— even so(1), just so(3), like this(1), so(5), this(1), this manner(2), this regard(1), thus(21).

3603. **כִּכָּר** **kikkar** (503b); from 3769; *a round, a round district, a round loaf, a round weight, a talent* (a measure of weight or money):— cake(1), cover(1), district(1), loaf(4), loaves(2), plain(4), talent(9), talents(38), valley(8).

3604. **כִּכַּר** **kikkar** (1098a); (Ara.) corr. to 3603; *a talent* (a measure of weight or money):— talents(1).

3605. **כֹּל** **kol** or

כּוֹל **kol** (481a); from 3634; *the whole, all:*— all(4045), all for every(2), all his and every(1), all his everything(1), all its the entire(1), all the and every(1), all the of every(1), all the everywhere(1), all the throughout(1), all your concerning everything(1), all your to every(1), all your throughout(1), all men(2), all these(1), all things(11), altogether(1), always*(15), annually*(2), any(176), any or by all(2), any*(5), anyone(12), anyone*(2), anything(31), anything*(6), anywhere(3), anywhere*(1), both(2), complete(2), completely(5), continually*(15), countryside*(1), during(1), each(4), each one(1), each*(1), earnestly*(1), else(1), entire(16), entirely(1), every(366), every and everyone(1), every in all(1), every of all(4), every of any(1), every pertaining to all(1), every man(1), every one(1), every one(12), every thing(1), every way(1), everyone(96), everyone's(3), everyone*(3), everything(52), everything*(4), everywhere(2), everywhere*(2), far(1), farthest(1), forever*(10), full(2), gaping(1), health*(1), just*(6), life*(1), lifetime*(1), long*(9), mere(1), much(1), no one(1), no*(33), none*(13), nothing*(12), one(3), only(1), perpetually*(2), plenty(1), something*(1), there is everywhere(1), throughout(20), throughout and all(1), throughout the whole(1), throughout all(1), throughout*(1), total(6), totally(2), utter(1), variety(1), whatever(24), whatever*(40), whenever(4), wherever*(20), whoever(45), whoever then any(1), whoever*(6), whoever...any(3), whole(125), whole and let all(1), whole and all(3), wholehearted*(1), wholly(2), whomever*(3).

3606. כֹּל **kol** (1097a); (Ara.) corr. to 3605; *the whole, all:*— all(46), all things(1), any(13), because*(4), entire(1), every(1), forasmuch*(1), inasmuch*(9), no*(6), none*(1), reason*(2), therefore*(4), whatever(1), whatever*(2), wherever*(1), whole(7).

3607. כָּלָא **kala** (476b); a prim. root; *to shut up, restrain, withhold:*— hold them back(1), kept(1), refuse(1), restrain(3), restrained(3), shut(4), stopped(1), withheld(2), withhold(1).

3608. כֶּלֶא **kele** (476c); from 3607; *confinement, restraint, imprisonment:*— prison(2), prison*(7), prisons(1).

3609. כִּלְאָב **Kilab** (476d); from 3607; a son of David:— Chileab(1).

3610. כִּלְאַיִם **kilayim** (476c); from 3607; *two kinds:*— two kinds(4).

3611. כֶּלֶב **keleb** (476d); of unc. der.; *a dog:*— dog(14), dog's(2), dogs(16).

3612. כָּלֵב **Kaleb** (477a); from the same as 3611; a son of Jephunneh and sent by Moses to spy out the land:— Caleb(31), Caleb's(4).

3613. כָּלֵב אֶפְרָתָה **Kaleb Ephrathah** (477a); from 3612 and 672; the place where Hezron died:— Caleb-ephrathah(1).

3614. כָּלִבּוֹ **Kalibbo** or

כָּלֵבִי **Kalebi** (477a); from 3612; desc. of Caleb:— Calebite(1).

3615. כָּלָה **kalah** (477b); a prim. root; *to be complete, at an end, finished, accomplished,* or *spent:*— accomplish(2), accomplished(1), annihilate(1), annihilated(2), been consumed(2), been spent(1), brings to pass(1), brought(1), came to an end(1), ceased(1), come to an end(5), complete(1), completed(10), completely gone(1), completion(1), consume(6), consumed(16), decided(3), demolish(1), destroy(10), destroyed(4), destroyed them all(1), destroys(1), destruction(1), determined(1), devoured(1), died(1), end(4), ended(3), ending(1), exhausted(2), exterminated(1), fail(10), failed(1), fails(2), faints(1), feed(1), finish(6), finished(67), finishes(1), fulfill(2), languish(1), languishes(1), longed(1), make an end(1), over(1), perish(1), perishing(1), plotted(1), put an end(2), ravage(1), settled(1), spend(3), spent(5), terminate(1), use(1), used(1), vanish(2), vanishes(1), waste away(1), wastes away(1), yearned(1).

3616. כָּלֶה **kaleh** (479a); from 3615; *a failing:*— yearn(1).

3617. כָּלָה **kalah** (478d); from 3615; *completion, complete destruction, consumption, annihilation:*— annihilation(1), complete destruction(5), complete end(4), completely(4), destroy*(2), destruction(2), end(1), entirely(1), full end(2).

3618. כַּלָּה **kallah** (483c); from an unused word; *daughter-in-law, bride:*— bride(15), brides(2), daughter-in-law(14), daughters-in-law(3).

3619. כְּלוּב **kelub** (477b); from the same as 3611; *a basket, cage:*— basket(2), cage(1).

3620. כְּלוּב **Kelub** (477b); from the same as 3611; two Isr.:— Chelub(2).

3621. כְּלוּבַי **Kelubay** (477b); from the same as 3611; a man of Judah:— Chelubai(1).

3622. כְּלוּהַי **Keluhi** (479a); from 3615; an Isr.:— Cheluhi(1).

3623. כְּלוּלָה **kelulah** (483c); from the same as 3618; *betrothal:*— betrothals(1).

3624. כֶּלַח **kelach** (480c); from an unused word; *firm* or *rugged strength:*— full vigor(1), vigor(1).

3625. כֶּלַח **Kelach** (480d); from the same as 3624; a city in Assyr.:— Calah(2).

3626. כָּל־חֹזֶה **Kol-chozeh** (480d); of unc. der.; an Isr. name:— Col-hozeh(2).

3627. כְּלִי **keli** (479b); from 3615; *an article, utensil, vessel:*— armor(24), armory*(1), article(10), articles(30), bag(2), baggage(12), bags(2), basket(1), bowls*(1), cargo(1), clothing(1), earthenware*(1), equipment(6), everything*(1), furnishings(10), furniture(4), gear(1), goods(6), implements(2), instruments(14), items(1), jar(2), jars(1), jars*(1), jewels(3), jewels*(1), object(3), pots(1), pottery(1), sack(1), something*(1), thing(5), things(3), tool(1), utensils(66), vessel(28), vessels(37), vessels of kinds(1), water(1), weapon(5), weapons(22), weapons of and equipment(1), yokes(1).

3628. כְּלִיא **keli** or

כְּלוּא **kelu** (476c); from 3607; *confinement, restraint, imprisonment:*— prison*(2).

3629. כִּלְיָה **kilyah** (480b); of unc. der.; *a kidney:*— feelings(1), finest*(1), heart(1), inmost being(1), inward parts(2), kidneys(18), mind(5), minds(1), within(1).

3630. כִּלְיוֹן **Kilyon** (479a); from 3615; a son of Naomi:— Chilion(3).

3631. כִּלָּיוֹן **killayon** (479a); from 3615; *failing, pining, annihilation:*— destruction(1), failing(1).

3632. כָּלִיל **kalil** (483a); from 3634; *entire, whole, a holocaust:*— all(2), burned entirely(1), completely(1), entirely(1), perfect(3), perfection(1), pure(1), whole(2), whole burnt offering(2), whole burnt offerings(1).

3633. כַּלְכֹּל **Kalkol** (465b); from 3557; an Isr. noted for his wisdom:— Calcol(2).

3634. כָּלַל **kalal** (480d); a prim. root; *to complete, perfect:*— perfected(2).

3635. כְּלַל **kelal** (1097a); (Ara.) corr. to 3634; *to complete:*— finish(2), finished(4), finishing(1).

3636. כְּלָל **Kelal** (483c); from the same as 3618; an Isr.:— Chelal(1).

3637. כָּלַם **kalam** (483d); a prim. root; *to be humiliated:*— ashamed(6), bear her shame(1), blush(2), brought us to dishonor(1), confounded(1), disgraced(1), dishonored(7), embarrassed(1), feel ashamed(1), feel humiliated(1), humiliated(10), humiliates(2), humiliating(1), insult(1), insulted(3), rebuke(1).

3638. כִּלְמַד **Kilmad** (484b); of for. or.; a place of unc. location:— Chilmad(1).

3639. כְּלִמָּה **kelimmah** (484a); from 3637; *insult, reproach, ignominy:*— disgrace(8), dishonor(6), humiliation(7), insults(5), reproach(1), reproaches(1), shame(2).

3640. כְּלִמּוּת **kelimmuth** (484b); from 3637; *ignominy:*— humiliation(1).

3641a. כַּלְנֵה **Kalneh** (484c); of for. or.; a place in Bab. (prob. the same as 3641b):— Calneh(1).

3641b. כַּלְנֵה **Kalneh** (484c); from the same as 3641a; a city conquered by Assyr.:— Calneh(1), Calno(1).

3642. כָּמַהּ **kamah** (484c); a prim. root; *to faint:*— yearns(1).

3643. כִּמְהָם **Kimham** (484c); from 3642; an attendant of David, also a place near Bethlehem:— Chimham(4).

3644. כְּמוֹ **kemo** or

כָּמוֹ **kamo** (455d); a pleonastic form of a prep. pref.; *like, as, when:*— alike(1), comparison(1), if(1), like(84), likewise(1), so(1), such(4), such*(1), thus(1), when(1).

3645. כְּמוֹשׁ **Kemosh** or

כְּמִישׁ **Kemish** (484d); of unc. der.; a god of the Moabites:— Chemosh(8).

3646. כַּמֹּן **kammon** (485a); of unc. der.; *cummin* (a plant grown as a condiment):— cummin(3).

3647. כָּמַס **kamas** (485a); a prim. root; *to store up:*— laid up in store(1).

3648. כָּמַר **kamar** (485a); a prim. root; *to grow warm and tender, to be* or *grow hot:*— become as hot(1), deeply*(1), kindled(1), stirred(2).

3649. כֹּמֶר **komer** (485c); from the same as 4364a; *a priest* (in idol worship):— idolatrous priests(3).

3650. כִּמְרִיר **kimrir** (485b); from an unused word; *darkness, gloominess:*— blackness(1).

3651. כֵּן **ken** (485d); a prim. adv.; *so, thus:*— accordingly(2), after*(1), afterward*(18), afterwards*(5), because*(1), case(1), correctly(1), enough(1), even(2), exactly(1), follows(1), hence(1), here(1), inasmuch*(5), like(3), like this(1), likewise(10), means*(2), more(4), nevertheless(1), now*(1), possessed*(1), practice*(1), reason*(4), right(1), same(8), same way(1), since*(1), so(226), so*(1), such(3), such a thing(2), such*(1), surely(2), then(1), thereafter*(1), therefore(190), therefore*(138), this(24), this is how(1), this account(1), this manner(1), this reason(1), thus(51), very well(2), yet(1).

3652. כֵּן **ken** (1097b); (Ara.) corr. to 3651; *thus, as follows:*— follows(5), thus(3).

3653a. כֵּן **ken** (467a); from 3559; *right, veritable, honest:*— false*(1), futile*(1), honest men(5), right(7), what is not right(1), who is steadfast(1), yes(1).

3653b. כֵּן **ken** (487c); from an unused word; *a base, pedestal, office:*— base(3), instead*(1), office(2), pedestal(2), place(3), stand(6).

3654. כֵּן **ken** (487d); of unc. der.; *gnat, gnats, a gnat swarm:*— gnats(6), manner(1).

3655. כָּנָה **kanah** (487b); a prim. root; *to title, give an epithet:*— flatter(2), given you a title(1), name with honor(1), title of honor(1).

3656. כַּנֵּה Kanneh (487c); from 3655; prob. a place in Bab.:— Canneh(1).

3657. כַּנָּה kannah (488a); from the same as 3654; *support:*— shoot(1).

3658. כִּנּוֹר kinnor (490a); of unc. der.; *a lyre:*— harp(9), harps(2), lyre(16), lyres(15).

3659. כָּנְיָהוּ Konyahu (220c); the same as 3078, q.v.

3660. כְּנֵמָא kenema (1097b); (Ara.) corr. to 3644; *accordingly, as follows:*— accordingly(1), follows(1), thus(2).

3661. כָּנַן kanan (not included); see 3657.

3662. כְּנָנִי Kenani (487d); from the same as 3653b; a Levite:— Chenani(1), thus(1).

3663. כְּנַנְיָה Kenanyah or

כְּנַנְיָהוּ Kenanyahu (487d); from 3653b and 3050; two Isr.:— Chenaniah(3).

3664. כָּנַס kanas (488a); a prim. root; *to gather, collect:*— assemble(1), collected(1), collecting(1), gather(4), gathered(1), gathers(2), wrap(1).

3665. כָּנַע kana (488b); a prim. root; *to be humble:*— becomes humbled(1), done(1), humble(4), humbled(12), humbled yourself(3), subdue(4), subdued(11).

3666. כִּנְעָה kinah (488c); from 3665; *a bundle, pack:*— bundle(1).

3667a. כְּנַעַן Kenaan (488c); from 3665; a son of Ham, also his desc. and their land W. of the Jordan:— Canaan(90).

3667b. כְּנַעַן kenaan (488d); from 3665; *a merchant:*— merchants(2), traders(1), tradesmen(1).

3668. כְּנַעֲנָה Kenaanah (489b); from 3665; two Isr.:— Chenaanah(5).

3669a. כְּנַעֲנִי Kenaani (489a); from 3667a; inhab. of Canaan:— Canaanite(26), Canaanite woman(1), Canaanites(43), Canaanitess(1).

3669b. כְּנַעֲנִי kenaani (489b); from 3665; *a trader, merchant:*— merchant(1), merchants(1).

3670. כָּנַף kanaph (489d); denom. vb. from 3671; *to be cornered* or *thrust into a corner:*— hide(1).

3671. כָּנָף kanaph (489b); from an unused word; *wing, extremity:*— bird*(1), corner(1), corners(4), covering(1), each other(1), edge(5), edges(1), ends(3), fold(2), garment(1), kind(3), skirt(3), skirts(1), sorts(1), wing(14), winged(5), wings(58), wings were each other(1), wingspan(1).

3672. כִּנֲרוֹת Kinaroth or

כִּנֶּרֶת Kinnereth (490b); from the same as 3658; a city in Galilee, also a lake near the city:— Chinnereth(4), Chinneroth(3).

3673. כְּנַשׁ kenash (1097b); (Ara.) corr. to 3664; *to gather:*— assemble(1), assembled(1), gathered around(1).

3674. כְּנָת kenath (490c); of unc. der.; *associate, colleague:*— colleagues(1).

3675. כְּנָת kenath (1097c); (Ara.) corr. to 3674; *an associate:*— colleagues(7).

3676. כֵּס kes (490c); appar. a contr. for 3678, q.v.

3677. כֶּסֶא kese or

כֶּסֶה keseh (490c); of unc. der.; *full moon:*— full moon(3).

3678. כִּסֵּא kisse or

כִּסֵּה kisseh (490c); from the same as 3677; *seat of honor, throne:*— authority(1), chair(1), official seat(1), seat(6), sworn*(1), throne(118), throne the thrones(1), thrones(5).

3679. כַּשְׂדִּים Kasdim (505a); the same as 3778, q.v.

3680. כָּסָה kasah (491b); a prim. root; *to cover:*— closed(2), clothed(1), conceal(1), conceals(8), cover(50), covered(51), covering(4), covers(20), engulfed(3), forgive(1), hidden(1), hide(2), keep(1), made a covering(1), overwhelm(2), overwhelmed(2), take refuge(1).

3681. כָּסוּי kasuy (492b); from 3680; *a covering:*— cover(1), covering(1).

3682. כְּסוּת kesuth (492b); from 3680; *a covering:*— clothing(1), covering(5), garment(1), vindication(1).

3683. כָּסַח kasach (492d); a prim. root; *to cut off* or *away:* cut(1), cut down(1).

3684. כְּסִיל kesil (493a); from 3688; *stupid fellow, dullard, fool:*— fool(35), fool's(2), foolish(6), foolish man's(1), fools(23), stupid(1), stupid man(1), stupid ones(1).

3685. כְּסִיל Kesil (493a); prob. from 3688; a heavenly constellation:— constellations(1), Orion(3).

3686. כְּסִיל Kesil (493b); from 3688; a place in S. Judah:— Chesil(1).

3687. כְּסִילוּת kesiluth (493a); from 3688; *stupidity:*— folly(1).

3688. כָּסַל kasal (492d); a prim. root; *to be* or *become stupid:*— foolish(1).

3689. כֶּסֶל kesel (492d); from 3688; *loins, stupidity, confidence:*— confidence(4), folly and the foolishness(1), foolish(1), loins(6), thighs(1).

3690. כִּסְלָה kislah (493a); from 3688; *stupidity, confidence:*— confidence(1), folly(1).

3691. כִּסְלֵו Kislev (493b); of for. or.; the ninth month of the Jewish calendar:— Chislev(2).

3692. כִּסְלוֹן Kislon (493b); from 3688; a Benjamite:— Chislon(1).

3693. כְּסָלוֹן Kesalon (493b); from 3688; a place on the border of Judah:— Chesalon(1).

3694. כְּסֻלּוֹת Kesulloth (493b); from 3688; a place in Issachar:— Chesulloth(1).

3695. כַּסְלֻחִים Kasluchim (493b); of unc. der.; a people desc. from Mizraim, prob. ancestors of the Philistines:— Casluh(1), Casluhim(1).

3696. כִּסְלֹת תָּבֹר Kisloth Tabor (493b); from 3688 and 8396; a place in Issachar:— Chisloth-tabor(1).

3697. כָּסַם kasam (493c); a prim. root; *to shear, clip:*— only trim(1).

3698. כֻּסֶּמֶת kussemeth (493c); from 3697; *spelt* (a kind of wheat):— rye(1), spelt(2).

3699. כָּסַס kasas (493c); a prim. root; *to compute:*— divide(1).

3700. כָּסַף kasaph (493d); a prim. root; *to long* (for):— eager(1), long(1), longed(1), longed greatly(1), shame(1).

3701. כֶּסֶף keseph (494a); from 3700; *silver, money:*— fine(2), fine silver(2), money(100), pay(1), price(10), property(1), purchase price(1), silver(284), silver from the money(1).

3702. כְּסַף kesaph (1097c); (Ara.) corr. to 3701; *silver:*— money(1), silver(12).

3703. כָּסִפְיָא Kasiphya (494d); perh. from 3700; a place in Bab.:— Casiphia(2).

3704. כֶּסֶת keseth (492c); from an unused word; *a band, fillet:*— bands(2).

3705. כְּעַן kean (1107b); (Ara.) prob. from 6032; *now:*— now(13).

3706. כְּעֶנֶת keeneth or

כְּעֶת keeth (1107b); (Ara.) fem. of 3705; *now:*— now(4).

3707. כָּעַס kaas (494d); a prim. root; *to be vexed* or *angry:*— anger(3), angry(4), demoralized*(1), make me angry(1), provoke(5), provoke him to anger(2), provoke me to anger(8), provoke them to anger(1), provoked(7), provoked him to anger(2), provoked me to anger(2), provoked the to anger(1), provoked to anger(1), provoking(7), provoking him to anger(2), provoking me to anger(4), provoking the to anger(1), spite(2), trouble(1), vexation(1), vexed(1).

3708a. כַּעַס kaas (495b); from 3707; *vexation, anger:*— anger(3), bitterly*(1), grief(4), grief and anger(1), grievous(1), indignation(1), provocation(7), provocations(1), sorrow(1), vexation(1), vexing(1).

3708b. כַּעַשׂ kaas (495b); from 3707; *vexation, anger:*— anger(1), grief(2).

3709. כַּף kaph (496a); from 3721; *hollow* or *flat of the hand, palm, sole* (of the foot), *a pan:*— branches(1), earnings*(1), footstep*(1), give pledges*(1), grasp(2), hand(46), handful*(1), handles(1), hands(69), hands*(1), hollow(1), hoof*(1), palm(8), palms(3), pan(12), pans(9), paws(1), pledge(1), pledges*(1), power(1), socket(4), sole(11), soles(6), spoons(3), together*(2).

3710. כֵּף keph (495b); perh. of for. or.; *a rock:*— rocks(2).

3711. כָּפָה kaphah (495c); a prim. root; *to subdue:*— subdues(1).

3712. כִּפָּה kippah (497a); fem. of 3709; *a branch, frond* (of a palm tree):— palm branch(3).

3713a. כְּפוֹר kephor (499b); from an unused word; *a bowl:*— bowls(5), each bowl(2).

3713b. כְּפוֹר kephor (499b); from the same as 3713a; *hoarfrost:*— frost(3).

3714. כָּפִיס kaphis (496a); from an unused word; *a rafter, girder:*— rafter(1).

3715. כְּפִיר kephir (498d); of unc. der.; *young lion:*— lion(5), lions(1), young(1), young lion(10), young lion's(1), young lions(11), young lions'(1).

3716a. כְּפִירָה Kephirah (499a); fem. of 3715; a city in Benjamin:— Chephirah(4).

3716b. כְּפִירִים Kephirim (499a); from the same as 3715; a city in Benjamin (prob. the same as 3716a):— Chephirim(1).

3717. כָּפַל kaphal (495c); a prim. root; *to double, double over:*— double over(1), doubled(1), folded double(3).

3718. כֶּפֶל kephel (495d); from 3717; *the double:*— double(2), two sides(1).

3719. כָּפַן kaphan (495d); a prim. root; *to be hungry, to hunger:*— bent(1).

3720. כָּפָן kaphan (495d); from 3719; *hunger, famine:*— famine(2).

3721. כָּפַף kaphaph (496a); a prim. root; *to bend, bend down, be bent* or *bowed:*— bow(1), bowed down(3), bowing(1).

3722a. כָּפַר kaphar (497b); denom. vb. from 3724a; *to cover over, pacify, make propitiation:*— appease(1), appease*(1), atone(3), atoned(2), atonement is made(1), atonement shall be made(1), atonement was made(1), atoning(1), canceled(1), expiation can be made(1), forgave(1), forgive(4), forgiven(5), made atonement(3), make atonement(71), makes atonement(2), making atonement(1), pardon(1).

3722b. כָּפַר kaphar (498d); denom. vb. from 3724b; *to pitch* (with pitch):— cover(1).

3723. כָּפָר kaphar (499a); from the same as 3715; *a village:*— villages(2).

3724a. כֹּפֶר kopher (497b); from an unused word; *the price of a life, ransom:*— bribe(1), bribes(1), ransom(11).

3724b. כֹּפֶר kopher (498d); of unc. der.; *pitch:*— pitch(1).

3724c. כֹּפֶר kopher (499a); from the same as 3715; (a shrub or low tree) *henna:*— henna(2).

3724d. כֹּפֶר kopher (499a); from the same as 3715; *village:*— villages(2).

3725. כִּפֻּר kippur (498c); from the same as 3724a; *atonement:*— atonement(8).

3726. כְּפַר הָעַמּוֹנִי Kephar Haammoni (499a); from 3723 and 5984; "a village of the Ammonites," a village in Benjamin:— Chepharammoni(1).

3727. כַּפֹּרֶת kapporeth (498c); from the same as 3724a; *propitiatory:*— mercy seat(27).

3728. כָּפַשׁ kaphash (499b); a prim. root; *to make bent, press* or *bend together:*— cower(1).

3729. כְּפַת kephath (1097c); (Ara.) a prim. root; *to bind:*— bound(1), tie(1), tied(2).

3730. כַּפְתֹּר kaphtor or

כַּפְתּוֹר kaphtor (499b); of unc. der.; *capital, knob, bulb:*— bulb(10), bulbs(6), capitals(1), tops of her pillars(1).

3731. כַּפְתֹּר Kaphtor or

כַּפְתּוֹר Kaphtor (499c); from the same as 3730; prob. a name for Crete:— Caphtor(3).

3732. כַּפְתֹּרִי Kaphtori (499c); from 3731; desc. of Mizraim, also their land:— Caphtor(1), Caphtorim(2).

3733a. כַּר kar (468b); from the same as 3564a; *basket-saddle:*— saddle(1).

3733b. כַּר kar (499c); of unc. der.; *a pasture:*— meadows(1), pasture(1), pastures(1).

3733c. כַּר kar (503a); from 3769; *a he-lamb, a battering ram:*— battering rams(3), lamb(1), lambs(8).

3734a. כֹּר kor (499d); from the same as 3733b; *kor* (a measure):— kor(1), kors(7).

3734b. כֹּר kor or

כּוֹר kor (1096d); (Ara.) corr. to 3734a; *kor* (a measure of wheat):— kors(1).

3735. כְּרָא kera (1097d); (Ara.) prob. corr. to 3738a; *to be distressed:*— distressed(1).

3736. כַּרְבֵּל karbel (499d); of unc. der.; *to be mantled:*— clothed(1).

3737. כַּרְבְּלָא karbela (1097d); (Ara.) corr. to 3736; *a helmet, cap:*— caps(1).

3738a. כָּרָה karah (500a); a prim. root; *to dig:*— cut(1), digs(3), dug(9), opened(1).

3738b. כָּרָה karah (500b); a prim. root; *to give a feast:*— prepared(1).

3739. כָּרָה karah (500b); a prim. root; *to trade, get by trade:*— bargain(1), barter(1), bought(1), purchase(1).

3740. כֵּרָה kerah (500c); from 3738b; *a feast:*— feast(1).

3741. כָּרָה karah (500b); from 3738a; *a cistern, well:*— caves(1).

3742. כְּרוּב kerub (500c); of unc. der.; prob. an order of angelic beings:— cherub(25), cherubim(65).

3743. כְּרוּב Kerub (500c); from the same as 3742; a place in Bab.:— Cherub(2).

3744. כָּרוֹז karoz (1097d); (Ara.) of for. or.; *a herald:*— herald(1).

3745. כְּרַז keraz (1097d); (Ara.) denom. vb. from 3744; *to make proclamation:*— issued a proclamation(1).

3746. כָּרִי Kari (501b); from 3738b; bodyguard of Jehoash:— Carites(2).

3747. כְּרִית Kerith (504d); from 3772; a brook where Elijah was hidden:— Cherith(2).

3748. כְּרִיתוּת kerithuth (504d); from 3772; *divorcement:*— divorce(4).

3749. כַּרְכֹּב karkob (501b); from an unused word; *border, rim* (of an altar):— ledge(2).

3750. כַּרְכֹּם karkom (501b); of unc. der.; *saffron:*— saffron(1).

3751. כַּרְכְּמִישׁ Karkemish (501c); of for. or.; a city on the Euphrates:— Carchemish(3).

3752. כַּרְכַּס Karkas (501c); of for. or.; a eunuch of Ahasuerus:— Carkas(1).

3753. כִּרְכָּרָה kirkarah (503a); from 3769; *dromedary:*— camels(1).

3754. כֶּרֶם kerem (501c); of unc. der.; *a vineyard:*— vineyard(47), vineyards(45).

3755. כֹּרֵם karam (501d); denom. vb. from 3754; *to tend vineyards, dress vines:*— vinedressers(5).

3756. כַּרְמִי Karmi (501d); from the same as 3754; two Isr.:— Carmi(8).

3757. כַּרְמִי Karmi (502a); from 3756; desc. of Carmi:— Carmites(1).

3758. כַּרְמִיל karmil (502b); prob. of for. or.; *crimson, carmine:*— crimson(3).

3759. כַּרְמֶל karmel (502a); from the same as 3754; *a plantation, garden land, fruit, garden growth:*— fertile field(5), fertile fields(1), fresh ears(1), fresh ears of grain(1), fruitful(1), fruitful field(3), fruitful garden(1), fruitful land(1), new growth(2), thickest(2).

3760. כַּרְמֶל Karmel (502a); from the same as 3754; a mountain promontory on the Mediterranean, also a city near Hebron:— Carmel(22).

3761. כַּרְמְלִי Karmeli (502b); from 3760; inhab. of Carmel:— Carmelite(3), Carmelitess(1).

3762. כַּרְמְלִית Karmelith (502b); fem. of 3761; a Carmelite woman:— Carmelitess(1).

3763. כְּרָן Keran (502b); of unc. der.; an Edomite:— Cheran(2).

3764. כָּרְסֵא korse (1097c); (Ara.) corr. to 3678; *a throne:*— throne(2), thrones(1).

3765. כִּרְסֵם kirsem (493c); from 3697; *to tear off:*— eats it away(1).

3766. כָּרַע kara (502c); a prim. root; *to bow down:*— bow(3), bow down(2), bowed(4), bowed down(9), bring him low(1), brought me very low(1), couches(2), crouch(1), feeble(1), fell(1), kneel down(2), kneeled down(1), kneeled*(1), kneeling(1), kneels*(1), sank(1), subdued(3), very low(1).

3767. כְּרָע kera (502d); from 3766; *a leg:*— legs(9).

3768. כַּרְפַּס karpas (502d); of for. or.; *cotton* or *fine linen:*— fine and linen(1).

3769. כָּרַר karar (502d); a prim. root; *to dance:*— dancing(2).

3770. כְּרֵשׂ kares (503c); from an unused word; *belly:*— stomach(1).

3771. כַּרְשְׁנָא Karshena (503c); of for. or.; a Pers. prince:— Carshena(1).

3772. כָּרַת karath (503c); a prim. root; *to cut off, cut down:*— beams(3), cease(1), chewed(1), completely cut off(1), covenanted(1), cut(10), cut her off(1), cut him off(5), cut it down(1), cut it off(1), cut them down(1), cut you down(1), cut you off(2), cut down(23), cut off(129), cuts(1), cuts off(4), cutter(1), destroy(1), destroyed(3), fail(1), kill(1), lack(8), made(52), make(31), makes(2), making(2), making an in writing(1), perish(1).

3773. כָּרֻתָה karuthah (503c); the same as 3772, q.v.

3774. כְּרֵתִי Kerethi (504d); from 3772; the for. bodyguard of King David:— Cherethites(10).

3775. כֶּשֶׂב keseb (461b); by transp. for 3532; *a lamb:*— lamb(3), lambs(3), sheep(6), sheep*(1).

3776. כִּשְׂבָּה kisbah (461b); fem. of 3775; *a ewe lamb:*— lamb(1).

3777. כֶּשֶׂד Kesed (505a); of unc. der.; a son of Nahor:— Chesed(1).

3778. כַּשְׂדִּי Kasdi or

כַּשְׂדִּימָה Kasdimah (505a); from 3777; a region of S. Bab. and its inhab.:— Chaldea(7), Chaldeans(71), Chaldeans'(1), Chaldees(1).

3779. כַּשְׂדָּי Kasday (1098a); (Ara.) corr. to 3778; inhab. of Chaldea:— Chaldean(3), Chaldeans(6).

3780. כָּשָׂה kasah (505b); a prim. root; *to be sated* or *gorged* (with food):— sleek(1).

3781. כַּשִּׁיל kashshil (506a); from 3782; *an axe:*— hatchet(1).

3782. כָּשַׁל kashal (505b); a prim. root; *to stumble, stagger, totter:*— bring you down(1), bring down(1), brought down(1), cast down(1), downfall(1), fail(1), failed(1), failing(1), fall(4), fall down(1), feeble(3), feeble*(1), overthrown(1), stumble(26), stumble badly(1), stumbled(12), stumbles(2), tottering(1), weak(1).

3783. כִּשָּׁלוֹן kishshalon (506a); from 3782; *a stumbling:*— stumbling(1).

3784. כָּשַׁף kashaph (506c); denom. vb. from 3785; *to practice sorcery:*— practiced sorcery(1), sorcerer(1), sorcerers(3), sorceress(1).

3785. כֶּשֶׁף kesheph (506c); from an unused word; *sorcery:*— sorceries(5), witchcrafts(1).

3786. כַּשָּׁף kashshaph (506d); from the same as 3785; *sorcerer:*— sorcerers(1).

3787. כָּשֵׁר kasher (506d); a prim. root; *to be advantageous, proper,* or *suitable, to succeed:*— giving success(1), proper(1), succeed(1).

3788. כִּשְׁרוֹן kishron (507a); from 3787; *skill, success:*— advantage(1), skill(2).

3789. כָּתַב kathab (507a); a prim. root; *to write:*— decreed(1), describe(3), described(1), inscribed(1), prescribed(2), record(3), recorded(7), registered(3), registers(1), sign(1), signed(2), write(31), write them down(1), write down(1), write...down(1), writes(2), writing(1), written(126), written down(4), wrote(27), wrote down(2).

3790. כְּתַב kethab (1098a); (Ara.) corr. to 3789; *to write:*— write down(1), writing(2), written(2), wrote(2), wrote the down(1).

3791. כְּתָב kethab (508b); from 3789; *a writing:*— decree(1), edict(2), letter(1), register(1), registration*(2), regulation(1), script(4), text(2), writing(3).

3792. **כְּתָב kethab** (1098a); (Ara.) corr. to 3791; *a writing:*— document(3), inscription(7), needed(1), written(1).

3793. **כְּתֹבֶת kethobeth** (508b); from 3789; *an imprint:*— marks(1), tattoo*(1).

3794. **כִּתִּי Kitti** or

כִּתִּיִּי Kittiyyi (508c); from an unused name; a son of Javan, also his desc. and their land:— Cyprus(3), Kittim(5).

3795. **כָּתִית kathith** (510c); from 3807; *beaten:*— beaten(5).

3796. **כֹּתֶל kothel** (508c); from an unused word; *wall* (of a house):— wall(2), walls(1).

3797. **כְּתַל kethal** (1098b); (Ara.) corr. to 3796; *a wall.*

3798. **כִּתְלִישׁ Kithlish** (508c); from the same as 3796; a city in Judah:— Chitlish(1)

3799. **כָּתַם katham** (508d); a prim. root; *to be stained:*— stain(1).

3800. **כֶּתֶם kethem** (508d); from an unused word; *gold:*— fine gold(2), gold(6), pure gold(1).

3801. **כְּתֹנֶת kethoneth** or

כֻּתֹּנֶת kuttoneth (509a); from an unused word; *a tunic:*— coat(2), dress(1), garment(2), garments(4), tunic(14), tunics(6).

3802. **כָּתֵף katheph** (509b); of unc. der.; *shoulder, shoulder blade, side:*— backs(1), flank(1), hands(1), next(1), shoulder(19), shoulders(7), side(26), sides(3), slope(4), slopes(1), supports(4).

3803. **כָּתַר kathar** (509c); a prim. root; *to surround:*— crowned(1), encircled(1), surround(2), surrounded(1), wait(1).

3804. **כֶּתֶר kether** (509d); from 3803; *a crown:*— crown(3).

3805. **כֹּתֶרֶת kothereth** (509d); from 3803; *capital* (of a pillar):— capital(11), capitals(12), crown(1).

3806. **כָּתַשׁ kathash** (509d); a prim. root; *to pound, pound fine, bray:*— pound(1).

3807. **כָּתַת kathath** (510a); a prim. root; *to beat, crush by beating:*— battered(1), beat(2), beat them down(1), broke in pieces(1), broken in pieces(1), crush(1), crushed(4), defeated(1), hammer(2), shattered(1), smashed(1), strike(1).

ל

3808. **לֹא lo** or

לוֹא lo or

לֹה loh (518b); a prim. adv.; *not:*— before(3), before*(5), behold(2), beyond(2), breathless*(1), cannot(81), cannot their nor(1), cannot*(47), carefully(1), cheaply*(1), disregarded*(1), except(1), failed*(1), false*(1), futile*(1), gone(1), ignorant*(1), illiterate*(1), impotent*(1), incapable*(1), indeed(2), injustice*(2), instead(2), many*(1), most assuredly*(1), neither(8), neither by nor(1), neither he nor(1), neither him nor(1), neither i nor(1), neither my nor(1), neither them nor(1), neither they nor(2), neither you nor(3), neither your nor(1), neither*(4), neither...nor(15), neither(2), never(64), never about nor(1), never*(25), no(525), no been nor(1), no to nor(1), no*(30), none(28), none*(19), nor(401), nor*(5), nothing(35), nothing*(27), nowhere*(1), or(10), or else(1), otherwise(4), pathless*(2), rather than(3), refrain(1), refuse*(1), refused*(1), ruthlessly*(1), so(11), so that we will no(1), such(1), surely*(27), too(1), truly*(2), unable*(10), unanswered*(1), unavoidable*(1), unaware*(1), unawares*(1), unceasingly*(1), unclean*(3), undivided*(1), undone*(1), ungodly*(1), unjustly*(1), unknown*(1), unless(1), unless*(7), unproductive*(1), unpunished*(1), unreliable*(1), unsearchable*(1), unsown*(1), unsparing*(1), untrained*(1), unvented*(1), unwilling*(3), unwise*(1), useless*(1), weak(1), whether*(1), without(61), worthless*(2).

3809. **לָא la** or

לָה lah (1098c); (Ara.) corr. to 3808; *not:*— disregarded*(1), ignorant*(1), neither(1), never*(1), no(8), no*(6), none*(1), nor(3), nothing(1), nothing*(1), without(5).

3810. **לֹא דְבָר Lo Debar** or

לוֹ דְבָר Lo Debar or

לִדְבִר Lidbir or

לְדְבָר Lodebar (520d); from 3808 and 1699a; "pastureless," a place in Gilead:— Lodebar(3), Lodebar(1).

3811. **לָאָה laah** (521a); a prim. root; *to be weary* or *impatient:*— become impatient(1), exhausted(1), find difficulty(1), impatient(1), parched(1), tired(2), try the patience(2), wearied(4), wearies(1), weary(5).

3812. **לֵאָה Leah** (521b); from 3811; "weary," a wife of Jacob:— Leah(28), Leah's(6).

3813. **לָאַט laat** (521b); a prim. root; *to cover:*— covered(1).

3814. **לָאט lat** (31d); from a prep. pref. and 328, q.v.

3815. **לָאֵל Lael** (522b); from a prep. pref. and 410; "belonging to God," a Levite:— Lael(1).

3816. **לְאֹם leom** or

לְאוֹם leom (522c); from an unused word; *people:*— nation(1), nations(11), other(1), people(4), peoples(17), peoples'(1).

3817. **לְאֻמִּים Leummim** (522c); pl. of 3816; desc. of Dedan:— Leummim(1).

3818. **לֹא עַמִּי Lo Ammi** (520d); from 3808 and 5971a; "not my people," symbolic name of Hosea's son:— Lo-ammi(1).

3819. **לֹא רֻחָמָה Lo Ruchamah** (520d); from 3808 and 7355; "without compassion," symbolic name of Hosea's daughter:— Lo-ruhamah(2).

3820. **לֵב leb** (524b); from the same as 3824; *inner man, mind, will, heart:*— accord(1), attention(4), attention*(1), bravest*(1), brokenhearted*(3), care*(2), celebrating*(1), chests*(1), completely*(1), concern*(1), concerned*(1), conscience(1), consider*(2), considered*(2), courage(1), decided*(1), determine*(1), discouraged*(1), discouraging*(1), doing*(1), double heart(1), encouragingly*(1), heart(396), heart's(2), hearts(40), Himself(1), himself(6), imagination(1), inspiration(2), intelligence(1), kindly(5), life(1), merry-hearted*(1), middle(2), midst(1), mind(36), minds(3), myself(6), obstinate*(2), planned*(1), presume*(1), pride*(1), recalls*(1), reflected*(1), regard*(1), self-exaltation*(1), sense(10), senseless*(1), seriously(1), skill*(1), skilled*(1), skillful man*(1), skillful men*(1), skillful persons*(1), skillful*(3), spirits(1), stouthearted*(1), stubborn-minded*(1), tenderly(2), thought(3), understanding(7), undivided*(1), well(2), willingly*(1), wisdom(2), yourself(1), yourselves(1).

3821. **לֵב leb** (1098d); (Ara.) corr. to 3820; *heart:*— myself(1).

3822. **לְבָאוֹת Lebaoth** (522d); from the same as 3833b; a city in S. Judah:— Lebaoth(1).

3823a. **לָבַב labab** (525d); denom. vb. from 3824; *to get a mind* or *to encourage:*— become intelligent(1), heart beat faster(2).

3823b. **לָבַב labab** (525d); denom. vb. from 3834; *to make cakes:*— made cakes(1), make(1).

3824. **לֵבָב lebab** (523b); from an unused word; *inner man, mind, will, heart:*— anger(1), breasts(1), conscientious*(1), consider*(5), courage(1), desire(1), encouragingly*(1), fainthearted*(3), heart(185), heart and the hearts(1), heart's(1), hearts(27), hearts like his heart(1), intelligence(1), intended(2), mind(8), purpose(1), thought(1), timid*(1), understanding(2), wholehearted*(1), wholeheartedly*(1), yourself(1).

3825. **לְבַב lebab** (1098d); (Ara.) corr. to 3824; *heart:*— heart(3), mind(4).

3826. **לִבָּה libbah** (525d); from the same as 3824; *heart:*— heart(1).

3827. **לַבָּה labbah** (529b); the same as 3852, q.v.

3828. **לְבוֹנָה lebonah** or

לְבֹנָה lebonah (526d); from 3835a; *frankincense:*— frankincense(13), incense(8).

3829. **לְבוֹנָה Lebonah** (526d); from 3835a; a place near Shiloh:— Lebonah(1).

3830. **לְבוּשׁ lebush** or

לְבֻשׁ lebush (528c); from 3847; *a garment, clothing, raiment:*— apparel(3), armor(1), attire*(1), clothed(2), clothing(12), dressed*(1), garment(5), garments(3), robe(3), robes(2).

3831. **לְבוּשׁ lebush** (1098d); (Ara.) corr. to 3830; *a garment:*— clothes(1), vesture(1).

3832. **לָבַט labat** (526a); a prim. root; *to thrust down, out,* or *away:*— ruined(3).

3833a. **לְבִי lebi** (522d); from the same as 3833b; *a lion:*— lions(1).

3833b. **לָבִיא labi** or

לְבִיָּא lebiyya or

לְבָאִים lebaim or

לְבָאוֹת lebaoth (522d); from an unused word; *a lion, lioness:*— lion(4), lioness(8), lionesses(1).

3834. **לָבִיבָה labibah** or

לְבִבָה lebibah (525d); from the same as 3824; *cakes:*— cakes(3).

3835a. **לָבֵן laben** (526a); a prim. root; *to be white:*— become white(1), make them pure(1), purified(1), white(1), whiter(1).

3835b. **לָבַן laban** (527c); denom. vb. from 3843; *to make brick:*— make brick(1), make bricks(1), making brick(1).

3836. **לָבָן laban** (526b); from 3835a; *white:*— white(24), white ones(1).

3837a. **לָבָן Laban** (526c); from 3835a; father-in-law of Jacob:— Laban(50), Laban's(4).

3837b. **לָבָן Laban** (526c); from 3835a; a place in the Sinai desert:— Laban(1).

3837c. **לַבֵּן labben** (527d); of unc. der.; perh. "to the son," part of a psalm title.

3838. **לְבָנָא Lebana** or

לְבָנָה Lebanah (526c); from 3835a; an Isr.:— Lebana(1), Lebanah(1).

3839. לִבְנֶה **libneh** (527b); from 3835a; *poplar:*— poplar(2).

3840. לִבְנָה **libnah** (527b); the same as 3843, q.v.

3841. לִבְנָה **Libnah** (526c); from 3835a; a city in S.W. Judah, also a place in the wilderness:— Libnah(18).

3842. לְבָנָה **lebanah** (526b); from 3835a; *moon:*— full moon(1), moon(2).

3843. לְבֵנָה **lebenah** (527b); from 3835a; *brick, tile:*— brick(2), bricks(7), pavement(1).

3844. לְבָנוֹן **Lebanon** (526d); from 3835a; a wooded mountain range on the N. border of Isr.:— Lebanon(71).

3845. לִבְנִי **Libni** (526d); from 3835a; two Levites:— Libni(5).

3846a. לִבְנִי **Libni** (526d); from 3845; desc. of Libni:— Libnites(2).

3846b. לֵב קָמָי **Leb Qamay** (525d); from 3820 and 6965; "the heart of (those who are) rising up against Me," cryptic name for Chaldea (Bab.):— Leb-kamai(1).

3847. לָבַשׁ **labash** or

לָבֵשׁ **labesh** (527d); a prim. root; *to put on, wear, clothe, be clothed:*— apparel(1), array(1), arrayed(3), attired(1), came(3), clothe(11), clothe yourself(3), clothe yourselves(1), clothed(36), dress(1), dressed(5), gave them clothes(1), put(36), put on clothing(1), putting(1), wear(5), worn(1).

3848. לְבֵשׁ **lebesh** (1098d); (Ara.) corr. to 3847; *to be clothed:*— clothed(3).

3849. לֹג **log** (528d); of unc. der.; *a log* (a liquid measure):— log(5).

3850a. לֹד **Lod** (528d); of unc. der.; a city in Benjamin near Joppa:— Lod(4).

3850b. לִדְבִר **Lidbir** (529a); another reading for 1688, q.v.

3851. לַהַב **lahab** (529a); from an unused word; *flame, blade:*— blade(2), flame(6), flames(1), flashing(2).

3852. לֶהָבָה **lehabah** or

לֶהֶבֶת **lahebeth** (529b); fem. of 3851; *flame, blade:*— blazing(1), blazing flame(1), flame(12), flames(1), flaming(4), head(1).

3853. לְהָבִים **Lehabim** (529c); from the same as 3851; a tribe desc. from Mizraim:— Lehab(1), Lehabim(1).

3854. לַהַג **lahag** (529c); from an unused word; *study, devotion* (to books):— excessive devotion(1).

3855. לַהַד **Lahad** (529c); of unc. der.; a man of Judah:— Lahad(1).

3856. לָהָה **lahah** (529c); a prim. root; *to languish, faint:*— languished(1).

3857. לָהַט **lahat** (529c); a prim. root; *to blaze up, flame:*— aflame(1), breathe forth fire(1), burned(1), burns(2), consumed(1), flaming(1), kindles(1), set him aflame(1), set them ablaze(1), sets on fire(1), sets the on fire(1).

3858a. לַהַט **lahat** (529d); from 3857; *a flame:*— flaming(1).

3858b. לִהְלֵהַּ **lihleah** (529c); from 3856; *to amaze, startle:*— madman(1).

3859. לָהַם **laham** (529d); a prim. root; *to swallow greedily:*— dainty morsels(2).

3860. לָהֵן **lahen** (530a); from a prep. pref. and 2005; *on this account, therefore:*— therefore(2).

3861a. לָהֵן **lahen** (1099a); (Ara.) corr. to 3860; *therefore:*— therefore(3).

3861b. לָהֵן **lahen** (1099a); (Ara.) corr. to 3860; *except, but:*— besides*(2), except(2), unless(1).

3862. לַהֲקָה **lahaqah** (530a); of unc. der.; *band, company:*— company(1).

3863. לוּא **lu** or

לֻא **lu** or

לוּ **lu** (530a); a prim. conjunc.; *if, oh that:*— if(8), if only(4), Oh(4), please(1), would(3).

3864. לוּבִים **Lubim** (530c); of unc. der.; inhab. of N. Africa:— Libya(1), Libyans(1), Lubim(3).

3865. לוּד **Lud** (530d); prob. of for. or.; a son of Shem, also his desc. and their land:— Lud(5).

3866. לוּדִים **Ludim** (530d); from the same as 3865; a tribe desc. from Mizraim:— Ludim(1), Lydians(1), people of Lud(1).

3867a. לָוָה **lavah** (530d); a prim. root; *to join, be joined:*— allied(1), become attached(1), join(5), joined(4), stand(1).

3867b. לָוָה **lavah** (531a); a prim. root; *to borrow:*— borrow(1), borrowed(1), borrower becomes the lender's(1), borrows(1), lend(4), lender like the borrower(1), lends(3).

3868. לוּז **luz** (531b); a prim. root; *to turn aside, depart:*— depart(1), devious(3), guile(1), vanish(1).

3869. לוּז **luz** (531c); prob. of for. or.; *almond tree, almond wood:*— almond(1).

3870. לוּז **Luz** (531c); prob. from the same as 3869; earlier name of Bethel, also a Hittite city:— Luz(8).

3871. לוּחַ **luach** or

לֻחַ **luach** (531d); from an unused word; *a tablet, board* or *plank, a plate:*— planks(4), plates(1), tablet(4), tablets(34).

3872. לוּחִית **Luchith** or

לֻחוֹת **Luchoth** (532a); from the same as 3871; a place in Moab:— Luhith(2).

3873. לוֹחֵשׁ **Lochesh** (538a); from 3907; "whisperer," a leader in Isr.:— Hallohesh(2).

3874. לוּט **lut** (532a); a prim. root; *to wrap closely* or *tightly, enwrap, envelop:*— wrapped(2).

3875. לוֹט **lot** (532b); from 3874; *envelope, covering:*— covering*(1).

3876. לוֹט **Lot** (532b); from 3874; Abraham's nephew:— lot(32), Lot's(1).

3877. לוֹטָן **Lotan** (532b); from 3874; a son of Seir:— Lotan(5), Lotan's(2).

3878. לֵוִי **Levi** (532b); of unc. der.; a son of Jacob, also the tribe descended from him:— Levi(65), Levi's(1).

3879. לֵוִי **Levay** (1099a); (Ara.) corr. to 3881; desc. of Levi:— Levites(4).

3880. לִוְיָה **livyah** (531b); from an unused word; *a wreath:*— garland(1), wreath(1).

3881. לֵוִיִּי **Leviyyi** or

לֵוִי **Levi** (532d); from 3878; desc. of Levi:— Levite(26), Levites(241), Levites'(1), Levites*(1), Levitical(15).

3882. לִוְיָתָן **Livyathan** (531b); from the same as 3880; "serpent," a sea monster or dragon:— Leviathan(6).

3883. לוּל **lul** (533b); of unc. der.; *a shaft* or *enclosed space with steps* or *ladder:*— winding stairs(1).

3884a. לוּלֵא **lule** or

לוּלֵי **lule** (530b); from 3863 and 3808; *if not, unless:*— if(5), if*(1), unless(2), unless*(1).

3884b. לֻלָאֹת **lulay** (533b); from an unused word; *a loop:*— loops(13).

3885a. לוּן **lun** or

לִין **lin** (533c); a prim. root; *to lodge, pass the night, abide:*— abide(2), dwell(1), endure(1), gazes(1), hang all night(1), last(1), left over(1), lies all night(2), lodge(9), lodged(6), lodges(3), night(2), pass(1), remain(1), remain with you all night(1), remain overnight(2), sleep(1), spend(2), spend the night(21), spent(3), spent the night(7).

3885b. לוּן **lun** (534a); a prim. root; *to murmur:*— growl(1), grumble(4), grumbled(7), grumbling(2), making(1).

3886a. לוּעַ **lua** (534b); a prim. root; *to swallow, swallow down:*— swallow(1).

3886b. לוּעַ **lua** or

לָעַע **laa** (534b); a prim. root; *to talk wildly:*— been rash(1), say rashly(1).

3887. לוּץ **luts** (539b); the same as 3917b, q.v.

3888. לוּשׁ **lush** (534c); a prim. root; *to knead:*— knead(2), kneaded(2), kneading(1).

3889. לוּשׁ **Lush** (539d); the same as 3919a, q.v.

3890. לְוָת **levath** (1099a); (Ara.) perh. from a root corr. to 3867a; *to, at, beside.*

3891. לְזוּת **lazuth** (531c); from 3868; *deviation, crookedness:*— devious(1).

3892. לַח **lach** (535a); from an unused word; *moist, fresh, new:*— fresh(4), green(2).

3893. לֵחַ **leach** (535a); from the same as 3892; *moisture, freshness:*— vigor(1).

3894. לְחוּם **lechum** (535d); from 3898b; *intestines, bowels:*— eating(1), flesh(1).

3895. לְחִי **lechi** (534d); from an unused word; *jaw, cheek:*— cheek(6), cheeks(4), jaw(1), jawbone(4), jaws(4), two cheeks(1).

3896. לְחִי **Lechi** (534d); from the same as 3895; a place prob. in Judah:— Lehi(4).

3897. לָחַךְ **lachak** (535a); a prim. root; *to lick:*— lick(4), licked(1), licks(1).

3898a. לָחַם **lacham** (535b); a prim. root; *to fight, do battle:*— conquer*(1), ever fight(1), fight(77), fighting(15), fights(2), fought(59), made war(1), make war(5), making war(1), overcome(1), waging war(1), war(1), warred(2), warring(3).

3898b. לָחַם **lacham** (536d); a prim. root; *to use as food, eat:*— consumed(1), dine(1), eat(4).

3899. לֶחֶם **lechem** (536d); from 3898b; *bread, food:*— bread(188), food(87), fruit(1), loaves(3), meal(7), meal*(1), meals(2), prey(1), provision(1), showbread*(4), something(1).

3900. לְחֶם **lechem** (1099b); (Ara.) corr. to 3899; *a feast:*— feast(1).

3901. לָחֶם **lachem** (535d); from 3898a; perh. *war:*— war(1).

3902. לַחְמִי **Lachmi** (537c); from 3898b; a brother of Goliath:— Lahmi(1).

3903. לַחְמָס Lachmas or

לַחְמָם Lachmam (537c); from 3898b; a place in Judah:— Lahmas(1).

3904. לְחֵנָה lechenah (1099b); (Ara.) of unc. der.; *a concubine:*— concubines(3).

3905. לָחַץ lachats (537d); a prim. root; *to squeeze, press, oppress:*— afflict(1), forced(1), hold the shut(1), oppress(2), oppressed(6), oppresses(1), oppressing(2), oppressors(3), pressed(2).

3906. לַחַץ lachats (537d); from 3905; *oppression, distress:*— oppression(8), sparingly(2).

3907. לָחַשׁ lachash (538a); a prim. root; *to whisper, charm:*— charmers(1), whisper(1), whispering(1).

3908. לַחַשׁ lachash (538a); from 3907; *a whispering, charming:*— amulets(1), charm(1), charmed(1), enchanter(1), whisper a prayer(1).

3909. לָט lat (532a); from 3874; *secrecy, mystery:*— secret arts(4), secretly(4).

3910. לֹט lot (538b); of unc. der.; *myrrh:*— myrrh(2).

3911. לְטָאָה letaah (538b); of unc. der.; (a kind of) *lizard:*— lizard(1).

3912. לְטוּשִׁם Letushim (538c); from 3913; "hammered ones," desc. of Abraham and Keturah:— Letushim(1).

3913. לָטַשׁ latash (538b); a prim. root; *to hammer, sharpen, whet:*— forger(1), glares*(1), sharp(1), sharpen(2).

3914. לִיָה loyah (531b); from the same as 3880; perh. *wreath:*— wreaths(3).

3915. לַיִל layil or

לֵיל lel or

לַיְלָה layelah (538c); of unc. der.; *night:*— midnight*(6), night(200), nights(14), nocturnal(1), overnight*(2), tonight(10).

3916. לֵילְיָא lela (1099b); (Ara.) corr. to 3915; *night:*— night(5).

3917a. לִילִית lilith (539b); from the same as 3915; a female night-demon:— night monster(1).

3917b. לִיץ lits (539b); a prim. root; *to scorn:*— carry on as scoffers(1), deride(1), envoys(1), interpreter(1), makes a mockery(1), mediator(1), mock(1), mocker(1), scoff(1), scoffer(10), scoffers(5), scoffs at the scoffers(1), scorner(1), spokesmen(1).

3918. לַיִשׁ layish (539d); from an unused word; *a lion:*— lion(3).

3919a. לַיִשׁ Layish (539d); from the same as 3918; "lion," a city and region in N. Canaan:— Laish(4).

3919b. לַיִשׁ Layish (539d); from the same as 3918; an Isr.:— Laish(2).

3919c. לַיְשָׁה Layeshah (539d); from the same as 3918; a place N. of Jer.:— Laishah(1).

3920. לָכַד lakad (539d); a prim. root; *to capture, seize, take:*— capture(9), captured(57), captures(4), captures at all(1), catch(2), caught(12), clasp(1), imprisoned(1), seized(1), take(6), taken(13), taken captive(2), takes(3), took(8).

3921. לֶכֶד leked (540b); from 3920; *a taking, capture:*— caught(1).

3922. לֵכָה Lekah (540b); of unc. der.; a place in Judah:— Lecah(1).

3923. לָכִישׁ Lachish (540b); of unc. der.; a Canaanite city S.W. of Jer.:— Lachish(24).

3924. לֻלָאָה lulaah (533b); the same as 3884b, q.v.

3925. לָמַד lamad (540c); a prim. root; *to exercise in, learn:*— accept(1), expert(1), instruct(1), instructors(1), learn(15), learned(5), really learn(1), skillful(1), taught(15), teach(30), teachers(1), teaches(3), teaching(1), teaching and again(1), train(1), trained(2), trains(3), untrained*(1).

3926. לְמוֹ lemo (518b); a form of a prep. pref.; *to* or *for.*

3927. לְמוּאֵל Lemuel or

לְמוֹאֵל Lemoel (541a); of unc. der.; king of Massa:— Lemuel(2).

3928. לִמּוּד limmud or

לִמֻּד limmud (541a); from 3925; *taught:*— accustomed(2), disciple(1), disciples(2), taught(1).

3929. לֶמֶךְ Lemek (541a); of unc. der.; a desc. of Cain, also a desc. of Seth:— Lamech(11).

3930. לֹעַ loa (534b); from 3886a; prob. *throat:*— throat(1).

3931. לָעַב laab (541b); a prim. root; *to jest:*— mocked(1).

3932. לָעַג laag (541b); a prim. root; *to mock, deride, stammer:*— laugh(1), mock(3), mocked(5), mocks(4), scoff(2), scoffs(1), sneer(1), stammering(1).

3933. לַעַג laag (541c); from 3932; *a mocking, derision:*— derision(4), scoffing(3).

3934. לָעֵג laeg (541d); from 3932; *mocking:*— jesters(1), stammering(1).

3935. לַעְדָּה Ladah (541d); of unc. der.; a man of Judah:— Laadah(1).

3936. לַעְדָּן Ladan (541d); from the same as 3935; an Ephraimite, also a Gershonite:— Ladan(7).

3937. לָעַז laaz (541d); a prim. root; *to talk indistinctly* or *unintelligibly:*— strange language(1).

3938. לָעַט laat (542a); a prim. root; *to swallow* (greedily):— have a swallow(1).

3939. לַעֲנָה laanah (542a); of unc. der.; *wormwood:*— wormwood(8).

3940. לַפִּיד lappid or

לַפִּד lappid (542a); of unc. der.; *a torch:*— burning torches(1), lightning flashes(1), torch(4), torches(7).

3941. לַפִּידוֹת Lappidoth (542b); from the same as 3940; husband of Deborah:— Lappidoth(1).

3942. לִפְנֵי liphnay (819b); from a prep. pref. and 6440, q.v.

3943. לָפַת laphath (542b); a prim. root; *to twist, turn, grasp with a twisting motion:*— bent forward(1), grasped(1), wind along(1).

3944. לָצוֹן latson (539c); from 3917b; *a scorning:*— scoffers*(1), scoffing(1), scorners*(1).

3945. לָצַץ latsats (539b); see 3917b.

3946. לַקּוּם Laqqum (542c); of unc. der.; a N. border town of Naphtali:— Lakkum(1).

3947. לָקַח laqach (542c); a prim. root; *to take:*— accept(8), accepted(3), accepts(2), bring(18), brought(13), buy(1), buys(1), capture(2), captured(2), carry(3), caught(2), exact(1), find(1), flashing(1), flashing forth(1), get(25), gets(1), got(2), has(1), keep(1), married(9), married*(6), marries(1), marry(5), obtain(1), placed(2), procured(2), put(1), raise(3), receive(20), received(12), receives(3), receiving(1), seize(3), seized(2), select(1), selected(1), sent(1), supply(1), take(355), taken(74), takes(15), taking(2), took(352), took away(1), use(1), used(1), wins(1).

3948. לֶקַח leqach (544b); from 3947; *a learning, teaching:*— instruction(1), learning(2), persuasions(1), persuasiveness(2), teaching(3).

3949. לִקְחִי Liqchi (544b); from 3947; a Manassite:— Likhi(1).

3950. לָקַט laqat (544c); a prim. root; *to pick* or *gather up, glean:*— gather(15), gathered(8), glean(8), gleaned(4), gleaning(1), picked(1).

3951. לֶקֶט leqet (545a); from 3950; *a gleaning:*— gleaning(1), gleanings(1).

3952. לָקַק laqaq (545a); a prim. root; *to lap, lick:*— lapped(2), laps(1), lick(1), licked(2).

3953. לָקַשׁ laqash (545c); denom. vb. from 3954; *to take the second crop, to take everything:*— glean(1)

3954. לֶקֶשׁ leqesh (545b); from an unused word; *the after-growth, spring crop:*— spring crop(2).

3955. לָשָׁד lashad (545c); from an unused word; *juice, juicy* or *dainty bit, a dainty:*— cakes baked(1), vitality(1).

3956. לָשׁוֹן lashon or

לָשֹׁן lashon or

לְשֹׁנָה leshonah (546a); from an unused word; *tongue:*— bar(2), bark*(1), bay(3), charmer*(1), language(14), languages(2), slanderer*(1), speech(1), tongue(84), tongues(5), word(1).

3957. לִשְׁכָּה lishkah (545c); of unc. der.; *room, chamber, hall, cell:*— chamber(13), chambers(27), hall(1), room(2), rooms(3).

3958. לֶשֶׁם leshem (545d); of unc. der.; (a precious stone) perh. *amber* or *jacinth:*— jacinth(2).

3959. לֶשֶׁם Leshem (546a); from the same as 3958; a place in N. Pal., the same as 3919a:— Leshem(2).

3960. לָשַׁן lashan (546d); denom. vb. from 3956; *to use the tongue, slander:*— slander(1), slanders(1).

3961. לִשָּׁן lishshan (1099b); (Ara.) corr. to 3956; *tongue:*— language(6), tongue(1).

3962. לֶשַׁע Lesha (546d); of unc. der.; a place on the boundary of Canaan:— Lasha(1).

3963. לֶתֶךְ lethek (547c); of unc. der.; a dry measure:— half(1).

מ

3964. מָא ma (1099d); (Ara.) the same as 4101, q.v.

3965. מַאֲבוּס maabus (7b); from 75; *granary:*— barns(1).

3966. מְאֹד meod (547b); from an unused word; *muchness, force, abundance:*— abundantly(1), all(1), almost(1), badly(3), carefully(1), closely(1), diligent(1), diligently(3), enough(1), especially(1), exceeding(1), exceedingly(14), exceedingly*(3), excessive(1), extremely*(1), far(1), firmly(1), fully(1), great(16), great abundance(1), greatly(52), greatly*(1), hard(1), harder*(1), highly(4), immense(1), louder(1), measure(2), might(2), more(2), more*(1), most(1), much*(1), quickly(1), richly(1), serious*(1), severely(1), so(2), so much(1), sorely(1), strongly(1), swiftly(1), too(2), utterly(1), utterly*(3), very(139), very well(1), very*(2), violently(1), violently*(1), well(2).

3967. מֵאָה meah or

מֵאיָה meyah (547d); a prim. root; *hundred:*— 1,100,000*(1), 1,200*(1), 1,222*(1), 1,247*(2), 1,254*(4), 1,290*(1), 1,335*(1), 1,400*(2), 1,700*(3), 1,760*(1), 1,775*(2), 100(14), 100,000*(7), 108,100*(2), 110*(1), 112*(3), 120*(4), 120,000*(5), 122*(2), 123*(2), 127*(3), 128*(4), 130*(1), 138*(1), 139*(1), 14,700*(1), 140*(1), 148*(1), 150*(4), 151,450*(2), 153,600*(2), 156*(1), 157,600*(2), 16,750*(1), 160*(1), 17,200*(1), 172*(1), 180*(1), 180,000*(3), 185,000*(2), 186,400*(2), 188*(1), 2,172*(2), 2,200*(1), 2,300*(1), 2,322*(1), 2,400*(2), 2,600*(2), 2,630*(1), 2,700*(1), 2,750*(1), 2,812*(1), 2,818*(1), 20,200*(1), 20,800*(1), 200(7), 200,000*(4), 212*(1), 218*(1), 22,200*(1), 22,273*(1), 22,600*(1), 220*(2), 223*(2), 232*(1), 242*(1), 245*(3), 25,100*(1), 250*(5), 250,000*(1), 273*(1), 28,600*(1), 280,000*(2), 284*(1), 288*(1), 3,200*(1), 3,300*(1), 3,600*(2), 3,630*(1), 3,700*(1), 3,930*(1), 30,500*(2), 300*(11), 300,000*(4), 307,500*(2), 32,200*(2), 32,500*(1), 320*(2), 323*(1), 324*(1), 328*(1), 337,500*(4), 345*(2), 35,400*(2), 372*(2), 392*(2), 4,500*(8), 4,600*(2), 40,500*(3), 400*(5), 400,000*(3), 41,500*(2), 410*(1), 42,360*(2), 43,730*(1), 435*(2), 44,760*(1), 45,400*(1), 45,600*(1), 45,650*(2), 450*(2), 454*(1), 46,500*(2), 468*(1), 470,000*(1), 5,400*(1), 500*(3), 500,000*(1), 52,700*(1), 53,400*(3), 530*(1), 54,400*(2), 57,400*(2), 59,300*(2), 6,200*(1), 6,720*(2), 6,800*(1), 60,500*(1), 600*(8), 600,000*(1), 601,730*(2), 603,550*(6), 62,700*(2), 621*(2), 623*(1), 628*(1), 64,300*(1), 64,400*(1), 642*(2), 648*(1), 650*(1), 652*(2), 655*(1), 666*(3), 667*(1), 675*(1), 675,000*(1), 690*(1), 7,100*(1), 7,337*(2), 7,500*(1), 7,700*(2), 700*(5), 721*(1), 725*(1), 730*(1), 736*(2), 74,600*(2), 743*(2), 745*(1), 76,500*(1), 760*(2), 775*(1), 8,580*(1), 8,600*(1), 800,000*(1), 822*(1), 832*(1), 845*(1), 928*(1), 945*(1), 956*(1), 973*(2), eleven*(3), hundred(220), hundredfold*(1), hundreds(27), hundredth(2), one hundred(1), two hundred(1).

3968. מֵאָה Meah (548c); from 3967; a tower on the N. wall of Jer.:— hundred(2).

3969. מְאָה meah (1099b); (Ara.) corr. to 3967; *hundred:*— 100(1), 120*(1), 200(1).

3970. מַאֲוַי maavay (16c); from the same as 336; *desire:*— desires(1).

3971. מאוּם mum or

מוּם mum (548c); from an unused word; *blemish, defect:*— defect(1), spot(1).

3972. מְאוּמָה meumah (548d); from the same as 3971; *anything:*— any sort(1), anything(13), anything*(1), fault(1), nothing*(11), something(1), thing(1), valuable(2).

3973. מָאוֹס maos (549d); from 3988a; *refuse:*— refuse(1).

3974. מָאוֹר maor or

מָאֹר maor or

מְאוֹרָה meorah or

מְאֹרָה meorah (22c); from 215; *a luminary:*— bright(1), light(12), lighting(2), lights(3), shining(1).

3975a. מְאוּרָה meurah (22d); from 215; *a hole for light:*— den(1).

3975b. מֵאָז meaz (23b); from 4480 and 227; *from that time:*— earlier(1), long ago(4), long since(2), old(1), once(1), past(1), since(4).

3976. מֹאזֵן mozen (24d); from 239; *balances, scales:*— balance(1), balances(5), scale(1), scales(8).

3977. מֹאזְנֵא mozanya (1079b); (Ara.) corr. to 3976; *a scale, balance:*— scales(1).

3978. מַאֲכָל maakal (38b); from 398; *food:*— eaten(1), food(26), fruit(2), provision(1), something to eat(1).

3979. מַאֲכֶלֶת maakeleth (38b); from 398; *a knife:*— knife(3), knives(1).

3980. מַאֲכֹלֶת maakoleth (38c); from 398; *fuel:*— fuel(2).

3981. מַאֲמָץ maamats (55c); from 553; *power, strength, force:*— forces(1).

3982. מַאֲמָר maamar (57d); from 559; *a word, command:*— command(2), what(1).

3983. מֵאמַר memar (1081b); (Ara.) corr. to 3982; *a word:*— command(1), request(1).

3984. מָאן man (1099c); (Ara.) perh. corr. to 579; *vessel, utensil:*— utensils(4), vessels(3).

3985. מָאֵן maen (549a); a prim. root; *to refuse:*— absolutely refuses(1), refuse(8), refused(26), refuses(4), refusing(2).

3986. מָאֵן maen (549b); from 3985; *refusing:*— refuse(3).

3987. מֵאֵן meen (549b); from 3985; *refusing:*— who refuse(1).

3988a. מָאַס maas (549b); a prim. root; *to reject:*— abhorred(1), cast them away(1), cast away(1), cast off(2), completely rejected(1), despise(6), despised(4), despises(2), despising(1), disdained(1), refuse(2), reject(8), rejected(37), rejects(1), reprobate(1), retract(1), utterly rejected(1), waste away(1).

3988b. מָאַס maas (549d); a prim. root; *to flow, run:*— flow(1), runs(1).

3989. מַאֲפֶה maapheh (66b); from 644; *something baked:*— baked(1).

3990. מַאֲפֵל maaphel (66d); from the same as 652; *darkness:*— darkness(1).

3991. מַאֲפֵלְיָה maapheleyah (66d); from the same as 652; *deep darkness:*— thick darkness(1).

3992. מָאַר maar (549d); a prim. root; *to prick, to pain:*— malignancy(2), malignant(1), prickling(1).

3993. מַאֲרָב maarab (70d); from 693; *an ambush:*— ambush(4), lurking places(1).

3994. מְאֵרָה meerah (76d); from the same as 779; *a curse:*— curse(3), curses(2).

3995. מִבְדָּלָה mibdalah (95d); from 914; *a separate place:*— set apart(1).

3996. מָבוֹא mabo (99d); from 935; *entrance, a coming in, entering:*— come(1), enter(1), entrance(13), entry(1), place of its setting(1), setting(5), sunset*(1), west*(1).

3997. מְבוֹאָה meboah (99d); the same as 3996, q.v.

3998. מְבוּכָה mebukah (100d); from 943; *confusion, confounding:*— confusion(2).

3999. מַבּוּל mabbul (550a); of unc. der.; *a flood:*— flood(13).

4000. מְבוֹנִים mabonim (108a); another reading for 995, q.v.

4001. מְבוּסָה mebusah (101b); from 947; *a treading down, subjugation:*— oppressive(2), subjugation(1).

4002. מַבּוּעַ mabbua (616a); from 5042; *a spring* (of water):— springs(2), well(1).

4003. מְבוּקָה mebuqah (101c); from the same as 950; *emptiness:*— desolate(1).

4004. מִבְחוֹר mibchor (104d); from 977; *choice:*— choice(3).

4005. מִבְחָר mibchar (104d); from 977; *choicest, best:*— choice(1), choice men(1), choicest(9).

4006. מִבְחָר Mibchar (104d); from 977; one of David's warriors:— Mibhar(1).

4007. מַבָּט mabbat or

מֶבָּט mebbat (613d); from 5027; *expectation:*— expectation(1), hope(2).

4008. מִבְטָא mibta (105a); from the same as 981; *rash utterance:*— rash statement(2).

4009. מִבְטָח mibtach (105c); from 982; *confidence:*— confidence(5), secure(1), security(1), trust(5), which they trust(1), who are the trust(1), whom you trust(1).

4010. מַבְלִיגִית mabligith (114d); from 1082; *smiling, cheerfulness, source of brightening:*— healing(1).

4011. מִבְנֶה mibneh (125d); from 1129; *structure:*— structure(1).

4012. מְבֻנַּי Mebunnay (125d); from 1129; one of David's heroes:— Mebunnai(1).

4013. מִבְצָר mibtsar or

מִבְצָרָה mibtsarah (131b); from 1219; *fortification:*— besieged(1), fortifications(5), fortified(17), fortified cities(1), fortified city(1), fortress(3), fortresses(1), strongest(1), strongholds(6), tester(1), well-fortified(1).

4014. מִבְצָר Mibtsar (550b); of unc. der.; an Edomite chief:— Mibzar(2).

4015. מִבְרָח mibrach (138b); another reading for 4005, q.v.

4016. מָבֻשׁ mabush or

מָבוּשׁ mabush (102b); from 954; *private parts, genitalia:*— genitals(1).

4017. מִבְשָׂם Mibsam (142a); from the same as 1314; a son of Ishmael, also a Simeonite:— Mibsam(3).

4018a. מְבַשְּׁלוֹת mebashsheloth (143b); from 1310; *cooking hearths:*— boiling places(1).

4018b. מַג mag (550b); see 7248.

4019. מַגְבִּישׁ Magbish (150d); from the same as 1378; an Isr. family:— Magbish(1).

4020. מִגְבָּלֹת migbaloth (148b); from the same as 1366; *twisted things,* i.e. *cords:*— twisted(1).

4021. מִגְבָּעוֹת migbaoth (149b); from the same as 1387; *headgear, a turban:*— caps(4).

4022. מֶגֶד meged (550c); from an unused word; *excellence:*— choice(5), choice things(3), fruits*(1).

4023a. מִגְדּוֹל migdol (154a); from 1431; *a tower:*— tower(1).

4023b. מְגִדּוֹן Megiddon or

מְגִדּוֹ Megiddo (151d); from 1413; a place in Manasseh:— Megiddo(12).

4024. מִגְדּוֹל Migdol or

מִגְדֹּל Migdol (154b); prob. from 1431; a city on the N.E. border of Eg.:— Migdol(6).

4025. מַגְדִּיאֵל Magdiel (550c); from 4022 and 410; "excellence of God," an Edomite chief:— Magdiel(2).

4026. מִגְדָּל migdal or

מִגְדָּלָה **migdalah** (153d); from 1431; *a tower:*— banks(1), podium(1), Tower(8), tower(23), towers(14), watchtower(2).

4027. מִגְדַּל־אֵל **Migdal-el** (154a); from 4026 and 410; "tower of God," a stronghold in Naphtali:— Migdal-el(1).

4028. מִגְדַּל־גָּד **Migdal-gad** (154a); from 4026 and 1408; "tower of Gad," a city in Judah:— Migdal-gad(1).

4029. מִגְדַּל־עֵדֶר **Migdal-eder** (154a); from 4026 and 5739; "flock tower," a tower near Bethlehem:— tower of Eder(1).

4030. מִגְדָּנָה **migdanah** (550c); from the same as 4022; *a choice* or *excellent thing:*— choice presents(1), precious things(2), valuables(1).

4031. מָגוֹג **Magog** (156a); from the same as 1463; perh. "land of Gog," a son of Japheth, also his desc. and their land:— Magog(4).

4032. מָגוֹר **magor** or
מָגוּר **magur** (159a); from 1481b; *fear, terror:*— panic(1), terror(6), terrors(1).

4033. מָגוֹר **magor** or
מָגוּר **magur** (158c); from 1481a; *a sojourning place, dwelling place, a sojourning:*— dwelling(1), pilgrimage(1), sojourning(2), sojournings(2), where he sojourned(1), where...had sojourned(1), where they sojourn(1), where they sojourned(1).

4034. מְגוֹרָה **megorah** (159a); fem. of 4032; *fear, terror:*— fears(1), what fears(1), what they dread(1).

4035. מְגוּרָה **megurah** (158c); from 1481a; *a storehouse, granary:*— barn(1).

4036. מָגוֹר מִסָּבִיב **Magor Missabib** (159a); from 4032 and 5439; "terror on every side," an expression coined by Jeremiah:— Magor-missabib(1).

4037. מַגְזֵרָה **magzerah** (160d); from 1504; *a cutting instrument, axe:*— axes(1).

4038. מַגָּל **maggal** (618c); from an unused word; *a sickle:*— sickle(2).

4039. מְגִלָּה **megillah** (166b); from 1556; *a scroll:*— scroll(18), scroll*(3).

4040. מְגִלָּה **megillah** (1086c); (Ara.) corr. to 4039; *a scroll:*— scroll(1).

4041. מְגַמָּה **megammah** (169d); from the same as 1571; perh. *assembling:*— horde(1).

4042. מָגַן **magan** (171c); denom. vb. from 4043; *to deliver up, deliver:*— delivered(2), present(1), surrender(1).

4043. מָגֵן **magen** or
מְגִנָּה **meginnah** (171b); from 1598; *a shield:*— armed(2), buckler(1), large(1), rulers(1), scales(1), shield(41), shields(16).

4044. מְגִנָּה **meginnah** (171c); from 1598; *a covering:*— hardness(1).

4045. מִגְעֶרֶת **migereth** (172b); from 1605; *a rebuke:*— rebuke(1).

4046. מַגֵּפָה **maggephah** (620a); from 5062; *a blow, slaughter, plague, pestilence:*— blow(1), calamity(1), plague(19), plagued(1), plagues(1), slaughter(3).

4047. מַגְפִּיעָשׁ **Magpiash** (550d); of unc. der.; an Isr.:— Magpiash(1).

4048. מָגַר **magar** (550d); a prim. root; *to cast, throw, toss:*— cast(1), delivered(1).

4049. מְגַר **megar** (1099c); (Ara.) corr. to 4048; *to overthrow:*— overthrow(1).

4050. מְגֵרָה **megerah** (176b); from 1641; *a saw:*— axes(1), saws(3).

4051. מִגְרוֹן **Migron** (550d); from 4048; an area near Gibeah, also a place N. of Michmash:— Migron(2).

4052. מִגְרָעָה **migraah** (175d); from 1639; *a recess, ledge:*— offsets(1).

4053. מֶגְרָפָה **megraphah** (175d); from 1640; *a shovel:*— clods(1).

4054. מִגְרָשׁ **migrash** or
מִגְרָשָׁה **migrashah** (177b); from 1644; *a common, common land, open land:*— open space(1), open spaces(2), pasture(2), pasture lands(109).

4055. מַד **mad** or
מֵד **med** (551b); from 4058; *a measure, cloth garment:*— armor(2), attire*(1), carpets(1), cloak(1), clothes(1), garment(1), garments(1), measure(1), measured(1), robe(1), stature(1).

4056. מַדְבַּח **madbach** (1087a); (Ara.) from 1684; *an altar:*— altar(1).

4057a. מִדְבָּר **midbar** (184c); from 1696; *mouth:*— mouth(1).

4057b. מִדְבָּר **midbar** (184d); from 1696; *wilderness:*— desert(11), deserts(1), wilderness(257).

4058. מָדַד **madad** (551a); a prim. root; *to measure:*— continues(1), measure(9), measured(41), stretched(1), surveyed(1).

4059. מִדַּד **middad** (551a); the same as 4058, q.v.

4060a. מִדָּה **middah** (551c); fem. of 4055; *measure, measurement, stature, size, a garment:*— area(1), extent(1), measure(6), measurement(7), measurements(13), measures of volume(1), measuring(10), robes(1), roomy(1), section(7), size(3), standard(1), stature(3).

4060b. מִדָּה **middah** (551d); of for. or.; *tribute:*— tax(1).

4061. מִדָּה **middah** or
מִנְדָּה **mindah** (1101b); (Ara.) corr. to 4060b; *tribute:*— tax(1), taxes(1), tribute(3).

4062. מַדְהֵבָה **madhebah** (923c); see 4787b.

4063. מֶדו **madu** (551d); of unc. der.; *a garment:*— garments(2).

4064. מַדְוֶה **madveh** (188c); from 1738; *sickness:*— diseases(2).

4065. מַדּוּחַ **madduach** (623b); from 5080; *something which draws aside, an enticement:*— misleading oracles(1).

4066. מָדוֹן **madon** (193b); from 1777; *strife, contention:*— contention(4), contentions(3), contentious(5), object of contention(1), strife(7).

4067. מָדוֹן **madon** (551c); see 4060a.

4068. מָדוֹן **Madon** (193c); from 1777; a royal city of the Canaanites:— Madon(2).

4069. מַדּוּעַ **maddua** or
מַדֻּעַ **maddua** (396c); from 4100 and 3045; *why? for what reason?:*— why(72).

4070. מְדוֹר **medor** or
מְדֹר **medor** or
מְדָר **medar** (1087b); (Ara.) from 1753; *a dwelling place:*— dwelling(1), dwelling place(3).

4071. מְדוּרָה **medurah** or
מְדֻרָה **medurah** (190b); from 1752; *a pile* (of wood):— pile(1), pyre(1).

4072. מִדְחֶה **midcheh** (191a); from 1760; *means* or *occasion of stumbling:*— ruin(1).

4073. מַדְחֵפָה **madchephah** (191b); from 1765; *a thrust:*— speedily(1).

4074. מָדַי **Maday** (552a); of for. or.; a son of Japheth, also his desc. and their land:— Madai(2), Medes(5), Media(8), Median(1).

4075. מָדַי **Maday** (552a); from 4074; an inhab. of Media:— Mede(1).

4076. מָדַי **Maday** (1099c); (Ara.) corr. to 4074; desc. of Japheth, also their land:— Medes(4), Media(1).

4077. מָדַי **Maday** (1099c); (Ara.) corr. to 4075; an inhab. of Media:— Mede(1).

4078. מַדַּי **madday** (552a); from 4100 and 1767, q.v.

4079. מִדְיָן **midyan** (193b); the same as 4066, q.v.

4080. מִדְיָן **Midyan** (193c); from the same as 4066; a son of Abraham and Keturah, also his desc. and the region where they settled :— Midian(54), Midianites(5).

4081. מִדִּין **Middin** (552a); of unc. der.; a city in the wilderness of Judah:— Middin(1).

4082. מְדִינָה **medinah** (193d); from 1777; *a province:*— each(3), each province(3), every province(2), province(10), provinces(28), realm(1).

4083. מְדִינָה **medinah** (1088c); (Ara.) corr. to 4082; *a district, province:*— province(8), provinces(3).

4084. מִדְיָנִי **Midyani** (193c); from 4080; a desc. of Midian:— Midianite(3), Midianite woman(2), Midianites(3).

4085. מְדֹכָה **medokah** (189a); from the same as 1743; *mortar:*— mortar(1).

4086. מַדְמֵן **Madmen** (199b); from the same as 1828; a place in Moab:— madmen(1).

4087. מַדְמֵנָה **madmenah** (199b); from the same as 1828; *place of dung, dung pit:*— manure pile(1).

4088. מַדְמֵנָה **Madmenah** (199b); from the same as 1828; a place in Benjamin:— Madmenah(1).

4089. מַדְמַנָּה **Madmannah** (199b); from the same as 1828; a city in S. Judah, also a desc. of Caleb:— Madmannah(2).

4090. מְדָן **medan** (193b); the same as 4066, q.v.:— strife(2).

4091. מְדָן **Medan** (193c); from 1777; a son of Abraham and Keturah:— Medan(2).

4092. מְדָנִי **Medani** (193c); the same as 4084, q.v.

4093. מַדָּע **madda** or
מַדַּע **madda** (396b); from 3045; *knowledge, thought:*— bedchamber(1), knowledge(5).

4094a. מַדְקָרָה **madqarah** (201b); from 1856; *a piercing, stab, thrust:*— thrusts(1).

4094b. מְדָר **medar** (1087b); (Ara.) from 1753; *dwelling place:*— place(1).

4095. מַדְרֵגָה **madregah** (201c); from an unused word; *steep place, a steep:*— steep pathway(1), steep pathways(1).

4096. מִדְרָךְ **midrak** (204a); from 1869; *a treading* or *stepping place:*— footstep*(1).

4097. מִדְרָשׁ **midrash** (205d); from 1875; *study, exposition, midrash:*— treatise(2).

4098. מְדֻשָׁה **medushshah** (190d); from 1758; *that which is threshed:*— threshed(1).

4099. מְדָתָא **Medatha** (241a); see 1992b.

4100. מָה **mah** or

מַ־ **ma-** or

מֶה **meh** (552b); a prim. interrogative and indefinite particle; *what? how? anything:*— anything(2), how(93), how long(2), how many(3), how many*(2), how often(2), how*(1), if*(1), many(1), nothing*(1), reason*(2), what(405), whatever(5), whatever*(2), where(3), where*(1), which(1), which*(3), who(2), why(196), why*(14).

4101. מָה **mah** (1099c); (Ara.) corr. to 4100; *what?:*— how(2), reason*(1), what(7), what*(1), whatever(2), why(1).

4102. מָהַהּ **mahah** (554c); a prim. root; *to linger, tarry:*— delay(2), delayed(2), delaying(1), hesitated(1), tarries(1), wait(2).

4103. מְהוּמָה **mehumah** (223b); from 1949; *tumult, confusion, disquietude, discomfiture:*— confusion(5), disturbances(1), panic(2), tumult(1), tumults(1), turmoil(2).

4104. מְהוּמָן **Mehuman** (54d); of for. or.; a eunuch of Ahasuerus:— Mehuman(1).

4105. מְהֵיטַבְאֵל **Mehetabel** (406b); from 3190 and 410; "God benefits," wife of an Edomite king, also an ancestor of the false prophet Shemaiah:— Mehetabel(3).

4106. מָהִיר **mahir** or

מָהִר **mahir** (555b); from 4116; *quick, prompt, ready, skilled:*— prompt(1), ready(1), skilled(2).

4107. מָהַל **mahal** (554c); a prim. root; *to circumcise, weaken:*— diluted(1).

4108. מַהְלֵךְ **mahlek** (237b); the same as 4109, q.v.

4109. מַהֲלָךְ **mahalak** (237b); from 1980; *a walk, journey, a going:*— free(1), journey(1), walk(3).

4110. מַהֲלָל **mahalal** (239c); from 1984b; *praise:*— praise(1).

4111. מַהֲלַלְאֵל **Mahalalel** (239d); from 4110 and 410; "praise of God," great-grandson of Seth, also a man of Judah:— Mahalalel(7).

4112. מַהֲלֻמּוֹת **mahalummoth** (240d); from 1986; *strokes, blows:*— blows(2).

4113. מַהֲמֹרָה **mahamorah** (243b); from an unused word; *a flood, watery pit:*— deep pits(1).

4114. מַהְפֵּכָה **mahpekah** (246b); from 2015; *an overthrow:*— overthrew(3), overthrow(2), overthrown(1).

4115. מַהְפֶּכֶת **mahpeketh** (246b); from 2015; *stocks* (instrument of punishment):— prison*(1), stocks(3).

4116. מָהַר **mahar** (554d); a prim. root; *to hasten:*— act quickly(1), anxious(1), bring quickly(2), bring...quickly(1), do quickly(1), haste(2), hasten(3), hastened(1), hastens(1), hastily(1), hasty(1), hurried(10), hurriedly(2), hurry(8), immediately(1), impetuous(1), impulsive(1), made haste(1), make haste(1), make speed(1), prepare(1), quickly(16), quickly thwarted(1), rapidly(1), soon(2), swift(3).

4117. מָהַר **mahar** (555c); denom. vb. from 4119; *to acquire by paying a purchase price:*— bartered(1), pay a dowry(1).

4118a. מַהֵר **maher** (555a); from 4116; *hastening, speedy, swift:*— coming...quickly(1).

4118b. מַהֵר **maher** (555b); from 4116; *quickly, speedily:*— hastily(1), quickly(16).

4119. מֹהַר **mohar** (555c); from an unused word; *purchase price* (of a wife):— bridal payment(1), dowry(2).

4120. מְהֵרָה **meherah** (555b); from 4116; *haste, speed:*— hurry(1), quickly(14), shortly(1), speed(1), speedily(2), swiftly(1).

4121. מַהֲרַי **Maharay** (555b); from 4116; one of David's heroes:— Maharai(3).

4122. מַהֵר שָׁלָל חָשׁ בַּז **Maher Shalal Chash Baz** (554d, 555b); from 4118a, 7998, 2363a, and 957; "swift (is) booty, speedy (is) prey," symbolic name of Isaiah's son:— Maher-shalal-hash-baz(1).

4123. מַהֲתַלּוֹת **mahathalloth** (251d, 1122c); from 2048; *deceptions:*— illusions(1).

4124. מוֹאָב **Moab** (555d); from a prefixed syllable and 1; a son of Lot,also his desc. and the territory where they settled:— Moab(168), Moab's(1), Moabites(12).

4125. מוֹאָבִי **Moabi** or

מוֹאֲבִיָּה **Moabiyyah** (555d); from 4124; desc. of Moab:— Moab(1), Moabite(6), Moabites(3), Moabitess(6).

4126. מוֹבָא **moba** (100a); by transp. for 3996; *a coming in, entrance:*— coming(1), entrances(1).

4127. מוּג **mug** (556a); a prim. root; *to melt:*— disheartened(1), dissolve(2), dissolved(2), melt(3), melted(2), melted away(4), melts(1), soften(1).

4128. מוֹד **mod** (551a, 556d); the same as 4058, q.v.

4129. מוֹדַע **moda** or

מֹדָע **moda** (396b); from 3045; *kinsman:*— intimate friend(1), kinsman(1).

4130. מוֹדַעַת **modaath** or

מֹדַעַת **modaath** (396b); from 3045; *kindred, kinship:*— kinsman(1).

4131. מוֹט **mot** (556d); a prim. root; *to totter, shake, slip:*— bring down(1), fall(1), falter(1), gives way(1), immovable*(1), moved(8), shake(1), shaken(11), shaken violently(1), slip(4), slipped(2), slips(1), staggering(1), totter(3), tottered(1), totters(1).

4132. מוֹט **mot** (557a); from 4131; *a shaking, pole, bar* (of a yoke):— carrying bars(2), pole(1), yoke bar(1).

4133. מוֹטָה **motah** (557b); fem. of 4132; *a pole, bar* (of a yoke):— bars(2), poles(1), yoke(5), yoke bars(1), yokes(3).

4134. מוּךְ **muk** (557b); a prim. root; *to be low* or *depressed, to grow poor:*— becomes poor(3), becomes poor(1), poorer(1).

4135. מוּל **mul** (557d); a prim. root; *to circumcise:*— circumcise(4), circumcised(25), circumcising(1), cut off(3), shafts(1), surely be circumcised(1).

4136. מוּל **mul** or

מוֹל **mol** or

מוֹאל **mol** or

מֻל **mul** (557b); a prim. root; *front, in front of:*— before(1), front(7), frontier(1), left(1), opposite(8), opposite*(2), over against(1), toward*(2).

4137. מוֹלָדָה **Moladah** (409d); from 3205; a city in Simeon:— Moladah(4).

4138. מוֹלֶדֶת **moledeth** (409d); from 3205; *kindred, birth, offspring:*— birth(7), born(3), kindred(3), native(2), offspring(1), relatives(6).

4139. מוּלָה **mulah** (558a); from 4135; *circumcision:*— circumcision(1).

4140a. מוֹלִיד **Molid** (410a); from 3205; a man of Judah:— Molid(1).

4140b. מוּם **mum** (548c); from the same as 3971; *blemish, defect:*— blemish(2), defect(14), injured*(1), injures*(1), insults(1).

4141. מוּסָב **musab** (687c); from 5437; perh. *encompassing, surrounding:*— surrounding(1).

4142. מוּסַבָּה **musabbah** or

מֻסַבָּה **musabbah** (685b); the same as 5437, q.v.

4143. מוּסָד **musad** (414b); from 3245; *foundation, foundation laying:*— foundation(2).

4144. מוֹסָד **mosad** (414c); from 3245; *foundation:*— foundations(13).

4145. מוּסָדָה **musadah** (414c); fem. of 4143; *foundation, appointment:*— foundations(1), punishment(1).

4146a. מוֹסָדָה **mosadah** or

מֹסָדָה **mosadah** (414c); the same as 4144, q.v.

4146b. מוּסָךְ **musak** (697b); from 5526a; *something covered:*— covered way(1).

4147. מוֹסֵר **moser** or

מוֹסֵרָה **moserah** or

מֹסֵרָה **moserah** (64c); from 631; *a band, bond:*— bands(1), bond(1), bonds(6), chains(1), fetters(2), shackles(1).

4148. מוּסָר **musar** (416b); from 3256; *discipline, chastening, correction:*— chastening(3), chastise(1), correction(3), discipline(18), disciplines(1), instruction(20), punishment(2), reproof(1), warning(1).

4149. מוֹסֵרָה **Moserah** or

מֹסֵרוֹת **Moseroth** (64c); fem. of 4147; a place in the wilderness where Aaron died:— Moserah(1), Moseroth(2).

4150. מוֹעֵד **moed** or

מֹעֵד **moed** or

מוֹעָדָה **moadah** (417b); from 3259; *appointed time, place,* or *meeting:*— appointed(3), appointed feast(3), appointed feasts(11), appointed festival(2), appointed meeting place(1), appointed place(1), appointed sign(1), appointed time(21), appointed times(8), appointment(1), assembly(2), definite time(1), feasts(2), festal assemblies(1), fixed festivals(3), meeting(147), meeting place(1), meeting places(1), season(4), seasons(3), set time(1), time(3), times(1), times appointed(1).

4151. מוֹעָד **moad** (418a); from 3259; *appointed place:*— ranks(1).

4152. מוּעָדָה **muadah** (418a); from 3259; *appointed:*— appointed(1).

4153. מוֹעַדְיָה **Moadyah** (588c); the same as 4573, q.v.

4154. מוּעֶדֶת **muedeth** (588c); the same as 4571, q.v.

4155. מוּעָף **muaph** (734a); from 5774b; *gloom:*— gloom(1).

4156. מוֹעֵצָה **moetsah** (420b); from 3289; *counsel, plan, principle, device:*— counsels(3), devices(4).

4157. מוּעָקָה **muaqah** (734c); from 5781; *compression, distress:*— oppressive burden(1).

4158. מוֹפַעַת **Mophaath** or

מֵיפַעַת **Mephaath** or

מֵפַעַת **Mephaath** (422b); from 3313; a Levitical city in Reuben:— Mephaath(4).

4159. מוֹפֵת **mopheth** or

מֹפֵת **mopheth** (68d); from an unused word; *a wonder, sign, portent:*— marvel(1), marvels(3), miracle(1), miracles(1), sign(8), symbol(1), token(1), wonder(4), wonders(17).

4160. מוּץ **muts** (568c); see 4671a.

4161. מוֹצָא **motsa** or

מֹצָא **motsa** (425d); from 3318; *a place* or *act of going forth, issue, export, source, spring:*— east(1), exits(3), fountains(1), going(2), going forth(1), import(1), imported(1), issuing(1), mine(1), outlet(1), proceeds(2), rising(1), seeds(1), spring(2), springs(2), starting places(2), utterance(2), what goes(1).

4162. מוֹצָא **Motsa** (426a); from 3318; a son of Caleb, also a desc. of Saul:— Moza(5).

4163. מוֹצָאָה **motsaah** (426a); fem. of 4161; *going forth:*— goings forth(1).

4164. מוּצַק **mutsaq** or

מוּצָק **mutsaq** (848a); from 6693; *constraint, distress:*— anguish(1), constraint(1), frozen(1).

4165. מוּצָק **mutsaq** (427c); from 3332; *a casting:*— casting(1), mass(1).

4166. מוּצֶקֶת **mutseqeth** (427c); from 3332; *a pipe, casting:*— piece(1), spouts(1).

4167. מוּק **muq** (558b); a prim. root; *to mock, deride:*— mock(1).

4168. מוֹקֵד **moqed** (428d); from 3344; *a burning mass:*— burning(1), hearth(1).

4169. מוֹקְדָה **moqedah** (429a); fem. of 4168; *hearth:*— hearth(1).

4170. מוֹקֵשׁ **moqesh** or

מֹקֵשׁ **moqesh** (430c); from 3369; *a bait* or *lure, a snare:*— bait(1), barbs(1), ensnared(2), snare(12), snares(8), trap(4).

4171. מוּר **mur** (558c); a prim. root; *to change:*— change(3), changed(3), does exchange(2), exchange(3), exchanged(1), exchanges(1).

4172. מוֹרָא **mora** or

מֹרָא **mora** or

מוֹרָה **morah** (432b); from 3372a; *a fear, terror:*— fear(3), respect(1), reverence(1), terror(3), terrors(1), what they fear(1), who is to be feared(1).

4173. מוֹרַג **morag** or

מֹרַג **morag** (558d); of for. or.; *a threshing sled:*— threshing sledge(1), threshing sledges(2).

4174. מוֹרָד **morad** (434b); from 3381; *a descent, slope:*— descent(3), hanging(1), steep place(1).

4175a. מוֹרֶה **moreh** (435c); from 3384; (early) *rain:*— early(1), early rain(2).

4175b. מוֹרֶה **moreh** (435d); from 3384; *a teacher:*— teacher(1), Teacher(2), teachers(1).

4176. מוֹרֶה **Moreh** or

מֹרֶה **Moreh** (435d); from 3384; a place near Shechem, also a hill of unc. location:— Moreh(3).

4177a. מוֹרָה **morah** (559a); of unc. der.; *a razor:*— razor(3).

4177b. מוֹרָה **morah** (432b); from 3372a; prob. *a terror:*— fear(1).

4178. מוֹרָט **morat** (598d); the same as 4803, q.v.

4179. מוֹרִיָּה **Moriyyah** or

מֹרִיָּה **Moriyyah** (559a); of unc. der.; a mountain where Isaac was to be sacrificed:— Moriah(2).

4180. מוֹרָשׁ **morash** (440c); from 3423; *a possession:*— possession(1), possessions(1), wishes(1).

4181. מוֹרָשָׁה **morashah** (440c); fem. of 4180; *a possession:*— possession(9).

4182. מוֹרֶשֶׁת גַּת **Moresheth Gath** (440d); from 3423 and 1661; "possession," a place near Gath:— Moresheth-gath(1).

4183. מוֹרַשְׁתִּי **Morashti** (440d); from 4182; inhab. of Moresheth-gath:— Moresheth(2).

4184. מוּשׁ **mush** (559b); a prim. root; *to feel:*— feel(3).

4185. מוּשׁ **mush** (559a); a prim. root; *to depart, remove:*— cease(1), depart(6), departed(1), departs(2), give way(1), left(1), move(2), remove(2), removed(2), removes(1), take away(1).

4186. מוֹשָׁב **moshab** or

מֹשָׁב **moshab** (444b); from 3427; *a seat, assembly, dwelling place, dwelling, dwellers:*— dwelling(3), dwelling place(1), dwelling places(5), dwellings(9), habitation(1), habitations(2), inhabited(3), inhabited places(1), lived(1), seat(8), seating(2), settlement(1), settlements(3), situation(1), time(1), where they lived(1), where you are to live(1).

4187. מוּשִׁי **Mushi** or

מֻשִׁי **Mushshi** (559b); from 4184; "sensitive," a Levite:— Mushi(8).

4188. מוּשִׁי **Mushi** (559b); from 4187; desc. of Mushi:— Mushites(2).

4189. מוֹשְׁכָה **moshekah** or

מֹשֶׁכֶת **mosheketh** (604d); from 4900; *a cord:*— cords(1).

4190. מוֹשָׁעָה **moshaah** (448a); from 3467; *saving acts:*— deliverances(1).

4191. מוּת **muth** (559b); a prim. root; *to die:*— body(1), bring about my death(1), bring death(1), caused the death(1), certainly die(1), certainly put(1), certainly put me to death(1), corpse(2), dead(104), dead man(1), dead*(2), deadly*(1), death(21), deceased(5), destroy(2), die(214), die shall be put(1), died(167), dies(30), dying(1), kill(13), killed(24), killing(2), kills(4), means kill(2), mortally(3), must die(1), perished*(1), put(4), put her to death(1), put him to death(1), put him to death(20), put his to death(1), put me to death(1), put me to death(3), put my to death(1), put some to death(1), put the to death(3), put their to death(1), put them to death(1), put them to death(8), put to death(62), put us to death(2), put you to death(6), puts him to death(1), putting to death(1), slay(7), surely be put to death(56), surely we will kill(1), surely will die(1), surely die(16), surely*(1), took life(2).

4192. מוּת **Muth** or

מוּת לַבֵּן **Muth Labben** (559b, 761c); from 4191 and 1121; "to die for the son," prob. a song title:— death(2).

4193. מוֹת **moth** (1099d); (Ara.) corr. to 4194; *death.*

4194. מָוֶת **maveth** (560c); from 4191; *death:*— dead(4), deadly(3), Death(2), death(129), die(7), died(9), dies(6), plague(1).

4195. מוֹתָר **mothar** (452d); from 3498; *abundance, preeminence:*— advantage(2), profit(1).

4196. מִזְבֵּחַ **mizbeach** (258a); from 2076; *an altar:*— altar(349), altars(52).

4197. מֶזֶג **mezeg** (561a); from an unused word; *a mixture:*— mixed wine(1).

4198. מָזֶה **mazeh** (561a); from an unused word; *sucked out, empty:*— wasted(1).

4199. מִזָּה **Mizzah** (561a); from the same as 4198; grandson of Esau:— Mizzah(3).

4200. מֶזֶו **mazu** (265a); from an unused word; *a granary:*— garners(1).

4201. מְזוּזָה **mezuzah** or

מְזֻזָה **mezuzah** (265b); from the same as 2123a; *a doorpost, gatepost:*— door post(2), door posts(1), doorpost(4), doorposts(10), post(1), posts(2).

4202. מָזוֹן **mazon** (266a); from 2109; *food, sustenance:*— food(1), sustenance(1).

4203. מָזוֹן **mazon** (1091b); (Ara.) corr. to 4202; *food:*— food(2).

4204. מָזוֹר **mazor** (561c); from an unused word; perh. *a net:*— ambush(1).

4205. מָזוֹר **mazor** or

מָזֹר **mazor** (267a); from 2115; *a wound:*— sore(1), wound(2).

4206a. מֵזַח **mezach** (561a); of unc. der.; *a girdle:*— belt(1), restraint(1).

4206b. מְזִיחַ **meziach** (561b); of unc. der.; *a girdle:*— belt(1).

4207a. מַזְלֵג **mazleg** (272c); from an unused word; a utensil used in offering sacrifices:— fork(2).

4207b. מִזְלָגָה **mizlagah** (272c); from the same as 4207a; an implement used in offering sacrifices:— flesh hooks(1), forks(4).

4208. מַזָּלוֹת **mazzaloth** (561b); of for. or.; *constellations,* perh. *signs of the zodiac:*— constellations(1).

4209. מְזִמָּה **mezimmah** (273c); from 2161; *purpose, discretion, device:*— devises evil(1), discretion(5), evil devices(1), intent(1), plans(1), plot(1), plots(1), purpose(2), purposes(1), schemer*(1), thoughts(1), vile deeds(1), wicked schemes(1), wickedly(1).

4210. מִזְמוֹר **mizmor** (274c); from 2167; *a melody.*

4211. מַזְמֵרָה **mazmerah** (275a); from 2168; *a pruning knife:*— pruning hooks(3), pruning knives(1).

4212. מְזַמֶּרֶת **mezammereth** (275a); from 2168; *snuffers:*— snuffers(5).

4213. מִזְעָר **mizar** (277d); from the same as 2191; *a little, a trifle, a few:*— few(1), very(2).

4214. מִזְרֶה **mizreh** (280a); from 2219; *a pitchfork:*— fork(2).

4215. מְזָרֶה **mezareh** (279d); the same as 2219, q.v.

4216. מַזָּרוֹת mazzaroth (561d); of unc. der.; perh. *a constellation:*— constellation(1).

4217. מִזְרָח mizrach (280d); from 2224; *place of sunrise, the east:*— east(41), east side(2), east side*(2), east*(9), eastern(2), eastward(5), rising(6), sunrise(3), sunrise*(3), sunrising(1).

4218. מִזְרָע mizra (283c); from 2232; *place of sowing:*— sown fields(1).

4219. מִזְרָק mizraq (284d); from 2236b; *bowl, basin:*— basin(1), basins(8), bowl(13), bowls(9), sacrificial bowls(1).

4220. מֵחַ meach (562d); from an unused word; *a fatling:*— fat beasts(1), wealthy(1).

4221. מֹחַ moach (562d); from the same as 4220; *marrow:*— marrow(1).

4222. מָחָא macha (561d); a prim. root; *to strike, clap:*— clap(2), clapped(1).

4223. מְחָא mecha (1099d); (Ara.) corr. to 4222; *to smite:*— impaled*(1), struck(2), ward off(1).

4224a. מַחֲבֵא machabe (285c); from 2244; *a hiding place:*— refuge(1).

4224b. מַחֲבֹא machabo (285c); from 2244; *a hiding place:*— hiding places(1).

4225. מַחְבֶּרֶת machbereth (289c); from 2266; *something joined, place of joining:*— place where(2), place where it is joined(1), place where it joined(1), set(6).

4226. מְחַבְּרָה mechabberah (289c); from 2266; *a binder, clamp, joint:*— clamps(1), couplings(1).

4227. מַחֲבַת machabath (290a); from the same as 2281; *a flat plate, pan, griddle:*— griddle(3), pan(1), plate(1).

4228. מַחֲגֹרֶת machagoreth (292b); from 2296; *girding, cincture:*— donning(1).

4229a. מָחָה machah (562a); a prim. root; *to wipe, wipe out:*— blot(12), blotted(11), destroys(1), utterly blot(1), wash off(1), wipe(1), wipe...away(1), wiped(1), wipes(3), wiping(1).

4229b. מָחָה machah (562b); a prim. root; *to strike:*— reach(1).

4229c. מָחָה machah (562d); denom. vb. from 4221; *to be full:*— marrow(1).

4230. מְחוּגָה mechugah (295b); from 2328; *a compass:*— compass(1).

4231. מָחוֹז machoz (562c); of for. or.; *a city:*— haven(1).

4232. מְחוּיָאֵל Mechuyael or
מְחִיּיָאֵל Mechiyyayel (562c); from 4229b and 410; "smitten of God," great-grandson of Cain:— Mehujael(2).

4233. מַחֲוִים Machavim (296a); of unc. der.; a description of Eliel:— Mahavite(1).

4234. מָחוֹל machol (298b); from 2342a; *a dance:*— dance(1), dances(1), dancing(4).

4235. מָחוֹל Machol (562d); from the same as 4231; father of Heman:— Mahol(1).

4236. מַחֲזֶה machazeh (303d); from 2372; *a vision:*— vision(4).

4237. מֶחֱזָה mechezah (303d); from 2372; *light, place of seeing, a window:*— window(4).

4238. מַחֲזִיאוֹת Machazioth (303d); from 2372; "visions," an Isr.:— Mahazioth(2).

4239. מְחִי mechi (562c); from 4229b; *a smiting:*— blow(1).

4240. מְחִידָא Mechida (563a); of unc. der.; an Isr.:— Mehida(2).

4241. מִחְיָה michyah (313c); from 2421a; *preservation of life, sustenance:*— maintenance(1), preserve life(1), quick(1), raw(1), recover(1), reviving(2), sustenance(1).

4242. מְחִיר mechir (564b); from the same as 4279; *price, hire:*— cost(2), payment(1), price(10), sale(1), wages(1).

4243. מְחִיר Mechir (564b); from the same as 4279; an Isr.:— Mehir(1).

4244. מַחְלָה Machlah (563a); of unc. der.; a daughter of Zelophehad, also a Gileadite:— Mahlah(5).

4245a. מַחֲלָה machalah (318b); from 2470a; *sickness, disease:*— diseases(1), sickness(3).

4245b. מַחֲלֶה machaleh (318b); from 2470a; *sickness, disease:*— disease(1), sickness(1).

4246. מְחֹלָה mecholah or
מְחוֹלָה mecholah (298b); fem. of 4234; *a dance:*— dance(1), danced(1), dances(2), dancing(4).

4247. מְחִלָּה mechillah (320a); from 2490a; *a hole:*— holes(1).

4248. מַחְלוֹן Machlon (563a); of unc. der.; the first husband of Ruth:— Mahlon(4).

4249. מַחְלִי Machli (563a); of unc. der.; a Levite, also a son of Mushi:— Mahli(12).

4250. מַחְלִי Machli (563a); from 4249; desc. of Mahli:— Mahlites(2).

4251. מַחֲלֻי machluy or
מַחֲלוּי machaluy (318c); from 2470a; *sickness, suffering* (caused by wounds):— sick(1).

4252. מַחֲלָף machalaph (322c); from 2498; *a knife:*— duplicates(1).

4253. מַחְלָפָה machalaphah (322c); from 2498; *a plait* (of hair):— locks(3).

4254. מַחֲלָצָה machalatsah (323a); from 2502a; *robe of state:*— festal robes(2).

4255a. מַחְלְקָה machleqah (1093b); (Ara.) corr. to 4256; *class, division:*— orders(1).

4255b. מַחְלְקוֹת machleqoth (325d); another reading for 4256, q.v.

4256. מַחֲלֹקֶת machaloqeth (324d); from 2505a; *division, course:*— division(17), divisions(24), escape(1), portions(1).

4257. מַחֲלַת Machalath (318d); from 2470a; in psalm titles, prob. the name of a tune.

4258. מַחֲלַת Machalath (563b); of unc. der.; daughter of Ishmael, also a granddaughter of David:— Mahalath(2).

4259. מְחֹלָתִי Mecholathi (563b); of unc. der.; inhab. of Abel-meholah:— Meholathite(2).

4260. מַחְמָאָה machamaah (563b); of unc. der.; *smoother than butter:*— butter(1).

4261. מַחְמָד machmad (326d); from 2530; *desire, desirable thing:*— desirable(2), desire(3), pleasant(1), precious ones(1), precious things(2), precious treasures(1), treasures(1), valuable(1).

4262. מַחְמֻד machmud or
מַחְמֹד machmod (327a); from 2530; *a desirable* or *precious thing:*— precious things(2).

4263a. מַחְמָל machmal (328c); from 2550; *a thing pitied, an object of compassion:*— delight(1).

4263b. מַחְמֶצֶת machmetseth (330a); from 2556a; *anything leavened:*— leavened(1), what is leavened(1).

4264. מַחֲנֶה machaneh (334a); from 2583; *an encampment, camp:*— armies(6), army(27), army camp(1), camp(158), camps(12), companies(3), company(5), fight(2), host(1).

4265. מַחֲנֵה־דָן Machaneh-dan (334b); from 4264 and 1835; "camp of Dan," a place where the Danites stayed:— Mahaneh-dan(2).

4266. מַחֲנַיִם Machanayim (334b); dual of 4264; "two camps," a place E. of the Jordan:— Mahanaim(13).

4267. מַחֲנָק machanaq (338b); from 2614; *strangling, suffocation:*— suffocation(1).

4268. מַחֲסֶה machaseh or
מַחְסֶה machseh (340b); from 2620; *refuge, shelter:*— refuge(19), shelter(1).

4269. מַחְסוֹם machsom (340d); from 2629; *a muzzle:*— muzzle(1).

4270. מַחְסוֹר machsor or
מַחְסֹר machsor (341d); from 2637; *a need, thing needed, poverty:*— lack(2), need(2), needs(1), poor(1), poverty(3), want(4).

4271. מַחְסֵיָה Machseyah (340c); from 4268 and 3050; "Yah is a refuge," an Isr.:— Mahseiah(2).

4272. מָחַץ machats (563c); a prim. root; *to smite through, wound severely, shatter:*— crush through(1), shatter(6), shattered(4), struck(1), wounded(1), wounds(1).

4273. מַחַץ machats (563d); from 4272; *a severe wound:*— bruise(1).

4274. מַחְצֵב machtseb (345b); from 2672; *a hewing:*— hewn(2), quarried(1).

4275. מֶחֱצָה mechetsah (345d); from 2673; *half:*— half(2).

4276. מַחֲצִית machatsith (345d); from 2673; *half, middle:*— half(11), half as much(1), half-tribe*(3), midday*(1).

4277. מָחַק machaq (563d); a prim. root; *to utterly destroy, annihilate:*— smashed(1).

4278. מֶחְקָר mechqar (350d); from 2713; *a range* (an area to explore):— depths(1).

4279. מָחָר machar (563d); from an unused word; *tomorrow, in time to come:*— later(1), later*(1), time to come(6), tomorrow(44).

4280. מַחֲרָאָה macharaah (351a, 1123c); from the same as 2716; *a cloaca, cesspool:*— latrine(1).

4281. מַחֲרֵשָׁה machareshah (361a); from 2790a; *a plowshare:*— hoe(1), plowshare(1), plowshares(1).

4282. מַחֲרֶשֶׁת macharesheth (361a); the same as 4281, q.v.

4283. מָחֳרָת mochorath or
מָחֳרָתָם mochoratham (564a); from the same as 4279; *the morrow:*— day after(5), following day(2), next(4), next day(18), next morning(3).

4284. מַחֲשָׁבָה machashabah or
מַחֲשֶׁבֶת machashebeth (364b); from 2803; *thought, device:*— design(1), designs(3), devised(1), intentions*(1), invented(1), inventive(1), plan(2), plans(14), plot(1), plots(1), plotting(1), purposes(3), scheme(2), schemes(4), thoughts(19), ways(1).

4285. מַחְשָׁךְ machshak (365b); from 2821; *dark place:*— dark place(1), dark places(4), darkness(2).

4286. מַחְשֹׂף machsoph; (362d); from 2834; *a laying bare, stripping:*— exposing(1).

4287. מַחַת Machath (367b); from 2846; two Levites:— Mahath(3).

4288. מְחִתָּה mechittah (369d); from 2865; *terror, destruction, ruin:*— object of terror(1), ruin(7), terror(3).

4289. מַחְתָּה machtah (367b); from 2846; *a fireholder, censer, snuff dish:*— censer(3), censers(4), firepan(3), firepans(9), trays(3).

4290. מַחְתֶּרֶת machtereth (369a); from 2864; *a breaking in, burglary:*— breaking(2).

4291. מְטָא meta or

מְטָה metah (1100a); (Ara.) appar. corr. to 4672; *to reach, attain:*— arrived(1), came(1), come(1), happened(1), reached(4).

4292. מַטְאֲטֵא matate (370a); from 2894; *broom, besom:*— broom(1).

4293. מַטְבֵּחַ matbeach (371a); from 2873; *a slaughtering place:*— place of slaughter(1).

4294. מַטֶּה matteh or

מַטָּה mattah (641c); from 5186; *a staff, rod, shaft, branch, a tribe:*— branch(3), branches(1), half-tribe*(13), rod(18), rods(6), scepter(2), spears(1), staff(33), staffs(1), supply(1), tribal(8), tribe(140), tribes(20).

4295. מַטָּה mattah (641b); from 5186; *downwards:*— below(2), beneath(2), bottom(2), downward(5), less(1), lower(2), under(1), underneath(1).

4296. מִטָּה mittah (641d); from 5186; *a couch, bed:*— bed(21), bedroom*(2), beds(1), bier(1), couch(3), couches(1).

4297. מֻטֶּה mutteh (642a); from 5186; *that which is perverted, perverted justice:*— perversion(1).

4298. מֻטָּה muttah (642a); from 5186; *spreading, outspreading:*— spread(1).

4299. מַטְוֶה matveh (376b); from 2901; *that which is spun, yarn:*— what they had spun(1).

4300. מְטִיל metil (564c); from an unused word; *a wrought metal rod:*— bars(1).

4301. מַטְמוֹן matmon or

מַטְמֹן matmon or

מַטְמֻן matmun (380c); from 2934; *hidden treasure, treasure:*— hidden(1), hidden treasures(2), hidden wealth(1), stores(1), treasure(1).

4302. מַטָּע matta (642d); from 5193; *place* or *act of planting, a plantation:*— planting(2), planting place(2), planting places(1), where it was planted(1).

4303. מַטְעַם matam or

מַטְעַמָּה matammah (381b); from 2938; *tasty* or *savory food, dainties:*— delicacies(2), savory dish(3), savory food(3).

4304. מִטְפַּחַת mitpachath (381c); from 2946; *a cloak:*— cloak(1), cloaks(1).

4305. מָטַר matar (565a); denom. vb. from 4306; *to rain:*— bring rain(1), rain(5), rained(5), rained down(1), send(1), send rain(3), sent rain(1).

4306. מָטָר matar (564d); a prim. root; *rain:*— downpour(1), rain(36).

4307. מַטָּרָא mattara or

מַטָּרָה mattarah (643c); from 5201; *a guard, ward, prison, target, mark:*— guard(6), guardhouse(7), target(3).

4308. מַטְרֵד Matred (382b); from 2956; an Edomite woman:— Matred(2).

4309. מַטְרִי Matri (565a); from 4306; a Benjamite family:— Matrite(1).

4310. מִי mi (566a); a prim. pron.; *who?:*— how(4), O(1), Oh(3), Oh that someone(3), Oh*(13), someone(1), what(19), which(4), who(285), whoever(12), whoever*(4), whom(48), whom*(1), whose(16), would*(7).

4311. מֵידְבָא Medeba (567d); of unc. der.; a city in Moab:— Medeba(5).

4312. מֵידָד Medad (392a); from the same as 3039; an Isr.:— Medad(2).

4313. מֵי הַיַּרְקוֹן Me Hayyarqon (566a); from 4325 and 3420; a place in Dan near Joppa:— Me-jarkon(1).

4314. מֵי זָהָב Me Zahab (566a); from 4325 and 2091; an Edomite:— Mezahab(2).

4315. מֵיטָב metab (406b); from 3190; *the best:*— best(6).

4316. מִיכָא Mika (567d); a var. for 4318; three Isr.:— Mica(5).

4317. מִיכָאֵל Mikael (567c); from 4310, a prep. pref. and 410; "Who is like God?" an angel, also a number of Isr.:— Michael(13).

4318. מִיכָה Mikah (567d); an abb. for 4320; the name of several Isr.:— Micah(28), Micah's(3), Micaiah(1).

4319. מִיכָהוּ Mikahu (567c); a contr. of 4321, q.v.

4320. מִיכָיָה Mikayah (567c); from 4310, 3588 and 3050; "Who is like Yah?" the name of several Isr.:— Micaiah(3).

4321. מִיכָיְהוּ Mikayehu or

מִכָיְהוּ Mikayehu (567c); from 4310, a prep. pref. and 3050; "Who is like Yah?" three Isr.:— Micah(2), Micaiah(19).

4322. מִיכָיָהוּ Mikayahu (567c); from 4310, a prep. pref. and 3050; "Who is like Yah?" an Isr., also an Isr. woman:— Micaiah(2).

4323. מִיכָל mikal (568a); of unc. der.; *a brook, stream:*— brook(1).

4324. מִיכַל Mikal (568a); of unc. der.; wife of David:— Michal(17).

4325. מַיִם mayim (565b); a prim. root; *waters, water:*— flood(1), loins(1), pool(1), Water(5), water(373), watering(1), waterless*(1), waters(192).

4326. מִיָּמִן Miyyamin (568a); of unc. der.; the name of several Isr.:— Mijamin(4).

4327. מִין min (568b); from an unused word; *kind, species:*— kind(21), kinds(10).

4328. מְיֻסָּדָה meyussadah (413d, 414c); fem. pass. part. of 3245, q.v.

4329. מֵיסָךְ mesak (697b); see 4146b.

4330. מִיץ mits (568c); from an unused word; *squeezing, pressing, wringing:*— churning(2), pressing(1).

4331. מֵישָׁא Mesha (568c); of unc. der.; a Benjamite:— Mesha(1), Mishael(1).

4332. מִישָׁאֵל Mishael (567d); from 4310 and 410; "Who is what God is?" three Isr.:— Mishael(7).

4333. מִישָׁאֵל Mishael (1100a); (Ara.) corr. to 4332; "Who is what God is?" a companion of Daniel.

4334. מִישׁוֹר mishor or

מִישֹׁר mishor (449d); from 3474; *a level place, uprightness:*— fairness(1), level(2), level place(1), plain(12), plains(1), plateau(2), plateau*(1), uprightness(3).

4335. מֵישַׁךְ Meshak (568d); of for. or.; a Bab. name given to Mishael:— Meshach(1).

4336. מֵישַׁךְ Meshak (1100a); (Ara.) of for. or.; a Bab. name:— Meshach(14).

4337. מֵישָׁע Mesha (448a); from 3467; "deliverance," a son of Caleb:— Mesha(1).

4338. מֵישַׁע Mesha (448a); from 3467; "deliverance," king of Moab:— Mesha(1).

4339. מֵישָׁר meshar (449d); from 3474; *evenness, uprightness, equity:*— equity(8), peaceful arrangement(1), right things(1), rightly(1), sincerity(1), smooth(1), smoothly(2), things that are upright(1), uprightly(1), uprightness(1), what is right(1).

4340. מֵיתָר methar (452d); from 3498; *cord, string:*— bowstrings(1), cords(7), ropes(1).

4341. מַכְאֹב makob or

מַכְאוֹב makob or

מַכְאֹבָה makobah (456b); from 3510; *pain:*— pain(10), painful(1), sorrow(1), sorrows(3), sufferings(1).

4342. מַכְבִּיר makbir (460b); from 3527, q.v.

4343. מַכְבֵּנָה Makbenah (460a); from the same as 3522; a desc. of Caleb:— Machbena(1).

4344. מַכְבַּנַּי Makbannay (460a); from 4343; one of David's heroes:— Machbannai(1).

4345. מַכְבֵּר makber (460d); from the same as 3523; *a netted cloth, coverlet:*— cover(1).

4346. מִכְבָּר mikbar (460d); from the same as 3523; *grating, lattice-work:*— grating(6).

4347. מַכָּה makkah or

מַכֶּה makkeh (646d); from 5221; *a blow, wound, slaughter:*— blow(1), casualties(1), crushed(1), disasters(1), inflicted(1), injury(1), plague(3), plagues(4), slaughter(14), stripes(1), strokes(2), wound(8), wounded(1), wounds(9).

4348. מִכְוָה mikvah (465a); from 3554; *a burnt spot, scar of a burn:*— burn(5).

4349. מָכוֹן makon (467c); from 3559; *a fixed* or *established place, foundation:*— area(1), dwelling place(1), foundation(3), foundations(1), place(11).

4350. מְכוֹנָה mekonah or

מְכֹנָה mekonah (467d); fem. of 4349; *a fixed resting place, base:*— foundation(1), pedestal(1), stand(7), stands(15).

4351. מְכוּרָה mekurah or

מְכֹרָה mekorah (468d); from 3564b; *origin:*— origin(3).

4352. מָכִי Maki (568d); of unc. der.; a Gadite:— Machi(1).

4353. מָכִיר Makir (569c); from 4376; two Isr.:— Machir(22).

4354. מָכִירִי Makiri (569d); from 4353; desc. of Machir:— Machirites(1).

4355. מָכַךְ makak (568d); a prim. root; *to be low* or *humiliated:*— brought low(1), sag(1), sank down(1).

4356. מִכְלָאָה miklaah or

מִכְלָה miklah (476c); from 3607; *an enclosure, fold:*— fold(1), folds(1), sheepfolds*(1).

4357. מִכְלָה miklah (479a); from 3615; *completeness, perfection:*— purest(1).

4358. מִכְלוֹל miklol (483b); from 3634; *perfection, gorgeous attire:*— magnificently(1), splendidly(1).

4359. מִכְלָל miklal (483b); from 3634; *completeness, perfection:*— perfection(1).

4360. מַכְלֻל maklul (483b); from 3634; *a thing made perfect,* prob. *a gorgeous garment:*— choice garments(1).

4361. מַכֹּלֶת makkoleth (38c); from 398; *foodstuff:*— food(1).

4362. מִכְמָן mikman (485a); from the same as 3646; *hidden stores:*— hidden treasures(1).

4363. מִכְמָס Mikmas or

מִכְמָשׂ Mikmash or

מִכְמַשׁ Mikmash (485a); from 3647; a city in Benjamin:— Michmas(2), Michmash(9).

4364a. מִכְמֹר makmor (485c); from an unused word; *a net, snare:*— nets(1).

4364b. מִכְמָר mikmar (485b); from the same as 4364a; *a net, snare:*— net(1).

4365a. מִכְמֶרֶת mikmereth (485c); from the same as 4364a; *a net, fishing net:*— fishing net(2).

4365b. מִכְמֹרֶת mikmoreth (485c); from the same as 4364a; *a net, fishing net:*— nets(1).

4366. מִכְמְתָת Mikmethath (485d); of unc. der.; a place in N.E. Ephraim:— Michmethath(2).

4367. מַכְנַדְבַי Maknadbay (569a); of unc. der.; an Isr.:— Machnadebai(1).

4368. מְכֹנָה Mekonah (569a); of unc. der.; a place in Judah:— Meconah(1).

4369. מְכֻנָה mekunah or

מְכוֹנָה mekonah (467d); the same as 4350, q.v.

4370. מִכְנָס miknas (488b); from 3664; *an undergarment:*— breeches(2), undergarments(3).

4371. מֶכֶס mekes (493d); from 3699; *computation, proportion to be paid, tax:*— levy(5), tax(1).

4372. מִכְסֶה mikseh (492c); from 3680; *a covering:*— covering(16).

4373. מִכְסָה miksah (493d); fem. of 4371; *a computation:*— amount(1), number(1).

4374. מְכַסֶּה mekasseh (492c); from 3680; *a covering:*— attire(1), awning(1), covering(2).

4375. מַכְפֵּלָה Makpelah (495d); from 3717; a place near Hebron:— Machpelah(6).

4376. מָכַר makar (569a); a prim. root; *to sell:*— certainly sell(1), destruction(1), make(1), merchants(1), offer yourselves for sale(1), sell(23), seller(3), selling(1), sells(8), sold(40).

4377. מֶכֶר meker (569c); from 4376; *merchandise, value:*— merchandise(1), price(1), worth(1).

4378. מַכָּר makkar (648c); from 5234; *acquaintance, friend:*— acquaintance(1), acquaintances(1).

4379. מִכְרֶה mikreh (500b); from 3738a; *a pit:*— pits(1).

4380. מְכֵרָה mekerah (468d); from 3564b; (prob. some kind of) *weapon:*— swords(1).

4381. מִכְרִי Mikri (569d); from 4376; a Benjamite:— Michri(1).

4382. מְכֵרָתִי Mekerathi (569d); from an unused name; a descriptive name for one of David's men:— Mecherathite(1).

4383. מִכְשׁוֹל mikshol or

מִכְשֹׁל mikshol (506a); from 3782; *a stumbling, means* or *occasion of stumbling, a stumbling block:*— fall(1), obstacle(2), occasion of stumbling(1), stumble(2), stumbling block(6), stumbling blocks(1), troubled(1).

4384. מַכְשֵׁלָה makshelah (506b); from 3782; *something overthrown, a stumbling block:*— ruins(2).

4385. מִכְתָּב miktab (508b); from 3789; *writing:*— letter(1), writing(7).

4386. מְכִתָּה mekittah (510c); from 3807; *something crushed* or *pulverized, crushed fragments:*— pieces(1).

4387. מִכְתָּם Miktam (508d); of unc. der.; a technical term in psalm titles.

4388. מַכְתֵּשׁ maktesh (509d); from 3806; *mortar:*— hollow(1), mortar(1).

4389. מַכְתֵּשׁ Maktesh (509d); from 4388; a place prob. in Jer.:— mortar(1).

4390. מָלֵא male or

מָלָא mala (569d); a prim. root; *to be full, to fill:*— accomplished(1), aloud(1), armed(1), become full(1), been completed(1), come(1), complete(3), completed(9), completion(1), confirm(1), consecrate*(3), consecrated*(4), covered(1), dedicate(1), drenched(1), drew(1), ended(1), endowed(1), expired(1), fill(38), filled(78), filling(5), fills(1), finished(1), fulfill(6), fulfilled(10), full(37), fullness(1), fully(8), gave in full(1), given fully(1), gratified(1), live(1), massed(1), messengers(1), mount*(1), mounted(1), ordain*(4), ordained*(4), ordination*(1), overflowing*(1), overflows*(1), passed(1), presume*(1), refresh(1), required(2), satisfied(1), satisfy(2), set(1), settings(2), space(1).

4391. מְלָא mela (1100a); (Ara.) corr. to 4390; *to fill:*— filled(2).

4392. מָלֵא male (570d); from 4390; *full:*— abundance(1), aloud(1), completely(1), filled(3), full(52), pregnant woman(1), strong(1), very old*(1), well(1), what is full(1), who were full(1).

4393. מְלֹא melo or

מְלוֹא melo or

מְלוֹ melo (571a); from 4390; *fullness, that which fills:*— all(2), all it contains(8), all its fullness(1), band(1), contains(1), fill(1), full(11), fullness(4), handful*(3), handfuls*(2), multitude(1), omerful*(2), which filled(1).

4394. מִלֻּא millu (571b); from 4390; *setting, installation:*— inlaid(1), ordination(8), ordination offering(3), setting(3).

4395. מְלֵאָה meleah (571b); from 4390; *fullness, full produce:*— all the produce(1), full produce(1), harvest(1).

4396. מִלֻּאָה milluah (571b); fem. of 4394; *setting* (of jewels):— filigree(1), mount*(1), mounted(1).

4397. מַלְאָךְ malak (521c); from an unused word; *a messenger:*— ambassadors(2), angel(101), angels(9), envoys(1), messenger(24), messengers(76).

4398. מַלְאַךְ malak (1098d); (Ara.) corr. to 4397; *an angel:*— angel(2).

4399. מְלָאכָה melakah (521d); from the same as 4397; *occupation, work:*— anything(4), article made(1), business(4), cattle(1), craftsmanship(3), details(1), duties(1), everything*(1), industrious*(1), laborer(1), material(1), occupation(1), performed(1), project(1), property(2), purpose(1), service(2), something(1), supplies(1), task(2), use(2), used(2), work(118), workers(1), workmanship(1), workmen(5), workmen*(5), works(1).

4400. מַלְאָכוּת malakuth (522b); from the same as 4397; *a message:*— commission(1).

4401. מַלְאָכִי Malaki (522b); from the same as 4397; "my messenger," an Isr. prophet:— Malachi(1).

4402. מִלֵּאת milleth (571c); from 4390; perh. *setting* or *border, rim:*— setting(1).

4403. מַלְבּוּשׁ malbush or

מַלְבֻשׁ malbush (528c); from 3847; *raiment, attire:*— attire(3), dress(1), garments(3), raiment(1).

4404. מַלְבֵּן malben (527c); from 3835b; *a brick mold, quadrangle:*— brick(1), brick mold(1), brickkiln(1).

4405. מִלָּה millah or

מִלֶּה milleh (576b); from 4448a; *a word, speech, utterance:*— answer*(1), anything to say(1), byword(1), said(1), speaking(1), speech(5), talking(1), utterances(1), what to say(1), word(2), words(22).

4406. מִלָּה millah (1100c); (Ara.) corr. to 4405; *a word, thing:*— anything(1), command(4), matter(5), message(2), revelation(1), statement(2), thing(1), things(1), word(2), words(3).

4407. מִלּוֹא Millo or

מִלֹּא Millo (571c); from 4390; a place near Shechem, also a citadel in Jer.:— Millo(7).

4408. מַלּוּחַ malluach (572a); from the same as 4417; *mallow:*— mallow(1).

4409. מַלּוּךְ Malluk or

מַלּוּכִי Malluki (576a); from the same as 4428; the name of several Isr.:— Malluch(6).

4410. מְלוּכָה melukah (574c); from the same as 4428; *kingship, royalty:*— king(1), kingdom(15), reign*(1), royal(6), royalty(1).

4411. מָלוֹן malon (533d); from 3885a; *a lodging place, inn, khan:*— lodging place(8).

4412. מְלוּנָה melunah (534a); from 3885a; *a lodge, hut:*— shack(1), watchman's hut(1).

4413. מַלּוֹתִי Mallothi (576c); from 4448a; a son of Heman:— Mallothi(2).

4414a. מָלַח malach (571d); a prim. root; *to tear away, dissipate:*— vanish(1).

4414b. מָלַח malach (572a); denom. vb. from 4417; *to salt, season:*— rubbed with salt(1), salted(1), season(1).

4415. מְלַח melach (1100b); (Ara.) denom. vb. from 4416; *to eat salt:*— service(1).

4416. מְלַח melach (1100a); (Ara.) corr. to 4417; *salt:*— salt(2).

4417. מֶלַח melach (571d); of unc. der.; *salt:*— salt(27).

4418. מֶלַח malach (571d); from 4414a; *a rag:*— rags(2).

4419. מַלָּח mallach (572a); from the same as 4417; *a mariner:*— sailors(4).

4420. מְלֵחָה **melechah** (572a); from the same as 4417; *saltiness, barrenness:*— salt(1), salt land(1), salt waste(1).

4421. מִלְחָמָה **milchamah** (536a); from 3898a; *a battle, war:*— attacked(1), battle(148), battle*(1), battles(6), fight(2), military(1), onslaught(1), soldiers*(3), time of war(1), wage war(1), war(136), warfare(1), warrior(4), warriors(4), wars(9), weapons of war(1).

4422. מָלַט **malat** (572b); a prim. root; *to slip away:*— certainly rescue(1), deliver(7), delivered(9), escape(26), escaped(25), escapes(3), gave birth(1), get away(1), lay(1), leap forth(1), left undisturbed(1), rescue(2), rescued(4), retain(1), save(8), saved(2).

4423. מֶלֶט **melet** (572d); from 4422; *mortar, cement:*— mortar(1).

4424a. מְלַטְיָה **Melatyah** (572d); from 4423 and 3050; "Yah delivered," a Gibeonite:— Melatiah(1).

4424b. מְלִיכוּ **Meliku** (576a); from the same as 4428; a priestly family:— Malluchi(1).

4425. מְלִילָה **melilah** (576c); from 4448b; *an ear* (of wheat):— heads(1).

4426. מְלִיצָה **melitsah** (539c); from 3917b; *satire, a mocking poem:*— figure(1), mockery(1).

4427a. מָלַךְ **malak** (573d); denom. vb. from 4428; *to be* or *become king* or *queen, to reign:*— actually going to reign(1), appoint(1), appointed(1), became king(123), become a king(1), become king(1), become king(2), becomes king(1), being king(1), being king(1), king(21), made(9), made a king(1), made queen(1), made king(24), made king(2), made...king(2), make...king(1), make...king(3), making...king(1), put on the throne(1), queen(1), reign(39), reigned(96), reigning(1), reigns(8), rule(2), set(2), set up kings(1), surely be king(1).

4427b. מָלַךְ **malak** (576a); a prim. root; *to counsel, advise:*— consulted(1).

4428. מֶלֶךְ **melek** (572d); from an unused word; *king:*— King(253), king(1730), King's(6), king's(241), kingdom(1), Kings(41), kings(241), kings'(2), royal(5).

4429. מֶלֶךְ **Melek** (574b); from the same as 4428; a Benjamite:— Melech(2).

4430. מֶלֶךְ **melek** (1100b); (Ara.) corr. to 4428; *king:*— King(20), king(127), king's(16), kings(14), royal(3).

4431. מְלַךְ **melek** (1100c); (Ara.) from a root corr. to 4427b; *counsel, advice:*— advice(1).

4432. מֹלֶךְ **Molek** (574c); from the same as 4428; a heathen god to whom Isr. sacrificed children:— Molech(8).

4433. מַלְכָּא **malka** or

מַלְכָּה **malkah** (1100b); (Ara.) corr. to 4436; *queen:*— queen(2).

4434. מַלְכֹּדֶת **malkodeth** (540b); from 3920; *a catching instrument, a snare, trap:*— trap(1).

4435. מִלְכָּה **Milkah** (574c); from the same as 4428; two Isr. women:— Milcah(11).

4436. מַלְכָּה **malkah** (573c); fem. of 4428; *queen:*— Queen(17), queen(14), queen's(2), queens(2).

4437. מַלְכוּ **malku** (1100b); (Ara.) corr. to 4438; *royalty, reign, kingdom:*— government affairs(1), kingdom(38), kingdoms(3), realm(4), reign(4), royal(3), sovereignty(4).

4438. מַלְכוּת **malkuth** or

מַלְכֻת **malkuth** or

מַלְכֻיָּה **malkuyyah** (574d); from the same as 4428; *royalty, royal power, reign, kingdom:*— kingdom(41), kingdoms(2), kingship(1), realm(3), reign(21), royal(15), royal position(1), royal robes(1), royalty(1), rule(1), sovereignty(2), throne(1).

4439. מַלְכִּיאֵל **Malkiel** (575c); from 4428 and 410; "my king is El," an Asherite:— Malchiel(3).

4440. מַלְכִּיאֵלִי **Malkieli** (575c); from 4439; desc. of Malchiel:— Malchielites(1).

4441. מַלְכִּיָּה **Malkiyyah** or

מַלְכִּיָּהוּ **Malkiyahu** (575c); from 4428 and 3050; "my king is Yah," the name of a number of Isr.:— Malchijah(16).

4442. מַלְכִּי־צֶדֶק **Malki-tsedeq** (575d); from 4428 and 6664; "my king is right," an early king of Salem:— Melchizedek(2).

4443. מַלְכִּירָם **Malkiram** (575d); from 4428 and 7311; "my king is high," a son of Jeconiah:— Malchiram(1).

4444. מַלְכִּישׁוּעַ **Malkishua** (575d); from 4428 and 7770b; "my king is wealth," a son of Saul:— Malchi-shua(5).

4445a. מַלְכָּם **Malkam** (575d); from the same as 4428; a Benjamite:— Malcam(3).

4445b. מִלְכֹּם **Milkom** (575d); from the same as 4428; a god of the Ammonites:— Milcom(4).

4446. מְלֶכֶת **meleketh** (573d); from the same as 4428; *queen:*— queen(5).

4447. מֹלֶכֶת **Moleketh** (574c); from the same as 4428; an Isr. woman:— Hammolecheth(1).

4448a. מָלַל **malal** (576a); a prim. root; *to speak, utter, say:*— say(1), speak(2).

4448b. מָלַל **malal** (576c); a prim. root; *to rub, scrape:*— signals(1).

4448c. מָלַל **malal** (576c); a prim. root; *to languish, wither, fade:*— cut off(2), fades(1), wither(1), withers(1).

4448d. מָלַל **malal** (576d); a prim. root; *to circumcise:*— headless(1).

4449. מְלַל **melal** (1100c); (Ara.) corr. to 4448a; *to speak, say:*— speak(1), speaking(1), spoke(1), uttering(2).

4450. מִלֲלַי **Milalay** (576c); from 4448a; an Isr. musician:— Milalai(1).

4451. מַלְמַד **malmad** (541a); from 3925; *an oxgoad:*— oxgoad(1).

4452. מָלַץ **malats** (576d); a prim. root; prob. *to be smooth* or *slippery:*— sweet(1).

4453. מֶלְצַר **meltsar** (576d); of for. or.; perh. *guardian:*— overseer(2).

4454. מָלַק **malaq** (577a); a prim. root; *to nip, nip off:*— nip(1), wring off(1).

4455a. מַלְקוֹחַ **malqoach** (544b); from 3947; *booty, prey:*— booty(3), prey(4).

4455b. מַלְקוֹחַ **malqoach** (544c); from 3947; *a jaw:*— jaws(1).

4456. מַלְקוֹשׁ **malqosh** (545b); from the same as 3954; *latter rain, spring rain:*— late(1), latter rain(1), rain*(1), spring rain(6).

4457. מֶלְקָח **melqach** or

מַלְקָח **malqach** (544c); from 3947; *tongs, snuffers:*— snuffers(3), tongs(3).

4458. מֶלְתָּחָה **meltachah** (547a); from an unused word; prob. *wardrobe, wearing apparel:*— wardrobe(1).

4459. מַלְתָּעָה **maltaah** (1069a); transp. for 4973, q.v.

4460. מַמְּגֻרָה **mammegurah** (158c); from 1481a; *granary, storehouse:*— barns(1).

4461. מֵמַד **memad** (551d); from 4058; *measurement:*— measurements(1).

4462. מְמוּכָן **Memukan** or

מוֹמְכָן **Momukan** (577a); of for. or.; a prince of Persia and Media:— Memucan(3).

4463. מָמוֹת **mamoth** (560d); from 4191; *death:*— deadly(1), death(1).

4464. מַמְזֵר **mamzer** (561c); from an unused word; *a bastard, child of incest:*— illegitimate birth(1), mongrel race(1), one of illegitimate birth(1).

4465. מִמְכָּר **mimkar** (569d); from 4376; *a sale, ware:*— merchandise(1), sale(6), what he has sold(1), what he sold(1), what...has sold(1).

4466. מִמְכֶּרֶת **mimkereth** (569d); fem. of 4465; *a sale:*— sale(1).

4467. מַמְלָכָה **mamlakah** (575a); from the same as 4428; *kingdom, sovereignty, dominion, reign:*— dominion(1), kingdom(58), kingdoms(48), reign(2), royal(6), rule(1), sovereignty(1).

4468. מַמְלָכוּת **mamlakuth** (575c); from the same as 4428; *kingdom, dominion, reign:*— kingdom(8), reign(1).

4469. מִמְסָךְ **mimsak** (587c); from 4537; *a mixed drink:*— mixed wine(2).

4470. מֶמֶר **memer** (601b); from 4843; *bitterness:*— bitterness(1).

4471. מַמְרֵא **Mamre** (577b); of unc. der.; a place in Pal., also an ally of Abraham:— Mamre(10).

4472. מַמְרֹר **mamror** (601b); from 4843; *a bitter thing:*— bitterness(1).

4473. מִמְשַׁח **mimshach** (603d); from 4886; perh. *expanded* or *far-reaching wings:*— anointed(1).

4474. מִמְשָׁל **mimshal** (606a); from 4910; *dominion, ruler:*— authority(1), ruled(1).

4475. מֶמְשָׁלָה **memshalah** (606a); fem. of 4474; *rule, dominion, realm:*— authority(1), domain(1), dominion(9), forces(1), govern(2), rule(4).

4476. מִמְשָׁק **mimshaq** (606c); from the same as 4943; perh. *possession:*— place possessed(1).

4477. מַמְתַקִּים **mamthaqqim** (609a); from 4985; *sweetness, sweet things:*— sweet(1), sweetness(1).

4478a. מָן **man** (577b); of unc. der.; *manna* (a kind of bread):— manna(13).

4478b. מָן **man** (577c); from the same as 4478a; *what?:*— what(1).

4479. מַן **man** (1100d); (Ara.) corr. to 4478b; *who?:*— what(2), who(2), whoever(2), whom*(1), whomever*(3).

4480. מִן **min** or

מִנִּי **minni** or

מִנֵּי **minne** (577d); a prim. prep.; *from:*— abandon*(1), about(4), above(17), above*(46), according(1), account(3), account*(2), across*(3), addition*(1), after(16), after*(5), against(13), against*(7), all(1), all alone*(1), all*(4), alone(2), alone*(2), aloof*(3), among(34), among*(1), any(35), any*(6), anything*(1), away(6), because(92), because*(86), before(12), before*(117), beforehand*(1), behind*(10), belongs(1), below(1), below*(10), beneath*(7), bereft*(1), beside*(6), besides(1), besides*(45), between(1), between*(2), beyond(1), beyond*(20), both(27), both sides*(1), both*(2), close*(1), concerning(1), concerning*(1), course*(2), devoid(2), dictated*(1), distance*(3), doing*(2), due(4), either(2), ever(1), exclusive(1), facing(2), far*(2), forever*(3), forsaking*(2), gone(2), Hamites*(1), help*(1), high*(1), hovered*(2), including(1), inside*(16), inward*(1), later*(1), leave*(7), left(1), mere(1), Mine(2), more(7), more...than(6), more than(43), more*(2), more...than(33), most(1), never*(2), no(10), no more(1), no*(1), nor(2), off(1), off*(6), one(4), openly*(1), opposite*(6), origin*(1), outermost*(1), outside*(52), over(4), over*(4), part(1), part*(1), presence*(1), previously*(1), promised*(1), rather than(7), recently*(1), regard(1), regarding*(1), removed(1), responsible*(1), result(1), said*(1), same(2), shared*(1), since(20), since*(2), so(12), so...cannot(8), so...no(4), so...none(1), so*(3), some(123), some*(1), than(224), than*(1), theirs*(2), there*(2), thereafter*(1), through(11), through...after(1), throughout(2), throughout*(1), too(51), top*(2), toward(6), toward*(3), under(3), unless*(1), when(3), where*(1), wherever*(1), whether(7), willingly*(1), within*(1), without(9), without*(6).

4481. מִן min (1100d); (Ara.) corr. to 4480; *from, out of, by, by reason of, at, more than:*— according(2), after*(1), among*(1), because(2), because*(2), before*(3), besides*(2), commanded*(1), more than(1), part(1), partly(6), some*(1), soon*(1), surely*(1), than(1).

4482a. מֵן men (577c); of unc. der.; *string* (of a harp):— stringed instruments(2).

4482b. מֵן men (585d); another reading for 4521, q.v.

4483. מְנָא mena or

מְנָה menah (1101b); (Ara.) corr. to 4487; *to number, reckon:*— appoint(1), appointed(3), numbered(1).

4484. מְנֵא mene (1101b); (Ara.) corr. to 4488; *maneh, mina* (a measure of weight):— MENE(3).

4485. מַנְגִּינָה manginah (618d); from 5059; (mocking, derisive) *song:*— mocking song(1).

4486. מַנְדַּע manda (1095b); (Ara.) corr. to 4093; *knowledge, the power of knowing:*— knowledge(2), reason(2).

4487. מָנָה manah (584a); a prim. root; *to count, number, reckon:*— appoint(1), appointed(9), count(3), counted(2), counts(1), destine(1), muster(1), number(4), numbered(5), numbers(1).

4488. מָנֶה maneh (584b); from 4487; *maneh, mina* (a measure of weight or money):— maneh(1), minas(4).

4489. מֹנֶה moneh (584c); from 4487; *a counted number, time:*— times(2).

4490. מָנָה manah (584b); from 4487; *part, portion:*— food(1), portion(5), portions(6).

4491. מִנְהָג minhag (624c); from 5090a; *driving* (a chariot):— driving(2).

4492. מִנְהָרָה minharah (626a); from 5102b; perh. *a cave, stronghold:*— dens(1).

4493. מָנוֹד manod (627b); from 5110; *a shaking, wagging:*— laughingstock*(1).

4494. מָנוֹחַ manoach (629d); from 5117; *a resting place, state* or *condition of rest:*— place(1), rest(2), rested(1), resting place(2), security(1).

4495. מָנוֹחַ Manoach (629d); from 5117; father of Samson:— Manoah(18).

4496. מְנוּחָה menuchah or

מְנֻחָה menuchah (629d); fem. of 4494; *resting place, rest:*— comforting(1), permanent(1), place(1), place of rest(1), quartermaster*(1), quiet(1), rest(8), resting(1), resting place(7), resting places(1).

4497. מָנוֹן manon (584d); of unc. der.; perh. *thankless one:*— son(1).

4498. מָנוֹס manos (631a); from 5127; *flight, place of escape* or *refuge:*— escape(2), flight(3), refuge(3).

4499. מְנוּסָה menusah or

מְנֻסָה menusah (631a); fem. of 4498; *flight:*— fugitives(1), though(1).

4500. מָנוֹר manor (644d); from an unused word; *a* (weaver's) *beam:*— beam(4).

4501. מְנוֹרָה menorah or

מְנֹרָה menorah (633a); from the same as 5216; *a lampstand:*— each lampstand(1), lampstand(33), lampstands(6).

4502. מִנְּזָר minzar (634d); from 5144a; perh. *consecrated ones, princes:*— guardsmen(1).

4503. מִנְחָה minchah (585a); from an unused word; *a gift, tribute, offering:*— gift(5), gifts(2), meal offering(7), meal offerings(1), offering(152), offering*(1), offerings(14), present(12), sacrifice(3), tribute(14).

4504. מִנְחָה minchah (1101c); (Ara.) corr. to 4503; *a gift, offering:*— offering(1), offerings(1).

4505. מְנַחֵם Menachem (637c); from 5162; "comforter," king of N. Isr.:— Menahem(8).

4506a. מָנַחַת Manachath (630a); from 5117; a desc. of Seir the Horite:— Manahath(2).

4506b. מָנַחַת Manachath (630a); from 5117; "resting place," a city of unknown location:— Manahath(1).

4506c. מָנַחְתִּי Manachti (630a); from 4506b; inhab. of Manahath:— Manahathites(2).

4507. מְנִי Meni (584c); from 4487; "award," a heathen god:— destiny(1).

4508. מִנִּי Minni (585d); of for. or.; a region of Armenia:— Minni(1).

4509. מִנְיָמִין Minyamin (568a); from 4480 and 3225; "from the right hand," the name of several Isr.:— Miniamin(3).

4510. מִנְיָן minyan (1101b); (Ara.) from 4483; *a number:*— number(1).

4511. מִנִּית Minnith (585d); from the same as 4482b; a place in Ammonite territory:— Minnith(2).

4512. מִנְלֶה minleh (649b); from 5239; perh. *gain, acquisition:*— grain(1).

4513. מָנַע mana (586a); a prim. root; *to withhold, hold back:*— held back(2), hinder(1), hold back(1), holds(1), keep(2), keep back(1), kept(1), refuse(2), restrain(1), restrained(2), restrains(1), withheld(8), withhold(5), withholds(1).

4514. מַנְעוּל manul or

מַנְעֻל manul (653b); from 5274a; *a bolt:*— bolt(1), bolts(5).

4515. מִנְעָל minal (653b); from 5274a; *a bolt:*— locks(1).

4516. מַנְעַמִּים manammim (654b); from 5276; *delicacies, dainties:*— delicacies(1).

4517. מְנַעַנְעַ menaanea (631c); from 5128; prob. (a kind of musical) *rattle:*— castanets(1).

4518. מְנַקִּית menaqqith (667d); from 5352; *a sacrificial bowl:*— bowls(2), drink offering bowls(1), sacrificial bowls(1).

4519. מְנַשֶּׁה Menashsheh (586b); from 5382; "causing to forget," a son of Joseph, also a tribe desc. from him, also a king of Judah , also two Isr.:— Manasseh(144), Manasseh's(2).

4520. מְנַשִּׁי Menashshi (586d); from 4519; desc. of Mannasseh:— Manassites(4).

4521. מְנָת menath (584c); from 4487; *portion:*— portion(6), portions(3), prey(1).

4522. מַס mas or

מִס mis (586d); of unc. der.; *body of forced laborers, forced service, taskworkers, taskwork, serfdom:*— forced(2), forced labor(13), forced laborer(1), forced laborers(5), laborers*(2), men subject to forced labor(1), taskmasters*(1), tribute(1).

4523. מָס mas (588a); from 4549; *despairing:*— despairing man(1).

4524. מֵסַב mesab or

מְסִבִּים mesibbim or

מְסִבּוֹת mesibboth (687b); from 5437; *that which surrounds* or *is round:*— changes direction(1), round about(1), surrounding area(1), table(1).

4525. מַסְגֵּר masger (689d); from 5462; *a locksmith, smith, a dungeon:*— dungeon(1), prison(2), smiths(4).

4526. מִסְגֶּרֶת misgereth (689d); from 5462; *border, rim, fastness:*— borders(8), fortresses(3), rim(6).

4527. מַסַּד massad (414c); from 3245; *foundation:*— foundation(1).

4528. מִסְדְּרוֹן misderon (690c); from the same as 5468; *a porch, colonnade:*— vestibule(1).

4529. מָסָה masah (587b); a prim. root; *to melt, dissolve, be liquefied:*— consume(1), dissolve(1), melt with fear(1), melts(1).

4530. מִסָּה missah or

מִסַּת missath (588b); of unc. der.; *sufficiency:*— tribute(1).

4531a. מַסָּה massah (588a); from 4549; *despair:*— despair(1).

4531b. מַסָּה massah (650b); from 5254; *a test, trial, proving:*— trials(3).

4532. מַסָּה Massah (650c); from 5254; a place in the desert where Isr. rebelled:— Massah(5).

4533. מַסְוֶה masveh (691d); from the same as 5497; *a veil:*— veil(3).

4534. מְסוּכָה mesukah (692b); from 5480b; *a hedge:*— thorn hedge(1).

4535. מַסָּח massach (587b); perh. from 5255; perh. *repulse, defense:*— defense(1).

4536. מִסְחָר mischar (695c); from 5503; prob. *merchandise:*— wares(1).

4537. מָסַךְ masak (587c); a prim. root; *to mix, produce by mixing:*— mingled(1), mixed(3), mixing(1).

4538. מֶסֶךְ mesek (587c); from 4537; *a mixture:*— mixed(1).

4539. מָסָךְ masak (697a); from 5526a; *a covering, screen:*— covering(2), defense(1), screen(16), screening(1), veil(5).

4540. מְסֻכָּה mesukkah (697b); from 5526a; *that with which one is covered, a covering:*— covering(1).

4541a. מַסֵּכָה massekah (651b); from 5258a; *a libation, molten metal* or *image:*— alliance(1), image(2), molten(5), molten image(8), molten images(9), molten metal(1).

4541b. מַסֵּכָה massekah (651b); from 5259; *woven stuff, web, covering:*— blanket(1), veil(1).

4542. מִסְכֵּן misken (587d); of unc. der.; *poor:*— poor(3), poor man(1).

4543. מִסְכְּנוֹת miskenoth (698b); from 5532a; *supply, storage:*— storage(4), store(2), storehouses(1).

4544. מִסְכֵּנֻת miskenuth (587d); from the same as 4542; *poverty, scarcity:*— scarcity(1).

4545. מַסֶּכֶת masseketh (651c); from 5259; *fabric on a loom:*— web(3).

4546. מְסִלָּה mesillah (700c); from 5549; *a highway:*— courses(1), highway(17), highways(7), path(1), steps(1).

4547. מַסְלוּל maslul (700c); from 5549; *a highway:*— highway(1).

4548. מַסְמֵר masmer or

מִסְמֵר mismer or

מַסְמְרָה masmerah or

מִסְמְרָה mismerah or

מַשְׂמְרָה masmerah (702c); perh. from 5568; *a nail:*— nails(5).

4549. מָסַס masas (587d); a prim. root; *to dissolve, melt:*— completely lose heart(1), drenched(1), dropped(1), melt(7), melt away(1), melted(5), melting(1), melts(1), wastes away(1), worthless(1).

4550. מַסַּע massa (652c); from 5265; *a pulling up, breaking* (camp), *setting out, a journey:*— journey(1), journeys(7), order of march(1), set(2), stages(1).

4551a. מַסָּע massa (652d); from 5265; *a quarry* or *quarrying:*— quarry(1).

4551b. מַסָּע massa (652d); from an unused word; *a missile, dart:*— dart(1).

4552. מִסְעָד misad (703c); from 5582; *support:*— supports(1).

4553. מִסְפֵּד misped (704d); from 5594; *a wailing:*— lament(1), lamentation(4), mourning(5), wailing(4).

4554. מִסְפּוֹא mispo (704c); from an unused word; *fodder:*— feed(2), fodder(3).

4555. מִסְפָּחָה mispachah (705d); from the same as 5597; *a long veil:*— veils(2).

4556. מִסְפַּחַת mispachath (705c); from the same as 5597; *scab:*— scab(3).

4557. מִסְפָּר mispar (708d); from the same as 5612; *number, tally:*— account(1), count(1), count*(1), counted(1), countless*(1), enumeration(1), few(7), infinite*(1), innumerable*(1), limit(1), list(2), many(2), measure(1), number(102), numbered(3), numbering(4), numbers(1), time*(1).

4558. מִסְפָּר Mispar (709a); from the same as 5612; an Isr.:— Mispar(1).

4559. מִסְפֶּרֶת Mispereth (709a); from the same as 5612; an Isr.:— Mispereth(1).

4560. מָסַר masar (588b); a prim. root; *to deliver up, offer:*— furnished(1), trespass*(1).

4561. מֹסָר mosar or

מוּסָר musar (416b); the same as 4148, q.v.

4562. מָסֹרֶת masoreth (64b); from 631; *bond* (of the covenant):— bond(1).

מִסַּת missath; see 4530.

4563. מִסְתּוֹר mistor (712c); from 5641; *place of shelter:*— protection(1).

4564. מַסְתֵּר master (712c); from 5641; *hiding, act of hiding:*— hide(1).

4565. מִסְתָּר mistar (712c); from 5641; *a secret place, hiding place:*— concealment(1), hiding place(1), hiding places(4), secret(2), secret places(2).

4566. מַעְבָּד mabad (716a); from 5647; *work:*— works(1).

4567. מַעְבָד maabad (1105a); (Ara.) corr. to 4566; *a work:*— works(1).

4568. מַעֲבֶה maabeh (716b); from 5666; *thickness, compactness:*— clay(2).

4569a. מַעֲבָר maabar (721b); from 5674a; *a ford, pass, passing:*— blow(1), ford(1), pass(1).

4569b. מַעְבָּרָה mabarah (721b); from 5674a; *a ford, pass, passage:*— fords(6), pass(1), passes(1).

4570. מַעְגָּל magal or

מַעְגָּלָה magalah (722d); from the same as 5695; *an entrenchment, track:*— circle of the camp(3), course(1), path(2), paths(5), tracks(2), ways(2), wayside(1).

4571. מָעַד maad (588c); a prim. root; *to slip, slide, totter, shake:*— shake(1), slip(2), slipped(2), unsteady(1), wavering(1).

4572. מַעֲדַי Maaday (588c); from 4571; an Isr.:— Maadai(1).

4573. מַעַדְיָה Maadyah (588c); from 4571 and 3050; an Isr. priest:— Maadiah(1), Moadiah(1).

4574. מַעֲדָן maadan or

מַעֲדַנָּה maadannah (726d); from the same as 5730a; *a dainty* (food), *delight:*— dainties(1), delicacies(1), delight(1).

4575a. מַעֲדַנּוֹת maadannoth (772c); by transp. from 6029; *bonds, bands:*— chains(1).

4575b. מַעֲדַנּוֹת maadannoth (588d); of unc. der.; perh. *in bonds* or *fetters:*— cheerfully(1).

4576. מַעְדֵּר mader (727c); from 5737b; *a hoe:*— hoe(1).

4577. מְעָה meah or

מְעָא mea (1101c); (Ara.) corr. to 4578; *belly:*— belly(1).

4578. מֵעֶה meeh (588d); of unc. der.; *internal organs, inward parts, belly:*— abdomen(1), body(4), bowels(4), children*(1), feelings(1), heart(4), inward parts(1), offspring*(1), own(1), soul(2), spirit(2), stomach(4), stomachs(1), within(1), womb(1).

4579. מְעָה maah (589a); from the same as 4578; *a grain* (of sand):— grains(1).

4580. מָעוֹג maog (728b); from the same as 5692; *a cake:*— bread(1), feast(1).

4581. מָעוֹז maoz or

מָעוּז mauz or

מָעֹז maoz or

מָעֻז mauz (731d); from 5756; *a place* or *means of safety, protection:*— defense(4), fortress(4), fortresses(3), helmet(2), protection(2), refuge(3), safety(2), strength(5), strong(1), stronghold(9), strongholds(1).

4582. מָעוֹךְ Maok (590d); from 4600; a Philistine:— Maoch(1).

4583. מָעוֹן maon or

מָעִין main (732d); from 5770b; *dwelling, habitation:*— den(1), dwelling(3), dwelling place(4), habitation(6), haunt(4).

4584. מָעוֹן Maon (733a); from 5770b; "habitation," a place in Judah, also a man of Judah, also an enemy of Isr.:— Maon(7), Maonites(1).

4585. מְעוֹנָה meonah or

מְעֹנָה meonah (733b); fem. of 4583; *habitation:*— den(2), dens(4), dwelling place(2), habitations(1).

4586. מְעוּנִים Meunim or

מְעִינִים Meinim (589b); of unc. der.; a people S.E. of the Dead Sea:— Meunim(2), Meunites(3).

4587. מְעוֹנֹתַי Meonothay (733b); from 5770b; a man of Judah:— Meonothai(2).

4588. מָעוּף mauph (734a); from 5774b; *gloom:*— gloom(1).

4589. מָעוֹר maor (735d); from 5783; *nakedness, pudendum:*— nakedness(1).

4590. מַעַזְיָה Maazyah or

מַעַזְיָהוּ Maazyahu (589b); of unc. der.; two Isr. priests:— Maaziah(2).

4591. מָעַט maat (589b); a prim. root; *to be* or *become small, diminished,* or *few:*— bring to nothing(1), decrease(2), diminish(2), diminished(2), dwindles(1), few(2), fewness(1), get a few(1), give less(1), had little(1), least(1), little(1), make so small(1), pay less(1), reduce(1), seem insignificant(1), small(1), take less(1).

4592. מְעַט meat or

מְעָט meat (589d); from 4591; *a little, fewness, a few:*— almost(2), brief(1), close(1), diminish(1), easily(1), enough(3), few(20), fewest(1), little(44), little while(8), many*(1), merely(1), quickly(1), scarcely(1), slight a thing(2), small(3), small matter(1), smaller(4), so small(1), some(1), soon(3).

4593. מְעֻטָּה miuttah (590c, 598d); scribal error, from 4803, q.v.

4594. מַעֲטֶה maateh (742a); from 5844a; *a wrap, mantle:*— mantle(1).

4595. מַעֲטָפָה maataphah (742c); from 5848b; *an overtunic:*— outer tunics(1).

4596. מְעִי mei (590c); of unc. der.; perh. *ruin heap:*— ruin(1).

4597. מָעַי Maay (590c); of unc. der.; an Isr. musician:— Maai(1).

4598. מְעִיל meil (591c); from 4603; *a robe:*— mantle(1), robe(23), robes(2).

4599. מַעְיָן mayan or

מַעְיְנוֹ mayeno or

מַעְיָנָה mayanah (745d); from 5869; *a spring:*— fountain(2), fountains(2), spring(8), springs(11).

4600. מָעַךְ maak (590c); a prim. root; *to press, squeeze:*— bruised(1), pressed(1), stuck(1).

4601. מַעֲכָה Maakah or

מַעֲכָת Maakath (590d); from 4600; an Isr. name, also a non-Isr. name, also a region in Syria:— Aram-maacah*(1), Maacah(21), Maacath(1).

4602. מַעֲכָתִי Maakathi (591a); from 4601; inhab. of Maacah:— Maacathite(4), Maacathites(4).

4603. מָעַל **maal** (591a); a prim. root; *to act unfaithfully* or *treacherously:*— act(1), acted(2), acted treacherously(2), acting(1), acting treacherously(1), acting unfaithfully(1), acts(2), became...unfaithful(1), been(1), been unfaithful(5), broke faith(1), committed(6), committing unfaithfulness(1), err(1), perpetrated(1), unfaithful(3), unfaithfulness they committed(1), violated(1).

4604. מַעַל **maal** (591b); from 4603; *an unfaithful* or *treacherous act:*— falsehood(1), treachery(2), trespass(1), trespass*(1), unfaithful(3), unfaithful act(4), unfaithful deeds(1), unfaithfully(6), unfaithfulness(6), very unfaithful(1).

4605. מַעַל **maal** (751c); from 5927; *above, upwards:*— above(7), above*(32), covered*(1), exceedingly(1), forward(2), greater(1), greatly(1), heaven(4), high above(1), high*(1), higher(4), highly(2), hovered*(2), older(2), onward(2), over(4), over*(1), severe(1), successive story(1), top(9), upside down(1), upward(53), upward by stages(1), upwards(2), very(3).

4606. מֶעָל **meal** (1106d); (Ara.) from 5954; *a going in:*— sunset*(1).

4607. מֹעַל **moal** (751b); from 5927; *a lifting:*— lifting(1).

4608. מַעֲלֶה **maaleh** (751b); from 5927; *an ascent:*— ascent(9), platform(1), slope(1), stairway(4), upper section(1).

4609a. מַעֲלָה **maalah** (752a); from 5927; *what comes up:*— thoughts*(1).

4609b. מַעֲלָה **maalah** (752a); from 5927; *a step, stair:*— go(1), high degree(1), stairway(6), steps(22), upper chambers(1).

4610. מַעֲלֵה עַקְרַבִּים **Maaleh Aqrabbim** (751b); from 4608 and 6137; "ascent of scorpions," a place on the S. border of Isr.:— ascent of Akrabbim(3).

4611. מַעֲלָל **maalal** (760b); from 5953a; *a deed, practice:*— actions(2), dealings(1), deeds(34), doings(1), practices(2), works(1).

4612. מַעֲמָד **maamad** (765b); from 5975; *office, function, service:*— attendance(2), office(1), station(1), stations(1).

4613. מָעֳמָד **moomad** (765c); from 5975; *a standing ground, foothold:*— foothold(1).

4614. מַעֲמָסָה **maamasah** (770c); from 6006; *a load, burden:*— heavy(1).

4615. מַעֲמַקִּים **maamaqqim** (771b); from 6009; *depths:*— deep(2), depths(3).

4616. מַעַן **maan** (775a); from 6030a; *purpose, intent:*— account(1), because(14), behalf(1), order(40), purpose(2), reason is so(1), sake(50), so(54), therefore(1), this reason(1).

4617. מַעֲנֶה **maaneh** (775a); from 6030a; *an answer, response:*— answer(6), purpose(1), response(1).

4618. מַעֲנָה **maanah** (776a); from 6030b; *place for* (doing) *a task; a field for plowing:*— furrow(1), furrows(1).

4619. מַעַץ **Maats** (591d); from an unused word; a man of Judah:— Maaz(1).

4620. מַעֲצֵבָה **maatsebah** (781a); from 6087a; *a place of pain:*— torment(1).

4621. מַעֲצָד **maatsad** (781b); from an unused word; *an axe:*— cutting tool(2).

4622. מַעְצוֹר **matsor** (784a); from 6113; *a restraint, hindrance:*— restrained(1).

4623. מַעְצָר **matsar** (784a); from 6113; *restraint, control:*— control(1).

4624. מַעֲקֶה **maaqeh** (785b); from an unused word; *a parapet:*— parapet(1).

4625. מַעֲקָשׁ **maaqash** (786a); from 6140; *a twisted* or *crooked place:*— rugged places(1).

4626. מַעַר **maar** (789a); from 6168; *a bare* or *naked place:*— clear space(1), Maareh-geba*(1), nakedness(1).

4627. מַעֲרָב **maarab** (786d); from 6148; *articles of exchange, merchandise:*— merchandise(9).

4628. מַעֲרָב **maarab** or

מַעֲרָבָה **maarabah** (788a); from the same as 6153; *west:*— setting(1), west(11), west side(2).

4629. מַעֲרֶה **maareh** (789a); the same as 4626, q.v.

4630. מַעֲרָה **maarah** (790a); see 4634.

4631. מְעָרָה **mearah** (792c); from an unused word; *a cave:*— cave(31), caves(5), den(1).

4632. מְעָרָה **Mearah** (792c); from the same as 4631; a cave region in Lebanon:— Mearah(1).

4633. מַעֲרָךְ **maarak** (790a); from 6186a; *an arrangement:*— plans(1).

4634. מַעֲרָכָה **maarakah** (790a); from 6186a; *row, rank, battle line:*— armies(3), army(3), arrangement(1), battle array(1), battle formation(1), battle line(5), battlefield*(1), orderly manner(1), ranks(3).

4635. מַעֲרֶכֶת **maareketh** (790b); from 6186a; *a row, line:*— row(2), rows(1), showbread(3), showbread*(4).

4636. מַעֲרֹם **maarom** (736a); from 5783; *something naked:*— naked ones(1).

4637. מַעֲרָצָה **maaratsah** (792b); from 6206; *an awful shock, a crash:*— terrible crash(1).

4638. מַעֲרָת **Maarath** (789b); from 6168; a place in Judah:— Maarath(1).

4639. מַעֲשֶׂה **maaseh** (795c); from 6213a; *a deed, work:*— accomplishments(1), achievements(1), act(1), act...did(1), actions(1), activities(2), activity(3), art(1), business(1), chainwork*(1), concern(1), conduct(1), deed(4), deeds(17), design(4), did(1), does(1), done(1), eventful(1), goods(2), just*(1), labors(2), made(2), occupation(2), practices(2), sculptured*(1), task(2), things(5), verses(1), vocation(1), what He has done(1), what is done(2), what is made(1), work(99), work quota(1), working(2), workmanship(10), works(42), wrought(1), yield(1).

4640. מַעֲשַׂי **Maasay** (796b); from 4639; "work of Yah," an Isr.:— Maasai(1).

4641. מַעֲשֵׂיָה **Maaseyah** or

מַעֲשֵׂיָהוּ **Maaseyahu** (796b); from 4639 and 3050; "work of Yah," the name of a number of Isr.:— Maaseiah(23).

4642. מַעֲשַׁקָּה **maashaqqah** (799a); from 6231; *extortionate act:*— oppressor(1), unjust*(1).

4643. מַעֲשֵׂר **maaser** or

מַעְשַׂר **maasar** or

מַעַשְׂרָה **maasrah** (798b); from the same as 6235; *tenth part, tithe:*— tenth(4), tenth part(1), tithe(17), tithes(9), tithing(1).

4644. מֹף **Moph** (592a); of for. or.; ancient capital of Eg.:— Memphis(1).

4645. מִפְגָּע **miphga** (803c); from 6293; *something hit, a mark:*— target(1).

4646. מַפָּח **mappach** (656a); from 5301; *a breathing out:*— breathe last(1).

4647. מַפֻּחַ **mappuach** (656b); from 5301; *a bellows:*— bellows(1).

4648. מְפִיבֹשֶׁת **Mephibosheth** or

מְפִבֹשֶׁת **Mephibosheth** (937c); from 6284 and 1322; "dispeller of shame," another name for 4807:— Mephibosheth(15).

4649. מֻפִּים **Muppim** (592b); of unc. der.; a family in Benjamin:— Muppim(1).

4650. מֵפִיץ **mephits** (807b); from 6327a; *scatterer, disperser:*— club(1), one who scatters(1).

4651. מַפָּל **mappal** (658c); from 5307; *refuse, hanging parts:*— folds(1), refuse(1), strong(1).

4652. מִפְלָאָה **miphlaah** (811a); from the same as 6382; *a wondrous work:*— wonders(1).

4653. מִפְלַגָּה **miphlaggah** (811b); from 6385; *a division:*— sections(1).

4654a. מַפָּלָה **mappalah** (658c); from 5307; *a ruin:*— fallen(1).

4654b. מַפֵּלָה **mappelah** (658c); from 5307; *a ruin:*— ruin(2).

4655. מִפְלָט **miphlat** (812d); from 6403; *an escape* or (place of) *escape:*— place of refuge(1).

4656. מִפְלֶצֶת **miphletseth** (814a); from 6426; *horrid thing:*— horrid image(4).

4657. מִפְלָשׂ **miphlas** (814a); from the same as 6425; *a swaying, poising:*— layers(1).

4658. מַפֶּלֶת **mappeleth** (658c); from 5307; *carcass, ruin, an overthrow:*— carcass(1), fall(5), overthrow(1), ruin(1).

4659a. מִפְעָל **miphal** or

מִפְעָלָה **miphalah** (821d); from 6466; *a work, something made:*— works(1).

4659b. מִפְעָלָה **miphalah** (821d); from 6466; *a deed:*— works(2).

4660. מַפָּץ **mappats** (658d); from 5310a; *a shattering:*— shattering(1).

4661. מַפֵּץ **mappets** (659a); from 5310a; *a war-club:*— war-club(1).

4662. מִפְקָד **miphqad** (824c); from 6485; *a muster, appointment, appointed place:*— appointed place(1), appointment(1), census(1), registration(1).

4663. מִפְקָד **Miphqad** (824c); from 4662; "appointed place," a gate in Jer.:— inspection(1).

4664. מִפְרָץ **miphrats** (830a); from 6555; *landing place:*— landings(1).

4665. מִפְרֶקֶת **miphreqeth** (830b); from 6561; *neck:*— neck(1).

4666. מִפְרָשׂ **miphras** (831c); from 6566; *a spreading out, something spread:*— sail(1), spreading(1).

4667. מִפְשָׂעָה **miphsaah** (832c); from 6585; *hip* or *buttock:*— hips(1).

4668. מַפְתֵּחַ **maphteach** (836b); from 6605a; *a key:*— key(2), opening(1).

4669. מִפְתָּח **miphtach** (836b); from 6605a; *an opening, utterance:*— opening(1).

4670. מִפְתָּן **miphtan** (837b); from the same as 6620; *threshold:*— threshold(8).

4671a. מֵץ **mets** (568c); from an unused word; *squeezer, extortioner:*— extortioner(1).

4671b. מֹץ mots or **מוֹץ mots** (558b); of unc. der.; *chaff:*— chaff(8).

4672. מָצָא matsa (592c); a prim. root; *to attain to, find:*— actually found(1), afford*(1), befall(1), befallen(2), befell(1), came(2), caught(5), come(6), comes(1), delivered(2), discover(8), discovered(4), discovery(1), enough(1), fall(1), find(109), finding(2), finds(17), found(231), going(1), had(2), handed(3), happen(1), happened(2), has(1), have(2), here(1), hit(1), invents(1), left(2), located(2), meet(2), met(3), overtake(2), overtook(1), pleases*(1), possessed(1), present(15), reached(3), reaped(1), requires(1), secured(1), seeking(1), spreads(1), strikes(1), sufficient(2), there(1), use(1).

4673. מַצָּב matstsab (662d); from 5324; *standing place, station, garrison:*— garrison(8), office(1), place where(1), place*(1), standing(2), where(2).

4674. מֻצָּב mutstsab (663a); from 5324; *palisade* or *entrenchment:*— siegeworks(1).

4675. מִצָּבָה mitstsabah (663a); fem. of 4673; perh. *a guard, watch:*— army(1).

4676. מַצֵּבָה matstsebah (663a); from 5324; *a pillar, stump:*— obelisks(1), pillar(19), pillars(16), stump(2).

4677. מְצֹבָיָה Metsobayah (594b); of unc. der.; descriptive title for one of David's men:— Mezobaite(1).

4678. מַצֶּבֶת matstsebeth (663a); the same as 4676, q.v.

4679. מְצַד metsad or **מְצָד metsad** or **מְצָדָה metsadah** (844d); from 6679; *fastness, a stronghold:*— impregnable(1), stronghold(3), strongholds(7).

4680. מָצָה matsah (594c); a prim. root; *to drain, drain out:*— drain(2), drained(4), drunk(1).

4681. מֹצָה Motsah (594c); of unc. der.; a place in Benjamin:— Mozah(1).

4682. מַצָּה matstsah (595b); from 4711; *unleavened bread* or *cake:*— unleavened(15), Unleavened Bread(10), unleavened bread(25), unleavened cakes(3).

4683. מַצָּה matstsah (663c); from 5327b; *strife, contention:*— strife(3).

4684. מִצְהָלָה mitshalah (843d); from 6670a; *a neighing:*— neighing(1), neighings(1).

4685a. מָצוֹד matsod (844d); from 6679; *siegeworks:*— siegeworks(1).

4685b. מָצוֹד matsod (844d); from 6679; *a hunting implement, net:*— booty(1), net(1), snares(1).

4685c. מְצוֹדָה metsodah (845a); from 6679; *a net:*— hunting nets(1), net(1).

4685d. מְצוֹדָה metsodah (845a); from 6679; *fastness, a stronghold:*— stronghold(1).

4686a. מְצוּדָה metsudah (845a); from 6679; *net, prey:*— hunted(1), net(1), snare(2).

4686b. מְצוּדָה metsudah (845a); from 6679; *a fastness, stronghold:*— fortress(6), inaccessible place(1), stronghold(10).

4687. מִצְוָה mitsvah (846b); from 6680; *commandment:*— command(15), commanded(7), commandment(34), commandments(118), commands(2), obligation(1), prescribed(2), terms(1), things(4), tradition*(1), what(1).

4688. מְצוֹלָה metsolah or **מְצֹלָה metsolah** or **מְצוּלָה metsulah** or **מְצֻלָה metsulah** (846d); from the same as 6683; *depth, deep:*— deep(4), depths(7).

4689. מָצוֹק matsoq (848a); from 6693; *straits, stress:*— anguish(1), distress(5).

4690. מָצוּק matsuq or **מָצֻק matsuq** (848b); from 6694; *molten support, pillar:*— pillars(1), rose(1).

4691. מְצוּקָה metsuqah or **מְצֻקָה metsuqah** (848a); from 6693; *straits, stress:*— anguish(1), distress(1), distresses(5).

4692. מָצוֹר matsor or **מָצוּר matsur** (848d); from 6696a; *siege enclosure, siege, entrenchment:*— besieged(3), defense(1), fortified(1), fortress(1), rampart(1), siege(17), siegeworks(1).

4693. מָצוֹר Matsor (596a); from the same as 4714; a country S.W. of the Red Sea:— Egypt(5).

4694. מְצוּרָה metsurah or **מְצֻרָה metsurah** (849a); from 6696a; *siegeworks, rampart:*— battle towers(1), fortified(5), fortress(1), fortresses(1).

4695. מַצּוּת matstsuth (663d); from 5327b; *strife, contention:*— quarrel(1).

4696. מֵצַח metsach (594d); of unc. der.; *brow, forehead:*— forehead(10), foreheads(2), stubborn*(1).

4697. מִצְחָה mitschah (595a); from the same as 4696; *greaves:*— greaves(1).

4698. מְצִלָּה metsillah (853a); from 6750; *a bell:*— bells(1).

4699. מְצֻלָּה metsullah (847a); from the same as 6683; *a basin* or *hollow:*— ravine(1).

4700. מְצִלְתַּיִם metsiltayim (853a); from 6750; *cymbals:*— cymbals(13).

4701. מִצְנֶפֶת mitsnepheth (857b); from 6801; *turban* (of the high priest):— turban(12).

4702. מַצָּע matstsa (427a); from 3331; *couch, bed:*— bed(1).

4703. מִצְעָד mitsad (857d); from 6805; *a step:*— heels(1), steps(2).

4704. מִצְּעִירָה mitstseirah (859a); see 6810.

4705. מִצְעָר mitsar (859b); from 6819; *a small thing:*— insignificant(1), little while(1), small(3).

4706. מִצְעָר Mitsar (859b); from 6819; a mountain near Hermon:— Mizar(1).

4707. מִצְפֶּה mitspeh (859d); from 6822; *watchtower:*— lookout(2), watchtower(1).

4708. מִצְפֶּה Mitspeh (859d); from 6822; the name of several places in Isr.:— Mizpah(4), Mizpeh(3).

4709. מִצְפָּה Mitspah (859d); from 6822; the name of several places in Isr.:— Mizpah(38), Mizpeh(1).

4710. מַצְפֻּן matspon (861b); from 6845; *hidden treasure, treasure:*— hidden treasures(1).

4711. מָצַץ matsats (595b); a prim. root; *to drain out:*— suck(1).

4712. מֵצַר metsar (865c); from 6887a; *straits, distress:*— distress(2), terrors(1).

4713. מִצְרִי Mitsri (596a); from the same as 4714; inhab. of Eg.:— Egypt(1), Egyptian(18), Egyptian's(4), Egyptians(7).

4714. מִצְרַיִם Mitsrayim (595c); of unc. der.; a son of Ham, also his desc. and their country in N.W. Africa:— Egypt(588), Egypt's(2), Egyptian(1), Egyptians(87), Mizraim(4).

4715. מַצְרֵף matsreph (864c); from 6884; *a crucible:*— crucible(1), refining pot(1).

4716. מַק maq (597a); from 4743; *decay, rottenness:*— putrefaction(1), rot(1).

4717. מַקֶּבֶת maqqebeth (666c); from 5344a; *a hammer:*— hammer(2), hammers(2).

4718. מַקֶּבֶת maqqebeth (666c); from 5344a; *a hole, excavation:*— quarry*(1).

4719. מַקֵּדָה Maqqedah (596b); of unc. der.; a place in Judah:— Makkedah(9).

4720. מִקְדָּשׁ miqdash or **מִקְּדָשׁ miqqedash** (874a); from the same as 6944; *a sacred place, sanctuary:*— holy(1), holy place(2), holy places(1), places(1), sacred part(1), sanctuaries(5), sanctuary(65).

4721. מַקְהֵל maqhel or **מַקְהֵלָה maqhelah** (875b); from the same as 6951; *an assembly:*— congregations(2).

4722. מַקְהֵלֹת Maqheloth (875b); from the same as 6951; "place of assembly," a place in the desert:— Makheloth(2).

4723a. מִקְוֶה miqveh or **מִקְוֵה miqveh** or **מִקְוֵא miqve** (876a); from 6960a; *a hope:*— Hope(1), hope(4).

4723b. מִקְוֶה miqveh (876c); from 6960b; *a collection, collected mass:*— collecting(1), gathering(1), reservoirs(1).

4724. מִקְוָה miqvah (876c); from 6960b; *reservoir:*— reservoir(1).

4725. מָקוֹם maqom or **מָקֹם maqom** or **מְקוֹמָה meqomah** or **מְקֹמָה meqomah** (879d); from 6965; *a standing place, place:*— anywhere*(1), area(1), country(1), direction(1), everywhere*(1), ground(2), home(7), hometown(1), localities(1), place(348), place suitable(1), places(16), position(1), room(3), seat*(2), site(4), sites(1), some(1), source(1), space(1), space*(1), where*(1), wherever(1), wherever*(2).

4726. מָקוֹר maqor or **מָקֹר maqor** (881b); from 6979; *a spring, fountain:*— flow(3), fountain(14), well(1).

4727. מִקָּח miqqach (544c); from 3947; *a taking, receiving:*— taking(1).

4728. מַקָּחָה maqqachah (544c); from 3947; *ware* (an article of merchandise):— wares(1).

4729a. מִקְטָר miqtar (883b); from the same as 6999; *place of sacrificial smoke:*— place for burning(1).

4729b. מֻקְטָר muqtar (883b); from the same as 6999; *incense:*— incense(1).

4729c. מְקַטְּרָה meqatterah (883b); from the same as 6999; *incense altar:*— incense altars(1).

4730. מִקְטֶרֶת miqtereth (883b); from the same as 6999; *a censer:*— censer(2).

4731. מַקֵּל maqqel or

מַקְּלָה maqqelah (596b); of unc. der.; *a rod, staff:*— rod(1), rods(6), staff(5), staffs(1), stick(2), sticks(1), wand(1), war clubs(1).

4732. מִקְלוֹת Miqloth (596c); from the same as 4731; a Benjamite, also an officer of David:— Mikloth(4).

4733. מִקְלָט miqlat (886a); from an unused word; *refuge, asylum:*— refuge(20).

4734. מִקְלַעַת miqlaath (887c); from 7049b; *carving:*— carved(1), carvings(1), engravings(1).

4735. מִקְנֶה miqneh (889b); from 7069; *cattle:*— acquired(1), cattle(10), cattle*(1), flocks(1), herds(1), livestock(54), possessions(3), purchased(1).

4736. מִקְנָה miqnah (889b); from 7069; *a purchase:*— bought(2), possession(1), price(2), purchase(6), purchased(1), who is bought(2), who were bought(1).

4737. מִקְנֵיָהוּ Miqneyahu (889c); from 4735 and 3050; "possession of Yah," a Levitical musician:— Mikneiah(2).

4738. מִקְסָם miqsam (890d); from the same as 7081; *divination:*— divination(2).

4739. מָקַץ Maqats (596d); from 7112; a place in Isr.:— Makaz(1).

4740. מִקְצוֹעַ miqtsoa or

מִקְצֹעַ miqtsoa or

מִקְצֹעָה miqtsoah (893a); from an unused word; *a corner buttress:*— Angle(4), corner buttress(1), corners(7), every corner(1).

4741. מַקְצֻעָה maqtsuah (893a); from 7106a; *a scraping tool:*— planes(1).

4742. מְקֻצְעָה mequtsah (893b); from 7106b, q.v.

4743. מָקַק maqaq (596d); a prim. root; *to decay, rot, fester, pine away:*— fester(1), rot(3), rot away(3), rotting away(1), waste away(1), wear away(1).

4744. מִקְרָא miqra (896d); from 7121; *a convocation, convoking, reading:*— assemblies(2), assembly(2), convocation(14), convocations(3), reading(1), summoning(1).

4745. מִקְרֶה miqreh (899d); from 7136a; *accident, chance, fortune:*— accident(1), chance(1), fate(6), happened*(1).

4746. מְקָרֶה meqareh (900a); from 7136a; *beam work:*— rafters(1).

4747. מְקֵרָה meqerah (903b); from 7174b; *coolness:*— cool(2).

4748. מִקְשֶׁה miqsheh (904d); from an unused word; (an artistic) *hairdo:*— well-set hair(1).

4749. מִקְשָׁה miqshah (904d); from the same as 4748; perh. *hammered work:*— hammered work(9).

4750. מִקְשָׁה miqshah (903d); from the same as 7180; *field of cucumbers:*— cucumber field(2).

4751. מַר mar or

מָרָה marah (600c); from 4843; *bitter, bitterness:*— bitter(15), bitter thing(1), bitterly(4), bitterness(11), discontented*(1), embittered(1), fierce(1), fierce*(2), great bitterness(1), greatly distressed(1).

4752. מַר mar (601c); from an unused word; *a drop:*— drop(1).

4753. מֹר mor or

מוֹר mor (600d); from 4843; *myrrh:*— myrrh(12).

4754. מָרָא mara (597a); a prim. root; perh. *to flap* (the wings):— lifts(1).

4755. מָרָא Mara (600d); from 4843; "bitter," symbolic name of Naomi:— Mara(1).

4756. מָרֵא mare (1101c); (Ara.) from a root corr. to 4754; *lord:*— Lord(2), lord(2).

4757. מְרֹאדַךְ בַּלְאֲדָן Merodak Baladan (597d); of for. or.; a king of Bab. (the same as 1255):— Merodach-baladan(1).

4758. מַרְאֶה mareh (909c); from 7200; *sight, appearance, vision:*— appear(1), appearance(48), appears(7), desires(1), face(2), form(2), good-looking*(1), impressive(1), like(2), looked(2), looking(1), openly(1), pattern(1), saw*(1), see*(1), sight(5), something(2), vision(10), what...see(2), who looked(1).

4759a. מַרְאָה marah (909b); from 7200; *vision:*— vision(6), visions(5).

4759b. מַרְאָה marah (909c); from 7200; *a mirror:*— mirrors(1).

4760. מֻרְאָה murah (597b); from the same as 4806; *crop* or *alimentary canal:*— crop(1).

4761. מַרְאָשָׁה marashah (912b); the same as 4763, q.v.

4762. מָרֵאשָׁה Mareshah or

מָרֵשָׁה Mareshah (601c); of unc. der.; a place in Judah, also two Isr.:— Mareshah(8).

4763. מְרַאֲשׁוֹת meraashoth (912b); from 7218; *a place at the head, head place:*— head(10).

4764. מֵרַב Merab (597b); from 7231; older daughter of Saul:— Merab(4).

4765. מַרְבַד marbad (915a); from 7234; *a spread, coverlet:*— coverings(2).

4766. מַרְבֶּה marbeh (916a); from 7235a; *abundance:*— abundant(1), increase(1).

4767. מִרְבָּה mirbah (916b); from 7235a; *much:*— much(1).

4768. מַרְבִּית marbith (916b); from 7235a; *increase, great number, greatness:*— gain(1), greatest part(1), greatness(1), increase(1), multitude(1).

4769. מַרְבֵּץ marbets (918c); from 7257; (place of) *lying down:*— resting place(2).

4770. מַרְבֵּק marbeq (918d); from an unused word; *a stall:*— fattened(2), stall(2).

4771. מַרְגּוֹעַ margoa (921b); from 7280b; *a rest:*— rest(1).

4772. מַרְגְּלוֹת margeloth (920b); from the same as 7272; *place of the feet, feet:*— feet(5).

4773. מַרְגֵּמָה margemah (920c); from 7275; *a sling:*— sling(1).

4774. מַרְגֵּעָה margeah (921c); from 7280b; *a rest, repose:*— repose(1).

4775. מָרַד marad (597c); a prim. root; *to rebel:*— rebel(8), rebelled(14), rebelling(1), rebellious(1), rebels(1).

4776. מְרַד merad (1101d); (Ara.) from a root corr. to 4775; *rebellion:*— rebellion(1).

4777. מֶרֶד mered (597d); from 4775; *rebellion, revolt:*— rebellion(1).

4778. מֶרֶד Mered (597d); from 4775; a man of Judah:— Mered(2).

4779a. מָרָד marad (1101d); (Ara.) from the same as 4776; *rebellious:*— rebellious(2).

4779b. מִרְדָּה mirdah (922a); another reading for 4783, q.v.

4780. מַרְדּוּת marduth (597d); from 4775; *rebellion, rebelliousness:*— rebellious(1).

4781. מְרֹדָךְ Merodak (597d); of for. or.; a god worshiped by the Bab.:— Marduk(1).

4782. מָרְדֳּכַי Mordekay (598a); of for. or.; a companion of Zerubbabel, also a cousin of Esther:— Mordecai(56), Mordecai's(3).

4783. מֻרְדָּף murdaph (923a); from 7291; *persecution:*— persecution(1).

4784. מָרָה marah (598a); a prim. root; *to be contentious* or *rebellious:*— became disobedient(1), bitter(1), disobedient(1), disobeyed(2), provocation(1), rebel(6), rebelled(18), rebellious(12), rebels(2), very rebellious(1).

4785. מָרָה Marah (600d); from 4843; a bitter spring in the Sinai peninsula:— Marah(5).

4786. מֹרָה morah (601a); from 4843; *bitterness:*— grief*(1).

4787a. מֹרָּה morrah (601a); from 4843; *bitterness:*— bitterness(1).

4787b. מַרְהֵבָה marhebah (923c); from 7292; *boisterous, raging behavior:*— fury(1).

4788. מָרוּד marud (924a); from 7300; *restlessness, straying:*— homeless(1), homelessness(1), wandering(1).

4789. מֵרוֹז Meroz (72d); perh. from the same as 730; a place in N. Pal.:— Meroz(1).

4790. מְרוֹחַ meroach (598c); of unc. der.; perh. *a rubbing away:*— crushed(1).

4791. מָרוֹם marom (928d); from 7311; *height:*— above*(1), exalted(1), exalted places(1), haughtily(2), heaven(1), heavens(1), height(4), heights(9), high(28), high places(2), loftiness(1), lofty(1), proudly(1).

4792. מֵרוֹם Merom (598c); of unc. der.; a place in Upper Galilee:— Merom(2).

4793. מֵרוֹץ merots (930c); from 7323; *a running, a race:*— race(1).

4794. מְרוּצָה merutsah or

מְרֻצָה merutsah (930c); from 7323; *a running, course:*— course(2), running(2).

4795. מָרוּק maruq (599d); from 4838; *a scraping, rubbing:*— beautification(1).

4796. מָרוֹת Maroth (598c); perh. from 4843; a place in Judah:— Maroth(1).

4797. מִרְזַח mirzach (931a); the same as 4798, q.v.

4798. מַרְזֵחַ marzeach (931a); from an unused word; *a cry:*— banqueting(1), mourning(1).

4799. מָרַח marach (598d); a prim. root; *to rub:*— apply(1).

4800. מֶרְחָב merchab (932c); from 7337; *a broad* or *roomy place:*— broad place(2), large field(1), large place(2), throughout(1).

4801. מֶרְחָק merchaq (935d); from 7368; *distant place, distance:*— afar(5), afar off(1), distant(3), far(3), far away(1), far countries(1), far-distant(1), last(1), remote place(1), remote places(1).

4802. מַרְחֶשֶׁת marchesheth (935d); from 7370; *a stewpan, saucepan:*— pan(2).

4803. מָרַט marat (598d); a prim. root; *to make smooth, bare* or *bald, to scour, polish:*— becomes bald(1), loses the hair(1), pluck out the beard(1), polished(6), pulled(1), pulled out hair(1), rubbed bare(1), smooth(2).

4804. **מְרַט** **merat** (1101d); (Ara.) corr. to 4803; *to pluck:*— plucked(1).

4805. **מְרִי** **meri** (598b); from 4784; *rebellion:*— rebellion(3), rebellious(16), rebellious man(1), rebellious ones(1), rebels(1).

4806. **מְרִיא** **meri** (597a); from an unused word; *a fatling, fatlings:*— fatling(2), fatlings(5), fed cattle(1).

4807. **מְרִיב בַּעַל** **Merib Baal** (937c); from 7378 and 1168a; perh. "Baal is advocate," a son of Jonathan:— Merib-baal(4).

4808. **מְרִיבָה** **meribah** (937b); from 7378; *strife, contention:*— strife(2).

4809. **מְרִיבָה** **Meribah** (937b); from 7378; "place of strife," two places in the desert:— Meribah(8), Meribah-kadesh*(1), Meribath-kadesh*(2).

4810. **מְרִי בַעַל** **Meri Baal** (937c); the same as 4807, q.v.

4811. **מְרָיָה** **Merayah** (599a); of unc. der.; an Isr. priest:— Meraiah(1).

4812. **מְרָיוֹת** **Merayoth** (599a); pl. of 4811; desc. of Aaron, also a priestly family:— Meraioth(7).

4813. **מִרְיָם** **Miryam** (599b); from the same as 4811; a sister of Aaron, also a man of Judah:— Miriam(15).

4814. **מְרִירוּת** **meriruth** (601b); from 4843; *bitterness:*— bitter grief(1).

4815. **מְרִירִי** **meriri** (601b); from 4843; *bitter:*— bitter(1).

4816. **מֹרֶךְ** **morek** (940b); perh. from 7401; *weakness:*— weakness(1).

4817. **מֶרְכָּב** **merkab** (939c); from 7392; *a chariot, riding seat:*— chariots(1), saddle(1), seat(1).

4818. **מֶרְכָּבָה** **merkabah** (939d); fem. of 4817; *a chariot:*— chariot(23), chariots(21).

4819. **מַרְכֹּלֶת** **markoleth** (940c); from 7402; prob. *place of trade, marketplace:*— merchandise(1).

4820. **מִרְמָה** **mirmah** (941b); from 7411b; *deceit, treachery:*— deceit(21), deceitful(6), deceitfully(2), deception(2), deceptive(1), dishonest(1), false(3), treacherous(1), treachery(2).

4821. **מִרְמָה** **Mirmah** (599b); of unc. der.; a Benjamite:— Mirmah(1).

4822. **מְרֵמוֹת** **Meremoth** (599b); from the same as 4821; two Isr. priests, also an Isr.:— Meremoth(6).

4823. **מִרְמָס** **mirmas** (942d); from 7429; *trampling place, trampling:*— trample(1), trample down(1), trampled(1), trampled down(1), trampled ground(1), trampling(1), tread down(1), what you tread down(1).

4824. **מֵרֹנֹתִי** **Meronothi** (599c); of unc. der.; inhab. of Meronoth:— Meronothite(2).

4825. **מֶרֶס** **Meres** (599c); of for. or.; a Persian noble:— Meres(1).

4826. **מַרְסְנָא** **Marsena** (599c); of for. or.; a Persian noble:— Marsena(1).

4827. **מֵרַע** **mera** (949b); from 7489a, q.v.

4828. **מֵרֵעַ** **merea** (946c); from 7462b; *friend, companion:*— adviser(1), companion(3), companions(1), friends(2).

4829. **מִרְעֶה** **mireh** (945c); from 7462a; *a pasturage, pasture:*— feeding place(1), pasture(11), pastures(1).

4830. **מַרְעִית** **marith** (945c); from 7462a; *a pasturing, shepherding, pasturage:*— flock(1), pasture(9).

4831. **מַרְעֲלָה** **Maralah** (599c); of unc. der.; a place on the border of Zebulun:— Maralah(1).

4832. **מַרְפֵּא** **marpe** (951b); from 7495; *a healing, cure, health:*— brings healing(1), composure(1), healing(8), health(1), incurable*(1), remedy(2), soothing(1), tranquil(1).

4833. **מִרְפָּשׂ** **marpes** (952c); from 7511; (water) *befouled:*— what you foul(1).

4834. **מָרַץ** **marats** (599c); a prim. root; *to be sick:*— painful(2), plagues(1), violent(1).

4835. **מְרֻצָה** **merutsah** or

מְרוּצָה **merutsah** (954d); from 7533; *a crushing, an oppression:*— extortion(1).

4836. **מַרְצֵעַ** **martsea** (954b); from 7527; *a boring instrument, awl:*— awl(2).

4837. **מַרְצֶפֶת** **martsepheth** (954b); from 7528; *pavement:*— pavement(1).

4838. **מָרַק** **maraq** (599d); a prim. root; *to scour, polish:*— polish(1), polished(1), scour(1), scoured(1).

4839. **מָרָק** **maraq** (600a); from an unused word; *juice* (stewed out of meat), *broth:*— broth(3).

4840. **מֶרְקָח** **merqach** (955c); from 7543; *spice, perfume:*— sweet-scented herbs(1).

4841. **מֶרְקָחָה** **merqachah** (955c); fem. of 4840; *an ointment pot:*— jar of ointment(1).

4842. **מִרְקַחַת** **mirqachath** (955c); from 7543; *an ointment mixture:*— mixing(1), mixture(1), perfumers'*(1).

4843. **מָרַר** **marar** (600a); a prim. root; *to be bitter:*— bitter(2), bitter weeping(1), bitterly(2), dealt...bitterly(1), embittered(2), enraged(2), had(1), harder*(1), made bitter(1), troubled(1), weep bitterly(1).

4844. **מְרֹר** **maror** or

מָרוֹר **maror** (601a); from 4843; *bitter thing, bitter herb:*— bitter herbs(2), bitterness(1).

4845. **מְרֵרָה** **mererah** (601a); from 4843; *gall:*— gall(2).

4846. **מְרֹרָה** **merorah** or

מְרוֹרָה **merorah** (601a); from 4843; *a bitter thing, gall, poison:*— bitter(1), bitter things(1), venom(1).

4847. **מְרָרִי** **Merari** (601b); from 4843; a son of Levi:— Merari(39).

4848. **מְרָרִי** **Merari** (601b); from 4847; desc. of Merari:— Merarites(1).

4849. **מִרְשַׁעַת** **mirshaath** (958a); from the same as 7563; *wickedness:*— wicked(1).

4850. **מְרָתַיִם** **Merathayim** (601c); perh. from 4784; perh. "double rebellion," another name for Bab.:— Merathaim(1).

4851. **מַשׁ** **Mash** (602a); of for. or.; a son of Aram:— Mash(1).

4852. **מֵשָׁא** **Mesha** (602a); of for. or.; one extremity of the territory of the Joktanites:— Mesha(1).

4853a. **מַשָּׂא** **massa** (672c); from 5375; *a load, burden, lifting, bearing, tribute:*— burden(10), carry(3), carrying(3), delight(1), load(10), loads(5), singing(3), things(1), tribute(1).

4853b. **מַשָּׂא** **massa** (672d); from 5375; *utterance, oracle:*— burden(3), oracle(25), oracles(1).

4854. **מַשָּׂא** **Massa** (601d); of unc. der.; a son of Ishmael, also the realm of King Lemuel:— Massa(2).

4855. **מַשָּׁא** **mashsha** (673d); from 5377; *lending on interest, usury:*— exaction(1), usury(2).

4856. **מַשֹּׂא** **masso** (673a); see 5375.

4857. **מַשְׁאָב** **mashab** (980c); from 7579; prob. *place of drawing* (water):— watering places(1).

4858. **מַשָּׂאָה** **massaah** (673a); from 5375; *the uplifted* (cloud):— smoke(1).

4859. **מַשָּׁאָה** **mashshaah** (673d); fem. of 4855; *a loan:*— debts(1), loan(1).

4860. **מַשָּׁאוֹן** **mashshaon** (674b); from 5378; *guile, dissimulation:*— guile(1).

4861. **מִשְׁאָל** **Mishal** (602b); from 7592; a place in Asher:— Mishal(2).

4862. **מִשְׁאָלָה** **mishalah** (982c); from 7592; *request, petition:*— desires(1), petitions(1).

4863. **מִשְׁאֶרֶת** **mishereth** (602b); of unc. der.; perh. *kneading trough:*— kneading bowl(2), kneading bowls(2).

4864. **מַשְׂאֵת** **maseth** (673a); from 5375; *an uprising, utterance, burden, portion:*— burden(1), cloud(2), gift(1), gifts(2), levy(2), lifting(1), portion(1), portions(1), present(1), signal(1), tribute(1).

4865. **מִשְׁבְּצָה** **mishbetsah** (990b); from 7660; *checkered* or *plaited work:*— filigree(8), interwoven(1).

4866. **מִשְׁבָּר** **mishbar** or

מַשְׁבֵּר **mashber** (991b); from 7665; *place of breach:*— birth(2), opening*(1), womb(1).

4867. **מִשְׁבָּר** **mishbar** (991c); from 7665; *a breaker* (of the sea):— breakers(3), waves(2).

4868. **מִשְׁבָּת** **mishbath** (992d); from 7673a; *cessation, annihilation:*— ruin(1).

4869. **מִשְׂגָּב** **misgab** (960d); from 7682; *a secure height, retreat, stronghold:*— lofty stronghold(1), refuge(1), stronghold(14), unassailable(1).

4870. **מִשְׁגֶּה** **mishgeh** (993b); from 7686; *a mistake:*— mistake(1).

4871. **מָשָׁה** **mashah** (602b); a prim. root; *to draw:*— drew(3).

4872. **מֹשֶׁה** **Mosheh** (602c); from 4871; a great Isr. leader, prophet and lawgiver:— Moses(748), Moses'(16).

4873. **מֹשֶׁה** **Mosheh** (1101d); (Ara.) corr. to 4872; a great Isr. leader, prophet and lawgiver:— Moses(1).

4874. **מַשֶּׁה** **mashsheh** (674c); from 5383; *a loan:*— creditor*(1).

4875. **מְשׁוֹאָה** **meshoah** or

מְשֹׁאָה **meshoah** (996c); from the same as 7722; *desolation:*— desolate(1), desolation(2).

4876. **מַשּׁוּאוֹת** **mashshuoth** (674b); from 5378; perh. *deceptions:*— ruins(1).

4877. **מְשׁוֹבָב** **Meshobab** (1000c); from 7725; a Simeonite:— Meshobab(1).

4878. **מְשׁוּבָה** **meshubah** or

מְשֻׁבָה **meshubah** (1000b); from 7725; *turning back, apostasy:*— apostasies(3), apostasy(2), faithless(4), faithlessness(1), turning(1), waywardness(1).

4879. **מְשׁוּגָה** **meshugah** (1000c); from an unused word; *error:*— error(1).

4880a. מָשׁוֹט mashot (1002b); from 7751a; *an oar:*— oar(1).

4880b. מִשּׁוֹט mishshot (1002b); from 7751a; *an oar:*— oars(1).

4881. מְשׂוּכָה mesukah or

מְשֻׂכָה mesukah (962b); from 7753; *a hedge:*— hedge(1).

4882. מְשׁוּסָה meshusah (1042d); the same as 4933, q.v.

4883. מַשּׂוֹר massor (673d); from an unused word; *a saw:*— saw(1).

4884. מְשׂוּרָה mesurah (601d); of unc. der.; *a measure:*— capacity(1), measure(2), volume(1).

4885. מָשׂוֹשׂ masos (965c); from 7797; *exultation, rejoicing:*— delight(1), exceedingly(1), gaiety(4), gladness(1), joy(7), joyful(1), rejoice(1), rejoices(1).

4886. מָשַׁח mashach (602d); a prim. root; *to smear, anoint:*— anoint(21), anointed(42), anointing(1), oil(1), painting(1), spread(4).

4887. מְשַׁח meshach (1101d); (Ara.) from a root corr. to 4886; *oil:*— anointing oil(1), oil(1).

4888a. מָשְׁחָה moshchah (603c); from 4886; *consecrated portion:*— portion(1).

4888b. מִשְׁחָה mishchah (603b); from 4886; *ointment, consecrated portion:*— anointing(22), which is consecrated(2).

4889. מַשְׁחִית mashchith (1008c); from 7843; *ruin, destruction:*— deathly pallor(1), destroy(2), destruction(3), trap(1), utterly(1).

4890. מִשְׂחָק mischaq (966a); from 7832; *object of derision:*— laughing(1).

4891. מִשְׁחָר mishchar (1007d); from the same as 7837; *dawn:*— dawn(1).

4892. מַשְׁחֵת mashcheth (1008c); from 7843; *ruin, destruction:*— destroying(1).

4893a. מָשְׁחָת moshchath (1008c); from 7843; *corruption* (ceremonial):— corruption(1).

4893b. מִשְׁחַת mishchath (1008c); from 7843; *disfigurement* (of face):— marred(1).

4894a. מִשְׁטוֹחַ mishtoach or

מִשְׁטַח mishtach (1009a); from 7849; *a spreading-place* (for drying fruit or nets):— place for the spreading(1).

4894b. מִשְׁטָח mishtach (1009a); from 7849; *a spreading-place* (for drying fruit or nets):— place for the spreading(2).

4895. מַשְׂטֵמָה mastemah (966b); from 7852; *animosity:*— hostility(2).

4896. מִשְׁטָר mishtar (1009c); from the same as 7860; *rule, authority:*— rule(1).

4897. מֶשִׁי meshi (603d); of unc. der.; (costly material for garments) perh. *silk:*— silk(2).

4898. מְשֵׁיזַבְאֵל Meshezabel (604a); from an equiv. of 7804 and from 410; "God delivers," an Isr. name:— Meshezabel(3).

4899. מָשִׁיחַ mashiach (603c); from 4886; *anointed:*— Anointed(1), anointed(34), anointed ones(2), Messiah(2).

4900. מָשַׁךְ mashak (604a); a prim. root; *to draw, drag:*— away(1), bore(1), continue(1), deferred(1), delayed(2), deployed(1), drag(1), drag me away(1), drags(1), draw(3), drawn(2), draws(1), drew(2), extend(1), follow(1), go(1), led(1), long blast(2), make a long blast(1), march(1), prolong(1), prolonged(1), pulled(3), sounds a long blast(1), sows(1), stimulate(1), stretched(1), tall(2), wield(1).

4901. מֶשֶׁךְ meshek (604d); from 4900; *a drawing, drawing up, a trail:*— acquisition(1), bag(1).

4902. מֶשֶׁךְ Meshek (604d); from 4900; a son of Japheth, also his desc. and their land:— Meshech(10).

4903. מִשְׁכַּב mishkab (1115b); (Ara.) corr. to 4904; *couch, bed:*— bed(6).

4904. מִשְׁכָּב mishkab (1012d); from 7901; *place of lying, a couch, act of lying:*— bed(25), bedroom*(3), beds(6), couch(1), health*(1), intimately*(3), lain*(1), lie(1), lying(1), rest(1), resting place(1), sleeping(1).

4905a. מְשֻׂכָּה mesukkah (968a); from an unused word; *a hedge:*— hedge(1).

4905b. מַשְׂכִּיל maskil (968d); from 7919a; *a contemplative poem:*— skillful psalm(1).

4906. מַשְׂכִּית maskith (967d); from the same as 7907; *a showpiece, figure, imagination:*— carved images(1), figured(1), figured stones(1), imagination(1), imaginations(1), settings(1).

4907a. מְשַׁכֶּלֶת meshakkeleth (1014a); another reading for 7921, q.v.

4907b. מִשְׁכַּן mishkan (1115c); (Ara.) corr. to 4908; *abode:*— dwelling(1).

4908. מִשְׁכָּן mishkan (1015c); from 7931; *dwelling place, tabernacle:*— dwelling(1), dwelling place(8), dwelling places(9), dwellings(9), resting place(1), tabernacle(109), tents(1), where...dwells(1).

4909. מַשְׂכֹּרֶת maskoreth (969b); from 7936; *wages:*— wages(4).

4910. מָשַׁל mashal (605c); a prim. root; *to rule, have dominion, reign:*— dominion(1), gain control(1), govern(1), had charge(1), have authority(1), master(1), obtain dominion(1), really going to rule(1), rule(27), ruled(5), ruler(18), ruler's(2), rulers(6), rules(9), ruling(3), wielded(1).

4911a. מָשַׁל mashal (605a); a prim. root; *to represent, be like:*— become like(4), compare(1), like(2).

4911b. מָשַׁל mashal (605b); denom. vb. from 4912; *to use a proverb, speak in parables* or *sentences of poetry:*— quotes proverbs(1), quotes proverbs(1), speak(2), speaking(1), use(1), use it as a proverb(1), use proverbs(1), using(1), will quote this proverb(1).

4912. מָשָׁל mashal (605a); from 4911a; *a proverb, parable:*— byword(3), discourse(9), parable(3), parables(1), proverb(15), proverbs(6), taunt(2), taunt-song(1).

4913. מָשָׁל Mashal (602b); of unc. der.; a place in Asher (the same as 4861):— Mashal(1).

4914. מְשֹׁל meshol (605c); from 4911a; *a byword:*— byword(1).

4915a. מֹשֶׁל moshel (606a); from 4910; *dominion:*— authority(1), dominion(1).

4915b. מֹשֶׁל moshel (605c); from 4911a; *likeness:*— like(1).

4916a. מִשְׁלָח mishlach (1020a); from 7971; *outstretching:*— place for pasturing(1), put(1), undertake*(2), undertakings*(3).

4916b. מִשְׁלֹחַ mishloach or

מִשְׁלוֹחַ mishloach (1020a); from 7971; *an outstretching, sending:*— possess*(1), sending(2).

4917. מִשְׁלַחַת mishlachath (1020a); from 7971; *a discharge, deputation, sending:*— band(1), discharge(1).

4918. מְשֻׁלָּם Meshullam (1024c); from 7999a; the name of a number of Isr.:— Meshullam(25).

4919. מְשִׁלֵּמוֹת Meshillemoth (1024c); from 7999a; an Ephraimite, also an Isr. priest:— Meshillemith(1), Meshillemoth(2).

4920. מְשֶׁלֶמְיָה Meshelemyah or

מְשֶׁלֶמְיָהוּ Meshelemyahu (1024c); from 7999a and 3050; a Levite:— Meshelemiah(4).

4921. מְשִׁלֵּמִית Meshillemith (1024c); the same as 4919, q.v.

4922. מְשֻׁלֶּמֶת Meshullemeth (1024c); from 7999a; mother of King Amon:— Meshullemeth(1).

4923. מְשַׁמָּה meshammah (1031d); from 8074; *devastation, waste, horror:*— desolate(2), object of horror(1), waste(4).

4924a. מִשְׁמָן mishman (1032d); from 8080; *fatness:*— fatness(1), richest(1), stout warriors(1), stoutest(1).

4924b. מַשְׁמָן mashman (1032d); from 8080; *a fat piece, tidbit:*— fat(1).

4925. מַשְׁמַנָּה Mashmannah (1032d); from 8080; one of David's heroes:— Mishmannah(1).

4926. מִשְׁמָע mishma (1036a); from 8085; *something heard:*— what...hear(1).

4927. מִשְׁמָע Mishma (1036a); from 8085; an Ishmaelite, also a Simeonite:— Mishma(4).

4928. מִשְׁמַעַת mishmaath (1036a); from 8085; *an obedient band, body of subjects:*— guard(3), subject(1).

4929. מִשְׁמָר mishmar (1038b); from 8104; *place of confinement, jail, prison, guard, watch, observance:*— confinement(4), custody(2), diligence(1), division(2), guard(8), keeping watch(1), post(1), prison(1), prison*(1), services(1).

4930. מַשְׂמְרָה masmerah (702c); the same as 4548, q.v.

4931. מִשְׁמֶרֶת mishmereth (1038b); fem. of 4929; *a guard, watch, charge, function:*— allegiance(1), charge(27), duties(15), duty(2), guard post(2), guard*(1), guards(2), keep(1), keep*(1), kept(5), obligation(4), obligations(4), offices(1), posts(1), safe(1), service(2), service divisions(1), watch(4), worship(1).

4932. מִשְׁנֶה mishneh (1041c); from 8138; *a double, copy, second:*— copy(2), double(6), doubly(1), fatlings(1), next(1), Second(3), second(16), second rank(1), twice(1), twice as much(1), twofold(2).

4933. מְשִׁסָּה meshissah (1042d); from 8155; *booty, plunder:*— plunder(3), spoil(3).

4934. מִשְׁעוֹל mishol (1043c); from the same as 8168; *a hollow passage:*— narrow path(1).

4935. מִשְׁעִי mishi (606b); from an unused word; *a cleansing:*— cleansing(1).

4936. מִשְׁעָם Misham (606c); from the same as 4935; a Benjamite:— Misham(1).

4937a. מִשְׁעָן mishan (1044a); from 8172; *a support, staff:*— stay(1), supply(2), support(1).

4937b. מַשְׁעֵן mishen (1044a); from 8172; *a support, staff:*— supply(1).

4938a. מַשְׁעֵנָה mashenah (1044a); from 8172; *a support, staff:*— support(1).

4938b. מִשְׁעֶנֶת misheneth (1044a); from 8172; *a staff:*— staff(10), staffs(1).

4939. **מִשְׂפָּח** **mispach** (705c); from the same as 5599a; prob. *outpouring, bloodshed:*— bloodshed(1).

4940. **מִשְׁפָּחָה** **mishpachah** (1046c); from the same as 8198; *a clan:*— clan(1), every family(3), families(170), family(120), kinds(1), relatives(4), tribes(1).

4941. **מִשְׁפָּט** **mishpat** (1048b); from 8199; *judgment:*— arrangements(1), case(5), case*(1), cause(7), charge(1), claim(1), court(2), crimes(1), custom(11), customs(2), decide(1), decision(2), decisions(1), deserving(1), destruction(1), due(1), injustice*(2), judge(1), judged(1), judgment(62), judgments(40), just(4), justice(118), justly(3), kind(1), manner(3), matters of justice(1), mode of life(1), order(1), ordinance(29), ordinances(79), plan(1), plans(1), practice(1), procedure(4), properly(2), regulation(1), right(8), rightful place(1), rights(2), rule(1), sentence(2), sentenced(1), standard(1), trial(1), unjustly*(1), verdict(1), way prescribed(2), what is right(2), worthy(1).

4942. **מִשְׁפְּתַיִם** **mishpethayim** (1046b); perh. from the same as 8239; perh. *fireplaces, ash heaps:*— sheepfolds(2).

4943. **מֶשֶׁק** **mesheq** (606c); of unc. der.; *acquisition, possession:*— heir*(1).

4944. **מַשָּׁק** **mashshaq** (1055b); from 8264; *a running, rushing:*— rushing about(1).

4945a. **מַשְׁקֶה** **mashqeh** (1052d); from 8248; *butler, cupbearer:*— cupbearer(10), cupbearers(2).

4945b. **מַשְׁקֶה** **mashqeh** (1052d); from 8248; *irrigation, drink:*— drink(1), drinking(2), liquid(1), office(1), watering places(1), well watered(1).

4946. **מִשְׁקוֹל** **mishqol** (1054a); from 8254; *heaviness, weight:*— weight(1).

4947. **מַשְׁקוֹף** **mashqoph** (1054d); from the same as 8260; prob. *lintel* (of a door):— lintel(3).

4948. **מִשְׁקָל** **mishqal** (1054a); from 8254; *weight:*— full(1), rationed amounts(1), weigh(1), weighed(4), weighing(3), weight(39).

4949. **מִשְׁקֶלֶת** **mishqeleth** or

מִשְׁקֹלֶת **mishqoleth** (1054a); fem. of 4948; *a leveling instrument, a level:*— level(1), plummet(1).

4950. **מִשְׁקָע** **mishqa** (1054b); from 8257; *what is settled* or *clarified:*— clear(1).

4951. **מִשְׂרָה** **misrah** (976a); from an unused word; *rule, dominion:*— government(2).

4952. **מִשְׁרָה** **mishrah** (1056a); from 8281; *juice:*— juice(1).

4953. **מַשְׁרוֹקִי** **mashroqi** (1117b); (Ara.) from a root corr. to 8319; *a* (musical) *pipe:*— flute(4).

4954. **מִשְׁרָעִי** **Mishrai** (606d); of unc. der.; a family of Kiriath-jearim:— Mishraites(1).

4955. **מִשְׂרָפָה** **misraphah** (977c); from 8313; *a burning:*— burned(2).

4956. **מִשְׂרְפוֹת מַיִם** **Misrephoth Mayim** (977c); from 4955 and 4325; "burning of water," a place in Isr. prob. near Sidon:— Misrephoth-maim(2).

4957. **מַשְׂרֵקָה** **Masreqah** (977d); from the same as 8320; a place in Edom:— Masrekah(2).

4958. **מַשְׂרֵת** **masreth** (602a); of unc. der.; prob. *pan, dish:*— pan(1).

4959. **מָשַׁשׁ** **mashash** (606d); a prim. root; *to feel, grope:*— feel(1), felt(2), felt through(2), grope(3), gropes(1).

4960. **מִשְׁתֶּה** **mishteh** (1059c); from 8354; *a feast, drink:*— banquet(16), banquets(1), drank(2), drink(3), drinking(1), feast(15), feasting(7), where they were drinking(1), which he drank(2).

4961. **מִשְׁתֵּי** **mishte** (1117c); (Ara.) corr. to 4960; *a feast:*— banquet(1).

4962. **מַת** **math** (607a); a prim. root; *male, man:*— associates(1), few(3), few men(1), men(14), men being few(1), number(2).

4963. **מַתְבֵּן** **mathben** (1062a); from the same as 8401; *a straw heap:*— straw(1).

4964. **מֶתֶג** **metheg** (607c); of unc. der.; *a bridle:*— bit(1), bridle(3), control(1).

4965. **מֶתֶג הָאַמָּה** **metheg haammah** (607c); a combination of 4964 and 522b, q.v.

4966. **מָתוֹק** **mathoq** or

מָתוּק **mathuq** (608d); from 4985; *sweet, sweetness:*— pleasant(2), something sweet(1), sweet(7), sweeter(2).

4967. **מְתוּשָׁאֵל** **Methushael** (607b); from 4962 and 410; "man of God," a desc. of Cain:— Methushael(2).

4968. **מְתוּשֶׁלַח** **Methushelach** (607b); perh. from 4962 and 7973; perh. "man of the dart," a desc. of Seth:— Methuselah(6).

4969. **מָתַח** **mathach** (607c); a prim. root; *to spread out:*— spreads(1).

4970. **מָתַי** **mathay** (607d); a prim. interrogative adv.; *when?:*— how(30), long*(27), when(13).

4971. **מַתְכֹנֶת** **mathkoneth** or

מַתְכֻנֶת **mathkuneth** (1067c); from 8505; *measurement, tally, proportion:*— proportions(2), quota(1), specifications(1), standard(1).

4972. **מַתְּלָאָה** **mattelaah** (521b); a combination of 4100 and 8513, q.v.

4973. **מְתַלְּעוֹת** **methalleoth** (1069a); from the same as 8438; *teeth:*— fangs(2), jaw teeth(1), jaws(1).

4974. **מְתֹם** **methom** (1071b); from 8552; *soundness:*— entire(1), sound(1), soundness(2).

4975. **מֹתֶן** **mothen** (608a); from an unused word; *loins:*— back(1), body(1), heart(1), herself(1), hips(1), loins(32), rooster(1), side(1), strutting*(1), waist(7).

4976. **מַתָּן** **mattan** (682b); from 5414; *a gift:*— gift(4), gifts(1).

4977. **מַתָּן** **Mattan** (682b); from 5414; a priest of Baal, also a man of Judah:— Mattan(3).

4978. **מַתְּנָא** **mattena** (1103d); (Ara.) corr. to 4979; *a gift:*— gifts(3).

4979. **מַתָּנָה** **mattanah** (682b); fem. of 4976; *a gift:*— bestowed(1), bribe(1), bribes(1), gift(3), gifts(10), give(1).

4980. **מַתָּנָה** **Mattanah** (682c); fem. of 4976; a place E. of the Jordan:— Mattanah(2).

4981. **מִתְנִי** **Mithni** (608c); of unc. der.; a descriptive title for one of David's men:— Mithnite(1).

4982. **מַתְּנַי** **Mattenay** (682d); from 5414; an Isr. priest, also two Isr.:— Mattenai(3).

4983. **מַתַּנְיָה** **Mattanyah** or

מַתַּנְיָהוּ **Mattanyahu** (682d); from 4976 and 3050; "gift of Yah," the last king of Judah, also a number of Isr.:— Mattaniah(16).

4984. **מִתְנַשֵּׂא** **mithnasse** (669d); from 5375, q.v.

4985. **מָתֹק** **mathoq** (608c); a prim. root; *to become* or *be sweet* or *pleasant:*— became sweet(1), feeds sweetly(1), gently cover(1), had sweet(1), sweet(2).

4986. **מֶתֶק** **metheq** (608d); from 4985; *sweetness:*— sweet(1), sweetness(1).

4987. **מֹתֶק** **motheq** (608d); from 4985; *sweetness:*— sweetness(1).

4988. **מָתָק** **mathaq** (608c); from 4985, q.v.

4989. **מִתְקָה** **Mithqah** (609a); from 4985; a place in the desert:— Mithkah(2).

4990. **מִתְרְדָת** **Mithredath** (609c); of for. or.; two Persians:— Mithredath(2).

4991. **מַתָּת** **mattath** (682c); from 5414; *a gift:*— gift(2), gifts(1), give(2), reward(1).

4992. **מַתַּתָּה** **Mattattah** (683a); from 4991; an Isr.:— Mattattah(1).

4993. **מַתִּתְיָה** **Mattithyah** or

מַתִּתְיָהוּ **Mattithyahu** (682d); from 4991 and 3050; "gift of Yah," the name of several Isr.:— Mattithiah(8).

נ

4994. **נָא** **na** (609a); a prim. particle of entreaty or exhortation; *I (we) pray, now:*— Ah(2), beg(1), beseech(1), come(3), implore(1), may(1), now(159), O(2), O may(1), Oh(10), Oh may(2), please(181), please*(1), pray(16).

4995. **נָא** **na** (644b); from an unused word; *raw:*— raw(1).

4996. **נֹא** **No** (609d); of for. or.; an Eg. city:— No-amon*(1), Thebes(4).

4997. **נֹאד** **nod** or

נֹאוד **nod** or

נֹאדָה **nodah** (609d); of unc. der.; *a skin bottle, skin:*— bottle(2), jug(1), wineskin(1), wineskins(2).

4998. **נָאָה** **naah** (610a); a prim. root; *to be comely* or *befitting:*— befits(1), lovely(2).

4999. **נָאָה** **naah** (627d); see 5116c:— habitations(2), pasture grounds(1), pastures(7).

5000. **נָאוֶה** **naveh** (610a); from 4998; *comely, seemly:*— becoming(2), comely(1), fitting(3), lovely(4).

5001. **נָאַם** **naam** (610c); denom. vb. from 5002; *to utter a prophecy, speak as a prophet:*— declare(1).

5002. **נְאֻם** **neum** (610b); from an unused word; *utterance:*— declared(1), declares(363), oracle(6), says(5), speaks(1).

5003. **נָאַף** **naaph** (610c); a prim. root; *to commit adultery:*— adulterer(3), adulterers(5), adulteress(3), adulteresses(2), adulteries(1), adulterous(1), adultery(1), commit adultery(6), commits adultery(3), committed adultery(5), committing of adultery(1).

5004. **נִאֻף** **niuph** (610d); from 5003; *adultery:*— adulteries(2).

5005. **נַאֲפוּף** **naaphuph** (610d); from 5003; *adultery:*— adultery(1).

5006. **נָאַץ** **naats** (610d); a prim. root; *to spurn, treat with contempt:*— blaspheme(1), blasphemed(1), despise(3), despised(5), given(1), rejects(1), spurn(3), spurned(8), spurns(1).

5007a. **נְאָצָה** **neatsah** (611a); from 5006; *contempt:*— rejection(2).

5007b. נְאָצָה neatsah (611a); from 5006; *contempt, blasphemy:*— blasphemies(2), revilings(1).

5008. נָאַק naaq (611a); a prim. root; *to groan:*— groan(2).

5009. נְאָקָה neaqah (611a); from 5008; *a groan, groaning:*— groaning(3), groanings(1).

5010. נָאַר naar (611b); a prim. root; prob. *to abhor, spurn:*— abandoned(1), spurned(1).

5011. נֹב Nob (611b); from 5010; a priestly city, perh. also a place N. of Jer.:— Nob(6).

5012. נָבָא naba (612a); denom. vb. from 5030; *to prophesy:*— prophesied(31), prophesies(8), prophesy(55), prophesying(19), raved(2).

5013. נְבָא neba (1101d); (Ara.) the same as 5029, q.v.

5014. נָבַב nabab (612c); a prim. root; *to hollow out:*— hollow(3), idiot*(1).

5015a. נְבוֹ Nebo (612d); from 5014; a city in Moab, also a mountain in Moab:— Nebo(12).

5015b. נְבוֹ Nebo (612d); from 5014; a Bab. god:— Nebo(1).

5016. נְבוּאָה nebuah (612c); from the same as 5030; *prophecy:*— prophecy(3).

5017. נְבוּאָה nebuah (1102a); (Ara.) corr. to 5016; *a prophesying:*— prophesying(1).

5018. נְבוּזַרְאֲדָן Nebuzaradan (613a); of for. or.; "Nebo has given seed," a Bab. general:— Nebuzaradan(15).

5019. נְבוּכַדְנֶאצַּר Nebukadnetstsar or
נְבֻכַדְנֶאצַּר Nebbukadnetstsar (613a); of for. or.; "Nebo, protect the boundary," a Bab. king:— Nebuchadnezzar(60).

5020. נְבוּכַדְנֶצַּר Nebukadnetstsar (1102a); (Ara.) corr. to 5019; a Bab. king:— Nebuchadnezzar(31).

5021. נְבוּשַׁזְבָּן Nebushaz-ban (613b); of for. or.; "O Nebo, deliver me," a Bab. officer:— Nebushazban(1).

5022. נָבוֹת Naboth (613b); of unc. der.; a Jezreelite:— Naboth(22).

5023. נְבִזְבָּה nebizbah(1102a); (Ara.) of unc. der.; *a reward:*— reward(1), rewards(1).

5024. נָבַח nabach (613b); a prim. root; *to bark:*— bark(1).

5025. נֹבַח Nobach (613b); from 5024; a place in Gilead, also a Manassite:— Nobah(3).

5026. נִבְחַז Nibchaz (613b); of for. or.; a god of the Avvites:— Nibhaz(1).

5027. נָבַט nabat (613c); a prim. root; *to look:*— beheld(1), behold(1), beholds(2), consider(2), depend(1), depended(1), gaze(1), gazed(1), look(34), look down(2), looked(11), looks(4), observe(1), observed(1), pay attention(1), regard(2), see(3).

5028. נְבָט Nebat (614a); from 5027; father of Jeroboam:— Nebat(25).

5029. נְבִיא nebi (1101d); (Ara.) corr. to 5030; *a prophet:*— prophesied(1), prophet(2), prophets(2).

5030. נָבִיא nabi (611c); from an unused word; *a spokesman, speaker, prophet:*— prophecy(1), prophesy(1), prophet(165), prophets(147).

5031. נְבִיאָה nebiah (612c); fem. of 5030; *a prophetess:*— prophetess(6).

5032. נְבָיוֹת Nebayoth or
נְבָיֹת Nebayoth (614a); from 5027; oldest son of Ishmael, also his desc.:— Nebaioth(5).

5033. נֵבֶךְ nebek (614a); of unc. der.; *a spring:*— springs(1).

5034a. נָבֵל nabal (614c); a prim. root; *to be senseless* or *foolish:*— been foolish(1), disgrace(1), make vile(1), scorned(1), treats...contemptuously(1).

5034b. נָבֵל nabel (615b); a prim. root; *to sink* or *drop down, languish, fade:*— crumbles away(1), fade(1), fade away(1), fades(2), fades away(1), fading(2), lose heart(1), surely wear(1), wither(4), wither away(1), withers(4).

5035a. נֵבֶל nebel (614b); of unc. der.; *a skin bottle, skin, jar, pitcher:*— jar(1), jars(2), jars*(1), jug(5), jugs(1), water jars(1).

5035b. נֵבֶל nebel or
נֶבֶל nebel (614b); of unc. der.; perh. *a harp* or *a lute, a guitar:*— harp(11), harps(16).

5036. נָבָל nabal (614d); from 5034a; *foolish, senseless:*— fool(9), foolish(5), foolish man(1), foolish women(1), fools(1), fools*(1).

5037. נָבָל Nabal (615a); from 5034a; a man of Carmel:— Nabal(19), Nabal's(3).

5038. נְבֵלָה nebelah (615c); from 5034b; *a carcass, corpse:*— body(11), carcass(10), carcasses(11), corpse(2), corpses(3), dead bodies(3), dead body(2), died a natural death(1), dies(1), natural death(1), what died(1), which dies(3).

5039. נְבָלָה nebalah (615a); from 5034a; *senselessness, disgrace:*— act of folly(2), disgraceful act(1), disgraceful acts(1), disgraceful thing(3), folly(3), foolishly(1), foolishness(1), nonsense(1).

5040. נַבְלוּת nabluth (615b); from 5034a; *immodesty, shamelessness:*— lewdness(1).

5041. נְבַלָּט Neballat (615d); of unc. der.; a place where Benjamites dwelt:— Neballat(1).

5042. נָבַע naba (615d); a prim. root; *to flow, spring, bubble up:*— belch forth(1), bubbling(1), eagerly utter(1), pour(1), pour forth(1), pours(1), pours forth(1), spouts(1), utter(2).

5043. נֶבְרְשָׁתָּא nebrashta (1102a); (Ara.) prob. of for. or.; *the candlestick:*— lampstand(1).

5044. נִבְשָׁן Nibshan (143c); from the same as 1316; a place in S. Judah:— Nibshan(1).

5045. נֶגֶב negeb (616a); from an unused word; *south country, the Negeb, south:*— Negev(36), South(11), south(45), south side(2), south*(3), southeast*(1), southern(2), southward(9).

5046. נָגַד nagad (616c); a prim. root; *to be conspicuous:*— answered(3), another(1), certainly told(1), confess(1), confront*(1), declare(46), declared(13), declares(6), declaring(4), denounce(2), describe(1), disclosed(1), display(1), explain(3), fully reported(1), give evidence(1), indeed tell(1), inform(3), informed(1), informs(2), know(1), known(1), made known(4), make...known(1), messenger(2), related(2), remind(1), report(2), reported(10), reported*(1), show(2), shown(2), surely report(1), surely tell(1), tell(101), telling(2), tells(3), told(131), told plainly(1), uttered(1).

5047. נְגַד negad (1102a); (Ara.) corr. to 5046; *to stream, flow:*— flowing(1).

5048. נֶגֶד neged (617a); from 5046; *in front of, in sight of, opposite to:*— against(3), aloof*(3), away(1), before(60), broad(1), demoralized*(1), directly(1), distance*(3), front(15), opposite(16), opposite*(5), other side(1), presence(13), resist*(1), risked*(1), sight(2), sight*(2), straight ahead(3), straight before(1), suitable(2), under(1).

5049. נֶגֶד neged (1102a); (Ara.) corr. to 5048; *in front, facing:*— toward(1).

5050. נָגַהּ nagah (618b); a prim. root; *to shine:*— gives...light(1), illumines(2), shed(1), shine(2).

5051. נֹגַהּ nogah (618b); from 5050; *brightness:*— bright(1), bright light(1), brightness(10), dawn(1), light(1), radiance(4), sunshine(1).

5052. נֹגַהּ Nogah (618b); from 5050; a son of David:— Nogah(2).

5053. נֹגַהּ nogah (1102a); (Ara.) corr. to 5051; *brightness, daylight:*— break of day(1).

5054. נְגֹהָה negohah (618c); from 5050; *brightness:*— brightness(1).

5055. נָגַח nagach (618c); a prim. root; *to push, thrust, gore:*— butting(1), collide(1), gore(2), gores(3), push(1), push back(1).

5056. נַגָּח naggach (618c); from 5055; *given to goring* (used of bulls):— habit of goring(2).

5057. נָגִיד nagid or
נָגִד nagid (617d); from 5046; *a leader, ruler, prince:*— chief(2), chief officer(3), commander(1), leader(14), noble things(1), nobles(1), officer(3), officers(1), officials(1), Prince(1), prince(5), princes(1), ruler(11).

5058. נְגִינָה neginah or
נְגִינַת neginath (618d); from 5059; *music:*— music(1), song(3), stringed instruments(2), taunt(1).

5059. נָגַן nagan (618d); a prim. root; *to touch* or *play a stringed instrument:*— minstrel(1), minstrel played(1), musician(1), musicians(1), play(5), play songs(1), player(1), playing(2), plays(1), pluck the strings(1).

5060. נָגַע naga (619a); a prim. root; *to touch, reach, strike:*— add(1), afford*(1), apply(1), arrive(1), arrived(4), attained(1), attains(1), bring down(1), brought down(1), came(6), cast(1), casts(1), close(2), come(2), draw near(1), drawn near(1), drew near(1), follows(1), happened(1), happens(2), plagued(1), pretended to be beaten(1), reach(4), reached(6), reaching(1), smitten(1), stricken(2), strike(1), strikes(1), struck(3), threw(1), touch(22), touched(20), touches(46), touching(6).

5061. נֶגַע nega (619c); from 5060; *a stroke, plague, mark:*— affliction(2), another(1), assault(2), infection(30), mark(32), plague(6), plagues(1), stripes(1), stroke(1), strokes(1), wounds(1).

5062. נָגַף nagaph (619d); a prim. root; *to strike, smite:*— beaten(1), defeated(17), hurts(1), plagued(1), routed(4), smite(3), smites(1), smote(3), strike(7), striking(1), struck(4), struck down(3), stumble(2), surely*(1).

5063. נֶגֶף negeph (620a); from 5062; *a blow, a striking:*— plague(6), strike(1).

5064. נָגַר nagar (620b); a prim. root; *to pour, flow, run:*— deliver(1), delivered(1), delivered over(1), flow(1), pour down(2), poured down(1), pours(1), spilled(1), stretched(1).

5065. נָגַשׂ nagas (620b); a prim. root; *to press, drive, oppress, exact:*— drive hard(1), driver(1), exact(2), exacted(1), hard-pressed(2), oppressed(2), oppressor(4), oppressors(2), overseers(1), ruler(1), taskmaster(1), taskmasters(5).

5066. נָגַשׁ nagash (620c); a prim. root; *to draw near, approach:*— approach(7), approached(12), bring(10), bring here(1), bring forth(1), bring forward(1), bring near(2), bringing(1), brought(10), brought close(2), came close(2), came closer(1), came forward(1), came near(18), come(3), come close(2), come closer(1), come forward(1), come near(14), coming near(1), draw near(7), drew near(5), go(2), go near(3), here(1), make room(1), near(1), offered*(1), overtake(2), present(4), presented(1), presenting(1), presents(1), put(1), set forth(1), stand(1), touch(1), went(1).

5067a. נֵד **ned** (622d); from an unused word; *a heap:*— heap(6).

5067b. נָדָא **nada** (621b); a prim. root; *to drive away, thrust aside:*— drove...away(1).

5068. נָדַב **nadab** (621c); a prim. root; *to incite, impel:*— freewill offering(1), given as a freewill offering(1), made offering(1), make offerings willingly(1), moved(2), moves(1), offer(1), offered(1), offered willingly(3), offerings willingly(1), volunteered(3), volunteers(1), willing(1), willingly offered(1).

5069. נְדַב **nedab** (1102b); (Ara.) corr. to 5068; *to volunteer, offer freely:*— freely offered(1), freewill offering(1), offered willingly(1), willing(1).

5070. נָדָב **Nadab** (621c); from 5068; an Isr. name:— Nadab(20).

5071. נְדָבָה **nedabah** (621d); from 5068; *voluntariness, freewill offering:*— freely(1), freewill offering(12), freewill offerings(9), plentiful(1), voluntarily(1), volunteer freely(1), willingly(1).

5072. נְדַבְיָה **Nedabyah** (622a); from 5068; "whom Yah impels," a son of Jeconiah:— Nedabiah(1).

5073. נִדְבָּךְ **nidbak** (1102b); (Ara.) of unc. der.; *a row* or *layer, course:*— layer(1), layers(1).

5074. נָדַד **nadad** (622b); a prim. root; *to retreat, flee, depart, stray, wander, flutter:*— chased(1), chased away(1), could(1), flapped(1), fled(6), flee(5), fleeing(1), fugitive(2), fugitives(1), shake(1), shrink(1), strayed(1), thrust away(1), wander(1), wanderers(1), wanders(3).

5075. נְדַד **nedad** (1102b); (Ara.) corr. to 5074; *to flee:*— fled(1).

5076. נָדֻד **nadud** or

נְדוּד **nedud** (622c); from 5074; *a tossing* (of sleeplessness):— tossing(1).

5077. נָדָה **nadah** or

נָדָא **nada** (622d); a prim. root; *to put away, exclude:*— exclude(1), put off(1).

5078. נֵדֶה **nedeh** (622d); from an unused word; *a gift:*— gifts(1).

5079. נִדָּה **niddah** (622c); from 5074; *impurity:*— abhorrent(1), abhorrent thing(2), impurity(8), menstrual(1), menstrual impurity(7), menstrual period(1), menstruation(2), menstruation*(1), period(1), time(1), unclean(1), unclean thing(1), uncleanness(2).

5080. נָדַח **nadach** (623a); a prim. root; *to impel, thrust, banish:*— banish(1), banished(3), banished one(3), bring down(1), dispersed(1), drawn away(2), drive(3), driven(11), driven away(5), hunted(1), led...astray(1), outcast(2), outcasts(6), scatter(1), scattered(4), seduce(2), seduced(1), seduces(1), straying away(1), swinging(1), swings(1), thrust(1), thrust down(1), will not be cast out(1).

5081. נָדִיב **nadib** (622a); from 5068; *inclined, generous, noble:*— generous man(1), moved(1), noble(3), noble man(1), nobleman(1), nobles(7), prince(2), prince's(1), princes(6), willing(2), willing man(1).

5082. נְדִיבָה **nedibah** (622a); from 5068; *nobility, nobleness:*— honor(1), noble plans(2), willing(1).

5083. נָדָן **nadan** (623c); of for. or.; *a gift:*— gifts(1).

5084. נָדָן **nadan** (623c); of for. or.; *a sheath:*— sheath(1).

5085. נִדְנֶה **nidneh** (1102b); (Ara.) corr. to 5084; *a sheath.*

5086. נָדַף **nadaph** (623c); a prim. root; *to drive, drive asunder:*— drive away(1), driven(2), driven away(2), drives away(1), fleeting(1), rout(1).

5087. נָדַר **nadar** (623d); a prim. root; *to vow:*— made(7), make(3), make vows(1), makes(2), takes(1), vow(6), vowed(8), vowing(1), vows(2), you will vow(1).

5088. נֶדֶר **neder** or

נֵדֶר **neder** (623d), from 5087; *a vow:*— votive(3), votive offering(1), votive offerings(5), vow(26), vows(24).

5089. נֹהַּ **noah** (627b); from an unused word; *eminency, distinction:*— eminent(1).

5090a. נָהַג **nahag** (624a); a prim. root; *to drive, conduct:*— carried off(1), carrying away(1), directed(2), drive(2), drive away(1), driven(1), drives(3), drove(2), drove away(1), guide(1), guided(1), guiding(1), lead(4), lead away(2), leading(1), led(3), led forth(1), led in procession(1), led away(1).

5090b. נָהַג **nahag** (624c); a prim. root; *to moan, lament:*— moaning(1).

5091. נָהָה **nahah** (624c); a prim. root; *to wail, lament:*— lamented(1), utter(1), wail(1).

5092. נְהִי **nehi** (624c); from 5091; *a wailing, lamentation, mourning song:*— lamentation(3), wailing(5).

5093. נִהְיָה **nihyah** (624d); from 5091; *a wailing, lamentation:*— bitter(1).

5094a. נְהִיר **nehir** or

נַהִירוּ **nehiru** (1102c); (Ara.) from a root corr. to 5102b; *a light:*— light(1).

5094b. נַהִירוּ **nahiru** (1102c); (Ara.) from the same as 5094a; *illumination, insight:*— illumination(2).

5095. נָהַל **nahal** (624d); a prim. root; *to lead* or *guide to a watering place, bring to a place of rest, refresh:*— fed(1), guide(3), guided(2), lead(1), leads(1), led(1), proceed(1).

5096. נַהֲלָל **Nahalal** or

נַהֲלֹל **Nahalol** (625b); from 5095; a place in Zebulun:— Nahalal(2), Nahalol(1).

5097. נַהֲלֹל **nahalol** (625b); from 5095; *a pasture:*— watering places(1).

5098. נָהַם **naham** (625b); a prim. root; *to growl, groan:*— groan(2), growl(1), growls(1), roaring(1).

5099. נַהַם **naham** (625b); from 5098; *growling* (of a lion):— growling(1), roaring(1).

5100. נְהָמָה **nehamah** (625b); from 5098; *a growling, groaning:*— agitation(1), roaring(1).

5101. נָהַק **nahaq** (625c); a prim. root; *to bray, cry:*— bray(1), cry(1).

5102a. נָהַר **nahar** (625c); a prim. root; *to flow, stream:*— stream(3).

5102b. נָהַר **nahar** (626a); a prim. root; *to shine, beam:*— radiant(3).

5103. נְהַר **nehar** (1102c); (Ara.) corr. to 5104; *a river:*— river(15).

5104. נָהָר **nahar** (625c); from 5102a; *a stream, river:*— canals(1), current(1), Euphrates(5), Euphrates river(1), floods(3), river(69), rivers(36), stream(1), streams(2).

5105. נְהָרָה **neharah** (626a); from 5102b; *a light, daylight:*— light(1).

5106. נוּא **nu** (626b); a prim. root; *to hinder, restrain, frustrate:*— discouraged*(1), discouraging*(1), forbid(2), forbidden(1), forbids(1), frustrates(1), refuse(1).

5107. נוּב **nub** (626b); a prim. root; *to bear fruit:*— flourish(1), flows(1), increase(1), yield fruit(1).

5108. נוֹב **nob** (626c); from 5107; *fruit:*— praise(1).

5109. נוֹבַי **Nobay** (626c); from 5108, an Isr. leader:— Nebai(1).

5110. נוּד **nud** (626c); a prim. root; *to move to and fro, wander, flutter, show grief:*— console(1), consoled(1), drive away(1), flee(2), flitting(1), grieve(1), grieving(1), mourn(4), shake(2), shaken(1), sympathize(1), sympathy(1), totters(1), wander(2), wandered(1), wanderer(2), waver(1).

5111. נוּד **nud** (1102c); (Ara.) corr. to 5110; *to flee:*— flee(1).

5112. נוֹד **nod** or

נֹד **nod** (627a); from 5110; *wandering* (of aimless fugitive):— wanderings(1).

5113. נוֹד **Nod** (627a); from 5110; a region into which Cain wandered:— Nod(1).

5114. נוֹדָב **Nodab** (622a); from 5068; an Arab tribe:— Nodab(1).

5115a. נָוָה **navah** (627b); a prim. root; *beautify:*— praise(1).

5115b. נָוָה **navah** (627d); denom. vb. from 5116a; *to dwell, abide:*— stay at home(1).

5116a. נָוֶה **naveh** (627c); from an unused word; *abode of shepherd* or *flocks, habitation:*— abode(3), dwelling(3), estate(1), fold(1), grazing ground(2), habitation(9), haunt(2), homestead(1), meadow(1), pasture(9), pasture land(1).

5116b. נָוֶה **naveh** (627d); from the same as 5116a; *dwelling, abiding:*— who remains(1).

5116c. נָוָה **navah** (627d); from the same as 5116a; *pasture, meadow:*— folds(1), pastures(2).

5117. נוּחַ **nuach** (628a); a prim. root; *to rest:*— abandon(2), allays(1), allow(1), appease(1), appeased(1), been at rest(1), calm(1), came to rest(1), camped(1), cast down(1), cast...down(1), deposit(3), deposited(1), down(1), enter into rest(1), find...rest(1), forsake(1), free(1), free space(2), give comfort(1), give rest(17), given rest(3), gives rest(1), had rest(1), idle*(1), laid(2), lay(8), lay down(1), laying(1), leave(8), left(7), let alone(4), let go*(1), permitted(2), place(2), placed(4), put(6), put it aside(1), put down(1), put aside(1), remain(3), resides(1), rest(14), rested(6), resting(1), rests(2), rid themselves(2), satisfy(1), set(4), set down(3), settle(2), settled(1), space*(1), spent(1), stationed(2), wait quietly(1), waited(1).

5118. נוּחַ **nuach** or

נֹחַ **noach** (629a); a form of 5117, q.v.

5119. נוֹחָה **Nochah** (629a); from 5117; a son of Benjamin:— Nohah(1).

5120. נוּט **nut** (630a); a prim. root; *to dangle, shake:*— shake(1).

5121. נָוִית Navith (627d); from the same as 5116a; an abode of prophets:— Naioth(6).

5122. נְוָלוּ nevalu or
נְוָלִי nevali (1102c); (Ara.) perh. of for. or.; *a refuse heap:*— refuse heap(1), rubbish heap(2).

5123. נוּם num (630b); a prim. root; *to be drowsy, slumber:*— sank(1), sleeping(1), slumber(3), slumbers(1).

5124. נוּמָה numah (630b); from 5123; *somnolence, indolence:*— drowsiness(1).

5125. נוּן nun (630c); a prim. root; *to propagate, increase:*— increase(1).

5126. נוּן Nun or
נוֹן Non (630c); from 5125; father of Joshua:— Non(1), Nun(29).

5127. נוּס nus (630c); a prim. root; *to flee, escape:*— abated(1), drives(1), escape(1), escaped(2), fled(78), flee(54), flee away(1), fleeing(5), flees(5), fugitive(2), fugitives(2), indeed flee(1), put to flight(1), run away(1), save(1), taken refuge(1).

5128. נוּעַ nua (631a); a prim. root; *to quiver, wave, waver, tremble, totter:*— disturb(1), moving(1), reels(1), scatter(1), set trembling(1), shake(4), shaken(4), shook(1), stagger(3), staggered(1), swing to and fro(1), to and fro(1), tremble(1), trembled(2), unstable(1), vagrant(2), wag(2), wander(5), wandered(2), wave(4).

5129. נוֹעַדְיָה Noadyah (418a); from 3259 and 3050; "meeting with Yah," a Levite, also a prophetess:— Noadiah(2).

5130. נוּף nuph (631d); a prim. root; *to move to and fro, wave, sprinkle:*— lifted(1), offer(1), present(5), presented(6), shake...back and forth(1), shakes(1), shed abroad(1), sprinkled(1), wave(13), waved(1), waving(1), wield(3), wielded(1), wielding(1), wields(1).

5131. נוֹף noph (632c); from an unused word; *elevation, height:*— elevation(1).

5132. נוּץ nuts (665b); see 5340b.

5133. נוֹצָה notsah or
נֹצָה notsah (663b); from 5327a; *plumage:*— feathers(1), plumage(3).

5134. נוּק nuq (632d); a prim. root; *to suckle, nurse:*— nursed(1).

5135. נוּר nur (1102c); (Ara.) from a root corr. to source of 5216; *a fire:*— fire(16).

5136. נוּשׁ nush (633b); a prim. root; *to be sick:*— sick(1).

5137a. נָזָה nazah (633b); a prim. root; *to spurt, spatter, sprinkle:*— splashed(1), splashes(1), sprinkle(16), sprinkled(4), sprinkles(1).

5137b. נָזָה nazah (633c); see 5137a.

5138. נָזִיד nazid (268a); from 2102; *something sodden* or *boiled, pottage:*— cooked food(1), stew(5).

5139. נָזִיר nazir or
נָזִר nazir (634c); from 5144a; *one consecrated, devoted:*— consecrated ones(1), Nazirite(9), Nazirites(2), one distinguished(2), untrimmed vines(2).

5140. נָזַל nazal (633c); a prim. root; *to flow, trickle, drop, distill:*— distill(1), flow(4), flowing(2), fresh water(1), pour down(2), quaked(1), streams(4), wafted(1).

5141. נֶזֶם nezem (633d); of unc. der.; *a ring* (worn as an ornament):— earring(3), earrings(4), ring(6), rings(4).

5142. נְזַק nezaq (1102c); (Ara.) corr. to the root of 5143; *to suffer injury:*— damage(1), damaging(1), detriment(1), suffer loss(1).

5143. נֵזֶק nezeq (634a); from the same as 5141; *injury, damage:*— annoyance(1).

5144a. נָזַר nazar (634a); a prim. root; *to dedicate, consecrate:*— abstain(1), careful(1), devoted(1), keep(1), separated(1), separates(1).

5144b. נָזַר nazar (634c); denom. vb. from 5145; *to be a Nazirite:*— abstain(1), dedicate(2), separated(1), separation(1).

5145. נֶזֶר nezer or
נֵזֶר nezer (634b); from 5144a; *consecration, crown, Naziriteship:*— consecration(1), crown(10), dedicated(4), hair(1), Nazirite(1), separation(8).

5146. נֹחַ Noach (629b); from 5117; "rest," patriarch who survived the flood:— Noah(44), Noah's(2).

5147. נַחְבִּי Nachbi (286a); from 2247; a Naphtalite:— Nahbi(1).

5148. נָחָה nachah (634d); a prim. root; *to lead, guide:*— brings(1), brought(1), guide(7), guided(6), guides(1), lead(14), leads(1), led(5), left(1), put(1), stationed(1).

5149. נְחוּם Nechum (637b); from 5162; "comfort," an Isr. of Nehemiah's time:— Nehum(1).

5150. נִחוּם nichum or
נִחֻם nichum (637b); from 5162; *comfort, compassion:*— comfort(1), comforting(1), compassions(1).

5151. נַחוּם Nachum (637b); from 5162; an Isr. prophet:— Nahum(1).

5152. נָחוֹר Nachor (637d); from the same as 5170a; grandfather of Abraham, also the brother of Abraham:— Nahor(16), Nahor's(2).

5153. נָחוּשׁ nachush (639a); from the same as 5178; *of bronze:*— bronze(1).

5154. נְחוּשָׁה nechushah or
נְחֻשָׁה nechushah (639a); fem. of 5153; *copper, bronze:*— bronze(9), copper(1).

5155. נְחִילָה nechilah (636a); perh. from 2485; perh. *flute* (a musical instrument).

5156. נָחִיר nachir (638a); from the same as 5170a; *a nostril:*— nostrils(1).

5157. נָחַל nachal (635c); denom. vb. from 5159; *to get* or *take as a possession:*— allotted(1), apportion(2), apportion for inheritance(1), apportion the inheritance(1), apportioned(1), apportioned for an inheritance(1), apportioning for inheritance(1), bequeath(2), distributed(1), divide(1), divide it for an inheritance(1), endow(1), endowed(1), gave(1), gave inheritance(1), give(1), give inheritance(1), give as a possession(1), give...possession(1), have(2), have an inheritance(2), inherit(16), inheritance(8), inherited(3), inherits(1), leaves an inheritance(1), possess(2), possess them as an inheritance(1), possessed(1), possesses(1), possession(2), receive inheritance(1), received(2), received inheritance(1), take(1), take possession(1), wills(1).

5158a. נַחַל nachal or
נַחְלָה nachlah or
נַחֲלָה nachalah (636a); of unc. der.; *torrent, torrent-valley, wadi:*— brook(44), brooks(5), flowing(1), ravine(2), ravines(2), river(13), rivers(5), shaft(1), stream(5), streams(5), torrent(7), torrents(3), valley(39), valleys(4), Wadi(1), wadi(1), wadis(3).

5158b. נַחַל nachal (636d); see 5158a.

5159. נַחֲלָה nachalah (635a); from an unused word; *possession, property, inheritance:*— gift(1), give(1), hereditary(1), heritage(14), heritages(1), inheritance(197), inheritances(1), portion(1), possession(7).

5160. נַחֲלִיאֵל Nachaliel (636d); from 5158a and 410; "valley of God," a place E. of the Dead Sea:— Nahaliel(2).

5161. נֶחֱלָמִי Nechelami (636d); from an unused name; descriptive title for a false prophet:— Nehelamite(3).

5162. נָחַם nacham (636d); a prim. root; *to be sorry, console oneself:*— am sorry(1), appeased(1), become a consolation(1), change mind(6), change minds(1), changed mind(4), comfort(30), comforted(18), comforter(2), comforters(4), comforts(2), console(3), consolers(1), consoling(1), give rest(1), have compassion(2), moved to pity(1), regret(1), regretted(1), relent(5), relented(4), relenting(3), relents(1), relieved(1), repent(3), repented(2), sorry(6), think better(1), when the time of mourning was ended(2).

5163. נַחַם Nacham (637b); from 5162; "comfort," a man of Judah:— Naham(1).

5164. נֹחַם nocham (637b); from 5162; *sorrow, repentance:*— compassion(1).

5165. נֶחָמָה nechamah (637c); from 5162; *comfort:*— comfort(1), consolation(1).

5166. נְחֶמְיָה Nechemyah (637c); from 5162 and 3050; "Yah comforts," three Isr.:— Nehemiah(8).

5167. נַחֲמָנִי Nachamani (637c); from 5162; "compassionate," an Isr. of Nehemiah's time:— Nahamani(1).

5168. נַחְנוּ nachnu (59d); from 587; *we:*— ourselves(1).

5169. נָחַץ nachats (637d); a prim. root; perh. *to urge:*— urgent(1).

5170a. נַחַר nachar (637d); from an unused word; *a snorting:*— snorting(1).

5170b. נַחֲרָה nacharah (637d); from the same as 5170a; *a snorting:*— snorting(1).

5171. נַחֲרַי Nacharay or
נַחְרַי Nachray (638a); from the same as 5170a; one of David's heroes:— Naharai(2).

5172. נָחַשׁ nachash (638c); a prim. root; *to practice divination, observe signs:*— divination(1), divined(1), enchantments(1), indeed practice divination(1), indeed uses(1), interprets omens(1), practice divination(1), took as an omen(1), used divination(2).

5173. נַחַשׁ nachash (638d); from 5172; *divination, enchantment:*— omen(1), omens(1).

5174. נְחָשׁ nechash (1102d); (Ara.) corr. to 5154; *copper, bronze:*— bronze(9).

5175. נָחָשׁ nachash (638a); from an unused word; *a serpent:*— serpent(24), serpent's(2), serpents(2), snake(1).

5176. **נָחָשׁ Nachash** (638b); from the same as 5175; the name of several non-Isr.:— Nahash(9).

5177. **נַחְשׁוֹן Nachshon** (638b); from the same as 5175; brother-in-law of Aaron:— Nahshon(10).

5178. **נְחֹשֶׁת nechosheth** (638d); of unc. der.; *copper, bronze:*— brass(2), bronze(130), bronze chains(1), bronze fetters(2), chain(1), copper(1), fetters(1), fetters of bronze(1).

5179a. **נְחֹשֶׁת nechosheth** (639b); from an unused word; perh. *lust, harlotry:*— lewdness(1).

5179b. **נְחֻשְׁתָּא Nechushta** (639b); from the same as 5178; mother of King Jehoiakin:— Nehushta(1).

5180. **נְחֻשְׁתָּן Nechushtan** (639b); from the same as 5178; the name of Moses' bronze serpent:— Nehushtan(1).

5181. **נָחֵת nacheth** (639b); a prim. root; *to go down, descend:*— bend(2), bring down(1), come down(1), go down(1), goes deeper(1), pressed down(1), settle(1), sunk deep(1).

5182. **נְחֵת necheth** (1102d); (Ara.) corr. to 5181; *to descend:*— deposed(1), deposit(1), descended(1), descending(1), put(1), stored(1).

5183a. **נַחַת nachath** (629b); from 5117; *quietness, rest:*— better(1), go down(1), quietness(1), rest(3), which was set(1).

5183b. **נַחַת nachath** (639c); from 5181; *descent:*— descending(1).

5184. **נַחַת Nachath** (639c); from 5181; an Edomite, also two Isr.:— Nahath(5).

5185. **נָחֵת nacheth** (639c); from 5181; *descending:*— coming down(1).

5186. **נָטָה natah** (639d); a prim. root; *to stretch out, spread out, extend, incline, bend:*— afternoon*(1), bend down(1), bent(1), bent down(1), bow(1), bowed(3), came to stumbling(1), cast down(1), decline(1), defraud(1), deprive(2), deviated(1), distort(1), distorts(1), entices(1), extend(1), extended(3), extends(2), followed*(2), held high(1), incline(27), inclined(7), intended(1), leaning(1), lengthen(1), lengthened(1), lengthens(1), let down(1), offer(1), outstretched(17), pervert(4), perverted(1), pitch(1), pitched(11), push aside(1), spread(3), stretch(28), stretched(32), stretched-out(1), stretches(5), stretching(2), thrust aside(1), took aside(3), turn(6), turn back(1), turn aside(9), turn away(3), turned(3), turned aside(6), turned away(4), turned...away(1), turning(1), turns(1), visited(1).

5187. **נָטִיל natil** (642b); from 5190; *laden:*— weigh(1).

5188. **נְטִיפָה netiphah** (643b); from 5197; *a drop, pendant:*— dangling earrings(1), pendants(1).

5189. **נְטִישָׁה netishah** (644a); from 5203; *a twig, tendril:*— branches(1), spreading branches(1), tendrils(1).

5190. **נָטַל natal** (642a); a prim. root; *to lift, bear:*— laid(1), lifted(1), lifts(1), offering(1).

5191. **נְטַל netal** (1102d); (Ara.) corr. to 5190; *to lift:*— lifted(1), raised(1).

5192. **נֵטֶל netel** (642b); from 5190; *burden, weight:*— weighty(1).

5193. **נָטַע nata** (642b); a prim. root; *to plant:*— establish(1), pitch(1), plant(31), planted(21), planters(1), plants(2), well-driven(1).

5194. **נֶטַע neta** (642c); from 5193; *plantation, planting, plant:*— plant(3), plants(1).

5195. **נָטִיעַ natia** (642d); from 5193; *a plant:*— plants(1).

5196. **נְטָעִים Netaim** (642d); from 5193; a place in Judah:— Netaim(1).

5197. **נָטַף nataph** (642d); a prim. root; *to drop, drip, discourse:*— drip(4), dripped(3), dripping(1), dropped(2), speak(7), spokesman(1).

5198a. **נָטָף nataph** (643a); from 5197; *a drop:*— drops(1).

5198b. **נָטָף nataph** (643b); from 5197; perh. *stacte,* a kind of gum:— stacte(1).

5199. **נְטֹפָה Netophah** (643b); from 5197; a place in Judah:— Netophah(2).

5200. **נְטֹפָתִי Netophathi** (643b); from 5199; inhab. of Netophah:— Netophathite(8), Netophathites(3).

5201. **נָטַר natar** (643b); a prim. root; *to keep:*— angry(2), bear any grudge(1), caretaker(1), caretakers(1), keep(1), reserves(1), take care(1), taken care(1).

5202. **נְטַר netar** (1102d); (Ara.) corr. to 5201; *to keep:*— kept(1).

5203. **נָטַשׁ natash** (643c); a prim. root; *to leave, forsake, permit:*— abandon(7), abandoned(5), allow(1), cast away(1), ceased(1), drawn(1), fall(1), forego(1), forsake(3), forsaken(2), forsook(1), hangs slack(1), leave(2), left(5), lie fallow(1), neglected(1), spread(6).

5204a. **נִי ni** (624d); another reading for 5092, q.v.

5204b. **נִיב nib** (626c); from 5107; *fruit:*— fruit(1).

5205. **נִיד nid** (627a); from 5110; *quivering motion* (of lips):— solace(1).

5206. **נִידָה nidah** (622c); from 5074; *impurity:*— unclean thing(1).

5207. **נִיחוֹחַ nichoach** or

נִיחֹחַ nichoach (629b); from 5117; *a quieting, soothing, tranquilizing:*— soothing(43).

5208. **נִיחוֹחַ nichoach** or

נִיחֹחַ nichoach (1102d); (Ara.) corr. to 5207; *soothing, tranquilizing:*— acceptable sacrifices(1), fragrant incense(1).

5209. **נִין nin** (630c); from 5125; *offspring, posterity:*— offspring(3).

5210. **נִינְוֵה Nineveh** (644b); of for. or; capital of Assyr.:— Nineveh(17).

5211. **נִיס nis** (630c); from 5127, q.v.

5212. **נִיסָן Nisan** (644c); of for. or.; first month of the Jewish religious year:— Nisan(2).

5213. **נִיצוֹץ nitsots** (665b); from 5340a; *a spark:*— spark(1).

5214. **נִיר nir** (644c); a prim. root; *to break up, freshly till:*— break(2).

5215a. **נִיר nir** (633a); from the same as 5216; *a lamp:*— lamp(5).

5215b. **נִיר nir** or

נִר nir (644c); from 5214; *tillable, untilled,* or *fallow ground:*— fallow ground(3).

5216. **נֵיר ner** or

נֵר ner (632d); from an unused word; *a lamp:*— lamp(18), lamps(25).

5217. **נָכָא naka** (644d); a prim. root; *to smite, scourge:*— scourged(1).

5218a. **נָכָא naka** (644d); from 5217; *stricken:*— who are stricken(1).

5218b. **נָכֵא nake** (644d); from 5217; *stricken:*— broken(3).

5219. **נְכֹאת nekoth** (644d); from 5217; (a spice) perh. *tragacanth gum:*— aromatic gum(2).

5220. **נֶכֶד neked** (645a); from an unused word; *progeny, posterity:*— posterity(3).

5221. **נָכָה nakah** (645a); a prim. root; *to smite:*— attack(5), attacked(6), attacks(3), beat(3), beat down(1), beaten(5), beating(1), blows(1), bothered(1), cast(1), clap(3), clapped(1), conquered(5), defeat(5), defeated(44), destroy(1), destroyed(2), drove(1), indeed defeated(1), inflicted(4), kill(11), kill*(1), killed(36), killing(3), kills(10), made(1), overthrown(1), pin(2), ruined(2), shoot(1), shot(1), slain(11), slapped(1), slaughter(1), slaughtered(1), slaughtering(2), slay(5), slayer(1), slayers(1), slaying(1), slays(1), slew(8), smashed(1), smite(12), smiter(1), smiting(1), smitten(7), smote(13), stricken(3), strike(49), strike down(9), strikes(9), strikes down(1), striking(4), striking down(2), struck(120), struck down(54), stuck(1), surely strike(1), take(5), taken(2), takes(2), thrust(1), troubled(1), wounded(5), wounding*(1).

5222. **נֵכֶה nekeh** (646d); from 5221; *smitten, stricken:*— smiters(1).

5223. **נָכֶה nakeh** (646d); from 5221; *smitten, stricken:*— contrite(1), crippled(2).

5224. **נְכוֹ Neko** (647a); prob. of for. or.; a king of Eg.:— Neco(3).

5225a. **נָכוֹן nakon** (646d); another reading for 3559, q.v.

5225b. **נָכוֹן Nakon** (467d); from 3559; an Isr.:— Nacon(1).

5226. **נֵכַח nekach** (647b); the same as 5227, q.v.

5227. **נֹכַח nokach** (647b); from an unused word; *in front of, opposite to:*— approval(1), before(2), behalf(1), directly ahead(1), front(4), opposite(9), over against(1), right before(3).

5228. **נָכֹחַ nakoach** (647c); from the same as 5227; *straight, right, straightness:*— right(2), straightforward(1), upright way(1), uprightness(2), what is right(2).

5229. **נְכֹחָה nekochah** (647c); fem.of 5228, q.v.

5230. **נָכַל nakal** (647c); a prim. root; *to be crafty, deceitful* or *knavish:*— deal craftily(1), deceived(1), plotted(1), swindler(1).

5231. **נֵכֶל nekel** (647d); from 5230; *wiliness, craft, knavery:*— tricks(1).

5232. **נְכַס nekas** (1103a); (Ara.) corr. to 5233; *riches, property:*— goods(1), treasury(1).

5233. **נֶכֶס nekes** (647d); prob. of for. or.; *riches, treasures:*— riches(1), wealth(4).

5234. **נָכַר nakar** (647d); a prim. root; *to regard, recognize:*— able(1), acknowledge(3), acknowledges(1), discern(1), distinguish(1), distinguishes(1), examine(1), examine and see(1), examined(1), familiar(1), know(2), knows(1), partial*(1), partiality*(3), perceived(1), point(1), recognize(7), recognized(8), regard(1), regards(2), show(3), take notice(1), took note(1), took notice(1).

5235a. **נָכַר nakar** (649a); denom. vb. from 5236; *to act* or *treat as foreign* or *strange, to disguise:*— another woman(2), delivered(1), disguised(1), disguises(1), made an alien(1), misjudge(1), pretend to be another woman(2).

5235b. **נֶכֶר neker** or

נֹכֶר noker (648c); from an unused word; *misfortune, calamity:*— disaster(1), misfortune(1).

5236. נֵכָר nekar (648c); from the same as 5235b; *that which is foreign, foreignness:*— aliens*(2), foreign(16), foreigner*(6), foreigners*(10), strange(1).

5237. נָכְרִי nokri (648d); from the same as 5235b; *foreign, alien:*— adulteress(2), adulterous woman(2), alien(2), aliens(1), extraordinary(1), foreign(16), foreigner(15), foreigners(5), stranger(1).

5238. נְכֹת nekoth (649b); of unc. der.; *treasure:*— treasure(2).

5239. נָלָה nalah (649b); prob. a prim. root; perh. *to obtain, attain:*— cease(1).

5240. נְמִבְזָה nemibzah (649c); another reading for 959, q.v.

5241. נְמוּאֵל Nemuel (649c); of unc. der.; two Isr.:— Nemuel(3).

5242. נְמוּאֵלִי Nemueli (649c); from 5241; desc. of Nemuel:— Nemuelites(1).

5243. נָמַל namal (557d); the same as 4135, q.v.

5244. נְמָלָה nemalah (649c); of unc. der.; *an ant:*— ant(1), ants(1).

5245. נְמַר nemar (1103a); (Ara.) corr. to 5246; *a leopard:*— leopard(1).

5246. נָמֵר namer (649d); from an unused word; *a leopard:*— leopard(4), leopards(2).

5247. נִמְרָה Nimrah (649d); from the same as 5246; "place of leopard," a place E. of the Jordan:— Nimrah(1).

5248. נִמְרוֹד Nimrod or

נִמְרֹד Nimrod (650a); prob. of for. or.; a son of Cush and founder of the Bab. kingdom:— Nimrod(4).

5249. נִמְרִים Nimrim (649d); from the same as 5246; a place in Moab:— Nimrim(2).

5250. נִמְשִׁי Nimshi (650a); of unc. der.; grandfather of Jehu:— Nimshi(5).

5251. נֵס nes (651d); from 5264; *a standard, ensign, signal, sign:*— banner(2), distinguishing mark(1), sail(1), signal(4), standard(12), warning(1).

5252. נְסִבָּה nesibbah (687c); from 5437; *turn of affairs:*— turn(1).

5253. נָסַג nasag (690d); the same as 5472, q.v.

5254. נָסָה nasah (650a); a prim. root; *to test, try:*— make a test(1), proved(1), put(1), put to the test(2), tempted(3), test(13), tested(9), testing(3), tried(1), try(1), venture(1), ventures(1).

5255. נָסַח nasach (650c); a prim. root; *to pull* or *tear away:*— tear away(1), tear down(1), torn(1), uprooted(1).

5256. נְסַח nesach (1103a); (Ara.) corr. to 5255; *to pull away:*— drawn(1).

5257a. נָסִיךְ nasik (651a); from 5258a; *a libation, molten image:*— drink offering(1), metal images(1).

5257b. נָסִיךְ nasik (651c); from 5258b; *a prince:*— chiefs(1), leaders(1), princes(2).

5258a. נָסַךְ nasak (650c); a prim. root; *to pour out:*— cast(1), casts(1), drink offerings(2), pour(5), pour out drink offerings(2), pour drink offerings(1), poured(9), pouring(3).

5258b. נָסַךְ nasak (651c); a prim. root; *to set, install:*— established(1), installed(1).

5259. נָסַךְ nasak (651b); a prim. root; *to weave:*— make(1), stretched(1).

5260. נְסַךְ nesak (1103a); (Ara.) corr. to 5258a; *to pour out:*— present(1).

5261. נְסַךְ nesak (1103a); (Ara.) corr. to 5262a; *a drink offering:*— drink offerings(1).

5262a. נֶסֶךְ nesek or

נֵסֶךְ nesek (651a); from 5258a; *a drink offering:*— drink(1), drink offering(29), drink offerings(29), libations(1).

5262b. נֶסֶךְ nesek (651a); from 5258a; *molten image:*— molten image(1), molten images(3).

5263. נָסַס nasas (651c); a prim. root; *to be sick:*— sick man(1).

5264. נָסַס nasas (651c); a prim. root; perh. *to be high* or *conspicuous:*— displayed(1), sparkling(1).

5265. נָסַע nasa (652a); a prim. root; *to pull out* or *up, set out, journey:*— blow(1), continuing*(1), departed(3), go about(1), go forward(1), journeyed(56), journeying(1), led(1), led forth(1), left(2), marching(1), move(2), moved(6), plucked(1), pulled(4), quarried(1), quarries(1), removed(1), set(53), set journey(1), set aside(1), sets(1), setting(1), take our journey(1), uprooted(1), wander(1), went forth(1).

5266. נָסַק nasaq (701b); the same as 5559a, q.v.

5267. נְסַק nesaq (1104b); (Ara.) the same as 5559b, q.v.

5268. נִסְרֹךְ Nisrok (652d); of for. or.; an Assyr. god:— Nisroch(2).

5269. נֵעָה Neah (631c); from 5128; a place in Zebulun:— Neah(1).

5270. נֹעָה Noah (631c); from 5128; a woman of Manasseh:— Noah(4).

5271. נָעוּר naur (655b); from the same as 5288; *youth, early life:*— youth(47).

5272a. נְעוּרוֹת neuroth (655c); from the same as 5288; *youth, early life:*— youth(1).

5272b. נְעִיאֵל Neiel (653a); of unc. der.; a place on the border of Asher:— Neiel(1).

5273a. נָעִים naim (653d); from 5276; *pleasant, delightful:*— compliments*(1), lovely(1), pleasant(7), pleasures(2).

5273b. נָעִים naim (654b); from an unused word; perh. *singing, sweetly sounding, musical:*— sweet(1), sweet sounding(1).

5274a. נָעַל naal (653a); a prim. root; *to bar, bolt, lock:*— lock(1), locked(5).

5274b. נָעַל naal (653b); denom. vb. from 5275; *to furnish with sandals, shoe:*— put sandals(1), sandals(1).

5275. נַעַל naal or

נַעֲלָה naalah (653a); from 5274a; *a sandal, shoe:*— dry-shod(1), sandal(7), sandals(9), shoe(2), shoes(3).

5276. נָעֵם naem (653c); a prim. root; *to be pleasant, delightful,* or *lovely:*— delight(1), delightful(1), pleasant(5), surpass in beauty(1).

5277. נַעַם Naam (653d); from 5276; a son of Caleb:— Naam(1).

5278. נֹעַם noam (653c); from 5276; *delightfulness, pleasantness:*— beauty(1), favor(3), pleasant(3).

5279a. נַעֲמָה Naamah (653d); from 5276; a sister of Tubal-cain, also an Ammonitess:— Naamah(4).

5279b. נַעֲמָה Naamah (654a); from 5276; a city in Judah:— Naamah(1).

5280. נַעֲמִי Naami (654b); from 5283; desc. of Naaman:— Naamites(1).

5281. נָעֳמִי Noomi (654a); from 5276; mother-in-law of Ruth:— Naomi(20), Naomi's(1).

5282. נַעֲמָן naaman (654a); from 5276; *pleasantness:*— delightful(1).

5283. נַעֲמָן Naaman (654a); from 5276; a desc. of Benjamin, also an Aramean (Syrian) general:— Naaman(15), Naaman's(1).

5284. נַעֲמָתִי Naamathi (654b); from an unused name; inhab. of Naamah:— Naamathite(4).

5285. נַעֲצוּץ naatsuts (654c); from an unused word; *a thorn bush:*— thorn bush(1), thorn bushes(1).

5286. נָעַר naar (654c); a prim. root; *to growl:*— growl(1).

5287. נָעַר naar (654c); a prim. root; *to shake, shake out* or *off:*— lose(1), overthrew(2), shake(2), shake free(1), shaken(2), shaken off(1), shakes(1), shook(1).

5288. נַעַר naar (654d); of unc. der.; *a boy, lad, youth, retainer:*— attendants(1), boy(19), boy's(1), boys(1), child(12), children(4), lad(36), lad's(2), lads(3), servant(34), servant's(1), servants(23), young(12), young man(33), young men(38), young people(1), youth(14), youths(2).

5289. נַעַר naar (654d); from 5287; *a shaking, scattering:*— scattered(1).

5290. נֹעַר noar (655a); from the same as 5288; *youth, early life:*— childhood(1), youth(3).

5291. נַעֲרָה naarah (655a); fem. of 5288; *a girl, maiden:*— each young lady(1), girl(21), girl's(11), maidens(8), maids(7), young(4), young ladies(1), young lady(4), young woman(2), young women(1), young...woman(1).

5292. נַעֲרָה Naarah (655c); from the same as 5288; an Isr. woman, also a place on the border of Ephraim:— Naarah(4).

5293. נַעֲרַי Naaray (655c); from the same as 5288; one of David's heroes:— Naarai(1).

5294. נְעַרְיָה Nearyah (655d); from the same as 5288 and 3050; two Isr.:— Neariah(3).

5295. נַעֲרָן Naaran (655d); from the same as 5288; a place in Ephraim:— Naaran(1).

5296. נְעֹרֶת neoreth (654d); from 5287; *tow* (for making thread):— tinder(1), tow(1).

5297. נֹף Noph (592a); of unc. der.; a city in Eg. (the same as 4644):— Memphis(7).

5298. נֶפֶג Nepheg (655d); of unc. der.; two Isr.:— Nepheg(4).

5299a. נָפָה naphah (632b); from 5130; *a sieve:*— sieve(1).

5299b. נָפָה naphah (632c); from the same as 5131; *height:*— height(1), heights(2).

5300. נְפוּשְׁסִים Nephushesim (656b); the same as 5304, q.v.

5301. נָפַח naphach (655d); a prim. root; *to breathe, blow:*— blow(3), blows(1), boiling(2), breathe(1), breathed(1), breathing is labored*(1), disdainfully sniff(1), lose(1), unfanned(1).

5302. נֹפַח Nophach (656a); from 5301; a city of Moab, perh. the same as 5025:— Nophah(1).

5303. נְפִלִים Nephilim or

נְפִילִים Nephilim (658c); from 5307; "giants," name of two peoples, one before the flood and one after the flood:— Nephilim(3).

5304. נְפִיסִים Nephisim (656b); of unc. der.; a family of returned exiles:— Nephisim(1), Nephushesim(1).

5305. נָפִישׁ Naphish (661c); from the same as 5315; a son of Ishmael:— Naphish(3).

5306. נֹפֶךְ nophek (656c); of unc. der.; (a precious stone) perh. *emerald:*— emeralds(1), turquoise(3).

5307. נָפַל naphal (656c); a prim. root; *to fall, lie:*— abandon(1), allot(1), allotted(2), anyone falls(1), apportioned(2), attacked(2), born(1), bring down(1), burst(1), came down(1), cast(16), cast down(5), casts(1), collapse(1), come(3), dash down(1), defect(1), defected(3), deserted(3), deserters(3), did(1), dismounted(1), divide by lot(2), divide it by lot(1), downfall(1), dropped(1), fail(1), fail*(1), failed(4), fall(130), fall down(4), fallen(55), fallen away(1), fallen down(4), falling(3), falling down(2), falls(22), falls away(1), fell(98), fell down(8), felled(1), felling(1), give birth(1), go over(1), going over(2), gone over(3), inferior(2), killed(1), knocks(1), lay(1), lay down(1), lay flat(1), lie down(1), look(1), lost(2), lying(5), making(1), perish(1), present(1), presenting(3), prostrating(1), remains(1), settled(1), surely fall(1), throw(2), topple(1), turns(1), void(1), waste away(3).

5308. נְפַל nephal (1103a); (Ara.) corr. to 5307; *to fall:*— came(1), fall down(5), fell(3), fell down(1), have occasion(1).

5309. נֶפֶל nephel or

נֵפֶל nephel (658b); from 5307; *miscarriage, abortion:*— miscarriage(2), miscarriages(1).

5310a. נָפַץ naphats (658c); a prim. root; *to shatter:*— broken(1), dash(1), dashes(1), pulverized(1), shatter(11), shattered(1), shattering(1), smashed(1).

5310b. נָפַץ naphats (659a); a prim. root; *to disperse, be scattered:*— disperse(1), dispersed(1), populated(1), scattering(1).

5311. נֶפֶץ nephets (658d); from 5310a; *a driving storm:*— cloudburst(1).

5312. נְפַק nephaq (1103b); (Ara.) a prim. root; *to go* or *come out* or *forth:*— came(1), come(1), coming(1), emerged(1), gone forth(1), here(1), taken(3), took(2), went forth(1).

5313. נִפְקָה niphqah (1103b); (Ara.) from 5312; *an outlay:*— cost(2).

5314. נָפַשׁ naphash (661c); denom. vb. from 5315; *to be refreshed:*— refresh(1), refreshed(2).

5315. נֶפֶשׁ nephesh (659b); from an unused word; *a soul, living being, life, self, person, desire, passion, appetite, emotion :*— any(1), anyone(2), anyone*(1), appetite(7), being(1), beings(3), body(1), breath(1), corpse(2), creature(6), creatures(3), dead(1), dead person(2), deadly(1), death(1), defenseless*(1), desire(12), desire*(2), discontented*(1), endure*(1), feelings(1), fierce*(2), greedy*(1), heart(5), heart's(2), herself(12), Himself(4), himself(19), human(1), human being(1), hunger(1), life(146), life*(1), lifeblood*(2), lives(34), living creature(1), longing*(1), man(4), man's(1), men*(2), mind(2), Myself(3), myself(2), number(1), ones(1), others(1), ourselves(3), own(1), passion*(1), people(2), people*(1), perfume*(1), person(68), person*(1), persons(19), slave(1), some(1), soul(238), soul's(1), souls(12), strength(1), themselves(6), thirst(1), throat(2), will(1), wish(1), wishes(1), yourself(11), yourselves(13).

5316. נֶפֶת Nepheth (632c); from the same as 5131; "height," a city belonging to Manasseh:— Napheth(1).

5317. נֹפֶת nopheth (661d); of unc. der.; *flowing honey, honey from the comb:*— drippings(1), honey(3), honey from the comb(1).

5318. נֶפְתּוֹחַ Nephtoach (836b); from 6605a; a place on the border of Judah and Benjamin:— Nephtoah(2).

5319. נַפְתּוּלִים naphtulim (836d); from 6617; *wrestlings:*— wrestlings(1).

5320. נַפְתֻּחִים Naphtuchim (661d); of for. or.; a tribe desc. from Mizraim:— Naphtuh(1), Naphtuhim(1).

5321. נַפְתָּלִי Naphtali (836d); from 6617; a son of Jacob, also his desc. and the district settled by them:— Kedesh-naphtali*(1), Naphtali(50).

5322a. נֵץ nets (665b); from 5340a; *a blossom:*— blossoms(1).

5322b. נֵץ nets (665c); from an unused word; *hawk, falcon* (a bird of prey):— hawk(3).

5323. נָצָא natsa (661d); another reading for 3318, q.v.

5324. נָצַב natsab (662a); a prim. root; *to take one's stand, stand:*— arises(1), attending(1), best(1), charge(2), deputies(4), deputy(1), erected(2), establish(2), established(1), fix(1), fixed(1), officers(1), pillar(1), present yourself(1), presiding(1), set(15), settled(1), stand(5), standing(14), stands(1), station myself(1), station yourself(1), stationed(1), stood(9), stood erect(1), takes stand(2), waiting(1).

5325. נִצָּב nitstsab (662c); from 5324; *haft, hilt* (of a sword):— handle(1).

5326. נִצְבָּה nitsbah (1103b); (Ara.) from a root corr. to 5324; *firmness:*— toughness(1).

5327a. נָצָה natsah (663b); a prim. root; perh. *to fly:*— fled(1).

5327b. נָצָה natsah (663c); a prim. root; *to struggle:*— contended(2), fighting(1), struggle(1), struggled(1), struggled together(1), struggling(1).

5327c. נָצָה natsah (663d); a prim. root; *to fall in ruins:*— destroyed(1), laid waste(2), ruinous(2), ruins(1).

5328. נִצָּה nitstsah (665b); from 5340a; *a blossom:*— flower(2).

5329. נָצַח natsach (663d); a prim. root; *preeminent* or *enduring:*— choir director(1), continual(1), lead(1), oversee(3), supervise(2), supervised(1), supervisors(1).

5330. נְצַח netsach (1103b); (Ara.) corr. to 5329; *to distinguish oneself:*— distinguishing(1).

5331. נֶצַח netsach or

נֵצַח netsach (664b); from 5329; *eminence, enduring, everlastingness, perpetuity:*— all time(1), always(3), end(1), eternally(1), ever(1), forever(22), Glory(1), limit(1), never*(6), perpetual(3), strength(1), victory(1).

5332. נֵצַח netsach (664c); from an unused word; *juice* (of grapes), *blood, gore:*— lifeblood(2).

5333. נְצִיב netsib or

נְצִב netsib (662d); from 5324; *a pillar, prefect, garrison, post:*— deputy(1), garrison(4), garrisons(5), officers(1), pillar(1).

5334. נְצִיב Netsib (662d); from 5324; a place in Judah:— Nezib(1).

5335. נְצִיחַ Netsiach (664c); from 5329; head of a family of Nethinim:— Neziah(2).

5336. נָצִיר natsir (666a); from 5341; *preserved:*— preserved(1).

5337. נָצַל natsal (664c); a prim. root; *to strip, plunder, deliver oneself, be delivered, snatch away, deliver:*— defended(2), deliver(103), deliver yourself(2), deliverance(1), delivered(46), delivered at all(1), deliverer(1), delivering(1), delivers(7), escape(1), escaped(1), plucked(1), plunder(1), plundered(1), preserved(1), recover(1), recovered(2), rescue(11), rescued(5), saves(1), separate(1), snatched(1), snatched away(1), snatches(1), spared(3), stripped(1), surely deliver(2), surely rescue(1), take(1), take away(1), taken away(2), took(1).

5338. נְצַל netsal (1103b); (Ara.) corr. to 5337; *to rescue, deliver:*— deliver(1), rescue(1), rescues(1).

5339. נִצָּן nitstsan (665b); from 5340a; *a blossom:*— flowers(1).

5340a. נָצַץ natsats (665a); a prim. root; *to shine, sparkle:*— gleamed(1).

5340b. נָצַץ natsats (665b); denom. vb. from 5328; *to bloom, blossom:*— bloomed(2), blossoms(1).

5341. נָצַר natsar (665c); a prim. root; *to watch, guard, keep:*— besieged(2), Besiegers(1), cunning(1), guard(2), guarding(1), guards(2), hidden things(1), keep(7), keep watch(1), keeper(1), keeps(3), kept(1), man(1), observe(10), observed(1), observes(1), preserve(10), preserves(1), reserve(1), secret places(1), tends(1), watch(4), watcher(1), watches(1), watchman(1), watchmen(1).

5342. נֵצֶר netser (666a); from 5341; *a sprout, shoot:*— branch(3), descendants(1).

5343. נְקֵא neqe (1103c); (Ara.) corr. to 5355a; *clean, pure:*— pure(1).

5344a. נָקַב naqab (666a); a prim. root; *to pierce:*— bored(1), designate(1), designated(6), distinguished(1), holes(1), name(1), pierce(4), pierced(1).

5344b. נָקַב naqab (666d); a prim. root; *to curse:*— blasphemes(2).

5345. נֶקֶב neqeb (666b); from 5344a; perh. *sockets* (technical term of jeweler's work):— sockets(1).

5346. נֶקֶב Neqeb (666c); from 5344a; see 129.

5347. נְקֵבָה neqebah (666c); from 5344a; *a female:*— female(20), woman(1), women(1).

5348. נָקֹד naqod (666d); from an unused word; *speckled:*— speckled(9).

5349. נֹקֵד noqed (667a); from an unused word; *sheep raiser, sheep dealer, sheep tender:*— sheep breeder(1), sheepherders(1).

5350. נִקֻּד niqqud or

נִקּוּד niqqud (666d); from the same as 5348; perh. *what is crumbled* or *easily crumbles, crumbs:*— cakes(1), crumbled(2).

5351. נְקֻדָּה nequddah (667a); from the same as 5348; *a point* or *drop:*— beads(1).

5352. נָקָה naqah (667a); a prim. root; *to be empty* or *clean:*— acquit(3), acquitted(2), avenge(1), avenged(1), blameless(1), by means clear(1), completely acquitted(1), completely free(1), completely free from punishment(1), deserted(1), free(4), free from punishment(1), go unpunished(8), immune(1), innocent(1), leave unpunished(2), means leave(4), by means leave unpunished(2), by means leave unpunished(2), purged(2), unpunished(1), without guilt(1).

5353. נְקוֹדָא Neqoda (667a); from the same as 5349; head of a family of Nethinim:— Nekoda(4).

5354. נָקַט naqat (876c); the same as 6962a, q.v.

5355a. נָקִי naqi (667c); from 5352; *clean, free from, exempt:*— clean(1), exempt(1), free(5), free of obligation(1), go unpunished(1), guiltless(1), innocent(31).

5355b. נָקִיא naqi (667d); from 5352; *innocency:*— innocent(2).

5356. נִקָּיוֹן niqqayon or

נִקָּיֹן niqqayon (667d); from 5352; *innocency:*— cleanness(1), innocence(4).

5357. נָקִיק naqiq (669b); from an unused word; *cleft* (of a rock):— clefts(1), crevice(1), ledges(1).

5358. נָקַם naqam (667d); a prim. root; *to avenge, take vengeance:*— avenge(9), avenged(5), avenger(2), avenging(2), exact(1), execute(1), punished(1), revengeful(1), take(2), take revenge(1), take vengeance(4), taken(1), takes vengeance(1), taking(1), vengeance shall be taken(1), vengeance will be taken(1).

5359. נָקָם naqam (668b); from 5358; *vengeance:*— vengeance(16).

5360. נְקָמָה neqamah (668c); fem. of 5359; *vengeance:*— avenged(1), full vengeance(2), revenge(2), vengeance(22).

5361. נָקַע naqa (668c); a prim. root; *to be alienated* or *estranged:*— alienated(2), become disgusted(1).

5362a. נָקַף naqaph (668d); a prim. root; *to strike off:*— cut down(1), destroyed(1).

5362b. נָקַף naqaph (668d); a prim. root; *to go around:*— circling(2), closed around(1), completed cycle(1), encircling(1), encompassed(3), go around(1), gone around(1), observe on schedule(1), round(1), surround(1), surround*(2), surrounded(1), surrounding(1).

5363. נֹקֶף noqeph (668d); from 5362a; *a striking off:*— shaking(2).

5364. נִקְפָּה niqpah (669a); from 5362b; *an encircling rope:*— rope(1).

5365. נָקַר naqar (669b); a prim. root; *to bore, pick, dig:*— dug(1), gouge(1), gouged(1), pick(1), pierces(1), put(1).

5366. נְקָרָה neqarah (669b); from 5365; *a hole, crevice:*— caverns(1), cleft(1).

5367. נָקַשׁ naqash (669b); a prim. root; *to knock, strike, hit, strike* or *bring down:*— ensnared(1), lay snares(1), laying a snare(1), seize(1), snared(1).

5368. נְקַשׁ neqash (1103c); (Ara.) corr. to 5367; *to knock:*— knocking(1).

5369. נֵר Ner (633a); from the same as 5216; father of Abner, also the father of Kish:— Ner(16).

5370. נֵרְגַּל Nergal (669c); of for. or.; a heathen god:— Nergal(1).

5371. נֵרְגַל שַׁרְאֶצֶר Nergal Sharetser (669c); from 5370 and 8272; a Bab. court official:— Nergal-sar-ezer(3).

5372. נִרְגָּן nirgan (920d); the same as 7279, q.v.

5373. נֵרְדְּ nerd (669d); of for. or.; *nard:*— nard(1), nard plants(1), perfume(1).

5374. נֵרִיָּה Neriyyah or

נֵרִיָּהוּ Neriyyahu (633a); from 5216 and 3050; "lamp of Yah," father of Baruch:— Neraiah(1), Neriah(9).

5375. נָשָׂא nasa or

נָסָה nasah (669d); a prim. root; *to lift, carry, take:*— accept*(3), accepted*(1), advanced(1), anything been taken(1), arises(1), assisted(1), bear(61), bearer(17), bearers(2), bearing(4), bears(1), become proud(2), bore(9), borne(5), bring(10), bring forth(1), bringing(7), brought(5), carried(45), carries(6), carry(45), carry away(1), carry off(2), carrying(20), contain(1), continued*(1), count*(1), desire(1), desire*(2), direct(1), ease(1), endure(4), endured(1), ever forgive(1), exalt(2), exalted(9), exalting(2), favor*(1), fetch(1), forgave(2), forget(1), forgive(8), forgiven(3), forgives(1), forgiving(2), found(3), grant(1), granted(1), have(1), high(1), honor*(1), honorable*(3), incur(2), laid(2), lift(64), lifted(67), lifts(4), load(2), loaded(3), lofty(1), longing*(1), looked*(2), make(1), married(1), must be carried(1), obtained(1), offer(3), pardon(2), pardons(1), partial*(2), partiality*(8), pick(1), picked(1), picks(3), promoted(1), protest(1), put(1), raise(5), raised(13), receive(2), receive*(2), receives(1), regard(1), released*(1), respected*(1), rise(2), rose(5), sets(1), shield-bearer*(1), shield-carrier*(1), show(5), showed(1), showing(1), shows(1), sing(1), spare(2), stirred(3), suffer(2), supplied(1), support(1), supported(1), sustain(2), swore*(12), sworn*(2), take(49), take away(1), taken(7), takes(3), took(37), towers(1), transporters*(1), upheaved(1), wearing(1), went(1), withhold(1), wore(1), worked(1).

5376. נְשָׂא nesa (1103c); (Ara.) corr. to 5375; *to lift, take, carry:*— carried(1), risen(1), take(1).

5377. נָשָׁא nasha (673d); a prim. root; *to lend on interest, be a creditor:*— debt(1), debtor(1), deceive(1), exacting(1), made(2).

5378. נָשָׁא nasha (674a); a prim. root; *to beguile, deceive:*— come deceitfully(1), deceive(8), deceived(3), deluded(1), utterly deceived(1).

5379. נִשֵּׂאת nisseth (669d, 672a); the same as 5375, q.v.

5380. נָשַׁב nashab (674b); a prim. root; *to blow:*— blow(1), blows(1), drove away(1).

5381. נָשַׂג nasag (673b); a prim. root; *to reach, overtake:*— able*(1), afford*(2), attained(1), becomes sufficient(1), caught(1), find(1), insufficient(2), last until(2), limited(1), means*(1), obtain(1), overtake(17), overtaken(2), overtakes(1), overtook(6), prospers(1), put(1), reach(1), reaches(1), recovers(1), remove(1), surely overtake(1), within(2).

5382. נָשָׁה nashah (674c); a prim. root; *to forget:*— forget(2), forgets(1), forgotten(2), surely forget(1).

5383. נָשָׁה nashah (674b); a prim. root; *to lend, become a creditor:*— creditor(4), creditors(1), exacting(1), lending(1), lent(2), loaned(1), make(1), make the loan(1).

5384. נָשֶׁה nasheh (674d); from 5382; *a vein* (or *nerve*) *in the thigh:*— hip(2).

5385. נְשׂוּאָה nesuah or

נְשֻׂאָה nesuah (672b); from 5375; *what is borne about:*— things that you carry(1).

5386. נְשִׁי neshi (674c); from 5383; *a debt:*— debt(1).

5387a. נָשִׂיא nasi or

נָשִׂא nasi (672b); from 5375; *one lifted up, a chief, prince:*— chief(2), chiefs(2), leader(43), leaders(32), officials(1), prince(30), prince's(1), princes(10), ruler(2), rulers(3).

5387b. נָשִׂיא nasi (672c); from 5375; *rising mist, vapor:*— clouds(3), vapors(1).

5388. נְשִׁיָּה neshiyyah (674d); from 5382; *forgetfulness, oblivion:*— forgetfulness(1).

5389. נָשִׁין nashin (1081d); (Ara.) corr. to pl. of 802; *wives:*— wives(1).

5390. נְשִׁיקָה neshiqah (676c); from 5401a; *a kiss:*— kisses(2).

5391a. נָשַׁךְ nashak (675a); a prim. root; *to bite:*— bit(2), bite(4), bites(4), bitten(1), creditors(1).

5391b. נָשַׁךְ nashak (675b); denom. vb. from 5392; *to pay* or *give interest:*— charge interest(3), loaned at interest(1).

5392. נֶשֶׁךְ neshek (675b); from 5391a; *interest, usury:*— interest(10).

5393. נִשְׁכָּה nishkah (675b); from 5391a; *a chamber:*— chambers(1), quarters(1), room(1).

5394. נָשַׁל nashal (675b); a prim. root; *to slip* or *drop off, draw off, clear away:*— clear away(1), cleared(1), clears away(1), drop off(1), remove(2), slips off(1).

5395. נָשַׁם nasham (675c); a prim. root; *to pant:*— gasp(1).

5396. נִשְׁמָה nishmah (1103c); (Ara.) corr. to 5397; *breath:*— life-breath(1).

5397. נְשָׁמָה neshamah (675c); from 5395; *breath:*— blast(2), breath(15), breathes(1), life(1), persons alive(1), spirit(2), who breathed(3).

5398. נָשַׁף nashaph (676a); a prim. root; *to blow:*— blew(1), blows(1).

5399. נֶשֶׁף nesheph (676a); from 5398; *twilight:*— dawn(2), dusky(1), evening(1), twilight(8).

5400. נָשַׂק nasaq (969c); the same as 8026b, q.v.

5401a. נָשַׁק nashaq (676b); a prim. root; *to kiss:*— do homage(2), kiss(8), kissed(18), kisses(2), threw a kiss(1), touching(1).

5401b. נָשַׁק nashaq (676c); a prim. root; prob. *to handle* or *be equipped with:*— armed(1), equipped(2).

5402. נֶשֶׁק nesheq or

נֵשֶׁק nesheq (676d); from 5401b; *equipment, weapons:*— armory(1), battle(1), weapon(1), weapons(7).

5403. נְשַׁר neshar (1103c); (Ara.) corr. to 5404; *an eagle:*— eagle(1), eagles'(1).

5404. נֶשֶׁר nesher (676d); a prim. root; *an eagle:*— eagle(19), eagle's(1), eagles(5), eagles'(1).

5405. נָשַׁת nashath (677a); a prim. root; *to be dry* or *parched:*— dry(1), exhausted(1), parched(1).

5406. נִשְׁתְּוָן nishtevan (677a); of for. or.; *a letter:*— decree(1), letter(1).

5407. נִשְׁתְּוָן nishtevan (1103c); (Ara.) corr. to 5406; *a letter:*— document(2), written reply(1).

5408. נָתַח nathach (677c); a prim. root; *to cut up, cut in pieces, divide by joints:*— cut(6), cut pieces(3).

5409. נֵתַח nethach (677c); from 5408; *a piece* (of a divided carcass):— piece(3), pieces(10).

5410a. נָתִיב nathib (677a); from an unused word; *path, pathway:*— path(4), pathway*(1), wake(1).

5410b. נְתִיבָה nethibah (677b); from the same as 5410a; *path, pathway:*— bypaths(1), path(5), paths(12), streets(1), travelers*(1).

5411. נְתִינִים nethinim (682a); from 5414; *temple servants:*— temple servants(16).

5412. נְתִינִין Nethinin (1103c); (Ara.) corr. to 5411; temple servants in Isr.:— Nethinim(1).

5413. נָתַךְ nathak (677c); a prim. root; *to pour forth, be poured out:*— emptied(2), melt(2), melted(3), pour(2), poured(11), rained(1).

5414. נָתַן nathan (678a); a prim. root; *to give, put, set:*— abandon(1), add(1), added(1), allow(14), allowed(3), applied(1), appoint(5), appointed(15), apportion(1), appropriated(1), ascribe(2), ascribed(2), assigned(5), bear(1), bestow(1), bestowed(2), blame*(1), bring(10), bring down(2), bringing(2), brings(2), brought(3), cast(3), cause(2), causes(1), certainly be given(1), certainly give(1), comes(1), commit(1), committed(1), conferred(1), consider(1), consign(1), contribute(1), cried(1), dedicated(1), defeat(1), deliver(26), delivered(26), delivers(3), designate(1), designated(1), direct(1), display(1), displayed(1), distribute(2), divide(1), enabled(1), entrust*(1), entrusted(2), entrusted*(1), establish(1), established(1), exchange(1), execute(1), executes(2), fasten(2), fastened(1), find(1), furnishing(1), gave(293), generously give(1), gift(1), give(491), given(259), gives(67), giving(37), grant(18), granted(11), growl*(1), had(3), hand over(2), hang(3), has had(1), have(2), have*(1), heap(1), held(1), hung(1), impose(1), imposed(3), indeed deliver(1), indeed give(1), inflict(2), inflicted(1), injured*(1), injures*(1), inserted(1), instilled(4), issued(5), kept giving(1), laid(5), lay(12), laying(1), lays(1), left(2), left hanging(1), lend(1), lends(1), let(7), lies*(1), lift(5), lifts(1), made(43), made turn(3), make(66), makes(3), making(3), marry off(1), offer(2), offered(4), Oh*(13), open*(1), over(1), paid(7), pay(6), performed(1), permit(2), pierce(1), pitch(1), place(13), placed(19), planted(1), pledged(2), pledged*(1), present(2), presented(1), prevent*(2), produces(1), provide(1), provided(2), provides(1), put(192), puts(4), putting(2), raised(2), reduces(1), render(2), repay(1), Requite(2), requited(1), roared loudly*(1), roared*(1), send(4), sends(1), sent(4), set(74), setting(5), show(2), showed(1), slander*(1), sounds forth(1), sparkles*(1), speaks forth(1), spend(1), spread(1), strike(1), submitted*(1), supplies(1), surely be given(1), surely give(2), take(2), taken(1), takes(1), to pay(1), took(1), traded(1), turned(6), used(1), utter(1), uttered(2), uttered forth(1), utters(5), wept*(1), wholly given(2), work(1), would*(7), yield(13), yield*(1), yielded(2), yields(2), yours(1).

5415. נְתַן nethan (1103d); (Ara.) corr. to 5414; *to give:*— bestows(3), give(1), pay(1), provide(2).

5416. נָתָן Nathan (681d); from 5414; the name of a number of Isr.:— Nathan(41).

5417. נְתַנְאֵל Nethanel (682a); from 5414 and 410; "given of God," the name of a number of Isr.:— Nethanel(14).

5418. נְתַנְיָה Nethanyah or

נְתַנְיָהוּ Nethanyahu (682b); from 5414 and 3050; "given of Yah," the name of several Isr.:— Nethaniah(20).

5419. נְתַן־מֶלֶךְ Nethan-melek (682a); from 5414 and 4428; "given of a king," a leader in Judah:— Nathan-melech(1).

5420. נָתַס nathas (683a); a prim. root; *to tear* or *break down:*— break(1).

5421. נָתַע natha (683a); a prim. root; *to break, break down,* or *out:*— broken(1).

5422. נָתַץ nathats (683a); a prim. root; *to pull down, break down:*— break(1), broke down(15), broken(1), broken down(2), demolish(1), destroy(1), pull down(1), pulled down(2), razed(1), smashed(1), tear down(6), tore down(6), torn down(4).

5423. נָתַק nathaq (683c); a prim. root; *to pull, draw,* or *tear away, apart,* or *off:*— break(1), broke apart(1), broken(2), burst(1), drag off(1), draw away(1), drawn away(3), lifted(1), pull(1), pull off(1), separated(1), snapped(2), snaps(1), tear(1), tear apart(1), tear off(2), tore off(1), torn(2), torn apart(3).

5424. נֶתֶק netheq (683d); from 5423; *scab:*— scale(13), scaly(1).

5425a. נָתַר nathar (684a); a prim. root; *to spring* or *start up:*— jump(1), leaps(1), startled(1).

5425b. נָתַר nathar (684a); a prim. root; *to be free* or *loose:*— loose(1), released(1), sets(2), undo(1).

5426. נְתַר nethar (1103d); (Ara.) corr. to 5425b; *to strip off:*— strip off(1).

5427. נֶתֶר nether (684a); from 5425b; *natron* or *carbonate of soda:*— lye(1), soda(1).

5428. נָתַשׁ nathash (684c); a prim. root; *to pull* or *pluck up, root out:*— pluck(3), plucked(2), root(1), rooted(1), snatched away(1), uproot(9), uprooted(4).

ס

5429. סְאָה seah (684b); of unc. der.; *seah* (a measure of flour or grain):— measure(3), measures(6).

5430. סְאוֹן seon (684b); prob. of for. or.; *sandal, boot* (of a soldier):— boot(1).

5431. סָאַן saan (684d); denom. vb. from 5430; *to tread, tramp:*— booted warrior(1), guarded(1).

5432. סַאסְאָה sese (684d); a prim. root; *to drive away:*— banishing(1).

5433a. סָבָא saba (684d); a prim. root; *to imbibe, drink largely:*— drink heavily(1), drunkard(1), drunken(1), heavy drinker(1), heavy drinkers(1).

5433b. סָבָא saba (685a); from 5433a; *drunkard:*— drunkards(1).

5434. סְבָא Seba (685b); from 5433a; son of Cush, also his desc. and their land:— Seba(4).

5435. סֹבֶא sobe (685a); from 5433a; *a drink, liquor:*— drink(2), liquor(1).

5436. סְבָאִים Sebaim (685b); from 5434; inhab. of Seba:— Sabeans(1).

5437. סָבַב sabab (685b); a prim. root; *to turn about, go around, surround:*— about(2), all around(1), around(2), around*(1), away*(1), bring back(1), bring...over(1), brought(2), brought around(2), brought about(1), change(1), changed(5), circle around(2), circled(2), circled around(1), circling(1), circuit(1), circumference*(3), come around(1), completely*(1), directed(1), driven(1), encircled(2), encircling(1), encompass(2), engulfed(2), escaped(1), faced*(2), flows around(2), form(1), gathered around(2), go about(3), go around(4), led around(2), made a circuit(1), make the rounds(2), march around(3), marched around(3), measured the circumference(1), opened(1), removed(2), returned(1), set(3), set*(1), sit(1), surround(7), surrounded(18), surrounding(2), surrounds(2), swinging(1), swirling(1), taken around(1), transferred(2), turn(13), turn around(2), turn aside(1), turn away(2), turn back(1), turned(12), turned about(4), turned around(2), turned aside(2), turned away(3), turned over(1), turned round(1), turning(5), turns(1), walk about(2), went about(1), went throughout(2).

5438. סִבָּה sibbah (686d); from 5437; *a turn* (of affairs):— turn(1).

5439. סָבִיב sabib or

סְבִיבָה sebibah (686d); from 5437; *circuit, round about:*— about(1), all(1), all around(68), all around about(1), all sides(3), all*(2), altogether*(1), around(114), around about(1), around*(1), circular courses(1), circumference*(2), completely(1), confines(1), encompassing(1), entirely(1), environs(5), every direction(2), every side(34), form(2), one surrounding(1), places around(1), round about(29), surround(10), surround*(2), surrounded(1), surrounding(17), surrounding area(1), surrounds(2), throughout(1).

5440. סָבַךְ sabak (687c); a prim. root; *to interweave:*— tangled(1), wrap around(1).

5441. סְבֹךְ sebok (687c); from 5440; *a thicket:*— forest(1), thicket(1).

5442. סְבָךְ sebak (687c); from 5440; *a thicket:*— thicket(1), thickets(2).

5443. סַבְּכָא sabbeka or

שַׂבְּכָא sabbeka (1113c); (Ara.) corr. to 5440; *trigon* (a musical instrument):— trigon(4).

5444. סִבְּכַי Sibbekay (687c); from 5440; one of David's captains:— Sibbecai(4).

5445. סָבַל sabal (687d); a prim. root; *to bear* (a heavy load):— bear(5), borne(1), carried(1), carry(1), drags(1).

5446. סְבַל sebal (1103d); (Ara.) corr. to 5445; *to bear, carry* (a load):— retained(1).

5447. סֵבֶל sebel (687d); from 5445; *a load, burden:*— burden(1), burdens(1), forced labor(1).

5448. סֹבֶל sobel or

סֻבָּל subbal (687d); from 5445; *a burden:*— burden(3).

5449. סַבָּל sabbal (688a); from 5445; *burden bearer:*— burden bearers(2), carry loads(2), transporters*(1).

5450. סִבְלָה siblah (688a); from 5445; *a burden:*— burdens(2), hard labor(1), hard labors(1), labors(2).

5451. סִבֹּלֶת sibboleth (688a); from 5445; prob. *an ear* (of wheat, etc.):— sibboleth(1).

5452. סְבַר sebar (1104a); (Ara.) a prim. root; *to think, intend:*— intend(1).

5453. סִבְרַיִם Sibrayim (688a); of for. or.; a city in Aram (Syria):— Sibraim(1).

5454. סַבְתָּא Sabta or

סַבְתָּה Sabtah (688b); prob. of for. or.; a son of Cush, also the territory settled by his desc.:— Sabta(1), Sabtah(1).

5455. סַבְתְּכָא Sabteka (688b); prob. of for. or.; a son of Cush, also the territory settled by his desc.:— Sabteca(2).

5456. סָגַד sagad (688b); a prim. root; *to prostrate oneself* (in worship):— bow down(1), fall down(1), falls down(2).

5457. סְגִד segid (1104a); (Ara.) corr. to 5456; *to do homage:*— did homage(1), worship(10), worshiped(1).

5458. סְגוֹר segor (689c); from 5462; *an enclosure, encasement:*— chests*(1), gold(1).

5459. סְגֻלָּה segullah (688c); from an unused word; *possession, property:*— possession(5), treasure(2), treasured possession(1).

5460. סְגַן segan (1104a); (Ara.) corr. to 5461; *a prefect:*— prefect(1), prefects(4).

5461. סָגָן sagan (688c); of for. or.; *a prefect, ruler:*— officials(11), prefects(3), rulers(3).

5462. סָגַר sagar (688d); a prim. root; *to shut, close:*— battle-axe(1), close(2), closed(9), confined(1), deliver(5), delivered(6), gave over(2), given(1), given over(1), hand over(1), hands over(1), imprison(1), imprisons(1), isolate(7), locked(1), pure(9), quarantine(3), quarantined(1), shut(31), shuts(2), surrender(4), tightly shut(1).

5463. סְגַר segar (1104a); (Ara.) corr. to 5462; *to shut:*— shut(1).

5464. סַגְרִיר sagrir (690a); from 5462; *steady* or *persistent rain:*— steady rain(1).

5465. סַד sad (690a); prob. of for. or.; *stocks* (for securing feet of prisoners):— stocks(2).

5466. סָדִין sadin (690b); perh. of for. or.; *linen garment:*— linen garments(1), linen wraps(2), undergarments(1).

5467. סְדֹם Sedom (690a); of unc. der.; a Canaanite city near the Dead Sea:— Sodom(39).

5468. סֶדֶר seder (690b); from an unused word; *arrangement, order:*— order(1).

5469. סַהַר sahar (690c); from an unused word; *roundness:*— round(1).

5470. סֹהַר sohar (690c); from the same as 5469; perh. *roundness:*— jail*(5), jailer*(3).

5471. סוֹא So (690c); of for. or.; an Eg. king:— so(1).

5472. סוּג sug (690d); a prim. root; *to move away, backslide:*— backslider(1), drawing(1), move(4), moves(1), remove(1), turn(2), turn back(1), turned(8), turned aside(1), turned back(3), turning away(1).

5473. סוּג sug (691b); a prim. root; *to fence about:*— carefully fence(1), fenced about(1).

5474. סוּגַר sugar (689c); from 5462; *a cage, prison:*— cage(1).

5475. סוֹד sod (691c); from an unused word; *council, counsel:*— circle(1), company(1), consultation(1), council(5), fellowship(1), friendship(1), gathering(1), intimate(1), plans(1), secret(2), secret counsel(3), secrets(2).

5476. סוֹדִי Sodi (691d); from the same as 5475; a Zebulunite:— Sodi(1).

5477. סוּחַ Suach (691d); from the same as 5478; an Asherite:— Suah(1).

5478. סוּחָה suchah (691d); of unc. der.; *offal:*— refuse(1).

5479. סוֹטַי Sotay (691d); of unc. der.; an Isr.:— Sotai(2).

5480a. סוּךְ suk (691d); a prim. root; *to pour* (in anointing), *anoint:*— anoint(4), anointed(3), poured(1), use any ointment(1).

5480b. סוּךְ suk (692a); a prim. root; *to hedge* or *fence about, shut in:*— enclosed(1), hedged(1).

5481. סוּמְפּוֹנְיָה sumponeyah or

סוּמְפֹּנְיָה **sumponeyah** or

סִיפֹּנְיָא **siphoneya** (1104a); (Ara.) of for. or.; *a bagpipe:*— bagpipe(4).

5482a. סְוֵנֵה Seveneh or

סְוֵנָה **Sevenah** or

סְוֵן **Seven** (692b); of for. or.; a city on the S. border of Eg.:— Syene(2).

5482b. סְוֵנִים Sevenim (692b); another reading for 5515, q.v.

5483a. סוּס sus or

סִס **sus** (692b); from the same as 5483b; *a swallow, swift* (type of bird):— swallow(1), swift(1).

5483b. סוּס sus (692b); prob. of for. or.; *a horse:*— horse(32), horse's(1), horseback(1), horseman*(2), horses(100), horses'(2).

5484. סוּסָה susah (692d); from the same as 5483b; *a mare:*— mare(1).

5485. סוּסִי Susi (692d); from the same as 5483b; a Manassite:— Susi(1).

5486. סוּף suph (692d); a prim. root; *to come to an end, cease:*— come to an end(2), completely remove(1), fade(1), remove(2), surely snatch(1), surely snatch away(1), swept away(1).

5487. סוּף suph (1104b); (Ara.) corr. to 5486; *to be fulfilled:*— fulfilled(1), put an end(1).

5488. סוּף suph (693a); prob. of for. or.; *reeds, rushes:*— red*(24), reeds(2), rushes(1), weeds(1).

5489. סוּף Suph (693b); from 5486; "reed," a place near which the law was given:— Suph(1).

5490. סוֹף soph (693a); from 5486; *an end:*— conclusion*(1), end(3), rear(1).

5491. סוֹף soph (1104b); (Ara.) corr. to 5490; *an end:*— end(2), ended(1), forever(2).

5492a. סוּפָה suphah (693a); from 5486; *a storm wind:*— gale(1), storm(3), tempest(2), whirlwind(8), windstorms(1).

5492b. סוּפָה Suphah (693b); from 5486; a place E. of the Jordan:— Suphah(1).

5493. סוּר sur or

שׂוּר **sur** (693b); a prim. root; *to turn aside:*— abolished(1), avoid(1), beheaded*(1), cut off(1), degenerate(1), depart(45), departed(7), deposed(1), deprives(2), do away(1), escape(1), get(1), go away(1), gone(1), keep away(1), keeps away(1), lacks(1), leave*(2), left(2), move(1), pardoning(1), pass away(1), past(1), put away(12), relieved(1), remove(45), removed(43), removing(1), retract(1), return(1), separated(1), strip away(1), swerve(1), take(2), take away(7), take off(1), taken away(14), takes away(1), took(3), took away(2), took off(2), turn(8), turn aside(25), turn away(12), turn...aside(1), turned(2), turned aside(24), turned away(3), turning aside(1), turning away(3), turns aside(1), turns away(3), undone*(1), wanderer(1), withdrawn(1).

5494. סוּר sur (694c); the same as 5493, q.v.

5495. סוּר Sur (694c); from 5493; "a turning aside," a gate of the temple:— Sur(1).

5496. סוּת suth (694c); a prim. root; *to incite, allure, instigate:*— diverted(1), entice(2), enticed(1), incited(3), inciting(1), induced(1), mislead(2), misleading(1), misleads(1), misled(1), moved(1), persuaded(2), stirred(1).

5497. סוּת suth (691d); from an unused word; *vesture:*— robes(1).

5498. סָחַב sachab (694d); a prim. root; *to drag:*— drag(2), drag off(2), dragged(1).

5499. סְחָבָה sechabah (695a); from 5498; *a rag:*— clothes(2).

5500. סָחָה sachah (695a); a prim. root; *to scrape:*— scrape(1).

5501a. סְחִי sechi (695a); from 5500; *offscouring:*— offscouring(1).

5501b. סָחִישׁ sachish (695a); of unc. der.; *something that grows by itself* (a kind of grain):— what springs(2).

5502. סָחַף sachaph (695a); a prim. root; *prostrate:*— become prostrate(1), driving(1).

5503. סָחַר sachar (695b); a prim. root; *to go around* or *about, travel about:*— commercial(1), customer(3), customers(2), merchant(1), merchants(6), roving about(1), throbs(1), trade(3), traders(2), trafficked(1).

5504. סַחַר sachar (695c); from 5503; *commerce, gain:*— gain(3), market(1), merchandise(1), profit(2).

5505. סָחָר sachar (695c); the same as 5504, q.v.

5506. סְחֹרָה sechorah (695c); from 5503; *merchandise:*— market(1).

5507. סֹחֵרָה socherah (695c); from 5503; *a buckler:*— bulwark(1).

5508. סֹחֶרֶת sochereth (695c); from 5503; *a stone* (used in paving):— precious stones(1).

5509. סִיג sig or

סוּג **sug** (691a); from 5472; *a moving back* or *away, dross:*— dross(8), gone aside(1).

5510. סִיוָן Sivan (695d); of for. or.; third month of the Jewish year:— Sivan(1).

5511. סִיחוֹן Sichon or

סִיחֹן **Sichon** (695d); of unc. der.; a king of the Amorites:— Sihon(37).

5512a. סִין Sin (695d); of for. or.; E. frontier city of Eg.:— Sin(6).

5512b. סִין Sin (695d); of for. or.; wilderness between Elim and Sinai.

5513. סִינִי Sini (696b); of unc. der.; a Canaanite people:— Sinite(1), Sinites(1).

5514. סִינַי Sinay (696a); prob. from the same as 5512a; the mountain where the law was given:— Sinai(35).

5515. סִינִים Sinim (696b); of unc.der.; inhab. of unc. location:— Sinim(1).

5516. סִיסְרָא Sisera (696b); of unc. der.; a general of the king of Hazor, also the father of some returning exiles:— Sisera(21).

5517. סִיעָא Sia or

סִיעֲהָא **Siaha** (696b); of unc. der.; father of some returning exiles:— Sia(1), Siaha(1).

5518a. סִיר sir or

סִירָה **sirah** or

סִרָה **sirah** (696c); prob. of for. or.; *a pot:*— cooking pot(1), cooking pots(1), pails(5), pot(14), pots(6).

5518b. סִיר sir (696c); from the same as 5518a; *a thorn, hook:*— hooks(1), thorn bushes(1), thorns(3).

5519. סָךְ sak (697c); from 5526b; *a throng:*— throng(1).

5520. סֹךְ sok (697c); from 5526b; *a thicket, covert, lair:*— hiding place(1), lair(1), tabernacle(2).

5521. סֻכָּה sukkah (697c); from 5526b; *a thicket, booth:*— booth(1), Booths(9), booths(8), canopies(1), canopy(1), hut(1), lair(1), pavilion(1), shelter(4), temporary shelters(3).

5522. סִכּוּת Sikkuth (696d); prob. of for. or.; a for. god:— Sikkuth(1).

5523. **סֻכּוֹת** **Sukkoth** or **סֻכֹּת** **Sukkoth** (697d); from 5526b; a city E. of the Jordan, also a place in Eg.:— Succoth(18).

5524. **סֻכּוֹת בְּנוֹת** **Sukkoth Benoth** (696d); from 5523 and 1323; "booths of daughters," an Assyr.-Bab. god:— Succoth-benoth(1).

5525. **סֻכִּיִּים** **Sukkiyyim** (696d); from an unused name, people in the army of Shishak:— Sukkiim(1).

5526a. **סָכַךְ** **sakak** or **שָׂכַךְ** **sakak** (696d); a prim. root; *to overshadow, screen, cover:*— cover(2), covered(4), covering(3), covers(1), incite(1), made a covering(1), relieve*(1), relieving*(1), screen(1), screened off(1), shelter(1), spurs(1).

5526b. **סָכַךְ** **sakak** (697b); a prim. root; *to weave together:*— knit together(1), wove(1).

5527a. **סֹכֵךְ** **sokek** (697d); from 5526b; *protector:*— mantelet(1).

5527b. **סְכָכָה** **Sekakah** (698a); from 5526b; a place in the wilderness of Judah:— Secacah(1).

5528. **סָכַל** **sakal** (698a); a prim. root; *to be foolish* or *a fool:*— acted foolishly(2), acted...foolishly(1), done*(1), done...foolishly(1), foolishly(1), foolishness(2), make(1), played the fool(1).

5529. **סֶכֶל** **sekel** (698a); from 5528; *folly:*— folly(1).

5530. **סָכָל** **sakal** (698a); from 5528; *a fool:*— fool(5), foolish(1), stupid(1).

5531. **סִכְלוּת** **sikluth** or **שִׂכְלוּת** **sikluth** (698a); from 5528; *folly:*— folly(5), foolishness(1).

5532a. **סָכַן** **sakan** (698b); a prim. root; *to be of use* or *service, benefit:*— advantage(1), ever been accustomed(1), intimately acquainted(1), nurse(2), profits(1), steward(1), use(1), useful(1), useless*(1), yield(1).

5532b. **סָכַן** **sakan** (698c); a prim. root; *to be poor:*— impoverished(1).

5533. **סָכַן** **sakan** (698b); a prim. root; *to incur danger:*— endangered(1).

5534a. **סָכַר** **sakar** (698c); a prim. root; *to shut up, stop up:*— closed(1), deliver(1), stopped(1).

5534b. **סָכַר** **sakar** (698d); a prim. root; *to hire:*— hired(1).

5535. **סָכַת** **sakath** (698d); a prim. root; *to be silent:*— silent(1).

5536. **סַל** **sal** (700d); from an unused word; *basket:*— basket(13), baskets(2).

5537. **סָלָא** **sala** (698d); a prim. root; *to weigh:*— weighed(1).

5538. **סִלָּא** **Silla** (698d); of unc. der.; a place in Jer.:— Silla(1).

5539. **סָלַד** **salad** (698d); a prim. root; *to spring:*— rejoice(1).

5540. **סֶלֶד** **Seled** (699a); from 5539; a man in Judah:— Seled(2).

5541a. **סָלָה** **salah** (699a); a prim. root; *to make light of, toss aside:*— rejected(2).

5541b. **סָלָה** **salah** (699a); a prim. root; *to weigh, balance:*— valued(2).

5542. **סֶלָה** **selah** (699d); from 5549; *to lift up, exalt:*— Selah(74).

5543a. **סַלּוּ** **Sallu** (699a); from 5541b; an Isr. priest:— Sallu(1).

5543b. **סַלּוּא** **Sallu** (699a); from 5541b; a Benjamite:— Sallu(2).

5543c. **סָלוּא** **Salu** (699a); from 5541b; a Simeonite:— Salu(1).

5544. **סִלּוֹן** **sillon** or **סַלּוֹן** **sallon** (699b); of unc. der.; *a briar:*— brier(1), thorns(1).

5545. **סָלַח** **salach** (699b); a prim. root; *to forgive, pardon:*— forgive(19), forgiven(13), pardon(12), pardoned(2), pardons(1).

5546a. **סַלָּח** **sallach** (699c); from 5545; *ready to forgive, forgiving:*— ready to forgive(1).

5546b. **סַלָּי** **Sallay** (699b); from 5541b; two Isr.:— Sallai(2).

5547. **סְלִיחָה** **selichah** (699c); from 5545; *forgiveness:*— forgiveness(3).

5548. **סַלְכָה** **Salkah** (699c); of unc. der.; a city on the E. border of Bashan:— Salecah(4).

5549. **סָלַל** **salal** (699c); a prim. root; *to lift up, cast up:*— build(6), exalt(1), highway(1), highway*(1), lift(1), pile(1), prize(1).

5550. **סֹלְלָה** **solelah** or **סוֹלְלָה** **solelah** (700c); from 5549; *a mound:*— ramp(2), ramps(2), siege ramp(4), siege ramps(2).

5551. **סֻלָּם** **sullam** (700c); from 5549; *a ladder:*— ladder(1).

5552. **סַלְסִלָּה** **salsillah** (700d); from the same as 5536; prob. *a branch:*— branches(1).

5553. **סֶלַע** **sela** (700d); from an unused word; *a crag, cliff:*— cliff(4), cliffs(4), crag(2), crags(3), mountain*(1), Rock(1), rock(39), rocks(4), rocky(1), Sela(1).

5554. **סֶלַע** **Sela** (701a); from the same as 5553; a city in Edom:— Sela(3).

5555. **סֶלַע הַמַּחְלְקוֹת** **Sela Hammachleqoth** (700d); see 5553 and 4256.

5556. **סָלְעָם** **solam** (701b); prob. from the same as 5553; *a locust:*— devastating locust(1).

5557. **סָלַף** **salaph** (701b); a prim. root; *to twist, pervert, overturn:*— overthrows(2), perverts(1), ruins(1), subverts(2), turning(1).

5558. **סֶלֶף** **seleph** (701b); from 5557; *crookedness, crooked dealing:*— crookedness(1), perversion(1).

5559a. **סָלַק** **saleq** (701b); of for. or.; *to ascend:*— ascend(1), carried(1).

5559b. **סְלִק** **seleq** (1104b); (Ara.) corr. to 5559a; *to come up:*— came(3), coming(1), taken(2), turned(1).

5560. **סֹלֶת** **soleth** (701c); of for. or.; *fine flour:*— fine(1), fine flour(51), fine...flour(1), flour*(1).

5561. **סַם** **sam** (702c); from an unused word; *spice* (used in incense):— fragrant(12), fragrant spices(1), spices(2), sweet(1).

5562. **סַמְגַּר נְבוֹ** **Samgar Nebo** (701c); of for. or.; a Bab. officer:— Samgar-nebu(1).

5563. **סְמָדַר** **semadar** (701d); of unc. der.; *blossom* (of the grape):— blossom(2), blossoms(1).

5564. **סָמַךְ** **samak** (701d); a prim. root; *to lean, lay, rest, support:*— braced(1), holds(1), laid(6), laid siege(1), lay(17), lean(1), leans(3), relied(1), rested(1), steadfast(1), support(1), sustain(3), sustained(2), sustainer(1), sustains(3), upheld(4), uphold(1).

5565. **סְמַכְיָהוּ** **Semakyahu** (702b); from 5564 and 3050; "Yah has sustained," a Korahite:— Semachiah(1).

5566. **סֶמֶל** **semel** or **סֵמֶל** **semel** (702b); of unc. der.; *an image, statue:*— figure(1), idol(4).

5567. **סָמַן** **saman** (702c); a prim. root; *appoint:*— place(1).

5568. **סָמַר** **samar** (702c); a prim. root; *to bristle up:*— bristled(1), trembles(1).

5569. **סָמָר** **samar** (702c); from 5568; *bristling, rough:*— bristly(1).

5570. **סְנָאָה** **Senaah** (702d); of unc. der.; a family of returning exiles:— Hassenaah(1), Senaah(2).

5571. **סַנְבַלַּט** **Sanballat** (702d); of for. or.; a Samaritan leader:— Sanballat(10).

5572. **סְנֶה** **seneh** (702d); of unc. der.; perh. *blackberry bush:*— bush(6).

5573. **סֶנֶּה** **Senneh** (702d); of unc. der.; a cliff in Isr.:— Seneh(1).

5574. **סְנוּאָה** **Senuah** or **סְנֻאָה** **Senuah** (703a); of unc. der.; an Isr.:— Hassenuah(2).

5575. **סַנְוֵרִים** **sanverim** (703a); of unc. der.; *sudden blindness:*— blindness(3).

5576. **סַנְחֵרִיב** **Sancherib** (703a); of for. or.; a king of Assyr.:— Sennacherib(13).

5577. **סַנְסִן** **sansin** (703b); of unc. der.; *fruit stalk* (of the date):— fruit stalks(1).

5578. **סַנְסַנָּה** **Sansannah** (703b); of unc. der.; a place in S. Judah:— Sansannah(1).

5579. **סְנַפִּיר** **senappir** (703b); of unc. der.; *a fin:*— fins(5).

5580. **סָס** **sas** (703b); of unc. der.; *a moth:*— grub(1).

5581. **סִסְמַי** **Sismay** (703b); of unc. der.; a man of Judah:— Sismai(2).

5582. **סָעַד** **saad** (703c); a prim. root; *to support, sustain, stay:*— hold(1), refresh(2), support(1), sustain(3), sustains(1), uphold(2), upholds(2).

5583. **סְעַד** **sead** (1104b); (Ara.) corr. to 5582; *to support, sustain:*— supporting(1).

5584. **סָעָה** **saah** (703c); a prim. root; *to rush* (of storm wind):— stormy(1).

5585. **סָעִיף** **saiph** (703d); from an unused word; *a cleft, branch:*— branches(2), cleft(2), clefts(2).

5586. **סָעַף** **saaph** (703d); denom. vb. from 5589a; *to lop off* (boughs):— lop off(1).

5587. **סָעִף** **saiph** or **שָׂעִף** **saiph** (704a); see 5589b.

5588. **סֵעֵף** **seeph** (704a); from the same as 5585; *divided, halfhearted:*— who are double-minded(1).

5589a. **סְעַפָּה** **seappah** (703d); from the same as 5585; *a bough, branch:*— boughs(2).

5589b. **סְעִפָּה** **seippah** (704a); from the same as 5585; *division, divided opinion:*— opinions(1).

5590. **סָעַר** **saar** (704a); a prim. root; *to storm, rage:*— blown away(1), enraged(1), scattered them with a storm wind(1), storm-tossed(1), stormed(1), stormier(1), stormy(1).

5591a. **סַעַר** **saar** (704b); from 5590; *a tempest:*— storm(4), tempest(4).

5591b. סְעָרָה searah (704b); from 5590; *a tempest, storm wind:*— storm(6), storm winds(1), stormy(2), tempest(2), violent(2), whirlwind(3).

5592a. סַף saph (706b); of unc. der.; *a basin, goblet:*— basin(2), basins(1), bowls(1), cup(1), cups(2).

5592b. סַף saph (706b); from the same as 5592a; *threshold, sill:*— door(1), doorkeeper*(1), doorkeepers*(4), gatekeepers*(1), temple(2), threshold(10), thresholds(6).

5593. סַף Saph (706c); from the same as 5592a; a Philistine (the same as 5598):— Saph(1).

5594. סָפַד saphad (704c); a prim. root; *to wail, lament:*— beat(1), lament(9), lamented(5), mourn(8), mourned(6), mourners(1), mourns(1).

5595. סָפָה saphah (705a); a prim. root; *to sweep* or *snatch away, catch up:*— add(2), captured(1), destroy(2), heap(1), perish(2), remove(1), snatched away(1), sweep away(2), swept away(6).

5596. סָפַח saphach or

שָׂפַח saphach (705b); a prim. root; *to join, attach to:*— assign(1), attach(1), attachment(1), gathered together(1), mix(1).

5597. סַפַּחַת sappachath (705c); of unc. der.; *an eruption, scab:*— scab(2).

5598. סִפַּי Sippay (706c); from the same as 5592a; a Philistine (the same as 5593):— Sippai(1).

5599a. סָפִיחַ saphiach (705b); from an unused word; *outpouring:*— torrents(1).

5599b. סָפִיחַ saphiach (705c); from the same as 5599a; *growth from spilled kernels:*— aftergrowth(2), what grows(2).

5600. סְפִינָה sephinah (706b); from 5603; *a vessel, ship:*— ship(1).

5601. סַפִּיר sappir (705d); of for. or.; *a sapphire:*— lapis lazuli(2), lapis lazuli*(1), sapphire(5), sapphires(3).

5602. סֵפֶל sephel (705d); of unc. der.; *a bowl:*— bowl(2).

5603. סָפַן saphan (706a); a prim. root; *to cover, cover in, panel:*— covered(1), paneled(3), paneling(1), reserved(1), treasures(1).

5604. סִפֻּן sippun (706a); from 5603; *a ceiling:*— ceiling*(1).

5605. סָפַף saphaph (706c); denom. vb. from 5592b; *to stand at* or *guard the threshold:*— stand at the threshold(1).

5606. סָפַק saphaq or

שָׂפַק saphaq (706c); a prim. root; *to slap, clap:*— clap(2), claps(1), smote(1), strike(2), strikes(1), struck together(1), wallow(1).

5607. סֶפֶק sepheq or

שֶׂפֶק sepheq (706d); from 5606; *handclapping, mockery:*— scoffing(1).

5608. סָפַר saphar (707d); denom. vb. from 5612; *to count, recount, relate:*— assigned(1), count(17), counted(6), counts(2), declare(6), declared(2), elapse(1), measuring(1), number(3), numbered(5), proclaim(1), recount(1), recounted(3), relate(3), related(9), relating(2), speak(1), state(1), surely(1), taken(1), taken account(1), talk(1), tell(23), telling(1), told(15), utter(1).

5609. סְפַר sephar (1104c); (Ara.) corr. to 5612; *a book:*— archives*(1), book(1), books(3).

5610. סְפָר sephar (708c); from the same as 5612; *enumeration, census:*— census(1).

5611. סְפָר Sephar (708c); from the same as 5612; a place in S. Arabia:— Sephar(1).

5612. סֵפֶר sepher (706d); prob. of for. or.; *a missive, document, writing, book:*— Book(47), book(79), books(2), certificate(3), deed(6), deeds(3), illiterate*(1), indictment(1), letter(14), letters(15), literate*(1), literature(2), read*(1), scroll(6), scroll*(3), writ(1).

5613a. סָפַר saphar (1104c); (Ara.) corr. to 5613b; *a secretary, scribe:*— scribe(6).

5613b. סֹפֵר sopher or

סוֹפֵר sopher (708b); from the same as 5612; *enumerator, secretary, scribe:*— learned(1), office(1), scribe(39), scribe's(2), scribes(5), secretaries(1), secretary(2), writer(1), writing(2).

5613c. סִפְרָה siphrah (707c); from the same as 5612; *a book:*— book(1).

5614. סְפָרַד Sephared (709b); of for. or.; the location of some exiles:— Sepharad(1).

5615. סְפֹרָה sephorah (708d); from the same as 5612; *a number:*— sum(1).

5616. סְפַרְוִי Sepharvi (709c); from 5617; inhab. of Sepharvaim:— Sepharvites(1).

5617. סְפַרְוַיִם Sepharvayim or

סְפָרִים Sepharim (709b); of for. or.; a city conquered by the king of Assyr.:— Sepharvaim(1), Sepharvaim(5).

5618. סֹפֶרֶת Sophereth (709a); from the same as 5612; father of some returning exiles:— Hassophereth(1), Sophereth(1).

5619. סָקַל saqal (709c); a prim. root; *to stone, put to death by stoning:*— cast(1), remove(1), removed stones(1), stone(7), stoned(6), stoning(1), surely be stoned(2), threw(1).

5620. סַר sar (711a); from 5637; *stubborn, resentful, sullen, implacable:*— sullen(3).

5621. סָרָב sarab (709d); of unc. der.; perh. *thorns:*— thistles(1).

5622. סַרְבַּל sarbal (1104c); (Ara.) prob. of for. or.; prob. *a mantle:*— trousers(2).

5623. סַרְגּוֹן Sargon (709d); of for. or.; a king of Assyr.:— Sargon(1).

5624. סֶרֶד Sered (710a); from an unused word; a son of Zebulun:— Sered(2).

5625. סַרְדִּי Sardi (710a); from 5624; desc. of Sered:— Seredites(1).

5626. סִרָה Sirah (92d); of unc. der.; the name of a cistern:— Sirah(1).

5627. סָרָה sarah (694c); from 5493; *turning aside, defection, apostasy, withdrawal:*— defected(1), rebellion(4), revolt(1), unceasing*(1), wrongdoing(1).

5628. סָרַח sarach (710a); a prim. root; *to go free, be unrestrained, overrun, exceed:*— decayed(1), flowing(1), lap(2), sprawl(1), sprawlers'(1), spreading(1).

5629. סֶרַח serach (710b); from 5628; *excess:*— overlapping part(1).

5630. סִרְיֹן siryon (710b); another spelling of 8302; *armor:*— scale-armor(2).

5631. סָרִיס saris or

סָרִס saris (710b); prob. of for. or.; *eunuch:*— court officers(1), court officials(1), eunuch(5), eunuchs(10), officer(5), officers(1), official(3), officials(16).

5632. סָרַךְ sarak (1104c); (Ara.) prob. of for. or.; *chief, overseer:*— commissioners(5).

5633a. סֶרֶן seren (710c); of for. or.; *tyrant, lord:*— lords(21).

5633b. סֶרֶן seren (710d); of unc. der.; *an axle:*— axles(1).

5634. סַרְעַפָּה sarappah (703d); from the same as 5585; *a bough:*— boughs(1).

5635. סָרַף saraph (976d); the same as 8313, q.v.

5636. סִרְפַּד sirpad (710d); of unc. der.; *nettle* (a desert plant):— nettle(1).

5637. סָרַר sarar (710d); a prim. root.; *stubborn* or *rebellious:*— rebellious(6), rebels(2), stubborn(8), stubbornly rebellious(1).

5638. סְתָו sethav (711a); of for. or.; *winter:*— winter(1).

5639. סְתוּר Sethur (712c); from 5641; an Asherite:— Sethur(1).

5640. סָתַם satham or

שָׂתַם satham (711a); a prim. root; *to stop up, shut up, keep close:*— closed(1), conceal(1), concealed(1), cut off(1), hidden part(1), keep the secret(1), secret(1), stop(1), stopped(5).

5641. סָתַר sathar (711b); a prim. root; *to hide, conceal:*— absent(1), conceal(3), concealed(4), cover(1), hid(11), hidden(16), hide(33), hides(4), hiding(3), placed(1), secret things(1), surely hide(1), undetected(1).

5642a. סְתַר sethar (1104c); (Ara.) corr. to 5641; *to hide:*— hidden things(1).

5642b. סְתַר sethar (1104d); (Ara.) corr. to 5641; *to destroy:*— destroyed(1).

5643a. סֵתֶר sether (712a); from 5641; *a covering, hiding place, secrecy:*— backbiting(1), covert(1), disguises*(1), hidden part(1), hiding place(6), secret(9), secret place(5), secretly(8), shelter(3).

5643b. סִתְרָה sithrah (712c); from 5641; *shelter, protection:*— hiding place(1).

5644. סִתְרִי Sithri (712c); from 5641; a Levite:— Sithri(1).

ע

5645. עָב ab (728a); from an unused word; *dark cloud, cloud mass, thicket:*— cloud(7), clouds(19), thick cloud(2), thick clouds(4), thickets(1).

5646. עָב ab or

עֹב ob (712b); of unc. der.; perh. *a landing:*— threshold(2), thresholds(1).

5647. עָבַד abad (712b); a prim. root; *to work, serve:*— become slaves(1), been slaves(1), bondage(2), burdened(2), cultivate(7), cultivated(2), cultivates(1), do(6), do the work(1), enslaved(3), given(1), holding in bondage(1), imposed(1), keep(2), labor(3), laborers*(2), make servant(1), make slaves(2), manufacturers(1), observe(1), perform(9), performed(2), plowed(1), rendered(1), serve(141), served(52), serves(2), serving(5), slave(1), slaves(1), subject(1), till(1), tiller(1), tiller*(1), tills(2), use as slaves(1), used(1), uses services(1), work(7), worked(2), workers(2), working(1), worship(7), worshipers(6).

5648. עֲבַד abad (1104d); (Ara.) corr. to 5647; *to make, do:*— carried(2), carrying(1), celebrated(1), committed(1), do(2), does(1), doing(1), done(4), executed(1), going(1), held(1), incited(1), made(4), make(1), observe(1), performs(1), torn(2), waging(1).

5649. עֲבַד abad (1105a); (Ara.) corr. to 5650; *slave, servant:*— servant(1), servants(6).

5650. עֶבֶד ebed (713d); from 5647; *slave, servant:*— attendants(1), bondage(2), male(24), male servant(7), male servants(5), male slaves(1), officers(1), official(2), Servant(6), servant(332), servant's(4), servant*(1), servants(353), servants'(2), servants*(12), slave(25), slave's(1), slave*(4), slavery(11), slaves(19), slaves*(8).

5651. עֶבֶד Ebed (714c); from 5647; "servant," two Isr.:— Ebed(6).

5652. עֲבָד abad (714d); from 5647; *a work:*— deeds(1).

5653. עַבְדָּא Abda (715a); from 5647; two Isr.:— Abda(2).

5654. עֹבֵד אֱדוֹם Obed Edom (714d); from 5647 and 112b; "servant of Edom," an Isr. name:— Obed-edom(20).

5655. עַבְדְּאֵל Abdeel (715a); from 5647 and 410; "servant of God," a man of Judah:— Abdeel(1).

5656. עֲבֹדָה abodah or

עֲבוֹדָה abodah (715a); from 5647; *labor, service:*— bondage(4), construction(2), construction work(1), job(2), kind of service(2), labor(9), laborious(12), labors(1), ministry(2), office(1), rite(3), rural(1), service(79), serving(1), servitude(2), tilled(1), use(1), work(18), workers(1).

5657. עֲבֻדָּה abuddah (715c); from 5647; *service:*— household(1), servants(1).

5658. עַבְדּוֹן Abdon (715c); from 5647; four Isr., also a Levitical city:— Abdon(8).

5659. עַבְדוּת abduth (715c); from 5647; *servitude, bondage:*— bondage(2), slavery(1).

5660. עַבְדִּי Abdi (715d); from 5647; two Isr.:— Abdi(3).

5661. עַבְדִיאֵל Abdiel (715d); from 5647 and 410; "servant of God," a Gadite:— Abdiel(1).

5662. עֹבַדְיָה Obadyah or

עֹבַדְיָהוּ Obadyahu (715d); act. part. of 5647 and 3050; "servant of Yah," the name of a number of Isr.:— Obadiah(20).

5663. עֶבֶד מֶלֶךְ Ebed Melek (715a); from 5650 and 4428; "servant of a king," an official under King Zedekiah:— Ebed-melech(6).

5664. עֲבֵד נְגוֹ Abed Nego (715a); of for. or.; "servant of Nebo," Bab. name of one of Daniel's companions:— Abed-nego(1).

5665. עֲבֵד נְגוֹ Abed Nego (1105a); (Ara.) of for. or.; "servant of Nebo," Bab. name of one of Daniel's companions:— Abed-nego(14).

5666. עָבָה abah (716a); a prim. root; *to be thick, fat,* or *gross:*— thick(1), thicker(2).

5667. עֲבוֹט abot or

עֲבֹט abot (716b); from an unused word; *a pledge, article pledged:*— pledge(4).

5668. עֲבוּר abur or

עֲבֻר abur (721a); from 5674a; *for the sake of, on account of, so that:*— account(9), because(8), order(5), reason(1), sake(10), so(7), while(1).

5669. עָבוּר abur (721a); from 5674a; *produce, yield:*— produce(1).

5670. עָבַט abat (716b); denom. vb. from 5667; *to take* or *give a pledge:*— borrow(1), deviate(1), generously lend(1), lend(1), take(1).

5671. עַבְטִיט abtit (716b); from the same as 5667; *weight of pledges, heavy debts:*— loans(1).

5672. עֲבִי abi or

עֳבִי obi (716a); from 5666; *thickness:*— massive*(1), thick(3), thickness(1).

5673. עֲבִידָה abidah (1105a); (Ara.) corr. to 5656; *work, service:*— administration(2), service(1), work(3).

5674a. עָבַר abar (716d); a prim. root; *to pass over, through,* or *by, pass on:*— accompanied(1), alienate(1), all*(1), avert(1), beyond*(1), blows away(1), bring(2), bring across(1), bring over(1), brought(1), brought over(1), came(2), carried over(1), carry over(1), charged(1), circulate(1), circulated(2), circulating(1), come(2), come around(1), come over(3), comes(3), continue(2), continued(13), continued through(1), contrary(2), cross(29), cross over(31), crossed(31), crossed over(17), crossing(5), crossing over(5), current(1), devote(1), drew across(1), drifting(1), enter(1), escapes the notice(1), ever bring(1), ever bring...over(1), excel(1), fail(2), flood(1), ford(1), forded(1), forth(1), freed(1), go(9), go on your way(1), go across(1), go along(1), go forward(1), go over(3), go through(3), go*(1), goes(1), going(2), going over(3), gone(1), gone over(1), gone through(1), laid aside(1), led across(1), led through(3), left(1), liquid(2), made(1), mates(1), means cross over(1), offer(1), over(4), overcome(1), overflow(1), overflowing(1), overlook(1), pass(72), pass along(2), pass away(5), pass over(7), pass through(29), passed(48), passed along(1), passed away(2), passed beyond(1), passed over(9), passed through(6), passed throughout(1), passer-by(2), passers-by(1), passes(18), passes through(7), passing(13), passing over(1), passing through(2), past(6), perish(1), proceed(1), proceeded(1), proceeding(2), put away(2), remove(1), removed(2), repealed(1), rolled(1), run riot(1), runs its course(1), send through(1), sent(2), sent across(2), sound(2), spare(2), spread beyond(1), standard(1), stretched across(1), survey(1), swept(3), take across(1), take away(5), taken away(1), taken away(2), through(1), through...we have gone(1), through...you passed(1), took(1), transfer(3), transgress(4), transgressed(11), transgressing(3), travel(1), traveler(1), turn away(2), use(2), vanish(1), visited(1), walk over(2), wayfaring(1), went(5), went away(1), went back(1), went forward(1), went over(1), went through(3).

5674b. עָבַר abar (720d); denom. vb. from 5678; *to be arrogant, become angry:*— angry(1), arrogant(1), been full(1), been full of wrath(1), filled with wrath(2), full of wrath(1), meddles(1), provokes him to anger(1).

5675. עֲבַר abar (1105a); (Ara.) corr. to 5676; *region across* or *beyond:*— beyond(12), region beyond(2).

5676. עֵבֶר eber (719b); from 5674a; *region across* or *beyond, side:*— across(10), across*(3), beside(1), beyond(33), beyond*(12), next*(1), other side(8), regions beyond(1), side(9), sides(2), space(1), straight*(3), way(1), west(2).

5677. עֵבֶר Eber (720a); from 5674a; "region beyond," a desc. of Shem, also the name of several Isr.:— Eber(15).

5678. עֶבְרָה ebrah (720c); fem. of 5676; *overflow, arrogance, fury:*— anger(1), fury(14), overflowings(1), rage(1), wrath(16).

5679. עֲבָרָה abarah (720b); from 5674a; *ford:*— ford(1), fords(1).

5680. עִבְרִי Ibri (720a); from 5677; perh. desc. of Eber, also another name for an Isr.:— Hebrew(9), Hebrew man(2), Hebrew man...woman(1), Hebrew woman(1), Hebrew women(3), Hebrews(17), Hebrews'(1).

5681. עִבְרִי Ibri (720b); from 5677; a Levite:— Ibri(1).

5682. עֲבָרִים Abarim (720d); from 5674a; "regions beyond," a mountainous region N. of the Dead Sea:— Abarim(5).

5683. עֶבְרֹן Ebron (720d); from 5674a; a place in Asher:— Ebron(1).

5684. עַבְרֹנָה Abronah (720d); from 5674a; a place in the desert:— Abronah(2).

5685. עָבַשׁ abash (721b); a prim. root; *to shrivel:*— shrivel(1).

5686. עָבַת abath (721b); a prim. root; *to wind, weave:*— weave it together(1).

5687. עָבֹת aboth or

עָבוֹת aboth (721c); from 5686; (having) *interwoven* (foliage), *leafy:*— leafy(4).

5688. עֲבֹת aboth or

עֲבוֹת aboth or

עֲבֹתָה abothah (721c); from 5686; *cord, rope, cordage:*— bonds(1), clouds(1), cordage(3), corded(1), cords(8), ropes(8).

5689. עָגַב agab (721d); a prim. root; *to have inordinate affection, lust:*— lovers(1), lusted(6).

5690. עֶגֶב agab (721d); from 5689; (sensuous) *love:*— lustful desires(1), sensual(1).

5691. עֲגָבָה agabah (721d); from 5689; *lustfulness:*— lust(1).

5692. עֻגָּה uggah (728a); from an unused word; *a disc* or *cake of bread:*— bread cake(2), bread cakes(1), cake(2), cakes(2).

5693. עָגוּר agur (723a); from an unused word; (a kind of bird) perh. *a crane:*— crane(1), thrush(1).

5694. עָגִיל agil (722d); from the same a 5695; *a hoop, ring:*— earrings(2).

5695. עֵגֶל egel (722a); from an unused word; *a calf:*— calf(22), calf's(1), calves(12).

5696. עָגֹל agol or

עָגוֹל agol (722c); from the same as 5695; *round:*— circular(3), round(3).

5697. עֶגְלָה eglah (722b); fem. of 5695; *a heifer:*— calf(1), heifer(10), heifer's(1).

5698. עֶגְלָה Eglah (722c); from the same as 5695; "heifer," a wife of David:— Eglah(2).

5699. עֲגָלָה agalah (722c); from the same as 5695; *a cart:*— cart(14), carts(4), cartwheel(1), chariots(1), wagon(1), wagons(4).

5700a. עֶגְלוֹן Eglon (722d); from the same as 5695; a king of Moab, also a city in Isr.:— Eglon(13).

5700b. עֶגְלַת Eglath (722c); from the same as 5695; a place near the S. border of Moab:— Eglath-shelishiyah*(2).

5701. עָגַם agam (723a); a prim. root; *to be grieved:*— grieved(1).

5702. עָגַן agan (723a); a prim. root; *to shut oneself in* or *off:*— refrain(1).

5703. עַד ad (723c); from 5710a; *perpetuity:*— all(1), continually(1), Eternal(1), ever(15), forever(26), forever*(1), forevermore*(2), old(1), perpetual(1).

5704. עַד ad (723d); from 5710a; *as far as, even to, up to, until, while:*— account(1), afar*(1), after(1), all the way(1), along(1), before(7), before*(3), beside*(1), beyond(2), beyond*(1), both*(1), completely*(1), either...or(1), equal(1), even(24), even including(1), exceedingly*(3), extremely*(1), far(131), far*(1), forever*(66), forevermore*(1), here*(2), how many*(2), including(1), like(2), little while*(1), long(23), long*(25), momentary*(1), never*(2), only(1), or(9), over(1), over there*(1), point(1), reaching(1), since*(1), so long(1), still*(1), there(1), threatened*(1), till(3), time(1), toward(1), unfathomable*(1), until(365), until the when(1), until*(43), utterly*(3), very(1), very*(2), violently*(1), when(1), when*(1), while(7), while i was still(1), within(1), without*(2), yet(1), yet*(1).

5705. עַד ad (1105b); (Ara.) corr. to 5704; *even to, until:*— before*(1), order*(1), until(3), until*(11).

5706. עַד ad (723d); from 5710a; *booty, prey:*— prey(2).

5707. עֵד ed (729c); from 5749a; *a witness:*— evidence(1), witness(45), witnesses(23).

5708. עֵד ed (723b); see 5713b.

5709. עֲדָא ada or

עֲדָה adah (1105b); (Ara.) corr. to 5710a; *to pass on* or *away:*— been removed(1), pass away(1), removes(1), revoked(2), taken away(3).

5710a. עָדָה adah (723c); a prim. root; *to pass on, advance:*— passed(1), takes off(1).

5710b. עָדָה adah (725c); a prim. root; *to ornament* or *deck oneself:*— adorn(1), adorn yourself(1), adorned(2), adorns(1), decorate(1), decorated yourselves(1), take(1).

5711. עָדָה Adah (725d); from 5710b; two non-Isr. women:— Adah(8).

5712. עֵדָה edah (417a); from 3259; *congregation:*— assembly(5), band(2), company(13), congregation(126), congregation's(1), herd(1), swarm(1).

5713a. עֵדָה edah (729d); fem. of 5707; *testimony, witness:*— witness(4).

5713b. עֵדָה edah (730a); from 5749a; *testimony:*— testimonies(21), testimony(1).

5713c. עִדָּה iddah (723b); from an unused word; *menstruation:*— filthy(1).

5714. עִדּוֹ Iddo or

עִדּוֹא Iddo or

עִדִּיא Iddi (723b); from the same as 5713c; "timely," the name of several Isr.:— Iddo(10).

5715. עֵדוּת eduth (730b); from 5749a; *testimony:*— admonitions(1), ordinance(1), testimonies(13), testimony(43), warnings(1).

5716. עֲדִי adi (725d); from 5710b; *ornaments:*— fine ornaments(1), jewels(1), ornaments(9), trappings(1), years(1).

5717. עֲדִיאֵל Adiel (726a); from 5716 and 410; "God is an ornament," three Isr.:— Adiel(3).

5718. עֲדָיָה Adayah or

עֲדָיָהוּ Adayahu (726a); from 5710b and 3050; "Yah has ornamented Himself," the name of a number of Isr.:— Adaiah(9).

5719. עָדִין adin (726d); from the same as 5730a; *voluptuous:*— sensual one(1).

5720. עָדִין Adin (726d); from the same as 5730a; an Isr.:— Adin(4).

5721. עֲדִינָא Adina (726d); from the same as 5730a; a Reubenite:— Adina(1).

5722. עֲדִינוֹ Adino (726d); from the same as 5730a; "voluptuous," one of David's heroes:— Adino(1).

5723. עֲדִיתַיִם Adithayim (726b); from 5710b; a city in Judah:— Adithaim(1).

5724. עַדְלַי Adlay (726b); from an unused word; the father of Shaphat:— Adlai(1).

5725. עֲדֻלָּם Adullam (726b); from an unused word; a Canaanite city:— Adullam(8).

5726. עֲדֻלָּמִי Adullami (726c); from 5725; inhab. of Adullam:— Adullamite(3).

5727. עָדַן adan (726c); denom. vb. from 5730a; *to luxuriate:*— reveled(1).

5728. עֲדֶן aden or

עֲדֶנָה adenah (725c); from 5710a; *hitherto, still:*— still(1).

5729. עֶדֶן Eden (727a); from the same as 5731; a territory conquered by Assyr.:— Eden(3).

5730a. עֵדֶן eden (726c); from an unused word; *a luxury, dainty, delight:*— delicacies(1), delights(1), luxuriously(1).

5730b. עֵדֶן Eden (726c); from the same as 5730a; a Levite:— Eden(2).

5731. עֵדֶן Eden (727a); from an unused word; the garden home of Adam and Eve:— Eden(14).

5732. עִדָּן iddan (1105c); (Ara.) corr. to 5713c; *time:*— moment(2), situation(1), time(8), times(2).

5733. עַדְנָא Adna (726c); from the same as 5730a; two Isr.:— Adna(2).

5734a. עַדְנָה Adnah (726d); from the same as 5730a; "pleasure," two Isr.:— Adnah(2).

5734b. עֶדְנָה ednah (726d); from the same as 5730a; *delight:*— pleasure(1).

5735. עַדְעָדָה Adadah (792d); from 3259; a city in Judah:— Adadah(1).

5736. עָדַף adaph (727a); a prim. root; *to remain over, be in excess:*— balance(1), excess(4), left over(4).

5737a. עָדַר adar (727b); a prim. root; *to help:*— helped(1).

5737b. עָדַר adar (727b); a prim. root; *to hoe:*— cultivated(1), hoed(1).

5737c. עָדַר adar (727c); a prim. root; *to be lacking, fail:*— fail(1), lacking(1), left...lacking(1), missing(3), remained(1).

5738. עֶדֶר Eder (727d); from 5737c; a Benjamite:— Eder(1).

5739. עֵדֶר eder (727c); from 5737c; *a flock, herd:*— droves(2), every drove(1), flock(15), flocks(15), herd(1), herds(3).

5740a. עֵדֶר Eder (727d); from 5737c; a Levite:— Eder(2).

5740b. עֵדֶר Eder (727d); from 5737c; a place in S. Judah:— Eder(1).

5741. עַדְרִיאֵל Adriel (727b); from 5737a; "my help is God," son-in-law of Saul:— Adriel(2).

5742. עֲדָשָׁה adashah (727d); of unc. der.; *a lentil:*— lentil(1), lentils(3).

5743. עוּב ub (728a); denom. vb. from 5645; *to becloud:*— cloud(1), covered(1).

5744. עוֹבֵד Obed (714d); from 5647; "worshiper," the name of several Isr.:— Obed(10).

5745. עוֹבָל Obal (716c); from an unused word; a son of Joktan, also his desc.:— Obal(1).

5746. עוּג ug (728b); denom. vb. from 5692; *to bake:*— baked(1).

5747. עוֹג Og (728b); from the same as 5692; king of Bashan:— Og(22).

5748. עוּגָב uggab or

עֻגָּב uggab (721d); perh. from 5689; (a reed musical instrument) perh. *a flute:*— flute(2), pipe(2).

5749a. עוּד ud (728c); a prim. root; *to return, go about, repeat, do again:*— encircled(1), stood upright(1), supports(2).

5749b. עוּד ud (729d); denom. vb. from 5713a; *to bear witness:*— admonish(2), admonished(6), call(5), called(1), gave witness(1), give warning(1), solemnly warn(2), solemnly warned(2), take(1), testified(3), testify(4), testimony(1), warn(1), warned(5), warning(2), witness(4).

5750. עוֹד od or

עֹד od (728c); from 5749a; *a going around, continuance, still, yet, again, beside:*— added(1), again(92), again*(9), again...more(1), all the more(1), all*(2), also(3), another(2), another*(1), any longer(15), any more(1), anymore(21), anymore*(1), back(1), besides(4), continue(1), continued(1), else(5), even(2), ever(1), farther(1), further(6), furthermore(3), life(2), long(1), long time(1), long*(2), longer(76), longer any(1), longer*(7), more(39), more*(5), moreover(2), never*(9), once more*(3), once*(1), other(8), since that time(1), soon(1), still(84), still more(1), while(6), while i was still(1), while the remains(1), within(3), yet(43), yet again(1), yet more(1).

5751. עוֹד od (1105c); (Ara.) corr. to 5750; *still:*— while(1).

5752. עוֹדֵד Oded or

עֹדֵד Oded (729c); from 5749a; "restorer," two Isr.:— Oded(3).

5753a. עָוָה avah (730c); a prim. root; *to bend, twist:*— bent(1), bewildered(1), distorts(1), made my crooked(1), perverse(2), perverted(2).

5753b. עָוָה avah (731c); denom. vb. from 5771; *to commit iniquity, do wrong:*— commits iniquity(1), committed iniquity(4), committing iniquity(1), did wrong(1), done wrong(1), wronged(1).

5754. עַוָּה avvah (730c); intens. from 5753a; *distortion, ruin:*— ruin(3).

5755. עִוָּה Ivvah or

עַוָּא Avva (731d); from the same as 5771; a city conquered by Assyr.:— Avva(1), Ivvah(3).

5756. עוּז uz (731d); a prim. root; *to take* or *seek refuge:*— bring(1), flee for safety(1), safety(1), seek refuge(1), sought refuge(1), take refuge(1).

5757. עַוִּי Avvi (731d); from 5755; inhab. of Avva:— Avvites(1).

5758. עִוְיָה avayah (1105c); (Ara.) corr. to 5753b; *iniquity:*— iniquities(1).

5759. עֲוִיל avil (732b); from an unused word; *a young boy:*— little ones(1), young children(1).

5760. עֲוִיל avil (732d); from the same as 5766; *unjust one:*— ruffians(1).

5761. עַוִּים Avvim (732a); of unc. der.; a city in Benjamin, also a people on the S.W. coast of the Mediterranean Sea:— Avvim(2), Avvite(1).

5762. עֲוִית Avith or **עַיּוֹת Ayyoth** or **עֲיּוּת Ayyuth** (732b); of unc. der.; a place in Edom:— Avith(2).

5763. עוּל ul (732b); a prim. root; *to nurse, give suck:*— ewes with suckling lambs(1), milch(1), nursing(2), suckling lambs(1).

5764. עוּל ul (732b); from 5763; *a sucking child, suckling:*— infant(1), nursing child(1).

5765. עָוַל aval (732c); denom. vb. from 5766; *to act wrongfully:*— deals unjustly(1), wrongdoer(1).

5766. עֶוֶל evel or **עָוֶל avel** or **עַוְלָה avlah** or **עוֹלָה olah** or **עֹלָה olah** (732b); from an unused word; *injustice, unrighteousness:*— iniquity(10), injustice(5), unjust(1), unjustly(2), unrighteousness(1), wrong(2).

5767a. עַוָּל avval (732d); from the same as 5766; *unjust, unrighteous one:*— unjust(3), wicked(2).

5767b. עַוְלָה avlah (732c); from the same as 5766; *injustice, unrighteousness, wrong:*— iniquity(3), injustice(4), injustices(1), unjust(1), unjustly(1), unrighteousness(9), violence(1), violent injustice(1), what is unjust(1), wicked*(3), wickedness(4), wrong(3), wrongdoers(1).

5768. עוֹלֵל olel or **עֹלָל olal** (760c); from an unused word; *a child:*— babes(1), child(2), children(6), infants(2), little ones(9).

5769. עוֹלָם olam or **עֹלָם olam** (761d); from an unused word; *long duration, antiquity, futurity:*— ages(1), all successive(1), always(1), ancient(13), ancient times(3), continual(1), days of old(1), eternal(2), eternity(3), ever(10), Everlasting(2), everlasting(110), forever(136), forever and ever(1), forever*(70), forevermore*(1), lasting(1), long(2), long ago(3), long past(1), long time(3), never*(17), old(11), permanent(10), permanently(1), perpetual(29), perpetually(1).

5770a. עָוַן avan (745a); see 5870b.

5770b. עוּן un (732d); another reading for 6030a, q.v.

5771. עָוֹן avon or **עָווֹן avon** (730d); from an unused word; *iniquity, guilt, punishment for iniquity:*— blame(1), guilt(21), guilty(1), iniquities(46), iniquity(143), punishment(12), punishment for the iniquity(3), punishment for their iniquity(3).

5772a. עוֹנָה onah (733b); from the same as 5771; *guilt:*— guilt(1).

5772b. עוֹנָה onah or **עֹנָה onah** (773b); from 6030a; *cohabitation:*— conjugal rights(1).

5773. עִוְעִים ivim (730c); from 5753a; *distorting, warping:*— distortion(1).

5774a. עוּף uph (733b); a prim. root; *to fly:*— brandish(1), flew(4), flies(3), flies away(2), fly(4), fly away(3), flying(6), set(1), swoop down(1).

5774b. עוּף uph (734a); another reading for 8591b, q.v.

5775. עוֹף oph (733d); from 5774a; *flying creatures:*— bird(17), birds(49), fowl(1), winged(3), wings(1).

5776. עוֹף oph (1105c); (Ara.) corr. to 5775; *fowl:*— bird(1), birds(1).

5777. עוֹפֶרֶת ophereth or **עֹפֶרֶת ophereth** (780b); from the same as 6082; *lead* (a metal):— lead(9).

5778. עוֹפַי Ophay (734a); from 5774b; an Isr.:— Ephai(1).

5779. עוּץ uts (734b); a prim. root; *to counsel, plan:*— devise(1), take counsel(1).

5780. עוּץ Uts (734b); from 5779; a son of Aram, also a son of Nahor, also an Edomite, also perh. a district E. of Pal.:— Uz(8).

5781. עוּק uq (734b); a prim. root; perh. *to totter, cause tottering:*— weighted down(2).

5782. עוּר ur (734d); a prim. root; *to rouse oneself, awake:*— arise(1), arouse(12), arouse or awaken(3), aroused(10), arouses(2), awake(15), awaken(2), awakened(2), awakens(2), awakes(1), exulted(1), lifted(1), raise(1), rouse(3), rouse yourself(2), roused(1), stir(7), stirred(7), stirs(2), swung(2).

5783. עוּר ur (735d); a prim. root; *to be exposed* or *bare:*— bare*(1), made(1), milch(1).

5784. עוּר ur (1105c); (Ara.) of unc. der.; *chaff:*— chaff(1).

5785. עוֹר or (736a); of unc. der.; *a skin:*— body(1), hide(4), hides(1), leather(15), skin(65), skins(13).

5786. עָוַר avar (734c); a prim. root; *to make blind, blind:*— blinded(2), blinds(2), put(1).

5787. עִוֵּר ivver (734c); from 5786; *blind:*— blind(22), blind man(1), blind men(1), blindness(1), who are blind(1).

5788a. עִוָּרוֹן ivvaron (734d); from 5786; *blindness:*— blindness(2).

5788b. עַוֶּרֶת avvereth (734d); from 5786; *blindness:*— blind(1).

5789. עוּשׁ ush (736b); a prim. root; *to lend aid, come to help:*— hasten(1).

5790. עוּת uth (736c); a prim. root; perh. *to help:*— sustain(1).

5791. עָוַת avath (736c); a prim. root; *to be bent* or *crooked:*— bent(1), cheat(1), crooked(1), defraud(1), pervert(3), stoop(1), subvert(1), thwarts(1), wronged(1).

5792. עַוָּתָה avvathah (736c); from 5791; *subversion:*— oppression(1).

5793. עוּתַי Uthay (736d); from 5790; two Isr.:— Uthai(2).

5794. עַז az (738c); from 5810; *strong, mighty, fierce:*— fierce(2), fierce men(1), greedy*(1), insolent*(1), mighty(2), power(1), raging(1), roughly(1), strong(10), strong ones(1), stronger(1).

5795. עֵז ez (777c); from an unused word; *female goat:*— female goat(2), female goats(3), goat(44), goat*(2), goats(13), goats'(9), young goat*(5), young goats*(3).

5796. עֵז ez (1107c); (Ara.) corr. to 5795; *female goat:*— goats(1).

5797. עֹז oz or **עוֹז oz** (738d); from 5810; *strength, might:*— fortress*(1), loud(1), might(3), mighty(4), power(12), stern(1), strength(53), strong(16), stronghold(2).

5798. עֻזָּא Uzza or **עֻזָּה Uzzah** (739b); from 5810; four Isr.:— Uzza(9), Uzzah(4).

5799. עֲזָאזֵל azazel (736d); from an unused word; *entire removal:*— scapegoat(4).

5800a. עָזַב azab (736d); a prim. root; *to leave, forsake, loose:*— abandon(3), abandoned(11), abandons(1), commits(1), deserted(1), failed(1), fails(1), forsake(48), forsaken(56), forsakes(2), forsaking(1), forsook(16), free(5), full*(1), give...vent(1), ignores(1), leave(26), leave them undone(1), leave your behind(1), leaves(2), leaving(1), left(22), left me behind(1), left the behind(1), left behind(1), let it go(1), neglect(2), stopped(1), surely release(1), withdrawn(1).

5800b. עָזַב azab (738a); denom. vb. from 5801; *to restore, repair:*— restore(1), restored(1).

5801. עִזָּבוֹן izzabon (738a); from 5800a; *wares:*— wares(7).

5802. עַזְבּוּק Azbuq (739d); from 5794 and the root of 950; an Isr.:— Azbuk(1).

5803. עַזְגָּד Azgad (739d); from 5794 and 1409; "Gad is mighty," an Isr. name:— Azgad(4).

5804a. עַזָּה Azzah (738a); of unc. der.; a Philistine city:— Gaza(20).

5804b. עזה Uzzah (739c); from 5810; "strong," an Isr. name:— Uzzah(1).

5805. עֲזוּבָה azubah (737d); from 5800a; *forsakenness, desolation:*— forsaken places(2).

5806. עֲזוּבָה Azubah (738a); from 5800a; two Isr. women:— Azubah(4).

5807. עֱזוּז ezuz (739b); from 5810; *strength, might, fierceness:*— fierceness(1), power(1), strength(1).

5808. עִזּוּז izzuz (739b); from 5810; *mighty, powerful:*— mighty man(1), strong(1).

5809. עַזּוּר Azzur or **עַזֻּר Azzur** (741a); from 5826; "helpful," three Isr.:— Azzur(3).

5810. עָזַז azaz (738b); a prim. root; *to be strong:*— became fixed(1), brazen(1), displays a bold(1), mighty(1), prevail(2), prevailed(1), prevailed*(1), show yourself strong(1), strengthens(1), strong(1).

5811. עָזָז Azaz (739b); from 5810; "strong," a Reubenite:— Azaz(1).

5812. עֲזַזְיָהוּ Azazyahu (739c); from 5810 and 3050; "Yah is mighty," three Isr.:— Azaziah(3).

5813. עֻזִּי Uzzi (739d); from 5810; "forceful," the name of several Isr.:— Uzzi(11).

5814. עֻזִּיָּא Uzziyya (739d); from 5810; one of David's heroes:— Uzzia(1).

5815. עֲזִיאֵל Aziel (739d); the same as 3268, q.v.:— Aziel(1).

5816. עֻזִּיאֵל Uzziel (739c); from 5797 and 410; "my strength is God," the name of several Isr.:— Uzziel(16).

5817. עָזִּיאֵלִי Ozzieli (739c); from 5816; desc. of Uzziel:— Uzzielites(2).

5818. עֻזִּיָּה Uzziyyah or **עֻזִּיָּהוּ Uzziyyahu** (739c); from 5797 and 3050; "my strength is Yah," the name of several Isr.:— Uzziah(26), Uzziah's(1).

5819. עֲזִיזָא Aziza (739c); from 5810; an Isr.:— Aziza(1).

5820a. עַזְמָוֶת **Azmaveth** (740a); from 5794 and 4194; "strong (one) of death," four Isr.:— Azmaveth(6).

5820b. עַזְמָוֶת **Azmaveth** (740a); from 5794 and 4194; a place near Jer.:— Azmaveth(2).

5821. עַזָּן **Azzan** (740a); from 5810; "strong," a man of Issachar:— Azzan(1).

5822. עָזְנִיָּה **ozniyyah** (740a); of unc. der.; (a bird of prey) perh. *vulture:*— buzzard(2).

5823. עָזַק **azaq** (740a); a prim. root; *to dig about:*— dug it all around(1).

5824. עִזְקָה **izqah** (1105d); (Ara.) from a root corr. to 5823; *a signet ring:*— signet ring(1), signet rings(1).

5825. עֲזֵקָה **Azeqah** (740a); from 5823; a place in Judah:— Azekah(7).

5826. עָזַר **azar** (740b); a prim. root; *to help, succor:*— ally(1), furthered(1), granted(1), help(38), helped(19), helper(6), helpers(2), helping(1), helps(8), protect(1), restrains(1), supporting(1).

5827. עֶזֶר **Ezer** (740d); from 5826; "help," two Isr.:— Ezer(2).

5828. עֵזֶר **ezer** (740c); from 5826; *a help, helper:*— help(18), helper(2), helpers(1).

5829. עֵזֶר **Ezer** (740d); from 5826; "help," three Isr.:— Ezer(3).

5830. עֶזְרָא **Ezra** (740d); from 5826; "help," three Isr.:— Ezra(22).

5831. עֶזְרָא **Ezra** (1105d); (Ara.) corr. to 5830; an Isr.:— Ezra(3).

5832. עֲזַרְאֵל **Azarel** (741a); from 5826 and 410; "God has helped," the name of several Isr.:— Azarel(6).

5833. עֶזְרָה **ezrah** or

עֶזְרָת **ezrath** (740d); fem. of 5828; *help, helper, assistance:*— assistance(2), help(22), helpers(1), support(1).

5834. עֶזְרָה **Ezrah** (741a); fem. of 5828; "help," a man in Judah:— Ezrah(1).

5835. עֲזָרָה **azarah** (741c); from an unused word; prob. *enclosure:*— court(3), court*(1), ledge(6).

5836. עֶזְרִי **Ezri** (741b); from 5828; "my help," an Isr.:— Ezri(1).

5837. עַזְרִיאֵל **Azriel** (741a); from 5828 and 410; "my help is God," three Isr.:— Azriel(3).

5838. עֲזַרְיָה **Azaryah** or

עֲזַרְיָהוּ **Azaryahu** (741a); from 5826 and 3050; "Yah has helped," the name of a number of Isr.:— Azariah(47), Azaryahu(1).

5839. עֲזַרְיָה **Azaryah** (1105d); (Ara.) corr. to 5838; one of Daniel's companions:— Azariah(1).

5840. עַזְרִיקָם **Azriqam** (741b); from 5828 and 6965; "my help has risen," four Isr.:— Azrikam(6).

5841. עַזָּתִי **Azzathi** (738b); from 5804a; inhab. of Gaza:— Gazite(1), Gazites(1).

5842. עֵט **et** (741c); of unc. der.; *a stylus:*— pen(2), stylus(2).

5843. עֵטָא **eta** (1096a); (Ara.) from 3272a; *counsel:*— discretion(1).

5844a. עָטָה **atah** (741d); a prim. root; *to wrap oneself, enwrap, envelop oneself:*— cover(5), covered(2), covering(1), covers(2), veils(1), wrap himself(1), wrapped(4), wraps himself(1).

5844b. עָטָה **atah** (742a); a prim. root; *to grasp:*— grasp you firmly(1).

5845. עֲטִין **atin** (742b); from an unused word; prob. *a pail, bucket:*— sides(1).

5846. עֲטִישָׁה **atishah** (743a); from an unused word; *a sneezing:*— sneezes(1).

5847. עֲטַלֵּף **atalleph** (742a); of unc. der.; *a bat:*— bat(2), bats(1).

5848a. עָטַף **ataph** (742b); a prim. root; *to turn aside:*— turns(1).

5848b. עָטַף **ataph** (742b); a prim. root; *to envelop oneself:*— covered(1), covers(1).

5848c. עָטַף **ataph** (742c); a prim. root; *to be feeble* or *faint:*— faint(4), fainted(1), fainting away(1), feeble(1), feebler(1), grow faint(1), grows faint(1), overwhelmed(2).

5849a. עָטַר **atar** (742c); a prim. root; *to surround:*— surround(1), surrounding(1).

5849b. עָטַר **atar** (742d); denom. vb. from 5850; *to crown:*— bestower of crowns(1), crown(1), crowned(2), crowns(1).

5850. עֲטָרָה **atarah** (742d); from 5849a; *a crown, wreath:*— crown(22), crowns(1).

5851. עֲטָרָה **Atarah** (742d); from 5849a; an Isr. woman:— Atarah(1).

5852. עֲטָרוֹת **Ataroth** or

עֲטָרֹת **Ataroth** (743a); pl. of 5850; the name of several places in Isr.:— Ataroth(4).

5853. עַטְרוֹת אַדָּר **Atroth Addar** (743a); from 5852 and 146; a place on the border between Ephraim and Benjamin:— Ataroth-addar(2).

5854. עַטְרוֹת בֵּית יוֹאָב **Atroth Beth Yoab** (743a); from the same as 5852, from 1004 and 3097; a place in Judah:— Atroth-beth-joab(1).

5855. עַטְרוֹת שׁוֹפָן **Atroth Shophan** (743a); from 5852 and 5603; a place in Isr.:— Atroth-shophan(1).

5856. עִי **i** (730c); from 5753a; *a ruin, heap of ruins:*— heap of ruins(3), ruins(2).

5857. עַי **Ay** or

עַיָּא **Ayya** or

עַיָּת **Ayyath** (743a); of unc. der.; a Canaanite city:— Ai(37), Aiath(1), Aija(1), Ayyah(1).

5858a. עֵיבָל **Ebal** (716c); from the same as 5745; an Edomite name:— Ebal(2).

5858b. עֵיבָל **Ebal** (716c); the same as 5745, q.v.:— Ebal(1).

5858c. עֵיבָל **Ebal** (716c); from the same as 5745; a mountain N. of Shechem:— Ebal(5).

5859. עִיּוֹן **Iyyon** (743b); of unc. der.; a place in Naphtali:— Ijon(3).

5860a. עִיט **it** (743b); a prim. root; *to scream, shriek:*— scorned(1).

5860b. עִיט **it** (743c); denom. vb. from 5861; *to dart greedily:*— rushed(2).

5861. עַיִט **ayit** (743c); from 5860a; *a bird of prey:*— bird of prey(3), birds of prey(4), predatory(1).

5862. עֵיטָם **Etam** (743c); from 5860a; three places in Isr.:— Etam(5).

5863. עִיֵּי הָעֲבָרִים **Iyye Haabarim** (743d); from 5864 and 5674a; a place on the E. border of Moab, also a city in S. Judah:— Iye-abarim(1), Iyeabarim(1).

5864. עִיִּים **Iyyim** (743d); of unc. der.; a place on the E. border of Moab:— Iim(1), Iyim(1).

5865. עֵילוֹם **elom** (761d); the same as 5769, q.v.

5866. עִילַי **Ilay** (743d); of unc. der.; one of David's heroes:— Ilai(1).

5867a. עֵילָם **Elam** or

עוֹלָם **Olam** (743d); of unc. der.; a son of Shem, also his desc. and their country:— Elam(17).

5867b. עֵילָם **Elam** (743d); from the same as 5867a; the name of several Isr.:— Elam(11).

5868. עֲיָם **ayam** (744a); of unc. der.; perh. *a glow:*— scorching(1).

5869. עַיִן **ayin** (744a); of unc. der.; *an eye:*— appearance(4), appeared*(1), before(3), broad(1), concern*(1), confidence(1), disdained*(1), displease*(2), displeased*(4), disregard*(1), eye(68), eyebrows*(1), eyelids*(1), eyes(372), eyesight(1), forehead*(5), generous*(1), glares*(1), gleam(3), humble person*(1), knowledge(1), like*(1), look(4), look*(3), looked*(3), looks*(1), maliciously*(1), notice(1), outward appearance(1), own eyes(1), please*(3), pleased*(14), pleases*(1), prefer*(2), presence(8), saw*(1), see(1), see*(1), seem(1), seemed*(1), selfish*(1), sight(277), sight*(1), sleep*(1), sparkles*(1), sparkling(1), spring(1), surface(4), think(2), thought(1), watch(1), watch*(1), whatever you like*(1), wish*(2), yourselves(2).

5870a. עַיִן **ayin** (1105d); (Ara.) corr. to 5869; *an eye:*— eye(1), eyes(4).

5870b. עִין **in** (745a); denom. vb. from 5869; *to eye:*— looked at with suspicion(1).

5871a. עַיִן **ayin** (745a); from the same as 5869; *a spring* (of water):— fountain(1), Fountain(3), fountains(1), spring(11), springs(4).

5871b. עַיִן **Ayin** (745b); from 5869; two places in Isr.:— Ain(5).

5872. עֵין גֶּדִי **En Gedi** (745b); from 5871a and 1423; "spring of a kid," a place on W. shore of the Dead Sea:— Engedi(6).

5873. עֵין גַּנִּים **En Gannim** (745c); from 5871a and 1588; "spring of a garden," two places in Isr.:— En-gannim(3).

5874. עֵין־דֹּאר **En-dor** or

עֵין דּוֹר **En Dor** or

עֵין־דֹּר **En-dor** (745c); from 5871a and 1755; "spring of dwelling," a town in Manasseh:— En-dor(3).

5875. עֵין הַקּוֹרֵא **En Haqqore** (896c); from 5871a and 7121; "spring of the one calling," location of a miraculous spring:— En-hakkore(1).

עֵינוֹן **Enon**; see 2703.

5876. עֵין חַדָּה **En Chaddah** (745c); from 5871a and 2300; "spring of sharpness," a place in Issachar:— En-haddah(1).

5877. עֵין חָצוֹר **En Chatsor** (745c); from 5871a and 2674; "a spring of Hazor," a city in Naphtali:— En-hazor(1).

5878. עֵין חֲרֹד **en Charod** (353d, 745a); see 5871a and 2730b.

5879a. עֵינַיִם **Enayim** (745d); from 5871a; "two springs," a place in Isr.:— Enaim(2).

5879b. עֵינָם **Enam** (745d); from 5871a; a city in Judah:— Enam(1).

5880. עֵין מִשְׁפָּט **En Mishpat** (745c); from 5871a and 4941; "spring of judgment," another name for a place called Kadesh:— En-mishpat(1).

5881. עֵינָן **Enan** (745d); from 5871a; "having fountains," a man of Naphtali:— Enan(5).

5882. עֵין עֶגְלַיִם En Eglayim (745c); from 5871a and 5695; "spring of two calves," a place on the Dead Sea:— Eneglaim(1).

5883. עֵין רֹגֵל En Rogel (745a); from 5869 and 7270; a place near Jer.:— En-rogel(4).

5884. עֵין רִמּוֹן En Rimmon (745c); from 5871a and 7416; "spring of a pomegranate," a place in Judah:— En-rimmon(1).

5885. עֵין שֶׁמֶשׁ En Shemesh (745d); from 5871a and 8121; "spring of (the) sun," a place on the border between Judah and Benjamin:— En-shemesh(2).

5886. עֵין תַּנִּים En Tannim (1072c); from 5871a and 8577; "spring of dragons," a place near Jer.:— Dragon's Well(1).

5887. עֵין תַּפּוּחַ En Tappuach (745d); from 5871a and 8598; "place of an apple tree," a city in Ephraim:— En-tappuah(1).

5888. עִיף iph (746a); a prim. root; *to be faint:*— became weary(1), exhausted(1), faint(1), weary(2).

5889. עָיֵף ayeph (746a); from 5888; *faint, weary:*— faint(2), famished(2), parched(2), weary(11).

5890. עֵיפָה ephah (734a); from 5774b; *darkness:*— darkness(1), utter gloom(1).

5891. עֵיפָה Ephah (734a); from 5774b; two Isr., also a Midianite:— ephah(5).

5892a. עִיר ir (735c); from 5782; *excitement:*— anguish(1), wrath(1).

5892b. עִיר ir or

עָר ar or

עָיַר ayar (746b); of unc. der.; *city, town:*— cities(420), cities each(1), city(643), city and its towns(1), each and city(3), each city(1), every city(1), inner room(1), town(5), towns(4).

5893. עִיר Ir (746d); from 5892b; an Isr.:— Ir(1).

5894. עִיר ir (1105d); (Ara.) from a root corr. to 5782; *waking* or *wakeful one:*— watcher(2), watchers(1).

5895. עַיִר ayir (747a); from an unused word; *a male donkey:*— colt(1), donkeys(3), foal(2), male donkeys(1), young donkeys(1).

5896. עִירָא Ira (747a); from the same as 5895; three Isr.:— Ira(6).

5897. עִירָד Irad (747a); of unc. der.; desc. of Cain:— Irad(2).

5898. עִיר הַמֶּלַח Ir Hammelach (746d); from 5892b and 4417; "city of salt," a place in the Judean desert:— City of Salt(1).

5899. עִיר הַתְּמָרִים ir hattemarim (746d); see 5892b and 8558.

5900. עִירוּ Iru (747a); from 5892b; "citizen," a man of Judah:— Iru(1).

5901. עִירִי Iri (747a); from 5892b; a Benjamite:— Iri(1).

5902. עִירָם Iram (747a); from 5892b; an Edomite:— Iram(2).

5903. עֵירֹם erom or

עֵרֹם erom (735d); from 5783; *naked, nakedness:*— naked(9), nakedness(1).

5904. עִיר נָחָשׁ Ir Nachash (638b); from 5892b and 5175; "city of a serpent," a city in Judah:— Ir-nahash(1).

5905. עִיר שֶׁמֶשׁ Ir Shemesh (746d); from 5892b and 8121; "city of the sun," a city in Dan:— Ir-shemesh(1).

5906. עַיִשׁ Ayish or

עָשׁ Ash (747a); of unc. der.; (a constellation) perh. *Great Bear:*— bear(2).

עַיָּת Ayyath; see 5857.

5907. עַכְבּוֹר Akbor or

עַכְבֹּר Akbor (747b); from the same as 5909; "mouse," an Isr., also an Edomite:— Achbor(7), come(1).

5908. עַכָּבִישׁ akkabish (747b); of unc. der.; *a spider:*— spider's(2).

5909. עַכְבָּר akbar (747b); of unc. der.; *a mouse:*— mice(5), mouse(1).

5910. עַכּוֹ Akko (747b); of unc. der.; a city in Asher:— Acco(1).

5911. עָכוֹר Akor (747d); from 5916; "disturbance," a valley on the border of Judah:— Achor(5).

5912. עָכָן Akan (747c); of unc. der.; an Isr. name:— Achan(6).

5913. עָכַס akas (747c); denom. vb. from 5914; *to shake bangles, rattle, tinkle:*— tinkle the bangles(1).

5914. עֶכֶס ekes (747c); from an unused word; *an anklet, bangle:*— anklets(1), fetters(1).

5915. עַכְסָה Aksah (747c); from the same as 5914; a daughter of Caleb:— Achsah(5).

5916. עָכַר akar (747d); a prim. root; *to stir up, disturb, trouble:*— bring trouble(1), brought trouble(1), does...harm(1), grew worse(1), trouble(3), troubled(3), troubler(2), troubles(2).

5917. עָכָר Akar (747c); from 5916; a man of Judah, perh. the same as 5912:— Achar(1).

5918. עָכְרָן Okran (747d); from 5916; an Asherite:— Ochran(5).

5919. עַכְשׁוּב akshub (747d); of unc. der.; *asp, viper:*— viper(1).

5920. עַל al (752b); from 5927; *height:*— high(2), upward(1).

5921. עַל al (752c); from 5927; *upon, above, over:*— about(27), about*(1), above(43), above*(16), accordance(2), accordance*(1), according(40), according*(2), account(11), account*(2), across*(1), addition(4), addition*(1), afflicted(1), after(14), after*(1), against(536), against*(1), along(11), alongside*(1), although(1), among(7), around(11), attention*(1), because(82), because*(49), before(10), before*(19), behalf(18), behind*(2), beside(47), beside*(6), besides(5), besiege*(1), besieged*(13), besieging(1), besieging*(5), better than(1), between(1), beyond(3), beyond*(1), bordered*(1), care(1), carried(1), charge(31), charge*(1), command(1), committed(1), concerning(97), concerning*(5), confront(1), confront*(1), connection(1), conquer*(1), consider*(3), considered*(2), contrary(1), corresponding(2), corresponding*(1), crowns(1), defiance*(1), despite(1), due(1), duty(1), east*(7), encouragingly*(2), engaged(1), even(1), everywhere*(1), faces*(1), facing*(1), far(2), forsaking*(1), full*(1), fully*(1), have charge(1), inasmuch*(5), instead*(1), leave*(1), length*(1), more than(2), much(1), named*(1), near(4), next(9), next*(13), now*(1), obliging*(1), off(6), off*(5), opposed(1), opposite(1), opposite*(4), ornamented*(1), over(538), over*(6), overflowing*(1), overflows*(1), overlooks*(3), part(1), planned*(1), pleased*(1), pleases*(2), presence(2), pressed*(1), prompts*(1), reason(2), reason*(6), received(1), regard(3), regarding(1), respect(1), responsibility(1), ruthlessly*(1), sake(4), sake*(1), sakes(2), settled*(1), since*(1), so(1), so*(2), sorrow(1), spite(2), steward*(4), surround*(1), sworn*(1), task(1), than(1), than were over(1), theirs*(1), therefore*(139), thereon(1), through(3), throughout(3), together(3), too(3), top(1), top*(2), toward(20), toward*(5), under(12), until(1), upright*(2), upside*(1), urged*(1), view(1), way(1), when(1), where(1), where*(5), wherever*(2), while(1), why*(10), within(13), within*(1), wore(1).

5922. עַל al (1106a); (Ara.) corr. to 5921; *upon, over, above:*— about(3), account(1), against(6), among(1), around(3), concerning(7), disregarded*(1), more(1), over(15), reason*(1), than*(1), therefore*(2), toward(1).

5923. עֹל ol or

עוֹל ol (760d); from 5953d; *a yoke:*— yoke(40).

5924. עֵלָּא ella (1106c); (Ara.) from 5922; *above:*— over(1).

5925. עֻלָּא Ulla (748a); of unc. der.; an Asherite:— Ulla(1).

5926. עִלֵּג illeg (748a); from an unused word; *speaking inarticulately:*— stammerers(1).

5927. עָלָה alah (748a); a prim. root; *to go up, ascend, climb:*— all means go(1), approach(1), arise(2), arose(1), ascend(12), ascended(10), ascending(2), ascends(2), ascent(1), attack(2), been(1), blow away(1), breaking(1), bring(33), bring them back(1), bringing(2), brings(1), brought(66), burn(2), burnt offerings(1), came(67), came back(1), carried(2), carried away(1), carry(3), cast(1), charging(1), chew(4), chews(5), climb(4), climbed(1), climbs(2), come(83), comes(2), coming(12), dawn*(1), dawned(1), depart(1), enter(1), entered(1), erected(1), evaporated(1), exalt(1), exalted(2), excel(1), falls(1), fell(2), get(1), get back(1), give off(1), go(140), goes(6), going(8), gone(18), gone away(2), got back(1), grew(3), grow(2), grow back(1), grows(1), imported*(2), incite(1), included(1), invaded(2), jump(1), lead(1), left(1), levied(3), lie(1), lift(1), lifted(10), lighted(1), made(1), marching(1), mating(2), mount(9), mounted(2), offer(29), offered(34), offering(10), offers(3), ornamented*(1), overgrown(1), placed(1), progressed(1), prompts*(1), put(2), raged(2), raised(1), raises(1), reached(1), reaches(1), recorded(1), restore(1), restored(1), rise(10), rises(7), rising(1), rose(4), scales(1), set(1), sets(2), sprang(1), spring(2), sprout(1), stacking(1), stirs(1), surely bring(1), take(3), take me away(1), taken(4), thrown(1), took(4), trims(1), using(4), vanish(1), wear(1), went(161), went away(1), withdraw(3), withdrawn(1), withdrew(1), worked(1).

5928. עֲלָה alah or

עֲלָת alath (1106a); (Ara.) corr. to 5930a; *a burnt offering:*— burnt offering(1).

5929. עָלֶה aleh (750a); from 5927; *leaf, leafage:*— branches(5), leaf(9), leaves(4).

5930a. עֹלָה olah or

עוֹלָה olah (750b); from 5927; *whole burnt offering:*— burnt offering(207), burnt offerings(80).

5930b. עֹלָה olah (751a); from 5927; *ascent, stairway:*— stairway(2).

5931. עִלָּה illah (1106c); (Ara.) from a root corr. to 5927; *matter, affair, occasion:*— ground of accusation(3).

5932. עַלְוָה **alvah** (732c); the same as 5767b, q.v.

5933. עַלְוָה **Alvah** or

עַלְיָה **Alyah** (759b); from 5927; an Edomite:— Aliah(1), Alvah(1).

5934. עֲלוּמִים **alumim** (761c); from the same as 5958; *youth, youthful vigor:*— youth(2), youthful vigor(2).

5935. עַלְוָן **Alvan** or

עַלְיָן **Alyan** (759b); from 5927; an Edomite:— Alian(1), Alvan(1).

5936. עֲלוּקָה **aluqah** (763c); from an unused word; *a leech:*— leech(1).

5937. עָלַז **alaz** (759c); a prim. root; *to exult:*— become jubilant(1), exult(11), exults(1), jubilant(1), rejoice(2).

5938. עָלֵז **alez** (759c); from 5937; *exultant, jubilant:*— jubilant(1).

5939. עֲלָטָה **alatah** (759c); of unc. der.; *thick darkness:*— dark(3), very dark(1).

5940. עֱלִי **eli** (750a); from 5927; *a pestle:*— pestle(1).

5941. עֵלִי **Eli** (750a); from 5927; a priest at Shiloh:— Eli(32), Eli's(1).

5942. עִלִּי **illi** (751a); from 5927; *upper:*— upper(2).

עִלִּי **illi**; see 5952.

5943. עִלַּי **Illay** (1106a); (Ara.) corr. to 5942; "highest," a name of God:— most high(10).

עַלְיָה **Alyah**; see 5933.

5944. עֲלִיָּה **aliyyah** (751a); from 5927; *a roof chamber:*— chamber over(1), roof chamber(4), upper chamber(4), upper chambers(2), upper room(4), upper rooms(4).

5945a. עֶלְיוֹן **elyon** (751b); from 5927; *high, upper:*— exalted(1), heap of ruins(1), high(2), highest(2), most(1), top(1), upper(15).

5945b. עֶלְיוֹן **Elyon** (751b); from 5927; "high," a name of God:— high(1), most high(30).

5946. עֶלְיוֹן **Elyon** (1106a); (Ara.) corr. to 5945b; "high," a name of God:— Highest One(4).

5947. עַלִּיז **alliz** (759c); from 5937; *exultant, jubilant:*— exultant(2), exulting ones(2), jubilant(2), revelers(1).

5948. עֲלִיל **alil** (760d); from 5953d; perh. *furnace, crucible:*— furnace(1).

5949. עֲלִילָה **alilah** or

עֲלִלָה **alilah** (760a); from 5953a; *wantonness, a deed:*— actions(3), acts(1), deeds(17), shameful(2).

5950. עֲלִילִיָּה **aliliyyah** (760b); from 5953a; *a deed:*— deed(1).

5951. עֲלִיצוּת **alitsuth** (763c); from 5970; *exultation:*— exultation(1).

5952. עַלִּית **allith** or

עִלִּי **illi** (1106a); (Ara.) from a root corr. to 5927; *a roof chamber:*— roof chamber(1).

5953a. עָלַל **alal** (759d); a prim. root; *to act severely:*— abuse(2), abused(1), bring pain(1), deal(1), dealt(2), made a mockery(2), make sport(1), practice deeds(1), severely dealt(2).

5953b. עָלַל **alal** (760a); denom. vb. from 5955; *to glean:*— caught(1), glean(1), go over(1), thoroughly glean(1).

5953c. עָלַל **alal** (760c); denom. vb. from 5768; *to act* or *play the child:*— children(1).

5953d. עָלַל **alal** (760d); a prim. root; *to insert, thrust in:*— thrust(1).

5954. עֲלַל **alal** (1106c); (Ara.) corr. to 5953d; *to go* or *come in:*— bring(2), brought(4), came(3), entered(2), take(1), went(2).

עֹלַל **olal**; see 5768.

עֲלִלָה **alilah**; see 5949.

5955. עֹלֵלוֹת **oleloth** or

עוֹלֵלוֹת **oleloth** (760a); from 5953a; *a gleaning:*— gatherers(1), gleaning(1), gleanings(4).

5956. עָלַם **alam** (761a); a prim. root; *to conceal:*— blind(1), disregard*(1), escapes(1), ever(1), hidden(10), hide(6), hides(1), melts(1), neglect(1), pay no attention(2), pretenders(1), secret(1), shuts(1).

5957. עָלַם **alam** (1106d); (Ara.) corr. to 5769; *perpetuity, antiquity:*— all ages(1), all ages to come(1), everlasting(4), forever(9), forever and ever(1), never*(1), past(2), perpetrated(1).

5958. עֶלֶם **elem** (761c); from an unused word; *a young man:*— youth(2).

עֹלָם **olam**; see 5769.

5959. עַלְמָה **almah** (761c); fem. of 5958; *a young woman, a virgin:*— girl(1), maid(1), maiden(1), maidens(3), virgin(1).

5960. עַלְמוֹן **Almon** (761b); from 5956; a city in Benjamin:— Almon(1).

5961. עֲלָמוֹת **alamoth** (761c); pl. of 5959; (soprano voices of) *young women:*— alamoth(1).

עַלְמוּת **almuth**; see 4191.

5962. עֵלְמָיֵא **Elmaye** (1106d); (Ara.) from a name corr. to 5867a; inhab. of Elam:— Elamites(1).

5963. עַלְמֹן דִּבְלָתָיְמָה **Almon Diblathayemah** (761b); from 5956 and 1690; a place in Moab (the same as 1015):— Almon-diblathaim(2).

5964. עָלֶמֶת **Alemeth** (761b); from 5956; a Benjamite name, also a Levitical city in Benjamin:— Alemeth(3), Allemeth(1).

5965. עָלַס **alas** (763a); a prim. root; *to rejoice:*— delight(1), enjoy(1), flap joyously(1).

5966. עָלַע **ala** (763a); a prim. root; perh. *to sip up:*— suck(1).

5967. עֲלַע **ala** (1106d); (Ara.) corr. to 6763; *a rib:*— ribs(1).

5968. עָלַף **alaph** (763b); a prim. root; *to cover:*— became faint(1), faint(1), fainted(1), inlaid(1), wilted away(1), wrapped(1).

5969. עֻלְפֶּה **ulpeh** (763b); the same as 5968, q.v.

5970. עָלַץ **alats** (763b); a prim. root; *to rejoice, exult:*— exult(5), exults(1), rejoices(1), triumph(1).

5971a. עַם **am** or

עָם **am** (766b); from an unused word; *people:*— Ammi(1), army(2), army*(1), citizens(3), creatures(1), each people(2), every people(2), fellow*(3), force(1), men(1), nation(1), nations(4), own people(1), people(1614), people's(4), people*(1), peoples(187), public*(1), throng(1), together(1), troops(2).

5971b. עַם **am** (769b); from 5973; *kinsman:*— people(32), peoples(1).

5972. עַם **am** (1107a); (Ara.) corr. to 5971a; *people:*— people(8), peoples(7).

5973. עִם **im** (767a); a prim. prep.; *with:*— against(50), alike(1), along(9), among(16), among my belongings(1), aside(1), because(1), before(5), before*(1), behalf(1), beside(1), besides(3), close(1), decided*(1), done*(1), has(1), have(1), leave*(1), like(3), Mine(1), near(7), own(1), presence(1), regard(3), side(1), take(1), terms(1), together(7), toward(5), toward*(1), tutored(1), well(1), while(2), within(2).

5974. עִם **im** (1107a); (Ara.) corr. to 5973; *with:*— like*(1), one another*(1).

5975. עָמַד **amad** (763c); a prim. root; *to take one's stand, stand:*— abiding(1), act(1), appoint(2), appointed(15), arise(11), arisen(1), arose(3), attend*(1), attended(1), broke(1), changed(1), confirmed(2), continue(1), defend(2), delay(2), endure(5), endures(4), enduring(1), enter(1), entered(2), erected(1), establish(1), established(2), establishing(1), fixed(1), fulfill(1), gives stability(1), halt(1), halted(1), hung(6), join(1), last(1), living(1), make a stand(1), oppose(1), opposed(2), persists(1), place(1), placed(2), present(3), presented(1), presented*(1), propped(2), quake(1), raise(2), raised(1), refrain(1), rely(1), remain(5), remained(4), remains(5), replaces*(1), represent(1), resist*(1), restore(2), restored(2), retains(1), rise(2), rose(1), serve(1), served(3), served*(4), service*(3), serving(1), set(12), sets(3), stand(121), stand still(1), standing(67), standing upright(2), stands(15), station(1), stationed(8), stay(8), stayed(2), staying(1), stood(110), stood firm(1), stood still(11), stop(3), stopped(9), survives(1), take a stand(1), take their stand(1), took his stand(1), took their stand(1), wait(1), waited(1), withstand(1), withstand*(1), withstanding(1).

5976. עָמַד **amad** (588c, 763c); see 4571.

5977. עֹמֶד **omed** (765a); from 5975; *a standing place:*— place(3), posts(1), stations(2), upright*(2), where i was standing(1).

5978. עִמָּד **immad** (767a); prol. for 5973, q.v.

עַמֻּד **ammud**; see 5982.

5979. עֶמְדָּה **emdah** (765a); from 5975; *standing ground:*— support(1).

5980. עֻמָּה **ummah** (769c); from 5973; *close by, side by side with:*— all alike(1), alongside(5), beside(3), close(5), close beside(2), close*(1), comparable(1), corresponded(1), corresponding(3), exactly(1), just(1), like(1), parallel(1), side(1), well(2).

5981. עֻמָּה **Ummah** (747b); of unc. der.; a city in Asher, perh. the same as 5910:— Ummah(1).

5982. עַמּוּד **ammud** or

עַמֻּד **ammud** (765a); from 5975; *a pillar, column:*— column(1), columns(2), pillar(29), pillars(77), posts(1).

5983. עַמּוֹן **Ammon** (769d); from 5973; a people living E. of the Jordan:— Ammon(98), Ammonites(1), Ammonites*(7).

5984. עַמּוֹנִי **Ammoni** (770a); from 5983; desc. of Ammon:— Ammonite(10), Ammonites(5).

5985. עַמּוֹנִית **Ammonith** (770a); fem. of 5984; an Ammonite woman:— Ammon(1), Ammonitess(4).

5986. עָמוֹס **Amos** (770c); from 6006; an Isr. prophet:— Amos(7).

5987. עָמוֹק **Amoq** (771b); from 6009; "deep," an Isr. priest:— Amok(2).

5988. עַמִּיאֵל **Ammiel** (770a); from 5971b and 410; "my kinsman is God," four Isr.:— Ammiel(6).

5989. עַמִּיהוּד **Ammihud** (770a); from 5971b and 1935; "my kinsman is majesty," four Isr., also a Geshurite:— Ammihud(10).

5990. עַמִּיזָבָד **Ammizabad** (770b); from 5971b and 2064; "my kinsman has bestowed," an Isr.:— Ammizabad(1).

5991. עַמִּיחוּר **Ammichur** (770b); see 5989.

5992. עַמִּינָדָב **Amminadab** (770b); from 5971b and 5081; "my kinsman is noble," the name of several Isr.:— Amminadab(13).

5993. עַמִּי נָדִיב **ammi nadib** (766b, 622a); from 5971a, q.v. and 5081, q.v.

5994. עֲמִיק **amiq** (1107a); (Ara.) corr. to 6012; *deep:*— profound(1).

5995. עָמִיר **amir** (771c); from the same as 6016a; *a swath, row of fallen grain:*— sheaf(1), sheaves(3).

5996. עַמִּישַׁדָּי **Ammishadday** (770b); from 5971b and 7706b; "my kinsman is Shaddai," a Danite:— Ammishaddai(5).

5997. עָמִית **amith** (765c); from an unused word; *an associate, fellow, relation:*— another(2), associate(1), companion(2), friend(2), friend's(1), neighbor(3), neighbor's(1).

5998. עָמַל **amal** (765c); a prim. root; *to labor, toil:*— does(1), labor(1), labored(4), laboriously(1), toils(2), work(1), works(1).

5999. עָמָל **amal** (765d); from 5998; *trouble, labor, toil:*— anguish(1), fruit of his labor(1), fruit of my labor(3), labor(16), mischief(9), misery(1), sorry(1), toil(3), toils(1), trouble(13), troublesome(1), unjust decisions(1), wickedness(2), work(1).

6000. עָמָל **Amal** (765d); from 5998; "trouble," an Asherite:— Amal(1).

6001a. עָמֵל **amel** (766a); from 5998; *a laborer, sufferer:*— who suffers(2), worker's(1), workmen's(1).

6001b. עָמֵל **amel** (766a); from 5998; *toiling:*— labored(2), laboring(1), labors(1), toils(1).

6002. עֲמָלֵק **Amaleq** (766a); from 5998; a desc. of Esau, also his posterity:— Amalek(25), Amalekites(14).

6003. עֲמָלֵקִי **Amaleqi** (766a); from 6002; desc. of Amalek:— Amalekite(3), Amalekites(9).

6004. עָמַם **amam** (770b); a prim. root; *to darken, dim:*— dark the has become(1), match(2).

6005. עִמָּנוּאֵל **Immanuel** (769b); from 5973 and 410; "with us is God," the name of a child:— Immanuel(2).

6006. עָמַס **amas** or
עָמַשׂ **amas** (770c); a prim. root; *to load, carry a load:*— bears our burden(1), borne(1), burdensome(1), lift(1), loaded(3), loading(1), took their load(1).

6007. עֲמַסְיָה **Amasyah** (770c); from 6006 and 3050; "Yah has loaded," a man of Judah:— Amasiah(1).

6008. עַמְעָד **Amad** (770c); of unc. der.; a place in Asher:— Amad(1).

6009. עָמַק **amoq** (770d); a prim. root; *to be deep:*— deep(1), deeply(2), depths(2), gone deep(2), made it deep(1), make it deep(1).

6010. עֵמֶק **emeq** (770d); from 6009; *a vale:*— Emek-keziz*(1), Valley(3), valley(55), valleys(10).

6011. עֹמֶק **omeq** (771b); from 6009; *depth:*— depth(1), depths(1).

6012. עָמֵק **ameq** (771b); from 6009; *deep, unfathomable:*— unintelligible(3).

6013. עָמֹק **amoq** (771b); from 6009; *deep:*— deep(6), deeper(8), exceedingly mysterious(1), mysteries(1).

6014a. עָמַר **amar** (771c); denom. vb. from 6016a; *to bind sheaves:*— binder of sheaves(1).

6014b. עָמַר **amar** (771c); a prim. root; *to deal tyrannically:*— deals with him violently(1), mistreat(1).

6015. עֲמַר **amar** (1107a); (Ara.) of unc. der.; *wool:*— wool(1).

6016a. עֹמֶר **omer** (771b); from an unused word; *a sheaf:*— sheaf(5), sheaves(3).

6016b. עֹמֶר **omer** (771c); from the same as 6016a; *an omer* (a measure):— omer(3), omerful*(2), omers(1).

6017. עֲמֹרָה **Amorah** (771d); from 6014b; a city in the Jordan Valley:— Gomorrah(19).

6018. עָמְרִי **Omri** (771d); from an unused word; a king of Isr., also several other Isr.:— Omri(18).

6019. עַמְרָם **Amram** (771d); from the same as 6018; the father of Moses, also an Isr.:— Amram(12), Amram's(2).

6020. עַמְרָמִי **Amrami** (771d); from 6019; desc. of Amram:— Amramites(2).

6021. עֲמָשָׂא **Amasa** (771d); of unc. der.; two Isr.:— Amasa(16).

6022. עֲמָשַׂי **Amasay** (772a); from the same as 6021; the name of several Isr.:— Amasai(5).

6023. עֲמַשְׁסַי **Amashsay** (772a); prob. from the same as 6021; an Isr. priest:— Amashsai(1).

6024. עֲנָב **Anab** (772a); from the same as 6025; "grape," a place in the hill country of Judah:— Anab(2).

6025. עֵנָב **enab** (772a); from an unused word; *a grape:*— grape(1), grapes(17), raisin*(1).

6026. עָנֹג **anog** (772b); a prim. root; *to be soft, delicate, dainty:*— dainty(1), delicateness(1), delight(4), delighted(1), jest(1), take delight(2).

6027. עֹנֶג **oneg** (772b); from 6026; *daintiness, exquisite delight:*— delight(1), luxurious(1).

6028. עָנֹג **anog** (772b); from 6026; *dainty:*— delicate(2), delicate woman(1).

6029. עָנַד **anad** (772c); a prim. root; *to bind* (around or upon):— bind(1), tie(1).

6030a. עָנָה **anah** (772c); a prim. root; *to answer, respond:*— accuse(1), accused(1), agrees to make(1), answer(94), answer*(1), answered(102), answering(1), answers(5), bear(2), bear witness(1), bears(1), bears witness(1), brought to answer(1), brought to give(1), continued(2), declare*(1), get...answer(1), give a answer(1), give an account(1), give him an answer(1), giving(1), go(1), grant them their petition(1), hailed(1), have(1), replied(29), replied*(1), respond(6), responded(3), responded*(7), said(1), said*(2), spoke(3), tell(1), testified(1), testifies(3), testify(5), testimony(1), unanswered*(1), witnessed(1).

6030b. עָנָה **anah** (775d); a prim. root; *to be occupied, busied:*— afflicted(1), keeps him occupied(1), occupy(1).

6031a. עָנָה **anah** (776a); a prim. root; *to be bowed down* or *afflicted:*— afflict(16), afflict him at all(1), afflicted(22), affliction(1), disturbed(1), do violence(1), force(1), humble(12), humbled(6), humbling(1), mistreat(1), oppressed(1), oppressors(1), ravish(1), ravished(2), silenced(1), submit(1), treated her harshly(1), violate(1), violated(5), weakened(1).

6031b. עָנָה **anah** (777b); a prim. root; *to sing:*— cry(3), howl(1), sang(2), sing(7), singing(1).

6032. עֲנָה **anah** (1107a); (Ara.) corr. to 6030a; *to answer:*— answered(7), reflected(1), replied(6), responded(5), said*(1), spoke(5).

6033. עֲנָה **anah** (1107c); see 6040b.

6034. עֲנָה **Anah** (777b); from 6031b; two Horites:— Anah(12).

עוֹנָה **onah**; see 5772a.

6035. עָנָו **anav** (776c); from 6031a; *poor, afflicted, humble, meek:*— afflicted(8), afflicted ones(1), humble(10), poor(1).

6036. עָנוּב **Anub** (772b); from the same as 6025; an Isr.:— Anub(1).

6037. עַנְוָה **anvah** (776c); the same as 6038, q.v.

6038. עֲנָוָה **anavah** (776c); from 6031a; *humility:*— gentleness(1), help(1), humility(4), meekness(1).

6039. עֱנוּת **enuth** (776d); from 6031a; *affliction:*— affliction(1).

6040a. עֳנִי **oni** (777a); from 6031a; *affliction, poverty:*— afflicted*(1), affliction(33), great pains(1), misery(2).

6040b. עֲנֵי **anay** (1107c); (Ara.) corr. to 6041; *poor, needy:*— poor(1).

6041. עָנִי **ani** (776d); from 6031a; *poor, afflicted, humble:*— afflicted(42), afflicted one(1), humble(3), lowly(1), needy(2), needy and poor(1), oppressed(1), poor(19), poor man(2), who is humble(1), wretched(1).

6042. עֻנִּי **Unni** (777d); of unc. der.; two Levites:— Unni(3).

6043. עֲנָיָה **Anayah** (777d); of unc. der.; an Isr.:— Anaiah(2).

6044. עָנִים **Anim** (745d); from the same as 5869; a place in the hill country of Judah:— Anim(1).

6045. עִנְיָן **inyan** (775d); from 6030b; *occupation, task:*— effort(1), investment(1), task(6).

6046. עָנֵם **Anem** (745c); of unc. der.; a city of Issachar, perh. the same as 5873:— Anem(1).

6047. עֲנָמִים **Anamim** (777d); of for. or.; a tribe desc. from Mizraim, prob. located in or near Eg.:— Anam(1), Anamim(1).

6048. עֲנַמֶּלֶךְ **Anammelek** (777d); of for. or.; an Assyr. god:— Anammelech(1).

6049a. עָנַן **anan** (778a); a prim. root; *to practice soothsaying:*— diviners'(1), fortune-tellers(1), practice witchcraft(1), practiced witchcraft(2), practices witchcraft(1), soothsayers(2), soothsaying(1), sorceress(1).

6049b. עָנַן **anan** (778a); denom. vb. from 6051; *to bring a cloud:*— bring(1).

6050. עֲנַן **anan** (1107c); (Ara.) corr. to 6051; *a cloud:*— clouds(1).

6051. עָנָן **anan** (777d); from an unused word; *a cloud mass, cloud:*— cloud(78), clouds(7), cloudy(1), heavy mist(1).

6052. עָנָן **Anan** (778b); from 6049a; an Isr.:— Anan(1).

6053. עֲנָנָה **ananah** (778a); from the same as 6051; *a cloud:*— cloud(1).

6054. עֲנָנִי **Anani** (778b); from 6049a; an Isr.:— Anani(1).

6055. עֲנַנְיָה **Ananyah** (778b); from 6049a; an Isr., also a place near Jer.:— Ananiah(2).

6056. עֲנַף anaph (1107c); (Ara.) corr. to 6057; *a bough:*— branches(4).

6057. עָנָף anaph (778c); from an unused word; *a branch, bough:*— boughs(3), branch(1), branches(3).

6058. עָנֵף aneph (778c); from the same as 6057; *full of branches:*— full of branches(1).

6059. עָנַק anaq (778d); denom. vb. from 6060; *to serve as a necklace:*— furnish him liberally(1), necklace(1).

6060. עֲנָק anaq (778d); from the same as 6061; *a necklace, neck pendant:*— neck bands(1), ornaments(1), strand(1).

6061. עֲנָק Anaq (778c); from an unused word; "neck," a Canaanite:— Anak(9).

6062. עֲנָק Anaq (778c); from the same as 6061; "neck," a giant people around Hebron and in Philistia:— Anakim(9).

6063. עָנֵר Aner (778d); of unc. der.; an ally of Abram, also a place in Manasseh:— Aner(3).

6064. עָנַשׁ anash (778d); denom. vb. from 6066; *to fine, mulct:*— fine(3), fined(1), imposed(1), pay the penalty(1), punished(2), surely be fined(1).

6065. עֲנָשׁ anash (1107c); (Ara.) corr. to 6064; *amercing, confiscation:*— confiscation(1).

6066. עֹנֶשׁ onesh (778d); from an unused word; *an indemnity, fine:*— fine(1), penalty(1).

6067. עֲנָת Anath (779a); of unc. der.; father of Shamgar:— Anath(2).

6068. עֲנָתוֹת Anathoth (779a); of unc. der.; a place near Jer., also two Isr.:— Anathoth(15).

6069. עַנְּתֹתִי Annethothi or
עַנְּתוֹתִי Annethothi (779a); from 6068; inhab. of Anathoth:— Anathoth(1), Anathothite(4).

6070. עַנְתֹתִיָּה Anthothiyyah (779a); of unc. der.; a Benjamite:— Anthothijah(1).

6071. עָסִיס asis (779b); from 6072; *sweet wine:*— juice(1), sweet wine(4).

6072. עָסַס asas (779a); a prim. root; *to press, crush, tread down:*— tread down(1).

6073. עֳפֶא ophe (779b); see 6074b.

6074a. עֳפִי ophi (1107c); (Ara.) corr. to 6074b; *leafage, foliage:*— foliage(3).

6074b. עֳפָיִם ophayim (779b); of unc. der.; *foliage:*— branches(1).

6075a. עָפַל aphal (779b); a prim. root; *to swell:*— proud(1).

6075b. עָפַל aphal (779c); a prim. root; perh. *to be heedless:*— heedlessly(1).

6076a. עֹפֶל ophel (779b); from 6075a; *a mound, hill:*— hill(3).

6076b. עֹפֶל ophel (779b); from 6075a; *a tumor:*— tumors(6).

6077. עֹפֶל Ophel (779b); from 6075a; a fortified mound or hill in Jer.:— Ophel(5).

6078. עָפְנִי Ophni (779c); from 6075b; a place in Benjamin:— Ophni(1).

6079. עַפְעַף aphaph (733d); from 5774a; *eyelid:*— breaking(1), eyelids(8), gaze(1).

6080. עָפַר aphar (780a); denom. vb. from 6083; *to throw dust:*— threw(1).

6081. עֵפֶר Epher (780a); from the same as 6082; two Isr., also a Midianite:— Epher(4).

6082. עֹפֶר opher (780a); from an unused word; *a young hart, stag:*— fawns(2), young(3).

6083. עָפָר aphar (779c); from an unused word; *dry earth, dust:*— ashes(2), debris(2), dirt(1), dry soil(1), dust(91), dusty(1), earth(5), ground(1), heap(2), loose earth(1), plaster(3), rubbish(1), rubble(1).

עֶפְרָה aphrah; see 1036.

6084. עָפְרָה Ophrah (780b); from the same as 6082; an Isr., also two places in Isr.:— Ophrah(8).

6085. עֶפְרוֹן Ephron (780b); from the same as 6082; a Hittite, also a mountain and a place in Isr.:— Ephron(13), Ephron's(1).

עֹפֶרֶת ophereth; see 5777.

6086. עֵץ ets (781c); from an unused word; *tree, trees, wood:*— carpenters*(4), framework(1), gallows(9), handle(1), logs(1), shaft(3), stalks(1), stick(8), sticks(3), timber(19), timbers(5), tree(74), trees(71), wild*(1), wood(111), wooden(6).

6087a. עָצַב atsab (780c); a prim. root; *to hurt, pain, grieve:*— crossed(1), distort(1), grieved(11), hurt(1), pain(1).

6087b. עָצַב atsab (781a); a prim. root; *to shape, fashion:*— fashioned(1), image(1).

6088. עֲצַב atsab (1107d); (Ara.) corr. to 6087a; *to pain, grieve:*— troubled(1).

6089a. עֶצֶב etseb (780d); from 6087a; *a hurt, pain, toil:*— hard-earned goods(1), harsh(1), labor(1), pain(1), painful labors(1), sorrow(1).

6089b. עֶצֶב etseb (781a); from 6087b; *a vessel:*— jar(1).

6090a. עֹצֶב otseb (780d); from 6087a; *a pain:*— hurtful(1), pain(2).

6090b. עֹצֶב otseb (781b); from 6087b; *an idol:*— idol(1).

6091. עָצָב atsab (781b); from 6087b; *an idol:*— idols(13), images(4).

6092. עָצֵב atseb or
עַצָּב atstsab (780d); from 6087a; *toiler:*— workers(1).

6093. עִצָּבוֹן itstsabon (781a); from 6087a; *a pain, toil:*— pain(1), toil(2).

6094. עַצֶּבֶת atstsebeth (781a); from 6087a; *a hurt, injury, pain:*— pains(1), sad(1), sorrows(1), trouble(1), wounds(1).

6095. עָצָה atsah (781b); a prim. root; *to shut:*— winks(1).

6096. עָצֶה atseh (782b); from an unused word; *spine:*— backbone(1).

6097. עֵצָה etsah (782a); from the same as 6086; *trees:*— trees(1).

6098. עֵצָה etsah (420a); from 3289; *counsel, advice:*— advice(11), consultation(2), counsel(52), counselor*(1), counselors*(1), counsels(1), designs(1), plan(8), plans(2), purpose(6), scheme(1), schemes(1), strategy(1).

6099. עָצוּם atsum (783a); from 6105a; *mighty, numerous:*— great(1), large number(1), mightier(6), mighty(14), mighty men(1), mighty ones(1), numerous(1), strong(5), stronger(1).

6100. עֶצְיוֹן גֶּבֶר Etsyon Geber (782b); from an unused word and 1397; a city on the shore of the Gulf of Aqaba:— Ezion-geber(7).

6101. עָצַל atsel (782b); a prim. root; *to be sluggish:*— delay(1).

6102. עָצֵל atsel (782b); from 6101; *sluggish, lazy:*— lazy(1), lazy one(1), sluggard(12).

6103. עַצְלָה atslah (782b); from 6101; *sluggishness:*— indolence(1), laziness(1).

6104. עַצְלוּת atsluth (782c); from 6101; *sluggishness:*— idleness(1).

6105a. עָצַם atsom (782c); a prim. root; *to be vast, mighty, numerous:*— became...mighty(2), gain power(1), made them stronger(1), mighty(2), numerous(6), powerful(2), strong(2), vast(1).

6105b. עָצַם atsam (783b); a prim. root; *to shut* (the eyes):— shut(1), shuts(1).

6105c. עָצַם atsam (783a, 1126a); denom. vb. from 6106; *to break bones:*— broken his bones(1).

6106. עֶצֶם etsem (782c); from 6105a; *bone, substance, self:*— body(3), bone(15), bone of my bones(1), bones(83), itself(1), limb(1), pains(1), same(7), strength(1), very(7), very same(4), wood(1).

6107. עֶצֶם Etsem (783a); from 6105a; "bone," a place in the Negev of Judah:— Ezem(3).

6108. עֹצֶם otsem (782c); from 6105a; *might, bones:*— frame(1), might(1), strength(1).

6109. עָצְמָה otsmah (782c); from 6105a; *might:*— might(1), power(2).

6110. עַצֻּמָה atsumah (783b); from an unused word; perh. *defense:*— strong(1).

6111. עַצְמוֹן Atsmon (783b); from 6105a; a place on the S. border of Canaan:— Azmon(3).

6112. עֶצְנִי Etsni (783b); of unc. der.; a descriptive title for one of David's men:— Eznite(1).

6113. עָצַר atsar (783c); a prim. root; *to restrain, retain:*— able*(2), bond(5), checked(3), closed fast(1), confined(3), could(1), detain(2), detained(1), held back(2), kept(1), prevail(1), prevented(1), recover(1), refrain(1), restrained(1), restrains(1), restricted(2), retain(2), retained(2), rule(1), shut(7), slow down(1), stayed(1), stop(1), stopped(1).

6114. עֶצֶר etser (783d); from 6113; perh. *restraint:*— ruler*(1).

6115. עֹצֶר otser (783d); from 6113; *restraint, coercion:*— barren(1), oppression(2).

6116. עֲצָרָה atsarah or
עֲצֶרֶת atsereth (783d); from 6113; *an assembly:*— assembly(2), solemn assemblies(1), solemn assembly(8).

6117. עָקַב aqab (784b); denom. vb. from 6119; *to follow at the heel, assail insidiously, circumvent, overreach:*— deals craftily(1), heel(1), restrain(1), supplanted(1), took(1).

6118. עֵקֶב eqeb (784c); from an unused word; *consequence, as a consequence of, because:*— because(3), because*(7), end(2), reward(2).

6119. עָקֵב aqeb (784a); from an unused word; *heel, footprint, hind part:*— footprints(1), footsteps(1), heel(4), heels(3), hoofs(1), rear guard(1), steps(1), trail(1).

6120. עָקֵב aqeb (784c); from the same as 6119; *overreacher:*— foes(1).

6121a. עָקֹב aqob (784c); from the same as 6119; *insidious, deceitful, tracked by footprints:*— deceitful(1), tracked(1).

6121b. עָקֹב aqob (784c); from the same as 6119; *steep, hilly:*— rough ground(1).

6122. עָקְבָה oqbah (784c); from the same as 6119; *insidiousness:*— cunning(1).

6123. עָקַד aqad (785b); a prim. root; *to bind:*— bound(1).

עֵקֶד eqed; see 1044.

6124. עָקֹד aqod (785b); from an unused word; *striped, streaked:*— striped(7).

6125. עָקָה aqah (734b); from 5781; *pressure:*— pressure(1).

6126. עַקּוּב Aqqub (784d); from the same as 6119; the name of several Isr.:— Akkub(8).

6127. עָקַל aqal (785b); a prim. root; *to bend, twist:*— perverted(1).

6128. עֲקַלְקַל aqalqal (785c); from 6127; *crooked:*— crooked ways(1), roundabout(1).

6129. עֲקַלָּתוֹן aqallathon (785c); from 6127; *crooked:*— twisted(1).

6130. עָקָן Aqan (785c); from 6127; a desc. of Esau:— Akan(1).

6131. עָקַר aqar (785c); denom. vb. from 6133; *to pluck* or *root up:*— uproot(1), uprooted(1).

6132. עֲקַר aqar (1107d); (Ara.) corr. to 6131; *to be rooted up:*— pulled out by the roots(1).

6133. עֵקֶר eqer (785c); from an unused word; *an offshoot, member:*— descendants(1).

6134. עֵקֶר Eqer (785d); from the same as 6133; a man of Judah:— Eker(1).

6135. עָקָר aqar (785d); from the same as 6133; *barren:*— barren(8), barren one(1), barren woman(1), barren woman(1).

6136a. עִקַּר iqqar (1107d); (Ara.) corr. to 6133; *root, stock:*— stump(3).

6136b. עִקֵּר iqqer (785c); denom. vb. from 6133; *to hamstring:*— hamstring(1), hamstrung(3), lamed(1).

6137. עַקְרָב aqrab (785d); from the same as 6133; *scorpion:*— scorpions(6).

6138. עֶקְרוֹן Eqron (785d); from the same as 6133; a Philistine city:— Ekron(22).

6139. עֶקְרוֹנִי Eqroni (785d); from 6138; inhab. of Ekron:— Ekronite(1), Ekronites(1).

6140. עָקַשׁ aqash (786a); a prim. root; *to twist:*— crooked*(1), declare me guilty(1), made their crooked(1), perverts(1), twist(1).

6141. עִקֵּשׁ iqqesh (786a); from 6140; *twisted, perverted:*— crooked(2), crooked*(1), perverse(4), perverted(2), who is perverse(1), who has(1), who has a crooked(1).

6142. עִקֵּשׁ Iqqesh (786a); from 6140; a Tekoan:— Ikkesh(3).

6143. עִקְּשׁוּת iqqeshuth (786a); from 6140; *crookedness:*— deceitful(1), perverse(1).

6144. עָר Ar (786b); of unc. der.; a place in Moab:— Ar(6).

6145. עָר ar (786b); from the same as 6144; perh. *adversary:*— adversary(1), enemies(1).

6146. עָר ar (1108a); (Ara.) corr. to 6145; *foe:*— adversaries(1).

6147. עֵר Er (735c); from 5782; two men of Judah:— Er(10).

6148. עָרַב arab (786c); a prim. root; *to take on pledge, give in pledge, exchange:*— associate(2), became surety(1), become guarantors(1), become surety(1), becomes(1), becomes surety(2), dare to risk(1), deal(1), dealers(1), guarantor(1), intermingled(1), make a bargain(2), mingled(1), mortgaging(1), security(1), share(1), surety(2).

6149. עָרֵב arab (787a); a prim. root; *to be sweet* or *pleasing:*— pleasant(1), please(1), pleasing(3), sweet(2), took pleasure(1).

6150. עָרַב arab (788a); denom. vb. from 6153; *to become evening, grow dark:*— close(1), evening(1), turns to gloom(1).

6151. עֲרַב arab (1107d); (Ara.) corr. to the root of 6154a; *to mix:*— combine(2), mixed(2).

6152a. עֲרָב Arab (787b); from an unused word; "steppe-dwellers," a country E. of Isr.:— Arabia(4), Arabs(1).

6152b. עֲרָב Arab (787a); from an unused word; "a desert plateau," a country E. of Isr.:— Arabia(2).

6153. עֶרֶב ereb (787d); from an unused word; *evening:*— evening(114), evening*(1), evenings(2), every evening(1), night(2), sunset(1), twilight(11).

6154a. עֵרֶב ereb (786b); from an unused word; *mixture, mixed company:*— foreign people(2), foreigners(2), mixed(1).

6154b. עֵרֶב ereb (786c); from the same as 6154a; *woof:*— woof(9).

6155. עָרָב arab or

עֲרָבָה arabah (788b); from the same as 6158; (a kind of tree) perh. *poplar,* also a wadi in Moab:— Arabim(1), poplars(1), willows(3).

6156. עָרֵב areb (787a); from 6149; *sweet, pleasant:*— sweet(2).

6157. עָרֹב arob (786c); from the same as 6154a; prob. *a swarm:*— swarm of flies(1), swarms(7), swarms of flies(1).

6158. עֹרֵב oreb (788b); from an unused word; *a raven:*— raven(6), ravens(4).

6159. עֹרֵב Oreb (1126a); from the same as 6153; a Midianite:— Oreb(7).

6160. עֲרָבָה arabah (787b); from the same as 6152b; *a steppe* or *desert plain,* also a desert valley running S. from the Sea of Galilee:— Arabah(28), desert(7), desert plain(2), desert plains(2), deserts(3), fords(1), plain(1), plains(15), wilderness(1).

6161. עֲרֻבָּה arubbah (786d); from the same as 6154a; *a thing exchanged, pledge, token:*— guarantor(1), news(1).

6162. עֵרָבוֹן erabon (786d); from 6148; *a pledge:*— pledge(4).

6163a. עַרְבִי Arbi (787b); from 6152a; inhab. of Arabia:— Arab(2), Arabians(2), Arabs(3).

6163b. עֲרָבִי Arabi (787b); from the same as 6152b; an inhab. of Arabia:— Arab(2).

6164. עַרְבָתִי Arbathi (112c); from 1026; inhab. of Arabah:— Arbathite(2).

6165. עָרַג arag (788b); a prim. root; *to long for:*— pant(1), pants(2).

6166a. עֲרָד Arad (788c); of unc. der.; a Canaanite city in the Negev:— Arad(4).

6166b. עֲרָד Arad (788c); from the same as 6166a; a Benjamite:— Arad(1).

6167. עֲרָד arad (1107d); (Ara.) corr. to 6171; *a wild donkey:*— wild donkeys(1).

6168. עָרָה arah (788c); a prim. root; *to be naked* or *bare:*— defenseless*(1), emptied(1), empty(1), laid bare(2), lay him open(1), leave(1), made naked(1), make their bare(1), make yourself naked(1), poured(2), raze(2), spreading(1), uncovered(1).

6169. עָרָה arah (788d); from 6168; *bare place:*— bulrushes(1).

6170. עֲרוּגָה arugah (788c); from 6165; *a garden terrace* or *bed:*— bed(1), beds(3).

6171. עָרוֹד arod (789b); prob. of for. or.; *a wild donkey:*— swift donkey(1).

6172. עֶרְוָה ervah (788d); from 6168; *nakedness:*— bare(1), indecency(1), indecent(1), nakedness(48), shame(1), undefended parts(2).

6173. עַרְוָה arvah (1107d); (Ara.) corr. to 6172; *dishonor:*— dishonor(1).

6174. עָרוֹם arom or

עָרֹם arom (736a); from 5783; *naked:*— naked(16).

6175. עָרוּם arum (791a); from 6191; *crafty, shrewd, sensible:*— crafty(2), prudent(2), prudent man(3), sensible(2), sensible man(1), shrewd(1).

6176. עֲרוֹעֵר aroer (792d); from 6209; (prob. a tree or bush) perh. *juniper:*— bush(1), juniper(1).

6177. עֲרוֹעֵר Aroer or

עֲרֹעֵר Aroer or

עַרְעֵר Aror (792d); from 6209; three cities in Isr.:— Aroer(16).

6178. עָרוּץ aruts (792a); from 6206; *dreadful:*— dreadful(1).

6179. עֵרִי Eri (735c); from 5782; a Gadite:— Eri(2).

6180. עֵרִי Eri (735d); from 6179; desc. of Eri:— Erites(1).

6181. עֶרְיָה eryah (789a); from 6168; *nakedness:*— bare(4), bare*(1), nakedness(1).

6182. עֲרִיסָה arisah (791b); of unc. der.; perh. *coarse meal:*— dough(4).

6183. עָרִיף ariph (791d); from 6201; *a cloud:*— clouds(1).

6184. עָרִיץ arits (792a); from 6206; *awe-inspiring, terror-striking:*— dread(1), most ruthless(2), ruthless(6), ruthless men(1), ruthless ones(1), tyrant(1), tyrants(4), violent(2), violent men(2).

6185. עֲרִירִי ariri (792d); from 6209; *stripped:*— childless(4).

6186a. עָרַךְ arak (789b); a prim. root; *to arrange* or *set in order:*— arrange(5), arranged(5), array(1), arrayed(13), battle lines(2), comparable(1), compare(2), draw(2), draw up in formation(3), draw up their battle lines(1), draw up your battle lines(1), drew(4), drew up in battle(2), drew up in formation(3), equal(2), handle(1), keep(1), keep it in order(2), keep the in order(1), laid in order(1), lay(1), line(1), Marshalled(1), order(3), ordered(1), prepare(2), prepared(2), present(1), ready(1), recount(1), set(5), set it in order(1), state the case in order(1).

6186b. עָרַךְ arak (790a); denom. vb. from 6187; *to value, tax:*— taxed(1), value(4), values(1).

6187. עֵרֶךְ erek (789d); from 6186a; *an order, row, estimate:*— arrangement(1), assessment(1), equal(1), frame(1), suit(1), valuation(25), value(2), what belongs(1).

6188. עָרֵל aral (790c); denom. vb. from 6190; *to count as foreskin* (as uncircumcised):— count(1), expose your own nakedness(1).

6189. עָרֵל arel (790c); from the same as 6190; *having foreskin* (uncircumcised):— closed(1), forbidden(1), uncircumcised(31), unskilled(2).

6190. עָרְלָה orlah (790b); from an unused word; *foreskin:*— forbidden(1), foreskin(7), foreskins(4), Gibeath-haaraloth*(1), uncircumcised(2).

6191. עָרַם arom (791a); a prim. root; *to be shrewd* or *crafty:*— become shrewd(1), make shrewd(1), sensible(1), very cunning(1).

6192. עָרַם aram (790d); a prim. root; *to be heaped up:*— piled(1).

6193. עֹרֶם orem (791a); from 6191; *craftiness:*— shrewdness(1).

עֵרֹם erom; see 5903.

עָרֹם arom; see 6174.

6194. עֲרֵמָה aremah (790d); from 6192; *a heap:*— heap(2), heap of grain(1), heaps(5), rubble(1), sacks of grain(1).

6195. עָרְמָה ormah (791a); from 6191; *craftiness, prudence:*— craftily(2), prudence(3).

6196. עַרְמוֹן armon (790d); from an unused word; *plane tree:*— plane trees(2).

6197. עֵרָן Eran (735d); from 5782; an Ephraimite:— Eran(1).

6198. עֵרָנִי Erani (735d); from 6197; desc. of Eran:— Eranites(1).

6199. עַרְעָר arar (792d); from 6209; *stripped, destitute:*— destitute(1).

עֲרֹעֵר Aroer; see 6177.

6200. עֲרֹעֵרִי Aroeri (793a); from 6177; inhab. of Aroer:— Aroerite(1).

6201. עָרַף araph (791c); a prim. root; *to drip, drop:*— drop(1), drop down(1).

6202. עָרַף araph (791c); denom. vb. from 6203; *to break the neck:*— break its neck(2), break the neck(1), break down(1), breaks a neck(1), neck was broken(1).

6203. עֹרֶף oreph (791b); from an unused word; *back of the neck, neck:*— back(5), backs(5), became stubborn*(2), neck(11), necks(2), obstinate*(4), stubborn*(2), stubbornness*(1).

6204. עָרְפָּה Orpah (791c); from the same as 6203; sister-in-law of Ruth:— Orpah(2).

6205. עֲרָפֶל araphel (791d); from 6201; *cloud, heavy cloud:*— deep darkness(1), gloom(1), gloomy(1), thick cloud(3), thick darkness(7), thick gloom(2).

6206. עָרַץ arats (791d); a prim. root; *to cause to tremble, tremble:*— cause(1), cause terror(1), cause trembling(1), dread(3), feared(2), make the tremble(2), shocked(1), stand in awe(1), tremble(4).

6207. עָרַק araq (792b); a prim. root; *to gnaw:*— gnaw(1), gnawing(1).

6208. עַרְקִי Arqi (792b); from 6207; desc. of Canaan, inhab. of the city of Arka:— Arkite(1), Arkites(1).

6209. עָרַר arar (792c); a prim. root; *to strip oneself:*— completely razed(1), stripped(1), undress(1).

6210. עֶרֶשׂ eres (793a); from an unused word; *a couch, divan:*— bed(1), bed*(1), bedstead(2), couch(4), couches(1), sickbed*(1).

6211. עָשׁ ash (799c); from 6244; *a moth:*— moth(5), moth-eaten*(1).

עָשׁ Ash; see 5906.

6212a. עֵשֶׂב eseb (793b); from an unused word; *herb, herbage:*— grass(8), herb(1), herbs(1), plant(9), plants(3), vegetation(11).

6212b. עֲשַׂב asab (1108a); (Ara.) corr. to 6212a; *herbage, grass:*— grass(5).

6213a. עָשָׂה asah (793c); a prim. root; *do, make:*— accomplish(8), accomplish much(1), accomplished(4), accomplishing(1), achieve(1), acquired(6), act(22), acted(13), acts(7), administer(1), administered(1), administered*(1), apply(1), appointed(3), artificial(1), attain(1), bear(4), bearing(2), behave(1), bestowed(1), bring(4), bring it about(1), bring about(1), bring forth(1), brought(1), brought about(4), brought forth(1), build*(1), built(3), busy(1), cared(1), carefully(3), carefully observing(1), carried(3), carries(2), carry(8), carved(5), cause(3), causing(1), celebrate(19), celebrated(12), celebrates(1), certainly carry(1), certainly make(1), certainly makes(1), certainly perform(2), commit(8), commits(7), commits and does(1), committed(35), committed and practices(1), committing(6), construct(3), deal(30), deals(1), dealt(22), desisting(1), destroy*(2), developing(1), did(310), did not do(1), displease*(1), do(479), do as has been done(1), do as i have done(1), doer(1), doers(1), does(48), doing(63), done(327), done you will do(1), done*(1), earns(1), established(1), establishes(1), evildoer*(2), evildoers*(1), execute(24), executed(10), executes(5), executing(1), exercise(1), exercises(1), exerted(1), fared(1), fashions(1), fit(1), follow(1), followed(1), fulfill(1), fulfilling(1), gather(1), gave(4), give you over(1), grant(1), granted(1), greedily(1), happen(1), happened(1), held(2), help(1), hold(1), imitate(1), imparted(1), inclines(1), indeed perform(1), industrious*(1), inflict(1), inflicted(1), inlaid(1), instituted(2), introduced(2), keep(1), kept(1), labored(1), laborers(1), made(369), maintain(6), maintained(1), make(200), make your ready(1), Maker(13), maker(4), makes(19), making(5), obey(1), observe(33), observe them carefully(1), observe to do(2), observe carefully(2), observed(12), observes(5), offer(35), offered(4), offering(1), oppressed*(1), ordained(1), perform(31), performed(23), performers(1), performing(2), performing the made(1), performs(3), practice(9), practice*(1), practiced(4), practices(6), practicing(1), prepare(26), prepared(19), preparing(2), present(5), presented(1), produce(4), produced(5), provide(13), provided(2), provides(1), punish(1), put(1), put into effect(1), put forth(1), ready(1), reign*(1), remade*(1), responsible(1), sacrifice(2), set(3), set*(1), show(16), showed(6), showing(2), shown(9), shows(3), spend(1), surely show(1), take action(6), thoroughly deal(1), treat(3), tried(1), trim(1), trimmed(1), truly practice(1), use(1), used(4), wage(2), waged(2), work(12), worked(7), worker(2), working(3), workmen*(5), works(6), woven(1), writing(1), wrought(2), yield(5), yielded(1), yields(1).

6213b. עָשָׂה asah (796b); a prim. root; *to press, squeeze:*— handled(3).

6214. עֲשָׂהאֵל Asahel (795c); from 6213a and 410; "God has made," four Isr.:— Asahel(18).

6215. עֵשָׂו Esav (796c); from 6213b; oldest son of Isaac:— Esau(84), Esau's(13).

6216. עָשׁוֹק ashoq (799a); from 6231; *oppressor, extortioner:*— oppressor(1).

6217. עֲשׁוּקִים ashuqim (799a); from 6231; *oppression, extortion:*— acts of oppression(1), oppressions(2).

6218. עָשׂוֹר asor or

עָשֹׂר asor (797c); from the same as 6235; *a ten, decade:*— ten(1), ten strings(2), ten-stringed(1), tenth(12).

6219. עָשׁוֹת ashoth (799d); from 6245a; perh. *smooth:*— wrought(1).

6220. עַשְׁוָת Ashvath (798b); of unc. der.; an Asherite:— Ashvath(1).

6221. עֲשִׂיאֵל Asiel (795c); from 6213a; a Simeonite:— Asiel(1).

6222. עֲשָׂיָה Asayah (795c); from 6213a; four Isr.:— Asaiah(8).

6223. עָשִׁיר ashir (799b); from 6238; *rich:*— rich(13), rich man(6), rich man's(2), rich men(2).

6224. עֲשִׂירִי asiri or

עֲשִׂירִיָּה asiriyyah or

עֲשִׂירִית asirith (798a); from the same as 6235; *tenth:*— one-tenth(1), tenth(27), tenth portion(1).

6225. עָשַׁן ashan (798c); denom. vb. from 6227; *to smoke, be angry:*— angry(1), burn(1), smoke(4).

6226. עָשֵׁן ashen (798c); from the same as 6227; *smoking:*— smoking(1), smoldering(1).

6227. עָשָׁן ashan (798c); from an unused word; *smoke:*— smoke(24), smoking(1).

6228. עָשָׁן Ashan (798c); from the same as 6227; a place in Judah and later in Simeon:— Ashan(4).

6229. עָשַׂק asaq (796c); a prim. root; *to contend:*— contended(1).

6230. עֵשֶׂק Eseq (796c); from 6229; "contention," a well in Gerar:— Esek(1).

6231. עָשַׁק ashaq (798d); a prim. root; *to oppress, wrong, extort:*— crushed(1), defrauded(2), extorted(1), got(1), laden(1), oppress(11), oppressed(9), oppresses(3), oppressor(2), oppressors(2), practiced(2), rages(1), rob(1).

6232. עֵשֶׁק Esheq (799a); from 6231; a Benjamite:— Eshek(1).

6233. עֹשֶׁק osheq (799a); from 6231; *oppression, extortion:*— extortion(2), oppressed*(1), oppression(12).

עָשֻׁק ashuq; see 6217.

6234. עָשְׁקָה oshqah (799a); from 6231; *oppression, distress:*— oppressed(1).

6235. עֶשֶׂר eser or

עֲשָׂרָה asarah (796d); from an unused word; *ten:*— 10(1), 10,000*(20), 110*(1), 20,000*(1), 410*(1), fifteen*(1), seventeen*(1), ten(147), ten shekels apiece(1), tens(3).

6236. עֲשַׂר asar or

עַשְׂרָה asrah (1108a); (Ara.) corr. to 6235; *ten:*— 12*(1), ten(4), twelve*(1).

6237. עָשַׂר asar (797c); denom. vb. from 6235; *to take the tenth of, tithe:*— paying(1), receive the tithes(1), receive tithes(1), surely give(1), surely give a tenth(1), surely tithe(1), take a tenth(2).

6238. עָשַׁר ashar (799b); a prim. root; *to be or become rich:*— become rich(4), becomes rich(1), enrich(2), enriched(1), gain(1), gain wealth(1), made...rich(1), makes rich(2), pretends to be rich(1), rich(3).

6239. עֹשֶׁר osher (799b); from 6238; *riches:*— fortune(1), riches(32), wealth(4).

6240. עָשָׂר asar or

עֶשְׂרֵה esreh (797a); from the same as 6235; *ten:*— 1,017*(2), 112*(3), 12*(2), 12,000*(8), 120,000*(1), 13*(1), 14,000*(1), 14,700*(1), 15*(1), 15,000*(1), 16,000*(2), 16,750*(1), 17,200*(1), 18*(2), 18,000*(6), 2,812*(1), 2,818*(1), 212*(1), 218*(1), eighteen*(8), eighteenth*(11), eleven*(15), eleventh*(17), fifteen*(14), fifteenth*(17), fourteen*(17), fourteenth*(23), nineteen*(3), nineteenth*(4), seventeen*(5), seventeenth*(6), sixteen*(18), sixteenth*(3), thirteen*(12), thirteenth*(11), twelfth*(22), twelve*(93).

6241. עִשָּׂרוֹן issaron (798a); from the same as 6235; *tenth part:*— one-tenth(1), tenth(5), three-tenths*(8), two-tenths*(11).

6242. עֶשְׂרִים esrim (797d); from the same as 6235; *twenty:*— 1,222*(1), 120*(4), 120,000*(5), 122*(2), 123*(2), 127*(3), 128*(4), 2,322*(1), 20(2), 20,000*(9), 20,200*(1), 20,800*(1), 22,000*(7), 22,034*(1), 22,200*(1), 22,273*(1), 22,600*(1), 220*(2), 223*(2), 23,000*(1), 24*(1), 24,000*(15), 25,000*(16), 25,100*(1), 26,000*(2), 27,000*(1), 28*(1), 28,600*(1), 29*(2), 3,023*(1), 320*(2), 323*(1), 324*(1), 328*(1), 6,720*(2), 621*(2), 623*(1), 628*(1), 721*(1), 725*(1), 822*(1), 928*(1), twentieth(9), twenty(111), twenty-eight*(4), twenty-fifth*(3), twenty-first*(4), twenty-five*(22), twenty-four*(3), twenty-fourth*(9), twenty-nine*(6), twenty-one*(4), twenty-second*(2), twenty-seven*(1), twenty-seventh*(6), twenty-sixth*(1), twenty-third*(7), twenty-three*(6), twenty-two*(9).

6243. עֶשְׂרִין esrin (1108a); (Ara.) corr. to 6242; *twenty:*— 120*(1).

6244. עָשֵׁשׁ ashesh (799c); a prim. root; *to waste away:*— wasted away(3).

6245a. עָשַׁת ashath (799c); a prim. root; *to be smooth* or *shiny:*— sleek(1).

6245b. עָשַׁת ashath (799d); a prim. root; *to think:*— concerned(1).

6246. עֲשִׁת ashith or

עֲשִׁית ashith (1108a); (Ara.) corr. to 6245b; *to think, plan:*— planned(1).

6247. עֶשֶׁת esheth (799d); from 6245a; *plate:*— carved(1).

6248. עַשְׁתּוּת ashtuth (799d); from 6245b; *thought:*— holds(1).

6249. עַשְׁתֵּי ashte (799d); from 6245b; *one:*— eleven*(6), eleventh*(13).

6250. עֶשְׁתֹּנָה eshtonah or

עֶשְׁתּוֹן eshton (799d); from 6245b; *thought:*— thoughts(1).

6251. עַשְׁתְּרוֹת ashtaroth (800b); from 6245b; perh. *young:*— young(4).

6252a. עַשְׁתָּרוֹת Ashtaroth (800b); from 6245b; a place E. of the Jordan:— Ashtaroth(6).

6252b. עַשְׁתֹּרֶת Ashtoreth or

עַשְׁתָּרוֹת Ashtaroth (800a); from 6245b; an ancient Near Eastern goddess:— Ashtaroth(6), Ashtoreth(3).

6253. עַשְׁתֹּרֶת Ashtoreth (800a); the same as 6252b, q.v.

6254. עַשְׁתְּרָתִי Ashterathi (800c); from 6252a; inhab. of Ashtaroth:— Ashterathite(1).

6255. עַשְׁתְּרֹת קַרְנַיִם Ashteroth Qarnayim (800b); from 6252a and 7161; "Ashtaroth of the double horns," a place E. of the Jordan:— Ashteroth-karnaim(1).

6256. עֵת eth (773b); prob. from 6030a; *time:*— always*(1), appointed time(1), circumstances(1), continually*(1), interval*(1), mealtime*(1), now(3), period(1), season(10), some(1), time(226), timely(1), times(27), when(8), whenever(1), year(2).

6257. עָתַד athod (800c); a prim. root; *to be ready:*— destined(1), make it ready(1).

עַתּוּד attud; see 6260.

6258. עַתָּה attah or

עַתָּה attah (773d); prob. from 6030a; *now:*— already(2), last*(1), now(411), so(1), then(5), this time(6), time(2), whereas(2), yet(1).

6259. עָתוּד athud (800c); the same as 6264, q.v.

6260. עַתּוּד attud (800c); from 6257; *male goat:*— goats(6), leaders(1), male goats(22).

6261. עִתִּי itti (774c); prob. from 6030a; *timely, ready:*— readiness(1).

6262. עַתַּי Attay (774c); prob. from 6030a; three Isr.:— Attai(4).

6263. עֲתִיד athid (1108a); (Ara.) corr. to 6264; *ready:*— ready(1).

6264. עָתִיד athid or

עָתוּד athud (800c); from 6257; *ready, prepared:*— impending things(1), prepared(1), ready(3), treasures(1).

6265. עֲתָיָה Athayah (800d); of unc. der.; an Isr.:— Athaiah(1).

6266. עָתִיק athiq (801b); from 6275; *eminent, surpassing, choice:*— choice(1).

6267. עַתִּיק attiq (801c); from 6275; *removed, old:*— ancient(1), taken(1).

6268. עַתִּיק Attiq (1108a); (Ara.) corr. to 6267; "aged," a part of a name of God:— Ancient(1), ancient(2).

6269. עֲתָךְ Athak (800d); of unc. der.; a place in Judah:— Athach(1).

6270. עַתְלַי Athlay (800d); the same as 6271, q.v.

6271. עֲתַלְיָה Athalyah or

עַתְלַי Athlay (800d); from an unused word; daughter of Ahab, also three Isr.:— Athaliah(17), Athlai(1).

6272. עָתַם atham (801a); a prim. root; perh. *to burn:*— burned(1).

6273. עָתְנִי Othni (801a); from 6272; a Levite:— Othni(1).

6274. עָתְנִיאֵל Othniel (801a); from 6272; a hero in Isr.:— Othniel(7).

6275. עָתַק atheq (801a); a prim. root; *to move, proceed, advance:*— become old(1), continue(1), failed(1), moved(1), moved away(1), moves(1), proceeded(1), removes(1), transcribed(1).

6276. עָתֵק atheq (801b); from 6275; *valuable, advanced, eminent, surpassing:*— enduring(1).

6277. עָתָק athaq (801b); from 6275; *forward, arrogant:*— arrogance(1), arrogantly(2), insolent(1).

6278. עֵת קָצִין Eth Qatsin (773d); from 6256 and 7101; "time of a ruler," a place on the border of Zebulun:— Eth-kazin(1).

6279. עָתַר athar (801c); a prim. root; *to pray, supplicate:*— answered(1), answered their prayers(1), entreat(2), entreated(2), listened to our entreaty(1), made supplication(2), make supplication(4), moved by his entreaty(1), moved by prayer(2), pray(2), prayed(2), respond(1).

6280. עָתַר athar (801d); a prim. root; *to be abundant:*— deceitful(1), multiplied(1).

6281. עֶתֶר Ether (801d); perh. from 6280; perh. "abundance," a place in Judah:— Ether(2).

6282a. עָתָר athar (801c); from 6279; *suppliant, worshiper:*— worshipers(1).

6282b. עָתָר athar (801d); of unc. der.; *an odor:*— fragrance(1).

6283. עֲתֶרֶת athereth (801d); from 6280; *abundance:*— abundance(1).

פ

פֹּא po; see 6311.

6284. פָּאָה paah (802a); a prim. root; *to cleave in pieces:*— cut them to pieces(1).

6285. פֵּאָה peah (802a); from 6284; *corner, side:*— boundary(1), corner(1), corners(6), edges(2), forehead(2), sector(1), side(69), side-growth(1), sides(1), temples(1).

6286. פָּאַר paar (802b); a prim. root; *to beautify, glorify:*— adorn(1), beautify(2), become boastful(1), boast(1), glorified(4), glorify(1), honor(1), show my glory(1), shows forth his glory(1).

6287a. פֵּאֵר peer (802d); denom. vb. from 6288; *to go over the boughs:*— go over(1), go over the boughs(1).

6287b. פְּאֵר peer (802c); from 6286; *headdress, turban:*— decorated(1), garland(2), headdresses(1), turban(1), turbans(2).

6288. פֹּארָה porah (802d); of unc. der.; *a bough:*— boughs(1), branches(5).

6289. פָּארוּר parur (802d); perh. from 6286; perh. *beauty:*— pale(2).

6290. פָּארָן Paran (803a); from the same as 6288; a place in Sinai:— Paran(11).

6291. פַּגָּה paggah (803a); from an unused word; *an early fig:*— figs(1).

6292. פִּגּוּל piggul (803b); from an unused word; *foul thing, refuse:*— offense(1), offensive thing(1), unclean(1), unclean meat(1).

6293. פָּגַע paga (803b); a prim. root; *to meet, encounter, reach:*— approach(1), attack(2), attacked(1), came(1), cut him down(1), entreat(2), fall(7), fell(4), happen(1), intercede(2), interceded(1), kill(1), make supplication(1), meet(3), meets(3), met(2), pleaded(1), reached(6), spare(1), strike the mark(1), touched(1), touched and reached(1), urge(1).

6294. פֶּגַע pega (803c); from 6293; *occurrence, chance:*— chance(1), misfortune*(1).

6295. פַּגְעִיאֵל Pagiel (803c); from 6293 and 410; "occurrence of God," an Asherite:— Pagiel(5).

6296. פָּגַר pagar (803c); a prim. root; *to be exhausted* or *faint:*— exhausted(2).

6297. פֶּגֶר peger (803d); from 6296; *corpse, carcass:*— carcasses(1), corpse(1), corpses(12), dead bodies(3), dead*(2), remains(2).

6298. פָּגַשׁ pagash (803d); a prim. root; *to meet, encounter:*— common bond(1), encounter(1), have a common bond(1), have this(1), have this in common(1), meet(3), meets(1), met(7).

6299. פָּדָה padah (804a); a prim. root; *to ransom:*— any means redeem(1), ransom(4), ransomed(7), redeem(24), redeemed(18), redeems(1), redemption price(1), rescued(1), surely redeem(1), way been redeemed(1).

6300. פְּדַהְאֵל Pedahel (804b); from 6299 and 410; "God has ransomed," a man of Naphtali:— Pedahel(1).

6301. פְּדָהצוּר Pedahtsur (804c); from 6299 and 6697; "the rock has ransomed," a Manassite:— Pedahzur(5).

6302a. פָּדוּי paduy (804a); pass. part. of 6299, q.v.

6302b. פְּדוּיִם peduyim (804b); from 6299; *a ransom:*— ransom(2).

6303. פָּדוֹן Padon (804b); from 6299; "ransom," head of a family of Nethinim:— Padon(2).

6304. פְּדוּת **peduth** (804b); from 6299; *ransom:*— division(1), ransom(1), redemption(2).

6305. פְּדָיָהוּ **Pedayahu** or

פְּדָיָה **Pedayah** (804c); from 6299 and 3050; "Yah has ransomed," the name of several Isr.:— Pedaiah(8).

6306a. פִּדְיוֹם **pidyom** (804b); another reading for 6299, q.v., and 6302b, q.v.

6306b. פִּדְיוֹן **pidyon** (804b); from 6299; *a ransom:*— redemption(2).

6307. פַּדָּן **Paddan** or

פַּדַּן אֲרָם **Paddan Aram** (804c); of unc. der.; the place where Rachel died:— Aram(1), Paddan(1), Paddan-aram(10).

6308. פָּדַע **pada** (804c); a prim. root; perh. *deliver:*— deliver(1).

6309. פֶּדֶר **peder** (804d); of unc. der.; *suet:*— suet(3).

פְּדֻת **peduth**; see 6304.

6310. פֶּה **peh** (804d); a prim. root; *mouth:*— accord(1), accordance(1), accordance*(1), accorded(1), according(9), according*(2), apt(1), beak(2), boast*(1), boasting(1), collar(1), command(45), commandment(6), counsel(1), dictated*(1), dictation(6), edge(37), edges(2), end(2), evidence(4), face(4), hunger(1), intent(1), jaws(1), just*(1), lips(5), mouth(275), mouths(14), much(3), one end(2), one end to the other(1), one end to another(1), opening(11), parts(1), portion(2), promised*(1), proportion(5), proportionate(2), said*(1), say(1), settled*(1), so(1), sound(1), speech(3), spoke(1), spoken*(1), spokesman(1), talking*(1), taste(1), terms(2), told*(1), two-edged(2), uniformly*(2), what they say(1), whenever(1), wishes(1), word(7), words(3).

6311. פֹּה **poh** or

פּוֹ **po** or

פֹּא **po** (805d); a prim. adv.; *here, hither:*— each side(16), here(45), side(2), side and on the other(1), thus(1).

6312. פּוּאָה **Puah** or

פֻּוָּה **Puvvah** (806a); from 6311; a man of Issachar:— Puah(2), Puvah(1), Puvvah(1).

6313. פּוּג **pug** (806a); a prim. root; *to grow numb:*— benumbed(1), ignored(1), stunned(1), weariness(1).

6314. פּוּגַת **pugath** (806b); from 6313; *benumbing, cessation:*— relief(1).

פֻּוָּה **Puvvah**; see 6312.

6315. פּוּחַ **puach** (806b); a prim. root; *to breathe, blow:*— blow(1), breathe(1), cool(2), hastens(1), longs(1), set a aflame(1), snorts(1), speaks(1), tells(2), utters(3).

6316. פּוּט **Put** (806c); of unc. der.; a son of Ham, also his desc. and their land:— put(8).

6317. פּוּטִיאֵל **Putiel** (806c); from 6316 and 410; Eleazar's father-in-law:— Putiel(1).

6318. פּוֹטִיפַר **Potiphar** (806c); of for. or.; Joseph's master:— Potiphar(2).

6319. פּוֹטִי פֶרַע **Poti Phera** (806c); of for. or.; Joseph's father-in-law:— Potiphera(3).

6320. פּוּךְ **puk** (806c); perh. of for. or.; *antimony, stibium:*— antimony(2), paint(1), painted*(1).

6321. פּוֹל **pol** (806d); of unc. der.; *beans:*— beans(2).

6322. פּוּל **Pul** (806d); of for. or.; an Assyr. king, the same as 8407:— Pul(3).

6323. פּוּן **pun** (806d); another reading for 647a, q.v.

6324. פּוּנִי **Puni** (806a); prob. from 6312; desc. of Puvah:— Punites(1).

6325. פּוּנֹן **Punon** (806d); perh. from 6323; a place where Isr. camped:— Punon(2).

6326. פּוּעָה **Puah** (806d); of unc. der.; an Isr. midwife:— Puah(1).

6327a. פּוּץ **puts** (806d); a prim. root; *to be dispersed* or *scattered:*— disperse yourselves(1), dispersed(2), dispersed*(1), disperses(1), harry(1), pour(1), scatter(16), scattered(33), scattering(2), scatters(1), sow(1), spread(2).

6327b. פּוּץ **puts** (807b); a prim. root; *to flow, overflow:*— overflow(1).

6328. פּוּק **puq** (807b); a prim. root; *to reel, totter:*— totter(2).

6329. פּוּק **puq** (807c); a prim. root; *to bring out, furnish, promote:*— furnishing(1), gains(1), give(1), obtain(1), obtains(2), promote(1).

6330. פּוּקָה **puqah** (807c); from 6328; *tottering, staggering:*— grief(1).

6331. פּוּר **pur** (830b); see 6565a.

6332. פּוּר **Pur** (807c); of unc. der.; "a lot," a Jewish feast:— Pur(3), Purim(5).

6333a. פּוּרָה **purah** (802d); from the same as 6288; *boughs:*— boughs(1).

6333b. פּוּרָה **purah** (807d); from an unused word; *wine press:*— measures(1), wine trough(1).

6334. פּוֹרָתָא **Poratha** (807d); prob. of for. or.; a son of Haman:— Poratha(1).

6335a. פּוּשׁ **push** (807d); a prim. root; prob. *to spring about:*— galloping(1), skip about(2).

6335b. פּוּשׁ **push** (807d); a prim. root; *to be scattered:*— scattered(1).

6336. פּוּתִי **Puthi** (807d); of unc. der.; a family in Judah:— Puthites(1).

6337. פָּז **paz** (808a); from 6338; *refined, pure gold:*— fine gold(5), pure gold(4).

6338. פָּזַז **pazaz** (808a); a prim. root; *to be refined:*— refined(1).

6339. פָּזַז **pazaz** (808a); a prim. root; *to be supple* or *agile:*— agile(1), leaping(1).

6340. פָּזַר **pazar** (808a); a prim. root; *to scatter:*— freely(1), scattered(7), scatters(2).

6341a. פַּח **pach** (809a); from an unused word; *a bird trap:*— snare(15), snares(4), trap(5).

6341b. פַּח **pach** (809a); from the same as 6341a; *a plate* (of metal):— sheets(2).

6342. פָּחַד **pachad** (808b); a prim. root; *to dread, be in dread* or *in awe:*— afraid(3), come in dread(1), come trembling(1), dread(6), fear(4), fears(1), shake(1), stands in awe(1), terrified(2), thrill(1), tremble(2), turned in fear(1).

6343. פַּחַד **pachad** (808b); from 6342; *dread:*— awe(1), disaster(1), dread(20), fear(9), great(1), great fear(1), great fear where fear(1), object of dread(1), panic(1), terror(10), terrors(1), unconcerned*(1), what(1).

6344. פַּחַד **pachad** (808c); prob. of for. or.; *thigh:*— thighs(1).

6345. פַּחְדָּה **pachdah** (808c); from 6342; *dread,* (religious) *awe:*— dread(1).

6346. פֶּחָה **pechah** (808d); of for. or.; *a governor:*— captains(1), governor(8), governor's(2), governors(15), official(2).

6347. פֶּחָה **pechah** (1108b); (Ara.) corr. to 6346; *a governor:*— governor(6), governors(4).

6348. פָּחַז **pachaz** (808d); a prim. root; *to be wanton* or *reckless:*— reckless(2).

6349. פַּחַז **pachaz** (808d); from 6348; *wantonness, recklessness:*— uncontrolled(1).

6350. פַּחֲזוּת **pachazuth** (808d); from 6348; *recklessness, extravagance:*— reckless boasting(1).

6351. פָּחַח **pachach** (809a); denom. vb. from 6341a; *to ensnare:*— trapped(1).

6352. פֶּחָם **pecham** (809b); from an unused word; *coal:*— charcoal(1), coals(2).

6353. פֶּחָר **pechar** (1108b); (Ara.) of unc. der.; *a potter:*— potter's(1).

6354. פַּחַת **pachath** (809b); from an unused word; *a pit:*— caves(1), chasm(1), pit(7), pitfall(1).

6355. פַּחַת מוֹאָב **Pachath Moab** (809b); from 6354 and 4124; a postexilic name:— Pahath-moab(6).

6356. פְּחֶתֶת **pechetheth** (809b); from the same as 6354; *a boring* or *eating out:*— eating away(1).

6357. פִּטְדָה **pitdah** (809b); prob. of for. or.; (a precious stone) perh. *topaz:*— topaz(4).

6358. פָּטוּר **patur** (809c); pass. part. of 6362, q.v.

6359. פָּטִיר **patir** (809c); see 6362.

6360. פַּטִּישׁ **pattish** (809c); of for. or.; *a forge hammer:*— hammer(3).

6361. פַּטֵּשׁ **petash** (1108b); (Ara.) of unc. der.; (a garment) perh. *leggings:*— coats(1).

6362. פָּטַר **patar** (809c); a prim. root; *to separate, remove, set free:*— dismiss(1), free(1), letting(1), open(4), separate(1), slipped away(1).

6363a. פֶּטֶר **peter** (809d); from 6362; *that which separates* or *first opens:*— first issue(2), first offspring(8).

6363b. פִּטְרָה **pitrah** (809d); from 6362; *that which separates* or *first opens:*— first issue(1).

6364. פִּי־בֶסֶת **Pi-beseth** (809d); of for. or.; a place in Eg.:— Pi-beseth(1).

6365. פִּיד **pid** (810a); from an unused word; *ruin, disaster:*— calamity(1), disaster(1), extinction(1), ruin(1).

6366. פֵּיָה **peh** (804d); the same as 6310, q.v.

6367. פִּי הַחִירֹת **Pi Hachiroth** (809d); of for. or.; a place on the E. border of Eg.:— Hahiroth(1), Pi-hahiroth(3).

6368. פִּיחַ **piach** (806b); from 6315; *soot:*— soot(2).

6369. פִּיכֹל **Pikol** (810a); from an unused word; commander of Abimelech's army:— Phicol(3).

6370. פִּילֶגֶשׁ **pilegesh** or

פִּלֶגֶשׁ **pilegesh** (811b); perh. of for. or.; *concubine:*— concubine(22), concubines(14), paramours(1).

6371a. פִּים **pim** (not listed); of unc. der.; (a measure of weight) *two-thirds of a shekel* (approximately):— two-thirds(1).

6371b. פִּימָה **pimah** (810a); from an unused word; *superabundance:*— flesh(1), heavy(1).

6372. פִּינְחָס **Pinechas** (810a); of unc. der.; three Isr.:— Phinehas(24), Phinehas'(1).

6373. פִּינֹן **Pinon** (810a); of unc. der.; an Edomite:— Pinon(2).

6374. פִּיפִיּוֹת piphiyyoth (804d); the same as 6310, q.v.

6375. פִּיק piq or

פָּק piq (807c); from 6328; *tottering, staggering:*— knocking(1).

6376. פִּישׁוֹן Pishon (810b); of unc. der.; one of the rivers of Eden:— Pishon(1).

6377. פִּיתוֹן Pithon (810b); of unc. der.; a desc. of Saul:— Pithon(2).

6378. פַּךְ pak (810b); from an unused word; *a vial, flask:*— flask(3).

6379. פָּכָה pakah (810b); perh. denom. vb. from 6378; *to trickle:*— trickling(1).

6380. פֹּכֶרֶת הַצְּבָיִים Pokereth Hatstsebayim (810b); from an unused word and 6643b; "bindress of the gazelles," head of a postexilic family:— Pochereth-hazzebaim(2).

6381. פָּלָא pala (810c); denom. vb. from 6382; *to be surpassing* or *extraordinary:*— bring extraordinary(1), deal marvelously(1), difficult(5), extraordinary degree(1), fulfill a special(3), made his wonderful(1), made marvelous(1), makes a difficult(1), makes a special(1), marvelous(1), marvelously(1), miracles(5), monstrous things(1), seemed hard(1), show your power(1), things...difficult(1), things...wonderful(1), too difficult(2), wonderful(4), wonderful acts(1), wonderful deeds(3), wonderful things(2), wonderful works(2), wonders(20), wondrous deeds(3), wondrous works(3), wondrously(2), wondrously marvelous(1).

6382. פֶּלֶא pele (810b); from an unused word; *a wonder:*— astonishingly(1), wonderful(2), wonders(9).

6383. פִּלְאִי pili or

פָּלִיא pali (811a); from the same as 6382; *wonderful, incomprehensible:*— wonderful(2).

6384a. פַּלֻּאִי Pallui (811a); from 6396; desc. of Pallu:— Palluites(1).

6384b. פְּלָאיָה Pelayah (811a); from the same as 6382; an Isr.:— Pelaiah(2).

פִּלְאֶסֶר Pileser; see 8407.

6385. פָּלַג palag (811a); a prim. root; *to split, divide:*— cleft(1), divide(1), divided(2).

6386. פְּלַג pelag (1108b); (Ara.) corr. to 6385; *to divide:*— divided(1).

6387. פְּלַג pelag (1108b); (Ara.) from 6386; *half:*— half(1).

6388. פֶּלֶג peleg (811b); from 6385; *a channel, canal:*— channels(1), stream(1), streams(8).

6389. פֶּלֶג Peleg (811b); from 6385; a son of Eber:— Peleg(7).

6390. פְּלַגָּה pelaggah (811b); from 6385; *a stream, division:*— divisions(2), streams(1).

6391. פְּלֻגָּה peluggah (811b); from 6385; *a division:*— sections(1).

6392. פְּלֻגָּה peluggah (1108c); (Ara.) from 6386; *a division:*— divisions(1).

פִּלֶגֶשׁ pilegesh; see 6370.

6393. פְּלָדָה peladah (811c); of unc. der.; prob. *iron, steel:*— steel(1).

6394. פִּלְדָּשׁ Pildash (811c); of unc. der.; a relative of Abraham:— Pildash(1).

6395. פָּלָה palah (811c); a prim. root; *to be separated* or *distinct:*— distinguished(1), make a distinction(1), makes a distinction(1), set apart(2), wonderfully(1), wondrously show(1).

6396. פַּלּוּא Pallu (811a); from the same as 6382; a son of Reuben:— Pallu(5).

6397. פְּלוֹנִי Peloni or

פְּלֹנִי Peloni (813d); of unc. der.; descriptive title of two of David's men:— Pelonite(3).

6398. פָּלַח palach (812a); a prim. root; *to cleave:*— bring forth(1), pierces through(1), plows(1), sliced(1), splits my open(1).

6399. פְּלַח pelach (1108c); (Ara.) corr. to 6398; *to pay reverence to, serve:*— servants(1), serve(9).

6400. פֶּלַח pelach (812a); from 6398; *cleavage, a millstone:*— millstone(1), piece(1), slice(2).

6401. פִּלְחָא Pilcha (812a); from 6398; a postexilic Isr.:— Pilha(1).

6402. פָּלְחָן polchan (1108c); (Ara.) from 6399; *service, worship:*— service(1).

6403. פָּלַט palat (812b); a prim. root; *to escape:*— calves(1), carries it off(1), deliver(5), delivered(4), deliverer(5), delivers(3), escape(1), preserve(2), rescue(3).

6404. פֶּלֶט Pelet (812b); from 6403; two Isr.:— Pelet(2).

פָּלֵט palet; see 6412b.

6405. פַּלֵּט pallet (812c); from 6403; *deliverance:*— cast them forth(1), deliverance(1).

פְּלֵטָה peletah; see 6413.

6406. פַּלְטִי Palti (812d); from 6403; "escape," two Isr.:— Palti(2).

6407. פַּלְטִי Palti (112c, 812c); from 6403; "escape," a descriptive title for one of David's men:— Paltite(1).

6408. פִּלְטָי Piltay (812d); from 6403; an Isr. priest:— Piltai(1).

6409. פַּלְטִיאֵל Paltiel (812d); from 6403; "deliverance of God," two Isr.:— Paltiel(2).

6410. פְּלַטְיָהוּ Pelatyahu or

פְּלַטְיָה Pelatyah (812d); from 6413; "Yah has delivered," three Isr.:— Pelatiah(5).

פָּלִא pali; see 6383.

6411. פְּלָיָה Pelayah (811a); from 6381; a man of Judah:— Pelaiah(1).

6412a. פָּלִיט palit (812c); from 6403; *escaped one, fugitive:*— escaped(1), fugitive(1), fugitives(4), one escape(1), refugee(1), refugees(4), survivors(1), who escape(2), who escaped(3), who escapes(1).

6412b. פָּלֵיט palet (812c); from 6403; *escaped one, fugitive:*— fugitives(1), refugees(2), survivors(1), who have escaped(1).

6413. פְּלֵיטָה peletah (812c); from 6403; *an escape:*— deliverance(2), escape(7), escaped(2), escaped remnant(3), escapes(1), fugitives(1), survivors(5), what has escaped(1), who have escaped(1), who escape(1), who escaped(2).

6414. פָּלִיל palil (813c); from 6419; *a judge:*— judge(1), judges(2).

6415. פְּלִילָה pelilah (813d); from 6419; *office of judge* or *umpire:*— decision(1).

6416. פְּלִילִי pelili (813d); from 6419; *for a judge, calling for judgment:*— judgment(1).

6417. פְּלִילִיָּה peliliyyah (813d); from 6419; *the giving of a decision:*— judgment(1).

6418. פֶּלֶךְ pelek (813a); from an unused word; *whorl of a spindle, a district:*— distaff(1), district(8), spindle(1).

6419. פָּלַל palal (813a); a prim. root; *to intervene, interpose:*— expected(1), intercede(2), interceded(1), interposed(1), made judgment favorable(1), make supplication(1), mediate(1), pray(36), prayed(28), praying(8), prays(4).

6420. פָּלָל Palal (813c); from 6419; a builder of the Jer. wall:— Palal(1).

6421. פְּלַלְיָה Pelalyah (813d); from 6419; "Yah has interposed," an Isr. priest:— Pelaliah(1).

6422. פַּלְמוֹנִי palmoni (811d); the same as 6423, q.v.

6423. פְּלֹנִי peloni (811d); from 6395; *a certain one:*— certain*(1), friend*(1), particular one(1), such(1).

6424. פָּלַס palas (814a); denom. vb. from 6425; *to weigh, make level:*— level(1), leveled(1), make(1), ponder(1), watch(1), watches(1), weigh(1).

6425. פֶּלֶס peles (813d); of unc. der.; *a balance, scale:*— balance(2).

פְּלֶסֶר Peleser; see 8407.

6426. פָּלַץ palats (814a); a prim. root; *to shudder:*— tremble(1).

6427. פַּלָּצוּת pallatsuth (814a); from 6426; *a shuddering:*— horror(3), shuddering(1).

6428. פָּלַשׁ palash (814b); a prim. root; (act of mourning) perh. *to roll in:*— roll(2), wallow(2).

6429. פְּלֶשֶׁת Pelesheth (814b); from 6428; a territory on the S. Mediterranean coast of Isr.:— Philistia(8).

6430. פְּלִשְׁתִּי Pelishti (814b); from 6429; inhab. of Philistia:— Philistine(33), Philistine's(2), Philistines(250), Philistines'(2).

6431. פֶּלֶת Peleth (814c); of unc. der.; two Isr.:— Peleth(2).

6432. פְּלֵתִי Pelethi (814c); from the same as 6431; some of David's soldiers:— Pelethites(7).

6433. פֻּם pum (1108c); (Ara.) prob. corr. to 6310; *mouth:*— mouth(5), mouths(1).

6434. פֵּן pen (819c); the same as 6438, q.v.

6435. פֶּן־ pen (814c); of unc. der.; *lest:*— because(2), fear(1), might(4), no(2), none(1), or(36), or else(6), otherwise(16), otherwise you might(1), perhaps(1), so(12).

6436. פַּנַּג pannag (815a); of unc. der.; (prob. a kind of food) perh. *cake:*— cakes(1).

6437. פָּנָה panah (815a); a prim. root; *to turn:*— approaches(1), clear(3), cleared(1), cleared away(1), considered(1), dawn*(1), dawns(1), declined(1), declines(1), empty(1), face(2), faced(2), faced*(1), faces(3), facing(11), facing back(1), have regard(2), look(4), looked(9), prepare(1), prepared(1), regard(2), regarded(1), regards(1), return*(1), toward(1), turn(26), turn back(2), turned(40), turned around(1), turned away(1), turned back(2), turns(3), turns away(2), turns back(1).

פָּנֶה paneh; see 6440.

6438. פִּנָּה pinnah (819c); of unc. der.; *a corner:*— chiefs(2), corner(16), corner towers(2), corners(7), cornerstone(3), cornerstone*(1).

6439. פְּנוּאֵל Penuel (819c); from 6440 and 410; "face of God," a place E. of the Jordan, also two Isr.:— Peniel(1), Penuel(8).

6440. פָּנִים **panim** or

פָּנֶה **paneh** (815d); from 6437; *face, faces:*— above(1), abroad*(1), accept*(3), accepted*(1), account(1), account*(2), across*(1), adjacent*(1), after*(1), again(1), against(6), against*(2), aged*(1), ahead(15), along*(1), anger(1), another*(1), appearance(2), appease*(1), around(1), attend(1), attend*(1), attended(1), attention(3), attitude(2), awaits(1), battle*(1), because*(80), before(868), before the in front(1), before*(137), condition(1), confront*(1), corresponding*(2), countenance(12), covering*(1), defer*(1), defiance*(1), direction(1), disposal(2), down(1), east(1), east*(6), edge(2), entertained*(1), expected*(1), face(259), face to the before(2), face you first(1), face before(1), face*(2), faced(6), faced*(4), faces(49), faces in the presence(1), faces toward(1), faces*(1), facing(7), facing*(4), favor(9), favor*(3), former times(2), formerly(14), forward(3), front(86), front line(1), gaze(1), ground*(1), head(2), headlong(1), honor*(1), honorable*(3), humiliation*(1), insolent*(1), intended(1), kindly(2), land(1), leading(1), led(1), length*(1), lifetime(1), long(2), meet(6), mind(4), mouth(1), old(1), open(15), openly*(1), opposite*(5), ours(1), outer(1), outran*(1), over(3), over*(1), overlooks*(2), own(1), partial*(3), partiality*(11), personal(2), personally(2), preceded(2), presence(131), presence and before(1), presence of the before(1), presence on the before(1), presented*(2), previously(1), prior(1), receive*(2), remain*(1), repulse*(2), request(1), respect(1), respected*(1), served*(4), service*(3), shame*(2), sight(26), sight*(1), straight*(3), stubborn*(1), surface(26), table(1), tops(1), toward*(4), under(1), upside*(1), vanguard(1), whole(1), withstand*(1).

6441. פְּנִימָה **penimah** (819b); from 6437; *toward the side* or *inside, within:*— inner(2), inner part(1), inside(3), inside*(2), within(4).

6442. פְּנִימִי **penimi** (819b); from 6437; *inner:*— inner(31), inside(1).

6443. פְּנִינִים **peninim** (819d); from the same as 6438; *corals:*— corals(1), jewels(4), pearls(1).

6444. פְּנִנָּה **Peninnah** (819d); from the same as 6438; wife of Elkanah:— Peninnah(3).

6445. פָּנַק **panaq** (819d); a prim. root; *to indulge, pamper:*— pampers(1).

6446. פַּס **pas** (821a); from an unused word; *flat* (of the hand or foot):— long-sleeved(2), varicolored(3).

6447. פַּס **pas** (1108d); (Ara.) corr. to 6446; *palm* (of the hand):— back(1).

6448. פָּסַג **pasag** (819d); a prim. root; *to pass between:*— go through(1).

6449. פִּסְגָּה **Pisgah** (820a); from 6448; "cleft," a mountain in Moab:— Pisgah(8).

6450. פַּס דַּמִּים **Pas Dammim** (67c); from 6446 and 1818; "palm of blood," a place in Judah (the same as 658b):— Pasdammim(1).

6451. פִּסָּה **pissah** (821a); from the same as 6446; prob. *abundance, plenty:*— abundance(1).

6452a. פָּסַח **pasach** (820a); a prim. root; *to pass* or *spring over:*— pass(2), pass over(1), passed(1).

6452b. פָּסַח **pasach** (820c); a prim. root; *to limp:*— became lame(1), hesitate(1), leaped(1).

6453. פֶּסַח **pesach** (820a); from 6452a; *passover:*— Passover(46), Passover offerings(3).

6454. פָּסֵחַ **Paseach** (820c); from 6452b; "limper," three Isr.:— Paseah(4).

6455. פִּסֵּחַ **pisseach** (820c); from 6452b; *lame:*— lame(12), lame man(1), lameness(1).

6456. פְּסִיל **pasil** (820d); from 6458; *an idol, image:*— carved images(6), engraved images(1), graven images(7), idols(8), images(1).

6457. פָּסַךְ **Pasak** (820d); from 6452b; an Asherite:— Pasach(1).

6458. פָּסַל **pasal** (820d); a prim. root; *to hew, hew into shape:*— carved(1), cut(5).

6459. פֶּסֶל **pesel** (820d); from 6458; *an idol, image:*— carved image(2), graven image(14), graven images(1), idol(10), idols(3), image(1).

6460. פְּסַנְטֵרִין **pesanterin** (1108c); (Ara.) of for. or.; (a triangular stringed instrument) perh. *trigon:*— psaltery(4).

6461. פָּסַס **pasas** (821a); a prim. root; *to disappear, vanish:*— disappear(1).

6462. פִּסְפָּה **Pispah** (821a); from 6461; an Asherite:— Pispa(1).

6463. פָּעָה **paah** (821a); a prim. root; *to groan:*— groan(1).

6464. פָּעוּ **Pau** or

פָּעִי **Pai** (821b); from 6463; a place in Edom:— Pai(1), Pau(1).

6465. פְּעוֹר **Peor** (822b); from 6473; a mountain in Moab, also a god worshiped there:— Peor(5).

פָּעִי **Pai**; see 6464.

6466. פָּעַל **paal** (821b); a prim. root; *do, make:*— accomplish(1), act(1), acted(1), carried(1), deal(1), did(2), do(15), doers(2), does(1), does his work(1), doing(1), done(6), made(3), Maker(1), makes(2), performed(2), work(4), workers(7), working(1), works(2), wrought(1).

6467. פֹּעַל **poal** (821c); from 6466; *doing, deed, work:*— acquisition(1), act(1), activity(1), conduct(2), deeds(4), doings(1), something(1), thing you are making(1), wages(2), what you have done(1), work(22).

6468. פְּעֻלָּה **peullah** (821c); from 6466; *a work, recompense:*— deeds(1), labor(1), recompense(3), reward(2), wages(2), work(3), works(1).

6469. פְּעֻלְּתַי **Peulletay** (821d); from 6466; "laborious," a Levite:— Peullethai(1).

6470. פָּעַם **paam** (821d); a prim. root; *to thrust, impel:*— anxious(1), stir(1), troubled(3).

6471. פַּעַם **paam** (821d); from 6470; *a beat, foot, anvil, occurrence:*— all(1), annual*(1), anvil(1), each story(1), feet(9), footsteps(3), hoofbeats(1), now(5), oftentimes*(1), once(1), once more(3), once*(4), other times(5), ranks(2), steps(3), stroke(1), this once(2), this time(4), thousand-fold*(1), time(13), times(42), twice(7), two times(1), usual(1).

6472. פַּעֲמֹן **paamon** (822b); from 6470; *bell* (on high priest's robe):— bell(3), bells(3).

6473. פָּעַר **paar** (822b); a prim. root; *to open wide* (the mouth):— gaped(1), opened(2), opened my wide(1).

6474. פַּעֲרַי **Paaray** (822b); from 6473; one of David's heroes:— Paarai(1).

6475. פָּצָה **patsah** (822c); a prim. root; *to part, open:*— given(2), open(1), open wide(1), opened(5), opens(2), rescue(2), rescues(1), uttered(1).

6476. פָּצַח **patsach** (822c); a prim. root; *to cause to break* or *burst forth, break forth with:*— break(1), break forth(7).

6477. פְּצִירָה **petsirah** (823a); from 6484; perh. *bluntness:*— charge(1).

6478. פָּצַל **patsal** (822d); a prim. root; *to peel:*— peeled(2).

6479. פְּצָלָה **pitslah** (822d); from 6478; *a peeled spot* or *stripe:*— stripes(1).

6480. פָּצַם **patsam** (822d); a prim. root; *to split open:*— split it open(1).

6481. פָּצַע **patsa** (822d); a prim. root; *to bruise, wound by bruising:*— emasculated*(1), one(1), wounded(1), wounding*(1).

6482. פֶּצַע **petsa** (822d); from 6481; *a bruise, wound:*— bruises(1), wound(3), wounding(1), wounds(3).

פַּצֵּץ **Patstsets**; see 1048.

6483a. פָּצַץ **patsats** (822d); a prim. root; *to break:*— shaken me to pieces(1), shattered(1), shatters(1).

6483b. פִּצֵּץ **Pitstsets** (823a); from 6483a; an Isr. priest:— Happizzez(1).

6484. פָּצַר **patsar** (823a); a prim. root; *to push, press:*— insubordination(1), pressed(1), urged(5).

6485. פָּקַד **paqad** (823b); a prim. root; *to attend to, visit, muster, appoint:*— am indeed concerned(1), any reason(1), any reason he is missing(1), appoint(12), appointed(19), appoints(1), assign(3), assigned(1), attend(1), attended(1), bring punishment(1), brought(1), call their to account(1), calls me to account(1), care(3), charge(1), commit(1), committed(3), concerned(1), counted(1), damage(1), deposited(3), deprived(1), empty(3), entrusted(1), examine(1), foremen(1), gave(1), had the oversight(1), lack(1), longed(1), look(1), made him overseer(2), made them overseers(1), miss(2), missed(3), misses me at all(1), missing(5), mustered(6), mustering(1), number(13), numbered(99), officers(2), oversight(3), punish(46), punished(6), put him in charge(1), put in charge(1), put under(1), put under the charge(1), register(2), see(1), sought(1), suffer(1), summoned(1), supervisors(1), surely take care(3), take care(1), take notice(1), took a census(1), took note(1), untouched*(1), visit(7), visited(6), visiting(4).

פִּקֻּד **piqqud**; see 6490.

6486. פְּקֻדָּה **pequddah** (824a); from 6485; *oversight, mustering, visitation, store:*— administrators(1), affairs(1), appointed(1), care(1), class(1), executioners(1), fate(1), muster(2), office(1), officers(1), offices(3), oversight(2), prison*(1), punishment(11), responsibility(2), stored(1).

6487. פִּקָּדוֹן **piqqadon** (824c); from 6485; *a deposit, store:*— deposit(2), reserve(1).

6488. פְּקִדֻת **peqiduth** (824b); from 6485; *oversight:*— guard(1).

6489. פְּקוֹד **Peqod** (824c); from 6485; a people in S.E. Bab.:— Pekod(2).

6490. פִּקּוּד **piqqud** (824b); from 6485; *a precept:*— precepts(24).

6491a. פְּקוּדִים **pequdim** (824b); from 6485; *musterings, expenses:*— number of the things(1).

6491b. פָּקַח **paqach** (824c); a prim. root; *to open* (eyes):— open(10), opened(7), opens(2), watch*(1).

6492. פֶּקַח **Peqach** (824d); from 6491b; "opening," a king of Isr.:— Pekah(11).

6493. פִּקֵּחַ **piqqeach** (824d); from 6491b; *seeing:*— clear-sighted(1), seeing(1).

6494. פְּקַחְיָה Peqachyah (824d); from 6491b; "Yah has opened (the eyes)," a king of Isr.:— Pekahiah(3).

6495. פְּקַח־קוֹחַ peqach-qoach (824d); from 6491b; *an opening:*— freedom(1).

6496. פָּקִיד paqid (824b); from 6485; *commissioner, deputy, overseer:*— leader(1), lieutenant(1), officer(3), overseer(6), overseers(3).

6497. פְּקָעִים peqaim (825a); from an unused word; *gourd* (shaped) *ornaments:*— gourds(3).

6498. פַּקֻּעֹת paqquoth (825a); from the same as 6497; *gourds:*— gourds(1).

6499. פַּר par (830d); from an unused word; *young bull, steer:*— bull(67), bull*(18), bulls(29), bulls*(5), fruit(1), heifer(6), ox(5), oxen(1), young bull(2), young bulls(4).

6500. פָּרָא para (826a); the same as 6509, q.v.

6501. פֶּרֶא pere (825b); from an unused word; *a wild donkey:*— wild donkey(6), wild donkeys(4).

6502. פִּרְאָם Piram (825b); from the same as 6501; a Canaanite king:— Piram(1).

6503. פַּרְבָּר parbar or

פַּרְוָר parvar (826c); of for. or.; prob. a structure on the W. side of Solomon's temple:— Parbar(2), precincts(1).

6504. פָּרַד parad (825b); a prim. root; *to divide:*— decides(1), dispersed(1), divided(1), go apart(1), joint(1), parted(1), parts(1), scattered(2), separate(1), separated(12), separates(3), spread(1).

6505. פֶּרֶד pered (825d); from an unused word; *a mule:*— mule(6), mules(8), mules'(1).

6506. פִּרְדָּה pirdah (825d); from the same as 6505; *a female mule:*— mule(3).

6507. פְּרֻדָה perudah (825c); from 6504; *grain:*— seeds(1).

6508. פַּרְדֵּס pardes (825d); of for. or.; *a preserve, park:*— forest(1), orchard(1), parks(1).

6509. פָּרָה parah (826a); a prim. root; *to bear fruit, be fruitful:*— bear fruit(2), bearing...fruit(1), become fruitful(1), flourishes(1), fruitful(18), fruitful tree(1), increased(1), made me fruitful(1), make him fruitful(1), make you fruitful(3).

6510. פָּרָה parah (831a); from the same as 6499; *a heifer, cow:*— cow(2), cows(18).

6511. פָּרָה Parah (831a); from the same as 6499; a place in Benjamin:— Parah(1).

6512. פֵּרָה perah (344a); from 2663c.

6513. פֻּרָה Purah (826c); from 6509; a servant of Gideon:— Purah(2).

6514. פְּרוּדָא Peruda or

פְּרִידָא Perida (825d); from 6504; an Isr.:— Perida(1), Peruda(1).

6515. פָּרוּחַ Paruach (827c); from 6524c; a man of Issachar:— Paruah(1).

6516. פַּרְוַיִם Parvayim (826c); of for. or.; a region from which Solomon obtained gold for the temple:— Parvaim(1).

6517. פָּרוּר parur (807d); from the same as 6333b; *a pot:*— pot(3).

6518. פָּרָז paraz or

פֶּרֶז perez (826d); of unc. der.; perh. *warriors:*— throngs(1).

6519. פְּרָזָה perazah (826d); from an unused word; *an open region, hamlet:*— rural(1), unwalled villages(1), without walls(1).

6520. פְּרָזוֹן perazon (826d); from the same as 6519; perh. *rural population:*— peasantry(2).

6521. פְּרָזִי perazi (826d); from the same as 6519; *hamlet dweller:*— country(1), rural areas(1), unwalled(1).

6522. פְּרִזִּי Perizzi (827a); perh. from the same as 6519; a people in the land of Canaan:— Perizzite(13), Perizzites(10).

6523. פַּרְזֶל parzel (1108d); (Ara.) corr. to 1270; *iron:*— iron(20).

6524a. פָּרַח parach (827a); a prim. root; *to bud, sprout, shoot:*— blossom(4), blossom profusely(1), blossomed(1), bring your to blossom(1), budded(2), budding(1), farther(1), flourish(8), sprout(2), sprouted(2), sprouts(1).

6524b. פָּרַח parach (827b); a prim. root; *to break out:*— breaking(3), breaks(2), broken(3), outbreak(1).

6524c. פָּרַח parach (827c); a prim. root; *to fly:*— birds(2).

6525. פֶּרַח perach (827b); from 6524a; *a bud, sprout:*— blossom(3), blossoms(1), bud(1), buds(1), flower(4), flowers(7).

6526. פִּרְחַח pirchach (827b); from 6524a; *a brood:*— brood(1).

6527. פָּרַט parat (827c); a prim. root; perh. *divide:*— improvise(1).

6528. פֶּרֶט peret (827c); from 6527; *the broken off:*— fallen fruit(1).

6529. פְּרִי peri (826b); from 6509; *fruit:*— earnings*(1), foliage(1), fruit(84), fruitful(2), fruits(2), fruits*(1), offspring(11), price(1), produce(12), product(1), results(2), reward(1).

6530. פָּרִיץ parits (829d); from 6555; *violent one:*— ones*(1), robbers(2), vicious(1), violent(3).

6531. פֶּרֶךְ perek (827d); from an unused word; *harshness, severity:*— rigorously(2), severity(4).

6532. פָּרֹכֶת paroketh (827d); from an unused word; *a curtain:*— curtain(1), veil(24).

6533. פָּרַם param (827d); a prim. root; *to tear* or *rend* (a garment):— tear(2), torn(1).

6534. פַּרְמַשְׁתָּא Parmashta (828a); of for. or.; a son of Haman:— Parmashta(1).

6535. פַּרְנָךְ Parnak (828a); of unc. der.; a man of Zebulun:— Parnach(1).

6536. פָּרַס paras (828a); a prim. root; *to break in two, divide:*— break(1), breaks(1), divide(8), divides(4), hoofs(1).

6537a. פְּרַס peras (1108d); (Ara.) corr. to 6536; *to break in two:*— been divided(1).

6537b. פְּרֵס peres (1108d); (Ara.) from 6537a; *half-mina:*— PERES(1), UPHARSIN(1).

6538. פֶּרֶס peres (828b); from 6536; (a bird of prey) perh. *bearded vulture:*— vulture(2).

6539. פָּרַס Paras (828a); of for. or.; a country in W. Asia which conquered Bab.:— Persia(28).

6540. פָּרַס Paras (1108d); (Ara.) corr. to 6539; a country in W. Asia which conquered Bab.:— Persia(2), Persians(4).

6541. פַּרְסָה parsah (828b); from 6536; *a hoof:*— hoof(13), hoofs(7).

6542. פַּרְסִי Parsi (828a); from 6539; inhab. of Persia:— Persian(1).

6543. פַּרְסַי Parsay (1108d); (Ara.) corr. to 6542; inhab. of Persia:— Persian(1).

6544a. פָּרַע para (828d); a prim. root; *let go, let alone:*— avoid(1), brought about a lack(1), control(1), draw the away(1), get out of control(1), go loose(1), lack of restraint(1), let(1), neglect(1), neglected(1), neglects(2), relent(1), uncover(2), uncovered(1), unrestrained(1).

6544b. פָּרַע para (828c); denom. vb. from 6546; perh. *act as a leader, lead:*— led(1).

6545. פֶּרַע pera (828d); from an unused word; *long hair, locks:*— locks(2).

6546. פֶּרַע pera (828c); from an unused word; perh. *leader:*— leaders(1), long-haired(1).

6547. פַּרְעֹה Paroh (829a); of for. or.; a title of Eg. kings:— Pharaoh(214), Pharaoh's(53).

6548. פַּרְעֹה חָפְרַע Paroh Chophra (344b); from 6547 and 2663b; an Eg. king:— Pharaoh Hophra(1).

6549. פַּרְעֹה נְכוֹ Paroh Neko or

פַּרְעֹה נְכֹה Paroh Nekoh (647a); from 6547 and 5224; an Eg. king:— Pharaoh Neco(5).

6550. פַּרְעֹשׁ parosh (829a); of unc. der.; *a flea:*— flea(2).

6551. פַּרְעֹשׁ Parosh (829b); from the same as 6550; two Isr.:— Parosh(6).

6552. פִּרְעָתוֹן Pirathon (828c); from the same as 6546; perh. "height," a place in Ephraim:— Pirathon(1).

6553. פִּרְעָתוֹנִי Pirathoni (828d); from 6552; inhab. of Pirathon:— Pirathonite(5).

6554. פַּרְפַּר Parpar (829b); of unc. der.; a river near Damascus:— Pharpar(1).

6555. פָּרַץ parats (829b); a prim. root; *to break through:*— became...prosperous(1), breaches(1), break(2), break their down(1), break down(1), break forth(1), breaker(1), breaking away(1), breaks through(2), broke(1), broke down(1), broken(3), broken down(5), broken through(2), destroyed(1), distributed(1), employ violence(1), everywhere(1), increase(1), increased(3), infrequent*(1), made(1), made an outburst(1), outburst*(2), overflow(1), sinks(1), spread(3), spread abroad(1), tear down(1), through(1), tore down(2), urged(4).

6556. פֶּרֶץ perets (829c); from 6555; *a bursting forth, breach:*— breach(10), breaches(3), breakthrough(2), gap(1), mishap(1), outburst*(2).

6557. פֶּרֶץ Perets (829d); from 6555; son of Judah and Tamar:— Perez(15).

6558. פַּרְצִי Partsi (829d); from 6557; desc. of Perez:— Perezites(1).

6559. פְּרָצִים Peratsim (829d); from 6555; a mountain in Isr.:— Perazim(1).

6560. פֶּרֶץ עֻזָּה Perets Uzzah (829d); from 6557 and 5798; a place near Jer.:— Perez-uzza(1), Perez-uzzah(1).

6561. פָּרַק paraq (830a); a prim. root; *to tear apart* or *away:*— break(1), deliver(1), dragging me away(1), rending(1), rescued(1), tear it off(1), tear off(2), tore off(1), torn off(1).

6562. פְּרַק peraq (1108d); (Ara.) corr. to 6561; *to tear away, break off:*— break away(1).

6563. פֶּרֶק pereq (830a); from 6561; *parting of ways, plunder:*— fork of the road(1), pillage(1).

6564. פָּרָק paraq (830a); another reading for 4839, q.v.

6565a. פָּרַר parar (830b); a prim. root; *to break, frustrate:*— annul(4), annulled(1), break(12), breaking(3), broke(4), broken(7), cease(1), do away(1), fail(1), frustrate(2), frustrated(2), frustrates(1), indeed annuls(2), ineffective(1), made my void(1), nullifies(1), shattered(1), thwart(2), thwarted(1).

6565b. פָּרַר **parar** (830c); a prim. root; *to split, divide:*— divided(1), split through(1).

6566. פָּרַשׂ **paras** (831a); a prim. root; *to spread out, spread:*— chop(1), dispersed(1), displays(1), extended(2), extends(1), scattered(2), spread(47), spreading(3), spreads(2), stretch(1), stretched(2), stretches(1), stretching(2).

6567a. פָּרַשׁ **parash** (831c); a prim. root; *to make distinct, declare:*— declared(1), made clear(1), scattered(1), translating(1).

6567b. פָּרַשׁ **parash** (831d); a prim. root; *to pierce, sting:*— stings(1).

6568. פְּרַשׁ **perash** (1109a); (Ara.) corr. to 6567a; *to make distinct:*— translated(1).

6569. פֶּרֶשׁ **peresh** (831d); from an unused word; *fecal matter:*— refuse(7).

6570. פֶּרֶשׁ **Peresh** (831d); from the same as 6569; a Manassite:— Peresh(1).

6571a. פָּרָשׁ **parash** (832a); from an unused word; *a horse, steed:*— horses(2), steeds(1), war horses(1).

6571b. פָּרָשׁ **parash** (832a); from the same as 6571a; *horseman:*— cavalry(2), horseman(1), horsemen(50).

6572. פַּרְשֶׁגֶן **parshegen** or

פַּתְשֶׁגֶן **pathshegen** (832b, 837d); of for. or.; *a copy:*— copy(4).

6573. פַּרְשֶׁגֶן **parshegen** (1109a); (Ara.) corr. to 6572; *a copy:*— copy(3).

6574. פַּרְשְׁדֹנָה **parshedonah** (832b); of unc. der.; perh. *crotch:*— refuse(1).

6575. פָּרָשָׁה **parashah** (831d); from 6567a; *exact statement:*— exact amount(1), full account(1).

6576. פַּרְשֵׁז **parsez** (831c); of unc. der.; *to spread:*— spreads(1).

6577. פַּרְשַׁנְדָּתָא **Parshandatha** (832b); of for. or.; a son of Haman:— Parshandatha(1).

6578. פְּרָת **Perath** (832b); of for. or.; a river of W. Asia:— Euphrates(18).

6579. פַּרְתְּמִים **partemim** (832c); of for. or.; *nobles:*— noble(1), nobles(2).

6580. פַּשׁ **pash** (832d); another reading for 6588, q.v.

6581. פָּשָׂה **pasah** (832c); a prim. root; *to spread:*— spread(14), spreads farther(4).

6582. פָּשַׁח **pashach** (832d); a prim. root; *to tear in pieces:*— torn me to pieces(1).

6583. פַּשְׁחוּר **Pashchur** (832d); from 6582; five Isr.:— Pashhur(14).

6584. פָּשַׁט **pashat** (832d); a prim. root; *to strip off, make a dash, raid:*— dashed(2), invaded(1), made a raid(5), made...raid(1), put off(1), raid(2), raided(2), removed(1), rush(1), rushed(1), skin(2), skinned(1), strip(8), strip the off(1), strip off(2), stripped(6), stripped off(2), strips(1), take off(2), taken off(1).

6585. פָּשַׂע **pasa** (832c); a prim. root; *to step, march:*— step(1).

6586. פָּשַׁע **pasha** (833b); a prim. root; *to rebel, transgress:*— been in rebellion(1), committed(1), offended(1), rebel(1), rebelled(6), rebellion(1), revolted(7), transgress(3), transgressed(10), transgressing(1), transgression(1), transgressors(8).

6587. פֶּשַׂע **pesa** (832c); from 6585; *a step:*— step(1).

6588. פֶּשַׁע **pesha** (833b); from 6586; *transgression:*— breach of trust(1), rebellion(6), rebellious(1), rebellious act(2), rebellious acts(2), transgression(37), transgressions(45).

6589. פָּשַׂק **pasaq** (832d); a prim. root; *to part, open wide:*— opens wide(1), spread(1).

6590. פְּשַׁר **peshar** (1109a); (Ara.) a prim. root; *to interpret:*— give interpretations(1), interpretation(1).

6591. פְּשַׁר **peshar** (1109a); (Ara.) from 6590; *interpretation:*— interpretation(30).

6592. פֵּשֶׁר **pesher** (833d); of for. or.; *solution, interpretation:*— interpretation(1).

6593. פֵּשֶׁת **pesheth** (833d); of unc. der.; *flax, linen:*— flax(6), linen(9), linen made from flax(1).

6594. פִּשְׁתָּה **pishtah** (834a); from the same as 6593; *flax:*— flax(2), wick(2).

6595. פַּת **path** (837d); from 6626; *fragment, bit, morsel:*— bits(1), bread(1), fragments(1), morsel(3), piece(6), piece of bread(1), pieces(1).

6596. פֹּת **poth** (834a); of unc. der.; perh. *a hinge:*— foreheads(1), hinges(1).

6597. פִּתְאֹם **pithom** (837b); from the same as 6621; *suddenness, suddenly:*— immediately(1), sudden(2), suddenly(22).

6598. פַּת־בַּג **path-bag** (834a); of for. or.; *portion, delicacies:*— choice food(6).

6599. פִּתְגָם **pithgam** (834a); of for. or.; *an edict, decree:*— edict(1), sentence(1).

6600. פִּתְגָם **pithgam** (1109b); (Ara.) corr. to 6599; *a command, word, affair:*— answer(1), answer...matter(1), answered*(1), edict(1), report(1), sentence(1).

6601a. פָּתָה **pathah** (834b); a prim. root; *to be spacious, wide* or *open:*— enlarge(1), gossip*(1).

6601b. פָּתָה **pathah** (834c); denom. vb. from 6612a; *to be simple:*— allure(1), became...enticed(1), deceive(2), deceived(5), entice(9), enticed(1), entices(1), persuaded(1), prevailed(2), seduces(1), silly(1), simple(1).

6602. פְּתוּאֵל **Pethuel** (834d); from 6601a; father of the prophet Joel:— Pethuel(1).

6603. פִּתּוּחַ **pittuach** (836c); from 6605b; *an engraving:*— carved engravings(1), carved work(1), engraves(1), engravings(6), inscription(1).

6604a. פְּתוֹר **Pethor** (834d); of for. or.; home of Balaam:— Pethor(2).

6604b. פְּתוֹת **pathoth** (837d); from 6626; *a fragment, bit, morsel* (of bread):— fragments(1).

6605a. פָּתַח **pathach** (834d); a prim. root; *to open:*— allow(1), break forth(1), deprive(1), drawn(2), express(1), free(1), freeing(1), freely open(2), loose(3), loosed(4), loosen(2), loosens(1), open(50), opened(46), opened wide(1), opens(4), release(1), set him free(1), set free(2), spread(1), takes it off(1), turn(1), undone(1), unguarded(1), unloaded(1), unstopped(1), unvented*(1).

6605b. פָּתַח **pathach** (836b); a prim. root; *to engrave:*— carved(1), engrave(4), engraved(2), make(1), make kinds of engravings(1).

6606. פְּתַח **pethach** (1109b); (Ara.) corr. to 6605a; *to open:*— open(1), opened(1).

6607. פֶּתַח **pethach** (835d); from 6605a; *opening, doorway, entrance:*— door(16), doors(6), doorway(81), doorway at the entrance(1), doorways(3), entrance(43), entrances(1), entry(1), gate(1), gates(1), gateway(1), gateway*(2), opening(1), openings(3).

6608. פֵּתַח **pethach** (836a); from 6605a; *an opening, unfolding:*— unfolding(1).

6609. פְּתִחָה **pethichah** or

פְּתִיחָה **pethichah** (836a); from 6605a; *a drawn sword:*— drawn swords(1).

6610. פִּתְחוֹן **pithchon** (836a); from 6605a; *an opening:*— open(1), open*(1).

6611. פְּתַחְיָה **Pethachyah** (836a); from 6605a; three Isr.:— Pethahiah(4).

6612a. פֶּתִי **pethi** (834b); from 6601a; *simple,* perh. *open-minded:*— folly(1), naive(12), naive ones(2), simple(3).

6612b. פְּתִי **pethi** (834c); from 6601a; *simplicity:*— simple-minded(1).

6613. פְּתָי **pethay** (1109b); (Ara.) from a root corr. to 6601a; *breadth:*— width(2).

6614. פְּתִיגִיל **pethigil** (836c); prob. of for. or.; perh. *an expensive robe:*— fine clothes(1).

6615. פְּתַיּוּת **pethiyyuth** (834c); from 6601a; *simplicity:*— naive(1).

6616. פָּתִיל **pathil** (836d); from 6617; *cord, thread:*— cord(6), cords(1), line(1), string(1), threads(1), tied down(1).

6617. פָּתַל **pathal** (836c); a prim. root; *to twist:*— crooked(1), cunning(1), show yourself astute(2), wrestled(1).

6618. פְּתַלְתֹּל **pethaltol** (836d); from 6617; *tortuous:*— crooked(1).

6619. פִּתֹם **Pithom** (837a); of for. or.; a place in Eg.:— Pithom(1).

6620. פֶּתֶן **pethen** (837a); from an unused word; (a venomous serpent) perh. *cobra:*— cobra(3), cobras(3).

6621. פֶּתַע **petha** (837b); of unc. der.; *suddenness:*— instant(1), instantly(2), suddenly(3), very(1).

6622. פָּתַר **pathar** (837c); a prim. root; *to interpret:*— interpret(4), interpreted(5).

6623. פִּתְרוֹן **pithron** (837c); from 6622; *interpretation:*— interpretation(4), interpretations(1).

6624. פַּתְרוֹס **Pathros** (837c); of for. or.; a designation of Upper Eg.:— Pathros(5).

6625. פַּתְרֻסִים **Pathrusim** (837d); from 6624; a tribe, desc. from Mizraim, which inhab. S. Eg.:— Pathrus(1), Pathrusim(1).

פַּתְשֶׁגֶן **pathshegen**; see 6572.

6626. פָּתַת **pathath** (837d); a prim. root; *to break up, crumble:*— break(1).

צ

6627. צֵאָה **tseah** (844b); from an unused word; *filth, human excrement:*— dung*(1), excrement(1).

6628. צֶאֱלִים **tseelim** (838a); of unc. der.; (a kind of) *lotus:*— lotus plants(2).

6629. צֹאן **tson** (838a); from an unused word; *small cattle, sheep and goats, flock:*— flock(102), flocks(58), lambs(1), lambs*(2), Sheep(3), sheep(99), sheepfolds*(3), sheepshearers*(1).

6630. צַאֲנָן **Tsaanan** (838c); from the same as 6629; a place perh. in the Shephelah of Judah:— Zaanan(1).

6631. צֶאֱצָא **tseetsa** (425c); from 3318; *issue, offspring, produce:*— crops(1), descendants(4), offspring(5), offspring*(1), springs(1).

6632a. צָב tsab (839d); from an unused word; *a litter:*— covered(1), litters(1).

6632b. צָב tsab (839d); from an unused word; *lizard:*— great lizard(1).

6633. צָבָא tsaba (838c); a prim. root; *to wage war, serve:*— gone to war(2), made war(1), mustered(2), perform(2), served(1), serving women served(1), wage war(4), war(1).

6634. צְבָא tseba (1109b); (Ara.) corr. to 6633; *to be inclined, desire, be pleased:*— desired(1), will(1), wished(4), wishes(4).

6635. צָבָא tsaba (838d); from 6633; *army, war, warfare:*— armies(23), army(79), army*(1), battle(1), combat(1), conflict(1), forced to labor(1), hardship(1), host(30), hosts(292), hosts is the army(1), most(1), service(10), struggle(1), trained(1), war(35), warfare(1).

6636. צְבֹאִים Tseboim or

צְבֹיִים Tseboyim (840b); from the same as 6643b; a place near Sodom:— Zeboiim(5).

6637. צֹבֵבָה Tsobebah (839d); from the same as 6632b; a man of Judah:— Zobebah(1).

6638. צָבָה tsabah (839d); a prim. root; *to swell, swell up:*— swell(2).

6639. צָבֶה tsabeh (839d); from 6638; *swelling, swollen:*— swell(1).

6640. צְבוּ tsebu (1109c); (Ara.) from 6634; *thing, anything:*— nothing*(1).

6641. צָבוּעַ tsabua (840c); from the same as 6648; *colored, variegated:*— speckled(1).

6642. צָבַט tsabat (840b); a prim. root; *to reach, hold out:*— served(1).

6643a. צְבִי tsebi (840a); from an unused word; *beauty, honor:*— Beautiful(3), beautiful(4), beauty(4), glorious beauty(2), glory(5).

6643b. צְבִי tsebi (840a); from an unused word; *gazelle:*— gazelle(9), gazelles(5).

6644. צִבְיָא Tsibya (840b); from the same as 6643b; a Benjamite:— Zibia(1).

6645. צִבְיָה Tsibyah (840b); from the same as 6643b; "gazelle," mother of Jehoash:— Zibiah(2).

6646. צְבִיָּה tsebiyyah (840b); fem. of 6643b; *female gazelle:*— gazelle(2).

6647. צְבַע tseba (1109c); (Ara.) corr. to the unused source of 6648; *to dip, wet:*— drenched(5).

6648. צֶבַע tseba (840c); from an unused word; *dye, dyed stuff:*— dyed work(3).

6649. צִבְעוֹן Tsibon (840d); from an unused word; "hyena," a Horite:— Zibeon(8).

6650. צְבֹעִים Tseboim (840d); from the same as 6649; a place prob. at S. end of the Dead Sea:— Zeboim(2).

6651. צָבַר tsabar (840d); a prim. root; *to heap up:*— amasses(1), heap(1), piled(2), piles(1), store(1), stored(1).

6652. צִבֻּר tsibbur or

צִבּוּר tsibbur (840d); from 6651; *a heap:*— heaps(1).

6653. צְבָתִים tsebathim (841a); from an unused word; *bundles* (of grain):— bundles(1).

6654. צַד tsad (841a); from an unused word; *a side:*— arms(1), beside*(4), hip(1), side(17), side on sides(1), side to the other(1), sides(7).

6655. צַד tsad (1109c); (Ara.) corr. to 6654; *side:*— against(1), regard(1).

6656. צְדָא tseda (1109c); (Ara.) from a root corr. to 6658a; *a purpose:*— true(1).

6657. צְדָד Tsedad (841a); from the same as 6654; a place on the N. border of Canaan:— Zedad(2).

6658a. צָדָה tsadah (841b); a prim. root; *to lie in wait:*— lie in wait(1), lying in wait(1).

6658b. צָדָה tsadah (841b); a prim. root; *to lay waste:*— laid waste(1).

6659. צָדוֹק Tsadoq (843b); from the same as 6664; the name of several Isr.:— Zadok(52), Zadok's(1).

6660. צְדִיָּה tsediyyah (841b); from 6658a; *a lying-in-wait:*— lying in wait(2).

6661. צִדִּים Tsiddim (841b); from the same as 6654; a place in Naphtali:— Ziddim(1).

6662. צַדִּיק tsaddiq (843a); from the same as 6664; *just, righteous:*— blameless(1), innocent(1), just(5), man that the righteous(1), one in the right(1), right(2), righteous(164), righteous man(19), righteous men(2), Righteous One(2), righteous one(2), righteous ones(3), righteously(1), who are in the right(1).

6663. צָדֵק tsadeq or

צָדֹק tsadoq (842c); denom. vb. from 6664; *to be just* or *righteous:*— acquit(1), acquitted(1), declare you right(1), do justice(1), give him justice(1), just(2), justified(5), justifies(1), justify(5), justifying(2), lead the to righteousness(1), made your appear righteous(2), properly restored(1), proved right(1), proved...righteous(1), right(4), righteous(9), vindicated(1), vindicates(1).

6664. צֶדֶק tsedeq (841c); from an unused word; *rightness, righteousness:*— accurate(1), fairly(1), just(10), just cause(1), justice(3), righteous(15), righteously(6), righteousness(76), righteousness'(1), rightly(1), vindication(1), what is right(3).

6665. צִדְקָה tsidqah (1109d); (Ara.) corr. to 6666; *right-doing:*— righteousness(1).

6666. צְדָקָה tsedaqah (842a); from the same as 6664; *righteousness:*— honesty(1), justice(1), merits(1), right(2), righteous(1), righteous acts(3), righteous deeds(7), righteously(1), righteousness(136), rights(1), vindication(3).

6667. צִדְקִיָּהוּ Tsidqiyyahu or

צִדְקִיָּה Tsidqiyyah (843b); from the same as 6664; "Yah is righteousness," six Isr.:— Zedekiah(63), Zedekiah's(1).

6668. צָהֵב tsaheb or

צָהֹב tsahob (843c); a prim. root; *to gleam:*— shiny(1).

6669. צָהֹב tsahob (843c); from 6668; *gleaming, yellow:*— yellowish(3).

6670a. צָהַל tsahal (843c); a prim. root; *to neigh, cry shrilly:*— cry(1), cry aloud(3), neigh(1), neighing(1), shout(1), shouted(1).

6670b. צָהַל tsahal (843d); a prim. root; *to make shining:*— glisten(1).

6671. צָהַר tsahar (844a); denom. vb. from 3323; *to press out oil:*— produce oil(1).

6672a. צֹהַר tsohar (843d); from an unused word; *midday, noon:*— midday(4), noon(16), noonday(3).

6672b. צֹהַר tsohar (844a); from the same as 6672a; prob. *roof:*— window(1).

6673. צַו tsav (846c); from 6680; perh. *command:*— command(1), order(8).

6674. צוֹא tso or

צֹאִי tsoi (844b); from the same as 6627; *filthy:*— filthy(2).

6675. צוֹאָה tsoah or

צֹאָה tsoah(844b); from the same as 6627; *filth:*— filth(1), filthiness(1), filthy(1).

6676. צַוַּאר tsavvar (1109d); (Ara.) corr. to 6677; *neck:*— neck(3).

6677. צַוָּאר tsavvar (848b); from an unused word; *neck, back of neck:*— headlong(1), neck(30), necks(8), pride(1), support*(1).

6678. צוֹבָא Tsoba or

צוֹבָה Tsobah (844b); of unc. der.; an Aramean (Syrian) kingdom:— Zobah(12).

6679. צוּד tsud (844c); a prim. root; *to hunt:*— catches(1), hunt(8), hunt down(2), hunted(2), hunted me down(1), hunts(2).

6680. צָוָה tsavah (845b); a prim. root; *to lay charge* (upon), *give charge* (to), *command, order:*— appoint(1), appointed(4), appoints(1), charge(5), charged(17), charging(1), command(56), commanded(332), commander(1), commanding(18), commands(6), commission(3), commissioned(4), commit(1), gave a command(1), gave them a charge(1), gave command(2), gave commandment(2), gave orders(2), give his charge(1), give you in commandment(1), give you charge(1), give orders(3), given(1), given a command(1), given it an order(1), given command(1), given commandment(1), giving(1), instructed(1), issued a command(2), laid(1), laid down(1), ordained(4), order(4), ordered(5), put(1), sent(1), set his in order(1), set your in order(2).

6681. צָוַח tsavach (846d); a prim. root; *to cry aloud:*— shout for joy(1).

6682. צְוָחָה tsevachah (846d); from 6681; *an outcry:*— cry(2), outcry(2).

6683. צוּלָה tsulah (846d); from an unused word; (ocean) *deep:*— depth of the sea(1).

6684. צוּם tsum (847a); a prim. root; *to abstain from food, fast:*— actually(1), fast(6), fasted(12), fasted*(1), fasting(1).

6685. צוֹם tsom (847b); from 6684; *fasting, a fast:*— fast(17), fasted*(1), fasting(7), times of fasting(1).

6686. צוּעָר Tsuar (859b); from 6819; "little one," a man of Issachar:— Zuar(5).

6687. צוּף tsuph (847b); a prim. root; *to flow, overflow:*— engulf(1), float(1), flowed(1).

6688. צוּף tsuph (847b); from 6687; (honey) *comb:*— honeycomb(1), honeycomb*(1).

6689. צוּף Tsuph (847c); from 6687; ancestor of Elkanah and Samuel:— Zophai(1), Zuph(3).

6690. צוֹפַח Tsophach (847c, 860c); from the same as 6835; an Asherite:— Zophah(2).

6691. צוֹפַר Tsophar or

צֹפַר Tsophar (862b); from the same as 6842; one of Job's friends:— Zophar(4).

6692a. צוּץ tsuts or

צִיץ tsits (847c); a prim. root; *to blossom, shine, sparkle:*— blossom(1), budded(1), flourish(1), flourished(1), flourishes(2), produced blossoms(1), shine(1).

6692b. צוּץ tsuts (847d); a prim. root; *to gaze, peep:*— peering(1).

6693. צוּק tsuq (847d); a prim. root; *to constrain, bring into straits, press upon:*— bring distress(1), constrains(1), distress(2), oppress(3), oppressor(2), pressed(1), pressed him so hard(1).

6694. צוּק tsuq (848b); a prim. root; *to pour out, melt:*— poured(1), smelted(1).

6695a. צוֹק tsoq (848a); from 6693; *constraint, distress:*— distress(1).

6695b. צוּקָה tsuqah (848a); from 6693; *pressure, distress:*— anguish(3).

6696a. צוּר tsur (848d); a prim. root; *to confine, bind, besiege:*— barricade(1), besiege(3), besiege*(1), besieged(1), besieged*(10), besieging*(5), bind(2), bound(1), enclosed(1), laid siege(1), lay siege(1), laying siege(1), set(1), stirring(1), tied(1).

6696b. צוּר tsur (849a); a prim. root; *to show hostility to, treat as foe:*— adversary(1), attack(1), harass(2).

6696c. צוּר tsur (849b); a prim. root; *to fashion, delineate:*— fashioned(2).

6697. צוּר tsur (849c); from an unused word; *rock, cliff:*— Rock(10), rock(54), rocks(7), rocky(1), stones(1), strength(1).

6698. צוּר Tsur (849d); from 6697; "rock," a Midianite, also a Gibeonite:— Zur(5).

6699. צוּרָה tsurah (849b); from 6696c; *form, fashion:*— design(2), designs(1).

6700. צוּרִיאֵל Tsuriel (849d); from 6697 and 410; "my rock is El," a Levite:— Zuriel(1).

6701a. צוּרִישַׁדָּי Tsurishadday (849d); from 6697 and 7706b; "my rock is the Almighty," a Simeonite:— Zurishaddai(5).

6701b. צַוָּרֹן tsavvaron (848c); from the same as 6677; *necklace:*— necklace(1).

6702. צוּת tsuth (428b); the same as 3341, q.v.

6703. צַח tsach (850a); from 6705; *dazzling, glowing, clear:*— clearly(1), dazzling(2), scorching(1).

6704. צִחֶה tsicheh (850a); from an unused word; *parched:*— parched(1).

6705. צָחַח tsachach (850a); a prim. root; *to be dazzling:*— whiter(1).

6706. צְחִיחַ tsachiach (850a); from 6705; *a shining or glaring surface:*— bare(4), exposed places(1).

6707. צְחִיחָה tsechichah (850b); from 6705; *scorched land:*— parched land(1).

6708. צְחִיחִי tsechichi (850a); see 6706.

6709. צַחֲנָה tsachanah (850b); from an unused word; *a stench:*— foul smell(1).

6710. צַחְצָחָה tsachtsachah (850b); from 6705; *a scorched region:*— scorched places(1).

6711. צָחַק tsachaq (850b); a prim. root; *to laugh:*— caressing(1), entertained*(1), jesting(1), laugh(4), laughed(2), make sport(2), mocking(1), play(1).

6712. צְחֹק tsechoq (850b); from 6711; *laughter:*— laughed(1), laughter(1).

6713. צַחַר tsachar (850c); from an unused word; *reddish-gray, tawny:*— white(1).

6714. צֹחַר Tsochar (850c); from the same as 6713; a Hittite, also two Isr.:— Zohar(4).

6715. צָחֹר tsachor (850c); from the same as 6713; *tawny:*— white(1).

6716a. צִי tsi (850d); of for. or.; *a ship:*— ship(1), ships(3).

6716b. צִי tsi (850d); of unc. der.; (a wild animal) perh. *desert dweller:*— desert creatures(4), nomads of the desert(1), wilderness(1).

6717. צִיבָא Tsiba or

צִבָא Tsiba (850d); of unc. der.; a servant in Saul's house:— Ziba(16).

6718a. צַיִד tsayid (844d); from 6679; *hunting, game:*— game(8), hunter(2), hunter*(1), hunting(2), prey(1).

6718b. צַיִד tsayid (845b); from an unused word; *provision, food:*— food(1), nourishment(1), provision(2), provisions(1).

6719a. צַיָּד tsayyad (844d); from 6679; *a hunter:*— hunters(1).

6719b. צִיד tsid (845b); denom. vb. from 6718b; *take as one's provision:*— took it for our provisions(1).

6720. צֵידָה tsedah (845b); from the same as 6718b; *provision, food:*— food(2), provisions(7).

6721. צִידוֹן Tsidon or

צִידֹן Tsidon (850d); of for. or.; a Phoenician city on the Mediterranean coast, also a son of Canaan:— Sidon(22).

6722. צִידֹנִי Tsidoni (851a); from 6721; an inhab. of Sidon:— Sidonian(1), Sidonians(15).

6723. צִיָּה tsiyyah (851a); from an unused word; *dryness, drought:*— desert(3), drought(2), dry(5), dry places(1), parched(4), parched land(1).

6724. צָיוֹן tsayon (851b); from the same as 6723; *dryness, parched ground:*— drought(1), dry country(1).

6725. צִיּוּן tsiyyun (846b); from 6680; *a signpost, monument:*— marker(1), monument(1), roadmarks(1).

6726. צִיּוֹן Tsiyyon (851b); from the same as 6723; a mountain in Jer., also a name for Jer.:— Zion(153), Zion's(1).

6727. צִיחָא Tsicha (851c); of unc. der.; an overseer of Nethinim, also an Isr. family:— Ziha(3).

6728. צִיִּי tsiyyi (850d); the same as 6716b, q.v.

6729. צִינֹק tsinoq (857b); from an unused word; *pillory:*— iron collar(1).

6730. צִיעֹר Tsior (859b); from 6819; a place near Hebron:— Zior(1).

6731a. צִיץ tsits (851c); of unc. der.; perh. *wings:*— wings(1).

6731b. צִיץ tsits (847c); from 6692a; *a blossom, flower, shining thing:*— flower(7), flowers(4), plate(3).

6732. צִיץ Tsits (851d); from the same as 6731a; a pass between the Dead Sea and Jer.:— Ziz(1).

6733. צִיצָה tsitsah (847c); see 6731b.

6734. צִיצִת tsitsith (851d); of unc. der.; *a tassel, lock:*— lock(1), tassel(2), tassels(1).

6735a. צִיר tsir (851d); from an unused word; *an envoy, messenger:*— envoy(3), envoys(2), messenger(1).

6735b. צִיר tsir (852a); from an unused word; *a pivot, hinge:*— hinges(1).

6735c. צִיר tsir (852a); from the same as 6735b; *a pang:*— anguish(1), pains(4).

6736. צִיר tsir (849c); from 6696c; *an image:*— form(1), idols(1).

6737. צִיַּר tsayar (845b); denom. vb. from 6735a; *to act as envoy:*— envoys(1).

6738. צֵל tsel (853b); from 6751; *a shadow:*— protection(4), shade(15), shadow(30), shadows(3), shelter(1).

6739. צְלָא tsela (1109d); (Ara.) a prim. root; *to pray:*— pray(1), praying(1).

6740. צָלָה tsalah (852a); a prim. root; *to roast* (flesh):— roast(1), roasting(1), roasts(1).

6741. צִלָּה Tsillah (853c); from 6751; wife of Lamech:— Zillah(3).

6742. צְלוּל tselul or

צְלִיל tselil (853d); from an unused word; *a cake, round loaf:*— loaf(1).

6743a. צָלַח tsalach (852b); a prim. root; *to rush:*— break forth(1), came upon him mightily(4), came upon mightily(1), came mightily(2), come upon you mightily(1), rushed(1).

6743b. צָלֵחַ tsaleach or

צָלַח tsalach (852b); a prim. root; *to advance, prosper:*— advanced(1), give us success(1), made his successful(1), make his successful(1), make your prosperous(1), make your successful(1), prosper(16), prospered(7), prosperous(1), prospers(2), send prosperity(1), succeed(10), succeeding(1), successful(4), successfully completed(1), thrive(2), useful(1), victoriously(1), worthless*(2).

6744. צְלַח tselach (1109d); (Ara.) corr. to 6743b; *to prosper:*— enjoyed success(1), prosper(1), succeeding(1), successful(1).

6745. צֵלָחָה tselachah (852c); from an unused word; *a pot* (for cooking):— pans(1).

6746. צְלֹחִית tselochith (852d); from the same as 6745; *a jar:*— jar(1).

6747. צַלַּחַת tsallachath (852c); from the same as 6745; *a dish:*— dish(3).

6748. צָלִי tsali (852a); from 6740; *roasted, a roast:*— roast(1), roasted(2).

6749. צָלַל tsalal (853a); a prim. root; *to sink, be submerged:*— sank(1).

6750. צָלַל tsalal (852d); a prim. root; *to tingle, quiver:*— quivered(1), tingle(3).

6751. צָלַל tsalal (853a); a prim. root; *to be or grow dark:*— grew dark(1), shade(1).

6752. צֵלֶל tselel (853b); from the same as 6738, q.v.

6753. צְלֶלְפּוֹנִי Tselelponi or

הַצְּלֶלְפּוֹנִי Hatstselelponi (853c); from 6751 and 6437; "give shade, you who turn to me!" an Isr. woman:— Hazzelelponi(1).

6754. צֶלֶם tselem (853d); from an unused word; *an image:*— form(1), image(5), images(6), likenesses(3), phantom(1).

6755. צְלֵם tselem (1109d); (Ara.) corr. to 6754; *an image:*— expression(1), image(11), statue(5).

6756a. צַלְמוֹן Tsalmon (854a); from the same as 6754; a mountain near Shechem, also perh. a snowcapped mountain of unc. location:— Zalmon(2).

6756b. צַלְמוֹן Tsalmon (854a); from the same as 6754; one of David's heroes:— Zalmon(1).

6757. צַלְמָוֶת tsalmaveth (853c); from 6738 and 4194; *death-like shadow, deep shadow:*— black gloom(1), dark(1), deep darkness(6), deep shadow(4), shadow of death(4), thick darkness(2).

6758. צַלְמֹנָה **Tsalmonah** (854a); fem. of 6756a; a place in the desert:— Zalmonah(2).

6759. צַלְמֻנָּע **Tsalmunna** (854a); from the same as 6754; a king of Midian:— Zalmunna(12).

6760. צָלַע **tsala** (854b); a prim. root; *to limp:*— lame(3), limping(1).

6761. צֶלַע **tsela** (854c); from 6760; *limping, stumbling:*— fall(2), stumbling(1).

6762. צֶלַע **Tsela** (854b); from the same as 6763; a place in Benjamin:— Zela(1), Zelah(1).

6763. צֵלָע **tsela** (854a); from an unused word; *rib, side:*— boards(3), chambers(1), hillside*(1), leaves(1), one...another(1), rib(1), ribs(1), side(15), side chamber(1), side chambers(10), sides(5), walls(1).

6764. צָלָף **Tsalaph** (854c); of unc. der.; father of one of the builders of the Jer. wall:— Zalaph(1).

6765. צְלָפְחָד **Tselophchad** (854c); of unc. der.; a man of Manasseh:— Zelophehad(11).

6766. צֶלְצַח **Tseltsach** (854c); of unc. der.; a place in Benjamin:— Zelzah(1).

6767a. צְלָצַל **tsiltsal** (852d); from 6750; *whirring, buzzing:*— whirring(1).

6767b. צִלְצַל **tsiltsal** (852d); from 6750; *a spear:*— spears(1).

6767c. צְלָצַל **tselatsal** (852d); from 6750; *a whirring locust:*— cricket(1).

6767d. צֶלְצְלִים **tseltselim** (852d); from 6750; (percussion musical instrument) perh. *cymbals:*— cymbals(3).

6768. צֶלֶק **Tseleq** (854c); of unc. der.; an Ammonite hero of David:— Zelek(2).

6769. צִלְּתַי **Tsillethay** (853c); from 6751; "shady," two Isr.:— Zillethai(2).

6770. צָמֵא **tsame** (854c); a prim. root; *to be thirsty:*— became...thirsty(1), thirst(3), thirsted(1), thirsts(2), thirsty(3).

6771. צָמֵא **tsame** (854d); from 6770; *thirsty:*— dry(1), thirsts(1), thirsty(6), thirsty man(1).

6772. צָמָא **tsama** (854d); from 6770; *thirst:*— parched ground(1), thirst(15), thirsty(1).

6773. צִמְאָה **tsimah** (854d); fem. of 6772; *parched condition:*— thirst(1).

6774. צִמָּאוֹן **tsimmaon** (855a); from 6770; *thirsty ground:*— thirsty ground(3).

6775. צָמַד **tsamad** (855a); a prim. root; *to bind, join:*— fastened(1), frames(1), joined(3).

6776. צֶמֶד **tsemed** (855a); from 6775; *a couple, pair:*— acre(1), acres(1), couple(1), pair(3), pairs(3), team(1), together(1), two(1), yoke(3).

6777. צַמָּה **tsammah** (855d); from an unused word; (woman's) *veil:*— veil(4).

6778. צִמּוּק **tsimmuq** (856a); from 6784; *bunch of raisins:*— bunches of raisins(1), clusters of raisins(3).

6779. צָמַח **tsamach** (855b); a prim. root; *to sprout, spring up:*— branch(1), grow(8), growing(1), grown(2), spring(5), spring forth(5), springs(1), sprout(4), sprouted(4), sprouts(1), unproductive*(1).

6780. צֶמַח **tsemach** (855c); from 6779; *a sprout, growth:*— Branch(5), growth(1), heads(1), plants(1), sprouting(1), sprouts(1), what grew(1), where it grew(1).

6781a. צָמִיד **tsamid** (855b); from 6775; *bracelet:*— bracelets(6).

6781b. צָמִיד **tsamid** (855b); from 6775; *a cover:*— covering(1).

6782. צַמִּים **tsammim** (855d); from the same as 6777; perh. *a snare, trap:*— schemer(1), trap(1).

6783. צְמִיתֻת **tsemithuth** (856c); from 6789; *completion, finality:*— permanently(2).

6784. צָמַק **tsamaq** (855d); a prim. root; *to dry up, shrivel:*— dry(1).

6785. צֶמֶר **tsemer** (856a); from an unused word; *wool:*— wool(16).

6786. צְמָרִי **Tsemari** (856a); from the same as 6785; a Canaanite people:— Zemarite(1), Zemarites(1).

6787. צְמָרַיִם **Tsemarayim** (856b); from the same as 6785; a place in Benjamin, also a mountain in Ephraim:— Zemaraim(2).

6788. צַמֶּרֶת **tsammereth** (856a); from the same as 6785; (tree) *top:*— top(5).

6789. צָמַת **tsamath** (856b); a prim. root; *to put an end to, exterminate:*— consumed(1), cut off(1), destroy(6), destroyed(4), silenced(2), silent(1).

6790. צִן **Tsin** (856c); of unc. der.; a desert area which included Kadesh-barnea:— Zin(10).

6791. צֵן **tsen** (856d); of unc. der.; perh. *a thorn, barb:*— thorns(2).

6792. צֹנֶה **tsoneh** or

צֹנְא **tsone** (856c); of unc. der.; *flocks:*— sheep(2).

6793a. צִנָּה **tsinnah** (856d); from the same as 6791; prob. *a hook, barb:*— meat hooks(1).

6793b. צִנָּה **tsinnah** (856d); from an unused word; *coolness:*— cold(1).

6793c. צִנָּה **tsinnah** (857a); from an unused word; (large) *shield:*— buckler(3), bucklers(1), large shield(3), large shields(3), shield(7), shield-bearer*(1), shield-carrier*(1), shields(1).

6794a. צָנוּעַ **tsanua** (857a); from 6800; *modest:*— humble(1).

6794b. צִנּוֹר **tsinnor** (857c); from an unused word; *a pipe, spout, conduit:*— water tunnel(1), waterfalls(1).

6795. צָנַח **tsanach** (856c); a prim. root; *to descend:*— alighted(2), went through(1).

6796. צָנִין **tsanin** (856d); from the same as 6791; *a thorn, prick:*— thorns(2).

6797. צָנִיף **tsaniph** (857b); from 6801; *a turban:*— diadem(1), turban(3), turbans(1).

6798. צָנַם **tsanam** (856d); a prim. root; *to dry up, harden:*— withered(1).

6799. צְנָן **Tsenan** (838c); from the same as 6629; a place in the Shephelah of Judah, perh. the same as 6630:— Zenan(1).

6800. צָנַע **tsana** (857a); a prim. root; *to be modest* or *humble:*— humbly(1).

6801. צָנַף **tsanaph** (857a); a prim. root; *to wrap* or *wind up together:*— attired(1), roll you tightly(1).

6802. צְנֵפָה **tsenephah** (857b); see 6801.

6803. צִנְצֶנֶת **tsintseneth** (857a); perh. from the same as 6793c; *a jar:*— jar(1).

6804. צַנְתְּרוֹת **tsanteroth** (857c); from the same as 6794b; *pipes:*— pipes(1).

6805. צָעַד **tsaad** (857c); a prim. root; *to step, march:*— gone(1), march(1), marched(3), run(1), takes(1), walk(1).

6806. צַעַד **tsaad** (857d); from 6805; *a step, pace:*— march(1), paces(1), steps(11), stride(1).

6807a. צְעָדָה **tseadah** (857d); fem. of 6806; *a marching:*— marching(2).

6807b. צְעָדָה **tseadah** (857d); of unc. der.; perh. *anklets:*— ankle chains(1).

6808. צָעָה **tsaah** (858a); a prim. root; *to stoop, bend, incline:*— exile(1), lain down(1), marching(1), tip(1), tip him over(1).

6809. צָעִיף **tsaiph** (858b); from an unused word; *a wrapper, shawl,* or *veil:*— veil(3).

6810. צָעִיר **tsair** (859a); from 6819; *little, insignificant, young:*— least(1), least one(1), little(1), little ones(3), servants(1), small(2), those younger(1), young(1), younger(7), youngest(4), youngest son(1).

6811. צָעִיר **Tsair** (859a); from 6820; a place on the border of Edom:— Zair(1).

6812. צְעִירָה **tseirah** (859a); fem. of 6810; *youth:*— youth(1).

6813. צָעַן **tsaan** (858a); a prim. root; *to wander, travel:*— folded(1).

6814. צֹעַן **Tsoan** (858a); from 6813; a place in Eg.:— Zoan(7).

6815. צַעֲנַנִּים **Tsaanannim** (858b); from 6813; a place on the border of Naphtali:— Zaanannim(2).

6816. צַעֲצֻעִים **tsaatsuim** (847b); from an unused word; *things formed, images:*— sculptured*(1).

6817. צָעַק **tsaaq** (858b); a prim. root; *to cry, cry out, call:*— appeal(1), appealed(1), called the together(1), cried(27), cries(1), cry(14), cry aloud(1), crying(2), summoned(6).

6818. צְעָקָה **tseaqah** (858c); from 6817; *a cry, outcry:*— cry(14), cry of distress(1), outcry(6).

6819. צָעַר **tsaar** (858d); a prim. root; *to be* or *grow insignificant:*— become insignificant(1), insignificant(1), little(1).

6820. צֹעַר **Tsoar** or

צוֹעַר **Tsoar** (858d); from 6819; "insignificance," a city at the S.E. end of the Dead Sea:— Zoar(10).

6821. צָפַד **tsaphad** (859b); a prim. root; *to draw together, contract:*— shriveled(1).

6822. צָפָה **tsaphah** (859b); a prim. root; *to look out* or *about, spy, keep watch:*— destined(1), keep watch(3), lookout(1), looks well(1), spies(1), watch(3), watch expectantly(1), watched(1), watching(2), watchman(14), watchman's(1), watchmen(5).

6823. צָפָה **tsaphah** (860a); a prim. root; *to lay out, lay over:*— adorned(1), overlaid(33), overlay(12), spread(1).

6824. צָפָה **tsaphah** (847c); from 6687; *an outflow:*— discharge(1).

6825. צְפוֹ **Tsepho** or

צְפִי **Tsephi** (859d); from 6822; perh. "gazing," an Edomite:— Zephi(1), Zepho(2).

6826. צִפּוּי **tsippuy** (860b); from 6823; (metal) *plating:*— overlaid(1), overlaying(2), plating(2).

6827. צְפוֹן **Tsephon** (859d); from 6822; perh. "gaze," a son of Gad, the same as 6837:— Zephon(1).

6828. צָפוֹן **tsaphon** (860d); from 6845; *north:*— North(8), north(125), north side(7), northern(1), northward(11).

6829. צָפוֹן **Tsaphon** (861b); from 6845; "north," a place on the E. bank of the Jordan:— Zaphon(2).

6830. צְפוֹנִי **tsephoni** (861a); from 6828; *northern:*— northern(1).

6831. צְפוֹנִי Tsephoni (859d); from 6827; desc. of Zephon:— Zephonites(1).

6832. צְפוּעַ tsephua or **צְפִיעַ tsaphia** (861c); from an unused word; *dung* (of cattle):— dung(1).

6833. צִפּוֹר tsippor or **צִפֹּר tsippor** (861d); from an unused word; *a bird:*— bird(26), bird's(1), birds(11), fowl(1), sparrow(1).

6834. צִפּוֹר Tsippor (862a); from the same as 6833; "bird," father of Balak:— Zippor(7).

6835. צַפַּחַת tsappachath (860b); from an unused word; *a jar, jug:*— jar(4), jug(3).

6836. צְפִיָּה tsippiyyah (859d); from 6822; *lookout post:*— watching(1).

6837. צִפְיוֹן Tsiphyon (859d); from 6822; perh. "gazing," a son of Gad, the same as 6827:— Ziphion(1).

6838. צַפִּיחִת tsappichith (860c); from the same as 6835; *a flat cake, wafer:*— wafers(1).

6839. צֹפִים Tsophim (859c); from 6822; "watchers," a field on the summit of Mount Pisgah:— Zophim(1).

6840. צָפִין tsaphin (860d); from 6845; *a treasure:*— treasure(1).

6841. צְפִיר tsephir (1110a); (Ara.) corr. to 6842; *male goat:*— male(1).

6842. צָפִיר tsaphir (862b); from an unused word; *male goat:*— goat(1), male(2), male goat(1), male goats(1).

6843. צְפִירָה tsephirah (862a); from an unused word; *a plait, chaplet,* perh. *doom:*— diadem(1), doom(2).

6844. צָפִית tsaphith (860b); from 6823; *a rug, carpet:*— cloth(1).

6845. צָפַן tsaphan (860c); a prim. root; *to hide, treasure up:*— ambush(2), authority(1), conceal(1), concealed(2), hid(1), hidden(1), hide(2), keep them secretly(1), kept(1), lurk(1), restrain her restrains(1), saved(1), secret place(1), stealthily watch(1), store(1), stored(5), stores(1), stores away(1), treasure(2), treasured(3), treasures(1).

6846. צְפַנְיָה Tsephanyah or **צְפַנְיָהוּ Tsephanyahu** (861b); from 6845 and 3050; "Yah has treasured," four Isr.:— Zephaniah(10).

6847. צָפְנַת פַּעְנֵחַ Tsaphenath Paneach (861b); of for. or.; "the god speaks and he lives," Joseph's Eg. name:— Zaphenath-paneah(1).

6848a. צֶפַע tsepha (861c); from an unused word; *a serpent:*— viper(1).

6848b. צִפְעוֹנִי tsiphoni (861c); from the same as 6848a; *a serpent:*— Adders(1), adders'(1), viper(1), viper's(1).

6849. צְפִיעָה tsephiah (861c); of unc. der.; perh. *offshoot:*— issue(1).

6850. צָפַף tsaphaph (861c); a prim. root; *to chirp, peep:*— chirped(1), twitter(1), whisper(2).

6851. צַפְצָפָה tsaphtsaphah (861d); from 6850; perh. *willow:*— willow(1).

6852. צָפַר tsaphar (861d); a prim. root; perh. *to depart:*— depart(1).

6853. צְפַר tsippar (1110a); (Ara.) corr. to 6833; *a bird:*— birds(3), birds'(1).

6854. צְפַרְדֵּעַ tsephardea (862c); of unc. der.; *frogs:*— frogs(13).

6855. צִפֹּרָה Tsipporah (862a); from the same as 6833; "bird," Moses' wife:— Zipporah(3).

6856. צִפֹּרֶן tsipporen (862b); from an unused word; *fingernail, stylus point:*— nails(1), point(1).

6857. צְפַת Tsephath (862c); of unc. der.; a Canaanite city:— Zephath(1).

6858. צֶפֶת tsepheth (860b); from 6823; prob. *plated capital* (of a pillar):— capital(1).

6859. צְפָתָה Tsephathah (862c); from the same as 6857; a valley in Judah:— Zephathah(1).

6860. צִקְלַג Tsiqelag (862c); of unc. der.; a city assigned to Judah, also to Simeon:— Ziklag(15).

6861. צִקְלֹן tsiqqalon (862d); of unc. der.; perh. *garment:*— sack(1).

6862a. צַר tsar (865a); from 6887a; *narrow, tight:*— cramped(1), limited(2), narrow(2), rushing(1), tight(1).

6862b. צַר tsar (865a); from 6887a; *straits, distress:*— afflicted(1), affliction(1), anguish(1), anguished(1), distress(17), privation(1), strait(1), trouble(7).

6862c. צַר tsar (865d); from 6887c; *adversary, foe:*— adversaries(40), adversary(15), distresses(1), enemies(5), enemy(2), foe(1), foes(3), oppressors(2).

6862d. צַר tsar (866a); from an unused word; *a hard pebble, flint:*— flint(1).

6863. צֵר Tser (862d); of unc. der.; a city in Naphtali:— Zer(1).

6864. צֹר tsor (866a); from the same as 6862d; *a hard pebble, flint:*— edge(1), flint(4).

6865. צֹר Tsor or **צוֹר Tsor** (862d); of for. or.; a Phoenician city:— Tyre(42).

6866a. צָרַב tsarab (863a); a prim. root; *to burn, scorch:*— burned(1).

6866b. צָרָב tsarab (863a); from 6866a; *burning, scorching:*— scorching(1).

6867. צָרֶבֶת tsarebeth (863a); from 6866a; *scab, scar* (of a sore):— scar(2).

6868a. צְרֵדָה Tseredah (863a); of unc. der.; a city in Ephraim:— Zeredah(1).

6868b. צְרֵדָתָה Tseredathah (866c); perh. the same as 6888, q.v.:— Zeredah(1).

6869a. צָרָה tsarah (865b); fem. of 6862b; *straits, distress:*— affliction(1), anguish(2), distress(34), distresses(1), trouble(22), troubles(11).

6869b. צָרָה tsarah (865d); from 6887c; *one who vexes, a rival wife:*— rival(1).

6870. צְרוּיָה Tseruyah (863b); from the same as 6875; an Isr. woman:— Zeruiah(26).

6871. צְרוּעָה Tseruah (864a); from the same as 6883; mother of Jeroboam:— Zeruah(1).

6872a. צְרוֹר tseror (865c); from 6887a; *a bundle, parcel, pouch, bag:*— bag(2), bundle(2), bundles(1), pouch(1), purse(1).

6872b. צְרוֹר tseror (866a); from the same as 6862d; *a pebble:*— kernel(1), small stone(1).

6872c. צְרוֹר Tseror (866c); from the same as 6862d; grandfather of Kish:— Zeror(1).

6873. צָרַח tsarach (863c); a prim. root; *to cry, roar:*— cries(1), raise a war cry(1), war cry(1).

6874. צְרִי Tseri (863b); from the same as 6875; an Isr. musician:— Zeri(1).

6875. צֳרִי tsori or **צְרִי tseri** or **צֳרִי tsori** (863b); from an unused word; (a kind of) *balsam:*— balm(6).

6876. צֹרִי Tsori (863a); from 6865; inhab. of Tyre:— men of Tyre(1), Tyre(1), Tyrian(1), Tyrians(2).

6877. צְרִיחַ tseriach (863c); from an unused word; perh. *excavation, underground chamber:*— cellars(1), inner chamber(3).

6878. צֹרֶךְ tsorek (863d); from an unused word; *a need:*— need(1).

6879. צָרַע tsara (863d); denom. vb. from 6883; *to be struck with leprosy, to be leprous:*— being a leper(1), leper(12), lepers(1), leprous(6).

6880. צִרְעָה tsirah (864a); from the same as 6883; *hornets:*— hornet(2), hornets(1).

6881. צָרְעָה Tsorah (864a); from the same as 6883; a city exchanged by Judah and Dan:— Zorah(10).

6882. צָרְעִי Tsori or **צָרְעָתִי Tsorathi** (864a); from 6881; inhab. of Zorah:— Zorathites(2), Zorites(1).

6883. צָרַעַת tsaraath (863d); from an unused word; *leprosy:*— leprosy(30), leprous(4), mark(1).

6884. צָרַף tsaraph (864a); a prim. root; *to smelt, refine, test:*— goldsmith(5), goldsmiths(2), pure(1), refine(3), refined(5), refiner's(1), refining goes(1), silversmith(2), smelt(1), smelter(2), smith(1), test(2), tested(4), tried(2).

6885. צֹרְפִי tsorephi (864c); from 6884; *goldsmiths:*— goldsmiths(1).

6886. צָרְפַת Tsarephath (864c); from 6884; "smelting place," a city S. of Sidon:— Zarephath(3).

6887a. צָרַר tsarar (864c); a prim. root; *to bind, tie up, be restricted, narrow, scant,* or *cramped:*— afflicted(1), besiege(3), besieges(1), bind(1), binds(1), bound(3), bring distress(1), cause them distress(1), cramped(2), distress(6), distressed(6), frustrated(1), impeded(1), mended(1), oppressed(1), shortened(1), shut(1), small(1), trouble(1), wrapped(1), wraps(2).

6887b. צָרַר tsarar (865b); denom. vb. from 6862b; *to suffer distress:*— distress(1), labor(2).

6887c. צָרַר tsarar (865c); a prim. root; *to show hostility toward, vex:*— adversaries(10), adversary(2), afflict(1), attacks(1), been hostile(1), distress(1), enemies(1), enemy(3), harass(2), hostile(1), persecuted(2), trouble(1).

6887d. צָרַר tsarar (865d); denom. vb. from 6869b; *to make a rival wife:*— rival(1).

6888. צְרֵרָה Tsererah (866c); from the same as 6862d; a city toward which Gideon's enemies fled:— Zererah(1).

6889. צֶרֶת Tsereth (866c); of unc. der.; a man of Judah:— Zereth(1).

6890. צֶרֶת הַשַּׁחַר Tsereth Hashshachar (866c); from 6889 and 7837; "Zereth of the dawn," a city in Reuben:— Zereth-shahar(1).

6891. צָרְתָן Tsarethan (866c); of unc. der.; a city in the Jordan Valley:— Zarethan(3).

ק

6892. קֵא qe (883c); from 7006a; *what is vomited up, vomit:*— vomit(1).

6893. **קָאַת** **qaath** or

קָאָת **qaath** (866b); of unc. der.; (a bird) perh. *pelican:*— pelican(5).

6894. **קַב** **qab** (866b); from an unused word; *kab* (a measure of capacity):— kab(1).

6895. **קָבַב** **qabab** (866d); a prim. root; *to utter a curse against, curse:*— blasphemed(1), curse(10), curse them at all(1), cursed(2).

6896. **קֵבָה** **qebah** (867a); from an unused word; *stomach, belly:*— body(1), stomach(1).

6897. **קֹבָה** **qobah** (867a); the same as 6896, q.v.

6898. **קֻבָּה** **qubbah** (866d); from the same as 6894; *a large vaulted tent:*— tent(1).

6899. **קִבּוּץ** **qibbuts** (868b); from 6908; *assemblage:*— collection(1).

6900. **קְבֻרָה** **qeburah** or

קְבוּרָה **qeburah** (869a); from 6912; *a grave, burial:*— burial(3), burial place(2), grave(7), tomb(2).

6901. **קָבַל** **qabal** (867a); a prim. root; *to receive, take:*— accept(4), accepted(1), made a custom(1), opposite(2), received(2), take(1), took(1), undertook(1).

6902. **קַבֵּל** **qabbel** (1110b); (Ara.) corr. to 6901; *to receive:*— receive(2), received(1).

6903. **קֳבֵל** **qobel** (1110a); (Ara.) corr. to 6904; *in front of, before, because of, because that:*— because(1), because*(4), before(1), forasmuch*(1), front(1), inasmuch*(9), just(1), opposite(1), presence(1), reason*(2), result(1), therefore*(4), though(1).

6904. **קֹבֶל** **qebol** (867b); from 6901; *something in front, a military siege engine:*— battering rams(1), before(1).

6905. **קָבָל** **qabal** (867b); the same as 6904, q.v.

6906. **קָבַע** **qaba** (867b); a prim. root; perh. *to rob:*— rob(2), robbed(1), robbing(2), take(1).

6907. **קֻבַּעַת** **qubbaath** (867c); from 6906; *a cup:*— chalice*(2), dregs(1).

6908. **קָבַץ** **qabats** (867c); a prim. root; *to gather, collect:*— assemble(7), assembled(7), brought the together(1), collect(1), collected(2), gather(52), gathered(45), gathers(4), grown(1), meet(1), rally(1), regather(1), surely gather(1), turn(1).

6909. **קַבְצְאֵל** **Qabtseel** (868b); from 6908 and 410; "God gathers," a city in S. Judah:— Jekabzeel(1), Kabzeel(3).

6910. **קְבֻצָה** **qebutsah** (868b); from 6908; *a gathering:*— gather(1).

6911. **קִבְצַיִם** **Qibtsayim** (868b); from 6908; "two heaps," a city in Ephraim:— Kibzaim(1).

6912. **קָבַר** **qabar** (868b); a prim. root; *to bury:*— burial(1), buried(93), buriers have buried(1), bury(30), burying(5), surely bury(1).

6913. **קֶבֶר** **qeber** (868d); from 6912; *a grave, sepulcher:*— burial(6), burial place(1), grave(28), graves(16), tomb(8), tombs(8).

6914. **קִבְרוֹת הַתַּאֲוָה** **Qibroth Hattaavah** (869a); from 6913 and 8378; "the graves of desire," a place in the desert:— Kibroth-hattaavah(5).

6915. **קָדַד** **qadad** (869a); a prim. root; *to bow down:*— bow low(1), bowed(7), bowed down(1), bowed low(6).

6916. **קִדָּה** **qiddah** (869b); from the same as 6936; *cassia:*— cassia(2).

6917. **קְדוּמִים** **qedumim** (870c); from the same as 6924a; perh. *ancient:*— ancient(1).

6918. **קָדוֹשׁ** **qadosh** (872c); from the same as 6944; *sacred, holy:*— consecrated(1), Holy(8), holy(50), Holy One(44), holy one(3), holy ones(6), one is holy(1), saints(2).

6919. **קָדַח** **qadach** (869b); a prim. root; *to be kindled, kindle:*— been kindled(1), kindle(1), kindled(2), kindles(1).

6920. **קַדַּחַת** **qaddachath** (869b); from 6919; *fever:*— fever(2).

6921. **קָדִים** **qadim** (870b); from the same as 6924a; *east, east wind:*— east(55), east side(1), east wind(10), forward(1).

6922. **קַדִּישׁ** **qaddish** (1110c); (Ara.) corr. to 6918; *holy:*— holy(4), holy one(2), holy ones(1), saints(6).

6923. **קָדַם** **qadam** (869d); denom. vb. from 6924a; *to come* or *be in front, meet:*— anticipate(1), before(2), come(2), come to meet(1), come before(3), comes before(1), confront(3), confronted(4), forestall(1), given(1), go(1), meet(5), receive(1), rise(1), went(1).

6924a. **קֶדֶם** **qedem** (869c); from an unused word; *front, east, formerly:*— ancient(4), ancient times(3), before(1), before his of old(1), earliest times(1), East(1), east(26), east side(1), eastward(1), eternal(1), everlasting(1), formerly(1), forward(1), gone(1), long ago(1), old(16), times*(2).

6924b. **קֵדֶם** **qedem** (870a); from the same as 6924a; *eastward, toward the east:*— east(9), east side(2), east*(2), eastern(1), eastward(10), side(1), southeast*(1).

6925. **קֳדָם** **qodam** (1110b); (Ara.) corr. to 6924a; *before:*— before(23), before*(3), presence(3), rose(1), toward(1).

6926. **קִדְמָה** **qidmah** (870b); from the same as 6924a; *front, east:*— east(4).

6927. **קַדְמָה** **qadmah** (870b); from the same as 6924a; *antiquity, former state:*— before(1), former state(2), formerly(1), origin is from antiquity(1).

6928. **קַדְמָה** **qadmah** (1110c); (Ara.) corr. to 6927; *former time:*— ago(1), previously(1).

6929. **קֵדְמָה** **Qedemah** (870b); from the same as 6924a; a son of Ishmael:— Kedemah(2).

6930. **קַדְמוֹן** **qadmon** (870c); from the same as 6924a; *eastern:*— eastern(1).

6931. **קַדְמוֹנִי** **qadmoni** or

קַדְמֹנִי **qadmoni** (870c); from the same as 6924a; *former, eastern:*— ancients(1), east(3), eastern(3), eastward(1), former(2), things of the past(1).

6932. **קְדֵמוֹת** **Qedemoth** or

קְדֵמֹת **Qedemoth** (870d); from the same as 6924a; a city in Reuben:— Kedemoth(4).

6933. **קַדְמַי** **qadmay** (1110c); (Ara.) corr. to 6931; *former, first:*— first(2), previous ones(1).

6934. **קַדְמִיאֵל** **Qadmiel** (870d); from 6924a and 410; "God is the ancient one," a Levite name:— Kadmiel(8).

6935. **קַדְמֹנִי** **Qadmoni** (870d); from the same as 6924a; "easterners," a tribe whose land Abraham was to inherit:— Kadmonite(1).

6936. **קָדְקֹד** **qodqod** (869a); from an unused word; *head, crown of the head:*— crown(1), crown of his head(2), crown of the head(3), crown of your head(2), pate(1), scalp(1), scalps(1).

6937. **קָדַר** **qadar** (871a); a prim. root; *to be dark:*— become dark(1), dark(1), darken(2), grew black(1), grow dark(2), mourn(3), mourning(6), sit(1), turbid(1).

6938. **קֵדָר** **Qedar** (871a); from 6937; perh. "swarthy," a son of Ishmael, also his desc.:— Kedar(12).

6939. **קִדְרוֹן** **Qidron** (871b); from 6937; perh. "dusky," a wadi E. of Jer.:— Kidron(11).

6940. **קַדְרוּת** **qadruth** (871a); from 6937; *darkness, gloom:*— blackness(1).

6941. **קְדֹרַנִּית** **qedorannith** (871a); from 6937; *as mourners:*— mourning(1).

6942. **קָדַשׁ** **qadash** (872d); denom. vb. from 6944; *to be set apart* or *consecrated:*— become consecrated(2), become defiled(1), become holy(1), consecrate(43), consecrated(35), consecrates(7), consecration(2), declare holy(1), dedicate(2), dedicated(8), dedicating(1), holier(1), holy(5), keep(1), keep it holy(2), keep the holy(3), made it holy(1), manifest my holiness(2), prepare(2), prove myself holy(2), proved himself holy(1), purified(1), regard as holy(1), sanctified(9), sanctifies(10), sanctify(12), set them apart(1), set apart(4), set apart the consecrated(2), show himself holy(1), transmit holiness(2), treat me as holy(3), treated as holy(1), vindicate the holiness(1), wholly dedicate(1).

6943. **קֶדֶשׁ** **Qedesh** (873d); from the same as 6944; "sanctuary," the name of several places in Isr.:— Kedesh(11), Kedesh-naphtali*(1).

6944. **קֹדֶשׁ** **qodesh** (871c); from an unused word; *apartness, sacredness:*— consecrated(2), consecrated thing(1), consecrated things(2), dedicated(1), dedicated gifts(2), dedicated things(5), holiness(9), Holy(6), holy(263), holies(6), holy ones(1), holy portion(3), holy thing(2), holy things(12), most holy(25), most holy place(6), most holy things(6), sacred(2), sacred gifts(2), sacred things(3), sacrifices(1), sacrificial(1), sanctuary(65), set apart(1), thing most holy(2), things that are most holy(1), things dedicated(1).

6945. **קָדֵשׁ** **qadesh** (873c); from the same as 6944; *a temple prostitute:*— cult prostitute(2), cult prostitutes(2), male cult prostitutes(2), sodomites(1), temple prostitute(3), temple prostitutes(1).

6946. **קָדֵשׁ** **Qadesh** (873d); from the same as 6944; "sacred," a place in the desert:— Kadesh(15), Meribah-kadesh*(1), Meribath-kadesh*(2).

6947. **קָדֵשׁ בַּרְנֵעַ** **Qadesh Barnea** (873d); from 6946 and a word of unc. der.; a place in the desert:— Kadesh-barnea(10).

6948. **קְדֵשָׁה** **qedeshah** (873c); fem. of 6945, q.v.

6949a. **קָהָה** **qahah** (874b); a prim. root; *to be blunt* or *dull:*— dull(1), set on edge(3).

6949b. **קֵהָיוֹן** **qehayon** (874c); another reading for 5356, q.v.

6950. **קָהַל** **qahal** (874d); denom. vb. from 6951; *to gather as an assembly* or *congregation:*— assemble(7), assembled(26), calls an assembly(1), convening(1), gathered(4).

6951. **קָהָל** **qahal** (874c); from an unused word; *assembly, convocation, congregation:*— army*(1), assembly(95), companies(1), company(15), congregation(8), crowd(1), horde(2).

6952. **קְהִלָּה** **qehillah** (875a); from the same as 6951; *assembly, congregation:*— assembly(2).

6953. קֹהֶלֶת Qoheleth (875a); from the same as 6951; "a collector (of sentences)," "a preacher," a son of David:— Preacher(7).

6954. קְהֵלָתָה Qehelathah (875b); from the same as 6951; "assembly," a place in the desert:— Kehelathah(2).

6955. קְהָת Qehath (875b); of unc. der.; a son of Levi:— Kohath(31), Kohath's(1).

6956. קְהָתִי Qehathi (875c); from 6955; desc. of Kohath:— Kohathite(2), Kohathites(13).

6957a. קַו qav (875c); see 6957b.

6957b. קַו qav (876a); from 6960a; *a line:*— circumference*(1), line(16), measuring line(3).

6958. קוֹא qo (883c); see 7006a.

6959. קוֹבַע qoba (875c); of unc. der.; *a helmet:*— helmet(2).

6960a. קָוָה qavah (875c); a prim. root; *to wait for:*— eagerly waits(1), expect(1), expected(3), hope(3), hoped(1), hopefully wait(1), hoping(1), look(1), look eagerly(1), looked(2), wait(22), waited(7), waited for you eagerly(1), waited patiently(1).

6960b. קָוָה qavah (876b); a prim. root; *to collect:*— gathered(2).

6961a. קָוֶה qaveh (876a); from 6960a; *a line:*— circumference*(1).

6961b. קְוֵה Qoveh or

קְוֵא Qove (875c); of unc. der.; an area in Cilicia:— Kue(4).

6962a. קוּט qut (876c); a prim. root; *to feel a loathing:*— loathe(6), loathed(1).

6962b. קוֹט qot (876c); a prim. root; perh. *break, snap:*— fragile(1).

6963. קוֹל qol (876d); from an unused word; *sound, voice:*— birds(1), bleating(1), crackling(2), cry(2), crying(1), growl*(1), listen(4), loudly(1), loudness(1), lowing(2), news(1), noise(21), obey*(14), obeyed*(5), outcry(1), proclamation(7), public(1), report(1), roared loudly*(1), roared*(1), screamed*(1), shout(1), sound(98), sound*(1), sounds(3), speaks(1), thunder(11), thunderbolt*(2), tinkling(1), voice(284), voice was like the sound(1), voices(14), wept*(1), what i say(1), what my are saying(1), what you say(2), witness(2).

6964. קוֹלָיָה Qolayah (877b); from 6963 and 3050; "voice of Yah," two Isr.:— Kolaiah(2).

6965. קוּם qum (877c); a prim. root; *to arise, stand up, stand:*— accomplished(1), accuses(1), arise(103), arise and let us go(1), arisen(1), arises(6), arose(136), assailants(1), assume(1), avail(1), brighter(1), build(1), carried(3), carry(4), caused(1), certainly help(1), certainly help him to raise(1), come(2), confirm(13), confirmed(3), confirming(1), confirms(1), deeded over(2), dim(1), endure(4), enemies(1), erect(2), erected(10), establish(20), established(11), fulfill(3), fulfilled(4), fulfillment(1), get(8), gets(1), go ahead(1), go ahead and confirm(1), got(2), grown(1), lift(2), make it good(1), obliging*(1), observed(2), opponent(1), pass(1), passes(1), posted(1), prepared(1), raise(29), raised(12), raises(3), raising(1), remained(1), restore(1), rise(73), risen(11), rises(10), rising(2), rose(36), rouse(2), set(22), setting(1), spent(1), stand(31), stands(2), station(1), stirred(1), stood(8), strengthen(1), succeed(1), surely stand(1), take his stand(1), taken(1).

6966. קוּם qum (1110d); (Ara.) corr. to 6965; *to arise, stand:*— appoint(2), appointed(2), arise(5), arose(2), endure(1), establish(2), establishes(2), made to stand(1), raised(1), set(10), sets(2), standing(3), stood(2).

6967. קוֹמָה qomah or

קֹמָה qomah (879b); from 6965; *height:*— height(26), height of his stature(1), high(9), length(1), stature(5), tall(2), very high(1).

6968. קוֹמְמִיּוּת qomemiyyuth (879c); from 6965; *uprightness:*— erect(1).

6969. קוֹנֵן qonen (884b); denom. vb. from 7015; *to chant an elegy* or *dirge:*— chant(3), chanted(2), chanted a lament(1), lament(1), mourning women(1).

6970. קוֹעַ Qoa (880c); of unc. der.; enemies of Jer.:— Koa(1).

6971. קוֹף qoph (880d); of for. or.; *an ape:*— apes(2).

6972. קוּץ quts (884d); see 7019b.

6973. קוּץ quts (880d); a prim. root; *to feel a loathing, abhorrence,* or *sickening dread:*— abhorred(2), dread(3), loathe(2), terrorize(1), tired(1).

6974. קוּץ quts (884c); see 7019a.

6975. קוֹץ qots (881a); from an unused word; *a thorn, thornbush:*— thorn(2), thorn bushes(1), thorns(9).

6976. קוֹץ Qots (881a); from the same as 6975; two Isr.:— Hakkoz(5), Koz(1).

6977. קְוֻצּוֹת qevutstsoth (881b); of unc. der.; *locks* (of hair):— locks(2).

6978. קַו־קָו qavqav (876a); from 6960a; perh. *might:*— powerful(2).

6979. קוּר qur (881b); a prim. root; *to bore, dig:*— dug(2).

6980. קוּר qur (881c); from an unused word; *thread, film:*— web(1), webs(1).

6981. קוֹרֵא Qore (896c); from 7121; "crier," two Levites:— Kore(3).

6982. קוֹרָה qorah (900a); from 7136a; *a rafter, beam:*— beam(2), beams(2), roof(1).

6983. קוֹשׁ qush (881c); a prim. root; *to lay bait* or *lure:*— ensnare(1).

6984. קוּשָׁיָהוּ Qushayahu (881c); from 6983 and 3050; a Levite:— Kushaiah(1).

6985. קַט qat (881c); of unc. der.; perh. *only:*— too(1).

6986. קֶטֶב qeteb (881c); from an unused word; *destruction:*— destruction(3), sting(1).

6987. קֹטֶב qoteb (881c); the same as 6986, q.v.

6988. קְטוֹרָה qetorah (882c); from the same as 7008; *smoke of sacrifice:*— incense(1).

6989. קְטוּרָה Qeturah (882c); from the same as 7008; a wife of Abraham:— Keturah(4).

6990. קָטַט qatat (876c); see 6962b.

6991. קָטַל qatal (881d); a prim. root; *to slay:*— kills(1), slay(2).

6992. קְטַל qetal (1111a); (Ara.) corr. to 6991; *to slay:*— kill(1), killed(1), slain(3), slay(1), slew(1).

6993. קֶטֶל qetel (881d); from 6991; *slaughter:*— slaughter(1).

6994. קָטֹן qaton (881d); a prim. root; *to be small* or *insignificant:*— insignificant(1), make the smaller(1), small thing(1), unworthy(1).

6995. קֹטֶן qeton (882b); from 6994; *little* (finger):— little finger(2).

6996a. קָטָן qatan (881d); from 6994; *small, young, unimportant:*— least(10), little(7), small(13), small things(1), smaller(1), smallest(1), young(3), younger(9), youngest(3).

6996b. קָטֹן qaton (882b); from 6994; *small, insignificant:*— all*(2), brief(1), lesser(1), little(6), minor(2), small(22), smallest one(1), young(1), younger(3), youngest(14).

6997. קָטָן Qatan (882a); from 6994; "the small," father of a postexilic Isr.:— Hakkatan(1).

6998. קָטַף qataph (882b); a prim. root; *to pluck off* or *out:*— cut down(1), pluck(3), plucked off(1).

6999. קָטַר qatar (882d); denom. vb. from 7004; *to make sacrifices smoke:*— burn(9), burn incense(17), burn sacrifices(3), burned(5), burned incense(17), burned sacrifices(3), burning incense(4), burning sacrifices(5), burns incense(1), burnt incense(1), offer(4), offer it up in smoke(12), offer them up in smoke(6), offer up in smoke(7), offer sacrifices(2), offered(3), offered it up in smoke(2), offered them up in smoke(4), offered up in smoke(2), offered incense(1), offered sacrifices(1), offered*(1), offering up in smoke(1), offering up sacrifices(1), perfumed(1), smoke(5), surely burn(1).

7000. קָטַר qatar (883b); a prim. root; perh. *to shut in, enclose:*— enclosed(1).

7001. קְטַר qetar (1111b); (Ara.) from a root corr. to 7000; *a joint, knot:*— difficult problems(2), joints(1).

7002. קִטֵּר qitter (883b); from the same as 7008; *incense:*— smoking sacrifices(1).

7003. קִטְרוֹן Qitron (883c); from the same as 7008; a city in Zebulun:— Kitron(1).

7004. קְטֹרֶת qetoreth (882c); from the same as 7008; *smoke, odor of* (burning) *sacrifice, incense:*— incense(58), perfume(1), smoke(1).

7005. קַטָּת Qattath (883c); of unc. der.; a city in Zebulun:— Kattah(1).

7006a. קִיא qi (883c); a prim. root; *to vomit up, spew out:*— spew(2), spewed(2), vomit(3), vomited(1).

7006b. קִיא qi (883c); from 7006a; *what is vomited up, vomit:*— vomit(3).

7006c. קָיָה qayah (883d); a prim. root; *to vomit:*— vomit(1).

7007. קַיִט qayit (1111b); (Ara.) corr. to 7019c; *summer:*— summer(1).

7008. קִיטוֹר qitor or

קִיטֹר qitor (882c); from an unused word; *thick smoke:*— clouds(1), smoke(3).

7009. קִים qim (879c); from 6965; *adversary:*— adversaries(1).

7010. קְיָם qeyam (1111a); (Ara.) from 6966; *a statute:*— statute(2).

7011. קַיָּם qayyam (1111a); (Ara.) from 6966; *enduring:*— assured(1), enduring(1).

7012. קִימָה qimah (879c); from 6965; *rising up:*— rising(1).

קִימוֹשׁ Qimosh; see 7057.

7013. קַיִן qayin (883d); from un unused word; *a spear:*— spear(1).

7014a. קַיִן Qayin (883d); from the same as 7013; a city in S. Judah:— Kain(2), Kenites(1).

7014b. קַיִן Qayin (884a); from the same as 7013; oldest son of Adam and Eve:— Cain(16).

7015. קִינָה qinah (884b); from the same as 7013; *an elegy, dirge:*— dirge(3), lament(1), lamentation(11), Lamentations(1), lamentations(2).

7016. **קִינָה Qinah** (884a); from the same as 7013; a city in S. Judah:— Kinah(1).

7017. **קֵינִי Qeni** or

קִינִי Qini (884a); from 7014a; members of the tribe of Kenites:— Kenite(7), Kenites(5).

7018. **קֵינָן Qenan** (884b); from the same as 7013; a desc. of Seth:— Kenan(6).

7019a. **קִיץ qits** (884c); a prim. root; *to awake:*— awake(13), awakened(2), awakens(2), awakes(1), awoke(2).

7019b. **קִיץ qits** (884d); from an unused word; *spend the summer:*— spend the summer(1).

7019c. **קַיִץ qayits** (884d); from the same as 7019b; *summer, summer fruit:*— fruit(1), summer(11), summer fruit(5), summer fruits(3).

7020. **קִיצוֹן qitson** (894a); from 7112; *at the end, outermost:*— outermost(4).

7021. **קִיקָיוֹן qiqayon** (884d); of unc. der.; (a plant) perh. *castor-oil plant:*— plant(5).

7022. **קִיקָלוֹן qiqalon** (887b); of unc. der.; *disgrace:*— utter disgrace(1).

7023. **קִיר qir** or

קִר qir or

קִירָה qirah (885a); of unc. der.; *a wall:*— ceiling(1), ceiling*(1), city(1), male*(6), masons*(1), Oh(1), side(2), sides(3), surface(1), wall(41), walled(1), walls(13).

7024a. **קִיר Qir** (885b); from the same as 7023; "wall," a city in Moab:— Kir(1).

7024b. **קִיר Qir** (885b); from the same as 7023; a place of exile in S. Bab.:— Kir(4).

7025. **קִיר חֶרֶשׂ Qir Cheres** or

קִיר חֲרֶשֶׂת Qir Chareseth (885b); from 7023 and 2789; "wall of earthenware," a fortified city in Moab:— Kir-hareseth(3), Kir-heres(2).

7026. **קֵירֹס Qeros** or

קֵרֹס Qeros (902b); from 7164; father of some postexilic temple servants:— Keros(2).

7027. **קִישׁ Qish** (885c); of unc. der.; father of Saul, also the name of several other Isr.:— Kish(21).

7028. **קִישׁוֹן Qishon** (885c); from 6983; a wadi in the plain of Megiddo:— Kishon(6).

7029. **קִישִׁי Qishi** (881c); prob. from 6983; a Levite, the same as 6984:— Kishi(1).

7030. **קִיתָרֹס qitharos** (1111b); (Ara.) of for. or.; *a lyre, zither:*— lyre(4).

7031. **קַל qal** (886d); from 7043; *light, swift, fleet:*— insignificant(1), swift(7), swift man(1), swift-footed*(1), swifter(1), swiftly(2).

7032a. **קָל qal** (1110d); (Ara.) corr. to 6963; *voice:*— sound(5), voice(2).

7032b. **קֹל qol** (887a); from 7043; *lightness, frivolity:*— lightness(1).

קֹל qol; see 6963.

7033. **קָלָה qalah** (885c); a prim. root; *to roast, parch:*— burning(1), parched(1), roasted(2).

7034. **קָלָה qalah** (885d); a prim. root; *to be lightly esteemed* or *dishonored:*— degraded(2), dishonors(1), inferior(1), lightly esteemed(2).

7035. **קָלַהּ qalah** (874d); the same as 6950, q.v.

7036. **קָלוֹן qalon** (885d); from 7034; *ignominy, dishonor:*— disgrace(4), dishonor(7), shame(6).

7037. **קַלַּחַת qallachath** (886a); of for. or.; *a caldron:*— caldron(1), kettle(1).

7038. **קָלַט qalat** (886a); a prim. root; *to be stunted:*— stunted(1).

7039. **קָלִי qali** or

קָלִיא qali (885d); from 7033; *parched* (grain):— parched(2), roasted grain(4).

7040. **קַלַּי Qallay** (887a); from 7043; an Isr. priest:— Kallai(1).

7041. **קֵלָיָה Qelayah** (886b); of unc. der.; a Levite, the same as 7042:— Kelaiah(1).

7042. **קְלִיטָא Qelita** (886b); from 7038; a Levite:— Kelita(3).

7043. **קָלַל qalal** (886b); a prim. root; *to be slight, swift* or *trifling:*— abated(2), accursed(1), brought a curse(1), contempt(1), contemptible(1), curse(15), cursed(16), curses(8), cursing(2), despise(1), despised(2), ease(1), easier(1), easy(2), insignificant(1), light a thing(1), lighten(5), lightly esteemed(2), make it lighter(2), moved to and fro(1), shakes(1), sharpen(1), slight thing(1), small a thing(1), superficially(2), swift(1), swifter(5), treat us with contempt(1), treated(1), treated and lightly(1), trivial(1), trivial thing(1).

7044. **קָלָל qalal** (887a); from 7043; *burnished:*— burnished(1), polished(1).

7045. **קְלָלָה qelalah** (887a); from 7043; *a curse:*— accursed(1), curse(27), curses(2), cursing(3), imprecation(2).

7046. **קָלַס qalas** (887b); a prim. root; *to mock, scoff:*— disdaining(1), mock(2), mocked(1).

7047. **קֶלֶס qeles** (887b); from 7046; *derision:*— derision(3).

7048. **קַלָּסָה qallasah** (887b); from 7046; *derision:*— mocking(1).

7049a. **קָלַע qala** (887b); a prim. root; *to sling, hurl forth:*— sling(2), slinging(1), slung(1).

7049b. **קָלַע qala** (887c); a prim. root; *to carve:*— carved(3).

7050a. **קֶלַע qela** (887c); from 7049a; *a sling:*— sling(5), slingstones*(1).

7050b. **קֶלַע qela** (887c); from 7049a; *a curtain, hanging:*— hangings(15), leaves(1).

7051. **קַלָּע qalla** (887c); from 7049a; *slinger:*— slingers(1).

7052. **קְלֹקֵל qeloqel** (887b); from 7043; *contemptible, worthless:*— miserable(1).

7053. **קִלְּשׁוֹן qilleshon** (887d); of unc. der.; perh. *fine point:*— forks*(1).

7054. **קָמָה qamah** (879b); from 6965; *standing grain:*— grown(2), standing grain(8).

7055. **קְמוּאֵל Qemuel** (887d); of unc. der.; a relative of Abraham, also two Isr.:— Kemuel(3).

7056. **קָמוֹן Qamon** (879c); from 6965; burial place of Jair:— Kamon(1).

7057. **קִמּוֹשׂ qimmos** (888b); of unc. der.; perh. *thistles:*— nettles(1), thistles(1), weeds(1).

7058. **קֶמַח qemach** (887d); from an unused word; *flour, meal:*— flour(7), flour cakes(1), flour*(1), grain(1), meal(4).

7059. **קָמַט qamat** (888a); a prim. root; *to seize:*— shriveled(1), snatched away(1).

7060. **קָמַל qamel** (888a); a prim. root; *to be decayed:*— rot away(1), withers(1).

7061. **קָמַץ qamats** (888a); a prim. root; *enclose with the hand, grasp:*— take(2), take a handful(1).

7062. **קֹמֶץ qomets** (888a); from 7061; *closed hand, fist:*— abundantly(1), handful(1), handful*(2).

7063. **קִמָּשׁוֹן qimmashon** (888b); the same as 7057, q.v.

7064. **קֵן qen** (890a); from an unused word; *a nest:*— nest(11), nestlings(1), rooms(1).

7065. **קָנָא qanah** (888c); denom. vb. from 7068; *to be jealous* or *zealous:*— became envious(1), became jealous(1), been very zealous(2), envied(1), envious(4), envy(2), jealous(14), jealousy(1), made him jealous(1), made me jealous(1), provoked him to jealousy(1), provokes to jealousy(1), zeal(1), zealous(1).

7066. **קְנָא qena** (1111b); (Ara.) corr. to 7069; *to acquire, buy:*— buy(1).

7067. **קַנָּא qanna** (888d); from the same as 7068; *jealous:*— jealous(6).

7068. **קִנְאָה qinah** (888b); from an unused word; *ardor, zeal, jealousy:*— anger(1), envy(1), jealousy(24), passion(1), rivalry(1), zeal(14).

7069. **קָנָה qanah** (888d); a prim. root; *to get, acquire:*— acquire(6), acquired(1), acquires(2), bought(20), buy(23), buyer(4), buying(2), buys(1), formed(1), gain acquisition(1), gained(1), get(3), gets(1), gotten(1), owner(1), possessed(1), possessor(2), purchased(3), purchaser(3), recover(1), redeemed(1), sold(1), surely buy(2).

7070. **קָנֶה qaneh** (889c); from an unused word; *a stalk, reed:*— branch(4), branches(18), calamus(1), cane(2), elbow(1), reed(5), reed...reeds(1), reeds(4), reeds by the reed(2), reeds with the reed(2), rod(11), scale(1), shaft(2), stalk(2), sweet cane(2).

7071. **קָנָה Qanah** (889d); from the same as 7070; a wadi between Ephraim and Manasseh, also a city in Asher:— Kanah(3).

7072. **קַנּוֹא qanno** (888d); from the same as 7068; *jealous:*— jealous(2).

7073. **קְנַז Qenaz** (889d); of unc. der.; an Edomite, also two Isr.:— Kenaz(11).

7074. **קְנִזִּי Qenizzi** (889d); from 7073; desc. of Kenaz:— Kenizzite(4).

7075. **קִנְיָן qinyan** (889a); from 7069; *something gotten* or *acquired, acquisition:*— acquired(1), acquiring(1), goods(3), possessions(2), property(3).

7076. **קִנָּמוֹן qinnamon** (890a); prob. of for. or.; *cinnamon:*— cinnamon(3).

7077. **קָנַן qanan** (890a); denom. vb. from 7064; *to make a nest:*— build their nests(1), make its nest(1), nested(2), nests(1).

7078. **קֶנֶץ qenets** (890b); from an unused word; *a snare, net:*— hunt*(1).

7079. **קְנָת Qenath** (890b); of unc. der.; a city E. of the Jordan:— Kenath(2).

7080. **קָסַם qasam** (890c); denom. vb. from 7081; *to practice divination:*— conjure(1), divination(2), divine(2), diviner(2), diviners(7), divining(1), practice(1), practiced(1), use(1), uses(1), utter...divinations(1).

7081. **קֶסֶם qesem** (890c); from an unused word; *divination:*—divination(10), divine decision(1).

7082. **קָסַס qasas** (890d); a prim. root; *to strip off:*— cut off(1).

7083. **קֶסֶת qeseth** (903c); from the same as 7184; *a pot* (for ink), *inkhorn:*— case(2), writing case(1).

7084. קְעִילָה Qeilah (890d); of unc. der.; a city in Judah:— Keilah(18).

7085. קַעֲקַע qaaqa (891a); from an unused word; *an incision, imprint, tattoo:*— tattoo*(1).

7086. קְעָרָה qearah (891a); from an unused word; *a dish, platter:*— dish(13), dishes(4).

קֹף qoph; see 6971.

7087a. קָפָא qapha (891a); a prim. root; *to thicken, condense, congeal:*— congealed(1), curdle(1), dwindle(1), stagnant(1).

7087b. קִפָּאוֹן qippaon (891b); another reading for 7087a, q.v.

7088. קָפַד qaphad (891b); a prim. root; *gather together, roll up:*— rolled(1).

7089. קְפָדָה qephadah (891c); from 7088; *a shuddering:*— anguish(1).

7090. קִפּוֹד qippod or

קִפֹּד qippod (891b); from 7088; *porcupine:*— hedgehog(3).

7091. קִפּוֹז qippoz (891c); from an unused word; perh. *arrow snake:*— tree snake(1).

7092. קָפַץ qaphats (891c); a prim. root; *draw together, shut:*— close(1), gathered(1), leaping(1), shut(2), shuts(1), withdrawn(1).

7093. קֵץ qets (893d); from 7112; *end:*— after(3), after*(1), course*(1), end(52), endless*(1), farthest(2), farthest border(1), goal(1), highest peak(1), interval*(1), later(1), limit(2).

קֹץ qots; see 6975.

7094. קָצַב qatsab (891d); a prim. root; *to cut off, shear:*— cut off(1), shorn(1).

7095. קֶצֶב qetseb (891d); from 7094; *a cut, shape, extremity:*— form(2), roots(1).

7096. קָצָה qatsah (891d); a prim. root; *to cut off:*— cut off(1), cuts off(1), cutting off(1), scrape off(1), scraped(1).

7097a. קָצֶה qatseh (892a); from 7096; *end, extremity:*— among(2), border(2), edge(12), end(46), ends(5), extreme(1), extreme end(2), extremity(2), frontiers(1), last one(1), most remote part(1), mouth(2), other(1), other*(3), outposts(1), outskirts(6), portion(1), quarter(1), remotest part(1).

7097b. קֵצֶה qetseh (892c); from 7096; *an end:*— countless*(1), end(2), limit(1), limits(1).

7098. קָצָה qatsah (892b); from 7096; *an end:*— all(2), among(1), corners(1), end(7), ends(19), fringes(1), outermost(1), outermost*(1), whole number(1).

7099. קֶצוּ qatsu (892c); from 7096; *end, boundary:*— borders(1), ends(2).

7100. קֶצַח qetsach (892d); from an unused word; *black cumin:*— dill(3).

7101. קָצִין qatsin (892d); from an unused word; *a chief, ruler:*— chief(3), chiefs(1), commander(1), ruler(3), rulers(4).

7102. קְצִיעָה qetsiah (893a); from 7106a; *cassia* (a powdered bark):— cassia(1).

7103. קְצִיעָה Qetsiah (893a); from 7106a; "cassia," a daughter of Job:— Keziah(1).

7104. קְצִיץ Qetsits (894a); perh. from 7112; a city in Benjamin:— Emek-keziz*(1).

7105a. קָצִיר qatsir (894c); from 7114b; *harvesting, harvest:*— gathering(1), Harvest(1), harvest(44), harvest time(1), harvest's(1), harvesting(1).

7105b. קָצִיר qatsir (894d); perh. from 7114b; *boughs, branches:*— branch(2), branches(1), limbs(1), sprigs(1).

7106a. קָצַע qatsa (892d); a prim. root; *to scrape, scrape off:*— scraped(1).

7106b. קָצַע qatsa (893b); denom. vb. from 4740; perh. *to corner:*— corners(1).

7107. קָצַף qatsaph (893b); a prim. root; *to be angry:*— angry(21), became angry(1), became...angry(1), become wrathful(1), enraged(1), furious(3), provoked(1), provoked him to wrath(1), provoked me to wrath(1), provoked the to wrath(2), wrath(1), wrathful(1).

7108. קְצַף qetsaph (1111c); (Ara.) corr. to 7107; *to be angry:*— furious(1).

7109. קְצַף qetsaph (1111c); (Ara.) from 7108; *wrath:*— wrath(1).

7110a. קֶצֶף qetseph (893c); from 7107; *wrath:*— anger(3), indignation(4), very(1), very*(1), wrath(19).

7110b. קֶצֶף qetseph (893c); from the same as 7111; prob. *a splinter:*— stick(1).

7111. קְצָפָה qetsaphah (893c); from an unused word; *snapping, splintering:*— splinters(1).

7112. קָצַץ qatsats (893c); a prim. root; *cut off:*— clip(1), cut(4), cut in pieces(1), cut in two(1), cut off(6), cuts the in two(1), pieces(1).

7113. קְצַץ qetsats (1127c); (Ara.) corr. to 7112; *cut off:*— cut off(1).

7114a. קָצַר qatsar (894a); a prim. root; *to be short:*— annoyed(1), became impatient(1), could bear(1), impatient(3), limited(1), no longer(1), short(3), shortened(3), smaller(1).

7114b. קָצַר qatsar (894b); a prim. root; *to reap, harvest:*— harvest(2), harvests(1), reap(18), reaped(2), reaper(3), reapers(7), reaping(1).

7115. קֹצֶר qotser (894b); from 7114a; *shortness:*— despondency*(1).

7116. קָצֵר qatser (894b); from 7114a; *short:*— quick-tempered*(2), short(2), short-lived*(1), who(1).

7117. קְצָת qetsath (892c); from 7096; *an end:*— end(3), ends(3), some*(1).

7118. קְצָת qetsath (1111c); (Ara.) corr. to 7117; *an end:*— end(1), later(1), some*(1).

7119. קַר qar (903b); from 7174b; *cool:*— cold(2), who has a cool(1).

קִר qir; see 7023.

7120. קֹר qor (903b); from 7174b; *cold:*— cold(1).

7121. קָרָא qara (894d); a prim. root; *to call, proclaim, read:*— become(1), become famous(1), call(121), called(301), calling(11), calls(17), cried(24), cries(1), cry(19), crying(2), dictated*(1), famous*(1), gave(4), given(1), gives(1), grasps(1), guests(4), invite(6), invited(14), live(1), made a proclamation(1), make a proclamation(1), men of renown(1), mentioned(3), name*(4), named(12), named*(62), offer it terms(1), proclaim(28), proclaimed(17), proclaiming(3), proclaims(2), read(35), reading(2), reads(1), screamed(2), screamed*(1), shouted(1), spoken(1), sues(1), summon(6), summoned(14), summoning(1), summons(2).

7122. קָרָא qara (896d); a prim. root; *to encounter, befall:*— against(16), befall(4), befallen(2), came(1), chance(1), come(1), down*(1), encounter(2), engage(1), event*(1), happen to come(1), happened(3), help(1), meet(87), met(6), opposite(1), right(1), seek(1), toward(3).

7123. קְרָא qera (1111c); (Ara.) corr. to 7121; *to call, read out* or *aloud:*— called(1), proclaimed(1), read(7), shouted(1), summoned(1).

7124. קֹרֵא qore (896c); from 7121; *a partridge:*— partridge(2).

7125. קִרְאָה qirah (896d); the same as 7122, q.v.

7126. קָרַב qarab (897b); a prim. root; *to come near, approach:*— accept(1), appear(1), approach(11), approach to offer(1), approached(9), approaches(3), approaching(2), assisted(1), bring(20), bring her near(1), bring him near(2), bring you near(1), bring near(4), brings(1), brought(11), brought his near(1), brought you near(1), brought your near(1), brought...near(1), came(3), came close(1), came forward(1), came near(12), came together(1), came*(1), come(7), come forward(1), come near(25), comes near(1), draw(2), draw near(9), drawn near(1), draws near(1), drew near(6), go near(3), join(2), joined(1), keep(1), made an offering(1), near(9), offer(43), offered(10), offering(2), offers(7), present(40), presented(16), presenting(3), presents(4), presents his shall present(1), soon(1).

7127. קְרֵב qereb (1111c); (Ara.) corr. to 7126; *to approach:*— approached(2), came forward(1), came near(1), come near(1), offer(2), offered(1), presented(1).

7128. קְרָב qerab (898b); from 7126; *a battle, war:*— battle(4), war(5).

7129. קְרָב qerab (1111d); (Ara.) corr. to 7128; *war:*— war(1).

7130. קֶרֶב qereb (899a); from an unused word; *inward part, midst:*— among(62), body(1), devoured*(2), entrails(20), heart(1), herself(1), inner thought(1), inside(1), inward feelings(1), inward part(1), inward thought(1), inwardly(2), middle(2), midst(81), within(35), within our land(2), within their land(2).

7131. קָרֵב qareb (898a); from 7126; *approaching:*— came(1), come near(2), comes near(5), coming near(1), nearer(1).

קָרֹב qarob; see 7138.

7132. קִרְבָה qirbah (898b); from 7126; *an approach:*— nearness(2).

7133a. קָרְבָּן qorban (898d); from 7126; *offering, oblation:*— offering(76), offering*(1), offerings(2), sacrifice(1).

7133b. קֻרְבָּן qurban (898d); from 7126; *offering:*— supply(2).

7134. קַרְדֹּם qardom (899c); of unc. der.; *an axe:*— axe(3), axes(2).

7135. קָרָה qarah (903b); from 7174b; *cold:*— cold(5).

7136a. קָרָה qarah (899c); a prim. root; *to encounter, meet, befall:*— befall(1), befalls(2), come(3), come true(1), grant me success(1), happen(2), happened(4), happened*(1), meet(1), met(4), overtake(1), select(1), take place(1).

7136b. קָרָה qarah (900a); denom. vb. from 6982; *to lay the beams of:*— laid its beams(2), lays the beams(1), make beams(2).

7137. קָרֶה qareh (899d); from 7136a; *chance, accident:*— emission(1).

קֹרָה qorah; see 6982.

7138. קָרוֹב qarob or

קָרֹב qarob (898b); from 7126; *near:*— about(1), close(2), close relative(1), closer(1), draws near(1), hand(1), kinsmen(1), lately(1), near(47), nearby(1), nearest(6), neighbors(2), ones near(1), related(1), relative(1), relatives(1), short(1), shortly(1), soon(2), who are near(2), who is near(1).

7139. קָרַח qarach (901a); a prim. root; *to make bald:*— bald*(1), baldness*(1), made bald(1), make(2), make yourself bald(1), shave his head(1).

7140. קֶרַח qerach (901c); of unc. der.; *frost, ice:*— crystal(1), frost(2), ice(4).

7141. קֹרַח Qorach (901b); from 7139; an Edomite name, also an Isr. name:— Korah(26).

7142. קֵרֵחַ qereach (901b); from 7139; *bald:*— bald(1), baldhead(2).

7143. קָרֵחַ Qareach (901b); from 7139; "bald one," a man of Judah:— Kareah(14).

7144. קָרְחָה qorchah or

קָרְחָא qorcha (901b); from 7139; *baldness, bald spot:*— bald(2), bald*(1), baldness(4), baldness*(1), plucked-out scalp(1), shave*(1), shaving the head(1).

7145. קָרְחִי Qorchi (901c); from 7141; desc. of Korah:— Korah(1), Korahite(1), Korahites(6).

7146. קָרַחַת qarachath (901b); from 7139; *baldness of head:*— bald head(2), bareness*(1), head(1), top(1).

7147. קְרִי qeri (899d); from 7136a; *opposition, contrariness:*— hostility(7).

7148. קָרִיא qari (896c); from 7121; *called, summoned:*— chosen(1), who were called(2).

7149. קִרְיָא qirya or

קִרְיָה qiryah (1111d); (Ara.) corr. to 7151; *a city:*— city(9).

7150. קְרִיאָה qeriah (896d); from 7121; *proclamation:*— proclamation(1).

7151. קִרְיָה qiryah (900a); from 7136a; *a town, city:*— cities(1), city(22), fortress*(1), town(5).

7152. קְרִיּוֹת Qeriyyoth (901a); pl. of 7151; a city in Judah, also a city in Moab:— Kerioth(3), Kerioth-hezron*(1).

7153. קִרְיַת אַרְבַּע Qiryath Arba or

קִרְיַת הָאַרְבַּע Qiryath Haarba (900b); from 7151 and 702; "city of the four," an older name of Hebron (2275a):— Kiriath-arba(9).

7154. קִרְיַת בַּעַל Qiryath Baal (900c); from 7151 and 1168a; "city of Baal," another name for Kiriath-jearim (7157):— Kiriath-baal(2).

7155. קִרְיַת חֻצוֹת Qiryath Chutsoth (900c); from 7151 and 2351; "city of streets," a city in Moab:— Kiriath-huzoth(1).

7156. קִרְיָתַיִם Qiryathayim (900b); from 7136a; a city in Moab, also a place in Naphtali:— Kiriathaim(6).

7157. קִרְיַת יְעָרִים Qiryath Yearim or

קִרְיַת עָרִים Qiryath Arim (900c); from 7151 and 3293a; "city of forests," a city given to Judah, then to Benjamin:— Kiriath(1), Kiriath-arim(1), Kiriath-jearim(18).

7158. קִרְיַת סַנָּה Qiryath Sannah or

קִרְיַת סֵפֶר Qiryath Sepher (900d); from 7151 and 5612; "city of writing," a city in Judah:— Kiriath-sannah(1), Kiriath-sepher(4).

7159. קָרַם qaram (901c); a prim. root; *to spread* or *lay* (something over):— cover(1), covered*(1).

7160. קָרַן qaran (902a); denom. vb. from 7161; *to send out rays:*— shone(3).

7161. קֶרֶן qeren (901d); from an unused word; *a horn:*— hill(1), horn(24), horns(46), might(1), rays(1), strength(1), tusks(1).

7162. קֶרֶן qeren (1111d); (Ara.) corr. to 7161; *a horn:*— horn(9), horns(5).

7163a. קֶרֶן הַפּוּךְ Qeren Happuk (902a); from 7161 and 6320; "horn of antimony," a daughter of Job:— Keren-happuch(1).

7163b. קַרְנַיִם Qarnayim (902b); from the same as 7161; a place prob. in Bashan:— Karnaim(1).

7164. קָרַס qaras (902b); a prim. root; *to bend down, stoop, crouch:*— stooped over(1), stoops over(1).

7165. קֶרֶס qeres (902b); from 7164; *a hook:*— clasps(9), hooks(1).

קֵרֹס Qeros; see 7026.

7166. קַרְסֹל qarsol (902b); from 7164; *ankle:*— feet(2).

7167. קָרַע qara (902b); a prim. root; *to tear:*— cut(2), enlarge(1), rend(3), slandered(1), split apart(2), surely tear(1), tear(7), tear apart(1), tear away(1), tore(26), tore the away(1), torn(16).

7168. קֶרַע qera (902d); from 7167; *torn piece* (of garment), *a rag:*— pieces(3), rags(1).

7169. קָרַץ qarats (902d); a prim. root; *to nip, pinch:*— compresses(1), formed(1), maliciously*(1), wink(1), winks(2).

7170. קְרַץ qerats (1111d); (Ara.) corr. to 7171; *a piece:*— charges(1), maliciously accused*(1).

7171. קֶרֶץ qerets (903a); from 7169; perh. *nipping:*— horsefly(1).

7172. קַרְקַע qarqa (903a); of unc. der.; *floor:*— floor(8).

7173. קַרְקַע Qarqa (903a); from the same as 7172; "floor," a place on S. border of Judah:— Karka(1).

7174a. קַרְקֹר Qarqor (903a); of unc. der.; a place E. of the Jordan:— Karkor(1).

7174b. קָרַר qarar (903a); a prim. root; *to be cold:*— keeps its fresh(1), keeps fresh(1).

7175a. קָרַר qarar (903b); a prim. root; perh. *to tear down:*— breaking down(1), tear down(1).

7175b. קֶרֶשׁ qeresh (903c); from an unused word; *board, boards:*— board(17), boards(32), deck(1), frames(1).

7176. קֶרֶת qereth (900d); from 7136a; *town, city:*— city(5).

7177. קַרְתָּה Qartah (900d); from 7136a; a city in Zebulun:— Kartah(1).

7178. קַרְתָּן Qartan (900b); from 7136a; a city in Naphtali:— Kartan(1).

7179. קַשׁ qash (905d); from an unused word; *stubble, chaff:*— chaff(5), straw(1), stubble(10).

7180. קִשֻּׁאָה qishshuah (903d); from an unused word; *a cucumber:*— cucumbers(1).

7181. קָשַׁב qashab (904a); a prim. root; *to incline* (ears), *attend:*— gave attention(1), give attention(3), give heed(9), give...heed(1), given heed(2), heed(2), incline(1), listen(10), listened(2), listening(1), listens(1), make your attentive(1), paid attention(3), paid...attention(1), pay attention(6), pay...attention(1), pays attention(1).

7182. קֶשֶׁב qesheb (904a); from 7181; *attentiveness:*— close(1), close attention(1), paid attention(1), response(1).

7183a. קַשָּׁב qashshab (904a); from 7181; *attentive:*— attentive(2).

7183b. קַשֻּׁב qashshub (904b); from 7181; *attentive:*— attentive(3).

7184. קָשָׂה qasah or

קְשׂוָה qasvah (903c); from an unused word; *jug, jar:*— jars(3), pitchers(1).

7185. קָשָׁה qashah (904b); a prim. root; *to be hard, severe* or *fierce:*— became stubborn*(2), cruel(1), defied*(1), hard(1), hard thing(1), hard-pressed(1), harden(2), hardened(1), hardens(2), harsher(1), made our hard(2), seem hard(1), severe(2), stiffen(2), stiffened(6), stubborn(1), suffered severe(1).

7186. קָשֶׁה qasheh (904c); from 7185; *hard, severe:*— cruel(2), difficult(2), fierce(2), hard(5), hardship(1), harsh(4), harshly(5), heavier(1), obstinate(1), obstinate*(5), oppressed(1), severe(2), stubborn(1), stubborn*(3), stubbornness*(1).

7187. קְשׁוֹט qeshot or

קְשֹׁט qeshot (1112a); (Ara.) corr. to 7189b; *truth:*— surely*(1), true(1).

7188. קָשַׁח qashach (905a); a prim. root; *to make hard, treat roughly:*— harden(1), treats her cruelly(1).

7189a. קֹשֶׁט qoshet (905a); another reading for 7189b, q.v.

7189b. קֹשְׁטְ qosht (905a); from an unused word; *truth:*— certainty(1), truth(1).

קֹשֹׁט qoshot; see 7187.

7190. קְשִׁי qeshi (904d); from 7185; *stubbornness:*— stubbornness(1).

7191. קִשְׁיוֹן Qishyon (904d); from 7185; a city in Issachar:— Kishion(2).

7192. קְשִׂיטָה qesitah (903c); of unc. der.; (unit of value), perh. *piece:*— piece of money(1), pieces of money(2).

7193. קַשְׂקֶשֶׂת qasqeseth (903d); from an unused word; *scale* (of fish):— scale-armor(1), scales(7).

7194. קָשַׁר qashar (905a); a prim. root; *to bind, league together, conspire:*— bind(9), bound(2), carried(1), conspirators(2), conspired(19), joined together(1), knit(1), made(3), stronger(2), tie(2), tied(2).

7195. קֶשֶׁר qesher (905c); from 7194; *conspiracy:*— conspiracy(10), treason(4).

7196. קִשֻּׁרִים qishshurim (905c); from 7194; *bands, sashes:*— attire(1), sashes(1).

7197a. קָשַׁשׁ qashash (905d); denom. vb. from 7179; *to gather stubble:*— gather(2), gathering(4).

7197b. קָשַׁשׁ qashash (905d); a prim. root; perh. *gather together:*— gather(2).

7198. קֶשֶׁת qesheth (905d); perh. from 6983; *a bow:*— archers*(3), arrows(1), bow(54), bowman*(1), bowmen(1), bows(13), bowshot*(1), rainbow(1).

7199. קַשָּׁת qashshath (906c); from the same as 7198; *bowman:*— archer*(1).

ר

7200. רָאָה raah (906b); a prim. root; *to see:*— access(1), advisers*(2), appear(21), appeared(43), appears(4), approve(2), became aware(1), became visible(1), become visible(1), behold(9), choice(1), consider(13), considered(1), display(1), displayed(1), distinguish(1), encountered(1), enjoy(1), enjoy*(3), examined(1), experience(1), exposed(1), face*(2), faced*(2), find(1), gaze(2), give attention(1), gloat(2), heed(1), indeed look(1), keep on looking(1), look(71), looked(59), looked and saw(1), looking(5), looks(11), make an inspection(2), make me see(1), makes an inspection(1), noticed(1), observe(1), observed(5), observing(1), perceive(2), perceived(2), presents(1), provide(3), provided(2), public(1), regard(2), regarded(2), regards(1), remained alive(1), saw(310), search(1), see(410), see as a sees(1), see plainly(1), seeing(5), seemed(1), seen(153), sees(32), select(1), selected(1), show(24), showed(15), shown(19), shows(1), sleep*(1), stare(2), staring(1), supervise(1), surely seen(1), take into consideration(1), take heed(1), tell(1), think(1), understand(1), view(1), vision(1), visit(1), watch(2).

7201. רָאָה **raah** (178d); scribal error for 1676, q.v.

7202. רָאֶה **raeh** (909a); from 7200; *seeing:*— conscious(1).

7203a. רֹאֶה **roeh** (909a); from 7200; *a seer:*— seer(10), seer's(1), seers(1).

7203b. רֹאֶה **roeh** (909b); from 7200; (prophetic) *vision:*— visions(1).

7204. רֹאֵה **Roeh** (909b); from 7203a; a man of Judah:— Haroeh(1).

7205. רְאוּבֵן **Reuben** (910a); from 7200 and 1121; "behold a son!" oldest son of Jacob, also his desc.:— Reuben(72).

7206. רְאוּבֵנִי **Reubeni** (910a); from 7205; desc. of Reuben:— Reuben(1), Reubenite(1), Reubenites(16).

7207. רַאֲוָה **raavah** (906b); the same as 7200, q.v.

7208. רְאוּמָה **Reumah** (910b); from 7213; concubine of Nahor:— Reumah(1).

7209. רְאִי **rei** (909b); from 7200; *a mirror:*— mirror(1).

7210. רֳאִי **roi** (909b); from 7200; *looking, seeing, sight:*— appearance(1), seeing(1), seen(1), sees(1), sight(1), spectacle(1), who(1).

7211. רְאָיָה **Reayah** (909d); from 7200 and 3050; "Yah has seen," three Isr.:— Reaiah(4).

7212. רְאִית **reith** or

רְאוּת **reuth** (909b); from 7200; *a look:*— look*(1).

7213. רָאַם **raam** (910b); a prim. root; *to rise:*— rise(1).

7214. רְאֵם **reem** or

רְאֵים **reem** or

רֵים **rem** or

רֵם **rem** (910b); from 7213; *a wild ox:*— wild ox(7), wild oxen(2).

7215. רָאמוֹת **ramoth** (910c); from 7213; perh. *corals:*— coral(2).

7216. רָאמוֹת **Ramoth** or

רָאמֹת **Ramoth** (928b); from 7311; "heights," the name of several cities in Isr.:— Ramoth(5).

7217. רֵאשׁ **resh** (1112a); (Ara.) corr. to 7218; *head:*— head(6), heads(1), mind(6), summary(1).

7218. רֹאשׁ **rosh** (910c); a prim. root; *head:*— bands(1), beginning(11), beheaded*(1), best(1), best things(1), bodyguard*(1), captains(3), census(7), chief(35), chief men(6), chiefs(3), companies(7), company(5), corner(1), count(1), distant(1), divisions(1), ends(2), every(1), faced*(1), favor*(1), finest(2), first(12), full(2), hair(3), head(256), heads(129), laughingstock*(1), leader(4), leaders(8), leading man(1), leading men(2), masters(1), released*(1), ridge(2), rivers(1), sum(2), summit(7), themselves(1), top(51), topmost(2), topmost*(1), tops(15).

7219. רֹאשׁ **rosh** or

רוֹשׁ **rosh** (912c); from 7218; (bitter and poisonous herb) *venom:*— bitterness(2), gall(1), poison(4), poisoned(2), poisonous(2), poisonous weeds(1).

7220a. רֹאשׁ **Rosh** (912c); from 7218; a son of Benjamin:— Rosh(1).

7220b. רֹאשׁ **Rosh** (911c); from 7218; a for. nation:— Rosh(4).

רֵאשׁ **resh**; see 7389.

7221. רִאשָׁה **rishah** (911c); from 7218; *beginning time, early time:*— first(1).

7222. רֹאשָׁה **roshah** (911c); fem. of 7218; *top:*— top(1).

7223. רִאשׁוֹן **rishon** or

רִאשֹׁן **rishon** (911c); from 7218; *former, first, chief:*— ancestors(3), before(4), beginning(2), chief(1), chiefs(1), earlier(4), earlier things(1), first(113), first one(2), first time(1), forefathers(1), foremost(1), former(25), former ones(4), former things(6), formerly(6), front(1), old(1), older(1), one in front(1), past(1), previous(1), previously(1).

7224. רִאשֹׁנִי **rishoni** (912a); from 7218; *first:*— first(1).

7225. רֵאשִׁית **reshith** (912a); from 7218; *beginning, chief:*— beginning(19), choice(2), choicest(3), finest(2), first(16), first fruits(7), foremost(2).

7226. רַאֲשׁוֹת **raashoth** (912b); the same as 4761, q.v.

7227a. רַב **rab** (912d); from 7231; *much, many, great:*— abound(1), abounding(4), abounds(1), abundance(1), abundant(15), abundantly(2), broad(1), enough(8), far enough(2), full(2), Great(2), great(83), great deal(1), greater(6), greatly(5), heavy(1), increased(2), large(6), larger(4), long(8), long enough(2), many(207), many things(1), many times(2), many...things(1), masses(1), mighty(7), more(5), more numerous(1), much(16), multitude(2), numerous(10), older(1), plentiful(1), plenty(2), populous(1), powerful(1), prevalent(1), severe(2), very(2), who are many(1), who was once great(1).

7227b. רַב **rab** (913c); from 7231; *chief:*— captain(24), captain*(1), Champion(1), chief(1), chief officers(1), leading officers(1), official(1).

7228. רַב **rab** (914d); from 7232b; *an archer:*— archer(1), arrows(1).

7229. רַב **rab** (1112a); (Ara.) corr. to 7227a; *great:*— boastful(1), captain(1), chief(3), great(15), large(2), larger(1).

רִב **rib**; see 7378.

7230. רֹב **rob** (913d); from 7231; *multitude, abundance, greatness:*— abundance(29), abundant(6), abundantly(2), age*(1), all(1), ample(1), common sort*(1), excellent(1), extensively(1), extent(1), great(13), great number(1), great numbers(1), great quantities(1), great quantity(1), greatly(1), greatness(12), grossness(1), harsh(1), immense(1), increased(1), large(1), large amount(1), large number(1), large numbers(1), large quantities(2), length(1), magnitude(1), many(25), mass(1), mighty(1), more(2), much(7), multiplied(1), multiply(1), multitude(11), number(3), numerous(5), plentiful(4), plenty(1), quantities(1), so many(1).

7231. רָבַב **rabab** (912c); a prim. root; *to be* or *become many* or *much:*— abound(1), become...numerous(1), been many(1), great(1), increase(1), increased(1), long(1), many(9), more(1), more in number(1), multiplied(2), multiply(1), numerous(1).

7232a. רָבַב **rabab** (1126c); denom. vb. from 7239; *to multiply ten thousand times:*— ten thousands(1).

7232b. רָבַב **rabab** (914d); a prim. root; *to shoot:*— shot(1).

7233. רְבָבָה **rebabah** (914b); from 7231; *multitude, myriad, ten thousand:*— myriad(1), numerous(1), ten thousand(6), ten thousands(7).

7234. רָבַד **rabad** (914d); a prim. root; *to spread over, deck:*— spread(1).

7235a. רָבָה **rabah** (915a); a prim. root; *to be* or *become much, many* or *great:*— abundance(2), abundant(2), abundantly(1), amounts(1), ask(1), became many(1), became...numerous(1), bitterly*(1), boast*(1), considerable(1), continue(1), continued(1), enlarge(1), excessively(2), gave numerous(1), give great(1), give many(1), give more(1), great(10), greater(1), greatly(1), greatly multiply(3), greatly*(1), grew(1), grow(1), grow...numerous(1), had gathered much(1), had many(2), heap(1), increase(14), increased(7), increases(5), large(1), larger(1), lavished(1), long(2), made their numerous(1), made many(1), make many(1), make more(1), makes me great(2), many(21), many which increase(1), more(3), more he made(1), much(15), much more(2), much*(1), multiplied(21), multiplies(5), multiply(45), numerous(3), often(2), outnumber(1), pay more(1), plenty(1), profited(1), provided in abundance(1), reared(2), repeatedly(1), risen(1), serious*(1), surpassed(1), take more(1), thoroughly(1), use much(1), very(2), wealth(1).

7235b. רָבָה **rabah** (916c); a prim. root; *to shoot:*— archer*(1).

7236. רְבָה **rebah** (1112b); (Ara.) corr. to 7235a; *to grow great:*— became large(1), become great(2), grew large(1), grown(1), promoted(1).

7237. רַבָּה **Rabbah** (913d); from 7231; two places in Isr.:— Rabbah(15).

7238. רְבוּ **rebu** (1112c); (Ara.) from 7236; *greatness:*— grandeur(2), greatness(2), majesty(1).

7239. רִבּוֹ **ribbo** or

רִבּוֹא **ribbo** (914b); from 7231; *ten thousand, myriad:*— 120,000*(1), 18,000*(1), 20,000*(2), 42,360*(2), 61,000*(1), myriads(1), ten thousand(1), tens of thousands(1).

7240. רִבּוֹ **ribbo** (1112b); (Ara.) corr. to 7239; *myriad:*— myriads(2).

7241. רְבִיבִים **rebibim** (914c); from 7231; *abundant showers:*— showers(6).

7242. רָבִיד **rabid** (914d); from an unused word; *a chain* (ornament for the neck):— necklace(2).

7243. רְבִיעִי **rebii** or

רְבִעִי **rebii** (917d); from the same as 702; *fourth:*— four-sided(1), fourth(51), one-fourth(1), square(1).

7244. רְבִיעִי **rebii** (1112c); (Ara.) corr. to 7243; *fourth:*— fourth(6).

7245. רַבִּית Rabbith (914c); from 7231; a place in Issachar:— Rabbith(1).

7246. רָבַךְ rabak (916c); a prim. root; *to mix, stir:*— stirred(2), well-mixed(1).

7247. רִבְלָה Riblah (916c); of unc. der.; a city in Hamath, also one on N.E. border of Isr.:— Riblah(11).

7248. רַב־מָג Rab-mag (913c); from 7227b and a word of for. or.; perh. "chief soothsayer," an official of the Bab. king:— Rab-mag(2).

7249. רַב־סָרִיס Rab-saris (913c); from 7227b and a word of for. or.; perh. "chief eunuch," an official of the Assyr. and Bab. kings:— Rab-saris(3).

7250. רָבַע raba (918a); a prim. root; *to lie stretched out, lie down:*— breed together(1), lying down(1), mate(2).

7251. רָבַע raba (917c), denom. vb. from 702; *to square:*— square(11), squared(1).

7252. רֶבַע reba (918a); the same as 7250, q.v.

7253. רֶבַע reba (917d); from the same as 702; *fourth part, four sides* (pl.):— directions(2), fourth(1), one-fourth(1), sides(3).

7254. רֶבַע Reba (918b); from 7250; a king of Midian:— Reba(2).

7255. רֹבַע roba (917d); from the same as 702; *fourth part:*— fourth(1), fourth part(1).

7256. רִבֵּעַ ribbea (918a); from the same as 702; *pertaining to the fourth:*— fourth(4).

רְבִעִי rebii; see 7243.

7257. רָבַץ rabats (918b); a prim. root; *stretch oneself out, lie down, lie stretched out:*— crouching(1), lay down(2), lead them to rest(1), lie down(15), lies(2), lies down(1), lying(3), lying down(1), rest(2), set(1), sitting(1).

7258. רֵבֶץ rebets (918c); from 7257; (place of) *lying down, resting place, dwelling place:*— resting place(4).

7259. רִבְקָה Ribqah (918d); from the same as 4770; wife of Isaac:— Rebekah(28), Rebekah's(2).

7260. רַבְרַב rabrab (1112a); (Ara.) the same as 7229, q.v.

7261. רַבְרְבָן rabreban (1112b); (Ara.) from the same as 7229; *lord, noble:*— nobles(8).

7262. רַבְשָׁקֵה Rabshaqeh (913c); from 7227b and 8248; perh. "chief of the officers," an Assyr. military leader:— Rabshakeh(16).

7263. רֶגֶב regeb (918d); of unc. der.; *a clod* (of earth):— clods(2).

7264. רָגַז ragaz (919a); a prim. root; *to be agitated, quiver, quake, be excited, perturbed:*— come trembling(1), deeply moved(1), disturbed(2), enraged(1), excited(1), moved(1), provoke(1), quake(1), quaked(2), quakes(2), quarrel(1), rages(1), raging(4), shakes(1), stirred(1), tremble(11), trembled(3), trembling(3), troubled(2), turmoil(1).

7265. רְגַז regaz (1112c); (Ara.) corr. to 7264; *to enrage:*— provoked(1), wrath(1).

7266. רְגַז regaz (1112c); (Ara.) from 7265; *a rage:*— rage(1).

7267. רֹגֶז rogez (919c); from 7264; *agitation, excitement, raging:*— rage(1), raging(1), thunder(1), turmoil(3), wrath(1).

7268. רַגָּז raggaz (919c); from 7264; *quivering, quaking:*— trembling(1).

7269. רָגְזָה rogzah (919c); fem. of 7267; *a quivering, quaking:*— quivering(1).

7270. רָגַל ragal (920a); denom. vb. from 7272; *to go about on foot:*— slander(1), slandered(1), spied(3), spies(11), spy(9), taught to walk(1).

7271. רְגַל regal (1112c); (Ara.) corr. to 7272; *foot:*— feet(7).

7272. רֶגֶל regel (919c); of unc. der.; *foot:*— accompany*(1), after(1), attended*(1), feet(139), follow(2), followed(2), following(1), foot(60), footstep*(1), footsteps(1), footstool*(6), four-footed*(1), haunt(1), heels(1), hoof*(1), journey(1), legs(5), pace(2), relieve*(1), relieving*(1), step(1), steps(2), swift-footed*(1), times(4), toes*(2), turned(1).

7273. רַגְלִי ragli (920b); from the same as 7272; *on foot:*— foot(6), foot soldiers(4), footmen(2), soldiers*(3).

7274. רֹגְלִים Rogelim (920c); from 7272; "(place of) fullers," a place in Gilead:— Rogelim(2).

7275. רָגַם ragam (920c); a prim. root; *to stone, kill by stoning:*— certainly stone(1), stone(7), stoned(7).

7276. רֶגֶם Regem (920d); from 7275; a desc. of Caleb:— Regem(1).

7277. רִגְמָה rigmah (920c); from 7275; *a heap* (of stones), *crowd* (of people):— throng(1).

7278. רֶגֶם מֶלֶךְ Regem Melek (920d); from 7276 and 4428; "king's heap," an Isr.:— Regemmelech(1).

7279. רָגַן ragan (920d); a prim. root; *to murmur, whisper:*— criticize(1), grumbled(2), slanderer(1), whisperer(3).

7280a. רָגַע raga (920d); a prim. root; *to disturb:*— instant(2), moment(1), quieted(1), stirs(2).

7280b. רָגַע raga (921b); a prim. root; *to be at rest, repose:*— bring rest(1), find its rest(1), find...rest(1), rest(1), set(1), settle(1).

7280c. רָגַע raga (921c); a prim. root; *to harden:*— hardens(1).

7281. רֶגַע rega (921a); from 7280a; *a moment:*— instant(1), instantly(2), moment(14), momentary*(1), suddenly(3), while(1).

7282. רָגֵעַ ragea (921b); from 7280b; *restful, quiet:*— who are quiet(1).

7283. רָגַשׁ ragash (921c); a prim. root; *to be in tumult* or *commotion:*— uproar(1).

7284. רְגַשׁ regash (1112c); (Ara.) corr. to 7283; *to be in tumult:*— came by agreement(3).

7285a. רֶגֶשׁ regesh (921c); from 7283; *a throng:*— throng(1).

7285b. רִגְשָׁה rigshah (921c); from 7283; *a throng:*— tumult(1).

7286. רָדַד radad (921d); a prim. root; *to beat out, beat down, subdue:*— gone(1), spread(1), subdue(1), subdues(1).

7287a. רָדָה radah (921d); a prim. root; *to have dominion, rule, dominate:*— dominated(1), had dominion(1), have dominion(1), prevailed(1), rule(12), ruled(4), ruling(1), subdued(1), subdues(1).

7287b. רָדָה radah (922a); a prim. root; *to scrape out:*— scraped(2).

7288. רַדַּי Radday (921d); from 7286; a son of Jesse:— Raddai(1).

7289. רָדִיד radid (921d); from 7286; *a wide wrapper, large veil:*— shawl(1), veils(1).

7290a. רָדַם radam (922b); a prim. root; *to be in* or *fall into heavy sleep:*— cast into a dead sleep(1), dead sleep(1), deep sleep(2), fallen sound asleep(1), fell into a deep sleep(1), sank into a deep sleep(1), sleeping(1), sleeps(1), sound asleep(1).

7290b. רֹדָן Rodan (922b); of unc. der.; another reading for 1719, q.v.

7290c. רֹדָנִים Rodanim or

רוֹדָנִים Rodanim (922c); of unc. der.; desc. of Japheth, the same as 1721:— Rodanim(1).

7291. רָדַף radaph (922c); a prim. root; *to pursue, chase, persecute:*— chase(6), chased(5), chases(1), follow(3), follow*(1), follows(1), hunts(1), passed(1), persecute(6), persecuted(5), persecutors(4), press(1), pursue(36), pursued(37), pursuer(1), pursuers(9), pursues(9), pursuing(13), puts to flight(1), took up the pursuit(1), went in pursuit(1).

7292. רָהַב rahab (923b); a prim. root; *to act stormily, boisterously* or *arrogantly:*— confused(1), importune(1), made me bold(1), storm(1).

7293. רַהַב Rahab (923c); from 7292; "storm," a sea monster:— Rahab(4).

7294. רַהַב Rahab (923c); from 7292; "storm," a name for Eg.:— Rahab(2).

7295. רָהָב rahab (923b); from 7292; *proud, defiant:*— proud(1).

7296. רֹהַב rohab (923b); from 7292; *pride:*— pride(1).

7297. רָהָה rahah (923c); another reading for 3385a, q.v.

7298a. רַהַט rahat (923d); from an unused word; *a trough:*— gutters(2), troughs(1).

7298b. רַהַט rahat (923d); from an unused word; perh. *lock* (of hair):— tresses(1).

7299. רֵו rev (1112a); (Ara.) from a root corr. to 7200; *appearance:*— appearance(2).

רוּב rub; see 7378.

7300. רוּד rud (923d); a prim. root; *to wander restlessly, roam:*— become restless(1), restless(1), roam(1), unruly(1).

7301. רָוָה ravah (924a); a prim. root; *to be saturated, drink one's fill:*— drench(1), drink(1), drink its fill(1), drink our fill(1), fill(2), filled(1), made me drunk(1), satiated(1), satisfy(2), soaked(1), water its abundantly(1), watering(1), waters(1).

7302. רָוֶה raveh (924b); from 7301; *watered:*— watered(3).

7303. רוֹהֲגָה Rohagah (923c); from an unused word; an Asherite:— Rohgah(1).

7304. רָוַח ravach (926b); a prim. root; *to be wide* or *spacious:*— get relief(1), refreshed(1), spacious(1).

7305. רֶוַח revach (926c); from 7304; *a space, interval, respite, relief:*— relief(1), space(1).

7306. רוּחַ ruach (926b); see 7381a.

7307. רוּחַ ruach (924c); from an unused word; *breath, wind, spirit:*— air(2), anger(1), blast(2), breath(31), breathless*(1), cool(1), courage(1), despondency*(1), exposed(1), grief*(1), heart(1), inspired(1), mind(3), motives(1), points(1), quick-tempered*(1), side(4), sides(2), Spirit(76), spirit(127), spirits(3), strength(1), temper(2), thoughts*(1), trustworthy*(1), wind(98), winds(7), windy(2), wrath(1).

7308. רוּחַ ruach (1112d); (Ara.) corr. to 7307; *wind, spirit:*— spirit(9), wind(1), winds(1).

7309. רְוָחָה revachah (926c); from 7304; *respite, relief:*— relief(2).

7310. רְוָיָה revayah (924b); from 7301; *saturation:*— abundance(1), hearts(1), overflows(1).

7311. רוּם **rum** (926c); a prim. root; *to be high* or *exalted, rise:*— aloud(1), became proud(1), become proud(1), boldly*(2), brought(1), contributed(5), defiantly*(1), display(1), exalt(11), exaltation(1), exalted(29), exalts(5), extol(5), extolled(1), haughty(5), heights(1), held(1), high(10), higher(2), levy(1), lift(19), lifted(11), lifting(1), lifts(4), lofty(6), loud(1), made it high(1), make(1), makes his on high(1), offer(5), offered(5), present(3), raise(6), raised(6), reared(1), rebelled*(2), remove(3), removed(2), rise(2), rose(1), set(2), set apart(3), stop(1), sworn*(1), take(5), take off(1), tall(4), taller(1), took(2), triumphant(1), turn(1), uplifted(1), went(1).

7312. רוּם **rum** or

רֻם **rum** (927d); from 7311; *height, haughtiness:*— haughtiness(2), haughty(1), height(1), loftiness(2), self-exaltation*(1).

7313. רוּם **rum** (1112d); (Ara.) corr. to 7311; *to rise:*— elevated(1), exalt(1), exalted(1), lifted(1).

7314. רוּם **rum** (1112d); (Ara.) from 7313; *height:*— height(5).

7315. רוֹם **rom** (927d); from 7311; *on high:*— high(1).

7316. רוּמָה **Rumah** (928a); from 7311; home of Pedaiah:— Rumah(1).

7317. רוֹמָה **romah** (928a); from 7311; *haughtily:*— haughtily(1).

7318. רוֹמָם **romam** (928c); from 7311; *extolling, praise:*— high praises(1).

7319. רוֹמֵמָה **romemah** (928c); the same as 7318, q.v.

7320a. רוֹמַמְתִּי עֶזֶר **Romamti Ezer** or

רֹמַמְתִּי עֶזֶר **Romamti Ezer** (928d); from 7311 and 5828; "I have made lofty help," a son of Heman:— Romamti-ezer(2).

7320b. רוּן **run** (929c); a prim. root; *to overcome:*— overcome(1).

7321. רוּעַ **rua** (929c); a prim. root; *to raise a shout, give a blast:*— battle cry(1), cry(1), cry aloud(1), crying(1), jubilant shouting(1), raise your battle cry(1), raised a war cry(1), raised the war cry(1), shout(9), shout for joy(1), shout in triumph(1), shout aloud(1), shout joyfully(8), shout loud(1), shouted(8), shouted for joy(1), shouting the cry(1), sound an alarm(3), sound the alarm(1), sounding an alarm(1), utter a shout(1).

7322. רוּף **ruph** (952c); see 7514a.

7323. רוּץ **ruts** (930a); a prim. root; *to run:*— carried them speedily(1), courier runs(1), courier runs to another(1), couriers(6), dash to and fro(1), guard(6), guards(7), guards'(2), hurriedly brought(1), outran*(1), quickly stretch(1), ran(25), run(34), runner(1), runners(1), running(6), runs(4), rushed(1), rushes(1), smashed(1).

7324. רוּק **ruq** (937d); see 7385a.

7325. רוּר **rur** (938b); see 7388a.

7326. רוּשׁ **rush** (930d); a prim. root; *to be in want* or *poor:*— am a poor(1), destitute(1), lack(1), poor(18), poor man(2), pretends to be poor(1).

רוֹשׁ **rosh**; see 7219.

7327. רוּת **Ruth** (946c); from 7462b; "friendship," a Moabite ancestress of David:— Ruth(12).

7328. רָז **raz** (1112d); (Ara.) of for. or.; *a secret:*— mysteries(3), mystery(6).

7329. רָזָה **razah** (930d); a prim. root; *to be* or *grow lean:*— become lean(1), starve(1).

7330. רָזֶה **razeh** (931a); from 7329; *lean:*— lean(2).

7331. רְזוֹן **Rezon** (931b); from 7336; an Aramean (Syrian) of Solomon's time:— Rezon(1).

7332. רָזוֹן **razon** (931a); from 7329; *leanness, wasting, scantness:*— short(1), wasting disease(2).

7333. רָזוֹן **razon** (931b); from 7336; *potentate:*— prince's(1).

7334. רָזִי **razi** (931a); from 7329; *leanness, wasting:*— woe(2).

7335. רָזַם **razam** (931b); a prim. root; *to wink, flash:*— flash(1).

7336. רָזַן **razan** (931b); a prim. root; *to be weighty, judicious* or *commanding:*— rulers(6).

7337. רָחַב **rachab** (931b); a prim. root; *to be* or *grow wide* or *large:*— enlarge(6), enlarged(2), enlarges(3), extend(1), extends(1), large(1), made your wide(1), made room(1), makes room(1), open your wide(1), open wide(1), opened their wide(1), rejoice(1), relieved(1), roomy(1), speaks boldly(1), wider(1).

7338. רַחַב **rachab** (931d); from 7337; *breadth, broad expanse:*— broad place(1), expanse(1).

7339. רְחֹב **rechob** or

רְחוֹב **rechob** (932a); from 7337; *a broad open place, plaza:*— open square(7), open squares(1), plaza(1), plazas(1), square(14), squares(4), street(1), streets(13), town squares(1).

7340. רְחֹב **Rechob** or

רְחוֹב **Rechob** (932b); from 7337; places in Aram (Syria) and Pal., also an Aramean (Syrian) and an Isr.:— Rehob(10).

7341. רֹחַב **rochab** (931d); from 7337; *breadth, width:*— breadth(4), depth(1), expanse(1), thick(1), thickness(3), wide(27), width(62).

7342. רָחָב **rachab** (932a); from 7337; *wide, broad:*— arrogant(2), broad(7), broader(1), extensive(1), large*(2), liberty(1), proud(1), spacious(1), spacious*(1), vast(1), wide(3).

7343. רָחָב **Rachab** (932a); from 7337; a harlot in Jericho:— Rahab(5).

7344. רְחֹבוֹת **Rechoboth** or

רְחֹבֹת **Rechoboth** (932c); from 7337; "broad places," a well dug by Isaac, also two cities of unc. location:— Rehoboth(3), Rehoboth-Ir(1).

7345. רְחַבְיָה **Rechabyah** or

רְחַבְיָהוּ **Rechabyahu** (932c); from 7337 and 3050; "Yah has enlarged," grandson of Moses:— Rehabiah(5).

7346. רְחַבְעָם **Rechabam** (932c); from 7337 and 5971a; "a people are enlarged," a king of Judah:— Rehoboam(48), Rehoboam's(1).

רְחֹבֹת **Rechoboth**; see 7344.

7347. רֵחֶה **recheh** (932d); from an unused word; (hand)*mill:*— handmill(1), millstones(4).

רְחוֹב **Rechob**; see 7339, 7340.

7348a. רְחוּם **Rechum** (933d); a form of 7349; "compassion," the name of several Isr.:— Rehum(4).

7348b. רְחוּם **Rechum** (1113a); (Ara.) of unc. der.; a Pers. official:— Rehum(4).

7349. רַחוּם **rachum** (933d); from the same as 7358; *compassionate:*— compassionate(11), merciful(2).

7350. רָחוֹק **rachoq** or

רָחֹק **rachoq** (935b); from 7368; *distant, far, a distance:*— afar(19), afar*(1), distance(11), distant(7), distant future(1), far(31), far away(1), far off(2), farthest(1), great while(1), great while to come(1), long ago(4), long*(1), off*(1), reach(1), remote(1), who are far(2), who are far away(1), who is far off(1).

7351. רָהִיט **rahit** (923d); from the same as 7298b; perh. *rafters, boards:*— rafters(1).

7352. רַחִיק **rechiq** (1113a); (Ara.) corr. to 7350; *far:*— keep away(1).

7353. רָחֵל **rachel** (932d); from an unused word; *ewe:*— ewes(3), sheep(1).

7354. רָחֵל **Rachel** (932d); from the same as 7353; a wife of Jacob:— Rachel(41), Rachel's(5).

7355. רָחַם **racham** (933c); denom. vb. from 7356; *to love, have compassion:*— compassion(1), compassionate(1), find compassion(1), finds mercy(1), had(2), had compassion(2), has compassion(4), have compassion(20), have had compassion(1), have mercy(2), have pity(1), have...compassion(3), have...mercy(2), love(1), mercy(1), obtained compassion(1), Ruhamah(1), show compassion(2), surely have mercy(1).

7356. רַחַם **racham** (933b); from the same as 7358; *compassion:*— compassion(30), compassions(1), deeply(1), deeply*(1), mercies(4), mercy(2).

7357. רַחַם **Racham** (933d); from the same as 7358; "pity," a man of Judah:— Raham(1).

7358. רֶחֶם **rechem** (933a); from an unused word; *womb:*— birth(3), born*(1), maiden(1), maidens(1), mother(1), womb(22), wombs(1).

7359. רְחֵם **rechem** (1113a); (Ara.) corr. to 7356; *compassion:*— compassion(1).

7360. רָחָם **racham** or

רָחָמָה **rachamah** (934b); from an unused word; *carrion vulture:*— carrion vulture(2).

7361. רַחֲמָה **rachamah** (933b); the same as 7358, q.v.

7362. רַחֲמָנִי **rachamani** (933d); from the same as 7358; *compassionate:*— compassionate(1).

7363a. רָחַף **rachaph** (934b); a prim. root; *to grow soft, relax:*— tremble(1).

7363b. רָחַף **rachaph** (934b); a prim. root; *to hover:*— hovers(1), moving(1).

7364. רָחַץ **rachats** (934b); a prim. root; *to wash, wash off* or *away, bathe:*— bathe(25), bathed(6), bathing(1), wash(24), washed(13), washed away(1), washing(2).

7365. רְחַץ **rechats** (1113a); (Ara.) corr. 7364; *to trust:*— put their trust(1).

7366. רַחַץ **rachats** (934d); from 7364; *a washing:*— washbowl(2).

7367. רַחְצָה **rachtsah** (934d); fem. of 7366; *a washing:*— washing(2).

7368. רָחַק **rachaq** (934d); a prim. root; *to be* or *become far* or *distant:*— abandon(1), away(1), distance(1), extended(2), fail(1), far(25), far has he removed(1), far away(1), go far(1), go...far(1), gone some distance(1), good distance(1), keep and far(1), keep your far(1), keep far(1), put it far away(1), put away(1), put...far(1), remove(1), remove it far(1), remove the army far(1), remove their far(1), remove them far(1), remove you far(1), remove...far(1), removed and far(1), removed my far(2), removed them far(1), removed...far(1), shun(1), stand aloof(1), went far(2).

7369. רָחֵק **racheq** (935b); from 7368; *removing, departing:*— far(1).

רָחֹק **rachoq**; see 7350.

7370. רָחַשׁ **rachash** (935d); a prim. root; *to keep moving, stir:*— overflows(1).

7371. רַחַת **rachath** (935d); of unc. der.; *winnowing shovel:*— shovel(1).

7372. רָטֹב **ratob** or

רָטֵב **rateb** (936a); a prim. root; *to be moist:*— wet(1).

7373a. רָטֹב **ratob** (936a); from 7372; *moist, juicy, fresh:*— thrives(1).

7373b. רָטָה **ratah** (936a); another reading for 3399, q.v.

7374. רֶטֶט **retet** (936a); from an unused word; *a trembling, panic:*— panic(1).

7375. רֻטֲפַשׁ **rutaphash** (936a); a prim. root; *to grow fresh:*— become fresher(1).

7376. רָטַשׁ **ratash** (936b); a prim. root; *to dash in pieces:*— dash in pieces(1), dashed in pieces(2), dashed to pieces(2), mow down(1).

7377. רִי **ri** (924b); from 7301; *moisture:*— moisture(1).

7378. רִיב **rib** or

רוּב **rub** (936b); a prim. root; *to strive, contend:*— argue(2), complain(2), contend(22), contended(9), contends(1), dispute(1), ever strive(1), filed(1), find fault(1), have a quarrel(1), judge(1), plead(9), plead my case(1), plead your case(1), pleaded(2), pleads(1), quarrel(2), quarreled(3), quarrels(1), reprimanded(2), strive(1), vigorously plead(1).

7379. רִיב **rib** or

רִב **rib** (936d); from 7378; *strife, dispute:*— adversary(1), case(11), cause(9), complaint(2), contend(1), contention(1), contentions(3), controversy(1), dispute(11), disputes(1), indictment(1), lawsuit(1), plea(1), plead his case(1), quarrel(2), strife(13), suit(2).

7380. רִיבַי **Ribay** (937a); from 7378; a Benjamite:— Ribai(2).

7381a. רִיחַ **riach** (926b); denom. vb. from 7381b; *to smell, perceive odor:*— accept(1), delight(2), scents(1), smell(3), smelled(2), touches(1), use as perfume(1).

7381b. רֵיחַ **reach** (926a); from the same as 7307; *scent, odor:*— aroma(43), aromas(1), fragrance(9), odious*(1), scent(1), smell(3).

7382. רֵיחַ **reach** (1112d); (Ara.) corr. to 7381b; *a smell:*— smell(1).

רֵים **rem**; see 7214.

רֵיעַ **rea**; see 7453.

7383. רִיפָה **riphah** or

רִפָה **riphah** (937d); of unc. der.; perh. *grain:*— crushed grain(1), grain(1).

7384. רִיפַת **Riphath** or

דִּיפַת **Diphath** (937d); prob. of for. or.; a son of Gomer, also his desc.:— Riphath(1).

7385a. רִיק **riq** (937d); a prim. root; *to make empty, empty out:*— draw(6), emptied(2), empty(3), emptying(1), keep the unsatisfied(1), led(1), pour(2), purified(1), unsheathe(2).

7385b. רִיק **riq** (938b); from 7385a; *emptiness, vanity:*— empty(1), nothing(1), nothing*(1), uselessly(2), vain(4), vain thing(1), what is worthless(1).

7386. רֵיק **req** or

רֵק **req** (938a); from 7385a; *empty, vain:*— emptied(1), empty(6), foolish ones(1), idle(1), satisfied(1), worthless(4).

7387. רֵיקָם **reqam** (938b); from 7385a; *emptily, vainly:*— empty(6), empty-handed(8), without cause(2).

7388a. רִיר **rir** (938b); a prim. root; *to flow* (like slime):— flow(1).

7388b. רִיר **rir** (938c); from 7388a; *slimy juice, spittle:*— saliva(1).

7389. רֵישׁ **resh** or

רֵאשׁ **resh** or

רִישׁ **rish** (930d); from 7326; *poverty:*— poverty(7).

7390. רַךְ **rak** (940a); from 7401; *tender, delicate, soft:*— frail(1), gentle(1), inexperienced(2), refined(2), soft(2), tender(3), tender one(1), timid*(1), weak(2).

7391. רֹךְ **rok** (940a); from 7401; *tenderness, delicacy:*— refinement(1).

7392. רָכַב **rakab** (938c); a prim. root; *to mount and ride, ride:*— carried(2), carried him in a chariot(1), chariot(1), drove(1), harness(1), horseman*(2), lead(1), led(1), mounted(4), pace(1), placed(1), put(2), ridden(2), ride(17), rider(7), riders(5), rides(5), riding(15), rode(9), rode in a chariot(1).

7393. רֶכֶב **rekeb** (939a); from 7392; *chariotry, chariot, millstone:*— chariot(19), chariot horses(2), charioteers(3), chariots(87), rider(1), riders(2), train(2), upper millstone(3).

7394. רֵכָב **Rekab** (939c); from 7392; perh. "band of riders," a Benjamite, also the head of a nomadic family:— Rechab(13).

7395. רַכָּב **rakkab** (939b); from 7392; *charioteer, horseman:*— driver of his chariot(1), driver of the chariot(1), horseman(1).

7396. רִכְבָּה **rikbah** (939b); from 7392; (act of) *riding:*— riding(1).

7397a. רֵכָבִי **Rekabi** (939c); from 7394; desc. of Rechab:— Rechabites(4).

7397b. רֵכָה **Rekah** (939d); of unc. der.; a place in Judah:— Recah(1).

7398. רְכוּב **rekub** (939c); from 7392; *a chariot:*— chariot(1).

7399. רְכוּשׁ **rekush** or

רְכֻשׁ **rekush** (940d); from 7408; *property, goods:*— equipment(1), goods(7), herds(1), plunder(1), possessions(12), property(5), wealth(1).

7400. רָכִיל **rakil** (940c); from 7402; *slander:*— slanderer(3), slanderous(1), talebearer(2).

7401. רָכַךְ **rakak** (939d); a prim. root; *to be tender, weak* or *soft:*— faint(1), fainthearted*(3), grow faint(1), softened(1), softer(1), tender(2).

7402. רָכַל **rakal** (940b); a prim. root; prob. *to go about:*— merchant(2), merchants(3), traded(4), traders(8).

7403. רָכָל **Rakal** (940b); from 7402; a city in S. Judah:— Racal(1).

7404. רְכֻלָּה **rekullah** (940b); from 7402; *traffic, merchandise:*— merchandise(1), trade(3).

7405. רָכַס **rakas** (940c); a prim. root; *to bind:*— bind(1), bound(1).

7406. רֶכֶס **rekes** (940c); from 7405; perh. *roughness:*— rugged terrain(1).

7407. רֹכֶס **rokes** (940c); from 7405; perh. *conspiracy:*— conspiracies(1).

7408. רָכַשׁ **rakash** (940d); a prim. root; *to collect, gather* (property):— accumulated(1), acquired(2), gathered(2).

7409. רֶכֶשׁ **rekesh** (940d); perh. from 7408; *steeds:*— horses(1), steeds(2), swift steeds(1).

רְכֻשׁ **rekush**; see 7399.

רֵם **rem**; see 7214.

7410. רָם **Ram** (928a); from 7311; two Isr., also family of Elihu:— ram(7).

רָם **rum**; see 7311.

7411a. רָמָה **ramah** (941a); a prim. root; *to cast, shoot.*— archers(1), bowman*(1), hurled(2).

7411b. רָמָה **ramah** (941a); a prim. root; *to beguile, deal treacherously with:*— betray(1), deceived(6), deceives(1).

7412. רְמָה **remah** (1113a); (Ara.) corr. to 7411a; *to cast, throw:*— cast(10), impose(1), set(1).

7413. רָמָה **ramah** (928a); from 7311; *height, high place:*— height(1), high place(3), high places(1).

7414. רָמָה **Ramah** (928a); from 7311; "height," the name of several places in Isr.:— Ramah(35).

7415. רִמָּה **rimmah** (942c); from an unused word; *a worm:*— maggot(1), maggots(1), worm(3), worms(2).

7416. רִמּוֹן **rimmon** or

רִמֹּן **rimmon** (941d); of for. or.; *a pomegranate:*— pomegranate(7), pomegranate tree(1), pomegranates(22).

7417a. רִמּוֹן **Rimmon** (942a); from the same as 7423b; a Syrian god:— Rimmon(3).

7417b. רִמּוֹן **Rimmon** (942a); from the same as 7423b; a Benjamite:— Rimmon(3).

7417c. רִמּוֹן **Rimmon** or

רִמּוֹנוֹ **Rimmono** (942a); from the same as 7423b; the name of several places in Isr.:— Rimmon(9), Rimmono(1).

רָמוֹת **Ramoth**; see 7418, 7433.

7418. רָמוֹת־נֶגֶב **Ramoth-negeb** (928b); from 7413 and 5045; "height of the south," a place in Simeon, prob. the same as 7437b:— Ramoth of the Negev(1).

7419. רָמוּת **ramuth** (928c); from 7311; *height, lofty stature:*— refuse(1).

7420. רֹמַח **romach** (942b); from an unused word; *a spear, lance:*— lances(1), spear(5), spears(9).

7421. רַמִּי **rammi** (74c); scribal error for 761, q.v.

7422. רַמְיָה **Ramyah** (941d); from the same as 7423b and from 3050; "Yah has loosened," an Isr. with a for. wife:— Ramiah(1).

7423a. רְמִיָּה **remiyyah** (941a); from 7411b; *deceit, treachery:*— deceit(4), deceitful(4), treacherous(1), what is deceitful(1).

7423b. רְמִיָּה **remiyyah** (941c); from an unused word; *laxness, slackness:*— idle(1), lazy man(1), negligent(1), negligently(1), slack(1).

7424. רַמָּךְ **rammak** (942b); of for. or.; perh. *a mare:*— royal stud(1).

7425. רְמַלְיָהוּ Remalyahu (942b); from an unused word and 3050; father of King Pekah of Isr.:— Remaliah(13).

7426a. רָמַם ramom (942c); a prim. root; *to be exalted:*— exalted(2), get away(1), rose(3).

7426b. רָמַם ramam (942c); denom. vb. from 7415; *to be wormy:*— bred(1).

7427. רֹמֵמֻת romemuth or

רוֹמֵמוּת romemuth (928c); from 7311; *uplifting, arising:*— lifting(1).

רִמֹּן rimmon; see 7416.

7428. רִמֹּן פֶּרֶץ Rimmon Parets (942a); from 7416 and 6556; "pomegranate of the breach," a place in the desert:— Rimmon-perez(2).

7429. רָמַס ramas (942c); a prim. root; *to trample:*— oppressors(1), trample(2), trample my down(1), trample down(1), trampled(7), trampled them down(1), tramples down(1), trampling(1), tread(1), tread down(1), treads(1), trodden(1).

7430. רָמַשׂ ramas (942d); a prim. root; *to creep, move lightly, move about:*— creep(1), creeps(7), moved(1), moves(6), prowl about(1), swarm(1).

7431. רֶמֶשׂ remes (943a); from 7430; *creeping things, moving things:*— creeping thing(5), creeping things(9), creeps(1), moving thing(1), swarms(1).

7432. רֶמֶת Remeth (928b); from 7311; a city in Issachar:— Remeth(1).

7433. רָמֹת גִּלְעָד Ramoth Gilad or

רָמוֹת גִּלְעָד Ramoth Gilad (928b); from 7413 and 1568; a city E. of the Jordan:— Ramoth-gilead(20).

7434. רָמַת הַמִּצְפֶּה Ramath Hammitspeh (928b); from 7413 and 4707; "height of the watchtower," a city on N. border of Gad:— Ramath-mizpeh(1).

7435. רָמָתִי Ramathi (928b); from 7414; inhab. of Ramah:— Ramathite(1).

7436. רָמָתַיִם צוֹפִים Ramathayim Tsophim (928a); from 7413 and 6822; "double height of watchers," a city in Ephraim:— Ramathaim-zophim(1).

7437a. רָמַת לֶחִי Ramath Lechi (928b); from 7413 and 3895; "height of a jawbone," a city in Judah:— Ramath-lehi(1).

7437b. רָמַת נֶגֶב Ramath Negeb (928b); from 7413 and 5045; "height of the south," a city in Simeon:— Ramah of the Negev(1).

רָן Ran; see 1028.

7438. רֹן ron (943c); from 7442; *a ringing cry:*— songs(1).

7439. רָנָה ranah (943a); a prim. root; *to rattle:*— rattles(1).

7440. רִנָּה rinnah (943c); from 7442; *a ringing cry:*— cry(12), joy(2), joyful shout(1), joyful shouting(9), joyful singing(1), rejoice(1), shout of joy(3), shouts of joy(3), singing(1).

7441. רִנָּה Rinnah (943d); from 7442; a man of Judah:— Rinnah(1).

7442. רָנַן ranan (943b); a prim. root; *to give a ringing cry:*— cries(1), cries of joy(1), cry aloud(1), joyfully sing(2), rejoice(1), sang(1), shout for joy(16), shout of joy(1), shout joyfully(4), shouted(1), shouts(1), sing for joy(18), sing aloud(3), sing aloud for joy(1), sings(1).

7443. רֶנֶן renen (943d); from 7442; (bird of) *piercing cries* (i.e. ostrich):— ostriches'(1).

7444. רַנֵּן rannen (943b); the same as 7442, q.v.

7445. רְנָנָה renanah (943c); from 7442; *a ringing cry:*— joyful(1), joyful shout(1), joyful singing(1), triumphing(1).

7446. רִסָּה Rissah (943d); of unc. der.; a place in the desert:— Rissah(2).

7447a. רָסִיס rasis (944a); from 7450; *a drop* (of dew):— damp(1).

7447b. רָסִיס rasis (944a); from an unused word; *a fragment:*— pieces(1).

7448. רֶסֶן resen (943d); from an unused word; *a halter, jaw:*— bridle(3), mail(1).

7449. רֶסֶן Resen (944a); from the same as 7448; a city in Assyr.:— Resen(1).

7450. רָסַס rasas (944a); a prim. root; *to moisten:*— moisten(1).

7451a. רַע ra (948a); from the same as 7455; *bad, evil:*— bad(23), bad*(2), badly(1), deadly(1), defamed*(1), defames*(1), defect*(1), destroying(1), displease*(1), displeased(1), displeasing(1), distressing(1), evil(124), evil man(3), evil men(4), evil things(4), evildoer(1), evildoers*(1), evils(1), great(1), grievous(4), harm*(1), harmful(3), man(1), miserable(1), misfortune*(1), sad(4), selfish*(1), serious(1), severe(2), sore(2), threats*(1), treacherous(1), trouble*(1), troubled(1), ugly(6), unpleasant(1), what is evil(2), what was evil(5), which is evil(3), wicked(15), wicked women(1), wild(5), worst(1), wretched(1).

7451b. רַע ra (948c); from the same as 7455; *evil, distress, misery, injury, calamity:*— adversity(7), calamity(4), disaster(2), evil(94), harm(2), harmful(1), hurt(1), ruin(3), surely(1), trouble(2), unpleasant(1), wickedly(1), wickedness(1).

7452. רֵעַ rea (929d); from 7321; perh. *shouting, roar:*— loudly(1), noise(1), shouted(1).

7453. רֵעַ rea or

רֵיעַ rea (945d); from 7462b; *friend, companion, fellow:*— another(27), another's(5), another*(1), companion(3), fellow(1), friend(30), friend's(1), friends(18), husband(1), kind(1), lover(1), lovers(1), mate(1), neighbor(64), neighbor's(23), neighbors(3), neighbors'(1), opponent(1), opponent's(1), other(6), together*(1).

7454. רֵעַ rea (946d); from an unused word; *purpose, aim:*— thought(1), thoughts(1).

7455. רֹעַ roa (947d); of unc. der.; *badness, evil:*— evil(10), rottenness(4), sad(1), sadness(1), ugliness(1), wickedness(2).

7456. רָעֵב raeb (944a); a prim. root; *to be hungry:*— famished(1), gets hungry(1), hunger(3), hungry(6), suffer hunger(2).

7457. רָעֵב raeb (944c); from 7456; *hungry:*— famished(3), hungry(16), hungry man(1).

7458. רָעָב raab (944b); from 7456; *famine, hunger:*— famine(94), famished(1), hunger(6).

7459. רְעָבוֹן reabon (944c); from 7456; *hunger, lack of food, famine:*— famine(3).

7460. רָעַד raad (944c); a prim. root; *to tremble, quake:*— trembles(1), trembling(2).

7461a. רַעַד raad (944c); from 7460; *a trembling:*— trembling(2).

7461b. רְעָדָה readah (944d); fem. of 7461a; *a trembling:*— panic(1), trembling(3).

7462a. רָעָה raah (944d); a prim. root; *to pasture, tend, graze:*— consume(1), devour(1), eat(3), fed(1), feed(16), feeding(4), feeds(4), graze(7), grazed(2), grazing(1), herdsmen(6), keeper(1), pasture(12), pastured(2), pastures(2), pasturing(5), rulers(1), shaved(1), Shepherd(5), shepherd(34), shepherd's(1), shepherded(1), shepherdess(1), shepherds(37), shepherds who are tending(1), shepherds will not feed(1), shepherds fed(1), shepherds feed(1), shepherds'(2), sweep away(1), sweep away your shepherds(1), tend(3), tending(3), wrongs(1).

7462b. רָעָה raah (945c); a prim. root; prob. *to associate with:*— associate(1), companion(2), cultivate(1), keeps company(1).

7462c. רָעָה raah (946b); denom. vb. from 7463b; *to be a special friend:*— friend(1).

7463a. רָעָה raah (949a); from the same as 7455; *evil, misery, distress, injury:*— adversities(1), adversity(7), afflictions(1), calamities(1), calamity(47), disaster(22), discomfort(1), distress(2), distresses(1), evil(112), evil deeds(1), evildoer*(1), evildoing(1), evils(5), great wickedness(1), harm(19), hurt(5), ill(1), injure(2), injury(1), misery(2), misfortune(6), misfortunes(1), pain(1), situation(1), sorrow(1), trouble(9), troubles(1), very*(1), wicked(3), wicked deeds(1), wickedly(1), wickedness(39), woe(1), wretchedness(1), wrong(4), wrongdoing(1).

7463b. רֵעֶה reeh (946b); from 7462b; *a friend:*— friend(3).

7464. רֵעָה reah (946b); from 7462b; *companion, attendant:*— companions(3).

7465. רֹעָה roah (949d); the same as 7489b, q.v.

7466a. רְעוּ Reu (946c); from 7462b; son of Peleg:— Reu(5).

7466b. רְעוּ reu (1113b); (Ara.) corr. to 7469; *good pleasure, will:*— decision(1), will(1).

7467. רְעוּאֵל Reuel (946c); from 7462b and 410; "friend of God," Moses' father-in-law, also an Edomite, a Gadite, and a Benjamite:— Reuel(10).

7468. רְעוּת reuth (946b); from 7462b; *fellow* (woman):— another(1), another's(1), kind(1), mate(1), neighbor(2).

7469. רְעוּת reuth (946d); from the same as 7454; *longing, striving:*— striving(7).

7470. רְעוּת reuth (1113b); see 7466b.

7471. רְעִי rei (945c); from 7462a; *a pasture:*— pasture-fed(1).

7472. רֵעִי Rei (946c); from 7462b; a courtier of King David:— Rei(1).

7473. רֹעִי roi (945c); from 7462a; *shepherd:*— shepherd(1), shepherd's(1).

7474. רַעְיָה rayah (946b); from 7462b; *a companion:*— darling(9).

7475. רַעְיוֹן rayon (946d); from the same as 7454; *longing, striving:*— striving(3).

7476. רַעְיוֹן rayon (1113b); (Ara.) corr. to 7475; *a thought:*— thoughts(6).

7477. רָעַל raal (947a); a prim. root; *to quiver, shake, reel:*— brandished(1).

7478. רַעַל raal (947a); from 7477; *a reeling:*— reeling(1).

7479. רַעֲלָה realah (947a); from 7477; prob. *a veil:*— veils(1).

7480. רְעֵלָיָה Reelayah (947a); from 7477 and 3050; companion of Zerubbabel:— Reelaiah(1).

7481. רָעַם raam (947b); denom. vb. from 7482; *to thunder:*— irritate(1), roar(3), thunder(2), thundered(3), thunders(3), troubled(1).

7482. רַעַם raam (947b); from an unused word; *thunder:*— thunder(6).

7483. רַעְמָה ramah (947c); from the same as 7482; perh. *vibration, quivering:*— mane(1).

7484. רַעְמָה Ramah or

רַעְמָא Rama (947c); from the same as 7482; "trembling," son of Cush, also a trading people:— Raama(1), Raamah(4).

7485. רַעַמְיָה Raamyah (947c); from 7482 and 3050; perh. "thunder of Yah," an Isr. who returned with Zerubbabel:— Raamiah(1).

7486. רַעְמְסֵס Raamses or

רַעַמְסֵס Rameses (947c); of for. or.; a city in Eg.:— Raamses(1), Rameses(4).

7487a. רָעַן raan (947d); a prim. root; *to be* or *grow luxuriant, fresh,* or *green:*— green(1).

7487b. רַעֲנַן raanan (1113b); (Ara.) corr. to 7488; *flourishing:*— flourishing(1).

7488. רַעֲנָן raanan (947d); from 7487a; *luxuriant, fresh:*— fresh(1), green(12), luxuriant(5), very green(1).

7489a. רָעַע raa (949b); denom. vb. from 7451b; *to be evil, bad:*— act so wickedly(1), act wickedly(1), acted wickedly(1), acted...wickedly(1), afflicted(3), badly(1), bring disaster(1), brought calamity(1), brought harm(1), damaged(1), disagreeable(1), displease*(1), displeased(2), displeased*(4), displeasing(6), distressed(2), do my harm(2), do us harm(1), do you harm(2), do evil(4), do harm(1), do...evil(1), do...harm(1), doing evil(1), done harm(2), done very wickedly(1), done wickedly(1), done wrong(1), evil(7), evildoer(2), evildoers(16), evildoing(1), grieved(1), hard(1), harm(1), harming(1), hostile(3), hurt(3), practiced evil(1), prefer*(2), sad(2), still do wickedly(1), suffer(1), suffer harm(1), treat me so badly(1), treat you worse(1), treated(1), treated us harshly(1), went hard(1), work calamity(1), worse(1).

7489b. רָעַע raa (949d); a prim. root; *to break:*— bad(1), break(1), breaks(1), broken(1), broken asunder(1), destroyed(1), ruin(1), smash(1), worthless(1).

7490. רְעַע rea (1113b); (Ara.) corr. to 7489b; *to crush, shatter:*— break in pieces(1), breaks in pieces(1).

7491. רָעַף raaph (950a); a prim. root; *to trickle, drip:*— drip(4), drip down(1).

7492. רָעַץ raats (950a); a prim. root; *to shatter:*— afflicted(1), shatters(1).

7493. רָעַשׁ raash (950a); a prim. root; *to quake, shake:*— leap(1), quake(4), quaked(5), quakes(3), quaking(1), shake(9), shaken(2), shook(2), tremble(2), wave(1).

7494. רַעַשׁ raash (950b); from 7493; *a quaking, shaking:*— commotion(1), earthquake(7), rattling(3), rumbling(2), shaking(1), trembling(1), tumult(2).

7495. רָפָא rapha (950c); a prim. root; *to heal:*— become fresh(3), completely healed(1), heal(24), healed(22), healer(1), healing(2), heals(3), physician(1), physicians(4), purified(2), reappeared(1), repaired(2), take care(1).

7496. רְפָאִים rapha (952b); from 7503; *shades, ghosts:*— dead(3), departed spirits(4), spirits of the dead(1).

7497. רָפָא Rapha (952b); from 7503; inhab. of an area E. of the Jordan:— Rephaim(18).

7498a. רָפָא Rapha (951a); from 7495; a Benjamite:— Rapha(1).

7498b. רָפָא rapha or

רָפָה raphah (952a); from 7503; *giant:*— giant(4), giants(3).

7499. רְפֻאָה rephuah (951b); from 7495; *remedy, medicine:*— healing(2), remedies(1).

7500. רִפְאוּת riphuth (951b); from 7495; *a healing:*— healing(1).

7501. רְפָאֵל Rephael (951b); from 7495 and 410; "God has cured," a Levite:— Rephael(1).

7502. רָפַד raphad (951c); a prim. root; *to spread:*— make(1), refresh(1), spreads(1).

7503. רָפָה raphah (951c); a prim. root; *sink, relax:*— abandon*(1), alone*(2), become helpless(1), become*(1), cease(2), collapses(1), courage*(1), discouraged*(2), discouraging*(1), drawn(1), dropped(2), fail(5), fall limp(2), feeble(1), forsake(1), hang limp(2), lazy(3), leave(1), let(2), let her alone(1), let him alone(1), let him go(1), let it go(1), let me alone(1), let us alone(1), let go(1), limp(1), loosens(1), lose courage*(1), lost(1), put off(1), relax(2), slack(2), subsided(1), wait(1).

7504a. רָפָה Rapha (951b); from 7495; an Isr. in the line of Saul:— Raphah(1).

7504b. רָפֶה rapheh (952a); from 7503; *slack:*— exhausted*(2), weak(2).

רָפָה raphah; see 7497, 7498b.

רִפָה riphah; see 7383.

7505. רָפוּא Raphu (951b); from 7495; "cured," a Benjamite:— Raphu(1).

7506. רֶפַח Rephach (952c); of unc. der.; an Ephraimite:— Rephah(1).

7507. רְפִידָה rephidah (951c); from 7502; perh. *a support:*— back(1).

7508. רְפִידִים Rephidim (951c); from 7502; a place in the desert:— Rephidim(5).

7509. רְפָיָה Rephayah (951b); from 7495 and 3050; "Yah has cured," five Isr.:— Rephaiah(5).

7510. רִפְיוֹן rippayon (952a); from 7503; *a sinking:*— limpness(1).

7511. רָפַס raphas or

רָפַשׂ raphas (952c); a prim. root; *to stamp, tread:*— foul(1), fouled(1), humble(1), trampled(1), trampling under foot(1).

7512. רְפַס rephas (1113b); (Ara.) corr. to 7511; *to tread, trample:*— trampled down(2).

7513. רַפְסֹדָה raphsodah (952c); from 7511; *a raft:*— rafts(1).

7514a. רָפַף raphaph (952c); a prim. root; *to shake, rock:*— tremble(1).

7514b. רָפַק raphaq (952d); a prim. root; *to support oneself, lean:*— leaning(1).

7515. רָפַשׂ raphas (952c); the same as 7511, q.v.

7516. רֶפֶשׁ rephesh (952d); from an unused word; *mire:*— refuse(1).

7517. רֶפֶת repheth (952d); of unc. der.; *stable, stall:*— stalls(1).

7518. רַץ rats (954d); from 7533; perh. *piece, bar:*— pieces(1).

7519. רָצָא ratsa (952d); a prim. root; *to run:*— ran(1).

7520. רָצַד ratsad (952d); a prim. root; *to watch* (stealthily):— look with envy(1).

7521. רָצָה ratsah (953a); a prim. root; *to be pleased with, accept favorably:*— accept(11), accepted(6), approve(1), approved(1), delight(4), delights(2), enjoy(2), enjoyed(1), favor(2), favorable(1), favored(2), favors(1), find pleasure(1), fulfills(1), make(1), make himself acceptable(1), make amends(1), making amends(1), please(1), pleased(6), pleasing(1), receive(1), received me favorably(1), removed(1), restored(1), showed favor(1), take delight(1), take pleasure(1), taken...delight(1), takes pleasure(1), took pleasure(1).

7522. רָצוֹן ratson or

רָצֹן ratson (953c); from 7521; *goodwill, favor, acceptance, will:*— acceptable(5), acceptance(1), accepted(8), delight(5), desire(2), desired(1), desires(1), earnestly*(1), favor(17), favorable(2), good will(1), please(1), pleased(1), pleases(3), self-will(1), what is acceptable(1), what they pleased(1), will(3).

7523. רָצַח ratsach (953d); a prim. root; *to murder, slay:*— killed(1), kills the manslayer(1), manslayer(18), murder(7), murdered(2), murderer(12), murderer shall be put(1), murderers(1), murders(1), put to death(1), slew(1).

7524. רֶצַח retsach (954a); from 7523; *a shattering:*— shattering(1), slaughter(1).

7525. רִצְיָא Ritsya (954a); of unc. der.; an Asherite:— Rizia(1).

7526. רְצִין Retsin (954a); of unc. der.; a king of Aram (Syria), also an Isr.:— Rezin(11).

7527. רָצַע ratsa (954a); a prim. root; *to bore, pierce:*— pierce(1).

7528. רָצַף ratsaph (954b); a prim. root; *to fit together, fit out:*— fitted(1).

7529. רֶצֶף retseph (954b); see 7531a.

7530. רֶצֶף Retseph (954b); from the same as 7531a; a place destroyed by Assyr.:— Rezeph(2).

7531a. רִצְפָּה ritspah (954b); from an unused word; *a glowing stone:*— burning coal(1), hot stones(1).

7531b. רִצְפָה ritsephah (954b); from 7528; *pavement:*— mosaic pavement(1), pavement(6).

7532. רִצְפָּה Ritspah (954c); from the same as 7531a; concubine of Saul:— Rizpah(4).

7533. רָצַץ ratsats (954c); a prim. root; *to crush:*— broke(1), bruised(1), crush(1), crushed(9), crushing(1), oppressed(5), struggled(1).

7534. רַק raq (956b); from an unused word; *thin, only, altogether, surely:*— alone*(4), except(4), except*(1), gaunt*(1), however(6), lean(2), moreover(1), never be anything(1), nevertheless(5), nothing(2), only(64), only*(1), sheer(1), still(1), surely(5), thin(1), those(1), though(1), yet(3).

7535. רַק raq (956b); the same as 7534, q.v.

7536. רֹק roq (956d); from 7556; *spittle:*— spitting(2), spittle(1).

7537. רָקֵב raqeb (955a); a prim. root; *to rot:*— rot(2).

7538. רָקָב raqab (955a); from 7537; *rottenness, decay:*— decay(1), rotten thing(1), rottenness(3).

7539. רִקָּבוֹן riqqabon (955a); from 7537; *rottenness, decay:*— rotten(1).

7540. רָקַד raqad (955a); a prim. root; *to skip about:*— bounding(1), dance(1), frolic(1), leap(1), leaping(1), skip(2), skip about(1), skipped(1).

7541. רַקָּה raqqah (956d); from the same as 7534; *the temple* (part of the head):— temple(3), temples(2).

7542. רַקּוֹן Raqqon (956d); from 7556; a city in Dan near Joppa:— Rakkon(1).

7543. רָקַח raqach (955b); a prim. root; *to mix* or *compound oil* or *ointment:*— blended(1), mix(1), mix in the spices(1), perfumer(3), perfumer's(1), perfumers'*(1), prepared(1).

7544. רֶקַח reqach (955b); from 7543; *spice:*— spiced(1).

7545. רֹקַח roqach (955b); from 7543; *spice mixture, perfume:*— perfume(2).

7546. רַקָּח raqqach (955c); from 7543; *ointment maker, perfumer:*— perfumers(1).

7547. רִקֻּחַ riqquach or

רִקּוּחַ riqquach (955c); from 7543; *perfumery:*— perfumes(1).

7548. רַקָּחָה raqqachah (955c); from 7543; (female) *ointment maker, perfumer:*— perfumers(1).

7549. רָקִיעַ raqia (956a); from 7554; *an extended surface, expanse:*— expanse(16), expanse of heaven(1).

7550. רָקִיק raqiq (956d); from the same as 7534; *thin cake, wafer:*— wafer(3), wafers(5).

7551. רָקַם raqam (955c); a prim. root; *to variegate:*— embroiderer(1), skillfully wrought(1), weaver(7).

7552. רֶקֶם Reqem (955d); from 7551; "having many colors," a Midianite king, also two Isr., also a city in Benjamin:— Rakem(1), Rekem(5).

7553. רִקְמָה riqmah (955d); from 7551; *variegated stuff:*— embroidered(4), embroidered cloth(2), embroidered work(3), embroidery(1), many colors(1), stones of various colors(1), various colors(1).

7554. רָקַע raqa (955d); a prim. root; *to beat, stamp, beat out, spread out:*— beaten(1), hammered(2), plates(1), spread(3), spreading(1), stamp(1), stamped(2).

7555. רִקֻּעַ riqqua or

רִקּוּעַ riqqua (956b); from 7554; *expansion:*— hammered(1).

7556. רָקַק raqaq (956d); a prim. root; *to spit:*— spits(1).

7557. רַקַּת Raqqath (957a); from 7556; a city in Naphtali:— Rakkath(1).

7558. רִשְׁיוֹן rishyon (957a); from an unused word; *permission:*— permission(1).

7559. רָשַׁם rasham (957a); a prim. root; *to inscribe, note:*— inscribed(1).

7560. רְשַׁם resham (1113b); (Ara.) corr. to 7559; *to inscribe, sign:*— sign(2), signed(3), written(2).

7561. רָשַׁע rasha (957d); denom. vb. from 7562; *to be wicked, act wickedly:*— act wickedly(3), acted wickedly(6), been wicked(1), behaved wickedly(1), condemn(10), condemned(2), condemning(1), condemns(3), do wickedly(1), guilty(1), inflicted punishment(1), wicked(3), wickedly departed(1).

7562. רֶשַׁע resha (957c); from the same as 7563; *wickedness:*— evil(2), Ill-gotten(1), wicked(4), wicked acts(1), wickedness(23).

7563. רָשָׁע rasha (957b); from an unused word; *wicked, criminal:*— evil(1), evil man(1), evil men(1), guilty(3), man(1), offender(1), ungodly(1), wicked(228), wicked man(21), wicked men(2), wicked one(1), wicked ones(3).

7564. רִשְׁעָה rishah (958a); from the same as 7563; *wickedness:*— evildoer*(1), guilt(1), wickedly(1), wickedness(11).

7565. רֶשֶׁף resheph (958a); from an unused word; *flame:*— bolts of lightning(1), flaming(1), flashes(2), plague(2), sparks*(1).

7566. רֶשֶׁף Resheph (958b); from the same as 7565; an Ephraimite:— Resheph(1).

7567. רָשַׁשׁ rashash (958b); a prim. root; *to beat down, shatter:*— beaten down(1), demolish(1).

7568. רֶשֶׁת resheth (440b); from 3423; *a net:*— net(20), network(2).

7569. רַתּוֹק rattoq (958d); from 7576; *a chain:*— chain(1), chains(1).

7570. רָתַח rathach (958b); a prim. root; *to boil:*— boil(2), seething(1).

7571. רֶתַח rethach (958c); from 7570; *a boiling:*— vigorously(1).

7572. רַתִּיקָה rattiqah (958d); see 7569.

7573. רָתַם ratham (958c); a prim. root; *to bind, attach:*— harness(1).

7574. רֶתֶם rethem or

רֹתֶם rothem (958c); from 7573; *broom plant, retem:*— broom shrub(1), broom tree(1), juniper tree(2).

7575. רִתְמָה Rithmah (958c); from 7573; a place in the desert:— Rithmah(2).

7576. רָתַק rathaq (958c); a prim. root; *to bind:*— bound(1), broken(1).

7577. רְתֻקָה rethuqah (958d); from 7576; *a chain:*— chains(1).

7578. רְתֵת retheth (958d); from an unused word; *a trembling:*— trembling(1).

ש

7579. שָׁאַב shaab (980b); a prim. root; *to draw* (water):— draw(9), draw water(1), drawers(3), draws(1), drew(5).

7580. שָׁאַג shaag (980c); a prim. root; *to roar:*— groan(1), roar(6), roar mightily(1), roared(3), roaring(4), roars(4).

7581. שְׁאָגָה sheagah (980d); from 7580; *a roaring:*— cries(1), groaning(2), roar(1), roaring(3).

7582. שָׁאָה shaah (980d); a prim. root; *to make a din* or *crash, crash into ruins:*— devastated(1), rumble(1), rush(1), turn(1), turn*(1).

7583. שָׁאָה shaah (981b); a prim. root; *to gaze:*— gazing(1).

7584. שַׁאֲוָה shaavah (981a); from 7582; *a devastating storm:*— storm(1).

7585. שְׁאוֹל sheol or

שְׁאֹל sheol (982d); of unc. der.; *underworld* (place to which people descend at death):— Sheol(66).

7586. שָׁאוּל Shaul (982b); from 7592; "asked (of Yah)," first king of Isr., also an Edomite and two Isr.:— Saul(357), Saul's(34), Shaul(9).

7587. שָׁאוּלִי Shauli (982c); from 7586; desc. of Shaul:— Shaulites(1).

7588. שָׁאוֹן shaon (981a); from 7582; *a roar* (of waters, etc.), *din, crash, uproar:*— big noise(1), clamor(1), destruction(1), din(1), noise(1), revelers*(1), riotous(1), roaring(2), rumbling(3), tumult(3), uproar(4).

7589. שְׁאָט sheat (1002b); from 7751c; *despite, contempt:*— scorn(3).

7590. שָׁאט shat (1002b); the same as 7751c, q.v.

7591. שְׁאִיָּה sheiyyah (981a); from 7582; *a ruin:*— ruins(1).

7592. שָׁאַל shaal (981b); a prim. root; *to ask, inquire:*— ask(45), asked(41), asking(5), asks(5), beg(1), begged(1), begs(1), borrow(1), borrowed(1), borrows(1), consult(2), consulting(1), consults(1), dedicated(2), dedicated*(1), demand(1), demanded(1), desired(1), desires(1), earnestly asked(1), earnestly asked leave(1), greet*(5), greeted*(1), inquire(6), inquired(18), inquires(1), making(2), medium*(1), pray(1), questioned(2), questioned particularly(1), request(2), request*(1), requested(7), require(1), required(1), sought(1), surely ask(1).

7593. שְׁאֵל sheel (1114a); (Ara.) corr. to 7592; *to ask:*— asked(3), demands(1), inquired(1), require(1).

7594. שְׁאָל Sheal (982b); from 7592; an Isr. with a for. wife:— Sheal(1).

שְׁאֹל sheol; see 7585.

7595. שְׁאֵלָה sheelah (1114b); (Ara.) from 7593; *affair:*— decision(1).

7596. שְׁאֵלָה sheelah or

שֵׁלָה shelah (982c); from 7592; *request, thing asked for:*— dedicated*(1), one(1), petition(8), request(4), request*(1).

7597. שְׁאַלְתִּיאֵל Shealtiel (982c); from 7592 and 410; "I have asked of God," an Isr. name:— Shealtiel(6).

7598. שְׁאַלְתִּיאֵל Shealtiel (not included); (Ara.) corr. to 7597; "I have asked of God," an Isr. name:— Shealtiel(1).

7599. שָׁאַן shaan (983b); a prim. root; *to be at ease* or *at peace, rest securely:*— been at ease(1), ease(3), secure(1).

7600. שַׁאֲנָן shaanan (983b); from 7599; *at ease, secure:*— arrogance(2), ease(3), those who are at ease(1), undisturbed(2), who are at ease(3).

7601. שָׁאַס shaas (1042c); see 8155.

7602a. שָׁאַף shaaph (983c); a prim. root; *to gasp, pant, pant after, long for:*— eager(1), hastening(1), long(1), pant(2), panted(1), pants(1), sniffs(1).

7602b. שָׁאַף shaaph (983c); a prim. root; *to crush, trample upon:*— crushed(1), pant(1), trample(1), trampled(2), tramples(1).

7603. שְׂאֹר seor (959a); from an unused word; *leaven:*— leaven(5).

7604. שָׁאַר shaar (983d); a prim. root; *to remain, be left over:*— bereft(1), have a left(1), have...left(1), leave(12), leave as a remnant(1), leaves(1), left(73), left behind(2), remain(10), remained(11), remains(6), remnant(2), reserved(1), rest(2), survive(1), survived(4), surviving remnant(2), survivor(1), survivors(1).

7605. שְׁאָר shear (984b); from 7604; *rest, residue, remnant:*— remainder(1), remnant(11), rest(13), survivors(1).

7606. שְׁאָר shear (1114b); (Ara.) corr. to 7605; *rest, remainder:*— remainder(2), rest(10).

7607. שְׁאֵר sheer (984d); from an unused word; *flesh:*— blood relative(4), blood relatives(2), body(1), flesh(4), food(1), himself(1), meat(2), relative(1), relatives(1).

7608. שְׁאָרָה shaarah (984d); fem. of 7607, q.v.

7609. שֶׁאֱרָה Sheerah (985a); from the same as 7607; an Ephraimite woman:— Sheerah(1).

7610. שְׁאָר יָשׁוּב Shear Yashub (984c); from 7605 and 7725; "a remnant shall return," son of Isaiah:— Shear-jashub(1).

7611. שְׁאֵרִית sheerith (984c); from 7604; *rest, residue, remnant, remainder:*— left(1), remnant(55), rest(7), survivors(2), those who had escaped(1).

7612. שֵׁאת sheth (981b); from 7582; perh. *devastation:*— devastation(1).

7613. שְׂאֵת seeth (673b); from 5375; *exaltation, dignity, swelling, uprising:*— authority(1), dignity(1), high position(1), lifted(1), majesty(2), raises(1), swelling(7).

7614. שְׁבָא Sheba (985a); of for. or.; a territory in S.W. Arabia, also the name of one or more desc. of Noah:— Sabeans(1), Sheba(22).

7615. שְׁבָאִי Shebai (985b); from 7614; desc. of Sheba:— Sabeans(1).

7616. שְׁבָבִים shebabim (985b); from an unused word; prob. *splinters:*— broken to pieces(1).

7617. שָׁבָה shabah (985c); a prim. root; *to take captive:*— captives(2), captors(2), captors captive(1), captured(4), carried(4), carried away captive(1), carried captive(1), carried off(1), driven away(1), keep(1), led them captive(1), led captive(1), take(3), take them away captive(1), take them captive(1), taken(8), taken captive(5), took(2), took them captive(2), took away(1), took captive(1).

7618. שְׁבוֹ shebo (986b); of unc. der.; (a precious stone) perh. *agate:*— agate(2).

7619. שְׁבוּאֵל Shebuel or

שְׁבֻאֵל Shebuel (986c); from 7617 (or 7725) and 410; "captive (or returned) of God," two Isr.:— Shebuel(3), Shubael(3).

7620. שָׁבוּעַ shabua (988d); from 7651; *a period of seven* (days, years), *heptad, week:*— seven(1), week(4), Weeks(5), weeks(14).

7621. שְׁבוּעָה shebuah or

שְׁבֻעָה shebuah (989d); from 7651; *an oath, curse:*— curse(1), oath(25), oaths(1), perjury*(1), swear(1), sworn(1).

7622. שְׁבוּת shebuth or

שְׁבִית shebith (986a); from 7617; *captivity, captives:*— captive(3), captivity(9), fortune(1), fortunes(18), own captivity(1).

7623a. שָׁבַח shabach (986c); a prim. root; *to soothe, still:*— holds(1), still(1), stills(1).

7623b. שָׁבַח shabach (986c); a prim. root; *to laud, praise:*— commended(1), congratulated(1), glory(2), Laud(1), praise(3).

7624. שְׁבַח shebach (1114b); (Ara.) corr. to 7623b; *to laud, praise:*— praise(2), praised(3).

7625. שְׁבַט shebat (1114b); (Ara.) corr. to 7626; *a tribe:*— tribes(1).

7626. שֵׁבֶט shebet (986d); from an unused word; *rod, staff, club, scepter, tribe:*— club(4), correction(1), half-tribe*(22), rod(27), scepter(11), scepters(1), spears(1), staff(1), tribe(40), tribes(83).

7627. שְׁבָט Shebat (987b); of for. or.; eleventh month in the Jewish calendar:— Shebat(1).

7628a. שָׁבִי shabi (985d); from 7617; *captive:*— captive(1).

7628b. שְׁבִי shebi (985d); from 7617; *captivity, captives:*— captive(16), captives(10), captivity(32), captured(2).

7629. שֹׁבִי Shobi (986b); from 7617; appar. an Ammonite prince:— Shobi(1).

7630. שֹׁבָי Shobay (986b); from 7617; head of a family of gatekeepers:— Shobai(2).

7631. שְׁבִיב shebib (1114b); (Ara.) corr. to 7632; *a flame:*— ablaze with flames(1), flame(1).

7632. שָׁבִיב shabib (985b); from an unused word; prob. *a flame:*— flame(1).

7633. שִׁבְיָה shibyah (986a); from 7617; *captivity, captives:*— captives(7), captivity(2).

7634. שָׁבְיָה Shobyah (967d); see 7914a.

7635. שְׁבִיל shebil or

שְׁבוּל shebul (987c); from the same as 7640; *a way, path:*— paths(2).

7636. שָׁבִיס shabis (987d); of unc. der.; *a headband:*— headbands(1).

7637. שְׁבִיעִי shebii or

שְׁבִיעִית shebiith (988c); from 7651; *seventh* (an ord. number):— fourth(1), seventh(96), seventh year(1).

שְׁבִית shebith; see 7622.

7638. שָׂבָךְ sabak (959b); the same as 7639, q.v.

שַׂבְּכָא sabbeka; see 5443.

7639. שְׂבָכָה sebakah (959a); from the same as 7730; *latticework, network:*— lattice(1), nets of network(1), network(8), networks(4), webbing(1).

7640. שֹׁבֶל shobel (987c); from an unused word; *flowing skirt, train:*— skirt(1).

7641. שִׁבֹּל shibbol or

שִׁבֹּלֶת shibboleth (987c); from the same as 7640; *ear* (of grain):— branches(1), ears(10), ears of grain(3), grain(1).

7642a. שַׁבְלוּל shablul (117d); from 1101a; *a snail:*— snail(1).

7642b. שִׁבֹּלֶת shibboleth (987c); from the same as 7640; *a flowing stream:*— flood(2), flowing stream(1), shibboleth(1).

שִׁבֹּלֶת shibboleth; see 7641.

7643. שְׂבָם Sebam (959b); of unc. der.; a place in Moab:— Sebam(1), Sibmah(5).

7644. שֶׁבְנָא Shebna or

שֶׁבְנָה Shebnah (987d); of unc. der.; secretary and majordomo of Hezekiah:— Shebna(7), Shebnah(2).

7645. שְׁבַנְיָה Shebanyah or

שְׁבַנְיָהוּ Shebanyahu (987d); from the same as 7644 and from 3050; the name of several Isr.:— Shebaniah(7).

7646. שָׂבַע saba or

שָׂבֵעַ sabea (959b); a prim. root; *to be sated, satisfied* or *surfeited:*— became satisfied(1), become weary(1), being satisfied(1), continually(1), drink their fill(1), enough(1), fed them to the full(1), filled(9), full(2), get enough(1), glutted(1), had enough(2), have his fill(1), have in plenty(1), have it in excess(1), have abundance(1), have enough(2), have plenty(2), plenty(1), ripe*(1), satiated(2), satisfied(49), satisfies(2), satisfy(10), saturates(1).

7647. שָׂבָע saba (960a); from 7646; *plenty, satiety:*— abundance(4), full stomach(1), plenty(3).

7648. שֹׂבַע soba (959d); from 7646; *satiety, abundance:*— abundance(1), fill(1), full(2), fullness(1), fully satisfied(1), satisfied(1), satisfy(1).

7649. שָׂבֵעַ sabea (960a); from 7646; *sated, satisfied, surfeited:*— full(4), ripe(1), sated(2), satisfied(3).

7650. שָׁבַע shaba (989a); denom. vb. from 7651; *to swear:*— adjure(6), curse(1), exchanged oaths(1), made a covenant(1), made an oath(1), promised on oath(1), promised them by oath(1), put the under oath(1), put them under oath(1), solemn(1), solemnly swear(1), strictly put(1), swear(40), swearer(1), swearing(1), swears(6), swore(62), sworn(41), take an oath(2), take the oath(1), take oath(1), takes(1), took an oath(3), took the oath(1), under oath(3), used(1), vow(1), vowed(6).

7651. שֶׁבַע sheba or

שִׁבְעָה shibah (987d); a prim. card. number; *seven:*— 1,017*(2), 1,247*(2), 1,700*(3), 1,760*(1), 1,775*(2), 127*(3), 14,700*(1), 157,600*(1), 16,750*(1), 17,200*(1), 2,067*(1), 2,700*(1), 2,750*(1), 27,000*(1), 3,700*(1), 307,500*(1), 337,500*(2), 37,000*(1), 43,730*(1), 44,760*(1), 52,700*(1), 57,400*(2), 6,720*(2), 601,730*(1), 603,550*(1), 62,700*(2), 667*(1), 67*(1), 7,000*(8), 7,100*(1), 7,337*(4), 7,500*(1), 7,700*(4), 700*(5), 721*(1), 725*(1), 730*(1), 736*(2), 743*(2), 745*(1), 760*(2), 77*(1), 775*(1), 87,000*(1), forty-seven*(1), seven(270), seven times(6), sevens(2), seventeen*(6), seventeenth*(6), seventh(8), thirty-seven*(4), thirty-seventh*(3), twenty-seven*(1), twenty-seventh*(6).

7652a. שֶׁבַע Sheba (989d); from 7651; two Isr.:— Sheba(9).

7652b. שֶׁבַע Sheba (989d); from 7651; a city in Simeon:— Sheba(1).

שָׁבֻעַ shabua; see 7620.

7653. שִׂבְעָה sibah (960a); the same as 7654, q.v.

7654. שָׂבְעָה sobah (960a); from 7646; *satiety:*— abundant(1), glutted(1), satisfied(2), satisfied*(1), sufficient(1), what does not satisfy(1).

שִׁבְעָה shibah; see 7651.

7655. שִׁבְעָה shibah or

שְׁבַע sheba (1114b); (Ara.) corr. to 7651; *seven:*— seven(7).

7656. שִׁבְעָה Shibah (988b); from 7651; a well in Beersheba:— Shibah(1).

שְׁבֻעָה shebuah; see 7620.

שְׁבִעִי shebii; see 7637.

7657. שִׁבְעִים shibim (988c); from 7651; *seventy* (a card. number):— 1,775*(2), 172*(1), 2,172*(1), 22,273*(1), 273*(1), 372*(2), 470,000*(1), 50,070*(1), 54,400*(1), 675*(1), 675,000*(1), 70(4), 70,000*(4), 72*(1), 72,000*(1), 74*(2), 74,600*(2), 75,000*(1), 76,500*(1), 77*(1), 775*(1), 973*(2), seventy(53), seventy-five(2), seventy-seven(2), seventy-sevenfold(1).

7658. שִׁבְעָנָה shibanah (988d); from 7651; *seven* (a card. number):— seven(1).

7659. שִׁבְעָתַיִם shibathayim (988d); from 7651; *sevenfold, seven times:*— seven times(2), sevenfold(4).

7660. שָׁבַץ shabats (990a); a prim. root; prob. *to weave in checker* (or *plaited*) *work:*— set(2), weave the of checkered(1), work(2).

7661. שָׁבָץ shabats (990b); perh. from 7660; perh. *cramp:*— agony(1).

7662. שְׁבַק shebaq (1114c); (Ara.) corr. to the root of 7733; *to leave, let alone:*— alone(1), leave(4), left(1).

7663a. שָׂבַר sabar (960b); a prim. root; *to inspect, examine:*— inspected(1), inspecting(1).

7663b. שָׂבַר sabar (960b); denom. vb. from 7664; *to wait, hope:*— hope(2), hoped(1), look(1), wait(2).

7664. שֵׂבֶר seber (960b); from 7663a; *a hope:*— hope(2).

7665. שָׁבַר shabar (990c); a prim. root; *to break, break in pieces:*— abolish(1), break(25), break down(1), breaking in pieces(1), breaks(5), breaks in pieces(1), bring to the point(1), broke(9), broke in pieces(6), broke the in pieces(1), broke down(1), broken(55), broken down(1), broken off(1), brokenhearted*(3), collapse(1), crush(2), crushed(2), demolished(1), destroy(2), fractured(1), hurt(2), injured(1), pieces(1), placed(1), point of birth(1), quench(1), shatter(2), shattered(13), smash(3), smashed(2), tore down(1), torn(2).

7666. שָׁבַר shabar (991c); denom. vb. from 7668; *to buy grain:*— bought(1), buy(12), buy grain(2), sell(3), sells(1), sold(2).

7667. שֶׁבֶר sheber or

שֵׁבֶר sheber (991a); from 7665; *a breaking, fracture, crushing, breach, crash:*— 2,172*(1), breaches(1), breakdown(1), broken(2), brokenness(3), collapse(1), crash(1), crashing(1), crushed(1), crushes(1), destruction(17), disaster(2), fracture(3), injury(2), interpretation(1), ruin(3), smashing(1).

7668. שֶׁבֶר sheber (991c); from 7665; *corn, grain:*— grain(9).

7669. שֶׁבֶר Sheber (991b); from 7665; a son of Caleb:— Sheber(1).

7670. שִׁבָּרוֹן shibbaron (991b); from 7665; *a breaking, crushing:*— breaking(1), destruction(1).

7671. שְׁבָרִים Shebarim (991b); pl. of 7667; perh. "quarries," a place near Ai:— Shebarim(1).

7672. שְׁבַשׁ shebash (1114c); (Ara.) a prim. root; *to be perplexed:*— perplexed(1).

7673a. שָׁבַת shabath (991d); a prim. root; *to cease, desist, rest:*— brought to an end(1), cease(21), ceased(7), ceases(3), did away(2), disappear(1), do away(1), eliminate(3), gone(1), hear...more(1), lacking(1), left you without(1), made an end(1), make an end(1), no*(1), observe(1), observe the rest(1), put a stop(3), put an end(3), puts an end(1), remove(2), removed(1), rest(3), rested(3), silence(1), stop(2), stopped(1).

7673b. שָׁבַת shabath (992c); denom. vb. from 7676; *to keep, observe* (sabbath):— have(1), keep(1), kept sabbath(1).

7674. שֶׁבֶת shebeth (992a); from 7673a; perh. *cessation:*— exterminated(1), keeping away(1), loss of time(1).

7675. שֶׁבֶת shebeth (443d); from 3427; *seat, dwelling, place:*— place(2), seat(1), seat*(2), site(1).

7676. שַׁבָּת shabbath (992a); from 7673a; *sabbath:*— every sabbath(2), sabbath(73), sabbaths(32).

7677. שַׁבָּתוֹן shabbathon (992d); from 7673a; *sabbath observance, sabbatism:*— complete rest(4), rest(4), sabbath observance(1), sabbatical(1), solemn rest(1).

7678. שַׁבְּתַי Shabbethay (992d); from 7673a; a Levite:— Shabbethai(3).

7679. שָׂגָא saga (960b); a prim. root; *to grow, grow great:*— exalt(1), makes the great(1).

7680. שְׂגָא sega (1113c); (Ara.) corr. to 7679; *to grow great:*— abound(2), increase(1).

7681. שָׁגֵא Shage or

שָׁגֶה Shageh (993b); from 7686; father of one of David's heroes:— Shagee(1).

7682. שָׂגַב sagab (960c); a prim. root; *to be* (inaccessibly) *high:*— exalted(7), high(4), lifted(1), raises(1), safe(1), securely on high(1), set him securely on high(1), set me securely on high(2), set you securely on high(1), sets the securely(1), unassailable(1).

7683. שָׁגַג shagag (992d); a prim. root; *to go astray, commit sin* or *error:*— because he also(1), goes astray(1), misled(1), sinned(1), went astray(1).

7684. שְׁגָגָה shegagah (993a); from 7683; *sin of error* or *inadvertance:*— error(5), mistake(1), unintentionally(14).

7685. שָׂגָה sagah (960d); a prim. root; *to grow, increase:*— grow(2), increase(1), increased(1).

7686. שָׁגָה shagah (993a); a prim. root; *to go astray, err:*— commits error(1), committed a error(1), erred(2), exhilarated(2), go astray(1), goes astray(1), intoxicated(1), leads the astray(1), misleader(1), misleads(1), reel(3), stray(1), unwittingly(1), wander(3), wandered(1).

7687. שְׂגוּב Segub (960d); from 7682; "exalted," two Isr.:— Segub(3).

7688. שָׁגַח shagach (993b); a prim. root; *to gaze:*— gaze(1), looking(1), looks(1).

7689. שַׂגִּיא saggi (960c); from 7679; *great:*— exalted(2).

7690. שַׂגִּיא saggi (1113c); (Ara.) corr. to 7689; *great, much:*— abundant(2), deeply(1), great(3), greatly(2), many(2), much(1), very(2).

7691. שְׁגִיאָה shegiah (993b); from 7686; *error:*— errors(1).

7692. שִׁגָּיוֹן Shiggayon or

שִׁגְיֹנָה Shiggayonah (993c); perh. from 7686; perh. a wild passionate song with rapid changes of rhythm:— Shigionoth(1).

7693. שָׁגַל shagel (993c); a prim. root; *to violate, ravish:*— ravished(2), violate(1), violated(1).

7694. שֵׁגָל shegal (993c); from 7693; (queen) *consort:*— queen(2).

7695. שֵׁגָל shegal (1114c); (Ara.) corr. to 7694; (royal) *consort:*— wives(3).

7696. שָׁגַע shaga (993c); a prim. root; *to be mad:*— act the madman(1), behaving as a madman(1), demented(1), driven mad(1), mad fellow(1), madman(1), madmen(1).

7697. שִׁגָּעוֹן shiggaon (993d); from 7696; *madness:*— furiously(1), madness(2).

7698. שֶׁגֶר sheger (993d); from an unused word; *offspring, young* (of beasts):— increase(4).

7699a. שַׁד shad (994c); from an unused word; (female) *breast:*— breast(2), breasts(18), nursing infants*(1).

7699b. שֹׁד shod (994d); from the same as 7699a; (female) *breast:*— breast(2), breasts(1).

7700. שֵׁד shed (993d); of for. or.; prob. *demon:*— demons(2).

7701. שֹׁד shod or

שׁוֹד shod (994c); from 7703; *violence, havoc, devastation, ruin:*— destroyed(1), destruction(12), devastation(7), violence(5).

7702. שָׂדַד sadad (961a); a prim. root; *to harrow:*— harrow(3).

7703. שָׁדַד shadad (994a); a prim. root; *to deal violently with, despoil, devastate, ruin:*— assaults(1), completely destroyed(1), dead(1), desolate(1), despoil(1), destroy(7), destroyed(12), destroyer(9), destroyer still destroys(1), destroyers(4), destroying(2), devastate(2), devastated(6), lays waste(1), robbers(1), ruined(6).

7704. שָׂדֶה sadeh (961b); from the same as 7706a; *field, land:*— agricultural(1), battlefield*(1), country(14), countryside(1), countryside*(1), field(235), fields(32), ground(3), ground*(1), land(16), lands(1), mainland(2), soil(2), territory(2), wild(7).

7705. שִׁדָּה shiddah (994d); from the same as 7699a; perh. *a mistress:*— many concubines(1).

7706a. שָׂדַי saday (961a); from an unused word; *field, land:*— country(1), field(12).

7706b. שַׁדַּי Shadday (994d); of unc. der.; perh. "the almighty," a title for God:— Almighty(48).

7707. שְׁדֵיאוּר Shedeur (994d); from the same as 7699a; a Reubenite:— Shedeur(5).

7708. שִׂדִּים Siddim (961a); from 7702; a valley near the Dead Sea:— Siddim(3).

7709. שְׁדֵמָה shedemah (995a); of unc. der.; *a field:*— fields(5).

7710. שָׁדַף shadaph (995b); a prim. root; *to scorch, blight:*— scorched(3).

7711a. שְׁדֵפָה shedephah (995b); from 7710; *blighted* or *blasted thing:*— scorched(2).

7711b. שִׁדָּפוֹן shiddaphon (995b); from 7710; *blight* (of crops):— blasting wind(1), blight(3), scorching(1).

7712. שְׁדַר shedar (1114c); (Ara.) a prim. root; *to struggle, strive:*— exerting(1).

7713. שְׂדֵרָה sederah (690b); from the same as 5468; *row, rank* (of soldiers):— planks(1), ranks(3).

7714. שַׁדְרַךְ Shadrak (995b); prob. of for. or.; Bab. name of one of Daniel's companions:— Shadrach(1).

7715. שַׁדְרַךְ Shadrak (1114c); (Ara.) corr. to 7714; Bab. name of one of Daniel's companions:— Shadrach(14).

7716. **שֶׂה** **seh** (961d); of unc. der.; *one of a flock, a sheep* (or *goat*):— flock(1), lamb(15), lambs(1), sheep(22), sheep and another(2), sheep and one(1), sheep*(1).

7717. **שָׂהֵד** **sahed** (962a); of for. or.; *a witness:*— advocate(1).

7718. **שֹׁהַם** **shoham** (995d); of unc. der.; (a gem) perh. *an onyx:*— onyx(11).

7719. **שֹׁהַם** **Shoham** (996a); from the same as 7718; a Levite:— Shoham(1).

7720. **שַׂהֲרֹן** **saharon** (962a); from an unused word; *moon, crescent:*— crescent ornaments(3).

7721. **שׂוֹא** **so** (669d); the same as 5375, q.v.

7722. **שׁוֹא** **sho** (996b); from an unused word; perh. *a ravage:*— ravages(1).

7723. **שָׁוְא** **shav** (996a); from an unused word; *emptiness, vanity:*— deceit(2), deceitful(1), deception(1), emptiness(2), empty(1), false(9), false visions(4), falsehood(7), lies(1), vain(18), vanity(3), worthless(4).

7724a. **שְׁוָא** **Sheva** (996a); of unc. der.; two Isr.:— Sheva(2).

7724b. **שׁוֹאָה** **shoah** or **שֹׁאָה** **shoah** (996b); from an unused word; *devastation, ruin, waste:*— destroy(1), destruction(4), devastation(1), onslaught(1), storm(1), tempest(1), waste(2).

7725. **שׁוּב** **shub** (996d); a prim. root; *to turn back, return:*— again(53), answer(4), answer*(5), answered(5), averted(1), back(7), back again(2), bring(1), bring her back(1), bring him back(2), bring it back(1), bring me back(2), bring the back(1), bring them again(1), bring them back(14), bring you back(5), bring back(14), bring presents(1), bring...back(4), bringing(1), bringing the back(1), brought(2), brought him again(2), brought him back(3), brought it back(3), brought me back(4), brought the again(1), brought them back(2), brought us back(1), brought again(1), brought back(17), brought...back(1), call(1), came again(1), came back(1), cause(1), certainly bring(1), certainly bring them back(1), come back(10), converted(1), deluded(1), desist(2), draw and turning(1), draw it back(1), drawn(1), drew back(1), drives(1), ever go back(1), fro(1), forth(1), gave...return(1), get(1), get it back(1), give(2), give a answer(1), give it back(1), give them back(1), give back(2), gives(2), go(1), go on back(1), go back(10), go*(1), going back(1), gone back(1), indeed(1), indeed bring(1), indeed bring me back(1), indeed return(2), indeed turn away(1), keeps(2), make them return(1), make restitution(1), paid(2), pass your again(1), pass away(1), pay(1), pays us back in full(2), punishing(1), put(3), put his back(1), put the back(1), put back(1), rebuilt*(2), recall(2), recalls*(1), receded(1), recompense(1), recompense*(1), recompensed(4), recovered(4), refreshes(1), refund(3), refuse(4), refute(1), regain(1), remade*(1), render(8), repaid(1), repay(5), repeatedly(2), repeats(1), repel(1), repent(6), repent and turn away(2), repentant(1), repented(1), replace(1), reply(6), reply*(1), reported(1), reported*(1), repulse*(2), rescue(1), respond(1), restitution may be made(1), restitution which is made(1), restore(58), restored(17), restorer(2), restores(7), restoring(1), restrain(2), restrained(2), retire(1), retreat(1), return(261), return and take back(1), return*(1), returned(151), returned*(1), returning(2), returns(9), reverse(1), revived(1), revoke(10), revoked(1), sent back(1), set(1), spent(1), still(3), subsides(2), surely return(4), take(4), take it back(1), take me back(1), take my back(2), take your back(1), take back(2), there(1), took back(2), turn(49), turn and and withdraw(1), turn her away(1), turn his away(1), turn it back(1), turn me into again(1), turn them back(1), turn to you again(1), turn you about(1), turn you around(1), turn you back(2), turn your away(1), turn again(1), turn aside(1), turn away(24), turn away and not repent(1), turn back(20), turn...back(1), turned(16), turned them back(1), turned around(1), turned away(9), turned back(16), turned...back(1), turning(2), turning away(1), turns(7), turns again(1), turns away(5), unleash(1), went back(5), went*(1), withdraw(4), withdrew(1).

שׁוּבָאֵל **Shubael**; see 7619.

7726. **שׁוֹבָב** **shobab** (1000a); from 7725; *turning back, recusant, apostate:*— faithless(2), turning away(1).

7727. **שׁוֹבָב** **Shobab** (1000a); from 7725; two Isr.:— Shobab(4).

7728. **שׁוֹבֵב** **shobeb** (1000a); from 7725; *turning back, apostate:*— apostate(1), backsliding(1), faithless(1).

7729. **שׁוּבָה** **shubah** (1000a); from 7725; *retirement, withdrawal:*— repentance(1).

7730. **שׂוֹבֶךְ** **sobek** (959a); from an unused word; *a network* (of boughs):— thick branches(1).

7731. **שׁוֹבָךְ** **Shobak** (1000c); of unc. der.; an Aramean (Syrian) general, the same as 7780:— Shobach(2).

7732. **שׁוֹבָל** **Shobal** (987c); from the same as 7640; "flowing," an Edomite, also two Isr.:— Shobal(9).

7733. **שׁוֹבֵק** **Shobeq** (990b); from an unused word; one who signed Nehemiah's covenant:— Shobek(1).

7734. **שׂוּג** **sug** (690d); the same as 5472, q.v.

7735. **שׂוּג** **sug** (691b); the same as 5473, q.v.

7736. **שׁוּד** **shud** (994a); see 7703.

שׁוֹד **shod**; see 7699b, 7701.

7737a. **שָׁוָה** **shavah** (1000d); a prim. root; *to agree with, be like, resemble:*— alike(1), commensurate(1), compare(1), compares(1), composed(2), equal(1), interest(1), level(1), like(1), liken(1), make me equal(1), placed(1), proper(1), satisfy(1).

7737b. **שָׁוָה** **shavah** (1001b); a prim. root; *to set, place:*— given(1), makes(2), place(1), produces(1), set(1).

7738. **שָׁוָה** **shavah** (996c); see 8663.

7739a. **שְׁוָה** **shevah** (1114d); (Ara.) corr. to 7737a; *to become like:*— like*(1), made(1).

7739b. **שְׁוָה** **shevah** (1114d); (Ara.) corr. to 7737b; *to be set* or *made:*— reduced(1).

7740. **שָׁוֵה** **Shaveh** (1001a); from 7737a; a valley near Salem:— Shaveh(1).

7741. **שָׁוֵה קִרְיָתַיִם** **Shaveh Qiryathayim** (1001a); from 7737a and 7151; a plain E. of the Jordan:— Shaveh-kiriathaim(1).

7742. **שׂוּחַ** **suach** (962b); of unc. der.; perh. *to muse:*— meditate(1).

7743. **שׁוּחַ** **shuach** (1001b); a prim. root; *to sink down:*— bowed down(1), sinks down(1), sunk down(1).

7744. **שׁוּחַ** **Shuach** (1001d); from 7743; a son of Abraham and Keturah.

7745. **שׁוּחָה** **shuchah** (1001c); from 7743; *a pit:*— pit(4), pits(1).

7746. **שׁוּחָה** **Shuchah** (1001d); from 7743; a desc. of Judah:— Shuhah(1).

7747. **שׁוּחִי** **Shuchi** (1001d); from 7744; desc. of Shuah:— Shuhite(5).

7748. **שׁוּחָם** **Shucham** (1001d); from 7743; a Danite:— Shuham(1).

7749. **שׁוּחָמִי** **Shuchami** (1001d); from 7748; desc. of Shuham:— Shuhamites(2).

7750. **שׂוּט** **sut** (962b); a prim. root; *to swerve, fall away:*— lapse(1).

7751a. **שׁוּט** **shut** (1001d); a prim. root; *to go* or *rove about:*— go to and fro(1), go about(2), go back(1), go back and forth(1), gone about(1), move to and fro(1), range to and fro(1), roam to and fro(1), roaming about(2), rush back(1), rush back and forth(1).

7751b. **שׁוּט** **shut** (1002b); denom. vb. from 7885; *to row:*— rowers(2).

7751c. **שׁוּט** **shut** (1002b); a prim. root; *to treat with despite:*— despise(1), scorn(1), scorned(1).

7752. **שׁוֹט** **shot** (1002a); from 7751a; *a scourge, whip:*— scourge(5), whip(2), whips(4).

7753. **שׂוּךְ** **suk** (962b); a prim. root; *to hedge* or *fence up* or *about:*— hedge(1), made a hedge(1).

7754a. שׂוֹךְ sok (962c); from an unused word; *branch, brushwood:*— branch(2).

7754b. שׂוֹכָה sokah (962c); from the same as 7754a; *branch, brushwood.*

7755. שׂוֹכֹה Sokoh or

שׂוֹכוֹ Soko (962c); from the same as 7754a; two places in Judah:— Soco(3), Socoh(5).

7756. שׂוּכָתִים Sukathim (962c); from the same as 7754a; a family of scribes:— Sucathites(1).

7757. שׁוּל shul (1002c); from an unused word; *skirt* (of a robe):— hem(4), hem of the robe(2), skirts(4), train of his robe(1).

7758. שׁוֹלָל sholal (1021d); from 7997a; *barefoot:*— barefoot(3).

7759. שׁוּלַמִּית Shulammith (1002c); of unc. der.; heroine of the Song of Solomon:— Shulammite(2).

7760. שׂוּם sum or

שִׂים sim (962c); a prim. root; *to put, place, set:*— appoint(9), appointed(9), assign(1), assigned(2), attached(1), bestowed(1), bring(1), brought(1), care*(2), changes(2), charge*(1), charged(1), charges(2), consider(4), consider*(6), considered*(2), determine*(1), determined(1), disguises*(1), establish(3), established(5), establishes(1), establishment(1), expected*(1), fasten(1), fix(1), formed and made(1), gave(2), give(7), grant(1), had(1), hunt*(1), impose(1), impress(1), impute(1), inflicted(1), insert(4), invoke(1), keeps(1), laid(19), lay(10), lay down(1), lays(1), leave(1), loaded(1), look*(2), made(45), make(67), makes(9), mark(3), named*(2), ordained(1), orders(1), paid(2), painted*(1), pay(1), pay attention(2), performed(3), place(15), placed(21), plant(1), prepare(1), preserve(1), put(123), puts(6), putting(2), really set(1), recite*(1), regard*(1), render(1), repaid(1), required(1), seized(1), seized*(2), serve(1), served(1), set(108), sets(3), shave*(1), shed(1), show(1), station(1), stationed(3), steadily(1), substitute(2), surely set(1), take(5), taken(1), takes(1), taking(1), throw(1), told*(1), took(3), transformed(1), treat(1), turn(1), turned(2), unobserved*(1), work(1), wrought(1).

7761. שׂוּם sum or

שִׂים sim (1113d); (Ara.) corr. to 7760; *to set, make:*— appointed(1), disregarded*(1), gave(1), issue(3), issued(11), laid(2), made(2), make(2), pays...attention(1), set(1).

7762a. שׁוּם shum (1002c); of unc. der.; *garlic:*— garlic(1).

7762b. שׂוּמָה sumah (965a); another reading for 7760, q.v.

7763. שׁוֹמֵר Shomer or

שֹׁמֵר Shomer (1037c); from 8104; two Isr.:— Shomer(2).

7764. שׁוּנִי Shuni (1002c); of unc. der.; a Gadite:— Shuni(2).

7765. שׁוּנִי Shuni (1002d); from 7764; desc. of Shuni:— Shunites(1).

7766. שׁוּנֵם Shunem (1002d); prob. from the same as 7764; a city in Issachar:— Shunem(3).

7767. שׁוּנַמִּית Shunammith (1002d); from 7766; female inhab. of Shunem:— Shunammite(8).

7768. שׁוַע shava (1002d); a prim. root; *to cry out* (for help):— call for help(2), cried(3), cried for help(3), cried to him for help(1), cried to you for help(1), cries for help(1), cry(5), cry for help(3), cry out for help(1), cry to you for help(1), help(3), shout for help(1).

7769. שׁוּעַ shua (1002d); from 7768; *a cry for help:*— cry out for help(1).

7770a. שׁוּעַ Shua (447c); from 3467; father of Judah's wife:— Shua(1), Shua's(1).

7770b. שׁוּעַ shua (447d); from 3467; perh. *opulence:*— riches(1).

7771a. שׁוֹעַ shoa (447c); from 3467; *independent, noble* (in station):— generous(1), rich(1).

7771b. שׁוֹעַ shoa (1003a); from 7768; *a cry:*— crying(1).

7772. שׁוֹעַ Shoa (1003a); from 7768; prob. nomads E. of the Tigris and in the Syrian desert:— Shoa(1).

7773. שֶׁוַע sheva (1002d); the same as 7769, q.v.:— help(1).

7774. שׁוּעָא Shua (447d); from 3467; "wealth," an Asherite woman:— Shua(1), Shuah(2).

7775. שַׁוְעָה shavah (1003a); from 7768; *a cry for help:*— cry(6), cry for help(5).

7776. שׁוּעָל shual (1043c); from an unused word; *fox,* perh. *jackal:*— fox(1), foxes(6).

7777a. שׁוּעָל Shual (1043c); from the same as 7776; "fox," a district in Isr.:— Shual(1).

7777b. שׁוּעָל Shual (1043c); from the same as 7776; "fox," an Asherite:— Shual(1).

7778. שׁוֹעֵר shoer or

שֹׁעֵר shoer (1045b); from the same as 8179; *a gatekeeper:*— gatekeeper(2), gatekeepers(33), gatekeepers*(1), keeper(1).

7779. שׁוּף shuph (1003a); a prim. root; *to bruise:*— bruise(2), bruises(1), overwhelm(1).

7780. שׁוֹפָךְ Shophak (1000c); from 8210; an Aramean (Syrian) general, the same as 7731:— Shophach(2).

7781. שׁוּפָמִי Shuphami (1051b); from 8197a; desc. of Shephupham:— Shuphamites(1).

7782. שׁוֹפָר shophar or

שֹׁפָר shophar (1051c); from 8231b; *a horn* (for blowing):— horn(4), horns(1), ram's horn(1), trumpet(46), trumpeter*(1), trumpets(19).

7783. שׁוּק shuq (1003b); a prim. root; prob. *to be abundant:*— overflow(3).

7784. שׁוּק shuq (1003b); from the same as 7785; *a street:*— street(3), streets(1).

7785. שׁוֹק shoq (1003b); from an unused word; *a leg:*— leg(2), legs(4), ruthlessly*(1), thigh(12).

7786. שׂוּר sur or

סוּר sur (693b); the same as 5493, q.v.

7787. שׂוּר sur (965a); a prim. root; *to saw:*— cut(1).

7788. שׁוּר shur (1003c); a prim. root; perh. *to travel, journey:*— carriers(1), journey down(1), journeyed(1).

7789. שׁוּר shur (1003d); a prim. root; *to behold, regard:*— behold(5), beholds(1), lie in wait(1), look(2), notices(1), regard(1), regards(1), see(1), watch(1).

7790. שׁוּר shur (1004a); from 7789; perh. *enemy:*— foes(1).

7791. שׁוּר shur (1004b); from the same as 7794; *a wall:*— wall(3), walls(1).

7792. שׁוּר shur (1114d); (Ara.) corr. to 7791; *a wall:*— walls(3).

7793. שׁוּר Shur (1004b); from the same as 7794; a desert region S.W. of Pal. on E. border of Eg.:— Shur(6).

7794. שׁוֹר shor (1004a); from an unused word; *a head of cattle* (bullock, ox, etc.):— bull(1), bulls(1), cattle(1), herd(1), ox(65), oxen(8).

7795a. שׂוֹרָה sorah (965a); perh. from 7787; perh. *a row:*— rows(1).

7795b. שׁוּרָה shurah (1004c); from the same as 7794; prob. *row* (of olive trees or vines):— vine rows(1).

שׂוֹרֵק soreq; see 8321a.

7796a. שׂוֹרֵק Soreq or

שֹׂרֵק Soreq (977d); from the same as 8320; "choice vines," a valley where Delilah lived:— Sorek(1).

7796b. שׁוֹרֵר shorer (1004a); from 7789; (treacherous) *watcher:*— foes(5).

7797. שׂוּשׂ sus or

שִׂישׂ sis (965a); a prim. root; *to exult, rejoice:*— delight(1), delighted(1), exult(3), glad(5), rejoice(9), rejoice greatly(1), rejoiced(2), rejoices(3).

7798. שַׁוְשָׁא Shavsha (1004c); of unc. der.; an Isr., perh. the same as 8304:— Shavsha(1).

7799. שׁוּשַׁן shushan or

שׁוֹשָׁן shoshan or

שׁוֹשַׁנָּה shoshannah (1004c); of unc. der.; prob. *lily* (or any lily-like flower):— lilies(6), lily(7).

7800. שׁוּשַׁן Shushan (1004d); from the same as 7799; residence of Pers. kings:— Susa(21).

7801. שׁוּשַׁנְכָיֵא Shushankaye (1114d); (Ara.) of for. or.; inhab. of Susa:— men of Susa(1).

7802. שׁוּשַׁן עֵדוּת Shushan Eduth or

שׁוֹשַׁנִּים עֵדוּת Shoshannim Eduth (1004c); from 7799 and 5715; perh. "lily of testimony," a song title.

שׁוּשַׁק Shushaq; see 7895.

7803. שׁוּתֶלַח Shuthelach (1004d); of unc. der.; an Ephraimite name:— Shuthelah(4).

7804. שְׁזַב shezab or

שֵׁיזִב shezib (1115a); (Ara.) corr. to 5800a; *to deliver:*— deliver(5), delivered(2), delivering(1), delivers(1).

7805. שָׁזַף shazaph (1004d); a prim. root; *to catch sight of, look on:*— burned(1), caught sight(1), saw(1).

7806. שָׁזַר shazar (1004d); a prim. root; *to be twisted:*— twisted(21).

7807. שַׁח shach (1006a); from 7817; *low, lowly:*— humble person*(1).

7808. שֵׂחַ seach (967b); from the same as 7879; *a thought:*— thoughts(1).

7809. שָׁחַד shachad (1005a); a prim. root; *to give a present, bribe:*— bribe(1), offer a bribe(1).

7810. שֹׁחַד shochad (1005a); from 7809; *a present, bribe:*— bribe(15), bribes(3), corrupt(1), gifts(1), present(2), reward(1).

7811. שָׂחָה sachah (965c); a prim. root; *to swim:*— swim(2), swimmer(1).

7812. שָׁחָה shachah (1005b); a prim. root; *to bow down:*— bow(5), bow ourselves down(1), bow yourselves down(1), bow down(21), bowed(16), bowed in worship(1), bowed themselves down(2), bowed down(14), bowing(1), bowing down(1), bows down(1), did homage(1), down in homage(1), homage(1), lie down(1), paid homage(3), prostrate(2), prostrated(13), prostrating(1), weighs it down(1), worship(47), worshiped(31), worshiping(3), worships(2).

7813. שָׂחוּ sachu (965c); from 7811; *swimming:*— swim(1).

7814. שְׂחוֹק sechoq or

שְׂחֹק sechoq (966a); from 7832; *laughter, derision, sport:*— enjoyment(1), joke(2), laughingstock(5), laughter(6), sport(1).

7815. שְׁחוֹר shechor (1007a); from 7835; *blackness:*— soot(1).

שִׁחוֹר Shichor; see 7883.

שָׁחוֹר shachor; see 7838.

7816. שְׁחוּת shechuth (1005c); from 7812; *a pit:*— pit(1).

7817. שָׁחַח shachach (1005d); a prim. root; *to bow, be bowed down, crouch:*— been humbled(1), bow down(1), bowed down(3), bowing(1), bows down(1), bring down(1), brought low(1), collapsed(1), crouch(2), despair(4), humbled(3), prostrate(1), sing softly(1).

7818. שָׂחַט sachat (965c); a prim. root; *to squeeze out:*— squeezed(1).

7819. שָׁחַט shachat (1006a); a prim. root; *to slaughter, beat:*— beaten(5), deadly(1), kill(2), killed(1), kills(1), offer(1), slain(5), slaughter(17), slaughtered(28), slaughtering(1), slaughters(2), slay(16), slew(5).

7820. שָׁחַט shachat (1006a); the same as 7819, q.v.

7821a. שַׁחֲטָה shachatah (1006b); from 7819; perh. *slaughtering:*— depravity(1).

7821b. שְׁחִיטָה shechitah (1006b); from 7819; (act of) *slaying:*— slaughter(1).

7822. שְׁחִין shechin (1006c); from an unused word; *a boil, eruption:*— boil(6), boils(7).

7823. שָׁחִיס shachis or

סָחִישׁ sachish (695a); the same as 5501b, q.v.

7824. שָׂחִיף sachiph (965d); of unc. der.; perh. *paneled:*— paneled(1).

7825. שְׁחִית shechith (1005d); from 7812; *a pit:*— destructions(1), pits(1).

7826. שַׁחַל shachal (1006c); from an unused word; *a lion:*— lion(7).

7827. שְׁחֵלֶת shecheleth (1006c); from the same as 7826; (an ingredient of the holy incense) perh. *onycha:*— onycha(1).

7828. שַׁחַף shachaph (1006d); from an unused word; *a sea mew, gull:*— sea gull(2).

7829. שַׁחֶפֶת shachepheth (1006d); from the same as 7828; (a wasting disease) *consumption:*— consumption(2).

7830. שַׁחַץ shachats (1006d); from an unused word; *dignity, pride:*— pride(1), proud(1).

7831. שַׁחֲצוֹם Shachatsom (1006d); from the same as 7830; a city in Issachar:— Shahazumah(1).

7832. שָׂחַק sachaq (965d); a prim. root; *to laugh:*— amuse(1), amusing(1), celebrate(2), celebrating(3), hold a contest(1), joking(1), laugh(6), laughed them to scorn(1), laughs(6), merrymakers(2), mock(1), mocked(1), play(2), played(1), playing(1), rejoicing(2), scorns(1), smiled(1), smiles(1), sport(1).

7833. שָׁחַק shachaq (1006d); a prim. root; *to rub away, beat fine, pulverize:*— beat(1), beat them fine(1), pulverized(1), wears away(1).

7834. שַׁחַק shachaq (1007a); from 7833; *dust, cloud:*— clouds(6), skies(12), sky(2), speck of dust(1).

שְׂחֹק sechoq; see 7814.

7835. שָׁחַר shachar (1007a); a prim. root; *to be black:*— turns black(1).

7836. שָׁחַר shachar (1007c); denom. vb. from 7837; *to look early* or *diligently for:*— diligently(1), diligently seek(1), diligently seeks(1), earnestly seek(1), searched diligently(1), seek(2), seek me diligently(1), seek you earnestly(1), seek your earnestly(1), seeking(1), seeks you diligently(1).

7837. שַׁחַר shachar (1007b); from an unused word; *dawn:*— charm away(1), dawn(16), dawn*(1), dawning of the day(1), daybreak(2), morning(2).

שִׁחֹר Shichor; see 7883.

7838. שָׁחֹר shachor (1007b); from 7835; *black:*— black(6).

7839. שַׁחֲרוּת shacharuth (1007b); from 7835; *blackness:*— prime of life(1).

7840. שְׁחַרְחֹרֶת shecharchoreth (1007b); from 7835; *blackish:*— swarthy(1).

7841. שְׁחַרְיָה Shecharyah (1007d); from 7836 and 3050; "Yah has sought," a Benjamite:— Shehariah(1).

7842. שַׁחֲרַיִם Shacharayim (1007d); from 7837; "two dawns," a Benjamite:— Shaharaim(1).

7843. שָׁחַת shachath (1007d); a prim. root; perh. *to go to ruin:*— act corruptly(4), act...corruptly(1), acted corruptly(3), acted...corruptly(1), acting corruptly(1), blemished animal(1), corrupt(8), corrupted(4), depravity(1), destroy(69), destroyed(14), destroyer(4), destroyers(1), destroying(7), destroys(5), destruction(2), devastate(1), felled(2), go to ruin(1), harm(2), jeopardize(1), laid waste(1), polluted(1), raiders(2), ravage(1), ravaged(1), ruin(1), ruined(4), set(1), spoiled(1), stifled(1), waste(1), wasted(1), wreaking destruction(1).

7844. שְׁחַת shechath (1115a); (Ara.) corr. to 7843; *to corrupt:*— corrupt(1), corruption(2).

7845. שַׁחַת shachath (1001c); from 7743; *a pit:*— destruction(1), dungeon(1), hole(1), pit(18), undergo decay(2).

7846. שֵׂט set or

סֵט set (962b); from 7750; *swerver,* perh. *revolter, deeds that swerve:*— revolters(1), those who fall away(1).

7847. שָׂטָה satah (966a); a prim. root; *to turn aside:*— goes astray(2), gone astray(2), turn aside(1), turn away(1).

7848. שִׁטָּה shittah (1008d); of unc. der.; *acacia* (a tree and a wood):— acacia(28).

7849. שָׁטַח shatach (1008d); a prim. root; *to spread, spread abroad:*— enlarges(1), scattered(1), spread(3).

7850. שֹׁטֵט shotet (1002b); from 7751a; *a scourge:*— whip(1).

7851. שִׁטִּים Shittim (1008d); from the same as 7848; a place E. of the Jordan, also a wadi perh. W. of Jer.:— Shittim(5).

7852. שָׂטַם satam (966b); a prim. root; *to bear a grudge* or *cherish animosity against:*— bear a grudge against(1), bears a grudge against(1), bore a grudge against(1), grudge against(3), harassed(1), hunted me down(1), persecute(1).

7853. שָׂטַן satan (966c); denom. vb. from 7854; *to be* or *act as adversary:*— accuse(1), accusers(2), act as my accusers(1), adversaries(1), oppose(1).

7854. שָׂטָן satan (966b); of unc. der.; *adversary,* also the name of the superhuman adversary of God:— accuser(1), adversary(8), Satan(18).

7855. שִׂטְנָה sitnah (966c); from the same as 7854; *accusation:*— accusation(1).

7856. שִׂטְנָה Sitnah (966c); from the same as 7854; "hostility," the name of a well near Gerar:— Sitnah(1).

7857. שָׁטַף shataph (1009a); a prim. root; *to overflow, rinse* or *wash off:*— charging(1), engulfed(1), flooded away(1), flooding(2), flowed(1), overflow(9), overflowing(6), overflows(1), overwhelming(2), rinsed(3), torrential(1), wash away(1), washed(1), washed off(1).

7858. שֶׁטֶף sheteph (1009b); from 7857; *a flood:*— flood(5), outburst(1), overflowing(1).

7859. שְׁטַר setar (1113d); (Ara.) of unc. der.; *a side:*— side(1).

7860. שֹׁטֵר shoter (1009c); from an unused word; *official, officer:*— foremen(5), officer(1), officers(17), official(1), officials(1).

7861. שִׁטְרַי Shitray (1009c); from the same as 7860; an official of David:— Shitrai(1).

7862. שַׁי shay (1009c); of unc. der.; *a gift* (offered as homage):— gift of homage(1), gifts(2).

7863. שִׂיא si (673b); from 5375; *loftiness:*— loftiness(1).

7864. שְׁיָא Sheya (996a); see 7724a.

7865. שִׂיאֹן Sion (673b); from 5375; another name for Mount Hermon:— Sion(1).

7866. שִׁיאֹן Shion (1009d); of unc. der.; a place in Issachar:— Shion(1).

7867. שִׂיב sib (966c); a prim. root; *to be hoary:*— gray(1), gray-haired(1).

7868. שִׂיב sib (1114a); (Ara.) corr. to 7867; *to be hoary:*— elders(5).

7869. שֵׂיב seb (966c); from 7867; (hoary) *age:*— age(1).

7870. שִׁיבָה shibah (1000a); another reading for 7622, q.v.

7871. שִׁיבָה shibah (444a); from 3427; *a sojourn:*— stayed(1).

7872. שֵׂיבָה sebah (966c); from 7867; *hoary head, old age:*— gray(1), gray hair(7), gray hairs(1), gray head(1), gray-haired(1), grayheaded(1), graying years(1), old age(6).

7873. שִׂיג sig (691a); the same as 5509, q.v.

7874. שִׂיד sid or

שׂוּד sud (966d); denom. vb. from 7875; *to whitewash:*— coat(2).

7875. שִׂיד sid (966d); from an unused word; *lime, whitewash:*— lime(4).

7876. שָׁיָה shayah (1009d); of unc. der.; *to forget:*— neglected(1).

7877. שִׁיזָא Shiza (1009d); of unc. der.; a Reubenite:— Shiza(1).

7878. שִׂיחַ siach (967a); denom. vb. from 7879; *to muse, complain, talk* (of):— complain(2), considered(1), meditate(7), meditates(1), muse(2), sigh(1), sing(1), speak(3), talk(2).

7879. שִׂיחַ **siach** (967a); from an unused word; *complaint, musing:—* complaining(1), complaint(8), concern(1), meditation(1), occupied(1), talk(1).

7880. שִׂיחַ **siach** (967b); from an unused word; *a bush, shrub, plant:—* bushes(3), shrub(1).

7881. שִׂיחָה **sichah** (967a); from an unused word; *complaint, musing:—* meditation(3).

7882. שִׁיחָה **shichah** (1001c); from 7743; *a pit:—* pit(1), pits(1).

7883. שִׁיחוֹר **Shichor** (1009d); of unc. der.; a stream on the border of Eg.:— Nile(2), Shihor(2).

7884. שִׁיחוֹר לִבְנָת **Shichor Libnath** (1009d); from the same as 7883 and from 3835a; a stream in Asher:— Shihor-libnath(1).

7885. שַׁיִט **shayit** (1002b); from 7751a; *a rowing:—* oars(1).

7886. שִׁילֹה **Shiloh** (1010a); of unc. der.; perh. "he whose it is," a Messianic title:— Shiloh(1).

7887. שִׁילֹה **Shiloh** or
שִׁלֹה **Shiloh** or
שִׁילוֹ **Shilo** or
שִׁלוֹ **Shilo** (1017d); from 7953; a city in Ephraim:— Shiloh(32).

7888. שִׁילוֹנִי **Shiloni** or
שִׁלֹנִי **Shiloni** or
שִׁלֹנִי **Shiloni** (1018a); from 7887; inhab. of Shiloh:— Shilonite(6), Shilonites(1).

שִׁילָל **shelal**; see 7758.

7889. שִׁימוֹן **Shimon** (1010a); of unc. der.; a man of Judah:— Shimon(1).

7890. שַׁיִן **shayin** or
שֵׁין **shen** (1010b); from an unused word; *urine:—* urine(2).

7891. שִׁיר **shir** (1010c); denom. vb. from 7892a; *to sing:—* sang(6), sing(32), singer(1), singers(34), singing(3), sings(1), song leaders(1), sung(2).

7892a. שִׁיר **shir** (1010b); of unc. der.; *song:—* music(3), musical(3), sing(1), singers(1), singing(2), Song(1), song(20), Songs(1), songs(14), songs*(1).

7892b. שִׁירָה **shirah** (1010c); from the same as 7892a; *song:—* song(1), song(10), songs(1).

שִׁישׁ **sis**; see 7797.

7893. שַׁיִשׁ **shayish** (1010d); perh. of for. or.; *alabaster:—* alabaster(1).

7894. שִׁישָׁא **Shisha** (1010d); from the same as 7893; father of Solomon's scribes:— Shisha(1).

7895. שִׁישַׁק **Shishaq** (1011a); of for. or.; an Eg. king:— Shishak(7).

7896. שִׁית **shith** (1011a); a prim. root; *to put, set:—* account(1), apply(1), appoint(1), appointed(1), bring(1), cast(1), close*(1), concern*(1), concerned*(1), consider*(1), demand(1), demanded(2), direct(1), fix(1), fixed positions(1), join(1), laid(5), lay(3), lays(1), made(5), make(11), make them turn(1), pay(2), perform(1), place(1), placed(1), put(9), reflected*(1), serve(1), set(17), sets(1), stop(1), take(2), took up fixed positions(1), turns(1), withdraw(1).

7897. שִׁית **shith** (1011c); from 7896; *a garment:—* dressed(1), garment(1).

7898. שַׁיִת **shayith** (1011d); perh. from 7896; *thornbushes:—* thorns(7).

7899. שֵׂךְ **sek** (968a); from an unused word; *a thorn:—* pricks(1).

7900. שֹׂךְ **sok** (968a); from 7917c; *booth, pavilion:—* tabernacle(1).

7901. שָׁכַב **shakab** (1011d); a prim. root; *to lie down:—* actually lies(1), has(1), laid(6), laid low(1), lain(3), lain down(2), lay(22), lay down(15), lie(26), lie down(31), lie still(1), lies(25), lies down(10), lodged(1), lying(7), lying down(4), make your bed(1), recline(1), rest(4), rested*(1), sleep(4), sleeps(1), slept(37), take...rest(1), taking(1), tip(1).

7902. שְׁכָבָה **shekabah** (1012c); from 7901; (act of) *lying, a layer:—* carnally*(1), emission(5), intercourse*(1), layer(2), seminal*(1).

7903. שְׁכֹבֶת **shekobeth** (1012d); from 7901; *copulation:—* intercourse(2), intercourse*(1), lies*(1).

7904. שָׁכָה **shakah** (1013a); a prim. root; perh. *to roam:—* lusty(1).

7905. שֻׂכָּה **sukkah** (968a); from the same as 7899; *a barb, spear:—* harpoons(1).

7906. שֵׂכוּ **Seku** (967d); of unc. der.; a city near Ramah:— Secu(1).

7907. שֶׂכְוִי **sekvi** (967c); from an unused word; perh. *appearance, phenomenon:—* mind(1).

7908. שְׁכוֹל **shekol** (1013d); from 7921; *bereavement, loss of children:—* bereavement(1), loss of children(2).

7909a. שַׁכּוּל **shakul** (1014a); from 7921; *childless:—* bereaved of my children(1).

7909b. שַׁכּוּל **shakul** (1014a); from 7921; *bereaved, robbed of offspring:—* childless(1), lost her young(2), robbed of her cubs(3).

7910. שִׁכּוֹר **shikkor** or
שִׁכֹּר **shikkor** (1016c); from 7937; *drunken:—* drunk(4), drunkard(2), drunkards(3), drunken(1), drunken man(3).

7911. שָׁכַח **shakach** (1013a); a prim. root; *to forget:—* ever forget(1), forget(47), forgets(3), forgot(10), forgotten(39), who forget(1).

7912. שְׁכַח **shekach** (1115b); (Ara.) corr. to 7911; *to find:—* discover(1), discovered(1), find(5), found(11).

7913. שָׁכֵחַ **shakeach** (1013c); from 7911; *forgetting, forgetful:—* who(1), who forget(2).

7914a. שְׂכִיָּה **Sakeyah** (967d); of unc. der.; a Benjamite:— Sachia(1).

7914b. שְׂכִיָּה **sekiyyah** (967c); from the same as 7907; perh. *ship:—* craft(1).

7915. שַׂכִּין **sakkin** (967d); of unc. der.; *a knife:—* knife(1).

7916. שָׂכִיר **sakir** (969b); from 7936; *hired:—* hired(1), hired man(11), hired servant(2), man hired(1), wage earner(1).

7917a. שְׂכִירָה **sekirah** (969b); fem. of 7916, q.v.:— hired(1), mercenaries(1).

7917b. שָׂכַךְ **sakak** (967d); a prim. root; *to cover, lay over:—* cover(1), yourselves(1).

7917c. שָׂכַךְ **sakak** (697b, 968a); see 5526b.

7918. שָׁכַךְ **shakak** (1013c); a prim. root; *to decrease, abate:—* lessen(1), lying in wait(1), subsided(3).

7919a. שָׂכַל **sakal** (968a); a prim. root; *to be prudent:—* act wisely(1), acts wisely(3), behaved himself wisely(1), comprehend(1), consider(1), considers(2), discern(1), expert(1), failed*(1), gain insight(2), give you insight(1), give heed(1), gives attention(1), giving attention(1), had...regard(1), have insight(4), have success(2), insight(1), instruct(2), instructed(1), instructs(1), intelligence(1), prosper(2), prospered(3), prospering(2), prospers(1), prudent(2), show discernment(1), showed(1), showing intelligence(1), succeed(1), understand(4), understanding(2), understands(2), understood(1), wisdom(1), wise(6), wise behavior(1).

7919b. שָׂכַל **sakal** (968d); a prim. root; *to lay crosswise:—* crossing(1).

7920. שְׂכַל **sekal** (1114a); (Ara.) corr. to 7919a; *to consider, contemplate:—* contemplating(1).

7921. שָׁכֹל **shakol** or
שָׁכַל **shakal** (1013c); a prim. root; *to be bereaved:—* abort(1), been(1), bereave(2), bereave them of children(2), bereave you of your children(1), bereave you of children(1), bereave your of children(1), bereaved(2), bereaved me of my children(1), bereaved of my children(1), bereaved your of children(1), cast(1), childless(1), depopulated(1), made...childless(1), miscarried(1), miscarrying(2), slays(1), unfruitful(1), unfruitfulness(1).

7922. שֶׂכֶל **sekel** or
שֵׂכֶל **sekel** (968c); from 7919a; *prudence, insight:—* discretion(3), insight(4), intelligent*(1), repute(1), sense(1), shrewdness(1), understanding(4), wisdom(1).

שַׁכֻּל **shakkul**; see 7909b.

שִׂכְלוּת **sikluth**; see 5531.

7923. שִׁכֻּלִים **shikkulim** (1014a); from 7921; *bereavement, childlessness:—* bereaved(1).

7924. שָׂכְלְתָנוּ **soklethanu** (1114a); (Ara.) from 7920; *insight:—* insight(3).

7925. שָׁכַם **shakam** (1014c); a prim. root; *to start* or *rise early:—* again(9), arise early(2), arisen early(1), arose(1), arose to early(1), arose early(16), eager(1), early(6), got up early(1), morning(1), persistently(1), rise up early(1), rise early(6), rising up early(2), rising early(1), rose up early(3), rose early(12), soon(1).

7926. שְׁכֶם **shekem** (1014a); from an unused word; *shoulder:—* back(2), portion(1), shoulder(12), shoulders(7), socket(1).

7927. שְׁכֶם **Shekem** (1014b); from the same as 7926; "ridge," a district in N. Pal., also a son of Hamor:— Shechem(61), Shechem's(2).

7928. שֶׁכֶם **Shekem** (1014c); from the same as 7926; a man of Manasseh:— Shechem(3).

7929. שִׁכְמָה **shikmah** (1014b); fem. of 7926, q.v.

7930. שִׁכְמִי **Shikmi** (1014c); from 7928; desc. of Shechem:— Shechemites(1).

7931. שָׁכַן **shakan** or
שָׁכֵן **shaken** (1014d); a prim. root; *to settle down, abide, dwell:—* abide(1), abide*(1), abides(1), camping(1), continue(1), dwell(56), dwellers(1), dwelling(7), dwells(11), dwelt(5), establish(5), inhabitants(1), inhabited(1), lay(1), lie(1), lies down(1), live(9), lived(3), lives(1), living(1), lying down(1), nest(2), pitched(1), remain(1), remained(2), remains(1), rest(1), rested(1), set(1), settle(2), settled(3), settled down(2), stands(1), stationed(1), stay(1), staying(1).

7932. שְׁכַן **sheken** (1115b); (Ara.) corr. to 7931; *to dwell:—* dwell(1), lodged(1).

7933. שֶׁכֶן **sheken** (1015c); another reading for 7931, q.v.

7934. שָׁכֵן **shaken** (1015c); from 7931; *inhabitant, neighbor:*— inhabitants(1), neighbor(4), neighbor women(1), neighbors(13), resident(1).

7935. שְׁכַנְיָה **Shekanyah** or

שְׁכַנְיָהוּ **Shekanyahu** (1016a); from 7931 and 3050; "Yah has taken up His abode," the name of several Isr.:— Shecaniah(10).

7936. שָׂכַר **sakar** (968d); a prim. root; *to hire:*— earns(2), hire(3), hired(11), hires(2), surely hired(1).

7937. שָׁכַר **shakar** (1016a); a prim. root; *to be* or *become drunk* or *drunken:*— became drunk(1), become drunk(5), drank freely(1), drunk(5), imbibe deeply(1), intoxicating(1), made him drunk(1), make(1), make him drunk(1), make them drunk(2), make yourself drunk(1).

7938. שֶׂכֶר **seker** (969a); from 7936; *hire, wages:*— hired(1), reward(1), wages(1).

7939. שָׂכָר **sakar** (969a); from 7936; *hire, wages:*— compensation(1), fare(1), hire(1), reward(6), rewarded(1), service(1), wage(2), wages(15).

7940. שָׂכָר **Sakar** (969b); from 7936; two Isr.:— Sacar(2).

7941. שֵׁכָר **shekar** (1016b); from 7937; *intoxicating drink, strong drink:*— drink(2), drink of strong(1), drink or strong(1), drunkards*(1), liquor(1), strong(2), strong drink(18).

שִׁכֹּר **shikkor**; see 7910.

7942. שִׁכְּרוֹן **Shikkeron** (1016c); from 7937; a city on N.W. border of Judah:— Shikkeron(1).

7943. שִׁכָּרוֹן **shikkaron** (1016c); from 7937; *drunkenness:*— drunk(1), drunkenness(2).

7944. שַׁל **shal** (1016d); of unc. der.; perh. *error:*— irreverence(1).

7945. שֶׁל **shel** or

שֶׁ· **she** (979b); a prim. rel. particle; *who, which, that:*— account(2), inasmuch(1), though*(1), very(1), whatever*(1), when(2), when*(1), where(1), which(28), which*(3), who(21), whom(8), whose(4).

7946. שַׁלְאֲנָן **shalanan** (983b, 1016d); the same as 7600, q.v.

7947. שָׁלַב **shalab** (1016d); a prim. root; *to be bound* or *joined:*— fitted(2).

7948. שְׁלַבִּים **shelabbim** (1016d); from 7947; *joining pieces* (of stands):— frames(3).

7949. שָׁלַג **shalag** (1017a); denom. vb. from 7950; *to snow:*— snowing(1).

7950. שֶׁלֶג **sheleg** (1017a); from an unused word; *snow:*— snow(18), snowy(2).

7951. שָׁלָה **shalah** or

שָׁלֵי **shale** (1017b); a prim. root; *to be quiet* or *at ease:*— deceive(1), ease(2), negligent(1), prosper(3).

7952. שָׁלָה **shalah** (1017b); the same as 7951, q.v.

7953. שָׁלָה **shalah** (1017d); a prim. root; *to draw out, extract:*— requires(1).

7954. שְׁלֵה **sheleh** (1115c); (Ara.) corr. to 7951; *at ease:*— ease(1).

שִׁלֹה **Shiloh**; see 7887.

7955. שָׁלָה **shalah** (1115c); (Ara.) see 7960.

שֵׁלָה **shelah**; see 7596.

7956. שֵׁלָה **Shelah** (1017c); from 7951; a son of Judah:— Shelah(8).

7957. שַׁלְהֶבֶת **shalhebeth** (529b); from the same as 3851; *flame:*— flame(2).

שָׁלֵו **shalav**; see 7951.

7958. שְׂלָו **selav** (969b); prob. of for. or.; *quail:*— quail(3), quails(1).

7959. שֶׁלֶו **shalu** (1017b); from 7951; *ease, prosperity:*— prosperity(1).

7960. שָׁלוּ **shalu** (1115c); (Ara.) from a root corr. to 7951; *neglect, remissness:*— fail(1), negligence(1), negligent(1), offensive(1).

7961. שָׁלֵו **shalev** or

שָׁלֵיו **shalev** or

שְׁלֵיו **shelev** (1017c); from 7951; *quiet, at ease:*— carefree(1), ease(3), peaceful(1), prosperous(1), quiet(1), satisfied(1).

7962. שַׁלְוָה **shalvah** (1017c); from 7951; *quietness, ease:*— complacency(1), ease(2), prosperity(2), quietness(1), time of tranquility(2).

7963. שְׁלֵוָה **shelevah** (1115c); (Ara.) corr. to 7962; *ease, prosperity:*— prosperity(1).

7964. שִׁלּוּחִים **shilluchim** (1019d); from 7971; *a sending away, parting gift:*— dowry(1), parting gifts(1).

7965. שָׁלוֹם **shalom** (1022d); from 7999a; *completeness, soundness, welfare, peace:*— close(2), ease(1), favorable(1), friend*(1), friendly terms(1), friends*(2), greet(1), greet*(5), greeted*(1), health(1), how(1), Peace(2), peace(153), peaceably(1), peaceful(2), peacefully(3), perfect peace(1), prosperity(3), rose(1), safe(2), safely(7), safety(6), secure(1), state(1), trusted(1), welfare(14), well(17), well-being(5), who were at peace(1), wholly(1).

7966. שִׁלּוּם **shillum** or

שִׁלֻּם **shillum** (1024b); from 7999a; *requital:*— bribe(1), recompense(1), retribution(1).

7967. שַׁלּוּם **Shallum** or

שַׁלֻּם **Shallum** (1024b); from 7999a; the name of a number of Isr.:— Shallum(27).

שְׁלוֹמִית **Shelomith**; see 8019a.

7968. שַׁלּוּן **Shallun** (1024c); of unc. der.; one of the postexilic wall builders:— Shallum(1).

7969. שָׁלוֹשׁ **shalosh** or

שָׁלֹשׁ **shalosh** or

שְׁלֹשָׁה **sheloshah** (1025c); of unc. der.; *a three, triad:*— 1,335*(1), 1,365*(1), 123*(2), 13*(1), 153,600*(1), 2,300*(1), 2,322*(1), 22,273*(1), 223*(2), 23,000*(1), 273*(1), 3,000*(11), 3,023*(2), 3,200*(1), 3,300*(2), 3,600*(2), 3,630*(1), 3,700*(1), 3,930*(1), 300*(11), 300,000*(4), 307,500*(1), 320*(2), 323*(2), 324*(1), 328*(1), 337,500*(2), 345*(2), 372*(2), 392*(2), 42,360*(2), 43,730*(1), 53,400*(3), 59,300*(2), 603,550*(2), 623*(1), 64,300*(1), 7,337*(2), 743*(2), 973*(2), forks*(1), oftentimes*(1), third(11), thirteen*(12), thirteenth*(11), thirty(2), thirty-three*(7), three(267), three things(6), three-pronged*(1), three-tenths*(8), three-year-old(1), twenty-third*(7), twenty-three*(6).

7970. שְׁלוֹשִׁים **sheloshim** or

שְׁלֹשִׁים **sheloshim** (1026c); from the same as 7969; *thirty:*— 1,335*(1), 130*(1), 138*(1), 139*(1), 2,630*(1), 22,034*(1), 232*(1), 3,630*(1), 3,930*(1), 30(4), 30,000*(5), 30,500*(2), 32*(1), 32,000*(2), 32,200*(2), 32,500*(1), 337,500*(2), 35,400*(2), 36,000*(3), 37,000*(1), 38,000*(1), 43,730*(1), 435*(2), 530*(1), 601,730*(1), 7,337*(2), 730*(1), 736*(2), 832*(1), thirtieth(1), thirty(88), thirty-eight*(1), thirty-eighth*(2), thirty-fifth*(1), thirty-first*(1), thirty-five*(4), thirty-four*(1), thirty-ninth*(3), thirty-one*(3), thirty-second*(2), thirty-seven*(4), thirty-seventh*(3), thirty-six*(1), thirty-sixth*(1), thirty-three*(7), thirty-two*(7).

שָׁלוּת **shaluth**; see 7960.

7971. שָׁלַח **shalach** (1018a); a prim. root; *to send:*— again(5), bade his farewell(1), burned*(1), cast(2), cast off(1), casting(1), certainly let(1), certainly let the go(1), delivered(1), direct(1), dismissed(2), dispatch(1), divorce(3), divorces(1), drive(1), driving them away(1), escort(1), escorted him away(1), extended(2), extends(1), forlorn(1), gave(1), gave them over(1), get rid(1), gets his own way(1), go(11), go away(1), go free(4), grow long(1), laid(2), lay(8), let(8), let her go(2), let him go(3), let me go(4), let my go(11), let my go free(1), let out freely(1), let the go(8), let them down(1), let them go(6), let you go(7), let your loose(1), let go(1), let loose(2), let...down(1), let...go(3), lets his loose(1), lets you go(1), letting the go(1), letting them go(1), letting us go(1), loot(1), pointing(1), put(10), put forth(7), puts(2), putting(1), reached(3), reached*(1), release(2), released(3), remove(1), rushed(1), scattered(1), send(139), send him away(2), send it away(2), send me away(4), send them away(1), send you away(2), send away(4), sending(13), sending me away(1), sending them and again(1), sends(10), sent(420), sent her away(5), sent him away(5), sent his away(1), sent me away(2), sent the away(3), sent them away(9), sent you away(3), sent your away(1), sent away(7), sent...away(3), set(12), set your free(1), set free(1), shot(1), spread(2), spreads(3), stretch(13), stretch forth(3), stretched(11), stretches(2), surely let(1), surely let me go(1), throw(1), thrown(1), thrust(1), urgently send(1), use(1), will(1).

7972. שְׁלַח **shelach** (1115c); (Ara.) corr. to 7971; *to send:*— attempts*(1), send(1), sent(12).

7973. שֶׁלַח **shelach** (1019c); from 7971; *a missile, weapon, sprout:*— defenses(1), Sheol(1), shoots(1), weapon(3), weapons(1).

7974. שֶׁלַח **Shelach** (1019d); from 7971; a desc. of Shem:— Shelah(9).

7975a. שֶׁלַח **Shelach** (1019d); from 7971; a reservoir in Jer.:— Shelah(1).

7975b. שִׁלֹחַ **Shiloach** (1019d); perh. from 7971; a fountain in S.E. Jer.:— Shiloah(1).

שִׁלֻּחַ **shilluach**; see 7964.

7976. שִׁלְחָה **shilluchah** or

שְׁלוּחָה **sheluchah** (1020a); from 7971; *a shoot, branch:*— tendrils(1).

7977. שִׁלְחִי **Shilchi** (1019d); from 7971; Jehoshaphat's grandfather:— Shilhi(2).

7978. שִׁלְחִים **Shilchim** (1019d); from 7971; a city in S. Judah:— Shilhim(1).

7979. שֻׁלְחָן **shulchan** (1020b); from an unused word; *a table:*— each table(1), table(55), tables(12).

7980. שָׁלַט **shalat** (1020c); a prim. root; *to domineer, be master of:*— control over(1), domineered(1), empowered(2), exercised authority(1), gain the mastery over(1), gained the mastery over(1), have dominion(1), mastery over(2).

7981. שְׁלֵט **shelet** (1115c); (Ara.) corr. to 7980; *to have power, rule:*— had...effect(1), have authority(2), made him ruler(1), overpowered(1), rule(2).

7982. שֶׁלֶט **shelet** (1020d); from an unused word; perh. *shield:*— quivers(1), shields(5), small shields(1).

7983. שִׁלְטוֹן **shilton** (1020d); from 7980; *mastery:*— authoritative(1), authority(1).

7984. שִׁלְטוֹן **shilton** or
שִׁלְטֹן **shilton** (1127c); (Ara.) corr. to 7983; *governor:*— rulers(2).

7985. שָׁלְטָן **sholtan** (1115d); (Ara.) from 7981; *dominion:*— dominion(13), dominions(1).

7986. שַׁלֶּטֶת **shalleteth** (1020c); the same as 7989, q.v.

7987. שְׁלִי **sheli** (1017b); from 7951; *quietness:*— privately(1).

7988. שִׁלְיָה **shilyah** (1017d); from 7953; *afterbirth:*— afterbirth(1).

שְׁלָיו **selayv**; see 7958.

שָׁלֵיו **shalev**; see 7961.

7989. שַׁלִּיט **shallit** (1020c); from 7980; *having mastery, domineering:*— bold-faced(1), has authority(1), ruler(2), rulers(1).

7990. שַׁלִּיט **shallit** (1115d); (Ara.) corr. to 7989; *having mastery, ruling:*— allowed(1), authority(1), commander(1), governing(1), ruler(5), rules(1).

7991a. שָׁלִישׁ **shalish** (1026c); from the same as 7969; *a third* (part):— large measure(1), measure(1).

7991b. שָׁלִישׁ **shalish** (1026c); from the same as 7969; (a musical instrument) perh. *a sistrum:*— musical instruments(1).

7991c. שָׁלִישׁ **shalish** (1026d); from the same as 7969; *adjutant, officer:*— captains(3), excellent things(1), officer(3), officers(4), royal officer(2), royal officers(2).

7992. שְׁלִישִׁי **shelishi** (1026a); from the same as 7969; *third* (an ord. number):— Eglath-shelishiyah*(2), one third(6), third(92), third part(1), third time(3), thirty(1), three(1).

7993. שָׁלַךְ **shalak** (1020d); a prim. root; *to throw, fling, cast:*— brings him down(1), cast(41), cast it away(1), cast me away(2), cast me off(1), cast them away(1), cast away(5), cast down(2), cast off(1), casts(1), dropped(1), fling(2), hurl(1), hurled(2), left(1), risked*(1), snatched(1), stretching(1), threw(29), threw her down(1), threw his down(1), threw them down(1), threw down(1), throw(13), throw it down(1), throw them away(1), throw away(1), thrown(8), thrown away(1), thrown down(1).

7994. שָׁלָךְ **shalak** (1021c); from 7993; (bird of prey) prob. *cormorant:*— cormorant(2).

7995. שַׁלֶּכֶת **shalleketh** (1021c); from 7993; *felling* (of a tree):— felled(1).

7996. שַׁלֶּכֶת **Shalleketh** (1021c); from 7993; "(gate of) casting forth," a temple gate on the W. side:— Shallecheth(1).

7997a. שָׁלַל **shalal** (1021c); a prim. root; *to draw out:*— purposely pull(1).

7997b. שָׁלַל **shalal** (1021d); a prim. root; *to spoil, plunder:*— capture(5), loot(1), looted(1), make a spoil(1), makes himself a prey(1), plunder(2), plundered(1), spoil of those who despoiled(1), take the spoil(1).

7998. שָׁלָל **shalal** (1021d); from 7997b; *a prey, spoil, plunder, booty:*— booty(11), gain(1), plunder(3), possessions(1), spoil(57), spoiler(1).

7999a. שָׁלֵם **shalem** (1022a); a prim. root; *to be complete* or *sound:*— completed(1), finished(3), fulfill(1), fully repay(1), make(2), make an end(2), make it good(2), make full restitution(1), make restitution(9), over(1), paid(1), pay(19), pay back(1), paying(1), pays(1), pays back(1), perform(2), performed(1), performing(1), performs(1), present(1), recompense(3), recompenses(1), render(2), rendering(2), repaid(3), repay(19), repays(3), restore(2), reward(3), rewarded(3), surely make restitution(2), surely pay(1), without harm(1).

7999b. שָׁלַם **shalam** (1023d); denom. vb. from 8002; *to be in a covenant of peace:*— friend(1), made peace(6), make peace(1), makes(1), peace(4), peaceable(1).

8000. שְׁלַם **shelem** (1115d); (Ara.) corr. to 7999a; *to be complete:*— completed(1), deliver in full(1), put an end(1).

8001. שְׁלָם **shelam** (1116a); (Ara.) corr. to 7965; *welfare, prosperity:*— peace(4).

8002. שֶׁלֶם **shelem** (1023b); from 7999a; *a sacrifice for alliance* or *friendship, peace offering:*— peace offering(2), peace offerings(85).

8003. שָׁלֵם **shalem** (1023d); from 7999a; *complete, safe, at peace:*— blameless(1), complete(1), completed(1), completely(1), entire(2), friendly(1), full(4), just(1), perfect(2), prepared(1), safely(1), uncut(2), whole(5), wholeheartedly*(1), wholly devoted(4).

8004. שָׁלֵם **Shalem** (1024a); from 7999a; "peaceful," an early name of Jer.:— Salem(2).

8005. שִׁלֵּם **shillem** (1024a); from 7999a; *recompense:*— retribution(1).

8006. שִׁלֵּם **Shillem** (1024b); from 7999a; a man of Naphtali:— Shillem(2).

8007. שַׂלְמָא **Salma** (969c); of unc. der.; father of Boaz, same as 8012, also the founder of Bethlehem:— Salma(4).

8008. שַׂלְמָה **salmah** (971a); from 8071 (by transposition); *a wrapper, mantle:*— cloak(5), clothes(6), clothing(1), garment(1), garments(3), robe*(1).

8009. שַׂלְמָה **Salmah** (969c); of unc. der.; father of Boaz, same as 8012:— Salmon(1).

8010. שְׁלֹמֹה **Shelomoh** (1024d); from 7999a; David's son and successor to his throne:— Solomon(266), Solomon's(21).

8011. שִׁלֻּמָה **shillumah** (1024b); from 7999a; *requital, retribution:*— recompense(1).

8012. שַׂלְמוֹן **Salmon** (969c); of unc. der.; father of Boaz, same as 8007 and 8009:— Salmon(1).

8013. שְׁלֹמוֹת **Shelomoth** (1024d); the same as 8019a, q.v.:— Shelomoth(5).

8014. שַׂלְמַי **Salmay** (969c); of unc. der.; head of a postexilic family:— Shalmai(2).

8015. שְׁלֹמִי **Shelomi** (1025a); from 7999a; an Asherite:— Shelomi(1).

8016. שִׁלֵּמִי **Shillemi** (1024b); from 8006; desc. of Shillem:— Shillemites(1).

8017. שְׁלֻמִיאֵל **Shelumiel** (1025a); from 7965 and 410; "peace of God," a Simeonite:— Shelumiel(5).

8018. שֶׁלֶמְיָה **Shelemyah** or
שֶׁלֶמְיָהוּ **shelemyahu** (1025a); from 8002 and 3050; "friend of Yah," the name of several Isr.:— Shelemiah(10).

8019a. שְׁלֹמִית **Shelomith** or
שְׁלוֹמִית **Shelomith** (1024d); from 7999a; the name of several Isr.:— Shelomith(3), Shelomoth(1).

8019b. שְׁלֹמִית **Shelomith** (1025a); from 7999a; the name of two Isr. women:— Shelomith(2).

8020. שַׁלְמַן **Shalman** (1025a); of for. or.; prob. a king of Assyr., perh. same as 8022:— Shalman(1).

8021. שַׁלְמֹן **shalmon** (1024b); from 7999a; *a reward, bribe:*— rewards(1).

8022. שַׁלְמַנְאֶסֶר **Shalmaneser** (1025b); of for. or.; a king of Assyr.:— Shalmaneser(2).

8023. שִׁלֹנִי **Shiloni** (1018a); the same as 7888, q.v.

8024. שֵׁלָנִי **Shelani** (1017c); from 7956; desc. of Shelah:— Shelanites(1).

8025. שָׁלַף **shalaph** (1025b); a prim. root; *to draw out* or *off:*— draw(9), drawn(4), drawn forth(1), drew(7), grows(1), removed(2), swordsmen*(1).

8026a. שֶׁלֶף **Sheleph** (1025c); from 8025; "drawn out," a son of Joktan and his desc.:— Sheleph(2).

8026b. שָׂלַק **salaq** (969c); a prim. root; *to kindle, burn:*— burn(1), kindled(1), makes a fire(1).

8027. שָׁלַשׁ **shalash** (1026a); denom. vb. from 7969; *to do a third time, divide into three parts:*— did it a third time(1), divide into three parts(1), do it a third time(1), stayed for three days(1), third time(2), three(2), three days(1), three parts(1), three year old(3).

8028. שֶׁלֶשׁ **Shelesh** (1026d); from the same as 7969; an Asherite:— Shelesh(1).

8029. שִׁלֵּשׁ **shillesh** (1026d); from the same as 7969; *pertaining to the third:*— third(5).

8030. שִׁלְשָׁה **Shilshah** (1027a); from the same as 7969; an Asherite:— Shilshah(1).

8031. שָׁלִשָׁה **Shalishah** (1027a); from the same as 7969; an area of Isr. searched by Saul:— Shalishah(1).

8032a. שִׁלְשׁוֹם **shilshom** or
שִׁלְשֹׁם **shilshom** (1026b); from the same as 7969; *three days ago, day before, yesterday:*— before*(3), beforehand*(1), formerly*(2), past*(2), previously*(12), time(1), time past(1), times*(2).

8032b. שַׁלְתִּיאֵל **Shaltiel** (1027a); of unc. der.; father of Zerubbabel:— Shealtiel(3).

8033. שָׁם **sham** (1027a); a prim. adv.; *there, thither:*— direction(1), everywhere*(1), here(3), place(1), rested*(1), there(609), there for ourselves where(1), there where there(1), there*(2), there...where(1), where(8), where there(2), where*(129), wherever(1), wherever*(6), which(2), whom*(1).

8034. שֵׁם **shem** (1027d); of unc. der.; *a name:*— byword(1), defamed*(1), defames*(1), fame(8), famous(3), famous*(1), memorial(1), Name(3), name(654), name's(11), name*(4), named(7), named*(66), names(80), renown(6), renowned(1), report(1), repute(1), same names(1).

8035. שֵׁם **Shem** (1028d); from the same as 8034; "name," oldest son of Noah:— Shem(17).

8036. שֻׁם **shum** (1116a); (Ara.) corr. to 8034; *a name:*— name(8), named(1), names(3).

8037. שַׁמָּא Shamma (1031c); from 8074; an Asherite:— Shamma(1).

8038. שֶׁמְאֵבֶר Shemeber (1028d); appar. from 8034 and 83; "name of pinion," king of Zeboiim:— Shemeber(1).

8039. שִׁמְאָה Shimah (1029a); of unc. der.; a Benjamite, same as 8043:— Shimeah(1).

8040. שְׂמֹאול semovl or

שְׂמֹאל semol (969d); of unc. der.; *the left:*— left(40), left hand(10), left side(1), north(3).

8041. שָׂמְאַל simel (970a); denom. vb. from 8040; *to take the left:*— go to the left(2), left(3).

8042. שְׂמָאלִי semali (970a); from the same as 8040; *left, on the left:*— left(9).

8043. שִׁמְאָם Shimam (1029a); from the same as 8039; a Benjamite, the same as 8039:— Shimeam(1).

8044. שַׁמְגַּר Shamgar (1029a); of unc. der.; an Isr. judge:— Shamgar(2).

8045. שָׁמַד shamad (1029b); a prim. root; *to be exterminated* or *destroyed:*— completely(1), demolish(2), destroy(36), destroyed(41), destruction(2), eradicated(1), exterminate(2), totally destroy(1), utterly destroyed(1), wipe(1).

8046a. שְׁמַד shemad (1116a); (Ara.) corr. to 8045; *to destroy:*— annihilated(1).

8046b. שֶׁמֶד Shamed (1029c); from 8045; a desc. of Benjamin:— Shemed(1).

8047. שַׁמָּה shammah (1031c); from 8074; *waste, horror:*— appalling(1), desolate(2), desolation(10), desolations(1), destroyed(1), destruction(1), dismay(1), horror(9), object of horror(10), waste(3).

8048. שַׁמָּה Shammah (1031c); from 8074; an Edomite, also several Isr.:— Shammah(8).

8049. שַׁמְהוּת Shamhuth (1030b); of unc. der.; a captain of Isr.:— Shamhuth(1).

8050. שְׁמוּאֵל Shemuel (1028d); from 8034 and 410; "name of God," a prophet of Isr.:— Samuel(140).

8051. שַׁמּוּעַ Shammua (1035b); from 8085; three Isr.:— Shammua(5).

8052. שְׁמוּעָה shemuah (1035b); from 8085; *a report:*— heard(1), message(3), news(6), report(10), rumor(4), rumors(1), tidings(1), what it means(1).

8053. שָׁמוּר Shamur or

שָׁמִיר Shamir (1039a); the same as 8069b, q.v.

8054. שַׁמּוֹת Shammoth (1031c); from 8074; one of David's heroes, the same as 8048:— Shammoth(1).

8055. שָׂמַח samach (970a); a prim. root; *rejoice, be glad:*— cheers(1), give them joy(1), give happiness(1), glad(53), gladden(1), gloated(1), happy(3), has...joy(1), joyful(1), made me glad(1), made you glad(1), make my glad(1), make the glad(2), make them joyful(1), make us glad(1), make glad(2), makes a glad(2), makes his glad(1), makes it glad(1), makes...glad(1), makes...merry(1), merry(1), pleased*(1), rejoice(48), rejoiced(17), rejoiced had given(1), rejoices(4), rejoicing(1), take pleasure(1), very happy(1).

8056. שָׂמֵחַ sameach (970c); from 8055; *glad, joyful, merry:*— glad(2), joyful(5), joyfully(1), merry-hearted*(1), pleased(1), rejoice(3), rejoiced(2), rejoices(1), rejoicing(4), who delight(1).

8057. שִׂמְחָה simchah (970d); from 8055; *joy, gladness, mirth:*— delight(1), exceeding joy(1), extremely*(1), festival(1), gladness(34), happiness(1), joy(38), mirth(1), pleasure(6), rejoice(1), rejoiced(1), rejoicing(6).

8058. שָׁמַט shamat (1030c); a prim. root; *to let drop:*— let it rest(1), let go(1), release(2), threw her down(1), throw her down(1), thrown down(1), upset(2).

8059. שְׁמִטָּה shemittah (1030d); from 8058; *a letting drop, a* (temporary) *remitting:*— remission(5).

8060. שַׁמַּי Shammay (1031d); from 8074; three men of Isr.:— Shammai(6).

8061. שְׁמִידָע Shemida (1029a); appar. from 8034 and 3045; "name of knowing," a man of Manasseh:— Shemida(3).

8062. שְׁמִידָעִי Shemidai (1029a); from 8061; desc. of Shemida:— Shemidaites(1).

8063. שְׂמִיכָה semikah (970d); of unc. der.; perh. *rug, thick coverlet.*— rug(1).

8064. שָׁמַיִם shamayim (1029c); from an unused word; *heaven, sky:*— astrologers*(1), compass(1), earth(1), heaven(191), heaven and the highest(2), heaven and the highest heavens(1), heaven of heavens(1), heavenly(3), heavens(151), heavens and the highest(1), highest heaven(1), highest heaven(1), highest heavens(4), horizons(1), other*(1), sky(50).

8065. שָׁמַיִן shamayin (1116a); (Ara.) corr. to 8064; *heavens:*— Heaven(1), heaven(29), heavens(2), sky(6).

8066. שְׁמִינִי shemini (1033a); from the same as 8083; *eighth* (an ord. number):— eighth(28), sheminith(1).

8067. שְׁמִינִית sheminith (1033a); fem. of 8066, q.v.

8068. שָׁמִיר shamir (1038d); from an unused word; *a thorn, adamant, flint:*— briars(8), diamond(1), emery(1), flint(1).

8069a. שָׁמִיר Shamir (1039a); from the same as 8068; a city in Judah, also a city in Ephraim:— Shamir(3).

8069b. שָׁמִיר Shamir (1039a); from the same as 8068; a Levite:— Shamir(1).

8070. שְׁמִירָמוֹת Shemiramoth (1029a); prob. from 8034 and 7413; prob. "name of heights," two Levites:— Shemiramoth(4).

8071. שִׂמְלָה simlah (971a); from an unused word; *a wrapper, mantle:*— cloak(4), cloth(1), clothes(9), clothing(5), garment(5), garments(5).

8072. שַׂמְלָה Samlah (971a); from the same as 8071; a king of Edom:— Samlah(4).

8073. שַׁמְלַי Shamlay (969c); scribal error for 8014, q.v.

8074. שָׁמֵם shamem (1030d); a prim. root; *to be desolated* or *appalled:*— appalled(13), astonished(8), astounded(1), become desolate(1), causes horror(1), causing consternation(1), desolate(22), desolated(4), desolating(1), desolation(5), desolations(3), destitute(1), destroy(1), devastations(1), horrified(2), laid desolate(1), laid waste(4), lie deserted(1), lies desolate(1), made me desolate(1), made you desolate(1), made desolate(3), make the desolate(2), make their desolate(2), make them desolate(1), make your desolate(1), make...appalled(1), make...desolate(1), makes desolate(2), ravaged(1), ruin(1), ruined(1), ruins(1).

8075. שְׁמַם shemam (1116b); (Ara.) corr. to 8074; *to be appalled:*— appalled(1).

8076. שָׁמֵם shamem (1031b); from 8074; *devastated:*— desolate(2).

8077. שְׁמָמָה shemamah or

שִׁמְמָה shimamah (1031b); from 8074; *devastation, waste:*— desolate(19), desolation(33), horror(1), utterly desolate(1), waste(1), waste and a desolation(1).

8078. שִׁמָּמוֹן shimmamon (1031d); from 8074; *horror:*— horror(2).

8079. שְׂמָמִית semamith (971b); of unc. der.; (a kind of) *lizard:*— lizard(1).

8080. שָׁמֵן shamen (1031d); a prim. root; *to grow fat:*— fat(1), grew fat(2), grown fat(1), insensitive(1), render(1).

8081. שֶׁמֶן shemen (1032a); from 8080; *fat, oil:*— choice(1), fatness(2), fertile(2), fertile*(1), lavish(1), oil(176), oils(3), ointment(1), olive(6), wild*(1).

8082a. שָׁמֵן shamen (1032a); from 8080; *fat, robust:*— fat(2), fertile(1), large(1), rich(4), robust(1).

8082b. שָׁמָן shaman (1032a); from 8080; *a fat* or *fertile place:*— fatness(1), fertility(1), plenteous(1).

8083. שְׁמֹנֶה shemoneh or

שְׁמֹנָה shemonah (1032d); of unc. der.; *eight* (a card. number):— 108,100*(1), 128*(4), 138*(1), 148*(1), 18*(2), 18,000*(7), 188*(1), 2,812*(1), 2,818*(2), 20,800*(1), 218*(1), 22,600*(1), 28*(1), 28,600*(1), 288*(1), 328*(1), 38,000*(1), 468*(1), 6,800*(1), 628*(1), 648*(1), 68*(1), 8,580*(1), 8,600*(1), 800,000*(1), 822*(1), 832*(1), 845*(1), 928*(1), 98*(2), eight(36), eighteen*(8), eighteenth*(11), eighth(3), forty-eight*(2), ninety-eight*(1), thirty-eight*(1), thirty-eighth*(2), twenty-eight*(4).

8084. שְׁמֹנִים shemonim (1033b); from the same as 8083; *an eighty:*— 180*(1), 180,000*(3), 185,000*(2), 186,400*(1), 188*(1), 280,000*(2), 284*(1), 288*(1), 8,580*(1), 80(2), 80,000*(3), 87,000*(1), eightieth(1), eighty(11), eighty-five(2), eighty-seven(1), eighty-six(1), eighty-three(1), eighty-two(2).

8085. שָׁמַע shama (1033b); a prim. root; *to hear:*— announce(2), announced(3), announces(3), completely(1), comprehends(1), diligently(1), discern(1), disregarded*(1), gave heed(2), give earnest heed(1), given heed(2), hear(270), hear*(1), heard(363), heard for certain(1), hearing(5), hears(33), heed(5), heeded(2), indeed obey(1), keep on listening(1), listen(226), listen attentively(1), listen carefully(3), listen closely(1), listen obediently(2), listened(52), listening(12), listens(7), loud-sounding(3), made a proclamation(1), make his heard(1), make their heard(1), make them known(1), make themselves heard(1), make your heard(1), obedient(1), obey(32), obey*(14), obeyed(21), obeyed*(5), obeying(6), obeys(1), overheard(1), pay heed(1), proclaim(15), proclaimed(6), proclaims(1), reported(3), sang(1), show(1), sound(2), sound*(1), sounded(1), summon(2), summoned(2), surely hear(1), surely heard(1), truly obey(1), understand(7), understanding(1), understood(1), witness(1).

8086. שְׁמַע shema (1116b); (Ara.) corr. to 8085; *to hear:*— hear(3), heard(4), hears(1), obey(1).

8087a. שֶׁמַע shema (1034d); from 8085; *a sound:*— loud(1).

8087b. שֶׁמַע Shema (1034d); from 8085; four Isr.:— Shema(5).

8088. שֵׁמַע shema (1034d); from 8085; *a hearing, report:*— about(1), fame(4), hear*(1), hearing(1), news(1), proclamation(1), report(8).

8089. שֹׁמַע **shoma** (1035a); from 8085; *a report:*— fame(2), report(2).

8090. שְׁמַע **Shema** (1035a); from 8085; a city in S. Judah:— Shema(1).

8091. שָׁמָע **Shama** (1035a); from 8085; one of David's heroes:— Shama(1).

8092. שִׁמְעָא **Shima** (1035a); from 8085; four Isr.:— Shimea(5).

8093. שִׁמְעָה **Shimah** (1035a); from 8085; a brother of David, same as 8092:— Shimeah(2).

8094. שְׁמָעָה **Shemaah** (1035a); from 8085; father of two of David's warriors:— Shemaah(1).

8095. שִׁמְעוֹן **Shimon** (1035b); from 8085; a son of Jacob, also his tribe, also an Isr. with a for. wife:— Shimeon(1), Simeon(43).

8096. שִׁמְעִי **Shimi** (1035c); from 8085; the name of a number of Isr.:— Shimei(44).

8097. שִׁמְעִי **Shimi** (1035c); from 8096; desc. of Shimei:— Shimeites(2).

8098. שְׁמַעְיָה **Shemayah** or

שְׁמַעְיָהוּ **Shemayahu** (1035d); from 8085 and 3050; "Yah hears," the name of a number of Isr.:— Shemaiah(41).

8099. שִׁמְעֹנִי **Shimoni** or

שִׁמְעוֹנִי **Shimoni** (1035c); from 8095; desc. of Simeon:— Simeonites(4).

8100. שִׁמְעָת **Shimath** (1035a); from 8085; an Ammonite woman:— Shimeath(2).

8101. שִׁמְעָתִים **Shimathim** (1035a); from 8085; a family of scribes:— Shimeathites(1).

8102. שֶׁמֶץ **shemets** (1036b); from an unused word; *a whisper:*— faint(1), whisper(1).

8103. שִׁמְצָה **shimtsah** (1036b); from the same as 8102; *whisper, derision:*— derision(1).

8104. שָׁמַר **shamar** (1036b); a prim. root; *to keep, watch, preserve:*— attend(4), being careful(1), beware(8), bodyguard*(1), careful(32), careful to keep(1), cares(1), charge(4), confine(1), confined(1), defending(1), did(1), diligently keep(1), doorkeeper*(1), doorkeepers*(4), gatekeepers*(1), give heed(2), giving heed(1), guard(20), guarded(7), guards(4), guardsmen(1), have charge(1), heed to yourself and keep(1), heeds(1), hoarded(1), indignant(1), keep(156), keeper(8), keepers(2), keeping(10), keeps(19), kept(38), kept watch(2), maintained(1), mark(2), observe(30), observed(6), observes(1), observing(1), officers(2), pay attention(1), perform(3), performed(1), performing(2), preserve(5), preserved(3), preserves(6), protect(4), protects(1), regard(3), regards(2), remains(1), reserved(1), secured(1), sentries(1), spare(1), spies(1), take care(1), take heed(5), take note(1), take...heed(1), waiting(1), waits(1), watch(11), watched(1), watches(3), watching(3), watchman(4), watchmen(7).

8105. שֶׁמֶר **shemer** (1038d); from an unused word; *lees, dregs:*— aged wine(2), dregs(2), spirit(1).

8106. שֶׁמֶר **Shemer** (1037c); from 8104; three Isr.:— Shemer(4).

8107. שִׁמֻּר **shimmur** (1037d); from 8104; *a watching, vigil:*— observed(2).

8108. שָׁמְרָה **shomrah** (1037c); from 8104; *a guard, watch:*— guard(1).

8109. שְׁמֻרָה **shemurah** (1037d); from 8104; *eyelid:*— eyelids*(1).

8110a. שִׁמְרוֹן **Shimron** (1038a); from 8104; a city of Canaan:— Shimron(2).

8110b. שִׁמְרוֹן **Shimron** (1038a); from 8104; a son of Issachar:— Shimron(3).

8111. שֹׁמְרוֹן **Shomron** (1037d); from 8104; capital of N. kingdom of Isr.:— Samaria(109).

8112. שִׁמְרוֹן מְראוֹן **Shimron Meron** (1038a); from 8104 and 4754; a Canaanite city conquered by Joshua, the same as 8110a:— Shimron-meron(1).

8113. שִׁמְרִי **Shimri** (1037c); from 8104; four Isr.:— Shimri(4).

8114. שְׁמַרְיָה **Shemaryah** or

שְׁמַרְיָהוּ **Shemaryahu** (1037d); from 8104 and 3050; "Yah has kept," three Isr.:— Shemariah(4).

8115. שָׁמְרַיִן **Shomrayin** (1116b); (Ara.) corr. to 8111; capital of N. kingdom of Isr.:— Samaria(2).

8116. שִׁמְרִית **Shimrith** (1037d); from 8104; a Moabite woman:— Shimrith(1).

8117. שִׁמְרֹנִי **Shimroni** (1038a); from 8110b; desc. of Shimron:— Shimronites(1).

8118. שֹׁמְרֹנִי **Shomeroni** (1038a); from 8111; inhab. of Samaria:— people of Samaria(1).

8119. שִׁמְרָת **Shimrath** (1037d); from 8104; a Benjamite:— Shimrath(1).

8120. שְׁמַשׁ **shemash** (1116b); (Ara.) corr. to the root of 8121; *to minister:*— attending(1).

8121. שֶׁמֶשׁ **shemesh** (1039a); from an unused word; *sun:*— battlements(1), daylight(1), daylight*(1), east side*(2), east*(7), sun(109), sun's(1), sundown*(1), sunrise*(3), sunset*(6), west*(1).

8122. שְׁמַשׁ **shemash** (1116b); (Ara.) corr. to 8121; *sun:*— sunset*(1).

8123. שִׁמְשׁוֹן **Shimshon** (1039c); from the same as 8121; a deliverer of Isr.:— Samson(35), Samson's(3).

8124. שִׁמְשַׁי **Shimshay** (1116c); (Ara.) from 8120; a scribe who opposed Isr.:— Shimshai(4).

8125. שַׁמְשְׁרַי **Shamsheray** (1039c); from the same as 8121; a Benjamite:— Shamsherai(1).

8126. שֻׁמָתִי **Shumathi** (1029c); of unc. der.; a family of Kiriath-jearim:— Shumathites(1).

8127. שֵׁן **shen** (1042a); from 8150; *tooth, ivory:*— crag(2), ivory(10), sharp(2), teeth(30), three-pronged*(1), tooth(9).

8128. שֵׁן **shen** (1116d); (Ara.) corr. to 8127; *tooth:*— teeth(3).

8129. שֵׁן **Shen** (1042b); from 8150; "tooth," a place near Mizpah:— Shen(1).

8130. שָׂנֵא **sane** (971b); a prim. root; *to hate:*— detest(1), enemy(3), enmity(1), foes(1), hate(78), hated(28), hated her intensely(1), hates(19), hating(2), hatred(1), turned against(1), turns against(2), unloved(7).

8131. שְׂנֵא **sena** (1114a); (Ara.) corr. to 8130; *to hate:*— hate(1).

8132. שָׁנָא **shana** or

שָׁנָה **shanah** (1039d); a prim. root; *to change:*— alter(1), beam(1), change(2), changed(4), changing(1), different(1), disguise(1), disguised(1), given to change(1), pervert(1), transferred(1), various(1).

8133. שְׁנָא **shena** (1116c); (Ara.) corr. to 8132; *to change:*— altered(1), change(1), changed(5), changes(1), damaged(1), different(5), grew even paler(1), grew pale(2), make alterations(1), pale(1), violates(1), violating(1).

8134. שִׁנְאָב **Shinab** (1039c); of unc. der.; a king of Admah:— Shinab(1).

8135. שִׂנְאָה **sinah** (971d); from 8130; *hating, hatred:*— hate(1), hated(1), hates(1), hatred(14).

8136. שִׁנְאָן **shinan** (1041d); from 8138; *repetition:*— thousands(1).

8137. שֶׁנְאַצַּר **Shenatstsar** (1039c); of unc. der.; uncle of Zerubbabel:— Shenazzar(1).

8138. שָׁנָה **shanah** (1040d); a prim. root; *to repeat, do again:*— again(1), did it a second time(1), do it a second time(1), do so again(1), repeating(1), repeats(2), second time(3), speak again(1).

8139. שְׁנָה **shenah** (1096b); (Ara.) corr. to 8142; *sleep:*— sleep(1).

8140. שְׁנָה **shenah** (1116d); (Ara.) corr. to 8141; *a year:*— age*(1), year(5), years(1).

8141. שָׁנָה **shanah** (1040a); from 8132; *a year:*— annual*(1), annually(2), annually*(4), count(2), every year(2), length(3), life(1), year(318), yearling(2), yearly(1), years(451), years the year(1).

8142. שֵׁנָה **shenah** or

שֵׁנָא **shena** (446a); from 3462; *sleep:*— asleep(1), sleep(22), sleep*(1).

8143. שֶׁנְהַבִּים **shenhabbim** (1042b); of unc. der.; *ivory:*— ivory(2).

8144. שָׁנִי **shani** (1040c); from an unused word; *scarlet:*— scarlet(42).

8145. שֵׁנִי **sheni** (1041b); from 8138; *second* (an ord. number):— again(2), another(8), another thing(1), besides(1), both(1), dependent(1), more(3), next(3), other(30), second(87), second time(19), two(2).

8146. שָׂנִיא **sani** (971d); from 8130; *hated, held in aversion:*— unloved(1).

8147. שְׁנַיִם **shenayim** or

שְׁתַּיִם **shettayim** (1040d); from 8138; *two* (a card. number):— 1,052*(2), 1,222*(1), 112*(3), 12*(2), 12,000*(8), 120,000*(1), 122*(2), 172*(1), 2,172*(2), 2,322*(1), 2,812*(1), 20,000*(2), 212*(1), 22,000*(7), 22,034*(1), 22,200*(1), 22,273*(1), 232*(1), 242*(1), 32*(1), 32,000*(2), 32,200*(2), 32,500*(1), 372*(2), 392*(2), 42*(2), 42,000*(1), 52*(2), 52,700*(1), 62*(1), 62,700*(2), 642*(2), 652*(2), 72*(1), 72,000*(1), 822*(1), 832*(1), both(62), both*(7), couple(2), double(7), each other(1), few(1), forty-two*(3), pair(7), second(11), second time(1), sixty-two*(4), thirty-second*(2), thirty-two*(7), twelfth*(22), twelve*(93), twenty-second*(2), twenty-two*(10), twice(5), two(424), two on opposite(2), two things(4), two-tenths*(11), twos(2).

8148. שְׁנִינָה **sheninah** (1042b); from 8150; *a sharp* (cutting) *word, taunt:*— byword(2), taunt(2).

8149. שְׁנִיר **Shenir** or

שְׂנִיר **Senir** (972a); of unc. der.; Amorite name for Mount Hermon:— Senir(4).

8150. שָׁנַן **shanan** (1041d); a prim. root; *to whet, sharpen:*— pierced(1), sharp(4), sharpen(2), sharpened(1), teach them diligently(1).

8151. שָׁנַס **shanas** (1042b); a prim. root; *to gird up:*— girded(1).

8152. שִׁנְעָר **Shinar** (1042b); prob. of for. or.; another name for Bab.:— Shinar(8).

8153. שְׁנָת **shenath** (446a); the same as 8142, q.v.

8154. שָׁסָה **shasah** or שָׁשָׂה **shasah** (1042c); a prim. root; *to spoil, plunder:*— despoiled(1), pillage(1), plunder(1), plundered(3), plunderers(2), plundering(1), taken spoil(1).

8155. שָׁסַס **shasas** (1042d); a prim. root; *to spoil, plunder:*— plunder(2), plundered(4).

8156. שָׁסַע **shasa** (1042d); a prim. root; *to divide, cleave:*— has the split(1), make a split(1), making a split(1), making split(1), persuaded(1), tear(1), tore him as one tears(1), two(1).

8157. שֶׁסַע **shesa** (1043a); from 8156; *cleft:*— hoof(1).

8158. שָׁסַף **shasaph** (1043a); a prim. root; *to hew in pieces:*— hewed to pieces(1).

8159. שָׁעָה **shaah** (1043a); a prim. root; *to gaze:*— gaze away(1), had regard(1), had...regard(1), have regard(3), look(3), looked(1), pay...attention(1), turn your eyes(1), turn your gaze(2), turn your gaze away(1).

8160. שָׁעָה **shaah** (1116d); (Ara.) from a root corr. to 8159; *a brief time, moment:*— immediately(3), suddenly(1), while(1).

8161. שַׁעֲטָה **shaatah** (1043b); from an unused word; *a stamping* (of hooves):— galloping(1).

8162. שַׁעַטְנֵז **shaatnez** (1043b); perh. of for. or.; *mixed stuff:*— material mixed(1), material mixed together(1).

8163a. שָׂעִיר **sair** or שָׂעִר **sair** (972c); from the same as 8181; *hairy:*— hairy(3), shaggy(2).

8163b. שָׂעִיר **sair** (972c); from the same as 8181; *male goat, buck:*— goat(6), goat*(1), goats(3), male(25), male goat(9), male goats(1).

8163c. שָׂעִיר **sair** (972d); from the same as 8181; *a satyr, demon:*— demons(1), satyrs(1).

8164. שָׂעִיר **sair** (973c); of unc. der.; *rain* (drop):— droplets(1).

8165. שֵׂעִיר **Seir** (973a); from the same as 8181; a mountain range in Edom, also its inhab., also a mountain in Judah:— Seir(39).

8166. שְׂעִירָה **seirah** (972c); fem. of 8163b; *female goat:*— goat(1), goat*(1).

8167. שְׂעִירָה **Seirah** (972c); from the same as 8181; "goat," a city in Ephraim:— Seirah(1).

8168. שֹׁעַל **shoal** (1043b); from an unused word; *hollow hand, handful:*— handfuls(2), hollow of his hand(1).

8169. שַׁעַלְבִים **Shaalbim** (1043c); from the same as 7776; perh. "(haunt of) foxes," a city in Dan:— Shaalabbin(1), Shaalbim(2).

8170. שַׁעַלְבֹנִי **Shaalboni** (1043d); from 8169; perh. an inhab. of Shaalbim:— Shaalbonite(2).

8171. שַׁעֲלִים **Shealim** (1043d); from the same as 7776; an area searched by Saul:— Shaalim(1).

8172. שָׁעַן **shaan** (1043d); a prim. root; *to lean, support oneself:*— lean(3), leaned(2), leaning(2), leans(2), relied(4), rely(4), rest yourselves(1), supported(1), trust(1), trusted(1), trusts(1).

8173a. שָׁעַע **shaa** (1044a); a prim. root; *to be smeared over, blinded:*— blind(2), blinded(1), dim(1).

8173b. שָׁעַע **shaa** (1044b); a prim. root; *to sport, take delight in, delight:*— delight(4), fondled(1), play(1).

8174a. שַׁעַף **Shaaph** (1044c); of unc. der.; two Calebites:— Shaaph(2).

8174b. שְׂעִפִּים **seippim** (972a); from an unused word; *disquieting* or *excited thoughts:*— disquieting thoughts(2).

8175a. שָׂעַר **saar** (973b); a prim. root; *to sweep* or *whirl away:*— away with a whirlwind(1), storm(1), sweep them away(1), tempestuous(1), whirls him away(1).

8175b. שָׂעַר **saar** (973b); a prim. root; perh. *to be acquainted with:*— dread(1).

8175c. שָׂעַר **saar** (972b); denom. vb. from 8181; *to bristle* (with horror):— afraid(2), shudder(1).

8176. שָׁעַר **shaar** (1045c); a prim. root; *to calculate, reckon:*— thinks(1).

8177. שְׂעַר **sear** (1114a); (Ara.) corr. to 8181; *hair:*— hair(3).

8178a. שַׂעַר **saar** (972c); from the same as 8181; *horror:*— horribly(2), horror(1).

8178b. שַׂעַר **saar** (973b); from 8175a; *a storm:*— tempest(1).

8179. שַׁעַר **shaar** (1044c); from an unused word; *a gate:*— cities(2), city(2), court(2), courts(1), each gate(1), every gate(1), every gate(1), Gate(49), gate(195), gatekeepers*(1), gates(88), gateway(4), gateway*(2), town(6), towns(13).

8180. שַׁעַר **shaar** (1045d); from 8176; *a measure:*— hundredfold*(1).

8181. שֵׂעָר **sear** (972b); from an unused word; *hair:*— hair(23), hairs(1), hairy(4).

8182. שֹׁעָר **shoar** (1045d); from an unused word; *horrid, disgusting:*— split-open(1).

8183. שְׂעָרָה **searah** (973b); fem. of 8178b; *a storm:*— storm(1), tempest(1).

8184. שְׂעֹרָה **seorah** (972d); from the same as 8181; *barley:*— barley(33).

8185. שַׂעֲרָה **saarah** (972b); from the same as 8181; *hair:*— hair(4), hairs(3).

8186a. שַׁעֲרוּרָה **shaarurah** (1045d); from the same as 8182; *a horror, horrible thing:*— horrible thing(2).

8186b. שַׁעֲרוּרִיָּה **shaaruriyyah** (1045d); from the same as 8182; *a horror, horrible thing:*— appalling thing(1), horrible thing(1).

8187. שְׁעַרְיָה **Shearyah** (1045c); from 8179 and 3050; perh. "gate of Yah," a Benjamite:— Sheariah(2).

8188. שְׂעֹרִים **Seorim** (972d); from the same as 8181; an Isr. priest:— Seorim(1).

8189. שַׁעֲרַיִם **Shaarayim** (1045c); from the same as 8179; two cities in Isr.:— maid(2), Shaaraim(3).

8190. שַׁעַשְׁגַז **Shaashgaz** (1045d); of for. or.; a Pers. eunuch:— Shaashgaz(1).

8191. שַׁעֲשֻׁעִים **shaashuim** (1044b); from 8173b; *a delight:*— delight(7), delightful(2).

8192. שָׁפָה **shaphah** (1045d); a prim. root; *to sweep bare:*— bare(1), stick(1).

8193. שָׂפָה **saphah** (973c); from an unused word; *lip, speech, edge:*— babbling(2), bank(10), binding(2), brim(9), edge(17), empty(2), gossip*(1), language(6), lip(1), lip service(1), lips(100), mere(1), seashore*(7), shore(1), speech(12), talk(1), talkative(1), words(2).

8194. שָׁפָה **shaphah** (1045d); from 8192; perh. *cream:*— cheese(1).

8195. שְׁפוֹ **Shepho** (1046a); from 8192; "bareness," an Edomite:— Shephi(1), Shepho(1).

8196. שְׁפוֹט **shephot** (1048b); from 8199; *judgment, act of judgment:*— judgment(1), judgments(1).

8197a. שְׁפוּפָם **Shephupham** (1051b); from the same as 8207; "serpent-like," a Benjamite:— Shephupham(1).

8197b. שְׁפוּפָן **Shephuphan** (1051b); from the same as 8207; "serpent-like," a Benjamite, perh. the same as 8197a:— Shephuphan(1).

8197c. שִׂפַּח **sippach** (705c); denom. vb. from 5597; *to cause a scab upon:*— afflict(1), scabs(1).

8198. שִׁפְחָה **shiphchah** (1046c); from an unused word; *maid, maidservant:*— female(9), female servant(3), female servants(5), maid(20), maids(5), maidservant(15), maidservants(1), servants*(6), slave(1), slave girl(1), slaves*(4), women(1).

8199. שָׁפַט **shaphat** (1047a); a prim. root; *to judge, govern:*— acting like a judge(1), already he is acting(1), argue our case(1), decide(1), defend(3), deliver(1), Dispense(1), enter into judgment(6), entered into judgment(1), entering into judgment(1), execute judgment(1), executing judgment(1), freed(2), handed down(1), has a controversy(1), Judge(5), judge(93), judged(22), judges(36), judges decide(1), judges governed(1), judges...judged(1), judging(5), plead(1), pleads(1), pronounce judgment(1), rule(2), rulers(1), rulers...ruled(1), vindicate(6).

8200. שְׁפַט **shephat** (1117a); (Ara.) corr. to 8199; *to judge:*— magistrates(1).

8201. שֶׁפֶט **shephet** (1048a); from 8199; *judgment:*— judgment(1), judgments(15).

8202. שָׁפָט **Shaphat** (1048b); from 8199; "he has judged," five Isr.:— Shaphat(8).

8203. שְׁפַטְיָה **Shephatyah** or שְׁפַטְיָהוּ **Shephatyahu** (1049b); from 8199 and 3050; "Yah has judged," the name of a number of Isr.:— Shephatiah(13).

8204. שִׁפְטָן **Shiphtan** (1049b); from 8199; "judgment," a prince of Ephraim:— Shiphtan(1).

8205. שְׁפִי **shephi** (1046a); from 8192; *bareness, a smooth* or *bare height:*— bare heights(8), bare hill(1).

8206. שֻׁפִּים **Shuppim** (1051b); of unc. der.; two Isr.:— Shuppim(3).

8207. שְׁפִיפֹן **shephiphon** (1051b); of unc. der.; *horned viper:*— horned snake(1).

8208. שָׁפִיר **Shaphir** (1051c); from 8231b; "beauty," a place perh. in Philistia:— Shaphir(1).

8209. שַׁפִּיר **shappir** (1117a); (Ara.) from a form corr. to 8208; *fair, beautiful:*— beautiful(2).

8210. שָׁפַךְ **shaphak** (1049b); a prim. root; *to pour out, pour:*— cast(5), cast up a siege(1), dump(1), gushed(1), pour(34), poured(26), pouring(1), pours(5), raise(1), shed(29), shedding(5), sheds(2), slipped(1), throw(2).

8211. שֶׁפֶךְ **shephek** (1050a); from 8210; (place of) *pouring:*— poured(2).

8212. שָׁפְכָה **shophkah** (1050a); from 8210; *male organ:*— male organ(1).

8213. שָׁפֵל **shaphel** (1050a); a prim. root; *to be* or *become low, to be abased:*— abase(4), abased(6), been abased(1), bring him low(1), bring down(1), brings down(1), brings low(1), brought low(1), cast down(1), go down(1), humbles(1), laid low(1), lay low(2), lays it low(2), lowly(1), made low(1), make him low(1), placed lower(1), puts down(1).

8214. שְׁפַל shephel (1117a); (Ara.) corr. to 8213; *to be low:*— humble(1), humbled(2), subdue(1).

8215. שְׁפַל shephal (1117a); (Ara.) from 8214; *low* (in station):— lowliest(1).

8216. שֵׁפֶל shephel (1050c); from 8213; *low estate* or *condition:*— humble places(1), low estate(1).

8217. שָׁפָל shaphal (1050c); from 8213; *low:*— abased(1), deeper(2), humble(3), low(3), lower(2), lowest(1), lowly(5), subjection(1), which is low(1).

8218. שִׁפְלָה shiphlah (1050c); from 8213; *humiliation:*— utterly(1).

8219. שְׁפֵלָה shephelah (1050c); from 8213; *lowland:*— foothills(1), lowland(17), Shephelah(2).

8220. שִׁפְלוּת shiphluth (1050d); from 8213; *a sinking:*— slackness*(1).

8221. שְׁפָם Shepham (1050d); of unc. der.; a place on the E. border of Isr.:— Shepham(2).

8222. שָׂפָם sapham (974a); from the same as 8193; *mustache:*— mouths(1), mustache(4).

8223. שָׁפָם Shapham (1050d); from the same as 8221; a Gadite:— Shapham(1).

8224. שִׂפְמוֹת Siphmoth or

שִׂפָמוֹת Shiphamoth (974a, 1050d); of unc. der.; a place in S. Judah:— Siphmoth(1).

8225. שִׁפְמִי Shiphmi (1050d); from 8221; inhab. of Shepham:— Shiphmite(1).

8226. שָׂפַן saphan (706a); the same as 5603, q.v.

8227a. שָׁפָן shaphan (1050d); from an unused word; *hyrax:*— shaphan(2), shephanim(2).

8227b. שָׁפָן Shaphan (1051a); from the same as 8227a; the name of several Isr.:— shaphan(30).

8228. שֶׁפַע shepha (1051a); from an unused word; *abundance:*— abundance(1).

8229. שִׁפְעָה shiphah (1051a); fem. of 8228; *abundance, quantity:*— abundance(2), company(2), multitude(2).

8230a. שִׁפְעִי Shiphi (1051b); from the same as 8228; a Simeonite:— Shiphi(1).

8230b. שָׂפַק saphaq (974a); a prim. root; *to suffice:*— suffice(1).

8231a. שֵׂפֶק sepheq (974b); from 8230b; *sufficiency, plenty:*— plenty(1).

8231b. שָׁפַר shaphar (1051c); a prim. root; *to be beautiful, fair* or *comely:*— beautiful(1).

8232. שְׁפַר shephar (1117a); (Ara.) corr. to 8231b; *to be fair* or *seemly:*— pleasing(1), seemed good(2).

8233. שֶׁפֶר shepher (1051c); from 8231b; *beauty, goodliness:*— beautiful(1).

8234. שֶׁפֶר Shepher (1051c); from 8231b; "beauty," a mountain in the desert:— Shepher(2).

8235. שִׁפְרָה shiphrah (1051c); from 8231b; *fairness, clearness* (of sky):— cleared(1).

8236. שִׁפְרָה Shiphrah (1051c); from 8231b; "fairness," a Heb. midwife:— Shiphrah(1).

8237. שַׁפְרוּר shaphrur or

שַׁפְרִיר shaphrir (1051d); from 8231b; perh. *splendor, pavilion, canopy:*— canopy(1).

8238. שְׁפַרְפַּר shepharpar (1117a); (Ara.) from a root corr. to 8231b; *dawn:*— dawn(1).

8239. שָׁפַת shaphath (1046b); from an unused word; *to set* (on the fire):— establish(1), lay(1), put(3).

8240a. שְׁפַתַּיִם shephattayim (1046b); from the same as 8239; perh. *fireplaces, ash heaps:*— sheepfolds(1).

8240b. שְׁפַתַיִם shephathayim (1052a); of unc. der.; prob. *hook-shaped pegs, hooks:*— double hooks(1).

8241. שֶׁצֶף shetseph (1009b); the same as 7858, q.v.

8242. שַׂק saq (974b); of unc. der.; *sack, sackcloth:*— sack(4), sackcloth(42), sacks(2).

8243. שָׁק shaq (1114d); (Ara.) corr. to 7785; (lower) *leg:*— legs(1).

8244. שָׂקַד saqad (974b); a prim. root; perh. *to bind on:*— bound(1).

8245. שָׁקַד shaqad (1052a); a prim. root; *to watch, wake:*— intent on doing(1), keep watch(1), keeps awake(1), kept the in store(1), lie awake(1), watch(2), watched(1), watching(4).

8246. שָׁקַד shaqad (1052b); denom. vb. from 8247; *to be shaped like almonds:*— shaped like almond(6).

8247. שָׁקֵד shaqed (1052b); from 8245; *almond* (tree):— almond tree(2), almonds(2).

8248. שָׁקָה shaqah (1052b); a prim. root; *cause to drink water, give to drink:*— drink(23), drinks were served(1), gave him a drink(2), gave me to drink(1), gave the a drink(1), gave them drink(2), give(5), give him to drink(1), give me to drink(2), give them to drink(1), give drink(2), given(1), given to drink(1), given us to drink(1), giving him a drink(1), irrigate(1), made them to drink(1), moist(1), provided him to drink(1), water(12), watered(5), waters(1).

8249. שִׁקֻּו shiqquv (1052c); the same as 8250, q.v.

8250. שִׁקּוּי shiqquy (1052c); from 8248; *a drink:*— drink(2), refreshment(1).

8251. שִׁקּוּץ shiqquts or

שִׁקֻּץ shiqquts (1055a); from the same as 8263; *detested thing:*— abominable idols(1), abomination(4), abominations(5), detestable(1), detestable idol(3), detestable idols(2), detestable things(10), detested things(1), filth(1).

8252. שָׁקַט shaqat (1052d); a prim. root; *to be quiet* or *undisturbed:*— been quiet(1), been undisturbed(1), calm(1), calmed(1), calms(1), careless(1), grant him relief(1), had rest(3), keep quiet(1), keeps quiet(1), pacified(1), peace(1), quiet(12), quietly(1), quietness(2), rest(2), still(3), undisturbed(7).

8253. שֶׁקֶט sheqet (1053b); from 8252; *quietness:*— quiet(1).

8254. שָׁקַל shaqal (1053b); a prim. root; *to weigh:*— actually weighed(1), pay(4), receive(1), spend(1), weigh(3), weighed(10), weighs(1).

8255. שֶׁקֶל sheqel (1053d); from 8254; (a measure of weight) *shekel:*— shekel(42), shekels(46).

8256. שִׁקְמָה shiqmah (1054a); of unc. der.; *sycamore tree:*— sycamore(1), sycamore trees(4), sycamores(2).

8257. שָׁקַע shaqa (1054b); a prim. root; *to sink, sink down:*— died(1), press down(1), settle(1), sink down(1), subside(1), subsides(1).

8258. שְׁקַעֲרוּרָה sheqaarurah (891a); from the same as 7086; *depression, hollow:*— depressions(1).

8259. שָׁקַף shaqaph (1054c); a prim. root; *to overhang, look out* or *down:*— grows(1), look down(1), looked(6), looked down(8), looks down(3), overlooks*(3).

8260. שֶׁקֶף sheqeph (1054d); from an unused word; *framework, casing* (of doors):— frames(1).

8261. שָׁקֻף shaquph or

שָׁקוּף shaquph (1054d); from the same as 8260; *frame, casing:*— frames(2).

8262. שָׁקַץ shaqats (1055a); denom. vb. from 8263; *to detest, make detestable:*— abhorred(1), detest(2), make...detestable(1), render...detestable(1), utterly detest(1).

8263. שֶׁקֶץ sheqets (1054d); from an unused word; *detestation, detestable thing:*— abhorrent(3), detestable(4), detestable thing(1), detestable things(3).

8264. שָׁקַק shaqaq (1055b); a prim. root; *to run, run about, rush:*— quenched(1), rush(1), rush about(1), rush wildly(1), rushing(1), thirsty(1).

8265. שָׂקַר saqar (974c); a prim. root; *to ogle:*— seductive(1).

8266. שָׁקַר shaqar (1055d); denom. vb. from 8267; *to do* or *deal falsely:*— deal falsely(4), dealt falsely(1), lie(2).

8267. שֶׁקֶר sheqer (1055b); from an unused word; *deception, disappointment, falsehood:*— deceit(2), deceitful(3), deceiving(4), deception(3), deceptive(3), false(17), false hope(1), falsehood(19), falsehoods(1), falsely(19), liar(1), lie(14), lies(5), lying(12), lying visions(1), perjury*(1), slander*(1), treacherously(1), useless(1), vain(1), wrongfully(3).

8268. שֹׁקֶת shoqeth (1052d); from 8248; *watering trough:*— trough(1), troughs(1).

8269. שַׂר sar (978a); from an unused word; *chieftain, chief, ruler, official, captain, prince:*— captain(22), captains(39), charge(1), chief(24), chief and commanders(1), chiefs(1), commander(40), commanders(49), governor(3), heads(1), leader(2), leaders(28), leading(3), officer(1), officers(14), official(9), officials(35), overseers(3), Prince(1), prince(9), prince of princes(1), princes(109), quartermaster*(1), ruler(1), rulers(10), taskmasters*(1).

8270. שֹׁר shor (1057a); from an unused word; *umbilical cord:*— body(1), navel(1), navel cord(1).

8271. שְׁרֵא shera (1117b); (Ara.) corr. to 8281; *to loosen, abide:*— began(1), dwells(1), loosed(1), solve(1), solving(1), went slack(1).

8272. שַׁרְאֶצֶר Sharetser or

שַׂרְאֶצֶר Saretser (974c); prob. of for. or.; an Assyr., also perh. an Isr.:— Sharezer(3).

8273. שָׁרָב sharab (1055d); from an unused word; *burning heat, parched ground:*— scorched land(1), scorching heat(1).

8274. שֵׁרֵבְיָה Sherebeyah (1055d); from 8273 and 3050; "Yah has sent burning heat," an Isr. name:— Sherebiah(8).

8275. שַׁרְבִיט sharbit (987b); from the same as 7626; *a scepter:*— scepter(4).

8276. שָׂרַג sarag (974d); a prim. root; *to be intertwined:*— knit together(2).

8277. שָׂרַד sarad (974d); a prim. root; *to escape:*— remained(1).

8278. **שְׂרָד** **serad** (975a); from an unused word; perh. *plaited* or *braided work:*— finely woven(1), woven(3).

8279. **שֶׂרֶד** **sered** (975b); from the same as 8278; *a stylus:*— chalk(1).

8280. **שָׂרָה** **sarah** (975b); a prim. root; *to persist, exert oneself, persevere:*— contended(1), striven(1), wrestled(1).

8281. **שָׁרָה** **sharah** (1056a); a prim. root; *to let loose:*— lets it loose(1), set you free(1).

8282. **שָׂרָה** **sarah** (979a); fem. of 8269; *princess, noble lady:*— ladies(1), princess(1), princesses(3).

8283. **שָׂרָה** **Sarah** (979a); from the same as 8269; "princess," a wife of Abraham:— Sarah(36), Sarah's(2).

8284. **שָׁרָה** **sharah** (1004b); fem. of 7791, q.v.

8285. **שֵׁרָה** **sherah** (1057a); from the same as 8270; *a bracelet:*— bracelets(1).

8286. **שְׂרוּג** **Serug** (974d); from 8276; a desc. of Peleg:— Serug(5).

8287. **שָׁרוּחֶן** **Sharuchen** (1056b); prob. from the same as 8302 and from 2580; a city in Simeon:— Sharuhen(1).

8288. **שְׂרוֹךְ** **serok** (976c); from 8308; (sandal) *thong:*— strap(1), thong(1).

8289. **שָׁרוֹן** **Sharon** (450a, 1056c); from 3474; a plain on the Mediterranean Sea, perh. also a region E. of the Jordan:— Lasharon(1), Sharon(6).

8290. **שָׁרוֹנִי** **Sharoni** (1056c); from 8289; inhab. of Sharon:— Sharonite(1).

8291. **שָׂרוּק** **saruq** or
שָׂרֹק **saroq** (977d); from the same as 8320; *vine tendrils* or *clusters:*— choice clusters(1).

8292. **שְׁרוּקָה** **sheruqah** or
שְׁרִיקָה **sheriqah** (1057a); from 8319; *hissing, whistling, piping:*— hissing(1), piping(1).

8293. **שֵׁרוּת** **sheruth** (1056a, 1056c); another form of 8281, q.v.

8294. **שֶׂרַח** **Serach** (976a); from the same as 4951; a daughter of Asher:— Serah(3).

8295. **שָׂרַט** **sarat** (976b); a prim. root; *to incise, scratch:*— make any cuts(1), severely injured(1).

8296a. **שֶׂרֶט** **seret** or
שָׂרֶטֶת **sareteth** (976b); from 8295; *incision:*— cuts(1).

8296b. **שָׂרֶטֶת** **sareteth** (976b); a form of 8295, q.v.

8297. **שָׂרַי** **Saray** (979c); from the same as 8269; a wife of Abram:— Sarai(16), Sarai's(1).

8298. **שָׁרַי** **Sharay** (1056c); of unc. der.; an Isr. with a for. wife:— Sharai(1).

8299. **שָׂרִיג** **sarig** (974d); from 8276; *tendril, twig:*— branches(3).

8300. **שָׂרִיד** **sarid** (975a); from 8277; *a survivor:*— left(1), remains(1), remnant(2), survived(1), survivor(13), survivors(8), who survived(2).

8301a. **שָׂרִיד** **Sarid** (975a); from 8277; a city on the border of Zebulun:— Sarid(2).

8301b. **שִׁרְיָה** **shiryah** (1056b); from an unused word; (a weapon) perh. *a lance, javelin:*— javelin(1).

8302. **שִׁרְיוֹן** **shiryon** or
שִׁרְיָן **shiryan** (1056b); from an unused word; *body armor:*— armor(3), body armor(1), breastplate(1), breastplates(1).

8303. **שִׂרְיֹן** **Siryon** (976b); of unc. der.; a Sidonian name for Mount Hermon:— Sirion(2).

8304. **שְׂרָיָה** **Serayah** or
שְׂרָיָהוּ **Serayahu** (976a); from 8280 and 3050; "Yah persists," the name of a number of Isr.:— Seraiah(20).

8305. **שָׂרִיק** **sariq** (977c); from an unused word; *carded* or *combed:*— combed(1).

8306. **שָׁרִיר** **sharir** (1057b); from the same as 8270; *sinew, muscle:*— muscles(1).

8307. **שְׁרִירוּת** **sheriruth** (1057b); from the same as 8270; *firmness, stubbornness:*— stubbornness(10).

8308. **שָׂרַךְ** **sarak** (976c); a prim. root; *to twist:*— entangling(1).

8309. **שְׁרֵמָה** **sheremah** (995b); scribal error for 7709, q.v.

8310. **שַׂרְסְכִים** **Sarsekim** (976c); of for. or.; one of Nebuchadnezzar's princes:— Sar-sekim(1).

8311. **שָׂרַע** **sara** (976c); a prim. root; *to extend:*— deformed(1), overgrown(1), stretch(1).

8312. **שַׂרְעַפִּים** **sarappim** (972a); from the same as 8174b; *disquieting thoughts:*— anxious thoughts(2).

8313. **שָׂרַף** **saraph** (976d); a prim. root; *to burn:*— brought(1), burn(35), burn it as he burned(1), burned(70), burns(5), completely burned(1), made(1), undertaker(1).

8314a. **שָׂרָף** **saraph** (977b); from 8313; *fiery serpent:*— fiery(1), fiery serpents(2), serpent(2).

8314b. **שָׂרָף** **saraph** (977b); from 8313; prob. one of an order of angelic beings:— seraphim(2).

8315. **שָׂרָף** **Saraph** (977b); from 8313; "burning," a man of Judah:— Saraph(1).

8316. **שְׂרֵפָה** **serephah** (977b); from 8313; *a burning:*— blaze(2), burned(1), burning(4), burnt(2), fire(3), thoroughly(1).

8317. **שָׁרַץ** **sharats** (1056c); a prim. root; *to swarm, teem:*— breed abundantly(1), increased greatly(1), populate the abundantly(1), swarm(3), swarmed(2), swarms(5), teem(1).

8318. **שֶׁרֶץ** **sherets** (1056d); from 8317; *swarmers, swarming things:*— insects(3), swarming thing(3), swarming things(5), swarms(1), teeming life(2), teeming things(1).

8319. **שָׁרַק** **sharaq** (1056d); a prim. root; *to hiss, whistle, pipe:*— hiss(9), whistle(3).

8320. **שָׂרֹק** **saroq** (977d); from an unused word; perh. *sorrel:*— sorrel(1).

8321a. **שֹׂרֵק** **soreq** (977d); from the same as 8320; (choice species of) *the vine:*— choice vine(1), choicest vine(1).

8321b. **שֹׂרֵקָה** **soreqah** (977d); from the same as 8320; (choice) *vine:*— choice vine(1).

8322. **שְׁרֵקָה** **shereqah** (1056d); from 8319; (object of derisive) *hissing:*— derision(1), hissing(6).

8323. **שָׂרַר** **sarar** (979a); denom. vb. from 8269; *to be* or *act as prince, rule:*— appointed princes(1), lord(1), master(1), rule(2), ruled(1).

8324. **שָׁרַר** **sharar** (1004a); see 7796b.

8325. **שָׁרָר** **Sharar** (1057b); from the same as 8270; father of one of David's heroes, the same as 7940:— Sharar(1).

8326. **שֹׁרֶר** **shorer** (1057a); the same as 8270, q.v.

8327. **שָׁרַשׁ** **sharash** (1057d); denom. vb. from 8328; *to deal with the roots:*— take root(1), taken root(2), taking root(1), took(1), uproot(2), uprooted(1).

8328. **שֹׁרֶשׁ** **shoresh** (1057c); from an unused word; *a root:*— base(1), deep root(1), depths(1), line(1), pretext(1), root(17), roots(10), soles(1).

8329. **שֶׁרֶשׁ** **Sheresh** (1058a); from the same as 8328; "root," a man of Manasseh:— Sheresh(1).

8330. **שֹׁרֶשׁ** **shoresh** (1117b); (Ara.) corr. to 8328; *a root:*— roots(3).

8331. **שַׁרְשָׁה** **sharshah** (1057b); the same as 8333, q.v.

8332. **שְׁרֹשׁוּ** **sheroshu** or
שְׁרֹשִׁי **sheroshi** (1117b); (Ara.) from a root corr. to that of 8328; *uprooting, banishment:*— banishment(1).

8333. **שַׁרְשְׁרָה** **sharsherah** (1057b); from the same as 8270; *chain:*— chains(7), chainwork*(1).

8334. **שָׁרַת** **sharath** (1058a); a prim. root; *to minister, serve:*— assist(1), attendant(4), attended(2), became his personal servant(1), minister(26), ministered(4), ministering(15), ministers(17), personal servant(1), servant(1), servant(2), serve(11), served(6), service(1), serving(1), take care(1), took care(1), used in temple service(2), waiters(1).

8335. **שָׁרֵת** **shareth** (1058b); from 8334; (religious) *ministry:*— service(2).

8336. **שֵׁשׁ** **shesh** (1058c); of for. or.; *byssus:*— fine linen(16), fine...linen(21), finely...linen(1).

8337a. **שֵׁשׁ** **shesh** or
שִׁשָּׁה **shishshah** (995c); from an unused word; *six* (a card. number):— 153,600*(1), 156*(1), 157,600*(1), 16,000*(2), 16,750*(1), 186,400*(1), 2,056*(1), 2,600*(2), 2,630*(1), 22,600*(1), 26,000*(2), 28,600*(1), 3,600*(2), 3,630*(1), 36,000*(3), 4,600*(2), 45,600*(1), 45,650*(2), 46,500*(2), 54,400*(1), 56*(1), 6,000*(3), 6,200*(1), 6,720*(2), 6,800*(1), 600*(8), 600,000*(1), 601,730*(1), 603,550*(3), 61,000*(1), 621*(2), 623*(1), 628*(1), 642*(2), 648*(1), 650*(1), 652*(2), 655*(1), 666*(6), 667*(1), 675*(1), 675,000*(1), 690*(1), 736*(2), 74,600*(2), 76,500*(1), 8,600*(1), 956*(1), 96*(1), ninety-six*(1), six(104), six things(1), sixteen*(18), sixteenth*(3), sixth(1), sixty-six*(2), thirty-six*(1), thirty-sixth*(1), twenty-sixth*(1).

8337b. **שֵׁשׁ** **shesh** (1010d); from the same as 7893; *alabaster:*— alabaster(1), marble(2).

8338. **שָׁשָׁא** **shasha** (1058c); a prim. root; prob. *to lead on:*— drive(1).

8339. **שֵׁשְׁבַּצַּר** **Sheshbatstsar** (1058c); of for. or; a prince of Judah:— Sheshbazzar(2).

8340. **שֵׁשְׁבַּצַּר** **Sheshbatstsar** (1117b, 1127c); (Ara.) corr. to 8339; a prince of Judah:— Sheshbazzar(2).

8341. **שִׁשָּׁה** **shishshah** (995d); denom. vb. from 8337a; *to give a sixth part of:*— sixth(1).

8342. **שָׂשׂוֹן** **sason** (965b); from 7797; *exultation, rejoicing:*— gaiety(1), gladness(3), joy(15), joyously(1), rejoicing(2).

8343. **שָׁשַׁי** **Shashay** (1058d); of unc. der.; an Isr. with a for. wife:— Shashai(1).

8344. **שֵׁשַׁי** **Sheshay** (1058d); of unc. der.; a son of Anak:— Sheshai(3).

8345. שִׁשִּׁי shishshi (995d); from the same as 8337a; *sixth:*— sixth(27), sixth part(1).

8346. שִׁשִּׁים shishshim (995d); from the same as 8337a; *sixty:*— 1,365*(1), 1,760*(1), 160*(1), 2,067*(1), 42,360*(2), 44,760*(1), 468*(1), 60(4), 60,000*(1), 60,500*(1), 61*(1), 61,000*(1), 62*(1), 62,700*(2), 64,300*(1), 64,400*(1), 65*(1), 666*(3), 667*(1), 67*(1), 68*(1), 760*(2), sixty(19), sixty-five*(3), sixty-nine*(1), sixty-six*(2), sixty-two*(4).

8347. שֵׁשַׁךְ Sheshak (1058d); of unc. der.; a name for Bab.:— Sheshach(1), Sheshak(1).

8348. שֵׁשָׁן Sheshan (1058d); of unc. der.; a man of Judah:— Sheshan(5).

8349. שָׁשַׁק Shashaq (1059a); of unc. der.; a Benjamite:— Shashak(2).

8350. שָׁשַׁר shasher (1059a); of unc. der.; *red color, vermilion:*— bright red(1), vermilion(1).

8351. שֵׁת sheth (1059d); from an unused word; *seat* (of the body), *buttocks:*— buttocks(1), hips(1).

8352. שֵׁת Sheth (1011c); from 7896; a son of Adam:— Seth(8), Sheth(1).

8353. שֵׁת sheth or

שִׁת shith (1114d); (Ara.) corr. to 8337a; *six:*— six(1), sixth(1).

8354. שָׁתָה shathah (1059a); a prim. root; *to drink:*— certainly drink(2), drank(27), drink(138), drink the will certainly(1), drink down(1), drinkers(1), drinking(18), drinks(9), drunk(11), drunkards*(1), feasted(1), surely drink(1), well-watered(2).

8355. שְׁתָה shethah (1117c); (Ara.) corr. to 8354; *to drink:*— drank(2), drink(1), drinking(2).

8356. שָׁתָה shathah or

שָׁת shath (1011d); from 7896; *foundation, stay* (of society):— foundations(1), pillars(1).

8357. שֵׁתָה shethah (1059d); the same as 8351, q.v.

8358. שְׁתִי shethi (1059c); from 8354; *a drinking, drinking bout:*— drunkenness(1).

8359. שְׁתִי shethi (1059d); from an unused word; *warp:*— warp(9).

8360. שְׁתִיָּה shethiyyah (1059c); fem. of 8358; *a drinking:*— drinking(1).

8361. שִׁתִּין shittin (1114d); (Ara.) corr. to 8346; *sixty:*— 60(2), sixty(1), sixty-two*(1).

8362. שָׁתַל shathal (1060a); a prim. root; *to transplant:*— plant(2), planted(8).

8363. שְׁתִל shethil or

שָׁתִיל shathil (1060a); from 8362; *a transplanted shoot, slip:*— plants(1).

8364. שֻׁתַלְחִי Shuthalchi (1004d); from 7803; desc. of Shuthelah:— Shuthelahites(1).

8365a. שָׂתַם satham (979c); a prim. root; prob. *to stop up:*— shuts(1).

8365b. שָׁתַם shatham (1060c); a prim. root; *open:*— opened(2).

8366. שָׁתַן shathan (1010b); denom. vb. from 7890; *to urinate:*— every(3), male*(6).

8367. שָׁתַק shathaq (1060c); a prim. root; *to be quiet:*— become calm(2), quiet(1), quiets down(1).

8368. שָׂתַר sathar (979c); a prim. root; *to burst* or *break out:*— broke(1).

8369. שֵׁתָר Shethar (1060c); of for. or.; a prince of Pers.:— Shethar(1).

8370. שְׁתַר בּוֹזְנַי Shethar Bozenay (1117c); (Ara.) of for. or.; a Pers. official:— Shethar-bozenai(4).

8371. שָׁתַת shathath (1060c); a prim. root; *to set, appoint:*— appointed(1).

ת

8372. תָּא ta (1060b); of unc. der.; *a chamber:*— guardroom(2), guardrooms(9), room(2).

8373. תָּאַב taab or

תָּאֵב taeb (1060b); a prim. root; *to long for:*— long(2).

8374. תָּאַב taab (1060b); from 8373; *to loathe:*— loathe(1).

8375. תַּאֲבָה taabah (1060b); from 8373; *a longing:*— longing(1).

8376. תָּאָה taah (1060d); a prim. root; prob. *to mark out:*— draw a line(1), draw your border line(1).

8377. תְּאוֹ teo (1060d); from 8376; *antelope:*— antelope(2).

8378. תַּאֲוָה taavah (16c); from the same as 183; *a desire:*— delight(1), desire(14), desires*(1), favorite(1), greedy(1), intensely(1), what is desirable(1).

8379. תַּאֲוָה taavah (1063b); from the same as 8420a; *a boundary:*— utmost bound(1).

8380. תָּאוֹם taom (1060d); see 8420b.

8381. תַּאֲלָה taalah (46d); from 422; *a curse:*— curse(1).

8382. תָּאַם taam (1060d); denom. vb. from 8420b; *to be double:*— bear twins(2), double(2).

8383. תְּאֻן teun (20b); from the same as 205; *toil:*— toil(1).

8384. תְּאֵנָה teenah (1061a); of unc. der.; *fig tree:*— fig(1), fig tree(17), fig trees(6), figs(14), figs on the fig tree(1).

8385a. תַּאֲנָה taanah (58c); from 579; *occasion* or *time of copulation:*— heat(1).

8385b. תֹּאֲנָה toanah (58c); from 579; *opportunity:*— occasion(1).

8386. תַּאֲנִיָּה taaniyyah (58b); from 578; *mourning:*— lamenting(1).

8387. תַּאֲנַת שִׁלֹה Taanath Shiloh (1061b); from 8385a and 7887; perh. "approach to Shiloh," a city of Ephraim:— Taanath-shiloh(1).

8388a. תָּאַר taar (1061b); a prim. root; prob. *to incline:*— curved(3), extended(2), stretches(1).

8388b. תָּאַר taar (1061c); denom. vb. from 8389; *to draw in outline, trace out:*— outlines(2).

8389. תֹּאַר toar (1061b); from 8388a; *outline, form:*— appearance(2), form(7), handsome(1), handsome*(1), resembling(1).

8390. תַּאֲרֵעַ Taarea (357c); of unc. der.; a desc. of Saul, the same as 8475:— Tarea(1).

8391. תְּאַשּׁוּר teashshur (81b); from 833; *boxtree:*— cypress(1), tree and the cypress(1).

8392. תֵּבָה tebah (1061c); prob. of for. or.; *a box, chest:*— ark(26), basket(2).

8393. תְּבוּאָה tebuah (100a); from 935; *product, revenue:*— crop(4), crops(6), gain(1), harvest(4), income(4), increase(3), produce(10), product(3), revenue(2), yield(5), yield may increase(1).

8394. תְּבוּנָה tebunah (108b); from 995; *an understanding:*— discernment(1), reasonings(1), skill(1), skillful(1), skillfully(1), understanding(37).

8395. תְּבוּסָה tebusah (101b); from 947; *a treading down, ruin, downfall:*— destruction(1).

8396. תָּבוֹר Tabor (1061d); of unc. der.; a mountain S.W. of the Sea of Galilee, also several other places in Isr.:— Tabor(10).

8397. תֶּבֶל tebel (117d); appar. from 1101a; *confusion:*— incest(1), perversion(1).

8398. תֵּבֵל tebel (385c); from 2986; *world:*— inhabited(1), inhabited world(1), world(34).

8399. תַּבְלִית tablith (115b); from 1086; *destruction:*— destruction(1).

8400. תְּבַלֻּל teballul (117d); from 1101a; *confusion, obscurity:*— defect(1).

8401. תֶּבֶן teben (1061d); of unc. der.; *straw:*— straw(17).

8402. תִּבְנִי Tibni (1062a); from the same as 8401; a rival of Omri:— Tibni(3).

8403. תַּבְנִית tabnith (125d); from 1129; *construction, pattern, figure:*— copy(1), form(4), image(1), likeness(5), model(2), pattern(4), plan(2).

8404. תַּבְעֵרָה Taberah (129c); from 1197a; "burning," a place in the desert:— Taberah(2).

8405. תֵּבֵץ Tebets (1062a); of unc. der.; a city near Shechem:— Thebez(3).

8406. תְּבַר tebar (1117c); (Ara.) corr. to 7665; *to break:*— brittle(1).

8407. תִּגְלַת פִּלְאֶסֶר Tiglath Pileser (1062a); of for. or.; an Assyr. king:— Tiglath-pileser(3), Tilgath-pilneser(3).

8408. תַּגְמוּל tagmul (168c); from 1580; *a benefit:*— benefits(1).

8409. תִּגְרָה tigrah (173d); from 1624; *contention, strife, hostility:*— opposition(1).

8410. תִּדְהָר tidhar (187b); from 1725; (name of a tree) prob. *elm:*— box(1), box tree(1), tree(1).

8411. תְּדִירָא tedira (1087b); (Ara.) from 1753; *continuance:*— constantly(2).

8412. תַּדְמֹר Tadmor or

תַּמֹּר Tammor (1062b); of unc. der.; a city built by Solomon:— Tadmor(1).

8413. תִּדְעָל Tidal (1062b); of unc. der.; perh. a Canaanite king:— Tidal(2).

8414. תֹּהוּ tohu (1062c); from an unused word; *formlessness, confusion, unreality, emptiness:*— chaos(1), confusion(1), desolation(1), emptiness(1), empty space(1), formless(2), futile(2), futile things(1), meaningless(2), meaningless arguments(1), nothing(2), waste(3), waste place(2).

8415. תְּהוֹם tehom or

תְּהֹם tehom (1062d); from an unused word; *deep, sea, abyss:*— deep(22), deeps(8), depths(4), ocean depths(1), springs(1).

8416. תְּהִלָּה tehillah (239d); from 1984b; *praise, song of praise:*— praise(47), praises(6), praising(1), song of praise(1).

8417. תָּהֳלָה toholah (1062d); of unc. der.; *error:*— error(1).

8418. תַּהֲלוּכָה tahalukah (237c); from 1980; *procession:*— proceeding(1).

8419. תַּהְפֻּכָה tahpukah (246c); from 2015; *perversity, perverse thing:*— perverse(2), perverse things(3), perversity(2), perverted(2), what is perverted(1).

8420a. תָּו tav (1063b); from an unused word; *a mark:*— mark(2), signature(1).

8420b. תּוֹאָם toam (1060d); from an unused word; *a twin:*— twins(4).

8421. תּוּב **tub** (1117d); (Ara.) corr. to 7725; *to return:*— answered*(1), give(1), replied(1), restored(1), returned(4).

8422. תּוּבַל **Tubal** or

תֻּבַל **Tubal** (1063a); prob. of for. or.; a son of Japheth, also his desc. and their land:— Tubal(8).

8423. תּוּבַל קַיִן **Tubal Qayin** (1063b); from 8422 and 7014b; a son of Lamech:— Tubal-cain(2).

8424. תּוּגָה **tugah** (387b); from 3013; *grief:*— grief(3), sorrow(1).

8425. תּוֹגַרְמָה **Togarmah** or

תֹּגַרְמָה **Togarmah** (1062b); prob. of for. or.; a son of Gomer, also his desc. and their land:— Beth-togarmah*(2), Togarmah(2).

8426. תּוֹדָה **todah** (392d); from 3034; *thanksgiving:*— choir(1), choirs(2), confession(1), hymns of thanksgiving(1), praise(1), sacrifices of thanksgiving(1), thank offering(2), thank offerings(4), thanksgiving(18).

8427. תָּוָה **tavah** (1063b); denom. vb. from 8420a; *to make* or *set a mark:*— put(1), scribbled(1).

8428. תָּוָה **tavah** (1063b); a prim. root; prob. *to pain, wound:*— pained(1).

8429. תְּוַהּ **tevah** (1117d); (Ara.) corr. to 8539; *to be startled* or *alarmed:*— astounded(1).

8430. תּוֹחַ **Toach** (1063c); of unc. der.; an ancestor of Samuel:— Toah(1).

8431. תּוֹחֶלֶת **tocheleth** (404b); from 3176; *a hope:*— expectation(1), hope(5).

8432. תָּוֶךְ **tavek** (1063c); of unc. der.; *midst:*— along(3), among(135), among*(1), between(2), center(10), high(1), home(2), inside(9), interior(1), internally(1), middle(32), middle part(1), midst(162), presence(1), reenter*(2), through(2), two(1), within(18).

8433a. תּוֹכֵחָה **tokechah** (407b); from 3198; *rebuke, correction:*— punishment(1), rebuke(3).

8433b. תּוֹכַחַת **tokachath** (407b); from 3198; *argument, reproof:*— argument(1), arguments(2), chastened(1), rebuke(1), rebukes(2), reproof(14), reproofs(2), reproved(1).

8434. תּוֹלָד **Tolad** (410a); from 3205; a city in Simeon:— Tolad(1).

תּוֹלָד **Tolad**; see 513.

8435. תּוֹלֵדוֹת **toledoth** (410a); from 3205; *generations:*— account(1), birth(1), genealogical registration(12), genealogies(3), generations(21), order of their birth(1).

8436. תּוּלוֹן **Tulon** or

תִּילוֹן **Tilon** (1066c); of unc. der.; a man of Judah:— Tilon(1).

8437. תּוֹלָל **tolal** (1064a); of unc. der.; perh. *to be wasted:*— tormentors(1).

8438. תּוֹלָע **tola** (1068d); from an unused word; *worm, scarlet stuff:*— crimson(1), purple(1), worms(1).

8439a. תּוֹלָע **Tola** (1069a); from the same as 8438; two men of Issachar:— Tola(6).

8439b. תּוֹלֵעָה **toleah** or

תּוֹלַעַת **tolaath** (1069a); from the same as 8438; *a worm:*— string(5), worm(6), worms(1).

8440. תּוֹלָעִי **Tolai** (1069a); from 8439a; desc. of Tola:— Tolaites(1).

8441. תּוֹעֵבָה **toebah** or

תֹּעֵבָה **toebah** (1072d); from an unused word; *abomination:*— abominable(5), abominable act(1), abomination(39), abominations(60), detestable(2), detestable act(1), detestable thing(3), detestable things(3), loathsome(2), object of loathing(1).

8442. תּוֹעָה **toah** (1073c); from the same as 8441; *a wandering, error:*— disturbance(1), error(1).

8443. תּוֹעָפָה **toaphah** (419b); from an unused word; *eminence:*— choice(1), horns(2), peaks(1).

8444. תּוֹצָאָה **totsaah** or

תֹּצָאָה **totsaah** (426a); from 3318; *an outgoing, extremity,* perh. *source, escape:*— borders(1), ended*(13), escapes(1), exits(1), farthest borders(1), springs(1), termination(5).

8445. תָּוֹקְהַת **Tovqhath** (876b); of unc. der.; father-in-law of Huldah, the same as 8616:— Tokhath(1).

8446. תּוּר **tur** (1064b); a prim. root; *to seek out, spy out, explore:*— explore(1), explored(1), explores(1), follow(1), guide(1), investigate(1), seek(2), selected(1), spied(5), spy(6), spying(2), traders*(2).

8447. תּוֹר **tor** or

תֹּר **tor** (1064c); from 8446; *a plait, turn:*— ornaments(2), standard(1), turn(2).

8448. תּוֹר **tor** (1064c); the same as 8447, q.v.

8449. תּוֹר **tor** or

תֹּר **tor** (1076a); of unc. der.; *turtledove:*— turtledove(5), turtledoves(9).

8450. תּוֹר **tor** (1117d); (Ara.) corr. to 7794; *a bullock:*— bulls(3), cattle(4).

8451. תּוֹרָה **torah** (435d); from 3384; *direction, instruction, law:*— custom(1), instruction(10), instructions(1), Law(1), law(188), laws(10), ruling(1), teaching(7), teachings(1).

8452. תּוֹרָה **torah** (1064c); prob. fem. of 8447, q.v.

8453. תּוֹשָׁב **toshab** (444c); from 3427; *a sojourner:*— foreign resident(1), settlers(1), sojourner(8), sojourners(2), sojourning(1), tenants(1).

8454. תּוּשִׁיָּה **tushiyyah** (444d); from an unused word; *sound, efficient wisdom, abiding success:*— deliverance(1), helpful insight(1), sound wisdom(7), success(1), wisdom(1).

8455. תּוֹתָח **tothach** (450c); from an unused word; (a weapon) perh. *club, mace:*— clubs(1).

8456. תָּזַז **tazaz** (1064d); a prim. root; *to strike away:*— cut away(1).

8457. תַּזְנוּת **taznuth** (276b); from 2181; *fornication:*— harlotries(14), harlotry(4), lust(1).

8458. תַּחְבֻּלָה **tachbulah** (287a); from 2254a; *direction, counsel:*— counsels(1), guidance(2), wise counsel(1), wise guidance(2).

8459. תֹּחוּ **Tochu** (1063c); from the same as 8430; an ancestor of Samuel, the same as 8430:— Tohu(1).

8460. תְּחוֹת **techoth** (1117d); (Ara.) corr. to 8478; *under:*— under(5).

8461. תַּחְכְּמֹנִי **Tachkemoni** (315d); from 2449; a descriptive title for one of David's men:— Tahchemonite(1).

8462. תְּחִלָּה **techillah** (321a); from 2490c; *a beginning:*— before(1), began(1), beginning(11), first(5), first time(2), previously(2).

8463. תַּחֲלוּא **tachalu** or

תַּחֲלֻא **tachalu** (316a); from 2456; *disease:*— diseases(4), pain(1).

8464. תַּחְמָס **tachmas** (329d); from 2554; *male ostrich:*— owl(2).

8465. תַּחַן **Tachan** (334c); from 2583; an Ephraimite:— Tahan(2).

8466. תַּחֲנָה **tachanah** (334c); from 2583; *an encamping, encampment:*— camp(1).

8467. תְּחִנָּה **techinnah** (337c); from 2603a; *favor, supplication for favor:*— grace(1), mercy(1), petition(4), supplication(18), supplications(1).

8468. תְּחִנָּה **Techinnah** (337c); from 2603a; "favor," a desc. of Judah: Tchinnah(1).

8469. תַּחֲנוּן **tachanun** (337c); from 2603a; *supplication for favor:*— supplication(3), supplications(15).

8470. תַּחֲנִי **Tachani** (334c); from 8465; desc. of Tahan:— Tahanites(1).

8471. תַּחְפַּנְחֵס **Tachpanches** or

תְּחַפְנְחֵס **Techaphneches** (1064d); of Eg. or.; a city in Eg.:— Tahpanhes(6), Tehaphnehes(1).

8472. תַּחְפְּנֵיס **Tachpenes** (1065a); from the same as 8471; an Eg. queen:— Tahpenes(3).

8473. תַּחְרָא **tachra** (1065a); of unc. der.; *a corselet:*— coat of mail(2).

8474. תַּחֲרָה **tacharah** (354a); the same as 2734, q.v.

8475. תַּחְרֵעַ **Tacharea** (357c); from an unused word; a desc. of Saul:— Tahrea(1).

8476. תַּחַשׁ **tachash** (1065a); of unc. der.; perh. *porpoise* (a kind of leather or skin):— porpoise(12), porpoise skin(2).

8477. תַּחַשׁ **Tachash** (1065a); from the same as 8476; a son of Nahor:— Tahash(1).

8478. תַּחַת **tachath** (1065a); a prim. root; *underneath, below, instead of:*— account(2), against*(4), allegiance*(1), Amid(1), among(2), because(1), because*(12), below(1), below*(10), beneath(13), beneath*(7), exchange(3), flat(2), foot(8), inasmuch*(1), instead(34), like(1), place(136), place*(1), places(1), replace*(1), replaces*(1), return(4), right where(1), site(1), sites(1), spot(1), stead(1), under(201), underneath(5), underparts(1), where(1), where they stand(1), whereas(1), whereas*(1), while she was mine(1), why*(1).

8479. תַּחַת **tachath** (1117d); (Ara.) see 8460.

8480. תַּחַת **Tachath** (1066c); from 8478; a place in the desert, also two Isr.:— Tahath(6).

8481. תַּחְתּוֹן **tachton** (1066b); from 8478; *lower, lowest:*— lower(11), lowest(2).

8482. תַּחְתִּי **tachti** (1066b); from 8478; *lower, lowest:*— beneath(3), depths(3), foot(1), lower(4), lower parts(3), lowest(2), lowest part(1), lowest parts(1), nether(1).

8483. תַּחְתִּים חָדְשִׁי **Tachtim Chodshi** (295a); prob. from 8478 and 2320; a place visited by Joab:— Tahtim-hodshi(1).

8484. תִּיכוֹן **tikon** or

תִּיכֹן **tikon** (1064a); from the same as 8432; *middle:*— lowest(1), middle(7), middle ones(2), second(1).

8485. תֵּימָא Tema (1066d); of unc. der.; a son of Ishmael, also his desc. and the region settled by them:— Tema(5).

8486. תֵּימָן teman (412c); from the same as 3225; *south, south wind:*— south(15), south side(2), south wind(1), south*(3), southward(1).

8487. תֵּימָן Teman (412d); from the same as 3225; a N. district of Edom, also an Edomite chief:— Teman(12).

8488. תֵּימְנִי Temeni (412d); from the same as 3225; a man of Judah:— Temeni(1).

8489. תֵּימָנִי Temani (412d); from 8487; inhab. of Teman:— Temanite(6), Temanites(2).

8490. תִּימָרָה timarah (1071d); from the same as 8560; (palm-like) *column:*— columns(2).

8491. תִּיצִי Titsi (1066d); of unc. der.; descriptive title of one of David's heroes:— Tizite(1).

8492. תִּירוֹשׁ tirosh (440d); from 3423; *must, fresh* or *new wine:*— fresh wine(1), grapes(1), new wine(33), wine(3).

8493. תִּירְיָא Tireya (432b, 1066d); from 3372a; a man of Judah:— Tiria(1).

8494. תִּירָס Tiras (1066d); of unc. der.; a son of Japheth and his desc.:— Tiras(2).

8495. תַּיִשׁ tayish (1066d); of unc. der.; *male goat:*— male goat(1), male goats(3).

8496. תֹּךְ tok or **תּוֹךְ tok** (1067a); from an unused word; *injury, oppression:*— oppression(3), oppressor*(1).

8497. תָּכָה takah (1067a); a prim. root; perh. *to follow:*— followed(1).

8498. תְּכוּנָה tekunah (1067c); see 8508.

8499. תְּכוּנָה tekunah (467d); from 3559; *arrangement, preparation, fixed place:*— seat(1), structure(1), treasure(1).

8500. תֻּכִּיִּים tukkiyyim (1067a); of unc. der.; *peacocks:*— peacocks(2).

8501. תָּכַךְ takak (1067a); the same as 8496, q.v.

8502. תִּכְלָה tiklah (479a); from 3615; *completeness, perfection:*— perfection(1).

8503. תַּכְלִית taklith (479b); from 3615; *end, completeness:*— boundary(1), end(1), limit(1), limits(1), utmost(1).

8504. תְּכֵלֶת tekeleth (1067b); of unc. der.; *violet, violet thread:*— blue(43), purple(1), violet(5).

8505. תָּכַן takan (1067b); a prim. root; *to regulate, measure, estimate:*— directed(1), firmly set(1), marked off(1), meted(1), right(9), weighed(2), weighs(3).

8506. תֹּכֶן token (1067c); from 8505; *a measurement:*— quantity(1), quota(1).

8507. תֹּכֶן Token (1067c); from 8505; "measurement," a city in Simeon:— Tochen(1).

8508. תָּכְנִית toknith (1067c); from 8505; *measurement, proportion:*— perfection(1), plan(1).

8509. תַּכְרִיךְ takrik (501b); from an unused word; *a robe:*— garment(1).

8510. תֵּל tel (1068b); from an unused word; *a mound:*— heap(2), mounds(1), ruin(2).

8511. תָּלָא tala (1067d); of unc. der.; *to hang:*— bent(1), hang(1).

8512. תֵּל אָבִיב Tel Abib (1068b); from 8510 and 24; "hill of grain," a place in Bab.:— Tel-abib(1).

8513. תְּלָאָה telaah (521b); from 3811; *weariness, hardship:*— hardship(4), tiresome(1).

8514. תַּלְאוּבָה talubah or **תַּלְאֻבָה talubah** (520d); from an unused word; *drought:*— drought(1).

8515. תְּלַאשָּׂר Telassar (1067d); of for. or.; a city in Mesopotamia:— Telassar(2).

8516. תִּלְבֹּשֶׁת tilbosheth (528d); from 3847; *raiment:*— clothing(1).

8517. תְּלַג telag (1117d); (Ara.) corr. to 7950; *snow:*— snow(1).

8518. תָּלָה talah (1067d); a prim. root; *to hang:*— hang(5), hanged(13), hanging(2), hangs(1), hung(7).

8519a. תָּלוּל talul (1068c); from the same as 8510; *exalted, lofty:*— lofty(1).

8519b. תְּלוּנָה telunah or **תְּלֻנָּה telunnah** (534b); from 3885b; *a murmuring:*— complaints(1), grumblings(7).

8520. תֶּלַח Telach (1068b); of unc. der.; an Ephraimite:— Telah(1).

8521. תֵּל חַרְשָׁא Tel Charsha (1068b); from 8510 and 2796; "mound of a craftsman," a city in Bab.:— Tel-harsha(2).

8522. תְּלִי teli (1068b); from 8518; *a quiver* (with its arrows):— quiver(1).

8523. תְּלִיתַי telithay (1118a); (Ara.) from 8532; *third:*— third(1).

8524. תָּלַל talal (1068c); a prim. root; *to mock, deceive, trifle with:*— cheated(1), deal deceitfully(1), deceive him as one deceives(1), deceived(4), deceives(1).

8525. תֶּלֶם telem (1068d); from an unused word; *a furrow:*— furrow(1), furrows(4).

8526. תַּלְמַי Talmay (1068d); from the same as 8525; "plowman," a father-in-law of David, also a desc. of Anak:— Talmai(6).

8527. תַּלְמִיד talmid (541a); from 3925; *a scholar:*— pupil(1).

8528. תֵּל מֶלַח Tel Melach (1068b); from 8510 and 4417; "mound of salt," a place in Bab.:— Tel-melah(2).

8529. תָּלַע tala (1069a); denom. vb. from 8438; *to clothe in scarlet:*— dressed in scarlet(1).

8530. תַּלְפִּיּוֹת talpiyyoth (1069b); from an unused word; perh. *weapons:*— rows of stones(1).

8531. תְּלַת telath (1118a); (Ara.) from 8532; *a third part:*— third(2).

8532. תְּלָת telath or **תְּלָתָה telathah** (1118a); (Ara.) corr. to 7969; *three:*— third(1), three(10).

8533a. תַּלְתִּי talti (1118a); (Ara.) from 8532; *third:*— third(1).

8533b. תְּלָתִין telathin (1118a); (Ara.) from 8532; *thirty:*— thirty(2).

8534. תַּלְתַּלִּים taltallim (1068c); from the same as 8510; perh. *locks* (of hair):— clusters of dates(1).

8535. תָּם tam (1070d); from 8552; *complete:*— blameless(5), blameless man(1), complete(2), guiltless(3), integrity(1), peaceful(1), perfect one(2).

8536. תַּם tam or **תַּמָּה tammah** (1118a); (Ara.) corr. to 8033; *there:*— there(3), where*(1).

8537. תֹּם tom (1070d); from 8552; *completeness, integrity,* also part of the high priest's breastplate:— blameless(1), full(1), full measure(1), innocently(1), integrity(16), random(2), upright(1).

8538. תֻּמָּה tummah (1070d); from 8552; *integrity:*— integrity(5).

8539. תָּמַהּ tamah (1069b); a prim. root; *to be astounded* or *dumbfounded:*— amazed(2), astonished(1), astonishment(2), astounded(1), look(1), looked(1), shocked(1), wait(1), wonder(1).

8540. תְּמַהּ temah (1118b); (Ara.) from a root corr. to 8539; *a wonder:*— wonders(3).

8541. תִּמָּהוֹן timmahon (1069b); from 8539; *bewilderment:*— bewilderment(2).

8542. תַּמּוּז Tammuz (1069c); of unc. der.; a Bab. god:— Tammuz(1).

8543. תְּמוֹל temol or **תְּמֹל temol** (1069d); of unc. der.; *yesterday, recently, formerly:*— before*(3), beforehand*(1), formerly(2), formerly*(1), past(1), past*(2), previously*(9), recently*(1), times*(2), yesterday(4), yesterday*(1).

8544. תְּמוּנָה temunah (568b); from the same as 4327; *likeness, form:*— form(7), likeness(3).

8545. תְּמוּרָה temurah (558d); from 4171; *exchange, recompense:*— exchange(1), exchanged(1), reward(1), substitute(2), trading(1).

8546. תְּמוּתָה timuthah (560d); from 4191; *death:*— death(1), die(1).

8547. תֶּמַח Tamach (1069c); of unc. der.; head of a postexilic family:— Temah(2).

8548. תָּמִיד tamid (556b); from an unused word; *continuity:*— all times(1), always(4), constantly(2), continual(26), continually(52), continuously(2), ever(2), perpetual(1), regular(3), regular sacrifice(5), regularly(5).

8549. תָּמִים tamim (1071a); from 8552; *complete, sound:*— blameless(22), blamelessly(1), complete(1), entire(1), full(1), intact(1), integrity(4), perfect(5), sincerity(1), unblemished(2), uprightly(1), who is perfect(1), whole(2), without blemish(12), without defect(36).

8550. תֻּמִּים Tummim (1070d); prob. the same as 8537, q.v.:— Thummim(5).

8551. תָּמַךְ tamak (1069c); a prim. root; *to grasp, support, attain:*— attain(1), attains(1), grasp(1), grasped(1), held(1), held fast(1), hold(1), hold her fast(1), hold fast(1), holds(2), obtain(1), support(2), supported(1), take hold(2), uphold(3), upholds(1).

8552. תָּמַם tamam (1070b); a prim. root; *to be complete* or *finished:*— all(1), all gone(1), all spent(2), been completed(1), blameless(1), blossoms(1), boil the well(1), came to an end(1), cease(1), come to an end(2), complete(2), completed(1), completely(3), consume(1), consumed(4), count(1), destroyed(6), end(1), ended(3), fail(1), finally(1), finish(1), finished(7), full(1), gone(1), lie(1), make an end(1), make your perfect(1), meet their end(4), met our end(1), perished(4), perished*(1), ready(1), run(1), show yourself blameless(2), spent(1), utterly(1).

8553. תִּמְנָה Timnah (584c); from 4487; "territory," two cities in Judah:— Timnah(12).

8554. תִּמְנִי Timni (584d); from 8553; inhab. of Timnah:— Timnite(1).

8555. תִּמְנָע Timna (586b); from 4513; an Edomite name:— Timna(6).

8556a. תִּמְנַת חֶרֶס Timnath Cheres (584d); from 8553 and 2775a; "territory of the sun," a village in the hill country of Ephraim:— Timnath-heres(1).

8556b. תִּמְנַת סֶרַח Timnath Serech (584d); from 8553 and 2775a; "territory of the sun," a village in the hill country of Ephraim, the same as 8556a:— Timnath-serah(2).

8557. תֶּמֶס temes (588a); from 4549; *a melting* (away):— melts away(1).

8558. תָּמָר tamar (1071c); from the same as 8560; *palm tree, date palm:*— date palms(1), palm(3), palm tree(3), palm trees(4), palms(1).

8559. תָּמָר Tamar (1071c); from the same as 8560; daughter-in-law of Judah, also two Isr. women, also a place S. of the Dead Sea :— Tamar(25).

8560. תֹּמֶר tomer (1071c); from an unused word; *palm tree, post:*— palm tree(1), scarecrow(1).

8561. תִּמֹּרָה timorah (1071c); from the same as 8560; *palm* (tree) *figure:*— palm tree(3), palm tree ornaments(6), palm trees(10).

8562. תַּמְרוּק tamruq (600a); from 4838; *a scraping, rubbing:*— cosmetics(3).

8563. תַּמְרוּר tamrur (601b); from 4843; *bitterness:*— bitter(2), most bitter(1).

8564. תַּמְרוּר tamrur (1071d); from the same root as 8560; perh. *signpost:*— guideposts(1).

8565. תַּן tan (1072b); from an unused word; *a jackal:*— jackals(14).

8566. תָּנָה tanah (1071d); a prim. root; *to hire:*— hire(1), hired(1).

8567. תָּנָה tanah (1072a); a prim. root; perh. *recount, rehearse:*— commemorate(1), recount(1).

8568. תַּנָּה tannah (1072b); fem. of 8565, q.v.

8569. תְּנוּאָה tenuah (626b); from 5106; *opposition:*— opposition(1), pretexts(1).

8570. תְּנוּבָה tenubah (626c); from 5107; *fruit, produce:*— fruit(2), fruits(1), produce(2).

8571. תְּנוּךְ tenuk (1072a); of unc. der.; *tip* or *lobe* (of the ear):— lobe(7), lobes(1).

8572. תְּנוּמָה tenumah (630b); from 5123; *slumber:*— slumber(5).

8573. תְּנוּפָה tenuphah (632b); from 5130; *a swinging, waving, wave offering, offering:*— brandishing weapons(1), offered by waving(2), offering(1), wave offering(24), wave offerings(1).

8574. תַּנּוּר tannur (1072a); from the same as 8571; (portable) *stove, firepot:*— furnace(2), Furnaces(2), oven(10), ovens(1).

8575. תַּנְחוּם tanchum (637c); from 5162; *consolation:*— comforting(1), consolation(2), consolations(2).

8576. תַּנְחֻמֶת Tanchumeth (637c); from 5162; father of Seraiah:— Tanhumeth(2).

8577. תַּנִּין tannin (1072c); from the same as 8565; *serpent, dragon, sea monster:*— dragon(2), monster(3), sea monster(1), sea monsters(3), serpent(3), serpents(2).

8578. תִּנְיָן tinyan (1118b); (Ara.) corr. to 8147; *second* (an ord. number):— second(1).

8579. תִּנְיָנוּת tinyanuth (1118b); (Ara.) from the same as 8578; *the second time:*— second time(1).

8580. תִּנְשֶׁמֶת tinshemeth (675d); from 5395; (an animal) perh. *owl, chameleon:*— chameleon(1), white owl(2).

8581. תָּעַב taab (1073a); denom. vb. from 8441; *to abhor:*— abhor(5), abhorred(3), abhorrent(1), abhors(1), acted...abominably(2), committed abominable(2), despise(1), detest(2), detestable(1), made your abominable(1), rejected(1), utterly abhor(1).

8582. תָּעָה taah (1073b); a prim. root; *to err:*— deceived(1), deceiving(1), err(2), go astray(3), goes astray(1), gone astray(3), lead my astray(1), lead you astray(1), leading them astray(1), leads them astray(1), leads to ruin(1), led my astray(2), led them astray(3), led...astray(2), misled(1), reels(1), seduced(1), stagger(3), staggers(1), stray(3), wander(5), wandered(4), wandering(1), wandering away(1), wanders(1), went astray(5).

8583. תֹּעוּ Tou or

תֹּעִי Toi (1073d); perh. from 8582; a king of Hamath:— Toi(3), Tou(2).

8584. תְּעוּדָה teudah (730c); from 5749a; *testimony, attestation:*— attestation(1), testimony(2).

8585a. תְּעָלָה tealah (752b); from 5927; *a watercourse:*— channel(1), channels(1), conduit(4), trench(3).

8585b. תְּעָלָה tealah (752b); from 5927; *a healing:*— healing(1), recovery(1).

8586. תַּעֲלוּלִים taalulim (760c); from 5953a; *wantonness, caprice:*— capricious children(1), punishments(1).

8587. תַּעֲלֻמָּה taalumah (761b); from 5956; *a hidden thing, secret:*— secrets(2), what is hidden(1).

8588. תַּעֲנוּג taanug (772c); from 6026; *daintiness, luxury, exquisite delight:*— charms(1), delight(1), luxury(1), pleasant(1), pleasures(1).

8589. תַּעֲנִית taanith (777a); from 6031a; *humiliation:*— humiliation(1).

8590. תַּעְנָךְ Tanak (1073d); of unc. der.; a Canaanite city assigned to Manasseh:— Taanach(7).

8591a. תָּעַע taa (1073d); a prim. root; *to mock:*— deceiver(1), scoffed(1).

8591b. תְּעֻפָה teuphah (734a); from 5774b; *gloom:*— darkness(1).

8592. תַּעֲצֻמָה taatsumah (783b); from 6105a; *might:*— power(1).

8593. תַּעַר taar (789b); from 6168; *a razor, sheath:*— knife(1), razor(5), sheath(7).

8594. תַּעֲרֻבָה taarubah (787a); from 6148; *a pledge:*— hostages(2).

8595. תַּעְתֻּעִים tatuim (1074a); from 8591a; *mockery:*— mockery(2).

8596. תֹּף toph (1074b); from an unused word; *a timbrel, tambourine:*— settings(1), tambourine(2), tambourines(7), timbrel(6), timbrels(1).

8597. תִּפְאָרָה tipharah (802c); from 6286; *beauty, glory:*— adornment(1), beautiful(8), beauty(7), boast(1), glorious(7), glory(17), honor(2), jewels*(1), pomp(1), pride(1), splendor(1).

8598. תַּפּוּחַ tappuach (656b); from 5301; *apple tree, apple:*— apple tree(3), apples(3).

8599. תַּפּוּחַ Tappuach (656b); from 5301; "apple," a city in Judah, also a city on the border between Ephraim and Manasseh:— Tappuah(5).

8600a. תְּפוֹצָה tephotsah (807b); from 6327a; *dispersion:*— dispersions(1).

8600b. תַּפֻּחַ Tappuach (656b); from 5301; a son of Hebron:— Tappuah(1).

8601. תֻּפִינִים tuphinim (1074a); perh. from 644; perh. *baked pieces:*— baked(1).

8602a. תָּפֵל taphel (1074a); from an unused word; *tasteless, unseasoned:*— foolish(1), something tasteless(1).

8602b. תָּפֵל taphel (1074b); from an unused word; *whitewash:*— whitewash(5).

8603. תֹּפֶל Tophel (1074b); from the same as 8602b; a place S.E. of the Dead Sea:— Tophel(1).

8604. תִּפְלָה tiphlah (1074b); from the same as 8602a; *unsavoriness, unseemliness:*— blame*(1), folly(1), offensive thing(1).

8605. תְּפִלָּה tephillah (813c); from 6419; *prayer:*— prayer(70), prayers(2).

8606. תִּפְלֶצֶת tiphletseth (814a); from 6426; *a shuddering, horror:*— terror(1).

8607. תִּפְסַח Tiphsach (820b); from 6452a; a place on the Euphrates:— Tiphsah(2).

8608. תָּפַף taphaph (1074c); denom. vb. from 8596; *to sound the timbrel, beat:*— beating(1), beating tambourines(1).

8609. תָּפַר taphar (1074c); a prim. root; *to sew together:*— sew(1), sew together(1), sewed(1), sewed...together(1).

8610. תָּפַשׂ taphas (1074c); a prim. root; *to lay hold of, wield:*— arrested(2), capture(2), captured(8), caught(5), grasp(1), grasps(1), handle(4), handled(1), hold(1), lay hold(1), lays hold(1), occupy(1), overlaid(1), play(1), profane(1), seize(5), seized(13), seizes(1), surely be captured(1), take(3), taken over(1), took(3), took hold(3), wielding(1), wields(1).

8611. תֹּפֶת topheth (1064b); from an unused word; (act of) *spitting:*— spit(1).

8612. תֹּפֶת Topheth (1075a); from 8610; a place S. of Jer.:— Topheth(9).

8613. תָּפְתֶּה Tophteh (1075a); from 8610; a place of burning, prob. the same as 8612:— Topheth(1).

8614. תִּפְתָּיֵא tiphtaye (1118b); (Ara.) of unc. der.; (title of an official) perh. *magistrates:*— magistrates(2).

8615a. תִּקְוָה tiqvah (876b); from 6960a; *cord:*— cord(2).

8615b. תִּקְוָה tiqvah (876b); from 6960a; *a hope:*— expectation(3), hope(28), longing(1).

8616. תִּקְוָה Tiqvah (876b); from 6960a; "hope," two Isr.:— Tikvah(2).

8617. תְּקוּמָה tequmah (879c); from 6965; *a standing, power to stand:*— stand(1).

8618. תְּקוֹמֵם teqomem (877c, 879d); the same as 6965, q.v.

8619. תָּקוֹעַ taqoa (1075d); from 8628; *a blast* or *wind instrument:*— trumpet(1).

8620. תְּקוֹעַ Teqoa (1075d); from 8628; a city in Judah:— Tekoa(7).

8621. תְּקוֹעִי Teqoi or

תְּקֹעִי Teqoi (1075d); from 8620; inhab. of Tekoa:— Tekoa(2), Tekoite(3), Tekoites(2).

8622. תְּקוּפָה tequphah (880d); from an unused word; *a coming round, circuit:*— circuit(1), due(1), turn(2).

8623. תַּקִּיף taqqiph (1076a); from 8630; *mighty:*— stronger(1).

8624. תַּקִּיף taqqiph (1118c); (Ara.) corr. to 8623; *strong, mighty:*— mighty(2), strong(3).

8625a. תְּקַל teqal (1118c); (Ara.) corr. to 8254; *to weigh:*— weighed(1).

8625b. תְּקֵל teqel (1118c); (Ara.) from 8625a; *a shekel:*— TEKEL(2).

8626. תָּקַן taqan (1075b); a prim. root; *to become straight:*— arranged(1), straighten(1), straightened(1).

8627. תְּקַן teqan (1118c); (Ara.) corr. to 8626; *to be in order:*— reestablished(1).

8628. תָּקַע taqa (1075b); a prim. root; *to thrust, clap, give a blow, blast:*— blew(19), blow(20), blowing(1), blown(7), blows(1), camped(1), clap(2), drive(1), driven(1), drove(2), fasten(1), fastened(3), give pledges*(1), given(1), guarantor(1), guarantor*(1), pitch(1), pitched(1), pledges*(1), thrust(2), trumpeter*(1).

8629. תֵּקַע teqa (1075d); from 8628; *blast* (of a horn):— sound(1).

8630. תָּקַף taqeph (1075d); a prim. root; *to prevail over, overpower:*— overpower(3).

8631. תְּקֵף teqeph (1118c); (Ara.) corr. to 8630; *to grow strong:*— became so proud(1), became strong(1), enforce(1), grew strong(1), grown strong(1).

8632a. תְּקָף teqaph (1118c); (Ara.) from 8631; *might:*— might(1).

8632b. תְּקֹף teqoph (1118c); (Ara.) corr. to 8633; *might:*— strength(1).

8633. תֹּקֶף toqeph (1076a); from 8630; *power, strength, energy:*— authority(2), power(1).

8634. תַּרְאֲלָה Taralah (1076a); of unc. der.; a city in Benjamin:— Taralah(1).

8635. תַּרְבּוּת tarbuth (916b); from 7235a; *an increase, brood:*— brood(1).

8636. תַּרְבִּית tarbith (916b); from 7235a; *increment, interest, usury:*— increase(3), profits(1), usurious(1), usury(1).

8637. תִּרְגַּל tirgal (920a); see 7270.

8638. תִּרְגַּם tirgam (1076b); perh. from 7275; *to interpret, translate:*— translated(1).

8639. תַּרְדֵּמָה tardemah (922b); from 7290a; *deep sleep:*— deep sleep(5), sound sleep(2).

8640. תִּרְהָקָה Tirhaqah (1076b); of for. or.; a king of Eg.:— Tirhakah(2).

8641. תְּרוּמָה terumah (929a); from 7311; *contribution, offering* (for sacred uses):— allotment(15), contribution(20), contributions(10), heave offering(4), offered by lifting(2), offering(20), offerings(4), who takes bribes(1).

8642. תְּרוּמִיָּה terumiyyah (929b); from 7311; *what belongs to a contribution, a contribution:*— allotment(1).

8643. תְּרוּעָה teruah (929d); from 7321; *a shout* or *blast of war, alarm,* or *joy:*— alarm(5), battle cry(2), blowing(1), blowing trumpets(1), joy(1), joyful sound(1), resounding(1), shout(10), shout of alarm(1), shout of joy(1), shouted(1), shouting(4), shouts of joy(1), signal(1), trumpet blast(1), war cries(2), war cry(1).

8644. תְּרוּפָה teruphah (930a); of unc. der.; *a healing:*— healing(1).

8645. תִּרְזָה tirzah (1076b); of unc. der.; (a tree) perh. *cypress:*— cypress(1).

8646. תֶּרַח Terach (1076b); of unc. der.; Abraham's father, also a place in the desert:— Terah(13).

8647. תִּרְחֲנָה Tirchanah (934b); of unc. der.; a child of Caleb:— Tirhanah(1).

8648. תְּרֵין teren (1118b); (Ara.) corr. to 8147; *two:*— 12*(1), second(1), sixty-two*(1), twelve*(1).

8649a. תָּרְמָה tormah (941b); from 7411b; perh. *treachery:*— deceitfully(1).

8649b. תַּרְמִית tarmith (941c); from 7411b; *deceitfulness:*— deceit(1), deceitful(1), deceitfulness(1), deception(2).

8650. תֹּרֶן toren (1076c); of unc. der.; *a mast:*— flag(1), mast(2).

8651. תְּרַע tera (1118d); (Ara.) corr. to 8179; *gate, door:*— court(1), door(1).

8652. תָּרָע tara (1118d); (Ara.) from the same as 8651; *doorkeeper:*— doorkeepers(1).

8653. תַּרְעֵלָה tarelah (947a); from 7477; *a reeling:*— reeling(2), stagger(1).

8654. תִּרְעָתִים Tirathim (1076c); of unc. der.; a Kenite family:— Tirathites(1).

8655. תְּרָפִים teraphim (1076c); of unc. der.; (a kind of idol) perh. *household idol:*— household idol(2), household idols(10), idolatry(1), teraphim(2).

8656. תִּרְצָה Tirtsah (953c); from 7521; daughter of Zelophehad, also a Canaanite city:— Tirzah(18).

8657. תֶּרֶשׁ Teresh (1076d); of for. or.; a eunuch of Ahasuerus:— Teresh(2).

8658. תַּרְשִׁישׁ tarshish (1076d); prob. of for. or.; (a precious stone) perh. *yellow jasper:*— beryl(6).

8659. תַּרְשִׁישׁ Tarshish (1076d); from the same as 8658; a son of Javan, his desc. and their land, also a port on the Mediterranean, also a Benjamite, also a Pers. noble:— Tarshish(29).

8660. תִּרְשָׁתָא tirshatha (1077a); of for. or.; (a Pers. title) *governor:*— governor(5).

8661. תַּרְתָּן Tartan (1077a); of for. or.; *general, commander* (title of an Assyr. general):— commander(1), Tartan(1).

8662. תַּרְתָּק Tartaq (1077b); of for. or.; a god of the Avvites:— Tartak(1).

8663. תְּשֻׁאָה teshuah (996c); from the same as 7722; *noise:*— noise(1), shoutings(1), shouts(1), storm(1), thundering(1).

8664a. תִּשְׁבֶּה Tishbeh (986c); another reading for 8664b, q.v.

8664b. תִּשְׁבִּי Tishbi (986c); from 8664a; inhab. of Tishbeh:— Tishbite(6).

8665. תַּשְׁבֵּץ tashbets (990b); from 7660; *checkered:*— checkered work(1).

8666. תְּשׁוּבָה teshubah (1000c); from 7725; *a return, answer:*— answers(2), return(1), spring(2), turn(3).

8667. תְּשׂוּמֶת tesumeth (965a); from 7760; *a pledge, security:*— security(1).

8668. תְּשׁוּעָה teshuah (448b); from 3467; *deliverance, salvation:*— deliverance(6), help*(1), salvation(16), victory(11).

8669. תְּשׁוּקָה teshuqah (1003c); from an unused word; *a longing:*— desire(3).

8670. תְּשׁוּרָה teshurah (1003d); from 7788; perh. *gift, present:*— present(1).

8671. תְּשִׁיעִי teshii (1077d); from the same as 8672; *ninth* (an ord. number):— ninth(18).

8672. תֵּשַׁע tesha or

תִּשְׁעָה tishah (1077c); of unc. der.; *a nine:*— 139*(1), 29*(2), 3,930*(1), 59,300*(2), 928*(1), 945*(1), 956*(1), 973*(2), forty-nine*(1), nine(21), nine-tenths(1), nineteen*(3), nineteenth*(4), ninety-nine*(2), ninth(5), sixty-nine*(1), thirty-ninth*(3), twenty-nine*(6).

8673. תִּשְׁעִים tishim (1077d); from the same as 8672; *ninety:*— 1,290*(1), 392*(2), 690*(1), 95*(2), 96*(1), 98*(2), ninety(5), ninety-eight*(1), ninety-five*(2), ninety-nine*(2), ninety-six*(1).

8674. תַּתְּנַי Tattenay (1118d); (Ara.) of for. or.; a Pers. prefect:— Tattenai(4).

VARIATIONS IN THE DIVISION OF CHAPTERS AND VERSES BETWEEN THE HEBREW TEXT AND ENGLISH TRANSLATIONS

	English		Hebrew
Genesis	31 : 55		32 : 1
	32 : 1-32		: 2-33
Exodus	8 : 1-4		7 : 26-29
	: 5-32		8 : 1-28
	22 : 1		21 : 37
	: 2-31		22 : 1-30
Leviticus	6 : 1-7		5 : 20-26
	: 8-30		6 : 1-23
Numbers	16 : 36-50		17 : 1-15
	17 : 1-13		: 16-28
	26 : 1	(first clause)	25 : 19
	26 : 1	(second clause)	26 : 1
	29 : 40		30 : 1
	30 : 1-16		: 2-17
Deuteronomy	12 : 32		13 : 1
	13 : 1-18		: 2-19
	22 : 30		23 : 1
	23 : 1-25		: 2-26
	29 : 1		28 : 69
	: 2-29		29 : 1-28
1 Samuel	20 : 42	(last sentence)	21 : 1
	21 : 1-15		: 2-16
	23 : 29		24 : 1
	24 : 1-22		: 2-23
2 Samuel	18 : 33		19 : 1
	19 : 1-43		: 2-44
1 Kings	4 : 21-34		5 : 1-14
	5 : 1-18		: 15-32
	18 : 33	(last half) ... (first half)	18 : 34
	20 : 2	(last half) ... (first half)	20 : 3
	22 : 22	(first clause) ... (last clause)	22 : 21
	: 43	(last half)	: 44
	: 44-53		: 45-54
2 Kings	11 : 21		12 : 1
	12 : 1-21		: 2-22
1 Chronicles	6 : 1-15		5 : 27-41
	: 16-81		6 : 1-66
	12 : 4	(last half)	12 : 5
	: 5-40		: 6-41
2 Chronicles	2 : 1		1 : 18
	: 2-18		2 : 1-17
	14 : 1		13 : 23
	: 2-15		14 : 1-14
Nehemiah	4 : 1-6		3 : 33-38
	: 7-23		4 : 1-17
	9 : 38		10 : 1
	10 : 1-39		: 2-40
Job	41 : 1-8		40 : 25-32
	: 9-34		41 : 1-26
Psalms	3 : *title*		3 : 1
	: 1-8		: 2-9
	4 : *title*		4 : 1
	: 1-8		: 2-9
	5 : *title*		5 : 1
	: 1-12		: 2-13
	6 : *title*		6 : 1
	: 1-10		: 2-11
	7 : *title*		7 : 1
	: 1-17		: 2-18
	8 : *title*		8 : 1
	: 1-9		: 2-10

	English		Hebrew
Psalms (cont.)	9 : *title*		9 : 1
	: 1-20		: 2-21
	11 : *title*	(first clause)	11 : 1
	12 : *title*		12 : 1
	: 1-8		: 2-9
	13 : *title*		13 : 1
	: 1-5		: 2-6
	: 6	(last half)	: 6
	14 : *title*	(first clause)	14 : 1
	15 : *title*	(first clause)	15 : 1
	16 : *title*	(first clause)	16 : 1
	17 : *title*	(first clause)	17 : 1
	18 : *title*	18 : 1(first clause)	: 2
	: 1-50		: 2-51
	19 : *title*		19 : 1
	: 1-14		: 2-15
	20 : *title*		20 : 1
	: 1-9		: 2-10
	21 : *title*		21 : 1
	: 1-13		: 2-14
	22 : *title*		22 : 1
	: 1-31		: 2-32
	23 : *title*	(first clause)	23 : 1
	24 : *title*	(first clause)	24 : 1
	25 : *title*	(first clause)	25 : 1
	26 : *title*	(first clause)	26 : 1
	27 : *title*	(first clause)	27 : 1
	28 : *title*	(first clause)	28 : 1
	29 : *title*	(first clause)	29 : 1
	30 : *title*		30 : 1
	: 1-12		: 2-13
	31 : *title*		31 : 1
	: 1-24		: 2-25
	32 : *title*	(first clause)	32 : 1
	34 : *title*		34 : 1
	: 1-22		: 2-23
	35 : *title*	(first word)	35 : 1
	36 : *title*		36 : 1
	: 1-12		: 2-13
	37 : *title*	(first word)	37 : 1
	38 : *title*		38 : 1
	: 1-22		: 2-23
	39 : *title*		39 : 1
	: 1-13		: 2-14
	40 : *title*		40 : 1
	: 1-17		: 2-18
	41 : *title*		41 : 1
	: 1-13		: 2-14
	42 : *title*		42 : 1
	: 1-11		: 2-12
	44 : *title*		44 : 1
	: 1-26		: 2-27
	45 : *title*		45 : 1
	: 1-17		: 2-18
	46 : *title*		46 : 1
	: 1-11		: 2-12
	47 : *title*		47 : 1
	: 1-9		: 2-10
	48 : *title*		48 : 1
	: 1-14		: 2-15
	49 : *title*		49 : 1
	: 1-20		: 2-21

	English		Hebrew
Psalms (cont.)	50 : *title*	(first clause)	50 : 1
	51 : *title*		51 : 1-2
	: 1-19		: 3-21
	52 : *title*		52 : 1-2
	: 1-9		: 3-11
	53 : *title*		53 : 1
	: 1-6		: 2-7
	54 : *title*		54 : 1-2
	: 1-7		: 3-9
	55 : *title*		55 : 1
	: 1-23		: 2-24
	56 : *title*		56 : 1
	: 1-13		: 2-14
	57 : *title*		57 : 1
	: 1-11		: 2-12
	58 : *title*		58 : 1
	: 1-11		: 2-12
	59 : *title*		59 : 1
	: 1-17		: 2-18
	60 : *title*		60 : 1-2
	: 1-12		: 3-14
	61 : *title*		61 : 1
	: 1-8		: 2-9
	62 : *title*		62 : 1
	: 1-12		: 2-13
	63 : *title*		63 : 1
	: 1-11		: 2-12
	64 : *title*		64 : 1
	: 1-10		: 2-11
	65 : *title*		65 : 1
	: 1-13		: 2-14
	66 : *title*	(first clause)	66 : 1
	67 : *title*		67 : 1
	: 1-7		: 2-8
	68 : *title*		68 : 1
	: 1-35		: 2-36
	69 : *title*		69 : 1
	: 1-36		: 2-37
	70 : *title*		70 : 1
	: 1-5		: 2-6
	72 : *title*	(first word)	72 : 1
	73 : *title*	(first clause)	73 : 1
	74 : *title*	(first clause)	74 : 1
	75 : *title*		75 : 1
	: 1-10		: 2-11
	76 : *title*		76 : 1
	: 1-12		: 2-13
	77 : *title*		77 : 1
	: 1-20		: 2-21
	78 : *title*	(first clause)	78 : 1
	79 : *title*	(first clause)	79 : 1
	80 : *title*		80 : 1
	: 1-19		: 2-20
	81 : *title*		81 : 1
	: 1-16		: 2-17
	82 : *title*	(first clause)	82 : 1
	83 : *title*		83 : 1
	: 1-18		: 2-19
	84 : *title*		84 : 1
	: 1-12		: 2-13
	85 : *title*		85 : 1
	: 1-13		: 2-14
	86 : *title*	(first clause)	86 : 1
	87 : *title*	(first clause)	87 : 1
	88 : *title*		88 : 1
	: 1-18		: 2-19
	89 : *title*		89 : 1
	: 1-52		: 2-53
	90 : *title*	(first clause)	90 : 1
	92 : *title*		92 : 1

	English		Hebrew
Psalms (cont.)	92 : 1-15		92 : 2-16
	98 : *title*	(first word)	98 : 1
	100 : *title*	(first clause)	100 : 1
	101 : *title*	(first clause)	101 : 1
	102 : *title*	(first clause)	102 : 1
	: 1-28		: 2-29
	103 : *title*	(first word)	103 : 1
	108 : *title*		108 : 1
	: 1-13		: 2-14
	109 : *title*	(first clause)	109 : 1
	110 : *title*	(first clause)	110 : 1
	120 : *title*	(first clause)	120 : 1
	121 : *title*	(first clause)	121 : 1
	122 : *title*	(first clause)	122 : 1
	123 : *title*	(first clause)	123 : 1
	124 : *title*	(first clause)	124 : 1
	125 : *title*	(first clause)	125 : 1
	126 : *title*	(first clause)	126 : 1
	127 : *title*	(first clause)	127 : 1
	128 : *title*	(first clause)	128 : 1
	129 : *title*	(first clause)	129 : 1
	130 : *title*	(first clause)	130 : 1
	131 : *title*	(first clause)	131 : 1
	132 : *title*	(first clause)	132 : 1
	133 : *title*	(first clause)	133 : 1
	134 : *title*	(first clause)	134 : 1
	138 : *title*	(first clause)	138 : 1
	139 : *title*	(first clause)	139 : 1
	140 : *title*		140 : 1
	: 1-13		: 2-14
	141 : *title*	(first clause)	141 : 1
	142 : *title*		142 : 1
	: 1-6		: 2-7
	143 : *title*	(first clause)	143 : 1
	144 : *title*	(first word)	144 : 1
	145 : *title*	(first clause)	145 : 1
Ecclesiastes	5 : 1		4 : 17
	: 2-20		5 : 1-19
Song of Solomon	6 : 13		7 : 1
	7 : 1-13		: 2-14
Isaiah	9 : 1		8 : 23
	: 2-21		9 : 1-20
	64 : 1		63 : 19
	: 2-12		64 : 1-11
Jeremiah	9 : 1		8 : 23
	: 2-26		9 : 1-25
Ezekiel	20 : 45-49		21 : 1-5
	21 : 1-32		: 6-37
Daniel	4 : 1-3		3 : 31-33
	: 4-37		4 : 1-34
	5 : 31		6 : 1
	6 : 1-28		: 2-29
Hosea	1 : 10-11		2 : 1-2
	2 : 1-23		: 3-25
	11 : 12		12 : 1
	12 : 1-14		: 2-15
	13 : 16		14 : 1
	14 : 1-9		: 2-10
Joel	2 : 28-32		3 : 1-5
	3 : 1-21		4 : 1-21
Jonah	1 : 17		2 : 1
	2 : 1-10		: 2-11
Micah	5 : 1		4 : 14
	: 2-15		5 : 1-14
Nahum	1 : 15		2 : 1
	2 : 1-13		: 2-14
Zechariah	1 : 18-21		2 : 1-4
	2 : 1-13		: 5-17
Malachi	4 : 1-6		3 : 19-24

GREEK DICTIONARY

OF THE
NEW AMERICAN STANDARD EXHAUSTIVE CONCORDANCE

Updated Edition

HOW TO USE THE GREEK DICTIONARY

The first three items in each entry are standard:

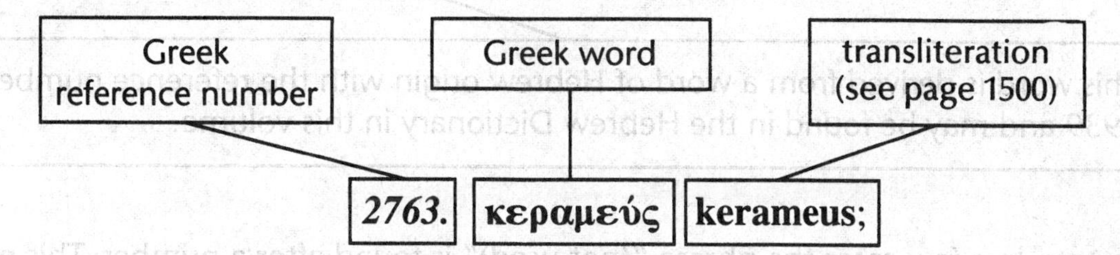

ORIGIN OR DERIVATION

Next, the word's origin or derivation is given on the basis of the standard Greek lexicons. This information is presented in the following ways:

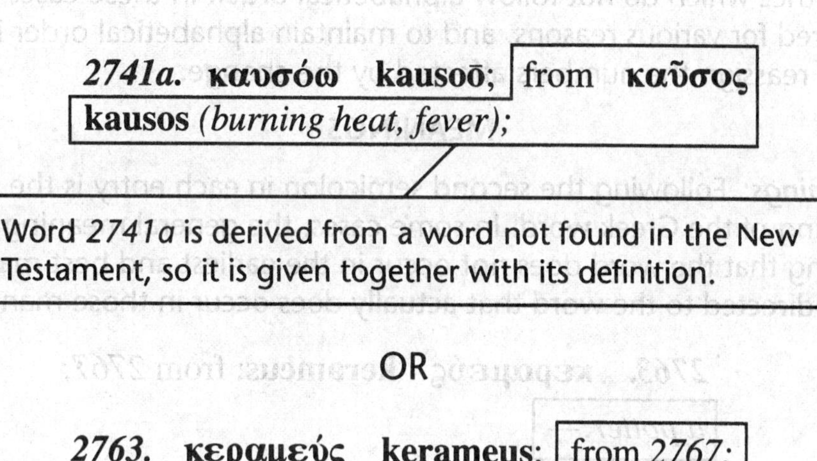

OR

2763. **κεραμεύς** **kerameus**; from *2767;*

This word is derived from word *2767* in this dictionary.

OR

1967. **ἐπιούσιος** **epiousios**; from the same as *1966;*

This word is derived from the same root or root word as word *1966* in this dictionary.

OR

869. **ἄφνω** **aphnō**; a prim. word;

This word is called primitive because it is not derived from any other known word in the Greek language.

OR

2748. **Κεδρών** **Kedrōn**; of Heb. or. [6939];

This word is derived from a word of Hebrew origin with the reference number 6939 and may be found in the Hebrew Dictionary in this volume.

Please note: In a few cases the phrase "(not used)" is found after a number. This means that the word referenced is not found in any reliable manuscript, or that the entry is obsolete for other reasons. The number has been retained for compatibility with Strong's system.

Two other irregularities occur for the same reason. First, the numbers 3203-3302 in the Greek dictionary are not used, because the same numbers are omitted in Strong's. Second, there are a few entries which do not follow alphabetical order. In these cases a formatting change was required for various reasons, and to maintain alphabetical order it would have been necessary to reassign the numbers affected by the change.

MEANINGS

General Meanings: Following the second semicolon in each entry is the section that gives the general meaning of the Greek word. In some cases, the general meaning will be followed by a note indicating that the word does not occur in the earliest and best manuscripts, and the reader will be directed to the word that actually does occur in those manuscripts.

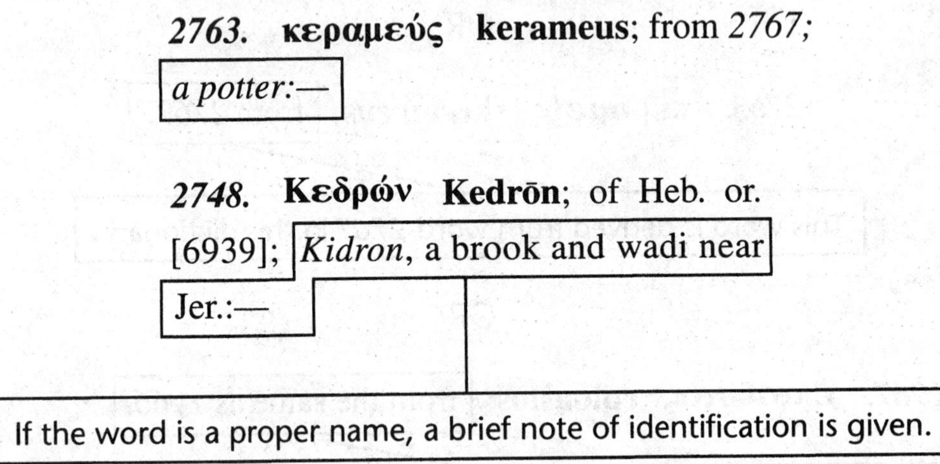

Specific Meanings: Specific meanings of words are dependent upon the context in which the words are found. Following the colon-dash (:—) in each entry is a list of NEW AMERICAN STANDARD BIBLE translations of the Greek word.

2763. **κεραμεύς** **kerameus**; from *2767*;
a potter:— potter(1), Potter's(2).

The number in parenthesis gives the number of times that English key word was used to translate the Greek word in the NEW AMERICAN STANDARD BIBLE Updated Edition.

SPECIAL SIGNS

An asterisk (*) indicates that the key word represents two or more Greek words. Refer to the English concordance listing of the key word for the additional Greek word numbers.

> ***3113.* μακρόθεν makrothen**; from *3117; from afar, afar:*—at a distance(8), distance (4), far away*(1), some distance away(1).

The phrase "var. reading" (for variant reading) means that the word cited is not found in the oldest and best Greek manuscripts, and a reference is given to the corresponding word in those manuscripts.*

In contrast to variant readings, the phrase "another reading" means that the entry is found in one or more reliable manuscripts, but that the corresponding word referenced has better manuscript support. Some entries of this type occur both in reliable and in inferior manuscripts.

* Usually the variant reading is found in the "Textus Receptus," a collation of several inferior Greek manuscripts edited in the 16th and 17th centuries. The variant reading may also occur in a large group of Greek manuscripts to which the name "Majority Text" has been given. These manuscripts usually agree with the Textus Receptus, and are likewise considered inferior by many scholars. A third possibility is that the variant reading is found in another manuscript or group of manuscripts whose value is questionable, such as the "Western Text" which is most often represented by manuscript D.

In a few instances a word in the preferred manuscripts referenced by a var. reading note is said to have come from the variant reading itself (see, for example, 217 and 251, 2045 and 2038a). While this might seem confusing at first, it is actually typical of such readings. Scribes who labored centuries after the New Testament was written sometimes changed a word of unfamiliar spelling to the corresponding form found in older, Classical Greek, thinking that they were making a correction. However, the word from the original manuscript being copied was in fact correct, because the spelling of this word had changed by New Testament times.

THE GREEK ALPHABET

Letter		Name	Classical[1] Pronunciation	Modern[2] Pronunciation	Transliteration
Α	α	alpha	ah	ah	a (also for ᾳ)
Β	β	beta	b	v[3]	b
Γ	γ	gamma	g in 'get'	y in 'yet'[3]	g
Δ	δ	delta	d	th in 'then'[3]	d
Ε	ε	epsilon	e in 'met'	e in 'met'	e
Ζ	ζ	zeta	dz	z	z
Η	η	eta	ey in 'they'	ee[4]	ē (also for ῃ)
Θ	θ	theta	th in 'thin'	th in 'thin'	th
Ι	ι	iota	short i in 'hit' ee (long) y in 'yet' (sometimes used before a vowel)	ee[4] y in 'yet' (sometimes before a vowel)	i
Κ	κ	kappa	k	k	k
Λ	λ	lambda	l	l	l
Μ	μ	mu	m	m	m
Ν	ν	nu	n	n	n
Ξ	ξ	xi	x (= ks)	x (= ks)	x
Ο	ο	omicron	o in 'box'	o in 'cloth'[5]	o
Π	π	pi	p	p	p
Ρ	ρ	rho	r or tongue flap[6]	tongue flap[6]	r
Σ	σ,ς[7]	sigma	s	s	s
Τ	τ	tau	t	t	t
Υ	υ	upsilon	oo (short) u in début (long)	ee[4] or f, v	u
Φ	φ	phi	ph (f)	ph (f)	ph
Χ	χ	chi	ch in 'Bach'[8]	similar to Classical[8]	ch
Ψ	ψ	psi	ps (Note that the 'p' sound is always pronounced, even when ψ is the first letter of a word.)	ps	ps
Ω	ω	omega	o in 'home'	o in 'cloth'[5]	ō (also for ῳ)

---

[1] I.e. the kind of pronunciation most often used in the study of ancient Greek. Sometimes a more authentic, archaic pronunciation is preferred. In that system the long vowels generally sound like the corresponding short vowels, but are held out longer. Also, spirantal consonants like θ and φ are pronounced like the corresponding "stop" consonants (e.g. 't' and 'p'), followed immediately by a strong 'h' sound.

[2] Note that these are approximations. One can detect subtle but important distinctions in the speech of a native speaker. For example, the vowels do not "glide" from one pitch to another as is typically done in English (e.g. 'ahee' for the pronoun 'I') but remain at the same pitch ('ee', 'ah', etc.), as is done in Spanish and many other languages.

[3] The 'stop' versions of these letters are still needed (i.e. b, g in 'get', and d), and are simulated in modern Greek by the combinations μπ, γκ, and ντ respectively.

[4] The fact that these vowels are pronounced alike in modern Greek is due to a phenomenon called 'iotacism'. As the language developed over the centuries, there was a tendency to emphasize the long ι 'ee' sound and even to use it for other vowels and diphthongs (see the next section). For υ as 'f' or 'v', see the next section, note 1.

[5] The modern Greek 'o' sound for both ο and ω may seem to some more like the 'o' in 'home', or an 'o' somewhere between 'cloth' and 'home'.

[6] A tongue flap, in which the tip of the tongue briefly touches the ridge behind the upper teeth, is similar to the single medial 'r' in Spanish (as in 'cara'). It is preferred for Classical pronunciation and mandatory for modern.

[7] This is a special form of sigma (called "final" sigma) which must be used if sigma occurs at the end of a word.

[8] I.e. a sound made by putting the back of the tongue to the roof of the mouth as if to make a 'k', but without actually touching the roof of the mouth with the tongue. In modern Greek the sound is sometimes the same as a strong 'h'.

DIPHTHONGS AND SYLLABLES

Diphthongs (Gr. for "with two sounds") are special combinations of two vowels which are pronounced together as one, and therefore form a single syllable in Greek. Otherwise, syllables are formed from single vowels. Two (or more) vowels together that are *not* diphthongs are treated as one syllable per vowel. A preceding or following consonant is usually part of a syllable, but a vowel must be present to form a syllable.

The following combinations of vowels are diphthongs. It is important to note that, with the exception of long vowels with iota subscripts (see below), no other combinations count as diphthongs. In fact, if the letters of any of the following pairs are switched (e.g. αι to ια), the result is no longer a diphthong but is instead two separate syllables.

Diphthong	Pronunciation Classical	Pronunciation Modern	Diphthong	Pronunciation Classical	Pronunciation Modern
αι	i in 'I' or 'bike'	e in 'met'	ηυ	eyoo (ey-oo)	--
αυ	ow in 'cow'	ahf (like 'off') or ahv[1]	οι	oi in 'oil'	ee[2]
ει	ey	ee[2]	ου	oo	oo
ευ	eoo (e in 'met')	ef or ev[1]	υι	wee in 'weep'	ee[2]

[1]In these diphthongs the υ assumes the consonantal sound of 'f' or 'v', much like the corresponding vowel/consonant in Latin.
[2]The sound of these diphthongs is the result of iotacism; see note 4 in the previous section.

In some words and grammatical constructions a long vowel (η, ω, or long α) has a small ι written underneath, called an "iota subscript." While this constitutes a diphthong, the long vowel is pronounced the same as if it did not have a iota subscript.

ACCENTS AND OTHER MARKS

Accents are used in Greek to indicate which syllable should be stressed in a word. In Classical Greek there are three accents which originally indicated differences in pitch: the acute (´), the circumflex (῀), and the grave (`). In most university settings today, the acute and circumflex are read the same way to stress a particular syllable. The grave accent is used only to replace an acute accent at the end of a word which is followed by another word, to indicate that the syllable is not to be stressed. Since it only occurs under these circumstances, the grave accent will not be seen in the Greek Dictionary.

Three other marks should be noted. There are two "breathing" marks, one of which must be used at the beginning of any word that begins with a vowel. A "rough" breathing mark (῾) indicates that the word is to be pronounced as if it began with an 'h'. A "smooth" breathing mark (᾿) indicates that no 'h' sound should be added; i.e., the word should be pronounced just as it is written. Finally, a dieresis over a vowel (e.g. ϋ) indicates that the vowel is to be pronounced as a separate syllable. These distinctions are usually observed in the study of ancient Greek.

The accents and breathing marks are treated quite differently in modern Greek than they are in the study of ancient Greek. In 1982 the Greek Ministry of Education issued a statement that one-syllable words were not to receive an accent (with a few exceptions), and that multi-syllable words were to receive only the acute. No breathing marks were to be used; they had already been ignored in modern Greek for some time.

ABBREVIATIONS USED IN THE GREEK DICTIONARY

abb.	abbreviated, abbreviation
acc.	accusative (case)
act.	active
adj.	adjective
adv.	adverb, adverbial
alt.	alternate
anal.	analogy
aor.	aorist
appar.	apparent, apparently
Ara.	Aramaic
Arab.	Arabic
art.	article
card.	cardinal
caus.	causative
Chr.	Christian
cf.	compare
comp.	compound
conjunc.	conjunction
contr.	contracted, contraction
cop.	copulative
cptv.	comparative, comparatively
dat.	dative (case)
def.	definite
der.	derivation, derivative, derived
desc.	descended, descendant(s)
dim.	diminutive
E.	east, eastern
Eg.	Egypt, Egyptian
equiv.	equivalent
esp.	especially
euph.	euphemism
ext.	extension
etc.	et cetera
fem.	feminine
fig.	figurative, figuratively
for.	foreign
fut.	future
gen.	genitive (case)
Gr.	Greek
Heb.	Hebrew
i.e.	id est, that is
imper.	imperative
imperf.	imperfect
impl.	implied, implication
incl.	including
ind.	indicative
indef.	indefinite
inf.	infinitive
inhab.	inhabited, inhabitant
intens.	intensive
interj.	interjection
interrog.	interrogative
Isr.	Israel, Israelite
Jer.	Jerusalem

Lat.	Latin
lit.	literal, literally
masc.	masculine
mean.	meaning
mid.	middle (voice)
mult.	multiplicative
N	north, northern
neg.	negative
neut.	neuter
nom.	nominative (case)
N.T.	New Testament
num.	number
obs.	obsolete
onomatop.	onomatopoeia, onomatopoeic
or.	origin
ord.	ordinal
O.T.	Old Testament
Pal.	Palestine
part.	participle
pass.	passive
perf.	perfect
perh.	perhaps
pers.	person, personal
Pers.	Persian
pl.	plural
poss.	possessive
pref.	prefix
prep.	preposition, prepositional
pres.	present
prim.	primary, primitive
prob.	probably
prol.	prolongated, prolongation
pron.	pronoun
q.v.	quod vide, which see
recip.	reciprocal
redupl.	reduplicated, reduplication
refl.	reflexive
rel.	relative
Rom.	Roman
S.	south, southern
sing.	singular
spec.	specifically
subst.	substantive
suff.	suffix
superl.	superlative
unc.	uncertain
var.	variant (reading)
vb.	verb
W.	west, western

The Symbol Greek II font used to print this work is available from Linguist's Software, Inc., PO Box 580, Edmonds, WA 98020-0580 USA tel (206) 775-1130.

A

1. **Α, α alpha**; first letter of the Greek alphabet; *alpha,* as num. *1* or *1000,* as pref. (1) negative (2) copulative (3) intensive (see also *256a).*

2. **Ἀαρών Aarōn**; of Heb. or. [175]; *Aaron,* the brother of Moses:— Aaron(4), Aaron's(1).

3. **Ἀβαδδών Abaddōn**; of Heb. or. [11]; *Abaddon,* the angel of the abyss:— Abaddon(1).

4. **ἀβαρής abarēs**; from *1* (as a neg. pref.) and *922; not burdensome:*— from being a burden(1).

5. **Ἀββά Abba**; of Ara. or. [2]; *Abba, father:*— Abba(3).

6. **Ἄβελ Habel**; of Heb. or. [1893]; *Abel,* a son of Adam:— Abel(4).

7. **Ἀβιά Abia**; of Heb. or. [29]; *Abijah, Abia,* the name of two Isr.:— Abijah(3).

8. **Ἀβιαθάρ Abiathar**; of Heb. or. [54]; *Abiathar,* an Isr.:— Abiathar(1).

9. **Ἀβιληνή Abilēnē**; of unc. or.; *Abilene,* territory northwest of Damascus:— Abilene(1).

10. **Ἀβιούδ Abioud**; of Heb. or. [31]; *Abiud, Abihud,* an Isr., the son of Zerubbabel:— Abihud(2).

11. **Ἀβραάμ Abraam**; of Heb. or. [85]; *Abraham,* the Heb. patriarch:— Abraham(66), Abraham's(7).

12. **ἄβυσσος abussos**; from *1* (as a neg. pref.) and **βυσσός bussos** = *1037; boundless, bottomless:*— abyss(7), bottomless(2).

13. **Ἄγαβος Agabos**; of unc. or.; *Agabus,* a Christian prophet:— Agabus(2).

14. **ἀγαθοεργέω agathoergeō**; from *18* and *2041; to do good:*— do good(1).

15. **ἀγαθοποιέω agathopoieō**; from *18* and *4160; to do good:*— do what is right(2), do good(4), do right(1), does good(1), doing what is right(1), doing right(1).

16. **ἀγαθοποιΐα agathopoiia**; from *17; welldoing:*— doing what(1), doing what is right(1).

17. **ἀγαθοποιός agathopoios**; from *18* and *4160; doing well.*

18. **ἀγαθός agathos**; of unc. or.; *good:*— generous(1), good(81), good man(2), good thing(6), good things(6), goodness(1), goods(2), kind(1), kindly(1), kindness(1).

19a. **ἀγαθουργέω agathourgeō**; contr. form of *14; to do good:*— did good(1).

19b. **ἀγαθωσύνη agathōsunē**; from *18; goodness:*— goodness(4).

20. **ἀγαλλίασις agalliasis**; from *21; exultation, exuberant joy:*— gladness(3), great joy(1), joy(1).

21. **ἀγαλλιάω agalliaō**; from **ἀγάλλομαι agallomai** *(to make glorious, exalt); to exult, rejoice greatly:*— exultation(1), exulted(1), glad(2), greatly rejoice(2), rejoice(1), rejoiced(2), rejoiced greatly(2).

22. **ἄγαμος agamos**; from *1* (as a neg. pref.) and *1062; unmarried:*— unmarried(4).

23. **ἀγανακτέω aganakteō**; of unc. or.; *to grieve much,* hence *to be indignant:*— feel indignant(1), indignant(5), indignantly(1).

24. **ἀγανάκτησις aganaktēsis**; from *23; indignation:*— indignation(1).

25. **ἀγαπάω agapaō**; of unc. or.; *to love:*— beloved(8), felt a love for(1), love(1), love(75), loved(38), loves(20).

26. **ἀγάπη agapē**; from *25; love, goodwill:*— beloved(1), love(1), love(112), love feasts(1), love's(1).

27. **ἀγαπητός agapētos**; from *25; beloved:*— beloved(60), very dear(1).

28. **Ἁγάρ Hagar**; of Heb. or. [1904]; *Hagar,* a concubine of Abraham:— Hagar(2).

29. **ἀγγαρεύω aggareuō**; of Pers. or., cf. [104]; *to impress, compel:*— forces(1), pressed into service(2).

30. **ἀγγεῖον aggeion**; from *32b; a vessel:*— flasks(1).

31a. **ἀγγελία aggelia**; from *32a; a message:*— message(2).

31b. **ἀγγέλλω aggellō**; from *32a; to announce, report:*— announcing(1).

32a. **ἄγγελος aggelos**; a prim. word; *a messenger, angel:*— angel(86), angel's(2), angelic(1), angels(80), messenger(4), messengers(3).

32b. **ἄγγος aggos**; a prim. word; *a vessel:*— containers(1).

33. **ἄγε age**; imper. of *71; come!:*— come(2).

34. **ἀγέλη agelē**; from *71; a herd:*— herd(7).

35. **ἀγενεαλόγητος agenealogētos**; from *1* (as a neg. pref.) and *1075; without genealogy:*— without genealogy(1).

36. **ἀγενής agenēs**; from *1* (as a neg. pref.) and *1085; unborn, of no family, ignoble:*— base things(1).

37. **ἁγιάζω hagiazō**; from *40; to make holy, consecrate, sanctify:*— hallowed(2), keep himself holy(1), sanctified(16), sanctifies(2), sanctify(7).

38. **ἁγιασμός hagiasmos**; from *37; consecration, sanctification:*— sanctification(8), sanctifying work(1), sanctity(1).

39. **ἅγιον hagion**; see *40.*

40. **ἅγιος hagios**; from a prim. root; *sacred, holy:*— Holy(92), holy(62), Holy of Holies(1), holy one(5), holy ones(1), holy place(7), most holy(1), saint(1), saints(59), saints'(1), sanctuary(2).

41. **ἁγιότης hagiotēs**; from *40; sanctity, holiness:*— holiness(2).

42. **ἁγιωσύνη hagiōsunē**; from *40; holiness:*— holiness(3).

43. **ἀγκάλη agkalē**; from **ἄγκος agkos** *(a bend); the bent arm:*— arms(1).

44. **ἄγκιστρον agkistron**; from the same as *43; a fishhook:*— hook(1).

45. **ἄγκυρα agkura**; from the same as *43; an anchor:*— anchor(1), anchors(3).

46. **ἄγναφος agnaphos**; from *1* (as a neg. pref.) and the same as *1102; uncarded, undressed:*— unshrunk(2).

47. **ἁγνεία hagneia**; from *53; purity:*— purity(2).

48. **ἁγνίζω hagnizō**; from *53; to purify, cleanse from defilement:*— purified(2), purifies(1), purify(3), purifying(1).

49. **ἁγνισμός hagnismos**; from *48; purification:*— purification(1).

50. **ἀγνοέω agnoeō**; from *1* (as a neg. pref.) and the same as *1097; to be ignorant, not to know:*— have no knowledge(1), ignorance(1), ignorant(2), ignorantly(1), know(2), knowing(2), recognize(1), recognized(1), recognizing(1), unaware(4), understand(2), uninformed(2), unknown(2).

51. **ἀγνόημα agnoēma**; from *50; a sin of ignorance:*— ignorance(1), sins(1).

52. **ἄγνοια agnoia**; from *50; ignorance:*— ignorance(4).

53. **ἁγνός hagnos**; from the same as *40; free from ceremonial defilement, holy, sacred:*— chaste(1), free from sin(1), innocent(1), pure(5).

54. **ἁγνότης hagnotēs**; from *53; purity, chastity:*— purity(2).

55. **ἁγνῶς hagnōs**; from *53; purely, with pure motives:*— pure motives(1).

56. **ἀγνωσία agnōsia**; from *1* (as a neg. pref.) and the same as *1097; ignorance:*— ignorance(1), no knowledge(1).

57. **ἄγνωστος agnōstos**; from *1* (as a neg. pref.) and the same as *1097; unknown:*— unknown(1).

58. **ἀγορά agora**; from **ἀγείρω ageirō** *(to bring together); an assembly, place of assembly:*— market place(5), market places(6).

59. **ἀγοράζω agorazō**; from *58; to buy in the marketplace, purchase:*— bought(9), buy(11), buying(3), buys(2), make the purchase(1), purchased(3), spend(1).

60. **ἀγοραῖος agoraios**; from *58; pertaining to the marketplace, an agitator:*— courts(1), market place(1).

61. **ἄγρα agra**; prob. akin to *68; a hunting, a catch:*— catch(2).

62. **ἀγράμματος agrammatos**; from *1* (as a neg. pref.) and *1125; without learning, unlettered:*— uneducated(1).

63. **ἀγραυλέω agrauleō**; from *68* and *833; to live in the fields:*— staying out in the fields(1).

64. **ἀγρεύω agreuō**; from *61; to catch, take by hunting:*— trap(1).

65. **ἀγριέλαιος agrielaios**; from *66* and *1636; of the wild olive:*— what(1), wild olive(1), wild olive tree(1).

66. **ἄγριος agrios**; from *68; living in the fields, wild, savage, fierce:*— wild(3).

67. **Ἀγρίππας Agrippas**; of unc. or.; *Agrippa,* the name of two desc. of Herod the Great:— Agrippa(11).

68. **ἀγρός agros**; a prim. word; *a field, the country:*— country(5), countryside(3), farm(1), farms(3), field(21), fields(2), piece of land(1), tract of land(1).

69. **ἀγρυπνέω agrupneō**; from *64* and *5258; to be sleepless, wakeful:*— alert(1), keep on the alert(2), keep watch(1).

70. **ἀγρυπνία agrupnia**; from *69; sleeplessness, watching:*— sleepless nights(1), sleeplessness(1).

71. **ἄγω agō**; a prim. vb.; *to lead, bring, carry:*— arrest(1), bring(11), bringing(3), brought(26), go(5), going(2), lead(1), leads(1), led(12), led away(1), session(1), taking(1), took away(1).

72. **ἀγωγή agōgē**; from *71; a carrying away, leading, guiding:*— conduct(1).

73. **ἀγών agōn**; from *71; a gathering, contest, struggle:*— conflict(1), fight(2), opposition(1), race(1), struggle(1).

74. **ἀγωνία agōnia**; from *73; a contest, great fear:*— agony(1).

75. **ἀγωνίζομαι agōnizomai**; from *73; to contend for a prize, struggle:*— competes in the games(1), fight(1), fighting(1), fought(1), laboring earnestly(1), strive(2), striving(1).

76. **Ἀδάμ Adam**; of Heb. or. [121]; *Adam,* the first man:— Adam(9).

77. **ἀδάπανος adapanos**; from *1* (as a neg. pref.) and *1160a; without expense:*— without charge(1).

78. **Ἀδδί Addi**; prob. of Heb. or., cf. [5716]; *Addi,* an Isr.:— Addi(1).

79. ἀδελφή adelphē; fem. from *80; sister:*— believing(1), sister(16), sisters(8).

80. ἀδελφός adelphos; from *1* (as a cop. pref.) and **δελφύς delphus** *(womb); a brother:*— believing husband(1), brethren(170), brethren*(13), brother(111), brother's(8), brothers(40).

81. ἀδελφότης adelphotēs; from *80; brotherhood:*— brethren(1), brotherhood(1).

82. ἄδηλος adēlos; from *1* (as a neg. pref.) and *1212; unseen, not manifest:*— concealed(1), indistinct(1).

83. ἀδηλότης adēlotēs; from *82; uncertainty:*— uncertainty(1).

84. ἀδήλως adēlōs; from *82; uncertainly:*— without aim(1).

85. ἀδημονέω adēmoneō; of unc. or.; *to be distressed:*— distressed(2), troubled(1).

86. ᾅδης hadēs; perh. from *1* (as a neg. pref.) and *1491a (3708); Hades,* the abode of departed spirits:— Hades(10).

87. ἀδιάκριτος adiakritos; from *1* (as a neg. pref.) and *1252; indistinguishable, without uncertainty:*— unwavering(1).

88. ἀδιάλειπτος adialeiptos; from *1* (as a neg. pref.) and *1257; incessant:*— constantly(1), unceasing(1).

89. ἀδιαλείπτως adialeiptōs; adv. from *88; incessantly:*— constantly(2), unceasingly(1), without ceasing(1).

90. ἀδιαφθορία adiaphthoria; var. reading for *862b,* q.v.

91. ἀδικέω adikeō; from *94; to do wrong, act wickedly:*— am a wrongdoer(1), damage(1), do harm(1), do wrong(1), does wrong(2), doing...wrong(1), done...wrong(2), harm(4), hurt(3), injure(2), injuring(1), offended(1), offender(1), treated unjustly(1), wrong(2), wrong...done(1), wronged(3).

92. ἀδίκημα adikēma; from *91; a wrong, injury:*— iniquities(1), misdeed(1), wrong(1).

93. ἀδικία adikia; from *94; injustice, unrighteousness:*— doing wrong(1), evildoers(1), iniquities(1), iniquity(2), injustice(1), unrighteous(2), unrighteousness(12), wickedness(4), wrong(1).

94. ἄδικος adikos; from *1* (as a neg. pref.) and *1349; unjust, unrighteous:*— unjust(3), unrighteous(8), wicked(1).

95. ἀδίκως adikōs; adv. from *94; unjustly:*— unjustly(1).

96a. Ἀδμίν Admin; of unc. or.; *Admin,* an Isr.:— Admin(1).

96b. ἀδόκιμος adokimos; from *1* (as a neg. pref.) and *1384; not standing the test, rejected:*— depraved(1), disqualified(1), fail the test(2), rejected(1), unapproved(1), worthless(2).

97. ἄδολος adolos; from *1* (as a neg. pref.) and *1388; guileless, genuine:*— pure(1).

98. Ἀδραμυττηνός Adramuttēnos; of unc. or.; *of Adramyttium,* a seaport of Mysia:— Adramyttian(1).

99. Ἀδρίας Adrias; of unc. or.; *the Adriatic,* the name of a sea:— Adriatic(1).

100. ἁδρότης hadrotēs; from **ἁδρός hadros** *(thick, well-grown); thickness, abundance:*— generous gift(1).

101. ἀδυνατέω adunateō; from *102; to be unable:*— impossible(2).

102. ἀδύνατος adunatos; from *1* (as a neg. pref.) and *1415; unable, powerless:*— impossible(6), no strength(1), things that are impossible(1), could not do(1), without strength(1).

103. ᾄδω adō; from **ἀείδω aeidō** *(to sing); to sing:*— sang(3), singing(2).

104. ἀεί aei; of unc. or.; *ever, unceasingly:*— always(6), constantly(1).

105. ἀετός aetos; a prim. word; *an eagle:*— eagle(3), vultures(2).

106. ἄζυμος azumos; from *1* (as a neg. pref.) and *2219; unleavened:*— unleavened(9).

107. Ἀζώρ Azōr; of Heb. or., cf. [5809]; *Azor,* an Isr.:— Azor(2).

108. Ἄζωτος Azōtos; of Heb. or. [795]; *Azotus* (i.e. Ashdod), a Philistine city:— Azotus(1).

109. ἀήρ aēr; from **ἄημι aēmi** *(to breathe, blow); air:*— air(7).

110. ἀθανασία athanasia; from *1* (as a neg. pref.) and *2288; immortality:*— immortality(3).

111. ἀθέμιτος athemitos; from *1* (as a neg. pref.) and **θεμιτός themitos** *(righteous); lawless:*— abominable(1), unlawful(1).

112. ἄθεος atheos; from *1* (as a neg. pref.) and *2316; godless, ungodly:*— without God(1).

113. ἄθεσμος athesmos; from *1* (as a neg. pref.) and **θεσμός thesmos** *(law, custom); lawless:*— unprincipled men(2).

114. ἀθετέω atheteō; from **ἄθετος athetos** *(without position* or *place);* from *1* (as a neg. pref.) and *5087; to do away with what has been laid down, set aside:*— nullify(1), refuse(1), reject(1), rejected(1), rejects(6), rejecting(1), set aside(3), sets...aside(1), setting aside(1).

115. ἀθέτησις athetēsis; from *114; a setting aside:*— put away(1), setting aside(1).

116. Ἀθῆναι Athēnai; from **Ἀθήνη Athēnē** (Gr. goddess of wisdom); *Athens,* capital of Attica in Greece:— Athens(4).

117. Ἀθηναῖος Athēnaios; from *116; Athenian:*— Athenians(1), Athens(1).

118. ἀθλέω athleō; from **ἄθλος athlos** *(a contest, struggle); to contend, wrestle:*— competes(1), competes as an athlete(1).

119. ἄθλησις athlēsis; from *118; a contest:*— conflict(1).

120a. ἀθροίζω athroizō; from **ἀθρόος athroos** *(assembled in crowds); to gather:*— gathered together(1).

120b. ἀθυμέω athumeō; from *1* (as a neg. pref.) and *2372; to be disheartened:*— lose heart(1).

121. ἀθῷος athōos; from *1* (as a neg. pref.) and **θωή thōē** *(a penalty); unpunished:*— innocent(2).

122. αἴγειος aigeios; from **αἴξ aix** *(a goat); of a goat:*— goatskins*(1).

123. αἰγιαλός aigialos; from **αἴξ aix** *(a wave); the seashore:*— beach(6).

124. Αἰγύπτιος Aiguptios; from *125; Egyptian:*— Egyptian(3), Egyptians(2).

125. Αἴγυπτος Aiguptos; of unc. or.; *Egypt,* the land of the Nile:— Egypt(25).

126. ἀΐδιος aidios; from *104; everlasting:*— eternal(2).

127. αἰδώς aidōs; from **αἰδέομαι aideomai** *(to be ashamed); a sense of shame:*— modestly(1).

128. Αἰθίοψ Aithiops; from **αἴθω aithō** *(to burn)* and **ὤψ ops** *(an eye); Ethiopian:*— Ethiopian(1), Ethiopians(1).

129. αἷμα haima; of unc. or.; *blood:*— blood(94), hemorrhage*(3).

130. αἱματεκχυσία haimatekchusia; from *129* and *1632b; shedding of blood:*— shedding of blood(1).

131. αἱμορροέω haimorroeō; from *129* and *4482; to lose blood:*— suffering from a hemorrhage(1).

132. Αἰνέας Aineas; of unc. or.; *Aeneas,* a paralytic cured by Peter:— Aeneas(2).

133. αἴνεσις ainesis; from *134; praise:*— praise(1).

134. αἰνέω aineō; from *136; to praise:*— give praise(1), praise(2), praising(5).

135. αἴνιγμα ainigma; from **αἰνίσσομαι ainissomai** *(to speak in riddles); a riddle:*—dimly(1).

136. αἶνος ainos; of unc. or.; *praise* (noun):— praise(2).

137. Αἰνών Ainōn; prob. of Ara. or., cf. [5871a]; *Aenon,* a place in the Jordan Valley:— Aenon(1).

138. αἱρέω haireō; a prim. vb.; *to take, choose:*— choose(1), choosing(1), chosen(1).

139. αἵρεσις hairesis; from *138; choice, opinion:*— factions(2), heresies(1), sect(6).

140. αἱρετίζω hairetizō; from *138; to choose:*— chosen(1).

141. αἱρετικός hairetikos; from *138; causing division:*— factious(1).

142. αἴρω airō; a prim. vb.; *to raise, take up, lift:*— away(5), bear(4), carried(1), carry(1), get(4), hoisted(1), keep(1), lifted(2), pick(9), picked(11), pulls away(2), put away(1), raised(2), remove(1), removed(3), suspense*(1), take(13), take away(5), take...away(4), taken(3), taken...away(1), taken away(12), takes away(7), taking(1), took(2), took...away(1), took away(3), weighed anchor(1).

143. αἰσθάνομαι aisthanomai; from **ἀΐω aiō** *(to perceive); to perceive:*— perceive(1).

144. αἴσθησις aisthēsis; from *143; perception:*— discernment(1).

145. αἰσθητήριον aisthētērion; from *143* and **-τηριον -tērion** (suff. denoting place); *organ of perception:*— senses(1).

146. αἰσχροκερδής aischrokerdēs; from *150* and *2771; greedy of base gain:*— fond of sordid gain(2), sordid gain(2).

147. αἰσχροκερδῶς aischrokerdōs; adv. from *146; from eagerness for base gain:*— sordid gain(1).

148. αἰσχρολογία aischrologia; from *150* and *3004; abusive language:*— abusive speech(1).

149. αἰσχρόν aischron; see *150.*

150. αἰσχρός aischros; from the same as *153; shameful:*— disgraceful(2), improper(1), sordid(1).

151. αἰσχρότης aischrotēs; from *150; baseness:*— filthiness(1).

152. αἰσχύνη aischunē; from the same as *153; shame:*— disgrace(1), shame(5).

153. αἰσχύνω aischunō; from **αἶσχος aischos** *(shame, disgrace); to dishonor, make ashamed:*— ashamed(2), put to shame(2), shame(1), shrink(1).

154. αἰτέω aiteō; a prim. vb.; *to ask, request:*— ask(36), asked(16), asking(7), asks(7), beg(1), called(1), making a request(1), requesting(1).

155. αἴτημα aitēma; from *154; a request:*— demand(1), requests(2).

156. **αἰτία aitia**; from *154; cause, reason:*— charge(1), charge against(2), charges(2), ground(2), guilt(3), reason(9), relationship(1).

157. **αἰτίαμα aitiama**; var. reading for *159b*, q.v.

158. **αἴτιον aition**; neut. of *159a*, q.v.

159a. **αἴτιος aitios**; from *156; causative of, responsible for:*— cause(1), guilt(3), source(1).

159b. **αἰτίωμα aitiōma**; from **αἰτιάομαι aitiaomai** *(to give as the cause* or *occasion); a charge:*— charges(1).

160. **αἰφνίδιος aiphnidios**; from **αἴφνης aiphnēs** *(suddenly); sudden:*— suddenly(2).

161. **αἰχμαλωσία aichmalōsia**; from *164; captivity:*— captivity(2), host of captives(1).

162. **αἰχμαλωτεύω aichmalōteuō**; from *164; to lead captive:*— led captive(1).

163. **αἰχμαλωτίζω aichmalōtizō**; from *164; to take* or *lead captive:*— captivate(1), led captive(1), making...a prisoner(1), taking...captive(1).

164. **αἰχμάλωτος aichmalōtos**; from **αἰχμή aichmē** *(a spear)* and **ἁλίσκομαι haliskomai** *(to be taken, conquered); captive:*— captives(1).

165. **αἰών aiōn**; from a prim. root appar. mean. *continued duration; a space of time, an age:*— age(20), ages(6), ancient time(1), beginning of time(1), course(1), eternal(2), eternity(1), ever*(2), forever(27), forever and ever(20), forevermore(2), long ago(1), never*(1), old(1), time(1), world(7), worlds(1).

166. **αἰώνιος aiōnios**; from *165; agelong, eternal:*— eternal(66), eternity(1), forever(1).

167. **ἀκαθαρσία akatharsia**; from *169; uncleanness:*— impurity(9), uncleanness(1).

168. **ἀκαθάρτης akathartēs**; var. reading for *169*, q.v.

169. **ἀκάθαρτος akathartos**; from *1* (as a neg. pref.) and *2508; unclean, impure:*— impure person(1), unclean(29), unclean things(1).

170. **ἀκαιρέομαι akaireomai**; from **ἄκαιρος akairos** *(unseasonable); to have no opportunity:*— lacked opportunity(1).

171. **ἀκαίρως akairōs**; from the same as *170; out of season:*— season(1).

172. **ἄκακος akakos**; from *1* (as a neg. pref.) and *2556; guileless:*— innocent(1), unsuspecting(1).

173. **ἄκανθα akantha**; from **ἀκή akē** *(a point, edge); a prickly plant, thorn:*— thorn(1), thorns(13).

174. **ἀκάνθινος akanthinos**; from *173; of thorns:*— thorns(2).

175. **ἄκαρπος akarpos**; from *1* (as a neg. pref.) and *2590; unfruitful:*— unfruitful(6), without fruit(1).

176. **ἀκατάγνωστος akatagnōstos**; from *1* (as a neg. pref.) and *2607; not to be condemned, beyond reproach:*— beyond reproach(2).

177. **ἀκατακάλυπτος akatakaluptos**; from *1* (as a neg. pref.) and *2619; uncovered:*— uncovered(2).

178. **ἀκατάκριτος akatakritos**; from *1* (as a neg. pref.) and *2632; uncondemned:*— uncondemned(1), without trial(1).

179. **ἀκατάλυτος akatalutos**; from *1* (as a neg. pref.) and *2647; indissoluble:*— indestructible(1).

180. **ἀκατάπαυστος akatapaustos**; from *1* (as a neg. pref.) and *2664; incessant:*— never cease(1).

181. **ἀκαταστασία akatastasia**; from *182; instability:*— confusion(1), disorder(1), disturbances(2), tumults(1).

182. **ἀκατάστατος akatastatos**; from *1* (as a neg. pref.) and *2525; unstable:*— restless(1), unstable(1).

183. **ἀκατάσχετος akataschetos**; var. reading for *182*, q.v.

184. **Ἁκελδαμάχ Hakeldamach**; of Ara. or.; *Hakeldama,* a field appar. located south of the valley of Hinnom:— Hakeldama(1).

185. **ἀκέραιος akeraios**; from *1* (as a neg. pref.) and *2767; unmixed, pure:*— innocent(3).

186. **ἀκλινής aklinēs**; from *1* (as a neg. pref.) and *2827; unbending:*— without wavering(1).

187. **ἀκμάζω akmazō**; from **ἀκμή akmē** *(a point, edge); to be at the prime:*— ripe(1).

188. **ἀκμήν akmēn**; acc. of the same as *187; at the present point of time:*— still(1).

189. **ἀκοή akoē**; from *191; hearing, the sense of hearing:*— ears(4), heard(2), hearing(8), keep(2), news(3), report(2), rumors(2).

190. **ἀκολουθέω akoloutheō**; from *1* (as a cop. pref.) and **κέλευθος keleuthos** *(a road, way); to follow:*— follow(35), followed(36), following(17), follows(1).

191. **ἀκούω akouō**; from a prim. word mean. *hearing; to hear, listen:*— come to...ears(1), every(1), give heed(2), grant(1), hear(115), heard(216), hearers(1), hearing(24), hears(21), heed(2), listen(24), listened(1), listeners(1), listening(14), listens(5), reached(1), reported(1), understand(1), understands(1).

192. **ἀκρασία akrasia**; from *193; want of power:*— lack of self-control(1), self-indulgence(1).

193. **ἀκρατής akratēs**; from *1* (as a neg. pref.) and *2904; powerless, impotent:*— without self-control(1).

194. **ἄκρατος akratos**; from *1* (as a neg. pref.) and *2767; unmixed:*— full strength(1).

195. **ἀκρίβεια akribeia**; from *198a; exactness:*— strictly(1).

196. **ἀκριβέστατος akribestatos**; superl. of *198a*, q.v.

197. **ἀκριβέστερον akribesteron**; adv. from the cptv. of *198a*, q.v.

198a. **ἀκριβής akribēs**; prob. from *206* and an unc. root; *exact, precise:*— strictest(1).

198b. **ἀκριβόω akriboō**; from *198a; to inquire with exactness:*— determined(2).

199. **ἀκριβῶς akribōs**; adv. from *198a; with exactness:*— accurately(1), careful*(1), carefully(2), full well(1), more accurately(1), more exact(1), more thorough investigation(1), more thoroughly(1).

200. **ἀκρίς akris**; a prim. word; *a locust:*— locusts(4).

201. **ἀκροατήριον akroatērion**; from **ἀκροάομαι akroaomai** *(to listen)* and **-τηριον -tērion** (suff. denoting place); *place of audience,* or *listening:*— auditorium(1).

202. **ἀκροατής akroatēs**; from the same as *201; a hearer:*— hearer(2), hearers(2).

203. **ἀκροβυστία akrobustia**; of unc. or.; *the prepuce, foreskin,* hence *uncircumcision:*— uncircumcised(10), uncircumcised man(1), uncircumcision(8), without being circumcised(1).

204. **ἀκρογωνιαῖος akrogōniaios**; from *206* and *1137; at the extreme angle* or *corner:*— corner(2).

205. **ἀκροθίνιον akrothinion**; from the same as *206* and **θίς this** *(a heap); the top of a heap,* i.e. *the best of the spoils:*— choicest spoils(1).

206. **ἄκρον akron**; from **ἄκρος akros**; from the same as *173; highest, extreme:*— end(1), farthest end(2), other(1), tip(1), top(1).

207. **Ἀκύλας Akulas**; of Lat. or.; *Aquila,* a Chr.:— Aquila(6).

208. **ἀκυρόω akuroō**; from *1* (as a neg. pref.) and **κῦρος kuros** *(authority); to revoke:*— invalidate(1), invalidated(1), invalidating(1).

209. **ἀκωλύτως akōlutōs**; from *1* (as a neg. pref.) and *2967; without hindrance:*— unhindered(1).

210. **ἄκων akōn**; contr. of *1* (as a neg. pref.) and *1635; unwilling:*— against my will(1).

211. **ἀλάβαστρον alabastron**; of for. or.; *a box of alabaster:*— alabaster vial(3), vial(1).

212. **ἀλαζονεία alazoneia**; from *213; boastfulness:*— arrogance(1), boastful pride(1).

213. **ἀλαζών alazōn**; from **ἄλη alē** *(wandering); vagabond,* hence *an impostor, boaster:*— boastful(2).

214. **ἀλαλάζω alalazō**; from **ἀλαλαί alalai** (a battle cry); *to raise a war cry:*— clanging(1), wailing(1).

215. **ἀλάλητος alalētos**; from *1* (as a neg. pref.) and *2980; inexpressible:*— too deep(1), too deep for words(1).

216. **ἄλαλος alalos**; from *1* (as a neg. pref.) and **λάλος lalos** *(talkative); mute, speechless:*— mute(3).

217. **ἅλας halas** and **ἅλα hala**; from *251; salt:*— salt(8).

218a. **ἁλεεύς haleeus**; another reading for *231*, q.v.

218b. **ἀλείφω aleiphō**; from the same root as **λίπος lipos** *(fat, oil); to anoint:*— anoint(3), anointed(3), anointing(3).

219. **ἀλεκτοροφωνία alektorophōnia**; from *220* and *5456; the crowing of a rooster:*— rooster crows(1).

220. **ἀλέκτωρ alektōr**; of unc. or.; *a rooster:*— rooster(11).

221. **Ἀλεξανδρεύς Alexandreus**; from **Ἀλεξάνδρεια Alexandreia** *(Alexandria); an Alexandrian:*— Alexandrian(1), Alexandrians(1).

222. **Ἀλεξανδρῖνος Alexandrinos**; from the same as *221; Alexandrian:*— Alexandrian(2).

223. **Ἀλέξανδρος Alexandros**; from **ἀλέξω alexō** *(to ward off)* and *435; Alexander,* a son of Simon of Cyrene, also a coppersmith, also two Jews:— Alexander(6).

224. **ἄλευρον aleuron**; from **ἀλέω aleō** *(to grind); meal:*— flour(2).

225. **ἀλήθεια alētheia**; from *227; truth:*— certainly*(2), most(1), rightly*(1), truly*(2), truth(104).

226. **ἀληθεύω alētheuō**; from *227; to speak the truth:*— speaking the truth(1), telling...the truth(1).

227. **ἀληθής alēthēs**; from *1* (as a neg. pref.) and **λήθω lēthō** = **λανθάνω lanthanō** *(to escape notice); true:*— real(1), true(21), truly(1), truth(1), truthful(2).

228. ἀληθινός alēthinos; from *227; true:*— sincere(1), true(26), true one(1).

229. ἀλήθω alēthō; from the same as *224; to grind:*— grinding(2).

230. ἀληθῶς alēthōs; adv. from *227; truly:*— certainly(2), indeed(2), really(2), sure(1), surely(2), truly(8), truthfully(1).

231. ἁλιεύς halieus; from **ἅλς hals** *(the sea); a fisherman:*— fishermen(3), fishers(2).

232. ἁλιεύω halieuō; from *231; to fish:*— fishing(1).

233. ἁλίζω halizō; from *251; to salt:*— made salty(1), salted(1).

234. ἀλίσγημα alisgēma; from **ἀλισγέω alisgeō** *(to pollute); pollution:*— things contaminated(1).

235. ἀλλά alla; adversative particle from *243; otherwise, on the other hand, but:*— besides(1), certainly(1), contrary(6), fact(2), however(9), indeed(4), indeed*(1), least*(1), nevertheless(5), no(1), rather(2), what(6), yes(1), yet(16).

236. ἀλλάσσω allassō; from *243; to change:*— alter(1), change(1), changed(3), exchanged(1).

237a. ἀλλαχόθεν allachothen; from *243; from another place:*— some other way(1).

237b. ἀλλαχοῦ allachou; from *243; elsewhere:*— somewhere else(1).

238. ἀλληγορέω allēgoreō; from *243* and **ἀγορεύω agoreuō** *(to speak in an assembly); to speak allegorically:*— allegorically speaking(1).

239. ἀλληλουϊά hallēlouia; of Heb. or., imper. of [1984b, 3050]; *hallelujah, alleluia* (an adoring exclamation):— Hallelujah(4).

240. ἀλλήλων allēlōn; a recip. pron.; *of one another:*— another(1), each(1), each other(1), one another(90), one another's(2), other's(1), themselves(1), together*(2), yourselves(1).

241. ἀλλογενής allogenēs; from *243* and *1085; of another race:*— foreigner(1).

242. ἅλλομαι hallomai; from a prim. root **ἁλ- hal-**; *to leap:*— leaped(1), leaping(1), springing(1).

243. ἄλλος allos; a prim. word; *other, another:*— another(50), another man(2), another woman(2), another's(1), else(4), more(5), one(3), one another(1), one else(1), other(35), other men(1), other women(1), others(41), some(2), some another(2), someone else(3).

244. ἀλλοτριεπίσκοπος allotriepiskopos; from *245* and *1985; one who meddles in things alien to his calling:*— troublesome meddler(1).

245. ἀλλότριος allotrios; from *243; belonging to another:*— another(2), another man's(1), another's(1), foreign(3), other men's(1), others(1), own(1), stranger(1), strangers(3).

246. ἀλλόφυλος allophulos; from *243* and **φῦλον phulon** *(a race, tribe); of another race:*— foreigner(1).

247. ἄλλως allōs; adv. from *243; otherwise:*— otherwise(1).

248. ἀλοάω aloaō; from *257; to thresh:*— thresher(1), threshing(2).

249. ἄλογος alogos; from *1* (as a neg. pref.) and *3056; without reason:*— absurd(1), unreasoning(2).

250. ἀλόη aloē; of unc. or.; *aloe:*— aloes(1).

251. ἅλς hals; var. reading for *217*, q.v.

252. ἁλυκός halukos; from *251; salt* (adj.):— salt(1).

253. ἀλυπότερος alupoteros; cptv. from *1* (as a neg. pref.) and *3077; having less grief:*— less concerned(1).

254. ἅλυσις halusis; of unc. or.; *a chain:*— chain(3), chains(8).

255. ἀλυσιτελής alusitelēs; from *1* (as a neg. pref.) and **λυσιτελέω lusiteleō** *(to pay dues, be useful); unprofitable:*— unprofitable(1).

256a. Ἄλφα Alpha; the first letter of the Gr. alphabet; *Alpha:*— Alpha(3).

256b. Ἁλφαῖος Halphaios; of Syr. or.; *Alphaeus,* the name of the fathers of two disciples:— Alphaeus(5).

257. ἅλων halōn; from **ἅλως halōs** *(a threshing floor); a threshing floor:*— threshing floor(2).

258. ἀλώπηξ alōpēx; of unc. or.; *a fox:*— fox(1), foxes(2).

259. ἅλωσις halōsis; from **ἁλίσκομαι haliskomai** *(to be taken, conquered); a taking, capture:*— captured(1).

260. ἅμα hama; a prim. word; *at once:*— early(1), same time(5), together(3).

261. ἀμαθής amathēs; from *1* (as a neg. pref.) and *3129; unlearned:*— untaught(1).

262. ἀμαράντινος amarantinos; from *263; unfading:*— unfading(1).

263. ἀμάραντος amarantos; from *1* (as a neg. pref.) and *3133; unfading:*— fade away(1).

264. ἁμαρτάνω hamartanō; from an early root **ἁμαρτ- hamart-**; *to miss the mark, do wrong, sin:*— commit sin(1), committed...offense(1), committing(1), sin(11), sinned(17), sinning(4), sins(8).

265. ἁμάρτημα hamartēma; from *264; a sin:*— sin(2), sins(2).

266. ἁμαρτία hamartia; from *264; a sin, failure:*— sin(96), sinful(2), sins(75).

267. ἀμάρτυρος amarturos; from *1* (as a neg. pref.) and *3144; without witness:*— without witness(1).

268. ἁμαρτωλός hamartōlos; from *264; sinful:*— sinful(4), sinner(12), sinners(31).

269. ἄμαχος amachos; from *1* (as a neg. pref.) and *3163; abstaining from fighting:*— peaceable(2).

270. ἀμάω amaō; of unc. or.; *to reap:*— mowed(1).

271. ἀμέθυστος amethustos; from *1* (as a neg. pref.) and *3184; amethyst:*— amethyst(1).

272. ἀμελέω ameleō; from *1* (as a neg. pref.) and *3199; to be careless:*— care(1), neglect(2), paid no attention(1).

273. ἄμεμπτος amemptos; from *1* (as a neg. pref.) and *3201; blameless:*— blameless(2), blamelessly(1), faultless(1), without blame(1).

274. ἀμέμπτως amemptōs; adv. from *273; blamelessly:*— blamelessly(1), without blame(1).

275. ἀμέριμνος amerimnos; from *1* (as a neg. pref.) and *3308; free from care:*— free from concern(1), trouble(1).

276. ἀμετάθετος ametathetos; from *1* (as a neg. pref.) and *3346a; immutable, unchangeable:*— unchangeable(1), unchangeableness(1).

277. ἀμετακίνητος ametakinētos; from *1* (as a neg. pref.) and *3334; immovable:*— immovable(1).

278. ἀμεταμέλητος ametamelētos; from *1* (as a neg. pref.) and *3338; not repented of:*— irrevocable(1), without regret(1).

279. ἀμετανόητος ametanoētos; from *1* (as a neg. pref.) and *3340; impenitent, unrepentant:*— unrepentant(1).

280. ἄμετρος ametros; from *1* (as a neg. pref.) and *3358; without measure:*— beyond*(2), measure(2).

281. ἀμήν amēn; adv. of Heb. or. [543]; *truly:*— Amen(30), truly(99).

282. ἀμήτωρ amētōr; from *1* (as a neg. pref.) and *3384; without a mother:*— without mother(1).

283. ἀμίαντος amiantos; from *1* (as a neg. pref.) and *3392; undefiled:*— undefiled(4).

284. Ἀμιναδάβ Aminadab; of Heb. or.; *Amminadab,* an Isr. ancestor of Christ:— Amminadab(3).

285. ἄμμος ammos; from **ψάμμος psammos** *(sand); sand:*— sand(5).

286. ἀμνός amnos; a prim. word; *a lamb:*— Lamb(2), lamb(2).

287. ἀμοιβή amoibē; from **ἀμείβομαι ameibomai** *(to repay); requital, recompense.*

288. ἄμπελος ampelos; of unc. or.; *vine:*— vine(9).

289. ἀμπελουργός ampelourgos; from *288* and *2041; a vinedresser:*— vineyard-keeper(1).

290. ἀμπελών ampelōn; from *288; a vineyard:*— vineyard(23).

291. Ἀμπλιᾶτος Ampliatos; of Lat. or.; *Ampliatus,* a Rom. Chr.:— Ampliatus(1).

292a. ἀμύνω amunō; from *1* (as an intens. pref.) and a prim. root **μυν- mun-**; *to ward off:*— defended(1).

292b. ἀμφιάζω amphiazō; from the same as *297; to clothe:*— clothes(1).

293a. ἀμφιβάλλω amphiballō; from the same as *297* and *906; to throw around:*— casting a net(1).

293b. ἀμφίβληστρον amphiblēstron; from *293a; something thrown around:*— net(1).

294. ἀμφιέννυμι amphiennumi; from the same as *297* and **ἕννυμι hennumi** *(to enrobe, clothe); to clothe:*— clothes(1), dressed(2).

295. Ἀμφίπολις Amphipolis; from the same as *297* and *4172; Amphipolis,* a city in Macedonia:— Amphipolis(1).

296. ἄμφοδον amphodon; from the same as *297* and *3598; a road around:*— street(1).

297. ἀμφότεροι amphoteroi; cptv. of **ἄμφω amphō** *(on both sides, around); both:*— all(2), both(12).

298. ἀμώμητος amōmētos; from *1* (as a neg. pref.) and *3469; blameless:*— blameless(1).

299a. ἄμωμον amōmon; of Indian or.; *amomum* (a fragrant plant of India):— spice(1).

299b. ἄμωμος amōmos; from *1* (as a neg. pref.) and *3470; without blemish:*— above reproach(1), blameless(5), unblemished(1), without blemish(1).

300. Ἀμών Amōn; of Heb. or. [526]; *Amon,* a king of Judah:— Amon(2).

301. Ἀμώς Amōs; of Heb. or. [531]; *Amos,* an Isr. ancestor of Christ:— Amos(1).

302. ἄν an; a prim. conditional particle; usually untranslatable, but generally denoting supposition, wish, possibility or uncertainty:— however*(1), if(4), unless*(1), what*(3), whatever*(9), whenever*(1), wherever*(1), whoever*(38), whomever*(5).

303. **ἀνά ana**; a prim. prep. and adv.; as a prep. denotes *upwards, up,* as a pref. denotes *up, again, back:*— among*(1), apiece(1), between*(1), each(3), each one(1), within*(1).

304. **ἀναβαθμός anabathmos**; from *305* and **βαθμός bathmos** *(a step); a going up, an ascent:*— stairs(2).

305. **ἀναβαίνω anabainō**; from *303* and the same as *939; to go up, ascend:*— arise(1), ascend(2), ascended(7), ascending(3), came(7), climbed(1), climbs(1), come(4), comes(2), coming(3), entered(2), go(6), goes(1), going(6), gone(3), got(2), grew(1), grows(1), rises(1), started on our way up(1), went(25).

306. **ἀναβάλλω anaballō**; from *303* and *906; to put off:*— put...off(1).

307. **ἀναβιβάζω anabibazō**; causal of *305; to make go up:*— drew(1).

308. **ἀναβλέπω anablepō**; from *303* and *991; to look up, recover sight:*— looked(4), looking(5), receive...sight(2), receive sight(2), received...sight(2), received sight(2), regain his sight(1), regain...sight(3), regained...sight(4).

309. **ἀνάβλεψις anablepsis**; from *308; recovery of sight:*— recovery of sight(1).

310. **ἀναβοάω anaboaō**; from *303* and *994; to cry out:*— cried(1).

311a. **ἀναβολή anabolē**; from *306; delay:*— delay(1).

311b. **ἀνάγαιον anagaion**; from *303* and *1093; above the ground,* i.e. *the second floor,* hence, *an upper room:*— upper room(2).

312. **ἀναγγέλλω anaggellō**; from *303* and *31b; to bring back word, announce:*— announce(1), announced(1), declare(1), declaring(2), disclose(3), disclosing(1), had...news(1), report(1), reported(2).

313. **ἀναγεννάω anagennaō**; from *303* and *1080; to beget again:*— born again(2).

314. **ἀναγινώσκω anaginōskō**; from *303* and *1097; to know certainly, know again, read:*— read(25), reader(2), reading(4), reads(1).

315. **ἀναγκάζω anagkazō**; from *318; to necessitate, compel:*— compel(3), compelled(2), force(1), forced(1), made(2).

316. **ἀναγκαῖος anagkaios**; from *318; necessary:*— close(1), more necessary(1), necessary(5), pressing(1).

317. **ἀναγκαστῶς anagkastōs**; adv. from **ἀναγκαστός anagkastos** *(forced, constrained); necessarily:*— under compulsion(1).

318. **ἀνάγκη anagkē**; from *303* and **ἄγχω agchō** *(to compress, press tight); necessity:*— compulsion(3), constraint(1), distress(3), distresses(1), hardships(1), inevitable(1), necessary(2), necessity(3), need(2), obliged*(1).

319. **ἀναγνωρίζω anagnōrizō**; another reading for *1107,* q.v.

320. **ἀνάγνωσις anagnōsis**; from *314; recognition, reading:*— reading(3).

321. **ἀνάγω anagō**; from *303* and *71; to lead up, bring up:*— bring(2), brought(5), launched(1), led(2), put out to sea(4), putting out to sea(1), set sail(7), setting sail(1).

322. **ἀναδείκνυμι anadeiknumi**; from *303* and *1166; to lift up and show, show forth:*— appointed(1), show(1).

323. **ἀνάδειξις anadeixis**; from *322; a showing forth:*— public appearance(1).

324. **ἀναδέχομαι anadechomai**; from *303* and *1209; to undertake, receive:*— received(1), welcomed(1).

325. **ἀναδίδωμι anadidōmi**; from *303* and *1325; to give up, yield:*— delivered(1).

326. **ἀναζάω anazaō**; from *303* and *2198; to live again:*— became alive(1), come to life again(1), life again(1).

327. **ἀναζητέω anazēteō**; from *303* and *2212; to seek carefully:*— look(1), looking(2).

328. **ἀναζώννυμι anazōnnumi**; from *303* and *2224; to gird up:*— prepare(1).

329. **ἀναζωπυρέω anazōpureō**; from *303* and a comp. of the root of *2226* and *4442; to kindle afresh:*— kindle afresh(1).

330. **ἀναθάλλω anathallō**; from *303* and **θάλλω thallō** *(to flourish); to revive:*— revived(1).

331. **ἀνάθεμα anathema**; from *394; that which is laid up,* i.e. *a votive offering:*— accursed(5), solemn(1).

332. **ἀναθεματίζω anathematizō**; from *331; to declare anathema, devote to destruction:*— bound...under...oath(1), bound...under a curse(2), bound...under an oath(2), curse(1), under...oath(1).

333. **ἀναθεωρέω anatheōreō**; from *303* and *2334; to observe carefully:*— considering(1), examining(1).

334. **ἀνάθημα anathēma**; from *394; a gift set up* (in a temple):— votive gifts(1).

335. **ἀναίδεια anaideia**; from *1* (as a neg. pref.) and *127; shamelessness:*— persistence(1).

336. **ἀναίρεσις anairesis**; from *337; a taking up, a destroying, slaying:*— putting...to death(1).

337. **ἀναιρέω anaireō**; from *303* and *138; to take up, take away, make an end:*— do away(1), executed(1), kill(4), killed(2), put...to death(8), put to death(3), slain(1), slay(3), slaying(1), slew(1), takes away(1), took...away(1).

338. **ἀναίτιος anaitios**; from *1* (as a neg. pref.) and *159a; guiltless:*— innocent(2).

339. **ἀνακαθίζω anakathizō**; from *303* and *2523; to set up, to sit up:*— sat(2).

340. **ἀνακαινίζω anakainizō**; from *341; to renew:*— renew(1).

341. **ἀνακαινόω anakainoō**; from *303* and *2537; to make new:*— renewed(2).

342. **ἀνακαίνωσις anakainōsis**; from *341; renewal:*— renewing(2).

343. **ἀνακαλύπτω anakaluptō**; from *303* and *2572; to unveil:*— unlifted(1), unveiled(1).

344. **ἀνακάμπτω anakamptō**; from *303* and *2578; to turn back, to return:*— return(4).

345. **ἀνάκειμαι anakeimai**; from *303* and *2749; to be laid up, to recline:*— dinner guests(3), reclined(1), reclines(2), reclining(7), seated(1).

346. **ἀνακεφαλαιόω anakephalaioō**; from *303* and *2775; to sum up, gather up:*— summed(1), summing(1).

347. **ἀνακλίνω anaklinō**; from *303* and *2827; to lay upon, lay down, to lie back:*— laid(1), recline(3), sit down(2).

348. **ἀνακόπτω anakoptō**; see *1465.*

349. **ἀνακράζω anakrazō**; from *303* and *2896; to cry out:*— cried(5).

350. **ἀνακρίνω anakrinō**; from *303* and *2919; to examine, investigate:*— appraised(2), appraises(1), asking questions(2), called to account(1), examine(2), examined(4), examines(1), examining(2), trial(1).

351. **ἀνάκρισις anakrisis**; from *350; an examination:*— investigation(1).

352a. **ἀνακυλίω anakuliō**; from *303* and *2947; to roll away* or *back:*— rolled away(1).

352b. **ἀνακύπτω anakuptō**; from *303* and *2955; to lift oneself up:*— straighten(2), straightened(1), straightening(1).

353. **ἀναλαμβάνω analambanō**; from *303* and *2983; to take up, raise:*— pick(1), received(1), take(1), take...on board(1), taken(5), taking(1), took(2), took...on board(1).

354. **ἀνάλημψις analēmpsis**; from *353; a taking up:*— ascension(1).

355. **ἀναλίσκω analiskō**; from *303* and **ἁλίσκω haliskō** *(to conquer); to expend, consume:*— consume(1), consumed(1).

356. **ἀναλογία analogia**; from *303* and *3056; proportion:*— proportion(1).

357. **ἀναλογίζομαι analogizomai**; from *303* and *3049; to consider:*— consider(1).

358. **ἄναλος analos**; from *1* (as a neg. pref.) and *251; saltless:*— unsalty(1).

359. **ἀνάλυσις analusis**; from *360; a loosing, departure:*— departure(1).

360. **ἀναλύω analuō**; from *303* and *3089; to unloose for departure:*— depart(1), returns(1).

361. **ἀναμάρτητος anamartētos**; from *1* (as a neg. pref.) and *264; unerring, faultless:*— without sin(1).

362. **ἀναμένω anamenō**; from *303* and *3306; to await:*— wait(1).

363. **ἀναμιμνήσκω anamimnēskō**; from *303* and *3403; to remind, call to one's remembrance:*— remember(1), remembered(1), remembers(1), remind(2), reminded(1).

364. **ἀνάμνησις anamnēsis**; from *363; remembrance:*— remembrance(3), reminder(1).

365. **ἀνανεόω ananeoō**; from *303* and *3501b; to renew:*— renewed(1).

366. **ἀνανήφω ananēphō**; from *303* and *3525; to return to soberness,* i.e. *regain one's senses:*— come to their senses(1).

367. **Ἀνανίας Ananias**; of Heb. or. [2608a]; *Ananias,* the name of three Isr.:— Ananias(11).

368. **ἀναντίρρητος anantirrētos**; from *1* (as a neg. pref.), *473* and **ῥητός rhētos** *(stated, specified); not to be contradicted:*— undeniable facts(1).

369. **ἀναντιρρήτως anantirrētōs**; adv. from *368; without contradiction:*— without...raising any objection(2).

370. **ἀνάξιος anaxios**; from *1* (as a neg. pref.) and *514; unworthy:*— competent(1).

371. **ἀναξίως anaxiōs**; adv. from *370; in an unworthy manner:*— unworthy manner(1).

372. **ἀνάπαυσις anapausis**; from *373; cessation, rest:*— cease(1), rest(4).

373. **ἀναπαύω anapauō**; from *303* and *3973; to give rest, give intermission from labor,* by impl. *refresh:*— give...rest(1), refresh(1), refreshed(3), rest(3), resting(2), rests(1), take your ease(1).

374a. **ἀναπείθω anapeithō**; from *303* and *3982; to persuade:*— persuades(1).

374b. ἀνάπειρος anapeiros; alt. form of **ἀνάπηρος anapēros**; from *303* and **πῆρος pēros** *(maimed); maimed.*

375. ἀναπέμπω anapempō; from *303* and *3992; to send up:*— send(1), sent(1), sent...back(3).

376a. ἀναπηδάω anapēdaō; from *303* and **πηδάω pēdaō** *(to leap); to leap up:*— jumped(1).

376b. ἀνάπηρος anapēros; var. reading for *374b*, q.v.:— crippled(2).

377. ἀναπίπτω anapiptō; from *303* and *4098; to fall back:*— leaned back(1), leaning back(1), recline(1), reclined(3), sat down(2), sit down(4).

378. ἀναπληρόω anaplēroō; from *303* and *4137; to fill up:*— complete(1), fill up the measure(1), fills(1), fulfill(1), fulfilled(1), supplied(1).

379. ἀναπολόγητος anapologētos; from *1* (as a neg. pref.) and *626; without excuse:*— no excuse(1), without excuse(1).

380. ἀναπτύσσω anaptussō; another reading for *455*, q.v.

381. ἀνάπτω anaptō; from *303* and *681; to kindle:*— kindled(1), set aflame(1).

382. ἀναρίθμητος anarithmētos; from *1* (as a neg. pref.) and *705; innumerable:*— innumerable(1).

383. ἀνασείω anaseiō; from *303* and *4579; to move to and fro, stir up:*— stirred(1), stirs(1).

384. ἀνασκευάζω anaskeuazō; from *303* and **σκευάζω skeuazō** *(to prepare, make ready); to pack up baggage, dismantle:*— unsettling(1).

385. ἀνασπάω anaspaō; from *303* and *4685; to draw up:*— drawn(1), pull(1).

386. ἀνάστασις anastasis; from *450; a standing up,* i.e. *a resurrection, a raising up, rising:*— resurrection(41), rise(1).

387. ἀναστατόω anastatoō; from **ἀνάστατος anastatos** *(driven from one's home); to stir up, unsettle:*— stirred up a revolt(1), troubling(1), upset(1).

388. ἀνασταυρόω anastauroō; from *303* and *4717; to crucify again:*— again crucify(1).

389. ἀναστενάζω anastenazō; from *303* and *4727; to sigh deeply:*— Sighing deeply(1).

390. ἀναστρέφω anastrephō; from *303* and *4762; to overturn, turn back:*— conduct(3), conducted(1), live(1), lived(1), return(1), returned(1), treated(1).

391. ἀναστροφή anastrophē; from *390; behavior, conduct:*— behavior(6), conduct(4), manner of life(2), way of life(1).

392. ἀνατάσσομαι anatassomai; from *303* and *5021; to arrange in order:*— compile(1).

393. ἀνατέλλω anatellō; from *303* and **τέλλω tellō** *(to make to arise); to cause to rise, to rise:*— arises(1), causes...to rise(1), dawned(1), descended(1), risen(3), rises(1), rising(1).

394. ἀνατίθημι anatithēmi; from *303* and *5087; to set up, set forth:*— laid(1), submitted(1).

395. ἀνατολή anatolē; from *393; a rising:*— east(7), east*(1), rising(1), Sunrise(1).

396. ἀνατρέπω anatrepō; from *303* and the same as *5157; to overturn, destroy:*— overturned(1), upset(1), upsetting(1).

397. ἀνατρέφω anatrephō; from *303* and *5142; to nurse up, nourish:*— brought(1), nurtured(2).

398. ἀναφαίνω anaphainō; from *303* and *5316; to bring to light, make to appear:*— appear(1), came in sight(1).

399. ἀναφέρω anapherō; from *303* and *5342; to carry up, lead up:*— bear(1), bore(1), brought(1), led(1), offer(3), offered(2).

400. ἀναφωνέω anaphōneō; from *303* and *5455; to cry out:*— cried(1).

401. ἀνάχυσις anachusis; from **ἀναχέω anacheō** *(to pour out); a pouring out, overflow:*— excesses(1).

402. ἀναχωρέω anachōreō; from *303* and *5562; to go back, withdraw:*— departed(1), gone(1), gone aside(1), leave(1), left(3), stepping aside(1), withdrew(6).

403. ἀνάψυξις anapsuxis; from *404; a recovery of breath, a refreshing:*— refreshing(1).

404. ἀναψύχω anapsuchō; from *303* and *5594; to refresh:*— refreshed(1).

405. ἀνδραποδιστής andrapodistēs; from **ἀνδράποδον andrapodon** *(a slave); a slave dealer:*— kidnappers(1).

406. Ἀνδρέας Andreas; from *435*; "manly," *Andrew,* one of the twelve apostles of Christ:— Andrew(13).

407. ἀνδρίζω andrizō; from *435; to behave like a man, to play the man:*— act like men(1).

408. Ἀνδρόνικος Andronikos; from *435* and *3534*; "man of victory," *Andronicus,* a Jewish Chr.:— Andronicus(1).

409. ἀνδροφόνος androphonos; from *435* and *5408; a manslayer:*— murderers(1).

410. ἀνέγκλητος anegklētos; from *1* (as a neg. pref.) and *1458; not to be called to account, unreprovable:*— above reproach(2), beyond reproach(2), blameless(1).

411. ἀνεκδιήγητος anekdiēgētos; from *1* (as a neg. pref.) and *1555; inexpressible:*— indescribable(1).

412. ἀνεκλάλητος aneklalētos; from *1* (as a neg. pref.) and *1583; unspeakable:*— inexpressible(1).

413. ἀνέκλειπτος anekleiptos; from *1* (as a neg. pref.) and *1587; unfailing:*— unfailing(1).

414. ἀνεκτότερος anektoteros; cptv. of **ἀνεκτός anektos** *(bearable, tolerable);* from *430; more tolerable:*— more tolerable(5).

415a. ἀνελεήμων aneleēmōn; from *1* (as a neg. pref.) and *1655; without mercy:*— unmerciful(1).

415b. ἀνέλεος aneleos; from *1* (as a neg. pref.) and *1656; merciless:*— merciless(1).

416. ἀνεμίζω anemizō; from *417; to drive by the wind:*— driven(1).

417. ἄνεμος anemos; from a prim. root **ἀνε- ane-** *(to blow, breathe); wind:*— wind(20), winds(11).

418. ἀνένδεκτος anendektos; from *1* (as a neg. pref.) and *1735; impossible:*— inevitable*(1).

419. ἀνεξεραύνητος anexeraunētos; from *1* (as a neg. pref.) and *1830; unsearchable:*— unsearchable(1).

420. ἀνεξίκακος anexikakos; from *430* and *2556; enduring evil:*— patient when wronged(1).

421. ἀνεξιχνίαστος anexichniastos; from *1* (as a neg. pref.) and **ἐξιχνιάζω exichniazō** *(to track out); that cannot be traced out:*— unfathomable(2).

422. ἀνεπαίσχυντος anepaischuntos; from *1* (as a neg. pref.) and *1870; not to be put to shame:*— does not need to be ashamed(1).

423. ἀνεπίλημπτος anepilēmptos; from *1* (as a neg. pref.) and *1949; without reproach:*— above reproach(2), reproach(1), without*(1).

424. ἀνέρχομαι anerchomai; from *303* and *2064; to go up:*— go(1), went(2).

425. ἄνεσις anesis; from *447; a loosening, relaxation:*— ease(1), freedom(1), relief(1), rest(2).

426. ἀνετάζω anetazō; from *303* and **ἐτάζω etazō** *(to examine); to examine judicially:*— examine(1), examined(1).

427. ἄνευ aneu; perh. akin to *1* (as a neg. pref.); *without* (prep.):— apart(1), without(2).

428. ἀνεύθετος aneuthetos; from *1* (as a neg. pref.) and *2111; not well placed:*— suitable(1).

429. ἀνευρίσκω aneuriskō; from *303* and *2147; to find out:*— found their way(1), looking(1).

430. ἀνέχω anechō; from *303* and *2192; to hold up, bear with:*— bear(3), bearing(2), endure(3), put(4), showing tolerance(1), tolerate(2).

431. ἀνεψιός anepsios; of unc. or.; *a cousin:*— cousin(1).

432. ἄνηθον anēthon; of unc. or.; *anise, dill:*— dill(1).

433. ἀνήκω anēkō; from *303* and *2240; to be fit, be proper:*— fitting(2), proper(1).

434. ἀνήμερος anēmeros; from *1* (as a neg. pref.) and **ἥμερος hēmeros** *(tame); not tame:*— brutal(1).

435. ἀνήρ anēr; a prim. word; *a man:*— brethren*(13), gentlemen(1), husband(39), husbands(13), man(71), man's(2), men(70), virgin*(1).

436. ἀνθίστημι anthistēmi; from *473* and *2476; to set against,* i.e. *withstand:*— cope(1), oppose(1), has opposed(1), opposed(4), opposing(1), resist(5), resists(2).

437. ἀνθομολογέομαι anthomologeomai; from *473* and *3670; to acknowledge fully, confess:*— giving thanks(1).

438. ἄνθος anthos; a prim. word; *a flower:*— flower(3), flowering(1).

439. ἀνθρακιά anthrakia; from *440; a heap of burning coals:*— charcoal fire(2).

440. ἄνθραξ anthrax; a prim. word; *coal, charcoal:*— coals(1).

441. ἀνθρωπάρεσκος anthrōpareskos; from *444* and **ἄρεσκος areskos** *(pleasing); man-pleasing:*— men-pleasers(1), please men(1), those who...please men(1).

442. ἀνθρώπινος anthrōpinos; from *444; human:*— human(5), human terms(1), such as is common to man(1).

443. ἀνθρωποκτόνος anthrōpoktonos; from *444* and **κτείνω kteinō** *(to kill); a manslayer:*— murderer(3).

444. ἄνθρωπος anthrōpos; prob. from *435* and **ὤψ ōps** *(eye); a man, human, mankind:*— any(1), anyone(1), child(1), enemy*(1), everyone*(1), fellow(1), friend(1), human(5), human judgment(1), human relations(1), king*(1), Man(89), man(232), man's(8), mankind(5), men(164), men's(2), nobleman*(1), one*(3), others(4), people(13), people*(1), person(2), persons(1), self(4).

445. ἀνθυπατεύω anthupateuō; var. reading for *446*, q.v.

446. **ἀνθύπατος anthupatos**; from *473* and **ὕπατος hupatos** *(highest); a consul, proconsul:*— proconsul(4), proconsuls(1).

447. **ἀνίημι aniēmi**; from *303* and **ἵημι hiēmi** *(to send); to send up, produce, send back:*— desert(1), give(1), loosening(1), unfastened(1).

448. **ἀνίλεως anileōs**; var. reading for *415b*, q.v.

449. **ἄνιπτος aniptos**; from *1* (as a neg. pref.) and *3538; unwashed:*— unwashed(2).

450. **ἀνίστημι anistēmi**; from *303* and *2476; to raise up, to rise:*— arise(4), arises(2), arose(4), get(15), getting(1), got(24), raise(7), raised(4), raised...up again(1), raised up again(1), raising(1), rise(3), rise again(10), risen(2), risen again(2), rises(1), rising(1), rose(6), rose again(1), stand(5), stood(13).

451. **Ἄννα Hanna**; of Heb. or. [2584]; *Anna*, a prophetess:— Anna(1).

452. **Ἄννας Hannas**; of Heb. or. [2608a]; *Annas*, a high priest:— Annas(4).

453. **ἀνόητος anoētos**; from *1* (as a neg. pref.) and **νοητός noētos** *(mental);* from *3539; not understanding:*— foolish(5), foolish men(1).

454. **ἄνοια anoia**; from *1* (as a neg. pref.) and *3563; folly, foolishness:*— folly(2), rage(1).

455. **ἀνοίγω anoigō**; from *303* and **οἴγω oigō** *(to open); to open:*— break(1), broke(7), open(22), opened(41), opening(2), opens(4), spoken freely(1).

456. **ἀνοικοδομέω anoikodomeō**; from *303* and *3618; to build again:*— rebuild(2).

457. **ἄνοιξις anoixis**; from *455; an opening:*— opening(1).

458. **ἀνομία anomia**; from *459; lawlessness:*— lawless deed(1), lawless deeds(2), lawlessness(12).

459. **ἄνομος anomos**; from *1* (as a neg. pref.) and *3551; lawless, without law:*— godless men(1), lawless(2), lawless one(1), transgressors(2), without the law(1), without law(1), without law(2).

460. **ἀνόμως anomōs**; adv. from *459; lawlessly:*— without the law(2).

461. **ἀνορθόω anorthoō**; from *303* and **ὀρθόω orthoō** *(to set straight, set up); to set upright, set straight again:*— made erect again(1), restore(1), strengthen(1).

462. **ἀνόσιος anosios**; from *1* (as a neg. pref.) and *3741; unholy:*— unholy(2).

463. **ἀνοχή anochē**; from *430; a delaying, forbearance:*— forbearance(1), tolerance(1).

464. **ἀνταγωνίζομαι antagōnizomai**; from *473* and *75; to struggle against:*— striving(1).

465. **ἀντάλλαγμα antallagma**; from *473* and *236; an exchange:*— exchange(2).

466. **ἀνταναπληρόω antanaplēroō**; from *473* and *378; to fill up in turn:*— filling(1), share(1).

467. **ἀνταποδίδωμι antapodidōmi**; from *473* and *591; to give back as an equivalent, recompense:*— paid back(1), render(1), repaid(1), repay(4), return(1).

468. **ἀνταπόδομα antapodoma**; from *467; requital:*— repayment(1), retribution(1).

469. **ἀνταπόδοσις antapodosis**; from *467; recompense:*— reward(1).

470. **ἀνταποκρίνομαι antapokrinomai**; from *473* and *611; to answer again:*— answers back(1), make...reply(1).

471. **ἀντεῖπον anteipon**; from *473* and *1513a; to speak against:*— refute(1), say in reply(1).

472. **ἀντέχω antechō**; from *473* and *2192; to hold against,* i.e. *to hold firmly to:*— devoted(2), help(1), holding fast(1).

473. **ἀντί anti**; a prim. prep., also a pref.; *over against, opposite,* hence *instead of,* in comp. denotes contrast, requital, substitution, correspondence:— accordingly(1), because*(4), instead(2), place(1), reason(1).

474. **ἀντιβάλλω antiballō**; from *473* and *906; to throw in turn, exchange:*— exchanging(1).

475. **ἀντιδιατίθημι antidiatithēmi**; from *473* and *1303; to oppose, set oneself in opposition:*— opposition(1).

476. **ἀντίδικος antidikos**; from *473* and *1349; an opponent, adversary:*— adversary(1), opponent(3), opponent at law(1).

477. **ἀντίθεσις antithesis**; from *473* and *5087; opposition:*— opposing arguments(1).

478. **ἀντικαθίστημι antikathistēmi**; from *473* and *2525; to set down against,* i.e. *to replace, oppose:*— resisted(1).

479. **ἀντικαλέω antikaleō**; from *473* and *2564; to invite in turn:*— invite...in return(1).

480. **ἀντίκειμαι antikeimai**; from *473* and *2749; to lie opposite,* i.e. *oppose, withstand:*— adversaries(1), contrary(1), enemy(1), opponents(3), opposes(1), opposition(1).

481. **ἄντικρυς antikrus**; from *473; over against:*— opposite(1).

482. **ἀντιλαμβάνω antilambanō**; from *473* and *2983; to take instead of, take hold of:*— given help(1), help(1), partake(1).

483. **ἀντιλέγω antilegō**; from *473* and *3004; to speak against,* hence *to contradict, oppose:*— argumentative(1), contradict(1), contradicting(1), objected(1), obstinate(1), opposed(1), opposes(1), say(1), spoken against(1).

484. **ἀντίλημψις antilēmpsis**; from *482; a laying hold of, help:*— helps(1).

485. **ἀντιλογία antilogia**; from *483; gainsaying, contradiction:*— dispute(2), hostility(1), rebellion(1).

486. **ἀντιλοιδορέω antiloidoreō**; from *473* and *3058; to revile in turn:*— revile in return(1).

487. **ἀντίλυτρον antilutron**; from *473* and *3083; a ransom:*— ransom(1).

488. **ἀντιμετρέω antimetreō**; from *473* and *3354; to measure in return:*— measured...in return(1).

489. **ἀντιμισθία antimisthia**; from **ἀντιμισθος antimisthos** *(as a reward); a reward:*— exchange(1), penalty(1).

490. **Ἀντιόχεια Antiocheia**; from **Ἀντίοχος Antiochos** *(Antiochus,* the name of a number of Syrian kings); *Antioch,* the name of two cities:— Antioch(18).

491. **Ἀντιοχεύς Antiocheus**; from *490; an Antiochian,* an inhab. of Antioch:— Antioch(1).

492. **ἀντιπαρέρχομαι antiparerchomai**; from *473* and *3928; to pass by opposite to:*— passed by on the other side(2).

493. **Ἀντίπας Antipas**; prob. a contr. of a comp. of *473* and *3962; Antipas,* a Chr. of Pergamum:— Antipas(1).

494. **Ἀντιπατρίς Antipatris**; from *473* and *3968; Antipatris,* a city between Joppa and Caesarea in Pal.:— Antipatris(1).

495. **ἀντιπέρα antipera**; from *473* and *4008; on the opposite side:*— opposite(1).

496. **ἀντιπίπτω antipiptō**; from *473* and *4098; to fall against, strive against:*— resisting(1).

497. **ἀντιστρατεύομαι antistrateuomai**; from *473* and *4754; to make war against:*— waging war against(1).

498. **ἀντιτάσσω antitassō**; from *473* and *5021; to range in battle against, to set oneself against:*— opposed(2), resist(1), resisted(1).

499. **ἀντίτυπος antitupos**; from *473* and *5179b; struck back, corresponding to:*— copy(1), corresponding(1).

500. **ἀντίχριστος antichristos**; from *473* and *5547; antichrist,* (one who opposes Christ):— antichrist(4), antichrists(1).

501. **ἀντλέω antleō**; from **ἄντλος antlos** *(a ship's hold, bilge water in a ship's hold); to bail out, draw water:*— draw(3), drawn(1).

502. **ἄντλημα antlēma**; from *501; a container to draw with:*— draw(1).

503. **ἀντοφθαλμέω antophthalmeō**; from *473* and *3788; to look in the face, look straight at:*— face(1).

504. **ἄνυδρος anudros**; from *1* (as a neg. pref.) and *5204; waterless:*— waterless(2), without water(2).

505. **ἀνυπόκριτος anupokritos**; from *1* (as a neg. pref.) and *5271; unhypocritical, unfeigned:*— genuine(1), sincere(3), without hypocrisy(2).

506. **ἀνυπότακτος anupotaktos**; from *1* (as a neg. pref.) and *5293; not subject to rule:*— rebellion(1), rebellious(1), rebellious men(1), subject(1).

507. **ἄνω anō**; adv. from *303; up, above:*— above(5), brim(1), upward(1).

508. **ἀνώγεον anōgeon**; var. reading for *311b*, q.v.

509. **ἄνωθεν anōthen**; from *507; from above:*— above(5), again(2), all over(1), beginning(1), long time(1), top(2).

510. **ἀνωτερικός anōterikos**; from *511; upper:*— upper(1).

511. **ἀνώτερος anōteros**; cptv. of *507; higher:*— above(1), higher(1).

512. **ἀνωφελής anōphelēs**; from *1* (as a neg. pref.) and *3786; unprofitable:*— unprofitable(1), uselessness(1).

513. **ἀξίνη axinē**; of unc. or.; *an axe:*— axe(2).

514. **ἄξιος axios**; from *71* (in the sense of *to weigh); of weight, of worth, worthy:*— appropriate(1), deserve(2), deserving(4), fitting(2), keeping(2), unworthy*(1), worthy(29).

515. **ἀξιόω axioō**; from *514; to deem worthy:*— consider...worthy(1), considered worthy(1), count...worthy(1), counted worthy(1), deserve(1), desire(1), insisting(1).

516. **ἀξίως axiōs**; adv. from *514; worthily:*— manner worthy(6).

517. **ἀόρατος aoratos**; from *1* (as a neg. pref.) and *3707; invisible:*— invisible(4), unseen(1).

518. **ἀπαγγέλλω apaggellō**; from *575* and *31b; to report, announce:*— announced(1), declared(1), declaring(3), proclaim(4), report(10), reported(22), take word(1), tell(1), told(3).

519. **ἀπάγχω apagchō**; from *575* and **ἄγχω agchō** *(to press, strangle); to strangle, hang oneself:*— hanged(1).

520. **ἀπάγω apagō**; from *575* and *71; to lead away:*— bringing(1), lead(1), lead...away(2), leads(2), led astray(1), led away(1), led...away(6), took(1), took...away(1).

521. **ἀπαίδευτος apaideutos**; from *1* (as a neg. pref.) and a der. of *3811; uninstructed:*— ignorant(1).

522. **ἀπαίρω apairō**; from *575* and *142; to lift off:*— taken away(3).

523. **ἀπαιτέω apaiteō**; from *575* and *154; to ask back:*— demand...back(1), required(3).

524. **ἀπαλγέω apalgeō**; from *575* and **ἀλγέω algeō** *(to feel pain, suffer); to cease to feel pain for:*— become callous(1).

525. **ἀπαλλάσσω apallassō**; from *575* and *236; to remove, release:*— free(1), left(1), settle(1).

526. **ἀπαλλοτριόω apallotrioō**; from *575* and *245; to alienate, estrange:*— alienated(1), excluded(2).

527. **ἁπαλός hapalos**; of unc. or.; *tender:*— tender(2).

528. **ἀπαντάω apantaō**; from *575* and **ἀντάω antaō** *(to come opposite to, meet face to face); to meet:*— meet(1), met(1).

529. **ἀπάντησις apantēsis**; from *528; a meeting:*— meet(3).

530. **ἅπαξ hapax**; from *1* (as a cop. pref.) and a prim. root **παγ- pag-**; *once:*— once(9), once for all(3), once more(2).

531. **ἀπαράβατος aparabatos**; from *1* (as a neg. pref.) and *3845; inviolable:*— permanently(1).

532. **ἀπαρασκεύαστος aparaskeuastos**; from *1* (as a neg. pref.) and *3903; unprepared:*— unprepared(1).

533. **ἀπαρνέομαι aparneomai**; from *575* and *720; to deny:*— denied(2), deny(9).

534. **ἀπάρτι aparti**; see *575* and *737*.

535. **ἀπαρτισμός Apartismos**; from **ἀπαρτίζω apartizō** *(to finish); completion:*— complete(1).

536. **ἀπαρχή aparchē**; from *575* and *746; the beginning of a sacrifice,* i.e. *the first fruit:*— first convert(1), first fruits(6), first piece(1).

537a. **ἅπας hapas**; from *1* (as a cop. pref.) and *3956; all, the whole:*— all(21), all things(2), everyone(1), everything(4), none*(1), perfect(1), whole(2).

537b. **ἀπασπάζομαι apaspazomai**; from *575* and *782; to take leave of:*— said farewell(1).

538. **ἀπατάω apataō**; from *539; to deceive:*— deceive(1), deceived(1), deceives(1).

539. **ἀπάτη apatē**; of unc. or.; *deceit:*— deceit(1), deceitfulness(3), deception(2), deceptions(1).

540. **ἀπάτωρ apatōr**; from *1* (as a neg. pref.) and *3962; fatherless:*— without father(1).

541. **ἀπαύγασμα apaugasma**; from *575* and *827; radiance:*— radiance(1).

542. **ἀπεῖδον apeidon**; see *872*.

543. **ἀπείθεια apeitheia**; from *545; disobedience:*— disobedience(6).

544. **ἀπειθέω apeitheō**; from *545; to disobey:*— disbelieved(1), disobedient(10), do not obey(1), obey(2).

545. **ἀπειθής apeithēs**; from *1* (as a neg. pref.) and *3982; disobedient:*— disobedience(1), disobedient(6).

546. **ἀπειλέω apeileō**; from *547; to threaten:*— uttered...threats(1), warn(1).

547. **ἀπειλή apeilē**; of unc. or.; *a threat:*— threatening(1), threats(2).

548. **ἄπειμι apeimi**; from *575* and *1510; to be away,* i.e. *to be absent:*— absent(5), am absent(1), remain absent(1).

549. **ἄπειμι apeimi**; from *575* and **εἶμι eimi** *(to go); to go away, depart:*— went(1).

550. **ἀπεῖπον apeipon**; from *575* and *1513a; to forbid, renounce:*— renounced(1).

551. **ἀπείραστος apeirastos**; from *1* (as a neg. pref.) and *3985; untried, untempted:*— cannot be tempted(1).

552. **ἄπειρος apeiros**; from *1* (as a neg. pref.) and *3984; without experience of:*— accustomed(1).

553. **ἀπεκδέχομαι apekdechomai**; from *575* and *1551; to await eagerly:*— awaiting eagerly(1), eagerly await(1), eagerly wait(1), wait eagerly(1), waiting(2), waiting eagerly(1), waits eagerly(1).

554. **ἀπεκδύομαι apekduomai**; from *575* and *1562; to strip off from oneself:*— disarmed(1), laid aside(1).

555. **ἀπέκδυσις apekdusis**; from *554; a stripping off:*— removal(1).

556. **ἀπελαύνω apelaunō**; from *575* and *1643; to drive away:*— drove...away(1).

557. **ἀπελεγμός apelegmos**; from *575* and *1649a; refutation,* i.e. by impl. *contempt:*— disrepute(1).

558. **ἀπελεύθερος apeleutheros**; from *575* and *1658; one freed away,* i.e. *a freedman:*— freedman(1).

559. **Ἀπελλῆς Apellēs**; from the same as *624; Apelles,* a Chr. at Rome:— Apelles(1).

560. **ἀπελπίζω apelpizō**; from *575* and *1679; to despair of:*— expecting in return(1).

561. **ἀπέναντι apenanti**; from *575* and *1725; over against, before:*— before(1), contrary(1), opposite(1), presence(1).

562. **ἀπέραντος aperantos**; from *1* (as a neg. pref.) and **περαίνω perainō** *(to complete, finish); unfinished,* i.e. *endless:*— endless(1).

563. **ἀπερισπάστως aperispastōs**; from *1* (as a neg. pref.) and *4049; without distraction:*— undistracted(1).

564. **ἀπερίτμητος aperitmētos**; from *1* (as a neg. pref.) and *4059; uncircumcised:*— uncircumcised(1).

565. **ἀπέρχομαι aperchomai**; from *575* and *2064; to go away, go after:*— came(1), depart(1), departed(3), drew(1), go(20), go away(6), go over(1), going away(1), going back(1), gone(2), gone away(4), leave(5), left(8), passed away(2), past(2), spread(1), went(16), went their way(1), went along(1), went away(37), went back(1), went off(3), withdrew*(1).

566. **ἀπέχει apechei**; third pers. sing. pres. ind. act. of *568*, q.v.

567. **ἀπέχομαι apechomai**; mid. of *568*, q.v.

568. **ἀπέχω apechō**; from *575* and *2192; to hold back, keep off, to be away, be distant:*— abstain(5), abstaining(1), away(1), away*(1), enough(1), have...back(1), have...in full(3), have received(1), have received in full(1), off(1), receiving...in full(1).

569. **ἀπιστέω apisteō**; from *571; to disbelieve, be faithless:*— believe(3), disbelieve(1), disbelieved(1), faithless(1), refused to believe(1), would not believe(1).

570. **ἀπιστία apistia**; from *571; unbelief:*— unbelief(10), unbelieving(1).

571. **ἄπιστος apistos**; from *1* (as a neg. pref.) and *4103; incredible, unbelieving:*— incredible(1), unbeliever(4), unbelievers(7), unbelieving(10), unbelieving one(1).

572. **ἁπλότης haplotēs**; from *573; singleness,* hence *simplicity:*— liberality(4), simplicity(1), sincerity(2).

573. **ἁπλοῦς haplous**; from *1* (as a cop. pref.) and perh. *4144; simple, single:*— clear(2).

574. **ἁπλῶς haplōs**; adv. from *573; simply, sincerely:*— generously(1).

575. **ἀπό apo**; a prep. and a prim. particle; *from, away from:*— after(1), against(4), ago(2), alike*(1), among(2), away(3), away*(1), because(9), before*(1), belonged(1), deserting*(1), distance(1), hereafter*(1), initiative(1), left(1), off(1), once*(1), since(11), since*(3), some(1), way(1).

576. **ἀποβαίνω apobainō**; from *575* and the same as *939; to step off, disembark:*— got(1), gotten(1), lead(1), turn(1).

577. **ἀποβάλλω apoballō**; from *575* and *906; to throw off:*— throw away(1), throwing aside(1).

578. **ἀποβλέπω apoblepō**; from *575* and *991; to look away from all else at an object:*— looking(1).

579. **ἀπόβλητος apoblētos**; from *577; to be thrown away,* i.e. *rejected:*— rejected(1).

580. **ἀποβολή apobolē**; from *577; a throwing away, rejection:*— loss(1), rejection(1).

581. **ἀπογίνομαι apoginomai**; from *575* and *1096; to be away, be removed from:*— die(1).

582. **ἀπογραφή apographē**; from *583; a register, enrollment:*— census(2).

583. **ἀπογράφω apographō**; from *575* and *1125; to copy, enroll:*— census be taken(1), enrolled(1), register(1), register for the census(1).

584. **ἀποδείκνυμι apodeiknumi**; from *575* and *1166; to bring out, show forth, declare:*— attested(1), displaying(1), exhibited(1), prove(1).

585. **ἀπόδειξις apodeixis**; from *584; a showing off, demonstration:*— demonstration(1).

586a. **ἀποδεκατεύω apodekateuō**; from *586b; to pay a tenth of:*— pay tithes(1).

586b. **ἀποδεκατόω apodekatoō**; from *575* and *1183; to pay a tenth of, tithe:*— collect a tenth(1), pay tithe(1), tithe(1).

587. **ἀπόδεκτος apodektos**; from *588; acceptable:*— acceptable(2).

588. **ἀποδέχομαι apodechomai**; from *575* and *1209; to accept gladly, welcome:*— acknowledge(1), received(2), welcome(1), welcomed(1), welcoming(2).

589. **ἀποδημέω apodēmeō**; from *590; to be or go abroad:*— go on a journey(1), went on a journey(4), went on his journey(1).

590. **ἀπόδημος apodēmos**; from *575* and *1218; gone abroad:*— away on a journey(1).

591. **ἀποδίδωμι apodidōmi**; from *575* and *1325; to give up, give back, return, restore:*— account*(1), award(1), fulfill(2), gave...back(2), give(4), give back(1), given(1), giving(1), make some return(1), must(1), paid(3), pay(2), pay...back(1), pay back(3), render(6), repay(8), repayment to be made(1), repays(1), returning(1), reward(3), sold(3), yielding(1), yields(1).

592. **ἀποδιορίζω apodiorizō**; from *575* and **διορίζω diorizō** *(to divide by limits, separate); to mark off:*— cause divisions(1).

593. **ἀποδοκιμάζω apodokimazō**; from *575* and *1381a; to reject:*— rejected(9).

594. **ἀποδοχή apodochē**; from *588; acceptance, approval:*— acceptance(2).

595. **ἀπόθεσις apothesis**; from *659; a putting away:*— laying aside(1), removal(1).

596. **ἀποθήκη apothēkē**; from *659; a place for putting away,* hence *a storehouse:*— barn(4), barns(2).

597. **ἀποθησαυρίζω apothēsaurizō**; from *575* and *2343; to treasure up, store away:*— storing(1), treasure(1).

598. **ἀποθλίβω apothlibō**; from *575* and *2346; to press hard:*— pressing(1).

599. **ἀποθνήσκω apothnēskō**; from *575* and *2348; to die:*— dead(5), death(1), death*(1), die(34), died(53), dies(12), dying(4), mortal(1), perished(1), put(1).

600. **ἀποκαθίστημι apokathistēmi**; from *575* and *2525; to restore, give back:*— restore(2), restored(5), restoring(1).

601. **ἀποκαλύπτω apokaluptō**; from *575* and *2572; to uncover, reveal:*— reveal(5), revealed(20), revelation is made(1).

602. **ἀποκάλυψις apokalupsis**; from *601; an uncovering:*— revealed(1), revealing(1), revelation(14), revelations(2).

603. **ἀποκαραδοκία apokaradokia**; from a comp. of *575*, **κάρα kara** *(the head)* and *1380; strained expectancy:*— anxious longing(1), earnest expectation(1).

604. **ἀποκαταλλάσσω apokatallassō**; from *575* and *2644; to reconcile completely:*— reconcile(2), reconciled(1).

605. **ἀποκατάστασις apokatastasis**; from *600; restoration:*— restoration(1).

606. **ἀπόκειμαι apokeimai**; from *575* and *2749; to be laid away, be laid up in store:*— appointed(1), laid(2), put away(1).

607. **ἀποκεφαλίζω apokephalizō**; from *575* and *2776; to behead:*— beheaded(4).

608. **ἀποκλείω apokleiō**; from *575* and *2808; to shut fast* or *completely:*— shuts(1).

609. **ἀποκόπτω apokoptō**; from *575* and *2875; to cut off:*— cut...off(2), cut away(1), cut off(2), mutilate(1).

610. **ἀπόκριμα apokrima**; from *611; a judicial sentence,* by ext. *an answer:*— sentence(1).

611. **ἀποκρίνομαι apokrinomai**; from *575* and *2919; to answer:*— answer(20), answered(169), answered answered(1), answering(8), answers(1), made...answer(1), replied(2), reply(1), respond(1), responded(2), response(1), said(1).

612. **ἀπόκρισις apokrisis**; from *611; an answering:*— answer(3), answers(1).

613. **ἀποκρύπτω apokruptō**; from *575* and *2928; to hide, conceal:*— hidden(4).

614. **ἀπόκρυφος apokruphos**; from *613; hidden:*— hidden(1), secret(2).

615. **ἀποκτείνω apokteinō** or **ἀποκτέννω apoktennō**; from *575* and **κτείνω kteinō** *(to kill); to kill:*— kill(33), killed(29), killing(1), kills(5), put...to death(2), put to death(4).

616. **ἀποκυέω apokueō**; from *575* and **κυέω kueō**, an older form of **κύω kuō** *(to be pregnant); to give birth to:*— brings forth(1), brought...forth(1).

617. **ἀποκυλίω apokuliō**; from *575* and *2947; to roll away:*— roll away(1), rolled away(2).

618. **ἀπολαμβάνω apolambanō**; from *575* and *2983; to receive from, receive as one's due:*— receive(3), receive back(1), received(1), received...back(1), receiving(2), took...aside(1).

619. **ἀπόλαυσις apolausis**; from **ἀπολαύω apolauō** *(to take of, enjoy); enjoyment:*— enjoy(1), enjoy the pleasures(1).

620. **ἀπολείπω apoleipō**; from *575* and *3007; to leave, leave behind:*— abandoned(1), left(3), remains(3).

621. **ἀπολείχω apoleichō**; var. reading for *1952b*, q.v.

622. **ἀπόλλυμι apollumi**; from *575* and same as *3639; to destroy, destroy utterly:*— bring(1), destroy(17), destroyed(9), dying(1), end(1), killed(1), lose(10), loses(7), lost(14), much(1), passed away(1), perish(14), perishable(1), perished(4), perishes(1), perishing(6), put to death(1), ruined(3).

623. **Ἀπολλύων Apolluōn**; act. part. of *622;* "a destroyer," *Apollyon,* the angel of the abyss:—Apollyon(1).

624. **Ἀπολλωνία Apollōnia**; from **Ἀπόλλων Apollōn** (name of the Gr. god *Apollo); Apollonia,* a city in Macedonia:— Apollonia(1).

625. **Ἀπολλῶς Apollōs**; prob. contr. from the adj. **Ἀπολλώνιος Apollōnios** *(of* or *belonging to Apollo); Apollos,* an Alexandrian Jewish Chr.:— Apollos(10).

626. **ἀπολογέομαι apologeomai**; from *575* and *3056; to give an account of oneself,* hence *to defend oneself:*— defend(1), defending(2), make a defense(1), make...defense(3), said in...defense(1), saying in...defense(1), speak in...defense(1).

627. **ἀπολογία apologia**; from *626; a speech in defense:*— defense(7), vindication(1).

628. **ἀπολούω apolouō**; from *575* and *3068; to wash off, wash away:*— wash away(1), washed(1).

629. **ἀπολύτρωσις apolutrōsis**; from **ἀπολυτρόω apolutroō** *(to release on payment of ransom); a release effected by payment of ransom:*— redemption(9), release(1).

630. **ἀπολύω apoluō**; from *575* and *3089; to set free, release:*— dismissed(1), divorce(3), divorced(2), divorces(5), freed(1), leaving(1), let...go(2), pardon(1), pardoned(1), release(20), released(8), releasing...to depart(1), send...away(9), sending...away(1), sending away(1), sends...away(1), sent...away(6), sent away(2), set free(1).

631. **ἀπομάσσω apomassō**; from *575* and **μάσσω massō** *(to handle, touch); to wipe off:*— wipe off(1).

632. **ἀπονέμω aponemō**; from *575* and the same as *3551; to assign, apportion:*— show(1).

633. **ἀπονίπτω aponiptō**; from *575* and *3538; to wash off:*— washed(1).

634. **ἀποπίπτω apopiptō**; from *575* and *4098; to fall off:*— fell(1).

635. **ἀποπλανάω apoplanaō**; from *575* and *4105; to cause to go astray:*— lead astray(1), wandered away(1).

636. **ἀποπλέω apopleō**; from *575* and *4126; to sail away:*— sail(1), sailed(2), sailing(1).

637. **ἀποπλύνω apoplunō**; var. reading for *4150*, q.v.

638. **ἀποπνίγω apopnigō**; from *575* and *4155; to choke:*— choked(2), drowned(1).

639. **ἀπορέω aporeō**; from *1* (as a neg. pref.) and **πόρος poros** *(a way, resource); to be at a loss, be perplexed:*— am perplexed(1), being at a loss(1), loss(1), perplexed(3).

640. **ἀπορία aporia**; from *639; perplexity:*—perplexity(1).

641. **ἀπορίπτω aporiptō**; from *575* and *4496; to throw away:*— jump overboard(1).

642. **ἀπορφανίζω aporphanizō**; from *575* and **ὀρφανίζω orphanizō** *(to make orphan, destitute); to be bereaved:*— taken away(1).

643. **ἀποσκευάζω aposkeuazō**; var. reading for *1980b*, q.v.

644. **ἀποσκίασμα aposkiasma**; from *575* and **σκιάζω skiazō** *(to overshadow, shade); a shadow:*— shadow(1).

645. **ἀποσπάω apospaō**; from *575* and *4685; to draw off, draw away:*— draw away(1), drew(1), parted(1), withdrew(1).

646. **ἀποστασία apostasia**; from *868; defection, revolt:*— apostasy(1), forsake(1).

647. **ἀποστάσιον apostasion**; from *868; a forsaking,* spec. (bill of) *divorce:*— certificate of divorce(1), divorce(2).

648. **ἀποστεγάζω apostegazō**; from *575* and **στεγάζω stegazō** *(to cover, roof* a building); to unroof:— removed(1).

649. **ἀποστέλλω apostellō**; from *575* and *4724; to send, send away:*— puts(1), send(17), send forth(3), sending(3), sends(1), sent(104), sent...away(1), set(1).

650. **ἀποστερέω apostereō**; from *575* and **στερέω stereō** *(to rob); to defraud, deprive of:*— defraud(2), defrauded(1), deprived(1), depriving(1).

651. **ἀποστολή apostolē**; from *649; a sending away:*— apostleship(4).

652. **ἀπόστολος apostolos**; from *649; a messenger, one sent on a mission, an apostle:*— apostle(19), apostles(52), apostles'(5), messenger(1), messengers(1), is sent(1).

653. **ἀποστοματίζω apostomatizō**; from *575* and *4750; to catechize,* i.e. *to question:*— question...closely(1).

654. **ἀποστρέφω apostrephō**; from *575* and *4762; to turn away, turn back:*— incites...to rebellion(1), put...back(1), remove(1), turn away(4), turned away(1), turning(1).

655. **ἀποστυγέω apostugeō**; from *575* and **στυγέω stugeō** *(to hate); to abhor:*— abhor(1).

656. **ἀποσυνάγωγος aposunagōgos**; from *575* and *4864; expelled from the congregation:*— outcasts from the synagogue(1), put out of the synagogue(2).

657. **ἀποτάσσω apotassō**; from *575* and *5021; to set apart, take leave of:*— bidding...farewell(1), give(1), say good-bye(1), taking...leave(1), taking leave(1), took leave(1).

658. **ἀποτελέω apoteleō**; from *575* and *5055; to bring to an end, complete:*— accomplished(1), perform(1).

659. **ἀποτίθημι apotithēmi**; from *575* and *5087; to put off, lay aside:*— laid aside(1), lay aside(3), laying aside(1), put(1), put...aside(1), putting aside(2).

660. **ἀποτινάσσω apotinassō**; from *575* and **τινάσσω tinassō** *(to shake, brandish); to shake off:*— shake...off(1), shook...off(1).

661. **ἀποτίνω apotinō**; from *575* and *5099; to pay off, repay:*— repay(1).

662. **ἀποτολμάω apotolmaō**; from *575* and *5111; to be very bold:*— very bold(1).

663. **ἀποτομία apotomia**; from *575* and the same as *664; sharpness, steepness:*— severity(2).

664. **ἀποτόμως apotomōs**; adv. from *575* and **τέμνω temnō** *(to cut); abruptly, curtly:*— severely(1), severity(1).

665. **ἀποτρέπω apotrepō**; from *575* and the same as *5157; to turn away:*— avoid(1).

666. **ἀπουσία apousia**; from fem. part. of *548; a being away,* i.e. *absence:*— absence(1).

667. **ἀποφέρω apopherō**; from *575* and *5342; to carry off, bear away:*— carried(1), carried...away(2), carried away(1), carry(1), led...away(1).

668. **ἀποφεύγω apopheugō**; from *575* and *5343; to flee from:*— escape(1), escaped(2).

669. **ἀποφθέγγομαι apophtheggomai**; from *575* and *5350; to speak forth:*— declared(1), utter(1), utterance(1).

670. **ἀποφορτίζομαι apophortizomai**; from *575* and *5412; to discharge a cargo:*— unload(1).

671. **ἀπόχρησις apochrēsis**; from a comp. of *575* and *5540; abuse, misuse:*— use(1).

672. **ἀποχωρέω apochōreō**; from *575* and *5562; to go away, depart:*— depart(1), leave(1), leaves(1), left(1).

673. **ἀποχωρίζω apochōrizō**; from *575* and *5563; to separate, part asunder:*— separated(1), split apart(1).

674. **ἀποψύχω apopsuchō**; from *575* and *5594; to leave off breathing,* i.e. *faint:*— fainting(1).

675. **Ἀππίου Φόρον Appiou phoron**; of Lat. or.; *Market of Appius,* the name of a city south of Rome:— Appius(1).

676. **ἀπρόσιτος aprositos**; from *1* (as a neg. pref.) and a comp. of *4314* and **εἶμι eimi** *(to go); unapproachable:*— unapproachable(1).

677. **ἀπρόσκοπος aproskopos**; from *1* (as a neg. pref.) and *4350; not causing to stumble, not stumbling:*— blameless(2), no offense(1).

678. **ἀπροσωπολήμπτως aprosōpolēmptōs**; adv. from a comp. of *1* (as a neg. pref.), *4383* and *2983; not accepting the person,* i.e. *without respect of persons:*— impartially(1).

679. **ἄπταιστος aptaistos**; from *1* (as a neg. pref.) and *4417; without stumbling:*— stumbling(1).

680. **ἅπτομαι haptomai**; mid. of *681,* q.v.

681. **ἅπτω haptō**; from a prim. root **ἁφ- haph-**; *to fasten to, lay hold of:*— clinging(1), handle(1), kindled(1), light(1), lighting(2), touch(13), touched(19), touching(1).

682. **Ἀπφία Apphia**; from a prim. root denoting endearment; *Apphia,* a Chr. woman in Colossae:— Apphia(1).

683. **ἀπωθέω apōtheō**; from *575* and **ὠθέω ōtheō** *(to thrust, push away); to thrust away:*— pushed...away(1), rejected(3), repudiate(1), repudiated(1).

684. **ἀπώλεια apōleia**; from *622; destruction, loss:*— destruction(13), destructive(1), perdition(1), perish(1), waste(1), wasted(1).

685. **ἀρά ara**; a prim. word; *a prayer, curse:*— cursing(1).

686. **ἄρα ara**; a prim. particle; *therefore* (an illative particle):— fact(1), perhaps(2), possible(1), so(4), so then(12), then(22), therefore(3), well then(1).

687. **ἆρα ara**; from *686;* an untranslatable interrog. particle implying anxiety or impatience.

688. **Ἀραβία Arabia**; of Heb. or. [6152b]; *Arabia,* a peninsula of Asia near Africa:— Arabia(2).

689. **Ἀράμ Aram**; of Heb. or. [7410]; *Ram,* an ancestor of Christ:— Ram(3).

690a. **ἄραφος araphos**; from a comp. of *1* (as a neg. pref.) and **ῥάπτω rhaptō** *(to sew); unsewn,* i.e. *without seam:*— seamless(1).

690b. **Ἄραψ Araps**; from *688; an Arab:*— Arabs(1).

691. **ἀργέω argeō**; from *692; to be idle:*— idle(1).

692. **ἀργός argos**; from *1* (as a neg. pref.) and *2041; inactive, idle:*— careless(1), idle(4), lazy(1), useless(2).

693. **ἀργυροῦς argurous**; from *696; of silver:*— silver(3).

694. **ἀργύριον argurion**; from *696; silvery,* by ext. *a piece of silver:*— money(10), pieces of silver(6), silver(5).

695. **ἀργυροκόπος argurokopos**; from *696* and *2875; a beater of silver,* i.e. *a silversmith:*— silversmith(1).

696. **ἄργυρος arguros**; from **ἀργός argos** *(shining); silver:*— silver(4).

697. **Ἄρειος Πάγος Areios Pagos**; from **Ἄρης Arēs** *(Ares,* the Gr. god of war) and **πάγος pagos** *(a rocky hill);* "the Hill of Ares," *Areopagus,* a hill in Athens:— Areopagus(2).

698. **Ἀρεοπαγίτης Areopagitēs**; from *697; a judge of the court of Areopagus:*— Areopagite(1).

699. **ἀρεσκία areskia**; from *700; a desire to please, pleasing:*— please(1).

700. **ἀρέσκω areskō**; from a prim. root **ἀρ- ar-** *(fit together); to please:*— found approval(1), please(12), pleased(2), pleasing(2).

701. **ἀρεστός arestos**; from *700; pleasing,* i.e. *fit:*— desirable(1), pleased(1), pleasing(1), things that are pleasing(1).

702. **Ἀρέτας Aretas**; of unc. or.; *Aretas,* an Arabian king:— Aretas(1).

703. **ἀρετή aretē**; of unc. or.; *moral goodness,* i.e. *virtue:*— excellence(2), excellencies(1), moral excellence(2).

704. **ἀρήν arēn**; a prim. word; *a lamb:*— lambs(1).

705. **ἀριθμέω arithmeō**; from *706; to number:*— count(1), numbered(2).

706. **ἀριθμός arithmos**; from a prim. root **ἀρι- ari-**; *a number:*— group(1), number(17).

707. **Ἀριμαθαία Harimathaia**; of Heb. or., cf. [7414]; *Arimathea,* prob. a city near Jer.:— Arimathea(4).

708. **Ἀρίσταρχος Aristarchos**; from **ἄριστος aristos** *(best)* and **ἄρχος archos** *(leader);* "best leader," *Aristarchus,* a Chr. of Thessalonica:— Aristarchus(5).

709. **ἀριστάω aristaō**; from *712; to breakfast,* hence *to take a meal:*— finished breakfast(1), have breakfast(1), have lunch(1).

710. **ἀριστερός aristeros**; cptv. adj. akin to **ἄριστος aristos** *(best); better,* euph. for *left, on the left:*— left(3), left hand(1).

711. **Ἀριστόβουλος Aristoboulos**; from the same as *708* and *1012;* "best-counseling," *Aristobulus,* a Chr. at Rome:— Aristobulus(1).

712. **ἄριστον ariston**; perh. from **ἦρι ēri** *(early)* and prim. root **ἐδ- ed-** *(eat,* see *2068); breakfast, dinner:*— dinner(1), luncheon(1), meal(1).

713. **ἀρκετός arketos**; from *714; sufficient:*— enough(2), sufficient(1).

714. **ἀρκέω arkeō**; a prim. vb.; to assist, suffice:— content(3), enough(2), satisfied(1), sufficient(2).

715. **ἄρκος arkos**; a prim. word; *a bear:*— bear(1).

716. **ἅρμα harma**; of unc. or.; a chariot:— chariot(3), chariots(1).

717. **Ἁρμαγεδών Harmagedōn**; of Heb. or. [2022 and 4023b]; *Har-Magedon,* a mountain of unc. location:— Har-Magedon(1).

718. **ἁρμόζω harmozō**; from *719; to fit, join,* hence *to join oneself to* (in marriage):— betrothed(1), suffer(1), treated(1).

719. **ἁρμός harmos**; from **ἀραρίσκω arariskō** *(to join together); a joining, joint:*— joints(1).

720. **ἀρνέομαι arneomai**; of unc. or.; *to deny, say no:*— denied(10), denies(5), deny(12), denying(2), disowned(3), refused(1).

721a. **Ἀρνί Arni**; prob. of Heb. or.; another reading for *689,* q.v.

721b. **ἀρνίον arnion**; dim. from *704; a little lamb:*— Lamb(27), lamb(1), Lamb's(1), lambs(1).

722. **ἀροτριάω arotriaō**; from *723; to plow:*— plow(1), plowing(1), plowman(1).

723. **ἄροτρον arotron**; from **ἀρόω aroō** *(to plow); a plow:*— plow(1).

724. **ἁρπαγή harpagē**; from *726; pillage, plundering:*— robbery(2), seizure(1).

725. **ἁρπαγμός harpagmos**; from *726; the act of seizing* or *the thing seized:*— thing to be grasped(1).

726. **ἁρπάζω harpazō**; from a prim. root **ἁρπ- harp-**; *to seize, catch up, snatch away:*— carry off(1), caught(4), snatch(2), snatched...away(1), snatches(1), snatches away(1), snatching(1), take...away...by force(1), take...by force(2).

727. **ἅρπαξ harpax**; from *726; rapacious:*— ravenous(1), swindler(1), swindlers(3).

728. **ἀρραβών arrabōn**; of Heb. or. [6162]; *an earnest* (a part payment in advance for security):— given as a pledge(1), pledge(2).

729. **ἄρραφος arraphos**; var. reading for *690a,* q.v.

730. **ἄρρην arrēn**; var. reading for *733b,* q.v.

731. **ἄρρητος arrētos**; from *1* (as a neg. pref.) and **ῥητος rhētos** *(stated); unspeakable:*— inexpressible(1).

732. **ἄρρωστος arrōstos**; from *1* (as a neg. pref.) and *4517; not strong,* i.e. *feeble, sickly:*— sick(3), sick people(2).

733a. **ἀρσενοκοίτης arsenokoitēs**; from *733b* and *2845; a sodomite:*— homosexuals(2).

733b. **ἄρσην arsēn**; a prim. word; *male:*— male(6), men(3).

734. **Ἀρτεμᾶς Artemas**; prob. a contr. from a comp. of *735* and *1435;* "gift of Artemis," *Artemas,* a friend of the apostle Paul:— Artemas(1).

735. **Ἄρτεμις Artemis**; of unc. or.; *Artemis,* the name of the Gr. goddess of the hunt:— Artemis(5).

736. **ἀρτέμων artemōn**; from **ἀρτάω artaō** *(to fasten to); something hung up* or *fastened,* i.e. *a foresail:*— foresail(1).

737. **ἄρτι arti**; of unc. or.; *just now:*— hereafter*(1), just(1), now(30), once(1), present(1), right now(1), this time(1).

738. **ἀρτιγέννητος artigennētos**; from *737* and *1080; newborn:*— newborn(1).

739. **ἄρτιος artios**; from *737; fitted, complete:*— adequate(1).

740. **ἄρτος artos**; of unc. or.; *bread, a loaf:*—bread(71), loaf(2), loaves(23), meal(1).

741. **ἀρτύω artuō**; prob. akin to same as *719; to make ready, to season* (food):— make...salty(1), seasoned(2).

742. **Ἀρφαξάδ Arphaxad**; of Heb. or. [775]; *Arphaxad*, a son of Shem and an ancestor of Christ:— Arphaxad(1).

743. **ἀρχάγγελος archaggelos**; from *757* and *32a; a chief angel*, i.e. *archangel:*— archangel(2).

744. **ἀρχαῖος archaios**; from *746; original, ancient:*— ancient(2), ancients(2), early(1), long standing(1), old(4), old things(1).

745. **Ἀρχέλαος Archelaos**; from *757* and *2992;* "people-ruling," *Archelaus*, a son of Herod the Great and king of Judea, Samaria and Idumea:— Archelaus(1).

746. **ἀρχή archē**; from *757; beginning, origin:*— beginning(38), corners(2), domain(1), elementary(1), elementary*(1), first(1), first preaching(1), principalities(1), rule(4), rulers(6).

747. **ἀρχηγός archēgos**; from *757* and *2233; founder, leader:*— author(2), Prince(1), prince(1).

748. **ἀρχιερατικός archieratikos**; from *749; high-priestly:*— high-priestly(1).

749. **ἀρχιερεύς archiereus**; from *757* and *2409; high priest:*— chief priest(1), chief priests(64), high priest(53), high priest's(1), high priesthood(1), high priests(2).

750. **ἀρχιποίμην archipoimēn**; from *757* and *4166; chief shepherd:*— Chief Shepherd(1).

751. **Ἄρχιππος Archippos**; from *757* and *2462;* "horse-ruler," *Archippus*, a Chr. at Colossae:— Archippus(2).

752. **ἀρχισυνάγωγος archisunagōgos**; from *757* and *4864; ruler of a synagogue:*— leader of the synagogue(2), synagogue official(5), synagogue officials(2).

753. **ἀρχιτέκτων architektōn**; from *757* and *5045; a master builder:*— master builder(1).

754. **ἀρχιτελώνης architelōnēs**; from *757* and *5057; a chief tax collector:*— chief tax collector(1).

755. **ἀρχιτρίκλινος architriklinos**; from *757* and **τρίκλινος triklinos** *(a dining room with three couches); the superintendent of a banquet:*— headwaiter(3).

756. **ἄρχομαι archomai**; mid. of *757*, q.v.

757. **ἄρχω archō**; a prim. vb.; *to rule, to begin:*— began(62), begin(7), beginning(8), begins(2), begun(1), proceed(1), rule(1), rulers(1), starting(2).

758. **ἄρχων archōn**; pres. part. of *757; ruler, chief:*— authorities(1), leaders(1), magistrate(1), official(2), official's(1), prince(1), ruler(1), ruler(13), rulers(16).

759. **ἄρωμα arōma**; of unc. or.; *a spice:*— spices(4).

760. **Ἀσάφ Asaph**; of Heb. or., cf. [623] and [609]; *Asa*, a king of Judah:— Asa(2).

761. **ἀσάλευτος asaleutos**; from *1* (as a neg. pref.) and *4531; unmoved:*— cannot be shaken(1), immovable(1).

762. **ἄσβεστος asbestos**; from *1* (as a neg. pref.) and **σβεστός sbestos** *(quenched, extinguished); unquenched, unquenchable:*— unquenchable(3).

763. **ἀσέβεια asebeia**; from *765; ungodliness, impiety:*— ungodliness(4), ungodly(3).

764. **ἀσεβέω asebeō**; from *765; to be impious*, i.e. *to be ungodly:*— done in an ungodly way(1), live ungodly(1), ungodly way(1).

765. **ἀσεβής asebēs**; from *1* (as a neg. pref.) and *4576; ungodly, impious:*— godless man(1), ungodly(6), ungodly persons(1).

766. **ἀσέλγεια aselgeia**; of unc. or.; *licentiousness, wantonness:*— licentiousness(1), sensual(1), sensuality(8).

767. **ἄσημος asēmos**; from *1* (as a neg. pref.) and the same as *4591; without mark:*— insignificant(1).

768. **Ἀσήρ Asēr**; of Heb. or. [836]; *Asher*, one of the twelve Isr. tribes:— Asher(2).

769. **ἀσθένεια astheneia**; from *772; weakness, frailty:*— ailments(1), diseases(1), ill(1), illness(1), infirmities(1), sickness(3), sicknesses(2), weak(1), weakness(9), weaknesses(4).

770. **ἀσθενέω astheneō**; from *772; to be weak, feeble:*— am weak(1), becoming weak(1), fell sick(1), sick(18), weak(12).

771. **ἀσθένημα asthenēma**; from *772; an infirmity:*— weaknesses(1).

772. **ἀσθενής asthenēs**; from *1* (as a neg. pref.) and **σθενής sthenēs** *(strong); without strength, weak:*— helpless(1), sick(6), unimpressive(1), weak(12), weak things(1), weaker(1), weakness(2).

773. **Ἀσία Asia**; of unc. or.; *Asia*, a Roman province:— Asia(18).

774. **Ἀσιανός Asianos**; from *773; Asian, of Asia:*— Asia(1).

775. **Ἀσιάρχης Asiarchēs**; from *773* and *757; an Asiarch*, an official of Asian cities:— Asiarchs(1).

776. **ἀσιτία asitia**; from *777; abstinence from food:*— time without food(1).

777. **ἄσιτος asitos**; from *1* (as a neg. pref.) and *4621; without eating, fasting:*— without eating(1).

778. **ἀσκέω askeō**; a prim. vb.; *to practice, endeavor:*— do my best(1).

779. **ἀσκός askos**; a prim. word; *a leather bottle, wineskin:*— skins(4), wineskins(8).

780. **ἀσμένως asmenōs**; adv. from **ἄσμενος asmenos** *(glad); gladly:*— gladly(1).

781. **ἄσοφος asophos**; from *1* (as a neg. pref.) and *4680; unwise:*— unwise men(1).

782. **ἀσπάζομαι aspazomai**; a prim. vb.; *to welcome, greet:*— acclaim(1), give...your greeting(1), greet(41), greeted(3), greeting(1), greets(5), paid their respects to(1), sends...greetings(4), taken...leave(1), welcomed(1).

783. **ἀσπασμός aspasmos**; from *782; a greeting, salutation:*— greeting(5), greetings(4), salutation(1).

784. **ἄσπιλος aspilos**; from *1* (as a neg. pref.) and *4696; spotless, unstained:*— spotless(2), stain(1), unstained(1), without*(1).

785. **ἀσπίς aspis**; a prim. word; *an asp:*— asps(1).

786. **ἄσπονδος aspondos**; from *1* (as a neg. pref.) and **σπονδή spondē** *(a libation); without libation*, i.e. *without truce*, hence *admitting of no truce:*— irreconcilable(1).

787. **ἀσσάριον assarion**; of Lat. or.; *an assarion, a farthing* (one tenth of a drachma):— cent(1), cents(1).

788. **ἆσσον asson**; cptv. adv. of **ἄγχι agchi** *(near); nearer:*— close(1).

789. **Ἄσσος Assos**; of unc. or.; *Assos*, a city on the W. coast of Asia Minor:— Assos(2).

790. **ἀστατέω astateō**; from *1* (as a neg. pref.) and *2476; to be unsettled*, i.e. *homeless:*— homeless(1).

791. **ἀστεῖος asteios**; from **ἄστυ astu** *(a city); of the town*, by impl. *courteous, elegant:*— beautiful(1), lovely(1).

792. **ἀστήρ astēr**; from a prim. root **στερ- ster-**; *a star:*— star(11), stars(13).

793. **ἀστήρικτος astēriktos**; from *1* (as a neg. pref.) and *4741; unstable, unsettled:*— unstable(2).

794. **ἄστοργος astorgos**; from *1* (as a neg. pref.) and **στοργή storgē** *(family affection); without natural affection:*— unloving(2).

795. **ἀστοχέω astocheō**; from *1* (as a neg. pref.) and **στόχος stochos** *(a mark); to miss the mark:*— gone astray(2), straying(1).

796. **ἀστραπή astrapē**; from *797; lightning, brightness:*— flashes of lightning(4), lightning(4), rays(1).

797. **ἀστράπτω astraptō**; of unc. or.; *to lighten, flash forth:*— dazzling(1), flashes(1).

798. **ἄστρον astron**; from *792; a star:*— star(1), stars(3).

799. **Ἀσύγκριτος Asugkritos**; from *1* (as a neg. pref.) and *4793;* "incomparable," *Asyncritus*, a Chr. at Rome:— Asyncritus(1).

800. **ἀσύμφωνος asumphōnos**; from *1* (as a neg. pref.) and *4859; dissonant, discordant:*— agree(1).

801. **ἀσύνετος asunetos**; from *1* (as a neg. pref.) and *4908; without understanding:*— foolish(1), lacking in understanding(2), without understanding(2).

802. **ἀσύνθετος asunthetos**; from *1* (as a neg. pref.) and *4934; not keeping covenant:*— untrustworthy(1).

803. **ἀσφάλεια asphaleia**; from *804; certainty, security:*— exact truth(1), safety(1), securely(1).

804. **ἀσφαλής asphalēs**; from *1* (as a neg. pref.) and **σφάλλω sphallō** *(to trip up); certain, secure:*— certain(1), definite(1), facts(1), safeguard(1), sure(1).

805. **ἀσφαλίζω asphalizō**; from *804; to make firm, secure:*— fastened(1), made...secure(1), made secure(1), make...secure(1).

806. **ἀσφαλῶς asphalōs**; adv. from *804; safely:*— certain(1), securely(1), under guard(1).

807. **ἀσχημονέω aschēmoneō**; from *809; to act unbecomingly:*— act unbecomingly(1), acting unbecomingly(1).

808. **ἀσχημοσύνη aschēmosunē**; from *809; unseemliness:*— indecent acts(1), shame(1).

809. **ἀσχήμων aschēmōn**; from *1* (as a neg. pref.) and *4976; shapeless*, i.e. fig. *unseemly:*— presentable(1).

810. **ἀσωτία asōtia**; from *1* (as a neg. pref.) and *4982; unsavedness*, i.e. *wastefulness:*— dissipation(3).

811. ἀσώτως asōtōs; adv. from the same comp. as *810; wastefully:*— loose(1).

812. ἀτακτέω atakteō; from *813; to be out of order, be remiss:*— act in an undisciplined manner(1), undisciplined manner(1).

813. ἄτακτος ataktos; from *1* (as a neg. pref.) and *5002; out of order, out of place:*— unruly(1).

814. ἀτάκτως ataktōs; adv. from *813; disorderly:*— undisciplined(1), unruly(1).

815. ἄτεκνος ateknos; from *1* (as a neg. pref.) and *5043; childless:*— childless(2).

816. ἀτενίζω atenizō; from *1* (as a cop. pref.) and **τείνω teinō** *(to stretch, extend); to look fixedly, gaze:*— fixed(1), fixed...gaze(4), fixing...gaze(2), gaze(1), gazed intently(1), gazing intently(1), look intently(2), looking intently(2).

817. ἄτερ ater; a prim. particle; *without:*— apart(1), without(1).

818. ἀτιμάζω atimazō; from *820; to dishonor:*— dishonor(2), dishonored(2), shame(1), shamefully(1), treated...shamefully(1).

819. ἀτιμία atimia; from *820; dishonor:*— common use(1), degrading(1), dishonor(4), shame(1).

820. ἄτιμος atimos; from *1* (as a neg. pref.) and *5092; without honor, dishonored:*— less(1), less honorable(1), without honor(3).

821. ἀτιμόω atimoō; var. reading for *818,* q.v.

822. ἀτμίς atmis; of unc. or.; vapor:— vapor(2).

823. ἄτομος atomos; from *1* (as a neg. pref.) and *5114; uncut, indivisible,* (an indivisible) *moment* (of time):— moment(1).

824. ἄτοπος atopos; from *1* (as a neg. pref.) and *5117; out of place, strange:*— perverse(1), unusual(1), wrong(2).

825. Ἀττάλεια Attaleia; from **Ἄτταλος Attalos** *(Attalus,* a king of Pergamum); *Attalia,* a city of Pamphylia:— Attalia(1).

826. αὐγάζω augazō; from *827; to shine forth:*— see(1).

827. αὐγή augē; a prim. word; *brightness,* spec. *daylight:*— daybreak(1).

828. Αὔγουστος Augoustos; of Lat. or.; *Augustus,* the name of a Rom. emperor:— Augustus(1).

829. αὐθάδης authadēs; from *846* and the same as *2237; self-pleasing:*— self-willed(2).

830. αὐθαίρετος authairetos; from *846* and *138; self-chosen,* i.e. *of one's own accord:*— himself(1), own accord(2).

831. αὐθεντέω authenteō; from *846* and a prim. root **σεν- sen-**; *to govern, exercise authority:*— exercise authority over(1).

832. αὐλέω auleō; from *836; to play on a flute:*— played on the flute(1), played the flute(2).

833. αὐλή aulē; of unc. or.; a courtyard, a court:— court(3), courtyard(5), fold(2), house(1), palace(1).

834. αὐλητής aulētēs; from *832; a flute player:*— flute-players(2).

835. αὐλίζομαι aulizomai; from *833; to lodge in the open, to lodge:*— spend the night(1), spent the night(1).

836. αὐλός aulos; prob. a prim. word; *a pipe, flute:*— flute(1).

837. αὐξάνω auxanō; a prol. form of a prim. vb.; *to make to grow, to grow:*— causes the growth(1), causing the growth(1), full grown(1), grew(1), grow(8), growing(2), grows(2), increase(2), increased(2), increasing(2), spreading(1).

838. αὔξησις auxēsis; from *837; growth:*— growth(2).

839. αὔριον aurion; adv. of unc. or.; *tomorrow:*— next day(3), tomorrow(11).

840. αὐστηρός austēros; from **αὔω hauō** *(to dry); harsh, severe:*— exacting(2).

841. αὐτάρκεια autarkeia; from *842; self-satisfaction,* i.e. *self-sufficiency:*— contentment(1), sufficiency(1).

842. αὐτάρκης autarkēs; from *846* and *714; self-sufficient, sufficient:*— content(1).

843. αὐτοκατάκριτος autokatakritos; from *846* and *2632; self-condemned:*— self-condemned(1).

844. αὐτόματος automatos; from *846* and perh. a suff. **ματ- mat-**; *acting of one's own will, of its own accord:*— itself(2).

845. αὐτόπτης autoptēs; from *846* and *3700; an eyewitness:*— eyewitnesses(1).

846. αὐτός autos; an intensive pron., a prim. word; (1) *self* (emphatic) (2) *he, she, it* (used for the third pers. pron.) (3) *the same:*— accompanied*(2), agree*(1), anyone(1), both*(1), city(2), even(1), here*(1), herself(5), himself(83), itself(7), just(1), lies(1), like(1), like-minded(1), money(1), myself(10), number(1), one(1), one's(2), other(1), ourselves(8), own(2), part(1), people(1), person(1), personally(1), righteousness(1), same(59), same things(4), same way(1), selves(1), sight(1), temple(1), theirs(3), themselves(23), there*(2), these(1), these things(2), this(1), those(2), together*(8), very(17), very one(1), very thing(4), well(1), who(3), whose(2), whose*(1), women(1), yourself(3), yourselves(14), yourselves*(3).

847. αὐτοῦ autou; adv. from *846; there, here:*— here(2), there(3).

848. αὑτοῦ hautou; see *1438:*— each other(1), himself(2), home(1), homes(1), themselves(1).

849a. αὐτόφωρος autophōros; from *846* and **φώρ phōr** *(a thief); the very act:*— very act(1).

849b. αὐτόχειρ autocheir; from *846* and *5495; with one's own hand:*— own hands(1).

850a. αὔχεω aucheō; from **αὐχή auchē** *(boasting); to boast:*— boasts(1).

850b. αὐχμηρός auchmēros; from **αὐχμός auchmos** *(drought); dry, squalid:*— dark(1).

851. ἀφαιρέω aphaireō; from *575* and *138; to take from, take away:*— cut off(3), take away(4), taken away(1), takes away(1), taking...away(1).

852. ἀφανής aphanēs; from *1* (as a neg. pref.) and *5316; unseen:*— hidden(1).

853. ἀφανίζω aphanizō; from *852; to make unseen,* i.e. *destroy:*— destroy(1), destroys(1), neglect(1), perish(1), vanishes away(1).

854. ἀφανισμός aphanismos; from *853; a vanishing:*— disappear(1).

855. ἄφαντος aphantos; from *1* (as a neg. pref.) and *5316; invisible:*— vanished(1).

856. ἀφεδρών aphedrōn; from *575* and *1476; a place of sitting apart,* i.e. *a privy, drain:*— eliminated*(2).

857. ἀφειδία apheidia; from *1* (as a neg. pref.) and *5339; unsparing treatment:*— severe treatment(1).

858. ἀφελότης aphelotēs; from **ἀφελής aphelēs** *(without a stone, even, smooth); simplicity:*— sincerity(1).

859. ἄφεσις aphesis; from *863; dismissal, release,* fig. *pardon:*— forgiveness(15), free*(1), release(1).

860. ἁφή haphē; from *681; a joint:*— joint(1), joints(1).

861. ἀφθαρσία aphtharsia; from *862a; incorruptibility:*— immortality(2), imperishable(4), incorruptible(1).

862a. ἄφθαρτος aphthartos; from *1* (as a neg. pref.) and *5351; undecaying,* i.e. *imperishable:*— immortal(1), imperishable(4), imperishable quality(1), incorruptible(1).

862b. ἀφθορία aphthoria; from *1* (as a neg. pref.) and *5351; incorruption:*— purity(1).

863. ἀφίημι aphiēmi; from *575* and **ἵημι hiēmi** *(to send); to send away, leave alone, permit:*— abandoned(1), allow(5), allowed(2), divorce(2), forgave(2), forgive(23), forgiven(23), forgives(1), gave...permission(1), leave(7), leaves(2), leaving(8), left(38), let(9), let...alone(6), let him have(1), neglected(1), neglecting(2), permit(6), permitted(1), permitting(1), send...away(1), tolerate(1), uttered(1), yielded(1).

864. ἀφικνέομαι aphikneomai; from *575* and the same as *2425; to arrive at:*— reached(1).

865. ἀφιλάγαθος aphilagathos; from *1* (as a neg. pref.) and *5358; without love of good:*— haters of good(1).

866. ἀφιλάργυρος aphilarguros; from *1* (as a neg. pref.) and *5366; without love of money:*— free from the love of money(1), free from the love(1).

867. ἄφιξις aphixis; from *864; arrival,* i.e. by impl. *departure:*— departure(1).

868. ἀφίστημι aphistēmi; from *575* and *2476; to lead away, to depart from:*— abstain(1), depart(1), departed(1), deserted(1), drew away(1), fall away(2), falls away(1), leave(1), left(2), let go(1), stay away(1), withdrew(1).

869. ἄφνω aphnō; a prim. word; *suddenly:*— suddenly(3).

870. ἀφόβως aphobōs; adv. from *1* (as a neg. pref.) and *5401; without fear:*— without cause(1), without cause to be afraid(1), without fear(3).

871. ἀφομοιόω aphomoioō; from *575* and *3666; to make like:*— made like(1).

872. ἀφοράω aphoraō; from *575* and *3708; to look away from all else at:*— fixing...eyes(1), see how(1).

873. ἀφορίζω aphorizō; from *575* and *3724; to mark off by boundaries from,* i.e. *set apart:*— hold...aloof(1), ostracize(1), separate(2), separates(1), set...apart(1), set apart(2), take(1), took away(1).

874. ἀφορμή aphormē; from *575* and *3729; a starting point,* i.e. fig. *an occasion:*— occasion(2), opportunity(5).

875. ἀφρίζω aphrizō; from *876; to foam at the mouth:*— foaming(1), foams(1).

876. ἀφρός aphros; a prim. word.; *foam:*— foaming(1).

877. ἀφροσύνη aphrosunē; from *878; foolishness:*— foolishness(4).

878. ἄφρων aphrōn; from *1* (as a neg. pref.) and *5424; without reason, foolish:*— fool(2), foolish(8), foolish ones(1).

879a. ἀφυπνόω aphupnoō; from *575* and *5258; to fall asleep:*— fell asleep(1).

879b. ἀφυστερέω aphustereō; from *575* and *5302*; *to be late,* spec. *to keep back:*— withheld(1).

880. ἄφωνος aphōnos; from *1* (as a neg. pref.) and *5456*; *without voice,* i.e. *speechless:*— mute(2), silent(1), without meaning(1).

881. Ἀχάζ Achaz; of Heb. or. [271]; *Ahaz,* a king of Judah:— Ahaz(2).

882. Ἀχαΐα Achaia; of unc. or.; *Achaia,* a Roman province incl. most of Greece:— Achaia(10).

883. Ἀχαϊκός Achaikos; from *882*; "an Achaian," *Achaicus,* a Chr. at Corinth:— Achaicus(1).

884. ἀχάριστος acharistos; from *1* (as a neg. pref.) and *5483*; *ungracious, ungrateful:*— ungrateful(2).

885. Ἀχίμ Achim; prob. of Heb. or., cf. [3137]; *Achim,* an ancestor of Christ:— Achim(2).

886. ἀχειροποίητος acheiropoiētos; from *1* (as a neg. pref.) and *5499*; *not made by hands:*— made with hands(1), made without hands(2).

887. ἀχλύς achlus; a prim. word; *a mist:*— mist(1).

888. ἀχρεῖος achreios; from *1* (as a neg. pref.) and **χρεῖος chreios** *(useful); useless:*— unworthy(1), worthless(1).

889. ἀχρειόω achreioō; from *888*; *to make useless:*— become useless(1).

890. ἄχρηστος achrēstos; from *1* (as a neg. pref.) and *5543*; *useless:*— useless(1).

891. ἄχρι achri or **ἄχρις achris**; a prim. particle, prep.; *until, as far as:*— even when(1), far(6), high(1), long(1), right(1), until(29), within(1).

892. ἄχυρον achuron; of unc. or.; *chaff:*— chaff(2).

893. ἀψευδής apseudēs; from *1* (as a neg. pref.) and *5571*; *free from falsehood:*— who cannot lie(1).

894. ἄψινθος apsinthos; of unc. or.; *wormwood:*— Wormwood(1), wormwood(1).

895. ἄψυχος apsuchos; from *1* (as a neg. pref.) and *5590*; *lifeless:*— lifeless things(1).

B

896. Βάαλ Baal; of Heb. or. [1168a]; *Baal,* a Canaanite deity:— Baal(1).

897. Βαβυλών Babulōn; of Akk. or., cf. [894]; "gate of god(s)," *Babylon,* a large city situated astride the Euphrates river:— Babylon(12).

898. βαθμός bathmos; from the same as *939*; *a step, degree:*— standing(1).

899. βάθος bathos; from *901*; *depth:*— deep(1), deep water(1), depth(5), depths(1).

900. βαθύνω bathunō; from *901*; *to deepen:*— deep(1).

901. βαθύς bathus; a prim. word; *deep:*— deep(2), deep things(1).

902. βαΐον baion; of Eg. or.; *a palm branch:*— branches(1).

903. Βαλαάμ Balaam; of Heb. or. [1109a]; *Balaam,* an unrighteous prophet:— Balaam(3).

904. Βαλάκ Balak; of Heb. or. [1111]; *Balak,* a king of the Moabites:— Balak(1).

905. βαλλάντιον ballantion; from a prim. root **βαλ- bal-**; *a purse:*— money belt(3), money belts(1).

906. βάλλω ballō; a prim. word; *to throw, cast:*— bring(2), cast(15), casting(3), casts(3), contributors(1), laid(1), lying(3), lying sick(1), place(1), poured(4), put(22), puts(2), putting(4), rushed(1), swung(2), threw(12), throw(16), thrown(27), tossing(1).

907. βαπτίζω baptizō; from *911*; *to dip, sink:*— Baptist(3), baptize(9), baptized(51), baptizes(1), baptizing(10), ceremonially washed(1), undergo(1).

908. βάπτισμα baptisma; from *907*; (the result of) *a dipping* or *sinking:*— baptism(20).

909. βαπτισμός baptismos; from *907*; (the act of) *a dipping* or *washing:*— washing(1), washings(2).

910. βαπτιστής baptistēs; from *907*; *a baptizer:*— Baptist(12).

911. βάπτω baptō; from a prim. root **βαφ- baph-**; *to dip:*— dip(2), dipped(2).

912. Βαραββᾶς Barabbas; of Ara. or. [1247] and *5*; "son of Abba," *Barabbas,* the Isr. robber released instead of Christ:— Barabbas(11).

913. Βαράκ Barak; of Heb. or. [1301]; *Barak,* a commander of the Isr.:— Barak(1).

914. Βαραχίας Barachias; of Heb. or. [1296]; *Barachiah,* the father of a man killed in the temple:— Berechiah(1).

915. βάρβαρος barbaros; of unc. or., but prob. onomatop. for unintelligible sounds; *barbarous, barbarian:*— barbarian(3), barbarians(1), natives(2).

916. βαρέω bareō; from *926*; *to weigh down:*— burdened(3), heavy(1), overcome(1), weighted down(1).

917. βαρέως bareōs; adv. from *926*; *heavily:*— scarcely(2).

918. Βαρθολομαῖος Bartholomaios; of Ara. or. [1247 and 8526]; "son of Tolmai," *Bartholomew,* one of the twelve apostles:— Bartholomew(4).

919. Βαριησοῦς Bariēsous; of Ara. or. [1247 and 3091]; "son of Joshua," *Bar-Jesus,* a false prophet:— Bar-Jesus(1).

920. Βαριωνᾶς Bariōnas; of Ara. or. [1247 and 3124]; "son of Jonah," *Bar-Jonah,* a surname of Peter:— Barjona(1).

921. Βαρνάβας Barnabas; prob. of Ara. or.; *Barnabas,* an Isr. companion of Paul:— Barnabas(27), Barnabas'(1).

922. βάρος baros; from *926*; *weight:*— asserted*(1), authority(1), burden(3), burdens(1), weight(1).

923. Βαρσαββᾶς Barsabbas; of Ara. or.; "son of Sabba," *Barsabbas,* the surname of two Isr. Chr.:— Barsabbas(2).

924. Βαρτιμαῖος Bartimaios; of Ara. or.; "son of Timaeus," *Bartimaeus,* a beggar:— Bartimaeus(1).

925. βαρύνω barunō; another reading for *916,* q.v.

926. βαρύς barus; a prim. word; *heavy:*— burdensome(1), heavy(1), savage(1), serious(1), weightier provisions(1), weighty(1).

927. βαρύτιμος barutimos; from *926* and *5092*; *of great value:*— very costly(1).

928. βασανίζω basanizō; from *931*; *to torture:*— battered(1), felt...tormented(1), pain(1), straining(1), torment(4), tormented(4).

929. βασανισμός basanismos; from *928*; *torture:*— torment(6).

930. βασανιστής basanistēs; from *928*; *a torturer:*— torturers(1).

931. βάσανος basanos; of Oriental or.; *a touchstone* (a dark stone used in testing metals), hence *examination by torture, torture:*— pains(1), torment(2).

932. βασιλεία basileia; from *936*; *kingdom, sovereignty, royal power:*— kingdom(159), kingdoms(3), reigns*(1).

933. βασίλειον basileion; from *934*; *a palace:*— royal palaces(1).

934. βασίλειος basileios; from *935*; *royal:*— royal(1).

935. βασιλεύς basileus; of unc. or.; *a king:*— king(82), King of kings(1), KING OF KINGS(1), king's(2), king*(1), kings(1), kings(24), kings'(1).

936. βασιλεύω basileuō; from *935*; *to be king, reign:*— become kings(2), kings(1), reign(12), reigned(4), reigning(1), reigns(1).

937. βασιλικός basilikos; from *935*; *royal:*— king's(1), royal(2), royal official(2).

938. βασίλισσα basilissa; fem. from *935*; *a queen:*— Queen(2), queen(2).

939. βάσις basis; from **βαίνω bainō** *(to walk, to go); a foot:*— feet(1).

940. βασκαίνω baskainō; from **βάσκανος baskanos** *(slanderous); to slander,* hence by ext. *to bewitch:*— bewitched(1).

941. βαστάζω bastazō; of unc. or.; *to take up, carry:*— bear(8), bearers(1), bearing(1), bore(1), borne(1), carried(2), carried...away(1), carried away(1), carries(1), carry(2), carrying(2), endured(1), picked(1), pilfer(1), remove(1), supports(1), tolerate(1).

942. βάτος batos; a prim. word; *a bramble bush:*— briar bush(1), bush(2), thorn bush(2).

943. βάτος batos; of Heb. or. [1324]; *a bath,* an Isr. liquid measure:— measures(1).

944. βάτραχος batrachos; of unc. or.; *a frog:*— frogs(1).

945. βατταλογέω battalogeō; from **βάττος battos** *(stammerer)* and *3056*; *to stammer:*— use meaningless repetition(1).

946. βδέλυγμα bdelugma; from *948*; *a detestable thing:*— abomination(3), abominations(2), detestable(1).

947. βδελυκτός bdeluktos; from *948*; *detestable:*— detestable(1).

948. βδελύσσομαι bdelussomai; from **βδέω bdeō** *(to stink); to detest:*— abhor(1), abominable(1).

949. βέβαιος bebaios; from the same as *939*; *firm, secure:*— certain(1), firm(2), firmly grounded(1), guaranteed(1), more sure(1), steadfast(1), unalterable(1), valid(1).

950. βεβαιόω bebaioō; from *949*; *to confirm, secure:*— confirm(2), confirmed(3), established(1), establishes(1), strengthened(1).

951. βεβαίωσις bebaiōsis; from *950*; *confirmation:*— confirmation(2).

952. βέβηλος bebēlos; from **βηλός bēlos** *(a threshold); permitted to be trodden,* by impl. *unhallowed:*— godless person(1), profane(1), worldly(3).

953. βεβηλόω bebēloō; from *952*; *to profane:*— break(1), desecrate(1).

954. Βεελζεβούλ Beelzeboul; of unc. or., cf. [1176]; *Beelzebul,* a name of Satan:— Beelzebul(7).

955. Βελιάρ Beliar; of unc. or.; "lord of the forest," *Beliar,* a name of Satan:— Belial(1).

956a. βελόνη belonē; akin to *956b; a needle:*— needle(1).

956b. βέλος belos; from *906; a missile:*— arrows(1).

957. βελτίων beltiōn; adv. from the cptv. of *18; better:*— very well(1).

958. Βενιαμίν Beniamin; of Heb. or. [1144]; *Benjamin,* one of the twelve Isr. tribes:— Benjamin(4).

959. Βερνίκη Bernikē; a Macedonian form of *5342* and *3529; Berenice, Bernice,* daughter of Herod Agrippa I:— Bernice(3).

960. Βέροια Beroia; of unc. or.; *Berea,* a city of Macedonia:— Berea(2).

961a. Βεροιαῖος Beroiaios; from *960; Berean,* a native of Berea:— Berea(1).

961b. Βεώρ beōr; of Heb. or. [1160]; *Beor,* father of Balaam:— Beor(1).

962. Βηθαβαρά Bēthabara; var. reading for *963,* q.v.

963. Βηθανία Bēthania; of Ara. or.; "house of affliction" or "house of dates," *Bethany,* the name of two cities in Pal.:— Bethany(12).

964. Βηθεσδά Bēthesda; prob. of Ara. or.; *Bethesda,* a pool in Jer.:— Bethesda(1).

965. Βηθλέεμ Bēthleem; of Heb. or. [1035]; "house of bread," *Bethlehem,* a city near Jer.:— Bethlehem(8).

966. Βηθσαϊδά Bēthsaida; of Ara. or.; "house of fish," *Bethsaida,* the name of two cities on the shore of the Sea of Galilee:— Bethsaida(7).

967. Βηθφαγή Bēthphagē; of Ara. or.; "house of unripe figs," *Bethphage,* a village on the Mt. of Olives:— Bethphage(3).

968. βῆμα bēma; from the same as *939; a step, raised place,* by impl. *a tribunal:*— ground(1), judgment seat(7), rostrum(1), tribunal(3).

969. βήρυλλος bērullos; of unc. or.; *beryl:*— beryl(1).

970. βία bia; a prim. word; *strength, force:*— force(1), violence(3).

971. βιάζω biazō; from *970; to force:*— forcing his way(1), suffers violence(1).

972. βίαιος biaios; from *970; violent:*— violent(1).

973. βιαστής biastēs; from *971; a violent man:*— violent men(1).

974. βιβλαρίδιον biblaridion; a dim. of *976; a little book:*— little book(3).

975. βιβλίον biblion; from *976; a paper, book:*— book(27), books(4), certificate(2), scroll(1).

976. βίβλος biblos; of unc. or.; (the inner) *bark* (of a papyrus plant), hence *a scroll,* spec. *a book:*— book(8), books(1), record(1).

977. βιβρώσκω bibrōskō; akin to **βορά bora** *(food); to eat:*— eaten(1).

978. Βιθυνία Bithunia; of unc. or.; *Bithynia,* a province in Asia Minor:— Bithynia(2).

979. βίος bios; a prim. word; *life, living:*— everyday life(1), goods(1), life(3), live(2), wealth(2).

980. βιόω bioō; from *979; to live:*— live(1).

981. βίωσις biōsis; from *980; manner of life:*— manner of life(1).

982. βιωτικός biōtikos; from *979; pertaining to life:*— life(1), matters of this life(2).

983. βλαβερός blaberos; from *984; hurtful:*— harmful(1).

984. βλάπτω blaptō; from a prim. root **βλαβ- blab-**; *to hurt:*— doing...harm(1), hurt(1).

985. βλαστάνω blastanō; from a prim. root **βλαστ- blast-**; *to sprout, produce:*— budded(1), produced(1), sprouted(1), sprouts(1).

986. Βλάστος Blastos; perh. from the same as *985; Blastus,* the chamberlain of Herod Agrippa I:— Blastus(1).

987. βλασφημέω blasphēmeō; from *989; to slander,* hence *to speak lightly* or *profanely of sacred things:*— be spoken of as evil(1), blaspheme(4), blasphemed(6), blasphemers(1), blasphemes(3), blaspheming(4), dishonored(1), hurling abuse(3), malign(2), maligned(1), revile(3), reviling(1), slandered(1), slanderously reported(1), spoken against(1), utter(1).

988. βλασφημία blasphēmia; from *989; slander:*— abusive language(1), blasphemies(4), blasphemous(2), blasphemy(6), railing(1), slander(3), slanders(1).

989. βλάσφημος blasphēmos; a comp. of a root of unc. or. and *5345; slanderous, evil-speaking:*— blasphemer(1), blasphemous(1), revilers(1), reviling(1).

990. βλέμμα blemma; from *991; a look:*— what he saw(1).

991. βλέπω blepō; a prim. vb.; *to look (at):*— beware(5), careful(1), careful*(1), consider(1), facing(1), guard(1), keep on seeing(2), look(7), looking(5), looks(1), partial*(2), saw(12), see(54), seeing(8), seen(8), sees(8), sight(2), take care(5), take heed(5), watch(1).

992. βλητέος blēteos; from *906;* (that which) *one must put:*— must be put(1).

993. Βοανηργές Boanērges; of Ara. or. [1123 and 7266]; *Boanerges,* an epithet applied to the two sons of Zebedee:— Boanerges(1).

994. βοάω boaō; from *995; to call out:*— called(1), cried(1), cry(1), crying(4), loudly declaring(1), shout(1), shouted(1), shouting(2).

995. βοή boē; a prim. word; *a cry:*— outcry(1).

996. βοήθεια boētheia; from *997; help:*— help(1), supporting cables(1).

997. βοηθέω boētheō; from *995* and **θέω theō** *(to run); to come to the aid of:*— come to...aid(1), come to the aid(1), help(4), helped(2).

998. βοηθός boēthos; from *997; helping, a helper:*— helper(1).

999. βόθυνος bothunos; prob. from *901; a pit:*— pit(3).

1000. βολή bolē; from *906; a throw:*— throw(1).

1001. βολίζω bolizō; from *1002; to heave the lead:*— took soundings(1), took...sounding(1).

1002. βολίς bolis; from *906; a dart, javelin.*

1003. Βόος Boos; of Heb. or. [1162]; *Boaz,* an Isr.:— Boaz(3).

1004. βόρβορος borboros; of unc. or.; *mud, filth:*— mire(1).

1005. βορρᾶς borras; of unc. or.; *north:*— north(2).

1006. βόσκω boskō; from the root **βοτ- bot-**; *to feed:*— feed(1), feeding(3), herdsmen(3), tend(2).

1007. Βοσόρ Bosor; of Heb. or. [1160]; var. reading for *961b,* q.v.

1008. βοτάνη botanē; from *1006; grass, fodder:*— vegetation(1).

1009. βότρυς botrus; a prim. word; *a cluster of grapes:*— clusters(1).

1010. βουλευτής bouleutēs; from *1011; a councilor:*— member of the council(2).

1011. βουλεύω bouleuō; from *1012; to take counsel, deliberate:*— consider(1), planned(1), planned together(1), purpose(2), resolved(1).

1012. βουλή boulē; from *1014; counsel:*— counsel(1), decision(1), motives(1), plan(4), purpose(5).

1013. βούλημα boulēma; from *1014; purpose, will:*— desire(1), intention(1), will(1).

1014. βούλομαι boulomai; a prim. vb.; *to will:*— am(1), desire(2), desires(1), desiring(1), intend(1), intended(3), intending(1), like(1), planned(1), unwilling*(1), want(7), wanted(3), wanting(2), will(1), willing(3), wills(3), wish(1), wished(1), wishes(1), wishing(3).

1015. βουνός bounos; prob. of for. or.; *a hill:*— hill(1), hills(1).

1016. βοῦς bous; a prim. word; *an ox, a cow:*— ox(4), oxen(4).

1017. βραβεῖον Brabeion; from **βραβεύς brabeus** *(an umpire); a prize:*— prize(2).

1018. βραβεύω brabeuō; from the same as *1017; to act as umpire:*— rule(1).

1019. βραδύνω bradunō; from *1021; to retard, to be slow:*— am delayed(1), slow(1).

1020. βραδυπλοέω braduploeō; from *1021* and a root akin to *4126; to sail slowly:*— sailed slowly(1).

1021. βραδύς bradus; of unc. or.; *slow:*— slow(3).

1022. βραδύτης bradutēs; from *1021; slowness:*— slowness(1).

1023. βραχίων brachiōn; cptv. of *1024; the arm:*— arm(3).

1024. βραχύς brachus; a prim. word; *short, little:*— briefly*(1), little(3), little while(2), short time(1).

1025. βρέφος brephos; a prim. word; *an unborn* or *a newborn child:*— babies(2), baby(4), childhood(1), infants(1).

1026. βρέχω brechō; a prim. word; *to send rain, to rain:*— fall(1), rain(2), rained(1), sends rain(1), wet(2).

1027. βροντή brontē; akin to **βρέμω bremō** *(to roar); thunder:*— peals of thunder(8), Thunder(1), thunder(2), thundered*(1).

1028. βροχή brochē; from *1026; a wetting:*— rain(2).

1029. βρόχος brochos; a prim. word; *a noose, halter:*— restraint(1).

1030. βρυγμός brugmos; from *1031; a biting, a gnashing of teeth:*— gnashing(7).

1031. βρύχω bruchō; a prim. word; *to bite, to gnash:*— gnashing(1).

1032. βρύω bruō; a prim. word; *to be full to bursting, to gush with:*— send(1).

1033. βρῶμα brōma; from *977; food:*— food(14), foods(3).

1034. βρώσιμος brōsimos; from *1035; edible:*— eat(1).

1035. βρῶσις brōsis; from *977; eating, food:*— eating(2), food(6), meal(1), rust(2).

1036. βυθίζω buthizō; from *1037; to sink, to cause to sink:*— plunge(1), sink(1).

1037. βυθός buthos; akin to *899; the bottom, the depth:*— deep(1).

1038. βυρσεύς burseus; from **βύρσα bursa** *(a hide); a tanner:*— tanner(3).

1039. **βύσσινος bussinos**; from *1040; fine linen:*— fine linen(5).

1040. **βύσσος bussos**; of Heb. or. [948]; *byssus* (a species of flax), also (the) *linen* (made from it):— fine linen(1).

1041. **βωμός bōmos**; from the same as *939; a platform, an altar:*— altar(1).

Γ

1042. **Γαββαθά Gabbatha**; of Ara. or.; *stone pavement:*— Gabbatha(1).

1043. **Γαβριήλ Gabriēl**; of Heb. or. [1403]; *Gabriel,* an angel:— Gabriel(2).

1044. **γάγγραινα gaggraina**; perh. from **γράω graō** *(to gnaw); a gangrene, an eating sore:*— gangrene(1).

1045. **Γάδ Gad**; of Heb. or. [1410]; *Gad,* a tribe of Isr.:— Gad(1).

1046. **Γαδαρηνός Gadarēnos**; from **Γαδαρά Gadara** *(Gadara,* the capital of Perea); *of Gadara, Gadarene:*— Gadarenes(1).

1047. **γάζα gaza**; of Pers. or.; *treasure:*— treasure(1).

1048. **Γάζα Gaza**; of Heb. or. [5804a]; *Gaza,* a Philistine city:— Gaza(1).

1049. **γαζοφυλάκιον gazophulakion**; from *1047* and *5438; treasury:*— treasury(5).

1050. **Γάϊος Gaios**; prob. of Lat. or.; *Gaius,* the name of several Chr.:— Gaius(5).

1051. **γάλα gala**; prob. from a prim. root **γλακτ- glakt-**; *milk:*— milk(5).

1052. **Γαλάτης Galatēs**; from *1053; a Galatian:*— Galatians(1).

1053. **Γαλατία Galatia**; of for. or.; *Galatia,* a district in Asia Minor or a larger Roman province including this district as well as others:— Galatia(4).

1054. **Γαλατικός Galatikos**; from *1053; belonging to Galatia:*— Galatian(2).

1055. **γαλήνη galēnē**; perh. akin to *1070; a calm:*— calm(3).

1056. **Γαλιλαία Galilaia**; of Heb. or. [1551]; *Galilee,* the northern region of Pal., also the name of a sea (same as *5085*):— Galilee(61).

1057. **Γαλιλαῖος Galilaios**; from *1056; Galilean:*— Galilean(4), Galileans(5), Galilee(2).

1058. **Γαλλίων Galliōn**; of Lat. or.; *Gallio,* proconsul of Asia:— Gallio(3).

1059. **Γαμαλιήλ Gamaliēl**; of Heb. or. [1583]; *Gamaliel,* a renowned teacher of the law:— Gamaliel(2).

1060. **γαμέω gameō**; from *1062; to marry:*— get married(2), marriage(1), married(7), marries(7), marry(9), marrying(2).

1061a. **γαμίζω gamizō**; from *1062; to give in marriage:*— give...in marriage(1), given in marriage(4), gives(1), giving in marriage(1), marriage(1).

1061b. **γαμίσκω gamiskō**; from *1062; to give in marriage:*— given in marriage(1).

1062. **γάμος gamos**; a prim. word; *a wedding:*— marriage(3), wedding(5), wedding feast(7).

1063. **γάρ gar**; a contr. of **γε ἄρα ge ara** *(verily then); for, indeed* (a conjunc. used to express cause, explanation, inference or continuation):— actually(1), after(1), after all(1), although(1), because(2), indeed(1), since(1), then(2), though(1), well(3), what(1), why(3), yes(2).

1064. **γαστήρ gastēr**; of unc. or.; *the belly:*—child*(4), gluttons(1), pregnant(3), womb(1).

1065. **γε ge**; a prim. encl. part.; emphasizes the word to which it is joined:— indeed(4), indeed*(1), least*(1), so(1), though*(1), well(1), yet(2).

1066. **Γεδεών Gedeōn**; of Heb. or. [1439]; *Gideon,* an Isr.:— Gideon(1).

1067. **γέεννα geenna**; of Heb. or. [1516 and 2011]; *Gehenna,* a valley W. and S. of Jer., also a symbolic name for the final place of punishment of the ungodly:— hell(12).

1068. **Γεθσημανί Gethsēmani**; of Heb. or. [1660 and 8081]; *Gethsemane,* an olive orchard on the Mt. of Olives:— Gethsemane(2).

1069. **γείτων geitōn**; from *1093; a neighbor:*— neighbors(4).

1070. **γελάω gelaō**; a prim. word; *to laugh:*— laugh(2).

1071. **γέλως gelōs**; from *1070; laughter:*— laughter(1).

1072. **γεμίζω gemizō**; from *1073; to fill:*— fill(1), filled(7), filling(1).

1073. **γέμω gemō**; a prim. word; *to be full:*— full(11).

1074. **γενεά genea**; from *1096; race, family, generation:*— generation(32), generations(10), kind(1).

1075. **γενεαλογέω genealogeō**; from *1096* and *3004* (in the sense of *reckon); to trace ancestry:*— genealogy is...traced(1).

1076. **γενεαλογία genealogia**; from *1096* and *3004* (in the sense of *reckon); the making of a pedigree, a genealogy:*— genealogies(2).

1077. **γενέσια genesia**; from *1078; a birthday celebration:*— birthday(2).

1078. **γένεσις genesis**; from *1096; origin, birth:*— birth(2), genealogy(1), life(1), natural(1).

1079a. **γενετή genetē**; from *1096; birth:*— birth(1).

1079b. **γένημα genēma**; from *1096; fruit, produce:*— fruit(3), harvest(1).

1080. **γεννάω gennaō**; from **γέννα genna** *(descent, birth); to beget, to bring forth:*— bear(1), bearing children(1), became the father of(4), became...father(1), begotten(4), bore(1), born(41), Child(1), conceived(1), father(37), Father(1), gave(1), gives birth(1), produce(1).

1081. **γέννημα gennēma**; from *1080; offspring:*— brood(4).

1082. **Γεννησαρέτ Gennēsaret**; of Heb. or., cf. [3672]; *Gennesaret,* a fertile plain on W. shore of the Sea of Galilee:— Gennesaret(3).

1083. **γέννησις gennēsis**; var. reading for *1078,* q.v.

1084. **γεννητός gennētos**; from *1080; begotten, born:*— born(2).

1085. **γένος genos**; from *1096; family, offspring:*— birth(2), countrymen(2), descendant(1), descent(1), family(2), kind(3), kinds(3), nation(1), native(1), race(3).

1086. **Γερασηνός Gerasēnos**; of unc. or.; *Gerasene, of Gerasa,* a city E. of the Jordan:— Gerasenes(3).

1087. **γερουσία gerousia**; from *1088; a council of elders:*— Senate(1).

1088. **γέρων gerōn**; a prim. word; *an old man:*— old(1).

1089. **γεύομαι geuomai**; a prim. vb.; *to taste, eat:*— eat(1), eaten(1), taste(8), tasted(4), tasting(1).

1090. **γεωργέω geōrgeō**; from *1092; to till:*— tilled(1).

1091. **γεώργιον geōrgion**; from *1092; cultivation:*— field(1).

1092. **γεωργός geōrgos**; from *1093* and *2041; a husbandman, vinedresser:*— farmer(2), vine-growers(16), vinedresser(1).

1093. **γῆ gē**; a prim. word; *the earth, land:*— country(2), earth(165), earthly(1), ground(20), land(46), soil(16).

1094. **γῆρας gēras**; a prim. word; *old age:*— old age(1).

1095. **γηράσκω gēraskō**; from *1094; to grow old:*— grow old(1), growing old(1).

1096. **γίνομαι ginomai**; from a prim. root **γεν- gen-**; *to come into being, to happen, to become:*— accomplished(1), appeared(3), arise(1), arises(2), arose(6), arrived(3), became(53), become(83), becomes(8), becoming(2), been(12), been brought(1), been done(1), been made(2), been...came(1), began(1), behaved(1), being(2), come into being(1), being carried(1), being done(2), being made(2), born(5), breaking*(1), came(45), came into being(2), came to pass(2), come(16), comes(1), comes to pass(1), coming(1), dawn(1), decided*(1), developing(1), done(20), drawing(1), during(1), elapsed(1), existed*(1), falling(1), feeling(1), fell(6), finished(1), followed(1), formed(3), found(2), get(4), give(1), got(1), granted(1), grown*(1), had(1), happen(6), happened(46), happening(5), happens(3), has(3), join*(1), joined(3), made(15), occur(3), occurred(18), performed(4), prove(7), proved(6), proving(1), put(1), reached(2), realized(1), results(2), show(1), spent(1), split(1), spoken(1), starting(1), take place(16), taken(2), taken place(5), takes place(1), taking place(3), there arose(1), thundered*(1), took place(7), turned(1), turns(3), would(1).

1097. **γινώσκω ginōskō**; from a prim. root **γνω- gnō-**; *to come to know, recognize, perceive:*— ascertaining(1), aware(7), certainty(1), come to know(1), comprehend(1), felt(1), find(3), found(2), kept...a virgin*(1), knew(13), know(104), know how(1), knowing(3), known(25), knows(14), learn(1), learned(1), perceived(1), perceiving(2), put(1), realize(3), recognize(7), recognized(1), recognizing(1), sure(4), take notice(1), unaware*(2), understand(11), understood(6), virgin*(1).

1098. **γλεῦκος gleukos**; from *1099; sweet new wine:*— sweet wine(1).

1099. **γλυκύς glukus**; a prim. word; *sweet:*— fresh(2), sweet(2).

1100. **γλῶσσα glōssa**; from a prim. root **γλωχ- glōch-** *(projecting point); the tongue, a language:*— tongue(25), tongues(25).

1101. **γλωσσόκομον glōssokomon**; from *1100* and the same as *2865; a case, a box:*— money box(2).

1102. **γναφεύς gnapheus**; from **κνάπτω knaptō** *(to card wool); one who cleans woolen cloth:*— launderer(1).

1103. **γνήσιος gnēsios**; from *1096; lawfully begotten, genuine:*— sincerity(1), true(3).

1104. **γνησίως gnēsiōs**; adv. from *1103; sincerely, truly:*— genuinely(1).

1105. **γνόφος gnophos**; from **δνόφος dnophos** *(darkness); darkness, gloom:*— darkness(1).

1106. **γνώμη gnōmē**; from *1097; purpose, opinion, consent, decision:*— consent(1), decided*(1), judgment(1), opinion(3), purpose(3).

1107. **γνωρίζω gnōrizō**; from *1097; to come to know, to make known:*— bring...information(1), have you know(1), inform(1), know(1), made...known(2), made known(11), make...known(2), make known(6), make...known(1).

1108. **γνῶσις gnōsis**; from *1097; a knowing, knowledge:*— knowing(1), knowledge(27), understanding way(1).

1109. **γνώστης gnōstēs**; from *1097; one who knows:*— expert(1).

1110. **γνωστός gnōstos**; from *1097; known:*— acquaintances(2), known(12), noteworthy(1).

1111. **γογγύζω gogguzō**; onomatop.; *to mutter, murmur:*— did(1), grumble(2), grumbled(2), grumbling(2), muttering(1).

1112. **γογγυσμός goggusmos**; from *1111; a muttering, murmuring:*— complaint(2), grumbling(2).

1113. **γογγυστής goggustēs**; from *1111; a murmurer:*— grumblers(1).

1114. **γόης goēs**; from **γοάω goaō** *(to wail); a wailer, a sorcerer, a swindler:*— impostors(1).

1115. **Γολγοθᾶ Golgotha**; of Ara. or.; *Golgotha,* a hill near Jer.:— Golgotha(3).

1116. **Γόμορρα Gomorra**; of Heb. or. [6017]; *Gomorrah,* one of the cities near the Dead Sea:— Gomorrah(4).

1117. **γόμος gomos**; from *1073; a ship's freight, cargo:*— cargo(1), cargoes(2).

1118. **γονεύς goneus**; from *1096; a parent:*— parents(20).

1119. **γόνυ gonu**; a prim. word; *the knee:*— down*(4), feet(1), knee(3), kneeling*(2), knees(3), knelt*(3).

1120. **γονυπετέω gonupeteō**; from *1119* and *4098; to fall on the knees:*— falling on his knees before(2), knees before(2), knelt before(1), knelt down(1).

1121. **γράμμα gramma**; from *1125; that which is drawn* or *written,* i.e. *a letter:*— bill(2), learning(1), letter(5), letters(3), writings(2).

1122. **γραμματεύς grammateus**; from *1121; a writer, scribe:*— scribe(4), scribes(59), town clerk(1).

1123. **γραπτός graptos**; from *1125; written:*— written(1).

1124. **γραφή graphē**; from *1125; a writing, scripture:*— Scripture(31), Scriptures(20).

1125. **γράφω graphō**; a prim. vb.; *to write:*— read(1), sent this letter(1), write(37), writes(1), writing(14), written(117), wrote(20).

1126. **γραώδης graōdēs**; from **γραῦς graus** *(an old woman)* and **-ωδης -ōdēs** (suff. denoting similarity); *characteristic of old women, anile:*— fit only(1), old women(1).

1127. **γρηγορέω grēgoreō**; formed from perf. of *1453; to be awake, to watch:*— alert(10), awake(1), keep(1), keep watch(4), keep watching(1), keeping alert(1), stay on the alert(1), stays awake(1), wake(2).

1128. **γυμνάζω gumnazō**; from *1131; to exercise naked, to train:*— discipline(1), trained(3).

1129. **γυμνασία gumnasia**; from *1128; exercise:*— discipline(1).

1130. **γυμνιτεύω gumniteuō**; from *1131; to be naked* or *poorly clothed:*— poorly clothed(1).

1131. **γυμνός gumnos**; a prim. word; *naked, poorly clothed:*— bare(1), naked(11), open(1), stripped(1), without clothing(1).

1132. **γυμνότης gumnotēs**; from *1131; nakedness:*— exposure(1), nakedness(2).

1133. **γυναικάριον gunaikarion**; dim. from *1135; a little woman,* (contemptuously) *a silly woman:*— weak women(1).

1134. **γυναικεῖος gunaikeios**; from *1135; female:*— woman(1).

1135. **γυνή gunē**; a prim. word; *a woman:*— bride(1), wife(71), wife's(1), wives(11), woman(96), woman's(1), women(33).

1136. **Γώγ Gōg**; of Heb. or. [1463]; *Gog,* associated with Magog:— Gog(1).

1137. **γωνία gōnia**; from *1119; an angle, a corner:*— corner(6), corners(3).

Δ

1138. **Δαβίδ Dabid**; var. reading for *1160b,* q.v.

1139. **δαιμονίζομαι daimonizomai**; from *1142; to be possessed by a demon:*— demon-possessed(11), demoniacs(2).

1140. **δαιμόνιον daimonion**; from *1142; an evil spirit, a demon:*— deities(1), demon(19), demons(43).

1141. **δαιμονιώδης daimoniōdēs**; from *1140* and **-ωδης -ōdēs** (suff. denoting similarity); *demon-like:*— demonic(1).

1142. **δαίμων daimōn**; perh. from **δαίω daiō** *(to distribute destinies); a demon:*— demons(1).

1143. **δάκνω daknō**; from a prim. root **δακ- dak-**; *to bite:*— bite(1).

1144. **δάκρυον dakruon**; a prim. word; *a teardrop:*— tear(2), tears(8).

1145. **δακρύω dakruō**; from *1144; to weep:*— wept(1).

1146. **δακτύλιος daktulios**; from *1147; a ring:*— ring(1).

1147. **δάκτυλος daktulos**; of unc. or.; *a finger:*— finger(6), fingers(2).

1148. **Δαλμανουθά Dalmanoutha**; of unc. or.; *Dalmanutha,* an unidentified place near the Sea of Galilee:— Dalmanutha(1).

1149. **Δαλματία Dalmatia**; of for. or.; *Dalmatia,* southern Illyricum on the Adriatic Sea:— Dalmatia(1).

1150. **δαμάζω damazō**; from a prim. root **δαμα- dama-**; *to tame:*— subdue(1), tame(1), tamed(2).

1151. **δάμαλις damalis**; from *1150; a heifer:*— heifer(1).

1152. **Δάμαρις Damaris**; from **δάμαρ damar** *(a wife); Damaris,* an Athenian woman:— Damaris(1).

1153. **Δαμασκηνός Damaskēnos**; from *1154; of Damascus:*— Damascenes(1).

1154. **Δαμασκός Damaskos**; of Heb. or. [1834]; *Damascus,* a city of Syria:— Damascus(15).

1155. **δανίζω danizō**; from **δάνος danos** *(a loan); to lend, borrow:*— borrow(1), lend(3).

1156. **δάνειον daneion**; from the same as *1155; a loan:*— debt(1).

1157. **δανιστής danistēs**; from *1155; a moneylender:*— moneylender(1).

1158. **Δανιήλ Daniēl**; of Heb. or. [1840]; *Daniel,* the prophet:— Daniel(1).

1159. **δαπανάω dapanaō**; from *1160a; to spend, spend freely:*— pay...expenses(1), spend(2), spent(2).

1160a. **δαπάνη dapanē**; from **δάπτω daptō** *(to devour); expense, cost:*— cost(1).

1160b. **Δαυίδ Dauid**; of Heb. or. [1732]; *David,* king of Isr.:— David(58), David's(1).

1161. **δέ de**; a prim. word; *but, and, now,* (a connective or adversative particle):— after(2), also(2), another*(8), even(4), even though(1), former*(1), however(6), moreover(1), moreover*(1), nevertheless(1), now(267), or(6), other(1), other hand(4), others*(3), partly(1), rather(1), so(12), suppose*(1), then(6), therefore(1), though(1), what(1), when(3), whereas(2), yes(1), yet(25).

1162. **δέησις deēsis**; from *1189a; a need, entreaty:*— entreaties(2), petition(3), prayer(6), prayers(6), supplication(1).

1163. **δεῖ dei**; a form of *1210; it is necessary:*— due(1), had(7), have(2), must(56), necessary(4), needed(1), ought(17), ought to(1), should(9).

1164. **δεῖγμα deigma**; from *1166; a thing shown, specimen:*— example(1).

1165. **δειγματίζω deigmatizō**; from *1164; to expose, make a show of:*— disgrace(1), made a display(1).

1166. **δείκνυμι deiknumi**; from a prim. root **δεικ- deik-**; *to show:*— bring(1), show(21), showed(8), shown(2), shows(1).

1167. **δειλία deilia**; from *1169; cowardice:*— timidity(1).

1168. **δειλιάω deiliaō**; from *1167; to be cowardly:*— fearful(1).

1169. **δειλός deilos**; from *1190a; cowardly, fearful:*— afraid(2), cowardly(1).

1170. **δεῖνα deina**; of unc. or.; *a certain one:*— certain man(1).

1171. **δεινῶς deinōs**; from the same as *1169; terribly, vehemently:*— business(1), fearfully(1), very(1).

1172. **δειπνέω deipneō**; from *1173; to eat, dine:*— dine(1), eat(2), eaten(1), supper(1).

1173. **δεῖπνον deipnon**; from the same as *1160a; dinner, supper:*— banquet(1), banquets(3), dinner(4), supper(8).

1174. **δεισιδαιμονέστερος Deisidaimonesteros**; cptv. Of **δεισιδαίμων deisidaimōn** *(fearing the gods);* from **δείδω deidō** *(to fear)* and *1142; very fearful of gods, religious, superstitious.*

1175. **δεισιδαιμονία deisidaimonia**; from same as *1174; a religion, superstition:*— religion(1), very religious(1).

1176. **δέκα deka**; a prim. num.; *ten:*— eighteen*(1), ten(24).

1177. **δεκαδύο dekaduo**; var. reading for *1427,* q.v.

1178a. **δεκαοκτώ dekaoktō**; from *1176* and *3638; eighteen:*— eighteen(2).

1178b. **δεκαπέντε dekapente**; from *1176* and *4002; fifteen:*— fifteen(2), two(1).

1179. **Δεκάπολις Dekapolis**; from *1176* and *4172; Decapolis,* a region E. of the Jordan:— Decapolis(3).

1180. **δεκατέσσαρες dekatessares**; from *1176* and *5064; fourteen:*— fourteen(5).

1181. **δεκάτη dekatē**; from *1176; a tenth part, a tithe:*— tenth(1), tenth part(1), tithes(2).

1182. **δέκατος dekatos**; from *1176; tenth:*— tenth(3).

1183. **δεκατόω dekatoō**; from *1181; to collect tithes:*— collected a tenth(1), paid tithes(1).

1184. **δεκτός dektos**; from *1209; acceptable:*— acceptable(2), favorable(1), welcome(2).

1185. **δελεάζω deleazō**; from **δέλεαρ delear** *(bait); to lure:*— entice(1), enticed(1), enticing(1).

1186. **δένδρον dendron**; of unc. or.; *a tree:*— tree(17), trees(8).

1187. **δεξιολάβος dexiolabos**; from *1188* and *2983;* prob. *a spearman* or *slinger:*— spearmen(1).

1188. **δεξιός dexios**; perh. a prim. word; *the right hand* or *side:*— right(22), right hand(31), right-hand(1).

1189a. **δέομαι deomai**; a form of *1210; to want, entreat:*— ask(1), beg(6), begged(1), begging(2), beseech(2), implored(1), making request(1), please(1), pray(2), prayed(3), praying(2).

1189b. **δέον deon**; a form of *1210; that which is needful:*— necessary(1), ought(1), things...proper(1).

1190a. **δέος deos**; from **δείδω deidō** *(to fear); fear, reverence:*— awe(1).

1190b. **Δερβαῖος Derbaios**; from *1191; of Derbe:*— Derbe(1).

1191. **Δέρβη Derbē**; of for. or.; *Derbe,* a city of Lycaonia:— Derbe(3).

1192. **δέρμα derma**; from *1194; the skin:*— goatskins*(1).

1193. **δερμάτινος dermatinos**; from *1192; made of skin, leathern:*— leather(2).

1194. **δέρω derō**; a prim. vb.; *to skin, to thrash:*— beat(5), beaten(1), beating(3), flogged(2), hits(1), receive(1), receive...lashes(1), strike(1).

1195. **δεσμεύω desmeuō**; from *1199; to bind together, to fetter:*— binding(1), bound(1), tie(1).

1196. **δεσμέω desmeō**; var. reading for *1195,* q.v.

1197. **δέσμη desmē**; from *1210; a bundle:*— bundles(1).

1198. **δέσμιος desmios**; from *1210; binding, bound:*— prisoner(12), prisoners(4).

1199. **δεσμός desmos**; from *1210; a band, bond:*— bond(1), bonds(3), chains(3), impediment(1), imprisonment(10).

1200. **δεσμοφύλαξ desmophulax**; from *1199* and *5441; a prison keeper:*— jailer(3).

1201. **δεσμωτήριον desmōtērion**; from *1199* and **-τηριον -tērion** (suff. denoting place); *a prison:*— imprisoned(1), prison house(3).

1202. **δεσμώτης desmōtēs**; from *1199; a prisoner:*— prisoners(2).

1203. **δεσπότης despotēs**; of unc. or.; *lord, master:*— Lord(3), Master(3), masters(4).

1204. **δεῦρο deuro**; of unc. or.; *until now, come here!:*— come(6), come here(2).

1205. **δεῦτε deute**; pl. of *1204; come!:*— come(9), come away(1), follow*(2).

1206. **δευτεραῖος deuteraios**; from *1208; on the second day:*— second day(1).

1207. (not used)

1208. **δεύτερος deuteros**; cptv. adj., perh. from *1417; second:*— second(30), second one(2), second time(10), subsequently(1), twice(1).

1209. **δέχομαι dechomai**; a prim. vb.; *to receive:*— accept(2), accepted(3), receive(16), received(12), receives(15), take(3), taken(1), took(1), welcome(2), welcomed(1).

1210. **δέω deō**; a prim. vb.; *to tie, bind:*— bind(7), binding(1), binds(2), bound(23), imprisoned(4), prisoners(1), put...in chains(1), tied(4).

1211. **δή dē**; a prim. particle akin to *2235; indeed, now* (used to give emphasis or urgency to a statement):— indeed(1), then(1), therefore(1).

1212. **δῆλος dēlos**; of unc. or.; *clear, evident:*— away*(1), evident(2).

1213. **δηλόω dēloō**; from *1212; to make plain, declare:*— denotes(1), indicating(1), informed(2), made clear(1), show(1), signifying(1).

1214. **Δημᾶς Dēmas**; prob. a short form of *1216; Demas,* a companion of Paul:— Demas(3).

1215. **δημηγορέω dēmēgoreō**; from **δημηγορός dēmēgoros** *(popular orator);* from *1218* and **ἀγορεύω agoreuo** *(to speak in the assembly, harangue); to deliver a public address:*— delivering an address(1).

1216. **Δημήτριος Dēmētrios**; from **Δημήτηρ Dēmētēr** (Gr. goddess of agriculture); *Demetrius,* the name of a silversmith and of a Chr.:— Demetrius(3).

1217. **δημιουργός dēmiourgos**; from *1218* and *2041; builder, maker, creator:*— builder(1).

1218. **δῆμος dēmos**; of unc. or.; *a district* or *country, the common people,* esp. *the people assembled:*— assembly(2), people(2).

1219. **δημόσιος dēmosios**; from *1218; public:*— public(3), publicly(1).

1220. **δηνάριον dēnarion**; of Lat. or.; *denarius* (a Rom. coin):— denarii(7), denarius(9).

1221. **δήποτε dēpote**; from *1211* and *4218; sometime:*— whatever*(1).

1222. **δήπου dēpou**; from *1211* and *4225; of course, surely:*— assuredly(1).

Δία Dia; see *2203.*

1223. **διά dia**; a prim. prep.; *through, on account of, because of:*— account(4), after(2), afterward(1), always*(2), because(111), between*(1), briefly*(1), charge*(1), constantly(1), continually*(6), during(1), forever*(1), gives(1), means(3), over(1), presence(1), reason(40), sake(41), sakes(5), since(1), so then*(1), so*(1), therefore*(16), this reason*(1), this*(1), though(1), through(225), through the agency(1), through*(1), view(2), way(3), what(1), why(3), why*(27).

1224. **διαβαίνω diabainō**; from *1223* and the same as *939; to step across:*— come over(2), passed through(1).

1225. **διαβάλλω diaballō**; from *1223* and *906; to bring charges* (usually with hostile intent):— reported(1).

1226. **διαβεβαιόομαι diabebaioomai**; from *1223* and *950; to affirm confidently:*— make confident assertions(1), speak confidently(1).

1227. **διαβλέπω diablepō**; from *1223* and *991; to look through, to see clearly:*— looked intently(1), see(1), see clearly(2).

1228. **διάβολος diabolos**; from *1225; slanderous, accusing falsely:*— devil(34), malicious gossips(3).

1229. **διαγγέλλω diaggellō**; from *1223* and *31b; to publish abroad, proclaim:*— giving notice(1), proclaim everywhere(1), proclaimed(1).

1230. **διαγίνομαι diaginomai**; from *1223* and *1096; to go through, to elapse:*— elapsed(1), over(1), passed(1).

1231. **διαγινώσκω diaginōskō**; from *1223* and *1097; to distinguish, to determine:*— decide(1), determine(1).

1232. **διαγνωρίζω diagnōrizō**; var. reading for *1107,* q.v.

1233. **διάγνωσις diagnōsis**; from *1231; a distinguishing, determination:*— decision(1).

1234. **διαγογγύζω diagogguzō**; from *1223* and *1111; to murmur among themselves:*— grumble(2).

1235. **διαγρηγορέω diagrēgoreō**; from *1223* and *1127; to keep awake, to be fully awake:*— fully awake(1).

1236. **διάγω diagō**; from *1223* and *71; to carry over, to pass:*— lead(1), spending...life(1).

1237. **διαδέχομαι diadechomai**; from *1223* and *1209; to receive in turn:*— received...in...turn(1).

1238. **διάδημα diadēma**; from **διαδέω diadeō** *(to bind around); a diadem, a crown:*— diadems(3).

1239. **διαδίδωμι diadidōmi**; from *1223* and *1325; to hand over, distribute:*— distribute(1), distributed(2), distributes(1).

1240. **διάδοχος diadochos**; from *1237; a successor:*— succeeded(1).

1241. **διαζώννυμι diazōnnumi**; from *1223* and *2224; to gird around:*— girded(2), put(1).

1242. **διαθήκη diathēkē**; from *1303; testament, will, covenant:*— covenant(30), covenants(3).

1243. **διαίρεσις diairesis**; from *1244; a division:*— varieties(3).

1244. **διαιρέω diaireō**; from *1223* and *138; to divide, to distribute:*— distributing(1), divided...between(1).

1245a. **διακαθαίρω diakathairō**; from *1223* and *2508; to cleanse thoroughly:*— thoroughly clear(1).

1245b. **διακαθαρίζω diakatharizō**; from *1223* and *2511; to cleanse thoroughly:*— thoroughly clear(1).

1246. **διακατελέγχομαι diakatelegchomai**; from *1223, 2596* and *1651; to confute completely:*— refuted(1).

1247. **διακονέω diakoneō**; from *1249; to serve, minister:*— administered(1), administration(1), cared(1), contributing...support(1), do...the serving(1), employ...in serving(1), minister(3), ministered(2), ministering(3), servant(1), serve(4), serve as deacons(1), served(2), served as deacons(1), serves(5), services...rendered(1), serving(4), take care(1), wait(1), waited(3).

1248. **διακονία diakonia**; from *1249; service, ministry:*— ministries(1), ministry(19), mission(1), preparations(1), relief(1), serve(1), service(7), serving(2), support(1).

1249. **διάκονος diakonos**; of unc. or.; *a servant, minister:*— deacons(3), minister(7), servant(10), servants(9).

1250. **διακόσιοι diakosioi**; pl. card. num. from *1364* and *1540; two hundred:*— one hundred(1), twelve hundred*(1), two hundred(6).

1251. **διακούω diakouō**; from *1223* and *191; to give a hearing to:*— give...a hearing(1).

1252. **διακρίνω diakrinō**; from *1223* and *2919; to distinguish, to judge:*— decide(1), discern(1), disputed(1), doubt(2), doubting(2), doubts(2), judge(1), judged(1), made distinctions(1), made...distinction(1), misgivings(2), pass judgment(1), regards...as superior(1), took issue(1), waver(1).

1253. **διάκρισις diakrisis**; from *1252; the act of judgment:*— discern(1), distinguishing(1), passing judgment(1).

1254. **διακωλύω diakōluō**; from *1223* and *2967; to hinder:*— prevent(1).

1255. **διαλαλέω dialaleō**; from *1223* and *2980; to discuss:*— discussed(1), talked about(1).

1256. **διαλέγομαι dialegomai**; from *1223* and *3004; to discuss, to address, to preach:*— addressed(1), argued(1), carrying on a discussion(1), discussed(1), discussing(1), reasoned(2), reasoning(4), talking(2).

1257. **διαλείπω dialeipō**; from *1223* and *3007; to leave off:*— ceased(1).

1258. **διάλεκτος dialektos**; from *1256; speech, language:*— dialect(3), language(3).

1259. **διαλλάσσω diallassō**; from *1223* and *236; change, exchange:*— reconciled(1).

1260. **διαλογίζομαι dialogizomai**; from *1223* and *3049; to consider:*— discuss(4), discussing(1), pondering(1), reason(1), reasoned(1), reasoning(7), wondering(1).

1261. **διαλογισμός dialogismos**; from *1260; a reasoning:*— argument(1), disputing(1), dissension(1), doubts(1), motives(1), opinions(1), reasonings(2), speculations(1), thoughts(3), what...were thinking(2).

1262. **διαλύω dialuō**; from *1223* and *3089; to break up:*— dispersed(1).

1263. **διαμαρτύρομαι diamarturomai**; from *1223* and *3143; to affirm solemnly:*— solemnly to testify(1), solemnly charge(3), solemnly testified(2), solemnly testifies(1), solemnly testifying(3), solemnly warned(1), solemnly witnessed(1), testified(1), testify solemnly(1), warn(1).

1264. **διαμάχομαι diamachomai**; from *1223* and *3164; to struggle against:*— argue heatedly(1).

1265. **διαμένω diamenō**; from *1223* and *3306; to remain, continue:*— continues(1), remain(2), remained(1), stood(1).

1266. **διαμερίζω diamerizō**; from *1223* and *3307; to distribute, to divide:*— distributing(1), divided(4), divided...among(1), divided up...among themselves(2), dividing up...among(1), share(1), sharing(1).

1267. **διαμερισμός diamerismos**; from *1266; a division:*— division(1).

1268. **διανέμω dianemō**; from *1223* and **νέμω nemō** *(to parcel out); to distribute, to disseminate:*— spread(1).

1269. **διανεύω dianeuō**; from *1223* and *3506; to wink at, nod to, beckon to:*— making signs(1).

1270. **διανόημα dianoēma**; from **διανοέομαι dianoeomai** *(to think);* from *1223* and *3539; a thought:*— thoughts(1).

1271. **διάνοια dianoia**; from *1223* and *3539; the mind, disposition, thought:*— mind(7), minds(2), thoughts(1), understanding(2).

1272. **διανοίγω dianoigō**; from *1223* and *455; to open up completely:*— explaining(2), opened(5), opens(1).

1273. **διανυκτερεύω dianuktereuō**; from *1223* and **νυκτερεύω nuktereuō** *(pass the night);* akin to *3571; to pass the night:*— spent the whole night(1), whole night(1).

1274. **διανύω dianuō**; from *1223* and **ἀνύω anuō** *(to effect); to accomplish fully:*— finished(1).

1275. **διαπαρατριβή diaparatribē**; from *1223* and **παρατριβή paratribē** *(friction, irritation); mutual irritation:*— constant friction(1).

1276. **διαπεράω diaperaō**; from *1223* and a der. of *4008; to cross over:*— cross over(1), crossed over(4), crossing over(1).

1277. **διαπλέω diapleō**; from *1223* and *4126; to sail across:*— sailed through(1).

1278. **διαπονέομαι diaponeomai**; from *1223* and **πονέομαι poneomai** *(to work hard); to toil through, to be worn out* or *annoyed:*— greatly annoyed(1), greatly disturbed(1).

1279. **διαπορεύομαι diaporeuomai**; from *1223* and *4198; to pass across, journey through:*— going(1), passing(2), passing through(2).

1280. **διαπορέω diaporeō**; from *1223* and *639; to be greatly perplexed* or *at a loss:*— great perplexity(1), greatly perplexed(3).

1281. **διαπραγματεύομαι diapragmateuomai**; from *1223* and *4231; to examine thoroughly, to gain by trading:*— business...done(1).

1282. **διαπρίω diapriō**; from *1223* and the same as *4249; to saw asunder, cut to the heart:*— cut(1), cut to the quick(1).

1283. **διαρπάζω diarpazō**; from *1223* and *726; to plunder:*— plunder(3).

1284. **διαρρήσσω diarrēssō**; from *1223* and *4486; to tear asunder:*— break(2), tearing(1), tore(2).

1285. **διασαφέω diasapheō**; from *1223* and **σαφής saphēs** *(clear); to make clear, explain fully:*— explain(1), reported(1).

1286. **διασείω diaseiō**; from *1223* and *4579; to shake violently, to intimidate:*— take money...by force(1).

1287. **διασκορπίζω diaskorpizō**; from *1223* and *4650;* generally *to separate,* spec. *to winnow,* fig. *to squander:*— scattered(6), scattered abroad(1), squandered(1), squandering(1).

1288. **διασπάω diaspaō**; from *1223* and *4685; to draw apart, tear asunder:*— torn to pieces(1), torn apart(1).

1289. **διασπείρω diaspeirō**; from *1223* and *4687; to sow throughout,* i.e. fig. *disperse* (in foreign lands):— scattered(3).

1290. **διασπορά diaspora**; from *1289; a dispersion* (Isr. in Gentile countries):— dispersed(1), Dispersion(1), scattered throughout(1).

1291. **διαστέλλω diastellō**; from *1223* and *4724; to set apart,* fig. *to distinguish, to charge expressly:*— command(1), gave...orders(3), gave...instruction(1), giving orders(1), ordered(1).

1292. **διάστημα diastēma**; from *1339; an interval:*— interval(1).

1293. **διαστολή diastolē**; from *1291; a separation, a difference:*— distinction(3).

1294. **διαστρέφω diastrephō**; from *1223* and *4762; to distort,* fig. *misinterpret, corrupt:*— make crooked(1), misleading(1), perverse(1), perverse things(1), perverted(2), turn...away(1).

1295. **διασῴζω diasōzō**; from *1223* and *4982; to bring safely through* (a danger), *to save thoroughly:*— bring...safely(1), bring...safely through(1), brought safely(2), brought safely through(1), cured(1), safely through(1), save the life(1), saved(1).

1296. **διαταγή diatagē**; from *1299; institution, ordinance:*— ordained(1), ordinance(1).

1297. **διάταγμα diatagma**; from *1299; an edict, mandate:*— edict(1).

1298. **διαταράσσω diatarassō**; from *1223* and *5015; to agitate greatly:*— very perplexed(1).

1299. **διατάσσω diatassō**; from *1223* and *5021; to arrange thoroughly,* i.e. *to charge, appoint:*— arrange(1), arranged(1), commanded(3), direct(1), directed(4), gave orders(2), giving instructions(1), ordained(1), ordered(1), orders(1).

1300. **διατελέω diateleō**; from *1223* and *5055; to accomplish thoroughly,* i.e. *to persist:*— constantly(1).

1301. **διατηρέω diatēreō**; from *1223* and *5083; to keep carefully:*— keep...free(1), treasured(1).

1302. **διατί diati**; another reading for *1223* and *5101,* q.v.

1303. **διατίθημι diatithēmi**; from *1223* and *5087; to place separately,* i.e. *dispose of by a will:*— grant(1), granted(1), made(3), make(2).

1304. **διατρίβω diatribō**; from *1223* and the same as *5147; to rub hard, rub away, to spend time:*— spending(1), spending time(2), spent(3), stayed(2), staying(1).

1305. **διατροφή diatrophē**; from *1223* and *5160; food, nourishment:*— food(1).

1306a. **διαυγάζω diaugazō**; from *1223* and *826; to shine through:*— dawns(1).

1306b. **διαυγής diaugēs**; from *1223* and *827; transparent:*— transparent(1).

1307. **διαφανής diaphanēs**; var. reading for *1306b,* q.v.

1308. **διαφέρω diapherō**; from *1223* and *5342; to carry through, carry about, to differ, make a difference, surpass:*— carry(1), differ(1), differs(1), driven about(1), essential(1), excellent(1), makes...difference(1), more valuable(3), spread(1), valuable(1), worth...more(1).

1309. **διαφεύγω diapheugō**; from *1223* and *5343; to flee through, escape:*— escape(1).

1310. **διαφημίζω diaphēmizō**; from *1223* and **φημίζω phēmizō** *(to spread a report);* from *5345; to spread abroad:*— spread...around(1), spread the news(1), widely spread(1).

1311. **διαφθείρω diaphtheirō**; from *1223* and *5351; to destroy utterly, to spoil, corrupt:*— decaying(1), depraved(1), destroy(2), destroyed(1), destroys(1).

1312. **διαφθορά diaphthora**; from *1311; destruction, corruption:*— decay(6).

1313. **διάφορος diaphoros**; from *1308; varying, excellent:*— differ(1), more excellent(2), various(1).

1314. **διαφυλάσσω diaphulassō**; from *1223* and *5442; to guard carefully:*— guard(1).

1315a. **διαχειρίζω diacheirizō**; from *1223* and **χειρίζω cheirizō** *(to handle);* from *5495; to have in hand,* thus *to lay hands on* (violently):— put...to death(1), put to death(1).

1315b. **διαχλευάζω diachleuazō**; from *1223* and *5512; to scoff, mock:*— mocking(1).

1316. **διαχωρίζω diachōrizō**; from *1223* and *5563; to separate entirely:*— leaving(1).

1317. **διδακτικός didaktikos**; from *1318; apt at teaching:*— able to teach(2).

1318. **διδακτός didaktos**; from *1321; instructed, taught:*— taught(3).

1319. **διδασκαλία didaskalia**; from *1320; instruction* (the function or the information):— doctrine(9), doctrines(3), instruction(1), teaching(7), teachings(1).

1320. **διδάσκαλος didaskalos**; from *1321; an instructor:*— Teacher(41), teacher(10), teachers(8).

1321. **διδάσκω didaskō**; a redupl. caus. form of **δάω daō** *(to learn); to teach:*— instructed(2), preaches(1), taught(13), teach(33), teaches(5), teaching(43).

1322. **διδαχή didachē**; from *1321; doctrine, teaching:*— instruction(2), teaching(27), teachings(1).

1323. **δίδραχμον didrachmon**; from *1364* and *1406; a double drachma:*— two-drachma(2).

1324. **Δίδυμος Didumos** *(double, twin);* "twin," *Didymus,* Gr. surname of the apostle Thomas (cf. *2381):*— Didymus(3).

1325. **δίδωμι didōmi**; redupl. from the root **δο- do-**; *to give* (in various senses lit. or fig.): add(1), allow(2), bestowed(4), cause(2), commanded*(1), dealing(1), drew(1), gave(79), give(122), given(117), gives(14), giving(12), grant(15), granted(10), granting(2), leave(1), make(1), offer(2), pass(1), pay(5), permitted(1), pour(1), poured(1), produce(1), produces(1), producing(1), put(6), puts(1), putting(1), show(1), struck*(1), utter(1), venture*(1), yielded(3).

1326. **διεγείρω diegeirō**; from *1223* and *1453; to arouse completely:*— got(2), stir(1), stirred(1), stirring(1), woke(1).

1327a. **διενθυμέομαι dienthumeomai**; from *1223* and *1760; to consider, reflect:*— reflecting(1).

1327b. **διέξοδος diexodos**; from *1223* and *1841; a way out through, an outlet:*— main(1).

1328. **διερμηνευτής diermēneutēs**; from *1329; an explainer, an interpreter:*— interpreter(1).

1329. **διερμηνεύω diermēneuō**; from *1223* and *2059; to explain thoroughly,* by impl. *to translate:*— explained(1), interpret(3), interprets(1), translated(1).

1330. **διέρχομαι dierchomai**; from *1223* and *2064; to go through, go about, to spread:*— come(1), coming(1), go(1), go across(1), go over(2), go straight(1), go through(1), going(1), going through(1), going throughout(1), gone through(2), made their way(1), pass(2), pass through(1), passed(1), passed through(7), passed...through(1), passes(2), passing(2), passing through(3), pierce(1), spread(1), spreading(1), through*(1), traveling through(2), went about(3).

1331. **διερωτάω dierōtaō**; from *1223* and *2065; to find by inquiry:*— asked directions(1).

1332. **διετής dietēs**; from *1364* and *2094; lasting two years, two years old:*— two years old(1).

1333. **διετία dietia**; from *1332; a space of two years:*— two years(1), two...years(1).

1334. **διηγέομαι diēgeomai**; from *1223* and *2233; to relate fully:*— describe(1), described(3), gave an account(1), relate(2), tell(1).

1335. **διήγησις diēgēsis**; from *1334; a narrative:*— account(1).

1336. **διηνεκής diēnekēs**; from the aor. of *1308; carried through, continuous:*— all time(2), continually(1), perpetually*(1).

1337. **διθάλασσος dithalassos**; from *1364* and *2281; divided into two seas, dividing the sea* (as a reef):— where two seas met(1).

1338. **διϊκνέομαι diikneomai**; from *1223* and the same as *2425; to go through, penetrate:*— piercing(1).

1339. **διΐστημι diistēmi**; from *1223* and *2476; to set apart, to intervene, make an interval:*— carried(1), farther(1), parted(1), passed(1).

1340. **διϊσχυρίζομαι diischurizomai**; from *1223* and **ἰσχυρίζομαι ischurizomai** *(to rely on* something, *feel confident);* from *2478; to lean upon, affirm confidently:*— insist(1), insisting(1).

1341. **δικαιοκρισία dikaiokrisia**; from *1342* and *2920; righteous judgment:*— righteous judgment(1).

1342. **δίκαιος dikaios**; from *1349; correct, righteous,* by impl. *innocent:*— innocent(1), just(6), justice(1), right(7), righteous(48), righteous man(8), righteous man's(1), righteous men(1), righteous one(4), righteous person(1), righteous persons(1).

1343. **δικαιοσύνη dikaiosunē**; from *1342; righteousness, justice:*— right(1), righteousness(90).

1344. **δικαιόω dikaioō**; from *1342; to show to be righteous, declare righteous:*— acknowledged...justice(1), acquitted(1), freed(3), justified(24), justifier(1), justifies(2), justify(4), vindicated(3).

1345. **δικαίωμα dikaiōma**; from *1344; an ordinance, a sentence of acquittal* or *condemnation, a righteous deed:*— act of righteousness(1), justification(1), ordinance(1), regulations(2), requirement(1), requirements(2), righteous acts(2).

1346. **δικαίως dikaiōs**; from *1342; righteously, justly:*— justly(1), ought(1), righteously(2), uprightly(1).

1347. **δικαίωσις dikaiōsis**; from *1344; the act of pronouncing righteous, acquittal:*— justification(2).

1348. **δικαστής dikastēs**; from **δικάζω dikazō** *(to judge); a judge:*— judge(2).

1349. **δίκη dikē**; a prim. word; *right* (as self-evident), *justice* (the principle, a decision or its execution):— justice(1), penalty(1), punishment(1).

1350. **δίκτυον diktuon**; from **δικεῖν dikein** *(to cast); a net:*— net(4), nets(8), nets nets(1).

1351. **δίλογος dilogos**; from *1364* and *3056; given to repetition, double-tongued:*— double-tongued(1).

1352. **διό dio**; from *1223* and *3739; wherefore, on which account:*— reason(1), so then(1), therefore(43), this reason(6), wherefore(1), why(1).

1353. **διοδεύω diodeuō**; from *1223* and *3593; to travel through:*— going around(1), traveled through(1).

1354. **Διονύσιος Dionusios**; from **Διόνυσος Dionusos** *(Dionysus,* Gr. god of wine and revelry); *Dionysius,* an Athenian:— Dionysius(1).

1355. **διόπερ dioper**; from *1352* and *4007a; for which very reason:*— therefore(2).

1356. **διοπετής diopetēs**; from **Διός Dios** *(of Zeus)* and the same as *4098; fallen from heaven:*— which fell down from heaven(1).

1357a. **διόρθωμα diorthōma**; from **διορθόω diorthoō** *(to make straight); a correction, a reform:*— reforms(1).

1357b. **διόρθωσις diorthōsis**; from the same as *1357a; a making straight, rectification:*— reformation(1).

1358. **διορύσσω diorussō**; from *1223* and *3736; to dig through* (as of breaking into a house):— break(2), broken(2).

Διός Dios; see *2203.*

1359. **Διόσκουροι Dioskouroi**; from **Διός Dios** (see *1356*) and pl. of **κοῦρος kouros** *(boy); the Dioscuri,* twin sons of Zeus (Castor and Pollux):— Twin brothers(1).

1360. **διότι dioti**; from *1223* and *3754; on the very account that, because, inasmuch as:*— because(14), therefore(2).

1361. **Διοτρέφης Diotrephēs**; from **Διός Dios** (see *1356*) and *5142;* "cherished by Zeus," *Diotrephes,* an opponent of the apostle John:— Diotrephes(1).

1362. **διπλοῦς diplous**; from *1364* and perh. *4144; twofold, double:*— double(1), double*(1), twice as much(2).

1363. **διπλόω diploō**; from *1362; to double:*— double*(1), give back(1).

1364. **δίς dis**; from *1417; twice:*— doubly(1), more*(2), twice(3).

1365a. **δισμυριάς dismurias**; from *1364* and *3463; twenty thousand:*— two hundred million*(1).

1365b. **διστάζω distazō**; from *1364; to duplicate, waver, doubt:*— doubt(1), doubtful(1).

1366. **δίστομος distomos**; from *1364* and *4750; double-mouthed, two-edged:*— two-edged(3).

1367. **δισχίλιοι dischilioi**; from *1364* and *5507; two thousand:*— two thousand(1).

1368. **διϋλίζω diulizō**; from *1223* and **ὑλίζω hulizō** *(to strain); to strain thoroughly, strain out:*— strain(1).

1369. **διχάζω dichazō**; from **δίχα dicha** *(apart); to cause a separation, separate,* fig. *alienate:*— set(1).

1370. **διχοστασία dichostasia**; from **διχοστατέω dichostateō** *(to stand apart); standing apart, dissension:*— dissensions(2).

1371. **διχοτομέω dichotomeō**; from the same as *1369* and **τέμνω temnō** *(to cut); to cut in two, cut asunder:*— cut...in pieces(2).

1372. **διψάω dipsaō**; from **δίψα dipsa** *(thirst); to thirst:*— am thirsty(1), thirst(5), thirsts(1), thirsty(9).

1373. **δίψος dipsos**; from the same as *1372; thirst:*— thirst(1).

1374. **δίψυχος dipsuchos**; from *1364* and *5590; of two minds, wavering:*— double-minded(2).

1375. **διωγμός diōgmos**; from *1377; persecution:*— persecution(5), persecutions(5).

1376. **διώκτης diōktēs**; from *1377; a persecutor:*— persecutor(1).

1377. **διώκω diōkō**; akin to a prim. vb. **δίω diō** *(put to flight); to put to flight, pursue,* by impl. *to persecute:*— persecute(10), persecuted(13), persecuting(7), persecutor(1), practicing(1), press(2), pursue(7), pursuing(2), run after(1), seek after(1).

1378. **δόγμα dogma**; from *1380; an opinion,* (a public) *decree:*— decree(1), decrees(3), ordinances(1).

1379. **δογματίζω dogmatizō**; from *1378; to decree, to subject oneself to an ordinance:*— submit...to decrees(1).

1380. **δοκέω dokeō**; from **δόκος dokos** *(opinion); to have an opinion, to seem:*— deem(1), expect(1), has a mind(1), inclined(1), recognized(1), regarded(1), reputation(3), reputed(1), seem(3), seemed best(1), seemed fitting(1), seemed good(4), seems(3), suppose(5), supposed(2), supposes(1), supposing(4), think(18), thinking(1), thinks(6), thought(4).

1381a. **δοκιμάζω dokimazō**; from *1384; to test,* by impl. *to approve:*— analyze(2), approve(3), approved(1), approves(1), examine(4), examines(1), prove(1), proving(1), see fit(1), test(2), tested(3), try(1), trying to learn(1).

1381b. **δοκιμασία dokimasia**; from *1381a; a testing, a proving:*— testing(1).

1382. **δοκιμή dokimē**; from *1384;* (the process or result of) *trial, proving, approval:*— ordeal(1), proof(2), proven character(2), proven worth(1), test(1).

1383. **δοκίμιον dokimion**; from *1384; a testing:*— proof(1), testing(1).

1384. **δόκιμος dokimos**; from *1209; tested, approved:*— approved(7).

1385. **δοκός dokos**; from *1209* (through the idea of holding up); *a beam of timber:*— log(6).

1386. **δόλιος dolios**; from *1388; deceitful:*— deceitful(1).

1387. **δολιόω dolioō**; from *1386; to deceive:*— deceiving(1).

1388. **δόλος dolos**; from the root **δελ- del-**; *a bait,* fig. *craft, deceit:*— deceit(9), stealth(2).

1389. **δολόω doloō**; from *1388; to ensnare,* fig. *to adulterate:*— adulterating(1).

1390. **δόμα doma**; from *1325; a gift:*— gift(1), gifts(3).

1391. **δόξα doxa**; from *1380; opinion* (always good in N.T.), hence *praise, honor, glory:*— approval(2), brightness(1), glories(1), glorious(5), glory(155), honor(1), majesties(2).

1392. **δοξάζω doxazō**; from *1391; to render* or *esteem glorious* (in a wide application):— full of glory(1), glorified(20), glorifies(1), glorify(19), glorifying(12), had glory(1), has...glory(1), honor(1), honored(2), magnify(1), praised(1), praising(1).

1393. **Δορκάς Dorkas**; from **δέρκομαι derkomai** *(to see clearly); "gazelle" (an animal with large bright eyes), Dorcas,* a Chr. woman:— Dorcas(2).

1394. **δόσις dosis**; from *1325; the act of giving, a gift:*— giving(1), thing given(1).

1395. **δότης dotēs**; from *1325; a giver:*— giver(1).

1396. **δουλαγωγέω doulagōgeō**; from *1401* and *71; to enslave,* fig. *subdue:*— make...slave(1).

1397. **δουλεία douleia**; from *1398; slavery:*— slavery(4), slaves(1).

1398. **δουλεύω douleuō**; from *1401; to be a slave, to serve:*— bondage(1), enslaved(3), render service(1), serve(10), served(1), serves(1), serving(4), slavery(1), slaves(3).

1399. **δούλη doulē**; fem. of *1401; female slave, bondmaid.*

1400. **δοῦλος doulos**; adj. from *1401; slavish, servile.*

1401. **δοῦλος doulos**; of unc. der.; *a slave:*— bond-servant(11), bond-servants(12), bondslave(3), bondslaves(8), both men and women(8), servants(1), slave(58), slave's(1), slaves(39).

1402. **δουλόω douloō**; from *1401; to enslave, bring under subjection:*— became slaves(1), enslaved(4), held in bondage(1), made a slave(1), under bondage(1).

1403. **δοχή dochē**; from *1209; a reception, a banquet:*— reception(2).

1404. **δράκων drakōn**; from an alt. form of **δέρκομαι derkomai** *(to look); a dragon* (a mythical monster):— dragon(13).

δραμεῖν dramein; see *5143.*

1405. **δράσσομαι drassomai**; a prim. vb.; *to grasp,* fig. *entrap:*— catches(1).

1406. **δραχμή drachmē**; from *1405; as much as one can hold in the hand, a drachma* (a Gr. coin made of silver):— coin(2), coins(1), silver coins(1).

1407. **δρέπανον drepanon**; from **δρέπω drepō** *(to pluck); a sickle, a pruning hook:*— sickle(8).

1408. **δρόμος dromos**; from **δραμεῖν dramein** *(to run); a course, race:*— course(3).

1409. **Δρούσιλλα Drousilla**; a fem. dim. of the Lat. *Drusus; Drusilla,* a member of the Herodian family:— Drusilla(1).

1410. **δύναμαι dunamai**; a prim. vb.; *to be able, to have power:*— able(50), am able(2), can(60), cannot(1), cannot*(59), could(24), may(1), might(3), power...has(1), unable*(7).

1411. **δύναμις dunamis**; from *1410;* (miraculous) *power, might, strength:*— ability(4), meaning(1), mightily(1), mighty(1), miracle(2), miracles(17), miraculous powers(3), power(83), powers(6), strength(2), wealth(1).

1412. **δυναμόω dunamoō**; from *1411; to make strong, enable:*— made strong(1), strengthened(1).

1413. **δυνάστης dunastēs**; from *1410; a ruler, a potentate:*— court official(1), rulers(1), Sovereign(1).

1414. **δυνατέω dunateō**; from *1415; to be able, be powerful:*— able(2), mighty(1).

1415. **δυνατός dunatos**; from *1410; strong, mighty, powerful:*— able(6), could(1), impossible*(1), influential men(1), man of power(1), mighty(3), mighty one(1), possible(12), power(1), powerful(1), strong(3), strong enough(1).

1416. **δύνω dunō**; a form of **δύω duō** *(to sink); to enter, to sink into:*— set(1), setting(1).

1417. **δύο duo**; a prim. num.; *two:*— both(1), forty-two*(2), pairs(2), twenty(1), two(124), two men(3).

1418. **δυσ- dus-**; a pref. of unc. der.; like *un-* or *mis-* (as in *unrest, misjudge*), nullifies good sense or increases bad sense of a word.

1419. **δυσβάστακτος dusbastaktos**; from *1418* and **βαστακτός bastaktos** *(borne);* from *941; hard to be borne, oppressive:*— hard to bear(1).

1420. **δυσεντέριον dusenterion**; from *1418* and **ἔντερον enteron** *(intestine); dysentery:*— dysentery(1).

1421. **δυσερμήνευτος dusermēneutos**; from *1418* and *2059; hard of interpretation:*— hard to explain(1).

1422a. **δύσις dusis**; from *1416; a sinking, setting.*

1422b. **δύσκολος duskolos**; from *1418* and **κόλον kolon** *(food); hard to satisfy with food,* hence generally *hard to please, difficult:*— hard(1).

1423. **δυσκόλως duskolōs**; adv. from *1422b; with difficulty:*— hard(3).

1424. **δυσμή dusmē**; from *1416; a setting* (as of the sun), by impl. (the) *western* (region):— west(5).

1425. **δυσνόητος dusnoētos**; from *1418* and the same as *453; hard to understand:*— hard to understand(1).

1426a. **δυσφημέω dusphēmeō**; from *1418* and *5345; to use evil words, to speak ill of:*— slandered(1).

1426b. **δυσφημία dusphēmia**; from *1418* and *5345; evil speaking, defamation:*— evil report(1).

δύω duō; see *1416.*

1427. **δώδεκα dōdeka**; from *1417* and *1176; two and ten,* i.e. *twelve:*— twelve(74).

1428. **δωδέκατος dōdekatos**; from *1427; twelfth:*— twelfth(1).

1429. **δωδεκάφυλον dōdekaphulon**; from adj. **δωδεκάφυλος dōdekaphulos** *(of twelve tribes);* from *1427* and *5443; the twelve tribes:*— twelve tribes(1).

1430. **δῶμα dōma**; from **δέμω demō** *(to build); a house, a housetop:*— housetop(4), housetops(2), roof(1).

1431. **δωρεά dōrea**; from *1325; a gift:*— freely(1), gift(12), needlessly(1), without a cause(1), without charge(1), without cost(2), without paying(1).

1432. **δωρεάν dōrean**; adv. from *1431; as a gift, to no purpose:*— freely(1).

1433. **δωρέομαι dōreomai**; from *1435; to give, present, bestow:*— granted(3).

1434. **δώρημα dōrēma**; from *1433; a gift, a bestowment:*— gift(2).

1435. **δῶρον dōron**; from *1325; a gift, present,* spec. *a sacrifice:*— gift(1), gifts(8), given(2), offering(8).

E

1436. **ἔα ea**; appar. imper. of *1439; ah! ha!* (interj. expressing surprise, indignation, fear):— let...alone(1).

1437. **ἐάν ean**; contr. from *1487* and *302; if* (a conditional particle used like *1487,* but usually with the Gr. subjunctive mood):— case(1), everyone(1), except*(1), if(222), if*(2), or*(1), though(2), unless*(34), whatever*(22), when(2), whenever*(2), wherever*(8), whether*(1), whoever*(17), whomever*(2).

1438. **ἑαυτοῦ heautou**; from a prim. pron. **ἕ he** *(him, her)* and gen. (dat. or acc.) of *846; of himself, herself, itself:*— aside*(1), conscious*(1), each other(2), herself(4), himself(91), itself(12), mind(1), none*(1), one another(13), oneself(1), ourselves(19), own(48), own estimation(2), own initiative(3), own persons(1), own...himself(1), senses(1), themselves(44), venture*(1), within*(1), yourselves(32).

1439. **ἐάω eaō**; a prim. vb., see also *1436; to let alone, leave:*— allow(2), allowed(2), leaving(1), left(1), let(2), permit(1), permitted(1), stop(1).

1440. **ἑβδομήκοντα hebdomēkonta**; from *1442* and a modified form of *1176; seventy:*— seventy(3), seventy-five*(1), seventy-six*(1).

1441. **ἑβδομηκοντάκις hebdomēkontakis**; mult. adv. from *1440; seventy times:*— seventy times(1).

1442. **ἕβδομος hebdomos**; ord. from *2033; seventh:*— seventh(9).

1443. **Ἔβερ Eber**; of Heb. or. [5677]; *Heber,* an ancestor of Christ:— Heber(1).

1444. **Ἑβραϊκός Hebraikos**; from *1443; Hebrew,* the Jewish language.

1445. **Ἑβραῖος Hebraios**; from *1443; a Hebrew* or *Jew:*— Hebrew of Hebrews(1), Hebrews(2).

1446. **Ἑβραΐς Hebrais**; from *1443; Hebrew,* the Ara. vernacular of Pal.:— Hebrew(3).

1447. **Ἑβραϊστί Hebraisti**; adv. from *1446; in Hebrew, in Aramaic:*— Hebrew(7).

1448. **ἐγγίζω eggizō**; from *1451; to make near,* refl. *to come near:*— approached(10), approaching(7), came(1), came close(1), came near(1), come near(2), comes near(2), coming near(1), draw near(3), drawing near(2), hand(7), near(5).

1449. **ἐγγράφω eggraphō**; from *1722* and *1125; to inscribe, to enter in a register:*— recorded(1), written(2).

1450. **ἔγγυος egguos**; from **ἐγγύη egguē** *(a security); under good security* (adj.), *guarantee* (noun):— guarantee(1).

1451. **ἐγγύς eggus**; of unc. or.; *near* (in place or time):— close(1), near(27), nearby(1), nearer(1), ready(1).

1452. **ἐγγύτερον egguteron**; adv. from neut. of cptv. of *1451,* q.v.:— get(1).

1453. **ἐγείρω egeirō**; a prim. vb.; *to waken, to raise up:*— arise(5), arisen(2), arises(1), awake(1), awaken(1), awoke(1), cause(1), get(17), gets(2), got(11), lift(1), raise(10), raised(61), raises(2), rise(5), rise again(2), risen(13), rose(1), rose again(1), stand(1), woke(3).

1454. **ἔγερσις egersis**; from *1453; a rousing, a rising* (from death):— resurrection(1).

1455. **ἐγκάθετος egkathetos**; from *1722* and a der. of *2524; hired to lie in wait, lying in wait:*— spies(1).

1456. **ἐγκαίνια egkainia**; neut. pl. comp. from *1722* and *2537; dedication, renewal* (of religious services):— feast of the Dedication(1).

1457a. **ἐγκανίζω egkanizō**; from *1456; to renew, inaugurate:*— inaugurated(2).

1457b. **ἐγκακέω egkakeō**; from *1722* and *2556; to lose heart:*— grow weary(1), lose heart(5).

1458. **ἐγκαλέω egkaleō**; from *1722* and *2564; to call in* (as a debt or demand), i.e. *bring to account:*— accused(4), accusing(1), bring a charge(1), bring charges against(1).

1459. **ἐγκαταλείπω egkataleipō**; from *1722* and *2641; to leave behind,* i.e. (in a good sense) *let remain over* or (in a bad sense) *desert:*— abandon(1), abandoned(1), deserted(2), forsake(1), forsaken(3), forsaking(1), left(1).

1460. **ἐγκατοικέω egkatoikeō**; from *1722* and *2730; to settle down in* (a place), *reside:*— living(1).

1461a. **ἐγκαυχάομαι egkauchaomai**; from *1722* and *2744; to take pride in, glory in:*—speak proudly(1).

1461b. **ἐγκεντρίζω egkentrizō**; from *1722* and **κεντρίζω kentrizō** *(to prick, goad); to ingraft, graft in:*— graft(1), grafted(5).

1462. **ἔγκλημα egklēma**; from *1458; an accusation:*— accusation(1), charges(1).

1463. **ἐγκομβόομαι egkomboomai**; from *1722* and **κομβόομαι komboomai** *(to gird oneself); to put on oneself* (as a garment):— clothe(1).

1464. **ἐγκοπή egkopē**; from *1465; a hindrance:*— hindrance(1).

1465. **ἐγκόπτω egkoptō**; from *1722* and *2875; to cut into,* i.e. fig. *impede, detain:*— hindered(3), prevented(1), weary(1).

1466. **ἐγκράτεια egkrateia**; from *1468; mastery, self-control:*— self-control(4).

1467. **ἐγκρατεύομαι egkrateuomai**; from *1468; to exercise self-control:*— exercises self-control(1), have self-control(1).

1468. **ἐγκρατής egkratēs**; from *1722* and *2904; strong, master of, self-controlled:*— self-controlled(1).

1469. **ἐγκρίνω egkrinō**; from *1722* and *2919; to judge in, to reckon among:*— class(1).

1470. **ἐγκρύπτω egkruptō**; from *1722* and *2928; to conceal in:*— hid(1).

1471. **ἔγκυος egkuos**; from *1722* and the same as *2949; pregnant:*— child(1).

1472. **ἐγχρίω egchriō**; from *1722* and *5548; to rub in* (oil):— anoint(1).

1473. **ἐγώ egō**; a prim. pron. of the first pers.; *I* (only expressed when emphatic):— have(2), mine(10), mine*(1), myself(11), number(1), ours(8), ourselves(4), part(2), say(1).

1474. **ἐδαφίζω edaphizō**; from *1475; to raze:*— level...to the ground(1).

1475. **ἔδαφος edaphos**; of unc. der.; *a basis, bottom, ground:*— ground(1).

1476. **ἑδραῖος hedraios**; from **ἕδρα hedra** *(a seat); sitting, steadfast:*— firm(1), steadfast(2).

1477. **ἑδραίωμα hedraiōma**; from *1476; a support,* fig. *a basis:*— support(1).

1478. **Ἐζεκίας Hezekias**; of Heb. or. [2396]; *Hezekiah,* a king of Judah:— Hezekiah(2).

1479. **ἐθελοθρησκία ethelothrēskia**; from an older form of *2309* and *2356; self-willed* (arbitrary and unwarranted) *piety:*— self-made religion(1).

1480. **ἐθίζω ethizō**; from *1485; to accustom,* i.e. *the established custom* (perf. pass. part.):— custom(1).

1481. **ἐθνάρχης ethnarchēs**; from *1484* and *757; an ethnarch,* a governor (not king) of a province:— ethnarch(1).

1482. **ἐθνικός ethnikos**; from *1484; national, foreign,* i.e. spec. *a Gentile:*— Gentile(1), Gentiles(3).

1483. **ἐθνικῶς ethnikōs**; adv. from *1482; as a Gentile:*— like the Gentiles(1).

1484. **ἔθνος ethnos**; prob. from a prim. root; *a race, a nation,* pl. *the nations* (as distinct from Isr.):— Gentiles(93), nation(30), nations(37), pagans(1), people(2).

1485. **ἔθος ethos**; from *1486; custom, a usage* (prescribed by habit or law):— custom(6), customs(5), habit(1).

1486. **ἔθω ethō**; a prim. vb.; *to be accustomed,* part. *custom:*— accustomed(1), custom(3).

1487. **εἰ ei**; a prim. particle; *if, whether* (a cond. part. introducing circumstances nec. for a given proposition to be true; sometimes used with a command or as an indirect question, etc.):— although*(1), if(341), no(1), only(1), only*(11), suppose*(1), though(7), though*(5), unless(2), unless*(5), until*(1), whatever*(1), whether(19), whoever*(3).

1488. **εἶ ei**; second pers. sing. pres. of *1510,* q.v.

1489. **εἴγε eige**; from *1487* and *1065; if indeed, seeing that, unless,* with neg. *otherwise:*— inasmuch(1).

1490a. **εἰδέα eidea**; from a form of *3708; form, appearance:*— appearance(1).

1490b. **εἰ δὲ μή(γε) ei de mē(ge)**; from *1487, 1161,* and *3361* (sometimes with *1065* added); *but if not:*— else(3), otherwise(7).

1491a. **εἶδον eidon**; a prim. vb. used only in certain tenses, see *3708.*

1491b. **εἶδος eidos**; from *1492; that which is seen, form:*— appearance(1), form(3), sight(1).

1492. **εἴδω eidō**; see *1491a* and *3609a.*

1493. **εἰδωλεῖον eidōleion**; from *1497; an idol's temple:*— idol's temple(1).

1494. **εἰδωλόθυτος eidōlothutos**; from *1497* and *2380; sacrificed to idols:*— sacrificed to an idol(1), sacrificed to idols(1), thing sacrificed(1), thing sacrificed to idols(1), things sacrificed(6), things sacrificed to idols(6).

1495. **εἰδωλολατρία eidōlolatria**; from *1497* and *2999; image worship:*— idolatries(1), idolatry(3).

1496. **εἰδωλολάτρης eidōlolatrēs**; from *1497* and **λάτρις latris** *(a hired servant); an image worshiper:*— idolater(2), idolaters(5).

1497. **εἴδωλον eidōlon**; from *1491b; an image* (i.e. for worship), by impl. *a false god:*— idol(4), idols(7).

1498. **εἴην eiēn**; optative (like English subjunctive) pres. of *1510,* q.v.

1499. **εἰ καί ei kai**; from *1487* and *2532,* q.v.

1500. **εἰκῇ eikē**; adv. prob. akin to *1635; without cause* or *reason, vainly:*— nothing(1), vain(4), without cause(1).

1501. **εἴκοσι eikosi**; a prim. word; *twenty:*— three*(1), twenty(3), twenty-four*(6), twenty-three*(1).

1502. **εἴκω eikō**; a prim. vb.; *to yield:*— yield(1).

1503. **εἴκω eikō**; see *1858a.*

1504. **εἰκών eikōn**; from *1503; an image,* i.e. lit. *statue,* fig. *representation:*— form(1), image(19), likeness(3).

1505. **εἰλικρίνεια eilikrineia**; from *1506; clearness,* by impl. *purity, sincerity:*— sincerity(3).

1506. **εἰλικρινής eilikrinēs**; of unc. or., perh. from **εἵλη heilē** *(the sun's ray)* and *2919; judged by sunlight, unalloyed, pure:*— sincere(2).

1507. **εἱλίσσω heilissō**; var. reading for *1667,* q.v.

1508. **εἰ μή ei mē**; from *1487* and *3361; if not:*— except(40), except*(1), more than(1), unless(1).

1509. **εἰ μήτι ei mēti**; from *1487* and *3385; if not somewhat:*— except(1).

1510. **εἰμί eimi**; a prol. form of a prim. and defective vb.; *I exist, I am:*— accompanied*(1), accompany*(2), am(138), amount(1), amounts(1), appear*(1), asserted*(1), become*(5), been(45), been*(1), being(26), belong(3), belonged*(1), belonging(1), belonging*(1), belongs(4), bring*(1), came(1), come(5), consist(1), crave*(1), depends*(1), do(1), done*(1), exist(3), existed(4), existed*(1), falls(1), found(1), had(8), happen(4), have(2), have come(1), lived(1), mean(1), mean*(2), means(7), meant(2), originate(1), owns(1), remain(3), remained(1), rest(1), sided(1), stayed(2), themselves(1), there(6), turn(1).

1511. **εἶναι einai**; pres. inf. of *1510,* q.v.

1512. **εἴπερ eiper**; from *1487* and *4007a; if perhaps:*— after all(1), if(2), if indeed(2), since indeed(1).

1513a. **εἶπον eipon**; see *3004*.

1513b. **εἴ πως ei pōs**; from *1487* and *4458; if somehow:*— order(1).

1514. **εἰρηνεύω eirēneuō**; from *1515; to bring to peace, to be at peace:*— live in peace(2), peace(2).

1515. **εἰρήνη eirēnē**; of unc. der., perh. from **εἴρω eirō** *(to join):* lit. or fig. *peace,* by impl. *welfare:*— peace(91), undisturbed*(1).

1516. **εἰρηνικός eirēnikos**; from *1515; peaceful:*— peaceable(1), peaceful(1).

1517. **εἰρηνοποιέω eirēnopoieō**; from *1518; to make peace:*— made peace(1).

1518. **εἰρηνοποιός eirēnopoios**; from *1515* and *4160; peacemaking, a peacemaker:*— peacemakers(1).

εἴρω eirō; see *3004*.

1519. **εἰς eis**; a prim. prep.; *to* or *into* (indicating the point reached or entered, of place, time, fig. purpose, result):— about(1), against(18), among(10), become*(5), before(2), before*(1), benefit(1), bestowed(1), beyond(1), beyond*(2), bring about(1), bring*(1), continually*(1), eliminated*(2), end(2), even(1), ever*(2), forever*(1), forward*(3), leading(2), leads(1), mine*(1), never*(1), next*(1), onto(2), over(1), perpetually*(1), reference(2), regard(3), relation(1), respect(2), result(3), resulted(2), resulting(10), sake(1), so(34), throughout(3), toward(23), until(4), view(3), why*(4).

1520. **εἷς heis** (masc.) or

μία mia (fem.) or

ἕν hen (neut.); a prim. num.; *one:*— agreement(1), alike*(1), alone(3), common(1), detail(1), first(9), individual(2), individually*(1), lone(1), man(1), nothing*(1), one(282), one another(1), one man(2), one thing(5), one*(2), person(1), single(1), smallest(1), someone(2), thirty-nine*(1), unity(1).

1521. **εἰσάγω eisagō**; from *1519* and *71; to bring in, to introduce:*— bring(1), brings(1), brought(9).

1522. **εἰσακούω eisakouō**; from *1519* and *191; to listen, to obey:*— heard(4), listen(1).

1523. **εἰσδέχομαι eisdechomai**; from *1519* and *1209; to admit, to receive* (into one's favor):— welcome(1).

1524. **εἴσειμι eiseimi**; from *1519* and **εἶμι eimi** *(to come* or *go); to go in, enter:*— entering(1), go(1), went(2).

1525. **εἰσέρχομαι eiserchomai**; from *1519* and *2064; to go in* (to), *enter:*— came(10), come(15), comes(3), coming(1), enter(66), entered(63), entering(6), enters(7), go(8), go*(1), gone(1), reached(1), started(1), went(8).

1526. **εἰσί eisi**; third pers. pl. pres. ind. of *1510,* q.v.

1527. **εἷς καθ' εἷς heis kath heis**; see *1520* and *2596*.

1528. **εἰσκαλέομαι eiskaleomai**; from *1519* and *2564; to call in:*— invited(1).

1529. **εἴσοδος eisodos**; from *1519* and *3598; an entrance, a means* or *place of entering:*— coming(1), coming*(1), enter(1), entrance(1), reception(1).

1530. **εἰσπηδάω eispēdaō**; from *1519* and **πηδάω pēdaō** *(to leap, spring); to rush in:*— rushed(1).

1531. **εἰσπορεύομαι eisporeuomai**; from *1519* and *4198;* lit. or fig. *to enter:*— came(1), come(1), enter(5), entered(2), entering(2), enters(1), go(1), goes(3), moving about freely*(1), went(1).

1532. **εἰστρέχω eistrechō**; from *1519* and *5143; to run in:*— ran(1).

1533. **εἰσφέρω eispherō**; from *1519* and *5342;* lit. or fig. *to carry inward:*— bring(3), bringing(1), brought(2), lead(2).

1534. **εἶτα eita**; a prim. particle; *then, next, therefore* (an adv. denoting sequence):— furthermore(1), then(12).

1535a. **εἴτε eite**; from *1487* and *5037; if*— if, whether— or:— either...or(1), if(11), or(22), or if(1), whether(13), whether...or(6), whether...or...or(2).

1535b. **εἶτεν eiten**; Ionic and Hellenistic for *1534; then:*— then(2).

1536. **εἴ τις ei tis**; see *1487* and *5100*.

1537. **ἐκ ek** or

ἐξ ex; a prim. prep. denoting or.; *from, from out of:*— after(1), against(1), among(18), based(5), basis(2), because(10), belonged*(1), belonging*(1), depends(1), depends*(1), derived(1), grudgingly*(1), heavenly*(1), inspired(1), means(1), over(1), reason(1), result(4), say*(1), since(1), some(3), through(1), under(1), utterly*(1), way(1), without*(1).

1538. **ἕκαστος hekastos**; a prim. word; *each, every:*— each(36), each man(4), each man's(3), each one(22), each one's(1), each person(2), every(1), every man(2), every one(2), every*(1), everyone(4), personal(1).

1539. **ἑκάστοτε hekastote**; from *1538; each time, always:*— any time(1).

1540. **ἑκατόν hekaton**; a prim. word; *a hundred:*— hundred(7), hundredfold(4), hundreds(1), one hundred(4).

1541. **ἑκατονταετής hekatontaetēs**; from *1540* and *2094; a hundred years old:*— hundred years old(1).

1542. **ἑκατονταπλασίων hekatontaplasiōn**; from *1540* and perh. a cptv. of *4183; a hundred times:*— hundred times(2), hundred times as great(1), hundred times as much(1).

1543. **ἑκατοντάρχης hekatontarchēs** or

ἑκατόνταρχος hekatontarchos; from *1540* and *757; a centurion, a captain of one hundred men:*— centurion(16), centurion's(1), centurions(3).

1544a. **ἐκβαίνω ekbainō**; from *1537* and the same as *939; to go out:*— impelled(1), went(1).

1544b. **ἐκβάλλω ekballō**; from *1537* and *906; to expel, to drive, cast* or *send out:*— brings(3), cast(28), casting(5), casts(5), drive(4), driven(1), drove(4), eliminated*(1), leads(1), leave(1), put(2), puts(1), puts forth(1), putting(1), scorn(1), send(2), sending...away(1), sent(3), sent...away(1), take(6), threw(3), throw(3), throwing(1), thrown(1), took(1).

1545. **ἔκβασις ekbasis**; from *1544a; an exit, outcome:*— result(1), way of escape(1).

1546. **ἐκβολή ekbolē**; from *1544b; a throwing out,* i.e. spec. *a throwing overboard* (of the cargo):— jettison the cargo(1).

1547. **ἐκγαμίζω ekgamizō**; var. reading for *1061a,* q.v.

1548. **ἐκγαμίσκω ekgamiskō**; var. reading for *1061b,* q.v.

1549. **ἔκγονος ekgonos**; der. of *1537* and the same as *1096; born of, a descendant,* i.e. *a grandchild:*— grandchildren(1).

1550. **ἐκδαπανάω ekdapanaō**; from *1537* and *1159; to expend wholly,* i.e. *to exhaust:*— expended(1).

1551. **ἐκδέχομαι ekdechomai**; from *1537* and *1209; to take* or *receive,* by impl. *to await, expect:*— expect(1), looking(1), wait(1), waiting(3), waits(1).

1552. **ἔκδηλος ekdēlos**; from *1537* and *1212; wholly evident:*— obvious(1).

1553. **ἐκδημέω ekdēmeō**; from *1537* and *1218; to be away from home, absent:*— absent(3).

1554. **ἐκδίδωμι ekdidōmi**; from *1537* and *1325; to give up, give out, let out for hire:*— rent(1), rented(3).

1555. **ἐκδιηγέομαι ekdiēgeomai**; from *1537* and *1334; to tell in detail:*— describe(1), describing in detail(1).

1556. **ἐκδικέω ekdikeō**; from *1558; to vindicate, to avenge:*— avenged(1), avenging(1), give...legal protection(2), legal protection(2), punish(1), take...revenge(1).

1557. **ἐκδίκησις ekdikēsis**; from *1556; vengeance, vindication:*— avenging of wrong(1), justice(2), punishment(1), retribution(1), vengeance(4).

1558. **ἔκδικος ekdikos**; from *1537* and *1349; exacting penalty from, avenging:*— avenger(2).

1559. **ἐκδιώκω ekdiōkō**; from *1537* and *1377; to pursue out,* i.e. *expel* or *persecute:*— drove(1).

1560. **ἔκδοτος ekdotos**; from *1537* and *1325; given out* or *over,* i.e. *surrendered:*— delivered(1).

1561. **ἐκδοχή ekdochē**; from *1551; a receiving from, expectation:*— expectation(1).

1562. **ἐκδύω ekduō**; from *1537* and the same as *1416; to take off, to put off:*— stripped(2), took...off(2), unclothed(1).

1563. **ἐκεῖ ekei**; of unc. der.; *there,* by ext. *to there:*— bystanders*(1), case(1), city(1), nearby(1), over there(1), place(2), place there(4), there(84).

1564. **ἐκεῖθεν ekeithen**; from *1563; from there:*— there(24), town(1).

1565. **ἐκεῖνος ekeinos**; from *1563; that one* (or neut. *that thing),* often intensified by the art. preceding:— once*(3), one(4), other(1), these(1), this(2), those(35), those things(1), very(1), what(1).

1566. **ἐκεῖσε ekeise**; from *1563; to there:*— there(2).

1567a. **ἐκζητέω ekzēteō**; from *1537* and *2212; to seek out, demand, inquire:*— charged(2), made careful*(1), searches(1), seek(2), seeks(1), sought(1).

1567b. **ἐκζήτησις ekzētēsis**; from *1567a; a questioning:*— speculation(1).

1568. **ἐκθαμβέω ekthambeō**; from *1569a; to amaze, to be amazed:*— amazed(3), very distressed(1).

1569a. **ἔκθαμβος ekthambos**; from *1537* and *2285; utterly astounded, amazed:*— full of amazement(1).

1569b. **ἐκθαυμάζω ekthaumazō**; from *1537* and *2296; to wonder greatly:*— amazed(1).

1570. **ἔκθετος ekthetos**; from *1620; cast out,* i.e. *exposed* (to perish):— expose*(1).

1571. **ἐκκαθαίρω ekkathairō**; from *1537* and *2508; to cleanse thoroughly:*— clean(1), cleanses(1).

1572. **ἐκκαίω ekkaiō**; from *1537* and *2545; to kindle, to be inflamed:*— burned(1).

1573. **ἐκκακέω ekkakeō**; var. reading for *1457b*, q.v.

1574. **ἐκκεντέω ekkenteō**; from *1537* and the same as *2759; to prick out, to pierce:*— pierced(2).

1575. **ἐκκλάω ekklaō**; from *1537* and *2806; to break off:*— broken off(3).

1576. **ἐκκλείω ekkleiō**; from *1537* and *2808; to shut out:*— excluded(1), shut(1).

1577. **ἐκκλησία ekklēsia**; from *1537* and *2564; an assembly, a* (religious) *congregation:*—assembly(3), church(74), churches(35), congregation(2).

1578. **ἐκκλίνω ekklinō**; from *1537* and *2827; to deviate, to turn away* (from someone or something):— turn away(2), turned aside(1).

1579. **ἐκκολυμβάω ekkolumbaō**; from *1537* and *2860; to swim out of:*— swim away(1).

1580. **ἐκκομίζω ekkomizō**; from *1537* and *2865; to carry out* (for burial):— carried(1).

1581. **ἐκκόπτω ekkoptō**; from *1537* and *2875; to cut off, cut down, cut out,* fig. *to frustrate:*— cut...off(5), cut down(5).

1582. **ἐκκρεμάννυμι ekkremannumi**; from *1537* and *2910; to hang from, hang upon* (the lips of a speaker), i.e. *to listen closely:*— hanging(1).

1583. **ἐκλαλέω eklaleō**; from *1537* and *2980; to speak out, divulge:*— tell(1).

1584. **ἐκλάμπω eklampō**; from *1537* and *2989; to shine out:*— shine forth(1).

1585. **ἐκλανθάνομαι eklanthanomai**; from *1537* and *2990; to forget utterly:*— forgotten(1).

1586. **ἐκλέγω eklegō**; from *1537* and *3004* (in the sense of *pick up*)*; to select:*— choose(4), chose(7), chosen(8), made a choice(1), picking(1), select(1).

1587. **ἐκλείπω ekleipō**; from *1537* and *3007; to leave out, leave off,* by impl. *to cease:*— come to an end(1), fail(1), fails(1), obscured(1).

1588. **ἐκλεκτός eklektos**; from *1586; select,* by impl. *favorite:*— choice(2), choice man(1), chosen(1), chosen(9), chosen one(1), elect(8).

1589. **ἐκλογή eklogē**; from *1586; a* (divine) *selection:*— choice(4), choosing(1), chosen(1), those who were chosen(1).

1590. **ἐκλύω ekluō**; from *1537* and *3089; to loose, release, to grow weary:*— faint(3), grow weary(1), lose(1).

1591. **ἐκμάσσω ekmasso**; from *1537* and **μάσσω masso** *(to knead); to knead out,* by anal. *to wipe dry:*— wipe(1), wiped(3), wiping(1).

1592. **ἐκμυκτηρίζω ekmuktērizō**; from *1537* and *3456; to hold up the nose in derision of:*— scoffing(1), sneering(1).

1593. **ἐκνεύω ekneuō**; from *1537* and *3506; to bend the head away, to withdraw:*— slipped away(1).

1594. **ἐκνήφω eknēphō**; from *1537* and *3525; to become sober* (after drunkenness):— become sober-minded(1).

1595. **ἑκούσιος hekousios**; from *1635; of free will, voluntary:*— free will(1).

1596. **ἑκουσίως hekousiōs**; from *1595; voluntarily:*— voluntarily(1), willfully(1).

1597. **ἔκπαλαι ekpalai**; from *1537* and *3819; long ago, for a long while:*— long ago(2).

1598. **ἐκπειράζω ekpeirazō**; from *1537* and *3985; to test thoroughly, tempt:*— put(2), put...to the test(1), test(2), try(1).

1599. **ἐκπέμπω ekpempō**; from *1537* and *3992; to send forth:*— sent(1), sent...away(1).

1600a. **ἐκπερισσῶς ekperissōs**; adv. from *1537* and *4057; more exceedingly:*— insistently(1).

1600b. **ἐκπετάννυμι ekpetannumi**; from *1537* and **πετάννυμι petannumi** *(to spread out); to spread out* (as a sail), *to stretch forth:*— stretched(1).

1601a. **ἐκπηδάω ekpēdaō**; from *1537* and **πηδάω pēdaō** *(to leap, spring); to leap out:*— rushed(1).

1601b. **ἐκπίπτω ekpiptō**; from *1537* and *4098; to drop away,* fig. *to lose, become inefficient:*— failed(1), fall(1), fall away(1), fallen(1), falls off(2), fell off(1), run aground(3).

1602. **ἐκπλέω ekpleō**; from *1537* and *4126; to sail away:*— put out to sea(1), sailed(1), sailed away(1).

1603. **ἐκπληρόω ekplēroō**; from *1537* and *4137; to fill full, to fulfill:*— fulfilled(1).

1604. **ἐκπλήρωσις ekplērōsis**; from *1603; a completion, fulfillment:*— completion(1).

1605. **ἐκπλήσσω ekplēssō**; from *1537* and *4141; to strike out,* hence *to strike with panic, to amaze:*— amazed(5), astonished(8).

1606. **ἐκπνέω ekpneō**; from *1537* and *4154; to breathe out, expire:*— breathed His last(3).

1607. **ἐκπορεύομαι ekporeuomai**; from *1537* and *4198; to make to go forth, to go forth:*— came(1), come(1), come forth(1), comes(1), coming(1), eliminated*(1), falling(1), flows(1), go(4), going(4), leave(1), leaving(2), moving about freely*(1), proceed(6), proceeded(1), proceeds(4), setting(1), spreading(1), went(1).

1608. **ἐκπορνεύω ekporneuō**; from *1537* and *4203;* mid. *to give oneself up to fornication:*— gross immorality(1), indulged in gross immorality(1).

1609. **ἐκπτύω ekptuō**; from *1537* and *4429; to spit out, to spurn:*— loathe(1).

1610. **ἐκριζόω ekrizoō**; from *1537* and *4492; to uproot:*— uproot(1), uprooted(3).

1611. **ἔκστασις ekstasis**; from *1839; a displacement* (of the mind), i.e. *bewilderment, ecstasy:*— amazement(1), astonishment(2), completely*(1), trance(3).

1612. **ἐκστρέφω ekstrephō**; from *1537* and *4762; to turn inside out,* fig. *to pervert:*— perverted(1).

1613. **ἐκταράσσω ektarassō**; from *1537* and *5015; to throw into great trouble:*— throwing...into confusion(1).

1614. **ἐκτείνω ekteinō**; from *1537* and **τείνω teinō** *(to stretch); to extend:*— extend(1), lay(2), reached(1), stretch(4), stretched(7), stretching(1).

1615. **ἐκτελέω ekteleō**; from *1537* and *5055; to complete fully:*— finish(2).

1616. **ἐκτένεια ekteneia**; from *1618; zeal, intentness:*— earnestly*(1).

1617. **ἐκτενέστερον ektenesteron**; neut. of the cptv. of *1618; more intently:*— very(1).

1618. **ἐκτενής ektenēs**; from *1614; stretched,* fig. *zealous, earnest:*— fervent(1).

1619. **ἐκτενῶς ektenōs**; adv. from *1618; intently, fervently:*— fervently(3).

1620. **ἐκτίθημι ektithēmi**; from *1537* and *5087; to set forth,* fig. *to declare:*— explain(1), explained(1), explaining(1), set outside(1).

1621. **ἐκτινάσσω ektinassō**; from *1537* and **τινάσσω tinassō** *(to swing); to shake off* or *out:*— shake...off(2), shook(1), shook off(1).

1622. **ἐκτός ektos**; from *1537; the exterior,* fig. (as a prep.) *aside from, besides:*— except*(1), excepted(1), outside(2).

1623. **ἕκτος hektos**; ord. from *1803; sixth:*— sixth(14).

1624. **ἐκτρέπω ektrepō**; from *1537* and the same as *5157; to turn away:*— avoiding(1), put out of joint(1), turn aside(1), turned aside(2).

1625. **ἐκτρέφω ektrephō**; from *1537* and *5142; to bring up to maturity, to nourish:*— bring(1), nourishes(1).

1626. **ἔκτρωμα ektrōma**; from *1537* and **τιτρώσκω titrōskō** *(to wound); untimely birth, miscarriage:*— one untimely born(1).

1627. **ἐκφέρω ekpherō**; from *1537* and *5342; to carry out, bring forth:*— bring(1), brought(1), carried(2), carry(1), carrying(1), take(1), yields(1).

1628. **ἐκφεύγω ekpheugō**; from *1537* and *5343; to flee away:*— escape(5), escaped(2), fled(1).

1629. **ἐκφοβέω ekphobeō**; from *1537* and *5399; to frighten away:*— terrify(1).

1630. **ἔκφοβος ekphobos**; from *1537* and *5401; terrified:*— full of fear(1), terrified(1).

1631. **ἐκφύω ekphuō**; from *1537* and *5453; to sprout up:*— puts forth(2).

1632a. **ἐκχέω ekcheō**; from *1537* and **χέω cheō** *(to pour); to pour out,* fig. *to bestow:*— pour(1), pour forth(2), poured(10), poured forth(1), pours(1), shed(1).

1632b. **ἐκχύννω ekchunnō**; from the same as *1632a; to pour out,* fig. *to bestow:*— gushed(1), poured(5), rushed headlong(1), shed(3), spilled(1).

1633. **ἐκχωρέω ekchōreō**; from *1537* and *5562; to depart, withdraw:*— leave(1).

1634. **ἐκψύχω ekpsuchō**; from *1537* and *5594; to expire, breathe one's last:*— breathed her last(1), breathed his last(1), died(1).

1635. **ἑκών hekōn**; from a prim. word; *of one's own free will, voluntary:*— voluntarily(1), willingly(1).

1636. **ἐλαία elaia**; a prim. word; *an olive* (the tree or the fruit):— olive tree(2), olive trees(1), olives(10).

1637. **ἔλαιον elaion**; from *1636; olive oil:*— oil(10), olive oil(1).

1638. **ἐλαιών elaiōn**; from *1636; an olive orchard,* i.e. spec. *the Mt. of Olives:*— Olivet(3).

1639. **Ἐλαμίτης Elamitēs**; of Heb. or. [5867a]; *an Elamite,* an inhab. of Elam:— Elamites(1).

1640. **ἐλάσσων elassōn** or **ἐλάττων elattōn**; cptv. of the same as *1646; smaller, less:*— less(1), lesser(1), poorer(1), younger(1).

1641. **ἐλαττονέω elattoneō**; from *1640; to be less:*— had...lack(1).

1642. ἐλαττόω elattoō; from *1640; to make less* (in rank or influence):— decrease(1), lower(2), made(2).

1643. ἐλαύνω elaunō; a prim. vb.; *to drive* or *push* (as wind, oars, or demoniacal power):— driven(3), oars(1), rowed(1).

1644. ἐλαφρία elaphria; from *1645; levity,* i.e. *fickleness:*— vacillating*(1).

1645. ἐλαφρός elaphros; a prim. word; *light, easy to bear:*— light(2).

1646. ἐλάχιστος elachistos; superl. of **ἔλαχυς elachus** *(little),* also used as superl. to *3398; least* (in size, amount, dignity, etc.):— least(6), smallest(1), very least(1), very little thing(4), very small(1), very small thing(1).

1647. ἐλαχιστότερος elachistoteros; cptv. of *1646,* q.v.

1648a. Ἐλεάζαρ Eleazar; of Heb. or. [499]; *Eleazar,* an Isr.:— Eleazar(2).

1648b. ἐλεάω eleaō; a form of *1653,* q.v.

1649a. ἐλεγμός elegmos; from *1651; reproof:*— reproof(1).

1649b. ἔλεγξις elegxis; from *1651; rebuke:*— rebuke(1).

1650. ἔλεγχος elegchos; from *1651; a proof, test:*— conviction(1).

1651. ἐλέγχω elegchō; a prim. vb.; *to expose, convict, reprove:*— convict(2), convicted(2), convicts(1), expose(1), exposed(2), rebuke(1), refute(1), reprimanded(1), reprove(4), reproved(1), show...fault(1).

1652. ἐλεεινός eleeinos; from *1656; pitiable:*— miserable(1), most to be pitied(1).

1653. ἐλεέω eleeō; from *1656; to have pity* or *mercy on, to show mercy:*— found mercy(1), had mercy(4), has mercy(2), have mercy(15), mercy(1), receive mercy(1), received mercy(3), show mercy(1), shown mercy(3), shows mercy(1).

1654. ἐλεημοσύνη eleēmosunē; from *1656; mercy, pity,* spec. *alms:*— alms(7), charity(3), giving(1).

1655. ἐλεήμων eleēmōn; from *1653; merciful:*— merciful(2).

1656. ἔλεος eleos; a prim. word; *mercy, pity, compassion:*— compassion(2), mercy(25).

1657. ἐλευθερία eleutheria; from *1658; liberty, freedom:*— freedom(7), liberty(4).

1658. ἐλεύθερος eleutheros; a prim. word; *free,* i.e. *not a slave* or *not under restraint:*— exempt(1), free(12), free man(2), free men(3), free woman(4), freeman(1).

1659. ἐλευθερόω eleutheroō; from *1658; to make free,* fig. *to exempt* (from liability):— freed(2), make...free(1), makes...free(1), set...free(2), set free(1).

1660. ἔλευσις eleusis; from alt. of *2064; a coming:*— coming(1).

1661. ἐλεφάντινος elephantinos; from **ἐλέφας elephas** *(elephant, ivory); of ivory:*— ivory(1).

1662. Ἐλιακίμ Eliakim; of Heb. or. [471]; *Eliakim,* two Isr.:— Eliakim(3).

1663. Ἐλιέζερ Eliezer; of Heb. or. [461]; *Eliezer,* an Isr.:— Eliezer(1).

1664. Ἐλιούδ Elioud; of Heb. or. [410 and 1935]; "God of majesty," *Eliud,* an Isr.:— Eliud(2).

1665. Ἐλισάβετ Elisabet; of Heb. or. [472]; *Elizabeth,* an Israelitess:— Elizabeth(9).

1666. Ἐλισαῖος Elisaios; of Heb. or. [477]; *Elisha,* an Isr. prophet:— Elisha(1).

1667. ἑλίσσω helissō; a form of *1507; to roll up, to coil:*— roll(1), rolled(1).

1668. ἕλκος helkos; prob. from a prim. root; *a wound, a sore, an ulcer:*— sore(1), sores(2).

1669. ἑλκόω helkoō; from *1668; to wound, to ulcerate,* pass. *to suffer from sores:*— covered with sores(1).

1670. ἕλκω helkō; a prim. vb.; *to drag:*— drag(1), dragged(2), draw(1), draws(1), drew(2), haul(1).

1671. Ἑλλάς Hellas; a prim. word; *Hellas,* i.e. *Greece,* a country of Europe:— Greece(1).

1672. Ἕλλην Hellēn; from *1671; a Greek,* usually a name for a Gentile:— Greek(9), Greeks(17).

1673. Ἑλληνικός Hellēnikos; from *1672; Hellenic,* i.e. *Grecian* (in language):— Greek(1).

1674. Ἑλληνίς Hellēnis; fem. of *1672; a Greek* (i.e. Gentile) *woman:*— Gentile(1), Greek(1).

1675. Ἑλληνιστής Hellēnistēs; from **Ἑλληνίζω Hellēnizō** *(to Hellenize); a Hellenist* (Greek-speaking Jew):— Hellenistic(2).

1676. Ἑλληνιστί Hellēnisti; adv. from the same as *1675; in Greek:*— Greek(2).

1677. ἐλλογέω ellogeō; from *1722* and *3056* (in the sense of *account, reckoning*); *to charge to one's account, impute:*— charge...to...account(1), imputed(1).

εἱλ- heil-; see *138.*

1678. Ἐλμαδάμ Elmadam; of Heb. or., perh. for [486]; *Elmadam,* an Isr.:— Elmadam(1).

1679. ἐλπίζω elpizō; from **ἔλπομαι elpomai** *(to anticipate, expect); to expect, to hope* (for) :— expect(1), expected(1), fix...hope(2), fixed...hope(2), hope(13), hoped(3), hopes(1), hoping(4), set...hope(2), trust(1).

1680. ἐλπίς elpis; from the same as *1679; expectation, hope:*— hope(53), hopes(1).

1681. Ἐλύμας Elumas; of Ara. or Arab. or.; *Elymas,* a magician:— Elymas(1).

1682. ἐλωΐ elōi; of Ara. or. [426] with pron. suff.; *my God:*— Eloi(2).

1683. ἐμαυτοῦ emautou; gen. reflex. pron. from *1700* and *846; of myself:*— myself(24), own(2), own initiative(6), own sake(1).

1684. ἐμβαίνω embainō; from *1722* and the same as *939; to walk on, to step into,* i.e. *embark:*— embarked(1), entered(1), get(2), getting(3), got(9), stepped(1), went on board(1).

1685. ἐμβάλλω emballō; from *1722* and *906; to cast into, subject to:*— cast(1).

1686. ἐμβάπτω embaptō; from *1722* and *911; to dip in:*— dipped(1), dips(1).

1687. ἐμβατεύω embateuō; perh. from *1684; to set foot upon:*— taking...stand(1).

1688. ἐμβιβάζω embibazō; caus. form of *1684; to place on, to put on board:*— put...aboard(1).

1689. ἐμβλέπω emblepō; from *1722* and *991; to look at,* fig. *to consider:*— look(1), looked(5), looking(3), see(1).

1690. ἐμβριμάομαι embrimaomai; from *1722* and **βριμάομαι brimaomai** *(to snort with anger); to be moved with anger, to admonish sternly:*— deeply moved(2), scolding(1), sternly warned(2).

1691. ἐμέ eme; emph. form of *3165,* see *1473.*

1692. ἐμέω emeō; a prim. word; *to vomit:*— spit(1).

1693. ἐμμαίνομαι emmainomai; from *1722* and *3105; to rage against:*— enraged(1).

1694. Ἐμμανουήλ Emmanouēl; of Heb. or. [6005]; "God with us," *Immanuel,* a name of Christ:— Immanuel(1).

1695. Ἐμμαούς Emmaous; prob. of Heb. or., cf. [3222]; *Emmaus,* a place 60 stadia (7.5 miles) west of Jer.:— Emmaus(1).

1696. ἐμμένω emmenō; from *1722* and *3306; to abide in,* fig. *to be true to, to persevere:*— abide(1), continue(2), stayed(1).

1697. Ἐμμώρ Hemmōr; of Heb. or. [2544]; *Emmor,* a Canaanite:— Hamor(1).

1698. ἐμοί emoi; emph. form of *3427,* see *1473.*

1699. ἐμός emos; from the oblique cases of *1473,* first pers. poss. pron.; *my:*— mine(14), own(11).

1700. ἐμοῦ emou; emph. form of *3450,* see *1473:*— mine(1).

1701a. ἐμπαιγμονή empaigmonē; from *1702; mockery:*— mocking(1).

1701b. ἐμπαιγμός empaigmos; from *1702; a mocking:*— mockings(1).

1702. ἐμπαίζω empaizō; from *1722* and *3815; to mock at:*— mock(2), mocked(5), mocking(4), ridicule(1), tricked(1).

1703. ἐμπαίκτης empaiktēs; from *1702; a mocker,* i.e. by impl. *a false teacher:*— mockers(2).

1704. ἐμπεριπατέω emperipateō; from *1722* and *4043; to walk about in* or *among:*— walk among(1).

1705a. ἐμπίπλημι empiplēmi; from *1722* and *4092a; to fill up,* by impl. *to satisfy:*— enjoyed(1), filled(2), satisfying(1), well-fed(1).

1705b. ἐμπίπρημι empiprēmi; from *1722* and *4092b; to set on fire:*— set...on fire(1).

1706. ἐμπίπτω empiptō; from *1722* and *4098; to fall into:*— fall(5), falls(1), fell(1).

1707. ἐμπλέκω emplekō; from *1722* and *4120; to weave in, to entwine,* i.e. *to involve with:*— entangled(1), entangles(1).

ἐμπλήθω emplēthō; see *1705a.*

1708. ἐμπλοκή emplokē; from *1707;* (elaborate) *braiding* (of the hair):— braiding(1).

1709. ἐμπνέω empneō; from *1722* and *4154; to breathe* (on), *to inhale:*— breathing(1).

1710. ἐμπορεύομαι emporeuomai; from *1722* and *4198; to travel in, to traffic,* by impl. *to trade:*— engage in business(1), exploit(1).

1711. ἐμπορία emporia; fem. from *1713; commerce, business, trade.*

1712. ἐμπόριον emporion; neut. from *1713; a trading place:*— business(1).

1713. ἔμπορος emporos; from *1722* and **πόρος poros** *(a journey); a passenger on shipboard, a merchant:*— merchant(1), merchants(4).

1714. ἐμπρήθω emprēthō; see *1705b.*

1715. ἔμπροσθεν emprosthen; from *1722* and *4314; before, in front of* (in place or time):— ahead(5), before(28), front(4), higher rank(2), presence(4), sight(3).

1716. ἐμπτύω emptuō; from *1722* and *4429; to spit upon:*— spat(2), spit(3), spitting(1).

1717. **ἐμφανής emphanēs**; from the comp. of *1722* and *5316*; *manifest:*— manifest(1), visible(1).

1718. **ἐμφανίζω emphanizō**; from *1717*; *to exhibit, appear* (in person), *to declare:*— appear(1), appeared(1), brought charges(3), disclose(2), make...clear(1), notified(1), notify(1).

1719. **ἔμφοβος emphobos**; from *1722* and *5401*; *terrible, in fear* (used of godly fear):— frightened(2), much alarmed(1), terrified(2).

1720. **ἐμφυσάω emphusaō**; from *1722* and **φυσάω phusaō** *(to blow); to breathe into* or *upon:*— breathed(1).

1721. **ἔμφυτος emphutos**; from **ἐμφύω emphuō** *(to implant); innate, implanted:*— implanted(1).

1722. **ἐν en**; a prim. prep. denoting position and by impl. instrumentality; *in, on, at, by, with:*— about(3), afterwards*(2), along(1), amid(1), among(124), among*(4), because(3), before(1), before*(3), besides(1), between*(1), case(2), child*(4), circumstance(1), circumstances(1), conscious*(1), death*(1), during(7), earnestly*(1), free*(1), had(1), here*(2), how*(1), means(1), outwardly*(1), over(1), there*(2), through(18), throughout(4), together(1), under(5), under...circumstances(1), undisturbed*(1), until*(1), way(4), when(19), when*(3), where*(2), while(19), while*(3), within(14), within*(1).

1723. **ἐναγκαλίζομαι enagkalizomai**; from *1722* and **ἀγκαλίζομαι agkalizomai** *(to embrace)*; from *43*; *to take into one's arms, to embrace:*— taking...in his arms(1), took...in his arms(1).

1724. **ἐνάλιος enalios**; from *1722* and **ἅλς hals** *(the sea); in* or *of the sea,* i.e. *marine creatures:*— creatures of the sea(1).

1725. **ἔναντι enanti**; adv. from *1722* and *473*; *before,* i.e. *in the presence of:*— before(2).

1726. **ἐναντίον enantion**; neut. of *1727*, used as prep. and adv.; *before, in the presence of.*

1727. **ἐναντίος enantios**; from *1722* and **ἀντίος antios** *(set against); opposite,* fig. *hostile, opposed:*— against(2), before(1), contrary(2), hostile(2), opponent(1), presence(1), right in front(1), sight(3).

1728. **ἐνάρχομαι enarchomai**; from *1722* and *757*; *to begin, to make a beginning:*— began(1), begun(1).

1729a. **ἔνατος enatos**; ord. from *1767*; *ninth:*— ninth(9), ninth hour(1).

1729b. **ἐνδεής endeēs**; from **ἐνδέω endeō** *(to fall short, be wanting* or *lacking)*; from *1722* and *1210*; *in want, needy:*— needy(1).

1730. **ἔνδειγμα endeigma**; from *1731*; *an indication, a proof:*— plain indication(1).

1731. **ἐνδείκνυμι endeiknumi**; from *1722* and *1166*; *to indicate* (by word or act), *to prove:*— demonstrate(4), did(1), show(4), showing(2), shown(1).

1732. **ἔνδειξις endeixis**; from *1731*; *a pointing out* or *indication, a proof:*— demonstration(1), proof(1), sign(1).

1733. **ἕνδεκα hendeka**; card. num. from the neut. of *1520* and *1176*; *eleven:*— eleven(6).

1734. **ἑνδέκατος hendekatos**; ord. num. from *1733*; *eleventh:*— eleventh(3).

1735. **ἐνδέχομαι endechomai**; from the comp. of *1722* and *1209*; *to admit, approve, to be possible:*— cannot*(1).

1736. **ἐνδημέω endēmeō**; from *1722* and *1218*; *to be in one's own country, to be at home:*— home(3).

1737. **ἐνδιδύσκω endiduskō**; a prol. form of *1746a*; *to put on, be clothed with:*— dressed(2).

1738. **ἔνδικος endikos**; from *1722* and *1349*; *righteous, just:*— just(2).

1739. **ἐνδόμησις endomēsis**; var. reading for *1746b*, q.v.

1740. **ἐνδοξάζομαι endoxazomai**; from *1741*; *to glorify:*— glorified(2).

1741. **ἔνδοξος endoxos**; from *1722* and *1391*; *held in honor, glorious:*— in all...glory(1), distinguished(1), glorious things(1), splendidly(1).

1742. **ἔνδυμα enduma**; from *1746a*; *apparel* (esp. the outer robe):— clothes(2), clothing(5), garment(1).

1743. **ἐνδυναμόω endunamoō**; from *1722* and *1412*; *to empower:*— grew strong(1), increasing in strength(1), strengthened(2), strengthens(1), strong(2).

1744. **ἐνδύνω endunō**; from *1722* and *1416*, see *1746a*.

1745. **ἔνδυσις endusis**; from *1746a*; *a putting on,* i.e. *investment* (with clothing):— putting(1).

1746a. **ἐνδύω enduō**; from *1722* and the same as *1416*; *to clothe* or *be clothed with* (in the sense of sinking into a garment):— clothed(6), dressed(1), enter(1), put(21).

1746b. **ἐνδώμησις endōmēsis**; from *1722* and **δωμάω dōmaō** *(to build); a building in* or *into, an interior structure:*— material(1).

ἐνεγκεῖν enegkein; see *5342*.

1747. **ἐνέδρα enedra**; from *1722* and **ἕδρα hedra** *(a seat); a lying in wait, an ambush:*— ambush(2).

1748. **ἐνεδρεύω enedreuō**; from *1747*; *to lie in wait for, to plot:*— lying in wait(1), plotting against(1).

1749. **ἔνεδρον enedron**; var. reading for *1747*, q.v.

1750. **ἐνειλέω eneileō**; from *1722* and **εἰλέω eileō** *(to wind); to roll in, to wind in:*— wrapped(1).

1751. **ἔνειμι eneimi**; from *1722* and *1510*, see also *1762*; *to be in, within:*— within(1).

1752a. **ἕνεκα heneka** or **ἕνεκεν heneken** or **εἵνεκεν heineken**; of unc. or.; *on account of, because of:*— because(2), because*(1), reason(4), sake(18).

1752b. **ἐνενήκοντα enenēkonta**; from *1767* and a modified form of *1176*; *ninety:*— ninety-nine*(4).

1753a. **ἐνεός eneos**; a prim. word; *mute, speechless:*— speechless(1).

1753b. **ἐνέργεια energeia**; from *1756*; *operative power:*— activity(1), exertion(1), influence(1), working(4).

1754. **ἐνεργέω energeō**; from *1756*; *to be at work, to work, to do:*— accomplish(1), brought about(1), effective(2), effectually worked(2), performs...work(1), work(6), working(2), works(7).

1755. **ἐνέργημα energēma**; from *1754*; *an effect, operation:*— effecting(1), effects(1).

1756. **ἐνεργής energēs**; from *1722* and *2041*; *at work, active:*— active(1), effective(2).

1757. **ἐνευλογέω eneulogeō**; from *1722* and *2127*; *to confer a benefit on, to bless:*— blessed(2).

1758. **ἐνέχω enechō**; from *1722* and *2192*; *to hold in* or *upon,* i.e. *to ensnare,* by impl. *to keep a grudge:*— grudge against(1), had a grudge against(1), hostile(1), subject(1).

1759a. **ἐνθάδε enthade**; adv. from a prol. form of *1722*; prop. *within,* i.e. (of place) *here, to here:*— here(7), there(1).

1759b. **ἔνθεν enthen**; from *1722*; *from here:*— here(2).

1760. **ἐνθυμέομαι enthumeomai**; from a comp. of *1722* and *2372*; *to reflect on, to ponder:*— considered(1), thinking(1).

1761. **ἐνθύμησις enthumēsis**; from *1760*; *deliberation, pondering,* pl. *thoughts:*— thought(1), thoughts(3).

1762. **ἔνι eni**; contr. for third pers. sing. pres. ind. of *1751*; *is in, has place, can be:*— neither*(3), there(6).

1763. **ἐνιαυτός eniautos**; of unc. or.; *a cycle of time, a year:*— year(15), years(2).

1764. **ἐνίστημι enistēmi**; from *1722* and *2476*; *to place in, to be at hand,* perf. part. *to be present:*— come(2), present(3), things present(2).

1765. **ἐνισχύω enischuō**; from *1722* and *2480*; *to strengthen:*— strengthened(1), strengthening(1).

1766. **ἔννατος ennatos**; var. reading for *1729a*, q.v.

1767. **ἐννέα ennea**; a prim. num.; *nine:*— nine(1), ninety-nine*(4).

1768. **ἐννενηκονταεννέα ennenēkontaennea**; var. reading for *1752b*, q.v.

1769. **ἐννεός enneos**; var. reading for *1753a*, q.v.

1770. **ἐννεύω enneuō**; from *1722* and *3506*; *to nod at,* i.e. *beckon* or *communicate by gesture:*— made signs(1).

1771. **ἔννοια ennoia**; from *1722* and *3563*; *thinking, thoughtfulness,* i.e. *moral understanding:*— intentions(1), purpose(1).

1772. **ἔννομος ennomos**; from *1722* and *3551*; *legal, subject to* (law):— lawful(1), under the law(1).

1773. **ἔννυχος ennuchos**; from *1722* and *3571*; *nightly,* neut. as adv. *by night:*— while it was... dark(1).

1774. **ἐνοικέω enoikeō**; from *1722* and *3611*; *to dwell in:*— dwell(2), dwells(2), dwelt(1).

1775a. **ἐνορκίζω enorkizō**; from *1722* and *3726*; *to adjure:*— adjure(1).

1775b. **ἑνότης henotēs**; from *1520*; *oneness,* i.e. *unanimity:*— unity(2).

1776. **ἐνοχλέω enochleō**; from *1722* and *3791*; *to crowd in,* i.e. *to annoy:*— causes trouble(1), troubled(1).

1777. **ἔνοχος enochos**; from *1758*; *held in, bound by, liable to* (a condition, penalty or imputation):— deserves(1), deserving(1), guilty(6), liable(1), subject(1).

1778. **ἔνταλμα entalma**; from *1781*; *an injunction,* i.e. *religious precept:*— commandments(1), precepts(2).

1779. **ἐνταφιάζω entaphiazō**; from a comp. of *1722* and *5028*; *to prepare for burial:*— burial(1), prepare...for burial(1).

1780. **ἐνταφιασμός entaphiasmos**; from *1779*; *preparation for burial:*— burial(2).

1781. **ἐντέλλομαι entellomai**; from *1722* and **τέλλομαι tellomai** *(to accomplish); to enjoin, to charge, command:*— command(6), commanded(7), gave orders(1), given orders(1).

1782. **ἐντεῦθεν enteuthen**; akin to *1759b; from here, on each side, thereupon:*— either side(2), here(4), source(1), this realm(1).

1783. **ἔντευξις enteuxis**; from *1793; a petition,* i.e. spec. *supplication:*— petitions(1), prayer(1).

1784. **ἔντιμος entimos**; from *1722* and *5092; valued, precious:*— high regard(1), highly regarded(1), more distinguished(1), precious(2).

1785. **ἐντολή entolē**; from *1781; an injunction, order, command:*— command(2), commanded*(1), commandment(38), commandments(23), instructions(1), orders(1), requirement(1).

1786. **ἐντόπιος entopios**; from *1722* and *5117; of a place, a resident:*— local residents(1).

1787. **ἐντός entos**; from *1722; within, among:*— inside(1), midst(1).

1788. **ἐντρέπω entrepō**; from *1722* and the same as *5157; to turn about, to reverence, to put to shame:*— put to shame(2), respect(5), respected(1), shame(1).

1789. **ἐντρέφω entrephō**; from *1722* and *5142; to train up:*— nourished(1).

1790. **ἔντρομος entromos**; from *1722* and *5156; terrified:*— shook with fear(1), trembling(1), trembling with fear(1).

1791. **ἐντροπή entropē**; from *1788; respect, shame:*— shame(2).

1792. **ἐντρυφάω entruphaō**; from *1722* and *5171; to revel in:*— reveling(1).

1793. **ἐντυγχάνω entugchanō**; from *1722* and *5177; to chance upon,* by impl. *confer with,* by ext. *entreat:*— appealed(1), intercedes(2), make intercession(1), pleads(1).

1794. **ἐντυλίσσω entulissō**; from *1722* and **τυλίσσω tulissō** *(to twist); to wrap up:*— rolled(1), wrapped(2).

1795. **ἐντυπόω entupoō**; from *1722* and *5179b; to imprint, engrave:*— engraved(1).

1796. **ἐνυβρίζω enubrizō**; from *1722* and *5195; to insult:*— insulted(1).

1797. **ἐνυπνιάζομαι enupniazomai**; from *1798; to dream:*— dream(1), dreaming(1).

1798. **ἐνύπνιον enupnion**; from *1722* and *5258; a dream:*— dreams(1).

1799. **ἐνώπιος enōpios**; from *1722* and **ὤψ ōps** *(the eye, face); in sight of, before:*— before(46), front(1), presence(20), sight(22).

1800. **Ἐνώς Enōs**; of Heb. or. [583]; *Enosh,* an antediluvian:— Enosh(1).

1801. **ἐνωτίζομαι enōtizomai**; from a comp. of *1722* and *3775; to give ear, to hearken:*— give heed(1).

1802. **Ἑνώχ Enōch**; of Heb. or. [2585]; *Enoch,* a patriarch:— Enoch(3).

ἐξ ex; see *1537.*

1803. **ἕξ hex**; a prim. card. num.; *six:*— forty-six*(1), seventy-six*(1), six(10), sixty-six*(1).

1804. **ἐξαγγέλλω exaggellō**; from *1537* and *31b; to tell out, proclaim:*— proclaim(1).

1805. **ἐξαγοράζω exagorazō**; from *1537* and *59; to buy up,* i.e. *ransom,* fig. *to rescue from loss:*— making the most(2), redeem(1), redeemed(1).

1806. **ἐξάγω exagō**; from *1537* and *71; to lead out:*— bring(1), brought(1), lead(1), leads(1), led(7), taking(1).

1807. **ἐξαιρέω exaireō**; from *1537* and *138; to take out, to deliver:*— pluck(1), rescue(2), rescued(3), rescuing(1), tear(1).

1808. **ἐξαίρω exairō**; from *1537* and *142; to lift up, to remove:*— remove(1).

1809. **ἐξαιτέω exaiteō**; from *1537* and *154; to ask for oneself* (mid.), *demand:*— demanded(1).

1810. **ἐξαίφνης exaiphnēs**; from *1537* and the same as *160; suddenly:*— suddenly(5).

1811. **ἐξακολουθέω exakoloutheō**; from *1537* and *190; to follow (out, up),* i.e. *to imitate:*— follow(2), followed(1).

1812. **ἑξακόσιοι hexakosioi**; pl. card. num. from *1803* and *1540; six hundred:*— six hundred(1), two(1).

1813. **ἐξαλείφω exaleiphō**; from *1537* and *218b; to wipe out, erase, obliterate:*— canceled(1), erase(1), wipe(1), wipe away(1), wiped away(1).

1814. **ἐξάλλομαι exallomai**; from *1537* and *242; to leap up:*— leap(1).

1815. **ἐξανάστασις exanastasis**; from *1817; a rising again:*— resurrection(1).

1816. **ἐξανατέλλω exanatellō**; from *1537* and *393; to spring up:*— sprang(2).

1817. **ἐξανίστημι exanistēmi**; from *1537* and *450; to raise up, to rise:*— raise(2), stood(1).

1818. **ἐξαπατάω exapataō**; from *1537* and *538; to seduce wholly, deceive:*— deceive(3), deceived(3).

1819. **ἐξάπινα exapina**; from *1537* and a der. of the same as *160; suddenly:*— all at once(1).

1820. **ἐξαπορέω exaporeō**; from *1537* and *639; to be utterly at a loss, be in despair:*— despaired(1), despairing(1).

1821. **ἐξαποστέλλω exapostellō**; from *1537* and *649; to send forth* or *away:*— send...away(1), sending forth(1), sent(3), sent...away(3), sent away(1), sent forth(3), sent...off(1).

1822. **ἐξαρτίζω exartizō**; from *1537* and **ἀρτίζω artizō** *(get ready, prepare); to complete, to equip fully:*— ended(1), equipped(1).

1823. **ἐξαστράπτω exastraptō**; from *1537* and *797; to flash* or *gleam like lightning, be radiant:*— gleaming(1).

1824. **ἐξαυτῆς exautēs**; from *1537* and gen. sing. fem. of *846; at once, forthwith:*— immediately(2), moment(1), once(3).

1825. **ἐξεγείρω exegeirō**; from *1537* and *1453; to raise up:*— raise(1), raised(1).

1826. **ἔξειμι exeimi**; from *1537* and **εἶμι eimi** *(to go); to go forth:*— get(1), going(1), leave(1), left(1).

1827. **ἐξελέγχω exelegchō**; var. reading for *1651,* q.v.

1828. **ἐξέλκω exelkō**; from *1537* and *1670; to draw out* or *away:*— carried away(1).

1829. **ἐξέραμα exerama**; from **ἐξεράω exeraō** *(to evacuate); vomit* (noun):— vomit(1).

1830. **ἐξεραυνάω exeraunaō**; from *1537* and *2038a; to search out:*— inquiries(1), made careful*(1).

1831. **ἐξέρχομαι exerchomai**; from *1537* and *2064; to go* or *come out of:*— came(33), came forth(4), come(22), come forth(3), comes(1), coming(7), departed(1), departing(1), descended*(1), eluded(1), get(2), go(21), go away(2), go*(1), goes(2), going(2), gone(13), gone forth(2), got(2), leave(4), left(15), proceeded forth(1), spread(3), went(61), went ashore(2), went away(3), went forth(5), went off(1).

1832. **ἔξεστι exesti**; from *1537* and *1510; it is permitted, lawful:*— lawful(26), may(3), permissible(1), permitted(2).

1833. **ἐξετάζω exetazō**; from *1537* and **ἐτάζω etazō** *(to examine); to examine closely:*— inquire(1), question(1), search(1).

1834. **ἐξηγέομαι exēgeomai**; from *1537* and *2233; to show the way:*— explained(2), related(2), related(1), relating(1).

1835. **ἑξήκοντα hexēkonta**; card. num. from *1803* and a modified form of *1176; sixty:*— seven(1), sixty(7), sixty-six*(1).

1836. **ἑξῆς hexēs**; from *2192; next:*— afterwards*(1), next(4), soon(1).

1837. **ἐξηχέω exēcheō**; from *1537* and *2278; to sound forth:*— sounded forth(1).

1838. **ἕξις hexis**; from *2192; habit, practice:*— practice(1).

1839. **ἐξίστημι existēmi**; from *1537* and *2476; to displace, to stand aside from:*— amazed(10), amazement(1), astonished(2), astonishing(1), astounded(1), beside ourselves(1), lost His senses(1).

1840. **ἐξισχύω exischuō**; from *1537* and *2480; to have strength enough:*— able(1).

1841. **ἔξοδος exodos**; from *1537* and *3598; a departure:*— departure(2), exodus(1).

1842. **ἐξολεθρεύω exolethreuō**; from *1537* and *3645; to destroy utterly:*— utterly destroyed(1).

1843. **ἐξομολογέω exomologeō**; from *1537* and *3670; to agree, confess:*— confess(2), confessed(1), confessing(2), consented(1), give praise(2), praise(2).

ἐξόν exon; see *1832.*

1844. **ἐξορκίζω exorkizō**; from *1537* and *3726; to administer an oath, to adjure:*— adjure(1).

1845. **ἐξορκιστής exorkistēs**; from *1844; an exorcist:*— exorcists(1).

1846. **ἐξορύσσω exorussō**; from *1537* and *3736; to dig out* or *up:*— dug(1), plucked(1).

1847. **ἐξουδενέω exoudeneō**; from *1537* and *3762; to despise, treat with contempt:*— treated with contempt(1).

1848. **ἐξουθενέω exoutheneō**; from *1847; to despise, treat with contempt:*— contemptible(1), despise(3), despised(1), no account(1), regard with contempt(1), regard...with contempt(1), rejected(1), treating...with contempt(1), viewed with contempt(1).

1849. **ἐξουσία exousia**; from *1832; power to act, authority:*— authorities(7), authority(65), charge(1), control(1), domain(2), dominion(1), jurisdiction(1), liberty(1), power(11), powers(1), right(11).

1850. **ἐξουσιάζω exousiazō**; from *1849; to exercise authority over:*— have authority over(3), mastered(1).

1851. **ἐξοχή exochē**; from **ἐξέχω exechō** *(to project from, be prominent);* from *1537* and *2192; a projection, eminence:*— prominent(1).

1852. **ἐξυπνίζω exupnizō**; from *1853; to awaken out of sleep:*— awaken...out of sleep(1).

1853. **ἔξυπνος exupnos**; from *1537* and *5258; roused out of sleep:*— awoke(1).

1854. **ἔξω exō**; from *1537; outside, without:*— away(2), foreign(1), forth(1), outer(1), outside(20), outsiders*(3).

1855. **ἔξωθεν exōthen**; from *1854; from without:*— external(1), outside(9), outwardly(1), without(1).

1856. **ἐξωθέω exōtheō**; from *1537* and **ὠθέω ōtheō** *(to push); to thrust out:*— drive(1), drove(1).

1857. **ἐξώτερος exōteros**; cptv. of *1854; outer:*— outer(3).

1858a. **ἔοικα eoika**; a prim. vb.; *to be like:*— like(2).

1858b. **ἑορτάζω heortazō**; from *1859; to celebrate a festival:*— celebrate the feast(1).

1859. **ἑορτή heortē**; of unc. der.; *a feast, a festival:*— feast(23), festival(3).

1860. **ἐπαγγελία epaggelia**; from *1861; a summons, a promise:*— promise(37), promised(1), promises(12), what was promised(2).

1861. **ἐπαγγέλλομαι epaggellomai**; from *1909* and *31b; to proclaim, to promise:*— made(1), made the promise(1), making a claim(1), professed(1), promise had been made(1), promised(9), promising(1).

1862. **ἐπάγγελμα epaggelma**; from *1861; a promise:*— promise(1), promises(1).

1863. **ἐπάγω epagō**; from *1909* and *71; to bring upon:*— bring(1), bringing(1), brought(1).

1864. **ἐπαγωνίζομαι epagōnizomai**; from *1909* and *75; to contend with* or *for:*— contend earnestly(1).

1865. **ἐπαθροίζω epathroizō**; from *1909* and **ἀθροίζω athroizō** *(to assemble); to assemble besides:*— increasing(1).

1866. **Ἐπαίνετος Epainetos**; from *1867;* "praiseworthy," *Epaenetus,* a Chr. of Rome:— Epaenetus(1).

1867. **ἐπαινέω epaineō**; from *1909* and *134; to praise:*— praise(5), praised(1).

1868. **ἔπαινος epainos**; from *1909* and *136; praise:*— fame(1), praise(9), worthy of praise(1).

1869. **ἐπαίρω epairō**; from *1909* and *142; to lift up:*— exalts(1), hoisting(1), lift(3), lifted(4), lifting(4), raised(5), turning(1).

1870. **ἐπαισχύνομαι epaischunomai**; from *1909* and *153; to be ashamed* (of):— am...ashamed(2), ashamed(9).

1871. **ἐπαιτέω epaiteō**; from *1909* and *154; to beg:*— beg(1), begging(1).

1872. **ἐπακολουθέω epakoloutheō**; from *1909* and *190; to follow after:*— devoted herself(1), follow(1), follow after(1), followed(1).

1873. **ἐπακούω epakouō**; from *1909* and *191; to listen to, to hearken to:*— listened(1).

1874. **ἐπακροάομαι epakroaomai**; from *1909* and the same as *201; to listen attentively:*—listening(1).

1875. **ἐπάν epan**; from *1893* and *302; after, when:*— when(3).

1876. **ἐπάναγκες epanagkes**; from *1909* and *318; necessary, of necessity:*— essentials(1).

1877. **ἐπανάγω epanagō**; from *1909* and *321; to put out* (to sea), *to return:*— put(2), returning(1).

1878. **ἐπαναμιμνήσκω epanamimnēskō**; from *1909* and *363; to remind again:*— remind...again(1).

1879. **ἐπαναπαύω epanapauō**; from *1909* and *373; to refresh, rest upon:*— rely(1), rest(1).

1880. **ἐπανέρχομαι epanerchomai**; from *1909* and *424; to return:*— return(1), returned(1).

1881. **ἐπανίστημι epanistēmi**; from *1909* and *450; to raise up against:*— rise(2).

1882. **ἐπανόρθωσις epanorthōsis**; from *1909* and *461; correction:*— correction(1).

1883. **ἐπάνω epanō**; from *1909* and *507; above, more than:*— above(3), more than(1), over(7).

1884a. **ἐπάρατος eparatos**; from **ἐπαράομαι eparaomai** *(to imprecate); accursed:*— accursed(1).

1884b. **ἐπαρκέω eparkeō**; from *1909* and *714; to help, aid:*— assist(2), assisted(1).

1885a. **ἐπαρχεία eparcheia**; from *1909* and *757; a province:*— province(2).

1885b. **ἐπάρχειος eparcheios**; another reading for *1885a,* q.v.

1886. **ἔπαυλις epaulis**; from *1909* and *833; a habitation:*— homestead(1).

1887. **ἐπαύριον epaurion**; from *1909* and *839; on the next day:*— day(1), following day(1), next day(16).

1888. **ἐπαυτοφώρῳ epautophōrō**; var. reading for *849a,* q.v.

1889. **Ἐπαφρᾶς Epaphras**; from *1891; Epaphras,* a Chr.:— Epaphras(3).

1890. **ἐπαφρίζω epaphrizō**; from *1909* and *875; to foam up:*— casting(1), like foam(1).

1891. **Ἐπαφρόδιτος Epaphroditos**; from *1909* and **Ἀφροδίτη Aphroditē** (name of Gr. goddess, *Venus* in Rom. myth.); Epaphroditus, a Chr.:— Epaphroditus(2).

1892. **ἐπεγείρω epegeirō**; from *1909* and *1453; to rouse up, excite:*— instigated(1), stirred(1).

1893. **ἐπεί epei**; from *1909* and *1487; when, because:*— because(5), otherwise(8), since(11).

1894. **ἐπειδή epeidē**; from *1893* and *1211; when now, seeing that:*— because(2), since(5), when(1).

1895. **ἐπειδήπερ epeidēper**; from *1894* and *4007a; inasmuch as:*— much(1).

1896. **ἐπεῖδον epeidon**; from *1909* and *1491a; to look upon:*— looked(1), take note(1).

1897a. **ἔπειμι epeimi**; from *1909* and the same as *1826; to come upon, come after:*— following(5).

1897b. **ἐπείπερ epeiper**; var. reading for *1512,* see *1893* and *4007a.*

1898a. **ἐπεισαγωγή epeisagōgē**; from **ἐπεισάγω epeisagō** *(to bring in besides);* from *1909* and *1521; a bringing in besides:*— bringing(1).

1898b. **ἐπεισέρχομαι epeiserchomai**; from *1909* and *1525; to come in upon:*— come(1).

1899. **ἔπειτα epeita**; from *1909* and *1534; thereafter:*— after(2), then(14).

1900. **ἐπέκεινα epekeina**; adv. from *1909* and *1565; farther on, beyond:*— beyond(1).

1901. **ἐπεκτείνω epekteinō**; from *1909* and *1614; to extend,* mid. *to stretch forward:*— reaching forward(1).

1902. **ἐπενδύομαι ependuomai**; from *1909* and *1746a; to have on over:*— clothed(2).

1903. **ἐπενδύτης ependutēs**; from *1902; an outer tunic:*— outer garment(1).

1904. **ἐπέρχομαι eperchomai**; from *1909* and *2064; to come to* or *upon:*— attacks(1), came(1), come(5), coming(2).

1905. **ἐπερωτάω eperōtaō**; from *1909* and *2065; to inquire of:*— ask(5), ask...question(1), ask...questions(1), asked(14), asked...a question(1), asking(2), asking...questions(1), question(3), questioned(18), questioning(9).

1906. **ἐπερώτημα eperōtēma**; from *1905; an inquiry, a demand:*— appeal(1).

1907. **ἐπέχω epechō**; from *1909* and *2192; to hold fast, to hold toward, to stop:*— give...attention(1), holding fast(1), noticed(1), pay close attention(1), stayed(1).

1908. **ἐπηρεάζω epēreazō**; from **ἐπήρεια epēreia** *(spiteful abuse); to revile:*— mistreat(1), revile(1).

1909. **ἐπί epi**; a prim. prep.; *on, upon:*— about(4), above(2), after(2), against(41), among(2), any(2), around(2), basis(4), because(2), because*(2), bedridden*(1), before(24), besides(1), beyond(1), certainly*(2), chamberlain*(1), charge(1), concerning(4), connection(1), embraced*(2), extent*(2), further*(3), inasmuch*(1), onto(1), over(57), passenger*(1), point(1), referring(1), time(3), together*(7), toward(5), truly*(2), under(1), under*(1), view(1), within(1).

1910. **ἐπιβαίνω epibainō**; from *1909* and the same as *939; to go aboard, to go up to:*— arrived(1), embarking(1), mounted(1), set foot(2), went aboard(1).

1911. **ἐπιβάλλω epiballō**; from *1909* and *906; to throw over, to throw oneself:*— breaking over(1), falls(1), laid(8), lay(2), put(2), puts(2), putting(1).

1912. **ἐπιβαρέω epibareō**; from *1909* and *916; to put a burden on:*— burden(2), say too much(1).

1913. **ἐπιβιβάζω epibibazō**; caus. form of *1910; to place upon:*— put(3).

1914. **ἐπιβλέπω epiblepō**; from *1909* and *991; to look on* (with favor):— had regard(1), look(1), pay special attention(1).

1915. **ἐπίβλημα epiblēma**; from *1911; that which is put on,* i.e. *a patch:*— patch(2), piece(1), piece of cloth(1).

1916. **ἐπιβοάω epiboaō**; var. reading for *994,* q.v.

1917. **ἐπιβουλή epiboulē**; from *1909* and *1012; a plan against:*— plot(2), plot...against(1), plots(1).

1918. **ἐπιγαμβρεύω epigambreuō**; from *1909* and **γαμβρός gambros** *(a connection by marriage); to marry:*— marry(1).

1919. **ἐπίγειος epigeios**; from *1909* and *1093; of the earth:*— earth(1), earthly(4), earthly things(2).

1920. **ἐπιγίνομαι epiginomai**; from *1909* and *1096; to come on, arrive:*— sprang(1).

1921. **ἐπιγινώσκω epiginōskō**; from *1909* and *1097; to know exactly, to recognize:*— acknowledge(1), ascertain(2), aware(2), find(1), found(2), fully known(1), know(7), know fully(1), known(2), knows(1), learned(3), perceiving(1), realized(1), recognize(5), recognized(6), recognizing(1), take note(1), taking note(1), understand(3), understood(1), well-known(1).

1922. **ἐπίγνωσις epignōsis**; from *1921; recognition, knowledge:*— acknowledge*(1), knowledge(14), real knowledge(1), true knowledge(4).

1923. **ἐπιγραφή epigraphē**; from *1924; an inscription:*— inscription(5).

1924. **ἐπιγράφω epigraphō**; from *1909* and *1125; to write upon:*— inscription(1), read(1), write(2), written(1).

1925. **ἐπιδείκνυμι epideiknumi**; from *1909* and *1166; to show, to prove:*— demonstrating(1), point(1), show(4), showing(1).

1926. **ἐπιδέχομαι epidechomai**; from *1909* and *1209; to accept as true, to receive besides:*— accept(1), receive(1).

1927. **ἐπιδημέω epidēmeō**; from *1909* and *1218; to be at home:*— visiting(1), visitors(1).

1928. **ἐπιδιατάσσομαι epidiatassomai**; from *1909* and *1299; to add provisions:*— adds conditions(1).

1929. **ἐπιδίδωμι epididōmi**; from *1909* and *1325; to give over, give way:*— delivered(1), gave(1), gave way(1), give(4), giving(1), handed(1).

1930. **ἐπιδιορθόω epidiorthoō**; from *1909 and the same as 1357a; to correct in addition:*—set in order(1).

1931. **ἐπιδύω epiduō**; from *1909* and *1416; to set* (of the sun):— go down(1).

1932. **ἐπιείκεια epieikeia**; from *1933; fairness, gentleness:*— gentleness(1), kindness(1).

1933. **ἐπιεικής epieikēs**; from *1909* and *1858a* (see also *1503); seemly, equitable, yielding:*— gentle(5).

1934. **ἐπιζητέω epizēteō**; from *1909* and *2212; to inquire for:*— craves(1), eagerly seek(2), searched(1), searching(1), seek(2), seeking(3), seeks after(1), sought(1), want(1).

1935. **ἐπιθανάτιος epithanatios**; from *1909* and *2288; condemned to death:*— men condemned(1), men condemned to death(1).

1936. **ἐπίθεσις epithesis**; from *2007; a laying on, an assault:*— laying(4).

1937. **ἐπιθυμέω epithumeō**; from *1909* and *2372; desire, lust after:*— covet(2), coveted(1), craved(1), desire(1), desired(2), desires(1), gladly(1), long(3), longing(1), lust(2), sets its desire(1).

1938. **ἐπιθυμητής epithumētēs**; from *1937; one who desires:*— crave*(1).

1939. **ἐπιθυμία epithumia**; from *1937; desire, passionate longing, lust:*— coveting(2), desire(4), desires(8), earnestly(1), impulses(1), long(1), lust(5), lustful(1), lusts(15).

1940. **ἐπικαθίζω epikathizō**; from *1909* and *2523; to sit upon:*— sat(1).

1941. **ἐπικαλέω epikaleō**; from *1909* and *2564; to call upon:*— address(1), appeal(2), appealed(4), call(7), called(14), calling(1), calls(1).

1942. **ἐπικάλυμμα epikalumma**; from *1943; a cover, veil:*— covering(1).

1943. **ἐπικαλύπτω epikaluptō**; from *1909* and *2572; to cover over* or *up:*— covered(1).

1944. **ἐπικατάρατος epikataratos**; from **ἐπικαταράομαι epikataraomai** *(to invoke curses on); accursed:*— cursed(2).

1945. **ἐπίκειμαι epikeimai**; from *1909* and *2749; to lie on:*— am under(1), assailing(1), imposed(1), insistent(1), lying(1), placed(1), pressing around(1).

1946a. **ἐπικέλλω epikellō**; from *1909* and a prim. vb. **κέλλω kellō** *(to drive* a ship *on); to run ashore:*— ran...aground(1).

1946b. **Ἐπικούρειος Epikoureios**; from **Ἐπίκουρος Epikouros** *(Epicurus,* a Gr. philosopher); *an Epicurean:*— Epicurean(1).

1947. **ἐπικουρία Epikouria**; from **ἐπίκουρος epikouros** *(helper, ally); aid, assistance:*— help(1).

1948. **ἐπικρίνω epikrinō**; from *1909* and *2919; to decree, give sentence:*— pronounced sentence(1).

1949. **ἐπιλαμβάνομαι epilambanomai**; from *1909* and *2983; to lay hold of:*— catch(2), give help(1), gives help(1), seized(2), take hold(2), taking(1), taking hold(1), took(4), took hold(5).

1950. **ἐπιλανθάνομαι epilanthanomai**; from *1909* and *2990; to forget, neglect:*— forget(1), forgetting(1), forgotten(4), neglect(2).

1951. **ἐπιλέγω epilegō**; from *1909* and *3004; to call* or *name, to choose:*— called(1), chose(1).

1952a. **ἐπιλείπω epileipō**; from *1909* and *3007; to fail:*— fail(1).

1952b. **ἐπιλείχω epileichō**; from *1909* and **λείχω leichō** *(to lick up); to lick over:*— licking(1).

1953. **ἐπιλησμονή epilēsmonē**; from *1950; forgetfulness:*— forgetful(1).

1954. **ἐπίλοιπος epiloipos**; from *1909* and *3062; still left:*— rest(1).

1955. **ἐπίλυσις epilusis**; from *1956; a release, an interpretation:*— interpretation(1).

1956. **ἐπιλύω epiluō**; from *1909* and *3089; to loose, to solve:*— explaining(1), settled(1).

1957. **ἐπιμαρτυρέω epimartureō**; from *1909* and *3140; to bear witness to:*— testifying(1).

1958. **ἐπιμέλεια epimeleia**; from *1959; attention, care:*— care(1).

1959. **ἐπιμελέομαι epimeleomai**; from *1909* and *3199; to take care of:*— take care(2), took care(1).

1960. **ἐπιμελῶς epimelōs**; adv. from **ἐπιμελής epimelēs** *(careful, anxious about);* akin to *1959; carefully:*— carefully(1).

1961. **ἐπιμένω epimenō**; from *1909* and *3306; to stay on:*— continue(4), continued(1), persevere(1), persisted(1), remain(4), stay(2), stayed(3), staying(1).

1962. **ἐπινεύω epineuō**; from *1909* and *3506; to nod approval:*— consent(1).

1963. **ἐπίνοια epinoia**; from *1909* and *3563; a thought, design:*— intention(1).

1964. **ἐπιορκέω epiorkeō**; from *1965; to swear falsely:*— make false vows(1).

1965. **ἐπίορκος epiorkos**; from *1909* and *3727; sworn falsely, a perjurer:*— perjurers(1).

1966. **ἐπιοῦσα epiousa**; see *1897a.*

1967. **ἐπιούσιος epiousios**; from *1897a; for the coming day, for subsistence:*— daily(2).

1968. **ἐπιπίπτω epipiptō**; from *1909* and *4098; to fall upon:*— embraced*(2), fallen(1), fell(6), gripped(1), pressed around(1).

1969. **ἐπιπλήσσω epiplēssō**; from *1909* and *4141; to strike at, to rebuke* (with words):— sharply rebuke(1).

1970. (not used)

1971. **ἐπιποθέω epipotheō**; from *1909* and **ποθέω potheō** *(to yearn); to long for:*— desires(1), long(3), longing(4), yearn(1).

1972. **ἐπιπόθησις epipothēsis**; from *1971; longing:*— longing(2).

1973. **ἐπιπόθητος epipothētos**; from *1971; greatly desired:*— whom I long(1).

1974. **ἐπιποθία epipothia**; from *1971; longing:*— longing(1).

1975. **ἐπιπορεύομαι epiporeuomai**; from *1909* and *4198; to travel:*— journeying(1).

1976. **ἐπιράπτω epiraptō**; from *1909* and the same as *4476; to sew upon:*— sews(1).

1977. **ἐπιρίπτω epiriptō**; from *1909* and *4496; to cast upon:*— casting(1), threw(1).

1978. **ἐπίσημος episēmos**; from *1909* and the same as *4591; bearing a mark, notable:*— notorious(1), outstanding(1).

1979. **ἐπισιτισμός Episitismos**; from **ἐπισιτίζομαι episitizomai** *(to supply with provisions); provisions:*— something to eat(1).

1980a. **ἐπισκέπτομαι episkeptomai**; from *1909* and the same as *4649; to inspect,* by ext. *to go to see:*— concerned...about(1), concerned about(1), select(1), visit(5), visited(3).

1980b. **ἐπισκευάζω episkeuazō**; from *1909* and **σκευάζω skeuazō** *(to prepare); to equip:*— got ready(1).

1981. **ἐπισκηνόω episkēnoō**; from *1909* and *4637; to tent upon,* fig. *abide:*— dwell(1).

1982. **ἐπισκιάζω episkiazō**; from *1909* and *4639; to overshadow:*— fall(1), overshadow(2), overshadowed(1), overshadowing(1).

1983. **ἐπισκοπέω episkopeō**; from *1909* and *4648; to look upon,* fig. *to care for:*— oversight(1), see(1).

1984. **ἐπισκοπή episkopē**; from *1980a; a visiting, an overseeing:*— office(1), office of overseer(1), visitation(2).

1985. **ἐπίσκοπος episkopos**; from *1909* and *4649; a superintendent, an overseer:*— guardian(1), overseer(2), overseers(2).

1986a. **ἐπισπάομαι epispaomai**; from *1909* and *4685; to draw over, to become as uncircumcised:*— become uncircumcised(1).

1986b. **ἐπισπείρω epispeirō**; from *1909* and *4687; to sow upon* or *besides:*— sowed(1).

1987. **ἐπίσταμαι epistamai**; from *2186; to know, to understand:*— being acquainted(1), know(6), know about(1), knowing(2), knows(1), understand(2), understands(1).

1988a. **ἐπίστασις epistasis**; from *2186; superintendence, attention:*— pressure(1), riot*(1).

1988b. **ἐπιστάτης epistatēs**; from *2186; a chief, commander:*— Master(7).

1989. **ἐπιστέλλω epistellō**; from *1909* and *4724; to send a message* (by letter):— write(1), written(1), wrote(1).

1990. **ἐπιστήμων epistēmōn**; from *1987; knowing, skilled:*— understanding(1).

1991. **ἐπιστηρίζω epistērizō**; from *1909* and *4741; to make stronger:*— strengthened(1), strengthening(2).

1992. **ἐπιστολή epistolē**; from *1989; an epistle, a letter:*— letter(16), letters(8).

1993. **ἐπιστομίζω epistomizō**; from *1909* and *4750; to stop the mouth:*— silenced(1).

1994. **ἐπιστρέφω epistrephō**; from *1909* and *4762; to turn, to return:*— back(2), back*(3), return(6), returned(3), returns(2), take back(1), turn(8), turn back(1), turned(6), turned again(1), turned around(1), turning(2), turning around(2), turns(2), turns...back(1).

1995. **ἐπιστροφή epistrophē**; from *1994; a turning about, conversion:*— conversion(1).

1996. **ἐπισυνάγω episunagō**; from *1909* and *4863; to gather together:*— gather...together(2), gather together(2), gathered(2), gathered together(1), gathers(1).

1997. **ἐπισυναγωγή episunagōgē**; from *1996; a gathering together, an assembly:*— assembling together(1), gathering together(1).

1998. **ἐπισυντρέχω episuntrechō**; from *1909* and *4936; to run together again:*— rapidly gathering(1).

1999. **ἐπισύστασις episustasis**; from *1909* and *4921;* var. reading for *1988a,* q.v.

2000. **ἐπισφαλής episphalēs**; from *1909* and **σφάλλω sphallō** *(to cause to fall); prone to fall:*— dangerous(1).

2001. **ἐπισχύω epischuō**; from *1909* and *2480; to grow stronger:*— insisting(1).

2002. **ἐπισωρεύω episōreuō**; from *1909* and *4987; to heap together:*— accumulate(1).

2003. **ἐπιταγή epitagē**; from *2004; a command:*— authority(1), command(3), commandment(3).

2004. **ἐπιτάσσω epitassō**; from *1909* and *5021; to arrange upon,* i.e. *to command:*— command(2), commanded(4), commands(3), order(1).

2005. **ἐπιτελέω epiteleō**; from *1909* and *5055; to complete, accomplish:*— accomplished(1), complete(1), completion(1), erect(1), finish(1), finished(1), perfect(1), perfected(1), perfecting(1), performing(1).

2006. **ἐπιτήδειος epitēdeios**; from **ἐπιτηδές epitēdes** *(enough); convenient, necessary:*— necessary(1).

2007. **ἐπιτίθημι epitithēmi**; from *1909* and *5087; to lay upon, to place upon:*— add(1), adds(1), applied(2), attack(1), beat*(1), gave(2), laid(9), lay(10), laying(5), lays(1), placed(1), placing(1), put(4), struck(1), supplied(1).

2008. **ἐπιτιμάω epitimaō**; from *1909* and *5091; to honor, to mete out due measure,* hence *to censure:*— rebuke(6), rebuked(13), rebuking(3), sternly telling(2), sternly told(1), warned(5).

2009. **ἐπιτιμία epitimia**; from *2008; punishment:*— punishment(1).

2010. **ἐπιτρέπω epitrepō**; from *1909* and the same as *5157; to turn to, entrust,* hence *to permit:*— allow(2), allowed(2), gave...permission(2), given...permission(1), granted permission(1), permit(4), permits(2), permitted(4).

2011. **ἐπιτροπή epitropē**; from *2010; authority:*— commission(1).

2012. **ἐπίτροπος epitropos**; from *2010; an administrator* (one having authority):— foreman(1), guardians(1), steward(1).

2013. **ἐπιτυγχάνω epitugchanō**; from *1909* and *5177; to light upon,* i.e. *to obtain:*— obtain(1), obtained(4).

2014. **ἐπιφαίνω epiphainō**; from *1909* and *5316; to show forth,* i.e. *to appear:*— appeared(3), shine(1).

2015. **ἐπιφάνεια epiphaneia**; from *2016; appearance:*— appearance(1), appearing(5).

2016. **ἐπιφανής epiphanēs**; from *2014; notable:*— glorious(1).

2017. **ἐπιφαύσκω epiphauskō**; from *2020; to shine forth:*— shine(1).

2018. **ἐπιφέρω epipherō**; from *1909* and *5342; to bring upon* or *against:*— inflicts(1), pronounce against(1).

2019. **ἐπιφωνέω epiphōneō**; from *1909* and *5455; to call out:*— calling(1), crying(1), shouting(2).

2020. **ἐπιφώσκω epiphōskō**; from *1909* and *5457; to let shine,* i.e. *to dawn:*— about to begin(1), dawn(1).

2021. **ἐπιχειρέω epicheireō;** from *1909* and *5495; to put one's hand to,* hence *to attempt:*— attempted(1), attempting(1), undertaken(1).

2022. **ἐπιχέω epicheō;** from *1909* and **χέω cheō** *(to pour); to pour upon:*— pouring(1).

2023. **ἐπιχορηγέω epichorēgeō**; from *1909* and *5524; to supply:*— provides(1), supplied(2), supplies(1), supply(1).

2024. **ἐπιχορηγία epichorēgia**; from *2023; a supply:*— provision(1), supplies(1).

2025. **ἐπιχρίω epichriō**; from *1909* and *5548; to spread on,* i.e. *to anoint:*— anointed(1).

2026. **ἐποικοδομέω epoikodomeō**; from *1909* and *3618; to build upon:*— building(2), builds(2), built(4).

2027. **ἐποκέλλω epokellō**; var. reading for *1946a,* q.v.

2028. **ἐπονομάζω eponomazō**; from *1909* and *3687; to call by name:*— bear the name(1).

2029. **ἐποπτεύω epopteuō**; from *2030; to look upon:*— observe(2).

2030. **ἐπόπτης epoptēs**; from *1909* and the fut. of *3708; a looker-on,* i.e. *a spectator:*— eyewitnesses(1).

2031. **ἔπος epos**; akin to *1513a,* see also *3004; a word:*— so*(1).

2032. **ἐπουράνιος epouranios**; from *1909* and *3772; of heaven:*— heaven(1), heavenly(14), heavenly one(1), heavenly things(3).

2033. **ἑπτά hepta**; a prim. word; *seven:*— seven(87), seventh(1).

2034. **ἑπτάκις heptakis**; adv. from *2033; seven times:*— seven times(4).

2035. **ἑπτακισχίλιοι heptakischilioi**; from *2034* and *5507; seven thousand:*— seven thousand(1).

2036. (not used)

2037. **Ἔραστος Erastos**; from **ἐράω eraō** *(to love);* "beloved," *Erastus,* the name of two Chr.:— Erastus(3).

2038a. **ἐραυνάω eraunaō**; from *2045; to search, examine.*

2038b. **ἐργάζομαι ergazomai**; from *2041; to work, labor:*— accomplish(1), accomplished(1), accomplishing(1), achieve(1), committing(1), do(1), do...work(1), does(3), doing(1), doing...work(1), done(2), make...living(1), perform(4), performed(1), performing(1), practice(1), produces(1), traded(1), work(9), work be done(1), work do...perform(1), working(7), works(1), wrought(1).

2039. **ἐργασία ergasia**; from *2041; work* (noun):— business(2), effort(1), practice(1), profit(2).

2040. **ἐργάτης ergatēs**; from *2038b; a workman:*— laborer(2), laborers(6), worker(1), workers(4), workman(1), workmen(1).

2041. **ἔργον ergon**; from a prim. vb. **ἔρδω erdō** *(to do); work:*— action(1), behavior(1), deed(13), deeds(52), doing(1), effectual(1), labor(1), result(1), task(1), what...done(1), work(34), works(62).

2042. **ἐρεθίζω erethizō**; from **ἐρέθω erethō** *(to stir to anger); to stir up:*— exasperate(1), stirred(1).

2043. **ἐρείδω ereidō**; a prim. word; *to prop, to fix firmly:*— stuck fast(1).

2044. **ἐρεύγομαι ereugomai**; a prim. vb.; *to spit,* by ext. *to speak aloud:*— utter(1).

2045. **ἐρευνάω ereunaō**; var. reading for *2038a,* q.v.:— search(2), searches(3), seeking to know(1).

2046. **ἐρέω ereō**; see *1513a* and *3004.*

2047. **ἐρημία erēmia**; from *2048; a solitude, a wilderness:*— deserts(1), desolate place(2), wilderness(1).

2048. **ἔρημος erēmos**; a prim. word; *solitary, desolate:*— desert(2), deserts(1), desolate(6), open pasture(1), secluded(5), unpopulated(1), wilderness(32).

2049. **ἐρημόω erēmoō**; from *2048; to desolate:*— desolate(1), laid waste(4).

2050. **ἐρήμωσις erēmōsis**; from *2049; a making desolate:*— desolation(3).

2051. **ἐρίζω erizō**; from *2054; to wrangle, strive:*— quarrel(1).

2052. **ἐριθεία eritheia**; from **ἔριθος erithos** *(day-laborer); rivalry,* hence *ambition:*—disputes(2), selfish ambition(3), selfishly ambitious(1), selfishness(1).

2053. **ἔριον erion**; from **εἶρος eiros** *(wool); wool:*— wool(2).

2054. **ἔρις eris**; a prim. word; *strife:*— quarrels(1), strife(8).

2055. **ἐρίφιον eriphion**; dim. of *2056; a little young goat:*— goats(1).

2056. **ἔριφος eriphos**; a prim. word; *a young goat:*— goats(1), young goat(1).

2057. **Ἑρμᾶς Hermas**; from *2060; Hermas,* a Chr. at Rome:— Hermas(1).

2058. **ἑρμηνεία hermēneia**; from *2059; interpretation:*— interpretation(2).

2059. **ἑρμηνεύω hermēneuō**; from *2060; to interpret:*— translated(2), translation(1).

2060. **Ἑρμῆς Hermēs**; of unc. or.; *Hermes,* the name of a Gr. god and a Chr. at Rome:— Hermes(2).

2061. **Ἑρμογένης Hermogenēs**; from *2060* and the same as *1096;* "born of Hermes," *Hermogenes,* one who deserted Paul:— Hermogenes(1).

2062. **ἑρπετόν Herpeton**; from **ἕρπω herpō** *(to crawl); a creeping thing:*— crawling creatures(3), reptiles(1).

2063. **ἐρυθρός eruthros**; a prim. word; *red:*— red(2).

2064. **ἔρχομαι erchomai**; a prim. vb.; *to come, go:*— arrival(1), arrived(1), brought(1), came(225), come(222), comes(64), coming(87), entered(2), expected(3), fall(2), falls(1), give(1), go(1), going(2), grown(1), lighting(1), next(1), turned(1), went(18).

2065. **ἐρωτάω erōtaō**; akin to **ἔρομαι eromai** *(to ask); to ask, question:*— ask(15), ask a question(1), asked(14), asking(11), asks(3), beg(1), begging(1), implored(1), imploring(1), make request(1), please(2), question(5), questioned(2), request(4), requesting(1), urging(1).

2066. **ἐσθής esthēs**; from **ἕννυμι hennumi** *(to clothe); clothing:*— apparel(1), clothes(3), clothing(1), garments(1), robe(1).

2067. **ἔσθησις esthēsis**; from **ἐσθέω estheō** *(to clothe); clothing:*— clothing(1).

2068. **ἐσθίω esthiō**; akin to **ἔδω edō** *(to eat); to eat:*— ate(21), consume(2), diet(1), dine(1), does so(1), eat(96), eaten(2), eating(19), eats(11), feed(2), use(1).

2069. **Ἑσλί Hesli**; of Heb. or.; *Hesli,* an Isr.:— Hesli(1).

2070. ἐσμέν esmen; first pers. pl. pres. ind. of *1510,* q.v.

2071. ἔσομαι esomai; fut. of *1510,* q.v.

2072. ἔσοπτρον esoptron; from *1519* and the fut. of *3708; a mirror* (i.e. an object for looking into):— mirror(2).

2073. ἑσπέρα hespera; fem. of **ἑσπερός hesperos** *(of evening); evening:*— evening(3).

2074. Ἑσρώμ Hesrōm; of Heb. or. [2696]; *Hezron,* an Isr.:— Hezron(3).

2075. ἐστέ este; second pers. pl. pres. ind. of *1510,* q.v.

2076. ἐστί esti; third pers. sing. pres. ind. of *1510,* q.v.

2077. ἔστω estō; imper. of *1510,* q.v.

2078. ἔσχατος eschatos; of unc. or.; *last, extreme:*— end(1), last(46), last of all(1), last man(1), last men(1), late(1), remotest part(1).

2079. ἐσχάτως eschatōs; adv. from *2078; extremely:*— point of death(1).

2080. ἔσω esō; adv. from *1519; within:*— inner(2), inner man(1), inside(2), within(1).

2081. ἔσωθεν esōthen; from *2080; from within:*— inside(6), inwardly(2), within(4).

2082. ἐσώτερος esōteros; cptv. of *2080; inner:*— inner(1), within(1).

2083. ἑταῖρος hetairos; from **ἔτης etēs** *(clansman, cousin); a companion:*— friend(3).

2084. ἑτερόγλωσσος heteroglōssos; from *2087* and *1100; of another tongue:*— men of strange tongues(1), strange tongues(1).

2085. ἑτεροδιδασκαλέω heterodidaskaleō; from *2087* and *1320; to teach other doctrine:*— advocates a different doctrine(1), children(2), different doctrine(1), teach strange doctrines(1).

2086. ἑτεροζυγέω heterozugeō; from *2087* and *2218; to be yoked up differently,* i.e. *to be unequally yoked:*— bound together(1).

2087. ἕτερος heteros; of unc. or.; *other:*— another(31), another man(1), another one(2), any other(1), different(6), else(2), neighbor(3), next(3), one(1), other(31), other person(1), others(13), someone else(1), strange(1), strangers(1).

2088. ἑτέρως heterōs; adv. from *2087; differently:*— different(1).

2089. ἔτι eti; a prim. adv.; *still, yet:*— after(1), any longer(7), anymore(4), besides(1), further(4), longer(15), more(6), moreover*(1), still(43), yes(2), yet(8).

2090. ἑτοιμάζω hetoimazō; from *2092; to prepare:*— get ready(1), get...ready(1), made ready(1), made...ready(1), make arrangements(1), make ready(4), prepare(11), prepared(20).

2091. ἑτοιμασία hetoimasia; from *2090; preparation:*— preparation(1).

2092. ἕτοιμος hetoimos; a prim. word; *prepared:*— accomplished(1), opportune(1), ready(15).

2093. ἑτοίμως hetoimōs; adv. from *2092; readily:*— ready(3).

2094. ἔτος etos; a prim. word; *a year:*— age(1), year(3), years(42), years of age(1).

2095. εὖ eu; adv. from **εὖς eus** *(good); well:*— done(1), good(1), well(2), well done(2).

2096. Εὕα Heua; of Heb. or. [2332]; *Eve,* the first woman:— Eve(2).

2097. εὐαγγελίζω euaggelizō; from *2095* and *32a; to announce good news:*— bring...good news(2), bring good news(1), brought...good news(1), good news(5), good news preached(2), gospel(2), gospel preached(2), preach(4), preach the gospel(11), preach...a gospel(1), preach...the good news(1), preached(11), preached the gospel(4), preaching(8), preaching the good news(1), preaching the gospel(4), preaching...a gospel(1).

2098. εὐαγγέλιον euaggelion; from the same as *2097; good news:*— good news(1), gospel(73), gospel's(2).

2099. εὐαγγελιστής euaggelistēs; from *2097; an evangelist, a bringer of good news:*— evangelist(2), evangelists(1).

2100. εὐαρεστέω euaresteō; from *2101; to be well-pleasing:*— please(1), pleased(1), pleasing(1).

2101. εὐάρεστος euarestos; from *2095* and **ἀρεστός arestos** *(acceptable, pleasing);* from *700; well-pleasing:*— acceptable(3), pleasing(3), well-pleasing(3).

2102. εὐαρέστως euarestōs; adv. from *2101; acceptably:*— acceptable(1).

2103. Εὔβουλος Euboulos; from *2095* and *1012;* "prudent," *Eubulus,* a Chr.:— Eubulus(1).

2104a. εὖγε euge; see *2095* and *1065.*

2104b. εὐγενής eugenēs; from *2095* and *1085; of noble race:*— more noble-minded(1), noble(1), nobleman*(1).

2105. εὐδία eudia; from **εὔδιος eudios** *(calm); fair weather:*— fair weather(1).

2106. εὐδοκέω eudokeō; from *2095* and *1380; to think well of,* i.e. *to be well-pleased:*— am well content(1), am well-pleased(5), been pleased(1), chosen gladly(1), good pleasure(1), has...pleasure(1), pleased(2), prefer(1), taken pleasure(1), taken...pleasure(1), thought it best(1), took pleasure(1), well-pleased(4).

2107. εὐδοκία eudokia; from *2106; good pleasure:*— desire(2), good pleasure(1), good will(1), kind intention(2), pleased(1), well-pleasing(2).

2108. εὐεργεσία euergesia; from *2110; a good deed:*— benefit(1), benefit done(1).

2109. εὐεργετέω euergeteō; from *2110; to do good:*— doing good(1).

2110. εὐεργέτης euergetēs; from *2095* and the same as *2041; a doer of good,* i.e. *a benefactor:*— benefactors(1).

2111. εὔθετος euthetos; from *2095* and *5087; well-placed,* i.e. *ready for use:*— fit(1), useful(1), useless*(1).

2112. εὐθέως eutheōs; adv. from *2117; at once, directly:*— immediately(32), shortly(1).

2113. εὐθυδρομέω euthudromeō; from *2117* and *1408; to run a straight course:*— ran a straight course(2), straight course(2).

2114. εὐθυμέω euthumeō; from *2115a; to be of good cheer:*— cheerful(1), keep up...courage(2).

2115a. εὔθυμος euthumos; from *2095* and *2372; of good cheer:*— encouraged(1).

2115b. εὐθύμως euthumōs; adv. from *2115a; cheerfully:*— cheerfully(1).

2116. εὐθύνω euthunō; from *2117; to make straight:*— make straight(1), pilot(1).

2117. εὐθύς euthus; a prim. word used as an adj. or adv.; *straight, straightway:*— early(1), immediately(52), just then(1), right(2), straight(6).

2118. εὐθύτης euthutēs; from *2117; uprightness:*— righteous(1).

2119. εὐκαιρέω eukaireō; from *2121; to have opportunity:*— have time(1), opportunity(1), spend...time(1).

2120. εὐκαιρία eukairia; from *2121; fitting time:*— good opportunity(2).

2121. εὔκαιρος eukairos; from *2095* and *2540; timely:*— strategic(1), time of need(1).

2122. εὐκαίρως eukairōs; adv. from *2121; in season:*— opportune time(1), season(1).

2123. εὐκοπώτερος eukopōteros; cptv. of **εὐκόπος eukopos** *(easy);* from *2095* and *2873; with easier labor:*— easier(7).

2124. εὐλάβεια eulabeia; from *2126; caution:*— piety(1), reverence(1).

2125. εὐλαβέομαι eulabeomai; from *2126; to be cautious:*— reverence(1).

2126. εὐλαβής eulabēs; from *2095* and *2983; cautious:*— devout(4).

2127. εὐλογέω eulogeō; from *2095* and *3056; to speak well of, praise:*— bless(9), blessed(25), blessing(3), giving a blessing(1), praise(1), praising(1), surely*(1).

2128. εὐλογητός eulogētos; from *2127; well spoken of,* i.e. *blessed:*— blessed(8).

2129. εὐλογία eulogia; from the same as *2127; praise, blessing:*— blessing(11), bountiful gift(2), bountifully(2), flattering speech(1).

2130. εὐμετάδοτος eumetadotos; from *2095* and *3330; ready to impart:*— generous(1).

2131. Εὐνίκη Eunikē; from *2095* and *3529;* "victorious," *Eunice,* the mother of Timothy:— Eunice(1).

2132. εὐνοέω eunoeō; from a comp. of *2095* and *3539; to think kindly of,* i.e. *to be favorable:*— make friends(1).

2133. εὔνοια eunoia; from the same as *2132; goodwill:*— good will(1).

2134. εὐνουχίζω eunouchizō; from *2135; to make a eunuch of:*— made eunuchs(1), made...eunuchs(1).

2135. εὐνοῦχος eunouchos; from **εὐνή eunē** *(a bed)* and *2192; a eunuch:*— eunuch(5), eunuchs(3).

2136. Εὐοδία Euodia; from the same as *2137;* perh. "success," *Euodia,* a Chr. at Philippi:— Euodia(1).

2137. εὐοδόω euodoō; from *2095* and *3598; to have a prosperous journey:*— prosper(2), prospers(1), succeed(1).

2138a. εὐπάρεδρος euparedros; from *2095* and **πάρεδρος paredros** *(sitting near); constantly attendant:*— devotion(1).

2138b. εὐπειθής eupeithēs; from *2095* and *3982; ready to obey:*— reasonable(1).

2139. εὐπερίστατος euperistatos; from *2095* and *4026; easily encircling:*— easily entangles(1).

2140. εὐποιΐα eupoiia; from *2095* and *4160; doing good:*— doing good(1).

2141. εὐπορέω euporeō; from a comp. of *2095* and the same as *4198; to prosper:*— had means(1).

2142. εὐπορία euporia; from the same as *2141; prosperity, plenty:*— prosperity(1).

2143. εὐπρέπεια euprepeia; from *2095* and a der. of *4241; goodly appearance:*— beauty(1).

2144. εὐπρόσδεκτος euprosdektos; from *2095* and *4327; acceptable:*— acceptable(5).

2145. εὐπρόσεδρος euprosedros; var. reading for *2138a,* q.v.

2146a. εὐπροσωπέω euprosōpeō; from a comp. of *2095* and *4383; to be of good counte-*

nance, i.e. *to look well:*— good showing(1), make a good showing(1).

2146b. **Εὐρακύλων Eurakulōn**; from **Εὖρος Euros** *(the east wind)* and the Lat. **Aquilo** *(the north wind); the Euraquilo,* a northeast wind:— Euraquilo(1).

2147. **εὑρίσκω heuriskō**; a prim. vb.; *to find:*— find(48), finding(9), finds(10), found(104), get(1), obtained(1), proved(1), regarded(1).

2148. **Εὐροκλύδων Eurokludōn**; var. reading for *2146b,* q.v.

2149. **εὐρύχωρος euruchōros**; from **εὐρύς eurus** *(broad, wide)* and *5561; spacious:*— broad(1).

2150. **εὐσέβεια eusebeia**; from *2152; piety:*— godliness(14), piety(1).

2151. **εὐσεβέω eusebeō**; from *2152; to show piety towards:*— practice piety(1), worship(1).

2152. **εὐσεβής eusebēs**; from *2095* and *4576; pious:*— devout(1), devout man(1), godly(1).

2153. **εὐσεβῶς eusebōs**; adv. from *2152; piously:*— godly(2).

2154. **εὔσημος eusēmos**; from *2095* and the same as *4591; clear:*— clear(1).

2155. **εὔσπλαγχνος eusplagchnos**; from *2095* and *4698; tenderhearted, compassionate:*— kindhearted(1), tender-hearted(1).

2156. **εὐσχημόνως euschēmonōs**; adv. from *2158; becomingly:*— properly(3).

2157. **εὐσχημοσύνη euschēmosunē**; from *2158; comeliness:*— presentable(1).

2158. **εὐσχήμων euschēmōn**; from *2095* and *4976; comely:*— appropriate(1), presentable(1), prominence(1), prominent(2).

2159. **εὐτόνως eutonōs**; from *2095* and **τείνω teinō** *(to stretch); in a well-strung manner,* fig. *vigorously:*— powerfully(1), vehemently(1).

2160. **εὐτραπελία eutrapelia**; from *2095* and the same as *5157; ready wit, coarse jesting:*— coarse jesting(1).

2161. **Εὔτυχος Eutuchos**; from *2095* and **τυχή tuchē** *(fortune, fate);* "well-fated," *Eutychus,* a young man restored to life by Paul:— Eutychus(1).

2162. **εὐφημία euphēmia**; from *2163; good report:*— good report(1).

2163. **εὔφημος euphēmos**; from *2095* and *5345; well reported of:*— good repute(1).

2164. **εὐφορέω euphoreō**; from *2095* and *5409; to bear well,* i.e. *to be fruitful:*— very productive(1).

2165. **εὐφραίνω euphrainō**; from *2095* and *5424; to cheer, make merry:*— celebrate(5), glad(1), joyously living(1), makes...glad(1), merry(1), rejoice(4), rejoicing(1).

2166. **Εὐφράτης Euphratēs**; of unc. or.; *Euphrates,* a river of Asia:— Euphrates(2).

2167. **εὐφροσύνη euphrosunē**; from a comp. of *2095* and *5424; gladness:*— gladness(2).

2168. **εὐχαριστέω eucharisteō**; from *2170; to be thankful:*— gave thanks(2), give...thanks(1), give thanks(8), given thanks(6), gives thanks(2), giving thanks(7), thank(9), thanked(1), thanks(1), thanks may be given(1).

2169. **εὐχαριστία eucharistia**; from *2170; thankfulness, giving of thanks:*— giving of thanks(3), gratefully*(1), gratitude(2), thankfulness(1), thanks(2), thanksgiving(4), thanksgivings(2).

2170. **εὐχάριστος eucharistos**; from *2095* and *5483; thankful:*— thankful(1).

2171. **εὐχή euchē**; from *2172; a prayer:*— prayer(1), vow(2).

2172. **εὔχομαι euchomai**; a prim. vb.; *to pray:*— pray(3), wish(1), wished(1), would wish(1).

2173. **εὔχρηστος euchrēstos**; from *2095* and *5543; useful:*— useful(3).

2174. **εὐψυχέω eupsucheō**; from a comp. of *2095* and *5590; to be of good courage:*— encouraged(1).

2175. **εὐωδία euōdia**; from *2095* and *3605; fragrance:*— fragrance(1), fragrant(2).

2176. **εὐώνυμος euōnumos**; from *2095* and *3686; of good name,* euph. for *left:*— left(9).

2177. **ἐφάλλομαι ephallomai**; from *1909* and *242; to leap upon:*— leaped(1).

2178. **ἐφάπαξ ephapax**; from *1909* and *530; once for all:*— once for all(4), one time(1).

2179. **Ἐφεσῖνος Ephesinos**; var. reading for *2181,* q.v.

2180. **Ἐφέσιος Ephesios**; from *2181; Ephesian:*— Ephesian(1), Ephesians(3).

2181. **Ἔφεσος Ephesos**; of unc. or.; *Ephesus,* a city in Asia Minor:— Ephesus(17).

2182. **ἐφευρετής epheuretēs**; from a comp. of *1909* and *2147; a discoverer,* hence *an inventor:*— inventors(1).

2183. **ἐφημερία ephēmeria**; from *2184; a class* (of priests detailed for service in the temple):— division(2).

2184. **ἐφήμερος ephēmeros**; from *1909* and *2250; for the day:*— daily(1).

2185. **ἐφικνέομαι ephikneomai**; from *1909* and the same as *2425; to arrive upon,* i.e. *to reach:*— reach(2).

2186. **ἐφίστημι ephistēmi**; from *1909* and *2476; to set upon, set up, to stand upon, be present:*— appeared(3), attacking(1), came(5), come(3), confronted(1), ready(1), set(1), standing(2), standing near(1), stood(1), stood before(1), stood near(1).

2187. **Ἐφραίμ Ephraim**; prob. of Heb. or.; *Ephraim,* a city near Jer.:— Ephraim(1).

2188. **ἐφφαθά ephphatha**; of Ara. or. [6606]; *be opened!:*— Ephphatha(1).

2189a. **ἐχθές echthes**; a prol. form of a prim. adv.; *yesterday:*— yesterday(3).

2189b. **ἔχθρα echthra**; from *2190; enmity:*— enemies(1), enmities(1), enmity(2), hostile(1), hostility(1).

2190. **ἐχθρός echthros**; from **ἔχθος echthos** *(hatred); hostile:*— enemies(20), enemy(10), enemy*(1), hostile(1).

2191. **ἔχιδνα echidna**; from **ἔχις echis** *(a viper, adder); a viper:*— viper(1), vipers(4).

2192. **ἔχω echō**; a prim. vb.; *to have, hold:*— ability(1), able(1), accompany(1), acknowledge*(1), am(2), become(1), been(3), being(1), being under(1), bringing(1), conceived*(1), consider(2), considered(2), could(2), derive(1), deriving(1), devoid*(1), enjoyed(1), experiencing(1), felt(1), following(1), get(2), gripped(1), had(80), has(134), have(283), have had(2), having(50), held(1), hold(5), holding(7), holds(2), ill*(5), incurring(1), involves(1), keep(3), keeping(3), kept(1), maintain(1), maintained(1), maintaining(1), meets(1), nearby(1), next(2), obliged*(1), obtain(2), obtained(1), owned(3), possess(2), possessed(4), possesses(1), receive(1), received(1), recover*(1), regard(2), regarded(1), reigns*(1), remember*(1), retain(1), seize(1), show(1), think*(1), unable*(1), under(1), under*(1), use(1), without*(3).

2193. **ἕως heōs**; a prim. particle used as a prep., adv. and conjunc.; *till, until:*— down(2), even(5), far(5), how(7), long(1), long*(7), no more(1), point(2), right(1), until(83), while(5).

Z

2194. **Ζαβουλών Zaboulōn**; of Heb. or. [2074]; *Zebulun,* a son of Jacob and one of the Isr. tribes:— Zebulun(3).

2195. **Ζακχαῖος Zakchaios**; of Heb. or. [2140]; *Zaccheus,* a tax collector:— Zaccheus(3).

2196. **Ζάρα Zara**; of Heb. or. [2226]; *Zerah,* an Isr.:— Zerah(1).

2197. **Ζαχαρίας Zacharias**; of Heb. or. [2148a]; *Zacharias,* the father of John the Baptist, *Zechariah,* the son of Barachiah:— Zacharias(9), Zechariah(2).

2198. **ζάω zaō**; from prim. roots **ζη- zē-** and **ζω- zō-**; *to live:*— alive(15), get their living(1), holding(1), life(6), life*(1), live(53), lived(3), lives(19), living(44).

2199. **Ζεβεδαῖος Zebedaios**; of Heb. or. [2069]; *Zebedee,* the father of the apostles James and John:— Zebedee(12).

2200. **ζεστός zestos**; from *2204; boiling hot:*— hot(3).

2201. **ζεῦγος zeugos**; from the same as *2218; a pair, a yoke:*— pair(1), yoke(1).

2202. **ζευκτηρία zeuktēria**; from **ζευκτήριος zeuktērios** *(fit for joining);* from the same as *2218; bands, ropes:*— ropes(1).

2203. **Ζεύς Zeus**; of unc. or.; *Zeus,* the greatest of the pagan Gk. gods:— Zeus(2).

2204. **ζέω zeō**; a prim. vb.; *to boil, be hot:*— being fervent(1), fervent(1).

2205a. **ζηλεύω zēleuō**; a late form of *2206; to have warmth of feeling for* or *against, to be zealous* or *jealous:*— zealous(1).

2205b. **ζῆλος zēlos**; prob. from *2204; zeal, jealousy:*— fury(1), jealousy(9), zeal(6).

2206. **ζηλόω zēloō**; from *2205b; to be jealous:*— am jealous(1), becoming jealous(1), desire earnestly(2), eagerly seek(1), eagerly sought(1), earnestly desire(1), envious(1), jealous(2), seek(1).

2207. **ζηλωτής zēlōtēs**; from *2206; zealous:*— zealous(6).

2208. **Ζηλωτής Zēlōtēs**; the same as *2207; the Zealot,* a member of a Jewish political party:— Zealot(2).

2209. **ζημία zēmia**; of unc. or.; *damage:*— loss(4).

2210. **ζημιόω zēmioō**; from *2209; to damage, suffer loss:*— forfeit(1), forfeits(2), suffer loss(2), suffered the loss of(1).

2211. **Ζηνᾶς Zēnas**; prob. a contr. of *2203* and *1435;* "Zeus-given," *Zenas,* a Chr. lawyer:— Zenas(1).

2212. **ζητέω zēteō**; of unc. or.; *to seek:*— deliberating(1), demanding(1), inquire(1), looking(11), made efforts(1), search(4), searched(1), seek(36), seek after(1), seeking(35), seeks(9), sought(4), striving(1), tried(1), trying(6), kept trying to obtain(2).

2213. **ζήτημα zētēma**; from *2212; an inquiry:*— issue(1), points of disagreement(1), questions(3).

2214. **ζήτησις zētēsis**; from *2212; a search, questioning:*— controversial questions(1), controversies(1), debate(2), discussion(1), how to investigate(1), speculations(1).

2215. ζιζάνιον zizanion; prob. of Sumer. or.; *zizanium* (a kind of darnel resembling wheat):— tares(8).

2216. Ζοροβαβέλ Zorobabel; of Heb. or. [2216]; *Zerubbabel*, an Isr.:— Zerubbabel(3).

2217. ζόφος zophos; akin to *1105; deep gloom:*— black(2), darkness(2), gloom(1).

2218. ζυγός zugos; from **ζεύγνυμι zeugnumi** *(to yoke); a yoke:*— pair of scales(1), yoke(5).

2219. ζύμη zumē; from a prim. root; *leaven:*— leaven(13).

2220. ζυμόω zumoō; from *2219; to leaven:*— leavened(2), leavens(2).

2221. ζωγρέω zōgreō; from the same as *2226* and *64; to catch alive:*— catching(1), held captive(1).

2222. ζωή zōē; from *2198; life:*— alive(1), life(133), living(1).

2223. ζώνη zōnē; from *2224; a belt:*— belt(5), belts(1), money belts(1), sash(1), sashes(1).

2224. ζώννυμι zōnnumi; a prim. vb.; *to gird:*— gird(3).

2225. ζωογονέω zōogoneō; from the same as *2226* and *1096; to preserve alive:*— gives life(1), preserve(1), survive(1).

2226. ζῷον zōon; from **ζωός zōos** *(alive); a living creature:*— animals(3), creature(4), living creature(3), living creatures(13).

2227. ζῳοποιέω zōopoieō; from the same as *2226* and *4160; to make alive:*— come to life(1), give life(1), gives...life(1), gives life(4), impart life(1), life-giving(1), made alive(2).

Η

2228. ἤ ē; a prim. conjunc. used disjunctively or cptv.; *or, than:*— either(4), nor(1), or(282), or else(4), other than(1), rather(1), rather than(2), than(36), than...or(1), whether(1).

2229. ἦ ē; var. reading for *1487*, q.v.

2230. ἡγεμονεύω hēgemoneuō; from *2232; to command:*— governor(2).

2231. ἡγεμονία hēgemonia; from *2232; rule:*— reign(1).

2232. ἡγεμών hēgemōn; from *2233; a leader, governor:*— governor(14), governor's(1), governors(4).

2233. ἡγέομαι hēgeomai; from *71; to lead, suppose:*— chief(1), consider(3), considered(2), considering(1), count(4), counted(1), esteem(1), governor(1), leader(1), leaders(3), leading(1), led(1), regard(5), regarded(1), Ruler(1), thought(2).

2234. ἡδέως hēdeōs; adv. From **ἡδύς hēdus** *(sweet); sweetly, gladly:*— enjoy(1), enjoyed(1), gladly(1), most gladly(2).

2235. ἤδη ēdē; a prim. adv. of time; *already:*— already(42), as soon as(1), now(14), soon*(1), this time(2).

2236. ἥδιστα hēdista; superl. from the same as *2234*, q.v.

2237. ἡδονή hēdonē; from **ἥδομαι hēdomai** *(to enjoy oneself); pleasure:*— pleasure(1), pleasures(4).

2238. ἡδύοσμον hēduosmon; from the same as *2234* and *3744; sweet smelling:*— mint(2).

2239. ἦθος ēthos; prol. form of *1485; custom:*— morals(1).

2240. ἥκω hēkō; a prim. vb.; *to have come, be present:*— come(17), comes(1), had come(1), has...come(1), has come(2), have come(3).

2241. ἠλί ēli; of Heb. or. [410] with pron. suff.; *my God:*— Eli(2).

2242. Ἠλί Ēli; of Heb. or. [5941]; *Eli*, an Isr.:— Eli(1).

2243. Ἠλίας Ēlias; of Heb. or. [452]; *Elijah*, an Isr. prophet:— Elijah(29).

2244. ἡλικία hēlikia; from **ἧλιξ hēlix** *(of the same age, mature); maturity*, i.e. *age:*— age(2), life(2), life's span(1), stature(3).

2245. ἡλίκος hēlikos; akin to root of *2244; how great, how small:*— how great(2), such a small(1).

2246. ἥλιος hēlios; a prim. word; *the sun:*— east*(1), sun(31).

2247. ἧλος hēlos; a prim. word; *a nail:*— nails(2).

2248. ἡμᾶς hēmas; acc. pl. of *1473*, q.v.

2249. ἡμεῖς hēmeis; nom. pl. of *1473*, q.v.:— ourselves(2).

2250. ἡμέρα hēmera; a prim. word; *day:*— always*(1), court(1), daily*(10), day(207), day's(1), day...another(1), daybreak(1), days(148), daytime(2), midday*(1), time(12), years(4).

2251. ἡμέτερος hēmeteros; poss. pron. from *2249; our:*— ours(1).

2252. ἤμην ēmēn; imperf. of *1510*, q.v.

2253. ἡμιθανής hēmithanēs; from the same as *2255* and *2348; half dead:*— half dead(1).

2254. ἡμῖν hēmin; dat. pl. of *1473*, q.v.

2255. ἥμισυς hēmisus; prol. form of **ἡμι- hēmi-** (a pref. mean. *half*); *half:*— half(5).

2256. ἡμιώριον hēmiōrion; from the root of *2255* and *5610; half an hour:*— half an hour(1).

2257. ἡμῶν hēmōn; gen. pl. of *1473*, q.v.

2258. ἦν ēn; imperf. of *1510*, q.v.

2259. ἡνίκα hēnika; adv. of unc. or.; *at which time:*— whenever*(2).

2260. ἤπερ ēper; see *2228* and *4007a*.

2261. ἤπιος ēpios; of unc. or.; *gentle, mild:*— gentle(1), kind(1).

2262. Ἤρ Ēr; of Heb. or. [6147]; *Er*, an Isr.:— Er(1).

2263. ἤρεμος ēremos; of unc. or.; *quiet:*— tranquil(1).

2264. Ἡρῴδης Hērōdēs; perh. from **ἥρως hērōs** *(hero)* and a patronymic suff.; perh. "son of a hero," *Herod*, the name of several kings of the Jews:— Herod(39), Herod's(4).

2265. Ἡρῳδιανοί Hērōdianoi; from *2264; Herodians*, partisans of Herod:— Herodians(3).

2266. Ἡρῳδιάς Hērōdias; from *2264; Herodias*, granddaughter of Herod the Great:— Herodias(6).

2267. Ἡρῳδίων Hērōdiōn; from *2264; Herodion*, a Chr. at Rome:— Herodion(1).

2268. Ἡσαΐας Ēsaias; of Heb. or. [3470b]; *Isaiah*, an Isr. prophet:— Isaiah(22).

2269a. Ἡσαῦ Ēsau; of Heb. or. [6215]; *Esau*, a son of Isaac:— Esau(3).

2269b. ἥσσων hēssōn; cptv. from **ἦκα ēka** *(slightly, a little); inferior, less:*— less(1), worse(1).

2270. ἡσυχάζω hēsuchazō; from the same as *2272; to be still, be silent:*— fell silent(1), kept silent(1), lead a quiet life(1), quiet life(1), quieted down(1), rested(1).

2271. ἡσυχία hēsuchia; from *2272; stillness:*— quiet(2), quiet fashion(1), quietly(1).

2272. ἡσύχιος hēsuchios; a prol. form of **ἥσυχος hēsuchos** *(still, quiet); tranquil:*— quiet(2).

2273. ἤτοι ētoi; from *2228* and *5104; whether:*— either(1).

2274. ἡττάομαι hēttaomai; from the same as *2269b; to be inferior:*— Israel(17), overcome(2), treated as inferior(1).

2275. ἥττημα hēttēma; from *2274; loss:*— defeat(1), failure(1).

2276. ἥττων hēttōn; var. reading for *2269b*, q.v.

2277. ἤτω ētō; imper. of *1510*, q.v.

2278. ἠχέω ēcheō; from *2279; to make a loud noise, to sound:*— noisy(1).

2279. ἦχος ēchos; a late form of a prim. word **ἠχή ēchē** *(noise, sound); a noise, sound:*— blast(1), noise(1), report(1), roaring(1).

Θ

2280a. θά tha; see *3134*.

2280b. Θαδδαῖος Thaddaios; of Ara. or.; *Thaddeus*, one of the twelve apostles:— Thaddaeus(2).

2281. θάλασσα thalassa; of unc. or.; *the sea:*— sea(86), seashore(5).

2282. θάλπω thalpō; a prim. vb.; *to warm*, hence *to cherish:*— cherishes(1), tenderly cares(1).

2283. Θαμάρ Thamar; of Heb. or. [8559]; *Tamar*, an Isr. woman:— Tamar(1).

2284. θαμβέω thambeō; from *2285; to astonish:*— amazed(3).

2285. θάμβος thambos; from a prim. root **θαφ- thaph-**; *amazement:*— amazement(2), wonder(1).

2286. θανάσιμος thanasimos; from *2288; deadly:*— deadly(1).

2287. θανατηφόρος thanatēphoros; from *2288* and *5342; death-bringing:*— deadly(1).

2288. θάνατος thanatos; from *2348; death:*— danger of death(1), death(112), fatal(2), pestilence(3).

2289. θανατόω thanatoō; from *2288; to put to death:*— cause...to be put to death(1), made to die(1), put...to death(3), putting to death(1).

2290. θάπτω thaptō; from a prim. root; *to bury:*— buried(7), bury(4).

2291. Θάρα Thara; of Heb. or. [8646]; *Terah*, the father of Abraham:— Terah(1).

2292. θαρρέω tharreō; a late form of *2293; to be of good courage:*— bold(2), confidently(1), good courage(2), have confidence(1).

2293. θαρσέω tharseō; from *2294; to be of good courage:*— take courage(7).

2294. θάρσος tharsos; from **θρασύς thrasus** *(bold); courage:*— courage(1).

2295. θαῦμα thauma; akin to *2300; a wonder:*— greatly*(1), wonder(1).

2296. θαυμάζω thaumazō; from *2295; to marvel, wonder:*— am amazed(1), amazed(15), amazement(1), astonished(3), being amazed(1), flattering(1), marvel(4), marveled(5), marveling(2), surprised(2), wonder(2), wondered(4), wondering(2).

2297. **θαυμάσιος thaumasios**; adj. from *2295; wonderful:*— wonderful things(1).

2298. **θαυμαστός thaumastos**; from *2296; wonderful:*— amazing thing(1), marvelous(5).

2299. **θεά thea**; fem. of *2316; a goddess:*— goddess(2).

2300. **θεάομαι theaomai**; of unc. or.; *to behold, look upon:*— look(1), look over(1), looked(1), noticed(3), saw(5), see(3), seeing(2), seen(5), watched(1).

2301. **θεατρίζω theatrizō**; from *2302; to make a spectacle of:*— made a public spectacle(1), public spectacle(1).

2302. **θέατρον theatron**; from *2300; a theater, a spectacle:*— spectacle(1), theater(2).

2303. **θεῖον theion**; of unc. or.; *brimstone:*—brimstone(7).

2304. **θεῖος theios**; from *2316; divine:*— divine(2), divine nature(1).

2305. **θειότης theiotēs**; from *2304; divinity, divine nature:*— divine nature(1).

2306. **θειώδης theiōdēs**; from *2303* and **-ωδης -ōdēs** (suff. denoting similarity); of brimstone:— brimstone(1).

2307. **θέλημα thelēma**; from *2309; will:*— desire(1), desires(1), will(57).

2308. **θέλησις thelēsis**; from *2309; will:*— will(1).

2309. **θέλω thelō**; a prim. vb.; *to will, wish:*— am...willing(1), am willing(3), delighting(1), delights(1), desire(14), desired(4), desires(4), desiring(2), intended(1), intending(1), like(3), maintain(1), mean(1), mean*(2), please(1), purposed(1), refused*(1), unwilling*(11), want(52), wanted(15), wanting(3), wants(8), will(5), willed(1), willing(15), wills(4), wish(24), wished(7), wishes(16), wishing(4), would(1).

2310a. **θεμέλιον themelion**; prob. from *2310b; of* or *for a foundation.*

2310b. **θεμέλιος themelios**; from *5087; of* or *for a foundation:*— foundation(11), foundation stone(1), foundation stones(2), foundations(2).

2311. **θεμελιόω themelioō**; from *2310b; to lay the foundation of:*— establish(1), firmly established(1), founded(1), grounded(1), laid the foundation(1).

2312. **θεοδίδακτος theodidaktos**; from *2316* and *1321; taught of God:*— taught by God(1).

2313. **θεομαχέω theomacheō**; from *2314; to fight against God.*

2314. **θεομάχος theomachos**; from *2316* and *3164; fighting against God:*— fighting against God(1).

2315. **θεόπνευστος theopneustos**; from *2316* and *4154; God-breathed,* i.e. *inspired by God:*— inspired by God(1).

2316. **θεός theos**; of unc. or.; *God, a god:*— divinely(1), God(1267), god(6), God's(27), God-fearing(1), godly(2), godly*(1), gods(8), Lord(1).

2317. **θεοσέβεια theosebeia**; from *2318; fear of God:*— godliness(1).

2318. **θεοσεβής theosebēs**; from *2316* and *4576; God-fearing:*— God-fearing(1).

2319. **θεοστυγής theostugēs**; from *2316* and the same as *4767; hating God:*— haters of God(1).

2320. **θεότης theotēs**; from *2316; deity:*— Deity(1).

2321. **Θεόφιλος Theophilos**; from *2316* and *5384;* "friend of God," *Theophilus,* the addressee of Luke and Acts:— Theophilus(2).

2322. **θεραπεία therapeia**; from *2323; attention, medical service:*— healing(2), servants(1).

2323. **θεραπεύω therapeuō**; from *2324; to serve, cure:*— cure(1), cured(4), get healed(1), getting cured(1), heal(9), healed(21), healing(5), served(1).

2324. **θεράπων therapōn**; a prim. word; *an attendant:*— servant(1).

2325. **θερίζω therizō**; from *2330; to reap:*— did the harvesting(1), reap(14), reaped(1), reaping(2), reaps(3).

2326. **θερισμός therismos**; from *2325; harvest:*— harvest(13).

2327. **θεριστής theristes**; from *2325; a reaper:*— reapers(2).

2328. **θερμαίνω thermainō**; from **θερμός thermos** *(hot);* from the same as *2330; to warm:*— warmed(1), warming(5).

2329. **θέρμη thermē**; prob. from the same as *2330; heat:*— heat(1).

2330. **θέρος theros**; from **θέρω therō** *(to heat); summer:*— summer(3).

2331. **Θεσσαλονικεύς Thessalonikeus**; from *2332; a Thessalonian:*— Thessalonians(3), Thessalonica(1).

2332. **Θεσσαλονίκη Thessalonikē**; perh. from **Θεσσαλός Thessalos** *(Thessalian)* and *3529; Thessalonica,* a city of Macedonia:— Thessalonica(5).

2333. **Θευδᾶς Theudas**; of unc. or.; *Theudas,* an Isr.:— Theudas(1).

2334. **θεωρέω theōreō**; from **θεωρός theōros** *(an envoy, spectator); to look at, gaze:*— beholds(1), look(1), looking(5), observe(3), observed(4), observing(3), perceive(2), saw(8), see(16), seeing(2), seen(1), sees(4), watched(1), watching(2).

2335. **θεωρία theōria**; from the same as *2334; a viewing,* hence *a spectacle:*— saw(1), spectacle(1).

2336. **θήκη thēkē**; from *5087; a receptacle:*— sheath(1).

2337. **θηλάζω thēlazō**; from **θηλή thēlē** *(a nipple); to suckle:*— nursed(1), nursing babies(4).

2338. **θῆλυς thēlus**; from prim. root **θη- thē-** *(to suckle); female:*— female(3), woman(1), women(1).

2339. **θήρα thēra**; from **θήρ thēr** *(a wild beast); a hunting, prey:*— trap(1).

2340. **θηρεύω thēreuō**; from *2339; to hunt:*— catch(1).

2341. **θηριομαχέω thēriomacheō**; from *2342* and *3164; to fight with wild beasts:*— fought with wild beasts(1), wild beasts(1).

2342. **θηρίον thērion**; dim. form of the same as *2339; a wild beast:*— beast(38), beasts(2), creature(2), wild beasts(3).

2343. **θησαυρίζω thēsaurizō**; from *2344; to lay up, store up:*— reserved(1), save(2), store(2), stored up...treasure(1), stores up treasure(1), storing(1).

2344. **θησαυρός thēsauros**; from the same as *5087* and a prim. root **αυρ- aur-**; treasure:— treasure(12), treasures(5).

2345. **θιγγάνω thigganō**; from a prim. root **θιγ- thig-**; *to touch:*— touch(2), touches(1).

2346. **θλίβω thlibō**; a prim. vb.; *to press, afflict:*— afflict(1), afflicted(5), crowd(2), distress(1), narrow(1), suffer affliction(1).

2347. **θλῖψις thlipsis**; from *2346; tribulation:*— affliction(14), afflictions(6), anguish(1), distress(2), persecution(1), tribulation(16), tribulations(4), trouble(1).

2348. **θνήσκω thnēskō**; from a prim. root **θαν- than-**; *to die:*— dead(7), died(2).

2349. **θνητός thnētos**; from *2348; subject to death:*— mortal(6).

2350a. **θορυβάζω thorubazō**; from *2351; to disturb:*— bothered(1).

2350b. **θορυβέω thorubeō**; from *2351; to make an uproar:*— make a commotion(1), noisy disorder(1), set(1), troubled(1), uproar(1).

2351. **θόρυβος thorubos**; from the same as *2360; an uproar:*— commotion(1), riot(3), uproar(3).

2352. **θραύω thrauō**; a prim. vb.; *to break in pieces:*— oppressed(1).

2353. **θρέμμα thremma**; from *5142; cattle:*— cattle(1).

2354. **θρηνέω thrēneō**; from *2355; to lament:*— lament(1), lamenting(1), sang a dirge(2).

2355. **θρῆνος thrēnos**; from **θρέομαι threomai** *(cry aloud, shriek); a lamentation.*

2356. **θρησκεία thrēskeia**; from a der. of *2357; religion:*— religion(3), worship(1).

2357. **θρῆσκος thrēskos** of unc. or.; *religious:*— religious(1).

2358. **θριαμβεύω thriambeuō**; from **θρίαμβος thriambos** (a festal hymn to Bacchus); *to triumph:*— leads...in triumph(1), triumphed over(1).

2359. **θρίξ thrix**; a prim. word; *hair:*— hair(13), hairs(2).

2360. **θροέω throeō**; from **θρόος throos** *(a noise, tumult); to be troubled:*— disturbed(1), frightened(2).

2361. **θρόμβος thrombos**; from *5142; a lump:*— drops(1).

2362. **θρόνος thronos**; prob. from **θρᾶνος thranos** *(bench); a throne:*— throne(53), thrones(8).

2363. **Θυάτειρα Thuateira**; of unc. or.; *Thyatira,* a city of Lydia:— Thyatira(4).

2364. **θυγάτηρ thugatēr**; a prim. word; *daughter:*— daughter(23), daughters(5).

2365. **θυγάτριον thugatrion**; dim. from *2364; a little daughter:*— little daughter(2).

2366. **θύελλα thuella**; from **θύω thuō** *(to rage, seethe); a whirlwind:*— whirlwind(1).

2367. **θύϊνος thuinos**; from **θύον thuon** *(citron wood,* containing an aromatic resin); *thyine, citron:*— citron(1).

2368. **θυμίαμα thumiama**; from *2370; incense:*— incense(6).

2369. **θυμιατήριον thumiatērion**; from *2370* and **-τηριον -tērion** (suff. denoting place); *altar of incense, a censer:*— altar of incense(1).

2370. **θυμιάω thumiaō**; from *2380; to burn incense:*— burn incense(1).

2371. **θυμομαχέω thumomacheō**; from *2372* and *3164; to fight desperately:*— very angry(1).

2372. **θυμός thumos**; from the same as *2366; passion:*— angry tempers(1), fierce(2), indignation(1), outbursts of anger(1), passion(2), rage(2), wrath(9).

***2373.* θυμόω thumoō**; from *2372; to be very angry:*— enraged(1).

***2374.* θύρα thura**; a prim. word; *a door:*— door(28), doors(6), entrance(3), gate(1), gates(1).

***2375.* θυρεός thureos**; from *2374; a shield:*— shield(1).

***2376.* θυρίς thuris**; dim. from *2374; a window:*— window(1), window sill(1).

***2377.* θυρωρός thurōros**; from *2374* and **οὖρος ouros** *(a guardian); a doorkeeper:*— doorkeeper(3), kept the door(1).

***2378.* θυσία thusia**; from *2380; a sacrifice:*— sacrifice(14), sacrifices(14).

***2379.* θυσιαστήριον thusiastērion**; from a der. of *2378* and **-τηριον -tērion** (suff. denoting place); *an altar:*— altar(23), altars(1).

***2380.* θύω thuō**; a prim. vb.; *to offer, sacrifice:*— butchered(1), kill(4), killed(2), offer sacrifice(1), offering sacrifice(1), sacrifice(2), sacrificed(3).

***2381.* Θωμᾶς Thōmas**; of Heb. or. [8420b]; "the twin," *Thomas,* one of the twelve apostles:—Thomas(11).

***2382.* θώραξ thōrax**; of unc. or.; a breastplate:— breastplate(2), breastplates(3).

I

***2383.* Ἰάϊρος Iairos**; of Heb. or. [2971]; *Jairus,* the ruler of a synagogue in Pal.:— Jairus(2).

***2384.* Ἰακώβ Iakōb**; of Heb. or. [3290]; *Jacob,* the son of Isaac, also the father of Joseph, Mary's husband:— Jacob(26), Jacob's(1).

***2385.* Ἰάκωβος Iakōbos**; from the same as *2384; James,* the name of several Isr.:— James(42).

***2386.* ἴαμα iama**; from *2390; a healing:*— healing(1), healings(2).

***2387.* Ἰαμβρῆς Iambrēs**; of unc. or.; *Jambres,* an Eg. sorcerer:— Jambres(1).

***2388.* Ἰανναί Iannai**; prob. of Heb. or.; *Jannai,* an Isr.:— Jannai(1).

***2389.* Ἰάννης Iannēs**; of unc. or.; *Jannes,* an Eg. sorcerer:— Jannes(1).

***2390.* ἰάομαι iaomai**; a prim. vb.; *to heal:*— curing(1), heal(4), healed(16), healing(2), heals(1), perform healing(2).

***2391.* Ἰάρετ Iaret**; of Heb. or. [3382]; *Jared,* the father of Enoch:— Jared(1).

***2392.* ἴασις iasis**; from *2390; a healing:*— cures(1), heal(1), healing(1).

***2393.* ἴασπις iaspis**; of Semitic or.; *jasper* (a translucent stone):— jasper(4).

***2394.* Ἰάσων Iasōn**; name of a legendary Greek; *Jason,* the name of one, perh. two, Chr.:— Jason(5).

***2395.* ἰατρός iatros**; from *2390; a physician:*— physician(5), physicians(1).

***2396.* ἴδε ide**; from *1491a,* used as an interj.; *see! behold!:*— behold(18), lo(1), look(4), see(5).

***2397.* ἰδέα idea**; var. reading for *1490a,* q.v.

***2398.* ἴδιος idios**; a prim. word; *one's own, distinct:*— due(1), friends(1), himself(4), home(1), individually(1), one's own(1), own(84), owner(1), private*(1), privately*(7), proper(4), themselves(3), themselves*(1).

***2399.* ἰδιώτης idiōtēs**; from *2398; a private* or *unskilled person:*— ungifted(1), ungifted man(1), ungifted men(1), unskilled(1), untrained(1).

***2400.* ἰδού idou**; from *1491a,* used as a demonstrative particle; *look, behold:*— assure(1), behold(145), here(3), lo(1), long(1), look(8), see(1), then(1), there(1), when(1), why(1), yet(1).

***2401.* Ἰδουμαία Idoumaia**; of Heb. or. [123]; *Idumea,* a region S. of Judea:— Idumea(1).

***2402.* ἱδρώς hidrōs**; from **ἶδος idos** *(sweat); sweat:*— sweat(1).

***2403.* Ἰεζάβελ Iezabel**; of Heb. or. [348]; *Jezebel,* the symbolic name of a false prophetess:— Jezebel(1).

***2404.* Ἱεράπολις Hierapolis**; from *2413* and *4172; Hierapolis,* a city in Asia:— Hierapolis(1).

***2405.* ἱερατεία hierateia**; from *2407; priesthood:*— priest's office(1), priestly office(1).

***2406.* ἱεράτευμα hierateuma**; from *2407; a priesthood:*— priesthood(2).

***2407.* ἱερατεύω hierateuō**; from *2409; to be a priest:*— performing...priestly service(1), priestly service(1).

***2408.* Ἱερεμίας Ieremias**; of Heb. or. [3414]; *Jeremiah,* an O.T. prophet:— Jeremiah(3).

***2409.* ἱερεύς hiereus**; from *2413; a priest:*— priest(16), priests(15).

***2410a.* Ἰεριχώ Ierichō**; of Heb. or. [3405]; *Jericho,* a city of Pal.:— Jericho(7).

***2410b.* ἱερόθυτος hierothutos**; from *2413* and *2380; offered in sacrifice:*— sacrificed to idols(1).

***2411.* ἱερόν hieron**; see *2413.*

***2412.* ἱεροπρεπής hieroprepēs**; from *2413* and *4241; reverent:*— reverent(1).

***2413.* ἱερός hieros**; a prim. word; *sacred, a sacred thing, a temple:*— sacred(1), sacred services(1), temple(71).

***2414.* Ἱεροσόλυμα Hierosoluma**; of Heb. or. [3389]; *Jerusalem,* the capital of united Isr. and Judah:— Jerusalem(63).

***2415.* Ἱεροσολυμίτης Hierosolumitēs**; from *2414;* an inhab. of Jer.:— people of Jerusalem(2).

***2416.* ἱεροσυλέω hierosuleō**; from *2417; to rob a temple:*— rob temples(1).

***2417.* ἱερόσυλος hierosulos**; from *2413* and *4813; robbing temples:*— robbers of temples(1).

***2418.* ἱερουργέω hierourgeō**; from a comp. of *2413* and *2041; to perform sacred rites:*— ministering as a priest(1).

***2419.* Ἰερουσαλήμ Ierousalēm**; of Heb. or. [3389]; *Jerusalem,* the capital of united Isr. and Judah, also a future heavenly city:— Jerusalem(76).

***2420.* ἱερωσύνη hierōsunē**; from *2413; priesthood:*— priesthood(3).

***2421.* Ἰεσσαί Iessai**; of Heb. or. [3448]; *Jesse,* the father of King David:— Jesse(5).

***2422.* Ἰεφθάε Iephthae**; of Heb. or. [3316]; *Jephthah,* a judge of Isr.:— Jephthah(1).

***2423.* Ἰεχονίας Iechonias**; of Heb. or. [3204]; *Jeconiah,* a king of Judah:— Jeconiah(2).

***2424.* Ἰησοῦς Iēsous**; of Heb. or. [3091]; *Jesus* or *Joshua,* the name of the Messiah, also three other Isr.:— Jesus(904), Jesus'(7), Joshua(3).

***2425.* ἱκανός hikanos**; from **ἱκνέομαι hikneomai** *(to come, reach, attain to); sufficient, fit:*— able(1), adequate(2), aloud(1), considerable(4), enough(1), fit(4), good many(1), large(1), large sum(1), length*(1), long(5), long while(1), many(9), number(1), pledge(1), satisfy*(1), sizeable(1), some(1), sufficient(1), very bright(1), worthy(2).

***2426.* ἱκανότης hikanotēs**; from *2425; sufficiency:*— adequacy(1).

***2427.* ἱκανόω hikanoō**; from *2425; to make sufficient:*— made...adequate(1), qualified(1).

***2428.* ἱκετηρία hiketēria**; from adj. **ἱκετήριος hiketērios**; from **ἱκέτης hiketēs** *(a suppliant); supplication:*— supplications(1).

***2429.* ἰκμάς ikmas**; a prim. word; *moisture:*— moisture(1).

***2430.* Ἰκόνιον Ikonion**; of unc. or.; *Iconium,* a city of Galatia:— Iconium(6).

***2431.* ἱλαρός hilaros**; from the same as *2436; cheerful:*— cheerful(1).

***2432.* ἱλαρότης hilarotēs**; from *2431; cheerfulness:*— cheerfulness(1).

***2433.* ἱλάσκομαι hilaskomai**; from the same as *2436; to be propitious, make propitiation for:*— make propitiation(1), merciful(1).

***2434.* ἱλασμός hilasmos**; from *2433; propitiation:*— propitiation(2).

***2435.* ἱλαστήριον hilastērion**; from **ἱλαστήριος hilastērios**; from *2433; propitiatory:*— mercy seat(1), propitiation(1).

***2436.* ἵλεως hileōs**; another spelling of **ἵλαος hilaos** *(propitious, gracious); propitious:*— god forbid(1), merciful(1).

***2437.* Ἰλλυρικόν Illurikon**; of unc. or.; *Illyricum,* a region adjacent to the Adriatic Sea:— Illyricum(1).

***2438.* ἱμάς himas**; of unc. or.; *a thong, strap:*— thong(3), thongs(1).

***2439.* ἱματίζω himatizō**; from *2440; to clothe:*— clothed(2).

***2440.* ἱμάτιον himation**; dim. form of **εἷμα heima** *(a garment); an outer garment, a cloak, robe:*— cloak(8), cloaks(1), clothes(1), clothing(2), coat(4), coats(8), dresses(1), garment(8), garments(18), outer garments(2), robe(4), robes(4).

***2441.* ἱματισμός himatismos**; from *2439; clothing:*— clothed(1), clothes(1), clothing(2), garments(1).

***2442.* ἱμείρομαι himeiromai**; var. reading for *3655b,* q.v.

***2443.* ἵνα hina**; a prim. conjunc. denoting purpose, definition or result; *in order that, that, so that:*— fear*(2), order(23), otherwise*(3), result(1), so(306), so*(12), why*(3).

***2444.* ἱνατί hinati**; from *2443* and *5101; for what purpose?:*— why(3).

***2445.* Ἰόππη Ioppē**; of Heb. or. [3305]; *Joppa,* a city of Pal.:— Joppa(10).

***2446.* Ἰορδάνης Iordanēs**; of Heb. or. [3383]; *the Jordan,* the largest river of Pal.:— Jordan(15).

***2447.* ἰός ios**; a prim. word; *rust, poison:*— poison(2), rust(1).

***2448.* Ἰούδα Iouda**; the same as *2455,* q.v.

***2449.* Ἰουδαία Ioudaia**; see *2453.*

***2450.* Ἰουδαΐζω Ioudaizō**; from *2453; to Judaize:*— live like Jews(1).

***2451.* Ἰουδαϊκός Ioudaikos**; from *2453; Jewish:*— Jewish(1).

***2452.* Ἰουδαϊκῶς Ioudaikōs**; adv. from *2451; in Jewish fashion:*— like the Jews(1).

2453. **Ἰουδαῖος Ioudaios**; from *2455; Jewish, a Jew, Judea:*— Jew(21), Jewess(1), Jewish(8), Jews(163), Judea(46).

2454. **Ἰουδαϊσμός Ioudaismos**; from *2450; Judaism:*— Judaism(2).

2455. **Ἰούδας Ioudas**; of Heb. or. [3063]; *Judah, Judas,* the name of several Isr., also one of the twelve tribes of Isr., also the Southern kingdom:— Judah(11), Judas(32), Jude(1).

2456. **Ἰουλία Ioulia**; fem. of *2457; Julia,* a Chr. at Rome:— Julia(1).

2457. **Ἰούλιος Ioulios**; of Lat. or.; *Julius,* a centurion:— Julius(2).

2458. **Ἰουνιᾶς Iounias**; of Lat. or.; *Junias,* a kinsman of Paul:— Junias(1).

2459. **Ἰοῦστος Ioustos**; of Lat. or.; *Justus,* the name of three Chr.:— Justus(3).

2460. **ἱππεύς hippeus**; from *2462; a horseman:*— horsemen(2).

2461. **ἱππικός hippikos**; from *2462; cavalry:*— horsemen(1).

2462. **ἵππος hippos**; a prim. word; *a horse:*— horse(7), horses(8), horses'(2).

2463. **ἶρις iris**; of unc. or.; *a rainbow:*— rainbow(2).

2464. **Ἰσαάκ Isaak**; of Heb. or. [3327]; *Isaac,* the son of Abraham:— Isaac(20).

2465. **ἰσάγγελος isaggelos**; from *2470* and *32a; equal to angels:*— like angels(1).

2466. **Ἰσαχάρ Isachar**; var. reading for *2475b,* q.v.

2467. (not used)

2468. **ἴσθι isthi**; imper. of *1510,* q.v.

2469. **Ἰσκαριώτης Iskariōtēs**; of Heb. or., prob. [377] and [7149]; *Iscariot,* surname of Judas and his father:— Iscariot(11).

2470. **ἴσος isos**; a prim. word; *equal:*— consistent(2), equal(3), equality(1), same(2).

2471. **ἰσότης isotēs**; from *2470; equality:*— equality(2), fairness(1).

2472. **ἰσότιμος isotimos**; from *2470* and *5092; held in equal honor:*— same kind(1).

2473. **ἰσόψυχος isopsuchos**; from *2470* and *5590; like-minded:*— kindred spirit(1).

2474. **Ἰσραήλ Israēl**; of Heb. or. [3478]; *Israel,* the name of the Jewish people and their land:— Israel(51).

2475a. **Ἰσραηλίτης Israēlitēs**; from *2474; an Israelite:*— Israel(5), Israelite(2), Israelites(2).

2475b. **Ἰσσαχάρ Issachar**; of Heb. or. [3485]; *Issachar,* one of the twelve tribes of Isr.:— Issachar(1).

2476. **ἵστημι histēmi**; from a redupl. of the prim. root **στα- sta-**; *to make to stand, to stand:*— brought(1), bystanders(1), bystanders*(1), came(1), came to a halt(1), come(1), confirmed(2), establish(3), fixed(1), hold(1), lying(1), make...stand(2), placed(1), put(1), put forward(2), set(4), stand(27), stand firm(4), standing(53), standing firm(1), stands(6), stood(27), stood still(1), stood upright(1), stop(1), stopped(5), taking his stand(1), weighed(1).

2477. **ἱστορέω historeō**; from **ἵστωρ histōr** *(one learned in); to inquire about, visit:*— become acquainted(1).

2478. **ἰσχυρός ischuros**; from *2480; strong, mighty:*— loud(1), mightier(3), mighty(3), mighty men(1), severe(1), strong(13), strong man(1), strong man's(1), strong man's(1), stronger(3).

2479. **ἰσχύς ischus**; of unc. or.; *strength, might:*— might(5), power(1), strength(4).

2480. **ἰσχύω ischuō**; from *2479; to be strong, have power:*— able(5), am...strong enough(1), been able(1), can(1), can do(1), could(8), force(1), good(1), healthy(2), means(1), overpowered(1), prevailing(1), strong enough(3), unable*(2).

2481. **ἴσως isōs**; adv. from *2470; perhaps:*— perhaps(1).

2482. **Ἰταλία Italia**; of Lat. or.; *Italy,* a region of western Europe:— Italy(4).

2483. **Ἰταλικός Italikos**; from *2482; Italian:*— Italian(1).

2484. **Ἰτουραῖος Itouraios**; of Heb. or. [3195]; *Ituraea,* a region N. of Pal.:— Ituraea(1).

2485. **ἰχθύδιον ichthudion**; dim. of *2486; a little fish:*— small fish(2).

2486. **ἰχθύς ichthus**; a prim. word; *a fish:*— fish(20).

2487. **ἴχνος ichnos**; a prim. word; *a track:*— steps(3).

2488. **Ἰωαθάμ Iōatham**; of Heb. or. [3147]; *Jotham,* a king of Judah:— Jotham(2).

2489a. **Ἰωανάν Iōanan**; of Heb. or. [3110]; *Joanan,* an Isr.:— Joanan(1).

2489b. **Ἰωάννα Iōanna**; of Ara. or.; *Joanna,* a follower of Jesus:— Joanna(2).

2490. **Ἰωαννᾶς Iōannas**; var. reading for *2489a,* q.v.

2491. **Ἰωάννης Iōannēs**; of Heb. or. [3110]; *John,* the name of several Isr.:— John(131), John's(4).

2492a. **Ἰώβ Iōb**; of Heb. or. [347]; *Job,* a patriarch:— Job(1).

2492b. **Ἰωβήδ Iōbēd**; of Heb. or. [5744]; *Obed,* the grandfather of King David:— Obed(3).

2493a. **Ἰωδά Iōda**; of Heb. or.; *Joda,* an Isr.:— Joda(1).

2493b. **Ἰωήλ Iōēl**; of Heb. or. [3100]; *Joel,* an Isr. prophet:— Joel(1).

2494. **Ἰωνάμ Iōnam**; of Heb. or.; *Jonam,* an Isr.:— Jonam(1).

2495. **Ἰωνᾶς Iōnas**; of Heb. or. [3124]; *Jonah,* an Isr. prophet:— Jonah(9).

2496. **Ἰωράμ Iōram**; of Heb. or. [3141]; *Joram,* an Isr.:— Joram(2).

2497. **Ἰωρίμ Iōrim**; of Heb. or.; *Jorim,* an Isr.:— Jorim(1).

2498. **Ἰωσαφάτ Iōsaphat**; of Heb. or. [3092]; *Jehoshaphat,* an Isr.:— Jehoshaphat(2).

2499. **Ἰωσή Iōsē**; var. reading for *2500,* q.v.

2500. **Ἰωσῆς Iōsēs**; perh. from *2501; Joses,* an Isr. name:— Joses(3).

2501. **Ἰωσήφ Iōsēph**; of Heb. or. [3130]; *Joseph,* the name of several Isr.:— Joseph(33), Joseph's(2).

2502a. **Ἰωσήχ Iōsēch**; of unc. der.; *Josech,* an Isr.:— Josech(1).

2502b. **Ἰωσίας Iōsias**; of Heb. or. [2977]; *Josiah,* a king of Judah:— Josiah(2).

2503. **ἰῶτα iōta**; of Semitic or.; name of the Gr. letter corresponding to the tenth Heb. letter, *yod; iota:*— letter(1).

K

2504. **κἀγώ kagō**; see *2532* and *1473.*

2505. **καθά katha**; from *2596* and *3739; according to which.*

2506. **καθαίρεσις kathairesis**; from *2507; a pulling down:*— destroying(1), destruction(1), tearing down(1).

2507. **καθαιρέω kathaireō**; from *2596* and *138; to take down, pull down:*— brought down(1), destroyed(1), destroying(1), dethroned(1), take...down(1), tear down(1), took...down(3).

2508. **καθαίρω kathairō**; from *2513; to cleanse:*— prunes(1).

2509. **καθάπερ kathaper**; from *2505* and *4007a; just as:*— even(1), just(11), like(2).

2510. **καθάπτω kathaptō**; from *2596* and *681; to lay hold of:*— fastened(1).

2511. **καθαρίζω katharizō**; from *2513; to cleanse:*— clean(3), cleanse(5), cleansed(16), cleanses(1), cleansing(1), declared...clean(1), make...clean(3), purify(1).

2512. **καθαρισμός katharismos**; from *2511; a cleansing:*— cleansing(2), purification(5).

2513. **καθαρός katharos**; a prim. word; *clean* (adj.):— clean(12), clear(3), innocent(1), pure(10).

2514. **καθαρότης katharotēs**; from *2513; cleanness:*— cleansing(1).

2515. **καθέδρα kathedra**; from *2596* and the same as *1476; a seat:*— chair(1), seats(2).

2516. **καθέζομαι kathezomai**; from *2596* and **ἕζομαι hezomai** *(to seat oneself, sit); to sit down:*— sit(1), sitting(5), stayed(1).

2517. **καθεξῆς kathexēs**; from *2596* and *1836; successively:*— afterwards*(1), consecutive order(1), orderly sequence(1), successively(1), successors onward(1).

2518. **καθεύδω katheudō**; from *2596* and **εὕδω heudō** *(to sleep); to sleep:*— asleep(8), do their sleeping(1), goes to bed(1), sleep(3), sleep do(1), sleeper(1), sleeping(8).

2519. **καθηγητής kathēgētēs**; from *2596* and *2233; a teacher:*— leader(1), leaders(1).

2520. **καθήκω kathēkō**; from *2596* and *2240; to be proper or fitting:*— proper(1), should...be allowed(1).

2521. **κάθημαι kathēmai**; from *2596* and **ἧμαι hēmai** *(to sit); to be seated:*— dwell(1), live(1), sat(15), sat down(4), seated(5), sit(16), sit down(1), sits(12), sitting(33), sitting down(3).

2522. **καθημερινός kathēmerinos**; from *2596* and *2250; daily:*— daily(1).

2523. **καθίζω kathizō**; another form of *2516; to make to sit down, to sit down:*— appoint(1), rested(1), sat(5), sat down(15), seat(1), seated(1), seated themselves(1), settled(1), sit(9), sit down(4), sitting down(1), stay(1), taken...seat(1), takes...seat(1), took...seat(3).

2524. **καθίημι kathiēmi**; from *2596* and **ἵημι hiēmi** *(to send); to let down:*— down(1), let...down(2), lowered(2), lowering*(1).

2525. **καθίστημι kathistēmi**; from *2596* and *2476; to set in order, appoint:*— appoint(1), appointed(4), appoints(1), escorted(1), made(5), makes(1), put...in charge(4), put in charge(3), render(1), set(1).

2526. **καθό katho**; from *2596* and *3739; according as:*— according(2), degree(1).

2527. **καθόλου katholou**; adv. from *2596* and *3650; in general:*— all(1).

2528. **καθοπλίζω kathoplizō**; from *2596* and *3695; to arm fully:*— fully armed(1).

2529. **καθοράω kathoraō**; from *2596* and *3708; to discern clearly:*— clearly seen(1).

2530. καθότι kathoti; from *2596, 3739* and *5100; according as, because:*— because(3), since(1).

2531a. καθώς kathōs; from *2596* and *5613; according as, just as:*— according(1), even(13), even so(1), how(2), just(92), only(1), proportion(1), so(2), what(1).

2531b. καθώσπερ kathōsper; from *2531a* and *4007a; even as:*— even(1).

2532. καί kai; a prim. conjunc.; *and, even, also:*— accompanied(1), actually(2), after(2), again(1), again*(1), along(4), also(535), although(1), although*(1), besides*(1), both(37), both*(1), certainly(1), continue(1), either(2), else(1), even(132), forty-six*(1), if(1), including(1), indeed(20), indeed*(2), just(3), likewise(1), more*(2), moving about freely*(1), nor(4), now(2), only(2), only*(1), or(11), same(1), so(30), than(2), than*(4), then(105), though(1), though*(6), together(1), too(34), until(1), very(3), well(13), when(7), whether(1), while(1), whose*(1), without*(4), yet(9).

2533. Καϊάφας Kaiaphas; of Ara. or.; *Caiaphas,* an Isr. high priest:— Caiaphas(9).

2534. καί γε kai ge; see *2532* and *1065.*

2535. Κάϊν Kain; of Heb. or. [7014b]; *Cain,* a son of Adam:— Cain(3).

2536. Καϊνάμ Kainam; of Heb. or. [7018]; *Cainan,* two ancestors of Christ:— Cainan(2).

2537. καινός kainos; a prim. word; *new, fresh:*— fresh(3), new(37), new things(1), things new(1).

2538. καινότης kainotēs; from *2537; newness:*— newness(2).

2539. καίπερ kaiper; from *2532* and *4007a; although:*— although(3), even though(1), though(1).

2540. καιρός kairos; a prim. word; *time, season:*— age(1), epochs(2), occasion(1), opportune time(1), opportunity(3), proper time(5), right time(1), season(1), seasons(4), short*(1), time(54), times(11), while(1).

2541. Καῖσαρ Kaisar; of Lat. or.; *Caesar,* a Roman emperor:— Caesar(21), Caesar's(8).

2542. Καισάρεια Kaisareia; from *2541; Caesarea,* the name of two cities in Pal.:— Caesarea(17).

2543. καίτοι kaitoi; from *2532* and *5104; and yet:*— although(1), yet(1).

2544. καίτοιγε kaitoige; from *2543* and *1065; and yet, indeed:*— although(1).

2545. καίω kaiō; a prim. vb.; *to kindle, burn:*— blazing(1), burned(2), burning(5), burns(2), light(1), lit(1).

2546. κἀκεῖ kakei; from *2532* and *1563; and there:*— house(1), there(7), there as well(1).

2547. κἀκεῖθεν kakeithen; from *2532* and *1564; and from there:*— there(9).

2548. κἀκεῖνος kakeinos; from *2532* and *1565; and that one:*— also(10), one(1), others(2), those(1), too(1).

2549. κακία kakia; from *2556; wickedness:*— evil(3), malice(5), trouble(1), wickedness(2).

2550. κακοήθεια kakoētheia; from *2556* and *2239; malevolence:*— malice(1).

2551. κακολογέω kakologeō; from a comp. of *2556* and *3056; to speak ill of:*— speak evil(1), speaking evil(1), speaks evil(2).

2552. κακοπάθεια kakopatheia; from a comp. of *2556* and *3806; affliction:*— suffering(1).

2553. κακοπαθέω kakopatheō; from the same as *2552; to suffer evil:*— endure hardship(1), suffer hardship(1), suffering(1).

2554. κακοποιέω kakopoieō; from *2556* and *4160; to do evil:*— do harm(2), does evil(1), doing what is wrong(1).

2555. κακοποιός kakopoios; from *2554; an evildoer:*— evildoer(1), evildoers(2).

2556. κακός kakos; a prim. word; *bad, evil:*— bad(1), bad things(1), evil(32), evil men(1), evil things(1), evildoer(1), harm(4), loathsome(1), wretches(1), wrong(5).

2557. κακοῦργος kakourgos; from *2556* and the same as *2041; a criminal:*— criminal(1), criminals(3).

2558. κακουχέω kakoucheō; from *2556* and *2192; to ill-treat:*— ill-treated(2).

2559. κακόω kakoō; from *2556; to ill-treat:*— embittered(1), harm(2), mistreat(1), mistreated(2).

2560. κακῶς kakōs; adv. from *2556; badly:*— cruelly(1), evil(1), ill*(5), sick(6), very(1), wretched(1), wrong motives(1), wrongly(1).

2561. κάκωσις kakōsis; from *2559; ill-treatment:*— oppression(1).

2562. καλάμη kalamē; appar. from *2563; stubble:*— straw(1).

2563. κάλαμος kalamos; a prim. word; *a reed:*— measuring rod(2), pen(1), reed(8), rod(1).

2564. καλέω kaleō; a prim. word; *to call:*— call(13), called(99), calling(2), calls(7), give(1), invite(2), invited(15), invited guests(1), invites(1), name given(1), named(2), so-called(1), summoned(2).

2565. καλλιέλαιος kallielaios; from the comp. of *2570* and *1636; a cultivated olive* (tree):— cultivated olive tree(1).

2566. κάλλιον kallion; see *2570.*

2567. καλοδιδάσκαλος kalodidaskalos; from *2570* and *1320; a teacher of good:*— teaching what(1), teaching what is good(1).

2568. Καλοὶ Λιμένες Kaloi Limenes; pl. of *2570* and *3040; Fair Havens,* a harbor in Crete:— Fair Havens(1).

2569. καλοποιέω kalopoieō; from *2570* and *4160; to do well:*— doing good(1).

2570. καλός kalos; a prim. word; *beautiful, good:*— beautiful(1), better(5), better*(2), commendable manner(1), excellent(1), fair(1), fine(2), good(79), high(1), honest(1), honorable(1), right thing(1), sound(1), treasure*(1), what is right(2).

2571. κάλυμμα kalumma; from *2572; a covering:*— veil(4).

2572. καλύπτω kaluptō; akin to **καλύβη kalubē** *(hut, cabin); to cover:*— being covered(1), concealed(1), cover(2), covers(2), veiled(2).

2573. καλῶς kalōs; adv. from *2570; well:*— beautifully(1), commendably(1), correctly(1), experts(1), good(4), honorably(1), kind enough(1), quite right(1), recover*(1), right(2), rightly(5), very well(1), well(16), well enough(1).

2574. κάμηλος kamēlos; of Heb. or. [1581]; *camel:*— camel(4), camel's(2).

2575. κάμινος kaminos; of unc. or.; *furnace:*— furnace(4).

2576. καμμύω kammuō; contr. of the comp. of *2596* and **μύω muō** *(to shut* the eyes); *to shut the eyes:*— closed(2).

2577. κάμνω kamnō; from a prim. root **καμ- kam-**; *to be weary:*— grow weary(1), sick(1).

2578. κάμπτω kamptō; from a prim. root **καμπ- kamp-**; *to bend:*— bow(3), bowed(1).

2579. κἄν kan; from *2532* and *1437; and if:*— even(1), even if(4), if(4), if even(1), just(2), least(1), or even(1), though(1), whether(1).

2580. Κανά Kana; of Heb. or.; *Cana,* a city in Galilee:— Cana(4).

2581. Καναναῖος Kananaios; of Ara. or.; *Cananaean,* Ara. for *Zealot,* surname of one of the twelve apostles:— Zealot(2).

2582. Κανδάκη Kandakē; of for. or.; *Candace,* a queen of Ethiopia:— Candace(1).

2583. κανών kanōn; from **κάννα kanna** *(a straight rod); a rule, standard:*— rule(1), sphere(3).

2584. Καπερναούμ Kapernaoum; var. reading for *2746b,* q.v.

2585. καπηλεύω kapēleuō; from **κάπηλος kapēlos** *(a huckster, peddler); to make a trade of:*— peddling(1).

2586. καπνός kapnos; a prim. word; *smoke:*— smoke(13).

2587. Καππαδοκία Kappadokia; of for. or.; *Cappadocia,* a province of Asia Minor:— Cappadocia(2).

2588. καρδία kardia; a prim. word; *heart:*— heart(102), heart's(1), hearts(49), mind(2), minds(1), quick(1), spirit(1).

2589. καρδιογνώστης kardiognōstēs; from *2588* and *1109; knower of hearts:*— who know(1), who know the hearts(1), who knows(1), who knows the heart(1).

2590. καρπός karpos; a prim. word; *fruit:*— benefit(2), crop(5), crops(2), descendants*(1), fruit(43), fruitful(1), fruits(4), grain(1), harvest(1), proceeds(1), produce(4), profit(1).

2591. Κάρπος Karpos; perh. the same as *2590; Carpus,* a Chr.:— Carpus(1).

2592. καρποφορέω karpophoreō; from *2593; to bear fruit:*— bear fruit(4), bearing fruit(2), bears fruit(1), produces crops(1).

2593. καρποφόρος karpophoros; from *2590* and *5342; fruitful:*— fruitful(1).

2594. καρτερέω kartereō; from a der. of *2904; to be steadfast:*— endured(1).

2595. κάρφος karphos; from **κάρφω karphō** *(to dry up, wither); a small dry stalk:*— speck(6).

2596. κατά kata; prep. of unc. or.; *down, against, according to:*— about(5), accord(1), accordance(12), according(140), accordingly(1), after(8), after another(1), against(52), along(1), along the coast(2), among(3), another(2), around(1), basis(1), because(2), before(1), beyond*(1), case*(2), certain(1), circumstances*(2), conforming(1), contrary(1), daily*(10), down(4), each(2), effect(1), every(10), every*(1), exactly*(1), excessively*(1), godly*(1), how*(1), inasmuch*(2), individually*(1), just(2), like(4), more(1), motives(1), natural*(1), off(2), one*(2), outwardly*(1), over(3), private*(1), privately*(7), reference(1), rightly*(1), standpoint(2), terms(2), through(1), throughout(6), together*(1), various(4), way(4), within(2).

2597. καταβαίνω katabainō; from *2596* and the same as *939; to go down:*— brought down(1), came down(12), come down(15), comes down(4), coming(1), coming down(9), descend(3), descended(6), descending(5), descends(1), falling down(1), fell(1), go(1), go down(4), go downstairs(1), going down(3), got(1), steps down(1), went(1), went down(11).

2598. καταβάλλω kataballō; from *2596* and *906; to cast down:*— laying(1), struck down(1).

2599a. καταβαρέω katabareō; from *2596* and *916; to weigh down:*— burden(1).

2599b. καταβαρύνω katabarunō; a prol. form of *2599a; to weigh down:*— heavy(1).

2600. κατάβασις katabasis; from *2597; descent:*— descent(1).

2601. καταβιβάζω katabibazō; from *2596* and the caus. form of the same as *939; to cause to go down.*

2602. καταβολή katabolē; from *2598; a laying down:*— conceive*(1), foundation(10).

2603. καταβραβεύω katabrabeuō; from *2596* and **βραβεύς brabeus** *(an umpire); to give judgment against:*— defrauding...of...prize(1).

2604. καταγγελεύς kataggeleus; from *2605; a proclaimer:*— proclaimer(1).

2605. καταγγέλλω kataggellō; from *2596* and *31b; to proclaim:*— announced(1), proclaim(7), proclaimed(5), proclaiming(5).

2606. καταγελάω katagelaō; from *2596* and *1070; to deride:*— laughing(3).

2607. καταγινώσκω kataginōskō; from *2596* and *1097; to blame:*— condemn(1), condemned(1), condemns(1).

2608a. κατάγνυμι katagnumi; from *2596* and **ἄγνυμι agnumi** *(to break, splinter); to break in pieces:*— break(2), broke(1), broken(1).

2608b. καταγράφω katagraphō; from *2596* and *1125; to trace:*— wrote(1).

2609. κατάγω katagō; from *2596* and *71; to bring down:*— bring...down(3), brought(1), brought...down(3), put(2).

2610. καταγωνίζομαι katagōnizomai; from *2596* and *75; to struggle against:*— conquered(1).

2611. καταδέω katadeō; from *2596* and *1210; to bind up:*— bandaged(1).

2612. κατάδηλος katadēlos; from *2596* and *1212; quite manifest:*— clearer(1).

2613a. καταδικάζω katadikazō; from *2613b; to pass sentence upon:*— condemn(1), condemned(4).

2613b. καταδίκη katadikē; from *2596* and *1349; sentence:*— sentence of condemnation(1).

2614. καταδιώκω katadiōkō; from *2596* and *1377; to pursue closely:*— searched(1).

2615. καταδουλόω katadouloō; from *2596* and *1402; to enslave:*— bring...into bondage(1), enslaves(1).

2616a. καταδυναστεύω katadunasteuō; from *2596* and **δυναστεύω dunasteuō** *(to hold power);* akin to *1413; to exercise power over:*— oppress(1), oppressed(1).

2616b. κατάθεμα katathema; from *2698; a curse:*— curse(1).

2617a. καταθεματίζω katathematizō; from *2616b; to curse vehemently:*— curse(1).

2617b. καταισχύνω kataischunō; from *2596* and *153; to put to shame, to disgrace:*— disappoint(1), disappointed(3), disgraces(2), humiliated(1), put to shame(3), shame(3).

2618. κατακαίω katakaiō; from *2596* and *2545; to burn up:*— burn(4), burned(8), burning(1).

2619. κατακαλύπτω katakaluptō; from *2596* and *2572; to cover up:*— cover(2), covered(1).

2620. κατακαυχάομαι katakauchaomai; from *2596* and *2744; to exult over:*— arrogant(2), arrogant toward(1), triumphs over(1).

2621. κατάκειμαι katakeimai; from *2596* and *2749; to lie down, recline:*— bedridden*(1), dining(1), lay(1), lying(4), lying sick(1), reclining(4).

2622. κατακλάω kataklaō; from *2596* and *2806; to break up:*— broke(2).

2623. κατακλείω katakleiō; from *2596* and *2808; to shut up:*— lock(1), locked(1).

2624. κατακληρονομέω kataklēronomeō; from *2596* and *2816; to distribute by lot:*— distributed(1), inheritance(1).

2625. κατακλίνω kataklinō; from *2596* and *2827; to make to lie down:*— reclined(2), sit down(2), take(1).

2626. κατακλύζω katakluzō; from *2596* and the same as *2830; to inundate:*— flooded(1).

2627. κατακλυσμός kataklusmos; from *2626; a flood:*— flood(4).

2628. κατακολουθέω katakoloutheō; from *2596* and *190; to follow after:*— followed(1), following after(1).

2629. κατακόπτω katakoptō; from *2596* and *2875; to cut up:*— gashing(1).

2630. κατακρημνίζω katakrēmnizō; from *2596* and *2911; to throw over a precipice:*— throw...down the cliff(1).

2631. κατάκριμα katakrima; from *2632; penalty:*— condemnation(3).

2632. κατακρίνω katakrinō; from *2596* and *2919; to give judgment against:*— condemn(9), condemned(8), condemns(1).

2633. κατάκρισις katakrisis; from *2632; condemnation:*— condemn(1), condemnation(1).

2634a. κατακύπτω katakuptō; from *2596* and *2955; to bend down:*— stooped down(1).

2634b. κατακυριεύω katakurieuō; from *2596* and *2961; to exercise dominion over:*— lord it over(2), lording it over(1), subdued(1).

2635. καταλαλέω katalaleō; from *2637; to speak evil of:*— slander(1), slandered(1), speak against(1), speaks against(2).

2636. καταλαλιά katalalia; from *2637; evil-speaking:*— slander(1), slanders(1).

2637. κατάλαλος katalalos; from *2596* and the same as *2980; a defamer:*— slanderers(1).

2638. καταλαμβάνω katalambanō; from *2596* and *2983; to lay hold of, seize:*— attained(1), caught(2), comprehend(2), found(1), laid hold(2), lay hold(1), overtake(2), seizes(1), understand(1), understood(1), win(1).

2639. καταλέγω katalegō; from *2596* and *3004; to lay down, choose out:*— put on the list(1).

2640. κατάλειμμα kataleimma; var. reading for *5275a,* q.v.

2641. καταλείπω kataleipō; from *2596* and *3007; to leave, leave behind:*— forsaking(1), kept(1), leave(4), leaves behind(1), leaving(3), leaving behind(1), left(8), left behind(1), left...behind(1), neglect(1), pulled free(1), remains(1).

2642. καταλιθάζω katalithazō; from *2596* and *3034; to cast stones at:*— stone...to death(1).

2643. καταλλαγή katallagē; from *2644; reconciliation:*— reconciliation(4).

2644. καταλλάσσω katallassō; from *2596* and *236; to reconcile:*— reconciled(5), reconciling(1).

2645. κατάλοιπος kataloipos; from *2596* and *3062; remaining:*— rest(1).

2646. κατάλυμα kataluma; from *2647* (in the sense of *to lodge); a lodging place:*— guest room(2), inn(1).

2647. καταλύω kataluō; from *2596* and *3089; to destroy, overthrow:*— abolish(2), destroy(5), destroyed(1), find lodging(1), guest(1), overthrow(1), overthrown(1), tear down(1), torn down(4).

2648. καταμανθάνω katamanthanō; from *2596* and *3129; to learn thoroughly:*— observe(1).

2649. καταμαρτυρέω katamartureō; from *2596* and *3140; to testify* or *bear witness against:*— testify against(1), testifying against(2).

2650. καταμένω katamenō; from *2596* and *3306; to remain:*— stay(1), staying(1).

2651. καταμόνας katamonas; see *3441.*

2652. κατανάθεμα katanathema; var. reading for *2616b,* q.v.

2653. καταναθεματίζω katanathematizō; var. reading for *2617a,* q.v.

2654. καταναλίσκω katanaliskō; from *2596* and *355; to use up:*— consuming(1).

2655. καταναρκάω katanarkaō; from *2596* and **ναρκάω narkaō** *(to grow numb); to grow numb:*— burden(3).

2656. κατανεύω kataneuō; from *2596* and *3506; to make a sign* (by nodding the head):— signaled(1).

2657. κατανοέω katanoeō; from *2596* and *3539; to take note of, perceive:*— consider(4), contemplated(1), detected(1), look(1), look more closely(1), looked(1), looks(1), notice(2), observe(1), observing(1).

2658. καταντάω katantaō; from *2596* and **ἀντάω antaō** *(to come opposite, meet face to face); to come down to, reach:*— arrived(4), attain(3), came(3), come(2), reach(1).

2659. κατάνυξις katanuxis; from *2660; stupefaction:*— stupor(1).

2660. κατανύσσω katanussō; from *2596* and *3572; to prick violently:*— pierced(1).

2661. καταξιόω kataxioō; from *2596* and *515; to deem worthy:*— considered worthy(3).

2662. καταπατέω katapateō; from *2596* and *3961; to tread down:*— stepping(1), trample...under(1), trampled under foot(3).

2663. κατάπαυσις katapausis; from *2664; rest:*— repose(1), rest(8).

2664. καταπαύω katapauō; from *2596* and *3973; to cause to cease, to rest:*— given...rest(1), rested(2), restrained(1).

2665. καταπέτασμα katapetasma; from *2596* and **πετάννυμι petannumi** *(to spread out); a curtain* (the inner veil of the temple):— veil(6).

2666. καταπίνω katapinō; from *2596* and *4095; to drink down:*— devour(1), drank(1), drowned(1), overwhelmed(1), swallow(1), swallowed(2).

2667. καταπίπτω katapiptō; from *2596* and *4098; to fall down:*— fall down(1), fallen(1), fell(1).

2668. καταπλέω katapleō; from *2596* and *4126; to sail down:*— sailed(1).

2669. καταπονέω kataponeō; from *2596* and *4192; to wear down:*— oppressed(2).

2670. καταποντίζω katapontizō; from *2596* and *4195* (in its ordinary use); *to throw into the sea:*— drowned(1), sink(1).

2671. κατάρα katara; from *2596* and *685; a curse:*— accursed(1), curse(3), cursed(1), cursing(1).

2672. **καταράομαι** **kataraomai**; from *2671; to curse:*— accursed(1), curse(3), cursed(1).

2673. **καταργέω** **katargeō**; from *2596* and *691; to render inoperative, abolish:*— abolished(4), abolishing(1), bring to an end(1), did away(1), do away(1), done away(4), fades away(1), fading(1), fading away(1), nullified(1), nullify(4), passing away(1), released(2), removed(1), render powerless(1), severed(1), use(1).

2674. **καταριθμέω** **katarithmeō**; from *2596* and *705; to number among:*— counted(1).

2675. **καταρτίζω** **katartizō**; from *2596* and **ἀρτίζω** **artizō** *(to get ready, prepare); to complete, prepare:*— complete(1), equip(1), fully trained(1), made complete(2), mending(2), perfect(1), prepared(4), restore(1).

2676. **κατάρτισις** **katartisis**; from *2675; a preparing, an equipping:*— made complete(1).

2677. **καταρτισμός** **katartismos**; from *2675; a preparing, an equipping:*— equipping(1).

2678. **κατασείω** **kataseiō**; from *2596* and *4579; to shake:*— motioned(2), motioning(2).

2679. **κατασκάπτω** **kataskaptō**; from *2596* and *4626; to dig down:*— torn down(1).

2680. **κατασκευάζω** **kataskeuazō**; from *2596* and **σκευάζω** **skeuazō** *(to prepare, make ready); to prepare:*— builder(2), built(1), construction(1), prepare(3), prepared(4).

2681. **κατασκηνόω** **kataskēnoō**; from *2596* and *4637; to pitch one's tent, encamp, dwell:*— live(1), nest(2), nested(1).

2682. **κατασκήνωσις** **kataskēnōsis**; from *2681; a lodging:*— nests(2).

2683. **κατασκιάζω** **kataskiazō**; from *2596* and **σκιάζω** **skiazō** *(to overshadow, shade);* from *4639; to overshadow:*— overshadowing(1).

2684. **κατασκοπέω** **kataskopeō**; from *2596* and **σκοπέω** **skopeō** *(to examine, inspect); to view closely, spy out:*— spy(1).

2685. **κατάσκοπος** **kataskopos**; prob. from *2684; a spy:*— spies(1).

2686. **κατασοφίζομαι** **katasophizomai**; from *2596* and *4679; to deal craftily with:*— took shrewd advantage(1).

2687. **καταστέλλω** **katastellō**; from *2596* and *4724; to keep down:*— keep calm(1), quieting(1).

2688. **κατάστημα** **katastēma**; from *2525; demeanor:*— behavior(1).

2689. **καταστολή** **katastolē**; from *2687; a garment:*— clothing(1).

2690. **καταστρέφω** **katastrephō**; from *2596* and *4762; to overturn:*— overturned(2), ruins(1).

2691. **καταστρηνιάω** **katastrēniaō**; from *2596* and *4763; to become wanton against:*— feel sensual desires(1), feel sensual desires in disregard of(1).

2692. **καταστροφή** **katastrophē**; from *2690; an overthrowing:*— destruction(1), ruin(1).

2693. **καταστρώννυμι** **katastrōnnumi**; from *2596* and *4766; to overthrow:*— laid low(1).

2694. **κατασύρω** **katasurō**; from *2596* and *4951; to drag away:*— drag(1).

2695. **κατασφάζω** **katasphazō**; from *2596* and *4969; to kill off:*— slay(1).

2696. **κατασφραγίζω** **katasphragizō**; from *2596* and *4972; to seal up:*— sealed(1).

2697. **κατάσχεσις** **kataschesis**; from *2722; a holding fast:*— dispossessing(1), possession(1).

2698. **κατατίθημι** **katatithēmi**; from *2596* and *5087; to lay down:*— do(2), laid(1).

2699. **κατατομή** **katatomē**; from *2596* and **τέμνω** **temnō** *(to cut); concision, mutilation:*— false circumcision(1).

2700. **κατατοξεύω** **katatoxeuō**; from *2596* and **τοξεύω** **toxeuō** *(to shoot with a bow);* from *5115; to strike down with an arrow.*

2701. **κατατρέχω** **katatrechō**; from *2596* and *5143; to run down:*— ran down(1).

2702. **καταφέρω** **katapherō**; from *2596* and *5342; to bring down:*— against(1), bringing(1), cast...against(1), overcome(1), sinking(1).

2703. **καταφεύγω** **katapheugō**; from *2596* and *5343; to flee for refuge:*— fled(1), taken refuge(1).

2704. **καταφθείρω** **kataphtheirō**; from *2596* and *5351; to destroy entirely:*— depraved(1).

2705. **καταφιλέω** **kataphileō**; from *2596* and *5368; to kiss fervently:*— kiss(1), kissed(4), kissing(1).

2706. **καταφρονέω** **kataphroneō**; from *2596* and *5426; to think little of:*— despise(5), despising(1), disrespectful(1), look down(1), think lightly(1).

2707. **καταφρονητής** **kataphronētēs**; from *2706; a despiser:*— scoffers(1).

2708. **καταχέω** **katacheō**; from *2596* and **χέω** **cheō** *(to pour); to pour down upon:*— poured(1), poured...over(1).

2709. **καταχθόνιος** **Katachthonios**; from *2596* and **χθών** **chthōn** *(the earth); under the earth:*— under the earth(1).

2710. **καταχράομαι** **katachraomai**; from *2596* and *5530; to make full use of:*— make full use(2).

2711. **καταψύχω** **katapsuchō**; from *2596* and *5594; to cool:*— cool(1).

2712. **κατείδωλος** **kateidōlos**; from *2596* and *1497; full of idols:*— full of idols(1).

2713. **κατέναντι** **katenanti**; adv. from *2596* and *1725; over against, opposite:*— ahead(1), front(1), opposite(4), presence(1), sight(2).

2714. **κατενώπιον** **katenōpion**; adv. from *2596* and *1799; over against:*— before(2), presence(1).

2715. **κατεξουσιάζω** **katexousiazō**; from *2596* and *1850; to exercise authority over:*— exercise authority over(2).

2716. **κατεργάζομαι** **katergazomai**; from *2596* and *2038b; to work out:*— accomplished(1), brings about(2), carried(1), committed(1), committing(1), does(1), doing(4), done(1), effecting(1), performed(1), prepared(1), produced(2), produces(2), producing(2), work(1).

2717. (not used)

2718. **κατέρχομαι** **katerchomai**; from *2596* and *2064; to come down:*— came down(6), comes down(1), down(1), landed(3), went down(4).

2719. **κατεσθίω** **katesthiō**; from *2596* and *2068; to eat up:*— ate(4), consume(1), devour(5), devoured(2), devours(2), eat(1).

2720. **κατευθύνω** **kateuthunō**; from *2596* and *2116; to make straight:*— direct(2), guide(1).

2721a. **κατευλογέω** **kateulogeō**; from *2596* and *2127; to bless fervently:*— blessing(1).

2721b. **κατεφίστημι** **katephistēmi**; from *2596* and *2186; to rise up against:*— rose up against(1).

2722. **κατέχω** **katechō**; from *2596* and *2192; to hold fast, hold back:*— afflicted(1), bound(1), heading(1), hold...fast(1), hold fast(5), hold firmly(1), keep(2), occupy(1), possess(1), possessing(1), restrains(2), suppress(1).

2723. **κατηγορέω** **katēgoreō**; from *2596* and **ἀγορεύω** **agoreuō** *(to speak in the assembly); to make accusation:*— accusation against(1), accuse(10), accused(3), accuses(2), accusing(3), bring against(1), charges they bring against(1), charges you make(1), make accusation(1), prosecute(1).

2724. **κατηγορία** **katēgoria**; prob. from *2723; an accusation:*— accusation(2), accused(1).

2725a. **κατήγορος** **katēgoros**; from the same as *2723; an accuser:*— accusers(5).

2725b. **κατήγωρ** **katēgōr**; a form of *2725a; an accuser:*— accuser(1).

2726. **κατήφεια** **katēpheia**; from **κατηφής** **katēphēs** *(with eyes downcast); dejection:*— gloom(1).

2727. **κατηχέω** **katēcheō**; from *2596* and *2278; to teach by word of mouth:*— instruct(1), instructed(2), taught(2), teaches(1), told(2).

2728. **κατιόω** **katioō**; from *2596* and *2447; to rust over:*— rusted(1).

2729. **κατισχύω** **katischuō**; from *2596* and *2480; to overpower:*— have strength(1), overpower(1), prevail(1).

2730. **κατοικέω** **katoikeō**; from *2596* and *3611; to inhabit, to settle:*— dwell(17), dwelling(1), dwells(3), dwells within(1), live(7), lived(8), living(4), residents(1), settled(2).

2731. **κατοίκησις** **katoikēsis**; from *2730; dwelling:*— dwelling(1).

2732. **κατοικητήριον** **katoikētērion**; from *2730* and **-τηριον** **-tērion** (suff. denoting place); *a habitation:*— dwelling(1), dwelling place(1).

2733a. **κατοικία** **katoikia**; from *2730; a dwelling:*— habitation(1).

2733b. **κατοικίζω** **katoikizō**; from *2730; to cause to dwell:*— made to dwell(1).

2734. **κατοπτρίζω** **katoptrizō**; from **κάτοπτρον** **katoptron** *(a mirror); to reflect as a mirror:*— beholding as in a mirror(1).

2735. **κατόρθωμα** **katorthōma**; var. reading for *1357a*, q.v.

2736. **κάτω** **katō**; adv. from *2596; down, below:*— below(3), bottom(2), down(4), under(1).

2737a. **κατώτερος** **katōteros**; cptv. of *2736; lower:*— lower(1).

2737b. **κατωτέρω** **katōterō**; adv. of *2737a; lower.*

2738. **καῦμα** **kauma**; from *2545; heat:*— heat(2).

2739. **καυματίζω** **kaumatizō**; from *2738; to burn up:*— scorch(1), scorched(3).

2740. **καῦσις** **kausis**; from *2545; burning:*— burned(1).

2741a. **καυσόω** **kausoō**; from **καῦσος** **kausos** *(burning heat, fever); to burn with great heat:*— intense heat(2).

2741b. **καυστηριάζω** **kaustēriazō**; from a der. of *2545; to mark by branding:*— branding iron(1), seared(1).

2742. **καύσων** **kausōn**; from *2545; burning heat:*— hot(1), scorching heat(1), scorching wind(1).

2743. **καυτηριάζω** **kautēriazō**; var. reading for *2741b*, q.v.

2744. καυχάομαι kauchaomai; of unc. or.; to boast:— boast(24), boasted(1), boasting(3), boasts(2), exult(3), glory(2), take pride(1).

2745. καύχημα kauchēma; from *2744; a boast:*— boast(3), boast about(1), boasting(3), proud(1), proud confidence(1), reason to be proud(1), reason to glory(1), something to boast about(1).

2746a. καύχησις kauchēsis; from *2744; a boasting:*— boasting(7), exultation(1), proud confidence(1), reason for boasting(2).

2746b. Καφαρναούμ Kapharnaoum; of Heb. or. [3723] and [5151]; *Capernaum,* a city of Galilee:— Capernaum(16).

2747. Κεγχρεαί Kegchreai; perh. from **κέγχρος kegchros** *(millet); Cenchrea,* a port of Corinth:— Cenchrea(2).

2748. Κεδρών Kedrōn; of Heb. or. [6939]; *Kidron,* a brook and wadi near Jer.:— Kidron(1).

2749. κεῖμαι keimai; a prim. vb.; *to be laid, lie:*— appointed(2), destined(1), laid(6), lain(1), lay(1), lies(2), lying(6), made(1), set(2), standing(2).

2750. κειρία keiria; of unc. or.; *a bandage, grave-clothes:*— wrappings(1).

2751. κείρω keirō; a prim. vb.; *to shear:*— cut(1), hair cut off(2), shearer(1).

2752. κέλευσμα keleusma; from *2753; a shout of command:*— shout(1).

2753. κελεύω keleuō; from **κέλομαι kelomai** *(to urge on); to command:*— command(2), commanded(4), gave orders(2), give orders(1), giving orders(1), order(2), ordered(12), ordering(2).

2754. κενοδοξία kenodoxia; from *2755; vainglory:*— empty conceit(1).

2755. κενόδοξος kenodoxos; from *2756* and *1391; vainglorious:*— boastful(1).

2756. κενός kenos; a prim. word; *empty:*— empty(2), empty-handed(4), foolish(1), futile things(1), vain(10).

2757. κενοφωνία kenophōnia; from *2756* and *5455; empty talk:*— empty chatter(2).

2758. κενόω kenoō; from *2756; to empty:*— emptied(1), made empty(1), made void(2), make...empty(1).

2759. κέντρον kentron; from **κεντέω kenteō** *(to prick); a sharp point:*— goads(1), sting(2), stings(1).

2760. κεντυρίων kenturiōn; of Lat. or.; *a centurion* (a Rom. army officer):— centurion(3).

2761. κενῶς kenōs; adv. from *2756; in vain:*— no purpose(1).

2762. κεραία keraia; from *2768; a little horn:*— stroke(1), stroke of a letter(1).

2763. κεραμεύς kerameus; from *2767; a potter:*— potter(1), Potter's(2).

2764. κεραμικός keramikos; from *2766; earthen:*— potter(1).

2765. κεράμιον keramion; from *2766; an earthen vessel:*— pitcher(2).

2766. κέραμος keramos; from *2767; a tile:*— tiles(1).

2767. κεράννυμι kerannumi; from a prim. word **κεράω keraō** *(to mix); to mix:*— mix(1), mixed(2).

2768. κέρας keras; a prim. word; *a horn:*— horn(1), horns(10).

2769. κεράτιον keration; dim. of *2768; a carob pod:*— pods(1).

2770. κερδαίνω kerdainō; from *2771; to gain:*— gain(2), gained(4), gains(2), incurred(1), profit(1), win(5), won(2).

2771. κέρδος kerdos; a prim. word; *gain:*— gain(3).

2772. κέρμα kerma; from *2751; a slice,* hence *a small coin:*— coins(1).

2773. κερματιστής kermatistēs; from a der. of *2772; a moneychanger:*— money changers(1).

2774. κεφάλαιον kephalaion; from *2776; of the head, the main point:*— main point(1), sum of money(1).

2775. κεφαλαιόω kephalaioō; from a dim. of *2776; to strike on the head:*— wounded...in the head(1).

2776. κεφαλή kephalē; a prim. word; *the head:*— chief(4), hair(1), head(50), heads(19), very(1).

2777. κεφαλίς kephalis; dim. of *2776; a little head, a roll:*— scroll(1).

2778a. κημόω kēmoō; from **κημός kēmos** *(a muzzle); to muzzle:*— muzzle(1).

2778b. κῆνσος kēnsos; of Lat. or.; *a poll tax:*— poll-tax(4).

2779. κῆπος kēpos; a prim. word; *a garden:*— garden(5).

2780. κηπουρός kēpouros; from *2779* and **οὖρος ouros** *(a watcher); a gardener:*— gardener(1).

2781. κηρίον kērion; from **κηρός kēros** *(wax); honeycomb.*

2782. κήρυγμα kērugma; from *2784; a proclamation:*— message preached(1), preaching(5), proclamation(2).

2783. κῆρυξ kērux; from *2784; a herald:*— preacher(3).

2784. κηρύσσω kērussō; of unc. or.; *to be a herald, proclaim:*— made proclamation(1), preach(16), preached(10), preacher(1), preaches(2), preaching(11), proclaim(8), proclaimed(6), proclaiming(6).

2785. κῆτος kētos; a prim. word; *a huge fish:*— sea monster(1).

2786. Κηφᾶς Kēphas; of Ara. or.; "a rock," *Cephas,* a name given to the apostle Peter:— Cephas(9).

2787. κιβωτός kibōtos; of unc. or.; *a wooden box:*— ark(6).

2788. κιθάρα kithara; a prim. word; *a lyre:*— harp(2), harps(2).

2789. κιθαρίζω kitharizō; from *2788; to play on the lyre:*— harp(1), playing(1).

2790. κιθαρῳδός kitharōdos; from *2788* and **ἀοιδός aoidos** *(a singer); one who plays and sings to the lyre:*— harpists(2).

2791. Κιλικία Kilikia; of unc. or.; *Cilicia,* a province of Asia Minor:— Cilicia(8).

2792. κινάμωμον kinamōmon; var. reading for *2796b,* q.v.

2793. κινδυνεύω kinduneuō; from *2794; to be in danger:*— danger(4).

2794. κίνδυνος kindunos; a prim. word; *danger:*— dangers(8), peril(1).

2795. κινέω kineō; a prim. vb.; *to move:*— move(2), moved(1), provoked(1), remove(1), stirs(1), wagging(2).

2796a. κίνησις kinēsis; from *2795; a moving:*— moving(1).

2796b. κιννάμωμον kinnamōmon; of Phoenician or.; *cinnamon:*— cinnamon(1).

2797. Κίς Kis; of Heb. or. [7027]; *Kish,* the father of King Saul:— Kish(1).

2798. κλάδος klados; from *2806; a branch:*— branch(2), branches(9).

2799. κλαίω klaiō; a prim. vb.; *to weep:*— weep(18), weeping(17), wept(4).

2800. κλάσις klasis; from *2806; a breaking:*— breaking(2).

2801. κλάσμα klasma; from *2806; a broken piece:*— broken pieces(7), fragments(2).

2802. Κλαῦδα Klauda; of unc. or.; *Clauda,* an island near Crete:— Clauda(1).

2803. Κλαυδία Klaudia; fem. of *2804; Claudia,* a Chr. woman:— Claudia(1).

2804. Κλαύδιος Klaudios; of Lat. or.; *Claudius,* the name of an Emperor, also an army officer:— Claudius(3).

2805. κλαυθμός klauthmos; from *2799; weeping:*— weep(1), weeping(9).

2806. κλάω klaō; a prim. vb.; *to break:*— break(2), breaking(3), broke(8), broken(1).

2807. κλείς kleis; from *2808; a key:*— key(4), keys(2).

2808. κλείω kleiō; of unc. or.; *to shut:*— close(1), closed(1), closes(1), locked(1), shut(11), shuts(1).

2809. κλέμμα klemma; from *2813; theft:*— thefts(1).

2810. Κλεοπᾶς Kleopas; abb. for **Κλεόπατρος Kleopatros** (*Cleopatros,* "celebration of the father"); *Cleopas,* a Chr.:— Cleopas(1).

2811. κλέος kleos; from **κλέω kleō** *(to celebrate); fame:*— credit(1).

2812. κλέπτης kleptēs; from *2813; a thief:*— thief(12), thieves(4).

2813. κλέπτω kleptō; a prim. vb.; *to steal:*— steal(10), steal...away(1), steals(1), stole...away(1).

2814. κλῆμα klēma; from *2806; a vine branch:*— branch(3), branches(1).

2815. Κλήμης Klēmēs; of Lat. or.; *Clement,* a Chr. at Philippi:— Clement(1).

2816. κληρονομέω klēronomeō; from *2818; to inherit:*— heir(1), inherit(16), inherited(1).

2817. κληρονομία klēronomia; from *2818; an inheritance:*— inheritance(14).

2818. κληρονόμος klēronomos; from *2819* and the same as *3551; an heir:*— heir(8), heirs(7).

2819. κλῆρος klēros; of unc. or.; *a lot:*— allotted to your charge(1), inheritance(2), lot(1), lots(5), portion(1), share(1).

2820. κληρόω klēroō; from *2819; to assign by lot:*— obtained an inheritance(1).

2821. κλῆσις klēsis; from *2564; a calling:*—call(1), calling(9), condition(1).

2822. κλητός klētos; from *2564; called:*— called(9), calling(1).

2823. κλίβανος klibanos; of unc. or.; *an oven:*— furnace(2).

2824. κλίμα klima; from *2827; a region:*— regions(3).

2825a. κλινάριον klinarion; dim. of *2825b; a small couch:*— cots(1).

2825b. κλίνη klinē; from *2827; a couch:*— bed(8).

2826. κλινίδιον klinidion; dim. of *2825b; a small couch:*— stretcher(2).

2827. **κλίνω klinō**; a prim. vb.; *to cause to bend:*— bowed(2), ending(1), lay(2), nearly over(1), put to flight(1).

2828. **κλισία klisia**; from *2827; a place for reclining:*— groups(1).

2829. **κλοπή klopē**; from *2813; theft:*— thefts(2).

2830. **κλύδων kludōn**; from **κλύζω kluzō** *(to wash over); a billow* (of water):— surf(1), surging waves(1).

2831. **κλυδωνίζομαι kludōnizomai**; from *2830; to be tossed by waves:*— tossed here and there by waves(1).

2832. **Κλωπᾶς Klōpas**; of Ara. or.; *Clopas,* an Isr.:— Clopas(1).

2833. **κνήθω knēthō**; a late form of **κνάω knaō** *(to scrape); to scratch, itch:*— tickled(1).

2834. **Κνίδος Knidos**; of unc. or.; *Cnidus,* a city on the S.W. coast of Asia Minor:— Cnidus(1).

2835. **κοδράντης kodrantēs**; of Lat. or.; *quadrans,* one-fourth of an *as* (a Rom. monetary unit):— cent(2).

2836. **κοιλία koilia**; from **κοῖλος koilos** *(hollow); belly:*— appetite(1), appetites(1), belly(1), innermost being(1), stomach(7), womb(11), wombs(1).

2837. **κοιμάω koimaō** from *2749; to put to sleep, fall asleep:*— asleep(3), dead(1), fallen asleep(7), fell asleep(3), sleep(2), sleeping(2).

2838. **κοίμησις koimēsis**; from *2837; a resting:*— literal(1).

2839. **κοινός koinos**; from *4862; common:*— common(3), common property(1), impure(2), unclean(5), unholy(5).

2840. **κοινόω koinoō**; from *2839; to make common:*— consider(2), defile(7), defiled(2), defiles(3).

2841. **κοινωνέω koinōneō**; from *2844; to have a share of:*— contributing(1), participates(1), share(4), shared(2).

2842. **κοινωνία koinōnia**; from *2844; fellowship:*— contribution(2), fellowship(12), participation(2), sharing(3).

2843. **κοινωνικός koinōnikos**; from *2842; ready to impart:*— ready to share(1).

2844. **κοινωνός koinōnos**; from *2839; a sharer:*— partaker(1), partakers(1), partner(2), partners(2), sharers(4).

2845. **κοίτη koitē**; from *2749; a bed:*— bed(2), conceived*(1), sexual promiscuity(1).

2846. **κοιτών koitōn**; from *2845; a bedchamber:*— chamberlain*(1).

2847. **κόκκινος kokkinos**; from *2848; scarlet:*— scarlet(6).

2848. **κόκκος kokkos**; a prim. word; *a grain:*— grain(2), seed(5).

2849. **κολάζω kolazō**; from **κόλος kolos** *(docked); to chastise:*— punish(1), punishment(1).

2850. **κολακεία kolakeia**; akin to **κόλαξ kolax** *(flatterer); flattery:*— flattering(1).

2851. **κόλασις kolasis**; from *2849; correction:*— punishment(2).

2852. **κολαφίζω kolaphizō**; from **κόλαφος kolaphos** *(a blow with the fist); to strike with the fist:*— beat...with their fists(2), harshly treated(1), roughly treated(1), torment(1).

2853. **κολλάω kollaō**; from **κόλλα kolla** *(glue); to glue, unite:*— associate(3), cling(1), clings(1), hired(1), join(1), joined(2), joins(2), piled(1).

2854. **κολλούριον kollourion**; see *2855b:*— eye salve(1).

2855a. **κολλυβιστής kollubistēs**; from **κόλλυβος kollubos** *(a small coin); a money-changer:*— money changers(3).

2855b. **κολλύριον kollurion**; dim. of **κολλύρα kollura,** prob. = **κόλλιξ kollix** *(a coarse bread roll); a small bread roll, an eye salve* (shaped like a roll).

2856. **κολοβόω koloboō**; from a der. of the same as *2849; to curtail:*— cut short(2), shortened(2).

2857. **Κολοσσαί Kolossai**; appar. akin to **κολοσσός kolossos** *(a colossus,* a huge statue); *Colossae,* a city in Phrygia:— Colossae(1).

2858. (not used)

2859. **κόλπος kolpos**; a prim. word; *the bosom:*— bay(1), bosom(4), lap(1).

2860. **κολυμβάω kolumbaō**; from **κόλυμβος kolumbos** *(a diver); to plunge into the sea:*— swim(1).

2861. **κολυμβήθρα kolumbēthra**; from *2860; a pool:*— pool(4).

2862. **κολωνία kolōnia**; of Lat. or.; *a colony* (a city settlement of soldiers disbanded from the Roman army):— colony(1).

2863. **κομάω komaō**; from *2864; to wear long hair:*— has long hair(2).

2864. **κόμη komē**; a prim. word; *hair:*— hair(1).

2865. **κομίζω komizō**; from **κομέω komeō** *(to take care of); to bear, carry:*— brought(1), obtaining(1), receive(4), receive back(1), received...back(2), receiving(1), recompensed(1).

2866. **κομψότερον kompsoteron**; comp. adv. of **κομψός kompsos** *(refined, gentlemanly); well-dressed:*— better(1).

2867. **κονιάω koniaō**; from **κονία konia** *(dust); to plaster over:*— whitewashed(2).

2868. **κονιορτός koniortos**; from the same as *2867* and **ὄρνυμι ornumi** *(to stir up); dust:*— dust(5).

2869. **κοπάζω kopazō**; from *2873; to grow weary:*— died down(1), stopped(2).

2870. **κοπετός kopetos**; from *2875; a beating of the head and breast:*— lamentation(1).

2871. **κοπή kopē**; from *2875; a cutting in pieces, slaughter:*— slaughter(1).

2872. **κοπιάω kopiaō**; from *2873; to grow weary, toil:*— diligently labor(1), grown weary(1), hard-working(1), labor(3), labored(4), labors(1), toil(4), wearied(1), weary(1), work hard(1), worked(2), worked hard(1), worked hard worked hard(1), workers(1), working hard(1).

2873. **κόπος kopos**; from *2875; laborious toil:*— bother*(3), bothers*(1), labor(7), labors(4), toil(2), trouble(1).

2874a. **κοπρία kopria**; from **κόπρος kopros** *(dung); a dunghill:*— manure pile(1).

2874b. **κόπριον koprion**; from the same as *2874a; dung:*— fertilizer(1).

2875. **κόπτω koptō**; from a prim. root **κοπ- kop-**; *to cut (off), strike,* by ext. *to mourn:*— cut(1), cutting(1), lament(1), lamenting(1), mourn(3), mourning(1).

2876. **κόραξ korax**; a prim. word; *a raven:*— ravens(1).

2877. **κοράσιον korasion**; dim. of **κορή korē** *(a maiden); girl:*— girl(7), little girl(1).

2878a. **κορβᾶν korban**; of Heb. or. [7133a]; *an offering:*— Corban(1).

2878b. **κορβανᾶς korbanas**; of Heb. or. [7133a]; *treasury:*— temple treasury(1).

2879. **Κορέ Kore**; of Heb. or. [7141]; *Korah,* an Isr.:— Korah(1).

2880. **κορέννυμι korennumi**; from **κόρος koros** *(surfeit); to satisfy:*— eaten(1), enough*(1), filled(1).

2881. **Κορίνθιος Korinthios**; adj. from *2882; Corinthian:*— Corinthians(2).

2882. **Κόρινθος Korinthos**; prob. named for a legendary king; *Corinth,* a city of Greece:— Corinth(6).

2883. **Κορνήλιος Kornēlios**; of Lat. or.; *Cornelius,* a Rom. centurion:— Cornelius(8).

2884. **κόρος koros**; of Heb. or. [3734a]; *a cor* (a Heb. measure equiv. to about 15 bushels):— measures(1).

2885. **κοσμέω kosmeō**; from *2889; to order, arrange:*— adorn(4), adorned(3), put in order(2), trimmed(1).

2886. **κοσμικός kosmikos**; from *2889; pertaining to the world:*— earthly(1), worldly(1).

2887. **κόσμιος kosmios**; from *2889; orderly:*— proper(1), respectable(1).

2888. **κοσμοκράτωρ kosmokratōr**; from *2889* and *2902; a ruler of this world:*— world forces(1).

2889. **κόσμος kosmos**; a prim. word; *order, the world:*— adornment(1), world(184), world's(1).

2890. **Κούαρτος Kouartos**; of Lat. or.; *Quartus,* a Chr. at Rome:— Quartus(1).

2891. **κοῦμ koum**; of Ara. or. [6966]; *arise:*— kum(1).

2892. **κουστωδία koustōdia**; of Lat. or.; *a guard:*— guard(3).

2893. **κουφίζω kouphizō**; from **κοῦφος kouphos** *(light); to make light* (in weight):— lighten(1).

2894. **κόφινος kophinos**; a prim. word; *a basket:*— baskets(6).

2895. **κράβαττος krabattos**; of Macedonian or.; *a camp bed:*— bedridden*(1), pallet(8), pallets(2).

2896. **κράζω krazō**; from a prim. root **κραγ- krag-**; *to scream, cry out:*— cried(20), cries(2), cry(5), crying(12), screaming(1), screams(1), shout(1), shouted(4), shouting(8).

2897. **κραιπάλη kraipalē**; a prim. word; *drunken nausea:*— dissipation(1).

2898. **κρανίον kranion**; from **κάρα kara** *(the head); a skull:*— Skull(4).

2899. **κράσπεδον kraspedon**; of unc. or.; *a border, tassel:*— fringe(4), tassels(1).

2900. **κραταιός krataios**; from *2904; strong:*— mighty(1).

2901. **κραταιόω krataioō**; from *2904; to strengthen:*— become strong(2), strengthened(1), strong(1).

2902. **κρατέω krateō**; from *2904; to be strong, rule:*— arrested(3), attained(1), clinging(1), held(1), hold(4), hold fast(4), holding back(1), holding fast(1), holds(1), laid hold(1), observe(1), observing(1), prevented(1), retain(1), retained(1), seize(8), seized(7), take custody(1), take hold(2), taking(2), took(3), took hold(1).

2903. **κράτιστος kratistos**; superl. from **κρατύς kratus** *(strong); strongest, noblest:*— most excellent(4).

2904. **κράτος kratos**; a prim. word; *strength, might:*— dominion(6), might(1), mightily(1), mighty deeds(1), power(1), strength(2).

2905. **κραυγάζω kraugazō**; from *2906; to cry out:*— cried(5), cry(1), crying(2), shout(1), shouting(1).

2906. **κραυγή kraugē**; from *2896; an outcry:*— clamor(1), crying(2), shout(1), uproar(1), voice(1).

2907. **κρέας kreas**; a prim. word; *flesh:*— meat(2).

2908. **κρεῖσσον kreisson**; see *2909.*

2909. **κρείττων kreittōn** or **κρείσσων kreissōn**; cptv. of the same as *2903; better:*— better(17), better things(1), greater(1).

2910. **κρεμάννυμι kremannumi**; from a prim. root **κρεμ- krem-**; *to hang:*— depend(1), hanged(1), hanging(3), hangs(1), hung(1).

2911. **κρημνός krēmnos**; from *2910; a steep bank:*— steep bank(3).

2912. **Κρής Krēs**; from *2914; a Cretan:*— Cretans(2).

2913. **Κρήσκης Krēskēs**; of Lat. or.; *Crescens,* a Chr.:— Crescens(1).

2914. **Κρήτη Krētē**; of unc. or.; *Crete,* an island in the Mediterranean:— Crete(5).

2915. **κριθή krithē**; a prim. word; *barley:*— barley(1).

2916. **κρίθινος krithinos**; adj. from *2915; of barley:*— barley(2).

2917. **κρίμα krima**; from *2919; a judgment:*— condemnation(8), judgment(15), judgments(1), lawsuits(1), sentence(1), sentence of condemnation(1), way(1).

2918. **κρίνον krinon**; a prim. word; *a lily:*— lilies(2).

2919. **κρίνω krinō**; a prim. vb.; *to judge, decide:*— act as...judge(1), concluded(1), condemn(1), condemning(1), considered(1), decided(8), determine(1), determined(2), go to law(1), goes to law(1), judge(42), judged(25), judges(10), judging(5), judgment(1), pass judgment(1), passes judgment(1), passing judgment(1), pronounced(1), regards(2), stand trial(2), sue(1), trial(3), tried(1), try(1).

2920. **κρίσις krisis**; from *2919; a decision, judgment:*— court(2), judgment(38), judgments(2), justice(4), sentence(1).

2921. **Κρίσπος Krispos**; of Lat. or.; *Crispus,* a Corinthian Chr.:— Crispus(2).

2922. **κριτήριον kritērion**; from *2923; a law court:*— court(1), law courts(2).

2923. **κριτής kritēs**; from *2919; a judge:*— judge(15), judges(4).

2924. **κριτικός kritikos**; from *2919; critical:*— able to judge(1).

2925. **κρούω krouō**; a prim. vb.; *to strike:*— knock(4), knocked(1), knocking(1), knocks(3).

2926. **κρύπτη kruptē**; fem. from *2927; a crypt:*— cellar(1).

2927. **κρυπτός kruptos**; from *2928; hidden:*— hidden(5), inwardly(1), secret(7), secrets(2), things hidden(2).

2928. **κρύπτω kruptō**; a prim. vb.; *to hide:*— concealed(1), hid(7), hidden(8), hide(1), secret(1), things hidden(1).

2929. **κρυσταλλίζω krustallizō**; from *2930; to shine like crystal:*— crystal-clear(1).

2930. **κρύσταλλος krustallos**; from **κρύος kruos** *(frost); crystal:*— crystal(2).

2931a. **κρυφαῖος kruphaios**; from *2931b; hidden, secret:*— secret(2).

2931b. **κρυφῇ kruphē**; adv. from *2928; secretly:*— secret(1).

2932. **κτάομαι ktaomai**; a prim. vb.; *to acquire:*— acquire(1), acquired(2), gain(1), get(1), obtain(1), possess(1).

2933. **κτῆμα ktēma**; from *2932; a possession:*— piece of property(1), property(3).

2934. **κτῆνος ktēnos**; from *2932; a beast of burden:*— beast(1), beasts(1), cattle(1), mounts(1).

2935. **κτήτωρ ktētōr**; from *2932; a possessor:*— owners(1).

2936. **κτίζω ktizō**; a prim. vb.; *to build, create:*— created(13), Creator(1), make(1).

2937. **κτίσις ktisis**; from *2936; creation* (the act or the product):— created thing(1), creation(14), creature(3), institution(1).

2938. **κτίσμα ktisma**; from *2936; a creature:*— created(1), created thing(1), creatures(2).

2939. **κτίστης ktistēs**; from *2936; a creator:*— Creator(1).

2940. **κυβεία kubeia**; from **κύβος kubos** *(a cube, die); dice playing:*— trickery(1).

2941. **κυβέρνησις kubernēsis**; from **κυβερνάω kubernaō** *(to steer, guide, govern); steering, government, administration:*— administrations(1).

2942. **κυβερνήτης kubernētēs**; from the same as *2941; a steersman, pilot:*— pilot(1), shipmaster(1).

2943a. **κυκλεύω kukleuō**; from the same as *2945; to encircle:*— surrounded(1).

2943b. **κυκλόθεν kuklothen**; from the same as *2945; round about:*— around(3).

2944. **κυκλόω kukloō**; from the same as *2945; to encircle:*— encircled(1), gathered around(1), stood around(1), surrounded(1).

2945. **κύκλῳ kuklō**; dat. from **κύκλος kuklos** *(a circle); around:*— around(3), around*(2), round about(1), surrounding(2).

2946. **κυλισμός kulismos**; from *2947; a rolling:*— wallowing(1).

2947. **κυλίω kuliō**; a late form of **κυλίνδω kulindō** *(to roll, roll along); to roll:*— rolling around(1).

2948. **κυλλός kullos**; a prim. word; *crippled:*— crippled(4).

2949. **κῦμα kuma**; from **κύω kuō** *(to be pregnant, swell); a wave:*— waves(4).

2950. **κύμβαλον kumbalon**; from **κύμβη kumbē** *(a cup); a cymbal:*— cymbal(1).

2951. **κύμινον kuminon**; of Semitic or., cf. [3646]; *cummin:*— cummin(1).

2952. **κυνάριον kunarion**; dim. of *2965; a little dog:*— dogs(4).

2953. **Κύπριος Kuprios**; from *2954; of Cyprus:*— Cyprian(1), Cyprus(2).

2954. **Κύπρος Kupros**; of unc. or.; *Cyprus,* an island at the east end of the Mediterranean Sea:— Cyprus(5).

2955. **κύπτω kuptō**; prob. from a prim. root **κυφ- kuph-**; *to stoop down:*— stoop down(1), stooped(1).

2956. **Κυρηναῖος Kurēnaios**; from *2957; of Cyrene:*— Cyrene(5), Cyrenians(1).

2957. **Κυρήνη Kurēnē**; of unc. or.; *Cyrene,* a city in N. Africa:— Cyrene(1).

2958. **Κυρήνιος Kurēnios**; of Lat. or.; *Quirinius,* a governor of Syria:— Quirinius(1).

2959. **κυρία kuria**; fem. of *2962; a lady:*— lady(2).

2960. **κυριακός kuriakos**; from *2962; of the Lord:*— Lord's(2).

2961. **κυριεύω kurieuō**; from *2962; to be lord of, rule:*— has jurisdiction over(1), Lord(1), lord it over(2), lords(1), master over(2).

2962. **κύριος kurios**; from **κῦρος kuros** *(authority); lord, master:*— lord(10), Lord(625), Lord of lords(2), Lord's(12), lords(1), master(38), master's(3), masters(8), masters'(1), owner(6), owners(1), sir(11), sirs(1).

2963. **κυριότης kuriotēs**; from *2962; lordship:*— authority(2), dominion(1), dominions(1).

2964. **κυρόω kuroō**; from the same as *2962; to make valid:*— ratified(1), reaffirm(1).

2965. **κύων kuōn**; a prim. word; *a dog:*— dog(1), dogs(4).

2966. **κῶλον kōlon**; a prim. word; *a limb* (of the body):— bodies(1).

2967. **κωλύω kōluō**; prob. from the same as *2849; to hinder:*— forbid(2), forbidden(1), forbidding(1), forbids(1), hinder(5), hindered(1), hindering(1), kept(1), prevent(3), prevented(2), prevents(1), refuse(1), restrained(1), stand in...way(1), withhold(1).

2968. **κώμη kōmē**; a prim. word; *a village:*— village(18), villages(9).

2969. **κωμόπολις kōmopolis**; from *2968* and *4172; a country town:*— towns(1).

2970. **κῶμος kōmos**; from *2968; a village festival, revel:*— carousing(3).

2971. **κώνωψ kōnōps**; prob. from **κῶνος kōnos** *(cone-shaped)* and **ὤψ ōps** *(eye, face); a gnat:*— gnat(1).

2972. **Κῶς Kōs**; of unc. or.; *Cos,* an island in the Aegean Sea:— Cos(1).

2973. **Κωσάμ Kōsam**; of Heb. or., cf. [7080]; *Cosam,* an Isr.:— Cosam(1).

2974. **κωφός kōphos**; of unc. or.; *blunt, dull:*— deaf(4), mute(6), mute man(3), one who(1), one who was deaf(1).

Λ

2975. **λαγχάνω lagchanō**; from a prim. root **λαχ- lach-**; *to obtain by lot:*— cast lots(1), chosen by lot(1), received(2).

2976. **Λάζαρος Lazaros**; contr. of Heb. [499]; *Lazarus,* the name of two Isr.:— Lazarus(15).

2977. **λάθρᾳ lathra**; from *2990; secretly:*— secretly(4).

2978. **λαῖλαψ lailaps**; prob. from intens. pref. **λαι- lai-** and a prim. root **λαπ- lap-**; *a hurricane:*— fierce gale(1), gale(1), storm(1).

2979a. **λακάω lakaō**; another form of *2997,* q.v.

2979b. **λακτίζω laktizō**; from **λάξ lax** *(with the foot); to kick:*— kick(1).

2980. **λαλέω laleō**; from **λαλός lalos** *(talkative); to talk:*— made(1), proclaiming(1), said(6), say(5), saying(7), says(2), speak(95), speak forth(1), speaking(54), speaks(25), spoke(44), spoken(38), stating(1), talked(1), talking(5), tell(1), telling(1), things spoken(2), told(7), uttered(1), whispered*(1).

2981. **λαλιά lalia**; from *2980; talk:*— said(1), way...talk(1), what...saying(1).

2982. **λαμά lama**; of Heb. or. [4100] with prep. pref. lamed *(for, to); why:*— lama(2).

2983. **λαμβάνω lambanō**; from a prim. root **λαβ- lab-**; *to take, receive:*— accept(1), accepting(1), attempted*(1), bring(2), caught(1), caught caught(1), collect(1), collected(1), conferred*(2), conspired*(1), consulted*(1), experienced*(1), forgotten*(1), gets(1), gripped(1), incur(1), married(2), marry(2), obtained(1), occupy(1), overtaken(1), partial*(1), picked(2), receive(63), received(48), receives(14), receiving(6), seizes(1), shows(1), struck(1), take(24), taken(7), takes(3), taking(9), took(50).

2984. **Λάμεχ Lamech**; of Heb. or. [3929]; *Lamech,* a patriarch and an ancestor of Christ:— Lamech(1).

2985. **λαμπάς lampas**; from *2989; a torch:*— lamps(7), torch(1), torches(1).

2986. **λαμπρός lampros**; from *2989; bright:*— bright(3), clear(1), fine(2), gorgeous(1), shining(1), splendid(1).

2987. **λαμπρότης lamprotēs**; from *2986; brightness:*— brighter(1).

2988. **λαμπρῶς lamprōs**; adv. from *2986; splendidly:*— splendor(1).

2989. **λάμπω lampō**; a prim. vb.; *to shine:*— gives light(1), shine(2), shines(1), shone(3).

2990. **λανθάνω lanthanō**; from a prim. root **λαθ- lath-**; *to escape notice:*— escape...notice(2), escape notice(1), escaped notice(1), escapes...notice(1), without knowing(1).

2991. **λαξευτός laxeutos**; from a comp. of **λᾶας laas** *(a stone)* and **ξέω xeō** *(to scrape); hewn* (in stone):— cut into the rock(1).

2992. **λαός laos**; a prim. word; *the people:*— people(134), peoples(8).

2993. **Λαοδίκεια Laodikeia**; from *2992* and *1349; Laodicea,* a city in Phrygia:— Laodicea(6).

2994. **Λαοδικεύς Laodikeus**; from *2993; Laodicean:*— Laodiceans(1).

2995. **λάρυγξ larugx**; a prim. word; *the throat:*— throat(1).

2996. **Λασαία Lasaia**; of unc. or.; *Lasea,* a city of Crete:— Lasea(1).

2997. **λάσκω laskō**; from a prim. root **λακ- lak-**, see *2979a; to crack noisily:*— burst open(1).

2998. **λατομέω latomeō**; from a comp. of **λᾶας laas** *(a stone)* and **τέμνω temnō** *(to cut); to hew out* (stones):— hewn(2).

2999. **λατρεία latreia**; from *3000; service:*— divine worship(2), service(2), service of worship(1).

3000. **λατρεύω latreuō**; from **λάτρις latris** *(a hired servant); to serve:*— offer(1), serve(15), served(1), service(1), serving(1), worship(1), worshiper(1), worshipers(1).

3001. **λάχανον lachanon**; from **λαχαίνω lachainō** *(to dig); a garden herb, a vegetable:*— garden herb(1), garden plants(2), vegetables(1).

3002. **Λεββαῖος Lebbaios**; var. reading for *2280b,* q.v.

3003. **λεγιών legiōn**; of Lat. or.; *a legion:*— legion(1), Legion(2), legions(1).

3004. **λέγω legō**; a prim. vb.; *to say:*— addressing(1), agree*(1), ask(1), asked(3), asking(4), bring charges(1), call(8), called(34), calling(1), calls(3), claimed(1), claiming(2), command(3), designated(1), follows(1), give(1), gives(1), greeted*(1), made(1), mean(2), means(3), meant(1), mention(1), named(3), ordered(2), quote(1), referred(1), remarking(1), said(1086), say(364), saying(440), says(102), shouting(1), so-called(3), speak(22), speaking(17), speaks(6), spoke(18), spoken(26), stated(1), stating(2), talking(5), tell(71), telling(18), thing spoken(1), things spoken(1), thought(1), told(35), using(1).

3005. **λεῖμμα leimma**; from *3007; a remnant:*— remnant(1).

3006. **λεῖος leios**; a prim. word; *smooth:*— smooth(1).

3007. **λείπω leipō**; a prim. vb.; *to leave, leave behind:*— lack(1), lacking(2), lacks(1), need(1), remains(1).

3008. **λειτουργέω leitourgeō**; from *3011; to serve the state,* i.e. by anal. *to perform religious service:*— minister(1), ministering(2).

3009. **λειτουργία leitourgia**; from *3008; a service, a ministry:*— ministry(2), priestly service(1), service(3).

3010. **λειτουργικός leitourgikos**; from *3011; of* or *for service:*— ministering(1).

3011. **λειτουργός leitourgos**; from *2992* and *2041; a public servant, a minister, a servant:*— minister(3), ministers(1), servants(1).

λεμά lema; see *2982.*

3012. **λέντιον lention**; of for. or.; *a linen cloth, a towel:*— towel(2).

3013. **λεπίς lepis**; from **λέπω lepō** *(to peel); a scale* (of a fish):— scales(1).

3014. **λέπρα lepra**; from *3013; leprosy:*— leprosy(4).

3015. **λεπρός lepros**; from *3013; scaly, leprous:*— leper(4), lepers(4), leprous(1).

3016. **λεπτός leptos**; from the same as *3013; peeled, fine, thin, small, light:*— cent(1), small copper coins(2).

3017. **Λευί Leui**; of Heb. or. [3878]; *Levi,* the name of several Isr.:— Levi(8).

3018. **Λευίς Leuis**; the same as *3017,* q.v.

3019. **Λευίτης Leuitēs**; from *3017; a Levite,* a desc. of Levi:— Levite(2), Levites(1).

3020. **Λευιτικός Leuitikos**; from *3019; Levitical:*— Levitical(1).

3021. **λευκαίνω leukainō**; from *3022; to whiten, to make white:*— made...white(1), whiten(1).

3022. **λευκός leukos**; a prim. adj.; *bright, white:*— white(25).

3023. **λέων leōn**; a prim. word; *a lion:*— lion(5), lion's(1), lions(3).

3024. **λήθη lēthē**; from *2990; forgetfulness:*— forgotten*(1).

3025a. **λῆμψις lēmpsis**; from *2983; receiving:*— receiving(1).

3025b. **ληνός lēnos**; a prim. word; *a trough,* i.e. *a* (wine) *vat:*— press(1), wine press(4), wine*(1).

3026. **λῆρος lēros**; a prim. word; *silly talk:*— nonsense(1).

3027. **λῃστής lēstēs**; from **ληΐς lēis** *(booty); a robber:*— robber(5), robbers(6), robbers'(4).

3028. **λῆψις lēpsis**; var. reading for *3025a,* q.v.

3029. **λίαν lian**; of unc. der.; *very, exceedingly:*— exceedingly(1), extremely(1), quite(1), still(1), utterly*(1), very(6), vigorously(1).

3030. **λίβανος libanos**; of Semitic or., cf. [3828]; *the frankincense tree, frankincense:*— frankincense(2).

3031. **λιβανωτός libanōtos**; from *3030; frankincense,* by ext. *a censer:*— censer(2).

3032. **Λιβερτῖνος Libertinos**; of Lat. or.; *Freedman,* the name of a synagogue:— Freedmen(1).

3033. **Λιβύη Libuē**; prob. from *3047;* "the west bank of the Nile," *Libya,* a region in N. Africa:— Libya(1).

3034. **λιθάζω lithazō**; from *3037; to throw stones, to stone:*— stone(4), stoned(4), stoning(1).

3035. **λίθινος lithinos**; from *3037; of stone:*— stone(3).

3036. **λιθοβολέω lithoboleō**; from *3037* and *906; to pelt with stones, to stone:*— stone(1), stoned(2), stones(2), stoning(1), went on stoning(1).

3037. **λίθος lithos**; a prim. word; *a stone:*— another(4), millstone*(1), stone(38), stone's(1), stones(15).

3038. **λιθόστρωτος lithostrōtos**; from *3037* and **στρωτός strōtos** *(spread, covered); stone pavement, mosaic:*— Pavement(1).

3039. **λικμάω likmaō**; from **λικμός likmos** *(a winnowing fan); to winnow, to scatter:*— like dust(2), scatter...like dust(2).

3040. **λιμήν limēn**; of unc. or.; *a harbor, a haven:*— harbor(2).

3041. **λίμνη limnē**; of unc. or.; a lake:— lake(11).

3042. **λιμός limos**; a prim. word; *hunger, famine:*— famine(7), famines(3), hunger(2).

3043. **λίνον linon**; a prim. word; *flax, linen:*— linen(1), wick(1).

3044. **Λίνος Linos**; the name of a mythical minstrel, perh. from *3043* (for the string of a musical instrument); *Linus,* a Chr.:— Linus(1).

3045. **λιπαρός liparos**; from **λίπος lipos** *(fat); oily, fatty,* fig. *rich:*— luxurious(1).

3046. **λίτρα litra**; of Lat. or.; *a pound* (in weight, by Rom. standards):— pound(1), pounds(1).

3047. **λίψ lips**; from **λείβω leibō** *(to pour); the southwest wind:*— southwest(1).

3048. **λογεία Logeia**; from **λογεύω logeuō** *(to collect); a collection:*— collection(1), collections(1).

3049. **λογίζομαι logizomai**; from *3056* (in the sense of an *account* or *reckoning*); *to reckon, to consider:*— consider(6), considered(2), counted(1), counting(1), credit(1), credited(9), credits(1), dwell(1), maintain(1), numbered(2), propose(1), reason(1), reckoned(2), regard(4), regarded(3), suppose(1), take into account(3), thinks(1).

3050. **λογικός logikos**; from *3056; reasonable, rational:*— spiritual(1), word(1).

3051. **λόγιον logion**; neut. of *3052; a saying, an oracle:*— oracles(3), utterances(1).

3052. **λόγιος logios**; from *3056; learned, eloquent:*— eloquent(1).

3053. **λογισμός logismos**; from *3049; a reasoning, a thought:*— speculations(1), thoughts(1).

3054. **λογομαχέω logomacheō**; from *3056* and *3164; to strive with words:*— wrangle about words(1).

3055. **λογομαχία logomachia**; from *3054; a strife of words:*— disputes about words(1).

3056. **λόγος logos**; from *3004; a word* (as embodying an idea), *a statement, a speech:*— account(7), account*(1), accounting(2), accounts(2), answer(1), appearance(1), complaint(1), exhortation*(1), have to do(1), instruction(1), length*(1), matter(4), matters(1), message(10), news(3), preaching(1), question(2), reason(2), reasonable(1), remark(1), report(1), said(1), say(1), saying(4), sayings(1), speaker(1), speech(10), statement(18), story(1), talk(1), teaching(2), thing(2), things(1), utterance(2), what he says(1), what*(1), word(179), words(61).

3057. **λόγχη logchē**; a prim. word; *a lance* or *spear:*— spear(1).

3058. **λοιδορέω loidoreō**; from *3060; to abuse, revile:*— revile(1), reviled(3).

3059. **λοιδορία loidoria**; from *3058; abuse, railing:*— insult(2), reproach(1).

3060. **λοίδορος loidoros**; of unc. or.; *abusive,* subst. *railer:*— reviler(1), revilers(1).

3061. **λοιμός loimos**; a prim. word; *pestilence, a pest:*— pest(1), plagues(1).

3062. **λοιπός loipos**; from *3007; the rest, the remaining:*— beyond(1), else(2), finally(6), future(1), moreover(1), now(2), other(1), other matters(1), other people(1), other things(1), other women(1), others(4), remaining(2), rest(26), still(2), then(1), things that remain(1), time onward(1).

3063. **λοιπόν loipon**; neut. sing. of *3062,* q.v.

3064. **λοιποῦ loipou**; gen. sing. of *3062,* q.v.

3065. **Λουκᾶς Loukas**; contr. from the Lat. *Lucanus; Luke,* a Chr.:— Luke(3).

3066. **Λούκιος Loukios**; of Lat. or.; *Lucius,* the name of two Chr.:— Lucius(2).

3067. **λουτρόν loutron**; from *3068; a washing, a bath:*— washing(2).

3068. **λούω louō**; a prim. vb.; *to bathe, to wash:*— bathed(1), washed(3), washing(1).

3069. **Λύδδα Ludda**; of Heb. or. [3850a]; *Lydda,* a city in Pal.:— Lydda(3).

3070. **Λυδία Ludia**; of for. or., fem. of **Λύδιος Ludios** *(of Lydia,* a region in Asia Minor); *Lydia,* a Chr. woman:— Lydia(2).

3071. **Λυκαονία Lukaonia**; perh. from *3074; Lycaonia,* a region in Asia Minor:— Lycaonia(1).

3072. **Λυκαονιστί Lukaonisti**; adv. from *3071; in Lycaonian* (speech):— Lycaonian language(1).

3073. **Λυκία Lukia**; perh. from *3074; Lycia,* a region of Asia Minor:— Lycia(1).

3074. **λύκος lukos**; a prim. word; *a wolf:*— wolf(2), wolves(4).

3075. **λυμαίνομαι lumainomai**; from **λύμη lumē** *(outrage); to outrage, to corrupt:*— ravaging(1).

3076. **λυπέω lupeō**; from *3077; to distress, to grieve:*— cause...sorrow(1), caused...sorrow(2), caused sorrow(2), distressed(1), grieve(3), grieved(7), grieving(2), hurt(1), made sorrowful(5), sorrow(1), sorrowful(1).

3077. **λύπη lupē**; a prim. word; *pain of body* or *mind, grief, sorrow:*— grief(2), grudgingly*(1), pain(1), sorrow(10), sorrowful(1), sorrows(1).

3078. **Λυσανίας Lusanias**; from *3089* and **ἀνία ania** *(trouble);* "ending sorrow," *Lysanias,* a governor of Abilene:— Lysanias(1).

3079. **Λυσίας Lusias**; of unc. or.; *Lysias,* a Rom.:— Lysias(3).

3080. **λύσις lusis**; from *3089; a loosing* (by divorce):— released(1).

3081. **λυσιτελέω lusiteleō**; from *3089* (in the sense of *paying* expenses, etc.) and *5056; to be advantageous, profitable:*— better(1).

3082. **Λύστρα Lustra**; of unc. or.; *Lystra,* a city of Lycaonia:— Lystra(6).

3083. **λύτρον lutron**; from *3089; a ransom:*— ransom(2).

3084. **λυτρόω lutroō**; from *3089; to release by paying a ransom, to redeem:*— redeem(2), redeemed(1).

3085. **λύτρωσις lutrōsis**; from *3084; a ransoming, a redemption:*— redemption(3).

3086. **λυτρωτής lutrōtēs**; from *3084; a redeemer, deliverer:*— deliverer(1).

3087. **λυχνία luchnia**; from *3088; a lampstand:*— lampstand(6), lampstands(6).

3088. **λύχνος luchnos**; a prim. word; *a* (portable) *lamp:*— lamp(13), lamps(1).

3089. **λύω luō**; a prim. vb.; *to loose, to release, to dissolve:*— annuls(1), break(1), breaking(1), broke down(1), broken(4), destroy(2), destroyed(3), loose(2), loosed(2), putting an end to(1), release(1), released(7), removed(1), take off(1), unbind(1), untie(8), untied(1), untying(4).

3090. **Λωΐς Lōis**; perh. Akin to **Λωΐων Lōiōn** *(more desirable, better); Lois,* a Chr. woman:— Lois(1).

3091. **Λώτ Lōt**; of Heb. or. [3876]; *Lot,* a patriarch:— lot(3), Lot's(1).

M

3092. **Μαάθ Maath**; prob. of Heb. or.; *Maath,* an Isr.:— Maath(1).

3093. **Μαγαδάν Magadan**; of unc. der.; *Magadan,* an unidentified place near the Sea of Galilee:— Magadan(1).

3094. **Μαγδαληνή Magdalēnē**; fem. of **Μαγδαληνός Magdalēnos**; Magdalene, of Magdala, a place on the coast of the Sea of Galilee near Tiberias:— Magdalene(12).

3095. **μαγεία mageia**; from *3096; magic:*— magic arts(1).

3096. **μαγεύω mageuō**; from *3097; to practice magic:*— practicing magic(1).

3097. **μάγος magos**; of Pers. or., cf. [7248]; *a Magian,* i.e. *an* (Oriental) *astrologer,* by impl. *a magician:*— magi(4), magician(2).

3098. **Μαγώγ Magōg**; of Heb. or. [4031]; *Magog,* a for. nation:— Magog(1).

3099. **Μαδιάμ Madiam**; of Heb. or. [4080]; *Midian,* a region of Arabia:— Midian(1).

3100. **μαθητεύω mathēteuō**; from *3101; to be a disciple, to make a disciple:*— become a disciple(2), made...disciples(1), make disciples(1).

3101. **μαθητής mathētēs**; from *3129; a disciple:*— disciple(26), disciples(233), disciples'(1), pupil(1).

3102a. **μαθήτρια mathētria**; fem. of *3101; a female disciple:*— disciple(1).

3102b. **Μαθθαῖος Maththaios**; of Heb. or.; *Matthew,* one of the twelve apostles:— Matthew(5).

3103a. **Μαθθάτ Maththat**; of Heb. or.; *Matthat,* an Isr.:— Matthat(1).

3103b. **Μαθθίας Maththias**; of Heb. or.; *Matthias,* a Chr.:— Matthias(2).

3103c. **Μαθουσάλα Mathousala**; of Heb. or. [4968]; *Methuselah,* a patriarch:— Methuselah(1).

3104. **Μαϊνάν Mainan**; var. reading for *3303b,* q.v.

3105. **μαίνομαι mainomai**; from the root **μαν- man-**; *to rage, be mad:*— am(1), insane(1), mad(1), mind(3).

3106. **μακαρίζω makarizō**; from *3107; to bless:*— count...blessed(2).

3107. **μακάριος makarios**; from **μάκαρ makar** *(happy); blessed, happy:*— blessed(1), blessed(46), fortunate(1), happier(1), happy(1).

3108. **μακαρισμός makarismos**; from *3106; a declaration of blessedness:*— blessing(2), sense of blessing(1).

3109. **Μακεδονία Makedonia**; from *3110; Macedonia,* a region of Greece:— Macedonia(22).

3110. **Μακεδών Makedōn**; of unc. or.; *a Macedonian,* an inhab. of Macedonia:— Macedonia(2), Macedonian(1), Macedonians(2).

3111. **μάκελλον makellon**; of for. or.; *a meat market:*— meat market(1).

3112. **μακράν makran**; fem. acc. sing. of *3117; a long way, far:*— distance(1), far(5), far away(1), far off(2), long way(1).

3113. **μακρόθεν makrothen**; from *3117; from afar, afar:*— away*(1), distance(11), far(1), great distance(1), some distance away(1).

3114. **μακροθυμέω makrothumeō**; from *3117* and *2372; to persevere, to be patient:*— delay long(1), have patience(2), patient(6), patiently waited(1).

3115. **μακροθυμία makrothumia**; from *3117* and *2372; patience, long-suffering:*— patience(14).

3116. **μακροθύμως makrothumōs**; adv. from **μακρόθυμος makrothumos** *(patient);* from *3117* and *2372; with forbearance, patiently:*— patiently(1).

3117. **μακρός makros**; from a prim. root; *long, far distant:*— distant(2), long(3).

3118. **μακροχρόνιος makrochronios**; from *3117* and *5550; of long duration:*— live long(1).

3119. **μαλακία malakia**; from *3120; softness, weakness:*— sickness(3).

3120. **μαλακός malakos**; a prim. word; *soft, effeminate:*— effeminate(1), soft(3).

3121. **Μαλελεήλ Maleleēl**; of Heb. or. [4111]; *Mahalaleel,* an antediluvian:— Mahalaleel(1).

3122. **μάλιστα malista**; superl. of a prim. adv. **μάλα mala** *(very); most:*— especially(12).

3123. **μᾶλλον mallon**; cptv. of the same as *3122; more:*— all the more(3), better*(2), especially(1), even farther(1), greater(1), instead(4), less(1), more(35), much(2), rather(25), still more(2), truer(1).

3124. **Μάλχος Malchos**; of Heb. or. [4429]; *Malchus,* a slave of the high priest:— Malchus(1).

3125. **μάμμη mammē**; a prim. word, onomatop.; *a grandmother:*— grandmother(1).

3126. **μαμωνᾶς mamōnas**; of Ara. or.; *riches:*— wealth(4).

3127. **Μαναήν Manaēn**; of unc. or.; *Manaen,* a Chr.:— Manaen(1).

3128. **Μανασσῆς Manassēs**; of Heb. or. [4519]; *Manasseh,* an Isr.:— Manasseh(3).

3129. **μανθάνω manthanō**; from the root **μαθ- math-**; *to learn:*— educated(1), find(1), learn(12), learned(9), learning(1), receive instruction(1).

3130. **μανία mania**; from *3105; frenzy, madness:*— mad(1).

3131. **μάννα manna**; of Heb. or. [4478a]; *manna:*— manna(4).

3132. **μαντεύομαι manteuomai**; from **μαντίς mantis** *(a seer); to divine:*— fortune-telling(1).

3133. **μαραίνω marainō**; a prim. word; *to quench, waste away:*— fade away(1).

3134. **μαράνα θᾶ marana tha**; transliterated Ara. phrase; (our) *Lord, come!:*— Maranatha(1).

3135. **μαργαρίτης margaritēs**; of for. or.; *a pearl:*— pearl(2), pearls(7).

3136. **Μάρθα Martha**; of Ara. or.; *Martha,* a Chr. woman:— Martha(13).

3137. **Μαρία Maria** or
Μαριάμ Mariam; of Heb. or. [4813]; *Mary,* the name of several Chr. women:— Mary(53), Mary's(1).

3138. **Μάρκος Markos**; of Lat. or.; *Mark,* a Chr.:— Mark(8).

3139. **μάρμαρος marmaros**; from **μαρμαίρω marmairō** *(to glisten); a crystalline stone,* esp. *marble:*— marble(1).

3140. **μαρτυρέω martureō**; from *3144; to bear witness, testify:*— add...testimony(1), attested(1), bear...witness(1), bear witness(1), continued to testify(1), gained approval(2), given(1), gives(1), good reputation(1), having a reputation(1), obtained the testimony(1), obtained the witness(1), received a good testimony(1), speaking well(1), testified(17), testifies(7), testify(25), testifying(5), testimony(5), well spoken(3), witness(1), witnessed(2), witnesses(1).

3141. **μαρτυρία marturia**; from *3140; testimony:*— reputation(1), testimony(30), witness(1).

3142. **μαρτύριον marturion**; from *3144; a testimony, a witness:*— testimony(19), witness(1).

3143. **μαρτύρομαι marturomai**; from *3144; to summon as witness, to affirm:*— affirm(1), imploring(1), testify(2), testifying(1).

3144. **μάρτυς martus**; a prim. word; *a witness:*— witness(12), witnesses(23).

3145. **μασάομαι masaomai**; of unc. or.; to chew:— gnawed(1).

3146. **μαστιγόω mastigoō**; from *3148; to scourge:*— scourge(4), scourged(2), scourges(1).

3147. **μαστίζω mastizō**; from *3148; to whip, scourge:*— scourge(1).

3148. **μάστιξ mastix**; of unc. or.; *a whip, scourge:*— affliction(2), afflictions(2), scourging(1), scourgings(1).

3149. **μαστός mastos**; der. from a prim. root **μα- ma-**; *the breast:*— breasts(2), chest(1).

3150. **ματαιολογία mataiologia**; from *3151; idle* or *foolish talk:*— fruitless discussion(1).

3151. **ματαιολόγος mataiologos**; from *3152* and *3004; talking idly:*— empty talkers(1).

3152. **μάταιος mataios**; from the same as *3155; vain, useless:*— futile(1), useless(1), vain things(1), worthless(3).

3153. **ματαιότης mataiotēs**; from *3152; vanity, emptiness:*— futility(2), vanity(1).

3154. **ματαιόω mataioō**; from *3152; to make vain, foolish:*— became futile(1).

3155. **μάτην matēn**; adv. from acc. of **μάτη matē** *(a folly); in vain, to no purpose:*— vain(2).

3156. **Ματθαῖος Matthaios**; var. reading for *3102b,* q.v.

3157. **Ματθάν Matthan**; of Heb. or. [4977]; *Matthan,* an Isr.:— Matthan(2).

3158. **Ματθάτ Matthat**; var. reading for *3103a,* q.v.:— Matthat(1).

3159. **Ματθίας Matthias**; var. reading for *3103b,* q.v.

3160. **Ματταθά Mattatha**; of Heb. or. [4992]; *Mattatha,* an Isr.:— Mattatha(1).

3161. **Ματταθίας Mattathias**; of Heb. or. [4993]; *Mattathias,* an Isr. name:— Mattathias(2).

3162. **μάχαιρα machaira**; perh. from *3164; a short sword* or *dagger:*— sword(23), swords(6).

3163. **μάχη machē**; from *3164; a fight:*— conflicts(2), disputes(1), quarrels(1).

3164. **μάχομαι machomai**; a prim. vb.; *to fight:*— argue(1), fight(1), fighting together(1), quarrelsome(1).

3165. **μέ me**; a form of *1691,* q.v.

3166. **μεγαλαυχέω megalaucheō**; var. reading for *3173* and *850a,* q.v.

3167. **μεγαλεῖος megaleios**; from *3173; magnificent, splendid:*— mighty deeds(1).

3168. **μεγαλειότης megaleiotēs**; from *3167; splendor, magnificence:*— greatness(1), magnificence(1), majesty(1).

3169. **μεγαλοπρεπής megaloprepēs**; from *3173* and *4241; befitting a great one:*— Majestic(1).

3170. **μεγαλύνω megalunō**; from *3173; to make* or *declare great:*— displayed...great(1), enlarged(1), exalted(1), exalting(1), exalts(1), held...in high esteem(1), high esteem(1), lengthen(1), magnified(1).

3171. **μεγάλως megalōs**; adv. from *3173; greatly:*— greatly(1).

3172. **μεγαλωσύνη megalōsunē**; from *3173; greatness, majesty:*— Majesty(3).

3173. **μέγας megas**; a prim. word; *great:*— abundant(1), all the more(1), arrogant(1), big(2), completely*(1), fierce(2), great(115), great men(2), great things(2), greater(30), greater things(1), greatest(10), greatly*(1), grown*(1), high(2), huge(1), large(8), larger(2), larger ones(1), long time(1), loud(42), mighty(1), more important(2), older(1), one greater(1), perfectly(2), severe(2), stricter(1), strong(1), surprising(1), terribly(1), too much(1), very much(1), wide(1).

3174. **μέγεθος megethos**; from *3173; greatness:*— greatness(1).

3175. **μεγιστάν megistan**; from *3176; the chief men:*— great men(2), lords(1).

3176. **μέγιστος megistos**; superl. of *3173; greatest:*— magnificent(1).

3177. **μεθερμηνεύω methermēneuō**; from *3326* and *2059; to translate, to interpret:*— translated(8).

3178. **μέθη methē**; a prim. word; *drunkenness:*— drunkenness(3).

3179. **μεθίστημι methistēmi**; from *3326* and *2476; to change, pervert:*— remove(1), removed(2), transferred(1), turned away(1).

3180. **μεθοδεία methodeia**; from **μεθοδεύω methodeuō** *(to employ craft); craft, deceit:*— schemes(1), scheming(1).

3181. **μεθόριον methorion**; var. reading for *3725,* q.v.

3182. **μεθύσκω methuskō**; caus. form of *3184; to make drunk:*— get drunk(3).

3183. **μέθυσος methusos**; from *3184; drunken:*— drunkard(1), drunkards(1).

3184. **μεθύω methuō**; from **μέθυ methu** *(wine); to be drunken:*— drunk(3), drunk freely(1), drunkards(1), get drunk(1), made drunk(1).

3185. **μεῖζον meizon**; neut. of *3187,* q.v.

3186. **μειζότερος meizoteros**; cptv. of *3173,* q.v.

3187. **μείζων meizōn**; cptv. of *3173,* q.v.

3188. **μέλαν melan**; neut. of *3189,* q.v.

3189. **μέλας melas**; a prim. word; *black:*— black(3), ink(3).

3190. **Μελεά Melea**; of Heb. or.; *Melea,* an Isr.:— Melea(1).

3191. **μελετάω meletaō**; from **μελέτη meletē** *(care); to care for, practice, study:*— devise(1), take pains(1).

3192. **μέλι meli**; a prim. word; *honey:*— honey(4).

3193. **μελίσσιος melissios**; from **μέλισσα melissa** *(a bee); made by bees.*

3194. **Μελίτη Melitē**; of unc. or.; *Melita* (Malta), an island in the Mediterranean:— Malta(1).

3195. **μέλλω mellō**; a prim. vb.; *to be about to:*— about(30), almost(1), am about(2), certainly(1), come(12), delay(1), future(1), going(19), intend(1), intending(8), later(1), must(1), next*(1), point(1), propose(1), ready(1), things to come(3), will(6), will certainly(1), would(3), would live...thereafter(1), would certainly(1).

3196. **μέλος melos**; a prim. word; *a member* or *limb* (of the body):— member(4), members(27), part(1), parts(2).

3197. **Μελχί Melchi**; of Heb. or. [4428]; *Melchi,* the name of two Isr.:— Melchi(2).

3198. **Μελχισέδεκ Melchisedek**; of Heb. or. [4442]; *Melchizedek,* O.T. king of Salem:— Melchizedek(8).

3199. **μέλω melō**; a prim. vb.; *to be an object of care:*— care(2), cares(1), concerned(4), defer(2), worry(1).

3200. **μεμβράνα membrana**; of Lat. or.; *parchment:*— parchments(1).

3201. **μέμφομαι memphomai**; a prim. vb.; *to blame, find fault:*— find fault(1), finding fault(1).

3202. **μεμψίμοιρος mempsimoiros**; from *3201* and **μοῖρα moira** *(fate); complaining of one's fate:*— finding fault(1).

3203-3302. (not used)

3303a. **μέν men**; a synonym of *3375;* shows affirmation or concession, usually followed by *1161* and a contrasting clause:— contrary*(1), however*(1), indeed(7), latter(1), one(1), one hand(4), one*(7), only(1), partly*(1), some*(13), sure(3), though(4), while(1).

3303b. **Μεννά Menna**; prob. of Heb. or.; *Menna,* an Isr.:— Menna(1).

3304. **μενοῦν menoun** and **μενοῦνγε menounge**; from *3303a, 3767* and *1065; rather, on the contrary:*— contrary(1), indeed(1), more than(1).

3305. **μέντοι mentoi**; from *3303a* and *5104; yet, however:*— however(1), nevertheless(1), nevertheless*(1), yet(4).

3306. **μένω menō**; a prim. vb.; *to stay, abide, remain:*— abide(16), abides(22), abiding(4), await(1), continue(4), continues(1), endures(3), enduring(1), lasting(2), lives(1), living(1), remain(20), remained(6), remaining(1), remains(8), stand(1), stay(11), stayed(11), staying(3), waiting(1).

3307. **μερίζω merizō**; from *3313; to divide:*— allotted(1), apportioned(2), assigned(1), divide(1), divided(9).

3308. **μέριμνα merimna**; of unc. or.; *care, anxiety:*— anxiety(1), concern(1), worries(3), worry(1).

3309. **μεριμνάω merimnaō**; from *3308; to be anxious, to care for:*— anxious(1), care(1), concerned(5), have...care(1), worried(4), worry(6), worrying(1).

3310. **μερίς meris**; fem. noun from *3313; a part, portion:*— common(1), district(1), part(2), share(1).

3311. **μερισμός merismos**; from *3307; a dividing, distribution:*— division(1), gifts(1).

3312. **μεριστής meristēs**; from *3307; a divider:*— arbitrator(1).

3313. **μέρος meros**; from **μείρομαι meiromai** *(to receive one's portion); a part, share, portion:*— case(2), country(1), detail(1), district(3), districts(2), group(1), individually(1), part(11), partial(2), partially(1), parts(3), party(1), piece(1), place(3), portion(1), regions(1), respect(1), share(1), side(1), some degree(1), some points(1), trade(1), turn(1), while(1).

3314. **μεσημβρία mesēmbria**; from *3319* and *2250; noon, the south:*— noontime(1), south(1).

3315. **μεσιτεύω mesiteuō**; from *3316; to interpose, mediate:*— interposed(1).

3316. **μεσίτης mesitēs**; from *3319; an arbitrator, a mediator:*— mediator(6).

3317. **μεσονύκτιον mesonuktion**; from **μεσονύκτιος mesonuktios** *(at midnight);* from *3319* and *3571; at midnight:*— midnight(4).

3318. **Μεσοποταμία Mesopotamia**; from *3319* and *4215; Mesopotamia,* a region through which the Tigris and Euphrates Rivers flow:— Mesopotamia(2).

3319. **μέσος mesos**; a prim. word; *middle, in the midst:*— among(3), among*(5), before*(3), between(1), between*(3), center(6), forward*(3), midday*(1), middle(6), midnight*(2), midst(19), two(1), way(2), within*(1).

3320. **μεσότοιχον mesotoichon**; from *3319* and *5109; a middle wall:*— dividing wall(1).

3321. **μεσουράνημα mesouranēma**; from *3319* and *3772*; the zenith, mid-heaven:— mid-heaven(3).

3322. **μεσόω mesoō**; from *3319; to be in the middle:*— midst(1).

3323. **Μεσσίας Messias**; of Heb. or. [4899]; *Messiah,* the O.T. title corresponding to *Christ:*— Messiah(2).

3324. **μεστός mestos**; of unc. or.; *full:*— full(9).

3325. **μεστόω mestoō**; from *3324; to fill:*— full(1).

3326. **μετά meta**; a prim. prep.; *with, among, after:*— accompanied(1), accompanied*(2), accompany*(1), after(82), afterward*(3), against(4), amid(1), among(5), away(1), before*(1), behind(1), companions*(5), end(1), follow*(1), gratefully*(1), hereafter*(1), later(12), now*(1), together(2), together*(1), toward(3), without*(2).

3327. **μεταβαίνω metabainō**; from *3326* and the same as *939; to pass over, withdraw, depart:*— depart(1), departed(1), departing(2), leave(2), left(1), move(2), moving(1), passed(2).

3328. **μεταβάλλω metaballō**; from *3326* and *906; to turn about, to change:*— changed their minds(1).

3329. **μετάγω metagō**; from *3326* and *71; to turn about, to direct:*— direct(1), directed(1).

3330. **μεταδίδωμι metadidōmi**; from *3326* and *1325; to give a share of:*— gives(1), impart(2), share(2).

3331. **μετάθεσις metathesis**; from *3346a; a change, removal:*— being taken(1), change(1), removing(1).

3332. **μεταίρω metairō**; from *3326* and *142; to remove, depart:*— departed(2).

3333. **μετακαλέω metakaleō**; from *3326* and *2564; to call from one place to another:*— called(1), invite(1), invited(1), summon(1).

3334. **μετακινέω metakineō**; from *3326* and *2795; to move away, remove:*— moved away(1).

3335. **μεταλαμβάνω metalambanō**; from *3326* and *2983; to partake of:*— find(1), receive his share(1), receives(1), share(1), take(2), taking...together(1).

3336. **μετάλημψις metalēmpsis**; from *3335; taking, receiving, sharing:*— shared(1).

3337. **μεταλλάσσω metallassō**; from *3326* and *236; to change, exchange:*— exchanged(2).

3338. **μεταμέλομαι metamelomai**; from *3326* and *3199; to regret, repent:*— change his mind(1), feel remorse(1), felt remorse(1), regret(2), regretted(1).

3339. **μεταμορφόω metamorphoō**; from *3326* and *3445; to transform:*— transfigured(2), transformed(2).

3340. **μετανοέω metanoeō**; from *3326* and *3539; to change one's mind* or *purpose:*— repent(26), repented(5), repents(3).

3341. **μετάνοια metanoia**; from *3340; change of mind, repentance:*— repentance(22).

3342. **μεταξύ metaxu**; from *3326* and **ξύν xun** (see *4862); between, after:*— alternately(1), between(5), Meanwhile(1), next(1).

3343. **μεταπέμπω metapempō**; from *3326* and *3992; to send after* or *for:*— brought(1), brought here(1), send(3), sent(4).

3344. **μεταστρέφω metastrephō**; from *3326* and *4762; to turn* (about), *to pervert:*— distort(1), turned(1).

3345. **μετασχηματίζω metaschēmatizō**; from *3326* and **σχηματίζω schēmatizō** *(to give* a certain *form to* something); *to change in fashion* or *appearance:*— disguise(1), disguises(1), disguising(1), figuratively applied(1), transform(1).

3346a. **μετατίθημι metatithēmi**; from *3326* and *5087; to transfer, change:*— changed(1), deserting*(1), removed(1), taken(1), took(1), turn(1).

3346b. **μετατρέπω metatrepō**; from *3326* and **τρέπω trepō** *(to turn); to turn about:*— turned(1).

3347. **μετέπειτα metepeita**; from *3326* and *1899; afterwards:*— afterwards(1).

3348. **μετέχω metechō**; from *3326* and *2192; to partake of, share in:*— belongs(1), partake(3), partakes(1), partook(1), share(1), sharing(1).

3349. **μετεωρίζω meteōrizō**; from **μετέωρος meteōros** *(buoyed up); to raise on high,* fig. *to be in suspense:*— worrying(1).

3350. **μετοικεσία metoikesia**; from **μετοικέω metoikeō** *(to change one's abode); change of abode:*— deportation(4).

3351. **μετοικίζω metoikizō**; from **μέτοικος metoikos** *(an emigrant); to cause to migrate:*— move(1), remove(1).

3352. **μετοχή metochē**; from *3348; sharing:*— partnership(1).

3353. **μέτοχος metochos**; from *3348; sharing in:*— companions(1), partakers(4), partners(1).

3354. **μετρέω metreō**; from *3358; to measure, measure out:*— measure(7), measured(3), it will be measured(1).

3355. **μετρητής metrētēs**; from *3354; a measurer, a measure:*— gallons(1).

3356. **μετριοπαθέω metriopatheō**; from the same as *3357* and *3806; to hold one's emotions in restraint:*— deal gently(1).

3357. **μετρίως metriōs**; adv. from **μέτριος metrios** *(moderate); moderately:*— greatly*(1).

3358. **μέτρον metron**; a prim. word; *a measure:*— measure(8), measurements(1), proper(1), standard(4).

3359. **μέτωπον metōpon**; from *3326* and **ὤψ ōps** *(an eye, face); the forehead:*— forehead(4), foreheads(4).

3360. **μέχρι mechri** or

μέχρις mechris; a prim. word; *as far as, until:*— even(1), far(1), point(2), until(10).

3361. **μή mē**; a prim. particle; *not, that...not, lest* (used for qualified negation):— all*(1), cannot(1), cannot*(6), case(1), certainly*(1), devoid*(1), ever*(3), except(2), fear*(2), inevitable*(1), keep(2), kept(1), lacks*(1), make(1), never(17), never*(16), no(67), no one(1), no*(11), none(2), none*(2), nothing(2), nothing*(3), only*(11), or(4), otherwise*(3), refrain(1), so(2), so that no(1), so*(12), stop(8), surely(4), than*(2), unable*(4), unless*(38), until*(1), without(6), without*(4).

3362. **ἐὰν μή ean mē**; see *1437* and *3361.*

3363. **ἵνα μή hina mē**; see *2443* and *3361.*

3364. **οὐ μή ou mē**; see *3756* and *3361.*

3365. **μηδαμῶς mēdamōs**; adv. from **μηδαμός mēdamos**; from *3366* and **ἀμός hamos** *(anyone); by no means:*— no means(2).

3366. **μηδέ mēde**; from *3361* and *1161; but not, and not:*— either(1), even(5), none(1), nor(16), or(21), or even(1), thereby(1).

3367. **μηδείς mēdeis,**

μηδεμία mēdemia,

μηδέν mēden; from *3366* and *1520; no one, nothing:*— all(1), any(7), anyone(8), anything(2), least(1), never(1), no(9), no at all(1), no basis(1), no man(1), no one(26), no way(1), nothing(22), without(4), without...any(1), without any(1).

3368. **μηδέποτε mēdepote**; adv. from *3366* and *4218; never:*— never(1).

3369. **μηδέπω mēdepō**; from *3366* and *4452; not yet:*— yet(1).

3370. **Μῆδος Mēdos**; of for. or.; *a Mede, Median,* an inhab. of Media:— Medes(1).

μηθείς mētheis and **μηθέν mēthen**; see *3367.*

3371. **μηκέτι mēketi**; from *3361* and *2089; no longer, not anymore:*— again(2), any longer(1), anymore(3), longer(1), no further(1), no longer(13), no more(1).

3372. μῆκος mēkos; from same as *3117; length:*— length(3).

3373. μηκύνω mēkunō; from *3372; to lengthen, grow:*— grows(1).

3374. μηλωτή mēlōtē; from **μῆλον mēlon** *(a sheep* or *goat); a sheepskin:*— sheepskins(1).

3375. μήν mēn; a strengthened form of *3303a; certainly:*— surely*(1).

3376. μήν mēn; a prim. word; *a month:*— month(4), months(14).

3377. μηνύω mēnuō; a prim. word; *to make known, report:*— informed(2), report(1), showed(1).

3378. μὴ οὐκ mē ouk; see *3361* and *3756.*

3379. μήποτε mēpote; from *3361* and *4218; never, lest ever:*— if(1), if perhaps(1), never(1), no(1), or(1), or else(1), otherwise(6), so(7), whether(1).

3380a. μή που mē pou; see *3361* and *4225; lest anywhere, lest perhaps.*

3380b. μήπω mēpō; from *3361* and *4452; not yet:*— yet(2).

3381. μή πως mē pōs; see *3361* and *4458; lest perhaps, whether perhaps:*— fear(2), otherwise(2).

3382. μηρός mēros; a prim. word; *the thigh:*— thigh(1).

3383. μήτε mēte; from *3361* and *5037; neither, nor:*— either(4), neither(2), neither...nor(3), no(1), nor(7), or(12).

3384. μήτηρ mētēr; a prim. word; *mother:*— mother(75), mother's(7), mothers(2).

3385. μήτι mēti; from *3361* and the neut. of *5100; can this be?* (interrog. particle expecting a neg. answer):— cannot(1), cannot*(1), perhaps(1), surely(4), surely no(1), unless*(2).

3386. μήτι γε mēti ge; see *3385* and *1065; let alone, much less, much more:*— how much more(1).

3387. μή τις mē tis; see *3361* and *5100.*

3388. μήτρα mētra; from *3384; the womb:*— womb(2).

3389. μητρολῴας mētrolōas; from *3384* and **ἀλοιάω aloiaō** *(to smite); a matricide:*— kill*(1), mothers(1).

3390. μητρόπολις mētropolis; from *3384* and *4172; a metropolis.*

3391. μία mia; fem. of *1520,* q.v.

3392. μιαίνω miainō; a prim. vb.; *to stain, defile:*— defile(1), defiled(4).

3393. μίασμα miasma; from *3392; a stain, defilement:*— defilements(1).

3394. μιασμός miasmos; from *3392; the act of defiling:*— corrupt(1).

3395. μίγμα migma; from *3396; a mixture:*— mixture(1).

3396. μίγνυμι mignumi; a prim. vb.; *to mix:*— mixed(4).

3397. μικρόν mikron; masc. or neut. sing. of *3398,* q.v.

3398. μικρός mikros; a prim. word; *small, little:*— least(4), less(1), little(13), little ones(6), little while(10), short(1), small(8), smaller(2), smallest(1).

3399. Μίλητος Milētos; of unc. or.; *Miletus,* a city in S.W. Asia Minor:— Miletus(3).

3400. μίλιον milion; of Lat. or.; *a Roman mile* (about 1618 yards):— mile(1).

3401. μιμέομαι mimeomai; from **μῖμος mimos** *(a mimic); to imitate:*— follow...example(2), imitate(2).

3402. μιμητής mimētēs; from *3401; an imitator:*— imitators(6).

3403. μιμνήσκω mimnēskō; from a prim. vb.; to remind, remember:— recall(1), remember(13), remembered(8), remembrance(1).

3404. μισέω miseō; from **μῖσος misos** *(hatred); to hate:*— hate(13), hated(12), hateful(1), hates(12), hating(2).

3405. μισθαποδοσία misthapodosia; from *3408* and *591; payment of wages:*— penalty(1), reward(2).

3406. μισθαποδότης misthapodotēs; from *3408* and *591; one who pays wages:*— rewarder(1).

3407. μίσθιος misthios; from *3408; a hired servant:*— hired men(2).

3408. μισθός misthos; a prim. word; *wages, hire:*— pay(2), price(1), reward(19), wage(1), wages(6).

3409. μισθόω misthoō; from *3408; to let for hire, to hire:*— hire(1), hired(1).

3410. μίσθωμα misthōma; from *3409; rent, a rented house:*— rented quarters(1).

3411. μισθωτός misthōtos; from *3409; hired, a hired servant:*— hired hand(2), hired servants(1).

3412. Μιτυλήνη Mitulēnē; late form of **Μυτιλήνη Mutilēnē**; Mitylene, the chief city of Lesbos:— Mitylene(1).

3413. Μιχαήλ Michaēl; of Heb. or. [4317]; *Michael,* the archangel:— Michael(2).

3414. μνᾶ mna; of Semitic or. [4488]; *a mina* (Gr. monetary unit):— mina(4), minas(5).

3415. μνάομαι mnaomai; var. reading for *3423,* q.v.

3416. Μνάσων Mnasōn; of unc. or.; *Mnason,* a Chr.:— Mnason(1).

3417. μνεία mneia; from *3403; remembrance, mention:*— mention(4), remember*(1), remembrance(1), think*(1).

3418. μνῆμα mnēma; from *3415* (in the sense of *to be mindful of); a memorial, a sepulcher:*— tomb(7), tombs(3).

3419. μνημεῖον mnēmeion; from *3420; a memorial, a monument:*— monuments(1), tomb(30), tombs(7).

3420. μνήμη mnēmē; from *3415* (in the sense of *to be mindful of); memory, remembrance:*— mind(1).

3421. μνημονεύω mnēmoneuō; from **μνήμων mnēmōn** *(mindful); to call to mind, to make mention of:*— bearing in mind(1), made mention(1), recall(1), remember(14), remembered(1), remembering(1), remembers(1), thinking(1).

3422. μνημόσυνον mnēmosunon; from the same as *3421; a memorial:*— memorial(1), memory(2).

3423. μνηστεύω mnēsteuō; from *3415* (in the sense of *to court* a bride); *to espouse, betroth:*— betrothed(1), engaged(2).

3424. μογιλάλος mogilalos; from *3425* and *2980; speaking with difficulty:*— spoke with difficulty(1).

3425. μόγις mogis; another reading for *3433,* q.v.

3426. μόδιος modios; of Lat. or.; *modius,* a dry measure of one peck:— basket(3).

3427. μοι moi; a simpler form of *1698,* see *1473.*

3428. μοιχαλίς moichalis; from the fem. of *3432; an adulteress:*— adulteress(2), adulteresses(1), adulterous(3), adultery(1).

3429. μοιχάω moichaō; from *3432; to commit adultery with:*— adultery(1), commits adultery(3).

3430. μοιχεία moicheia; from *3431; adultery:*— adulteries(2), adultery(1).

3431. μοιχεύω moicheuō; from *3432; to commit adultery:*— adultery(1), commit adultery(11), commits adultery(2), committed adultery(1), committing(1).

3432. μοιχός moichos; a prim. word; *an adulterer:*— adulterers(3).

3433. μόλις molis; from **μόλος molos** *(toil); with difficulty:*— difficulty(4), hardly(1), only with difficulty(1), scarcely(1).

3434. Μολόχ Moloch; of Heb. or. [4432]; *Moloch,* the god of the Ammonites:— Moloch(1).

3435. μολύνω molunō; of unc. or.; *to stain, defile:*— defiled(2), soiled(1).

3436. μολυσμός molusmos; from *3435; defilement:*— defilement(1).

3437. μομφή momphē; from *3201; blame:*— complaint(1).

3438. μονή monē; from *3306; an abiding, an abode:*— abode(1), dwelling places(1).

3439. μονογενής monogenēs; from *3441* and *1085; only begotten:*— only(3), only begotten(6).

3440. μόνον monon; adv. from *3441; merely:*— only(53), simply(2).

3441. μόνος monos; a prim. word; *alone:*— alone(31), even(1), just(2), mere(1), merely(2), only(18), only one(1), only thing(1), private(1), themselves*(1).

3442. μονόφθαλμος monophthalmos; from *3441* and *3788; having one eye:*— one eye(2).

3443. μονόω monoō; from *3441; to leave alone, forsake:*— left alone(1).

3444. μορφή morphē; a prim. word; *form, shape:*— form(3).

3445. μορφόω morphoō; from *3444; to form:*— formed(1).

3446. μόρφωσις morphōsis; from *3445; a forming, a form:*— embodiment(1), form(1).

3447. μοσχοποιέω moschopoieō; from *3448* and *4160; to make a calf* (as an image):— made a calf(1).

3448. μόσχος moschos; a prim. word; *a young shoot, a calf:*— calf(4), calves(2).

3449. μόχθος mochthos; akin to *3425; toil, hardship:*— hardship(3).

3450. μου mou; a simpler form of *1700,* see *1473.*

3451. μουσικός mousikos; from **Μοῦσα Mousa** *(a Muse); skilled in the arts* (esp. music):— musicians(1).

3452. μυελός muelos; a prim. word; *marrow:*— marrow(1).

3453. μυέω mueō; from **μύω muō** *(to shut the eyes* or *mouth); to initiate into the mysteries,* hence *to instruct:*— learned the secret(1).

3454. μῦθος muthos; a prim. word; *a speech, story,* i.e. *a fable:*— fables(1), myths(3), tales(1).

3455. μυκάομαι mukaomai; a prim. word, onomatop.; *to roar:*— roars(1).

3456. **μυκτηρίζω muktērizō**; from **μυκτήρ muktēr** *(nostril); to turn up the nose* or *sneer at:*— mocked(1).

3457a. **μυλικός Mulikos**; from **μύλη mulē** *(a mill); of a mill:*— millstone*(1).

3457b. **μύλινος mulinos**; from *3458; of a mill:*— millstone(1).

3458. **μύλος mulos**; from the same as *3457a; a mill, a millstone:*— mill(2), millstone(2).

3459. **μύλων mulōn**; var. reading for *3458*, q.v.

3460. **Μύρα Mura**; of unc. or.; *Myra,* a city of Lycia:— Myra(1).

3461. **μυριάς murias**; from *3463; ten thousand, a myriad:*— fifty*(1), many thousands(2), myriads(3), thousand(1), thousands(1), two hundred million*(1).

3462. **μυρίζω murizō**; from *3464; to anoint:*— anointed(1).

3463. **μυρίος murios**; a prim. word; *countless,* pl. *ten thousand:*— countless(1), ten thousand(2).

3464. **μύρον muron**; a prim. word; *ointment:*— ointment(1), perfume(12), perfumes(1).

3465. **Μυσία Musia**; of unc. or.; *Mysia,* a province of Asia Minor:— Mysia(2).

3466. **μυστήριον mustērion**; from **μύστης mustēs** *(one initiated);* from *3453; a mystery* or *secret doctrine:*— mysteries(5), mystery(22).

3467. **μυωπάζω muōpazō**; from **μύωψ muōps** *(shortsighted); to be shortsighted:*— short-sighted(1).

3468. **μώλωψ mōlōps**; of unc. or.; a bruise:— wounds(1).

3469. **μωμάομαι mōmaomai**; from *3470; to find fault with:*— discredit(1), discredited(1).

3470. **μῶμος mōmos**; a prim. word; *blame, disgrace, blemish:*— blemishes(1).

3471. **μωραίνω mōrainō**; from *3474; to be foolish:*— became fools(1), become tasteless(2), made foolish(1).

3472. **μωρία mōria**; from *3474; foolishness:*— foolishness(5).

3473. **μωρολογία mōrologia**; from *3474* and *3004; foolish talking:*— silly talk(1).

3474. **μωρός mōros**; a prim. word; *dull, stupid, foolish:*— fool(1), foolish(7), foolish things(1), foolishness(1), fools(2).

3475. **Μωϋσῆς Mōusēs**; of Heb. or. [4872]; *Moses,* a leader of Isr.:— Moses(80).

N

3476. **Ναασσών Naassōn**; of Heb. or. [5177]; *Nahshon,* an Isr.:— Nahshon(3).

3477. **Ναγγαί Naggai**; prob. of Heb. or., cf. [5052]; *Naggai,* an Isr.:— Naggai(1).

3478. **Ναζαρά Nazara** or
Ναζαρέτ Nazaret or
Ναζαρέθ Nazareth; of unc. der.; *Nazareth,* a city in Galilee:— Nazareth(12).

3479. **Ναζαρηνός Nazarēnos**; prob. from *3478; a Nazarene,* an inhab. of Nazareth:— Nazarene(4), Nazareth(2).

3480. **Ναζωραῖος Nazōraios**; prob. from *3478; a Nazarene,* an inhab. of Nazareth:— Nazarene(9), Nazarenes(1), Nazareth(3).

3481. **Ναθάμ Natham**; of Heb. or. [5416]; *Nathan,* an Isr.:— Nathan(1).

3482. **Ναθαναήλ Nathanaēl**; of Heb. or. [5417]; *Nathanael* (prob. the same as Bartholomew, see *918):*— Nathanael(6).

3483a. **ναί nai**; a prim. particle of strong affirmation; *yes (indeed), certainly:*— indeed(1), so(1), yes(32).

3483b. **Ναιμάν Naiman**; of Heb. or. [5283]; *Naaman,* a Syrian:— Naaman(1).

3484. **Ναΐν Nain**; of Heb. or., cf. [4998]; *Nain,* a village of Galilee:— Nain(1).

3485. **ναός naos**; prob. akin to **ναίω naiō** *(to inhabit); a temple:*— shrines(1), temple(42), temple sanctuary(1), temples(1).

3486. **Ναούμ Naoum**; of Heb. or. [5151]; *Nahum,* an Isr.:— Nahum(1).

3487. **νάρδος nardos**; of for. or., cf. [5373]; *nard, ointment of nard:*— nard(2).

3488. **Νάρκισσος Narkissos**; from **νάρκη narkē** *(numbness); Narcissus,* a Rom.:— Narcissus(1).

3489. **ναυαγέω nauageō**; from *3491* and **ἄγνυμι agnumi** *(to break); to suffer shipwreck:*— shipwrecked(1), suffered shipwreck(1).

3490. **ναύκληρος nauklēros**; from *3491* and *2819; a shipowner, shipmaster:*— captain of the ship(1).

3491. **ναῦς naus**; a prim. word; *a ship:*— vessel(1).

3492. **ναύτης nautēs**; from *3491; a seaman:*— sailor(1), sailors(2).

3493. **Ναχώρ Nachōr**; of Heb. or. [5152]; *Nahor,* the grandfather of Abraham:— Nahor(1).

3494. **νεανίας neanias**; from *3501b; a young man:*— young man(3).

3495. **νεανίσκος neaniskos**; from *3494; a young man, a youth:*— young man(7), young men(4).

3496. **Νέα Πόλις Nea Polis**; see *3501b* and *4172; Neapolis,* a city of Macedonia:— Neapolis(1).

3497. **Νεεμάν Neeman**; var. reading for *3483b,* q.v.

3498. **νεκρός nekros**; a prim. word, the same as **νέκυς nekus** *(a dead body); dead:*— corpse(1), dead(122), dead man(3), dead men(1), dead men's(1).

3499. **νεκρόω nekroō**; from *3498; to put to death:*— consider(1), dead(3).

3500. **νέκρωσις nekrōsis**; from *3499; a putting to death, a state of death:*— deadness(1), dying(1).

3501a. **νεομηνία neomēnia**; from *3501b* and *3376; a new moon:*— new moon(1).

3501b. **νέος neos,**
νεώτερος neōteros (cptv.); a prim. word; *young, new:*— new(10), new self(1), young men(2), young women(1), younger(6), younger men(2), youngest(1).

3502. **νεοσσός neossos**; var. reading for *3556b,* q.v.

3503. **νεότης neotēs**; from *3501b; youth:*— youth(3), youthfulness(1).

3504. **νεόφυτος neophutos**; from *3501b* and *5453; newly planted:*— new convert(1).

3505. (not used)

3506. **νεύω neuō**; a prim. vb.; *to nod* or *beckon* (as a sign):— gestured(1), nodded(1).

3507. **νεφέλη nephelē**; from *3509; a cloud:*— cloud(18), clouds(7).

3508. **Νεφθαλίμ Nephthalim**; of Heb. or. [5321]; *Naphtali,* a tribe of Isr.:— Naphtali(3).

3509. **νέφος nephos**; a prim. word; *a mass of clouds, a cloud:*— cloud(1).

3510. **νεφρός nephros**; a prim. word; *a kidney,* fig. *the* (inmost) *mind:*— minds(1).

3511. **νεωκόρος neōkoros**; from a form of *3485* and **κορέω koreō** *(to sweep); a temple keeper:*— guardian of the temple(1).

3512. **νεωτερικός neōterikos**; from the cptv. of *3501b; youthful:*— youthful(1).

νεώτερος neōteros; see *3501b.*

3513. **νή nē**; prob. an intens. form of *3483a; by* (a particle of affirmation employed in oaths):— affirm(1).

3514. **νήθω nēthō**; from **νέω neō** *(to spin); to spin:*— spin(2).

3515. **νηπιάζω nēpiazō**; from *3516; to be an infant:*— infants(1).

3516. **νήπιος nēpios**; of unc. or.; *an infant,* fig. *a simple-minded* or *immature person:*— child(5), childish(1), children(2), immature(1), infant(1), infants(4).

3517. **Νηρεύς Nēreus**; of unc. or., name of a mythological sea god; *Nereus,* a Chr.:— Nereus(1).

3518. **Νηρί Nēri**; of Heb. or. [5374]; *Neri,* an Isr.:— Neri(1).

3519. **νησίον nēsion**; dim. of *3520; a small island:*— small island(1).

3520. **νῆσος nēsos**; of unc. or.; an island:— island(9).

3521. **νηστεία nēsteia**; from *3522; fasting, a fast:*— fast(1), fasting(2), fastings(1), hunger(1), without food(1).

3522. **νηστεύω nēsteuō**; from *3523; to fast:*— fast(14), fasted(2), fasting(4).

3523. **νῆστις nēstis**; from **νη- nē-** (implying negation) and the same as *2068; not eating:*— hungry(2).

3524. **νηφάλιος nēphalios**; from *3525; sober:*— temperate(3).

3525. **νήφω nēphō**; a prim. word; *to be sober, to abstain from wine:*— keep sober(1), sober(5).

3526. **Νίγερ Niger**; of Lat. or. *(dark in color); Niger,* a Chr.:— Niger(1).

3527. **Νικάνωρ Nikanōr**; prob. from *3528* and *435; Nicanor,* a Chr.:— Nicanor(1).

3528. **νικάω nikaō**; from *3529; to conquer, prevail:*— conquer(1), conquering(1), overcame(2), overcome(11), overcomes(10), overpowers(1), prevail(1), victorious(1).

3529. **νίκη nikē**; a prim. word; *victory:*— victory(1).

3530. **Νικόδημος Nikodēmos**; from *3534* and *1218; Nicodemus,* an Isr.:— Nicodemus(5).

3531. **Νικολαΐτης Nikolaitēs**; from *3532; a Nicolaitan,* a follower of Nicolaus, who prob. was not the same as *3532:*— Nicolaitans(2).

3532. **Νικόλαος Nikolaos**; from *3534* and *2992; Nicolaus,* a Chr., prob. not connected with the sect bearing the same name:— Nicolas(1).

3533. **Νικόπολις Nikopolis**; from *3534* and *4172;* "victorious city," *Nicopolis,* a city in Achaia:— Nicopolis(1).

3534. **νῖκος nikos**; a late form of *3529; victory:*— victory(4).

3535. **Νινευΐ Nineui**; of Heb. or. [5210]; var. reading for *3536*, q.v.

3536. **Νινευίτης Nineuitēs**; from *3535; a Ninevite,* an inhab. of Ninevah:— Nineveh(2), Ninevites(1).

3537. **νιπτήρ niptēr**; from *3538; a basin:*— basin(1).

3538. **νίπτω niptō**; a late form of **νίζω nizō** *(to cleanse); to wash:*— wash(11), washed(6).

3539. **νοέω noeō**; from *3563; to perceive, think:*— consider(1), perceive(1), see(1), think(1), understand(9), understood(1).

3540. **νόημα noēma**; from *3539; thought, purpose:*— minds(4), schemes(1), thought(1).

3541. **νόθος nothos**; a prim. word; *a bastard, baseborn:*— illegitimate children(1).

3542. **νομή nomē**; from the same as *3551; a pasture, a grazing:*— pasture(1), spread(1).

3543. **νομίζω nomizō**; from *3551; to practice, consider:*— suppose(1), supposed(4), supposing(3), think(4), thinks(1), thought(2).

3544. **νομικός nomikos**; from *3551; relating to law, learned in the law:*— Law(1), lawyer(3), lawyers(5).

3545. **νομίμως nomimōs**; from **νόμιμος nomimos** *(conformable to law); rightly, lawfully:*— lawfully(1), rules(1).

3546. **νόμισμα nomisma**; from *3543; a custom, current coin:*— coin(1).

3547. **νομοδιδάσκαλος nomodidaskalos**; from *3551* and *1320; a teacher of the law:*— teacher of the Law(1), teachers of the Law(2).

3548. **νομοθεσία nomothesia**; from *3550; legislation, lawgiving:*— giving of the law(1).

3549. **νομοθετέω nomotheteō**; from *3550; to make law, to ordain by law:*— enacted(1), received the Law(1).

3550. **νομοθέτης nomothetēs**; from *3551* and *5087; a lawgiver:*— Lawgiver(1).

3551. **νόμος nomos**; from **νέμω nemō** *(to parcel out); that which is assigned,* hence *usage, law:*— Law(193), laws(2), principle(1).

3552. **νοσέω noseō**; from *3554; to be sick:*— has a morbid interest(1), morbid interest(1).

3553. **νόσημα nosēma**; from *3552; sickness:*— disease(1).

3554. **νόσος nosos**; a prim. word; *disease, sickness:*— disease(3), diseases(8).

3555. **νοσσιά nossia**; from *3556b; a brood of young birds:*— brood(1).

3556a. **νοσσίον nossion**; dim. of *3556b; a young bird:*— chicks(1).

3556b. **νοσσός nossos**; shortened from of *3502; a young bird:*— young(1).

3557. **νοσφίζω nosphizō**; from **νόσφι nosphi** *(apart); to abandon, to set apart:*— keep back(1), kept back(1), pilfering(1).

3558. **νότος notos**; a prim. word; *the south wind,* hence *the southern quarter:*— south(4), south wind(3).

3559. **νουθεσία nouthesia**; from *3560; admonition:*— instruction(2), warning(1).

3560. **νουθετέω noutheteō**; from *3563* and *5087; to admonish, exhort:*— admonish(5), admonishing(2), give...instruction(1).

3561. **νουμηνία noumēnia**; var. reading for *3501a*, q.v.

3562. **νουνεχῶς nounechōs**; from *3563* and *2192; sensibly, discreetly:*— intelligently(1).

3563. **νοῦς nous**; contr. of a prim. word **νόος noos** *(mind); mind, understanding, reason:*— composure(1), comprehension(1), mind(20), minds(1), understanding(1).

3564. **Νύμφα Numpha**; from *3565; Nympha,* a Chr. of Laodicea:— Nympha(1).

3565. **νύμφη numphē**; a prim. word; *a bride, a young woman:*— bride(5), daughter-in-law(3).

3566. **νυμφίος numphios**; from *3565; a bridegroom:*— bridegroom(15), bridegroom's(1).

3567. **νυμφών numphōn**; from *3565; the bridechamber:*— bridegroom(3), wedding hall(1).

3568. **νῦν nun**; a prim. particle of pres. time; *now, the present:*— actually(1), just now(1), now(130), present(11), present case(1), since(1), this time(1).

3569. **τανῦν tanun** or
τὰ νῦν ta nun; see *3588* and *3568*.

3570. **νυνί nuni**; a strengthened form of *3568; now:*— now(18).

3571. **νύξ nux**; a prim. word; *night, by night:*— evening(1), midnight*(2), night(55), night night(1), nights(3).

3572. **νύσσω nussō**; a prim. word; *to pierce:*— pierced(1).

3573. **νυστάζω nustazō**; of unc. or.; *to nod in sleep, to fall asleep:*— asleep(1), got drowsy(1).

3574. **νυχθήμερον nuchthēmeron**; from *3571* and *2250; lasting a night and a day:*— a night and a day(1).

3575. **Νῶε Nōe**; of Heb. or. [5146]; *Noah,* a patriarch:— Noah(8).

3576. **νωθρός nōthros**; akin to **νωθής nōthēs** *(sluggish, slothful); sluggish, slothful:*— dull(1), sluggish(1).

3577. **νῶτος nōtos**; of unc. or.; *the back:*— backs(1).

Ξ

3578. **ξενία xenia**; from *3581; hospitality, a lodging place:*— lodging(2).

3579. **ξενίζω xenizō**; from *3581; to receive as a guest, to surprise:*— entertained(2), gave...lodging(1), lodge(1), staying(3), strange things(1), surprised(2).

3580. **ξενοδοχέω xenodocheō**; from *3581* and *1209; to entertain strangers:*— shown hospitality(1), shown hospitality to strangers(1).

3581. **ξένος xenos**; a prim. word; *foreign, a foreigner, guest:*— host(1), strange(2), strange thing(1), stranger(4), strangers(6).

3582. **ξέστης xestēs**; of Lat. or.; *a sextarius* (about a pint), *a pitcher* (of wood or stone):— pitchers(1).

3583. **ξηραίνω xērainō**; from *3584; to dry up, waste away:*— dried(2), dries(1), ripe(1), stiffens(1), wither(1), withered(4), withered away(3), withers(2).

3584. **ξηρός xēros**; a prim. word; *dry:*— dry(2), land(1), withered(5).

3585. **ξύλινος xulinos**; from *3586; wooden:*— wood(2).

3586. **ξύλον xulon**; a prim. word; *wood:*— clubs(5), cross(4), stocks(1), tree(7), wood(3).

3587a. **ξυράω xuraō**; a late form of *3587b; to shave:*— shaved(1).

3587b. **ξυρέω xureō**; from **ξυρόν xuron** *(a razor); to shave:*— shave(1), shaved(1).

Ο

3588. **ὁ ho,**
ἡ hē,
τό to; the def. art.; *the:*— about(2), all(5), case*(3), cause*(1), circumstances*(3), companions*(8), condition*(1), experiences(2), far(1), followers*(1), former*(1), meat(1), one(6), one who(1), one*(1), others(4), others*(1), outsiders*(3), people(1), sight(1), some(7), some*(5), suitable(1), these(4), things(1), this(31), those(406), those who(17), together*(8), under*(1), welfare(1), what(47), what had happened(1), what*(1), which(14), who(52), whoever(8), whom(4).
ὅ ho; see *3739*.

3589. **ὀγδοήκοντα ogdoēkonta**; card. num. from *3590* and a modified form of *1176; eighty:*— eighty(1), eighty-four*(1).

3590. **ὄγδοος ogdoos**; ord. num. from *3638; the eighth:*— eighth(4), seven others(1).

3591. **ὄγκος ogkos**; of unc. or.; *bulk, an encumbrance:*— encumbrance(1).

3592. **ὅδε hode,**
ἥδε hēde,
τόδε tode; from *3588* and *1161; this* (referring to what is present):— such(2), this(7), this is what(1).

3593. **ὁδεύω hodeuō**; from *3598; to travel:*— journey(1).

3594. **ὁδηγέω hodēgeō**; from *3595; to lead, guide, teach:*— guide(3), guides(2).

3595. **ὁδηγός hodēgos**; from *3598* and *2233; a leader, guide:*— guide(2), guides(3).

3596. **ὁδοιπορέω hodoiporeō**; from **ὁδοιπόρος hodoiporos** *(a traveler); to travel:*— way(1).

3597. **ὁδοιπορία hodoiporia**; from the same as *3596; a journey:*— journey(1), journeys(1).

3598. **ὁδός hodos**; a prim. word; *a way, road:*— highways(2), journey(7), path(1), paths(1), road(24), roads(1), streets(1), way(54), ways(9).

3599. **ὀδούς odous**; a prim. word; *a tooth:*— teeth(10), tooth(2).

3600. **ὀδυνάω odunaō**; from *3601; to cause* or *suffer pain:*— agony(1), am in agony(1), anxiously(1), grieving(1).

3601. **ὀδύνη odunē**; a prim. word; *pain, distress:*— grief(1), griefs(1).

3602. **ὀδυρμός odurmos**; from **ὀδύρομαι oduromai** *(to lament); lamentation:*— mourning(2).

3603. **ὅ ἐστι ho esti**; see *3739* and *1510*.

3604. **Ὀζίας Ozias**; of Heb. or. [5818]; *Uzziah,* an Isr.:— Uzziah(2).

3605. **ὄζω ozō**; a prim. vb.; *to* (emit a) *smell:*— stench(1).

3606. **ὅθεν hothen**; from *3739; from where, for which reason:*— so(3), there(1), therefore(4), this(1), where(2), which(4).

3607. **ὀθόνη othonē**; of unc. or.; *fine linen,* hence *a sheet* or *sail:*— sheet(2).

3608. **ὀθόνιον othonion**; dim. of *3607; a piece of fine linen:*— linen wrappings(5).

3609a. **οἶδα oida**; perf. of *1491a; to have seen* or *perceived,* hence *to know:*— appreciate(1), aware(3), become learned(1), conscious*(1), having a knowledge(1), knew(16), knew...about(1), know(216), know about(1), know how(9), knowing(36), known(4), known about(1), knows(15), knows how(1), realize(1), realizing(2), recognize(3), unaware*(1), understand(5), understanding(1).

3609b. **οἰκεῖος oikeios**; from *3624; in* or *of the house:*— household(3).

3610a. **οἰκετεία oiketeia**; from *3610b; a household* (of servants):— household(1).

3610b. **οἰκέτης oiketēs**; from *3611; a house servant:*— servant(2), servants(2).

3611. **οἰκέω oikeō**; from *3624; to inhabit, to dwell:*— dwells(7), live(2).

3612. **οἴκημα oikēma**; from *3611; a dwelling:*— cell(1).

3613. **οἰκητήριον oikētērion**; from **οἰκητήρ oikētēr** *(an inhabitant); a habitation:*— abode(1), dwelling(1).

3614. **οἰκία oikia**; from *3624; a house, dwelling:*— home(6), house(75), household(5), households(1), houses(7).

3615. **οἰκιακός oikiakos**; from *3614; belonging to the household:*— household(2).

3616. **οἰκοδεσποτέω oikodespoteō**; from *3617; to rule a household:*— keep house(1).

3617. **οἰκοδεσπότης oikodespotēs**; from *3624* and *1203; the master of a house:*— head of a household(1), head of the house(4), head of the household(1), landowner(4), owner(1), owner of the house(1).

3618. **οἰκοδομέω oikodomeō**; from *3620b; to build a house:*— build(13), builders(4), building(2), built(10), edified(1), edifies(3), edify(1), rebuild(4), strengthened(1).

3619. **οἰκοδομή oikodomē**; from *3624* and the same as *1430;* (the act of) *building, a building:*— building(8), buildings(3), edification(5), edifying(1), upbuilding(1).

3620a. **οἰκοδομία oikodomia**; var. reading for *3622,* q.v.

3620b. **οἰκοδόμος oikodomos**; from *3624* and the same as *1430; a builder:*— builders(1).

3621. **οἰκονομέω oikonomeō**; from *3623; to be a steward, to manage:*— manager(1).

3622. **οἰκονομία oikonomia**; from *3621; stewardship, administration:*— administration(3), management(3), stewardship(3).

3623. **οἰκονόμος oikonomos**; from *3624* and **νέμω nemō** *(to manage); the manager of a household:*— manager(3), managers(1), steward(2), stewards(3), treasurer(1).

3624. **οἶκος oikos**; a prim. word; *a house, a dwelling:*— descendants(1), families(1), family(1), home(18), homes(2), house(79), household(14), households(1), itself(1), palaces(1), place(1).

3625. **οἰκουμένη oikoumenē**; the fem. pres. pass. part. of *3611; the inhabited earth:*— inhabited earth(1), world(14).

3626. **οἰκουργός oikourgos**; from *3624* and *2041; working at home:*— workers at home(1).

3627. **οἰκτίρω oiktirō**; from **οἶκτος oiktos** *(pity); to pity, to have compassion on:*— have compassion(2).

3628. **οἰκτιρμός oiktirmos**; from *3627; compassion, pity:*— compassion(2), mercies(2), mercy(1).

3629. **οἰκτίρμων oiktirmōn**; from *3627; merciful:*— merciful(3).

οἶμαι oimai; see *3633.*

3630. **οἰνοπότης oinopotēs**; from *3631* and **πότης potēs** *(a drinker); a wine drinker:*— drunkard(2).

3631. **οἶνος oinos**; a prim. word; *wine:*— wine(33), wine*(1).

3632. **οἰνοφλυγία oinophlugia**; from *3631* and the same as *5397; drunkenness, debauchery:*— drunkenness(1).

3633. **οἴομαι oiomai** and **οἶμαι oimai**; a prim. vb.; *to suppose, expect:*— expect(1), suppose(1), thinking(1).

3634. **οἷος hoios**; related to *3588, 3739* and *3745; what sort* or *manner of:*— such(4), what(4), what kind(1), what kind of men(1), which(1).

οἴσω oisō; see *5342.*

3635. **ὀκνέω okneō**; from **ὄκνος oknos** *(shrinking, hesitation); to shrink* (from doing), *to hesitate* (to do):— delay(1).

3636. **ὀκνηρός oknēros**; from *3635; shrinking, timid,* hence *idle, lazy, troublesome:*— lagging behind(1), lazy(1), trouble(1).

3637. **ὀκταήμερος oktaēmeros**; from *3638* and *2250; of the eighth day, eight days old:*— eighth day(1).

3638. **ὀκτώ oktō**; a prim. card. num.; *eight:*—eight(6), eighteen*(1), thirty-eight*(1).

3639. **ὄλεθρος olethros**; from **ὄλλυμι ollumi** *(to destroy); destruction, death:*— destroyed(1), destruction(3), ruin(1).

3640a. **ὀλιγοπιστία oligopistia**; from *3641* and *4102; little faith:*— littleness of...faith(1).

3640b. **ὀλιγόπιστος oligopistos**; from the same as *3640a; of little faith:*— little faith(5), men of little faith(3).

3641. **ὀλίγος oligos**; a prim. word; *few, little, small:*— brief(1), briefly(1), few(11), few things(3), great*(1), little(7), little way(1), little while(4), long*(1), number*(2), short(3), short time(1), small(3), while(1).

3642. **ὀλιγόψυχος oligopsuchos**; from *3641* and *5590; fainthearted:*— fainthearted(1).

3643a. **ὀλιγωρέω oligōreō**; from *3641* and **ὥρα ōra** *(care); to esteem lightly:*— regard lightly(1).

3643b. **ὀλίγως oligōs**; adv. from *3641; a little, almost:*— barely(1).

3644. **ὀλοθρευτής olothreutēs**; from *3645; a destroyer:*— destroyer(1).

3645. **ὀλοθρεύω olothreuō**; from **ὀλεθρεύω olethreuō**; prob. from *3639; to destroy, ruin.*

3646. **ὁλοκαύτωμα holokautōma**; from *3650* and *2545; a whole burnt offering:*— burnt offerings(1), whole burnt offerings(2).

3647. **ὁλοκληρία holoklēria**; from *3648; completeness, soundness:*— perfect health(1).

3648. **ὁλόκληρος holoklēros**; from *3650* and *2819; complete, entire:*— complete(2).

3649. **ὀλολύζω ololuzō**; from a prim. word, onomatop.; *to cry aloud:*— howl(1).

3650. **ὅλος holos**; a prim. word; *whole, complete:*— all(49), all all(1), completely(1), entire(5), entirely(1), full(1), one piece(1), throughout(1), whole(49), wholly(1).

3651. **ὁλοτελής holotelēs**; from *3650* and *5056; complete, perfect:*— entirely(1).

3652. **Ὀλυμπᾶς Olumpas**; shortened form from a comp. with **Ὄλυμπος Olumpos**; *Olympas,* a Chr.:— Olympas(1).

3653. **ὄλυνθος olunthos**; of unc. or.; *an unripe fig:*— unripe figs(1).

3654. **ὅλως holōs**; adv. from *3650; altogether, assuredly:*— actually(2), all(2).

3655a. **ὄμβρος ombros**; a prim. word; *a rainstorm:*— shower(1).

3655b. **ὁμείρομαι homeiromai**; of unc. or.; *to desire earnestly:*— having...fond an affection(2).

3656. **ὁμιλέω homileō**; from **ὅμιλος homilos** *(a crowd, throng); to consort with,* hence *to converse with:*— converse(1), talked(1), talking(2).

3657. **ὁμιλία homilia**; from the same as *3656; company, association:*— company(1).

3658. **ὁμίχλη homichlē**; a prim. word; *a mist* or *fog:*— mists(1).

3659. **ὄμμα omma**; prob. akin to **ὄψ ops** *(the eye); an eye:*— eyes(2).

3660. **ὀμνύω omnuō**; and **ὄμνυμι omnumi**; a prim. vb.; *to swear, take an oath:*— make an oath(1), make...oath(1), swear(6), swears(10), swore(6), sworn(2).

3661. **ὁμοθυμαδόν homothumadon**; from the same as *3674* and *2372; with one mind:*— one accord(7), one impulse(1), one mind(3).

3662. **ὁμοιάζω homoiazō**; var. reading for *3945,* q.v.

3663. **ὁμοιοπαθής homoiopathēs**; from *3664* and *3958; of like feelings* or *affections:*— nature like(1), same nature(1).

3664. **ὅμοιος homoios**; from the same as *3674; like, resembling, the same as:*— like(43), one like(2), same(1).

3665. **ὁμοιότης homoiotēs**; from *3664; likeness, in like manner:*— likeness(1).

3666. **ὁμοιόω homoioō**; from *3664; to make like:*— become like(1), comparable(1), compare(4), compared(4), like(2), made like(1), picture(1), resembled(1).

3667. **ὁμοίωμα homoiōma**; from *3666; that which is made like* (something):— appearance(1), form(1), likeness(4).

3668. **ὁμοίως homoiōs**; adv. from *3664; likewise, in like manner:*— like manner(1), likewise(12), same(3), same thing(1), same way(11), similar way(1), so(2), way(1).

3669. **ὁμοίωσις homoiōsis**; from *3666; a making like, likeness:*— likeness(1).

3670. **ὁμολογέω homologeō**; from **ὁμόλογος homologos** *(of one mind); to speak the same, to agree:*— acknowledge(2), admit(1), assured(1), confess(6), confessed(4), confesses(6), confessing(1), declare(1), give thanks(1), made(1), profess(1), promised(1).

3671. **ὁμολογία homologia**; from *3670; an agreement, confession:*— confession(6).

3672. **ὁμολογουμένως homologoumenōs**; adv. from *3670; as agreed, by common consent:*— common confession(1).

3673. **ὁμότεχνος homotechnos**; from the same as *3674* and *5078; of the same trade:*— same trade(1).

3674. **ὁμοῦ homou**; adv. from gen. of **ὁμός homos** *(the same); together:*— together(4).

3675. **ὁμόφρων homophrōn**; from the same as *3674* and *5424; agreeing:*— harmonious(1).

3676. **ὅμως homōs**; adv. from the same as *3674; yet, but yet:*— even though(1), nevertheless*(1), yet(2).

3677. **ὄναρ onar**; a prim. word; *a dream, in a dream:*— dream(6).

3678. **ὀνάριον onarion**; dim. of *3688; a little donkey:*— young donkey(1).

3679. ὀνειδίζω oneidizō; from *3681; to reproach:*— denounce(1), insult(2), insulting(2), reproach(1), reproached(2), reviled(1).

3680. ὀνειδισμός oneidismos; from *3679; a reproach:*— reproach(3), reproaches(2).

3681. ὄνειδος oneidos; a prim. word; *reproach, disgrace:*— disgrace(1).

3682. Ὀνήσιμος Onēsimos; from **ὄνησις onēsis** *(use, profit, advantage);* "useful," *Onesimus,* a Chr.:— Onesimus(2).

3683. Ὀνησίφορος Onēsiphoros; from the same as *3682* and *5342;* "bringing advantage," *Onesiphorus,* a Chr.:— Onesiphorus(2).

3684. ὀνικός onikos; from *3688; of* or *for a donkey:*— heavy(2).

3685. ὀνίνημι oninēmi; a prim. vb.; *to profit, help:*— benefit(1).

3686. ὄνομα onoma; a prim. word; *a name, authority, cause:*— called(1), name(175), name's(7), named(34), names(8), people(1), people*(1), persons(1).

3687. ὀνομάζω onomazō; from *3686; to name, to give a name:*— derives its name(1), name(1), named(5), names(1), so-called(1).

3688. ὄνος onos; a prim. word; *a donkey:*— donkey(4), donkey's(1).

3689. ὄντως ontōs; from the part. of *1510; really, truly:*— certainly(2), indeed(6), real(1), really(1).

3690. ὄξος oxos; from *3691; sour wine:*— sour wine(6).

3691. ὀξύς oxus; a prim. word; *sharp, swift:*— sharp(7), swift(1).

3692. ὀπή opē; prob. from a prim. root **ὀπ- op-** (cf. *3708); an opening, a hole:*— holes(1), opening(1).

3693. ὄπισθεν opisthen; prob. from **ὄπις opis** *(back); behind, after:*— back(1), behind(5).

3694. ὀπίσω opisō; from the same as *3693; back, behind, after:*— after(18), around(1), back(2), back*(3), behind(5), follow(2), follow*(2), withdrew*(1).

3695. ὁπλίζω hoplizō; from *3696; to make ready, to equip:*— arm(1).

3696. ὅπλον hoplon; a prim. word; *a tool, implement, weapon:*— armor(1), instruments(2), weapons(3).

3697. ὁποῖος hopoios; from *3739* and *4169; of what sort:*— quality(1), what(1), what kind(2), what kind of person(1).

3698. ὁπότε hopote; var. reading for *3739* and *4218,* q.v.:— when(1).

3699. ὅπου hopou; from *3739* and *4225; where:*— above(1), place(1), since(1), there(2), whenever(1), where(61), whereas(1), wherever(3), wherever*(8), which(5).

3700. ὀπτάνομαι optanomai; from a prim. root **ὀπ- op-** (cf. *3708); to appear:*— appearing(1).

3701. ὀπτασία optasia; from **ὀπτάζομαι optazomai** *(to be seen); an appearing:*— vision(3), visions(1).

3702. ὀπτός optos; a prim. word; *roasted:*— broiled(1).

3703. ὀπώρα opōra; perh. from the same as *3693* and *5610; late summer, ripe fruits:*— fruit(1).

3704. ὅπως hopōs; from *3739* and *4459; as, how, that:*— end(1), how(4), order(2), so(26), what(1).

3705. ὅραμα horama; from *3708; that which is seen:*— sight(1), vision(11).

3706. ὅρασις horasis; from *3708; the act of seeing, a vision, appearance:*— appearance(2), vision(1), visions(1).

3707. ὁρατός horatos; from *3708; visible:*—visible(1).

3708. ὁράω horaō; a prim. vb.; *to see, perceive, attend to:*— appear(2), appeared(21), appearing(1), behold(3), beware(1), certainly seen(1), do(2), look(5), look after(1), looked(12), perceive(3), recognizing(1), saw(180), see(129), seeing(20), seen(63), seen...see(1), sees(2), suffer(1), undergo(3), underwent(1), watch(2), witnessed(1).

3709. ὀργή orgē; a prim. word; *impulse, wrath:*— anger(6), wrath(30).

3710. ὀργίζω orgizō; from *3709; to make angry:*— angry(4), enraged(3), moved with anger(1).

3711. ὀργίλος orgilos; from *3709; inclined to anger, passionate:*— quick-tempered(1).

3712. ὀργυιά orguia; from *3713; a fathom* (the length of the outstretched arms):— fathoms(2).

3713. ὀρέγω oregō; a prim. vb.; *to stretch out, to reach after, to yearn for:*— aspires(1), desire(1), longing(1).

3714. ὀρεινός oreinos; from *3735; mountainous, the hill country:*— hill country(2).

3715. ὄρεξις orexis; from the mid. of *3713; desire, longing:*— desire(1).

3716. ὀρθοποδέω orthopodeō; from *3717* and *4228; to walk straight:*— straightforward(1).

3717. ὀρθός orthos; a prim. word; *straight, upright:*— straight(1), upright(1).

3718. ὀρθοτομέω orthotomeō; from *3717* and **τέμνω temnō** *(to cut); to cut straight:*— accurately handling(1).

3719. ὀρθρίζω orthrizō; from *3722; to rise early:*— get early in the morning(1).

3720. ὀρθρινός orthrinos; from *3722; early:*— early in the morning(1).

3721. ὄρθριος orthrios; var. reading for *3720,* q.v.

3722. ὄρθρος orthros; a prim. word; *daybreak, dawn:*— daybreak(1), early in the morning(1), early dawn(1).

3723. ὀρθῶς orthōs; from *3717; rightly:*— correctly(3), plainly(1).

3724. ὁρίζω horizō; from the same as *3725; to mark off by boundaries, to determine:*— appointed(2), declared(1), determined(3), fixes(1), predetermined(1).

3725. ὅριον horion; from **ὅρος horos** *(a boundary); a boundary:*— district(1), region(10), vicinity(1).

3726. ὁρκίζω horkizō; from *3727; to make* (one) *swear, to adjure:*— adjure(1), implore(1).

3727. ὅρκος horkos; akin to **ἕρκος erkos** *(fence, enclosure); an oath:*— oath(7), oaths(2), vows(1).

3728. ὁρκωμοσία horkōmosia; from **ὁρκόω horkoō** *(to make* (one) *swear); affirmation on oath:*— oath(4).

3729. ὁρμάω hormaō; from *3730; to set in motion, to hasten on:*— rushed(5).

3730. ὁρμή hormē; a prim. word; *a rapid motion forwards, onrush, assault:*— attempt(1), inclination(1).

3731. ὅρμημα hormēma; from *3729; a rush:*— violence(1).

3732. ὄρνεον orneon; from *3733; a bird:*— bird(1), birds(2).

3733. ὄρνις ornis; a prim. word; *a bird,* spec. *a rooster* or *hen:*— hen(2).

3734. ὁροθεσία horothesia; from the same as *3725* and *5087; a setting of boundaries:*— boundaries(1).

3735. ὄρος oros; a prim. word; *a mountain:*— hill(2), mount(3), Mount(15), mountain(31), mountains(12).

3736. ὀρύσσω orussō; a prim. vb.; *to dig:*— dug(3).

3737. ὀρφανός orphanos; a prim. word; *an orphan:*— orphans(2).

3738. ὀρχέομαι orcheomai; of unc. or.; *to dance:*— dance(2), danced(2).

3739. ὅς hos,
ἥ hē,
ὅ ho; a prim. pron.; usually rel. *who, which, that,* also demonstrative *this, that:*— another*(8), any(1), because*(7), deeds*(1), just(1), just*(1), once*(1), one(11), one*(6), other(2), others*(2), same(2), since*(3), so(1), some(7), some*(8), someone(1), such(1), there(1), these(6), these things(3), thing(1), things(4), third(1), this(22), this is what(1), those whom(1), until*(1), what(101), what*(2), whatever(5), whatever*(28), when(9), when*(3), where(1), where*(2), which(404), while*(3), who(158), whoever(4), whoever*(51), whom(218), whomever*(6), whose(38), why*(3).

3740. ὁσάκις hosakis; adv. from *3745; as often as:*— often(3).

3741. ὅσιος hosios; a prim. word; *righteous, pious, holy:*— devout(1), holy(4), Holy One(3).

3742. ὁσιότης hosiotēs; from *3741; piety, holiness:*— holiness(2).

3743. ὁσίως hosiōs; adv. from *3741; piously, holily:*— devoutly(1).

3744. ὀσμή osmē; from *3605; a smell:*— aroma(4), fragrance(1), sweet aroma(1).

3745. ὅσος hosos; from *3739; how much, how many:*— all(9), all...who(5), all things(1), all who(6), all*(1), degree(1), extent*(2), great(1), how much(2), inasmuch*(3), long(2), many(11), more(1), much(3), so(1), so much(1), those who(3), those whom(1), very...while(1), what(2), what great things(4), whatever(14), whatever*(4), which(3), while(1), who(6).

3746. ὅσπερ hosper; see *3739* and *4007a.*

3747. ὀστέον osteon; a prim. word; *a bone:*— bone(1), bones(3).

3748. ὅστις hostis,
ἥτις hētis,
ὅ τι ho ti; from *3739* and *5100; whoever, anyone who:*— after(1), because(1), everyone who(1), one who(1), ones who(1), these(2), these...matters which(1), this(3), what(1), whatever things(1), which(29), who(61), whoever(9), whoever*(3), yet(1).

3749. ὀστράκινος ostrakinos; from **ὄστρακον ostrakon** *(an earthen vessel); earthen:*— earthen(1), earthenware(1).

3750. ὄσφρησις osphrēsis; from **ὀσφραίνομαι osphrainomai** *(to smell); the sense of smell, smelling:*— sense of smell(1).

3751. ὀσφύς osphus; a prim. word; *the loin:*— descendants*(1), descended*(1), loins(2), waist(2).

3752. **ὅταν hotan**; from *3753* and *302; whenever:*— after(2), soon*(1), until*(1), when(107), whenever(9), while(2).

3753. **ὅτε hote**; from *3739* and *5037; when:*— after(5), soon(1), when(90), while(4).

3754. **ὅτι hoti**; conjunc. from neut. of *3748; that, because:*— because(212), fact(3), how(2), saying(1), since(10), so(1), then(1), though(1), what(1).

3755. **ὅτου hotou**; gen. of *3748*, q.v.

3756. **οὐ ou,**
οὐκ ouk,
οὐχ ouch; a prim. word; *not, no:*— all*(1), any the less(2), before*(1), cannot(1), cannot*(49), certainly*(1), ever*(3), except(1), failed(1), few*(1), great*(1), greatly*(1), impossible*(1), incessantly*(1), kept...a virgin*(1), kept right*(1), long*(1), neither(2), neither*(3), never(6), never*(17), no(147), no*(22), none(4), none*(3), nor(3), nothing(8), nothing*(13), nowhere*(2), number(1), number*(2), only*(5), rather(2), rather than(1), refrain(1), refused*(1), than*(2), unable*(6), unaware*(3), unwilling*(12), unworthy*(1), virgin*(1), without(2), without*(6).

3757. **οὗ hou**; gen. of *3739; where* (adv. of place):— there(1), where(21), wherever*(1), which(1).

3758. **οὐά oua**; a prim. interj.; *ah! ha!* (an expression of wonder or surprise):— Ha(1).

3759. **οὐαί ouai**; a prim. interj.; *alas! woe!* (an expression of grief or denunciation):— woe(46), woes(1).

3760. **οὐδαμῶς oudamōs**; from **οὐδαμός oudamos** *(not even one,* cf. *3365); by no means:*— no means(1).

3761. **οὐδέ oude**; from *3756* and *1161; and not, neither:*— all(2), cannot*(3), either(4), even(37), neither(4), no(4), no*(1), nor(64), nothing*(1), or(20), then(1).

3762. **οὐδείς oudeis** and **οὐθείς outheis,**
οὐδεμία oudemia,
οὐδέν ouden and **οὐθέν outhen**; from *3761* and *1520; no one, none:*— all(1), any(7), anyone(9), anything(7), cannot*(1), never*(1), no(26), no...anything(1), no such thing(1), no man(3), no one(87), no one's(1), no respect(1), no*(6), nobody(1), none(12), none*(1), nothing(45), nothing at all(1), nothing nothing(1), nothing*(7), one(10), one*(3), useless*(1), worthless(1).

3763. **οὐδέποτε oudepote**; from *3761* and *4218; never:*— ever(1), never(14), nothing(1), nothing...ever(1).

3764. **οὐδέπω oudepō**; from *3761* and *4452; not yet:*— yet(4).

3765. **οὐκέτι ouketi**; from *3756* and *2089; no longer, no more:*— again(4), another(1), any longer(1), any more(2), anymore(3), further(1), more(1), never...again(1), no longer(33), no*(1), then(1).

3766. **οὐκοῦν oukoun**; from *3756* and *3767; therefore, so then:*— so(1).

3767. **οὖν oun**; a prim. word; *therefore, then, (and) so:*— contrary*(1), however*(1), now(5), so(153), so then(9), so...then(1), then(141), therefore(178).

3768. **οὔπω oupō**; from *3756* and *4452; not yet:*— ever(1), still...no(1), yet(24), yet...ever(1).

3769. **οὐρά oura**; appar. a prim. word; *a tail:*— tail(1), tails(4).

3770. **οὐράνιος ouranios**; from *3772; of* or *in heaven:*— heaven(1), heavenly(8).

3771. **οὐρανόθεν ouranothen**; from *3772; from heaven:*— heaven(2).

3772. **οὐρανός ouranos**; a prim. word; *heaven:*— air(9), heaven(218), heavenly*(1), heavens(24), sky(22).

3773. **Οὐρβανός Ourbanos**; of Lat. or. *(of the city, polished,* etc.); *Urbanus,* a Chr.:— Urbanus(1).

3774. **Οὐρίας Ourias**; of Heb. or. [223a]; *Uriah,* a Hittite:— Uriah(1).

3775. **οὖς ous**; a prim. word; *the ear:*— ear(12), ears(23), hearing(1), whispered*(1).

3776. **οὐσία ousia**; from **οὖσα ousa** (fem. part. of *1510); substance, property:*— estate(2).

3777. **οὔτε oute**; from *3756* and *5037; and not, neither:*— either(4), neither(11), neither...nor(4), neither...nor(11), neither...nor...nor(1), never*(1), no...either(1), nor(32), nothing(1), or(9), useless*(1).

3778. **οὗτος houtos,**
αὕτη hautē,
τοῦτο touto; prob. from a redupl. of *3588, used as a demonstrative pron.; this:*— afterward*(3), especially(1), fact(2), follow*(1), here*(1), hereafter*(1), man(1), now*(1), one(2), one whom(1), partly*(1), person(1), present(1), same(1), so(1), so then*(1), so*(1), some(2), such(2), therefore*(16), these(179), these...things(1), these men(10), these people(1), these things(192), this(737), this man(56), this man's(2), this one(4), this reason*(1), this thing(2), this way(1), this woman(4), this*(1), this...thing(1), those(2), those things(1), very(3), very thing(2), who(2), whom(1).

3779. **οὕτω houtō** and **οὕτως houtōs**; adv. from *3778; in this way, thus:*— even so(1), exactly(2), exactly*(1), follows(2), in such a manner(1), in such a way(4), just(2), like this(5), like*(1), same(2), same manner(1), same way(5), so(125), such(2), then(1), thereby(1), this(1), this is the way(2), this is how(1), this effect(1), this manner(4), this respect(1), this way(22), thus(7), way(7), way this(1).

3780. **οὐχί ouchi**; intens. of *3756; not, not at all:*— fail(1), no(6), no indeed(1).

3781. **ὀφειλέτης opheiletēs**; from *3784; a debtor:*— culprits(1), debtors(1), indebted(1), owed(1), under obligation(3).

3782. **ὀφειλή opheilē**; from *3784; a debt:*— debt(1), duty(1), what is due(1).

3783. **ὀφείλημα opheilēma**; from *3784; that which is owed, a debt:*— debts(1), what is due(1).

3784. **ὀφείλω opheilō**; a prim. word; *to owe:*— had(1), have(1), indebted(2), must(1), obligated(3), ought(15), owe(4), owed(4), owes(1), responsible(1), should(2).

3785. **ὄφελον ophelon**; from *3784; would that* (used to express an unattainable wish):— wish(4).

3786. **ὄφελος ophelos**; from **ὀφέλλω ophellō** *(to increase); advantage, help:*— profit(1), use(2).

3787. **ὀφθαλμοδουλία ophthalmodoulia**; from *3788* and *1397; eye service:*— external service(1), eyeservice(1).

3788. **ὀφθαλμός ophthalmos**; from a prim. root **οπ- op-** and an unc. root; *the eye:*— envy*(1), eye(29), eyes(68), gaze(1), sight(1).

3789. **ὄφις ophis**; a prim. word; *a snake:*— serpent(6), serpents(6), snake(2).

3790. **ὀφρύς ophrus**; a prim. word; *an eyebrow:*— brow(1).

3791. **ὀχλέω ochleō**; from *3793; to disturb, trouble:*— afflicted(1).

3792. **ὀχλοποιέω ochlopoieō**; from *3793* and *4160; to gather a crowd:*— formed a mob(1).

3793. **ὄχλος ochlos**; a prim. word; *a crowd, multitude, the common people:*— crowd(87), crowds(47), gathering(1), many(1), mob(1), multitude(3), multitudes(1), number of people(1), numbers(2), people(27), riot*(1).

3794. **ὀχύρωμα ochurōma**; from **ὀχυρόω ochuroō** *(to fortify); a stronghold, fortress:*— fortresses(1).

3795. **ὀψάριον opsarion**; dim. of **ὄψον opson** *(cooked food); fish:*— fish(5).

3796. **ὀψέ opse**; from the same as *3693; long after, late:*— after(1), evening(2), late(1).

3797. **ὄψιμος opsimos**; from *3796; the latter rain:*— late(1).

3798. **ὄψιος opsios**; from *3796; evening:*— evening(14).

3799. **ὄψις opsis**; from **ὄπωπα opōpa** (perf. of *3708); the act of seeing, the sense of sight:*— appearance(1), face(2).

3800. **ὀψώνιον opsōnion**; from the same as *3795* and *5608; provisions, wages:*— expense(1), wages(3).

3801. **ὁ ὢν καὶ ὁ ἦν καὶ ὁ ἐρχόμενος ho ōn kai ho ēn kai ho erchomenos**; see *3588, 1510, 2532* and *2064.*

Π

3802. **παγιδεύω pagideuō**; from *3803; to set a trap:*— trap(1).

3803. **παγίς pagis**; from *4078; a trap, snare:*— snare(4), trap(1).

Πάγος Pagos; see *697.*

3804. **πάθημα pathēma**; from *3958; that which befalls one,* i.e. *a suffering, a passion:*— passions(2), suffering(2), sufferings(12).

3805. **παθητός pathētos**; from *3958; one who has suffered* or *is subject to suffering:*— suffer(1).

3806. **πάθος pathos**; from *3958; that which befalls one, a passion, a suffering:*— passion(2), passions(1).

3807. **παιδαγωγός paidagōgos**; from *3816* and *71; a trainer of boys,* i.e. *a tutor:*— tutor(2), tutors(1).

3808. **παιδάριον paidarion**; dim. of *3816; a little boy:*— lad(1).

3809. **παιδεία paideia**; from *3811; the rearing of a child, training, discipline:*— discipline(5), training(1).

3810. **παιδευτής paideutēs**; from *3811; a teacher, one who disciplines:*— corrector(1), discipline(1).

3811. **παιδεύω paideuō**; from *3816; to train children, to chasten, correct:*— correcting(1), discipline(2), disciplined(2), disciplines(1), educated(2), instructing(1), punish(2), punished(1), taught(1).

3812. **παιδιόθεν paidiothen**; from *3813; from childhood:*— childhood(1).

3813. **παιδίον paidion**; dim. of *3816; a young child:*— boy's(1), Child(10), child(21), child's(2), children(17), children's(1).

3814. **παιδίσκη paidiskē**; dim. of *3816; a young girl, maidservant:*— bondwoman(5), servant-girl(4), servant-girls(1), slave-girl(2), slaves*(1), women(1).

3815. **παίζω paizō**; from *3816; to play as a child:*— play(1).

3816. **παῖς pais**; a prim. word; *a child, boy, youth:*— boy(4), child(1), children(1), girl's(1), male children(1), men(1), servant(12), servants(2), slaves*(1), son(1).

3817. **παίω paiō**; a prim. vb.; *to strike,* spec. *to sting:*— hit(2), stings(1), struck(2).

3818. (not used)

3819. **πάλαι palai**; a prim. word; *long ago, of old:*— all this time(1), former(1), long(1), long ago(3).

3820. **παλαιός palaios**; from *3819; old, ancient:*— old(19).

3821. **παλαιότης palaiotēs**; from *3820; oldness:*— oldness(1).

3822. **παλαιόω palaioō**; from *3820; to make* or *declare old:*— become old(1), becoming obsolete(1), made...obsolete(1), wear(1).

3823. **πάλη palē**; from **πάλλω pallō** *(to sway); wrestling,* generally *fight:*— struggle(1).

3824. **παλιγγενεσία paliggenesia**; from *3825* and *1078; regeneration, renewal:*— regeneration(2).

3825. **πάλιν palin**; a prim. word; *back* (of place), *again* (of time), *further:*— again(127), again*(1), another(1), back(4), once more(4), other hand(3).

3826. **παμπληθεί pamplēthei**; from *3956* and *4128; with the whole multitude:*— all together(1).

3827. **πάμπολυς pampolus**; var. reading from *3956* and *4183,* q.v.

3828. **Παμφυλία Pamphulia**; from a comp. of *3956* and *5443; Pamphylia,* a province of Asia Minor:— Pamphylia(5).

3829. **πανδοχεῖον pandocheion**; from *3830; an inn:*— inn(1).

3830. **πανδοχεύς pandocheus**; from *3956* and *1209; an innkeeper, a host:*— innkeeper(1).

3831. **πανήγυρις panēguris**; from *3956* and a der. of *58; a festal assembly:*— general assembly(1).

3832. **πανοικεί panoikei**; from *3956* and *3624; with all the household:*— whole household(1).

3833. **πανοπλία panoplia**; from *3956* and *3696; full armor:*— all...armor(1), full armor(2).

3834. **πανουργία panourgia**; from *3835; cleverness, craftiness:*— craftiness(4), trickery(1).

3835. **πανοῦργος panourgos**; from *3956* and *2041; ready to do anything, crafty, skillful:*— crafty(1).

3836a. **πανταχῇ pantachē**; from the same as *3837; everywhere:*— everywhere(1).

3836b. **πανταχόθεν pantachothen**; from *3837; from all sides.*

3837. **πανταχοῦ pantachou**; from a presumed der. of *3956; everywhere:*— everywhere(7).

3838. **παντελής pantelēs**; from *3956* and *5056; all complete, entire:*— all(1), forever*(1).

3839. **πάντῃ pantē**; adv. from *3956; every way, entirely:*— every way(1).

3840. **πάντοθεν pantothen**; adv. from *3956; from all sides:*— all sides(1), every side(1), everywhere(1).

3841. **παντοκράτωρ pantokratōr**; from *3956* and *2902; almighty:*— Almighty(10).

3842. **πάντοτε pantote**; from *3956* and *5119; at all times:*— all times(1), always(40).

3843. **πάντως pantōs**; adv. from *3956; altogether, by all means:*— all(3), all means(1), altogether(1), certainly(1), no doubt(1), undoubtedly(1).

3844. **παρά para**; a prim. prep.; *from beside, by the side of, by, beside:*— above(2), along(1), among(4), anyone's*(1), aside*(1), before(4), beside(6), beyond(2), contrary(5), give(1), had(1), rather than(2), reason(2), riverside*(1), sent(1), side(1), sight(2), than(12), thirty-nine*(1), together(1), under*(1), unnatural*(1).

3845. **παραβαίνω parabainō**; from *3844* and the same as *939; to go by the side of, to go past:*— break(1), transgress(1), turned aside(1).

3846. **παραβάλλω paraballō**; from *3844* and *906; to throw beside:*— crossed over(1).

3847. **παράβασις parabasis**; from *3845; a going aside, a transgression:*— breaking(1), offense(1), transgression(2), transgressions(2), violation(1).

3848. **παραβάτης parabatēs**; from *3845; one who stands beside:*— transgressor(4), transgressors(1).

3849. **παραβιάζομαι parabiazomai**; from *3844* and *971; to force against* (nature):— prevailed(1), urged(1).

3850a. **παραβολεύομαι paraboleuomai**; from *3846; to expose oneself to danger:*— risking(1).

3850b. **παραβολή parabolē**; from *3846; a placing beside, a comparison:*— parable(31), parables(16), proverb(1), symbol(1), type(1).

3851. **παραβουλεύομαι parabouleuomai**; var. reading for *3850a,* q.v.

3852. **παραγγελία paraggelia**; from *3853; an instruction, a command:*— command(2), commandments(1), instruction(1), strict orders(1).

3853. **παραγγέλλω paraggellō**; from *3844* and *31b; to transmit a message, to order:*— charge(1), command(4), commanded(4), commanding(1), direct(1), directed(2), gave(1), give...order(1), give instructions(1), giving...instruction(1), instruct(2), instructed(3), instructing(3), ordered(3), Prescribe(2).

3854. **παραγίνομαι paraginomai**; from *3844* and *1096; to be beside, to arrive:*— appeared(2), arrive(2), arrived(10), came(13), come(4), come here(1), coming(1), present(1), supported(1), when...arrived(1).

3855. **παράγω paragō**; from *3844* and *71; to lead by, to pass by* or *away:*— going along(1), passed(2), passer-by(1), passing(1), passing away(3), went(2).

3856. **παραδειγματίζω paradeigmatizō**; from *3844* and *1165; to set forth as an example:*— put...to open shame(1).

3857. **παράδεισος paradeisos**; of Pers. or. *(enclosure); a park, a garden, a paradise:*— Paradise(3).

3858. **παραδέχομαι paradechomai**; from *3844* and *1209; to receive, admit:*— accept(3), receive(1), received(1), receives(1).

3859. **παραδιατριβή paradiatribē**; var. reading for *1275,* q.v.

3860. **παραδίδωμι paradidōmi**; from *3844* and *1325; to hand over, to give* or *deliver over, to betray:*— betray(17), betrayed(10), betraying(9), betrays(3), commended(1), committed(3), deliver(6), delivered(21), delivered over(1), delivering(3), entrusted(3), entrusting(1), gave(4), gave...over(3), given...over(1), hand(6), handed(9), handed...over(1), handed down(4), handed over(4), hands(1), permits(1), put(1), putting(1), risked(1), surrender(1), taken into custody(2), turn...over(1).

3861. **παράδοξος paradoxos**; from *3844* and *1391; contrary to opinion* or *expectation:*— remarkable things(1).

3862. **παράδοσις paradosis**; from *3860; a handing down* or *over, a tradition:*— tradition(1), tradition(8), traditions(4).

3863. **παραζηλόω parazēloō**; from *3844* and *2206; to provoke to jealousy:*— make...jealous(2), move to jealousy(1), provoke...to jealousy(1).

3864. **παραθαλάσσιος parathalassios**; from *3844* and *2281; by the sea:*— sea(1).

3865. **παραθεωρέω paratheōreō**; from *3844* and *2334; to compare, to overlook:*— overlooked(1).

3866. **παραθήκη parathēkē**; from *3908; a deposit* or *trust:*— entrusted(1), treasure*(1), what has been entrusted(1), what...have entrusted(1).

3867. **παραινέω paraineō**; from *3844* and *134; to exhort, advise:*— admonish(1), urge(1).

3868. **παραιτέομαι paraiteomai**; from *3844* and *154; to beg from, to beg off:*— begged(1), excused(2), have nothing to do with(1), make excuses(1), refuse(4), refused(1), reject(1), requested(1).

3869a. **παρακαθέζομαι parakathezomai**; from *3844* and *2516; to sit down beside:*— seated(1).

3869b. **παρακαθίζω parakathizō**; from *3844* and *2523; to set beside.*

3870. **παρακαλέω parakaleō**; from *3844* and *2564; to call to* or *for, to exhort, to encourage:*— appeal(4), appealed(1), appealing(2), beg(1), begging(2), beseeching(1), comfort(5), comforted(11), comforts(2), conciliate(1), encourage(6), encouraged(4), encouraging(3), entreat(1), exhort(8), exhortation*(1), exhortations(1), exhorted(2), exhorting(3), exhorts(1), given(1), implore(4), implored(9), imploring(5), invited(2), making an appeal(1), plead(1), pleaded(1), pleading(1), preach(1), requested(1), urge(17), urged(5), urging(1).

3871. **παρακαλύπτω parakaluptō**; from *3844* and *2572; to cover* (by hanging something beside), *to hide:*— concealed(1).

3872. **παρακαταθήκη parakatathēkē**; from a comp. of *3844* and *2698; a trust* or *deposit.*

3873. **παράκειμαι parakeimai**; from *3844* and *2749; to lie beside, be present:*— present(2).

3874. **παράκλησις paraklēsis**; from *3870; a calling to one's aid,* i.e. *encouragement, comfort:*— appeal(1), comfort(13), consolation(1), encouragement(6), exhortation(7), urging(1).

3875. **παράκλητος paraklētos**; from *3870; called to one's aid:*— Advocate(1), Helper(4).

3876. **παρακοή parakoē**; from *3878; a hearing amiss,* by impl. *disobedience:*— disobedience(3).

3877. **παρακολουθέω parakoloutheō**; from *3844* and *190; to follow closely, to investigate:*— accompany(1), followed(1), following(1), investigated(1).

3878. **παρακούω parakouō**; from *3844* and *191; to overhear, to hear amiss, to take no heed:*— overhearing(1), refuses to listen(2).

3879. **παρακύπτω parakuptō**; from *3844* and *2955; to stoop sideways, to stoop to look:*— look(1), looks intently(1), stooped and looked(1), stooping and looking(2).

3880. **παραλαμβάνω paralambanō**; from *3844* and *2983; to receive from:*— receive(3), received(12), take(5), taken(5), takes(1), takes along(1), taking(1), took(16), took...along(1), took...aside(2), took along(3).

3881. **παραλέγομαι paralegomai**; from *3844* and *3004; to sail past* or *coast along:*— sailing along(1), sailing past(1).

3882. **παράλιος paralios**; from *3844* and the same as *231; by the sea, the sea coast:*— coastal region(1).

3883. **παραλλαγή parallagē**; from a comp. of *3844* and *236; change:*— variation(1).

3884. **παραλογίζομαι paralogizomai**; from *3844* and *3049; to miscalculate, to reason falsely:*— delude(2).

3885. **παραλυτικός paralutikos**; from *3886; paralytic:*— paralytic(8), paralytics(1), paralyzed(1).

3886. **παραλύω paraluō**; from *3844* and *3089; to loose from the side:*— feeble(1), paralytic(1), paralyzed(3).

3887. **παραμένω paramenō**; from *3844* and *3306; to remain beside* or *near:*— abides(1), continue(1), continuing(1).

3888. **παραμυθέομαι paramutheomai**; from *3844* and **μυθέομαι mutheomai** *(to speak); to encourge, comfort:*— console(1), consoling(1), encourage(1), encouraging(1).

3889. **παραμυθία paramuthia**; from *3888; encouragement, exhortation, comfort:*— consolation(1).

3890. **παραμύθιον paramuthion**; from *3888; exhortation, encouragement:*— consolation(1).

3891. **παρανομέω paranomeō**; from a comp. of *3844* and *3551; to transgress the law:*— in violation of the law(1).

3892. **παρανομία paranomia**; from the same as *3891; lawbreaking:*— transgression(1).

3893. **παραπικραίνω parapikrainō**; from *3844* and *4087; to embitter, provoke:*— provoked(1).

3894. **παραπικρασμός parapikrasmos**; from *3893; provocation:*— provoked(2).

3895. **παραπίπτω parapiptō**; from *3844* and *4098; to fall in, into* or *away, to fail:*— fallen away(1).

3896. **παραπλέω parapleō**; from *3844* and *4126; to sail by* or *past:*— sail past(1).

3897. **παραπλήσιος paraplēsios**; from a comp. of *3844* and the same as *4139; coming near, nearly resembling:*— point(1).

3898. **παραπλησίως paraplēsiōs**; adv. from *3897; in like manner:*— likewise(1).

3899. **παραπορεύομαι paraporeuomai**; from *3844* and *4198; to go beside* or *past:*— go(1), passing(4).

3900. **παράπτωμα paraptōma**; from *3895; a false step, a trespass:*— transgression(7), transgressions(9), trespass(1), trespasses(3).

3901. **παραρρέω pararreō**; from *3844* and *4482; to flow by,* hence *slip away:*— drift away(1).

3902. **παράσημος parasēmos**; from *3844* and **σῆμα sēma** *(a sign, mark); marked amiss, marked at the side, marked with a sign:*— figurehead(1), had(1).

3903. **παρασκευάζω paraskeuazō**; from *3844* and **σκευάζω skeuazō** *(to prepare, make ready); to prepare, make ready:*— making preparations(1), prepare(1), prepared(2).

3904. **παρασκευή paraskeuē**; from *3903; preparation, the day of preparation* (for a Sabbath or feast):— day(1), day of preparation(3), preparation(2), preparation day(1).

3905. **παρατείνω parateinō**; from *3844* and **τείνω teinō** *(to stretch); to extend, prolong:*— prolonged(1).

3906. **παρατηρέω paratēreō**; from *3844* and *5083; to watch closely, to observe scrupulously:*— observe(1), watched(1), watching(2), watching...closely(2).

3907. **παρατήρησις paratērēsis**; from *3906; observation:*— signs to be observed(1).

3908. **παρατίθημι paratithēmi**; from *3844* and *5087; to place beside, to set before:*— commend(1), commended(1), commit(1), entrust(3), entrusted(1), giving evidence(1), presented(2), serve(1), served(2), set before(5), set...before(1).

3909. **παρατυγχάνω paratugchanō**; from *3844* and *5177; to happen to be near* or *present:*— happened to be present(1).

3910. **παραυτίκα parautika**; from **πάραυτα parauta** *(immediately); immediately, for a moment:*— momentary(1).

3911. **παραφέρω parapherō**; from *3844* and *5342; to bring to, to carry away:*— carried along(1), carried away(1), remove(2).

3912. **παραφρονέω paraphroneō**; from *3844* and *5426; to be beside oneself, to be deranged:*— insane(1).

3913. **παραφρονία Paraphronia**; from *3912; madness:*— madness(1).

3914. **παραχειμάζω paracheimazō**; from *3844* and *5492; to winter at:*— spend the winter(3), wintered(1).

3915. **παραχειμασία paracheimasia**; from *3914; a wintering:*— wintering(1).

3916. **παραχρῆμα parachrēma**; from *3844* and *5536; instantly:*— immediately(14), once(3).

3917. **πάρδαλις pardalis**; of unc. or.; *a panther, leopard:*— leopard(1).

3918a. **παρεδρεύω paredreuō**; from **πάρεδρος paredros** *(sitting beside); to sit constantly beside:*— attend regularly(1), here(1).

3918b. **πάρειμι pareimi**; from *3844* and *1510; to be present, to have come:*— am present(1), been present(1), came(1), come(4), have(1), have come(1), here(1), here present(1), lacks*(1), moment(1), present(10).

3919. **παρεισάγω pareisagō**; from *3844* and *1521; to introduce, to bring in secretly:*— secretly introduce(1).

3920. **παρείσακτος pareisaktos**; from *3919; brought in secretly:*— secretly brought(1), sneaked(1).

3921. **παρεισδύω pareisduō**; from *3844* and a comp. of *1519* and *1416; to settle in alongside:*— crept in unnoticed(1).

3922. **παρεισέρχομαι pareiserchomai**; from *3844* and *1525; to come in beside:*— came(1).

3923. **παρεισφέρω pareispherō**; from *3844* and *1533; to bring in, to supply besides:*— applying(1).

3924. **παρεκτός parektos**; from *3844* and *1622; in addition, except:*— except(2), external(1).

3925a. **παρεμβάλλω paremballō**; from *3844* and *1685; to put in beside* or *between, interpose:*— throw(1).

3925b. **παρεμβολή parembolē**; from *3925a; an insertion, an army in battle array, barracks:*— armies(1), barracks(6), camp(3).

3926. **παρενοχλέω parenochleō**; from *3844* and *1776; to annoy:*— trouble(1).

3927. **παρεπίδημος parepidēmos**; from *3844* and **ἐπίδημος epidēmos** *(sojourning in); sojourning in a strange place:*— exiles(1), reside as aliens(1), strangers(1).

3928. **παρέρχομαι parerchomai**; from *3844* and *2064; to pass by, to come to:*— came along(1), come(2), disregard(1), late(1), neglected(1), over(1), pass(5), pass away(14), passed away(1), passing(2), past(1).

3929. **πάρεσις paresis**; from *3935; a letting go:*— passed over(1).

3930. **παρέχω parechō**; from *3844* and *2192; to furnish, to present:*— became(1), bother*(3), bothers*(1), bringing(2), cause(1), furnished(1), give rise(1), grant(2), offer(1), show(1), showed(1), supplies(1).

3931. **παρηγορία parēgoria**; from **παρηγορέω parēgoreō** *(to address); exhortation, comfort:*— encouragement(1).

3932. **παρθενία parthenia**; from *3933; virginity:*— marriage(1).

3933. **παρθένος parthenos**; of unc. or.; *a maiden, a virgin:*— chaste(1), virgin(9), virgin's(1), virgins(4).

3934. **Πάρθος Parthos**; of for. or.; *a Parthian,* an inhab. of Parthia:— Parthians(1).

3935. **παρίημι pariēmi**; from *3844* and **ἵημι hiēmi** *(to send); to pass by* or *over, to relax:*— neglecting(1), weak(1).

3936. **παρίστημι paristēmi**; from *3844* and *2476; to place beside, to present, stand by, appear:*— bystanders(5), come(1), commend(1), help(1), present(11), presented(4), presenting(1), prove(1), provide(1), put at...disposal(1), stand before(2), standing(1), standing beside(1), standing nearby(2), stands(1), stands here(1), stood(2), stood before(1), stood beside(2), took their stand(1).

3937. **Παρμενᾶς Parmenas**; prob. a contr. for **Παρμενίδης Parmenidēs** (from a comp. of *3844* and *3306)* or a similar name; "constant," *Parmenas,* a Chr.:— Parmenas(1).

3938. **πάροδος parodos**; from *3844* and *3598; a passing* or *passage:*— passing(1).

3939. **παροικέω paroikeō**; from *3844* and *3611; to dwell near,* i.e. *reside as a foreigner:*— lived as an alien(1), visiting(1).

3940. **παροικία paroikia**; from *3941; a sojourning:*— stay(2).

3941. **πάροικος paroikos**; from *3844* and *3624; dwelling near, foreign:*— alien(1), aliens(3).

3942. **παροιμία paroimia**; from **πάροιμος paroimos** *(by the way); a byword, a parable, an allegory:*— figurative language(2), figure of speech(2), proverb(1).

3943. πάροινος paroinos; from *3844* and *3631; given to wine, drunken:*— addicted to wine(2).

3944. παροίχομαι paroichomai; from *3844* and **οἴχομαι oichomai** *(to depart); to have passed by:*— gone(1).

3945. παρομοιάζω paromoiazō; from *3946; to be like:*— like(1).

3946. παρόμοιος paromoios; from *3844* and *3664; much like:*— such(1).

3947. παροξύνω paroxunō; from *3844* and **ὀξύνω oxunō** *(to sharpen); to sharpen,* fig. *to stimulate, to provoke:*— provoked(2).

3948. παροξυσμός paroxusmos; from *3947; stimulation, provocation:*— sharp disagreement(1), stimulate(1).

3949. παροργίζω parorgizō; from *3844* and *3710; to provoke to anger:*— anger(1), provoke...to anger(1).

3950. παροργισμός Parorgismos; from *3949; irritation:*— anger(1).

3951. παροτρύνω parotrunō; from *3844* and **ὀτρύνω otrunō** *(to spur); to urge on, to stir up:*— incited(1).

3952. παρουσία parousia; from the pres. part. of *3918b; a presence, a coming:*— coming(22), presence(2).

3953. παροψίς paropsis; from *3844* and the same as *3795; a side dish of delicacies:*— dish(2).

3954. παρρησία parrēsia; from *3956* and **ῥῆσις rhēsis** *(speech); freedom of speech, confidence:*— boldness(4), boldness in...speech(1), confidence(13), confidently(1), openly(2), openness(1), plainly(5), public(1), publicly(3).

3955. παρρησιάζομαι parrēsiazomai; from *3954; to speak freely* or *boldly:*— confidence(1), had the boldness(1), speak out boldly(1), speak boldly(1), speaking out boldly(2), speaking boldly(1), spoke out boldly(1), spoken out boldly(1).

3956. πᾶς pas; a prim. word; *all, every:*— all(731), all the things(7), all...things(1), all kinds(1), all men(14), all people(4), all respects(3), all things(126), all*(1), always*(3), any(16), any at all(1), anyone(3), anything(3), anything*(1), continually*(6), entire(4), every(128), every form(1), every kind(9), every respect(1), every way(2), everyone(71), everyone's(1), everyone*(1), everything(45), forever*(1), full(2), great(2), no*(15), none*(1), nothing(1), nothing*(1), one(4), perfectly(1), quite(1), whatever(3), whatever*(1), whoever(7), whole(18).

3957. πάσχα pascha; of Ara. or., cf. [6453]; *the Passover, the Passover supper* or *lamb:*— Passover(29).

3958. πάσχω paschō; akin to *3997; to suffer, to be acted on:*— endured(1), endured...sufferings(1), suffer(22), suffered(10), suffering(4), suffers(2).

3959. Πάταρα Patara; prob. of for. or.; *Patara,* a city of Lycia:— Patara(1).

3960. πατάσσω patassō; of unc. or.; *to beat* (of the heart), *to strike:*— strike(2), strike down(3), striking down(1), struck(4).

3961. πατέω pateō; from **πάτος patos** *(trodden); to tread* or *tread on:*— trampled under(1), tread(1), tread under foot(1), treads(1), trodden(1).

3962. πατήρ patēr; a prim. word; *a father:*— father(348), father's(13), fathers(53), parents(1).

3963. Πάτμος Patmos; of unc. or.; *Patmos,* an island in the Aegean Sea:— Patmos(1).

3964. πατραλῴας patralōas; var. reading for *3970a,* q.v.

3965. πατριά patria; from *3962; lineage, family:*— families(1), family(2).

3966. πατριάρχης patriarchēs; from *3965* and *757; a patriarch:*— patriarch(2), patriarchs(2).

3967. πατρικός patrikos; from *3962; paternal, ancestral:*— ancestral(1).

3968. πατρίς patris; from *3962; of one's fathers, fatherland:*— country(1), country of their own(1), hometown(6).

3969. Πατροβᾶς Patrobas; for **Πατρόβιος Patrobios** (a comp. of *3962* and *979*); "father's life," *Patrobas,* a Chr.:— Patrobas(1).

3970a. πατρολῴας patrolōas; from *3962* and **ἀλοιάω aloiaō** *(to strike); one who kills one's father:*— fathers(1), kill*(1).

3970b. πατροπαράδοτος patroparadotos; from *3962* and *3860; handed down from one's fathers:*— inherited from...forefathers(1).

3971. πατρῷος patrōos; from *3962; of one's fathers, received from one's fathers:*— fathers(3).

3972. Παῦλος Paulos; of Lat. or.; (Sergius) *Paulus* (a Rom. proconsul), also *Paul* (an apostle):— Paul(152), Paul's(5), Paulus(1).

3973. παύω pauō; a prim. word; *to make to cease, hinder:*— cease(4), ceased(4), finished(2), incessantly*(1), keep(1), kept right*(1), stopped(2).

3974. Πάφος Paphos; of unc. or.; *Paphos,* a city in Cyprus:— Paphos(2).

3975. παχύνω pachunō; from **παχύς pachus** *(thick); to thicken, to fatten,* fig. *to make dull:*— become dull(2).

3976. πέδη pedē; from **πέζα peza** *(the instep); a fetter, shackle:*— shackles(3).

3977. πεδινός pedinos; from **πεδίον pedion** *(a plain); level, plain:*— level(1).

3978. πεζεύω pezeuō; from *3979b; to travel on foot* or *by land:*— go by land(1).

3979a. πεζῇ pezē; adv. from *3979b; on foot, by land:*— foot(2).

3979b. πεζός pezos; from *4228; on foot, by land.*

3980. πειθαρχέω peitharcheō; from a comp. of *3982* and *757; to obey authority:*— followed...advice(1), obedient(1), obey(2).

3981. πειθός peithos; from *3982; persuasive:*— persuasive(1).

3982. πείθω peithō; a prim. vb.; *to persuade, to have confidence:*— assure(1), confident(3), convinced(7), followed(2), have confidence(2), having confidence(2), listen(1), obey(3), obeying(1), persuade(4), persuaded(8), persuading(1), put...trust(1), put confidence(1), put...confidence(1), relied(1), seeking the favor(1), sure(2), took...advice(1), trust(2), trusted(1), trusting(1), trusts(1), urging(1), win...over(1), won over(2).

3983. πεινάω peinaō; from **πεῖνα peina** *(hunger); to hunger, be hungry:*— going hungry(1), hunger(4), hungry(18).

3984. πεῖρα peira; a prim. word; *a trial, an experiment:*— attempted*(1), experienced*(1).

3985. πειράζω peirazō; from *3984; to make proof of, to attempt, test, tempt:*— did(1), put(1), put to the test(2), tempt(2), tempted(13), tempter(2), test(6), tested(2), testing(7), tried(2), trying(2).

3986. πειρασμός peirasmos; from *3985; an experiment, a trial, temptation:*— temptation(12), testing(2), trial(3), trials(4).

3987. πειράομαι peiraomai; from *3984; to try, attempt:*— tried(1).

3988. πεισμονή peismonē; from *3982; persuasion:*— persuasion(1).

3989. πέλαγος pelagos; a prim. word; *the deep, the deep sea:*— depth(1), sea(1).

3990. πελεκίζω pelekizō; from **πέλεκυς pelekus** *(a battle-ax); to cut off with an ax,* esp. *to behead:*— beheaded(1).

3991. πέμπτος pemptos; an ord. num. from *4002; fifth:*— fifth(4).

3992. πέμπω pempō; a prim. word; *to send:*— dispatch(1), put(2), send(24), sending(2), sent(50).

3993. πένης penēs; from **πένομαι penomai** *(to work for one's daily bread); one who works for his living:*— poor(1).

3994. πενθερά penthera; fem. of *3995; a mother-in-law:*— mother-in-law(6).

3995. πενθερός pentheros; a prim. word; *a father-in-law:*— father-in-law(1).

3996. πενθέω pentheō; from *3997; to mourn, lament:*— mourn(6), mourned(1), mourning(3).

3997. πένθος penthos; a prim. word; *mourning:*— mourning(5).

3998. πενιχρός penichros; from the same as *3993; needy, poor:*— poor(1).

3999. πεντάκις pentakis; adv. from *4002; five times:*— five times(1).

4000. πεντακισχίλιοι pentakischilioi; a card. num. from *3999* and *5507; five thousand:*— five(1), five thousand(6).

4001. πεντακόσιοι pentakosioi; pl. card. num. from *4002* and *1540; five hundred:*— five hundred(2).

4002. πέντε pente; a prim. card. num.; *five:*— fifty*(1), five(34), seventy-five*(1), three*(1).

4003. πεντεκαιδέκατος pentekaidekatos; an ord. num. from *4002, 2532* and *1182; fifteenth:*— fifteenth(1).

4004. πεντήκοντα pentēkonta; a card. num. from *4002* and a modified form of *1176; fifty:*— fifties(1), fifty(5), fifty-three*(1).

4005. πεντηκοστή pentēkostē; from **πεντηκοστός pentēkostos**; an ord. num. from *4004; fiftieth, Pentecost,* the second of the three great Jewish feasts:— Pentecost(3).

4006. πεποίθησις pepoithēsis; from *3982; confidence:*— confidence(5), confident(1).

4007a. περ per; enclitic particle akin to *4012; indeed* (adds force to the preceding word):— if*(2).

4007b. περαιτέρω peraiterō; cptv. adv. from **πέρα pera** *(beyond); beyond:*— beyond(1).

4008. πέραν peran; akin to **πέρα pera** *(on the further side); on the other side:*— beyond(8), cross(1), other side(13), over(1).

4009. πέρας peras; akin to **πεῖραρ peirar** *(end, limit); a limit:*— end(1), ends(3).

4010. Πέργαμος Pergamos; from *4444; Pergamum,* a city of Mysia:— Pergamum(2).

4011. Πέργη Pergē; prob. from the same as *4010; Perga,* a city of Pamphylia:— Perga(3).

4012. περί peri; a prim. prep.; *about, concerning, around* (denotes place, cause or subject):— about(103), about*(1), against(4), all around(1), around(12), around*(1), because(2), behalf(4), case*(1), cause*(1), circumstances*(1), companions*(1), concerning(48), condition*(1), connection(2), followers*(1), help(1), neighborhood(1), over(1), over...about(1), refers(1), regard(3), regarding(4), vicinity(1).

4013. περιάγω periagō; from *4012* and *71; to lead around, to go about:*— around*(1), going(1), going through(1), going throughout(1), take along(1), travel around(1), went about(1).

4014. περιαιρέω periaireō; from *4012* and *138; to take away* (that which surrounds):— abandoned(1), casting off(1), take away(1), taken away(1).

4015a. περιάπτω periaptō; from *4012* and *681; to tie around:*— kindled(1).

4015b. περιαστράπτω periastraptō; from *4012* and *797; to flash around:*— flashed(1), flashed around(1).

4016. περιβάλλω periballō; from *4012* and *906; to throw around, put on:*— clothe(4), clothed(13), dressed(1), wear for clothing(1), wearing(2), wrap...around(1).

4017. περιβλέπω periblepō; from *4012* and *991; to look around:*— looked around(2), looking about(1), looking around(4).

4018. περιβόλαιον peribolaion; from *4016; that which is thrown around, a covering:*— covering(1), mantle(1).

4019. περιδέω perideō; from *4012* and *1210; to tie around:*— wrapped around(1).

4020. περιεργάζομαι periergazomai; from *4012* and *2038b; to waste one's labor about* (a thing):— acting like busybodies(1).

4021. περίεργος periergos; from *4012* and *2041; overly careful, curious, meddling,* subst. *a busybody:*— busybodies(1), magic(1).

4022. περιέρχομαι perierchomai; from *4012* and *2064; to go about:*— go around(1), sailed around(1), went from place to place(1), went about(1).

4023. περιέχω periechō; from *4012* and *2192; to surround:*— contained(1), seized(1).

4024. περιζώννυμι perizōnnumi; from *4012* and *2224; to gird:*— clothe(1), dressed in readiness(1), gird(1), girded(3).

4025. περίθεσις perithesis; from *4060; a putting around:*— wearing(1).

4026. περιΐστημι periistēmi; from *4012* and *2476; to stand around, turn around* (to avoid):— avoid(2), standing around(1), stood around(1).

4027. περικάθαρμα perikatharma; from a comp. of *4012* and *2508; that which is cleaned off, refuse:*— scum(1).

4028. περικαλύπτω perikaluptō; from *4012* and *2572; to cover around:*— blindfold(1), blindfolded(1), covered(1).

4029. περίκειμαι perikeimai; from *4012* and *2749; to lie around:*— beset(1), hung(2), surrounding(1), wearing(1).

4030. περικεφαλαία perikephalaia; from *4012* and *2776; a helmet:*— helmet(2).

4031. περικρατής perikratēs; from *4012* and *2904; having full command of:*— under control(1).

4032. περικρύπτω perikruptō; from *4012* and *2928; to conceal entirely:*— kept...in seclusion(1).

4033. περικυκλόω perikukloō; from *4012* and *2944; to encircle:*— surround(1).

4034. περιλάμπω perilampō; from *4012* and *2989; to shine around:*— shining...around(1), shone around(1).

4035. περιλείπομαι perileipomai; from *4012* and *3007; to be left remaining:*— remain(2).

4036. περίλυπος perilupos; from *4012* and *3077; very sad:*— deeply grieved(2), very sad(1), very sorry(1).

4037. περιμένω perimenō; from *4012* and *3306; to wait for:*— wait(1).

4038. πέριξ perix; adv. from *4012; (all) around:*— vicinity(1).

4039. περιοικέω perioikeō; from *4012* and *3611; to dwell around:*— living around(1).

4040. περίοικος perioikos; from *4012* and *3624; dwelling around, a neighbor:*— neighbors(1).

4041. περιούσιος periousios; from a comp. of *4012* and *1510; of one's own possession:*— possession(1).

4042. περιοχή periochē; from *4023; circumference, a portion circumscribed:*— passage(1).

4043. περιπατέω peripateō; from *4012* and *3961; to walk:*— behave(2), conduct ourselves(1), conduct yourselves(1), leading...life(1), leads...life(1), prowls around(1), so occupied(1), walk(50), walk about(1), walk around(2), walked(7), walking(21), walking around(1), walks(5).

4044. περιπείρω peripeirō; from *4012* and **πείρω peirō** *(to pierce through); to put on a spit,* hence *to pierce:*— pierced(1).

4045. περιπίπτω peripiptō; from *4012* and *4098; to fall around:*— encounter(1), fell among(1), striking(1).

4046. περιποιέω peripoieō; from *4012* and *4160; to preserve, get possession of:*— keep(1), obtain(1), purchased(1).

4047. περιποίησις peripoiēsis; from *4046; preservation, acquisition:*— gain(1), obtaining(1), possession(2), preserving(1).

4048. περιρήγνυμι perirēgnumi; from *4012* and *4486; to tear off all around:*— tore...off(1).

4049. περισπάω perispaō; from *4012* and *4685; to draw away:*— distracted(1).

4050. περισσεία perisseia; from *4052; superfluity:*— abundance(2), more(1), remains(1).

4051. περίσσευμα perisseuma; from *4052; superfluity:*— abundance(2), full of what was left over(1), which fills(2).

4052. περισσεύω perisseuō; from *4053; to be over and above, to abound:*— abound(10), abounded(1), abounding(1), abundance(2), abundant(1), better(1), cause(1), cause*(1), excel(2), has an abundance(1), have an abundance(3), have more than enough(1), having abundance(1), increasing(1), lavished(1), left over(4), leftover(1), live in prosperity(1), make...abound(1), overflowed(1), overflowing(2), surpasses(1), surplus(2).

4053. περισσός perissos; from *4012; abundant:*— abounds all(1), abounds all the more(1), abundantly(1), advantage(1), all the more(2), beyond(1), especially(2), even more(2), excessive(1), further(1), greater(3), John(1), more(5), more abundant(2), more extremely(1), much more(1), superfluous(1), utterly*(1), widely(1).

4054. περισσότερον perissoteron; neut. of *4055,* q.v.

4055. περισσότερος perissoteros; cptv. from *4053; greater, more.*

4056. περισσοτέρως perissoterōs adv. from *4055; (even) more, especially.*

4057. περισσῶς perissōs; adv. from *4053; abundantly:*— all the more(3), even more(1), even...more(1), far more(3), furiously(1), more(2), much closer(1).

4058. περιστερά peristera; of unc. or.; *a dove:*— dove(4), doves(5), pigeons(1).

4059. περιτέμνω peritemnō; from *4012* and the same as *5114; to cut around, circumcise:*— circumcise(4), circumcised(10), circumcision(1), receive circumcision(1), receives circumcision(1).

4060. περιτίθημι peritithēmi; from *4012* and *5087; to place around:*— bestow(1), put(5), put...around(2).

4061. περιτομή peritomē; from *4059; circumcision:*— circumcised(11), circumcision(25).

4062. περιτρέπω peritrepō; from *4012* and the same as *5157; to turn about:*— driving(1).

4063. περιτρέχω peritrechō; from *4012* and *5143; to run about:*— ran about(1).

4064. περιφέρω peripherō; from *4012* and *5342; to carry about:*— carried about(1), carry here and there(1), carrying about(1).

4065. περιφρονέω periphroneō; from *4012* and *5426; to examine on all sides, to despise:*— disregard(1).

4066. περίχωρος perichōros; from *4012* and *5561; neighboring:*— country(1), district around(2), surrounding district(6), surrounding region(1).

4067. περίψημα peripsēma; from *4012* and **ψάω psaō** *(to wipe off); offscouring:*— dregs(1).

4068. περπερεύομαι perpereuomai; from **πέρπερος perperos** *(vainglorious); to boast:*— brag(1).

4069. Περσίς Persis; fem. noun from **Περσικός Persikos** *(Persian); Persis,* a Chr. at Rome:— Persis(1).

4070. πέρυσι perusi; a prim. adv.; *last year:*— last year(1), year ago(1).

4071. πετεινόν peteinon; from **πετεινός peteinos**; from *4072; winged:*— birds(14).

4072. πέτομαι petomai; a prim. vb.; *to fly:*— fly(2), flying(3).

4073. πέτρα petra; a prim. word; *a* (large mass of) *rock:*— rock(10), rocks(3), rocky(2).

4074. Πέτρος Petros; a noun akin to *4073,* used as a proper name; "a stone" or "a boulder," *Peter,* one of the twelve apostles:— Peter(150), Peter's(5).

4075. πετρώδης petrōdēs; from *4073* and **-ωδης -ōdēs** (suff. denoting similarity); *rock-like:*— rocky(4).

4076. πήγανον pēganon; perh. from *4078; rue* (a plant with thick, fleshy leaves):— rue(1).

4077. πηγή pēgē; a prim. word; *a spring* (of water):— flow(1), fountain(1), spring(1), springs(5), well(3).

4078. πήγνυμι pēgnumi; a prim. vb.; *to make fast:*— pitched(1).

4079. πηδάλιον pēdalion; from **πηδόν pēdon** *(the blade of an oar); a rudder:*— rudder(1), rudders(1).

4080. πηλίκος pēlikos; from the same as *2245; how large? how great?:*— how great(1), what large(1).

4081. **πηλός pēlos**; a prim. word; *clay:*— clay(6).

4082. **πήρα pēra**; a prim. word; *a leather pouch:*— bag(6).

4083. **πῆχυς pēchus**; a prim. word; *the forearm,* i.e. *a cubit:*— hour(2), yards(2).

4084. **πιάζω piazō**; a late form of *4085; to lay hold of, to take:*— caught(2), seize(6), seized(3), seizing(1).

4085. **πιέζω piezō**; of unc. or.; *to press down:*— pressed down(1).

4086. **πιθανολογία pithanologia**; from a der. of *3982* and *3056; persuasive speech:*— persuasive argument(1).

4087. **πικραίνω pikrainō**; from *4089; to make bitter:*— embittered(1), made bitter(2), make...bitter(1).

4088. **πικρία pikria**; from *4089; bitterness:*— bitterness(4).

4089. **πικρός pikros**; a prim. word; *bitter, sharp:*— bitter(2).

4090. **πικρῶς pikrōs**; adv. from *4089; bitterly:*— bitterly(2).

4091. **Πιλᾶτος Pilatos**; of Lat. or.; *Pilate,* a Rom. procurator of Judea:— Pilate(55).

4092a. **πίμπλημι pimplēmi**; perh. from a prim. root **πλη- plē-**; *to fill full of:*— come(1), completed(2), ended(1), filled(18), fulfilled(1), passed(1).

4092b. **πίμπρημι pimprēmi**; perh. from a prim. root **πρη- prē-**; *to burn, swell:*— swell(1).

4093. **πινακίδιον pinakidion**; dim. of *4094; a writing tablet:*— tablet(1).

4094. **πίναξ pinax**; a prim. word; *a board, dish:*— platter(5).

4095. **πίνω pinō**; a prim. word; *to drink:*— drank(5), drink(49), drinking(11), drinks(8), drunk(1).

4096. **πιότης piotēs**; from **πίων piōn** *(fat); fatness:*— rich(1).

4097. **πιπράσκω pipraskō**; from **πέρνημι pernēmi** *(to export for sale); to sell:*— sales(1), selling(1), sold(7).

4098. **πίπτω piptō**; from a redupl. of the prim. root **πετ- pet-**; *to fall:*— beat down(1), fail(1), fails(1), fall(15), fall down(2), fallen(8), falling(3), falls(8), fell(46), fell down(6).

4099. **Πισιδία Pisidia**; of unc. or.; *Pisidia,* a region of Asia Minor:— Pisidia(1), Pisidian(1).

4100. **πιστεύω pisteuō**; from *4102; to believe, entrust:*— believe(118), believed(73), believers(3), believes(29), believing(10), do(1), entrust(1), entrusted(6), entrusting(1), has faith(1).

4101. **πιστικός pistikos**; from *4102; trustworthy:*— pure(2).

4102. **πίστις pistis**; from *3982; faith, faithfulness:*— faith(238), faithfulness(3), pledge(1), proof(1).

4103. **πιστός pistos**; from *3982; faithful, reliable:*— believe(2), believer(4), believers(5), believing(1), faithful(44), faithful one(1), faithfully(1), sure(1), trustworthy(7), who believe(1).

4104. **πιστόω pistoō**; from *4103; to make trustworthy,* hence *to establish:*— convinced(1).

4105. **πλανάω planaō**; from *4106; to cause to wander, to wander:*— deceive(3), deceived(9), deceives(3), deceiving(2), go astray(1), gone astray(3), leads...astray(2), led astray(1), misguided(1), mislead(4), misleads(2), misled(1), mistaken(3), straying(2), strays(1), wandering(1).

4106. **πλάνη planē**; fem. of *4108; a wandering:*— deceitful(1), deception(1), deluding(1), error(7).

4107. **πλανήτης planētēs**; from *4105; a wanderer:*— wandering(1).

4108. **πλάνος planos**; a prim. word; *wandering, leading astray* (adj.), *a deceiver* (subst.):— deceitful(1), deceiver(2), deceivers(2).

4109. **πλάξ plax**; a prim. word; *anything flat and broad,* hence *a flat stone:*— tables(1), tablets(2).

4110. **πλάσμα plasma**; from *4111; that which is molded:*— thing molded(1).

4111. **πλάσσω plassō**; a prim. vb.; *to form:*— created(1), molder(1).

4112. **πλαστός plastos**; from *4111; formed, molded:*— false(1).

4113. **πλατεῖα plateia**; fem. of *4116; a wide road, street.*

4114. **πλάτος platos**; from *4116; breadth:*— breadth(1), broad plain(1), width(2).

4115. **πλατύνω platunō**; from *4116; to make broad:*— broaden(1), open wide(1), opened wide(1).

4116. **πλατύς platus**; a prim. word; *broad,* subst. *a street:*— street(4), streets(5), wide(1).

4117. **πλέγμα plegma**; from *4120; a braiding:*— braided hair(1).

4118. **πλεῖστος pleistos**; superl. of *4183,* q.v.

4119. **πλείων pleiōn**; cptv. of *4183,* q.v.

4120. **πλέκω plekō**; a prim. vb.; *to plait:*— twisted(1), twisting(2).

4121. **πλεονάζω pleonazō**; from the cptv. of *4183; to superabound, to make to abound:*— cause*(1), grows...greater(1), have too much(1), increase(3), increased(1), increases(1), increasing(1), spreading(1).

4122. **πλεονεκτέω pleonekteō**; from *4123; to have more, to overreach:*— advantage would be taken of(1), defraud(1), take any advantage(1), taken advantage(1), took advantage(1).

4123. **πλεονέκτης pleonektēs**; from the cptv. of *4183* and *2192; one desirous of having more:*— covetous(3), covetous man(1).

4124. **πλεονεξία pleonexia**; from *4123; advantage, covetousness:*— covetousness(1), deeds of coveting(1), greed(7), greediness(1).

4125. **πλευρά pleura**; a prim. word; *the side:*— side(5).

4126. **πλέω pleō**; a prim. word; *to sail:*— passenger*(1), sail(1), sailing(4).

4127. **πληγή plēgē**; from *4141; a blow, wound:*— beat*(1), beaten(1), beatings(1), blows(1), flogging(1), plague(3), plagues(10), wound(3), wounds(1).

4128. **πλῆθος plēthos**; from **πλήθω plēthō** *(to be full); a great number:*— assembly(1), body(1), bundle(1), congregation(4), crowd(3), great number(1), multitude(7), multitudes(1), number(1), number of people(2), people(6), quantity(1), throng(1).

4129. **πληθύνω plēthunō**; from *4128; to increase, to be increased:*— fullest measure(1), increase(2), increased(1), increasing(1), multiplied(4), multiply(1), surely multiply(1).

4130. (not used)

4131. **πλήκτης plēktēs**; from *4141; a striker:*— pugnacious(2).

4132. **πλήμμυρα plēmmura**; of unc. or.; a flood:— flood(1).

4133. **πλήν plēn**; adv. from the cptv. form of *4183; yet, except:*— besides(1), except(2), however(3), nevertheless(8), only(1), than(1), yet(3).

4134. **πλήρης plērēs**; from a der. of **πλήθω plēthō** *(to be full); full:*— abounding(1), covered(1), filled(1), full(12), mature(1).

4135. **πληροφορέω plērophoreō**; from *4134* and *5409; to bring in full measure, to fulfill:*— accomplished(1), fulfill(1), fully accomplished(1), fully assured(2), fully convinced(1).

4136. **πληροφορία plērophoria**; from *4135; full assurance:*— conviction(1), full assurance(3).

4137. **πληρόω plēroō**; from *4134; to make full, to complete:*— accomplish(1), accomplished(1), amply supplied(1), approaching(1), complete(1), completed(3), completing(1), elapsed(1), fill(3), filled(16), fills(1), finished(1), fulfill(20), fulfilled(20), fully carry(1), fully come(1), fully preached(1), increasing(1), made complete(2), made full(5), make...full(1), make...complete(1), passed(2), supply(1).

4138. **πλήρωμα plērōma**; from *4137; fullness, a filling up:*— all...contains(1), fulfillment(2), full(2), fullness(10), patch(2).

4139. **πλησίον plēsion**; adv. from **πλησίος plēsios**; from **πέλας pelas** *(near); near, neighboring:*— near(1), neighbor(16).

4140. **πλησμονή plēsmonē**; from **πλήθω plēthō** *(to be full); a filling up:*— indulgence(1).

4141. **πλήσσω plēssō**; of unc. der.; *to strike:*— struck(1).

4142. **πλοιάριον ploiarion**; dim. of *4143; a little boat:*— boat(1), boats(1), little boat(1), small boat(1), small boats(2).

4143. **πλοῖον ploion**; from *4126; a boat:*— boat(40), boats(4), ship(18), ship's(1), ships(3).

4144. **πλόος ploos** or **πλοῦς plous**; from *4126; a voyage:*— voyage(3).

4145. **πλούσιος plousios**; from *4149; wealthy:*— people(1), rich(19), rich man(7), rich man's(1), rich people(1).

4146. **πλουσίως plousiōs**; adv. from *4145; richly:*— abundantly(1), richly(3).

4147. **πλουτέω plouteō**; from *4149; to be rich:*— abounding in riches(1), become rich(4), become wealthy(1), get rich(1), rich(5).

4148. **πλουτίζω ploutizō**; from *4149; to make rich:*— enriched(2), making...rich(1).

4149. **πλοῦτος ploutos**; prob. from *4126* in an early sense of *to flow, abound; wealth:*— riches(18), wealth(4).

4150. **πλύνω plunō**; a prim. vb.; *to wash:*— wash(1), washed(1), washing(1).

4151. **πνεῦμα pneuma**; from *4154; wind, spirit:*— breath(3), Spirit(241), spirit(101), spirits(32), spiritual(1), wind(1), winds(1).

4152. **πνευματικός pneumatikos**; from *4151; spiritual:*— spiritual(23), spiritual men(1), spiritual things(2).

4153. **πνευματικῶς pneumatikōs**; adv. from *4152; spiritually:*— mystically(1), spiritually(1).

4154. **πνέω pneō**; a prim. vb.; *to blow:*— blew(2), blow(1), blowing(2), blows(1), wind(1).

4155. **πνίγω pnigō**; a prim. vb.; *to choke:*— choke(1), drowned(1).

4156. **πνικτός pniktos**; from *4155; strangled:*— strangled(2), things strangled(1).

4157. **πνοή pnoē**; from *4154; a blowing, wind, breath:*— breath(1), wind(1).

4158. **ποδήρης podērēs**; from *4228* and an unc. root or suff.; *reaching to the feet:*— robe reaching(1), robe reaching to the feet(1).

4159. **πόθεν pothen**; adv. from the same as *4214; from where:*— how(3), what(1), what...source(1), what sense(1), where(22).

4160. **ποιέω poieō**; a prim. word; *to make, do:*— accomplished(1), act(4), acted(3), acting(1), acts(2), appointed(3), away*(1), bear(5), bearing(1), bears(3), become(1), bore(1), bring(1), bring...to pass(1), bring about(2), bringing(1), brings forth(1), call(1), carried(1), carries(1), carry(1), cause(3), causes(2), causing(1), commit(2), commits(2), committed(4), composed(1), consider(1), created things(1), dealt(1), did(33), did...do(2), do(170), does(16), does...do(1), doing(38), done(43), establishing(1), execute(4), exercises(1), expose*(1), formed(1), formed a conspiracy(1), forms(1), gave(4), give(4), gives(1), giving(1), have(2), have kept(1), having(1), held(1), indulging(1), keep(3), keeps(1), kept(1), made(38), make(47), makes(7), making(9), observe(2), offer(1), offering(1), perform(4), performed(8), performing(7), performs(1), practice(5), practices(11), practicing(1), present(1), proceeding(1), produce(3), produced(1), produces(2), producing(1), provide(1), put(1), satisfy*(1), setting(1), show(2), showed(1), shown(1), spend(1), spent(4), took(1), treat(6), treated(1), weaker(1), worked(1), working(1).

4161. **ποίημα poiēma**; from *4160; a work:*— what has been made(1), workmanship(1).

4162. **ποίησις poiēsis**; from *4160; a making, a doing:*— what...does(1).

4163. **ποιητής poiētēs**; from *4160; a maker, a doer:*— doer(3), doers(2), poets(1).

4164. **ποικίλος poikilos**; a prim. word; *many colored:*— manifold(1), varied(1), various(8).

4165. **ποιμαίνω poimainō**; from *4166; to act as a shepherd:*— caring(1), rule(3), shepherd(5), tending sheep(1), tends(1).

4166. **ποιμήν poimēn**; of unc. or.; *a shepherd:*— pastors(1), shepherd(13), shepherds(4).

4167. **ποίμνη poimnē**; prob. from *4166; a flock:*— flock(5).

4168. **ποίμνιον poimnion**; from *4167; a flock:*— flock(5).

4169. **ποῖος poios**; from the same as *4214; of what sort?:*— any(1), kind of...by which(1), what(21), what kind(6), what things(1), which(3), which ones(1).

4170. **πολεμέω polemeō**; from *4171; to make war:*— make war(1), quarrel(1), wage war(2), waged(1), wages war(1), waging(1).

4171. **πόλεμος polemos**; a prim. word; *war:*— battle(4), quarrels(1), war(10), wars(5).

4172. **πόλις polis**; a prim. word; *a city:*— cities(20), city(142).

4173. **πολιτάρχης politarchēs**; from *4172* and *757; the ruler of a city:*— city authorities(2).

4174. **πολιτεία politeia**; from *4176; citizenship:*— citizenship(1), commonwealth(1).

4175. **πολίτευμα politeuma**; from *4176; a form of government, citizenship:*— citizenship(1).

4176. **πολιτεύομαι politeuomai**; from *4177; to live as a citizen:*— conduct(1), lived...life(1).

4177. **πολίτης politēs**; from *4172; a citizen:*— citizen(1), citizens(2), fellow citizen(1).

4178. **πολλάκις pollakis**; adv. from *4183; often:*— frequent(1), many(1), often(15), time after time(1).

4179. **πολλαπλασίων pollaplasiōn**; from *4183* and perh. a cptv. of the same; *many times more:*— many times(2), many times as much(2).

4180. **πολυλογία polulogia**; from *4183* and *3056; much speaking:*— many words(1).

4181. **πολυμερῶς polumerōs**; adv. from a comp. of *4183* and *3313; in many parts:*— many portions(1).

4182. **πολυποίκιλος polupoikilos**; from *4183* and *4164; of differing colors:*— manifold(1).

4183. **πολύς polus**; a prim. word; *much, many:*— all(3), better(1), deep(1), earnestly(3), enough(1), even more(1), few*(1), freely(1), full(1), further(1), further*(3), great(33), greater(4), greater numbers(1), greatly(5), hard(2), harshly(1), heartily(1), high price(1), large(30), large numbers(1), large sums(1), larger(1), late*(2), lengthy(1), long(5), longer(1), loudly(1), majority(3), many(181), many more(1), many people(1), many subjects(1), many things(17), many...things(4), more(25), more numerous(1), most(8), most people's(1), much(50), often(1), plentiful(2), quite(2), several(1), some(1), something greater(2), strict(1), terrible(1), very(1), very large(1), very long(1), very much(1).

4184. **πολύσπλαγχνος polusplagchnos**; from *4183* and *4698; very compassionate:*— full of compassion(1).

4185. **πολυτελής polutelēs**; from *4183* and *5056; very costly:*— costly(1), precious(1), very costly(1).

4186. **πολύτιμος polutimos**; from *4183* and *5092; very precious:*— great value(1), more precious(1), very costly(1).

4187. **πολυτρόπως polutropōs**; adv. from a comp. of *4183* and *5158; in many ways:*— many ways(1).

4188. **πόμα poma**; from *4095; a drink:*— drink(2).

4189. **πονηρία ponēria**; from *4190; iniquity:*— malice(1), wicked ways(1), wickedness(5).

4190. **πονηρός ponēros**; from **πονέω poneō** *(to toil); toilsome, bad:*— bad(5), crimes(1), envious(1), envy*(1), evil(50), evil one(5), evil things(1), malignant(1), more evil(1), more wicked(1), vicious(1), wicked(6), wicked man(1), wicked things(1), worthless(1).

4191. **πονηρότερος ponēroteros**; cptv. of *4190,* q.v.

4192. **πόνος ponos**; from **πένομαι penomai** *(to toil); labor:*— concern(1), pain(2), pains(1).

4193. **Ποντικός Pontikos**; from *4195; of Pontus:*— Pontus(1).

4194. **Πόντιος Pontios**; of Lat. or.; *Pontius* (Pilate), a governor of Judea:— Pontius(3).

4195. **Πόντος Pontos**; a prim. word used as proper name; "a sea," *Pontus,* a region of Asia Minor:— Pontus(2).

4196. **Πόπλιος Poplios**; of Lat. or.; *Publius,* an inhab. of Malta:— Publius(2).

4197. **πορεία poreia**; from *4198; a journey:*— pursuits(1), way(1).

4198. **πορεύομαι poreuomai**; from **πόρος poros** *(a ford, passage); to go:*— accompany*(1), am on my way(1), depart(1), departed(1), departure(1), following(3), go(69), go on their way(1), go away(1), goes(7), going(15), going away(2), gone(3), indulge(1), journey(1), journeying(2), leave(1), proceed(1), proceeded(2), pursued a course(1), sets(1), started(3), traveling(3), walking(1), way(6), went(22), went His way(1), went on their way(1), went their way(1).

4199. **πορθέω portheō**; from **πέρθω perthō** *(to ravage); to destroy:*— destroy(2), destroyed(1).

4200. **πορισμός porismos**; from **πορίζω porizō** *(to procure); a providing, a means of gain:*— means of gain(2).

4201. **Πόρκιος Porkios**; of Lat. or.; *Porcius* (Festus), a governor of Judea:— Porcius(1).

4202. **πορνεία porneia**; from *4203; fornication:*— fornication(4), fornications(2), immoralities(1), immorality(16), sexual immorality(1), unchastity(1).

4203. **πορνεύω porneuō**; from *4204; to commit fornication:*— act immorally(1), commit...immorality(2), committed...immorality(3), did(1), immoral(1).

4204. **πόρνη pornē**; prob. from **πέρνημι pernēmi** *(to export for sale); a prostitute:*— harlot(6), harlots(1), prostitute(2), prostitutes(3).

4205. **πόρνος pornos**; akin to *4204; a fornicator:*— fornicators(2), immoral(2), immoral men(1), immoral people(2), immoral person(1), immoral persons(2).

4206. **πόρρω porrō**; an alt. form of **πρόσω prosō** *(far from); far off:*— away*(1), far(2), far away(1), farther(1).

4207. **πόρρωθεν porrōthen**; adv. from *4206* with adv. suff. of source; *from afar:*— distance(2).

4208. **πορρωτέρον porrōteron**; cptv. adv. from *4206,* q.v.

4209. **πορφύρα porphura**; prob. from a redupl. der. of **φύρω phurō** *(to mix dry with wet); purple fish, purple dye, purple cloth:*— purple(3), purple robe(1).

4210. **πορφυροῦς porphurous**; from *4209; purple:*— purple(4).

4211. **πορφυρόπωλις porphuropōlis**; from *4209* and *4453; a seller of purple fabrics:*— purple fabrics(1), seller of purple fabrics(1).

4212. **ποσάκις posakis**; interrog. adv. from *4214; how often?:*— how often(3).

4213. **πόσις posis**; from *4095; a drinking, a drink:*— drink(2), drinking(1).

4214. **πόσος posos**; interrog. adj. from a prim. root; *how much? how great?:*— how(1), how great(1), how many(10), how many things(1), how much(13), what(1).

4215. **ποταμός potamos**; from *4095; a river:*— floods(2), River(2), river(6), rivers(4), riverside*(1), torrent(2).

4216. **ποταμοφόρητος potamophorētos**; from *4215* and **φορητός phorētos** *(carried); carried away by a stream:*— swept away(1), swept away with the flood(1).

4217. **ποταπός potapos**; from prim. roots **ποδ-** and **-απας**; *from what country?:*— how great(1), what kind(2), what sort(2), what sort of person(1), what wonderful(2).

4218. **ποτέ pote**; enclitic particle from the same as *4214* and *5037; once, ever:*— any time(1), ever(4), former(1), former times(1), formerly(8), last(2), never*(2), once(8), when(1), when once(1).

4219. **πότε pote**; interrog. adv. from the same as *4218; when?:*— long*(7), when(14).

4220. **πότερον poteron**; from **πότερος poteros,** a cptv. of the same as *4214; which of two:*— whether(1).

4221. **ποτήριον potērion**; a dim. form der. from *4095; a wine cup:*— cup(30), cups(1).

4222. **ποτίζω potizō**; from **ποτός potos** *(drink, for drinking); to give to drink:*— drink(2), gave...a drink(2), gave...to drink(5), gives(2), made...drink(1), made to drink(1), water(1), watered(1), waters(2).

4223. **Ποτίολοι Potioloi**; of Lat.or.; *Puteoli,* a city on the Bay of Naples:— Puteoli(1).

4224. **πότος potos**; from *4095; a drinking bout:*— drinking parties(1).

4225. **πού pou**; enclitic particle from the same as *4214; somewhere:*— about(1), somewhere(3).

4226. **ποῦ pou**; interrog. adv. from the same as *4214; where?:*— nowhere*(2), place(1), what(1), where(44).

4227. **Πούδης Poudēs**; of Lat. or.; *Pudens,* a Chr.:— Pudens(1).

4228. **πούς pous**; a prim. word; *a foot:*— feet(83), foot(9), under*(1).

4229. **πρᾶγμα pragma**; from *4238; a deed, a matter:*— anything*(1), case(1), deed(1), matter(3), thing(1), things(4).

4230. **πραγματεία pragmateia**; from *4231; careful application, hard work:*— affairs(1).

4231. **πραγματεύομαι pragmateuomai**; from *4229; to busy oneself:*— do business(1).

4232. **πραιτώριον praitōrion**; of Lat. or.; *Praetorium* (official residence of a governor), *praetorian guard:*— praetorian guard(1), Praetorium(7).

4233. **πράκτωρ praktōr**; from *4238; one who does* or *accomplishes:*— officer(2).

4234. **πρᾶξις praxis**; from *4238; a deed, function:*— action(1), deeds(2), function(1), practices(2).

4235. **πρᾶος praos**; var. reading for *4239b,* q.v.

4236. **πραότης praotēs**; var. reading for *4240,* q.v.

4237. **πρασιά prasia**; from **πράσον prason** *(a leek); a garden bed:*— groups(1).

4238. **πράσσω prassō**; a prim. vb.; *to do, practice:*— act(1), acted(1), attend(1), collect(1), collected(1), committed(3), deeds*(1), do(7), does(1), doing(2), done(6), performing(1), practice(9), practiced(2), practices(1), practicing(1).

4239a. **πραϋπαθία praupathia**; from *4239b* and *3958; meekness:*— gentleness(1).

4239b. **πραΰς praus**; of unc. or.; *gentle:*— gentle(4).

4240. **πραΰτης prautēs**; from *4239b; gentleness:*— consideration(1), gentleness(8), humility(1), meekness(1).

4241. **πρέπω prepō**; a prim. vb.; *to be fitting, proper, suitable:*— fitting(4), proper(3).

4242. **πρεσβεία presbeia**; from *4243; age, seniority:*— delegation(2).

4243. **πρεσβεύω presbeuō**; from the same as *4245; to be the elder, to take precedence:*— am an ambassador(1), ambassadors(1).

4244. **πρεσβυτέριον presbuterion**; from *4245; a body of elders:*— council of the elders(1), council of elders(1), presbytery(1).

4245. **πρεσβύτερος presbuteros**; a cptv. of **πρέσβυς presbus** *(an old man); elder:*— elder(3), elders(57), men of old(1), old men(1), older(1), older man(1), older ones(1), older women(1), women(1).

4246. **πρεσβύτης presbutēs**; from the same as *4245; an old man:*— aged(1), old man(1), older men(1).

4247. **πρεσβῦτις presbutis**; fem. of *4246; an aged woman:*— older women(1).

4248. **πρηνής prēnēs**; from a modified form of *4253; headlong:*— headlong(1).

4249. **πρίζω prizō**; alt. form of a prim. vb. **πρίω priō** *(to saw); to saw (in two):*— sawn in two(1).

4250. **πρίν prin**; a prim. adv. akin to *4253; before:*— before(13).

4251. **Πρίσκα Priska**; of Lat. or.; *Prisca,* a Chr. and the wife of Aquila:— Prisca(3), Priscilla(3).

4252. **Πρίσκιλλα Priskilla**; dim. of *4251* (indicating endearment); *Priscilla,* the same person as *Prisca.*

4253. **πρό pro**; a prim. prep.; *before:*— above(2), ago(4), ahead(2), ahead*(2), before(30), front(2), just outside(1), prior(1), right(1).

4254. **προάγω proagō**; from *4253* and *71; to lead forth, to go before:*— before(1), bring(1), bring...forward(1), brought(1), brought...before(1), former(1), get(1), go ahead(4), goes too far(1), going ahead(3), going before(1), led the way(1), previously made(1), walking on ahead(1), went in front(1), went on before(1).

4255. **προαιρέω proaireō**; from *4253* and *138; to bring forth* or *forward:*— purposed(1).

4256. **προαιτιάομαι proaitiaomai**; from *4253* and a der. of *156; to accuse beforehand:*— already charged(1).

4257. **προακούω proakouō**; from *4253* and *191; to hear beforehand:*— previously heard(1).

4258. **προαμαρτάνω proamartanō**; from *4253* and *264; to sin before:*— sinned in the past(2).

4259. **προαύλιον proaulion**; from *4253* and *833; a vestibule:*— porch(1).

4260. **προβαίνω probainō**; from *4253* and the same as *939; to go forward:*— advanced(3), going(1), going on...farther(1).

4261. **προβάλλω proballō**; from *4253* and *906; to throw before:*— put...forward(1), put forth(1).

4262. **προβατικός probatikos**; from *4263b; of sheep:*— sheep(1).

4263a. **προβάτιον probation**; dim. from *4263b; a little sheep:*— sheep(2).

4263b. **πρόβατον probaton**; from *4260; small animals* in a herd, esp. *sheep:*— sheep(36), sheep's(1).

4264. **προβιβάζω probibazō**; caus. form of *4260; to lead forward, lead on:*— prompted(1).

4265. **προβλέπω problepō**; from *4253* and *991; to foresee:*— provided(1).

4266. **προγίνομαι proginomai**; from *4253* and *1096; to happen before:*— previously committed(1).

4267. **προγινώσκω proginōskō**; from *4253* and *1097; to know beforehand:*— foreknew(2), foreknown(1), knowing...beforehand(1), known(1).

4268. **πρόγνωσις prognōsis**; from *4267; foreknowledge:*— foreknowledge(2).

4269. **πρόγονος progonos**; from *4266; born before:*— forefathers(1), parents(1).

4270. **προγράφω prographō**; from *4253* and *1125; to write before:*— beforehand marked(1), earlier times(1), publicly portrayed(1), written in earlier times(1), wrote before(1).

4271. **πρόδηλος prodēlos**; from *4253* and *1212; evident beforehand:*— evident(1), quite evident(2).

4272. **προδίδωμι prodidōmi**; from *4253* and *1325; to give before, give first:*— first given(1).

4273. **προδότης prodotēs**; from *4272; a betrayer:*— betrayers(1), traitor(1), treacherous(1).

4274. **πρόδρομος prodromos**; from *4390; a running forward, going in advance:*— forerunner(1).

4275a. **προεῖδον proeidon**; from *4253* and *1491a; to foresee:*— foreseeing(1), looked ahead(1).

4275b. **προεῖπον proeipon**; from *4253* and *1513a,* used as 2 aor. of *4302; to say before:*— foretold(2), forewarned(1), previously said(1), said before(3), spoken beforehand(2), told...in advance(2), told...before(1).

4276. **προελπίζω proelpizō**; from *4253* and *1679; to hope before:*— first to hope(1).

4277. (not used)

4278. **προενάρχομαι proenarchomai**; from *4253* and *1728; to begin before:*— first to begin(1), previously made(1), previously made a beginning(1).

4279. **προεπαγγέλλω proepaggellō**; from *4253* and *1861; to announce before:*— previously promised(1), promised beforehand(1).

4280. **προερέω proereō**; fut. of *4275b,* q.v.

4281. **προέρχομαι Proerchomai**; from *4253* and *2064; to go forward, go on:*— go(1), go on ahead(1), going ahead(1), gone on ahead(1), got there ahead(1), preceding(1), went...beyond(2), went along(1).

4282. **προετοιμάζω proetoimazō**; from *4253* and *2090; to prepare before:*— prepared beforehand(2).

4283. **προευαγγελίζομαι proeuaggelizomai**; from *4253* and *2097; to announce good news beforehand:*— gospel beforehand(1), preached the gospel beforehand(1).

4284. **προέχω proechō**; from *4253* and *2192; to hold before:*— better(1).

4285. **προηγέομαι proēgeomai**; from *4253* and *2233; to go before* (as a leader):— give preference(1).

4286. **πρόθεσις prothesis**; from *4388; a setting forth,* i.e. fig. *proposal,* spec. *the showbread, sacred* (bread):— consecrated(3), purpose(7), resolute(1), sacred(1).

4287. **προθεσμία prothesmia**; from **προθέσμιος prothesmios**; from *4253* and **θέσμιος thesmios** *(fixed, settled); appointed beforehand:*— date set(1).

4288. **προθυμία prothumia**; from *4289; eagerness:*— eagerness(1), readiness(4).

4289. **πρόθυμος prothumos**; from *4253* and *2372; willing, ready:*— eager(1), willing(2).

4290. **προθύμως prothumōs**; adv. from *4289; eagerly:*— eagerness(1).

4291a. **πρόϊμος proimos**; an alt. form of *4406; early:*— early(1).

4291b. **προΐστημι proistēmi**; from *4253* and *2476; to put before, to set over, to rule:*— engage(2), have charge over(1), leads(1), manage(1), managers(1), manages(1), rule(1).

4292. **προκαλέω prokaleō**; from *4253* and *2564; to call forth, challenge:*— challenging(1).

4293. **προκαταγγέλλω prokataggellō**; from *4253* and *2605; to announce beforehand:*— announced beforehand(1), previously announced(1).

4294. **προκαταρτίζω prokatartizō**; from *4253* and *2675; to make ready beforehand:*— arrange beforehand(1).

4295. **πρόκειμαι prokeimai**; from *4253* and *2749; to be set before, to be set forth:*— exhibited(1), present(1), set before(3).

4296. **προκηρύσσω prokērussō**; from *4253* and *2784; to proclaim* (by herald):— proclaimed(1).

4297. **προκοπή prokopē**; from *4298; progress:*— progress(3).

4298. **προκόπτω prokoptō**; from *4253* and *2875; to cut forward* (a way), *advance:*— advancing(1), almost gone(1), increasing(1), lead(1), make...progress(1), proceed(1).

4299. **πρόκριμα prokrima**; from a comp. of *4253* and *2919; a prejudice:*— bias(1).

4300. **προκυρόω prokuroō**; from *4253* and *2964; to establish beforehand:*— previously ratified(1).

4301. **προλαμβάνω prolambanō**; from *4253* and *2983; to take beforehand:*— beforehand(1), caught(1), takes...first(1).

4302. **προλέγω prolegō**; from *4253* and *3004; to say beforehand,* i.e. *to predict:*— forewarn(1), say in advance(1), telling...in advance(1).

4303. **προμαρτύρομαι promarturomai**; from *4253* and *3143; to say beforehand:*— predicted(1).

4304. **προμελετάω promeletaō**; from *4253* and *3191; to premeditate:*— prepare beforehand(1).

4305. **προμεριμνάω promerimnaō**; from *4253* and *3309; to be anxious beforehand:*— worry beforehand(1).

4306. **προνοέω pronoeō**; from *4253* and *3539; to foresee:*— have regard(1), provide(1), respect(1).

4307. **πρόνοια pronoia**; from *4306; foresight, forethought:*— providence(1), provision(1).

4308. **προοράω prooraō**; from *4253* and *3708; to see before:*— previously seen(1), saw(1).

4309. **προορίζω proorizō**; from *4253* and *3724; to predetermine, foreordain:*— predestined(6).

4310a. **προπάσχω propaschō**: from *4253* and *3958; to suffer before:*— already suffered(1).

4310b. **προπάτωρ propatōr**; from *4253* and *3962; a forefather:*— forefather(1).

4311. **προπέμπω propempō**; from *4253* and *3992; to send before, send forth:*— accompanying(1), escorted(1), help(1), helped on my journey(1), helped on my way(1), journey(1), send...on his way(1), send...on my way(1), send...on their way(2), way(1).

4312. **προπετής propetēs**; from a comp. of *4253* and *4098; falling forward, headlong:*— rash(1), reckless(1).

4313. **προπορεύομαι proporeuomai**; from *4253* and *4198; to make to go before, to cause to go before:*— go(1), go before(1).

4314. **πρός pros**; a prim. prep.; *advantageous for, at* (denotes local proximity), *toward* (denotes motion toward a place):— about(1), accord(1), according(1), across(1), against(21), among(5), around(2), because(2), before(9), beside(1), end(1), near(4), order(1), pertaining(4), promote(1), regard(1), so(5), terms(1), together*(1), toward(9), whispered*(1).

4315. **προσάββατον prosabbaton**; from *4253* and *4521; the day before the Sabbath:*— day before(1), day before the Sabbath(1).

4316. **προσαγορεύω prosagoreuō**; from *4314* and **ἀγορεύω agoreuō** *(to speak in the assembly); to address,* hence *to call by name:*— designated(1).

4317. **προσάγω prosagō**; from *4314* and *71; to bring* or *lead to:*— approaching(1), bring(2), brought(2).

4318. **προσαγωγή prosagōgē**; from *4317; a bringing to:*— access(2), introduction(1).

4319a. **προσαιτέω prosaiteō**; from *4314* and *154; to ask besides:*— beg(1).

4319b. **προσαίτης prosaitēs**; from *4319a; a beggar:*— beggar(2).

4320. **προσαναβαίνω prosanabainō**; from *4314* and *305; to go up besides:*— move(1).

4321. **προσαναλίσκω prosanaliskō**; from *4314* and *355; to spend besides.*

4322. **προσαναπληρόω prosanaplēroō**; from *4314* and *378; to fill up by adding to:*— fully supplied(1), fully supplying(1).

4323. **προσανατίθημι prosanatithēmi**; from *4314* and *394; to lay on besides,* hence *to undertake besides* (mid.):— consult(1), contributed(1).

4324. **προσαπειλέω prosapeileō**; from *4314* and *546; to threaten further:*— threatened...further(1).

4325. **προσδαπανάω prosdapanaō**; from *4314* and *1159; to spend besides:*— more...spend(1).

4326. **προσδέομαι prosdeomai**; from *4314* and *1189a; to want further:*— needed(1).

4327. **προσδέχομαι prosdechomai**; from *4314* and *1209; to receive to oneself:*— accepted(1), accepting(1), cherish(1), looking(3), receive(2), receives(1), waiting(5), waiting anxiously(1).

4328. **προσδοκάω prosdokaō**; from *4314* and **δοκεύω dokeuō** *(to watch); to await, expect:*— expect(2), expecting(2), look(4), looking(2), state of expectation(1), waited(1), waiting(2), watching(1).

4329. **προσδοκία prosdokia**; from *4328; expectation:*— expectation(1), expecting(1).

4330. **προσεάω proseaō**; from *4314* and *1439; to permit further:*— permit...to go farther(1).

4331. **προσεγγίζω proseggizō**; late or var. reading for *4374,* q.v.

4332. **προσεδρεύω prosedreuō**; var. reading for *3918a,* q.v.

4333. **προσεργάζομαι prosergazomai**; from *4314* and *2038b; to work besides, to gain besides:*— made...more(1).

4334. **προσέρχομαι proserchomai**; from *4314* and *2064; to approach, to draw near:*— agree(1), approached(2), approaching(1), came(64), came forward(2), come(2), comes(1), coming(3), draw near(4), go(1), visit(1), went(6).

4335. **προσευχή proseuchē**; from *4336; prayer:*— earnestly(1), place of prayer(2), prayer(20), prayers(14).

4336. **προσεύχομαι proseuchomai**; from *4314* and *2172; to pray:*— make...prayers(1), offer...prayers(2), pray(44), prayed(14), prayer(1), praying(24), prays(1).

4337. **προσέχω prosechō**; from *4314* and *2192; to hold to, turn to, attend to:*— addicted(1), beware(8), give attention(1), giving...attention(1), giving attention(2), guard(3), officiated(1), pay attention(2), pay...attention(1), paying attention(2), respond(1), take care(1).

4338. **προσηλόω prosēloō**; from *4314* and a der. of *2247; to nail to:*— nailed(1).

4339. **προσήλυτος prosēlutos**; from *4334; one who has arrived* (at Judaism), *a proselyte:*— proselyte(2), proselytes(2).

4340. **πρόσκαιρος proskairos**; from *4314* and *2540; in season,* i.e. *temporary:*— passing(1), temporal(1), temporary(2).

4341. **προσκαλέω proskaleo**; from *4314* and *2564; to call to:*— call(2), called(13), calling(3), summoned(8), summoning(3).

4342. **προσκαρτερέω proskartereō**; from *4314* and *2594; to attend constantly:*— continually devoting themselves(2), continued(1), continuing(1), devote ourselves(1), devote yourselves(1), devoted(1), devoting themselves(1), personal attendants(1), stand ready(1).

4343. **προσκαρτέρησις proskarterēsis**; from *4342; steadfastness:*— perseverance(1).

4344. **προσκεφάλαιον proskephalaion**; from a comp. of *4314* and a der. of *2776; a pillow:*— cushion(1).

4345. **προσκληρόω prosklēroō**; from *4314* and *2820; to allot to:*— joined(1).

4346a. **προσκλίνω prosklinō**; from *4314* and *2827; to cause to lean against:*— joined(1).

4346b. **πρόσκλισις prosklisis**; from *4346a; inclination:*— partiality(1).

4347. **προσκολλάω proskollaō**; from *4314* and *2853; to glue to,* fig. *to cleave to:*— joined(1).

4348. **πρόσκομμα proskomma**; from *4350; a stumbling, an occasion of stumbling:*— obstacle(1), offense(1), stumbling(3), stumbling block(1).

4349. **προσκοπή proskopē**; from *4350; an occasion of stumbling:*— cause for offense(1).

4350. **προσκόπτω proskoptō**; from *4314* and *2875; to strike against, to stumble:*— slammed against(1), strike(2), stumble(2), stumbled over(1), stumbles(2).

4351. **προσκυλίω proskuliō**; from *4314* and *2947; to roll to:*— rolled(2).

4352. **προσκυνέω proskuneō**; from *4314* and **κυνέω kuneō** *(to kiss); to do reverence to:*— bow down(1), bow down before(1), bowed down(1), bowed down before(2), bowing before(1), bowing down(1), prostrated himself before(1), worship(32), worshiped(17), worshipers(1), worshiping(1), worships(1).

4353. **προσκυνητής proskunētēs**; from *4352; a worshiper:*— worshipers(1).

4354. **προσλαλέω proslaleō**; from *4314* and *2980; to speak to:*— speak(1), speaking(1).

4355. **προσλαμβάνω proslambanō**; from *4314* and *2983; to take in addition:*— accept(3), accepted(2), received(1), taken(1), taking along(1), took(1), took...aside(3).

4356. **πρόσλημψις proslēmpsis**; from *4355; a receiving:*— acceptance(1).

4357. προσμένω prosmenō; from *4314* and *3306; to wait longer:*— continue(1), continues(1), remain(2), remained(3).

4358. προσορμίζω prosormizō; from *4314* and **ὅρμος hormos** *(an anchorage); to bring* (a ship) *to anchor at:*— moored(1).

4359. προσοφείλω prosopheilō; from *4314* and *3784; to owe besides:*— owe(1), well(1).

4360. προσοχθίζω prosochthizō; from *4314* and **ὀχθέω ochtheō** *(to be sorely angered); to be angry with:*— angry(2).

4361. πρόσπεινος prospeinos; from *4314* and the same as *3983; hungry:*— hungry(1).

4362. προσπήγνυμι prospēgnumi; from *4314* and *4078; to fasten to* (spec. to a cross):— nailed to a cross(1).

4363. προσπίπτω prospiptō; from *4314* and *4098; to fall upon, fall prostrate before:*— fall down before(1), fell(1), fell before(1), fell down(1), fell down before(3), slammed against(1).

4364. προσποιέω prospoieō; from *4314* and *4160; to attach to, take to oneself,* hence *to pretend:*— acted as though(1).

4365. προσπορεύομαι prosporeuomai; from *4314* and *4198; to come near:*— came(1).

4366. προσρήγνυμι prosrēgnumi; from *4314* and *4486; to break against:*— burst against(2).

4367. προστάσσω prostassō; from *4314* and *5021; to place at, give a command:*— appointed(1), commanded(5), ordered(1).

4368. προστάτις prostatis; fem. of a der. of *4291b; a patroness, protectress:*— helper(1).

4369. προστίθημι prostithēmi; from *4314* and *5087; to put to, add:*— add(2), added(6), adding(1), brought(1), further be spoken(1), increase(1), laid(1), more will be given...besides(1), proceeded(3), went(1).

4370. προστρέχω prostrechō; from *4314* and *5143; to run to:*— ran(2), running(1).

4371. προσφάγιον prosphagion; from *4314* and *5315a* ; *a relish* (eaten with bread), spec. *fish:*— fish(1).

4372. πρόσφατος prosphatos; from *4314* and a prim. root **φέν- phen-** *(to slay, kill); freshly slain,* generally *new:*— new(1).

4373. προσφάτως prosphatōs; adv. from *4372; recently:*— recently(1).

4374. προσφέρω prospherō; from *4314* and *5342; to bring to,* i.e. *to offer:*— bringing(2), brought(12), deals(1), get(1), make an offering(1), offer(8), offered(12), offering(4), offers(1), present(2), presented(1), presenting(1).

4375. προσφιλής prosphilēs; from *4314* and *5368; pleasing, agreeable:*— lovely(1).

4376. προσφορά prosphora; from *4374; an offering:*— offering(6), offerings(2), sacrifice(1).

4377. προσφωνέω prosphōneō; from *4314* and *5455; to call to:*— addressed(1), addressing(1), call(2), called(1), called...over(1), spoke(1).

4378. πρόσχυσις proschusis; from a comp. of *4314* and **χέω cheō** *(to pour); a pouring upon:*— sprinkling(1).

4379. προσψαύω prospsauō; from *4314* and **ψαύω psauō** *(to touch); to touch:*— touch(1).

4380. προσωπολημπτέω prosōpolēmpteō; from *4381; to have respect of persons:*— show partiality(1).

4381. προσωπολήμπτης prosōpolēmptēs; from *4383* and *2983; an accepter of a face,* i.e. *a respecter of persons:*— one to show partiality(1), show partiality(1).

4382. προσωποληмψία prosōpolēmpsia; from *4381; respect of persons:*— partiality(3), personal favoritism(1).

4383. πρόσωπον prosōpon; from *4314* and **ὤψ ōps** *(an eye, face); the face:*— ahead*(2), appearance(5), before*(2), coming*(1), face(37), faces(5), openly(1), outwardly*(1), partial*(3), partiality(1), people(1), person(1), persons(1), presence(11), sight(1).

4384. προτάσσω protassō; var. reading for *4367,* q.v.

4385. προτείνω proteinō; from *4253* and **τείνω teinō** *(to stretch); to stretch out:*— stretched(1).

4386. πρότερον proteron; adv. from *4387,* q.v.

4387. πρότερος proteros; cptv. adj. from *4253; before:*— before(2), first(2), first time(1), former(3), formerly(2), one(1), previously(1).

4388. προτίθημι protithēmi; from *4253* and *5087; to set before,* i.e. *propose:*— displayed publicly(1), planned(1), purposed(1).

4389. προτρέπω protrepō; from *4253* and the same as *5157; to turn forward, urge forward:*— encouraged(1).

4390. προτρέχω protrechō; from *4253* and *5143; to run forward,* i.e. *run in advance:*— ran(1), ran ahead(1).

4391. προϋπάρχω prouparchō; from *4253* and *5225; to exist beforehand:*— been*(1), before(1), formerly(1).

4392. πρόφασις prophasis; from *4253* and *5316; a pretense:*— appearance's sake(2), excuse(1), pretense(3), pretext(1).

4393. προφέρω propherō; from *4253* and *5342; to bring forth:*— brings forth(2).

4394. προφητεία prophēteia; from *4395; prophecy:*— prophecies(1), prophecy(15), prophesying(1), prophetic utterance(1), prophetic utterances(1).

4395. προφητεύω prophēteuō; from *4396; to foretell, tell forth, prophesy:*— prophesied(5), prophesies(3), prophesy(16), prophesying(3), prophetesses(1).

4396. προφήτης prophētēs; from a comp. of *4253* and *5346; a prophet* (an interpreter or forth-teller of the divine will):— prophet(63), prophets(81).

4397. προφητικός prophētikos; from *4396; prophetic:*— prophetic(1), prophets(1).

4398. προφῆτις prophētis; fem. of *4396; a prophetess:*— prophetess(2).

4399. προφθάνω prophthanō; from *4253* and *5348; to anticipate:*— first(1).

4400. προχειρίζω procheirizō; from a comp. of *4253* and *5495; to put into the hand, to take into one's hand,* hence *to determine:*— appoint(1), appointed(2).

4401. προχειροτονέω procheirotoneō; from *4253* and *5500; to appoint beforehand:*— chosen beforehand(1).

4402. Πρόχορος Prochoros; from *4253* and *5525; Prochorus,* a Chr. at Jer.:— Prochorus(1).

4403. πρύμνα prumna; fem. of **πρύμνος prumnos** *(the hindmost); the stern* (of a ship):— stern(3).

4404. πρωΐ prōi; adv. from *4253; early:*— early(4), early morning(1), morning(7).

4405. πρωΐα prōia; fem. of **πρώϊος prōios** *(at early morning); (early) morning.*

4406. πρώϊμος prōimos; var. reading for *4291a,* q.v.

4407. πρωϊνός prōinos; from *4404; at early morning:*— day(1), morning(3), breaking*(1).

4408. πρῷρα prōra; of unc. der.; the prow (of a ship):— bow(1), prow(1).

4409. πρωτεύω prōteuō; from *4413; to have the first place:*— have first place(1).

4410. πρωτοκαθεδρία prōtokathedria; from *4413* and *2515; the chief seat:*— chief seats(4).

4411. πρωτοκλισία prōtoklisia; from *4413* and *2828; the chief place* (at the table):— place of honor(2), places of honor(3).

4412. πρῶτον prōton; adv. from *4413,* q.v.

4413. πρῶτος prōtos; contr. superl. of *4253; first, chief:*— before(3), best(1), first(128), first of all(2), first importance(1), first man(1), first one(1), first things(1), first time(1), foremost(5), leading(2), leading man(1), leading men(5), outer(3), previous(1).

4414. πρωτοστάτης prōtostatēs; from *4413* and *2476; one who stands first* (of soldiers), hence *a leader:*— ringleader(1).

4415. πρωτοτόκια prōtotokia; from *4416a; the rights of the first-born:*— birthright(1).

4416a. πρωτότοκος prōtotokos; from *4413* and **τόκος tokos** *(childbirth, offspring);* from *5088; first-born:*— firstborn(8).

4416b. πρώτως prōtōs; adv. from *4413; first:*— first(1).

4417. πταίω ptaiō; a prim. word; *to cause to stumble, to stumble:*— stumble(4), stumbles(1).

4418. πτέρνα pterna; a prim. word; *the heel:*— heel(1).

4419. πτερύγιον pterugion; dim. of *4420; a little wing,* hence (anything like a wing) *a battlement:*— pinnacle(2).

4420. πτέρυξ pterux; from **πτερόν pteron** *(feather, bird's wing);* from *4072; a wing:*— wings(5).

4421. πτηνός ptēnos; from *4072; winged:*— birds(1).

4422. πτοέω ptoeō; a prim. word; *to terrify:*— startled(1), terrified(1).

4423. πτόησις ptoēsis; from *4422; a fluttering, excitement,* hence *terror:*— fear(1).

4424. Πτολεμαΐς Ptolemais; from **Πτολεμαῖος Ptolemaios** *(Ptolemy,* a king of Egypt); *Ptolemais,* a seaport south of Tyre:— Ptolemais(1).

4425. πτύον ptuon; a prim. word; *a winnowing shovel:*— winnowing fork(2).

4426. πτύρω pturō; of unc. or.; *to be frightened:*— alarmed(1).

4427. πτύσμα ptusma; from *4429; spittle:*— spittle(1).

4428. πτύσσω ptussō; a prim. vb.; *to fold,* i.e. *roll up:*— closed(1).

4429. πτύω ptuō; a prim. word; *to spit:*— spat(1), spitting(2).

4430. πτῶμα ptōma; from *4098; a fall,* hence *a misfortune, ruin:*— body(3), corpse(1), dead bodies(3).

4431. πτῶσις ptōsis; from *4098; a fall:*— fall(2).

4432. **πτωχεία ptōcheia**; from *4433; beggary,* i.e. *destitution:*— poverty(3).

4433. **πτωχεύω ptōcheuō**; from *4434; to be a beggar, be destitute:*— became(1).

4434. **πτωχός ptōchos**; adj. from **πτώσσω ptōssō** *(to crouch, cower);* (of one who crouches and cowers, hence) *beggarly, poor:*— poor(29), poor man(5), worthless(1).

4435. **πυγμή pugmē**; from **πύξ pux** *(the fist); the fist:*— carefully(1).

4436. **πύθων puthōn**; from **Πυθώ Puthō** *(Pytho,* an area of Greece); *Python,* a mythical serpent slain by Apollo, *divination:*— divination(1).

4437. **πυκνός puknos**; from the same as *4435; close,* i.e. *frequent:*— frequent(1), often(1), quite often(1).

4438. **πυκτεύω pukteuō**; from **πύκτης puktēs** *(a pugilist), to box:*— box(1).

4439. **πύλη pulē**; a prim. word; *a gate:*— gate(8), gates(2).

4440. **πυλών pulōn**; from *4439; a porch, gateway:*— gate(5), gates(12), gateway(1).

4441. **πυνθάνομαι punthanomai**; from a prim. root **πυθ- puth-**; *to inquire,* by impl. *to learn:*— ask(1), asking(2), inquire(4), inquired(2), inquiring(1), learned(1).

4442. **πῦρ pur**; a prim. word; *fire:*— burning(2), fiery(2), fire(69).

4443. **πυρά pura**; from *4442; a fire:*— fire(2).

4444. **πύργος purgos**; a prim. word; *a tower:*— tower(4).

4445. **πυρέσσω puressō**; from *4442; to be on fire, to be ill of a fever:*— fever(2).

4446. **πυρετός puretos**; from *4442; a fever:*— fever(6).

4447. **πύρινος purinos**; from *4442; fiery:*— fire(1).

4448. **πυρόω puroō**; from *4442; to set on fire,* i.e. *to burn* (pass.):— burn(1), burning(1), flaming(1), intense concern(1), made to glow(1), refined(1).

4449. **πυρράζω purrazō**; from *4450a; to be fiery red:*— red(2).

4450a. **πυρρός purros**; from *4442; fiery red:*— red(2).

4450b. **Πύρρος Purros**; prob. the same as *4450a; Pyrrhus,* the father of one of Paul's companions:— Pyrrhus(1).

4451. **πύρωσις purōsis**; from *4448; a burning,* hence *a refining:*— burning(2), fiery ordeal(1).

4452. **-πω -pō**; enclitic particle used as suffix or prefix, see *3369, 3380b, 3764, 3768,* and *4455.*

4453. **πωλέω pōleō**; a prim. word; *to exchange* or *barter, to sell:*— dealers(1), sell(7), selling(8), sells(1), sold(5).

4454. **πῶλος pōlos**; a prim. word; *a foal:*— colt(12).

4455. **πώποτε pōpote**; adv. from *4452* and *4218; ever yet:*— any time(3), never*(1), yet(1), yet...ever(1).

4456. **πωρόω pōroō**; from **πῶρος pōros** *(a stone, a callous); to petrify,* i.e. *to harden:*— hardened(5).

4457. **πώρωσις pōrōsis**; from *4456; a covering with a callous,* fig. *blindness:*— hardening(1), hardness(2).

4458. **πως pōs**; an enclitic particle from the same as *4459,* see also *1513b* and *3381; at all:*— perhaps(4), somehow(3).

4459. **πῶς pōs**; interrog. adv. from the same as *4214; how?:*— how(101), what(1), why(1).

Ρ

4460. **Ῥαάβ Rhaab**; of Heb. or. [7343]; *Rahab,* a Canaanitess and an ancestor of Christ:— Rahab(3).

4461. **ῥαββί rhabbi**; of Heb. or. [7227b]; *my master, my teacher:*— Rabbi(15).

4462. **ῥαββουνί rhabbouni**; of Ara. or., cf. [7227b]; *my master, my teacher:*— Rabboni(2).

4463. **ῥαβδίζω rhabdizō**; from *4464; to beat with a rod:*— beaten with rods(2).

4464. **ῥάβδος rhabdos**; a prim. word; *a staff, rod:*— rod(5), scepter(2), staff(5).

4465. **ῥαβδοῦχος rhabdouchos**; from *4464* and *2192, a rod holder,* i.e. (a Roman) *lictor* (one holding the rod of office):— policemen(2).

4466. **Ῥαγαύ Rhagau**; of Heb. or. [7466a]; *Reu,* an ancestor of Christ:— Reu(1).

4467. **ῥᾳδιούργημα rhadiourgēma**; from a comp. of **ῥᾴδιος rhadios** *(easy, reckless)* and *2041; a reckless act, a crime:*— crime(1).

4468. **ῥᾳδιουργία rhadiourgia**; from the same as *4467; ease in doing, laziness, recklessness,* hence *wickedness:*— fraud(1).

4469. **ῥακά rhaka**; of Ara. or. [7387]; *empty* (an expression of contempt):— good-for-nothing(1).

4470. **ῥάκος rhakos**; a prim. word; *a rag:*— cloth(2).

4471. **Ῥαμά Rhama**; of Heb. or. [7414]; *Ramah,* a city N. of Jer.:— Ramah(1).

4472. **ῥαντίζω rhantizō**; from **ῥαίνω rhainō** *(to sprinkle); to sprinkle:*— cleanse(1), sprinkled(3), sprinkling(1).

4473. **ῥαντισμός rhantismos**; from *4472; sprinkling:*— sprinkled(2).

4474. **ῥαπίζω rhapizō**; from a der. of *4464; to strike with a rod,* hence *to strike with the palm of the hand:*— slapped(1), slaps(1).

4475. **ῥάπισμα rhapisma**; from *4474; a blow* (with a stick or the palm of the hand):— slaps(2), struck*(1).

4476. **ῥαφίς rhaphis**; from **ῥάπτω rhaptō** *(to sew); a needle:*— needle(2).

4477. **Ῥαχάβ Rhachab**; from the same as *4460,* q.v.

4478. **Ῥαχήλ Rhachēl**; of Heb. or. [7354]; *Rachel,* the wife of Jacob:— Rachel(1).

4479. **Ῥεβέκκα Rhebekka**; of Heb. or. [7259]; *Rebecca,* the wife of Isaac:— Rebekah(1).

4480. **ῥέδη rhedē**; of Gallic or.; *a chariot:*— chariots(1).

4481. **Ῥεμφάν Rhemphan**; var. reading for *4501a,* q.v.

4482. **ῥέω rheō**; a prim. vb.; *to flow:*— flow(1).

4483. (not used)

4484. **Ῥήγιον Rhēgion**; of Lat. or.; *Rhegium,* a city in southern Italy:— Rhegium(1).

4485. **ῥῆγμα rhēgma**; from *4486; a fracture,* hence *a ruin:*— ruin(1).

4486. **ῥήγνυμι rhēgnumi**; prol. vb. from a prim. root **ρηγ- rēg-**; *to break apart,* by ext. *to throw down:*— break forth(1), burst(3), slammed(1), slams(1), tear...to pieces(1).

4487. **ῥῆμα rhēma**; from a modified form of *2046; a word,* by impl. *a matter:*— charge(1), discourse(1), fact(2), matters(1), message(2), nothing*(1), remark(1), say(1), say say(1), saying(1), sayings(3), statement(6), thing(2), things(4), word(18), words(22).

4488. **Ῥησά Rhēsa**; prob. of Heb. or.; *Rhesa,* an Isr.:— Rhesa(1).

4489. **ῥήτωρ rhētōr**; from a modified form of *2046; a public speaker:*— attorney(1).

4490. **ῥητῶς rhētōs**; adv. from **ῥητός rhētos** *(stated); in stated terms:*— explicitly(1).

4491. **ῥίζα rhiza**; a prim. word; *a root:*— root(16), roots(1).

4492. **ῥιζόω rhizoō**; from *4491; to cause to take root:*— firmly rooted(1), rooted(1).

4493. **ῥιπή rhipē**; from *4496;* any rapid movement, spec. *a twinkling* (of lights or the eye):— twinkling(1).

4494. **ῥιπίζω rhipizō**; from **ῥιπίς rhipis** *(a fan); to fan,* generally *to make a breeze:*— tossed by the wind(1).

4495. **ῥιπτέω rhipteō**; see *4496.*

4496. **ῥίπτω rhiptō**; a prim. vb.; *to throw, cast,* spec. *to throw off, toss:*— cast(1), dispirited(1), laid...down(1), threw(2), throwing off(1), thrown(1), had thrown...down(1).

4497. **Ῥοβοάμ Rhoboam**; of Heb. or. [7346]; *Rehoboam,* a king of Judah:— Rehoboam(2).

4498. **Ῥόδη Rhodē**; from **ῥόδον rhodon** *(a rose); Rhoda,* a servant girl:— Rhoda(1).

4499. **Ῥόδος Rhodos**; prob. from the same as *4498; Rhodes,* an island in the Mediterranean:— Rhodes(1).

4500. **ῥοιζηδόν rhoizēdon**; adv. from **ῥοῖζος rhoizos** *(the whistling of an arrow); with a rushing sound:*— roar(1).

4501a. **Ῥομφά Rhompha**; of Eg. or.; *Rompha, Rephan,* the name of an Eg. god:— Rompha(1).

4501b. **ῥομφαία rhomphaia**; of for. or.; *a large broad sword,* generally *a sword:*— sword(7).

4502. **Ῥουβήν Rhoubēn**; of Heb. or. [7205]; *Reuben,* a son of Jacob, also a tribe of Isr.:— Reuben(1).

4503. **Ῥούθ Rhouth**; of Heb. or. [7327]; *Ruth,* a Moabitess and an ancestor of Christ:— Ruth(1).

4504. **Ῥοῦφος Rhouphos**; of Lat. or.; "red," *Rufus,* a Chr. at Rome:— Rufus(2).

4505. **ῥύμη rhumē**; prob. akin to **ῥεῦμα rheuma** *(that which flows, current);* from *4482; the rush* (of a moving body), hence *a* (crowded) *street:*— lanes(1), street(2), streets(1).

4506. **ῥύομαι rhuomai**; akin to **ἐρύω eruō** *(to drag); to draw to oneself,* i.e. *deliver:*— deliver(3), delivered(1), Deliverer(1), rescue(3), rescued(7), rescues(1), set...free(1).

4507a. **ῥυπαίνω rhupainō**; from *4509; to make filthy:*— filthy(1).

4507b. **ῥυπαρία rhuparia**; from *4508;* fig. *filthiness:*— filthiness(1).

4508. **ῥυπαρός rhuparos**; from *4509; filthy:*— dirty(1), filthy(1).

4509. **ῥύπος rhupos**; a prim. word; *filth:*— dirt(1).

4510. **ῥυπόω rhupoō**; var. reading for *4507a,* q.v.

4511. **ῥύσις rhusis**; from *4482; a flowing:*— hemorrhage*(3).

4512. **ῥυτίς rhutis**; prob. from **ῥυσός rhusos** *(shrivelled, wrinkled); a wrinkle:*— wrinkle(1).

4513. **Ῥωμαϊκός Rhōmaikos**; var. reading for *4515* q.v.

4514. **Ῥωμαῖος Rhōmaios**; from *4516; Roman:*— Roman(5), Romans(6), Rome(1).

4515. **Ῥωμαϊστί Rhōmaisti**; adv. from *4514; in Latin:*— Latin(1).

4516. **Ῥώμη Rhōmē**; of Lat. or.; *Rome,* the capital of Italy and the Rom. Empire (named after Romulus, the legendary founder):— Rome(8).

4517. **ῥώννυμι rhōnnumi**; prob. from **ῥώομαι rhōomai** *(to move with speed); to strengthen, be strong:*— farewell(1).

Σ

4518. **σαβαχθάνι sabachthani**; of Ara. or. [7662] with pron. suff.; *you have forsaken me:*— sabachthani(2).

4519. **σαβαώθ sabaōth**; of Heb. or. [6635] in fem. pl.; *Sabaoth,* i.e. *armies:*— Sabaoth(2).

4520. **σαββατισμός sabbatismos**; from a der. of *4521; a sabbath rest:*— Sabbath rest(1).

4521. **σάββατον sabbaton**; of Heb. or. [7676]; *the Sabbath,* i.e. *the seventh day* (of the week):— Sabbath(58), Sabbaths(1), week(9).

4522. **σαγήνη sagēnē**; of unc. or.; *a dragnet:*— dragnet(1).

4523. **Σαδδουκαῖος Saddoukaios**; prob. of Heb. or. [6659]; *a Sadducee,* a member of a Jewish religious sect:— Sadducees(14).

4524. **Σαδώκ Sadōk**; of Heb. or. [6659]; *Zadok,* an Isr.:— Zadok(2).

4525. **σαίνω sainō**; a prim. vb.; *to wag the tail,* hence *to greet, flatter, disturb:*— disturbed(1).

4526. **σάκκος sakkos**; perh. of Phoenician or.; *sackcloth:*— sackcloth(4).

4527. **Σαλά Sala**; of Heb. or. [7974]; *Shelah,* an ancestor of Christ, also *Salmon,* an ancestor of Christ:— Shelah(1).

4528. **Σαλαθιήλ Salathiēl**; of Heb. or. [7597]; *Shealtiel,* an Isr.:— Shealtiel(3).

4529. **Σαλαμίς Salamis**; perh. akin to *4535; Salamis,* the chief city of Cyprus:— Salamis(1).

4530. **Σαλείμ Saleim**; prob. from the same as *4532; Salim,* a place in Pal.:— Salim(1).

4531. **σαλεύω saleuō**; from *4535; to agitate, shake,* by ext. *to cast down:*— agitating(1), shake(1), shaken(11), shaken together(1), shook(1).

4532. **Σαλήμ Salēm**; of Heb. or. [8004]; *Salem,* the home of Melchizedek:— Salem(2).

4533. **Σαλμών Salmōn**; of Heb. or. [8012]; *Salmon,* an Isr.:— Salmon(3).

4534. **Σαλμώνη Salmōnē**; of unc. or.; *Salmone,* a promontory of Crete:— Salmone(1).

4535. **σάλος salos**; a prim. word; *a tossing,* spec. *the swell* (of the sea):— waves(1).

4536. **σάλπιγξ salpigx**; from *4537; a trumpet:*— bugle(1), trumpet(8), trumpets(2).

4537. **σαλπίζω salpizō**; of unc. or.; *to sound a trumpet:*— sound(3), sound a trumpet(1), sounded(7), trumpet will sound(1).

4538. **σαλπιστής salpistēs**; from *4537; a trumpeter:*— trumpeters(1).

4539. **Σαλώμη Salōmē**; of Heb. or. [8004]; *Salome,* the mother of the apostles James and John:— Salome(2).

4540. **Σαμάρεια Samareia**; of Heb. or. [8111]; *Samaria,* the name of both a city and a region in Pal.:— Samaria(11).

4541. **Σαμαρίτης Samaritēs**; from *4540; a Samaritan,* an inhab. of the region of Samaria:— Samaritan(3), Samaritans(6).

4542. **Σαμαρῖτις Samaritis**; fem. of *4541;* (the region of) *Samaria, a Samaritan woman:*— Samaritan(2).

4543. **Σαμοθράκη Samothrakē**; from *4544* and **Θράκη Thrakē** *(Thrace);* "Samos of Thrace," *Samothrace,* an island in the Aegean:— Samothrace(1).

4544. **Σάμος Samos**; of unc. or.; *Samos,* an island in the Aegean:— Samos(1).

4545. **Σαμουήλ Samouēl**; of Heb. or. [8050]; *Samuel,* a prophet and judge in Isr.:— Samuel(3).

4546. **Σαμψών Sampsōn**; of Heb. or. [8123]; *Samson,* a judge in Isr.:— Samson(1).

4547. **σανδάλιον sandalion**; dim. of **σάνδαλον sandalon** *(a wooden sole, sandal); a sandal:*— sandals(2).

4548. **σανίς sanis**; a prim. word; *a board:*— planks(1).

4549. **Σαούλ Saoul**; of Heb. or. [7586]; *Saul,* the first Isr. king, also the Jewish name of Paul:— Saul(9).

4550. **σαπρός sapros**; from *4595; rotten, worthless:*— bad(7), unwholesome(1).

4551. **Σαπφίρη Sapphirē**; of Ara. or., cf. [5601]; *Sapphira,* a Chr. woman:— Sapphira(1).

4552. **σάπφιρος sapphiros**; of Semitic or., cf. [5601]; *sapphire,* perh. *lapis lazuli:*— sapphire(1).

4553. **σαργάνη sarganē**; of unc. or., cf. [8276]; *a plaited rope,* hence *a hamper, basket:*— basket(1).

4554. **Σάρδεις Sardeis**; of unc. or.; *Sardis,* the chief city of Lydia:— Sardis(3).

4555. **σάρδινος sardinos**; var. reading for *4556,* q.v.

4556. **σάρδιον sardion**; of unc. or.; *sard, a sardian* (stone):— sardius(2).

4557. **σαρδόνυξ sardonux**; from *4556* and **ὄνυξ onux** *(a gem); sardonyx:*— sardonyx(1).

4558. **Σάρεπτα Sarepta**; of Heb. or. [6886]; *Sarepta,* a city near Sidon:— Zarephath(1).

4559. **σαρκικός sarkikos**; from *4561; pertaining to the flesh, carnal:*— flesh(1), fleshly(4), material things(2).

4560. **σάρκινος sarkinos**; from *4561; of the flesh:*— flesh(1), human(1), men of flesh(1), physical(1).

4561. **σάρξ sarx**; a prim. word; *flesh:*— bodily(1), bodily condition(1), body(2), earth(1), earthly(1), fellow countrymen(1), flesh(129), fleshly(4), life(3), man(1), mankind(1), nation(1), personally(1).

4562. **Σαρούχ Sarouch**; var. reading for *4588b,* q.v.

4563. **σαρόω saroō**; from **σαίρω sairō** *(to sweep); to sweep:*— sweep(1), swept(2).

4564. **Σάρρα Sarra**; of Heb. or. [8283]; *Sarah,* the wife of Abraham:— Sarah(3), Sarah's(1).

4565. **Σάρων Sarōn**; of Heb. or. [8289]; *Sharon,* a plain in Pal.:— Sharon(1).

4566. **Σατάν Satan**; var. reading for *4567,* q.v.

4567. **Σατανᾶς Satanas**; of Heb. or. [7854]; *the adversary, Satan,* i.e. *the devil:*— Satan(35), Satan's(1).

4568. **σάτον saton**; of Ara. or., cf. [5429]; *seah, a* (Heb.) *measure* (equiv. to about one and a half pecks):— pecks(2).

4569. **Σαῦλος Saulos**; a modified form of *4549; Saul,* the Jewish name of the apostle Paul:— Saul(15).

4570. **σβέννυμι sbennumi**; a prim. vb.; *to quench:*— extinguish(1), going(1), put(1), quench(1), quenched(4).

4571. **σέ se**; acc. sing. of *4771,* q.v.

4572. **σεαυτοῦ seautou**; refl. pron. from *4771* and *846; of (to, for) yourself:*— own conviction(1), own self(1), yourself(38).

4573. **σεβάζομαι sebazomai**; from a der. of *4576; to fear,* spec. *to have reverential awe:*— worshiped(1).

4574. **σέβασμα sebasma**; from *4573; an object of worship:*— object of worship(1), objects of...worship(1).

4575. **σεβαστός sebastos**; from *4573; reverend, august,* hence *Augustus,* a Rom. emperor:— Augustan(1), Emperor(1), Emperor's(1).

4576. **σέβω sebō**; a prim. vb.; *to worship:*— devout(1), God-fearing(3), worship(4), worshiper(2).

4577. **σειρά seira**; var. reading for *4618a,* q.v.

4578. **σεισμός seismos**; from *4579; a commotion, shaking:*— earthquake(10), earthquakes(3), storm(1).

4579. **σείω seiō**; a prim. vb.; *to shake:*— shake(1), shaken(1), shook(2), stirred(1).

4580. **Σεκοῦνδος Sekoundos**; of Lat. or.; "second," *Secundus,* a Chr. of Thessalonica:— Secundus(1).

4581. **Σελεύκεια Seleukeia**; from **Σέλευκος Seleukos** *(Seleucus,* a Syrian king); *Seleucia,* a city of Syria:— Seleucia(1).

4582. **σελήνη selēnē**; from **σέλας selas** *(a bright flame); the moon:*— moon(9).

4583. **σεληνιάζομαι selēniazomai**; from *4582; to be moonstruck,* spec. *be epileptic* (supposedly influenced by the moon):— epileptics(1), lunatic(1).

4584. **Σεμεΐν Semein**; of Heb. or. [8096]; *Semein,* an Isr.:— Semein(1).

4585. **σεμίδαλις semidalis**; of unc. or.; *fine wheat flour:*— fine flour(1).

4586. **σεμνός semnos**; from *4576; reverend,* i.e. *venerable,* spec. *serious:*— dignified(2), honorable(1), men of dignity(1).

4587. **σεμνότης semnotēs**; from *4586; seriousness:*— dignified(1), dignity(2).

4588a. **Σέργιος Sergios**; of Lat. or.; *Sergius,* a Rom. proconsul of Cyprus:— Sergius(1).

4588b. **Σερούχ Serouch**; of Heb. or. [8286]; *Serug,* an ancestor of Christ:— Serug(1).

4589. **Σήθ Sēth**; of Heb. or. [8352]; *Seth,* a son of Adam:— Seth(1).

4590. **Σήμ Sēm**; of Heb. or. [8035]; *Shem,* a son of Noah:— Shem(1).

4591. **σημαίνω sēmainō**; from **σῆμα sēma** *(a sign, mark); to give a sign:*— communicated(1), indicate(3), signifying(2).

4592. **σημεῖον sēmeion**; from the same as *4591; a sign:*— distinguishing mark(1), miracle(2), sign(35), signs(39).

4593. **σημειόω sēmeioō**; from *4592; to mark, note:*— take special note(1).

4594. **σήμερον sēmeron**; adv. from *2250* with a prefixed **σ- s-** (from a prim. stem meaning *this); today:*— last night(1), this(1), this day(6), this very(2), today(29), today's(1), very(1).

4595. **σήπω sēpō**; a prim. vb.; *to make corrupt,* pass. *become corrupt:*— rotted(1).

4596. **σηρικός sērikos**; var. reading for *4617b,* q.v.:— silk(1).

4597. **σής sēs**; a prim. word; *a moth:*— moth(3).

4598. **σητόβρωτος sētobrōtos**; from *4597* and *977; moth-eaten:*— moth-eaten(1).

4599. **σθενόω sthenoō**; from **σθένος sthenos** *(strength); to strengthen:* strengthen(1).

4600. **σιαγών siagōn**; of unc. or.; *a jawbone,* by impl. *cheek:*— cheek(2).

4601. **σιγάω sigaō**; from *4602; to keep silent, to keep secret:*— became silent(1), keep silent(3), kept secret(1), kept silent(2), quiet(1), silent(1), stopped speaking(1).

4602. **σιγή sigē**; a prim. word; *silence:*— hush(1), silence(1).

4603. **σίδηρος sidēros**; a prim. word; *iron:*— iron(5).

4604. **σιδηροῦς sidērous**; from *4603; of iron:*— iron(1).

4605. **Σιδών Sidōn**; of Heb. or. [6721]; *Sidon,* a maritime city of Phoenicia:— Sidon(9).

4606. **Σιδώνιος Sidōnios**; adj. from *4605; of Sidon:*— Sidon(2).

4607. **σικάριος sikarios**; of Lat. or., *sica (a dagger); an assassin:*— Assassins(1).

4608. **σίκερα sikera**; of Heb. or. [7941]; *fermented liquor:*— liquor(1).

4609. **Σιλᾶς Silas**; of Ara. or.; *Silas,* a fellow missionary of Paul:— Silas(13).

4610. **Σιλουανός Silouanos**; a Lat. form of *4609;* "sylvan," *Silvanus,* alt. form of the name Silas:— Silvanus(4).

4611. **Σιλωάμ Silōam**; of Heb. or. [7975a]; *Siloam,* a pool in Jer.:— Siloam(3).

4612. **σιμικίνθιον simikinthion**; of Lat. or.; (a workman's) *apron:*— aprons(1).

4613. **Σίμων Simōn**; of unc. or.; *Simon,* the name of several Isr.:— Simon(71), Simon Simon(1), Simon's(5).

4614. **Σινά Sina**; of Heb. or. [5514]; *Sinai,* a mountain prob. on the Sinai Peninsula:— Sinai(4).

4615. **σίναπι sinapi**; of Eg. or.; *mustard* (a plant):— mustard(5).

4616. **σινδών sindōn**; of unc. der.; fine linen cloth:— linen cloth(4), linen sheet(2).

4617a. **σινιάζω siniazō**; from **σινίον sinion** *(a sieve); to sift:*— sift(1).

4617b. **σιρικός sirikos**; from **σηρικός sērikos**; from **Σήρ Sēr** (the *Seres,* i.e. the Chinese people, from whom silk was obtained); *Seric,* i.e. *silk.*

4618a. **σιρός siros**; a prim. word; *a pit* (for grain storage):— pits(1).

4618b. **σιτευτός siteutos**; from a der. of *4621; well-fed,* i.e. *fattened:*— fattened(3).

4619a. **σιτίον sition**; dim. of *4621; grain:*— grain(1).

4619b. **σιτιστός sitistos**; from a der. of *4621; fattened:*— fattened livestock(1).

4620. **σιτομέτριον sitometrion**; from a comp. of *4621* and *3354; a measured portion of food:*— rations(1).

4621. **σῖτος sitos**; a prim. word; *grain:*— grain(2), wheat(12).

4622. **Σιών Siōn**; of Heb. or. [6726]; *Zion,* a mountain of Jer. or the city of Jer.:— Zion(7).

4623. **σιωπάω siōpaō**; from **σιωπή siōpē** *(silence); to be silent:*— become silent(1), hush(1), kept silent(4), quiet(2), silent(2).

4624. **σκανδαλίζω skandalizō**; from *4625; to put a snare* (in the way), hence *to cause to stumble, to give offense:*— cause(1), cause...to stumble(2), causes(2), causes...to stumble(6), fall away(7), falls away(1), led into sin(1), makes...stumble(2), offend(1), offended(1), stumble(3), stumbling(1), take(1), take offense(1), took offense(2).

4625. **σκάνδαλον skandalon**; of unc. or.; *a stick for bait* (of a trap), generally *a snare, a stumbling block, an offense:*— cause for stumbling(1), hindrances(1), offense(2), stumbling block(7), stumbling blocks(4).

4626. **σκάπτω skaptō**; from a prim. root **σκαφ- skaph-**; *to dig:*— dig(2), dug(1).

4627. **σκάφη skaphē**; from *4626; anything scooped out,* spec. *a light boat:*— boat(3).

4628. **σκέλος skelos**; a prim. word; *the leg* (from the hip down):— legs(3).

4629. **σκέπασμα skepasma**; from **σκεπάζω skepazō** *(to cover); a covering:*— covering(1).

4630. **Σκευᾶς Skeuas**; perh. of Lat. or.; *Sceva,* a Jewish chief priest:— Sceva(1).

4631. **σκευή skeuē**; from *4632; equipment:*— tackle(1).

4632. **σκεῦος skeuos**; a prim. word; *a vessel, implement,* pl. *goods:*— article(2), container(1), goods(1), instrument(1), jar(1), merchandise(1), object(3), property(2), sea anchor(1), someone(1), vessel(3), vessels(6).

4633. **σκηνή skēnē**; a prim. word; *a tent:*— dwellings(1), tabernacle(15), tabernacles(3), tents(1).

4634. **σκηνοπηγία skēnopēgia**; from *4633* and *4078; the setting up of tents:*— feast of Booths(1).

4635. **σκηνοποιός skēnopoios**; from *4633* and *4160; making tents:*— tent-makers(1).

4636. **σκῆνος skēnos**; from *4633; a tent,* fig. for *the body:*— tent(2).

4637. **σκηνόω skēnoō**; from *4633; to have one's tent, dwell:*— dwell(3), dwelt(1), spread His tabernacle(1).

4638. **σκήνωμα skēnōma**; from *4637; a tent:*— dwelling(2), dwelling place(1).

4639. **σκιά skia**; a prim. word; *shadow:*— shade(1), shadow(6).

4640. **σκιρτάω skirtaō**; from **σκαίρω skairō** *(to skip); to leap:*— leap(1), leaped(2).

4641. **σκληροκαρδία sklērokardia**; from *4642* and *2588; hardness of heart:*— hardness of heart(3).

4642. **σκληρός sklēros**; from **σκέλλω skellō** *(to dry); hard, rough:*— difficult(1), hard(2), harsh things(1), strong(1).

4643. **σκληρότης sklērotēs**; from *4642; hardness:*— stubbornness(1).

4644. **σκληροτράχηλος sklērotrachēlos**; from *4642* and *5137; stiff-necked:*— stiff-necked(1).

4645. **σκληρύνω sklērunō**; from *4642; to harden:*— becoming hardened(1), harden(3), hardened(1), hardens(1).

4646. **σκολιός skolios**; a prim. word; *curved, winding,* hence *crooked:*— crooked(2), perverse(1), unreasonable(1).

4647. **σκόλοψ skolops**; a prim. word; anything pointed, spec. *a stake, thorn:*— thorn(1).

4648. **σκοπέω skopeō**; from *4649; to look at, contemplate:*— keep your eye on(1), look(2), looking(1), observe(1), watch(1).

4649. **σκοπός skopos**; from **σκέπτομαι skeptomai** *(to look carefully, consider); a watchman, a mark* (on which to fix the eye):— goal(1).

4650. **σκορπίζω skorpizō**; of unc. or.; *to scatter:*— scattered(2), scatters(3).

4651. **σκορπίος skorpios**; of unc. or.; *a scorpion:*— scorpion(2), scorpions(3).

4652. **σκοτεινός skoteinos**; from *4655; dark:*— dark(1), full of darkness(2).

4653. **σκοτία skotia**; from *4655; darkness:*— dark(3), darkness(14).

4654. **σκοτίζω skotizō**; from *4655; to darken:*— darkened(5).

4655. **σκότος skotos**; a prim. word; *darkness:*— darkness(30).

4656. **σκοτόω skotoō**; from *4655; to darken:*— darkened(3).

4657. **σκύβαλον skubalon**; of unc. or.; *refuse:*— rubbish(1).

4658. **Σκύθης Skuthēs**; of unc. or.; *a Scythian,* an inhab. of Scythia (considered the wildest of barbarians):— Scythian(1).

4659. **σκυθρωπός skuthrōpos**; from **σκυθρός skuthros** *(sullen)* and **ὤψ ōps** *(eye); with a gloomy look:*— gloomy face(1), looking sad(1).

4660. **σκύλλω skullō**; a prim. vb.; *to skin,* fig. *to trouble:*— distressed(1), trouble(3).

4661. **σκῦλον skulon**; perh. from *4660; arms stripped from a foe,* i.e. *spoils:*— plunder(1).

4662. **σκωληκόβρωτος skōlēkobrōtos**; from *4663* and *977; eaten by worms:*— eaten by worms(1).

4663. **σκώληξ skōlēx**; of unc. or.; *a worm:*— worm(3).

4664. **σμαράγδινος smaragdinos**; from *4665; of emerald, emerald green:*— emerald(1).

4665. **σμάραγδος smaragdos**; of unc. or.; *an emerald:*— emerald(1).

4666. **σμύρνα smurna**; of for. or.; *myrrh* (used as an ointment and for embalming):— myrrh(2).

4667. **Σμύρνα Smurna**; the same as *4666;* "myrrh," *Smyrna,* an Ionian city in Asia Minor:— Smyrna(2).

4668. **Σμυρναῖος Smurnaios**; from *4667; of Smyrna.*

4669. **σμυρνίζω smurnizō**; from *4666; to be like myrrh, to mingle with myrrh:*— mixed with myrrh(1).

4670. **Σόδομα Sodoma**; of Heb. or. [5467]; *Sodom,* an unidentified city in the Jordan Valley:— Sodom(9).

4671. **σοί soi**; dat. of *4771,* q.v.

4672. Σολομών Solomōn; of Heb. or. [8010]; *Solomon,* a son of David and king of Isr.:— Solomon(11), Solomon's(1).

4673. σορός soros; a prim. word; *a cinerary urn,* by anal. *a coffin:*— coffin(1).

4674. σός sos; poss. pron. from *4771; your:*— people(1), yours(9).

4675. σοῦ sou; gen. of *4771,* q.v.

4676. σουδάριον soudarion; of Lat. or.; *a handkerchief, a head cloth* (for the dead):— cloth(1), face-cloth(1), handkerchief(1), handkerchiefs(1).

4677. Σουσάννα Sousanna; of Heb. or. [7799]; "lily," *Susanna,* one of the women accompanying Jesus on His journeys:— Susanna(1).

4678. σοφία sophia; from *4680; skill, wisdom:*— cleverness(1), learning(1), wisdom(49).

4679. σοφίζω sophizō; from *4680; to make wise:*— cleverly devised(1), give...wisdom(1).

4680. σοφός sophos; a prim. word; *skilled, wise:*— wise(16), wise man(2), wise men(1), wiser(1).

4681. Σπανία Spania; of for. or.; *Spain,* a peninsula of S.W. Europe:— Spain(2).

4682. σπαράσσω sparassō; akin to **σπαίρω spairō** *(to gasp); to mangle, convulse:*— throwing...into...convulsions(2), throws...into a convulsion(1).

4683. σπαργανόω sparganoō; from **σπάργανον sparganon** *(a swathing band); to wrap in swaddling clothes:*— wrapped...in cloths(1), wrapped in cloths(1).

4684. σπαταλάω spatalaō; from **σπατάλη spatalē** *(lewdness, luxury); to live riotously:*— gives herself(1), led a life of wanton pleasure(1), wanton pleasure(1).

4685. σπάω spaō; a prim. vb.; *to draw* (a sword):— drew(2).

4686. σπεῖρα speira; of Lat. or.; anything wound up or coiled, by ext. *a body* (of soldiers), i.e. *a cohort:*— cohort(7).

4687. σπείρω speirō; a prim. vb.; *to sow* (seed):— sow(13), sowed(6), sower(5), sower sows(1), sowing(1), sown(17), sows(8).

4688. σπεκουλάτωρ spekoulatōr; of Lat. or.; *a scout,* by ext. *an executioner:*— executioner(1).

4689. σπένδω spendō; a prim. vb.; *to pour out* (as a drink offering), *to make a libation:*— drink offering(2), poured out as a drink(2).

4690. σπέρμα sperma; from *4687; that which is sown,* i.e. *seed:*— children(7), conceive*(1), descendant(4), descendants(16), posterity(1), seed(10), seeds(4).

4691. σπερμολόγος spermologos; from *4690* and **λέγω legō** *(to pick out,* same vb. as *3004* but with a different mean.); *a seed picker,* fig. *one who picks up scraps of knowledge:*— idle babbler(1).

4692. σπεύδω speudō; a prim. word; *to hasten, urge on:*— hastening(1), hurried(1), hurry(2), hurrying(1), make haste(1).

4693. σπήλαιον spēlaion; from **σπέος speos** *(a cave); a cave:*— cave(1), caves(2), den(3).

4694. σπιλάς spilas; a prim. word; *a ledge of rock* (over which the sea dashes), i.e. *a reef:*— hidden reefs(1).

4695. σπιλόω spiloō; from *4696; to stain, defile:*— defiles(1), polluted(1).

4696. σπίλος spilos; a prim. word; *a spot, stain:*— spot(1), stains(1).

4697. σπλαγχνίζομαι splagchnizomai; from *4698; to be moved in the inward parts,* i.e. *to feel compassion:*— feel compassion(2), felt compassion(7), moved with compassion(2), take pity(1).

4698. σπλάγχνον splagchnon; of unc. or.; *the inward parts* (heart, liver, lungs, etc.), fig. *the emotions:*— affection(3), affections(1), heart(4), hearts(1), intestines(1), tender(1).

4699. σπόγγος spoggos; a prim. word; *a sponge:*— sponge(3).

4700. σποδός spodos; a prim. word; *ashes:*— ashes(3).

4701. σπορά spora; from *4687; a sowing,* by impl. *seed:*— seed(1).

4702. σπόριμος sporimos; from *4687; sown,* i.e. *a sown field:*— grainfields(3).

4703. σπόρος sporos; from *4687; a sowing,* i.e. *seed* (sown):— seed(5).

4704. σπουδάζω spoudazō; from *4710; to make haste,* hence *to give diligence:*— diligent(6), eager(2), make every effort(3).

4705. σπουδαῖος spoudaios; from *4710; hasty, eager, diligent:*— diligent(2), earnest(1).

4706. σπουδαιότερον spoudaioteron; adv. from the cptv. of *4705,* var. reading for *4709,* q.v.

4707. σπουδαιότερος spoudaioteros; cptv. of *4705,* q.v.

4708. σπουδαιοτέρως spoudaioterōs; adv. from *4707,* another reading for *4709,* q.v.

4709. σπουδαίως spoudaiōs; adv. from *4705; with haste, diligently:*— all the more eagerly(1), diligently(1), eagerly(1), earnestly(1), more eagerly(1).

4710. σπουδή spoudē; from *4692; haste, diligence:*— diligence(4), earnestness(5), effort(1), hurry(2).

4711. σπυρίς spuris; of unc. or.; *a* (large, flexible) *basket* (for carrying provisions):— large basket(1), large baskets(4).

4712. στάδιον stadion; from the same as *2476; a stadium* (a Gr. measure of length), by impl. *a racecourse:*— distance(1), miles(5), race(1).

4713. στάμνος stamnos; from the same as *2476; an earthen jar* (for racking off wine):— jar(1).

4714a. στασιαστής stasiastēs; from **στασιάζω stasiazō** *(to rebel); a rebel, revolutionist:*— insurrectionists(1).

4714b. στάσις stasis; from *2476; a standing,* by impl. *an insurrection,* fig. *strife:*— dissension(4), insurrection(3), riot(1), standing(1).

4715. στατήρ statēr; from the same as *2476; a stater* (a coin):— shekel(1).

4716. σταυρός stauros; from the same as *2476; an upright stake,* hence *a cross* (the Rom. instrument of crucifixion):— cross(27).

4717. σταυρόω stauroō; from *4716; to fence with stakes, to crucify:*— crucified(29), crucifixion(1), crucify(16).

4718. σταφυλή staphulē; of unc. or.; *a bunch of grapes:*— grapes(3).

4719. στάχυς stachus; a prim. word; *a head of grain:*— head(2), heads(2), heads of grain(1).

4720. Στάχυς Stachus; the same as *4719; Stachys,* a Chr. at Rome:— Stachys(1).

4721. στέγη stegē; from *4722; a roof:*— roof(3).

4722. στέγω stegō; a prim. word; *to cover closely* (so as to keep water out), generally *to bear up under:*— bears(1), endure(3).

4723. στεῖρα steira; from **στεῖρος steiros** *(barren); barren:*— barren(3), barren woman(1).

4724. στέλλω stellō; a prim. vb.; *to arrange, prepare, gather up,* hence *to restrain:*— keep away(1), taking precaution(1).

4725. στέμμα stemma; from the same as *4735; a wreath:*— garlands(1).

4726. στεναγμός stenagmos; from *4727; a groaning:*— groanings(1), groans(1).

4727. στενάζω stenazō; from **στένω stenō** *(to moan, sigh, groan); to groan* (within oneself):— complain(1), deep sigh(1), grief(1), groan(3).

4728. στενός stenos; a prim. word; *narrow:*— narrow(2), small(1).

4729. στενοχωρέω stenochōreō; from *4728* and *5562; to be made narrow, to compress:*— crushed(1), restrained(2).

4730. στενοχωρία stenochōria; from *4728* and **χῶρος chōros** *(space); narrowness of space,* fig. *difficulty:*— difficulties(1), distress(2), distresses(1).

4731. στερεός stereos; a prim. word; *hard, firm:*— firm(2), solid(2).

4732. στερεόω stereoō; from *4731; to make firm, strengthen:*— strengthened(3).

4733. στερέωμα stereōma; from *4732; a solid body, a support, strength, firmness:*— stability(1).

4734. Στεφανᾶς Stephanas; of unc. der., perh. a modified form of *4736;* "crowned," *Stephanas,* a Chr. at Corinth:— Stephanas(3).

4735. στέφανος stephanos; from **στέφω stephō** *(to encircle); that which surrounds,* i.e. *a crown:*— crown(14), crowns(3), wreath(1).

4736. Στέφανος Stephanos; the same as *4735;* "crown," *Stephen,* the first Chr. martyr:— Stephen(7).

4737. στεφανόω stephanoō; from *4735; to crown:*— crowned(2), win the prize(1).

4738. στῆθος stēthos; a prim. word; *the breast:*— bosom(2), breast(1), breasts(1), chests(1).

4739. στήκω stēkō; from the perf. tense of *2476; to stand,* spec. *stand firm:*— stand(2), stand firm(4), standing(1), standing firm(2), stands(2).

4740. στηριγμός stērigmos; from *4741; a setting firmly, steadfastness:*— steadfastness(1).

4741. στηρίζω stērizō; akin to **στῆριγξ stērigx** *(support, prop); to make fast, establish:*— confirm(1), determined(1), establish(2), established(2), fixed(1), strengthen(6), strengthening(1).

4742a. στιβάς stibas; from **στείβω steibō** *(to tread under foot); a bed of leaves* or *rushes:*— leafy branches(1).

4742b. στίγμα stigma; from **στίζω stizō** *(to prick); a tattoo mark* or *brand:*— brand-marks(1).

4743. στιγμή stigmē; from the same as *4742b; a point,* i.e. *a moment:*— moment(1).

4744. στίλβω stilbō; a prim. vb.; *to shine:*— radiant(1).

4745. στοά stoa; a prim. word; *a portico:*— portico(3), porticoes(1).

4746a. στοιβάς stoibas; var. reading for *4742a,* q.v.

4746b. Στοϊκός Stoikos; from *4745; Stoic,* i.e. belonging to the Stoic school of thought.

4747. **στοιχεῖον stoicheion**; from the same as *4748; one of a row,* hence *a letter* (of the alphabet), by ext. *the elements* (of knowledge):— elemental things(2), elementary principles(2), elementary*(1), elements(2), principles(1).

4748. **στοιχέω stoicheō**; from **στοῖχος stoichos** *(a row); to be in rows,* fig. *to walk by rule:*— follow(1), living(1), walk(2), walk orderly(1).

4749. **στολή stolē**; from *4724; equipment, apparel:*— long robes(2), robe(3), robes(4).

4750. **στόμα stoma**; a prim. word; *the mouth:*— edge(2), face(4), lips(1), mouth(60), mouths(5), say*(1), testimony(1), utterance(1), voice(1), words(1).

4751. **στόμαχος stomachos**; from *4750; an opening, the stomach:*— stomach(1).

4752. **στρατεία strateia**; from *4754; a campaign, expedition,* hence *warfare:*— fight(1), warfare(1).

4753. **στράτευμα strateuma**; from *4754; an expedition, an army, a company of soldiers:*—armies(4), army(1), soldiers(1), troops(2).

4754. **στρατεύω strateuō**; from **στρατός stratos** *(an encamped army); to make war,* hence *to serve as a soldier:*— active service(1), fight(1), serves as a soldier(1), soldier in active service(1), soldiers(1), wage war(2), war(1).

4755. **στρατηγός stratēgos**; from the same as *4754* and from *71; a general, governor:*— captain(3), chief magistrates(5), officers(2).

4756. **στρατιά stratia**; from the same as *4754; an army:*— host(2).

4757. **στρατιώτης stratiōtēs**; from *4756; a soldier:*— soldier(4), soldiers(21), soldiers'(1).

4758. **στρατολογέω stratologeō**; from the same as *4754* and *3004* (in the sense of *pick up* or *choose*); *to enlist soldiers:*— enlisted...as a soldier(1).

4759. (not used)

4760. **στρατόπεδον stratopedon**; from the same as *4754* and **πέδον pedon** *(ground, a site); a military camp,* i.e. *an army:*— armies(1).

4761. **στρεβλόω strebloō**; from **στρεβλός streblos** *(twisted); to twist:*— distort(1).

4762. **στρέφω strephō**; a prim. vb.; *to turn,* i.e. *to change:*— converted(2), returned(1), turn(3), turned(8), turned away(1), turned back(1), turning(5).

4763. **στρηνιάω strēniaō**; from the same as *4764; to run riot:*— lived sensuously(2).

4764. **στρῆνος strēnos**; from **στρηνής strēnēs** *(hard, strong); insolent luxury:*— sensuality(1).

4765. **στρουθίον strouthion**; dim. of **στρουθός strouthos** *(a sparrow); a sparrow:*— sparrows(4).

4766. **στρωννύω strōnnuō**; from a prim. root **στορ- stor-**; *to spread:*— furnished(2), make...bed(1), spread(2), spreading(1).

4767. **στυγητός stugētos**; from **στυγέω stugeō** *(to hate); hateful:*— hateful(1).

4768. **στυγνάζω stugnazō**; from **στυγνός stugnos** *(hated, gloomy);* from *4767; to have a gloomy appearance:*— saddened(1), threatening(1).

4769. **στῦλος stulos**; a prim. word; *a pillar:*— pillar(2), pillars(2).

4770. **Στωϊκός Stōikos**; var. reading for *4746b,* q.v.:— Stoic(1).

4771. **σύ su**; second pers. sing. pers. pron.; *you* (early mod. Eng. *thou):*— number(1), yours(17), yourself(4), yourselves(20), yourselves*(3).

4772. **συγγένεια suggeneia**; from *4773a; kinship,* hence *kinfolk, relatives:*— relatives(3).

4773a. **συγγενής suggenēs**; from *4862* and *1085; congenital,* hence *akin to,* subst. *a kinsman, relative:*— kinsman(1), kinsmen(3), relative(1), relatives(6).

4773b. **συγγενίς suggenis**; fem. from *4773a; a kinswoman:*— relative(1).

4774. **συγγνώμη suggnōmē**; from *4862* and *1097; confession, fellow feeling:*— concession(1).

4775. **συγκάθημαι sugkathēmai**; from *4862* and *2521; to sit together* or *with:*— sitting(2).

4776. **συγκαθίζω sugkathizō**; from *4862* and *2523; to make to sit together, to sit together:*— sat down together(1), seated(1).

4777. **συγκακοπαθέω sugkakopatheō**; from *4862* and *2553; to bear evil treatment along with:*— join with...in suffering(1), suffer hardship(1).

4778. **συγκακουχέομαι sugkakoucheomai**; from *4862* and *2558; to endure adversity with* (pass.):— endure ill-treatment(1).

4779. **συγκαλέω sugkaleō**; from *4862* and *2564; to call together:*— called...together(2), called together(3), calls together(2), summoned(1).

4780. **συγκαλύπτω sugkaluptō**; from *4862* and *2572; to cover completely:*— covered(1).

4781. **συγκάμπτω sugkamptō**; from *4862* and *2578; to bend together:*— bend(1).

4782. **συγκαταβαίνω sugkatabainō**; from *4862* and *2597; to go down with:*— go(1).

4783. **συγκατάθεσις sugkatathesis**; from *4784; a putting down together,* i.e. *agreement:*— agreement(1).

4784. **συγκατατίθημι sugkatatithēmi**; from *4862* and *2698; to deposit together,* hence *to agree with:*— consented(1).

4785. **συγκαταψηφίζομαι sugkatapsēphizomai**; from *4862* and a comp. of *2596* and *5585; to condemn with,* spec. *to vote* (one) *a place among:*— added(1).

4786. **συγκεράννυμι sugkerannumi**; from *4862* and *2767; to mix together,* hence *to agree with:*— composed(1), united(1).

4787. **συγκινέω sugkineō**; from *4862* and *2795; to move together,* fig. *to stir up:*— stirred(1).

4788. **συγκλείω sugkleiō**; from *4862* and *2808; to shut together,* i.e. *enclose:*— enclosed(1), shut(3).

4789. **συγκληρονόμος sugklēronomos**; from *4862* and *2818; a co-inheritor:*— fellow heir(1), fellow heirs(3).

4790. **συγκοινωνέω sugkoinōneō**; from *4862* and *2841; to have fellowship with:*— participate(2), share(1).

4791. **συγκοινωνός sugkoinōnos**; from *4862* and *2844; partaking jointly of:*— fellow partaker(2), partaker(1), partakers(1).

4792. **συγκομίζω sugkomizō**; from *4862* and *2865; to bring together,* spec. *to take up* (a body for burial):— buried(1).

4793. **συγκρίνω sugkrinō**; from *4862* and *2919; to combine, compare:*— combining(1), compare(2).

4794. **συγκύπτω sugkuptō**; from *4862* and *2955; to bend forwards, bow down:*— bent double(1).

4795. **συγκυρία sugkuria**; from a comp. of *4862* and **κυρέω kureō** *(to happen); chance:*— chance(1).

4796. **συγχαίρω sugchairō**; from *4862* and *5463; to rejoice with:*— rejoice(3), rejoices(1), rejoicing(1), share...joy(2).

4797. **συγχέω sugcheō** or **συγχύννω sugchunnō**; from *4862* and **χέω cheō** *(to pour); to pour together,* i.e. *to confuse, throw into confusion:*— bewildered(1), confounding(1), confusion(2), stir(1).

4798. **συγχράομαι sugchraomai**; from *4862* and *5530; to use together with,* fig. *to associate with:*— have...dealings(1).

4799. **σύγχυσις sugchusis**; from *4797; confusion:*— confusion(1).

4800. **συζάω suzaō**; from *4862* and *2198; to live with:*— live(2), live together(1).

4801. **συζεύγνυμι suzeugnumi**; from *4862* and the same as *2218; to yoke together:*— joined together(2).

4802. **συζητέω suzēteō**; from *4862* and *2212; to examine together,* hence *to dispute:*— argue(1), argued(1), arguing(3), debated(1), discuss(1), discussing(3).

4803. **συζήτησις suzētēsis**; from *4802; disputation:*— dispute(1).

4804. **συζητητής suzētētēs**; from *4802; a disputer:*— debater(1).

4805. **σύζυγος suzugos**; from *4801; a yokefellow:*— companion(1).

4806. **συζωοποιέω suzōopoieō**; from *4862* and *2227; to make alive together with:*— alive together(2), made...alive together(2).

4807. **συκάμινος sukaminos**; of Heb. or. [8256]; *the mulberry tree, the sycamine:*— mulberry tree(1).

4808. **συκῆ sukē**; from *4810; a fig tree:*— fig tree(16).

4809. **συκομορέα sukomorea**; from *4810* and **μόρον moron** *(the black mulberry); the fig-mulberry tree, sycamore fig:*— sycamore tree(1).

4810. **σῦκον sukon**; a prim. word; *a fig:*— figs(4).

4811. **συκοφαντέω sukophanteō**; from *4810* and *5316; to accuse falsely:*— accuse...falsely(1), defrauded(1).

4812. **συλαγωγέω sulagōgeō**; from the same as *4813* and *71; to carry off as spoil:*— takes...captive(1).

4813. **συλάω sulaō**; from **σύλη sulē** *(booty); to plunder:*— robbed(1).

4814. **συλλαλέω sullaleō**; from *4862* and *2980; to talk together:*— conferred(1), discussed(1), talking(4).

4815. **συλλαμβάνω sullambanō**; from *4862* and *2983; to collect,* i.e. *to take,* by impl. *to take part with,* spec. *to conceive:*— arrest(3), arrested(4), became pregnant(1), conceive(1), conceived(3), help(2), seized(1), taken(1).

4816. **συλλέγω sullegō**; from *4862* and *3004; to collect:*— gather(4), gathered(3), gathering(1).

4817. **συλλογίζομαι sullogizomai**; from *4862* and *3049; to reckon, to compute,* i.e. *to reason:*— reasoned(1).

4818. **συλλυπέω sullupeō**; from *4862* and *3076; to be moved to grief with* (pass.):— grieved(1).

4819. **συμβαίνω sumbainō**; from *4862* and the same as *939; to come together,* i.e. (of events) *to come to pass:*— came(1), happen(1), happened(3), happening(1), taken place(1).

4820. **συμβάλλω sumballō**; from *4862* and *906; to throw together,* hence *to discuss, consider, meet with:*— confer(1), conversing(1), helped(1), meet(1), met(1), pondering(1).

4821. **συμβασιλεύω sumbasileuō**; from *4862* and *936; to reign with:*— reign(2).

4822. **συμβιβάζω sumbibazō**; from *4862* and the caus. form of the same as *939; to join together,* hence *to consider,* by ext. *to teach:*— concluded(1), concluding(1), held(1), held together(1), instruct(1), knit together(1), proving(1), together*(1).

4823. **συμβουλεύω sumbouleuō**; from *4862* and *1011; to take counsel together, advise:*— advise(1), advised(1), plotted together(2).

4824. **συμβούλιον sumboulion**; from *4825; counsel,* by impl. *a council:*— conferred*(2), conspired*(1), conspiring(1), consultation(1), consulted*(1), council(1), plotted together(1), together(2).

4825. **σύμβουλος sumboulos**; from *4862* and *1012; a counselor:*— counselor(1).

4826. **Συμεών Sumeōn**; of Semitic or., cf. [8095]; *Symeon, Simeon,* the name of several Isr., also a tribe of Isr.:— Simeon(6).

4827. **συμμαθητής summathētēs**; from a comp. of *4862* and *3101; a fellow disciple:*— fellow disciples(1).

4828. **συμμαρτυρέω summartureō**; from *4862* and *3140; to testify* or *bear witness with:*— bearing witness(1), testifies(2).

4829. **συμμερίζω summerizō**; from *4862* and *3307; to have a share in* (mid.):— have...share(1).

4830. **συμμέτοχος summetochos**; from *4862* and *3353; partaking with,* subst. *a joint partaker:*— fellow partakers(1), partakers(1).

4831. **συμμιμητής summimētēs**; from *4862* and *3402; a fellow imitator:*— following...example(1), join*(1).

4832a. **συμμορφίζω summorphizō**; from *4832b; to conform to:*— conformed(1).

4832b. **σύμμορφος summorphos**; from *4862* and *3444; conformed to:*— conformed(1), conformity(1).

4833. **συμμορφόω summorphoō**; var. reading for *4832a,* q.v.

4834. **συμπαθέω sumpatheō**; from *4835; to have a fellow feeling with,* i.e. *sympathize with:*— showed sympathy(1), sympathize(1).

4835. **συμπαθής sumpathēs**; from *4862* and *3958; sympathetic:*— sympathetic(1).

4836. **συμπαραγίνομαι sumparaginomai**; from *4862* and *3854; to be present together:*— came together(1).

4837. **συμπαρακαλέω sumparakaleō**; from *4862* and *3870; to exhort together,* pass. *to be strengthened with:*— encouraged together(1).

4838. **συμπαραλαμβάνω sumparalambanō**; from *4862* and *3880; to take along with:*— along(1), take(1), take...along(1), taking along(1), taking...along(1).

4839. **συμπαραμένω sumparamenō**; var. reading for *3887,* q.v.

4840. **συμπάρειμι sumpareimi**; from *4862* and *3918b; to be present together:*— here present(1).

4841. **συμπάσχω sumpaschō**; from *4862* and *3958; to suffer with:*— suffer(2).

4842. **συμπέμπω sumpempō**; from *4862* and *3992; to send with:*— sent(1), sent along(1).

4843. **συμπεριλαμβάνω sumperilambanō**; from *4862* and a comp. of *4012* and *2983; to enclose, embrace:*— embracing(1).

4844a. **συμπίνω sumpinō**; from *4862* and *4095; to drink with:*— drank(1).

4844b. **συμπίπτω sumpiptō**; from *4862* and *4098; to fall together:*— collapsed(1).

4845. **συμπληρόω sumplēroō**; from *4862* and *4137; to fill up completely,* hence *to fulfill:*— approaching(1), come(1), swamped(1).

4846. **συμπνίγω sumpnigō**; from *4862* and *4155; to choke:*— choke(2), choked(2), pressing against(1).

4847. **συμπολίτης sumpolitēs**; from *4862* and *4177; a fellow citizen:*— fellow citizens(1).

4848. **συμπορεύομαι sumporeuomai**; from *4862* and *4198; to journey together,* hence *to come together:*— gathered(1), going along(2), traveling(1).

4849. **συμπόσιον sumposion**; from *4844a; a drinking party, company* (guests at a party):— groups(1).

4850. **συμπρεσβύτερος sumpresbuteros**; from *4862* and *4245; a fellow elder:*— fellow elder(1).

4851a. **συμφέρω sumpherō**; from *4862* and *5342; to bring together, to be profitable:*— advantage(2), better(4), brought...together(1), common good(1), expedient(2), good(1), profitable(4).

4851b. **σύμφορος sumphoros**; from *4851a; profitable, useful:*— benefit(1), profit(1).

4852. **σύμφημι sumphēmi**; from *4862* and *5346; to say together,* i.e. *consent:*— agree(1).

4853. **συμφυλέτης sumphuletēs**; from *4862* and *5443; a fellow tribesman* or *countryman:*— countrymen(1).

4854. **σύμφυτος sumphutos**; from *4855; congenital,* hence *united with:*— united(1).

4855. **συμφύω sumphuō**; from *4862* and *5453; to grow together* (pass.):— grew(1).

4856. **συμφωνέω sumphōneō**; from *4859; to call out with, to be in harmony,* generally *to agree:*— agree(3), agreed(1), agreed together(1), match(1).

4857. **συμφώνησις sumphōnēsis**; from *4856; agreement:*— harmony(1).

4858. **συμφωνία sumphōnia**; from *4859; symphony,* i.e. *music:*— music(1).

4859. **σύμφωνος sumphōnos**; from *4862* and *5456; calling out together,* i.e. *agreeing:*— agreement(1).

4860. **συμψηφίζω sumpsēphizō**; from *4862* and *5585; to reckon together:*— counted(1).

4861. **σύμψυχος sumpsuchos**; from *4862* and *5590; of one mind:*— united in spirit(1).

4862. **σύν sun**; a prim. prep.; *with, together with* (expresses association with):— accompanied(1), accompanied*(1), accompany*(2), along(10), associates(2), besides*(1), companions*(2), including(1), together(1).

4863. **συνάγω sunagō**; from *4862* and *71; to lead together,* i.e. *bring together,* hence *come together* (pass.), *entertain:*— assemble(1), assembled(5), came together(1), convened(1), gather(10), gather...together(2), gather together(1), gathered(9), gathered...together(3), gathered together(14), gathered...together(1), gathering(3), gathering together(1), invite(2), invited(1), met(2), store(2).

4864. **συναγωγή sunagōgē**; from *4863; a bringing together,* by ext. *an assembling,* hence *a synagogue:*— assembly(1), synagogue(31), synagogues(24).

4865. **συναγωνίζομαι sunagōnizomai**; from *4862* and *75; to strive with:*— strive together(1).

4866. **συναθλέω sunathleō**; from *4862* and *118; to strive with:*— shared...struggle(1), striving together(1).

4867. **συναθροίζω sunathroizō**; from *4862* and *120a*; to gather together:— gathered together(2).

4868. **συναίρω sunairō**; from *4862* and *142; to take up together,* i.e. *settle accounts:*— settle(2), settled(1).

4869. **συναιχμάλωτος sunaichmalōtos**; from *4862* and *164; a fellow prisoner:*— fellow prisoner(2), fellow prisoners(1).

4870. **συνακολουθέω sunakoloutheō**; from *4862* and *190; to follow along with:*— accompanied(1), accompany(1), following(1).

4871a. **συναλίζω sunalizō**; from *4862* and **ἁλίζω halizō** *(to gather together); to assemble with:*— gathering...together(1).

4871b. **συναλλάσσω sunallassō**; from *4862* and *236; to reconcile:*— reconcile(1).

4872. **συναναβαίνω sunanabainō**; from *4862* and *305; to go up with:*— came(2).

4873. **συνανάκειμαι sunanakeimai**; from *4862* and *345; to recline with* (at table):— dining(2), dinner guests(2), reclining(2), table(1).

4874. **συναναμίγνυμι sunanamignumi**; from *4862* and a comp. of *303* and *3396; to mix up together,* hence *to associate with:*— associate(3).

4875. **συναναπαύομαι sunanapauomai**; from *4862* and the mid. of *373; to lie down to rest with,* fig. *to be refreshed in spirit with:*— find...rest(1).

4876. **συναντάω sunantaō**; from *4862* and **ἀντάω antaō** *(to come opposite, meet face to face); to meet with,* hence *to befall:*— happen(1), meet(1), met(4).

4877. **συνάντησις sunantēsis**; late or var. reading for *5222,* q.v.

4878. **συναντιλαμβάνομαι sunantilambanomai**; from *4862* and *482; to take hold with at the side,* hence *to take a share in,* generally *to help:*— help(1), helps(1).

4879. **συναπάγω sunapagō**; from *4862* and *520; to lead away with,* fig. *to be carried away with* (pass.):— associate(1), carried away(2).

4880. **συναποθνήσκω sunapothnēskō**; from *4862* and *599; to die with:*— die(1), die together(1), died(1).

4881. **συναπόλλυμι sunapollumi**; from *4862* and *622; to destroy with,* mid. *to perish together:*— perish along(1).

4882. **συναποστέλλω sunapostellō**; from *4862* and *649; to send along with:*— sent(1).

4883. **συναρμολογέω sunarmologeō**; from *4862* and a comp. of *719* and *3004* (in the sense of *to pick up*); *to fit together:*— fitted(1), fitted together(1), together*(1).

4884. **συναρπάζω sunarpazo**; from *4862* and *726; to seize and carry away:*— caught(1), dragged...away(1), dragging along(1), seized(1).

4885. **συναυξάνω sunauxanō**; from *4862* and *837; to cause to grow together,* pass. *to grow together:*— grow together(1).

συνβ- sunb-; see **συμβ- sumb-**.

συνγ- sung-; see **συγγ- sugg-**.

4886. **σύνδεσμος sundesmos**; from *4887; that which binds together,* i.e. *a bond:*— bond(1), bond of unity(1), bondage(1), ligaments(1).

4887. **συνδέω sundeō**; from *4862* and *1210; to bind together:*— prison(1).

4888. **συνδοξάζω sundoxazō**; from *4862* and *1392; to join in approving,* hence *to glorify together:*— glorified(1).

4889. **σύνδουλος sundoulos**; from *4862* and *1401; a fellow servant:*— fellow bond-servant(2), fellow servant(2), fellow servants(1), fellow slave(2), fellow slaves(3).

4890. **συνδρομή sundromē**; from *4936; a running together,* i.e. *a concourse* (esp. of a riotous gathering):— rushed together(1).

4891. **συνεγείρω sunegeirō**; from *4862* and *1453; to raise together:*— raised(3).

4892. **συνέδριον sunedrion**; from *4862* and the same as *1476; a sitting together,* hence *a council,* spec. *the Sanhedrin:*— council(19), courts(2), supreme court(1).

4893. **συνείδησις suneidēsis**; from *4894; consciousness,* spec. *conscience:*— conscience(24), conscience'(4), consciences(1), consciousness(1).

4894. **συνεῖδον suneidon**; from *4862* and *1491a; to see together,* hence *to comprehend:*— aware(1), realized(1).

4895. **σύνειμι suneimi**; from *4862* and *1510; to be with.*

4896. **σύνειμι suneimi**; from *4862* and **εἶμι eimi** *(to go); to come together:*— coming together(1).

4897. **συνεισέρχομαι suneiserchomai**; from *4862* and *1525; to enter together:*— entered(2).

4898. **συνέκδημος sunekdēmos**; from *4862* and a comp. of *1537* and *1218; a fellow traveler:*— travel(1), traveling companions(1).

4899. **συνεκλεκτός suneklektos**; from *4862* and *1586; chosen together with:*— chosen together(1).

4900. **συνελαύνω sunelaunō**; var. reading for *4871b,* q.v.

4901. **συνεπιμαρτυρέω sunepimartureō**; from *4862* and *1957; to testify* or *bear witness together with.*

4902a. **συνεπιτίθημι sunepitithēmi**; from *4862* and *2007; to help in putting on:*— joined in the attack(1).

4902b. **συνέπομαι sunepomai**; from *4862* and a prim. vb. **ἕπομαι hepomai** *(to follow); to follow with:*— accompanied(1).

4903. **συνεργέω sunergeō**; from *4904; to work together:*— causes to work(1), helps in the work(1), work together(1), worked(1), working(1), working together(1).

4904. **συνεργός sunergos**; from *4862* and the same as *2041; a fellow worker:*— fellow worker(6), fellow workers(6), workers(1).

4905. **συνέρχομαι sunerchomai**; from *4862* and *2064; to come together,* by ext. *to accompany:*— accompanied(2), assemble(2), assembled(3), assembles(1), came(3), came together(3), come(1), come together(7), coming together(1), gathered(1), gathered together(1), gathering(1), go(1), gone(1), meet(1), went(1).

4906. **συνεσθίω sunesthiō**; from *4862* and *2068; to eat with:*— ate(2), eat(2), eats(1).

4907. **σύνεσις sunesis**; from *4920; a running together,* spec. *understanding:*— cleverness(1), insight(1), understanding(5).

4908. **συνετός sunetos**; from *4920; intelligent:*— clever(1), intelligence(1), intelligent(2).

4909. **συνευδοκέω suneudokeō**; from *4862* and *2106; to join in approving:*— approve(1), approving(1), consents(2), give hearty approval(1), hearty agreement(1).

4910. **συνευωχέομαι suneuōcheomai**; from *4862* and **εὐωχέω euōcheō** *(to entertain sumptuously, feast); to entertain together,* pass. *feast together:*— carouse(1), feast(1).

4911. **συνεφίστημι sunephistēmi**; from *4862* and *2186; to place over, rise together:*— rose up together(1).

4912. **συνέχω sunechō**; from *4862* and *2192; to hold together, to hold fast,* pass. *to be seized* (by illness):— afflicted(1), controls(1), covered(1), crowding(1), devoting...completely(1), distressed(1), gripped(1), hard-pressed(1), hem(1), holding...in custody(1), suffering(2).

συνζ- sunz-; see **συζ- suz-**.

4913. **συνήδομαι sunēdomai**; from *4862* and the same as *2237; to rejoice together:*— joyfully concur(1).

4914. **συνήθεια sunētheia**; from *4862* and *2239; habit, habitual use:*— accustomed(1), custom(1), practice(1).

4915. **συνηλικιώτης sunēlikiōtēs**; from *4862* and *2244; one of the same age:*— contemporaries(1).

4916. **συνθάπτω sunthaptō**; from *4862* and *2290; to bury with:*— buried(2).

4917. **συνθλάω sunthlaō**; from *4862* and **θλάω thlaō** *(to crush); to crush together:*— broken to pieces(2).

4918. **συνθλίβω sunthlibō**; from *4862* and *2346; to press together:*— pressing(2).

4919. **συνθρύπτω sunthruptō**; from *4862* and **θρύπτω thruptō** *(to break in pieces); to break in pieces, crush:*— breaking(1).

4920. **συνίημι suniēmi**; from *4862* and **ἵημι hiēmi** *(to send); to set together,* fig. *to understand:*— gained...insight(1), understand(17), understanding(1), understands(2), understood(5).

4921. **συνίστημι sunistēmi** and **συνίστανω sunistanō**; from *4862* and *2476; to commend, establish, stand near, consist:*— commend(3), commended(1), commending(3), commends(2), demonstrated(1), demonstrates(2), formed(1), hold together(1), prove(1), standing(1).

συνκ- sunk-; see **συγκ- sugk-**.

συνλ- sunl-; see **συλλ- sull-**.

συνμ- sunm-; see **συμμ- summ-**.

4922. **συνοδεύω sunodeuō**; from *4862* and *3593; to journey with:*— traveled(1).

4923. **συνοδία sunodia**; from *4862* and *3598; a journey in company,* by ext. *a company* (of travelers):— caravan(1).

4924a. **σύνοιδα sunoida**; from *4862* and *3609a; to share the knowledge of:*— am conscious(1), full knowledge(1).

4924b. **συνοικέω sunoikeō**; from *4862* and *3611; to dwell together:*— live(1).

4925. **συνοικοδομέω sunoikodomeō**; from *4862* and *3618; to build together,* fig. *to build up together:*— built together(1).

4926. **συνομιλέω sunomileō**; from *4862* and *3656; to converse with:*— talked(1).

4927. **συνομορέω sunomoreō**; from *4862* and **ὁμορέω homoreō** *(to border upon); to border on:*— next(1).

4928. **συνοχή sunochē**; from *4912; a holding together,* fig. *distress:*— anguish(1), dismay(1).

συνπ- sunp-; see **συμπ- sump-**.

συνσ- suns-; see **συσσ- suss-**.

4929. **συντάσσω suntassō**; from *4862* and *5021; to arrange* (together):— directed(2), instructed(1).

4930. **συντέλεια sunteleia**; from *4931; a joint payment* (for public service), *joint action,* spec. *completion:*— consummation(1), end(5).

4931. **συντελέω sunteleō**; from *4862* and *5055; to complete, accomplish:*— effect(1), ended(1), finished(1), fulfilled(1), over(1), thoroughly(1).

4932. **συντέμνω suntemnō**; from *4862* and the same as *5114; to cut in pieces:*— quickly(1).

4933. **συντηρέω suntēreō**; from *4862* and *5083; to keep close,* i.e. *preserve:*— kept...safe(1), preserved(1), treasured(1).

4934. **συντίθημι suntithēmi**; from *4862* and *5087; to place together,* hence *observe, agree:*— agreed(3).

4935. **συντόμως suntomōs**; adv. from **σύντομος suntomos** *(cut short);* from *4932; briefly:*— brief(1).

4936. **συντρέχω suntrechō**; from *4862* and *5143; to run with:*— ran together(1), ran...together(1), run(1).

4937. **συντρίβω suntribō**; from *4862* and the same as *5147; to break in pieces, crush:*— battered(1), broke(1), broken(1), broken in pieces(1), broken to pieces(1), crush(1), mauling(1).

4938. **σύντριμμα suntrimma**; from *4937; a fracture,* fig. *a calamity:*— destruction(1).

4939. **σύντροφος suntrophos**; from *4862* and *5142; one brought up with,* i.e. *a foster brother* or *an intimate friend:*— brought(1).

4940. **συντυγχάνω suntugchanō**; from *4862* and *5177; to meet with:*— get(1).

4941. **Συντύχη Suntuchē**; from *4940;* "happy event," *Syntyche,* a Chr. woman at Philippi:— Syntyche(1).

4942. **συνυποκρίνομαι sunupokrinomai**; from *4862* and *5271; to play a part with:*— joined...in hypocrisy(1).

4943. **συνυπουργέω sunupourgeō**; from *4862* and **ὑπουργέω hupourgeō** *(to render service, assist); to help together:*— joining in helping(1).

συνφ- sunph-; see **συμφ- sumph-**.

συνχ- sunch-; see **συγχ- sugch-**.

συνψ- sunps-; see **συμψ- sumps-**.

4944. **συνωδίνω sunōdinō**; from *4862* and *5605; to be in travail together:*— suffers the pains of childbirth(2), together*(1).

4945. **συνωμοσία sunōmosia**; from **συνόμνυμι sunomnumi** *(to swear together); from 4862* and *3660; a swearing together,* i.e. *a conspiracy:*— plot(1).

4946. **Συράκουσαι Surakousai**; of unc. or.; *Syracuse,* a large maritime city of Sicily:— Syracuse(1).

4947. **Συρία Suria**; of unc. or., perh. related to [6865]; *Syria,* a region N. and E. of Pal.:— Syria(8).

4948. **Σύρος Suros**; from *4947; Syrian:—* Syrian(1).

4949. **Συροφοινίκισσα Surophoinikissa**; fem. of a comp. of *4948* and *5403; a Syrophoenician* (woman):— Syrophoenician(1).

4950. **Σύρτις Surtis**; from *4951;* "shoal," *Syrtis,* the name of two large sandbanks on the Lybian coast:— Syrtis(1).

4951. **σύρω surō**; a prim. word; *to draw, drag:—* dragged(1), dragging(3), swept away(1).

4952. **συσπαράσσω susparassō**; from *4862* and *4682; to convulse completely:—* threw...into a convulsion(2).

4953. **σύσσημον sussēmon**; from *4862* and the same as *4591; a fixed sign:—* signal(1).

4954. **σύσσωμος sussōmos**; from *4862* and *4983; of the same body:—* fellow members(1), fellow members of the body(1).

4955. **συστασιαστής sustasiastēs**; var. reading for *4714a,* q.v.

4956. **συστατικός sustatikos**; from *4921; constructive, commendatory:—* commendation(1).

4957. **συσταυρόω sustauroō**; from *4862* and *4717; to crucify together with:—* crucified(5).

4958. **συστέλλω sustellō**; from *4862* and *4724; to draw together,* hence *wrap up:—* covered(1), shortened(1).

4959. **συστενάζω sustenazō**; from *4862* and *4727; to groan together:—* groans(1), together*(1).

4960. **συστοιχέω sustoicheō**; from *4862* and *4748; to stand in the same rank,* fig. *correspond to:—* corresponds(1).

4961. **συστρατιώτης sustratiōtēs**; from *4862* and *4757; a fellow soldier:—* fellow soldier(2).

4962. **συστρέφω sustrephō**; from *4862* and *4762; to twist together,* hence *to gather together* (pass.):— gathered(1), gathering together(1).

4963. **συστροφή sustrophē**; from *4962; a twisting together,* hence *a concourse* or *conspiracy:—* disorderly gathering(1).

4964. **συσχηματίζω suschēmatizō**; from *4862* and **σχηματίζω schēmatizō** *(to assume a certain form, figure); to conform to:—* conformed(2).

4965. **Συχάρ Suchar**; of Heb. or. [7941]; *Sychar,* a city in Samaria:— Sychar(1).

4966. **Συχέμ Suchem**; of Heb. or. [7927]; *Shechem,* a city in Samaria:— Shechem(2).

4967. **σφαγή sphagē**; from *4969; slaughter:—* slaughter(2), slaughtered(1).

4968. **σφάγιον sphagion**; from *4967; a victim* (for slaughter):— victims(1).

4969. **σφάζω sphazō**; from a prim. root **σφαγ- sphag-**; *to slay, slaughter:—* slain(7), slay(2), slew(1).

4970. **σφόδρα sphodra**; adv. from **σφοδρός sphodros** *(excessive, violent); very much:—* deeply(3), exceedingly(1), extremely(3), greatly(1), very(2).

4971. **σφοδρῶς sphodrōs**; adv. from the same as *4970; exceedingly:—* violently(1).

4972. **σφραγίζω sphragizō**; from *4973; to seal:—* put...seal on(1), seal(2), sealed(9), set a seal on(1), set...seal to(2).

4973. **σφραγίς sphragis**; a prim. word; *a seal, a signet:—* seal(11), seals(5).

4974. **σφυδρόν sphudron**; from **σφυρόν sphuron** *(the ankle); the ankle:—* ankles(1).

4975. **σχεδόν schedon**; adv. from *2192; near, nearly:—* almost(2), nearly(1).

4976. **σχῆμα schēma**; from *2192; figure, shape:—* appearance(1), form(1).

4977. **σχίζω schizō**; from a prim. root **σχιδ- schid-**; *to cleave, split:—* divided(2), opening(1), split(1), tear(2), tears(1), torn(4).

4978. **σχίσμα schisma**; from *4977; a split,* fig. *division:—* division(4), divisions(2), tear(2).

4979. **σχοινίον schoinion**; dim. of **σχοῖνος schoinos** *(a rush); a rope* (made of rushes):— cords(1), ropes(1).

4980. **σχολάζω scholazō**; from *4981; to be at leisure,* hence *to devote oneself to:—* devote yourselves(1), unoccupied(1).

4981. **σχολή scholē**; a prim. word; *leisure,* hence *disputation* (that for which leisure is used), by ext. *school:—* school(1).

4982. **σῴζω sōzō**; from **σῶς sōs** *(safe, well); to save:—* bring...safely(1), cured(1), ensure salvation(1), get(1), get well(2), made...well(6), made well(5), preserved(1), recover(1), restore(1), save(36), saved(50), saves(1), saving(1).

4983. **σῶμα sōma**; of unc. or.; *a body:—* bodies(11), body(128), personal(1), slaves(1), substance(1).

4984. **σωματικός sōmatikos**; from *4983; of the body:—* bodily(2).

4985. **σωματικῶς sōmatikōs**; adv. from *4984; bodily:—* bodily form(1).

4986. **Σώπατρος Sōpatros**; from the same as *4982* and from *3962;* "of a safe father," *Sopater,* a Chr. from Berea:— Sopater(1).

4987. **σωρεύω sōreuō**; from **σωρός sōros** *(a heap); to heap on:—* heap(1), weighed down(1).

4988. **Σωσθένης Sōsthenēs**; from the same as *4982* and *4599;* "of safe strength," *Sosthenes,* the name of a ruler of a synagogue and of a Chr.:— Sosthenes(2).

4989. **Σωσίπατρος Sōsipatros**; a prol. form of *4986;* "of a safe father," *Sosipater,* a Chr., perh. the same as *4986:—* Sosipater(1).

4990. **σωτήρ sōtēr**; from *4982; a savior, deliverer:—* Savior(24).

4991. **σωτηρία sōtēria**; from *4990; deliverance, salvation:—* deliverance(2), preservation(1), salvation(42).

4992. **σωτήριος sōtērios**; from *4990; saving, bringing salvation:—* bringing salvation(1), salvation(1), salvation(3).

4993. **σωφρονέω sōphroneō**; from *4998; to be of sound mind,* i.e. *to be temperate:—* have sound judgment(1), right mind(2), sensible(1), sound judgment(1), sound mind(1).

4994. **σωφρονίζω sōphronizō**; from *4998; to recall one to his senses, admonish:—* encourage(1).

4995. **σωφρονισμός sōphronismos**; from *4994; self-control:—* discipline(1).

4996. **σωφρόνως sōphronōs**; adv. from *4998; with sound mind:—* sensibly(1).

4997. **σωφροσύνη sōphrosunē**; from *4998; soundness of mind, self-control:—* discreetly(1), self-restraint(1), sober(1).

4998. **σώφρων sōphrōn**; from the same as *4982* and from *5424; of sound mind, self-controlled:—* prudent(1), sensible(3).

T

4999. **ταβέρνη tabernē**; of Lat. or.; "hut," *a tavern,* spec. *Treis Tabernai,* "Three Taverns," a stopping place on the Appian Way:— Inns(1).

5000. **Ταβιθά Tabitha**; of Ara. or.; "gazelle," *Tabitha* (also called Dorcas, see *1393),* a Chr. woman:— Tabitha(2).

5001. **τάγμα tagma**; from *5021; that which has been arranged in order,* spec. *a division, rank:—* order(1).

5002. **τακτός taktos**; from *5021; ordered, stated:—* appointed(1).

5003. **ταλαιπωρέω talaipōreō**; from *5005; to suffer hardship* or *distress:—* miserable(1).

5004. **ταλαιπωρία talaipōria**; from *5005; hard work, hardship, distress:—* miseries(1), misery(1).

5005. **ταλαίπωρος talaipōros**; prob. from a root **ταλα- tala-** *(patient, stedfast)* and **πωρέω pōreō** = *3996; distressed, miserable:—* wretched(2).

5006. **ταλαντιαῖος talantiaios**; from *5007; worth a talent,* i.e. *of a talent's weight:—* one hundred pounds(1).

5007. **τάλαντον talanton**; from a prim. root; *a balance,* hence *that which is weighed,* i.e. *a talent* (about 3000 shekels in weight, cf. [3603]):— talent(3), talents(11).

5008. **ταλιθά talitha**; of Ara. or.; *maiden:—* Talitha(1).

5009. **ταμεῖον tameion**; later form of **ταμιεῖον tamieion** *(treasury); an inner chamber:—* inner room(1), inner rooms(2), storeroom(1).

5010. **τάξις taxis**; from *5021; an arranging, order:—* good discipline(1), order(7), orderly manner(1).

5011. **ταπεινός tapeinos**; a prim. word; *low-lying,* fig. *lowly,* hence *lowly in spirit:—* depressed(1), humble(5), lowly(1), meek(1).

5012a. **ταπεινοφροσύνη tapeinophrosunē**; from *5012b; lowliness of mind, humility:—* humility(4), humility of mind(1), self-abasement(2).

5012b. **ταπεινόφρων tapeinophrōn**; from *5011* and *5424; humble-minded:—* humble in spirit(1).

5013. **ταπεινόω tapeinoō**; from *5011; to make low,* fig. *to humble:—* brought low(1), get along(1), humble(2), humble means(1), humbled(4), humbles(4), humbling(1), humiliate(1).

5014. **ταπείνωσις tapeinōsis**; from *5013; low estate, humiliation:—* humble state(2), humiliation(2).

5015. **ταράσσω tarassō**; from a prim. root **ταραχ- tarach-**; *to stir up, to trouble:—* disturbed(1), disturbing(2), stirred(3), stirring(1), terrified(2), troubled(9).

5016. **ταραχή tarachē**; from 5015; a disturbance, stirring up:— stirring(1).

5017. **τάραχος tarachos**; a later form of **ταραχή tarachē** *(disorder); disturbance, trouble:—* disturbance(2).

5018. **Ταρσεύς Tarseus**; from *5019; of Tarsus:*— Tarsus(2).

5019. **Ταρσός Tarsos**; of unc. or.; *Tarsus,* a city of Cilicia:— Tarsus(3).

5020. **ταρταρόω tartaroō**; from **Τάρταρος Tartaros** (a Gr. name for the abode of the damned); *to cast into hell:*— cast...into hell(1).

5021. **τάσσω tassō**; from a prim. root **ταγ- tag-**; *to draw up in order, arrange:*— appointed(2), designated(1), determined(1), devoted(1), established(1), set(1).

5022. **ταῦρος tauros**; a prim. word; *a bull:*— bulls(2), oxen(2).

5023. **ταῦτα tauta**; nom. or acc. neut. pl. of *3778,* q.v.

5024. **ταὐτά tauta**; variant reading from contr. of *3588* and *846,* q.v.

5025. **ταύταις tautais** and

ταύτας tautas; dat. and acc. fem. pl. respectively of *3778,* q.v.

5026. **ταύτῃ tautē** and

ταύτην tautēn and

ταύτης tautēs; dat., acc. and gen. fem. sing. respectively of *3778,* q.v.

5027. **ταφή taphē**; from *2290; burial:*— burial place(1).

5028. **τάφος taphos**; from *2290; a burial,* hence *a grave:*— grave(5), tombs(2).

5029. **τάχα tacha**; adv. from *5036; quickly, perhaps:*— perhaps(2).

5030. **ταχέως tacheōs**; adv. from *5036; quickly, hastily:*— hastily(1), once(1), quickly(4), shortly(2), soon(2).

5031. **ταχινός tachinos**; late form of *5036; swift:*— imminent(1), swift(1).

5032. **τάχιον tachion**; cptv. adv. from *5036,* q.v.

5033. **τάχιστα tachista**; superl. of *5036,* q.v.

5034. **τάχος tachos**; from *5036; speed:*— quickly(3), shortly(1), soon(3).

5035. **ταχύ tachu**; neut. of *5036; quickly:*— before long(1), possible(1), quickly(11), soon afterward(1).

5036. **ταχύς tachus**; a prim. word; *quick, swift:*— faster(1), quick(1), quickly(1), soon(2), sooner(1).

5037. **τε te**; a prim. enclitic particle; *and* (denotes addition or connection):— alike(1), along(1), also(7), both(37), even(1), only(1), only*(1), or(2), well(2), whether(1).

5038. **τεῖχος teichos**; of unc. or.; *a wall:*— wall(8), walls(1).

5039. **τεκμήριον tekmērion**; from a prim. word **τέκμαρ tekmar** *(a mark, sign); a sure sign:*— convincing proofs(1).

5040. **τεκνίον teknion**; dim. of *5043; a little child:*— little children(8).

5041. **τεκνογονέω teknogoneō**; from a comp. of *5043* and **γόνος gonos** *(offspring, child); to beget children:*— bear children(1).

5042. **τεκνογονία teknogonia**; from the same as *5041; childbearing:*— bearing of children(1).

5043. **τέκνον teknon**; from *5088; a child* (of either sex):— child(13), children(76), children's(2), son(8), sons(1).

5044. **τεκνοτροφέω teknotropheō**; from a comp. of *5043* and a der. of *5142; to rear children:*— brought up children(1).

5045. **τέκτων tektōn**; from a prim. root **τεκτ- tekt-**; *a craftsman,* spec. *a carpenter:*— carpenter(1), carpenter's(1).

5046. **τέλειος teleios**; from *5056; having reached its end,* i.e. *complete,* by ext. *perfect:*— complete(2), mature(4), more perfect(1), perfect(12).

5047. **τελειότης teleiotēs**; from *5046; completeness, perfection:*— maturity(1), perfect(1).

5048. **τελειόω teleioō**; from *5046; to bring to an end, to complete, perfect:*— accomplish(2), accomplished(1), finish(1), fulfill(1), full number(1), made perfect(4), made...perfect(1), make...perfect(1), make perfect(1), perfect(2), perfected(7), reach...goal(1), spending the full number(1).

5049. **τελείως teleiōs**; adv. from *5046; completely:*— completely(1).

5050. **τελείωσις teleiōsis**; from *5048; completion, perfection:*— fulfillment(1), perfection(1).

5051. **τελειωτής teleiōtēs**; from *5048; a completer, finisher:*— perfecter(1).

5052. **τελεσφορέω telesphoreō**; from *5056* and *5409; to bring fruit to perfection,* hence *to bear perfect offspring:*— bring...fruit to maturity(1).

5053. **τελευτάω teleutaō**; from *5054; to complete, to come to an end,* hence *to die:*— deceased(1), die(4), died(5), dying(1), put(2).

5054. **τελευτή teleutē**; from *5055; a finishing, end,* i.e. *death:*— death(1).

5055. **τελέω teleō**; from *5056; to bring to an end, complete, fulfill:*— accomplished(3), carried(1), carry(1), completed(3), finish(1), finished(11), fulfilled(2), fulfilling(1), keeps(1), pay(2), perfected(1), performed(1).

5056. **τέλος telos**; a prim. word; *an end, a toll:*— continually*(1), custom(2), customs(1), end(24), ends(2), finished(1), fulfillment(1), goal(1), outcome(6), sum(1), utmost(1).

5057. **τελώνης telōnēs**; from *5056* and *5608; a farmer of taxes,* i.e. *a tax collector:*— collector(1), tax collector(5), tax collectors(15).

5058. **τελώνιον telōnion**; from *5057; a place of* (collecting) *toll:*— tax(1), tax booth(2), tax collector's booth(1).

5059. **τέρας teras**; a prim. word; *a wonder, marvel:*— wonders(16).

5060. **Τέρτιος Tertios**; of Lat. or.; "third," *Tertius,* a Chr. to whom Paul dictated Romans:—Tertius(1).

5061. **Τέρτυλλος Tertullos**; of unc. or.; *Tertullus,* prob. a Rom.:— Tertullus(2).

5062. **τεσσαράκοντα tessarakonta**; var. reading for *5065b,* q.v.

5063. **τεσσαρακονταετής tessarakontaetēs**; var. reading for *5066a,* q.v.

5064. **τέσσαρες tessares**; a prim. card. num.; *four:*— eighty-four*(1), forty-four*(3), four(29), four men(1), twenty-four*(6).

5065a. **τεσσαρεσκαιδέκατος tessareskaidekatos**; from *5064, 2532* and *1182; fourteenth:*— fourteenth(2).

5065b. **τεσσεράκοντα tesserakonta**; from *5064* and a modified form of *1176; forty:*— forty(14), forty-four*(3), forty-six*(1), forty-two*(2), thirty-nine*(1).

5066a. **τεσσερακονταετής tesserakontaetēs**; from *5065b* and *2094; of forty years:*— forty(1), forty years(1).

5066b. **τεταρταῖος tetartaios**; from *5067a; of the fourth day:*— four days(1).

5067a. **τέταρτος tetartos**; ord. num. from *5064; fourth:*— four(1), fourth(9).

5067b. **τετρααρχέω tetraarcheō**; from *5068a; to be tetrarch:*— tetrarch(3).

5068a. **τετραάρχης tetraarchēs**; from *5064* and *757; a tetrarch* (the governor of a fourth part of a region):— tetrarch(4).

5068b. **τετράγωνος tetragōnos**; from *5064* and *1137; four-cornered,* i.e. *square:*— square(1).

5069. **τετράδιον tetradion**; from *5064; a group of four, a quaternion* (a guard of four soldiers):— squads(1).

5070. **τετρακισχίλιοι tetrakischilioi**; from an adv. der. of *5064* and *5507; four thousand:*— four thousand(5).

5071. **τετρακόσιοι tetrakosioi**; pl. card. num. from *5064* and *1540; four hundred:*— four hundred(4).

5072. **τετράμηνος tetramēnos**; from *5064* and *3376; of four months:*— four months(1).

5073. **τετραπλοῦς tetraplous**; from *5064* and perh. *4144; fourfold:*— four times(1), four times as much(1).

5074. **τετράπους tetrapous**; from *5064* and *4228; four-footed:*— four-footed animals(3).

5075. **τετραρχέω tetrarcheō**; var. reading for *5067b,* q.v.

5076. **τετραρχής tetrarchēs**; var. reading for *5068a,* q.v.

5077. **τεφρόω tephroō**; from a prim. word **τέφρα tephra** *(ashes); to burn to ashes:*— reducing...to ashes(1).

5078. **τέχνη technē**; from *5045; art, craft, trade:*— art(1), craft(1), trade(1).

5079. **τεχνίτης technitēs**; from *5078; a craftsman, artificer:*— architect(1), craftsman(1), craftsmen(2).

5080. **τήκω tēkō**; from a root **τακ- tak-**; *to melt (down), to melt away:*— melt(1).

5081. **τηλαυγῶς tēlaugōs**; adv. from **τῆλε tēle** *(afar)* and *827; at a distance clearly:*— clearly(1).

5082. **τηλικοῦτος tēlikoutos**; from a comp. of *3588* with *2245* and *3778; such as this,* of persons *so old,* of things *so great:*— so(1), so great(3).

5083. **τηρέω tēreō**; from a prim. word **τηρός tēros** *(a guard); to watch over, to guard:*— continue(1), guard(1), guards(1), heed(2), heeds(1), held in custody(1), keep(27), keep watch over(1), keeping(1), keeping guard over(1), keeps(9), kept(12), kept in custody(3), observe(3), preserve(1), preserved(1), reserved(4), watching over(1).

τῇ tē and

τήν tēn and

τῆς tēs; dat., acc. and gen. fem. sing. of *3588,* q.v.

5084. **τήρησις tērēsis**; from *5083; a watching,* hence *imprisonment, a keeping:*— jail(2), keeping(1).

5085. **Τιβεριάς Tiberias**; from *5086; Tiberias,* a city of Galilee, also another name for the Sea of Galilee (*1056*):— Tiberias(3).

5086. **Τιβέριος Tiberios**; of Lat. or.; *Tiberius,* a Rom. emperor:— Tiberius(1).

5087. **τίθημι tithēmi**; from a prim. root **θε- the-**; *to place, lay, set:*— appointed(6), assign(2), committed(1), conceived(1), destined(1), down*(4), falling(1), fixed(1), kept(1), kneeling*(2), knelt*(3), laid(22), laid aside(1), laid down(1), lay(4), lay...down(2), lay down(8), laying(2), lays down(1), made(4), make(4), offer(1), placed(4), present(1), purposed(1), put(15), puts(2), puts...away(1), putting(1), reached(1), serves(1), set...down(1), set down(1), sink(1).

5088. **τίκτω tiktō**; from a prim. root **τεκ- tek-**; *to beget, bring forth:*— bear(4), birth(1), born(2), brings forth(1), gave birth(5), give birth(4), gives birth(1), labor(1).

5089. **τίλλω tillō**; a prim. word; *to pluck, to pluck off:*— pick(1), picking(2).

5090. **Τιμαῖος Timaios**; prob. from *5091;* "highly prized," *Timaeus,* an Isr.:— Timaeus(1).

5091. **τιμάω timaō**; from *5092; to fix the value, to price:*— had been set(1), honor(16), honored(1), honors(2), price(1).

5092. **τιμή timē**; akin to **τίω tiō** *(to value, honor); a valuing, a price:*— honor(28), honorable use(1), marks of respect(1), precious value(1), price(7), proceeds(1), sum(1), value(1).

5093. **τίμιος timios**; from *5092; valued, precious:*— dear(1), honor(1), precious(8), respected(1), very costly(2).

5094. **τιμιότης timiotēs**; from *5093; preciousness, worth:*— wealth(1).

5095. **Τιμόθεος Timotheos**; from *5092* and *2316; Timothy,* a Chr.:— Timothy(24).

5096. **Τίμων Timōn**; from *5092; Timon,* a Chr.:— Timon(1).

5097. **τιμωρέω timōreō**; perh. from *5092* and **ἄρνυμαι arnumai** *(to exact* atonement); *to punish, avenge:*— punished(2).

5098. **τιμωρία timōria**; from *5097; punishment, vengeance:*— punishment(1).

5099. **τίνω tinō**; a prim. vb.; *to pay, to pay a penalty:*— pay(1).

5100. **τις tis**; a prim. enclitic indef. pron.; *a certain one, someone, anyone:*— any(36), any man(9), any man's(2), any one(4), any way(1), any woman(1), anyone(90), anyone's(1), anyone's*(1), anyone...anything(1), anything(40), anything...anyone(1), certain(6), certain man(1), certain men(2), few(1), in any way(1), high(1), kind(1), man(10), man's(2), matter(1), no*(5), none*(3), nothing*(8), one(45), one...another(1), ones(1), others(1), person(2), several(2), some(104), some men(3), some people(1), some things(1), somebody(1), someone(27), something(15), somewhat(2), such(1), various things(1), whatever(1), whatever*(6), who(1), whoever*(4), whomever*(1).

5101. **τίς tis**; an interrog. pron. related to *5100; who? which? what?:*— anything(1), how(7), how*(2), person(1), something(3), suppose one(2), what(266), what each(1), what*(5), which(24), which one(3), who(128), whom(16), whose(6), why(70), why*(33).

5102a. **Τίτιος Titios**; of Lat. or.; *Titius* (surnamed Justus), a Chr.:— Titius(1).

5102b. **τίτλος titlos**; of Lat. or.; *a title, an inscription:*— inscription(2).

5103. **Τίτος Titos**; of Lat. or.; *Titus,* a Chr.:— Titus(13).

5104. **τοι toi**; ethical dat. of *4771;* an enclitic particle of asseveration used as a pref. or suff. in the N.T.

5105. **τοιγαροῦν toigaroun**; from *5104, 1063* and *3767; wherefore then, so therefore:*— so(1), therefore(1).

5106. **τοίνυν toinun**; from *5104* and *3568; accordingly, therefore:*— so(1), then(1), therefore(1).

5107. **τοιόσδε toiosde**; from **τοῖος toios** *(such, such-like)* and *1161; such:*— such(1).

5108. **τοιοῦτος toioutos**; from **τοῖος toios** *(such, such-like)* and *3778; such as this, such:*— like this(1), men like(1), other(1), similar(1), so(2), such(16), such a fellow(1), such a kind(1), such a man(3), such a one(5), such a person(2), such as these(4), such men(5), such people(1), such persons(2), such thing(1), such things(7), such women(1).

5109. **τοῖχος toichos**; alt. form of *5038; a wall:*— wall(1).

5110. **τόκος tokos**; from *5088; a bringing forth, birth,* fig. *interest, usury:*— interest(2).

5111. **τολμάω tolmaō**; from **τόλμα tolma** *(boldness); to have courage, to be bold:* am...bold(1), bold(2), courageous(1), dare(4), dared(1), gathered up courage(1), have courage(1), have...courage(1), presume(1), venture(2), ventured(1).

5112. **τολμηρότερον tolmēroteron**; adv. from cptv. of **τολμηρός tolmēros** *(bold); boldly:*— very boldly(1).

5113. **τολμητής tolmētēs**; from *5111; a bold, daring man:*— Daring(1).

5114. **τομός tomos**; from a prim. word **τέμνω temnō** *(to cut); sharp:*— sharper(1).

5115. **τόξον toxon**; a prim. word; *a bow:*— bow(1).

5116. **τοπάζιον topazion**; of unc. or.; *a topaz:*— topaz(1).

5117. **τόπος topos**; a prim. word; *a place:*— areas(1), locality(1), occasion(1), opportunity(2), parts(1), passenger*(1), place(75), places(6), reef(1), regions(1), room(3).

5118. **τοσοῦτος tosoutos**; from **τόσος tosos** *(so much)* and *3778; so great, so much,* pl. *so many:*— all(1), great many(1), long*(1), much(1), price(1), same degree(1), so(2), so great(1), so long(1), so many(4), so many people(1), so many things(1), so much(1), such(1), such and such a price(1), such great(3).

5119. **τότε tote**; from the neut. of *3588* and *3753; then, at that time:*— then(146), time(10).

5120. **τοῦ tou**; the gen. of *3588,* q.v.

5121. **τοὐναντίον tounantion**; adv. from contr. of *3588* and *1726; on the contrary:*— contrary(2), instead(1).

5122. **τοὔνομα tounoma**; contr. for the neut. of *3588* and *3686; by name:*— named(1).

5123. **τουτέστι toutesti**; var. reading, comb. of *5124* and *2076,* q.v.

5124. **τοῦτο touto**; neut. sing. nom. or acc. of *3778,* q.v.

5125. **τούτοις toutois**; dat. pl. masc. or neut. of *3778,* q.v.

5126. **τοῦτον touton**; acc. sing. masc. of *3778,* q.v.

5127. **τούτου toutou**; gen. sing. masc. or neut. of *3778,* q.v.

5128. **τούτους toutous**; acc. pl. masc. of *3778,* q.v.

5129. **τούτῳ toutō**; dat. sing. masc. or neut. of *3778,* q.v.

5130. **τούτων toutōn**; gen. pl. masc., fem., or neut. of *3778,* q.v.

5131. **τράγος tragos**; from *5176; a male goat:*— goats(4).

5132. **τράπεζα trapeza**; from modified forms of *5064* and *3979; a table, dining table:*— bank(1), food(1), table(9), tables(4).

5133. **τραπεζίτης trapezitēs**; from *5132; a money-changer, banker:*— bank(1).

5134. **τραῦμα trauma**; of unc. or.; *a wound:*— wounds(1).

5135. **τραυματίζω traumatizō**; from *5134; to wound:*— wounded(2).

5136. **τραχηλίζω trachēlizō**; from *5137; to take by the throat, to overthrow:*— laid bare(1).

5137. **τράχηλος trachēlos**; prob. from *5138; the neck:*— embraced*(2), neck(4), necks(1).

5138. **τραχύς trachus**; a prim. word; *rough:*— rocks(1), rough(1).

5139. **Τραχωνῖτις Trachōnitis**; from *5138; Trachonitis,* a rough region S. of Damascus:— Trachonitis(1).

5140. **τρεῖς treis** and
τρία tria; a prim. card. num.; *three:*— fifty-three*(1), thirty(1), three(66), twenty-three*(1).

5141. **τρέμω tremō**; a prim. vb.; *to tremble* (esp. with fear):— tremble(1), trembling(2).

5142. **τρέφω trephō**; a prim. vb.; *to make to grow, to nourish, feed:*— brought(1), fattened(1), fed(1), feed(1), feeds(2), nourished(2), nursed(1).

5143. **τρέχω trechō**; a prim. vb.; *to run:*— ran(7), run(7), running(3), runs(1), rushing(1), spread rapidly(1).

5144a. **τρῆμα trēma**; from **τετραίνω tetrainō** *(to pierce); a hole:*— eye(2).

5144b. **τριάκοντα triakonta**; card. num. from *5140* and a modification of *1176; thirty:*— thirty(9), thirty-eight*(1).

5145. **τριακόσιοι triakosioi**; pl. card. num. from *5140* and *1540; three hundred:*— three hundred(2).

5146. **τρίβολος tribolos**; from *5140* and *956b; a thistle:*— thistles(2).

5147. **τρίβος tribos**; from **τρίβω tribō** *(to rub, thresh out); a beaten track, a path:*— paths(3).

5148. **τριετία trietia**; from *5140* and *2094; a period of three years:*— period of three years(1), three years(1).

5149. **τρίζω trizō**; from a root **τριγ- trig-**; *to cry, chirp, to grind the teeth:*— grinds(1).

5150. **τρίμηνον trimēnon**; neut. of a comp. of *5140* and *3376; of three months:*— three months(1).

5151. **τρίς tris**; adv. from *5140; three times:*— three times(12).

5152. **τρίστεγον tristegon**; from **τρίστεγος tristegos** *(of three stories);* from *5140* and *4721; the third story:*— third floor(1).

5153. **τρισχίλιοι trischilioi**; from *5151* and *5507; three thousand:*— three thousand(1).

5154. **τρίτος tritos**; ord. num. from *5140; third:*— third(47), third one(1), third time(8).

τρίχες triches; see *2359.*

5155. **τρίχινος trichinos**; from *2359; of hair:*— hair(1).

5156. **τρόμος tromos**; from *5141; trembling, quaking:*— trembling(5).

5157. **τροπή tropē**; from **τρέπω trepō** *(to turn); a turning:*— shifting(1).

5158. **τρόπος tropos**; from the same as *5157; a way, manner, fashion:*— character(1), circumstance(1), exactly*(1), just*(1), respect(1), same way(1), way(5).

5159. **τροποφορέω tropophoreō**; from *5158* and *5409; to bear with another's manners:*— put(1).

5160. **τροφή trophē**; from *5142; nourishment, food:*— enough*(1), food(13), meals(1), support(1).

5161. **Τρόφιμος Trophimos**; from *5160; Trophimus,* a Chr.:— Trophimus(3).

5162. **τροφός trophos**; from *5142; a nurse:*— nursing(1).

5163. **τροχιά trochia**; from *5164; the track of a wheel,* hence *a track, path:*— paths(1).

5164. **τροχός trochos**; from *5143; a wheel:*— course(1).

5165. **τρύβλιον trublion**; of unc. or.; *a bowl, dish:*— bowl(2).

5166. **τρυγάω trugaō**; from **τρύγη trugē** *(ripe); to gather in:*— gather(1), gathered(1), pick(1).

5167. **τρυγών trugōn**; from **τρύζω truzō** *(to murmur, coo); a turtledove:*— turtledoves(1).

5168. **τρυμαλιά trumalia**; from **τρύω truō** *(to wear away); a hole, eye* (of a needle):— eye(1).

5169. **τρύπημα trupēma**; var. reading for *5144a,* q.v.

5170. **Τρύφαινα Truphaina**; from *5172; Tryphaena,* a Chr. woman:— Tryphaena(1).

5171. **τρυφάω truphaō**; from *5172; to live luxuriously:*— lived luxuriously(1).

5172. **τρυφή truphē**; from **θρύπτω thruptō** *(to break); softness, daintiness, luxuriousness:*— luxury(1), revel(1).

5173. **Τρυφῶσα Truphōsa**; from *5172; Tryphosa,* a Chr. woman:— Tryphosa(1).

5174. **Τρῳάς Trōas**; from **Τρωϊάς Trōias** *(Trojan); Troas,* a city near the Hellespont (i.e. Dardanelles):— Troas(6).

5175. **Τρωγύλλιον Trōgullion**; of unc. or.; *Trogyllium,* a place in Ionia.

5176. **τρώγω trōgō**; a prim. word; *to gnaw, munch, crunch:*— eating(1), eats(5).

5177. **τυγχάνω tugchanō**; from a prim. root **τυχ- tuch-**; *to hit, hit upon, meet, happen:*— attain(1), attained(1), extraordinary(2), obtain(2), obtained(2), perhaps(3), receive(1).

5178. **τυμπανίζω tumpanizō**; from **τύμπανον tumpanon** *(a kettle drum); to beat a drum, to torture by beating:*— tortured(1).

5179a. **τυπικῶς tupikōs**; from *5179b; typically:*— example(1).

5179b. **τύπος tupos**; from *5180; the mark* (of a blow), *an impression, stamp* (made by a die):— example(3), examples(2), form(2), images(1), imprint(1), model(1), pattern(3), type(1).

5180. **τύπτω tuptō**; a prim. vb.; *to strike, smite, beat:*— beat(3), beating(5), hits(1), strike(2), struck(1), wounding(1).

5181. **Τύραννος Turannos**; of for. or.; "absolute ruler," *Tyrannus,* an Ephesian:— Tyrannus(1).

5182. **τυρβάζω turbazō**; from **τύρβη turbē** *(disorder, confusion); to disturb, to trouble.*

5183. **Τύριος Turios**; from *5184; a Tyrian,* an inhab. of Tyre:— Tyre(1).

5184. **Τύρος Turos**; of for. or., cf. [6865]; *Tyre,* a city of Phoenicia:— Tyre(11).

5185. **τυφλός tuphlos**; of unc. or.; *blind:*— blind(34), blind man(10), blind men(5), person...blind(1).

5186. **τυφλόω tuphloō**; from *5185; to blind, to make blind:*— blinded(3).

5187. **τυφόω tuphoō**; from **τῦφος tuphos** *(vanity, arrogance); to be conceited, foolish:*— conceited(3).

5188. **τύφω tuphō**; a prim. word; *to raise smoke:*— smoldering(1).

5189. **τυφωνικός tuphōnikos**; from **τυφῶν tuphōn** *(a hurricane); tempestuous:*— violent(1).

5190. **Τύχικος Tuchikos**; from **Τυχή tuchē** *(fortune, fate);* "fortuitous," *Tychicus,* a Chr.:— Tychicus(5).

Υ

5191. **ὑακίνθινος huakinthinos**; from *5192; of hyacinth, hyacinthine:*— hyacinth(1).

5192. **ὑάκινθος huakinthos**; of unc. or.; *hyacinth:*— jacinth(1).

5193. **ὑάλινος hualinos**; from *5194; of glass, glassy:*— glass(3).

5194. **ὕαλος hualos**; prob. of for. or.; *a clear transparent stone, glass:*— glass(2).

5195. **ὑβρίζω hubrizō**; from *5196; to run riot, to outrage, insult:*— insult(1), mistreat(1), mistreated(3).

5196. **ὕβρις hubris**; a prim. word; *wantonness, insolence, an act of wanton violence:*— damage(2), insults(1).

5197. **ὑβριστής hubristēs**; from *5195; a violent, insolent man:*— insolent(1), violent aggressor(1).

5198. **ὑγιαίνω hugiainō**; from *5199; to be sound, healthy:*— good health(2), safe and sound(1), sound(8), well(1).

5199. **ὑγιής hugiēs**; a prim. word; *sound, whole, healthy:*— good health(1), healed(1), normal(1), restored(1), sound(1), well(7).

5200. **ὑγρός hugros**; a prim. word; *wet, moist,* of wood *sappy:*— green(1).

5201. **ὑδρία hudria**; from *5204; a water pot, a pot* or *jar:*— waterpot(1), waterpots(2).

5202. **ὑδροποτέω hudropoteō**; from *5204* and *4095; to drink water:*— drink water(1).

5203. **ὑδρωπικός hudrōpikos**; from **ὕδρωψ hudrōps** *(dropsy); suffering from edema:*— suffering from dropsy(1).

5204. **ὕδωρ hudōr**; a prim. word; *water:*— water(63), waters(13).

5205. **ὑετός huetos**; from **ὕω huō** *(to rain); rain:*— rain(4), rains(1).

5206. **υἱοθεσία huiothesia**; prob. from a comp. of *5207* and a der. of *5087; adoption:*— adoption as sons(5).

5207. **υἱός huios**; a prim. word; *a son:*— attendants(3), foal(1), man(1), son(1), son(307), sons(68).

5208. **ὕλη hulē**; a prim. word; *wood, timber, forest:*— forest(1).

5209. **ὑμᾶς humas**; acc. of *5210,* q.v.

5210. **ὑμεῖς humeis**; nom. pl. of *4771,* q.v.

5211. **Ὑμέναιος Humenaios**; from **Ὑμήν Humēn** *(Hymen,* the Gr. god of weddings); *Hymenaeus,* a heretical teacher at Ephesus:— Hymenaeus(2).

5212. **ὑμέτερος humeteros**; poss. pron. from *5210; your, yours:*— yours(2).

5213. **ὑμῖν humin**; dat. of *5210,* q.v.

5214. **ὑμνέω humneō**; from *5215; to sing to, to laud:*— sing...praise(1), singing a hymn(2), singing hymns(1), singing hymns of praise(1).

5215. **ὕμνος humnos**; a prim. word; *a hymn:*— hymns(2).

5216. **ὑμῶν humōn**; gen. of *5210,* q.v.

5217. **ὑπάγω hupagō**; from *5259* and *71; to lead* or *bring under, to lead on slowly, to depart:*— get(2), go(45), go their way(1), go away(3), goes(5), going(20), going away(1), going back(1), went(1).

5218. **ὑπακοή hupakoē**; from *5219; obedience:*— obedience(13), obedient(1), obey(1).

5219. **ὑπακούω hupakouō**; from *5259* and *191; to listen, attend to:*— answer(1), became obedient(1), becoming obedient(1), heed(1), obedient(2), obey(12), obeyed(3).

5220. **ὕπανδρος hupandros**; from *5259* and *435; under the power of* or *subject to a man:*— married(1).

5221. **ὑπαντάω hupantaō**; from *5259* and **ἀντάω antaō** *(to meet face to face, meet with); to go to meet, to meet:*— encounter(1), met(7), went and met(1), went to meet(1).

5222. **ὑπάντησις hupantēsis**; from *5221; a going to meet:*— meet(3).

5223. **ὕπαρξις huparxis**; from *5225; subsistence, existence, property:*— possession(1), possessions(1).

5224. **ὑπάρχοντα huparchonta**; neut. pl. of pres. act. part. of *5225,* q.v.

5225. **ὑπάρχω huparchō**; from *5259* and *757; to begin, to be ready* or *at hand, to be:*— been(2), being(9), belonging(1), exist(1), existed(1), gone(1), live(1), owned(1), possess(1), possessions(11), private means(1), property(1).

5226. **ὑπείκω hupeikō**; from *5259* and **εἴκω eikō** *(to yield); to retire, withdraw, submit:*— submit(1).

5227. **ὑπεναντίος hupenantios**; from *5259* and *1727; set over against, opposite:*— adversaries(1), hostile(1).

5228. **ὑπέρ huper**; a prim. prep.; *over, beyond,* fig. *on behalf of, for the sake of, concerning:*— about(5), above(4), behalf(22), beyond(4), concerning(3), exceed(1), more so(1), more than(5), over(2), regard(1), sake(9), sakes(1), than(3).

5229. **ὑπεραίρω huperairō**; from *5228* and *142; to lift* or *raise over,* mid. *to uplift oneself:*— exalting(2), exalts(1).

5230. **ὑπέρακμος huperakmos**; from *5228* and the same as *187; past the bloom of youth:*— past her youth(1).

5231. **ὑπεράνω huperanō**; prep. from *5228* and *507; (high) above:*— above(1), far above(2).

5232. **ὑπεραυξάνω huperauxanō**; from *5228* and *837; to increase beyond measure:*— greatly enlarged(1).

5233. **ὑπερβαίνω huperbainō**; from *5228* and the same as *939; to step over, transgress:*— transgress(1).

5234. **ὑπερβαλλόντως huperballontōs**; adv. from pres. act. part. of *5235; above measure:*— times without number(1).

5235. **ὑπερβάλλω huperballō**; from *5228* and *906; to throw over* or *beyond, to run beyond:*— surpasses(2), surpassing(3).

5236. ὑπερβολή huperbolē; from *5235; a throwing beyond, excess, superiority:*— all comparison(1), beyond*(1), excessively*(1), far...all comparison(1), measure(1), more excellent(1), surpassing greatness(2), utterly(1).

5237. ὑπερεῖδον hupereidon; from *5228* and *1491a; to overlook:*— overlooked(1).

5238a. ὑπερέκεινα huperekeina; adv. from *5228* and *1565; beyond:*— beyond(1).

5238b. ὑπερεκπερισσοῦ huperekperissou; from *5228, 1537* and *4053; superabundantly:*— far more abundantly(1), most earnestly(1).

5239a. ὑπερεκπερισσῶς huperekperiss ōs; from *5228, 1537* and *4057; beyond measure, exceedingly:*— very highly(1).

5239b. ὑπερεκτείνω huperekteinō; from *5228* and *1614; to stretch beyond measure:*— overextending(1).

5240. ὑπερεκχύννω huperekchunnō; from *5228* and *1632b; to pour out over, to overflow:*— running over(1).

5241. ὑπερεντυγχάνω huperentugchanō; from *5228* and *1793; to intercede, to make petition for:*— intercedes(1).

5242. ὑπερέχω huperechō; from *5228* and *2192; to hold above, to rise above, to be superior:*— authority(1), governing(1), more important(1), surpasses(1), surpassing value(1).

5243. ὑπερηφανία huperēphania; from *5244a; haughtiness, disdain:*— pride(1).

5244a. ὑπερήφανος huperēphanos; from *5228* and *5316; showing oneself above others:*— arrogant(2), proud(3).

5244b. ὑπερλίαν huperlian; from *5228* and *3029; exceedingly, preeminently:*— most eminent(2).

5245. ὑπερνικάω hupernikaō; from *5228* and *3528; to be more than conqueror:*— overwhelmingly conquer(1).

5246. ὑπέρογκος huperogkos; from *5228* and *3591; of excessive weight* or *size:*— arrogant(1), arrogantly(1).

5247. ὑπεροχή huperochē; from *5242; a projection, eminence:*— authority(1), superiority(1).

5248. ὑπερπερισσεύω huperperisseuō; from *5228* and *4052; to abound more exceedingly:*— abounded all(1), abounded all the more(1), overflowing(1).

5249. ὑπερπερισσῶς huperperissōs; from *5228* and *4057; beyond measure, exceedingly:*— utterly(1).

5250. ὑπερπλεονάζω huperpleonazō; from *5228* and *4121; to abound exceedingly:*— more than abundant(1).

5251. ὑπερυψόω huperupsoō; from *5228* and *5312; to exalt beyond measure:*— highly exalted(1).

5252. ὑπερφρονέω huperphroneō; from *5228* and *5426; to be overly proud, to have high thoughts:*— think more highly(1).

5253. ὑπερῷον huperōon; neut. of **ὑπερῷος huperōos** *(upper); the upper story, the upper rooms:*— upper room(4).

5254. ὑπέχω hupechō; from *5259* and *2192; to hold* or *put under,* fig. *to undergo:*— undergoing(1).

5255. ὑπήκοος hupēkoos; from *5219; giving ear, obedient:*— obedient(3).

5256. ὑπηρετέω hupēreteō; from *5257; to serve as a rower, to minister to, serve:*— ministered(1), ministering(1), served(1).

5257. ὑπηρέτης hupēretēs; from *5259* and **ἐρέτης eretēs** *(a rower); an underling, servant:*— attendant(1), helper(1), minister(1), officer(1), officers(13), servants(3).

5258. ὕπνος hupnos; a prim. word; *sleep:*— sleep(6).

5259. ὑπό hupo; a prim. prep.; *by, under:*— about(1), hands(3), power(1), under(46).

5260. ὑποβάλλω hupoballō; from *5259* and *906; to throw* or *put under:*— secretly induced(1).

5261. ὑπογραμμός hupogrammos; from **ὑπογράφω hupographō** *(to trace in outline, sketch out);* from *5259* and *1125; a writing to be copied, an example:*— example(1).

5262. ὑπόδειγμα hupodeigma; from *5263; a figure, copy, example:*— copies(1), copy(1), example(4).

5263. ὑποδείκνυμι hupodeiknumi; from *5259* and *1166; to show secretly, to show by tracing out, to teach, make known:*— show(2), showed(1), warn(1), warned(2).

5264. ὑποδέχομαι hupodechomai; from *5259 and 1209; to receive under one's roof, to receive as a guest:*— received(2), welcomed(2).

5265. ὑποδέω hupodeō; from *5259* and *1210; to bind under:*— put(1), shod(1), wear(1).

5266. ὑπόδημα hupodēma; from *5265; a sole bound under* (the foot), *a sandal:*— sandal(1), sandals(8), shoes(1).

5267. ὑπόδικος hupodikos; from *5259* and *1349; brought to trial, answerable to:*— accountable(1).

5268. ὑποζύγιον hupozugion; from *5259* and *2218; a beast of burden* or *draught:*— beast of burden(1), donkey(1).

5269. ὑποζώννυμι hupozōnnumi; from *5259* and *2224; to undergird:*— undergirding(1).

5270. ὑποκάτω hupokatō; from *5259* and *2736; below, under:*— beneath(2), soles(1), under(7), underneath(1).

5271. ὑποκρίνομαι hupokrinomai; from *5259* and *2919; to answer, reply, to answer on a stage, to pretend:*— pretended(1).

5272. ὑπόκρισις hupokrisis; from *5271; a reply, answer, playacting, hypocrisy:*— hypocrisy(6).

5273. ὑποκριτής hupokritēs; from *5271; one who answers, an actor, a hypocrite:*— hypocrite(2), hypocrites(16).

5274. ὑπολαμβάνω hupolambanō; from *5259* and *2983; to take* or *bear up, to receive, to assume:*— received(1), replied(1), support(1), suppose(2).

5275a. ὑπόλειμμα hupoleimma; from *5259* and *3005; a remnant:*— remnant(1).

5275b. ὑπολείπω hupoleipō; from *5259* and *3007; to leave remaining:*— left(1).

5276. ὑπολήνιον hupolēnion; from *5259* and *3025b; a vessel* or *trough beneath a winepress* (to receive the juice):— vat under(1), wine press(1).

5277. ὑπολιμπάνω hupolimpanō; a collateral form of *5275b; to leave behind:*— leaving(1).

5278. ὑπομένω hupomenō; from *5259* and *3306; to stay behind, to await, endure:*— endure(3), endure...with patience(1), endured(5), endures(3), patiently endure(1), perseveres(1), persevering(1), remained(1), stayed behind(1).

5279. ὑπομιμνήσκω hupomimnēskō; from *5259* and *3403; to cause* (one) *to remember, to remind:*— bring to...remembrance(1), call attention(1), remembered(1), remind(4).

5280. ὑπόμνησις hupomnēsis; from *5279; a reminding, reminder:*— mindful(1), reminder(2).

5281. ὑπομονή hupomonē; from *5278; a remaining behind, a patient enduring:*— endurance(7), patient enduring(1), perseverance(21), steadfastness(3).

5282. ὑπονοέω huponoeō; from *5259* and *3539; to suspect, conjecture:*— expecting(1), suppose(1), surmise(1).

5283. ὑπόνοια huponoia; from *5282; a suspicion:*— suspicions(1).

5284. ὑποπλέω hupopleō; from *5259* and *4126; to sail under* (i.e. under the lee of):— sailed under(2), sailed under the shelter(2).

5285. ὑποπνέω hupopneō; from *5259* and *4154; to blow underneath:*— moderate...came(1).

5286. ὑποπόδιον hupopodion; from *5259* and the dim. of *4228; a footstool:*— footstool(7).

5287. ὑπόστασις hupostasis; from *5259* and *2476; a support, substance, steadiness,* hence *assurance:*— assurance(2), confidence(2), nature(1).

5288. ὑποστέλλω hupostellō; from *5259* and *4724; to draw in, let down, draw back:*— shrink(2), shrinks back(1), withdraw(1).

5289. ὑποστολή hupostolē; from *5288; a letting down, a shrinking back:*— shrink back(1).

5290. ὑποστρέφω hupostrephō; from *5259* and *4762; to turn back, return:*— return(6), returned(22), returning(3), started back(1), turn away(1), turned back(1), went back(1).

5291. ὑποστρωννύω hupostrōnnuō; from *5259* and *4766; to spread under:*— spreading(1).

5292. ὑποταγή hupotagē; from *5293; subjection:*— control(1), obedience(1), subjection(1), submissiveness(1).

5293. ὑποτάσσω hupotassō; from *5259* and *5021; to place* or *rank under, to subject,* mid. *to obey:*— put in subjection(5), subject(16), subjected(7), subjecting(1), subjection(4), submissive(3), submit(2).

5294. ὑποτίθημι hupotithēmi; from *5259* and *5087; to place under, lay down,* mid. *to suggest:*— pointing(1), risked(1).

5295. ὑποτρέχω hupotrechō; from *5259* and *5143; to run in under:*— running under(1), running under the shelter(1).

5296. ὑποτύπωσις hupotupōsis; from **ὑποτυπόω hupotupoō** *(to delineate); an outline, sketch,* fig. *an example:*— example(1), standard(1).

5297. ὑποφέρω hupopherō; from *5259* and *5342; to bear by being under, to endure:*— bears up under(1), endure(1), endured(1).

5298. ὑποχωρέω hupochōreō; from *5259* and *5562; to go back, retire:*— slip away(1), withdrew(1).

5299. ὑπωπιάζω hupōpiazō; from **ὑπώπιον hupōpion** *(the part of the face under the eyes); to strike under the eye:*— discipline(1), wear(1).

5300. ὗς hus; a prim. word; *a hog:*— sow(1).

5301. ὕσσωπος hussōpos; of Semitic or., cf. [231]; *hyssop:*— hyssop(2).

5302. **ὑστερέω hustereō**; from *5306; to come late, be behind, come short:*— am...lacking(1), come short(1), comes short(1), destitute(1), fall short(1), impoverished(1), inferior(2), lack(2), lacked(1), lacking(1), need(1), ran(1), suffering need(1), worse(1).

5303. **ὑστέρημα husterēma**; from *5302; that which is lacking, need:*— lacking(1), need(3), needs(1), poverty(1), what is lacking(1), what was deficient(1), what was lacking(1).

5304. **ὑστέρησις husterēsis**; from *5302; need, want:*— poverty(1), want(1).

5305. **ὕστερον husteron**; neut. of *5306; afterwards, later:*— afterward(4), afterwards(1), last(1), later(3).

5306. **ὕστερος husteros**; from a prim. root and cptv. suff.; *latter, later:*— finally(1), later(1), then(1).

5307. **ὑφαντός huphantos**; from **ὑφαίνω huphainō**; a prim. vb. *(to weave); woven:*— woven(1).

5308. **ὑψηλός hupsēlos**; from *5311; high, lofty:*— conceited*(1), exalted(1), haughty(1), high(6), highly esteemed(1), uplifted(1).

5309. **ὑψηλοφρονέω hupsēlophroneō**; from *5308* and *5426; to be high-minded:*— conceited(1).

5310. **ὕψιστος hupsistos**; superl. akin to **ὕψι- hupsi-** *(on high); highest, most high:*— highest(4), most high(9).

5311. **ὕψος hupsos**; from **ὕψι hupsi** *(on high, aloft); height:*— height(2), high(3), high position(1).

5312. **ὑψόω hupsoō**; from *5311; to lift* or *raise up, to exalt, uplift:*— exalt(2), exalted(9), exalts(3), lift(1), lifted(4), made...great(1).

5313. **ὕψωμα hupsōma**; from *5312; height, that which is lifted up:*— height(1), lofty thing(1).

Φ

5314. **φάγος phagos**; from *5315a; a glutton:*— gluttonous(2).

5315a. **φάγομαι phagomai**; fut. tense of *2068*, q.v.

5315b. **φαιλόνης phailonēs**; for **φαινόλης phainolēs** *(a cloak); a cloak:*— cloak(1).

5316. **φαίνω phainō**; from a prim. root; *to bring to light, to cause to appear:*— appear(5), appeared(7), appears(1), became evident(1), become(1), flashes(1), noticed(2), seem(1), seen(2), shine(3), shines(1), shining(4), shown(1), visible(1).

5317. **Φάλεκ Phalek**; of Heb. or. [6389]; *Peleg,* a patriarch:— Peleg(1).

5318. **φανερός phaneros**; from *5316; visible, manifest:*— apparent(1), disclosed(2), evident(6), light(2), obvious(1), outward(1), outwardly*(1), tell(2), well known(2).

5319. **φανερόω phaneroō**; from *5318; to make visible, make clear:*— appear(1), appeared(6), appears(3), become visible(1), becomes visible(1), disclose(1), disclosed(1), displayed(1), made...evident(2), made known(1), made manifest(2), make...clear(1), manifested(18), manifests(1), revealed(7), show(1), shown(1).

5320. **φανερῶς phanerōs**; adv. from *5318; manifestly, openly:*— clearly(1), publicly(2).

5321. **φανέρωσις phanerōsis**; from *5319; manifestation:*— manifestation(2).

5322. **φανός phanos**; from *5316; a torch* or *lantern:*— lanterns(1).

5323. **Φανουήλ Phanouēl**; of Heb. or. [6439]; *Phanuel,* an Isr.:— Phanuel(1).

5324. **φαντάζω phantazō**; from a der. of *5316; to make visible, to become visible:*— sight(1).

5325. **φαντασία phantasia**; from *5324; imagination, show, display:*— pomp(1).

5326. **φάντασμα phantasma**; from *5324; an appearance, apparition:*— ghost(2).

5327. **φάραγξ pharagx**; of unc. or.; *a chasm, ravine:*— ravine(1).

5328. **Φαραώ Pharaō**; of Eg. or. *(great house); Pharaoh,* an Eg. king:— Pharaoh(3), Pharaoh's(2).

5329. **Φαρές Phares**; of Heb. or. [6557], *Perez,* an Isr.:— Perez(3).

5330. **Φαρισαῖος Pharisaios**; of Heb. or., cf. [6567a]; *a Pharisee,* member of a Jewish religious sect:— Pharisaic(1), Pharisee(10), Pharisee's(2), Pharisees(86).

5331. **φαρμακεία pharmakeia**; from **φαρμακεύω pharmakeuō** *(to administer drugs); the use of medicine, drugs* or *spells:*— sorceries(1), sorcery(2).

5332. **φαρμακεύς pharmakeus**; var. reading for *5333*, q.v.

5333. **φάρμακος pharmakos**; from **φάρμακον pharmakon** *(a drug); a poisoner, sorcerer, magician:*— sorcerers(2).

5334. **φάσις phasis**; from *5346; information, a report:*— report(1).

5335. **φάσκω phaskō**; prob. from the same as *5346; to affirm, assert:*— asserted(1), asserting(1), professing(1).

5336. **φάτνη phatnē**; a prim. word; a manger:— manger(3), stall(1).

5337. **φαῦλος phaulos**; a prim. word; *worthless, bad:*— bad(3), evil(3).

5338. **φέγγος pheggos**; a prim. word; *light, brightness:*— light(3).

5339. **φείδομαι pheidomai**; a prim. vb.; *to spare, forbear:*— refrain(1), spare(8), sparing(1).

5340. **φειδομένως pheidomenōs**; adv. from a part. of *5339; sparingly:*— sparingly(2).

5341. **φελόνης phelonēs**; see *5315b.*

5342. **φέρω pherō**; a prim. word; *to bear, carry, bring forth:*— bear(6), bearing(1), bears(3), bring(16), bringing(7), brought(14), carry(1), carrying(1), driven(2), endured(1), leads(1), made(3), moved(1), press(1), produce(2), produced(1), reach(2), rushing(1), take(1), took(1), upholds(1).

5343. **φεύγω pheugō**; a prim. vb.; *to flee:*— escape(2), escaped(2), fled(5), fled away(2), flee(13), flees(2), ran away(3).

5344. **Φῆλιξ Phēlix**; of Lat. or.; "fortunate," *Felix,* a governor of Judea:— Felix(9).

5345. **φήμη phēmē**; from *5346; a saying* or *report:*— news(2).

5346. **φημί phēmi**; from a prim. root **φα- pha-**; *to declare, say:*— claim(1), mean(1), replied(1), said(57), say(4), says(2), stated(1).

5347. **Φῆστος Phēstos**; of Lat. or.; *Festus,* a governor of Judea:— Festus(13).

5348. **φθάνω phthanō**; a prim. vb.; *to come before* (another), *anticipate, arrive:*— arrive(1), attained(1), come(3), first to come(1), precede(1).

5349. **φθαρτός phthartos**; from *5351; perishable, corruptible:*— corruptible(1), perishable(3), perishable things(1), which is perishable(1).

5350. **φθέγγομαι phtheggomai**; a prim. word; *to utter:*— speak(1), speaking(2).

5351. **φθείρω phtheirō**; from a prim. root **φθερ- phther-**; *to destroy, corrupt, spoil:*— corrupted(2), corrupting(1), corrupts(1), destroy(1), destroyed(2), destroys(1), led astray(1).

5352. **φθινοπωρινός phthinopōrinos**; from **φθινόπωρον phthinopōron** *(late autumn); autumnal:*— autumn(1).

5353. **φθόγγος phthoggos**; from *5350; a sound:*— tones(1), voice(1).

5354. **φθονέω phthoneō**; from *5355; to envy:*— envying(1).

5355. **φθόνος phthonos**; a prim. word; *envy:*— envy(7), envying(1), jealously(1).

5356. **φθορά phthora**; from *5351; destruction, corruption:*— corruption(4), destruction(1), killed(1), perish(1), perishable(2).

5357. **φιάλη phialē**; of unc. or.; *a* (shallow) *bowl:*— bowl(7), bowls(5).

5358. **φιλάγαθος philagathos**; from *5384* and *18; loving that which is good:*— loving what(1), loving what is good(1).

5359. **Φιλαδέλφεια Philadelpheia**; from *5361; Philadelphia,* a city of Lydia:— Philadelphia(2).

5360. **φιλαδελφία philadelphia**; from *5361; the love of brothers, brotherly love:*— brotherly kindness(2), brotherly love(1), love of the brethren(3).

5361. **φιλάδελφος philadelphos**; from *5384* and *80; loving one's brother:*— brotherly(1).

5362. **φίλανδρος philandros**; from *5384* and *435; loving men,* (of a wife) *loving her husband:*— love their husbands(1).

5363. **φιλανθρωπία philanthrōpia**; from *5384* and *444; love for mankind, kindness:*— kindness(1), love for mankind(1).

5364. **φιλανθρώπως philanthrōpōs**; adv. from **φιλάνθρωπος philanthrōpos** *(humane, kind);* from the same as *5363; humanely, kindly:*— consideration(1).

5365. **φιλαργυρία philarguria**; from *5366; love of money, avarice:*— love of money(1).

5366. **φιλάργυρος philarguros**; from *5384* and *696; loving money:*— lovers of money(2).

5367. **φίλαυτος philautos**; from *5384* and *846; loving oneself:*— lovers of self(1).

5368. **φιλέω phileō**; from *5384; to love:*— kiss(3), love(13), loved(3), loves(6).

5369. **φιλήδονος philēdonos**; from *5384* and *2237; loving pleasure:*— lovers of pleasure(1).

5370. **φίλημα philēma**; from *5368; a kiss:*— kiss(7).

5371. **Φιλήμων Philēmōn**; from *5368;* "kindly," *Philemon,* a Chr.:— Philemon(1).

5372. **Φίλητος Philētos**; from *5368;* "worthy of love," *Philetus,* an erring Chr. at Ephesus:— Philetus(1).

5373. **φιλία philia**; from *5384; friendship:*— friendship(1).

5374. **Φιλιππήσιος Philippēsios**; from *5375; a Philippian:*— Philippians(1).

5375. **Φίλιπποι Philippoi**; from *5376; Philippi,* a city of Macedonia:— Philippi(4).

5376. Φίλιππος Philippos; from *5384* and *2462;* "horse-loving," *Philip,* two sons of Herod the Great, also two Chr.:— Philip(35), Philippi(2).

5377. φιλόθεος philotheos; from *5384* and *2316; loving God:*— lovers of God(1).

5378. Φιλόλογος Philologos; from *5384* and *3056;* "student, scholar," *Philologus,* a Chr.:— Philologus(1).

5379. φιλονεικία philoneikia; from *5380; love of strife:*— dispute(1).

5380. φιλόνεικος philoneikos; from *5384* and **νεῖκος neikos** *(strife); fond of strife:*— contentious(1).

5381. φιλοξενία philoxenia; from *5382; love of strangers:*— hospitality(1), hospitality to strangers(1).

5382. φιλόξενος philoxenos; from *5384* and *3581; loving strangers:*— hospitable(3).

5383. φιλοπρωτεύω philoprōteuō; from a comp. of *5384* and *4413; to strive to be first:*— loves to be first(1).

5384. φίλος philos; a prim. word; *beloved, dear, friendly:*— friend(12), friends(17).

5385. φιλοσοφία philosophia; from *5386; the love* or *pursuit of wisdom:*— philosophy(1).

5386. φιλόσοφος philosophos; from *5384* and *4680; a philosopher:*— philosophers(1).

5387. φιλόστοργος philostorgos; from *5384* and **στοργή storgē** *(family affection); tenderly loving:*— devoted(1).

5388. φιλότεκνος philoteknos; from *5384* and *5043; loving one's children:*— love their children(1).

5389. φιλοτιμέομαι philotimeomai; mid. from a comp. of *5384* and *5092; to love* or *seek after honor:*— aspired(1), have as our ambition(1), make it your ambition(1).

5390. φιλοφρόνως philophronōs; from *5391; kindly:*— courteously(1).

5391. φιλόφρων philophrōn; var. reading for *5012b,* q.v.

5392. φιμόω phimoō; from **φιμός phimos** *(a muzzle); to muzzle, to put to silence:*— muzzle(1), quiet(2), silence(1), silenced(1), speechless(1), still(1).

5393. Φλέγων Phlegōn; from the same as *5395; Phlegon,* a Chr.:— Phlegon(1).

5394. φλογίζω phlogizō from *5395; to set on fire, burn:*— set on fire(1), sets on fire(1).

5395. φλόξ phlox; from **φλέγω phlegō** *(to burn); a flame:*— flame(6), flaming(1).

5396. φλυαρέω phluareō; from *5397; to talk nonsense:*— unjustly accusing(1).

5397. φλύαρος phluaros; from **φλύω phluō** *(to babble); babbling:*— gossips(1).

5398. φοβερός phoberos; from *5399; fearful:*— terrible(1), terrifying(1), terrifying thing(1).

5399. φοβέω phobeō; from *5401; to put to flight, to terrify, frighten:*— afraid(39), am afraid(2), awestruck(1), fear(27), feared(5), fearful(2), fearing(6), fears(2), frightened(7), have...fear(1), respects(1), terrified(1).

5400. φόβητρον phobētron; from **φόβητρος phobētros** (something *to be feared); from 5399; a* (cause of) *terror:*— terrors(1).

5401. φόβος phobos; from **φέβομαι phebomai** *(to be put to flight); panic flight, fear, the causing of fear, terror:*— cause of fear(1), fear(37), fearful(1), fears(1), intimidation(1), respect(1), respectful(1), reverence(1), sense of awe(1).

5402. Φοίβη Phoibē; fem. of **φοῖβος phoibos** *(bright); Phoebe,* a deaconess:— Phoebe(1).

5403. Φοινίκη Phoinikē; prob. from *5404; Phoenicia,* a region N. of Galilee:— Phoenicia(3).

5404. φοῖνιξ phoinix; of unc. or.; *the date palm, a palm:*— palm branches(1), palm trees(1).

5405. Φοῖνιξ Phoinix; from the same as *5403; a Phoenician* (an inhab. of Phoenicia), *Phoenix* (a city of Crete):— Phoenix(1).

5406. φονεύς phoneus; from *5408; a murderer:*— murderer(3), murderers(4).

5407. φονεύω phoneuō; from *5406; to kill, murder:*— commit murder(5), commits murder(1), murder(3), murdered(2), put to death(1).

5408. φόνος phonos; from **φεν- phen-** *(to slay); a murder:*— death*(1), murder(5), murders(3).

5409. φορέω phoreō; from *5342; to bear constantly, to wear:*— bear(2), borne(1), wear(1), wearing(2).

5410. φόρον phoron; of Lat. or., only in combination with *675,* q.v.:— market(1).

5411. φόρος phoros; from *5342; tribute:*— tax(2), taxes(3).

5412. φορτίζω phortizō; from the same as *5413; to load:*— heavy-laden(1), weigh...down(1).

5413. φορτίον phortion; dim. of *5414 (load, cargo);* from *5342; a burden:*— burden(1), burdens(3), cargo(1), load(1).

5414. φόρτος phortos; var. reading for *5413,* q.v.

5415. Φορτουνάτος Phortounatos; of Lat. or.; "prosperous, lucky," *Fortunatus,* a Chr.:— Fortunatus(1).

5416. φραγέλλιον phragellion; of Lat. or.; *a scourge:*— scourge(1).

5417. φραγελλόω phragelloō; of Lat. or.; *to scourge:*— scourged(2).

5418. φραγμός phragmos; from *5420; a fencing in, a fence:*— barrier(1), hedges(1), wall(2).

5419. φράζω phrazō; from a root **φραδ- phrad-**; *to show forth, tell:*— explain(1).

5420. φράσσω phrassō; from a root **φραγ- phrag-**; *to fence in, to stop:*— closed(1), shut(1), stopped(1).

5421. φρέαρ phrear; a prim. word; *a well:*— pit(4), well(3).

5422. φρεναπατάω phrenapataō; from *5423; to deceive the mind:*— deceives(1).

5423. φρεναπάτης phrenapatēs; from *5424* and *539; self-deceiving:*— deceivers(1).

5424. φρήν phrēn; a prim. word; *midriff, heart, mind, thought:*— thinking(2).

5425. φρίσσω phrissō; a prim. vb.; *to be rough, to shiver, shudder:*— shudder(1).

5426. φρονέω phroneō; from *5424; to have understanding, to think:*— adopt...view(1), conceited*(1), concern(1), concerned(1), feel(1), have...attitude(3), intent on...purpose(1), live in harmony(1), mind(4), observes(2), set their minds(2), set your mind(1), setting your mind(2), think(3), views(1).

5427. φρόνημα phronēma; from *5426; the thought* (that which is in the mind):— mind(1), mind set(3).

5428. φρόνησις phronēsis; from *5426; understanding, practical wisdom:*— attitude(1), insight(1).

5429. φρόνιμος phronimos; from *5426; practically wise, sensible:*— more shrewd(1), prudent(5), sensible(2), shrewd(1), wise(4), wise men(1).

5430. φρονίμως phronimōs; adv. from *5429; sensibly:*— shrewdly(1).

5431. φροντίζω phrontizō; from **φροντίς phrontis** *(thought); to give heed, take thought:*— careful(1).

5432. φρουρέω phroureō; from **φρουρός phrouros** *(a guard); to guard:*— guard(1), guarding(1), kept in custody(1), protected(1).

5433. φρυάσσω phruassō; of unc. der.; *to neigh, whinny,* fig. *to be wanton:*— rage(1).

5434. φρύγανον phruganon; from a prim. vb. **φρύγω phrugō** *(to parch); a dry stick:*— sticks(1).

5435. Φρυγία Phrugia; prob. of for. or.; *Phrygia,* a region of Asia Minor:— Phrygia(2), Phrygian(1).

5436. Φύγελος Phugelos; prob. of for. or.; *Phygelus,* one who deserted Paul:— Phygelus(1).

5437. φυγή phugē; from *5343; flight:*— flight(1).

5438. φυλακή phulakē; from *5442; a guarding, guard, watch:*— guard(1), imprisonment(1), imprisonments(2), prison(34), prisons(3), time of the night(1), watch(4).

5439. φυλακίζω phulakizō; from *5441; to imprison:*— imprison(1).

5440. φυλακτήριον phulaktērion; from the same as *5442* and **-τηριον -tērion** (suff. denoting place); *an outpost, fortification, an amulet:*— phylacteries(1).

5441. φύλαξ phulax; from *5442; a guard, keeper:*— guards(3).

5442. φυλάσσω phulassō; from a root **φυλακ- phulak-**; *to guard, watch:*— abstain(1), guard(8), guarded(1), guarding(1), guards(1), keep(5), keeping(2), keeps(1), kept(4), kept under guard(1), maintain(1), observe(2), preserved(1), protect(1), watching(1).

5443. φυλή phulē; from *5453; a clan* or *tribe:*— tribe(23), tribes(8).

5444. φύλλον phullon; a prim. word; *a leaf:*— leaf(1), leaves(5).

5445. φύραμα phurama; from **φυράω phuraō** *(to mix); that which is mixed:*— lump(5).

5446. φυσικός phusikos; from *5449; natural, according to nature:*— creatures of instinct(1), natural(2).

5447. φυσικῶς phusikōs; adv. from *5446; naturally, by nature:*— instinct(1).

5448. φυσιόω phusioō; from **φῦσα phusa** *(bellows); to puff* or *blow up:*— arrogant(5), inflated(1), makes arrogant(1).

5449. φύσις phusis; from *5453; nature:*— instinctively(1), natural(1), natural*(1), nature(7), physically(1), race(1), species(1), unnatural*(1).

5450. φυσίωσις phusiōsis; from *5448; a puffing up:*— arrogance(1).

5451. φυτεία phuteia; from *5452; a planting:*— plant(1).

5452. φυτεύω phuteuō; from **φυτόν phuton** *(a plant); to plant:*— plant(1), planted(6), planting(1), plants(3).

5453. φύω phuō; a prim. vb.; *to bring forth, produce:*— grew(2), springing(1).

5454. **φωλεός phōleos**; of unc. or.; *a hole, den:*— holes(2).

5455. **φωνέω phōneō**; from *5456; to call out:*— call(4), called(13), calling(6), calls(1), cried(3), crow(2), crowed(4), crows(5), crying(1), invite(1), summoned(2).

5456. **φωνή phōnē**; prob. from *5346; a voice, sound:*— blasts(1), cry(1), language(1), languages(1), outcry(1), sound(15), sounds(4), statement(1), tone(1), utterance(3), utterances(1), voice(102), voices(7).

5457. **φῶς phōs**; cont. of **φάος phaos** *(light, daylight);* from the same as *5316; light:*— fire(1), firelight(1), light(68), lights(2).

5458. **φωστήρ phōstēr**; from *5457; a luminary, light:*— brilliance(1), lights(1).

5459. **φωσφόρος phōsphoros**; from *5457* and *5342; light-bringing, the morning star:*— morning star(1).

5460. **φωτεινός phōteinos**; from *5457; bright, light:*— bright(1), full of light(3), illumined(1).

5461. **φωτίζω phōtizō**; from *5457; to shine, give light:*— bring to light(2), brought(1), enlightened(3), enlightens(1), illumine(1), illumined(2), illumines(1), light(1).

5462. **φωτισμός phōtismos**; from *5461; illumination:*— light(2).

X

5463. **χαίρω chairō**; a prim. vb.; *to rejoice, be glad:*— am glad(1), glad(7), gladly(1), greeted*(1), greeting(2), greetings(4), hail(4), joyfully(1), make(1), rejoice(33), rejoiced(8), rejoices(2), rejoicing(10).

5464. **χάλαζα chalaza**; a prim. word; *hailstone:*— hail(2), hailstones(1), hailstorm(1).

5465. **χαλάω chalaō**; a prim. word; *to slacken:*— let down(6), let down let down(1), lowering*(1).

5466. **Χαλδαῖος Chaldaios**; of Semitic or., cf. [3778]; *a Chaldean,* an inhab. of Chaldea:— Chaldeans(1).

5467. **χαλεπός chalepos**; a prim. word; *hard (to do* or *bear):*— difficult(1), violent(1).

5468. **χαλιναγωγέω chalinagōgeō**; from *5469* and *71; to lead with a bridle:*— bridle(2).

5469. **χαλινός chalinos**; of unc. or.; *a bridle:*— bits(1), bridles(1).

5470. **χαλκοῦς chalkous**; from *5475; brazen* (i.e. of copper, bronze, brass):— brass(1).

5471. **χαλκεύς chalkeus**; from *5475; a worker in metal:*— coppersmith(1).

5472. **χαλκηδών chalkēdōn**; of unc. or.; *chalcedony* (a precious stone):— chalcedony(1).

5473. **χαλκίον chalkion**; from *5475; a brazen* (i.e. of copper, bronze, brass) *vessel:*— copper pots(1).

5474. **χαλκολίβανον chalkolibanon**; from *5475* and *3030; chalcolibanus* (fine copper, bronze or brass):— burnished bronze(2).

5475. **χαλκός chalkos**; a prim. word; *copper* or *bronze:*— bronze(1), copper(1), gong(1), money(2).

5476. **χαμαί chamai**; a prim. adv.; *on* or *to the ground:*— ground(2).

5477. **Χαναάν Chanaan**; of Heb. or. [3667a]; *Canaan,* earlier name of Pal.:— Canaan(2).

5478. **Χαναναῖος Chananaios**; from *5477; Canaanite,* a Gentile of Pal.:— Canaanite(1).

5479. **χαρά chara**; from *5463; joy, delight:*— greatly(1), joy(54), joyful(1), joyfully(1), joyously(1), rejoicing(1).

5480. **χάραγμα charagma**; from **χαράσσω charassō** *(to sharpen, to engrave); a stamp, impress:*— image formed(1), mark(7).

5481. **χαρακτήρ charaktēr**; from the same as *5480; a tool for engraving:*— exact representation(1).

5482. **χάραξ charax**; from the same as *5480; a pointed stake, a rampart:*— barricade(1).

5483. **χαρίζομαι charizomai**; from *5485; to show favor, give freely:*— bestowed(1), forgave(2), forgive(3), forgiven(4), forgiving(2), freely give(1), gave(1), given(1), graciously forgave(1), granted(4), hand(2), things freely given(1).

5484. **χάριν charin**; acc. of *5485,* used as prep.; *in favor of, for the pleasure of:*— because(1), reason(5), sake(2).

5485. **χάρις charis**; a prim. word; *grace, kindness:*— blessing(1), concession(1), credit(3), favor(11), gift(1), grace(122), gracious(2), gracious work(3), gratitude(1), thank(3), thankfulness(2), thanks(6).

5486. **χάρισμα charisma**; from *5483; a gift of grace, a free gift:*— favor(1), free gift(3), gift(5), gifts(7), spiritual gift(1).

5487. **χαριτόω charitoō**; from *5485; to make graceful, endow with grace:*— favored(1), freely bestowed(1).

5488. **Χαρράν Charran**; of Semitic or., cf. [2771a]; *Haran,* a city in northwest Mesopotamia:— Haran(2).

5489. **χάρτης chartēs**; of unc. or.; a sheet of *paper* (made of papyrus strips):— paper(1).

5490. **χάσμα chasma**; from **χάσκω chaskō** *(to yawn); a chasm, wide space:*— chasm(1).

5491. **χεῖλος cheilos**; a prim. word; *a lip, an edge:*— lips(6).

5492. **χειμάζω cheimazō**; from **χεῖμα cheima** *(winter cold); to expose to winter cold, to drive with storm:*— storm-tossed(1).

5493. **χείμαρρος cheimarros**; from the same as *5492* and *4482; flowing in winter, a torrent:*— ravine(1).

5494. **χειμών cheimōn**; from the same as *5492; winter, a storm:*— storm(2), winter(4).

5495. **χείρ cheir**; a prim. word; *the hand:*— agency(1), charge*(1), grasp(1), hand(82), hands(88), help(1).

5496. **χειραγωγέω cheiragōgeō**; from *5497; to lead by the hand:*— leading...by the hand(1), led by the hand(1).

5497. **χειραγωγός cheiragōgos**; from *5495* and *71; leading by the hand:*— lead...by the hand(1).

5498. **χειρόγραφον cheirographon**; from *5495* and *1125; a (handwritten) document, legal note, bond:*— certificate of debt(1).

5499. **χειροποίητος cheiropoiētos**; from *5495* and *4160; made by hand:*— human hands(1), made by human hands(1), made with hands(4), performed(1).

5500. **χειροτονέω cheirotoneō**; from *5495* and **τείνω teinō** *(to stretch); to vote by stretching out the hand, to appoint:*— appointed(2).

5501. **χείρων cheirōn**; from a prim. root **χερ- cher-**, used as cptv. of *2556; worse:*— severer(1), worse(10).

5502. **Χερουβίν Cheroubin**; of Heb. or., pl. of [3742]; *Cherubim,* heavenly beings who serve God:— cherubim(1).

5503. **χήρα chēra**; of unc. der.; *a widow:*— widow(13), widows(11), widows'(3).

5504. **χθές chthes**; var. reading for *2189a,* q.v.

5505. **χιλιάς chilias**; from *5507; one thousand:*— thousand(20), thousands(2).

5506. **χιλίαρχος chiliarchos**; from *5507* and **ἄρχος archos** *(leader); a chiliarch, a commander of a thousand:*— commander(18), commanders(3), military commanders(1).

5507. **χίλιοι chilioi**; a prim. word; *a thousand:*— one thousand(1), thousand(8), twelve hundred*(1).

5508. **Χίος Chios**; of unc. or.; *Chios,* an island in the Aegean Sea:— Chios(1).

5509. **χιτών chitōn**; of Semitic or., cf. [3801]; *a tunic:*— clothes(1), coats(1), garment(1), shirt(2), tunic(2), tunics(4).

5510. **χιών chiōn**; from the root **χι- chi-**; *snow:*— snow(2).

5511. **χλαμύς chlamus**; a prim. word; *a chlamys* or *short cloak:*— robe(2).

5512. **χλευάζω chleuazō**; from **χλεύη chleuē** *(a jest); to jest, mock, jeer:*— sneer(1).

5513. **χλιαρός chliaros**; from **χλίω chliō** *(to become warm); tepid, warm:*— lukewarm(1).

5514. **Χλόη Chloē** a prim. word; *young foliage (Verdant,* epithet of the pagan goddess Demeter), *Chloe,* a Chr. woman:— Chloe's(1).

5515. **χλωρός chlōros**; akin to *5514* (in its ordinary usage); *pale green, pale:*— ashen(1), green(2), green thing(1).

5516. **χξς' chxs**; i.e. **chi xi sigma**; abb. for *six hundred sixty-six,* var. reading for *1812, 1835, 1803,* q.v.

5517. **χοϊκός choikos**; from *5529b; earthy, made of dust:*— earthy(4).

5518. **χοῖνιξ choinix**; of unc. or.; *a choenix* (a dry measure of less than a quart):— quart(1), quarts(1).

5519. **χοῖρος choiros**; a prim. word; *a swine:*— swine(12).

5520. **χολάω cholaō**; from *5521; to be melancholy, mad, angry:*— angry(1).

5521. **χολή cholē**; a prim. word; *gall* (a bitter herb):— gall(2).

5522. **χόος choos**; see *5529b.*

5523. **Χοραζίν Chorazin**; of unc. or.; *Chorazin,* a city of Galilee:— Chorazin(2).

5524. **χορηγέω chorēgeō**; from *5525* and *71; to lead a chorus* (i.e. a group of performers), *to defray the cost of a chorus:*— supplies(1), supply(1).

5525. **χορός choros**; a prim. word; *a dance, chorus:*— dancing(1).

5526. **χορτάζω chortazō**; from *5528; to feed, fatten, fill, satisfy:*— fed(1), filled(4), satisfied(8), satisfy(2).

5527. **χόρτασμα chortasma**; from *5526; fodder:*— food(1).

5528. **χόρτος chortos**; a prim. word; *a feeding place, food, grass:*— blade(1), grass(12), hay(1), wheat(1).

5529a. **Χουζᾶς Chouzas**; prob. of Ara. or.; *Chuza,* an officer of Herod:— Chuza(1).

5529b. **χοῦς chous**; contr. of a der. of **χέω cheō** *(to pour); earth, soil:*— dust(2).

5530. **χράομαι chraomai**; akin to *5534; to use, make use of:*— do(1), treated(1), use(5), used(2), uses(1), vacillating*(1).

5531. **χράω chraō** or **κίχρημι kichrēmi**; akin to *5534; to lend:*— lend(1).

5532. **χρεία chreia**; akin to *5530; need, business:*— necessary(1), need(40), needed(1), needs(6), task(1).

5533. **χρεοφειλέτης chreopheiletēs**; prob. a comp. of **χρέος chreos** *(debt)* and *3781; a debtor:*— debtors(2).

5534. **χρή chrē**; a prim. word; *it is necessary, fitting:*— ought(1).

5535. **χρῄζω chrēzō**; from *5534; to need, have need of:*— have need(1), need(3), needs(1).

5536. **χρῆμα chrēma**; from *5530; a thing that one uses* or *needs:*— money(4), wealthy(2).

5537. **χρηματίζω chrēmatizō**; from *5536; to transact business, to make answer:*— called(2), directed(1), revealed(1), warned(5).

5538. **χρηματισμός chrēmatismos**; from *5537; a divine response, an oracle:*— divine response(1).

5539. **χρήσιμος chrēsimos**; from *5530; useful:*— useless*(1).

5540. **χρῆσις chrēsis**; from *5530; use* (as in a sexual sense):— function(2).

5541. **χρηστεύομαι chrēsteuomai**; from *5543; to be kind:*— kind(1).

5542. **χρηστολογία chrēstologia**; from *5543* and *3004; smooth speech:*— smooth(1).

5543. **χρηστός chrēstos**; adj. from *5530; serviceable, good:*— easy(1), good(2), kind(2), kindness(2).

5544. **χρηστότης chrēstotēs**; from *5543; goodness, excellence, uprightness:*— good(1), kindness(9).

5545. **χρῖσμα chrisma**; from *5548; an anointing, unction:*— anointing(3).

5546. **Χριστιανός Christianos**; from *5547; a Christian:*— Christian(2), Christians(1).

5547. **Χριστός Christos**; from *5548; the Anointed One, Messiah, Christ:*— Christ(516), Christ's(11), Messiah(4).

5548. **χρίω chriō**; a prim. word; *to anoint:*— anointed(5).

5549. **χρονίζω chronizō**; from *5550; to spend* or *take time, delay:*— is not coming for a long time(1), delay(2), delaying(1), long time(2).

5550. **χρόνος chronos**; a prim. word; *time:*— age(1), all(1), delay(1), exact time(1), long(5), long ages(2), long*(1), period(2), time(30), times(5), while(5).

5551. **χρονοτριβέω chronotribeō**; from *5550* and the same as *5147; to spend time:*— spend time(1).

5552. **χρυσοῦς chrusous**; from *5557; golden:*— gold(4), golden(14).

5553. **χρυσίον chrusion**; dim. of *5557; a piece of gold, gold:*— gold(12), gold jewelry(1).

5554. **χρυσοδακτύλιος chrusodaktulios**; from *5557* and *1146; with a gold ring:*— gold ring(1).

5555. **χρυσόλιθος chrusolithos**; from *5557* and *3037; a chrysolite* (a yellow gem):— chrysolite(1).

5556. **χρυσόπρασος chrusoprasos**; from *5557* and a prim. word **πράσον prason** *(a leek); a chrysoprase* (a greenish-yellow gem):— chrysoprase(1).

5557. **χρυσός chrusos**; a prim. word; *gold:*— gold(9).

5558. **χρυσόω chrusoō**; from *5557; to gild, to cover with gold:*— adorned(2).

5559. **χρώς chrōs**; a prim. word; *the surface of the body, skin:*— body(1).

5560. **χωλός chōlos**; a prim. word; *lame, halt, maimed:*— lame(14).

5561. **χώρα chōra**; a prim. word; *a space, place, land:*— country(15), fields(2), land(4), region(6), regions(1).

5562. **χωρέω chōreō**; from **χῶρος chōros** *(a definite space, place); to make room, advance, hold:*— accept(3), come(1), contain(1), containing(1), has...place(1), make room(1), passes(1), room(1).

5563. **χωρίζω chōrizō**; from *5565; to separate, divide:*— leave(5), leaves(1), left(1), separate(4), separated(2).

5564. **χωρίον chōrion**; dim. of *5561; a place, property:*— field(3), land(3), lands(1), parcel of ground(1), place(2).

5565. **χωρίς chōris**; adv. akin to **χῆρος chēros** *(bereaved); separately, separate from:*— apart(10), besides(2), independent(2), itself(1), separate(1), without(25).

5566. **χῶρος chōros**; of Lat. or.; *the northwest wind:*— northwest(1).

Ψ

5567. **ψάλλω psallō**; from **ψάω psaō** *(to rub); to pull, twitch, twang, play, sing:*— making melody(1), sing(3), sing praises(1).

5568. **ψαλμός psalmos**; from *5567; a striking* (of musical strings), *a psalm:*— Psalm(1), psalm(1), Psalms(3), psalms(2).

5569. **ψευδάδελφος pseudadelphos**; from *5571* and *80; a false brother:*— false brethren(2).

5570. **ψευδαπόστολος pseudapostolos**; from *5571* and *652; a false apostle:*— false apostles(1).

5571. **ψευδής pseudēs**; from *5574; lying, false:*— false(2), liars(1).

5572. **ψευδοδιδάσκαλος pseudodidaskalos**; from *5571* and *1320; a false teacher:*— false teachers(1).

5573. **ψευδολόγος pseudologos**; from *5571* and *3056; speaking falsely, lying:*— liars(1).

5574. **ψεύδομαι pseudomai**; from a root **ψευδ- pseud-**; *to lie:*— falsely(1), lie(6), lied(1), lying(4).

5575. (not used)

5576. **ψευδομαρτυρέω pseudomartureō**; from *5577b; to bear false witness, give false testimony:*— bear false witness(3), give false testimony(1), giving false testimony(1).

5577a. **ψευδομαρτυρία pseudomarturia**; from *5577b; false witness, false testimony:*— false testimony(1), false witness(1), testified(1).

5577b. **ψευδόμαρτυς pseudomartus**; from *5571* and *3144; a false witness:*— false witnesses(2).

5578. **ψευδοπροφήτης pseudoprophētēs**; from *5571* and *4396; a false prophet:*— false prophet(4), false prophets(7).

5579. **ψεῦδος pseudos**; from *5574; a falsehood, untruth, lie:*— false(1), falsehood(1), lie(5), lying(2), what is false(1).

5580. **ψευδόχριστος pseudochristos**; from *5571* and *5547; a false Christ* or *Messiah:*— false Christs(2).

5581. **ψευδώνυμος pseudōnumos**; from *5571* and *3686; under a false name, falsely called:*— falsely called(1).

5582. **ψεῦσμα pseusma**; from *5574; a lie, falsehood:*— lie(1).

5583. **ψεύστης pseustēs** from the same as *5574; a liar:*— liar(8), liars(2).

5584. **ψηλαφάω psēlaphaō**; prob. from *5567* and **ἁφάω haphaō** *(to handle); to feel* or *grope about:*— grope(1), touch(1), touched(2).

5585. **ψηφίζω psēphizō**; from *5586; to count, calculate:*— calculate(2).

5586. **ψῆφος psēphos**; from the same as *5567; a small smooth stone, a pebble:*— stone(2), vote(1).

5587. **ψιθυρισμός psithurismos**; from **ψιθυρίζω psithurizō** *(to whisper); a whispering:*— gossip(1).

5588. **ψιθυριστής psithuristēs**; from the same as *5587; a whisperer:*— gossips(1).

5589. **ψιχίον psichion**; from a prim. word **ψίξ psix** *(a crumb); a crumb* (of bread):— crumbs(2).

5590. **ψυχή psuchē**; of unc. or.; breath, the soul:— heart(2), heartily(1), life(36), lives(7), mind(1), minds(1), person(1), persons(3), soul(33), souls(14), suspense*(1), thing(1).

5591. **ψυχικός psuchikos**; from *5590; natural, of the soul* or *mind:*— natural(5), worldly-minded(1).

5592. **ψύχος psuchos**; from *5594; cold:*— cold(3).

5593. **ψυχρός psuchros**; from *5592; cold:*— cold(4).

5594. **ψύχω psuchō**; a prim. vb.; *to breathe, blow, to make cool:*— grow cold(1).

5595. **ψωμίζω psōmizō**; from *5596; to feed with morsels:*— feed(2), give(1).

5596. **ψωμίον psōmion**; dim. of **ψωμός psōmos** *(a fragment, morsel); a fragment, morsel:*— morsel(4).

5597. **ψώχω psōchō**; collateral form of **ψάω psaō** *(to rub); to rub:*— rubbing(1).

Ω

5598. **Ω Ō**; i.e. **ὦμεγα ōmega**; the last letter of the Gr. alphabet:— Omega(3).

5599. **ὦ ō**; a prim. interj.; *O, oh!:*— O(7), Oh(1).

5600. **ὦ ō**; the subjunctive of *1510,* q.v.

5601. **Ὠβήδ Ōbēd**; var. reading for *2492b,* q.v.

5602. **ὧδε hōde**; demonstrative adv. from *3592; so, to here, here:*— here(56), there(1), this case(2), this place(1).

5603. **ᾠδή ōdē**; contr. from **ἀοιδή aoidē** *(a song);* from the same as *103; a song, ode:*— song(5), songs(2).

5604. **ὠδίν ōdin**; akin to *3601; a birth pang:*— agony(1), birth pangs(2), labor pains(1).

5605. **ὠδίνω ōdinō**; from *5604; to have birth pangs, to travail:*— am in labor(1), labor(2).

5606. **ὦμος ōmos**; a prim. word; *the shoulder:*— shoulders(2).

5607. **ὤν ōn,**
οὖσα ousa,
ὄν on; masc., fem. and neut. pres. part. of *1510,* q.v.

5608. **ὠνέομαι ōneomai**; from a prim. word **ὦνος ōnos** *(a price); to buy:*— purchased(1).

5609. **ᾠόν ōon**; a prim. word; *an egg:*— egg(1).

5610. **ὥρα hōra**; a prim. word; *a time* or *period, an hour:*— hour(84), hours(3), late*(2), moment(3), once*(3), short*(1), time(6), while(4).

5611. **ὡραῖος hōraios**; from *5610; seasonable, timely:*— beautiful(4).

5612. **ὠρύομαι ōruomai**; onomatop., a prim. vb.; *to roar, howl:*— roaring(1).

5613. **ὡς hōs**; adv. from *3739; as, like as, even as, when, since, as long as:*— about(20), according(2), affected(1), after(2), appear*(1), appeared(1), effect(1), how(20), however*(1), if(10), just(6), just like(1), like(106), like*(1), namely(1), one(2), same way(1), seeing(1), since(2), size(1), so(3), so*(1), though(15), way(1), when(53), whenever*(1), where(1), while(10).

5614. **ὡσαννά hōsanna**; of Heb. or. [3467] and [4994]; *save, we pray:*— Hosanna(6).

5615. **ὡσαύτως hōsautōs**; adv. from *5613* and a der. of *846; in like manner:*— likewise(8), same manner(1), same thing(4), same way(4).

5616. **ὡσεί hōsei**; adv. from *5613* and *1487; as if, as it were, like:*— about(10), about*(1), like(3), much like(1), some(1).

5617. **Ὡσηέ Hōsēe**; of Heb. or. [1954]; *Hosea,* an Isr. prophet:— Hosea(1).

5618. **ὥσπερ hōsper**; from *5613* and *4007a; just as, even as:*— indeed(1), just(13), just like(3), like(4).

5619. **ὡσπερεί hōsperei**; from *5618* and *1487; as, as it were.*

5620. **ὥστε hōste**; from *5613* and *5037; so as to, so then, therefore:*— order(1), result(2), so(43), so then(9), such an extent(3), therefore(16).

5621a. **ὠτάριον ōtarion**; from *5621b; an ear:*— ear(2).

5621b. **ὠτίον ōtion**; dim. of *3775; an ear:*— ear(3).

5622. **ὠφέλεια ōpheleia**; from *5623; assistance, profit, benefit:*— advantage(1), benefit(1).

5623. **ὠφελέω ōpheleō**; from *3786; to help, benefit, do good:*— accomplishing(1), benefit(1), benefited(1), doing...good(1), help(2), helped(1), profit(4), profited(1), profits(2), value(1).

5624. **ὠφέλιμος ōphelimos**; from *5623; useful, profitable:*— profit(1), profitable(3).

VARIATIONS IN VERSIFICATION BETWEEN THE GREEK NEW TESTAMENT AND ENGLISH BIBLES

	English			Greek
Matthew	2 : 1	(last word)	(first word)	2 : 2
	25 : 16	(first word)	(last word)	25 : 15
Mark	12 : 15	(first sentence)	(last sentence)	12 : 14
Luke	7 : 19	(first clause)	(last clause)	7 : 18
	22 : 66	(last word)	(first word)	22 : 67
John	4 : 36	(first word)	(last word)	4 : 35
Acts	3 : 19	(second half)	(first half)	3 : 20
	5 : 40	(first clause)	(last clause)	5 : 39
	13 : 39	(last half)	(last half)	13 : 38
	19 : 41		(last sentence)	19 : 40
	24 : 18	(last clause)	(first clause)	24 : 19
Romans	9 : 11	(last 2 phrases)	(first half)	9 : 12
2 Corinthians	10 : 5	(first clause)	(last clause)	10 : 4
	13 : 13		(last sentence)	13 : 12
	13 : 14			13 : 13
Galatians	2 : 20	(first clause)	(last clause)	2 : 19
Ephesians	2 : 15	(first phrase)	(last phrase)	2 : 14
	5 : 13	(last clause)	(first sentence)	5 : 14
Philippians	2 : 8	(first clause)	(last clause)	2 : 7
1 Thessalonians	1 : 3	(first word)	(last word)	1 : 2
	2 : 6	(last clause)	(first phrase)	2 : 7
	2 : 11	(middle)	(first half)	2 : 12
Hebrews	3 : 9	(last 2 words)	(first 2 words)	3 : 10
	7 : 21	(first clause)	(last half)	7 : 20
	12 : 23	(first 4 words)	(last word)	12 : 22
1 John	2 : 13	(last sentence)	(first sentence)	2 : 14
Revelation	2 : 27	(last clause)	(first half)	2 : 28
	13 : 1	(first sentence)		12 : 18
	17 : 10	(first clause)	(last clause)	17 : 9

A SELECT BIBLIOGRAPHY OF WORKS CONSULTED FOR THE UPDATED EDITION

Greek-English Lexicon compiled by Henry George Liddell and Robert Scott; revised and augmented throughout by Sir Henry Stuart Jones with the assistance of Roderick McKenzie and with the cooperation of many scholars; with a Revised Supplement 1996 (Oxford and New York: Oxford University Press, 1996).

A Greek-English Lexicon of the New Testament and Other Early Christian Literature; a translation and adaptation of the fourth revised and augmented edition of Walter Bauer's Griechisch-Deutsches Wörterbuch zu den Schriften des Neuen Testaments und der übrigen urchristlichen Literatur by William F. Arndt and F. Wilbur Gingrich; second edition revised and augmented by F. Wilbur Gingrich and Frederick W. Danker from Walter Bauer's Fifth Edition, 1958 (Chicago and London: The University of Chicago Press, 1979).

A Manual Greek Lexicon of the New Testament by G. Abbott-Smith (Edinburgh: T. & T. Clark, 1973).

The New Brown-Driver-Briggs-Gesenius Hebrew and English Lexicon, with an appendix containing the Biblical Aramaic by Francis Brown, with the cooperation of S. R. Driver and Charles A. Briggs (Lafayette, Indiana: Associated Publishers and Authors, Inc., 1978).

Theological Dictionary of the New Testament edited by Gerhard Kittel, Geoffrey Bromiley, and Gerhard Friedrich, 10 volumes (Grand Rapids, Michigan: Wm. B. Eerdmans Publishing Company, 1964-1976).

Theological Dictionary of the Old Testament edited by G. Johannes Botterweck and Helmer Ringgren, revised edition, 5 volumes (Grand Rapids, Michigan: Wm. B. Eerdmans Publishing Company, 1974-1986).

Theological Wordbook of the Old Testament edited by R. Laird Harris, Gleason L. Archer, and Bruce K. Waltke, 4 volumes (Chicago: Moody Press, 1980).

A SELECT BIBLIOGRAPHY OF WORKS USING THE SAME HEBREW-ARAMAIC AND GREEK REFERENCE NUMBERS AS FOUND IN THE NEW AMERICAN STANDARD EXHAUSTIVE CONCORDANCE

Gesenius' Hebrew and Chaldee Lexicon to the Old Testament Scriptures (Grand Rapids, Michigan: Baker Book House, 1979).

A Greek-English Lexicon of the New Testament by Joseph Henry Thayer (Grand Rapids, Michigan: Baker Book House, 1977; reprinted by Broadman Press, Nashville, Tennessee, n.d.).

The New Brown-Driver-Briggs-Gesenius Hebrew and English Lexicon (see above).

The New Englishman's Greek Concordance of the New Testament (Lafayette, Indiana: Associated Publishers and Authors, Inc., 1976).

Theological Dictionary of the New Testament (see above).

Theological Wordbook of the Old Testament (see above).

The Word Study Concordance by George V. Wigram and Ralph D. Winter (Pasadena, California: William Carey Library, 1972, 1978) and *The Word Study New Testament* by Ralph D. Winter and Roberta H. Winter (Pasadena, California: William Carey Library, 1978). The second of these has a table with which the Greek word represented by each reference number can be located in *A Greek-English Lexicon of the New Testament and Other Early Christian Literature* and in the *Concordance to the Greek New Testament* by Moulton and Geden.

We want to hear from you. Please send your comments about this book to us in care of zreview@zondervan.com. Thank you.